A GREEK-ENGLISH LEXICON OF THE NEW TESTAMENT AND OTHER EARLY CHRISTIAN LITERATURE

A
GREEK-ENGLISH LEXICON
OF THE
NEW TESTAMENT
and Other Early Christian Literature

A translation and adaptation of the
fourth revised and augmented edition of
WALTER BAUER'S
Griechisch-Deutsches Wörterbuch zu den Schriften
des Neuen Testaments und der übrigen
urchristlichen Literatur

by
WILLIAM F. ARNDT
and
F. WILBUR GINGRICH

SECOND EDITION
REVISED AND AUGMENTED BY
F. WILBUR GINGRICH AND FREDERICK W. DANKER
FROM WALTER BAUER'S FIFTH EDITION, 1958

THE UNIVERSITY OF CHICAGO PRESS

CHICAGO AND LONDON

PUBLISHED BY

THE UNIVERSITY OF CHICAGO PRESS

THE UNIVERSITY OF CHICAGO PRESS, CHICAGO 60637
The University of Chicago Press, Ltd., London

Library of Congress Cataloging in Publication Data

Bauer, Walter, 1877–1960.
  A Greek-English lexicon of the New Testament and other
early Christian literature.

  Includes bibliographical references.
  1. Greek language, Biblical—Dictionaries—English.
I. Arndt, William, 1880–1957.   II. Gingrich, Felix
Wilbur.   III. Danker, Frederick W.   IV. Title.
PA881.B38   1979   487'.4   78-14293
ISBN 0-226-03932-3

FOREWORD TO THE FIRST EDITION

The history of dictionaries specifically intended for the Greek New Testament opens with a Greek-Latin glossary of seventy-five unnumbered pages in the first volume of the Complutensian Polyglot of 1522, including the words of the New Testament, Ecclesiasticus, and the Wisdom of Solomon. The incompleteness, inaccuracy, and elementary character of this glossary reflect the low state of Greek studies at the time it was published, but it was the first in a long and useful succession of New Testament lexical works.

The first NT dictionary with scholarly pretensions was the *Lexicon Graeco-Latinum in Novum Testamentum* by Georg Pasor, published in 1619 at Herborn in Nassau. Ludovicus Lucius put out his *Dictionarium Novi Testamenti* at Basel in 1640 with its words arranged for the first time in strict alphabetic order instead of by word-roots.

Many faults of contemporary NT lexicons were pointed out by Johann Friedrich Fischer in his *Prolusiones de Vitiis Lexicorum Novi Testamenti* (Leipzig, 1791); among these defects were neglect of the smaller words whose frequent use makes them extremely difficult to analyze and classify, the inclusion of too few or too many meanings, lack of logical arrangement, and insufficient attention to the background of NT words in Hebrew, the LXX, and secular Greek.

Among the works that showed the effect of Fischer's criticism was CAWahl's Greek-Latin lexicon of 1822 (Leipzig). This was translated into English by Edward Robinson, the eminent American Biblical scholar, in 1825; Robinson brought out his own Greek-English dictionary of the NT in 1836 (Boston).

Up to this time it was customary for dictionaries intended for serious scholarly use to give the meanings of the words in Latin, though Edward Leigh in his *Critica Sacra* (London, 1639) had made a partial and apologetic attempt to give them in English, and John Parkhurst had published a Greek-English lexicon in 1769.

CLWGrimm published in 1868 (Leipzig) a thorough revision of CGWilke's Greek-Latin *Clavis Novi Testamenti*. Joseph Henry Thayer of Harvard University, after twenty-two years of arduous labor in translating and augmenting Grimm's work, put out his *Greek-English Lexicon of the N.T.* (New York and Edinburgh) in 1886.

The first dictionary to appear after the epoch-making discoveries of papyri, etc., beginning about 1890, was Erwin Preuschen's Greek-German lexicon of 1910. Much to the disappointment of many reviewers, it failed to make much use of the new material, though it did include for the first time the words of the Apostolic Fathers.

Upon Preuschen's untimely death in 1920, the revision of his lexicon was entrusted to Walter Bauer of Göttingen. Now, more than thirty years later, we may say that Professor Bauer stands pre-eminent in the history of NT lexicography. When his revision appeared in 1928 (Giessen) as the second edition of Preuschen, it was hailed as the best thing in its field. A third edition, thoroughly revised and reset, came out in 1937 (Berlin), with Bauer's name alone on the title-page.

In preparing for the fourth edition, Bauer undertook a systematic search in Greek literature down to Byzantine times for parallels to the language of the NT. The magnitude of this task and the greatness of the achievement have been well characterized in a review by HvonCampenhausen (ThLZ 75, 1950, 349) of its first three fascicles: We are here dealing with a work 'which, when considered as the performance of one man, strikes one as almost fabulous. Not only was there a gigantic amount of material to be mastered, involving the most minute acquaintance with the whole body of Christian literature, but this task required at the same time the gift of combining and relating facts, and of preserving an adequate scholarly alertness which is granted to but few people; one thinks of the difficulty of immediately recognizing parallels in the respective authors and making proper use of them. This art is all the more admirable because its achievements manifest themselves only in the apparently insignificant form of articles in a lexicon, which purposely are kept as brief and factual as possible; most of the readers will normally not become aware of what has been accomplished.'

To this we may add that Bauer's analysis and arrangement of the small words so frequently used is a great improvement over anything of its kind previously done.*

It is this fourth edition of Bauer's *Griechisch-Deutsches Wörterbuch zu den Schriften des Neuen Testaments und der übrigen urchristlichen Literatur* (Berlin, 1949–52) that we are privileged to present here in English dress, with some adaptations and additions. It has not been our purpose to make a literal translation, which would indeed have been impossible. The difficulties of translation being what they are, those who wish to know exactly what Bauer says about any word will have to consult the German original. On the other hand, our departures from the general sense of Bauer's work have been few and far between.

We give here a representative, though not exhaustive, list of words in the treatment of which we have made more or less significant adaptations or additions:

ἀγαπάω 1αβ, ἀγενής, ἀγρός, αἰών 1b, ἀκίνητος, ἀκρίς, ἀναιρέω 2, ἀνατρέφω, ἀντίτυπος 1, ἀπειθέω 3, ἀπέχω 1, ἀπλότης, ἀπλῶς, ἄρα, βελόνη, βόρβορος, διανύω, δίκαιος 3; 4, δικαιόω 3b, διϋλίζω, δοῦλος, εἰδέα, εἰς 6a, ἐκδίκησις, ἐκεῖσε, ἐκλεκτός, ἐλαιών, ἐμβατεύω, ἐν II 3, ἐντός, ἐξουσία 4c; 5, ἐπερώτημα 2, ἐπίνοια, ἑτοιμασία, εὐδοκία, εὐθύς, θεομακαρίτης, θερισμός, ἱλαστήριον, ἵνα III 1, καλάμη, καλῶς, καταλαμβάνω 1a, καταργέω 2, κατέχω 1αγ, κατώτερος, κεφαλή 2b, κοιλία 3, κόσμος 5b, κράσπεδον 1, κρίσις 3, λέπρα, λῃστής, λίμνη, μάκελλον, μεθίστημι, μονογενής, μυστήριον 2 (Eph 5: 32), νικάω 2a (Dg 5: 10), οἶνος, ὁμοθυμαδόν, ὀρθοτομέω, οὖν 2c; 3; 4, ὄχλος 1, παιδαγωγός, πάντως 2; 3; 4, παραβολή 1, παρεκτός 1, παρεμβολή 1, παρέχω 2c, πηγή 1, Πιλᾶτος, πιστεύω 2αδ, πλεονεκτέω 1b, πληροφορέω 1a, πνεῦμα 5b, πρεσβύτερος 2b, πρηνής, προέχω 3, πρόθεσις 1, προσευχή 2, προσπίπτω 1 (Lk 5: 8), πρῶτος 1cα (Eph 6: 2), πύθων, ῥύπος 1, σήμερον (w. ref. to ἐπιούσιος), σκεῦος 2, σπερμολόγος, στοιχεῖον 1; 3, συγγινώσκω, συγχρωτίζομαι, συναρμόζω 3, συνεργέω (Ro 8: 28), συντριβή, τέλος 3, τηρέω 2b (1 Cor 7: 37), υἱός 1cγ (Mt 5: 9), ὑποκρίνομαι, φαιλόνης, φάραγξ, Φίλιππος 2, φύσις, χαίρω, χάρις 3 (2 Cor 1: 15).

We have included a few words that are not in Bauer⁴; most of them are those found in the fragments of Papias (e.g. ῥίς); all the words of these fragments are dealt with in this lexicon. Other additions are words like εὐπερίσπαστος, εὐσχημονέω and ξαίνω, which appear in the apparatus of the latest editions of the Nestle text, and for which we gratefully acknowledge the aid of Dr. Erwin Nestle, its editor. One interesting conjecture, ἀπαρτί, has been included for the first time.

Various other minor changes and additions will be evident to anyone who compares this book with the German original. Slight adjustments have been made in the arrangement of

* See FWGingrich, The Contributions of Professor Walter Bauer to NT Lexicography, NTS 9, '62/'63, 3–10.

entries, which, we hope, will smooth the way for the user of this lexicon. We have corrected typographical and other small errors in the original, varying from wrong punctuation or accent to a faulty NT reference. We can only hope that we have not made too many fresh mistakes of our own. We have also included more irregular verb-forms than Bauer has.

The notations M-M. and B. at the end of an entry mean that the word is treated in Moulton and Milligan's invaluable *Vocabulary of the Greek New Testament* and CDBuck's *Dictionary of Selected Synonyms in the Principal Indo-European Languages*; the latter will partially make up for the paucity of etymological information deplored by Bauer in the foreword to his third edition of 1937; we may add that Buck's monumental work deserves to be better known. References are likewise given to all the words treated by EJGoodspeed in his *Problems of NT Translation*, and to some from FField's *Notes on the Translation of the NT*. The NT grammars of JHMoulton, Moulton-Howard, and Robertson are referred to when this is possible. All this is largely in addition to the bibliographical notices given in Bauer⁴.

References to the *New (Oxford) English Dictionary* will be found under these words: διαθήκη, διϋλίζω, δοῦλος, ἐξαγοράζω, θάλασσα, Ἰάκωβος, ἱλαστήριον, παιδαγωγός, πραΰς, πρεσβύτερος, πύθων, σπλάγχνον, τράπεζα, ὑάκινθος.

The references to scholarly periodical literature have been brought up to the latter part of 1954. We have made other additions to the bibliographical notices as our allowance of time and other resources (extremely generous but, of course, not unlimited) permitted. If the user finds them insufficient, he is referred to the excellent bibliographies found in *Biblica* (by PNober), in the *Internationale Zeitschriftenschau für Bibelwissenschaft und Grenzgebiete*, vol. I (Heft I 1951f; Heft II, also covering 1951f, publ. 1954) edited by FStier of Tübingen, in the *Theologische Literaturzeitung*, in *NT Literature, An Annotated Bibliography* (1943–5 inclusive) publ. 1948 by WNLyons and MMParvis, in BMMetzger's *Index of Articles on the NT and Early Church Published in Festschriften* (1951), and in many other places. It is also taken for granted that much use will be made of the standard commentaries and other handbooks.

The history of our work should be briefly recounted. When in 1947 the Lutheran Church-Missouri Synod observed its centennial, a part of the thank-offering gathered was set aside as a fund for scholarly research. The Lutheran Academy of Scholarship, Dr. MHScharlemann president, had a prominent part in the discussions that led to this decision. The committee, appointed by Dr. JWBehnken, the president of the church, to administer the fund, resolved to have Bauer's *Wörterbuch* done into English, with such adaptations and additions as would be required. Since the University of Chicago Press had been in negotiation with Dr. Bauer on this subject, the committee of the Church turned to this publishing house and enlisted its co-operation and services. The translation rights were duly obtained. Professor FWGingrich of Albright College, Reading, Pa., was engaged to give his full time to the undertaking, having been granted a leave of absence in September 1949. Professor WFArndt of Concordia Seminary, St. Louis, Mo., an institution of the Lutheran Church-Missouri Synod, was appointed to be the director of the venture. The manuscript was finished in January 1955. This dictionary in its English dress constitutes a gift of the Lutheran Church-Missouri Synod to the English-speaking world, presented in the hope that the work may assist in the interpretation and dissemination of the Divine Word which lives and abides for ever.

Various officials of the University of Chicago Press have rendered valuable assistance in the complicated negotiations required to set this project in motion. Among them we may mention particularly Dr. Mitford M. Mathews, head of the Dictionary Department of the Press and editor of the *Dictionary of Americanisms*. His wise counsel has helped us in every stage of our work.

We have been aided from the beginning of our project by an advisory committee composed of the following scholars: HJCadbury, ECColwell, CHDodd, FVFilson, MHFranzmann, EJGoodspeed, FCGrant, BMMetzger, PSchubert, WWente, APWikgren. CHKraeling advised us on archaeological matters, and AHeidel (d. June 1955) checked the Semitic language materials in our manuscript.

We have also received valued assistance from the following: VBartling, WBeck, HGreeven, WHPHatch, WRHutton, PKatz, PEKretzmann, JRMantey, RMarcus, ENestle, MMParvis, OAPiper, JMRife, and JDYoder. Neither these gentlemen nor those of the advisory committee are to be held responsible for the opinions expressed in this lexicon. The editors accept responsibility for all errors, and invite users of the lexicon to draw attention to any they may find.

Regarding the question whether to enter the contract verbs in their contracted or uncontracted form, we recognize the validity of DJGeorgacas' arguments in *Classical Philology* 47, '52, 167-9, but have retained the uncontracted forms to avoid confusing the student, who almost invariably learns them in those forms. The references to Biblical literature and Josephus have been checked by Messrs. RStallmann and CFroehlich. In the spelling of proper names we have generally followed the usage of the Revised Standard Version. Finally we express warm thanks to the staff of Cambridge University Press, and especially its typesetters and proofreaders, for their splendid co-operation and assistance.

SOLI DEO GLORIA

W. F. ARNDT
F. W. GINGRICH

FOREWORD TO THE SECOND EDITION

When the English translation of Walter Bauer's *Wörterbuch* was published on 29 January 1957, Professor Bauer was completing work on the fifth edition of his book, which came out in nine fascicles during 1957 and 1958. This contained so much new material that a revision of our work was made inevitable. Our second revised edition contains Bauer's additions as well as a number of changes and additions of our own.

In the foreword to the first edition we invited those who found errors in our work to call them to our attention. As a result, we had replies from as far away as Africa and New Guinea, as well as a large number from our own country. Many, if not most, of these errors were corrected in subsequent reprintings, notably the sixth of 1963 and the tenth of 1967, and we wish to express our gratitude to those users of this book. We now extend the same invitation to the users of the second edition.

We also acknowledge a debt of gratitude to the many scholars who sent us valuable suggestions, whether solicited or unsolicited. Two young men did valiant service in checking and correcting the asterisks at the end of many entries; they are John Recks for the New Testament and Almon D. Baird, Jr., for the Apostolic Fathers. As a result of their painstaking work, the asterisks now present a much more accurate picture of the usage than they ever did before. Others who rendered sustained and valuable assistance are Theodore Eisold, Robert Stockman, William Reader, and Donald Wicke.

The enormous current proliferation of books and articles has made it impossible to continue the fullness of citation that some of Bauer's entries exhibited. Furthermore, ready access to bibliographical data banks, such as the annual *Internationale Zeitschriftenschau für Bibelwissenschaft und Grenzgebiete* (Patmos-Verlag, Düsseldorf, 1951ff) or *New Testament Abstracts*, published three times a year by the Weston School of Theology, now at Cambridge, Massachusetts (1956ff), suggests that it would not be discreet even to make the attempt. Instead, we have been at pains to add discussions where previously there had been none, and the number of such and other supplemental references to scholarly literature runs well into four figures (apart from Bauer's own additions), and extends into 1973.

More important, the classics, papyri, and inscriptions have yielded fresh formal and semantic parallels, in some cases necessitating rearrangement of patterns of definition. References to the literature of Qumran and to texts of portions of the New Testament published since our first edition are frequent. Indeed, the number of new words and other variants that have been incorporated reflects the contribution made especially by the Bodmer Papyri to the study of the New Testament. Among the new entries are: ἀπονεύω (Bauer), γοργός, ἐθελο- compounds (Bauer), εἶμι, θερεία, κοινῶς, λεπράω, Λίβανος, νεῖκος, νευης, ποδονιπτήρ (Bauer), πρεσβευτής, πυρκαϊά, ὑπερασπίζω, ὑσσός.

It has also proved impossible to list all available translations of foreign-language publications. Fortunately, the section numbers in the standard grammar of F. Blass and A. Debrunner remain the same in the translation and revision by Robert W. Funk, *A Greek Grammar of the New Testament and Other Early Christian Literature* (Chicago, 1961); and the publishers of G. W. Bromiley's translation of the Kittel-Friedrich *Theologisches Wörterbuch*, the *Theological Dictionary of the New Testament* (Grand Rapids, Michigan, 1964ff), are to be congratulated for maintaining in the main the pagination of that monumental German work. The student is urged to consult these and all other standard reference works, whether we cite them specifically or not.

To Professor Lorman M. Petersen of Concordia Theological Seminary, Springfield, Illinois, and the Committee for Scholarly Research (Lutheran Church-Missouri Synod) under his direction go our warmest thanks for their continuing interest in and support of a costly undertaking. At the same time we record with sorrow the death of our mentor, Professor Walter Bauer (b. 8 August 1877, d. 17 November 1960) and of our esteemed coworker, Professor William F. Arndt (b. 1 December 1880, d. 25 February 1957).

F. WILBUR GINGRICH
FREDERICK W. DANKER

AN INTRODUCTION TO THE LEXICON OF
THE GREEK NEW TESTAMENT*

WALTER BAUER

The second edition of the *Griechisch-deutsches Wörterbuch zu den Schriften des Neuen Testaments und der übrigen urchristlichen Literatur* of 1928, which reached its fourth edition in 1952, contained in its opening pages a short 'introduction' to its use. The exigencies of space and the desire to keep the price of the book as reasonable as possible caused the omission of these pages in the later editions. This was deplored by certain scholars whose judgment on the lexicon was favorable, among them ADeissmann in the *Deutsche Literaturzeitung* (1937), p. 520. Their ranks were joined by AFridrichsen, the editor of the series 'Coniectanea Neotestamentica,' who declared himself ready to give the introduction a new home in his series. The publishers also gave their consent, for which they deserve our gratitude. Accordingly, it is here presented once more, with some corrections and a supplement.

The earliest Christian literature, with which this book deals, is made up of a number of writings which were composed in the Greek language. It is not the Greek of more ancient times, least of all that of the Golden Age of Athens which is now taught in the institutions of higher learning and occupies the most prominent place in the dictionaries used in them. A comparison reveals, on the contrary, differences in phonology and morphology, in syntax and style, and, not least of all, in the vocabulary as well. These divergences are too plain to have remained unnoticed. When in the seventeenth century the learned controversy about the purity of New Testament Greek arose, the so-called 'Hebraists' tried to explain the peculiarities of this Greek as due to the influence of the Hebrew. Although they shot wide of the mark in some of their conclusions, their recognition of the special character of the New Testament language constituted a strong impetus in the right direction, when compared with the conception of their opponents, the 'purists,' whose attempt to demonstrate that the Holy Spirit inspired the New Testament writers with as fine and pure a Greek as any classical author ever wrote could not maintain itself indefinitely.

However, neither did the Hebraists achieve a real grasp of the situation. This was due largely to the fact that philology at that time knew the Greek language only from its literature and consequently fell into the error of equating Greek with the Greek literary language. In addition, the writings contemporaneous with the New Testament—upon which they based their judgments—were deeply colored by Atticism, an artificial revival of the classical language. This prevented recognition of the truth that Greek had been developing since the days of the Attic orators and Plato, as any living language must.

This judgment, one-sided to say the least, was destined to hold the field as long as formal literature was almost the only source of our knowledge. But the situation took a decided change when, in the 1890's, there began to appear in great abundance those volumes which make available to the learned world the Greek papyri found in Egypt. As a result, interest was awakened, too, in the earlier isolated publications of a similar nature, and it spread to the other non-literary sources—the ostraca (fragments of broken pottery which served as

* The German original was published as No. xv of 'Coniectanea Neotestamentica,' 1955, under the title *Zur Einführung in das Wörterbuch zum Neuen Testament*. Translated and published here with permission of the author, the editor, Harald Riesenfeld, and the publishers, CWKGleerup, Lund and Ejnar Munksgaard, København.

cheap writing materials) and inscriptions. In all of them we have witnesses of the speech of daily life, especially in its colloquial form, in so far as they avoid the influence of custom, formula, and school—and infinitely many do just that! Here, at length, was discovered the proper background for a truly scientific view of the language of the oldest Christian literature. The honor of having been discoverer and pathfinder in this field belongs to Adolf Deissmann, who, beginning in 1895, demonstrated to us more and more clearly—both in numerous single investigations and in comprehensive works—that our literature on the whole represents the late Greek colloquial language, which, to be sure, some authors used with more literary polish, others with less. The upper and lower limits for our literature in this respect are marked by Hb, MPol, and Dg on the literary side, and Rv on the colloquial. *

While theology in particular became interested in these discoveries, so recently made or appreciated, because they provided the possibility of arriving at a better understanding of the language of the Greek Bible, this newly discovered field appeared no less attractive to classical philology as well. As a matter of fact, the philologists now had the opportunity—of which they made good use—to investigate thoroughly what was known even in ancient times as the 'Koine,' ἡ κοινὴ διάλεκτος, 'the common language.'

This 'common language' was formed from the old dialects (Ionic, Attic, Doric, Aeolic) by a mixture to which, as one might expect, the Attic made the greatest contribution. Then, in almost complete homogeneity, it conquered the Hellenistic world.

Peculiarities characteristic of the Koine are met first in the fifth century B.C. Perhaps, indeed, we may speak of a Koine, or at least its beginnings, in this early period when (in the time of the first Athenian maritime empire) the need was felt of a common Greek language for purposes of communication. Complete development and displacement of the dialects, however, were not achieved by the common language until toward the end of the fourth century B.C., when, through the agency of Alexander the Great of Macedonia, not Attic, nor Ionic, but Greek conquered the Eastern world. In the kingdoms of the Diadochi it expanded and confirmed its domain, while the Romans, their successors in the rule of the East, preserved it carefully and made it serve their own interests. Furthermore, the Romans did not need to visit this part of the world to learn the nature and significance of Greek. This language had been used in Greek colonies in the West for centuries; it was heard a great deal in the capital city itself and was quite generally spoken there by the educated classes (cf. HLietzmann, 'Das Problem der Spätantike,' SAB [1927], p. 347).

The writings of our literature arose in this period, when the Greek language ruled over the East and many parts of the West. They were written by men who spoke the common language of communication in their day more or less colloquially. Hence, in order to understand their works, we must make ourselves familiar with that stage in the development of the Greek language which we call the 'Koine.' The sources from which we gain our knowledge are, in the first place, the afore-mentioned non-literary evidences (papyri, ostraca, inscriptions). But in addition to these there are a number of authors who were more or less able to avoid the spell of antiquarianism which we know as 'Atticism' (Polybius, Diodorus Siculus, Strabo, Plutarch, Epictetus, Artemidorus, Pseudo-Apollodorus, Vettius Valens, et al.). The representatives of Jewish Hellenism are especially important for the investigation of our literature because of the close similarity in the

---

* Cf. JRos, *De studie van het Bijbelgrieksch van Hugo Grotius tot Adolf Deissmann* (1940). Of course, Deissmann's methods are capable of further refinement, and the investigations which he inspired attempt to go beyond his own achievements.

content of their works; included here are Philo, Josephus, the Epistle of Aristeas, and, above all, the Septuagint, which not only contains original Greek words of the late period but also uses the contemporary tongue even when it translates. Ancient Christian writings, too, outside the scope of our literature, like the Apocryphal Acts of the Apostles and old legends,* are valuable as witnesses of the colloquial common speech. Finally, the contribution of medieval and modern Greek is not to be neglected, because the Koine finds in them its lineal descendants (cf. GNHatzidakis, *Einleitung in die neugriechische Grammatik* [1892]; AThumb, *Handbuch der neugriechischen Volkssprache* [1895; 2nd ed., 1910]; ANJannaris, *An Historical Greek Grammar* [1897]).

On the basis of these sources, what conception can we gain of this common speech? Even though we recognize the Attic dialect as the main factor in its origin, that dialect had to sacrifice much to the common cause—so much, in fact, that some investigators are not willing to regard it as the main element (cf. PKretschmer, 'Die Entstehung der Κοινή,' *Sitzungsbericht der Wiener Akad., Phil.-hist. Klasse*, Vol. CXLIII [1900]. For the opposite view, see Mlt., 33f).† In this connection we need not chiefly call to mind the classical writers, nor regretfully note the absence of their elegance in periodic sentence structure, in the use of particles, in the employment of the moods, in the change of prepositions or negatives. The Attic had to give up the characteristics which differentiated it from all or most of the other dialects, e.g. ττ instead of σσ (cf. Bl-D. §34, 1), ρρ instead of ρσ (cf. Bl-D. §34, 2 and see ἄρσην, θαρρέω and θαρσέω), ξυν instead of συν (cf. Bl-D. §34, 4). It gave up the dual altogether and used the optative very modestly. The Attic second declension ekes out a miserable existence, represented in the New Testament only by ἵλεως (*q.v.*); the Attic future is in process of dying out and maintains itself in the New Testament only in the case of several verbs in -ίζω, even there predominantly in quotations from the LXX (Bl-D. §74, 1). The Attic ἕνεκα (*q.v.*) is attested unanimously only in one New Testament passage. Where, as in this case, the tradition is divided, it is impossible to escape the suspicion that scribes under the influence of Atticism have subsequently restored to classical Greek what, according to their view, presumably belonged to it. In this way the Attic future has got into some manuscripts (Bl-D. §74, 1), or, for instance, the Attic forms πανδοκεῖον and πανδοκεύς force their way into the text of Lk 10: 34, 35 (s. πανδοχεῖον, πανδοχεύς). Cf. WMichaelis, 'Der Attizismus und das NT,' *ZNW*, XXII [1923], 91–121.

Just as noticeable as the losses suffered by the Attic are the influences taken over from other dialects. Of Doric origin are: ἀμφιάζω (*q.v.*), which, together with the similarly Hellenistic form ἀμφιέζω, takes the place of the older ἀμφιέννυμι (Bl-D. §73), πιάζω (*q.v.*), and προσαχέω (*q.v.*). Likewise ἀλέκτωρ (Ion.-Att. ἀλεκτρυών), βουνός (*q.v.*), ἔναντι as well as ἀπέναντι and κατέναντι (Bl.-D. §214, 4), ἐνδιδύσκω (?Bl.-D. §73), λαός and ναός (for Att. λεώς and νεώς; cf. Bl-D. §44, 1), μοιχάομαι, μαρυκάομαι (*q.v.*), οἰκοδομή (*q.v.*), ὀρκίζω (EFraenkel, *Geschichte der griechischen nomina agentis auf -τήρ, -τωρ, -της*, I [1910], 180), ὀρκωμοσία (*q.v.*), ὄρνιξ (*q.v.*). On the pass. ἐγενήθην as the aor. of γίνομαι s. that entry.

Ionic, as the dialect most closely related to Attic, offers a richer contribution. Here belong uncontracted noun forms like νεομηνία (*q.v.*) and ἐπαοιδός; on the other side, contractions like ἱερωσύνη (Att. ἱερεωσύνη); the disappearance of the vowel before

---

* See especially those edited by HUsener, of St. Pelagia (1879), St. Marina and St. Christopher (1886), St. Tychon (1907); also GBjörck, 'Der Fluch des Christen Sabinus'; *Pap. Ups.*, No. 8 (1938).

† The abbreviations here and in what follows are those of the lexicon.

another vowel in νοσσός (for νεοσσός), βαθμός (Att. βασμός), and κλίβανος (q.v.; Att. κρίβανος). Likewise the forms τέσσερα and τεσσεράκοντα (for τέσσαρα [q.v.] and τεσσαράκοντα [q.v.]), ἔσω (Att. εἴσω), ἕνεκεν as well as εἵνεκεν (Att. ἕνεκα), εἶτεν (Att. εἶτα, q.v. end). Further, Hellenistic Greek shares a number of verbal forms with the Ionic, e.g.: ἐλεύσομαι as future of ἔρχομαι (Att. εἶμι); ἔζησα (Att. ἐβίων); ἐκέρδησα (Att. ἐκέρδανα and ἐκέρδηνα); ἐπόθησα (Att. ἐπόθεσα); τέτευχα (Att. τετύχηκα). The Ionic may also be responsible for the inflection of -μι verbs in -ω or in -ῶ (cf. Mlt. 38). Cf. γογγύζω (q.v.); πρὶν ἤ (s. πρίν).

Most of the peculiarities of the Koine in comparison with the classical languages can be referred to no definite dialect. So it is when forms appear like εἶδα, εἴδαμεν, εἴδατε, εἶδαν (s. εἶδον); ἤνεγκα with the ptc. ἐνέγκας (s. φέρω); ἔπεσα beside ἔπεσον (s. πίπτω), in which the two aorists are mingled. Further, the imperfect with endings of the first aorist: εἴχαμεν, εἶχαν (s. ἔχω); ἔλεγαν (s. λέγω). Perf. with aorist endings (inscr. and pap. since II BC): ἔγνωκαν (s. γινώσκω); τετήρηκαν (J 17: 6); γέγοναν (s. γίνομαι); εἴρηκαν (s. εἶπον); πέπτωκαν (s. πίπτω). The ending -σαν expands its territory and is especially noticeable in the imperfect and 2 aor.: εἴχοσαν (s. ἔχω); παρελάβοσαν (s. παραλαμβάνω); ἐξῆλθοσαν (Mk 8: 11 D). Or the types of inflection in -ᾶν and -εῖν become confused (cf. ἐλλογέω). While among Attic writers many active verbs form a middle future—at least as the regular form—the Koine insists on the active, although not quite inflexibly: ἀκούσω (s. ἀκούω); ἁμαρτήσω (Mt 18: 21; cf. Hm 4, 1, 1; 2); ἀπαντήσω (Mk 14: 13) and συναντήσω (Lk 22: 10; Ac 20: 22); ἁρπάσω (J 10: 28); γελάσω (s. γελάω); κλαύσω (s. κλαίω); ῥεύσω (J 7: 38). Correspondingly, it prefers the 'regular' first aorist to the second aor., which was formerly the favorite: ἡμάρτησα (s. ἁμαρτάνω); ἐβίωσα (s. βιόω); ἐβλάστησα (s. βλαστάνω); ἔκραξα (s. κράζω). In deponents the common dialect values the aor. and fut. passive more highly than the middle: ἀπεκρίθην (s. ἀποκρίνομαι) and διεκρίθην (as aor. of the mid. διακρίνομαι; s. διακρίνω 2, mid.); ἐθαυμάσθην and θαυμασθήσομαι (s. θαυμάζω 2). Yet it also uses middle forms where the Attic dialect has the passive: ἠρνησάμην (s. ἀρνέομαι); διελεξάμην (s. διαλέγομαι).

Far more than its grammatical structure, the vocabulary and use of words in the Greek language suffered radical changes in the course of centuries. Instead of classical middles or deponents, the common speech employs the corresponding actives: ἀτενίζω (q.v.); εὐαγγελίζω (q.v.). Above all, however, it resorts to new formations (s. the respective articles in the lexicon), which in part take the place of related forms in more ancient times.

Of verbs in -ίζω: αἱρετίζω, αἰχμαλωτίζω, ἀνακαθίζω, ἀνεμίζω (Att. ἀνεμόω), ἀπελπίζω, ἀποθησαυρίζω, ἀποκεφαλίζω, ἀσφαλίζομαι, γαμίζω, διασκορπίζω and σκορπίζω, διαφημίζω, ἐξαρτίζω, ἐξερίζω, ἐξυπνίζω, εὐνουχίζω, ἰουδαΐζω, καθαρίζω (for καθαίρω), κατασοφίζομαι, κατοπτρίζω, κλυδωνίζομαι, ὀξίζω, παρορίζω and προορίζω, πελεκίζω, προελπίζω, προσεγγίζω, ῥαντίζω (for ῥαίνω), σκοτίζω, συμμερίζω.— -ιάζω: ἁγιάζω (for ἁγίζω), ἐνταφιάζω, καυστηριάζω, νηπιάζω, σεληνιάζομαι, σινιάζω.— -ματίζω (from neuters in -μα): ἀναθεματίζω and καταθεματίζω, δειγματίζω and παραδειγματίζω, δογματίζω, ἱματίζω, καυματίζω.— -άζω: ἀνετάζω, ἀποσκευάζομαι, διαυγάζω, ἑδράζω, ἐκθαυμάζω, ἐξαγοράζω, μονάζω (from μόνος), στυγνάζω (from στυγνός).— -όω: ἀκυρόω, ἀναστατόω, ἁπλόω, ἀποδεκατόω, ἀφιερόω (religious technical term), ἀφυπνόω, ἀχρειόω, βεβηλόω, δυναμόω, ἐκριζόω, ἑνόω, ἐντυπόω, ἐξαπλόω, καθηλόω, κατιόω, καυσόω, κραταιόω (class. κρατύνω), μεταμορφόω and μορφόω, νεκρόω, προδηλόω, προσκληρόω, σαρόω (class.

σαίρω), σημειόω, σπιλόω, χαριτόω.— -έω: ἀθετέω, ἀναθεωρέω, ἀναισθητέω, ἀναντλέω, ἀνομέω, ἀντιλοιδορέω, ἀντιμετρέω, ἀντοφθαλμέω, ἀποκυέω, ἀπολαλέω,
ἀστοχέω, αὐθεντέω (together with αὐθέντης and αὐθεντικός), ἀφυστερέω, ἐγκακέω,
εἰσκαλέομαι, ἐκδικέω, ἐκζητέω, ἐκκακέω, ἐλλογέω (commercial technical term),
ἐνειλέω, ἐξαπορέομαι, ἐξουδενέω, ἐπιχορηγέω, κατηχέω, λατομέω, συγγνωμονέω,
συγκρατέω, συλλαλέω, συνομιλέω.— -άω: ἀναζάω, ἀροτριάω (for ἀρόω), δειλιάω,
(ἐξ)εραυνάω (for [ἐξ]ερευνάω), λικμάω, μηνιάω, ξυράω (q.v.), προσδαπανάω, σπαταλάω, στρηνιάω, συγχράομαι.— -εύω: αἰχμαλωτεύω, ἀκριβεύομαι, γυμνιτεύω,
ἐγκρατεύομαι, ἱερατεύω, κατακυριεύω, κατασκοπεύω, κυκλεύω (for κυκλόω), μαθητεύω, μεθοδεύω, μεσιτεύω, ὀλοθρεύω, παραβολεύομαι, παροδεύω, περπερεύομαι,
συμβασιλεύω, συνοδεύω, σωρεύω and ἐπισωρεύω.—Cf. also ἀνακυλίω and ἀποκυλίω, ἀναζώννυμι, ἀναθάλλω, ἀνατάσσομαι, ἀπολείχω, ἀποτάσσομαι (mid.), ἐκπλέκω, ἐπιφώσκω, καμμύω, κνήθω, κρύβω (for κρύπτω), ὀμείρομαι, ὀπτάνομαι, περιλάμπω, περιπείρω, προαμαρτάνω, προβλέπω, στήκω, χύν(ν)ω (present for χέω; Bl-D.
§73).

Of substantives in -μός: ἁγνισμός, ἀπαρτισμός, ἁρπαγμός, ἀφανισμός, βαπτισμός,
γογγυσμός, διαλογισμός, ἐνταφιασμός, ἱλασμός, ἱματισμός, καθαρισμός, καταρτισμός, κυλισμός, μιασμός, μολυσμός, ὀνειδισμός, πειρασμός, πλατυσμός, πορισμός, συγκλεισμός, σωφρονισμός, ψιθυρισμός.— -μα (the Ionic shows a marked
preference for this form): ἁγίασμα, ἀγνόημα, αἰτίωμα (for αἰτίαμα), ἀνόμημα,
ἄντλημα, ἀπαύγασμα, ἀπόκριμα, γένημα, διάταγμα, ἔκτρωμα, ἐλάττωμα, ἕλιγμα,
ἐνέργημα, ἔνταλμα, ἐξέραμα, θέλημα, κατάκριμα and πρόκριμα, κατάλυμα, καταπέτασμα, κατάχυμα, κατόρθωμα, κένωμα, κτίσμα, παράπτωμα, περίσσευμα,
πρόσκομμα, ῥάντισμα, ῥάπισμα, σέβασμα, χόρτασμα. If the ending of the stem before
the suffixes -σις and -της (-τος) is short, the Koine introduces the short ending of the
stem in the corresponding forms in -μα as well (Bl-D. §109, 3): δόμα, θέμα, ἀνάθεμα (for
the class. ἀνάθημα) and κατάθεμα, κλίμα, κρίμα, πόμα (as early as Pindar and Hdt.;
the classic writers used πῶμα); see also s.v. εὕρημα and κατάστημα.— -σις: ἀθέτησις,
ἄθλησις, ἀνάδειξις, ἀνάχυσις, ἀνάψυξις, ἀπάντησις, ἀποκάλυψις, ἀπολύτρωσις
and λύτρωσις (technical business terms), ἀπόχρησις, βίωσις, διάταξις, ἐκδίκησις,
ἐκπέτασις, ἐκπλήρωσις, ἔλεγξις, ἔλευσις, ἐξομολόγησις and ὁμολόγησις, ἐρήμωσις,
θέλησις, θλῖψις, κατάκρισις, κατάνυξις, κατάρτισις, κατασκήνωσις, καύχησις,
μείωσις, μόρφωσις, νέκρωσις, ὅρασις, παρατήρησις, πεποίθησις, περίθεσις, περιποίησις, προσκαρτέρησις, πρόσκλισις, σημείωσις, συζήτησις, συνείδησις, συνέλευσις.— -ότης: ἀγαθότης, ἁγιότης, ἁγνότης, ἀδελφότης, ἀδηλότης, ἁδρότης,
ἀφελότης, γυμνότης, δολιότης, εἰκαιότης, θειότης, θεότης, ἱλαρότης, ἰσχυρότης,
ματαιότης, μεγαλειότης, ποσότης.— -σύνη: ἀκεραιοσύνη, ἐλεημοσύνη; with
lengthening of the ο after a short syllable ἁγιωσύνη, μεγαλωσύνη.— -ία: ἀβροχία,
αἰχμαλωσία, ἀμεριμνία, ἀνοδία, ἀποστασία, (class. ἀπόστασις), ἀποτομία, ἀφειδία,
ἀφθαρσία, ἐλαφρία, ἐπιχορηγία, ἐτοιμασία, κατοικία, λυχνία (for λυχνεῖον), μετοικεσία, ὀπτασία, παραχειμασία, πρωΐα, σκοτία (for σκότος), συνοδία.— -εία: ἐριθεία,
ἱερατεία, λογεία, μαθητεία, μεθοδεία, περισσεία, προφητεία.— -εια: ἀπώλεια, ἀρέσκεια, ἐκτένεια.— -ή: ἁρμογή, βροχή and ἐμβροχή, διαταγή and ἐπιταγή, ἐγκοπή,
κοπή, προκοπή, προσκοπή and συγκοπή, κατ' ἐξοχήν, ἐπισκοπή, μηλωτή, ὀφειλή,
πεισμονή, περιοχή, προσευχή.— -της (agent nouns): ἀποστάτης, βαπτιστής, βιαστής, γνώστης, διωγμίτης, ἐξορκιστής, καθηγητής, καταφρονητής, μεριστής, μεσίτης, προσαίτης, προσκυνητής, σαλπιστής, στασιαστής, συμμύστης, χρεώστης,

ψιθυριστής.— -ωρ: ἀντιλήπτωρ, κατήγωρ, κτήτωρ.— -ων: ἀμπελών, ἐλαιών, καύσων, κοιτών, λαμπηδών, νυμφών, πυλών.— -τήριον: ἀγνευτήριον, ἀκροατή-ριον, ἱλαστήριον (religious technical term).—The feminine forms βασίλισσα (q.v.) and Συροφοινίκισσα are Hellenistic, also μοιχαλίς, συγγενίς, μαθήτρια and some diminu-tives, whose actual diminutive force is certainly no longer felt in many cases; animals: ἐρίφιον, ὀνάριον (ἀρνίον, ἰχθύδιον, κυνάριον, προβάτιον are taken over from the older language); parts of the body: ὠτίον and ὠτάριον. Cf. ἀγρίδιον, βιβλίδιον (βιβλαρίδιον and βιβλιδάριον), κλινίδιον (κλινάριον is older), κοράσιον, νησίον, πτερύγιον, ῥαβδίον, ψωμίον.—Formations in -ιον that are not diminutive: γεώργιον, δοκίμιον, δυσεντέριον, ὀψώνιον, προαύλιον, προσφάγιον, συμβούλιον, τελώνιον, ὑποπόδιον. —Finally, a large group of other nouns, like ἀγάπη, ἄρκος (for ἄρκτος), βασιλίσκος, βραβεῖον, βυρσεύς, γρόνθος, καταγγελεύς, καταιγίς, κειρία, κρύπτη, κύθρα, λα-τόμος, λειτουργός, ληνός, μάμμη, μύλος (for μύλη), νῖκος (for νίκη), ὁδηγός, περι-κεφαλαία, πινακίς, πλήμμυρα, πολιά, ῥομφαία, σαγήνη, σκύβαλον, σπίλος, στρῆ-νος, συγκληρονόμος (legal t.t.), συμπολίτης (in one passage in Euripides), σύνοδος, ταμεῖον (for ταμιεῖον).

Of adjectives in -ιος: ἐπιθανάτιος, ἐπιούσιος (q.v.), μετακόσμιος, παρόδιος, περιού-σιος, σεβάσμιος.— -ικός (-ιακός): ἀγγελικός, αἱρετικός, ἀνατολικός, ἀρσενικός, ἀρχοντικός, αὐθεντικός, δαιμονικός, διδακτικός, ἐθνικός, καθολικός, κυριακός, λαϊ-κός, λειτουργικός, λογικός (a philosophical t.t. Aristot.+), νεωτερικός, οἰκιακός, ὀνικός, προβατικός, προφητικός, σαρκικός, σηρικός, χοϊκός.— -ινος: ἀμαράντινος, δερμά-τινος, καθημερινός, καρπάσινος, κόκκινος, μύλινος, ὀρθρινός, ὀστράκινος, πρωϊνός, ταχινός.— -τος: ἀρκετός, δεκτός, διαβόητος, ἔκπληκτος, ἐπήλυτος, ἐπιπόθητος and ποθητός, κατάκριτος, οἰκοδομητός, παθητός, σεβαστός, σιτιστός.—Cf. also γραώ-δης, ἔγγραφος, ἔκτρομος and ἔντρομος, ἐνάρετος (Stoic t.t.), ἔξυπνος, ἐπάλληλος, ἐπίμονος, ἤρεμος, θηλυκός, πρόσκαιρος, σύμμορφος, σύμψυχος, σύνδενδρος, ὕπαν-δρος.—Double comparison for the purpose of attaining greater clarity is occasionally found in classical times (Kühner-Bl. I 373), and becomes very popular with Hellenistic writers (Bl-D. §61, 2; Mlt. 236; Mayser I 301, 1; Crönert 190): διπλότερος (s. διπλοῦς), ἐλαχιστότερος (s. ἐλάχιστος, beg.), μειζότερος (s. μέγας, beg.).

In general, it becomes a very common custom to put new life into certain forms that show the wear and tear of time—that is, have become indistinct in meaning—by compounding them with other words. This explains in part the preference of the Koine for compounds, of which the previous lists exhibit a considerable number, even in the simplest speech. Where the older language does very well with a simple form, Hellenistic Greek likes to prefix a preposition (cf. GBWiner's five reports [Programme], *De verborum cum praepos. compositorum in Novo Testamento usu* [Leipzig, 1834-43]): ἀνανήφω and ἐκνήφω, ἀνατρέφομαι, ἀποδεκατεύω, ἀποτυφλόω, ἀποφθέγγομαι, διανεύω, δια-νυκτερεύω, διερμηνεύω and μεθερμηνεύω, ἐγκαυχάομαι, ἐγχρίω, ἐκλιπαρέω, ἐκπει-ράζω, ἐναγκαλίζομαι, ἐνδοξάζομαι, ἐνορκίζω, ἐξακολουθέω and κατακολουθέω, ἐξηχέω, ἐξισχύω, ἐξομολογέω, ἐπαγωνίζομαι, ἐπαθροίζω, ἐπιβαρέω and κατα-βαρέω, ἐπιπορεύομαι, ἐπισκηνόω, ἐπισπουδάζω (?q.v.), ἐπισφραγίζω, καταντάω, καταπιστεύω, παραβιάζομαι, προσεγγίζω, προσονομάζω.—ἐπίγνωσις.—ἀπό-κενος, περίπικρος.—ἔκπαλαι, ἐπαύριον, ὑπεράγαν, ὑπεράνω, ὑπερεκπερισσοῦ, ὑπερλίαν, ὑπερπερισσῶς.

Compare also the great number of multiple compounds, by which the classical store of such forms is increased (cf. ARieder, 'Die mit mehr als einer Präposition zusammengesetzten Verba [und überhaupt Wörter] des N [und A] T,' *Programm Gumbinnen* [1876]): ἀντιδιατίθημι, ἀντιπαρέρχομαι, ἀπεκδέχομαι, ἀπεκδύομαι, ἐμπεριπατέω, ἐπανα- παύομαι, ἐπανατρέχω, ἐπενδύομαι, ἐπιδιορθόω, ἐπισυνάγω, καταδιαιρέω, παρεισ- έρχομαι, παρεκφέρω, παρενθυμέομαι, παρεπιδημέω, προεπαγγέλλω and προκα- ταγγέλλω, συγκατανεύω, συγκαταψηφίζομαι, συναντιλαμβάνομαι, συνεπέρχο- μαι, συνεπιμαρτυρέω, συνυποκρίνομαι.—διαπαρατριβή, ἐγκατάλειμμα, ἐπισυνα- γωγή, ἐπισύστασις, συγκατάθεσις.—ἐπικατάρατος, παρείσακτος, παρεπίδημος, συνέκδημος.

But the common speech uses various other combinations as well. Verbal adjectives with ἀ-privative prefixed: ἀδιάκριτος, ἀδιάλειπτος, ἀκατάγνωστος, ἀκατακάλυπτος, ἀκατάληπτος, ἀκατάλυτος, ἀκατάπαυστος, ἀκατάστατος (also ἀκαταστατέω and ἀκαταστασία), ἀκατάσχετος, ἀλάλητος, ἀμάραντος, ἀμετάθετος, ἀμετανόητος, ἀναντίρρητος, ἀναπάρτιστος, ἀναπολόγητος, ἀνεκλάλητος, ἀνέκλειπτος, ἀνεξ- ιχνίαστος, ἀνεπαίσχυντος, ἀνυπόκριτος, ἀνυπότακτος, ἀπαράβατος, ἀπερινόητος, ἀπερίσπαστος, ἀπρόσιτος, ἄσκυλτος, ἀστήρικτος, ἀστομάχητος, ἀσύγκριτος, ἄτρε- πτος, ἄφθαρτος, ἄψευστος, ἀψηλάφητος. (Cf. also ἀδρανής, ἄθεσμος, ἀμέριμνος, ἀπροσδεής, ἀπρόσκοπος, ἄσπιλος, ἄτονος);—with δυσ- prefixed: δυσβάστακτος, δυσερμήνευτος, δυσνόητος;—with εὐ- prefixed: εὐάρεστος (also εὐαρεστέω and εὐα- ρέστησις), εὐλογητός, εὐμετάδοτος, εὐοικονόμητος, εὐπρόσδεκτος, εὐσυνείδητος. (Cf. other combinations with εὐ- in the Koine: εὐδοκέω and συνευδοκέω, εὐδόκησις, εὐδοκία, εὐκαιρέω, εὔκοπος, εὔλαλος, εὐποΐα, εὐπροσωπέω, εὐστάθεια, εὐσταθέω, εὐψυχέω);—with a noun prefixed: θεόπνευστος, πατροπαράδοτος, ποταμοφόρητος.

Compounds of various other kinds: ἀγαθοποιέω and ἀγαθοποιός, ἀλεκτοροφωνία, ἀλλογενής, ἀμνησίκακος, ἀνθρωπόμορφος, ἀργυροκόπος, ἀρσενοκοίτης, ἀρτιγέν- νητος, ἀρχάγγελος, ἀρχέγονος, ἀρχιποίμην, ἀρχισυνάγωγος, ἀρχιτρίκλινος, αὐτο- κατάκριτος, γαζοφυλάκιον, γονυπετέω, δεσμοφύλαξ, διετία, διθάλασσος, δικαιο- κρισία, δικαιοπραγία, δωροφορία, ἐθνάρχης, ἑτερόγλωσσος, ἑτερογνώμων, ἡδύο- σμον, ἡμιθανής, ἡμίξηρος, θεομάχος (θεομαχέω is older), θεοπρεπής, θεοσεβέω (θεοσέβεια and θεοσεβής are older), θυμομαχέω, ἱερουργέω, ἰσάγγελος, ἰσότιμος, ἰσχυροποιέω, κακουχέω, καλοποιέω, κενοδοξέω, κενοδοξία and κενόδοξος, κενό- σπουδος, κενοφωνία, κοινωφελής, κοσμοκράτωρ, κωμόπολις, λειποτακτέω, λιθο- βολέω, μακροθυμία, μακροθυμέω and μακρόθυμος; μακροχρόνιος, ματαιολογία and ματαιολόγος, ματαιοπονία, μεγαλο(ρ)ρημονέω and μεγαλο(ρ)ρημοσύνη, μεσουρά- νημα, μετριοπαθέω, μογιλάλος, νεκροφόρος, νυχθήμερον, οἰκοδεσπότης and οἰκοδε- σποτέω, οἰνόμελι, ὁλοκληρία (ὁλόκληρος is older), ὁλοτελής, ὁροθεσία, πανάρετος, πάνσεμνος, παντεπόπτης, παντοκράτωρ, πληροφορία (πληροφορέω is earlier, in isolated cases), πολιτάρχης, πολύτιμος, πρωτότοκος, ῥαδιούργημα, σαρδόνυξ, σιτο- μέτριον, στενοχωρέω, συλαγωγέω, υἱοθεσία, φιλαργυρέω (also ἀφιλάργυρος, while φιλάργυρος is attested even earlier), φίλαυτος, φιλήδονος, φιλόθεος, φιλοπρωτεύω, φρεναπάτης, χειραγωγέω and χειραγωγός, χειρόγραφον, χρεοφειλέτης. Cf. also the contractions κἀκεῖ, κἀκεῖθεν, κἀκεῖνος, κἀκεῖσε.

Adverbs of Hellenistic Greek: ἀντιπέρα; ἀπέναντι, ἔναντι and κατέναντι (Doric; see p. xiii above); ἐνώπιον, ἐξάπινα, ἐφάπαξ, καθά, καθεξῆς, καθώς, μακρόθεν, παιδιό- θεν, παμπληθεί, πανοικεί, πάντοτε, ῥητῶς, ῥοιζηδόν, ὑπέρ (q.v. 3).—Adjectival comparison of adverbs: ἐξώτερος, ἐσώτερος, κατώτερος.

Another way in which a language can be made more expressive is by adopting foreign words. The Koine had demonstrably incorporated many such terms, now found in our literature, before the New Testament period: ἀγγαρεύω, ἀσσάριον, βάϊον, βύσσος, γάζα, δηνάριον, εὐρακύλων, θριαμβεύω, Καῖσαρ, καλάνδαι, καμάρα, κεντυρίων, κερβικάριον, κῆνσος, κολωνία, κουστωδία, κράβαττος, κύμινον, λεγιών, λέντιον, λιβερτῖνος, λίτρα, μάκελλον (but see this entry), μίλιον, μόδιος, νάρδος, ξέστης(?), πραιτώριον, σάκκος, σάπφειρος, στατίων, συκάμινος, φαιλόνης (but see this entry also). The same may confidently be assumed of not a few others: ἄκκεπτα, δεπόσιτα, δεσέρτωρ, ἐξεμπλάριον, ζιζάνιον, καροῦχα, κοδράντης, κομφέκτωρ, μεμβράνα, ῥέδη, σικάριος, σιμικίνθιον, σουδάριον, σπεκουλάτωρ, συμψέλιον, τίτλος, φραγέλλιον and φραγελλόω, χῶρος (q.v. II).

The words quoted above are all clearly shown by secular witnesses to be part of the Hellenistic vocabulary (s. Bl-D. §5, 1). Naturally, it is possible that some of them were used in more ancient times, as in the case of θριαμβεύω, used by Ctesias.

A language improves not only through new formations and the appropriation of foreign words but also through the process by which terms which have long been available develop new possibilities of usage. Much-used words acquire a new meaning beside the older one, and sometimes repress the earlier meaning or even exclude it altogether. The change often consists in the rise of specialized or technical terms: ἀδελφός as a member of a religious community (s. ἀδελφός 2); ἀνακλίνω=to cause to recline at table (s. ἀνακλίνω 1b); ἀναπίπτω=lie down (at a meal—s. ἀναπίπτω 1); ἀναστροφή (q.v.)=way of life; ἀντιλαμβάνεσθαι=notice (q.v. 2); ἀντιλέγω=oppose (q.v. 2); ἀντίλημψις=help (q.v.); ἀπαρτίζω=accomplish (q.v.); ἀπέχω as a commercial technical term (q.v. 1); ἀποκόπτω=emasculate (q.v. 2); ἀποτάσσω in the middle (q.v. 1; 2); ἀρετή=a demonstration of divine power, miracle (q.v. 3); ἄριστον=noon meal, or meal in general (q.v. 2); ἄρτι of the present time in general (q.v. 3); τὴν ἀρχήν at all (s. ἀρχή 1b); αὐτάρκεια=contentment, a technical term of the Cynic-Stoic teaching concerning virtue (q.v. 2); βαρύτιμος=very expensive; βίος=way of life (q.v. 2); γενέσια=birthday celebration (q.v.); δαιμόνιον and δαίμων=evil spirit; δαιμονίζομαι=be possessed by an evil spirit; διαθήκη exclusively=last will and testament; διάκονος as a cult technical term; διαπονέομαι=be angry; δύναμις=personal supernatural being (q.v. 6); δῶμα=roof; ἐμβατεύω as a t.t. of the mystery religions (q.v. 4); ἐμβλέπω=observe with the eyes of the spirit (q.v. 2); ἐμβριμάομαι=scold (q.v.); ἐπαγγελία=promise; ἐπιθυμητής in the bad sense; ἐπιστρέφομαι=be converted (s. ἐπιστρέφω 2b); ἐπιτιμάω=punish (q.v. 2); ἐπιφάνεια, of the process by which the hidden divinity becomes visible; ἐπόπτης as a t.t. of the mysteries; ἐρεύγομαι=proclaim; ἐρωτάω=request; εὐαγγέλιον=good news, occasionally with a religious tinge (s. this and εὐαγγελιστής); εὐσχήμων=distinguished, of high repute; εὐχαριστέω=give thanks, sometimes to a deity (q.v. 2); θυρεός=a shield (large as a door); κεφαλίς=book in the form of a scroll; κοίμησις of death (q.v. 2); κρύσταλλος=rock-crystal; λαλιά no longer exclusively in the bad sense; λειτουργέω and derivatives, of religious service; μάρμαρος=marble; μέθυσος of males; μνημεῖον=grave (q.v. 2); νήφω in the metaphorical sense; ὀψάριον=fish; παρακαλέω=request (q.v. 3); παρουσία in the technical sense (q.v. 2b); παρρησία=frankness, joyousness (q.v. 3a, b); περισπάω=occupy fully (q.v. 2); πήρα=beggar's knapsack (q.v.); πλῆθος=community (q.v. 2bδ); πνεῦμα and ψυχή as contrasting terms (s. πνευματικός 2aγ); ποιμήν as a religious t.t. (q.v. 2bγ); πρεσβύτερος as the designation of an official (q.v. 2b); πτῶμα=corpse; πύργος=farm or business building (q.v. 2); ῥύμη=street; σεβάζομαι of religious reverence; σταυρόω=crucify; στέγω=endure; στενοχωρία in the metaphorical sense; στόμαχος=stomach; συνίστημι=show, prove (q.v. I 1c); σχολή=school; φθάνω=arrive (q.v. 2).

A considerable number of older words have been appropriated as technical terms from the Roman civil and military administration: ἀπογραφή = census; ἑκατόνταρχος (ἑκατοντάρχης) = centurio; ἔπαρχος = praefectus; ἐπίτροπος = procurator; ἡγεμών and ἡγεμονεύειν of the imperial governor; ῥαβδοῦχος = lictor; σεβαστός = Augustus; σπεῖρα = cohors; στρατηγοί = duumviri coloniae; στρατόπεδον = legio; χιλίαρχος = tribunus militum; κράτιστος = vir egregius; τὸ ἱκανὸν ποιεῖν τινι = satisfacere alicui; λαμβάνειν τὸ ἱκανόν = satis accipere (s. ἱκανός 1c). Other terms of this kind appear for the first time in the Hellenistic period: ἀνθύπατος = proconsul (ἀνθυπατεύειν); ἐπαρχεία and ἡ ἐπάρχειος = provincia (from the older ἔπαρχος).

We have yet to consider those words which our literature, primarily the New Testament, either shares with the LXX alone, or for which it is the only witness, and which for this reason play a unique role as 'voces biblicae' in the philology of the Greek Bible. Before the systematic investigation of the popular speech, their number was much larger. The fact that the advances in our knowledge have freed one after another of these words from their isolation and demonstrated that they were part of the living language forces upon us the conclusion that the great mass of biblical words for which we do not yet have secular evidence also belong to that language. * Of course, there are some formations with regard to which it is not only possible, but in some instances very probable, that the translators of the Old Testament formed them for their own purposes and then handed them on to the composers of our literature, while the latter, in turn, created other terms to satisfy their own needs. The Hellenistic spirit, however, makes itself felt even in these cases through the fact that those forms are preferred for which we have been able to establish a preference in the common speech. Here belong, for instance, ἀγαλλιάομαι and ἀγαλλίασις,† ἁγιασμός, αἴνεσις, ἀλίσγημα, ἀλλοτριεπίσκοπος, ἀνθρωπαρεσκέω and ἀνθρωπάρεσκος, ἀνταπόδομα and ἀνταποδότης, ἀντιμισθία, ἀξιαγάπητος and other combinations with ἄξιος in Ignatius, ἀποκαταλλάσσω, ἐθελοθρησκία, ἑτεροδιδασκαλέω, ἑτεροζυγέω, θεοδρόμος, θεομακάριστος, θεομακαρίτης, θεοπρεσβευτής, θυσιαστήριον, κακοδιδασκαλία, καλοδιδάσκαλος, καρδιογνώστης, κατακληρονομέω, λυτρωτής, μισθαποδοσία and μισθαποδότης, νομοδιδάσκαλος, ὀλιγοπιστία and ὀλιγόπιστος, ὀλοθρευτής, ὀφθαλμοδουλία, πατριάρχης, πολυσπλαγχνία and πολύσπλαγχνος, πρεσβυτέριον, πρωτοκαθεδρίτης, σκανδαλίζω and σκάνδαλον, σκληροκαρδία, σπλαγχνίζομαι, ψευδάδελφος, ψευδοδιδασκαλία and ψευδοδιδάσκαλος, ψευδοπροφήτης.

Likewise it is certain that there are specific expressions for biblical or Jewish or primitive Christian things which, like the things they denote, are limited to the Old Testament (and Jewish writers influenced by it) and our literature (together with the Christian writings dependent upon it): ἀκροβυστία and ἀκρόβυστος, ἀντίχριστος, ἀπερίτμητος, ἀποσυνάγωγος, βάπτισμα, ἐγκαίνια, εἰδωλεῖον, εἰδωλόθυτος; εἰδωλολατρία, εἰδωλολατρέω, εἰδωλολάτρης; κατείδωλος, μοσχοποιέω, ὀλοκαύτωμα, χριστέμπορος, χριστομαθία, χριστόνομος, ψευδαπόστολος, ψευδόχριστος.

* The following lists have become noticeably shorter when compared with those of 1928. The words that have been omitted are now demonstrably part of the common language; we need no longer rely on conjecture.

† There are no secular occurrences of ἀγαλλίασις. The reference to Ps.-Callisthenes in Liddell-Scott is based on the inadequate edition of CMüller (1846), where it is found at the end of 2, 22. In the oldest form attainable of the *Historia Alex. Mag.* of Ps.-Callisthenes, prepared by WKroll in 1926, the word is found nowhere, not even in the apparatus. It belongs, evidently, to one of the many later reworkings of the original text of Ps.-Callisthenes. But this reworking obviously took place under biblical influence. In addition to other things, 2, 42 (which also is omitted in Kroll) has Alexander say: εἰς τὴν Ἰουδαίαν παρήμην γῆν. Οἵτινες (οἱ ἐκεῖσε) ζῶντι θεῷ ἔδοξαν λατρεύειν, ὃς ἐμὲ ἐποίησε πρὸς αὐτοὺς ἀγαθὴν ἔχειν γνώμην, καὶ ὅλη μου ἡ ψυχὴ πρὸς αὐτὸν ἦν.... Κἀκεῖσε [in Alexandria] πάντας τοὺς θεοὺς ἐξουθένισα, ὡς οὐκ ὄντας θεούς. τὸν δὲ ἐπὶ τῶν Σεραφὶμ θεὸν ἀνεκήρυξα.

In the case of most of the words found only in the LXX and our literature, it is highly improbable that they originated in Jewish or early Christian circles. This is, at any rate, a totally unwarranted assumption when secular speech exhibits closely related forms and there is nothing specifically Jewish or early Christian or even religious about these 'biblical' words. Due allowance must be made for the chance which has preserved one word while allowing another to disappear. It is pure accident that προσευχή = prayer, so common in the LXX and our literature, has come to light in only one pagan papyrus. If this had not turned up, we would have had another 'vox biblica.' Why should παροικία be 'biblical' when πάροικος in the same sense is quite common? Who would be so rash as to deduce a rule from the fact that καταλιθάζω is found only in Christian writers, while in the LXX it is καταλιθοβολέω, and in secular writers καταλιθόω?

In my judgment, the following 'biblical words,' for example, belong to the common language: ἀγαθωσύνη, ἀδιαφθορία, ἀκρογωνιαῖος, ἀνακαίνωσις, ἀπάρτισμα, ἀπελεγμός, ἀποδεκατόω, ἀποκαραδοκία, ἀφθορία, ἀφιλάγαθος, γόγγυσος and γογγυστής, διενθυμέομαι, διώκτης, ἑδραίωμα, εἰρηνοποιέω, ἐκμυκτηρίζω, ἐλεγμός, ἐμπαιγμονή and ἐμπαίκτης, ἐπιδιατάσσομαι, ἐπικαταλλάσσομαι, ἐπιπόθησις and ἐπιποθία, εὐνουχία, ἥττημα, ἱεράτευμα, καταλαλιά, κατοικητήριον, κερματιστής, κρυσταλλίζω, λαξευτός, λογομαχέω, ματαίωμα, μέθυσμα, ὀξυχολία, ὀρθοποδέω, ὀρθοτομέω, ὀχλοποιέω, παγιδεύω, παιδοφθορέω, παραπικραίνω and παραπικρασμός, παραφρονία, παροργισμός, προενάρχομαι, πρόσχυσις, ῥαντισμός, σινιάζω, συζητητής, φρεναπατάω, φυλακίζω.

More important than the appearance of newly formed words is the fact that our literature, sometimes following the LXX, sometimes apart from it, uses many words of the older or even of the common Greek in new meanings: τὰ ἄζυμα (s. ἄζυμος 1); ἀνάθεμα (q.v. 2); ἀναφέρω as a t.t. of sacrificial practice (q.v. 2); ἀπαρχή = first convert (q.v. 2); ἀποκαλύπτω of divine revelations of every possible kind; ἀπόστολος as t.t. (q.v. 3); βαπτίζω = baptize (q.v. 2); δέησις exclusively = prayer; διάβολος = devil (q.v. 2); διασπορά (q.v.); ἐπισκέπτομαι of a visitation of divine grace (q.v. 3); ἐπισκοπή = visitation and = office of overseer (q.v. 2 and 3); εὐλογέω and εὐλογία in the sense of 'blessing' and 'consecrating'; κιβωτός = ark and = ark of the covenant; μάρτυς = martyr (q.v. 3); μετάνοια with definite religious coloring; παιδεύω = discipline, punish (q.v. 2); παράδεισος (q.v.); παρασκευή = day of preparation; παρουσία of the coming of Christ (q.v. 2b); πεντηκοστή = Pentecost; προσήλυτος as a t.t.; σκηνή (τοῦ μαρτυρίου); φυλακτήριον = phylactery; χήρα as a t.t. (q.v. 2).—Cf. also the words used by Christian piety with a connotation of its own, like δικαιόω and πιστεύω together with their derivatives; πνεῦμα, χάρις and the like.*

Sometimes it is plainly Hebrew influence which gives special meaning to words and expressions in the LXX and our literature. τὰ ἔθνη = 'the heathen, Gentiles' comes about when that plural form is used to translate גוֹים, a rendering that was more natural for the translators of the LXX, because among the Greeks it had become customary to call foreigners ἔθνη (s. ἔθνος 2). πρόσωπον λαμβάνειν is נָשָׂא פָנִים and there are found in our literature in addition to this expression (borrowed from the LXX) the forms προσωπολημπτέω, προσωπολήμπτης, and προσωπολημψία (s. πρόσωπον 1b and cf. there under b-e still other O.T. expressions using πρόσωπον). Cf. ῥῆμα = thing (q.v. 2); ῥίζα = root-shoot, sprout (q.v. 2); σάκκος = mourning garment; πᾶσα σάρξ (s. σάρξ 3); στόμα

---

* S. FWGingrich, Prolegomena to a Study of the Christian Element in the Vocabulary of the NT and Apost. Fathers, in Search the Scriptures, memorial vol. for RTStamm, Leiden, '69, 173-8.

μαχαίρης (s. στόμα 2); υἱός with a genitive of the thing, like υἱὸς γεέννης (s. υἱός 1cδ). Cf. also τέκνον (q.v. 2f).

The Semitic coloring is especially plain where Hebrew and Aramaic words or expressions, Hellenized or not, appear as a foreign element: ἀλληλούϊα, ἀμήν, βάτος = bath (Hebrew measure), γέεννα, κόρος, μάννα, πάσχα, Σαβαώθ, σάββατον, σατάν and σατανᾶς, σάτον, σίκερα, ὕσσωπος, ὡσαννά.

A special place must be accorded those expressions which originated not in the Old Testament but in the Aramaic basis of the gospel tradition or from the religious language of the primitive community: ἀββᾶ; ἐλωΐ; ἐφφαθά; κορβᾶν and κορβανᾶς; λαμά; μαμωνᾶς; μαρὰν ἀθά; ῥαββί; ῥαββουνί; ῥαβιθά (q.v.); ῥακά; σαβαχθάνι; ταλιθὰ κούμ.

Spoken Jewish-Greek as an entity to be clearly differentiated from the language of the people in general is something that can rarely be established, though more often suspected (cf. Bl-D. §4, 3). As for the influence of the LXX, every page of this lexicon shows that it outweighs all other influences on our literature. In the body of the work will also be found references to the important recent literature for lexicographical investigations, as occasion requires. Cf. also U. von Wilamowitz, *Geschichte der griechischen Sprache* (1928).

It is the purpose of this lexicon to facilitate the understanding of texts that were composed in the Late Greek described above. This kind of Greek was the mother-tongue of those who wrote them (CCTorrey, *The Four Gospels* [1933], p. 243; GBjörck, Ἡν Διδασκων [1940], pp. 123f), no matter how well they may have been acquainted with Semitic idiom. Likewise, those who heard and read their messages spoke the same kind of Greek. They, at least, were no longer conscious of Semitic originals upon which, in one form or another, some of those writings were based. With regard to the authors, too, we do well to maintain a cautious reserve on this question, since the solution of the problem of Semitic influence* is burdened with so much uncertainty at the present time (s. Björck, *loc. cit.*).† We shall do well to have recourse to Semitic originals only in cases where the Greek of our literature either cannot be understood from the background of the contemporary language at all or at least not sufficiently well.

In the Greek world to which the early Christian writings belong there were not only gentile literary men, but Jewish authors as well; this fact militates against the unity of later Greek literature at a point that is important for its understanding. We are incomparably better informed concerning the language of Hellenistic Judaism than we are about its gentile counterpart. How easy it is, comparatively speaking, to gain a conception of the language of the LXX, Philo, and the Epistle of Aristeas, of the Greek Enoch and the Testaments of the 12 Patriarchs! Because of the work already done, we can learn a good deal about Ps.-Phocylides and Josephus without too great an expenditure of time. These works comprise the greater part of the available sources. On the other hand, for gentile writers we must depend on chance references in the lexicons, on sections from the ancient gatherers of annotations that have survived in literature, and what modern studies‡ have contributed to New Testament philology or to the Koine. This means that we are comparing two entities, which, when viewed together, must present a distorted picture;

* For references on this subject see Bl-D. §4 w. app.

† Especially the handling of the problem of whether and to what extent we are able to recover the living speech of Jesus which was behind the Greek reports of his teaching must be left to the daring and the specialized work of the small group of those really qualified to do it.

‡ Because of their fragmentary character, these studies are only partly available even to those who industriously seek them out.

only the one can be seen in its proper dimensions, while the other has been woefully retarded in its development. It is all too easy to yield to the inclination to assume that Jewish influence is present, when, in reality, a typical Greek sentiment may be expressed in a Jewish-Greek source. In this case we can bring about a greater degree of equality by giving gentile Greek literature more of a chance to speak for itself than it has had in the past.

This will serve to indicate the general direction in which the third and fourth editions (of Bauer's *Wörterbuch*) have departed from the second. Yet, as is easy to understand, only a beginning has been made so far. Systematic, connected reading of secular Greek literature can and must bring to light with still greater clarity its relation to the Greek used by the earliest Christians. A few observations, made while the fourth edition was in process of being published, but too late to be included in it, may serve to demonstrate how far even the latest edition is from being exhaustive in this respect, and how far removed it is from forcing upon a (possible) collaborator the unwanted role of mere gleaner in this wide field. This or that item submitted here may contribute a little to an understanding of pertinent facts. Yet how important is this result, too, when we wish to know what effect our literature produced on people who were thoroughly steeped in pagan thought, feeling, and custom!

The following linguistic phenomena, not included in the fourth edition, are to be found in non-Christian Greek literature.

αἰσχρολογία='obscene speech,' Diod. S. 5, 4, 7;
  αἰσχρός= 'obscene,' Ps.-Demetr., Eloc. 151.
βιβλίδιον = 'letter,' Polyaenus 7, 33, 1.
γένος (1 at Rv 22: 16) τινός of a single offspring: Hom.; Soph., Ant. 1117; esp. Epimenides [VI BC] no. 457 fgm. 3 Jac. ἐγὼ (Musaeus) γένος εἰμὶ Σελήνης.
ἐγείρω (1aγ) τὸν λίθον='lift' or 'move a stone from its place': Seleucus of Alexandria [I AD] no. 341 fgm. 4 Jac.
εἰμί (I 5) the short clause of J 10: 22 is like Polyaenus 7, 44, 2 πόλεμος ἦν.
ἐκλείπω Lk 22: 32 of faith: 'fail, die out.' So Plut., Lyc. 31, 8 of a race of men.
ἐλπίζω (1) τὰ ἐλπιζόμενα: Polyaenus 3, 9, 11.
θηρεύω 'go on a hunting expedition' after statements of someone, in order to use them against him: Pla., Gorg. 489B ὀνόματα θηρεύειν...ἐάν τις ῥήματι ἀμάρτῃ.
ἴδε (4) 'hear': schol. on Pla. 130c Ἀλκιβιάδης, ἴδε, τί λέγει.
καταπατέω (1b on Lk 12: 1) Polyaenus 4, 3, 21 ὑπ' ἀλλήλων καταπατούμενοι.
κέραμος (2 on Lk 5: 19)='roof-tile': Pausanias 1, 13, 8.
κρίνω (4aα) κρίνομαι ἐπί τινος='be judged before someone': schol. on Hes., Op. 9.
μαρτυρία (2c, end) God's 'good testimony': Dio Chrys. 16[33], 12 τῆς μεγίστης ἔτυχε μαρτυρίας παρὰ τοῦ δαιμονίου.
μάρτυς (2c) of a man as witness for a divine message: Epict. 3, 24, 112f; 3, 26, 28.
ὁμολογέω (5) τινί 'praise someone': Dio Chrys. 10[11], 147.
πόσος (1) πόσῳ foll. by comp.: Polyaenus 3, 9, 25 πόσῳ ἡμεῖς ἐκείνοις φοβερώτεροι;
ῥιζόω (end) ῥιζοῦσθαι ἐν='be firmly rooted in': Nicander, Theriaca 183.
ὑδρία λιθίνη J 2: 6: Athen. 13 p. 589B.
χωλός symbolically: Pla., Leg. 1 p. 634A; Plut., Cim. 16, 10.

Other characteristics which appeared in the fourth edition as Jewish peculiarities have now been found in pagan sources.

ἅγιος (1bα) of a pagan: Ramsay, Phrygia no. 232, 8 Γάϊος, ὡς ἅγιος, ὡς ἀγαθός.

ἀθλητής fig. as early as Gorgias (EScheel, *De Gorgianae disciplinae vestigiis* [Diss., Rostock, 1890], p. 13). Also Dio Chrys. 2, 18.

ἀκοῇ (1b) ἀκούω occurs in the New Testament only as a quot. from the Old Testament but can hardly be called a 'reproduction of the Hebrew,' since it is also found in Polyaenus, Exc. 55, 2.

ἀποχωρέω='fall away, desert': Sb 7835 [I BC] the cult brotherhood of Zeus Hypsistos forbids its members to desert the (monarchic) ἡγούμενος, to whom they all owe obedience, and thus to cause σχίσματα.

ἀρνέομαι (3d)='deny, reject,' with a thing as object: Lycophron 348.

διάκονος (2) as fem.: Epict. 3, 7, 28; 2, 23, 8.

εἰσακούω (2a)='hear, grant' of God: Quintus Smyrnaeus 12, 154.

ἐκχέω (1, at Ac 1: 18) of the entrails: Quintus Smyrnaeus 8, 302; 9, 190.

ἐξέρχομαι ἔξω τινός (s.v. ἔξω 2b) Polyaenus 3, 7, 3.

ἐπιστρέφεσθαι (2b) πρός τινα='turn to someone': Diog. L. 3, 25.

ἡσυχάζω (4)='have rest': Diog. L. 3, 21.

κάμνω (3)='die': Crinagoras [I BC–I AD] 25, 1 [ed. M. Rubensohn (1888)] καμοῦσιν ὡς ζωοῖς 'for dead as well as for living'; Dionys. Byz. [200 AD] §109; 110 [ed. RGüngerich (1927)]; Epigr. Gr. 321, 8.

καρδία (1bβ) as the seat of the intellect, as early as an 'ancient poet,' perhaps Hesiod: fgm. 247 Rzach.

κρίμα (2)='decree': *Explor. arch. de la Galatie* etc., par GPerrot, etc., I [1872], inscr. no. 25 [II AD].

λύτρον ὑπέρ τινος Lucian, Dial. Deor. 4, 2.

λύω (2a) τι ἀπό τινος at Lk 13: 15: Quintus Smyrnaeus 4, 373.

μανθάνω (1) w. inf. foll.: Aristoxenus [300 BC] fgm. 96 [ed. FWehrli (1945)].

μανθάνω (4) at Hb 5: 8: schol. on Pla. 222B ἐὰν μὴ πάθῃς, οὐ μὴ μάθῃς.

μέμφομαι (end) at Ro 9: 19 'find fault, complain': Ps.-Pla., Axiochus 7 p. 368A.

νεφέλη as a medium for snatching a person away as Ac 1: 9; I Th 4: 17; better parallels than those quoted from Josephus are to be found: Dosiadas [III BC] no. 458 fgm. 5 Jac. νέφος ἥρπασεν αὐτὸν (Ganymede) εἰς οὐρανόν; Ps.-Apollodorus 2, 7, 7, 12 (Heracles).

οἰκία (3)='household' at Phil 4: 22: Diog. L. 5, 75 on Demetrius of Phalerum ἦν ἐκ τῆς Κόνωνος οἰκίας.

ὁράω (1aβ, end)='perceive' in the sense 'hear': Polyaenus 7, 14, 2; schol. on Nicander, Ther. 165 ὁρῶ οἷα λέγεις.

πειράζω (2) of God putting men to the test: Ps.-Apollodorus 3, 7, 7, 4.

πληρόω (4a) of the fulfilment of divine prophecy: Polyaenus 1, 18 τοῦ λογίου πεπληρω-μένου.

ποιέω of God as the Creator of the universe (s.v. κόσμος 2, end): Epict. 4, 7, 6. As far as I know, the same meaning cannot be quoted for κτίζω from secular sources today. But it certainly is not insignificant that κτίστης in this sense was used of pagan divinities even in pre-Christian times.

φεύγω (5) ἀπὸ τοῦ προσώπου at Rv 20: 11: Ctesias, Pers. 2 φυγεῖν ἀπὸ προσώπου Κυρίου; schol. on Nicander, Ther. 377. Herodas the writer of mimes 8, 59 has, in a passage inaccurately cited by this scholion, ἔρρ' ἐκ προσώπου 'get out of my sight.'

φρονέω (1) ἄλλο='have a different opinion': Hdt. 7, 205, 3.

The closer Judaism and Hellenism approach each other in relation to the understanding of early Christianity, the more insistent becomes the question of how we may give proper credit to both of them. The use of the same words here and there does not mean that the language is identical. Both sides present their own challenge, and the author of a lexicon that seeks to shed light on primitive Christianity from the Greek world should have an ear for both. He must reckon with the possibility that what, for instance, Paul said, conditioned as he was by his Jewish past, was not always understood in the same terms by his gentile Christian hearers, who were also unable to dissociate themselves entirely from their previous ways of thought. Certainly, speaker and hearer were better attuned to each other when Paul addressed himself to Christians among whom he had worked, and the apostle was more certain to be understood correctly under these circumstances than when he wrote to people who did not know him personally. Yet even in Corinth, where Paul worked so long, there was a notable lack of understanding. It was not only that the old immorality lived on uncontrolled in some circles. The state of 'being long accustomed to idols' (I Cor 8: 7) had not yet died out for some of them. In general, there is much in I Cor that we can begin to understand only after we have made an effort to form some conception of pagan Greek life and thought.

When Paul speaks of sacrifice, of the wrath of God or the δικαιοσύνη θεοῦ, it is quite correct to understand his words from the standpoint of Judaism. But what about his public, who have heard these words before, but with different connotations and associations? His hearers certainly did not feel themselves challenged to make an eschatological decision as often as the apostle summoned them to it. With this in mind we might conclude that sometimes there are two meanings for the same passage, one from the standpoint of the writer and another which becomes evident when one puts one's self in the place of the recipient, intellectually and spiritually; the lexicographer naturally feels an obligation to draw the proper conclusions. The way a passage is understood by its first readers has an immediate effect upon its later interpretation. We know how hard it was to understand Paul's letters (2 Pt 3: 15, 16), and in what manifold and sometimes contradictory fashion they have been interpreted.

I give herewith a few examples (not found in the fourth edition) to illustrate the possibility that different meanings have been associated with similar words.

On πολίτευμα Phil 3: 20: Epict. 2, 23, 38; 39 'you have gone on a journey to return thither where you were born, and where you are a πολίτης' (39=εἰς τὴν πατρίδα 38). Olympiodorus in Platonis Phaedonem [ed. WNorvin (1913)] p. 122, 8 says of the wise man συμπολιτεύεσθαι τοῖς θεοῖς καὶ συνοικονομεῖν.

On κρίνω (4bβ) 1 Cor 6: 2, on the saints as fellow-rulers with God: Epict., Ench. 15; Sallustius 21 p. 36, 14 [ed. ADNock (1926)] τὸν ὅλον κόσμον συνδιοικοῦσιν ἐκείνοις (the pious with the gods).

On εἰρήνη (3) τοῦ θεοῦ: Epict. 3, 13, 12 εἰρήνη ὑπὸ τοῦ θεοῦ κεκηρυγμένη διὰ τοῦ λόγου (=philosophy).

On I Cor 7: 34f: Epict. 3, 22, 69 ἀπερίσπαστον εἶναι δεῖ τὸν Κυνικὸν ὅλον πρὸς τῇ διακονίᾳ τοῦ θεοῦ, coupled with an exhortation to keep one's self free from marriage and other earthly bonds. In such a case would a Greek not feel himself deeply moved by the apostle's preaching? Would he not receive its words with connotations familiar to him, and so pass them on to others?

Sometimes one gets the distinct impression that the Greek must have failed to understand the basic meaning of a New Testament author. He may have been led in another direction by his own background and have lacked a knowledge of Jewish and Old Testament matters which the author took for granted.

On Mt 1: 17, a better parallel than can be found in rabbinic literature may be pointed out in the numerological statements found as early as Hellanicus [400 B.C.] with γενεαί (no. 323a fgm. 22a Jac.): ἐννέα γενεαῖς ὕστερον . . . ἐξ γενεαῖς ὕστερον . . . τρισὶ γενεαῖς ὕστερον . . . .

Βοανηργές Mk 3: 17 has less light shed on it by the unsatisfactory explanations of the word's meaning than by the fact that, among the Greeks, pairs of brothers or sisters are often referred to by a special name: Apollodorus no. 244 fgm. 210 Jac. Σταγόνιον καὶ "Ανθις ἀδελφαί· αὗται 'Αφύαι ἐκαλοῦντο, ὅτι λευκαὶ κτλ. In Diog. L. 2, 52 Gryllus and Diodorus, the two sons of Xenophon, Διόσκουροι ἐπεκαλοῦντο. In schol. on Pla. 118E Ξάνθιππος καὶ Πάραλος οἱ Περικλέους υἱοί, οὓς καὶ βλιττομάμμας ἐκάλουν.

On Mt 15: 27=Mk 7: 28: Aelius Dionysius [II AD] α, 159 [ed. HErbse (1950)] ψωμὸς εἰς ὃν ἐκματτόμενοι τὰς χεῖρας μετὰ τὸ δεῖπνον ἐρρίπτουν τοῖς κυσίν.

On Lk 6: 15; Ac 1: 13: the word ζηλωτής as a surname of the second Simon may have been meant by the author to have the sense 'zealot'; his readers were much more likely to understand it as meaning 'enthusiastic adherent,' which it has so often meant (Polyaenus 5, 2, 22; Diog. L. 2, 113 al.).

At Mt 18: 22 the number ἑβδομηκοντάκις ἑπτά probably comes from Gen 4: 24. But Gentiles did not need to know this in order to understand that Mt means to indicate a number that is large out of all proportion. In a story taken from older accounts, Plut., Mor. 245D uses the number 7,777 for the same purpose (cf. Polyaenus 8, 33).

On Ro 13: 1b: here Paul was possibly thinking of Wisdom 6: 3 and similar Jewish sayings. But the Roman Christians were probably more impressed and encouraged by the 'old saying' (Artemidorus 2, 36 p. 135, 24, also 2, 69 p. 161, 17) τὸ κρατοῦν δύναμιν ἔχει θεοῦ 'the government derives its power from God.' Similar sentiments are found as early as Hesiod, Theogony 96. This was an old Greek belief (HFränkel, *Dichtung und Philosophie des frühen Griechentums* [1951], p. 141, 5).

On 1 Cor 9: 9: the apostle quotes the Law of Moses. But in connection with the words immediately following, the Greeks might easily think of their own proverb τῶν δ᾽ ὄνων οὔ μοι μέλει (Aelius Dionysius τ, 35).

On 1 Cor 15: 32: the writer certainly has Is 22: 13 in mind, but it is just as certain that his readers are reminded of a very common and primitive piece of worldly wisdom brought to their attention by the tombs along the roads (e.g., *Explor.*, etc., par Perrot, etc. [see p. xxiii above], inscr. no. 78, 11).

The writer of the Revelation, too, is no exception. When in his vision (10: 9f) he swallows a book that 'makes' his stomach 'bitter,' the concept comes without doubt from Ezk 2: 8; 3: 1-3. But would the gentile Christians of Asia Minor not rather be reminded of the dream-books that interpreted ἐσθίειν βιβλία to mean an early death (Artem. of Ephesus 2, 45 p. 149, 6)?

And in connection with Babylon the Harlot (Rv 17: 4) would they not think of something like the image portrayed on the painting of Cebes [I AD] 5, 1? Sitting on the throne is the beautifully adorned woman 'Απάτη, ἣ ἐν τῇ χειρὶ ἔχει ποτήριόν τι. She gives men wine to drink (ποτίζει Cebes 5, 2 as Rv 14: 8) and thus leads them astray (πλανάω as Rv 18: 23).

Artemidorus 2, 70 p. 167, 25 asks the readers of his books μήτε προσθεῖναι μήτε τι τῶν ὄντων ἀφελεῖν, and in 168, 2ff he commends his work to the protection of Apollo, who commissioned him to write it and who helped him carry it to completion. Is this not a pagan commentary on Rv 22: 18, 19 (and 1: 9ff), and is it not worth more for a living understanding of these passages than the Old Testament parallels printed in heavy type in the editions?

What we can learn here and there about communal meals among the Greeks will, perhaps, shed some light on the observance of the Lord's Supper in Corinth. The references that we have come from the vicinity of that city, and they illuminate both the observance and the words used in connection with it. In order to gain a proper insight into this point it seems to me that we must do more than point out that rabbinical literature permits us to trace a Hebrew expression for 'sacred cup' back to about 300 A.D.*

Diog. L. 8, 35 has Pythagoras say that the εἶς ἄρτος (cf. 1 Cor 10: 17) had served as a symbol of the bond between φίλοι. Theopompus (in Athen. 4, 31 p. 149D) tells us about banquets in Arcadia at which the diners gathered about *one* table on which the food for all of them was set; likewise, they all drank from the same jar. κοινωνία with the genitive (1 Cor 10: 16) is the common possession or enjoyment of something (Diog. L. 7, 124 al.). The eating together of the *one* loaf, which means the body of Christ (11: 24), brings the many together in *one* body (10: 17). We read of communal meals in Crete in the historian Pyrgion (Hellenistic times; no. 467 fgm. 1 Jac.) that they were consecrated by the offering of a libation with prayer (μετ' εὐφημίας) at the beginning of them. When the offering has been made, the food is distributed to all present. The νεώτατοι waited on the tables.

Is it too bold to look upon the Corinthian sacral meal as a Christianized communal dinner at which the consecration was brought about by a calling to mind of what had happened on the last evening of Jesus' life? The unseemly conduct that Paul condemned (11: 17–22) had a strong 'heathen' tone to it. And similar occurrences were a cause for concern to serious-minded Greeks long before this time. Dicaearchus [300 BC] fgm. 59 [ed. FWehrli (1944)] complains of carelessness and encroachment upon the rights of others at common meals, which should really serve to make brothers of those who eat together. Eratosthenes [III BC] no. 241 fgm. 16 Jac. waxes bitter over the fact that at the festival of the Lagynophoria each one eats what he has brought along and drinks from his own (ἴδιος as 1 Cor 11: 21) bottle, which he has brought with him. His judgment is as severe as that of the apostle: 'such a festal meeting is a dirty thing, ἀνάγκη γὰρ τὴν σύνοδον γίνεσθαι παμμιγοῦς ὄχλου.'

There is at least something comparable to the unworthy partaking of the Eucharist and its results (1 Cor 11: 29f). Simplicius in Epict. p. 93, 51–3 Düb. tells in detail how the divine power (ἐνέργεια) passes over to first-fruits that are offered with a pure heart. Someone, so he says, has asserted that he was cured of his epilepsy by eating such first-fruits. With the unseemly conduct described by Paul we may contrast the conduct ἀπὸ ζωῆς καθαρᾶς in Simplicius 1. 49. Just as the eating of the consecrated food, laden with divine power, can bring healing when it is accompanied by a pure life, so in Corinth participation in the Lord's Supper, coupled with the wrong kind of conduct, can bring illness or even death.

Finally, one more proposal, which may possibly illuminate the meaning ἀγάπη (II) 'love-feast.' Scholia on Pla. 112B: the common meals of the Lacedaemonians καλεῖται

---

* Similarly, the importance of the word in the services of the church at Corinth cannot be understood from the viewpoint of the synagogue (WBauer, *Der Wortgottesdienst der ältesten Christen* [1930], pp. 19ff). On the other hand, it is from 1 Cor that we learn how tolerant Paul could be of heathen customs (eating meat offered to idols, baptism for the dead). And the same letter proclaims as one of the basic principles of his mission to the Gentiles: 'To those who do not know the Mosaic law I became as one who does not concern himself about it, in order to win them' (9: 21).

φιλίτια, ἐπεὶ φιλίας συναγωγά ἐστιν. If it is permissible to see in ἀγάπη a transfer of φιλία into the Christian realm, this passage can shed light on the custom as well as the vocabulary of the Christians.

At times the information in the fourth edition (of Bauer's *Wörterbuch*) seems in need of correction or supplementation.

On ἁρπάζω (2b, end) τι Mt 11: 12. The meaning 'plunder, pillage something thoroughly' is also possible: Libanius, Or. 1 p. 147, 4 F. κώμας ἁρπάζειν; Polyaenus 8, 11 τῆς πόλεως ἁρπαγή.

On ἱκανός (1c) Mk 15: 15 τὸ ἱκανὸν ποιεῖν τινι better: 'do someone a favor' Diog. L. 4, 50.

On καρτερέω Hb 11: 27. The translation 'endure, hold out' is hardly correct. This is apart from the question whether this quality is particularly characteristic of Moses. The participle with καρτερεῖν does not express an accompanying circumstance, but the respect in which someone is 'enduring' or 'constant.' Diod. Sic. 14, 65, 4 μέχρι τίνος καρτερή-σομεν ταῦτα πάσχοντες; 'how long will we continue to endure this?' Arrian, Anab. 7, 8, 3 οὐκοῦν σιγῇ ἔχοντες ἐκαρτέρησαν='they therefore continued in silence.' Ps.-Dicaear-chus, Βίος Ἑλλάδος [ed. MFuhr (1841), p. 141, 1. 11=CMüller, Geogr. Gr. min. I (1855) p. 99 I] ἀκούων καρτ.='keep on listening.' So in Hb 11: 27, giving the reason for his fearlessness: 'for he kept his eyes constantly upon Him who is unseen.'

On ῥύομαι 2 Cor 1: 10a. ῥ. ἐκ τοῦ θανάτου does not mean 'preserve from death' in general, but 'rescue from a(n actual) situation in which death was threatened': Aristoxenus [300 BC] fgm. 113 [ed. FWehrli (1945)] ῥύεσθαι καὶ ἐρύεσθαι διαφορὰν ἔχει πρὸς ἄλληλα.—τὸ μὲν γὰρ ῥύεσθαι ἐκ θανάτου ἕλκειν, τὸ δὲ ἐρύεσθαι φυλάττειν.

On λυπέω (1) abs.: in 2 Cor 2: 5 it is more than 'vex' or 'cause grief.' Polyaenus 8, 47 uses it of the severe humiliation felt by a king whose subjects have deposed him.

On πῶλος I have presented material which I hope is significant and more to the point in a study that appeared in the *Journal of Biblical Literature*, LXXII (1953), 220-9.

In the case of certain entries, new and better examples have turned up.

On ἀδελφός (1). There is no longer any doubt in my mind that ἀδελφοί can mean 'brothers and sisters' in any number. There are passages that scarcely permit any other interpretation. Ptolemaeus, Apotelesm. 3, 5 has as its subject περὶ γονέων and 3, 6 περὶ ἀδελφῶν, divided into male and female. The meaning is so clear that FERobbins [1948] rightly translates the second title 'Of Brothers and Sisters.' Likewise Diog. L. 7, 108; 120 al.

On ἀπό (II 3a) Jd 14: Diog. L. 3, 1 in the list of descendants Plato is ἕκτος ἀπὸ Σόλωνος.

On σὺ εἶπας (εἶπον 1) Mt 26: 25, 64: schol. on Pla. 112ε Socrates says in declining or yielding: σὺ ταῦτα εἶπες, οὐκ ἐγώ.

εὐνουχίζω (literally) as early as Clearchus IV/III BC fgm. 49 [ed. FWehrli (1948)].

φαντάζομαι of a theophany (Athena) in Ps.-Aristotle, Mirabilia 108.

φωτισμός in Strato of Lamps. [300 BC] fgm. 76 [ed. FWehrli (1950)].

I shall add some passages here in which the subject matter is of interest, as well as the words themselves.

On ἀναγινώσκω (2): at the end of the sixth letter of Plato we read ταύτην τὴν ἐπιστολὴν πάντας ὑμᾶς ἀναγνῶναι χρή, just as I Th 5: 27.

On Γαλατία: for Memnon of Asia Minor, a slightly older contemporary of Paul, the Galatians (of whom he speaks now and again: no. 434 fgm. 1, 11ff Jac.) are the people who came from Europe to Asia Minor, with a very definite national composition and tone. He would certainly never address Lycaonians as Γαλάται. For him, Γαλατία is the land of these particular people (e.g., fgm. 1, 20, 2).

On ἐγώ εἰμί J 8: 58. Ammonius Hermiae (Comm. in Aristot. IV 5 ed. ABusse [1897]) c. 9 p. 136, 20f: in the Timaeus (37ε) it is written that one should not say of the gods τὸ ἦν, ἢ τὸ ἔσται, μεταβολῆς τινος ὄντα σημαντικά, μόνον δὲ τὸ ἔστι.

On ἐξέλκω Js 1: 14: Pla., Ep. 7 p. 325β εἷλκεν δέ με ἡ ἐπιθυμία.

On ἱλάσκομαι Lk 18: 13: Sb 8511, 7 ἱλαθί μοι, Μανδοῦλι (a divinity), σῶζέ με.

On κεράτιον Lk 15: 16: fodder for swine as Lycophron, Al. 675–8.

On πᾶσα Ἱεροσόλυμα Mt 2: 3: of the inhabitants as Pla., Ep. 7 p. 348α πᾶσα Σικελία; Demosth. 18, 18 ἡ Πελοπόννησος ἅπασα.

On Ac 9: 1: Saul breathing out murder has a parallel in Theocr. 22, 82: the two opponents φόνον ἀλλήλοισι πνέοντες.

The parallel in language can be absent entirely, and yet there may be significant similarities in subject matter. This is especially true of some passages from Diogenes Laërtius.

Diog. L. 2, 14 has a story of Hieronymus of Rhodes concerning the trial of Anaxagoras. Pericles puts on a scene with the latter, his teacher, in order to arouse the sympathy of the judges. In Nicol. Dam. no. 90 fgm. 68, 4 Jac., in connection with the fall of Croesus, Cyrus lets a woeful spectacle take its course βουλόμενος καὶ τοὺς Πέρσας οἶκτόν τινα λαβεῖν αὐτοῦ. Compare the Ecce Homo J 19: 5.

Diog. L. 2, 48 Socrates stops Xenophon at their very first meeting and says: 'ἕπου καὶ μάνθανε.' καὶ τοὐντεῦθεν ἀκροατὴς Σωκράτους ἦν. Cf. ἀκολουθέω (3).

Diog. L. 2, 127 Menedemus the philosopher [300 bc], in whose presence someone has acted in an unseemly manner, διέγραφεν εἰς τοὔδαφος. By doing this he shames him. Cf. J 8: 6, 8.

Diog. L. 3, 19 Plato awaits a verdict before the popular assembly on the island of Aegina that could mean death, but says not a word (μηδ᾽ ὁτιοῦν φθέγξασθαι). Cf. Mt 26: 63; Mk 14: 61, and σιωπάω (1).

Diog. L. 6, 97 Crates the Cynic goes about with his like-minded wife, seeking adherents for his cause. Cf. 1 Cor 9: 5.

Now and then everything is clear from a linguistic point of view, but the subject matter poses questions for which an answer should at least be sought among the Greeks.

Why does Mt (13: 55) say of Jesus τοῦ τέκτονος υἱός for Mark's ὁ τέκτων (6: 3)? Aristoxenus [300 bc] fgm. 115 (ed FWehrli [1945]) describes Sophillus, the father of Sophocles, as τέκτων. The Vita Sophoclis 1 rejects this and will only admit that he owned τέκτονες as slaves.

Why do we read in 1 Cor 15: 5 of οἱ δώδεκα, when Judas the traitor has disappeared from the scene? The variant ἔνδεκα shows that the problem was felt. 'The Twelve' is a fixed expression, like οἱ τριάκοντα in Athens. Xenophon, Hell. still refers to them in these terms in 2, 4, 23, despite the fact that 2, 4, 19 tells of the deaths of Critias and Hippomachus.

These examples must suffice. They represent a small sampling from the work of gathering parallels during the years 1951 and 1952. No one need fear that the task is almost finished and that there are no more parallels to be found. One who gives himself to this task with any devotion at all cannot escape the feeling thus expressed: how great is the ocean, and how tiny the shell with which we dip!

ABBREVIATIONS

1. The New Testament, the Apostolic Fathers, and the other Early Christian Literature dealt with in this Lexicon

The basic text for the NT is the one by Erwin Nestle and Kurt Aland[25], 1963; for the Apostolic Fathers, the Didache, the Epistle to Diognetus and the Martyrdom of Polycarp, the smaller edition of the Patres Apostolici by OvGebhardt, AvHarnack and ThZahn[6] 1920; for the rest of the literature the editions noted in each case. Readings which are not received into the text of these editions are nearly always treated as variants.

* at the end of an entry means that all the passages in which the word occurs in our literature are given in this entry; ** means that all the NT passages are given.

Ac= Acts of the Apostles
Agr= Agraphon (EPreuschen, Antilegomena[2] 1905, 26–31: Herrenlose Herrnworte, i.e. non-canonical sayings of Jesus)
AP= Apocalypse of Peter (Kl. T. [see table 5] 3, 1908 [reprinted 1933], 8–13)
B= Barnabas
1 Cl= 1 Clement
2 Cl= 2 Clement
Col= Colossians
1 Cor= 1 Corinthians
2 Cor= 2 Corinthians
D= Didache
Dg= Diognetus
Eph= Ephesians
Epil Mosq= Epilogus Mosquensis to the Martyrdom of Polycarp (p. 128 in Gebh., Har., and Zahn)
Gal= Galatians
GEb= Gospel of the Ebionites (Kl. T. 8[3], 1929, 12–15)
GEg= Gospel according to the Egyptians (Kl. T. 8[3], 15f)
GH= Gospel according to the Hebrews (Kl. T. 8[3], 5–12)
GNaass= Gospel of the Naassenes (Preuschen, op. cit. 12f)
GOxy= Gospel Fragment from POxy. V 840 (Kl. T. 31, 1908 [reprinted 1924], 4f)
GP= Gospel of Peter (Kl. T. 3, 4–8)
H= Hermas
  m= Mandate
  s = Similitude
  v = Vision
Hb= Hebrews
[I]= Ignatius
  IEph= I. to the Ephesians
  IMg= I. to the Magnesians
  IPhld= I. to the Philadelphians

IPol= I. to Polycarp
IRo= I. to the Romans
ISm= I. to the Smyrnaeans
ITr= I. to the Trallians
J= John
1J= 1 John
2J= 2 John
3J= 3 John
Jd= Jude
Js= James
LJ= Logia Jesu (Kl. T. 8[3], 19–22)
Lk= Luke
Mk= Mark
  Ending of Mk in the Freer ms.: Kl. T. 31, 10; cf. also Nestle ad loc.
MPol= Martyrdom of Polycarp
Mt= Matthew
Papias= Fragments of Papias
Phil= Philippians
Phlm= Philemon
PK= Petruskerygma (Preaching of Peter: Kl. T. 3, 13–16)
Pol= Polycarp to the Philippians
1 Pt= 1 Peter
2 Pt= 2 Peter
Ro= Romans
Rv= Revelation
1 Th= 1 Thessalonians
2 Th= 2 Thessalonians
1 Ti= 1 Timothy
2 Ti= 2 Timothy
Tit= Titus
UGosp= Fragments of an Unknown Gospel, ed. by HIBell and TCSkeat 1935, 1–41

2. The Old Testament and Apocrypha

The OT literature is cited according to the LXX in the edition of ARahlfs 1935 [reprinted 1949], unless it is expressly stated that the quotation is from the translation of Aq[uila], Sym[machus], or Theod[otion]. References from the Psalms are given in the LXX numbering exclusively. For discrepancies in the numbering of Prov and Jer see the table 'Loci Collati' in the insert in the Rahlfs LXX.

Am= Amos
Bar= Baruch
Bel= Bel and the Dragon
1 Ch= 1 Chronicles
2 Ch= 2 Chronicles
Da= Daniel
Dt= Deuteronomy
Eccl= Ecclesiastes
EpJer= Epistle of Jeremiah
1 Esdr= 1 Esdras (apocryphal book)
2 Esdr= 2 Esdras (chs. 1-10=Hebr. Ezra; 11-23=Nehemiah
Esth= Esther
Ex= Exodus
Ezk= Ezekiel
Gen= Genesis
Hab= Habakkuk
Hg= Haggai
Hos= Hosea
Is= Isaiah
Jdth= Judith
Jer= Jeremiah
Jo= Joel
Job (unabbreviated)
Jon= Jonah
Josh= Joshua
Judg= Judges

1 Km= 1 Kingdoms (Hebr. 1 Samuel)
2 Km= 2 Kingdoms (Hebr. 2 Samuel)
3 Km= 3 Kingdoms (Hebr. 1 Kings)
4 Km= 4 Kingdoms (Hebr. 2 Kings)
La= Lamentations
Lev= Leviticus
1 Macc= 1 Maccabees
2 Macc= 2 Maccabees
3 Macc= 3 Maccabees
4 Macc= 4 Maccabees
Mal= Malachi
Mi= Micah
Na= Nahum
Nehemiah—see 2 Esdras
Num= Numbers
Ob= Obadiah
Pr= Proverbs
Ps= Psalms
PsSol= Psalms of Solomon
Sir= Jesus Sirach
SSol= Song of Solomon
Sus= Susanna
Tob= Tobit
Wsd= Wisdom of Solomon
Zech= Zechariah
Zeph= Zephaniah

The following papyri include some readings not found in Nestle-Aland[25]:

$\mathfrak{P}^{66}$= Papyrus Bodmer II, Evangile de Jean chap. 1-14, ed. VMartin 1956; Supplément, Jean chap. 14-21, ed. VMartin et JWBBarns 1962.

$\mathfrak{P}^{72}$= Papyrus Bodmer VII-IX: VII L'Epître de Jude; VIII Les deux Epîtres de Pierre; IX Les Psaumes 33 et 34, ed. MTestuz, 1959.

$\mathfrak{P}^{74}$= Papyrus Bodmer XVII: Actes des Apôtres, Epîtres de Jacques, Pierre, Jean et Jude, ed. RKasser 1961.

$\mathfrak{P}^{75}$= PBodmer XIV: Evangile de Luc chap. 3-24, ed.

VMartin et RKasser 1961; PBodmer XV: Ev. de Jean chap. 1-15, 1961.

Third Corinthians= PBodmer X: Correspondance Apocryphe des Corinthiens et de l'apôtre Paul, ed. MTestuz 1959 (cf. EHennecke, NT Apokryphen³ II, 1964, ed. WSchneemelcher, 258ff; Eng. transl. RMcLWilson, 1964, 374ff).

The Qumran Literature

CD= The Zadokite Document.
IQS= The Manual of Discipline.
IQM= War of the Sons of Light and the Sons of Darkness.

IQH= Psalms of Thanksgiving (Hôdāyôt).
IQpHab= The Habakkuk Commentary.
IQIs^a= St. Mark's Isaiah Scroll.

3. Published Collections of Inscriptions and Papyri
(in addition to those that are unmistakably indicated in the text)

Aberciusinschr(ift) ed. EPreuschen, Analecta² I 1909 pp. 26ff—II AD.

ASP= American Studies in Papyrology, vol. VI: Michigan Collection, ed. GMBrowne 1970.

Audollent, Defix. Tab.= AAud., Defixionum Tabellae 1904.

BASP= Bulletin of the American Society of Papyrologists 1963ff.

Berl(iner) Klassikertexte I-VII 1904-23.

BGU= Aegyptische Urkunden aus den Museen zu Berlin: Griech. Urkunden I-VIII 1895-1933.

CIA= Corpus Inscriptionum Atticarum 1873-97.

CIG= Corpus Inscriptionum Graecarum 1828-77.

CII= Corpus Inscriptionum Iudaicarum I 1936. II 1952.

CIL= Corpus Inscriptionum Latinarum 1863-1909.

Dialekt-Inschr.= Sammlung der griechischen Dialekt-Inschriften, ed. HCollitz and OHoffmann, 4 vols. 1884-1915.

Dit., Or.= Orientis Graeci Inscriptiones Selectae, ed. WDittenberger, 2 vols. 1903-5.

Dit., Syll.= Sylloge Inscriptionum Graecarum, ed. Dittenberger³, 4 vols. 1915-24. The second edition, 3 vols. 1898-1901, was used when an item from the second ed. was not taken over into the third.

Enteux.= Ἐντεύξεις I ed. OGuéraud 1931.

Epigr. Gr.=Epigrammata Graeca ex Lapidibus Conlecta, ed. GKaibel 1878.

Fluchtaf.= RWünsch, Antike Fluchtafeln: Kleine Texte 20², 1912.

Hatch= WHPHatch, Some Illustrations of NT Usage from Greek Inscriptions of Asia Minor: JBL (see table 5) 27, 1908, 134-46.

Hauser= KH., Gramm. d. griech. Inschr. Lykiens. Diss. Zürich 1916.

IG= Inscriptiones Graecae 1873ff.

IG²= editio minor of the above, 1913ff.

Inscr. Gal.= Exploration archéol. de la Galatie et de Bithynie par GPerrot et al. I 1872.

Inschr. v. Hierap.= Die Inschriften v. Hierapolis in: Jahrb. d. Kaiserl. Dtsch. Archäol. Inst. 4. Ergzgsheft 1898, pp. 67-180, ed. WJudeich.

Inschr. v. Magn.=Die Inschriften von Magnesia am Mäander, ed. OKern 1900.

Inschr. v. Perg.= Die Inschriften von Pergamon, ed. MFränkel 1890; 1895.

Inschr. v. Priene= Die Inschriften von Priene, ed. FHiller von Gaertringen 1906.

Inscr. gr.=Recueil d'Inscriptions grecques, éd. ChMichel 1900; 1912.

Inscr. Rom.= Inscriptiones Graecae ad res Romanas pertinentes ed. RCagnat I-IV 1911-14.

Isishymnus v. Andros u. verwandte Texte, by WPeek 1930.

JJP= Journal of Juristic Papyrology 1946ff.

Kyr.-Inschr.= D. Augustus-Inschr. auf d. Marktplatz v. Kyrene, ed. JStroux and LWenger in Abh. d. Bayer. Ak. d. W., phil.-hist. Kl. XXXIV 2, 1928 [7/6 BC and 4 BC],

also= Suppl. Epigr. Gr. IX 1938 no. 8.

Lind. Tempelchr.= D. Lindische Tempelchronik, ed. ChrBlinkenberg: Kl. T. 131 (1915).

Maspéro=JMasp., Pap. grecs d'époque Byzantine I-III 1910-16.

Mitteis, Chrest.=LMitteis, Chrestomathie der Papyruskunde 1912.

Moses, 8th Book of (ADieterich, Abraxas 1891, 167-205)= PGM (s. below) 13.

Ostraka= UWilcken, Griechische Ostraka I, II, 1899 (I contains the commentary, II the texts).

PAmh.= BPGrenfell and ASHunt, The Amherst Papyri I, II, 1900f.

PBerlin 5025; 5026= PGM (s. below) 1; 2.

PBrem.= Die Bremer Papyri, ed. UWilcken 1936.

PEleph.= ORubensohn, Elephantine-Papyri 1907.

PFay.= Grenfell, Hunt and DGHogarth, Fayûm Towns and their Papyri 1900.

PFlor.= GVitelli and DComparetti, Papiri Fiorentini I-III 1906-15.

PFrankf.= HLewald, Griech. Papyri aus Frankfurt (Sitzgsber. d. Hdlbg. Ak. d. Wiss. 1920, Abh. 14).

PGenève= JNicole, Les Papyrus de Genève I 1896ff.

PGiess.= OEger, EKornemann and PMMeyer, Griech. Pap. zu Giessen 1910-12.

PGM= KPreisendanz, Papyri Graecae Magicae; D. Griech. Zauberpapyri I 1928; II 1931. Esp. important are: 1 and 2 (= PBerlin 5025; 5026); 3 (PMimaut); 4 (Paris Magic Pap.); 5 (PLond. 46); 7 (PLond. 121); 12 (PLeid. V); 13 (PLeid. W); 36 (POsl. 1).

PGoodspeed=EJGoodsp., Greek Pap. from the Cairo Museum 1902.

PGrenf. I= An Alexandrian Erotic Fragment and other Greek Pap., chiefly Ptolemaic, ed. Grenfell 1896.

PGrenf. II= New Classical Fragments, ed. Grenfell and Hunt 1897.

PHal.= Dikaiomata herausgeg. v. der Graeca Halensis 1913.

PHamb.= PMMeyer, Griech. Papyrusurkunden der Hamburger Stadtbibliothek 1911-24.

PHermopol.= CWessely, Corpus Papyrorum Hermopolitanorum (Studien z. Paläographie u. Papyruskunde V) 1905.

PHib.= Grenfell and Hunt, The Hibeh Papyri I 1906.

PHolm.= Papyrus Graecus Holmiensis, ed. OLagercrantz 1913.

PIand.= Papyri Iandanae, ed. CKalbfleisch cum discipulis 1912ff.

PLeid.= CLeemans, Papyri Graeci Musei Antiquarii Publici Lugduni-Batavi I 1843; II 1885; quoted as UPZ (s. below) and PGM 12; 13.

PLeipz.= LMitteis, Griech. Urkunden der Papyrussammlung zu Leipzig 1906.

PLille= PJouguet, Papyrus grecs de Lille I 1907-23.

PLond.= FGKenyon and HIBell, Greek Papyri in the British Museum I-V 1893-1917; s. PGM 5; 7.

PMagd.= JLesquier, Papyrus de Magdola 1912.

PMerton= PWilfred Merton, 3 vols. 1948-67, ed. HIBell et al.

PMich.= Michigan Papyri (Zenon Pap. ed. CCEdgar) 1931; II (pap. from Tebtunis I ed. AERBoak) 1933; III (Miscell. Pap. ed. JGWinter) 1936.

PMimaut= PGM 3.

POsl.= Papyri Osloenses, ed. SEitrem and LAmundsen I-III 1925-36. No. 1= PGM 36.

POxy.= Grenfell and Hunt, The Oxyrhynchus Papyri I-XVII 1898-1927.

PPar.=Paris pap. in Notices et Extraits XVIII 2, éd. Brunet de Presle 1865. Most of them are quoted as UPZ (s. below).—The great Paris magical papyrus (Bibl. nat. no. 574 of the Supplément grec) PGM 4.

PPetr.= JPMahaffy and JGSmyly, The Flinders Petrie Papyri I-III 1891-1905.

PRainer= CWessely, Corpus Papyrorum Raineri 1895.

PReinach=ThRein., Pap. Grecs et démotiques 1905.

PRev.= Revenue Laws of Ptolemy Philadelphus, ed. BPGrenfell and JPMahaffy 1896.

PRyl.= Catalogue of the Greek Papyri in the John Rylands Library, Manchester, Eng. I; II 1911-15.

PSI=Pubblicazioni della Società Italiana: Papiri Greci e Latini I-XI 1912-35.

PStrassb.= FPreisigke, Griech. Papyrus zu Strassburg I; II 1906-20.

PTebt.= Grenfell, Hunt, Goodspeed and Smyly, The Tebtunis Papyri I-III 1, 1902-33.

PThéad.=PJouguet, Pap. de Théadelphie 1911.

PTurin= APeyron, Papyri Graeci Regii Taurinensis Musei Aegyptii I; II 1826; 1827.

PUps. 8=GBjörck, D. Fluch des Christen Sabinus, Pap. Upsaliensis 8, 1938. VI AD.

PWarr.= The Warren Papyri 1941.

PWien Bosw.= EBoswinckel, Einige Wiener Pap. 1942.

PYale= Yale Papyri, ed. JFOates et al.= ASP vol. II, 1967.

Rouffiac= JR., Recherches sur les caractères du Grec dans le NT d'après les inscriptions de Priène 1911.

Sb= Sammelbuch; s. table 5 under Preisigke.

Suppl. Epigr. Gr.= Supplementum Epigraphicum Graecum ed. JJEHondius I-IX 1923-38.

Thieme=GTh., D. Inschriften v. Magnesia am Mäander u. d. NT, Diss. Heidelberg 1905.

UPZ=Urkunden der Ptolemäerzeit, ed. UWilcken I; II 1927ff.

Wadd.= WHWaddington, Inscriptions Grecques et Latines de la Syrie 1870.

Wilcken, Grundzüge | =UWilcken, Grundzüge u. Chre-
Wilcken, Chrest. | stomathie der Papyruskunde I; II 1912.

Witkowski= StW., Epistulae Privatae Graecae² 1911.

Zen.-P.= Zenon Papyri. Most of them are found in the PSI IV-VII, PMich. I, P. of Columbia Univ. I; II 1934-40 and, edited by CCEdgar, in the Catalogue Général des Antiquités Égypt. du Musée du Caire 79 (1925); 82 (1926); 85 (1928); 90 (1931); some of the Cairo Zen.-P. are also in the Sb III pp. 86ff, nos. 6707-820.

ZPE=Zeitschrift für Papyrologie u. Epigraphik 1967ff.

4. WRITERS AND WRITINGS OF ANTIQUITY

(including names that are not abbreviated. Some indication of time is given; in the case of authors this denotes the period of their literary activity. Roman numerals indicate the century, Arabic numerals the year).

Achilles Tat(ius) ed. RHercher 1858 . .	IV AD
Achmes, Oneirocriton, a secular text reworked from a Christian viewpoint, ed. FDrexl 1925, cited by page and line . . .	c. 900 AD
Aelian(us) ed. RHercher 1864 . . .	II AD
Ael(ius) Aristid(es) II ed. BKeil 1898, the rest ed. WDindorf 1829	II AD
Ael(ius) Dion(ysius) II AD and Paus(anias) II AD, two Atticists, ed. HErbse, Untersuchungen zu den attizist. Lexika 1950, pp. 95-151; 152-221	
Aeneas Tact(icus) ed. RSchöne 1911, cited by prose lines	IV BC
Aeschin(es)	IV BC
spurious Letters (ed. EDrerup 1904) . .	II AD
Aeschyl(us)	V BC
Aesop	uncertain
Aëtius, Treatment of Diseases of the Eye (Augenheilkunde) ed. JHirschberg 1899 .	VI AD
Alcaeus, s. Anth. Lyr. Gr. . . .	VII-VI BC
Alciphr(on) ed. MASchepers 1905 . . .	c. 200 AD

Alex(ander) Aphr(odisiensis):	
Scripta Minora=Supplementum Aristotelicum II 1, 2 ed. IBruns 1887. 1892: (De) An(ima) Mant(issa), (De) An(ima), Quaest(iones), (De) Fat(o), (De) Mixt(ione) .	c. 200 AD
Alexis Com.	IV BC
Anacr(eon), s. Anth. Lyr. Gr. . . .	VI BC
Anacreontea Carmina (Anacreontics) ed. CPreisendanz 1912	post-Christian
Ananius, s. Anth. Lyr. Gr. . . .	VI BC
Anaxandrides	IV BC
Anaximander s. Vorsokrat. . . .	VI BC
Andoc(ides)	c. 400 BC
Anecd(ota) Gr(aeca) ed. IBekker 1814-21; the vols. are paginated consecutively	
Anna Comn(ena), Alexias ed. AReiffenscheid, Leipzig 1884	1148 AD
Anth(ologia) Lyr(ica) Gr(aeca) ed. EDiehl² 1936-42	
Anth(ologia) Pal(atina) ed. FDübner 1864-72	
Antig(onus of) Car(ystus) ed. OKeller: Rer.	

Nat. Scr. 1877	III BC
Antiphanes Com.	IV BC
Antipho (the Orator) and Antipho Soph(ista) both	V BC
Anton(inus) Lib(eralis) ed. EMartini 1896 .	II AD
Apollon(ius) Dysc(olus)=Grammatici Graeci II 1, 2, 3 ed. RSchneider and GUhlig 1878– 1910	II AD
Apollon(ius) Paradox(ographus) ed. OKeller (s. Antig. Car. above) . . .	uncertain
Apollon(ius of) Rhod(es)	III BC
Appian(us) ed. PViereck and AGRoos I 1936; II 1905	II AD
Apuleius	II AD
Arat(us)	III BC
Archilochus Lyr. ed. EDiehl²	VII BC
Aretaeus, ed. CHude: CMG II 1923 .	II AD
Aristaen(etus) s. Ep(istola) . . .	V AD
Aristoph(anes)	V–IV BC
Aristot(le)	IV BC
De Mundo (spurious) . . .	I AD
Aristoxenus, ed. FWehrli 1945 . .	IV–III BC
Arrian(us), ed. AGRoos I 1907; II 1928 .	II AD
Artem(idorus) ed. RHercher 1864 . .	II AD
Astrampsychus, Oraculorum Decades CIII ed. RHercher 1863. Probably Christian, but containing secular material . .	V AD
Athen(aeus), ed. GKaibel I–III (1887–1890) .	III AD
Babrius, ed. OCrusius 1897 . .	c. 200 AD
Bacchylides, ed. BSnell 1949 . .	V BC
Batr(achomyomachia) . . .	uncertain
Berosus no. 680 Jac.	IV–III BC
Biogr.=Βιογραφοι. Vitarum Scriptores Gr. Minores, ed. AWestermann 1845 (cited by page)	
Bion Bucol.	II BC
Caecilius Calactinus, ed. EOfenloch 1907 .	I BC–I AD
Callim(achus)	III BC
Callinus, s. Anth. Lyr. Gr. . . .	VII BC
Callisth(enes) no. 124 Jac. . . .	IV BC
Cass(ius) Dio, ed. UPBoissevain 1895–1931 .	II–III AD
Cat. Cod. Astr.=Catalogus Codicum Astrologorum Graecorum Iff, 1898ff	
Cebes, ed. KPraechter 1893 . . .	I AD
Cecaumen(us), ed. Wassiljewsky-Jernstedt, Petersburg 1896	XI AD
Celsus in Origen, C. Celsum, ed. PKoetschau 1899	II AD
Chaeremon (Historicus) ed. H-RSchwyzer 1932	I AD
Charito, ed. RHercher 1859 . .	I–II AD
Chio Ep(istolographus), s. Ep(istola) .	I–II AD
Chrysipp(us)	III BC
Clearch(us), ed. FWehrli 1948 . .	IV–III BC
CMG=Corpus Medicorum Graecorum appearing since 1908; quoted by vol., page, line	
Coll(ectanea Alexandrina), ed. IUPowell 1925	
Comicorum Att. Fragmenta, ed. ThKock, 3 vols. 1881–8	
Cornutus, Theologiae Gr. Comp., ed. CLang 1881	I AD

Cosmas, s. Kosmas	
Cratinus Com.	V BC
Crinagoras, ed. MRubensohn 1888 . .	I BC–I AD
Critias, s. Vorsokrat.	V BC
Ctesias, ed. CMüller 1844 (ed. after Herodotus by GDindorf	c. 400 BC
Cyranides, s. Kyraniden	
Cyrill(us of) Scyth(opolis), ed. ESchwartz 1939 (=TU 49, 2)	VI AD
Delph(ic) Orac(le), ed. Parke-Wormell I. II, Oxford 1956	
Demetr(ius of) Phaler(um), ed. FWehrli 1949 (no. 228 Jac.)	IV BC
Democr(itus)	c. 400 BC
Demosth(enes)	IV BC
Dicaearchus, ed. FWehrli 1944. The writings wrongly attributed to him are found in MFuhr, Dic. Quae Supersunt 1841 .	IV BC
Dinarchus the Orator	IV BC
Dio Cassius, s. Cassius Dio	
Dio Chrys(ostom) ed. GdeBudé 1916–19 . .	I–II AD
Diocles: Die Fragmente der sikel. Ärzte Akron, Philistion, Diokles v. Karystos, ed. MWellmann 1901	IV BC
Diod(orus) S(iculus), ed. [LDindorf-] FVogel-CTFischer [1866ff] 1888ff . . .	I BC
Diog(enes) L(aertius), ed. CGCobet 1850. .	III AD
Diogenian(us) Epicureus, ed. AGercke, Jahrb. für klass. Phil. Suppl. 14, 1885, 748ff .	II AD
Dionys(ius) Byz(antius), Anaplus Bospori ed. RGüngerich 1927. Cited by §§ . .	c. 200 AD
Dionys(ius of) Hal(icarnassus) . .	I BC
Dionys(ius) Soph(ista), s. Ep(istola) .	VI AD
Diosc(urides)	I AD
Diphilus Com.	IV–III BC
Dositheus, Ars Grammatica, ed. JTolkiehn 1913	IV AD(?)
Doxogr(aphi) Gr(aeci), coll. HDiels 1879	
En(och), s. Henoch	
Epicharmus s. Vorsokrat. and Com. Graec. p. 91ff	V BC
Epici=Epicorum Graecorum Fragmenta ed. GKinkel 1877	
Epict(etus), ed. HSchenkl 1894 . .	I–II AD
Epicurus	c. 300 BC
Epimenides s. Vorsokrat. . . .	VI BC
Ep(istle of) Arist(eas), ed. PWendland 1900 .	II BC
Ep(istola): unless a special edition is used (Aeschines, Alciphron, Apollonius of Tyana, Demosthenes, Epicurus, Julian, Philostratus, Plato, Socrates), the letter is found in the Epistolographi Graeci, ed. RHercher 1873	
Eratosth(enes), ed. AOlivieri 1897 . .	III BC
Erotici (Scriptores) ed. RHercher, Leipzig 1858. 1859	
Eth(ica) Epic(urea), ed. WSchmid 1939= Studia Herculanensia 1	
Etym(ologicum) Gud(ianum), ed. EAloysius de Stefani I 1909; II 1920	
Etym(ologicum) Mag(num), ed. TGaisford 1848	

Eubul(us) Com..   IV BC

Eunap(ius), Vi(tae) Soph(istarum), ed. JFBoissonade 1822; cited by page   IV-V AD

Eupolis Com.   V BC

Eur(ipides)   V BC

Eustath(ius)   XII AD

Eutecnius on [Ps.-]Oppian's Cynegetica, ed. OTueselmann: GGAbh., n.F. IV 1, 1900

Ezechiel Trag. ed. JWieneke, Diss. Phil. Münster 1931   II BC

Galen   II AD

Geogr(aphi) Graec(i) Minor(es) ed. CMüller, Paris 1882

Geopon(ica), a collection of older pieces, put together   X AD

Gorgias of Leontini   V BC

Harpocration, ed. WDindorf 1853.   II AD

Hecataeus Mil(esius) no. 1 Jac.   VI-V BC

— (Abderita) no. 264 Jac.   IV BC

Hdt. = Herodotus   V BC

Heliod(orus)   III AD

Henoch = En(och) chapters 1-32; 89, 42-9, ed. LRadermacher 1901; chapter 97, 6-104; 106f, ed. CBonner 1937

Heraclid(es) Pont(icus), ed. FWehrli 1953   IV BC

— (Criticus) s. Geogr. (I 97ff)   uncertain

— (Lembus?) pol. s. Fgm. Hist. Graec. II 208ff = Aristot. Fgm., ed. VRose, Leipzig 1886 p. 370ff   uncertain

Heraclitus, ed. HDiels (Vorsokrat. 22)   V BC

Heraclit(us) Sto(icus), Quaestiones Homericae ed. Soc. Philol. Bonn 1910   I BC-I AD

Herm(etic) Wr(itings): unless a different edition is specified, cited according to WScott, Hermetica I 1924 (-IV 1936). Cf. also ed. ADNock and A-JFestugière 1945   imperial times

Hermippus Com.   V BC

Hermogenes Rhet.   II AD

Hero Alex(andrinus), ed. WSchmidt et al.; vols. I-V 1899-1914   I BC-I AD

Herodian(us) Gramm(aticus), ed. ALentz 1867-70   II AD

— Historicus, ed. KStavenhagen 1921 (when the name Herodian is used alone, this one is meant).   III AD

Hero(n)das, ed. OCrusius⁵ 1914   III BC

Hes(iod)   VII BC

Hesychius, ed. MSchmidt 1858-68; ed. KLatte I [A -Δ] 1953 with a text that differs widely   V AD

Hierocles, Commentarius in Aureum Carmen: FWAMullach, Fragmenta Philosophorum Graecorum I 1860 p. 416-84   IV-V AD

Himerius, Declamationes et Orationes rec. AColonna 1951. The earlier method of citation (from the time of FDübner 1849) when it differs, is given in square brackets   IV AD

Hippiatr. = Corpus Hippiatricorum Graecorum, ed. EOder and CHoppe I 1924; II 1927

Hippocr(ates) = Corpus Hippocraticum .   V-IV BC

Hipponax, s. Anth. Lyr. Gr..   VI BC

Hom(er)   perh. VIII-VI BC

Hom(eric) Hymns   fr. VII BC on

Horapollo, Hieroglyphica, ed. CLeemans 1835 .   IV AD

Hyperid(es), ed. ChJensen 1917   IV BC

Iambl(ichus)   c. 300 AD

Iambl(ichus) Erot(icus), ed. RHercher 1858   II AD

Il. = Iliad

Isaeus   IV BC

Isocr(ates)   IV BC

Jac. = Die Fragmente der griech. Historiker, by FJacoby 1923ff; cited by number of author and number of fragment

Jo(annes) Lydus.   VI AD

— Philopon(us) s. Commentaria in Aristot. vols. 13-17, Berlin 1887ff .   VI AD

Joseph and Aseneth, ed. MPhilonenko, 1968 .   uncertain

Joseph(us), ed. BNiese 1887-95, cited as Jos., with book and §   I AD

Julian, Letters, ed. JBidez 1922   IV AD

Kephal(aia) = Manichaean manuscripts I 1935ff

Kleopatra = Kl. und die Philosophen, ed. RReitzenstein: Nachr. d. Gött. Ges., Phil.-hist. Kl. 1919, pp. 14ff. The pagan Gk. in it dates   III AD

Kos(mas) und Dam(ian), ed. LDeubner 1907

Kyraniden, die: ed. Ch-ERuelle, Les lapidaires Grecs II 1898.   IV AD(?)

Laud(atio) Therap(ontis) in LDeubner, De Incubatione 1900 pp. 120-34   VII AD

Leo(nis Imper.) Strategemata as appendix to Polyaenus (q.v.) pp. 503-40 (a very close connection with Polyaenus is unmistakable)

Leonidas Tarent(inus), ed. JGeffcken, Leipzig 1896   c. 300 BC

Leontius (of Neapolis), Life of St. John the Merciful ed. HGelzer 1893   VII AD

Lex(icon) Vind(obonense) rec. ANauck 1867

Libanius, ed. RFörster, 12 vols. 1903-23.   IV AD

Longus   II AD

Lucian   II AD

Lycon, ed. FWehrli 1952   III BC

Lycophron   III BC

Lyric Poets, s. Anth(ologia) Lyr(ica) Gr(aeca)

Lysias   V-IV BC

Manetho (from Jos., C. Ap.), ed. WGWaddell 1948   III BC

— Apotelesmatica (astrol.), ed. AKöchly 1858 .   fr. III AD

M(arcus) Ant(oninus) = Marcus Aurelius, ed. HSchenkl 1913   II AD

Maximus Tyr(ius), ed. HHobein 1910   II AD

Menand(er Athen.) ed. ChJensen 1929 (Kö = Körte-Thierfelder 1957, 1959) and Com. Att. Fgm. III 1888.—Mon(osticha), ed. AMeineke, Com. Graec. IV 340ff.—Dyskolos, ed. EWHandley 1965.—Sikyonius, ed. RKassel 1965 = Kl. Texte 185   IV BC

— Ephes(ius) no. 783 Jac.   II BC

— Protector ed. LDindorf, Hist. Graeci Min. II 1ff   VI AD

Mesomedes, Hymnen, ed. KHorna (Sitzgsber.
d. Wiener Ak. d. W., vol. 207, 1) 1928. . II AD
Mimnermus, s. Anth. Lyr. Gr. . . . VI BC
Moeris, ed. JPierson 1759 . . . II AD
Moschus, Bucolicus . . . . . II BC
Musaeus s. Vorsokrat. . . . . uncertain
— Hero and Leander ed. ALudwich= Kl. T. 98
1929 . . . . V AD
Musonius (Rufus), ed. OHense 1905 . . I AD
Nicander . . . . II BC
Nicetas Eugen(ianus) s. Erotici II 437ff . XII AD
Nicol(aus) Dam(ascenus) . . . . I BC
Numenius of Apamea . . . . . II AD
Ocellus Luc(anus), ed. RHarder 1926 . . II BC
Od. = Odyssey
Oenomaus (Cynicus) ed. PValette 1908 after
Euseb., Praep. Ev. 5, 18, 6-5, 36, 4; 6, 7,
1-6, 7, 42 . . . . . II AD (Hadrian)
Olympiodorus . . . . . . VI AD
Oppian(us) . . . . . . II AD
Cynegetica (spurious) . . . . III AD
Oracula Sibyllina, ed. JGeffcken 1902
Oribasius . . . . . . IV AD
Orphica, ed. EAbel 1885; the Hymns, ed.
WQuandt 1941 . . . . . uncertain
Palaeph(atus), ed. NFesta 1902 . . uncertain
Paradoxogr(aphi) Flor(entini), anon. opuscu-
lum de aquis mirabilibus, ed. HÖhler (Diss.
Tübingen) 1913 . . . . I AD
Paradoxogr(aphus) Vat(icanus) s. Antig. Car. . uncertain
Parmenides, ed. HDiels (Vorsokrat. 28 B) . VI-V BC
Paroem. Gr. = Paroemiographi Graeci, ed.
ELvLeutsch and FGSchneidewin I 1839; II
1851
Parthenius, ed. EMartini 1902 . . . I BC
Paus(anias) . . . . . . II AD
Paus(anias) the Atticist s. Ael. Dion. above
Pel(agia)-Leg(enden)= Legenden der hl. Pela-
gia, ed. HUsener 1879
Peripl(us Maris) Eryth(raei), ed. HFrisk 1927 . I AD
Περὶ ὕψους (De Sublimitate) . . . I AD
Petosiris (and Nechepso), astrolog. writings.
Collection of fragments by ERiess, Philol.
Suppl. VI 1891/93, pp. 327-94 . . II BC
Philemo Com. (Com. Att. Fgm. vol. II) . IV-III BC
Philistion, physician s. Diocles . . . IV BC
—, a composer of mimes . . . . I AD
Philo (of Alexandria), ed. LCohn and PWend-
land 1896ff, cited by book and §. Vol. VII
1930 contains the indices by JLeisegang . I AD
Philo Mech(anicus), ed. RSchöne 1893 . III BC
Philod(emus) . . . . . . I BC
Philosophenspr(üche) sayings of various kinds
in Fgm. Philos. Graec. ed. FWAMullach I
1860 pp. 485-509 (cited by page and number)
Philostrat(us), ed. KLKayser 1870 . . III AD
Phlegon (of Tralles) . . . II AD (Hadrian)
Philumen(us), ed. MWellmann: CMG X 1, 1,
1908 . . . . II AD
Photius, ed. SANaber 1864-5 . . . IX AD

Phryn(ichus), ed. CALobeck 1820 . . . II AD
Physiogn. = Scriptores Physiognomici, ed.
RFörster 1893
Pind(ar), ed. OSchröder 1900; BSnell 1955 . V BC
Pla(to)
spurious: Def. = Definitiones, and certain
Dialogues (Timaeus of Locri, Alcib., then
Axioch[us] I BC et al.) . . . IV BC
Pliny the Elder (natural history) . . I AD
Pliny the Younger (letters) . . . I-II AD
Plotinus . . . . . . III AD
Plut(arch) . . . . . . I-II AD
Poet(arum) Philos(ophorum Fragmenta) ed.
HDiels, Berlin 1901
Polemo Soph., ed. HHinck 1873 . . II AD (Trajan)
Pollux, ed. EBethe 1900-37 . . . II AD
Polyaenus, ed. JMelber 1887; unless exc(erpta)
accompanies the ref., the main work,
Strategemata, is meant . . . II AD
Polyb(ius), ed. ThBüttner-Wobst 1882-1904 . II BC
Polystrat(us Epicureus), ed. CWilke 1905 . III BC
Porphyr(y) . . . . . . III AD
Posidippus Com. . . . . . III BC
—, Epigrams, ed. PSchott, Berlin 1905 . III BC
Posidonius no. 87 Jac. . . . . II-I BC
Pre-Socr(atic Philosophers), s. Vorsokrat.
Proclus (Diadochus) . . . . V AD
his work, Theol. = Στοιχείωσις λογική ed.
ERDodds 1933
Procop(ius), Hist. . . . . . VI AD
—, Soph(ista) s. Ep(istola) . . . V-VI AD
Psellus, History ed. CSathas 1899 . . XI AD
Ps.-Apollod(orus), ed. RWagner 1894 . II AD
Ps.-Callisth(enes)= Historia Alex. Magni, ed.
WKroll 1926 . . . . . 200 AD
Ps.-Demetr(ius), De Eloc(utione) . . . I AD
Ps.-Demetrius, Form(ae) Ep(istolicae) and
Ps.-Libanius, Charact(eres) Ep(istolares) are
cited according to: Demetrii et Libanii qui
feruntur Τύποι ἐπιστολικοί et Ἐπιστολι-
μαῖοι Χαρακτῆρες, ed. ValWeichert 1910
(by page and line)
Ps.-Phoc(ylides), ed. EDiehl (=Anthol. Lyr.
Gr. I² 1936). . . . . Hellenistic times
Ptolem(aeus) . . . . . . II AD
—, Apotel(esmatica) astrol. ed. FBoll-AeBoer
1940
Pythag(oras) . . . . . . VI BC
Quint(us) Smyrn(aeus), ed. AZimmerman 1891 IV AD
Rhet(ores) Gr(aeci), ed. ChWalz 1832-6 (a
mixture of pagan and Christian works).—
The collection of the Rhet. Gr. put out since
1853 by LSpengel et al. is cited according to
ancient authors and modern editors.
Rhinthon s. Com. Graec. p. 183ff . . III BC
Sallust(ius), περὶ θεῶν κ. κόσμου, ed. ADNock
1926 . . . . IV AD
Sappho, s. Anth. Lyr. Gr. . . . VII-VI BC
Schol(ia) on Apollon(ius of) Rhod(es), ed.
KWendel 1935

— on Aeschyl(us), ed. WDindorf 1838
— on Aristoph(anes), ed. WDindorf 1838
— on Eur(ipides), ed. ESchwartz 1887–91
— on Lucian, ed. HRabe 1906
— on Pind(ar), ed. ABDrachmann 1903–27
— on Pla(to), ed. GCGreene 1938
— on Soph(ocles), ed. PNPapageorgius, Leipzig 1888
Scymnus Chius s. Geogr. (I 196ff) . . .   II BC
Semonides of Amorgos . . . .   VII BC
Sext(us) Emp(iricus) . . . .   II AD
Sextus (Pyth.), Sententiae, a Christian reworking of a pagan original, ed. AElter, Academica Bonn 1891–2; 1892 . . . end of II AD
Sib. Or., s. Oracula Sibyllina
Simonides of Ceos . . . .   VI–V BC
Simplicius, (Commentarius) In Epict(eti Enchiridion) ed. FDübner 1840. Cited by page and line . . . . .   VI AD
Socrat., Ep. = Die Briefe des Sokrates u. der Sokratiker, by Liselotte Köhler: Philologus Suppl. 20, 2, 1928
Solon, s. Anth. Lyr. Gr. . . .   VII–VI BC
Soph(ocles) . . . . .   V BC
Soranus, ed. JIlberg: CMG IV 1927 . .   II AD
Sotades, s. Anth. Lyr. Gr. . . .   III BC
Stephan(us) Byz(antius) . . . .   VI AD
Stesichorus, s. Anth. Lyr. Gr. . . .   VII–VI BC
Stob(aeus), ed. CWachsmuth and OHense, 5 vols. 1884–1923 . . . .   V AD
Stoic. = Stoicorum Veterum Fragmenta; coll. JvArnim I–IV 1903–24
Strabo . . . . .   I BC–I AD
Suidas (= Suda), ed. Ada Adler 1928–35. .   X AD
Synes(ius) (the letters: Epistolographi Gr. [s. Ep. above]; the Opuscula ed. NTerzaghi 1944).—The chapter numbers are given according to Terzaghi; the numbers at the side are those of the ed. by Pettau, which Terz. notes in the margin . . .   c. 400 AD
Syntipas, ed. VJernstedt-PNikition: Mémoires

de l'Acad. impériale des sciences hist.-phil. tome XI 8me série, Pétersbourg 1912 pp. 1–200. Cited by page and line
Teles, ed. OHense² 1909 . . .   III BC
Test. Reub., Sim., etc. = Test(aments of the) 12 Patr(iarchs) ed. RHCharles 1908
Test(ament) Abraham = The Testament of Abraham, ed. MRJames 1892
Tetrast(icha) Iamb(ica); Babrius, ed. Crusius pp. 264–96
Themist(ius), Orationes, ed. WDindorf 1832 .   IV AD
Theocr(itus) . . . . .   III BC
Theod(orus) Prodr(omus) s. Erotici (II 287ff) .   XII AD
Theognis . . . . . .   VI BC
Theophanes Conf(essor), ed. CdeBoor, Leipzig 1883–1885 . . . . .   VIII AD
Theophr(astus), ed. FWimmer 1854ff . .   IV BC
Theophyl(actus) Sim(ocatta) . . .   VII AD
Theosophien, Fragmente griechischer, ed. HErbse (Diss. Hamburg) 1941
Thom(as) Mag(ister), ed. FRitschl 1832 . .   XIV AD
Thu(cydides) . . . . . .   V BC
Timaeus no. 566 Jac. . . . .   IV–III BC
Timon s. Poet. Philos. (pp. 173ff) . .   III BC
Trag. = tragic writer(s) or tragedy
Vett(ius) Val(ens), ed. WKroll; cited by page and line . . . . . .   II AD
Vi(tae) Aesopi, ed. AEberhard 1872
Vit(ae) Homeri et Hesiodi, ed. UvWilamowitz = Kl. T. 137, reprinted 1929
Vorsokrat(iker), their fragments ed. by HDiels, 5th ed. by WKranz I–III 1934–7; 6th ed. 1951ff
Xenophanes, s. Anth. Lyr. Gr. and Vorsokrat. .   VI BC
X(enophon) . . . . . .   IV BC
  spurious: Constitution of the Athenians (by the 'Old Oligarch') . . .   V BC
  Cynegetica . . . . .   IV BC
Xenophon Eph(esius) ed. RHercher 1858 .   II AD
Zeno the Stoic . . . . .   IV–III BC

5. Periodicals, Collections, Modern Authors and Literature

ABA = Abhandlungen der Berliner Ak. d. Wissensch. (Phil.-hist. Klasse).
Abel = F-MAbel, Grammaire du Grec Biblique 1927.
AGG = GGAbh.
AJPh = The American Journal of Philology 1880ff.
AJTh = The American Journal of Theology 1897ff.
Anz = HA., Subsidia ad Recognoscendum Graecorum Sermonem Vulgarem e Pentateuchi Versione Alexandrina Repetita: Dissert. Philolog. Halenses XII 1894, 259–387.
APF = Archiv für Papyrusforschung 1901ff.
ARW = Archiv für Religionswissenschaft 1898ff.
ATR = Anglican Theological Review 1918ff.
B. = CDBuck, A Dictionary of Selected Synonyms in the Principal Indo-European Languages: A Contribution to the History of Ideas 1949.
Baedeker (K), Palästina u. Syrien⁷ 1910.
Beginn. = The Beginnings of Christianity, ed. by FJFoakes-Jackson and KLake, Part I, 5 vols. (Acts) 1920–33.

BFChTh = Beiträge zur Förderung christlicher Theologie 1897ff.
Bibel-Lexikon, ed. by DSchenkel, 5 vols. 1869–75.
Bibelwörterbuch, Kurzes, ed. HGuthe 1903.
Billerb. = (HLStrack and) PBillerbeck, Kommentar z. NT aus Talmud u. Midrasch, 4 vols. 1922–8.
Black, Aramaic Approach = MBl., An Aramaic Approach to the Gospels and Acts² 1953; ³1967.
Bl-D. = FBlass, Grammatik d. ntl. Griechisch, bearbeitet v. ADebrunner⁹ 1954; cited by §§; app. = appendix; in the ninth ed. the material of the app. is placed in the text, immediately after the main articles. English translation by R. W. Funk, A Greek Grammar of the New Testament and Other Early Christian Literature (1961); the §-numbers are the same as in the German original.
Boll = FB., Aus der Offenb. Johannis 1914.
Bousset, Rel. = WB., D. Religion des Judentums im ntl. Zeitalter³ 1926.

BPhW= Berliner Philologische Wochenschrift 1881ff.

Breusing= AB., D. Nautik d. Alten 1886.

Buhl (F), Geographie v. Palästina 1896.

Bull. de corr. hell.= Bulletin de correspondance hellénique 1877ff.

Buttmann (A), Grammatik des ntl. Sprachgebrauchs 1859.

ByzZ= Byzantinische Zeitschrift 1892ff.

BZ= Biblische Zeitschrift 1903ff.

CBQ= Catholic Biblical Quarterly 1947ff.

CCD= The NT, Translated from the Latin Vulgate, etc., under the patronage of the Episcopal Committee of the Confraternity of Christian Doctrine 1941.

C(h)QR= The Church Quarterly Review 1875ff.

Clemen= CCl., Religionsgesch. Erklärung des NT² 1924.

ClR= The Classical Review 1887ff.

Congr. d'Hist. du Christ.= Congrès d'Histoire du Christianisme. Jubilé ALoisy, 3 vols. 1928.

Con(iectanea) Neot(estamentica) cur. AFridrichsen et al. 1ff. 1935ff.

CPJ= Corpus Papyrorum Judaicarum, 3 vols. 1957-64.

Crönert= WCr., Memoria Graeca Herculanensis 1903.

CTM= Concordia Theological Monthly 1930ff.

Cumont= FC., D. oriental. Religionen im röm. Heidentum³ 1931.

Dalman (G), Arbeit= Arbeit u. Sitte in Palästina, 7 vols. 1928-42.

—, Gramm.= Grammatik d. jüd.-palästin. Aramäisch² 1905.

—, Jesus= Jesus-Jeschua 1922.

—, Orte= Orte u. Wege Jesu³ 1924.

—, Worte= D. Worte Jesu 1898,² 1930.

Dana and Mantey= HED. and JRM., A Manual Grammar of the Greek NT 1927.

Dibelius, Geisterwelt= MD., D. Geisterw. im Glauben des Paulus 1909.

Dict. d'Arch.= Dictionnaire d'Archéologie chrétienne et de Liturgie by FCabrol and HLeclercq 1903ff.

Dictionary of the Bible, 4 vols. and extra vol. 1898-1904. Dict. of Christ and the Gospels, 2 vols. 1906; 1908. Dict. of the Apostolic Church, 2 vols. 1915; 1918. All ed. by JHastings.

Dictionnaire de la Bible, ed. by LVigouroux, 5 vols. 1895-1912; the Supplement to it, ed. by LPirot 1928ff.

Dodd= CHD., The Bible and the Greeks 1935.

Dssm. (ADeissmann), B= Bibelstudien 1895.

— NB= Neue Bibelstudien 1897. BS= Bible Studies, Eng. transl. of the two preceding, by AGrieve 1901.

— LO= Licht vom Osten⁴ 1923. LAE= Light from the Ancient East, Engl. transl. by LRMStrachan² 1927.

Elbogen= IE., Der jüd. Gottesdienst² 1924; ³1931.

Encyclopaedia Biblica, ed. by TKCheyne and JSBlack, 4 vols. 1899-1903.

Encyclopaedia of Religion and Ethics, ed. by JHastings, 13 vols. 1908-26.

Eranos: Acta Philologica Suecana 1896ff.

ET= The Expository Times 1890ff.

Exp.= The Expositor 1875ff.

Festschr.= Festschrift, without regard to the exact title in each case, unless misunderstanding may be caused thereby.

Field, Notes= FF., Notes on the Translation of the NT 1899.

FRL= Forschungen z. Rel. und Lit. des A u. NT 1903ff.

Gbh.= OvGebhardt.

Gdspd., Probs.= EJGoodspeed, Problems of NT Translation 1945.

GGA= Göttingische Gelehrte Anzeigen.

GGAbh.= Abhandlungen der Gesellschaft d. Wissenschaften zu Göttingen (Philol.-hist. Klasse).

Hahn= LH., Rom u. Romanismus im griech.-röm. Osten 1906.

Handwörterbuch des Bibl. Altertums, ed. ERiehm, 2 vols.² 1893f.

Hatch(E) and Redpath(HA), A Concordance to the Septuagint and the Other Greek Versions of the OT 1897; 1900.

HDB, see Dictionary of the Bible.

Hdb.= Handbuch zum NT, ed HLietzmann.

Helbing= RH., Grammatik der LXX: Laut- u. Wortlehre 1907.

Her.= Hermes, Zeitschr. für klass. Philologie 1866ff.

Hobart= WKH., The Medical Language of St. Luke 1882.

HTR= The Harvard Theological Review 1908ff.

HUCA= Hebrew Union College Annual 1924ff.

ICC= International Critical Commentary.

IDB= Interpreter's Dictionary of the Bible 1962.

IndogF= Indogermanische Forschungen 1891ff.

Jannaris(AN), An Historical Greek Grammar, London 1897.

JB= Jerusalem Bible 1966.

JBL= Journal of Biblical Literature 1881ff.

JHS= The Journal of Hellenic Studies 1880ff.

Johannessohn= MJ., D. Gebrauch der Präpositionen in LXX: NGG, Beiheft 1926.

JPh= The Journal of Philology 1868ff.

JQR= The Jewish Quarterly Review 1888ff.

JTS= The Journal of Theological Studies 1900ff.

Jülicher, Gleichn.= AJ., D. Gleichnisreden Jesu II 1899.

Kalt(E), Biblisches Reallexikon, 2 vols. 1931; 2nd ed. 1938ff.

KEK= Kritisch-exegetischer Kommentar über das NT, HAWMeyer, 1829ff.

Kl. T.= Kleine Texte, ed. HLietzmann.

Krüger(KW), Griech. Sprachlehre⁵ 1875-9.

Kühner-Bl. and Kühner-G.= RK., Ausf. Gramm. d. griech. Sprache³ by FBlass and BGerth 1890-1904.

L.= KLachmann.

Lexikon für Theologie u. Kirche, ed. MBuchberger, 10 vols. 1930-8.

Lghtf.= JBLightfoot.

L-S-J (lex.)= HGLiddell and RScott, A Greek-English Lexicon; New Edition by HSJones, 2 vols. 1925-40.

Ltzm.= HLietzmann.

Magie= DMagie, De Romanorum Juris Publici Sacrique Vocabulis Sollemnibus in Graecum Sermonem Conversis 1905.

Mayser= EM., Gramm. der griech. Pap. aus der Ptolemäerzeit I; II 1906-34. If the vol. number is omitted, vol. I is meant. Parts of ed.² are noted in each case.

Μεγα Λεξικον της Ελληνικης Γλωσσης (JSZerbos), 9 vols. 1950.

Meisterhans-Schw.= KM., Gramm. der attisch. Inschr., 3. Aufl. von ESchwyzer 1900.

Meyer(E)= EdMeyer, Ursprung u. Anfänge des Christentums, 3 vols. 1921-3.

Mlt.= JHMoulton, A Grammar of NT Greek, vol. I Prolegomena³ 1908; reprinted 1949.

Mlt.-H.= JHMoulton and WFHoward, A Grammar of NT

Greek, vol. II Accidence and Word-Formation, w. an appendix on Semitisms 1919-29.

Mlt.-Turner= JHMoulton and NTurner, A Grammar of NT Greek, vol. 3 Syntax 1963.

M-M.= JHMoulton and GMilligan, The Vocabulary of the Greek NT Illustrated from the Papyri and Other Non-Literary Sources 1914-30.

Murray(JAH et al.), A New Engl(ish) Dict(ionary on Historical Principles) 1888-1933.

Mus. Helv.= Museum Helveticum 1944ff.

N.= Nestle.

Nägeli= ThN., Der Wortschatz des Apostels Paulus 1905.

NEB= The New English Bible 1970.

NGG= Nachrichten der Gesellsch. der Wissenschaften zu Göttingen.

NJklA= Neue Jahrbücher f. d. klass. Altertum 1898ff.

NKZ= Neue Kirchliche Zeitschrift 1890f.

Norden, Agn. Th.= EN., Agnostos Theos 1913.

NovT= Novum Testamentum 1956ff.

NThSt= Nieuwe Theologische Studiën 1918ff.

NThT= Nieuw Theologisch Tijdschrift 1912ff.

NTS= New Testament Studies 1954ff.

OLZ= Orientalische Literaturzeitung 1898ff.

Passow(F), Handwörterbuch der griech. Sprache, 5th ed. by VChFRost, FPalm et al., 2 vols. in 4 parts 1841-57.—Completely revised by WCrönert, so far 3 fascicles 1912; 1913.

Pauly-W.= Pauly, Real-Encyclopädie der klass. Altertumswissensch. New revision in progress since 1892 by GWissowa, then by WKroll, KMittelhaus et al.

PEF= Palestine Exploration Fund 1870ff.

Philol(ogus), Zeitschr. f. d. klass. Altertum 1847ff.

Pj= Palästinajahrbuch 1905ff.

PJ= Preussische Jahrbücher 1858ff.

PM= Protestantische Monatshefte 1897ff.

Preisigke(F), Fachwörter= Fachw. des öffentl. Verwaltungsdienstes Ägyptens in den griech. Papyrusurkunden d. ptol. u. röm. Zeit 1915.

—, Namenbuch 1922.

—, Sb= Sammelbuch griech. Urkunden aus Ägypten I 1915; II 1922; III-V 1927-50 by FBilabel.

—, Wörterbuch der griech. Papyrusurkunden (finished by EKiessling), 3 vols. 1925-31.

Prümm(K), Religionsgeschichtl. Handbuch f. d. Raum der altchr. Umwelt 1943.

Psaltes= StBPsaltes, Grammatik der Byzantinischen Chroniken (Forschungen zur griech. u. lat. Gramm. 2) 1913.

PTR= Princeton Theological Review 1903ff.

RAC= Reallexikon für Antike u. Christentum, ed. ThKlauser 1941ff.

Ramsay(WM), Bearing= The Bearing of Recent Discovery on the Trustworthiness of the NT 1915.

—, Church= The Church in the Roman Empire[5] 1897.

—, Hist. Geogr.= The Historical Geography of Asia Minor 1890.

—, Letters= The Letters to the Seven Churches of Asia 1905.

—, Phrygia= The Cities and Bishoprics of Phrygia, 2 vols. 1895-7.

RB= Revue Biblique 1892ff, n.s. 1904ff.

Rdm.= LRadermacher, Neutest. Grammatik[2] 1925.

RE= Realencyclopädie für protest. Theol. und Kirche, 24 vols.[3], ed. AHauck 1896-1913.

Reallexikon der Vorgeschichte, 15 vols. 1924-32.

Rech de Sc rel= Recherches de Science religieuse 1910ff.

Reinhold= HR., De Graecitate Patrum Apostolicorum Librorumque Apocryphorum NTi Quaestiones Grammaticae, Diss. Phil. Hal. XIV 1 1898, 1-115.

RGG= Die Religion in Geschichte u. Gegenwart, 5 vols. and index vol.[2] 1927-32.

RhM= Rheinisches Museum für Philologie, n. F. 1842ff.

RHPhr= Revue d'Histoire et de Philosophie religieuses 1921ff.

Rob.= ATRobertson, A Grammar of the Greek NT in the Light of Historical Research[4] 1923.

RSphth= Revue des Sciences philosophiques et théologiques 1907ff.

RSV= The Revised Standard Version of the NT 1946.

RThPh= Revue de théologie et de philosophie 1868ff. n.s. 1913ff.

Rtzst. (RReitzenstein), Erlösungsmyst.= D. iranische Erlösungsmysterium 1921.

Rtzst., Herr der Grösse= D. mandäische Buch des Herrn der Grösse 1919.

—, Hist.Mon.= Historia Monachorum und Historia Lausiaca 1916.

—, Mysterienrel.= Die hellenistischen Mysterienreligionen[3] 1927.

—, Poim.= Poimandres 1904.

—, Taufe= D. Vorgeschichte der christl. Taufe 1929.

RVV= Religionsgesch. Versuche und Vorarbeiten 1903ff.

SAB= Sitzungsber. der Preussischen Akad. der Wissenschaften z. Berlin (Phil.-hist. Klasse).

Schmid= WSch., D. Attizismus in s. Hauptvertretern, 5 vols. 1887-97.

Schmidt= WSch., De Fl. Josephi Elocutione: Fleckeisens Jahrbücher f. klass. Philol., Suppl. XX 1894, pp. 341-550.

SchThZ= Schweizerische Theolog. Zeitschrift 1884ff.

Schürer= ESch., Geschichte des jüdischen Volkes[4], 3 vols. 1901-11.

StKr= Theolog. Studien u. Kritiken 1828ff.

Symb. Osl.= Symbolae Osloenses 1922ff.

Tdf.= CvTischendorf.

Thackeray= HStJTh., A Grammar of the OT in Greek according to the Septuagint I 1909.

ThBl= Theologische Blätter 1922ff.

ThGl= Theologie u. Glaube 1909ff.

ThLZ= Theolog. Literaturzeitung 1876ff.

ThQ= Theolog. Quartalschrift 1819ff.

ThSt= Theologische Studiën 1883ff.

ThT= Theologisch Tijdschrift 1867ff.

Thumb= ATh., D. griech. Sprache im Zeitalter des Hellenismus 1901.

ThZ= Theologische Zeitschrift, ed. by the Theol. Faculty of the Univ. of Basel 1945ff.

TU= Texte u. Untersuchungen 1882ff.

TW= Theologisches Wörterbuch zum NT, ed. by GerhKittel (d. 1948; succeeded by GFriedrich) I 1933; II 1935; III 1938; IV 1942; V 1954; VI 1 1954. English translation by G. W. Bromiley, Theological Dictionary of the New Testament (1964 ff.).

Ursing, UU., Studien zur griech. Fabel; Diss. Lund 1930.

Vetus T = Vetus Testamentum 1951ff.
Vivre et Penser = RB 1941-4.
W-H. = BFWestcott and FJAHort.
Winer(GB), Gramm. d. ntl. Sprachidioms⁷ 1867.
Wlh. = JWellhausen; Einl. = Einleitung in d. drei ersten Ev.² 1911.
W-S. = Winer, Gramm. d. ntl. Sprachidioms, 8th ed. by PWSchmiedel 1894ff; cited by §§.
Wuthnow = HW., Die semit. Menschennamen in griech. Inschr. u. Pap. des vord. Orients 1930.
Zahn(Th), Einl. = Einleitung in d. NT³, 2 vols. 1906f.
— Forsch. = Forschungen z. Gesch. d. ntl. Kanons 1881ff.
— GK. = Geschichte d. ntl. Kanons I; II 1888-92.

ZAW = Zeitschr. f. die Atl. Wissenschaft 1881ff.
ZDMG = Zeitschr. d. Deutschen Morgenländischen Gesell-schaft 1847ff.
ZDPV = Zeitschr. d. Deutschen Palästina-Vereins 1878ff.
ZKG = Zeitschr. f. Kirchengeschichte 1877ff.
ZkTh = Zeitschr. f. kathol. Theologie 1877ff.
ZMR = Zeitschr. f. Missionskunde u. Religionswissenschaft 1886ff.
ZNW = Zeitschr. f. die Ntl. Wissenschaft 1900ff.
Zorell(F), Novi Testamenti Lexicon Graecum² 1931.
ZsystTh = Zeitschr. f. systematische Theol. 1923ff.
ZThK = Zeitschr. f. Theol. u. Kirche 1891ff; n. F. 1920ff.
ZWTh = Zeitschr. f. Wissenschaftl. Theologie 1858ff.

6. OTHER ABBREVIATIONS

abs. = absolute
acc. = accusative
acc. to = according to
act. = active
AD = Anno Domini
adj. = adjective
ad loc. = ad locum (to or at the place under consideration)
adv. = adverb
al. = alibi (elsewhere), aliter (otherwise), alii (others)
aor. = aorist
app. = appendix
approx. = approximately
art. = article
Att. = Attic
attrib. = attribute, -butive
augm. = augment
BC = Before Christ
beg. = beginning
betw. = between
bibl. = biblical
c. = circa (about)
cf. = confer (compare)
cj. = conjecture(d by)
class. = classical
cod., codd. = codex, -ices
colloq. = colloquial
comm. = commentary, -aries
comp. = comparative(ly)
conj. = conjunction
connot. = connotation
constr. = construction
contr. = contracted, -action
correl. = correlative(ly)
corresp. = corresponding(ly)
cpd. = compound
dat. = dative
demonstr. = demonstrative
dep. = deponent
deriv. = derived, -ation, -ative
difft. = different(ly)
dim. = diminutive
dir. = direct
dub. l. = dubia lectio (doubtful reading)
eccl. = ecclesiastical

ed. = edited (by), edition
e.g. = exempli gratia (for example)
ellipt. = elliptical(ly)
elsewh. = elsewhere
enclit. = enclitic
equiv. = equivalent
esp. = especially
et al. = et alii (and others), etc.
eth. = ethics, etc.
etym. = etymological
euphem. = euphemism, -istic
ex., exx. = example, -ples
exc. = except; excursus
exclam. = exclamation
expl. = explanation, -plained
expr. = expression
f, ff = following
f(em). = feminine
fgm. = fragment
fig. = figurative(ly)
foll. = followed
foreg. = foregoing
fr. = from
freq. = frequent(ly)
fut. = future
gen. = genitive
gener. = general(ly)
Gk. = Greek
gov. = governed
H.Gk. = Hellenistic Greek
hist. = historical
ibid. = ibidem (in the same place or book)
i.e. = id est (that is)
I.-E. = Indo-European
imper. = imperative
impers. = impersonal(ly)
impf. = imperfect
incl. = including
indecl. = indeclinable
indef. = indefinite
indic. = indicative
indir. = indirect
inf. = infinitive
infl. = influence(d)

inscr. = inscription(s)
instr. = instrumental
interpol. = interpolated
interpr. = interpreted, -pretation
interrog. = interrogative
intr. = intransitive
irreg. = irregular
iterat. = iterative
KJ = King James version, 1611
l. = line
Lat. = Latin
l.c., loc. cit. = loco citato (in the place already quoted)
likew. = likewise
lit. = literal(ly); literature, references to (scholarly) literature
loanw. = loanword
m(asc). = masculine
metaph. = metaphor(ically)
mg. = margin
mid. = middle
mng. = meaning
Mod. Gk. = Modern Greek
ms., mss. = manuscript(s)
n(eut). = neuter
neg. = negative
n.m. = nomen masc.
nom. = nominative
n.s. = new series
num. = numeral
obj. = object
occas. = occasionally
oft. = often
op. cit. = opere citato (in the work already quoted)
opp. = opposed to
orig. = original(ly)
otherw. = otherwise
p., pp. = page(s)
pap. = papyrus, -yri
par. = parallel
partic. = particular(ly)
pass. = passive; passage
pecul. = peculiar
perf. = perfect
perh. = perhaps
pers. = person(s)
personif. = personified
pf. = perfect
phr. = phrase
pl. = plural
plpf. = pluperfect
pos. = positive
poss. = possible, -bly
possess. = possessive
prec. = preceding
pred. = predicate
predom. = predominant(ly)
pref. = prefix
prep. = preposition(al)
pres. = present

prob. = probable
pron. = pronoun
prop. = properly
prov. = proverbial(ly)
ptc. = participle
quot. = quotation
q.v. = quod vide (which see)
rabb. = rabbinical literature, etc.
rdg. = reading
ref., reff. = reference(s)
reflex. = reflexive
regul. = regular(ly)
relat. = relative
relig. = religious
repres. = represents, -enting
rest. = restoration, -ored
rhet. = rhetorical
s. = see
sc. = scilicet (you may understand; supply)
schol. = scholia(st)
sg. = singular
sic = so, thus, indicating an error transcribed from the original
signf. = signification
sim. = similar(ly)
sing. = singular
somet. = sometimes
someth. = something
specif. = specifically
subj. = subjunctive; subject
subscr. = subscription
subst. = substantive(ly)
suf. = suffix
superl. = superlative
superscr. = superscription
suppl. = supplement
susp. = suspected
s.v. = sub voce (under the word)
syll. = syllable
synon. = synonymous
thr. = through
t.r. = textus receptus
trag. = tragic writers, tragedy
trans. = transitive
transf. = transferred
transl. = translate, etc.
translit. = transliteration, etc.
t.t. = technical term
usu. = usually
var. = various
viz. = videlicet (namely)
v.l., vv.ll. = varia(e) lectio(nes) (variant reading[s])
voc. = vocative
vs., vss. = verse(s)
Vulg. = Vulgate
w. = with
wr. = writers, writings

A GREEK-ENGLISH LEXICON OF
THE NEW TESTAMENT
AND OTHER EARLY CHRISTIAN LITERATURE

A, α *alpha* first letter of the Gk. alphabet. α'=1 (cf. Sib. Or. 5, 15) or *first* in titles of letters: 1 Cor; 1 Th; 1 Ti; 1 Pt; 1 J; 1 Cl; ἐντολή Hm 1, title. As a symbolic letter Α signifies the beginning, Ω the end (FBoll, Sphaera '03, 469ff). The two came to designate the universe and every kind of divine and demonic power. Cf. Rtzst., Poim. 256ff, Erlösungsmyst. 244; FBoll, Aus d. Offb. Joh. '14, 26f. In the expr. ἐγώ εἰμι τὸ ἄλφα καὶ τὸ ὦ the letters are explained as *beginning* and *end* Rv 1: 8 t.r.; 21: 6 (s. OWeinreich, ARW 19, '19, 180f); as *first* and *last* 1: 11 v.l., and as both 22: 13.—S. on Ω and FCabrol, Dict. d'Arch. I, 1, 1–25; FDornseiff, D. Alphabet in Mystik u. Magie² '25, 17f; 122ff; RHCharles, HDB I 70; GerhKittel, TW I 1–3; GStuhlfauth, Protestantenbl. 69, '36, 372-4, ThBl 18, '39, 210-12.*

Ἀαρών, ὁ indecl. (אַהֲרֹן) (LXX, Philo.—In Joseph. Ἀαρών, ῶνος [Ant. 3, 54]) *Aaron,* brother of Moses (Ex 4: 14), Ac 7: 40 (Ex 32: 1). Represents the priesthood (Ex 28: 1; Num 3: 10) Hb 5: 4; 7: 11; θυγατέρες Ἀ. Lk 1: 5.—GEb 1. The strife of Aaron and Miriam w. Moses (Num 12) 1 Cl 4: 11; the test of the rods (Num 17) 43: 5; Hb 9: 4.*

Ἀβαδδών, ὁ indecl. (אֲבַדּוֹן Pr 15: 11; Ps 87: 12; Theod. Job 26: 6; 28: 22=ἀπώλεια LXX) *Abaddon* name of the ruling angel in hell Rv 9: 11, explained as Ἀπολλύων *Destroyer* (cf. אָבַד). This name for the ἄγγελος τῆς ἀβύσσου and its transl. are based on the OT passages above, in which ἀπώλεια is parallel to ᾅδης=שְׁאוֹל Theod. Job 26: 6; Pr 15: 11 and to τάφος Ps 87: 12. In Theod. Job 28: 22 it is personified, together with θάνατος. —PKatz, Vet. Test. 8, '58, 272.*

ἀβαναύσως adv. of uncertain mng.; *not in narrow-minded fashion, unselfishly, nobly* are poss.; λειτουργεῖν ἀ. beside ἀμέμπτως, μετὰ ταπεινοφροσύνης and ἡσύχως 1 Cl 44: 3. The adj. ἀβάναυσος stands betw. εὐσπλαγχνος and ἀγαπητικός Const. Apost. 2, 3, 3 and is understood by the Syrian of the Didasc. Apost. Syr. (p. 35 Lewis) as חנן *kind;* cf. Clem. Alex., Paed. 3, 34 φιλανθρώπως, οὐ βαναύσως.*

ἀβαρής, ές, gen. οῦς (Aristot.+; cf. Nägeli 38) lit. *light in weight,* only fig. *not burdensome* (CIG 5361, 15 [I bc] ἀ. ἑαυτὸν παρέσχηται; BGU 248, 26 [II ad] ἐάν σοι ἀβαρὲς ᾖ; 1080, 17; POxy. 933, 29) ἀβαρῆ ἐμαυτὸν ὑμῖν ἐτήρησα *I kept myself fr. being a burden to you* 2 Cor 11: 9. M-M.*

ἀββά (Aram. אַבָּא vocative form, secondarily and erroneously equated with the determinate state [status emphaticus; Dalman, Gramm. 90f] and hence translated ὁ πατήρ [instead of πάτερ μου]) *father,* translit. *abba,* Aram. form used in prayer (Dalman, Worte 157) and in the family circle, taken over by Greek-speaking Christians (Ltzm., Hdb. on Ro 8: 15), transl. ὁ πατήρ Mk 14: 36; Ro 8: 15; Gal 4: 6.—JWackernagel, Anredeformen '12, 12, 18; CFabricius, RSeeberg-Festschr. '29, I 21–41; Gerh Kittel, TW I 4–6, D. Religionsgesch. u. d. Urchristentum '32, 92ff, Lexicographia Sacra (Engl.) '38, 14–16; SV McCasland, JBL 72, '53, 79–91; JoachJeremias, Abba '66, 15–67; Engl., Central Message of the NT '65, 9–30;

against him, JCGreig, Studia Evangelica 5, '68, 5–10.— There is a possibility that the word may be found in the Cyprian Glosses (OHoffmann, D. griechischen Dialekte I '91 pp. 104-26). Cf. p. 105 ἀβάθ. διδάσκαλος, Κύπριοι. Cf. Μανασσῆς.*

Ἀβ(ε)ιρών, ὁ indecl. (אֲבִירָם) (LXX.—In Joseph. Ἀβίραμος, ου [Ant. 4, 19]) *Abiram,* son of Eliab, w. Dathan and On leader of a rebellion of the sons of Reuben against Moses and Aaron (Num 16); ex. of fatal jealousy 1 Cl 4: 12.*

Ἄβελ, ὁ indecl. (הֶבֶל, in pause הָבֶל) (LXX, Philo, Test. 12 Patr.—In Joseph. Ἄβελος, ου [Ant. 1, 67]), *Abel,* son of Adam (Gen 4); Abel's blood Mt 23: 35; Lk 11: 51; Hb 12: 24 (En. 22, 7); his sacrifice 11: 4; 1 Cl 4: 1f; cf. 6.— VAptowitzer, Kain u. Abel '22.*

Ἀβιά, ὁ indecl. (אֲבִיָּה) *Abijah.*—1. Son of Rehoboam (1 Ch 3: 10), an ancestor of Jesus Mt 1: 7ab.

2. Founder of the class of priests to which Zechariah belonged (1 Ch 24: 10; 2 Esdr 22 [Neh 12]: 16f; the name Zacharias occurs in the latter pass.) Lk 1: 5. Cf. ἐφημερία, Ζαχαρίας.*

Ἀβιαθάρ, ὁ indecl. (אֶבְיָתָר) (in Joseph. Ἀβιάθαρος, ου [Ant. 7, 110]) *Abiathar,* priest at Nob (1 Km 22: 20ff), son of Ahimelech (1 Km 21: 2, 7) Mk 2: 26, where he is mentioned in place of his father.*

Ἀβιληνή, ῆς, ἡ *Abilene,* the territory around the city of Abila (τὰ Ἄβιλα) at the southern end of the Anti-Lebanon range, northwest of Damascus; ruled over by Lysanias the tetrarch. Lk 3: 1.—S. lit. on Λυσανίας.*

Ἀβιούδ, ὁ indecl. (אֲבִיהוּד) (Philo.—In Joseph. Ἀβιοῦς) *Abiud,* son of Zerubbabel (not mentioned in 1 Ch 3: 19; 8: 3 the name occurs as that of a member of a Benjamite family), in genealogy of Jesus Mt 1: 13ab; Lk 3: 23ff D.*

Ἀβραάμ, ὁ indecl. (אַבְרָהָם 'father of a multitude') (LXX, Philo, Test. 12 Patr.; Sib. Or. 2, 246; PGM 7, 315; 13, 817 δύναμιν τοῦ Ἀβραάμ, Ἰσὰκ καὶ τοῦ Ἰακώβ; 35: 14 τοῦ θεοῦ τοῦ Ἀβρὰμ καὶ Ἰσακὰ καὶ Ἰακώβ. Indecl. also in Apollonius Molon [I bc], an opponent of the Jews: Euseb., Pr. Ev. 9, 19, 2; 3.—In the Jew Artapanus [II bc]: Euseb. 9, 18, in Ps.-Hecataeus: 264 fgm. 24 Jac. in a work Κατ' Ἄβραμον καὶ τοὺς Αἰγυπτίους and in Joseph. Ἄβραμος, ου [Ant. 1, 148]; cf. Ep. Arist. 49; BGU 585 II, 3 [212 ad]; Damasc., Vi. Isid. 141.—Nicol. Dam. [in Jos., Ant. 1, 159f] Ἀβράμης, ου. Charax of Pergam. [II ad]: 103 Jac. ἀπὸ Ἀβράμωνος.—In Hesychius 1, 81 we find Ἀβραμίας, obviously a Hellenized form of Abraham, as the name of a throw in dice-playing. Personal names were frequently used for this purpose: Eubulus, Com. fgm. 57K. Dssm., NB 15 [BS 187]; Bl-D. §260, 2 app.) *Abraham* in the genealogy of Jesus Mt 1: 1, 2, 17; Lk 3: 34; father of the Israelite nation (Jos., Ant. 1, 158 ὁ πατὴρ ἡμῶν Ἀ.), and of the Christians, as the true Israel Mt 3: 9; Lk 1: 73; 3: 8; J 8: 39, 53, 56; Ac 7: 2; Ro 4: 1; Js 2: 21. Hence the people of Israel are called A.'s seed J 8: 33, 37; Ro 9: 7; 11: 1; 2 Cor 11: 22; Gal 3: 29; Hb 2: 16.—A. as bearer of the

1

promise Ac 3: 25; 7: 17; Ro 4: 13; Gal 3: 8, 14, 16, 18; Hb 6: 13. His faith Ro 4: 3 (Gen 15: 6), 9, 12, 16; Gal 3: 6 (Gen 15: 6), 9; 1 Cl 10: 6 (Gen 15: 6); Js 2: 23. Here and 1 Cl 10: 1; 17: 2 called a friend of God (cf. Is 41: 8; 2 Ch 20: 7; Da 3: 35. But only Sym Is 41: 8 and, indirectly, Ex 33: 11 use the word φίλος. LXX Is 41: 8 and the other passages use a form of ἀγαπάω; cf. EPeterson, ZKG 42, '23, 172ff. Philo quotes Gen 18: 17 φίλος μου Sobr. 56 [s. PKatz, Philo's Bible, '50, 85]; cf. Wsd 7: 27; Book of Jubilees 19, 9; 30, 20); occupies a place of prominence in the next life Lk 16: 22ff (s. on κόλπος 1), like Isaac, Jacob, and the prophets 13: 28. God is designated as God of Abraham, Isaac and Jacob (Ex 3: 6.—MRist, The God of A., I., and J.: JBL 57, '38, 289–303) Mt 22: 32; Mk 12: 26; Lk 20: 37; Ac 3: 13; 7: 32; B 6: 8. W. Isaac and Jacob at the banquet in the Kingdom Mt 8: 11; listed among the great men of God (cf. Sib. Or. 2, 245-8) B 8: 4; IPhld 9: 1 (on the triad s. above and s.v. 'Ιακώβ). Points typologically to Jesus B 9: 7f.—OSchmitz, Abr. im Spätjudent. u. im Urchristent.: ASchlatter-Festschr. '22, 99–123; Billerb. (s. index of persons and things: IV 1213); JoachJeremias, TW I 7-9; MColacci, Il Semen Abrahae alla luce del V e del NT: Biblica 21, '40, 1-27. M-M.*

ἀβροχία, ας, ἡ *drought* (Dit., Or. 56, 15 [III BC]; pap. since 238 BC [Mayser I² 3, p. 27, 39; Wilcken, Grundz. index b; SWaszynski, D. Bodenpacht '05, 130ff]; LXX; Sib. Or. 3, 540) ἀ. γίνεται *a drought comes* Hs 2: 8.*

ἄβρωτος, ον (Ctesias, Menand.+; Pr 24: 22e; Philo, Spec. Leg. 3, 144; Jos., Ant. 5, 219; loanw. in rabb.) of wood *not eaten* by worms (Theophr., Hist. Pl. 5, 1, 2) ῥάβδοι Hs 8, 4, 6.*

ἄβυσσος, ου, ἡ (orig. adj., Aeschyl., Hdt.+) *abyss, depth, underworld* (Diog. L. 4, 5, 27; Iambl., Myst. 6, 5 p. 245, 15 Parthey; Herm. Wr. 3, 1; 16, 5; PGM 1, 343; 3, 554; 4, 1148; 1350; 2835; 7, 261; 517; LXX; En. 21, 7; Philo, Op. M. 29; Sib. Or. 1, 223).
   1. gener., contrasted w. sky and earth 1 Cl 28: 3 (pl. as Dt 8: 7; Ps 32: 7; 76: 17al.; Test. Levi 3: 9; Cat. Cod. Astr. VIII 2 p. 173, 29); Dg 7: 2. Dark (Gen 1: 2), hence unfathomable to the human eye 1 Cl 20: 5, and discernible only by God 59: 3.
   2. esp. the abode of the dead Ro 10: 7 (Ps 106: 26) and of demons Lk 8: 31; dungeon where the devil is kept Rv 20: 3; abode of the θηρίον, the Antichrist 11: 7; 17: 8; of Abaddon (q.v.), the angel of the underworld 9: 11 (cf. PGM 13, 169 and s. Ael. Aristid. 38 p. 724 D. on Philip: ἀνὴρ ὑβριστὴς ἐκ τοῦ βαράθρου τ. γῆς ὁρμώμενος κακῇ μοίρᾳ τ. Ἑλλήνων); φρέαρ τῆς ἀ. 9: 1f; capable of being sealed 9: 1; 20: 1, 3.—JKroll, Gott u. Hölle '32; Käthe Schneider, RAC I 60-2. M-M.*

Ἄγαβος, ου, ὁ *Agabus* (a Palmyr. inscr. [Répert. d'épigraphie sémitique II '14 no. 1086] has 'Agaba [עגבא] as a woman's name), a Christian prophet fr. Judaea Ac 11: 28; 21: 10.*

ἀγαγεῖν s. ἄγω.

ἀγαθά, ῶν, τά subst. neut. of ἀγαθός (q.v. 2b).

ἀγαθοεργέω (Pythag., Ep. 10 p. 607; contr. ἀγαθουργέω Ac 14: 17; the verb is quite rare, but ἀγαθουργός and ἀγαθουργίη go back to Hdt.) *do good* of the rich 1 Ti 6: 18. Of God *confer benefits* Ac 14: 17.*

ἀγαθοεργός, όν (Plut., Mor. 370E; 1015E; Physiogn. I 364, 13; Julian, Or. 4, 144D; Proclus on Pla., Tim. III p. 313, 17 Diehl; Theol. 122 p. 108, 21) *doing good*, subst.

(opp. ὁ κακός) Ro 13: 3 v.l. (WLLorimer, NTS 12, '66, 389f)*

ἀγαθόν, οῦ, τό subst. neut. of ἀγαθός (q.v. 2a).

ἀγαθοποιέω 1 aor. inf. ἀγαθοποιῆσαι *do good* (Sext. Emp., Math. 11, 70; Aesop 66 Halm; LXX; Ep. Arist. 242; Test. Benj. 5: 2).
   1. lit. (opp. κακοποιέω) Mk 3: 4 v.l.; Lk 6: 9. Of persons, w. pers. obj. ἀ. τινά *do good to someone* (Tob 12: 13 BA) Lk 6: 33; abs. (Zeph 1: 12) 6: 35.
   2. *do what is right* in the sense of fulfilling the Christian moral law, *be a good citizen*, opp. πονηρεύεσθαι Hs 9, 18, 1f; Dg 5: 16. Opp. ἁμαρτάνειν 1 Pt 2: 20; cf. vs. 15.—3: 6, 17; 3 J 11; 2 Cl 10: 2; Hv 3, 5, 4; 3, 9, 5.*

ἀγαθοποίησις, εως, ἡ *doing good* Hm 8: 10; προθυμίαν ἔχειν τῆς ἀ. *be zealous to do good* Hs 5, 3, 4 (found elsewh. only in very late wr.).*

ἀγαθοποιΐα, ας, ἡ (Ptolem., Apotel. 1, 18, 4 ed. FBoll-AeBoer '40; Vett. Val. 164, 17; Vi. Aesopi III p. 309, 8) *doing good* (Test. Jos. 18, 2 v.l.) κτίστῃ παρατίθεσθαι τὰς ψυχὰς ἐν ἀγαθοποιΐᾳ (𝔓⁷² et al. ἀγαθοποιΐαις) *entrust their souls to the creator while* (or *by*) *doing good*, which can be taken gener. or as meaning specif. acts (so, if pl.) 1 Pt 4: 19; πόθος εἰς ἀ. *a longing to do good* 1 Cl 2: 2. —cf. 2: 7; 33: 1; πρόθυμος εἰς ἀ. *eager to do good* 34: 2.*

ἀγαθοποιός, όν (late word [e.g. Sext. Emp., Math. 5, 29f; PGM 4, 2678; 5, 48], w. var. mngs.) *doing good, upright* (Plut., Is. et Osir. 42 p. 368a; Physiogn. II 342, 31 al.; Sir 42: 14); subst. (CWessely, Stud. z. Paläogr. u. Papyrusk. 20, '21, no. 293 II, 8) ὁ ἀ. *one who does good* 1 Pt 2: 14 (opp. κακοποιός, as Artem. 4, 59 p. 238; 9, 11; Porphyr., Ep. ad Aneb. [GParthey, Iambl. De Myst. Lb. 1857 pp. xxix-xlv] c. 6; PGM 4, 2872ff; 13, 1028ff). M-M.*

Ἀγαθόπους, ποδος, acc. Ἀγαθόπουν, ὁ *Agathopus*, epithet of 'Ρέος (q.v.) IPhld 11: 1; I Sm 10: 1. Freq. as name of slaves and freedmen, s. Hdb. ad loc.; Preisigke, Namenbuch '22; inscr. in Rev. archéol. 5. sér. 22, '25, p. 363 no. 97; Clem. Alex., Strom. III 7, 59, 3.*

ἀγαθός, ή, όν (Hom.+; inscr., pap., LXX, Ep. Arist., Philo, Joseph., Test. 12 Patr.) Comp. ἀμείνων (not in NT, but e.g. PGM 5, 50; 6, 2; Jos., Bell. 5, 19, Ant. 11, 296) 1 Cl 57: 2; I Eph 13: 2; 15: 1; βελτίων, also κρείσσων, colloq. ἀγαθώτερος (Diod. S. 8 fgm. 12, 8; Judg 11: 25 B; 15: 2 B) Hm 8: 9, 11. Superl. ἄριστος (Jos., C. Ap. 2, 156, Ant. 16, 142); colloq. ἀγαθώτατος (Diod. S. 16, 85, 7; Philo Bybl. [c. 100 AD] s. below 1ba; Heliod. 5, 15, 2; Synes., Ep. 143; Jos., Bell. 2, 277) Hv 1, 2, 3;—Ael. Dion. a, 10 rejects the forms ἀγαθώτερος, -τατος as wholly foreign to Greek. Bl-D. §61, 1 *good*.
   1. adj.—a. in external sense *fit, capable, useful.*
      α. of pers. δοῦλος (Heraclitus, Ep. 9, 3) Mt 25: 21, 23; Lk 19: 17. ἀνήρ (Teles p. 16, 6; Diod. S. 20, 58, 1; Epict. 3, 24, 51 al.; PLond. 113, 1; 27; 2 Macc 15: 12; 4 Macc 4: 1; Jos., Bell. 5, 413, Ant. 18, 117; JGerlach, ΑΝΗΡ ΑΓΑΘΟΣ, Diss. Munich '32) Lk 23: 50; Ac 11: 24; νέαι Tit 2: 5. ἀπόστολοι 1 Cl 5: 3.
      β. of things καρποί (Procop. Soph., Ep. 27; Sir 6: 19; Da 4: 12 LXX) Js 3: 17. δένδρον Mt 7: 17f. γῆ fertile soil (X., Oec. 16, 7 γῆ ἀ.—γῆ κακή; Diod. S. 5, 41, 6; Arrian, Anab. 4, 28, 3; Jos., Ant. 5, 178) Lk 8: 8; B 6: 8, 10. δόματα *beneficial* (Sir 18: 17) Mt 7: 11; Lk 11: 13. δόσις Js 1: 17; λόγος ἀ. πρὸς οἰκοδομήν *useful for edification* Eph 4: 29 (cf. X., Mem. 4, 6, 11; Chio, Ep. 3, 6 πρὸς ἀνδρείαν ἀμείνους; Isocr. 15, 284 ἄριστα πρὸς ἀρετήν);

γνώμη ἀ. *a gracious declaration* 1 Cl 8: 2; ἡμέραι ἀ. *happy* (Cass. Dio 51, 19; PGenève 61, 10; Sir 14: 14; 1 Macc 10: 55) 1 Pt 3: 10; 1 Cl 22: 2 (both Ps 33: 13; 34: 12); cf. 50: 4.

b. of inner worth, esp. moral (so Pind.+).

a. of pers. *perfect* of God (Dio Chrys. 80[30], 26 οἱ θεοί; Zoroaster in Philo Bybl. [Euseb., Pr. Ev. 1, 10, 52]: God is ἀγαθῶν ἀγαθώτατος; Sallust. c. 1 πᾶς θεὸς ἀγαθός.— Cf. WPPaton and ELHicks, The Inscr. of Cos 1891 no. 92, which calls Nero ἀ. θεός, ἀγαθὸς δαίμων [Dit., Or. 666, 3; POxy. 1021, 8—both referring to Nero—POxy. 1449, 4; cf. also JKroll, D. Lehren d. Hermes Trismeg. '14, 90; Rtzst., Erlösungsmyst. 189; 191ff] and Sb 349 θεῷ ἀγαθῷ Διὶ Ἡλίῳ; Philo, Leg. All. 1, 47 al.; Celsus 4, 14) Mt 19: 17b (in Cleanthes [Euseb., Pr. Ev. 13, 13, 37] a description of God follows the question τἀγαθὸν ἐρωτᾷς μ' οἷόν ἐστ';); Mk 10: 18b (JoachJeremias, Unknown Sayings of Jesus, tr. Fuller, '57, 33-36); Lk 18: 19b; Dg 8: 8 (on these passages cf. Simonides, fgm. 4, 6f χαλεπὸν ἐσθλὸν [=ἀγαθός 1. 10] ἔμμεναι, 7 θεὸς ἂν μόνος τοῦτ' ἔχοι γέρας); μόνος ἀ. ἐστιν ibid.; πατὴρ ἀ. 1 Cl 56: 16 (Philo, Op. M. 21 ἀγ. εἶναι τὸν πατέρα κ. ποιητήν); ἀ. ἐν τ. ὁρωμένοις *good in the visible world* 60: 1.—Of Christ Mk 10: 17, 18a; Lk 18: 18, 19a (WWagner, ZNW 8, '07, 143-61; FSpitta, ibid. 9, '08, 12-20; BBWarfield, PTR 12, '14, 177-228; WCaspari, Christent. u. Wissensch. 8, '32, 218-31; s. below.—Cf. also the saying of Pythagoras in Diog. L., Prooem. 12, who does not wish to be called σοφός because: μηδένα εἶναι σοφὸν ἀλλ' ἢ θεόν); *upright* J 7: 12.—Of men Mt 12: 35; Ro 5: 7; D 3: 8; νομοθέται B 21: 4; πονηροί τε καὶ ἀ. *good and bad* designating a crowd gathered at random Mt 22: 10. Same contrast 5: 45 (cf. Jos., Ant. 8, 314). βελτίονα ποιεῖν *make better* 1 Cl 19: 1; βελτίω γενέσθαι *become better* Dg 1; *kind, generous* (X., Cyr. 3, 3, 4; CIG 37, 49) Mt 20: 15 (in Mk 10: 17f=Lk 18: 18 [s. above] it is understood as *kind* by Wlh., EKlostermann, Billerb., Wagner, Spitta, Dalman [Worte 277], EHirsch [D. Werden des Mk '41, 246]); δεσπόται *benevolent* 1 Pt 2: 18 (cf. PLeipz. 40 II, 19, where a slave says ὁ ἀγαθὸς δεσπότης μου).

β. of things πνεῦμα Lk 11: 13 v.l.; ἐντολή Ro 7: 12 (Archytas [IV BC] in Stob., Ecl. 4, 138 vol. IV p. 85, 17 H. νόμος ἀγ. καὶ καλός); ἀγγελία (Pr 25: 25) Hv 3, 13, 2; παιδεία s 6, 3, 6; μνεία ἀ. *kindly remembrance* 1 Th 3: 6 (2 Macc 7: 20 μνήμη ἀ.); ἐλπὶς *dependable* (Pla., Rep. 331A; Charito 7, 5; Jos., Ant. 14, 96) 2 Th 2: 16; μερὶς ἀ. *the better part* Lk 10: 42; πρᾶξις (Democr. 177 πρῆξις) 1 Cl 30: 7; συνείδησις *clear* Ac 23: 1; 1 Ti 1: 5, 19; 1 Pt 2: 19 𝔓⁷² et al.; 3: 16, 21; 1 Cl 41: 1; διάνοια Hm 5, 2, 7; ἐπιθυμία (Pr 11: 23; 13: 12) *pure* (i.e., directed toward pure things) *desire* m 12, 1, 1f; 2: 4f; 3: 1; γνώμη ἀ. *good intention* B 21: 2, ἀ. ἐν Χριστῷ ἀναστροφή *good Christian conduct* 1 Pt 3: 16; ἀ. θησαυρὸς Mt 12: 35; Lk 6: 45; καρδία καλὴ καὶ ἀ. 8: 15; ἔργον (Thu. 5, 63, 3; Maspéro 151, 237) *a good deed* 2 Cor 9: 8; Col 1: 10; 1 Ti 5: 10; 2 Ti 2: 21; 3: 17; Tit 1: 16; 3: 1; 1 Cl 2: 7; 33: 1; 34: 4. Pl. ἔργα ἀ. (Empedocles [V BC] 112, 2) 1 Ti 2: 10; also specif. of benefactions (w. ἐλεημοσύναι) Ac 9: 36; 1 Cl 33: 7; ἐν παντὶ ἔργῳ κ. λόγῳ ἀ. (λόγος 2 3; 3 Km 8: 56; 4 Km 20: 19; Is 39: 8) 2 Th 2: 17; ὑπομονὴ ἔργου ἀ. *persistency in doing right* Ro 2: 7.

2. used as a pure subst. (Hom.+; inscr., pap., LXX).

a. ἀγαθόν, οὗ, τό *the good, what is good, right* (Diog L. 1, 105 ἀγαθόν τε καὶ φαῦλον=a good thing and a bad thing at the same time).

a. what is intrinsically valuable, morally good ἐργάζεσθαι τὸ ἀ. *do what is good* Ro 2: 10; Hm 4, 2, 2; 7: 4; also specif. of benefaction Gal 6: 10 and of honest work

Eph 4: 28; Hm 2: 4; τὸ ἀ. ποιεῖν (cf. Jos., Bell. 1, 392) Ro 13: 3b; Hm 8: 12; cf. 6, 2, 8.—Mt 19: 17a; Ro 7: 13; 12: 9; 16: 19; 1Th 5: 15; 1 Pt 3: 13; 1 Cl 21: 6; 2 Cl 13: 1; Hm 8: 2, 7.

β. *advantage, good* εἰς (τὸ) ἀ. (Theognis 162 τὸ κακὸν γίνεται εἰς ἀ.; Sir 7: 13; 39: 27) *for good, to advantage* Lk 7: 16 v.l.; Ro 8: 28; 13: 4; 15: 2.

γ. In Ro 14: 16 it is uncertain whether τὸ ἀ. means the gospel as a *good thing* or Christian freedom as a *right* or *privilege*.

b. ἀγαθά, ῶν, τά *good things*—a. quite gener. τὰ ἀγαθά σου Lk 16: 25 (cf. Job 21: 13; the opp. of τὰ κακά as Ephor. of Cyme [IV BC] περὶ ἀγαθῶν κ. κακῶν: 70 Test. 1 Jac.; Diod. S. 18, 53, 1 ἀγαθῶν τε καὶ κακῶν μεταλαμβάνων; Job 2: 10); τοιαῦτα ἀ. *such fine things* Hs 9, 10, 1.—1 Cl 61: 3.

β. *possessions, treasures* (Hdt. 2, 172 al.; PRyl. 28, 182 δεσπότης πολλῶν ἀγαθῶν κ. κτημάτων; Sir 14: 4; Wsd 7: 11; Sib. Or. 3, 660; 750) Lk 1: 53 (Ps 106: 9.—Comic poet Amphis [IV BC] in Athen. 3, 56 p. 100A χορτάζομαι ἐν ἅπασιν ἀγαθοῖς; Sb 7517, 4 [211/12 AD] ἀγαθῶν πεπληρῶσθαι); Gal 6: 6; Hv 3, 9, 6; τὰ ἀ. τῆς γῆς 1 Cl 8: 4 (Is 1: 19); esp. of crops (Diod. S. 3, 46, 1 τὰ ἀγ.='the good gifts', specifically 'products of nature'. Likewise 19, 26, 3. Even more generally Synes., Kingship 16 p. 17D τὰ ἀγ.= food; Philo, Op. M. 167, Mos. 1, 6) Lk 12: 18f.

γ. possessions of a higher order (Dio Chrys. 64 [14], 1 ἐλευθερία as μέγιστον τ. ἀγαθῶν; Ael. Aristid. 24, 4 K.= 44 p. 825 D.: ὁμόνοια as μέγ. τῶν ἀ.; 45, 18 K.= 8 p. 89 D.: τὰ τῆς ψυχῆς ἀγ. Diog. L. 6, 4 the priest promises the initiate into the Orphic mysteries πολλὰ ἐν ᾅδου ἀγαθά) Ro 3: 8; 10: 15 (Is 52: 7).—Hb 9: 11; 10: 1; 2 Cl 6: 6; 15: 5.

δ. τὰ ἀ. *good deeds* J 5: 29; cf. Hm 10, 3, 1. M-M. B. 1176.

ἀγαθότης, ητος, ἡ *goodness* (Philo, Leg. All. 1, 59 ἡ γενικωτάτη ἀρετή, ἥν τινες ἀγαθότητα καλοῦσιν) of God (Sallust. 3 p. 4, 4; c. 7 p. 14, 1 al.; Themist., Or. 1, p. 8, 28; Procl. on Pla., Rep. I p. 27, 10; 28, 4 al. WKroll; Simplicius in Epict. p. 12, 7; Cat. Cod. Astr. VIII 2 p. 156, 16; Sb 2034, 7; Wsd 7: 26; 12: 22; Philo, Deus Imm. 73 al.) and of men (Wsd 1: 1; Sir 45: 23; Test. Asher 3: 1; Benj. 8: 1), as 2 Cl 13: 4.*

ἀγαθουργέω Ac 14: 17, s. ἀγαθοεργέω.*

ἀγαθωσύνη, ης, ἡ (Thom. Mag. p. 391, 12; for the formation s. W-S §16b note 14; Rob. 201) as a characteristic of men (2 Ch 24: 16; Ps 51: 5; Physiogn. II 342, 17 ἀγαθωσύνη) *goodness, uprightness* Ro 15: 14; Eph 5: 9; 2 Th 1: 11; *generosity* Gal 5: 22. Of God (2 Esdr 19[Neh 9]: 25, 35) ἀ. τοῦ πατρὸς ἡμῶν B 2: 9.*

ἀγαλλίασις, εως, ἡ (only in Bibl. [incl. En. 5, 9; Test. 12 Patr.] and eccl. wr.; esp. freq. in Ps. Not in secular writers [s. the foreword to this lexicon, p. xix, note.]) *exultation* (esp. messianic) ἦν πολλὴ ἀ. Ac 11: 28 D; w. χαρά Lk 1: 14; 1 Cl 63: 2; MPol 18: 2; w. εὐφροσύνη 1 Cl 18: 8; B 1: 6; ἐν ἀ. *full of exultation, joy* Lk 1: 44; Ac 2: 46; Jd 24; MPol 18: 2. ἔλαιον ἀγαλλιάσεως *oil of gladness* Hb 1: 9 (Ps 44: 8 שָׂשׂוֹן i.e., the oil w. which people anointed themselves at festivals). ἀπόδος μοι τὴν ἀ. τοῦ σωτηρίου σου *restore to me the joy of thy salvation* 1 Cl 18: 12 (Ps 50: 14).—BReicke, Diakonie, Festfreude u. Zelos, usw. '51, 165-229.*

ἀγαλλιάω (new formation in H. Gk., found only in Bibl. and eccl. wr., for ἀγάλλω) seldom act. (Bl-D. §101;

Mlt.-H. 225f): ἀγαλλιᾶτε 1 Pt 1: 8 v.l. (for ἀγαλλιᾶσθε); Rv 19: 7 ἀγαλλιῶμεν (v.l. ἀγαλλιώμεθα); 1 aor. (as POxy. 1592, 4 [IV AD]) ἠγαλλίασεν Lk 1: 47 (ἐπὶ τ. θεῷ, cf. Hab 3: 18 v.l.); usu. dep. ἀγαλλιάομαι (Syntipas p. 75, 28) w. 1 aor. mid. ἠγαλλιασάμην or pass. ἠγαλλιάθην v.l. ἠγαλλιάσθην (Bl-D. §78; Mlt-H. 225) exult, be glad, overjoyed (oft. LXX; Test. 12 Patr.) abs. 1 Pt 1: 6 (ἀγαλλιάσαντες 𝔓72); 1 Cl 18: 8 (Ps 50: 10; Hm 5, 1, 2; 5, 2, 3; s 1: 6; MPol 19: 2; my tongue exults Ac 2: 26 (Ps 15: 9); as here w. εὐφραίνεσθαι (Ps 30: 8; 31: 11; Is 25: 9) Hm 5, 1, 2; s 9, 18, 4; χαίρειν καὶ ἀ. (Tob 13: 15 BA) Mt 5: 12; Rv 19: 7; cf. ἵνα χαρῆτε ἀγαλλιώμενοι that you might shout for joy 1 Pt 4: 13; cf. IMg 1: 1; Hs 1: 6. W. complementary ptc. ἠγαλλιάσατο πεπιστευκώς he was overjoyed because he had become a Christian Ac 16: 34. W. ἵνα foll. (s. ἵνα II 1aα): ἀ., ἵνα ἴδῃ he was overjoyed to see J 8: 56 (Bl-D. §392, 1a app.). The one who causes the joy is given in the dat. ἀ. τῷ πνεύματι τῷ ἁγίῳ Lk 10: 21; w. ἐν and dat. ibid. v.l.—W. dat. of cause ἀ. χαρᾷ ἀνεκλαλήτῳ exult w. unspeakable joy 1 Pt 1: 8. οἷς ἀγαλλιῶμαι I rejoice in this IEph 9: 2 (cf. Quint. Smyrn. 9, 118 παισὶν ἀγαλλόμενος = rejoicing aloud over his sons). The object of the joy is indicated by ἐπί τινι (Ps 9: 15; 20: 2; Sir 30: 3 al.; Bl-D. §196 w. app.): Hs 8, 1, 18; 9, 24, 2. Also ἔν τινι (Ps 88: 17) J 5: 35; ἀ. ἐν τῷ πάθει rejoice in the Passion IPhld inscr.; the acc. occurs once ἀ. τὴν δικαιοσύνην rejoice in righteousness 1 Cl 18: 15 (Ps 50: 16).—RBultmann, TW I 18-20; Gdspd., Probs. 192-4; WNauck, Freude im Leiden, ZNW 46, '55, 68-80.*

ἀγάλλομαι (Hom.+; Jos., Ant. 18, 66; Sib. Or. 3, 785) be glad, rejoice ἐπί τινι in someth. (Thu. 3, 82, 7; Polemo, Decl. 2, 17 p. 22, 1; Aesop., Fab. 74 P.= 128 H.; Philo, Somn. 2, 211; Jos., Ant. 17, 112) 1 Cl 33: 2 (A reads ἀγαλλιᾶται).*

ἄγαμος, ου, ὁ and ἡ (Hom.+; BGU 86, 15; 113, 4; PRyl. 28, 29) an unmarried man or woman: of both 1 Cor 7: 8 (opp. γεγαμηκότες vs. 10, as X., Symp. 9, 7). Of men vs. 32; Agr 18; of women (Hyperid. 2, 12) 1 Cor 7: 34; AP 11: 26 (restored; the adv. ἀγάμως is also poss.); of divorced women 1 Cor 7: 11. There is a curious usage in Mt 22: 10 v.l. in ms. C. M-M.*

ἀγανακτέω 1 aor. ἠγανάκτησα (since Thu. 8, 43, 4; inscr., pap., LXX) be aroused, indignant, angry (Bel 28 Theod.; Jos., Ant. 2, 284) Mt 21: 15; 26: 8; Mk 10: 14; 2 Cl 19: 2. W. the pers mentioned ἀ. περί τινος at someone Mt 20: 24; Mk 10: 41 (cf. Pla., Ep. 7, p. 349D; Jos., Ant. 14, 182; Bl-D. §229, 2). ἀ. ἐπί τινι (Lysias 1, 1; Isocr. 16, 49; PLond. 44, 20[II BC] ἀγανακτοῦντα ἐφ' οἷς διετελοῦντο ἐν τοιούτῳ ἱερῷ; Wsd 12: 27) at someone GP 4: 14; at someth. (Diod. S. 4, 63, 3 ἐπὶ τῷ γεγονότι; Appian, Macedon. 1 §3) 1 Cl 56: 2; Mk 14: 4 ἦσαν δέ τινες ἀγανακτοῦντες πρὸς ἑαυτούς is difficult; perh. some expressed their displeasure to each other (but elsewh. πρός introduces the one against whom the displeasure is directed: Dio Chrys. 13[7], 43 ὁ ἄρχων ἠγανάκτησε πρός με; Socrat., Ep. 6, 7.—D reads οἱ δὲ μαθηταὶ αὐτοῦ διεπονοῦντο καὶ ἔλεγον). The reason for the displeasure is added w. ὅτι (Herodian 3, 2, 3) Lk 13: 14. M-M.*

ἀγανάκτησις, εως, ἡ (since Thu. 2, 41, 3; Appian, Bell. Civ. 1, 10 §39; 4, 124 §521; PGrenf. II 82, 17f; Esth 8: 12 i v.l.; Jos., Bell. 4, 342) indignation 2 Cor 7: 11. M-M.*

ἀγαπάω impf. ἠγάπων; fut. ἀγαπήσω; 1 aor. ἠγάπησα; pf. ἠγάπηκα, ptc. ἠγαπηκώς; pf. pass. ptc. ἠγαπημένος; 1 fut. pass. ἀγαπηθήσομαι (in var. mngs. Hom.+; inscr., pap.; LXX; Ep. Arist.; Philo; Jos., e.g.

Vi. 198 [alternating w. φιλέω]; Test. 12 Patr.—STromp de Ruiter, Gebruik en beteekenis van ἀγαπᾶν in de Grieksche Litteratuur '30; CCRichardson, Love: Greek and Christian in Journ. of Rel. 23, '43, 173-85) love, cherish.

1. of affection for persons—a. by human beings—α. to persons; w. obj. given γυναῖκας Eph 5: 25, 28, 33; Col 3: 19; ὡς ἀδελφήν Hv 1, 1, 1. τὸν πλησίον Mt 5: 43; 19: 19; 22: 39; Mk 12: 31, 33 (on 33b s. Aristaen., Ep. 2, 13, end φιλῶ σε ὡς ἐμαυτήν); Ro 13: 9; Gal 5: 14; Js 2: 8; B 19: 5 (all quots. fr. Lev 19: 18); s. πλησίον 1; τὸν ἕτερον Ro 13: 8. τὸν ἀδελφόν 1 J 2: 10; 3: 10; 4: 20f. τοὺς ἀδελφούς 3: 14. τὰ τέκνα τοῦ θεοῦ 5: 2. ἀλλήλους J 13: 34; 15: 12, 17; 1 J 3: 11, 23; 4: 7, 11f; 2 J 5; Ro 13: 8; 1 Th 4: 9. τοὺς ἀγαπῶντας Mt 5: 46; Lk 6: 32. τὸ ἔθνος ἡμῶν 7: 5. τοὺς ἐχθρούς Mt 5: 44; Lk 6: 27, 35; cf. WCvanUnnik, Nov T 8, '66, 284-300, and s. ἐχθρός 2bβ; ἀ. τινα ὑπὲρ τὴν ψυχήν love someone more than one's own life B 1: 4; 4: 6; 19: 5; D 2: 7 (cf. Philo, Rer. Div. Her. 42 ὑπερφυῶς ἀ.; Epigr. Gr. 716, 5 φίλους ὑπὲρ ἀτὸν [=αὐτὸν] ἐτίμα). εἰ περισσοτέρως ὑμᾶς ἀγαπῶ, ἧσσον ἀγαπῶμαι; if I love you more, am I to be loved less? 2 Cor 12: 15; ἀ. πολύ, ὀλίγον show much or little love Lk 7: 47; cf. πλεῖον ἀγαπήσει αὐτόν will love him more vs. 42 (on the love-hate pair s. AFridrichsen, Svensk Exegetisk Årsbok 5, '40, 152-62.—The meaning be grateful is suggested for Lk 7: 42 by HGWood, ET 66, '55, 319, after JoachJeremias. See Jos. Bell. 1, 392 and Ps 114: 1 LXX). Abs. ἡμεῖς ἀγαπῶμεν 1 J 4: 19. πᾶς ὁ ἀγαπῶν vs. 7. ὁ μὴ ἀγαπῶν vs. 8. W. indication of the kind of love: ἀ. ἐν Ἰησοῦ Χρ. I Mg 6: 2. Opp. μισεῖν (Dt 21: 15-17) Mt 6: 24; Lk 16: 13.

β. to supernatural beings: to Jesus 1 Pt 1: 8. Esp. in J: 8: 42; 14: 15, 21, 23f; 21: 15f (always spoken by Jesus.—On the last passage cf. AFridrichsen, Symb. Osl. 14, '35, 46-9; EAMcDowell, Rev. and Exp. 32, '35, 422-41; Gdspd., Probs. 116-18; JAScott, Class. Weekly 39, '45-'46, 71f; 40, '46-'47, 60f; M-EBoismard, RB 54, '47, 486f.—ἀ. and φιλέω seem to be used interchangeably here; cf. the freq. interchange of synonyms elsewh. in the same chapter [βόσκειν-ποιμαίνειν, ἀρνία-προβάτια, ἑλκύειν-σύρειν]).—To God (Dio Chrys. 11[12], 61; Sextus 442; 444; LXX; Philo, Post. Caini 69; Jos., Ant. 7, 269; Test. Benj. 3: 1; 4: 5) Mt 22: 37; Mk 12: 30, 33; Lk 10: 27 (all Dt 6: 5); Ro 8: 28; 1 Cor 2: 9; 8: 3. Of love to the Creator B 19: 2.

b. of the love of supernatural beings—α. to human beings: God's love to men (Dio Chrys. 3, 60 ἀγαπώμενος ὑπὸ θεῶν; 79[28], 13; CIG 5159 Βρουτταρᾶτος, ὃν ἀγαπᾷ ἡ Φαρία Ἴσις; Norden, Agn. Th. 225 ὃν Ἄμμων ἀγαπᾷ; 226 [= Dit., Or. 90, 4]; s. 1d below; LXX; Jos., Ant. 8, 173; 314; Test. Napht. 8: 4, 10) Ro 8: 37; 9: 13 (Mal 1: 2); 2 Th 2: 16; Hb 12: 6 (Pr 3: 12); J 14: 21 (τηρη θήσεται 𝔓75); 1 J 4: 10, 19; 1 Cl 56: 4 (Pr 3: 12). ἱλαρὸν δότην 2 Cor 9: 7.—Jesus' love for men Ι. ἠγάπησεν αὐτόν J. became fond of him Mk 10: 21 (caressed him is also poss.; cf. X., Cyr. 7, 5, 50; Plut., Pericl. 1, 1 al.).—Gal 2: 20; Eph 5: 2; J 11: 5; 15: 9; B 1: 1. Of the beloved disciple J 13: 23; 19: 26; 21: 7, 20; s. Hdb.[3] on J 13: 23, also JAMaynard, Journ. of the Soc. of Oriental Research 13, '29, 155-9; Bultmann 369-71 al.; AKragerud, Der Lieblingsjünger im Johannesevangelium, '59; LJohnson, ET 77, '66, 157f; see also μαθητής 2ba.

β. to other supernatural beings: God's love for Jesus J 3: 35; 10: 17; 17: 26, from before creation 17: 24.—Jesus' love for God J 14: 31.

c. of the practice of love: prove one's love J 13: 1, 34 (perh. an allusion to the agape or love-feast). Abs. w. indication of the means μὴ ἀγαπῶμεν λόγῳ μηδὲ τῇ γλώσσῃ ἀλλὰ ἐν ἔργῳ *let us show our love not with word or w. tongue, but w. deeds* (Test. Gad 6: 1 ἀγαπήσατε ἀλλήλους ἐν ἔργῳ) 1 J 3: 18; cf. ἀ. τῷ στόματι *love w. the mouth* 1 Cl 15: 4 (Ps 77: 36 Swete).

d. pf. pass. ptc. *the one loved* by God (cf. Dt 32: 15; 33: 5, 26; Is 44: 2) as designation of Jesus (cf. Odes of Sol. 3, 8; Ascension of Isaiah 1, 3 al.; Dit., Or. 90, 4 [II BC] an Egyptian king is ἠγαπημένος ὑπὸ τοῦ Φθᾶ; Wilcken, Chrest. 109, 12 [III BC] a king ἠγαπημένος ὑπὸ τ. Ἴσιδος) Eph 1: 6; B 3: 6; 4: 3, 8. ἠγαπημένος παῖς αὐτοῦ 1 Cl 59: 2f; υἱὸς ἠ. Hs 9, 12, 5. Of Jerusalem τὴν πόλιν τὴν ἠ. (Sir 24: 11) Rv 20: 9. Of the Christians ἀδελφοὶ ἠ. ὑπὸ τ. θεοῦ (cf. Sir 45: 1; 46: 13) 1 Th 1: 4; 2 Th 2: 13; ἅγιοι καὶ ἠ. Col 3: 12; τοῖς ἐν θεῷ πατρὶ ἠγαπημένος Jd 1; ἐκκλησία ἠ. ITr inscr.; IRo inscr.— Ro 9: 25 (Hos 2: 25 v.l.).—S. the lit. on φιλέω 1a.

2. of the love for things; denoting high esteem for or satisfaction with something (Aesop, Fab. 156 P.—Appian, Mithrid. 57 §230 τὰ προτεινόμενα = the proffered terms), or striving after them (Theopomp. [IV BC]: 115 fgm. 124 Jac. τιμήν; Diod. S. 11, 46, 2 τ. πλοῦτον; Appian, Bell. Civ. 1, 49 §215 citizenship; Dit., Syll.³ 1268 I, 9 [III BC] φιλίαν ἀγάπα; pap. of early Ptolemaic times in WCrönert, NGG '22, 31; Ps 39: 17; Sir 3: 26) τὴν πρωτοκαθεδρίαν καὶ τοὺς ἀσπασμούς Lk 11: 43. μισθὸν ἀδικίας 2 Pt 2: 15. τὸν κόσμον 1 J 2: 15. τὸν νῦν αἰῶνα 2 Ti 4: 10; Pol 9: 2. δικαιοσύνην (Wsd 1: 1) Hb 1: 9 (Ps 44: 8). σεμνότητα Hm 5, 2, 8. τὴν ἀλήθειαν (Jos., C. Ap. 2, 296; Test. Reub. 3: 9) 1 Cl 18: 6 (Ps 50: 8); Hm 3: 1. Opp. ἀ. ψεύδη B 20: 2. ὅρκον ψευδῆ 2: 8 (Zech 8: 17). μᾶλλον τὸ σκότος ἢ τὸ φῶς J 3: 19 (on ἀγ. μᾶλλον w. acc. cf. Jos., Ant. 5, 350 and see μᾶλλον 3c); ἀ. τὴν δόξαν τ. ἀνθρώπων μᾶλλον ἥπερ τ. δ. τοῦ θεοῦ *value the approval of men more highly than that of God* 12: 43 (cf. Pla., Phaedr. 257E). ζωήν *enjoy life* (Sir 4: 12) 1 Pt 3: 10; also τὴν ψυχήν (Sir 30: 23 v.l.) Rv 12: 11.—Hence *long for* τὶ *someth.* (Ps 39: 17) τὴν ἐπιφάνειαν αὐτοῦ *his appearing* 2 Ti 4: 8. W. inf. fol. *wish* (Anton. Lib. 40, 1 ἠγάπησεν ἀεὶ παρθένος εἶναι). ἡμέρας ἰδεῖν ἀγαθάς *to see good days* 1 Cl 22: 2 (Ps 33: 13). τὸ παθεῖν *wish for martyrdom* ITr 4: 2.—ἀγάπην ἀ. (2 Km 13: 15) *show love* J 17: 26; Eph 2: 4; *show one's love* τὰ δεσμά *for my bonds* IPol 2: 3 (not *kiss*; there is so far no evidence for that mng. of ἀ.).—ISm 7: 1 the context seems to require for ἀ. the sense ἀγάπην ποιεῖν (8: 2)= *hold a love-feast*, but so far this mng. cannot be confirmed lexically. But since the noun ἀγάπη is used absolutely in 6: 2, it may be that ἀγαπᾶν in 7: 1 refers to *acts of love*. M-M. B. 1110.

ἀγάπη, ης, ἡ—I. *love* (an unquestioned example fr. a pagan source was lacking for a long time [s. critical art. by EPeterson, BZ 20, '32, 378–82]. Now we have an inscr. that is surely pagan [Suppl. Epigr. Gr. VIII '37, 11, 6—III AD], in the light of which such exx. as PBerl. 9869= Berl. Klassikertexte II '05 p. 55 [II BC]; Philod., παρρ. col. 13a, 3 Oliv.; POxy. 1380, 28; 109 [II AD] and others fr. paganism [s. Ltzm., exc. after 1 Cor 13; L-S-J lex.; ACeresa-Gastaldo, Ἀγάπη nei documenti anteriori al NT: Aegyptus 31, '51, 269–306 has a new pap. and a new inscr. ex. fr. III AD secular sources; in Rivista di Filologia 31, '53, 347–56 the same author shows it restored in an inscr. of 27 BC, also in various later texts] take on new mng. In Jewish sources: LXX, esp. SSol, also PsSol 18: 3; Ep. Arist. 229; Philo, Deus Imm. 69; Test. Gad 4: 7; 5: 2, Benj. 8: 2; Sib. Or. 2, 65. Cf. ACarr, ET 10, '99, 321–30).

1. of human love—a. without indication of the pers. who is the object of the love (cf. Eccl 9: 1, 6; Sir 48: 11 v.l.): ἀ. as subj. ἡ ἀ. οἰκοδομεῖ 1 Cor 8: 1.—13: 4, 8 (on 1

Cor 13 cf. AHarnack, SAB '11, 132–63, esp. 152f; ELehmann and AFridrichsen, 1 Cor 13 e. christl.-stoische Diatribe: StKr Sonderheft '22, 55–95 [Maximus Tyr. 20, 2 praise of ἔρως, what it is not and what it is]; EHoffmann, Pauli Hymnus auf d. Liebe: Dtsche Vierteljahrsschrift für Literaturwiss. u. Geistesgesch. 4, '26, 58–73; NWLund, JBL 50, '31, 266–76; GRudberg, Hellas och Nya Testamentet '34, 149f; HRiesenfeld, Con. Neot. 5, '41, 1–32, Nuntius 6, '52, 47f); Phil 1: 9. ἡ ἀ. κακὸν οὐκ ἐργάζεται Ro 13: 10; πλήρωμα νόμου ἡ ἀ. ibid.; ψυγήσεται ἡ ἀ. τ. πολλῶν Mt 24: 12; ἡ ἀ. ἀνυπόκριτος *let love be genuine* Ro 12: 9, cf. 2 Cor 6: 6. As predicate 1 Ti 1: 5; 1 J 4: 16b. As obj. ἀγάπην ἔχειν 1 Cor 13: 1–3; Phil 2: 2; διώκειν 1 Cor 14: 1; 1 Ti 6: 11; 2 Ti 2: 22; ἐνδύσασθαι τὴν ἀ. Col 3: 14.—2 Pt 1: 7; Col 1: 8. In gen. case ὁ κόπος τῆς ἀ. 1 Th 1: 3; τὸ τ. ὑμετέρας ἀ. γνήσιον *the genuineness of your love* 2 Cor 8: 8. ἔνδειξις τῆς ἀ. vs. 24.—Hb 10: 24; Phil 2: 1; 1 Pt 5: 14; 1 Cl 49: 2.—In prep. phrases ἐξ ἀγάπης *out of love* Phil 1: 16; παράκλησις ἐμὶ τῇ ἀ. *sou comfort from your love* Phlm 7; περιπατεῖν κατὰ ἀ., ἐν ἀ. Ro 14: 15; Eph 5: 2; ἐν ἀ. ἔρχεσθαι (opp. ἐν ῥάβδῳ) 1 Cor 4: 21; ἀληθεύειν ἐν ἀ. Eph 4: 15. Other verbal combinations w. ἐν ἀ., 1 Cor 16: 14; Eph 3: 17; 4: 2; Col 2: 2; 1 Th 5: 13; cf. Eph 4: 16. διὰ τῆς ἀ. δουλεύετε ἀλλήλοις Gal 5: 13. πίστις δι' ἀγάπης ἐνεργουμένη 5: 6. διὰ τὴν ἀ. παρακαλῶ *for love's sake I appeal* Phlm 9. μετὰ ἀγάπης πολιτεύεσθαι *live in love* 1 Cl 51: 2.—W. πίστις 1 Th 3: 6; 5: 8; 1 Ti 1: 14; 2 Ti 1: 13; Phlm 5; B 11: 8; IEph 1: 1; 9: 1; 14: 1 al. W. πίστις and other concepts on the same plane Eph 6: 23; 1 Ti 2: 15; 4: 12; 6: 11; 2 Ti 2: 22; 3: 10; Tit 2: 2; Rv 2: 19; Hm 8: 9; cf. v 3, 8, 2–5. The triad πίστις, ἐλπίς, ἀγάπη 1 Cor 13: 13; s. also Col 1: 4f; 1 Th 1: 3; 5: 8; B 1: 4 (cf. Porphyr., Ad Marcellam 24 τέσσαρα στοιχεῖα μάλιστα κεκρατύνθω περὶ θεοῦ· πίστις, ἀλήθεια, ἔρως, ἐλπίς and s. Rtzst., Hist. Mon. '16, 242ff; NGG '16, 367ff; '17, 130ff, Hist. Zeitschr. 116, '16, 189ff; AHarnack, PJ 164, '16, 5ff= Aus d. Friedens- u. Kriegsarbeit '16, 1ff; PCorssen, Sokrates 7, '19, 18ff; Annemarie Brieger, D. urchr. Trias Gl., Lbe, Hoff., Heidelb. Diss. '25; WTheiler, D. Vorbereitung d. Neuplatonismus '30, 148f). W. δύναμις and σωφρονισμός 2 Ti 1: 7. Cf. B 1: 6.—Attributes of love: ἀνυπόκριτος Ro 12: 9; 2 Cor 6: 6. γνησία 1 Cl 62: 2. φιλόθεος and φιλάνθρωπος Agr 7. σύμφωνος IEph 4: 1; ἄοκνος IPol 7: 2. ἐκτενής 1 Pt 4: 8. It is a *fruit of the Spirit* καρπὸς τοῦ πνεύματος Gal 5: 22, and takes first rank among the fruits. ἀ. τοῦ πνεύματος Ro 15: 30; cf. Col 1: 8. In the sense *alms, charity* ISm 6: 2 (cf. ἀ. λαμβάνειν 'receive alms' PGenève 14, 7).—ἀσπάζεται ὑμᾶς ἡ ἀγάπη τῶν ἀδελφῶν *the beloved brothers greet you*, i.e., *the church greets you* IPhld 11: 2; ISm 12: 1, cf. ITr 13: 1; IRo 9: 3. In these passages the object of the love is often made plain by the context; in others it is

b. expressly mentioned—α. impers. ἀ. τῆς ἀληθείας 2 Th 2: 10; ἀ. τῆς πατρίδος 1 Cl 55: 5.

β. human beings ἀ. εἴς τινα *love for someone* εἰς πάντας τοὺς ἁγίους Eph 1: 15; Col 1: 4. εἰς ἀλλήλους καὶ εἰς πάντας 1 Th 3: 12; 2 Th 1: 3; cf. 2 Cor 2: 4, 8; 1 Pt 4: 8. ἐν ἀλλήλοις J 13: 35. ἐξ ἡμῶν ἐν ὑμῖν 2 Cor 8: 7; ἡ ἀ. μου μετὰ ὑμῶν 1 Cor 16: 24.

γ. God or Christ ἀ. τοῦ θεοῦ *love toward God* (but in many cases the gen. may be subjective) Lk 11: 42; J 5: 42; 2 Th 3: 5; 1 J 2: 5, 15; 3: 17; 4: 12; 5: 3; 2 Cor 7: 1 v.l. (for φόβος); ἀ. εἰς θεὸν καὶ Χριστὸν καὶ εἰς τὸν πλησίον Pol 3: 3; ἀ. εἰς τὸ ὄνομα θεοῦ Hb 6: 10.

2. of the love of God and Christ—a. to men. Of God (cf. Wsd 3: 9): ἐν ἡμῖν 1 J 4: 9, 16. εἰς ἡμᾶς Ro 5: 8, cf. vs. 5. ἀγάπην διδόναι *bestow love* 1 J 3: 1; ἐν ἀ. προορίσας ἡμᾶς εἰς υἱοθεσίαν Eph 1: 4f; cf. 2: 4.—2 Cor 13: 13; Jd

5

2. God is the source of love 1 J 4: 7, the θεὸς τῆς ἀ. 2 Cor 13: 11 and therefore *God is love* 1 J 4: 8, 16. Christians, embraced by his love, are τέκνα ἀγάπης B 9: 7; 21: 9.— Of Jesus' love J 15: 9, 10a, 13 (cf. MDibelius, Joh 15: 13: Deissmann-Festschr. '27, 168-86); Ro 8: 35; 2 Cor 5: 14; cf. Eph 3: 19. Perh. the ἀληθὴς ἀγάπη of Pol 1: 1 is a designation of Jesus.

b. of the relation betw. God and Christ J 15: 10b; 17: 26 (on the constr. cf. Pel.-Leg. 12, 21 ὁ πλοῦτος ὄν με ἐπλούτισεν ὁ σατανᾶς). τοῦ υἱοῦ τῆς ἀ. αὐτοῦ *of the son of his love*, i.e., *of his beloved son* Col 1: 13 (s. PsSol 13: 9 υἱὸς ἀγαπήσεως).—WLütgert, D. L. im NT 1905; BBWarfield, PTR 16, '18, 1-45; 153-203; JMoffatt, Love in the NT '29; HPreisker, StKr 95, '24, 272-94, D. urchr. Botschaft v. der L. Gottes '30; EStauffer, TW I 20-55; RSchütz, D. Vorgeschichte der joh. Formel ὁ θεὸς ἀγ. ἐστίν Kiel Diss. '17; CRBowen, Love in the Fourth Gosp.: Journ. of Rel. 13, '33, 39-49; GEichholz, Glaube u. L. im 1 J: Ev. Theol. '37, 411-37. On ἔρως and ἀ. s. Harnack, SAB '18, 81-94; ANygren, Eros u. Agape I '30, II '37 (Eng. transl. Agape and Eros, AGHebert and PSWatson '32, '39; on this JATRobinson, Theology 48, '45, 98-104); LGrünhut, Eros u. Ag. '31. Cf. CCTarelli, Ἀγάπη, JTS n.s. 1, '50, 64-7; EKLee, Love and Righteousness: ET 62, '50f, 28-31; AŠuštar, Verbum Domini 28, '50, 110-19; 122-40; 193-213; 257-70; 321-40; TOhm, D. Liebe zu Gott in d. nichtchristl. Religionen, '50; WHarrelson, The Idea of Agape, Journ. of Rel. 31, '51, 169-82; VWarnach, Agape: Die Liebe als Grundmotiv der ntl. Theol. 1951; JESteinmueller, Ἐρᾶν, Φιλεῖν, Ἀγαπᾶν in Extrabiblical and Bibl. Sources: Studia Anselmiana 27f, '51, 404-23.—Full bibliog. in HRiesenfeld, Étude bibliographique sur la notion biblique d'ἀγάπη, surtout dans 1 Cor 13: Con. Neot. 5, '41, 1-32, Nuntius 6, '52, 47f; CSpicq, Agapè, 3 vols., '58/'59; Eng. transl. by McNamara and Richter, 3 vols., '63/'66 without footnotes.

II. *a love-feast*, a common meal eaten by early Christians in connection w. their church services, for the purpose of fostering and expressing brotherly love (cf. Acta Pauli et Theclae 25; Clem. Alex., Paed. 2, 1, 4, Strom. 3, 2, 10; Pass. Perp. et Felic. 17, 1; Tertull., Apolog. 39, De Jejun. 17; s. also ἀγαπάω 1c on J 13: 1, 34) Jd 12 (v.l. ἀπάταις; 2 Pt 2: 13 ἀγάπαις is v.l. for ἀπάταις; the same v.l. Eccl 9: 6 S, where ἀπάτη is meaningless; cf. RSchütz, ZNW 18, '18, 224). ἀγάπη ἄφθαρτος IRo 7: 3. ἀγάπην ποιεῖν hold a love-feast ISm 8: 2, in both pass. w. poss. ref. to the eucharist (s. ἀγαπάω 2).—Meals accompanied by religious rites and in a religious context were conducted by various social groups among the Greeks from early times (s. the foreword to this lexicon, pp. xxvi f.). A scholion on Pla. 122в says of such meals among the Lacedaemonians that they were called φιλίτια, because they φιλίας συναγωγά ἐστιν. Is ἀγ. perhaps a translation of φιλία into Christian terminology?—JFKeating, The Ag. and the Eucharist in the Early Church '01; HLeclercq, Dict. d'Arch. I '03, 775-848; FXFunk, Kirchengesch. Abhdlgen. 3, '07, 1-41; EBaumgartner, Eucharistie u. Ag. im Urchr. '09; RLCole, Love Feasts, a History of the Christian Ag. '16; GPWetter, Altchr. Liturgien II '21; HLietzmann, Messe u. Herrenmahl '26 (on this ALoisy, Congr. d'Hist. du Christ. I '28, 77-95); KVölker, Mysterium u. Ag. '27; DTambolleo, Le Agapi '31; BReicke, Diakonie, Festfreude u. Zelos in Verbindung mit der altchristlichen Agapenfeier, '51, M-M.

ἀγαπητός, ή, όν (verbal adj. of ἀγαπάω, fixed as an adj. Bl-D. §65, 3; Rob. 1096).

1. *beloved,* inclining strongly toward the mng. *only-beloved* (common Hom.+; Pollux 3, 19 καλοῖτο ἂν υἱὸς ἀγ. ὁ μόνος ὢν πατρί; LXX Gen 22: 2, 12, 16 al.; Philo, Ebr. 30 μόνος κ. ἀγ. υἱός) of Christ's (cf. the messianic usage in Test. Benj. 11: 2) relationship to God ὁ υἱός μου ὁ ἀ. Mt 3: 17 (BWBacon, Jesus' Voice fr. Heaven: AJT 9, '05, 451-73)=GEb 3b; Mt 17: 5; Mk 1: 11=GEb 3a; Mk 9: 7, cf. 12: 6 (CHTurner, JTS 27, '26, 113-29; 28, '27, 362 would translate *only*; cf. ASouter, ibid. 28, '27, 59f); Lk 3: 22; 9: 35 v.l.; cf. 20: 13; 2 Pt 1: 17.—Mt 12: 18; MPol 14: 1, 3; Dg 8: 11.

2. *dear, beloved* (pap., LXX; Jos., Bell. 1, 240, Ant. 15, 15; Test. 12 Patr.) indicating a close relationship, esp. that betw. parent and child υἱός (Artem. 5, 37) Hs 5, 2, 6. W. τέκνον 1 Cor 4: 17, τέκνα vs. 14; Eph 5: 1; ἀδελφός Phlm 16. W. proper names (POxy. 235, 2 [I вс] Τρύφων ἀγαπητέ) Ro 16: 12; Phlm 1; Ac 15: 25; 3 J 1; w. proper names and ἀδελφός Eph 6: 21; Col 4: 7, 9; 2 Pt 3: 15; w. σύνδουλος Col 1: 7; w. τέκνον 2 Ti 1: 2; w. ἰατρός Col 4: 14; w. gen. of the pers. pron. and a proper name Ἐπαίνετον τὸν ἀ. μου Ro 16: 5; cf. vs. 8f; IPol 8: 2.—Oft. in dir. address 3 J 2, 5, 11 (cf. Tob 10: 13); mostly pl. *dear friends* Ro 12: 19; 2 Cor 7: 1; 12: 19; Hb 6: 9; 1 Pt 2: 11; 4: 12; 2 Pt 3: 1, 8, 14, 17; 1 J 2: 7; 3: 2, 21; 4: 1, 7, 11; Jd 3, 17, 20; 1 Cl 1: 1; 7: 1; 12: 8; 21: 1; 24: 1f al.; ἀ. μου 1 Cor 10: 14; Phil 2: 12; IMg 11: 1. ἄνδρες ἀγαπητοί 1 Cl 16: 17; ἀδελφοί μου ἀ. 1 Cor 15: 58; Js 1: 16, 19; 2: 5; ἀδελφοί μου ἀ. καὶ ἐπιπόθητοι Phil 4: 1.—Of members of a Christian group ἀ. θεοῦ Ro 1: 7 (cf. Ps 59: 7; 107: 7). The Jews are κατὰ τὴν ἐκλογὴν ἀ. 11: 28. Of the prophets IPhld 9: 2.—ἀγαπητοὶ ἡμῖν ἐγενήθητε *you have become dear to us* 1 Th 2: 8; cf. 1 Ti 6: 2 (perh.= *worthy of love,* as X., Mem. 3, 10, 5); ἀ. λίαν ἔχειν τινά *hold someone very dear* IPol 7: 2.—EHvan Leeuwen, Ἀγαπητοί: ThSt 21, '03, 139-51. M-M.**

Ἀγάρ, ἡ indecl. (הָגָר) (LXX, Philo.—In Jos. Ἀγάρη, ης [Ant. 1, 215]) *Hagar,* a concubine of Abraham, mother of Ishmael (Gen 16); taken allegorically by Paul as a type of Judaism Gal 4: 24. In vs. 25 τὸ δὲ Ἀγὰρ Σινᾶ ὄρος ἐστὶν ἐν τῇ Ἀραβίᾳ the ms. readings vary considerably (Zahn, Gal exc. II p. 296-9). Perh. this is a play on names, since Arab. 'hajar' means 'stone', and names compounded w. it are found on the Sinai peninsula. The sense is: Hagar is a type of the Mosaic law, since Ἀγάρ=Σινᾶ.*

ἀγγαρεύω fut. ἀγγαρεύσω; 1 aor. ἠγγάρευσα (since Menand., Sicyon 4; pap. since 252 вс [Mayser I¹ p. 42 and I² 3 p. 139, 3]; Dit., Or. 665, 24; Jos., Ant. 13, 52. For the v.l. ἐγγαρεύω cf. Bl-D. §42, 2; Mlt.-H. 67.—Persian loanw., perh. orig. Babylonian [CFries, Klio 3, '03, 169f; 4, '04, 117ff]. Also in rabbin. lit. [PFiebig, ZNW 18, '18, 64-72], and in Lat. as 'angariare': Ulpian, Dig. XLIX 18, 4) *requisition* (orig. for the Pers. royal post), *press into service,* and so *force, compel* w. obj. τοῦτον ἠγγάρευσαν, ἵνα ἄρῃ τὸν σταυρόν *they pressed him into service, to carry the cross* Mt 27: 32; cf. Mk 15: 21. ὅστις σε ἀγγαρεύσει μίλιον ἕν (sc. ὑπάγειν) *whoever forces you to go one mile* Mt 5: 41; D 1: 4.—MRostovtzeff, Klio 6, '06, 249ff; Wilcken, Grundzüge 372ff, APF 4, '08, 228; FZucker SAB '11, 803ff; Preisigke, Klio 7, '07, 241ff, Fachwörter '15. M-M.*

ἀγγεῖον, ου, τό (Hdt.+; inscr., pap., LXX) *vessel, flask, container* e.g. for oil (BGU 248, 40 [I AD]; Num 4: 9; Philo; Jos., Bell. 3, 272, Ant. 9, 48) Mt 25: 4. Of containers for fish (cf. PSI 553, 11 [III вс] for edible snails) 13: 48 v.l. for ἄγγη. Fig., of the body (Hippocr.+; Dio Chrys. 11[12],

59; M. Ant. 3, 3, 6; Stob. I 414, 9; Philo, Post. Cain. 137, Migr. Abr. 193; 197) as the home of spirits (w. ἄγγος) Hm 5, 2, 5. M-M.*

ἀγγελία, ας, ἡ (Hom.+; LXX)—1. *message* (Jos., Ant. 17, 332, Vi. 380; Test. Napht. 2: 1) gener. *ἀ. ἀγαθή* (Pr 12: 25; 25: 25) *good news* Hv 3, 13, 2; of the gospel 1 J 1: 5, where the content is indicated by a *ὅτι*-clause.
2. *command* to love one's brothers in Christ 3: 11, w. *ἵνα* foll. M-M.*

ἀγγελικός, ή, όν (Pollux 4, 103) *pertaining to an angel* (Theosophien §14; Hierocles, Carm. Aur. 2, p. 423 Mullach; Proclus on Plato, Rep., index Kroll; schol. on Pla. 216A; Simplicius in Epict. p. 42, 53 *ἀρεταὶ ἀγγελικαί*; 45, 54; 80, 7) *τοποθεσίαι ἀ. places of the angels* ITr 5: 2.*

ἀγγέλλω 1 aor. *ἤγγειλα* (Hom.+; inscr., pap. [seldom], LXX in several pass., e.g. Jer 4: 15 as v.l.; Jos., Vi. 301 al.) *announce τινί to someone*, of the Easter message brought by Mary Magdalene J 20: 18. Abs. 4: 51 v.l. M-M. B. 1278.*

ἄγγελος, ου, ὁ (Hom.+; inscr., pap., LXX) *messenger*—
1. of human messengers: *an envoy, one who is sent*
  a. by men (Hom.+; inscr., pap.; Gen 32: 4, 7; Jdth 1: 11; 3: 1; 1 Macc 1: 44; 7: 10; Jos., Ant. 14, 451, Vi. 89): in his earthly ministry Jesus *ἀπέστειλεν ἀγγέλους* Lk 9: 52; of John the Baptist's disciples 7: 24; of Joshua's scouts Js 2: 25 (cf. Josh 7: 22).
  b. by God (prophets Hg 1: 13; Mal subscr.; a priest Mal 2: 7.—1 Esdr 1: 48f. Cf. also Theognis 1, 769, where the poet is *Μουσέων ἄγγελος*; Epict. 3, 22, 23; 38; Ael. Aristid. 37 K.=1 p. 15 D.; Maximus Tyr. 11, 9c Plato, as the one who brings us information about God, is called *ὁ ἐξ Ἀκαδημίας ἄγγ.*; Oenomaus in Euseb., Pr. Ev. 5, 20, 3; 5 Carnus the soothsayer is *ἄγγ.* of the gods.) of the forerunner of the Messiah Mt 11: 10; Mk 1: 2; Lk 7: 27 (all Mal 3: 1; cf. Ex 23: 20).
2. of supernatural powers (*ἄ.* as a spirit-being that is oft. connected w. the underworld, in pagan sources [EZiebarth, Neue attische Fluchtafeln: NGG 1899, 105ff no. 24; IG XII 3, 933-74. Other material in Dibelius, Geisterwelt 209ff. Cf. also the oracles: Theosophien §13 p. 169, 31; Porphyr., Ad Marcellam 21 *ἄγγελοι θεῖοί τε κ. ἀγαθοὶ δαίμονες.—ἄ.* w. *θεοί* and *δαίμονες* Damascius—V/VI AD—183 Ruelle; *ἄ.* w. *δαίμονες* and *ἥρωες* Proclus, Rep. II 243 Kroll, Tim. III 109 Diehl.—FCumont, Rev. d'Hist. des Rel. 72, '15, 159-82; FAndres, D. Engellehre d. griech. Apologeten '14 and in Pauly-W. Suppl. III '18, 101ff; Rtzst., Myst. 171, 2; Bousset, ARW 18, '15, 170ff] and as a supernatural power in Judaism [LXX; En. 10, 7; 20, 1; 99, 3 al.; Essenes in Jos., Bell. 2, 142; Philo, cf. Schürer III⁴ 706ff w. lit.; Joseph.; Test. 12 Patr.; Prayers for vengeance fr. Rheneia 9f *κύριε ὁ πάντα ἐφορῶν καὶ οἱ ἄγγελοι θεοῦ*; on this Dssm. LO 353f; 357-LAE 414; 418f; Dit., Syll.³ 1181 w. note 2; PFouad 203, 3f [I AD]; on this PBenoit, RB 58, '51, 549-65; PKatz, ThZ 9, '53, 228-31. Loanw. in rabb.—Bousset, Rel. 320ff; J-BFrey, L'Angélologie juive au temps de J-Chr.: RSphth 5, '11, 75-110; HBKuhn, JBL 67, '48, 217-32 Jewish apocalypses], likewise in the magical pap., w. their mixture of heathen and Jewish infl. [PGM 1, 76 an *ἄ.* as a star fr. heaven; 4, 570ff; 998; 1112; 13, 329; 585; 609; 744]. Cf. the inscr. in the APF 3, '06, p. 445 no. 67; p. 451 no. 94)
  a. *angels* as messengers of God (LXX; Philo, Somn. 1, 190; the supernatural messengers of the gods in Hom. are not intermediary beings. Yet perh. the description of

Hermes, the *κῆρυξ τῶν θεῶν*, as their *ἄγγελος ἄριστος* [Diod. S. 5, 75, 2] may have made it easier for the Gentiles to understand *ἄγγ.* as God's heavenly messenger.) mostly w. gen.: *κυρίου* (Gen 16: 10f al.) Mt 1: 20; 2: 13, 19; Lk 1: 11; 2: 9; Ac 5: 19; 12: 7, 23. *τοῦ θεοῦ* (Gen 31: 11; 32: 2 al.; Philo, Deus Imm. 1; Jos., Bell. 5, 388) Lk 12: 8f; 15: 10; J 1: 51 (HWindisch, ZNW 30, '31, 215-33). *ἄ. θεοῦ* (Gen 21: 17 A; Judg 13: 6 B; Jos., Ant. 1, 73) Gal 4: 14; Hb 1: 6 (Ps 96: 7; Dt 32: 43); 1 Cl 29: 2 (Dt 32: 8). Abs. (Num 20: 16; Judg 13: 11; Tob 6: 4ff al.) Lk 1: 13, 18, 38; 2: 10, 13, 15, 21; J 20: 12; Ac 7: 53; 1 Ti 3: 16; 1 Pt 1: 12 (on the superiority of men to angels s. Sextus 32) al.; *ἅγιοι ἄ.* (PGM 4, 1934; 1938) Mk 8: 38; Lk 9: 26; Ac 10: 22; Rv 14: 10; 1 Cl 39: 7 (Job 5: 1); Hv 2, 2, 7; *ἐκλεκτοὶ ἄ.* 1 Ti 5: 21 (*ἄ.* as witnesses as Test. Levi 19: 3 and Dit., Syll.³ 1181, 10=Dssm. LO 351-62 [LAE 413-24]; cf. Jos., Bell. 2, 401); *ἄ. ἰσχυρός* (cf. Da 4: 13; Ps 102: 20) Rv 5: 2; 18: 21. Their abode is heaven, and so they are *ἄ. τῶν οὐρανῶν* Mt 24: 36 (unless *οὐρ.=θεοῦ*); *ἄ. ἐν τοῖς οὐρανοῖς* Mk 12: 25; *ἄ. ἐν οὐρανῷ* 13: 32; *ἄ. ἐξ οὐρανοῦ* Gal 1: 8, cf. Mt 22: 30; 28: 2; Lk 22: 43. They return to heaven when they have fulfilled their mission on earth 2: 15. Hence *ἄ. φωτός* (opp. *Σατανᾶς*) 2 Cor 11: 14; *ἄ. φωταγωγοί* B 18: 1. There the good are united w. them after death Hv 2, 2, 7; s 9, 27, 3. They appear in dazzling light Lk 2: 9; Ac 7: 30 (Ex 3: 2); ISm 6: 1; cf. the 'shining face' of Ac 6: 15; in white garments J 20: 12; cf. Mt 28: 3; Lk 24: 4. Called *πνεύματα* Hb 1: 7; 1 Cl 36: 3 (both after Ps 103: 4). *πνεύματα λειτουργικά serving spirits* Hb 1: 14. Their voice is like thunder J 12: 29; *γλῶσσαι τῶν ἀ. language of angels* 1 Cor 13: 1 (after the analogy of the languages of the gods, Plato in Clem. Alex., Str. 1, 143; cf. 2 Cor 12: 4; Rv 14: 2f; Test. Job 48-50: Texts and Studies V 1, 1897, 135; GSteindorff, Apk. d. Elias: TU 17, 3a, 1899, 153). They bring messages fr. God to men Lk 1: 11f; Mt 28: 2ff, and were also active in the giving of the law *νόμος διαταγεὶς δι' ἀγγέλων* Gal 3: 19; cf. Ac 7: 38, 53; Hb 2: 2 (Jos., Ant. 15, 136 *τῶν ἐν τοῖς νόμοις δι' ἀγγέλων παρὰ τ. θεοῦ μαθόντων*). As guardian angels of individuals (Tob 5: 6, 22; cf. PGM 1, 172ff; Ael. Aristid. 50, 57 K.=26 p. 519 D.: *ὁ σὸς Ἑρμῆς ἐστιν*, to whom Aristid. has been entrusted since his birth) Mt 18: 10 (Barry, ET 23, '12, 182); Ac 12: 15 (JHMoulton, JTS 3, '02, 514-27, ET 14, '03, 5ff); Lk 4: 10 (Ps 90: 11); Hv 5: 1f. They conduct the blessed dead into heaven Lk 16: 22 (Hermes does this acc. to Pythag. [Diog. L. 8, 31])); instruct men to do good Hv 3, 5, 4; *δικαιοσύνης* m 6, 2, 1; rejoice at the repentance of a sinner Lk 15: 10; cf. the *ἄ. τῆς μετανοίας* Hm 12, 4, 7; 12, 6, 1 al. They preside over various realms *ἄ. ὁ ἔχων ἐξουσίαν ἐπὶ τοῦ πυρός* Rv 14: 18; *ἄ. τῶν ὑδάτων* 16: 5; the four winds 7: 1. An angel, Thegri, rules the animal world Hv 4, 2, 4 (Synes., Ep. 57 p. 192B *δαίμονες* as leaders of the grasshoppers). *ἄ. τοῦ προφητικοῦ πνεύματος* m 11: 9; *τὸν ἄ. τὸν τιμωρητήν* s 7: 6.—On *ἄ. τῶν ἐκκλησιῶν* Rv 1: 20, cf. 2: 1, 8, 12, 18; 3: 1, 7, 14 and s. on *ἀστήρ.*—Subordinate to Christ Mt 4: 11; 13: 41; 16: 27; Hb 1: 4ff (Ps 96: 7); 1 Pt 3: 22; Rv 5: 11f; *δώδεκα λεγιῶνας ἀ.* Mt 26: 53; *μυριάσιν ἀ.* Hb 12: 22; cf. Rv 5: 11. Seven principal angels (Tob 12: 15) Rv 8: 2, 6; 15: 1, 6; 16: 1; 17: 1; 21: 9 (GHDix, The Seven Archangels and the Seven Spirits: JTS 28, '27, 233-50). Six angels, created first, to whom the management of all creation is entrusted Hv 3, 4, 1. Angels at the Parousia Mt 24: 31; 2 Th 1: 7. *Μιχαὴλ καὶ οἱ ἄ. αὐτοῦ* Rv 12: 7. Revered by men (Celsus 1, 26 *Ἰουδαίους σέβειν ἀγγέλους*; 5, 6) *θρησκεία τῶν ἀ. worship of angels* Col 2: 18; *λατρεύειν ἀγγέλοις* as a sign of Jewish piety PK 2 p. 14, 26.

Christ as σεμνότατος ἄ. Hv 5: 2; m 5, 1, 7; cf. ὁ ἅγιος ἄ. s 5, 4, 4; ὁ ἔνδοξος ἄ. s 7, 1ff; 8, 1, 2. ὁ ἄ. κυρίου s 7: 5; 8, 1, 2ff; called Michael in s 8, 3, 3, where it is to be noted that Michael was the guardian angel of the Jewish nation (WLueken, D. Erzengel Michael 1900; MDibelius, Hdb. exc. on Hs 5, 6, 8 p. 575f).

b. intermediary beings gener., w. no ref. to their relation to God (opp. ἄνθρωποι) 1 Cor 4: 9 (cf. Test. Jos. 19: 9 ἔχαιρον ἐπ' αὐτῷ οἱ ἄγγελοι κ. οἱ ἄνθρωποι κ. πᾶσα ἡ γῆ).—Ro 8: 38 ἄ. as serving spirit-powers seem to be differentiated fr. the ἀρχαί, who rule.

c. evil spirits (Lactant., Inst. 2, 15, 8 daemonas Trismegistus ἀγγέλους πονηρούς appellat. Cf. also Job 1: 6; 2: 1; Philo, Gig. 16; Test. Ash. 6: 4; PGM 4, 2701; ADieterich, Nekyia 1893, 60f) τῷ διαβόλῳ καὶ τοῖς ἀγγέλοις αὐτοῦ Mt 25: 41; cf. Rv 12: 9. ὁ δράκων καὶ οἱ ἄ. αὐτοῦ vs. 7; ἄ. τῆς ἀβύσσου 9: 11 (s. 'Αβαδδών); ἄ. πονηρός B 9: 4; ἄ. τῆς πονηρίας in contrast to the guardian angels Hm 6, 2, 1; ἄ. Σατανᾶ, which causes physical pain 2 Cor 12: 7; esp. called ἄ. τρυφῆς καὶ ἀπάτης Hs 6, 2, 1f; leading men into evil B 18: 1. Of the angels' fall and their punishment (cf., in the opinion of many, Gen 6: 2; En. 6ff; 54; Book of Jubilees 5; ApocBar 56: 13; LJung, Fallen Angels in Jewish, Christian, and Mohammedan Lit. '26; ALods, Congr. d'Hist. du Christ. I 29–54) ὁ θεὸς ἀγγέλων ἁμαρτησάντων οὐκ ἐφείσατο 2 Pt 2: 4; ἄ. τοὺς μὴ τηρήσαντας τὴν ἑαυτῶν ἀρχήν who did not keep to their proper domain (s. ἀρχή 4) Jd 6. From the pass. already quoted above, w. Gen. 6: 2 (cf. also Test. Reub. 5: 3; Jos., Ant. 1, 73 ἄγγελοι θεοῦ γυναιξὶ συνιόντες. Also the pagan concept of erotic desires of demons: HUsener, Weihnachtsfest² '11, 74f; Rtzst., Poim. 228ff. Herr der Grösse 14f and Protev. Jacobi 14, 1) some conclude that the angels were subject to erotic desires; this is held to explain the regulation that women are to wear a veil in the church services, since angels are present (cf. Origen, Orat. 31 and Ps 137: 1 ἐναντίον ἀγγέλων ψαλῶ σοι) 1 Cor 11: 10 (for another view and for the lit. s. ἐξουσία 5; cf. also JAFitzmyer, [Qumrân angelology] NTS 4, '57/'58, 48–58). In 6: 3 οὐκ οἴδατε, ὅτι ἀγγέλους κρινοῦμεν; it is not certain whether only fallen angels are meant.—OEverling, D. paulinische Angelologie u. Dämonologie 1888; Dibelius, Geisterwelt '09; GKurze, D. Engels- u. Teufels-glaube d. Ap. Pls '15; MJones, St Paul and the Angels: Exp. 8 Ser. XVI '21, 356–70; 412–25; EPeterson, D. Buch von den Engeln '35; JMichl, D. Engelvorstellungen in Apk I '37; ELangton, The Angel Teaching of the NT '37; JBBernardin, JBL 57, '38, 273–9; ESchick, D. Botschaft der Engel im NT '40; WMichaelis, Z. Engelchristol. im Urchristent. '42; GNHatzidakis, Ἄγγελος u. Verwandtes: SAWien 173, '14. M-M. B. 1486.

ἄγγος, ους, τό (Hom.+; CIG 3573; Inscr. gr. 1361, 4f; LXX; Philo, Post. Cai. 130; Jos., Ant. 8, 322) vessel, container B 8: 1. Of containers for fish Mt 13: 48 (v.l. ἀγγεῖα, q.v.). Fig., of the body as the home of evil spirits Hm 5, 2, 5 (w. ἀγγεῖον). M-M., s.v. ἀγγεῖον.*

ἄγε present imper. of ἄγω, used as an interjection (since Hom., who uses it for the pl.; LXX; Sib. Or. 3, 562) come! ἄγε νῦν (oft. in comedy) w. imp. foll. (Hom.) Js 5: 1.—4: 13; ἄ. δή (Aeschyl.+) come then Dg 2: 1.*

ἀγέλη, ης, ἡ (Hom.+; inscr., pap., LXX, Philo; Jos., Ant. 8, 294) herd of swine (as Eudoxus Rhod. [IIBC]

in Aelian, N.A. 10, 16) Mt 8: 30–2; Mk 5: 11, 13; Lk 8: 32f. M-M.*

ἀγενεαλόγητος, ον without genealogy, of Melchizedek (w. ἀπάτωρ and ἀμήτωρ) Hb 7: 3 (found elsewh. only w. ref. to this pass.). M-M.*

ἀγενής, ές gen. οὖς lit. not of noble birth (opp. εὐγενής; in this sense since X., Pla.; POxy. 33 V, 5 [IIAD]= Wilcken, Chrest. 20 V, 5; Jos., Bell. 4, 148) but more commonly base, low, insignificant (Soph., fgm. 84 Pears., opp. ἀγαθός; Philo, Conf. Lingu. 43; POxy. 79, 3; Dit., Syll.² 855, 11; 862, 22) which is most probably its mng. in 1 Cor 1: 28. M-M.*

ἀγέννητος, ον (Soph.+) unborn, lit. unbegotten (so of God, Herm. Wr. 2, 4; 5, 2; 14, 2 al.; Philo, Mos. 2, 171 v.l. [for ἀγένητος]. Written ἀγένητος: Thales in Diog. L. 1, 35; Zoroaster in Philo Bybl. [c. 100 AD]: Euseb., Pr. Ev. 1, 10, 52; PGM 13, 842; Philo; Jos., C. Ap. 2, 167; Sib. Or., fgm. 1, 7; 17) w. γεννητός, of Christ (cf. Act. Phil. 141 p. 76, 27 B.) IEph 7: 2 (v.l. ἀγένητος); cf. Lghtf., Apost. Fath. II 2² 1889, p. 90–4.—PStiegele, D. Agennesiebegriff in d. griech. Theol. d. 4 Jh. '13; LPrestige, JTS 24, '23, 486–96; JLebreton, 'Αγέννητος dans la Tradition philos. et dans la Litt. chrét. du IIe siècle: Rech de Sc rel 16, '26, 431–43.*

ἄγια, ων s. on ἅγιος 2b.

ἁγιάζω 1 aor. ἡγίασα, imper. ἁγίασον; pf. pass. ἡγίασμαι, ptc. ἡγιασμένος; 1 aor. pass. ἡγιάσθην, imper. ἁγιάσθητω; 1 fut. pass. ἁγιασθήσομαι 1 Cl 46: 2 make holy, consecrate, sanctify (LXX; Philo, Leg. All. 1, 18, Spec. Leg. 1, 67. Quite rare in extra-Bibl. usage, where ἁγίζω is the usual form; but s. PGM 4, 522 ἁγιασθείς; Cat. Cod. Astr. VII 178, 1; 27; Anecd. Gr. p. 328, 1ff and Herm. Wr. 1, 32 συναγιάζειν. Cf. also καθαγιάζειν under 3 below).

1. of things: set them aside or make them suitable for ritual purposes (Ex 29: 27, 37, 44 al.) ἄ. τὸ δῶρον the sacrifice Mt 23: 19; 1 Ti 4: 5 (Act. Thom. 79 τὴν προσφορὰν ἄ.); of profane things make holy by contact w. someth. holy ἄ. τὸν χρυσόν the gold in the temple Mt 23: 17.

2. of pers. consecrate, dedicate, sanctify, i.e., include in the inner circle of what is holy, in both relig. and moral uses of the word (cf. Ex 28: 41; Sir 33: 12; 45: 4; Zeph 1: 7). So of the Christians, who are consecrated by baptism; w. ἀπολούσασθαι 1 Cor 6: 11. Of the church ἵνα αὐτὴν ἁγιάσῃ καθαρίσας τῷ λουτρῷ τοῦ ὕδατος Eph 5: 26; sanctify by the blood of a sacrifice, i.e., atone for sins Hb 9: 13. Of Christ ἵνα ἁγιάσῃ διὰ τοῦ ἰδίου αἵματος τὸν λαόν 13: 12 (ἄ. τὸν λαόν Josh 7: 13; Ezk 46: 20; ἄ. by blood Ex 29: 21); cf. 2: 11; 10: 10, 29; consecrate, sanctify by contact w. what is holy: unbelievers by a Christian marriage 1 Cor 7: 14. Hence Christians are ἡγιασμένοι (cf. Dt 33: 3; 4 Macc 17: 19) Hb 10: 14; Ac 20: 32; 26: 18; IEph 2: 2; ἡ. ἐν Χριστῷ Ἰησοῦ 1 Cor 1: 2; ἡ. ἐν ἀληθείᾳ J 17: 19b (cf. Sir 45: 4 ἐν πίστει); of Gentile Christians ἐν πνεύματι ἁγίῳ Ro 15: 16; the church ἁγιασθεῖσα=ἁγία D 10: 5; κλητοὶ ἡ. 1 Cl inscr.; of an individual σκεῦος ἡγιασμένον 2 Ti 2: 21; Paul ἡγιασμένος IEph 12: 2. God consecrates his own, incl. Christ J 10: 36 (s. Hdb.³ ad loc.), and Christians (cf. schol. on Apollon. Rhod. 3, 62 ἐλεήσας αὐτὸν ὁ Ζεὺς ἁγνίζει=Zeus absolves him, takes away his guilt) 17: 17; 1 Th 5: 23, the latter through Christ 1 Cl 59: 3. Of Jesus ὑπὲρ αὐτῶν (ἐγὼ) ἁγιάζω ἐμαυτόν I

dedicate myself for them (the disciples) as an offering J 17: 19a (ἀ. of an offering Ex 13: 2; Dt 15: 19).

3. *treat as holy, reverence* of pers. κύριον δὲ τὸν Χριστὸν ἀγιάσατε 1 Pt 3: 15 (Is 8: 13); of things: ἀγιασθήτω τὸ ὄνομά σου *may thy name be held in reverence* (cf. Is 29: 23; Ezk 36: 23; PGM 4, 1119f τὸ ὄνομα τὸ ἅγιον τὸ καθηγιασμένον ὑπὸ τ. ἀγγέλων πάντων; 1, 206; Ps.-Clem., Hom. 13, 4) Mt 6: 9; Lk 11: 2; D 8: 2 (AFridrichsen, Geheiligt werde dein Name: Teologisk Tidsskrift 8, '17, 1-16; LBrun, Harnack-Ehrung '21, 22-31; RAsting, D. Heiligkeit im Urchristentum '30, 75-85 w. lit.). τὸ σάββατον B 15: 1, 3, 6f (Ex 20: 8-11). ἀγιασθῆναι *keep oneself holy* Rv 22: 11.

4. *purify* (Num 6: 11 al.) ἀ. ἀπὸ πάσης πονηρίας καὶ ἀπὸ πάσης σκολιότητος Hv 3, 9, 1. This mng. is also poss. in such pass. as Ro 15: 16; 1 Cor 1: 2; 1 Th 5: 23. M-M.*

ἀγίασμα, ατος, τό (almost excl. Bibl. and Christian, but also Philo, Plant. 50; PGM 4, 522) *sanctuary* (1 Macc 1: 21, 36ff; 5: 1; Sir 36: 12; 49: 6; 50: 11; Test. Dan 5: 9) τὰ δεξιὰ μέρη τοῦ ἀ. Hv 3, 2, 1.*

ἀγιασμός, οῦ, ὁ (LXX.—Diod. S. 4, 39, 1 has ἁγισμός) *holiness, consecration, sanctification*; the use in a moral sense for a process or, more often, its result (the state of being made holy) is peculiar to our lit. (cf. Jer 6: 16 v.l.; Test. Benj. 10, 11) εἰς ἀγιασμόν *for consecration* (opp. εἰς ἀνομίαν) Ro 6: 19, 22 (Act. Thom. 121). Opp. ἀκαθαρσία 1 Th 4: 7; w. τιμῇ vs. 4, cf. vs. 3; w. πίστις and ἀγάπη 1 Ti 2: 15; w. εἰρήνη Hb 12: 14. ἐν ἀ. πνεύματος *in consecration through the Spirit* 2 Th 2: 13; 1 Pt 1: 2 (Test. Levi 18: 7 πνεῦμα ἀγιασμοῦ). Christ described as ἁ. w. δικαιοσύνη and ἀπολύτρωσις (abstr. for concr. *author of holiness*) 1 Cor 1: 30. ποιεῖν τὰ τοῦ ἁ. *do everything that belongs to holiness* 1 Cl 30: 1; ἐγκράτεια ἐν ἀ. *self-control with consecration* 35: 2.—EGaugler, D. Heiligung in d. Ethik des Ap. Pls: Internat. kirchl. Ztschr. 15, '25, 100-20; MSEnslin, The Ethics of Paul '30; SDjukanovič, Heiligkt u. Heiligg b. Pls, Diss. Bern '39.*

ἅγιοι, ων, οἱ s. ἅγιος 2d.

ἅγιον, ου, τό s. ἅγιος 2a.

ἀγιοπρεπής, ές *fitting* or *proper for one who is holy*, or simply *holy* λόγοι ἀ. *holy words* 1 Cl 13: 3; δεσμοὶ ἀ. *bonds fitting for a saint* Pol 1: 1.*

ἅγιος, ία, ον orig. a cultic concept, of the quality possessed by things and persons that could approach a divinity (so among the trag. poets only Thespis, fgm. 4 p. 833 Nauck² βωμῶν ἀγίων, but found since V BC as a cultic term in Ion. and Att., e.g. ἱρόν Hdt. 2, 41; 44; Pla., Critias 116c, τόπος Leg. 904E; τελεταί Aristoph., Nub. 304 and Demosth. 25, 11 [ἀγιώταται τ.]; above all in the mysteries [GWobbermin, Rel. gesch. Studien 1896, 59ff, cf. Dit., Or. 721, 1 τῶν ἀγιωτάτων Ἐλευσῖνι μυστηρίων]; LXX [HSGehman, Vet. Test. 4, '54, 337-48]; Ep. Arist.; Philo; Joseph.; Test. 12 Patr.; Sib. Or.).

1. adj.—a. `of things—a. in the cultic sense *dedicated to God, holy, sacred*, i.e., reserved for God and his service: ἀ. πόλις of Jerusalem (Appian, Syr. 50, §250: Jerus. is called the ἁγιωτάτη πόλις of the Jews; also Mithrid. 106 §498; Is 48: 2; 52: 1; 66: 20; 2 Esdr 21 [Neh 11]: 1; Da 3: 28; 1 Macc 2: 7 al.) Mt 4: 5; 27: 53; Rv 11: 2; of the heavenly Jerusalem 21: 2, 10; 22: 19; τόπος ἄ. of the temple (2 Macc 2: 18; 8: 17; 3 Macc 2: 14) Mt 24: 15; Ac 6: 13; 21:

28, but of the next life 1 Cl 5: 7, like ὁ ἄ. αἰών *the holy age*=αἰὼν μέλλων (cf. in the addition to the Lat. transl. of Sir 17: 27 'aevum sanctum') B 10: 11; γῇ ἀ. (2 Macc 1: 7) Ac 7: 33 (Ex 3: 5); ὄρος ἄ. (Wsd 9: 8; Ps 14: 1 al.—Appian, Bell. Civ. 1, 1 §2 τὸ ὄρος τὸ ἀπὸ τοῦδε [i.e., something extremely significant occurred] κληζόμενον ἱερόν) of the mountain of Transfiguration 2 Pt 1: 18; σκεύη (1 Esdr 8: 57; 1 Macc 4: 49) GOxy 14; 21; 29; σκηνή Hb 9: 2 (JSwetnam, CBQ 32, '70, 205-21, defends the Vulgate transl.). διαθήκη (Da 11: 28ff Theod.; 1 Macc 1: 15) Lk 1: 72; γραφαί Ro 1: 2 (cf. 1 Macc 12: 9; Philo, Rer. Div. Her. 159). λόγος 1 Cl 13: 3; 56: 3; Dg 7: 2 (cf. Herm. Wr. 1: 18 ὁ θεὸς εἶπεν ἀγίῳ λόγῳ). Since the Christians are called 'holy ones' (s. 2dβ), their κλῆσις is also ἀ. 2 Ti 1: 9; so also of the ἐντολή given them 2 Pt 2: 21. Their community forms an ἐκκλησία ἀ. ITr inscr.; Hv 1, 1, 6; 1, 3, 4; cf. 4, 1, 3, as well as a ἱεράτευμα ἀ. 1 Pt 2: 5 and an ἔθνος ἄ. (Wsd 17: 2) vs. 9. For φίλημα ἀ. s. φίλημα.—πίστις is ἀγιωτάτη *most holy* Jd 20 (for the superl. cf. Pla., Leg. 729E al., also Dit., Syll.³ 339, 14; 768, 16 [31 BC]; Jos., Ant. 16, 115; ἀγιώτατος θεός: Dit., Or. 755, 1; 756, 3; cf. PGM 4, 668).

β. shading over into the mng. *holy= pure, perfect, worthy of God* (Stephan. Byz. s. v. Παλική: ὅρκος ἅγιος) θυσία Ro 12: 1. ἀναστροφαί 2 Pt 3: 11. Of the divine law Ro 7: 12; ἀπαρχή (cf. Ezk 48: 9ff) 11: 16a; ναός (Ps 10: 4; 17: 7 al.; Jos., Bell. 7, 379; cf. ἱερὸν ἄ.: Hdt. 2, 41; Diod. S. 5, 72; Paus., 10, 32, 13) 1 Cor 3: 17; Eph 2: 21.

b. of persons—a. of human beings *consecrated to God, holy* (Ramsay, Phrygia I 2 p. 386 no. 232, 8 [early III AD] of a pagan: Γάϊος, ὡς ἅγιος, ὡς ἀγαθός) prophets (Wsd 11: 1) Lk 1: 70; Ac 3: 21; 2 Pt 3: 2. John the Baptist (w. δίκαιος) Mk 6: 20; apostles Eph 3: 5; Polycarp, Epil Mosq 1; 2; 4; αἱ ἄ. γυναῖκες 1 Pt 3: 5. Israel a λαὸς ἄ. (Is 62: 12; Sir 49: 12 v.l.; Da 7: 27) 1 Cl 8: 3; cf. B 14: 6; πᾶν ἄρσεν τῷ κυρίῳ Lk 2: 23.—The Christians Ro 1: 7; 1 Pt 1: 16a (Lev 19: 2); ἀδελφοὶ ἄ. Hb 3: 1; their children 1 Cor 7: 14 (GDelling, Studien zum NT, '70, 270-80, 281-87). W. ἄμωμος Eph 1: 4; 5: 27; Col 1: 22; ἄ. ἐν ἀναστροφῇ 1 Pt 1: 15, cf. D 10: 6.

β. of angels *holy* (Job 5: 1; Tob 11: 14; 12: 15; cf. Bousset, Rel.³ 321; Cat. Cod. Astr. VIII 2 p. 176, 19; cf. PGM 4, 668) Mk 8: 38; Lk 9: 26; Ac 10: 22; Col 1: 12 (cf. 1 QS 11, 7f); Rv 14: 10; 1 Cl 39: 7; Hv 2, 2, 7; 3, 4, 1f; ἐν ἀ. μυριάσιν αὐτοῦ w. *his holy myriads* Jd 14 (w. ἄγγελος 𝔓⁷²; cf. En. 1, 9).

γ. of Christ *holy* τὸν ἅγιον παῖδά σου Ac 4: 27, 30; τὸ γεννώμενον ἄ. κληθήσεται Lk 1: 35 (ἄ. belongs to the pred.).

δ. of God (Aristoph., Av. 522; Pla., Soph. 248E; Dit., Or. 262, 25; 378, 1 [19 AD] θεῷ ἀγίῳ ὑψίστῳ; 590, 1; 620, 2 [98 AD]; UPZ 79, 22 [159 BC] of Isis; likew. POxy. 1380, 34; 36; 89; Audollent, Defix. Tab. 242 τὸν ἄ. Ἑρμῆν; Herm. Wr. 1, 31; PGM 1, 198; 3, 312; 4, 851; 2093. Further exx. in Wobbermin 70; Cumont³ 266.—LXX; Philo, Sacr. Abel. 101; Sib. Or. 3, 478) *holy* J 17: 11; 1 Pt 1: 16b (Lev 19: 2); Rv 4: 8 (Is 6: 3.—The threefold ἅγιος serves to emphasize the idea, as the twofold καλὸν καλόν=indescribably beautiful Theocr. 8, 73); 6: 10. Of the name of God (LXX; PGM 4, 1190; 13, 638) Lk 1: 49; 1 Cl 64.—On the Holy Spirit cf. πνεῦμα 5c.

2. used as a pure subst.—a. ἄ. ἅγιον, ου, τό *what is holy*.

a. concrete *sacrificial meat* (Lev 22: 14.—Also concr. θύειν τὸ ἱερόν: 67th letter of Apollon. of Ty. [Philostrat. I 363, 30 K.]) μὴ δῶτε τὸ ἄ. τοῖς κυσίν Mt 7: 6; cf. D 9: 5 (IZolli, Religio 13, '37, 272-7; HJEWesterman

Holstijn, Mt 7: 6: Onder Eig. Vaandel 15, '40, 259-67; MBlack, Aramaic Approach³, '67, 200-202.).

β. *sanctuary* (Dit., Or. 56, 59 [239 вс]; UPZ 119, 12 [156 вс]; Num 3: 38; Ezk 45: 18; 1 Esdr 1: 5 v.l.; 1 Macc 10: 42; Philo, Leg. All. 3, 125; Jos., Ant. 3, 125) τὸ ἅ. κοσμικόν Hb 9: 1.

b. ἅγια, ων, τά *sanctuary* (Jdth 4: 12; 16: 20; 1 Macc. 3: 43, 59 al.; Philo, Fuga 93 οἶς [sc. ἡ Λευιτικὴ φύλη] ἡ τῶν ἁγίων ἀνάκειται λειτουργία; Jos., Bell. 2, 341) Hb 8: 2; 9: 24f; 13: 11. Also the front, or outer part of the temple, *the holy place* (3 Km 8: 8; Philo, Rer. Div. Her. 226) Hb 9: 2. τὰ ἅ. of the heavenly sanctuary (Sib. Or. 3, 308) vs. 12; 10: 19.—(τὰ) ἅγια (τῶν) ἁγίων *the holy of holies* (3 Km 8: 6; 2 Ch 4: 22; 5: 7; Philo, Leg. All. 2, 56.—Formed like κακὰ κακῶν Soph., Oed. C. 1238, ἄρρητ' ἀρρήτων Oed. R. 465; ἔσχατα ἐσχάτων Ael. Aristid. 46 p. 260 D.) Hb 9: 3; IPhld 9: 1. Of the Christians 1 Cl 29: 3 (cf. 2 Ch 31: 14; Ezk 48: 12).

c. ἅγιος, ου, ὁ *the Holy One*—**a.** of God 1 J 2: 20 (β is also poss.).

β. of Christ ὁ ἅ. Rv 3: 7; 1 Cl 23: 5; Dg 9: 2; ὁ ἅ. καὶ δίκαιος Ac 3: 14. ὁ ἅ. τοῦ θεοῦ Mk 1: 24; Lk 4: 34; J 6: 69 (cf. Ps 105: 16 ὁ ἅ. κυρίου of Aaron).

d. ἅγιοι, ων, οἱ *the holy ones*—**a.** of the angels (Zech 14: 5; Ps 88: 6; En. 1, 9; PGM 1, 198; 4, 1345; 1347) perh. 1 Th 3: 13; 2 Th 1: 10; Col 1: 12, but β is also poss.

β. *saints* of Christians as consecrated to God (cf. Is 4: 3; Tob 8: 15; Ps 33: 10; Da 7: 18, 21) Ac 9: 13, 32; Ro 8: 27; 12: 13; 15: 25 (Ltzm., exc. ad loc.); 1 Cor 6: 1f; 2 Cor 1: 1; Eph 2: 19; 3: 8; Phil 4: 22; Col 1: 4; 1 Ti 5: 10; Hb 6: 10; D 16: 7; 1 Cl 46: 2; Hv 1, 1, 9 al. κλητοὶ ἅ. Ro 1: 7; 1 Cor 1: 2; οἱ ἅ. αὐτοῦ Col 1: 26; cf. Ac 9: 13; Hv 3, 8, 8; οἱ ἅ. καὶ πιστοὶ αὐτοῦ ISm 1: 2.

γ. of other men esp. close to God (Dionys. Soph., Ep. 70 σωφροσύνη . . . προσήγαγέ σε θεῷ . . . τοῖς ἁγίοις παρέστησεν) Mt 27: 52; cf. Rv 18: 20, 24.—FJDölger ΙΧΘΤΣ '10, 180-3; WLink, De vocis 'sanctus' usu pagano, Diss. Königsb. '10; AFridrichsen, Hagios-Qadoš '16; EWilliger, Hagios '22; JDillersberger, Das Heilige im NT '26; HDelehaye, Sanctus '27;² '33; RAsting, D. Heiligkeit im Urchristentum '30; UBunzel, D. Begriff der Heiligkeit im AT, Diss. Breslau '14; JHänel, D. Religion d. Heiligkeit '31; PChantraine et OMasson, Debrunner-Festschr., '54, 85-107; FNötscher, Vom Alten Zum NT, '62, 126-74 (Qumran); OProksch and KGKuhn, TW I 87-116. M-M. B. 1475.

ἁγιότης, ητος, ἡ *holiness* (schol. Aristoph., Plut. 682; PAmh. 151, 16; PGiess. 55, 5; 2 Macc 15: 2; Ps 28: 2 in one transl. of the Hexapla; Test. Levi 3: 4 ὑπεράνω πάσης ἁγιότητος) μεταλαβεῖν τῆς ἁ. *share in his holy character* Hb 12: 10. Of moral purity w. εἰλικρίνεια 2 Cor 1: 12 (v.l. ἁπλότητι, πραότητι). M-M.*

ἁγιοφόρος, ον *bearing holy things* (cultic vessels in processions) of persons (ἀγιαφόρος IG III 162 of pers. engaged in Isis-worship); in Christian use only fig. (cf. Plut., Is. et Osir. 3 p. 352в: the ἱεραφόροι in the Isis cult are those who bear the teaching about the gods, purified from all superstition, in their souls as in a cabinet, or as an adornment) w. ναοφόροι et al. IEph 9: 2. Of the church ISm inscr., cf. Lghtft. ad loc.*

ἁγιωσύνη, ης, ἡ (also ἀγιοσύνη) *holiness* (Herodian Gr. I 335; 18; schol. [Plato,] Axioch. 371D; LXX Ps and 2 Macc 3: 12; Pel.-Leg. p. 10, 2; Act. Thom. 58; 97; 104 al.; PMMeyer, Griech. Texte aus Ägypten ['16] 24, 2) of Christ κατὰ πνεῦμα ἁγιωσύνης (πν. ἁγ. as Test. Levi 18: 11)

Ro 1: 4 (opp. κατὰ σάρκα)=πνεῦμα ἅγιον like רוּחַ הַקֹּדֶשׁ (Ps 51: 13; Is 63: 10, 11). Of Christians ἐπιτελεῖν ἁγιωσύνην *to perfect holiness*=become perfectly holy 2 Cor 7: 1. ἐν ἁγιωσύνῃ *in holiness* (Act. Thom. 85; 86) 1 Th 3: 13.—BSchneider, Biblica 48, '67, 359-87; OProksch, TW I, 116.*

ἀγκάλη, ης, ἡ (trag., Hdt.+; inscr., pap., LXX, mostly pl.) *arm*, bent as to receive someth.; δέξασθαι εἰς τὰς ἀ. *take into one's arms* (Jos., Ant. 8, 28 τὸ παιδίον . . . εἰς τὰς ἀ. μου τίθησι; Dit., Or. 56, 60 of an idol τὶς τῶν ἱερέων οἴσει ἐν ταῖς ἀγκάλαις) Lk 2: 28 (Mk 9: 36 uses ἐναγκαλίσασθαι). M-M and suppl.*

ἄγκιστρον, ου τό (Hom.+; LXX, e.g., Is 19: 8) *fishhook*—**1.** lit. βάλλειν ἄ. εἰς θάλασσαν Mt 17: 27.

2. fig. (Polyaenus, Exc. 1 "golden fishhooks") ἐμπεσεῖν εἰς τὰ ἄ. τῆς κενοδοξίας *be caught on the fishhooks of error* IMg 11. B 897; 899.*

ἄγκυρα, ας, ἡ *anchor* (Alcaeus+; Dit., Syll.² 588, 168; 171; Zen.-P. 59287, 64 [III вс]; PLond. 1164h, 9; 1714, 31; Jos., Vi. 167.—Sym. Jer 52: 18 in special mng.).

1. lit., of a ship's anchor ῥίπτειν ἀ. *let go* or *drop an anchor* Ac 27: 29. ἀ. ἐκτείνειν *run out an anchor* vs. 30 (Breusing 195; LCasson, Ships and Seamanship in the Anc. World, '71, 256). ἀ. περιαιρεῖν vs. 40 (s. περιαιρέω 1).

2. fig. (Eur., Hec. 80 ἄ. οἴκων; Soph., fgm. 623 ἄ. βίου; Heliod. 7, 25, 4 πᾶσα ἐλπίδος ἄ.; IG XII, VII 123b, 3 ἄ. γήρως) of hope (Marinus, Vi. Procli 29) ἣν ὡς ἄγκυραν ἔχομεν τῆς ψυχῆς Hb 6: 19. M-M. B. 737.*

ἀγκών, ῶνος, ὁ (Hom.+; pap., LXX; Jos., Ant. 17, 187) *the bent arm* αἴρειν τινὰ τῶν ἀ. *take someone by the arms* Hv 1, 4, 3. B. 238.*

ἄγναφος, ον (Peripl. Eryth. c. 6; Moeris p. 31 under ἄκναπτον; Thomas Mag. p. 12, 14; Cair. Zen.-P. 92, 16 [III вс]; PLond. 193 verso, 22 [II AD] κιτῶνα ἄγναφον; PHamburg 10, 32) *unbleached, unshrunken, unsized, new* (s. PMMeyer on the Hamb. pap. above) ἐπίβλημα ῥάκους ἀγνάφου *a patch of new cloth* Mt 9: 16; Mk 2: 21. M-M.*

ἁγνεία, ας, ἡ (Soph., Oed. R. 864 ἁ. λόγων ἔργων τε πάντων; Pla.; inscr. [e.g. fr. Epidaurus in Porphyr., Abst. 2, 19 ἁγνὸν χρὴ ναοῖο θυώδεος ἐντὸς ἰόντα ἔμμεναι· ἁγνεία δ' ἐστὶ φρονεῖν ὅσια; Wadd. 2034; 2203]; pap., LXX, Ep. Arist., Philo, Joseph.) *purity;* of a pure mind (s. inscr. fr. Epidaurus above; Jos., Ant. 19, 331) specif. *chastity* (Diod. S. 10, 21, 2 ἁγνεία τ. σώματος; Philo, Abr. 98 ἁ. τῆς γυναικός; Jos., Ant. 3, 78) ἐν πάσῃ ἁ. w. *all propriety* 1 Ti 5: 2. W. πίστις and ἀγάπη Pol 4: 2. W. δικαιοσύνη Hs 9, 16, 7. W. σεμνότης (Diod. S. 4, 24, 5) Hs 5, 6, 5. W. σωφροσύνη (Test. Jos. 10: 2) IEph 10: 3. W. other virtues 1 Ti 4: 12; 1 Cl 21: 7; 64; Hs 9, 15, 2; Hm 6, 2, 3 (Act. Jo. 29; Act. Phil. 3; 37; Act. Thom. 104). As first duty of youth Pol 5: 3; ἐν ἁ. μένειν *remain chaste* IPol 5: 2 (Act. Phil. 119). ἐν ἁ. κατοικεῖν Hm 4, 3, 2 (cf. Act. Thom. 131); ἁ. φυλάσσειν (cf. Philo, Vi. Cont. 68) 4, 1, 1=ἁ. τηρεῖν 4, 4, 3.—JMüller, D. Keuschheitsideen in ihrer gesch. Entwicklung 1897; EFehrle, D. kult. Keuschh. im Altertum '10, 42ff. M-M.*

ἀγνευτήριον, ου, τό (Chaeremon Hist. [I AD] in Porphyr., De Abst. 4, 6) lit. *place of purification*, perh. *sanctuary* of the part of the temple precinct in which the ἅγια σκεύη were kept GOxy (POxy. 840) 8; 13. JoachJeremias, Unbekannte Jesusworte '48, p. 39 n. 3; 43 (Unknown Sayings of Jesus, tr. Fuller, '57, p. 37 n. 2; 41-43: 'inner court, court of the Israelites'). M-M s.v. ἀγνεία.*

ἀγνεύω fut. ἀγνεύσω (Aeschyl., Hdt.+; inscr.; BGU 1201, 6; PTebt. 298, 68; Philo; Jos., Bell. 5, 227, Ant. 14, 285) be pure ὑπὲρ τῆς ψυχῆς for your soul's sake B 19: 8 (cf. Diod. S. 10, 9, 6 [Exc. De Virt. II 201 Vogel] τ. ψυχὴν ἀγνεύουσαν; Philo, Mut. Nom. 44).*

ἀγνίζω 1 Aor. ἥγνισα; pf. ptc. ἡγνικώς, pass. ἡγνισμένος; 1 aor. imper. pass. ἀγνίσθητι, ptc. ἀγνισθείς (Aeschyl., Hdt.+; LXX, Joseph.; Sib. Or. 3, 592).
1. purify—a. of the cultic lustrations and rites of atonement (so in trag., also Lind. Tempelchr. D 74; Plut., Mor. 263E τὸ πῦρ καθαίρει κ. τὸ ὕδωρ ἀγνίζει), of the Jews before Passover J 11: 55 (cf. Ex 19: 10; 2 Chr 31: 17f; Jos., Bell. 6, 425, Ant. 12, 145).
b. fig. καρδίας Js 4: 8; ψυχάς 1 Pt 1: 22; ἑαυτόν 1 J 3: 3. Pass. ἀ. τῇ ἀφέσει τ. ἁμαρτιῶν become pure through forgiveness of sins B 5: 1. Also ἀ. ἀπὸ τῶν ἁμαρτιῶν 8: 1.
2. mid. (w. pass. aor.)—a. purify oneself (Plut., Mor. 1105B; Josh 3: 5) of the lustrations with the Nazirite oath (cf. Num 6: 3) Ac 21: 24, 26; 24: 18.
b. dedicate oneself i.e. give oneself up as a propitiation ὑπὲρ ὑμῶν for you IEph 8: 1. ἀγνίζεται ὑπὲρ ὑμῶν τὸ ἐμὸν πνεῦμα my spirit dedicates itself for you ITr 13: 3. M-M.*

ἀγνισμός, οῦ, ὁ purification (Dionys. Hal. 3, 22; Plut., Mor. 418B al.; Dit., Syll.³ 1219, 19).
1. of the purification customs when a vow was accomplished τῶν ἡμερῶν τοῦ ἀ. Ac 21: 26 (πᾶσαι αἱ ἡμέραι τοῦ ἀ. Num 6: 5).
2. in the moral sense (s. ἀγνίζω 1b) ὁ ἀ. τῆς καρδίας B 8: 3, w. forgiveness of sins. M-M.*

ἀγνοέω impf. ἠγνόουν; 1 aor. ἠγνόησα (Hom.+; inscr., pap., LXX, Philo, Joseph.).
1. not to know, be ignorant w. ὅτι foll. (Περὶ ὕψους 33, 3 [οὐδὲ ἐκεῖνο ἀγνοῶ ὅτι=nor do I fail to recognize this, namely that...]; PGiess. 11, 17 [118 AD]) Ro 2: 4; 6: 3; 7: 1; MPol 17: 2. A favorite is the formula οὐ θέλω ὑμᾶς ἀγνοεῖν (cf. Theophr., C. Pl. 2, 4, 8; 3, 9, 5; PTebt. 314, 3 [II AD] πιστεύω σε μὴ ἀγνοεῖν; Philo, Opif. M. 87 χρὴ μηδ' ἐκεῖνο ἀγνοεῖν ὅτι; Jos., Ant. 13, 354 οὐ γὰρ ἀγνοεῖν βούλομαι σε) I want you to know w. ὅτι foll. Ro 1: 13; 1 Cor 10: 1; cf. 2 Cl 14: 2; w. περί τινος 1 Cor 12: 1; 1 Th 4: 13; w. ὑπέρ τινος and ὅτι foll. 2 Cor 1: 8; w. acc. foll. Ro 11: 25; cf. οὐ γὰρ αὐτοῦ τὰ νοήματα ἀγνοοῦμεν we know his designs quite well 2 Cor 2: 11 (cf. Diod. S. 3, 66, 4; Appian, Samn. 4 §14 οὐκ ἀγνοεῖν ὅτι=know very well that; Athen. 4, 73 p. 172F οὐκ ἀγνοῶ ἅ...; Wsd 12: 10; Jos., Bell. 1, 608, Ant. 6, 253; 7, 217; PGM 7, 245 οὐκ ἀγνοοῦμεν); w. indir. question foll. 2 Cl 10: 4; MPol 10: 1. Abs. ἀγνοῶν ἐποίησα I did it in ignorance 1 Ti 1: 13 (Test. Jud. 12: 5).
2. not to know w. acc. of the pers. (PGiess. 69, 4 Χαιρήμονα οὐκ ἀγνοεῖς; PPetr. III 53n, 4 [III BC]; Herm. Wr. 11, 21b ἀ. τὸν θεόν [codd. τὸ θεῖον]) or thing (Dit., Syll.³ 336, 9 ἀ. τοὺς τῆς πόλεως νόμους; 881, 2; Wilcken, Chrest. 57, 6 [II BC]; Jos., Vi. 107) τοῦτον ἀγνοήσαντες Ac 13: 27. τὴν τοῦ θεοῦ δικαιοσύνην Ro 10: 3 (here perh.=disregard). παράπτωμα Hm 9: 7. τὸ χάρισμα IEph 17: 2; cf. MPol 11: 2. Abs. ὁ ἀγνοοῦντες εὐσεβεῖτε what you worship without knowing it (on the subject matter Maximus Tyr. 11, 5e: all sorts of philosophers ἴσασιν οὐκ

ἑκόντες καὶ λέγουσιν ἄκοντες sc. τὸ θεῖον=they know and name God without wishing to do so) Ac 17: 23; cf. ISm 5: 1. ὁ ἀγνοῶν the man who does not know it ITr 6: 2. Pass. (Jos., Ant. 1, 286) ἀγνοοῦνται (the Christians) are not well known Dg 5: 12; ἀγνοούμενοι (opp. ἐπιγινωσκόμενοι 2 Cor 6: 9; ἀγνοούμενος τῷ προσώπῳ ταῖς ἐκκλησίαις unknown to the churches by face (= personally, dat. of relation Bl-D. §197; manner, Rob. 530) Gal 1: 22.—Practically not to recognize, disregard (cf. Ro 10: 3 above) εἴ τις ἀγνοεῖ, ἀγνοεῖται if anyone disregards (it),he is disregarded (by God) 1 Cor 14: 38 (v.l. ἀγνοείτω let him remain ignorant—For the juxtaposition of act. and pass. s. Alex. Aphr., Fat. 31, II 2 p. 202, 18 ἀγνοῶν καὶ ἀγνοούμενος).
3. not to understand w. acc. τὸ ῥῆμα Mk 9: 32; Lk 9: 45. ἐν οἷς (=ἐν τούτοις, ἅ) ἀγνοοῦσιν βλασφημοῦντες deriding what they do not understand 2 Pt 2: 12 (cf. PTebt. 43, 25 [118 BC] ὑφ' ἡμῶν ἔν τισιν ἠγνοηκότων).
4. do wrong, sin in ignorance (class.; Polyb. 1, 67, 5; Diod. S. 1, 70, 7 ὑπὲρ τῶν ἀγνοουμένων; 11, 16, 1 τὰ ἠγνοημένα=lapses; 17, 73, 6; Sir 5: 15; 2 Macc 11: 31; PTebt. 23, 12 [II BC] τὰ προηγνοημένα the former sins) w. πλανᾶσθαι Hb 5: 2. M-M.*

ἀγνόημα, ατος, τό (since Gorgias, Helena 19 [V BC]) sin committed in ignorance (Diod. S. 1, 71, 3 ἐλάχιστα ἀ.; 13, 90, 7; Dit., Or. 116, 2; UPZ 111, 3 [163 BC]; PTebt. 5, 3 [118 BC] ἀγνοήματα, ἁμαρτήματα, ἐνκλήματα, καταγνώσματα [APF 2, '03, 483ff; PMMeyer, Jurist. Pap. '20, 69; KLatte, ARW 20, '21, p. 287, 1]; BGU 1185, 7; 1 Macc 13: 39; Tob 3: 3; Sir 23: 2) Hb 9: 7. Forgiven by God Hs 5, 7, 3f. M-M.*

ἄγνοια, ας, ἡ (since Aeschyl. and Thu. 8, 92, 11; inscr., pap., LXX; Ep. Arist. 130; Philo; Jos., Bell. 4, 29, Ant. 18, 335, C. Ap. 1, 73; Test. 12 Patr.) ignorance.
1. gener. κατὰ ἄγνοιαν ἐπράξατε you acted in ignorance Ac 3: 17 (Polyb. 12, 12, 4; 5 κατ' ἄ. παραπαίειν; Plut., Mor. 551E; Philo, Leg. All. 1, 35; Jos., Ant. 11, 130; Inscr. 14 in FSteinleitner, D. Beicht '13; POxy. 237 VIII, 36; BGU 619, 4). As v.l. for ἀγνωσία 1 Pt 2: 15 𝔓⁷². ἄχρι τῆς ἀγνοίας as long as he knows nothing of it Hm 4, 1, 5.—PK 2 p. 14, 11; 3 p. 15, 26.
2. esp. in religious sense, almost=sin (so LXX, e.g. Sir 23: 3 [in parallelism with ἁμαρτίαι]; 28: 7; Test. Levi 3: 5, Zeb. 1: 5; Philo, Ebr. 154ff; but cf. also Pla., Theaet. 176C; Stoic in Diog. L. 7, 93; Diod. S. 14, 1, 2 τ. ἰδίαν ἄγνοιαν=one's own mistaken conduct; Epict. 1, 26, 6; Herm. Wr. 13, 8; 11, 21 ἡ τελεία κακία τὸ ἀγνοεῖν τὸ θεῖον, also 10, 9; PTebt. 24, 33 [II BC] of evildoers: λήγοντες τῆς ἀγνοίας;—Diod. S. 4, 11, 2 ἄ. is the "delusion" that drove Heracles to commit murder); IEph 19: 3. τοὺς χρόνους τῆς ἀγνοίας Ac 17: 30 (Test. Gad 5: 7 μετάνοια ἀναιρεῖ τὴν ἄ.). διὰ τὴν ἄγνοιαν (Diod. S. 11, 10, 2; Dit., Syll.³ 904, 6; cf. Alex. Aphr., Fat. 19, II 2 p. 189, 16 διὰ ἄγνοιαν ἁμαρτάνειν) Eph 4: 18. ἐν τῇ ἀγνοίᾳ ὑμῶν 1 Pt 1: 14. ἀ. προτέρα Hs 5, 7, 3. The pl. as v.l. for ἀπάταις 2 Pt 2: 13. M-M.*

ἀγνός, ή, όν (Hom.+; inscr., pap., LXX, Ep. Arist., Philo) pure, holy, cultic word, orig. an attribute of the divinity and everything belonging to it (Suppl. Epigr. Gr. VIII 550, 2 [I BC] Ἰσι ἀγνή ἁγία; GBjörck, Der Fluch d. Christ. Sabinus '38: inscr. [p. 25-38] no. 14 [pre-Christian] τῇ Ἁγνῇ Θεᾷ), then transferred to moral sense (Clem. Alex., Str. defines it 7, 27, 2 πᾶς ἀ. ἐστιν ὁ μηδὲν ἑαυτῷ κακὸν συνειδώς).

1. of pers. (Diog. L. 7, 119: acc. to the Stoics the wise men are ἀγνοί, ὅσιοι, δίκαιοι; POxy. 41, 29f; ἀγνοὶ πιστοὶ σύνδικοι; Sb 4117): of Christ or God 1 J 3: 3 (Sib. Or. 3, 49 of the Messiah). σεαυτὸν ἀ. τήρει keep yourself pure (fr. sins) 1 Ti 5: 22; ἀ. ἐν τῇ σαρκί 1 Cl 38: 2; ἀ. ἐν ἔργοις 48: 5.—Innocent (Pla., Leg. 6, 759c ἀ. τοῦ φόνου) συνεστήσατε ἑαυτοὺς ἁγνοὺς εἶναι you have shown that you were innocent 2 Cor 7: 11, where τῷ πράγματι is to be connected w. ἁγνούς.—Esp. of women chaste, pure (since Aeschyl., fgm. 238 N.; Pla., Leg. 840D, also Dit., Syll.³ 985, 35; Sb 2481 Ἰουλία ἀγνή; PGM 36, 289) παρθένος (Herodian 1, 11, 4; Dit., Syll.³ 797, 20 [37 AD]; Aberciusinschr. 14; 4 Macc 18: 7; Philo, Spec. Leg. 1, 107) 2 Cor 11: 2; cf. Tit 2: 5.

2. of things ὅσα ἁγνά everything that is pure Phil 4: 8; ἔργα ἁ. (Pr 21: 8) Hv 3, 8, 7. χεῖρες (Eur., Hipp. 316f, Or. 1604) 1 Cl 29: 1; ἀ. ἀναστροφή 1 Pt 3: 2. ἀγωγή 1 Cl 48: 1. συνείδησις clear conscience (w. ἄμωμος, σεμνός) 1: 3; Pol 5: 3. ἀγάπη holy love 1 Cl 21: 8. Of liturgical matters (cf. Herm. Wr. 1, 31 θυσίας ἀ.): (w. ἀμίαντον) τὸ βάπτισμα ἀ. τηρεῖν keep oneself pure after baptism 2 Cl 6: 9. Of the wisdom from above Js 3: 17. M-M.*

ἁγνότης, ητος, ἡ purity, sincerity (Cornutus 32 p. 67, 2; IG IV 588, 15 [II AD] δικαιοσύνης ἕνεκεν καὶ ἁγνότητος) ἐν ἁγνότητι 2 Cor 6: 6; in 11: 3 it is a doubtful reading, though w. very ancient attestation. ἀ. τῆς ἀληθείας true purity Hv 3, 7, 3; πορεύεσθαι ἐν ἀ. lead a pure life m 4, 4, 4.*

ἁγνῶς adv. (Hes.+; Dit., Or. 485, 14; 524, 6, Syll.³ 986, 8; 16; Ep. Arist. 317; PGM 4, 2639; 12, 38 ἀ. καὶ καθαρῶς) purely, sincerely μένειν abide in purity B 2: 3. πολιτεύεσθαι lead a pure life Hs 5, 6, 6. Also ἀναστρέφεσθαι s 9, 27, 2. διακονεῖν in sincerity v 3, 5, 1; cf. s 9, 26, 2. διδάσκειν σεμνῶς καὶ ἀ. teach seriously and sincerely s 9, 25, 2; τὸν Χριστὸν καταγγέλλουσιν οὐχ ἀ. not from pure motives Phil 1: 17.*

ἀγνωσία, ας, ἡ (Eur., Thu.+; pap., LXX, Test. Levi 18: 9, Judah 19: 3.) ignorance, not predominantly in the intellectual sense but, as in the speech of the mysteries (Herm. Wr. 1, 27 ἀ. τοῦ θεοῦ; 7, 1; 10, 8) a lack of religious experience or lack of spiritual discernment (cf. Rtzst., Mysterienrel.³ 292f) ἀγνωσίαν θεοῦ τινες ἔχουσιν some have no knowledge of God (cf. Wsd 13: 1; APF 5, '13, 383) 1 Cor 15: 34. καλεῖν ἀπὸ ἀ. εἰς ἐπίγνωσιν δόξης ὀνόματος αὐτοῦ 1 Cl 59: 2; φιμοῦν τὴν τῶν ἀφρόνων ἀνθρώπων ἀ. silence the ignorant talk of foolish men 1 Pt 2: 15 (ἄγνοια 𝔓⁷²). M-M.*

ἄγνωστος, ον (Hom.+; pap. [PGiess. 3, 2f [117 AD] ἥκω σοι, ὦ δῆμε, οὐκ ἄγνωστος Φοῖβος θεός]; LXX; Philo; Jos., C. Ap. 2, 167 [of God's οὐσία] al.) unknown in the inscr. on an altar in Athens ἀγνώστῳ θεῷ Ac 17: 23 (Paus. 1, 4: ἐπὶ τῇ Φαληρῷ ... Ἀθηνᾶς ναός ἐστιν ... βωμοὶ θεῶν τε ὀνομαζομένων ἀγνώστων καὶ ἡρώων; cf. 5, 14, 8 and a Pergamene inscr. [HHepding, Ath. Mitteilungen 35, '10, 454–57]). Cf. also Diog. L. 1, 110 ἔτι καὶ νῦν ἔστι εὑρεῖν κατὰ τοὺς δήμους τ. Ἀθηναίων βωμοὺς ἀνωνύμους. Norden, Agn. Th. '13, 115–25 thinks that this expr. comes fr. a speech by Apollonius of Tyana (cf. Philostrat., Vi. Apoll. 6, 3, 19 ἀγνώστων δαιμόνων βωμοὶ ἵδρυνται). S. AHarnack, TU 39, 1, '13, 1–46; Rtzst., NJklA 31, '13, 146ff; 393ff; PCorssen, ZNW 14, '13, 309ff; FCBurkitt, JTS 15, '14, 455–64; ThBirt, RhM 69, '14, 342ff; OWeinreich, De Dis Ignotis: ARW 18, '15, 1–52; AWikenhauser, D.

Apostelgesch. '21, 369–94; EMeyer III '23, 96–8; Clemen 290–300; Dssm., Paulus² '25, 226–9 (Eng. tr. Paul '26, 287–91); KLake: Beginn. I 5, '33, 240–6; WGöber, Pauly-W. 2. R. V '34, 1988–94; MDibelius, Pls. auf d. Areopag '39=ch. 2 in Studies in the Acts, ed. HGreeven, '56. BGärtner, The Areopagus Speech and Natural Revelation, '55, 242–47 (lit.). For further lit. see s.v. Ἄρειος πάγος. M-M.*

ἀγορά, ᾶς, ἡ (in var. mngs. Hom.+; inscr., pap., LXX, Jos., Bell. 5, 513 al.; loanw. in rabb.) market place as a place for children to play Mt 11: 16; Lk 7: 32. Place for men seeking work and for idlers (Harpocration, s.v. Κολωνέτας: the μισθωτοὶ are standing in the market-place) Mt 20: 3; cf. 23: 7; Mk 12: 38; Lk 11: 43; 20: 46. Scene of public events, incl. the healings of Jesus ἐν ταῖς ἀ. ἐτίθεσαν τοὺς ἀσθενοῦντας Mk 6: 56. Scene of a lawsuit (so as early as Hom.; cf. Demosth. 43, 36 τῶν ἀρχόντων) against Paul Ac 16: 19, 35 D. Of the Agora in Athens (in the Ceramicus), the center of public life 17: 17 (cf. ECurtius, Paulus in Athen: SAB 1893, 925ff; Suzanne Halstead, Paul in the Agora: Quantulacumque [KLake-Festschr.] '37, 139–43). ἀπ' ἀγορᾶς (+ὅταν ἔλθωσιν [D it] is the correct interpr.) ἐὰν μὴ ῥαντίσωνται οὐκ ἐσθίουσιν when they return fr. the market place they do not eat unless they wash themselves (pregnant constr. as Vi. Aesopi I c. 40 πιεῖν ἀπὸ τοῦ βαλανείου=after returning from the bath; PHolm. 20, 26 μετὰ τὴν κάμινον=after burning in the oven. Cf. also Epict. 3, 19, 5 φαγεῖν ἐκ βαλανείου; Sir 34: 25 βαπτιζόμενος ἀπὸ νεκροῦ) Mk 7: 4. Since the mid. form ῥαντ. expresses someth. about the persons of those who eat, the words ἀπ' ἀγ. prob. refer to them, too, and so the interpr. of ἀπ' ἀγ. = '(of) the things sold in the market', though linguistically poss. (ἀ. in this sense X.+; simply='food': Memnon [I BC/I AD] no. 434 fgm. 1, 29, 9 Jac.; Appian, Sicil. 2 §10 and 4; Polyaenus 3, 10, 10; 5, 2, 10; Jos., Bell. 1, 308, Ant. 14, 472) is untenable. M-M. B. 822.*

ἀγοράζω impf. ἠγόραζον; 1 aor. ἠγόρασα, pass. ἠγοράσθην buy, purchase (so, trans., Aristoph.+; inscr., pap., LXX; Jos., Ant. 12, 175; Test. 12 Patr.).

1. lit., w. acc. of the thing (X., An. 1, 5, 10; Gen 42: 7; 2 Ch 34: 11) τὸν ἀγρὸν ἐκεῖνον Mt 13: 44; Lk 14: 18; αὐτόν (i.e. μαργαρίτην) Mt 13: 46; σινδόνα Mk 15: 46; ἀρώματα 16: 1; μάχαιραν Lk 22: 36; cf. 14: 19; J 4: 8; 6: 5. τὸν γόμον αὐτῶν Rv 18: 11. W. rel. clause as obj.: ἀ. ὧν χρείαν ἔχομεν what we need J 13: 29. Of fields and fig. of souls=win Hs 1: 8f. W. dat. of pers. and acc. of thing (Gen 43: 4; 44: 25) ἑαυτοῖς βρώματα Mt 14: 15; cf. Mk 6: 36. W. dat. of pers. only Mt 25: 9. ἀ. τι εἴς τινα someth. for someone Lk 9: 13. Abs. (Gen 42: 5; 2 Ch 1: 16) Mt 25: 10; 1 Cor 7: 30. W. πωλεῖν (Aristoph., Ach. 625; Dit., Syll.³ 330, 19; Is 24: 2; 1 Macc 13: 49; Jos., Bell. 2, 127) Rv 13: 17; cf. Mt 21: 12; Mk 11: 15; Lk 17: 28; 19: 45 v.l. W. price given in genit. (PPar. 59, 6; Dt 2: 6; Bar 1: 10; cf. Bl-D. §179; Rob. 510f) δηναρίων διακοσίων ἄρτους buy 200 denarii worth of bread Mk 6: 37. Also ἐκ (pap. in Kuhring [s. ἀνά, beg.] 27f; EpJer 24) ἠγόρασαν ἐξ αὐτῶν (i.e. w. the 30 shekels of silver) τὸν ἀγρόν Mt 27: 7. W. the seller mentioned παρά τινος (Isocr. 2, 54; PLond. 882, 24; 1208, 10; POxy. 1149, 5; Dt 2: 6; 2 Esdr 20: 32 [Neh 10: 31]) ἀ. παρ' ἐμοῦ χρυσίον Rv 3: 18.

2. fig., based on the analogy of religious law which in reality bestowed freedom on a slave purchased by a divinity (ἀ. of the purchase of a slave Dit., Or. 338,

23; POxy. 1149, 5f. Dit., Syll.³ 845, 1 has ἐπρίατο in a manumission. S. LMitteis, Reichsrecht u. Volksrecht 1891, 374ff; Dssm. LO 275, n. 9 [LAE 322ff]; for the opp. view WElert, ThLZ 72, '47, 265–70) buy, acquire as property of believers, for whom Christ has paid the price w. his blood: w. gen. of price ἠγοράσθητε τιμῆς you were bought for a price 1 Cor 6: 20; 7: 23 (s. τιμή 1). τινά 2 Pt 2: 1. W. dat. of the possessor and ἐν of the price (Bl-D. §219, 3; cf. 1 Ch 21: 24): ἠγόρασας τῷ θεῷ ἐν τῷ αἵματί σου Rv 5: 9. W. ἀπό τινος to indicate from whom or from what the purchase separates ἠγορασμένοι ἀπὸ τῆς γῆς Rv 14: 3; cf. vs. 4. M-M. B. 818.*

ἀγοραῖος, ον (Aeschyl., Hdt.+; inscr., pap.) pertaining to a market used only as subst.

1. οἱ ἀ. market people, specif. the crowd in the market place, and so rabble (Gramm. Ammonius ἀγοραῖος σημαίνει τ. πονηρόν, τὸν ἐν ἀγορᾷ τεθραμμένον, cf. Aristoph., Ran. 1015; Pla., Prot. 347c; Theophr., Char. 6, 2; Dio Chrys. 49[66], 25; Plut., Aemil. Paul. 38, 4 ἀνθρώπους ἀγεννεῖς καὶ δεδουλευκότας, ἀγοραίους δὲ καὶ δυναμένους ὄχλον συναγαγεῖν al.) Ac 17: 5.

2. αἱ ἀγοραῖοι (sc. ἡμέραι or σύνοδοι) court days or sessions ἀ. ἄγονται the courts are in session 19: 38 (Jos., Ant. 14, 245 ἄγειν τὴν ἀγοραῖον; Ephemeris Epigraphica VII p. 436, no. 44, 10 [II AD] ἡ ἀγοραῖος ἤχθη; Strabo 13, 4, 12 τὰς ἀ. ποιεῖσθαι=Lat. conventus forenses agere; Bl-D. §5, 3b). M-M.*

ἄγρα, ας, ἡ (Hom.+; Test. Zeb. 6: 6; Jos., Ant. 8, 40)—
1. act. catching (Ctesias, Ind. 22; Alciphr. 1, 15, 1; Aesop, Fab. 21 P.=24 H.; 191 P.=260 H.) εἰς ἄ. to catch someth. (Eur., Suppl. 885 ἐς ἄγρας ἱέναι) Lk 5: 4; likew. vs. 9 w. the v.l. ὧν συνέλαβον BD.

2. pass. a catch (what is caught) (Solon 23, 3 Diehl²; X., Cyr. 2, 4, 19; Lycophron v. 665; Appian, Bell. Civ. 4, 129 §545; Iambl. Erot. 34) w. the rdg. ᾗ=ἣν συνέλαβον א A in the same vs.*

ἀγράμματος, ον unable to write, illiterate (since X., Mem. 4, 2, 20; Epict. 2, 2, 22; BGU 118; 152; POxy. 71; 133; 134; 137; 139 al.—EMajer-Leonhard, Ἀγράμματοι, Diss. Marb. '13) and also uneducated, illiterate (since Pla., Tim. 23B; ἄνθρωποι Epicurus in Philod., Rhet. 1, 141; Philo, Omn. Prob. Lib. 51) of Peter and John ἄνθρωποι ἀ. καὶ ἰδιῶται Ac 4: 13 (WWuellner, The Mng. of 'Fishers of Men' '67, 45–63 ἀγράμ.=lacking in expertise concerning the law). M-M.*

ἀγραυλέω live out of doors (Aristot.+; Plut., Num. 4, 1. Of shepherds Bryso in Stob. 4, 28, 15; Parthenius 29, 1; cf. Il. 18, 162 ποιμένες ἄγραυλοι) Lk 2: 8.*

ἀγρεύω 1 aor. ἤγρευσα catch (Soph., Hdt.+; pap., LXX) in NT only fig. (Soph., fgm. 510; Pr 5: 22; 6: 25f) ἵνα αὐτὸν ἀγρεύσωσιν λόγῳ that they might catch him in a(n unguarded) statement Mk 12: 13. M-M.*

ἀγρίδιον, ου, τό (Diod. S. 13, 84, 4; Epict. 2, 22, 10 al.; M. Ant. 4, 3, 9; Sb 5230, 28 [I AD] a little farm or country house MPol 5: 1; 6: 1.*

ἀγριέλαιος really an adj. (Bl-D. §120, 3 w. app.; Rob. 168, cf. 166) and so perh. Ro 11: 17 (as Erycius in Anth. Pal. 9, 237; Theocr., Idyll 25, 257). But it may also be taken as a subst., as we say 'oak' of a piece of furniture (see below).*

ἀγριέλαιος, ου, ἡ wild olive tree (Theophr., Hist. Pl. 2, 2, 5; Theocr. 7, 18; Nicol. Dam.: 90 fgm. 66, 40 Jac.; Zen.-P. 100 [=Sb 6815], 7 [255 BC]. As masc. in schol. on

Apollon. Rhod. 2, 843, 848–50a) fig., of the heathen Ro 11: 17, 24 (opp. καλλιέλαιος).—ThFischer, D. Ölbaum '04; WMRamsay, The Olive-Tree and the Wild-Olive: Exp. 6th Ser. XI '05, 16–34; 152–60; EFickendey, D. Ölbaum in Kleinasien '22; SLinder, D. Pfropfen m. wilden Ölzweigen (Ro 11: 17); Pj 26, '30, 40–3; FJBruijel, De Olijfboom: Geref. Theol. Tijdschr. 35, '35, 273–80. M-M.*

ἄγριος, ία, ον (Hom.+; inscr., pap., LXX, Ep. Arist., Philo; Jos., Ant. 2, 246; Test. 12 Patr.; loanw. in rabb.) found in the open field, wild.

1. lit., of plants (Diod. S. 5, 2, 4; Artem. 4, 57; Jos., Bell. 5, 437) Hs 9, 26, 4. Of animals (so Diod. S. 4, 17, 4 ζῷα; 4, 17, 5 θηρία; Arrian, Ind. 11, 11; 13, 1; PSI 406, 42; 409, 18 [III BC]; BGU 1252, 4; as a rule LXX; Jos., C. Ap. 2, 139) 1 Cl 56: 11f (Job 5: 22f); μέλι ἄ. honey fr. wild bees (Iambl. Erot. p. 222, 16 μέλιτται ἄγριαι w. their μέλι; Cat. Cod. Astr. X 86b, 6 ἀγριομέλισσα.—Others think of a plant product; cf. Ps.-Aristot., Mirab. 19 ἐν Λυδίᾳ ἀπὸ τῶν δένδρων τὸ μέλι συλλέγεσθαι πολύ; Diod. S. 19, 94, 10 φύεται παρ' αὐτοῖς [i.e. the Nabataeans] ἀπὸ τ. δένδρων μέλι πολὺ τὸ καλούμενον ἄγριον, ᾧ χρῶνται ποτῷ μεθ' ὕδατος; Jos., Bell. 4, 468) Mt 3: 4; Mk 1: 6; GEb 2.

2. fig. of persons wild in appearance of women in black w. flowing hair Hs 9, 9, 5; more completely ἄ. τῇ ἰδέᾳ of a shepherd 6, 2, 5. Of desires savage, fierce (Pla., Rep. 572B) Hm 12, 1, 2; cf. 12, 4, 6. τὸ ἄγριον cruelty (Pla., Rep. 571c et al.; Herm. Wr. 486, 38; 492, 4 Sc.) IEph 10: 2 (opp. ἥμερος). Of nat. phen. stormy (Aeschyl., Hdt.+) κύματα ἄ. θαλάσσης (Wsd 14: 1; Sib. Or. 3, 778) Jd 13. M-M.*

ἀγριότης, ητος, ἡ (X.+; 2 Macc 15: 21; Philo; Jos., Ant. 16, 363 θυμὸς καὶ ἀ.) wildness, savagery of desires Hm 12, 1, 2.*

ἀγριόω make wild (trag., X.+; 3 Macc 5: 2). Pass., fig., become wild of men Hs 9, 26, 4 (Diod. S. 19, 6, 6; Appian, Iber. 96 §417; the act.='cause to become wild' Test. Sim. 4: 8 ἀγριοῖ τοῦτο τ. ψυχήν).*

Ἀγρίππας, α, ὁ Agrippa (lit. [Diod. S. 12, 30, 1; also Philo, Joseph.]; inscr., pap., coins).

1. Herod Agrippa I (10 BC–44 AD), son of Aristobulus, grandson of Herod the Great; ruler first (37) of Gaulanitis, Trachonitis, Batanaea, Panias, then (39) also of Abilene, Galilee, and Peraea, finally (41) also of Judaea and Samaria; called Herod in Ac 12: 1ff.—Schürer I⁴ 549ff (sources and lit.); ESchwartz, NGG '07, 263ff; Rosenberg in Pauly-W. X 1, '17, 143–6; EMeyer I 42f; 167f; 541f. 541f.

2. Herod Agrippa II (27–92/93 AD), son of 1, ruled over various parts of Palestine fr. 53 to his death. For his part in Paul's trial s. Ac 25: 13ff (he is mentioned 25: 13, 22–4, 26; 26: 1f, 7 v.l., 19, 27f, 32).—Schürer I⁴ 585ff (sources and lit.); Rosenberg in Pauly-W. X 1, '17, 146–50.—On both s. WOtto and HWillrich on Ἡρῴδης, beg.*

ἀγρός, οῦ, ὁ (Hom.+; inscr., pap., LXX, Philo, Joseph., Test. 12 Patr.).

1. field a plot of ground used mainly for agriculture (X., Mem. 1, 1, 8) Mt 13: 24, 27, 31, 38; Hv 3, 1, 3. In it grow τὰ κρίνα τοῦ ἀ. wild lilies Mt 6: 28; χόρτος τοῦ ἀ. (Gen 3: 18; 4 Km 19: 26) vs. 30; ζιζάνια τοῦ ἀ. weeds in the field 13: 36; παμβότανον τοῦ ἀ. 1 Cl 56: 14 (Job 5: 25). ἐν (τῷ) ἀγρῷ in the field (PAmh. 134, 5; 2 Km 2: 18; 10: 8 al.) Mt 24: 18; Lk 17: 31. εἰς τὸν ἀγρόν in the field Mk

13

13: 16. εἶναι ἐν (τῷ) ἀ. Mt 24: 40; Lk 15: 25 (17: 36); ἔρχεσθαι εἰς τὸν ἀ. go (out) into the field Hv 3, 1, 2. εἰσέρχεσθαι ἐκ τοῦ ἀ. (cf. PEleph. 13, 6 οὔπω εἰσελήλυθεν ἐξ ἀγροῦ; Gen 30: 16; Jos., Ant. 5, 141) Lk 17: 7.— Bl-D. §255, 1 w. app.; Mlt. 82.—Viewed primarily as a piece of property Mt 19: 29; Mk 10: 29f; Lk 14: 18; Ac 4: 37.—Used to hide treasure Mt 13: 44; ἀ. τοῦ κεραμέως potter's field Mt 27: 7f, 10.

2. the country as opposed to city or village Hv 2, 1, 4; πορεύεσθαι εἰς ἀ. (Timaeus Hist. [IV/III BC] no. 566 fgm. 48 Jac.; Ruth 2: 2) Mk 16: 12 or ὑπάγειν εἰς ἀ. Hv 4, 1, 2; περιπατεῖν εἰς τὸν ἀ. s 2: 1. ἔρχεσθαι ἀπ' ἀγροῦ come in fr. the country Mk 15: 21; Lk 23: 26; cf. πάρεστιν ἀπ' ἀγροῦ 11: 6 D. B. 1304.

3. in the pl. ἀ. can mean farm(s), hamlet(s) (cf. Josh 19: 6; Jos., Ant. 17, 193) Lk 15: 15. W. πόλις: ἀπήγγειλαν εἰς τὴν πόλιν καὶ εἰς τοὺς ἀγρούς Mk 5: 14; Lk 8: 34; w. κῶμαι (Dio Chrys. 13[7], 42) Mk 6: 36; Lk 9: 12; w. κῶμαι and πόλεις Mk 6: 56.—KDieterich, RhM 59, '04, 226ff. M-M.

ἀγρυπνέω—1. lit. keep oneself awake, be awake (Theognis+; pap., LXX; Philo, Aet. M. 70) fig. ἀγρυπνεῖτε be on the alert Mk 13: 33; Lk 21: 36 (cf. 1 Esdr 8: 58; 2 Esdr [Ezra] 8: 29).

2. metaph. keep watch over someth. = guard, care for it (Plut., Mor. 337B; Dit., Or. 521, 6; Da 9: 14 ἀ. ἐπὶ τὰ κακά) ἀ. ὑπὲρ τῶν ψυχῶν Hb 13: 17; εἰς αὐτό Eph 6: 18; ἀ. οὐκ εἰς τὸ ἀγαθὸν ἀλλ' εἰς τὸ πονηρόν D 5: 2; οὐκ εἰς φόβον θεοῦ ἀλλὰ ἐπὶ τὸ πονηρόν B 20: 2. M-M. and suppl.*

ἀγρυπνία, ας, ἡ (Hdt.+; BGU 1764, 9 [I BC]; Sir 31: 2; 38: 26 al.; 2 Macc 2: 26; Jos., Bell. 3, 318) wakefulness.

1. lit., only pl. (Dit., Syll.³ 1169, 50) ἐν ἀγρυπνίαις with sleepless nights (and other hardships, as X., Mem. 4, 5, 9; Plut., Mor. p. 135E, Sertor. 13, 2 πόνοι, ὁδοιπορίαι, ἀγρυπνίαι, Sulla 28, 14 ἀγρυπνίαι κ. κόποι. Cf. AFridrichsen, Symb. Osl. 7, '28, 25-9; 8, '29, 78-82; K. Hum. Vetensk.-Samfundet i. Upps. Årsbok '43, 31-4) 2 Cor 6: 5; 11: 27.

2. fig. care, which causes sleeplessness (Sir 42: 9) B 21: 7 (w. ἐπιθυμία). M-M.*

ἄγω fut. ἄξω; 2 aor. ἤγαγον; impf. pass. ἠγόμην; 1 aor. pass. ἤχθην; 1 fut. pass. ἀχθήσομαι; see the pres. act. imper. ἄγε as a separate entry (Hom.+; inscr., pap., LXX; En. 103, 15; Ep. Arist., Philo, Joseph., Test. 12 Patr.).

1. lead—a. lit. lead, bring w. acc. τὴν ὄνον καὶ τὸν πῶλον Mt 21: 7; γυναῖκα J 8: 3; παῖδα Ac 20: 12. W. acc. and indication of the goal πρὸς αὐτόν Lk 4: 40; 18: 40; cf. 19: 35; J 9: 13; Ac 9: 27; 23: 18. πρὸς τὸ συμψέλιον Hv 3, 1, 7. εἰς τὴν ἔρημον B 7: 8. ἐπὶ σφαγήν to be slaughtered Ac 8: 32; 1 Cl 16: 7; B 5: 2 (all three Is 53: 7). ἔξω J 19: 4, 13; ὧδε Lk 19: 27. W. dat. of pers. (1 Macc 7: 2) ἀγάγετέ μοι bring it to me Mt 21: 2. τινὰ σύν τινι (cf. PGM 1, 179) 1 Th 4: 14. Fig., of Jesus as shepherd J 10: 16; ὁ θεὸς ἤγαγεν τῷ Ἰσραὴλ σωτῆρα Ἰησοῦν God brought Jesus to Israel as savior Ac 13: 23.

b. bring or take along (Jos., Ant. 10, 179) εἰς Ἀντιόχειαν Ac 11: 26. ἕως Ἀθηνῶν 17: 15. ἐπὶ τὸν Ἄρειον πάγον vs. 19; ἄγοντες παρ' ᾧ ξενισθῶμεν Μνάσωνι (= πρὸς Μνάσωνα) ἵνα παρ' αὐτῷ ξενισθῶμεν 21: 16 (cf. on this ξενίζω and Bl-D. §294, 5 app.; Rob. 719). ἄγε μετὰ σεαυτοῦ bring (him) along 2 Ti 4: 11 (PPetr. II 32[2a], 13 ἄγων μεθ' αὑτοῦ).

c. fig. lead (X., Mem. 1, 6, 14; Demosth. 25, 76 εἰς

ἔλεον; 18, 316 εἰς ἀχαριστίαν; Jos., Ant. 2, 174; Pr 18: 6) τινὰ εἰς μετάνοιαν Ro 2: 4 (Polyb. 5, 16, 2 εἰς μετάνοιαν ἄξειν τ. βασιλέα; Ep. Arist. 188; Jos., Ant. 4, 144). εἰς δόξαν Hb 2: 10. Of jealousy ἄ. εἰς θάνατον 1 Cl 9: 1.

2. legal t.t. lead away, take into custody, arrest w. acc. Mk 13: 11; Lk 22: 54; J 7: 45; Ac 5: 26. ὅπως δεδεμένους ἀγάγῃ εἰς Ἰερουσαλήμ 9: 2; cf. 22: 5. Of arraignment and trial w. ἐπί and acc. (BGU 22, 34ff; PTebt. 331, 16f) ἐπὶ ἡγεμόνας Mt 10: 18. ἐπὶ τὸ βῆμα Ac 18: 12. ἐπ' ἐξουσίαν Hs 9, 28, 4. εἰς τὸ συνέδριον Ac 6: 12. Abs. 25: 6, 17, 23. Of the transport of a prisoner 23: 31; J 18: 28. εἰς τὴν παρεμβολήν take away to the barracks Ac 21: 34; 23: 10. Of leading away to execution (cf. Diod. S. 13, 102, 1; Appian, Bell. Civ. 5, §36; Lucian, Syr. Dea 25; 2 Macc 6: 29; 7: 18) Lk 23: 32.

3. fig., of the working of the Spirit on man lead, guide, pass. be led. allow oneself to be led πνεύματι θεοῦ ἄγεσθαι Ro 8: 14; cf. Gal 5: 18; Lk 4: 1, 9. γυναικάρια ἀγόμενα ἐπιθυμίαις ποικίλαις 2 Ti 3: 6 (Aristot., Nic. Eth. 7, 3, 10 p. 1147a, 34 ἡ ἐπιθυμία ἄγει. Cf. Eur., Med. 310 σε θυμὸς ἦγεν; Pla., Prot. 355A ὑπὸ τ. ἡδονῶν ἀγόμενος; Demosth. 18, 9 τοῖς ἔξωθεν λόγοις ἡγμένος; Parthenius 29, 2 ἄγειν εἰς ἐπιθυμίαν = entice to desire). 1 Cor 12: 2 is difficult: ὅτι πρὸς τὰ εἴδωλα τὰ ἄφωνα ὡς ἂν ἤγεσθε ἀπαγόμενοι may be transl. how you were attracted, carried away again and again to dumb idols, where ἄν denotes repetition, and ὡς takes up the preceding ὅτι; for another expl., presupposing the rdg. ὡς ἀνήγεσθε, s. J. Weiss ad loc.; s. also ICC ad loc. (Psellus p. 96, 33 offers a choice between ἂν ἀγάγοι and ἀναγάγοι; Herodas 6, 73 ἂν εὑρήσεις RHerzog or ἀνευρήσεις ADKnox; Ramsay, Phrygia I 2 p. 390 no. 248 ὃς ἂν ὀρύξει or ὃς ἀνορύξει).

4. of time spend (Eur., Hdt.+; Aberciusinschr. 18; LXX) ἀ. τὴν ἡμέραν τὴν ὀγδόην εἰς εὐφροσύνην celebrate the eighth day as a festival of joy B 15: 9 (cf. Dit., Or. 90, 47 [196 BC] ἄγειν τὰς ἡμέρας ταύτας ἑορτάς; PGoodspeed 3, 18 [III BC] ἡμέραν καλὴν ἤγαγον). Perh. impers. τρίτην ταύτην ἡμέραν ἄγει this is the third day Lk 24: 21; but, since this expr. cannot be found elsewhere, it is prob. better to supply Ἰησοῦς as subj. (Bl-D. §129 app.) lit. Jesus is spending the third day (cf. Galen XIII 581 Kühn τετάρτην ἡμέραν ἄγων ἀνώδυνος ἦν, XI 65 K. πόσην ἄγει τὴν ἀπὸ τοῦ νοσεῖν ἡμέραν ὁ ἄνθρωπος). Of festivals celebrate, observe (Hdt.+; Aesop, Fab. 389 P. γενέθλιον ἄγειν; Jos., Ant. 11, 77 = IEsdr 4: 50) γενέσια Mt 14: 6 v.l.; τὸ σάββατον PK 2 p. 14, 28; νεομηνίαν ibid. 1. 29. Of meetings (like Lat. agere) συμβούλιον ἄγειν hold a meeting IPol 7: 2. Pass. ἀγοραῖοι ἄγονται (s. ἀγοραῖος 2) Ac 19: 38.

5. intr. go (X.+) ἄγωμεν let us go (so Vi. Aesopi Ic. 77; loanw. in rabb.) Mt 26: 46; Mk 14: 42; J 11: 16. W. the goal given (Ael. Aristid. 51, 28 K. = 27 p. 541 D.: εἰς τὸ ἱερόν; Epict. 3, 22, 55 ἄγωμεν ἐπὶ τ. ἀνθύπατον) εἰς τὰς κωμοπόλεις Mk 1: 38. εἰς τὴν Ἰουδαίαν J 11: 7. εἰς τὸ ὄρος AP 4. εἰς ἀγρόν Hs 6, 1, 5; πρὸς αὐτόν J 11: 15. πρὸς τὸν πύργον Hs 9, 5, 6. W. the point of departure given ἐντεῦθεν J 14: 31.—JAFitzmyer, The Use of Agein and Pherein in the Synoptics, FWGingrich-Festschr., ed. EHBarth and RECocroft, '72, 147-60. M-M. B. 711; 713.

ἀγωγή, ῆς, ἡ (Aeschyl., Hdt.+; inscr., pap., LXX) way of life, conduct (so X., Eq. 3, 4; Polyb. 4, 74, 1; 4 ἀ. τοῦ βίου; Diod. S. 13, 82, 7; M. Ant. 1, 6; Inschr. v. Magn. 164, 3 ἤθει καὶ ἀγωγῇ κόσμιον; Dit., Or. 223, 15 [III BC]; 474, 9; 485, 3; UPZ 113, 12 [156 BC]; PTebt. 24, 57 [117 BC]; Esth 2: 20; 2 Macc 11: 24; Ep. Arist., Philo; Jos.,

Ant. 14, 195; cf. Nägeli 34) 2 Ti 3: 10. ἡ ἐν Χριστῷ ἀ. *the Christian way of life* 1 Cl 47: 6. σεμνὴ ... ἀγνὴ ἀ. 48: 1. M-M.*

ἀγών, ἀγῶνος, ὁ (w. many mngs. Hom.+; inscr., pap., LXX; Ep. Arist. 14; Philo; Jos., Ant. 17, 92; 185 al.; loanw. in rabb.).
  1. an athletic *contest* only fig. (cf. Wsd 4: 2) τρέχωμεν τὸν προκείμενον ἡμῖν ἀγῶνα *let us run the race that lies before us* Hb 12: 1 (Cf. Eur., Or. 847; Hdt. 9, 60, 1 ἀγῶνος μεγίστου προκειμένου, cf. 7, 11, 3; Lucian, Gymnas. 15; Epict. 3, 25, 3.—Hdt. 8, 102 πολλοὺς ἀγῶνας δραμέονται οἱ Ἕλληνες; Dionys. Hal. 7, 48). Cf. 1 Cl 7: 1.
  2. gener. *struggle, fight* only fig. of suffering for the gospel Phil 1: 30 and struggle in its service ἐν πολλῷ ἀ. *under a great strain* or *in the face of great opposition* 1 Th 2: 2. ἀ. ἀγωνίζομαι (Socrat., Ep. 14, 4; Epict. 1, 9, 12; Appian, Bell. Civ. 1, 110 §515; Dit., Syll.³ 434/5, 10; Inscr. of the Brit. Mus. III 604, 7f ἠγωνίσατο ἀ. τρεῖς, ἐστέφθη δύο; Philo; Herm. Wr. 10, 19a) *fight a fight, engage in a contest* 1 Ti 6: 12; 2 Ti 4: 7 (cf. Thu. 7, 68, 3 καλὸς ὁ ἀ.; Synes., Ad. Paeon. 3 p. 309c ὡς ἀγῶνα καλὸν ὑπὲρ ἡμῶν ἀγωνίξῃ= that you fight ...); ὁ τῆς ἀφθαρσίας ἀ. 2 Cl 7: 5. Also ἄφθαρτος ἀ. vs. 3; opp. φθαρτὸς ἀ. vs. 1 (s. καταπλέω), 4.—*Anxiety, concern* (Eur., Phoen. 1350; Thu. 7, 71, 1; Polyb. 4, 56, 4; Plut., Tit. Flamin. 16, 1 ἀγῶνα καὶ πόνον; BGU 1139, 17; Is 7: 13) ὑπέρ τινος Col 2: 1; cf. 1 Cl 2: 4.—FJDölger, Antike u. Christentum II ’30, 294ff; III ’32, 177ff; VCPfitzner, Paul and the Agon Motif, athletic imagery in the Pauline lit., ’67, M-M.*

ἀγωνία, ας, ἡ (Pind., Hdt. and other ancient writers= ἀγών) in later times (ἀγωνιάω underwent a similar change) *agony, anxiety* (so Hyperid., fgm. 203; Demosth. 18, 33 φόβος καὶ ἀ., esp. Stoics: Chrysipp.: Stoic. II 248; Epict. 2, 13, 10; also schol. on Apollon. Rhod. 3, 471 ἐτετάρακτο καὶ ἐν ἀγωνίᾳ ἦν; BGU 884, 6; PTebt. 423, 13f εἰς ἀ. γενέσθαι; 2 Macc 3: 14, 16; Philo; Jos., Bell. 4, 90, Ant. 11, 326 ἦν ἐν ἀγωνίᾳ κ. δέει) γενόμενος ἐν ἀ. Lk 22: 44.—Field, Notes 77f. M-M.*

ἀγωνιάω impf. ἠγωνίων *be in anxiety* (so in later writers, including Dio Chrys. 4, 55 [w. μή foll.]; inscr.; pap. [Witkowski index]; LXX; Jos., Ant. 9, 32) ἀγωνιῶντες μεγάλως (PGiess. 19, 3; 2 Macc 3: 21; cf. συναγωνιάω 'be in fearful suspense' Polyb. 3, 43, 7 and 8) *full of great anxiety* GP 11: 45; w. indir. quest. foll. μήποτε (UPZ 62, 30 [161/60 BC]) 5: 15.*

ἀγωνίζομαι impf. ἠγωνιζόμην; 1 aor. ἠγωνισάμην; pf. ἠγώνισμαι (Eur., Hdt.+; inscr., pap., LXX; Jos., Bell. 3, 194, Ant. 5, 246; Test. Jos. 2: 2).
  1. of a(n athletic) contest, lit. and fig. *engage in a contest* πᾶς ὁ ἀγωνιζόμενος 1 Cor 9: 25 (AEhrhardt, ZNW 48, ’57, 101-10); cf. 2 Cl 7: 1ff.
  2. gener. *to fight, struggle*—a. lit., w. weapons (Polyb. 1, 45, 9; Plut., Marcell. 10, 4; 2 Macc 8: 16) ἠγωνίζοντο ἄν, ἵνα παραδοθῶ J 18: 36.
  b. fig. of any struggle κοπιῶ ἀγωνιζόμενος *I labor, striving* Col 1: 29; cf. 1 Ti 4: 10. Of wrestling in prayer ἀ. ὑπὲρ ὑμῶν Col 4: 12 (ἀ. ὑπέρ τινος: Diod. S. 13, 14, 3; Dit., Syll.³ 317, 20; 386, 19; 409, 33; Jos., Ant. 13, 193). ἀ. ἀγῶνα (s. ἀγών 2) 1 Ti 6: 12; 2 Ti 4: 7. W. inf. foll. (Thu. 8, 89, 4 ἠγωνίζετο εἷς ἕκαστος αὐτὸς πρῶτος προστάτης τοῦ δήμου γενέσθαι; Diod. S. 31, 19, 8 ὥστε τὸ πατὴρ ἐξίστασθαι τῆς ὅλης ἀρχῆς ἠγωνίζετο τῷ παιδί; PLond. 1338.—ἀγ. simply='take pains, exert

oneself': Alex. Aphr., Fat. 31, II 2 p. 203, 9) ἀγωνίζεσθε εἰσελθεῖν *strain every nerve to enter* Lk 13: 24; cf. 1 Cl 35: 4; B 4: 11. M-M.**

Ἀδάμ. ὁ indecl. (אָדָם) (LXX, Philo, Sib. Or.—In Joseph. Ἄδαμος, ου [Ant. 1, 66]) *Adam*, the first man 1 Ti 2: 13 (cf. Gen 1: 27ff). Formed from the earth B 6: 9. Ancestor of mankind Ro 5: 14; Jd 14; 1 Cl 50: 3. Hence πατὴρ ἡμῶν 6: 3; men are υἱοὶ Ἀ. 29: 2 (cf. Dt 32: 8). In the genealogy of Jesus Lk 3: 38. His fall Ro 5: 14; 1 Ti 2: 14. Some hold there existed the conception that at the end of the world the events of the beginning will repeat themselves, and that hence the all-destroyer Adam is contrasted w. Christ, who gives life to all 1 Cor 15: 22 (HGunkel, Schöpfung u. Chaos 1895). The parallel betw. Adam and Christ and the designation of Christ as future Ro 5: 14 or last Adam 1 Cor 15: 45 is held in some quarters to show the influence of the well-known myth of the first man as a redeemer-god (cf. Bousset, Kyrios Christos² ’21, 140-5; Rtzst., Erlösungsmyst. 107ff and s. on ἄνθρωπος 2d).— BMurmelstein, Adam. E. Beitrag z. Messiaslehre: Wiener Ztschr. f. d. Kunde d. Morgenlandes 35, ’28, 242-75; 36, ’29, 51-86; Ltzm., exc. on 1 Cor 15: 45-9; AVitti, Christus-Adam: Biblica 7, ’26, 121-45; 270-85; 384-401; AEJRawlinson, The NT Doctrine of the Christ ’26, 124ff; CKraeling, Anthropos and the Son of Man, ’27; AMarmorstein, ZNW 30, ’31, 271-7; OKuss, Ro 5: 12-21. D. Adam-Christusparallele, Diss. Bresl. ’30; GCWestberg, The Two Adams: Bibl. Sacra 94, ’37, 37-50; ARöder, D. Gesch.-philos. des Ap. Pls., Diss. Frb. ’38; SHanson, Unity of the Church in the NT, ’46, 66-73; EBrandenburger, Adam u. Christus, ’62; RScroggs, The Last Adam, ’66 [bibliog. 123-28].*

ἀδάπανος, ον (Aristoph., Pax 593; Teles 7, 8 al.; Inscr. Gr. 1006, 21 [II BC] ἀδάπανον τὴν συμμορίαν καθιστάνει) *free of charge* ἵνα ἀ. θήσω τὸ εὐαγγέλιον *that I might offer the gospel free of charge* 1 Cor 9: 18. M-M.*

Ἀδδί, ὁ indecl. *Addi* in the genealogy of Jesus Lk 3: 28.*

ἀδελφή, ῆς, ἡ (Aeschyl.+; inscr., pap., LXX, Philo; Jos., Ant. 18, 130, Vi. 186 al.; Test. 12 Patr.) *sister*.
  1. lit. Mt 19: 29; Mk 10: 29f; Lk 10: 39f; 14: 26; J 11: 1; 3, 5, 28, 39; 19: 25; Ro 16: 15; 1 Ti 5: 2. Of Jesus' *sisters* (s. on ἀδελφός 1) Mt 13: 56; Mk 3: 32; 6: 3. Paul's sister Ac 23: 16. Used by Jesus for a spiritual, rather than a natural relationship Mt 12: 50; Mk 3: 35; ἀγαπᾶν ὡς ἀ. Hv 1, 1, 1; ἐντρέπεσθαι ὡς ἀ. v 1, 1, 7.
  2. fig. of grief: ἀδελφή ἐστιν τῆς διψυχίας *is a sister of doubt* Hm 10, 1, 1f (Alcaeus 142 Diehl: poverty and helplessness as sisters; Paroem. Gr. Append. 3, 12 ἡ μωρία ἀ. πονηρίας; Pla., Rep. 3, 404B; Cebes 16, 2 ἐγκράτεια and καρτερία as ἀδελφαί; Herm. Wr. 9, 1c ἡ νόησις ἀ. τοῦ λόγου).
  3. fig. of a *sister* in the faith (as Hebr. אָחוֹת; sister= countrywoman Num 25: 18; s. ἀδελφός 2 and cf. PGM 4, 1135ff χαίρετε, εἰς τὸ χαίρειν ἐν εὐλογίᾳ δίδοται, ἀδελφοῖς καὶ ἀδελφαῖς, ὁσίοις καὶ ὁσίαις) Ro 16: 1; 1 Cor 7: 15; 9: 5; Phlm 2; Js 2: 15; IPol 5: 1; 2 Cl 12: 5; Hv 2, 2, 3; 2, 3, 1. In address w. ἀδελφοί 2 Cl 19: 1; 20: 2.
  4. fig., of the close relationship of similar communities (Dit., Or. 536) 2 J 13 (s. κυρία). M-M.*

ἀδελφοκτονία, ας, ἡ (Philo, De Jos. 13; Jos., Bell. 1, 606, Ant. 17, 60; 91) *fratricide* of Cain (Philo, Agric. 21) 1 Cl 4: 7.*

ἀδελφός, οῦ, ὁ (since Hom. [ἀδελφεός]; inscr., pap.,

LXX, Philo; Jos., Vi. 190 al.; Test. 12 Patr. [the vocative ἄδελφε should be accented on the antepenult in Ac 9: 17; 21: 20 contrary to the practice of the editions; also GP 2: 5; Bl-D-Funk §13]) *brother*.

1. lit. Mt 1: 2, 11; 4: 18, 21 al.; τὸν ἀ. τ. ἴδιον J 1: 41 (s. Jos., Ant. 11, 300). Of Jesus' brothers (passages like Gen 13: 8; 14: 14; 24: 48; 29: 12; Lev 10: 4; 1 Ch 9: 6 do not establish the mng. 'cousin' for ἀ.; they only show that in rendering the Hebr. אח ἀ. is used loosely in isolated cases to designate masc. relatives of various degrees. The case of ἀδελφή [q.v. 1] is similar Gen 24: 59f; Tob 8: 4, 7 [cf. 7: 15]; Jos., Ant. 1, 211 [ἀδελφή=ἀδελφοῦ παῖς]. Sim. M. Ant., who [1, 14, 1] uses ἀ. for his brother-in-law Severus; the same use is found occas. in the pap.: JJCollins, Theological Studies 5, '44, 484-94; cf. HTR '42, 25-44) Mt 12: 46f; 13: 55; Mk 3: 31f; J 2: 12; 7: 3, 5; Ac 1: 14; 1 Cor 9: 5. James ὁ ἀδελφὸς τοῦ κυρίου Gal 1: 19. Cf. ThZahn, Forschungen 6, '00, 225-364; TNicklin, Gospel Gleanings '50, 191-202; for the Catholic view M-JLagrange, Marc⁴ '29, 72-89; JSickenberger, Lex. f. Theol. u. Kirche II '31, 580-2.—The pl. can also mean *brothers and sisters* (Eur., El. 536; Andoc. 1, 47 ἡ μήτηρ ἡ ἐκείνου κ. ὁ πατὴρ ὁ ἐμὸς ἀδελφοί; Anton. Diog. 3 [Erot. Gr. I 233, 23; 26 Hercher]; POxy. 713, 21f [97 AD] ἀδελφοῖς μου Διοδώρῳ κ. Θαΐδι; schol. on Nicander, Ther. 11 [p. 5, 9] δύο ἐγένοντο ἀδελφοί, Φάλαγξ μὲν ἄρσην, θήλεια δὲ Ἀράχνη τοὔνομα. The θεοὶ Ἀδελφοί, a married couple consisting of brother and sister on the throne of the Ptolemies: Dit., Or. 50, 2 [III BC] and pap. [Wilcken, Grundz. 99, Chrest. nos. 103-7, III BC]). In all these cases only *one* brother and *one* sister are involved. Yet there are also passages in which ἀδελφοί means *brothers and sisters*, and in whatever sequence the writer chooses (Polyb. 10, 18, 15 ποιήσεσθαι πρόνοιαν ὡς ἰδίων ἀδελφῶν καὶ τέκνων; Epict. 1, 12, 20 ἀδ. beside γονεῖς, τέκνα, γείτονες; 1, 22, 10; 4, 1, 111; Artem. 3, 31; Ptolem., Apotel. 3, 6; Diog. L. 7, 108; 120; 10, 18. In PMich. 214, 12 [296 AD] οἱ ἀδελφοί σου seems to be even more general = 'your relatives'. So in Lk 21: 16 there is no doubt that ἀδελφοί = *brothers and sisters*. There is more room for uncertainty in the case of the ἀδελφοί of Jesus in Mt 12: 46f; Mk 3: 31; J 2: 12; 7: 3, 5; Ac 1: 14.

2. fig.: Jesus calls everyone who is devoted to him *brother* Mt 12: 50; Mk 3: 35, esp. the disciples Mt 28: 10; J 20: 17. Hence gener. for those in such spiritual communion Mt 25: 40; Hb 2: 12 (Ps 21: 23), 17 al. Of a relationship w. a woman other than that of husband Hs 9, 11, 3 al.—Of the members of a relig. community (PPar. 20 [II BC] al. of the hermit at the Serapeum in Memphis; UPZ 162 I, 20 [117 BC] ἀδελφοὶ οἱ τὰς λειτουργίας ἐν ταῖς νεκρίαις παρεχόμενοι; IGSic. It. 956Β, 11f ἀ.=member of the ἱερὰ ξυστικὴ σύνοδος; BLatyschev, Inscr. Pont. Eux. II 449f εἰσποιητοὶ ἀ. σεβόμενοι θεὸν Ὕψιστον [Ltzm. ZWTh 55, '13, 121]. Mystery pap. [III AD]: APF 13, '39, 212. Essenes in Jos., Bell. 2, 122. Vett. Val. 172, 31; Kleopatra 1. 94. Cf. GMilligan '08 on 1 Th 1: 4; Ltzm. Hdb. on Ro 1: 13 [lit.]; Dssm. B 82f, 140 [BS 87f, 142]; Nägeli 38; Cumont³ 276). Hence used by Christians in their relations w. each other Ro 8: 29, 1 Cor 5: 11; Eph 6: 23; 1 Ti 6: 2; Ac 6: 3; 9: 30; 10: 23; Rv 1: 9; 12: 10; IEph 3: 1; ISm 12: 1 al. So esp. w. proper names (for ἀδ. in a figurative sense used with a name, cf. the address of a letter PMich. 162 verso [II AD] ἀπὸ Ἀπλωναρίου ἀδελφοῦ) to indicate membership in the Church Ro 16: 23; 1 Cor 1: 1; 16: 12; 2 Cor 1: 1; Phil 2: 25; Col 1: 1; 4: 7, 9; 1 Th 3: 2; Phlm 1; 1 Pt 5: 12; 2 Pt 3: 15. Completely ἀδελφὸς ἐν κυρίῳ Phil 1: 14. Oft. in direct address 1 Cl 1: 1; 4: 7; 13: 1; 33: 1; 2 Cl 20: 2 al.; B 2: 10; 3: 6 al.; IRo 6:

2; Hv 2, 4, 1; 3, 1, 1; 4. ἀδελφοί μου B 4: 14; 5: 5; 6: 15; IEph 16: 1; ἄνδρες ἀ. Ac 1: 16; 15: 7, 13; 1 Cl 14: 1; 37: 1; 43: 4; 62: 1.

3. *fellow countryman* (cf. Pla., Menex. 239A ἡμεῖς δὲ καὶ οἱ ἡμέτεροι, μιᾶς μητρὸς πάντες ἀδελφοὶ φύντες; Lev 10: 4; Dt 15: 3, 12; 17: 15 al.; Philo, Spec. Leg. 2, 79f 'ἀ.' τὸν ὁμόφυλον εἶπεν; Jos., Ant. 10, 201; 7, 371 after 1 Ch 28: 2) Ac 2: 29; 3: 17, 22 (Dt 18: 15); 7: 2, 23 (Ex 2: 11), 25f al.; Ro 9: 3.

4. without ref. to a common nationality or faith *neighbor* (of an intimate friend X., An. 7, 2, 25; 38. Specif. in the sense 'neighbor' Gen 9: 5; Lev 19: 17 al.) Mt 5: 22ff; 7: 3ff; 18: 15, 21, 35; Lk 6: 41f; 17: 3; B 19: 4; Hm 2: 2 al.

5. Form of address used by a king to persons in very high position (Dit., Or. 138, 3; 168, 26; 36 [both II BC]; Jos., Ant. 13, 45; 126) Herod says ἄδελφε Πιλᾶτε GP 2: 5.—JO'Callaghan, El vocativo sing. de ἀδελφός, Biblica 52, '71, 217-25. M-M. B. 107.

ἀδελφότης, ητος, ἡ (Bl-D. §110, 1; Mlt.-H. 367)—1. *a brotherhood* (group of fellow-believers; cf. 4 Macc 9: 23; 10: 3, 15; Phryg. inscr. [III AD, in Harnack, Mission⁴ '24, 773 n.] εἰρήνη πᾶσι τ. ἀδελφοῖς, εἰρήνη πάσῃ τ. ἀδελφότητι) of the Christian community, whose members are ἀδελφοί and ἀδελφαί 1 Pt 5: 9; 1 Cl 2: 4. τὴν ἀ. ἀγαπᾶν 1 Pt 2: 17 (ThSpörri, D. Gemeindegedanke im 1 Pt '25).

2. *brotherliness* (Dio Chrys. 21 [38], 15; Vett. Val. p. 2, 28; 4, 5; 1 Macc 12: 10, 17; 4 Macc 13: 27) ἀ. συντηρεῖν Hm 8: 10. M-M.*

ἀδεῶς adv. (Hdt.+; Aristoph., Vesp. 359; IG IV 597 [II AD]; 3 Macc 2: 32; Philo, Cherub. 99; Jos., Ant. 6, 313; 18, 370) *without fear* or *disturbance* προσεύχεσθαι MPol 7: 2; λαμβάνειν ITr 6: 2.*

ἄδηλος, ον (Hes.+; inscr.; PLond. 940, 23; POxy. 118, 5f; PLeipz. 37, 23; PGM 4, 3048; LXX, Philo; Jos., Bell. 7, 115, Ant. 1, 268; 13, 151).

1. *not clear, unseen* (Soph.+; Dit., Or. 218, 129 [III BC]) τὰ μνημεῖα τὰ ἄ. *graves which are not seen* Lk 11: 44. τὰ ἄ. δηλοῦν *reveal what is unseen* 1 Cl 18: 6 (Ps 50: 8).

2. *indistinct* (Polyb. 8, 1, 2 ἄ. ἐλπίδες=vague hopes; likew. Maximus Tyr. 36, 4a) of a trumpet ἄ. φωνὴν διδόναι *give out an indistinct sound*, so that the signal cannot be recognized 1 Cor 14: 8. M-M.*

ἀδηλότης, ητος, ἡ *uncertainty* (Protagoras [V BC]+; Polyb., Plut., Philo al.) ἐλπίζειν ἐπὶ πλούτου ἀδηλότητι *in uncertain wealth* 1 Ti 6: 17 (Bl-D. §165).*

ἀδήλως adv. (Thu.+; Plut.; Aelian, V.H. 1, 21 p. 10, 4; Philo, Conf. Lingu. 119) *uncertainly* (Ps.-Phoc. 25; 117) of a race οὕτως τρέχω ὡς οὐκ ἀδήλως *not aimlessly*, i.e., not as one who has no fixed goal 1 Cor 9: 26 (cf. Ps.-Phoc. 28 ἄδηλος πλοῦς).*

ἀδημονέω (Hippocr.+; Pla., X.; Jos., Ant. 15, 211; 388; POxy. 298, 45 [I AD] λίαν ἀδημονοῦμεν χάριν τῆς θρεπτῆς Σαραποῦτος; Aq. Job 18: 20; Sym. Ps 60: 3 al.) *be in anxiety, be distressed, troubled* w. λυπεῖσθαι Mt 26: 37; w. ἐκθαμβεῖσθαι Mk 14: 33; foll. by διότι *because* Phil 2: 26. M-M.*

ἅδης, ου, ὁ (w. var. spellings Hom.+; inscr.; PGM 1, 345; 12, 241; LXX, Philo; Jos., Ant. 6, 332; Test. 12 Patr.; Sib. Or.).

1. *Hades* (orig. proper noun, name of god of the underworld), *the underworld* as the place of the dead Ac 2: 27, 31 (Ps 15: 10; Eccl 9: 10; PGM 1, 179; 16, 8; Philo, Mos. 1, 195; Jos., Bell. 1, 596, Ant. 6, 332). In the depths,

contrasted w. heaven Mt 11: 23; Lk 10: 15 (cf. Is 14: 11, 15); 16: 23. Accessible by gates (but the pl. is also used [e.g. Hom., X., Ael. Aristid. 47, 20 K.=23 p. 450 D.] when only one gate is meant), hence πύλαι ἅδου (since II. 5, 646; Is 38: 10; Wsd 16: 13; 3 Macc 5: 51; PsSol 16, 2.— Lucian, Menipp. 6 the magicians can open τοῦ Ἅιδου τὰς πύλας and conduct people in and out safely) Mt 16: 18 (s. on πέτρα 1b and πύλη 1); locked ἔχω τὰς κλεῖς τοῦ θανάτου καὶ τοῦ ἅδου Rv 1: 18 (the genitives are either obj. [Ps.-Apollod. 3, 12, 6, 10 Aeacus, the son of Zeus holds the κλεῖς τοῦ Ἅιδου; Suppl. Epigr. Gr. VIII 574, 3 [III ᴀᴅ] τῷ τὰς κλεῖδας ἔχοντι τῶν καθ' Ἅιδου] or poss.; in the latter case death and Hades are personif.; s. 2). ὠδῖνες τοῦ ἅδου (Ps 17: 6) Pol 1: 2 (cf. Ac 2: 24, where D, Latins, Pesh. also read ἅδου for θανάτου). εἰς ἅδου (sc. δόμους, Hom.+; Bar 3: 11, 19; Tob 3: 10) Ac 2: 31 v.l.; 1 Cl 4: 12; 51: 4 (Iambl., Vi. Pyth. 30, 179 ἐν ἅδου κεῖσθαι τὴν κρίσιν; Hierocles 14 p. 451 τὰ ἐν ἅδου κολαστήρια; Simplicius in Epict. p. 108, 14 punishments for sinners ἐν ἅδου).

2. personif., w. θάνατος (cf. Is 28: 15; Job 38: 17) Rv 6: 8; 20: 13f; 1 Cor 15: 55 v.l.—GBeer, D. bibl. Hades: HJHoltzmann Festschr. '02, 1–30; (Stade-) ABertholet, Bibl. Theol. II '11, 397f; ERohde, Psyche⁴ I 54ff; 309ff; ADieterich, Nekyia 1893; Bousset, Rel.³ 285f; 293ff; Billerb. IV 1016–29; JoachJeremias, TW I 146–50; AHeidel, The Gilgamesh Epic and OT Parallels², '49, 173–91; LESullivan, Theological Studies (Woodstock, Md.) 10, '49, 62ff. S. also s.v. πνεῦμα 2 and 4c. M-M. B. 1485.*

ἀδιάκριτος, ον (Hippocr.+; Polyb. 15, 12, 9; Dit., Or. 509, 8; LXX Pr 25: 1; Sym. Gen 1: 2; Philo, Spec. Leg. 3, 57 al.; var. mngs in Lghtf. on IEph 3: 2.—As a human virtue also in Ptolem., Apotel. 3, 14, 29) can designate someth. in which there is no discord or uncertainty, *unwavering* (cf. Js 1: 6) or *impartial* Js 3: 17; *inseparable* or *unshakable* IEph 3: 2; IMg 15: ITr 1: 1; M-M.*

ἀδιακρίτως adv. (Anecd. Gr. 352; Proclus on Pla., Crat. p. 91, 13; schol. on Apollon. Rhod. 2, 62; Philo, fgm. 105 Harris [1886]; Test. Zeb. 7: 2; POxy. 715, 36 [131 ᴀᴅ]= Wilcken, APF 4, '08, 254) *without wavering* IRo inscr.; IPhld inscr. (s. ἀδιάκριτος).*

ἀδιάλειπτος, ον (Ps.-Pla., Tim. Locr. 98ᴇ al.; Dit., Syll.³ 1104, 35; PTebt. 27, 45 [113 ʙᴄ]; PGM 8, 32; Ep. Arist. 84; Jos., Bell. 2, 155; 5, 31) *unceasing, constant* ὀδύνη Ro 9: 2; μνεία 2 Ti 1: 3; προσευχαί IPol 1: 3; ἀ. ἔχειν ὕδωρ *without failing* Hs 2: 8; ἵνα ἀ. γένηται ἐν τῇ ζωῇ αὐτοῦ *that he might lack nothing in his life* 2: 6 (s. MDibelius ad loc.). M-M.*

ἀδιαλείπτως adv. (since Metrodorus Philos. [IV/III ʙᴄ]: Pap. Hercul. 831, 8; Polyb. 9, 3, 8; Dit., Syll.³ 1104, 15; 1171, 4; pap. fr. II ʙᴄ on [Mayser 458]; 1, 2, 3 Macc; Ep. Arist. 92; 294; Aristobulus in Euseb., Pr. Ev. 13, 12, 4; Test. Levi 13: 2, Jos., Bell. 3, 164; 241) *constantly, unceasingly* μνείαν ποιεῖσθαι Ro 1: 9; 1 Th 1: 2. εὐχαριστεῖν 2: 13. προσεύχεσθαι 5: 17; IEph 10: 1; Hs 9, 11, 7; cf. Pol 4: 3. προσκαρτερεῖν τῇ ἐλπίδι Pol 8: 1. διδόναι (of God) Hs 5, 4, 4. σκεπάζειν s 9, 27, 2.*

ἀδιαφθορία, ας, ἡ (the subst. is not found elsewhere, but ἀδιάφθορος is common enough since Plato; also Philo) *sincerity, integrity* Tit 2: 7 t.r. for ἀφθορία, q.v. M-M. s.v. -os.*

ἀδιήγητος, ον *indescribable* (so X.+; Ael. Aristid. 33, 30

K.=51 p. 581 D.; PGM 1, 164; Ep. Arist. 89; 99) ὁ ἐν ἀγάπῃ ἀ. *a man of inexpressible love* IEph 1: 3.*

ἀδικέω fut. ἀδικήσω; 1 aor. ἠδίκησα; pf. ἠδίκηκα; 1 aor. pass. ἠδικήθην (Hom. Hymns+; inscr., pap., LXX, Joseph., Test. 12 Patr.).

1. intrans.—a. *do wrong* of any violation of human or divine law (defined Aristot., Rhet. 1, 10: ἔστι τὸ ἀδικεῖν τὸ βλάπτειν ἑκόντα παρὰ τὸν νόμον; Philo, Dec. 66) ὁ ἀδικῶν *the evildoer* (Diod. S. 8, 15, 1; Dit., Syll.³ 635, 22) ὁ ἀδικῶν ἀδικησάτω ἔτι Rv 22: 11. Cf. Col 3: 25a; also 25b κομίσεται ὃ ἠδίκησεν *he will reap the reward of his wrongdoing* (cf. BGU 1138, 13 ὃ ἠδίκησεν ἐμαρτύρησεν).

b. *be in the wrong* (Ex 2: 13) εἰ ἀδικῶ Ac 25: 11.

2. trans.—a. *do wrong* (τινά) *to someone, treat someone unjustly* (58th letter of Apollonius of Tyana [Philostrat. I 361, 25 K.] τὸν υἱόν) οὐκ ἀδικῶ σε *I am not cheating you* Mt 20: 13. ἱνατί ἀδικεῖτε ἀλλήλους; Ac 7: 26. τὸν πλησίον vs. 27; οὐδένα 2 Cor 7: 2; ἀδελφούς 1 Cor 6: 8; νηπίους 1 Cl 57: 7 (Pr 1: 32). W. acc. to be supplied 2 Cor 7: 12a. W. double acc. (Demosth. 21, 129; Epict. 3, 24, 81; Jos., Ant. 2, 138; Lev 5: 21; Pr 24: 29) οὐδέν με ἠδικήσατε *you have done me no wrong* Gal 4: 12; cf. Ac 25: 10; MPol 9: 3.—Pass. (Bl-D. §314; Rob. 808; 816) *be wronged, be unjustly treated* (Ael. Aristid. 45 p. 81 D.; ἀδικεῖσθαι βέλτιον ἢ ἀδικεῖν; Jos., Bell. 5, 377) 1 Cl 8: 4 (Is 1: 17); Dg 6: 5. ἰδών τινα ἀδικούμενον Ac 7: 24. ὁ ἀδικηθείς 2 Cor 7: 12b. τίς πλέον ἀδικηθείς; *who has suffered more injustice?* IEph 10: 3; *let oneself be wronged* 1 Cor 6: 7.

b. *injure* (Thu., Antipho+; Tob 6: 15; Jdth 11: 4) w. acc. of the pers. (Jos., Ant. 17, 109) με (Appian, Bell. Civ. 4, 69 §291 ἀδικεῖν με) IRo 1: 2. τοὺς ἀνθρώπους (Ep. Arist. 146) Rv 9: 10; αὐτούς 11: 5. W. acc. of the thing (Dio Chrys. 14 [31], 54 τὸν τόπον; Bull. de corr. hell. 26, '02, 217 ἐάν τις τὴν στήλην ἀδικήσει; Dit., Syll.³ 635, 8; 9) *damage, spoil* τὴν γῆν Rv 7: 2f; τὸν χόρτον τῆς γῆς 9: 4; τὸ ἔλαιον καὶ τὸν οἶνον 6: 6. W. double acc. (Demosth., Ep. 2, 16 οὔτε ἠδίκηχ' ὑμᾶς οὐδέν) οὐδὲν ὑμᾶς οὐ μὴ ἀδικήσει Lk 10: 19 (in case οὐδέν is not the subj.—Bl-D. §431, 3 app.); *if he has caused you any loss* Phlm 18 (PMich. 8, 492, 21f). W. ἐν of the means by which the harm results ἐν αὐταῖς (i.e. οὐραῖς) ἀδικοῦσιν Rv 9: 19.—Pass. foll. by ἐκ of the source fr. which the harm comes οὐ μὴ ἀδικηθῇ ἐκ τοῦ θανάτου τοῦ δευτέρου *he will not be harmed by the second death*, Rv 2: 11. ἀδικούμενοι μισθὸν ἀδικίας *damaged in respect to* (i.e. *cheated out of*) *the reward of unrighteousness* 2 Pt 2: 13 (the readings vary [s. κομίζω 2a] and the text is uncertain; Bl-D. §351, 2 app.; PSkehan, Biblica 41, '60, 69–71, takes ἀδικούμενοι with the phrase that precedes; GSchrenk, TW I 157). M-M.*

ἀδίκημα, ατος, τό (Hdt.+; inscr., pap., LXX, En., Philo, Joseph.) *a wrong, crime, misdeed* (Aristot., Nic. Eth. 5, 7 τὸ ἄδικον ... ὅταν πραχθῇ, ἀ. ἐστιν; Jos., Ant. 3, 321; 5, 234) Ac 18: 14; 24: 20; Rv 18: 5.—Pl. *mistreatment* (Diod. S. 14, 2, 2; PHal. 1, 193) IRo 5: 1. M-M.*

ἀδικία, ας, ἡ (Anaximander, Hdt.+; LXX, En., Ep. Arist., Philo; Jos., C. Ap. 2, 217 al.; Test. 12 Patr.).

1. *wrongdoing* (opp. δικαιοσύνη, as Aristot. p. 10b, 13 and 20) Hb 1: 9 v.l. (Ps 44: 8 v.l.); 2 Cl 19: 2. W. ἀνομία (Epict. 2, 16, 44; Is 33: 15) 1 Cl 35: 5 v.l.; χαρίσασθέ μοι τὴν ἀδικίαν ταύτην *pardon me for this wrong* (ironic) 2 Cor 12: 13; ἀπέχεσθαι πάσης ἀ. Pol 2: 2. Pl. *misdeeds* (Sir 17: 20; Bar 3: 8; Tob 13: 5 al.;

Philo, Conf. Lingu. 21, Migr. Abr. 60; Jos., Bell. 7, 260) Hb 8: 12 (Jer 38[31]: 34). W. ἀνομίαι et al. 1 Cl 60: 1.

2. *unrighteousness, wickedness, injustice* (Isocr. 8, 35; Herm. Wr. 13, 9; LXX; Jos., C. Ap. 2, 291 [opp. δικαιοσύνη]) Dg 9: 1f. Said to be sin 1 J 5: 17 (but 1 is also poss.), hence impossible in God Ro 9: 14 and at enmity w. truth ἐπὶ ἀδικίαν ἀνθρώπων τῶν τὴν ἀλήθειαν ἐν ἀ. κατεχόντων 1: 18; the same contrast betw. ἀ. and ἀληθής (cf. 1 Esdr 4: 37) J 7: 18; cf. also πείθεσθαι τῇ ἀ. *follow the wrong* Ro 2: 8; χαίρειν ἐπὶ τῇ ἀ. 1 Cor 13: 6; εὐδοκεῖν τῇ ἀ. *take pleasure in wickedness* 2 Th 2: 12; ἀφιστάναι ἀπὸ ἀ. ἡμᾶς *in wickedness* 2 Th 2: 12; ἀφιστάναι ἀπὸ ἀ. (Sir 35: 3; Test. Dan 6: 10) 2 Ti 2: 19. καθαρίζειν ἡμᾶς ἀπὸ πάσης ἀ. 1 J 1: 9; πεπληρωμένος πάσῃ ἀ. Ro 1: 29; cf. 3: 5. ἐν πάσῃ ἀπάτῃ ἀδικίας lit. *with every kind of deception of wickedness* i.e. w. all the arts of deception that the wicked one can devise 2 Th 2: 10. ὅπλα ἀδικίας *weapons of unrighteousness* Ro 6: 13.—The gen. is oft. found as in Sem. lang. (cf. 2 Km 3: 34; 7: 10; Hos 12: 8), but also in secular Gk. (ENachmanson, Eranos 9, '09, 63-6; Mlt. 73f; Rdm. 108f.—Polyaenus 1, 19 στρατήγημα τῆς ἀπάτης=deceitful military stratagem) in place of the adj. οἰκονόμος τῆς ἀ. Lk 16: 8; κριτὴς τῆς ἀ. 18: 6; μαμωνᾶς τῆς ἀ. 16: 9 (also μ. ἄδικος vs. 11); cf. NSchlögl, BZ 14, '17, 41-3; μισθὸς ἀ. *reward for wickedness* 2 Pt 2: 13, 15; cf. Ac 1: 18 (of a single misdeed: Arrian, Anab. 3, 25, 8, a murder; cf. Ezk 14: 4 κόλασις τ. ἀδικίας). On κόσμος τῆς ἀ. Js 3: 6 s. κόσμος 8, on σύνδεσμος Ac 8: 23 s. σύνδεσμος; also B 3: 3 (Is 58: 6). In ἐργάται ἀ. (cf. 1 Macc 3: 6 ἐργάται τ. ἀνομίας) the gen. represents the obj. acc.= ἐργαζόμενοι τὴν ἀ. *evildoers* Lk 13: 27 (1 Macc 9: 23; cf. Ps 6: 9; 13: 4).—BAvanGroningen, Ἀδικία: Mnemosyne, n.s. 55, '27, 260-2. M-M.*

ἀδικοκρίτης, ου, ὁ (opp. δικαιοκρίτης 2 Macc 12: 41; PRyl. 113, 35 [II AD]; ἀδικοκρισία in Hephaestion Astrol. [IV AD] 3, 34: Cat. Cod. Astr. V 3 p. 81, 7) *an unjust judge* Tit 1: 9 v.l.*

ἄδικος, ον (Hes.+; inscr., pap., LXX, Philo, Joseph., Test. 12 Patr.) *unjust.*
1. of pers.: doing contrary to what is right, opp. δίκαιος (Aristot. p. 10b, 15 al.; Epict. 2, 11, 5; Aesop, Fab. 173 P.=308 H.; Philo, Abr. 33; Jos., Bell. 2, 139; 5, 407) Mt 5: 45; Ac 24: 15; 1 Pt 3: 18; Dg 9: 2; Hm 6, 1, 1f. W. ἄνομος (X., Mem. 4, 4, 13) 1 Cl 56: 11 (Job 5: 22). W. ἅρπαγες and μοιχοί Lk 18: 11. Negative of God Ro 3: 5; Hb 6: 10. The ἄ. is excluded fr. the Kingdom 1 Cor 6: 9; ἄ. become rich 2 Cl 20: 1. Of pagan judges κρίνεσθαι ἐπὶ τῶν ἀ. *go to law before the unjust* 1 Cor 6: 1 (Maximus Tyr. 3, 4c ὡς ἐπὶ δικαστῶν; ἀλλὰ ἄδικοι). Of an unjust (pagan) judge MPol 19: 2. Opp. εὐσεβής 2 Pt 2: 9 (cf. Jos., Ant. 8, 251 ἄδ. κ. ἀσεβής); *dishonest, untrustworthy* (opp. πιστός) ὁ ἐν ἐλαχίστῳ ἄ. καὶ ἐν πολλῷ ἄ. ἐστιν Lk 16: 10.
2. of things (Phalaris, Ep. 70 κέρδος ἄ.; Pr 15: 26; Jos., Vi. 299) *unjust* μαμωνᾶς Lk 16: 9D, 11 (cf. πλοῦτος ἄ. of ill-gotten gains: Charito 3, 3, 11; Philo, Spec. Leg. 4, 158 and the opp. πλοῦτος δίκαιος Sib. Or. 3, 783); κρίσις ἄ. (Test. Jos. 14: 1) Pol 6: 1; ἄ. βίος (w. ἄνομος) MPol 3; ζῆλος ἄ. 1 Cl 3: 4; 5: 4; 45: 4; ἄ. συγγραφή B 3: 3 (Is 58: 6). M-M.*

ἀδίκως adv. (Aeschyl., Hdt.+; inscr., pap., LXX; Philo, Joseph., Test. 12 Patr.) *unjustly* (opp. δικαίως as Menand., Sam. 311 διαφέρει οὐδὲ γρῦ ἀδίκως παθεῖν

ταῦτ' ἢ δικαίως; Ael. Aristid. 46 p. 223 D.) B 5: 4 (Pr 1: 17); μισεῖν τινα ἀ. 1 Cl 60: 3; *undeservedly* (Plut., Mor. 216D; ἀ. πάσχειν Jos., Ant. 10, 115. Opp. δικαίως πάσχειν Ael. Aristid. 35 p. 671 D.; Test. Sim. 4: 3) πάσχων ἀ. 1 Pt 2: 19. Vs. 23 has the v.l. τῷ κρίνοντι ἀδίκως (applied to Pilate; defended by Harnack, Beiträge VII '16 p. 89f. Cf. UHolzmeister, Comm. p. 270ff; EGSelwyn, 1 Pt '46 ad loc.).*

ἀδιστάκτως adv.—1. act. *without doubting, without hesitating* (Philod., Rhet I 133 Sudh.) αἰτεῖσθαι ask confidently Hm 9: 2, 4, 6. ἐπιχορηγεῖν πάντα τῷ πένητι *provide everything for the poor without hesitating* s 2: 5, cf. 7; cf. 9, 24, 2 (w. ἀνονειδίστως). μετανοεῖν *repent without delay* s 8, 10, 3.
2. pass. *without doubt, securely* (Apollon. Dysc.: Gramm. Graeci II 2 p. 213, 5 U.; Anth. Pal. 12, 151; PGM 4, 2511) κατοικεῖν *live* s 9, 29, 2.*

Ἀδμίν, ὁ indecl. *Admin*, son of Arni, in the genealogy of Jesus Lk 3: 33 (the name is lacking in the t.r.; v.l. Ἀδάμ).*

ἀδόκιμος, ον (Democr.+; also Polyb. 6, 25, 8; 16, 14, 9; inscr., pap., Pr 25: 4; Is 1: 22) *not standing the test*, then *unqualified, worthless, base* of pers. (X., De Rep. Lac. 3, 3; Plut., Lib. Educ. 7 p. 4c ἀνθρώποις ἀδοκίμοις ἐγχειρίζουσι τ. παῖδας; Herodian 7, 7, 5; Jos., C. Ap. 2, 236 ἀ. σοφισταί) 2 Cor 13: 5-7; ITr 12: 3; *disqualified* 1 Cor 9: 27; ἀνήρ ἀ. ἀπείραστος *a man who is not tempted is unproved* Agr 21. W. indication of the respect in which the test is not met ἀδόκιμοι περὶ τὴν πίστιν 2 Ti 3: 8; πρὸς πᾶν ἔργον ἀγαθὸν ἀ. *unfit for any good deed* Tit 1: 16.—Of things (Philo, Conf. Lingu. 198) barren soil Hb 6: 8. Of the pagan νοῦς in a play on words w. οὐ δοκιμάζειν Ro 1: 28.*

ἄδολος, ον *without deceit* (Pind.+, but mostly act., 'honest', so also as adv. Wsd 7: 13 and Jos., Ant. 1, 212) pass. *unadulterated* (esp. in pap. and inscr. since III BC; e.g. PHib. 85, 16f [261 BC]; 98, 19 [261 BC]; POxy. 729, 19; BGU 290, 13; 1005, 5; 1015, 13; PTebt. 105; Dit., Syll.³ 736, 100; Philo, Rer. Div. Her. 95) of milk 1 Pt 2: 2.—FJDölger, Antike u. Christentum I '29, p. 170, 39. M-M.*

ἄδοξος, ον *without reputation, obscure* (so X.+; Dit., Or. 5, 64 [311 BC]; POxy. 79 II, 4 [II AD]; Sir 10: 31; Jos., Vi. 278) 1 Cl 3: 3; MPol 8: 1 (both times as opp. of ἔνδοξος, as Ael. Aristid. 26, 39 K.=14 p. 338 D.; Diog. L. 7, 117).*

Ἀδραμυττηνός, ή, όν (Ἀδραμυντηνός W-H.; for the spelling cf. Stephan. Byz. s.v. Ἀδραμύττειον; W-S. §5, 26d; Bl-D. §42, 3 app.; Rob. 210; 223) *of Adramyttium* (Ἀτραμύττειον Hdt. 7, 42 al., later Ἀδραμύττειον. The adj. e.g. Strabo 13, 1, 61; 62; Plut., Cic. 4, 5; Dit., Or. 238, 4), a seaport in Mysia (n.w. Asia Minor) on the Aegean Sea Ac 27: 2. Cf. RHarris, Adramyttium (Ac 27: 2): Contemp. Rev. '25, 194-202.*

ἀδρανής, ές (since Posidippus [c. 280 BC]: Anth. Pal. 9, 359; Plut.; Dio Chrys. 11[12], 31; Philostrat., Vi. Apoll. 3, 39; Wsd 13: 19) *powerless* (w. ἀδύνατος; cf. Proclus, Theol. 149 p. 130, 25) πνεύματα ἐπίγεια ἀ. Hm 11: 19.*

Ἀδρίας, ου, ὁ (class.; inscr. since 325 BC Meisterhans³-Schw.; Bl-D. §261, 8) *the Adriatic Sea* (the sea betw. Crete and Sicily is included in it: Eudoxus [III BC]: 79 fgm. 1 Jac.; Ptolem. 3, 4, 1; 17, 1; Ael. Aristid. 48, 66 K.=24 p. 483 D.; Jos., Vi. 15) Ac 27: 27.*

ἀδρότης, ητος, ἡ (Il. 24, 6; Theophr. and Epicurus [Diog.

L. 10, 83]) *abundance* ἐν τῇ ἁ. ταύτῃ *in this lavish gift* (the collection) 2 Cor 8: 20. M-M.*

ἀδυνατέω fut. ἀδυνατήσω lit. *be powerless, be disabled* (so since Epicharmus [c. 480 BC], who uses it personally [Vorsokrat.⁵ 23 B, 23 ἀδυνατεῖ δ᾽ οὐδὲν θεός]; also UPZ 110, 13 and 89 [164 BC]; 6, 36 [163 BC]; Herm. Wr. 10, 18; Philo; Jos., Ant. 15, 211); in NT only impers. (Philod., Ira p. 98 W.; Job 10: 13; 42: 2; 2 Ch 14: 10; Wsd 13: 16) *it is impossible* οὐδὲν ἀδυνατήσει ὑμῖν Mt 17: 20; οὐκ ἀδ. παρὰ τοῦ θεοῦ (v.l. π. τῷ θεῷ) πᾶν ῥῆμα *nothing will be impossible w. God (as far as God is concerned)* Lk 1: 37 (Gen 18: 14; Dt 17: 8.—The idea that nothing is impossible for the gods is also found among the Greeks from early times: Od. 16, 211f; Hes., Works 5f; Alcaeus 78, 7 Diehl). M-M.*

ἀδύνατος, ον—1. act. *powerless, impotent* (since Epicharmus, Hdt., Eur.; inscr., pap., LXX).
   a. adj., of spirit beings Hm 11: 19c. W. dat. ἀνὴρ ἀ. τοῖς ποσίν Ac 14: 8 (cf. PLond. 678, 6 [99/98 BC] ἀ. ὄμμασι, also PStrassb. 81, 17 [II BC]; Tob S 2: 10; 5: 10).
   b. subst. οἱ ἀδύνατοι (Hyperid. 2, 10 contrasted w. δυνάμενοι εἰπεῖν, of those who cannot speak) of those weak in faith (opp. οἱ δυνατοί) Ro 15: 1.—τὰ ἀδύνατα *what is powerless* Dg 9: 6b.—τὸ ἀδύνατον *inability* εἰς τὸ τυχεῖν 6a; τὸ καθ᾽ ἑαυτοὺς ἀδύνατον εἰσελθεῖν *our own inability to enter* 9: 1.
   2. pass. *impossible* (Pind., Hdt.+; LXX, Philo, Joseph.).
   a. adj. ἀ. w. and without ἐστίν *it is impossible* Hm 11: 19a, b; παρὰ ἀνθρώποις τοῦτο ἀ. ἐστιν Mt 19: 26; Mk 10: 27 (cf. Philo, Spec. Leg. 1, 282; Jos., Ant. 10, 196; dedicatory inscr. fr. Phrygia [JZingerle, Hlg. Recht: Österr. Jh. 23, '26, Beibl. p. 11] Μητρὶ Λητῷ ὅτι ἐξ ἀδυνάτων δυνατὰ ποιεῖ.—Ps.-Pla., Alcyon c. 3 ἀδύνατος and δυνατός of that which God cannot do and what he can); οὐδὲν ἀ. παρὰ τῷ θεῷ 1 Cl 27: 2; cf. Lk 18: 27. W. inf. foll. and acc. w. the inf. (Wsd 16: 15; 2 Macc 4: 6; Jos., Ant. 5, 109) Hb 6: 4, 18; 10: 4; 11: 6; Hs 9, 26, 6; MPol 6: 1. οὐκ ἔστιν ἀ. ὑπὲρ ὀνόματος θεοῦ (sc. τοῦτο ποιεῖν) IPhld 10: 2.
   b. subst. (Bl-D. §263, 2; Rob. 372; Mitteis, Chrest. 372 V, 24: ἐπιχειρεῖς τοῖς ἀδυνάτοις; Jos., Ant. 11, 195) τὸ ἀ. τ. νόμου *what was impossible for the law* (God has done) Ro 8: 3. M-M.*

ᾄδω (since Hom., but there in the uncontracted form ἀείδω; inscr., pap., LXX) *sing* abs. (w. χορεύειν, ὀρχεῖσθαι) Hs 9, 11, 5. W. dat. of the pers. (LXX; Philostrat., Imag. 1, 11, 780; Heliod. 5, 15, 3 ἐμβατήρια ᾄδ. τ. Διονύσῳ; cf. Diod. S. 2, 47, 3 ὕμνους λέγειν τῷ θεῷ; Nägeli 42f) ᾄ. διὰ Ἰ. Χρ. τῷ πατρί IEph 4: 2; τῷ πατρὶ ἐν Χρ. Ἰ. IRo 2: 2; ᾄ. ἐν ταῖς καρδίαις ὑμῶν τ. θεῷ Col 3: 16; ᾄδοντες καὶ ψάλλοντες (+ἐν v.l.) τῇ καρδίᾳ ὑμῶν τῷ κυρίῳ *singing and playing in your hearts to the Lord* Eph 5: 19. W. acc. foll., of the song that is sung (Polycrates: no. 588 fgm. 1 Jac.; Jos., Ant. 3, 64 ὕμνους) ᾠδὴν καινήν (Ps 143: 9; cf. Philo, Mos. 1, 255 ᾁ. ᾆσμα καινόν) Rv 5: 9. (ὡς) ᾠδὴν καινήν 14: 3. τὴν ᾠδὴν Μωυσέως 15: 3 (Dt 31: 30; cf. Ex 15: 1). Pass. Ἰησοῦς Χριστὸς ᾄδεται (praise of) *Jesus Christ is being sung* IEph 4: 1. ᾄδω τὰς ἐκκλησίας *I sing the praise of the churches* IMg 1: 2 (Funk, in the text). φόβος νόμου ᾄδεται *the fear of the law is sung* Dg 11: 6 (but s. Philo, Sacr. Abel. 131 λόγος ᾄδεται=a teaching is presented; Aelian, N.A. 17, 5 Φύλαρχος ᾄδει [=says] τοιαῦτα; Arrian, Anab. 4, 9, 5 'proclaim'. Likewise Epict., fgm. Stob. ᾄδειν τὰ λόγια; Plut., Thes. 19, 1; Maximus Tyr. 32, 1b).—JKroll, D.

christl. Hymnodik bis zu Klemens v. Al.: Beigabe z. Vorlesungsverz. v. Braunsberg SS. 1921 and WS. 1921/22. M-M. B. 1249.*

ἀεί adv. (Hom.+; inscr., pap. [Mayser 103f], LXX, Ep. Arist.; Jos., Vi. 87 al.).
   1. *always* ἀ. χαίροντες 2 Cor 6: 10; ἕτοιμοι ἀ. πρὸς ἀπολογίαν *always prepared to make a defense* 1 Pt 3: 15; cf. Dg 8: 8; 11: 5; 12: 8; Pol 6: 1; IEph 11: 2; εἰς ἀ. *forever* (Dio Chrys. 21[38], 51; Ael. Aristid. 43, 9 K.=1 p. 3 D.; BGU 180, 24; 316, 22; POxy. 67, 22; PLeipz. 4. 24; Jos., C. Ap. 2, 156) IPol 2: 2.
   2. *from the beginning* (Pla., Gorg. 523A καὶ ἀεὶ καὶ νῦν ='from time immemorial to the present'; Diod. S. 20, 24, 2) Κρῆτες ἀ. ψεῦσται *Cretans have always been liars* Tit 1: 12.
   3. of a freq. recurring action or situation, *continually, constantly* (Diod. S. 19, 39, 1 allies were coming on 'from time to time'; PRyl. 114, 26 ἐμὲ τὴν χήραν ἀ. ἀποστερεῖν; Ep. Arist. 196) ἀ. εἰς θάνατον παραδιδόμεθα 2 Cor 4: 11; ἀ. τῷ πνεύματι τῷ ἁγίῳ ἀντιπίπτετε Ac 7: 51; ἀ. ὑμᾶς ὑπομιμνήσκειν *from time to time* 2 Pt 1: 12; ἀ. πλανῶνται Hb 3: 10 (Ps 94: 10). καθὼς ἀ. ἐποίει *as he was accustomed to do* Mk 15: 8 v.l. Cf. MPol 13: 2. B. 985.*

ἀέναος, ον (in var. spellings—mostly w. one ν—Hes., Hdt.+; inscr., pap., LXX).
   1. lit. *ever-flowing* of springs (Hes., Opera 595; Simonides in Diog. L. 1, 90; Epict. in Stob., fgm. 2 p. 463 Sch.; M. Ant. 8, 51; Wsd 11: 6; Philo, Spec. Leg. 1, 303; Jos., Bell. 3, 45, Ant. 3, 258; Sib. Or. 4, 15) 1 Cl 20: 10.
   2. fig. *eternal* (Pind.+; LXX; Sib. Or. 3, 698; Herm. Wr. 18, 14a; PGM 13, 842) God (Sb 8141, 22 [inscr. I BC] θεοῦ μεγάλου ἔκγονος ἀενάου) PK 2. τὴν ἀ. τοῦ κόσμου σύστασιν *the everlasting constitution of the universe* 1 Cl 60: 1 (cf. Dit., Or. 56, 48 εἰς τὸν ἀ. κόσμον).*

ἀετός, οῦ, ὁ (since Hom., who writes αἰετός like many after him [cf. Jos., Bell. 5, 48]; inscr., pap., LXX; Jos., Bell. 1, 650f, Ant. 17, 151; Test. 12 Patr.) *eagle* symbol of swiftness Rv 12: 14 (s. Ezk 17: 3, 7); cf. 4: 7; 8: 13 (s. Boll 37f; 113f—ἀ. πετόμενος as Job 9: 26). Eating carrion, in the proverb (cf. Job 39: 30) ἐκεῖ (ἐπι)συναχθήσονται οἱ ἀ. Mt 24: 28; Lk 17: 37 (where the *vulture* is meant; Aristot., Hist. An. 9, 32 and Pliny, Hist. Nat. 10, 3 also class the vulture among the eagles; TWManson, Sayings of Jesus '54, 147, emphasizes the swiftness of the coming of the Day of the Son of Man). The Jews are forbidden to eat its flesh B 10: 1, 4 (Dt 14: 12; Lev 11: 13). M-M.*

Ἀζαρίας, ου, ὁ (Joseph.) *Azariah*, in Da 1: 6f; 3: 23ff one of the three youths in the fiery furnace 1 Cl 45: 7.*

ἄζυμος, ον *without fermentation* (Pla., Tim. 74D σάρξ unfermented=firm, solid, of sinews; ἄρτος made without yeast, *unleavened*: Hippocr., περὶ διαίτης 2, 42; 3, 79; Trypho of Alex. [I BC] in Ath. 3 p. 109B ἄρτοι ἄζυμοι; Galen: CMG V 4, 2 p. 220, 1; 3 of country people who ἑορτάζοντες make loaves of bread which they call ἄζυμοι; Pollux 6, 32; Athen. 3, 74; LXX).
   1. subst. τὰ ἄζυμα—a. *unleavened bread* in the form of flat cakes, *matzoth* (מַצּוֹת; [the Gk. word μάζα, ἡ='dough, bread' Hdt.+; Harmodius–III BC—no. 319 Jac. fgm. 1 μάζας καὶ ἄρτους; Antig. Car. 173]; τὰ ἄ. Ex 12: 8, 15 al.; 23: 15; Philo, Congr. Erud. Gr. 161; Jos., Ant. 3, 249b; 17, 213; λάγανα 'flat cakes' Lev 2: 4; Num 6: 15, as ἄρτοι ἄ. Ex 29: 2; Lev 2: 5; Jos., Ant. 3, 142) eaten by the

Jews at Passover. In the NT only fig., ἑορτάζειν ἐν ἀ. εἰλικρινείας καὶ ἀληθείας *celebrate the festival w. the unleavened bread of purity and truth*, i.e., a pure and true life 1 Cor 5: 8.

b. *the festival of unleavened bread* (s. πάσχα 1; GBeer, Pesachim '12 [p. 1, 1 lit.]. On the pl. cf. W-S. §27, 4b; Bl-D. §141, 3) PK 2 p. 14, 29; w. πάσχα (1 Esdr 1: 17; cf. Jos., Ant. 14, 21 κατὰ τὸν καιρὸν τῆς τ. ἀζύμων ἑορτῆς, ἣν πάσχα λέγομεν; 18, 29 and Lk 22: 7 s. below) Mk 14: 1; ἡ ἑορτὴ τῶν ἀ. (Ex 23: 15; 34: 18; Dt 16: 16; Jos., Ant. 2, 317; 14, 21 s. above; Inschr. v. Hierap. no. 342) Lk 2: 42 D; 22: 1; ἡ ἡμέρα τῶν ἀ., ᾗ ἔδει θύεσθαι τὸ πάσχα vs. 7 (s. above); αἱ ἡμέραι τῶν ἀ. Ac 12: 3; 20: 6 (cf. FStrobel, Nov T 2, '58, 216, note 2). τῇ πρώτῃ ἡμέρᾳ τῶν ἀ. Mk 14: 12; cf. Mt 26: 17 (LDieu, Ephem. theol. Lov. 14, '38, 657-67). πρὸ μιᾶς τῶν ἀ. *one day before the festival of unleavened bread* GP 2: 5 (on this use s. WSchulze, Graeca Latina '01, 14f; Bl-D. §213 w. app.; Mlt. 100f).

2. fig. of men in whom sin has been overcome in principle καθώς ἐστε ἄ. 1 Cor 5: 7.*

Ἀζώρ, ὁ indecl. *Azor*, in the genealogy of Jesus Mt 1: 13f; Lk 3: 23ff D.*

Ἄζωτος, ου, ἡ (since Hdt. 2, 157; also Diod. S. 19, 85, 1; LXX; Jos., Index Niese) *Azotus*, the OT (Is 20: 1) *Ashdod*, one of the five Philistine cities, on the coast of S. Palestine Ac 8: 40.—Schürer II⁴ 125f (lit.).*

ἀηδής, ές (Hippocr., Hdt.+) *unpleasant, odious*. Comp. ἀηδέστερος, α, ον *more loathsome* Papias 3.*

ἀηδία, ας, ἡ *enmity*, lit. *unpleasantness* (so Demosth.+; UPZ 72, 8 [152 BC]; 119, 23; BGU 22, 14f; LXX Pr 23: 29; Aq. Sym. Jer 15: 10; Philo; Jos., Ant. 17, 307; Test. Dan 4: 3) ὄντες ἐν ἀηδίᾳ Lk 23: 12 D (ἐν ἀ. εἶναι Ael. Aristid. 47, 10 K.= 23 p. 447 D.). M-M.*

ἀηδῶς adv. *unwillingly, reluctantly* (so X., Pla.+; BGU 801, 4 λίαν ἀηδῶς; Jos., Ant. 11, 149; 12, 174) ἀ. ἔχειν (Demosth. 20, 142; 37, 11; BGU 665 III, 10f [I AD] ἀηδῶς ἔσχον περὶ τοῦ ἵππου; PGiess. 20, 9) *be displeased* (w. ἀγανακτεῖν) 2 Cl 19: 2.*

ἀήρ, έρος, ὁ (Hom.+; pap., LXX; Ep. Arist. 70; Philo; Jos., Ant. 14, 473; Test. Reub. 2: 5; Sib. Or. 2, 207; loanw. in rabb.) *air*, w. the sun Rv 9: 2; as an element w. fire and water (PGM 12, 251; 17b, 15) Dg 7: 2. To indicate the direction 'up' (Achilles Tat. 7, 15, 3 ἐξάλλομαι εἰς ἀέρα; PPar. 21b, 16 ἀπὸ ἐδάφους μέχρι ἀέρος; PLond. 991, 10; PGM 13, 832 εἰς ἀέρα βλέπων; Jos., Ant. 7, 327) βάλλειν εἰς τὸν ἀ. *throw into the air* Ac 22: 23; ἁρπάζεσθαι εἰς ἀ. 1 Th 4: 17 (cf. PGM 1, 179); ἐκχέειν ἐπὶ τὸν ἀ. Rv 16: 17. In figures of speech: ἀέρα δέρειν *beat the air* fr. the language of the arena, of a gladiator who misses a stroke 1 Cor 9: 26 (s. δέρω; Vergil, Aen. 5, 377 verberat ictibus auras; 6, 294; sim. Quint. Smyrn. 9, 259f ἐς κενεὴν τύψας ἠέρα); proverb. (AOtto, D. Sprichwörter d. Röm. 1890, 364) εἰς ἀ. λαλεῖν *talk to the wind* 14: 9 (Ovid, Am. 1, 6, 42 dare verba in ventos; Lucret. 4, 931).—Of space (Artem. 2, 8 p. 91, 10ff; 2, 36 p. 138, 2 οἱ ὑπὲρ ἀέρα ἀστέρες; Cyranides p. 49, 7 τὰ ἐν οὐρανῷ κ. ἐν ἀέρι) πετεινὰ τ. ἀέρος PK 2 p. 14, 17; ἶρις ἐν ἀ. AP 10.—Of the kgdm. of the air, in which spirit beings live (Ocellus Luc. c. 40: the gods live in heaven, men live on earth, the δαίμονες in the ἀέριος τόπος; Diog. L. 8, 32 after Pythagoras εἶναί τε πάντα τὸν ἀέρα ψυχῶν ἔμπλεον, καὶ τούτους δαίμονάς τε καὶ ἥρωας νομίζεσθαι; Plut., Mor. 274B; Celsus 8, 35; PGM 13, 278 πνεῦμα ἐν

ἀέρι φοιτώμενον; 4, 1134; 2699; 3042 ἀέριον 'air-spirit'; likew. 7, 314.—1, 129 a supernat. being as μόνος κύριος τοῦ ἀέρος; Fluchtaf. no. 4, 37 p. 19 ἀέρος τὴν ἐξουσίαν ἔχοντα Ωη Ιαω; SEitrem and AFridrichsen, E. christl. Amulett auf Pap. '21, p. 31. 5; p. 13f; Philo, Plant. 14, Gig. 6f, Conf. Lingu. 174 al.) ὁ ἄρχων τῆς ἐξουσίας τοῦ ἀ. *the ruler of the kingdom of the air* i.e. Satan, Eph 2: 2 (cf. Ascension of Isaiah 11, 23; Slav. En. 31; Test. Benj. 3: 4 ἀέριον πνεῦμα τοῦ Βελίαρ).—OEverling, D. paulinische Angelologie 1888, 107f; Dibelius, Geisterwelt 156f; FPfister, Philol. 69, '10, 416ff; Cumont³ 289, 55. M-M. and suppl. B. 63.*

ἀθᾶ s. μαρὰν ἀθᾶ.

ἀθανασία, ας, ἡ (Isocr., Pla.+; Vett. Val. 221; 330; Dit., Syll.³ 798, 4; Sb 4127, 14; PGM 4, 477; Wsd, 4 Macc, Philo; Jos., Bell. 7, 348, Ant. 17, 354; Sib. Or. 2, 41; 150; loanw. in rabb.) *immortality* (w. γνῶσις, πίστις) D 10: 2. ἐνδύσασθαι ἀ. *put on immortality*=be clothed w. an immortal body 1 Cor 15: 53f; God ὁ μόνος ἔχων ἀ. 1 Ti 6: 16; ζωὴ ἐν ἀ. 1 Cl 35: 2. In accord w. widespread medical terminology (ThSchermann, ThQ 92, '10, 6ff) the Lord's Supper is called a φάρμακον ἀθανασίας (syn. ἀντίδοτος τοῦ μὴ ἀποθανεῖν) *medicine of immortality* IEph 20: 2 (Diod. S. 1, 25 τὸ τῆς ἀ. φάρμακον). M-M.*

ἀθάνατος, ον (Hom.+; inscr., pap., LXX; Ps.-Phoc. 115; Jos., Ant. 11, 56, C. Ap. 2, 277) *immortal* of God (Philo, Aet. M. 44; Sib. Or. 3, 276; 582; οἱ ἀ. Hom.+) 1 Ti 1: 17 v.l. Of the soul (acc. to Diog. L. 1, 24 since Thales and Choerilus Ep. [V BC]; cf. further Pla., Ep. 7 p. 335A; Diod. S. 5, 28, 6; Paus. 4, 32, 4; Herm. Wr. 8, 1; Vett. Val. 242, 16; Iambl., Vi. Pyth. 30, 173; Philo, Op. M. 119.—MPNilsson, The Immortality of the Soul in Gk. Rel.: Eranos 39, '41, 1-16) Dg 6: 8. Of γνῶσις (cf. the combin. w. χάρις Demosth., Ep. 4, 9; Dit., Syll.³ 798, 7; w. κρίσις Dit., Or. 383, 207) 1 Cl 36: 2. τὸν ἀ. τῆς ἀναστάσεως καρπὸν τρυγᾶν 2 Cl 19: 3. Subst. of Jesus ὁ ἀ. Dg 9: 2 (opp. οἱ θνητοί); τὸ ἀ. *that which is immortal* (opp. τὸ θνητόν, like Philo, Rer. Div. Her. 265) D 4: 8 (cf. Alexis 158 τὸ ἀ. in contrast to σῶμα). M-M. s.v. ἀθανασία.*

ἀθέμιστος Dg 4: 2 s. the foll.

ἀθέμιτος, ον (Hom. and other early wr. ἀθέμιστος; since Antipho, more and more commonly in the Koine, incl. LXX and Jos. [e.g. Bell. 4, 562, Vi. 26]; UPZ 162 II, 22 [117 BC] ἀθέμιτος) *unlawful, lawless, wanton* εἰδωλολατρίαι 1 Pt 4: 3. ὀργή 1 Cl 63: 2. ἀθέμιτον *it is unlawful* w. inf. foll. (Plut., Mor. 150F; Jos., Bell. 1, 650) Ac 10: 28. πῶς οὐκ ἀθέμιστον; Dg 4: 2.—Subst. ἀ. ποιεῖν (X., Mem. 1, 1, 9) *commit lawless acts* D 16: 4. M-M.*

ἄθεος, ον (Aeschyl.+; Diog. L. 7, 119; Stoic. III p. 157, 606; Vett. Val. ind.; PGM 36, 319; 337; Cat. Cod. Astr. II 98, 15; 108, 3; 109, 12; Philo, Leg. All. 1, 49 al.—HIBell, Jews and Christians in Egypt '24) *without God, godless.*

1. without censure (Artem. 1, 8 p. 14, 4 οὐδὲν ἔθνος ἄθεον; Maximus Tyr. 30, 2d δι' ἀμαθίαν ἄθεοι of those who, through no fault of their own, have never heard of gods), of pagans ἄ. ἐν τῷ κόσμῳ Eph 2: 12. So also, if it is correctly restored, LJ 1: 5.

2. of one who disdains or denies God or the gods and their laws (Euhemerus and other Gk. thinkers are so called in Sext. Emp., Math. 9, 50 and 9, 17; Diogenes, Epicurus et al. in Aelian, V.H. 2, 31.—Nicol. Dam.: 90 fgm. 16 Jac. οἷα ἀθέους ἐπόντωσεν; Ptolem., Apotel. 3, 14, 28 in a catalogue of vices).

a. in the mouth of pagans against Christians (also Jews:

Jos., C. Ap. 2, 148) αἶρε τοὺς ἀ. *away w. the atheists!* MPol 3; 9: 2a (cf. Justin, Apol. I 6, 1; 13, 1 al.; Dit., Or. 569, 22; ThMommsen, Hist. Ztschr. 64, 1890, 407; ABDrachmann, Atheism in Pagan Antiquity '22). **b.** in the mouth of Christians, w. ref. to pagans MPol 9: 2b (likew. Sib. Or. 8, 395; Ps.-Clem., Hom. 15, 4; Clem. Alex., Paed. 3, 11, 80). Of heterodox Christians ITr 10 and hence prob. also 3: 2 (cf. Third Corinthians 3: 37). M-M.*

ἄθεσμος, ον (Diod. S. 1, 14; Plut., Caes. 10, 5; POxy. 129, 8; PLond. 1678, 5; PGM 4, 2607; 2670; Philo, Mos. 2, 198; Jos., Bell. 7, 264; 3 Macc 5: 12; 6: 26) *lawless, unprincipled* (opp. δίκαιος). Subst. ὁ ἄ. *the lawless man* (Philo, Praem. 126; Sib. Or. 5, 177) 2 Pt 2: 7; 3: 17. M-M.*

ἀθετέω fut. ἀθετήσω; 1 aor. ἠθέτησα (Polyb.+; inscr., pap., LXX, Joseph. [but only Ant. 15, 26 v.l.]; Test. 12 Patr.).
1. trans.—**a.** *declare invalid, nullify, set aside* (BGU 1123, 11 [I BC]; Ps 88: 35; 1 Macc 11: 36; 2 Macc 13: 25 al.) a will Gal 3: 15. τὴν ἐντολὴν τοῦ θεοῦ Mk 7: 9 (cf. Act. Phil. 142). τὴν βουλὴν τοῦ θεοῦ Lk 7: 30 (cf. Ps 32: 10). νόμον Μωϋσέως Hb 10: 28 (cf. Ezk 22: 26). τὴν χάριν τοῦ θεοῦ Gal 2: 21. τὴν πρώτην πίστιν *break their first pledge* 1 Ti 5: 12 (πίστιν ἀ. Polyb. 8, 2, 5; 11, 29, 3; Diod. S. 21, 20 al.); *thwart, confound* (Ps 32: 10) τὴν σύνεσιν τῶν συνετῶν 1 Cor 1: 19.
b. *reject, not recognize* (POxy. 1120, 8; PGiess. 34, 8) Christ J 12: 48 (cf. Third Corinthians 3: 3 κύριος Χρ. ἀθετούμενος); God 1 Th 4: 8 (cf. Act. Jo. 3; 41); both, together w. the apostles Lk 10: 16. κυριότητα Jd 8. τὸν κύριον Hm 3: 2. Gener.: οὐκ ἠθέλησεν ἀθετῆσαι αὐτήν he did not want to refuse (perh. *break faith w.*: Is 1: 2; Polyb. 3, 29, 2) her Mk 6: 26.—Pass. of Christ τίς ἀθετηθείς; IEph 10: 3.
2. intr. (so oft. LXX; Maspéro 151, 251) *commit an offense* εἰς τὸν θεόν Hv 2, 2, 2 (cf. 3 Km 12: 19; Ezk 39: 23). M-M.*

ἀθέτησις, εως, ἡ (Cicero, Ad Att. 6, 9, 3; Diog. L. 3, 39, 66 al.; pap., LXX).
1. *annulment* legal t.t. (BGU 44, 16 [102 AD]; 196, 21; 281, 18 al.) ἀ. γίνεται προαγούσης ἐντολῆς *a former commandment is annulled* Hb 7: 18.
2. gener. *removal* (Sext. Emp., Math. 8, 142 w. ἀναίρεσις) εἰς ἀ. τῆς ἁμαρτίας Hb 9: 26.—Dssm., NB 55f [BS 228f]. M-M.*

Ἀθῆναι, ῶν, αἱ, (Hom.+; Philo, Joseph.) *Athens,* capital of Attica Ac 17: 15f; 18: 1; 1 Th 3: 1 (also in the ms. notes after 1 and 2 Th and Hb). Cf. EHaenchen on Ac 17: 15 (lit.); OBroneer, Bibl. Archaeologist 21, '58, 2-28.*

Ἀθηναῖος, α, ον (Hom.+; Philo, Joseph.) *Athenian;* subst. ὁ Ἀ. *the Athenian* Ac 17: 21; in dir. address: ἄνδρες Ἀθηναῖοι *gentlemen of Athens* (Demosth. 8, 35; 18, 27; Diod. S. 13, 102, 2 al.) vs. 22.*

ἄθικτος, ον *inviolable, sacred* (so trag.+; Dit., Syll.³ 569, 16; Sb 7202, 68 [III BC]; Sym. Lev 8: 9; 21: 12) τὰ ἄ. ἀρχεῖα IPhld 8: 2.*

ἀθλέω 1 aor. ἤθλησα (Hom.+; Philo) *compete in a contest* in the arena 2 Ti 2: 5; νομίμως *according to the rules* ibid. (Epict. 3, 10, 8; Galen, Ad Hippocr. Aphor. 18 οἱ γυμνασταὶ κ. οἱ νομίμως ἀθλοῦντες). Of the apostles ἕως θανάτου ἤθλησαν *they contended unto death* 1 Cl 5: 2. Gener. θεοῦ ζῶντος πεῖραν ἀ. (w. γυμνάζεσθαι) *we are competing in a contest of a living God* 2 Cl 20: 2.*

ἄθλησις, εως, ἡ (since Polyb. 5, 64, 6; Bull. de corr. hell. 23, 1899, 557 [II BC]; IG XIV 1102 [II AD]; Dit., Syll.³ 1073, 24; PHermopol. 119в III, 13; Philo) *contest,* in NT only fig. of temptations and suffering which, so to speak, fight against men: πολλὴν ἄ. ὑπεμείνατε παθημάτων *you have had to endure a hard struggle w. suffering* Hb 10: 32. M-M.*

ἀθλητής, οῦ, ὁ (since Pind. [ἀεθλητής]; inscr., pap., 4 Macc, Philo; Jos., Ant. 13, 327; 17, 259; loanw. in rabb.) *contender, athlete,* in our lit. only fig. (since Gorgias [EScheel, De Gorgianae Disciplinae Vestigiis, Diss. Rostock 1890, 13], also Diod. S. 9, 1, 1 ἀ. πάσης ἀρετῆς; Dio Chrys. 2, 18; 4 Macc 6: 10; 17: 15f) of the martyrs οἱ ἔγγιστα γενόμενοι ἀ. 1 Cl 5: 1. Of one practised in suffering τέλειος ἀ. *master athlete* IPol 1: 3; μέγας ἀ. 3: 1; θεοῦ ἀ. 2: 3.*

ἄθραυστος, ον (Eur.+; Dit., Syll.³ 970, 15; Sb 8960, 20 ἄ. βίος) *unbroken* ἄ. διαφυλάσσειν τὸν ἀριθμὸν τῶν ἐκλεκτῶν *to preserve unbroken the number of the elect* 1 Cl 59: 2.*

ἀθροίζω pf. pass. ptc. ἠθροισμένος (trag., Hdt.+; Dit., Or. 764, 9; UPZ 12, 42 [158 BC]; LXX; Philo, De Jos. 158; Jos., Ant. 3, 300 Μωϋσῆς εἰς ἐκκλησίαν ἀθροίζει τὸ πλῆθος) *collect, gather* Lk 24: 33. M-M.*

ἀθυμέω (since Aeschyl., Thu. 5, 91, 1; PAmh. 37, 7; 10 [II BC]; PGiess. 79 III, 11; LXX, Philo; Jos., Bell. 6, 94, Ant. 9, 87) *be discouraged, lose heart* of children (Hyperid., fgm. 144) ἵνα μὴ ἀθυμῶσιν *that they may not lose heart* Col 3: 21. M-M.*

ἀθυμία, ας, ἡ (Soph., Hdt.+; UPZ 19, 14 [163 BC], LXX, Philo; Jos., Bell. 3, 182, Ant. 12, 357, C. Ap. 1, 236) *discouragement* εἰς ἀ. βάλλειν τινά *plunge someone into disc.* 1 Cl 46: 9 (cf. Aeschin. 3, 177 εἰς τὴν ἐσχάτην ἀ. ἐμβαλεῖν).*

ἀθῷος, ον (Eur.+; Dit., Syll.³ 1157, 59; 1217, 6; PTebt. 44, 28; LXX, Philo; Jos., Ant. 4, 271; 8, 15) *innocent* αἷμα ἀ. (oft. LXX; Philo, Spec. Leg. 1, 204; Test. Lev. 16: 3; Test. Zeb. 2: 2) Mt 27: 4. Of pers.: ἀ. εἶναι ἀπό τινος (Bl-D. §182, 3; cf. Gen 24; 41; Num 5: 19, 31) *be innocent of someth.* vs. 24; 1 Cl 59: 2. μετὰ ἀνδρὸς ἀθῴου ἀ. ἔσῃ 1 Cl 46: 3 (Ps 17: 26). W. δίκαιος vs. 4 (cf. Ex 23: 7); *guiltless* of the almsgiver, so far as he has fulfilled the commandment D 1: 5; Hm 2: 6. M-M. B. 1446.*

αἴγειος, εία, ειον (Hom.+; inscr., pap., LXX; Jos., Ant. 3, 102) *of a goat;* of the clothing of the prophets: ἐν αἰγείοις δέρμασιν (PFay. 107, 2f δέρματα αἴγεια) *in goatskins* Hb 11: 37; 1 Cl 17: 1 (w. μηλωταῖς). Of the clothing of the angel of punishment Hs 6, 2, 5; of the shepherd Hv 5: 1 v.l. M-M.*

αἰγιαλός, οῦ, ὁ *shore, beach* (Hom.+, mostly of the sea, as Dit., Or. 199, 21; Judg 5: 17 A; Philo, Aet. M. 42; Jos., Ant. 14, 292; Test. Zeb. 6: 3, but also of lakes: PTebt. 79 [148 BC]; 82; 83; PFay. 82, 3; Jos., Bell. 3, 521 [Lake Gennesaret]) gener. ἑστάναι ἐπὶ τὸν αἰ. Mt 13: 2; ἑστάναι εἰς τὸν αἰ. J 21: 4; ἀναβιβάζειν ἐπὶ τὸν αἰ. Mt 13: 48; cf. Ac 21: 5. Suitable for beaching ships κόλπον ἔχοντα αἰ. *a bay with a (good) beach* 27: 39 (cf. X., An. 6, 4, 4 λιμὴν αἰγιαλὸν ἔχων); κατέχειν εἰς τ. αἰ. *to head for the beach* (s. κατέχω 2) vs. 40. M-M. B. 32.*

Αἰγύπτιος, ία, ιον (Hom.+; inscr., pap., LXX, Ep. Arist., Philo, Joseph., Test. 12 Patr., Sib. Or.) *Egyptian* τὸ Αἰ. εὐαγγέλιον Kl. T. 8³, p. 15, 8.—Subst. only as a national name *the Egyptian* Ac 7: 24; Hb 11: 23 D (both Ex 2: 12; cf. Ezek. Trag. in Euseb., Pr. Ev. 9, 28); Ac 7: 28; 1 Cl 4: 10 (both Ex 2: 14). Their wisdom Ac 7: 22. Of a certain unnamed Egyptian 21: 38 (cf. Jos., Ant. 20, 171; 172). οἱ Αἰγύπτιοι of the Pharaoh of the Exodus and his army Hb 11: 29. Of the nation as a whole B 9: 6; τὸ κατ' Αἰγυπτίους εὐαγγ. Kl. T. 8³, p. 4, 14; 15, 19; 16, 5; 9. M-M.*

Αἴγυπτος, ου, ἡ (Hom.+; inscr., LXX, Ep. Arist., Philo, Joseph., Test. 12 Patr., Sib. Or.; except for Ac 7: 11; 1 Cl 25: 3, always without the art. [W-S. §18, 5d; Bl-D. §261, 7]) *Egypt* Mt 2: 13f, 15 (Hos 11: 1), 19; Ac 2: 10; 7: 9ff, 34 (Ex 3: 7, 10), 39; Hb 3: 16; 11: 26f; 1 Cl 4: 10; 25: 3; 51: 5a. More fully γῆ Αἰγύπτου Ac 7: 36 (Ex 7: 3), 40; 13: 17; Hb 8: 9 (Jer 38: 32); Jd 5; 1 Cl 51: 5b; 53: 2; B 14: 3 (the two last Ex 32: 7; Dt 9: 12); B 2: 7 (Jer 7: 22); 4: 8 (Ex 32: 7). Country for people 1 Cl 17: 5.—As symbolic name (w. Sodom) of a city; the addition of ὅπου καὶ ὁ κύριος αὐτῶν ἐσταυρώθη shows that Jerusalem is meant Rv 11: 8.*

αἰδέομαι 1 aor. ἠδέσθην (Hom.+; inscr., pap., LXX; Jos., Bell. 1, 8; 319, Ant. 15, 28; Test. 12 Patr.; cf. Nägeli 57) *respect* τινά someone (Callinus [VII BC], fgm. 1, 2 Diehl²; Apollon. Rhod. 4, 796 ἐμέ=me, i.e., Hera; Diod. S. 5, 31, 5 Ἄρης αἰδεῖται τὰς Μούσας) τοὺς προηγουμένους 1 Cl 21: 6; *have regard for* (Appian, Maced. 9 §6; Dio Chrys. 71 [21], 13) αἰδέσθητί σου τὴν ἡλικίαν *have some regard for your age* MPol 9: 2 (cf. 4 Macc 5: 7; Philo, Spec. Leg. 2, 238). M-M. s.v. αἰδώς.*

ἀΐδιος, ον (Hom. Hymns, Hes.+; inscr.; Wsd 7: 26; 4 Macc 10: 15; a favorite w. Philo: Op. M. 7; 171, Cher. 2; 4; 9, Post. Caini 39, Fuga 173; Jos., Ant. 4, 178; 17, 152) *eternal* ἡ ἀ. αὐτοῦ (of God) δύναμις Ro 1: 20 (Zoroaster in Philo Bybl. [Euseb., Pr. Ev. 1, 10, 52], 58th letter of Apollonius of Tyana [Philostrat. I 360, 29 K.] and Sib. Or. 5, 66 θεὸς ἀ.). ζωή (Philo, Fug. 97) IEph 19: 3; δεσμοῖς ἀ. Jd 6 (PGM 4, 1466 πυλωρὲ κλείθρων ἀϊδίων). M-M.*

αἰδοῖον, ου, τό (Hom.+; LXX) *private part(s)* Papias 3.*

αἰδώς, οῦς, ἡ (Hom.+; Epict.; Dit., Or. 507, 8; pap., LXX; Jos., Bell. 2, 325; Test. Jud. 14: 7; Sib. Or. 1, 35).
1. *modesty* of women (Diod. S. 13, 55, 4.—With σωφροσύνη) μετὰ αἰ. 1 Ti 2: 9 (cf. Jos., Ant. 2, 52).
2. *reverence, respect* (Pind. et al.; Plut., Timol. 7, 1; Jos., Ant. 6, 262) w. εὐλάβεια (as Philo, Leg. ad Gai. 352) Hb 12: 28 v.l. (cf. Appian, Bell. Civ. 1, 71 §331 αἰδὼς θεῶν).—RSchultz, ΑΙΔΩΣ, Diss. Rostock '10; CEvErffa, ΑΙΔΩΣ: Philol. Suppl. 30, 2, '37. M-M. B. 1141.*

Αἰθίοψ, οπος, ὁ (Hom.+; inscr., pap., LXX; Philo, Deus Imm. 174; Joseph.; Ep. Arist. 13; Sib. Or.) *Ethiopian* βασίλισσα Αἰθιόπων Ac 8: 27; as adj. w. ἀνήρ (Stephan. Byz. s.v. Αἰθίοψ acc. to Favorinus) ibid.—For lit. s. on Κανδάκη.*

αἰκία, ίας, ἡ (w. var. spellings Aeschyl.+; pap.; 2 and 3 Macc; Joseph.) *mistreatment, torture*, w. painful death (Andoc. 1, 138; Polyb. 1, 85, 2; Ps.-Pla., Axioch 372A) 1 Cl 6: 1 (w. βάσανος; cf. Jos., Bell. 3, 321). εἰς αἰ. περιβαλεῖν (Lghtft. cj. παραβαλεῖν) *torture* 45: 7 (cf. 3 Macc 6: 26; Ep. Arist. 208). αἰκίαις περιπίπτειν *be tortured, tormented* 51: 2.*

αἴκισμα, ατος, τό (trag.+; Lysias 6, 26; Pollux 6, 183) *mistreatment, torment* 1 Cl 6: 2; (w. μάστιγες) 17: 5.*

αἰκισμός, οῦ, ὁ (since Ctesias [400 BC]; Pollux 8, 79; pap., LXX) *mistreatment* (PHal. 1, 118; 2 and 4 Macc), (w.

κόλασις) *punishment* (Plut., Mor. 8F) εἰς αἰ. τιθέναι=αἰκίζειν *punish* 1 Cl 11: 1.*

Αἰλαμίτης s. Ἐλαμίτης.

αἴλουρος, ου, ὁ, ἡ (since Hdt. 2, 66 [αἰέλουρος]) *cat* (Hdt., Aristot., Diod. S. 20, 58, 2; Ptolem., Apotel. 3, 9, 2 κυνῶν ἢ αἰλούρων; Aelian; Plut., Mor. 144c; Cyranides p. 59, 13 αἰ. ἤτοι κάττα; EpJer 21) PK 2 p. 14, 19.*

αἷμα, ατος, τό (Hom.+; inscr., pap., LXX, En., Ep. Arist., Philo, Joseph., Test. 12 Patr., Sib. Or.) *blood*.
1. lit.—a. of human blood J 19: 34 (PHaupt, Blood and Water: AJPh 45, '24, 53-5; FJDölger, Ant. u. Christent. II '30, 117ff). ὅταν ἐκ ξύλου αἰ. στάξῃ *when blood drips from a tree* B 12: 1 (cf. 4 Ezra 5: 5). ῥύσις αἵματος *hemorrhage* (cf. Lev 15: 25; 20: 18) as a woman's disease Mk 5: 25; Lk 8: 43f; πηγὴ τοῦ αἷ. Mk 5: 29; θρόμβοι αἵματος Lk 22: 44.—Esp. as a principal component of the human body, w. σάρξ; σὰρξ καὶ αἷμα=man, w. strong emphasis on his ephemeral character, his shortsightedness and moral weakness (Sir 14: 18; 17: 31; Philo, Rer. Div. Her. 57. Freq. in rabb. as בָּשָׂר וָדָם, s. Billerb. I 730f; Polyaenus 3, 11, 1 of human beings in contrast to gods: αἷμα καὶ σάρκας ἔχοντες; Herm. in Stob., Floril. I 461, 12 W.=510, 27 Sc. of souls σαρκὶ καὶ αἷμ. βεβαπτισμέναι) Mt 16: 17; 1 Cor 15: 50; Gal 1: 16; Eph 6: 12. κοινωνεῖν αἵματος καὶ σαρκός *share in* (the) *human nature* (of their parents) Hb 2: 14.—Pl. τὰ αἵματα (pl. in trag.; Polyb. 15, 33, 1; LXX; Ep. Arist. 88; 90; Bl-D. §141, 6) *descent* ἐξ αἱμάτων γεννηθῆναι (w. ἐκ θελήματος σαρκός, opp. ἐκ θεοῦ)=owe one's descent to the physical nature J 1: 13 (cf. Aeschyl., Choëph. 284 ἐκ τ. πατρῴων αἱμάτων; Lycophron v. 1249 τῶν Ἡρακλείων ἐκγεγῶτες αἱμάτων; inscr. [Ramsay, Phryg. I 2 p. 537 no. 394 τέκνα ἐκ τ. αἵματός μου, cf. p. 472 no. 315 ἀπὸ τοῦ αἷμ.; PLeipz. 28, 16ff [381 AD] υἱὸν ἐξ ἰδίου αἵματος γεννηθέντα. Cf. HJCadbury, The Ancient Physiological Notions Underlying J 1: 13a, Hb 11: 11: Exp. 9th Ser. II '24, 430-9). ἐξ ἑνὸς αἵματος fr. the blood of one man Ac 17: 26 t.r. (cf. Musonius, Ep. 1, 10 ἐξ αἵματος; Jos., Ant. 20, 226).
b. of the blood of animals Hb 9: 7, 18, 25 αἰ. τράγων (cf. Is 1: 11) vs. 12; ταύρων vs. 13; B 2: 5; τῶν μόσχων Hb 9: 12, 19; ζῴων τὸ αἰ. 13: 11; πρόσχυσις τοῦ αἷ. 11: 28; cf. 12: 24. Its use as food is forbidden (cf. Lev 3: 17; 7: 26f; 17: 10) in the apostolic decree Ac 15: 20, 29; 21: 25 (representatives of this point of view in Haenchen on Ac 15: 21, p. 396; s. HJSchoeps, Theol. u. Gesch. d. Judenchristent. '49, 191-3; others [e.g. GResch; Harnack; Six; Zahn, Ac II 546ff; lit. on πνικτός] on the basis of a 'western' rdg. interpret ἀπέχεσθαι τ. αἵματος as a command not to shed blood; αἰ. act. *shedding of blood* in Paus. Attic. μ, 14; Maximus Tyr. 24, 4k w. σφαγή; Herodian 2, 6, 14; Wsd 14: 25 αἷμα κ. φόνος).
2. fig.—a. as the seat of life (Lev 17: 11; Wsd 7: 2; Jos., Ant. 1, 102) αἰ. ἐκχύννειν or ἐκχέειν *shed blood=kill* (Aeschyl.; Gen 9: 6; 37: 22; Lev 17: 4, 13; 1 Km 25: 31 al.; prayers for vengeance fr. Rheneia: Dssm., LO 351ff [LAE 423ff] and Dit., Syll.³ 1181, 5f) Lk 11: 50; Ac 22: 20; Ro 3: 15 (Ps 13: 3; Is 59: 7) Rv 16: 6; αἰ. Ἄβελ, Ζαχαρίου Mt 23: 35; Lk 11: 51. τῶν προφητῶν Mt 23: 30. ἁγίων καὶ προφητῶν Rv 16: 6; 18: 24; ἁγ. κ. μαρτύρων 17: 6. τῶν δούλων αὐτοῦ 19: 2 (4 Km 9: 7); cf. 6: 10; Pol 2: 1; αἰ. ἀθῷον Mt 27: 4, 24 (s. ἀθῷος). οὔπω μέχρις αἵματος ἀντικατέστητε you have not yet resisted as far as blood i.e., so that your blood was shed Hb 12: 4 (cf. Heliod. 7, 8, 2 τῆς μέχρις αἵματος στάσεως). τιμὴ αἵματος *the reward for a bloody deed* (αἰ.=bloody deed, murder Diod.

S. 18, 56, 4; Paroem. Gr. I p. 18: Zenobius 1, 47 Αἰσώ-πειον αἷμα=the murder of Aesop; Pr 1: 11) Mt 27: 6 (cf. Test. Zeb. 3: 3; UPZ 77 II, 9 λάβε τοὺς χαλκοὺς τοῦ αἵματος). ἀγρὸς αἵματος *a field bought with blood-money* vs. 8; differently Ac 1: 19 χωρίον αἱ.=a field soaked w. blood. αἱ. ἐκζητεῖν (oft. LXX) *demand the blood* Lk 11: 50. ἐκδικεῖν (Dt 32: 43; 4 Km 9: 7; prayers for vengeance fr. Rheneia, s. above) Rv 6: 10; 19: 2. τὸ αἷμα αὐτοῦ ἐφ' ἡμᾶς Mt 27: 25; cf. 23: 35; Ac 5: 28; 18: 6 (2 Km 1: 16; Test. Levi 16: 3 τὸ ἀθῷον αἱ. ἐπὶ τῆς κεφαλῆς ὑμῶν ἀναδεχόμενοι. For a judgment on one's head [Ac 18: 6] and children [Mt 27: 25] cf. 2 Km 1: 16; Ezk 33: 4 and the saying of the Pythia in Aelian, V.H. 3, 43 ἀλλ' αὐτῶν κεφαλῆσι καὶ ἐν σφετέροισι τέκεσσιν εἱλεῖται); καθαρὸς ἀπὸ τοῦ αἱ. πάντων (Sus 46 Theod.) Ac 20: 26. Also αἵματα 1 Cl 18: 14 (Ps 50: 16).

b. blood and life as an expiatory sacrifice 1 Cl 55: 1.—Esp. of the blood of Jesus as a means of expiation ἱλαστήριον ἐν τῷ αὐτοῦ αἱ. Ro 3: 25. ἀπολύτρωσις διὰ τοῦ αἱ. αὐτοῦ Eph 1: 7 (Col 1: 14 v.l.). Of the high-priestly sacrifice of Jesus Hb 9: 12, 14; 10: 19; 1 J 1: 7; Rv 1: 5; 5: 9; B 5: 1; ῥαντισμὸς αἱ. *sprinkling w. blood* 1 Pt 1: 2; αἱ. τοῦ ἀρνίου Rv 7: 14; 12: 11. ἀμνοῦ 1 Pt 1: 19. As the means of freeing from guilt Ro 5: 9; 1 Cl 7: 4; 12: 7; 21: 6; 49: 6. Hence πιστεύειν εἰς τὸ αἱ. Χρ. ISm 6: 1; αἱ. τῆς διαθήκης Hb 10: 29; 13: 20 (Test. Benj. 3: 8; cf. Ex 24: 8). Esp. in the words of institution of the Lord's Supper (cf. διαθήκη 2 and end) Mt 26: 28; Mk 14: 24; Lk 22: 20; 1 Cor 11: 25; cf. 10: 16; J 6: 53-5; 1 J 5: 6, 8. Of fellowship in the Lord's Supper ποτήριον εἰς ἕνωσιν τοῦ αἱ. αὐτοῦ IPhld 4. Described as bringing about a fellowship Ac 20: 28 (on αἱ. τοῦ ἰδίου s. CFDeVine, The Blood of God: CBQ 9, '47, 381-408); Eph 2: 13; cf. εἰρηνοποιήσας διὰ τοῦ αἱ. τοῦ σταυροῦ αὐτοῦ Col 1: 20. Love descr. as the blood of Jesus ITr 8: 1; IRo 7: 3, cf. ISm 1: 1; αἱ. θεοῦ IEph 1: 1 (cf. Hdb., and on Ac 20: 28 above).—FRüsche, Blut, Leben u. Seele '30; AAnwander, D. Blut in rel.-gesch. Schau: ThGl 26, '34, 414-27; OSchmitz, D. Opferanschauung d. späteren Judentums u. d. Opferaussagen d. NT '10; ARScott, Christianity acc. to St. Paul '27, 85ff; JSchneider, D. Passionsmystik d. Pls '29, 28ff; 120ff; HWindisch, Hdb. Exc. on Hb 9: 22 (² '31; lit. here).

3. of the (apocalyptic) red color, whose appearance in heaven indicates disaster (cf. MWMüller, ZNW 8, '07, 290ff; Eva Wunderlich, D. Bed. d. roten Farbe im Kult d. Griechen u. Römer '25): w. fire and smoke Ac 2: 19 (Jo 3: 3). So the world will end δι' αἵματος καὶ πυρός Hv 4, 3, 3. W. fire and hail Rv 8: 7. Of the color of water vs. 8; 11: 6 (Jos., Ant. 3, 17, the water turned to blood is not potable); cf, 16: 3f. Of the color of the moon Ac 2: 20 (Jo 3: 4); Rv 6: 12. The figure 'blood of the grape' (Gen 49: 11; Dt 32: 14; Sir 39: 26) used apocalypt. in ἐξῆλθεν αἱ. ἐκ τῆς ληνοῦ 14: 20 (cf. Is 63: 1-3). On the role of blood with other frightful portents, cf. Appian, Bell. Civ. 2, 36 §144; 4, 4 §14.—On the whole JBehm, TW I 171-6; LMorris, JTS n.s. 3, '52, 216-27; LDewar, ibid. 4, '53, 204-8. M-M. B. 206.

αἱματεκχυσία, ας, ἡ (fr. αἷμα and ἐκχέω, s. αἷμα 2a) *the shedding* or *pouring out* (so TCGThornton, JTS n.s. 15, '64, 63-65, w. ref. to such passages as Lev 4: 7, 18, 25 al.) *of blood* (found only in Christian wr., e.g. Byz. Chroniclers in Psaltas p. 349, but cf. ἔκχυσις αἵματος 3 Km 18: 28; Sir 27: 15; Charax of Pergamum [II/III AD]: 103 fgm. 5 Jac.) χωρὶς αἱ. οὐ γίνεται ἄφεσις *without the shedding of blood there is no forgiveness* Hb 9: 22.*

αἱματώδης, ες (Thu.+) *blood-red* (schol. on Nicander,

Ther. 228; Cat. Cod. Astr. VIII 2 p. 174, 3 Ἄρες αἱ.), i.e. dark red Hv 4, 1, 10 (as apocal. color w. black, yellow, and white; cf. αἷμα 3); w. πυροειδής (q.v.) *red as fire*, i.e. light red 4, 3, 3.*

αἱμορροέω (Hippocr.+; Lev 15: 33) *suffer with hemorrhage*, or *bloody flux* Mt 9: 20. M-M.*

Αἰνέας, ου, ὁ (lit.; inscr. [e.g. Wadd. 1929; 2238, also fr. Palestine: Suppl. Epigr. Gr. VIII 255—112/11 BC]; pap. [Preisigke, Namenbuch]) *Aeneas* Ac 9: 33f.*

αἴνεσις, εως, ἡ (Philod., παρρ. col. 8a, 10 Oliv.; LXX; Philo, Spec. Leg. 1, 224) *praise* ἀναφέρειν θυσίαν αἰνέσεως *offer a sacrifice of praise* Hb 13: 15 (cf. זֶבַח תּוֹדָה Lev 7: 12, 13, 15); cf. 1 Cl 35: 12 (Ps 49: 23); 52: 3 (Ps 49: 14); ἀναγγέλλειν τὴν αἱ. τινος *proclaim the praise of someone* 1 Cl 18: 15 (Ps 50: 17).*

αἰνέω *to praise* (so Hom.+; LXX) in our lit. used only of the praise of God (Diog. L. 1, 39; very oft. LXX; PGM 4, 1146) αἱ. τὸν θεόν Lk 2: 13, 20; 19: 37; 24: 53 D; Ac 2: 47; 3: 8f; cf. MPol 14: 3. τὸν κύριον Ro 15: 11 (Ps 116: 1). τῷ θεῷ ἡμῶν Rv 19: 5 (the dat. corresp. to לְ w. הוֹדָה and הִלֵּל LXX e.g. Jer 20: 13; 1 Ch 16: 36; 2 Ch 5: 13; Bl-D. §187, 4 app.); cf. B 7: 1. W. εὐλογεῖν (Da 5: 23) Lk 24: 53 v.l. Of praise of the gods by the heathen Dg 2: 7 (cf. Judg 16: 24 A; Da 5: 23). M-M.*

αἴνιγμα, ατος, τό (Pind., Aeschyl.+; LXX, Philo; Jos., C. Ap. 1, 114f; Sib. Or. 3, 812) lit. *riddle* PK 4 p. 15, 31, then *indirect* or *indistinct image* βλέπομεν δι' ἐσόπτρου ἐν αἰνίγματι *we see by reflection, dimly in a mirror* 1 Cor 13: 12 (cf. Num. 12: 8; Plut., Mor. 382A αἱ. τοῦ θείου of an indirect or indistinct divine revelation.—(ἐν) αἰν.=speak 'indistinctly' or 'in allegories': Mor. 12D; 672E).—αἴνιγμα =intimation: Sallust. c. 6 p. 12, 10.—Lit. s.v. ἀγάπη I 1a and ἔσοπτρον.*

αἶνος, ου, ὁ (Hom.+; inscr., LXX) *praise* αἶνον διδόναι τῷ θεῷ *to praise God* Lk 18: 43; 2 Cl 1: 5; 9: 10. καταρτίζεσθαι αἶνον *bring praise* for oneself Mt 21: 16 (Ps 8: 3). M-M.*

Αἰνών, ἡ indecl. *Aenon* place where John the Baptist was baptizing J 3: 23. M-JLagrange, RB 4, 1895, 506ff, also Comm.³ '27, and FMAbel, RB 23, '13, 222ff, who follow ancient church tradition (Euseb., Onom. p. 41), place it in the Jordan valley 8 mi. south of Scythopolis. Cf. ThZahn, NKZ 18, '07, 593-608; CKopp, Holy Places of the Gospels, '63, 129-37, and s. Σαλίμ.*

αἴξ, αἰγός, ὁ, ἡ *goat* (Hom.+; inscr., pap., LXX; Philo, Omn. Prob. Lib. 30; Jos., Ant. 6, 217; 295; Test. Zeb. 4: 9; Sib Or. 3, 627) ἔριφος ἐξ αἰγῶν (Gen 38: 20) Lk 15: 29 D. B. 165.*

αἵρεσις, έσεως, ἡ (Aeschyl., Hdt.+; inscr., pap., LXX; Ep. Arist. 7; Philo, Joseph.).

1. *sect, party, school* (of schools of philos. Diod. S. 2, 29, 6; Dionys. Hal., Comp. Verb. 2 τ. Στωϊκῆς αἱ.; Diog. L. 1, 18 and 19, al.; Iambl., Vi. Pyth. 34, 241; HDiels, Doxographi Graeci 1879, index; Aristobulus in Euseb., Pr. Ev. 13, 12, 10; Nägeli 51).

a. of the Sadducees Ac 5: 17 (Jos., Ant. 13, 171; 20, 199). Of the Pharisees 15: 5 (Jos., Vi. 10; 12; 191 al.). The latter described as ἡ ἀκριβεστάτη αἱ. τῆς ἡμετέρας θρησκείας *the strictest sect of our religion* 26: 5. Of the Christians αἵρεσις τῶν Ναζωραίων 24: 5; cf. vs. 14 and 28: 22. The last three exx. incline toward sense b.

b. in the later sense, *heretical sect* (also in Dit., Syll.³

675, 28 [II BC] αἵ. is used in malam partem: γίνωνται δὲ καὶ ἄλλοι ζηλωταὶ τῆς αὐτῆς αἱρέσεως IEph 6: 2; ITr 6: 1; Epil Mosq 1. Cf. also the agraphon from Justin, Trypho 35 in JoachJeremias, Unknown Sayings of Jesus (tr. Fuller), '57, 59–61. In general, WBauer, Rechtgläubigkeit u. Ketzerei im Aeltesten Christentum '34, 2d ed. w. supplement, GStrecker, '64.

c. *dissension, a faction* 1 Cor 11: 19; Gal 5: 20.

2. *opinion, dogma* (Philo, Plant. 151 κυνικὴ αἵ.) αἱ. ἀπωλείας *destructive opinions* 2 Pt 2: 1 (perh. also 1b).—*Way of thinking* (UPZ 20, 26 [163 BC]; 144, 10) αἵ. ἔχειν *hold to a way of thinking* Hs 9, 23, 5 (*inclination* is also possible: Dialekt-Inschr. 2746, 14; 2800, 7, both from Delphi). M-M.*

αἱρετίζω 1 aor. ἡρέτισα (Hippocr.+; Dit., Syll.³ 1042, 2; UPZ 109, 4 [98 BC]; LXX) act. *choose* Mt 12: 18 (Hg 2: 23; perh. in the specif. sense 'adopt' as 1 Ch 28: 6; Mal 3: 17; Epigr. Gr. 252).—Mid. (since Ctesias, Pers. c. 9; LXX) *choose for oneself* w. inf. foll. (1 Macc 9: 30) 2 Cl 14: 1. M-M. and suppl.*

αἱρετικός, ή, όν (in Ps.-Pla., Definit. 412A; Aelian, N.A. 6, 59; Hierocles Stoic. [I/II AD] Eth. 9, 5; here 7 and Diog. L. 7, 126 also the adv.) *factious, causing divisions* perh. *heretical* Tit 3: 10 (s. αἵρεσις 1b, c).*

αἱρετός, ή, όν comp. αἱρετώτερος *desirable* (so Hdt.+; LXX) αἱρετώτερον ἦν αὐτοῖς w. inf. foll. (X., Cyr. 3, 3, 51; Diod. S. 14, 45, 3; Polyaenus 4, 6, 6; Aesop, Fab. 261 P.=273 H.; cf. Sextus 362) *it would have been better for them* Hv 4, 2, 6.*

αἱρέω fut. mid. αἱρήσομαι; 2 aor. εἱλόμην and εἱλάμην 2 Th 2: 13; Hs 5, 6, 6 (Hom.+; inscr., pap., LXX, Philo, Joseph.).

1. act. *take* καρπὸν αἱρῶν *if you pick fruit* Dg 12: 8 (text uncertain; s. Bihlmeyer ad loc.).

2. mid. (so exclus. in NT) *choose* (cf. Nägeli 19f) w. double acc. (Hdt. 1, 96; Jos., Ant. 9, 106) Hs 5, 6, 6. τινὰ εἴς τι *someone for someth.* 2 Th 2: 13. W. acc. *prefer* (Diod. S. 17, 29, 3; 17, 48, 2; Jos., Bell. 6, 330) Phil 1: 22; likew. μᾶλλον αἱ. w. inf. foll. and ἤ w. inf. (class. Diod. S. 11, 11, 1 μᾶλλον εἵλοντο τελευτᾶν ἢ ζῆν; Περὶ ὕψους 33, 5; Appian, Bell. Civ. 4, 117 §491) Hb 11: 25. M-M. B. 743.*

αἴρω fut. ἀρῶ; 1 aor. ἦρα; pf. ἦρκα (Col 2: 14); pf. pass. ἦρμαι (J 20: 1; Hs 9, 5, 4); 1 aor. ἤρθην; 1 fut. ἀρθήσομαι (Hom.+; he, like some later wr., has ἀείρω; inscr., pap., LXX, Ep. Arist., Philo, Joseph., Test. 12 Patr.).

1. *lift up, take up, pick up*—a. lit., of stones (Dio Chrys. 12[13], 2) J 8: 59 (cf. Jos., Vi. 303); Rv 18: 21; Hs 9, 4, 7. A fish Mt 17: 27. A coffin 1 Cl 25: 3. A hand (X., An. 7, 3, 6) Rv 10: 5 (Dt 32: 40). The hands, in prayer 1 Cl 29: 1 (Ael. Aristid. 24, 50 K.=44 p. 840 D.; 54 p. 691; GBjörck, D. Fluch des Christen Sabinus, '38: inscr. [pp. 25–38] no. 14 [pre-Christian] Θεογένης αἴρει τὰς χεῖρας τῷ Ἡλίῳ; Sb 1323 [II AD] θεῷ ὑψίστῳ καὶ πάντων ἐπόπτῃ καὶ Ἡλίῳ καὶ Νεμέσεσι αἴρει Ἀρσεινόη ἄωρος τὰς χεῖρας). But αἵ. τὴν χεῖρα ἀπό τινος *withdraw one's hand fr. someone* =*renounce* or *withdraw fr. someone* B 19: 5; D 4: 9. Of snakes *pick up* Mk 16: 18. κλίνην Mt 9: 6. κλινίδιον Lk 5: 24. κράβατον Mk 2: 9; J 5: 8–12. Of a boat that is pulled on board Ac 27: 17. Of a spirit that carries a man away Hv 2, 1, 1. αἵ. σύσσημον *raise a standard* ISm 1: 2 (Is 5: 26). αἵ. τινὰ τῶν ἀγκώνων *take someone on one's arms* Hv 1, 4, 3. Abs. *weigh anchor, depart* (Thu.+; Philo, Mos. 1, 85; Jos., Ant. 7, 97; 9, 229; 13, 86 ἄρας ἀπὸ τῆς

Κρήτης κατέπλευσεν εἰς Κιλικίαν) Ac 27: 13.—Pass. 2 Cl 7: 4. ἄρθητι (of mountains) *arise* Mt 21: 21; Mk 11: 23. ἤρθη νεκρός Ac 20: 9.

b. fig. αἵ. τοὺς ὀφθαλμοὺς ἄνω *look upward* (in prayer, as Ps 122: 1; Is 51: 6 al.) J 11: 41; αἵ. τὴν ψυχήν τινος *keep someone in suspense* 10: 24 (Nicetas, De Manuele Comm. 3, 5 [Migne, S. Gr. 139 p. 460A]: ἕως τίνος αἴρεις, Σαρακηνέ, τὰς ψυχὰς ἡμῶν; The expr. αἵ. τὴν ψυχήν w. different mng. Ps 24: 1; 85: 4; 142: 8; Jos., Ant. 3, 48); αἵ. φωνήν *raise one's voice, cry out loudly* (1 Km 11: 4; 30: 4; 2 Km 3: 32 al.) Lk 17: 13. πρός τινα Ac 4: 24.

2. (*lift up and*) *take* or *carry* (*along*) lit. w. obj. acc. σταυρόν Mt 16: 24; 27: 32; Mk 8: 34; 15: 21; Lk 9: 23. ζυγόν (La 3: 27) Mt 11: 29. τινὰ ἐπὶ χειρῶν 4: 6; Lk 4: 11 (both Ps 90: 12). Pass. Mk 2: 3. αἵ. τι εἰς ὁδόν *take someth. along for the journey* 6: 8; Lk 9: 3, cf. 22: 36.—Fig. δόξαν ἐφ' ἑαυτὸν αἵ. *claim honor for oneself* B 19: 3.

3. (*lift up and*) *carry away, remove* lit. ταῦτα ἐντεῦθεν J 2: 16 (inscr. [218 BC]: ΕΛΛΗΝΙΚΑ 7, '34, p. 179, 15 ταῦτα αἱρέσθω). The crucified body 19: 38; cf. 20: 2, 13, 15; of John the Baptist Mt 14: 12; Mk 6: 29. A stone from a grave-opening J 11: 39; pass. 20: 1. τὸ περισσεῦον *the remainder* Mt 14: 20; 15: 37; cf. Lk 9: 17. περισσεύματα Mk 8: 8. κλάσματα *fragments* 6: 43; *baskets* 8: 19f. ζώνην *take off* Ac 21: 11; *take*: τὸ σόν *what belongs to you* Mt 20: 14; τὰ ἀρκοῦντα *what was sufficient for him* Hs 5, 2, 9. αἵ. τι ἐκ τῆς οἰκίας *get someth. fr. the house* Mk 13: 15; cf. Mt 24: 17; *take τινὰ ἐκ τοῦ κόσμου* J 17: 15.

4. *take away, remove* w. no suggestion of lifting up. By force, even by killing: abs. ἆρον, ἆρον *away, away* (with him)! J 19: 15 (cf. POxy. 119, 10 [Dssm., LO 168; LAE 188 n. 22]; Philo, In Flacc. 144; ἆρον twice also La 2: 19 v.l., in different sense). W. obj. αἶρε τοῦτον Lk 23: 18; cf. Ac 21: 36; 22: 22. αἶρε τοὺς ἀθέους (s. ἄθεος 2a) MPol 3; 9: 2 (twice); *sweep away* Mt 24: 39. W. the connot. of force and/or injustice (Epict. 1, 18, 13; PTebt. 278 [I AD]; SSol 5: 7): τὸ ἱμάτιον Lk 6: 29; cf. vs. 30; D 1: 4. τὴν πανοπλίαν *all his weapons* Lk 11: 22. Pass. Mk 4: 25. *Conquer, take over* (Diod. S. 11, 65, 3 πόλιν) τόπον, ἔθνος J 11: 48. αἵρεις ὃ οὐκ ἔθηκας Lk 19: 21f. αἵ. τὴν ψυχὴν ἀπό τινος J 10: 18 (cf. EFascher, Deutsche Theol. '41, 37–66). Pass. ἀπὸ τῆς Ac 8: 33b (Is 53: 8). ἀφ' ὑμῶν ἡ βασιλεία Mt 21: 43.—ἐξ ὑμῶν πᾶσαν ὑπόκρισιν *remove hypocrisy fr. yourselves* B 21: 4; ἀπὸ τῆς καρδίας τὰς διψυχίας αἵ. *put away doubt fr. their heart* Hv 2, 2, 4. αἵ. ἀφ' ἑαυτοῦ *put away fr. oneself* Hm 9: 1; 10, 1, 1; 10, 2, 5; 12, 1, 1. αἵ. ἐκ (τοῦ) μέσου *remove, expel* (fr. among) (Epict. 3, 3, 15; Plut., Mor. 519D; BGU 388 II, 23 ἆρον ταῦτα ἐκ τοῦ μέσου; PHib. 73, 14; Is 57: 2) 1 Cor 5: 2 (v.l. ἐξαρθῇ); a bond, note αἵ. ἐκ τοῦ μέσου *destroy* Col 2: 14. Of branches *cut off* J 15: 2. Prob. not intrans., since other exx. are lacking, but w. 'something' supplied αἴρει τὸ πλήρωμα ἀπὸ τοῦ ἱματίου *the patch takes someth. away fr. the garment* Mt 9: 16; cf. Mk 2: 21. *Remove, take away, blot out* (Eur., El. 942 κακά; Hippocr., Epid. 5, 49 pain; cf. Job 6: 2; IG II 467, 81 ζημίας; Epict. 1, 7, 5 τὰ ψευδῆ; Dit., Syll.³ 578, 42 τ. νόμον; Pr 1: 12; Ep. Arist. 215) τὴν ἁμαρτίαν τ. κόσμου J 1: 29 (ERiggenbach, NKZ 18, '07, 295–307); 1 J 3: 5 (Aquila Is 53: 12, s. PKatz, Vetus Test. 8, '58, 272; cf. 1 Km 15: 25; 25: 28). Pass. Eph. 4: 31. Fig. *take*, in order to make someth. out of the obj. 1 Cor 6: 15. M-M. B. 669f.

αἰσθάνομαι 2 aor. ἠσθόμην, subj. αἴσθωμαι (Aeschyl. +; inscr., pap., LXX, Philo; Jos., Ant. 1, 333; 13, 25 al.).

1. *possess the power of perception, notice* (Cleanthes [s.

2, end]; Appian, Liby. 120 §568; Test. Jud. 15: 1) Dg 2: 8 (cf. EpJer 19; 23).
  2. *understand* (X., Cyr. 1, 5, 4 al.; Pr 17: 10; 24: 14) ῥῆμα Lk 9: 45 (opp. ἀγνοέω). γνώμην B 2: 9. W. ὅτι foll. (Dio Chrys. 52[69], 2; Is 49: 26) 6: 18. αἰσθάνεσθε (*you*) *notice* w. indir. quest. foll. (Epict. 1, 6, 41; 3, 23, 16) 11: 8; cf. 13: 3.—Both meanings are included by Cleanthes [IV/III BC] in Diog. L. 7, 172 in a play on words, when he says to his pupil: οὐκ αἰσθάνομαι, ὅτι αἰσθάνῃ=I do not notice that you understand. M-M. B. 1020.*

αἴσθησις, εως, ἡ (Pre-Socr., Eur.+; Epict., Herm. Wr.; LXX, esp. Pr; Philo; Jos., Bell. 7, 69, C. Ap. 2, 178; Test. 12 Patr.; Sib. Or. fgm. 3, 23) *insight, experience,* denoting moral understanding (cf. αἰσθητήριον and ABonhöffer, Epikt. u. d. NT '11, 105), beside ἐπίγνωσις, which means intellectual perception; of love: περισσεύειν ἐν πάσῃ αἰσθήσει *become rich in every* (moral) *experience* Phil 1: 9. *Feeling, perception* (Ep. Arist. 213) Dg 2: 9 (w. λογισμός 'reasoning'). M-M. B 1020.*

αἰσθητήριον, ου, τό (Hippocr.+; Herm. Wr. 7, 3; Jer 4: 19; 4 Macc 2: 22; Philo) lit. 'organ of sense'; fig. *sense, faculty* of the ability to make moral decisions (cf. PLinde, De Epicuri Vocab., Bresl. Philol. Abh. X 3, 1906, 32) τὰ αἰσθητήρια γεγυμνασμένα ἔχειν πρὸς διάκρισιν καλοῦ τε καὶ κακοῦ *have one's faculties trained to distinguish betw. good and evil* Hb 5: 14 (Galen, De Dign. Puls. 3, 2 vol. VIII 892 K. αἰσθητήριον ἔχειν γεγυμνασμένον). M-M.*

αἰσχροκερδής, ές (since Eur., And. 451, Hdt. 1, 187; Philo, Sacr. Abel. 32 end; Test. Jud. 16: 1) *fond of dishonest gain, greedy for money* (cf. Lysias 12, 19) 1 Ti 3: 8 (3 t.r.); Tit 1: 7. (also in a catalogue of vices Ptolem., Apotel. 3, 14, 15).*

αἰσχροκερδῶς adv. *in fondness for dishonest gain, greedily* (opp. προθύμως) 1 Pt 5: 2.*

αἰσχρολογία, ας, ἡ (X.+; Polyb., Diod. S., Plut., Epict.; POxy. 410, 77) *evil speech* in the sense of *obscene speech* (Clem. Alex., Paed. 2, 6, 52 αἰ. εἰκότως ἂν καλοῖτο ἡ περὶ τῶν τῆς κακίας ἔργων λογοποιία, οἷον τὸ περὶ μοιχείας ἢ παιδεραστίας; αἰσχρός=obscene: Ps.-Demetr. Eloc. 151) or *abusive speech* (Polyb. 8, 11, 8; 31, 6, 4; BGU 909, 11f) Col 3: 8; D 5: 1.—AWikenhauser, BZ 8, 1910, 270. M-M.*

αἰσχρολόγος, ου, ὁ (Pollux 6, 123; 8, 80f) *a foulmouthed person* (s. αἰσχρολογία) D 3: 3. M-M s.v. αἰσχρολογία.*

αἰσχρός, ά, όν (Hom.+; inscr., pap., LXX, Philo) *ugly, shameful, base* only fig. αἰσχρόν κέρδος *dishonest gain* Tit 1: 11 (Theognis 466; Polyb. 6, 46, 3). ῥῆμα (PFlor. 309, 4) Hv 1, 1, 7. Neut. in the expr. αἰσχρόν ἐστί τινι w. inf. foll. *it is disgraceful for someone* (cf. 4 Macc 16: 17; Jdth 12: 12): for a woman to cut her hair 1 Cor 11: 6; to speak in a meeting 14: 35. Without the person Eph 5: 12. Also the pl. αἰσχρά (sc. ἐστιν) 1 Cl 47: 6 (for the doubling cf. Demosth. 25, 28 μιαρόν, μιαρὸν τὸ θηρίον; Caecil. Calact., fgm. 61 p. 42f; Maximus Tyr. 41, 3a; Bl-D. §493, 1 w. app.; Rob. 1200). M-M. B. 1195.*

αἰσχρότης, ητος, ἡ *ugliness, wickedness* (Pla., Gorg. 525A; Artem. 4, 2 p. 204, 8), then abstr. for concr.= αἰσχρολογία (q.v.) Eph 5: 4 (KGKuhn, NTS 7, '61, 339 [Qumran]).*

αἰσχύνη, ης, ἡ (Theognis, Aeschyl.+; pap., LXX).
  1. *modesty, shame,* a feeling that one has (Aristoxenus,

fgm. 42a; Diod. S. 2, 4, 3; Plut., Mor. 248B; PGM 17a, 8; Jos., Ant. 5, 147) τὸ τῆς αἰσχύνης ἔνδυμα πατεῖν prob. to throw off and *tread under foot the garment of shame* (which men have worn since the awakening of modesty, i.e. the fall, Gen 3: 7, cf. 2: 25) GEg 2; τὰ κρυπτὰ τῆς αἰ. *what one conceals fr. a feeling of shame* 2 Cor 4: 2. *Modesty, reverence* (w. φόβος) of slaves toward masters D 4: 11; B 19: 7 (cf. X., Cyr. 6, 1, 35; Soph., Ajax 1079; Demosth. 25, 24).
  2. *shame, disgrace, ignominy,* an experience which comes to someone (Diod. S. 2, 23, 2; Appian, Samn. 4 §11; PEleph. 1, 6; PTebt. 104, 30; POxy. 471, 78; Sir 25: 22; Ep. Arist. 206; Philo; Test. Levi 15: 2): ἡ αἰ. τῆς γυμνότητος *shameful nakedness* Rv 3: 18. καταφρονεῖν αἰσχύνης *despise the shame* Hb 12: 2. ἡ δόξα ἐν τῇ αἰσχύνῃ αὐτῶν *they find their glory in that which causes them shame* Phil 3: 19. μετὰ αἰσχύνης *in disgrace* (Demosth. 20, 16; Polyb. 3, 81, 6; 1 Esdr 8: 74; Philo, Det. Pot. Ins. 51; Jos., Ant. 12, 179) Lk 14: 9.
  3. *a shameful deed,* which one commits; pl. (Eur., Herc. 1423; Isocr. 14, 50; Aeschin. 1, 154; Jos., Ant. 4, 260) ἐπαφρίζειν τὰς αἰσχύνας *casting up their shameful deeds like* (waves casting up) *foam* Jd 13.—MAKlopfenstein, Scham u. Schande nach d. AT, '72. M-M. B. 1141.*

αἰσχυντηρός, ά, όν (Pla.+; Sir 26: 15; 32: 10; 41: 27) *modest* (w. τρυφερός, πραΰς, ἡσύχιος) of the angel of righteousness Hm 6, 2, 3.*

αἰσχύνω in our lit. only mid. and pass.; impf. ἠσχυνόμην; 1 aor. pass. subj. αἰσχυνθῶ, 1 fut. αἰσχυνθήσομαι (Hom.+; inscr. pap., LXX, Test. of 12 Patr.).
  1. *be ashamed* (Dit., Syll.³ 1168, 122; UPZ 62, 27 [161 BC] οὐκέτι ἥκει πρὸς ἐμὲ αἰσχυνθείς; Philo, Spec. Leg. 1, 321) w. inf. foll. (Aeschyl., Hdt.; UPZ 62, 24; Sir 4: 26; 22: 25; Sus 11 Theod.; Jos., Ant. 13, 327) ἐπαιτεῖν Lk 16: 3. μετ' αὐτῶν μένειν Hs 9, 11, 3. ἐξ αὐτῶν λέγεσθαι *be called one of them* IRo 9: 2. Abs. (Gen 2: 25) 1 Pt 3: 16 ᴾ⁷²; 4: 16; IRo 1: 6; IEph 11: 1 (perh. *be reverent*).
  2. *be put to shame, disgraced* i.e. (as LXX for בּוֹשׁ) be disappointed in a hope (opp. παρρησία) Phil 1: 20; 2 Cor 10: 8. ἀπό τινος (Is 1: 29; Jer 12: 13; cf. Sir 41: 17) *before someone* 1 J 2: 28. M-M.*

αἰτέω imper. αἴτει IPol 2: 2, mid. αἰτοῦ IPol 1: 3; fut. αἰτήσω; 1 aor. ᾔτησα, pf. ᾔτηκα 1 J 5: 15; impf. mid. ᾐτούμην; 1 aor. ᾐτησάμην, imper. αἴτησαι; fut. αἰτήσομαι (Hom.+; inscr., pap., LXX, Philo; Jos., Ant. 15, 197 al.; Test. 12 Patr.) *ask, ask for, demand* (without any real distinction betw. act. and mid. The distinc. betw. act. ['ask' outright] and mid. ['ask' as a loan] found by ancient grammarians has only very limited validity for our lit. [Bl-D. §316, 2; Mlt. 160f]; cf. Js 4: 2f, where they seem to be used interchangeably) w. acc. of the person or thing asked for (Lucian, Dial. Mer. 7, 2 αἰ. τὸ δίδραχμον) ἰχθύν Mt 7: 10; τὸ σῶμα τοῦ Ἰησοῦ 27: 58 (Appian, Syr. 63 §335 αἰτήσας τὸ σῶμα, i.e., for burial); Mk 15: 43; Lk 23: 52. πινακίδιον Lk 1: 63. εἰρήνην Ac 12: 20. φῶτα 16: 29. σημεῖα 1 Cor 1: 22. τὸν Βαραββᾶν Mt 27: 20 (Appian, Bell. Civ. 4, 18 §71 and 72; Synes., Provid. 2, 3 p. 121C Ὄσιριν ᾔτουν=they asked for O.). βασιλέα (Jos., Ant. 6, 88) Ac 13: 21. Gener. τί Mk 6: 24; 10: 38; Mt 20: 22. ὅ 1 J 3: 22. πράγματος οὗ ἐὰν αἰτήσωνται (w. attraction of the relative) *for which they wish to ask* Mt 18: 19, cf. Eph 3: 20 (s. Judg 8: 26). W. acc. of the thing and indication of the purpose αἰ. τι πρός τι: αἰ. τὸ σῶμα τοῦ κυρίου πρὸς ταφήν GP 2: 3; τινί τι αἰ. *pray for someth. for someone* IRo 3: 2. W. acc. of the pers. who is asked Mt 5: 42; 6: 8; 7: 11; Lk 6: 30; 11: 13; J 4: 10; Ac 13: 28. W.

double acc. *ask someone for someth.* (Hom.+; Diod. S. 14, 108, 1; Eunap., Vi. Soph. p. 31 αἰ. τοὺς θεούς τι; PFay. 109, 12; PGM 4, 777; Josh 14: 12; 1 Esdr 6: 11; Jos., Ant. 12, 24) Mk 6: 22f (Diog. L. 6, 38 αἴτησόν με ὃ θέλεις [Alex. to Diogenes]; Aesop. Fab. 287b H. αὐτῇ δοῦναι, ὃ ἂν αἰτήσῃ); 10: 35; J 11: 22; 15: 16; 16: 23; Mt 7: 9; Lk 11: 11; cf. vs. 12. αἰ. τινὰ λόγον *demand an accounting fr. someone, call someone to account* (Pla., Pol. 285E; cf. BGU 747, 21) 1 Pt 3: 15. τὶ ἀπό τινος *request someth. fr. someone* (Plut., Galb. 20, 6) Mt 20: 20; 1 J 5: 15 (both w. παρά as v.l.); cf. Lk 12: 20 𝔓⁷⁵. τὶ παρά τινος (Appian, Bell. Civ. 3, 7 §23; Apollon. Paradox. 5; Paradoxogr. Vat. 43 αἰτεῖται παρὰ τῶν θεῶν οὐδέν; PFay. 121, 12ff; PGM 12, 277; oft. LXX; Jos., Ant. 13, 63) *alms* Ac 3: 2. Abs. αἴτησαι παρ' ἐμοῦ *ask me* Ac 13: 33 D; 1 Cl 36: 4 (both Ps 2: 8); cf. Hm 9: 1 (rdg. uncertain), 2, 4; J 4: 9; Ac 9: 2; Js 1: 5. αἰ. χάριν *ask a favor* B 21: 7. αἰτούμενοι χάριν κατ' αὐτοῦ *they requested a favor against him* i.e., one directed against him (Paul) Ac 25: 3. αἰτούμενοι κατ' αὐτοῦ καταδίκην *asking for his conviction* vs. 15; αἰ. περί τινος *pray for someone* IRo 8: 3. W. the manner of asking more exactly described: κακῶς Js 4: 3b; ἐν τῇ προσευχῇ Mt 21: 22. Also δεήσεσιν αἰ. τὸν θεόν *beseech God w. supplications* Pol 7: 2 (cf. Dit., Syll.³ 1168, 11); in the same sense ὅσα προσεύχεσθε κ. αἰτεῖσθε *whatever you ask in prayer* Mk 11: 24; ἐν πίστει Js 1: 6. ἐν τῷ ὀνόματί μου J 14: 13f; 15: 16; 16: 24, 26. τὶ κατὰ τὸ θέλημα αὐτοῦ *someth. in accord w. his will* 1 J 5: 14. Elliptically: αἰτεῖσθαι καθὼς ἐποίει αὐτοῖς *ask (to do) as he was accustomed to do for them* Mk 15: 8. Foll. by acc. and inf. (Dit., Syll.³ 1168, 11; 3 Km 19: 4) αὐτὸν σταυρωθῆναι Lk 23: 23; cf. Ac 3: 14. W. inf. (Aristoph., Plut. 240; X., An. 2, 3, 18; Appian, Liby. 82, §386) πεῖν αἰτεῖς J 4: 9 (Jos., Ant. 18, 192). ᾐτήσατο εὑρεῖν σκήνωμα *he asked to be permitted to find an abode* Ac 7: 46. αἰ. θεοῦ ἐπιτυχεῖν *ask to reach the presence of God* ITr 12: 2; cf. IRo 1: 1. Neg. αἰτοῦμαι μὴ ἐγκακεῖν Eph 3: 13. W. ἵνα foll. (w. προσεύχεσθαι) Col 1: 9 (cf. Ps.-Apollod. 1, 106). Abs. (Arrian, Anab. 2, 14, 8 αἴτει καὶ λάμβανε) Mt 7: 7f; Lk 11: 9f; J 16: 24; Js 4: 3; 1 J 5: 16. Mid. Mk 6: 25. M-M. B. 1270f.

αἴτημα, τος, τό *request* (so Pla.+; POxy. 1273, 28; LXX; Philo, Spec. Leg. 1, 43; Jos., Ant. 8, 24; if rightly restored, Dit., Syll.³ 888, 62) Hm 9: 4. τὰ αἰ. γνωριζέσθω πρὸς τὸν θεόν *let your requests be made known to God* Phil 4: 6. αἰτεῖσθαι τὸ αἰ. (Judg 8: 24 B; 1 Km 1: 27) *make a request* Hm 9: 7, 8. τὸ αἴτημα γενέσθαι *their demand should be granted* Lk 23: 24; ἔχειν τὰ αἰ. *obtain the requests* 1 J 5: 15; λαμβάνεσθαι τὰ αἰ. *receive what one requests* Hs 4: 6; cf. m 9: 5, 7. τὸ αἰ. τῆς ψυχῆς σου πληροφορήσει *he will fulfill the petition of your soul* Hm 9: 2 (πληροφορεῖν=πληροῦν, Ps 19: 5). M-M.*

αἴτησις, εως, ἡ *request* (Hdt.+; Aristaen., Ep. 2, 7 p. 162: τὴν αἴτησιν ἐπλήρου; inscr., pap., LXX, Philo; Jos., Ant. 10, 27; 17, 232) πληρῶσαι τὴν αἰ. ITr 13: 3; cf. IPol 7: 1 v.l.*

αἰτία, ας, ἡ (Pind.+; inscr., pap., LXX, Philo, Joseph.).
1. *cause, reason* Dg 5: 17; gov. by διά: διὰ ταύτην τὴν αἰτίαν *for this reason* (Iambl., Vi. Pyth. 10, 52; 2 Macc 12: 40; Jos., Ant. 3, 279; Dit., Syll.³ 700, 15; 826G, 21; Inscr. gr. 456, 14 διὰ ταύτας τὰς αἰτίας) Ac 28: 20; cf. 10: 21; 1 Cl 44: 2; 2 Cl 10: 3; Hs 9, 8, 3. οὐ δι' ἄλλην τινὰ αἰ.... ἀλλά *for no other reason ... than* 1 Cl 51: 5. δι' ἣν αἰτίαν (Dit., Syll.³ 630, 6f; PLeid. 16, 33, 15; 1 Esdr 2: 17; Wsd 18: 18; oft. 2 Macc) in indir. quest. *why* Lk 8: 47; Ac

22: 24; at beg. of a sentence as causal conj. (Bl-D. §456, 4) *for this reason, therefore* (Diod. S. 4, 80, 4; 13, 11, 2; 2 Macc 4: 28; Philo, Op. M. 100; Jos., Ant. 17, 202) 2 Ti 1: 6, 12; Tit 1: 13; Hb 2: 11. κατὰ πᾶσαν αἰτίαν *for any and every cause* (Appian, Bell. Civ. 3, 25 §94 κατὰ μηδεμίαν αἰτίαν; BGU 136, 26 [II AD] κατὰ ταύτην τ. αἰτίαν; Jos., Ant. 4, 249; 253) Mt 19: 3.—*Relationship, case* (Latinism =causa Bl-D. §5, 3b; cf. PRyl. 63, 2 τίς δὲ ἡ αἰτία τούτων τῶν εἰδώλων;) εἰ οὕτως ἐστὶν ἡ αἰτία τοῦ ἀνθρώπου μετὰ τῆς γυναικός *if the relationship of a man with his wife is like this* Mt 19: 10.
2. *legal t.t.* (Diod. S. 20, 62, 5 ἐν αἰτίαις ἔχειν τινά= bring charges against someone)—a. *charge, ground for complaint* Ac 23: 28. αἰ. εὑρίσκειν (ἔν τινι) J 18: 38; 19: 4, 6. αἰτία θανάτου=Lat. causa capitalis, *reason for capital punishment* Ac 13: 28; 28: 18. The charge specified Mt 27: 37; Mk 15: 26.
b. *accusation* (Athen. 12 p. 542E αἰτίαν φέρειν *bring an accusation* Ac 25: 18 (Jos., Ant. 20, 47); t.r. has αἰ. ἐπιφέρειν (q.v. 3). αἰ. κατ' αὐτοῦ αἰ. *the (formal) charges against him* vs. 27. M-M. B. 1183; 1244.*

αἰτίαμα, τος, τό (s. αἰτίωμα) Ac 25: 7 t.r.*

αἰτιάομαι (Hom.+; Dit., Or. 484, 30; PTebt. 35, 19; Philo, Decal. 87; Jos., Ant. 14, 44; LXX) *blame, accuse* w. acc. of the pers. (Hom.+; Dit., Syll.³ 1236, 5f; PLeipz. 37, 7; Jos., Ant. 15, 31) σεαυτόν Hm 9: 8. τὸν κύριον Hs 6, 3, 5 (cf. Libanius, Or. 6 p. 354, 6 F. αἰτιᾶται τὴν θεόν; Pr 19: 3).—*To charge* w. acc. and inf. foll. Ro 3: 9 v.l. M-M.*

αἰτίζω 1 aor. pass. ᾐτίσθην (Hom.+) *beg* μή τι αἰτισθῶσιν ὑπ' αὐτῶν *that they might be begged for someth. by them* Hs 9, 20, 2.*

αἴτιος, ία, ον (Hom.+; inscr., pap., LXX, Philo, Joseph.) *responsible, guilty,* in our lit. only subst.
1. ὁ αἴ. *the cause, source* αἴ. σωτηρίας Hb 5: 9 (class.; Diod. S. 4, 82 αἴ. ἐγένετο τῆς σωτηρίας; Dit., Syll.³ 1109, 80; Philo, Agr. 96, Spec. Leg. 1, 252 θεὸν τ. σωτηρίας αἴτιον al.; Jos., Ant. 14, 136; Bel 42; 2 Macc 4: 47; 13: 4; Ep. Arist. 205).
2. neut. τὸ αἴτ.=αἰτία 2a *guilt, complaint* αἴ. εὑρίσκειν ἔν τινι Lk 23: 4, 14. αἴ. θανάτου *reason for capital punishment* vs. 22. Also simply *cause* (class.; PHib. 73, 18 [243/2 BC]; BGU 1121, 27; 29; Philo; Jos., Ant. 7, 75; 12, 84) μηδενὸς αἰ. ὑπάρχοντος Ac 19: 40. M-M.*

αἰτίωμα, τος, τό (PFay. 111, 8[95 AD]; class. [Aeschyl., Thu.+] αἰτίαμα W-S. §5, 21d; Mlt.-H. 354) *charge, complaint* αἰ. καταφέρειν *bring charges* Ac 25: 7. M-M.*

αἰφνίδιος, ον (Aeschyl., Thu.+; inscr., PFay. 123, 21; Wsd 17: 14; 2 Macc 14: 17; 3 Macc 3: 24; Jos., Ant. 3, 207, Vi. 253) *sudden* Lk 21: 34; 1 Th 5: 3. αἰ. συμφοραί 1 Cl 1: 1 (cf. Dit., Syll.³ 730, 20). S. also εὐθέως. M-M.*

αἰχμαλωσία, ας, ἡ (Polyb. 5, 102, 5; Diod. S., Plut., Vett. Val.; Inscr. gr. 965, 6; LXX, Joseph., Test. 12 Patr.).
1. *captivity,* mostly in war (Am 1: 15; Jos., Ant. 10, 68) 2 Cl 6: 8. W. πόλεμος 1 Cl 3: 2. εἴ τις εἰς αἰ. (sc. ἀπάγει, as t.r. does), εἰς αἰ. ὑπάγει *whoever leads (others) into capt. is led capt. himself* Rv 13: 10 (cf. Jer 15: 2).
2. abstr. for concr. *prisoners of war* (Diod. S. 17, 70; Num 31: 12; Jdth 2: 9; 1 Esdr 6: 5, 8; 1 Macc 9: 70, 72; 2 Macc 8: 10; Jos., Ant. 11, 1) Hb 7: 1 v.l.; αἰχμαλωτεύειν αἰ. Eph 4: 8 (Ps 67: 19).*

αἰχμαλωτεύω 1 aor. ᾐχμαλώτευσα (Ps.-Callisth. p. 50, 16; 69, 3; Phryn. p. 442 Lob.; LXX; Ep. Arist. 23; Test. Zeb. 9: 6; Suidas II p. 187, 387; Etym. Gud. 59, 10) *capture, take captive* in war, fig. 2 Ti 3: 6 t.r.; αἰχμαλω-σίαν αἰ. Eph 4: 8 (Ps 67: 19).*

αἰχμαλωτίζω, 1 aor. pass. ἠχμαλωτίσθην; 1 fut. pass. αἰχμαλωτισθήσομαι (since Diod. S. 14, 37; Plut., Mor. 233c; Epict. 1, 28, 26; Ps.-Callisth. 2, 4, 3; 2, 6, 5 [pass.]; 3, 4, 6 [pass.]; Dit., Syll.³ 763, 7; 10 [64 BC]; LXX; Ep. Arist. 12; Test. 12 Patr.; Jos., Bell. 1, 433 [mid.], Ant. 10, 153 [pass.]; cf. Nägeli 29) *capture,* in war.

1. lit. εἰς τὰ ἔθνη πάντα *be scattered as captives among all nations* Lk 21: 24 (αἰ. εἰς as Tob 1: 10; 1 Macc 10: 33).

2. fig. (so Dio Chrys. 15[32], 90 αἰχμάλωτος and αἰχ-μαλωσία) *make captive* of the ἕτερος νόμος: αἰχμαλω-τίζοντά με ἐν τῷ νόμῳ τῆς ἁμαρτίας *makes me a prisoner to the law of sin* Ro 7: 23. αἰχμαλωτίζοντες πᾶν νόημα εἰς τὴν ὑπακοὴν τοῦ Χριστοῦ *we take every thought captive and make it obey Christ* 2 Cor 10: 5. Of the devil μὴ αἰχμαλωτίσῃ ὑμᾶς ἐκ τοῦ προκειμένου ζῆν *lest he lead you captive from the life which lies before you* IEph 17: 1.

3. the figure may fade so that αἰ. means *carry away= mislead, deceive* (Jdth 16: 9 αἰ. ψυχήν; Irenaeus I Praef. 1) αἰ. γυναικάρια 2 Ti 3: 6; τινά τινι αἰ. *mislead someone w. someth.* IPhld 2: 2 (w. dat., and acc. to be supplied Test. Reub. 5: 3.).*

αἰχμαλωτισμός, οῦ, ὁ (Simplicius in Epict. p. 35, 31; schol. on Aristoph., Nub. 186) *captivity* (w. θάνατος) αἰ. ἑαυτῷ ἐπισπᾶσθαι *bring captivity on oneself* Hv 1, 1, 8.*

αἰχμάλωτος, ώτου, ὁ *captive* (Aeschyl.+; inscr.; PLille 3, 66; PPetr. II 29e, 1; LXX; Jos., Bell. 4, 116, Ant. 10, 180, Vi. 354; Test. 12 Patr.) with beggars, blind men, and oppressed as examples of misery Lk 4: 18; B 14: 9 (both Is 61: 1). M-M. B. 1414.*

αἰών, ῶνος, ὁ (Hom.+; Herm. Wr.; inscr., pap., LXX, En., Philo, Joseph., Test. 12 Patr., Sib. Or.) *time, age.*

1. *very long time, eternity*—a. of time gone by, *the past, earliest times,* then *eternity* οἱ ἅγιοι ἀπ' αἰῶνος προ-φῆται *the holy prophets fr. ages long past* (cf. Hes., Theog. 609; Περὶ ὕψους 34, 4 τοὺς ἀπ' αἰ. ῥήτορας; Cass. Dio 63, 20 τῶν ἀπὸ τοῦ αἰ. Ῥωμαίων; Inschr. v. Magn. 180, 4; Dit., Syll.³ index; Gen 6: 4; Tob 4: 12; Sir 14: 17; 51: 8; En. 14, 1; 99, 14; Jos., Bell. 1, 12) Lk 1: 70; Ac 3: 21; *to make known from of old* Ac 15: 18; πρὸ παντὸς τ. αἰ. *before time began* Jd 25a (for the combination with πᾶς cf. Sallust. c. 20 p. 36, 5 τὸν πάντα αἰῶνα=through all eternity); pl. πρὸ τῶν αἰ. 1 Cor 2: 7 (cf. Ps 54: 20 θεὸς ὁ ὑπάρχων πρὸ τῶν αἰ. [PGM 4, 3067 ἀπὸ τ. ἱερῶν αἰώνων]); ἐξ αἰ. *since the beginning* D 16: 4 (Diod. S. 1, 6 al.; Sext. Emp., Math. 9, 62; Dit., Or. 669, 61; Philo, Somn. 1, 19; Jos., Bell. 5, 442; Sir 1: 4; Sib. Or., fgm. 1, 16 of God μόνος εἰς αἰῶνα κ. ἐξ αἰῶνος). W. neg. foll. ἐκ τοῦ αἰῶνος οὐκ ἠκούσθη *never has it been heard* J 9: 32.

b. of time to come which, if it has no end, is also known as *eternity* (so commonly in Gk. lit. Pla.+); εἰς τὸν αἰῶνα (since Isocr. 10, 62; Dit., Syll.³ 814, 50 and Or., index VIII; POxy. 41; also Diod. S. 1, 56, 1 εἰς τ. αἰ.=εἰς ἅπαντα τ. χρόνον; 4, 1, 4; PGM 8, 33; 4, 1051 [εἰς αἰ.]; LXX; En. 12, 6; 102, 3; Jos., Ant. 7, 356 [εἰς αἰ.]) *to eternity, eternally, in perpetuity:* live J 6: 51, 58; B 6: 3; remain J 8: 35ab; 12: 34; 1 Pt 1: 23 t.r., 25 (Is 40: 8); 1 J 2: 17; 2 J 2; be with someone J 14: 16. W. neg.=*never, not at all, never again* (Ps 124: 1; Ezk 27: 36 al.) Mt 21: 19; Mk 3: 29; 11: 14; 1 Cor 8: 13. ἕως αἰῶνος (LXX) 1 Cl 10: 4 (Gen 13: 15); Hv 2, 3, 3; s 9, 24, 4. εἰς τὸν αἰ. τοῦ αἰῶνος (Ps 44: 18; 82: 18 al.) Hb 1: 8 (Ps 44: 7). ἕως αἰῶνος Lk 1: 55 v.l.—The pl.

is also used (Emped., fgm. 129, 6 αἰῶνες=generations; Theocr. 16, 43 μακροὺς αἰῶνας=long periods of time; Sext. Emp., Phys. 1, 62 εἰς αἰῶνας διαμένει; Sib. Or. 3, 767.—Bl-D. §141, 1), esp. in doxologies: εἰς τοὺς αἰῶνας (Ps 60: 5; 76: 8) Mt 6: 13 v.l.; Lk 1: 33 (cf. Wsd 3: 8); Hb 13: 8; εἰς πάντας τοὺς αἰ. (Tob 13: 4; Da 3: 52b; En. 9, 4; Sib. Or. 3, 50) Jd 25b. εὐλογητὸς εἰς τοὺς αἰῶνας *to all eternity* (cf. Ps 88: 53) Ro 1: 25; 9: 5; 2 Cor 11: 31; αὐτῷ ἡ δόξα εἰς τοὺς αἰ. Ro 11: 36; more fully εἰς τοὺς αἰ. τῶν αἰώνων (Ps 83: 5; PGM 4, 1038; 22b, 15) *for evermore* in doxologies 16: 27; Gal 1: 5; Phil 4: 20; 1 Ti 1: 17; 2 Ti 4: 18; Hb 13: 21; 1 Pt 4: 11; 5: 11; 1 Cl 20: 12; 32: 4; 38: 4; 43: 6; Rv 1: 6; 5: 13; 7: 12 al. εἰς πάσας τὰς γενεὰς τοῦ αἰῶνος τῶν αἰ. Eph 3: 21 (cf. Tob 1: 4; 13: 12; En. 103, 4; 104, 5). Of God ὁ ζῶν εἰς τοὺς αἰ. (cf. Tob 13: 2; Sir 18: 1; Da 6: 27 Theod.) Rv 4: 9f; 10: 6; 15: 7.—κατὰ πρόθεσιν τῶν αἰώνων *according to the eternal purpose* Eph 3: 11. All-inclusive ἀπὸ αἰώνων καὶ εἰς τ. αἰῶνας *from (past) eternity to (future) eternity* B 18: 2 (cf. Ps 40: 14 and Ps.-Aristot., De Mundo 7 p. 401a, 16 ἐξ αἰῶνος ἀτέρμονος εἰς ἕτερον αἰῶνα; M. Ant. 9, 28, 1 ἐξ αἰῶνος εἰς αἰῶνα; Sib. Or., fgm. 1, 16 of God μόνος εἰς αἰῶνα κ. ἐξ αἰῶνος).

2. *a segment of time, age*—a. ὁ αἰὼν οὗτος (הָעוֹלָם הַזֶּה) *the present age* (nearing its end) (cf. Bousset, Rel. 243ff; Dalman, Worte 120ff; Schürer II⁴ 636ff; NMessel, D. Einheitlichkeit d. jüd. Eschatol. '15, 44-60) contrasted w. the age to come (Philo and Joseph. do not have the two aeons) Mt 12: 32. A time of sin and misery Hv 1, 1, 8; s 3: 1ff; ending of Mk in the Freer ms. 2; ἡ μέριμνα τοῦ αἰ. (sc. τούτου) *the cares of the present age* Mt 13: 22; cf. Mk 4: 19. πλοῦτος *earthly riches* Hv 3, 6, 5. ματαιώματα *vain, futile things* Hm 9: 4; s 5, 3, 6. πραγματεῖαι m 10, 1, 4. ἐπιθυμία m 11: 8; s 6, 2, 3; 7: 2; 8, 11, 3. πονηρία s 6, 1, 4. ἀπάται s 6, 3, 3. οἱ υἱοὶ τοῦ αἰ. τούτου *the sons of this age, the people of the world* (opp. sons of light, enlightened ones) Lk 16: 8; cf. 20: 34.—The earthly kingdoms βασιλεῖαι τοῦ αἰ. τούτου IRo 6: 1. συσχηματίζεσθαι τῷ αἰ. τούτῳ *be conformed to this world* Ro 12: 2. As well as everything non-Christian, it includes the striving after worldly wisdom: συζητητὴς τοῦ αἰ. τούτου *searcher after the wisdom of this world* 1 Cor 1: 20. σοφία τοῦ αἰ. τούτου 2: 6. ἐν τῷ αἰ. τούτῳ 3: 18 prob. belongs to what follows: *he must become a fool in the* (estimation of) *this age.* The ruler of this age is the devil: ὁ θεὸς τοῦ αἰ. τούτου 2 Cor 4: 4 (θεὸς 5). ἄρχων τοῦ αἰ. τούτου IEph 17: 1; 19: 1; IMg 1: 3; ITr 4: 2; IRo 7: 1; IPhld 6: 2; his subordinate spirits are the ἄρχοντες τοῦ αἰ. τούτου 1 Cor 2: 6, 8 (ἄρχων 3).—Also ὁ νῦν αἰών: πλούσιοι ἐν τῷ νῦν αἰ. 1 Ti 6: 17; ἀγαπᾶν τὸν νῦν αἰ. 2 Ti 4: 10; Pol 9: 2. Cf. Tit 2: 12. Or ὁ αἰ. ὁ ἐνεστὼς *the present age* Gal 1: 4 (cf. Dit., Syll.³ 797, 9 [37 AD] αἰῶνος νῦν ἐνεστῶτος). The end of this period (cf. Sib. Or. 3, 756 μέχρι τέρματος αἰῶνος) συντέλεια (τοῦ) αἰ. Mt 13: 39f, 49; 24: 3; 28: 20; συντέλεια τῶν αἰ. Hb 9: 26.

b. ὁ αἰὼν μέλλων (הָעוֹלָם הַבָּא) *the age to come,* the Messianic period (on the expr. cf. Demosth. 18, 199; Hippocr., Ep. 10, 6 ὁ μ. αἰ.=the future, all future time; Ael. Aristid. 46, p. 310 D.: ἡ τοῦ παρελθόντος χρόνου μνεία κ. ὁ τοῦ μέλλοντος αἰῶνος λόγος; Jos., Ant. 18, 287), in 2 Cl 6: 3, cf. Hs 4: 2ff, opposed to the αἰὼν οὗτος both in time and quality, cf. Mt 12: 32; Eph 1: 21; δυνάμεις μέλλοντος αἰ. Hb 6: 5. Also αἰ. ἐκεῖνος: τοῦ αἰ. ἐκείνου τυχεῖν *take part in the age to come* Lk 20: 35. ὁ αἰ. ὁ ἐρχόμενος Mk 10: 30; Lk 18: 30; Hs 4: 8. ὁ αἰ. ὁ ἐπερχόμενος Hv 4, 3, 5; pl. ἐν τοῖς αἰῶσιν τοῖς ἐπερχο-μένοις *in the ages to come* Eph 2: 7. As a holy age ὁ ἅγιος αἰ. (opp. οὗτος ὁ κόσμος) B 10: 11 and as a time of perfection αἰ. ἀλύπητος *an age free from sorrow* 2 Cl 19: 4, while the present αἰών is an 'aeon of pain' (Slav. Enoch 65, 8).—The plurals 1 Cor 10: 11 have been explained by some as referring to both ages, i.e., the end-point of the first and beginning of the second; this view urges that the earliest Christians believed that the two ages came together during their own lifetimes: *we, upon whom the ends of the ages have come* (JWeiss. A Greek would not refer to the beginning as τέλος. The Gordian knot has οὔτε τέλος οὔτε ἀρχή: Arrian, Anab. 2, 3, 7). But since τὰ τέλη can also mean 'end' in the singular (Ael. Aristid. 44, 17 K.=17 p. 406 D.: σώματος ἀρχαὶ κ. τέλη='beginning and end': 39 p. 737 D.: τὰ τέλη . . . δράματος; Longus 1, 23, 1 ms. ἧρος τέλη; Vi. Thu. II 2 τέλη τοῦ πολέμου; Aëtius, Eye Diseases p. 120, 25 Hirschb. after Galen: τὰ τέλη τ. λόγου=the close of the section; Philo, Virt. 182) and, on the other hand, the pl. αἰῶνες is often purely formal (s. above 1a and b, 2a at end) τὰ τέλη τῶν αἰ. can perh. be regarded as equal to τέλος αἰώνων (Sib. Or. 8, 311)=*the end of the age(s)*. Cf. Test. Levi 14: 1 ἐπὶ τὰ τέλη τῶν αἰώνων.—For the essential equivalence of sing. and pl. cf. Maximus Tyr. 14, 8b τὰ τῆς κολακείας τέλη beside τέλος τῆς σπουδῆς. Cf. also τέλος 3.

3. *the world* as a spatial concept (αἰ. in sg. and pl. [Bl-D. §141, 1]: Hippocr., Ep. 17, 34; Diod. S. 1, 1, 3 God rules ἅπαντα τὸν αἰῶνα; Ael. Aristid. 20, 13 K.=21 p. 434 D.: ἐκ τοῦ παντὸς αἰῶνος; Maximus Tyr. 11, 5e; Isisaretal. from Cyrene 4 [103 AD] in WPeek, D. Isishymnus etc. '30, 129; Ps 65: 7; Ex 15: 18 [cf. Philo, Plant. 47; 51]; Wsd 13: 9; 14: 16: 18: 4) AP 14. Created by God through the Son Hb 1: 2; through God's word 11: 3. Hence God is βασιλεὺς τῶν αἰ. 1 Ti 1: 17; 1Cl 61: 2 (cf. PGM 12, 247 αἰώνων βασιλεῦ; Tob 13: 7, 11, cf. Act. Phil. 2; 11 Bonnet); πατὴρ τῶν αἰ. 35: 3 (cf. Justin, Apol. I 41, 2; Act. Phil. 144, p. 84, 9); θεὸς τῶν αἰ. 55: 6 (cf. Sir 36: 17; PGM 4, 1163; ThSchermann, Griech. Zauber-pap. 23; Act. Jo. 82). But it is poss. that many of these belong under 4.

4. *the Aeon as a person* (Rtzst., Erlösungsmyst. 268 index under Aion, Taufe 391 index; Epict. 2, 5, 13 οὐ γάρ εἰμι αἰών, ἀλλ᾽ ἄνθρωπος=I am not a being that lasts forever, but a man [and therefore I know that whatever is must pass away]; Mesomedes 1, 17; Simplicius in Epict. p. 81, 15 οἱ αἰῶνες beside the μήτηρ τῆς ζωῆς and the δημιουργός; En. 9, 4 κύριος τ. κυρίων καὶ θεὸς τ. θεῶν κ. βασιλεὺς τ. αἰώνων; PGM 4, 520; 1169; 2198; 2314; 3169; 5, 468; Act. Phil. 132, p. 63, 4f; Kephalaia I p. 24, 6; 45, 7) ὁ αἰ. τοῦ κόσμου τούτου Eph 2: 2. The secret hidden from the Aeons Col 1: 26; Eph 3: 9 (Rtzst., Erlösungsmyst. 235f); IEph 19: 2 (Rtzst., op. cit. 86, 3); cf. 8: 1 (Rtzst. 236, 2). Various other meanings are poss. in these passages.—CLackeit, Aion I, Diss. Königsbg. '16; EDBurton, ICC Gal '21, 426-32; HJunker, Iran. Quellen d. hellenist. Aionvorstellung: Vortr. d. Bibl. Warburg I '23, 125ff; ENorden, D. Geburt des Kindes '24; JKaerst, Gesch. d. Hellenismus II² '26, 239-42; MZepf, D. Gott Αιων in d. hellenist. Theologie: ARW 25, '27, 225-44; HSasse TW I 197-208; ADNock, HTR 27, '34, 78-99= Essays on Religion etc. I, '72, 377-96; RLöwe, Kosmos u. Aion '35; ECEOwen, αἰών and αἰώνιος: JTS 37, '36, 265-83; 390-404; OCullmann, Christus u. d. Zeit, '46, 38-42; Eng. tr. '50, 44-9; GStadtmüller, Saeculum, 2, '51, 315-20; EJenni, Das Wort 'ōlām im AT: ZAW 64, '52, 197-248; 65, '53, 1-35; KDeichgräber, RGG I³ 193-95. M-M. B. 13.

αἰώνιος (ια Pla., Tim. 38B; Jer 39: 40; Ezk 37: 26; 2 Th 2: 16; Hb 9: 12; as v.l. Ac 13: 48; 2 Pt 1: 11; Bl-D. §59, 2; Mlt.-H. 157), ον *eternal* (since Hyperid. 6, 27; Pla.; inscr.;

pap., LXX; Ps.-Phoc. 112; Test. 12 Patr.; standing epithet for princely, esp. imperial power: Dit., Or. Index VIII; BGU 176; 303; 309; Sb 7517, 5 [211/2 AD] κύριος αἰ.; al. in pap.; Jos., Ant. 7, 352).

1. *without beginning* χρόνοις αἰ. *long ages ago* Ro 16: 25; πρὸ χρόνων αἰ. *before time began* 2 Ti 1: 9; Tit 1: 2 (on χρόνος αἰ. cf. Dit., Or. 248, 54; 383, 10).

2. *without beginning or end; of God* (Ps.-Pla., Tim. Locr. 96c θεὸν τ. αἰώνιον; Inscr. in the Brit. Mus. 894 al. κ. ἀθάνατος; Gen 21: 33; Is 26: 4; 40: 28; Bar 4: 8 al.; Philo, Plant. 8; 74; Sib. Or., fgm. 3, 17 and 4; PGM 1, 309; 13, 280) Ro 16: 26; of the Holy Spirit in Christ Hb 9: 14. θρόνος αἰ. 1 Cl 65: 2 (cf. 1 Macc 2: 57).

3. *without end* (Diod. S. 1, 1, 5; 5, 73, 1; 15, 66, 1 δόξα αἰ. everlasting fame; in Diod. S. 1, 93, 1 the Egyptian dead are said to have passed to their αἰ. οἴκησις; Arrian, Peripl. 1, 4 ἐς αἰώνην μνήμην αἰ.; Jos., Bell. 4, 461 αἰ. χάρις= a gracious gift for all future time; Dit., Or. 383, 10 [I BC] εἰς χρόνον αἰ.; ECEOwen, οἶκος αἰ.: JTS 38, '37, 248-50) of the next life σκηναὶ αἰ. Lk 16: 9 (cf. En. 39, 5). οἰκία, contrasted w. the οἰκία ἐπίγειος, of the glorified body 2 Cor 5: 1. διαθήκη (Gen 9: 16; 17: 7; Lev 24: 8; 2 Km 23: 5 al.) Hb 13: 20. εὐαγγέλιον Rv 14: 6; κράτος in a doxolog. formula (=εἰς τοὺς αἰῶνας) 1 Ti 6: 16. παράκλησις 2 Th 2: 16. λύτρωσις Hb 9: 12. κληρονομία (Esth 4: 17 m) vs. 15; αἰ. ἀπέχειν τινά (opp. πρὸς ὥραν) *keep someone forever* Phlm 15 (cf. Job 40: 28). Very often of God's judgment (Diod. S. 4, 63, 4 διὰ τὴν ἀσέβειαν ἐν ἄδου διατελεῖν τιμωρίας αἰωνίου τυγχάνοντα; similarly 4, 69, 5; Jer 23: 40; Da 12: 2; Ps 76: 6; 4 Macc 9: 9; 13: 15) κόλασις αἰ. (Test. Reub. 5: 5) Mt 25: 46; 2 Cl 6: 7; κρίμα αἰ. Hb 6: 2; θάνατος B 20: 1. ὄλεθρον (4 Macc 10: 15) 2 Th 1: 9. πῦρ (4 Macc 12: 12.—Sib. Or. 8, 401 φῶς αἰ.) Mt 18: 8; 25: 41; Jd 7; Dg 10: 7 (1QS 2, 8). ἁμάρτημα Mk 3: 29 (v.l. κρίσεως and ἁμαρτίας). On the other hand of *eternal life* (Maximus Tyr. 6, 1d θεοῦ ζωὴ αἰ.; Diod. S. 8, 15, 3 life μετὰ τὸν θάνατον lasts εἰς ἅπαντα αἰῶνα; Da 12: 2; 4 Macc 15: 3; PsSol 3, 12; Philo, Fuga 78; Jos., Bell. 1, 650; Sib. Or. 2, 336) in the Kingdom of God: ζωὴ αἰ. Mt 19: 16, 29; 25: 46; Mk 10: 17, 30; Lk 10: 25; 18: 18, 30; Ac 13: 46, 48; Ro 2: 7; 5: 21 al.; J 3: 15f, 36; 4: 14, 36 al.; 1 J 1: 2; 2: 25 al.—D 10: 3; 2 Cl 5: 5; 8: 4, 6; IEph 18: 1; Hv 2, 3, 2; 3, 8, 4 al. Also βασιλεία αἰ. 2 Pt 1: 11 (cf. Da 4: 3; 7: 27; Philo, Somn. 2, 285; Dit., Or. 569, 24 ὑπὲρ τῆς αἰωνίου καὶ ἀφθάρτου βασιλείας ὑμῶν; Dssm. B 279f, BS 363). Of the glory in the next life δόξα αἰ. 2 Ti 2: 10 (cf. Wsd 10: 14; Jos., Ant. 15, 376.—Sib. Or. 8, 410). αἰώνιον βάρος δόξης 2 Cor 4: 17; σωτηρία αἰ. (Is 45: 17; Ps.-Clem., Hom. 1, 19) Hb 5: 9; short ending of Mk. Of heavenly glory in contrast to the transitory world of the senses τὰ μὴ βλεπόμενα αἰώνια 2 Cor 4: 18.—χαρά IPhld inscr.; δοξάζεσθαι αἰωνίῳ ἔργῳ *be glorified by an everlasting deed* IPol 8: 1. DHill, Gk. Words and Hebr. Mngs. '67, 186-201. M-M.

ἀκαθαρσία, ας, ἡ (Hippocr., Pla.+; pap., LXX, Test. 12 Patr.) *impurity, dirt.*

1. lit. *refuse* (BGU 1117, 27 [13 BC]; POxy. 912, 26; 1128, 25) of the contents of graves, causing ceremonial impurity Mt 23: 27 (cf. Num 19: 13).

2. fig., in a moral sense, of men (Epict. 4, 11, 5; 8; Pr 6: 16; 24: 9; Wsd 2: 16; 3 Macc 2: 17; 1 Esdr 1: 40; Ep. Arist. 166; En. 10, 20; Philo, Leg. All. 2, 29) *immorality, viciousness* esp. of sexual sins (Vett. Val. p. 2, 19; En. 10, 11) w. πορνεία 2 Cor 12: 21; Gal 5: 19; Col 3: 5; Eph 5: 3. Opp. ἁγιασμός 1 Th 4: 7; Ro 6: 19. Of unnatural vices: παραδιδόναι εἰς ἀ. *give over to viciousness* Ro 1: 24. δι᾽ ἀκαθαρσίαν *with immoral intent* B 10: 8. εἰς ἐργασίαν

ἀκαθαρσίας πάσης to the practice of every kind of immorality Eph 4: 19. Of impure motive (Demosth. 21, 119; BGU 393, 16 [168 AD]) 1 Th 2: 3 (w. πλάνη and δόλος). ἐν ἀ. τινῶν B 19: 4 is uncertain; prob. in the presence of impure men. M-M.*

ἀκαθάρτης, ητος, ἡ uncleanness τ. πορνείας Rv 17: 4 t.r. (s. ἀκάθαρτος 2).*

ἀκάθαρτος, ον (Soph., Hippocr.+; inscr.; pap., LXX, Ep. Arist., Philo, Joseph., Test. 12 Patr.) impure, unclean.

1. in the cultic sense, that which may not be brought into contact w. the divinity (so mostly LXX, also Jos., C. Ap. 1, 307; Dit., Syll.³ 1042, 3): of foods (w. κοινός) πᾶν κοινὸν καὶ ἀ. anything common or unclean Ac 10: 14, cf. 11: 8; w. μεμισημένος of birds (Lev 11: 4ff; Dt 14: 7ff) Rv 18: 2; (τὸ) ἀ. what is unclean 2 Cor 6: 17 (Is 52: 11).—Esp. of everything connected w. idolatry, which defiles whatever it touches (Am 7: 17; Is 52: 1 ἀπερίτμητος κ. ἀ.; Sib. Or. 5, 264) of pagans ἄνθρωπος κοινὸς ἢ ἀ. Ac 10: 28; τέκνα ἀ. (opp. ἄγια) 1 Cor 7: 14 (on the question of child baptism cf. τέκνον 1aa).

2. as the ceremonial mng. fades, the moral sense becomes predominant (since Pla., Leg. 4, 716E; Is 6: 5; 64: 5; Sir 51: 5; Pr 3: 32 al.; Philo, Deus Imm. 132, Spec. Leg. 3, 209; Jos., Bell. 4, 562) unclean, impure, vicious (cf. ἀκαθαρσία 2) B 10: 8. W. πόρνος (Plut., Oth. 2, 2 ἐν γυναιξὶ πόρναις κ. ἀκαθάρτοις. Cf. Vett. Val. 76, 1), πλεονέκτης and εἰδωλολάτρης Eph 5: 5.—τὰ ἀ. (w. πονηρά) impure things Hv 1, 1, 7. τὰ ἀ. τῆς πορνείας the impurities of vice Rv 17: 4 (ἀ. of vice Test. Jos. 4: 6; on the constr. cf. Bl-D. §136, 1).—Esp. of evil spirits πνεῦμα, πνεύματα ἀ. (cf. Zech 13: 2; Test. Benj. 5: 2; Cat. Cod. Astr. X 179, 19; 181, 5) Mt 10: 1; 12: 43; Mk 1: 23, 26f; 3: 11, 30; 5: 2, 8, 13; 6: 7; 7: 25; 9: 25. Ending of Mk in Freer ms. 3; Lk 4: 36; 6: 18; 8: 29; 9: 42; 11: 24; Ac 5: 16; 8: 7; Rv 16: 13; 18: 2. πνεῦμα δαιμονίου ἀκαθάρτου Lk 4: 33 (cf. PGM 4, 1238). On ἐν πνεύματι ἀ. s. GBjörck, Con. Neot. 7, '42, 1–3. M-M. B. 1081.*

ἀκαιρέομαι impf. ἠκαιρούμην; 1 aor. ἠκαιρέθην (act. Diod. S. 10, 7, 3; pass., Corpus Glossariorum Lat. 2, 137) to have no time, no opportunity abs. ἠκαιρεῖσθε you had no opportunity to show your love to me Phil 4: 10. μικρὸν ἔχω ἀκαιρεθῆναι I am busy for a little while Hs 9, 10, 5 (Bl-D. §307 app.; Mlt.-H. 390).*

ἄκαιρος, ον (Aeschyl.+; Thu. 5, 65, 2; Dit., Syll.³ 1102, 12 [II BC]; Sir 20: 19; 22: 6; Jos., Ant. 12, 6 [after Agatharchides]) untimely, ill-timed. εὔνοια ἄκαιρος an ill-timed kindness (proverbial expr., ἄκαιρος εὔνοι' οὐδὲν ἔχθρας διαφέρει Zenob., Paroem. 1, 50), which becomes burdensome or dangerous IRo 4: 1 (cf. Lghtf. ad loc.).*

ἀκαίρως adv. (Aeschyl.+; BGU 846, 14 [II AD]; Sir 32: 4; Philo, Mos. 2, 206; Jos., Ant. 6, 137) in a play on words εὐκαίρως ἀ. in season, out of season (i.e. whether or not the preaching comes at a convenient time for the hearers) 2 Ti 4: 2. M-M.*

ἀκακία, ας, ἡ innocence, guilelessness (Aristot.+; Diog. L. 4, 19; LXX) 1 Cl 14: 5 (Ps 36: 37); w. ἁπλότης (as Philo, Op. M. 156; 170; Test. Iss. 5: 1) Hv 1, 2, 4; 2, 3, 2; 3, 9, 1. ἐνδύσασθαι ἀκακίαν put on innocence (opp. αἴρειν τ. πονηρίαν) s 9, 29, 3; personif. as a Christian virtue v 3, 8, 5; 7; s 9, 15, 2.*

ἄκακος, ον innocent, guileless (so Aeschyl.+; Polyb., Diod. S., Plut., LXX; Philo, Spec. Leg. 3, 119) 1 Cl 14: 4

(Pr 2: 21); Hs 9, 30, 2. ἄκακον γίνεσθαι m 2: 1. τὰς καρδίας τῶν ἀ. ἐξαπατᾶν deceive the hearts of the unsuspecting Ro 16: 18; (w. μακρόθυμος, ἐλεήμων et al.) D 3: 8; Dg 9: 2; (w. ἁπλοῦς [Diod. S. 13, 76 ἄ. καὶ τὴν ψυχὴν ἁπλοῦς; cf. Philo on ἀκακία], μακάριος) Hs 9, 24, 2, cf. 9, 30, 3; of Christ (w. ὅσιος, ἀμίαντος) Hb 7: 26. M-M.*

ἄκανθα, ης, ἡ thorn-plant (since Od. 5, 328; pap., LXX; Jos., Bell. 5, 51) of such plants in general, esp. the common weed Ononis spinosa, cammock (cf. LFonck, Streifzüge durch d. bibl. Flora '00, 195) in contrast to useful plants (w. τρίβολος, cf. Gen 3: 18; Hos 10: 8) Mt 7: 16; Lk 6: 44 (cf. Jer 12: 13). It is found on cultivated land and is thus harmful to the grain (GDalman, Pj 22, '26, 126ff) Mt 13: 7, 22; Mk 4: 7, 18; Lk 8: 7, 14 (on the interpr. of the ἄκανθαι cf. Philo, Leg. All. 3, 248); B 9: 5 (Jer 4: 3).—στέφανος ἐξ ἀ. crown of thorns Mt 27: 29; J 19: 2 (Fonck 51; 99; FLundgreen, D. Bäume im NT: NKZ 27, '16, 827–42; EHa-Reubéni, RB 42, '33, 230–4. S. also ἀκάνθινος).—W. thistles (τρίβολοι, s. above) as signs of a neglected field Hb 6: 8; Hs 6, 2, 6f; 9, 1, 5; 9, 20, 1. W. other weeds Hm 10, 1, 5.—In the description of the rites of atonement B 7: 11 ἄ. means the thornbush on which the wool was placed, cf. ῥάχος, ῥαχία. M-M.*

ἀκάνθινος, η, ον (Hdt.+; pap.) thorny, (so Is 34: 13) ἀ. στέφανος Mk 15: 17; J 19: 5; GP 3: 8. S. HStJHart, JTS n.s. 3, '52, 66–75; CBonner, HTR 46, '53, 47f; ER Goodenough and CBWelles, ibid. 46, '53, 241f.*

ἀκανθώδης, ες (since Hdt. 1, 126, also Agathocles [III BC] no. 472, fgm. 4 Jac.) thorny, covered w. thornbushes ὁδός Hm 6, 1, 3f; τόπος Hs 6, 2, 6; 9, 1, 5 FL.*

ἄκαρπος, ον (Aeschyl.+; pap., LXX; Jos., Ant. 2, 213; 15, 300) unfruitful, fruitless.

1. lit. πτελέα ξύλον ἄ. the elm is an unfruitful (i.e., bearing no edible fruit, cf. Pollux I 234) tree Hs 2: 3. δένδρα ἄ. (Theophyl. Sim., Ep. 11) unfruitful trees (w. φθινοπωρινά) as a type of heretical teachers Jd 12, cf. Hs 4: 4. Of a mountain, on which nothing grows (Jos., Bell. 4, 452) ὄρος ἄ. unfruitful, barren Hs 9, 19, 2.

2. fig. useless, unproductive (Jos., Bell. 6, 36) of seed (preaching) Mt 13: 22; Mk 4: 19 (Pla., Phaedr. 277A λόγοι ἄ.; Synes., Dio 3 p. 39C λόγος ἄ.). Of deeds ἔργα ἄ. τοῦ σκότους useless deeds of darkness Eph 5: 11. Of men who do no good deeds (Philostrat., Gymn. 42 p. 284, 11) Tit 3: 14; 2 Pt 1: 8. Of speaking in tongues νοῦς ἄ. ἐστιν (my) mind is unproductive, because it is not active 1 Cor 14: 14. M-M.*

ἀκατάγνωστος, ον (Rhet. Gr. I 597; Syntipas p. 129, 12; exx. fr. inscr. and pap. in Nägeli 47) not condemned (2 Macc 4: 47), beyond reproach λόγον ἀ. preaching that is beyond repr. Tit 2: 8. M-M.*

ἀκατακάλυπτος, ον (Polyb. 15, 27, 2; Lev 13: 45; Act. Phil. 60 p. 25, 13 B.) uncovered ἀ. τῇ κεφαλῇ (Philo, Spec. Leg. 3, 60) with unc. head (of praying women; cf. Dit., Syll.³ 999, 10; 736, 22; Philostrat. Jun. [III AD]: APF 14, '41, p. 8; 19 l. 60f: γυναῖκες ἀκαλύπτοι in a solemn procession) 1 Cor 11: 5. In short γυναῖκα ἀ. a woman without head-covering vs. 13.*

ἀκατάκριτος, ον (Corpus Gloss. Lat. 2, 80) uncondemned, without a proper trial Ac 16: 37; 22: 25. M-M.*

ἀκατάληπτος, ον (Aristot.+; Jos., Bell. 3, 159) incomprehensible (so Diog. L. 7, 46; 9, 91; Plut., Mor 1056E;

Epict., fgm. 1 Schenkl; Ep. Arist. 160; Philo, Spec. Leg. 1, 47, Mut. Nom. 10) of God's wisdom σύνεσις 1 Cl 33: 3. Of God himself PK 2.*

ἀκατάλυτος, ον indestructible, hence endless (Dionys. Hal. 10, 31, 5; Chio, Ep. 14, 1; 4 Macc 10: 11) ζωή Hb 7: 16.*

ἀκατάπαστος s. next. M-M.

ἀκατάπαυστος, ον (Polyb. 4, 17, 4; Diod. S. 11, 67; Plut., Caes. 57, 1, Mor. 114ϝ; Heliod. 1, 13, 5; PSI 28, 52; PGM 4, 2364) unceasing, restless w. gen. (Bl-D. §182, 3; cf. Rob. 503f) ὀφθαλμοὶ ἀ. ἁμαρτίας eyes unceasingly looking for sin 2 Pt 2: 14 (v.l. ἀκαταπάστους, which cannot be explained w. certainty [perh. = 'insatiable'] and may be due to a scribal error).*

ἀκαταστασία, ας, ἡ (Polyb. 7, 4, 8; 14, 9, 6; Diog. L. 7, 110; Epict. 3, 19, 3; Vett. Val. index; PGrenf. I 1, 4 [173 ʙᴄ]; Astrol. Pap. I fr. Munich: APF 1, '01, 494; Tob 4: 13; Pr 26: 28).
1. disturbance (schol. on Apollon. Rhod. 1, 916, 18b) Hs 6, 3, 4. Pl. (Dionys. Hal. 6, 31) 2 Cor 6: 5; 2 Cl 11: 4 (quot. of unknown orig.).
2. disorder, unruliness (Nicol. Dam.: 90 fgm. 130, 110 Jac. ἐν ἀ. πραγμάτων; Cat. Cod. Astr. VIII 3, 182, 8; 187, 2) 1 Cl 14: 1 (w. ἀλαζονεία); cf. 3: 2; 43: 6; (w. φαῦλον πρᾶγμα) Js 3: 16; (opp. εἰρήνη) 1 Cor 14: 33 (EKäsemann, NTS 1, '54/'55, 248-60). Pl. (Cat. Cod. Astr. VII 126, 13; VIII 3, 175, 9) 2 Cor 12: 20; (w. πόλεμος) insurrections (Maspéro 4, 6) Lk 21: 9.—Boll 130f. M-M.*

ἀκαταστατέω (Epict. 2, 1, 12; Vett. Val. index; Cat. Cod. Astr. VII 134, 18; 138, 25; Tob 1: 15 BA; Gen 4: 12 Aq.) be unsettled or vacillating; the man possessed by evil spirits is unsettled Hm 5, 2, 7. W. dat. ἀ. ταῖς βουλαῖς be vacillating in their purposes Hs 6, 3, 5.*

ἀκατάστατος, ον (Hippocr.+; Polyb. 7, 4, 6; Plut., Mor. 437ᴅ; Audollent, Defix. Tab. 4b, 12; Sib. Or. 1, 164; Is 54: 11 LXX; Gen 4: 12 and La 4: 14 Sym.; Test. of Job 36) unstable, restless, of vacillating persons ἀ. ἐν πάσαις ταῖς ὁδοῖς αὐτοῦ unstable in all his actions Js 1: 8. Of the tongue ἀ. κακόν a restless evil 3: 8 (v.l. ἀκατάσχετον). Of slander personified ἀκατάστατον δαιμόνιον a restless demon Hm 2: 3. M-M.*

ἀκατάσχετος, ον (Hipparch. in Stob. 4, 44, 81; Diod. S. 17, 38; Plut., Mar. 44, 10; Aelian, N.A. 4, 48 ἀ. ὀρμῇ; Xenophon Eph. 1, 3, 4 ἔρως; POxy. 684, 19 [restored]; Philo, Det. Pot. Ins. 110, Deus Imm. 138, Somn. 2, 275; Jos., Bell. 2, 407; Ps.-Phoc. 96; Job 31: 11; 3 Macc 6: 17) uncontrollable ἀκατασχέτῳ θυμῷ w. uncontr. anger MPol 12: 2; Js 3: 8 v.l. (s. ἀκατάστατος).*

ἀκαυχησία, ας, ἡ (found only here) freedom fr. boasting ἐν ἀ. without boasting IPol 5: 2.*

Ἀκελδαμάχ (v.l. Ακελδαιμαχ, Ακελδαμα, Ακελδαμακ, Αχελδαμαχ), Aram. חֲקַל דְּמָא (= field of blood) Akeldama, expl. as χωρίον αἵματος (Mt 27: 8 ἀγρὸς αἵματος) Field of Blood, of the field bought w. Judas' money Ac 1: 19 (formerly called the potter's field Mt 27: 7); located by tradition south of the valley of Hinnom. Cf. EKautzsch, Gramm. d. Bibl.-Aramäischen 1884, 8; Dalman, Gramm.² 137, 1; 202, 2; JSickenberger, Judas als Stifter des Blutackers: BZ 18, '29, 69-71; MWilcox, The Semitisms of Ac, '65, 87-89.*

ἀκέραιος, ον (Eur., Hdt.+; inscr., pap., Ep. Arist.; Jos.,

Bell. 1, 621, Ant. 1, 61; 5, 47) pure, innocent (lit. 'unmixed') only fig. (cf. Pla., Rep. 3, 409ᴀ ἀ. κακῶν ἠθῶν; Epict. 3, 23, 15; Esth 8: 12f; Ep. Arist. 31; 264) (w. φρόνιμος) Mt 10: 16, quoted IPol 2: 2; (w. σοφὸς εἰς τὸ ἀγαθόν) ἀ. εἰς τὸ κακόν innocent as far as evil is concerned Ro 16: 19; (w. ἄμεμπτος) Phil 2: 15; (w. εἰλικρινής) 1 Cl 2: 5. τὸ ἀ. τῆς πραΰτητος βούλημα the pure purpose of meekness 1 Cl 21: 7. M-M.*

ἀκεραιοσύνη, ης, ἡ (only in Suidas) purity ἐν ἀ. πιστεύειν believe in all purity (of heart) B 3: 6. ἐν ἀ. περιπατεῖν 10: 4.*

ἀκηδεμονέω (found nowhere else) for ἀδημονέω (q.v.) Mk 14: 33 D.*

ἀκηδία, ας, ἡ (Hippocr.+; LXX) indifference, apathy (pl. = sing. Bl-D. §142; Rob. 408) παραδιδόναι ἑαυτὸν εἰς τὰς ἀ. give oneself over to indifference Hv 3, 11, 3.*

ἀκίνητος, ον (Pind.+; inscr., pap., LXX, Philo; Jos., Ant. 15, 364; 399) without movement.
1. lit. immovable πέτρα ἀ. IPol 1: 1. Of idols unable to move Dg 2: 4.
2. fig. πίστις ISm 1: 1; unmoved (by passions) τὸ ἀκίνητον (Dionys. Byz. §23 p. 10, 5; Philo, Op. M. 101) steadfast character IPhld 1: 2.*

ἄκκεπτα, ων, τά Lat. loanw. 'accepta' savings, back pay, t.t. of military finance: a sum credited to the Roman soldier and paid upon his discharge IPol 6: 2 (s. δεπόσιτα).*

ἀκλινής, ές (Pla.+; Meleager [I ʙᴄ]: Anth. Pal. 12, 158, 4 φιλία; Lucian, Encom. Demosth. 33 ἀ. τὴν ψυχήν; Aelian, V.H. 12, 64; POxy. 904, 9; Philo, Mos. 1, 30, Virtut. 158, Spec. Leg. 2, 2 ὅρκος ἀ.; 4 Macc 6: 7; 7: 3) without wavering τὴν ὁμολογίαν ἀ. κατέχειν hold fast the confession without wavering Hb 10: 23. M-M.*

ἀκμάζω 1 aor. ἤκμασα (Aeschyl., Hdt.+; Dit., Syll.³ 814, 17; 4 Macc 2: 3; Philo, Aet. M. 63; 73; Jos., Ant. 13, 2, C. Ap. 2, 253) be ripe (so since Thu. 2, 19, 1; Dit., Syll.³ 866, 21f; PGM 5, 231) of grapes (Plut., Mor. 671ᴅ) Rv 14: 18. M-M.*

ἀκμήν adverbial acc. (Bl-D. §160 app.; Rob. 294; 487f; KKrumbacher, Ztschr. f. vergleich. Sprachforsch. 27, 1885, 498-521; 29, 1888, 188f) even yet, still Mt 15: 16; Hb 5: 13 v.l. (Hyperid., fgm. 116; X., An. 4, 3, 26; Polyb. 1, 13, 12; 4, 36, 8; Plut., Mor. 346ᴄ; Dit., Or. 201, 13; PGenève 14, 13 et al.; Jos., Ant. 19, 118; Phryn. p. 123 Lob.).*

ἄκμων, ονος, ὁ (Hom.+; PGdspd. 30, 22, 11; 18) anvil, type of firmness (Aeschyl., Pers. 51; Aristopho [IV ʙᴄ] 4 Kock ὑπομένειν πληγὰς ἄκμων; Job 41: 16), ἄ. τυπτόμενος an anvil when it is beaten IPol 3: 1. B. 607.*

ἀκοή, ῆς, ἡ (in form ἀκουή as early as Hom.; freq., incl. inscr., pap., LXX, Ep. Arist., Philo, Joseph., Test. 12 Patr.).
1. that by which one hears—a. the faculty of hearing (Philo, Rer. Div. Her. 12 of images οἷς ὦτα μέν ἐστιν, ἀκοαὶ δ᾽ οὐκ ἔνεισιν) 1 Cor 12: 17; but mng. c is also poss.
b. the act of hearing, listening (Pla., Theaet. 142ᴅ λόγος ἄξιος ἀκοῆς; Antig. Car. 129 ἀκοῆς ἄξια; BGU 1080, 6; Ep. Arist. 142 w. ὅρασις; Jos., Ant. 8, 171; w. ὄψις 172) w. βλέμμα 2 Pt 2: 8. ἀκοῇ ἀκούειν (Polyaenus, Exc. 55, 2; LXX) Mt 13: 14; Ac 28: 26 (both Is 6: 9); B 9: 2 (cf. Ex 15: 26). εἰς ἀ. ὠτίου ὑπακούειν obey upon hearing

ακοή – ακούω

with the ear, i.e., *as soon as one hears* B 9: 1 (Ps 17: 45; cf. 2 Km 22: 45).

c. the organ w. which one hears, *the ear* (Sappho+; POxy. 129, 4; PGM 4, 306; 323; 2 Macc 15: 39; Ep. Arist. 166) esp. pl. (Dio Chrys. 15[32], 11; Aelian, V.H. 3, 1 p. 39, 21; oft. Philo; Jos., Ant. 8, 172; Sib. Or. 4, 172) αἱ ἀκοαί Mk 7: 35. εἰσφέρειν εἰς τὰς ἀ. *bring to someone's ears* Ac 17: 20 (cf. Soph., Ajax 147). εἰς τὰς ἀ. τινος *in someone's ears* Lk 7: 1. νωθρὸς (q.v.) ταῖς ἀ. Hb 5: 11; κνήθεσθαι τὴν ἀ. *have itching ears* 2 Ti 4: 3, cf. vs. 4. Fig. περιτέμνειν τὰς ἀ. *circumcise the ears*= make someone attentive B 9: 4; 10: 12.

2. that which is heard—a. *fame, report, rumor* (Hom. +; 1 Km 2: 24; 2 Km 13: 30; 3 Km 2: 28; 10: 7) Mt 4: 24; 14: 1; 24: 6; Mk 1: 28; 13: 7; 1 Cl 47: 7.

b. *account, report, preaching* (Thu. 1, 20, 1 ἀκοὴν δέχεσθαι πιστεύειν τῇ ἀ. (cf. Jos., C. Ap. 2, 14) J 12: 38; Ro 10: 16f; 1 Cl 16: 3 (all three Is 53: 1). ἐξ ἀ. πίστεως *as the result of preaching which demanded (only) faith* Gal 3: 2, 5. λόγος τῆς ἀκοῆς *the word of preaching* Hb 4: 2. λόγος ἀκοῆς παρ' ἡμῶν τοῦ θεοῦ *the word of divine preaching that goes out from us* 1 Th 2: 13 (RSchippers, Novum Testamentum 8, '66, 223–34 *tradition*). The mng. 'instruction' is also possible for some of these passages; cf. Test. Reuben 2, 5.—AOepke, Dis Missionspredigt d. Ap. Pls. '20, 40ff. M-M.*

ἀκοίμητος, ον (since Aeschyl., Pr. 139; Aelian, N.A. 11, 3 πῦρ ἄσβεστον καὶ ἀ.; POxy. 1468, 7; Wsd 7: 10; Philo; Sib. Or. 2, 181) *not to be put to sleep* σκώληκες ἀ. *restless worms* AP 27; ἀ. πνεῦμα IPol 1: 3.*

ἀκολουθέω imper. ἀκολούθει; impf. ἠκολούθουν; fut. ἀκολουθήσω; 1 aor. ἠκολούθησα; pf. ἠκολούθηκα Mk 10: 28 (Thu., Aristoph.+; inscr., pap., LXX; Philo, Aet. M. 84; 145 al.; Jos., Ant. 9, 108 al.) *follow.*

1. lit. *come after* abs. (Diod. S. 13, 75, 7) οἱ προάγοντες κ. οἱ ἀκολουθοῦντες Mt 21: 9; Mk 11: 9; cf. J 21: 20; Ac 21: 36; 1 Cor 10: 4; Rv 14: 8. W. dat. of the pers. (X., Hell. 5, 2, 26; Herodian 6, 7, 8) Mt 9: 19; 26: 58; Mk 14: 13; Lk 22: 10; J 10: 4f; 11: 31; IPhld 11: 1; Hv 3, 8, 4; 7. ἠκολούθει τῷ Ἰησοῦ Σίμων Πέτρος κ. ἄλλος μαθητής J 18: 15 (more than one subject with a verb in the sing. as Appian, Bell. Civ. 3, 72 §296 ὑπερόψεταί με Λέπιδος κ. Πλάγκος.

2. *accompany, go along with*, oft. of the crowd following Jesus ἠκολούθησαν αὐτῷ ὄχλοι πολλοί (s. ὄχλος 1) Mt 4: 25; 8: 1; 12: 15; 14: 13; Mk 5: 24; Lk 7: 9; 9: 11; J 6: 2. μετά τινος *someone* (Thu. 7, 57, 9; Phryn. 353 L.; Bl-D. §193, 1) Rv 6: 8 (Lk 9: 49 οὐκ ἀκολουθεῖ [sc. σοι] μεθ' ἡμῶν is different, *he does not follow as your disciple with us*). For this we have Hebraistically ὀπίσω τινός (3 Km 19: 20; Is 45: 14; Ezk 29: 16) Mt 10: 38; Mk 8: 34 v.l.—Of the deeds that follow one into the next world Rv 14: 13 τὰ ἔργα αὐτῶν ἀκολουθεῖ μετ' αὐτῶν *they take with them the record of their deeds* (NEB) (cf. Diod. S. 13, 105 νομίσαντες . . . ἑαυτοῖς τὴν μέμψιν ἀκολουθήσειν).

3. w. transition to the fig. mng. *follow someone as a disciple* (Diog. L. 9, 21 of Parmenides: ἀκούσας Ξενοφάνους οὐκ ἠκολούθησεν αὐτῷ; Palaeph. 2 p. 6, 16) ἀκολούθει μοι *follow me*= *be my disciple* Mt 9: 9 (in Diog. L. 2, 48 Socrates stops Xenophon at their first meeting and says: "ἕπου καὶ μάνθανε". καὶ τοὐντεῦθεν ἀκροατὴς Σωκράτους ἦν; cf. 8: 19; 19: 21 (Aristoxenus, fgm. 17: Simichos the tyrant hears Pythagoras, divests himself of his kingly power, disposes of his χρήματα [Mt 19: 22 v.l.], and attaches himself to him; Sextus 264a ἀφεὶς ἃ κέκτησαι ἀκολούθει τῷ ὀρθῷ λόγῳ); 27f; Mk 1: 18 (on the call

of a disciple directly fr. his work s. Jos., Ant. 8, 354 εὐθέως . . . καταλιπὼν τ. βόας ἠκολούθησεν Ἡλίᾳ . . . μαθητής [after 3 Km 19: 20f]); Mk 2: 14; 8: 34; Lk 5: 11, 27f al. The transition may be observed in J 1, where ἀ. has sense 2 in vss. 37f, but sense 3 in vss. 40, 43 (OCullmann, ThZ 4, '48, 367).—TArvedson, Svensk Teol. Kvartalskrift 7, '31, 134–61; ASchulz, Nachfolgen u. Nachahmen, '62; TAerts, Suivre Jésus, Ephemerides Theol. Lovanienses 42, '66, 476–512; ESchweizer, Lordship and Discipleship, '60.

4. gener. *follow, obey* (Thu. 3, 38, 6 γνώμῃ; Ps.-Andoc. 4, 19; Demosth. 26, 5; BGU 1079, 10 ἀκολούθει Πτολλαρίωνι πᾶσαν ὥραν; l. 26; 2 Macc 8: 36 νόμοις; cf. Jdth 2: 3.—M. Ant. 7, 31 θεῷ; Jdth 5: 7 τοῖς θεοῖς) τοῖς ἔθεσιν *customs* Dg 5: 4. τοῖς νομίμοις τ. δεσπότου *obey the statutes of the Master* 1 Cl 40: 4. τῇ ὁδῷ τῆς ἀληθείας 35: 5 (cf. Test. Ash. 6: 1 ἀ. τῇ ἀληθείᾳ); the bishop ISm 8: 1; a schismatic IPhld 3: 3.—Hm 6, 2, 9. M-M. B. 699.

ἀκόλουθος, ον (Bacchylides, Soph.+; inscr., pap., LXX, Ep. Arist., Philo, Joseph.) *following* (so Demosth. et al.; 2 Macc 4: 17) καὶ τῶν λοιπῶν τῶν ἀκολούθων πάντων *and of all the other things that followed* Hs 5, 5, 1. W. gen. (Ps.-Demosth. 59, 8 τὰ ἀ. αὐτῶν) τὰ ἀ. τούτων *what follows them* Hm 8: 4, 10; cf. s 9, 15, 3. W. dat. (Lucian, Hermotim. 74; Ps.-Lucian: Anth. Pal. 11, 401, 4) τὰ τούτοις ἀ. (1 Esdr 8: 14; Jos., Ant. 14, 1) *and so forth* MPol 8: 2; 9: 2.—Abs. ἀ. ἐστιν *they follow* from them (Dit., Or. 669, 32; PTebt. 296, 14) IEph 14: 1; *it is suitable* (Demosth 46, 17; Ael. Aristid. 13 p. 172 D. al.; PTebt. 304 τὸ ἀ. 'what is suitable') ὅπου καὶ ἀ. ἦν *where it was suitable*=*at a suitable place* MPol 18: 1.*

ἀκόρεστος, ον (Aeschyl.+—in Hom. ἀκόρητος; Maspéro 89 III, 6) *insatiable* fig. (X., Symp. 8, 15 φιλία; Philo, Somn. 1, 50 ἵμερος, Ebr. 4) πόθος *desire* 1 Cl 2: 2.*

ἀκουστός, ή, όν *audible* (Hom. Hymns+; LXX, Philo) ἀκουστὸν ἐγένετο τοῖς ἀποστόλοις ὅτι *it came to the apostles' ears that* Ac 11: 1 D (ἀ. γίνεσθαι as Isocr. 3, 49; Gen 45: 2; Dt 4: 36; Is 48: 20).*

ἀκουτίζω fut. ἀκουτιῶ (LXX; Syntipas p. 73, 1; Aesop. mss. [Ursing 78f]; Suidas s.v. δογματίζω; Etym. Mag. p. 51, 32; Etym. Gud. 71, 3; Anecd. Gr. p. 366, 3) *cause to hear* ἀ. με ἀγαλλίασιν 1 Cl 18: 8 (Ps 50: 10).*

ἀκούω fut. ἀκούσω (Sib. Or. 4, 175) Mt 12: 19; 13: 14 (Is 6: 9); J 5: 25, 28; 10: 16, ἀκούσομαι (Ep. Arist. 5) Ac 3: 22 (Dt 18: 15); 28: 28; 1 aor. ἤκουσα; pf. ἀκήκοα; 1 aor. pass. ἠκούσθην (Hom.+; inscr., pap., LXX; Philo, Aet. M. 142 al.; Joseph.; Test. 12 Patr.) *hear*, as a passive respondent to λέγω.

1. lit., of sense perception—a. abs. τὰ ὦτα ἀκούουσιν Mt 13: 16; κωφοὶ ἀ. 11: 5; cf. Mk 7: 37; Lk 7: 22; τοῖς ὠσὶν βαρέως ἀ. *be hard of hearing* Mt 13: 15 (Is 6: 10); ἀκοῇ ἀ. Mt 13: 14; Ac 28: 26 (both Is 6: 9). ἀκούοντες οὐκ ἀκούουσιν *they hear and yet do not hear* Mt 13: 13 (s. Aeschyl., Prom. 448 κλύοντες οὐκ ἤκουον; Demosth., Against Aristogeiton 1, 89), cf. Mk 8: 18 (Ezk 12: 2) and s. 7 below. A challenge to the hearers, by which their attention is drawn to a special difficulty: ὁ ἔχων ὦτα (οὖς) ἀκούειν ἀκουέτω, w. variations (Arrian, Ind. 5, 1 ὅστις ἐθέλει φράζειν . . . , φραζέτω) Mt 11: 15; 13: 9; Mk 4: 23; Rv 2: 7, 11, 17, 29; 3: 6, 13, 22; 13: 9.

b. w. obj. (on the syntax Bl-D. §173; 416, 1; Rob. 506f; on the LXX s. MJohannessohn, D. Gebr. d. Kasus in LXX, Diss. Berl. '10, 36; RHelbing, D. Kasussyntax d. Verba b. den LXX, '28, 150ff).

31

α. foll. by a thing as obj. in acc. (Diod. S. 8, 32, 1 τὶ something) Mt 11: 4; 13: 17ff; Lk 7: 22; 1 J 1: 1, 3. τὴν φωνήν (UPZ 77 I, 25) Mt 12: 19; J 3: 8; Ac 22: 9 (but see 7 below); 1 Cl 39: 3 (Job 4: 16); (pass. Mt 2: 18 [Jer 38: 15]; Rv 18: 22). τὸν λόγον Mt 13: 20ff; J 5: 24. τοὺς λόγους, τὰ ῥήματα Mt 10: 14; J 8: 47; Ac 2: 22. πολέμους καὶ ἀκοὰς πολέμων Mt 24: 6. τὴν βλασφημίαν 26: 65. τὸν ἀσπασμόν Lk 1: 41. ἄρρητα ῥήματα 2 Cor 12: 4. τὸν ἀριθμόν Rv 9: 16. τὴν ἀποκάλυψιν Hv 3, 12, 2. Pass. τὰ ἀκουσθέντα what has been heard i.e., the message Hb 2: 1. ἠκούσθη ὁ λόγος εἰς τὰ ὦτα τῆς ἐκκλησίας τῆς οὔσης ἐν Ἰερουσαλήμ the report reached the ears of the church in Jerusalem Ac 11: 22. Oft. the obj. is to be supplied fr. context Mt 13: 17; Mk 4: 15; καθὼς ἀκούω=ἃ ἀ. J 5: 30; Ac 2: 37; 8: 30; 9: 21; J 6: 60; Ro 10: 14.

β. τί τινος hear someth. fr. someone τὴν ἐπαγγελίαν, ἣν ἠκούσατέ μου the promise which you heard from me Ac 1: 4. Still other constrs. occur, which are also poss. when the hearing is not directly fr. the mouth of the informant, but involves a report which one has received fr. him in any way at all (s. below 3d). τὶ ἔκ τινος (Od. 15, 374; Hdt. 3, 62 ἐκ τοῦ κήρυκος) 2 Cor 12: 6. τὶ παρά τινος (Soph., Oed. Rex 7 παρ' ἀγγέλων; Pla., Rep. 6 p. 506D; Demosth. 6, 26; Jer 30: 8; Jos., Bell. 1, 529) J 8: 26, 40 (τὴν ἀλήθειαν ἀ. as Diod. S. 16, 50, 2); 15: 15; Ac 10: 22; 28: 22; 2 Ti 2: 2; w. attraction of the relative λόγων ὧν παρ' ἐμοῦ ἤκουσας teachings which you have heard from me 1: 13; τὶ ἀπό τινος (Thu. 1, 125, 1) 1 J 1: 5. Hebraistically ἀπὸ τ. στόματός τινος Lk 22: 71 (cf. ἐκ τ. στόμ. τ. Ex 23: 13; Ezk 3: 17; 33: 7).

γ. foll. by a thing as obj. in gen. (Hdt. 8, 135; X., Cyr. 3, 1, 8; Demosth. 18, 3; Bl-D. §173, 2; Rob. 507) hear someth. τῆς βλασφημίας (=τὴν βλ. Mt 26: 65) Mk 14: 64. συμφωνίας καὶ χορῶν Lk 15: 25; τῆς φωνῆς J 5: 25, 28; Ac 9: 7 (on the experience of Paul and his companions cf. Maximus Tyr. 9, 7d-f: some see a divine figure, others see nothing but hear a voice, still others both see and hear); 11: 7; 22: 7 (HRMoehring, Novum Testamentum 3, '59, 80-99). But cf. Rob. 506 for the view that the difference in cases betw. 9: 7 and 22: 9 is important. τ. λόγων Lk 6: 47; τῶν ῥημάτων J 12: 47.

c. hear, listen to w. gen. of the pers. and a ptc. (Pla., Prot. 320B; X., Symp. 3, 13; Herm. Wr. 12, 8; Jos., Ant. 10, 105 ἤκουσε τοῦ προφήτου ταῦτα λέγοντος): ἠκούσαμεν αὐτοῦ λέγοντος we have heard him say Mk 14: 58. ἤκουον εἷς ἕκαστος . . . λαλούντων αὐτῶν each one heard them speaking Ac 2: 6, 11; Rv 16: 5, 7 (in vs. 7 the altar speaks); Hv 1, 3, 3. W. acc. instead of gen. πᾶν κτίσμα . . . καὶ τὰ ἐν αὐτοῖς πάντα ἤκουσα λέγοντας (v.l. λέγοντα) Rv 5: 13. Used without ptc. w. pronoun only; μου (Dio Chrys. 79[28], 14) Mk 7: 14; Ac 26: 3. αὐτῶν Lk 2: 46. αὐτοῦ vs. 47; 15: 1; 19: 48; 21: 38; J 3: 29 etc. ἡμῶν Ac 24: 4.—ἀ. τινὸς περί τινος (since Hdt. 7, 209; IG II 168 [338 BC]) hear someone (speak) about someth. Ac 17: 32. ἤκουσεν αὐτοῦ περὶ τῆς . . . πίστεως he heard him speak about faith Ac 24: 24, cf. Hm 11: 7.—W. ὅτι foll. (X., Cyr. 3, 3, 18) J 14: 28; Ac 22: 2.—Abs. οἱ ἀκούοντες the hearers (Diod. S. 4, 7, 4) Lk 6: 27; MPol 7: 2. Esp. imper. ἄκουε listen! Mk 12: 29 (Dt 6: 4); Hs 5, 1, 3; pl. Mk 4: 3. ἀκούσατε Ac 7: 2; 13: 16. W. συνίετε listen and try to understand Mt 15: 10.

2. legal t.t. give someone a hearing (X., Hell. 1, 7, 9 al.; PAmh. 135, 14; PIand. 9, 10; 15; BGU 511 II, 2; POxy. 1032, 59) w. παρά τινος: ἐὰν μὴ ἀκούσῃ πρῶτον παρ' αὐτοῦ without first giving him a hearing J 7: 51 (SPancaro, Biblica 53, '72, 340-61).—Ac 25: 22.

3. learn or be informed about someth.—**a.** abs. ἀκού-σας δὲ ὁ Ἰησοῦς when Jesus learned about it (the death of J. Bapt.) Mt 14: 13.—Mk 3: 21; 6: 14 (cf. HLjungvik, ZNW 33, '34, 90-2); Ro 10: 18. W. ἀναγγέλλειν 15: 21 (Is 52: 15).

b. w. gen. of the person οὗ οὐκ ἤκουσαν of whom they have not heard Ro 10: 14a.—W. acc. of the thing (X., Cyr. 1, 1, 4; Diod. S. 19, 8, 4; Chio, Ep. 12 ἀκ. τὴν τυραννίδα; Herodian 4, 4, 8) learn of τὴν ἀγάπην Phlm 5. τὴν ἀναστροφήν Gal 1: 13. τὰ ἔργα τοῦ Χριστοῦ Mt 11: 2. τὴν ἐνέδραν the ambush Ac 23: 16; Χριστιανισμὸν ἀ. hear Christianity IPhld 6: 1; τὴν οἰκονομίαν Eph 3: 2. τὴν πίστιν 1: 15; Col 1: 4. τὴν ὑπομονήν Js 5: 11.—Pass. ἀκούεται ἐν ὑμῖν πορνεία it is reported that there is immorality among you 1 Cor 5: 1 (schol. on Nicander, Ther. 139 τοῦτο ἐξακούεται=this report is heard). ἐὰν ἀκουσθῇ τοῦτο ἐπὶ τοῦ ἡγεμόνος if this should come to the procurator's ears Mt 28: 14.

c. ἀ. τι περί τινος (since Hdt. 2, 43) learn someth. about someone Lk 9: 9; 16: 2.—ἀ. περί τινος (Jos., Vi. 246) Lk 7: 3.

d. w. prep., to denote the author or source of the information (s. 1bβ above) ἀ. τι παρά τινος: τῶν ἀκου-σάντων παρὰ Ἰωάννου who had learned fr. John (who Jesus was) J 1: 40, cf. 6: 45 (Simplicius in Epict. p. 110, 35 τὸ ἀκοῦσαι παρὰ θεοῦ, ὅτι ἀθάνατός ἐστιν ἡ ψυχή); ἀ. τι ἔκ τινος: ἠκούσαμεν ἐκ τοῦ νόμου we have heard from the law (when it was read in the synagogue) J 12: 34, where ἀ. approaches the technical sense learn (a body of authoritative teaching), as 1 J 1: 5 (s. above); 2: 7, 24 et al. (OAPiper, JBL 66, '47, 437 n. 1). ἀ. ἀπό τινος περί τινος Ac 9: 13.

e. w. ὅτι foll. (class., also Dit., Syll.³ 370, 21; PTebt. 416, 8; BGU 246, 19; Josh 10: 1; Da 5: 14 Theod.; 1 Macc 6: 55; 4 Macc 4: 22) Mt 2: 22; 4: 12 al.—Pass. ἠκούσθη ὅτι ἐν οἴκῳ ἐστίν it became known that he was in the house Mk 2: 1. οὐκ ἠκούσθη ὅτι it is unheard of that J 9: 32.

f. w. acc. and inf. foll. (Hom.+; Jos., Ant. 11, 165; 13, 292) J 12: 18; 1 Cor 11: 18. W. acc. and ptc. (X., Cyr. 2, 4, 12; Herodian 2, 12, 4) Ac 7: 12; 3 J 4.

4. ἀ. τινός listen to someone, follow someone (Hom.+) ἀκούετε αὐτοῦ Mt 17: 5; Lk 9: 35; Ac 3: 22 (all three Dt 18: 15); cf. Mt 18: 15; Lk 16: 29, 31; J 10: 8; Ac 4: 19. W. acc. J 8: 47.—Abs. obey, listen αὐτοὶ καὶ ἀκούσονται Ac 28: 28; cf. Mt 18: 16; J 5: 25b; agree 9: 27a.

5. ἀ. τινός listen to someone or someth. (Wilcken, Chrest. 14, 18; 461, 6) Mk 6: 11; J 6: 60b. Of God (Hom.+) Ac 7: 34 (Ex 3: 7); J 9: 31; 11: 41f; 1 J 5: 14f.—Abs. καθὼς ἠδύναντο ἀ. as they were able to listen Mk 4: 33 (EMolland, Symb. Osl. 8, '29, 83-91; s. also 7 below).

6. be called (Demosth. 18, 46 κόλακες ἀκούουσι; Diog. L. 2, 111 a derisive nickname; 2, 140) ἤκουσαν προδόται γονέων they were called betrayers of their parents Hv 2, 2, 2.

7. understand (Teles p. 47, 12; Galen: CMG Suppl. I p. 12, 29; Aelian, V.H. 13, 46; Apollon. Dysc., Gramm. Gr. II 2 p. 424, 5 U. ἀκούειν=συνιέναι τῶν ἠκουσμένων; Sext. Emp., Math. 1, 37 τὸ μὴ πάντας πάντων ἀκούειν; Julian, Orat. 4 p. 147A; PGM 3, 453 ἀκούσεις τὰ ὄρνεα λαλοῦντα; Philo, Leg. All. 2, 35) abs. (Is 36: 11) 1 Cor 14: 2. Perh. also Mk 4: 33 (s. above, and cf. Epict. 1, 29, 66 τ. δυναμένοις αὐτὰ ἀκοῦσαι). W. acc. τὸν νόμον understand the law Gal 4: 21; perh. Ac 22: 9; 26: 14 (s. 1ba above) belong here. Cf. also the play on words (1a above) ἀκούοντες οὐκ ἀκούουσιν Mt 13: 13.

ἀκούω is occasionally used as a perfective present: I hear=I have heard (so as early as Il. 24, 543; Aristoph., Frogs 426; X., An. 2, 5, 13, Mem. 2, 4, 1; 3, 5, 26; Pla.,

Rep. 583D; Theocr. 15, 23) Lk 9: 9; 1 Cor 11: 18; 2 Th 3: 11. Bl-D. §322. M-M. B. 1037; 1339.

ἀκρασία, ας, ἡ (Pre-Socr.+;=ἀκράτεια Phryn. p. 524f Lob.) *lack of self-control, self-indulgence* (so in X. et al.; Philo; Jos., Bell. 1, 34; Sib. Or. 1, 35); w. ref. to sex (X., Symp. 8, 27; Diod. S. 3, 65, 2; 19, 33, 2 δι' ἀκρασίαν; Musonius p. 66 H.; Jos., Ant. 8, 191 τ. ἀφροδισίων ἀκ.) ἵνα μὴ πειράζῃ ὑμᾶς ὁ σατανᾶς διὰ τὴν ἀ. ὑμῶν *because of your lack of self-control* (cf. Jos., C. Ap. 1, 319; 2, 244) 1 Cor 7: 5; Mt 23: 25 (the v.l. ἀκαθαρσίας, ἀδικίας, πλεονεξίας, πονηρίας do not go well w. ἁρπαγῆς, but 'intemperance' corresponds to the 'cup'). Personif. as a vice Hs 9, 15, 3.*

ἀκρατής, ές (Aesch., Thu.+; Vett. Val. 39, 33; inscr.; Pr 27: 20a; Ep. Arist. 277; Philo; Jos., Ant. 16, 399) *without self-control, dissolute* 2 Ti 3: 3 (in a list of vices). M-M.*

ἄκρατος, ον (since Hom., who has ἄκρητος; LXX; Philo; Jos., Ant. 17, 103) *unmixed* οἶνος (Od. 24, 73; Hdt. 1, 207; Posidon.: 87 fgm. 15, 4 Jac. 22; 3 Macc 5: 2) fig. (cf. POxy. 237 VII, 40 ἄκρατος τῶν νόμων ἀποτομία) of God's anger *in full strength* Rv 14: 10 (cf. Jer 32: 15; Ps 74: 9; PsSol 8, 14. ἀκρ. is found w. ὀργή Aeschyl., Prom. 678; Alcidamas [IV BC] in Aristot., Rhet. 1406a, 10; Jos., Ant. 5, 150; 17, 148). M-M.*

ἀκρίβεια, ας, ἡ *exactness* (so Thu.+; UPZ 110, 46 [164 BC]; POxy. 471, 11ff [II AD]; 237 VIII, 39 [II AD]; LXX; Ep. Arist. 103; Philo; Jos., Ant. 4, 309; 9, 208 al.) πεπαιδευμένος κατὰ ἀ. τοῦ πατρῴου νόμου *educated strictly according to our ancestral law* Ac 22: 3 (Isocr. 7, 40 ἀ. νόμων; Jos., Vi. 191). M-M.*

ἀκριβεύομαι (περί τινος Sext. Emp., Math. 1, 71; the active PAmh. 154, 7) *pay strict attention* περὶ τῆς σωτηρίας B 2: 10.*

ἀκριβής, ές (Heraclitus+; inscr., pap., LXX, Philo, Jos., Ant. 2, 60) *exact, strict* κατὰ τὴν ἀκριβεστάτην αἵρεσιν *according to the strictest school* Ac 26: 5. M-M.*

ἀκριβόω 1 aor. ἠκρίβωσα (since Eur., X., Pla.; Aq. Is 30: 8; 49: 16; Philo) *ascertain (exactly)* (so Aristot., Gen. Anim. 5, 1; Vett. Val. 265, 3; Philo, Op. M. 77; Jos., Bell. 1, 648, Vi. 365) τί παρά τινος: παρ' αὐτῶν τὸν χρόνον Mt 2: 7; cf. vs. 16. M-M.*

ἀκριβῶς adv. (Aeschyl., Hdt.+; inscr., pap., LXX, Ep. Arist., Philo, Joseph.) *accurately, carefully, well* βλέπειν (POxy. 1381, 111f [I/II]) Eph 5: 15. ἀκούειν (Thu. 1, 134, 1) Hm 3: 4; 4, 3, 7. προσέχειν *pay close attention* B 7: 4. γινώσκειν (Antiphanes 196, 15 Kock al.; Diod. S. 11, 41, 5) Hs 9, 5, 5. κατανοεῖν (Herm. Wr. 11, 6b) s 9, 6, 3. εἰδέναι (Aeschyl., Pr. 328 al.; Epict. 1, 27, 17; 2, 22, 36; PPetr. II 15[1], 11) 1 Th 5: 2. διδάσκειν Ac 18: 25; Pol 3: 2. γράφειν Papias 2: 15. ἐξετάζειν (Isocr. 7, 63; Demosth. 6, 37; Galen ed. Kühn XIV, 210; Dt 19: 18; Jos., Ant. 3, 70) Mt 2: 8; Hs 9, 13, 6. παρακολουθεῖν *follow carefully* Lk 1: 3 (cf. Herodian 1, 1, 3 μετὰ πάσης ἀκριβείας ἤθροισα ἐς συγγραφήν; Stephan. Byz. s.v. Χαράκμωβα: Οὐράνιος ἐν τοῖς Ἀραβικοῖς—ἀξιόπιστος δ' ἀνήρ . . . σπουδὴν γὰρ ἔθετο ἱστορῆσαι ἀκριβῶς . . .).—Comp. ἀκριβέστερον *more exactly* (POxy. 1102, 12; BGU 388 II, 41; Philo, Joseph.) ἀ. ἐκτίθεσθαι *explain more exactly* Ac 18: 26, cf. 23: 15, 20; also *more accurately* (PPetr. II 16, 13 [205 BC]; Epict. 1, 24, 10) 24: 22. ἀ. αὐτὰ γνωσόμεθα *we will find it out more exactly* Hv 3, 10, 10. μανθάνειν (Herm. Wr. 10, 25; Jos., Ant. 8, 402) s 9, 1, 3. M-M.*

ἀκρίς, ίδος, ἡ (Hom.+; PTebt. 772, 2 [236 BC]; LXX, Philo; Jos., Ant. 2, 306; Sib. Or. 5, 454) *grasshopper, locust*, even today commonly eaten by the poorer people in Arabia, Africa, and Syria (cf. Aristoph., Ach. 1116; Diod. S. 3, 29, 1f Vogel; Strabo 16, 4, 12; Theophyl. Sim., Ep. 14; Pliny the Elder 6, 35; Lev 11: 22): used as food by John the Baptist (other, less prob. interpr. of ἀ. in ELohmeyer, Joh. d. T. '32, p. 50, 4) Mt 3: 4; Mk 1: 6; the widespread notion that the ἀ. were carob pods (St. John's-bread; so TK Cheyne, Encycl. Bibl. '03 s.v. 'husks') is supported neither by good linguistic evidence nor by probability (cf. JHastings, Dict. of the Bible '04 s.v. 'husks' and 'locust'); cf. also ἐγκρίς. They appear at the fifth trumpet Rv 9: 3, 7. Fiery locusts (in an apocalyptic vision) Hv 4, 1, 6.—SKrauss, Z. Kenntnis d. Heuschrecken in Palästina: ZDPV 50, '27, 244–9; HGrégoire, Les Sauterelles de St Jean: Byzantion 5, '30, 109–28.—On Rv: Boll 68–77; 145f; against him JFreundorfer, D. Apk. d. Ap. J. u. d. hellenist. Kosmologie u. Astrologie '29.*

ἀκροατήριον, ου, τό *audience room* (Lat. auditorium) of the procurator, in which hearings were held and justice was privately dispensed (Mommsen, Röm. Strafrecht 1899, 362) Ac 25: 23. Since the proceedings described here are not strictly a trial, the word can mean simply *auditorium* (so Philo, Congr. Erud. Grat. 64; Dio Chrys. 15[32], 8; Plut., Mor. 45F; Epict. 3, 23, 8).*

ἀκροατής, οῦ, ὁ (Thu.+; Is 3: 3; Sir 3: 29; Ep. Arist. 266) *a hearer* Dg 2: 1. ἀ. λόγου (cf. Philo, Congr. Erud. Grat. 70) Js 1: 23; pl. (Diod. S. 4, 7, 4) vs. 22 (Thu., 3, 38, 4 a similar reproach directed against the θεαταὶ μὲν τῶν λόγων, ἀκροαταὶ δὲ τῶν ἔργων). ἀ. νόμου Ro 2: 13 (cf. Jos., Ant. 5, 107; 132 νόμων ἀκροαταί). ἀ. ἐπιλησμονῆς *a forgetful hearer* Js 1: 25. γενοῦ ἀ. *listen* Hv 1, 3, 3. M-M.*

ἀκροβυστία, ας, ἡ (prob. from ἀκροποσθία [Hippocrates, Aph. 6, 19; Aristot., H. An. 1, 13 p. 493a, 29], connected by popular etymology w. βύειν; Bl-D. §120, 4; Mlt.-H. 277; found only in Bibl. and eccl. Gk.; Etym. Magn. p. 53, 47) *foreskin* (opp. περιτομή).

1. lit. ἄνδρες ἀ. ἔχοντες *uncircumcised men* (=Gentiles; cf. Gen 34: 14) Ac 11: 3.—1 Cor 7: 18f. ἀπερίτμητος ἀκροβυστίαν w. *uncircumcised foreskin* B 9: 5.

2. fig. *uncircumcision* as a state of being Ro 2: 25ff; Gal 5: 6; 6: 15. πιστεύειν δι' ἀκροβυστίας *to believe as an uncircumcised man*, i.e., *as a Gentile* Ro 4: 11; B 13: 7; cf. Ro 4: 10–12. W. ref. to the sins of paganism νεκροὶ . . . τῇ ἀ. τῆς σαρκὸς ὑμῶν *dead through your uncircumcised* (i.e., full of vice, in the pagan manner) *flesh* Col 2: 13 (cf. Gen 17: 11 σὰρξ τῆς ἀ.).

3. abstr. for concr. *heathenism, the Gentiles* (beside περιτομή) Ro 3: 30; 4: 9; Col 3: 11; Eph 2: 11. τὸ εὐαγγέλιον τῆς ἀ. *the gospel for the Gentile world* (gospel of uncircumcision is also poss.) Gal 2: 7. M-M.*

ἀκρόβυστος, ου, ὁ (not LXX, but used by other translators of the OT) *an uncircumcised man, a Gentile* (Christian) IPhld 6: 1.*

ἀκρογωνιαῖος, α, ον (purely Biblical) *lying at the extreme corner* ἀ. λίθος *cornerstone* or *capstone* (RJMcKelvey, NTS 8, '61/'62, 352–59 rejects *capstone*), only fig., of Christ Eph 2: 20; w. ref. to the preciousness of the material λίθον ἐκλεκτὸν ἀ. ἔντιμον 1 Pt 2: 6; B 6: 2 (both Is 28: 16); s. lit. on κεφαλή 2b. M-M.*

ἀκροθίνιον, ου, τό oft. pl., *first-fruits*, usu. (Hdt. 1, 86; Thu. 1, 132, 2 al.; Dit., Syll.³ 23; 605A, 5) of the best part of the booty, which is reserved for the divinity, also prob. *booty, spoils* gener. Hb 7: 4. M-M.*

ἄκρον, ου, τό (Hom.+; inscr., pap., LXX, Philo, Joseph.; really neut. of ἄκρος W-S. §20, 12c; Rob. 775) *high point, top* ὄρους *of a mountain* (Ex 34: 2) Hs 9, 1, 4; ἐπ' ἄκρον ὄρους ὑψηλοῦ[s] *on the top of a high mountain* (Is 28: 4) LJ 1: 7. τὸ ἄ. τῆς ῥάβδου *the top of his staff* Hb 11: 21 (Gen 47: 31). τὸ ἄ. τοῦ δακτύλου (schol. on Nicander, Ther. 383 τὰ ἄκρα τῶν δακτύλων; cf. 4 Macc 10: 7; Philo, De Prov. in Euseb., Pr. Ev. 8, 14, 65; Jos., Ant. 11, 234) *a finger tip* Lk 16: 24; of the *tip* of a stick Hs 8, 1, 14; 8, 10, 1.—*Extreme limit, end* (Pla., Phaedo 109D ἄ. τῆς θαλάσσης; POxy. 43 verso I, 17; PThéad. 19, 12; Jos., Ant. 14, 299): ἀπ' ἄ. οὐρανῶν ἕως ἄ. αὐτῶν *from one end of heaven to the other* Mt 24: 31 (Dt 30: 4; Ps 18: 7; cf. Dt 4: 32; Jos., Ant. 19, 6 ἀπ' ἄκρων ἐπ' ἄκρα). The expr. found in the OT pass. mentioned is mixed w. the one found in Dt 13: 8 and Jer 12: 12 in ἀπ' ἄ. γῆς ἕως ἄ. οὐρανοῦ Mk 13: 27. B. 854; 856.*

ἀκτίν (so Herodian Gr. index Lentz; Corp. Gloss. Lat. 3, 278; Kephalaia I, 166, 4; 165, 30) AP 7 (Bl-D. §46, 4; cf. Mlt.-H. 135 ὠδίν); s. the foll.

ἀκτίς, ῖνος, ἡ (Hom.+; inscr. [e.g. Isis of Andros 8 Peek]; LXX; Sib. Or. 3, 803; later form ἀκτίν, s. the foregoing) *ray, beam* of the sun (Strato of Lamps. [300 BC], fgm. 65a Wehrli ['50] τοῦ ἡλίου ἀκτῖνες; Ps.-Pla., Axioch. 13 p. 371D; Diod. S. 3, 48, 3; Wsd 2: 4; 16: 27; Sir 43: 4; Philo, Conf. Lingu. 157; Jos., Ant. 19, 344; Herm. Wr. 10, 4b) B 5: 10; AP 15. Of the heavenly radiance of angels AP 7 (cf. En. 106, 5). ⟨ἀκτῖν⟩ες πυρός 26 (restored by Diels).*

'Ακύλας, acc. -αν, ὁ *Aquila* (Brutus, Ep. 61; 63; 64; Philostrat., Vi. Soph. 2, 11, 1; Dit., Or. 533, 84; 544, 9; PGiess. 73, 5; BGU 71, 21; 484, 6; Jos., Ant. 19, 110; 283 [Dssm., NB 15; BS 187]) a Jewish workman (s. σκηνοποιός) from Pontus (an Aq. fr. Pontus in an inscr. of Sinope: AJPh 27, '06, p. 269), friend of Paul, who esteemed him and his wife Priscilla highly, Ac 18: 2, 18, 21 v.l., 26; Ro 16: 3; 1 Cor 16: 19; 2 Ti 4: 19. Cf. RSchumacher, Aquila u. Priscilla: ThGl 12, '20, 86-99; FXPölzl, D. Mitarbeiter des Weltap. Pls '11, 371-81; Billerb. III 486-93; AHarnack, SAB '00, 2-13= Studien I '31, 48-61; on this FMSchiele, ZMR 15, '00, 353-60. M-M.*

ἄκυρος, ον (Thu.+; inscr., pap., Pr, Philo; Jos., Ant. 13, 262; 16, 38) *void, of no effect* ἄκυρον ποιεῖν *disregard* (Pla., Prot. 356D et al.; Pr 5: 7) τὰς βουλάς 1 Cl 57: 4 (Pr 1: 25).*

ἀκυρόω 1 aor. ἠκύρωσα *make void* (so Dinarchus 1, 63; Diod. S. 16, 24 al. [Nägeli 29]; Dit., Syll.³ 742, 30 [86 BC]; BGU 944, 11; 1167, 26; LXX; Philo, Ebr. 197, Conf. Lingu. 193; Jos., Ant. 18, 304 ἐντολάς; 20, 183; Third Corinthians 3: 12) τὸν λόγον τοῦ θεοῦ Mt 15: 6; Mk 7: 13. As legal t.t. (OEger, ZNW 18, '18, 92f) διαθήκην (POxy. 491 [126 AD]; cf. 494; 495) Gal 3: 17. M-M.*

ἀκωλύτως adv. (Pla.+; freq. in pap. as legal t.t.: POxy. 502; BGU 917, 14; PLeipz. 26, 11; 30, 9; Sym. Job 34: 31; Jos., Ant. 12, 104; 16, 41 ἀ. τὴν πάτριον εὐσέβειαν διαφυλάττειν) *without let or hindrance* διδάσκειν ἀ. Ac 28: 31. M-M.*

ἄκων, ἄκουσα, ἆκον (since Hom., who has ἀέκων; inscr., pap.; 4 Macc 11: 12; Jos., Bell. 2, 123, Ant. 16, 256) *unwilling*; to be transl. as adv. *unwillingly* πράσσειν 1 Cor 9: 17 (cf. Philo, Omn. Prob. Lib. 61 ἄ. ποιεῖν). ἀ. ἁμαρτάνειν *sin inadvertently* (Soph., fgm. 604 Nauck²;

Pla., Rep. 336E ἄκοντες ἡμαρτάνομεν; Dio Chrys. 17[34], 13; Ael. Aristid. 34, 5 K.=50 p. 547 D.—See also Ps.-Callisth. 1, 9, 2 ἁμαρτήσασα οὐχ ἥμαρτες) 1 Cl 2: 3 (cf. Job 14: 17). See IRo 5: 2 v.l. M-M.*

ἄλα s. **ἅλας**.

ἀλάβαστρος, ου, ὁ and ἡ, also **ἀλάβαστρον, τό** (s. Mk 14: 3 w. its variants; cf. Theocr. 15, 114; Delian inscr. [III BC]: IG XI [2], 161B, 9; 4 Km 21: 13 with v.l. and Bl-D. §49, 1; Mlt.-H. 122) *alabaster*, then an *alabaster flask* for ointment, a vessel w. a rather long neck which was broken off when the contents were used; a container for spikenard ointment (so Hdt.+); also a loanword in Lat.: Pliny, Nat. H. 13, 3 unguenta optime servantur in alabastris) Mt 26: 7; Mk 14: 3; Lk 7: 37 (ἀλ. μύρου as Hdt. 3, 20; Lucian, Dial. Mer. 14, 2; Dionys. Hal. 7, 9; PSI 333, 6; 628, 8).—Avan Veldhuizen, De alabasten flesch: ThSt 24, '06, 170-2. M-M.*

ἀλαζονεία, ας, ἡ (Aristoph., Pla.+; Wsd 5: 8; 4 Macc 1: 26; 2: 15; 8: 19; Test. Jos. 17: 8; Philo, Virt. 162ff; Jos., Ant. 6, 179; 14, 111; pap. [HIBell, Jews and Christians in Egypt '24]; on the spelling s. Kühner-Bl. II p. 275; Rob. 196f) *pretension, arrogance* in word and deed καυχᾶσθαι ἐν ταῖς ἀλαζονείαις *boast in arrogance* Js 4: 16. ἐγκαυχᾶσθαι ἐν ἀ. τοῦ λόγου *boast w. arrogant words* 1 Cl 21: 5. ἀποτίθεσθαι ἀ. (w. τύφος [as Ep. 3 of Apollonius of Tyana: Philostrat. I 345, 22 K.], ἀφροσύνη, ὀργαί) 13: 1; (w. ἀκαταστασία) 14: 1; (w. ὑπερηφανία) 16: 2. W. other vices 35: 5; Hm 6, 2, 5; 8: 5; D 5: 1. Of Jewish pride Dg 4: 1, 6. ἡ ἀ. τοῦ βίου *pride in one's possessions* 1 J 2: 16 (cf. X., Hell. 7, 1, 38; Polyb. 6, 57, 6 ἀ. περὶ τοὺς βίους; Wsd 5: 8).—PJoüon, Rech de Sc rel 28, '38, 311-14. TW I 227f. M-M.*

ἀλαζονεύομαι (Aristoph., Lysias+; Philo, Fug. 33; Jos., Bell. 4, 122) *boast, be boastful* w. acc. *about someth.* (Aeschin, 3, 218; Herodian 2, 7, 2 χρήματα; Wsd 2: 16) μηδέν 1 Cl 2: 1. τὴν μείωσιν τῆς σαρκός Dg 4: 4. Abs. (Timaeus Hist. [IV-III BC] no. 566 fgm. 132 Jac.; Dio Chrys. 26[43], 2) 1 Cl 38: 2.*

ἀλαζών, όνος, ὁ (Cratinus, Aristoph.+; Job 28: 8; Philo, Mos. 2, 240) *boaster, braggart* Ro 1: 30; 2 Ti 3: 2.—Also (like Hdt. 6, 12; Philostrat., Vi. Soph. 2, 9, 2 p. 87, 11; Hab 2: 5; Jos., Ant. 8, 264; Plut., Mor. 523E) as adj. (w. ὑπερήφανος, as Syntipas p. 126, 9) ἡ ἀ. αὐθάδεια *boastful presumption* 1 Cl 57: 2.—ORibbeck, Alazon 1882.*

ἀλαλάζω (Pind.+; LXX; Jos., Ant. 5, 225; 6, 191 al.) *cry out loudly* of people over one who has died ἀ. πολλά (w. κλαίειν) *wail loudly* Mk 5: 38 (cf. Eur., El. 483; Jer 32: 34.—PHeinisch, D. Trauergebräuche b. d. Israeliten '31). Gener. of shrill tones (Nonnus, Dionys. 12, 354 of the screeching sound of the wine-press) κύμβαλον ἀλαλάζον *a clashing cymbal* 1 Cor 13: 1 (Ps 150: 5 ἐν κυμβάλοις ἀλαλαγμοῦ). Gdspd., Probs. 160f. TW I 228.—S. κύμβαλον.*

ἀλάλητος, ον (Philod.; Anth. Pal. 5, 4; Cyranides p. 19, 19) *unexpressed, wordless* στεναγμοὶ ἀ. *sighs too deep for words* (so the Syr. and Armen. tr.; the Vulgate renders it 'inenarrabilis', *inexpressible*) Ro 8: 26.*

ἄλαλος, ον (Aeschyl.+, also IG XIV 1627; LXX; Sib. Or. 4, 7) *mute, dumb* ἄ. γίνεσθαι *be struck dumb* of deceitful lips 1 Cl 15: 5 (Ps 30: 19); πνεῦμα ἄ. (Plut., Or. Def. 51 p. 438B of the Pythia: ἀλάλου καὶ κακοῦ πνεύματος πλήρης. Paris ms. 2316 leaf 318 in Rtzst., Poim. 293, 1 πνεῦμα ... ἄλαλον) *a dumb spirit*, which robs men of their speech Mk 9: 17; acc. to vs. 25 the πν. ἄ. is also deaf (ἄ. w. κωφός Alex. Aphr., Probl. 1, 138; Artem. 1, 76; Ps 37: 14).—ὁ ἄ. *a mute person* (Ps 37: 14) ποιεῖ ἀ. λαλεῖν 7: 37.*

ἅλας, ατος, τό (Aristot.+; pap. since III BC [Mayser 286; Nägeli 58, 1]; LXX [Helbing 49; Thackeray 152]. For the v.l. ἅλα Mt 5: 13 al. [Sb 8030, 21 [47 AD], prob. a back-formation fr. ἅλατ- on the model of σῶμα, ατος] s. W.-S. §9, note 7; Bl-D. §47, 4 w. app.; Mlt-H. 132f. From the class. form ἅλς only ἁλί [cf. Lev 2: 13] as v.l. in Mk 9: 49 and ἁλός 1 Cl 11: 2 [Gen 19: 26]) *salt.*
1. lit. as seasoning for food or as fertilizer Mt 5: 13b; Mk 9: 50 ab; Lk 14: 34 (EPDeatrick, Biblical Archaeologist 25, '62, 41–48).
2. fig., of the spiritual qualities of the disciples τὸ ἄ. τῆς γῆς Mt 5: 13a; cf. Mk 9: 50c (Jülicher, Gleichn. 67–79; LFonck, D. Parabeln⁴'27, 782ff; GAicher, Mt 5: 13: BZ 5, '07, 48–59 [against him Fonck, ZkTh 31, '07, 553–8]; WSWood, JTS 25, '24, 167–72; NDColeman, ET 48, '36/37, 360–62; LKöhler, ZDPV 59, '36, 133f=Kleine Lichter, '45, 73–6, cf. GRDriver, JTS 47, '46, 75; WNauck, Studia Theologica 6, '53, 165–78; OCullmann, RHPhR 37, '57, 36–43: salt a symbol of sacrifice; RSchnackenburg, Schriften zum NT, '71, 177–200; GBertram, TW IV 842–4). Of speech, which is winsome or witty (Plut., Mor. 514EF; 685A: life seasoned with words) ὁ λόγος ἅλατι ἠρτυμένος (sc. ἔστω) *let your speech be seasoned w. salt* Col 4: 6. (Diog. L. 4, 67: Timon [III BC] says the speech of the Academics is ἀνάλιστος) M-M. B. 382.*

Ἄλασσα Ac 27: 8 v.l.; s. Λασαία.*

ἀλατόμητος, ον *uncut* Hs 9, 16, 7.*

ἀλγέω (Hom.+; inscr., pap., LXX; Philo, Leg. All. 3, 200; 211; Jos., Ant. 15, 58) *feel pain* ἀλγεῖν ποιεῖ *causes pain*=sends suffering 1 Cl 56: 6 (Job 5: 18). ὁ ἀλγῶν σάρκα *the one who is ill in body* B 8: 6 (cf. Pla., Rep. 7 p. 515E τὰ ὄμματα; Artem. 4, 24 p. 218, 7 τὴν κεφαλήν; Jos., Vi. 420 τὴν ψυχήν).*

ἀλεεῖς, οἱ s. ἀλιεύς.

ἀλείφω 1 aor. ἤλειψα, 1 aor. mid. imper. ἄλειψαι (Hom.+; inscr., pap., LXX; Jos., Bell. 2, 123) *anoint*
1. lit. (Diod. S. 17, 90, 2) τοὺς πόδας μύρῳ *anoint his feet w. perfume* Lk 7: 38, 46 (KWeiss, ZNW 46, '55, 241–45); J 12: 3; cf. 11: 2. Those who were ill were anointed w. oil (household remedy; cf. Cat. Cod. Astr. VII p. 178, 3; 28) Mk 6: 13; Js 5: 14 (MMeinertz, D. Krankensalbung Jk 5: 14f: BZ 20, '32, 23–36; CArmerding, Biblioth. Sacra 95, '38, 195–201; HFriesenhahn, BZ 24, '40, 185–90. Cf. ἔλαιον 1 and κάμνω 2, 3). Of the dead, w. spices Mk 16: 1. Mid. *anoint oneself* (Jos., Bell. 5, 565) τὴν κεφαλήν Mt 6: 17 (w. washing of the face as Plut., Mor. 142A).
2. fig. (Philo, Conf. Lingu. 91, Mos. 1, 298) pass. ἀ. δυσωδίαν *let oneself be besmeared w. filth* of accepting false doctrine IEph 17: 1 (ἀ. w. acc. of that which one applies, as 2 Km 14: 2; Mi 6: 15 al.). S. χρίω. M-M.*

ἀλεκτοροφωνία, ας, ἡ (Strabo 7, 35; Aesop., Fab. 55 P.; Phryn. 229 Lob.; Bl-D. §123, 1; Mlt.-H. 271) *the crowing of a cock* ἀλεκτοροφωνίας at cockcrow, name of the third watch of the night (12–3 A.M.) Mt 26: 34 v.l. (s. PKatz, ThLZ 80, '55, 737); Mk 13: 35 (on the gen. cf. Bl-D. §186, 2; Rob. 471).—On chickens in Judaea and Jerusalem s. KHRengstorf on Tosefta Yebamoth 3, 4 (Rabb. Texte I 3, '33, p. 36f).—Dalman, Arbeit VII (s. οἰκία 1).*

ἀλεκτρυών, όνος, ὁ *cock, rooster* (since Theognis 864;

Cratinus 108, κοκκύζει 311; POxy. 1207, 8; Inscr. gr. 692, 5 [I AD]; Dit., Syll.³ 1173, 16; 3 Macc 5: 23; PGM 3, 693; 701) Gospel fgm. from the Fayum (Kl. T. 8³, p. 23, 10). B. 174.*

ἀλέκτωρ, ορος, ὁ *cock, rooster* (for class. times cf. WG Rutherford, New Phryn., 1881, 307; Lycophron v. 1094; Batr. 192; PTebt. 140 [72 BC]; PFay. 119, 29 [c. 100 AD]; BGU 269, 4; 1067, 11; PGM 2, 73; 4, 2190; Pr 30: 31) φωνεῖ Mt 26: 34, 74f; Mk 14: 30, 68 v.l., 72; Lk 22: 34, 60f; J 13: 38; 18: 27. M-M.*

Ἀλεξανδρεύς, έως, ὁ *an Alexandrian* (Plut., Pomp. 49, 6; Dit., Or. index II; 3 Macc 2: 30; 3: 21; Philo, Joseph., Sib. Or.; cf. Wilcken, Grundzüge 15, Chrestom. 82) of Apollos Ac 18: 24 (on Jews as Ἀ. cf. Jos., C. Ap. 2, 38). συναγωγή Ἀ. (Schürer II⁴ 87; 502; 524) 6: 9.*

Ἀλεξανδρῖνος, η, ον (on the accent s. Kühner-Bl. II 296; Mlt.-H. 359.—Polyb. 34, 8, 7; BGU 142, 5; 143, 3; 741, 4 κλάση Ἀλεξανδρίνη=Lat. classis Alexandrina; cf. Wilcken, Grundzüge 379) *Alexandrian* πλοῖον Ἀ. Ac 27: 6; 28: 11.—Subst. 6: 9 v.l.*

Ἀλέξανδρος, ου, ὁ *Alexander* a favorite name w. Jews as well as Gentiles (Joseph.—ET 10, 1899, 527).
1. son of Simon of Cyrene Mk 15: 21.
2. a Jew of the high priestly family Ac 4: 6.
3. a Jew of Ephesus 19: 33.—4. an apostate 1 Ti 1: 20, presumably the smith of 2 Ti 4: 14.*

ἀλεσμός, οῦ, ὁ *grinding* (Jos., Ant. 3, 252 v.l.) fig. ἀλεσμοὶ ὅλου τοῦ σώματος *grinding* (s. 4: 1) *of the whole body* of torture in martyrdom IRo 5: 3 (cf. Lghtf. ad loc.—Of a partic. kind of torture, Eunap., Vi. Soph. 59 cod.; cf. 312).*

ἄλευρον, ου, τό (Hdt.+; PGM 7, 539 and elsewh. in pap.; LXX; Jos., Ant. 3, 142; 8, 322; Sib. Or. 8, 14) *wheat flour* used for making bread Mt 13: 33; Lk 13: 21. M-M. B. 361.*

ἀλήθεια, ας, ἡ (since Hom., who uses it in the form ἀληθείη; inscr., pap., LXX, Ep. Arist., Philo, Joseph., Test. 12 Patr.).
1. *truthfulness, dependability, uprightness* in thought and deed (Alcaeus 57; Mimnermus 8 al.) of God (Gen 24: 27 al.) Ro 3: 7; 15: 8. Of men (Pittacus in Diog. L. 1, 78; Arrian, Anab. 7, 30, 3; Lucian, Dial. Mort. 11, 6; 4 Km 20: 3; Judg 9: 15f al.; Ep. Arist. 206) ἐν ἀ. λαλεῖν *speak truthfully* 2 Cor 7: 14; (w. εἰλικρίνεια) 1 Cor 5: 8; (w. ἀγαθωσύνη and δικαιοσύνη) Eph 5: 9; 1 Cl 19: 1; 31: 2; 35: 2; Pol 2: 1; ἐν πάσῃ ἀ. w. *perfect fidelity* 4: 2.—Hm 8: 9; 12, 3, 1; s 9, 15, 2.
2. *truth* (opp. ψεῦδος)—a. gener. ἀ. λαλεῖν *tell the truth* (Zech 8: 16) Eph 4: 25; Hm 3: 5; 2 Cl 12: 3. ἀ. λέγειν (Hdt. 2, 115 al.; PGiess. 84, 14 [II AD] τὴν ἀ. εἰπεῖν) Ro 9: 1; 1 Ti 2: 7. Fut. ἀ. ἐρῶ 2 Cor 12: 6. ἀ. ἀγαπᾶν Hm 3: 1. Opp. ψεύδεσθαι κατὰ τῆς ἀ. *lie against the truth* Js 3: 14; εἶπεν αὐτῷ πᾶσαν τὴν ἀ. *she told him the whole truth* Mk 5: 33 (cf. Hdt. 9, 89; Thu. 6, 87, 1 al.; Kleopatra l. 88; POxy. 283, 13f [45 AD] γνωσθῆναι πᾶσαν τὴν ἀ.; Jos., Bell. 7, 31 πυθόμενος παρ' αὐτοῦ πᾶσαν τὴν ἀ.). ἐν λόγῳ ἀληθείας *by truthful speech* 2 Cor 6: 7; ῥήματα ἀληθείας Ac 26: 25; μόρφωσις τῆς γνώσεως καὶ τῆς ἀ. *embodiment of knowledge and truth* Ro 2: 20; ἡ ἁγνότης τῆς ἀ. *the purity that belongs to truth* Hv 3, 7, 3. ἔξωθεν τῆς ἀ.=ψευδής 3, 4, 3.
b. esp. of the content of Christianity as the absolute truth (cf. Plut., Is. et Os. 2 p. 351E ἀ. περὶ θεῶν; Philo,

Spec. Leg. 4, 178, the proselyte is a μετανάστας εἰς ἀ.)
Eph 4: 21 (CAScott, Exp. 8th Ser. III '12, 178–85;
RBultmann, ZNW 27, '28, 128; FJBriggs, ET 39, '28, 526).
ὁ λόγος τῆς ἀ. the word of truth Eph 1: 13; Col 1: 5; 2 Ti
2: 15; Js 1: 18. ἡ ἀ. τοῦ εὐαγγελίου Gal 2: 5, 14. ὁ περὶ ἀ.
λόγος Pol 3: 2; πείθεσθαι τῇ ἀ. Gal 5: 7; πιστεύειν τῇ ἀ.
2 Th 2: 12; hence πίστει ἀληθείας belief in the truth vs.
13; περιπατεῖν ἐν ἀ. 2 J 4; 3 J 3f (cf. 4 Km 20: 3); ζῆν
κατὰ ἀ. IEph 6: 2; πορεύεσθαι κατὰ τὴν ἀ. Pol 5: 2; ἐν
ἀ. (3 Km 2: 4) Hm 3: 4; gird oneself w. truth Eph 6: 14; cf.
Hm 11: 4.—Truth has a strongly practical side, which
expresses itself in virtues like righteousness and holiness,
Eph 4: 24 (Nicol. Dam.: 90 fgm. 67, 1 Jac. δικαιοσύνην κ.
ἀλ.). Hence it is contrasted w. ἀδικία 1 Cor 13: 6; Ro 1:
18; 2: 8. In the last-named passage a negative attitude
toward the truth is called ἀπειθεῖν τῇ ἀ. Also πλανᾶσθαι ἀπὸ τῆς ἀ. wander from the truth Js 5: 19; κατα-
στρέφειν ἀπὸ τῆς ἀ. Hs 6, 2, 1, cf. 4; ἀποστερεῖσθαι
τῆς ἀ. 1 Ti 6: 5; ἐρευνᾶν περὶ τῆς ἀ. make inquiries about
the truth Hm 10, 1, 4; 6; ἀνθίστασθαι τῇ ἀ. oppose the
truth (i.e., the gospel) 2 Ti 3: 8. Opp. μῦθοι 4: 4. Truth can
be communicated: φανερώσει τῆς ἀ. by a clear statement
of the truth 2 Cor 4: 2 (cf. POxy. 925, 5 φανέρωσόν μοι
τὴν παρὰ σοὶ ἀλ.); is taught D 11: 10; recognized 1 Ti 4:
3; Hv 3, 6, 2; cf. ἐπίγνωσις τῆς ἀληθείας (Alex. Aphr.,
Quaest. 3, 12, II 2 p. 102, 3 γνῶσις τ. ἀληθείας) 1 Ti 2: 4;
2 Ti 2: 25; 3: 7; Tit 1: 1; Hb 10: 26; ὁδὸς τῆς ἀ. 2 Pt 2: 2; 1
Cl 35: 5 (cf. Pind., P. 3, 103; Eur., fgm. 289; Gen 24: 48
al.); ὑπακοὴ τῆς ἀ. 1 Pt 1: 22; ἀγάπη τῆς ἀ. 2 Th 2: 10.
God is πατὴρ τῆς ἀ. 2 Cl 3: 1; 20: 5; φῶς ἀληθείας IPhld
2: 1 (cf. Ps 42: 3); θεὸς τῆς ἀ. (1 Esdr 4: 40) 2 Cl 19: 1; cf. 1
Cl 60: 2. The reverse genitival constr. in ἀ. τοῦ θεοῦ Ro 1:
25, is best rendered adjectively divine truth='the true
God', though its exact mng. is uncertain.—'A. is a favorite
word of the Joh. lit., and plays a great role in it. God's word
is truth J 17: 17 (Ps 118: 142). Truth w. χάρις 1: 14, 17; w.
πνεῦμα 4: 23f. The Spirit leads into truth 16: 13; hence
πνεῦμα τῆς ἀ. 14: 17; 15: 26; 16: 13; 1 J 4: 6 (cf. Hm 3: 4).
πνεῦμα is identified w. ἀ. 1 J 5: 6; it is mediated through
Christ J 1: 17, who calls himself truth 14: 6 (cf. PGM 5, 148
ἐγώ εἰμι ἡ ἀλήθεια, on the other hand POxy. 1380, 63
[early II AD] Isis is called ἀ.; Apollonaretal. Berl. Gr. Pap.
11517 [II AD]: Her 55, '20, 188–95 l. 52 Apollo as the
ἀψευδὴς ἀλ.; M. Ant., 9, 1, 2 God=Nature ἀλήθεια
ὀνομάζεται; Lucian, How to Write History 61 says of a
good history-writer: ἦν ἀλήθεια ἐπὶ πᾶσι). He who possesses Christ knows truth (γινώσκ. τὴν ἀλ. as Jos., Ant.
13, 291; ἀληθείας γνῶσις Maximus Tyr. 26, 5b) 8: 32 (cf.
1QS 5, 10); 2 J 1; he does the truth J 3: 21, cf. 1 J 1: 6
(ποιεῖν τὴν ἀ. Gen 32: 11; 47: 29; Is 26: 10 al.; Test.
Reub. 6: 9, Benj. 10: 3); stands in the truth J 8: 44; is of the
truth 18: 37; cf. 1 J 2: 21; 3: 19 (ἐκ τῆς ἀληθείας=corre-
sponding to the truth P. Turin I, 6, 13). The truth sets him
free J 8: 32. Christ proclaims this truth: λέγειν (Jos., Ant.
10, 124) 8: 45f; 16: 7; λαλεῖν 8: 40 (also λαλεῖν ἐν ἀ.
IEph 6: 2); μαρτυρεῖν τῇ ἀλ. J 18: 37. As John the Baptist
witnesses to Jesus, he witnesses to the truth 5: 33; cf.
μαρτυρούντων σου τῇ ἀληθείᾳ bear witness to your
(fidelity to the) truth 3 J 3; ἵνα συνεργοὶ γινώμεθα τῇ ἀ.
vs. 8. In Pilate's skeptical question τί ἐστιν ἀ.; J 18: 38
the worldly man speaks. Opp. θάνατος ISm 5: 1.—On ἀ.
in J s. CKBarrett, JTS new ser. I '50, 8.—Mlt.-Turner 177f.

3. reality (Diod. S. 2, 8, 4) as opposed to mere appear-
ance (opp. πρόφασις) Phil 1: 18. κατὰ ἀλήθειαν rightly
Ro 2: 2 (cf. Diod. S. 4, 64, 2 οἱ κατ' ἀλήθειαν γονεῖς; M.
Ant. 2, 11, 3; 4, 11; Damianus of Larissa p. 20, 2 [ed.
Schöne 1897]; Zen.-P. Cairo 59 202, 7 [254 BC]; Ep. Arist.
140; 4 Macc 5: 18; PGM 12, 235). ἐν ἀληθείᾳ indeed, truly

(Jer 33: 15) Mt 22: 16; J 17: 19; 1 Cl 63: 1. ἐπιγινώσκειν
τὴν χάριν ἐν ἀλ. Col 1: 6; οὓς ἐγὼ ἀγαπῶ ἐν ἀλ. 2 J 1,
cf. 3 J 1 belongs here (like the epist. formulas PFay. 118,
26; 119, 26 [100–110 AD] τοὺς φιλοῦντας ἡμᾶς πρὸς ἀ.=
'really and truly'). ἐπ' ἀληθείας in accordance w. the
truth, truly (Demosth. 18, 17; Dit., Syll.³ 495, 174 [III BC];
PAmh. 68, 33; POxy. 480, 9; Job; Da; Philo, Leg. ad Gai.
60; 248): διδάσκειν Mk 12: 14; Lk 20: 21; εἰπεῖν Mk 12:
32; λέγειν Lk 4: 25; συνάγεσθαι Ac 4: 27; κατα-
λαμβάνεσθαι 10: 34; τελειοῦν 1 Cl 23: 5; ἐπιστέλλειν
47: 3; ἐπ' ἀ. καὶ οὗτος μετ' αὐτοῦ ἦν certainly this man
was with him, too Lk 22: 59.—GStorz, Gebr. u. Be-
deutungsentwicklg v. ἀλήθεια u. begriffsverwandten Wör-
tern, Diss. Tüb. '22; Dodd 65–75; WLuther, 'Wahrheit' u.
'Lüge' im ältest. Griechentum '35; FBüchsel, D. Begriff d.
Wahrheit in dem Ev. u. den Briefen des J. '11; ASchlatter,
D. Glaube im NT⁴ '27, 551–61; Hans v Soden, Was ist
Wahrheit? '27; FNötscher, Vom Alten zum NT, '62, 112–
25 (Qumran); JBecker, Das Heil Gottes '64 (Qumran);
HBraun, Qumran und d. NT II '66, 118–44; I de la
Potterie, TU 73, '59, 277–94 (John); ABöhlig, Mysterion u.
Wahrheit, '68, 3–40; BHJackayya, CTM 41, '70, 171–75
(John); YIbuki, D. Wahrheit im J, '72; RBultmann, Unter-
suchungen z. J. Ἀλήθεια: ZNW 27, '28, 113–63, TW I
239–51. M-M.

ἀληθεύω (Pre-Socr., Aeschyl.+; PAmh. 142, 1; LXX;
Jos., C. Ap. 1, 223) be truthful, tell the truth τινί to
someone (Philo, Cher. 15) Gal 4: 16. Abs. (Solon in Stob.
III p. 114, 10 H.; Philostrat., Vi. Apoll. 4, 16 p. 135, 2; 8,
26 p. 339, 27; Jos., Bell. 3, 322, Vi. 132) ἀληθεύοντες ἐν
ἀγάπῃ, i.e., in such a way that the spirit of love is
maintained Eph 4: 15 (cf. Pr 21: 3). M-M.*

ἀληθής, ές (Hom.+; inscr., pap., LXX, Philo, Joseph.,
Test. 12 Patr.) true.

1. of pers. truthful, righteous, honest (Aeschyl., Thu.+;
IG XIV 1071; BGU 1024 VI, 17; 2 Esdr 17: 2 [Neh 7: 2];
Wsd 1: 6; Jos., Ant. 8, 234) of Jesus Mt 22: 16; Mk 12: 14; J
7: 18. Of God (Wsd 15: 1; Philo, Spec. Leg. 1, 36; Jos.,
Bell. 7, 323; Sib. Or. fgm. 1, 10; 5, 499) J 3: 33; 7: 28 𝔓⁶⁶ et
al.; 8: 26; Ro 3: 4; Dg 8: 8. Gener. (opp. πλάνοι) 2 Cor 6:
8. Of bishops and deacons D 15: 1.

2. of things: true (Gen 41: 32) Hm 3: 3f; 11: 3.
γνῶσις Dg 12: 6. παροιμία (Soph., Ajax 664) 2 Pt 2: 22.
ἀληθῆ λέγειν (Soph., Ph. 345; Ps.-Demosth. 7, 43; POxy.
37, 12 [I AD]; PStrassb. 41, 18 [c. 250 AD] τὰ ἀληθῆ λέγειν;
3 Macc 7: 12; Jos., Vi. 286) J 19: 35. τοῦτο ἀληθές (v.l.
ἀληθῶς) εἴρηκας you have said this truly (lit., 'as someth.
true'; cf. Pla.; Ps.-Demosth. 59, 34 ταῦτ' ἀληθῆ λέγω;
Lucian, Fugit. 1) 4: 18; cf. 10: 41 (πάντα ὅσα . . . ἀλ. like
Jos., Ant. 8, 242). οὐδὲν ἀληθές Ac 14: 19 v.l. (Oenomaus
the Cynic in Euseb., Pr. Ev. 5, 26, 4 says that in the oracles
there is μηδὲν ἀληθὲς ἢ ἔνθεον) τἀληθῆ διδάσκειν
Papias 2: 3. ὅσα ἐστὶν ἀληθῆ Phil 4: 8. ἀληθές ἐστιν καὶ
οὐκ ἔστιν ψεῦδος (the contrast as Pla., Ep. 7 p. 344B;
Philo, Rer. Div. Her. 132) 1 J 2: 27, cf. vs. 8; Hv 3, 4, 3.
γραφαί 1 Cl 45: 2. λόγος (since Pind., O. 1, 28, also
Galen, in Hippocratis De Natura Hom., 29 p. 17, 26f
Mewaldt; Dt 13: 15; Jdth 11: 10; Wsd 2: 17; Philo) Dg 12:
7. Dependable μαρτυρία (PHal. 1, 227 ἀληθῆ μαρτυρεῖν;
Jos., Ant. 4, 219 μαρτυρία) J 5: 31f, 17; 21: 24; 3 J 12; Tit
1: 13. κρίσις J 8: 16 𝔓⁶⁶ et al.

3. real, genuine (Thu. et al.; PTebt. 285, 3; 293, 17; Pr 1:
3; Wsd 12: 27) ἀγάπη Pol 1: 1; MPol 1: 2. χάρις 1 Pt 5:
12. ζωή (Philo, Poster. Cai. 45) Dg 12: 4. βρῶσις, πόσις of
the body and blood of Jesus J 6: 55. ἵνα τὸ πνεῦμα ἀληθὲς
εὑρεθῇ Hm 3: 1. ἀ. ἐστιν τὸ γινόμενον διὰ τ. ἀγγέλου

36

what was done by the angel is a reality Ac 12: 9. On μαθητὴς ἀ. IRo 4: 2 s. ἀληθῶς 2. M-M. B. 1169.*

ἀληθινός, ή, όν (Heraclitus, X., Pla. et al.; inscr., pap., LXX, En., Philo, Joseph., Test. 12 Patr.) *true.*

1. *true, dependable* (X., An. 1, 9, 17; LXX) of God (Ex 34: 6; Num 14: 18; 1 Esdr 8: 86; 3 Macc 2: 11; Jos., Ant. 11, 55) perh. J 7: 28 (s. 3 below); Rv 6: 10 (w. ἅγιος); (w. ἀψευδής) MPol 14: 2. More exactly defined ὁ κύριος ἀ. ἐν παντὶ ῥήματι Hm 3: 1 (opp. ψεῦδος). Of Christ, the judge of the world, w. ἅγιος Rv 3: 7; w. πιστός 3: 14; 19: 11. Of Job 1 Cl 17: 3 (Job 1: 1). ἀ. καρδία (Is 38: 3; Test. Dan 5: 3) Hb 10: 22.

2. *true, in accordance w. truth* Hm 3: 5. λόγος (Pla., Rep. 7 p. 522A al.; 3 Km 10: 6; 2 Ch 9: 5; Da 6: 13, 10: 1 Theod.) J 4: 37. λόγοι (2 Km 7: 28; En. 99, 2) Rv 19: 9; (w. πιστός) 21: 5; 22: 6. μαρτυρία *dependable* J 19: 35; κρίσις ἀ. (Tob 3: 2BA; Is 59: 4; En. 27, 3) *judgment*, by which the truth is brought to light 8: 16 (ἀληθὴς 𝔓⁶⁶ et al.); pl. (w. δίκαιος) Rv 16: 7; 19: 2. ὁδοί 15: 3; cf. Hv 3, 7, 1.

3. *genuine, real* (X., Oec. 10, 3; Pla., Rep. 6 p. 499c; Dio Chrys. 47[64], 21 αἷμα ἀλ.; POxy. 465, 108 ἄγαλμα κυάνου ἀ.=a statue of genuine lapis lazuli; PGM 8, 20; 41; 43 οἶδά σου καὶ τ. βαρβαρικὰ ὀνόματα . . . τὸ δὲ ἀ. ὄνομά σου; Fluchtaf.² p. 19f; PGM 4, 278; 5, 115) ἀ. φῶς (Ael. Aristid. 23, 15 K.=42 p. 772 D. [Asclep.]; Plotinus, Enn. 6, 9, 4) J 1: 9; 1 J 2: 8; ἀ. τ. θεοῦ δύναμις ending of Mk in the Freer ms. 3f; ἄμπελος J 15: 1. ἄρτος *the real bread* of the Lord's Supper 6: 32. ζωή (Philo, Leg. All. 1, 32) IEph 7: 2; cf. 11: 1; ITr 9: 2; ISm 4: 1. Of God in contrast to other gods, who are not *real* (PGM 7, 634f πέμψον μοι τὸν ἀ. Ἀσκληπιὸν δίχα τινὸς ἀντιθέου πλανοδαίμονος; Philo, Leg. ad Gai. 366; Sib. Or., fgm. 1, 20; Is 65: 16; 3 Macc 6: 18) J 17: 3 (s. μόνος 1aδ); 1 J 5: 20 (s. AHarnack, SAB '15, 538f=Studien I '31, 110f); 1 Th 1: 9; 1 Cl 43: 6; ἀ. ὁ πέμψας με J 7: 28. Of human beings (Demosth. 9, 12; 53, 8; 12 ἀ. φίλος; Polyb. 1, 6, 5; 1, 80, 2; 3, 12, 6; Epict. 4, 1, 154; 172; PHamb. 37, 6 ἀ. φιλόσοφος; PGiess. 40 II, 27 ἀ. Αἰγύπτιοι) προσκυνηταί J 4: 23. προφῆται in contrast to the false prophets D 11: 11; cf. 13: 1. διδάσκαλος in contrast to the false teachers D 13: 2.—πάθος *the real suffering* (opp. Docetism) IEph inscr.; *true* in the sense of the reality possessed only by the archetype, not by its copies (X., Mem. 3, 10, 7; Pla., Leg. 1 p. 643c of toys ὄργανα σμικρά, τῶν ἀ. μιμήματα. Of the real body in contrast to its artistic representation: Alcidamas [IV BC], Soph. 28 Blass; Theocr., Epigr. no. 18 Gow =Anth. Pal. 9, 600; Athen. 6 p. 253E): σκηνὴ ἀ. *the true tabernacle*, the heavenly sanctuary Hb 8: 2; the temple ἀντίτυπα τῶν ἀ. *copy of the true sanctuary* 9: 24.—τὸ ἀ. what is really good (contrasted w. the supposed good, the ἄδικος μαμωνᾶς) πιστεύειν τὸ ἀ. *entrust the true* (*riches*) Lk 16: 11 (cf. Philo, Praem. 104 ὁ ἀ. πλοῦτος ἐν οὐρανῷ). M-M.*

ἀλήθω (Hippocr.; Theophr. 4, 12, 13; Diod. S. 3, 13, 2; POxy. 908, 26; 34 [II AD]; PGM 4, 3097; LXX; Jos., Ant. 3, 270 has ἀλέω which acc. to Phryn. p. 151 Lob. is Att. for ἀλήθω) grind ἐν τῷ μύλῳ (Num 11: 8) *with the hand-mill* Mt 24: 41 (on the ptc. s. HRiesenfeld, Con. Neot. 13, '49, 12–16). Also ἀ. ἐπὶ τὸ αὐτό g. *at the same place* since the mills are usu. operated by two women Lk 17: 35. Used fig. of martyrdom by Ign., who would like to be ground as God's wheat by the teeth of wild beasts IRo 4: 1. B. 362.*

ἀληθῶς adv. (Aeschyl., Hdt.+; inscr., pap., LXX, Ep. Arist. 219, Philo, Joseph.) *truly, in truth, really, actually.*

1. as a real adv. modifying a verb λέγειν *tell truly* (Dio Chrys. 33[50], 7; PFay. 123, 24) Lk 9: 27; IRo 8: 2; λαλεῖν

ibid.; γινώσκειν *really know* J 7: 26; 17: 8. εἰδέναι Ac 12: 11. ἀ. τετελείωται *is truly perfected* 1 J 2: 5. κτᾶσθαι IEph 15: 2. πέμπειν 17: 2. πράσσειν IMg 11. ἐγείρεσθαι ITr 9: 2; cf. vs. 1. ἐκλέγεσθαι Pol 1: 1. φρονεῖν (w. καλῶς) Hm 3: 4. βλέπειν B 1: 3. κατοικεῖν 16: 8. ζῆν (Charito 8, 6, 8) Dg 10: 7; ἀ. καθηλωμένος *in truth nailed* ISm 1: 2; ἀ. θεοῦ υἱὸς εἶ *you are really God's Son* (cf. Aeschyl., Suppl. 585) Mt 14: 33; cf. 27: 54.—26: 73; Mk 11: 32 D; 14: 70; 15: 39; J 4: 42; 6: 14; 7: 40; GP 11: 45; B 7: 9; Dg 7: 2; I Sm 1: 1; 2: 1. As a formula of affirmation w. λέγω (s. ἀμήν 2), *truly, I tell you* Lk 12: 44; 21: 3.

2. in attributive relation w. substantives (Pla., Phaedo 129E ἐκεῖνός ἐστιν ὁ ἀληθῶς οὐρανός; Plut., Is. et Os. 3 p. 352c; Dit., Syll.³ 834, 6; Ruth 3: 12 ἀληθῶς ἀγχιστεὺς ἐγώ εἰμι; 4 Macc 11: 23; Jos., Ant. 9, 256 ὁ ἀ. θεός) ἴδε ἀ. Ἰσραηλίτης *here is a real Israelite* (lit. 'really an Is.') J 1: 47; ἀ. μαθηταί μού ἐστε *you are real disciples of mine* 8: 31; cf. IRo 4: 2, where μαθητὴς ἀληθῶς τ. Χριστοῦ (so Lake) is to be read (s. ἀληθής 3).—ἀ. οἰκοδομητὸς ναὸς διὰ χειρός *a temple really built w. hands* B 16: 7. καθὼς ἀ. ἐστιν (for which ὡς ἀ. is also found, cf. 4 Macc 6: 5) *as it really is* 1 Th 2: 13.*

ἁλιεύς, έως, ὁ (on the form ἁλεεῖς, found also Arrian, Anab. 6, 23, 3 [with ἁλεέας twice as v.l.]; PFlor. 127, 15 [256 AD]; BGU 1035, 6; Is 19: 8; Ezk 47: 10, for which ἁλιεῖς is a v.l. in all NT passages, cf. Bl-D. §29, 5 w. app.; Mlt.-H. 76; 142) *fisherman* (Hom.+) lit. Mt 4: 18; Mk 1: 16; Lk 5: 2. Fig., of the disciples ποιήσω ὑμᾶς ἁ. ἀνθρώπων *I will make you fish for men* Mt 4: 19; Mk 1: 17 (CWFSmith, HTR 52, '59, 187–203), allegorically connecting their present and future vocations (Lk 5: 10 has for this ἀνθρώπους ἔσῃ ζωγρῶν, s. ζωγρέω). The figure and expr. are also found in ancient wr. (RhM n.F. 35, 1880, 413 no. 12.—See also Diog. L. 4, 16, 17 θηράω=hunt down, in the sense "catch someone for one's point of view". In 8, 36 Diog. L. has Timon [fgm. 58 Diels] say of Pythagoras that he went out θήρῃ ἐπ' ἀνθρώπων=on a hunt for men).—WWuellner, The Mng. of 'Fishers of Men' '67. S. also the lit. s.v. ἀμφιβάλλω. M-M. B. 184.*

ἁλιεύω (as act. IG XII 5, 126 [II/I BC]; Plut., Ant. 29, 5 al.; PFlor. 275, 24; Jer 16: 16; Test. Zeb. 6: 3, 7, 8. As mid. Philo, Agr. 24, Plant. 102) *to fish* ὑπάγω ἁλιεύειν *I am going fishing* J 21: 3. M-M.*

ἁλίζω pass.: 1 fut. ἁλισθήσομαι; 1 aor. ἡλίσθην (Aristot.+; LXX) *to salt* ἐν τίνι ἁλισθήσεται; *how will it* (the salt) *be made salty again?* Mt 5: 13 (but s. on ἐν I 6). In Mk 9: 49 the ms. trad. is uncertain and the mng. obscure; there are 3 rdgs.: 1. πᾶς γὰρ πυρὶ ἁλισθήσεται. 2. πᾶσα γὰρ θυσία ἁλὶ ἁλισθ. 3. πᾶς γὰρ πυρὶ ἁλισθ. καὶ πᾶσα θυσία ἁλὶ ἁλισθ. Of these, 2=3b is an OT requirement for sacrifice (Lev 2: 13), in 1=3a the fire serves as a symbol of the suffering and sacrifice by which the disciple is tested. Cf. lit. on ἅλας 2 and πῦρ 2. Of similar apocalyptic obscurity is the saying of Heraclitus fgm. 66 πάντα τὸ πῦρ ἐπελθὸν κρινεῖ καὶ καταλήψεται. Also fig. ἁλίζεσθαι ἐν αὐτῷ (Χριστῷ) *be salted by him*, i.e. appropriate his power to prevent corruption IMg 10: 2.*

ἁλίσγημα, ατος, τό (Anecd. Gr. p. 377, 1; Hesychius; Suidas; from ἁλισγέω 'make ceremonially impure' LXX) *pollution* ἀπέχεσθαι ἀ. τῶν εἰδώλων *avoid pollution* (pl. denotes separate acts) *by idols* Ac 15: 20.*

Ἄλκη, ης, ἡ *Alce* (Isaeus 6, 19; 20; 55; Diod. S. 5, 49, 3; CIG 3268 [Smyrna]; 7064; Lat. Alce is more freq. [CIL III 2477; VI 20852; IX 3201 al.]) a woman of Smyrna ISm 13: 2; IPol 8: 3; MPol 17: 2.*

ἀλλά

ἀλλά (Hom.+ gener.; inscr., pap., LXX, Ep. Arist., Philo, Joseph., Test. 12 Patr.) adversative particle indicating a difference with or contrast to what precedes, in the case of individual clauses as well as whole sentences *but, yet, rather, nevertheless, at least.*

1. after a negative—**a.** introducing a contrast οὐκ ἦλθον καταλῦσαι, ἀλλὰ πληρῶσαι Mt 5: 17. οὐ πᾶς ὁ λέγων ... ἀλλ᾽ ὁ ποιῶν 7: 21. οὐκ ἀπέθανεν, ἀλλὰ καθεύδει Mk 5: 39. οὐκ ἔστι θεὸς νεκρῶν ἀλλὰ ζώντων Mt 22: 32; Mk 12: 27; Lk 20: 38.—W. ascensive force (Bl-D. §448; Rob. 1187) οὐ μόνον ... ἀλλὰ καί *not only ..., but also* (Ep. Arist. oft.; Jos., Bell. 3, 102) οὐ μόνον δεθῆναι, ἀλλὰ καὶ ἀποθανεῖν Ac 21: 13. οὐ μόνον σὲ ἀλλὰ καὶ πάντας τοὺς ἀκούοντας 26: 29; cf. 27: 10; Ro 1: 32; 4: 12, 16; 9: 24; 13: 5; 2 Cor 8: 10, 21; 9: 12; Eph 1: 21; Phil 1: 29; 1 Th 1: 5; 2: 8; Hb 12: 26; 1 Pt 2: 18. W. the first member shortened οὐ μόνον δέ, ἀλλὰ καί *not only this* (is the case), *but also:* οὐ μόνον δέ (sc. καυχώμεθα ἐπὶ τούτῳ), ἀλλὰ καὶ καυχώμεθα ἐν ταῖς θλίψεσιν Ro 5: 3, cf. vs. 11; 8: 23; 9: 10; 2 Cor 8: 19.—Introducing the main point after a question expressed or implied, which has been answered in the negative οὐχί, ἀλλὰ κληθήσεται Ἰωάννης *no; rather his name shall be John* Lk 1: 60. οὐχί, λέγω ὑμῖν, ἀλλὰ ἐὰν μὴ μετανοῆτε *no! I tell you; rather, if you do not repent* 13: 3, 5; cf. 16: 30; J 7: 12; Ac 16: 37; Ro 3: 27; after μὴ γένοιτο, which serves as a strong negation 3: 31; 7: 7, 13; cf. 1 Cor 7: 21. The neg. answer is omitted as obvious: (*no,*) *instead of that* 6: 6 (as a declaration). Instead of ἀ.: ἀλλ᾽ ἤ Lk 12: 51; B 2: 8. Also after a negative and ἄλλος, as in class. (Kühner-G. II 284f; IG IV 951, 76 [320 BC]; PPetr. II 46a, 5 [200 BC]; Bl-D. §448, 8): *except* οὐ γὰρ ἄλλα γράφομεν ὑμῖν ἀλλ᾽ ἢ ἃ ἀναγινώσκετε *for we write you nothing* (else) *except what you* (really) *read* 2 Cor 1: 13. This construction οὐκ ἄλλος ἀλλ᾽ ἤ is a combination of οὐκ ἄλλος ..., ἀλλά (PTebt. 104, 19 [92 BC] μὴ ἐξέστω Φιλίσκωνι γυναῖκα ἄλλην ἐπαγαγέσθαι, ἀλλὰ Ἀπολλωνίαν) 1 Cl 51: 5, and οὐκ ἄλλος ἤ ... (Ps.-Clem., Hom. 16, 20).

b. within the same clause, used to contrast single words οὐ ... δικαίους ἀλλ᾽ ἁμαρτωλούς Mt 9: 13; Lk 5: 32. οὐκ ἐμὲ δέχεται ἀλλὰ τὸν ἀποστείλαντά με Mk 9: 37. ἀλλ᾽ οὐ τί ἐγὼ θέλω ἀλλὰ τί σύ 14: 36, cf. J 5: 30; 6: 38. ἡ ἐμὴ διδαχὴ οὐκ ἔστιν ἐμὴ ἀλλὰ τοῦ πέμψαντός με 7: 16. οὐκ ἐγὼ ἀλλὰ ὁ κύριος 1 Cor 7: 10. οὐ τῇ πορνείᾳ, ἀλλὰ τῷ κυρίῳ 6: 13. οὐκ εἰς τὸ κρεῖσσον ἀλλὰ εἰς τὸ ἧσσον 11: 17. οὐκ ἔστιν ἓν μέλος ἀλλὰ πολλά 12: 14. οὐκ εἰς τὸ ἀγαθὸν ἀλλ᾽ εἰς τὸ πονηρόν D 5: 2. οὐχ ὡς διδάσκαλος ἀλλ᾽ ὡς εἷς ἐξ ὑμῶν B 1: 8 and oft. In Mt 20: 23, οὐκ ἔστιν ἐμὸν τοῦτο δοῦναι, ἀλλ᾽ οἷς ἡτοίμασται ὑπὸ τοῦ πατρός μου has been shortened from οὐκ ἐμὸν ... ἀλλὰ τοῦ πατρός, ὃς δώσει οἷς ἡτοίμασται ὑπ᾽ αὐτοῦ.—But s. WBeck, CTM 21, ᾽50, 606–10 for the mng. *except* for Mt 20: 23=Mk 10: 40, and Mk 4: 22, also 9: 8 v.l. (for εἰ μή); D 9: 5. So also Bl-D. §448, 8; Mlt.-Turner 330; MBlack, An Aramaic Approach³, ᾽67, 113f.—After μέν, to indicate that a limiting phrase is to follow πάντα μὲν καθαρά, ἀλλὰ κακὸν τῷ ἀνθρώπῳ Ro 14: 20. σὺ μὲν γὰρ καλῶς εὐχαριστεῖς, ἀλλ᾽ ὁ ἕτερος οὐκ οἰκοδομεῖται I Cor 14: 17.—The use of ἀλλά in the Johannine lit. is noteworthy, in that the parts contrasted are not always of equal standing grammatically: οὐκ ἦν ἐκεῖνος τὸ φῶς ἀλλ᾽ ἵνα μαρτυρήσῃ περὶ τοῦ φωτός=ἀλλὰ μαρτυρῶν π. τ. φ. 1: 8; οὐκ ᾔδειν αὐτόν ἀλλ᾽ ... ἦλθον *although I did not know him, yet I came* vs. 31. εἶπον· οὐκ εἰμὶ ἐγὼ ὁ Χριστός, ἀλλ᾽ ὅτι I said, 'I am not the Christ; rather, I was sent before him' 3: 28. οὔτε οὗτος ἥμαρτεν οὔτε οἱ γονεῖς αὐτοῦ, ἀλλ᾽ ἵνα φανερωθῇ *neither this man has*

sinned, nor his parents, but (he was born blind) *that... might be revealed* 9: 3.

2. when whole clauses are compared, ἀλλά can indicate a transition to someth. different or contrasted: *but, yet.* δεῖ γὰρ γενέσθαι, ἀλλ᾽ οὔπω ἐστὶν τὸ τέλος Mt 24: 6, cf. Lk 21: 9. κεκοίμηται· ἀλλὰ πορεύομαι ἵνα ἐξυπνίσω αὐτόν J 11: 11, cf. vs. 15; 16: 20; Lk 22: 36; J 4: 23; 6: 36, 64; 8: 37; Ac 9: 6; Ro 10: 18f. ἁμαρτία οὐκ ἐλλογεῖται ... ἀλλὰ ... *sin is not charged; nevertheless ...* 5: 13f. Introducing an objection ἀλλὰ ἐρεῖ τις (Jos., Bell. 7, 363 ἀλλὰ φήσει τις) 1 Cor 15: 35; Js 2: 18. Taking back or limiting a preceding statement παρένεγκε τὸ ποτήριον τοῦτο ἀπ᾽ ἐμοῦ· ἀλλ᾽ οὐ τί ἐγὼ θέλω Mk 14: 36. ἀλλ᾽ οὐχ ὡς τὸ παράπτωμα, οὕτως καὶ τὸ χάρισμα Ro 5: 15. ἀλλ᾽ οὐκ ἐχρησάμεθα τῇ ἐξουσίᾳ ταύτῃ 1 Cor 9: 12. ἀλλὰ ἕκαστος ἴδιον ἔχει χάρισμα 7: 7. ἀλλὰ καὶ περὶ τούτου δὲ εἴρηται D 1: 6.—In ἀλλ᾽ οὐ πάντες οἱ ἐξελθόντες ...; in Hb 3: 16 ἀλλ᾽, in the opinion of some, seems to owe its origin solely to a misunderstanding of the preceding τίνες as τινές by an early copyist (Bl-D. §448, 4 w. app.), but here ἀλλά may convey strong asseveration *surely* (so NEB). See 3 below.

3. before independent clauses, to indicate that the preceding is to be regarded as a settled matter, thus forming a transition to someth. new ἀλλὰ ὁ ὄχλος οὗτος ... ἐπάρατοί εἰσιν *but this rabble ... is accursed* J 7: 49. ἀλλ᾽ ἐν τούτοις πᾶσιν ὑπερνικῶμεν (no, not at all!) *but in all these we are more than conquerors* Ro 8: 37. ἀλλ᾽ ὅτι ἃ θύουσιν, δαιμονίοις ... θύουσιν (no!) *but they* (the heathen) *offer what they sacrifice to demons* 1 Cor 10: 20. Cf. Gal 2: 3 and Mt 11: 7f ἀλλὰ τί ἐξήλθατε ἰδεῖν; (you could not have wanted to see that;) *but what did you go out to see?* Also to be explained elliptically is the ascensive ἀλλὰ καί (and not only this,) *but also* Lk 12: 7; 16: 21; 24: 22; Phil 1: 18; negative ἀλλ᾽ οὐδέ Lk 23: 15; Ac 19: 2; 1 Cor 3: 2; 4: 3; strengthened ἀλλά γε καί *indeed* Lk 24: 21; ἀλλὰ μὲν οὖν γε καί Phil 3: 8; Hb 3: 16 (s. 2 above) may well be rendered (as NEB) *all those, surely, whom Moses had led out of Egypt* (cf. Dio Chrys. 33, 36; 47, 3).

4. in the apodosis of conditional sentences *yet, certainly, at least* εἰ καὶ πάντες σκανδαλισθήσονται, ἀλλ᾽ οὐκ ἐγώ *certainly I will not* Mk 14: 29; cf. 1 Cor 8: 6; 2 Cor 4: 16; 5: 16; 11: 6; strengthened ἀλλὰ καί: εἰ γὰρ σύμφυτοι γεγόναμεν ..., ἀλλὰ καὶ τῆς ἀναστάσεως (sc. σύμφυτοι) ἐσόμεθα *we shall certainly be united w. him in his resurrection* Ro 6: 5; limited by γε: εἰ ἄλλοις οὐκ εἰμὶ ἀπόστολος, ἀλλά γε ὑμῖν *at least I am one to you* 1 Cor 9: 2 (cf. X., Cyr. 1, 3, 6; Bl-D. §439, 2; Dana and Mantey §211). ἐὰν γὰρ μυρίους παιδαγωγοὺς ἔχητε ἐν Χριστῷ, ἀλλ᾽ οὐ πολλοὺς πατέρας *certainly not many fathers* 1 Cor 4: 15.

5. rhetorically ascensive: (not only this,) *but rather* πόσην κατειργάσατο ὑμῖν σπουδήν, ἀλλὰ ἀπολογίαν, ἀλλὰ ἀγανάκτησιν, ἀλλὰ φόβον, ἀλλὰ ἐπιπόθησιν, ἀλλὰ ζῆλον, ἀλλὰ ἐκδίκησιν *even* 2 Cor 7: 11.

6. w. an imper. to strengthen the command: *now, then* (Arrian, Anab. 5, 26, 4 ἀλλὰ παραμείνατε=so hold on! Jos., Ant. 4, 145; Sib. Or. 3, 624; 632): ἀλλὰ ἐλθὼν ἐπίθες τὴν χεῖρά σου *now come and lay your hand on her* Mt 9: 18. ἀλλ᾽ εἴ τι δύνῃ, βοήθησον *now help me, if you can* (in any way) Mk 9: 22. ἀλλὰ ὑπάγετε εἴπατε *now go and tell* 16: 7. ἀλλὰ ἀναστὰς κατάβηθι Ac 10: 20. ἀλλὰ ἀνάστηθι 26: 16.—In same sense w. subjunctive ἀλλ᾽ ... ἀπειλησώμεθα αὐτοῖς μηκέτι λαλεῖν *now let us warn them not to speak any longer* 4: 17. ἀλλ᾽ ὥσπερ ἐν παντὶ περισσεύετε ... ἵνα καὶ ἐν ταύτῃ τῇ χάριτι περισσεύητε 2 Cor 8: 7. Eph 5: 24 is prob. to be understood in this way as an ellipsis, and can be expanded thus: *then just as the church is subject to Christ, wives should also be subject to their husbands.* Yet ἀλλά is also used to introduce an inference from what precedes: *so, therefore, accordingly* (e.g., Aristoph., Ach. 1189 ὁδὶ δὲ καὐτός. Ἀλλ᾽ ἄνοιγε τὴν θύραν='here he is in person. So open the door', Birds 1718; Herodas 7, 89; Artem. 4, 27 p. 219, 22). M-M.

ἀλλαγή, ῆς, ἡ (Aeschyl. +; pap.; Wsd 7: 18) *a change* τὰς τῶν καιρῶν ἀλλαγὰς καταδιαιρεῖν *make a distinction betw. the changes of the seasons* Dg 4: 5 (cf. Wsd 7: 18; Sib. Or. 2, 257).*

ἀλλάσσω fut. ἀλλάξω; 1 aor. ἤλλαξα; 2 fut. pass. ἀλλαγήσομαι (Aeschyl.+; inscr., pap., LXX, Joseph.).
1. *change, alter* τὴν φωνήν μου *change my tone* Gal 4: 20 (Artem. 2, 20 of ravens πολλάκις ἀλλάσσειν τ. φωνήν; Test. Jos. 14: 2 ἀλλ. τὸν λόγον). Of the hyena τὴν φύσιν *change its nature* B 10: 7 (cf. Windisch, Hdb. ad loc.). τὰς χρόας *change colors* of stones Hs 9, 4, 5; 8. Of Jesus on the Judgment Day ἀλλάξει τὸν ἥλιον καὶ τὴν σελήνην καὶ τοὺς ἀστέρας *he will change the sun, the moon, and the stars,* so that they lose their radiance B 15: 5. τὰ ἔθη *change the customs* Ac 6: 14 (Diod. S. 1, 73, 3 τὰς τῶν θεῶν τιμὰς ἀλλάττειν).—Pass. (Dionys. Perieg. [Geogr. Gr. Min. ed. CMüller II 1861 p. 127, v. 392]; Herm. Wr. 1, 4; 13, 5; Jos., Ant. 2, 97 v.l.; Sib. Or. 3, 638; 5, 273 ἕως κόσμος ἀλλαγῇ of the last times): of the change in the bodily condition of the Christian on the Last Day *be changed* 1 Cor 15: 51f (cf. MEDahl, The Resurrection of the Body '62, 103-5); of the change to be wrought by Christ in the heavens when the world is destroyed Hb 1: 12 (Ps 101: 27).
2. *exchange* (Aeschyl.+; POxy. 729, 43; BGU 1141, 41; 44; Jer 2: 11; Jos., Ant. 18, 237) ἤλλαξαν (v.l. ἠλλάξαντο, as in Attic usage) τὴν δόξαν τοῦ ἀφθάρτου θεοῦ ἐν ὁμοιώματι εἰκόνος *they exchanged the glory of the immortal God for* . . . Ro 1: 23 (ἀ. ἔν τινι after Ps 105: 20, where it renders בְּ; but cf. ἐν IV 5). Of bad stones in a bldg. Hs 9, 5, 2. Of changing clothes (Appian, Bell. Civ. 5, 122 §504 τὴν ἐσθῆτα ἤλλαξεν; Gen 35: 2; 2 Km 12: 20) GOxy 19. M-M. B. 913.*

ἀλλαχόθεν adv. of place (since Antipho 3, 4, 3 Thalh.; Appian, Liby. 126; Plut., Fab. 6, 9, Mor. 1086D; 1129E; Jos., Ant. 2, 198; 4, 236; 18, 316; PRainer 232, 28; POxy. 237 V, 15 [186 AD]; 4 Macc 1: 7) *from another place* ἀναβαίνειν *climb over at some other place* (opp. εἰσέρχεσθαι διὰ τῆς θύρας) J 10: 1. M-M.*

ἀλλαχοῦ adv. of place *elsewhere* (so Soph., X.+), also *in another direction* (Epict. 3, 23, 22; 3, 26, 4; Dio Chrys. 21[38], 15; Polyaenus 1, 12; 1, 46; 4, 2, 21; Dit., Syll.³ 888, 38 [238 AD]; Phryn., 43f L.) ἀ. ἄγειν εἰς τὰς ἐχομένας κωμοπόλεις *go in another direction to* . . . Mk 1: 38. M-M.*

ἀλληγορέω (Athen. 2 p. 69c; Plut., Is. et Os. 32 p. 363D; Porphyr., Vi. Pyth. 12 Nauck; schol. on Pind., Ol. 10, 13a; Philo, Cher. 25, Somn. 2, 31, Vi. Cont. 28; Jos., Ant. 1, 24) *speak allegorically* ἅτινά ἐστιν ἀλληγορούμενα Gal 4: 24.—FWehrli, Z. Gesch. der allegor. Deutung Homers Diss. Basel '28: this kind of mythical interpretation was practiced at least as early as the Vth cent. BC. On allegorical interpretation among Greeks and Jews cf. Heraclit. Sto., Allegoriae= Quaestiones Homericae and,

of course, Philo of Alexandria.—FBüchsel TW I 260-4 (lit.). M-M. suppl.*

ἀλληλουϊά (הַלְלוּ־יָהּ) lit. *praise Yahweh,* transliterated *hallelujah,* liturg. formula of Jewish (Ps; Tob 13: 18; 3 Macc 7: 13) and then of Christian worship. Used as such Rv 19: 1, 3, 6; w. ἀμήν (cf. the Hebr. of Ps 106: 48; PGM 7, 271; a Christian amulet PBerol. 6096 in Wilcken, APF 1, '01, 430; ESchaefer in Pland. I p. 29) vs. 4. M-M.*

ἀλλήλων gen. of the reciprocal pron.; dat. ἀλλήλοις; acc. ἀλλήλους (Hom.+ gener.; inscr., pap., LXX, Joseph., Test. 12 Patr.) *each other, one another, mutually,* ἀλλήλων μέλη *members of one another* Ro 12: 5; Eph 4: 25; 1 Cl 46: 7. ἀ. τὰ βάρη Gal 6: 2. καταλαλεῖν ἀ. *slander each other* Js 4: 11; ἀνέχεσθαι ἀ. Col 3: 13; ἀπ᾽ ἀ. Mt 25: 32; Ac 15: 39; κατ᾽ ἀ. (Appian, Bell. Civ. 5, 24 §95) Js 5: 9; μετ᾽ ἀ. J 6: 43; 11: 56; 16: 19; ITr 12: 2; μεταξὺ ἀ. Ro 2: 15; παρὰ ἀ. J 5: 44; ὑπὲρ ἀ. 1 Cor 12: 25; ὑπ᾽ ἀ. (Appian, Bell. Civ. 5, 22 §89) Gal 5: 15.—ἀλλήλοις ἀντίκειται Gal 5: 17; ἐγκαλεῖν ἀ. Ac 19: 38; ἐν ἀ. (Jos., Bell. 2, 127, Ant. 9, 240) εἰρηνεύειν Mk 9: 50; cf. J 13: 35; Ro 15: 5.—ἀλλήλους: ἀγαπᾶν ἀ. J 13: 34; Ro 13: 8; 1 Th 4: 9; 1 J 3: 11; 2 J 5; 2 Cl 9: 6; παραδιδόναι ἀ. Mt 24: 10; πρὸς ἀ. (Ael. Aristid. 46 p. 404 D.; En. 6, 2; Jos., Ant. 2, 108) Mk 4: 41; 8: 16; εἰς ἀ. J 13: 22; Ro 12: 10 (cf. ἑαυτούς 1 Pt 4: 9).

ἀλλογενής, ές (Dit., Or. 598 [I AD], the famous Jerus. temple inscr. μηδένα ἀλλογενῆ εἰσπορεύεσθαι; see M-M and Schürer⁴ II, 329); Sb 6235, 6; LXX, Philo; Jos., Bell. 2, 417) *foreign* of the grateful Samaritan εἰ μὴ ὁ ἀ. οὗτος *except this foreigner* Lk 17: 18. M-M.*

ἀλλοιόω 1 aor. ἠλλοίωσα, pass. ἠλλοιώθην (Pre-Socr.+; LXX) *change* τὸ ῥηθέν *the word* (Gen 2: 23), so that it becomes null and void 1 Cl 6: 3. Of the earth μηδὲ ἀλλοιοῦσά τι τῶν δεδογματισμένων ὑπ᾽ αὐτοῦ *changing none of the things he ordained* 20: 4 (cf. Da 2: 21; 6: 9 Theod.; En. 2, 1; 2).—Pass. *be changed* (Thu. 2, 59, 1; Antig. Car. 25, 164; Polyb. 8, 27, 2; Dio Chrys. 35[52], 13) Lk 9: 29 D. ἠλλοιώθη ἡ ἰδέα αὐτοῦ Hv 5: 4. ἡ μορφὴ αὐτοῦ ἠλλοιώθη Hm 12, 4, 1 (cf. Da Theod. 5: 6; 7: 28).—s 8, 5, 1.*

ἄλλομαι 1 aor. ἡλάμην (Hom.+; LXX; Jos., Bell. 5, 330, Ant. 20, 61) *leap, spring up.*
1. lit., of quick movement by living beings (PRyl. 138, 15): of the lame man when healed (Is 35: 6) περιπατῶν καὶ ἀλλόμενος *walking and leaping* i.e., showing by slow and fast movement that he was really healed Ac 3: 8. ἥλατο καὶ περιεπάτει *he leaped up and could walk* 14: 10.
2. fig., of the quick movement of inanimate things (since Il. 4, 125): of water *well up, bubble up* (as Lat. salire Vergil, Ecl. 5, 47; Suet., Octav. 82) πηγὴ ὕδατος ἀλλομένου *a spring of water welling up* J 4: 14. M-M.*

ἄλλος, η, ο (Hom.+; inscr., pap., LXX, Ep. Arist., Philo, Joseph., Test. 12 Patr.) adj. and subst.
1. *other*—a. different fr. the subject who is speaking or who is logically understood μήπως ἄλλοις κηρύξας αὐτὸς ἀδόκιμος γένωμαι *lest after I have preached to others I myself might be rejected* 1 Cor 9: 27. ἄ. ἐστιν ὁ μαρτυρῶν J 5: 32 (ἄλλος of God as Epict. 3, 13, 13). ἄλλη συνείδησις (=ἄλλου συν.) *another man's conscientious scruples* 1 Cor 10: 29. ἄλλους ἔσωσεν, ἑαυτὸν οὐ δύναται σῶσαι *others he saved, himself he cannot save* Mt 27: 42; Mk 15: 31, cf. Lk 23: 35.
b. different fr.—α. a previously mentioned subj. or obj.

ἄλλα δὲ ἔπεσεν ἐπὶ κτλ. Mt 13: 5, 7f. ἄλλην παραβολήν vss. 24, 31, 33; 21: 33. ἄλλους ἑστῶτας 20: 3, 6.— Freq. the subj. or obj. is not expressly mentioned, but can be supplied fr. what precedes δι' ἄλλης ὁδοῦ ἀνεχώρησαν 2: 12 (cf. 3 Km 13: 10) al.

β. different fr. the subj. in a following contrasting phrase ἄλλοι κεκοπιάκασιν, καὶ ὑμεῖς εἰς τὸν κόπον αὐτῶν εἰσεληλύθατε J 4: 38 (JATRobinson, TU 73, '59, 510-15 [identity]).

c. used correlatively in contrast οἱ μὲν—ἄλλοι (δέ) some—others J 7: 12. Indefinite τινὲς—ἄλλοι 9: 16. Also ὁ ὄχλος—ἄλλοι the crowd—others 12: 29. ὁ πλεῖστος ὄχλος—ἄλλοι δέ Mt 21: 8. With no mention of the first part, and the other parts introd. by ἄλλοι—ἄλλοι Mk 6: 15; 8: 28; Lk 9: 19; J 9: 9.—In enumerations, w. ὁ μέν in the first part, continued by ἄλλος δέ (somet. ἕτερος takes the place of ἄλλος, as Hb 11: 35f; Libanius, Or. 32, p. 155, 18 F. ἄλλοι . . . ἕτεροι; Ps.-Clem., Hom. 19, 9; UPZ 42, 32f [162 BC]; s. e below) 1 Cor 12: 8ff. οἱ πέντε—ὁ εἷς—ὁ ἄλλος=the last one Rv 17: 10. οἱ ἄλλοι w. a noun expressed or understood (X., Cyr. 3, 3, 4; Herodian 2, 4, 4) the other(s), the rest (Ps.-Callisth. 3, 35 τὰ ἄλλα λ' [ἔτη]= the rest of the thirty years) J 20: 25; 21: 8; 1 Cor 14: 29.— Various cases of ἄ. in juxtapos. (Epictetus index Schenkl; Hippocr., Ep. 17, 31 ἀλλὰ ἄλλος ἄλλου; Maximus Tyr., 3, 1d ἀλλὰ ἄλλον ἄλλο; 21, 7b; Sallust. 4 p. 6, 19; Jos., Bell. 7, 389; 396, Ant. 7, 325) ἄ. πρὸς ἄ. λέγοντες one said to the other Ac 2: 12. ἄλλοι μὲν οὖν ἄλλο τι ἔκραζον now some were shouting one thing, some another (X., An. 2, 1, 15 ἄλλος ἄλλα λέγει) 19: 32; cf. 21: 34.

d. ἄλλος τις some other, any other μήτε ἄλλον τινὰ ὅρκον Js 5: 12. ἄ. τις διϊσχυρίζετο another man maintained Lk 22: 59. Esp. εἴ τις ἄ. (1 Macc 13: 39) 1 Cor 1: 16; Phil 3: 4.—οὐδεὶς ἄλλος no one else (cf. Jos., Vi. 196) J 15: 24.

e. in comparisons another, different (from, compared with).

α. different in kind 1 Cor 15: 39ff; 2 Cor 11: 4 (interchanging w. ἕτερος; s. below β Gal 1: 7 and c above).

β. another (except, besides) οὐκ ἔστιν ἄ. πλὴν αὐτοῦ there is none (i.e. no other God) but he Mk 12: 32 (cf. Ex 8: 6; Is 45: 21; Pr 7: 1a). W. ἀλλά foll. 1 Cl 51: 5; ἀλλ' ἤ 2 Cor 1: 13; εἰ μή J 6: 22; παρά w. acc. (Philostrat., Vi. Apoll. 5, 30 p. 188, 30) 1 Cor 3: 11. Gal 1: 6, 7 (Bl-D. §306, 4; Mlt. 80 n. 1; 246; EDBurton, ICC Gal., 420-2) belongs in this section (s. ἕτερος 1bγ).

γ. ἄλλος ἐστὶν ὁ σπείρων καὶ ἄλλος ὁ θερίζων one sows, another reaps J 4: 37.

δ. ἄλλος καὶ ἄλλος each one a different, or simply different Hs 9, 1, 4; 10; 9, 17, 1; 2; 9, 28, 1.

2. more (Pla., Leg. 5 p. 745A ἄλλο τοσοῦτον μέρος) w. cardinal numbers (Stephan. Byz. s.v. Ἐορδαῖαι: ἄλλαι δύο χῶραι; Diog. L. 1, 115 Ἐπιμενίδαι ἄλλοι δύο; Gen 41: 3, 6, 23; Jos., Ant. 1, 92) ἄ. δύο ἀδελφούς two more brothers Mt 4: 21; ἄ. πέντε τάλαντα (cf. Dit., Syll.³ 201, 17 [356 BC] ἄλλας τριάκοντα μνᾶς; PBouriant 23, 7 [II AD]; 1 Esdr 4: 52; 1 Macc 15: 31) 25: 20, cf. vs. 22. μετ' αὐτοῦ ἄ. δύο J 19: 18.

3. w. art. the other of the two (Soph., El. 739; Eur., Iph. T. 962f; Pla., Leg. 1 p. 629D; Dit., Syll.³ 736, 91 [92 BC]; UPZ 162 VIII, 34 [117 BC]; BGU 456, 10ff; PRain. 22, 15 [II AD] τὸ ἄλλο ἥμισυ, also Tob 8: 21 S; cf. also 1 Km 14: 4. The strictly correct word would be ἕτερος): the healed hand is ὑγιὴς ὡς ἡ ἄλλη Mt 12: 13. ἡ ἄ. Μαρία (to differentiate her fr. Mary Magdalene, as Appian, Basil. 1a §4 Αἰνείας ἄλλος; Arrian, Anab. 5, 21, 3; 5 ὁ ἄλλος Πῶρος) 27: 61; 28: 1. στρέψον αὐτῷ καὶ τὴν ἄ. turn the

other (i.e. the left cheek) to him, too Mt 5: 39; cf. Lk 6: 29. ὁ μαθητὴς ὁ ἄλλος J 18: 16 (cf. 20: 2ff); τοῦ ἄ. τοῦ συσταυρωθέντος 19: 32. M-M.

ἀλλοτριεπίσκοπος (t.r. ἀλλοτριοεπίσκοπος, s. Mlt.-H. 272; Bl-D. §124), ου, ὁ (elsewh. only Dionys. Areop., Ep. 8 p. 783) a word whose meaning has not yet been determined w. certainty; w. φονεύς, κλέπτης, κακοποιός 1 Pt 4: 15 (ἀλλοτρίοις ἐπίσκοπος 𝔓⁷²). The proximity of κλέπτης has led to the conjecture concealer of stolen goods; for spy, informer (Lat. delator) s. AHilgenfeld, Einl. 1875, 630. EZeller, SAB 1893, 129ff, referring to the claim by Cynic preachers to be overseers (ἐπίσκοποι) of all men (Epict. 3, 22, 97 οὐ τὰ ἀλλότρια πολυπραγμονεῖ ὅταν τὰ ἀνθρώπινα ἐπισκοπῇ ἀλλὰ τὰ ἴδια), interprets the word as mng. one who meddles in things that do not concern him, a busybody (cf. PWendland, Kultur² '12, 82, 1; Zahn, Einl. II 39f; EGSelwyn, Comm. '46 ad loc.). Dssm., NB 51, 5; BS 224, 4 (BGU 531 II, 22 [II AD] οὔτε εἰμὶ ἄδικος οὔτε ἀλλοτρίων ἐπιθυμητής) suggests revolutionist (cf. A Bischoff, ZNW 7, '06, 271-4; 9, '08, 171; PSchmidt, ZWTh 50, '08, 26ff). New English Bible, NT: infringing the rights of others. KErbes, ZNW 19, '20, 39-44; 20, '21, 249 considers it a Christian coinage, aimed at neglectful bishops. Tertullian, Scorp. 12 'alieni speculator'. Cyprian, Test. 3, 37 'curas alienas agens'. Vulg. 'alienorum adpetitor'.—HWBeyer, TW II '35, 617-19. M-M.*

ἀλλότριος, ία, ον (Hom.+; inscr., pap., LXX; Philo, Aet. M. 40; Jos., Ant. 11, 41; Test. 12 Patr.; Sib. Or. 3, 464).

1. belonging to another (ἄλλος), not one's own, strange (opp. ἴδιος; Περὶ ὕψους 4, 1; Epict. 2, 4, 10; 3, 2, 4, 3f; Proverb. Aesopi 114 P.; Dit., Syll.³ 982, 4ff; BGU 1121, 22 [5 BC] μήτε ἴδια μήτ' ἀλλότρια; 15, 15; Jos., Ant. 18, 46; 19, 305).

a. adj. ἀ. οἰκέτης another man's servant (Dio Chrys. 14[31], 34 ἀλλ. οἰκ.; Jos., Ant. 18, 47.—ἀ. δοῦλος as early as Pla., Leg. 9, 9 p. 868A; cf. Diod. S. 36, 2, 2) Ro 14: 4; γυνὴ ἀ. (Charito 6, 3, 7; POxy. 1067, 6ff) Hm 4, 1, 1; 12, 2, 1. καυχᾶσθαι ἐν ἀ. κόποις boast about work done by others 2 Cor 10: 15 (cf. Epict. 1, 28, 23 ἀλλότριον ἔργον=another man's deed); κοινωνεῖν ἁμαρτίαις ἀ. participate in other men's sins 1 Ti 5: 22. ἐν ἀ. κανόνι καυχᾶσθαι boast (of work already done) in another man's field 2 Cor 10: 16. πάντα ἀ. ἐστι (w. ὑπ' ἐξουσίαν ἑτέρου) Hs 1: 3. ἀ. αἷμα Hb 9: 25. θεμέλιον Ro 15: 20. ἐντολαί Papias 2: 3. ἀλλοτρίας σάρκας καταφαγεῖν B 10: 4b. Of lands (Suppl. Epigr. Gr. VIII 548, 31 [I BC]) strange, foreign πάροικον ἐν γῇ ἀ. Ac 7: 6 (Ex 2: 22). παροικεῖν εἰς γῆν . . . ὡς ἀ. sojourn in a land as if it were foreign Hb 11: 9. ἀ. τοῦ θεοῦ ὄντες aliens to God 1 Cl 7: 7 (cf. Herm. Wr. 2, 16); so τὰ κοσμικὰ ὡς ἀ. ἡγεῖσθαι, i.e. to look on them as someth. that does not concern Christians 2 Cl 5: 6.

b. subst.—α. τὸ ἀ. other people's property (Epict. 2, 6, 8; Jos., C. Ap. 2, 216) B 10: 4a. ἐν τῷ ἀ. πιστοὶ faithful w. what belongs to another Lk 16: 12 (the wealth of this world is foreign to the Christian, cf. Epict. 4, 5, 15 of temporal goods: οὐδὲν ἴδιον τῷ ἀνθρώπῳ ἐστίν, ἀλλὰ πάντα ἀλλότρια; also 2, 6, 8; 24.—S. ἡμέτερος. ἀλλοτρίοις ἐπίσκοπος 1 Pt 4: 15 𝔓⁷², 'meddling in other people's affairs'. τοῦ ἀ. ἅψασθαι Hs 1: 11; ἀλλοτρίων ἐπιθυμεῖν ibid.

β. ὁ ἀ. the stranger (='one who is unknown' cf. Sir 8: 18) J 10: 5a. οἱ ἀλλότριοι strange people vs. 5b; specif. aliens (LXX; Jos., Bell. 7, 266) Mt 17: 25f (opp. οἱ υἱοί).

2. alien, unsuitable (cf. POxy. 282, 9) στάσις ἀ., explained by ξένη τοῖς ἐκλεκτοῖς τοῦ θεοῦ 1 Cl 1: 1. ἀ.

γνώμη strange=false doctrine IPhld 3: 3; ἀ. βοτάνη ITr 6: 1; χρῶμα IRo inscr.

3. hostile, enemy (Hom.+; Polyb. 27, 15, 13 et al.; Diod. S. 11, 27, 1; 1 Macc 1: 38; 2: 7; cf. Dit., Or. 90, 91) παρεμβολὰς κλίνειν ἀλλοτρίων Hb 11: 34. M-M.*

ἀλλόφυλος, ον (Aeschyl., Thu.+; BGU 34; 411; 419; 858; LXX; Philo, Leg. ad Gai. 200; Jos., Bell. 5, 194, Ant. 1, 338 al.; Test. 12 Patr.) foreign, hence fr. the Jewish viewpoint= Gentile, heathen, subst. a Gentile (opp. ἀνὴρ Ἰουδαῖος; cf. Jos., Ant. 4, 183) κολλᾶσθαι ἢ προσέρχεσθαι ἀ. associate w. or approach a Gentile Ac 10: 28; cf. 13: 19 D. Esp. (as LXX) of the Philistines 1 Cl 4: 13 or Amalekites B 12: 2. ἡ παρεμβολὴ τῶν ἀ. the camp of the heathen (cf. 1 Km 14: 19; 17: 46; 28: 5) 1 Cl 55: 4. Of Christians in relation to Jews Dg 5: 17. M-M.*

ἄλλως adv. (Hom.+; inscr., pap., LXX; Jos., Bell. 2, 113) otherwise, in another way Hs 7: 3; 9, 12, 5f; 9, 13, 2; 9, 16, 2. τὰ ἄ. ἔχοντα κρυβῆναι οὐ δύνανται if they are not (good, evident) they cannot (in the end) remain hidden 1 Ti 5: 25. M-M.*

ἀλοάω (Aristoph., Pla., X.+) thresh (so Pla., X.; Theocr. 10, 48; PFrankf. 2, 27; 70 [III bc]; PLond. 131, 502; 576 al. [78 ad]; LXX) mostly done w. oxen, which were driven over the threshing-floor 1 Cor 9: 9; 1 Ti 5: 18 (both Dt 25: 4); on this s. IBenzinger, Hebr. Archäologie² '07, §30, 2; GDalman, Arbeit u. Sitte in Palästina III: Von der Ernte z. Mehl usw. '33. ὁ ἀλοῶν (sc. ἀλοᾷ) ἐπ' ἐλπίδι τοῦ μετέχειν he who threshes, (does so) in hope of a share in the crop 1 Cor 9: 10. M-M.*

ἄλογος, ον (Pre-Socr.+; pap., LXX)—1. without reason of animals ὡς ἄ. ζῷα like unreasoning animals 2 Pt 2: 12; Jd 10 (so Democr. A 116; B 164; X., Hiero 7, 3 al; Herm. Wr. 1, 11; 10, 19; 22 al.; Wsd 11: 15; 4 Macc 14: 14, 18; Philo, Leg. All. 3, 30 al.; Jos., C. Ap. 2, 213, Ant. 10, 262; Plut., Mor. 493d).

2. contrary to reason (Thu.+; Jos., Ant. 1, 24 al.) ἄλογόν μοι δοκεῖ it seems absurd to me Ac 25: 27 (cf. BGU 74, 8). M-M.*

ἀλόη, ης ἡ (Plut., Mor. p. 141f; 693c; Diosc. 3, 22 al.; PLeid. II X 12, 36) aloes, the strongly aromatic, quick-drying sap of a tree (Aquillaria), mixed w. myrrh (ἀ. w. σμύρνα PGM 7, 434; SSol 4: 14), used for embalming J 19: 39 (Ps.-Callisth. 3, 34, 4 ἀλόη and μύρρα [so] are used to embalm Alexander's corpse).*

ἅλς, ἁλός, ὁ (Hom.+; Lev 2: 13; Philo, Spec. Leg. 1, 289 al.; Jos., Ant. 3, 227; cf. ἄλας) salt πᾶσα θυσία ἀλὶ ἀλισθήσεται Mk 9: 49 v.l. (s. ἀλίζω). στήλη ἁλός a pillar of salt 1 Cl 11: 2 (Gen 19: 26).*

ἁλυκός, ή, όν (Aristoph., Hippocr.+; BGU 14 IV, 22; LXX) salty; in οὔτε ἁλυκὸν γλυκὺ ποιῆσαι ὕδωρ Js 3: 12 ἀ. is usu. understood as salt spring (so ἁλυκίς Strabo 4, 1, 7): nor can a salt spring give sweet water; but perh. the text is defective (HWindisch and MDibelius ad loc.—Theophr., H. Pl. 4, 3, 5 contrasts ἀ. ὕδωρ w. ὕδωρ γλυκύ. Lycus Hist. [IV-III bc] no. 570 fgm. 8 Jac. of the River Himera in Sicily: τὸν δὲ Ἱμέραν ἐκ μιᾶς πηγῆς σχιζόμενον τὸ μὲν ἁλυκὸν τῶν ῥείθρων ἔχειν, τὸ δὲ ποτιμόν). M-M.*

ἀλύπητος, ον without sorrow (Soph.; Theopomp. [IV bc] 115 fgm. 399 Jac.) εὐφρανθήσεται εἰς τὸν ἀ. αἰῶνα he will rejoice through an eternity free from sorrow 2 Cl 19: 4 (cf. Soph., Trach. 168 τὸ λοιπὸν ἤδη ζῆν ἀλυπήτῳ βίῳ).*

ἄλυπος, ον pass. free from anxiety (so Soph.+; X., Hiero 9, 9; Epict.; Lucian; Herm Wr. 482, 9 Sc.; Wadd. 1835; 1851 al.; PPetr II 13, 13 [c. 250 bc]; BGU 246, 17 [II/III ad]; Philo, Cher. 86) ἵνα κἀγὼ ἀλυπότερος ὦ in order that I might be less anxious (than now=free from all anxiety) Phil 2: 28. M-M.*

ἄλυσις, εως, ἡ (for the breathing cf. W-S. §5, 10e; Mlt.-H. 100).
    1. lit. chain (Hdt.+; Dit., Syll.² 586, 86; 588, 32; PSI 240, 12; PGM 4, 3092; 13, 294; Philo, Leg. All. 1, 28; Jos., Ant. 3, 170), esp. handcuffs Ac 28: 20. δῆσαί τινα ἀλύσει (since Thu. 4, 100, 2; Wsd 17: 16; Jos., Ant. 19, 294) bind someone w. chains of a demoniac Mk 5: 3, cf. vs. 4. δεσμεύειν ἁλύσεσιν (w. πέδαις, as Polyb. 3, 82, 8; Dionys. Hal. 6, 26, 2; 6, 27, 3; Mk 5: 4) Lk 8: 29. Double chains Ac 12: 6f; 21: 33. At the beginning of the 'Thousand Years' Satan will be bound w. a chain Rv 20: 1f.
    2. gener. of imprisonment πρεσβεύω ἐν ἀλύσει in chains=as a prisoner Eph 6: 20; causing disgrace 2 Ti 1: 16. M-M.*

ἀλυσιτελής, ές (Hippocr., Pla., X.+; PSI 441, 21 [III bc]; PTebt. 68, 31 [117/16 bc]; Philo) unprofitable ἀλυσιτελὲς ὑμῖν τοῦτο that would be unprofitable for you Hb 13: 17; but ἀ. can also be used positively, harmful (Polyb. 11, 4, 7; 28, 6, 4 al.; Philo, Spec. Leg. 1, 100 ἡ οἴνου χρῆσις ἀ.). M-M.*

ἄλφα, τό indecl. (Pla., Cratyl. 431e; Aeneas Tact. 1500; 1505; Herodas 3, 22) alpha s. entry A.

Ἁλφαῖος, ου, ὁ (Syr. חַלְפַי, Hebr. חַלְפַי; MLidzbarski, Handb. d. nordsem. Epigraphik 1898, 275; ThNöldeke, Beiträge z. semit. Sprachwissenschaft '04, 98; Procop. Gaz., Ep. 99) Alphaeus.
    1. father of Levi the tax-collector Λευὶν τὸν τοῦ Ἁ. Mk 2: 14; Lk 5: 27 D; GP 14: 60.
    2. father of one of the 12 disciples, who is called Ἰάκωβος ὁ τοῦ Ἁ. to distinguish him from the son of Zebedee Mt 10: 3; Mk 3: 18, also simply Ἰ. Ἁλφαίου Lk 6: 15; Ac 1: 13.—On him, and the attempts to equate 2 w. Clopas, as well as 1 w. 2, s. Zahn, Forsch. 6, 1900, 323f; JChapman, JTS 7, '06, 412ff; FMaier, BZ 4, '06, 164ff; 255ff.*

ἅλων, ωνος, ἡ (a by-form, found since Aristot., also in pap. [Mayser 287; Crönert p. ix]; LXX; Jos. [Ant. 20, 181] for Att. [since Aeschyl.] ἅλως, gen. ἅλω or ἅλωος, found 1 Cl 29: 3 [prob. after LXX] and in inscr. [Dit., Syll.³ 631, 7; 671a, 9], pap. [Mayser 258f; PGM 4, 2746], LXX and Jos., Ant. 4, 281; cf. Bl-D. §44, 1; 52; Mlt.-H. 121; 127) threshing floor.
    1. lit. γεννήματα ληνοῦ καὶ ἅλωνος products of winepress and threshing floor D 13: 3 (cf. Num 18: 30). θημωνιὰ ἅλωνος a heap on the threshing floor 1 Cl 56: 15 (Job 5: 26).
    2. fig. of the threshed grain still lying on the threshing floor (PRyl. 122, 10; 20 [II ad]; Job 39: 12) διακαθαίρειν τὴν ἅλωνα cleanse (winnow) what he has threshed Mt 3: 12; Lk 3: 17. M-M.*

ἀλώπηξ, εκος, ἡ (since Archilochus [VII bc], Hdt.; Sb 7223; LXX; Jos., Ant. 5, 295 [after Judg 15: 4]; Sib. Or. 8, 41) fox.
    1. lit. αἱ ἀ. φωλεοὺς ἔχουσιν Mt 8: 20; Lk 9: 58.
    2. fig., of crafty people (Alcaeus [VII-VI bc] 42, 6 Diehl²; Theocr. 5, 112; Plut., Solon 30, 2, Sulla 28, 5; Epict. 1, 3, 7; Artem. 2, 12 p. 104, 9.—Billerb. II 678) of

Herod Antipas εἴπατε τῇ ἀλώπεκι ταύτῃ 13: 32. B. 186.*

ἄλως s. ἅλων.

ἅλωσις, εως, ἡ (Pind., Hdt.+; Jer 27: 46; Jos., Ant. 2, 250; 5, 261; Sib. Or. 4, 89) *capture, catching* of animals for food (so Aristot.; Epict. 4, 1, 29) γεγεννημένα εἰς ἅ. καὶ φθοράν *born to be caught and killed* 2 Pt 2: 12.*

ἅμα (Hom.+; inscr., pap., LXX)—1. adv.—a. denoting the coincidence of two actions in time (Bl-D. §425, 2; Rob. index) *at the same time, together* B 8: 6; w. ptc. (Is 41: 7; Jos., Bell. 3, 497) ἅ. ἀνέντες τὰς ζευκτηρίας *while at the same time* Ac 27: 40; cf. 16: 4 D. W. finite verb *everything at once* Dg 8: 11. ἅ. (δὲ) καί (*but) at the same time also, besides* ἅ. καὶ ἐλπίζων Ac 24: 26 (Jos., Ant. 18, 246 ἅ. καὶ ἀγόμενος). ἅ. δὲ καὶ ἀργαὶ μανθάνουσιν 1 Ti 5: 13. ἅ. δὲ καὶ ἑτοίμαζε Phlm 22.—Postpositive προσευχόμενοι ἅμα καὶ περὶ ἡμῶν Col 4: 3.
b. denoting coincidence in place *together* ἅ. ἠχρεώθησαν (like יַחְדָּו) Ro 3: 12 (Ps 13: 3; 52: 4).
2. improper prep. w. dat. *together with* (Hom.+; Dit., Syll.³ 958, 21f; 1168, 6; PReinach 26, 14; POxy. 658, 13; 975; PFlor. 21, 15; Wsd 18: 11; 1 Esdr 1: 43 al.) ἐκριζώσητε αὐτοῖς Mt 13: 29. ἅ. 'Ρέῳ IPhld 11: 1; cf. IEph 2: 1; 19: 2; IMg 15 al. Seemingly pleonastic w. σύν (cf. Alex. Aphr., An. 83, 19 ἅ. αἰσθομένη σὺν αὐτῷ; En. 9, 7; Jos., Ant. 4, 309; cf. Dit., Syll.³ 705, 57 ἅμα μετ' αὐτῶν) to denote what belongs together in time and place (about like Lat. una cum): ἅ. σὺν αὐτοῖς ἁρπαγησόμεθα 1 Th 4: 17. ἅ. σὺν αὐτῷ ζήσωμεν 5: 10.—Also w. adv. of time (POxy. 1025, 16 [III AD] ἅμ' αὔριον; cf. Jos., Ant. 6, 40 ἅ. ἕῳ) ἅ. πρωῒ *early in the morning* Mt 20: 1 (Theophanes Continuatus 719, 7 [IBekker 1838]; cf. Ep. Arist. 304 ἅ. τῇ πρωΐᾳ). M-M.**

ἀμαθής, ές (Hdt., Eur., Aristoph.+; Epict., Ench. 48, 3; Sym. Ps 48: 11; Philo; Jos., Ant. 12, 191) *ignorant* (w. ἀστήρικτος) of heretics 2 Pt 3: 16 (cf. Plut., Mor. 25c ἐν πᾶσιν ἁμαρτωλὸν εἶναι τὸν ἀμαθῆ). M-M.*

'Αμαλήκ, ὁ indecl. (LXX, Philo; Test. Sim. 6: 3; Sib. Or. 8, 252.—In Joseph. 'Αμάληκος, ου [Ant. 2, 6]) *Amalek,* a Semitic tribe in the Sinai desert (cf. Ex 17: 8ff) B 12: 9.*

ἄμαξα, ης, ἡ (Hom.+; LXX) *wagon* Papias 3.*

ἀμαράντινος, η, ον *unfading* in our lit. only fig. of eternal life τῆς δόξης στέφανον *the unfading crown of glory* (στεφ. ἅ. also Philostrat., Her. 19, 14 p. 208, 18; perh. CIG 155, 39) 1 Pt 5: 4. Possibly a wreath of amaranths (Diosc. 4, 57 and Aesop, Fab. 369 P.=384 H.= Babrius 178 τὸ ἀμάραντον or Artem. 1, 77 p. 70, 19 ὁ ἀμάραντος the flower that μέχρι παντὸς διαφυλάττει), or strawflowers (everlastings) is meant; its unfading quality may typify eternal glory.*

ἀμάραντος, ον *unfading* (Diosc. 4, 57; Lucian, Dom. 9; schol. on Apollon. Rhod. 2, 399-401a; inscr. fr. II BC APF 1, '01, 220; CIG II 2942c, 4; Wsd 6: 12).
1. lit. ἅ. ἄνθη *unfading flowers* (as they bloom in the next world) AP 15.
2. fig. (w. ἄφθαρτος and ἀμίαντος) of eternal bliss ἅ. κληρονομία 1 Pt 1: 4 (cf. Sib. Or. 8, 411 ζωὴ ἅ.). M-M.*

ἀμαρτάνω fut. ἁμαρτήσω Mt 18: 21, cf. Hm 4, 1, 1f (W-S. §13, 8; Mlt.-H. 227); 2 aor. (class.) ἥμαρτον, subj. ἁμάρτω Lk 17: 3; 1 aor. (H.Gk.) ἡμάρτησα, subj. ἁμαρτήσω (Mt 18: 15; Lk 17: 4; Ro 6: 15, ptc. ἁμαρτήσας Ro 5: 14, 16; Hb 3: 17; 2 Pt 2: 4 (Bl-D. §75; 77;

Mlt.-H. 214; on the LXX forms cf. Thackeray 259) (in the sense *transgress, sin* against divinity, custom, or law since Hom., esp. LXX, also En., Ep. Arist., Philo, Joseph., Test. 12 Patr., Herm. Wr.; class. also 'miss the mark') *do wrong, sin* of offenses against the relig. and moral law of God.
1. abs. (Menand., fgm. 499 K. ἄνθρωπος ὢν ἥμαρτον; Herodas 5, 27) Mt 18: 15; Lk 17: 3; J 5: 14; 9: 2f; Ro 3: 23; 5: 12 (s. the lit. on ἁμαρτία 3); 1 Cor 7: 28, 36; Eph 4: 26 (Ps 4: 5); Tit 3: 11; 1 Pt 2: 20; 1 Cl 4: 4 (Gen 4: 7); 56: 13 (Job 5: 24); 2 Cl 1: 2; B 10: 10; Hv 3, 5, 5; m 4, 1, 4f; 8; 4, 2, 2 al. Of sinning angels (En. 106, 14; cf. 7, 5) 2 Pt 2: 4. Of the devil 1 J 3: 8.
2. w. fuller indication of that in which the sin consists, by means of a supplementary ptc. (Bl-D. §414, 5; cf. Hipponax [VI BC] 70 Diehl οὐχ ἁμαρτάνω κόπτων=I don't miss when I strike; Jos., Ant. 3, 174) ἥμαρτον παραδοὺς αἷμα ἀθῷον *I have committed a sin by betraying innocent blood* Mt 27: 4.
3. w. indication of the manner of sinning ἀνόμως ἁ. Ro 2: 12; opp. ἐν νόμῳ ἁ. ibid.; ἑκουσίως ἁ. (cf. Job 31: 33) Hb 10: 26. Opp εἴ τι ἄκοντες ἡμάρτετε 1 Cl 2: 3 (s. ἄκων). Also w. acc. (epigr. in Demosth. 18, 289 μηδὲν ἁμαρτεῖν ἐστι θεῶν=; ἁ. ἁμαρτίαν (= חֵטְא חָטָא Ex 32: 30f al.; cf. Soph., Phil. 1249; Pla., Phaedo 113E) *commit a sin* 1 J 5: 16a; ἁμαρτίας ἁ. Hv 2, 2, 4; also τοσαῦτα Hm 9: 1 (Cornutus 10 τοιαῦτα ἁ.).—ὑπὸ χεῖρα ἁ. *sin repeatedly* Hm 4, 3, 6 (Bl-D. §232, 1 app.).
4. w. indication of the pers. against whom the sin is committed—a. in the dat. (M. Ant. 4, 26; 9, 4 ἑαυτῷ ἁμαρτάνει; Ps 77: 17; Bar 1: 13; 2: 5) σοὶ μόνῳ ἥμαρτον *against thee only* 1 Cl 18: 4 (Ps 50: 6).
b. ἁ. εἴς τινα (Soph., fgm. 21 εἰς θεούς; likew. X., Hell. 1, 7, 19; Pla., Phaedr. 242c εἰς τὸ θεῖον; Jdth 5: 20; 11: 10; Sir 7: 7; EpJer 12; Jos., Ant. 7, 320 εἰς τ. θεόν) Mt 18: 21; Lk 17: 4. εἰς Χριστόν 1 Cor 8: 12. εἰς τοὺς ἀδελφούς ibid. εἰς τὸ ἴδιον σῶμα 1 Cor 6: 18.—εἰς τὸν οὐρανόν *against God* Lk 15: 18, 21. ἁ. εἴς τινά τι (M. Ant. 7, 26; BGU 1141, 14ff [13 BC] ἡμάρτηκά τι εἰς σέ) Ac 25: 8.
c. ἁ. ἐνώπιόν τινος (1 Km 7: 6; 20: 1; Tob 3: 3; Bl-D. §214, 6): ἐνώπιόν σου Lk 15: 18, 21.
5. w. indication of the result ἁ. μὴ πρὸς θάνατον *commit a sin that does not lead to death* (like חֵטְא לָמוּת Num 18: 22 λαβεῖν ἁμαρτίαν θανατηφόρον; Dt 22: 26 ἁμάρτημα θανάτου) 1 J 5: 16b (RSeeberg, LIhmels-Festschr. '28, 19-31; OBauernfeind, VSchultze-Festschr. '31, 43-54).—EDBurton, ICC Gal., 436-43; OHey, 'Αμαρτία: Philol. 83, '27, 1-17; 137-63; FSteinleitner, D. Beicht '13; KLatte, Schuld u. Sünde in d. griech. Rel.: ARW 20, '21, 254-98. M-M.

ἁμάρτημα, τος, τό (Pre-Socr., Soph.+; Diod. S. 14, 76, 4 εἰς θεοὺς ἁμαρτήματα; POxy. 34 III, 13; PTebt. 5, 3 [s. ἀγνόημα]; PPar. 63 XIII, 2ff; BGU 1141, 8; 1185, 7; LXX; En.; Ep. Arist. 297; Philo; Jos., Bell. 4, 348, Ant. 1, 22, 3; 221 al.) *sin, transgression* Ro 5: 16 v.l.; αἰώνιον ἁ. *an everlasting sin* Mk 3: 29; τὰ προγεγονότα ἁμαρτήματα Ro 3: 25 (s. Eunap. p. 76 τὰ προγεγενημένα τῶν ἁμαρτημάτων); cf. τῶν πάλαι αὐτοῦ ἁμαρτημάτων 2 Pt 1: 9 v.l.; ἐξαλείφειν τὰ πρότερα ἁ. *wipe out our former sins* 2 Cl 13: 1; καθαρίζεσθαι ἀπὸ τῶν ἁ. *be cleansed fr. sins* Hv 3, 2, 2; ποιεῖν ἁ. (Hdt. 7, 194; Jdth 11: 17; 13: 16) 1 Cor 6: 18. ἀφιέναι τινὶ τὰ ἁ. (1 Macc 13: 39) *forgive someone's sins* Mk 3: 28; PK 3 p. 15, 27; for this ἰᾶσθαι τὰ ἁ. (Pla., Gorg. 525B ἰάσιμα ἁμαρτήματα ἁμαρτάνειν) Hv 1, 1, 9; s 9, 23, 5; ποιεῖν ἴασιν τοῖς προτέροις ἁ. m 12, 6, 2; τελειοῦν τὰ ἁ. GP 5: 17. ἵνα κἀκεῖνοι τελειωθῶσιν τοῖς ἁ. *in order that they might be perfected in their sins=that the measure of their* (i.e. the Jews') *sins might be filled* B 14: 5. μετανοεῖν ἐπὶ τοῖς ἁ. *repent of sins* 1 Cl 7: 7 (Wsd 12: 19 ἐπὶ ἁμαρτήμασιν μετάνοια. Cf. Appian, Bell. Civ. 2, 63 §261f ἐπὶ μετάνοιαν . . . τὸ ἁμάρτημα). ἐφήδεσθαι τοῖς ἁ. *delight in sins* Dg 9: 1. M-M.*

ἁμάρτησις, εως, ἡ *sin* ἐὰν . . . ἔτι ἁ. γένηται *if there is any more sinning* Hv 2, 2, 5.*

ἁμαρτία, ίας, ἡ (Aeschyl., Antipho, Democr.+; inscr. fr. Cyzicus JHS 27, '07, p. 63 [III BC] ἁμαρτίαν μετανόει; PLeipzig 119 r., 3; POxy. 1119, 11; LXX; En.; Ep. Arist. 192; Philo; Jos., Ant. 13, 69 al.; Test. 12 Patr.; cf. CIR 24, '10, p. 88; 234; 25, '11, 195-7) *sin.*

1. The action itself (ἁμάρτησις), as well as its result (ἁμάρτημα), every departure fr. the way of righteousness, both human and divine πᾶσα ἀδικία ἁ. ἐστίν 1 J 5: 17 (cf. Eur., Or. 649; Gen 50: 17). ἁ. w. ἀνομήματα Hv 1, 3, 1; descr. as ἀνομία (cf. Ps 58: 3) 1 J 3: 4; but he who loves is far from sin Pol 3: 3, cf. Js 5: 20; 1 Pt 4: 8, 1 Cl 49: 5; Agr 13. ἀναπληρῶσαι τὰς ἁ. *fill up the measure of sins* (Gen 15: 16) 1 Th 2: 16. κοινωνεῖν ἁ. ἀλλοτρίαις 1 Ti 5: 22. ποιεῖν ἁ. *commit a sin* (Tob 12: 10; 14: 7S; Dt 9: 21) 2 Cor 11: 7; 1 Pt 2: 22; Js 5: 15; 1 J 3: 4, 8. For this ἁμαρτάνειν ἁ. (Ex 32: 30; La 1: 8) 1 J 5: 16; ἐργάζεσθαι ἁ. Js 2: 9; Hm 4, 1, 2 (LXX oft. ἐργάζ. ἀδικίαν or ἀνομίαν). μεγάλην ἁ. ἐργάζεσθαι *commit a great sin* m 4, 1, 1; 8: 2. Pl. (cf. Pla., Ep. 7 p. 335A τὰ μεγάλα ἁμαρτήματα κ. ἀδικήματα) s 7: 2. ἐπιφέρειν ἁ. τινί Hv 1, 2, 4. ἑαυτῷ ἁ. ἐπιφέρειν *bring sin upon oneself* m 11: 4; for this ἁ. ἐπισπᾶσθαί τινι m 4, 1, 8 (cf. Is 5: 18). προστιθέναι ταῖς ἁ. *add to one's sins* Hv 5: 7; m 4, 3, 7; s 6, 2, 3; 8, 11, 3; φέρειν ἁ. 1 Cl 16: 4 (Is 53: 4). ἀναφέρειν vs. 14 (Is 53: 12). γέμειν ἁμαρτιῶν B 11: 11. εἶναι ἐν ταῖς ἁμαρτίαις 1 Cor 15: 17 (cf. Alex. Aphr., Eth. Probl. 9 II 2 p. 129, 13 ἐν ἁμαρτήμασιν εἶναι).—Of God or Christ ἀφιέναι τὰς ἁ. *let go=forgive sins* (Lev 4: 20 al.) Mt 9: 2, 5f; Mk 2: 5, 7, 9f; Lk 5: 20ff; Hv 2, 2; 1 Cl 50: 5; 53: 5 (Ex 32: 32) al. (ἀφίημι 2); hence ἄφεσις (τῶν) ἁμαρτιῶν *forgiveness of sins* Mt 26: 28; Mk 1: 4; Lk 1: 77; 3: 3; 24: 47; Ac 2: 38; 5: 31; 10: 43; 13: 38; Hm 4, 3, 2; B 5: 1; 6: 11; 8: 3; 11: 1; 16: 8. λαβεῖν ἄφεσιν ἁ. *receive forgiveness of sins* Ac 26: 18; καθαρίζειν τὰς ἁ. *cleanse the sins* (thought of as a stain) Hs 5, 6, 3; καθαρίζειν ἀπὸ ἁ. 1 Cl 18: 3 (Ps 50: 4; cf. Sir 23: 10); also καθαρισμὸν ποιεῖσθαι τῶν ἁ. Hb 1: 3; ἀπολούεσθαι τὰς ἁ. Ac 22: 16 (w. βαπτίζειν); λύτρον ἁ. *ransom for sins* B 19: 10.—αἴρειν J 1: 29; περιελεῖν ἁ. Hb 10: 11; ἀφαιρεῖν (Ex 34: 9; Is 27; 9) vs. 4; Hs 9, 28, 3; ῥυσθῆναι ἀπὸ ἁ. 1 Cl 60: 3. Sin as a burden αἱ ἁ. κατεβάρησαν Hs 9, 28, 6; as a disease ἰᾶσθαι s 9, 28, 5 (cf. Dt 30: 3); s. also the verbs in question.—Looked upon as an entry in a ledger; hence ἐξαλείφεται ἡ ἁ. *wiped away, cancelled* (Ps 108: 14; Jer 18: 23; Is 43: 25) Ac 3: 19.—Opp. στῆσαι τὴν ἁ. Ac 7: 60; λογίζεσθαι ἁ. *take account of sin* (as a debt) Ro 4: 8 (Ps 31: 2); 1 Cl 60: 2. Pass. ἁ. οὐκ ἐλλογεῖται *is not entered in the account* Ro 5: 13 (GFriedrich, ThLZ 77, '52, 523-8). Of sinners ὀφειλέτης ἁ. Pol 6: 1 (cf. Dit., Syll.³ 1042, 14ff [II AD] ὃς ἂν δὲ πολυπραγμονήσῃ τὰ τοῦ θεοῦ ἢ περιεργάσηται, ἁμαρτίαν ὀφιλέτω Μηνὶ Τυράννωι, ἣν οὐ μὴ δύνηται ἐξειλάσασθαι).—γινώσκειν ἁ. (cf. Num 32: 23) Ro 7: 7; Hm 4, 1, 5. ἐπίγνωσις ἁμαρτίας Ro 3: 20; ὁμολογεῖν τὰς ἁ. 1 J 1: 9; ἐξομολογεῖσθε ἐπὶ ταῖς ἁ. B 19: 12; ἐξομολογεῖσθε ἁ. Mk 1: 5; Hv 3, 1, 5f; s 9, 23, 4; ἐξομολογεῖσθε ἀλλήλοις τὰς ἁ. *confess your sins to each other* Js 5: 16.—ἐλέγχειν τινὰ περὶ ἁ.

convict someone of sin J 8: 46; cf. ἵνα σου τὰς ἁ. ἐλέγξω πρὸς τὸν κύριον *that I might reveal your sins before the Lord* Hv 1, 1, 5.—σεσωρευμένος ἁμαρτίαις *loaded down w. sins* 2 Ti 3: 6; cf. ἐπισωρεύειν ταῖς ἁ. B 4: 6; ἔνοχος τῆς ἁ. *involved in the sin* Hm 2: 2; 4, 1, 5. μέτοχος τῆς ἁ. m 4, 1, 9.

2. In Johannine usage ἁ. is conceived as a condition or characteristic quality, *sinfulness,* and is opposed to ἀλήθεια; hence ἁ. ἔχειν J 9: 41; 15: 24; 1 J 1: 8. μείζονα ἁ. ἔχειν J 19: 11; ἁ. μένει 9: 41. γεννᾶσθαι ἐν ἁμαρτίαις *be born in sin* 9: 34 (ἐν ἁμαρτίᾳ 𝔓⁶⁶ et al.); opp. ἐν ἁ. ἀποθανεῖν *die in sin* 8: 21, 24. ἁ. ἐν αὐτῷ οὐκ ἔστιν 1 J 3: 5.

3. Paul thinks of sin almost in pers. terms (cf. Sir 27: 10; PGM 4, 1448 w. other divinities of the underworld, also Ἀμαρτίαι χθόνιαι; Dibelius, Geisterwelt 119ff) as a ruling power. Sin came into the world Ro 5: 12 (JFreundorfer, Erbsünde u. Erbtod b. Ap. Pls '27; ELohmeyer, ZNW 29, '30, 1-59; JSchnitzer, D. Erbsünde im Lichte d. Religionsgesch. '31; ROtto, Sünde u. Urschuld '32; FW Danker, Ro 5: 12: Sin under Law, NTS 14, '67/'68, 424-39), reigns there vs. 21; 6: 14; everything was subject to it Gal 3: 22; men serve it Ro 6: 6; are its slaves vss. 17, 20; are sold into its service 7: 14 or set free from it 6: 22; it has its law 7: 23; 8: 2; it revives (ἀνέζησεν) Ro 7: 9 or is dead vs. 8; it pays its wages, viz., death 6: 23, cf. 5: 12 (see lit. s.v. ἐπί II 1bγ). As a pers. principle it dwells in man Ro 7: 17, 20, viz., in the flesh (cf. σάρξ 7) 8: 3; cf. vs. 2; 7: 25. The earthly body is hence a σῶμα τῆς ἁ. 6: 6 (Col 2: 11 t.r.).—As abstr. for concr. τὸν μὴ γνόντα ἁ. ὑπὲρ ἡμῶν ἁμαρτίαν ἐποίησεν (God) *has made him to be sin* (i.e., subject to death) *who knew no sin, for our sakes* 2 Cor 5: 21. Or ἁ. may=*sin-offering* here, as Lev 4: 24 (cf. APlummer, ICC ad loc.; NHSnaith, Vetus Testamentum 7, '57, 316f); or Jesus is viewed as representative and bearer of the world's sin (cf. Expos. Gk. NT ad loc.).

4. In Hb (as in OT) sin appears as the power that deceives men and leads them to destruction, whose influence and activity can be ended only by sacrifices: ἀπάτη τῆς ἁ. Hb 3: 13; sin is atoned for (ἱλάσκεσθαι τὰς ἁ. 2: 17) by sacrifices θυσίαι ὑπὲρ ἁ. 5: 1 (cf. 1 Cl 41: 2). προσφορὰ περὶ ἁ. *sin-offering* 10: 18; also simply περὶ ἁ. (Lev 5: 11; 7: 37) vss. 6, 8 (both Ps 39: 7; cf. 1 Pt 3: 18; προσφέρειν περὶ ἁ. *bring a sin-offering* Hb 5: 3; cf. 10: 12; 13: 11. Christ has made the perfect sacrifice for sin 9: 23ff; συνείδησις ἁ. *consciousness of sin* 10: 2; ἀνάμνησις ἁ. *a reminder of sins* of the feast of atonement vs. 3.

5. special sins: πρὸς θάνατον *that leads to death* 1 J 5: 16 (ἁμαρτάνω 5); opp. οὐ πρὸς θάνατον vs. 17. μεγάλη ἁ. *a great sin* Hv 1, 1, 8 al. (Gen 20: 9; Ex 32: 30 al.). μείζων ἁ. m 11: 4; ἥττων 1 Cl 47: 4. μεγάλη κ. ἀνίατος Hm 5, 2, 4; τέλειαι ἁ. Hv 2, 1; B 8: 1, cf. τὸ τέλειον τῶν ἁ. 5: 11 (Philo, Mos. 1, 96 κατὰ τῶν τέλεια ἡμαρτηκότων); ἡ προτέρα ἁ. (Arrian, Anab. 7, 23, 8 εἴ τι πρότερον ἡμάρτηκας) sin committed before baptism Hm 4, 1, 11; 4, 3, 3; s 8, 11, 3; cf. v 2, 1, 2.—On the whole word s. ἁμαρτάνω, end. JKöberle, Sünde u. Gnade im relig. Leben d. Volkes Israel bis auf Chr. '05; JHempel, Sünde u. Offenbarung nach atl. u. ntl. Ansch.: Ztschr. f. syst. Theol. 10, '33, 163-99; GFMoore, Judaism I '27, 445-52; ABüchler, Studies in Sin and Atonement in the Rabb. Lit. of the I Cent. '28; WKnuth, D. Begriff der Sünde b. Philon v. Alex., Diss. Jena '34; EThomas, The Problem of Sin in the NT '27; TW I 267-320; Dodd 76-81; DDaube, Sin, Ignorance and Forgiveness in the Bible, '61; AMDubarle, The Bibl. Doctrine of Original Sin [Eng. tr.] '64; AGelin and ADescamps, Sin in the Bible, '65; SLyonnet, Sin, Redemption and Sacrifice, '70.—On the special question 'The Christian and Sin' see PWernle 1897; HWindisch '08; EHedström '11; RBultmann, ZNW 23, '24, 123-40; Windisch, ibid. 265-81; EGaugler, Internat. kirchl. Ztschr. 15, '25, 100-20; WMundle, Ztschr. f. syst. Th. 4, '27, 456-82; JSchnitzer, Paulus und die Sünde des Christen: Religio 10, '34, 539-45; OMoe, Tidsskr. f. Teol. og K. 11, '40, 33-40; RSchulz, D. Frage nach der Selbsttätigkt. d. Menschen im sittl. Leben b. Pls., Diss. Hdlb. '40; AKirchgässner, D. Chr. u. d. Sü. b. Pls., Diss. Frbg. '42.—JTAddison, ATR 33, '51, 137-48; KGKuhn, πειρασμός ἁμαρτία σάρξ im NT: ZThK 49, '52, 200-22. M-M. B. 1182.

ἀμάρτυρος, ον (since Thu. 2, 41, 4, also Callim., fgm. 442 Schn. ἀμάρτυρον οὐδὲν ἀείδω=I announce nothing that is not attested; Herodian 1, 1, 3; Inscr. Ariassi 58, 8 [Bull. de corr. hell. 16, 1892, p. 428]; PRain. 232, 30; PFlor. 59, 13 [III AD]ἵνα μὴ ἀμάρτυρον ᾖ; Philo, Sacr. Abel. 34; Jos., Ant. 14, 111) without witness; of God οὐκ ἀμάρτυρον αὐτὸν ἀφῆκεν God has not left himself without witness= plainly revealed (in his works) Ac 14: 17 (Philostrat., Vi. Apoll. 6, 1 p. 204, 3 ἀμ. means simply 'unknown'). M-M.*

ἁμαρτωλός, όν—1. adj. (Aristoph., Th. 1111; Aristot., Eth. Nicom. 2, 9; Philod., Ira p. 73 W.; Plut., Mor. 25c; LXX) sinful ἀνὴρ ἁ. (Sir 15: 12; 27: 30; 1 Macc 2: 62) a sinner Lk 5: 8; 19: 7; ἄνθρωπος ἁ. (Sir 11: 32; 32: 17) J 9: 16; pl. (Num 32: 14) Lk 24: 7. ἐν τῇ γενεᾷ ταύτῃ τῇ μοιχαλίδι καὶ ἁ. in this adulterous (=unfaithful) and sinful generation Mk 8: 38. ἵνα γένηται καθ' ὑπερβολὴν ἁ. ἡ ἁμαρτία that sin might become sinful in the extreme Ro 7: 13.

2. subst. ὁ ἁ. the sinner (inscr. from Lycia ἁ. θεοῖς 'sinner against the gods' [OBenndorf et al., Reisen im südw. Kleinasien I 1884, 30 No. 7; CIG 4307; Lyc. inscr.: ARW 19, '19, 284] or ἁ. θεῶν [Reisen etc. II 1889, 36 No. 58; Dit., Or. 55, 31f; CIG 4259; other inscr.: Steinleitner [see ἁμαρτάνω, end] p. 84f; LXX; En.; Test. 12 Patr.) ἁ. παρὰ πάντας τοὺς Γαλιλαίους greater sinners than all the other Galileans Lk 13: 2; (opp. δίκαιος as En. 104, 6) οὐκ ἦλθον καλέσαι δικαίους, ἀλλὰ ἁ. Mt 9: 13; Mk 2: 17; Lk 5: 32; 2 Cl 2: 4; B 5: 9; cf. Hs 3: 2f; 4: 2ff. W. ἀσεβής (En. 5, 6) 1 Ti 1: 9; 1 Pt 4: 18 (Pr 11: 31); B 11: 7 (Ps 1: 5); w. πονηρός (Gen 13: 13) 4: 2; w. ἄπιστος Rv 21: 8 v.l.; ἁ. εἰμι Hm 4, 2, 3. οὗτος ὁ ἄνθρωπος ἁ. ἐστιν J 9: 24; cf. vs. 25. ἁ. μετανοῶν a sinner who repents Lk 15: 7, 10. μετάνοια τῶν ἁ. Hs 8, 6, 6. ἁμαρτωλοὺς προσδέχεσθαι Lk 15: 2. ἁ. ἐπιστρέφειν 1 Ti 1: 15; ἐπιστρέφειν 5: 20; ἱλάσθητί μοι τῷ ἁ. Lk 18: 13. ἁμαρτωλῶν οὐκ ἀκούει of God J 9: 31. ἡ ἁμαρτωλός the sinful woman Lk 7: 37, 39 (PJoüon, Rech de sc rel 29, '39, 615-19).—W. τελώνης (IAbrahams, Publicans and Sinners: Stud. in Pharisaism and the Gospels I '17, 54ff; JoachJeremias, ZNW 30, '31, 293-300; WHRaney, Jour. of Rel. 10, '30, 578-91; Gdspd., Probs. 28f) irreligious, unobservant people, of those who did not observe the Law in detail Mt 9: 10f; 11: 19; Mk 2: 15f; Lk 5: 30; 7: 34; 15: 1.—Lk 6: 32 has ἁ., while its parallel Mt 5: 46 has τελώνης. W. ἔθνη Hs 4: 4; more exactly ἡμεῖς οὐκ ἐξ ἐθνῶν ἁμαρτωλοί, which means, in the usage of Jews and Jewish Christians, no 'sinners' of Gentile descent Gal 2: 15. Gener. a favorite term for heathen (Is 14: 5; Tob 13: 8; 1 Macc 1: 34 al.); hence perh. heathen in ὁ υἱὸς τ. ἀνθρώπου παραδίδοται εἰς (τὰς) χεῖρας (τῶν) ἁ. Mt 26: 45; Mk 14: 41 (on χεῖρ. ἁ. cf. Ps 70: 4; 81: 4; 96: 10); cf. Lk 6: 32ff, whose parallel Mt 5: 47 has ἐθνικός. (ἡ) ὁδὸς ἁμαρτωλῶν the way of sinners B 10: 10 (Ps 1: 1). Its adj. character is wholly lost in Jd 15, where it is itself modif. by ἀσεβεῖς (En. 1, 9).—Of

the state of the man who is not yet reconciled ἔτι ἁ. ὄντων ἡμῶν Ro 5: 8. ἁ. κατεστάθησαν οἱ πολλοί the many (i.e. 'humanity'; opp., 'the one', Adam) were made sinners 5: 19. Opp. κεχωρισμένος ἀπὸ τῶν ἁ. separated from sinners of Jesus Hb 7: 26.—ESjöberg, Gott u. die Sünder im paläst. Judentum '38. KH Rengstorf, TW I 320-39. M-M.

Ἀμασίας, ου, ὁ (אֲמַצְיָה) Amaziah (2 Ch 25: 1; 4 Km 14: 1; Jos., Ant. 9, 186) in genealogy of Jesus Mt 1: 8 v.l.; Lk 3: 23ff D.*

ἀμαύρωσις, εως, ἡ darkening, dimness (Hippocr.+; Plut., Anton. 71, 8; Vett. Val. 109, 31; 110, 36; Herm. Wr. 3, 4), in our lit. only fig. of perception (Aristot., De Anima 408b, 20 of mental dullness.—W. ἀχλύς as Jos., Ant. 9, 57) ἀμαύρωσιν περικείμενοι afflicted w. dimness of sight 2 Cl 1: 6.*

ἄμαχος, ον act. (as X.,+; Jos., Ant. 15, 115) peaceable (so Epigr. Gr. 387, 6 ἄ. ἐβίωσα μετὰ φίλων; WRPaton and ELHicks, Inscr. of Cos 1891, 325, 9. The adv. ἀμάχως Sir 19: 6 v.l.) of Christians gener. Tit 3: 2; of bishops 1 Ti 3: 3. M-M.*

ἀμάω 1 aor. ptc. ἀμήσας (Hom.+; Philostrat., Gymn. 43 p. 285, 2; PHib. 47, 12 [256 BC] θερίζειν δὲ καὶ ἀμᾶν; PStrassb. 35, 14; LXX; Jos., Ant. 4, 231) mow fields Js 5: 4. M-M. B. 506.*

ἀμβλυωπέω (Hippocr., X.+; Plut., Mor. 53F; 3 Km 12: 24i.—PGM 7, 245 ἀμβλυωπός) be dim-sighted (opp. ὀξυωπεῖν Theophr., Sens. 8) in our lit. only fig. ἐν τῇ πίστει see poorly in the things of faith 1 Cl 3: 4.*

ἀμέθυστος, ου, ἡ (Pliny, H.N. 37, 121; Plut., Mor. 15B) or **ὁ** (PGraec. Holm. [ed. Lagercrantz '13] δ3) amethyst (Ex 28: 19; Ezk 28: 13; Jos., Bell. 5, 234 [ἀμέθυστος], Ant. 3, 168 [ἀμέθυσος as Mich. Psellus 4: Les lapidaires Gr. 1898 p. 201 and Rv 21: 20 v.l.]) Rv 21: 20.—MBauer, Edelsteinkunde (3rd ed. by KSchlossmacher) '32; EFJourdain, The Twelve Stones in the Apc.: ET 22, '11, 448-50; JLMyres, Precious Stones: Encycl. Bibl. 4799-812; CWCooper, The Precious Stones of the Bible '25.*

ἀμείβομαι fut. ἀμείψομαι (Hom.+; inscr., pap.; Sym. 2 Km 1: 6; Aq., Theod. Pr 11: 17) to reward, w. acc. of the pers. (12th letter of Apollonius of Tyana: Philostrat. I 348, 32; Jos., Ant. 12, 139; Dit., Syll.³ 898, 23; 902, 15) ISm 12: 1. On 9: 2 s. ἀμοιβή. B. 913.*

ἀμείνων, ον comp. of ἀγαθός, q.v.

ἀμέλεια, ας, ἡ (Eur., Thu.+; Dit., Syll.³ 784, 7; 837, 14; POxy. 62, 9; 1220; Sym. Ps 89: 8; Ep. Arist. 248; Jos., Ant. 6, 316; 12, 164) neglect ἄμπελος ἀμελείας τυγχάνουσα a vine that meets w. neglect Hs 9, 26, 4; cf. m 10, 1, 5.*

ἀμελέω 1 aor. ἠμέλησα (fut. ἀμελήσω 2 Pt 1: 12 t.r. for διὸ μελλήσω); pass. imper. ἀμελείσθω (Hom.+, also inscr., pap., LXX) to neglect, be unconcerned τινός about someone or someth. (Il.; trag.; Appian, fgm. [I p. 532-36 Viereck-R.] 21; UPZ 81 col. 3, 4 τοῦ ἱεροῦ; Wsd 3: 10; 2 Macc 4: 14; Philo, Exs. 156; Jos., Ant. 4, 67) κἀγὼ ἠμέλησα αὐτῶν Hb 8: 9 (Jer 38: 32); χήρας Pol 6: 1; w. the same noun in pass. be neglected IPol 4: 1. τηλικαύτης ἀμελήσαντες σωτηρίας if we disregard so great a salvation Hb 2: 3. μὴ ἀμέλει τοῦ ἐν σοὶ χαρίσματος do not neglect the spiritual gift that is in you 1 Ti 4: 14. ἀμελήσαντες τῆς ἐντολῆς τοῦ θεοῦ who cared nothing for God's command AP 15: 30. ἁ. ἡμῶν ἐδόκει (w.

ἀφρονιστεῖν) Dg 8: 10.—Abs. (Epict. 3, 24, 113; PTebt. 37, 23ff [73 BC]; POxy. 742, 14 [2 BC]; PGiess. 13, 22f; Jos., Bell. 4, 168) ἀμελήσαντες ἀπῆλθον they paid no attention and went away Mt 22: 5. M-M.*

ἀμελής, ές careless, negligent (so Aristoph., X., Pla.+; Epict. 2, 6, 2; Plut., Mor. 34D; 64F; PGiess. 79 II, 9; Jos., Ant. 11, 20) οὐχ εὑρεθήσομαι ἀ. Hs 8, 2, 7; κἀγὼ ἀ. δόξω εἶναι 9, 7, 6.*

ἄμεμπτος, ον (since trag., Pla., X.; freq. in inscr. and pap. [Nägeli 54], LXX, Philo; Jos., Ant. 3, 278; 4, 230) blameless, faultless of the Mosaic covenant Hb 8: 7. Of hearts ἄ. ἐν ἁγιωσύνῃ blameless in holiness 1 Th 3: 13. Otherw. only of pers. (Ael. Aristid. 33 p. 637 D.; 45 p. 91 παρὰ θεοῖς ἄ.; 46 p. 319) γενόμενος ἄ. Phil 3: 6 (cf. Gen 17: 1—MGoguel, JBL 53, '34, 257-67). πορευόμενοι . . . ἄμεμπτοι (for ἀμέμπτως, cf. Bl-D. §243; Rob. 659) Lk 1: 6. W. ἀκέραιος Phil 2: 15; w. δίκαιος of Job 1 Cl 17: 3 (Job 1: 1). ἀ. ἀπὸ τῶν ἔργων blameless in (lit. because of) his works (cf. Bl-D. §210, 1; Rob. 579f) 39: 4 (Job 4: 17). Of deacons Pol 5: 2; ἄ. ἐν πᾶσιν in all respects 5: 3. M-M.*

ἀμέμπτως adv. (Aeschyl.+; inscr., pap., Esth 3: 13d; Philo, Migr. Abr. 129) blamelessly (w. ὁσίως and δικαίως) γενηθῆναι behave blamelessly 1 Th 2: 10; ἀ. τηρεῖσθαι be kept blameless 5: 23; ἀναστρέφεσθαι ἀ. conduct oneself blamelessly 1 Cl 63: 3; δουλεύειν τῷ κυρίῳ ἀ. Hv 4, 2, 5; δουλεύειν τῷ πνεύματι ἀ. s 5, 6, 7 (text restored). λειτουργεῖν ἀ. (UPZ 20, 62 [163 BC]) 1 Cl 44: 3; προσφέρειν ἀ. 44: 4; μετάγειν ἐκ τῆς ἀ. αὐτοῖς τετιμημένης λειτουργίας remove them from the office which they filled blamelessly 44: 6 (on the text see Knopf, Hdb.). 1 Th 3: 13 v.l.*

ἀμεριμνία, ας, ἡ (Plut., Mor. 830A; Appian, Liby. 65 §290; Secundus [II AD], Sententiae 8b; Herodian 2, 4, 6; inscr. and pap. in many mngs., incl. techn.) freedom from care=confidence (Appian, Syr. 61 §321; Jos., Bell. 1, 627.—Ps 107: 10 Sym. has ἀ. for ἐλπίς LXX) ἐν ἀ. θεοῦ w. God-given freedom fr. care IPol 7: 1.*

ἀμέριμνος, ον free from care (so since the new comedy [Philemo 114; Menand., fgm. 1083], also grave inscr.: Eranos 13, '13, 87 No. 9, 5ff; pap.; Wsd 6: 15; 7: 23; cf. Nägeli 37, 1).
1. of pers. θέλω ὑμᾶς ἀ. εἶναι I want you to be free from care (Appian, Maced. 19, §3 ἀμέριμνός εἰμι; Vett. Val. 355, 34 w. ἀλύπητος; Sext. Emp., Adv. Ethic. 117 syn. χωρὶς ταραχῆς) 1 Cor 7: 32 (cf. Theophrastus [Jerome, Adv. Jovin. 1, 47=Seneca, fgm. 13, 47 Haase], who recommends celibacy because it makes one free for contemplation; PFay. 117, 22 [108 AD] ἵνα ἀ. ᾖς). ἀμέριμνον ποιεῖν τινα keep someone out of trouble (cf. PMich. 211, 8 [c. 200 AD]) Mt 28: 14.
2. of personal characteristics μακροθυμία Hm 5, 2, 3. M-M.*

ἀμέριστος, ον (since Pla., Tim. 35A, also Philo, mostly= 'indivisible') undivided (Dit., Syll.³ 783, 35f. of a married couple: παρ' ἀμφοτέροις ἀμέριστος ὁμόνοια) ἀγαπᾶν ἐν ἀ. καρδίᾳ to love w. undivided heart ITr 13: 2; cf. IPhld 6: 2.*

ἀμετάθετος, ον—1. unchangeable (since the Stoics Zeno and Chrysippus, also Polyb. 2, 32, 5; 30, 19, 2 al.; Diod. S. 1, 23, 8 et al.; Dit., Or. 331, 58 [II BC]; 335, 73 [II/I BC]; POxy. 75, 15; 482, 35; 636, 12 [of a will]; 3 Macc 5: 1, 12; Jos., C. Ap. 2, 189) πράγματα ἀ. Hb 6: 18.—The neut. as subst. τὸ ἀ. τῆς βουλῆς αὐτοῦ the unchangeableness of his purpose Hb 6: 17 (cf. PGM 4, 527f κατὰ δόγμα θεοῦ ἀμετάθετον).—2. impossible MPol 11: 1. M-M.*

ἀμετακίνητος, ον (Pla., Ep. 7 p. 343A; Dionys. Hal. 8, 74; inscr. [RB 40, '31, p. 544, 5]; PHamb. 62, 18 [123 AD]; Jos., C. Ap. 2, 169; 234; 254, Ant. 1, 8) immovable (w. ἑδραῖος) γίνεσθε ἀ. 1 Cor 15: 58. M-M.*

ἀμεταμέλητος, ον—1. pass. not to be regretted, without regret (so Pla., Tim. 59D; Polyb. 21, 11, 11; 23, 16, 11; Dionys. Hal. 11, 13; Plut., Mor. 137B) μετάνοια ἀ. a repentance not to be regretted 2 Cor 7: 10; πολιτεία ἀ. 1 Cl 54: 4. ἔσται ἀμεταμέλητα ὑμῖν you will have nothing to regret 58: 2. Hence also irrevocable, of someth. one does not take back (ὀργή ἀ.: Epist. Claud. [= PLond. 1912, 4, 78-41 AD] p. 8 StLösch '30, also in Loeb Class. Library, Select Papyri II '34, 78ff; so in wills LMitteis, Chrest. 319 [VI AD]; OEger, ZNW 18, '18, p. 91, 1) χαρίσματα, κλῆσις τ. θεοῦ Ro 11: 29 (CSpicq, RB 67, '60, 210-19).
2. act., feeling no remorse, having no regret (Aristot., Eth. Nic. 9, 4) 1 Cl 2: 7.*

ἀμεταμελήτως adv. (Aesop. 40d, 7 Chambry; Themist., Or. 19 p. 281, 14) without feeling regret 1 Cl 58: 2 (cf. Inschr. v. Priene 114 [I BC]).*

ἀμετανόητος, ον (mostly [Lucian, Vett. Val., Plotinus] pass. 'irrevocable', so also in pap.) act. unrepentant Ro 2: 5 (cf. Test. Gad 7: 5; Epict., fgm. 25 Sch.). M-M.*

ἄμετρος, ον (Pla., X.+; Dit., Or. 669, 51; Philo; Jos., Bell. 4, 350) immeasurable εἰς τὰ ἄ. καυχᾶσθαι boast beyond limits 2 Cor 10: 13, 15 (Epict., Ench. 33, 14 ἀμέτρως of self-praise). M-M.*

ἀμήν (LXX occas. for אָמֵן, usu. transl. by γένοιτο; taken over by Christians; in pap. symbol. expressed by the number 99 [α=1+μ=40+η=8+ν=50; ESchaefer, PIand. I 29], but also as ἀμήν [POxy. 1058; SEitrem and AFridrichsen, E. christl. Amulett '21, 3]. Inscr.: Wadd. 1918; MvOppenheim-HLucas, ByzZ 14, '05, p. 34ff nos. 36, 39, 46, 84) so let it be, truly, amen.
1. liturg. formula, at the end of the liturgy, spoken by the congregation (cf. 1 Ch 16: 36; 2 Esdr 15: 13; 18: 6 [Neh 5: 13; 8: 6]); hence τὸ ἀ. λέγειν 1 Cor 14: 16, cf. Rv 5: 14. At the end of a doxology (cf. 3 Macc 7: 23; 4 Macc 18: 24) Mt 6: 13 v.l.; Ro 1: 25; 9: 5; 11: 36; 15: 33; 16: 24 v.l., 27; Gal 1: 5; 6: 18; Eph 3: 21; Phil 4: 20, 23 v.l.; 1 Ti 1: 17; 6: 16; 2 Ti 4: 18; Hb 13: 21, 25 v.l.; 1 Pt 4: 11; 5: 11; Jd 25; Rv 1: 6; 7: 12; 1 Cl 20: 12; 32: 4; 38: 4; 43: 6; 45: 8; 50: 7; 58: 2; 61: 3; 65: 2; 2 Cl 20: 5. W. its transl. ναί, ἀ., even so, amen Rv 1: 7.—Accord. to later custom (cf. Tob; 3 and 4 Macc; Cyranides p. 124, 18 Ἀμήν· τέλος· ἀμήν· ἀμήν) was almost always put at the end of books, but not in the older mss. (and hence v.l.) Mt 28: 20; Mk 16: 20; Lk 24: 53; J 21: 25; Ac 28: 31; 1 Cor 16: 24; 2 Cor 13: 13 al. The liturg. formula is extended to ἀ. ἀλληλουϊά (q.v.) after the doxology Rv 19: 4; to ἀ. ἔρχου κύριε Ἰησοῦ (cf. μαρὰν ἀθά) 22: 20 or μαρὰν ἀθά ἀ. D 10: 6.—At beginning and end of a doxology Rv 7: 12.—Hence
2. asseverative particle, truly, always w. λέγω, beginning a solemn declaration but used only by Jesus Mt 5: 18, 26; 6: 2, 5, 16; 8: 10 (31 times, but 18: 19 is bracketed). Mk 3: 28; 8: 12; 9: 1, 41 (13 times). Lk 4: 24; 12: 37; 18: 17 (6 times; JCO'Neill, JTS 10, '59, 1-9). For this J always has ἀμὴν ἀμὴν λέγω (cf. OT אָמֵן וְאָמֵן [Num 5: 22; 2 Esdr 18: 6 (Neh 8: 6); Ps 41: 14; 72: 19], Gk. mostly γένοιτο, γένοιτο, but 2 Esdr 18: 6 ἀμήν and in the corresp. passage 1 Esdr 9: 47 likew., w. the v.l. ἀμ. ἀμ. [like PGM 22b, 21; 25], only to strengthen a preceding statement) 1: 51; 3: 3,

5, 11; 5: 19, 24f (25 times). On the emphatic force of repetition s. Rdm.² 68, 1. Cf. Aristaen., Ep. 1, 24 εὐθὺς εὐ.; 2, 13 οἶδα οἷ.

3. τὸ ἀ. (w. τὸ ναί): διὸ καὶ δι᾿ αὐτοῦ τὸ ἀ. τῷ θεῷ πρὸς δόξαν therefore the 'amen' is spoken through him to the glory of God (w. ref. to the liturgical use of 'amen') 2 Cor 1: 20; s. 1 Cor 14: 16, in 1 above.

4. ὁ ἀ. of Christ, only in the enigmatic lang. of Rv, explained as ὁ μάρτυς ὁ πιστὸς κ. ἀληθινός 3: 14 (Ps 88: 38); LGillet, ET 56, '44/'45, 134–6; LHSilbermann, JBL 82, '63, 213–15.—On the word gener. Dalman, Worte 185; Jesus 27f (Eng. transl. '29, 30); PGlaue, Amen: ZKG, n.F. 7, '25, 184–98; EPeterson, Εἷς Θεός, '26, index; DDaube JTS 45, '44, 27–31; Gdspd., Probs., 96–8; GDelling, D. Gottesdienst im NT '52, 73–75; JoachJeremias, Wikenhauser-Festschr., '53, 86–93; FASchilling, ATR 38, '56, 175–81; AStuiber, Jahrb. f. Antike u. Christ. I, '58, 153–59; JCGreig, Studia Evangelica. 5, '68, 10–13; KBerger, Die Amen-Worte Jesu, '70, ZNW 63, '72, 45–75; HSchlier, TW I, 339–42. M-M.

ἀμήτωρ, ορος (since Pre-Socr., trag., Hdt. in var. mngs.; denotes origin without a mother in Ps.-Oppian, Cyneg. 2, 567 ἀμήτορα φῦλα [fish, originating fr. slime]; Philostrat., Vi. Apoll. 2, 14 p. 57, 32 [of vipers]; Pla., Symp. 180D [of the heavenly Aphrodite]; Eur., Phoen. 666; Philo, Op. M. 100, Leg. All. 1, 15, Mos. 2, 210; Celsus 6, 42 [of Pallas Ath.]; Jo. Lydus, De Mens. 2, 11; oracle of Apollo: Theosophia §13 p. 169=Lactant., Inst. 1, 7, 1, also 4, 13, 2 [of God]; Philo, Ebr. 61 [of Sara]. Cf. ἀπάτωρ) *without a mother* (w. ἀπάτωρ [like Eur., Ion 109; Nonnus, Dionys. 41; 53] and ἀγενεαλόγητος) of Melchizedek, either to indicate that his genealogy is not given in the OT, or to ascribe to him heavenly origin Hb 7: 3. M-M.*

ἀμίαντος, ον (Pind.+; Wsd., 2 Macc., Philo; PGM 4, 289) *undefiled* only fig. (Pla., Leg. 6, 777E; Plut., Nic. 9, 5 al.), *pure* in relig. and moral sense.

1. of things κοίτη ἀ. (parall. τίμιος γάμος; cf. Epigr. Gr. 204 [I BC]; Plut., Numa 9, 5; Wsd 3: 13) Hb 13: 4; w. καθαρός (Cornutus 20 p. 36, 9; Plut., Pericl. 39, 2, Mor. 383B; 395E; Jos., Bell. 6, 99; Test. Jos. 4: 6) θρησκεία ἀ. Js 1: 27 (cf. Wsd 4: 2). καρδία Hm 2: 7. σάρξ s 5, 7, 1 (cf. Wsd 8: 20 σῶμα ἀ.); w. ἁγνός: βάπτισμα 2 Cl 6: 9; χεῖρες ἀ. 1 Cl 29: 1; w. ἄσπιλος: σάρξ Hs 5, 6, 7; w. ἄφθαρτος and ἀμάραντος: κληρονομία 1 Pt 1: 4.

2. of pers.: w. ὅσιος, ἄκακος of Christ Hb 7: 26. M-M.*

Ἀμιναδάβ, ὁ indecl. (עַמִּינָדָב) (Philo, Poster. Cai. 76 Ἀμινάδαμ.—In Joseph. Ἀμινάδαβος, ου [Ant. 6, 18]) *Amminadab*, son of Aram (Lk. Admin), father of Nahshon; in the genealogy of Jesus (cf. Ex 6: 23; Num 1: 7; 1 Ch 2: 10; Ruth 4: 19f) Mt 1: 4; Lk 3: 33.*

ἄμμον, ου, τό *sand* τὸ ἄ. τῆς θαλάσσης Ro 4: 18 v.l.*

ἄμμος, ου, ἡ (Pla., X.+; pap., LXX; En. 101, 6; Sib. Or. 3, 363) *sand* ἡ ἄ. τῆς θαλάσσης=seashore Rv 12: 18. Of a sandy subsoil Mt 7: 26. Cf. Ac 7: 24 D.—Mostly fig., of things that cannot be counted (LXX; Philo, Somn. 1, 175) Ro 9: 27 (Is 10: 22); Rv 20: 8. More specif. ἡ ἄ. ἡ παρὰ τὸ χεῖλος τῆς θ. (Gen 22: 17; Da 3: 36; 1 Macc 11: 1) *the sand on the seashore* Hb 11: 12; in same sense ἄ. τῆς γῆς 1 Cl 10: 5 (Gen 13: 16). M-M. B. 22.*

ἀμνησίκακος, ον (Philo, De Jos. 246.—Nicol. Dam.: 90 fgm. 130, 59 p. 402, 19 Jac. μνησίκακος; 130, 117 p. 415, 25 ἀμνησικακεῖν) *bearing no malice, forgiving* (w. εἰλικρινής, ἀκέραιος) εἰς ἀλλήλους *bearing no malice toward each other* 1 Cl 2: 5. ἀμνησίκακον εἶναι Hm 8: 10; of God 9: 3.*

ἀμνησικάκως adv. (Diod. S. 31, 8) *without bearing malice* ὁμονοεῖν ἀ. 1 Cl 62: 2.*

ἀμνός, οῦ, ὁ (Soph., Aristoph.+; Dit., Syll.³ 1024, 9 [III BC]; LXX; Philo, Mut. Nom. 159; Jos., Ant. 7, 382) *lamb* (acc. to Istros [III BC] no. 334 fgm. 23 Jac., a sheep one year old; acc. to a schol. on Nicander, Alexiph. 151 ὁ μηδέπω κέρατα ἔχων. Acc. to Ex 12: 5 the passover lamb must be one year old); in our lit. used only of Christ or referring to him (so also the Christian addition to Test. Jos. 19). Sacrificial lamb without blemish 1 Pt 1: 19. ὁ ἀ. τοῦ θεοῦ J 1: 29, 36 (PFederkiewicz, Verb. Dom 12, '32; JoachJeremias, ZNW 34, '35, 115–23; PJoüon, Nouv. Rev. Théol. 67, '40, 318–21; CKBarrett, NTS 1, '54/'55, 210–18; FGryglewicz, D. Lamm Gottes, NTS 13, '66/7, 133–46). Symbol of patience ἀ. ἐναντίον τοῦ κείροντος Ac 8: 32; 1 Cl 16: 7; B 5: 2 (all Is 53: 7).—FSpitta, Streitfragen d. Gesch. Jesu '07, 172–224; H. Wenschkewitz, D. Spiritualisierung d. Kultusbegriffe Tempel, Priester u. Opfer im NT '32. M-M. B. 159.*

ἀμοιβή, ῆς, ἡ (Hom.+; inscr., pap., Aq., Sym.; Philo, Aet. M. 108) *a return, recompense* (so freq. in honorary inscr., e.g. fr. Priene, 119, 27; 113, 120; 112, 17; Jos., Ant. 4, 266) ἀμοιβὰς ἀποδιδόναι τοῖς προγόνοις *make a return to those who brought them up* 1 Ti 5: 4 (ἀ. ἀποδιδόναι Democr. B 92; PLond. 1729, 22; Jos., Ant. 5, 13). ἀμοιβή is also to be read ISm 9: 2, with the new pap. (Berl. Klassikertexte VI '10, p. 3ff; so also Lake in Loeb series). M-M.*

ἄμορφος, ον *misshapen, ugly* (so Eur., Hdt.+; Aelian, N.A. 16, 24 p. 402, 10; Ps.-Apollod. 1, 4, 2, 1; Philo) of the εἴδωλα 1 Cor 12: 2 v.l.*

ἄμπελος, ου, ἡ (Hom.+; inscr., pap., LXX, Ep. Arist., Philo; Jos., Ant. 12, 75 κλήματα ἀμπέλων σὺν βότρυσιν) *vine, grapevine.*

1. lit. 1 Cl 23: 4=2 Cl 11: 3 (quot. of unknown orig.); Hs 5, 2, 5; 5, 2; 19, 26, 4. τὸ γένημα τῆς ἀ. (cf. Is 32: 12) Mt 26: 29; Mk 14: 25; Lk 22: 18. μὴ δύναται ποιῆσαι ἄ. σῦκα; *can a grapevine yield figs?* Js 3: 12 (Plut., Mor. 472E τὴν ἄμπελον σῦκα φέρειν οὐκ ἀξιοῦμεν; Epict. 2, 20, 18 πῶς δύναται ἄμπελος μὴ ἀμπελικῶς κινεῖσθαι, ἀλλ᾿ ἐλαϊκῶς κτλ.;). Trained on elm trees Hs 2: 1ff. τρυγᾶν τοὺς βότρυας τῆς ἀ. τῆς γῆς *to harvest the grapes fr. the vine of the earth* (i.e., fr. the earth, symbol. repr. as a grapevine) Rv 14: 18f; perh., however, ἀ. has taken on the meaning of ἀμπελών, as oft. in pap., possibly PHib. 70b, 2 [III BC]; PTebt. 24, 3; PAmh. 79, 56; PFlor. 50, 2; Greek Parchments fr. Avroman in Medina (JHS 34, '14); Aelian, N.A. 11, 32 p. 286, 12 Hercher acc. to the mss. (see p. xl); Themistius 21 p. 245D; Aesop mss. (Ursing 77f).—Lit. on οἶνος 1 and συκῆ. HFLutz, Viticulture . . . in the Ancient Orient '22; ILöw, D. Flora d. Juden I '28, 48–189.

2. fig. of Christ and his disciples: he is the vine, they the branches J 15: 1, 4f (cf. Cornutus 27 p. 51, 3, where the pleasant state for the ἄμπ. is τὸ πολυφόρον κ. καθαρόν; Sir 24: 17 of wisdom: ἐγὼ ὡς ἄ. ἐβλάστησα χάριν). The words of the eucharistic prayer over the cup in D 9: 2 cannot be explained w. certainty εὐχαριστοῦμέν σοι . . . ὑπὲρ τῆς ἁγίας ἀ. Δαβὶδ τοῦ παιδός σου, ἧς ἐγνώρισας ἡμῖν διὰ Ἰησοῦ τοῦ παιδός σου (cf. AHarnack, TU II 1f, 1884 ad loc.; PDrews in Hdb. z. d. ntl. Apokr. '04, 269f; EvdGoltz, D. Gebet in d. ältesten Christenh. '01, 214ff; ThSchermann, Knöpfler-Festschr. '06, 225ff; GKlein, ZNW 9, '08, 132ff; GLoeschcke, ZWTh 54, '12, 193ff; RKnopf, Hdb. ad loc.). M-M.*

ἀμπελουργός, οῦ, ὁ (Aristoph., Hippocr.+; Lucian, Philops. 11; inscr., pap., LXX; Philo, Plant. 1) vine-dresser, gardener Lk 13: 7. M-M.*

ἀμπελών, ῶνος, ὁ (Theophr., Hist. Pl. 9, 10, 3; PEleph. 14, 2; PHib. 151; PPetr. II 140 [III BC] and later, also LXX; Philo; Jos., Ant. 8, 359) vineyard φυτεύειν ἀ. (Gen 9: 20 al.; Philo, Virt. 28, Exs. 128) plant a vineyard 1 Cor 9: 7 (cf. Dt 20: 6); Hs 5, 2, 2; 5, 6, 2; ἀ. καλοί well-culti-vated v. m 10, 1, 5; χαρακοῦν ἀ. fence a vineyard s 5, 2, 3; cf. 5, 4, 1ff; σκάπτειν ἀ. (Diod. S. 4, 31) spade up a v. 5, 2, 4. In the parables: Mt 20: 1ff; 21: 28ff; Mk 12: 1ff (WGKümmel, MGoguel-Festschr., '50, 120–31; MHengel, ZNW 59, '68, 1–39); Lk 20: 9ff (BMFvanIersel, 'D. Sohn' in den synopt. Jesusworten '61, 124–45,' '64; JDMDerrett, Law in the NT, '70, 286–312). Cf. 13: 6, where it may mean orchard. Symbol of the Christian people Hs 5, 5, 3. M-M.*

Ἀμπλιᾶτος, ου, ὁ (by-form Ἀμπλιάς [Ro 16: 8 as v.l.], more correctly accented Ἀμπλιᾶς; s. W-S. §6, 7g; Bl-D. §125, 1 and 2) Ampliatus (common slave name: CIL II 3771 [Spain]; VI 14918; 15509 [Rome]; IV 1182; 1183 [Pompeii]; IG III 1161, 8; 1892 [Athens]; CIL III 436 [Ephesus]) recipient of a greeting, designated as ἀγαπη-τὸς ἐν κυρίῳ Ro 16: 8 (cf. Lghtf., Phil. 1891, 172; Rouffiac 90; Ltzm., Hdb. ad loc.). M-M. s.v. Ἀμπλιάς.*

ἀμύνομαι 1 aor. ἠμυνάμην (Hom.+; LXX, but here just as rare as in the inscr. [e.g. Dit., Syll.³ 780, 35; Isisaretal. fr. Cyme 37] and the pap. [e.g. APF 3, '06, p. 418, 71].—Jos., Bell. 1, 319; 5, 129, Ant. 9, 9 al.) retaliate abs. (as Epict. 4, 13, 7) w. ἐκδίκησιν ποιεῖν of Moses, who killed the Egyptian Ac 7: 24; but help, come to the aid of someone (Is 59: 16) is perh. to be preferred (for Att. ἀμύνω Bl-D. §316, 1). M-M.*

ἀμφιάζω (Plut., C. Gracch. 2, 3 Z. v.l.; Vett. Val. 64, 9; Alciphr. 3, 6, 3; Dit., Or. 200, 24; Sb 6949, 24; PIand. 62, 14; LXX; Jos., Bell. 7, 131, Ant. 10, 11) by-form with ἀμφιέζω (which is H. Gk.; JACramer, Anecd. Ox. 1835–7, II 338 τὸ μὲν ἀμφιέζω ἐστὶ κοινῶς, τὸ δὲ ἀμφιάζω δωρικόν) clothe Lk 12: 28 (the mss. vary betw. ἀ., ἀμφιέζει, ἀμφιέννυσιν). Cf. Bl-D. §29, 2; 73; 101; Mlt.-H. 68; 228; Rdm. 44; 225. M-M. s.v. ἀμφιέννυμι.*

ἀμφιβάλλω (in var. mngs. Hom.+; pap.; Hab 1: 17) cast, a t.t. for the throwing out of the circular casting-net (δίκτυον Geopon. 20, 12; ἀμφιβλήστρον Hab 1: 17); abs. εἶδεν Σίμωνα κ. Ἀνδρέαν ἀμφιβάλλοντας ἐν τῇ θαλάσσῃ he saw them casting their net(s) in the sea Mk 1: 16 (cf. PFlor. 119, 3 [254 AD] οἱ ἁλιεῖς ... ἀμφιβάλλουσι, but the words indicated by periods cannot be restored w. certainty, and hence it remains doubtful whether the word is used abs.).—HermvSoden, Reisebriefe aus Palästina² '01, 162; FDunkel, D. Fischerei am See Gennesareth u. d. NT: Biblica 5, '24, 375–90; Dalman, Arbeit VI: Zeltleben, Vieh- u. Milchwirtschaft, Jagd, Fischfang '39; LBuns-mann, De piscatorum in Graec. atque Rom. litteris usu, Diss. Münst. '10. M-M.*

ἀμφίβληστρον, ου, τό (Hes., Hdt.+; Artem. 2, 14 p. 107, 13; LXX) a (circular) casting-net used in fishing. βάλλειν ἀ. throw out a casting-net (Aesop., Fab. 11 P.=27 H. βάλλειν τὸ ἀμφ.) Mt 4: 18; Mk 1: 16 v.l.; s. ἀμφιβάλλω.*

ἀμφιβολία, ας, ἡ (Hdt.+ in var. mngs.; Aristot.; Dit., Syll.³ 728 V, 6; PLond. 1716, 8; Jos., Bell. 3, 434) a quarrel ἀ. ἔχειν μετά τινος D 14: 2. B. 1244.*

ἀμφιέζω s. ἀμφιάζω.

ἀμφιέννυμι pf. pass ptc. ἠμφιεσμένος (Aelian, N.A. 4, 46 p. 102, 17; Jos., Ant. 8, 186; cf. Bl-D. §69, 1; Mlt.-H. 192) (Hom.+; inscr.; BGU 388, 41) clothe, dress w. acc. of what is clothed τὸν χόρτον Mt 6: 30 (cf. Third Corinthians 3: 26). Pass. (Jos., Bell. 4, 473, Ant. 15, 403) ἐν μαλακοῖς (ἱματίοις) ἡ. dressed in soft garments Mt 11: 8; Lk 7: 25 (on the construction Bl-D. §159, 1). On Lk 12: 28 s. ἀμφιάζω. M-M.*

Ἀμφίπολις, εως, ἡ Amphipolis, capital of southeast Macedonia, so called because the Strymon R. flows around it (Thu. 4, 102, 4; Appian, Bell. Civ. 4, 104 §437; 4, 107 §447), a military post on the Via Egnatia, the main road from Rome to Asia. Paul went through Ἀ. on a journey from Philippi to Thessalonica Ac 17: 1.—OHirschfeld in Pauly-W. I 1949ff.*

ἄμφοδον, ου, τό (Aristoph.; Hyperid., fgm. 137; inscr. [Dit., Syll.³ 961 w. note, Or. 483, 80] and pap. [UPZ 77 I, 6–163 BC; PLond. 208, 7; 225, 4; 247b, 5 al.; cf. Preisigke, Fachwörter 1915] since II BC; Jer 17: 27; 30: 33) a city quarter, surrounded and crossed by streets, then street (Hesychius explains ἄμφοδα· αἱ ῥύμαι. ἀγυιαί. δίοδοι) ἔξω ἐπὶ τοῦ ἀ. outside, in the street Mk 11: 4 (exx. for ἐπὶ τοῦ ἀ. in pap. in Mayser 261, 1). τρέχειν εἰς τὸ ἀ. run into the street Ac 19: 28 D. M-M.*

ἀμφότεροι, αι, α (Hom.+; inscr., pap., LXX).

1. both (Jos., Ant. 16, 125) Dg 9: 6. ἀ. συντηροῦνται both (i.e. wine and skins) are preserved Mt 9: 17; Lk 5: 38 t.r.; ἀ. εἰς βόθυνον (ἐμ-)πεσοῦνται both (the guide and the one whom he leads) will fall into the pit Mt 15: 14; Lk 6: 39. Cf. Mt 13: 30.—ἦσαν δίκαιοι ἀ. Lk 1: 6; cf. vs. 7 (the masc. form for a married couple, Ammonius, Vi. Aristot. p. 10, 6 Westerm.). ἀμφοτέροις ἐχαρίσατο 7: 42; κατέβησαν ἀ. Ac 8: 38; ἀ. οἱ νεανίσκοι GP 9: 37; ἀ. τὰ πλοῖα Lk 5: 7; τὸν ἐπ᾽ ἀμφοτέροις θεόν God who is over both B 19: 7; D 4: 10.—οἱ ἀ. both together (Lat. utrique; οἱ δύο 'each one of both', Lat. uterque, cf. Bl-D. §275, 8) ἀποκαταλλάσσειν τοὺς ἀ. τῷ θεῷ to reconcile both of them w. God Eph 2: 16. οἱ ἀ. ἐν ἑνὶ πνεύματι vs. 18; τὰ ἀ. ἕν ποιεῖν vs. 14. Either D 7: 3.

2. all, even when more than two are involved (Diod. S. 1, 75, 1 πρὸς ἀμφότερα=for everything, in every respect; PLond. 336, 13 [167 AD]; PThéad. 26. 4 [296 AD]; PGenève 67, 5; 69, 4) Ac 19: 16. Φαρισαῖοι ὁμολογοῦσιν τὰ ἀ. believe in them all 23: 8. JBury, CR 11, 1897, 393ff; 15, '01, 440, ByzZ 7, 1898, 469; 11, '02, 111; Mlt. 80; Rdm. 77f. M-M.**

ἀμώμητος, ον (Hom.+; Diod. S. 33, 7, 3; Plut., Mor. 489A; Ep. Arist. 93; Philo, Aet. M. 41; Wadd. 2007; Sb 332; 367; PGM 13, 89; 603) blameless, unblemished, of Christians 2 Pt 3: 14 (w. ἄσπιλος); Phil 2: 15 v.l. M-M.*

ἄμωμον, ου, τό (Hippocr.+; Theophr., Hist. Pl. 9, 7, 2; Diosc. 1, 15; PGM 4, 1311; Jos., Ant. 20, 25) amomum, an Indian spice-plant, w. κιννάμωμον, θυμιάματα, μύρον and other spices Rv 18: 13.*

ἄμωμος, ον (Hes.+; Arrian: 156 fgm. 121 Jac.; CIG 1974; inscr. of Herod: APF 1, '01, 220; LXX; Philo, Congr. Erud. Grat. 106; Jos., Bell. 5, 229 al.).

1. unblemished of the absence of defects in sacrificial animals (Num 6: 14; 19: 2 al.; Philo, Sacr. Abel. 51, Somn. 1, 62), hence of Christ as sacrificial lamb ὡς ἀμνοῦ ἀ. καὶ ἀσπίλου 1 Pt 1: 19. Cf. ἑαυτὸν προσήνεγκεν ἄ. τῷ θεῷ presented himself as an offering without blemish to God Hb 9: 14.

2. *blameless,* in moral and relig. sense (Aeschyl., Pers. 185; Hdt. 2, 177; Theocr. 18, 25; 2 Km 22: 24; Ps 14: 2; 17: 24 al.).

a. of pers. (Sb 625; Sir 31: 8; 40: 19; Philo, Mut. Nom 60; Jos., Ant. 3, 279 w. καθαρός): of the Christian community Eph 1: 4; 5: 27; (w. ἅγιος, ἀνέγκλητος) Col 1: 22; (w. ἄσπιλος) 2 Pt 3: 14 v.l.; τέκνα θεοῦ ἄ. Phil 2: 15; ἄ. εἰσιν Rv 14: 5; cf. Jd 24; 1 Cl 50: 2; ITr 13: 3.

b. of divine and human characteristics (Jos., Ant. 3, 278f δίαιτα = way of life): βούλησις 1 Cl 35: 5. ὄψις 36: 2. πρόσωπον IPol 1: 1. χεῖρες (w. ἱεραί) 1 Cl 33: 4. διάνοια ITr 1: 1. καρδία (w. καθαρά) Hv 4, 2, 5 (cf. Ps 118: 80). πρόθεσις (w. ὅσιος) 1 Cl 45: 7. συνείδησις (w. σεμνός, ἁγνός) 1: 3; cf. Pol 5: 3. χαρά IEph inscr.; IMg 7: 1. ἑνότης IEph 4: 2; προστάγματα 1 Cl 37: 1.—The Holy Spirit πνεῦμα ἄ. ISm inscr. ἄμωμον παθεῖν *suffer as a blameless person* (of Christ) MPol 17: 2. M-M.*

ἀμώμως adv. *blamelessly, without blame* χαίρειν IRo inscr.*

᾿Αμών, ὁ indecl. (אָמוֹן) (in Jos., Ant. 10, 46–8 ᾿Αμμών, ῶνα) *Amon,* in genealogy of Jesus Mt 1: 10 v.l. (text has ᾿Αμώς, q.v. 2), son of Manasseh, father of Josiah (cf. 1 Ch 3: 14 and 4 Km 21: 18–26 w. the vv. ll.).*

᾿Αμώς, ὁ indecl. (on the corresp. Hebr. name s. ENestle, ZNW 4, ’03, 188) *Amos* in genealogy of Jesus.

1. father of Mattathias, son of Nahum Lk 3: 25.

2. son of Manasseh, father of Josiah Mt 1: 10 (v.l. ᾿Αμών, q.v.); Lk 3: 23ff D.*

ἄν (after relatives ἐάν [q.v.] is oft. used for ἄν, but the mss. vary greatly, cf. Bl-D. §107; 377; Mlt. 165ff; Mayser 152f; Crönert 130f; Thackeray 67; Dssm., NB 30ff [BS 202ff]). A particle peculiar to Gk. (Hom. +; LXX), incapable of translation by a single English word; it denotes that the action of the verb is dependent on some circumstance or condition; the effect of ἄν upon the meaning of its clause depends on the mood and tense of the verb w. which it is used. The NT use of ἄν corresponds in the main to the classical, although the rich variety of its employment is limited, as is generally the case in later Greek.

1. ἄν w. aor. or imperf. indic.—**a.** denoting repeated action in past time, but only under certain given conditions, esp. after relatives (Bl-D. §367; Rob. index): aor. (Gen 30: 42; Num 9: 17; 1 Km 14: 47; Ezk 10: 11) ὅσοι ἂν ἥψαντο αὐτοῦ, ἐσῴζοντο *whoever touched him was cured* Mk 6: 56. Imperf. (Ezk 1: 20; 1 Macc 13: 20; Tob 7: 11) ὅπου ἂν εἰσεπορεύετο εἰς κώμας *wherever he went* (as he was accustomed to do.—ADebrunner, D. hellenist. Nebensatziterativpräteritum mit ἄν: Glotta 11, ’20, 1–28) *into villages* Mk 6: 56. καθότι ἄν τις χρείαν εἶχεν *as anyone was in need* Ac 2: 45; 4: 35. Similarly ὡς ἂν ἤγεσθε, unless ἀνήγεσθε is the correct reading, 1 Cor 12: 2. Cf. also ὅταν 2c and d.

b. in the apodosis of a contrary to fact (unreal) condition (Bl-D. §360; but ἄν is not always used: §360, 1; Mlt. 199ff; PMelcher, De sermone Epicteteo ’05, 75); it is found **a.** w. imperf. (4 Macc 17: 7; Bar 3: 13) οὗτος εἰ ἦν προφήτης, ἐγίνωσκεν ἄν *if he were a prophet, he would* (now) *know* (but he does not) Lk 7: 39. εἰ ἔχετε πίστιν . . . , ἐλέγετε ἄν *if you had faith . . . , you would say* 17: 6. εἰ ἐπιστεύετε Μωϋσεῖ, ἐπιστεύετε ἂν ἐμοί J 5: 46. εἰ ἐμὲ ᾔδειτε, καὶ τὸν πατέρα μου ἂν ᾔδειτε 8: 19; cf. vs. 42; 9: 41; 15: 19. εἰ ἔτι ἀνθρώποις ἤρεσκον, Χριστοῦ δοῦλος οὐκ ἂν ἤμην Gal 1: 10; cf. 3: 21. εἰ ἑαυτοὺς διεκρίνομεν, οὐκ ἂν ἐκρινόμεθα 1 Cor 11: 31. εἰ ἦν ἐπὶ

γῆς, οὐδ᾿ ἂν ἦν ἱερεύς *if he were on earth, he would not even be a priest* Hb 8: 4; cf. 4: 8; 8: 7; 11: 15.

β. w. aor., placing the assumption in the past (Gen 30: 27; Wsd 11: 25; Jdth 11: 2; 4 Macc 2: 20; PGiess. 47, 17; PLond. II 278) εἰ ἐγένοντο αἱ δυνάμεις, πάλαι ἂν . . . μετενόησαν *if the miracles had been performed, they would long ago have repented* Mt 11: 21. εἰ ἔγνωσαν, οὐκ ἂν ἐσταύρωσαν 1 Cor 2: 8; cf. Ro 9: 29 (Is 1: 9). εἰ ἐγνώκειτε, οὐκ ἂν κατεδικάσατε *if you had recognized, you would not have condemned* Mt 12: 7. εἰ ἠγαπᾶτέ με, ἐχάρητε ἄν *if you loved me, you would have rejoiced* J 14: 28. The pluperf. for aor. indic. (PGiess. 79 II, 6 εἰ δυνατόν μοι ἦν, οὐκ ἂν ὠκνήκειν; BGU 1141, 27f εἰ ἦσαν μεμενήκεισαν ἄν 1 J 2: 19; cf. J 11: 21 v.l.—In κἀγὼ ἐλθὼν σὺν τόκῳ ἂν αὐτὸ ἔπραξα Lk 19: 23, ἐλθών takes the place, as it were, of an unreal-temporal protasis (Bl-D. §360, 2); cf. καὶ ἐλθὼν ἐγὼ ἐκομισάμην ἂν τὸ ἐμόν Mt 25: 27. Sim. ἐπεὶ οὐκ ἂν ἐπαύσαντο προσφερόμεναι; where ἐπεί takes over the role of the protasis, *otherwise* (i.e., if the sacrifices had really brought about a lasting atonement) *would they not have ceased to offer sacrifices?* Hb 10: 2.

2. ἄν w. subjunc. after relatives, the rel. clause forming virtually the protasis of a conditional sentence (Bl-D. §380, 1) of the future more vivid or present general type.

a. w. fut. or impf. in apodosis, to show that the condition and its results are thought of as in the future, of single and repeated action (IG XIV 865 [VI BC]) ὃς δ᾿ ἄν με κλέψῃ, τυφλὸς ἔσται). ὃς δ᾿ ἂν ποιήσῃ καὶ διδάξῃ, οὗτος μέγας κληθήσεται *but whoever does and teaches=* if he does and teaches it Mt 5: 19. ὃς ἂν ἐσθίῃ . . . , ἔνοχος ἔσται 1 Cor 11: 27. οὓς ἐὰν (v.l. ἄν) δοκιμάσητε, τούτους πέμψω 16: 3.—Mt 10: 11; 1 Cor 16: 2.

b. w. pres. in apodosis, to show that the condition and its results involve repeated action, regardless of the time element: ἃ ἂν ἐκεῖνος ποιῇ, ταῦτα καὶ ὁ υἱὸς ὁμοίως ποιεῖ *whatever he does, the Son does likewise* J 5: 19. ὅπου ἐὰν (v.l. ἄν) αὐτὸν καταλάβῃ, ῥήσσει αὐτόν *wherever it seizes him* Mk 9: 18. ὑμῖν ἐστιν ἡ ἐπαγγελία . . . , ὅσους ἂν προσκαλέσηται κύριος Ac 2: 39. ὃς ἐὰν (v.l. ἄν) βουληθῇ φίλος εἶναι τοῦ κόσμου, ἐχθρὸς τοῦ θεοῦ καθίσταται *whoever wishes to be a friend of the world* Js 4: 4.—Where ὅς or ὅστις appears without ἄν (but cf. IG XII 1, 671 ὃς ἀνασπαράξῃ τ. τάφον; PRainer 24; 25; Act. Thom. 93; Is 7: 2; 31: 4), the reading that gives the fut. ind. is poss. the right one: ὅστις τηρήσῃ אBC, τηρήσει AKLP Js 2: 10. ὅσοι (without ἄν PPetr. I 13; PRain. 237; Inschr. v. Perg. 249, 26 ὅσοι ἐγλίπωσι τὴν πόλιν. Vett. Val. 125, 16): ὅσοι μετανοήσωσι καὶ καθαρίσωσι Hs 8, 11, 3 is the result of a conjecture by vGebhardt; the ms. has καθαρίσουσι, and the Michigan Pap. ed. CBonner ’34, p. 114, yields no sure result. Cf. Reinhold 108; Bl-D. §380, 4.

3. In temporal clauses ἄν is found w. the subjunct. when an event is to be described which can and will occur, but whose occurrence cannot yet be assumed w. certainty. So

a. ὅταν (=ὅτε ἄν; cf. ὅταν) w. pres. subjunct. to indicate regularly recurring action (Wsd 12: 18): ὅταν ἄρτον ἐσθίωσιν *whenever they eat bread* Mt 15: 2. ὅταν λαλῇ τὸ ψεῦδος *whenever he tells a lie* J 8: 44. ὅταν λέγῃ τις *whenever anyone says* 1 Cor 3: 4.—W. aor. subjunct. to express action in the future which is thought of as already completed (Sir pref. l. 22; Tob 8: 21) ὅταν ποιήσητε πάντα *when you have done* Lk 17: 10. ὅταν ἔλθῃ ὁ κύριος *when the owner has come* Mt 21: 40; ὅταν ἔλθῃ ἐν τῇ δόξῃ Mk 8: 38; cf. J 4: 25; 16: 13; Ac 23: 35. ὅταν πάλιν εἰσαγάγῃ τὸν πρωτότοκον Hb 1: 6.

b. ἡνίκα ἄν *every time that* (Ex 1: 10; 33: 22; 34: 24 al.;

POxy. 104, 26 [96 AD]; PTebt. 317, 18[174/5] ἡνίκα ἐὰν εἰς τὸν νόμον παραγένηται). ἡνίκα ἄν (so AB א C 17ψ⁴⁶; ἄν omitted by DFG t.r.) ἀναγινώσκηται Μωϋσῆς *every time that Moses is read aloud* 2 Cor 3: 15. ἡνίκα δὲ ἐάν (A א * ψ⁴⁶, δ᾽ ἄν B א ᶜ DFG rel) ἐπιστρέψῃ vs. 16.

c. ὁσάκις ἄν *as often as*: ὁσάκις ἐάν (so B א C 17, ἄν DFG 47 KL) πίνητε 1 Cor 11: 25. ὁσάκις ἐάν (AB א C 17, ἄν DFG 37; 47 KLP) ἐσθίητε vs. 26.

d. ὡς ἄν *as soon as* (PHib. 59, 1 [c. 245 BC] ὡς ἂν λάβῃς; 66, 4; PEleph. 9, 3 [III BC]; PPar. 46, 18 [143 BC]; BGU 1209, 13 [23 BC]; Josh 2: 14; Jdth 11: 15; 1 Macc 15: 9): ὡς ἂν πορεύωμαι *as soon as I travel* Ro 15: 24. ὡς ἂν ἔλθω *as soon as I come* 1 Cor 11: 34. ὡς ἂν ἀφίδω τὰ περὶ ἐμέ *as soon as I see how it will go with me* Phil 2: 23. ὡς ἐάν (PFay. 111, 16[95/6]) Hv 3, 8, 9; 3, 13, 2.—ἀφ᾽ οὗ ἄν *after* Lk 13: 25.—In the case of temporal particles indicating a goal, viz. ἕως οὗ, ἄχρις (οὗ), μέχρις (οὗ), the mss. show considerable variation; the addition of ἄν is prob. correct only in rare cases (see Bl-D. §383, 2). Only ἕως ἄν (PPetr. II 40a, 28 [III BC] ἕως ἂν ὑγιαίνοντας ὑμᾶς ἴδωμεν; Gen 24: 14, 19; 49: 10; Ex 23: 30 al.) has certain attestation: μείνατε ἕως ἂν ἐξέλθητε *stay until you go away* Mt 10: 11. ἕως ἂν ἴδωσιν τὴν βασιλείαν τοῦ θεοῦ Lk 9: 27.—Mt 2: 13; 5: 26. ἕως ἄν (א 13: 31, οὗ 68 al.; in ABKL al. only ἕως) λάβῃ Js 5: 7.—ἄχρι οὗ (ἄν א ᶜ Dᶜ37; 47 KLP, omitted by AB א *CD*FG 17) ἔλθῃ 1 Cor 11: 26. ἄχρις οὗ (ἄν א ᶜ Dᵇ37; 47 KL) θῇ 15: 25. ἄχρι οὗ ἄν (omitted by 38) ἥξω Rv 2: 25. ἄχρις ἂν ἔλθῃ (cf. BGU 830, 13 [I AD] ἄχρις ἄν σοι ἔλθω) Gal 3: 19 (so B.—ψ⁴⁶ א AD t.r. have ἄχ. οὗ).—πρὶν ἄν: πρὶν ἂν (πρὶν ἤ AD א ᵃ 1, πρὶν ἤ ἂν BR(L)X 33, πρὶν alone 69, ἕως ἂν א *) ἴδῃ τὸν Χριστόν Lk 2: 26 (Bl-D. §383, 3).

4. In purpose clauses the Attic (EHermann, Griech. Forschungen I, ᾽12, 267f; JKnuenz, De enuntiatis Graec. finalibus ᾽13, 13ff; 26ff) ὅπως ἄν, esp. freq. in earlier inscr. (Meisterhans³-Schw. 254) has become quite rare (LXX still rather often: Gen 18: 19; 50: 20; Ex 33: 13; Jer 7: 23 al.) ὅπως ἂν ἀποκαλυφθῶσιν διαλογισμοί Lk 2: 35. ὅπως ἂν ἔλθωσιν καιροί Ac 3: 20.—15: 17 (Am 9: 12 v.l.); Ro 3: 4 (Ps 50: 6).

5. The opt. w. ἄν in a main clause (potential opt.) has almost wholly disappeared; a rare ex. is εὐξαίμην (εὐξάμην א * 61 HL) ἄν Ac 26: 29 in Paul's speech before Agrippa (literary usage; cf. Bl-D. §385, 1; cf. Rob. 938; Themist. 6 p. 80 D.—On the rarity of the potential opt. in pap., LXX, Apost. Fathers see CHarsing, De Optat. in Chartis Aeg. Usu, Diss. Bonn ᾽10, 28; Reinhold 111). Cf.—also in the literary lang. of Lk—direct rhetor. questions (Gen 23: 15; Job 19: 23; Sir 25: 3; 4 Macc 7: 22; 14: 10 v.l.) πῶς γὰρ ἂν δυναίμην; Ac 8: 31. τί ἂν θέλοι οὗτος λέγειν; 17: 18. Dg has also preserved the opt. as a mark of elegant style (2: 3, 10; 3: 3f; 4: 5; 7: 2f; 8: 3). MPol 2: 2 has τίς οὐκ ἂν θαυμάσειεν;—More freq. in an indirect question, after an imperf. or histor. pres. (Bl-D. §386, 1; Rob. 938f) τὸ τί ἂν θέλοι καλεῖσθαι αὐτό *what he wanted the child's name to be* Lk 1: 62. τὸ τίς ἂν εἴη μείζων αὐτῶν *which of them was the greatest* 9: 46. τί ἂν ποιήσαιεν τῷ Ἰησοῦ *what they should do to Jesus* 6: 11. τί ἂν γένοιτο τοῦτο Ac 5: 24. τί ἂν εἴη τὸ ὅραμα 10: 17. (Inschr. v. Magn. 215 [I AD] ἐπερωτᾷ τί ἂν ποιήσας ἀδεῶς διατελοίη) Esth 3: 13c πυθομένου δέ μου . . . πῶς ἂν ἀχθείη τοῦτο).

6. The use of ἄν w. inf. and ptc., freq. in class. Gk., is not found in the NT at all (Bl-D. §396); ἵνα μὴ δόξω ὡς ἄν (or ὡσάν, q.v.) ἐκφοβεῖν ὑμᾶς 2 Cor 10: 9 is surely to be expl. in such a way that ὡς ἄν=Lat. quasi: *I would not want it to appear as if I were frightening you*; cf. Bl-D.

§453, 3; Mlt. 167.—On εἰ μήτι ἂν (sc. γένηται) ἐκ συμφώνου *except perhaps by agreement* 1 Cor 7: 5 cf. Bl-D. §376 app.; Mlt. 169. M-M.

ἄν for ἐάν is rare in H. Gk. (Bl-D. §107; Mlt. 43 n. 2; cf. Hyperid. 4, 5; 5, 15; Teles p. 31, 6; Plut., Mor. 547A; Epict., index Schenkl; pap. [Mayser 152]; inscr., esp. of the Aegean Sea [Rdm.² 198, 3; s. also Dit., Syll.³ ind. IV p. 204]; 1 Esdr 2: 16; 4 Macc 16: 11; Jos., Ant. 4, 70; 219; Test. 12 Patr.), offered by individ. mss. and occas. taken into the text: J 5: 19a (ἂν μή); 12: 32 B; 13: 20; 16: 23; 20: 23; Ac 9: 2 א E; IMg 10: 1.

ἀνά prep. w. acc.

Special lit. on the prepositions: Bl-D. §203 to 240; Rdm.² p. 137-46; Mlt.-H. 292-332; Rob. 553-649; Mayser II 2., p. 152-68; 337-543.—MJohannessohn, D. Gebrauch d. Präpositionen in LXX: NGG, Beiheft ᾽26.—PF Regard, Contribution à l'Étude des Prépositions dans la langue du NT ᾽19.—FKrebs, D. Präpositionen b. Polybius, Diss. Würzb. 1882; FKrumbholz, De praepos. usu Appianeo, Diss. Jena 1885; PMelcher, De sermone Epict. (Diss. philol. Halenses 17, 1) ᾽05) JKäser, D. Präpos. b. Dionys. Hal., Diss. Erl. ᾽15; HTeykowski, D. Präpositions-gebr. b. Menander, Diss. Bonn ᾽40.—RGünther, D. Präpos. in d. griech. Dialektinschriften: IndogF 20, ᾽06, 1-163; ENachmanson, Eranos 9, ᾽09, 66ff.—WKuhring, De praepos. Graec. in chartis Aeg. usu, Diss. Bonn ᾽06; KRossberg, De praepos. Graec. in chart. Aeg. Ptolem. aetatis usu, Diss. Jena ᾽09.—GRudberg, Ad usum circumscribentem praepositionum graec.: Eranos 19, ᾽22, 173-206.

ἀνά (Hom.+), rare in later Gk.

1. ἀνὰ μέσον (Aristot. et al.; Polyb., Diod. S., inscr., pap., LXX, Ep. Arist. [ref. in ELohmeyer, Diatheke ᾽13, 86, 1; Nägeli 30; Rossberg 34; Johannessohn 170-3, esp. 170, 6]) w. gen.

a. *among, in the midst of* (PGM 36, 302) ἀ. μ. τοῦ σίτου Mt 13: 25; ἀ. μ. τῶν ὁρίων Δεκαπόλεως *into the* (*midst of the*) *district of Decapolis* Mk 7: 31.

b. (*in the middle*) *between* (Diod. S. 11, 90, 3 ἀνὰ μέσον ποταμῶν δυοῖν; 12, 9, 2; 14, 80, 2; 17, 52, 1; Strabo 4, 4, 2) GP 4: 10; Hs 9, 2, 3; 9, 15, 2. With breviloquence—if the text is undamaged, which Mlt. 99 and JWeiss ad loc. doubt—διακρῖναι ἀ. μ. τοῦ ἀδελφοῦ αὐτοῦ *decide between his brother* (*and his opponent*) 1 Cor 6: 5 (on the shortening cf. Sir 25: 18 v.l. ἀ. μ. τοῦ πλησίον αὐτοῦ ἀναπεσεῖται ὁ ἀνήρ. S. also on μέσος 2 beg.—Lawsuits ἀ. μ. Ἑλλήνων: Kyr.-Inschr. l. 64); *in the midst of* (Antiatt.: IBekker, Anecd. I 1814, 80, 24 ἀ. μέσον· ἀντὶ τοῦ ἐν μέσῳ. Cf. Diod. S. 1, 30, 4 ἀνὰ μ. τῆς Κοίλης Συρίας; PPetr. III 37a II, 18; Ex 26: 28; Josh 16: 9; 19: 1) τὸ ἀρνίον τὸ ἀ. μ. τοῦ θρόνου *in the center of the throne* Rv 7: 17. ἀ. μ. ἐκκλησίας *in the midst of the congregation* B 6: 16.

2. ἀνὰ μέρος *in turn* (Aristot., Pol. 1287a, 17; Polyb. 4, 20, 10 ἀνὰ μέρος ᾄδειν; Kyr.-Inschr. 122) 1 Cor 14: 27.

3. distributive, w. numbers, *each, apiece* (Aristoph., Ran. 554f; X., An. 4, 6, 4; Kyr.-Inschr. 27; PAmh. II 88 [128 AD]; POxy. 819 [I AD] al.; Gen 24: 22; 3 Km 18: 13; 1 Ch 15: 26; En. 10, 19; Jos., Ant. 8, 179; 17, 172; Rdm. 20) ἀνὰ δηνάριον *a denarius apiece* Mt 20: 9f. ἀπέστειλεν αὐτοὺς ἀνὰ δύο *he sent them out two by two* Lk 10: 1. κλισίας ὡσεὶ ἀνὰ πεντήκοντα *by fifties* 9: 14; ἀνὰ μετρητὰς δύο ἢ τρεῖς *two or three measures apiece* J 2: 6 (Diod. S. 3, 13, 2 ἀνὰ τρεῖς ἢ δύο).—Lk 9: 3; Rv 4: 8; GP 9: 35. ἀνὰ μέσον αὐτῶν ἀνὰ δύο παρθένοι *between them*

(the maidens at the four corners) *two maidens apiece* Hs 9, 2, 3 (see MDibelius, Hdb. ad loc.).—In ἀνὰ δύο παρθένοι ἀ. has become fixed as an adverb. Likew. ἀνὰ εἷς ἕκαστος τῶν πυλώνων Rv 21: 21 (Bl-D. §204; 305; Rob. 571). On ἀνὰ δύο δύο Lk 10: 1 v.l., cf. Ac. Philippi 142 p. 79, 6 Bonnet and δύο 5. M-M.*

ἀναβαθμός, οῦ, ὁ (Hdt.+; Aelian, N.A. 6, 61; 11, 31; Cass. Dio 65, 21; 68, 5; Philo, Leg. ad Gai. 77; PSI 546, 3; LXX) *step*, pl. *flight of stairs*. Of the stairs that led fr. the temple court to the tower Antonia: ὅτε ἐγένετο ἐπὶ τοὺς ἀ. *when he came to the steps* Ac 21: 35; ἑστὼς ἐπὶ τῶν ἀ. (cf. 2 Ch 9: 19) vs. 40. M-M.*

ἀναβαίνω 2 aor. ἀνέβην, imper. ἀνάβα Rv 4: 1, pl. ἀνάβατε 11: 12 (W-S. §13, 22; Mlt.-H. 209f); fut. ἀναβήσομαι; pf. ἀναβέβηκα (Hom.+; inscr., pap., LXX; Philo, Aet. M. 58; Joseph.; Test. 12 Patr.).

1. lit. *go up, ascend*—a. of living beings—α. of actual going: εἰς τὸ ὑπερῷον (cf. Jos., Vi. 146) Ac 1: 13; εἰς τὸ ὄρος (Ex 19: 3, 12 al.; Jos., C. Ap. 2, 25) Mt 5: 1; 14: 23; 15: 29; Mk 3: 13; Lk 9: 28. Esp. of the road to Jerusalem, located on high ground (like עָלָה; cf. 2 Esdr [Ezra] 1: 3; 1 Esdr 2: 5; 1 Macc 13: 2 Jos., Bell. 2, 40, Ant. 14, 270) Mt 20: 17f; Mk 10: 32f; Lk 18: 31; 19: 28; J 2: 13; 5: 1; 11: 55; Ac 11: 2; 21: 12, 15; 24: 11; 25: 1, 9; Gal 2: 1. εἰς τὸ ἱερόν, since the temple lies on a height (UPZ 41, 5; 42, 4 [162 BC] ἀ. εἰς τὸ ἱερὸν θυσιάσαι; 70, 19f [152/1 BC]; Is 37: 1, 14 v.l.; 38: 22; Jos., Ant. 12, 164f ἀναβὰς εἰς τὸ ἱερὸν . . . καταβὰς ἐκ τ. ἱεροῦ) Lk 18: 10; J 7: 14; Ac 3: 1.—ἀ. εἰς τὴν ἑορτήν *go up* to Jerusalem *to the festival* J 7: 8, 10 (cf. BGU 48, 19 [III AD] ἐὰν ἀναβῇς τῇ ἑορτῇ; Sb 7994, 21).— W. ἐπί τι (X., Cyr. 6, 4, 9; Jos., Bell. 6, 285) ἐπὶ τὸ δῶμα (Josh 2: 8; Judg 9: 51) Lk 5: 19; Ac 10: 9.—πρός τινα (UPZ 62, 31 [161 BC]) πρὸς τοὺς ἀποστόλους καὶ πρεσβυτέρους εἰς Ἱερουσαλὴμ περὶ τοῦ ζητήματος τούτου Ac 15: 2. W. indication of the place from which one goes up ἀπό τινος (X., Hell. 6, 5, 26; Polyb. 10, 4, 6; Dio Chrys. 79[28], 1) ἀπὸ τοῦ ὕδατος in baptism Mt 3: 16; for this ἔκ τινος (X., Hell. 5, 4, 58) ἐκ τοῦ ὕδατος Mk 1: 10; Ac 8: 39. δι' ὕδατος Hs 9, 16, 2. Of the journey to Judaea ἀπὸ τῆς Γαλιλαίας εἰς τὴν Ἰουδαίαν Lk 2: 4. Gener. ἀλλαχόθεν J 10: 1. Of ships, *embark, get (into)* (Appian, Bell. Civ. 2, 85 §358 v.l. ἀ. ἐς τὸ σκάφος) εἰς τὸ πλοῖον (Jon 1: 3 v.l.) Mt 14: 32; Mk 6: 51; Lk 8: 22 𝔓75; J 6: 24 𝔓75 et al.—Abs. ἀναβάς *he went up* again to the third story Ac 20: 11; to Jerusalem (Sir 48: 18; 1 Esdr 1: 38; 5: 1; 1 Macc 3: 15; sim. ἀ. of a journey to the capital Epict. 3, 7, 13; POxy. 935, 13; 1157, ll. 7, 25; BGU 1097, 3) 18: 22.

β. of any upward movement *ascend, go up* εἰς (τοὺς) οὐρανούς or εἰς τ. οὐρανόν (Charito 3, 2, 5 to Zeus; Polyaenus 7, 22 to Hera; Artem. 4, 72 τὸ ἀ. εἰς οὐρανόν means the ὑπερβάλλουσα εὐδαιμονία; Diogenes, Ep. 33, 4 ἀ. ἐπὶ τὸν οὐ.; Herm. Wr. 10, 25; 11, 21a; PGM 4, 546; Sib. Or. 5, 72; cf. Ascens. of Isaiah 2, 16=PAmh. 1) Ac 2: 34; Ro 10: 6 (Dt 30: 12) J 3: 13; Rv 11: 12; B 15: 9; for this εἰς ὕψος Eph 4: 8f (Ps 67: 19); ὑπεράνω πάντων τῶν οὐρανῶν vs. 10; paraphrased ἀ. ὅπου ἦν τὸ πρότερον J 6: 62; ὧδε Rv 4: 1; 11: 12; ἐπὶ τὸ πλάτος τῆς γῆς 20: 9. W. indication of the place from which ἐκ τῆς ἀβύσσου 11: 7; 17: 8; ἐκ τῆς θαλάσσης (cf. Da 7: 3) 13: 1; ἐκ τῆς γῆς vs. 11. Abs. of angels ἀγγέλους τοῦ θεοῦ ἀναβαίνοντας καὶ καταβαίνοντας J 1: 51 (cf. Gen 28: 12 and see on ἄγγελος 2a, also WThüsing s.v. δόξα, end; JGDavies, He Ascended into Heaven, '58).—*Climb up* ἐπὶ συκομορέαν Lk 19: 4 (Diod. S. 3, 24, 2 ἐπὶ τὰ δένδρα; Aesop, Fab. 32 P.=48 H.; Dit., Syll.³ 1168, 91 ἐπὶ δένδρον ἀ.).—Repres. a passive (Wlh., Einl.² 19.—Synes., Ep. 67 p.

215D a burden 'is laid' ἐπί τι) τὸν ἀναβάντα πρῶτον ἰχθύν the *first fish that you catch* Mt 17: 27 (Bl-D. §315).

b. of things: smoke (Ex 19: 18; Josh 8: 21; Is 34: 10) Rv 8: 4; 9: 2; 19: 3; rocks ἐκ τοῦ πεδίου Hs 9, 2, 1; stones ἐκ βυθοῦ 9, 3, 3; of vines, which cling to elm trees *climb up* Hs 2: 3. Of plants also *come up* (Theophr., Hist. Pl. 8, 3, 2): thorn bushes (cf. Is 5: 6; 32: 13) Mt 13: 7; Mk 4: 7. ὅταν σπαρῇ ἀναβαίνει vs. 32; w. αὐξάνεσθαι vs. 8. Trees *grow up* B 11: 10.—Prayers *ascend* to heaven (Ex 2: 23; 1 Macc 5: 31; 3 Macc 5: 9; En. 9, 10 στεναγμός; Proverbia Aesopi 79 P.: ἀγαθῷ θεῷ λίβανος οὐκ ἀναβαίνει) Ac 10: 4.

2. fig. ἀνέβη φάσις τῷ χιλιάρχῳ *a report came up to the tribune* Ac 21: 31.—Semitism (4 Km 12: 5 A; Jer 3: 16; 51: 21; Is 65: 16; MWilcox, The Semitisms of Acts. '65, 63.) οὐκ ἀ. ἐπὶ καρδίαν *it has never entered our minds*, since the heart was regarded as the organ of thinking (=עַל לֵב עָלָה—The Greek said ἐπὶ νοῦν ἀναβαίνει [Synes., Ep. 44 p. 182c] or ἦλθεν [Marinus, Vi. Procli 17 Boiss.]) 1 Cor 2: 9 (MPhilonenko, ThZ 15, '59, 51f); Hv 1, 1, 8; 3, 7, 2 al. (s. καρδία 1bβ). Also ἀ. ἐν τῇ καρδίᾳ s 5, 1, 5. διαλογισμοὶ ἀναβαίνουσιν ἐν τῇ καρδίᾳ *doubts arise in (your) hearts* Lk 24: 38. M-M.

ἀναβάλλω (Hom.+ in var. mngs.; LXX) act. and mid. *postpone* (mid.: Hes., Works 410 one should not ἀναβάλλεσθαι anything ἐς αὔριον; Nicol. Dam.: 90 fgm. 130, 43 Jac.; Syntipas p. 52, 2; Jos., Ant. 4, 288; 14, 28); legal t.t. *adjourn* a trial, etc. (Hdt., Demosth. et al.; PTebt. 22, 9 [112 BC]; Jos., Ant. 14, 177) τινά *remand someone, adjourn (his trial)* (like ampliare alqm. Cicero, Verr. 1, 29) ἀνεβάλετο αὐτοὺς ὁ Φῆλιξ Ac 24: 22. M-M.*

ἀναβάτης, ου, ὁ (Pla., X. et al.; LXX) ἅρματα καὶ ἀναβάται αὐτῶν leaves the question open whether αὐτῶν refers to ἅρματα, in which case ἀ. would mean *drivers* (of the chariots), or to the Egyptians. In the latter case ἀ. would retain its usu. mng. *rider*, which it has in the OT pass. (Ex 14: 23, 26, 28) forming the basis for 1 Cl 51: 5.*

ἀναβιβάζω (Hdt.+; Zen.-P. 59736, 36 [III BC]; POxy. 513, 27; LXX; Philo, De Jos. 120; Jos., Ant. 20, 60) *bring up* of a net ἀναβιβάσαντες ἐπὶ τὸν αἰγιαλόν *they pulled it up on the shore* Mt 13: 48 (cf. Maximus Tyr. 29, 6a ἀναβ. ἐπὶ ἵππους ἱππέας=cause riders to mount horses; X., Hell. 1, 1, 2 πρὸς τ. γῆν ἀνεβίβαζε τὰς τριήρεις). M-M.*

ἀναβιόω (Aristoph., Andoc., Pla. et al., also Artapanus in Euseb., Pr. Ev. 9, 27, 25) *come to life again* (Artem. 2, 62; 4, 82; Palaeph. p. 60, 6; Philostrat., Vi. Apoll. 1, 1, 1; 8, 7 p. 324, 27, Heroicus 1, 4; Jos., Ant. 18, 14) 2 Cl 19: 4.*

ἀναβλέπω 1 aor. ἀνέβλεψα, imper. ἀνάβλεψον (Pre-Socr., Hdt., Eur.+; pap., LXX; Jos., Ant. 10, 270) *look up, see again*.

1. lit. ἀ. εἰς τὸν οὐρανόν *look up to heaven* (X., Cyr. 6, 4, 9; Ps.-Pla., Axioch. 370B; Charito 8, 7, 2 εἰς τ. οὐρανόν ἀναβλέψας εὐφήμει τ. θεούς; Dt 4: 19; Job 35: 5; Jos., Ant. 11, 64) Mt 14: 19; Mk 6: 41; 7: 34; Lk 9: 16; 1 Cl 10: 6 (Gen 15: 5); MPol 9: 2; 14: 1.—*Look up* Mk 8: 24. ἀ. τοῖς ὀφθαλμοῖς 1 Cl 10: 4 (Gen 13: 14; cf. X., Hell. 7, 1, 30 ἀν. ὀρθοῖς ὄμμασιν); MPol 2: 3. ἀναβλέψασαι θεωροῦσιν *when they looked up, they saw* Mk 16: 4; Lk 16: 5; 21: 1. ἀνάβλεψον *look up* Ac 22: 13a. W. εἰς αὐτόν to show the direction of the glance (Jos., Ant. 12, 24) 22: 13b; but perh. this vs. belongs under 2a.

2. *gain sight*—a. lit.—α. of blind persons, who were formerly able to see, *regain sight* (Hdt. 2, 111; Aristoph., Plut. 126; Pla., Phaedr. 234B; Ps-Apollod. 1, 4, 3, 3; Dit.,

Syll.³ 1173, 4 and 17 [138 AD]; Tob 14: 2; Philo, Cher. 62) Mt 11: 5; Lk 7: 22; Ac 9: 12, 17f. εὐθέως ἀνέβλεψαν they regained their sight at once Mt 20: 34; cf. Mk 10: 52. (θέλω), ἵνα ἀναβλέψω I want to regain my sight Mk 10: 51; Lk 18: 41ff.

β. w. total loss of the force of ἀνά again (cf. ἀναζάω 1b; Aristoph., Plut. 95; 117 πάλιν ἀν.; Philostrat., Vi. Soph. 2, 1, 2) of one born blind receive sight, become able to see (Paus. 4, 12, [7] 10 συνέβη τὸν Ὀφιονέα . . . τὸν ἐκ γενετῆς τυφλὸν ἀναβλέψαι) J 9: 11, 15, 18.

b. fig., of spiritual sight (Herm. Wr. 7, 3; 1a) ἐν τίνι ἀνεβλέψατε; in what (state) did you receive sight? 2 Cl 9: 2; cf. 1: 6. M-M.*

ἀνάβλεψις, εως, ἡ (Aristot. et al.) recovery of sight κηρῦξαι τυφλοῖς ἀνάβλεψιν Lk 4: 18; B 14: 9 (both Is 61: 1).*

ἀναβοάω 1 aor. ἀνεβόησα (Aeschyl., Hdt.+; Antig. Car. 1; LXX; Jos., Bell. 5, 120, Ant. 19, 345; rare in pap.: POxy. 33 III, 7; PGM 36, 141) cry out Mk 15: 8 v.l.; Lk 9: 38 v.l.; ἀ. φωνῇ μεγάλῃ (1 Km 28: 12; Jdth 7: 23; Bel 41 Theod.; 3 Macc 5: 51) Mt 27: 46; Lk 1: 42 v.l. ἀνεβόησε λέγων (Jos., Ant. 9, 10) GP 5: 19. M-M.*

ἀναβολή, ῆς, ἡ (Hdt.+ in various mngs.: inscr., pap., LXX) delay (Hdt. et al.; Dit., Syll.³ 546, 22 [III BC]; PAmh. 3a II, 7; POxy. 888, 5; PTebt. 24, 22; Jos., Bell. 7, 69, Ant. 17, 75; ἀ. ποιεῖσθαι: Thu. 2, 42, 4; Dionys. Hal. 11, 33; Plut., Camill. 35, 3; Jos., Ant. 19, 70) legal t.t. postponement (PAmh. 34d, 5 [c. 157 BC]) ἀ. μηδεμίαν ποιησάμενος I did not postpone the matter Ac 25: 17; cf. ἀναβάλλω. M-M.*

ἀνάγαιον, ου, τό a room upstairs (Varro, De Lingua Lat. 5, 162; PPar. 21c, 19; PSI 709, 17 [both VI AD]) Mk 14: 15; Lk 22: 12 (both places have ἀνώγαιον and ἀνώγεον as v.l., cf. Phryn. 297f). Cf. Bl-D. §25; 35, 2; 44, 1; Mlt.-H. 70; 76; 296. M-M.*

ἀναγγέλλω fut. ἀναγγελῶ; 1 aor. ἀνήγγειλα, inf. ἀναγγεῖλαι; 2 aor. pass. ἀνηγγέλην (Bl-D. §76, 1; Mlt.-H. 226). Anz 283f (Aeschyl., Thu.+; inscr., pap., LXX, Joseph., Test. 12 Patr.).

1. lit. to report, of pers. returning fr. a place (X., An. 1, 3, 21; Gen 9: 22; Jdth 11: 15) τινί τι: ἀναγγέλλων ἡμῖν τὴν ὑμῶν ἐπιπόθησιν 2 Cor 7: 7. ἀ. ὅσα ἐποίησεν ὁ θεός they reported what God had done Ac 14: 27; cf. 15: 4.

2. gener. disclose, announce, proclaim, teach (=Att. ἀπαγγέλλω, a usage widely quotable fr. inscr. and pap., but found as early as Aeschyl., Prom. 661, X., et al. On the LXX cf. Anz 283) αἴνεσιν the praise of God 1 Cl 18: 15; (Ps 50: 17). ποίησιν χειρῶν the work of his hands 27: 7 (Ps 18: 2). τινί τι (En. 13, 10; Jos., Bell. 1, 663, Ant. 5, 114) ἀ. ταῦτα τοῖς ἐκλεκτοῖς Hv 2, 1, 3; cf. 3, 3, 1. ἀ. τοῖς λοιποῖς τὰ γενόμενα MPol 15: 1.—W. ἐξομολογεῖσθαι: ἀ. τὰς πράξεις αὐτῶν make their deeds known Ac 19: 18.—Of a report to officials Mt 28: 11 v.l.; J 5: 15 v.l.—Of the proclamation of what is to come in the future (Is 41: 22f) through the Spirit τὰ ἐρχόμενα ἀ. ὑμῖν he will proclaim to you what is to come J 16: 13; cf. vss. 14f, 4: 25 (PJoüon, Rech de Sc rel 28, '38, 234f: ἀν.=report what one has heard).—Of didactic speaking: preach w. διδάσκειν Ac 20: 20; cf. ἀ. πᾶσαν τὴν βουλὴν τοῦ θεοῦ vs. 27 (cf. Dt 24: 8 τὸν νόμον). ἃ νῦν ἀνηγγέλη ὑμῖν which have now been proclaimed to you 1 Pt 1: 12; 1 J 1: 5. ἀνηγγείλαμεν ἐναντίον αὐτοῦ we proclaimed before him 1 Cl 16: 3 (Is 53: 2); cf. GEb 4. περί τινος Ro 15: 21 (Is 52: 15); 2 Cl 17: 5. M-M.*

ἀναγεννάω 1 aor. ἀνεγέννησα; pf. pass. ptc. ἀναγεγεννημένος (Philod., Ira p. 18 W.; Sir Prol. l. 28 v.l.) beget again, cause to be born again fig. of the spiritual rebirth of Christians.—Of God ὁ ἀναγεννήσας ἡμᾶς εἰς ἐλπίδα ζῶσαν who has caused us to be born again to a living hope 1 Pt 1: 3. ἀναγεγεννημένοι οὐκ ἐκ σπορᾶς φθαρτῆς born again not of perishable seed vs. 23 (Herm. Wr. 13, 1 Sc. ἀγνοῶ, ὦ τρισμέγιστε, ἐξ οἵας μήτρας ἄνθρωπος ἀναγεννηθείη ἄν, σπορᾶς δὲ ποίας the rdg. ἀναγ. is not certain, but Sallust. 4 p. 8, 24 uses the word in describing mysteries).—Cf. RPerdelwitz, D. Mysterienreligion u. d. Problem des 1 Pt '11, 37ff; HWindisch, Hdb. Exc. on 1 Pt 2: 2 and the entry παλιγγενεσία. M-M.*

ἀναγινώσκω (class. -γιγν-) fut. ἀναγνώσομαι; 2 aor. ἀνέγνων, inf. ἀναγνῶναι Lk 4: 16, ptc. ἀναγνούς; 1 aor. pass. ἀνεγνώσθην (Hom.+; inscr., pap., LXX).

1. read (Pind., Thu.+; PEleph. 9, 3 [222 BC]; 13, 3; BGU 1079, 6ff [I AD]; Dit., Syll.³ 785, 1f [I AD]; LXX; Philo, Spec. Leg. 4, 160; 161; Jos., Ant. 11, 98) w. indication of that in which one reads ἐν τῇ βίβλῳ (Test. Dan 5: 6) Mk 12: 26; ἐν τῷ νόμῳ Mt 12: 5; ἐν ταῖς γραφαῖς 21: 42. W. acc. (Jos., Ant. 20, 44 τὸν νόμον; Test. Levi 13: 2) τὸ ῥηθέν Mt 22: 31; τὴν γραφὴν ταύτην Mk 12: 10; cf. Ac 8: 32; τὸν τίτλον the inscription on the cross J 19: 20; Ἡσαΐαν Ac 8: 28, 30 (the eunuch read aloud to himself); ἐπιστολήν (Diod. S. 15, 8, 4 ἀναγνοὺς τὴν ἐπιστολήν; Jos., Vi. 227) Col 4: 16; τοῦτο Lk 6: 3.—βιβλαρίδιον Hv 2, 1, 3.—W. ὅτι foll. Mt 19: 4; 21: 16.—W. question foll. ἀ. τί ἐποίησεν Δαυίδ Mt 12: 3; Mk 2: 25.—πῶς ἀναγινώσκεις; Lk 10: 26.—Plays on words (cf. Pla., Ep. 2 p. 312D ἵνα ὁ ἀναγνοὺς μὴ γνῷ; Polyb. 23, 11, 1 μὴ μόνον ἀναγινώσκειν τὰς τραγῳδίας . . . ἀλλὰ καὶ γινώσκειν; POxy. 1062, 13 [II AD] αὐτὴν δέ σοι τὴν ἐπιστολὴν πέμψω διὰ Σύρου, ἵνα αὐτὴν ἀναγνοῖς νήφων καὶ σαυτοῦ καταγνοῖς) γινώσκεις ἃ ἀναγινώσκεις; do you understand what you are reading? Ac 8: 30; ἐπιστολὴ γινωσκομένη καὶ ἀναγινωσκομένη ὑπὸ πάντων ἀνθρώπων known and read by everybody 2 Cor 3: 2; cf. 1: 13.—Abs. ὁ ἀναγινώσκων (so PFay. 20, 23; Sb 1019; 1020 al.; Sir Prol. l. 4) νοείτω let the reader consider (this) Mt 24: 15, Mk 13: 14 (mng. 2 is also poss. here and in Rv 1: 3, μακάριος ὁ ἀ. blessed is the reader [of this book]). The obj. is usu. easy to supply: ἀναγνόντες (i.e. τὴν ἐπιστολήν) ἐχάρησαν Ac 15: 31. ἀναγνοὺς (i.e. τὴν ἐπιστολήν) καὶ ἐπερωτήσας 23: 34. δύνασθε ἀναγινώσκοντες (i.e. ἃ προέγραψα) νοῆσαι Eph 3: 4. ἵνα καὶ ὑμεῖς ἀναγνῶτε (i.e. τὴν ἐπιστολήν) Col 4: 16.

2. read aloud in public (X., Cyr. 4, 5, 26 al.; PGrenf. I 37, 15 [II BC]; POxy. 59, 8; PCairo 29 III, 1 Gdspd. '02; Dit., Syll.³ 883, 27; 789, 48; LXX; En. 13, 4; Ep. Arist. 310; Jos., Ant. 4, 209 ἀ. τοὺς νόμους ἅπασι, cf. 12, 52) of scripture reading in the services of synagogue and Christian church (cf. Sb 7336, 29 [III AD] ἀναγνώστῃ=for the reader at a Serapis festival, who prob. read accounts of Serapis-miracles [Ael. Aristid. 45, 29fK.]). Of Jesus ἀνέστη ἀναγνῶναι he stood up to read the scripture (G Dalman, Jesus-Jeshua, Eng. transl. '29, 38-55; cf. Strack-Billerb. IV, 1, 153-88) Lk 4: 16. Μωϋσῆς κατὰ πᾶν σάββατον ἀναγινωσκόμενος read aloud every Sabbath Ac 15: 21; cf. 13: 27. ἡνίκα ἂν ἀναγινώσκηται Μωϋσῆς whenever Moses is read 2 Cor 3: 15. Letters of the apostles were read in Christian meetings at an early period (cf. Diod. S. 15, 10, 2 τὴν ἐπιστολὴν ἀναγνόντες=after they had read the letter aloud); cf. POxy. 2787, 14 and 15 [II AD]) Col 4: 16; 1 Th 5: 27 (the close of the 6th letter of Plato [p. 323C]) makes this request: ταύτην τ. ἐπιστολὴν

πάντας ὑμᾶς ἀναγνῶναι χρή). ἀναγινώσκω ὑμῖν ἔντευξιν 2 Cl 19: 1; παραβολάς Hv 5: 5 (mng. 1 is also poss. here). Abs. v 1, 3, 3; 2, 4, 3. ἐτέλεσεν ἀναγινώσκουσα she stopped reading (aloud) v 1, 4, 1.—P Glaue, Die Vorlesung hl. Schriften im Gottesdienste I '07. M-M. B. 1284.*

ἀναγκάζω impf. ἠνάγκαζον; 1 aor. ἠνάγκασα, imper. ἀνάγκασον; 1 aor. pass. ἠναγκάσθην (Soph., Hdt., Thu.+; inscr., pap., LXX, Ep. Arist.; Philo, Aet. M. 136; Joseph.).
1. *compel, force* of inner and outer compulsion; w. inf. foll. (Ps.-Pla., Sisyphus 1 p. 387B ξυμβουλεύειν αὐτοῖς ἠνάγκαζόν με=they tried to compel me to make common cause with them; Jos., Ant. 12, 384f) 1 Cl 4: 10. ἠνάγκαζον βλασφημεῖν *I tried to force them to blaspheme* Ac 26: 11. τὰ ἔθνη ἀ. ἰουδαΐζειν *compel the Gentiles to live in the Jewish manner* Gal 2: 14. οὐκ ἠναγκάσθη περιτμηθῆναι *he was not compelled to be circumcised* 2: 3 (see Jos., Vi. 113); cf. 6: 12, where mng. 2 is poss. ἠναγκάσθην ἐπικαλέσασθαι Καίσαρα *I was obliged to appeal to Caesar* Ac 28: 19 (cf. BGU 180, 16). ἀ. αὐτοὺς πεισθῆναί σοι *I will compel them to obey you* Hm 12, 3, 3. W. εἴς τι for the inf. ἀναγκάζομαι εἰς τοῦτο *I am forced to do this* B 1: 4. W. inf. understood 2 Cor 12: 11.
2. weakened *invite (urgently)*, *urge (strongly)* (POxy. 1069, 2; 20; cf. HPernot, Études sur la langue des Évang. '27; ET 38, '27, 103-8) w. acc. and inf. (Diog. L. 1, 1, 4 τ. μητρὸς ἀναγκαζούσης αὐτὸν γῆμαι) ἠνάγκασεν τ. μαθητὰς ἐμβῆναι *he made the disciples embark* Mt 14: 22; Mk 6: 45. W. acc. supplied Lk 14: 23 (FANorwood, Religion in Life 23, '54, 516-27).—EFascher, Lk 14: 23: D. evangel. Diaspora 27, '56, 1-16. M-M.*

ἀναγκαῖος, α, ον (Hom.+ in var. mngs.; inscr., pap., LXX; En. 103, 2; Ep. Arist.; Philo; Jos., Vi. 144 al.).
1. *necessary (physically)* τὰ μέλη τοῦ σώματος ἀ. ἐστιν *the members of the body are nec.* 1 Cor 12: 22; cf. 1 Cl 37: 5; αἱ ἀ. χρεῖαι (Diod. S. 1, 34; Inschr. v. Priene 108, 80 [c. 129 BC]; POxy. 56, 6; 1068, 16; Philo, Omn. Prob. Lib. 76) *pressing needs* Tit 3: 14. Of relieving nature Papias 3.—Neut. ἀναγκαῖόν ἐστιν *it is necessary* w. inf. (and acc.) foll. (PFlor. 132, 11 ὅπερ ἀναγκαῖόν σε ἦν γνῶναι. Philo, Migr. Abr. 82; Jos., Vi. 413) Ac 13: 46. ἀ. ἡγοῦμαι (PFay. 111, 19; Dit., Syll.³ 867, 9 ἀναγκαῖον ἡγησάμην ... φανερὸν ποιῆσαι. 2 Macc 9: 21) *I consider it necessary* 2 Cor 9: 5; Phil 2: 25. ἀ. ἐστιν, μηδὲν πράσσειν ὑμᾶς ITr 2: 2. ὃ ἐστιν ἀναγκαῖον *to be supplied*, as Ep. Arist. 197; 205) ἔχειν τι τοῦτον *so this one must have someth.* Hb 8: 3.—Comp. (PLond. 24, 31; Witkowski 36, 21) ἀναγκαιότερόν ἐστιν *it is more necessary* Phil 1: 24.
2. as Lat. necessarius of relatives and friends τοὺς ἀ. φίλους *close friends* Ac 10: 24 (cf. Eur., Andr. 671; Dio Chrys. 3, 120; Dit., Syll.³ 1109, 51; POsl. 60, 5 [II AD]; PFlor. 142, 2; BGU 625, 26; Jos., Ant. 7, 350; 11, 254). M-M.*

ἀναγκαστῶς adv. (Hdt.+; Ps.-Pla., Axioch. 366A; Jos., Ant. 18, 37) *by compulsion* (opp. ἑκουσίως) ποιμαίνειν 1 Pt 5: 2. M-M.*

ἀνάγκη, ης, ἡ (Hom.+; inscr., pap., LXX, En., Philo, Joseph.).
1. *necessity, compulsion* of any kind, outer or inner, brought about by the nature of things, a divine dispensation, some hoped-for advantage, custom, duty, etc. (Appian, Bell. Civ. 5, 17 §68 ἀ. νόμων; Sib. Or. 3, 101; 296) ἄνευ ζυγοῦ ἀνάγκης *without the yoke of necessity* B 2: 6.

ἀνάγκη (sc. ἐστὶν) *it is necessary, inevitable, one must* w. inf., or acc. and inf. (Hdt. 2, 35; Dit., Syll.³ 888, 79; BGU 665 II, 16) ἀ. (ἐστὶν [v.l.]) ἐλθεῖν τὰ σκάνδαλα *temptations must come* Mt 18: 7. διὸ ἀ. (sc. ἐστὶν) *therefore it is nec. (for you) to be subject* Ro 13: 5. θάνατον ἀ. (sc. ἐστὶν) φέρεσθαι τοῦ διαθεμένου *the death of the testator must be announced* Hb 9: 16; cf. vs. 23. W. ἐστί and without inf. εἰ ἀ. ἐστί Hs 9, 9, 3. ἐὰν ᾖ ἀ. D 12: 2.—ἀ. ἔχω w. inf. (Plut., Cato Min. 24, 6; Jos., Ant. 16, 290, Vi. 171 et al.; POxy. 1061, 4 [22 BC]; PFlor. 278 IV, 23) *I must* ἰδεῖν αὐτόν Lk 14: 18; ἀναγκαίαν 23: 17 t.r.; γράψαι ὑμῖν Jd 3; θυσίας ἀναφέρειν Hb 7: 27; αἰτεῖσθαι Hs 5, 4, 5; ἐρωτᾶν 9, 14, 4; cf. 9, 16, 2. Without inf. μὴ ἔχων ἀ. 1 Cor 7: 37.—ἀ. μοι ἐπίκειται (Il. 6, 458) *I am under compulsion* 9: 16.—W. prep. ἐξ ἀνάγκης *under compulsion* (trag., Thu., Epict. 2, 20, 1; Jos., Bell. 5, 568; POxy. 237 IV, 33; PIand. 19, 1) [22 Cor 9: 7; *necessarily (logically)* (Diod. S. 1, 80, 3; Dio Chrys. 21[38], 31; 34; Philo, Aet. M. 21; 52) Hb 7: 12; Hs 7: 3. For this pleonastically δεῖ ἐξ ἀ. m 6, 2, 8; s 9, 9, 2. ὡς κατὰ ἀνάγκην (opp. κατὰ ἑκούσιον) *as it were, by compulsion* Phlm 14 (cf. X., Cyr. 4, 3, 7; Artem. 5, 23; Ep. Arist. 104; 2 Macc 15: 2; Jos., Ant. 3, 223; Maspéro 66, 2).
2. *distress, calamity* (Diod. S. 10, 4, 6 [mortal danger]; Appian, Bell. Civ. 5, 40 §167 ἐσχάτη ἀ.; Musaeus v. 289; LXX; Jos., Bell. 5, 571; Ant. 2, 67. So as loanw. in rabb.) of the distress in the last days ἀ. μεγάλη Lk 21: 23. ἡ ἐνεστῶσα ἀ. *the present distress* 1 Cor 7: 26 (the expr. 'present distress' is found in Epict. 3, 26, 7; 3 Macc 1: 16 v.l. and PGM 4, 526f. In Antipho 6, 25 the present calamity is called ἡ παροῦσα ἀνάγκη.—See KBenz, ThGl 10, '18, 388ff; PTischleder, ibid. 12, '20, 225ff). W. θλῖψις (like Job 15: 24) 1 Th 3: 7. Pl. *calamities* (Antipho 6, 25; Herodas 5, 59; Diod. S. 4, 43; Dit., Syll.³ 521, 23 [III BC]; Cat. Cod. Astr. VII 143, 23; VIII 3, 182, 17; 185, 27; LXX; Philo, Rer. Div. Her. 41; Jos., Ant. 16, 253; Test. Jos. 2, 4) w. θλίψεις, στενοχωρίαι et al. 2 Cor 6: 4; w. διωγμοί and στενοχωρίαι 12: 10 (but see 3 below). ἐξ ἀναγκῶν ἐξαιρεῖσθαι *rescue from calamities* 1 Cl 56: 8 (Job 5: 19). For this ἐξ ἀναγκῶν λυτροῦσθαι τοὺς δούλους τοῦ θεοῦ Hm 8: 10.
3. concr. for abstr. *the means of compulsion, (instruments of) torture* (ref. in AFridrichsen, Con. Neot. 9, '44, 28f and L-S-J s.v. 3); this mng. is poss. in some passages, e.g. 2 Cor 12: 10.—HSchreckenburg, Ananke, '64. M-M. B. 638.*

ἄναγνος, ον (trag.+; Ramsay, Phryg. I 1 p. 149 no. 41 [=ritually unclean]; Philo, Cher. 94; Jos., C. Ap. 1, 306; Sib. Or. 3, 496f) *unchaste* (w. μιαρός as Antipho, Tetral. 1, 1, 10 Blass μιαρὸν κἄναγνον) συμπλοκαί *embraces in sexual intercourse* 1 Cl 30: 1 (cf. Ptolem., Apotel. 3, 14, 17 τὰς συνουσίας ἀνάγνους).*

ἀναγνωρίζω 1 aor. ἀνεγνωρισάμην (Pla., Polit. 258A; Herm. Wr. 1, 18; LXX) *learn to know again, see again* ταύτην Hv 1, 1, 1. ἀνεγνωρίσθη Ἰωσὴφ τ. ἀδελφοῖς αὐτοῦ Ac 7: 13 v.l. (Gen 45: 1).*

ἀνάγνωσις, εως, ἡ (Hdt.+; LXX, Ep. Arist., Philo; Jos., C. Ap. 2, 147).
1. *reading, public reading* (Pla.; Dit., Syll.³ 695, 81; pap.; LXX; Ep. Arist. 127; 283; 305) of the reading of the law and prophets in the synagogue (cf. the synag. inscr. in Jerusalem, Suppl. Epigr. Gr. VIII 170, 4 συναγωγὴν εἰς ἀνάγνωσιν νόμου) μετὰ τὴν ἀ. τ. νόμου καὶ τ. προφητῶν Ac 13: 15. ἡ ἀ. τῆς παλαιᾶς διαθήκης *the public reading of the OT* 2 Cor 3: 14. The Christian church also knew public reading πρόσεχε τῇ ἀ., τῇ παρακλήσει, τῇ

διδασκαλίᾳ devote yourself to (public) reading, exhorting, teaching 1 Ti 4: 13. Cf. WBauer, D. Wortgottesdienst d. ältesten Christen '30, 39–54.

2. reading=what is read ἤρεσέν σοι ἡ ἀ. μου; did my reading (=what I read) please you? Hv 1, 4, 2. M-M.*

ἀναγραφή, ῆς, ἡ (Pla., X.+; inscr., pap., Ep. Arist., Philo) pl. public records (Polyb.; Diod. S. 1, 31, 7 ἐν ταῖς ἱεραῖς ἀναγραφαῖς; Plut.; Jos., C. Ap. 1, 28; 2 Macc 2, 13; Sammlg. d. griech. Dialektinschr. 1743, 10 Collitz) ἐπισκέπτεσθαι τὰς ἀ. τῶν χρόνων examine the records of the dates 1 Cl 25: 5 (Diod. S. 16, 51, 2 of the ancient documents in Egyptian temples).*

ἀναγράφω (Hdt.+; inscr., pap., LXX, Ep. Arist.; Philo, Abr. 17, Deus Imm. 137; Jos., Ant. 10, 271; Test. Benj. 11: 4) record, register εἰ αὕτη μοι ἡ ἁμαρτία ἀναγράφεται if this sin is recorded against me (in the judgment-book—Aesop, Fab. 317, 17 P.=Babr. 75, 17 of recording in books in the underworld) Hv 1, 2, 1.*

ἀνάγω 2 aor. ἀνήγαγον, 1 aor. pass. ἀνήχθην (Hom.+; inscr., pap., LXX, Philo, Joseph., Test. 12 Patr.) lead or bring up.
1. lit., from a lower to a higher point: Lk 4: 5 (εἰς ὄρος ὑψηλόν t.r.); Mt 17: 1 D; εἰς Ἱεροσόλυμα Lk 2: 22 (Jos., Bell. 1, 96). ἀνήχθη εἰς τὴν ἔρημον he was led up into the desert, from the Jordan (below sea level) into the highland Mt 4: 1, unless it be thought that he was 'snatched away' (cf. 1 Cor 12: 2, if ὡς ἀνήγεσθε is the right rdg. there). εἰς τὸ ὑπερῷον to the room upstairs Ac 9: 39. εἰς τὸν οἶκον into the house proper, since the rooms in the cellar served as the prison 16: 34.—ἀ. ἐκ νεκρῶν bring up from the (realm of the) dead, represented as subterranean Ro 10: 7; Hb 13: 20 (cf. Lucian, Dial. Mort. 23, 6; 1 Km 2: 6; 28: 11; Tob 13: 2; Ps 29: 4).—Bring before (Dit., Syll.³ 799, 24 [38 AD] ἀναχθέντα εἰς τ. δῆμον; PMagd. 33, 8; PTebt. 43, 19) τινά τινι (Jos., Ant. 12, 390) Ac 12: 4.
2. fig. (with εἴς τι, as Joannes Sard., Comm. in Aphth. p. 4, 10 Rabe ['28]) of love τὸ ὕψος εἰς ὃ ἀνάγει ἡ ἀγάπη 1 Cl 49: 4.—ἀ. θυσίαν bring an offering (cf. Hdt. 2, 60; 6, 111; Dit., Or. 764, 47 (c. 127 BC) ἀναγαγὼν ... ταύρους δύο; 3 Km 3: 15; Philo, Agr. 127, Mos. 2, 73 al.) Ac 7: 41.
3. as a nautical t.t. (ἀ. τὴν ναῦν put a ship to sea), mid. or pass. ἀνάγεσθαι put out to sea (class., also Polyb. 1, 21, 4; 1, 23, 3 al.; pap. [Mayser 380]; Jos., Bell. 3, 502): ἀνήχθημεν ἐν πλοίῳ we put to sea in a ship Ac 28: 11. ἀ. ἀπὸ τῆς Πάφου (cf. Epict. 3, 21, 12 ἀ. ἀπὸ λιμένος) put out from Paphos Ac 13: 13; cf. 16: 11; 18: 21; 27: 21. ἐκεῖθεν (Jos., Ant. 14, 377) 27: 4, 12. W. the course given εἰς τὴν Συρίαν 20: 3 (cf. BGU 1200, 14 [I BC] ἀ. εἰς Ἰταλίαν). ἐπὶ τὴν Ἄσσον vs. 13. Abs. ἀνήχθησαν they set sail Lk 8: 22, cf. Ac 21: 1f; 27: 2; 28: 10.
4. fig. restore, bring back (in pap. of improvement of the soil) τοὺς ἀσθενοῦντας περὶ τὸ ἀγαθόν restore those who are weak in goodness 2 Cl 17: 2. M-M.*

ἀναγωγεύς, έως, ὁ one who leads upward (Proclus, on Pla., Tim. I p. 34, 20 Diehl, of Hermes, Hymni 1, 34 [Orphica p. 277 Abel], of Helios ψυχῶν ἀναγωγεύς), only fig. ἡ πίστις ὑμῶν ἀ. ὑμῶν IEph 9: 1 (cf. Hdb. ad loc.); the 'windlass' of Ltft. et al. seems quite unlikely.*

ἀναδείκνυμι 1 aor. ἀνέδειξα (Soph., Hdt.+; inscr., LXX; Philo, Sacr. Abel. 35; Joseph.) show forth.
1. show clearly, reveal someth. hidden (cf. Isisaretal. v. Ios 19 Peek; POxy. 1081, 31; 2 Macc 2: 8; Sib. Or. 3, 15; Third Corinthians 3: 17) τινά Ac 1: 24.
2. appoint, commission someone to a position (Polyb. 4, 48, 3; 4, 51, 3; Diod. S. 1, 66, 1; 13, 98, 1; Plut., Caes. 37,

2; Dit., Or. 625, 7; Da 1: 11, 20; 1 Esdr 8: 23; 2 Macc 9: 23, 25 al.; Jos., Ant. 14, 280; 20, 227) ἀνέδειξεν (ἐνέδ. 𝔓⁷⁵) ὁ κύριος ἑτέρους ἑβδομήκοντα Lk 10: 1.—EPeterson, Deissmann-Festschr. '27, 320–6. M-M.*

ἀνάδειξις, εως, ἡ (Polyb. et al.; ESRoberts and EAGardner, Introd. to Gk. Epigraphy II '05, 119; Sir 43: 6) commissioning, installation (Polyb. 15, 26, 7; Plut., Mar. 8, 5; s. ἀναδείκνυμι 2) ἕως ἡμέρας ἀναδείξεως αὐτοῦ πρὸς τὸν Ἰσραήλ until the day when he was manifested before Israel as forerunner of the Messiah (cf. Lk 3: 2) Lk 1: 80.—EBickerman, Ἀνάδειξις: Mélanges EBoisacq I '37, 117–24. HSahlin, D. Messias u. d. Gottesvolk '45, 178–82.*

ἀναδέχομαι 1 aor. ἀνεδεξάμην (Hom.+; 2 Macc; Joseph.).
1. accept, receive (Dit., Syll.³ 962, 65 [IV BC]; PEleph. 29, 12 [III BC]; PTebt. 329, 19; BGU 194, 11 al.; 2 Macc 6: 19; 8: 36) τὰς ἐπαγγελίας Hb 11: 17. Take a burden upon oneself (Diod. S. 15, 51, 1 ἀ. τ. πόλεμον; Plut., Eumen. 6, 3; Epict. 3, 24, 64; Dit., Syll.³ 685, 30 [139 BC] ἀ. πᾶσαν κακοπαθίαν; Jos., Bell. 3, 4; 14) τὸ βάρος Dg 10: 6; τὰς ἁμαρτίας 9: 2 (cf. Demosth. 19, 36 ἁμαρτήματα).
2. receive, welcome of guests (Dit., Or. 339, 20 [II BC] τάς τε πρεσβείας ἀνεδέχετο προθύμως; 441, 9) Ac 28: 7. M-M.*

ἀναδίδωμι 2 aor. ptc. ἀναδούς (Pind.+; inscr., pap.; Sir 1: 23; Joseph.) deliver, hand over τινί τι (Philo, Aet. M. 62; Jos., Ant. 1, 249) ἀ. τὴν ἐπιστολὴν τῷ ἡγεμόνι Ac 23: 33 (the same expr. in Polyb. 29, 10, 7; Diod. S. 11, 45, 3; Inscr. Graec. Sic. It. 830, 22; PTebt. 448; PFay. 130, 15). M-M.*

ἀναζάω 1 aor. ἀνέζησα (Nicander [II BC] in Athen. 4, 11 p. 133D; Charito 3, 8, 9; Artem. 4, 82; Paradox. Flor. 6; CIG 2566; Dssm., LO 75f [LAE 94ff]; Nägeli 47) come to life again.
1. lit.—a. come to life again (so in the places cited above) of the dead Rv 20: 5 t.r., of Christ Ro 14: 9 v.l.
b. spring into life (with loss of the force of ἀνά; cf. ἀναβλέπω 2aβ) ἡ ἁμαρτία ἀνέζησεν sin became alive Ro 7: 9.
2. fig., of one morally and spiritually dead ὁ υἱός μου νεκρὸς ἦν καὶ ἀνέζησεν Lk 15: 24 (v.l. ἔζησεν); 32 v.l. (ἔζησεν in the text). M-M.*

ἀναζέω intr. (so Soph., Hippocr.+; Περὶ ὕψους p. 67, 5v; Plut., Artax. 16, 6, Mor. 728B; Ex 9: 9, 10; 2 Macc 9: 9) boil up of the mud, etc., in hell AP 16: 31.*

ἀναζητέω impf. ἀνεζήτουν (Hdt. 1, 137; Thu. 2, 8, 3; inscr., pap., LXX; Philo, Somn. 2, 61; Joseph.) look, search τινά for someone (in pap. of criminals and fugitive slaves: PHib. 71, 9 [245/4 BC]; PReinach 17, 13; PFlor. 83, 12; also 2 Macc 13: 21; Jos., Bell. 3, 340, Ant. 9, 134) Σαῦλον Ac 11: 25. ἀνεζήτουν αὐτόν Lk 2: 44; cf. 45 (in the latter passage v.l. ζητοῦντες). A lost work of literature MPol 22: 3. M-M.*

ἀναζώννυμι 1 aor. mid. ἀνεζωσάμην (Didym. Gramm. [I BC/I AD] in Athen. 4, 17 p. 139E; Pr 31: 17 τὴν ὀσφύν; Judg 18: 16B; Philo, Leg. All. 2, 28; 3, 153) bind up, gird up the long Oriental robes to facilitate work or walking (Dio Chrys. 55[72], 2 ἀνεζωσμένοι; Achilles Tat. 8, 12, 1). Fig., ἀναζωσάμενοι τὰς ὀσφύας τῆς διανοίας ὑμῶν when you have girded the loins of your mind, i.e., prepared your mind for action 1 Pt 1: 13; Pol 2: 1.*

ἀναζωπυρέω 1 aor. ἀνεζωπύρησα.

1. trans. (Pla., X.+) *rekindle, kindle, inflame* τὶ *something* usu. fig. (Plut., Pericl. 1, 4, Pomp. 49, 5; Iambl., Vi. Pyth. 16, 70; PGM 13, 739; Jos., Bell. 1, 444 [Pass. ὁ ἔρως], Ant. 8, 234) τὸ χάρισμα τοῦ θεοῦ *rekindle the gift of God* 2 Ti 1: 6.

2. intr. (Dionys. Hal. 7, 54; Plut., Timol. 24, 1, Pomp. 41, 2; Gen 45: 27; 1 Macc 13: 7; Jos., Ant. 11, 240) *be rekindled, take on new life* ἀναζωπυρήσαντες ἐν αἵματι θεοῦ *taking on new life through the blood of God* IEph 1: 1. ἀναζωπυρησάτω ἡ πίστις αὐτοῦ *let faith in him be rekindled* 1 Cl 27: 3.—Cf. Anz 284. M-M for pap. ref.*

ἀναθάλλω 2 aor. ἀνέθαλον (Bl-D. §101 s.v. θάλλειν; Rob. 348).

1. intr. *grow up again, bloom again* (lit. of plants, e.g., schol. to Nicander, Ther. 677. Also Oenomaus in Euseb., Pr. Ev. 5, 34, 14 end γῆ ἀνέθαλεν=the earth bloomed again) also fig. (Aelian, V.H. 5, 4; PGM 4, 1611; Ps 27: 7; Wsd 4: 4; Sir 46: 12; 49: 10) ἡ ἐσκοτωμένη διάνοια ἡμῶν ἀναθάλλει εἰς τὸ φῶς *our darkened mind grows up again into the light* (like a plant) 1 Cl 36: 2.

2. factitive *cause to grow* or *bloom again* (lit. Sir 50: 10; Ezk 17: 24 and fig. Sir 1: 18; 11: 22)—Phil 4: 10 both mngs. are poss. ἀνεθάλετε τὸ ὑπὲρ ἐμοῦ φρονεῖν either: *you have revived, as far as your care for me is concerned* or: *you have revived your care for me.* M-M.*

ἀνάθεμα, ατος, τό=ἀνατεθειμένον 'something placed' or 'set up', H.Gk. form for the class. ἀνάθημα (Moeris 188; Phryn. 249 L.; cf. Dit., Syll. Index).

1. *a votive offering* set up in a temple (Plut., Pelop. 25, 7; 2 Macc 2: 13; Philo, Mos. 1, 253) Lk 21: 5 ‭א‬AD.

2. LXX as a rule= חֵרֶם: what is 'devoted to the divinity' can be either consecrated or accursed. The mng. of the word in the other NT passages moves definitely in the direction of the latter (like Num 21: 3; Dt 7: 26; Josh 6: 17; 7: 12; Judg 1: 17; Zech 14: 11, but also the curse-tablets from Megara [Fluchtaf. 1]).

a. object of a curse οὐδεὶς ἐν πνεύματι θεοῦ λαλῶν λέγει· ἀνάθεμα Ἰησοῦς *no one who speaks by the Spirit of God says 'Jesus be cursed'* 1 Cor 12: 3 (on this subject Laud. Therap. 22 ὅταν ὁ δαίμων ἀλλοιώσας τὸν ἐνεργούμενον, ἐκεῖνος ὅλος λαλεῖ, τὸ στόμα τοῦ πάσχοντος ἴδιον τεχναζόμενος ὄργανον=when the demon has altered the one who is under his influence, then it is altogether he [the demon] who speaks, since he has made the victim's mouth his tool, by means of his [evil] skill). As a formula ἀνάθεμα ἔστω Gal 1: 8f. For this ἤτω ἀ. 1 Cor 16: 22. Likew. ηὐχόμην ἀνάθεμα εἶναι αὐτὸς ἐγὼ ἀπὸ τοῦ Χριστοῦ *I could wish that I myself would be accursed (and therefore separated) from Christ* Ro 9: 3 (CSchneider, D. Volks- u. Heimatgefühl b. Pls: Christentum u. Wissensch. 8, '32, 1–14; PBratsiotis, Eine Notiz zu Ro 9: 3 u. 10: 1, Nov T 5, '62, 299f).

b. the expr. ἀναθέματι ἀνεθεματίσαμεν ἑαυτοὺς μηδενὸς γεύσασθαι Ac 23: 14 means that the conspirators bound themselves to the plot with a dreadful oath, so that if they failed the curse would fall upon them (ἀ. ἀναθεματίζειν as Dt 13: 15; 20: 17). Cf. Dssm. ZNW 2, '01, 342, LO 74 (LAE 92f); Nägeli 49; Schürer II⁴ 508f; Billerb. IV 293–333; D. Synagogenbann.—S. also ἀνάθημα, a spelling that oft. alternates w. ἀνάθεμα in the texts, in so far as the fine distinction betw. ἀνάθημα= 'votive offering' and ἀνάθεμα='a thing accursed' is not observed.—GBornkamm, Das Ende des Gesetzes⁴ '63, 123–32. M-M.*

ἀναθεματίζω 1 aor. ἀνεθεμάτισα (LXX mostly=carry out a curse: Num 21: 2f; Dt 13: 16; 20: 17; Josh 6: 21 al.).

1. *bind with an oath*, or *under a curse* τινά *someone* (cf. curse-tablets from Megara, s. ἀνάθεμα 2) pleonastically ἀναθέματι ἀ. ἑαυτόν Ac 23: 14 s. ἀνάθεμα 2b; ἀ. ἑαυτόν vss. 12, 21, 13 v.l. (cf. En. 6, 4 ἀναθεματίσωμεν πάντες ἀλλήλους μὴ . . . μέχρις οὗ . . . 5).

2. intr. *curse* ἤρξατο ἀναθεματίζειν καὶ ὀμνύναι *he began to curse and to swear* Mk 14: 71 (OJFSeitz, TU 73, '59, 516–19; HMerkel, CFDMoule-Festschr., '70, 66–71). M-M.*

ἀναθεωρέω *look at again and again=examine, observe carefully* (so both lit. and fig. Theophr., Hist. Pl. 8, 6, 2; Diod. S. 12, 15, 1 ἐξ ἐπιπολῆς θεωρούμενος 'examining superficially' in contrast to ἀναθεωρούμενος καὶ μετ' ἀκριβείας ἐξεταζόμενος; 2, 5, 5; 14, 109, 2; Lucian, Vit. Auct. 2, Necyom. 15; Plut., Cato Min. 14, 3, Mor. 1119B).

1. lit. ἀναθεωρῶν τὰ σεβάσματα ὑμῶν *I looked carefully at the objects of your worship* Ac 17: 23.

2. fig. of spiritual things τὶ (Philostrat., Vi. Apollon. 2, 39 p. 81, 17) ὧν ἀναθεωροῦντες τὴν ἔκβασιν τῆς ἀναστροφῆς *considering the outcome of their lives* Hb 13: 7.*

ἀνάθημα, ατος, τό (Hom.+) *a votive offering* (since Soph., Ant. 286; Hdt. 1, 14; 92; inscr., pap.; 3 Macc 3: 17; Jdth 16: 19; Ep. Arist. 40; Philo; Jos., Bell. 6, 335, Ant. 17, 156 al.) Lk 21: 5 (the expr. used here, ἀναθήμασι κοσμεῖν: Hdt. 1, 183; Ps.-Pla., Alcib. 2, 12 p. 148c; Epict. in Stob. 59 Sch.; 2 Macc 9: 16). Cf. ἀνάθεμα. M-M.*

ἀναίδεια, ας, ἡ (Hom.+; Zen.-P. 59534, 21 [III BC]; Sir 25: 22; Jos., Bell. 1, 224, Ant. 17, 119; Sib. Or. 4, 36; on the spelling s. Kühner-Bl. II 276, 1. Bl-D. §23 app.) *persistence, impudence*, lit. *shamelessness* Lk 11: 8 (differently NLevison, Exp. 9 S. III '25, 456–60 and AFridrichsen, Symb. Osl. 13, '34, 40–3). M-M.*

ἀναιδεύομαι 1 aor. ptc. ἀναιδευσάμενος (Aristoph., Eq. 397; Philod., Rhet. I 251 Sudh.; Phryn. 66f L.; PRyl. 141, 19 [37 AD]; Pr 7: 13 Theod.) *be unabashed, bold*, lit. *shameless* ἀ. αὐτὴν ἐπηρώτησα *unabashed, I asked her* Hv 3, 7, 5.*

ἀναιδής, ές (Hom.+; Dit., Or. 665, 16 [adv.]; PLond. 342, 14 [185 AD]; LXX; Test. 12 Patr.) *shameless, bold* (Jos., Bell. 6, 337) ἀ. εἰ *you are shameless* Hv 3, 3, 2; w. ἰταμός (as Menand., Epitr. 310) and πολύλαλος m 11: 12.*

ἀναίρεσις, εως, ἡ (Eur., Thu.+; Philo, Aet. M. 5 al.) *murder, killing* (X., Hell. 6, 3, 5; Plut., Mor. 1051D; Herodian 2, 13, 1; Num 11: 15; Jdth 15: 4; 2 Macc 5: 13; Jos., Ant. 5, 165, Vi. 21; Test. Jud. 23: 3) ἦν συνευδοκῶν τῇ ἀναιρέσει αὐτοῦ (*Saul*) *consented to his murder* Ac 8: 1 (22: 20 v.l. infl. by 8: 1); 13: 28D. M-M.*

ἀναιρέω fut. ἀναιρήσω and ἀνελῶ (Bl-D. §74, 3), the latter (Dionys. Hal. 11, 18, 2; Jdth 7: 13) formed after 2 aor. ἀνεῖλον, which appears also in the forms (Bl-D. §81, 3 app.) ἀνεῖλα (ἀνείλατε Ac 2: 23, ἀνεῖλαν 10: 39); subj. ἀνέλω, mid. ἀνειλόμην and ἀνειλάμην (ἀνείλατο 7: 21; cf. CIG 4137, 3; Ex 2: 5, 10; Bl-D. §81, 3 app.; cf. Mlt.-H. 226 s.v. αἱρέω); 1 aor. pass ἀνῃρέθην (Hom.+; inscr., pap., LXX, Ep. Arist., Philo, Joseph., Test. 12 Patr.).

1. act. *take away, do away with, destroy.*

a. of pers. τινά *someone*, mostly of killing by violence, in battle, by execution, murder, or assassination (trag.,

54

ἀναιρέω – ἀνακεφαλαιόω

Hdt. +; Dit., Syll.³ 226, 20; 709, 35; PAmh. 142, 8; LXX; Ep. Arist. 166; Jos., Bell. 1, 389, Ant. 17, 44) ἀ. πάντας τοὺς παῖδας Mt 2: 16 (PSaintyves, Le massacre des Innocents: Congr. d'Hist. du Christ. I 229–72). ἐζήτουν τὸ πῶς ἀνέλωσιν αὐτόν they sought a way to put him to death Lk 22: 2. τοῦτον Ac 2: 23; cf. 5: 33; 7: 28 (Ex 2: 14); 9: 23f, 29; 22: 20; 23: 15, 21; 25: 3; 1 Cl 4: 10 (Ex 2: 14). ἀ. ἑαυτόν commit suicide (Parthenius 17, 7; Jos., Ant. 20, 80) Ac 16: 27. Of execution (Charito 4, 3, 5) Lk 23: 32; Ac 10: 39; 12: 2; 13: 28. Synon. w. θανατοῦν 1 Cl 39: 7 (Job 5: 2). Of the destruction of the Antichrist ὃν ὁ Κύριος Ἰησοῦς ἀνελεῖ (v.l. ἀναλοῖ, ἀναλώσει) τῷ πνεύματι τοῦ στόματος αὐτοῦ whom the Lord Jesus will slay with the breath of his mouth 2 Th 2: 8 (after Is 11: 4). Pregnant constr., of martyrs ἀναιρούμενοι εἰς θεόν those who come to God by a violent death IEph 12: 2. Of the tree of knowledge: kill οὐ τὸ τῆς γνώσεως (sc. ξύλον) ἀναιρεῖ ἀλλ' ἡ παρακοὴ ἀναιρεῖ Dg 12: 2.—Pass. Ac 23: 27. ἀναιρεθῆναι 5: 36; 13: 28; 26: 10.

b. of things take away πνοήν 1 Cl 21: 9. Do away with, abolish Hb 10: 9 (opp. στῆσαι). Take up a martyr's bones MPol 18: 1.

2. mid. take up (for oneself) Jos., Ant. 5, 20) of the baby Moses, whom Pharaoh's daughter rescued from the river (Ex 2: 5, 10; Philo, Mos. 1, 17) Ac 7: 21; the context strongly favors the mng. adopt here, although not all the passages cited for this mng. will support it in the full sense. Cf. Aristocritus [III BC] no. 493 Fgm. 3 Jac.; Dio Chrys. 65[15], 9 ἀλλότρια εὑρόντες ἐν τῇ ὁδῷ παιδία ἀνελόμενοι ἔτρεφον ὡς αὑτῶν. Aristoph., Nub. 531; Epict. 1, 23, 7; Plut., Anton. 36, 3, Mor. 320E al.; PSI 203, 3; POxy. 37, 6 (act.) and 38, 6 (mid.), both 49 AD; the pap. exx. involve exposed children taken up and reared as slaves. M-M.*

ἀναισθητέω (Demosth. 18, 221; Plut., Mor. 1103D; 1105A; Philo, Ebr. 6; 154) be unfeeling, insensible τινός toward something (Plut., Mor. 1062c; Jos., Bell. 4, 165, Ant. 11, 176) τῆς χρηστότητος αὐτοῦ having no feeling for his goodness IMg 10: 1. Abs. (Epicurus, Ep. 1 p. 21 Us.) lack perception Dg 2: 8f.*

ἀναίσθητος, ον (Thu. +, Philo; Jos., Ant. 11, 41) without feeling or perception (Thrasymachus [IV BC]: Vorsokrat. B 1, vol. II⁵ 322, 11; Pla., Tim. 75E; Philostrat., Imag. 1, 23 p. 326, 20; Herm. Wr. 9, 9 ὁ θεὸς οὐκ ἀ.) of idols Dg 2: 4; 3: 3.*

ἀναίτιος, ον innocent (Hom. +; PTebt. 43, 32 [II BC]; Philo; Jos., Bell. 4, 543, Ant. 17, 174; LXX only in the expr. ἀ. αἷμα, which occurs also in the prayers for vengeance from Rheneia [Dssm., LO 352-4 [LAE 423ff]= Dit., Syll.³ 1181, 7; 12]) Ac 16: 37 D. ψυχή 2 Cl 10: 5; ἀ. εἶναι Mt 12: 5, 7. M-M.*

ἀνακαθίζω 1 aor. ἀνεκάθισα sit up, upright (Ps.-Xenophon, Cyn. 5, 7; 19; Plut., Alex. 14, 4; POxy. 939, 25; in medical writers [Hobart 11f], also Hippiatr. I 177, 24; Gen 48: 2 v.l. [ed. ARahlfs '26]); ἀνεκάθισεν ὁ νεκρός the dead man sat up Lk 7: 15 (v.l. ἐκάθισεν); cf. Ac 9: 40. M-M.*

ἀνακαινίζω 1 aor. ἀνεκαίνισα (Isocr. +; Plut., Marcell. 6, 3; Appian, Mithridates 37 §144; Ps.-Lucian, Philopatris 12 δι' ὕδατος ἡμᾶς ἀνεκαίνισεν [prob. against the Christians]; Philo, Leg. ad Gai. 85 v.l.; Jos., Ant. 9, 161; 13, 57; Ps 38: 3; 102: 5; 103: 30; La 5: 21; 1 Macc 6: 9) renew, restore ἀ. εἰς μετάνοιαν restore to repentance Hb 6: 6. ἀνακαινίσας ἡμᾶς ἐν τῇ ἀφέσει τῶν ἁμαρτιῶν

since he made us new by forgiveness of sins (in baptism) B 6: 11; ἀ. τὸ πνεῦμα renew our spirit Hs 9, 14, 3; cf. 8, 6, 3.*

ἀνακαινόω (mid. in Heliod. Philos., In Eth. Nicom. Paraphr. 221, 13 Heylbut) renew only in Paul, in pass., and fig. of the spiritual rebirth of the Christian (opp. διαφθείρειν) ὁ ἔσω ἡμῶν (ἄνθρωπος) ἀνακαινοῦται our inner (spiritual) man is being renewed 2 Cor 4: 16. ἀ. εἰς ἐπίγνωσιν renew for full knowledge Col 3: 10. M-M.*

ἀνακαίνωσις, εως, ἡ (not quotable outside Christian lit.; Nägeli 52.—καίνωσις Jos., Ant. 18, 230) renewal; of the spiritual rebirth of men μεταμορφοῦσθαι τῇ ἀ. τοῦ νοός be changed by the renewal of your minds Ro 12: 2. λουτρὸν ἀ. πνεύματος ἁγίου washing of renewal through the Holy Spirit (w. παλιγγενεσία) Tit 3: 5. ἀ. τῶν πνευμάτων ὑμῶν the renewal of your spirit of the imparting of a new spirit Hv 3, 8, 9.*

ἀνακαλύπτω pf. pass. ἀνακεκάλυμμαι (Eur., X. +; Polyb., Plut.; Dit., Syll.³ 1169, 62; POxy. 1297, 7; LXX; En. 16, 3; 98, 6; Philo, Congr. Erud. Grat. 124 ἀ. πρόσωπον=unveil) uncover, unveil ἀνακεκαλυμμένῳ προσώπῳ w. unveiled face (w. ref. to Ex 34: 34, of the relation betw. the Christian and his Lord) 2 Cor 3: 18 (ἀνακεκαλυμμένῳ πρ. like Pel.-Leg. 4, 14). κάλυμμα μένει μὴ ἀνακαλυπτόμενον a veil remains unlifted vs. 14 (cf. Test. Judah 14: 5; Dt 23: 1 v.l. ἀνακαλύψει κάλυμμα; PGM 57, 17 ἀνακάλυψον τὸν ἱερὸν πέπλον; Maximus Tyr. 26, 2c ἀποκαλύψαντες τὰ προκαλύμματα). (WCvanUnnik, Novum Testamentum 6, '63, 153–69) M-M.*

ἀνακάμπτω fut. ἀνακάμψω; 1 aor. ἀνέκαμψα (Hdt. 2, 8+; LXX; cf. Anz 314f) intr.

1. return—a. lit. (Diod. S. 16, 3, 6; 16, 8, 1 al.; PMagd. 8, 10; Zen.-P. 34 [=Sb 6740], 5 [255/4 BC]; Ex 32: 27; Philo, Aet. M. 58; cf. 31 [w. πρός and acc.]; Jos., Bell. 2, 116; Sib. Or. 5, 33) μὴ ἀ. πρὸς Ἡρῴδην Mt 2: 12. πρὸς ὑμᾶς Ac 18: 21. Abs. Hb 11: 15.

b. fig. (cf. BGU 896, 6 πάντα τὰ ἐμὰ ἀνακάμψει εἰς τὴν θυγατέρα) of a religious greeting ἐφ' ὑμᾶς ἀνακάμψει it will return to you Lk 10: 6 (ἀ. ἐπί w. acc. as Pla., Phaedo 72B; Περὶ ὕψους p. 57, 8V; M. Ant. 4, 16).

2. turn back again ἀπό τ. παραδοθείσης ἐντολῆς 2 Pt 2: 21 v.l. M-M.*

ἀνάκειμαι impf. ἀνεκείμην (Pind., Hdt. +; inscr., pap., LXX; Jos., Ant. 3, 38 al.) lie, recline.

1. gener. (opp. ἑστηκέναι) Mk 5: 40 v.l.; Hv 3, 12, 2.

2. otherw. always of reclining at table= be at table (Aristot. and Diphilus [300 BC] in Athen. 1 p. 23c; Polyb. 13, 6, 8; BGU 344; 1 Esdr 4: 11; cf. Phryn. 216f Lob.) αὐτοῦ ἀνακειμένου ἐν τῇ οἰκίᾳ as he was at table in the house Mt 9: 10.—26: 7; Mk 14: 18; 16: 14. ἀ. μετά τινος Mt 26: 20. σὺν τινι J 12: 2; ἀ. ἐν τῷ κόλπῳ τινός lean on someone's breast= take the place of honor, in case it was the breast of the head of the house 13: 23 (cf. Lk 16: 23, where sc. ἀνακείμενον [some mss. supply ἀναπαυόμενον]). Pliny, Epist. 4, 22, 4 cenabat Nerva cum paucis; Veiento proximus atque etiam in sinu recumbebat.—ὁ ἀνακείμενος the one who is reclining, the guest Mt 22: 10f; Mk 6: 26; Lk 22: 27 (opp. ὁ διακονῶν); J 6: 11; 13: 28.—For pictures on ancient reliefs and vases cf. e.g. JJung, Leben u. Sitten d. Römer I 1883, 24; ABaumeister, Denkmäler d. klass. Altert. I 1885, 365f. M-M.*

ἀνακεφαλαιόω 1 aor. mid. ἀνεκεφαλαιωσάμην (Aristot. +; in OT only Theod. and the Quinta to Ps 71: 20)

55

sum up. recapitulate (Aristot., fgm. 123, 1499a, 33; Dionys. Hal. 1, 90; Quintil. 6, 1 rerum repetitio et congregatio, quae graece ἀνακεφαλαίωσις dicitur; cf. Protev. Jac. 13: 1). Of individual commandments ἐν τῷ λόγῳ τούτῳ ἀνακεφαλαιοῦται everything *is summed up in this word* (the command. of love) Ro 13: 9. ἀνακεφαλαιώσασθαι τὰ πάντα ἐν τῷ Χριστῷ *to bring everything together in Christ* Eph 1: 10 (Ps.-Aristot., De Mundo 4, 1 τὰ ἀναγκαῖα ἀνακεφαλαιούμενοι= sum up the necessary points). ἀ. τὸ τέλειον τῶν ἁμαρτιῶν *complete the total of the sins* B 5: 11.—HSchlier, TW III 681f; SHanson, Unity of the Church in the NT '46, 123-6. M-M.*

ἀνακλίνω fut. ἀνακλινῶ; 1 aor. ἀνέκλινα; 1 aor. pass. ἀνεκλίθην, 1 fut. ἀνακλιθήσομαι (Hom.+; 3 Macc 5: 16; Sib. Or., fgm. 3, 37).
   1. act.—a. *lay* (*down*), *put to bed* of a child ἀ. αὐτὸν ἐν φάτνῃ Lk 2: 7.
   b. *cause to lie down, recline* (Polyb. 30, 26, 5; Test. Gad 1: 5) ἐμὲ ἀνέκλιναν εἰς τὸ μέσον αὐτῶν they caused me to lie down in their midst Hs 9, 11, 7. ἀνακλινεῖ αὐτοὺς he will have them recline Lk 12: 37 (normally it is vice versa: Lucian, Ep. Sat. 1, 22; 3, 32); cf. 9: 15 t.r.—Mk 6: 39 v.l. (Bl-D. §392, 4 app.).
   2. pass. *lie down, recline* at a meal, abs. Lk 7: 36 t.r. ἐπὶ τ. χόρτου *on the grass* Mt 14: 19. ἐπὶ τ. χλωρῷ χόρτῳ *on the green grass* Mk 6: 39. ἀνακλίνεσθαι εἰς τοὺς ἐξέχοντας τόπους *recline in the preferred places* Mt 20: 28 D=Agr 22. Fig., of the Messianic banquet Mt 8: 11; Lk 13: 29 (DZeller, BZ 15, '71, 222-37). M-M.*

ἀνακοινόω (X.+; pap., usu. in mid., as Diod. S. 4, 40, 2; Zen.-P. 59520, 6 [III BC]; 2 Macc 14: 20; Jos., Ant. 19, 19) *communicate τινί* (*τι*) (*something*) *to someone* Dg 8: 9 (ἀνακοινοῦν τινί τι Syntipas p. 9, 17; 47, 8).*

ἀνακόπτω (Hom.+; Jos., Ant. 2, 338; Third Corinthians 3: 19) *hinder, restrain* (so Plut.; Lucian; Philo, Spec. Leg. 1, 67; Jos., Bell. 1, 180; PFlor. 36, 3; Wsd 18: 23; 4 Macc 13: 6) Gal 5: 7 t.r. (s. ἐγκόπτω). Of desires *restrain* (Procop. Soph., Ep. 117 σωφροσύνη νεότητος ἀλόγους ὁρμὰς ἀνακόπτουσα=moderation, which restrains the irrational impulses of youth) mid. *abstain* ἀνακόπτεσθαι ἀπὸ τῶν ἐπιθυμιῶν Pol 5: 3. M-M.*

ἀνακράζω 1 aor. ἀνέκραξα (BGU 1201, 11 [II AD]; Judg 7: 20; Mk 1: 23); 2 aor. ἀνέκραγον (Hom.+; Polyb., Plut., pap., LXX) *cry out* (Jos., Ant. 2, 235) of the cry of demoniacs (of the departing demon himself: Neo-plat. Damascius [VI AD], Vi. Isidori 56 Westerm.) Mk 1: 23, w. φωνῇ μεγάλῃ (בְּקוֹל גָּדוֹל; 1 Km 4: 5; 1 Macc 2: 27. But also Phlegon: 257 'fgm. 36, 3, 9 Jac.: ἀνεκεκράγει μεγάλῃ τῇ φωνῇ λέγων) added, *with a loud voice* Lk 4: 33, cf. 8: 28; of the cries of frightened men Mk 6: 49; of an aroused multitude Lk 23: 18.—Of the loud speech of an angry person ἀ. φωνῇ μεγάλῃ Hv 3, 8, 9. M-M.*

ἀνακραυγάζω (Epict. 2, 19, 15) *cry out* Lk 4: 35 D.*

ἀνακρίνω 1 aor. ἀνέκρινα, pass. ἀνεκρίθην (Thu.+; inscr., pap., LXX).
   1. *question, examine*—a. of general questions (Epict. 1, 1, 20; 2, 20, 27 τὴν Πυθίαν; 1 Km 20: 12; Sus 13; Jos., Ant. 5, 329) ἀ. τὰς γραφάς *examine the Scriptures* Ac 17: 11 (ἀ. εἰ as Jos., Ant. 8, 267; 12, 197). μηδὲν ἀνακρίνοντες *without asking questions* 1 Cor 10: 25, 27; Ac 11: 12 v.l. (for διακρίνω). ἀ. τοὺς λόγους *inquire about the words* Papias 2: 4.
   b. of judicial hearings, w. acc. of the person examined (Dit., Syll.³ 953, 46 [II BC] ἀνακρινάντω δὲ καὶ τ.

μάρτυρας; Sus 51 Theod.; Jos., Ant. 17, 131) ἀ. τοὺς φύλακας *examine the guards* Ac 12: 19.—28: 18; 1 Cor 4: 3f; 9: 3; pass. 4: 3. Abs. *conduct an examination* (Sus 48) Lk 23: 14. W. indication of the thing investigated ἀ. περὶ πάντων τούτων *about all these things* Ac 24: 8.—W. the reasons for the hearing given ἐπὶ εὐεργεσίᾳ *because of a good deed* 4: 9.
   2. *examine and judge, call to account, discern* (Demosth. 57, 66; 70; POxy. 1209, 19; 1706, 20) πάντα 1 Cor 2: 15; pass. vs. 14f; 14: 24 (w. ἐλέγχειν). M-M.*

ἀνάκρισις, εως, ἡ *investigation, hearing,* esp. *preliminary hearing* (X., Symp. 5, 2; Pla., Leg. p. 766D; Isaeus 6, 13; Dit., Syll.³ 780, 28, Or. 374, 6; PSI 392 [III BC]; PTebt. 86, 1 ff; PLeipz. 4, 15; PLond. 251; 3 Macc 7: 5; Jos., Ant. 17, 121) τῆς ἀ. γενομένης Ac 25: 26. M-M.*

ἀνακτάομαι 1 aor. ἀνεκτησάμην (trag., Hdt.+; inscr., pap.; Sym. 1 Km 30: 12 al.) w. ἑαυτόν *regain one's strength, renew one's energy* (Epict. 3, 25, 4; PFay. 106, 18 ὅπως δυνηθῶ ἐμαυτὸν ἀνακτήσασθαι; Jos., Ant. 9, 123; 15, 365; Ode of Solomon 11: 11). ἀνακτήσασθε (ἑαυτοὺς ἐν πίστει) ITr 8: 1 is Cotelier's conjecture for the ἀνακτίσασθε of the mss.*

ἀνακτίζω (Strabo 9, 2, 5; Aq. Ps 50: 12; Jos., Bell. 1, 165, Ant. 11, 12) *create anew;* mid. *have oneself created anew* ITr 8: 1; s. ἀνακτάομαι.*

ἀνακυλίω pf. pass. ἀνακεκύλισμαι (Alexis in Athen. 6 p. 237c; Lucian, De Luctu 8 al.) *roll away* of the stone at the grave Mk 16: 4.*

ἀνακύπτω 1 aor. ἀνέκυψα, imper. ἀνάκυψον *raise oneself up, stand erect, straighten oneself.*
   1. lit. (X., De Re Equ. 7, 10 et al.; Sus 35; Jos., Ant. 19, 346) J 8: 7, 10. Of a body bent by disease μὴ δυναμένη ἀνακύψαι Lk 13: 11 (medical t.t., acc. to Hobart 20ff).
   2. fig. (as Hdt. 5, 91; X., Oec. 11, 5; UPZ 70, 23 [152/1 BC] ἀ. ὑπὸ τῆς αἰσχύνης; Job 10: 15; Philo, In Flacc. 160; Jos., Bell. 6, 401) Lk 21: 28 (w. ἐπαίρειν τὴν κεφαλήν). M-M.*

ἀναλαμβάνω 2 aor. ἀνέλαβον; pf. ἀνείληφα; 1 aor. pass. ἀνελήμφθην; Bl-D. §101 λαμβ.; Mlt.-H. 246f (Hdt.+, inscr., pap., LXX, Test. of Job 34, 12, Philo, Joseph.).
   1. *take up* εἰς τὸν οὐρανόν (4 Km 2: 10f; 1 Macc 2: 58; Philo, Mos. 2, 291; cf. Justin Martyr, Dialogue w. Trypho 80, 4) pass. of Christ Mk 16: 19; Ac 1: 11. In same sense without εἰς τ. οὐ. (cf. Sir 48: 9; 49: 14) Ac 1: 2 (PAvan Stempvoort, NTS 5, '58/'59, 30–42 takes Ac 1: 2 to refer to the death of Christ; JDupont, NTS, '61/'62, 154–57, to his ascension. Cf. also BMMetzger, The Mng. of Christ's Ascension, RTStamm-memorial vol., '69, 118–28), 22; 1 Ti 3: 16; GP 5: 19. Perh. of a deceased woman (Christian inscr. ἀνελήμφθη='has died', like our 'is in heaven': Byzantion 2, '26, 330; Ramsay, Phrygia I p. 561 No. 454) Hv 1, 1, 5 (see handbooks ad loc.). Of a sheet Ac 10: 16.
   2. *take up* in order to *carry* ἀ. τὴν σκηνὴν τοῦ Μολόχ *you took up the tent of Moloch* Ac 7: 43 (Am 5: 26).—Of weapons *take* (Hdt. 3, 78; 9, 53 al.; Dit., Syll.³ 742, 45; 49; 2 Macc 10: 27; Jdth 6: 12; 7: 5; 14: 3 ἀναλαβόντες τὰς πανοπλίας; Jos., Ant. 20, 110 πανοπλ. ἀναλ. 121) τὴν πανοπλίαν τοῦ θεοῦ Eph 6: 13. τὸν θυρεὸν τῆς πίστεως vs. 16.
   3. *take to one's self, adopt* τὴν πραϋπάθειαν ITr 8: 1. ζῆλον ἄδικον καὶ ἀσεβῆ 1 Cl 3: 4; *accept* παιδείαν 56: 2. μιαρὸν καὶ ἄδικον ζῆλον 45: 4.—ἀ. τὴν διαθήκην ἐπὶ στόματός σου *take the covenant in your mouth* 35: 7 (Ps

49: 16).—τὴν δύναμίν τινος *take back someone's power* Hs 9, 14, 2. τὴν ζωήν *receive life* s 9, 16, 3.

4. *take along* of a travel companion (Thu., X.; 2 Macc 12: 38; Jos., Bell. 2, 551, Ant. 4, 85; Test. Jos. 16, 5) 2 Ti 4: 11; of Paul's escort Ac 23: 31.—*Take on board* (Thu. 7, 25, 4) 20: 13f.

5. *take in hand* (books Polyb. 3, 9, 3; βιβλίον 1 Esdr 9: 45) τὴν ἐπιστολὴν τ. μακαρίου Παύλου 1 Cl 47: 1. M-M.*

ἀναλημφθείς s. ἀναλαμβάνω.

ἀνάλημψις, εως, ἡ (Hippocr.+ in var. mngs.; inscr., pap., Philo; on spelling cf. Bl-D. §101 λαμβ.; Mlt.-H. 246f) in the Gk. Bible only Lk 9: 51 αἱ ἡμέραι τῆς ἀ. αὐτοῦ. Here it is usu. interpr. to mean *ascension* (into heaven); this is its mng. in PK 4 p. 15, 35; Test. Levi 18: 3 v.l.; Assumpt. Mos. 10, 12 (cf. ἀναλαμβάνω 1); also obviously in the inscr. at the end of Mk in the Ferrar family (Min. 13 et al. See on 'Ρωμαϊστί ἐγράφη ιβ' ἔτη τῆς ἀναλήψεως τ. κυρίου.—But ἀ. can also mean *death, decease* (cf. PsSol 4: 18 τὸ γῆρας αὐτοῦ εἰς ἀνάλημψιν; Christian inscr. from Aphrodisias: Byzantion 2, '26, 331; Ps.-Clem., Hom. 3, 47). M-M.*

ἀναλίσκω (Pr 24: 22d; Ezk 15: 4; Jos., Ant. 3, 236; 19, 352) or **ἀναλόω** (Bel 12 Theod., cf. EpJer 9; Jos., Bell. 7, 321) 1 aor. ἀνήλωσα, pass. ἀνηλώθην (Pind., Thu.+; inscr., pap.) *consume* τινά of fire Lk 9: 54 (like Alex. Aphr., An. Mant. 111, 20, Quaest. 2, 23 p. 73, 17, Mixt. 9, p. 223, 5 Bruns; Jo 1: 19; 2: 3; Ezk 19: 12; 2 Macc 2: 10; Philo, Prov. 2, 32 ed. Mangey II p. 642; Jos., Bell. 7, 321). Fig., of annihilation (cf. Gen 41: 30; Pr 23: 28; En. 103, 9; Sib. Or. 3, 646; Jos., Ant. 2, 287) βλέπετε μὴ ὑπ' ἀλλήλων ἀναλωθῆτε *see to it that your are not consumed by one another* Gal 5: 15 (w. κατεσθίειν as Pr 30: 14); 2 Th 2: 8 v.l. (ἀναιρέω 1a. Ael. Dion. a, 121 ἀναλοῦντες· ἀντὶ τοῦ ἀναιροῦντες). M-M.*

ἀνάλλομαι (Aristoph., X.+; PGM 36, 138) *jump up* ἀνήλατο Ac 14: 10 D.*

ἀναλογία, ας, ἡ (Pre-Socr.+; Philo; Jos., Ant. 15, 396) *right relationship, proportion* κατὰ (τὴν) ἀναλογίαν *in right relationship to, in agreement w., or in proportion to* (Pla., Polit. 257B; PFlor. 50, 15; 91 [III AD]; Lev 27: 18 acc. to Field, Hexapla κατὰ ἀναλογίαν τῶν ἐτῶν. Cf. Philo, Virtut. 95) κατὰ τὴν ἀ. τῆς πίστεως *in agreement w. (or proportion to) the faith* Ro 12: 6 (s. also πίστις 3). M-M.*

ἀναλογίζομαι 1 aor. ἀνελογισάμην (Thu. 8, 83, 3+; Stoic. III p. 246, 15; Polyb. 10, 37, 10; Diod. S. 20, 8, 1; Plut., Anton. 75, 6; Lucian, Toxar. 17; PTebt. 183; 3 Macc 7: 7; Wsd 17: 12 v.l.; Jos., Ant. 4, 312) *consider* τινά (Diod. S. 4, 83, 2) Hb 12: 3. Abs. ἀναλογισώμεθα *let us consider* 1 Cl 38: 3. M-M.*

ἄναλος, ον (Aristot., Probl. 21, 5, 1; Plut., Mor. 684F; Aq. Ezk 13: 10; 22: 28) *without salt, deprived of its salt content* Mk 9: 50. Salt produced by natural evaporation on the shores of the Dead Sea is never pure; when dampness decomposes it, the residue is useless.—FPerles, La parab. du Sel sourd: Rev. d. Ét. juives 82, '26, 119–23; Jde Zwaan, Het smakelooze zout bij Mc 9: 50: NThSt 11, '28, 176–8; cf. ἅλας 2.*

ἀναλόω s. ἀναλίσκω.

ἀνάλυσις, εως, ἡ (Soph.+) lit. *loosing*; then, like our 'breaking up', *departure* (Philo, In Flacc. 115; Jos., Ant. 19, 239); fig., of departure from life, *death* (Philo, In

Flacc. 187 τ. ἐκ τοῦ βίου τελευταίαν ἀνάλυσιν. ἀνάλυσις alone='death' in contrast to γένεσις in Joannes Sard., Comm. in Aphth. p. 87, 4 Rabe) καιρὸς τῆς ἀ. μου 2 Ti 4: 6. ἔγκαρπον καὶ τελείαν ἔχειν τ. ἀνάλυσιν *a fruitful and perfect departure* (i.e., after a fruitful and perfect life) 1 Cl 44: 5; s. ἀναλύω 2.*

ἀναλύω 1 aor. ἀνέλυσα (Hom.+; pap., LXX, Philo, Joseph.).

1. trans. *loose, untie* (Callim., Del. 237 ζώνην; Isishymn. v. Andr. 144f δεσμῶν ἀνάγκαν) pass. τὰ δεσμὰ ἀνελύθη Ac 16: 26 v.l.

2. intr. *depart, return* (Polyb.; pap. in APF 1, '01, p. 59 l. 10; Tob 2: 9; 2 Macc 8: 25; 12: 7; Jos., Ant. 6, 52; 11, 34 [after dinner]) ἔκ τινος *from something* (Aelian, V.H. 4, 23 v.l. ἐκ συμποσίου; Wsd 2: 1; 2 Macc 9: 1) ἐκ τῶν γάμων Lk 12: 36.—Fig., *depart* (sc. ἐκ τοῦ ζῆν) euphemistic for *die* (Lucian, Philops. 14 ὀκτωκαιδεκαέτης ὢν ἀνέλυεν; Socrat., Ep. 27, 5; IG XIV 1794, 2; Inscr. Oenoand. 58 I, 11 [Bull. de corr. hell. 21, 1897 p. 401] ἀ. ἐκ τοῦ ζῆν) ἐπιθυμίαν ἔχων εἰς τὸ ἀναλῦσαι Phil 1: 23 (GOsnes, Tidsskr. f. Teol. og K. 11, '40, 148–59).*

ἀναμάρτητος, ον (Hdt. 5, 39, 2+; Musonius 6, 16 H.; Epict. 4, 8, 6; 4, 12, 19; Plut., Mor. 419A; Appian, Liby. 51 §224 πρὸς τ. θεούς; inscr. [LAMuratori, Nov. Thes. vet. inscr. IV 1742, p. 2062, 6 Ναρκίσσῳ τέκνῳ ἀναμαρτήτῳ]; pap.; Dt 29: 19; 2 Macc 8: 4; 12: 42; En. 99, 2; Ep. Arist. 252; Philo, Mut. Nom. 51; Jos., Bell. 7, 329 πρὸς τ. θεόν) *without sin*, i.e., not having sinned (Teles p. 55, 13=ἐκτὸς ἁμαρτίας) ὁ ἀ. ὑμῶν J 8: 7. M-M.*

ἀναμαρυκάομαι (Lucian, Gall. 8; Lev 11: 26 v.l.; Dt 14: 8 v.l.) *ruminate* fig., w. ref. to Lev 11: 3; Dt 14: 6 τὸν λόγον κυρίου *ruminate on the word of the Lord*, i.e., think on it again and again B 10: 11.—S. μαρυκάομαι.*

ἀναμένω 1 aor. ἀνέμεινα, imper. ἀνάμεινον (Hom.+; pap., LXX).

1. gener. abs. (Ps.-Callisth. 2, 19, 5; POxy. 1773, 32) ἀνάμεινον *wait* Hs 8, 1, 4.

2. *wait for, expect* someone or something (Attic wr.; Epict. 4, 8, 42; Jdth 8: 17; Sir 2: 7; Is 59: 11; Jos., Bell. 3, 72), esp. the Messiah ἀ. τ. υἱὸν αὐτοῦ ἐκ τῶν οὐρανῶν *wait for his Son (coming) from heaven* 1 Th 1: 10. ὃν δικαίως ἀνέμενον IMg 9: 3. W. εἰς αὐτὸν ἐλπίζειν IPhld 5: 2.—Fig., of time μακάριος αὐτὸν ἀναμένει χρόνος *a blessed time awaits him* 2 Cl 19: 4 (cf. Test. Ash. 5: 2). P-ÉLangevin, Jésus Seigneur '67, 67–73. M-M.*

ἀναμέσον s. ἀνά 1.

ἀναμιμνῄσκω fut. ἀναμνήσω; 1 aor. pass. ἀνεμνήσθην (Hom.+; inscr., pap., LXX; En. 103, 15; 104, 1; Philo; Joseph.) *remind* τινά τι *someone of something* (X., An. 3, 2, 11; Diod. S. 17, 10, 6) ὃς ὑμᾶς ἀναμνήσει τὰς ὁδούς μου *who will remind you of my ways* 1 Cor 4: 17. τινά w. inf. ἀ. σε ἀναζωπυρεῖν *I remind you to rekindle* 2 Ti 1: 6.—Pass. *be reminded, remember* (Dit., Syll.³ 557, 26; PGrenf. I 1 Col. 1, 2; 22) w. acc. of the thing (X., An. 7, 1, 26; Pla., Phaedo 72E; Jos., Bell. 3, 396; Bl-D. §175; Rob. 509) ἀνεμνήσθη ὁ Πέτρος τὸ ῥῆμα *Peter remembered the word* Mk 14: 72. ἀ. τὴν ὑπακοήν 2 Cor 7: 15. ἀ. τὰς πρότερον ἡμέρας Hb 10: 32. Cf. Ac 16: 35 D.—W. gen. (Thu. 2, 54, 2; 2 Esdr 19 [Neh 9]: 17; Jos., Bell. 4, 174, Ant. 2, 137; Maspéro 2 III, 6) τῆς περυσινῆς ὁράσεως *the vision of the previous year* Hv 2, 1, 1.—Abs. (Hdt. 3, 51, 1 ὁ δὲ ἀναμνησθεὶς εἶπε) ἀναμνησθεὶς ὁ Πέτρος λέγει Mk 11: 21. M-M.*

ἀνάμνησις, εως, ἡ (Pla.+; inscr., LXX, Philo; Jos., Ant. 4, 189) *reminder, remembrance* τινός *of something* (Diod. S. 20, 93, 7 τῆς φιλίας ἀν.; Wsd 16: 6; Jos., Bell. 3, 394) ἀ. ἁμαρτιῶν *a reminder of sins,* of the sacrifices repeated every year Hb 10: 3. In the account of the Lord's Supper εἰς τὴν ἐμὴν ἀνάμνησιν *in remembrance* (*memory*) *of me* 1 Cor 11: 24f; Lk 22: 19 (εἰς ἀ. Appian, Hann. 1 §2; Hierocles 11 p. 440 εἰς ἀν. τοῦ νόμου, p. 441 εἰς ἀν. τοῦ ὀρθοῦ λόγου= remember it; Lev 24: 7; Ps 37: 1; 69: 1; Jos., Ant. 19, 318. Cf. μνήμη 2. In Diod. S. 3, 57, 8 Basileia is honored as a goddess by the people from whose midst she has disappeared. And when they offer sacrifices or show other honors to her, they beat kettledrums and cymbals, as Basileia did, and put on a representation [ἀπομιμουμένους] of her experiences; POxy. 494, 22ff; Wilcken, Chrest. 500; Ltzm., Messe u. Herrenmahl '26; ELohmeyer, JBL 56, '37, 244f; JoachJeremias, D. Abendmahlsworte Jesu² '48; DJones, JTS 6, '55, 183–91; HKosmala, NovT 4, '60, 81–94.—For the mng. *memorial sacrifice,* cf. Num 10: 10 and s. L-S-J, but s. GBCaird, JTS 19, '68, 458; cf. EHPeters, CBQ 10, '48, 248f).—πρὸς ἀ. γράφειν *to remind* (*you*) 1 Cl 53: 1. M-M.*

ἀνανεόω 1 aor. ἀνενέωσα (trag.+; inscr., pap., LXX; Jos., Ant. 12, 321).
1. trans. *renew.* The act. is not found very oft. w. this mng. (Aristonous Corinth. [III BC]: Anth. Lyr. Gr. II 6 p. 139 D.² Δελφοὶ ἀνενέωσαν τὰν πάτριον προξενίαν; M. Ant. 4, 3, 3 σεαυτόν; 6, 15, 1; Herm. Wr. 9, 6; inscr.; pap.; Job 33: 24; 1 Macc 12: 1) ἀ. τὴν ζωήν (of the angel of repentance) *restore life* Hs 9, 14, 3. Much more freq. is (Thu. 7, 33, 4+) the mid. (Diod. S. 33, 28a, 3 Dind.; 37, 15, 2; Chio, Ep. 16, 8; Appian, Maced. 11 §6; Dit., Syll.³ 721, 13; 475, 10; 654, 6f, cf. index; Dit., Or. 90, 35; Esth 3: 13b; 1 Macc 12: 3, 10, 16 al.; Jos., Bell. 1, 283, Ant. 1, 290), which seems not to have the reflexive sense 'renew oneself'. Hence ἀνανεοῦσθαι τῷ πνεύματι τοῦ νοός is better taken as a pass. *be renewed= get* (*yourselves*) *renewed in the spirit of your minds* Eph 4: 23 (on the figure Cornutus 33 p. 70, 10 ἀνανεάζειν ἐκ τῶν νόσων καὶ ἐκδύεσθαι τὸ γῆρας). ἀνανεοῦται τὸ πνεῦμα *his spirit is renewed* Hv 3, 12, 2; 3, 13, 2, cf. 3, 12, 3.
2. intr. *become young again* μηκέτι ἔχοντες ἐλπίδα τοῦ ἀνανεῶσαι v 3, 11, 3. M-M.*

ἀνανέωσις, εως, ἡ (Thu. et al; Herm. Wr. 3, 4; Dit., Syll.³ 1059 II, 9; POxy. 274, 20; PStrassb. 52, 7; 1 Macc 12: 17; Jos., Ant. 9, 161; 12, 324) *renewal* of the Christian ἀ. λαμβάνειν τῶν πνευμάτων *renewal of the spirit* (pl., since several pers. are involved) Hv 3, 13, 2. ἐλπὶς ἀνανεώσεώς τινος *hope of some renewal* s 6, 2, 4. M-M s.v. -όω and suppl.*

ἀνανήφω 1 aor. ἀνένηψα (Aristot.+) *become sober* (rather oft. transferred to the spiritual, esp. ethical realm in post-class. times: Cebes 9, 3; Dio Chrys. 4, 77; Ps.-Lucian, Salt. 84; M. Ant. 6, 31; Philo, Leg. All. 2, 60 ἀνανήφει, τοῦτο δ' ἐστὶ μετανοεῖ; Jos., Ant. 6, 241; cf. Nägeli 30) *come to one's senses again* ἀ. ἐκ τῆς τοῦ διαβόλου παγίδος *come to one's s. and escape from the snare of the devil* 2 Ti 2: 26. Abs. ἀνανῆψαι *become sober again* ISm 9: 1.*

Ἀνανίας (חֲנַנְיָה), ου, ὁ (Ep. Arist. 48; Joseph.—Diod. S. 20, 97, 7 Ἀνανίας is the name of a Rhodian general. See also Athen. 12, 3 p. 511 C Ἀνάνιος or Ἄνανις). *Ananias.*
1. one of the three youths in the fiery furnace 1 Cl 45: 7 (cf. Da 3: 24 acc. to LXX).
2. a member of the Christian church at Jerusalem, husband of Sapphira Ac 5: 1, 3, 5 (cf. the scene in Jos.,

Ant. 8, 266–73).—WBornemann, A. u. S.: Christl. Welt 13, '99, 987–91. RSchumacher, A. u. S.: ThGl 5, '13, 824–30. P-HMenoud, Goguel-Festschr., '50, 146–54; E Haenchen, Apostelgeschichte '56, 196–201 (Eng. tr. '71, 236–41).
3. a Christian in Damascus, who instructed Paul in Christianity and baptized him 9: 10, 12f, 17; 22: 12 (E Fascher, Z. Taufe des Paulus: ThLZ 80, '55, 643–48).
4. a Jewish high priest, son of Nedebaeus, in office c. 47–59 (Jos., Ant. 20, 103; 131; 205; 208–10; 213, Bell. 2, 243; 426; 429; 441f) Ac 22: 5 v.l.; 23: 2; 24: 1. Cf. Schürer II⁴ 272.*

ἀναντίρρητος, ον (ἀναντίρητος W-H.; W-S. §5, 266) pass. (Polyb.; Plut.; Dit., Or. 335, 138 [II/I BC w. one ρ]; Job 11: 2 Sym.) *not to be contradicted, undeniable* (Herm. Wr. 2, 11 ἀ. ὁ λόγος; Jos., C. Ap. 1, 160) ἀ. ὄντων τούτων *since this is undeniable* Ac 19: 36. βραβεῖον ἀ. ἀποφέρεσθαι *carry off an incontestable prize* MPol 17: 1. M-M.*

ἀναντιρρήτως adv., in NT only in act. mng. (Polyb. 23, 8, 11; Diod. S.; pap.; Job 33: 13 Sym.) *without raising any objection* ἔρχεσθαι Ac 10: 29.*

ἀναντλέω 1 aor. ἀνήντλησα lit. *draw up* of water, *drain out, empty;* fig., of toil or hardships *bear patiently* (Dionys. Hal. 8, 51 πόνους; Phalaris, Ep. 19 πόνους; Dio Chrys. 11[12], 51; UPZ 60, 14[168 BC] τοιούτους καιροὺς ἀνηντληκυῖα) ταῦτα πάντα 1 Cl 26: 3 (Job 19: 26). κόπους Hs 5, 6, 2 (acc. to the Mich.-Pap. ed. CBonner '34, 58).*

ἀνάξιος, ον (Soph., Hdt.+; Epict. 2, 8, 18; PStrass. 5, 8 [262 AD]; Sir 25: 8; Philo, Aet. M. 85; Jos., Ant. 6, 17) *unworthy* τινός: ἀνάξιοί ἐστε κριτηρίων ἐλαχίστων; *are you not good enough* or *not competent to settle trivial cases?* 1 Cor 6: 2 (Simplicius in Epict. p. 60, 33 τοὺς μηδὲ ἀξίους ὄντας τῶν τοιούτων κριτάς). πράσσειν ἀ. (Hippocr., Ep. 9, 1; Herm. Wr. 478, 33 Sc.; Ep. Arist. 205; 217) θεοῦ IEph 7: 1. ἀ. ζωῆς *unworthy of* (eternal) *life* Dg 9: 1. τῆς ἐν Χριστῷ ἀγωγῆς 1 Cl 47: 6. ἀνάξιοι *unworthy people* Hs 6, 3, 4. M-M.*

ἀναξίως (Soph., Hdt.+; Teles p. 56, 9; Sb 1267, 5; 2 Macc 14: 42) adv. *in an unworthy* or *careless manner* ἐσθίειν, πίνειν of the Lord's Supper 1 Cor 11: 27 (29 v.l.). For partaking of the Lord's Supper in an improper manner, and the results thereof, cf. Con. Neot. 15, '55, p. 27f.*

ἀναπάρτιστος, ον (Diog. L. 7, 63) *imperfect* ὡς ἔτι ὢν ἀ. *as one who is not yet perfected* IPhld 5: 1 (v.l. ἀνάρπαστος; s. the text-crit. notes in Zahn, Lghtf., Bihlmeyer).*

ἀνάπαυσις, εως, ἡ (Mimnermus, Pind.+; inscr.; PFlor. 57, 56; BGU 180, 5; LXX).
1. *stopping, ceasing* ἀνάπαυσιν οὐκ ἔχουσιν λέγοντες *they say without ceasing* Rv 4: 8; cf. 14: 11.
2. *rest* (Diocles, fgm. 142 p. 186, 13; LXX; Ep. Arist. 94; Philo, Fuga 174 ἡ ἐν θεῷ ἀ.; Jos., Ant. 3, 281 al.) εὑρίσκειν ἀ. (Sir 6: 28; 11: 19; 22: 13; Is 34: 14; La 1: 3) εὑρίσκειν ἀ. ταῖς ψυχαῖς Mt 11: 29 (as in Sir 51: 27), cf. 2 Cl 6: 7. ἀ. διδόναι τινί (Ps 131: 4; Aristobul. in Euseb., Pr. Ev. 13, 12, 9; Jos., Bell. 4, 88) *give someone rest* Hs 6, 2, 7.—ἀ. τῆς μελλούσης βασιλείας καὶ ζωῆς αἰωνίου *rest in the coming kingdom and in eternal life* 2 Cl 5: 5.
3. *a resting-place* (Gen 8: 9; Num 10: 33; Ps 131: 8) ζητεῖν ἀ. (Ruth 3: 1; Sir 24: 7) *seek a resting-place* Mt 12: 43; Lk 11: 24. M-M.*

ἀναπαύω fut. ἀναπαύσω; 1 aor. ἀνέπαυσα, imper. ἀνάπαυσον, pf. mid. and pass. ἀναπέπαυμαι; 1 aor. pass.

ἀνεπαύθην Hs 9, 5, 1f; fut. mid. ἀναπαύσομαι; 2 fut. pass. ἀναπαήσομαι Rv 14: 13, LJ 2: 2 cf. Bl-D. §78 (Hom.+, inscr., pap., LXX, Philo, Joseph., Test. 12 Patr.).

1. trans. *cause to rest, give* (someone) *rest, refresh, revive* w. acc. (X., Cyr. 7, 1, 4; Appian, Mithrid. 45 §176; Arrian, Anab. 3, 7, 6 τὸν στρατόν; 1 Ch 22: 18; Pr 29: 17; Sir 3: 6; Jos., Ant. 3, 61) κἀγὼ ἀναπαύσω ὑμᾶς *and I will give you rest* Mt 11: 28. ἀ. τὸ πνεῦμα 1 Cor 16: 18. τὴν ψυχήν *set at rest* Hs 9, 5, 4. ἀνάπαυσόν μου τὰ σπλάγχνα *refresh, cheer my heart* Phlm 20 (cf. Nägeli 64f). κατὰ πάντα *in every way* IEph 2: 1; Mg 15; Tr 12: 1; Sm 9: 2; 10: 1; 12: 1. Abs. IRo 10: 2. Mid. τὸ πνεῦμα ἀναπέπαυται 1 Pt 4: 14 v.l.—Pass. ἀναπέπαυται τὸ πνεῦμα αὐτοῦ *his spirit has been set at rest* 2 Cor 7: 13. τὰ σπλάγχνα ἀναπέπαυται (their) *hearts have been refreshed* Phlm 7.

2. mid. *rest, take one's rest* (Cornutus 32 p. 69, 17; Artem. 1, 8 p. 14, 7; Plotinus, Enn. 6, 9, 9 ἀναπαύεται ψυχή; Julian, Letters 97 p. 382D; Herm. Wr. 408, 27 Sc.; Ex 23: 12; Is 14: 30; 57: 20; Esth 9: 17f; Philo; Jos., Vi. 249) of persons who are drowsy ἀναπαύεσθε Mt 26: 45; Mk 14: 41 (s. λοιπός 3aα); who have just eaten B 10: 11; who are tired Mk 6: 31; Hs 9, 5, 1f. ἀ. ἐκ τῶν κόπων *rest from their labors* Rv 14: 13 (cf. Pla., Critias 106A ἐκ μακρᾶς ἀναπεπαυμένος ὁδοῦ; Arrian, Anab. 3, 9, 1 ἐκ τῆς ὁδοῦ; Jos., Ant. 3, 91 ἀ. ἀπὸ παντὸς ἔργου). *Take one's ease* Lk 12: 19; 16: 23D. Of sheep Hs 9, 1, 9.—ἀ. χρόνον μικρόν *remain quiet* (i.e., wait) *for a short time* (Da 12: 13) Rv 6: 11.—*Rest upon* (Is 11: 2 ἀναπαύσεται ἐπ' αὐτὸν πνεῦμα τ. θεοῦ) τὸ τ. θεοῦ πνεῦμα ἐφ' ὑμᾶς ἀναπαύεται 1 Pt 4: 14.—Of God ἅγιος ἐν ἁγίοις ἀναπαυόμενος *holy, abiding among the holy* 1 Cl 59: 3 (Is 57: 15). M-M.*

ἀναπαφλάζω (Eutecnius 1 p. 13, 9; Hesychius; Ps.-Caesarius of Naz., Dial. 3, 146 [Migne, S. Gr. XXXVIII 1096] of the Tigris) *boil, bubble up* AP 9: 24.*

ἀναπείθω 1 aor. pass. ἀνεπείσθην (Hdt.+; inscr., pap., LXX) *persuade,* in malam partem *induce, incite* (so Hdt. 3, 148; 5, 66; X., Cyr. 1, 5, 3; PMagd. 14, 3f [221 BC]; POxy. 1295, 10; Jer 36: 8; 1 Macc 1: 11) τινά w. inf. foll. (cf. Philo, Leg. All. 3, 212; Jos., Bell. 7, 438, Ant. 14, 285; 15, 72) ἀ. τοὺς ἀνθρώπους Ac 18: 13. Pass. Hs 9, 13, 8. M-M.*

ἀνάπειρος, ον (Tob 14: 2 S= ℵ) Lk 14: 13, 21 ℵABD for ἀνάπηρος, q.v. LXX mss. (2 Macc 8: 24) also have both forms (Thackeray 83). Phryn., Praep. Soph. p. 13, 4f Borries ['11] διὰ τοῦ τὴν τρίτην, οὐ διὰ τῆς διφθόγγου ὡς οἱ ἀμαθεῖς. Cf. Bl-D. §24 app.; Mlt.-H. 72.*

ἀναπέμπω fut. ἀναπέμψω; 1 aor. ἀνέπεμψα (Pind., Aeschyl.+; inscr., pap., Joseph.).

1. *send up*—a. lit. (Ps.-Aristot., Mirabilia 114 φλόγα πυρός) toward heaven (Bias in Diog. L. 1, 88 εἰς θεοὺς ἀνάπεμπε) τὸ ἀμήν MPol 15: 1.

b. fig. *send* (up, i.e., to one in a higher position: Plut., Marius 17, 3; Jos., Bell. 2, 571; Dit., Or. 329, 51; PHib. 1, 57 [III BC]; PTebt. 7, 7; hence t.t. for sending to the proper pers. or gov. agency [Jos., Ant. 4, 218; Nägeli 34]) τινὰ πρός τινα Lk 23: 7 (HHoehner, CFDMoule-Festschr., '70, 84-90 [Antipas]); Ac 25: 21; for this τινά τινι 27: 1 v.l.

2. *send back* (Plut., Sol. 4, 6; PPar. 13, 22 [157 BC]; POxy. 1032, 50 [162 AD]) τινά τινι Lk 23: 11 (πέμπω 𝔓75 et al.); Phlm 12; τινὰ πρός τινα Lk 23: 15; 1 Cl 65: 1. M-M.*

ἀνάπεσε, εῖν s. ἀναπίπτω.

ἀναπηδάω 1 aor. ἀνεπήδησα (Hom.+; LXX; Jos., Vi. 265) *jump up,* also w. weakened force *stand up* (Epict. 3, 4, 4; Tob 2: 4; 7: 6; PGM 1, 93; Jos., Ant. 8, 360) Mk 10: 50.*

ἀνάπηρος, ον (Soph.+; Jos., Ant. 7, 61) *crippled,* subst. *a cripple* w. πτωχός, χωλός, τυφλός (Pla., Crito 53A χωλοὶ καὶ τυφλοὶ καὶ ἄλλοι ἀνάπηροι; Aelian, V.H. 11, 9 p. 115, 23; Diog. L. 6, 33) Lk 14: 13, 21; s. ἀνάπειρος.*

ἀναπίπτω 2 aor. ἀνέπεσον and H.Gk. ἀνέπεσα (Bl-D. §81, 3; Mlt.-H. 208) (trag.+; pap., LXX; Jos., Ant. 8, 256).

1. *lie down, recline* esp. at a meal (Alexis in Athen. 1, 23E; Diod. S. 4, 59; Ps.-Lucian, Asin. 23; PGM 1, 24; Tob 2: 1; 7: 9S; Jdth 12: 16; cf. Anz 301f) Lk 11: 37; 17: 7; 22: 14; J 13: 12. ἀ. εἰς τὸν ἔσχατον τόπον *occupy the humblest place* Lk 14: 10; Mt 20: 28D=Agr 22. ἀνέπεσαν πρασιαὶ *they took their places in groups* to eat Mk 6: 40; cf. J 6: 10. ἀ. ἐπὶ τῆς γῆς *take their places on the ground* Mk 8: 6 (Diod. S. 4, 59, 5 ἐπί τινος κλίνης; Syntipas 48, 29 ἀ. ἐπὶ τ. κλίνης). ἀ. ἐπὶ τὴν γῆν Mt 15: 35.

2. *lean, lean back* (Pla., Phaedr. 254B and E; Polyb. 1, 21, 2) J 13: 25 (ἐπιπίπτω 𝔓66 et al.); 21: 20. M-M.*

ἀναπλάσσω 1 aor. mid. ἀνεπλασάμην (Hdt.+; PHal. 1, 183 [III BC]; Jos., C. Ap. 2, 248) *form, mold again.*

1. lit. of a potter, who reshapes a vessel which he has spoiled πάλιν αὐτὸ ἀ. 2 Cl 8: 2 (cf. Wsd 15: 7).

2. fig., of spiritual transformation of a person B 6: 11, 14.*

ἀναπληρόω fut. ἀναπληρώσω; 1 aor. ἀνεπλήρωσα (Eur.+; inscr., pap., LXX).

1. *make complete* fig. (Appian, Bell. Civ. 3, 47 §191 a body of troops, 4, 89 §374 of outstanding obligations; schol. on Nicander, Ther. 447 τὴν ἡλικίαν=period of childhood; Ep. Arist. 75) ἀ. αὐτῶν τὰς ἁμαρτίας (Gen 15: 16) *fill up the measure of their sins* 1 Th 2: 16.

2. *fulfill* (A contract: UPZ 112 V) 3 [203/2 BC]; Ostraka I 532. A duty: POxy. 1121, 11. An order for work: Jos., Ant. 8, 58) of prophecies (1 Esdr 1: 54 εἰς ἀναπλήρωσιν τ. ῥήματος τ. κυρίου) ἀναπληροῦται αὐτοῖς ἡ προφητεία *in them the prophecy is being fulfilled* Mt 13: 14. Of claims upon one: ἀ. τὸν νόμον τ. Χριστοῦ Gal 6: 2. ἀ. πᾶσαν ἐντολήν B 21: 8.

3. *fill a gap, replace* (Pla., Symp. 188E; Dit., Syll.³ 364, 62, Or. 56, 46; Jos., Bell. 4, 198, Ant. 5, 214) τὸ ὑστέρημα (Herm. Wr. 13, 1 τὰ ὑστερήματα ἀναπλήρωσον; Test. Benj. 11: 5) w. gen. of the pers. *make up for someone's absence or lack, represent one who is absent* (AHeisenberg and LWenger, Byz. Pap. '14, no. 14, 18 τῷ βικαρίῳ Ἑρμώνθεως ἀναπληροῦντι τὸν τόπον τοῦ τοποτηρητοῦ) 1 Cor 16: 17; Phil 2: 30; 1 Cl 38: 2. τὸν τ. ὑπακοῆς τόπον ἀναπληρῶσαι *take the attitude of obedience* 1 Cl 63: 1. τοὺς τύπους τῶν λίθων ἀ. *fill up the impressions left by the stones* (cf. Ep. Arist. 75) Hs 9, 10, 1.

4. ὁ ἀναπληρῶν τ. τόπον τ. ἰδιώτου 1 Cor 14: 16, because of the ἰδ. of vss. 23f, cannot mean 'the man who occupies the position (for this mng. of τόπος see s.v. 1e; ἀναπληρ. in such a connection: Jos., Bell. 5, 88; Ps.-Clem., Hom. 3, 60) of a layman', i.e., in contrast to those speaking with tongues, one who is not so gifted (PhBachmann; Ltzm.; JSickenberger; H-DWendland). Rather ἀ. τὸν τόπον τινὸς means *take* or *fill someone's place* (cf. Diod. S. 19, 22, 2 τὸν τόπον ἀ.; Hero Alex. I p. 8, 20 τὸν κενωθέντα τόπον ἀ.; Pla., Tim. 79B ἀ. τὴν ἕδραν; Epict.

2, 4, 5 ἀ. τὴν χώραν), and *place* here means the place actually reserved for the ἰδιώτης in the meeting (GHeinrici; JWeiss; most Eng. translators do not share this view). S. ἰδιώτης 2 and GHWhitaker, JTS 22, '21, 268. M-M.*

ἀναπολόγητος, ον (Polyb. 29, 10, 5; Dionys. Hal. 7, 46; Plut., Brut. 46, 2; Cicero, Ad Att. 16, 7 et al.; Jos., C. Ap. 2, 137) *without excuse, inexcusable* (Polyb. 12, 21, 10; Dio Chrys. 2, 39) εἰς τὸ εἶναι αὐτοὺς ἀναπολογήτους *so that they are without excuse* Ro 1: 20; ἀ. εἶ 2: 1.*

ἀναπράσσω (Thu.+, inscr., pap.) *demand, exact* of a payment Lk 19: 23 v.l.*

ἀναπτύσσω 1 aor. ἀνέπτυξα *unroll* of a book in scroll form (so Hdt.+; Epict. 1, 17, 21; 4 Km 19: 14; Jos., Vi. 223) Lk 4: 17 v.l.; PK 4 p. 15, 30.*

ἀνάπτω 1 aor. pass. ἀνήφθην *kindle* (so Eur., Hdt.+; PGiess. 3, 8; PGM 13, 681; 2 Ch 13: 11) ὕλην (cf. Philo, Aet. M. 127) *a forest* Js 3: 5. Cf. Ac 28: 2 t.r. Of fire (Eur., Or. 1137; Jos., Ant. 3, 207) ἀνήφθη *has been kindled*= is now burning Lk 12: 49 (Diod. S. 13, 84, 2 ὅταν ἀναφθῇ πῦρ=when a fire would be kindled, or would burn). M-M.*

ἀναρίθμητος, ον (Pind., Hdt.+; LXX; Jos., Ant. 17, 214) *innumerable* of the grains of sand on the seashore Hb 11: 12.*

ἀνασείω (Hes.+; PTebt. 28, 20 [II BC]; Jos., Bell. 5, 120) *stir* (lit. shake) *up, incite* (so Diod. S. 13, 91; 14, 10; 17, 62; 18, 10; Is 36: 18 Aq., Sym.) w. acc. τ. ὄχλον Mk 15: 11. τ. λαόν Lk 23: 5 (cf. Dionys. Hal. 8, 81 τὸ πλῆθος; Philod., Rhet. II 290 Sudh.). M-M.*

ἀνασκευάζω (Thu.+ in var. mngs.; POxy. 745, 5 [I AD]; Jos., Bell. 6, 282, Ant. 14, 406; 418) *tear down, upset, unsettle* fig., w. ταράσσειν (cf. Vett. Val. 212, 20 ἀνασκευασθήσεται καὶ ἐπιτάραχον γενήσεται) ἀνασκευάζειν τὰς ψυχάς Ac 15: 24. M-M.*

ἀνασπάω fut. ἀνασπάσω; 1 aor. pass. ἀνεσπάσθην (Hom.+; PTebt. 420, 25; BGU 1041, 8; PGM 4, 2498; 2973; Hab 1: 15; Da 6: 18; Bel 42 Theod.; Jos., Ant. 2, 259 al.) *draw, pull up* Lk 14: 5. Of the sheet, which Peter saw in his vision ἀνεσπάσθη εἰς τ. οὐρανόν Ac 11: 10. M-M.*

ἀνάστα s. ἀνίστημι.

ἀνάστασις, εως, ἡ (Aeschyl., Hdt.+ in var. mngs.; inscr., pap., LXX; Jos., Bell. 6, 339, Ant. 11, 19).

1. *rise* (La 3: 63; Zech 3: 8; Jos., Ant. 17, 212; 18, 301 [here of the 'erection' of a statue]) κεῖται εἰς πτῶσιν καὶ ἀ. πολλῶν *he is destined for the fall and rise of many* of Jesus Lk 2: 34, i.e., because of him many will fall and others will rise, w. transfer to religious sense (for contrast w. πτῶσις cf. Evagrius Pont., Cent. 5, 19 p. 327 Frankenberg: ἡ μικρὰ τ. σώματος ἀνάστασίς ἐστιν ἡ μετάθεσις αὐτοῦ ἐκ πτώσεως τ. ἀσελγείας εἰς τὴν τ. ἁγιασμοῦ ἀνάστασιν).—Esp.

2. *resurrection* from the dead (Aeschyl., Eum. 648 ἅπαξ θανόντος οὔτις ἐστ᾽ ἀ.; Ps.-Lucian, De Salt. 45; Ael. Aristid. 32, 25 K.=12 p. 142 D.; 46 p. 300 D.; Inscr. Rom. IV 743 οἱ δείλαιοι πάντες εἰς ἀνάστασιν βλέποντες; 2 Macc 7: 14; 12: 43), and so

a. in the past: of Jesus' resurrection Ac 1: 22; 2: 31; 4: 33; Ro 6: 5; Phil 3: 10 (JAFitzmyer, BRigaux-Festschr., '70, 411-25); 1 Pt 3: 21; 1 Cl 42: 3; ISm 3: 1, 3; in more detail ἀ. ἐκ νεκρῶν 1 Pt 1: 3; ἀ. νεκρῶν res. *from the dead* Ro 1: 4; w. the passion of Jesus IEph 20: 1; Mg 11; Tr inscr.; Phld inscr.; 8: 2; 9: 2; Sm 7: 2; 12: 2; cf. 1: 2. τὸν

Ἰησοῦν καὶ τὴν ἀ. εὐαγγελίζεσθαι *preach about Jesus and the resurrection* i.e., his res., and in consequence, the possibility of a general res. Ac 17: 18 (τὸν Ἰησοῦν καὶ τὴν ἀνάστασιν could also mean 'the resurrection of Jesus', as perh. Nicol Dam.: 90 fgm. 130, 18 p. 400, 17 Jac. μνήμη τἀνδρὸς καὶ φιλοστοργίας='. . . the love of the husband'); cf. vs. 32 and 4: 2. Of the raisings from the dead by Elijah and Elisha ἔλαβον γυναῖκες ἐξ ἀ. τοὺς νεκροὺς αὐτῶν *women* (i.e., the widow of Zarephath and the Shunammite woman 3 Km 17: 23; 4 Km 4: 36) *received their dead by resurrection* Hb 11: 35.

b. of the future resurrection, at the Judgment Day: described as ἀ. νεκρῶν Mt 22: 31; Ac 23: 6; 24: 15, 21; 26: 23; 1 Cor 15: 12f; Hb 6: 2; D 16: 6; or ἀ. ἐκ νεκρῶν Lk 20: 35; B 5: 6; cf. IPol 7: 1; Pol 7: 1; MPol 14: 2. Of Jesus: τὴν ἀ. ποιεῖν *bring about the res.* (of the dead) B 5: 7. Jesus' Passion as our res. ISm 5: 3. ἀθάνατος τῆς ἀ. καρπός 2 Cl 19: 3. Described as ἀ. κρείττων Hb 11: 35 in contrast w. the res. of the past, because the latter was, after all, followed by death. ἡ μέλλουσα ἀ. ἔσεσθαι *the future res.* 1 Cl 24: 1. ἡ κατὰ καιρὸν γινομένη ἀ. *the res. that comes at regular intervals* (i.e., seasons, day and night), as a type of the future res. 24: 2.—More details in J, who mentions an ἀ. ἐν τῇ ἐσχάτῃ ἡμέρᾳ *on the Last Day* J 11: 24 and differentiates betw. the ἀ. κρίσεως *res. for judgment* for the wicked and the ἀ. ζωῆς *res. to life* for those who do good 5: 29. Christ calls himself (J 11: 25) ἡ ἀ. and ἡ ζωή, since he mediates both to men.—Paul seeks to demonstrate the validity of belief in Jesus' resurrection in terms of the res. of the dead in general 1 Cor 15: 12ff (MDahl, The Res. of the Body. A Study of 1 Cor 15, '62).—Lk 14: 14 mentions only a resurrection of the just, as in Jewish belief; likew. B 21: 1. Hebraistically υἱοὶ τῆς ἀ. (w. υἱοὶ θεοῦ) *children of the res.*=sharers in the res. Lk 20: 36. A second res. is presupposed by the ἀ. ἡ πρώτη of Rv 20: 5f. Denial of the res. by the Sadducees Mt 22: 23, 28, 30f; Mk 12: 18, 23; Lk 20: 27, 33, 35f (on this see Schürer II⁴ 459; 485); by the Epicureans Ac 17: 18 (ERohde, Psyche³ '03 II 331-5; cf. the inscr. 2 above); and by Christians 1 Cor 15: 12 (prob. in the sense of Justin, Dial. 80 λέγουσι μὴ εἶναι νεκρῶν ἀνάστασιν, ἀλλ᾽ ἅμα τῷ ἀποθνήσκειν τὰς ψυχὰς αὐτῶν ἀναλαμβάνεσθαι εἰς τ. οὐρανόν; cf. JHWilson, ZNW 59, '68, 90-107); 2 Ti 2: 18 (perh. like Menander in Iren. 1, 23, 5 resurrectionem enim per id, quod est in eum baptisma, accipere eius discipulos, et ultra non posse mori, sed perseverare non senescentes et immortales; cf. Justin, Ap. 1, 26, 4; Valent. in Clem. of Alex., Str. 4, 13, 91; Tertull., Carn. Resurr. 25 agnitio sacramenti [=ἡ τοῦ μυστηρίου γνῶσις] resurrectio). The expr. ἀ. σαρκός Third Corinthians 3: 24, is not found in the NT.—FNötscher, Altoriental. u. atl. Auferstehungsglaube '26; JLeipoldt, Sterbende u. auferstehende Götter '23; Cumont³ '31; ATNikolainen, D. Auferstehungsglauben in d. Bibel u. in ihrer Umwelt. I Relgesch. Teil '44. II NT '46.—WBousset, Rel.³, '26, 269-74 al.; Billerb. IV '28, 1166-98.—AMeyer, D. Auferstehung Christi '05; KLake, The Historical Evidence for the Res. of Jesus Christ '07; LBrun, D. Auferst. Christi in d. urchr. Überl. '25; PGardner-Smith, The Narratives of the Resurrection '26; SV McCasland, The Res. of Jesus '32; MGoguel, La foi à la résurr. de Jésus dans le Christianisme primitif '33; EFascher, ZNW 26, '27, 1-26; EFuchs, ZKG 51, '32, 1-20; AThomson, Did Jesus Rise from the Dead? '40; EHirsch, D. Auferstehungsgeschichten u. d. chr. Glaube '40; PAlthaus, D. Wahrheit des kirchl. Osterglaubens² '41; WMichaelis, D. Erscheinungen des Auferstandenen '44; AMRamsey, The Res. of Christ '45; JLeipoldt, Zu den Auferstehungsgeschichten: ThLZ 73, '48, 737-42 (rel.-

hist.); KHRengstorf, Die Auferstehung Jesu² '54; GKoch, Die Auferstehung J. Christi '59; HGrass, Ostergeschehen u. Osterberichte, '56; ELohse, Die Auferstehung J. Chr. im Zeugnis des Lk '61; HvCampenhausen, Tradition and Life in the Early Church, '68, 42–89. S. also τάφος 1.— KDeissner, Auferstehungshoffnung u. Pneumagedanke b. Pls '12; GVos, The Pauline Doctrine of the Res.: PTR 27, '29, 1–35; 193–226; FGuntermann, D. Eschatologie d. hl. Pls '32; HMolitor, Die Auferstehung d. Christen und Nichtchristen nach d. Ap. Pls '33; LSimeone, Resurrectionis iustorum doctr. in ep. S. Pauli '38; DMStanley, Christ's Resurrection in Pauline Soteriology '61; CFD Moule, NTS 12, '65/'66, 106–23.—RMGrant, Miracle and Nat. Law '52, 221–63. M-M.

ἀναστατόω 1 aor. ἀνεστάτωσα (H.Gk.: pap., e.g. BGU 1858, 12 [I вс]; POxy. 119, 10; PGM 4, 2244; LXX, Aq., Sym. [Nägeli 47f]) *disturb, trouble, upset* τὴν οἰκουμένην Ac 17: 6. Of the leaders of the party disturbing the church Gal 5: 12 (cf. BGU 1079, 20 [41 AD] μὴ ἵνα ἀναστατώσῃς ἡμᾶς). Abs. ὁ ἀναστατώσας *the man who raised a revolt* Ac 21: 38 M-M.*

ἀνασταυρόω (Hdt.+) in extra-Bibl. Gk. always simply *crucify* (ἀνά=up; cf. Pla., Gorg. 473c; Polyb. 1, 11, 5; 1, 24, 6; Diod. S. 2, 1, 10; 2, 44, 2; 13, 111, 5; 14, 53, 5; Plut., Fab. 6, 5, Cleom. 39, 2; Charito 4, 2, 6; Aesop., Fab. 152 P. [=σταυρόω 264H.]; POxy. 842, col. 18, 22; Jos., Bell. 2, 306; 5, 449, Ant. 2, 73; 11, 246, Vi. 420); hence Hb 6: 6 ἀνασταυροῦντας ἑαυτοῖς τὸν υἱὸν τ. θεοῦ may mean *since, to their own hurt, they crucify the Son of God,* of apostate Christians; but the context seems to require the fig. mng. *crucify again* (ἀνά=again), and the ancient translators and Gk. fathers understood it so; cf. L-S-J s.v.—AMVitti, Verb. Dom. 22, '42, 174–82.*

ἀναστενάζω 1 aor. ἀνεστέναξα (Aeschyl., Choëph. 335+; Hdt. 1, 86; PGM 4, 2493; Sir 25: 18; La 1: 4; Sus 22 Theod.) *sigh deeply* ἀναστενάξας τῷ πνεύματι αὐτοῦ λέγει *he sighed deeply in his spirit* (= to himself; cf. Mk 2: 8) *and said* Mk 8: 12 (cf. 2 Macc 6: 29).—CBonner, HTR 20, '27, 171–81.*

ἀνάστηθι s. ἀνίστημι.

ἀναστρέφω 1 aor. ἀνέστρεψα; 2 aor. pass. ἀνεστράφην, ptc. ἀναστραφείς (Hom.+ in var. mngs.; inscr., pap., LXX, Philo, Joseph.)

1. trans. *upset, overturn* (Polyb. 5, 9, 3; Ps.-Apollod. 3, 8, 1; Dionys. Hal. 9, 6, 2, all acc. to the mss.) τὶ *something* τὰς τραπέζας *overturn the tables* J 2: 15 v.l. (s. Hdb. ad loc.).

2. pass., reflex. *turn back and forth.*
   a. of place *stay, live* ἐν (Pla., Rep. 8 p. 558A μένειν καὶ ἀ. ἐν; X., Hell. 6, 4, 16; Polyb. 3, 33, 18; Epict. 1, 2, 26; Plut., Fab. 9, 5; Josh 5: 6; Ezk 19: 6. Cf. PKatz, JTS 47, '46, 31) Mt 17: 22 v.l.
   b. fig., of human conduct *act, behave, conduct oneself,* or *live* in the sense of the practice of certain principles (X.+; Polyb. 1, 9, 7; 1, 74, 13 al.; Chio, Ep. 7, 1; Crates, Ep. 35, 2 p. 216 H.; Vett. Val. index; inscr., pap. Dssm. B 83, NB 22 [BS 88; 194], LO 264f [LAE 315]; Nägeli 38; Thieme 14; Hatch 136; Pr 20: 7; Ezk 22: 30; Jos., Ant. 15, 190); always with the kind of behavior more exactly described
   α. by an adv. (Ael. Dion. σ, 41 ἀμαθῶς ἀναστρέφεσθαι; Dit., Syll. and Or. indices; Jos., Ant. 19, 72 εὐπρεπῶς) ἁγνῶς (Hatch, op. cit. III 73 Cilic. inscr.) Hs 9, 27, 2. ἰσχυρῶς καὶ ἀνδρείως ἀ. *conduct oneself w. strength and courage* 5, 6, 6. καλῶς ἀ. (Dit., Syll.³ 717, 95, Or.

322, 8) Hb 13: 18. ἀμέμπτως (Dit., Or. 323, 5) 1 Cl 63: 3; ὁσίως (Dit., Syll.³ 800, 21) 2 Cl 5: 6.
   β. by prep. phrases (X., Ages. 9, 4 ἀ. ἐν μέσαις εὐφροσύναις; Ep. Arist. 252) ἐν ταῖς ἐπιθυμίαις τῆς σαρκός *live in the passions of the flesh*=be a slave to physical passion Eph 2: 3. ἐν παλαιοῖς πράγμασιν *according to ancient* (i.e., Jewish) *customs* IMg 9: 1. ἐν τρυφαῖς πολλαῖς Hm 11: 12. ἐν πλάνῃ 2 Pt 2: 18. ἀ. ἐν οἴκῳ θεοῦ *conduct oneself in the household of God* 1 Ti 3: 15. ἐν φόβῳ ἀ. *live in fear* 1 Pt 1: 17.
   γ. w. adv. and prep. phrase (Simplicius in Epict. p. 24, 16 ἀλύτως ἐν τούτοις ἀναστρεφώμεθα; Jos., Vi. 273) ὁσίως ἀ. ἐν καθαρᾷ διανοίᾳ *live in holiness w. a pure mind* 1 Cl 21: 8.
   δ. w. more than one ἐν in var. mngs. ἐν ἁγιότητι τοῦ θεοῦ, οὐκ ἐν σοφίᾳ σαρκικῇ ἀλλ' ἐν χάριτι θεοῦ ἀνεστράφημεν ἐν τῷ κόσμῳ *we have conducted ourselves in the world in holiness before God, not w. earthly wisdom, but in the grace of God* 2 Cor 1: 12.—Somewhat as the phrase ἀ. ἐν τῷ κόσμῳ above—i.e., not in the active sense of practising something—οὕτως ἀ. Hb 10: 33 *to live in such a way* (i.e. amid reproach and affliction) means *to be treated in such a way.*

3. intr.—**a.** *associate* (cf. Epict. 4, 1, 116 πρός τινα with someone; Jos., Ant. 1, 55) μετά τινος B 19: 6; D 3: 9.
   b. *return, come back* (Appian, Bell. Civ. 5, 51 §215; Polyaenus 1, 48, 1; 8, 12; Sus 49 Theod.; Jdth 15: 7; 1 Macc 5: 8; 10: 52, 55 v.l.; Jos., Ant. 7, 226) Ac 5: 22; 15: 16. M-M.*

ἀναστροφή, ῆς, ἡ (Aeschyl., Pre-Socr.+; inscr., pap., LXX; Jos., Ant. 18, 359 al.) *way of life, conduct, behavior* (Polyb. 4, 82, 1 [FKälker, Quaest. de elocut. Polyb.= Leipz. Stud. III 2, '80, 301]; Teles p. 41, 2; Diog. L.; Epict. 1, 9, 24; 1, 22, 13; inscr.: Dit., Syll. index; IG Mar. Aeg. 1032, 6 [II вс], Magn. 91, Perg. 86, Brit. Mus. 200, 24 Hicks; Tob 4: 14; 2 Macc 6: 23; Ep. Arist. 130; 216) ἠκούσατε τ. ἐμὴν ἀ. ποτε ἐν τῷ Ἰουδαϊσμῷ *you have heard of my conduct when I was still in Judaism* Gal 1: 13. κατὰ τὴν προτέραν ἀ. *according to your former* (i.e., pre-Christian) *way of life* Eph 4: 22 (Dialekt-Inschr. 4320, 5 κατὰ τὰν ἄλλαν ἀναστροφάν [Rhodes]). ἡ ἐν φόβῳ ἁγνὴ ἀ. 1 Pt 3: 2; cf. vs. 1. ἡ ἀγαθὴ ἐν Χριστῷ ἀ. vs. 16. ἡ καλὴ ἀ. Js 3: 13; 1 Pt 2: 12. ἡ ματαία ἀ. πατροπαράδοτος *the futile* (i.e., directed toward futile ends) *way of life handed down by your fathers* 1: 18. ἡ ἐν ἀσελγείᾳ ἀ. 2 Pt 2: 7. ἡ ἔκβασις τῆς ἀ. Hb 13: 7. ἅγιον ἐν πάσῃ ἀ. γίνεσθαι *be holy in all your conduct* 1 Pt 1: 15. W. λόγος, ἀγάπη κτλ. 1 Ti 4: 12. Pl. ἅγιαι ἀ. καὶ εὐσέβειαι *holy conduct and piety* (pl. to include all varieties; cf. Ep. Arist. 130) 2 Pt 3: 11.—DDaube, Alexandrian Methods of Interpretation and the Rabbis: Festschr. HLewald '53, 27–44, M-M.*

ἀνασῴζω (Soph., Hdt.+; Hippocr., Ep. 11, 3 ἀνασῴζω τι; inscr.; Jer 27: 29; Zech 2: 11; Jos., Ant. 5, 214; 6, 364; 365) *save* pass. τοὺς ἀνασῳζομένους Hb 10: 14 𝔓⁴⁶ (for τ. ἁγιαζομένους).*

ἀνατάσσομαι 1 aor. ἀνεταξάμην lit. arrange in proper order; fig., *repeat in proper order* (Plut., Mor. 968c; Iren. 3, 21, 2) διήγησιν ἀ. *reproduce a narrative* (in writing) Lk 1: 1; but ἀ. is also taken as synon. w. συντάσσεσθαι *draw up, compile* (Syr., Copt., Goth. versions; Athanasius' 39th Festival Letter: EPreuschen, Analecta² II '10, p. 43, 9; so Hippiatr. 1, 1 in a prologue reminiscent of Lk 1: 1; Ep. Arist. 144). Cf. PCorssen, GGA '99, 317f; Zahn on Lk 1: 1; PScheller, De hellenist. conscribendae historiae arte, Diss. Lpz. '11, 23; JMansion, Serta Leodiensia '30, 261–7;

HJCadbury, JBL 52, '33, 56-8. S. also on παρακολουθέω 3. M-M.*

ἀνατεθραμμένος s. ἀνατρέφω

ἀνατέλλω fut. ἀνατελῶ; 1 aor. ἀνέτειλα; pf. ἀνατέταλκα.

1. trans. (Hom.+; Philo, Conf. Ling. 63; Gen 3: 18; cf. Anz 265f) *cause to spring up* or *rise* (Jos., Ant. 1, 31) ξύλον *a tree* Dg 12: 1 (Aeschyl., fgm. 300 Αἴγυπτος Δήμητρος ἀνατέλλει στάχυν). τροφὴν τοῖς ζῴοις *cause food to grow for the living creatures* 1 Cl 20: 4. ἥλιον *cause the sun to rise* Mt 5: 45; GNaass 2 (cf. Nicephorus: Rhet. Gr. I p. 500, 2 μετὰ τόκον ἀστέρα καινὸν ἀνέτειλε).

2. intr. (Soph., Hdt.+; LXX, Joseph.) *rise, spring up* of the sun (oft. in secular lit.; also Inscr. Gr. 466, 10 ἅμα τῷ ἡλίῳ ἀνατέλλοντι; PHib. 27, 52; Gen 32: 31; Ex 22: 3; Sir 26: 16; Philo) Mt 13: 6; Mk 4: 6; 16: 2; Js 1: 11. Of a light *dawn* Mt 4: 16 (cf. Is 58: 10; Esth 1: 1k). Fig., of the robes of the righteous *shine brightly* B 3: 4 (cf. Is 58: 8; on the text, s. Hdb. ad loc.; cf. also Mk 9: 3). Of Christ ἕως οὗ φωσφόρος ἀνατείλῃ ἐν ταῖς καρδίαις ὑμῶν *until the morning star rises in your hearts* 2 Pt 1: 19. Of a cloud *come up* Lk 12: 54. Of one's origin *be descended* Hb 7: 14 (cf. Test. Sim. 7, 1; Jer 23: 5 ἀναστήσω τῷ Δαυὶδ ἀνατολὴν δικαίαν; Apollon. Rhod. 1, 810). As a greatly weakened figure *spring forth* (Jos., Bell. 1, 406 πηγαί) of horns B 4: 5. Fig. ἡ ζωὴ ἡμῶν ἀνέτειλεν *our life has arisen* IMg 9: 1. Death is likened to the setting, resurr. to the rising, of a heavenly body IRo 2: 2. M-M.*

ἀνατίθημι 2 aor. mid. ἀνεθέμην (Hom.+ w. var. mngs.; inscr., pap., LXX, Philo, Joseph.) lit. *place upon.*

1. act. *ascribe, attribute* τινί τι *something to someone* (schol. on Eur., Hippol. 264 τὸ μηδὲν ἄγαν τῷ Χίλωνι) τῷ θεῷ τὴν κατὰ πάντων ἐξουσίαν *ascr. to God power over all things* MPol 2: 1 (cf. Alex. Aphr., Fat. 30, II 2 p. 201, 26 πρόγνωσιν ἀνατιθέναι τοῖς θεοῖς; Jos., Ant. 1, 15, C. Apion. 2, 165).

2. otherw. only mid. *declare, communicate, refer* w. the added idea that the pers. to whom a thing is ref. is asked for his opinion *lay someth. before someone for consideration* (Polyb. 21, 46, 11; Diog. L. 2, 141; Alciphr. 3, 23, 2; PPar. 69ᴅ, 23; 2 Macc 3: 9) τινί τι (Plut., Mor. 772ᴅ τὴν πρᾶξιν ἀνέθετο τ. ἑταίρων τισί; Artem. 2, 59 v.l. ἀ. τινι τὸ ὄναρ; Mi 7: 5) ὁ Φῆστος τῷ βασιλεῖ ἀνέθετο τὰ κατὰ τὸν Παῦλον Ac 25: 14. ἀνεθέμην αὐτοῖς τὸ εὐαγγέλιον *I laid my gospel before them* Gal 2: 2. Cf. Nägeli 45. M-M.*

ἀνατολή, ῆς, ἡ (Hom. [ἀντ-]+; inscr., pap., LXX, En., Philo, Joseph., Test. 12 Patr.).

1. *rising* of stars (Aeschyl.+; PHib. 27, 45 πρὸς τ. δύσεις καὶ ἀνατολὰς τ. ἄστρων; PTebt. 276, 38; PGM 13, 1027; 1037; Philo, Spec. Leg. 3, 187) ἐν τῇ ἀνατολῇ *in its rising, when it rose* Mt 2: 2, because of the sg. and the article in contrast to ἀπὸ ἀνατολῶν, vs. 1, prob. not a geograph. expr. like the latter, but rather astronomical; likew. vs. 9 (cf. Petosiris, fgm. 6 l. 31 of the moon ἅμα τῇ ἀνατολῇ=simultaneously with its rising; 12 l. 133 ἐν τῇ τοῦ ἄστρου ἀνατολῇ; Basilius, Hom. 25 p. 510 τὴν τοῦ ἀστέρος ἀ.; FBoll, ZNW 18, '18, 44f; a distinction is also made by PGM 36, 239 ἐξ ἀνατολῆς τ. χωρίου πλησίον ἀνατολῶν ἡλίου. Cf. EJHodous, CBQ 6, '44, 81f ['near the horizon'], and L-S-J s.v. 2).

2. *rising* of the sun, *east, orient* (Hdt.+; LXX).

a. sg. (cf. Aeschyl., Pr. 707) ἀπὸ ἀ. ἡλίου *from the east* Rv 7: 2; 16: 12; simply ἀπὸ ἀ. (Dit., Syll.³, 1112, 25) 21: 13; (opp. δύσις; cf. Appian, Mithrid. 68 §288 ἀπό τε δύσεως καὶ ἐξ ἀνατολῆς; Dit., Or. 199, 32; Jos., Bell. 6,

301) short ending of Mk; πρὸς τὴν ἀ. *toward the east* (Jos., Ant. 1, 37, C. Ap. 1, 77) Hv 1, 4, 1; 3.

b. pl. (Hdt.+; Diod. S. 5, 42, 3; Jos., C. Ap. 1, 65; Bl-D. §141, 2; Rob. 408) 1 Cl 10: 4 (Gen 13: 14). ἀπὸ ἀνατολῶν *from the east* (Gk. Parchments fr. Avroman IIᴀ, 8; JHS 35, '15, p. 30 ἀπὸ τ. ἀνατολῶν; Num 23: 7) μάγοι ἀπὸ ἀ. Mt 2: 1. ἐξέρχεσθαι ἀπὸ ἀ. *come from the east* (of lightning) Mt 24: 27. ἀπὸ ἀ. καὶ δυσμῶν (this contrast Apollon. Rhod. 1, 85; Epict. 3, 13, 9; Sb 385, 2; Mal 1: 11; Zech 8: 7; Is 59: 19; Philo, In Flacc. 45) *from east and west*=fr. the whole world Mt 8: 11. The four points of the compass Lk 13: 29 (Ps 106: 3). Gener. of the orient (opp. δύσις) 1 Cl 5: 6; IRo 2: 2.

3. fig., of the coming of the Messiah (cf. Damasc., Vi. Isidori 244 φέρειν τ. θείαν ἀνατολήν; Epigr. Gr. 978 ἀνέτειλε σωτήρ) ἀ. ἐξ ὕψους *the dawn from heaven* Lk 1: 78, interpr. by AJacoby, ZNW 20, '21, 205ff. as *sprout* or *scion* of God, and sim. by Billerb. II, '24, 113 as *Messiah of Yahweh*.—FJDölger, Sol Salutis², '25, 149ff. M-M. B. 871.*

ἀνατολικός, ή, όν (Epicurus, fgm. 346ᴮ; Strabo 2, 3, 2; Plut., Mor. 888ᴀ; Herodian 3, 2, 2; 3, 4, 3; Philo, Leg. ad Gai. 289; Jos., Ant. 20, 220; PFlor. 278 V, 1; Sym. Job 1: 3 al.) *eastern* Ac 19: 1 v.l. ἐν τοῖς ἀ. τόποις *in the eastern lands* 1 Cl 25: 1.*

ἀνατομή, ῆς, ἡ (Aristot., Plut., Philo) *cutting up, mutilation* of the body; pl. of tortures IRo 5: 3 (text uncertain; cf. the text-crit. notes of Lghtf., Hilgenfeld, Bihlmeyer ad loc.).*

ἀνατρέπω 1 aor. ἀνέτρεψα (Aeschyl.+; inscr., pap., LXX; Philo, Mut. Nom. 239; Jos., Bell. 4, 318, Vi. 250) *cause to fall, overturn, destroy.*

1. lit. τὰς τραπέζας (Teles p. 18, 9H.; Plut., Galba 5, 3; Ps.-Lucian, Asin. 40; Ps.-Apollod. 3, 7, 7, 6) *overturn* J 2: 15 (v.l. ἀνέστρεψεν; cf. ἀναστρέφω 1 and Hdb. ad loc.).

2. fig. (Pla., Ep. 7 p. 336ᴮ; Appian, Bell. Civ. 4, 131 §550 ἐλπίδα; Test. Ash. 1, 7) ἀνατρέπουσιν τὴν τινων πίστιν *they are upsetting the faith of some* 2 Ti 2: 18 (Third Corinthians 1: 2; ἀ. πίστιν also Diod. S. 1, 77, 2). ὅλους οἴκους ἀ. *they ruin whole families,* i.e., by false teachings Tit 1: 11 (cf. Plut., Mor. 490ᴮ; UPZ 144 IX, 37 [II ʙᴄ] τῆς πατρικῆς οἰκίας ἀνατετραμμένης). M-M.*

ἀνατρέφω 1 aor. ἀνέθρεψα, mid. ἀνεθρεψάμην; pf. pass. ἀνατέθραμμαι; 2 aor. pass. ἀνετράφην (Aeschyl.+; LXX, Joseph.).

1. of physical nurture *bring up, care for* (X., Mem. 4, 3, 10 et al.; PLeipz. 28, 12; Wsd 7: 4) of the infant Moses Ac 7: 20 (cf. Jos., Ant. 9, 142; Eutecnius 4 p. 41, 18 Διόνυσον ἐκ τοῦ κιβωτίου δεξάμενος ἀνεθρέψατο). Of Jesus Lk 4: 16 v.l., where it may also have sense 2. Pass. *be nourished* of the worm generated within the body of the phoenix 1 Cl 25: 3

2. of mental and spiritual nurture *bring up, rear, train* (Epict. 2, 22, 26; 3, 1, 35; Herodian 1, 2, 1; 4 Macc 10: 2) ἀνεθρέψατο αὐτὸν ἑαυτῇ εἰς υἱόν *she brought him up as her own son* Ac 7: 21 (Jos., Ant. 2, 232). ἀνατεθραμμένος ἐν τ. πόλει ταύτῃ 22: 3. WCvanUnnik, Tarsus or Jerusalem '62.*

ἀνατρέχω 2 aor. ἀνέδραμον (Hom.+; PTebt. 711, 10; Philo, Ebr. 8, Aet. M. 33) (lit. 'run back') *make up for, make amends for* (Plut., Mor. 2c; Lucian, Adv. Ind. 4) w. acc. of the thing ἵν' ὃ οὐκ εἰργάσαντο, νῦν ἀναδράμωσιν *that they may now make up for what they neglected to do* Hs 9, 20, 4.*

ἀνατυλίσσω 1 aor. ἀνετύλιξα (Lucian) unroll; fig., think over or call to mind again τὶ (Lucian, Nig. 7 τ. λόγους, οὓς τότε ἤκουσα συναγείρων καὶ πρὸς ἐμαυτὸν ἀνατυλίττων) τὰ ἀπ᾽ ἀρχῆς γενόμενα 1 Cl 31: 1.*

ἀναφαίνω 1 aor. (Dor.) ἀνέφανα (Bl-D. §72; Mlt.-H. 214f) (Hom. +; LXX) light up, cause to appear ἀναφάναντες (only this rdg. is poss., not the 2 aor. pass. ἀναφανέντες) τὴν Κύπρον we came within sight of Cyprus, i.e., we sighted it Ac 21: 3 (Bl-D. §309, 1 app.; Rob. 817), prob. a nautical t.t. (cf. Lucian, D. Mar. 10, 1; Philostrat., Her. 19, 6 p. 212, 10 τὴν νῆσον; Theophanes, Chronograph. I p. 721 Classen [Corpus Script. Hist. Byz.] οἱ Ἄραβες περιεφέροντο ἐν τῷ πελάγει. ἀναφανέντων δὲ αὐτῶν τὴν γῆν, εἶδον αὐτοὺς οἱ στρατηγοί). Pass. appear (Job 13: 18; 40: 8; Philo; Jos., Ant. 2, 339; 7, 333; PGM 36, 107) Lk 19: 11. M-M.*

ἀναφέρω 2 aor. ἀνήνεγκα (H.Gk.) and ἀνήνεγκον (Bl-D. §80; 81; Mlt.-H. 263) (Hom. + in var. mngs.; inscr., pap., LXX; Philo, Aet. M. 64; Jos., Bell. 1, 234, C. Ap. 1, 232) bring or take up.
1. lit. ἀ. αὐτοὺς εἰς ὄρος ὑψηλόν he led them up a high mountain Mt 17: 1; Mk 9: 2. Pass. ἀνεφέρετο εἰς τ. οὐρανόν he was taken up into heaven (of Romulus: Plut., Numa 2, 4; of Endymion: Hes., fgm. 148 Rz. τὸν Ἐνδυμίωνα ἀνενεχθῆναι εἰς οὐρανόν; schol. on Apollon. Rhod. 4, 57 and 58 p. 264, 17) Lk 24: 51 𝔓[75] et al. ἀναφερόμενοι εἰς τὰ ὕψη IEph 9: 1.
2. specif. a t.t. of the sacrificial system (Lev 17: 5; 1 Esdr 5: 49; Is 57: 6; 2 Macc 1: 18; 2: 9 al.) ἀ. θυσίας ὑπέρ τινος offer sacrifices for someth. Hb 7: 27. ἀ. τινα ἐπὶ τὸ θυσιαστήριον (Gen 8: 20; Lev 14: 20; Bar 1: 10; 1 Macc 4: 53) offer up someone on the altar Js 2: 21. Of Christ's sacrifice: ἑαυτὸν ἀνενέγκας when he offered up himself Hb 7: 27. τὰς ἁμαρτίας ἡμῶν αὐτὸς ἀνήνεγκεν ἐν τῷ σώματι αὐτοῦ ἐπὶ τὸ ξύλον he himself brought our sins in his body to the cross 1 Pt 2: 24 (cf. Dssm., B 83ff [BS 88f]). Pol 8: 1 (Is 53: 12).—Fig. (schol. on Apollon. Rhod. 2, 214b χάριν = render thanks to the divinity) ἀ. θυσίαν αἰνέσεως offer up a sacr. of praise Hb 13: 15 (cf. 2 Ch 29: 31). ἀ. πνευματικὰς θυσίας 1 Pt 2: 5. ἀ. προσευχὰς offer prayers 2 Cl 2: 2. ἀ. δέησιν περί τινος offer up a petition for someth. B 12: 7.
3. In Is 53: 11 ἀ. is used to translate סָבַל, in vs. 12 for נָשָׂא, and in the corresponding passages in our lit. ἀ. is often rendered 'bear' or 'take away'. But ἀ. seems not to have these meanings. Very often, on the contrary, it has a sense that gives ἀνα- its full force: lay or impose a burden on someone, give something to someone to bear, as a rule, in fact, to someone who is not obligated to bear it (Aeschyl., Choeph. 841 ἄχθος; Polyb. 1, 36, 3; 4, 45, 9; Diod. S. 15, 48, 4; 32, 26, 1; Appian, Liby. 93; Syr. 41, where the other defendants were τὴν αἰτίαν ἐς τὸν Ἐπαμεινώνδαν ἀναφέροντες, i.e., putting the blame on Epaminondas. The Lex. Vind. p. 12, 3 sees in Eur., Or. 76 ἐς Φοῖβον ἀναφέρουσα τ. ἁμαρτίαν and in Procop. Soph., Ep. 7 p. 535 H. proof that ἀναφέρειν is used ἀντὶ τοῦ τὴν αἰτίαν εἰς ἕτερον τιθέναι. In a case in which a man takes upon himself the burden that another should have borne, then ἀ. = take upon oneself (Thu. 3, 38, 3 ἡ πόλις τὰ μὲν ἆθλα ἑτέροις δίδουσιν, αὐτὴ δὲ τοὺς κινδύνους ἀναφέρει = the city gives the prizes to others, but she takes the dangers upon herself). Christ was once for all offered up in this respect (εἰς 5) that he took upon himself the sins of many Hb 9: 28. Cf. 1 Cl 16: 12, 14. M-M.*

ἀναφωνέω 1 aor. ἀνεφώνησα (Epicurus p. 24, 16 Us.; Polyb. 3, 33, 4; Ps.-Aristot., De Mundo 6 p. 400a, 18;

Artem. I, 58; PFay. 14, 2; 1 Ch 15: 28 al; 2 Ch 5: 13) cry out. ἀ. κραυγῇ μεγάλῃ cry out loudly Lk 1: 42. M-M.*

ἀναχθείς s. ἀνάγω.

ἀνάχυσις, εως, ἡ (Strabo 3, 1, 9; Plut., Mar. 25, 5; Philo Decal. 41, Aet. M. 102, Spec. Leg. 1, 34; Somn. 2, 278) lit. pouring out, then wide stream Ocellus Luc. c. 41 of the sea; Maximus Tyr. 26, 1a; 38, 3e ἀ. θαλάττης; only fig. ἡ τῆς ἀσωτίας ἀ. flood of dissipation 1 Pt 4: 4. M-M.*

ἀναχωρέω 1 aor. ἀνεχώρησα; pf. ἀνακεχώρηκα (Hom. +; inscr., pap., LXX).
1. go away (Epict. 2, 1, 8; 2, 12, 6; 4, 1, 96; Herodian 1, 12, 2; 2 Macc 10: 13; Jos., Vi. 151) Mt 2: 13; 9: 24; 27: 5; Hv 3, 1, 8; s 9, 5, 1f. μικρόν a little way s 9, 5, 1. ἀπό τινος s 9, 11, 2. τόπος ἀνακεχωρηκώς a secluded place v 3, 1, 3.
2. in special senses—a. return (εἰς Polyb. 1, 11, 15; Dit., Syll.³ 1168, 117, Or. 335, 121; Jos., Bell. 2, 407, Ant. 17, 58) εἰς τ. χώραν αὐτῶν to their own country Mt 2: 12.
b. withdraw, retire, take refuge (POxy. 251, 10 εἰς τὴν ξένην; 252, 9 [19/20]; PLille 3, 76 [241 BC]; Wilcken, APF 5, '08, 222; Ex 2: 15; 2 Macc 5: 27 εἰς) εἰς Αἴγυπτον Mt 2: 14. εἰς τὰ μέρη τῆς Γαλιλαίας 2: 22; cf. 15: 21. εἰς τὴν Γαλιλαίαν 4: 12. εἴς τινα τόπον to a certain place Hv 2, 1, 4. πρὸς (Tdf. εἰς) τὴν θάλασσαν to the sea Mk 3: 7 (ἀ. πρός w. acc. as Jos., Ant. 1, 85). εἰς τὸ ὄρος J 6: 15. ἀπό τ. Ἀθηνῶν Ac 18: 1 D. ἐκεῖθεν Mt 12: 15. ἐκεῖθεν εἰς ἔρημον τόπον from there to a lonely place 14: 13; κατ' ἰδίαν ibid. Ac 23: 19. Abs. 26: 31. M-M.*

ἀνάψας s. ἀνάπτω.

ἀνάψυξις, εως, ἡ (Diocles, fgm. 15; Strabo 10, 2, 19; Heraclit. Sto. 10 p. 17, 17; Herm. Wr. 512, 4 Sc.; Philo, De Abrah. 152; Ex 8: 11; pap. [s. Witkowski Index]) breathing space, relaxation, relief fig., of the Messianic age καιροὶ ἀναψύξεως times of rest Ac 3: 20. Cf. ADieterich, Nekyia 1893, 95f.*

ἀναψύχω 1 aor. ἀνέψυξα.
1. trans. (Hom. +; Plut.; Jos., Ant. 15, 54. [Nägeli 16; Anz 303]) give someone a breathing space, revive, refresh τινά IEph 2: 1; Tr 12: 2. πολλάκις με ἀνέψυξεν he often refreshed me 2 Ti 1: 16.
2. intr. (Diphilus [c. 300 BC] 81; POsl. 153, 10 [early II AD]; POxy. 1296, 7; Sb 3939, 28; 1 Km 16: 23; Ps 38: 14; En. 103, 13) be refreshed μετά τινος together with someone Ro 15: 32 D. M-M.*

ἀνδραποδιστής, οῦ, ὁ (Aristoph., Pla., X. +; Demosth. 4, 47; Polyb. 13, 6, 4; Dio Chrys. 52[69], 9; Charito 5, 7, 4; Philo, Spec. Leg. 4, 13) slave-dealer, kidnapper 1 Ti 1: 10 (here perh. w. the mng. 'procurer'. Vulg. plagiarius). M-M.*

Ἀνδρέας, ου, ὁ a good Gk. name (Diod. S. 8, 24; Dit., Syll.³ 649, 5; Ep. Arist.; Joseph.; a Jew Ἀ. also in Cass. Dio 68, 32, 2) Andrew, brother of Simon Peter; acc. to J 1: 44 he was from Bethsaida on the Sea of Galilee, and, (s. vss. 35, 40) was orig. a disciple of John the Baptist. Mt 4: 18; 10: 2; Mk 1: 16, 29; 3: 18; 13: 3; Lk 6: 14; J 6: 8; 12: 22; Ac 1: 13; GP 14: 60; GEb 2; Papias 2: 4 (PMPeterson, Andrew, Brother of Simon '58).*

ἀνδρεῖος, εία, εῖον (trag., Hdt. +; inscr.; PLeipz. 119 II, 3; LXX; Jos., C. Ap. 2, 292; Test. 12 Patr.) manly, strong subst. τὰ ἀνδρεῖα heroic deeds worthy of a brave man (Philo, Mut. Nom. 146) ἐπιτελεῖσθαι πολλὰ ἀ. do many heroic deeds of famous women (like Aristot., Pol. 1277ᵇ, 22) 1 Cl 55: 3.*

ἀνδρείως (Aristoph., Pax 498; 1 Macc 9: 10 v.l.; 2 Macc 6: 27; Philo, Mos. 2, 184; Jos., Ant. 12, 302) adv. *in a manly* (i.e. *brave*) *way* ἀ. ἀναστρέφεσθαι conduct oneself bravely (w. ἰσχυρῶς) Hs 5, 6, 6. ἀ. ἑστηκέναι stand firm of maidens s 9, 2, 5.*

ἀνδρίζομαι (Pla., X.+; Lucian, De Gymn. 15 et al.; PSI 402, 3; 512, 29; PPetr. II 40a, 12 [c. 233 BC] μὴ οὖν ὀλιγοψυχήσητε, ἀλλʼ ἀνδρίζεσθε; LXX; Jos., Bell. 6, 50) conduct oneself in a manly or courageous way w. κραταιοῦσθαι (like חֲזַק וֶאֱמָץ; cf. 2 Km 10: 12; Ps 26: 14; 30: 25) 1 Cor 16: 13; w. ἰσχύειν (Dt 31: 6, 7, 23; Josh 1: 6, 7 al.) MPol 9: 1. ἀνδρίζου be a man! Hv 1, 4, 3. Of an old man, whose hope in life has been renewed v 3, 12, 2. Even of a woman who is girded and of manly appearance v 3, 8, 4. M-M.*

Ἀνδρόνικος, ου, ὁ a name freq. found (Diod. S. 19, 59, 2; Appian, Maced. 16; Dit., Syll.² and Or. index; Inschr. v. Priene 313 [I BC]; Preisigke, Namenbuch; 2 Macc 4: 31, 32, 34, 38; 5: 23; Jos., Ant. 13, 75; 78) *Andronicus,* greeted in Ro 16: 7; w. Junias described by Paul as συγγενεῖς μου καὶ συναιχμάλωτοι and called ἐπίσημοι ἐν τ. ἀποστόλοις.—BWBacon, ET 42, ʼ31, 300–4. GABarton, ibid. 43, ʼ32, 359–61.*

ἀνδροφόνος, ου, ὁ (Hom.+; Dit., Or. 218, 99 [III BC]; Epigr. Gr. 184, 6 [III BC]; POsl. 18, 4 [162 AD]; 2 Macc 9: 28; Philo) *murderer* (Lex. Vind. p. 192, 13: also a murderer of women and children) 1 Ti 1: 9. M-M.*

ἀνέβην s. ἀναβαίνω.

ἀνεγκλησία, ας, ἡ (pap. oft.=indemnity) *blamelessness* (Bardesanes in Euseb., Praep. Ev. 6, 10, 10 p. 274D) ἀ. τοῦ θεοῦ *bl. before God* Phil 3: 14 v.l.*

ἀνέγκλητος, ον (Pla., X.+; Epict. 1, 28, 10; Dit., Syll.³ 911, 25 [III BC]; 556D, 5 [207/6 BC]; pap.; 3 Macc 5: 31; Jos., Ant. 10, 281; 17, 289) *blameless, irreproachable* of Christians gener. ὃς βεβαιώσει ὑμᾶς ἀ. ἐν τ. ἡμέρᾳ τ. κυρίου *who will establish you as blameless in the day of the Lord*=so that you will be bl. when it comes 1 Cor 1: 8; w. ἅγιος and ἄμωμος Col 1: 22. Of eccl. leaders 1 Ti 3: 10; Tit 1: 6f. M-M.*

ἀνέγνων s. ἀναγινώσκω.

ἀνεθέμην s. ἀνατίθημι.

ἀνέθην, ἀνείς s. ἀνίημι.

ἀνεθρεψάμην s. ἀνατρέφω.

ἀνεῖλα, ἀνεῖλον s. ἀναιρέω.

ἀνεκδιήγητος, ον (Rhet. Gr. III 747, 8; Hesychius; Ep. Arist. 99 v.l.) *indescribable* in good sense ἐπὶ τῇ ἀ. αὐτοῦ δωρεᾷ 2 Cor 9: 15. Of God's power ἀ. κράτος 1 Cl 61: 1. τὸ ὕψος, εἰς ὃ ἀνάγει ἡ ἀγάπη, ἀ. ἐστι 49: 4. νερτέρων ἀ. κρίματα (so the mss.; κλίματα is an unnecessary emendation) *the indescribable judgments of the underworld* 20: 5 (s. Knopf, Hdb. ad loc.). M-M.*

ἀνεκλάλητος, ον (Diosc., Eup. preface Wellm.; Heliod. 6, 15, 4; Ps.-Callisth. 1, 40, 5; Herm Wr. 1, 4, 31; Eunap. 486) *inexpressible* χαρᾷ ἀ. καὶ δεδοξασμένῃ 1 Pt 1: 8; Pol 1: 3. φῶς ἀ. of the radiance of the star at Jesus' birth IEph 19: 2.*

ἀνέκλειπτος, ον (Hyperid.+; Diod. S. 1, 36, 1; 4, 84, 2; Plut., Mor. 438D; Dit., Or. 383, 70 [I BC]; PLond. 1166, 7 [42 AD]; Ep. Arist. 89; 185) *unfailing, inexhaustible* of the treasure of good works θησαυρὸς ἀ. (cf. Wsd 7: 14; 8: 18) Lk 12: 33. M-M.*

ἀνεκτός, όν (Hom.+; Dit., Syll.² 793; Inscr. Rom. IV 293 II, 4 [II BC, Pergam.]; Jos., Bell. 7, 68, Ant. 18, 348) *bearable, endurable* ἀνεκτὸν ἦν, εἰ it could be endured, if 2 Cl 10: 5.—Comp. (Memnon [I BC/I AD] no. 434, fgm. 1, 2, 1; 1, 6, 3 Jac. ἀνεκτότερον; Cicero, Att. 12, 45, 2; Christian letter POxy. 939, 25 ἀνεκτότερον ἐσχηκέναι) Τύρῳ καὶ Σιδῶνι ἀνεκτότερον ἔσται *it will be more tolerable for Tyre and Sidon* Mt 11: 22; Lk 10: 14. ἀ. ἔ. γῇ Σοδόμων Mt 10: 15; 11: 24; cf. Mk 6: 11 t.r.; Lk 10: 12. M-M.*

ἀνελεήμων, ον (Aristot. 1442a, 13; Cat. Cod. Astr. II 173; Pr 5: 9; Job 30: 21 al.) *unmerciful* Ro 1: 31; Tit 1: 9 v.l. (in a catalogue of vices in Ptolem., Apotel. 3, 14, 28).*

ἀνελεῖν, ἀνελῶ s. ἀναιρέω.

ἀνέλεος, ον (for Att. ἀνηλεής; cf. Phryn. 710L.; Bl-D. §120, 2) *merciless* κρίσις ἀ. *judgment is merciless* Js 2: 13 (t.r. ἀνίλεως). M-M.*

ἀνελήμφθην s. ἀναλαμβάνω.

ἀνεμίζω (for Att. ἀνεμόω) pass. *be moved by the wind* (schol. on Od. 12, 336) κλύδων ἀνεμιζόμενος καὶ ῥιπιζόμενος *surf moved and tossed by the wind* Js 1: 6. M-M.*

ἄνεμος, ου, ὁ (Hom.+; inscr., pap., LXX; Philo, Aet. M. 125 al.; Joseph.) *wind.*
1. lit.—a. the wind itself: blowing Rv 7: 1; playing among the reeds Mt 11: 7; Lk 7: 24; scattering chaff B 11: 7 (Ps 1: 4); desired by the sailor IPol 2: 3, or not ἐναντίος ἀ. *a contrary wind* Mt 14: 24; Mk 6: 48; cf. Ac 27: 7. ὁ ἄ. *the storm* Mt 14: 30 (ἀ. ἰσχυρός t.r.); cf. vs. 32; Mk 6: 51. ἄ. μέγας *a strong wind* J 6: 18; Rv 6: 13. ἄ. τυφωνικός *a violent, hurricane-like wind* Ac 27: 14, cf. 15. For this, λαῖλαψ ἀνέμου *a storm-wind* Mk 4: 37; Lk 8: 23, cf. Mk 4: 41; Lk 8: 24 (on the stilling of the storm POxy. 1383, 1 [III AD] κελεύειν ἀνέμοις.—WFiedler, Antik. Wetterzauber ʼ31, esp. 17–23).—Pl. without the art. (Jos., Bell. 4, 286) Js 3: 4. οἱ ἄ. (Jos., Bell. 4, 299; also thought of as personified, cf. Fluchtaf. 4, 6 τὸν θεὸν τῶν ἀνέμων καὶ πνευμάτων Λαιλαμ) Mt 7: 25, 27; 8: 26f (the par. Mk 4: 39 has the sg.). Lk 8: 25; Jd 12; ἄ. ἐναντίοι *contrary winds* Ac 27: 4. οἱ τέσσαρες ἄ. τῆς γῆς Rv 7: 1 (cf. Zech 6: 5; Jer 25: 16; Da 7: 2; on the angels of the winds cf. PGM 15, 14; 16, and on control of the winds Diod. S. 20, 101, 3 Aeolus as κύριος τῶν ἀνέμων; Ps.-Apollod., Epit. 7, 10 Zeus has appointed Aeolus as ἐπιμελητὴς τῶν ἀνέμων, καὶ παύειν καὶ προΐεσθαι; Ael. Aristid. 45, 29 K.; Isisaretal. v. Kyme 39; POxy. 1383, 9 ἀπέκλειε τὰ πνεύματα).
b. οἱ τέσσαρες ἄ. can also be *the four directions,* or *cardinal points* (Annales du service des antiquités de l'Égypte 19, ʼ20, p. 40, 20 [93 BC]; PRainer 115, 6; PFlor. 50, 104 ἐκ τῶν τεσσ. ἀ.; Ezk 37: 9 v.l.; Zech 2: 10; 1 Ch 9: 24; Jos., Bell. 301, Ant. 8, 80; PGM 3, 496; 4, 1607) Mt 24: 31; Mk 13: 27; D 10: 5. ἀνέμων σταθμοὶ *stations or quarters* of the wind 1 Cl 20: 10 (Job 28: 25; s. Lghtft. and Knopf ad loc.).
2. fig. (cf. 4 Macc 15: 32), of tendencies in religion περιφερόμενοι παντὶ ἀ. τ. διδασκαλίας *driven about by every wind of doctrine* Eph 4: 14. M-M. B. 64.*

ἀνεμπόδιστος, ον (Aristot. et al.; Epict. 3, 22, 41; 4, 4, 5; Vett. Val. 246, 5; Dit., Syll.² 517, 32 [³ 955, 32 restores this passage difftly.], Or. 383, 129; UPZ 191, 13; 192, 23; 193, 23; PAmh. 38, 12; Wsd 17: 19; 19: 7) *unhindered* only adv.

ἀνεμποδίστως (Aristot., Nicom. 7, 12, 13; Diod. S. 1, 36,

10; PTebt. 6, 48; 43, 40 [118 BC] al. in pap.; Jos., Ant. 16, 172) κλῆρον ἀ. ἀπολαβεῖν *receive my lot unhindered* IRo 1: 2.*

ἀνένδεκτος, ον (Artem. 2, 70; Diog. L. 7, 50; PLond. 1404, 8) *impossible* ἀ. ἐστιν *it is imp.* Lk 17: 1 (cf. Bl-D. §400, 4; Mlt.-H. 305; Rob. 1171).*

ἀνένεγκαι s. ἀναφέρω.

ἀνεξεραύνητος, ον *unfathomable,* lit. *unsearchable* of God's judgments τὰ κρίματα αὐτοῦ Ro 11: 33 (H.Gk. form for ἀνεξερεύνητος—so Heraclitus in Clem. Alex., Str. 2, 17, 4 Stählin; Cass. Dio 69, 14; Sym. Pr 25: 3; Jer 17: 9. Cf. Bl-D. §30, 4; Nägeli 16; 23; Mlt. 46). M-M.*

ἀνεξίκακος, ον (Lucian, Jud. Voc. 9; Vett. Val. 38, 21; Cat. Cod. Astr. VIII 2 p. 156, 15; Pollux 5, 138; PTebt. 272, 19 [II AD].—ἀνεξικακία Epict., Ench. 10; Wsd 2: 19; Jos., Bell. 1, 624) *bearing evil without resentment, patient* of Christians 2 Ti 2: 24 (w. ἤπιος, διδακτικός). M-M.*

ἀνεξιχνίαστος, ον (Cat. Cod. Astr. VIII 2 p. 156, 16; Etym. Mag. p. 709, 50; Job 5: 9; 9: 10; 34: 24; Prayer of Manasseh [=Ode 12] 6) *inscrutable, incomprehensible,* lit. 'not to be tracked out', of God's ways Ro 11: 33. Of the riches in Christ *fathomless* Eph 3: 8 (REThomas, ET 39, '28, 283). ἀ. δημιουργία *inscrutable creation* Dg 9: 5.—1 Cl 20: 5. Cf. FPfister, SAHeidelb. 1914, Nr. 11, p. 8.*

ἀνεπαίσχυντος, ον (Jos., Ant. 18, 243; Agapetus, De Offic. Boni Princ. 57 p. 174 Groebel) *who does not need to be ashamed* of a bishop: ἐργάτης ἀ. 2 Ti 2: 15. M-M.*

ἀνέπεσα s. ἀναπίπτω.

ἀνεπιδεής, ές (Pla., Leg. 12 p. 947E; Lucian, Dial. Mort. 26, 2) *who lacks nothing* of God (Philo, Plant. 35) PK 2 p. 13, 25.*

ἀνεπίλημπτος, ον (Eur., Thu.+; Lucian, Pisc. 8; Ps.-Lucian, Salt. 81; Dio Chrys. 11[12], 66; PTebt. 5, 48; 61b, 237f; 72, 176; Inscr. Or. Sept. Pont. Eux. II 52, 8 Latyschev) *irreproachable* 1 Ti 3: 2; 5: 7; w. ἄσπιλος 6: 14. ἀ. πολιτεία *irrepr. conduct* (Philo, Spec. Leg. 3, 24; cf. PGiess. 55, 10 ἀ. βίον ἔχειν) MPol 17: 1. M-M.*

ἀνέρχομαι 2 aor. ἀνῆλθον (Hom.+; inscr., pap., LXX; Philo, Mos. 2, 70 al.; Joseph.; Test. 12 Patr.) *go up, come up* from a lower place to a higher (X., Hell. 2, 4, 39 εἰς τ. ἀκρόπολιν; 3 Km 13: 12; Jos., Ant. 6, 314) εἰς τὸ ὄρος J 6: 3 (on the journey to Jerusalem cf. ἀναβαίνω 1aα) ἀ. εἰς Ἱεροσόλυμα Gal 1: 17f (of the journey to the capital Epict. 1, 11, 32 νῦν ἐν Ῥώμῃ ἀνέρχῃ; PTebt. 412, 3 ἄνελθε εἰς μητρόπολιν; 411, 5; Jos., Ant. 16, 91 εἰς τ. Ῥώμην). Of coming up out of a river ἀ. ἀπὸ ὕδατος GEb 3. M-M.*

ἀνερωτάω (Hom.+) *ask* τινά (Dio Chrys. 13[7], 5; Ael. Aristid. 36, 48 K.=48 p. 457 D.) MPol 9: 2.*

ἄνεσις, εως, ἡ (Hdt. 5, 28+; Dit., Syll.³ 880, 53; 884, 16; pap.; LXX; Ep. Arist. 284) *relaxing.*

1. lit. of relaxation of custody ἀ. ἔχειν *have some freedom* Ac 24: 23 (cf. Jos., Ant. 18, 235 φυλακὴ μὲν γὰρ καὶ τήρησις ἦν, μετὰ μέντοι ἀνέσεως).

2. *rest, relaxation, relief* (Pla., Leg. 4, 724A; Strabo 10, 3, 9; M. Ant. 1, 16, 6; Philo, Rer. Div. Her. 156) ἵνα ἄλλοις ἄ. (sc. ᾖ), ὑμῖν θλῖψις *that others should have relief, and you be burdened* 2 Cor 8: 13. ἀ. ἔχειν (Jos., Bell. 3, 319) 2: 13; 7: 5. ἄνεσιν διδόναι τινί (Diod. S. 19, 26, 10 αὐτῷ δοὺς ἄνεσιν; 2 Ch 23: 15; 1 Esdr 4: 62; Jos., Ant. 3, 254; 281) B

4: 2. ἀνταποδοῦναι τ. θλιβομένοις ἄνεσιν *grant, in turn, rest to those who are oppressed* 2 Th 1: 7. M-M.*

ἀνέστην s. ἀνίστημι.

ἀνετάζω (PSI 380, 9 [249 BC]; POxy. 34 I, 13 [127 AD]; Judg 6: 29A; Sus 14 Theod.) *give someone* (τινά) *a hearing* judicial t.t. (Anaphora Pilati A 6 p. 417 Tischendorf) Ac 22: 29. μάστιξιν ἀ. *give a hearing, and use torture* (in the form of a lashing) *in connection w. it,* vs. 24. M-M.*

ἄνευ prep. w. gen. (Hom.+; inscr., pap., LXX; Witkowski 60 and cf. lit. s.v. ἀνά) *without* (cf. ἄτερ, χωρίς, fr. which it can scarcely be distinguished in usage).

1. of pers. *without the knowledge and consent of* (Od. 2, 372 and Appian, Bell. Civ. 5, 100 §416; Ael. Aristid. 28, 105 K.=49 p. 525 D.: ἄνευ θεοῦ; UPZ 69, 4 [152 BC] ἄνευ τ. θεῶν οὐθὲν γίνεται; PPetr. II Append. p. 3; Ostraka I 559f). ἄ. τοῦ πατρὸς ὑμῶν Mt 10: 29 (cf. Am 3: 5); cf. B 19: 6; IMg 7: 1; ITr 2: 2; IPol 4: 1.

2. of things (Jos., Bell. 2, 1, Ant. 7, 72, Vi. 167) ἄ. λόγου *without a word* (opp. διὰ τῆς ἀναστροφῆς) 1 Pt 3: 1. ἄ. γογγυσμοῦ *without complaining* 4: 9. ἄ. χειρῶν (Da 2: 34) *built without hands* Mk 13: 2 D W. χωρίς: οὐ δύναται κεφαλὴ χωρὶς γεννηθῆναι ἄ. μελῶν *the head cannot be born separately, without limbs* ITr 11: 2; cf. B 2: 6; Dg 12: 4, 5, 6. M-M and suppl.*

ἀνεύθετος, ον (Hesychius; Suidas; beginning of the lexicon of Photius ed. RReitzenstein '07; Anecd. Gr. p. 399, 11) *poor, unfavorably situated* of a harbor λιμὴν ἀ. πρὸς παραχειμασίαν *not suitable for wintering* in Ac 27: 12 (of the harbor Καλοὶ Λιμένες on Crete). M-M.*

ἀνευρίσκω 2 aor. ἀνεῦρα Lk 2: 16 (ἀνεῦρον א AB³PR al.; εὗρον D, 1, 69; εὗραν L; cf. W-S. §13, 13), ptc. ἀνευρών (Aeschyl., Hdt.+; inscr., pap.; 4 Macc 3: 14; Philo, Aet. M. 2; Jos., Bell. 7, 114) *look* or *search for* (w. finding presupposed) τινά: τὴν Μαριὰμ καὶ τὸν Ἰωσὴφ καὶ τὸ βρέφος Lk 2: 16. τοὺς μαθητάς Ac 21: 4. M-M.*

ἀνευφημέω impf. ἀνευφήμουν (Soph., Pla.+; Jos., Bell. 2, 608; 4, 113) *praise loudly* τ. κύριον θεόν AP 5: 19 (cf. Ps 62: 8 Sym.; Achilles Tat. 3, 5, 6 τ. θεοὺς ἀ.).*

ἀνέχω in our lit. only mid.: impf. ἀνειχόμην; fut. ἀνέξομαι; 2 aor. ἀνεσχόμην Ac 18: 14; v.l. ἠνεσχόμην; on the augm. s. Bl-D. §69, 2; Rob. 368. (Hom.+; inscr., pap., LXX, Philo, Joseph.)

1. *endure, bear with, put up with*; on its constr. cf. Bl-D. §176, 1; Rob. 508.

a. τινός *someone* (Pla., Polit. 8 p. 564E; Teles p. 18, 6; Gen 45: 1; Is 63: 15; 3 Macc 1: 22) Hm 4, 4, 1. ὑμῶν Mt 17: 17; Mk 9: 19; Lk 9: 41. μου 2 Cor 11: 1b (Appian, Samn. 4 §10 τίς ἀνέξεταί μου). πάντων IPol 1: 2. ἀλλήλων ἐν ἀγάπῃ *bear w. one another in love* Eph 4: 2; cf. Col 3: 13. τῶν ἀφρόνων *foolish people* 2 Cor 11: 19.

b. *something:* w. acc. (Procop. Soph., Ep. 161 p. 597 κακά; Is 1: 13; Job 6: 26) or w. gen. (Od. 22, 423; Polyaenus 8, 10, 1; Job 6: 26 v.l.; 2 Macc 9: 12) of the thing πάντα 1 Cl 49: 5. τὰ σάββατα *Sabbath-observances* B 2: 5; 15: 8 (Is 1: 13). ταῦτα Dg 2: 9. ἀ. μου μικρόν τι ἀφροσύνης *put up w. a little foolishness from me* 2 Cor 11: 1a (Ltzm. ad loc.—Appian, Bell. Civ. 1, 103 §480 ἀνέχεσθαι=be pleased with something, consent). ἐν ταῖς θλίψεσιν αἷς ἀνέχεσθε *in the trials which you endure* (αἷς can be attraction for ἅς as well as for ὧν, cf. W-S §24, 4e; Rob. 716) 2 Th 1: 4.

c. abs.; but the obj. is easily supplied fr. the context (Vi. Aesopi Ic3; Is 42: 14; Job 6: 11) *forbear, put up with*

Dg 9: 1f. διωκόμενοι ἀνεχόμεθα when we are persecuted we endure it 1 Cor 4: 12 (use w. ptc. is quite common Thu.+; cf. e.g. Epict. Index Schenkl). W. adv. καλῶς ἀνέχεσθε you put up with it quite easily 2 Cor 11: 4 (cf. εὖ ἀ. PAmh. 3a II, 14 and s. καλῶς 5 [lit.]). W. εἰ foll. 11: 20.

2. endure, in the sense hear or listen to willingly, put up with w. gen. (Synes., Prov. 2, 6 p. 226c ἀνέχεσθαι φαύλων εἰκόνων =put up with poor pictures; Philo, Omn. Prob. Lib. 36; Jos., C. Ap. 2, 126) τ. λόγου τ. παρακλήσεως listen willingly to the word of exhortation Hb 13: 22. τῆς ὑγιαινούσης διδασκαλίας 2 Ti 4: 3. W. acc. (Appian, Bell. Civ. 2, 63 §264 Καῖσαρ οὐδὲ τοῦτ' ἀνασχόμενος; Job 6: 26; Jos., Ant. 19: 12) ὀλίγα μου ῥήματα ἔτι ἀνάσχου put up w. a few more words from me Hm 4, 2, 1.—Legal t.t. accept a complaint κατὰ λόγον ἂν ἀνεσχόμην ὑμῶν I would have been justified in accepting your complaint Ac 18: 14. M-M.*

ἀνεψιός, οῦ, ὁ (Hom.+) cousin (IG IV² 1, 693, 4 [III AD]; Wadd. 2053c; PLond. 1164κ, 20; PTebt. 323, 13; Sb 176 ἀ. πρὸς πατρός; Num 36: 11; Tob 7: 2; Philo, Leg. ad Gai. 67; Jos., Bell. 1, 662, Ant. 1, 290; 15, 250 al.) Μᾶρκος ὁ ἀ. Βαρναβᾶ Col 4: 10. Cf. JKalitsunakis, Mittel- u. neugriech. Erklärungen bei Eustathius '19, 42ff. M-M. B. 116; 118.*

ἀνέῳγα, ἀνέῳξα s. ἀνοίγω.

ἀνήγαγον s. ἀνάγω.

ἀνήγγειλα, ἀνηγγέλην s. ἀναγγέλλω.

ἄνηθον, ου, τό (since Aristoph., Nub. 982; Theocr. 15, 119; Dit., Syll.³ 1170, 26; pap.) dill, a plant used for seasoning, w. ἡ δύοσμον and πρὸς κύμινον (s. Hippiatr. II 164, 13 πήγανον, κύμινον, ἄνηθον), acc. to rabb. tradition (Maaseroth 4, 5) subject to the tithe Mt 23: 23; Lk 11: 42 𝔓⁴⁵ et al. Gdspd, Probs. 37f. M-M.*

ἀνῆκα s. ἀνίημι.

ἀνήκω (Soph., Hdt.+; inscr., pap., LXX).
1. refer, relate, belong εἴς τι to someth. (Demosth. 60, 6; Dit., Syll.³ 589, 63 ἀ ἀνήκει εἰς τ. τροφήν; 742, 15; BGU 1120, 32 [I BC]; Sir Prol. l. 12; Jos., Ant. 4, 198) διακονία εἰς τὸ κοινὸν ἀνήκουσα a service related to the church, a service to the church IPhld 1: 1. τὰ ἀνήκοντα εἰς τ. ἐκκλησίαν what concerns the church ISm 8: 1. τὰ ἀ. εἰς σωτηρίαν what relates to salvation 1 Cl 45: 1; B 17: 1. οἰκοδομὴ εἰς τ. κύριον ἡμῶν ἀνήκουσα edification that pertains to our Lord Pol 13: 2. Instead of the prep., τινί to someth. (BGU 300, 7; 638, 14 al.) τὰ ἀ. τῇ θρησκείᾳ ἡμῶν what pertains to our religion 1 Cl 62: 1. τὰ ἀ. τῇ βουλήσει θεοῦ what is in harmony w. God's will 35: 5. εὐποιΐα θεῷ ἀνήκουσα a good deed which concerns God IPol 7: 3. τὰ ἀ. ταῖς ψυχαῖς what your souls need D 16: 2. παραβολὴ ἀνήκουσα τῇ νηστείᾳ a parable that has to do w. fasting Hs 5, 2, 1.
2. impers. (Nägeli 48; Thieme 15) ἀνήκει it is proper, fitting (Ael. Dion. α, 138 ἀνήκει· Ἀντιφῶν [fgm. 103 Blass] ἀντὶ τοῦ καθήκει; BGU 417, 17 ὅτι καὶ σοὶ τοῦτο ἀνήκει καὶ συμφέρει; 1 Macc 10: 42) ὡς ἀνῆκεν as is fitting Col 3: 18 (on the use of the impf. Bl-D. §358, 2; Rob. 920; Mlt.-Turner 90f, but s. Lohmeyer ad loc.). ἃ οὐκ ἀνῆκεν Eph 5: 4 (τὰ οὐκ ἀνήκοντα t.r.). τὸ ἀνῆκον what is proper, one's duty (Inschr. v. Magn. 53, 65 [III BC] τὰ ἀνήκοντα τῇ πόλει what one owes the city; PFay. 94; PTebt. 6, 41; 1 Macc 11: 35; 2 Macc 14: 8) ἐπιτάσσειν σοι τὸ ἀνῆκον order you (to do) your duty Phlm 8. τὰ

ἀνήκοντα τῇ ἀρχῇ what belongs to the authorities UGosp 1. 49. M-M.*

ἀνήμερος, ον (since Anacr. 1, 7; Epict. 1, 3, 7; Dio Chrys. 11[12], 51; Aelian, N.A. 15, 25; Ep. Arist. 289; Philo et al. [Nägeli 16; 25]) savage, brutal, lit. untamed, w. other undesirable qualities 2 Ti 3: 3. M-M.*

ἀνήνεγκον s. ἀναφέρω.

ἀνήρ, ἀνδρός, ὁ (Hom.+, common in all the mngs. known to our lit. and LXX) man.
1. in contrast to woman (Pla., Gorg. 514E; X., Hell. 4, 5, 5; Dio Chrys. 1, 14; Ex 21: 29; 35: 22, 29 and oft.; Philo, Abr. 137) Mt 14: 21; 15: 38; Mk 6: 44; Lk 9: 14; J 1: 13; Ac 4: 4; 8: 3, 12; 1 Cor 11: 3, 7ff; Hm 5, 2, 2; 6, 2, 7; 12, 2, 1 and oft. Hence ἄνδρα γινώσκειν (אִישׁ יָדְעָה Gen 19: 8; Judg 11: 39) of a woman have sexual intercourse w. a man Lk 1: 34. Esp. husband (Hom.+; Diod. S. 2, 8, 6; Sir 4: 10; Jos., Ant. 18, 149) Mt 1: 16, 19; Mk 10: 2, 12; Lk 2: 36; J 4: 16ff; Ac 5: 9f; Ro 7: 2f (Sb 8010, 21 [pap. I AD] μέχρι οὗ ἐὰν συνέρχωμαι ἑτέρῳ ἀνδρί; PLond. 1731, 16 [VI AD] κολλᾶσθαι ἑτέρῳ ἀνδρί); 1 Cor 7: 2ff, 10ff; 14: 35; Gal 4: 27; Eph 5: 22ff; Col 3: 18f; 1 Ti 3: 2, 12; 5: 9; Tit 1: 6 (on the four last ref. εἷς 2b, the comm. and JFischer, Weidenauer Studien 1, '06, 177-226; comparison w. non-Christian sources in J-BFrey, Signification des termes μονάνδρα et Univira: Rech de Sc rel 20, '30, 48-60; GDelling, Pls' Stellung z. Frau u. Ehe '31, 136ff; BS Easton, Past. Epistles, '47, 216ff; WASchulze, Kerygma und Dogma [Göttingen] 4, '58, 287-300) 2: 5; 1 Pt 3: 1, 5, 7; Hm 4, 1, 4ff; 1 Cl 6: 3; Pol 4: 2.—1 Ti 2: 12 (cf. Ocellus Luc. c. 49: the wife wishes ἄρχειν τοῦ ἀνδρὸς παρὰ τὸν τῆς φύσεως νόμον). Even a bridegroom can be so called (cf. אִישׁ Dt 22: 23) ὡς νύμφην κεκοσμημένην τῷ ἀνδρὶ αὐτῆς Rv 21: 2. Freq. in address: ἄνδρες men, gentlemen (X., An. 1, 4, 14; 1 Esdr 3: 18; 4: 14, 34) Ac 14: 15; 19: 25; 27: 10, 21, 25. ἄνδρες ἀδελφοί brethren (4 Macc 8: 19; cf. X., An. 1, 6, 6 ἄ. φίλοι) Ac 15: 7, 13; 23: 1, 6; 28: 17; 1 Cl 14: 1; 37: 1; 43: 4; 62: 1. ἀ. ἀδελφοὶ καὶ πατέρες Ac 7: 2. Of soldiers (1 Macc 5: 17; 16: 15) οἱ ἄ. οἱ συνέχοντες αὐτόν the men who were holding him Lk 22: 63.—But cf. Ac 17: 34, where ἀνήρ=ἄνθρωπος.
2. man in contrast to boy (Tob 1: 9) ὅτε γέγονα ἀ. when I became a man 1 Cor 13: 11. ἀ. τέλειος a full-grown man (X., Cyr. 1, 2, 4) Eph 4: 13; in eth. sense perfect Js 3: 2.
3. used w. a word indicating national or local origin, calling attention to a single individual, or even individualizing the pl.; hence in address (X., An. 1, 7, 3 ὦ ἄ. Ἕλληνες; Jdth 4: 9; 15: 13; 1 Macc 2: 23); the sg. is omitted in transl., the pl. rendered men, gentlemen of a certain place: ἀνὴρ Αἰθίοψ Ac 8: 27 (X., An. 1, 8, 1 ἀ. Πέρσης; Palaeph. 5; Maximus Tyr. 5, 1a ἀ. Φρύξ). ἄ. Ἀθηναῖοι (Lysias 6, 8) 17: 22; ἄ. Γαλιλαῖοι 1, 11; ἄ. Ἐφέσιοι 19: 35; ἀ. Ἰουδαῖος 10: 28; ἄ. Ἰουδαῖοι (Jos., Ant. 11, 169) 2: 14; ἄ. Ἰσραηλῖται (Jos., Ant. 3, 189) 2: 22; 5: 35; 13: 16; 21: 28; ἄ. Κύπριοι καὶ Κυρηναῖοι 11: 20; ἀ. Μακεδών 16: 9. (Cf. Bl-D. §242).
4. used w. adj. to emphasize the dominant characteristic of a man: ἀ. ἀγαθός Ac 11: 24; ἀ. ἀγαθὸς καὶ δίκαιος Lk 23: 50; δεδοκιμασμένοι ἄ. 1 Cl 44: 2; δίκαιος Hm 4, 1, 3; 11, 9, 13f; δίκαιος καὶ ἅγιος Mk 6: 20; ἀ. δίψυχος, ἀκατάστατος Js 1: 8; ἀ. ἐλλόγιμος 1 Cl 44: 3; ἀ. εὔδοξος Hv 5: 1; ἀ. εὐλαβής Ac 8: 2; 22: 12; ἀ. λόγιος 18: 24; ἀ. μεμαρτυρημένος IPhld 11: 1; ἀ. πιστὸς καὶ ἐλλογιμώτατος 1 Cl 62: 3; ἀ. πονηρός Ac 17: 5; ἀ. πραΰς D 15: 1; ἀ. συνετός Ac 13: 7; ἀ. φρόνιμος Mt 7: 24; ἀ. μωρός vs. 26.—Oft. in circumlocutions for nouns ἀ. πλήρης λέπρας =a leper (in serious condition) Lk 5: 12; cf. οἱ ἄνδρες τοῦ

τόπου (Gen 26: 7) Mt 14: 35; ἀ. πλήρης πίστεως Ac 6: 5, 11: 24. In such combinations as ἀ. ἁμαρτωλός (Sir 12: 14; 27: 30 al.), ἀ. is wholly pleonastic (like Heb. אִישׁ) a sinner Lk 5: 8; 19: 7. Esp. is this true of noun combinations (Ps.-Pla., Axioch. 12 p. 371A ἀ. μάγος; Chio, Ep. 14, 4 ἀ. δεσπότης; Maximus Tyr. 19, 2a ποιμὴν ἀ.) ἀ. προφήτης (Judg 6: 8) a prophet 24: 19. ἀ. πρεσβύτης (s. πρεσβύτης) MPol 7: 2.

5. man w. special emphasis on manliness (Hom.+; Philostrat., Vi. Apoll. 1, 16 p. 17, 2) of the apostles 1 Cl 6: 1.

6. equiv. to τὶς someone (Theognis 1, 199 Diehl[2]; X., Cyr. 2, 2, 22; Sir 27: 7) Lk 9: 38; 19: 2; J 1: 30. Pl. some people (1 Macc 12: 1; 13: 34) Lk 5: 18; Ac 6: 11. ἀνήρ τις, where τις is pleonastic a man Lk 8: 27; Ac 10: 1. ἀνήρ ὅς Lat. is qui (like אִישׁ אֲשֶׁר; cf. 1 Macc 7: 7 and as early as Pind., Pyth. 9, 87 ἀνήρ τις ὅς . . .) Ro 4: 8 (Ps 31: 2); Js 1: 12. οἱ κατ᾿ ἄνδρα (Dio Chrys. 15[32], 6) man for man, individually IEph 4: 2 (but s. JAKleist, note ad loc., rank and file); 20: 2; ITr 13: 2; ISm 5: 1; 12: 2; IPol 1: 3.

7. a figure of a man of heavenly beings who resemble men (Or. Sib. 3, 137 the Titans are so called) GP 9: 36; 10: 39.

8. of Jesus as the judge of the world, appointed by God: ὁ θεὸς . . . μέλλει κρίνειν τὴν οἰκουμένην ἐν ἀνδρὶ ᾧ ὥρισεν Ac 17: 31 (cf. Oenomaus in Euseb., Pr. Ev. 5, 19, 3 Minos is the ἀνήρ, ὃν ἀποδεικνύναι ἐμέλλετε κοινὸν ἀνθρώπων δικαστήν=whom you [gods] intended to make the common judge of mankind). M-M. B. 81; 96.

ἀνῃρέθην s. ἀναιρέω.

ἀνήφθην s. ἀνάπτω.

ἀνήχθην s. ἀνάγω.

ἀνθέξομαι s. ἀντέχω.

ἀνθέω (Hom.+; LXX; Jos., Ant. 1, 171; 288; Test. Sim. 3: 3; 6: 2; Sib. Or. 4, 103) bloom τὴν γῆν ἀνθοῦσαν ἀμαράντοις ἄνθεσι blooming w. unfading flowers AP 5: 15 (w. the dat. ἄνθεσι as Hom. Hymn Ap. 139).*

ἀνθηρός, ά, όν (Soph.+; Cornutus 30 p. 59, 16; Longus 1, 15, 3) of hair splendid, brilliant AP 3: 10.*

ἀνθίστημι 2 aor. ἀντέστην; pf. ἀνθέστηκα; 1 aor. pass. ἀντεστάθην Hm 12, 2, 3 (Hom.+; pap., LXX; Jos., Bell. 7, 246, C. Ap. 2, 23 ἀνθίστασθαί τινι) set against; the forms occurring in our lit. have the mid. sense set oneself against, oppose, resist, withstand.

1. τινί someone (PGiess. 65, 9) Mt 5: 39; Ac 13: 8; κατὰ πρόσωπον αὐτῷ ἀντέστην (Dt 7: 24; 9: 2; 11: 25) I opposed him to his face Gal 2: 11; ἀ. Μωϋσεῖ 2 Ti 3: 8; ἀ. τῷ διαβόλῳ Js 4: 7; cf. 1 Pt 5: 9; Hm 12, 5, 2 and ἀ. ἀντιστήτω μοι let him oppose me B 6: 1 (Is 50: 8).

2. τινί used impers. τῇ σοφίᾳ Lk 21: 15; Ac 6: 10. τ. βουλήματι αὐτοῦ Ro 9: 19 (cf. Demosth. 18, 49 τοὺς ἀνθισταμένους τ. ὑμετέροις βουλήμασι). θεοῦ διαταγῇ 13: 2a. τῷ κράτει τῆς ἰσχύος αὐτοῦ 1 Cl 27: 5 (cf. Wsd 11: 21). τῇ ἀληθείᾳ 2 Ti 3: 8. τοῖς ἡμετέροις λόγοις 4: 15 (cf. Jdth 8: 28). ἐπιθυμίαις Hm 12, 2, 3f. ἀ. τῇ ὀξυχολίᾳ resist ill temper m 5, 2, 8.

3. abs. (BGU 747 II, 10; Esth 9: 2; 3 Macc 6: 19) ἵνα δυνηθῆτε ἀντιστῆναι that you might be able to stand your ground Eph 6: 13 (cf. PPetr. II 37, 2a 14 [III BC] οὐ δύναμαι ἀνθιστάνειν). ἀντιστῶμεν let us take a firm stand B 4: 9. οἱ ἀνθεστηκότες those who resist Ro 13: 2b (sc. τ. διαταγῇ). M-M.*

ἀνθομολογέομαι impf. ἀνθωμολογούμην (w. many mngs.

Demosth.+; pap., LXX; Jos., Ant. 8, 257; 362) praise, thank (publicly express: thanks Plut., Aemil. Paul. 11, 1; recognition: Diod. S. 1, 70) τῷ θεῷ (Ps 78: 13; Da 4: 37 [here alternating w. ἐξομολογοῦμαι; cf. Sir 17: 27, 28]; 3 Macc 6: 33) Lk 2: 38. M-M and suppl.*

ἄνθος, ους, τό (Hom.+; LXX; Philo, Aet. M. 64; Jos., Ant. 15, 394; 19, 192; Sib. Or. 5, 261).

1. blossom, flower specif., of a grape blossom 1 Cl 23: 4. Type of that which does not last (Quint. Smyrn. 14, 207 ἀνδρῶν γὰρ γένος ἐστὶν ὁμοῖιον ἄνθεσι ποίης=like the flowers of the grass; Aristaen., Ep. 2, 1 πέπαυται τὰ ἄνθη) ἀ. χόρτου wild flower Js 1: 10, cf. vs. 11. 1 Pt 1: 24ab (both Is 40: 6f). Colorful splendor AP 3: 10 (descr. of κόμη like Anacr., fgm. 46 Diehl.[2] Pap. from Chicago col. 3, 9f: Coll. p. 83). ἄ. ἀμάραντα unfading flowers 15.

2. fragrance of flowers AP 5: 16. M-M. B. 527.*

ἀνθρακιά, ᾶς, ἡ (Hom.+; Sir 11: 32; 4 Macc 9: 20) a charcoal fire ἀ. ποιεῖν make a ch. f. (PGM 4, 2468) J 18: 18. ἀ. κειμένη a charcoal fire on the ground 21: 9 (itala incensos=ἀ. καιομένη would mean: a pile of burning charcoal). For ἀνθ. used in preparing fish, and the connection with J 21: 9, cf. Creophylus of Ephesus [400 BC] No. 416 fgm. 1 Jac. ἁλιέας ἀριστοποιεῖσθαι . . . τῶν ἰχθύων . . . σὺν ἀνθρακιᾷ.*

ἄνθραξ, ακος, ὁ (Thu., Aristoph.+; inscr., pap., LXX, Ep. Arist., Philo) charcoal only in the proverb ἄνθρακας πυρὸς σωρεύειν ἐπὶ τὴν κεφαλήν τινος heap burning embers on someone's head Ro 12: 20, i.e., prob., cause him to blush w. shame and remorse (Pr 25: 22). Cf. A Wright, Interpreter 16, '20, 159. EJRoberts and FJarrat, ibid. 239; ATFryer, ET 36, '25, 478; SBartstra NThT 23, '34, 61-8; SMorenz, ThLZ 78, '53, 187-92; KStendahl, HTR 55, '62, 343-55, esp. 346-48 (Qumran); WKlassen, NTS 9, '63, 337-50. M-M.*

ἀνθρωπαρεσκέω (hapax legomenon) court the favor of men, be a man-pleaser οὐ θέλω ὑμᾶς ἀνθρωπαρεσκῆσαι IRo 2: 1 (cf. Gal 1: 10).*

ἀνθρωπάρεσκος, ον (Ps 52: 6; PsSol 4: 7, 8, 19; cf. Nägeli 61; ADebrunner, Griech. Wortbildungslehre, '17, 51) as subst., one who tries to please men at the sacrifice of principle, a men-pleaser Eph 6: 6; Col 3: 22. W. ἑαυτῷ ἀρέσκειν 2 Cl 13: 1 (WCvanUnnik, ZNW Beiheft 26, '60, 221-34). M-M.*

ἀνθρώπινος, η, ον (Pre-Socr., Hdt.+; inscr., pap., LXX, Philo; Jos., Ant. 8, 419 al.) human.

1. gener. (ἀνθρώπινόν τι πάσχειν=die: PPetr. I 11, 9ff; PGenève 21, 15; BGU 1149, 34; Dit., Syll.[3] 1042, 13) ἀ. ἔργα the deeds of men 1 Cl 59: 3; φόβοι ἀ. human fears i.e., such as man is heir to 2 Cl 10: 3; συνήθεια ἀ. IEph 5: 1; σάρξ ἀ. (Wsd 12: 5; Philo, Spec. Leg. 4, 103) IPhld 7: 2; πειρασμὸς ἀ. a temptation common to man (cf. Epict. 1, 9, 30, Ench. 26; Num 5: 6), i.e., bearable (Pollux 3, 27, 131 also mentions among the concepts which form a contrast to ὃ οὐκ ἄν τις ὑπομένειεν, the expr. τὸ ἀνθρώπινον) 1 Cor 10: 13. ἀνθρώπινον λέγειν speak in human terms i.e., as people do in daily life Ro 6: 19 (cf. Plut., Mor. 13c; Philo, Somn. 2, 288); ἀ. ὁ λόγος the saying is commonly accepted 1 Ti 3: 1 D, cf. 1: 15 v.l. (favored by Zahn, Einl. I 487; GWohlenberg ad loc.; EKühl, Erläuterung d. paul. Briefe II '09, 179; WLock, ICC ad loc. and Intr. xxxvi, 'true to human needs').

2. in contrast to animal (Diod. S. 3, 35, 5; Ezk 4: 15; Da 7: 4, 8) δεδάμασται τῇ φύσει τῇ ἀ. has been tamed by human nature or humankind Js 3: 7.

3. in contrast to the divine (Maximus Tyr. 38, 5e; Dit., Syll.³ 526, 29f [III вс]; 721, 33; 798, 10 [c. 37 AD]; Job 10: 5; 4 Macc 1: 16f; 4: 13; Jos., Bell. 6, 429) ἀ. μυστήρια (merely) *human secrets* Dg 7: 1. ὑπὸ χειρῶν ἀ. θεραπεύεται Ac 17: 25 (χ. ἀ. Jos., Bell. 5, 387; 400). ἀ. σοφία *human wisdom* (Philo, Rer. Div. Her. 126.—Jos., Ant. 3, 223 σύνεσις ἀ.) 1 Cor 2: 13 (t.r. also 2: 4). ἀ. ἡμέρα *a human court* 4: 3. πρόσκλισις ἀ. *human partiality* 1 Cl 50: 2. δόγμα ἀ. *human doctrine* Dg 5: 3. ἀ. κτίσις *human institution* of the authorities 1 Pt 2: 13. M-M.*

ἀνθρωπίνως adv. (Thu. et al., Jos., Ant. 19, 4) *as a man* θεοῦ ἀ. φανερουμένου *since God showed himself in human form* IEph 19: 3.*

ἀνθρωποκτόνος, ου, ὁ (quite rare: Eur., Cycl. 127, Iph. T. 389, both times as adj.; Ps.-Plut., De Fluv. 1165A; Nicetas Eugen. 8, 225H.) *murderer* of the one who hates his brother 1 J 3: 15 (cf. Mt 5: 21f). Of the devil ἀ. ἦν ἀπ᾽ ἀρχῆς *he was a murderer from the beginning,* not w. ref. to the murder of Abel, but to designate the devil as the one who brought death into the world by misleading Adam (Wsd 2: 24) J 8: 44. M-M.*

ἀνθρωπόμορφος, ον (Epicur., fgm. 353 Us. θεός; [acc. to Diod. S. 40, 3, 4 Moses refused to believe in a θ. ἀνθρωπόμορφος]; Diod. S. 3, 62, 2 [Dionysus]; 22, 9, 4 θεοὶ ἀ.; Strabo 16, 2, 35 τὸ θεῖον; Cornutus 27 p. 49, 7; Diog. L.; Plut., Mor. 149c; 167D; Philo, Op. M. 69) *in human form* θηρία ἀ. *wild beasts in human form* (Philo, Abr. 33) of heretics ISm 4: 1.*

ἀνθρωποποίητος, ον *man-made* προσφορὰ ἀ. *an offering made by man* B 2: 6.*

ἄνθρωπος, ου, ὁ (Hom.+; inscr., pap., LXX, En., Ep. Arist., Philo, Joseph., Test. 12 Patr.; loanw. in rabb.) *human being, man.*

1. gener.—**a.** as a class—α. ἐγεννήθη ἄ. J 16: 21; εἰς χεῖρας ἀ. Mk 9: 31; ψυχὴ ἀνθρώπου Ro 2: 9; συνείδησις ἀ. 2 Cor 4: 2; μέτρον ἀ. Rv 21: 17.
β. in contrast to animals, plants, etc. Mt 4: 19; 12: 12; Mk 1: 17; Lk 5: 10; 1 Cor 15: 39; 2 Pt 2: 16; Rv 9: 4, 7; 13: 18 al. To angels (cf. Aristaen. 1, 24, end σάτυροι οὐκ ἄνθρωποι) 1 Cor 4: 9; 13: 1. To God (Aeschyl., Ag. 663 θεός τις οὐκ ἄνθ.; Aeschines 3, 137 θεοὶ κ. δαίμονες; Ael. Aristid. 30 p. 578 D.; Herm. Wr. 14, 8 θεοὺς κ. ἀνθρ.) Hb 13: 6 (Ps 117: 6); Mt 10: 32f; 19: 6; Mk 10: 9; J 10: 33 (ἄνθ. ὤν = 'as a mortal man' is a favorite formula: X., An. 7, 6, 11; Menand., Epitr. 528, fgm. 51; 460, 2; 549, 1; Alexis Com., fgm. 150; Polyb. 3, 31, 3; Charito 4, 4, 8 [WEBlake '38]; Heliod. 6, 9, 3; As early as Eur., Hipp. 472ff ἄνθρωπος οὖσα...κρείσσω δαιμόνων εἶναι θέλειν); Ac 10: 26; 12: 22; 14: 11, 15; 1 Th 2: 13; Phil 2: 7. ἐντάλματα ἀνθρώπων *precepts of men* Mt 15: 9; Mk 7: 7; (Is 29: 13); w. οὐρανός (=God) Mt 21: 25; Mk 11: 30. ἀδύνατα παρὰ ἀνθρώποις Lk 18: 27, cf. Mt 19: 26. δοῦλοι ἀνθρώπων *slaves to men* 1 Cor 7: 23. πείθειν and ἀρέσκειν ἀ. Gal 1: 10. μεσίτης θεοῦ καὶ ἀ. 1 Ti 2: 5 al. θεὸς πάντας ἀνθρώπους θέλει σωθῆναι 1 Ti 2: 4 (cf. Epict. 3, 24, 2 ὁ θεὸς πάντας ἀνθρώπους ἐπὶ τὸ εὐδαιμονεῖν ἐποίησεν).
γ. in address ἄνθρωπε *friend* (X., Cyr. 2, 2, 7; Plut., Mor. 553E) indicating a close relationship between the speaker and the one addressed Lk 5: 20. W. a reproachful connotation, *man!* (Diogenes the Cynic in Diog. L. 6, 56; Diod. S. 33, 7, 4; Charito 6, 7, 9; Ps.-Callisth. 1, 31, 1) 12: 14; 22: 58, 60. Also in rhetorical address, in a letter Ro 2: 1, 3; 9: 20 (Pla., Gorg. 452в σὺ δὲ . . . τίς εἶ, ὦ ἄνθρωπε); Js 2: 20. (Cf. Pla., Apol. 16 p. 28в; Epict. Index Schenkl; Mi 6: 8; Ps 54: 14.—JWackernagel, Über einige antike Anredeformen: Progr. Gött. '12).

δ. in pl. w. gener. mng. οἱ ἄ. *people,* also one's *fellow men* (Jos., Ant. 9, 28) Mt 5: 13, 16; 6: 1f, 5, 14, 18; 7: 12; 8: 27; 23: 5; Mk 8: 27 and very oft. οἱ τότε ἄ. *the people of that time* Pol 3: 2.—οἱ υἱοὶ τῶν ἀνθρώπων *the sons of men* (Gen 11: 5; 1 Esdr 4: 37; Ps 10: 4) Mk 3: 28; Eph 3: 5.
b. as a physical being Js 5: 17; subject to death Hb 9: 27; Rv 8: 11; Ro 5: 12; sunken in sin (Menand., fgm. 499 K. ἄνθρωπος ὢν ἥμαρτον; Herodas 5, 27 ἄνθρωπός εἰμι, ἥμαρτον; schol. on Apollon. Rhod. 4, 1015–17a σὺ ἄνθρωπος εἶ, οἷς τὸ ἁμαρτάνειν γίνεται ῥαδίως) 5: 18f al., hence judged to be inferior Gal 1: 1, 11f; Col 2: 8, 22 (Is 29: 13) or even carefully to be avoided προσέχειν ἀπὸ τ. ἀ. *beware of* (evil) *men* Mt 10: 17; cf. Lk 6: 22, 26.
c. κατὰ ἄνθρωπον (Aeschyl., Sept. 425; Pla., Phileb. 370F; Diod. S. 16, 11, 2; Athen. 10 p. 444в; Plut., Mor. 1042A; Witkowski 8, 5 [252 вс]) *in a human way, from a human standpoint* emphasizes the inferiority of man in comparison w. God; λαλεῖν 1 Cor 9: 8; λέγειν Ro 3: 5; Gal 3: 15; περιπατεῖν 1 Cor 3: 3. κ. ἄ. ἐθηριομάχησα perh. *like an ordinary man* (opp. as a Christian sure of the resurrection) 15: 32. Of the gospel οὐκ ἔστιν κ. ἄ. Gal 1: 11. Pl. κ. ἀνθρώπους (opp. κ. θεόν) 1 Pt 4: 6.
2. in special combinations and mngs.
a. w. gen. ἄνθρωποι εὐδοκίας Lk 2: 14 (εὐδοκία 1). ὁ ἄ. τῆς ἀνομίας (v.l. ἁμαρτίας) 2 Th 2: 3. ἄ. (τοῦ) θεοῦ *man of God* 1 Ti 6: 11; 2 Ti 3: 17; 2 Pt 1: 21 t.r. (3 Km 12: 22; 13: 1; 17: 24; 4 Km 1: 9ff; 2 Ch 8: 14 al.; Ep. Arist. 140; Philo, Gig. 61, Deus Imm. 138f. But also Sextus 2; 3; Herm. Wr. 1, 32; 13, 20; PGM 4, 1177, where no comma is needed betw. ἄ. and θ.).
b. the context requires such mngs. as—α. *man,* adult male (Pla., Prot. 6 p. 314E, Phaedo 66 p. 117E) Mt 11: 8; Lk 7: 25. σκληρὸς εἶ ἄ. Mt 25: 24; cf. Lk 19: 21f. In contrast to woman (Achilles Tat. 5, 22, 2; PGM 36, 225f; 1 Esdr 9: 40; Tob 6: 8) Mt 19: 5; Eph 5: 31 (both Gen 2: 24); 1 Cor 7: 1; GOxy l. 39.—β. *husband* Mt 19: 10.—γ. *son,* opp. father (Sir 3: 11) Mt 10: 35.—δ. *slave* (X., Mem. 2, 1, 15, Vect. 4, 14; Herodas 5, 78; BGU 830, 4; POxy. 1067, 30; 1159, 16) Lk 12: 36. οἱ τοῦ πυρὸς ἄ. *the slaves in charge of the fire* MPol 15: 1.—ε. *a human figure* of a heavenly being that looked like a person GP 11: 44.
c. Pauline and Post-Pauline thought differentiates betw. var. aspects of man:
α. betw. the two sides of human nature as ὁ ἔξω ἄ. *the outer man,* i.e., man in his material, transitory, and sinful aspects 2 Cor 4: 16, and, on the other hand, ὁ ἔσω ἄ. *the inner man,* i.e., man in his spiritual, immortal aspects, striving toward God Ro 7: 22; 2 Cor 4: 16; Eph 3: 16 (cf. Pla., Rep. 9, 589A ὁ ἐντὸς ἄνθρωπος; Plotinus, Enn. 5, 1, 10 ὁ εἴσω ἄ.; Philo, Plant. 42 ὁ ἐν ἡμῖν πρὸς ἀλήθειαν ἄ., τουτέστιν ὁ νοῦς, Congr. Erud. Grat. 97, Det. Pot. Insid. 23; Zosimus in Rtzst., Poim. 104 ἔσω αὐτοῦ ἄνθρωπος πνευματικός. Cf. Rtzst., Mysterienrel.³ 354f; WGutbrod, D. paulin. Anthropologie '34; KTSchäfer, FTillmann-Festschr. '34, 25–35; RJewett, Paul's Anthropological Terms, '71, 391–401). Similar in mng. is ὁ κρυπτὸς τῆς καρδίας ἄ. *the hidden man of the heart*=ὁ ἔσω ἄ. 1 Pt 3: 4.
β. from another viewpoint, betw. παλαιὸς and καινὸς (νέος) ἄ. Ro 6: 6; Eph 4: 22, 24; Col 3: 9 (cf. Dg 2: 1; Jesus as καινὸς ἄ. IEph 20: 1 is the *new man,* who is really God), or betw. ὁ ψυχικὸς ἄ. and ὁ πνευματικὸς ἄ. 1 Cor 2: 14f (cf. πνευματικός 2aγ).
d. Jesus Christ is called ἄ. 1 Ti 2: 5; Hb 2: 6a (Ps 8: 5a).

He is opp. to Adam Ro 5: 15; 1 Cor 15: 21, the πρῶτος ἄ. 1 Cor 15: 45, 47 (cf. Philo, Abr. 56) as δεύτερος ἄ. vs. 47. On the nature and origin of this concept cf. Ltzm. and JWeiss on 1 Cor 15: 45ff; WBousset, Kyrios Christos² '21, 120ff, Jesus der Herr '16, 67ff; Rtzst., Mysterienrel.³ 343ff, Erlösungsmyst. 107ff; AEJRawlinson, The NT Doctrine of the Christ '26, 124ff; BAStegmann, Christ, the 'Man from Heaven', a Study of 1 Cor 15: 45-7: The Cath. Univ., Washington '27; CHKraeling, Anthropos and Son of Man '27. S. on Ἀδάμ and on οὐρανός 2b.—On ὁ υἱὸς τοῦ ἀ. as a self-designation of Jesus s. υἱός 2c.

3. almost equiv. to the indef. pron., w. the basic mng. of ἄ. greatly weakened.

a. without the art.—α. used w. τις: ἐὰν γένηταί τινι ἀνθρώπῳ Mt 18: 12. ἄνθρωπός τις κατέβαινεν a man was going down Lk 10: 30. ἀνθρώπου τινὸς πλουσίου 12: 16. ἄ. τις ἦν ὑδρωπικός 14: 2, cf. vs. 16; 15: 11; 16: 1, 19: 12. ἦν τις ἄ. ἐκεῖ J 5: 5. τινῶν ἀ. αἱ ἁμαρτίαι 1 Ti 5: 24.

β. without τις, and somet. nearly equiv. to it (Paus. 5, 7, 3 ἐξ ἀνθρώπου=from someone) εἷς ἄ.=εἷς τις an individual J 11: 50, cf. 18: 14. εἶδεν ἄνθρωπον καθήμενον he saw a man sitting Mt 9: 9. λαβὼν ἄ. a man took 13: 31; cf. Mk 1: 23; 3: 1; 4: 26; 5: 2; 7: 11; 10: 7 (Gen 2: 24); Lk 2: 25; 4: 33; 5: 18; 6: 48f; 13: 19; J 3: 4, 27 al. Used w. negatives ἄ. οὐκ ἔχω I have nobody J 5: 7. οὐδέποτε ἐλάλησεν οὕτως ἄ. nobody has ever spoken thus (no [mere] man has ever spoken thus is also poss.) 7: 46.

γ. in indef. and at the same time general sense, oft.= one (Ger. man, Fr. on) οὕτως ἡμᾶς λογιζέσθω ἄ. lit. this is how one (i.e., you) should regard us 1 Cor 4: 1; cf. Mt 16: 26; Ro 3: 28; 1 Cor 7: 26; 11: 28; Gal 2: 16; 6: 7; Js 2: 24.

δ. w. relative foll. ἴδετε ἄ. ὃς εἶπέν μοι see a man who told me J 4: 29. ἄ., ὃς τὴν ἀλήθειαν ὑμῖν λελάληκα 8: 40. ὁ ἄ., ἐν ᾧ ἦν τὸ πνεῦμα τὸ πονηρόν Ac 19: 16.

ε. used pleonastically w. a noun (Il. 16, 263; Lev 21: 9; Sir 8: 1; 1 Macc 7: 14) ἄ. φάγος a glutton Mt 11: 19; Lk 7: 34; ἄ. ἔμπορος a merchant Mt 13: 45 v.l.; ἄ. οἰκοδεσπότης vs. 52; 21: 33; ἄ. βασιλεύς (Horapollo 2, 85; Jos., Ant. 6, 142) 18: 23; 22: 2.—Likew. w. names indicating local or national origin (X., An. 6, 4, 23; Ex 2: 11 ἄ. Αἰγύπτιος) ἄ. Κυρηναῖος a Cyrenaean 27: 32; ἄ. Ἰουδαῖος Ac 21: 39; ἄ. Ῥωμαῖος 16: 37; 22: 25. W. adj., giving them the character of nouns (Menand., fgm. 630 ἄ. φίλος; PFlor. 61, 60; PAmh. 78, 13 ἄ. αὐθάδης; PStrassb. 41, 40 πρεσβύτης ἄ. εἰμι; Sir 8: 2 and al.) ἄ. τυφλός (EpJer 36) a blind man J 9: 1; ἄ. ἁμαρτωλός (Sir 11: 32; 32: 17) vs. 16; ἄ. αἱρετικός Tit 3: 10. Likew. w. ptc. ἄ. σπείρων a sower Mt 13: 24.

ζ. pleonastic are also the combinations τίς ἄ.; who? Mt 7: 9; Lk 15: 4; πᾶς ἄ. everyone J 2: 10; Js 1: 19; πάντες ἄ. all men Ac 22: 15, everyone 1 Cor 7: 7; εἷς ἄ. J 11: 50; δύο ἄ. Lk 18: 10. Likew. the partitive gen. ἀνθρώπων w. οὐδείς (cf. Mimnermus 1, 15f Diehl² οὐ δέ τίς ἐστιν ἀνθρώπων) Mk 11: 2; Lk 19: 30, μηδείς Ac 4: 17, τίς 19: 35; 1 Cor 2: 11.—MBlack, An Aramaic Approach³, '67, 106f.

b. w. the generic art. (Wsd 2: 23; 4 Macc 2: 21) ὁ ἀγαθὸς ἄ. the good man, opp. ὁ πονηρὸς ἄ. the evil man Mt 12: 35. οὐκ ἐπ' ἄρτῳ ζήσεται ὁ ἄ. no one can live on bread (Dt 8: 3) 4: 4. κοινοῖ τὸν ἄ. defiles a person 15: 11, 18; cf. Mk 7: 15, 20; τὸ σάββατον διὰ τὸν ἄ. ἐγένετο 2: 27; τί ἦν ἐν τῷ ἀ. J 2: 25; κρίνειν τὸν ἄ. 7: 51; ὁ νόμος κυριεύει τοῦ ἀ. Ro 7: 1; ὁ ποιήσας ἄ. everyone who does it 10: 5 (Lev 18: 5; 2 Esdr 19 [Neh 9]: 29); κακὸν τῷ ἀ. τῷ διὰ προσκόμματος ἐσθίοντι wrong for everyone who eats w. misgivings Ro 14: 20 al.

4. w. the art., ἄ. designates—

a. the person who has just been mentioned (Diod. S. 37, 18 ὁ ἄνθ. εἶπε) Mt 12: 13; Mk 3: 5; 5: 8; J 4: 50 al.

b. a certain person, w. a connotation of contempt (Diogenianus Epicureus [II AD] in Euseb., Pr. Ev. 6, 8, 30 calls Chrysippus, his opponent, contemptuously ὁ ἄνθ.; Artem. 5, 67 ἡ ἄνθρωπος of a prostitute; UPZ 72, 6 [152 BC]; BGU 1208 I, 25; Plut., Mor 870c.—ASvensson [ὁ, ἡ, τό beg.]; AWilhelm, Anzeigen der Ak. d. W. in Wien, phil.-hist. Kl. '37 [XXIII-XXVI 83-6]) οὐκ οἶδα τὸν ἄ. I don't know the fellow (of Jesus, as oft. in these exx.) Mt 26: 72, 74; Mk 14: 71. προσηνέγκατέ μοι τὸν ἄ. τοῦτον Lk 23: 14. εἰ ὁ ἄ. Γαλιλαῖός ἐστιν vs. 6. τίς ἐστιν ὁ ἄ. J 5: 12. ἰδοὺ ὁ ἄ. here is the man! 19: 5 (on the attempt to arouse pity, cf. Nicol. Dam.: 90 fgm. 68, 4 Jac. Cyrus in connection w. the downfall of Croesus; Diog. L. 2: 13 Pericles in the interest of Anaxagoras, his teacher; Jos., Ant. 19, 35f). μὴ οἰέσθω ὁ ἄ. ἐκεῖνος such a person must not expect Js 1: 7.—JMNielen, D. Mensch in der Verkünd. der Ev.: FTillmann-Festschr. '34, 14-24; Gutbrod op. cit. 2cα; WGKümmel, Man in the NT, tr. JJVincent, '63. M.-M. B. 80.

ἀνθυπατεύω (Plut., Cic. 52, 7; Herodian 7, 5, 2; Dit., Or. 517, 10) be proconsul Ac 18: 12 t.r. ἀνθυπατεύοντος Στατίου Κοδράτου when Statius Quadratus was proconsul MPol 21.*

ἀνθύπατος, ου, ὁ (Polyb.+; freq. in lit.; Jos., Ant. 14, 236; 244 al.; inscr., pap.) proconsul, head of the govt. in a senatorial province (cf. Hahn 39f; 115; 259, w. lit.). Those mentioned are the proconsul of Cyprus, Sergius Paulus Ac 13: 7, cf. vss. 8 and 12; of Achaia, Gallio 18: 12; cf. 19: 38; of Asia MPol 3f; 9: 2, 3 FL; 10: 2; 11: 1; 12: 1. M.-M.*

ἀνίατος, ον (Hippocr., Pla.+; IG III add. 171a.; pap., LXX; Jos., Ant. 19, 325 [adv.]) incurable only fig. (Aeschines 3, 156 κακά; Test. Reub. 6: 3) ἁμαρτία μεγάλη καὶ ἀ. a great and unforgivable sin Hm 5, 2, 4 (cf. Philo, Somn. 1, 87 τὰ ἀνίατα τ. ἁμαρτημάτων; Pla., Gorg. 525c διὰ τοιαῦτα ἀδικήματα ἀνίατοι).*

ἀνίημι 1 aor. ἀνῆκα; 2 aor. subj. ἀνῶ, ptc. ἀνείς; 1 aor. pass. ἀνέθην (no augm., Bl-D. §67, 2 app.) (Hom.+; inscr., pap., LXX, Joseph.; cf. Nägeli 16; 20).

1. loosen, unfasten of chains (Od. 8, 359; Callim., Hec. 1, 2, 13 δεσμά; Plut., Alex. M. 73, 9 τοὺς δεσμούς) πάντων τὰ δεσμὰ ἀνέθη Ac 16: 26. Of ropes ἀ. τὰς ζευκτηρίας 27: 40.

2. abandon, desert τινά someone οὐ μή σε ἀνῶ (word for word like Philo, Conf. Lingu. 166; cf. PKatz, Biblica 33, '52, 523-25) I will never desert you Hb 13: 5.

3. give up, cease from τι someth. (Thu. 3, 10, 4; Plut., Alex. M. 70, 6 τὴν ὀργήν; Jos., Ant. 14, 286) ἀ. τὴν ἀπειλήν give up threatening Eph 6: 9. M.-M.*

ἀνίλεως, gen. ω merciless (Herodian, Epim. 257 Boiss.; Test. Gad 5: 11) κρίσις Js 2: 13 t.r. (v.l. for ἀνέλεος, q.v.).*

ἀνίπταμαι (Maximus Tyr. 20, 6d; Cass. Dio 56, 42, 3; Themist. 27 p. 406, 11; Cyranides 3 p. 100, 11; on the form [for ἀναπέτομαι] Kühner-Bl. II 450) fly up, flutter about νοσσοὶ ἀνιπτάμενοι B 11: 3 (Is 16: 2).*

ἄνιπτος, ον (Hom.+) unwashed χεῖρες (Il. 6, 266; Philo, Spec. Leg. 2, 6) Mt 15: 20. κοιναῖς χερσίν, τουτέστιν ἀνίπτοις Mk 7: 2, 5 t.r. Acc. to a rabb. rule, going beyond the Torah, it was necessary to wash one's hands before a meal; see Schürer II⁴ 565.*

ἀνίστημι fut. ἀναστήσω; 1 aor. ἀνέστησα; 2 aor. ἀνέστην, imper. ἀνάστηθι and ἀνάστα Eph 5: 14; Ac 12: 7 (9: 11; 11: 7 v.l.), ptc. ἀναστάς, Bl-D. §95, 3; fut. mid. ἀναστήσομαι (Hom.+; inscr., pap., LXX, En., Philo, Joseph., Test. 12 Patr.).

1. trans. (fut. and 1 aor. act) *raise, erect, raise up* (oft. of statues. Dit., Syll.³ 867, 68; 1073, 45; BGU 362 VI, 4).

a. lit. of idols PK 2 p. 14, 16.—Of one lying down (Artem. 2, 37 p. 139, 23 τοὺς νοσοῦντας ἀνίστησιν; Jos., Ant. 7, 193) δοὺς αὐτῇ χεῖρα ἀνέστησεν αὐτήν *he gave her his hand and raised her up* Ac 9: 41; esp. of the dead *raise up, bring to life* (Ps.-X., Cyn. 1, 6; Paus. 2, 26, 5 [Asclepius] ἀνίστησι τεθνεῶτας; Ael. Aristid. 45, 29 K.= 8 p. 95 D.: [Sarapis] κειμένους ἀνέστησεν; Palaeph. p. 35, 8; Himerius, Or. [Ecl.] 5, 32; 2 Macc 7: 9) J 6: 39f, 44, 54; in full ἀ. ἐκ νεκρῶν Ac 13: 34 (Herodas 1, 43 ἐκ νερτέρων ἀνίστημί τινα). Esp. of Jesus' resurrection Ac 2: 24, 32; 3: 26; 13: 33f; 17: 31. Ign. says of Jesus ἀνέστησεν ἑαυτόν Sm 2 (cf. Theodore Prodr. 5, 88H. ἂν . . . ἑαυτὸν αὐτὸς ἐξαναστήσῃ πάλιν).

b. fig. *raise up* in the sense *cause to appear* or *be born* (Plut., Marcell. 27, 2; Synes., Ep. 67 p. 210c; EpJer 52) προφήτην ὑμῖν Ac 3: 22 (after Dt 18: 15); σπέρμα τῷ ἀδελφῷ *children for his brother* Mt 22: 24 (Gen 38: 8) w. ref. to levirate marriage.

c. of a building *put up* (Jos., Ant. 19, 329 ναούς) Mk 14: 58 D.

2. intr. (2 aor. and all mid. forms) *rise, stand up, get up.*

a. lit. of one sitting or lying down: *rise to speak* (X., An. 3, 2, 34 ἀναστὰς εἶπε) ἀναστὰς ὁ ἀρχιερεὺς εἶπεν Mt 26: 62; cf. Mk 14: 57, 60; out of bed (2 Km 11: 2) Lk 11: 7, 8. *Rise* and come together for consultation (PTebt. 285, 15—APF 5, '08, 232—ἀναστὰς εἰς συμβούλιον καὶ σκεψάμενος μετὰ τῶν . . .) Ac 26: 30. Of one recovered from illness Mk 9: 27 or come back to life (Proverbia Aesopi 101 P.) ἀνέστη τὸ κοράσιον Mk 5: 42; cf. Lk 8: 55. W. inf. foll. to show purpose ἀ. ἀναγνῶναι *stand up to read* (scripture) Lk 4: 16; ἀ. παίζειν 1 Cor 10: 7 (Ex 32: 6); ἀ. ἄρχειν Ro 15: 12; Is 11: 10). Short for *stand up and go* (Sus 34) ἀναστὰς ὁ ἀρχιερεὺς εἰς μέσον *he stood up and went before them* Mk 14: 60; ἀ. ἀπὸ τῆς συναγωγῆς Lk 4: 38; ἀ. ἀπὸ τῆς προσευχῆς 22: 45. Of a tree that is bent over and rises again B 12: 1.—Used esp. oft. of the dead (Il. 21, 56; Hdt. 3, 62; J 11: 23f; 1 Cor 15: 51 v.l. (PBrandhuber, D. sekund. LAA b. 1 Cor 15: 51: Bibl. 18, '37, 303–33; 418–38); 1 Th 4: 16; IRo 4: 3; Sm 7: 1; B 11: 7 (Ps 1: 5); 2 Cl 9: 1; in full ἐκ νεκρῶν ἀ. (Phlegon: 257 fgm. 36, 3, 3 Jac. ἀνέστη ὁ Βούπλαγος ἐκ τῶν νεκρῶν) Mk 9: 10; 12: 25; Lk 16: 30 w. ἀπό א. Partic. of Jesus' resurrection (cf. Hos 6: 2 ἐν τῇ ἡμέρᾳ τῇ τρίτῃ ἀναστησόμεθα: 1 Cor 15: 4) Mt 17: 9; 20: 19 (both v.l.); Mk 8: 31; 9: 9f, 31; 10: 34; 16: 9; Lk 18: 33; 24: 7, 46; J 20: 9; Ac 17: 3; 1 Th 4: 14; IRo 6: 1; B 15: 9. Intr. used for the pass. ὑπὸ τ. θεοῦ ἀναστάντα *raised by God* (from the dead) Pol 9: 2. Fig., of a spiritual reawakening ἀνάστα ἐκ τ. νεκρῶν *arise from the dead* Eph 5: 14 (cf. Kleopatra l. 127f and Rtzst., Erlösungsmyst. 6; 135ff).—For lit. s. ἀνάστασις, end.

b. *arise to help the poor*, of God 1 Cl 15: 6 (Ps 11: 6).—

c. *rise up, arise* in the sense *appear, come* (1 Macc 2: 1; 14: 41; Jdth 8: 18; 1 Esdr 5: 40) of a king Ac 7: 18 (Ex 1: 8). Of a priest Hb 7: 11, 15. Of accusers in court Mt 12: 41; Lk 11: 32 (both w. ἐν τῇ κρίσει; cf. ἐγείρω 2e); Mk 14: 57. Of a questioner who appears in a group of disciples Lk 10: 25, cf. Ac 6: 9 (s. 2 Ch 20: 5). Of an enemy ἀ. ἐπί τινα (Gen 4: 8; 2 Ch 20: 23; Sus 61 Theod.) *rise up* or *rebel against someone* Mk 3: 26.

d. gener., w. weakened basic mng., to indicate the beginning of an action (usu. motion) expr. by another verb: *rise, set out, get ready* (X., Cyr. 5, 2, 14; Gen 13: 17; 19: 14; 1 Macc 16: 5; Tob 8: 10; 10: 10; Sus 19 Theod.; Jos., Ant. 14, 452) ἀναστὰς ἠκολούθησεν αὐτῷ *he got ready and followed him* Mt 9: 9; Lk 5: 28; Mk 2: 14. ἀ. ἐξῆλθεν 1: 35; ἀ. ἀπῆλθεν 7: 24; ἀ. ἔρχεται 10: 1; ἀναστᾶσα ἐπορεύθη (cf. Gen 43: 8) Lk 1: 39, cf. 15: 18. ἀναστάντες ἐξέβαλον 4: 29; ἀναστᾶσα διηκόνει vs. 39; ἀ. ἔστη 6: 8; ἀ. ἦλθεν 15: 20; ἀνάστηθι καὶ πορεύου get up and go Ac 8: 26, cf. 27. For this ἀναστὰς πορεύθητι (but v.l. ἀνάστα πορ.) 9: 11. ἀνάστηθι καὶ εἴσελθε vs. 6. ἀνάστηθι καὶ στρῶσον vs. 34. ἀναστὰς κατάβηθι 10: 20 al.

e. of a building *rise* Mk 13: 2 v.l.—Dalman, Worte 18f. M-M. B. 668.

Ἄννα, ας, ἡ (חַנָּה) (1 Km 1: 2ff; Philo, Deus Imm. 5ff, Ebr. 145ff, Mut. Nom. 143f, Somn. 1, 254; Jos., Ant. 5, 342; 344–7; Bull. de corr. hell. 3, 1879, p. 344, 23; Wadd. 1965; oft. pap.) *Anna* Lk 2: 36; cf. Bl-D. §39, 3; 40; 53, 3; Rob. 225.*

Ἄννας, α, ὁ (Herodas 8, 14; 43; 66 [as a man's name, accented Ἀννᾶς by the editions]; PGenève 42, 8; Cyprian inscr. from an Egyptian temple: Κυπρ. I p. 293 no. 21) *Annas* (cf. Bl-D. §40; 53, 2; Rob. 225; short for Ἄνανος, חֲנַנְיָה), high priest 6–15 AD, Lk 3: 2; J 18: 13; Ac 4: 6. Father-in-law of Caiaphas J 18: 13. Cf. Jos., Ant. 18, 26; 20, 197. Schürer II⁴ 256; 270; 274f; PGaechter, Petrus u. seine Zeit, '58, 67–104.*

ἀνοδία, ας, ἡ (Polyb. 5, 13, 6 al.; Diod. S. 19, 5, 3; Plut., Mar. 37, 9, Mor. 508D; Sym. Job 12: 24) *a place with no roads* Hv 1, 1, 3. Opp. ὁδός (Philo, Somn. 2, 161, Mos. 2, 138) 3, 2, 9. Pl. (Jos., Bell. 4, 109) 3, 7, 1; m 6, 1, 3.*

ἀνόητος, ον (predom., and in our lit., always in active sense, as in Pre-Socr., Soph.; Pla., Gorg. 464D et al.; LXX; Ep. Arist. 136; Philo; Jos., Ant. 9, 225, C. Ap. 2, 255) *unintelligent, foolish.*

1. of pers., opp. σοφός (cf. Pr 17: 28) Ro 1: 14; w. ἄφρων (Plut., Mor. 22c τοῖς ἄφροσι καὶ ἀνοήτοις; Epict. 2, 21, 1) 1 Cl 21: 5; w. βραδὺς τ. καρδίᾳ Lk 24: 25. In address (Diog. L. 2, 117 ἀνόητε=you fool!; 4 Macc 8: 17) 1 Cl 23: 4; 2 Cl 11: 3; Hm 10, 2, 1.—Gal 3: 1 (Charito 6, 7, 9; Alciphr. 4, 7, 4; Philostrat., Vi. Apoll. 8, 7 p. 307, 13 ὦ ἀνόητοι; Philo, Somn. 2, 181 ὦ ἀνόητε); 3 (Charito 5, 7, 3 οὕτως ἀ.; Maximus Tyr. 36, 4 τίς οὕτως ἀ.; Jos., Ant. 9, 255). Of the intellectual and spiritual condition of men before becoming Christians ἦμεν γάρ ποτε καὶ ἡμεῖς ἀ. Tit 3: 3 (cf. Herm. Wr. 1, 23 τοῖς ἀνοήτοις πόρρωθέν εἰμι).

2. w. a noun denoting a thing (Soph., Ajax 162 γνῶμαι; Pla., Phileb. 12D δόξαι; Herm. Wr. 6, 3b) ἐπιθυμίας ἀ. *foolish desires* 1 Ti 6: 9 (v.l. ἀνονήτους). M-M. B. 1215.*

ἄνοια, ας, ἡ (Theognis 453+; Pla., Tim. 86B δύο ἀνοίας γένη, τὸ μὲν μανία, τὸ δ' ἀμαθία; Herm. Wr. 14, 8; LXX; Philo; Jos., Bell. 2, 110, C. Ap. 210) *folly* of heretical teachers 2 Ti 3: 9 (Third Corinthians 1: 16). Gener. of human ignorance w. πονηρία (Jos., Ant. 8, 318) 2 Cl 13: 1. Of angry men ἐπλήσθησαν ἀνοίας *they were filled w. fury* Lk 6: 11.*

ἀνοίγω on this alternate form of ἀνοίγνυμι see Kühner-Bl. II p. 496f; Bl-D. §101; Rob. 1212f; Mayser 404. Fut. ἀνοίξω; 1 aor. ἀνέῳξα J 9: 14 (v.l. ἠνέῳξα, ἤνοιξα), ἠνέῳξα vs. 17 (BX; ἤνοιξα אAD al.; ἀνέῳξα KL), mostly ἤνοιξα Ac 5: 19; 9: 40 al.; 2 pf. (intrans.) ἀνέῳγα; pf.

pass. ἀνέῳγμαι (ἠνέῳγμαι 2 Cor 2: 12 acc. to DEP), ptc. ἀνεῳγμένος; 1 aor. pass. ἀνεῴχθην Mt 3: 16, ἠνεῴχθην (Mt 3: 16B; 9: 30BD) J 9: 10; ἠνοίχθην Ac 16: 26 (ἠνεῴχθην BCD); inf. ἀνεῳχθῆναι Lk 3: 21 (ἀνοιχθῆναι D); 1 fut. pass. ἀνοιχθήσομαι Lk 11: 9 ([A]DEF al.); 2 aor. pass. ἠνοίγην Mk 7: 35; Ac 12: 10; Hv 1, 1, 4 (Dssm. NB 17 [BS 189]); 2 fut. ἀνοιγήσομαι Mt 7: 7. The same situation prevails in LXX: Helbing 78f; 83ff; 95f; 102f. Thackeray 202ff. (Hom+; inscr., LXX, En., Philo, Joseph., Test. 12 Patr.; Sib. Or. 3, 769).

1. trans. *open*—**a.** *a door* (Menand., Epitr. 643; Polyb. 16, 25, 7; Dit., Or. 222, 36; 332, 28, Syll.³ 798, 19; 1 Km 3: 15; Jos., Ant. 13, 92 ἀ. τ. πύλας, Vi. 246) τὰς θύρας (really the wings of a double door) Ac 5: 19; 12: 10 (see 2 below); 16: 26f (cf. OWeinreich, Türöffnung im Wunder-, Prodigien -u. Zauberglauben d. Antike, d. Judentums u. Christentums: WSchmid-Festschr. '29, 200–452). ἀ. τὸν πυλῶνα *open the outer door* of the house Ac 12: 14. τ. θύραν τ. ναοῦ fig., of the mouth of the believer, who is the temple of God B 16: 9 (with this figure cf. Philosophenspr. p. 488, ὁ τοῦ σοφοῦ στόματος ἀνοιχθέντος, καθάπερ ἱεροῦ=when the mouth of the wise man opens as a temple). Without *door* as obj. acc., or as subject of a verb in the pass., easily supplied from the context Mt 7: 7f; Lk 11: 9f; Mt 25: 11; Lk 13: 25.—Used fig. in var. ways (PTebt. 383, 29 [46 AD]; Epict. Schenkl index θύρα: ἡ θύρα ἤνοικται=I am free to go anywhere) Rv 3: 20, cf. 3: 7f (s. Is 22: 22; Job 12: 14). πύλη δικαιοσύνης 1 Cl 48: 2, cf. 4. Of preaching that wins attention ἤνοιξεν τοῖς ἔθνεσιν θύραν πίστεως *he made it possible for the heathen to become Christians* Ac 14: 27. Cf. θύρας μοι ἀνεῳγμένης *since a door was opened for me*, i.e., I was given an opportunity to work 2 Cor 2: 12 (for 1 Cor 16: 9 s. 2 below). Likew. ἀ. θύραν τοῦ λόγου Col 4: 3.

b. closed places, whose interior is thereby made accessible: a sanctuary 1 Cl 43: 5; pass. Rv 11: 19; 15: 5 heaven (Epigr. Gr. 882 [III AD] οὐρανὸν ἀνθρώποις εἶδον ἀνοιγόμενον; PGM 4, 1180; 36, 298; Is 64: 1; Ezk 1: 1; cf. 3 Macc 6: 18) Mt 3: 16; Lk 3: 21; Ac 10: 11; Rv 19: 11; GEb 3; Hv 1, 1, 4; the underworld Rv 9: 2; graves (Dit., Syll.³ 1237, 3 ἀνοίξαι τόδε τὸ μνῆμα; Ezk 37: 12, 13) Mt 27: 52. Fig., of the throat of the impious τάφος ἀνεῳγμένος ὁ λάρυγξ αὐτῶν *their gullet is an open grave* (breathing out putrefaction?) Ro 3: 13 (Ps 5: 10; 13: 3).

c. objects locked, closed, or shut τ. θησαυρούς (Dit., Syll.² 587, 302 τῷ τ. θησαυροὺς ἀνοίξαντι; 601, 32; 653, 93; Eur., Ion 923; Arrian, Cyneg. 34, 2 ἀνοίγνυται ὁ θησαυρός; Is 45: 3; Sir 43: 14; Philo, Leg. All. 3, 105) *treasure chests* Mt 2: 11. κεράμιον οἴνου ἢ ἐλαίου *open a jar of wine or oil* D 13: 6. ἀ. βιβλίον *open a book* in scroll form (Diod. S. 14, 55, 1 βιβλίον ἐπεσφραγισμένον ... ἀνοίγειν; 2 Esdr 18 [Neh 8]: 5; Da 7: 10) Lk 4: 17; Rv 5: 2ff; 10: 2, 8 (cf. 2 Esdr 16 [Neh 6]: 5); 20: 12.

d. seals (X., De Rep. Lac. 6, 4; Dit., Syll.³ 1157, 47 [I AD] τὰς σφραγίδας ἀνοιξάτω) Rv 5: 9; 6: 1–12; 8: 1.

e. parts of the body—**α.** the mouth ἀ. τὸ στόμα *open the mouth* of another person 1 Cl 18: 15 (cf. Ps 50: 17); of a fish, to take something out Mt 17: 27; of a mute (Wsd 10: 21) Lk 1: 64.—*Open* one's own *mouth* to speak (oft. in OT; Sib. Or. 3, 497, but e.g. also Aristoph., Av. 1719) Mt 5: 2; 6: 8D; Ac 8: 35; 10: 34; 18: 14; GEb 2. More specif. ἐν παραβολαῖς=he spoke *in parables* Mt 13: 35 (Ps 77: 2; cf. Lucian, Philops. 33 ὁ Μέμνων αὐτὸς ἀνοίξας τὸ στόμα ἐν ἔπεσιν ἑπτά). εἰς βλασφημίας to blaspheme Rv 13: 6.—*Not to open* one's *mouth*, remain silent Ac 8: 32; 1 Cl 16: 7 (both Is 53: 7).—Fig., of the earth when it opens to swallow something Rv 12: 16 (cf. Num 16: 30; 26: 10; Dt 11: 6).

β. the eyes ἀ. τοὺς ὀφθαλμούς of a blind man (Is 35: 5; 42: 7; Tob 11: 7) Mt 9: 30; 20: 33; J 9: 10, 14, 17, 21, 26, 30, 32; 10: 21; B 14: 7 (Is 42: 7).—One's own eyes, to see (Epict. 2, 23, 9 and 12; PGM 4, 624) Ac 9: 8, 40.—Fig., of spiritual sight Lk 24: 31 v.l.; Ac 26: 18. τοὺς ὀφθαλμοὺς τ. καρδίας 1 Cl 36: 2; 59: 3.

γ. the ears (PGM 7, 329) of a deaf man Mk 7: 35.

δ. the heart ἀ. τ. καρδίαν πρὸς τ. κύριον *open one's heart to the Lord* Hv 4, 2, 4.

2. intr. (only 2 pf., except that the 2 aor. pass. ἠνοίγη Ac 12: 10 is the practical equivalent of an intr. Other exx. of 2 pf.: Hippocr., Morb. 4, 39 ed. Littré VII 558; Plut., Mor. 693D, Coriol. 37, 2; Lucian, Nav. 4; Polyaenus 2, 28, 1) *open* τ. οὐρανὸν ἀνεῳγότα J 1: 51. θύρα μοι ἀνέῳγεν 1 Cor 16: 9 (s. above 1a; Lucian, Soloec. 8 ἡ θύρα ἀνέῳγέ σοι τῆς γνωρίσεως αὐτῶν). τὸ στόμα ἡμῶν ἀνέῳγεν πρὸς ὑμᾶς *our mouth is open toward you*, i.e., I have spoken freely and openly 2 Cor 6: 11 (cf. Ezk 16: 63; 29: 21 and ἄνοιξις). M-M. B. 847.

ἀνοικοδομέω fut. ἀνοικοδομήσω (Hdt., Aristoph.+; inscr., pap., LXX; Ep. Arist. 100; Jos., Ant. 2, 203 al. in mngs. 'build' and 'build again') *build up again* (so Ephoros [IV BC]: 70 fgm. 132 Jac.; PPetr. II 12, 1, 15; Wilcken, Chrest. 96 VIII, 4; Dit., Syll.³ 454, 12 τῶν τειχῶν τ. πεπτωκότων συνεπεμελήθη ὅπως ἀνοικοδομηθεῖ) τ. σκηνὴν Δαυίδ *the tabernacle of David* Ac 15: 16a (Am 9: 11); τὰ κατεστραμμένα αὐτῆς *its ruins* vs. 16b; the temple B 16: 4. Fig., mid. ἀγαπητοί ἀνοικοδομεῖσθε Jd 20ᵖ⁷². M-M.*

ἄνοιξις, εως, ἡ (since Thu. 4, 68, 5; Plut., Mor. 738c χειλῶν; PGM 5, 285; 36, 312; Jos., Ant. 18, 30) the act of *opening* ἵνα μοι δοθῇ λόγος ἐν ἀνοίξει τ. στόματός μου *that I may be given a message when I open my mouth* Eph 6: 19 (cf. ἀνοίγω 2). M-M.*

ἀνοίσω s. ἀναφέρω.

ἀνοιχθήσομαι s. ἀνοίγω.

ἀνομέω 1 aor. ἠνόμησα, ptc. ἀνομήσας (Hdt. 1, 144; UPZ 5, 47=6, 34 [163 BC]; LXX; RHelbing, Kasussyntax '28, 12) *be lawless, sin* εἴς τινα (Num 32: 15; Ps 118: 78) *against someone* Hv 1, 3, 1. Abs. 1 Cl 53: 2; B 4: 8; 14: 3 (all three Ex 32: 7).*

ἀνόμημα, ατος, τό (Stoic. III 136; Diod. S. 17, 5, 4; PGM 4, 3099; LXX; En. 9, 10; Jos., Ant. 8, 251; CSchmidt and WSchubart, Altchr. Texte '10, p. 111) *lawless action, iniquity* w. ἁμαρτία Hv 1, 3, 1; w. ἀνομία and ἁμαρτία 1 Cl 18: 2f (Ps 50: 3f).*

ἀνομία, ας, ἡ (Eur., Hdt., Pre-Socr.+; pap., LXX, En., Philo; Jos., Bell. 1, 493, Ant. 15, 348; Test. 12 Patr.) *lawlessness.*

1. as a frame of mind, opp. δικαιοσύνη (Hdt. 1, 96; X., Mem. 1, 2, 24 ἀνομίᾳ μᾶλλον ἢ δικαιοσύνῃ χρώμενοι) Ro 6: 19a; 2 Cor 6: 14; Dg 9: 5; Hm 4, 1, 3; w. ὑπόκρισις Mt 23: 28; oft. (as Ps 58: 3) w. ἁμαρτία, w. which it is identified 1 J 3: 4: cf. 1 Cl 8: 3; 15: 5; 18: 3 (Ps 50: 4; 30: 19; 102: 10); Hs 7: 2. ἔργα τῆς ἀ. *lawless deeds*, which originate in this frame of mind B 4: 1; Hs 8, 10, 3. υἱοὶ τῆς ἀ. *lawless men*, those who despise the law (cf. Ps 88: 23) Hv 3, 6, 1; AP 1: 3. ἀ. characterizes this aeon as Satan's domain, ending of Mk in the Freer ms. 2. ὁ ἄνθρωπος τῆς ἀ. (v.l. ἁμαρτίας) of Antichrist 2 Th 2: 3 (regarded as transl. of Beliar by Bousset, D. Antichr. 1895, 86; s. also Ps 93: 20 θρόνος ἀνομίας and cf. 1QH 5: 36; but see BRigaux, Les Épîtres aux Thess. '56, 656–67). μυστήριον τῆς ἀ. *the secret of lawlessness*, secret because (and as long as) the Antichrist has not made his appearance vs. 7; on the ἀ. in the last days Mt 24: 12; D 16: 4. μέθυσμα ἀνομίας wanton drunkenness Hm 8: 3. ἡ τῆς πλάνης ἀ. lawless deceit B 14: 5. ὁ καιρὸς ὁ νῦν τῆς ἀ. the present time, when lawlessness reigns 18: 2; cf. 15: 7. Of God μισεῖν ἀ. (Ps 44: 8) Hb 1: 9 (v.l. ἀδικίαν).

2. a lawless deed Ro 6: 19b. λυτρώσασθαι ἀπὸ πάσης ἀ. (Ps 129: 8) redeem fr. all lawlessness, i.e., l. deeds Tit 2: 14. ἐργάζεσθαι ἀ. (oft. LXX) Mt 7: 23; Hm 10, 3, 2; ἐργάτης ἀ. 2 Cl 4: 5; ἀ. ποιεῖν (Hos 6: 9; Is 5: 7 al.) Mt 13: 41; 1 J 3: 4; 1 Cl 16: 10 (Is 53: 9); more specif. ἐν στόματι commit sin with the mouth B 10: 8. ἁρπάζειν ἐν ἀ. seize lawlessly 10: 4. Pl. lawless deeds, transgressions (POxy. 1121, 20; Herm. Wr. 1, 23; oft. LXX) Ro 4: 7 (Ps 31: 1); Hb 8: 12 t.r.; 10: 17; 1 Cl 16: 5, 9 (Is 53: 8); 18: 5, 9 (Ps 50: 7, 11); 50: 6 (Ps 31: 1); 60: 1; B 5: 2 (Is 53: 5); Hv 2, 2, 2; 3, 6, 4; s 5, 5, 3. (In ms. tradition ἀ. is oft. interchanged w. synonyms; so Hb 1: 9 [ἀδικία]; 2 Th 2: 3 [ἁμαρτία]; 1 Cl 35: 5 as v.l. for πονηρία). Dodd 76-81. M-M.*

ἀνόμοιος, ον (Pind., Pla.+; POxy. 237 VI, 29; Wsd 2: 15; Philo) unlike w. dat. (Pla., Gorg. 513в; Wsd) of a star πόθεν ἡ καινότης ἡ ἀ. αὐτοῖς whence the new thing, unlike them (the other stars), might come IEph 19: 2.*

ἄνομος, ον (Soph., Hdt., Thu.+; POxy. 237 VII, 11 [II AD]; PGM 58, 8; LXX, En., Test. 12 Patr.) lawless.
1. w. ref. to any law ἄ. κριτής an unjust judge, who cares nothing for the law B 20: 2; D 5: 2.
2. w. ref. to the Mosaic law, used of Gentiles.
a. as persons who do not know it, w. no criticism implied (Pla., Polit. 302ε [Nägeli 14]; Esth 4: 17u) τοῖς ἀ. ὡς ἀ. to the Gentiles as a Gentile 1 Cor 9: 21.
b. w. the connotation of godlessness, so that it approaches mng. 3 (Wsd 17: 2) διὰ χειρὸς ἀνόμων Ac 2: 23. οἱ ἄνομοι MPol 16: 1. τὰ ἀ. ἔθνη (3 Macc 6: 9) the godless heathen 9: 2.
3. w. ref. to God's moral law. μὴ ὢν ἀ. θεοῦ though I do not reject God's law 1 Cor 9: 21 (opp. ἔννομος, in the constr. of ἄ. θεοῦ s. Mlt. 236). Hence godless, wicked in gener. (oft. LXX) Dg 9: 4f; w. ἀνυπότακτος 1 Ti 1: 9; w. ἀσεβής (1 Macc 7: 5; PGM 58, 11; Audollent, Defix. Tab. 188) 1 Cl 18: 13 (Ps 50: 15); cf. 35: 9 (Ps 49: 21); w. ἄδικος (PLond. 358, 13 ἄνομα καὶ ἄδικα) 56: 11 (Job 5: 22). Opp. δίκαιος (Pr 21: 18) 45: 4; ἅγιος Dg 9: 2. μετὰ ἀνόμων λογισθῆναι be classed among the criminals Mk 15: 28 t.r.; Lk 22: 37 (SGHall, Studia Evangelica '59, 499-501); cf. 1 Cl 16: 13 (all three Is 53: 12). ὑπὲρ πᾶσαν ἁμαρτίαν ἀνομώτερος wicked beyond measure B 5: 9. τὸ γένος ἄ. the wicked kind Hs 9, 19, 1.—Of things ἄ. βίος w. ἄδικος MPol 3; ἄ. ἔργα 2 Pt 2: 8 (Nicol. Dam.: 90 fgm. 58, 2 Jac. ἔργον ἄνομον ἐργάσασθαι). ὁ ἄ. καιρός wicked time B 4: 9 (cf. 18: 2).
4. ὁ ἄ. the lawless one (Ezk 18: 24; 33: 8) of the Antichrist 2 Th 2: 8 (cf. vs. 3). This prob. explains ὁ καιρὸς τοῦ ἀ. B 15: 5. M-M.*

ἀνόμως adv. (Eur., Thu.+, but usu.=impiously; PMagd. 6, 11; BGU 1200, 20; 2 Macc 8: 17; Philo, Leg. All. 1, 35 v.l.; Jos., C. Ap. 1, 147; 2, 151, Ant. 15, 59) without the law ὅσοι ἥμαρτον ἀ. καὶ ἀπολοῦνται those who sinned without the law will also be lost without the law Ro 2: 12 (=χωρὶς νόμου 7: 9; cf. Isocr. 4, 39 ἀ. ζῆν=live in ignorance of the law. Likew. Jos., C. Ap. 2, 151).*

ἀνονειδίστως adv. (Nicol. Dam.: 90 fgm. 130, 62 Jac. ἀνονείδιστα) without reproaching w. ἀδιστάκτως: χορηγεῖν τινι Hs 9, 24, 2.*

ἀνόνητος, ον (Soph., Pla.+; Mitteis, Chrest. 88 IV, 9;

Wsd 3: 11; 4 Macc 16: 7, 9; Jos., Bell. 1, 464, Vi. 422 al.) useless ἐπιθυμίαι ἀ. w. βλαβεραί 1 Ti 6: 9 v.l. (for ἀνοήτους).*

ἀνορθόω fut. ἀνορθώσω; 1 aor. pass. ἀνορθώθην Lk 13: 13 (ἀνωρθώθη t.r., W-H.; cf. Bl-D. §67, 2 app.; Helbing p. 72f) (Eur., Hdt.+; LXX) rebuild, restore, lit., of a fallen structure (Hdt. 1, 19 τὸν νηόν; Dit., Or. 710, 4 [II AD] τὸ προπύλαιον χρόνῳ διαφθαρὲν ἀνώρθωσεν; 2 Km 7: 26 v.l.; 1 Ch 17: 24) Ac 15: 16. Of a crippled woman, who was healed, pass. ἀνορθώθη she became erect once more Lk 13: 13 (Hobart 22). τὰ παραλελυμένα γόνατα ἀ. strengthen the weakened knees Hb 12: 12. M-M.*

ἀνόσιος, ον (Aeschyl., Hdt.+; inscr., pap., LXX, Philo; Jos., Bell. 6, 399, C. Ap. 2, 201 al.) unholy, wicked.
1. of pers. (PBrem. 1, 4 [116 AD]; PGiess. 41 II, 4 [both ἀνόσιοι Ἰουδαῖοι]; PGM 4, 2476; 2 Macc 7: 34; 8: 32; 4 Macc 12: 11; Ep. Arist. 289) 1 Ti 1: 9; cf. 2 Ti 3: 2; w. ἄνομος 1 Cl 45: 4.
2. of things (Diod. S. 34+35, fgm. 14 πρᾶξις; Wsd 12: 4; 3 Macc 5: 8) ἀ. στάσις unholy discord 1 Cl 1: 1. αἰκίσματα δεινὰ καὶ ἀ. terrible and wicked tortures 6: 2. M-M.*

ἀνοχή, ῆς, ἡ (X.+)—1. holding back, delay, pause (1 Macc 12: 25; Jos., Bell. 1, 173, Ant. 6, 72; w. ἔχειν (Diod. S. 11, 36, 4 ἀνοχὴν ἔχειν; POxy. 1068, 15 ἡμερῶν ἀνοχὴν ἔχω) ἀνοχὴν οὐκ ἔχειν have no relief Hs 6, 3, 1. ἀ. τῆς οἰκοδομῆς a pause in the building s 9, 5, 1; 9, 14, 2.
2. forbearance, clemency (Epict. 1, 29, 62 ἀ. ἔχω I enjoy clemency; PSI 632, 13 [III BC]; cf. Nägeli 45) ἐν τῇ ἀ. τοῦ θεοῦ in God's forbearance Ro 3: 26 (for a neg. expression of this idea s. Dit., Syll.³ 985, 34f [I AD]: καὶ τοὺς παραβαίνοντας τὰ παρα[γέλματα οὐκ ἀνέ]ξονται [said of the great gods], FWDanker in FWGingrich-Festschr., '72, 102f). W. μακροθυμία 2: 4.*

ἀνταγωνίζομαι (Thu.+; 4 Macc 17: 14; Jos., C. Ap. 1, 56; w. πρός τινα Inschr. v. Priene 17, 15 [III BC]) struggle ἀ. πρὸς τ. ἁμαρτίαν in your struggle against sin Hb 12: 4. M-M.*

ἀντακούω fut. ἀντακούσομαι (trag.+; X., An. 2, 5, 16; Philostrat., Imag. 1, 28 p. 333, 24; PLond. 1708, 57) hear in turn ὁ τὰ πολλὰ λέγων καὶ ἀντακούσεται he who speaks much hears much in return 1 Cl 30: 4 (Job 11: 2).*

ἀνταλλαγή, ῆς, ἡ (Maximus Tyr. 39, 1c v.l.; Hesychius; Simplicius, in Aristot., Phys. 1350, 32; Theophilus Antecessor [VI AD] 2, 6 p. 281 [ed. OReitz 1751]) exchange ὦ τῆς γλυκείας ἀ. what a sweet exchange (from being sinners to righteous men) Dg 9: 5.*

ἀντάλλαγμα, ατος, τό (Eur.+; Ruth 4: 7; Job 28: 15; Jer 15: 13; Sir 6: 15; Philo, fgm. 110 Harris; Jos., Bell. 1, 355, Ant. 14, 484) someth. given in exchange τί δώσει ἄνθρωπος ἀ. τ. ψυχῆς αὐτοῦ; what shall a man give in exchange for his soul? there is nothing that would compensate for such a loss Mt 16: 26; Mk 8: 37.*

ἀνταναιρέω 2 aor. ἀντανεῖλον (Demosth.+; pap., LXX) take away as a punishment τὶ ἀπό τινος 1 Cl 18: 11 (Ps 50: 13).*

ἀντιαναπληρόω (Demosth. 14, 16 and 17; Cass. Dio 44, 48; Apollon. Dysc., Constr. ed. GUhlig '10 p. 21, 5; 158, 1; 365, 3; 487, 1) fill up, complete for someone else τὰ ὑστερήματα τῶν θλίψεων I fill up what is lacking in suffering Col 1: 24. The Christian must suffer to be like Christ (2 Cor 1: 5; 4: 10; 1 Th 3: 3). Paul is glad, by means of the suffering which he vicariously endures for the church, to unite the latter for its own benefit w. Christ; he supplies whatever lack may still exist in its proper share of suffering. Cf. WRGMoir, Col 1: 24: ET 42, '31 479f; EPercy, Die Probleme der Kolosser- und Epheserbriefe '46, 128–34; ELohse, Märtyrer u. Gottesknecht '55, 202ff; JKremer, Was an den Leiden Christi noch mangelt: Bonner Biblische Beiträge 12, '56; HGustafson, Biblical Research 8, '63, 28–42 and lit. on πάθημα 1. M-M.*

ἀνταποδίδωμι fut. ἀνταποδώσω; 2 aor. inf. ἀνταποδοῦναι; 1 fut. pass. ἀνταποδοθήσομαι (Hdt.+; Suppl. Epigr. Gr. VIII 549, 33 [I BC]; PSI 386, 23 [245 BC]; UPZ 120, 22 [II BC]; LXX; Test. Jud. 13: 8) *give back, repay, return.*
1. in good sense τινί τι (PLond. 413, 8 ἵν' ἀνταποδώσω σοι τὴν ἀγάπην; Pr 25: 22; Sir 30: 6; 1 Macc 10: 27) εὐχαριστίαν τῷ θεῷ ἀ. *return thanks to God* 1 Th 3: 9; without obj. οὐκ ἔχουσιν ἀ. σοι *they have no way to repay you* Lk 14: 14 (cf. EpJer 33). Pass. (Jos., Ant. 14, 212) ἀνταποδοθήσεται αὐτῷ *it will be paid back to him* Ro 11: 35 (Is 40: 14 v.l.).
2. in bad sense, of punishment or revenge τινί τι (PGM 3, 115; Lev 18: 25; Ps 7: 5; 34: 12 al.) ἀ. τοῖς θλίβουσιν ὑμᾶς θλῖψιν 2 Th 1: 6. Abs. ἐγὼ ἀνταποδώσω *I will repay* Ro 12: 19; Hb 10: 30 (both Dt 32: 35). M-M.*

ἀνταπόδομα, ατος, τό (LXX) *repayment,* as a *reward* (Is 1: 23; Sir 20: 10) B 20: 2; D 5: 2. μὴ γένηταί ἀ. σοι *that no repayment may come to you* Lk 14: 12.—As punishment, as mostly in LXX (w. σκάνδαλον) εἰς ἀ. αὐτοῖς *as retribution for them* Ro 11: 9.—Neutrally, of the last judgment, *recompense,* which dispenses both reward and punishment (w. ἀνάστασις) B 21: 1.*

ἀνταπόδοσις, εως, ἡ (Thu.+ [cf. Nägeli 36]: inscr., pap., LXX, mostly sensu malo) *repaying, reward* ἀπολαμβάνειν τὴν ἀ. τῆς κληρονομίας *receive the inheritance as a reward* Col 3: 24 (cf. Judg 9: 16 B; Ps 18: 12). ἡμέρα τῆς ἀ. (Is 63: 4) *day of recompense* of divine judgment B 14: 9 (Is 61: 2); cf. Ro 2: 5 A. M-M.*

ἀνταποδότης, ου, ὁ (Jer 28: 56 Sym.) *paymaster* ὁ τοῦ μισθοῦ καλὸς ἀ. *the good paymaster* D 4: 7; B 19: 11.*

ἀνταποκρίνομαι 1 aor. pass. ἀνταπεκρίθην (mathematical t.t. = correspond to [Nicomachus Gerasenus—II AD—, Arithmet. 1, 8, 10fHoche]; LXX) *answer in turn* (Aesop 301a, 6 [ed. Chambry '25]; schol. on Pind., Pyth. 9, 65; Syntipas p. 80, 12; Leontios 35 p. 68, 23 τινί; Judg 5: 29 A; Job) οὐκ ἴσχυσαν ἀ. πρὸς ταῦτα *they could make no reply to this* Lk 14: 6 (cf. Job 32: 12). ὁ ἀνταποκρινόμενος τῷ θεῷ *one who answers back to God* Ro 9: 20 (cf. Job 16: 8; Pind., Pyth. 2, 88 χρὴ δὲ πρὸς θεὸν οὐκ ἐρίζειν = one must not contend against God).*

ἀντασπάζομαι 1 aor. ἀντησπασάμην (X.; Plut., Tim. 38, 6) *greet in return* τινά *someone* Hv 4, 2, 2; 5: 1.*

ἀντεῖπον 2 aor., used in place of the missing aor. of ἀντιλέγω (Aeschyl., Thu.+; LXX; Jos., Ant. 1, 11; 19, 208; Sib. Or. 2, 276) *say against* or *in return* ἀ. τινι (PMich. 219, 9) *contradict someone* Lk 21: 15; Hm 3: 3. οὐδὲν εἶχον ἀντειπεῖν *they had nothing to say in reply* Ac 4: 14 (cf. Aeschyl., Prom. 51 οὐδὲν ἀντειπεῖν ἔχω; POxy. 237 V, 13 [186 AD] ἐσιώπησεν οὐδὲν ἀντειπεῖν δυνάμενος).*

ἀντέχω fut. ἀνθέξομαι (in our lit. only in the mid., which is quotable fr. Pindar's time, and common in coll. H. Gk. [Nägeli 54]).
1. *cling to, hold fast to* someth. or *someone, be devoted to* τινός (PTebt. 40, 9; POxy. 1230, 30; PStrassb. 74, 18; Is 56: 2, 4, 6; Jer 2: 8; 1 Macc 15: 34 [hold fast to]; Pr 4: 6; Jer 8: 2 [be devoted to]; Jos., Bell. 4, 323) ἑνὸς ἀνθέξεται *he will be devoted to the one* Mt 6: 24; Lk 16: 13 (cf. Pind., Nem. 1, 33 ἀντ. Ἡρακλέος). τῶν ἀγαθῶν τ. μελλόντων *hold fast to the good things to come* Hv 1, 1, 8. τοῦ πιστοῦ λόγου *cling to the trustworthy message* Tit 1: 9 (cf. Ael. Aristid. 36, 112 K. = 48 p. 484 D.: ἀληθείας ἀντέχεσθαι). Since the last passage concerns a bishop, who might be expected to do more than hold fast to true doctrine, perh. mng. 2 is to be preferred.
2. *take an interest in, pay attention to,* hence *help* τινός *someone* or *someth.* (Diod. S. 2, 33, 3; 3, 71, 4; 14, 4, 5 al.; UPZ 170 [127/6 BC] A, 24 = B, 23 οὐθενὸς δικαίου ἀντεχόμενοι; Dt 32: 41; Pr 3: 18; Zeph 1: 6; Jos., Ant. 20, 120) ἀ. τῶν ἀσθενῶν 1 Th 5: 14. M-M.*

ἀντί prep. w. gen. (Hom.+; inscr., pap., LXX; Jos., Ant. 16, 158; for lit. s. on ἀνά, beg.); orig. mng. local, *opposite.* Figurative
1. in order to indicate that one person or thing is, or is to be, replaced by another *instead of, in place of* ἀντὶ τοῦ πατρὸς αὐτοῦ Ἡρῴδου *in place of his father Herod* Mt 2: 22 (cf. Hdt. 1, 108; X., An. 1, 1, 4; Appian, Mithrid. 7 §23 Νικομήδης ἀντὶ Προυσίου ἐβασίλευε, Syr. 69 §364; 3 Km 11: 43; Tob 1: 15, 21; 1 Macc 3: 1; 9: 31 al.; Jos., Ant. 15, 9). ἀ. ἰχθύος ὄφιν *instead of a fish, a snake* Lk 11: 11 (Paroem. Gr.: Zenobius [Hadr.] 1, 88 ἀντὶ πέρκης σκορπίον, prob. from Attic comedy: Kock III 678 [Adesp.]; Paus. 9, 41, 3 Cronos receives ἀντὶ Διὸς πέτρον to swallow). Cf. Eur., Alc. 524.). ἀ. τῆς προκειμένης αὐτῷ χαρᾶς ὑπέμεινεν σταυρόν Hb 12: 2 (cf. PHib. 170 [247 BC] ἀντὶ φιλίας ἔχθραν; 3 Macc 4: 6, 8); sense 3 is also poss., depending on the mng. of πρόκειμαι (q.v. 2 and 3). Cf. Hs 1: 8; 9, 29, 4.
2. in order to indicate that one thing is equiv. to another *for, as, in place of* (Diod. S. 3, 30, 3) κόμη ἀ. περιβολαίου *hair as a covering* 1 Cor 11: 15. ὀφθαλμὸν ἀ. ὀφθαλμοῦ καὶ ὀδόντα ἀ. ὀδόντος Mt 5: 38 (Ex 21: 24). κακὸν ἀ. κακοῦ ἀποδίδωμι (cf. Ael. Aristid. 38 p. 711 D.: ἴσα ἀντ' ἴσων ἀποδ.; Pr 17: 13.—Dit., Syll.³ 145, 5 τὰ κακὰ ἀντὶ τ. ἀγαθῶν) Ro 12: 17; 1 Th 5: 15; 1 Pt 3: 9. λοιδορίαν ἀ. λοιδορίας ibid. (Dionys. Soph., Ep. 40 χάριν ἀντὶ χάριτος = gift in return for gift). Differently to be understood is χάριν ἀ. χάριτος *grace after* or *upon grace* (i.e., grace pours forth in ever new streams; cf. Philo, Poster. Cain. 145 διὰ τὰς πρώτας χάριτας . . . ἑτέρας ἀντ' ἐκείνων καὶ τρίτας ἀντὶ τ. δευτέρων καὶ ἀεὶ νέας ἀντὶ παλαιοτέρων . . . ἐπιδίδωσι. Theognis 344 ἀντ' ἀνίας ἀνίας) J 1: 16 (JMBover, Biblica 6, '25, 454–60; PJoüon, Rech de Sc rel 22, '32, 206; WLNewton, CBQ 1, '39, 160–3).
3. Gen 44: 33 shows how the mng. *in place of* can develop into *in behalf of, for* someone, so that ἀ. becomes = ὑπέρ (cf. Rossberg [s.v. ἀνά] 18.—Diod. S. 20, 33, 7 αὐτὸν ἀντ' ἐκείνου τὴν τιμωρίαν ὑπέχειν = he would have to take the punishment for him [i.e., his son]; Ael. Aristid. 51, 24 K. = 27 p. 540 D.: Φιλουμένη ψυχὴν ἀντὶ ψυχῆς κ. σῶμα ἀντὶ σώματος ἀντέδωκεν, τὰ αὐτῆς ἀντὶ τῶν ἐμῶν) δοῦναι ἀ. ἐμοῦ καὶ σοῦ *pay (it) for me and for yourself* Mt 17: 27. λύτρον ἀ. πολλῶν *a ransom for many* 20: 28; Mk 10: 45 (Appian, Syr. 60 §314 διδόναι τι ἀντὶ τῆς σωτηρίας, Bell. Civ. 5, 39 §166 ἐμοὶ ἀντὶ πάντων ὑμῶν καταχρήσασθαι = inflict punishment on me in place of all of you; Jos., Ant. 14, 107 τὴν δοκὸν αὐτῷ τὴν χρυσῆν λύτρον ἀ. πάντων ἔδωκεν; cf. Eur., Alc. 524). S. the lit. on λύτρον.—ἀ. τούτου *for this reason* Eph 5: 31. W. attraction of the rel. ἀνθ' ὧν *in return for which* = *because* (Soph., Ant. 1068; X., An. 1, 3, 4; Dit., Or. 90,

35 [196 BC]; PLeid. DI, 21; LXX; Jos., Ant. 17, 201; Sib. Or. 5, 68) Lk 1: 20; 19: 44; Ac 12: 23; 2 Th 2: 10; *therefore* (Aeschyl., Prom. 31; Thu. 6, 83, 1; 4 Macc 18: 3; Jdth 9: 3; Jos., Ant. 4, 318) Lk 12: 3.—W. articular inf. (Ael. Aristid. 34 p. 654 D.; Jos., Ant. 16, 107) ἀ. τοῦ λέγειν ὑμᾶς *instead of* (*your*) *saying* Js 4: 15 (Bl-D. §403; Rob. 574; Mlt.-Turner 258).—Replacing the gen. of price (even in class. Kühner-G. I 454; cf. Hdt. 3, 59 νῆσον ἀντὶ χρημάτων παρέλαβον. Pla., Rep. 371D; Jos., Ant. 4, 118) ἀ. βρώσεως μιᾶς ἀπέδοτο (*in exchange*) *for a single meal* Hb 12: 16. So perh. also vs. 2 (s. 1 above). M-M.**

ἀντιβάλλω (Thu.+; pap., LXX) lit. *put* or *place against* τὶ πρός τινα (2 Macc 11: 13 ἀ. πρὸς ἑαυτόν) τίνες οἱ λόγοι οὒς ἀντιβάλλετε πρὸς ἀλλήλους; *what are the words you are exchanging with each other?* i.e. *what is the subject of your discussion?* Lk 24: 17 (Theophanes Conf. [VIII AD], Chron. 461, 18 de Boor ἀντιβάλλειν πρὸς ἀλλήλους = dispute).*

ἀντιβλέπω (X.+; PGM 5, 323; Jos., Ant. 6, 10, C. Ap. 2, 235) *look at* πρός τινα (cf. Plut., Pomp. 69, 5; Aelian, N. A. 3, 33) *someone* AP 3: 6.*

ἀντίγραφον, ου, τό (Lysias, Demosth. et al.; Strabo 8, 6, 15; inscr., pap., LXX, Ep. Arist.; Jos., Ant. 13, 126; 17, 145; Test. 12 Patr.) *a copy* of a book MPol 22: 2; Epil Mosq 4.*

ἀντιδιατίθημι (post-class. word of the higher Koine [Nägeli 30]) mid. *oppose oneself, be opposed* (Περὶ ὕψους 17, 1 πρὸς τὴν πειθὼ τ. λόγων πάντως ἀντιδιατίθεται) παιδεύειν τοὺς ἀντιδιατιθεμένους *correct his opponents* 2 Ti 2: 25. M-M.*

ἀντίδικος, ου, ὁ *opponent* in a lawsuit (so X.+; Dit., Syll.³ 656, 24; 953, 5 and 15; very oft. pap., e.g. POxy. 37 I, 8; 237 VII, 24, 32, VIII, 12; BGU 592, 7; Pr 18: 17; Jer 27: 34; Philo, Aet. M. 142; Jos., Ant. 8, 30; loanw. in rabb.) Mt 5: 25; Lk 12: 58; 18: 3. Of the devil, since he appears in court as an accuser 1 Pt 5: 8 (cf. Rv 12: 10; Job 1: 6ff; Zech 3: 1); but here and in Lk 18: 3 it could mean *enemy, opponent* in gener. (so Aeschyl., Ag. 41; Philod., Ira p. 65 W.; PGM 3, 6; 1 Km 2: 10; Is 41: 11; Sir 36: 6; Jos., Ant. 13, 413). This would corresp. to the designation of the devil as ἐχθρός Test. Dan 6: 3f. M-M. B. 1432.*

ἀντίδοτος, ου, ἡ (Strabo [II AD]: Anth. Pal. 12, 13; Diosc. 2, 110, 1 W.; Galen: CMG V 4, 2 p. 147, 15; 191, 21; Philumen. p. 21, 1 al.) *antidote* (w. φάρμακον) ἀ. τοῦ μὴ ἀποθανεῖν *against death* IEph 20: 2.*

ἀντίζηλος, ου, ὁ (adj., Vett. Val. 198, 11; Lev 18: 18; Sir 26: 6; 37: 11) *the jealous one* (Test. Jos. 7: 5 ἡ ἀντίζηλός σου) w. βάσκανος and πονηρός of the devil MPol 17: 1.*

ἀντίθεσις, εως, ἡ (Pre-Socr.+; Plut., Mor. 953B; Lucian, Dial. Mort. 10, 10; Herm. Wr. 10, 10; Philo, Ebr. 187) *opposition, objection, contradiction* ἀ. τῆς ψευδωνύμου γνώσεως 1 Ti 6: 20 (γνῶσις 3). M-M.*

ἀντικαθίστημι 2 aor. (intr.) ἀντικατέστην *place against*; intr. *oppose, resist* (so Thu. 1, 62, 5; 1, 71, 1+; POxy. 97, 9 [II AD]; BGU 168, 11; Mi 2: 8 A) μέχρις αἵματος ἀ. *resist unto death* Hb 12: 4. M-M.*

ἀντικαλέω 1 aor. ἀντεκάλεσα *invite in return* τινά *someone* of an invitation to a meal in return for a previous invitation (so X., Symp. 1, 15) Lk 14: 12.*

ἀντίκειμαι (Hdt.+ in the mng. 'be opposite, form a contrast to'; cf. Nägeli 39. So also Jos., Bell. 4, 454) *be*

opposed, in opposition τινί *to someone* (Cass. Dio 39, 8 ἀλλ' ἐκείνῳ τε ὁ Μίλων ἀντέκειτο): ταῦτα ἀλλήλοις ἀντίκειται *these things are in opposition to each other* Gal 5: 17. ἀ. τῇ ὑγιαινούσῃ διδασκαλίᾳ 1 Ti 1: 10.—ὁ ἀντικείμενος *the opponent, enemy* (UPZ 69, 6 [152 BC] Μενέδημον ἀντικείμενον ἡμῖν. Ex 23: 22; Esth 9: 2; 2 Macc 10: 26 al. LXX; Ep. Arist. 266) w. dat. of the pers. Lk 13: 17; 21: 15. Abs. 1 Cor 16: 9; Phil 1: 28. Of the Antichrist *adversary* 2 Th 2: 4 ('anteciminus', Ps.-Philo, Liber Antiq. Bibl. 45, 6). Of the devil (Berl. Kopt. Urk. 6, 25) 1 Cl 51: 1; MPol 17: 1; perh. also 1 Ti 5: 14. M-M.*

ἀντικνήμιον, ου, τό (Hipponax [VI BC] 49; Aristoph., Hippocr., X. et al.; oft. pap.) *shin* MPol 8: 3.*

ἄντικρυς adv. (Hom.+; oft. Joseph.; on its form see Kühner-Bl. I p. 298f; Bl-D. §21; Mlt.-H. 328; Thackeray p. 136) *opposite*, used as improper prep. w. gen. (Themistocl., Ep. 20 ἄ. τοῦ θρόνου. POxy. 43 verso III, 20 ἄ. οἰκίας Ἐπιμάχου. PTebt. 395, 4; 3 Macc 5: 16; Philo, Op. M. 79; Jos., Ant. 15, 410) ἄ. Xίου Ac 20: 15; ἄ. αὐτῶν AP 11: 26 (cf. POxy. 471, 81 ἄ. τοῦ δεῖνα). M-M.*

ἀντιλαμβάνω in our lit. only mid. (which is common Thu.+; LXX, Philo, Joseph.) 2 aor. ἀντελαβόμην.

1. *take someone's part, help, come to the aid of* τινός (Diod. S. 11, 13, 1; Cass. Dio 40, 27; 46, 45; Plut., Pyrrh. 25, 2; Dit., Or. 51, 9f; 697, 1; PPetr. II 3b, 7; UPZ 47, 23 [II BC]; LXX) ἀντελάβετο Ἰσραὴλ παιδὸς αὐτοῦ *he has helped his servant Israel* Lk 1: 54 (cf. Is 41: 8f). ἀ. τῶν ἀσθενούντων *help the weak* Ac 20: 35 (cf. 2 Ch 28: 15). ἀ. ἀλλήλων Hv 3, 9, 2.

2. of things *take part in, devote oneself to, practice* (X., Cyr. 2, 3, 6 τ. πραγμάτων. PReinach 47, 4 τῆς γεωργίας. PLond. 301, 6ff τῆς χρείας = the office; likew. POxy. 1196, 12ff. Dit., Or. 339, 32 τῆς εὐσχημοσύνης. Is 26: 3; Bar 3: 21; Jos., Ant. 5, 194; 19, 238) οἱ τῆς εὐεργεσίας ἀντιλαμβανόμενοι *who devote themselves to kindness* 1 Ti 6: 2 (s. also mng. 3).

3. *perceive, notice* τινός someth. (Ps.-Pla., Axioch. 370A; cf. MMeister, Axioch. Dial., Diss. Breslau '15, 43) εὐωδίας ἀ. *notice a fragrance* MPol 15: 2 (Philo, Leg. All. 3, 56, Det. Pot. Ins. 101: tones). Many Eng.-speaking scholars expand this mng. into *enjoy, benefit by* for 1 Ti 6: 2, which fits well into the context (cf. Field, Notes 210; WLock, ICC ad loc.). M-M.*

ἀντιλέγω 2 aor. ἀντεῖπον (s. as separate entry) (trag., Hdt.+; inscr., pap., LXX).

1. *speak against, contradict* τινί someone or someth. (Thu. et al.; Sir 4: 25; Jos., Ant. 3, 217 μηδὲν ἀ. δύνασθαι τούτοις = be able to say nothing against them) τοῖς ὑπὸ Παύλου λαλουμένοις Ac 13: 45. Abs. (Thu. 8, 53, 2b οἱ ἀντιλέγοντες. Ep. Arist. 266; Jos., Ant. 1, 338) τοὺς ἀντιλέγοντας ἐλέγχειν *refute those who contradict* Tit 1: 9; μὴ ἀντιλέγοντες 2: 9 (cf. 3 Macc 2: 28).—Ac 28: 19, 22.—Foll. by μή w. inf. *deny* (Dio Chrys. 21[38], 14; this constr. is found in the sense 'speak out against a thing' Thu. 3, 41) ἀ. ἀνάστασιν μὴ εἶναι *they deny that there is a resurrection* Lk 20: 27.

2. *oppose, refuse* (Appian, Liby. 94, §442; Lucian, Abdic. 24, Dial. Mort. 30, 3; Achilles Tat. 5, 27; POxy. 1148, 5ff; pap. letter in Dssm., LO 160, 23 [LAE 194, 23]; Is 22: 22; 4 Macc 8: 2) ἀ. τῷ Καίσαρι J 19: 12. λαὸν ἀντιλέγοντα ὁδῷ δικαίᾳ μου *that opposes my righteous way* B 12: 4 (cf. Is 65: 2). τῇ δωρεᾷ τοῦ θεοῦ *refuse the gift of God* ISm 7: 1. Abs. (Diod. S. 18, 2, 3 οἱ ἀντιλέγοντες = the opponents) λαὸν ἀπειθοῦντα καὶ ἀντιλέγοντα *a disobedient and obstinate people* Ro 10: 21 (Is 65: 2).—

σημεῖον ἀντιλεγόμενον *a sign that is opposed* Lk 2: 34.—*reject* a writing as spurious: Plut., Mor. 839c Aphareus composed 37 tragedies, ὧν ἀντιλέγονται δύο. On the other hand, in Plut., Mor. 839ϝ, of the 64 λόγοι of Isaeus 50 are γνήσιοι= genuine. M-M.*

ἀντίλημψις, εως, ἡ (Thu.+in var. mngs.; on the spelling w. or without μ cf. W-S. §5, 30; Mayser 194f; WSchulze, Orthographica 1894 I p. xivff) *help* (so UPZ 42, 40 [162 ʙᴄ]; PAmh. 35, 57; BGU 1187, 27; LXX; Jos., Ant. 18, 4; cf. Dssm B 87 [BS p. 92]; Nägeli 39) ἀντιλήμψεις *helpful deeds* 1 Cor 12: 28 (for the pl. cf. 2 Macc 8: 19; 3 Macc 5: 50). M-M.*

ἀντιλήπτωρ, ορος, ὁ (BGU 1138, 19 of a Rom. official: τὸν πάντων σωτῆρα κ. ἀντιλήπτορα. UPZ 14, 17f [158 ʙᴄ] the royal couple: ὑμᾶς τ. θεοὺς μεγίστους καὶ ἀντιλήμπτορας; LXX of God; En. 103, 9) *helper, protector* ὁ βοηθὸς καὶ ἀ. ἡμῶν *our helper and protector* 1 Cl 59: 4 (ἀ. and βοηθός Ps 118: 114; 17: 3; 58: 17).*

ἀντίληψις s. ἀντίλημψις.

ἀντιλογία, ας, ἡ (Hdt.+; inscr., pap., LXX).
1. *contradiction, dispute* χωρὶς πάσης ἀντιλογίας (BGU 1133, 15; PStrassb. 75, 10; PLond. 310, 16) *beyond all doubt* Hb 7: 7. πάσης ἀ. πέρας 6: 16.
2. *hostility, rebellion* (PPetr. II 17[3], 7 [III ʙᴄ]; Pr 17: 11; Jos., Ant. 2, 43; 17, 313) ἡ εἰς ἑαυτὸν ἀ. *hostility toward himself* Hb 12: 3. τῇ ἀντιλογίᾳ τοῦ Κόρε *in the rebellion of Korah* Jd 11. M-M.*

ἀντιλοιδορέω (Plut., Anton. 42, 5, Mor. 88ᴇ; Lucian, Conviv. 40; PPetr. III 21g, 20 [III ʙᴄ] ἐμοῦ δέ σε ἀντιλοιδοροῦντος foll. by ἐλοιδόρησας φαμένη) *revile in return*, of Christ λοιδορούμενος οὐκ ἀντελοιδόρει 1 Pt 2: 23. M-M.*

ἀντίλυτρον, ου, τό (Polyaenus, Exc. 52, 7 Melber; Orphica Lithica 593 πάντων ἀ.; schol. on Nicander, Alexiph. 560 ἀντ. . . . . ὑπὲρ τῶν βοῶν; Origen, Hexapla II 170 Field on Ps 48: 9; Hesychius; Cosmas and Damian 40, 30; PLond. 1343, 31 [VIII ᴀᴅ]) *ransom* ἀ. ὑπὲρ πάντων 1 Ti 2: 6 (cf. Mlt. 105; Jos., Ant. 14, 107 λύτρον ἀντὶ πάντων).*

ἀντιμετρέω fut. pass. ἀντιμετρηθήσομαι (perh. as early as Caecilius Calactinus p. 147 Ofenloch; then Ps.-Lucian, Amor. 19; Rhet. Gr. I 523, 12 [mid.]) *measure in return* τινί *to someone* Lk 6: 38; Pol 2: 3. M-M.*

ἀντιμιμέομαι (Appian, Bell. Civ. 5, 41 §174; 5, 94 §393) *follow the example* τινά *of someone* IEph 10: 2.*

ἀντιμισθία, ας, ἡ (so far found only in Christian writers; Theoph., Ad Autol. 2, 9; Clem. Alex.) *reward*, also in the mng. *penalty*, w. emphasis on the reciprocal nature of the transaction (ἀντί), *exchange* τὴν αὐτὴν ἀ. πλατύνθητε καὶ ὑμεῖς *widen your hearts in the same way in exchange* 2 Cor 6: 13 (on the acc. cf. Bl-D. §154; Rob. 486f).—ἀπολαμβάνειν τὴν ἀ. *receive the penalty* Ro 1: 27 (FWDanker, FWGingrich-Festschr., '72, 95). ἀ. διδόναι τινί *make a return* 2 Cl 1: 3; 9: 7. ἀντιμισθίας ἀποδιδόναι τινί 11: 6; 15: 2. μισθὸν ἀντιμισθίας διδόναι *give a recompense in return* 1: 5. M-M.*

Ἀντιόχεια, ας, ἡ (lit., inscr., Joseph., Sib. Or.) *Antioch*.
1. *A. on the Orontes*, the largest city in Syria (Jos., Ant. 16, 148), capital of the Seleucid Empire, later seat of the Rom. legate. Many Jews lived there (Jos., Bell. 7, 43). Of the origin of the Christian Church in A. we know only what is reported in Ac 11: 19-26. Paul labored there Ac 13: 1;

14: 26; 15: 22ff; 18: 22, and had a difference of opinion w. Peter Gal 2: 11. Ignatius, bishop of the church there, mentions the city IPhld 10: 1; ISm 11: 1; IPol 7: 1.—OMüller, Antiquitates Antiochenae 1839; ThMommsen, Röm. Gesch. V 456ff; RFörster, A. am Orontes: Jahrb. d. K. D. Arch. Inst. 12, 1897, 103-49; HLeclerq, Antioche: Dict. d'Arch. Chrét. I 2359-427; KBauer, A. in der ältesten Kirchengesch. '19; HDieckmann, Antiochien '20; KPieper, A. am Orontes im ap. Zeitalter: ThGL 22, '30, 710-28; VSchultze, Antiocheia '30; LMEnfrey, Antioche '30; CHKraeling, The Jewish Commun. at Antioch: JBL 51, '32, 130-60; MCTenney, Bibliotheca Sacra 107, '50, 298-310; JKollwitz, RAC I '50, 461-69; GDowney, A History of Antioch in Syria from Seleucus to the Arab Conquest, '61.
2. *Pisidian A.* (Strabo 12, 8, 14; Pliny the Elder, Nat. Hist. 5, 94; Dit., Or. 536), belonging to the province of Galatia, seat of the civil and military administration in S. Galatia. Visited several times by Paul Ac 13: 14; 14: 19, 21; 2 Ti 3: 11.—Ramsay, Bearing 282ff; JWeiss, RE X 559f; WMCalder, Journ. of Rom. Stud. II '12, 79-109; P Gaechter, Petrus u. seine Zeit, '58, 155-212.

Ἀντιοχεύς, έως, ὁ (lit., inscr., Joseph.) *a man from Antioch* in Syria, of the proselyte Nicolaus Ac 6: 5.*

ἀντιπαλαίω 1 aor. ἀντεπάλαισα, inf. ἀντιπαλαῖσαι (POxy.1099; schol.on Aristoph., Ach.570; schol.on Thu.2, 89) *wrestle* τινί w. someone (opp. καταπαλαίω) τῷ διαβόλῳ Hs 8, 3, 6; abs. m 12, 5, 2.*

ἀντιπαρέλκω only pass. *let oneself be dragged over to the opposite side* 2 Cl 17: 3.*

ἀντιπαρέρχομαι 2 aor. ἀντιπαρῆλθον (Strato: Anth. Pal. 12, 8[7] Jacobs; Wsd 16: 10) *pass by on the opposite side* Lk 10: 31f. M-M.*

Ἀντιπᾶς, ᾶ, ὁ (Sb 4206, 65; 255 [I ʙᴄ]; prob. short for Ἀντίπατρος [cf. Jos., Ant. 14, 10], found Inschr. v. Perg. 524, 2 et aliter) *Antipas* martyr (μάρτυς 3) in Pergamum Rv 2: 13.—WSchulze, Kl. Schr. 61, 275 A. 1.*

Ἀντιπατρίς, ίδος, ἡ *Antipatris* city in Judaea founded by Herod the Great and named after his father (Jos., Ant. 16, 143, Bell. 1, 417), on the road fr. Lydda to Caesarea Mt 13: 54 ℵ. Paul went through the city while being taken as captive to Caesarea Ac 23: 31.—Schürer II⁴ 202-4.*

ἀντιπέρα adv. (Bl-D. §26 app.; Rob. 638f; Jos. only Ant. 2, 341 τὴν ἀντιπέραν γῆν) *opposite*, as improper prep. w. gen. (Polyb. 4, 43, 4; Diod. S. 2, 47, 1; POsl 26, 8 [5/4 ʙᴄ]; as ἀντιπέρας as early as Thu. 2, 66, 1) Gerasa ἀ. τῆς Γαλιλαίας *opposite Galilee*, i.e., on the east shore of the Lake of Gennesaret Lk 8: 26. M-M.*

ἀντιπίπτω (Aristot.+) *resist, oppose* (so since Polyb. 24, 11, 5; oft. in Plut., also UPZ 36, 21 [162/1 ʙᴄ]; Num 27: 14; cf. Anz 343) w. dat. (Polyb., loc. cit.; BGU 1300, 22 [III/II ʙᴄ]; UPZ 81 III, 6 the divine command) τῷ πνεύματι τ. ἁγίῳ Ac 7: 51. M-M.*

ἀντιστῆναι s. ἀνθίστημι.

ἀντιστρατεύομαι (X., Cyr. 8, 8, 26; Diod. S. 22, 13, 2 Dind.; this is also the act., as Jos., Ant. 2, 240.—Nägeli 18; 23) *be at war with* τινί, only fig. (cf. Aristaen. 2, 1 Ἔρωτες ἀντ. τοῖς ὑπερηφανοῦσι), of sin regarded as a ruling power ἀ. τῷ νόμῳ τοῦ νοός μου *at war w. the law of my mind* Ro 7: 23.*

ἀντιτάσσω (Aeschyl., Hdt.+; in our lit., as LXX; Jos., Bell. 2, 194; 3, 15, Vi. 202, only mid.) *oppose, resist* w. dat. of pers. or thing opposed. Of pers. (3 Km 11: 34; Hos 1: 6) ὑπερηφάνοις Js 4: 6; 1 Pt 5: 5; 1 Cl 30: 2; IEph 5: 3 (all Pr 3: 34). οὐκ ἀ. ὑμῖν *he offers you no resistance* Js 5: 6. τῇ ἐξουσίᾳ Ro 13: 2. μηδενί (w. ἡσύχιον εἶναι) Hm 8: 10.—Of things (Esth 3: 4; 4 Macc 16: 23S) τῷ θελήματι θεοῦ *oppose the will of God* 1 Cl 36: 6. τῷ νόμῳ Hs 1: 6. ταῖς ἡδοναῖς *oppose their pleasures* (Procop. Soph., Ep. 117 ἀντιτάξει τ. ἡδοναῖς) Dg 6: 5. Abs. Ac 18: 6. M-M.*

ἀντίτυπος, ον (Anaximander+; IG XIV 1320; Esth 3: 13d v.l.).
    1. adj. *corresponding to* someth. that has gone before. The ἀ. is usu. regarded as secondary to the τύπος (cf. the oracular saying in Diod. S. 9, 36, 3 τύπος ἀντίτυπος and Ex 25: 40), but since τύπος can mean both 'original' and 'copy' (see s.v. 2 and 5), ἀ. is also ambiguous (Polyb. 6, 31, 8 ἀντίτυπος τίθεμαί τινι I am placed opposite someth.). Thus in 1 Pt 3: 21 ὅ (i.e., ὕδωρ) ὑμᾶς ἀ. νῦν σώζει βάπτισμα means *baptism, which is a fulfilment* (of the type), *now saves you*, i.e., the saving of Noah fr. the flood is a τύπος, or 'foreshadowing' (hardly the 'original' in the full Platonic sense 2 below), and baptism corresponds to it (so PLundberg, La Typologie Baptismale dans l'ancienne Église, '42, 110ff; EGSelwyn, The First Epistle of St Peter, '46, 298f; difftly. BReicke, The Disobedient Spirits and Christian Baptism, '46, 144f).
    2. subst. τὸ ἀ. *copy, antitype, representation* (Wadd. 1855; Plotin. 2, 9, 6; Proclus on Pla., Cratyl. p. 76, 28 Pasquali), acc. to Platonic doctrine, w. ref. to the world of things about us, as opposed to the true heavenly originals, or ideas (the αὐθεντικόν). So χειροποίητα ἅγια, ἀ. τῶν ἀληθινῶν *a sanctuary made w. hands, a (mere) copy of the true (sanctuary)* Hb 9: 24. The flesh is ἀντίτυπος τοῦ πνεύματος 2 Cl 14: 3a; the spirit, on the other hand, is τὸ αὐθεντικόν vs. 3b. M-M.*

ἀντίχριστος, ου, ὁ (cf. ἀντίθεος: Heliod. 4, 7, 13; Iambl., Myst. 3, 31; PGM 7, 635 πέμψον μοι τὸν ἀληθινὸν Ἀσκληπιὸν δίχα τινὸς ἀντιθέου πλανοδαίμονος; Philo, Somn. 2, 183) *the Antichrist* the adversary of the Messiah, to appear in the last days 1 J 2: 18, 22; 4: 3; 2 J 7; Pol 7: 1. Pl. ἀ. πολλοί 1 J 2: 18. The word is not found outside Christian circles; the concept is. For the general idea in the NT without the word cf. 2 Th 2: 1-12 and Rv 12-14. Cf. WBousset, Der Antichrist 1895, Rel.³ 254-6 al.; KErbes, Der A. in d. Schriften d. NTs 1897; JGeffcken, D. Sage v. Antichrist: PJ 102, '00, 385ff; MFriedländer, Der Antichrist in d. vorchr. jüd. Quellen '01, AJeremias, D. Antichrist in Gesch. u. Gegenwart '30; PBRigaux, L'Antéchrist '32; HSchlier, KBarth-Festschr. '36, 110-23; OA Piper, JBL 66, '47, 444f; MDibelius, Hdb.³ 11, '37, 47-51; RHCharles, ICC Rv II, '50, 76-87; ELohmeyer, RAC I '50, 450-57; RSchütz, RGG³ I, 431f (lit). M-M.*

ἀντίψυχον, ου, τό *ransom* (cf. 4 Macc 6: 29; 17: 21. The adj. ἀντίψυχος, ον=someth. given in return for sparing one's life: Lucian, Lex. 10 χρήματα ἀντίψυχα διδόναι; Cass. Dio 59, 8, 3 ἀντίψυχοι) IEph 21: 1; ISm 10: 2; IPol 2: 3; 6: 1.*

ἀντλέω 1 aor. ἤντλησα (Theognis, Hdt.+).
    1. *draw,* water (so Hdt.+; POxy. 985; PLond. 1177, 66; LXX; Jos., Bell. 4, 472) w. acc. (Biogr. p. 428; Gen 24: 13; Is 12: 3) J 2: 9; 4: 7. Abs. (Hdt. 6, 119; Diog. L. 7, 168 and 169) 2: 8; 4: 15.
    2. fig. *endure* (trag. and later; Lucian, De Merc. Cond. 17 δουλείαν) πολλοὺς κόπους ἀ. Hs 5, 6, 2 (s. ἀναντλέω). M-M.*

ἄντλημα, ατος, τό *a bucket* for drawing water (Plut., Mor. 974E; schol. on Aristoph., Ran. 1297; PFlor. 384, 17) J 4: 11.*

ἀντοφθαλμέω (oft. in Polyb., w. whom it is a characteristic word, in var. mngs.) *look directly at* of the sun εἰς τὰς ἀκτῖνας αὐτοῦ B 5: 10 (cf. Antig. Car. 46; Gk. Apoc. Bar. 7). τινί *look someone in the face* τῷ ἐργοπαρέκτῃ his *employer* 1 Cl 34: 1. ἀ. τῇ ἀληθείᾳ *look the truth in the face* honestly or defiantly (Περὶ ὕψους 34, 4 ἀντ. τοῖς ἐκείνου πάθεσιν=the passions of that man; Wsd 12: 14) Ac 6: 10 D. Fig., of a ship τοῦ πλοίου μὴ δυναμένοι ἀ. τῷ ἀνέμῳ *since the ship was not able to face the wind* Ac 27: 15 (cf. Breusing 167f; ChVoigt, Hansa 53, '16, 728). M-M.*

ἀνυβρίστως adv. *without being insulted* or *injured* (so pass. Ps.-Phoc. 157; adj. PRyl. 117, 26 [III AD]); perh. act., *without insolence, decorously* (Democr. 73; Jos., Ant. 17, 308) ἀ. ἀγαλλιᾶσθαι Hs 1: 6.*

ἄνυδρος, ον (since Hes., fgm. 24 Rz.; Eur., Hdt.; Dit., Or. 199, 21; POxy. 918 II, 10; LXX; Jos., C. Ap. 1, 277) *waterless, dry* τόποι ἄ. *waterless places* (Plut., Lucull. 36, 3; Ps.-Callisth. 2, 9, 1; cf. Pr 9: 12c; Is 44: 3; Jos., C. Ap. 2, 25) as the abode of demons (cf. Is 13: 21; Bar 4: 35; Rv 18: 2) Mt 12: 43; Lk 11: 24. Fig. πηγαὶ ἄ. *springs without water* of sinners 2 Pt 2: 17. νεφέλαι ἄ. (cf. Pr 25: 14 Hebr.; Vergil, Georg. 3, 197 arida nubila) *clouds that yield no rain* Jd 12. M-M.*

ἀνυπέρβλητος, ον (X., Pla.+; Polyb. 8, 12, 12; Diod. S. 1, 55, 10; 13, 56, 5; Dio Chrys. 58[75], 8; Ael. Aristid. 25, 18 K.=43 p. 803 D.; Herm. Wr. 6, 3; 11, 5; Dit., Syll³ 839, 9; 893, 16f; PGM 2, 150; 4, 1201; 1873; 3172; Jdth 16: 13; Ep. Arist. 92; Philo, Mos. 2, 207; Jos., Bell. 2, 198, Ant. 11, 44) *unsurpassable, unexcelled* τελειότης *perfection* 1 Cl 53: 5. εὔνοια MPol 17: 3.*

ἀνυπόκριτος, ον (schol. on Aristoph., Av. 798; Iambl., Vi. Pyth. §69, 188 αἰδώς; Ps.-Demetr., De Eloc. 194; Wsd 5: 18; 18: 15) *genuine, sincere,* lit. *without hypocrisy* ἀγάπη Ro 12: 9; 2 Cor 6: 6. φιλαδελφία 1 Pt 1: 22. πίστις 1 Ti 1: 5; 2 Ti 1: 5. *Free from insincerity* σοφία Js 3: 17.*

ἀνυποκρίτως adv. (M.Ant. 8, 5, 2) *with no insincerity* or *hypocrisy* 2 Cl 12: 3.*

ἀνυπότακτος, ον (since Polyb. 3, 36, 4).
    1. *not made subject, independent* (Epict. 2, 10, 1; 4, 1, 161; Artem. 2, 30; Vett. Val. 9, 18; 41, 3 al.; PGM 4, 1366; Philo, Rer. Div. Her. 4; Jos., Ant. 11, 217) οὐδὲν ἀφῆκεν αὐτῷ ἀ. *he has left nothing that was not made subject to him* i.e., he has withheld nothing from his sovereignty Hb 2: 8.
    2. *undisciplined, disobedient, rebellious* (Ptolem., Apotel. 2, 3, 13; 18; 45; 4, 5, 3; 5; Sym. 1 Km 2: 12; 10: 27; Moeris p. 34 Pierson groups ἀ. with ἀφηνιαστής 'rebel' and ὑπερήφανος; PGM 4, 1367; Maspéro 97 II, 49) w. ἄνομος 1 Ti 1: 9. Of refractory church members Tit 1: 10. Of spoiled children 1: 6. M-M.*

ἀνυστέρητος, ον *not lacking* w. gen. *in anything* ἐκκλησίᾳ ἀ. οὔσῃ παντὸς χαρίσματος *not lacking in any spiritual gift* ISm inscr.; ἀπὸ πάντων τῶν αἰτημάτων σου ἀ. ἔσῃ *all your requests will be granted* Hm 9: 4.*

ἄνω adv. of place (Hom.+; inscr., pap., LXX).
    1. *above* (opp. κάτω as Aristot. p. 6a, 13; Aeneas Tact. 1674; Philo, Conf. Ling. 139, Deus Imm. 175 al.; Jos., C. Ap. 1, 77) ἐν τ. οὐρανῷ ἄ. *in the heaven above* Ac 2: 19 (Jo

3: 3 v.l.; cf. Ex 20: 4; Dt 4: 39; 5: 8 al.; Herm. Wr. in Stobaeus I 407, 23 W.=Sc. 494, 28), where ἄ. is seemingly pleonastic. ἕως ἄ. (2 Ch 26: 8) γεμίζειν *fill to the brim* J 2: 7. Cf. 2 Cl 19: 4; Hs 2: 5.—As adj. (Diod. S. 4, 55, 7 οἱ ἄνω τόποι; Appian, Syr. 12 §47 ἡ Ἀσία ἡ ἄνω; Arrian, Ind. 5, 13; UPZ 162 V, 28 [117 bc]; Jos. Ant. 12, 135 οἱ ἄνω τόποι, 147; 13, 223 ἡ ἄ. Συρία, Vi. 67) ἡ ἄ. Ἰερουσαλήμ (opp. ἡ νῦν Ἰ.) *the Jerus. above, the heavenly Jerus.* Gal 4: 26 (s. Ἱεροσόλυμα 2 and cf. Jos., Bell. 5, 400 ὁ ἄ. δικαστής of God).—As subst. τὰ ἄ. *what is above*=heaven (cf. Herm. Wr. 4, 11 τὴν πρὸς τὰ ἄνω ὁδόν) ἐγὼ ἐκ τῶν ἄ. εἰμί *I am from the world above* J 8: 23. τὰ ἄ. ζητεῖν *seek what is above* (heavenly) Col 3: 1. τὰ ἄ. φρονεῖν vs. 2.

2. *upward(s), up* (Alex. Aphr., Fat. 27, II 2 p. 198, 28 ἄνω φέρεσθαι=raise oneself upward; POxy. 744, 8 [I bc]; I Esdr 9: 47; Philo, Spec. Leg. 1, 207 ἀπὸ γῆς ἄνω πρὸς οὐρανόν) ἄ. ὁρᾶν *look upward* Dg 10: 2 (in prayer as ἄνω βλέπω in Moschus, fgm. 4 p. 139 v. Wilam. ['06]; cf. Herm. Wr. 406, 19 Sc. ἄ. βλέπειν; Celsus 3, 62). For this ἦρεν τοὺς ὀφθαλμοὺς ἄνω, where ἄ. is superfluous J 11: 41. ῥίζα ἄ. φύουσα *a root growing up* Hb 12: 15 (Dt 29: 17). ἡ ἄνω κλῆσις *the upward call* Phil 3: 14 (cf. Gk. Apoc. Bar. 4 p. 87, 33 James ἐν αὐτῷ μέλλουσιν τ. ἄνω κλῆσιν προσλαβεῖν, καὶ τ. εἰς παράδεισον εἴσοδον). M-M.*

ἀνῶ s. ἀνίημι.

ἀνώγαιον and ἀνώγεον s. ἀνάγαιον.

ἄνωθεν adv. of place (trag., Hdt.+; inscr., pap., LXX).
1. locally *from above* (Dit., Syll.³ 969, 63; PHib. 110, 66; 107; 109; Gen 49: 25; Josh 3: 16; EpJer 61; En. 28, 2; Philo, Rer. Div. Her. 64; 184, Fug. 138, Somn, 2, 142; Jos., Ant. 3, 158) σχισθῆναι ἀπ᾽ ἄ. ἕως κάτω *be torn fr. top to bottom* Mk 15: 38. For this ἄ. ἕως κάτω Mt 27: 51 (where ἀπ᾽ is added by most witnesses, foll. Mk). ἐκ τῶν ἄ. ὑφαντὸς δι᾽ ὅλου *woven from the top in one piece* (i.e., altogether without seam) J 19: 23. Esp. *from heaven* (cf. ἄνω 1 and schol. on Pla. 856E of the seer: ἄνωθεν λαμβάνειν τὸ πνεῦμα; Philo, Mos. 2, 69) ἄ. ἐκ τ. οὐρανοῦ J 3: 27 v.l. ὁ ἄ. ἐρχόμενος *he who comes from heaven* (explained in the same vs. by ὁ ἐκ τοῦ οὐρανοῦ ἐρχόμενος) 3: 31. Of the Holy Spirit πνεῦμα ἄ. ἐρχόμενον Hm 11: 21; for this simply τὸ πνεῦμα τὸ ἄ. 11: 8. ἡ δύναμις ἡ ἄ. ἐρχομένη 11: 20. ἡ σοφία ἄ. κατερχομένη Js 3: 15. For this ἡ ἄ. σοφία vs. 17. ἄ. εἶναι *come from above* Hm 9: 11; 11: 5; Js 1: 17. Opp. νῦν (cf. ἄνω 1) 2 Cl 14: 2. ἄ. δεδομένον *bestowed from above* (i.e., by God; cf. Procop. Soph., Ep. 109 θεοῦ ἄ. ἐπινεύοντος) J 19: 11.
2. *temporally*—a. *from the beginning* (Pla.; Demosth. 44, 69; Dit., Syll.³ 1104, 11; POxy. 237 VIII, 31; En. 98, 5; Philo, Mos. 2, 48) παρακολουθεῖν ἄ. *follow from the beginning* Lk 1: 3; mng. b is also poss.
b. *for a long time* (Dit., Syll.³ 685, 81 and 91; 748, 2; PTebt. 59, 7 and 10; Jos., Ant. 15, 250) προγινώσκειν ἄ. *know for a long time* Ac 26: 5 (Ael. Aristid. 50, 78 K.=26 p. 525 D. ἄ. Ἀριστείδην γιγνώσκω). For Lk 1: 3 s. a above.
3. *again, anew* (Pla., Ep. 2 p. 310E ἄ. ἀρξάμενος; Epict. 2, 17, 27; Jos., Ant. 1, 263; IG VII 2712, 58; BGU 595, 5ff) ἄ. ἐπιδεικνύναι MPol 1: 1. Oft. strengthened by πάλιν (CIG 1625, 60; Wsd 19: 6) Gal 4: 9—ἄ. γεννηθῆναι is purposely ambiguous and means both *born from above* and *born again* J 3: 3, 7 (ἄ. γεννᾶσθαι also Artem. 1, 13; Epict. 1, 13, 3: all men are begotten of their forefather Zeus ἐκ τῶν αὐτῶν σπερμάτων καὶ τῆς αὐτῆς ἄνωθεν [from above] καταβολῆς). JLouw, NThSt 23, '40, 53-6; OCullmann ThZ 4, '48, 364f; ESjöberg, Wiedergeburt u.

Neuschöpfung im paläst. Judentum: Studia Theologica 4, '51, 44-85. M-M.*

ἀνωτερικός, ή, όν (Hippocr.; Galen [Hobart 148]; Hippiatr. I 69, 22) *upper* τὰ ἀ. μέρη *the upper,* i.e., *inland country, the interior* Ac 19: 1 (like ἄνω for the interior, Jdth 1: 8; 2: 21 al. LXX).*

ἀνώτερος, έρα, ον in our lit. only neut. as adv. (Aristot.+; Dit., Syll.³ 674, 55; Lev 11: 21; 2 Esdr 13 [Neh 3]: 28; cf. Bl-D. §62; Rob. 298).
1. *higher* προσαναβαίνω ἀ. *go up higher,* i.e., to a better place Lk 14: 10.
2. *above, earlier* (as we say *above* in a citation when referring to someth. stated previously; Zen.-P. 59631, 10 [III bc] ἀνώτερον γεγράφαμεν; Polyb. 3, 1, 1 τρίτῃ ἀνώτερον βίβλῳ; Jos., Ant. 19, 212 καθάπερ ἀν. ἔφην; cf. AHeisenberg and LWenger, Byz. Pap. in d. Staatsbibl. zu München '14, No. 7, 47) ἀ. λέγειν Hb 10: 8. M-M.*

ἀνωφελής, ές (Aeschyl., Thu.+; LXX; Ep. Arist. 253; Philo).
1. *useless* (PLond. 908, 31, cf. 28; Wsd 1: 11; Is 44: 10; Jer 2: 8; Jos., Ant. 4, 191) νηστεία Hs 5, 1, 3. τὸ ἀνωφελές *uselessness* (Lucian, Dial. Mort. 15, 4) διὰ τὸ ἀσθενὲς καὶ ἀ. *because of its weakness and usel.* Hb 7: 18.
2. *harmful* (Pla., Protag. 21 p. 334A; Pr 28: 3; PsSol 16: 8 ἁμαρτία ἀ.) of controversies Tit 3: 9 (ἀν. with μάταιος as Is 44: 9f). Of myths IMg 8: 1. M-M.*

ἀξιαγάπητος, ον *worthy of love* of pers. (w. ἀξιοθαύμαστος) IPhld 5: 2.—Of things ὄνομα 1 Cl 1: 1; ἦθος 21: 7.*

ἀξίαγνος s. ἀξιόαγνος.

ἀξιέπαινος, ον (X. et al.; Appian, Ital. 6, Liby. 51 §224; Aelian, N.A. 2, 57) *worthy of praise* of the Roman church IRo inscr.*

ἀξίνη, ης, ἡ (Hom.+; BGU 1529, 4 [III bc]; Zen.-P. 59783; LXX) *ax* used for cutting wood (X., An. 1, 5, 12; Jer 26: 22) Mt 3: 10; Lk 3: 9; 13: 7 D. M-M. B. 561.*

ἀξιόαγνος, ον *worthy of sanctification* IRo inscr. (Lghtf. ἀξίαγνος).*

ἀξιοεπίτευκτος, ον *worthy of success* IRo inscr. (s. Lghtf. ad loc.).*

ἀξιοθαύμαστος, ον (X., Mem. 1, 4, 4; Appian, Bell. Civ. 1, 6 §24; Herm. Wr. 458, 16 Sc.; Ep. Arist. 282) *worthy of admiration* (w. ἀξιαγάπητος) IPhld 5: 2.*

ἀξιόθεος, ον *worthy of God* (Oenomaus [II AD] in Euseb., Pr. Ev. 5, 34, 4; Studia Pontica III No. 173 τῇ ἀξιοθέᾳ μητρί) of the church at Tralles ITr inscr.; at Rome IRo inscr. Of pers. Mg 2: 1; Sm 12: 2; τὰ ἀ. πρόσωπα IRo 1: 1.*

ἀξιομακάριστος, ον (X., Apol. 34; Cyrillus of Scyth. p. 235, 27) *worthy of blessing* IEph inscr.; IRo inscr. and 10: 1; of Paul IEph 12: 2.*

ἀξιονόμαστος, ον *worthy of the name* πρεσβυτέριον IEph 4: 1.*

ἀξιόπιστος, ον—1. *trustworthy* (X., Pla. et al.; pap.; Pr 28: 20; 2 Macc 15: 11; Jos., C. Ap. 1, 4) οἱ δοκοῦντες ἀ. εἶναι καὶ ἑτεροδιδασκαλοῦντες *who seem to be worthy of confidence and yet teach error* IPol 3: 1.
2. ironically, in a bad sense, *betraying confidence, pretentious, specious* (Lucian, Alex. 4; Charito 6, 9, 7; so the

adv. Jos., Bell. 1, 508) φιλόσοφοι Dg 8: 2; λύκοι ἀ. IPhld 2: 2.—Suidas: ἀξιόπιστος οὐχὶ ὁ κατάπλαστος λέγεται ὑπὸ τῶν παλαιῶν καὶ τεραταία χρώμενος, ἀλλ᾽ ὁ πιστὸς καὶ δόκιμος καὶ ἀξιόχρεως.*

ἀξιόπλοκος, ον worthily woven στέφανος, fig., of a group of worthy pers. IMg 13: 1.*

ἀξιοπρεπής, ές (X., Symp. 8, 40; Sym. Ps 89: 16) worthy of honor of the Roman church IRo inscr.; of pers. ἀξιοπρεπέστατος ἐπίσκοπος most esteemed bishop IMg 13: 1.*

ἄξιος, ία, ον (Hom.+; inscr., pap., LXX, Ep. Arist., Philo, Joseph.; loanw. in rabb.).
1. of things, in relation to other things, corresponding, comparable, worthy.
  a. of price equal in value (Eur., Alc. 300; Ps.-Demosth. 13, 10; Herodian 2, 3 [of the value of a thing]; Pr 3: 15; 8: 11; Sir 26: 15; cf. Nägeli 62) οὐκ ἄξια τὰ παθήματα πρὸς τ. μέλλουσαν δόξαν the sufferings are not to be compared w. the glory to come Ro 8: 18 (Arrian, Anab. 6, 24, 1 οὐδὲ τὰ ξύμπαντα... ξυμβληθῆναι ἄξια εἶναι τοῖς... πόνοις=all [the trials] are not worthy to be compared with the miseries). οὐδενὸς ἄ. λόγου worthy of no consideration Dg 4: 1 (λόγου ἄξ. Hdt. 4, 28; Pla., Ep. 7 p. 334E; Diod. S. 13, 65, 3 οὐδὲν ἄξιον λόγου πράξας; Dionys. Hal. 1, 22, 5; Dio Chrys. 22[39], 1; Vit. Hom. et Hes. 4); cf. vs. 4.
  b. gener., of any other relation (Diod. S. 4, 11, 1 ἄξιον τῆς ἀρετῆς=worthy of his valor; Jos., Vi. 250 βοὴ εὐνοίας ἀξία) καρποὶ ἄ. τῆς μετανοίας fruits in keeping with your repentance Lk 3: 8; Mt 3: 8. For this ἄ. τῆς μετανοίας ἔργα Ac 26: 20. καρπὸς ἄ. οὗ ἔδωκεν fruit which corresponds to what he gave us 2 Cl 1: 3. ἄ. πρᾶγμα ISm 11: 3. ἄκκεπτα IPol 6: 2. ἔργα ἄ. τῶν ῥημάτων deeds corresponding to the words 2 Cl 13: 3. πάσης ἀποδοχῆς ἄ. worthy of full acceptance 1 Ti 1: 15; 4: 9 (Ps.-Dicaearch. p. 144 l. 10 F. πάσης ἄξιος φιλίας). οὐδὲν ἄ. θανάτου nothing deserving death (cf. ἄξιον... τι θανάτου Plut., Marcus Cato 21, p. 349A) Lk 23: 15; Ac 25: 11, 25. θανάτου ἢ δεσμῶν ἄ. nothing deserving death or imprisonment 26: 31 (cf. Hyperid. 3, 14; Appian, Iber. 31 §124 ἄξια θανάτου; Jos., Ant. 11, 144; Herm. Wr. 1, 20 ἄ. τοῦ θανάτου). Foll. by rel. clause ἄ. ὧν ἐπράξαμεν Lk 23: 41.
  c. impers. ἄξιόν ἐστι it is worth while, fitting, proper (Hyperid. 2, 3; 6, 3; 4 Macc 17: 8; Ep. Arist. 4; 282) w. articular inf. foll. (Bl-D. §400, 2; Rob. 1059) τοῦ πορεύεσθαι 1 Cor 16: 4. καθὼς ἄ. ἐστιν 2 Th 1: 3.
2. of pers. worthy, fit.—a. in a good sense, w. gen. of the thing of which one is worthy τῆς τροφῆς entitled to his food Mt 10: 10; D 13: 1f. τῆς αἰωνίου ζωῆς Ac 13: 46. τοῦ μισθοῦ Lk 10: 7; 1 Ti 5: 18. πάσης τιμῆς 6: 1 (Dio Chrys. 14[31], 93; Lucian, Tox. 3 τιμῆς ἄ. παρὰ πάντων). ἄ. μετανοίας Hs 8, 6, 1.—W. gen. of the pers. οὐκ ἔστιν μου ἄ. he is not worthy of me= does not deserve to belong to me (perh. 'is not suited to me', s. 1 above) Mt 10: 37f; cf. PK 3 p. 15, 17; D 15: 1; ἄ. θεοῦ (Wsd 3: 5) IEph 2: 1; 4: 1; cf. 15: 1; IRo 10: 2; ὧν οὐκ ἦν ἄ. ὁ κόσμος of whom the world was not worthy=did not deserve to possess them Hb 11: 38.—W. inf. foll. (M. Ant. 8, 42 οὐκ εἰμι ἄξιος with inf.; BGU 1141, 15 [13 BC]; Jos., Ant. 4, 179) οὐκέτι εἰμὶ ἄ. κληθῆναι υἱός σου I am no longer fit to be called your son Lk 15: 19, 21; cf. Ac 13: 25; Rv 4: 11; 5: 2, 4, 9, 12 (WCvUnnik, BRigaux-Festschr. ’70, 445-61); B 14: 1; IEph 1: 3; Mg 14; Tr 13: 1; Sm 11: 1; Hs 8, 2, 5.—W. gen. of the inf. MPol 10: 2. Foll. by ἵνα (Bl-D. §393, 4; Rob. 658) ἄ. ἵνα λύσω τὸν ἱμάντα good enough to untie the thong J 1: 27 (ἱκανός 𝔓⁶⁶ ⁷⁵). Foll. by a rel. clause ἄ. ἐστιν ᾧ παρέξῃ τοῦτο Lk 7: 4 (Bl-D. §5, 3b; 379; Rob. 724).

Abs. (PPetr. II 15[3], 8 ἄ. γάρ ἐστιν ὁ ἄνθρωπος; 2 Macc 15: 21) ἄ. εἰσιν they deserve to Rv 3: 4; 16: 6; Mt 10: 11, 13; 22: 8; IEph 2: 2; Mg 12; Tr 4: 2; IRo 9: 2; ISm 9: 2; cf. IPol 8: 1; Hs 6, 3, 3; 8, 11, 1; B 9: 9; 14: 4; 21: 8. ἄ. τινα ἡγεῖσθαι (Job 30: 1) Hv 2, 1, 2; 3, 3, 4; 4, 1, 3; m 4, 2, 1; s 7: 5; w. ἵνα foll. Hs 9, 28, 5. As an epithet of persons IMg 2.
  b. in a bad sense (Ael. Aristid. 34 p. 650 D. ἄ. ὀργῆς) ἄ. πληγῶν (Dt 25: 2; cf. Jos., Ant. 13, 294) deserving blows Lk 12: 48. ἄ. θανάτου (Nicol. Dam.: 90 fgm. 4 p. 335, 12f Jac.; Appian, Bell. Civ. 2, 108 §452) Ac 23: 29; Ro 1: 32. Comp. ἀξιώτερος (Dit., Syll.³ 218, 25) Hv 3, 4, 3.—JA Kleist, ‘Axios’ in the Gospels: CBQ 6, ’44, 342-6; KStendahl, Nuntius 7, ’52, 53f. M-M.*

ἀξιόω impf. ἠξίουν; fut. ἀξιώσω; 1 aor. ἠξίωσα; pres. imper. pass. ἀξιούσθω; 1 aor. pass. ἠξιώθην; 1 fut. pass. ἀξιωθήσομαι; pf. pass. ἠξίωμαι (trag., Hdt.+; inscr., pap., LXX, Ep. Arist., Philo, Joseph.).
1.—a. consider worthy, deserving τινά τινος (Diod. S. 17, 76, 3 τιμῆς ἠξίωσαν αὐτόν; schol. on Nicander, Alex. 8; 2 Macc 9: 15; Jos., Vi. 231) someone of someth. σὲ λόγου (Eur., Med. 962 ἡμᾶς ἀξιοῖ λόγου) you of a discussion MPol 10: 2; cf. 14: 2. Pass. (Diod. S. 16, 59, 2 τ. στρατηγίας ἠξιωμένος; schol. on Apollon. Rhod. 4, 1212-14a; Jos., Ant. 2, 258 τιμῆς) διπλῆς τιμῆς ἀξιοῦσθαι 1 Ti 5: 17. δόξης Hb 3: 3. In a bad sense (Hdt. 3, 145; Diod. S. 16, 64, 1 ὑπὸ τοῦ δαιμονίου τιμωρίας ἠξιώθησαν) χείρονος τιμωρίας 10: 29 (Diod. S. 34+35, fgm. 3 τῆς αὐτῆς τιμωρίας ἀξιῶσαί τινα). W. inf. foll. οὐδὲ ἐμαυτὸν ἠξίωσα πρὸς σὲ ἐλθεῖν I did not consider myself worthy to come to you Lk 7: 7; MPol 20: 1. Pass. be considered worthy w. inf. foll. (Simplicius in Epict. p. 110, 37 ἀξιοῦσθαι μανθάνειν; Gen 31: 28) IEph 9: 2; 21: 2; IMg 2: 14; IRo 1: 1.
  b. make worthy τινά τινος someone of someth. ἵνα ὑμᾶς ἀξιώσῃ τ. κλήσεως ὁ θεός that God may make you worthy of the call which your are already heeding 2 Th 1: 11. Pass. Dg 9: 1.
2.—a. consider suitable, fitting (Appian, Bell. Civ. 1, 34 §154; Philo, Spec. Leg. 1, 319; Jos., Ant. 1, 307), hence desire, request w. inf. foll. (EpJer 40) ἠξίου, μὴ συμπαραλαμβάνειν τοῦτον he insisted (impf.) that they should not take him along Ac 15: 38. ἀξιοῦμεν παρὰ σοῦ ἀκοῦσαι we desire to hear from you 28: 22; cf. Dg 3: 2; 7: 1.
  b. gener. ask, request, pray (X., Mem. 3, 11, 12; Herodas 6, 79; so mostly LXX) w. inf. foll. (Alex. Aphr., An. Mant. II 1 p. 184, 2 ἄ. παρὰ θεῶν μαθεῖν=ask to learn from the gods; Jos., Ant. 1, 338) Ac 13: 42f v.l.; 1 Cl 51: 1; 53: 5; 59: 4. W. acc. of the pers. and ἵνα foll. Hv 4, 1, 3. Only w. acc. of the pers. 1 Cl 55: 6. In the passages from 1 Cl and H the request is directed to God (so UPZ 78, 22 [159 BC]. Prayers for vengeance from Rheneia in Dssm., LO 352, 354 [LAE 423ff]=Dit., Syll.³ 1181, 1 [II/I BC] ἐπικαλοῦμαι καὶ ἀξιῶ τ. θεὸν τὸν ὕψιστον. Jer 7: 16; 11: 14; Ep. Arist. 245). M-M.*

ἀξίως adv. (Soph., Hdt.+; inscr., pap., LXX; Ep. Arist. 32; 39) worthily, in a manner worthy of, suitably w. gen. of the pers. foll. τοῦ θεοῦ (Hyperid. 3: 25 τῆς θεοῦ) 1 Th 2: 12; 3 J 6; cf. Pol 5: 2; 1 Cl 21: 1. τοῦ κυρίου Col 1: 10 (cf. on these formulas, which have many counterparts in the inscr., Dssm. NB 75f [BS 248f]; Nägeli 54; Thieme 21). τῶν ἁγίων Ro 16: 2. ὑπηρετῶν Dg 11: 1. W. gen. of the thing (Diod. S. 1, 51, 7 τῆς ἀληθείας ἀ.; Appian, Bell. Civ. 5, 36 §146 ἀ. τῆς ἀνάγκης=in a manner corresponding to the necessity; Wsd 7: 15) τοῦ εὐαγγελίου Phil 1: 27. τῆς κλήσεως Eph 4: 1. τῆς ἐντολῆς Pol 5: 1. Without such a gen. ἀγαπᾶν τινα ἀ. love someone in a suitable manner

(='as he deserves'; cf. Thu. 3, 40, 8 κολάσατε ἀξίως τούτους. Wsd 16: 1; Sir 14: 11) MPol 17: 3. M-M. s.v. ἄξιος.*

ἀοίκητος, ον (Hes., Hdt.+; LXX) *uninhabited* Papias 3.*

ἄοκνος, ον (Hes.+; pap.; Pr 6: 11a) *untiring* ἀγάπη IPol 7: 2. ὃν ἀγαπητὸν λίαν ἔχετε καὶ ἄοκνον *whom you hold esp. dear to you, and who is resolute* (lit. 'without hesitation') ibid.*

ἀόκνως adv. (Hippocr. et al.; Dit., Syll.³ 762, 30; PSI 621, 6 [III BC]; UPZ 145, 46 [164 BC]; Jos., Ant. 5, 238) *without hesitation* προσέρχεσθαί τινι 1 Cl 33: 8.*

ἀόρατος, ον (Isocr.+; LXX) *unseen, invisible* of God (Diod. S. 2, 21, 7; Cornutus 5 p. 5, 3; Maximus Tyr. 2, 10a; 11, 9d; PGM 5, 123; 12, 265; 13, 71; Herm. Wr. 11, 22; 14, 3; Philo, Op. Mundi 69, Mos. 2, 65, Spec. Leg. 1, 18; 20; 46 al.; Jos., Bell. 7, 346; Sib. Or. fgm. 1, 8. HDaxer, Ro 1: 18–2: 20 im Verh. z. spätjüd. Lehrauffassung, Diss. Rostock '14, 11. Cf. Ltzm., Hdb. on Ro 1: 20 [lit.]. FBoll, Studien über Claud. Ptolem. 1894, 68. RBultmann, ZNW 29, '30, 169–92. EFascher, Deus invisibilis: Marb. Theol. Studien '31, 41–77) Col 1: 15; 1 Ti 1: 17; Hb 11: 27; 2 Cl 20: 5; PK 2 p. 13, 24; Dg 7: 2. Of divine attributes δύναμις (cf. Philo, Somn. 2, 291) Hv 1, 3, 4; 3, 3, 5. τὰ ἀ. τοῦ θεοῦ *God's invisible attributes* Ro 1: 20. Of Christ, who is described as ἀ. ἐπίσκοπος IMg 3: 2 or as ὁ ἀ., ὁ δι' ἡμᾶς ὁρατός IPol 3: 2. τὰ ἀ. *the invisible world* (opp. τὰ ὁρατά the visible world, like Philo, Congr. Erud. Gr. 25) Col 1: 16; ITr 5: 2; IRo 5: 3; IPol 2: 2. ἄρχοντες ὁρατοί καὶ ἀ. *rulers visible and invisible* ISm 6: 1. θησαυροὶ ἀ. B 11: 4 (Is 45: 3). ψυχή (Philo, Virt. 57, 172) Dg 6: 4. θεοσέβεια ibid. M-M.*

ἀόργητος, ον (Aristot.+; Stoic t.t. in sense 'without passions'; cf. Philo, Praem. 77 [Moses]) *free from anger* of God (w. χρηστός, ἀγαθός and ἀληθής) Dg 8: 8. ἀ. ὑπάρχει πρὸς πᾶσαν τ. κτίσιν αὐτοῦ *he is free from wrath toward all his creation* 1 Cl 19: 3. τὸ ἀόργητον αὐτοῦ *his freedom from passion* IPhld 1: 2 (τὸ ἀ. Epict. 3, 20, 9; M. Ant. 1, 1).*

ἀπαγγέλλω impf. ἀπήγγελλον; fut. ἀπαγγελῶ; 1 aor. ἀπήγγειλα; 2 aor. pass. ἀπηγγέλην Bl-D. §76, 1; Mlt.-H. 226 (Hom.+; inscr., pap., LXX).
1. *report, announce, tell* (Jos., Vi. 62 al.) w. dat. of the pers. Mt 2: 8; 14: 12; 28: 8; Mk 16: 10, 13; Ac 22: 26; 23: 16. W. dat. of the pers. and acc. of the thing (Gen 37: 5; 42: 29; 44: 24 al.) Mt 28: 11; Mk 6: 30 al.; 1 Cl 65: 1; Hs 5, 2, 11. Only w. acc. of the thing: πάντα Mt 8: 33. περί τινος 1 Th 1: 9. τὶ περί τινος Ac 28: 21. τινὶ περί τινος (X., An. 1, 7, 2; Gen 26: 32; Esth 6: 2; 1 Macc 14: 21) Lk 7: 18; 13: 1 (Plut., Mor. 509c; J 16: 25. τὶ πρός τινα (Hyperid. 3, 14; Epict. 3, 4, 1; 2 Km 15: 13) Ac 16: 36, 38D; ἀ. εἰς τὴν πόλιν *bring a report into the city* (X., Hell. 2, 2, 14) Mk 5: 14; Lk 8: 34 (cf. Jos., Ant. 5, 357 ἀπαγγελθείσης τῆς ἥττης εἰς τὴν Σιλώ; Am 4: 13; 1 Macc 6: 5). Used w. λέγων J 4: 51 t.r.; Ac 5: 22. W. dat. of the pers. foll. by acc. and inf. IPhld 10: 1. Foll. by a relative clause Mt 11: 4; Lk 7: 22; Ac 4: 23; 23: 19. W. πῶς foll. Lk 8: 36; Ac 11: 13. W. ὅτι foll. Lk 18: 37. W. acc. and inf. Ac 12: 14. W. ὡς foll. (1 Esdr 5: 37) Lk 8: 47 (Bl-D. §396; Rob. 726).
2. *proclaim* (of someth. in the present or fut.) κρίσιν τοῖς ἔθνεσιν Mt 12: 18; (w. μαρτυρεῖν) τὴν ζωήν 1 J 1: 2; cf. vs. 3; τὸ ὄνομά σου τοῖς ἀδελφοῖς Hb 2: 12; ἀ. ἐνώπιόν τινος (Ps 141: 3) in the sense *tell openly* or *frankly* (Gen 12: 18; 1 Km 9: 19) ἀπήγγειλεν ἐνώπιον

παντὸς τοῦ λαοῦ *she confessed before all the people* Lk 8: 47; cf. 1 Cor 14: 25. W. dat. and inf. foll. τ. ἔθνεσιν ἀ. μετανοεῖν καὶ ἐπιστρέφειν *they declared to the Gentiles that they should repent...* Ac 26: 20. Foll. by ἵνα to introduce a command which is to be transmitted to another Mt 28: 10 (cf. Polyaenus 7, 15, 2 Xerxes' command: ἄπιτε κ. τοῖς Ἕλλησιν ἀπαγγείλατε, ὅσα ἑωράκατε).—JSchniewind, TW I 64–6. M-M.

ἀπάγχω 1 aor. mid. ἀπηγξάμην (Hom.+; Jos., Ant. 12, 256; 15, 176) mid. *hang oneself* (so since Aeschyl., Hdt.; Epict.; PSI 177, 10; PGM 4, 1911; 2 Km 17: 23; Tob 3: 10.—Mlt. 155) of Judas Mt 27: 5 (ἀπελθὼν ἀπήγξατο like Epict. 1, 2, 3). S. Ἰούδας 6.*

ἀπάγω 2 aor. ἀπήγαγον; 1 aor. pass. ἀπήχθην Ac 12: 19 (Hom.+; inscr., pap., LXX; Philo; Jos., C. Ap. 2, 271; Test. 12 Patr.) *lead away*.
1. gener., to water Lk 13: 15. W. acc. of the pers. and indication of the goal (Ps 59: 11; 3 Km 1: 38) με εἰς τὴν Ἀρκαδίαν Hs 9, 1, 4 (Diod. S. 5, 51, 4 Διόνυσος ἀπήγαγε τὴν Ἀριάδνην εἰς τὸ ὄρος).
2. legal t.t.—a. *bring before* πρὸς Καϊάφαν Mt 26: 57. πρὸς τὸν ἀρχιερέα Mk 14: 53.—Mt 27: 2. Of a witness Ac 23: 17.
b. *lead away* a prisoner or condemned man (cf. Andoc. 4, 181; Demosth. 23, 80; PPetr. II 10[2], 7; PLille 7, 13 οὗτος ἀπήγαγέν με εἰς τὸ δεσμοτήριον; Dit., Or. 90, 14; Gen 39: 22; Philo, De Jos. 154) Mk 14: 44; 15: 16.
c. *lead away* to execution (Diod. S. 13, 102, 3; POxy. 33; Sus 45 Theod.; EpJer 17; Jos., Bell. 6, 155, Ant. 19, 269) ἀ. εἰς τὸ σταυρῶσαι *to crucify* (him) Mt 27: 31. With no addition (Aesop., Fab. 56 P.; Esth 1: 1o) Lk 23: 26; J 19: 16 ℵ, but s. also 𝔓⁶⁶ ed. VMartin, Papyrus Bodmer II, Supplement, '58, 38. Pass. ἐκέλευσεν ἀπαχθῆναι *he ordered that they be led away* (Polyaenus 5, 2, 16 ἀπαχθῆναι προσέταξεν) to execution Ac 12: 19. εἰς Ῥώμην IEph 21: 2.
3. intr. of a road *lead* (like Lat. ducere) εἴς τι (Stephanus Byzantius [VI AD], Ethnica ed. AMeineke I [1849] p. 287 Εὔτρησις, κώμη... κεῖται παρὰ τ. ὁδὸν τὴν ἐκ Θεσπιῶν εἰς Πλαταιὰς ἀπάγουσαν) εἰς τ. ἀπώλειαν *to destruction* Mt 7: 13. εἰς τ. ζωήν vs. 14.
4. pass. *be misled, carried away* (Lucian, Catapl. 26 πρὸς ὕβριν) πρὸς τὰ εἴδωλα *led astray to idols* 1 Cor 12: 2. ἡδοναῖς καὶ ἐπιθυμίαις ἀπαγόμενοι *carried away by pleasures and desires* Dg 9: 1. M-M.

ἀπαθής, ές *incapable of suffering* (so Pla. et al; Teles p. 56: 14; Porphyr., Abst. 2, 61; Herm. Wr. 2, 12; Philo; Jos., Bell. 5, 417.—Jos., Ant. 1, 284=without having suffered, also Dio Chrys. 19[36], 40; Appian, Liby. 111 §522) of Christ (opp. παθητός like Proclus, Theol. 80 p. 74, 33) IEph 7: 2; IPol 3: 2.*

ἀπαίδευτος, ον (Eur., Pla.+; LXX; Philo; Jos., Ant. 2, 285, C. Ap. 2, 37; Sib. Or. 3, 670, mostly of pers.) *uninstructed, uneducated* (w. ἄφρων, ἀσύνετος, μωρός) 1 Cl 39: 1. ζητήσεις *stupid speculations* 2 Ti 2: 23 (cf. Xenophon, Ep. 2 Ad Crit. p. 789 γνώμη ἀ.; Pla., Phaedr. 269B ῥῆμα ἀ.). M-M.*

ἀπαίρω 1 aor. pass. ἀπήρθην (Eur., Hdt.+; LXX; Jos., Bell. 4, 87, Vi. 422) *take away* τινὰ ἀπό τινος, in our lit. only pass. ὅταν ἀπαρθῇ ἀπ' αὐτῶν ὁ νυμφίος *when the bridegroom is taken away from them* Mt 9: 15; Mk 2: 20 (GBraumann, Novum Testamentum 6, '63, 264–67); Lk 5: 35. Yet there is no need to assume the necessity of force Ac 1: 9D (PPetr. II 13[5], 5 [III BC] ἀπηρμένος=gone on a journey. Cf. PLeipz. 47, 12 [IV AD]). M-M.*

ἀπαιτέω (trag., Hdt.+; inscr., pap., LXX, Philo, Joseph.).

1. ask for or demand something back, e.g. a loan or stolen property (Theophr., Char. 10, 2; Phalaris, Ep. 83, 1; 2; Dit., Syll.³ 955, 18; BGU 183, 8; Sir 20: 15; Philo, De Jos. 227) τὶ ἀπό τινος Lk 6: 30. W. obj. supplied from the context ἀπό τινος Hs 8, 1, 5; cf. D 1: 4. Abs. 1: 5. Using the concept of life as a loan (Cicero, De Rep. 1, 3, 4; cf. Epict. 4, 1, 172; Wsd 15: 8) τὴν ψυχὴν ἀπαιτοῦσιν ἀπὸ σοῦ they are demanding your soul fr. you, i.e., your soul will be demanded of you Lk 12: 20 (v.l. αἰτοῦσιν).

2. gener. demand, desire (Diod. S. 16, 56, 3; Jos., Ant. 12, 181; PBerl. 11, 662, 26 [I AD. BOlsson, Pap.briefe aus d. frühest. Römerzeit, Diss. Ups. '25, p. 100] ὁ τόπος ἀπαιτεῖ=the place demands) ὁ καιρὸς ἀπαιτεῖ σε the time demands you, i.e., a man like you IPol 2: 3 (Procop. Soph., Ep. 54 καιρὸς γράμματα ἀπαιτῶν=time that demands a letter). 1 Pt 3: 15 v.l. M-M.*

ἀπαλγέω pf. ἀπήλγηκα (Thu. 2, 61, 4+; Philo, Exs. 135) become callous, languish (Polyb. 1, 35, 5 ἀπηλγηκυίας ψυχάς; 16, 12, 7; Cass. Dio 48, 37; cf. Nägeli 34) ἀπηλγηκότες Eph 4: 19 (v.l. ἀπηλπικότες).*

ἀπαλλάσσω 1 aor. ἀπήλλαξα; pf. pass. ἀπήλλαγμαι; 2 aor. pass. ἀπηλλάγην (Aeschyl., Hdt.+; inscr., pap., LXX, Philo, Joseph.).

1. act. trans. free, release τούτους Hb 2: 15 (cf. Jos., Ant. 11, 270; 13, 363). αὐτόν from an evil spirit Lk 9: 40 D.

2. pass.—a. be released, be cured (PTebt. 104, 31; POxy. 104, 26; PGenève 21, 12; Philo, Spec. Leg. 3, 107) δὸς ἐργασίαν ἀπηλλάχθαι ἀπ᾽ αὐτοῦ do your best to come to a settlement w. him lit., get rid of him Lk 12: 58. Sick people are cured ἀπὸ πάσης ἀσθενείας Ac 5: 15D (Jos., Ant. 2, 33).

b. intr. leave, depart (Philo, Spec. Leg. 2, 85; Jos., Ant. 5, 143) ἀπό τινος (X., An. 7, 1, 4; Phlegon: 257 fgm. 36, 1, 2 Jac.; Mitteis, Chrest. 284, 12; PRyl. 154, 26 ἀπαλλασσομένης ἀπ᾽ αὐτοῦ) of diseases Ac 19: 12 (cf. Ps.-Pla., Eryx. 401c εἰ αἱ νόσοι ἀπαλλαγείησαν ἐκ τ. σωμάτων; PGM 13, 245). τοῦ κόσμου depart from the world euphem. for die 1 Cl 5: 7. For this τοῦ βίου (Eur., Hel. 102; PFay. 19, 19 ἀπαλλάσσομαι τοῦ βίου) MPol 3. εἰς οἶκον go home GP 14: 59; 2 Cl 17: 3. M-M.*

ἀπαλλοτριόω 1 aor. ἀπηλλοτρίωσα; pf. pass. ptc. ἀπηλλοτριωμένος (Hippocr., Pla.+; inscr., pap., LXX) estrange, alienate τινά τινος (Dit., Syll.³ 495, 164 [III BC]; Sir 11: 34; Jos., Ant. 4, 3) γαμετὰς ἀνδρῶν wives from their husbands 1 Cl 6: 3. ἡμᾶς τοῦ καλῶς ἔχοντος us from what is right 14: 2.—Pass. (Polyb. 1, 79, 6; Ezk 14: 5, 7; 3 Macc 1: 3; Test. Benj. 10: 10; Herm. Wr. 13, 1 τ. κόσμου) ἀπηλλοτριωμένοι τῆς ζωῆς τοῦ θεοῦ estranged from the life of God Eph 4: 18. τῆς πολιτείας τοῦ Ἰσραήλ excluded from the commonwealth of Israel 2: 12. W. ἐχθρός Col 1: 21. M-M.*

ἀπαλός, ή, όν (Hom.+; Zen.-P. 22, 9=Sb 6728 [257/6 BC]; LXX; Jos., Bell. 2, 120) tender of the young shoots of the fig tree ὅταν ὁ κλάδος αὐτῆς ἀ. γένηται when its branch becomes tender, i.e. sprouts Mt 24: 32; Mk 13: 28 (a favorite expression w. plants in Theocr. 5, 55; 8, 67; 11, 57; 15, 113).*

ἀπαναίνομαι (Hom.+; LXX) reject, disown w. acc. (Hippocr., Mul. 2, 179 the wife τὸν ἄνδρα ἀπαναίνεται) νουθέτημα παντοκράτορος 1 Cl 56: 6 (Job 5: 17).*

ἀπάνθρωπος, ον (trag.+; Jos., Ant. 8, 117; 16, 42; pap.) inhuman βασανισταί MPol 2: 3.*

ἀπαντάω fut. ἀπαντήσω; 1 aor. ἀπήντησα (Eur., Hdt. +; inscr., pap., LXX; Ep. Arist. 36; Philo, Migr. Abr. 82; Joseph.; cf. Anz 351) meet τινί someone (Appian, Liby. 109 §515, Bell. Civ. 4, 36 §152; 1 Km 25: 20; Jos., Ant. 1, 179; 6, 189) Mk 14: 13; Ac 16: 16 t.r. Without obj. (Hyperid., fgm. 205) ἀπήντησαν δέκα λεπροὶ ἄνδρες ten lepers came toward him Lk 17: 12 (v.l. ὑπήντησαν; gener. in the mss. ὑπαντάω is interchanged w. ἀ., as Mt 28: 9; Mk 5: 2; Lk 14: 31; J 4: 51; Ac 16: 16).—οὐδέν σοι ἀπήντησεν; did nothing meet you? Hv 4, 2, 3 (fr. the context=come toward, not=happen to. ἀπ. has the latter mng. Polyb. 4, 38, 10; Diod. S. 15, 58, 4; Gen 49: 1; Jer 13: 22; Sir 31: 22; 33: 1). M-M. B. 1366.*

ἀπάντησις, εως, ἡ (Soph.+; Polyb. 5, 26, 8; Diod. S. 18, 59, 3 et al.; inscr., pap., LXX; Ep. Arist. 91; Jos., Ant. 7, 276; cf. Nägeli 30; Mlt. 14, note 4; 242; loanw. in rabb. [TW I 380]) meeting only in the formula εἰς ἀπάντησιν (LXX freq. in friendly and hostile mng.) to meet. Abs. (PTebt. 43 I, 7 [118 BC] παρεγενήθημεν εἰς ἀπ.; 1 Km 13: 15) ἐξέρχεσθαι εἰς ἀ. Mt 25: 6 (vv. ll. add a gen. or dat. [so also J 12: 13 v.l.]). W. dat. (1 Km 4: 1; 13: 10; 1 Ch 14: 8; Jos., Ant. 13, 101) ἔρχεσθαι εἰς ἀ. τινι (Jdth 5: 4) Ac 28: 15. W. gen. (Pel.-Leg. p. 19; 1 Km 30: 21; 2 Km 19: 26) Mt 27: 32D. ἁρπάζεσθαι εἰς ἀ. τοῦ κυρίου εἰς ἀέρα be snatched up to meet the Lord in the air 1 Th 4: 17 (s. EPeterson, D. Einholung des Kyrios: ZsystTh 7, '30, 682–702.—Diod. S. 34+35, fgm. 33, 2 of the bringing in of the Great Mother of the gods by the Romans). M-M.*

ἅπαξ adv. (Hom.+; inscr., pap., LXX, Philo; Jos., Vi 82) once.

1. as an actual numer. concept ἅ. ἐλιθάσθην I was stoned once 2 Cor 11: 25. ἅ. πεφανέρωται Hb 9: 26. ἅ. ἀποθανεῖν vs. 27 (Proverbia Aesopi 141P.: πλέον ἢ ἅπαξ οὐδεὶς ἄνθρωπος θνῄσκει); cf. 1 Pt 3: 18. ἅ. προσενεχθείς Hb 9: 28. W. gen. foll. ἅ. τοῦ ἐνιαυτοῦ (Hdt. 2, 59; Ex 30: 10; Lev 16: 34) once a year Hb 9: 7. ἔτι ἅ. (2 Macc 3: 37; Judg 16: 18, 28) once more=for the last time (Aeschyl., Ag. 1322; Judg 6: 39) 12: 26f (Hg 2: 6). ἅ. καὶ δίς (Dionys. Hal. 8, 56, 1 οὐχ ἅ. ἀλλὰ καὶ δίς; Ael. Aristid. 36, 91 K.:=48 p. 474 D.: ἅ. ἢ δίς. Anna Comn., Alexias 3, 3 ed. Reiff. I 102, 17 καὶ ἅ. καὶ δίς; 1 Km 17: 39; 2 Esdr 23 [Neh 13]: 20; 1 Macc 3: 30) again and again, more than once (LMorris, Novum Testamentum 1, '56, 205–8) Phil 4: 16; 1 Th 2: 18; 1 Cl 53: 3 (Dt 9: 13). W. weakening of the numer. idea ἐπεὶ ἅ. (Thu. 7, 44, 7; X., An. 1, 9, 10; Menand., Pap. Did. 36 J.; Chio, Ep. 14, 1; POxy. 1102, 8 ἐπεὶ ἅ. προσῆλθε τῇ κληρονομίᾳ) since for once Hv 3, 3, 4; m 4, 4, 1; so prob. once in Hb 6: 4.

2. once for all (Hippocr., Ep. 27, 41; Aelian, V.H. 2, 30; Philostrat., Ep. 7, 2; PLeipz. 34, 20; 35, 19; Ps 88: 36; PsSol 12: 6; Philo, Ebr. 198; Jos., Bell. 2, 158, Ant. 4, 140) Hb 10: 2; Jd 3, 5. M-M and suppl.*

ἀπαράβατος, ον (belonging to H.Gk. [Phryn. p. 313 L.]; not LXX) in Hb 7: 24 is usu. interpr. without a successor. But this mng. is found nowhere else. ἀ. rather has the sense permanent, unchangeable (Stoic. II 266; 293; Plut., Mor. 410F; 745D; Epict. 2, 15, 1, Ench. 51, 2; Herm. Wr. 494, 26 Sc.; Philo, Aet. M. 112; Jos., Ant. 18, 266, C. Ap. 2, 293; PRyl. 65, 18 [I BC]; PLond. 1015, 12 ἄτρωτα καὶ ἀσάλευτα καὶ ἀπαράβατα). M-M.*

ἀπαρασκεύαστος, ον (X.+; Jos., Ant. 4, 293; Nägeli 16) not ready, unprepared (actually a military t.t.) εὑρεῖν τινα ἀ. find someone not in readiness 2 Cor 9: 4.*

ἀπαρθῇ s. ἀπαίρω.

ἀπαρνέομαι fut. ἀπαρνήσομαι; 1 aor. ἀπηρνησάμην; pf. pass. ἀπήρνημαι ISm 5: 2; 1 fut. pass. ἀπαρνηθήσομαι (Bl-D. §78; 311); irreg. act. aor. ἀπαρνῆσαι Hs 1: 5 (Soph., Hdt.+) *deny τινά* (Is 31: 7) Christ (of Peter's denial; MGoguel, Did Peter Deny his Lord? HTR 25, '32, 1–27) Mt 26: 34f, 75; Mk 14: 30f, 72; Lk 22: 61. In full ἕως τρὶς με ἀπαρνήσῃ μὴ εἰδέναι *until you have denied three times that you know me* vs. 34 (on the constr. cf. Soph., Ant. 422 κατάρνῃ μὴ δεδρακέναι τάδε;). τὸν κύριον Hv 3, 6, 5. ISm 5: 2 (Lucian, M. Peregr. 13 p. 337 θεούς). Abs. (but sc. τὸν κύριον) Hs 8, 8, 2; τ. νόμον s 1: 5 (Diod. S. 20, 63, 4 ἀ. τὴν ἐπιστήμην=deny, refuse to acknowledge his [former] trade [as a potter]—opp. καυχάομαι=be proud of it; Sib. Or. 4, 27f νηοὺς κ. βωμούς). ἀ. ἑαυτόν *deny himself*=act in a wholly selfless manner, give up his personality Mt 16: 24; Mk 8: 34 (Lk 9: 23 v.l.). AFridrichsen, 'S. selbst verleugnen': Con. Neot. 2, '36, 1–8. 6, '42, 94–6, Sv. exeg. Årsbok 5, '40, 158–62; JLebreton, La doctrine du renoncement dans le NT: Nouv. Rev. théol. 65, '38, 385–412. Pass. (Soph., Philoct. 527; Pla., 7th Letter p. 338E; Herodas 4, 74) ἀπαρνηθήσεται ἐνώπιον τῶν ἀγγέλων *he will be denied* (i.e., not recognized) *before the angels* Lk 12: 9 (Ps.-Callisth. 2, 8, 10 ἀπαρνέομαι=reject, wish to know nothing of). M-M.*

ἀπαρτί adv. (Hdt., Hippocr.+; Teleclides [V BC]) *exactly, certainly* (ἀ.=ἀπηρτισμένως, τελείως, ἀκριβῶς Phryn. 20f Lob.; cf. Suidas s.v. and Bekker, Anecd. Gr. 418, 15; this mng. is also poss. for Aristoph., Pl. 388) may be the correct rdg. for ἀπ' ἄρτι Rv 14: 13; if ναί is rejected as a gloss; also Mt 26: 29, 64 (Bl-D. §12 app.; ADebrunner, after AFridrichsen, Coniect. Neot. XI, '47, 45–9).*

ἀπάρτι s. ἀπ' ἄρτι s.v. ἄρτι 3.

ἀπαρτίζω 1 aor. ἀπήρτισα; pf. pass. ἀπήρτισμαι, ptc. ἀπηρτισμένος (Aeschyl., Hippocr.+; pap.) *finish, complete* (Polyb. 31, 12, 10; 31, 13, 1; Diod. S. 1, 11, 6 et al.; POxy. 908, 23; 936, 22; PLeipz. 105, 11; 3 Km 9: 25 A; Jos., Ant. 3, 146; 8, 130) τὶ· ἔργον τελείως ἀ. *complete a task perfectly* IEph 1: 1. τὸν ἴδιον κλῆρον *fulfill his own destiny* MPol 6: 2. ὅταν αὐτὸ ἀπαρτίσητε *when you complete it* IPol 7: 3. Of God ὁ ἀπαρτίσας αὐτά *who perfected them* Hs 5, 5, 2. Also τινά (POxy. 724, 11 [II AD] ἐὰν αὐτὸν ἀπαρτίσῃς) *make someone complete* με ἀπαρτίσει IPhld 5: 1. Pass. παρὰ θεῷ ἀπηρτισμένος IEph 19: 3. ἀπήρτισμαι ἐν Ἰ. Χριστῷ S 3: 1. M-M. s.v. ἀπαρτισμός.

ἀπάρτισμα, ατος, τό (3 Km 7: 9 Sym.) *completion* ἀ. ἀφθαρσίας *consummation of immortality* IPhld 9: 2.*

ἀπαρτισμός, οῦ, ὁ (Chrysippus: Stoic. II 164; Dionys. Hal., De Comp. Verb. 24; Apollon. Dysc., De Adv. p. 532, 8; pap., in Mitteis, Chrestomathie 88 IV, 25 [II AD]; PGiess. 67, 8ff) *completion* ἀ. (sc. πύργου) Lk 14: 28. M-M.*

ἀπαρχή, ῆς, ἡ (Soph., Hdt.+; inscr. pap., LXX, Philo, Joseph., Test. 12 Patr.; Celsus 8, 33) 1. sacrificial t.t. *first-fruits* of any kind (incl. animals, both domesticated and wild [for the latter Arrian, Cyneg. 33, 1]), which were holy to the divinity and were consecrated before the rest could be put to secular use (cf. Theopomp. [IV BC]; 115 fgm. 334 Jac.; Cornutus 28 p. 55, 9; Ael. Aristid. 45 p. 136 D.; Theophyl. Sym., Ep. 29 Π ἀνὶ τοῦ ποιμνίου τὰς ἀπαρχάς; Dit., Or. 179 [I BC]; PSI 690, 11; Porphyr., Abst. 2, 61 θεοῖς ἀρίστη μὲν ἀπαρχὴ νοῦς καθαρός). a. lit. εἰ ἡ ἀ. ἀγία, καὶ τὸ φύραμα *if the firstfruits (of dough) are holy, so is the whole lump* Ro 11: 16 (on

first-fruits of bread dough, Num 15: 18–21, cf. D. Mischna ed. Beer-Holtzmann I 9: Challa by KAlbrecht '13). In full ἀ. γεννημάτων ληνοῦ καὶ ἅλωνος, βοῶν τε καὶ προβάτων *the first-fruits of the produce of wine-press and threshing-floor, of cattle and sheep* D 13: 3, cf. 5f (s. Ex 22: 28); ἀ. τῆς ἅλω 1 Cl 29: 3. Assigned to the prophet, as to the priests and seers among the Gentiles (Artem. 3, 3) and in the OT to the priest D 13: 3, 6f.
b. fig.—α. of persons *first-fruits* of Christians ἀ. τῆς Ἀσίας, i.e., the first convert in Asia Ro 16: 5. ἀ. τῆς Ἀχαΐας 1 Cor 16: 15. Perh. 2 Th 2: 13 (ἀπαρχήν acc. to cod. BFGP 33) the first converts of Thessalonica (so Harnack, SAB '10, 575ff); pl. 1 Cl 42: 4. Gener. ἀ. τις τῶν αὐτοῦ κτισμάτων *a kind of first-fruits of his creatures* Js 1: 18 (cf. Philo, Spec. Leg. 4, 180 of the Jews: τοῦ σύμπαντος ἀνθρώπων γένους ἀπενεμήθη οἷά τις ἀπαρχὴ τῷ ποιητῇ καὶ πατρί; Alex. Aphr., Fat. 1, II 2 p. 164, 10 τινὰ ἀπαρχὴν τῶν ἡμετέρων καρπῶν=a sort of first-fruit of our [spiritual] harvest. LEElliott-Binns, NTS 3, '56/'57, 148–61). Here as Rv 14: 4 the emphasis is less on chronological sequence than on quality (schol. on Eur., Or. 96 ἀπαρχὴ ἐλέγετο οὐ μόνον τ. πρῶτον τῇ τάξει, ἀλλὰ καὶ τ. πρῶτον τ. τιμῇ). The orig. mng. is greatly weakened, so that ἀ. becomes almost=πρῶτος; of Christ ἀ. τῶν κεκοιμημένων *the first of those who have fallen asleep* 1 Cor 15: 20; cf. vs. 23 (HMontefiore, When did Jesus Die? ET 62, '60, 53f); 1 Cl 24: 1.
β. of things (Dio Chrys. 54[71], 2 ἀπαρχαὶ τῆς σοφίας) τὴν ἀ. τοῦ πνεύματος ἔχοντες *since we possess the first-fruits of the Spirit*, i.e., as much of the Spirit as has been poured out so far Ro 8: 23 (cf. Thieme 25f), but s. 2 below. διδόναι ἀπαρχὰς γεύσεώς τινος *give a foretaste of someth.* B 1: 7.
2. *birth-certificate* also suits the context of Ro 8: 23; cf. Mitteis, Chrest. 372, col 4, 7; PFlor. 57, 81; 86; 89; PTebt. 316, 10; 49; 82; HSJones, JTS 23, '22, 282f; RTaubenschlag, Opera Minora 2, '59, 220–21 (identification card); L-S-J s.v. 7.—HBeer, Ἀπαρχή; Diss., Würzb. '14, M-M.*

ἅπας, ασα, αν (Hom.+; inscr., pap., LXX, Philo; Jos., Ant. 14, 28 al.; Sib. Or. fgm. 1, 9. Beside πᾶς in Attic after consonants; for πᾶς after vowels, cf. HDiels, GGA 1894, 298ff; but the distinction is not maintained in the NT Bl-D. §275; Rob. 771; s. also Mayser 161f. On its use w. the art. W.-S. §20, 11).
1. used w. a noun and the art. ἅ. τὸν λαόν (cf. Jos., Ant. 7, 63; 211) *the whole people* (opp. an individual) Lk 3: 21; cf. GP 8: 28. ἅ. τὸ πλῆθος Lk 8: 37; 19: 37; 23: 1; Ac 25: 24. ἅ. τὸν βίον Lk 21: 4 v.l. (for πάντα). ἅ. τὰ γενόμενα *all that had happened* Mt 28: 11. τὴν ἐξουσίαν ταύτην ἅπασαν *this whole domain* Lk 4: 6. ὁ λαὸς ἅ. (Jos., Ant. 6, 199; 8, 101) 19: 48.
2. without a noun. masc. ἅπαντες *all, everybody* Mt 24: 39; Lk 5: 26; 7: 16 v.l.; 9: 15; 21: 4 v.l.; Ac 2: 7 v.l.; 4: 31; 5: 12 v.l., 16; 16: 3, 28; 27: 33; Gal 3: 28 v.l.; Js 3: 2.—Neut. ἅπαντα *everything* Mk 8: 25; Lk 2: 39 v.l.; 15: 13 v.l. ἔχειν ἅ. κοινά *have everything in common* Ac 2: 44; 4: 32 v.l. χρῄζειν τούτων ἅ. *need all this* Mt 6: 32. Cf. D 3: 2–6. M-M.

ἀπασπάζομαι 1 aor. ἀπησπασάμην (Tob 10: 12 S; Himerius, Eclog. in Phot. 11, 1 p. 194) *take leave of, say farewell to τινά someone* (Charito 3, 5, 8 ἀπησπασάμεθα ἀλλήλους *we said farewell to one another* Ac 21: 6. Abs. 20: 1 D (s. FBlass, Acta apost. 1895 ad loc.).*

ἀπατάω 1 aor. pass. ἠπατήθην (Hom.+; not in inscr.; rare in pap. [e.g. PSI 152, 24 [II AD]; PLond. 1345, 13];

Epicurus p. 298, 29 Us.; Plut.; Epict. 4, 5, 32; Herodian 2, 1, 10; LXX; Philo, Aet. M. 117; Joseph.; Test. 12 Patr.).

1. *deceive, cheat, mislead* τινά τινι (Is 36: 14) *someone with someth.* μηδεὶς ὑμᾶς ἀπατάτω κενοῖς λόγοις *let nobody deceive you w. empty words* Eph 5: 6 (cf. Test. Napht. 3: 1; Jos., Vi. 302 λόγοις ἀ. τινά). ἀπατῶν αὐτοὺς τ. ἐπιθυμίαις τ. πονηραῖς Hs 6, 2, 1. ἀ. καρδίαν ἑαυτοῦ *deceive oneself* Js 1: 26 (cf. Job 31: 27); Hs 6, 4, 1 and 4. W. acc. of the pers. Dg 2: 1; Hm 11: 13. Pass. (Jos., Ant. 12, 20; w. the mng. 'be led astray' C. Ap. 2, 245) Ἀδὰμ οὐκ ἠπατήθη 1 Ti 2: 14 (v.l. has the simplex also in ref. to Eve). ἀπατηθεὶς τῷ κάλλει τῶν γυναικῶν τούτων *led astray by the beauty of these women* Hs 9, 13, 9 (Test. Jud. 12: 3 ἠπάτησέ με τὸ κάλλος αὐτῆς.—ἀ.=seduce sexually as early as Eratosth. p. 22, 10).

2. mid. *enjoy oneself, live pleasurably* (w. τρυφᾶν cf. Sir 14: 16 and s. ἀπάτη 2) Hs 6, 4, 1; 6, 5, 3f. M-M.*

ἀπάτη, ης, ἡ (Hom.+; inscr., pap., LXX, Philo, Joseph., Test. 12 Patr.).

1. *deception, deceitfulness* (Jdth 9: 10, 13; 4 Macc 18: 8; Jos., Ant. 2, 300; Sib. Or. 5, 405 ἀ. ψυχῶν) ἡ ἀ. τοῦ πλούτου *the seduction which comes from wealth* Mt 13: 22; Mk 4: 19; ἀ. τῆς ἁμαρτίας *deceitfulness of sin* Hb 3: 13 (note that mng. 2 is also poss., even probable, for the synoptic passages, and poss. for Hb 3: 13). ἀ. τοῦ κόσμου Dg 10: 7 (cf. Herm. Wr. 13, 1 ἡ τοῦ κόσμου ἀπάτη). (w. φιλοσοφία) κενὴ ἀ. *empty deceit* Col 2: 8. ἐν πάσῃ ἀ. ἀδικίας w. *every kind of wicked deception* 2 Th 2: 10 (of deceptive trickery, like Jos., Ant. 2, 284). ἐπιθυμία τ. ἀπάτης *deceptive desire* Eph 4: 22. W. φιλαργυρία 2 Cl 6: 4; w. εἰκαιότης Dg 4: 6; listed w. other sins Hm 8: 5. Personified (Hes., Theog. 224; Lucian, De Merc. Cond. 42) Hs 9, 15, 3.

2. esp. (since Polyb. 2, 56, 12; 4, 20, 5; Inschr. v. Priene 113, 64 [84 BC; cf. Rouffiac 38f]; Moeris p. 65 ἀπάτη· ἡ πλάνη παρ' Ἀττικοῖς... ἡ τέρψις παρ' Ἕλλησιν; Philo, Dec. 55) *pleasure, pleasantness* that involves one in sin, w. τρυφή Hs 6, 2, 1; 6, 4, 4; 6, 5, 1 and 3f; pl. (Ps.-Dicaearch. p. 104F. ψυχῆς ἀπάται) Hm 11: 12; s 6, 2, 2 and 4; (w. ἐπιθυμίαι) ἀπάται τοῦ αἰῶνος τούτου Hs 6, 3, 3; cf. 6, 5, 6. Hence ἐντρυφῶντες ἐν ταῖς ἀ. (v.l. ἀγάπαις; the same variant Mk 4: 19; Eccl 9: 6 v.l. See AvHarnack, Z. Revision d. Prinzipien d. ntl. Textkritik '16, 109f and ἀγάπη II) *reveling in their lusts* 2 Pt 2: 13. M-M.*

ἀπάτωρ, ορος (Soph.+; oft. in pap.) *fatherless, without a father* of children who are orphaned, abandoned, estranged, or born out of wedlock; in our lit. only of Melchizedek (Gen 14: 18ff) w. ἀμήτωρ, ἀγενεαλόγητος Hb 7: 3. This may mean simply that no genealogy is recorded for M., or that he was a kind of angelic being (as Pollux, Onom. 3, 26 ὁ οὐκ ἔχων μητέρα ἀμήτωρ, καθάπερ ἡ Ἀθηνᾶ, καὶ ὁ οὐκ ἔχων πατέρα ἀπάτωρ ὡς ὁ Ἥφαιστος; Anth. Pal. 15, 26; schol. on Theocr. 1, 3/4d Wendel ['14] of Pan; PGM 5, 282 of the god Horus; s. also ἀμήτωρ). M-M.*

ἀπαύγασμα, ατος, τό (Heliod. 5, 27, 4 φωτὸς ἀ.; Philo; Wsd 7: 26; Plut. has ἀπαυγασμός Mor. 83D and 934D; PGM 4, 1130 καταύγασμα) act. *radiance, effulgence*; pass., *reflection*. The mng. cannot always be determined w. certainty. The pass. is prob. to be preferred in Plut. The act. seems preferable for Wsd and Philo (Op. Mundi 146, Spec. Leg. 4, 123, Plant. 50), corresp. to Hesychius: ἀ.= ἡλίου φέγγος. Philo uses the word of the relation of the Logos to God. Christ is described as ἀ. τῆς δόξης *radiance of his glory* Hb 1: 3 (the act. mng. in the Gk. fathers Orig.;

Gregory of Nyssa; Theodoret; Chrysostom: φῶς ἐκ φωτός. Likew. Theodore of Mopsu.; Severian of Gabala; Gennadius of Constantinople: KStaab, Pauluskommentare '33, 201; 346; 421). For this ἀ. τῆς μεγαλωσύνης 1 Cl 36: 2.—FJDölger, Sonne u. Sonnenstrahl als Gleichnis in d. Logostheologie d. Altertums: Antike u. Christent. I '29, 269ff.*

ἀπαφρίζω (Galen, CMG V 4, 2 p. 120, 3; 125, 21; Oribas. 5, 33, 4; Geopon. 8, 29; 32) *cast off like foam* τὶ Jd 13 P⁷² et al.*

ἀπέβην s. ἀποβαίνω.

ἀπέδετο H.Gk. for ἀπέδοτο; s. ἀποδίδωμι.

ἀπέθανον s. ἀποθνήσκω.

ἀπεῖδον s. ἀφοράω.

ἀπείθεια, ας, ἡ (X., Mem. 3, 5, 5+; inscr.; pap.; 4 Macc 8: 9, 18: 12: 4) *disobedience*, in our lit. always of disob. toward God (cf. Jos., Ant. 3, 316); somet. w. the connotation of *disbelief* in the Christian gospel (see ἀπειθέω 3). Those who oppose God are called υἱοὶ τῆς ἀ. Eph 2: 2; 5: 6; Col 3: 6 v.l. (KGKuhn, NTS 7, '61, 339 for Qumran parallels). Of disobed. of the Jews Ro 11: 30; Hb 4: 6, 11; of all men gener. Ro 11: 32. Personified Hs 9, 15, 3. M-M.*

ἀπειθέω 1 aor. ἠπείθησα (for ἀπιθέω [Hom.] since Aeschyl., Pla.; inscr.; pap.; LXX; Ep. Arist. 25; Jos., Bell. 2, 320, Vi. 109; Test. 12 Patr.) *disobey, be disobedient* (for the mng. *disbelieve, be an unbeliever* see 3 below); in our lit. the disobedience is always toward God or his ordinances (like Eur., Or. 31; Pla., Leg. 741D; Lucian, Dial. Deor. 8, 1; Dit., Syll.³ 736, 40 [92 BC] τὸν δὲ ἀπειθοῦντα ἢ ἀπρεπῶς ἀναστρεφόμενον εἰς τὸ θεῖον μαστιγούντω οἱ ἱεροί; Dt 1: 26; 9: 23; Josh 5: 6; Is 36: 5; 63: 10; Bar 1: 18f).

1. w. dat. of the pers. (Num 14: 43 κυρίῳ) τῷ θεῷ (Diod. S. 5, 74, 4 ἀ. τοῖς θεοῖς; Hierocles 24 p. 473 τῷ θεῷ; Jos., Ant. 9, 249) Ro 11: 30, cf. Pol 2: 1. τῷ υἱῷ J 3: 36.—W. dat. of the thing (Diod. S. 5, 71, 5 τοῖς νόμοις) τῇ ἀληθείᾳ Ro 2: 8. τῷ εὐαγγελίῳ 1 Pt 4: 17. τῷ λόγῳ 2: 8; 3: 1. τοῖς εἰρημένοις 1 Cl 59: 1. τοῖς ἐμοῖς ἐλέγχοις 57: 4 (Pr 1: 25).

2. abs. (Dicaearchus in Athen. 13 p. 603B ἀπειθήσας= disobedient) of the Jews Ac 19: 9; Ro 11: 31; 15: 31. οἱ ἀπειθήσαντες Ἰουδαῖοι *the disobedient* (but see 3 below) *Jews* Ac 14: 2. λαὸς ἀπειθῶν Ro 10: 21; B 12: 4 Funk (Is 65: 2). οἱ ἀπειθοῦντες IMg 8: 2; 1 Cl 58: 1. Of Gentiles οἱ ἀπειθήσαντες Hb 11: 31.—Gener. 3: 18; 1 Pt 3: 20.

3. since, in the view of the early Christians, the supreme disobedience was a refusal to believe their gospel, ἀ. may be restricted in some passages to the mng. *disbelieve, be an unbeliever*. This sense, though greatly disputed (it is not found outside our lit.), seems most probable in J 3: 36; Ac 14: 2; 19: 9; Ro 15: 31, and only slightly less prob. in Ro 2: 8; 1 Pt 2: 8; 3: 1, perh. also vs. 20; 4: 17; IMg 8: 2. M-M.*

ἀπειθής, ές *disobedient* (so Thu.+; LXX; Jos., Ant. 17, 186).

1. w. dat. of the pers. γονεῦσιν *to parents* Ro 1: 30; 2 Ti 3: 2 (cf. Dt 21: 18).—W. dat. of the thing τῇ οὐρανίῳ ὀπτασίᾳ *to the heavenly vision* Ac 26: 19.

2. abs. (Num 20: 10) opp. δίκαιος Lk 1: 17; w. βδελυκτός Tit 1: 16; w. ἀνόητος, πλανώμενος 3: 3. Of the Jews λαὸς ἀ. B 12: 4 (cf. Is 30: 9; Sib. Or. 3, 668). M-M.*

ἀπειλέω impf. ἠπείλουν; 1 aor. mid. ἠπειλησάμην (on

the mid. cf. Bl-D. §316, 1) (Hom.+; pap., LXX; Jos., Ant. 5, 144; Test. 12 Patr.) *threaten, warn* τινί someone, foll. by μή and inf. *warn (them) no longer* to Ac 4: 17 (t.r. adds ἀπειλῇ). τὶ (4 Macc 9: 5; Jos., Ant. 13, 143 πόλεμον) *with someth.* πῦρ MPol 11: 2. Abs., of Christ πάσχων οὐκ ἠπείλει *although he suffered he did not threaten* 1 Pt 2: 23. M-M. B. 1279.*

ἀπειλή, ῆς, ἡ (Hom.+; pap., LXX; Jos., Bell. 6, 257, Ant. 8, 362) *threat* ἐμπνέων ἀπειλῆς κ. φόνου *breathing murderous threats* Ac 9: 1 (CBurchard, ZNW 61, '70, 163–65). ἀνιέναι τὴν ἀ. *stop threatening* Eph 6: 9. ἡ ἀ. τοῦ διαβόλου Hm 12, 6, 2. ἀπειλῇ ἀπειλεῖσθαι μή w. inf. *warn sharply* Ac 4: 17 t.r. Pl. (Sib. Or. 3, 71; 97) φυγεῖν τὰς ἀ. *escape the threats* 1 Cl 58: 1. ἐφορᾶν ἐπὶ τὰς ἀ. Ac 4: 29. M-M.*

I. **ἄπειμι** ptc. ἀπών (fr. εἰμί. Hom.+; inscr., pap., LXX; Jos., C. Ap. 2, 212) *be absent* or *away* πόρρω ἀ. ἀπό τινος *be far away fr. someone* 1 Cl 15: 2; 2 Cl 3: 5; cf. 1 Cl 3: 4 Funk. Opp. παρών (Socrat., Ep. 7, 1; Ael. Aristid. 13, p. 222 D.; Dit., Syll.³ 1044, 43; PTebt. 317, 32; BGU 1080, 6ff; Wsd 11: 11; 14: 17) 2 Cor 10: 11; 13: 2; cf. Pol 3: 2. ἀπὼν θαρρῶ 2 Cor 10: 1; ἀ. γράφω 13: 10; ἀ. ἀκούω Phil 1: 27. More specif. ἀ. τῷ σώματι *be absent in body* 1 Cor 5: 3. For this τῇ σαρκὶ ἀ. Col 2: 5. M-M.*

II. **ἄπειμι** impf. ἀπῄειν (fr. εἶμι. Hom.+; inscr., pap., LXX; Jos., Bell. 7, 17 and 69, Ant. 1, 59; 4, 126) *go away* ἀπό τινος *fr. someth.* (Dit., Syll.³ 1218, 19) Hs 9, 7, 3. Simply *go, come* (Jos., Ant. 14, 289) εἰς τ. συναγωγήν Ac 17: 10. ἀ. οὗ ἐὰν βούλησθε *wherever you wish* 1 Cl 54: 2. Of the day *depart* (cf. Inschr. 10, 1: Eranos 13, '13, p. 87) 24: 3.*

ἀπεῖπον 2 aor., to which (since Hdt.; Ostraka II 1156; LXX; Nägeli 23) the mid. ἀπειπάμην belongs (on the form cf. W-S. §13, 13 note); in our lit. only mid. *disown, renounce* τὶ (cf. Hdt. 4, 120 συμμαχίην; Polyb. 33, 12, 5 φιλίαν; Job 6: 14) ἀπειπάμεθα τὰ κρυπτὰ τ. αἰσχύνης *we have renounced the things that one hides from a sense of shame* 2 Cor 4: 2. M-M.*

ἀπείραστος, ον (Philod., Rhet. I p. 45, 3 Sudh.; Empirikerschule p. 91, 18 KDeichgräber ['30]; Galen: CMG V 4, 1, 1 p. 62, 30; Alciphron 2, 35, 3 Sch. after Cobet; Jos., Bell. 5, 364 and 7, 262 codd.) for the older ἀπείρατος (Pind.+) *without temptation*, either active=who does not tempt, or passive=who cannot be tempted. Of God ὁ θεὸς ἀ. ἐστιν κακῶν Js 1: 13, certainly pass. because δέ in the next clause introduces a new thought, *God cannot be tempted to do evil* (Leontios 8 p. 17, 3 of God as One who cannot and dare not be tempted; for the gen. κακῶν cf. X., Cyr. 3, 3, 55 ἀπαίδευτος ἀρετῆς, and s. Bl-D. §182, 3; Rob. 516). Of men ἀνὴρ ἀδόκιμος ἀπείραστος (παρὰ θεῷ is added by Const. Apost. II 8, 2) *an untempted man is untried* Agr 21. M-M.*

I. **ἄπειρος, ον** (fr. πειράομαι) *unacquainted with, unaccustomed to* (Pind., Hdt.+; Epict. 2, 24, 3; Dit., Or. 669, 11; PSI 522, 4; LXX; Philo, Agr. 160 [a beginner is ἄ.], Op. M. 171; Jos., Bell. 6, 291), of an immature Christian ἄ. λόγου δικαιοσύνης *unacquainted w. the teaching about righteousness* Hb 5: 13 (the gen. as freq., e.g. PGiess. 68, 17 ἄ. τῶν τόπων; Jos., Ant. 7, 336). M-M.*

II. **ἄπειρος, ον** (fr. πέρας; cf. ἀπέραντος) *boundless* (Pind., Hdt.+; Dit., Or. 383, 43 and 113 [I BC]; Herm. Wr. 3, 1; Philo; Jos., Ant. 4, 163; Test. Judah 13: 4; Sib. Or. 3, 236) θάλασσα 1 Cl 20: 6.*

ἀπεκατέστην s. ἀποκαθίστημι.

ἀπεκδέχομαι impf. ἀπεξεδεχόμην *await eagerly* (so Alciphr. 3, 4, 6; Heliod. 2, 35, 3; 7, 23, 5; Sext. Emp., Math. 2, 73) τινά or τί; in our lit. always of Christian hope w. its var. objects: σωτῆρα Phil 3: 20; Christ Hb 9: 28.—τὴν ἀποκάλυψιν τῶν υἱῶν τοῦ θεοῦ *the revelation of the sons of God* Ro 8: 19; cf. 1 Cor 1: 7. υἱοθεσίαν Ro 8: 23 (for this and other passages JSwetnam suggests *infer, understand in a certain sense*: Biblica 48, '67, 102–8). ἐλπίδα δικαιοσύνης Gal 5: 5.—Abs. *wait* δι' ὑπομονῆς *wait patiently* Ro 8: 25. Of God's forbearance 1 Pt 3: 20. M-M.*

ἀπεκδύομαι 1 aor. ptc. ἀπεκδυσάμενος (Proclus on Pla., Rep. I p. 16, 10 WKroll; Jos., Ant. 6, 330 Cod. Marc.; Eustath. ad Il., p. 664, 23).
   1. *take off, strip off* of clothes (opp. ἐπενδύομαι) only fig. (of σῶμα Dox. Gr. 573, 22) τὸν παλαιὸν ἄνθρωπον *the old man*, i.e., sinful human nature Col 3: 9 (cf. Philo, Mut. Nom. 233 ἐκδύεσθαι τὰ ἁμαρτήματα).
   2 *disarm* τινά (on the mid. for the act. s. Bl-D. §316, 1; Rob. 805) τὰς ἀρχὰς καὶ τ. ἐξουσίας *the principalities and powers* Col 2: 15.—S. on θριαμβεύω.*

ἀπέκδυσις, εως, ἡ (found nowhere independently of Paul; does not reappear until Eustath. ad Il. p. 91, 28; cf. Nägeli 50) *removal, stripping off* of clothes; only fig. ἐν τῇ ἀ. τοῦ σώματος τ. σαρκός *in stripping off your fleshly* (i.e. sinful) *body*, because Christians have, as it were, a new body (with no material circumcision that cuts flesh from the body Moffatt) Col 2: 11. M-M.*

ἀπεκτάνθην s. ἀποκτείνω.

ἀπελαύνω 1 aor. ἀπήλασα (trag., Hdt.+; Cyranides p. 101, 2 δαίμονας; pap.; LXX; Joseph.) *drive away* τινὰ ἀπό τινος (X., Cyr. 3, 2, 16; Ezk 34: 12) αὐτοὺς ἀπὸ τοῦ βήματος *them away from the tribunal* Ac 18: 16 (v.l. ἀπέλυσε.—Cf. Jos., Bell. 1, 245 τ. λοιποὺς ἀπήλασεν). M-M.*

ἀπελεγμός, οῦ, ὁ (found only in Christian writings) *refutation, exposure, discredit* εἰς ἀ. ἐλθεῖν (Lat. in redargutionem venire) *come into disrepute* Ac 19: 27 [GDKilpatrick, JTS 10, '59, 327 [reproof, public criticism]]. M-M.*

ἀπελεύθερος, ου, ὁ (since Ps.-X., De Rep. Athen. 1, 10; X.; Pla.; oft. in pap. and inscr.; Jos., Ant. 7, 263; 14, 75; cf. Hahn 241, 10; 244, 4; 246, 3; Thalheim in Pauly-W. VII 95ff; JBaunack, Philol. 69, '10, 473ff) *freedman* only fig., of Christians ἀ. κυρίου *a freedman of the Lord*, because he has freed us fr. the powers of darkness, the slaveholders of this age 1 Cor 7: 22. Likew. ἀ. Ἰησοῦ Χριστοῦ IRo 4: 3 (Epict. 1, 19, 9 ἐμέ ὁ Ζεὺς ἐλεύθερον ἀφῆκεν.—Dssm., LO 277; 323 [LAE 332f]; Magie 70; JWeiss on 1 Cor 7: 22). WElert, ThLZ 72, '47, 265ff. M-M.*

ἀπεληλύθειν, ἀπελθών s. ἀπέρχομαι.

Ἀπελλῆς, οῦ, ὁ (Dit., Or. 265, 12; 444, 7; Inschr. v. Priene 248; Philo, Leg. ad Gai. 203ff; Jos., Ant. 12, 270) *Apelles*, greeted in Ro 16: 10. The name was common among Jews (cf. credat Judaeus Apella: Hor., Sat. 1, 5, 100). Ac 18: 24; 19: 1 have Ἀ. for Ἀπολλῶς in א; cf. Bl-D. §29, 4; 125, 1. M-M.*

ἀπελπίζω pf. ptc. ἀφηλπικώς Hv 3, 12, 2, cf. Reinhold 36; BGU 1844, 13 I BC (Hyperid. 5, 35; Epicurus p. 62, 6 Us.; Polyb. 1, 19, 12; Diod. S. 17, 106, 7 et al.; Dit., Syll.³

1173, 5; Zen.-P. 59642, 4 [III BC]; LXX; Jos., Bell. 4, 397; 5, 354) *despair* abs. Eph 4: 19 v.l. ἀ. ἑαυτόν *despair of oneself* Hv 3, 12, 2. Pass. (En. 103, 10) ἀπηλπισμένος (Is 29: 19) *despairing* 1 Cl 59: 3.—Lk 6: 35 δανείζετε μηδὲν ἀπελπίζοντες, because of the contrast w. παρ' ὧν ἐλπίζετε λαβεῖν vs. 34, demands the meaning *lend, expecting nothing in return* which, although it is contrary to contemporary usage, is quotable fr. Gk. lit. at least since Chrysostom, and then introduced widely through the Vulg. W. the v.l. μηδένα *without disappointing anyone.* M-M.*

ἀπέναντι improper prep. w. gen. (Polyb. 1, 86, 3+; pap. since III BC [PPetr. II 17(3), 3; cf. Mayser 242; 459]; inscr. since II BC [Priene]; LXX; JWackernagel, Hellenistica '07, 3ff).

1. *opposite* someone or someth.—a. strictly of place καθήμεναι ἀ. τοῦ τάφου *opposite the tomb* Mt 27: 61, cf. Mk 12: 41 v.l. (Dit., Syll.³ 756, 17 ἀ. τῆς εἰσόδου; PGrenf. I 21, 14; Jdth 3: 9; 7: 3, 18); *before, in the presence of* someone (cf. 1 Macc 6: 32) ἀ. τοῦ ὄχλου *before the crowd* Mt 27: 24 v.l. (for κατέναντι); ἀ. πάντων ὑμῶν Ac 3: 16. βλέπω ἀ. μου *I see before me* Hv 2, 1, 3.

b. fig. ἀ. τῶν ὀφθαλμῶν αὐτῶν *before their eyes* (לְנֶגֶד עֵינָי)=with them Ro 3: 18 (Ps 13: 3 LXX; 35: 2). ἀ. τ. ὀ. μου (cf. Sir 27: 23)=so that I see it 1 Cl 8: 4 (Is 1: 16); cf. Pol 6: 2.

2. *against, contrary to* (Sir 37: 4) ἀ. τῶν δογμάτων Καίσαρος πράσσειν *act contrary to the decrees of Caesar* Ac 17: 7. M-M.*

ἀπενεγκεῖν s. ἀποφέρω.

ἀπέραντος, ον (Pind., Thu.+; Herm. Wr. 1, 11; 4, 8; Job 36: 26; 3 Macc 2: 9; Philo, Congr. Erud. Gr. 53; Jos., Ant. 17, 131) *endless, limitless* γενεαλογίαι 1 Ti 1: 4 (Polyb. 1, 57, 3 of the tiresome enumeration of details). ὠκεανὸς ἀ. ἀνθρώποις *the ocean, impassable for men* 1 Cl 20: 8 (cf. 3 Macc 2: 9).*

ἀπερινόητος, ον (Epicurus p. 10, 5 Us.; Sext. Emp., Pyrrh. 2, 70 ed. Mutschm. v.l.; Damascius, De Princ. 4; Philo, Mut. Nom. 15 [of God]; PGM 4, 1138) *incomprehensible* of the divine λόγος Dg 7: 2.*

ἀπερίσπαστος, ον (Polyb.+; Diod. S. 17, 9, 4; BGU 1057, 22 [I BC]; POxy. 898, 15; PLond. 932, 9; Wsd 16: 11; Sir 41: 1; cf. Nägeli 30) *not distracted* ἀ. διανοίᾳ *with undisturbed mind* IEph 20: 2. (Epict. 3, 22, 69 ἀπερίσπαστον εἶναι δεῖ τὸν Κυνικὸν ὅλον πρὸς τῇ διακονίᾳ τοῦ θεοῦ; for this reason he should keep himself free from marriage and all other earthly obligations. In Diod. S. 40, 3, 7 Moses places the priests on a higher economic level than the laymen, ἵνα ἀπερίσπαστοι προσεδρεύωσι ταῖς τοῦ θεοῦ τιμαῖς).*

ἀπερισπάστως adv. (Polyb. 2, 20, 10; 4, 18, 6; Epict. 1, 29, 59) *without distraction* πρὸς τὸ εὐπάρεδρον τ. κυρίῳ ἀ. *that you might adhere faithfully to the Lord without distraction* 1 Cor 7: 35. M-M.*

ἀπερίτμητος, ον (oft. LXX; Philo; Jos., Bell. 1, 34, Ant. 20, 45; in Plut., Mor. 495c=unmutilated) *uncircumcised.*

1. lit. (so also Zen.-P. 84=Sb 6790, 14 [257 BC]) ἔθνη ἀπερίτμητα ἀκροβυστίαν *heathen w. uncircumcised foreskin* B 9: 5a (Jer 9: 25).

2. fig. ἀ. καρδίαις καὶ τοῖς ὠσὶν uncir. (=obdurate) *in heart and ears* Ac 7: 51 (after Lev 26: 41; Jer 6: 10; Ezk 44: 7, 9); ἀ. καρδίας B 9: 5b (Jer 9: 25b). Cf. Dssm., B 151 (BS 153). M-M.*

ἀπέρχομαι fut. ἀπελεύσομαι; 2 aor. ἀπῆλθον; pf. ἀπελήλυθα Js 1: 24; Hs 9, 5, 4; plpf. ἀπεληλύθειν J 4: 8; cf. Bl-D. §101 ἔρχεσθαι (Hom.+; inscr., pap., LXX, Joseph., Test. 12 Patr.).

1. *go away, depart*—a. lit., w. no indication of place (1 Macc 9: 36; 2 Macc 14: 34; 1 Esdr 4: 11) Mt 8: 21; 13: 25; 16: 4; Ac 10: 7; 28: 29 v.l.; Js 1: 24.—Ptc. ἀπελθών w. ind., subj., or imper. of another verb=*go away and* (Epict. Index Sch.; Gen 21: 14, 16 al.) Mt 13: 28, 46; 18: 30; 25: 18, 25; Mk 6: 27, 37; Lk 5: 14.—W. indication of place or person ἀπό τινος (Thu. 8, 92, 2; UPZ 61, 7 [161 BC] ἀφ' ὑμῶν ἀπελήλυθα; Epict. 3, 15, 11; 3 Km 21: 36; Tob 14: 8): ἀπὸ τ. ὁρίων αὐτῶν Mk 5: 17. ἀπ' αὐτῆς Lk 1: 38. ἀπ' αὐτῶν 2: 15; 8: 37.—ἔξω τοῦ συνεδρίου Ac 4: 15 (cf. Jdth 6: 12). In a ship J 6: 22.

b. fig., of diseases, etc. (Cebes 14, 3 οὐ μὴ ἀπέλθῃ ἀπ' αὐτῶν ἡ κακία; Ex 8: 25) ἀπῆλθεν ἀπ' αὐτοῦ ἡ λέπρα *the leprosy left him* Mk 1: 42; Lk 5: 13; ἡ ὀπώρα ἀ. ἀπὸ σοῦ *the fruit has gone from you* Rv 18: 14.—Gener. pass away (SSol 2: 11) Rv 9: 12; 11: 14; 21: 1, 4.

2. *go* w. indication of place εἰς (Simplicius in Epict. p. 134, 51 ἀ. εἰς τὸ ἱερόν): εἰς ἔρημον τόπον Mk 1: 35; cf. 6: 36, 46; 7: 24; Mt 8: 33; 14: 15; εἰς τὸν οἶκον Mt 9: 7; Mk 7: 30; Lk 1: 23; Hs 9, 11, 2; εἰς τ. Γαλιλαίαν Mt 28: 10; J 4: 3. εἰς Σπανίαν Ro 15: 28; cf. 2 Cor 1: 16 v.l. (for διελθεῖν). Gal 1: 17. ἐπί τι (Jos., Vi. 151): ἐπὶ τὸ μνημεῖον Lk 24: 24 (cf. 3 Km 19: 19 v.l.; Epict. 4, 7, 30). ἐν· Hs 1: 6 (cf. Pel.-Leg. p. 7, 3; Epict. 2, 20, 33 ἀπελθεῖν ἐν βαλανείῳ). W. the simple dat. (PFay. 113, 12 [100 AD] τῇ πόλει πέμψας) ποίῳ τόπῳ ἀπῆλθεν Hv 4, 3, 7.—Of demons (Thrasyllus [I AD] in Ps-Plut., Fluv. 16, 2; PGM 13, 244) ἀ. εἰς τοὺς χοίρους Mt 8: 32.—ἀ. πρός τινα (PFay. 123, 19 [100 AD]; BGU 884 II, 13f; 1 Km 25: 5; 1 Macc 7: 20) *come or go to someone* Mk 3: 13; Rv 10: 9. πρὸς αὐτόν *go home* Lk 24: 12; pl. J 20: 10.—J 16: 7 πρὸς τὸν πατέρα is to be supplied from the context (PPetr. II 13[19], 7 [252 BC] εἰς θεοὺς ἀπελθεῖν).—Also of a journey in a boat εἰς τὸ πέραν *go over to the opposite side* Mt 8: 18; Mk 8: 13. εἰς ἔρημον τόπον Mk 6: 32. W. no place indicated (the context supplies the goal as POxford [EP Wegener '42] 16, 16: to a festival) Lk 17: 23.—Fig., of stones *go* εἰς τ. οἰκοδομήν *into the building* Hs 9, 5, 3 and 4.

3. of a report *go out and spread* εἰς ὅλην τ. Συρίαν Mt 4: 24.

4. ἀ. ὀπίσω τινός (Job 21: 33) *go after, follow someone* of the disciples Mk 1: 20; of the world J 12: 19; of the Sodomites ἀ. ὀπίσω σαρκὸς ἑτέρας *go after strange flesh*, i.e., practice unnatural vice Jd 7.—Abs. ἀ. εἰς τὰ ὀπίσω *draw back* J 18: 6; almost=*desert* 6: 66. M-M.

ἀπεστάλην, ἀπέσταλκα, ἀπέστειλα s. ἀποστέλλω.

ἀπέστην s. ἀφίστημι.

ἀπεστράφην s. ἀποστρέφω.

ἀπέχω fut. mid. ἀφέξομαι (Hom.+; inscr., pap., LXX, Philo, Joseph., Test. 12 Patr.).

1. act., commercial t.t. *receive a sum in full* and give a receipt for it (Dit., Syll.² 845, 7 [200 BC] τὰν τιμὰν ἀπέχει; M. Ant. 9, 42 ἀπέχει τὸ ἴδιον; oft. pap. and ostraca; cf. Dssm., NB 56 [BS 229]; LO 88ff [LAE 110f]; Erman, APF 1, '01, 77ff; Mayser 487; Ostraka I 86; Nägeli 54f; Anz 318; Gen 43: 23; Num 32: 19; Jos., Bell. 1, 596 ἀ. τῆς ἀσεβείας τὸ ἐπιτίμιον) τὸν μισθόν (Plut., Sol. 22, 4, Mor. 334A) Mt 6: 2, 5, 16; τὴν παράκλησιν Lk 6: 24; πάντα Phil 4: 18; τὸ τέλειον τῆς γνώσεως *perfect knowledge* B 13: 7; ἀ. τὴν ἀποκάλυψιν *to have received the revelation*

Hv 3, 13, 4.—Sim. Phlm 15 ἵνα αἰώνιον αὐτὸν ἀπέχῃς *that you might keep him forever* (opp. χωρίζεσθαι πρὸς ὥραν). Here perh. belongs the difficult impers. ἀπέχει in the sense *the account is closed* Mk 14: 41; cf. JdeZwaan, Exp. 6 S. XII '05, 459–72, who takes the traitor of vs. 42 as the subj. *he has received the money.* Vulg. has for it 'sufficit' *it is enough,* which is supported by some comparatively late evidence (Anacreontea 15[28], 33 Bergk PLG III; PStrassb. 4, 19 note [550 AD]; PLond. 1343, 38 [709 AD] dub. l.); this is perh. to be preferred. The rather freq. expr. οὐδὲν ἀπέχει='nothing hinders' (Pla., Cra. 23 p. 407B; Plut., Mor. 433A; 680E) would suggest for ἀπέχει *that is a hindrance,* referring to the extreme drowsiness of the disciples at the decisive moment. D has ἀ. τὸ τέλος *this is the end* (Bl-D. §129 app.; JWackernagel, Syntax. I² '26, 119. Cf. Epigr. Gr. 259 [II AD] ἀπέσχε τέλος [=death]. MBlack, An Aramaic Approach, '46, 161f, suggests an Aram. background).—GHBoobyer, NTS 2, '55, 44–48 'he (Judas) is taking possession of' me.

2. intr. *be distant* (Hdt.+; PStrassb. 57, 6; PLille 1, 5; 2, 2; Jos., Ant. 5, 161) αὐτοῦ μακρὰν ἀπέχοντος *when he was still far away* Lk 15: 20 (Diod. S. 12, 33, 4 μακρὰν ἀπ.; Gen 44: 4; Jo 4: 8; En. 32, 2); W. indication of the place from which (as 1 Macc 8: 4; 2 Macc 11: 5) οὐ μακρὰν ἀπέχων ἀπὸ τ. οἰκίας *being not far fr. the house* Lk 7: 6; cf. MPol 5: 1; of a ship at some distance from the land Mt 14: 24 (as Inscr. Gr. 466, 9 ἀπέχον ἀπὸ τῆς γῆς). W. the exact distance given (so since Thu. 2, 5, 2) κώμη ἀπέχουσα σταδίους ἑξήκοντα ἀπὸ Ἰερουσαλήμ *sixty stades fr. Jerusalem* Lk 24: 13 (Demetr. of Kallatis [200 BC]: 85 fgm. 2 Jac. ἀπεχούσης τῆς νήσου ἀπὸ τῆς ἠπείρου σταδίους υʹ. Cf. the comic poet Euphro [III BC] 11, 3 Kock; 2 Macc 12: 29; Jos., Bell. 2, 516).—Fig. πόρρω ἀ. ἀπό τινος (= רָחַק מִן) *be far from someone* Mt 15: 8; Mk 7: 6 (both Is 29: 13).

3. mid. *keep away, abstain* w. gen. of the thing (Hom.+; Dit., Syll.³ 768, 16 [31 BC]; PHermopol. 52, 21; 1 Esdr 6: 26; Wsd 2: 16; Jos., Bell. 2, 581, Ant. 11, 101) εἰδωλοθύτων καὶ αἵματος καὶ πνικτῶν καὶ πορνείας *abstain fr. things offered to idols, blood, things strangled, and sexual vice* Ac 15: 29, cf. vs. 20 (s. αἷμα 1b). πάσης ἀδικίας (Hyperid., fgm. 210 τ. ἀδικημάτων; Dit., Syll.³ 1268 I, 18 [III BC] κακίας ἀπέχου) Pol 2: 2; cf. 6: 1, 3; Hv 1, 2, 4; 2, 2, 3; 3, 8, 4; m 3: 5; Dg 4: 6. τῶν κακῶν βοτανῶν IPhld 3: 1; cf. ITr 6: 1. βρωμάτων 1 Ti 4: 3. εὐχαριστίας κ. προσευχῆς *keep away fr. the Lord's Supper and prayer* ISm 7: 1, cf. 2. τῶν σαρκικῶν ἐπιθυμιῶν 1 Pt 2: 11; D 1: 4. τῆς γλώσσης=*control the tongue* Hv 2, 2, 3. λατρείας Dg 3: 2.—W. ἀπό τινος (oft. LXX; En. 104, 6; Ep. Arist. 143): ἀπὸ τῆς πορνείας 1 Th 4: 3; cf. Ac 15: 20 t.r.; ἀπὸ παντὸς εἴδους πονηροῦ *fr. every kind of evil* 1 Th 5: 22. ἀπὸ παντὸς κακοῦ 1 Cl 17: 3 (Job 1: 1, 8; 2: 3). ἀπέχεσθε ἀπὸ τ. ἀνθρώπων *keep hands off the men* Ac 5: 39 D.—Pol 5: 3; Hm 2: 3; 4, 1, 3 and 9; 5, 1, 7; 5, 2, 8; 7: 3; 9: 12; 11: 4, 8, 21; 12, 1, 3; 12, 2, 2; s 4: 5. M-M and suppl.*

ἀπῇεσαν s. ἄπειμι 2.

ἀπήλασα s. ἀπελαύνω.

ἀπῆλθα and ἀπῆλθον s. ἀπέρχομαι.

ἀπηλλάχθαι s. ἀπαλλάσσω.

ἀπίδω s. ἀφοράω.

ἀπιστέω impf. ἠπίστουν; 1 aor. ἠπίστησα (Hom.+; LXX, Philo).

1. *disbelieve, refuse to believe*—a. gener. (POxy. 471, 4 [II AD]; Jos., Ant. 2, 58; Third Corinthians 3: 25) Mk 16:

11; Lk 24: 41. ἠπίστουν *refused to believe* Ac 28: 24; ἀ. τινι *someone* (Jos., Ant. 2, 330) Lk 24: 11.—Dit., Syll.³ 1168, 24; 30; 31; Philo, Mos. 1, 212; 2, 261 show the transition to

b. the relig. sense (Iambl., Vi. Pyth. 28, 148 περὶ θεῶν μηδὲν θαυμαστὸν ἀπιστεῖν. Herm. Wr. 9, 10; Wsd. 1: 2; 10: 7; 18: 13; 2 Macc 8: 13; Jos., Ant. 2, 270) Mk 16: 16. οἱ ἀπιστοῦντες *the unbelievers* (Iambl., Vi. Pyth. 28, 139) of pagans and Jews 1 Pt 2: 7; IEph 18: 1.

2 *be unfaithful* (X., An. 2, 6, 19 of disloyal soldiers) Ro 3: 3; 2 Ti 2: 13. M-M.*

ἀπιστία, ας, ἡ (Hes., Hdt.+; LXX, Philo, Joseph.; cf. Mayser 11f, 130).

1. *unfaithfulness* (X., An. 3, 2, 4+; UPZ 18, 5 [163 BC]; Wsd 14: 25; Philo, Spec. Leg. 2, 8, Decal. 172; Jos., Ant. 14, 349) Ro 3: 3 (JGGriffiths, ET 53, '41, 118).

2. *unbelief, lack of belief* (Wilcken, Chrest. 155, 11; Jos., Ant. 2, 327; 19, 127).

a. of the Jews at Nazareth Mt 13: 58; Mk 6: 6 and other people 9: 24, toward Jesus.

b. in an expressly relig. sense (Cercidas Iamb. [III BC] 72 Knox '29 p. 234; Plut., Coriol. 38, 4, Alex. 75, 2 ἀ. πρὸς τὰ θεῖα καὶ καταφρόνησις αὐτῶν, De Superstit. 2 p. 165B; Ael. Aristid. 47, 66 K.=23 p. 462 D.; Philo, Leg ad Gai. 118 ἀ. πρὸς τὸν τοῦ κόσμου παντὸς εὐεργέτην, Mut. Nom. 201 al.; Jos., Ant. 10, 142) of the disciples Mt 17: 20 t.r. (w. CDSin. Syr.). Of the Jews toward God Ro 11: 20 (τῇ ἀπιστίᾳ=because of their unbelief; ACharue, L'Incrédulité des Juifs dans le NT '29; on the dat. of cause Schmid III 57; IV 59; M. Ant. 3, 1; inscr. in ENachmanson, Eranos II, '11, 220–5), 23; Hb 3: 19. διακρίνεσθαι τῇ ἀπιστίᾳ *waver in disbelief* Ro 4: 20. ἐποίησα ἐν ἀ. *while I was still an unbeliever* 1 Ti 1: 13. καρδία πονηρὰ ἀπιστίας *an evil, unbelieving heart* Hb 3: 12.—Among Christians w. διψυχία 2 Cl 19: 2. Personif. as one of the chief sins Hs 9, 15, 3. (Opp. πίστις) IEph 8: 2.—As a characteristic of this age (w. ἀνομία) ending of Mark in the Freer Ms. l. 2. M-M.*

ἄπιστος, ον (Hom.+; LXX, Philo, Joseph.).

1. *unbelievable, incredible* (Bacchylides 17, 117; X., Cyr. 3, 1, 26; Pla., Theag. 130D; Herm. Wr. 9, 10; Ep. Arist. 296; Philo, Op. M. 114 al.; Jos., Ant. 6, 198) τί ἄπιστον κρίνεται παρ' ὑμῖν; *why does it seem incredible to you?* Ac 26: 8 (Jos., Ant. 18, 76 ἄπιστα αὐτὰ κρίνειν).

2. *faithless, unbelieving* (w. relig. coloring as early as Dit., Syll.³ 1168, 33 [c. 320 BC]; Is 17: 10; Pr 28: 25 v.l.; Philo, Leg. All. 3, 164, Leg ad Gai. 3) γενεά Mt 17: 17; Mk 9: 19; Lk 9: 41; of Thomas J 20: 27.—Esp. of the heathen οἱ ἄ. 1 Cor 6: 6; 7: 15; 10: 27; 14: 22; 2 Cl 17: 5; Dg 11: 2; MPol 16: 1; IMg 5: 2; condemned at the Last Judgment Lk 12: 46 (cf. Paroem. Gr.: Zenob. [II AD] 2, 6 p. 33, 4f. αἱ ἀμυήτων ψυχαί are tormented in Hades); w. ἰδιώτης 1 Cor 14: 23f; ἄ. γυνή 7: 12, 14; ἀνήρ vs. 13f (cf. JKöhne, Die Ehen zw. Christen u. Heiden in d. ersten christl. Jahrhunderten '31). W. the connotation of evildoing 2 Cor 6: 14f; 1 Ti 5: 8; w. μεμιαμμένοι Tit 1: 15; cf. Rv 21: 8.—Of teachers of error ITr 10; ISm 2: 5; 3.—ἐν οἷς ὁ θεὸς τ. αἰῶνος ἐτύφλωσεν τὰ νοήματα τῶν ἀ. 2 Cor 4: 4 can best be transl. *in their case, the god of this age has blinded their unbelieving minds.* M-M.*

ἀπλότης, ητος, ἡ (X., Pla., et al.; Dit., Or. 764, 1; LXX; Philo; Joseph.; cf. Nägeli 52).

1. *simplicity, sincerity, uprightness, frankness* ἐν ἀ. τῆς καρδίας ὑπακούειν *obey w. a sincere heart* Eph 6: 5; cf. Col 3: 22 (Diod. S. 5, 66, 4 ἀπλότης τῆς ψυχῆς; 1 Ch 29: 17; Wsd 1: 1; Test. Reub. 4: 1, Sim. 4: 5, Levi 13: 1); 2 Cor

1: 12 v.l.; 1 Cl 60: 2 v.l. ἐν ἁ. λέγειν *speak simply, plainly* B 8: 2 (cf. Dionys. Hal., Ars Rhet. 9, 14). ἐν ἁ. δηλῶσαι 17: 1. ἐν ἁ. εὑρίσκεσθαι *be found upright* Hm 2: 7. ἡ ἁ. ἡ εἰς Χριστόν *sincere devotion to Christ* 2 Cor 11: 3 (WSWood, Exp. 9 S. II '25, 450-3).—Hermas is esp. fond of this word, mng. simple goodness, which gives itself without reserve (Jos., Bell. 5, 319, Ant. 7, 332): w. ἀκακία (Philo, Op. M. 170) Hv 1, 2, 4; 3, 9, 1. W. ἐγκράτεια Hv 2, 3, 2. W. νηπιότης s 9, 24, 3. ἐμμένειν τῇ ἁ. *continue in your sincerity* Hv 3, 1, 9. For this ἁ. ἔχειν m 2: 1. Personif. w. other Christian virtues Hv 3, 8, 5 and 7; s 9, 15, 2. This mng. is readily restricted (cf. esp. Hs 9, 24, 3) to

2. *generosity, liberality* (Test. Iss. 3: 8, cf. RHCharles, Test. of 12 Patr., '08, on Test. Iss. 3: 1, 2, 8; Epigr. Gr. 716, 5=IG 14, 1517 [s. L-S-J s.v. II 3]) Ro 12: 8; 2 Cor 8: 2; 9: 11, 13. This sense is in dispute, however, and it is possible that the mng. *sincere concern* is sufficient for the passages under 2.—JAmstutz, ΑΠΛΟΤΗΣ '68 does not favor *generosity,* etc. M-M.*

ἁπλοῦς, ῆ, οῦν (Aeschyl., Thu.+; inscr.; pap.; Pr 11: 25; Philo; Jos., C. Ap. 2, 190) *single, simple, sincere* εἶναι ἁ. τῇ καρδίᾳ *be simple in heart* B 19: 2 (cf. Dit., Syll.³ 1042, 12 ἁ. τῇ ψυχῇ; Pr 11: 25; Ps.-Phoc. 50). ἁ. διάνοια *a sincere mind* 1 Cl 23: 1. W. ἄκακος (Diod. S. 13, 76; Nicol. Dam.: 90 fgm. 61, 2 Jac.) Hs 9, 24, 2. Of the eye (Damasc., Vi. Isid. 16) *clear, sound, healthy,* w. the connotation *generous* (s. ἁπλότης 2; opp. πονηρός, whose mng. is apparent fr. Mt 20: 15; Mk 7: 22. Cf. Test. Iss. 3: 4 πορευόμενος ἐν ἁπλότητι ὀφθαλμῶν) Mt 6: 22; Lk 11: 34 (s. Jülicher, Gleichn. 98ff; WBrandt, ZNW 14, '13, 189ff; CEdlund, D. Auge der Einfalt: Acta Sem. NT Ups. 19, '52, 51-122; HJCadbury, The Single Eye: HTR 47, '54, 69-74 holds out strongly for *generous;* opposed by TThienemann, Gordon Review 1, '55, 10-22. Cf. also λύχνος 2, ὀφθαλμός 1, πονηρός 1aα and bβ).—As of animals gener. (Aristot., Hist. An. 9, 1), so the superl. ἁπλούστατος (the form in X., Mem. 4, 2, 16; Polyb. 9, 10, 5; Strabo 7, 3, 7; Philo, Vi. Cont. 82) *quite simple, guileless,* of doves Mt 10: 16 D.— The comp. ἁπλούστερον *very simply* B 6: 5.—CSpicq, La vertu de Simplicité dans l'A. et le N. Test.: RSphth 22, '33, 1-26; ESjöberg, Studia Theologica 5, '51, 89-105; HBacht, Geist u. Leben 29, '56, 416-26. M-M.*

ἁπλόω (Hero Alex. III p. 130, 7; Cornutus 32 p. 66, 7; Soranus p. 76, 16; Aelian, N.A. 12, 27; Ps.-Callisth. p. 36, 10; Herm. Wr. 486, 8 Sc.; Anth. Pal. 11, 107; Job 22: 3) *make single, unfold* pass. (Aelian, N.A. 14, 26 p. 359, 13) χάρις ἁπλουμένη *unfolding grace* Dg 11: 5.*

ἄπλυτος, ον (Semonides 7, 5; Dio Chrys. 11[12], 43; Galen XIII 664 K.) *unwashed* τὸ ἔντερον ἄ. φαγεῖν *eat the entrails unwashed* B 7: 4.*

ἁπλῶς adv. (Aeschyl.+; inscr., pap.; Pr 10: 9; Philo).
1. *simply, sincerely, openly* (Demosth. 23, 178; Epict. 2, 2, 13; Philo, Ebr. 76) ἁ. τι τελέσαι *fulfill someth. sincerely* Hm 2: 6a, cf. b. προσευχὰς ἀναφέρειν 2 Cl 2: 2. Comp. ἁπλούστερον (Isaeus 4, 2) γράφειν *write very plainly* B 6: 5.
2. w. διδόναι *generously, without reserve* Js 1: 5 (cf. MDibelius ad loc.; HRiesenfeld, Con. Neot. 9, '44, 33-41); Hm 2: 4 (cf. ἁπλότης 2).
3. *simply, at all* w. neg. expr. (ref. in Riesenf., op. cit. 37f, and Theopomp. [IV BC]: 115 fgm. 224 Jac. ἁ. οὐδείς; Diod. S. 3, 8, 5 ἁ. οὐ) ἁ. οὐ δύναμαι ἐξηγήσασθαι *I simply cannot describe* AP 3: 9.
4. *in short, in a word* (Eur., Rhesus 851; Epict. 3, 22, 96) ἁ. εἰπεῖν *to put it briefly* Dg 6: 1; the mng. *frankly*

(Epict. 3, 15, 3; M. Ant. 5, 7, 2; schol. on Apollon. Rhod. 2, 844-47a ἁπλῶς κ. κατὰ ἀλήθειαν ἐξειπεῖν) is also poss. here. M-M. and suppl.*

ἀπό (Hom.+; inscr., pap., LXX, Philo, Joseph., Test. 12 Patr.) prep. w. gen. (see the lit. on ἀνά, beg., also for ἀπό: KDieterich, IndogF 24, '09, 93-158). Basic mng. *separation from someone* or *someth.,* fr. which the other mngs. have developed. In the NT it has encroached on the domain of Att. ἐκ, ὑπό, παρά, and the gen. of separation; cf. Mlt. 102; 246; Mlt.-Turner 258f.
I. Of place, exclusively, *from, away from.*
1. w. all verbs denoting motion, esp. those compounded w. ἀπό, ἀπάγεσθαι, ἀπαλλάσσεσθαι, ἀπελαύνειν, ἀπέρχεσθαι, ἀπολύεσθαι, ἀποπλανᾶσθαι, ἀποχωρεῖν, ἀποχωρίζεσθαι; but also w. διαστῆναι, διέρχεσθαι, ἐκδημεῖν, ἐκκινεῖν, ἐκπλεῖν, ἐκπορεύεσθαι, ἐξέρχεσθαι, ἐξωθεῖν, μεταβαίνειν, μετατίθεσθαι, νοσφίζειν, παραγίνεσθαι, πλανᾶσθαι, πορεύεσθαι, ὑπάγειν, ὑποστρέφειν, φεύγειν; s. the entries in question.
2. w. all verbs expressing the idea of separation ἐκβάλλειν τὸ κάρφος ἀ. τοῦ ὀφθαλμοῦ *remove the splinter fr. the eye* Mt 7: 4 v.l. (for ἐκ). ἀπολύεσθαι ἀ. ἀνδρός *be divorced fr. her husband* Lk 16: 18, cf. Ac 15: 33. ἀποκυλίειν, ἀπολαμβάνεσθαι, ἀποστρέφειν, ἐπιστρέφεσθαι, ἐπανάγειν, αἴρειν, ἀφαιρεῖν, ἀπολέσθαι et al., see the pertinent entries. So also κενὸς ἀ. τινος Hs 9, 19, 2. ἔρημος ἀ. τινος (Jer 51: 2) 2 Cl 2: 3. W. verbs which express the concept of separation in the wider sense, like loose, free, acquit et al. ἀπορφανίζειν, διεγείρεσθαι, δικαιοῦν, ἐκδικοῦν, ἐλευθεροῦν, λούειν, λύειν, λυτροῦν, ῥαντίζειν, σαλεύειν, στέλλειν, σῴζειν, φθείρειν, s. the entries; hence also ἀθῷος (Sus 46 Theod. v.l.) Mt 27: 24. καθαρὸς ἀ. τινος (Tob 3: 14; but s. Dssm. NB 24 [BS 196; 216]) Ac 20: 26; cf. Kuhring '06, 54.
3. Verbs meaning *be on guard, be ashamed,* etc., take ἀπό to express the object of their caution, shame, or fear; so αἰσχύνεσθαι, βλέπειν, μετανοεῖν, προσέχειν, φοβεῖσθαι, φυλάσσειν, φυλάσσεσθαι; see these entries and V 3 below.
4. W. verbs of *concealing, hiding, hindering,* the pers. *from* whom someth. is concealed is found w. ἀπό; so κρύπτειν τι ἀπό τινος, παρακαλύπτειν τι ἀπό τινος, κωλύειν τι ἀπό τινος; s. the entries.
5. in pregnant constr. like ἀνάθεμα εἶναι ἀ. τοῦ Χριστοῦ *be separated fr. Christ by a curse* Ro 9: 3. μετανοεῖν ἀ. τ. κακίας (Jer 8: 6) Ac 8: 22. ἀποθνῄσκειν ἀ. τινος *through death become free from* Col 2: 20. φθείρεσθαι ἀ. τ. ἁπλότητος *be ruined and lose devotion* 2 Cor 11: 3. Cf. Hs 6, 2, 4.
6. as a substitute for the partitive gen. (Hdt. 6, 27; Thu. 7, 87, 6; PPetr. III 11, 20; PIand. 8, 6; Kuhring 20; Rossberg 22; Johannessohn 17) τίνα ἀ. τῶν δύο; Mt 27: 21, cf. Lk 9: 38; 19: 39 (like PTebt. 299, 13; 1 Macc 1: 13; 3: 24; Sir 6: 6; 46: 8). τὰ ἀ. τοῦ πλοίου *pieces of the ship* Ac 27: 44. ἐκχεῶ ἀ. τοῦ πνεύματός μου Ac 2: 17f (Jo 3: 1f). λαμβάνειν ἀ. τ. καρπῶν *get a share of the vintage* Mk 12: 2.—Of foods (like Da 1: 13, 4: 33a; 2 Macc 7: 1) ἐσθίειν ἀ. τ. ψιχίων *eat some of the crumbs* Mt 15: 27; Mk 7: 28. χορτάζεσθαι ἀ. τινος *eat one's fill of someth.* Lk 16: 21. αἴρειν ἀ. τῶν ἰχθύων *pick up the remnants of the fish* Mk 6: 43. ἐνέγκατε ἀ. τ. ὀψαρίων *bring some of the fish* J 21: 10.—Of drink (like Sir 26: 12) πίνειν ἀπὸ τ. γενήματος τῆς ἀμπέλου *drink the product of the vine* Lk 22: 18.
II. To denote the point from which someth. begins, in lit. and fig. mng.
1. of place *from, out from* σημεῖον ἀ. τ. οὐρανοῦ *a sign*

fr. heaven Mk 8: 11. ἀ. πόλεως εἰς πόλιν *from one city to another* Mt 23: 34. ἀπ' ἄκρων οὐρανῶν ἕως ἄκρων αὐτῶν (Dt 30: 4; Ps 18: 7) *from one end of heaven to the other* 24: 31, cf. Mk 13: 27. ἀπ' ἄνωθεν ἕως κάτω *from top to bottom* Mt 27: 51. ἀρξάμενοι ἀ. Ἰερουσαλήμ *beginning in Jerusalem* Lk 24: 47 (inclusive use, as in 3 below; s. also Lk 23: 5; Ac 1: 22; 10: 37). ἀφ' ὑμῶν ἐξήχηται ὁ λόγος τ. κυρίου *the word of the Lord has gone out from you and sounded forth* 1 Th 1: 8. ἀπὸ βορρᾶ, ἀπὸ νότου *in the north, in the south* (PGoodspeed 6, 5 [129 BC] ἐν τῷ ἀπὸ νότου πεδίῳ; Wilcken, Chrest. 11A Col. 1, 12 [123 BC] τὸ ἀπὸ νότου τῆς πόλεως χῶμα, 7 ἀπὸ βορρᾶ τῆς πόλεως, 70, 16 al.; Josh 18: 5; 19: 34; 1 Km 14: 5) Rv 21: 13.

2. of time *from—(on), since* (POxy. 523, 4; cf. Kuhring 54ff).

a. ἀ. τῶν ἡμερῶν Ἰωάννου *from the days of John* Mt 11: 12. ἀ. τῆς ὥρας ἐκείνης 9: 22. ἀπ' ἐκείνης τ. ἡμέρας (Jos., Bell. 4, 318, Ant. 7, 382) Mt 22: 46; J 11: 53. ἔτη ἑπτὰ ἀ. τῆς παρθενίας αὐτῆς *for seven years fr. the time she was a virgin* Lk 2: 36. ἀ. ἐτῶν δώδεκα *for 12 years* 8: 43. ἀ. τρίτης ὥρας τῆς νυκτός Ac 23: 23. ἀ. κτίσεως κόσμου Ro 1: 20. ἀ. πέρυσι *since last year, a year ago* 2 Cor 8: 10; 9: 2.—ἀπ' αἰῶνος, ἀπ' ἀρχῆς, ἀπ' ἄρτι, ἀπὸ καταβολῆς κόσμου, ἀπὸ τότε, ἀπὸ τοῦ νῦν; s. the pertinent entries.

b. w. the limits defined, forward and backward: ἀπὸ-ἕως (Jos., Ant. 6, 364) Mt 27: 45. ἀπὸ-ἄχρι Phil 1: 5. ἀπὸ-μέχρι Ac 10: 30; Ro 5: 14; 15: 19.

c. ἀφ' ἧς (sc. ὥρας or ἡμέρας, which is found Col 1: 6, 9; but ἀφ' ἧς became a fixed formula: Plut., Pelop. 15, 5; cf. Bl-D. §241, 2 app.) *since* Lk 7: 45; Ac 24: 11; 2 Pt 3: 4 (cf. X., Hell. 4, 6, 6; 1 Macc 1: 11). ἀφ' οὖ (sc.—like X., Cyr. 1, 2, 13—χρόνου; Att. inscr. in Meisterhans.³-Schw. and s. Witkowski. ἀφ' οὖ is also a formula) *since, when once* (X., Symp. 4, 62; Lucian, Dial. Mar. 15, 1) Lk 13: 25; 24: 21; Rv 16: 18 (cf. Da 12: 1; 1 Macc 9: 29; 16: 24; 2 Macc 1: 7; Jos., Ant. 4, 78). τρία ἔτη ἀφ' οὖ (cf. Tob 5: 35) Lk 13: 7.

3. indicating the beg. of a series *from—(on)*.

a. ἀρξάμενος ἀ. Μωϋσέως καὶ ἀ. πάντων τ. προφητῶν *beginning w. Moses and all the prophets* Lk 24: 27. ἕβδομος ἀ. Ἀδάμ Jd 14 (Diod. S. 1, 50, 3 ὄγδοος ὁ ἀπὸ τοῦ πατρός [ancestor]; Appian, Mithrid. 9 §29 τὸν ἕκτον ἀπὸ τοῦ πρώτου Μιθριδάτην; Arrian, Anab. 7, 12, 4; Diog. L. 3, 1: Plato in the line of descent was ἕκτος ἀπὸ Σόλωνος; Biogr. p. 31: Homer δέκατος ἀπὸ Μουσαίου). ἀ. διετοῦς καὶ κατωτέρω Mt 2: 16 (cf. Num 1: 20; 2 Esdr [Ezra] 3: 8).

b. w. both beg. and end given ἀπὸ-ἕως (Sir 18: 26; 1 Macc 9: 13) Mt 1: 17; 23: 35; Ac 8: 10. Sim., ἀ. δόξης εἰς δόξαν *fr. glory to glory* 2 Cor 3: 18.

III. To indicate distance fr. a point *away from*; for μακρὰν ἀ. τινος *far fr. someone*, ἀπὸ μακρόθεν *fr. a great distance* s. μακράν, μακρόθεν. ἀπέχειν ἀπὸ τινος s. ἀπέχω 2. W. detailed measurements (corresp. to Lat. 'a', cf. Bl-D. §161, 1; Rob. 575; WSchulze, Graeca Latina '01, 15ff; Hdb. on J 11: 18; Appian, Bell. Civ. 3, 12 §42; Ramsay, Phrygia I 2 p. 390 no. 248) ἦν Βηθανία ἐγγὺς τῶν Ἱεροσολύμων ὡς ἀπὸ σταδίων δεκατέντε *Bethany was near Jerusalem, about 15 stades away* J 11: 18. ὡς ἀπὸ πηχῶν διακοσίων *about 200 cubits* 21: 8. ἀπὸ σταδίων χιλίων ἑξακοσίων Rv 14: 20; cf. Hv 4, 1, 5.—Hebraistically ἀπὸ προσώπου τινός (פְּנֵי־מִן Gen 16: 6; Jer 4: 26; Jdth 2: 14; Sir 21: 2; 1 Macc 5: 34)=פְּנֵי־מִן *(away) from the presence of someone* 2 Th 1: 9 (Is 2: 10, 19, 21; Rv 12: 14 (Bl-D. §140; 217, 1; Mlt.-H. 466).

IV. To indicate origin or source *from.*

1. lit.—a. with verbs of motion—α. *down from* πίπτειν ἀ. τραπέζης Mt 15: 27. καθεῖλεν δυνάστας ἀ. θρόνων *he has dethroned rulers* Lk 1: 52.

β. *from* ἔρχεσθαι ἀ. θεοῦ J 3: 2; cf. 13: 3; 16: 30. παραγίνεται ἀ. τῆς Γαλιλαίας Mt 3: 13; ἀ. ἀνατολῶν ἥξουσιν 8: 11 (Is 49: 12; 59: 19); ἀ. τοῦ ἱεροῦ ἐπορεύετο 24: 1; ἀ. Παμφυλίας Ac 15: 38. ἐγείρεσθαι ἀ. τ. νεκρῶν *be raised from the dead* Mt 14: 2.

b. to indicate someone's local origin *from* (Hom.+; Soph., El. 701; Hdt. 8, 114; inscr. [Rev. archéol. 4 sér. IV '04 p. 9 ἀπὸ Θεσσαλονίκης]. PFlor. 14, 2; 15, 5; 17, 4; 22, 13 al.; Judg 12: 8; 13: 2; 17: 1 [all three acc. to B]; 2 Km 23: 20 al.; Jos., Bell. 3, 422, Vi. 217; cf. Bl-D. §209, 3; Rob. 578) ἦν ἀ. Βηθσαϊδά *he was from B.* J 1: 44; cf. 12: 21. ὄχλοι ἀ. τῆς Γαλιλαίας *crowds fr. Galilee* Mt 4: 25. ἄνδρες ἀ. παντὸς ἔθνους Ac 2: 5. ἀνὴρ ἀ. τοῦ ὄχλου *a man fr. the crowd* Lk 9: 38. ὁ προφήτης ὁ ἀ. Ναζαρέθ Mt 21: 11. οἱ ἀ. Κιλικίας *the Cilicians* Ac 6: 9. οἱ ἀδελφοὶ οἱ ἀ. Ἰόππης 10: 23 (Musaeus v. 153 παρθένοι ἀπ' Ἀρκαδίας). οἱ ἀ. Θεσσαλονίκης Ἰουδαῖοι 17: 13. οἱ ἀ. τῆς Ἰταλίας *the Italians* Hb 13: 24, who could be inside as well as outside Italy (cf. Dssm., Her 33, 1898, 344, LO 167, 1 [LAE 200, 3]; Mlt. 237; Bl-D. §437).—Rather denoting membership οἱ ἀ. τῆς ἐκκλησίας *church members* Ac 12: 1; likew. 15: 5 (cf. Plut., Cato Min. 4, 2 οἱ ἀπὸ τ. στοᾶς φιλόσοφοι; Ps.-Demetr. c. 68 οἱ ἀπ' αὐτοῦ= his [Isocrates'] pupils; Synes., Ep. 4 p. 162B; 66 p. 206C; PTebt. 33, 3 [112 BC] Ῥωμαῖος τῶν ἀπὸ συγκλήτου).— To indicate origin in the sense of material fr. which someth. is made (Hdt. 7, 65; Theocr. 15, 117; Inschr. γ. Priene 117, 72 ἀπὸ χρυσοῦ; 1 Esdr 8: 56; Sir 43: 20 v.l.) ἔνδυμα ἀ. τριχῶν καμήλου *clothing made of camel's hair* Mt 3: 4.

2. fig.—a. w. verbs of asking, desiring, to denote the pers. *of* or *from* whom a thing is asked: δανίσασθαι ἀπό τινος *borrow fr. someone* Mt 5: 42. ἐκζητεῖν ἀ. τῆς γενεᾶς ταύτης Lk 11: 51. ἀπαιτεῖν τι ἀπό τινος Lk 12: 20. ζητεῖν τι ἀπό τινος 1 Th 2: 6. λαμβάνειν τι ἀπό τινος Mt 17: 25f; 3 J 7.

b. w. verbs of perceiving, to indicate what has been perceived (Lysias, Andoc. 6; Ps.-Aristot., De Mundo 6 p. 399b ἀπ' αὐτῶν τῶν ἔργων θεωρεῖται ὁ θεός; Appian, Liby. 104 §493 ἀπὸ τῆς σφραγῖδος = [recognize a corpse] by the seal-ring). ἀ. τῶν καρπῶν αὐτῶν ἐπιγνώσεσθε αὐτούς *by their fruits you will know them* Mt 7: 16, 20. μανθάνειν παραβολὴν ἀ. τῆς συκῆς *learn a lesson from the fig tree* 24: 32; Mk 13: 28.—Also μανθάνειν τι ἀπό τινος *learn someth. fr. someone* Gal 3: 2; Col 1: 7.

c. γράψαι ἀφ' ὧν ἠδυνήθην, lit., *write from what I was able,* i.e., *as well as I could* B 21: 9.

V. To indicate cause, means, or outcome.

1. gener., to show the reason for someth. *because of, as a result of, for* (numerous ref. in FBleek on Hb 5: 7; PFay. 111, 4; Jdth 2: 20; Jos., Ant. 9, 56) οὐκ ἠδύνατο ἀ. τοῦ ὄχλου *he could not because of the crowd* Lk 19: 3; cf. Mk 2: 4 v.l. οὐκ ἐνέβλεπον ἀπὸ τῆς δόξης τοῦ φωτός *I could not see because of the brilliance of the light* Ac 22: 11. ἀ. τοῦ πλήθους τ. ἰχθύων J 21: 6. ἀ. τοῦ ὕδατος *for the water* Hs 8, 2, 8. ἀ. τῆς θλίψεως *because of the persecution* Ac 11: 19. οὐαὶ τῷ κόσμῳ ἀ. τ. σκανδάλων Mt 18: 7 (cf. Bl-D. §176, 1; Mlt. 246). εἰσακουσθεὶς ἀ. τῆς εὐλαβείας *heard because of his piety* Hb 5: 7 (but the text may be corrupt; at any rate it is obscure and variously interpr.; s. comm.; Bl-D. §211 app.; Rob. 580; and on εὐλάβεια).

2. to indicate means *with the help of, with* (Hdt. et al.; Ael. Aristid. 37, 23 K.=2 p. 25 D.; PGM 4, 2128 σφράγιζε ἀπὸ ῥύπου=seal with dirt; En. 97, 8) γεμίσαι

τὴν κοιλίαν ἀ. τ. κερατίων *fill one's stomach w. the husks* Lk 15: 16 v.l. (cf. Pr 18: 20). οἱ πλουτήσαντες ἀπ' αὐτῆς Rv 18: 15 (cf. Sir 11: 18).

3. to indicate motive or reason *for, from, with* (Appian, Bell. Civ. 5, 13 §52 ἀπ' εὐνοίας=with goodwill; 1 Macc 6: 10; papyrus exx. in Kuhring 35) κοιμᾶσθαι ἀ. τῆς λύπης *sleep from sorrow* Lk 22: 45. ἀ. τῆς χαρᾶς αὐτοῦ Mt 13: 44; cf. Lk 24: 41; Ac 12: 14. ἀ. τοῦ φόβου κράζειν Mk 14: 26. ἀ. φόβου καὶ προσδοκίας *with fear and expectation* Lk 21: 26. Hence verbs of fearing, etc., take ἀ. to show the cause of the fear (s. above I 3) μὴ φοβεῖσθαι ἀ. τ. ἀποκτεννόντων τὸ σῶμα *not be afraid of those who kill only the body* Mt 10: 28; Lk 12: 4 (cf. Jdth 5: 23; 1 Macc 2: 62; 3: 22; 8: 12).

4. to indicate the originator of the action denoted by the verb *from* (trag., Hdt.+) ἀ. σοῦ σημεῖον ἰδεῖν Mt 12: 38. γινώσκειν ἀπό τινος *learn fr. someone* Mk 15: 45. ἀκούειν ἀ. τοῦ στόματός τινος *hear fr. someone's mouth*, i. e., fr. him personally Lk 22: 71 (Dionys. Hal. 3, 8 ἀ. στόματος ἤκουσεν); cf. Ac 9: 13; 1 J 1: 5. τὴν ἀ. σοῦ ἐπαγγελίαν *a promise given by you* Ac 23: 21. ἀφ' ἑνὸς ἐγενήθησαν Hb 11: 12. Prob. παραλαμβάνειν ἀ. τοῦ κυρίου 1 Cor 11: 23 is to be understood in the same way; Paul is convinced that he is taught by the Lord himself (for direct teaching s. EBröse, Die Präp. ἀπό 1 Cor 11: 23: StKr 71, 1898, 351-60; Dssm.; BWeiss; H-DWendland. On the other hand, for indirect communication: Zahn, PFeine, JWeiss, PhBachmann, Ltzm., OHoltzmann, Sickenberger, Schlatter).—Of the more remote cause ἀπ' ἀνθρώπων *from men* (w. δι' ἀνθρώπου) Gal 1: 1. ἀ. κυρίου πνεύματος *fr. the Lord, who is the Spirit* 2 Cor 3: 18. ἔχειν τι ἀπό τινος *have (received) someth. fr. someone* 1 Cor 6: 19; 1 Ti 3: 7; 1 J 2: 20; 4: 21.—In salutation formulas εἰρήνη ἀ. θεοῦ πατρός *peace that comes from God, the Father* Ro 1: 7; 1 Cor 1: 3; 2 Cor 1: 2; Gal 1: 3; Eph 1: 2; cf. 6: 23; Phil 1: 2; Col 1: 2; 1 Th 1: 1 t.r.; 2 Th 1: 2; 1 Ti 1: 2; 2 Ti 1: 2; Tit 1: 4; Phlm 3. σοφία ἀ. θεοῦ *wisdom that comes fr. God* 1 Cor 1: 30. ἔπαινος ἀ. θεοῦ *praise fr. God* 4: 5. καὶ τοῦτο ἀ. θεοῦ *and that brought about by God* Phil 1: 28. The expr. εἰρήνη ἀπὸ 'ὁ ὢν καὶ ὁ ἦν καὶ ὁ ἐρχόμενος' Rv 1: 4 is quite extraordinary. It may be an interpretation of the name Yahweh already current, or an attempt to show reverence for the divine name by preserving it unchanged, or simply one more of the grammatical peculiarities so frequent in Rv (Meyer⁶-Bousset '06, 159ff; Hadorn, '28, 28; Mlt. 9, note 1; cf. PPar. 51, 33 ἀπὸ ἀπηλιότης).

5. As in class. usage (Thu. 5, 60, 1; X., Mem. 2, 10, 3; Andoc., Orat. 2, 4 οὗτοι οὐκ ἀφ' αὑτῶν ταῦτα πράττουσιν; Diod. S. 17, 56; Num 16: 28; 4 Macc 11: 3), the expr. ἀφ' ἑαυτοῦ (pl. ἀφ' ἑαυτῶν) *of himself* and ἀπ' ἐμαυτοῦ *of myself* are common Lk 12: 57; 21: 30; 2 Cor 3: 5, esp. so in J: 5: 19, 30; 8: 28; 10: 18; 15: 4.—7: 17f; 11: 51; 14: 10; 16: 13; 18: 34. So also ἀπ' ἐμαυτοῦ οὐκ ἐλήλυθα *I did not come of myself* (opp. the Father sent me) 7: 28; 8: 42.

6. W. verbs in the passive voice or passive mng. ὑπό is somet. replaced by ἀπό (in isolated cases in class. [Kühner-G. I p. 457f]; Polyb. 1, 79, 14; Hero I 152, 6; 388, 11; Nicol. Dam.: 90 fgm. 130, 130 Jac.; IG XII 5, 29; Dit., Syll.³ 820, 9; PLond. 1173, 12; BGU 1185, 26; PFlor. 150, 6 ἀ. τῶν μυῶν κατεσθιόμενα; PGM 4, 256; Kuhring 36f; 1 Macc 15: 17; Sir 16: 4; Philo, Leg. All. 3, 62. Cf. Bl-D. §210; Rob. 820; GNHatzidakis, Einl. in d. neugriech. Gramm. 1892, 211; ANJannaris, An Histor. Gk. Grammar 1897, §1507). Yet just at this point the textual tradition varies considerably, and the choice of prep. is prob. at times influenced by the wish to express special nuances of

mng. Lk 8: 29, 43b (both ὑπ' v.l.); 10: 22D; ἀποδεδειγμένος ἀ. τ. θεοῦ *attested by God* Ac 2: 22. ἐπικληθεὶς Βαρναβᾶς ἀ. (ὑπό t.r.) τ. ἀποστόλων *named B. by the apostles* 4: 36. κατενεχθεὶς ἀ. τοῦ ὕπνου *overcome by sleep* 20: 9. Freq. in such cases ἀπό denotes the one who indirectly originates an action, and can be transl. *at the hands of, by command of*: πολλὰ παθεῖν ἀ. τ. πρεσβυτέρων *suffer much at the hands of the elders* Mt 16: 21; cf. Lk 9: 22; 17: 25, where the emphasis is to be placed on παθεῖν, not on ἀποδοκιμασθῆναι. In ἀ. θεοῦ πειράζομαι the thought is that the temptation is caused by God, though not actually carried out by him Js 1: 13. ἡτοιμασμένος ἀ. τοῦ θεοῦ *prepared by God's command*, not by himself Rv 12: 6.

VI. In a few expr. ἀπό helps to take the place of an adverb. ἀπὸ μέρους, s. μέρος 1c.—ἀπὸ μιᾶς (acc. to Wlh., Einl.² 26, an Aramaism, min ch'da=at once [cf. MBlack, An Aramaic Approach³, '67, 113]; this does not explain the fem. gender, found also in the formula ἐπὶ μιᾶς En. 99, 9, and in Mod. Gk. μὲ μιᾶς *at once* [AThumb, Hdb. d. neugriech. Volkssprache² '10, §162 note 2]. PSI 286, 22 uses ἀπὸ μιᾶς of a payment made 'at once'. Orig. γνώμης might have been a part of the expr. [Philo, Spec. Leg. 3, 73], or ὁρμῆς [Thu. 7, 71, 6], or γλώσσης [Cass. Dio 44, 36, 2], or φωνῆς [Herodian 1, 4, 8]; cf. Bl-D. §241, 6 app.) *unanimously, alike, in concert* Lk 14: 18. Sim. ἀπὸ τ. καρδιῶν *fr. (your) hearts, sincerely* Mt 18: 35.—Himerius, Or. 39 [=Or. 5], 6 has as a formula διὰ μιᾶς, probably=continuously, uninterruptedly, Or. 44 [Or. 8], 2 fuller διὰ μιᾶς τῆς σπουδῆς=with one and the same, or with quite similar zeal. M-M and suppl.

ἀποβαίνω fut. ἀποβήσομαι; 2 aor. ἀπέβην (Hom.+; inscr., pap., LXX).

1. lit. *go away, get out* e.g. from a ship to the land (X., An. 5, 7, 9 ἀ. εἰς τ. χώραν; Diogenes, Ep. 37, 1) ἀ. εἰς τὴν γῆν J 21: 9. Abs. (Thu. 1, 116, 2; Jos., Bell. 4, 660) ἀποβάντες *when they had gotten out* Lk 5: 2.

2. fig. *turn out, lead* (to) (Hdt.+; Artem. 3, 66; Dit., Syll.³ 851, 10 εἰ καὶ ἑτέρως τοῦτο ἀπέβη; PPetr. III 42ʜ (8) f, 5=Witkowski p. 15; Job 30: 31 εἰς πάθος; Jos., Ant. 1, 20 ἀ. εἰς μαρτύριον) ἀ. εἰς μαρτύριον *lead to testifying* Lk 21: 13. ἀ. εἰς σωτηρίαν *turn out to salvation* Phil 1: 19 (Job 13: 16). M-M.*

ἀποβάλλω fut. ἀποβαλῶ; 2 aor. ἀπέβαλον; pf. ἀποβέβληκα, pass. ptc. ἀποβεβλημένος; 1 aor. ἀπεβλήθην (Hom.+; inscr., pap., LXX).

1. *throw away, take off*—a. lit., a garment Mk 10: 50. Of a tree ἀ. τὰ φύλλα (Is 1: 30) *shed (its) leaves* Hs 3: 3 (ἀποβ.=drop, let fall [unintentionally]: Ps.-Demetr. c. 65). ἀ. λίθους *reject* or *throw away stones* Hv 3, 2, 7; 3, 5, 5; pass., 3, 7, 5; 9, 8, 4ff; 9, 9, 4; 9, 13, 3, and 6 and 9; 9, 30, 1. ἀποβάλλεσθαι ἀπὸ τοῦ πύργου s 9, 8, 3; ἀπὸ τοῦ οἴκου s 9, 13, 9; ἐκ τῆς οἰκοδομῆς s 9, 7, 1; 9, 9, 5. W. indication of the goal ἀποβάλλεσθαι εἰς τὸν ἴδιον τόπον *be put back in their place* s 9, 12, 4. ἀποβάλλεσθαι πρὸς τ. λοιπούς *be thrown away w. the rest* s 9, 8, 7.

b. fig.—α. *take off* (schol. on Nicander, Alexiph. 450 τὸν ὕπνον ἀποβ.=shake off) of characteristics, which can be put on and taken off like a garment (w. ἐνδύσασθαι) Hm 10, 3, 4; ἀ. τὰς πονηρίας s 6, 1, 4; ἀ. πᾶσαν λύπην v 4, 3, 4; ἀ. πονηρίαν ἀπὸ σεαυτοῦ *take off all wickedness* m 1: 2; ἀ. τὰς ἐπιθυμίας s 9, 14, 1; τὰ ἔργα τούτων τ. γυναικῶν s 9, 14, 2.

β. *reject* τινά (Theocr. 11, 19; Hippocr., Ep. 10, 4) 2 Cl 4: 5. Mid. ἐσκανδαλισμένους ἀπὸ τ. πίστεως ἀ. *reject those who are offended in the faith* Hm 8: 10. Pass 1 Cl 45: 3; Hs 9, 18, 3f; 9, 22, 3.

ἀποβάλλω–ἀποδεκατόω

2. *lose* τὶ *someth.* (Hdt. et al.; Epict. 2, 10, 15 ἀ. αἰδῶ; Dio Chrys. 17[34], 39 ἀ. τὴν παρρησίαν; Dt 26: 5; Philo, Abr. 235; 236, Spec. Leg. 3, 202; Jos., Bell. 1, 90, Ant. 8, 225; 14, 77) τ. παρρησίαν Hb 10: 35 (but the mng. *throw away* [Lucian, Dial. Mort. 10, 1; Aelian, V.H. 10, 13 et al.] is also poss.). Of gold ἀποβάλλει τὴν σκωρίαν *puts away, loses its dross* Hv 4, 3, 4. ἐὰν μὴ . . . ἀποβάλῃ ἐξ αὐτοῦ τι *if he does not lose,* or *take away, anything of it* v 3, 6, 6.

3. *remove, depose* τινά τινος: ἀ. τῆς ἐπισκοπῆς *depose from the office of a bishop* (cf. Ltzm. ZWTh 55, '13, 135) 1 Cl 44: 4. Pass. ἀ. τῆς λειτουργίας *be removed fr. his office* 44: 3.

4. mid.=1bα Ro 13: 12 v.l. M-M.*

ἀποβλέπω impf. ἀπέβλεπον (trag., Hdt.+; inscr., pap., LXX) *look, pay attention* εἴς τι *at* or *to someth.* (Epict. 1, 6, 37; Dit., Syll.³ 867, 10; PSI 414, 9; Ps 9: 29; 10: 4; Philo, Spec. Leg. 1, 293) fig., of Moses ἀ. εἰς τ. μισθαποδοσίαν *his attention was on the reward* Hb 11: 26 (cf. Jos., Bell. 2, 311, Ant. 20, 61). M-M.*

ἀπόβλητος, ον verbal adj. of ἀποβάλλω (Hom.+; pap., Aq., Sym.; Philo, Spec. Leg. 2, 169 [cf. Nägeli 25]) *rejected* (Herm. Wr. 6, 1)=unclean (opp. καλός) 1 Ti 4: 4.*

ἀποβολή, ῆς, ἡ (Pla.+; PLond. 1659, 10) corresp. to the var. mngs. of ἀποβάλλω.

1. *rejection* of the rejection of the Jews by God (Jos., Ant. 4, 314) Ro 11: 15 (opp. πρόσλημψις).

2. *loss* (55th letter of Apollonius of Tyana [Philostrat. I 358, 19] by death; Philo, Praem. 33 of a ship; Jos., Ant. 2, 147; Sextus 257) ἀ. ψυχῆς οὐδεμία ἔσται ἐξ ὑμῶν *not a single one of you will be lost* Ac 27: 22 (Strato of Lamps., fgm. 124 ἀ. ζωῆς).*

ἀπογίνομαι 2 aor. ἀπεγενόμην (opp. ζῆν) *die* (Hdt., Thu. [cf. 1, 39, 3 τῶν ἁμαρτημάτων ἀπογενόμενοι, in the sense 'have no part in'], Teles 59, 11f; Dionys. Hal. 4, 15; Dit., Syll.³ 1099, 15; ²850, 12; PMagd. 29, 3; PRyl. 65, 9; PGrenf. II 69, 10; PLeipz. 29, 9; 10; 13; PGM 4, 719; cf. Jos., Ant. 5, 1) 1 Pt 2: 24. M-M.*

ἀπογινώσκω pf. ἀπέγνωκα *give up as hopeless, despair* (so Lysias et al.; Dit., Syll.³ 326, 30; 2 Macc 9: 22; Jdth 9: 11) τὶ *of someth.* (Aristot., Eth. Nic. 1115b, 2 et al.; PGiess. 72, 12 τοῦτο ἀπέγνων; Jos., Ant. 2, 140 τ. σωτηρίαν; 336 al.): ἀ. ἑαυτόν (Polyb. 22, 9, 14; Plut., Tib. Gracch. 13, 6; Philo, Somn. 1, 60; Jos., Bell. 5, 537) *despair of oneself* Hv 1, 1, 9; s 9, 26, 4. τὴν ζωήν *of life* m 12, 6, 2 (cf. Philo, Leg. ad Gai. 352 τὸ ζῆν ἀ.).*

ἀπογνωρίζω *reject, dispossess* pass. ἀπογνωρίζεσθαι ἀπὸ τ. ζωῆς *be dispossessed of one's life* Hv 2, 2, 8.*

ἀπογραφή, ῆς, ἡ (Lysias, Pla. et al.; Dit., Syll.³ 1023, 45; 71; 1109, 34; 1157, 33, Or. 338, 11; 34; very freq. pap.; LXX, Ep. Arist., Joseph.) *list, inventory* of the statistical reports and declarations of citizens for the purpose of completing the tax lists and family registers (cf. Wilcken, Grundz. 175f; 178; 202ff; 225ff; Chrest. no. 198ff, esp. 202, the census edict of C. Vibius Maximus, 104 AD; on this Dssm., LO 231f [LAE 268f]). Lk 2: 2 the word means *census, registration,* of the census taken by Quirinius. Joseph. puts a census taken by Q. in 6/7 AD (cf. Jos., Bell. 7, 253, Ant. 18, 3). Presumably Ac 5: 37 ἐν τ. ἡμέραις τ. ἀπογραφῆς also refers to this census. The chronology is full of problems, on which see the commentaries and lit. Cf. Schürer I⁴ 508-43 (the older lit. is given here); Ramsay, Bearing 238ff; Zahn, Lk 129-35 and Exk. IV; EKloster-mann, Hdb. on Lk 2: 1-3; M-JLagrange, RB n.s. 8, '11, 60-84; EGroag, Prosopogr. Beitr. VII (Jahresh. d. Österr. Arch. Inst. 21/22, '24 Beiblatt, cols. 445-78); HWindisch, NThT 16, '27, 106-24; Av Premerstein, Ztschr. d. Savigny-Stiftg. f. Rechtsgeschichte 48, '28, Rom. Abt. 449ff; LR Taylor, AJPh 54, '33, 120-33; EWSeraphin, CBQ 7, '45, 91-6; FHauck, Theol. Hndkomm., Lk p. 37; Gdspd., Probs. 71f; EStauffer, Jesus, Gestalt u. Geschichte, '57, Die Dauer des Census Augusti: Studien zum NT u. zur Patristik, '61, 9-34; HUInstinsky, D. Jahr der Geburt Christi, '57; HBraunert, Cives Romani und ΚΑΤ' ΟΙ-ΚΙΑΝ ΑΠΟΓΡΑΦΑΙ: Antidoron MDavid in Papyrologica Lugd.-Bat. vol. 17, '68, 11-21 (lit.). S. also on ἡγεμονεύω and Κυρήνιος. M-M.*

ἀπογράφω 1 aor. mid. ἀπεγραψάμην; pf. pass. ptc. ἀπογεγραμμένος (Hdt.+; inscr., pap., LXX) *register, record.*

1. of official registration in the tax lists (Philol. 71, '12, 24; POxy. 249, 5; 250, 1 et al.; cf. ἀπογραφή) mid. *register* (*oneself*) (Arrian, Anab. 3, 19, 6) Lk 2: 3, 5; pass. vs. 1.

2. fig., of the records kept by God (the Book of Life; cf. En. 98, 7; 8; Apoc. of Paul p. 39f Tischendorf πάντα τὰ πραττόμενα παρ' ὑμῶν καθ' ἡμέραν ἄγγελοι ἀπογράφονται ἐν οὐρανοῖς) πρωτότοκοι ἀπογεγραμμένοι ἐν οὐρανοῖς Hb 12: 23. M-M.*

ἀποδείκνυμι 1 aor. ἀπέδειξα; pf. pass. ptc. ἀποδεδειγμένος (Pind., Hdt.+; inscr., pap., LXX; Philo, Aet. M. 112; 116).

1. *make, render, proclaim, appoint* w. double acc. (X., Cyr. 1, 2, 5 παῖδας βελτίστους ἀ.; Socrat., Ep. 28, 11; Diod. S. 2, 26, 6; Arrian, Anab. 6, 2, 1; Da 2: 48; 2 Macc 14: 26 [Swete]; Jos., Ant. 8, 162) of God (Jos., Ant. 11, 3; Test. Jos. 2: 7) ἡμᾶς τοὺς ἀποστόλους ἐσχάτους ἀπέδειξεν *he has made,* or *exhibited, us* (*as*) *the last ones* perh. in a triumphal procession 1 Cor 4: 9. W. ὅτι foll. instead of the second acc. ἀποδεικνύντα ἑαυτὸν ὅτι ἔστιν θεός *proclaiming that he himself is God* 2 Th 2: 4. Pass. (Diod. S. 3, 59, 2) διάκονοι, ἀποδεδειγμένοι ἐν γνώμῃ Ἰησοῦ *deacons, appointed w. the approval of Jesus* IPhld inscr. (cf. PPetr. III 36a verso, 17 ἀποδεδειγμένοι ἐπίσκοποι; PGenève 36, 2; Jos., Ant. 7, 356).

2. *show forth, display* (PLond. 904, 34; BGU 388 II, 19) τὸ ἀκέραιον τῆς πραὔτητος αὐτῶν βούλημα ἀποδειξάτωσαν *let them display a sincere and gentle disposition* 1 Cl 21: 7. Pass. ἄνδρα ἀποδεδειγμένον ἀπὸ τοῦ θεοῦ *attested by God* Ac 2: 22 (cf. Esth 3: 13c; also Diod. S. 20, 40, 6 ἀποδεδειγμένος εἰς τ. πόλιν=well-liked in the city).—**3.** *prove* τὶ *someth.* (4 Macc 1: 8) Ac 25: 7.—EPeterson, Deissmann-Festschr., '26, 320ff. M-M.*

ἀπόδειξις, εως, ἡ (Pre-Socr., Hdt.+; inscr., pap.; 3 Macc 4: 20; Ep. Arist. 102; Philo; Jos., C. Ap. 1, 155, Ant. 17, 99; Test. Jos. 14: 5) *proof* (esp. of or for an intervention by a divinity, as Diod. S. 15, 49, 4) ἀ. πνεύματος καὶ δυνάμεως lit. *proof of spirit and power,* i.e. proof consisting in possession of the Spirit and power (opp. πειθοὶ λόγοι) 1 Cor 2: 4 (Philo, Mos. 1, 95 ἀ. διὰ σημείων κ. τεράτων in contrast to διὰ τ. λόγων). M-M.*

ἀποδεκατεύω (Alexis in Athen. 6 p. 216A; Suppl. Epigr. Gr. IX 72, 56 τῷ θεῷ) *tithe, give one tenth* τὶ (*of*) *someth.* πάντα Lk 18: 12.*

ἀποδεκατόω inf. ἀποδεκατοῦν, not ἀποδεκατοῖν Hb 7: 5 𝔓⁴⁶ BD* (Bl-D. §91 app.; Mlt. 53; Rob. 343).

1. *tithe, give one tenth* τὶ (*of*) *someth.* (Gen 28: 22) Mt 23: 23; Lk 11: 42.—**2.** *collect a tithe* (*one tenth*) (1 Km 8: 15, 16, 17) τινά fr. someone τὸν λαόν Hb 7: 5.*

ἀπόδεκτος, ον is accented thus almost exclusively in the NT tradition (but s. CRGregory, Prolegomena to Tdf. NT⁸ 1894, 100f), but ἀποδεκτός elsewhere (Plut., Mor. 1061A; Sext. Emp., Math. 11, 83; Dit., Or. 441, 100). Strictly speaking, ἀποδεκτός means *acceptable* and ἀποδέκτος *pleasing* (W-S. §6, 4; Mlt.-H. 58). The former is given Dg 8: 3; the latter is to be preferred in 1 Ti 2: 3; 5: 4. M-M.*

ἀποδέχομαι 1 aor. ἀπεδεξάμην; pass. ἀπεδέχθην (Hom. +; inscr., pap., LXX, Ep. Arist., Philo, Joseph.).
1. τινά *welcome someone, receive someone favorably* (Polyb. 21, 35, 5; Diod. S. 1, 18, 5; Dit., Syll.³ 601, 9; POxy. 939, 11; 2 Macc 3: 9; 13: 24) Lk 8: 40; 9: 11; Ac 18: 27; 21: 17; 28: 30; IEph 1: 1; ITr 1: 2.—*Accept* τί (En. 103, 14; Philo, Abr. 90; Jos., Ant. 9, 176) τ. λόγον (this expr. in Pla. et al.) Ac 2: 41; cf. Dg 8: 2.
2. *recognize, acknowledge, praise* someone or someth. (Diod. S. 4, 31, 8 τὴν ἀνδρείαν; Appian, Bell. Civ. 2, 82 §347; Aesop, Fab. 173 P.=308 H.; Himerius, Or. 65 [=Or. 19], 2; IG II 481, 60; 4 Macc 3: 20; Ep. Arist. 194; 274 al.; Philo, Gig, 37; Jos., Ant. 9, 176; 20, 264) Ac 24: 3 (sc. ταῦτα); τινά IPol 1: 1. τινά τινος *receive someone for someth.* (POxy. 705, 59 ἀποδεχόμεθά σε ταύτης τ. ἐπιδόσεως; Jos., Ant. 6, 340; 7, 160) τῆς προθυμίας σε ταύτης *I praise you for this eagerness* Dg 1. M-M.*

ἀποδημέω 1 aor. ἀπεδήμησα (Pind., Hdt.+; inscr., pap.; Ezk 19: 3 A).
1. *go on a journey* εἰς χώραν μακράν *to a distant country* (cf. PSI 436, 2 [248 BC]; 413, 22) Lk 15: 13. Abs. (PSI 416, 3 [III BC]; Jos., Ant. 6, 227, C. Ap. 2, 259) Mt 21: 33; 25: 15; Mk 12: 1; Lk 20: 9. ἄνθρωπος ἀποδημῶν *a man who was about to go on a journey* Mt 25: 14 (Epict. 4, 1, 58 of the κύριος of a δοῦλος who [the κύριος] ἀποδημεῖ but ἥξει).—Fig., euphem. ἀ. τῆς σαρκός *be absent fr. the flesh*=die (cf. ἤδη ἄγγελοι ἦσαν vs. 3), or perh.=be in a trance MPol 2: 2 (=die: Epict. 3, 24, 88; cf. MMeister, Axioch. Dial., Diss. Breslau '15, 87, 1).
2. *be away, absent* (Pind.+) ἀπὸ τ. κυρίου *fr. the Lord* 2 Cor 5: 6 DG (cf. PTebt. 104, 17 ἐνδημῶν [q.v.] κ. ἀποδημῶν). M-M.*

ἀποδημία, ας, ἡ (Hdt.+; Dit., Syll.³ 1109, 50; POxy. 471, 134; PTebt. 330, 3; Jos., Ant. 17, 69) *absence, journey* Hs 5, 5, 3. εἰς ἀ. ἐξέρχεσθαι *go on a journey* 5, 2, 2.*

ἀπόδημος, ον (Pind.+; Plut., Mor. 799E; Dit., Syll.³ 279, 24; 524, 30; POxy. 1446, 84; 89; 1547, 23; Jos., Ant. 2, 165) *away on a journey* ἄνθρωπος ἀ. *a man who is away on a journey* Mk 13: 34 (JDupont, BRigaux-Festschr. '70, 89–116). M-M.*

ἀποδιδράσκω 2 aor. ἀπέδραν, 3 sg. ἀπέδρα; in late Gk. the subj. ἀποδράσῃ is found (Hom.+; pap., LXX; En. 102, 1; Philo, Post. Cai. 43; Jos., Ant. 12, 378; Sib. Or. 4, 124) *run away, escape* ἀπό τινος (Jdth 11: 3; Test. Benj. 5: 3; Kleopatra l. 126) *fr. someone* 1 Cl 28: 4. ἀπὸ προσώπου τινός (Gen 16: 6; Jdth 10: 12; 11: 16) 4: 8.*

ἀποδίδωμι ptc. ἀποδιδοῦν (for -δόν) Rv 22: 2 (Bl-D. §94, 1 app.; Rob. 312); impf. ἀπεδίδουν Ac 4: 33; fut. ἀποδώσω; 1 aor. ἀπέδωκα; 2 aor. subj. 2 sg. ἀποδῷς, 3 sg. ἀποδῷ, imper. ἀπόδος, ἀπόδοτε; 2 aor. mid. ἀπεδόμην, 3 sg. ἀπέδοτο Hb 12: 16; 1 aor. pass. ἀπεδόθην, inf. ἀποδοθῆναι (the ms. tradition varies in the aor. subj. act., cf. Bl-D. §95, 2) (Hom.+; inscr., pap., LXX, Ep. Arist., Philo, Joseph., Test. 12 Patr.).
1. *give away, give up, give out* τὸ σῶμα Mt 27: 58 (Diod. S. 14, 84, 2 τοὺς νεκροὺς ἀπέδωκαν). τὸν μισθόν (X.,

An. 1, 2, 12; Dio Chrys. 13[7], 12; Dit., Syll.³ 127, 27; Sb 3924, 20 [19 AD]; Tob 2: 12; Jer 22: 13; Philo, Virt. 88) *pay out wages* Mt 20: 8; 2 Cl 20: 4; B 11: 8. τὴν ἀντιμισθίαν τινὶ ἀ. 2 Cl 11: 6; 15: 2. Fig., στέφανον ἀ. *award a crown* 2 Ti 4: 8. Of proceeds, *give* Mt 21: 41. Of taxes, *pay* (Philo, Op. M. 85) 22: 21; Mk 12: 17; Lk 20: 25 (cf. Sextus 20). ἀ. τῷ ὑψίστῳ τὰς εὐχάς *pay vows to the Highest* 1 Cl 52: 3 (Ps 49: 14; cf. Dt 23: 22; Jos., Ant. 11, 9 τ. εὐχὰς ἀπέδοσαν τ. θεῷ; X., Mem. 2, 2, 10 τ. θεοῖς εὐχὰς ἀ.; Diod. S. 4, 48, 7; 4, 49, 2; 8 τὰς εὐχὰς ἀποδοῦναι τοῖς θεοῖς; 14, 13, 5 Ἄμμωνι; PGiess. 27, 10 [II AD] ἵνα τ. θεοῖς τ. ὀφειλομένας σπονδὰς ἀποδῶ). τὴν ὀφειλήν τινι ἀ. *fulfill one's duty to someone* 1 Cor 7: 3; pl. Ro 13: 7. Of God, *bestow, grant, fulfil* τινί τι 1 Cl 23: 1; B 5: 7; Hv 1, 3, 4. καρπόν *yield fruit* (POxy. 53, 11 καρποὺς ἀ.; Lev 26: 4) Rv 22: 2; Hs 2: 8; fig., Hb 12: 11. τοὺς ὅρκους ἀ. *keep oaths* Mt 5: 33 (cf. POxy. 1026, 6). μαρτύριον ἀ. (4 Macc 6: 32) *give testimony* Ac 4: 33. λόγον ἀ. *give account* (s. λόγος 2a) Mt 12: 36; Lk 16: 2; Ac 19: 40; Ro 14: 12 v.l.; Hb 13: 17; 1 Pt 4: 5; Hv 3, 9, 10; m 2: 5.
2. *give back, return* τί (Philo, Spec. Leg. 4, 67; Jos., Vi. 335) Hm 3: 2. τινί τι (X., Hell. 2, 2, 9 et al.) Lk 9: 42; Hs 2: 7. τινί τι, 3. τῷ ὑπηρέτῃ Lk 4: 20. *Pay back a debt* Mt 5: 26; 18: 25ff, 34; Lk 7: 42; 12: 59; D 1: 5; *repay an advance* Lk 10: 35; *give back* taxes unjustly collected 19: 8 (cf. Num 5: 7f).
3. *render, reward, recompense*, in good and bad senses, like ἀνταποδίδωμι, of God Mt 6: 4, 6, 18. ἑκάστῳ κατὰ τὰ ἔργα αὐτοῦ Ro 2: 6 (Ps 61: 13; Pr 24: 12); cf. 2 Ti 4: 14; Rv 22: 12; 1 Cl 34: 3. ἑκάστῳ κατὰ τ. πρᾶξιν αὐτοῦ Mt 16: 27 (Sir 35: 22). τινί τι 1 Cl 18: 12 (Ps 50: 14). κακὸν ἀντὶ κακοῦ (cf. Pr 17: 13) Ro 12: 17 (cf. IQS 10, 17); 1 Th 5: 15; 1 Pt 3: 9; Pol 2: 2. ἀμοιβὰς ἀ. (Dionys. Hal. 6, 73; POxy. 705, 61 ἀποδιδοὺς ἀμοιβήν; Aq. Ps 27: 4) *make a return* 1 Ti 5: 4. Abs. ἀπόδοτε αὐτῇ ὡς καὶ αὐτὴ ἀπέδωκεν *render to her as she herself has rendered to others* Rv 18: 6 (cf. Ps 136: 8).
4. mid.—a. *sell* (Hdt. 1, 70+; inscr., pap.) τὸν Ἰωσήφ Ac 7: 9 (Gen 37: 28; 45: 4; Philo, De Jos. 15; 238). τί τινος *someth. for someth.* (Pla., Phaedo 98B; X., Hell. 2, 3, 48) τοσούτου τὸ χωρίον *sell the piece of ground for so much* Ac 5: 8 (ἀ. τὸ χ. as Jos., Ant. 3, 283).
b. *give up* τὸν ἴδιον υἱὸν λύτρον *his own son as a ransom* Dg 9: 2. τὶ ἀντί τινος (as Test. Iss. 2: 2) Hb 12: 16 (*sell*, s. 4a, also poss.).—c. *give back* τὰς ῥάβδους Hs 8, 1, 5. M-M.*

ἀποδιορίζω (Aristot., Pol. 4, 4, 13 p. 1290b, 25; Herm. Wr. 3, 2a codd.) *divide, separate* (opp. ἐποικοδομεῖν) abs. οὗτοί εἰσιν οἱ ἀποδιορίζοντες *these are the ones who cause a division* Jd 19. M-M.*

ἀποδιϋλίζω (s. Lghtft. ad loc.) *strain* or *filter clear* ἀπὸ παντὸς ἀλλοτρίου χρώματος *of every foreign color*, fig., of the true teaching IRo inscr.*

ἀποδιϋλισμός, οῦ, ὁ (s. ἀποδιϋλίζω) *filtering*; fig., *purification* fr. evil elements (opp. μερισμός) IPhld 3: 1.*

ἀποδοκιμάζω 1 aor. ἀπεδοκίμασα, pass. ἀπεδοκιμάσθην; pf. pass. ptc. ἀποδεδοκιμασμένος (Solon+; Hdt. 6, 130; Vett. Val. 278, 18; 313, 26; LXX) *reject* (after scrutiny), *declare useless*.
1. *of things* (Epicurus in Diog. L. 10, 31; Appian, Bell. Civ. 5, 32 §126; Ps.-Demetr. c. 200; Dit., Syll.³ 306, 52; PGiess. 47, 14ff; Jer 6: 30; Jos., Ant. 15, 321) of stones Mt 21: 42; Mk 12: 10; Lk 20: 17; 1 Pt 2: 4, 7; B 6: 4 (all aforementioned passages after Ps 117: 22); Hs 9, 7, 4; 9,

90

23, 3. λίθους ἀ. ἐκ τ. οἰκοδομῆς *reject stones fr. the building* 9, 12, 7. Of coins *reject as counterfeit* Agr 11 (of a τραπεζίτης Epict. 3, 3, 3; cf. Theophr., Char. 4, 11 ἀργύριον; Jer 6: 30).

2. of pers. (Pla., Theaet. 181в; X., Mem. 2, 2, 13) pass., *be rejected* (Aristoxenus, fgm. 18) of Jesus Mk 8: 31; Lk 9: 22; 17: 25. Gener., *be rejected* by God (Jer 6: 30; 7: 29; 14: 19 al.) Hb 12: 17. IRo 8: 3 (in latter pass.= not to become a martyr, opp. παθεῖν). M-M.*

ἀποδοχή, ῆς, ἡ (Thu.+) *acceptance, approval* (so since Polyb. 1, 5, 5 ὁ λόγος ἀποδοχῆς τυγχάνει; Letter 2 of Apollonius of Tyana [Philostrat. I 345, 12] ἀποδοχῆς ἄξιον; Diog. L. 5, 64; Hierocles in Stob., Ecl. 4, 27, 20 p. 662 H. ἔργον πολλῆς ἄξιον ἀποδοχῆς; Inschr. v. Priene 108, 312; Dit., Syll.³ 867, 21 ἀνδρὸς πάσης τειμῆς καὶ ἀποδοχῆς ἀξίου; Ep. Arist. 257; 308; Jos., Ant. 6, 347. Cf. Nägeli 34f) of a saying πάσης ἀ. ἄξιος 1 Ti 1: 15; 4: 9. M-M.*

ἀποδύομαι 1 aor. ἀπεδυσάμην (Hom.+; Jos., Bell. 1, 452 codd.) *take off* τὸ ἔνδυμα Hs 9, 13, 8 (cf. Athen. 11 p. 507ε as a saying of Plato: τὸν τῆς δόξης χιτῶνα ἀποδυόμεθα; PLeipz. 40 III, 22 τὸ ἱμάτιον).*

ἀποδώῃ, ἀποδῷς, s. ἀποδίδωμι.

ἀποθανοῦμαι s. ἀποθνήσκω.

ἀπόθεσις, εως, ἡ (Hippocr., Pla.+ in var. mngs.; inscr., pap.) *removal, getting rid of,* only fig. ἀ. ῥύπου *of dirt* in baptism 1 Pt 3: 21. ἡ ἀ. τ. σκηνώματός μου *of my tent* euphem. *for death* 2 Pt 1: 14. M-M.*

ἀποθήκη, ης, ἡ (Thu. 6, 97, 5+; Dit., Syll.³ 1106, 84; PRyl. 97, 11; PTebt. 347, 1; 5; BGU 32, 3; 816, 5; 931, 2; LXX; Jos., Ant. 9, 274; loanw. in rabb.) *storehouse, barn* συνάγειν εἰς τὴν ἀ. *gather into the barn* Mt 3: 12; 6: 26; 13: 30; Lk 3: 17. S. on ἀλοάω.—12: 18; w. ταμιεῖον (Jos., loc. cit.) 12: 24; *cellar* for oil and wine Hm 11: 15. M-M. B. 492.*

ἀποθησαυρίζω (Diod. S. 3, 31, 3; 5, 75, 4; Epict. 3, 22, 50; Lucian, Alex. 23; Aelian, N.A. 14, 18; Artem. 1, 73 p. 66, 22; Vett. Val. 16, 21; 18: 12; Jos., Bell. 7, 299 et al. [Nägeli 30]; Sir 3: 4) *store up, lay up* fig. ἀ. θεμέλιον καλόν *lay up a good foundation* 1 Ti 6: 19. M-M.*

ἀποθλίβω (Eur.+ in var. mngs.; pap. [Mayser 381]; Num 22: 25; Jos., Ant. 2, 64; 6, 118) *press upon, crowd* (UPZ 162 II, 13 [117 bc]) τινά *someone,* of a throng (w. συνέχειν) Lk 8: 45. M-M.*

ἀποθνήσκω impf. ἀπέθνησκον; fut. ἀποθανοῦμαι; 2 aor. ἀπέθανον (Hom.+; inscr., pap., LXX, En., Philo, Joseph., Test. 12 Patr.; on the η s. Bl-D. §26 app.; Rob. 194).

1. *die*—**a.** lit., of natural death
α. of pers. Mt 9: 24; 22: 24 (Dt 25: 5), 27; Mk 5: 35, 39; 9: 26; Lk 8: 42 (ἀπέθνησκεν *was about to die,* like Jos., Ant. 5, 4), 52; Ro 6: 10; 7: 2f (Artem. 4, 71 p. 246, 2 πάντων ὁ θάνατός ἐστι λυτικός); Phil 1: 21; Hb 9: 27 (Archinus: Orat. Att. II p. 167 πᾶσι ἀνθρώποις ὀφείλεται ἀποθανεῖν); GEg 1 and oft. Of violent death (also as pass. of ἀποκτείνω=be killed: Hdt. 1, 137; 7, 154; Lycurgus 93; Pla., Ap. 29ᴅ; 32ᴅ; Nicol. Dam.: 90 fgm. 30 Jac.; Lucian, Dial. Mort. 4, 4 ὑπὸ τοῦ παιδὸς ἀποθανῶν; Iambl., Vi. Pyth. 28, 143 ἱεροσυλῶν ἐλήφθη κ. ἀπέθανε; Josh 20: 3) Mt 26: 35 (for κἂν δέῃ ἀποθανεῖν cf. Lucian, Timon 43; Jos., Ant. 6, 108) J 19: 7; Ac 25: 11. θανάτῳ ἀ. (Od. 11, 412; Gen 2: 17; 3: 4) J 12: 33; 18: 32; cf. Hs 8, 7, 3.

W. ἐπί τινι *on the basis of* (Dio Chrys. 47[64], 3) ἐπὶ δυσὶν ἢ τρισὶν μάρτυσιν ἀ. *suffer death on the basis of* (the testimony of) *two or three witnesses* Hb 10: 28 (Dt 17: 6). W. ὑπέρ τινος *for* (Epict. 2, 7, 3 ὑπὲρ αὐτοῦ; Lucian, Peregr. 23; 33: Per. dies ὑπὲρ τ. ἀνθρώπων; 2 Macc 7: 9; 8: 21; 4 Macc 1: 8, 10; Jos., Ant. 13, 5; 6) J 11: 50f; Ac 21: 13; Ro 5: 6ff. διά (4 Macc 6: 27; 16: 25) Ἰησοῦν Χριστὸν ἀ. IRo 6: 1 v.l. (the rdg. varies betw. διά, εἰς, ἐν). Esp. of Christ's death Ro 5: 8; 14: 15; 1 Cor 15: 3; 2 Cor 5: 14f; ITr 2: 1; IRo 6: 1; Pol 9: 2. ἀ. ἐν κυρίῳ *die in the Lord* of martyrs Rv 14: 13. For this ὑπὲρ θεοῦ ἀ. IRo 4: 1. Not specif. of a martyr's death τῷ κυρίῳ ἀ. *die for the Lord* Ro 14: 8 (cf. Alciphr. 4, 10, 5 δεῖ γὰρ αὐτὸν ἢ ἐμοὶ ζῆν ἢ τεθνάναι Θετταλῇ). W. the reason given ἀ. ἔκ τινος *die because of someth.* (Hdt. 2, 63 ἐκ τ. τρωμάτων) Rv 8: 11. The extraordinary expr. ἀ. εἰς τὸ αὐτοῦ (i.e., Jesus') πάθος may be transl. *die in order to share his passion* (= *his death;*—also s. JKleist, note ad loc.) IMg 5: 2.

β. of animals and plants ἀ. ἐν τοῖς ὕδασιν *drown* Mt 8: 32. Of grains of wheat placed in the ground *decay* J 12: 24; 1 Cor 15: 36; w. regard to what is being illustrated, this is called *dying.* Of trees *die* Jd 12.

b. fig.—**α.** of losing the true, eternal life Ro 8: 13; Rv 3: 2. So almost always in J: 6: 50, 58; 8: 21, 24; 11: 26 al. ἡ ἁμαρτία ἀνέζησεν, ἐγὼ δὲ ἀπέθανον *sin revived, and I died* Ro 7: 9, 10.

β. of mystical death with Christ ἀπεθάνομεν σὺν Χριστῷ Ro 6: 8 (EKlaar, ZNW 59, '68, 131–34). Cf. 2 Cor 5: 14; Col 3: 3.

γ. w. dat. of the pers. or thing fr. which one is separated by death, however death may be understood: τ. θεῷ Hs 9, 28, 5; νόμῳ Gal 2: 19; τ. ἁμαρτίᾳ Ro 6: 2; ἀ. (τούτῳ) ἐν ᾧ κατειχόμεθα *dead to that which held us captive* 7: 6 (Plut., Agis et Cleom. 819ϝ; see s.v. ζάω 3b and CFD Moule, BRigaux-Festschr., '70, 367–75).—W. ἀπό τινος instead of the dat. Col 2: 20 (cf. Porphyr., Abst. 1, 41 ἀπὸ τ. παθῶν).

2. *be about to die, face death, be mortal* (Phalaris, Ep. 52 ἀποθνήσκοντες=be in danger of death; Philosophenspr. p. 495, 125 ὁ τῶν ἀσώτων βίος ὥσπερ καθ᾽ ἡμέραν ἀποθνήσκων ἐκφέρεται; Athen. 12 p. 552в καθ᾽ ἑκάστην ἡμέραν ἀποθνήσκειν; Seneca, Ep. 24, 20; Philo, In Flacc. 175; PGiess. 17, 9 ἀποθνήσκομεν ὅτι οὐ βλέπομέν σε καθ᾽ ἡμέραν) καθ᾽ ἡμέραν ἀ. *I face death every day* 1 Cor 15: 31 (cf. Ps 43: 23). ὡς ἀποθνήσκοντες καὶ ἰδοὺ ζῶμεν 2 Cor 6: 9. ἀποθνήσκοντες ἄνθρωποι *mortal men* Hb 7: 8. M-M. B. 287.

ἀποίητος, ον (Pind.+) *uncreated* of God PK 2.*

ἀποκαθίστημι and **ἀποκαθιστάνω** (the latter form in Dit., Syll.³ 588, 55 [196 вc]; Polyb. 3, 98, 9; Jos., Ant. 16, 170; Mk 9: 12; Ac 1: 6; Bl-D. §93 w. app.; Rob. 1216) fut. ἀποκαταστήσω; 2 aor. ἀπεκατέστην; 1 fut. pass. ἀποκατασταθήσομαι; 1 aor. pass. ἀπεκατεστάθην (on the double augm.—PTebt. 413, 4—cf. Bl-D. §69, 3; Rob. 368; KBrugmann⁴-AThumb, Griech. Gramm. '13, p. 311) X.+; inscr., pap., LXX; Anz 330f.

1. *restore, reëstablish* (Dit., Or. 90, 18; Demosth. 18, 90; Dionys. Hal. 3, 23; Herodian 2, 6, 11; PGM 4, 629f; Gen 29: 3; Ezk 16: 55; 1 Macc 15: 3) of Elijah (Mal 3: 23) πάντα Mt 17: 11; Mk 9: 12 (cf. Schürer II⁴ 610ff; Bousset, Rel.³ 232f; Billerb. IV 764–98). τινί τι (Diod. S. 16, 45, 9; 20, 32, 2 τ. πολίταις τ. δημοκρατίαν ἀποκατέστησε) ἀ. τὴν βασιλείαν τῷ Ἰσραήλ Ac 1: 6. Abs. 1 Cl 56: 6 (Job 5: 18).—Medical t.t. *cure* (Diosc., Mat. Med. I 64, 4; Vi. Aesopi I c. 7 ἀ. τὴν φωνήν= restore the voice of a mute; Ex 4: 7; Lev 13: 16) intr. ἀπεκατέστη *he was cured* (Ep.

Arist. 316) Mk 8: 25. Pass. ἀπεκατεστάθη ὑγιής *it was restored* Mt 12: 13; Mk 3: 5; Lk 6: 10. ἀπεκατεστάθη τὸ οὖς 22: 51 D. Fig., of the tortured body of a persecuted church ISm 11: 2.

2. *bring back*—**a.** lit. τινὰ εἴς τι (Polyb. 8, 29, 6; 1 Esdr 6: 25; Jer 16: 15; 23: 8; Jos., Ant. 11, 2, Vi. 183) εἰς τ. οἶκον Hs 7: 6.

b. fig. ἐπὶ τ. σεμνὴν τ. φιλαδελφίας ἀγωγήν *to the holy practice of brotherly love* 1 Cl 48: 1.

3. *give back, restore* (Polyb. 3, 98, 7; Diod. S. 18, 65, 1; POxy. 38, 12 ὑφ' οὗ καὶ ἀποκατεστάθη μοι ὁ υἱός al. in pap.; 2 Km 9: 7; Job 8: 6; 2 Macc 11: 25; Jos., Ant. 15, 195) ἵνα ἀποκατασταθῶ ὑμῖν *that I might be restored to you* Hb 13: 19. M-M. B. 751.*

ἀποκαλύπτω fut. ἀποκαλύψω; 1 aor. ἀπεκάλυψα, pass. ἀπεκαλύφθην; 1 fut. pass. ἀποκαλυφθήσομαι (Hdt.+; pap., LXX; Jos., Bell. 5, 350, Ant. 14, 406; Test. 12 Patr.) *uncover, reveal,* in our lit. only fig.

1. gener. *reveal, disclose, bring to light* pass. *be revealed* (opp. καλύπτω) Mt 10: 26; Lk 12: 2; J 12: 38 and 1 Cl 16: 3 (Is 53: 1); Ro 1: 17 (cf. Ps 97: 2), 18; Lk 2: 35 (cf. Josh 2: 20; Sir 27: 16f; Ezk 16: 57; 1 Macc 7: 31).

2. esp. of divine revelation of certain supernatural secrets (Ps 97: 2; Da 2: 19, 22 [both Theod.], 28; 1 Km 2: 27; 3: 21; Is 56: 1) ἀ. τινί τι *reveal someth. to someone* (Test. Jos. 6: 6) Mt 11: 25; 16: 17; Lk 10: 21; Phil 3: 15; IEph 20: 1; w. ὅτι foll. (Test. Levi 1: 2) 1 Pt 1: 12. The revealers are Christ Mt 11: 27; Lk 10: 22, and the Holy Spirit 1 Cor 2: 10; 14: 30; Eph 3: 5. For Gal 1: 16 s. on ἐν IV 4a and s. AMDenis, RB 64, '57, 335-62; 481-515. Abs. (w. φανεροῦν) ἀ. διά τινος Dg 8: 11. τὰ ἀποκαλυφθέντα ἡμῖν *the revelations that have come to us* 11: 8.

3. of the interpr. of prophetic visions ἀ. τινί Hv 2, 2, 4; 2, 4, 1; 3, 3, 2ff; 3, 4, 3; 3, 8, 10; 3, 13, 4. ἀ. τινὶ ἀποκάλυψιν *impart a revelation to someone* v 3, 12, 2. ἀ. τινὶ περί τινος *give someone a revelation about someth.* (Test. Reub. 3: 15) v 3, 10, 2. ἀπεκαλύφθη μοι ἡ γνῶσις τῆς γραφῆς *a knowledge of the scripture was disclosed to me* v 2, 2, 1.

4. in the eschatolog. sense of the revelation of certain pers. and circumstances (Da 10: 1 Theod.): of Christ's coming again Lk 17: 30. Of the Antichrist 2 Th 2: 3, 6, 8. Of the Judgment Day 1 Cor 3: 13. ἡ μέλλουσα δόξα ἀποκαλυφθῆναι *the glory that is about to be revealed* Ro 8: 18; cf. 1 Pt 5: 1. σωτηρία 1: 5. πίστις Gal 3: 23. The disciples say to the risen Lord ἀποκάλυψον σοῦ τὴν δικαιοσύνην ἤδη *reveal thy righteousness just now* Ending of Mk in the Freer ms.—RBultmann, D. Begriff d. Offenbarung im NT '29. EFScott, The NT Idea of Rev. '35. AOepke TW III 365-97. EGSelwyn, I Peter, '46, 250-2; HSchulte, D. Begriff d. Offenbarung im NT, Diss. Heidelberg '47; WBulst, Offenbarung: Bibl. u. Theolog. Begriff '60; BVawter, CBQ 22, '60, 33-46. M-M.*

ἀποκάλυψις, εως, ἡ (Philod., περὶ κακιῶν p. 38 Jensen) *revelation, disclosure* (Plut., Cato Mai. 20, 8, Aemil. 14, 3, Mor. 70F ἀ. τῆς ἁμαρτίας; Sir 11: 27; 22: 22; 41: 26 v.l.) in our lit. only fig.

1. of the revelation of truth gener., w. obj. gen. Ro 16: 25. πνεῦμα σοφίας κ. ἀ. Eph 1: 17. φῶς εἰς ἀ. ἐθνῶν *a light of revelation for the Gentiles* Lk 2: 32.

2. of revelations of a particular kind, through visions, etc.: w. gen. of the author ἀ. Ἰησοῦ Χριστοῦ Gal 1: 12; Rv 1: 1; (w. ὀπτασία) ἀ. κυρίου 2 Cor 12: 1. κατὰ ἀποκάλυψιν *because of a rev.* Gal 2: 2; MPol 22: 3, Epil Mosq 4. κατὰ ἀ. ἐγνωρίσθη μοι τὸ μυστήριον *the secret was made known to me by revelation* Eph 3: 3. Cf. 1 Cor 2: 4D; 14: 6, 26; 2 Cor 12: 7.—In the visions of Hermas the ἀ.

are not only supernatural rev. for eye and ear, but also the interpretations given to such rev. The ἀ. is ὁλοτελής *complete* only when it is explained and understood v 3, 10, 9; 3, 13, 4a. W. ὁράματα 4, 1, 3. Cf. 3, 1, 2; 3, 3, 2; 3, 3, 6-9; 3, 12, 2; 3, 13, 4b; v 5 inscr.—MBuber, Ekstatische Konfessionen '09.

3. in the eschatolog. sense of the disclosure of secrets belonging to the last days ἀ. τῆς δόξης τοῦ Χριστοῦ 1 Pt 4: 13. Of the parousia ἐν ἀποκαλύψει Ἰ. Χ. 1 Pt 1: 7, 13; cf. 1 Cor 1: 7; 2 Th 1: 7. τὴν ἀ. τ. υἱῶν τ. θεοῦ ἀπεκδέχεσθαι *wait for the revealing of the sons of God,* i.e., for the time when they will be revealed Ro 8: 19. ἀ. δικαιοκρισίας τ. θεοῦ 2: 5.

4. in book form (Porphyr., Vi. Plot. 16 συγγράμματα . . . , ἀποκαλύψεις Ζωροάστρου κ. Ζωστριανοῦ κτλ.) ἀ. Ἰωάννου Rv inscr. M-M.*

ἀποκαραδοκία, ας, ἡ (only in Christian writers—also Hesychius; Suidas; Anecd. Gr. p. 428, 14; Etym. Gud. 171, 14—however ἀποκαραδοκέω in Polyb. 16, 2, 8; 18, 48, 4 ἀ. τὴν Ἀντιόχου παρουσίαν; 22, 19, 3; Sostratus [I BC] in Stob. 4, 20, 70=vol. I p. 187 Jac.; Jos., Bell. 3, 264; Ps 36: 7 Aq.) *eager expectation* ἡ ἀ. τῆς κτίσεως=ἡ ἀποκαραδοκοῦσα κτίσις *the eagerly awaiting creation* Ro 8: 19 (GSchläger, D. ängstl. Harren d. Kreatur: NThT 19, '30, 353-60). κατὰ τὴν ἀ. μου (w. ἐλπίς) *according to my eager expectation* Phil 1: 20. (GBertram, ZNW 49, '58, 264-70). M-M.*

ἀποκαταλλάσσω 1 aor. ἀποκατήλλαξα; 2 aor. pass. ἀποκατηλλάγην (found only in Christian writers; cf. Nägeli 52) *reconcile* (Anecd. Gr. p. 428, 15=φιλοποιῆσαι) ἀ. τὰ πάντα εἰς αὐτόν *reconcile everything in his own person,* i.e., the universe is to form a unity, which has its goal in Christ Col 1: 20 (cf. MDibelius, Hdb. ad loc.); many prefer to transl. *reconcile everything to himself* (i.e., God). ἀ. τοὺς ἀμφοτέρους τῷ θεῷ Eph 2: 16. Abs. ἀποκατήλλαξεν Col 1: 22 (v.l. ἀποκατηλλάγητε and ἀποκαταλλαγέντες).*

ἀποκατάστασις, εως, ἡ (Aristot. p. 1204b, 36; Epicurus 8, 9 Us.; Polyb.; Diod. S. 20, 34, 5 al., also inscr., pap.; Herm. Wr. 8, 4; 11, 2; τέλειος λόγος in Lact., Inst. 7, 18, 3; Iambl., Myst. 1, 10; Ep. Arist. 123; Philo, Rer. Div. Her. 293; Jos., Ant. 11, 63; 98) *restoration,* which can be var. understood ἄχρι χρόνων ἀποκαταστάσεως πάντων *until the time for restoring everything* to perfection or, as of stars in their orbits, to their starting-points (Diod. S. 12, 36, 2) Ac 3: 21.—AMéhat, Apocatastase (Origen, Clem. Alex., Ac 3: 21) Vigiliae Christianae 10, '56, 196-214. M-M.*

ἀπόκειμαι (Pind.+) *be put away, stored up* (so X.+; pap., LXX).

1. lit. (POxy. 69, 5 ἀπὸ τῶν ἐν τ. οἰκίᾳ ἀποκειμένων; BGU 275, 9; PTebt. 340, 13; Job 38: 23; Philo, Det. Pot. Ins. 128; Jos., Vi. 119) ἡ μνᾶ, ἣν εἶχον ἀποκειμένην ἐν σουδαρίῳ *the mina, which I kept laid away in a napkin* Lk 19: 20.

2. fig. διὰ τὴν ἐλπίδα τ. ἀποκειμένην ὑμῖν ἐν τ. οὐρανοῖς *because of the hope that is laid up for you in heaven* Col 1: 5. ἀπόκειται μοι . . . στέφανος *a crown is reserved for me* 2 Ti 4: 8 (cf. Iambl., Myst. 8, 7 p. 270 P. τὰ ἀπὸ τ. εἱμαρμένης ἀποκείμενα κακά; Demophilus, Similitud. 22 p. 6 Orelli; Dit., Or. 383, 189 οἷς ἀποκείσεται παρὰ θεῶν χάρις εὐσεβείας; UPZ 144, 47 [II BC] ἀπόκειται παρὰ θεοῦ μῆνις τοῖς . . . ; 2 Macc 12: 45; Jos., Ant. 6, 368). FPfister, ZNW 15, '14, 94-6.—Impers. ἀπόκειταί τινι *it is reserved* or *certain for someone, one is* *destined* (Ael. Aristid. 39 p. 764 D.) w. inf. foll. ἅπαξ ἀποθανεῖν Hb 9: 27 (cf. Epigr. Gr. 416, 6 ὡς εἰδώς, ὅτι πᾶσι βροτοῖς τὸ θανεῖν ἀπόκειται; 4 Macc 8: 11). M-M.*

ἀπόκενος, ον (Diosc. 5, 36 W. et al.) *quite empty* (Hero, Spiritalia 2, 24; Zen.-P. 59680, 3 [III BC]) w. δίψυχος Hm 5, 2, 1; 12, 5, 2ff.*

ἀποκεφαλίζω 1 aor. ἀπεκεφάλισα (Philod., περὶ σημ. 13, 29 G.; Epict. 1, 1, 19; 24 al.; Artem. 1, 35; Cass. Dio 71, 28, 1; pap.; Ps 151: 7; Phryn. p. 341 L.) *behead* Ἰωάννην Mt 14: 10; Mk 6: 16, 27; Lk 9: 9.*

ἀποκλείω 1 aor. ἀπέκλεισα (trag., Hdt.+; pap., LXX) *close, shut* τὴν θύραν (Iambl., Myst. 2, 8; Achilles Tat. 6, 10, 6; POxy. 1272, 5; Gen 19: 10; 2 Km 13: 17f al.; En. 101, 2; Jos., Vi. 246) Lk 13: 25. M-M.*

ἀποκνέω fut. ἀποκνήσω (Thu. et al.; Ael. Aristid. 34 p. 664, 9 D. al.; Zen-P. 59416, 3 [III BC]) *hesitate, have misgivings* LJ 2: 4.*

ἀποκομίζω 1 aor. subj. ἀποκομίσω (Hdt. et al.; inscr., pap., LXX) *take along* (Polyb. 28, 10, 7) γράμματα *a letter* Pol 13: 1.*

ἀποκόπτω fut. ἀποκόψω; 1 aor. ἀπέκοψα; 2 aor. pass. inf. ἀποκοπῆναι (Hom.+; pap., LXX, Philo, Joseph.).
1. *cut off* of limbs or parts of the body (Hom.+; Hdt. 6, 91 χεῖρας; Diod. S. 17, 20, 7 ἀπέκοψε τὴν χεῖρα; Dt 25: 12; Judg 1: 6f; Jos., Bell. 6, 164, Vi. 177) Mk 9: 43, 45 (Epict. 2, 5, 24 of ἀποκόπτειν the foot ὑπὲρ τοῦ ὅλου; cf. Ael. Aristid. 48, 27 K.=24 p. 472 D.: παρατέμνειν one limb ὑπὲρ σωτηρίας of the whole body); J 18: 10, 26. τὰ σχοινία *cut the ropes* (cf. Od. 10, 127; X., Hell. 1, 6, 21; Polyaenus 5, 8, 2; 6, 8) Ac 27: 32. πολὺ δεῖ ἀπ᾽ αὐτῶν ἀποκοπῆναι *a great deal must be cut away from them* Hs 9, 9, 2.
2. *make a eunuch of, castrate* (Lucian, Eunuch. 8; Cass. Dio 79, 11; Dt 23: 2; Philo, Leg. All. 3, 8, Spec. Leg. 1, 325) mid. (Epict. 2, 20, 19; Bl-D. §317; Rob. 809) ὄφελον καὶ ἀποκόψονται *would that they might make eunuchs of themselves* Gal 5: 12. So interpr. by many since Chrysostom and Ambrosiaster, also PDebouxhtay, Revue des Études Grecques 39, '26, 323–6 (against ChBruston, ibid. 36, '23, 193f) GSDuncan, Gal '34, 154; 161; GStählin, TW III 853–5. M-M. and suppl.*

ἀπόκριμα, ατος, τό (quotable since Polyb., Excerpta Vaticana 12, 26b, 1 as a t.t., esp. freq. in inscr. [Dssm., NB 85 (BS 257); Nägeli 30]; PTebt. 286, 1; Jos., Ant. 14, 210. Cf. Wilcken, Her 55, '20, p. 32, 1) *official report, decision* ἀ. τ. θανάτου 2 Cor 1: 9 (Theodoret III 291 N. ἀ. δὲ θανάτου τὴν τοῦ θανάτου ψῆφον ἐκάλεσε). M-M.*

ἀποκρίνομαι 1 aor. mid. ἀπεκρινάμην (7 times in NT, but the usual form in Joseph.), pass. ἀπεκρίθην (195 times; in Jos. only Ant. 9, 35; in so far as there is a difference in mng., ἀπεκρινάμην implies solemn [Lk 3: 16] or legal [Mt 27: 12] utterance; see M-M) 1 fut. pass. ἀποκριθήσομαι (cf. Bl-D. §78; Rob. 334; Mayser I 2², 158; Thackeray 239).
1. *answer, reply* (so occas. in Hdt. and fr. Thu. on; inscr., pap., LXX; En. 106, 9; Ep. Arist.; Philo, e.g. Aet. M. 4 [ἀπεκρίνατο] τινί and in Lk πρός τινα *to someone* (Thu. 5, 42, 2; Iambl., Myster. 7, 5 at end) Lk 4: 4; 6: 3; Ac 3: 12; 25: 16. To a question Mt 11: 4; 13: 11; 19: 4; Mk 12: 28, 34; Lk 3: 11; 7: 22; J 1: 21, 26, 48; 3: 5 al. To requests, exhortations, commands, etc., the answer being quoted directly Mt 4: 4; 12: 39; 13: 37; 1 Cl 12: 4 al. Freq.

in Hermas: v 1, 1, 5 and 7; 3, 3, 1; 3, 4, 1 and 3; 3, 6, 5f al. Not preceded by a question expressed or implied, when the sentence is related in content to what precedes and forms a contrast to it, *reply* (as a reaction) Mt 3: 15; 8: 8; 12: 48; 14: 28; 15: 24, 28; Mk 7: 28; J 2: 18; 3: 9; Ac 25: 4 al. τινί τι Mt 15: 23; 22: 46; Mk 14: 40; Lk 23: 9 (cf. Epict. 2, 24, 1 πολλάκις ἐπιθυμῶν σου ἀκοῦσαι ἦλθον πρός σε καὶ οὐδέποτέ μοι ἀπεκρίνω). οὐ γὰρ ᾔδει τί ἀποκριθῇ Mk 9: 6; οὐδέν Mt 26: 62; 27: 12; Mk 14: 61; πρός τι *to someth.* (Pla., Protag. 338D) οὐκ ἀπεκρίθη αὐτῷ πρὸς οὐδὲ ἓν ῥῆμα *he made no reply to him, not even to a single word* or *charge* Mt 27: 14 (cf. Jesus, son of Ananias, before the procurator Albinus: πρὸς ταῦτα οὐδ᾽ ὁτιοῦν ἀπεκρίνατο Jos., Bell. 6, 305; Eupolis Com. [V BC] K. ὡς ὑμῖν ἐγὼ πάντως ἀποκρινοῦμαι πρὸς τὰ κατηγορούμενα.— Artem. 3, 20 ὁ μηδὲν ἀποκρινόμενος μάντις . . . καὶ ἡ σιγὴ ἀπόκρισις ἀλλ᾽ ἀπαγορευτική= . . . a negative answer, to be sure). W. inf. foll. Lk 20: 7; w. acc. and inf. foll. (X., Hell. 2, 2, 18) Ac 25: 4; foll. by ὅτι and direct discourse Mk 8: 4; Ac 25: 16; IPhld 8: 2; foll. by dir. disc. without ὅτι Mk 9: 17; J 1: 21.
2. Hebraistically of the continuation of discourse like וַיַּעַן וַיֹּאמֶר עָנָה) *continue* Mt 11: 25; 12: 38; 15: 15; 22: 1; 26: 25; Mk 10: 24; *begin, speak up* Mt 26: 63 v.l.; Mk 9: 5; 10: 51; 11: 14; 12: 35; Lk 1: 19; 13: 14; 14: 3; J 5: 19; Ac 5: 8 (cf. Dt 21: 7; 26: 5; Is 14: 10; Zech 1: 10; 3: 4; 1 Macc 2: 17; 8: 19; 2 Macc 15: 14). Used as a formula w. εἰπεῖν or λέγειν, and oft. left untransl. 2 Cl 5: 3. ἀπεκρίθη καὶ εἶπεν J 2: 19. ἀποκριθεὶς εἶπεν Mt 16: 16 and oft. ἀποκριθεὶς ἔφη Lk 23: 3; GP 11: 46. ἀπεκριθη καὶ λέγει Mk 7: 28. ἀποκριθήσονται λέγοντες Mt 25: 37 (cf. Hdt. 5, 67, 2 χρᾷ φάσα=[the Pythia] declared and said; Test. Levi 19: 2; Bl-D. §420, 1; Mlt. 131; Dalman, Worte 19f [Eng. 24f]; PJoüon, 'Respondit et dixit': Biblica 13, '32, 309–14). M-M. B. 1266.

ἀπόκρισις, εως, ἡ (Theognis, Hdt.+; Dit., Syll.³ 344, 62; 591, 28; pap., LXX; Ep. Arist.; Jos., Ant. 7, 119) *answer* Lk 2: 47; 20: 26. ἀ. διδόναι τινί (Dit., Syll.³ 683, 15; Job 32: 4; 33: 5; 35: 4 al.; without dat. Diod. S. 16, 25, 2; 18, 48, 3; Jos., Ant. 20, 89) J 1: 22; 19: 9. M-M.*

ἀποκρύπτω fut. ἀποκρύψω; 1 aor. ἀπέκρυψα; pf. pass. ptc. ἀποκεκρυμμένος (Hom.+; Vett. Val. 15, 26; PSI 169, 13 [II BC]; PStrassb. 42, 17; LXX; En. 98, 6; Jos., Bell. 2, 446, Ant. 3, 73; Sib. Or. 4, 75) *hide, conceal* by digging Mt 25: 18 v.l. τὶ ἀπό τινος (Is 40: 27; Jer 39: 17) Lk 10: 21; Hs 9, 11, 9. ἀποκεκρυμμένος *hidden, kept secret* (Pla., Phaedr. 273C ἀποκεκρυμμένη τέχνη; Ps.-Demetr. c. 155 κατηγορίαι ἀποκεκρυμμέναι) 1 Cor 2: 7; Eph 3: 9; Col 1: 26. M-M.*

ἀπόκρυφος, ον (Pre-Socr., Eur.+; Vita Philonidis [Crönert, SAB '00, 942ff], fgm. 3; Vett. Val. Index; Epigr. Gr. 1028, 10; PGM 4, 1115; 12, 321; 13, 343f; 730f; LXX; En.; Jos., Bell. 3, 340) *hidden* of treasures (Da 11: 43 Theod.; 1 Macc 1: 23=Jos., Ant. 12, 250), fig., of secret wisdom (Isishymn. v. And. [I BC] p. 15, 10ff ἀπόκρυφα σύμβολα; Philo, Sacr. Abel. 62 ἐν ἀποκρύφοις αὐτῶν ἐθησαυρίσαντο) θησαυροὶ ἀ. Col 2: 3; B 11: 4 (Is 45: 3). Opp. φανερός (Philo, Abr. 147) Mk 4: 22; Lk 8: 17.—Cf. A Oepke and RMeyer, TW III 979–99: Canonical and apocryphal. M-M.*

ἀποκτείνω or **ἀποκτέννω** (the latter form Mt 10: 28; Mk 12: 5; Lk 12: 4; 2 Cor 3: 6 v.l.; Rv 6: 11; 2 Cl 5: 4; cf. Bl-D. §73 w. app.; Rob. 1213; W-S. §15 s.v. κτείνω; mss. rdgs. vary greatly betw. ἀποκτέννω, ἀποκτένω, ἀποκτεννύω, ἀποκτιννύω) fut. ἀποκτενῶ; 1 aor. ἀπέκτεινα, pass.

ἀπεκτάνθην (cf. Bl-D. §76, 2; 315) (Hom.+; inscr., pap., LXX, En., Joseph., Test. 12 Patr.) *kill τινά some-one.*
1. lit., of any way of depriving a person of life.
a. of natural life Mt 14: 5; 16: 21; 17: 23; 21: 35, 38, 39; Mk 6: 19; 9: 31ab; Lk 11: 47; J 16: 2 (killing of an unbeliever considered by the Jews a service to God: Synes., Ep. 4 p. 160A.—Lycophron v. 1172 δῆμος τὸν κτανόντ᾽ ἐπαινέσει by public decree every Trojan who kills one of the accursed Locrians is publicly praised. Thereupon blood-lust breaks out against these unfortunates.); 18: 31 (Ltzm., SAB '31 XIV; ZNW 30, '31, 211-15; ibid. 31, '32, 78-84; FBüchsel, ibid. 30, '31, 202-10; 33, '34, 84-7; MGoguel, ibid. 31, '32, 289-301; PFiebig, StKr 104, '32, 213-28; UHolzmeister, Biblica 19, '38, 43-59; 151-74; HEWvanHille, Mnemosyne 10, '42, 241-50; JBlinzler, D. Prozess Jesu '51; JoachJeremias ZNW 43, '51, 145-50 [lit.]) Rv 6: 8; 9: 5 al. Of God ὁ ἀποκτείνων κ. ζῆν ποιῶν 1 Cl 59: 3. ἀ. ἑαυτόν commit suicide (Dio Chrys. 47[64], 3; Artem. 2, 49 p. 151, 13; Jos., Ant. 9, 39) J 8: 22. Also of things as causing death: of a falling tower Lk 13: 4; of plagues Rv 9: 18.—Mk 3: 4; Lk 6: 9 t.r. ἀποκτείναι is either abs. or to be taken w. ψυχήν (like Eur., Tro. 1214).
b. of true spiritual life Ro 7: 11. τὸ γράμμα ἀ. *the letter* (of the law) *kills,* in so far as the law causes men to die 2 Cor 3: 6. ἀ. τὴν ψυχήν Mt 10: 28 (s. ψυχή 1c; cf. Epict. 3, 23, 21 [after Pla., Apol. p. 30c] ἐμὲ ἀποκτεῖναι μὲν δύνανται, βλάψαι δ᾽ οὔ).
2. fig. *put to death* (Eur., Hipp. 1064 τὸ σεμνόν; Philippus [=Demosth. 12] 9 φιλίαν) τὴν ἔχθραν *the enmity* Eph 2: 16. M-M. B. 288.

ἀποκυέω 1 aor. ἀπεκύησα (because the aor. is found in this form [not ἀπέκυσα] Js 1: 18, 1: 15 should be accented ἀποκυεῖ, without reference to the collateral form ἀποκύω; cf. W-S §15 p. 129. Aristot., fgm. 76 Rose; Dionys. Hal. 1, 70 [interpol.]; Plut., Sull. 37, 7; Lucian, Dial. Mar. 10, 1; Aelian, V.H. 5, 4 et al.; Herm. Wr. 1, 16; BGU 665 II, 19 [I AD]; APF 3, '06, 370 II, 4; Sb 6611, 15; 4 Macc 15: 17; Philo, Ebr. 30 al.) *give birth to, bear* in our lit. only fig. of sin, personif., ἡ ἁμαρτία ἀ. θάνατον *sin brings forth death* Js 1: 15. But it is not confined to the female principle (cf. Herm Wr. 1, 9); of God (cf. γεννάω) ἀπεκύησεν ἡμᾶς λόγῳ ἀληθείας *he has brought us into being through the word of truth* Js 1: 18.—C-MEdsman, Schöpferwille u. Geburt Jk 1: 18: ZNW 38, '39, 11-44. M-M.*

ἀποκυλίω fut. ἀποκυλίσω; pf. pass. ἀποκεκύλισμαι (cf. Bl-D. §101 p. 46) (Diod. S. 14, 116, 6; Ps.-Apollod. 3, 15, 7; Lucian, Rhet. Praec. 3; Jos., Ant. 4, 284; 5, 359; LXX) *roll away* τὶ (Ἀρχαιολ. Ἐφημερίς '23, 39 [IV BC] λίθους) ἀ. τὸν λίθον (Gen 29: 3, 8, 10) Mt 28: 2; GP 12: 53; ἀ. τ. λίθον ἐκ τ. θύρας *roll the stone away from the entrance* Mk 16: 3; cf. vs. 4 v.l. λίθος ἀποκεκυλισμένος ἀπὸ τ. μνημείου Lk 24: 2 (the passive also has the same mng. as the intrans. *roll away*: Diod. S. 20, 14, 6).*

ἀπολακτίζω 1 aor. ἀπελάκτισα (Theognis+) intr. *kick up* (as a saying of Plato in Diog. L. 5, 2; M. Ant. 10, 28, 1; Ps.-Lucian, Asin. 18). So lit. 1 Cl 3: 1 (Dt 32: 15), but the fig. mng. *spurn* is also poss. (cf. Aeschyl., Prom. 651; Plut., Ant. 36, 2 τὰ καλά).*

ἀπολαλέω impf. 3 sg. ἀπελάλει (Lucian, Nigrin. 22 blurt out) *speak out freely* (Jos., Ant. 6, 178) Ac 18: 25 D.*

ἀπολαμβάνω fut. ἀπολή(μ)ψομαι; 2 aor. ἀπέλαβον; 2 aor. mid. ptc. ἀπολαβόμενος (Eur., Hdt.+; inscr., pap., LXX; Ep. Arist. 14; Joseph.).

1. *receive* τὶ: τ. υἱοθεσίαν *adoption* Gal 4: 5. τὴν ἐπαγγελίαν B 15: 7; pl. Hv 2, 2, 6, cf. 5: 7. πάντα Hm 9: 4. τ. ἐκκλησίαν 2 Cl 14: 3. τ. αἰώνιον ζωήν 8: 6.—As commercial t.t. (cf. ἀπέχω) *receive* (UPZ 162 VIII, 28 [117 BC] τ. τιμὴν ἀπολαβεῖν) τὰ ἀγαθά σου *you have already received your good things* Lk 16: 25 (otherw. KBornhäuser, NKZ 39, '28, 838f); cf. 2 Cl 11: 4. Esp. of wages (since Hdt. 8, 137 μισθόν; Sb 7438, 13 [VI AD] μισθόν) ἀ. πολλαπλασίονα *receive many times more* Lk 18: 30 v.l.; ἄξια ἀ. 23: 41; τ. μισθόν 2 Cl 9: 5; Hs 5, 6, 7; μισθὸν πλήρη 2 J 8; ἀντιμισθίαν ἀ. Ro 1: 27; ἀπὸ κυρίου ἀ. τ. ἀνταπόδοσιν Col 3: 24; τ. κλῆρον ἀ. *obtain one's lot* IRo 1: 2; τ. μέλλοντα αἰῶνα *the future age* (w. its glory) Pol 5: 2; τ. τῆς ἀφθαρσίας στέφανον MPol 19: 2. It is used abs. GOxy 4. where its mng. is doubtful; EPreuschen, ZNW 9, '08, 4.

2. *receive in return, recover, get back* (Jos., Ant. 5, 19) τὰ ἴσα *the same amount* Lk 6: 34 (Sb 7516, 24 [II AD] τὰ ὀφειλόμενα). ὑγιαίνοντα αὐτὸν ἀπέλαβεν *he has gotten him back safe and sound* 15: 27. Fig. τ. λαὸν καθαρόν *take his people back pure* Hs 9, 18, 4. τὸ ἴδιον μέγεθος ISm 11: 2.

3. *take aside* of persons (so since Hdt. 1, 209; Aristoph., Ran. 78 αὐτὸν μόνον; PLond. 42, 12ff; PVat. A, 10 in Witkowski² p. 65; Jos., Bell. 2, 109 ἀπολαβόμενος αὐτὸν κατ᾽ ἰδίαν; 2 Macc 6: 21) mid. ἀπολαβόμενος αὐτὸν ἀπὸ τ. ὄχλου κατ᾽ ἰδίαν *he took him aside, away fr. the crowd, by himself* Mk 7: 33.

4. *welcome* (PLeipz. 110, 6; PIand. 13, 17 ἵνα μετὰ χαρᾶς σε ἀπολάβωμεν) 3 J 8 v.l.; τὴν πολυπληθίαν ὑμῶν *your whole congregation* IEph 1: 3. ὃν ἐξεμπλάριον τ. ἀφ᾽ ὑμῶν ἀγάπης ἀπέλαβον *whom I have welcomed as a living example of your love* 2: 1. M-M.*

ἀπόλαυσις, εως, ἡ (Eur., Thu.+; Dit., Or. 383, 12 and 150; 404, 10; pap.; 3 Macc 7: 16; Philo, Mos. 2, 70; Jos., Ant. 2, 52; 174 εἰς ἀ. ἀγαθῶν) *enjoyment* πρόσκαιρον ἔχειν ἁμαρτίας ἀπόλαυσιν *enjoy the short-lived pleasures of sin* Hb 11: 25. (Opp. ἐπαγγελία) ἡ ἐνθάδε ἀ. 2 Cl 10: 3f. πρὸς ἀπόλαυσιν (Clearchus, fgm. 44; Palaeph. p. 84, 13; Dit., Or. 669, 8; IG XII, III 326, 12) *for enjoyment* 1 Cl 20: 10, a H.Gk. expression, like εἰς ἀ. (Diod. S. 14, 80, 2; Nägeli 30): εἰς ἀ. διδόναι τί τινι D 10: 3. εἰς ἀ. παρέχειν τί τινι 1 Ti 6: 17. M-M.*

ἀπολείπω impf. ἀπέλειπον; 2 aor. ἀπέλιπον (Hom.+; inscr., pap., LXX; Philo, Aet. M. 7; 8; Joseph.).
1. *leave behind* (cf. Nägeli 23) τινά or τὶ ἔν τινι (1 Macc 9: 65) 2 Ti 4: 13, 20; Tit 1: 5.
2. pass. *remain* ἀ. σαββατισμός *a Sabbath rest remains* Hb 4: 9 (Polyb. 6, 58, 9 ἐλπὶς ἀπολείπεται σωτηρίας). ἀ. θυσία *a sacrifice remains*=can be made 10: 26 (cf. Polyb. 3, 39, 12; Diog. L. 7, 85 ἀ. λέγειν). Abs. ἀ. w. inf. and acc. foll. (Bl-D. §393, 6) *it is reserved* or *certain* 4: 6.
3. *desert* (Apollon. Rhod. 4, 752 δώματα=[leave] a house; Appian, Bell. Civ. 3, 92 §377, 380; UPZ 19, 6 [163 BC]; Job 11: 20; Jos., Ant. 1, 20) τὸ ἴδιον οἰκητήριον *their own abode* Jd 6.
4. *put aside, give up* (Polycrates: no. 588 fgm. 1 Jac.; Dio Chrys. 45[62], 2; Socrat., Ep. 6, 2 οὐδέν; Sir 17: 25; Pr 9: 6), also *leave behind, overcome* (Isocr., Panegyr. 50, Panathen. 159; Harpocration p. 47, 6 Dind.: ἀπολελοιπότες· ἀντὶ τοῦ νενικηκότες; Lex. Vind. p. 7, 33) τὸν φόβον τοῦ θεοῦ *abandon the fear of God* 1 Cl 3: 4. τὰς κενὰς φροντίδας *empty cares* 7: 2. τὴν ματαιοπονίαν 9: 1. μιαρὰς ἐπιθυμίας 28: 1. τ. κενὴν ματαιολογίαν Pol 2: 1; cf. 7: 2. M-M.*

ἀπολεῖται, -ολέσαι, -ολέσῃ s. ἀπόλλυμι.

ἀπολείχω impf. ἀπέλειχον (Apollon. Rhod. 4, 478; Athen. 6, 13 p. 250A) *lick, lick off* Lk 16: 21 v.l.*

ἀπολιμπάνω an Aeolic and H.Gk. by-form of ἀπολείπω, q.v. 1 Pt 2: 21 as v.l. in 𝔓⁷² for ὑπολιμπάνω, q.v.*

ἀπόλλυμι for its conj. s. Bl-D. §101 (s.v. ὅλλυμι); Rob. 317; fut. ἀπολέσω Hs 8, 7, 5, Att. ἀπολῶ 1 Cor 1: 19 (Is 29: 14); 1 aor. ἀπώλεσα; 1 pf. ἀπολώλεκα; fut. mid. ἀπολοῦμαι Lk 13: 3; 2 aor. ἀπωλόμην; the 2 pf. ἀπόλωλα serves as a pf. mid., ptc. ἀπολωλώς (Hom.+; inscr., pap., LXX, En., Philo, Joseph., Test. 12 Patr.).

1. act.—a. *ruin, destroy.*

a. of pers. (Sir 10: 3) Mk 1: 24; Lk 4: 34. W. ref. to eternal destruction μὴ ἐκεῖνον ἀπόλλυε *do not bring about his ruin* Ro 14: 15. Esp. *kill, put to death* (Gen 20: 4; Esth 9: 6 v.l.; 1 Macc 2: 37; Jos., C. Ap. 1, 122) Hs 9, 26, 7. παιδίον Mt 2: 13; Jesus 12: 14; 27: 20; Mk 3: 6; 11: 18; Lk 19: 47; B 12: 5; the wicked tenants κακοὺς κακῶς ἀ. (s. κακός 1a) *he will put the evildoers to a miserable death* Mt 21: 41. τοὺς γεωργούς Mk 12: 9; Lk 20: 16; τ. φονεῖς Mt 22: 7; τ. μὴ πιστεύσαντας *those who did not believe* Jd 5; πάντας Lk 17: 27, 29. W. σῶσαι (like Charito 2, 8, 1) Js 4: 12; Hs 9, 23, 4. Of eternal death (Herm. Wr. 4, 7) ψυχὴν κ. σῶμα ἀ. ἐν γεέννῃ Mt 10: 28; ψυχήν B 20: 1; τ. ψυχάς Hs 9, 26, 3 (cf. Sir 20: 22).

β. w. impers. obj. ἀ. τ. σοφίαν τ. σοφῶν *destroy the wisdom of the wise* 1 Cor 1: 19 (Is 29: 14). ἀ. τ. διάνοιαν *destroy the understanding* Hm 11: 1.—**γ.** without obj. J 10: 10.

b. *lose* (X., Pla.+; PPetr. III 51, 5; POxy. 743, 23; PFay. 111, 3ff; Sir 6: 3; 9: 6; 27: 16 et al.; Tob 7: 6BA; 4 Macc 2: 14) τ. μισθόν *lose the reward* Mt 10: 42; Mk 9: 41; Hs 5, 6, 7. δραχμήν (Dio Chrys. 70[20], 25) Lk 15: 8f; ἀ. ἃ ἠργασάμεθα *lose what we have worked for* 2 J 8. διαθήκην B 4: 6, 8. τὴν ζωὴν τ. ἀνθρώπων Hm 2: 1; cf. s 8, 6, 6; 8, 7, 5; 8, 8, 2f and 5. τὴν ἐλπίδα m 5, 1, 7.—W. Semitic flavoring ἵνα πᾶν ὃ δέδωκέν μοι μὴ ἀπολέσω ἐξ αὐτοῦ *that I should lose nothing of all that he has given me* J 6: 39 (Bl-D. §466, 3; Rob. 437; 753).—ἀ. τὴν ψυχήν (cf. Sir 20: 22) *lose one's life* Mt 10: 39; 16: 25; Mk 8: 35; Lk 9: 24; 17: 33; cf. J 12: 25. For this ἀ. ἑαυτόν *lose oneself* Lk 9: 25 (similar in form is Tyrtaeus Lyr. [VII BC], fgm. 8 Diehl² lines 12ff: 'The man who risks his life in battle has the best chance of saving it; the one who flees to save it is most likely to lose it').

2. mid.—a. *be destroyed, ruined.*

a. of pers. *perish, die* (schol. on Nicander, Ther. 188 ἀπόλυται ὁ ἀνήρ=the man dies) 1 Cl 51: 5; 55: 6; B 5: 4, 12; D 16: 5; Hs 6, 2, 1f. As a cry of anguish ἀπολλύμεθα *we are perishing!* (PPetr. II 4, 4 νυνὶ δὲ ἀπολλύμεθα) Mt 8: 25; Mk 4: 38; Lk 8: 24 (Arrian, Peripl. 3, 3 of disaster that the stormy sea brings to the seafarer). ἐν μαχαίρῃ ἀ. *die by the sword* Mt 26: 52. λιμῷ *of hunger* (Ezk 34: 29) Lk 15: 17. τῇ ἀντιλογίᾳ τοῦ Κόρε Jd 11c (because of 11a and b it should perh.=*be corrupted;* cf. Polyb. 32, 23, 6). ὑπό τινος (Hdt. 5, 126; Dio Chrys. 13[7], 12) ὑπὸ τ. ὄφεων *killed by the snakes* 1 Cor 10: 9; cf. vs. 10. Abs. of a people *perish* J 11: 50. Of individuals (Lev 23: 30) Ac 5: 37; 2 Pt 3: 9; 1 Cl 12: 6; 39: 5 (Job 4: 20).—Esp. of eternal death (cf. Ps 9: 6f; 36: 20; 67: 3; 91: 10; Is 41: 11) J 3: 16; 17: 12. ἀπολέσθαι εἰς τὸν αἰῶνα *perish forever* 10: 28 (Bar 3: 3 ἡμεῖς ἀπολλύμενοι τὸν αἰῶνα). ἀνόμως ἀ. Ro 2: 12; μωρῶς ἀ. IEph 17: 2; ἐν καυχήσει *because of boasting* ITr 4: 1; cf. IPol 5: 2. Abs. 1 Cor 8: 11; 15: 18; 2 Cl 17: 1.—οἱ ἀπολλύμενοι (opp. οἱ σωζόμενοι, like Plut., Mor. 469D) *those who are lost* 1 Cor 1: 18; 2 Cor 2: 15; 4: 3; 2 Th 2: 10; 2 Cl 1: 4; 2: 5. For this τὸ ἀπολωλός Lk 19: 10 (Mt 18: 11—Ezk 34: 4, 16). τὰ ἀπολλύμενα 2 Cl 2: 7 (cf. Dit.,

Syll.³ 417, 9 τὰ τε ἀπολωλότα ἐκ τ. ἱεροῦ ἀνέσωσαν).

β. of things *be lost, pass away, be ruined* (Jos., Bell. 2, 650 of Jerusalem) of bursting wineskins Mk 9: 17; Mk 2: 22; Lk 5: 37; fading beauty Js 1: 11; transitory beauty of gold 1 Pt 1: 7; passing splendor Rv 18: 14 (w. ἀπό as Jer 10: 11; Da 7: 17). Of earthly food J 6: 27; spoiled honey Hm 5, 1, 5. Of the heavens which, like the earth, will pass away Hb 1: 11 (Ps 101: 27). Of the end of the world Hv 4, 3, 3, Of the way of the godless, which is lost in darkness B 11: 7 (Ps 1: 6).

b. *be lost* (Antipho 54 Diels, Vorsokrat. ἀπολόμενον ἀργύριον; X., Symp. 1, 5; 1 Km 9: 3) ISm 10: 1. Of falling hair Lk 21: 18; Ac 27: 34; a member or organ of the body Mt 5: 29f; remnants of food J 6: 12. Of wine that has lost its flavor Hm 12, 5, 3.—Of sheep gone astray Mt 10: 6; 15: 24; Lk 15: 4, 6; B 5: 12 (cf. Jer 27: 6; Ezk 34: 4; Ps 118: 176). Of a lost son Lk 15: 24 (Artem. 4, 33 ἡ γυνή...τ. υἱὸν ἀπώλεσε και...εὗρεν αὐτόν.—JSchniewind, D. Gleichn. vom verl. Sohn '40). ἀ. θεῷ *be lost to God* Hs 8, 6, 4. M-M. B. 758; 766.

Ἀπολλύων, ονος, ὁ *Apollyon, the Destroyer,* transl. of Ἀβαδδών (q.v.) Rv 9: 11 (Archilochus Lyr. [VII BC], fgm. 30 Ἄπολλον ... ὄλλυ' ὥσπερ ὀλλύεις=Apollo, you destroyer-god, destroy them [the guilty ones]).—A Oepke, TW I 396.*

Ἀπολλωνία, ας, ἡ *Apollonia,* a city in Macedonia (lit., inscr.), which Paul passed through Ac 17: 1.*

Ἀπολλώνιος, ου, ὁ *Apollonius,* a name freq. found (Dit., Syll. and Or., Inschr. v. Magn. indices; Joseph.); of a presbyter in Magnesia IMg 2: 1.—Ac 18: 24 D s. Ἀπολλῶς.*

Ἀπολλῶς, ῶ, ὁ (Ostraka II 1319; 1577; very oft. in pap., e.g. PLond. 929, 44 and 66; 1233, 8) *Apollos* a Christian born and educated at Alexandria, who worked in Ephesus and Corinth Ac 18: 24; 19: 1; 1 Cor 1: 12 (cf. Epict. 1, 9, 1–4: not Ἀθηναῖος ἢ Κορίνθιος, ἀλλὰ κόσμιος); 3: 4–6, 22; 4: 6; 16: 12; Tit 3: 13; 1 Cl 47: 3. On the form of the name, which is short for Ἀπολλώνιος (as this man is called Ac 18: 24 D), and prob. also for Ἀπολλόδωρος and Ἀπολλωνίδης, cf. Rob. 172; 189; 260; Bl-D. §125, 1; Ltzm., Hdb., exc. on 1 Cor 16: 18 and s. on Ἀπελλῆς.— RSchumacher, D. Alexandriner Apollos '16; GABarton, Some Influences of Apollos in the NT: JBL 43, '24, 207–23; EBuonaiuti, Paolo ed Apollo: Ricerche Religiose 1, '25, 14–34; HPreisker, Ap. u. d. Johannesjünger in Ac 18: 24-19: 6: ZNW 30, '31, 301–4; SBugge, Norsk Teol. Tidsskr. 44, '43, 83–97. M-M.*

ἀπολογέομαι impf. ἀπελογούμην; 1 aor. ἀπελογησάμην; 1 aor. pass. inf. ἀπολογηθῆναι Lk 21: 14 (Eur., Hdt.+; Dit., Or. 609, 39; PStrassb. 5, 15 al.; pap., LXX, Joseph.) *speak in one's own defense, defend oneself* (Jos., Ant. 4, 169; 15, 35). Abs. (opp. κατηγορέω) Ro 2: 15; Lk 21: 14. ὁ Παῦλος ἀπελογεῖτο Ac 26: 1. Ending of Mark in the Freer ms. 1. W. acc. ταῦτα αὐτοῦ ἀπολογουμένου *as he spoke thus in his defense* Ac 26: 24. πῶς ἢ τί ἀπολογήσησθε *how or what you should answer* Lk 12: 11. τὰ περὶ ἐμαυτοῦ ἀ. *I make my defense* Ac 24: 10. ἀ. περί τινος *defend oneself against someth.* (Demosth. 19, 214; Diod. S. 4, 53, 1) 26: 1f (ἐπί τινος *before someone*).—W. dat. of the pers. (Pla., Prot. 359A; esp. later writers [Nägeli 43]; Epict. 2, 16, 42 σοί [God] ἀπολογήσομαι [ὑπέρ τινος πρός τινα=in a matter before someone]; Maximus Tyr. 3, 7a; Vett. Val. 209, 13 βασιλεῖ ἀπολογήσεται). τῷ δήμῳ *make a defense before the people* Ac 19: 33; ὑμῖν ἀ. 2 Cor 12: 19; αὐτοῖς MPol 10: 2.—W. ὅτι foll. τοῦ

Παύλου ἀπολογουμένου, ὅτι when Paul said in his defense (direct quot. foll.) Ac 25: 8. M-M.*

ἀπολογία, ας, ἡ (Pre-Socr., Thu.+; BGU 531, 21 [I AD]; PLeipz. 58, 18; Wsd 6: 10; Jos., C. Ap. 2, 147) defense.
1. as a thing: a speech of defense, reply ἀκούσατέ μου τῆς πρὸς ὑμᾶς νυνὶ ἀπολογίας hear the defense which I now make to you Ac 22: 1 (ἀ. πρός τινα as X., Mem. 4, 8, 5). ἡ ἐμὴ ἀ. τοῖς ἐμὲ ἀνακρίνουσιν my reply to those who sit in judgment over me 1 Cor 9: 3.
2. as an action—a. in court (Jos., Bell. 1, 621) ἐν τ. πρώτῃ μου ἀ. at my first defense 2 Ti 4: 16 (s. πρῶτος 1a). τόπον ἀπολογίας λαμβάνειν περί τινος receive an opportunity to defend himself concerning someth. Ac 25: 16.
b. gener. of eagerness to defend oneself 2 Cor 7: 11. Of defending the gospel Phil 1: 7, 16. ἕτοιμοι πρὸς ἀπολογίαν παντί ready to make a defense to anyone 1 Pt 3: 15.
3. excuse ἔχειν ἀπολογίαν εἰπεῖν be able to say as an excuse PK 3 p. 15, 23. M-M.*

ἀπολούω 1 aor. mid. ἀπελουσάμην (Hom.+; Job 9: 30). The NT knows only the mid. in the sense wash oneself, fig. (as Philo, Mut. Nom. 49; Lucian, Cataplus 24 ἀπάσας τ. κηλῖδας τῆς ψυχῆς ἀπελουσάμην) τὰς ἁμαρτίας wash away one's sins Ac 22: 16. Abs. (w. ἁγιάζεσθαι) 1 Cor 6: 11.*

ἀπόλυσις, εως, ἡ (Hdt.+; pap., 3 Macc, Ep. Arist.; Jos., Ant. 17, 204 as release, deliverance; in Polyb. oft. as departure) euphem. for death (Theophr., Hist. Pl. 9, 16, 8; Dio Chrys. 60+61[77+78], 45; Diog. L. 5, 71) γίνεσθαι πρὸς ἀ. τοῦ ἀποθανεῖν come to the dissolution of death, 1 Cl 25: 2.*

ἀπολύτρωσις, εως, ἡ orig. buying back a slave or captive, making him free by payment of a ransom (λύτρον, q.v.). The word is comp. rare (Diod. S., fgm. 37, 5, 3 p. 149, 6 Dind.; Plut., Pomp. 24, 5; Ep. Arist. 12; 33; Philo, Omn. Prob. Lib. 114; Jos., Ant. 12, 27; Da 4: 34. An inscr. fr. Cos so designates sacral manumission of slaves: RHerzog, Koische Forschungen u. Funde 1899, 39f. Dssm., LO 278 [LAE 331]; KLatte, Heiliges Recht '20), and usage often diverges freely fr. the orig. mng.
1. lit. release, offered in return for apostasy (Philo, loc. cit.; for the story 2 Macc 7: 24; 4 Macc 8: 4-14) Hb 11: 35.
2. fig., of the release fr. sin and finiteness that comes through Christ.
a. redemption, acquittal, also the state of being redeemed διὰ τῆς ἀ. τῆς ἐν Χριστῷ Ἰησοῦ Ro 3: 24. εἰς ἀ. τῶν παραβάσεων for redemption fr. the transgressions Hb 9: 15. ἐγγίζει ἡ ἀ. ὑμῶν Lk 21: 28. ἡ ἀ. τοῦ σώματος ἡμῶν the freeing of our body fr. earthly limitations or redemption of our body (σῶμα=σάρξ as 2 Cor 5: 8) Ro 8: 23. ἔχομεν τὴν ἀ. διὰ τ. αἵματος αὐτοῦ Eph 1: 7; Col 1: 14. ἐσφραγίσθητε εἰς ἡμέραν ἀπολυτρώσεως you have been sealed for the day of redemption Eph 4: 30. εἰς ἀ. τῆς περιποιήσεως for a redemption, through which you become God's property 1: 14.
b. abstr. for concr. redeemer Christ ἐγενήθη ἡμῖν ἀ. 1 Cor 1: 30.—JWirtz, D. Lehre von d. Apolytrosis '06. JJStamm, Erlösen u. Vergeben im AT '40. BBWarfield, The NT Terminol. of 'Redemption': PTR 15, '17, 201-49. ELohmeyer, D. Begriff d. Erlösung im Urchristentum '28. EvDobschütz, ThBl 8, '29, 34-6; 99f; OProcksch and FBüchsel, TW IV 330-7; 343-59. JBohatec, ThZ 4, '48, 268-70; DaConchas, Verbum Domini 30, '52, 14-29; 81-91; 154-69; ELohse, Märtyrer u. Gottesknecht, '55; DEHWhitely, JTS 8, '57, 240-55; DHill, Gk. Words and

Hebr. Mngs. '67, 49-81; SLyonnet, Sin, Redemption, and Sacrifice '70, 79-103.*

ἀπολύω impf. ἀπέλυον; fut. ἀπολύσω; 1 aor. ἀπέλυσα, inf. ἀπολῦσαι; pf. pass. ἀπολέλυμαι; 1 aor. pass. ἀπελύθην; fut. ἀπολυθήσομαι (Hom.+; inscr., pap., LXX, Ep. Arist., Joseph.).
1. set free, release, pardon τινά a prisoner (PGiess. 65a, 4; 66, 11; POxy. 1271, 5; 2 Macc 4: 47; 12: 25; 4 Macc 8: 2; Jos., Bell. 2, 4) ἀ. ἕνα ὄχλῳ δέσμιον release a prisoner for the crowd (JMerkel, D. Begnadigung am Passahfeste: ZNW 6, '05, 293-316; CBChavel, JBL 60, '41, 273-8;—ἀπολύω=pardon: Diod. S. 3, 71, 5; Appian, Bell. Civ. 5, 4 §15; Dit., Or. 90, 14 [196 BC]; UPZ 111, 2 [163 BC]) Mt 27: 15-26; cf. Mk 15: 6-15; Lk 23: 16-25; J 18: 39; 19: 10, 12; Ac 3: 13; 5: 40; 16: 35f; 26: 32; 28: 18; release against Mt 18: 27. Abs. ἀπολύετε καὶ ἀπολυθήσεσθε pardon (your debtors) and you will be pardoned Lk 6: 37.—Pass. be freed (Tob 3: 6; 2 Macc 12: 45; Jos., Ant. 2, 65 τ. δεσμῶν) of diseases (Diog. L. 3, 6; Jos., Ant. 3, 264 τ. νόσου) ἀπολέλυσαι (v.l.+ἀπό) τῆς ἀσθενείας σου Lk 13: 12.
2. let go, send away, dismiss—a. divorce, send away τὴν γυναῖκα one's wife, or betrothed (1 Esdr 9: 36; cf. Dt 24: 1ff; the expr. ἀ. τ. γυν. Dionys. Hal. 2, 25, 7) Mt 1: 19; 5: 31f; 19: 3, 7-9; Mk 10: 2, 4, 11 (GDelling, Nov T 1, '56, 263-74); Lk 16: 18; Hm 4, 1, 6. Of the woman ἀ. τὸν ἄνδρα divorce her husband (Diod. S. 12, 18, 1) Mk 10: 12. This is in accord not w. Jewish (Jos., Ant. 15, 259), but w. Greco-Rom. custom (D has simply ἐξελθεῖν ἀπὸ τοῦ ἀνδρός). Cf. on divorce ThEngert, Ehe -u. Familienrecht d. Hebräer '05. AOtt, D. Auslegung d. ntl. Texte über d. Ehescheidung '10. HNordin, D. ehel. Ethik d. Juden z. Zt. Jesu '11. AEberharter, D. Ehe- u. Familienrecht d. Hebräer '14. LBlau, D. jüd. Ehescheidung u. d. jüd. Scheidebrief '11/12. RHCharles, The Teaching of the NT on Divorce '21; Billerb. I 303-21 al.; SEJohnson, Jesus' Teaching on Divorce '45; FLCirlot, Christ and Divorce '45; JDMDerrett, Law in the NT, '70, 363-88.
b. dismiss, send away (X., Hell. 6, 5, 21; UPZ 62, 18 [161 BC]; Tob 10: 12 S; 1 Macc 11: 38; 2 Macc 14: 23; Jos., Ant. 5, 97) of a crowd (Jos., Ant. 11, 337 ἀ. τὸ πλῆθος) Mt 14: 15, 22; 15: 32, 39; Mk 6: 36, 45; 8: 9 al.; ἀ. τὴν ἐκκλησίαν dismiss the assembly Ac 19: 40. Also of individuals Mt 15: 23; Lk 8: 38; 14: 4. W. the goal indicated (Jos., Vi. 271 εἰς) εἰς οἶκον (send them away) to their homes Mk 8: 3. εἰς τὰ τείχη let (them) go into the building Hs 8, 2, 5; cf. 8, 2, 1. Pass. be dismissed, take leave, depart (Philo, In Flacc. 96; Jos., Ant. 5, 99) Ac 4: 23; 15: 30, 33, also Hb 13: 23, unless the ref. is to a release fr. imprisonment (s. 1 above) or simply mng. 3 (cf. WWrede, D. Literar. Rätsel d. Hb '06, 57ff).—Euphem. for let die (Ps.-Plut., Consol. ad Apoll. 13 p. 108c ἕως ἂν ὁ θεὸς ἀπολύσῃ ἡμᾶς; M. Ant. 12, 36; a veteran's gravestone [Sb 2477] Ἡλιόδωρε ἐντείμως ἀπολελυμένε, εὐψύχει; Gen 15: 2; Num 20: 29; Tob 3: 6; 2 Macc 7: 9) νῦν ἀπολύεις τὸν δοῦλόν σου Lk 2: 29 (some interpret this as modal now mayest thou... JAKleist, Mk '36, 147-50 and AFridrichsen, Con. Neot. 7, '42, 5f; cf. also Gdspd., Probs. 77-9). Perh. discharge fr. Simeon's long vigil (vs. 26); cf. POxy. 2760, 2f (179/80 AD), of a cavalryman's discharge.
3. mid. go away (Thu., Polyb.; PHal. 1, 174 [III BC]; Ex 33: 11; Ep. Arist. 304; Anz 285) Ac 28: 25; perh. Hb 13: 23. M-M. B. 768.

ἀπολῶ, ἀπολωλός s. ἀπόλλυμι.

ἀπομάσσω (Aristoph.+; POxy. 1381, 133; Tob 7: 16 S)

wipe off, mid. *oneself* (Galen, Protr. 10 p. 34, 5 John; Ps.-Callisth. 1, 18, 10) τὸν κονιορτὸν ἀπομασσόμεθα ὑμῖν *we wipe off the dust (in protest) against you* Lk 10: 11. S. on ἐκτινάσσω 1.*

ἀπομένω (very late pap. [VIII AD]=stay at a place. W. doubtful mng. PFlor. 378, 6 [V AD]) *remain behind* (so Alciphr. 3, 24, 2) Lk 2: 43 D.*

ἀπομνημονεύω 1 aor. ἀπεμνημόνευσα (Pla.+; Lucian) *remember* Papias 2: 15.*

ἀπονέμω (Simonides, Pind.+; Dit., Or. 90, 19; 116, 19; BGU 168, 4; POxy. 71 II, 3; 1185, 6; LXX; Ep. Arist. 24; Philo, Spec. Leg. 1, 148) *assign, show, pay* τινὶ τιμήν (Pla., Laws 8, 837c; Isocr., Paneg. 178; Herodian 1, 8, 1; Jos., Ant. 1, 156) *show honor to someone* 1 Pt 3: 7; 1 Cl 1: 3; MPol 10: 2. τινὶ πᾶσαν ἐντροπήν *show all respect to someone* IMg 3: 1. M-M.*

ἀπονεύω (Pla., Theophr. et al.) w. ἀπό τινος *withdraw, turn away from* (Epict. 4, 10, 2; 4, 12, 18). Of Jesus: ἀπένευσεν ἀπ᾽ [αὐτῶν] *he withdrew from* [them] UGosp 31.*

ἀπονίζω (Hom.+) and later ἀπονίπτω (Od. 18, 179 v.l.; Diod. S. 4, 59, 4; LXX) 1 aor. mid. ἀπενιψάμην (this formation is class. [s. νίπτω, beg.], also Dit., Syll.³ 1168, 63 [III BC]) *wash off* mid. (*for*) *oneself* (Plut., Phoc. 18, 3; Philostrat., Vi. Apoll. 8, 3 p. 330, 26; Achilles Tat. 8, 3, 2 μὲ ἀ. τὸ πρόσωπον) τ. χεῖρας (Theophr., Char. 16, 2) as a sign of innocence (Jewish, not Roman custom acc. to Origen, Comm. on Mt., Ser. Lat. 124 [ed. EKlostermann '33, 259]; cf. Dt 21: 6f=Jos., Ant. 4, 222; Ps 25: 6; 72: 13; Ep. Arist. 305f=Jos., Ant. 12, 106; Sota 9, 6.—Anticlides Hist. [III BC] no. 40 fgm. 6 Jac. in Supplement III B p. 743 says of the Greeks that acc. to an old custom still practiced ὅταν ἢ φόνον ἀνθρώπων ἢ καὶ ἄλλας σφαγὰς ἐποίουν, ὕδατι ἀεννάῳ τὰς χεῖρας ἀπονίπτειν εἰς τοῦ μιάσματος κάθαρσιν) Mt 27: 24. M-M.*

ἀπόνοια, ας, ἡ (Thu.+; inscr., pap., LXX, Philo; Jos., Bell. 7, 267, C. Ap. 2, 148, Ant. 14, 321) *madness, frenzy* εἰς τοσοῦτον ἀπονοίας *to such a degree of madness* 1 Cl 1: 1 (w. στάσις, as Cat. Cod. Astr. II 18). εἰς τοσαύτην ἀ. ἔρχεσθαι 46: 7 (cf. Dit., Syll.³ 643, 19 [171 BC] εἰς τοῦτο ἦλθεν ἀπονοίας; Philo, Somn. 2, 277 ἐπὶ τοσοῦτον ἀπονοίας).—W. ὥστε foll. as Hyperid. 2, 5.*

ἀποπέμπω (Hom.+) *send out* J 17: 3 𝔓⁶⁶.*

ἀποπίπτω aor. ἀπέπεσα (Hom.+; UPZ 70, 27 [II BC]; LXX) *fall away* ἀπό τινος (Hdt. 3, 130; Job 24: 24) or w. gen. (Hdt. 3, 64; Jdth 11: 6) *fr. someth.*
  1. lit. (Jos., Ant. 6, 2) ἀ. αὐτοῦ ἀπὸ τ. ὀφθαλμῶν *there fell fr. his eyes* Ac 9: 18.
  2. fig. (Polyb.; Diod. S.; Jdth 11: 6; Jos., Bell. 1, 527) ἀ. τῆς ὁδοῦ τ. δικαίας *fall from the right way* 2 Cl 5: 7 (cf. Proclus, Inst. 13 ἀ. τἀγαθοῦ). M-M.*

ἀποπλανάω 1 aor. pass. ἀπεπλανήθην (Hippocr.+; Ps.-Pla., Axioch. 369D; Polyb. 3, 57, 4; Dionys. Hal.; Plut.; Epict. 4, 6, 38; LXX) *mislead* τινά (2 Ch 21: 11; Pr 7: 21; Sir 13: 6; En. 98, 15) only fig. of false teachers ἀ. τ. ἐκλεκτούς *mislead the elect* Mk 13: 22; cf. Hm 5, 2, 1; Pol 6: 3. Pass. (Sir 4: 19; 13: 8; 2 Macc 2: 2) ἀποπλανᾶσθαι ἀπό τινος *wander away fr. someone* or *someth.* ἀ. ἀπὸ τ. πίστεως *they have gone astray fr. the faith* 1 Ti 6: 10 (Dionys. Hal., Comp. Verb. 4 ἀπὸ τ. ἀληθείας). ἀποπλανώμενος ἀπὸ τ. θεοῦ *wandered away fr. God* Hs 6, 3, 3; ἀ. ἀπὸ τ. διανοίας αὐτῶν *wander away fr. their*

understanding Hm 10, 1, 5. Abs. *be led into error* (En. 8, 2) s 9, 20, 2. τὰ ἀποπεπλανημένα=τοὺς ἀ. *those who have gone astray* Pol 6: 1.*

ἀποπλέω 1 aor. ἀπέπλευσα (Hom.+; PLille 3, 5 [III BC]; Jos., Ant. 16, 16 al.) nautical t.t. *sail away* ἐκεῖθεν Ac 20: 15. W. εἰς to indicate destination (Thu. 6, 61, 6; Zen.-P. 6, 3=Sb 6712 [258/7 BC]) 13: 4; 14: 26; 27: 1.*

ἀποπλύνω impf. ἀπέπλυνον; 1 aor. ἀπέπλυνα (Hom.+; Epict.; Philostrat., Vi. Apoll. 8, 22 p. 337, 14; LXX; Jos., Ant. 3, 114; 8, 417) *wash off* or *out* Lk 5: 2 v.l. (for ἔπλυνον).*

ἀποπνίγω 1 aor. ἀπέπνιξα; 2 aor. pass. ἀπεπνίγην (Hdt., Aristoph.+; pap., LXX) *choke* trans. (Bull. de corr. hell. 16, 1892, p. 384 No. 81; Na 2: 13; Tob 3: 8 BA; Jos., Bell. 1, 551) of rank weeds (Theophr.) ἄκανθαι ἀ. αὐτά Mt 13: 7; Lk 8: 7.—*Drown* (Diod. 3, 57, 5; Syntipas p. 19, 4) pass., lit. ἡ ἀγέλη ἀπεπνίγη *the drove drowned* 8: 33 (cf. Demosth. 32, 6; Epict. 2, 5, 12; Diog. L. 9, 12). M-M.*

ἀπορέω impf. ἠπόρουν (Pre-Socr., Hdt.+; inscr., pap., LXX; cf. Bl-D. §101; 307) *be at a loss, in doubt, uncertain* act. (Thu. 5, 40, 3; X., Hell. 6, 1, 4; POxy. 472, 8; 939, 23f; Wsd 11: 17; Philo, Leg. All. 1, 70; Jos., Ant. 2, 271 and 304, Vi. 161) πολλὰ ἠπόρει *he was very much disturbed* Mk 6: 20 (so Gdspd., Probs. 58f; but cf. FZorell, Lex. s.v. and CBonner, HTR 37, '44, 41–4, 336 'he was wont to raise many questions'; s. also L-S-J s.v. I 2).—Elsewh. in our lit. mid. (X., An. 6, 1, 21; 7, 3, 29 et al.; Dit., Syll.³ 226, 35; 1 Macc 3: 31; Jos., Bell. 4, 226) περί τινος *about someth.* Lk 24: 4; Hs 8, 3, 1; w. indir. question foll. ἀπορούμενοι περὶ τίνος λέγει *uncertain as to which one he meant* J 13: 22. πρός τι UGosp l. 63. W. acc. foll. ἀπορούμενος τὴν περὶ τούτων ζήτησιν *since I was at a loss how to investigate these matters* Ac 25: 20 (Bl-D. §148, 2 app.; Rob. 472). ἔν τινι *because of someone* Gal 4: 20. Abs. 2 Cor 4: 8. M-M.*

ἀπο(ρ)ρήγνυμι pf. ἀπέρρηγα, ptc. ἀπερρηγώς (Hom.+; Philo, Aet. M. 118; Jos., Ant. 17, 320; on the spelling cf. Bl-D. §11, 1) *break up* τόπος κρημνώδης καὶ ἀ. ἀπὸ τ. ὑδάτων *a steep place broken up by the waters* Hv 1, 1, 3.*

ἀπορία, ας, ἡ (Pind., Hdt.+; inscr., pap., LXX; Jos., Bell. 1, 198, Ant. 8, 328) *perplexity, anxiety* ἀ. ἤχους θαλάσσης *anxiety because of the roaring of the sea* Lk 21: 25 (cf. Herodian 4, 14, 1 ἀ. τοῦ πρακτέου). M-M.*

ἀπο(ρ)ρίπτω 1 aor. ἀπέριψα (mss. ἀπέρριψα Bl-D. §11, 1); 2 aor. pass. ἀπερίφην Hv 3, 5, 5; 3, 6, 1 (Hom.+; pap., LXX; Philo, Ebr. 7; Joseph.).
  1. trans. *throw down* or *away.*
    a. lit. (Jon 2: 4) pass. ἀπὸ τοῦ πύργου Hs 9, 23, 3; cf. v 3, 5, 5; 3, 6, 1.
    b. fig. *drive* or *scare away* (Himerius, Or. [Ecl.] 36, 1 τινὰ εἴς τι) μὴ ἀποριψῃς με ἀπὸ τοῦ προσώπου σου *do not drive me away fr. thy presence* 1 Cl 18: 11 (Ps 50: 13; gener. freq. in LXX; Jos., Bell. 1, 624 ἀ.=*drive away from.*—ἀ.=*reject,* of God, in Celsus 3, 71.—Procop. Soph., Ep. 77 ἀπερριμμένοι=rejected ones; 94). μέριμναν ἀποριψαντες *casting care* 1 Pt 5: 7 𝔓⁷². ἀ. ἀφ᾽ ἑαυτῶν πᾶσαν ἀδικίαν *casting away fr. ourselves all unrighteousness* 1 Cl 35: 5 (cf. Ezk 18: 31; 20: 7f; Sib. Or. 1, 338 ἀ. ἐκ κραδίης κακίας; of the *casting off* of a garment Jos., Bell. 1, 197, Ant. 6, 113).
    2. intr. (Lucian, Ver. Hist. 1, 30; Charito 3, 5, 6; cf. Moulton, CR 20, '06, 216) *throw oneself down* Ac 27: 43 (cf. Bl-D. §308; Rob. 797). M-M.*

ἀπορρέω fut. ἀπορυήσομαι (trag., Hdt.+; Eudoxos-Pap. [=PPar. 1] 14, 17 [II BC]; LXX) *flow down* fig., of leaves (Demosth. 22, 70) *fall down* B 11: 6, 8 (Ps 1: 3).*

ἀπορφανίζω 1 aor. pass. ptc. ἀπορφανισθείς (Aeschyl.; Bull. de corr. hell. 46, '22, 345; Philo [Nägeli 25]) *make an orphan of* someone, fig., of the apostle separated fr. his church ἀπορφανισθέντες ἀφ' ὑμῶν *made orphans by separation fr. you* 1 Th 2: 17.*

ἀποσκευάζω 1 aor. ἀπεσκευασάμην (mostly mid.; Polyb.+; cf. Dit., Syll.³ 588, 54 [196 BC]; 633, 68; Lev 14: 36; Philo, Deus Imm. 135) *lay aside, get rid of* τὶ (Jos., Bell. 1, 260; 618) τ. συνήθειαν *lay aside the habit* Dg 2: 1. Ac 21: 15 t.r., ἀ. prob. means *pack up and leave.* M-M.*

ἀποσκίασμα, ατος, τό (Aëtius [100 AD] 2, 30, 3: Dox. Gr. 361b, 21.—ἀποσκιασμοί Plut., Pericl. 6, 5) *shadow* τροπῆς ἀ. *a shadow cast by variation* (in position of heavenly bodies) Js 1: 17 (Theopomp. [?]: 115 fgm. 400 Jac. τὸ ἀποσκίασμα τῆς τοῦ ἡλίου ἀνταυγείας). JH Ropes, ICC ad loc. and Gdspd, Probs. 189f prefer the rdg. of B ℵ* POxy. 1229 et al. (παρ.) ἢ τροπῆς ἀποσκιάσματος '(no variation) of changing shadow'. MDibelius, Meyer⁷ '21 ad loc. would emend to put both nouns in the genitive and transl. the clause 'who is without change and knows neither turning nor darkness'. M-M.*

ἀποσπάω 1 aor. ἀπέσπασα, pass. ἀπεσπάσθην (Pind., Hdt.+; pap., LXX) *draw* or *pull away.*
1. lit., *draw out* ἀ. τ. μάχαιραν *draw a sword* Mt 26: 51. ἀ. τοὺς ἥλους ἀπὸ τ. χειρῶν *draw out the nails fr. the hands* GP 6: 21.
2. fig., of pers. *draw* or *tear away, attract* (cf. Artem. 5, 43 τινά τινος someone from someone; Josh 8: 6; Jer 12: 14; Jos., Vi. 321, Ant. 8, 277 ἀπὸ τ. θεοῦ) ἀπὸ τ. εἰδώλων *fr. idols* 2 Cl 17: 1 (cf. Polyaenus 8, 51 of the bringing out of one who has fled to a temple for refuge; cf. ἀπὸ τ. ἁμαρτιῶν ἀποσπασθῆναι Third Corinthians 3: 9). ἀ. τοὺς μαθητὰς ὀπίσω ἑαυτῶν *draw away the disciples after them* (and thereby alienate them) Ac 20: 30 (cf. Aelian, V.H. 13: 32; Diog. L. 2, 113 ἀ. τινὰ ἀπό τινος *alienate pupils from someone*; PPetr. III 43[3], 12; BGU 1125, 9 [13 BC] οὐκ ἀποσπάσω αὐτὸν ἀπὸ σοῦ).
3. pass. ἀ. ἀπό τινος *be parted fr. someone* Ac 21: 1; Hs 6, 2, 3.—*Withdraw* (Diod. S. 20, 39; POxy. 275, 22 [66 AD]; Job 41: 9; Jos., Bell. 2, 498; 6, 379) ἀπό τινος Lk 22: 41. M-M.*

ἀποσταλῶ, ἀποσταλείς s. ἀποστέλλω.

ἀποστασία, ας, ἡ (a form quotable since Diod. S. outside the Bible [Nägeli 31] for class. ἀπόστασις [Phryn. 528 L.]) *rebellion, abandonment* in relig. sense, *apostasy* (Josh 22: 22; 2 Ch 29: 19; 1 Macc 2: 15) ἀπό τινος (Plu., Galb. 1, 9 Z. v.l. ἀπὸ Νέρωνος ἀ.; Jos., Vi. 43) ἀποστασίαν διδάσκεις ἀπὸ Μωϋσέως *you teach (Jews) to abandon Moses* Ac 21: 21. Of the rebellion caused by the Antichrist in the last days 2 Th 2: 3. M-M.*

ἀποστάσιον, ου, τό a legal t.t. found as early as Lysias, Hyperid. [fgm. Or. 17] and Demosth., and freq. in pap. since PHib. 96, 3 [258 BC]; PSI 551, 9 [III BC] (cf. Wilcken, APF 2, '03, 143 and 388f; 4, '08, 183 and 456f; Preisigke, Fachwörter '15) in the sense of relinquishment of property after sale, abandonment, etc. The consequent giving up of one's claim explains the meaning which the word acquires in Jewish circles: δοῦναι βιβλίον ἀποστασίου (Jer 3: 8) *give (one's wife) a certificate of divorce* Mt 19: 7. διδόναι ἀποστάσιον, w. the same mng. 5: 31. For this γράφειν β.

ἀ. (Dt 24: 1, 3) Mk 10: 4.—S. lit. on ἀπολύω 2a and Tractate Giṭṭin (Certificates of Divorce). M-M.*

ἀποστάτης, ου, ὁ (Polyb.+; Dit., Syll.³ 705, 50 [112 BC]; PAmh. 30, 33ff; Witkowski p. 96, 12; LXX; Berosus in Jos., Ant. 10, 221=C. Ap. 1, 136) *deserter, apostate* w. ἔθνη Hv 1, 4, 2; w. προδότης s 8, 6, 4; w. βλάσφημος and προδότης s 9, 19, 1. W. obj. gen. (Polyb. 5, 57, 4 and Diod. S. 15, 18, 1 τ. βασιλέως) νόμου *from the law* (2 Macc 5: 8 τ. νόμων ἀ.) Js 2: 11 v.l.*

ἀποστεγάζω 1 aor. ἀπεστέγασα (rare and in var. mngs.; Jer 49: 10 Sym.) *unroof* τ. στέγην *remove the roof* Mk 2: 4 (so Strabo 4, 4, 6; 8, 3, 30; Artem. 2, 36 p. 137, 26; Dit., Syll.³ 852, 30 στοὰ ἀπεστέγασται ὅλη).—S. lit. on στέγη.*

ἀποστέλλω fut. ἀποστελῶ; 1 aor. ἀπέστειλα; ἀποστείλω Ac 7: 34 (Ex 3: 10) is perh. not hortat. subj. but pres. ind. as in the Pontic dial. (Thumb 18, cf. M-M); pf. ἀπέσταλκα, pass. ἀπέσταλμαι; 2 aor. pass. ἀπεστάλην (Soph., Hdt.+; inscr., pap., LXX, Ep. Arist., Philo, Joseph., Test. 12 Patr.).
1. *send away* or *out* τινά someone.
a. w. the obj. given alone Mt 13: 41; Mk 11: 1; 12: 5 al.
b. more exactly defined—α. w. indication of the pers. to whom someone is sent: by the dat. (PPar. 32, 20) Mt 22: 16; Ac 28: 28. εἴς τινα Mt 15: 24; Lk 11: 49; Ac 26: 17. πρός τινα (Epict. 3, 22, 74; Jos., Ant. 7, 334) Mt 21: 34, 37; 23: 34, 37; 27: 19; Mk 3: 31; 12: 4, 6; J 1: 19 al.
β. w. indication of the place to which someone is sent, w. εἰς: Mt 14: 35; 20: 2; Mk 8: 26; Lk 1: 26; 10: 1; J 3: 17 al. W. ἐν (4 Km 17: 25; 2 Ch 7: 13) ἐν μέσῳ λύκων Mt 10: 16; Lk 10: 3 (cf. Jer 32: 27). ἔξω τ. χώρας *outside the country* Mk 5: 10. W. ὧδε *here* Mk 11: 3. ἀ. πρεσβείαν ὀπίσω τινός *send an embassy after someone* Lk 19: 14 (cf. 4 Km 14: 19). ἀ. ἔμπροσθέν τινος (cf. Gen 45: 5, 7; 46: 28) *send before someone* J 3: 28; cf. ἀ. ἄγγελον πρὸ προσώπου σου Mt 11: 10; Mk 1: 2 (Ex 23: 20; cf. Mal 3: 1); cf. Lk 9: 52; 10: 1.
γ. w. the purpose of the sending indicated by ἵνα (Gen 30: 25) Mk 12: 2, 13; Lk 20: 10; J 1: 19; 3: 17; 7: 32; Hv 5: 2 al. By ὅπως (1 Macc 16: 18) Ac 9: 17. By the inf. (Num 16: 12; 31: 4) Mt 22: 3; Mk 3: 14; Lk 1: 19; 4: 18a (Is 61: 1); 9: 2; 14: 17; J 4: 38; Ac 5: 21; 1 Cor 1: 17; Rv 22: 6; B 14: 9 (Is 61: 1); Hm 12, 6, 1. By ἐπί w. acc. (Apollon. Paradox. 1; PFlor. 126, 8; Sb 174 [III BC] ἀ. ἐπὶ τ. θήραν τ. ἐλεφάντων) ἐπὶ τοῦτο *for this purpose* Lk 4: 43. εἰς διακονίαν *to render service* Hb 1: 14 (cf. Jdth 11: 7; Gen 45: 5). By the simple acc. τοῦτον ἄρχοντα καὶ λυτρωτὴν ἀπέσταλκεν *this man he sent as leader and deliverer* Ac 7: 35. ἀ. τὸν υἱὸν αὐτοῦ ἱλασμὸν 1 J 4: 10. ἀ. τ. υἱὸν σωτῆρα vs. 14.
δ. in pass. ἀποστέλλεσθαι παρὰ θεοῦ (Vi. Aesopi I c. 31 p. 295, 1 ed. Eberh. ἀπεστάλην παρὰ τ. θεοῦ μου; cf. Sir 15: 9; 34: 6) J 1: 6. ἀπὸ τ. θεοῦ (Epict. 3, 22, 23 ἀπὸ τοῦ Διός; Vi. Aesopi P. I c. 119: the prophets of Heliupolis say ἡμεῖς ἀπεστάλημεν ἀπὸ τοῦ θεοῦ) Lk 1: 26; cf. 1 Cl 65: 1. ἀπὸ Κορνηλίου πρὸς αὐτόν Ac 10: 21 v.l. ἀπὸ Καισαρείας 11: 11 (cf. 1 Macc 15: 1). ἀπ' οὐρανοῦ 1 Pt 1: 12.
c. esp. of the sending out of the disciples by Jesus Mt 10: 5; Mk 3: 14; 6: 7; Lk 9: 2; J 4: 38; 17: 18, as well as the sending forth of Jesus by God (of the divine mission, esp. of prophets, very oft. in LXX; on the Heb. חלשׁ see LKopf, Vetus Testamentum 7, '58, 207-9.—Philo, Migr. Abr. 22. The Cynic ἀπὸ τ. Διὸς ἀπέσταλται Epict. 3, 22, 23; cf. 46.—Cornutus 16 p. 30, 19 ὁ Ἑρμῆς ὁ λόγος ὤν, ὃν ἀπέστειλαν πρὸς ἡμᾶς ἐξ οὐρανοῦ οἱ θεοί) Mt 15: 24;

Mk 9: 37; Lk 9: 48; J 3: 17, 34; 5: 36, 38; 6: 29, 57; 7: 29; 8: 42; 11: 42; 17: 3 (ἀποπέμπω 𝔓⁶⁶), 8, 21, 23, 25; 20: 21; Ac 3: 20. Σιλωάμ transl. ἀπεσταλμένος J 9: 7 (cf. Philo, Poster. Cai. 73). John the Baptist ἀπεσταλμένος παρὰ θεοῦ 1: 6.—Also of the Holy Spirit 1 Pt 1: 12 (cf. Jdth 16: 14; Ex 15: 10).—Of angels Hv 4, 2, 4 (cf. Da 4: 13, 23; 2 Macc 11: 6; 15: 22f; Tob 3: 17).

d. When used w. other verbs, it often means simply that the action in question has been performed by someone else, like have (cf. Gen 31: 4; 41: 8, 14; Ex 9: 27; 2 Km 11: 5 al.; X., Cyr. 3, 1, 6; Plut., Mor. 11c μεταπέμψας ἀνεῖλε τ. Θεόκριτον) ἀποστείλας ἀνεῖλεν he had (them) killed Mt 2: 16. ἀ. ἐκράτησεν τ. Ἰωάννην he had John arrested Mk 6: 17. ἀ. μετεκαλέσατο he had (him) summoned Ac 7: 14. ἐσήμανεν ἀ. διὰ τ. ἀγγέλου αὐτοῦ he had it made known by his angel Rv 1: 1. Sim. ἀπέστειλαν αἱ ἀδελφαὶ πρὸς αὐτὸν λέγουσαι the sisters had word brought to him J 11: 3. ἀ. ἐν ἀφέσει set free Lk 4: 18b (Is 58: 6).

2. w. impers. obj.: μάστιγας Hv 4, 2, 6. ἀ. τὸ δρέπανον (cf. Jo 3: 13) put in the sickle (Field, Notes 26), unless δρέπ. is fig. = reapers Mk 4: 29. ἀ. αὐτούς, i.e., donkeys Mt 21: 3. ἀ. τὸν λόγον send out a message (Ps 106: 20; 147: 7; cf. PLeipz. 64, 42 τὸ περὶ τούτου ἀποσταλὲν πρόσταγμα) Ac 10: 36; 13: 26 v.l.; cf. Lk 24: 49 𝔓⁷⁵ et al. Pass., 28: 28.—See lit. s.v. ἀπόστολος. M-M. B. 710.

ἀποστερέω 1 aor. ἀπεστέρησα; perf. pass. ptc. ἀπεστερημένος (Aeschyl., Hdt.+; inscr., pap., LXX) steal, rob τινά someone (UPZ 32, 33 [162/1 bc] ἀποστεροῦντες ἡμᾶς; Jos., Vi. 128) ἀποστερεῖτε, καὶ τοῦτο ἀδελφούς you defraud (people), even your own brothers 1 Cor 6: 8. Fig., μὴ ἀποστερεῖτε ἀλλήλους do not deprive each other of marital rights 7: 5 (cf. Ex 21: 10 and s. Nägeli 20). W. gen. of the thing (PRyl. 116, 16 βουλόμενοι ἀποστερέσαι τῶν ἐμῶν; Sir 29: 6; Jos., Ant. 2, 303 τῆς ἐπιμελείας τῆς ἀληθείας 1 Ti 6: 5. W. acc. of the thing and gen. of the pers. (Herm. Wr. 5, 8; Sir 34: 1; 34: 21) ἀ. τὴν ζωὴν ὑμῶν rob you of (eternal) life Hv 3, 9, 9. Abs. (UPZ 42, 35 [163/2 bc]) μὴ ἀποστερήσῃς do not steal Mk 10: 19 (perh. w. ref. to property held on deposit: CCCoulter, . . . the Bithynian Christians, Classical Philology 35, '40, 60–63; Pliny, Ep. to Trajan 96, 7; Lev 6: 2–5 [=5: 20–25 LXX]).—Pass. ὁ μισθὸς ὁ ἀπεστερημένος (Sir 34: 22; Mal 3: 5; cf. Philo, Mos. 1, 142; Jos., Ant. 4, 288.—Dit., Syll.³ 1199, 5: ἀ. = acquire illegally, embezzle) wages stolen or held back fr. the workers Js 5: 4 v.l. τίς πλέον ἀποστερηθείς; who has suffered greater loss? IEph 10: 3. Let oneself be robbed 1 Cor 6: 7. W. gen. lose someth. (Jos., Vi. 205) Ac 16: 19 D. M-M.*

ἀποστέρησις, εως, ἡ (since Thu. 7, 70, 6; POxy. 71, 10; Jos., Ant. 18, 7) robbery, fraud (Diod. S. 4, 33, 1 ἀποστέρησις τοῦ μισθοῦ) in a catalogue of vices Hm 8: 5.*

ἀποστερητής, οῦ, ὁ (Pla., Rep. 5 p. 344b et al.; POxy. 745, 7 [I bc]) robber, classed w. other sinners Hs 6, 5, 5. οἱ ψευδόμενοι γίνονται ἀποστερηταὶ τοῦ κυρίου liars become defrauders of the Lord m 3: 2.*

ἀποστῇ, ἀποστῆναι, etc. s. ἀφίστημι.

ἀποστιβάζω (s. στιβάζω) occurs only here, as it seems, ἀ. τ. ἀποθήκην empty the storeroom Hm 11: 15.*

ἀποστολή, ῆς, ἡ (Eur., Thu.+ in var. mngs.; Diod. S. 36, 1 [ἀ. στρατιωτῶν='sending out' of troops]; inscr., pap., LXX; Ep. Arist. 15; Jos., Ant. 20, 50, Vi. 268) in our lit. only of apostleship, office of an apostle, w. διακονία

Ac 1: 25. Used esp. by Paul to designate his position: ἡ σφραγίς μου τ. ἀποστολῆς the seal (official confirmation) of my apostleship 1 Cor 9: 2. ἐνεργεῖν τινι εἰς ἀ. make someone capable of being an apostle Gal 2: 8. λαμβάνειν ἀποστολὴν εἰς ὑπακοὴν πίστεως receive apostleship, to bring about obedience to the faith or obedience consisting in faith Ro 1: 5. M-M.*

ἀποστολικός, ή, όν (schol. on Pind., Pyth. 2, 6b, Isth. 2 inscr. a; Proclus in Phot., Bibl. p. 322b; Athen. 14 p. 631d[?]) apostolic ἐν ἀ. χαρακτῆρι in apostolic fashion= as the apostles did in their letters ITr inscr. διδάσκαλος ἀ. καὶ προφητικός an apost. and prophetic teacher of Polycarp MPol 16: 2.*

ἀπόστολος, ου, ὁ In class. Gk. (Lysias, Demosth.) and later (e.g. Posidon. 87 fgm. 53 Jac.) ὁ ἀ. is a naval expedition, prob. also its commander (Anecd. Gr. 217, 26). τὸ ἀπόστολον with (Pla., Ep. 7 p. 346a) or without (Vi. Hom. 19) πλοῖον means a ship ready for departure. In its single occurrence in Jos. (Ant. 17, 300; it is not found elsewh. in Jewish-Gk. lit.) it prob. means 'sending out'; in pap. mostly 'bill of lading', less freq. (Gnomon 64 [II ad]) 'passport'. It can also be 'dispatch, letter': Wilcken, Chrest. 443, 10 (15 ad); PHermopol. 6, 11f (cf. Dig. 49, 6, 1 litteras dimissorias sive apostolos). In contrast, in isolated cases it means ambassador, delegate, messenger (Hdt. 1, 21; 5, 38; Synesius, Providence 2, 3 p. 122a ἀπόστολοι of ordinary messengers; Sb 7241, 48; BGU 1741, 6 [64 bc]; 3 Km 14: 6A; Is 18: 2 Sym.). Cf. KLake, The Word 'Α.: Beginn. I 5, '33, 46–52.

1. In the NT, ἀ. can also mean delegate, envoy, messenger (opp. ὁ πέμψας) J 13: 16. Of Epaphroditus, messenger of the Philippians Phil 2: 25.—2 Cor 8: 23, perh. missionary.

2. esp. of God's messengers (cf. Epict. 3, 22, 23 of Cynic wise men: ἄγγελος ἀπὸ τ. Διὸς ἀπέσταλται) w. the prophets Lk 11: 49; Rv 18: 20; cf. 2: 2; Eph 3: 5. Even of Christ (w. ἀρχιερεύς) Hb 3: 1 (cf. the firman [decree] Sb 7240, 4f οὐκ ἔστιν θεὸς εἰ μὴ ὁ θεὸς μόνος. Μααμετ ἀπόστολος θεοῦ). GPWetter, 'D. Sohn Gottes' '16, 26ff.

3. But our lit. uses ἀ. predom. for the apostles, a group of highly honored believers, who had a special function. Even Judaism had an office known as apostle (שָׁלִיחַ; Schürer III⁴ 119f w. sources and lit.; Billerb. III '26, 2–4; JWTruron, Theology 51, '48, 166–70; 341–3; GDix, ibid. 249–56; 385f). From it the expr. may have been borrowed to designate one esp. commissioned. At first it denoted one who proclaimed the gospel, and was not strictly limited: Paul freq. calls himself an ἀ.: Ro 1: 1; 11: 13; 1 Cor 1: 1; 9: 1f; 15: 9; 2 Cor 1: 1; Gal 1: 1; Eph 1: 1; Col 1: 1; 1 Ti 1: 1; 2: 7; 2 Ti 1: 1, 11; Tit 1: 1.—1 Cl 47: 1. Of Barnabas Ac 14: 14. Of Andronicus and Junias (either apostles or honored by the apostles) Ro 16: 7. Of James, the Lord's brother Gal 1: 19. Of Peter 1 Pt 1: 1; 2 Pt 1: 1. Then esp. of the 12 apostles οἱ δώδεκα ἀ. Mt 10: 2; Mk 3: 14 v.l.; Lk 22: 14; cf. 6: 13; 9: 10; 17: 5; Ac 1: 26 (P-HMenoud, RHPhr 37 '57, 71–80); Rv 21: 14; PK 3 p. 15, 18. Peter and the apostles Ac 5: 29. Paul and apostles Pol 9: 1. Gener. the apostles 1 Cor 4: 9; 9: 5; 15: 7; 2 Cor 11: 13; 1 Th 2: 7; Ac 1: 2; 4: 42f; 4: 33, 35, 37; 5: 2, 12, 18, 40; 6: 6; 8: 1, 14, 18; 9: 27; 11: 1; 2 Pt 3: 2; Jd 17; IEph 11: 2; IMg 7: 1; 13: 2; ITr 2: 2; 3: 1; 7: 1; IPhld 5: 1; ISm 8: 1; D inscr.; 11: 3, 6. As a governing board, w. the elders Ac 15: 2, 4, 6, 22f; 16: 4. As possessors of the most important spiritual gift 1 Cor 12: 28f. Preachers of the gospel 1 Cl 42: 1f; B 5: 9; Hs 9, 17, 1. Prophesying strife 1 Cl 44: 1. Working miracles 2 Cor 12: 12. W. bishops, teachers and deacons Hv 3, 5, 1; s 9, 15, 4; w. teachers s 9,

25, 2; w. the teachers, preaching to those who had fallen asleep s 9, 16, 5; w. deacons and presbyters IMg 6: 1; w. prophets Eph 2: 20; D 11: 3; Pol 6: 3. Christ and the apostles as the foundation of the church IMg 13: 1; ITr 12: 2; cf. Eph 2: 20. οἱ ἀ. and ἡ ἐκκλησία w. the three patriarchs and the prophets IPhld 9: 1. The Holy Scriptures named w. the ap. 2 Cl 14: 2. Paul ironically refers to his opponents (or the original apostles; s. s.v. ὑπερλίαν) as οἱ ὑπερλίαν ἀ. the super-apostles 2 Cor 11: 5; 12: 11. The orig. apostles he calls οἱ πρὸ ἐμοῦ ἀ. Gal 1: 17.—Harnack, Mission⁴ I '23, 332ff (Eng. tr. I 319-31). WSeufert, D. Urspr. u. d. Bed. d. Apostolates 1887. EHaupt, Z. Verständnis d. Apostolates im NT 1896. EHMonnier, La notion de l'Apostolat des origines à Irénée '03. PBatiffol, RB n.s. 3, '06, 520-32. Wlh., Einleitung², '11, 138-47. EDBurton, AJT 16, '12, 561-88, Gal. '21, 363-84. RSchütz, Apostel u. Jünger '21. EMeyer I 265ff; III 255ff. HVogelstein, Development of the Apostolate in Judaism, etc., Hebrew Union Coll. Annual II, '25, 99-123. JWagenmann, D. Stellg. d. Ap. Pls neben den Zwölf '26. WMundle, D. Apostelbild der AG: ZNW 27, '28, 36-54. KHRengstorf, TW I 406-46 (s. critique by HConzelmann, The Theol. of St. Luke '60, 216, n. 1), Apost. u. Predigtamt '34. J-LLeuba, Rech. exégét. rel. à l'apostolat dans le NT, Diss. Neuchâtel '36. PSaintyves, Deux mythes évangéliques, Les 12 apôtres et les 72 disciples '38. GSass, Apostelamt u. Kirche...paulin. Apostelbegr. '39. EKäsemann, ZNW 40, '41, 33-71; KKertelge, Das Apostelamt des Paulus, BZ 14, '70, 161-81; RLiechtenhan, D. urchr. Mission '46. E Schweizer, D. Leben d. Herrn in d. Gemeinde u. ihren Diensten '46. AFridrichsen, The Apostle and his Message '47. HvCampenhausen, D. urchristl. Apostelbegr.: Studia Theologica 1, '47, 96-130; HMosbech, ibid. 2, '48, 166-200; ELohse, Ursprung u. Prägung des christl. Apostolates: ThZ 9, '53, 259-75. CFDMoule, Col and Phlm '57, 155-159; GKlein, Die 12 Apostel, '60; FHahn, Mission in the NT, tr. FClarke, '65; WSchmithals, The Office of the Apostle, tr. JESteely, '69. S. also ἐκκλησία, end, esp. Holl and Kattenbusch. M-M.

ἀποστοματίζω is found since Pla. (Euthyd. 276c; 277ᴀ) w. the mngs. 'teach by dictation' or 'repeat from memory' (ἀπὸ στόματος), which do not fit the context of Lk 11: 53 (note that the passage is not text-critically certain; D and Sin. Syr. differ greatly fr. the text). Here usu. transl. question closely, interrogate τινὰ περί τινος (so L-S-J s.v. I 2; cf. Pla. in Pollux 1, 102 [pass.]); but s. Wlh. ad loc. Ancient commentators interpreted it (prob. correctly) as catch (him) in someth. he says= vs. 54; then approx. watch his utterances closely. M-M.*

ἀποστρέφω fut. ἀποστρέψω; 1 aor. ἀπέστρεψα; pf. pass. ἀπέστραμμαι; 2 aor. pass. ἀπεστράφην (Hom.+; inscr., pap., LXX; En. 6, 4; Ep. Arist.; Philo; Joseph.).
  1. trans.—a. turn away τὶ ἀπό τινος (BGU 955, 1; Ex 23: 25; Job 33: 17; Pr 4: 27; Sir 4: 5 al.).
  α. lit. ἀπὸ τ. ἀληθείας τ. ἀκοὴν ἀ. turn away one's ear fr. the truth= be unwilling to listen to the truth 2 Ti 4: 4. ἀ. τὸ πρόσωπον (oft. LXX) turn away one's face 1 Cl 18: 9 (Ps 50: 11). ἀπέστραπται τὸ πρόσωπον αὐτοῦ his face is turned away 16: 3 (Is 53: 3). ἀπεστραμμένοι ἦσαν they (i.e., their faces) were turned away Hv 3, 10, 1.
  β. fig. ἀ. τὸν λαόν mislead the people, cause them to revolt Lk 23: 14 (cf. 2 Ch 18: 31; Jer 48: 10); Ac 20: 30D (foll. by ὀπίσω ἑαυτῶν). τ. γυναῖκας κ. τὰ τέκνα mislead, alienate Lk 23: 2 Marcion. τ. ὀργήν ἀπό τινος (cf. 1 Macc 3: 8) turn away wrath fr. someone Hv 4, 2, 6. ἀ. ψυχὴν εἰς τὸ σωθῆναι turn a soul to salvation 2 Cl 15: 1.

ἀποστρέψει ἀσεβείας ἀπὸ Ἰακώβ he will remove ungodliness fr. Jacob Ro 11: 26 (Is 59: 20).
  b. return, put back τὶ Mt 27: 3 t.r.; ἀ. τ. μάχαιραν εἰς τ. τόπον αὐτῆς Mt 26: 52 (cf. Jer 35: 3).
  2. intr. turn away ἀπό τινος fr. someth. (Ezk 3: 18, 19, 20; Sir 8: 5; 17: 26; Bl-D. §308; Rob. 800) Ac 3: 26; but the trans. is also poss. (cf. Job 33: 17).
  3. mid. (also 2 aor. pass.)—a. ἀ. τινά or τὶ turn away from someone or someth., reject or repudiate someone (so w. acc. since Aristoph., Pax 683; X., Cyr. 5, 5, 36; PSI 392, 11 [III ʙᴄ] ὁ δεῖνα οὐκ ἀπεστρεμμένος αὐτόν; PGM 13, 620 Σάραπι, . . . μὴ ἀποστραφῇς με; Hos 8: 3; Jer 15: 6; 3 Macc 3: 23; 4 Macc 5: 9; Ep. Arist. 236; Philo, Det. Pot. Ins. 93 al.; Jos., Ant. 4, 135; 6, 340; 20, 166) ἀ. με πάντες everybody has turned away fr. me 2 Ti 1: 15; ἀ. τὸν ἐν δεόμενον turn away fr. the needy D 4: 8; 5: 2; B 20: 2. ἀ. τὸν θέλοντα ἀπὸ σοῦ δανείσασθαι turn away fr. him who wants to borrow fr. you Mt 5: 42; ἀ. τὸν ἀπ' οὐρανῶν reject the one fr. heaven Hb 12: 25. τὴν ἀλήθειαν Tit 1: 14 (Appian, Bell. Civ. 5, 25 §99 τὴν πολιτείαν=reject the form of government; Jos., Ant. 2, 48 τὴν ἀξίωσιν; 4, 135).
  b. turn back (Heraclides Pont., fgm. 49 Wehrli: the statue of Hera ἀπεστράφη=turned around) fig. ἀπεστράφησαν ἐν τ. καρδίαις εἰς Αἴγυπτον Ac 7: 39 D. M-M.*

ἀποστροφή, ῆς, ἡ (Hdt.+; PLond. 1344, 4; LXX; Philo; Jos., Bell. 2, 212, Ant. 19, 131) turning, return πρὸς σὲ ἡ ἀ. αὐτοῦ he shall turn to you 1 Cl 4: 5 (Gen 4: 7).*

ἀποστυγέω (trag.; Hdt. 2, 47; 6, 129; Parthenius 20, 2; 36, 2) hate, abhor τὸ πονηρόν the evil (opp. κολλᾶσθαι τ. ἀγαθῷ) Ro 12: 9.*

ἀποσυνάγωγος, ον (unknown to secular writers and LXX) expelled from the synagogue, excommunicated, put under the curse or ban (חֵרֶם) ἀ. ποιεῖν expel fr. the synagogue J 16: 2; ἀ. γενέσθαι be excommunicated 9: 22; 12: 42.—Schürer II⁴ 507-9; 543f; Billerb. IV 293-333; JDöller, ZkTh 37, '13, 1-24; KLCarroll, Bulletin of the JRylands Library 40, '57, 19-32. M-M.*

ἀποσυνέχω (found only in this passage) apparently hold, keep ἑαυτὸν εἰς ὁδὸν σκότους hold to the way of darkness B 5: 4 (ensnare, tr. RAKraft, Didache and Barnabas, '65, 93).*

ἀποσύρω 1 aor. inf. ἀποσῦραι (Thu.+; 4 Macc 9: 28; Jos., Bell. 3, 243, C. Ap. 2, 114) tear or scrape the skin off τὶ someth. (Alciphr. 3, 32, 2 τὸ δέρμα τ. κεφαλῆς) MPol 8: 3.*

ἀποτάσσω 1 aor. ἀπεταξάμην in our lit. only mid., as in later usage gener. (cf. Eccl 2: 20).
  1. say farewell (to), take leave (of) τινί (Vi. Aesopi I c. 124; POxy. 298, 31 [I ᴀᴅ]; BGU 884 II, 12 [II/III ᴀᴅ]; Jos., Ant. 8, 354; cf. Nägeli 39) τοῖς ἀδελφοῖς Ac 18: 18. αὐτοῖς 2 Cor 2: 13. τοῖς εἰς τ. οἶκόν μου to my people at home Lk 9: 61; cf. Mk 6: 46. (Opp. ἀκολουθεῖν τινι) τ. ἀγγέλῳ τ. πονηρίας say farewell to the angel of wickedness Hm 6, 2, 9. τῷ βίῳ to life IPhld 11: 1 (cf. Cat. Cod. Astr. VIII 3 p. 136, 17). Abs. Ac 18: 21; 21: 15 D.
  2. fig., w. impers. obj. renounce, give up (POxy. 904; Philo, Leg. All. 3, 142 al.; cf. Rtzst., Hist. Mon. 104; Jos., Ant. 11, 232) 2 Cl 6: 4f (opp. χρᾶσθαι). ταῖς ἡδυπαθείαις 16: 2. πᾶσιν τοῖς ἑαυτοῦ ὑπάρχουσιν Lk 14: 33. M-M.*

ἀποτελέω fut. ἀποτελοῦμαι Lk 13: 32 D; 1 aor. ἀπετέ-

λεσα, pass. ἀπετελέσθην (Hdt., X.+; pap., LXX; Philo, Aet. M. 41 al., De Prov. in Euseb., Pr. Ev. 7, 21, 2).
1. *bring to completion, finish* (1 Esdr 5: 70 v.l.; Jos., C. Ap. 1, 154) of the constr. of a tower Hs 9, 5, 1f; 9, 26, 6. τὰ ῥήματα πάντα *finish all the words* v 2, 4, 2. Fig., pass. *come to completion, be fully formed* (Synesius, Dio 1 p. 36 Petavius Δίων φιλόσοφος ἀπετελέσθη) ἡ ἁμαρτία ἀποτελεσθεῖσα *sin, when it has run its course* Js 1: 15 (in the sense of being completed in action: Pla., Leg. 823D ἀ. τὰ προσταχθέντα, 7th Letter p. 336c ἀ. βουλήσεις).
2. without special reference to a beginning *perform* (Pla., Gorg. 503D; X., Cyr. 5, 1, 14; PTebt. 276, 14; 2 Macc 15: 39; Jos., C. Ap. 2, 179) ἰάσεις *cures* Lk 13: 32 (v.l. ἐπιτελῶ; for D s. above). M-M.*

ἀποτίθημι 2 aor. mid. ἀπεθέμην; 1 aor. pass. ἀπετέθην (Hom.+; inscr., pap., LXX; in our lit. the act. does not occur) *put off.*
1. *take off*—**a.** lit., of clothes (Teles p. 16, 7 ἱμάτιον; Alciphr. 3, 6, 2; 2 Macc 8: 35; Jos., Ant. 8, 266) τὰ ἱμάτια ἀ. MPol 13: 2; *take off and lay down* Ac 7: 58.
b. fig. *lay aside, rid oneself of* τὰ ἔργα τ. σκότους Ro 13: 12. ἀλαζονείαν 1 Cl 13: 1. αὐθάδειαν 57: 2. τὰς μαλακίας Hv 3, 12, 3. τὴν νέκρωσιν τ. ζωῆς s 9, 16, 2f. τὰ πάντα, ὀργὴν κτλ. Col 3: 8 (Plut., Cor. 19, 4 ὀργήν). νέφος 2 Cl 1: 6. τὸν παλαιὸν ἄνθρωπον Eph 4: 22 (w. acc. of a pers. in Callim., Epigr. 21, 6; Maximus Tyr. 1 4e in the theater ἀποθέμενος τὸν θεατὴν ἀγωνιστὴς γενέσθαι=stop being a spectator and become a contestant). τὸ ψεῦδος vs. 25. πᾶσαν ῥυπαρίαν Js 1: 21. πᾶσαν κακίαν 1 Pt 2: 1. ὄγκον πάντα καὶ τὴν ἁμαρτίαν Hb 12: 1 (of vices since Demosth. 8, 46; Lucian, Dial. Mort. 10, 8f; Ep. Arist. 122 et al. [Nägeli 20]).—αἵρεσιν *give up a way of thinking* Hs 9, 23, 5; *lose cracks* s 8, 5, 1.
2. *lay down, put away* (PFlor. 125, 2; PRyl. 125, 14; Jos., Ant. 11, 11 v.l.) a martyr's bones MPol 18: 1 (Appian, Syr. 63 §336 ἀπέθετο of the 'laying away' or 'depositing' of the remains [τὰ λείψανα] of a cremated body); rods 1 Cl 43: 2; *put back* (opp. αἴρω) stones Hs 9, 5, 4; 9, 9, 4 (cf. 1 Macc 4: 46).—ἀ. τινὰ ἐν φυλακῇ *put someone in prison* Mt 14: 3 (cf. Polyb. 24, 8, 8; Diod. S. 4, 49, 3; PEleph. 12, 2[223/2 BC] ἀποθέσθαι αὐτοὺς εἰς τ. φυλακήν; Lev 24: 12; Num 15: 34; 2 Ch 18: 26). M-M.*

ἀποτίκτω (Pla., Plut.; Artem. 1, 16; 4 Macc 13: 21; 14: 16; Philo, Virt. 139, Aet. M. 60) *bring to birth* τὰ ἀποτικτόμενα *children* born after a full-term pregnancy (in contrast to premature births or abortions) AP fgm. 3 p. 12, 31.*

ἀποτινάσσω 1 aor. ἀπετίναξα (Eur., Bacch. 253; Galen VI 821 K.; LXX) *shake off* τὶ, of a snake which has bitten a hand τὸ θηρίον εἰς τὸ πῦρ Ac 28: 5. τὸν κονιορτὸν (Amulet of Parisinus 2316 leaf 318 verso ff: Rtzst., Poim. 297f κονιορτὸν ἀποτινάξαι) ἀπὸ τ. ποδῶν ἀ. *shake the dust fr. one's feet* Lk 9: 5 (s. on ἐκτινάσσω 1).*

ἀποτίνω fut. ἀποτίσω (Hom.+; inscr. [Dit., Syll. Ind.]; pap. [POxy. 275, 27 and oft. in pap.; OGradenwitz, Einführg. in die Pap.kunde '00, 85]; LXX; Jos., Ant. 4, 282, Vi. 298; Sib. Or. 5, 191) legal t.t. *make compensation, pay the damages* abs. ἐγὼ ἀποτίσω (better ἀποτείσω, Bl-D. §23) *I will pay the damages* (BGU 759, 23 and oft. PPetr.) Phlm 19. M-M. B. 796f.*

ἀποτολμάω (Thu.+; Polyb.; Diod. S.; Plut.; Dit., Syll.³ 1169, 94; PLond. 1343, 42; Philo, Post. Cai. 42; Jos., C. Ap. 2, 180) *be bold* abs. Ἡσαΐας ἀποτολμᾷ καὶ λέγει *Isaiah is so bold as to say* Ro 10: 20 (cf. Demosth. 19, 199 τολμήσει. . . καὶ ἐρεῖ).*

ἀποτομία, ας, ἡ (Diod. S. 12, 16, 3; Dionys. Hal. 8, 61; Plut., Mor. 13D τὴν ἀ. τῇ πραότητι μιγνύναι; Ps.-Demetrius, Eloc. 292 Roberts; POxy. 237 VII, 40; BGU 1024 V, 13; Na 3: 1 Sym.; Philo, Spec. Leg. 2, 94, In Flacc. 95) *severity* (opp. χρηστότης) ἀ. θεοῦ Ro 11: 22. M-M.*

ἀπότομος, ον (Soph., Hdt.+; LXX) *relentless* ἐν κρίσει *in judgment* Pol 6: 1 (cf. in this fig. mng. [lit. 'steep'] Wsd 6: 5 al.; Diod. S. 1, 76, 1; 2, 57, 5; Περὶ ὕψους 27, 1 ἀπειλή; Jos., Ant. 19, 329 τιμωρία).*

ἀποτόμως adv. (Isocr.+; Polyb. 18, 11, 2; Plut., Mor. 131c; Cic., Att. 10, 11, 5; Wsd 5: 22) *severely, rigorously* ἔλεγχε αὐτοὺς ἀ. *correct them rigorously* Tit 1: 13. ἵνα μὴ ἀ. χρήσωμαι=ἀποτομίᾳ χρ. *that I may not have to deal sharply* 2 Cor 13: 10. M-M.*

ἀποτρέπω pres. mid. imper. ἀποτρέπου (Hom.+; Jos., Bell. 3, 500, Ant. 18, 283; Third Corinthians 3: 21, 39) mid. *turn away from, avoid* w. acc. (so trag., Polyb., Plut. [Nägeli 25]; 4 Macc 1: 33) 2 Ti 3: 5. M-M.*

ἀποτρέχω (Hdt.+; inscr., pap., LXX; En. 107, 2) *hurry* (lit. *run*) *away* Hv 3, 3, 1.*

ἀποτυγχάνω 2 aor. subj. ἀποτύχω (Hippocr., X., Pla.+; pap.; Job 31: 16; Test. 12 Patr.; Ep. Arist. 191; 192) *fail, have no success* w. gen. (Diod. S. 1, 75, 3 τῆς προαιρέσεως =in the intention; Appian, Hann. 43, §183 τ. πείρας=in the attempt; PSI 96, 5 τ. παρακλήσεως; Jos., Ant. 19, 289) ἡ διψυχία πάντων ἀ. τῶν ἔργων αὐτῆς *double-mindedness fails in all its works* Hm 9: 10; cf. 10, 2, 2. W. inf. foll. τοῦ πεῖσαι αὐτόν *they failed to persuade him* MPol 8: 3.*

ἀποτυφλόω (Aristot.; Diod. S. 3, 37, 9; Plut., Arat. 10, 4, Mor. 1107c; LXX lit. and fig.) *to blind* pass., fig. (Epict. 1, 16, 19) ἀ. ἀπὸ τ. διανοίας τ. ἀγαθῆς *be blinded and cease to have good intentions* Hm 5, 2, 7.*

ἀπουσία, ας, ἡ (Aeschyl., Thu., Plut. [Nägeli 16]; Philo, Leg. All. 3, 113; Jos., Ant. 2, 56; PAmh. 135, 5 [II AD]; BGU 195, 38; 242, 8) *absence* ἐν τῇ ἀ. μου *while I am absent* Phil 2: 12 (opp. παρουσία as Aristoxenus, fgm. 37; Ps.-Demetr., Form. Ep. p. 12, 15f). M-M.*

ἀποφαίνομαι (Pind., Hdt.+; inscr., pap., LXX, Ep. Arist.; Jos., Ant. 11, 37) *show, declare, pronounce* (some creature) θεόν Dg 3: 3.*

ἀποφέρω aor. ἀπήνεγκα, inf. ἀπενεγκεῖν; 1 aor. pass. ἀπηνέχθην (Hom.+; inscr., pap., LXX).
1. act.—**a.** *carry away, take away*—**α.** someone or someth. to a place Lk 16: 22; Hv 3, 10, 1ab; s 9, 4, 7; 9, 8, 3; 9, 9, 5f. Of being transported in or by the spirit Rv 17: 3; cf. 21: 10; Hv 1, 1, 3; 2, 1, 1; GH 5.
β. *lead away* by force (POxy. 37 I, 18; BGU 22, 29ff; Da 11: 8) of a prisoner Mk 15: 1; J 21: 18 v.l.
b. *take, bring* someth. fr. one place to another ἀ. τὴν χάριν ὑμῶν εἰς Ἱερουσαλήμ *take your gift to Jer.* 1 Cor 16: 3. τὶ ἐπί τινα Ac 19: 12; or τινί Lk 19: 24 D.
2. mid.—**a.** *carry off, win* (Diod. S. 4, 76, 5 δόξαν; Jos., Ant. 4, 234) βραβεῖον a prize MPol 17: 1 (Thu.+ in sim. connections; Diod. S. 17, 6, 1 τὸ πρωτεῖον ἀπηνέγκατο; Lev 20: 19; Ep. Arist. 39; Jos., Vi. 360).—**b.** *take away* by force Hs 9, 21, 4. M-M.*

ἀποφεύγω 2 aor. ἀπέφυγον (Pind., Hdt.+; PRyl. 77, 39 [192 AD]; Sir 22: 22).
1. *escape, escape from* w. acc. of pers. or thing fr. which one escapes (Alex. Aphr. Fat. 8 II 2 p. 173, 9) 2 Pt 2: 18, 20. W. gen. of the thing (cf. Aesop 80d, 8 Chambry v.l.

τούτων ἐκφεύγειν; Third Corinthians 3: 21) τῆς ἐν τ. κόσμῳ ἐν ἐπιθυμίᾳ φθορᾶς *from the destruction in the world caused by desire* 1: 4.

2. *avoid, shun* τινά someone Hm 11: 13 (opp. ἐγγίζειν). M-M.*

ἀποφθέγγομαι *speak out, declare* boldly or loudly (of the speech of the wise man Diog. L. 1, 63; 73; 79; but also of the oracle-giver, diviner, prophet, exorcist, and other 'inspired' persons Diod. S. 16, 27, 1; Plut., Pyth. Or. 23 [Mor. 405ᴇ]; Vett. Val. 73, 24; 112, 15; 113, 1; Philostrat., Vi. Apollon. 1, 19 p. 20, 7; Mi 5: 11; Zech 10: 2; Ezk 13: 9, 19; Philo, Mos. 2, 33) τὶ: σωφροσύνης ῥήματα Ac 26: 25; ἀ. τινι *declare to someone w. enthusiasm* 2: 14, also abs. vs. 4. M-M.*

ἀποφορτίζομαι nautical t.t. (fig. Jos., Bell. 1, 172; 266), mostly of 'jettisoning' the cargo in a storm (Athen. 2, 5 p. 37cf; Philo, Praem. 33; Pollux 1, 99), but also of regular unloading (Dionys. Hal. 3, 44 αἱ μείζους νῆες ἀπογεμίζονται καὶ ἀποφορτίζονται σκάφαις) *unload* τ. γόμον *the cargo* Ac 21: 3 (Mod. Gk. ἀποφορτώνω).*

ἀπόχρησις, εως, ἡ *consuming, using up* (so Dionys. Hal. 1, 58; Plut., Mor. 267ꜰ; PStrassb. 35, 6.—ἀποχράομαι Polyb. 1, 45, 2; PHib. 52, 7 [c. 245 ʙᴄ]) ἐστὶν εἰς φθορὰν τῇ ἀποχρήσει *are meant for destruction by being consumed* (εἰς κόπρον γὰρ ἅπαντα μεταβάλλεται Theodoret III p. 491 N.) Col 2: 22. M-M.*

ἀποχωρέω 1 aor. ἀπεχώρησα (Eur., Thu.+; pap., LXX; Jos., Bell. 1, 24, Ant. 1, 261) *go away* ἀπό τινος *fr. someone* Hv 3, 6, 3. Also more strongly in the sense *leave, desert* (Sb. 7835, 14 [I ʙᴄ] ἀ. ἐκ . . . εἰς=desert from . . . to; 3 Macc 2: 33) Ac 13: 13 or *depart* (Jer 26: 5; 2 Macc 4: 33) ἀποχωρεῖτε ἀπ᾽ ἐμοῦ *depart from me!* Mt 7: 23 (Vi. Aesopi Ic, 6 p. 239, 19 ἀποχώρει=away w. you!), also of defeated opponents (Jos., Ant. 15, 149) Lk 20: 20 v.l. Of spirits *withdraw fr. someone* Lk 9: 39. Hm 5, 2, 6; of the devil m 12, 5, 4. M-M.*

ἀποχωρίζω 1 aor. pass. ἀπεχωρίσθην (Pla.+; pap.; Ezk 43: 21) *separate* Mt 19: 6 D.—Pass. *be separated* ἀπό τινος (PLond. 1731, 11) Ac 15: 39. ὁ οὐρανὸς ἀπεχωρίσθη *the sky was split* Rv 6: 14 (cf. Boll 17. 9, 1).*

ἀποψύχω *breathe out, stop breathing,* hence either *faint* (Od. 24, 348) or *die* (Soph., Thu.+; 4 Macc 15: 18; Philo, Aet. M. 128; Jos., Ant. 19, 114) ἀπὸ φόβου *of* or *from fear* Lk 21: 26.*

Ἀππίου φόρον *Appii Forum, the Forum of Appius,* a market town on the Appian Way, 43 Rom. miles fr. Rome (CIL X 6825; Itin. Anton. p. 107 Wess.); acc. to Horace, Sat. I 5, 1ff, full of sailors and rascals; cf. Cicero, Ad Att. 2, 10. Paul was met there on his journey to Rome by some fellow-Christians Ac 28: 15.*

ἀπρεπής, ές *not fitting* (fig. Thu.; Lucian, Dial. Deor. 13, 1; Aelian, V.H. 14, 19; PAmh. 142, 8; 4 Macc 6: 17; Philo, Cher. 92; Jos., Ant. 18, 314, Vi. 146) lit. (Artem. 2, 3 p. 88, 6 ἀ. ἐσθῆτες) λίθοι ἀ. ἐν τ. οἰκοδομῇ *stones that are not suitable for the building* Hs 9, 4, 6f.*

ἀπροσδεής, ές (H. Gk.) *needing nothing, self-sufficient* of God (Philod., περὶ θεῶν [ed. H. Diels, ABA '16f] 3, 13; Plut., Aristid. et Cat. 4, 2; 2 Macc 14: 35; 3 Macc 2: 9; Ep. Arist. 211; Philo, Deus Imm. 56; Jos., Ant. 8, 111) 1 Cl 52: 1 (cf. Norden, Agn. Th. 13f).*

ἀπροσδόκητος, ον (Aeschyl., Hdt.+; Dit., Syll.³ 742, 9; 814, 9; PFay. 19, 3; Wsd 17: 14; 3 Macc 3: 8 al.; Philo, De

Prov. in Euseb., Pr. Ev. 8, 14, 60; Jos., Ant. 12, 308) *unexpected* ἀ. εὐεργεσίαι Dg 9: 5.*

ἀπρόσιτος, ον (since Ctesias, Pers. 41; Polyb. 3, 49, 7; Diod. S. 1, 32, 1; Dio Chrys. 13[7], 51; Lucian; Philo, Mos. 2, 70; Jos., Bell. 7, 280, Ant. 3, 76) *unapproachable* of God φῶς οἰκεῖν ἀπρόσιτον *dwell in unapproachable light* 1 Ti 6: 16.*

ἀπρόσκοπος, ον *without offense*—1. *undamaged, blameless* (PGiess. 17, 7; 22, 9; Ep. Arist. 210) w. εἰλικρινής: ἀ. εἰς ἡμέραν Χριστοῦ *blameless for the day of Christ* Phil 1: 10; ἀ. συνείδησις *a clear conscience* Ac 24: 16.

2. *giving no offense* (Sext. Emp., Math. 1, 195; Sir 32: 21) ἀ. τινι γίνεσθαι 1 Cor 10: 32. Cf. Nägeli 43. M-M and suppl.*

ἀπροσκόπως adv. (PGiess. 79 IV, 8 ἀπροσκόπως ἐξέλθωμεν ἀπ᾽ αὐτῶν) *without stumbling* (w. ὁμαλῶς) περιπατεῖν Hm 6, 1, 4; *without disturbance* λειτουργίαν ἐπιτελεῖν 1 Cl 20: 10; *blamelessly* διέπειν τ. ἡγεμονίαν 61: 1.*

ἀπροσωπολήμπτως adv. (on the form -λημπ- cf. W-S. §5, 30; Reinhold §7) (-λημπτος Cosmas and Dam. 1, 17) *impartially* κρίνειν 1 Pt 1: 17; B 4: 12; ἀ. πάντα ποιεῖν 1 Cl 1: 3. Cf. προσωπολημπτέω, -λήμπτης, -λημψία, πρόσωπον λαμβάνειν. M-M.*

ἄπταιστος, ον (X., Equ. 1, 6+ [of a horse]; fig., Epict. [Stob., Flor. 9, 44] no. 52 p. 475 Sch.; M. Ant. 5, 9, 5; Vett. Val. Ind.; 3 Macc 6: 39; Ep. Arist. 187; Philo, Agr. 177, Ebr. 199; Sib. Or. 3, 289) *without stumbling* φυλάξαι ὑμᾶς ἀ. *keep you from stumbling* Jd 24.*

ἄπτω 1 aor. ἧψα, ptc. ἅψας; 1 aor. mid. ἡψάμην (Hom.+; inscr., pap., LXX).

1. *light, kindle* (Aeschyl., Hdt.; PGM 7, 543; POxy. 1297, 4; 7; 13; Joseph.) λύχνον ἄ. (Herodas 8, 6; Epict. 1, 20, 19; Diog. L. 6, 41; Philo, Gig. 33 [mid.]; Jos., Ant. 3, 199) Lk 8: 16; 11: 33; 15: 8. ἄ. πῦρ *kindle a fire* (Eur., Hel. 503; Phalaris, Ep. 122, 2; Jdth 13: 13; Jos., Ant. 4, 55) Lk 22: 55 t.r. (v.l. πυράν). Ac 28: 2. Pass. Mk 4: 21 v.l. (cf. PGM 13, 683 λύχνους ἡμμένους).

2. mid. *touch, take hold of, hold* τινός someone or someth. (Hom.+; Jos., Ant. 6, 308).

a. lit. Lk 7: 39; IRo 5: 2. Dg 12: 8. MPol 13: 2. Hs 1: 11; the sky by throwing a stone m 11: 18. μή μου ἅπτου *stop clinging to me!* (cf. BHaensler, BZ 11, '13, 172-7; K Kastner, ibid. 13, '15, 344-53; KRösch, ibid. 14, '17, 333-7; BViolet, ZNW 24, '25, 78-80; FPerles, ibid. 25, '26, 287; WEPCotter, ET 43, '32, 45f; TNicklin, ibid. 51, '39/'40, 478; JMaiworm, ThGl '38, 540-6) J 20: 17 (Arrian, Anab. 6, 13, 3: Alexander has been severely wounded in the chest by an arrow and his soldiers cannot believe that he is still alive. When he appears among them, recovered from his wound, they take hold [ἁπτόμενοι] of his hands, knees, and clothing in astonishment and delight); cf. GH 22=ISm 3: 2.—Of intercourse w. a woman (Pla., Leg. 8, 840ᴀ; Plut., Alex. M. 21, 9; M. Ant. 1, 17, 13; Jos., Ant. 1, 163; Gen 20: 6; Pr 6: 29) γυναικὸς μὴ ἅ. 1 Cor 7: 1 (ἅπτεσθαι w. gen. of 'touching' a woman in general: Vi. Aesopi I c. 103).—Of contact w. unclean things 2 Cor 6: 17 (Num 16: 26; Is 52: 11). The abs. μὴ ἅψῃ *you must not touch* or *handle* Col 2: 21 can be interpreted in this sense. On the other hand, ἅπτεσθαι can mean *eat,* like our 'touch food' (Od. 4, 60; Plut., Anton. 17 [923]; Charito 6, 2, 8 οὐχ ἥπτετο τροφῆς; Aelian, V.H. 12, 37 ἐπ᾽ ἀπορίᾳ τροφῶν ἥψατο τῶν καμήλων=he seized [and ate] the camels; Diog. L. 6, 73 κρεῶν; Philostrat., Vi. Apoll. 3, 27 p. 105, 9; Philo, Exs.

134; Jos., Ant. 4, 234; 8, 362; 13, 276). We would then have in this passage the anticlimax *eat, taste, touch.* Finally, θιγγάνω, like ἄπτ. and γεύομαι (q.v. 1) can mean *eat* (cf. Iambl., Vi. Pyth. 31, 191 κυάμων μὴ θιγγάνειν; 13, 61 γεύεσθαι=Porphyr., Vi. Pyth. 24 θιγγάνειν; POxy. 1185, 10f [c. 200 AD], where three diff. expr. for 'eat' are grouped together: τὸν παῖδα· δεῖ ἄρτον ἐσθίειν, ἅλας ἐπιτρώγειν, ὀψαρίου μὴ θιγγάνειν; [eat, eat [with], not eat at all]). The combination ἐσθ., τρωγ., θιγγ. might corresp. to Col 2: 21 ἅπτ., γεύ., θιγγ., taken to mean *eat, enjoy, consume* (ἅ. and γεύ. together, both='eat' in Teles p. 34, 5). The verbs perh. connected w. var. foods (s. POxy.) by the false spirits are effectively combined by Paul, in order to picture the feeling of dread which he castigates.— *Touch* someone's chest, spontaneously, of one who is speaking Hv 1, 4, 2; cf. 3, 1, 6. Fig. οὐ μὴ ἅψηταί σου κακόν *no evil shall touch you* 1 Cl 56: 8 (Job 5: 19).

b. freq. of touching as a means of conveying a blessing (divine working by a touch of the hand: Anton. Lib. 4, 7 Ἀπόλλων ἁψάμενος αὐτοῦ τῇ χειρὶ πέτρον ἐποίησεν; Ps.-Apollod. 2, 1, 3, 1 Zeus transforms by touching [ἅπτεσθαι]) Mk 10: 13; Lk 18: 15 (here perh. *hold*). Esp. to bring about a healing (Dit., Syll.³ 1169, 62). Gener. of touching persons who are ill Mt 8: 3; 17: 7; Mk 1: 41; 8: 22; Lk 5: 13. ἅψαι αὐτῆς ἐκ τ. χειρῶν σου Mk 5: 23 D. Esp. of touching parts of the body (Dit., Syll.³ 1170, 23 ἡψάτό μου τῆς δεξιᾶς χιρός) τ. γλώσσης (cf. Philo, De Prov. in Euseb., Pr. Ev. 8, 14, 18) Mk 7: 33. τ. ὀφθαλμῶν Mt 9: 29; cf. 20: 34; 8: 15; Lk 22: 51. Likew. τῆς σοροῦ *touch the coffin,* if the purpose was to raise the dead man, not simply to halt the bearers (cf. Aphrodite touching a chariot Pind., Pyth. 9, 11) Lk 7: 14. Of those who are ill, touching the healer Mk 3: 10; 6: 56; Lk 6: 19; 8: 45ff. Also of touching the clothes of the healer (cf. Athen. 5 p. 212ϝ ἐκάστου σπεύδοντος κἂν προσάψασθαι τῆς ἐσθῆτος) ἅ. τ. ἱματίου *touch his cloak* Mt 9: 21; Mk 5: 27; 6: 56. τ. ἱματίων 5: 28, 30f. τ. κρασπέδου *the hem* or *tassel* Mt 9: 20; 14: 36; Lk 8: 44.

c. fig. *take hold of* τ. βασιλείας *the Kingdom* B 7: 11.—JBBauer, Agraphon 90 Resch, ZNW 62, '71, 301–3.

d. *touch* for the purpose of harming, *injure* (Diod. S. 1, 84; Arrian, Alex. Anab. 4, 4, 2 AGRoos ['07]; Ps 104: 15; 1 Ch 16: 22; Zech 2: 12) ὁ πονηρὸς οὐχ ἅπτεται αὐτοῦ *the evil one cannot harm him* (or *cannot even touch him;* cf. 1 Esdr 4: 28 and s. above a., at end) 1 J 5: 18.—OWHeick, Hapto in the NT: Luth. Church Quart. 12, '39, 90–5. M-M. B 76; 1061.*

Ἀπφία, ας, ἡ (a name freq. found in western Asia Minor [KBuresch, Aus Lydien 1898, 44; Lghtf., Col. and Phlm. 304f; Thieme 9; 39], also in Colossae, CIG III p. 1168 No. 4380κ, 3) *Apphia,* the name of a Christian woman, prob. wife of Philemon, at Colossae, Phlm 2; inscr. v.l.; subscr. v.l. M-M.*

ἀπωθέω 1 aor. ἀπωσάμην (Hom.+; PFay. 124, 19 al. in pap.; LXX; Philo, Aet. M. 74; Joseph.) in our lit. only mid. *push aside.*

1. lit., w. acc. (4 Km 4: 27; Jos., Ant. 17, 91) ἀπώσατο αὐτόν *he pushed him aside* Ac 7: 27 (like POxy. 1206, 10).

2. fig., *reject, repudiate* (sc. Moses) Ac 7: 39. τὶ *something* (Appian, Syr. 5 §21; Quint. Smyrn. 9, 96) the word of God (Jer 23: 17) 13: 46; a good conscience 1 Ti 1: 19 (cf. Jos., Ant. 4, 123). Esp. of God: *repudiate* the people Israel Ro 11: 1f (Ps 93: 14; cf. 94: 4 v.l. and oft. in LXX); of men gener. Dg 9: 2. τινὰ ἀπό τινος (Ps 118: 10) *force someone out of someth.* B 4: 13. M-M.*

ἀπώλεια, ας, ἡ (Demades [IV BC] in the sense 'loss'; later

writers; inscr., pap., oft. LXX; En.; Test. 12 Patr.) *destruction.*

1. trans., the *destruction* that one causes, *waste* (Polyb. 6, 11a, 10 opp. τήρησις; PTebt. 276, 34) εἰς τί ἡ ἀ. αὕτη τ. μύρου; *why this waste of the ointment?* Mk 14: 4; cf. Mt 26: 8.

2. intrans. the *destruction* that one experiences, *annihilation* both complete and in process, *ruin* (so usu. LXX; Ep. Arist. 167; Philo, Aet. M. 20; 74; Jos., Ant. 15, 62, Vi. 272; Test. Dan 4: 5; but also in Polyb., Plut., Epict. et al. [Nägeli 35]; Diod. S. 15, 48, 1 with φθορά; Herm. Wr. 12, 16; PGM 4, 1247f παραδίδωμι σε εἰς τὸ μέλαν χάος ἐν τ. ἀπωλείαις) Ac 25: 16 t.r.; (w. ὄλεθρον) βυθίζειν εἰς ὄ. καὶ ἀ. *plunge into utter destruction* 1 Ti 6: 9; εἶναι εἰς ἀ. *perish* Ac 8: 20 (Da 2: 5 and 3: 96 Theod.); πρὸς τ. ἰδίαν αὐτῶν ἀ. *to their own ruin* 2 Pt 3: 16; (w. πλάνη) 2 Cl 1: 7. Esp. of eternal destruction as punishment for the wicked: Mt 7: 13; εἰς ἀ. ὑπάγειν *go to destr.* Rv 17: 8, 11. (Opp. περιποίησις ψυχῆς) Hb 10: 39. (Opp. σωτηρία) Phil 1: 28. ἡμέρα κρίσεως καὶ ἀπωλείας (Job 21: 30) τ. ἀσεβῶν ἀνθρώπων *day of judgment and* (consequent) *destruction of wicked men* 2 Pt 3: 7. Hence the end of the wicked is described as ἀ. Phil 3: 19. σκεύη ὀργῆς, κατηρτισμένα εἰς ἀ. *objects of* (his) *anger, ready for destruction* Ro 9: 22 (Is 54: 16). It will come quickly 2 Pt 2: 1, is not sleeping vs. 3. Appears as a consequence of death (cf. Job 28, 22): ὁ θάνατος ἀ. ἔχει αἰώνιον Hs 6, 2, 4; God laughs at it 1 Cl 57: 4 (Pr 1: 26). Those destined to destruction are υἱοὶ τῆς ἀ. J 17: 12; AP 1: 2. The Antichrist is also υἱὸς τῆς ἀ. 2 Th 2: 3. αἱρέσεις ἀπωλείας *heresies that lead to destr.* 2 Pt 2: 1; δόγματα τῆς ἀ. AP 1: 1. M-M.*

ἀπώλεσε, ἀπώλετο s. ἀπόλλυμι.

ἀπωσάμην s. ἀπωθέω.

Ἄρ s. Ἀρμαγεδ(δ)ών.

ἀρά, ᾶς, ἡ (Hom.+; Dit., Or. 383, 236; Inschr. v. Magn. 105, 53; LXX; Philo; Jos., Ant. 17, 3 and 88, Vi. 101) *curse* (w. πικρία) τὸ στόμα ἀρᾶς γέμει Ro 3: 14 (Ps 9: 28; 13: 3). M-M.*

ἄρα (Hom.+ [cf. Kühner-G. II p. 317ff]; inscr., pap., LXX) inferential (illative) particle; in class. usage never at the beginning of its clause. Strengthened to ἄρα γε Gen 26: 9; Mt 7: 20; 17: 26; Ac 17: 27.—Rob. 1189f and index.

1. *so, then, consequently, you see* (Bl-D. §451, 2) εὑρίσκω ἄ. τὸν νόμον so I find the law Ro 7: 21. οὐδὲν ἄρα νῦν κατάκριμα so there is no condemnation now 8: 1. γινώσκετε ἄρα you may be sure, then Gal 3: 7. After ἐπεί: for otherwise (Bl-D. 456, 3) 1 Cor 5: 10; 7: 14. After εἰ: if then, if on the other hand (Dit., Syll.³ 834, 12; Gen 18: 3; cf. Bl-D. §454, 2 app.) 15: 15 (εἴπερ ἄρα—really is also poss. here); Hv 3, 4, 3; 3, 7, 5; s 6, 4, 1; 8, 3, 3; 9, 5, 7.

2. freq. in questions which draw an inference fr. what precedes; but oft. simply to enliven the question (Jos., Ant. 6, 200; Bl-D. §440, 2 w. app.) τίς ἄρα who then Mt 18: 1; 19: 25; 24: ▓▓▓▓ Lk 8: 25; 12: 42; 22: 23. τί ἄ. what then ▓▓▓▓ 66; Ac 12: 18; Hm 11: 2. εἰ ἄρα then (X▓▓▓▓ t.r.; οὐκ ἄ. are you *not,* then A▓▓▓ After οὖν 1 Cl 35: 3; B 15: ▓▓▓ (PPetr▓▓▓▓ ▓▓ ἄ. whether (perhaps) ▓▓: 13; Ac 5: 8D; 8: 22; 17:▓▓▓

3. in th▓▓▓▓▓▓ conditional sentences, to emphasize the result, *then, as a result* (Herm. Wr. 11, 13 ed. Nock; Bl-D. §451, 2d) Mt 12: 28; Lk 11: 20; 1 Cor 15: 14; 2 Cor 5: 14; Gal ▓: 21; 3: 29; 5: 11; Hb 12: 8; 2 Cl 14: 4; B 6: 19;

IEph 8: 1. Also 1 Cor 15: 18 ἅ. is used to emphasize a further result, and continues the apodosis of vs. 17.

4. at the beg. of a sentence: *so, as a result, consequently* Mt 7: 20; 17: 26; Lk 11: 48; Ro 10: 17; 2 Cor 7: 12; Hb 4: 9. Strengthened to ἄρα οὖν (never elided) *so then*; here ἄ. expresses the inference and οὖν the transition Ro 5: 18; 7: 3, 25 (s. ἄρα); 8: 12; 9: 16, 18; 14: 12, 19; Gal 6: 10; Eph 2: 19; 1 Th 5: 6; 2 Th 2: 15; 2 Cl 8: 6; 14: 3; B 9: 6; 10: 2; ITr 10.—KWClark, FWGingrich-Festschr., ed. EHBarth and RECocroft, '72, 70-84: in addition to its inferential mng., ἄρα is employed in the context of the tentative, the uncertain, the unresolved, the contingent, e.g. *perhaps* Ac 17: 27; *possibly* 12: 18; *conceivably* Mk 4: 41, or it may be rendered by a phrase: *would you say?* Mt 24: 45 and others. Good survey from LXX to Mod. Gk. M-M.*

ἆρα (Pind.+ [cf. Kühner-G. II p. 527f]; POxy. 33 IV, 7; 120 II, 10; in Sym. more oft. than in the other transl. of the OT) interrog. particle indicating anxiety or impatience, introducing only direct questions (Bl-D. §440, 2 w. app.; Rob. 1176); usu. incapable of direct transl. ἆ. εὑρήσει τ. πίστιν; *will he find faith?* Lk 18: 8; ἆ. Χριστὸς ἁμαρτίας διάκονος; *is Christ, then, a servant of sin?* Gal 2: 17 (s. Bl-D., loc. cit.). In a question which forms the apodosis of a conditional sentence Hm 4, 1, 4. Strengthened ἆρά γε (Aristoph., X.+; Gen 37: 10; Jer 4: 10 Swete; Jos., Bell. 6, 330) Ac 8: 30; Dg 7: 3. Zahn, Komm. 370f, also takes Ro 7: 25 (s. ἄρα 4) as a question: ἆρα οὖν; (Περὶ ὕψους 33, 4; Ael. Aristid. 32 p. 607 D. [twice]; 34 p. 660; 39 p. 745; Maximus Tyr. 8, 6c; Jos., C. Ap. 2, 232). M-M.*

Ἀραβία, ας, ἡ (Hdt. 3, 107 et al.; Ep. Arist. 119; Philo; Joseph. On Ἀ. w. and without the art. cf. Bl-D. §261, 6 app.; PFlor. 278 στρατηγῷ Ἀραβίας) *Arabia* as a geogr. concept includes the territory west of Mesopotamia, east and south of Syria and Palestine, to the isthmus of Suez. In Roman times independent kingdoms arose like that of the Nabataeans south of Damascus, which could be called simply Arabia (Diod. S. 19, 94, 1 χώρα τῶν Ἀράβων τῶν καλουμένων Ναβαταίων; Stephan. Byz. s.v. Γοαρήνη: χώρα Ἀραβίας πλησίον Δαμασκοῦ; Appian, Bell. Civ. 2, 71 §294 describes Ἄραβες and Ἑβραῖοι as neighbors), and is regularly so called by Joseph. This seems to have been the country visited by Paul after his conversion Gal 1: 17 (CWBriggs, The Ap. Paul in Arabia: Biblical World 41, '13, 255-9). Of Arabia in the narrower sense, w. special ref. to the Sinai peninsula Gal 4: 25. As the home of the phoenix 1 Cl 25: 1.—BMoritz, Arabien '23; HSPhilby, Arabia '30; JMontgomery, A. and the Bible '34. M-M.*

Ἀραβικός, ή, όν (Diod. S. 19, 94, 4; Diosc. 1, 17; Plut., Anton. 69, 4; PGenève 29, 8 [II AD]; Jos., Bell. 1, 267, Ant. 16, 288) *Arabian* ἡ Ἀ. χώρα *Arabia* 1 Cl 25: 3.*

Ἄραβοι Ac 2: 11D could have been wrongly formed fr. the gen. pl. Ἀράβων (Appian, Syr. 51 §257 ἐξ Ἀράβων; Ps 71: 10; Ep. Arist. 114; Jos., Ant. 2, §213) of Ἄραψ (q.v.), perh. as ἅλα fr. ἅλατος (s. ἅλας, be⬛⬛⬛

ἀραβών s. ἀρραβών.

ἄραγε s. ἄρα.

ἆραι s. αἴρω.

Ἀράμ (רָם), ὁ inde⬛. Ara⬛⬛⬛⬛⬛⬛1: 3f; Lk 3: 33 t.r. (cf. 1 Ch 2: 9f⬛

ἄραφος, ον (ἄρραφος.—Galen, De Usu Part. II 177, 18; 179, 14 Helmreich of bones=without sutures) *seamless* J 19: 23 (cf. Jos., Ant. 3, 161 the high priest's χιτών is not

ραπτός).—PRieger, Versuch e. Technologie u. Terminol. d. Handwerke in d. Mischna, Diss. Bresl. 1894, 36ff; FCConybeare, Exp. IX '04, 458-60; JRepond, Le costume du Christ: Biblica 3, '22, 3-14; Bultmann, J 519, 10.*

Ἄραψ, βος, ὁ an *Arab* (Strabo 1, 2, 34; Appian, Syr. 51 §256; UPZ 72, 2 [152 BC]; Ep. Arist. 114; Philo; Sib. Or.; oft. Joseph.) Ac 2: 11 (s. Κρής); B 9: 6.*

ἀργέω 1 aor. ἤργησα (Soph., Hippocr.+; pap. fr. PPetr. II 4[9], 4 [225/4 BC] on; LXX; Jos., C. Ap. 2, 282) *be idle, grow weary* (w. ἐγκαταλείπειν) ἀπὸ τῆς ἀγαθοποιΐας 1 Cl 33: 1. Abs. (Agatharchides in Jos., C. Ap. 1, 209) τὸ κρίμα ἔκπαλαι οὐκ ἀργεῖ *from ancient times (their) condemnation has not been idle* i.e., it is being prepared 2 Pt 2: 3 (cf. 1 Esdr 2: 26 [30] ἤργει ἡ οἰκοδομή=the construction was delayed). M-M.*

ἀργός, ή, όν (Aeschyl., Hdt.+; Herm. Wr. 11, 5; inscr., pap., LXX; Philo; Joseph.; on the number of endings cf. Nägeli 31).

1. *unemployed, idle, w. nothing to do* (BGU 1078, 6ff [39 AD] οὐ γὰρ ἀργὸν δεῖ με καθῆσθαι). Of men in the market-place Mt 20: 3, 6 (Aesop, Fab. 291 P.=Babr. 20 ἀργὸς εἱστήκει=stood idle). μὴ ἀ. μεθ' ὑμῶν ζήσεται Χριστιανός D 12: 4.

2. *idle, lazy* (Sir 37: 11) 1 Cl 34: 4; of widows 1 Ti 5: 13ab. ἀ. πρὸς τ. ἔντευξιν *neglectful of, careless in prayer* Hs 5, 4, 3f (ἀ. πρός τι as Vi. Aesopi I c. 15 p. 268, 2; Wsd 15: 15). ὄρνεα ἀ. καθήμενα B 10: 4. Of Cretans γαστέρες ἀργαί *lazy gluttons* Tit 1: 12 (fr. Epimenides? cf. Vorsokr.⁵ I p. 31f; s. MDibelius, Hdb. ad loc.—With this unfavorable description of persons cf. Diod. S. 19, 41, 1 ὦ κακαὶ κεφαλαί).

3. *useless, unproductive* (Dit., Syll.³ 884, 23f; PAmh. 97, 9f; Wsd 14: 5; 15: 15; Philo, Spec. Leg. 2, 86; 88; Jos., Ant. 12, 378) ἡ πίστις χωρὶς τ. ἔργων ἀ. ἐστιν *faith without deeds is useless* Js 2: 20 (νεκρά v.l. and κενή 𝔓⁷⁴); ἀ. εἰς τ. Χριστοῦ ἐπίγνωσιν (w. ἄκαρπος) 2 Pt 1: 8 (cf. Ode of Solomon 11, 23); ῥῆμα ἀ. *a careless word* which, because of its worthlessness, had better been left unspoken (Pythagoras in Stob., Flor. III 34, 11 p. 684 W. αἱρετώτερόν σοι ἔστω λίθον εἰκῇ βαλεῖν ἢ λόγον ἀργόν; cf. Jos., Ant. 15, 224) Mt 12: 36 (EbNestle; Jülicher, Gleichn. 126; JViteau, La Vie spirituelle '31, 16-28: abuse, slander; EStauffer, Von jedem unnützen Wort, EFascher-Festschr., '58, 94-102). M-M. B. 315.*

ἀργύρεος s. ἀργυροῦς.

ἀργύριον, ου, τό (Hdt., Aristoph.+; inscr., pap., LXX, Ep. Arist.; Jos., Vi. 199 al.; Test. 12 Patr.) *silver*.

1. *as a material* 1 Cor 3: 12 (s. ἄργυρος).—**2.** *as money* —**a.** silver money beside gold (Gen 24: 35; Num 31: 22 al.; En. 97, 8; 98, 2; Jos., Ant. 15, 5) Ac 3: 6; 20: 33; cf. 1 Pt 1: 18. ᾧ ὠνήσατο Ἀβραὰμ τιμῆς ἀργυρίου *which Abraham had bought for a sum of silver* Ac 7: 16 (cf. Gen 23: 16).

b. *money* gener. (Gen 42: 25, 35; Aristoph., Plut. 131; Appian, Artem. 1, 2 p. 4, 16 al.; Diog. L. 6, 95; Alex. Aphr., Fat. 8 II 2 p. 172, 30; Synes., Ep. 6 p. 169 A.) Lk 9: 3; Ac 8: 20 D 13: 7; ἀργύριον τὸ ἀ. Mt 25: 18; ἀ. αἰτεῖν *ask for money* D 11: 6; ἀ. δοῦναί τινι *give* or *pay money to someone* Mk 14: 11; Lk 22: 5; cf. D 11: 12. Otherw. διδόναι τὸ ἀ. *give the money*=entrust Lk 19: 15. διδόναι τὸ ἀ. ἐπὶ τράπεζαν *put money into a bank* vs. 23. For this τὰ ἀ. (cf. Aristoph., Av. 600; Demosth. 25, 41 v.l.; cf. Pollux 3, 86) Mt 25: 27. διδόναι ἀ. ἱκανά *give a sum of money* Mt 28: 12; λαμβάνειν ἀ. (Appian, Iber. 34 §138 ἀργ. λαμβάνειν; Gen 23: 13) vs. 15 (=allow oneself to be bribed, as Artem. 4, 82).

c. of particular silver coins (so as loanw. in rabb. ἀργύρια=silver coins: Pla., Leg. 5 p. 742D; Pollux 3, 86; 9, 89f; PGM 4, 2439) τριάκοντα ἀργύρια *30 silver shekels* (each worth about 4 drachmas; s. below) Mt 26: 15; 27: 3, 9; cf. vs. 5f (= שֶׁקֶל כֶּסֶף or simply כֶּסֶף, cf. Zech 11: 12f). ἀργυρίου μυριάδας πέντε 50,000 (Attic silver) *drachmas* (each worth normally 18 to 20 cents, eight or nine pence) Ac 19: 19 (cf. Jos., Ant. 17, 189).—FPrat, Le cours des Monnaies en Palest. au temps de J.-Chr.: Rech de Sc rel 15, '25, 441-8; ORoller, Münzen, Geld u. Vermögensverhältnisse in den Evv. '29; Billerb. I 290-4. CSeltmann, Greek Coins '33; AReifenberg, Ancient Jewish Coins², '47. M-M. B. 773.*

ἀργυροκόπος, ου, ὁ (Plut., Mor. 830E; Dit., Syll.³ 1263, 1 [fr. Smyrna]; BGU 781 IV, 5; PGiess. 47, 22; POxy. 1146, 12; PLond. 983, 1; Jer 6: 29) *silversmith* (Judg 17: 4 B) Ac 19: 24; Dg 2: 3. M-M.*

ἄργυρος, ου, ὁ (Hom.+; inscr., pap., LXX, but much less freq. than ἀργύριον) *silver.*
   1. *as money* (w. χρυσός: Herodian 2, 6, 8; Jos., Ant. 6, 201, C. Ap. 2, 217) Mt 10: 9 (s. ἀργύριον 2).
   2. *as a material* (Diod. S. 2, 16, 4; 2, 36, 2; Appian, Bell. Civ. 4, 75 §320) w. gold (Jos., Ant. 9, 85; Test. Levi 13: 7) Ac 17: 29; Rv 18: 12; MPol 15: 2; 1 Cor 3: 12 v.l. (s. ἀργύριον 1). W. still other materials (Diod. S. 4, 46, 4; 5, 74, 2) 2 Cl 1: 6; PK 2 p. 14, 14; Dg 2: 2. It rusts acc. to Js 5: 3. M-M. B. 610.*

ἀργυροῦς, ᾶ, οῦν (*made of*) *silver.* The contracted form of this word (common Hom.+; freq. in LXX [cf. Helbing 34f]) predominates in our lit. and the pap., and is found Jos., Ant. 3, 221.—σκεύη χρυσᾶ καὶ ἀ. (Gen 24: 53 al.) 2 Ti 2: 20; ναοὶ ἀ. Ac 19: 24 (Artem. 4, 31 ἀργυροῦς νεώς); τὰ εἴδωλα τὰ ἀ. Rv 9: 20 (cf. Da 5: 4, 23 LXX+ Theod.). —ἀργύρεος (Dit., Syll.³ 579, 3; 1168, 39; PLond. 1007, 3; 9): θεοὶ ἀ. *gods made of silver* Dg 2: 7 (cf. Ex 20: 23; EpJer 3; 10; 29). M-M.*

Ἄρειος πάγος, ὁ (Hdt. 8, 52 et al.; Diod. S. 11, 77, 6; Paus., Attic. 1, 28, 5; Meisterhans³-Schw. 43, 3; 47, 21; Dit., Syll.³ Ind IV) *the Areopagus* or *Hill of Ares* (Ares, the Gk. god of war=Rom. Mars, hence the older 'Mars' Hill'), northwest of the Acropolis in Athens Ac 17: 19, 22. But the A. is to be understood here less as a place (where speakers were permitted to hold forth freely, and listeners were always at hand) than as the council, which met on the hill (ἐπὶ τὸν Ἄ.=*before the A.*; cf. 16: 19, 17: 6). For the opp. view s. MDibelius below. In Rom. times it was the most important governmental body in Athens; among its many functions was that of supervising education, particularly of controlling the many visiting lecturers (Thalheim [s. below] 632; Gärtner [s. below] 56ff), and it is not improbable that Paul was brought before it for this reason.—Thalheim in Pauly-W. II 1896, 627ff; ECurtius, Pls in Athen: SAB 1893, 925ff; WSFerguson, Klio 9, '09, 325-30; Ramsay, Bearing 101ff; AWikenhauser, Die AG '21, 351ff; Beginn. IV '33, 212f; JMAdams, Paul at Athens: Rev. and Exp. 32, '35, 50-6; MDibelius, Pls auf d. Areopag '39; WSchmid, Philol. 95, '42, 79-120; MPohlenz, Pls. u. d. Stoa: ZNW 42, '49, 69-104; NBStonehouse, The Areopagus Address '49; HHommel, Neue Forschungen zur Areopagrede: ZNW 46, '55, 145-78; BGärtner, The Areopagus Speech and Natural Revelation '55; EHaenchen AG '56, 457-74; WNauck, ZThK 53, '56, 11-52.*

Ἀρεοπαγίτης, ου, ὁ (Lobeck on Phryn. 697f; Bl-D. §30, 2 w. app.; Mlt.-H. 277; 366; Aeschin. 1, 81; Menand., Fab. 11 J.; Alciphr. 1, 16, 1; Dit., Syll.³ 334, 35.—Inscr. Gr. 687,

52 [III BC]; 823, 7 [220 BC] the form Ἀρευπαγίτης is found) *Areopagite,* member of the council or court of the Areopagus (s. preced.); of Dionysius Ac 17: 34. (Tdf. Ἀρεοπαγείτης as Dit., Syll.³ 856, 8).*

ἀρεσκεία, ας, ἡ (ἀρέσκεια L-S-J et al.; s. Mlt.-H 339; Aristot., Theophr.+, mostly in bad sense: obsequiousness. In good sense: that by which one gains favor, Pr 31: 30; of human conduct Latyschev, Inscr. Orae Sept. Ponti Eux. II 5 χάριν τῆς εἰς τ. πόλιν ἀρεσκείας; Inschr. v. Priene 113, 73; POxy. 729, 24 πρὸς ἀ. τοῦ Σαραπίωνος. Of one's relation w. God Philo, Op. M. 144, Fuga 88 ἕνεκα ἀ. θεοῦ, Spec. Leg. 1, 176) *desire to please* εἰς πᾶσαν ἀ. *to please* (him) *in all respects* Col 1: 10. M-M.*

ἀρέσκω impf. ἤρεσκον; fut. ἀρέσω; 1 aor. ἤρεσα (Hom. +; inscr., pap., LXX).
   1. *strive to please, accommodate* (conduct, activity, oft. almost *serve*; Nägeli 40) τινί *someone* τῷ πλησίον Ro 15: 2; ἀνθρώποις (Pla., Ep. 4 p. 321B; Simplicius in Epict. p. 118, 30 ἀρέσκειν ἀνθρώποις βουλόμενος) Gal 1: 10 a, b (conative imperfect); 1 Th 2: 4. πάντα πᾶσιν ἀ. *everyone in all respects* 1 Cor 10: 33 (Demosth., Ep. 3, 27 πᾶσιν ἀ.). For this κατὰ πάντα τρόπον πᾶσιν ἀ. ITr 2: 3; ἀ. θεῷ 1 Th 4: 1; IRo 2: 1; cf. IPol 6: 2; ἑαυτῷ ἀ. Ro 15: 1, 3; 2 Cl 13: 1; Hs 9, 22, 1.
   2. *please, be pleasing* (condition; cf. POxy. 1153, 25 ἐὰν αὐτῷ ἀρέσκῃ; PGiess. 20, 15) τινί (to) *someone.*
      a. of pleasure caused by pers. ἀ. θεῷ (Theopomp. [IV BC]: 115 fgm. 344 Jac. τ. θεοῖς ἀ.; Num 23: 27; Ps 68: 32; Jos., Ant. 6, 164; 13, 289) Ro 8: 8; 1 Th 2: 15; cf. Hs 5, 2, 7; ἀ. τ. κυρίῳ 1 Cor 7: 32; 1 Cl 52: 2 (Mal 3: 4). ἀ. τ. γυναικί 1 Cor 7: 33; cf. vs. 34; 2 Ti 2: 4. τῷ Ἡρῴδῃ Mt 14: 6; Mk 6: 22. Cf. Od. 22, 55.
      b. of pleasure in things (Ael. Aristid. 46 p. 380 D.: θεοῖς ἀρέσκοντα) Hv 1, 4, 2; s 5, 6, 6. ἤρεσεν ὁ λόγος ἐνώπιον (for בְּעֵינֵי or לִפְנֵי) τοῦ πλήθους (=τῷ πλήθει) *the saying pleased the whole group* (cf. 2 Ch 30: 4; 1 Macc 6: 60; 8: 21; Jos., Vi. 238) Ac 6: 5 (Bl-D. §4, p. 4, 5; 187, 2; 214, 6).
   3. impers. (Philo, Aet. M. 87; Jos., Ant. 14, 205; 207) ἀρέσκει μοι *it pleases me* (=mihi placet) w. inf. foll. (Hdt. 8, 19; Josh 24: 15; 1 Macc 14: 23; 15: 19; Jos., Ant. 14, 352) Hm 6, 1, 5. M-M. B, 1099.*

ἀρεστός, ή, όν (Semonides, Hdt.+; inscr., pap., LXX, Joseph.) *pleasing* τὰ ἀ. τ. θεῷ ποιεῖν (the Pythagorean Ecphantus in Stob. 4, 7, 65 H.; Porphyr., Abst. 1, 25; Sir 48: 22) *do what is pleasing to God* J 8: 29. Also ἐνώπιον τοῦ θεοῦ (Is 38: 3; Tob 4: 21; Da 4: 37a) 1 J 3: 22 (s. ἀρέσκω 2b). ἔστιν ἀ. τῷ θεῷ B 19: 2; τ. κυρίῳ D 4: 12.—Of men (Aristoxenus, fgm. 70 πλήθει [=the masses] ἀρεστὸν εἶναι; Sb 6649, 5; Tob 4: 3; 2 Esdr 19 [Neh 9]: 37; Jos., Ant. 16, 135) τ. Ἰουδαίοις Ac 12: 3; οὐκ ἀ. ἐστιν w. acc. and inf. foll. *it is not desirable* 6: 2 (Bl-D. §408). M-M.*

Ἀρέτας, α, ὁ (on the spelling s. Dssm. NB 11 [BS 183f]) *Aretas,* a name which, in the form Ḥâriṭat, is often found in Nabataean inscriptions and among the Arabs, and was borne by Nabataean kings (Joseph. Index). The one named 2 Cor 11: 32 was Aretas IV (c. 9 BC to 40 AD). Cf. Schürer I⁴ 726ff; 738ff; ASteinmann, Aretas IV: BZ 7, '09, 174-84, 312-41; also sep. '09; Ltzm., Hdb. Exk. on 2 Cor 11: 32f; HWindisch in Meyer⁹ '24 ad loc. (lit.). JStarcky, Dict. de la Bible, Suppl. VII '66, 913-16. M-M.*

ἀρετή, ῆς, ἡ (Hom.+; inscr., pap., LXX).
   1. in its usual mng. *moral excellence, virtue* (Theognis 1, 147; Herm. Wr. 9, 4; 10, 9; Wsd 2, 3, 4 Macc; Ep. Arist.; Philo; Jos., Ant. 1, 113 al.) Phil 4: 8. W. πίστις (as Dit.,

Or. 438, 6ff ἄνδρα διενένκαντα πίστει καὶ ἀρετῇ καὶ δικαιοσύνῃ καὶ εὐσεβείαι, cf. Dssm., LO 270 [LAE 322]) 2 Pt 1: 5. ἐνδύσασθαι πᾶσαν ἀ. δικαιοσύνης *put on every virtue of righteousness* (=every Christian virtue) Hm 1: 2; s 6, 1, 4. ἐργάζεσθαι πᾶσαν ἀ. καὶ δικαιοσύνην s 8, 10, 3; cf. m 12, 3, 1; διώκειν τὴν ἀ. 2 Cl 10: 1; ἀ. ἔνδοξος m 6, 2, 3.

2. in accordance w. a usage that treats ἀ. and δόξα as synonyms, which finds expression outside the OT (Is 42: 8, 12) in the juxtaposition of the two concepts (Wettstein on 2 Pt 1: 3), the LXX transl. הוֹד glory (Hab 3: 3; Zech 6: 13) and also תְּהִלָּה *praise* (Is) with ἀ. The latter mng. (pl.= laudes) can be the correct one for 1 Pt 2: 9, which may be influenced by Is 42: 12; 43: 21. But another sense is poss., namely

3. *manifestation of divine power, miracle* (Oenom. in Euseb., Pr. Ev. 5, 22, 4; Dit., Syll.³ 1151, 2; 1172, 10 πλείονας ἀρετὰς τ. θεοῦ, see on this note 8 w. further exx. and lit.; 1173, 5; Mitteil. des Deut. Arch. Inst. Athen. Abt. 21, 1896, 77; POxy. 1382 [II AD]; Sb 8026, 1; PGM 5, 419; Philo, Somn. 1, 256; Jos., Ant. 17, 130; cf. Dssm., B 90–3 [BS 95f]; Nägeli 69; OWeinreich, Neue Urkunden z. Sarapisrel. '19, Index; SReiter, Ἐπιτύμβιον, presented in honor of HSwoboda '27, 228–37), also that which causes such things, *the power of God* (IG IV² 128, 79 [280 BC]; PGM 4, 3205; Herm. Wr. 10, 17; Jos., Ant. 17, 130 ἀ. τοῦ θείου; cf. 1, 100). So also, in all probability, 2 Pt 1: 3 (Dssm., B 277ff. [BS 360ff]).—AKiefer, Aretalogische Studien, Diss. Freib. '29. M-M.*

ἄρη s. αἴρω.

ἀρήν, ἀρνός, ὁ nom. found only in early inscr. (VII–VI BC, HMSearles, A Lexicograph. Study of the Gk. Inscr. 1898, 21; Meisterhans³-Schw. §58, 1; Kühner-Bl. I p. 429, 14; cf. L-S-J s.v.), but the oblique cases Hom.+; inscr., pap., LXX; Philo, Leg. ad Gai. 317; Jos., Ant. 3, 239 al. Gen. pl. ἀρνῶν; acc. ἄρνας *lamb* as an animal for slaughter B 2: 5 (Is 1: 11). As a type of weakness ὡς ἄρνας ἐν μέσῳ λύκων Lk 10: 3 (cf. Epigr. Gr. 1038, 38 ὡς ἄρνας κατέχουσι λύκοι; Is 65: 25.—The contrast is as old as Hom. [Il. 22, 263]). M-M.*

ἀριθμέω 1 aor. ἠρίθμησα, imper. ἀρίθμησον; pf. pass. ἠρίθμημαι (Hom.+; inscr., pap., LXX; Jos., Ant. 10, 243; 14, 194) *count* ὄχλον Rv 7: 9; ἀστέρας 1 Cl 10: 6 (Gen 15: 5); pass. Mt 10: 30; Lk 12: 7. M-M.*

ἀριθμός, οῦ, ὁ (Hom.+; inscr., pap., LXX, Philo, Joseph.) *number.*

1. lit. ὄντα ἐκ τοῦ ἀριθμοῦ τῶν δώδεκα (like Lat. e numero esse) lit. *belonging to the number of the twelve,* i.e., to the twelve Lk 22: 3; cf. εὑρεθῆναι ἐν τῷ ἀ. τινος be *found among the number* 1 Cl 35: 4; sim. 58: 2; MPol 14: 2; Hs 5, 3, 2; 9, 24, 4. W. specif. numbers ἀ. τῶν ἀνδρῶν Ac 4: 4; 5: 36. τὸν ἀριθμὸν ὡς πεντακισχίλιοι *about 5,000 in number* (class.; Dit., Syll.³ 495, 115 [III BC]; POxy. 1117, 15; PFlor. 53, 7; 16; PGenève 16, 22 ἀδελφοὶ ὄντες τ. ἀριθμὸν πέντε; 2 Macc 8: 16; 3 Macc 5: 2; Jos., Vi. 15) J 6: 10; cf. Rv 5: 11; 7: 4; 9: 16. W. non-specif. numbers Ro 9: 27; Rv 20: 8 (both Is 10: 22).—Rv 13: 17f, 15: 2 refer to numerology, which was quite familiar to the people of ancient times; acc. to it, since each Gk. letter has a numerical value, a name could be replaced by a number representing the total of the numerical values of the letters making up the name (cf. PGM 13, 155=466 σὺ εἶ ὁ ἀριθμὸς τ. ἐνιαυτοῦ Ἀβρασάξ [α=1+β=2+ρ=100+α=1+σ=200+α=1+ξ=60 makes 365, the number of days in a year]; Inscr. Rom. IV 743, 7f ἰσόψηφος δυσὶ τούτοις

Γάϊος ὡς ἅγιος ὡς ἀγαθὸς προλέγω [the name and both adjs. each have a num. value of 284]; PGM 1, 325 κλήζω δ᾽ οὔνομα σὸν Μοίραις αὐταῖς ἰσάριθμον; 2, 128; 8, 44ff; Sib. Or. 1, 141–5; Dssm., LO 237f [LAE 276f]; FBücheler, RhM n.F. 61, '06, 307f; ORühle, TW I 461–4); on the interpr. of the number 666 s. χξϛ'.

2. *number, total* (Dt 26: 5; 28: 62) ἀ. τῶν ἐκλεκτῶν *the number of the elect* 1 Cl 2: 4; cf. 59: 2. ἐπληθύνετο ὁ ἀ. *the total continued to grow* Ac 6: 7; περισσεύειν τῷ ἀ. 16: 5; πολὺς ἀ. (Diod. S. 13, 27; 14, 43, 3; Sir 51: 28) 11: 21. κατὰ ἀριθμὸν ἀγγέλων acc. *to the number of angels* 1 Cl 29: 2 (Dt 32: 8). M-M. B. 917.*

'Αριμαθαία, ας, ἡ *Arimathaea,* a city in Judaea (acc. to Dalman, Orte³ 139 and PThomsen, Philol. Wochenschr. 49, '29, 246=Rentis); home of Joseph (s. Ἰωσήφ 6) Mt 27: 57; Mk 15: 43; Lk 23: 51; J 19: 38.*

Ἄριος πάγος s. Ἄρειος πάγος.

'Αρίσταρχος, ου, ὁ (common name: Dit., Syll. and Or., Index; Preisigke, Namenbuch) *Aristarchus* of Thessalonica, Ac 20: 4, cf. 19: 29, accompanied Paul on his collection-journey and when he left for Rome 27: 2; Phlm 24, named as Paul's συνεργός; Col 4: 10 as his συναιχμάλωτος.*

ἀριστάω 1 aor. ἠρίστησα (s. ἄριστον).

1. *eat breakfast* (oft. so since X., Cyr. 6, 4, 1) J 21: 12, 15 (cf. vs. 4)—2. of the main meal (Aelian, V.H. 9, 19; Gen 43: 25), and of any meal *eat a meal, dine* (3 Km 13: 7; Jos., Ant. 6, 362; 8, 240) Lk 11: 37; 15: 29 D.*

ἀριστερός, ά, όν (Hom.+; inscr., pap., LXX; Jos., Vi. 173) *left* (opp. to right) ὅπλα δεξιὰ καὶ ἀ. weapons used w. the right hand, and those used w. the left=*weapons for offense and defense* (cf. Plut, Mor. 201D; Polyaenus 8, 16, 4 ἀριστερά and δεξιά of weapons for defense and offense) 2 Cor 6: 7. ἡ ἀριστερά sc. χείρ Bl-D. §241, 6; Rob. 652) *the left hand* Mt 6: 3 (cf. Damasc., Vi. Isid. 283 the proverb: give not w. one hand, but w. both). τὰ ἀ. μέρη *the left side* (on the pl. Bl-D. §141, 2) Hv 3, 1, 9; 3, 2, 1; hence ἐξ ἀριστερῶν (sc. μερῶν) *on the left* (Diogenes the Cynic in Diog. L. 6, 48; UPZ 121, 7 [156 BC]; BGU 86, 27; LXX) Mk 10: 37; Lk 23: 33; Hs 9, 6, 2. γνῶναι δεξιὰν καὶ ἀριστεράν *distinguish right fr. left* i.e., good fr. evil D 12: 1 (Jon 4: 11). M-M. B. 866.*

'Αριστίων, ωνος, ὁ *Aristion,* an early Christian, called 'a disciple of the Lord' Papias 2: 4.*

'Αριστόβουλος, ου, ὁ (common name: Dit., Syll. and Or., Index; Preisigke, Namenbuch; Joseph.) *Aristobulus:* οἱ ἐκ τῶν Ἀριστοβούλου those who belong to (the household of) *A.* Ro 16: 10.—PFeine, Die Abfassung d. Phil. in Ephesus '16, 128–30. M-M.*

ἄριστον, ου, τό (s. ἀριστάω).

1. *breakfast* (so Hom.+; Dialekt-Inschr. 5495, 45 [Ionic]; POxy. 519, 17; 736, 28; PTebt. 116, 36; Sus 13 Theod., cf. 12 LXX) Lk 14: 12 differentiated fr. δεῖπνον (as Polyaenus 4, 3, 32 ἄριστον κ. δεῖπνον; Jos., Ant. 8, 356).

2. *noon meal* (Athen. 1, 9, 10 p. 11B δεῖπνον μεσημβρινόν, cf. 2 Km 24: 15; Tob 2: 1; Jos., Ant. 5, 190) Mt 22: 4 and *meal* gener. (PTebt. 120, 82 [I BC]; Tob 12: 13; Bel 34; 37; Jos., Ant. 2, 2) Lk 11: 38; 14: 15 v.l.—In both mngs. loanw. in rabb. M-M. B. 354.*

'Αρκαδία, ας, ἡ (Hom.+; inscr.) *Arcadia,* a province in the interior of the Peloponnesus in Greece, to which Hermas was taken in a vision Hs 9, 1, 4.—Rtzst., Poim. 33; MDibelius, Harnack-Ehrung '21, 116; Hdb. ad loc.*

ἀρκετός, ή, όν (Bl-D. §187, 8; 405, 2; Rob. 80) *enough, sufficient, adequate* (Chrysippus Tyanensis [I AD] in Athen. 3, 79 p. 113B; Vett. Val. 304, 25; Herm. Wr. in Stob. I 49, 44=p. 464, 18 Sc.; Anth. Pal. 4, 18, 10 ἀρκετὸν οἴνῳ αἴθεσθαι κραδίην; BGU 33, 5; 531 II, 24 [I AD]; Epigr. Gr., Praef. 288c, 10; Dt 25: 2 Aq.; Jos., Bell. 3, 130) τίς ἀ. ἐξειπεῖν; *who is in a position to declare?* 1 Cl 49: 3. τινί *for someone* or *someth.* w. inf. foll. ἀ. (v.l. ἡμῖν or ὑμῖν) ὁ παρεληλυθὼς χρόνος . . . κατειργάσθαι 1 Pt 4: 3. ἀρκετή σοι ἡ ὑπόμνησις αὕτη *this reminder is enough for you* Hv 3, 8, 9. τὴν αὐτάρκειαν τὴν ἀ. σοι *an adequate competence* Hs 1: 6. ἀρκετὸν (Bl-D. §131) τῇ ἡμέρᾳ ἡ κακία αὐτῆς Mt 6: 34 (s. κακία 2). W. ἵνα foll. (cf. Bl-D. §393, 2) ἀ. τῷ μαθητῇ *it is* (=must be) *enough for the disciple* Mt 10: 25.—As a substantive τὸ ἀ. τ. τροφῆς *an adequate amount of food* Hv 3, 9, 3. M-M. B. 927.*

ἀρκέω 1 aor. ἤρκεσα; 1 fut. pass. ἀρκεσθήσομαι 1 Ti 6: 8.
1. act. *be enough, sufficient, adequate* (trag., Thu.+; pap.; Num 11: 22; 3 Km 8: 27; Wsd 14: 22; Jos., Ant. 9, 266) ἀρκεῖ τινί τι *someth. is enough for someone* (Epict. 2, 19, 19; Jos., Ant. 13, 291) ἀ. σοι ἡ χάρις μου *my grace is sufficient for you* (=you need nothing more than my grace) 2 Cor 12: 9. ἀρκοῦσίν σοι αἱ ἀποκαλύψεις αὗται *these revelations are enough for you* Hv 3, 10, 8. μή ποτε οὐ μὴ ἀρκέσῃ (sc. τὸ ἔλαιον) ἡμῖν καὶ ὑμῖν *there may not be enough for us and you* Mt 25: 9. ἄρτοι οὐκ ἀ. αὐτοῖς, ἵνα (*loaves of*) *bread is* (*are*) *not enough, so that* J 6: 7. τὰ ἀρκοῦντα αὐτῷ *what was enough for him* Hs 5, 2, 9 (cf. PLond. 1833, 4 τὸ ἀρκοῦν=a sufficient quantity).—Impers. (Ael. Aristid. 47, 23 K.=23 p. 451 D. and Vi. Aesopi W. c. 64: ἀρκεῖ) ἀρκεῖ ἡμῖν *it is enough for us* J 14: 8 (cf. PLond. 964, 13, ἵνα ἀρκέσῃ ἡμῖν).
2. pass. ἀρκέομαί τινι *be satisfied* or *content with someth.* (Hdt., X.+; Epict., pap. [Nägeli 55]; Pr 30: 15; 2 Macc 5: 15; 4 Macc 6: 28; Jos., Ant. 12, 294) 1 Ti 6: 8. ἀρκεῖσθε τοῖς ὀψωνίοις ὑμῶν *be content w. your wages* Lk 3: 14. ἀ. τοῖς παροῦσιν (this expr. in Democrit., fgm. 191 Diels; Teles 11, 5; 38, 10; 41, 12; Cassius Dio 38, 8; 38; 56, 33; cf. GAGerhard, Phoinix v. Kolophon '09, 56f) *be content w. what one has* Hb 13: 5; τοῖς ἐφοδίοις τ. θεοῦ (or τ. Χριστοῦ) ἀ. *be satisfied w. the travel-allowance which God* (*or Christ*) *has given us* 1 Cl 2: 1; τοῖς συμβίοις ἀ. *be content w. their husbands* IPol 5: 1.—W. ἐπί τινι (PLond. 45, 13; UPZ 162 II, 18 [117 BC] οὐκ ἀρκεσθέντες δὲ ἐπὶ τῷ ἐνοικεῖν ἐν τ. ἐμῇ οἰκίᾳ; Bl-D. §235, 2 app.): μὴ ἀρκούμενος ἐπὶ τούτοις (i.e. λόγοις) *not be satisfied w. words* (opp. deeds) 3 J 10 (UPZ 19, 20 [165 BC] οὐκ ἀρκεσθεῖσα ἐπὶ τούτοις). M-M.*

ἄρκος, ου, ὁ, ἡ (on this form, found also Heraclides, Pol. 38; Aelian, N.A. 1, 31; Inscr. Graec. Sic. It. 1302; 2325; 2328; 2334; Audollent, Defix. Tab. 249 [I AD]; Anth. Pal. 11, 231; LXX; Jos., Ant. 6, 183; Test. Jud. 2: 4 instead of ἄρκτος [Hom.+; Herm. Wr. 5, 4; Philo; Sib. Or. 3, 26] cf. W-S. §5, 31) *bear* Rv 13: 2 (Da 7: 5). M-M. B. 186.*

ἀρκούντως adv. fr. pres. ptc. of ἀρκέω (Aeschyl., Thu.+; Jos., Ant. 13, 73) *sufficiently* ἀ. μανθάνειν Dg 4: 6.*

ἄρκτος s. ἄρκος.

ἅρμα, ατος, τό (Hom.+; inscr., pap., LXX, Philo, Joseph.) *carriage, traveling-chariot* (Dio Chrys. 64[14], 20 and Ps.-Apollod. 3, 5, 7, 5 ἐφ᾽ ἅρματος; Gen 41: 43; 46: 29; Jos., Ant. 8, 386 ἐφ᾽ ἅρματος καθεζομένῳ) Ac 8: 28f, 38. Esp.

war chariot (X., Cyr. 6, 3, 8; Jos., Ant. 2, 324) Rv 9: 9 (cf. Jo 2: 5); 1 Cl 51: 5 (cf. Ex 14: 23, 26, 28; 15: 19). M-M.*

Ἁρμαγεδ(δ)ών (W-H. Ἁρ Μαγεδών) indecl. *Armageddon*, a mystic place-name, said to be Hebrew Rv 16: 16; it has been identified w. Megiddo and Jerusalem, but its interpr. is beset w. difficulties that have not yet been surmounted. See comm., and JoachJeremias, ZNW 31, '32, 73-7; BViolet, ibid. 205f; CCTorrey, HTR 31, '38, 237-50; JHMichael, JTS 38, '37, 168-72.*

ἁρμογή, ῆς, ἡ (Polyb. et al.) *joint in masonry*, where one stone touches the others (Jos., Ant. 15, 399) Hv 3, 2, 6; 3, 5, 1f; s 9, 9, 7.*

ἁρμόζω 1 aor. mid. ἡρμοσάμην; pf. pass. ἥρμοσμαι; 1 aor. pass. ἡρμόσθην (Hom.+; inscr., pap., LXX, Ep. Arist., Philo, Joseph.; on the spelling cf. Crönert 135; 245).
1. intr. *fit, fit in* τινί *with someth.* (Diod. S. 23, 12, 1; PSI 442, 12 [III BC]; Jos., Bell. 3, 516; cf. C. Ap. 2, 188) of stones in a building ἀ. τοῖς λοιποῖς *fit in w. the others* Hs 9, 7, 2; cf. v 3, 7, 6. For this ἀ. μετὰ τῶν λοιπῶν λίθων s 9, 7, 4; ἀ. εἴς τι *fit into someth.* v 3, 2, 8; 3, 6, 5; 3, 7, 5; s 9, 9, 3.
2. trans. *fit together, join* (Maximus Tyr. 15, 3a λίθους; Jos., Ant. 6, 189 a stone into a sling) τὶ εἴς τι Hs 9, 8, 4. Pass. Hv 3, 2, 6; s 9, 4, 2f; 9, 8, 5ff; 9, 9, 4; 9, 15, 4.—*Harmonize*, pass. *be harmonized* μετακόσμια ἁρμόζεται *are harmonized* Dg 12: 9. τὰ πρὸς τ. πυρὰν ἡρμοσμένα ὄργανα *the material* (wood) *or instruments of wood prepared for the pyre* MPol 13: 3.
3. *join* or *give in marriage, betroth* (t.t. Pind., Hdt.+ [Nägeli 25]; Pr 19: 14; Jos., Ant. 20, 140), mid. ἁρμόζεσθαι τ. θυγατέρα τινός *become engaged to someone's daughter* (cf. POxy. 906, 7). The mid. is used for the act. in one isolated case (Bl-D. §316, 1) ἡρμοσάμην ὑμᾶς ἑνὶ ἀνδρὶ *I betrothed you to one man* 2 Cor 11: 2 (cf. Parthenius 6, 3; Philo, Leg. All. 2, 67 τὸν πιστόν, ᾧ τὴν Αἰθιόπισσαν αὐτὸς ὁ θεὸς ἡρμόσατο, Abr. 100; Mlt. 160).—RABatey, NT Nuptial Imagery, '71. M-M.*

ἁρμός, οῦ, ὁ (Soph., X.+; Dit., Syll.³ 970, 9; 972, 106; Sir 27: 2; Ep. Arist. 71; Jos., Ant. 1, 78 v.l.) *joint* (Schol. on Nicander, Ther. 781; 4 Macc 10: 5; Test. Zeb. 2: 5) Hb 4: 12. M-M.*

ἄρνας s. ἀρήν.

ἀρνέομαι fut. ἀρνήσομαι; 1 aor. ἠρνησάμην (Bl-D. §78; BGU 195, 22); pf. ἤρνημαι (Hom.+; inscr., pap., LXX, Joseph.).
1. *refuse, disdain* (Hes., Works 408; Appian, Syr. 5 §19; Artem. 1, 78 p. 72, 26; 5, 9; Diog. L. 2, 115; 6, 36; Jos., Ant. 4, 86; 5, 236, Vi. 222) w. inf. foll. (Hdt. 6, 13; Wsd 12: 27; 17: 9) ἠρνήσατο λέγεσθαι υἱός *he refused to be known as the son* Hb 11: 24 (JFeather, ET 43, '32, 423-5).
2. *deny* (opp. ὁμολογεῖν=admit, say 'yes', as Diog. L. 6, 40; Jos., Ant. 6, 151) w. ὅτι foll.: ἀ. ὅτι Ἰησ. οὐκ ἔστιν ὁ Χριστός 1 J 2: 22 (the neg. is redundant as Demosth. 9, 54 ἀ. ὡς οὐκ εἰσὶ τοιοῦτοι; Alciphr. 4, 17, 4 v.l.). W. acc. and inf. foll. PK 2 p. 14, 22. W. inf. foll. (Epict. 3, 24, 81; Wsd 16: 16) ἠρνησάμην δεδωκέναι *I said that I had not given* (it) Hv 2, 4, 2; τὶ *someth.* (Jos., Ant. 6, 151 τ. ἁμαρτίαν, Vi. 255) IMg 9: 2; abs. (Dit., Syll.³ 780, 25; Gen 18: 15) Lk 8: 45; J 1: 20; Ac 4: 16.
3. *deny, repudiate, disown* w. acc. *someone* or *someth.*, or abs., with obj. supplied fr. the context Ac 7: 35; usu. of apostasy fr. the Christian faith.
a. of denying Christ ἀ. με ἔμπροσθεν τ. ἀνθρώπων Mt 10: 33; Lk 12: 9; ἀ. (αὐτὸν) κατὰ πρόσωπον Πιλάτου Ac

3: 13; cf. vs. 14; ἀ. τὸν κύριον Hv 2, 2, 8; s 9, 26, 6; 9, 28, 8; Dg 7: 7. τὸν Ἰησοῦν 2 Cl 17: 7; cf. 3: 1. Ἰησοῦν Χριστόν Jd 4. τὸν υἱόν 1 J 2: 23. τὸν δεσπότην (s. below b) 2 Pt 2: 1; cf. ISm 5: 1. Of Peter's denial (MGoguel, Did Peter Deny his Lord? HTR 25, '32, 1–27) Mt 26: 70, 72; Mk 14: 68, 70; Lk 22: 57; J 13: 38; 18: 25, 27. ἀ. τὴν ζωήν=τὸν Χριστόν Hv 2, 2, 7.

b. of denying God (Aesop, Fab. 323 P.=Babrius 152 Crus. τὸν πρότερόν σου δεσπότην [Apollo] ἠρνήσω) ἀ. θεὸν τοῖς ἔργοις disown God by deeds Tit 1: 16. ἀ. τὸν πατέρα καὶ τ. υἱόν 1 J 2: 22.

c. of denial of Christ by men (cf. the Egypt. inscr. HTR 33, '40, 318 τοῦτον ἀπηρνήσαντο θεοί) Mt 10: 33; 2 Ti 2: 12.

d. w. impers. obj. refuse, reject, decline someth. (Lycophron v. 348 γάμους=marriage; Himerius, Or. 18 [Ecl. 19], 2 the χάρις of a god, the gracious gift offered by him; 4 Macc 8: 7; 10: 15; Nägeli 23) ἀ. τὴν πίστιν repudiate the (Christian) faith 1 Ti 5: 8; Rv 2: 13. τὸ ὄνομά μου 3: 8. τὸν νόμον Hs 8, 3, 7.

e. gener. ἀ. ποικίλαις ἀρνήσεσι deny in many different ways Hs 8, 8, 4.

4. ἀ. ἑαυτόν deny, disregard oneself=act in a wholly selfless way Lk 9: 23 (s. on ἀπαρνέομαι). But ἀ. ἑαυτόν be untrue to oneself 2 Ti 2: 13. ἀ. τὴν δύναμιν εὐσεβείας deny the power of religion (by irreligious conduct) 3: 5. τὴν ἀσέβειαν ἀ. renounce godlessness Tit 2: 12.—HRiesenfeld, The Mng. of the Verb ἀρνεῖσθαι: Coniect. Neot. XI, '47, 207–19; CMasson, Le reniement de Pierre RHPhr 37, '57, 24–35; cf. lit. s.v. ἀπαρνέομαι. M-M. B. 1269; 1273.**

ἄρνησις, εως, ἡ (Aeschyl.+; pap.; Job 16: 8 Aq.; Jos., Ant. 16, 216, C. Ap. 2, 276) denial (opp. ὁμολόγησις) Hs 9, 28, 7; 8, 8, 4 (cf. ἀρνέομαι 3e). εἰς ἄ. τινα τρέπειν bring someone to a denial (of his faith) MPol 2: 4.*

Ἀρνί n. m. indecl. Arni, in the genealogy of Jesus Lk 3: 33 (Ἀράμ t.r.).*

ἀρνίον, ου, τό (dim. of ἀρήν, but no longer felt to be a dim. in NT times. Lysias+; BGU 377, 2; 7; PStrassb. 24, 7f; PGenève 68, 7; LXX [rare]; Philo, Leg. ad Gai. 362; Jos., Ant. 3, 221; 226) sheep, lamb; in Rv a designation of Christ 5: 6, 8, 12f; 6: 1, 16; 7: 9f, 14, 17; 12: 11; 13: 8; 14: 1, 4, 10; 15: 3; 17: 14; 19: 7, 9; 21: 9, 14, 22f, 27; 22: 1, 3; cf. 13: 11. τὰ ἀ. (as πρόβατα elsewh.) of the Christian community J 21: 15. As a type of weakness 2 Cl 5: 2ff. Cf. Boll 45, 6; FSpitta, Streitfragen d. Gesch. Jesu '07, 174; HWindisch, D. messian. Krieg '09, 70; ELohmeyer, Hdb., exc. on Rv 5: 6; THoltz, D. Christologie der Apokalypse, Diss. Halle '59. M-M. B. 159.*

ἀρνῶν s. ἀρήν.

ἄρον s. αἴρω.

ἀροτριάω (Theophr.+[Nägeli 31]; PPetr. III 31, 7 et al.; pap.; LXX; Jos., Bell. 2, 113) to plow (w. ποιμαίνειν) Lk 17: 7. ὀφείλει ἐπ' ἐλπίδι ὁ ἀροτριῶν ἀροτριᾶν the plowman should plow in hope (of reaping a crop) 1 Cor 9: 10. M-M.*

ἄροτρον, ου, τό (Hom.+; PReinach 17, 20; PFlor. 134, 1; PStrassb. 32, 3; LXX; Jos., Ant. 2, 84 al.) a plow ἐπιβάλλειν τ. χεῖρα ἐπ' ἄ. put one's hand to the plow Lk 9: 62 (cf. Hes., Works 467 ἀρχόμενος ἀρότρου ἄκρον ἐχέτλης χειρὶ λαβών=when you begin the plowing take hold of the plowhandle. M-M. B. 495.*

ἁρπαγή, ῆς, ἡ (since Solon 3, 13 Diehl², Aeschyl.; inscr., pap., LXX, Jos., C. Ap. 2, 200).

1. robbery, plunder (Aeschyl.; Thu. 4, 104, 2; Dit., Syll.³ 679, 85; BGU 871, 5; PLeipz. 64, 53; 4 Macc 4: 10; Jos., Ant. 5, 25; Test. Judah 23: 3) of forcible confiscation of property in a persecution Hb 10: 34. καθῆσθαι εἰς ἁρπαγήν sit (waiting) for prey B 10: 10. Pl. robberies (1 Macc 13: 34) D 5: 1; B 20: 1.

2. what has been stolen, plunder (so trag.; Thu. 8, 62, 2; mostly LXX; Jos., Vi. 380) of cup and dish ἔσωθεν γέμουσιν ἐξ ἁρπαγῆς Mt 23: 25. The Lucan parallel refers not to the cup, but to the Pharisees themselves, so that ἁ. takes on mng. 3, which is also poss. for the Mt passage.

3. greediness, rapacity (w. πονηρία) Lk 11: 39 (X., Cyr. 5, 2, 17). M-M.*

ἁρπαγμός, οῦ, ὁ (quite rare in secular Gk.; not found at all in the Gk. transl. of the OT).

1. robbery (Plut., Mor. 12A; Vett. Val. 122, 1; Phryn., Appar. Soph.: Anecd. Gr. I 36. Also Plut., Mor. 644A ἁρπασμός), which is next to impossible in Phil 2: 6 (W-S. §28, 3: the state of being equal w. God cannot be equated w. the act of robbery).

2. As equal to ἅρπαγμα, w. change fr. abstr. to concr. (as θερισμός Rv 14: 15, cf. J 4: 35; ἱματισμός J 19: 24). This mng. cannot be quoted fr. non-Christian lit., but is grammatically justifiable (Kühner-Bl. II p. 272; RALipsius, Hand-Comment. ad loc.). Christian exx. are Euseb., In Luc. 6 (AMai, Nova Patr. Bibl. IV 165), where Peter regards death on the cross as ἁρπαγμός 'a prize to be grasped eagerly', and Cyrill. Alex., De Ador. 1, 25 (Migne, Ser. Gr. LXVIII 172c). Lot does not regard the angels' demand as a ἁρπαγμός 'prize'.—But acc. to FEVokes, on Phil 2: 5–11 in Studia Evangelica 2, '64, 670-75, forms in -μα may approach -μος forms in mng., but not vice versa, cf. πορισμός 1 Ti 6: 5.

a. This can be taken 'sensu malo' to mean prize, booty (so LXX), and only the context and an understanding of Paul's thought in general can decide whether it means holding fast to a prize already obtained (ἁ.='res rapta'; so the Gk. fathers) or the appropriation to oneself of a prize which is sought after (ἁ.='res rapienda').

b. However, a good sense is also poss., a piece of good fortune, windfall (Heliod. 7, 11, 7; 7, 20, 2 [=ἕρμαιον]; 8, 7, 1; Plut., Mor. 330D; Diod. S. 3, 61, 6; Nägeli 43f)=ἕρμαιον (Isid. Pelus., Ep. 4, 22); again it remains an open question whether the windfall has already been seized and is waiting to be used, or whether it has not yet been appropriated.

3. another less probable mng., is (mystical) rapture, cf. ἁρπάζω 2b and LHammerich, An Ancient Misunderstanding (Phil 2: 6 'robbery'), '66, who would translate the phrase 'considered that to be like God was no rapture'; a similar view was expressed by PFlorensky (1915), quoted in Dictionnaire de la Bible, Suppl. V, '57, col. 24 s.v. kénose.—LSaint-Paul, RB n.s. 8, '11, 550ff (pretext, opportunity). WJaeger, Her. 50, '15, 537–53 (w. further support, RHoover, HTR 64, '71, 95–119); AJülicher, ZNW 17, '16, 1–17; PWSchmidt, PM 20, '16, 171–86; HSchumacher, Christus in s. Präexistenz u. Kenose nach Phil 2: 5–8, I '14, II '21; FLoofs, StKr 100, '27/8, 1–102; ELohmeyer, Kyrios Jesus: s. the Heidelb. Ak. d. W. '27/8, 4 Abh.; WFoerster, ZNW 29, '30, 115–28; FKattenbusch, StKr 104, '32, 373–420; EBarnikol, Mensch u. Messias '32, Philipper 2, '32; KBornhäuser, NKZ 44, '33, 428–34; 453–62; SMowinckel, Norsk Teol. Tidssk. 40, '39, 208–11; AAStephenson, CBQ 1, '39, 301–8; AFeuillet, Vivre et Penser, Sér. 2, '42, 61f; AFridrichsen: AKaritz-Festschr. '46, 197ff; HAlmqvist, Plut. u. d. NT, '46, 117f; JHering,

D. bibl. Grundlagen des Christl. Humanismus '46, 31f.; AATEhrhardt, JTS 46, '45, 49-51 (cf. Plut., Mor. 330D; Diod. S. 3, 61, 6); EKäsemann, ZThK 47, '50, 313-60; HKruse, Verbum Domini 27, '49, 355-60; 29, '51, 206-14; LBouyer, Rech de Sc rel 39, '51, 281-8; DRGriffiths, ET 69, '57/'58, 237-39.—S. also s.v. κενόω 1. M-M.*

ἁρπάζω fut. ἁρπάσω (J 10: 28); 1 aor. ἥρπασα; 1 aor. pass. ἡρπάσθην (Rv 12: 5; cf. Jos., Bell. 2, 69); 2 aor. ἡρπάγην (2 Cor 12: 2, 4; Wsd 4: 11; Jos., Ant. 6, 14; 12, 144); 2 fut. ἁρπαγήσομαι (1 Th 4: 17) (Hom.+; inscr., pap., LXX; Philo, Cher. 93, Agr. 151; Joseph.; Test. 12 Patr.) snatch, seize, i.e., take suddenly and vehemently, or take away in the sense of

1. *steal, carry off, drag away* (so mostly LXX; En. 102, 9) τὶ someth. of wild animals (Gen 37: 33; Ps 7: 3) J 10: 12 (X., Mem. 2, 7, 14); 1 Cl 35: 11 (Ps 49: 22). Of thieving men (Dit., Syll.³ 1168, 111 [IV BC]; Jos., Ant. 20, 214) τὰ σκεύη his property Mt 12: 29. τὰ ἀλλότρια *other people's property* B 10: 4.

2. *snatch* or *take away*—a. forcefully τινά *someone* (Appian, Bell. Civ. 4, 113 §474; Polyaenus 8, 34; Ps.-Apollod. 1, 5, 1, 1 of Persephone; Judg 21: 21) ἀ. αὐτόν *take him away* J 6: 15 (cf. Jos., Bell. 4, 259, Ant. 19, 162; Philogonius, who ἐκ μέσης τ. ἀγορᾶς ἁρπασθείς was made a bishop [Chrysostom I p. 495D Montf.]; Act. Thom. 165); Ac 23: 24 v.l. Of an arrest ἀ. τινα ἐκ μέσου αὐτῶν *take someone away fr. among them* Ac 23: 10. Of seed already sown *tear out* Mt 13: 19. ἀ. ἐκ τ. χειρός *snatch fr. the hand* (cf. 2 Km 23: 21) J 10: 28f; Hv 2, 1, 4. Of rescue from a threatening danger ἐκ πυρὸς ἀ. *snatch fr. the fire* Jd 23.

b. in such a way that no resistance is offered (Herodian 1, 11, 5; Quint. Smyrn. 11, 291 [Aphrodite 'snatches away' Aeneas, who is in danger]; Wsd 4: 11; cf. Jos., Ant. 7, 113), esp. of the Holy Spirit, which carries someone away Ac 8: 39 (v.l. has ἄγγελος κυρίου.—On the word πνεῦμα, which means both 'spirit' and 'wind', cf. Apollon. Rhod. 3, 1114, where ἀναρπάζειν is used of winds which transport a person from one place to another far away). Pass. ἁρπαγῆναι ἕως τρίτου οὐρανοῦ *be caught up to the third heaven* 2 Cor 12: 2 (Hesych. Miles. [VI AD], Vir. Ill. C. 66 JFlach [1880]: the pagan Tribonian says of Emperor Justinian ὅτι οὐκ ἀποθανεῖται, ἀλλὰ μετὰ σαρκὸς εἰς οὐρανοὺς ἁρπαγήσεται); ἀ. εἰς τ. παράδεισον vs. 4; ἀ. ἐν νεφέλαις εἰς ἀέρα 1 Th 4: 17; ἀ. πρὸς τ. θεόν Rv 12: 5.—The mng. of ἀ. τὴν βασιλείαν τ. οὐρανῶν Mt 11: 12 is difficult to determine; ἀ. beside βιάζειν (as Plut., Mor. 203c et al.; s. HAlmqvist, Plut. u. d. NT, '46, 38; 117f) prob. means someth. like *seize* or *claim for oneself* (cf. X., An. 6, 5, 18; 6, 6, 6; Epict. 4, 7, 22; Plut., Mor. 81c; s. WLKnox, HTR 41, '48, 237). Another possiblilty is *plunder* (Libanius, Or. 1 p. 147, 4 F. κώμας ἀ.; Polyaenus 8, 11 τ. πόλεως ἁρπαγή=the plundering of the city).—Finally ἀ. τι *grasp something quickly, eagerly, with desire* (Musonius in Stob. 3, 7, 23 vol. III p. 315, 4 H. ἅρπαζε τὸ καλῶς ἀποθνῄσκειν; Aelian, N. An. 2, 50; Libanius, Declam. 4, 81 vol. V p. 281, 16 F. ἀ. τὴν δωρεάν). M-M. B. 744.*

ἅρπαξ, αγος adj. (Hes.+; X., LXX).
1. *rapacious, ravenous* of wolves (Gen 49: 27) Mt 7: 15.
—2. subst., ὁ ἄ. *robber* (Jos., Bell. 6, 203); to differentiate it fr. λῃστής perh. better *swindler* or *rogue* (Dssm., LO 269, 4 [LAE 321, 1]; ἅρπαξ and λῃστής in juxtaposition: Artem. 4, 56 p. 234, 18) w. ἄδικοι, μοιχοί Lk 18: 11; cf. 1 Cor 5: 10f; 6: 10; Tit 1: 9 v.l.; D 2: 6. M-M.*

ἀρραβών, ῶνος, ὁ (Semit. loanw.; Hebr. עֵרָבוֹן Gen 38: 17-

20=ἀρραβῶν LXX; Lat. arra or arrabo [Thesaur. Linguae Lat. II 633]. For the spelling ἀραβῶν cf. Bl-D. §40; Thackeray 119; M-M.) legal and commercial t.t. (since Isaeus 8, 23 and Aristot., freq. inscr., pap., ostraca [Nägeli 55; Preisigke, Fachw.]) *first instalment, deposit, down payment, pledge,* that pays a part of the purchase price in advance, and so secures a legal claim to the article in question, or makes a contract valid (UPZ 67, 13 [153 BC]; PLond. 143, 13; PFay. 91, 14; POxy. 299, 2f; BGU 446, 5); in any case, ἀ. is a payment which obligates the contracting party to make further payments. It is also used fig. (Aristot., Pol. 1, 11; Stob. IV 418, 13 H. ἔχειν ἀρραβῶνα τ. τέχνην τοῦ ζῆν) δοὺς τὸν ἀ. τοῦ πνεύματος ἐν ταῖς καρδίαις ἡμῶν *has deposited the first instalment of the Spirit in our hearts* 2 Cor 1: 22 (on association w. baptism: EDinkler, OCullmann-Festschr. '62, 188f; cf. 5: 5. The Spirit is the *first instalment* τῆς κληρονομίας Eph 1: 14. Jesus Christ is ἀ. τῆς δικαιοσύνης ἡμῶν *pledge of our righteousness* Pol 8: 1.—S. BAhern, CBQ 9, '47, 179-89. M-M and suppl. B. 799.*

ἄρραφος s. ἄραφος.

ἄρρην s. ἄρσην.

ἄρρητος, ον (Hom.+; Philo; Jos., Bell. 7, 262; on the spelling s. Bl-D. §11, 1) *inexpressible, not to be spoken.*
1. of someth. that cannot be expressed, since it is beyond human powers (Pla., Symp. 189B; Plut., Mor. 564F; Herm. Wr. 1, 31; PGM 13, 763 explains it: ἐν ἀνθρώπου στόματι λαληθῆναι οὐ δύναται).
2. of someth. that must not be expressed, since it is holy (since Eur., Bacch. 472; Hdt. 5, 83; Thessalus [I AD] adjures Asclepius δι' ἀρρήτων ὀνομάτων: Cat. Cod. Astr. VIII 3, 137. Not infreq. on sacral inscr. [Nägeli 55]. PGM 3, 205; 12, 237; Vett. Val. 19, 1; Plut., Is. et Osir. 25 p. 360F; Philo, Det. Pot. Ins. 175) ἄ. ῥήματα *words too sacred to tell* 2 Cor 12: 4 (cf. Lucian, Epigr. 11). M-M.*

ἀρρωστέω (since Heraclit. 58; inscr., pap.; Sir 18: 21; Jos., Ant. 10, 221, C. Ap. 1, 136; Test. 12 Patr.) *be ill, sick* Mt 14: 14 D (οἱ ἀρρωστοῦντες as Diod. S. 14, 71, 4).*

ἄρρωστος, ον (for spelling Bl-D. §11, 1) *sick, ill,* lit. powerless (so Hippocr.+; Dit., Syll.² 858, 17; Zen.-P. 4, 5=Sb 6710 [259/8 BC]; Sir 7: 35; Mal 1: 8; Jos., Bell. 5, 526) 1 Cor 11: 30 (w. ἀσθενής).—Mt 14: 14; Mk 6: 5, 13; 16: 18. M-M. B. 298; 302.*

ἀρσενικός, ή, όν (Callim., Epigr. 27; PLille 1, 10 [III BC]; POxy. 38, 7; PGM 4, 2519; oft. LXX) *male* φρονεῖν τι ἀ. περί τινος *think of someone as a male* w. women as subj. 2 Cl 12: 5.*

ἀρσενοκοίτης, ου, ὁ (Bardesanes in Euseb., Pr. Ev. 6, 10, 25.—Anth. Pal. 9, 686, 5 and Cat. Cod. Astr. VIII 4 p. 196, 6; 8 ἀρρενοκοίτης.—ἀρσενοκοιτεῖν Sib. Or. 2, 73) *a male who practices homosexuality, pederast, sodomite* 1 Cor 6: 9; 1 Ti 1: 10; Pol 5: 3. Cf. Ro 1: 27. DSBailey, Homosexuality and the Western Christian Tradition, '55. M-M.*

ἄρσην, εν, gen. **ενος** (Hom.+; Dit., Syll.³ 1033; 1044, 3; 13; PSI 569, 6; 7 [III BC]; PGM 15, 18; LXX; Ep. Arist. 152; Sib. Or. 3, 133. The Attic form ἄρρην [oft. pap., also Philo, Joseph.] Ac 7: 19 v.l.; GEg 2; B 10: 7. Cf. Bl-D. §34, 2 w. app.; Mlt-H. 103f) *male* (opp. θῆλυς, as Pla., Leg. 2, 9 p. 665c; PGM 15, 18) subst. τὸ ἄ. W. strong emphasis on sex (syn. ἀνήρ) Ro 1: 27a, b, c (cf. Jos., C. Ap. 2, 199). ἄρσεν καὶ θῆλυν ἐποίησεν αὐτούς *God created them male and female* (Gen 1: 27; cf. PGM 5, 105) Mt 19: 4; Mk 10: 6; 1 Cl 33: 5; 2 Cl 14: 2. οὐκ ἔνι ἄρσεν καὶ θῆλυ Gal 3: 28;

cf. GEg 2; 2 Cl 12: 2, 5; GNaass 1; πᾶν ἄρσεν Lk 2: 23. The neut. ἄρσεν Rv 12: 5, otherw. vs. 13, comes fr. Is 66: 7 and is in apposition to υἱόν. Of the juxtaposition s. FBoll, ZNW 15, '14, 253; BOlsson, Glotta 23, '34, 112. M-M. B. 84.*

'Αρτεμᾶς, ᾶ, ὁ (CALobeck, Pathologiae Sermonis Graeci Prolegomena 1843, 505f; Dit., Syll.³ 851, 16; Inschr. v. Magn. 122d, 13; BGU 1205, 25 [28 BC]; POxy. 745, 2 [1 AD]) Artemas, a friend of Paul (short for 'Αρτεμίδωρος Bl-D. §125, 1) Tit 3: 12.*

Ἄρτεμις, ιδος, ἡ (Hom.+) Artemis a goddess whose worship was widespread (Diana is her Roman name). The center of her worship in Asia Minor was at Ephesus (DGHogarth, Excav. at Eph. The Archaic Artemisia '08; CPicard, Ephèse et Claros '22.—Jos., Ant. 15, 89; Sib. Or. 5, 293) Ac 19: 24, 27f, 34f. As here, A. is called 'The Great' in the lit. (Xenophon Eph. 1, 11, 5) and in inscr. fr. Ephesus (CIG 2963c; Gk. Inscr. Brit. Mus. III 1890, no. 481, 324; JTWood, Discoveries at Ephesus 1877 app., Inscr. fr. the Theater no. 1 col. 1, 9; 4, 48) and elsewh. (IG XII 2 no. 270; 514; cf. PGM 4, 2720 to 2722). Cf. BMüller, ΜΕΓΑΣ ΘΕΟΣ '13 (=Dissert. Phil. Hal. 21, 3) 331-3.— Jessen, Ephesia: Pauly-W. V '05, 2753-71; AWikenhauser, D. AG '21, 363-7; JdeJongh, Jr., De tempel te Ephese en het beeld van Diana: Geref. Theol. Tijdschr. 26, '26, 461-75; Beginn. V, '33, 251-6; HThiersch, Artemis Ephesia I: AGG III 12, '35. S. on Ἔφεσος.*

ἀρτέμων, ωνος, ὁ sail, prob. foresail ἐπαίρειν τὸν ἀ. hoist the foresail (cf. Plut., Mor. 870B τὰ ἱστία ἐπαίρ.) Ac 27: 40. Cf. Breusing 79f; HBalmer, D. Romfahrt d. Ap. Pls. '05; LCasson, Ships and Seamanship, '71, 240, n. 70. M-M.*

ἀρτηρία, ας, ἡ (Soph., Hippocr.+; Philo) artery MPol 2: 2.*

ἄρτι adv. (Pind.+; inscr., pap., LXX) now, just.
1. as class. (Phryn. p. 18 Lob.; 2 Macc 3: 28), of the immediate past just (Dio Chrys. 4, 61; Ael. Aristid. 48, 35 K.=24 p. 474 D.) ἄ. ἐτελεύτησεν she has just died Mt 9: 18. ἄ. ἐγένετο ἡ σωτηρία salvation has just now come Rv 12: 10.—GH 5.
2. also as class., of the immediate present at once, immediately, now (cf. Hippocr., Ep. 9, 2; Lucian, Soloec. 1 p. 553; Jdth 9: 1; 2 Macc 10: 28) παραστήσει μοι ἄ. at once he will put at my disposal Mt 26: 53; ἀκολουθεῖν ἄ. follow immediately J 13: 37; ἄφες ἄ. let it be so now (on the position of ἄ. cf. Bl-D. §474, 3) Mt 3: 15.
3. Later Gk. uses ἄ. of the present in general now, at the present time (Jos., Ant. 1, 125 alternating w. νῦν; 15, 18; Epict. 2, 17, 15; BGU 294, 5; PLond. 937b, 8ff οὐ δύναμαι ἄρτι ἐλθεῖν πρὸς σέ) ἄ. βλέπει now he can see J 9: 19, 25; cf. 13: 7, 33 (πλὴν ἄρτι 𝔓⁶⁶); 16: 12, 31; 1 Cor 13: 12; 16: 7; Gal 1: 9f; 4: 20; 1 Th 3: 6; 2 Th 2: 7; 1 Pt 1: 6, 8; 2 Cl 17: 3. After an aor. Hs 5, 5, 1.—Used w. prep. ἀπ' ἄρτι fr. now on (Plato Com., fgm. 143 K. ἀπαρτί for ἄρτι ἀπὸ νῦν) ἀπ' ἄ. λέγω J 13: 19; ἀπ' ἄ. γινώσκετε 14: 7; ἀποθνῄσκοντες ἀπ' ἄ. Rv 14: 13 (see s.v. ἀπαρτί and Bl-D. §12 app.); w. fut. (Aristoph., Plut. 388 ἀπαρτὶ πλουτήσαι ποιήσω) ἀπ' ἄ. ὄψεσθε Mt 26: 64; J 1: 51 t.r.; ἀπ' ἄ. ἕως up to the present time, until now (POxy. 936, 23; Sb 7036, 4) Mt 11: 12; J 2: 10; 5: 17; 16: 24; 1 Cor 4: 13; 8: 7; 15: 6; 1 J 2: 9.—In attributive position ἄ. has adj. mng. as in class. (Jos., Ant. 9, 264 ὁ ἄ. βίος) ἄχρι τῆς ἄ. ὥρας up to the present moment 1 Cor 4: 11 (cf. PGM 4, 1469 ἐν τῇ ἄ. ὥρᾳ; 1581;

1935; 5, 195; 7, 373; 546). μέχρι τῆς ἄρτι ὥρας Ac 10: 30 D. Nägeli 36, 1. M-M.*

ἀρτιγέννητος, ον (Lucian, Alex. 13; Longus 1, 9, 1; 2, 4, 3) new born βρέφη babes 1 Pt 2: 2 (Lucian, Dial. Marit. 12, 1 βρέφος ἀρτιγέννητον).—RPerdelwitz, D. Mysterienrel. u. d. Problem d. 1 Pt '11, 16ff; WBornemann, 1 Pt e. Taufrede d. Silvanus: ZNW 19, '20, 143-65. M-M.*

ἄρτιος, ία, ον (Hom.+; Epict. 1, 28, 3; IG XIV 889, 7 ἄ. εἴς τι; Philo) complete, capable, proficient=able to meet all demands 2 Ti 3: 17. M-M.*

ἄρτος, ου, ὁ (Hom.+; inscr., pap., LXX, Philo, Joseph., Test. 12 Patr.) bread.
1. lit. and specif., of bread as a food—a. gener. bread, also loaf (of bread) Mt 4: 4 (Dt 8: 3); 14: 17, 19; 15: 26, 33f; 16: 8ff; Mk 6: 38, 44, 52 (QQuesnell, The Mind of Mark, '69); 7: 27; 8: 4ff, 14 (JManek, Novum Testamentum 7, '64, 10-14), 16f; Lk 4: 4 (Dt 8: 3); 9: 13; 11: 5; J 6: 5, 23, 26; 21: 9; 2 Cor 9: 10 (Is 55: 10). Opp. λίθος Mt 4: 3 and Lk 4: 3 (Ps.-Clem., Hom. 2, 32 Simon Mag. ἐκ λίθων ἄρτους ποιεῖ); Mt 7: 9; Lk 11: 11 v.l. W. water (Dt 9: 18; Sir 29: 21; Hos 2: 7) Hs 5, 3, 7. The father of the household opened a meal (s. Billerb. IV 620ff) by taking a loaf of bread, giving thanks, breaking it, and distributing it: λαμβάνειν τὸν ἄ., (κατα)κλάσαι τὸν ἄ. (Jer 16: 7) Mt 14: 19; 15: 36; Mk 6: 41; 8: 19; Lk 9: 16; 24: 30; J 6: 11; 21: 13; Ac 20: 11; 27: 35. Cf. Lk 24: 35. Usu. taken along on journeys Mk 6: 8; Lk 9: 3; cf. Mt 16: 5, 7; Mk 8: 14. W. gen. of price διακοσίων δηναρίων ἄρτοι J 6: 7; Mk 6: 37. ἄρτοι κρίθινοι (Judg 7: 13; 4 Km 4: 42) loaves of barley bread J 6: 9, 13. The martyr's body in the fire is compared to baking bread MPol 15: 2.—Dalman, Arbeit IV: Brot, Öl u. Wein '35.
b. of a bread-offering ἄρτοι τῆς προθέσεως (Ex 40: 23; 1 Km 21: 7; 1 Ch 9: 32; 23: 29; 2 Ch 4: 19; cf. 2 Ch 13: 11; 2 Macc 10: 3; Dssm B 155f. Cf. Dit., Or. 56, 73; UPZ 149, 21 [III BC] πρόθεσις τ. ἄρτων in a temple l. 31; Wilcken p. 640) consecrated bread, lit. loaves of presentation (Billerb. III 719-33) Mt 12: 4; Mk 2: 26; Lk 6: 4; Hb 9: 2.
c. of the bread of the Lord's Supper, which likew. was broken after giving thanks, and then eaten Mt 26: 26; Mk 14: 22; Lk 22: 19; Ac 2: 42, 46; 20: 7; 1 Cor 10: 16f (the acc. τὸν ἄρτον vs. 16 is by attraction to the rel. ὅν; cf. Gen 31: 16); 11: 23, 26ff; D 14: 1; IEph 20: 2 (s. κλάω, κατακλάω, εὐχαριστέω 2, εὐχαριστία 3 and Abercius-inschr. 16.—Diog. L. 8, 35: acc. to Pythagoras the εἷς ἄρτος [1 Cor 10: 17] has served as a symbol of the union of the φίλοι from time immemorial to the present. Partaking of the same bread and wine [τ. αὐτὸν ἄρτον, οἶνον] as proof of the most intimate communion: Theodor. Prodr. 8, 400ff H.; Herodas 4, 93f: in the temple of Asclepius those who offer a sacrifice—in this case women—receive consecrated bread called ὑγίη [ὑγίεια] to eat; Athen. 3 p. 155A ὑγίεια καλεῖται ἡ διδομένη ἐν ταῖς θυσίαις μᾶζα ἵνα ἀπογεύσωνται; Anecd. Gr. p. 313, 13).—PdeBoer, Divine Bread, Studies in the Rel. of Anc. Israel, '72, 27-36.
2. food gener. (since bread is the most important food; cf. לֶחֶם e.g. Is 65: 25) περισσεύεσθαι ἄρτων have more than enough bread, i.e., plenty to eat Lk 15: 17 (cf. Pr 20: 13). διαθρύπτειν πεινῶσι τὸν ἄ. break bread for the hungry, i.e., give them someth. to eat B 3: 3, cf. 5 (Is 58: 7, 10). Hence ἄ. ἐσθίειν eat, dine, eat a meal (Gen 37: 25; 2 Km 12: 20; Eccl 9: 7) Mt 15: 2; Mk 3: 20; 7: 2, 5; Lk 14: 1. δωρεὰν ἄ. φαγεῖν παρά τινος eat someone's bread without paying 2 Th 3: 8. Opp. τὸν ἑαυτοῦ ἄρτον ἐσθίειν vs. 12. Of an ascetic way of life μὴ ἐσθίων ἄρτον μήτε πίνων οἶνον neither eating bread nor drinking wine, i.e.,

fasting Lk 7: 33 (cf. 1 Esdr. 9: 2). On ἄ. ἐπιούσιος Mt 6: 11; Lk 11: 3; D 8: 2 s. ἐπιούσιος.—τρώγειν τινὸς τὸν ἄ. *be the guest of someone* J 13: 18 (cf. Ps 40: 10). Since according to a concept widespread among Jews and pagans, eternal bliss was to be enjoyed in the form of a banquet, φαγεῖν ἄ. ἐν τῇ βασιλείᾳ τοῦ θεοῦ=share eternal bliss, or salvation Lk 14: 15.—In J ἄ. ἐκ τ. οὐρανοῦ (after Ps 77: 24; cf. Ex 16: 4; 2 Esdr 19 [Neh 9]: 15; Ps 104: 40; Wsd 16: 20; Sib. Or. fgm. 3, 49) is Christ and his body in the eucharist J 6: 31ff, 41, 50, 58 or simply Christ himself. For this ἄ. τῆς ζωῆς vs. 35, 48; ὁ ἄ. ὁ ζῶν vs. 51. Sim. ἄ. τ. θεοῦ IEph 5: 2; IRo 7: 3; ἄ. τ. Χριστοῦ 4: 1.—BGärtner, J 6 and the Jewish Passover, Con. Neot. 17, '59; GVermes, MBlack-Festschr., '69, 256–63.

3. *support, livelihood* τὸν ἄ. λαμβάνειν take his bread (i.e., support) D 11: 6.

4. *reward, proceeds* λαμβάνειν τὸν ἄ. τοῦ ἔργου receive the reward of (one's) labor 1 Cl 34: 1. M-M. B. 357.*

ἀρτύω fut. ἀρτύσω; pf. pass. ἤρτυμαι, 1 fut. ἀρτυθήσομαι (Hom.+; Polyb 15, 25, 2; Jos., Bell. 2, 614) *prepare,* specif. *season* (Hippocr.; Aristot., Nic. Eth. 3, 13 p. 1118a, 29 τὰ ὄψα; Theophr., De Odor. 51 [fgm. 4, 11] ἠρτυμένος οἶνος, cf. SSol 8: 2 Sym.; Athen. 3, 79 p. 113b; PTebt. 375, 27; POxy. 1454, 4) lit. *season, salt* Mk 9: 50; Lk 14: 34 (JWackernagel, ThLZ 33, '08, 36). Fig., λόγος ἅλατι ἠρτυμένος *speech seasoned w. salt* to make it interesting and fruitful Col 4: 6 (cf. MDibelius, Hdb. ad loc.). M-M.*

Ἀρφαξάδ, ὁ indecl. (אַרְפַּכְשַׁד), in Jos., Ant. 1, 146 Ἀρφαξάδης, ου, *Arphaxad,* son of Shem (Gen 10: 22, 24), in genealogy of Jesus Lk 3: 36.*

ἀρχάγγελος, ου, ὁ (En. 20, 8; Philo, Confus. Lingu. 146, Rer. Div. Her. 205, Somn. 1, 157; Porphyr., Ep. Ad Anebonem [GParthey, Iambl. De Myst. Lib. 1857 p. xxix-xlv c. 10; Iambl., Myst. 2, 3 p. 70, 10; Theologumena Arithmetica ed. VdeFalco '22, p. 57, 7; Agathias: Anth. Pal. 1, 36, 1; inscr. in Ramsay, Phrygia I 2 p. 557 no. 434 ὁ θεὸς τῶν ἀρχαγγέλων; Gnost. inscr. CIG 2895; PGM 1, 208; 3, 339; 4, 1203; 2357; 3052; 7, 257 τῷ κυρίῳ μου τῷ ἀρχαγγέλῳ Μιχαήλ; 13, 257; 328; 744) *archangel* a member of the higher ranks in the heavenly host PK 2 p. 14, 27. Michael (En. 20, 5; 8) is one of them Jd 9. He is also prob. the archangel who will appear at the Last Judgment 1 Th 4: 16 (the anonymous sing. as PGM 4, 483, where the archangel appears as a helper of Helios Mithras).—Cf. WLueken, D. Erzengel Michael 1898; Rtzst., Mysterienrel.³ 171, 2; UHolzmeister, Verb. Dom. 23, '43, 176–86 and s. on ἄγγελος. M-M.*

ἀρχαῖος, αία, αῖον (Pind., Hdt.+; inscr., pap., LXX, Philo, Joseph.) *ancient, old.*

1. *of what has existed fr. the beginning, or for a very long time* (Sir 9: 10; 2 Macc 6: 22) ὁ ὄφις ὁ ἀ. *the ancient serpent* Rv 12: 9; 20: 2. Of a Christian church βεβαιοτάτη καὶ ἀ. *old, established* 1 Cl 47: 6; ἀ. μαθητής *a disciple of long standing* (perh. *original disc.*) Ac 21: 16 (cf. Inschr. v. Magn. 215b, 3 [I AD] ἀρχαῖος μύστης; Thieme 26; Sir 9: 10 φίλος ἀ.).

2. *of what was in former times, long ago* (Ps 78: 8; 88: 50; Sir 16: 7; Jos., Ant. 9, 264) ἀ. ὑποδείγματα *examples from ancient times* 1 Cl 5: 1; ἀ. κόσμος *the world before the deluge* 2 Pt 2: 5. Of ages past (Diod. S. 1, 6, 2) ἀφ' ἡμερῶν ἀ. (Is 37: 26; La 1: 7; 2: 17) Ac 15: 7; ἐκ γενεῶν ἀ. (Sir 2: 10) 15: 21; ἐξ ἀ. χρόνων (Sb 7172, 12 [217 BC]) Pol 1: 2.—οἱ ἀρχαῖοι *men of ancient times, of old* (Thu. 2, 16, 1; Cornutus p. 2, 18; 4, 9; Ps.-Demetr. c. 175 [here ἀρχαῖοι is used to intensify παλαιοί: very old—old]; Sir 39: 1; 3

Km 5: 10; Philo, Rer. Div. Her. 181 [w. ref. to Plato]; Jos., Ant. 7, 171) Mt 5: 21, 27 t.r.; 33 (grammatically, τοῖς ἀρχαίοις can mean *by the men of old* as well as *to the men of old*; since Hdt. 6, 123; Thu. 1, 51; 118 the dat. w. the passive often replaces ὑπό w. gen., esp. in later writers such as Polyb. and Arrian. Cf. Lk 23: 15 πράσσω 1a). Of the ancient prophets (cf. Jos., Ant. 12, 413) Lk 9: 8, 19; D 11: 11. ἀ. ἀνήρ of Papias in Papias I 4 (Funk)=Eus., H.E. III 39, 1. τὰ ἀρχαῖα (Ps 138: 5; Wsd 8: 8; Is 43: 18) *what is old* 2 Cor 5: 17 (cf. τὸ ἀρχαῖον=the old state of things Dit., Or. 672, 9; Sb 5233, 17; Is 23: 17). M-M. B. 959.*

ἀρχέγονος, ον philosoph. and theol. term *original author, originator, source* τινός *of someth.* (Heraclit. Sto. 22 p. 32, 20 ἀ. ἁπάντων; Ps.-Aristot., De Mundo 6; Damoxenus in Athen. 3 p. 102A ἡ φύσις ἀρχέγονον πάσης τέχνης; Cornutus 8 p. 8, 11 ἀ. πάντων; Proclus, Theol. 152 p. 134, 21 τῶν ὅλων ἀ.; Philo, Poster. Cai. 63 [of God]; PGM 4, 1459) of the name of God ἀ. πάσης κτίσεως 1 Cl 59: 3.*

ἀρχεῖον, ου, τό lit. (X.+; inscr., pap.; Jos., Vi. 38, C. Ap. 1, 143; Inschr. v. Hierapolis 212, 6 ἐν τῷ ἀρχίῳ τ. Ἰουδαίων; loanw. in rabb.) the government building, in which the official records were kept, hence also *archives,* and the *official records, original documents* themselves (so Dionys. Hal., Ant. 2, 26; Jul. Africanus in Euseb., H.E. 1, 7, 13; Euseb., H.E. 1, 13, 5) ἐὰν μὴ ἐν τοῖς ἀρχείοις εὕρω *if I do not find it in the original documents* (prob.=the OT) IPhld 8: 2. ἐμοὶ δὲ ἀρχεῖά ἐστιν Ἰ. Χρ., τὰ ἄθικτα ἀρχεῖα ὁ σταυρὸς αὐτοῦ *for me the original documents are Jesus Christ, the holy original documents are his cross* ibid.*

Ἀρχέλαος, ου, ὁ *Archelaus,* a common (Diod. S. 18, 37, 4; Dit., Syll. and Or. Index; Preisigke, Namenbuch) name; in NT, the son of Herod I, ethnarch of Judaea, Idumaea and Samaria fr. his father's death in 4 B.C. to A.D. 6 when he was deposed by the Emperor Augustus; noted for his cruelty (Jos., Ant. 17, 342ff, Bell. 1, 668ff) Mt 2: 22.—Schürer I⁴ 449ff (sources and lit.).*

ἀρχή, ῆς, ἡ (Hom.+; inscr., pap., LXX, Philo, Joseph.).

1. *beginning*—a. concrete, pl. *corners* of a sheet Ac 10: 11; 11: 5 (cf. Hdt. 4, 60; Diod. S. 1, 35, 10).

b. *beginning* (opp. τέλος; cf. Diod. S. 16, 1, 1 ἀπ' ἀρχῆς μεχρὶ τοῦ τέλους; Ael. Aristid. 30, 24 K.=10 p. 123 D.: ἐξ ἀ. εἰς τέλος; Appian, Bell. Civ. 5, 9, §36; Wsd 7: 18) B 1: 6; IEph 14: 1; IMg 13: 1; IRo 1: 2, cf. 1. τὰ στοιχεῖα τῆς ἀ. *elementary principles* Hb 5: 12. ὁ τῆς ἀ. τοῦ Χ. λόγος *elementary Christian teaching* 6: 1. W. gen. foll. ἡμέρας ὀγδόης B 15: 8; ἡμερῶν (2 Km 14: 26) Hb 7: 3; τῶν σημείων *first of the signs* J 2: 11 (cf. Isocr., Paneg. 10: 38 Blass ἀλλ' ἀρχὴν μὲν ταύτην ἐποιήσατο τῶν εὐεργεσιῶν, τροφὴν τοῖς δεομένοις εὑρεῖν; Pr 8: 22; Jos., Ant. 8, 229 ἀ. κακῶν); ὠδίνων Mt 24: 8; Mk 13: 8; κακῶν ISm 7: 2. As the beginning of a book (Ion of Chios [V BC] no. 392 fgm. 24 Jac. ἀρχὴ τοῦ λόγου; Polystrat. p. 28; Diod. S. 17, 1, 1 ἡ βύβλος τὴν ἀ. ἔσχε ἀπό . . . ; Ael. Aristid. 23, 2 K.=42 p. 768 D.: ἐπ' ἀρχῇ τοῦ συγγράμματος; Diog. L. 3, 37 ἡ ἀρχὴ τῆς Πολιτείας; cf. Sb 7696, 53; 58 [250 AD]) ἀ. τοῦ εὐαγγελίου Ἰ. Χ. *beginning of the gospel of J. C.* Mk 1: 1 (cf. Hos 1: 2 ἀ. λόγου κυρίου πρὸς Ὠσηέ); cf. RHarris, Exp. '19, 113–19; '20, 142–50; 334–50; FEDaubanton, NThSt 2, '19, 168–70; AvanVeldhuizen, ibid., 171–5; EEidem, Ingressen til Mkevangeliet: FBuhl-Festschr. '25, 35–49; NFFreese, StKr 104, '32, 429–38; AWikgren, JBL 61, '42, 11–20 [review of interpr.]; LEKeck, NTS 12, '65/'66, 352–70). ἀ. τῆς ὑποστάσεως *original conviction* Hb 3: 14. ἀρχὴν ἔχειν w. gen. of the inf. *begin to be someth.* IEph 3: 1. ἀρχὴν λαμβάνειν *begin* (Polyb.; Aelian, V.H. 2, 28; 12, 53; Diog. L., Prooem. 3, 4; Sext. Emp., Phys. 1, 366; Philo, Mos. 1, 81) λαλεῖσθαι *be proclaimed at first* Hb 2: 3, cf. IEph 19: 3.—W. prep. ἀπ᾽ ἀρχῆς *from the beginning* (Paus. 3, 18, 2; Dit., Syll.³ 741, 20; UPZ 160, 15 [119 bc]; BGU 1141, 44; Jos., Ant. 8, 350; 9, 30) J 15: 27; 1 J 2: 7, 24; 3: 11; 2 J 5f; Ac 26: 4; MPol 17: 1; Hs 9, 11, 9; Dg 12: 3. οἱ ἀπ᾽ ἀ. αὐτόπται *those who fr. the beginning were eyewitnesses* Lk 1: 2. Also ἐξ ἀρχῆς (Dit., Syll.³ 547, 9; 634, 4; PGenève 7, 8; BGU 1118, 21; Jos., Bell. 7, 358) J 6: 64; 16: 4; 1 Cl 19: 2; Pol 7: 2; Dg 2: 1. πάλιν ἐξ ἀ. (Ael. Aristid. 21, 10 K.=22 p. 443 D.; Dit., Syll.³ 972, 174) *again fr. the beginning* B 16: 8. ἐν ἀρχῇ (Diod. S. 19, 110, 5; Palaeph. p. 2, 3; Dit., Or. 56, 57; PPetr. II 37, 2b verso 4; POxy. 1151, 15; BGU 954, 26) *at the beginning, at first* Ac 11: 15. ἐν ἀ. τοῦ εὐαγγελίου *when the gospel was first preached* Phil 4: 15; sim., word for word, w. ref. to beg. of 1 Cor, 1 Cl 47: 2.—τὴν ἀ. J 8: 25, as nearly all the Gk. fathers understood it, is used adverbially=ὅλως *at all* (Plut., Mor. 115b; Dio Chrys. 10[11], 12; 14[31], 5; 133; Lucian, Eunuch. 6 al.; Ps.-Lucian, Salt. 3; POxy. 472, 17 [c. 130 ad]; Philo, Spec. Leg. 3, 121; Jos., Ant. 1, 100; 15, 235 al.; as a rule in neg. clauses, but the negation can inhere in the sense; 48th letter of Apollonius of Tyana [Philostrat. I 356, 17]; Philo, Abrah. 116, Decal. 89; Ps.-Clem., Hom. 6, 11; cf. Field, Notes, 93f) τὴν ἀ. ὅτι καὶ λαλῶ ὑμῖν (*how is it) that I even speak to you at all?* Another possible mng. is, *To begin with, why do I as much as speak to you!* 𝔓⁶⁶ reads εἶπον ὑμῖν before τ. ἀρχήν, yielding the sense *I told you at the beginning what I am also telling you now* (RWFunk, HTR 51, ᾽58, 95–100).

c. *beginning, origin* in the abs. sense ἀ. πάντων χαλεπῶν Pol 4: 1 (cf. 1 Ti 6: 10, which has ῥίζα for ἀ., and s. passages like Ps 110: 10; Sir 10: 13); ἀ. κόσμου B 15: 8; ἀ. πάντων PK 2, p. 13, 21; ἀπ᾽ ἀρχῆς *fr. the very beginning* (Is 43: 13; Wsd 9: 8; 12: 11; Sir 24: 9 al.) Mt 19: 4, 8; J 8: 44; 1 J 1: 1 (of the histor. beg. of Christianity: HHWendt, D. Johannesbriefe u. d. joh. Christent. ᾽25, 31f; HWindisch, Hdb. ad loc.; differently, HConzelmann, RBultmann-Festschr., ᾽54, 194–201); 3: 8; 2 Th 2: 13 v.l.; ὁ ἀπ᾽ ἀ. 1 J 2: 13f; Dg 11: 4; οἱ ἀπ᾽ ἀ. *the first men* 12: 3; τὰ ἀπ᾽ ἀ. γενόμενα 1 Cl 31: 1; ἀπ᾽ ἀ. κτίσεως Mk 10: 6; 13: 19; 2 Pt 3: 4 (on ἀ. κτίσεως cf. En. 15, 9); ἀπ᾽ ἀ. κόσμου Mt 24: 21. Also ἐξ ἀ. (X., Mem. 1, 4, 5; Ael. Aristid. 43, 9 K.= 1 p. 3 D. [of the existence of Zeus]; Philo, Aet. M. 42, Spec. Leg. 1, 300) Dg 8: 11; ἐν ἀ. *in the beginning* (Simplicius in Epict. p. 104, 2) J 1: 1f; ἐν ἀ. τῆς κτίσεως B 15: 3. κατ᾽ ἀρχάς *in the beg.* Hb 1: 10 (Ps 101: 26; cf. Hdt. 3, 153 et al.; Diod. S.; Plut.; Philo, Leg. All. 3, 92, Det. Pot. Insid. 118; Ps 118: 152).

d. fig., of pers. (Gen 49: 3 Ῥουβὴν σὺ ἀρχὴ τέκνων μου; Dt 21: 17): of Christ Col 1: 18. W. τέλος of God or Christ Rv 1: 8 v.l.; 21: 6; 22: 13 (Hymn to Selene 35 ἀ. καὶ τέλος εἶ: Orphica p. 294, likew. PGM 4, 2836; 13, 362; 687; Philo, Plant. 93; Jos., Ant. 8, 280; others in Rtzst., Poim. 270ff and cf. Dit., Syll.³ 1125, 10 Αἰών, ἀρχὴν μεσότητα τέλος οὐκ ἔχων).

2. *the first cause* (philos. t.t. ODittrich, D. Systeme d. Moral I ᾽23, 360a.;—Ael. Aristid. 43, 9 K.=1 p. 3 D.: ἀρχὴ ἀπάντων Ζεύς τε καὶ ἐκ Διὸς πάντα; Jos., C. Ap. 2, 190 God as ἀρχὴ κ. μέσα κ. τέλος τῶν πάντων) of Christ ἡ ἀ. τῆς κτίσεως Rv 3: 14; but the mng. *beginning*=first created is linguistically poss. (s. above 1b and Job 40: 19); cf. CFBurney, Christ as the Ἀρχή of Creation: JTS 27, ᾽26, 160–77.

3. *ruler, authority* (Aeschyl., Thu.+; inscr.; e.g. PHal. 1, 226 μαρτυρείτω ἐπὶ τῇ ἀρχῇ καὶ ἐπὶ τῷ δικαστηρίῳ;

Gen 40: 13, 21; 41: 13; 2 Macc 4: 10, 50 al., cf. Magie 26; so as a loanw. in rabb.) w. ἐξουσία Lk 20: 20; pl. (Oenomaus in Euseb., Pr. Ev. 6, 7, 26 ἀρχαὶ κ. ἐξουσίαι; 4 Macc 8: 7; Jos., Ant. 4, 220) Lk 12: 11; Tit 3: 1; MPol 10: 2 (αἱ ἀρχαί can also be *the officials* as persons, as those who took part in the funeral procession of Sulla: Appian, Bell. Civ. 1, 106 §497.—The same mng. 2, 106 §442; 2, 118 §498 al. Likewise Diod. S. 34+35 fgm. 2, 31).—Also of angelic and demonic powers, since they were thought of as having a political organization (Damascius, Princ. 96 R.) Ro 8: 38; 1 Cor 15: 24; Eph 1: 21; 3: 10; 6: 12; Col 1: 16; 2: 10, 15. Cf. Justin, Dial. 120 at end.

4. *rule, office* (Diod. S. 3, 53, 1; Appian, Bell. Civ. 1, 13 §57; Jos., C. Ap. 2, 177, Ant. 19, 273), or better *domain, sphere of influence* (Procop. Soph., Ep. 139) of the angels Jd 6.—Cf. the lit. on ἄγγελος and HSchlier, Mächte u. Gewalten im NT: ThBl 9, ᾽30, 289–97. M-M.*

ἀρχηγός, οῦ, ὁ—1. *leader, ruler, prince* (Aeschyl.+; POxy. 41, 5; 6 and mostly LXX) ἀ. καὶ σωτήρ Ac 5: 31 (this combin. also 2 Cl 20: 5).—τ. ζωῆς 3: 15, where mng. 3 is also poss.

2. *one who begins* someth. as first in a series and thus supplies the impetus (Aristot., Metaph. 1, 3 of Thales ὁ τῆς τοιαύτης ἀρχηγὸς φιλοσοφίας; Aristoxenus, fgm. 83 Ὄλυμπος ἀ. γενέσθαι τ. Ἑλληνικῆς μουσικῆς; Polyb. 5, 10, 1; Plut., Mor. 958d; 1135b; Dit., Or. 219, 26 ἀ. τοῦ γένους; 1 Macc 9: 61; 10: 47; Mi 1: 13; Jos., C. Ap. 1, 130 [of Moses]) in bad sense *instigator* 1 Cl 14: 1 ζήλους; ἀ. στάσεως 51: 1 (cf. Herodian 7, 1, 11 ἀ. τ. ἀποστάσεως).

3. *originator, founder* (Diod. S. 15, 81, 2 ἀ. τῆς νίκης= originator; 16, 3, 5 τῆς βασιλείας ἀ.=founder; Jos., Ant. 7, 207. Oft. of God: Pla., Tim. 21e al.; Isocr. 4, 61 τῶν ἀγαθῶν; Diod. S. 5, 64, 5; Dit., Or. 90, 47, Syll.³ 711l, 13 Apollo ἀ. τ. εὐσεβείας) ἀ. τῆς ἀφθαρσίας 2 Cl 20: 5; ἀ. τῆς σωτηρίας Hb 2: 10; τῆς πίστεως ἀ. 12: 2. M-M.*

ἀρχιερατικός, όν (CIG 4363; Dit., Or. 470, 21; Jahresh. d. Österr. Archäol. Inst. 15, 51; Jos., Bell. 4, 164, Ant. 4, 83; 6, 115) *highpriestly* γένος ἀ. (Jos., Ant. 15, 40) *the high priest's family* Ac 4: 6 (on this Schürer II⁴ 274ff). M-M.*

ἀρχιερεύς, έως, ὁ (Hdt.+; inscr., pap., LXX, Ep. Arist., Philo, Joseph.; on the use of the title in pagan cults s. Brandis in Pauly-W. II 471–83; Magie 64).

1. lit.—a. pagan; *high priest* MPol 21=Ἀσιάρχης (q.v.) 12: 2.

b. Jewish; *high priest,* president of the Sanhedrin (Schürer II⁴ 255ff): in Jesus' trial Mt 26: 57, 62f, 65; Mk 14: 60f, 63; J 18: 19, 22, 24. Those named are Ἀβιαθάρ, Ἀνανίας, Ἄννας, Καϊάφας, Σκευᾶς; see these entries. The pl. is used in the NT and in Joseph. (Schürer II⁴ 275, 27; 276, 36) to denote members of the Sanhedrin who belonged to highpriestly families: ruling high priests, those who had been deposed, and adult male members of the most prominent priestly families (Schürer II⁴ 274ff; a different view in JoachJeremias, Jerusalem II B 1, ᾽29, 34ff [Coniect. Neotest. XI, ᾽47, 99–101]: holders of such priestly offices as treasurer, captain of police). ἀρχιερεῖς w. ἄρχοντες Lk 23: 13; 24: 20; w. γραμματεῖς and πρεσβύτεροι Mt 16: 21; 27: 41; Mk 8: 31; 11: 27; 14: 43, 53; 15: 1; Lk 9: 22; w. γραμματεῖς (Inschr. v. Magn. 197, 11f; 193, 10; Thieme 21f) Mt 2: 4; 20: 18; 21: 15; Mk 10: 33; 11: 18; 14: 1; 15: 31; Lk 20: 19; 22: 2, 66; 23: 10; w. πρεσβύτεροι Mt 21: 23; 26: 3, 47; 27: 1, 3, 12, 20; Ac 4: 23; 23: 14; 25: 15; ἀ. καὶ τὸ συνέδριον ὅλον Mt 26: 59; Mk 14: 55; Ac 22: 30 (πᾶν τὸ συν.). οἱ ἀρχιερεῖς alone=*the Sanhedrin* Ac 9: 14. Cf. 1 Cl 40: 5; 41: 2.—On ἀ. τ. ἐνιαυτοῦ ἐκ. J 11: 49, 51; 18: 13 cf. ἐνιαυτός 1.

2. fig.—a. of Christ, who has made atonement for the sins of men Hb 2: 17; 3: 1 (w. ἀπόστολος); 5: 10; 6: 20; 7: 26; 8: 1; 9: 11; 1 Cl 61: 3; 64; ἀ. μέγας (1 Macc 13: 42; Philo, Somn. 1, 219; Inscr. Gr. 1231; cf. also the ἀ. μέγιστος=pontifex maximus of imperial inscr.) Hb 4: 14 (GFriedrich, ThZ 18, '62, 95-115); ἀ. τῶν προσφορῶν 1 Cl 36: 1. Cf. ANairne, The Epistle of Priesthood '13, 135ff; HWindisch, Hdb., exc. on Hb 9: 14; JThUbbink, NThSt 22, '39, 172-84 (on Hb); MDibelius, D. himml. Kultus nach Hb: ThBl 21, '42, 1-11; HWenschkewitz, D. Spiritualisierung d. Kultusbegriffe Tempel, Priester u. Opfer im NT '32; OMoe, D. Priestert. Christi im NT ausserhalb des Hb: ThLZ 72, '47, 335-8; GSchille, Erwägungen zur Hohepriesterlehre des Hb: ZNW 56, '55, 81-109; AJansen, Schwäche u. Vollkommenheit des H-priesters Christus, Diss. Rome, '57.

b. of Christian prophets D 13: 3 and AP 20 acc. to Harnack's text (Wilamowitz ἀδελφῶν, Schubert ἀρχηγῶν).—GSchrenk, TW III 265-84. M-M.

ἀρχιλῃστής, οῦ, ὁ (Herodian Gr. I 82, 26; Ps.-Callisth. 1, 36; Maspéro 2 III, 22; Jos., Bell. 1, 204, Vi. 105; loanw. in rabb.) *robber chieftain* J 18: 40 v.l.*

ἀρχιποίμην, ενος, ὁ (Herodian Gr. I 16, 19; wooden tablet of imperial times in Dssm., LO 77f [LAE 97ff]=Sb 3507; PLeipz. 97 XI, 4 Κάμητι ἀρχιποίμενι; PSI 286, 6; 4 Km 3: 4 Sym.; Test. Judah 8: 1: cited in WJost, ΠΟΙΜΗΝ, Diss. Giessen, '39, 47-50) *chief shepherd* of Christ 1 Pt 5: 4 (cf. the ποιμὴν μέγας Hb 13: 20 and the ἀρχιβουκόλος of the Dionysus mysteries; RPerdelwitz, D. Mysterienrel. u. d. Problem d. 1 Pt '11, 100f). M-M and suppl.*

Ἄρχιππος, ου, ὁ *Archippus* a common name (Diod. S. 18, 58, 1; Dit., Syll. Index; PHib. 124-6; 130), found also in west. Asia Minor (CIG 3143; 3224 Smyrna). Of a Christian in Colossae Col 4: 17, called συστρατιώτης of Paul and Ti, Phlm 2. Cf. also inscr. v.l. and subscr. v.l.*

ἀρχισυνάγωγος, ου, ὁ (exx. fr. inscr. and lit. in Schürer II⁴ 509-12; Sb 5959, 3 [time of Augustus]; Suppl. Epigr. Gr. VIII 170; on this ZNW 20, '21, 171; Dssm., LO 378-80 w. lit.) *leader* or *president of a synagogue*, a term found also in pagan religions and given simply as a title (Schürer 512), in our lit. only w. ref. to the Jewish synagogue, of an official whose duty it was esp. to take care of the physical arrangements for the worship services (Hebr. רֹאשׁ הַכְּנֶסֶת) Mk 5: 22, 35f, 38; Lk 8: 49; 13: 14; Ac 13: 15; 14: 2D; 18: 8, 17. Those named are Ἰάϊρος, Κρίσπος and Σωσθένης; s. these entries. M-M.*

ἀρχιτέκτων, ονος, ὁ (Hdt.+; inscr., pap., LXX, Philo; Jos., Vi. 156; loanw. in rabb.) *master builder* σοφὸς ἀ. (Is 3: 3; cf. Philo, Somn. 2, 8) 1 Cor 3: 10 (Pla., Amat. 135ᴮ τέκτονα μὲν ἂν πρίαιο πέντε ἢ ἓξ μνῶν ἄκρον, ἀρχιτέκτονα δ᾽ οὐδ᾽ ἂν μυρίων δραχμῶν. 10,000 drachmas =100 minas). M-M.*

ἀρχιτελώνης, ου, ὁ (not found elsewh.) *chief tax collector* Lk 19: 2.*

ἀρχιτρίκλινος, ου, ὁ (Heliod. 7, 27, 7 ἀρχιτρίκλινοι καὶ οἰνοχόοι) *head waiter, butler,* the slave who was responsible for managing a banquet; in Lat architriclinus, tricliniarcha. In the context of J 2: 8f it may= συμποσίαρχος *toastmaster, master of the feast* (cf. ἡγούμενος Sir 32: 1f).*

ἀρχοντικός, ή, όν (Herm. Wr. 1, 25; Anth. Pal. 9, 763; Vett. Val. 14, 24f; 70, 8; 355, 33; pap.) *pertaining to the archon,* or *ruler* (s. ἄρχων 3; used of angels ἀρχοντικός

Celsus 6, 27; 35; Kephal. I 53, 7) συστάσεις ἀ. *associations of the (angelic) rulers* ITr 5: 2.*

ἄρχω fut. mid. ἄρξομαι; 1 aor. ἠρξάμην (Hom.+; inscr., pap., LXX, Ep. Arist., Philo, Joseph., Test. 12 Patr.) lit. *be first.*

1. act. *rule* w. gen. *over someth.* or *someone* (Hom.+; class.; UPZ 81 col. 2, 18 [II ʙᴄ] as an epithet of Isis: τῶν ἐν τῷ κόσμῳ ἄρχουσα; En. 9, 7; Ep. Arist. 190; Philo, Congr. Erud. Gr. 6) τῶν ἐθνῶν Mk 10: 42; Ro 15: 12 (Is 11: 10). τῶν θηρίων τ. γῆς B 6: 12 (cf. Gen 1: 26, 28).

2. mid. *begin*—**a.** w. pres. inf. (DCHesseling, Z. Syntax v. ἄρχομαι: ByzZ 20, '11, 147-64; JAKleist, Mk '36, 154-61 Marcan ἤρξατο).

α. lit., to denote what one begins to do, in pres. inf. (Polyaenus 3, 9, 40 σφαγιάζειν) λέγειν (Jos., Ant. 8, 276; 18, 289) Mt 11: 7; ὀνειδίζειν vs. 20; τύπτειν 24: 49; κηρύσσειν 4: 17; Mk 5: 20; παίζειν Hs 9, 11, 5 al.; εἶναι IRo 5: 3. Emphasis can be laid on the beginning Lk 15: 14; 21: 28, Ac 2: 4; 11: 15, or a contrast can be implied, as w. continuation Mk 6: 7; 8: 31; IEph 20: 1; w. completion Mt 14: 30; J 13: 5; w. an interruption Mt 12: 1; 26: 22; Ac 27: 35.—μὴ ἄρξησθε λέγειν ἐν ἑαυτοῖς *do not begin to think* =do not cherish the unfortunate thought Lk 3: 8.

β. Oft. ἄ. only means that the pers. in question has been doing something else, and that his activity now takes a new turn Mt 26: 37, 74; Lk 4: 21; 5: 21; 7: 15, 24, 38, 49 al. In such cases it is freq. almost superfluous, in accordance w. late Jewish usage (Jos., Ant. 11, 131; 200; Dalman, Worte 21f; cf. JWHunkin, 'Pleonastic' ἄρχομαι in NT: JTS 25, '24, 390-402). So ὧν ἤρξατο ὁ Ἰησ. ποιεῖν Ac 1: 1=simply *what Jesus did* (sim. Lat. coepio).

b. abs. (sc. the inf. fr. the context) ἦν Ἰησοῦς ἀρχόμενος ὡσεὶ ἐτῶν τριάκοντα Lk 3: 23 prob. *Jesus was about 30 years old when he began his work.* In ἀρξάμενος Πέτρος ἐξετίθετο (Aesop, Fab. 100 P. Μῶμος ἀρξάμενος ἔλεγε; Xenophon Eph. 5, 7, 9 ἀρξαμένη κατέχομαι) ἀ. receives its content fr. the foll. καθεξῆς: P. *began and explained in order* Ac 11: 4.

c. w. indication of the starting point ἄ. ἀπὸ τότε *begin fr. that time* Mt 4: 17; 16: 21; ἄ. ἀπό τινος (class., also Arrian, Cyneg. 36, 4; PMMeyer, Griech. Texte aus Ägypt. '16, 24, 3; Ezk 9: 6; Jos., Ant. 7, 255 ἀπὸ σοῦ; in local sense Dit., Syll.³ 969, 5; PTebt. 526; Jos., Ant. 13, 390) ἀρξάμενος ἀπὸ Μωϋσέως *beginning w. Moses* Lk 24: 27; ἀ. ἀπὸ τῆς γραφῆς ταύτης *beginning with this passage of Scripture* Ac 8: 35; J 8: 9; 1 Pt 4: 17. Locally Ac 10: 37. With both starting point and end-point given (Lucian, Somn. 15 ἀπὸ τῆς ἕω ἀρξάμενος ἄχρι πρὸς ἑσπέραν; Gen 44: 12) ἀπό τινος ἕως τινός: ἀπὸ τ. ἐσχάτων ἕως τῶν πρώτων Mt 20: 8; Ac 1: 22; local Lk 23: 5. M-M. B. 976; 1319.

ἄρχων, οντος, ὁ (Aeschyl., Hdt.+; inscr., pap., LXX; Ep. Arist. 281; Philo, Joseph.) actually ptc. of ἄρχω, used as subst.

1. *ruler, lord, prince* of Christ ὁ ἄ. τ. βασιλέων τ. γῆς *the ruler of the kings of the earth* Rv 1: 5; οἱ ἄ. τῶν ἐθνῶν Mt 20: 25; cf. B 9: 3 (Is 1: 10) οἱ ἄ. *the rulers* Ac 4: 26 (Ps 2: 2). W. δικαστής of Moses 7: 27, 35 (Ex 2: 14).

2. gener. of those in authority (so loanw. in rabb.) *authorities, officials* Ro 13: 3; Tit 1: 9 v.l. For 1 Cor 2: 6-8 s. 3 below.

a. of Jewish authorities (Schürer, index; PLond. 1177, 57 [113 ᴀᴅ] ἀρχόντων Ἰουδαίων προσευχῆς Θηβαίων; Inscr. Rom. 1024, 21; Jos., Ant 20, 11) of the high priest Ac 23: 5 (Ex 22: 27). Of those in charge of the synagogue (Inscr. Graec. Sic. It. 949) Mt 9: 18, 23; cf. ἄ. τῆς συναγωγῆς Lk 8: 41; Ac 14: 2 D. Of members of the

Sanhedrin Lk 18: 18; 23: 13, 35; 24: 20; ἄ. τ. Ἰουδαίων (cf. Epict. 3, 7, 30 κριτὴς τῶν Ἑλλήνων) J 3: 1; cf. 7: 26, 48; 12: 42; Ac 3: 17; 4: 5, 8 (ἄρχοντες καὶ πρεσβύτεροι as 1 Macc 1: 26); 13: 27; 14: 5. τὶς τῶν ἀρχόντων τ. Φαρισαίων a member of the Sanhedrin who was a Pharisee Lk 14: 1. Of a judge Lk 12: 58.

b. of pagan officials (Diod. S. 18, 65, 6; cf. the indices to Dit., Syll. and Or.) Ac 16: 19; 1 Cl 60: 2, 4 (Funk); MPol 17: 2. W. ἡγούμενοι 1 Cl 61: 1. W. βασιλεῖς and ἡγούμενοι 1 Cl 32: 2.

3. esp. of evil spirits (Kephal. I p. 50, 22; 24; 51, 25 al.), whose hierarchies resembled human polit. institutions. The devil is ἄ. τ. δαιμονίων Mt 9: 34; 12: 24; Mk 3: 22; Lk 11: 15 (cf. Βεεζεβούλ.—Porphyr. [in Euseb., Pr. Ev. 4, 22, 15] names Sarapis and Hecate as τοὺς ἄρχοντας τ. πονηρῶν δαιμόνων) or ἄ. τοῦ κόσμου τούτου J 12: 31; 14: 30; 16: 11; ἄ. καιροῦ τοῦ νῦν τῆς ἀνομίας B 18: 2; ὁ ἄ. τοῦ αἰῶνος τούτου IEph 17: 1; 19: 1; IMg 1: 3; ITr 4: 2; IRo 7: 1; IPhld 6: 2. (Cf. Ascension of Isaiah 1, 3; 10, 29; Third Corinthians 3, 11 in the Acts of Paul [EHennecke, NT Apoc. II, 376] the 'prince of the world' and s. ASchlatter, D. Evglst. Joh. '30, 271f). Many would also class the ἄρχοντες τοῦ αἰῶνος τούτου 1 Cor 2: 6–8 in this category (so from Origen to H-DWendland ad loc.), but the pass. may belong under mng. 2 above (TLing, ET 68, '56/'57, 26; WTPBoyd, ibid. 68, '57/'58, 158). ὁ πονηρὸς ἄ. B 4: 13; ὁ ἄδικος ἄ. MPol 19: 2 (cf. ὁ ἄρχων τ. πλάνης Test. Sim. 2: 7, Judah 19: 4). ὁ ἄ. τῆς ἐξουσίας τοῦ ἀέρος Eph 2: 2 (s. ἀήρ, end). W. ἄγγελος as a messenger of God and representative of the spirit world (Porphyr., Ep. ad Aneb. [s. ἀρχάγγελος] c. 10) Dg 7: 2; οἱ ἄ. ὁρατοί τε καὶ ἀόρατοι the visible and invisible rulers ISm 6: 1. M-M. B. 1324.*

ἄρωμα, ατος, τό (Hippocr. +) nearly always pl. (X., An. 1, 5, 1; Dit., Syll.³ 999, 17, Or. 383, 143; POxy. 1211, 10; BGU 149, 1; LXX; Ep. Arist.; Philo, Leg. All. 1, 42; Jos., Ant. 14, 72), in our lit. exclusively so spices, aromatic oils or salves, perfumery, esp. used in embalming the dead (Diod. S. 18, 26, 3 [the ἀρώματα in Alexander's coffin were put there to preserve the corpse]; Charito 1, 8, 2; Plut., Sulla 38, 3; 2 Ch 16: 14) Mk 16: 1; Lk 23: 56; 24: 1; J 19: 40; 1 Cl 25: 2. τίμια ἀ. precious perfumes MPol 15: 2. Of aromatic herbs AP 5: 15. M-M.*

ἀσάλευτος, ον (Eur., Pla.+; Jos., Bell. 1, 405; inscr.; pap.; LXX in special sense) immovable, unshaken.

1. lit., of part of a ship that has run aground ἡ πρῷρα ἔμεινεν ἀ. the bow remained immovable Ac 27: 41.

2. fig. (so Polystrat. p. 10 [πίστις]; Diod. S. 2, 48, 4 [ἐλευθερία]; 3, 47, 8; 5, 15, 3 al.; Plut., Mor. p. 83E; Philo, Mos. 2, 14; Inschr. v. Magn. 116, 36f [διάταξις]; Epigr. Gr. 855, 3; 1028, 4; PLeipz. 34, 18; 35, 20) βασιλεία ἀ. a kingdom that cannot be shaken Hb 12: 28. M-M.*

Ἀσάφ (אָסָף 1 Ch 3: 10), ὁ indecl. (cf. Jos., Ant. 11, 80 οἱ Ἀσάφου παῖδες) Asa(ph), in genealogy of Jesus Mt 1: 7f (v.l. Ἀσά both times); Lk 3: 23ff D.*

ἄσβεστος, ον (Hom.+; Jos., Bell. 2, 245).

1. inextinguishable (syn. αἰώνιος Mt 18: 8; 25: 41) πῦρ ἄ. (this combin. also Dionys. Hal. 1, 76; Strabo 15, 3, 15; Plut., Num 9, 15, Mor. 410B; 411C; Ael. Aristid. 26, 99 K. = 14 p. 365 D.; Aelian, N.A. 5, 3; Philo, Spec. Leg. 1, 285, Ebr. 134; Job 20, 26 v.l.; PGM 4, 3070; PWarr. 21, 2, 21) Mt 3: 12; Mk 9: 43, 45 t.r.; Lk 3: 17; 2 Cl 17: 7; IEph 16: 2.

2. ἡ ἄ. unslaked lime (Diosc. 5, 115 W.; Plut., Sert. 17, 3) Hs 9, 10, 1.*

ἀσβόλη, ης, ἡ (Semonides 7, 61 Diehl; Diosc. 5, 161 W.; La 4: 8 for ἡ ἄσβολος; Galen XVI 623, 8 ὑπὸ τ. πολλῶν ἀσβόλην, ἣν ἄσβολον οἱ Ἕλληνες. Cf. Lobeck, Phryn. p. 113) soot, typical of blackness Hs 9, 1, 5; 9, 6, 4.*

ἀσέβεια, ας, ἡ (Eur., X., Pla.+; Diod. S. 1, 44, 3 εἰς τοὺς θεοὺς ἀσέβεια; Epict., inscr.; PEleph. 23, 1; 9f; GPlaumann, Griech. Pap. d. Samml. Gradenwitz [1914] 4, 20; LXX; Ep. Arist. 166; Philo; Jos., Ant. 9, 266, C. Ap. 2, 291; Test. 12 Patr.) godlessness, impiety, in thought and act ἐπὶ πλεῖον προκόπτειν ἀσεβείας progress further in ungodliness 2 Ti 2: 16; ἀρνεῖσθαι τὴν ἀ. Tit 2: 12; φυγεῖν τὴν ἀ. 2 Cl 10: 1; ἔργα ἀσεβείας Jd 15 (En. 1, 9). Of the relig. condition of the heathen Ro 1: 18 (cf. Dt 9: 5). ἀσεβείας ὑπόδειγμα Papias 3. Fig. τῆς ἀ. πλησθήσονται they will be sated w. their impiety 1 Cl 57: 6 (Pr 1: 31).—Pl. (Pla., Leg. 890A; LXX; Jos., Bell. 7, 260) ἀποστρέψει ἀσεβείας ἀπὸ Ἰακώβ Ro 11: 26 (Is 59: 20). ἐπιθυμίαι τ. ἀσεβειῶν godless desires Jd 18 (cf. En. 13, 2 ἔργα τ. ἀσεβειῶν).—Dodd 76–81; BGärtner, The Areopagus Speech and Natural Revelation '55, 73ff. M-M.*

ἀσεβέω 1 aor. ἠσέβησα (Aeschyl., Hdt.+; inscr.; LXX; Philo; Jos., Ant. 9, 262; 11, 91, C. Apion. 2, 194; Test. 12 Patr.) act impiously 2 Pt 2: 6; 2 Cl 17: 6. ἔργα ἀσεβείας ἀσεβεῖν commit impious deeds Jd 15 (En. 1, 9). M-M.*

ἀσεβής, ές acc. sing. ἀσεβῆν Ro 4: 5 אDFG, Bl-D. §46, 1 (Aeschyl., Thu.+; Epict.; Paus. 4, 8, 1 θεῶν ἀσεβής; inscr., pap., LXX, Philo, Joseph.) godless, impious.

1. of pers. ἁμαρτωλός ἀ. Jd 15 (En. 1: 9). οἱ ἀ. ἄνθρωποι (UPZ 162 III, 8 [117 BC] ὑπὸ ἀσεβῶν ἀνθρώπων) 2 Pt 3: 7. Mostly subst. ὁ ἀ. the godless (man) (Diod. S. 1, 96, 5; 3, 61, 5; 5, 71, 2; 6; Dit., Or. 90, 23; 26; LXX; Test. Zeb. 10: 3) Ro 5: 6; 2 Pt 2: 5; 2: 6 ℘⁷² et al.; Jd 4, 15; 1 Cl 14: 5 (Ps 36: 35); 18: 13 (Ps 50: 15); 57: 7 (Pr 1: 32); B 10: 10 (Ps 1: 1); 11: 7 (Ps 1: 4ff); (w. ἁμαρτωλός) 1 Ti 1: 9; (w. ἄνομος) B 15: 5; Dg 9: 4; (w. κεκριμένοι τῷ θανάτῳ) B 10: 5; οἱ κρινόμενοι ἀ. the wicked who are (already) condemned 2 Cl 18: 1. Punished w. eternal fire MPol 11: 2 (Diod. S. 4, 74, 2 the ἀσεβεῖς in everlasting torment in a subterranean place of punishment).—The collective sg. (as Lucian, Bacch. 7 ὁ γέρων=οἱ γέροντες; Ep. Arist. 13) Ro 4: 5; 1 Pt 4: 18 (Pr 11: 31).—AVStröm, Vetekornet, Studier över individ och kollektiv i NT '44.

2. of human characteristics (w. ἄδικος, as Philo, Rer. Div. Her. 90; Jos., Ant. 8, 251) ζῆλος ἀ. 1 Cl 3: 4. Impers. (Epict. 4, 7, 11; Dit., Syll.³ 204, 52 ὅπως ἂν μηδὲν ἀσεβὲς γίγνηται) πῶς οὐκ ἀσεβές; how is it not impious? Dg 4: 3. M-M.*

ἀσέλγεια, ας, ἡ (Pla., Isaeus et al.; Polyb. 1, 6, 5; 5, 28, 9 al.; Plut., Alcib. 8, 2; Lucian, Gall. 32; PMagd. 24, 2; PLond. 1711, 34; Wsd 14: 26; 3 Macc 2: 26; Jos., Ant. 4, 151; 8, 252; 318; 20, 112; Test. Judah 23: 1) licentiousness, debauchery, sensuality in sg. and pl. ἑαυτὸν παραδιδόναι τῇ ἀ. give oneself over to debauchery Eph 4: 19; πορεύεσθαι ἐν ἀσελγείαις live licentiously 1 Pt 4: 3; cf. Hm 12, 4, 6. τὴν χάριτα μετατιθέναι εἰς ἀ. pervert favor into licentiousness Jd 4 (here ἀσ. is perh. rather insolence, as Diod. S. 16, 87, 1, where it is used of the insolence of a scoffer); ἐξακολουθεῖν ταῖς ἀ. follow the inclination to sensuality 2 Pt 2: 2. Cf. Hv 2, 2, 2. Esp. of sexual excesses (Philo, Mos. 1, 305) w. κοῖται Ro 13: 13; w. ἀκαθαρσία and πορνεία 2 Cor 12: 21; Gal 5: 19, in a long catalogue of vices, like Mk 7: 22; Hs 9, 15, 3. ἡ ἐν ἀ. ἀναστροφή *indecent conduct* 2 Pt 2: 7; cf. vs. 18. αἱ ἐπιθυμίαι τῆς ἀ. *licentious desires* Hv 3, 7, 2 (cf. Polyb. 36, 15, 4 ἀ. περὶ τ. σωματικὰς ἐπιθυμίας). M-M.*

ἄσημος, ον (trag., Hdt.+; inscr., pap., LXX) *without (distinguishing) mark.*
1. *unintelligible* (Aeschyl., Prom. 662 χρησμοί; Hdt. 1, 86, 4; Philo, Migr. Abr. 79) τὰ γεγραμμένα Dg 12: 3.
2. *obscure, insignificant* (Gen 30: 42; 3 Macc 1: 3; Philo, Virt. 222; Jos., Bell. 6, 81, Ant. 16, 243 οὐκ ἄ., Vi. 1 οὐκ ἄ.) οὐκ ἄ. πόλις *no unimportant city* Ac 21: 39 (Eur., Ion 8 οὐκ ἄσημος πόλις, likewise Strabo 8, 6, 15; a favorite expr., s. Wettstein ad loc.). M-M.*

ἄσηπτος, ον (Hippocr.+; LXX almost always w. ξύλον) *not rotted* of sticks Hs 8, 6, 5, fr. the context here obviously in the mng. *not worm-eaten.* *

Ἀσήρ (אָשֵׁר), ὁ indecl. (LXX, Philo, Test. 12 Patr.—In Joseph. Ἄσηρος, ου [Ant. 7, 59]) *Asher*, son of Jacob (Gen 30: 13; 49: 20; 2 Ch 30: 11), ancestor of the tribe to which the prophetess Anna belonged Lk 2: 36. In the list of the 12 tribes Rv 7: 6.*

ἀσθένεια, ας, ἡ (Hdt., Thu.+; inscr., pap., LXX, Philo, Joseph., Test. 12 Patr.) *weakness.*
1. lit.—a. of bodily weakness Hv 3, 11, 4; 3, 12, 2. Oft. *sickness, disease* (X., Mem. 4, 2, 32; Appian, Bell. Civ. 5, 16 §5; Herodian 1, 4, 7; pap.; 2 Macc 9: 21f; Jos., Bell. 1, 76, Ant. 15, 359) Ac 5, 15D; w. νόσος Mt 8: 17; ἔχειν ἀ. *be ill* Ac 28: 9; ἀσθένειαν τῇ σαρκὶ αὐτῶν ἐπισπῶνται Hv 3, 9, 3; θεραπεύεσθαι ἀπὸ τῶν ἀ. Lk 5: 15. For this ἀπολύεσθαι τῆς ἀ. 13: 12; ἔτη ἔχειν ἐν ἀ. (s. ἔτος, end) J 5: 5, cf. 11: 4; Hs 6, 3, 4. δι᾽ ἀσθένειαν τῆς σαρκός *because of a bodily ailment* (Dio Chrys. 28 [45], 1 σώματος ἀσθ., likew. Ael. Aristid. 27, 2 K.=16 p. 382 D.— PLond. 971, 4 ἀδύνατος γάρ ἐστιν ἡ γυνὴ διὰ ἀσθένιαν τῆς φύσεως, cf. also PFlor. 51, 5 σωματικῆς ἀσθενείας) Gal 4: 13. ἀσθένειαι (pl., as 2 Cor 12: 5, 9f) *times of weakness, weaknesses* 1 Ti 5: 23. Caused by demons, the πνεύματα ἀσθενείας, Lk 8: 2; 13: 11.
b. gener., of any kind of weakness (opp. δύναμις. Diod. S. 4, 8, 3: many do not believe the writers of history when they relate the marvelous deeds of one like Heracles, because they judge the δύναμις of the divine hero in comparison with the ἀσθένεια of contemporary men) 1 Cor 15: 43. δυναμοῦσθαι ἀπὸ ἀ. *come out of weakness to strength* Hb 11: 34. In Paul's ἀ., which appears in τὰ τῆς ἀ. μου 2 Cor 11: 30 or αἱ ἀσθένειαι (s. a above) 12: 5, 9f, God's δύναμις manifests itself 12: 9 (s. τελέω 1, end).
c. gener., of the frailty to which all human flesh is heir (Pla., Leg. 854A ἀ. τ. ἀνθρωπίνης φύσεως; Diod. S. 1, 2, 3 ἡ τῆς φύσεως ἀ.; 13, 24, 4; 6) of Christ ἐσταυρώθη ἐξ ἀ. (opp. ἐκ δυνάμεως θεοῦ) *he was crucified as a result of his weakness* (his weak nature) 2 Cor 13: 4. περίκειται ἀσθένειαν Hb 5: 2. For this ἀ. ἔχειν 7: 28.
2. fig., of *timidity* (w. φόβος and τρόμος) 1 Cor 2: 3. Of weakness in judgment τῆς σαρκός Ro 6: 19. Of the lack of relig. insight 8: 26. Of moral weakness 1 Cl 36: 1; Hm 4, 3, 4. συμπαθῆσαι ταῖς ἀ. *sympathize w. weaknesses* Hb 4: 15. M-M.*

ἀσθενέω 1 aor. ἠσθένησα (Eur., Thu.+; inscr., pap., LXX, Test. 12 Patr.) *be weak, powerless.*
1. lit.—a. of bodily weakness *be sick* (Dit., Syll.³ 596, 16 ἰατρὸν τὸν θεραπεύσοντα τοὺς ἀσθενοῦντας; 620, 43; POxy. 725, 40; BGU 844, 13; PLond. 144 al.) Mt 25: 39; Lk 7: 10 v.l.; J 4: 46; 11: 1, 2, 3, 6; Phil 2: 26f; 2 Ti 4: 20; Js 5: 14; ἀ. νόσοις ποικίλαις *suffer from various diseases* Lk

4: 40.—Pres. ptc. oft. as subst. *the sick person* J 5: 7, 13 v.l.; mostly pl., Mt. 10: 8; Mk 6: 56; Lk 9: 2 v.l.; J 5: 3; 6: 2; Ac 19: 12; 1 Cl 59: 4.—The aor. means *I was sick* Mt 25: 36 or *I have become sick* Ac 9: 37 (Palaeph. p. 44, 2 ἡ Ἕλλη ἀσθενήσασα ἀπέθανεν).
b. of weakness of any kind 2 Cor 12: 10; ἀ. εἴς τινα (opp. δυνατεῖν ἔν τινι) *be weak toward someone* 2 Cor 13: 3; cf. vss. 4, 9; *be weakened, disabled* (Oenomaus in Euseb., Pr. Ev. 5, 24, 3; Jos., Bell. 2, 329, Ant. 6, 370; Sb 5113, 19) of the law's weakness: ἐν ᾧ ἠσθένει *because it was weakened* Ro 8: 3. Of weakness caused by fear or caution 2 Cor 11: 21.
2. fig., of relig. and moral weakness Ro 14: 2; 1 Cor 8: 11f; 2 Cl 17: 2. W. σκανδαλίζεσθαι Ro 14: 21 v.l.; ἀ. τῇ πίστει *be weak in faith* 4: 19; 14: 1 (i.e., over-scrupulous). Gener. of faint-heartedness and fearfulness 2 Cor 11: 29.
3. *be weak economically, be in need* (Eur.; Aristoph., Pax 636; PHib. 113, 17; PTebt. 188 [I BC]) Ac 20: 35 (s. ἀσθενής 2c). M-M.*

ἀσθένημα, ατος, τό (Aristot. 638a, 37; 726a, 15; the rdg. is not certain in BGU 903, 15 [II AD]) *weakness*; pl., of conscientious scruples caused by weakness of faith (cf. ἀσθενέω 2) Ro 15: 1. M-M.*

ἀσθενής, ές (Pind., Hdt.+; inscr., pap., LXX, Philo; Jos., Ant. 3, 11; 7, 344; Test. 12 Patr.; loanw. in rabb.) *weak, powerless.*
1. lit.—a. *sick, ill* ἄνθρωπος ἀ. Ac 4: 9. Subst. ὁ ἀ. *the sick person* (Diod. S. 1, 34, 4) Mt 25: 43f; Lk 10: 9; Ac 5: 15f; 1 Cl 59: 4; Pol 6: 1. W. ἄρρωστος 1 Cor 11: 30 (on the connection betw. wrongdoing and disease cf. PMich. Inv. 3690, 7-11 [ZPE 4, '69, 123]); ἀ. τῷ σώματι *physically weak* (PFlor. 382, 41) 1 Cl 6: 2; ἀ. τῇ σαρκί Hs 9, 1, 2.
b. gener., of any weakness. Opp. ἰσχυρός (cf. Ael. Aristid. 36 p. 690 D.; Philo, Aet. M. 58) 1 Cl 38: 2; cf. Hv 3, 11, 4; ἡ σὰρξ ἀ. *the flesh is weak*, gives up too easily Mt 26: 41; Mk 14: 38; Pol 7: 2. Of woman (PAmh. 141, 15; PFlor. 58, 14 γυνὴ ἀσθενής; Ep. Arist. 250) ἀσθενέστερον σκεῦος *weaker vessel*, i.e. sex 1 Pt 3: 7. ἡ παρουσία τοῦ σώματος ἀ. *his personal presence is weak* i.e. unimpressive 2 Cor 10: 10. Acc. to many modern scholars, of spirit beings that can do nothing (w. πτωχός) τὰ ἀ. στοιχεῖα *the weak elementary spirits* Gal 4: 9 (S. στοιχεῖον 3).
2. fig.—a. *weak, feeble, miserable* ἡμεῖς ἀ. 1 Cor 4: 10; τὰ μέλη ἀσθενέστερα *the weaker, less important members* 12: 22. W. φθαρτός the heart B 16: 7.—τὸ ἀσθενές=ἡ ἀσθένεια (Thu. 2, 61, 2; POxy. 71 II, 4 τὸ τῆς φύσεως ἀ.; Jos., Ant. 13, 430) w. τὸ ἀνωφελές Hb 7: 18; τὸ ἀ. τοῦ θεοῦ *the weakness of God*: even *what is weak* acc. to human standards becomes effective as soon as it comes *fr. God* 1 Cor 1: 25.—τὰ ἀ. τοῦ κόσμου *what is weak in* (the eyes of) *the world* 1: 27.
b. *morally weak* ὄντων ἡμῶν ἀ. (=ἁμαρτωλῶν vs. 8) Ro 5: 6. Of a weakness in faith, which, through lack of advanced knowledge, considers externals of the greatest importance (cf. Epict. 1, 8, 8 ἀπαιδεύτοις κ. ἀσθενέσι) 1 Cor 8: 7, 9f (WJMcGarry, Eccl. Rev. 94, '37, 609-17). ἐγενόμην τοῖς ἀ. ἀ. *to those who are weak in faith I became as they are* 1 Cor 9: 22; ἀντέχεσθαι τῶν ἀ. *take care of the weak* 1 Th 5: 14.—ERiggenbach, StKr 66, 1893, 649-78; MRauer, D. 'Schwachen' in Korinth u. Rom nach den Pls-briefen '23.
c. *weak, without influence* συγγένεια 1 Cl 10: 2. οἱ ἀσθενέστεροι Dg 10: 5 (but here ἀ. could have the mng. *economically weak, poor*, as PHib. 113, 17; PThéad. 20, 15 τὰς ἀσθενεστέρας κώμας).

d. comp., of stones *too weak*, i.e. incapable of standing great strain Hs 9, 8, 4; 6. M-M. B. 298.*

'Ασία, ας, ἡ (Pind., Hdt.+; inscr., LXX, Philo, Joseph.) *Asia*, a Rom. province (Asia proprie dicta) in western Asia Minor, formed in 133-130 BC, from the time of Augustus ruled by proconsuls. Ac 2: 9; 16: 6; 19: 1D, 10, 22, 26f; 20: 4 v.l., 16, 18; 21: 27; 24: 19; 27: 2; 6: 9 καὶ 'Ασίας is lacking in AD*.—Ro 16: 5; 1 Cor 16: 19; 2 Cor 1: 8; 2 Ti 1: 15; 1 Pt 1: 1; Rv 1: 4; IEph inscr.; ITr inscr.; IPhld inscr.; ISm inscr.; MPol 12: 2.—Cf. JMarquardt, Röm. Staatsverwaltung I² 1881, 339-49; Mommsen, Röm. Geschichte V 299ff; Brandis, Pauly-W. II 1538ff; JWeiss, RE X 537ff; VChapot, La province romaine procons. d'Asie '04.*

'Ασιανός, οῦ, ὁ (Thu. et al.; Philo) *a man from the* Rom. province of *Asia*, of Tychicus and Trophimus Ac 20: 4.*

'Ασιάρχης, ου, ὁ (Strabo 14, 1, 42; inscr.) *Asiarch*, plainly equiv. to the ἀρχιερεὺς 'Ασίας (cf. Ramsay, Phrygia I 2 p. 465 no. 299, where ἀρχιερεῖς is used in the sense 'Asiarchs') MPol 12: 2 (cf. 21). Many would understand it so also in Ac 19: 31 (JMarquardt, Röm. Staatsverwaltung I² 1881, 513ff; Lghtf., Ign. and Pol. III² 1889, 404ff; Ramsay, Bearing 88; also Wendt, Hoennicke, Preuschen, Zahn, EJacquier, Steinmann ad loc.). But the titles are sometimes differentiated (Dit., Syll.³ 900, 5), and the pl. in Ac rather favors a ref. to deputies of the κοινὸν 'Ασίας, the assembly of Asia, which met in Ephesus (so finally Beyer; Bauernfeind). Cf. Brandis, Pauly-W. II 1564ff (lit.); JWeiss RE X 538f; Thieme 17; LRTaylor: Beginnings I 5, '33, 256-62; DMagie, Roman Rule in Asia Minor, '50, 449f, 1298-1301, 1526; EHaenchen, AG '56, p. 514, 4). M-M.*

ἀσιτία, ας, ἡ (Eur., Hdt.+; Jos., Ant. 12, 290; PRyl. 10, 6 and 12 in the sense 'a fast, hunger'; so ἀσιτέω Esth 4: 16; 1 Macc 3: 17) *lack of appetite* (Hippocr., Aphor. 7, 6; Hippiatr. I 54, 10; ἄσιτος='without appetite' in Ostr. 2, 35 in Preisendanz, PGM II p. 210) πολλῆς ἀ. ὑπαρχούσης *since almost nobody wanted to eat* because of anxiety or seasickness (seasickness: Ael. Aristid. 48, 68 K.=24 p. 483 D. ἀσιτίαι οὐκ ὀλίγαι in a storm.—JRMadan, JTS 6, '05, 116-21.—Hippiatr. I 3, 7 ἀσιτίας μενούσης) Ac 27: 21. M-M.*

ἄσιτος, ον (Hom.+; Arrian, Anab. 4, 9, 4) *without eating, fasting* Ac 27: 33 (Galen XI 242 K. ἄ. διετέλεσε; cf. Jos., Ant. 10, 258). M-M.*

ἀσκέω impf. ἤσκουν (Hom.+; inscr., pap., Ep. Arist., Philo; Jos., Ant. 3, 309; 4, 294) *practice, engage in* τὶ someth. (so trag., Hdt.+; cf. 2 Macc 15: 4) ἐμπορίαν ἀ. *engage in business* w. θεοσέβειαν *practice piety* 2 Cl 20: 4 (UPZ 144, 24 [164 BC] εὐσέβειαν ἀσκήσαντα; cf. Sib. Or. 4, 170.—Eur., Bacch. 476 ἀσέβειαν; Philo, Cher. 42 εὐσ., Virt. 94 ἀσ.); ἀ. πᾶσαν ὑπομονήν *practice patience to the limit* Pol 9: 1; δικαιοσύνην ἀ. (Hdt. 1, 96; Pla., Gorg. 527ε; Nicol. Dam.: 90 fgm. 103m, 2 Jac. ἀσκοῦντες εὐσέβειαν κ. δικαιοσύνην; 103w, 2; Ep. Arist. 168) Hm 8: 10; βίον παράσημον ἀ. *lead a peculiar kind of life* Dg 5: 2 (cf. Sb 5100, 4 epitaph for Abbot David: τὸν μοναδικὸν ἀσκήσας βίον). ἡ εἰς ζωὴν ἀσκουμένη γνῶσις *knowledge which is applied to life* 12: 5 (Eur., Electra 1073 γυνή...ἥτις ἐκ δόμων ἐς κάλλος ἀσκεῖ=who, outside of her home, pays too much attention to beautifying herself). Abs. ἐν τούτῳ ἀσκῶ w. inf. foll. *therefore I do my best* Ac 24: 16 (cf. X., Cyr. 5, 5, 12, Mem. 2, 1, 6; Epict. 3, 12, 10).—HDressler, Ἀσκέω and its cognates in Gk. Documents to 100 AD, Diss. Cath. Univ. of America '47. M-M.*

ἄσκησις, εως, ἡ (Thu.+; 4 Macc 13: 22; Philo, Migr. Abr. 31, Vi. Cont. 28; Jos., C. Ap. 2, 171) *practice* lit., of athletes, transferred to martyrs, w. ἑτοιμασία MPol 18: 2.—FPfister, Deissmann-Festschr. '27, 76-81.*

ἀσκός, οῦ, ὁ (Hom.+; inscr., pap., LXX) *a leather bag*, esp. *wine-skin* (Dio Chrys. 13[7], 46; Ps.-Apollod., Epit. 7, 4; Jos., Ant. 6, 55 ἀ. οἴνου) Mt 9: 17; Mk 2: 22; Lk 5: 37f. M-M.*

ἄσκυλτος, ον *not tortured, untroubled* (so Act. Thom. 12 p. 118, 6 Bonnet. In pap. freq. *undisturbed*: BGU 638, 13 [II AD]; 650, 20; PFlor. 39, 11; POxy. 125, 15 al.). In our lit. only in one passage, where *unmoved, without moving* seems to be the sense ἄσκυλτον ἐπιμεῖναι MPol 13: 3.*

ἀσμένως adv. (Aeschyl.+; Dit., Syll.³ 742, 52; PGrenf. II 14, 17f; 2 and 3 Macc; Ep. Arist. 5; Jos., Bell. 1, 309 al.; ἄσμενος Hom.+) *gladly* ἀ. ἀποδέχεσθαι *receive someone gladly* (Cebes 26, 1 ἀσμ. ὑποδέχεσθαί τινα; Philo, Rer. Div. Her. 295 v.l.; Jos., Ant. 4, 131 ἀ. δέχ. τ. λόγους) Ac 2: 41 t.r.; 21: 17. M-M.*

ἄσοφος, ον (Theognis, Pind.+; PRyl. 62, 12; Pr 9: 8 v.l.) *unwise, foolish* subst. ὁ ἄ. (Philostrat., Vi. Apoll. 6, 39 p. 250, 10) 2 Cl 19: 2. Opp. σοφός (Philostrat., op. cit. 3, 43 p. 117, 26f) Eph 5: 15. M-M.*

ἀσπάζομαι 1 aor. ἠσπασάμην (Hom.+; inscr., pap., LXX, Ep. Arist., Philo, Joseph.) *greet*.

1. τινά *someone*—a. lit., of those entering a house Mt 10: 12; Lk 1: 40; Ac 21: 19; Hv 5: 1. Of those meeting others (Jos., Ant. 8, 321) Lk 10: 4; *welcome, greet someone* (Philostrat., Vi. Apoll. 1, 12) Mk 9: 15; Hv 1, 1, 4; 1, 2, 2; 4, 2, 2. Of those departing *take leave of* (X., An. 7, 1, 8; Nicol. Dam.: 90 fgm. 68, 7 Jac.; Plut., Aemil. P. 29, 1 ἀσπασάμενος ἀνέζευξεν) Ac 20: 1, 12D; 21: 6 v.l.—Mt 5: 47 ἀ. certainly means more than 'greet'; *be fond of, cherish, be devoted to, like* are better (X., Cyr. 1, 4, 1; Ael. Aristid. 31, 6 K.=11 p. 128 D.; Aelian, V.H. 9, 4; Appian, Bell. Civ. 3, 79 §322 τ. ἐναντίους); w. ἀγαπάω, of which it is almost a synonym (as Plut., Mor. 143B; s. HAlmqvist, Plut. u. das NT, '46, 34; Ptolem., Apotel. 1, 3, 17.—W. φιλέω: Hierocles 19 p. 460; opp. μισέω: Simplicius in Epict. p. 31, 6). S. FXPorporato, Verb. Domini 11, '31, 15-22.—Freq. in written greetings (cf. the exx. in Ltzm., Griech. Papyri [Kleine Texte 14]² '10, nos. 7, 8, 9, 10, 11, 13.—FZiemann, De Epistularum Graec. Formulis Soll., Diss. Halle '11, 325ff; FXJExler, The Form of the Ancient Gk. Letter '23; ORoller, D. Formular d. paul. Briefe '33, 67ff); the imper. may be transl. *greetings to* (*someone*) or *remember me to* (*someone*); other moods than imperative may be rendered *wish to be remembered, greet, send greetings* Ro 16: 3, 5ff; 1 Cor 16: 19f; 2 Cor 13: 12; Phil 4: 21f; Col 4: 10, 12, 14f; 2 Ti 4: 19, 21; Tit 3: 15; Phlm 23; Hb 13: 24; 1 Pt 5: 13f; 2 J 13; 3 J 15; IMg inscr.; 15; ITr inscr.; 12: 1; 13: 1; IRo inscr.; 9: 3; IPhld inscr.; 11: 2; ISm 11: 1; 12: 1f; 13: 1f; IPol 8: 2f. Another person than the writer of the letter sometimes adds greetings of his own Ro 16: 22 (sim. POxy. 1067, 25 κἀγὼ Ἀλέξανδρος ἀσπάζομαι ὑμᾶς πολλά). ἀ. πολλά (beside the pap. just mentioned also PPar. 18, 3 [Dssm., B 215]; POxy. 930; 935; PGrenf. II 73 [=Ltzm. nos. 13, 14, 15]) *greet warmly* 1 Cor 16: 19; ἀ. κατ' ὄνομα (PPar. 18 [Dssm., B 216]; POxy. 930 [=Ltzm. no. 13]) *greet by name* 3 J 15; ISm 13: 2 (πάντας κατ' ὄνομα as PMich. 206, 20ff [II AD]; ἄσπασαι τοὺς φιλοῦντας ἡμᾶς ἐν πίστει (PFay. 119, 26 ἀσπάζου τοὺς φιλοῦντες [sic] ἡμᾶς πρὸς ἀλήθιαν. Sim. BGU 814, 39) Tit 3: 15. Among friends the greeting is accompanied by a kiss (Ps.-Lucian, De Asin. 17 φιλήμασιν ἠσπάζοντο ἀλλήλους; Heliod.

10, 6), hence: ἀ. ἐν φιλήματι Ro 16: 16; 1 Cor 16: 20; 2 Cor 13: 12; 1 Th 5: 26; 1 Pt 5: 14. Of homage to a king *hail, acclaim* (Dionys. Hal. 4, 39; Plut., Pomp. 12, 4; 13, 7; cf. Jos., Ant. 10, 211) Mk 15: 18 (cf. Philo, In Flacc. 38).

b. of short visits Ac 18: 22; 21: 7; IRo 1: 1. Of official visits *pay one's respects to* (Sb 8247, 13; 15 [II AD]; BGU 248, 12; 347 I 3, II 2; 376 I, 3; Jos., Ant. 1, 290: 6, 207) Ac 25: 13.

2. fig., of things *greet, welcome* someth. (Eur., Ion 587; Charito 6, 7, 12; Alciphr. 1, 3, 3; POxy. 41, 17 τὴν παρ᾽ ὑμῶν τιμήν; PRainer 30 II, 39; Philo, Det. Pot. Ins. 21; Jos., Ant. 6, 82; 7, 187; Test. Gad 3: 3) τὰς ἐπαγγελίας the promises Hb 11: 13. M-M.*

ἀσπασμός, οῦ, ὁ (Theognis+; Epict. 4, 4, 3; 37; POxy. 471, 67; Ep. Arist. 246; 304; Jos., Ant. 15, 210) *greeting.*

1. of formal salutations Lk 1: 29, 41, 44; φιλεῖν etc. Mt 23: 7; Mk 12: 38; Lk 11: 43; 20: 46.

2. of written greetings ὁ ἀ. τῇ ἐμῇ χειρὶ Παύλου 1 Cor 16: 21; Col 4: 18; 2 Th 3: 17. M-M.*

ἄσπιλος, ον (since IG II 5, 1054c, 4 [c. 300 BC; Eleusis]; Nägeli 38) *spotless, without blemish.*

1. lit. (ἵππος Herodian 5, 6, 7; μῆλον Antiphil. [I AD]: Anth. Pal. 6, 252, 3; ἀλέκτωρ PGM 2, 25; 3, 693; 13, 370; Cyranides p. 25, 26 λίθος; 36, 27) ἀμνὸς ἄμωμος καὶ ἄ. *a lamb spotless and without blemish* 1 Pt 1: 19.

2. fig. in moral sense (Job 15: 15 Sym.) of Christians (w. ἀμώμητος) 2 Pt 3: 14, cf. Jd 25 P⁷² et al. W. καθαρός Hv 4, 3, 5.—Of flesh (=person) w. ἀμίαντος Hs 5, 6, 7. ἄσπιλον ἑαυτὸν τηρεῖν ἀπό τ. κόσμου *keep oneself unspotted by the world* Js 1: 27 (on the constr. w. ἀπό s. PGM 12, 260); τηρεῖν τὴν ἐντολήν ἄ. 1 Ti 6: 14; τηρεῖν τὴν σφραγῖδα ἄ. 2 Cl 8: 6. M-M.*

ἀσπίς, ίδος, ἡ (Hdt.+; Antig. Car. 16; Aelian, N.A. 2, 24; 6, 38; Plut., Is. et Osir. 74 p. 380F; Ps.-Oppian, Cyn. 3, 433; Dit., Or. 90, 43; PGM 4, 2116; LXX; Philo; Jos., C. Ap. 2, 86; Sib. Or. 3, 794) *asp, Egyptian cobra* gener. of venomous snakes ἰὸς ἀσπίδων *venom of asps* Ro 3: 13 (Ps 13: 3; 139: 4). M-M.*

ἄσπλαγχνος, ον (Soph.+) *merciless* (so Aq. Dt 32: 33; Sym. Ezk 31: 12; Pr 17: 11) w. πικρός Hs 6, 3, 2.*

ἄσπονδος, ον *irreconcilable* (so Aeschyl.+; Demosth. 18, 262; Polyb. 1, 65, 6; Cicero, Ad Att. 9, 10, 5; Philo, Virt. 131, Mos. 1, 242; Jos., Ant. 4, 264) in a list of vices Ro 1: 31 t.r.; 2 Ti 3: 3 (in both passages w. ἄστοργος, as schol. on Nicander, Ther. 367). M-M.*

ἀσσάριον, ου, τό (Lat. loanw.: assarius [nummus]; s. Hahn index; Dit., Or. II p. 108 note 14; Kubitschek in Pauly-W. II 1742ff., end) the *as* or *assarion*, a Roman copper coin, worth about one-sixteenth of a denarius (s. δηνάριον), or a similar native coin ἀσσαρίου πωλεῖσθαι *be sold for a cent* (half-penny) Mt 10: 29; Lk 12: 6. M-M.*

Ἀσσάρων, ωνος Ac 9: 35 t.r.; s. Σαρων.*

ἆσσον adv. (comp. of ἄγχι) *nearer* (Hom.+; Jos., Ant. 1, 328; 19, 198) ἆσσον παρελέγοντο τὴν Κρήτην *they sailed along closer (close* is also poss.—Bl-D. §244, 2) *to Crete* Ac 27: 13. (The Vulg. understands Ἆσσον, q.v.).*

Ἆσσος, ου, ἡ *Assos,* a city on the coast of Mysia, in the Rom. province of Asia (Stephan. Byz. s.v. Ἆσσος after Alexander Cornelius Polyhistor) Ac 20: 13f.*

ἀστατέω (Plut., Crass. 17, 1; Vett. Val. 116, 30; Anth. Pal. App. 3, 146, 4 I App. Nova Epigrammatum ed. ECougny 1890]; mostly=*be unsteady;* Nägeli 44) *be unsettled, home-*less, *a vagabond* (Is 58: 7 Aq.) of Paul's way of life 1 Cor 4: 11.—Field, Notes 170. M-M.*

ἄστατος, ον (Aristot.+; inscr., pap. in various mngs.) *unsteady, unstable,* (Polyb.+) *unweighed* (Nicander, Ther. 602; IG I 32B, 25 al.). In UGosp 62, in a fragmentary context, (the first half of the line is missing entirely) the second half of the line is restored thus: τ̣ὸ̣ βάρος αὐτοῦ ἄστατο(ν). The editors translate it (p. 28): 'its weight unweighed(?)'.*

ἄστεγος, ον (Manetho 1, 173; Appian, Iber. 78 §336; Philo, Fuga 189; Ps.-Phoc. 24 Diehl) *homeless* B 3: 3 (Is 58: 7).*

ἀστεῖος, α, ον (lit. *pertaining to the city,* Lat. urbanus, fr. ἄστυ; Aristoph.+; X., Pla.; PHib. 54, 16; LXX, Philo; Jos., Ant. 7, 147).

1. *beautiful, well-formed* of bodily grace and charm (Judg 3: 17; Jdth 11: 23; Sus 7) Hb 11: 23 (Ex 2: 2). However, this adj. applied to Moses in scripture seems also to have been understood (as the addition of τ. θεῷ shows) in the sense

2. *acceptable, well-pleasing* (Num 22: 32; Philo, Spec. Leg. 1, 284 ἄξιον αὐτὸν παρεχέτω τῶν εὐπραγιῶν ἀστεῖος ὤν) ἀ. τῷ θεῷ Ac 7: 20. For the possibility that τ. θεῷ functions as a superl. (Jon 3: 3) s. θεός 3gβ. M-M.*

ἀστήρ, έρος, ὁ (Hom.+; Epict. 1, 28, 3; Vett. Val. 244, 20; Herodian 1, 14, 1; Herm. Wr. 5, 3; Dit., Syll.³ 241, 111, Or. 194, 19; a few times in astron. and magic. pap. [e.g. PGM 4, 574; 580; 2891; 2894; 2939]; LXX; En. 18, 4; Philo [e.g. Plant. 12] ἀστέρες as livings beings endowed w. reason; loanw. in rabb.) *star, single star* (Achilles, Comm. in Arat. p. 41 ἀστήρ ἐστιν εἷς ἀριθμῷ; schol. on Pind., Ol. 1, 9d) IEph 19: 2. Of the star of the Magi Mt 2: 2, 7, 9f (FBoll, ZNW 18, '18, 40-8. Diod. S. 16, 66, 3: a marvelous, divinely sent heavenly body leads the fleet of Timoleon toward Italy. When he and his companions noticed this heavenly manifestation, περιχαρεῖς ἦσαν [16, 66, 5].—On the star s. on μάγος 1). Falling fr. heaven in the last tribulation Mt 24: 29; Mk 13: 25; Rv 6: 13 (all three Is 13: 10; cf. Artem. 2, 36 p. 137, 15 καταπίπτοντες εἰς γῆν οἱ ἀστέρες). Single stars 8: 10; 9: 1 (cf. Artem. 5, 23 τ. οὐρανοῦ ἀστέρα ἐκπεσεῖν; Ps.-Callisth. 3, 33, 26: at the death of Alexander μέγας ἀστὴρ πεσὼν ἐκ τ. οὐρανοῦ ἐπὶ τὴν θάλασσαν.—Boll, Offb. 135). Changed at Christ's parousia B 15: 5. W. sun and moon (Dt 4: 19; Test. Napht. 3: 2) 1 Cor 15: 41; Rv 8: 12; 12: 1 (Eratosth. 33 ἔχει ἀστέρας ἐπὶ τ. κεφαλῆς); 1 Cl 20: 3; B 15: 5. Of the stars as numberless (Gen 22: 17; 1 Ch 27: 23 al.) 1 Cl 10: 6 (Gen 15: 5); 32: 2 (Gen 22: 17).—As to the seven stars which the Son of Man holds in his right hand Rv 1: 16; 2: 1; 3: 1 it has been conjectured that the metaphor is based on a constellation, prob. that of the Great Bear (Strabo 1, 1, 21 τοὺς ἑπτὰ τῆς μεγάλης ἄρκτου ἀστέρας; almost the same thing in Diod. S. 3, 48, 1.—Philo, Op. M. 114, Leg. All. 1, 8; PGM 4, 700; ADieterich, Mithraslit. '03, 14; 16f; 72f; Boll, Offb. 21f). In 1: 20 they are interpr. to mean the ἄγγελοι (PGM 1, 74f star=angel; 154; Chrysipp., Stoic. II 1076 and Diod. S. 2, 30, 6 stars=gods; En. 18, 14=heavenly beings) of the seven churches, by which according to some are meant the guardian angels (so fr. Origen, Hom. 12 and 13 In Luc., De Orat. 11, to Bousset, Charles, Lohmeyer; JSickenberger, Röm. Quartalschr. 35, '27, 135-49; Behm); more commonly they are held to signify the overseers or bishops (so fr. Primasius and Bede to Zahn, JWeiss, Billerb., Allo.—... to designate a prominent man: Plut., Marcell. 30, 8 ὁ μέγας πατρίδος ἀ.). ἀ. ὁ πρωϊνός *the morning star* (Venus) likened to Christ 22: 16; δώσω αὐτῷ τὸν ἀ. τὸν πρωϊνόν 2: 28 (cf. on both passages Boll, Offb. 47-50). Other pass. reflecting the same point of view, going back largely, as some hold, to Babyl. apocalyptic are 8: 11, 12; 12: 1, 4, which also contain the word ἀ.— ἀστέρες πλανῆται wandering stars (Cicero, De Nat. Deor. of stars 'quae falso vocantur errantes'), perh. meteors, typical of heret. teachers Jd 13 (cf. En. 18: 14; also chap. 21).—FBoll, Sternglaube u. Sterndeutung⁴ '31 (lit.). M-M. B. 56.*

ἀστήρικτος, ον (Περὶ ὕψους 2, 2; Anth. Pal. 6, 203, 11; Vett. Val., Ind.; Galen, De Usu Part. II 459 Helmr. [ind.]) unstable, weak ψυχαὶ ἀ. unst. souls 2 Pt 2: 14. Subst. οἱ ἀ. (w. ἀμαθεῖς) 3: 16. M-M.*

ἀστομάχητος, ον (Alciphr. 4, 17, 2; CIG 6647; FBilabel, Badische Pap. '23 no. 35, 17 [87 AD]) not easily angered (w. μακρόθυμος) Hv 1, 2, 3.*

ἄστοργος, ον (Aeschin.+; Hellenist. poets; Plut.; M. Ant. [Nägeli 17]; Athen. 14 p. 655c; Epigr. Gr. 146, 6; 1028, 44) unloving in a catalogue of vices Ro 1: 31; 2 Ti 3: 3. M-M.*

ἀστοχέω (fr. III BC, Polyb. et al.; inscr., pap., LXX; Jos., Bell. 4, 116; cf. Nägeli 31) orig. miss the mark then miss, fail, deviate, depart w. gen. fr. someth. (Plut., Def. Orac. p. 414F; Dit., Syll.³ 543, 28 [214 BC]; POxy. 219, 21; UPZ 6, 26 [163 BC] ἀστοχήσαντες τοῦ καλῶς ἔχοντος; Sir 7: 19; 8: 9) 1 Ti 1: 6; ἀ. περί τι (Plut., Mor. p. 46A; 705c) περὶ τὴν πίστιν miss the mark w. regard to the faith 6: 21; ἀ. περὶ τὴν ἀλήθειαν 2 Ti 2: 18. κατά τινος wrong someone D 15: 3. Abs. (BGU 531 II, 19 [I AD]) οἱ ἀστοχήσαντες those who have gone astray (in word and deed) w. ἀρνησάμενοι 2 Cl 17: 7. M-M.*

ἀστραπή, ῆς, ἡ (Aeschyl., Hdt.+; PGM 7, 785; LXX; Jos., Ant. 2, 343; 5, 201) lightning, illuminating the whole sky Mt 24: 27. Proceeding fr. God's throne Rv 4: 5 (cf. Ezk 1: 13; PGM 4, 703). Accompanying cosmic phenomena 8: 5; 11: 19; 16: 18 (cf. PGM 4, 681f; 694ff. The combin. w. βρονταί also Diod. S. 4, 2, 3; Epict. 2, 18, 30; hymn to Isis POxy. 1380, 238; Jos., Ant. 3, 184). Type of the greatest speed Lk 10: 18 (FSpitta, ZNW 9, '08, 160-3) and brilliance 17: 24; Mt 28: 3 (cf. Na 2: 5). Of a lamp light (Aeschyl., fgm. 386) Lk 11: 36. ἀ. πυρός fiery lightning AP fgm. 1. M-M. B. 56.*

ἀστράπτω (Hom.+; Epict. 1, 29, 61; PGM 5, 150; 7, 234; 8, 92; LXX; Philo, Aet. M. 86) flash, gleam ἀστραπὴ ἀστράπτουσα (cf. Ps 143: 6) lightning flashing Lk 17: 24. Of clothing gleam like lightning 24: 4. M-M.*

ἄστρον, ου, τό (Hom.+; inscr., pap., LXX; En. 18, 14; Philo; Jos., Ant. 1, 31, C. Ap. 2, 117) star, constellation, also single star (=ἀστήρ: Posidon. in Stob., Flor. 1, 24 p. 518 [HDiels, Doxogr. Graec. 1879 p. 466, 20] διαφέρειν ἀστέρα ἄστρου. εἰ μὲν γὰρ τίς ἐστιν ἀστήρ, καὶ ἄστρον ὀνομασθήσεται δεόντως. οὐ μὴν ἀνάπαλιν; PGM 1, 75; Galen XVIIA p. 16, 6ff K.; cf. Boll, ZNW 18, '18, 41ff) w. sun and moon (Pla., Leg. 10 p. 898D; Dio Chrys. 80[30], 28; Epict. 2, 16, 32; 3, 13, 16 al.; Jo 2: 10; Ezk 32: 7) Lk 21: 25; Dg 4: 5; 7: 2 (w. ἀστήρ) IEph 19: 2. Normally showing sailors the way at night Ac 27: 20. Typical of a large number Hb 11: 12 (Ex 32: 13; Dt 1: 10; 10: 22 al.; Philo, Rer. Div. Her. 86; Jos., Ant. 1, 183). τὸ ἄ. τοῦ θεοῦ Ῥομφά the constellation of the god Rompha Ac 7: 43 (Am 5: 26) s. Ῥομφά. M-M.*

ἀσυγκρασία, ας, ἡ (not found elsewh.) lack of sharing or community spirit Hv 3, 9, 4.*

ἀσύγκριτος, ον incomparable (Theophr.+; Epicurus [in

Diog. L. 10, 83]; Plut., Marcell. 17, 7; Herm. Wr. 6, 5; Dialekt-Inschr. 4481, 8 [Laconia]; Inschr. Gal. no 110, 8; BGU 613, 20; PGenève 55, 4ff; POxy. 1298, 1; Philo; Test. Levi 2, 9; Jewish inscr.: RGarrucci, Dissert. Archeol. II 1865, p. 179; 182) ISm 13: 2 (here w. εὔτεκνος, scarcely a proper name; s. the foll. entry) πρᾶξις ἀ. conduct beyond compare Hm 7: 1.*

Ἀσύγκριτος, ου, ὁ (CIL VI 12565 [Rome]; IX 114; 224; XII 3192; PLeipz. 98 I, 2; 40 II, 10; POxy. vol. XII, perh. also IG III 1093h, 5) Asyncritus Ro 16: 14. S. the preceding entry. M-M.*

ἀσύμφορος, ον (Hes., Thu.+; Dio Chrys. 3, 91; 10[11], 13; Pr 25: 20; Philo) not advantageous, harmful ἀ. ἐστί τινι it is harmful for someone 2 Cl 6: 1; Hm 4, 3, 6; 5, 1, 4; 5, 2, 2; 6, 2, 6; s 1: 10; w. inf. foll. 1: 5.*

ἀσύμφωνος, ον (Pla.+; Bel 17; Philo) not harmonious, lit. (cf. Wsd 18: 10), and fig.=at variance (Pla., Gorg. 482c; Plut., Agis 10, 8; Jos., C. Ap. 1, 38; cf. Vett. Val., Ind. II) ἀ. ὄντες πρὸς ἀλλήλους (Diod. S. 4, 1) being at variance w. each other Ac 28: 25. M-M.*

ἀσύνετος, ον (Hdt.+; POxy. 471, 89; LXX; Jos., Bell. 6, 170, Ant. 1, 117) senseless, foolish, implying also a lack of high moral quality (Epigr. Gr. 225, 3; Sir 15: 7; Test. Levi 7, 2).

1. of pers. (as Job 13: 2) Mt 15: 16; Mk 7: 18; B 2: 9; Hv 3, 10, 9; m 10, 1, 2f; ἀ. ἄνθρωπος Hv 3, 8, 9; ἔθνος ἀ. Ro 10: 19 (Dt 32: 21); ἀσύνετόν τινα ποιεῖν Hv 3, 10, 9. In a play on words σύνιε ἀσύνετε understand, foolish man s 9, 12, 1 and ἀσυνέτους ἀσυνθέτους senseless, faithless Ro 1: 31 (ἀ. in a list of vices also Dio Chrys. 2, 75. W. ἀσύνθετος [and ἄφρων] Maspéro 97 II, 84). W. ἄφρων Hs 9, 14, 4 (cf. Ps 91: 7). ἀ. εἰς τὰ μέλλοντα without understanding of the future B 5: 3. W. μωρός Hv 3, 6, 5; s 9, 22, 4. W. ἄφρων, μωρός and other characteristics 1 Cl 39: 1. W. ἄφρων, δίψυχος Hm 12, 4, 2.

2. used w. an impers. noun (Aristoph., Av. 456 φρήν ἀ.) καρδία Ro 1: 21; 1 Cl 51: 5 (cf. Ps 75: 6); ἡ ἀ. καὶ ἐσκοτωμένη διάνοια the foolish and darkened mind 1 Cl 36: 2; (w. πονηρός) διψυχία Hm 9: 9. M-M.*

ἀσύνθετος, ον (Pla.+; Eth. Epicur. col. 19, 19; Herm. Wr. 14, 6) faithless, lit. covenant-breaking (Hesychius and Suidas explain ἀ.: μὴ ἐμμένων ταῖς συνθήκαις. Cf. Demosth. 19, 136; Jer 3: 7-11) or undutiful (Maspéro 97 II, 84 ἀ. παῖς) in a list of vices (as Ptolem., Apotel. 3, 14, 35 Boll-B.) Ro 1: 31 (s. also ἀσύνετος 1).—AFridrichsen, Con. Neot. 9, '44, 47f: 'self-willed'. M-M.*

ἀσύνκ., s. ἀσύγκ.

ἀσφάλεια, ας, ἡ (Aeschyl.+; inscr., pap., LXX, Ep. Arist., Joseph., loanw. in rabb.)

1. firmness—a. lit. κεκλεισμένος ἐν πάσῃ ἀ. securely locked Ac 5: 23 (Jos., Bell. 3, 398 φρουρεῖν μετὰ πάσης ἀσφαλείας; Dit., Syll.³ 547, 30; 2 Macc 3: 22). χωρὶς τῆς ὑμετέρας ἐκ τῶν ἥλων ἀσφαλείας without being fastened w. nails by you MPol 13: 3.

b. fig. certainty, truth τ. λόγων Lk 1: 4 (X., Mem. 4, 6, 15 ἀ. λόγου; ἀ. is also a legal t.t.='security' [Epict. 2, 13, 7; PAmh. 78, 16 ἀσφάλιαν γραπτήν; PTebt. 293, 19].—JH Ropes, St Luke's Preface; ἀσφάλεια and παρακολουθεῖν: JTS 25, '24, 67-71; FVogel, NKZ 44, '33, 203ff; CFD Moule, memorial volume for TWManson '59, 165-79).

2. safety, security (Jos., Ant. 2, 245) w. εἰρήνη 1 Th 5: 3 (X., Mem. 3, 12, 7; Epict. 1, 9, 7. In inscr. w. ἀσυλία and ἀτέλεια, s. Dit., Syll. and Or., Ind.; LXX). M-M.*

ἀσφαλής, ές (Hom.+; Epict., inscr., pap., LXX, Philo, Joseph.).

1. *firm*—a. lit. ἄγκυρα Hb 6: 19 (w. βέβαιος, like Cebes 18, 3; 31, 1; Sext. Emp., Adv. Log. 2, 374; BGU 419, 18; Wsd 7: 23; Dio Chrys. 34, 17 and 37; cf. 33, 17). τὸν ἀ. θεμέλιον *the sure foundation* 1 Cl 33: 3 (cf. Wsd 4: 3).

b. fig. (Philo, Exs. 153; Jos., Bell. 2, 524) *sure, certain* ἀσφαλές τι γράφειν *write someth. definite* Ac 25: 26; τὸ ἀ. *the certainty=the truth* (Wilcken, Chrest. 17, 8 [Traj.] ἵνα τὸ ἀ. ἐπιγνῶ) γνῶναι 21: 34; 22: 30; ἡ ἀ. γνῶσις 1 Cl 1: 2; Dg 12: 4.

2. *safe, secure* (Demosth. 10, 70 βίος ἀ.; Jos., Ant. 3, 41 ἀ. καὶ σῶφρον=the safest and wisest) ὑμῖν (ἐστιν) ἀσφαλές *it is (a) safe (course) for you* Phil 3: 1. ἀσφαλὲς εἶναι ISm 8: 2. M-M. B. 756; 1237.*

ἀσφαλίζω 1 aor. pass. ἠσφαλίσθην; in our lit. the mid. is used for the act., as oft. since Epicurus 215 p. 164, 22; Polyb. 6, 22, 4; 9, 3, 3 (e.g. Diod. S. 18, 52, 4; Dit., Or. 613, 4; PTebt. 53, 29; POxy. 1033, 13; LXX; Ep. Arist. 104; Jos., Ant. 13, 22; 183).

1. lit. *guard τινά someone* so that he cannot escape (PTebt. 283, 19 [I BC] τὸν προγεγραμμένον Π. ἀσφαλίσασθαι [actively]; PRyl. 68, 19) Ac 16: 30D; τοὺς πόδας εἰς τὸ ξύλον *fasten (their) feet in the stocks* 16: 24; τ. τάφον (PHamb. 29, 12 κέλλα ἠσφαλισμένη) Mt 27: 64ff.

2. fig. ἀ. τινα *safeguard, watch over someone* (Epicurus [see above]; Is 41: 10) IPhld 5: 1. M-M.*

ἀσφαλῶς adv. (Hom.+; Epict. 2, 13, 21; 2, 17, 33; inscr. [e.g. Dit., Syll., ind.]; PGiess. 19, 14; PHib. 53, 3; POxy. 742, 5f; LXX; Ep. Arist. 46; 312; Joseph.) *securely*.

1. lit. ἀ. τηρεῖν τινα *guard someone securely* Ac 16: 23; ἀπάγειν ἀ. *lead away under guard* Mk 14: 44.

2. fig. (Appian, Bell. Civ. 2, 125 §521; Ep. Arist. 312; Jos., Ant. 1, 106) ἀ. γινώσκειν *know beyond a doubt* Ac 2: 36 (cf. Wsd 18: 6).*

ἀσχημονέω (Eur.+; X., Pla., pap., oft.=suffer someth. disgraceful, indecent; so LXX).

1. *behave disgracefully, dishonorably, indecently* (X.+; Dionys. Hal. 4, 65; Plut., Cat. Min. 24, 6; Vett. Val. 64, 10; 67, 7; 81, 25; PTebt. 44, 17 [114 BC]; Philo, Cher. 94) 1 Cor 13: 5 (v.l. εὐσχημονεῖ, q.v.). εἴ τις ἀσχημονεῖν ἐπὶ τὴν παρθένον αὐτοῦ νομίζει *if anyone thinks he is behaving dishonorably toward his maiden* 7: 36 (s. γαμίζω 1).

2. *to feel that one ought to be ashamed* (Epict. 3, 22, 15; 52; Dt 25: 3; Ezk 16: 7), but this mng. is hardly poss. in 1 Cor 7: 36. M-M.*

ἀσχημοσύνη, ης, ἡ—1. *shameless deed* (Anacharsis [600 BC] in Diog. L. 1, 103 in pl.; Pla.; Epict. 2, 5, 23; Vett. Val. 61, 31; Sir 26: 8; 30: 13; Philo, Leg. All. 2, 66; 3, 158; Jos., Ant. 16, 223; Sib. Or. 5, 389) Ro 1: 27.

2. *shame=private parts* (Ex 20: 26; Dt 23: 14; Lev 18: 6ff) βλέπειν τὴν ἀ. Rv 16: 15; Papias 3. M-M.*

ἀσχήμων, ον (Eur., Hdt.+; Epict. 2, 16, 18; 4, 9, 5; Vett. Val. 62, 16; Dit., Syll.³ 736, 4; BGU 1247, 10; PRyl. 144, 18; 150, 11; LXX; Ep. Arist. 211; Jos., Ant. 16, 363) *shameful, unpresentable, indecent* (opp. εὐσχήμων). The word is applied esp. to sexual life in Dio Chrys. 23[40], 29; LXX Gen 34: 7, Dt 24: 1; Theod. Sus 63 (s. ἀσχημοσύνη 2). Hence τὰ ἀ. (it is prob. unnecessary to supply μέλη) *the unpresentable*, i.e. *private, parts* 1 Cor 12: 23. M-M. and suppl.*

ἀσώματος, ον (Pla.+; Philostrat., Vi. Apoll. 8, 18 p. 333, 26; Plotinus 4, 7, 8 ed. Volkm. II 130, 27; Herm. Wr. 2, 4b θεῖον ἢ θεός; Celsus 3, 32; PGM 4, 1777; Philo) *bodiless* δαιμόνιον (q.v. 2) ISm 3: 2; w. δαιμονικός ISm 2.*

ἀσωτία, ας, ἡ (Pla.+; Polyb. 32, 11, 10; 39, 7, 7; PFay. 12, 24 [103 BC]; Pr 28: 7; 2 Macc 6: 4; Test. Jud. 16: 1) *debauchery, dissipation, profligacy*, lit. incorrigibility (Athen. 11 p. 485A ἀπὸ τῶν εἰς τ. μέθας κ. τ. ἀσωτίας πολλὰ ἀναλισκότων; cf. Aristot., Eth. N. 4, 1, 29) Eph 5: 18; Tit 1: 6; τῆς ἀ. ἀνάχυσις 1 Pt 4: 4. M-M.*

ἀσώτως adv. (Theopomp. [IV BC]: 115 fgm. 224 Jac.; Demosth. 40, 58; adj. ἄσωτος Soph.+; Pr 7: 11; Test. 12 Patr.; loanw. in rabb.) *dissolutely, loosely* ζῆν of debauched, profligate living (Lucian, Catapl. 17; Athen. 4 p. 167c ζῆν ἀ.; 168E πάντα γὰρ ἀνήλωσε τὰ πατρῷα εἰς ἀσωτίαν; Jos., Ant. 12, 203) Lk 15: 13 (PFlor. 99, 6ff ἐπεὶ ὁ υἱὸς ἡμῶν Κάστωρ μεθ' ἑτέρων [Zahn ἑταιρῶν, cf. Lk 15: 30] ἀσωτευόμενος ἐσπάνισε τὰ αὐτοῦ πάντα καὶ ἐπὶ τὰ ἡμῶν μεταβὰς βούλεται ἀπολέσαι κτλ.; Philo, De Prov., in Euseb., Pr. Ev. 8, 14, 4 τῶν ἀσώτων υἱέων οὐ περιορῶσιν οἱ τοκέες) GH 15.*

ἀτακτέω 1 aor. ἠτάκτησα in our lit. only 2 Th 3: 7, where the context demands the mng. *be idle, lazy* (s. X., Cyr. 8, 1, 22; Demosth. 3, 11; Plut., Mor. 184F; IG IV² 1, 68, 83 [IV BC]; PEleph. 2, 13 [III BC]; BGU 1125, 8; POxy. 275, 25 [66 AD]; 725, 40). CSpicq, Studia Theologica 10, '56, 1–13. M-M.*

ἄτακτος, ον *not in proper order* (3 Macc 1: 19; Philo; Jos., Bell. 2, 517; 649, Ant. 15, 152; Test. Napht. 2: 9; ἀταξία ibid. 3: 2; loanw. in rabb.).

1. *undisciplined* φορά *impulse* Dg 9: 1 (cf. Pla., Leg. 2 p. 660B ἄτακτον ἡδοναί; Plut., Mor. p. 5A likew.).

2. of pers. *disorderly, insubordinate* (Hdt., Thu.+; PFlor. 332, 4; Philo, Sacr. Abel. 32) 1 Th 5: 14, though the sense *idle, lazy* is to be preferred here (s. ἀτακτέω and ἀτάκτως 2, also the orator Lycurgus 39 Blass ἄτακτος= 'not at one's post'). M-M.*

ἀτάκτως (since Thu. 3, 108, 3; PFay. 337, 16 [II AD]; POxy. 842; PGM 4, 2628; Philo, Sacr. Abel. 45; Jos., C. Ap. 2, 151) adv. of ἄτακτος in the sense of insufficient inclination to disciplined work *in a disorderly* or *an irresponsible manner*.

1. lit., of irregular religious services 1 Cl 40: 2.—2. fig. ἀ. περιπατεῖν *live in idleness* (s. ἀτακτέω, ἄτακτος 2) 2 Th 3: 6, 11 (Isocr. 2, 31 ἀ. ζῆν).*

ἀταράχως (Epicurus, Ep. 1 p. 14 Us.; Diod. S. 17, 54, 1; Jos., Ant. 14, 157) adv. of ἀτάραχος (Aristot.+; LXX; Ep. Arist. 213) *without confusion, undisturbed* 1 Cl 48: 4.*

ἄτεκνος, ον (Hes.+; Polyb. 20, 6, 5; Plut.; Lucian; inscr. [Dit., Syll.² 838, 6 [II BC]; 858, 13; epitaphs 11 and 22, 7: ZNW 22, '23, 281; 283]; pap. [PLond. 23, 13 et al.]; LXX; En. 98, 5; Philo in Euseb., Pr. Ev. 8, 11, 13; Jos., Bell. 1, 563, Ant. 4, 254; Test. Jud. 19: 2) *childless* Lk 20: 28f. M-M.*

ἀτενίζω 1 aor. ἠτένισα (Hippocr.+) *look intently at someth.* or *someone* εἴς τι (Polyb. 6, 11, 5; Lucian, Charon 16; 3 Macc 2: 26; Jos., Bell. 5, 517) Ac 1: 10; 7: 55; 2 Cor 3: 7, 13; 1 Cl 7: 4; 17: 2; 36: 2. εἴς τινα (Diog. L. 6, 6, 61; Sext. Emp., Math. 1, 306) Ac 3: 4; 6: 15; 11: 6; 13: 9; 1 Cl 9: 2; 19: 2. W. dat. of the pers. (PGM 4, 556; 711) Lk 4: 20; 22: 56; Ac 3: 5 v.l., 12; 10: 4; 14: 9; 23: 1. Abs. (Herm. Wr. 13, 3) 3: 3 D.—FSolmsen, Beiträge z. griech. Wortforschung I '09, 22. M-M.*

ἄτερ prep. w. gen. *without* (Hom.+, but in prose first Inschr. v. Priene 109, 106 [c. 120 BC], then in imperial times [Bl-D. §216, 2]: Dionys. Hal. 3, 10; Plut., Num. 14, 7, Cato Min. 5, 6; Vett. Val. 136, 9; 271, 9; 341, 3; POxy. 936, 18; PGM 13, 56; 2 Macc 12: 15) ἄ. ὄχλου *apart fr. the crowd*, perh. *without a disturbance* Lk 22: 6; ἄ. βαλλαν-τίου *without a purse* vs. 35; ἄ. γραφῆς PK 4 p. 16, 6; ἄ. θεοῦ *without God, apart fr. God's will* D 3: 10 (Polyaenus 6, 53 θεῶν ἄτερ); ἄ. ἀλλήλων Hs 5, 7, 4; cf. 5, 4, 5; 5, 6, 2; 9, 12, 8; 9, 27, 2; ἄ. ἀνάγκης B 2: 6 v.l. (Funk). M-M.*

ἀτιμάζω 1 aor. ἠτίμασα, pass. ἠτιμάσθην (Hom.+; Epict., inscr., pap., LXX; Jos., Ant. 15, 31) *dishonor, treat shamefully, insult* (Ael. Aristid. 53 p. 620 D.: τὰ τῶν θεῶν ἀ.) τινά *someone* Mk 12: 4 (s. ἀτιμάω and ἀτιμόω); Lk 20: 11; J 8: 49; Ro 2: 23; Js 2: 6 (cf. Pr 14: 21); IPhld 11: 1.—Pass. Ac 5: 41; Dg 11: 3. τοῦ ἀτιμάζεσθαι τὰ σώματα αὐτῶν *that their bodies might be degraded* Ro 1: 24. ἠτιμάσθη καὶ οὐκ ἐλογίσθη *he was dishonored and despised* 1 Cl 16: 3 (Is 53: 3). M-M.*

ἀτιμάω 1 aor. ἠτίμησα (Hom.+; Philostrat., Ep. 28 p. 240, 10). Mng. same as ἀτιμάζω (q.v.); ἠτίμησαν Mk 12: 4 D (s. also ἀτιμόω).*

ἀτιμία, ας, ἡ (Hom.+; Epict. 4, 1, 60; PGiess. 40 II, 5; LXX; En. 98, 3; Philo; Jos., Ant. 4, 229; 15, 24; Test. 12 Patr.) *dishonor, disgrace, shame* 2 Cor 6: 8 (opp. δόξα); ἐν ταῖς ἀτιμίαις δοξάζονται *in dishonor* (or *by shameful treatment*) *they are glorified* Dg 5: 14 (pl. as Pla., Pol. 309A; Demosth. 18, 205). πάθη ἀτιμίας *shameful passions* Ro 1: 26; ἀ. αὐτῷ ἐστιν *it is a disgrace for him* 1 Cor 11: 14; ἐν ἀ. *in humiliation* (opp. δόξα) 15: 43; εἰς ἀ. *for (a) dishonor(able use)* Ro 9: 21; 2 Ti 2: 20. κατὰ ἀ. λέγω *to my shame I must confess* 2 Cor 11: 21. M-M.*

ἄτιμος, ον (Hom.+; Epict. 4, 6, 3; Dit., Or. 218, 103; 140; 338, 29; 527, 8; pap.; LXX; Philo; Jos., Ant. 4, 136, C. Ap. 2, 191) *unhonored, dishonored.*
1. lit. 1 Cor 4: 10 (opp. ἔνδοξος); 1 Cl 3: 3 (opp. ἔντιμος as Synes., Ep. 79 p. 226D; cf. Is 3: 5); *despised* εἶδος 16: 3 (Is 53: 3); οὐκ ἄ. εἰ μή *honored everywhere, except* Mt 13: 57; Mk 6: 4.
2. fig. *insignificant, less honorable* μέλη 1 Cor 12: 23 (of parts of the body also Aristot. 672b, 21 τὸ τιμιώτερον κ. ἀτιμότερον). Artem. 4, 25. On the subject-matter cf. Heraclit. Sto. 19 p. 29, 3 ἡ κεφαλὴ ἐν τῷ σώματι τὴν κυριωτάτην εἰληχυῖα τάξιν; line 9 κυριώτατον μέρος. S. also εὐσχήμων 1). ἀτιμοτάτη ὑπηρεσία *the lowliest service* Dg 2: 2. M-M.*

ἀτιμόω pf. pass. ptc. ἠτιμωμένος (Aeschyl., Hdt.+; Dit., Syll.³ 64, 6; 112, 10; LXX). Mng. same as ἀτιμάζω (q.v.). Pass. *be disgraced* ἀπέστειλαν ἠτιμωμένον Mk 12: 4 AC (s. ἀτιμάω); Dg 5: 14. M-M.*

ἀτμίς, ίδος, ἡ (since Hdt. 4, 75, Pla., Tim., p. 86E; Zen.-P. 59 354, 7 [III BC]; PGM 7, 639; 743; LXX) *mist, vapor* ἀ. καπνοῦ *smoky vapor* Ac 2: 19 (Jo 3: 3). Typical of what passes away Js 4: 14 (cf. Eccl 1: 2; 12: 8 Aq.). ἀ. ἀπὸ κύθρας *steam that rises from a pot*, typical of nothingness 1 Cl 17: 6 (quot. of unknown orig.; cf. RHarris, JBL 29, '10, 190–5). M-M.*

ἄτομος, ον (Pre-Socr.+; Philo) *uncut* (τέμνω), *indivisible* because of smallness (Is 54: 8 Sym. ἐν ἀτόμῳ ὀργῆς *in a short outburst of wrath*=LXX ἐν θυμῷ μικρῷ), used of time by Aristot. (Phys. 236a, 6 ἐν ἀτόμῳ) ἐν ἀ. *in a moment* 1 Cor 15: 52 (Nägeli 31). M-M.*

ἄτονος, ον (Theophr., H. Plant. 3, 18, 11; Plut.; Epict. 3, 16, 7; Vett. Val. 233, 12; 15; 337, 19; PStrassb. 95, 11;

Aq. Job 5: 16; Sym. Ps 81: 3; Jos., Bell. 1, 203; 3, 114) *slack, powerless* of the devil's threats ἄ. ὥσπερ νεκροῦ νεῦρα *as powerless as the sinews of a corpse* Hm 12, 6, 2 (ἄ. w. νεκρός as Epict., loc. cit.).*

ἄτοπος, ον (Eur., Pre-Socr.+; pap., LXX, Philo, Joseph.) *out of place* (τόπος).
1. *unusual, surprising* (Thu. 3, 38, 5; Pla., Leg. 1 p. 646B) in the sense of someth. harmful (Thu. 2, 49, 2; Herodian 4, 11, 4; Jos., Ant. 11, 134) μηδὲν ἄ. εἰς αὐτὸν γινόμενον *nothing unusual happened to him* Ac 28: 6.
2. morally *evil, wrong, improper* (Plut., Mor. 27F; PPetr. II 19(1a), 5f; UPZ 5, 12 [163 BC]; Philo, Leg. All. 3, 53; Jos., Ant. 6, 88; Job 11: 11; 35: 13) (w. πονηρός) ἄνθρωποι 2 Th 3: 2; ποιεῖν τὰ ἄ. (Polyb. 5, 11, 1; Job 34: 12) *do what is improper* Pol 5: 3; οὐδὲν ἄ. ἔπραξεν (ἄ. πράσσειν): Dio Chrys. 10[11], 65; Aristipp. in Diog. L. 2, 93; PPetr. III 43(3), 17f [III BC]; BGU 757, 21 [12 AD]; Job 27: 6; Pr 30: 20; 2 Macc 14: 23) Lk 23: 41; cf. Ac 25: 5. ἄτοπόν ἐστιν *it is wrong, absurd* (Philo, Mos. 1, 308) IMg 10: 3. M-M.*

ἄτρεπτος, ον (Chrysipp.+ [Stoic. II 158]; Plut.; Aelian; Herm. Wr.; IG IX 2, 317; Sym. Job 15: 15; Philo, Leg. All. 1, 51 al.; Jos., Ant. 11, 57) *unchangeable* δόξα IEph inscr.*

Ἀττάλεια, ας, ἡ *Attalia*, a seaport in Pamphylia Ac 14: 25.—Ramsay, Hist. Geogr. 420.*

Ἄτταλος, ου, ὁ *Attalus*, a Christian in Smyrna IPol 8: 2. The name was common in Asia Minor; specif. in Smyrna CIG 3141; 3142; 3239; 3288 al.*

αὐγάζω 1 aor. inf. αὐγάσαι.—1. *see* (so in poets Soph.+; Lycophron v. 941 αὐγάζων φάος=seeing the light; Philod.: Anth. Pal. 5, 123, 3 and Philo, Mos. 2, 139; cf. Nägeli 25f) τι *someth.* Fig., of the gospel's light 2 Cor 4: 4 (s. φωτισμός 1). This is the most likely interpr. (see, for example, Ltzm., Windisch, H-DWendland, RSV).
2. intr. *shine forth* (PGM 3, 143; 4, 1636; 2558; Lev 13: 24ff; 14: 56) suggested by some for 2 Cor 4: 4 (s. 1)—so, for example, Sickenberger—can hardly do without αὐτοῖς, which is actually added to the t.r. M-M.*

αὐγή, ῆς, ἡ (Hom.+; Epict. 3, 3, 20; 21; Vett. Val., Ind. II; Dit., Syll.³ 798, 3; PGM 4, 2243; 13, 476; Philo; Jos., Bell. 2, 148, Ant. 3, 184; Sib. Or. 3, 287) *dawn* (Polyaenus 4, 6, 18 κατὰ τὴν πρώτην αὐγὴν τ. ἡμέρας; Is 59: 9) ἄχρι αὐ. *until daybreak* Ac 20: 11.—Orig. 'light', esp. 'daylight'. M-M. B. 993.*

Αὔγουστος, ου, ὁ *Augustus*, title (usu. transl. Σεβαστός, q.v.) given Octavian, first Rom. emperor (31 BC–14 AD) in 27 BC; Lk 2: 1.—HDieckmann, Kaisernamen u. Kaiserbezeichnungen b. Lk: ZkTh 33, '19, 213–34; EPeterson, Kaiser A. im Urteil d. antiken Christent.: Hochland 30, '33, 289ff.*

αὐθάδεια, ας, ἡ (Pla.+; Is 24: 8; Philo, Rer. Div. Her. 21; Jos., Bell. 4, 94, Ant. 12, 29; 15, 101); the poet. form αὐθαδία (Aeschyl.+) becomes prominent in later colloq. Gk. (Crönert 32), and is predom. in inscr. and pap. *arrogance, willfulness, stubbornness* 1 Cl 30: 8 (w. θράσος, cf. Pr 21: 24); ὑπερήφανος αὐ. *proud willfulness* 57: 2; Hs 9, 22, 2f. In a list of vices D 5: 1; B 20: 1.*

αὐθάδης, ες (Aeschyl., Hdt.+; Polyb. 4, 21; Plut., Lycurg. 11, 6, Lucull. 7, 2; PAmh. 78, 13f; Sb 4284, 9; Gen 49: 3, 7; Pr 21: 24; Jos., Ant. 1, 189; 4, 263) *self-willed, stubborn, arrogant* Tit 1: 7; 2 Pt 2: 10; 1 Cl 1: 1 (w.

προπετής); Hs 5, 4, 2; 5, 5, 1; 9, 22, 1; D 3: 6. Field, Notes, 219. M-M.*

αὐθαίρετος, ον (trag., Thu.+; Dit., Or. 583, 8; pap.; Sym. Ex 35: 5, 22; Philo, Mos. 1, 50 v.l.; Jos., Bell. 6, 310) *of one's own accord* 2 Cor 8: 3, 17. M-M.*

αὐθαιρέτως adv. (Plut., Pel. 24, 8; Philostrat., Vi. Apoll. 8, 7 p. 306, 22; Inschr. v. Magn. 163, 15ff; PLond. 280, 7; BGU 581, 6; 2 Macc 6: 19; 3 Macc·6: 6; 7: 10) *voluntarily* ἀποθανεῖν IMg 5: 2.*

αὐθεντέω (Philod., Rhet. II p. 133, 14 Sudh.; Jo. Lydus, Mag. 3, 42; Moeris p. 58; Hesychius; Thom. Mag. p. 18, 8; schol. in Aeschyl., Eum. 42; BGU 103, 3; 8; 1208, 38 [27 BC]) *have authority, domineer* τινός *over someone* (Ptolem., Apotel. 3, 14, 10 Boll-B.; Cat. Cod. Astr. VIII 1 p. 177, 7; Bl-D. §177) ἀνδρός 1 Ti 2: 12 (Mich. Glykas 270, 10 IBekker [1836] αἱ γυναῖκες αὐθεντοῦσι τ. ἀνδρῶν. According to Diod. S. 1, 27, 2 there was a well-documented law in Egypt: κυριεύειν τὴν γυναῖκα τἀνδρός). M-M.*

αὐθέντης, ου, ὁ (on the mng. s. PKretschmer, Glotta 3, '12, 289–93; the adj. is a loanw. in rabb., and the noun is the source of Turk. 'effendi'; cf. Jos., Bell. 2, 240) *master* (Eur., Suppl. 442; Sb 6754, 15; PGM 13, 258) τοῦ πύργου Hs 9, 5, 6.*

αὐθεντικός, ή, όν (POxy. 260, 20; 719, 30; 33 al. in pap.) *original* τὸ αὐ. (opp. ἀντίτυπον) 2 Cl 14: 3 (so PGiess. 34, 4 τὰ αὐθεντικά; the adj. in the pap. passages above, not used as subst., has the same mng.).*

αὐθεντικῶς adv. (Cicero, Att. 9, 14, 2; 10, 9, 1) w. *perfect clarity* PK 4 p. 15, 31.*

αὐλέω 1 aor. ηὔλησα (Alcman, Hdt.+; Dit., Syll.³ 1084–8 al.; CWessely, Stud. z. Paläograph. und Pap.-kunde 22, '22, no. 47, 5) *play the flute* τινί (X., Symp. 2, 8) *for someone* (to dance) Mt 11: 17; Lk 7: 32 (Aesop 27 H. ὅτε ηὔλουν, οὐκ ὠρχεῖσθε; similarly 134 H.; Proverbia Aesopi 115 P.). τὸ αὐλούμενον *what is played on the flute* 1 Cor 14: 7.*

αὐλή, ῆς, ἡ (Hom.+; inscr., pap., LXX, Ep. Arist., Joseph.).
 1. *courtyard,* an enclosed space, open to the sky, near a house, or surrounded by buildings (Dio Chrys. 60 and 61[77+78], 35 περὶ τὰς αὐλὰς κ. πρόθυρα; PLond. 45, 15; BGU 275, 6f; POxy. 104; 105 al.; PFay. 31; 32 al.; Tob 2: 9; Jos., Ant. 1, 196) Mt 26: 58, 69; Mk 14: 54, 66; Lk 22: 55; J 18: 15. Used also as a *fold* for sheep (Il. 4, 433; PHib. 36, 4; POxy. 75) J 10: 1, 16.
 2. *farm, house* (Dionys. Hal. 6, 50; PGiess. 32, 7; 19; PFlor. 81, 8; cf. FLuckhard, D. Privathaus, Diss. Giess. '14, 79) Lk 11: 21, where *palace* (s. 4 below) is also poss.
 3. (*outer*) *court* of the temple (αὐ. τοῦ ἱεροῦ Dit., Syll.³ 485, 28; 547, 46 al; Ex 27: 9 al.) Rv 11: 2; B 2: 5 (Is 1: 12).
 4. the 'court' of a prince (lit., inscr., pap.), then *palace* (Suidas αὐλή· ἡ τοῦ βασιλέως οἰκία. So Polyb. et al.; Diod. S. 16, 93, 7; Epict. 1, 10, 3; 4; 1 Macc 11: 46; 3 Macc 2: 27; 5: 46; Jos., Bell. 2, 328, Vi. 66; 295) Mt 26: 3; Mk 15: 16 (=πραιτώριον). M-M. B. 463.*

αὐλητής, οῦ, ὁ (Theognis, Hdt.+; inscr., pap.) *flute-player* for festive occasions Rv 18: 22, and for mourning (Jos., Bell. 3, 437) Mt 9: 23. M-M.*

αὐλητρίς, ίδος, ἡ (Simonides+; X., Pla., inscr., pap.) *flute-girl*; in pl. immoral women w. πόρναι GOxy 36; cf.

GH 15 (Euhem. in Athen. 14, 77 p. 658F αὐ. τοῦ βασιλέως in the sense 'concubine'. Phylarch. [III BC]: 81 fgm. 42 Jac. and Dio Chrys. 53[70], 9 pl. w. ἑταῖραι; Theophyl. Sim., Ep. 12 αὐ. as πορνίδιον).*

αὐλίζομαι impf. ηὐλιζόμην; 1 aor. pass. ηὐλίσθην (Hom.+; Dit., Or. 730, 7 [III BC]; pap.; LXX; Joseph.).
 1. *spend the night, find lodging* (Eupolis [V BC] 322; Nicol. Dam.: 90 fgm. 4 p. 332, 17 Jac.; Arrian, Anab. 6, 25, 5; Judg 19: 6f, 10f; 20: 4B; Ruth 3: 13 αὐλίσθητι τὴν νύκτα al. LXX; Jos., Ant. 1, 279) ἐκεῖ (Judg 19: 7; Tob 6: 1BA) Mt 21: 17; εἴς τι Lk 21: 37 (cf. Tob 14: 9BA μηκέτι αὐλισθῆτε εἰς Νινευή, but the mng. here is 'stay', cf. 2 below; *spend some time* is also poss. for the Lk pass.). ἕως οὗ αὐλισθῇ *until he finds lodging* (again) D 11: 6.
 2. *live, stay* (Ps.-Demetr., Eloc. §216 [after Ctesias]; Epict., fgm. Stob. 47; Himerius, Or. 54[15], 1 αὐλίζ. ἡμέραν μίαν, accordingly not at night; Sir 51: 23; Jos., Bell. 1, 334; 2, 301) 1 Cl 4: 11. M-M.*

αὐλός. οῦ, ὁ (Hom.+; PHib. 54, 6 [c. 245 BC]; LXX) *flute* 1 Cor 14: 7 (w. κιθάρα, as Dio Chrys. 16[33], 35; Ps.-Lucian, Salt. 16; Himerius, Or. 8[23], 11; Is 30: 32).—S. lit. on κύμβαλον. M-M.*

αὐξάνω and **αὔξω** (both forms as early as Pindar with the latter predominating, as usu. in the earlier lit.; later the longer form becomes more freq., and the shorter one [Epict.; Heraclit. Sto. p. 2, 7; 78, 12; Hierocles the Stoic [II AD]: Berl. Klassikertexte IV p. 28f col. 6, 16; Dit., Syll. Index, Or. 51, 12; 56, 9 and 22; POxy. 1450, 3; 21; 4 Macc 13: 22; Ep. Arist. 208; Philo, Aet. M. 71; Jos., Ant. 1, 61; 4, 59] becomes rare; both in the same sentence Aëtius 132, 13 αὐξανομένου τ. πάθους αὔξει κ. τὰ συμπτώματα) Bl-D. §101; Meisterhans³-Schw. p. 176; Mayser 465. Fut. αὐξήσω; 1 aor. ηὔξησα, pass. ηὐξήθην.
 1. trans. *grow, cause to grow, increase* (class.; inscr.; pap.; LXX; Jos., Ant. 2, 205 [Nägeli 35]) the fruits of righteousness 2 Cor 9: 10. Abs. 1 Cor 3: 6f; Hv 1, 1, 6; 3, 4, 1.
 2. pass. *grow, increase* (Hes., Hdt.+; LXX; Jos., Ant. 18, 129, Vi. 193) of the human race 1 Cl 33: 6; B 6: 12, 18 (Gen 1: 28). Of children (Hdt. 5, 92, 5; Gen 21: 8; 25; 27) 1 Pt 2: 2. Of plants (Ps.-Phoc. 38) Mt 13: 32; Mk 4: 8; καρπὸς αὐξανόμενος ibid. v.l. (Diosc., Mat. Med. 2, 199 add. πρὸ τοῦ τὸν καρπὸν αὐξηθῆναι).—Fig. (Pind., Nem. 8, 40 αὔξεται δ'ἀρετά=ἀρετή grows) of the gospel Col 1: 6. Of faith 2 Cor 10: 15. Of knowledge Col 1: 10. Of unrighteousness D 16: 4.
 3. The use of the act. in the same intrans. sense belongs to later Gk. (Aristot.; Polyb.; Diod. S.; Maximus Tyr. 6, 4f; Olympiodor., Comm. in Alcib. Plat. 18 ed. Creuzer 1821: αὐξούσης τ. σελήνης; PGM 4, 2553; 13, 65; Ep. Arist. 208; Jos., Ant. 2, 189; 4, 59; not LXX) lit. of plants Mt 6: 28; Lk 12: 27 v.l.; Gospel fgm. POxy. 655=Kl. Texte 8³, p. 23 (on the last 3 passages cf. ξαίνω); Lk 13: 19. ἐκ τοῦ ἑνὸς πλείονα fr. one (grain) many grow 1 Cl 24: 5. Of children Lk 1: 80; 2: 40. Of a people Ac 7: 17. Of a house εἰς ναόν Eph 2: 21. Of the word of God Ac 6: 7; 12: 24; 19: 20. αὐ. τὴν αὔξησιν Col 2: 19; ἔν τινι 2 Pt 3: 18; αὐ. εἰς Χριστόν grow up into (union w.) *Christ* Eph 4: 15. Abs. Mt 20: 28 D=Agr 22. Of Jesus *increase* J 3: 30. This is usu. considered a direct ref. to success in attracting followers. But αὐ. can also be used of the increase of sunlight (Kalendarium of Antiochus [c. 200 AD] on Dec. 25 Ἡλίου γενέθλιον· αὔξει φῶς [FBoll, SA Heidelbg. '10, 16; Abh. p. 40ff]; Cosmas of Jerusalem [FCumont, Natalis Invicti: Extr. des compt. rend. de l'Ac. des Inscr. et Bell. Lett. '11,

292f]). Cf. 3: 19–21, where φῶς occurs five times, and is the leading concept. May this not also be true of 3: 30? At any rate the Gk. and Lat. fathers understood 3: 30 in the solar sense. S. also on ἐλαττοῦσθαι and cf. ENorden, D. Geburt des Kindes '24, 99–112. M-M. B. 876.*

αὔξησις, εως, ἡ (Pre-Socr., Hdt.+; Epict. 1, 14, 14; inscr. [57/6 BC] in Wilcken, Chrest. no. 70, 12; Sb 1161, 18; 4224, 23; 2 Macc 5: 16; Philo; Jos., Ant. 1, 60; 4, 261) *growth, increase* αὔ. ποιεῖσθαι *cause growth* (Aristot., H.A. 6, 12) εἴς τι Eph 4: 16. αὔξειν τὴν αὔ. τοῦ θεοῦ *grows w. divine growth* Col 2: 19 (cf. Herm. Wr. 3, 3 εἰς τὸ αὐξάνεσθαι ἐν αὐξήσει; Ode of Solomon 11, 19). M-M.*

αὔξω s. αὐξάνω.

αὔρα, ας, ἡ (Hom.+; Philo) *breeze* 1 Cl 39: 3 (Job 4: 16).*

αὔριον adv. (Hom.+; inscr., pap., LXX) *tomorrow.*

1. of the *next day* Ac 23: 15 v.l., 20; 25: 22; σήμερον ἤ αὔ. Js 4: 13. W. art., w. ἡμέρα to be supplied (as Soph., Trach. 945; Diod. S. 19, 32, 2 ἡ αὔ.; PFlor. 118, 5 μετὰ τὴν αὔριον; PTebt. 417, 7 al.; Ex 8: 19; 32: 30; 1 Km 11: 11 al.; Jos., Ant. 17, 91) ἡ αὔ. Mt 6: 34b; Js 4: 14; εἰς τὴν αὔ. (Aristo of Ceos [IV BC], fgm. 24 [ed. Wehrli '52]; BGU 511 I, 18; Esth 5: 12; 3 Macc 5: 38; Jos., Ant. 3, 231) Mt 6: 34a (Epict. 1, 9, 19 discourages care περὶ τῆς αὔριον, πόθεν φάγητε; Artem. 4, 84 περὶ τῆς αὔριον φοβεῖσθαι ἢ ἐλπίζειν.—The opposite of Mt 6: 34 among the Pythagoreans: Philosophenspr. p. 504, 1: διδάσκει ἀεὶ τι τοῦ παρόντος εἰς τὸ μέλλον καταλιπεῖν, καὶ τῆς αὔρ. ἐν τῇ σήμερον μνημονεύειν); Ac 4: 3; Hs 6, 5, 3; μέχρι τῆς αὔριον 9, 11, 7; ἐπὶ τὴν αὔ. *on the next day* Lk 10: 35; Ac 4: 5; ἐπὶ τὴν αὔ. ἡμέραν 4: 5 D (ἡ αὔριον ἡμέρα as Zen.-P. 59 078, 7).

2. in the sense *soon, in a short time* 1 Cor 15: 32 (Is 22: 13). σήμ. . . . *soon* αὔρ. *now* . . . soon Mt 6: 30; Lk 12: 28. This extended mng. is prob. also valid for 13: 32f (on σήμ. καὶ αὔ. καὶ τῇ τρίτῃ vs. 32 cf. Ex 19: 10f and τρίτος 1, end). M-M. B. 999.*

αὐστηρός, ά, όν (Hippocr., Pla.+; inscr., pap., Philo) of pers. *severe, austere, exacting, strict* both in favorable and unfav. senses (Polyb. 4, 20, 7; Plut., Mor. 300D; Vett. Val. 75, 11; Diog. L. 7, 26; 117; PTebt. 315, 19 [II AD] of a govt. finance inspector ὁ γὰρ ἄνθρωπος λείαν ἐστὶν αὐστηρός; grave inscr. ZNW 22, '23, 280 αὔ. παράκοιτις; 2 Macc 14: 30) Lk 19: 21f. M-M.*

αὐτάρκεια, ας, ἡ—1. *sufficiency, a competence* (Pla.+ αὐ. means the state of one who supports himself without aid fr. others, but POxy. 729, 10 it is 'sufficient supply') Hs 1: 6; πᾶσαν αὔ. ἔχειν (PFlor. 242, 8 ἵνα δυνηθῇς ἔχειν τ. αὐτάρκιαν) *have enough of everything* 2 Cor 9: 8.

2. *contentment, self-sufficiency,* a favorite virtue of the Cynics and Stoics (Epicurus in Diog. L. 10, 130; Stoic. III p. 67, 3; 68, 5; Stob. III p. 101, 16 [Epict.]; 265, 13 H.; Teles p. 5, 1; cf. 11, 5; 38, 10f H.; Sextus 98. Cf. GAGerhard, Phoinix v. Kolophon '09, 57ff) 1 Ti 6: 6; Hm 6, 2, 3. M-M.*

αὐτάρκης, ες (Aeschyl., Hdt.+; inscr., pap., LXX; Philo, Op. M. 146; Jos., C. Ap. 2, 190 [of God]) of pers. *content, self-sufficient* (Pla., Rep. 369B; Polyb. 6, 48, 7; Diog. L. 2, 24 of Socrates αὐτάρκης καὶ σεμνός; Sir 40: 18; Philo; Jos., C. Ap. 2, 291) εἶναι *be content,* perh. *self-sufficient* Phil 4: 11. M-M.*

αὐτεπαινετός, όν (not yet found elsewhere) *praising oneself* subst. 1 Cl 30: 6.*

αὐτοκατάκριτος, ον (in Philo in the fgm. fr. the Sacra Parallela ed. Mangey II 652; cf. RHarris, Fragments of Philo 1886. Otherw. only in Christian writers) *self-condemned* Tit 3: 11. M-M.*

αὐτολεξεί adv. (Philo, Leg. ad Gai. 353) *expressly, in the very words* PK 4 p. 15, 32.*

αὐτόματος, η, ον, also w. two endings (Crönert 183) *by itself* (of someth. that happens without visible cause) (Hom.+; Josh 6: 5; Job 24: 24; Wsd 17: 6; Philo; Jos., Ant. 1, 54. Loanw. in rabb.) of doors opening by themselves (Il. 5, 749; X., Hell. 6, 4, 7; Apollon. Rhod. 4, 41; Plut., Timol. 12, 9; Cass. Dio 44, 17; Artapanus de Judaeis in Euseb., Pr. Ev. 9, 27, 23 νυκτός. . .τὰς θύρας πάσας αὐτομ. ἀνοιχθῆναι τοῦ δεσμωτηρίου. S. ἀνοίγω 1a) Ac 12: 10. Of plants growing without help (Hes., Works 118 and Hdt.+; Theophr., Hist. Pl. 4, 8, 8; Diod. S. 1, 8, 1; Lev 25: 5, 11; Philo, Op. M. 167; Jos., Ant. 12, 317, Vi. 11) Mk 4: 28 (on this parable s. KWeiss, Voll Zuversicht '22; BZ 18, '29, 45–67; JFreundorfer, BZ 17, '26, 51–62; 68; TWManson, JTS 38, '37, 399f; KWClark, Class. Weekly 36, '42, 27–9; GHarder, Theologia Viatorum 1, '48/'49, 51–70.). M-M.*

αὐτομολέω (Hdt., Aristoph.+; LXX; Philo, Aet. M. 76; Jos., Bell. 4, 380, Vi. 107; 239) *desert* ἀπό τινος (fr.) *someone* 1 Cl 28: 2.*

αὐτόπτης, ου, ὁ (Hdt.+; Polyb. 3, 4, 13; Vett. Val. 260, 30; POxy. 1154, 8 [I AD]; Jos., Bell. 3, 432) *eyewitness* αὐ. γενόμενος (Dionys. Hal., Pomp. 6, 3; Maximus Tyr. 16, 3h; Jos., Ant. 18, 342; 19, 125, C. Ap. 1, 55) Lk 1: 2. M-M.*

αὐτός, ή, ό (Hom.+; inscr., pap., LXX, En., Ep. Arist., Philo, Joseph.) W-S. §22; Bl-D. index.

1. *self,* intensive, setting the individual off fr. everything else, emphasizing and contrasting; used in all pers., genders, and numbers.

a. used w. a subject (noun or pron.)—a. specif. named (X., Cyr. 1, 4, 6; Plut., Caes. 7, 9 αὐ. Κικέρων; 2 Macc 11: 12) αὐτὸς Δαυίδ *David himself* Mk 12: 36f; Lk 20: 42; αὐτὸς ὁ Ἰησοῦς short ending of Mk.

β. or otherw. exactly designated αὐ. ὁ θεός (Jos., Bell. 7, 346) Rv 21: 3; αὐ. τ. ἐπουράνια Hb 9: 23 (cf. 4 Macc 17: 17; Sir 46: 3); αὐ. ἐγώ *I myself* Ro 15: 14 (cf. 3 Macc 3: 13; POxy. 294 [22 AD]); αὐτὸς ἐγὼ Παῦλος 2 Cor 10: 1; αὐτοὶ ὑμεῖς J 3: 28 (cf. 4 Macc 6: 19); αὐτοὶ οὗτοι (Thu. 6, 33, 6) Ac 24: 15; ἐν ὑμῖν αὐτοῖς *among yourselves* 1 Cor 11: 13.

b. to emphasize a subject already known: of Jesus Mt 8: 24; Mk 8: 29; Lk 5: 16f; 9: 51; 10: 38; 24: 36 (cf. the Pythagorean αὐτὸς ἔφα). Of God Hb 13: 5 (cf. Wsd 6: 7; 7: 17; Sir 15: 12; 1 Macc 3: 22 and oft. LXX).

c. differentiating fr. other subjects or pointing out a contrast w. them αὐ. καὶ οἱ μετ' αὐτοῦ Mk 2: 25; J 2: 12; 4: 53; 18: 1; Lk 24: 15; 1 Cor 3: 15. αὐτοὶ οὐκ εἰσήλθατε καὶ τοὺς εἰσερχομένους ἐκωλύσατε *you yourselves did not come in* etc. Lk 11: 52; cf. vs. 46.—J 9: 21; Mt 23: 4; Lk 6: 11; Ac 18: 15; 1 Th 1: 9; 1 Cor 2: 15. αὐτὸς μόνος *he alone* (cf. μόνος 1aβ) Mk 6: 47; J 6: 15. αὐτὸς ἐγώ *I alone* 2 Cor 12: 13. εἰ μὴ αὐτός *except himself* Rv 19: 12. αὐτὸς ὄγδοός ἐστιν *he is the eighth* 17: 11.

d. *self=in person* (Philo, De Jos. 238; Jos. to his brothers αὐ. εἰμι ἐγώ) J 4: 2; Lk 24: 36, 39.

e. *of himself, ourselves* (Hyperid. 1, 19, 11; 3, 2) without help J 2: 25; 4: 42; 6: 6; Ac 20: 34; αὐ. ᾠκοδόμησεν *he built at his own expense* Lk 7: 5; αὐ. ὁ πατὴρ φιλεῖ ὑμᾶς *the Father loves you of himself* J 16: 27.

f. *thrown on one's own resources* αὐ. ἐγὼ τῷ νοΐ δουλεύω νόμῳ θεοῦ *thrown on my own resources I can only serve the law of God as a slave with my mind* Ro 7: 25 (JWeiss, Beitr. zur Paulin. Rhetorik, in BWeiss-Festschr., 1897, 233f; JKürzinger, BZ 7, '63, 270–74).—Cf. Mk 6: 31; Ro 9: 3.

g. intensifying καὶ αὐτός *even* (Sir Prol. l. 24 καὶ αὐ. ὁ νόμος *even the law*; 4 Macc 17: 1) καὶ αὐτὴ ἡ κτίσις *even the created world* Ro 8: 21. καὶ αὐτὴ Σάρρα *even Sara* Hb 11: 11 (on the rdg. here cf. Windisch ad loc. and Bl-D. §194, 1; Rob. 686; Mlt-Turner 220; cf. Ps.-Callisth. 1, 10, 3 καὶ αὐτὸν τὸν Φίλιππον=and even Philip; but the text of the Hb passage is not in order; s. καταβολή). οὐδὲ ἡ φύσις αὐτὴ διδάσκει; 1 Cor 11: 14.

h. the mng. *even, very* directs attention to a certain pers. or thing to the exclusion of the others, so that αὐ. can almost take on demonstrative sense (cf. 2, end, below, also Aeschyl., 7 against Thebes 528; Hes., Works 350): αὐ. τὰ ἔργα *the very deeds* J 5: 36; αὐ. ὁ Ἰωάννης (POxy. 745 [I AD]) αὐ. τὸν Ἀντ᾿αν) *this very* (or *same*) John Mt 3: 4 (s. Mlt. 91); ἐν αὐ. τ. καιρῷ (cf. Tob 3: 17BA; 2: 9; Dit., Syll.³ 1173, 1 αὐταῖς τ. ἡμέραις) *just at that time* Lk 13: 1.—23: 12; 24: 13.—2: 38; 10: 21; 12: 12.—10: 7. αὐτὸ τοῦτο *just this, the very same thing* (Oenomaus in Euseb., Pr. Ev. 5, 22, 3; PRyl. 77, 39; POxy. 1119, 11; cf. Phoenix of Colophon p. 6, 82 Gerh.; also p. 115; 2 Cor 7: 11; Gal 2: 10; Phil 1: 6; εἰς αὐ. τοῦτο Ro 9: 17; 13: 6; 2 Cor 5: 5; Eph 6: 22; Col 4: 8. The phrases τοῦτο αὐ. 2 Cor 2: 3 and αὐ. τοῦτο 2 Pt 1: 5 are adverbial accusatives *for this very reason* (Pla., Prot. 310ε; X., An. 1, 9, 21; PGrenf. I 1, 14).

2. αὐτός refers w. more or less emphasis to a subject, oft. resuming one already mentioned: αὐτοὶ παρακληθή-σονται *they* (not others) *shall be comforted* Mt 5: 4; cf. vs. 5ff. οὐκ αὐτοὶ βλασφημοῦσιν; Js 2: 7. αὐτὸς σώσει Mt 1: 21 (cf. Ps 129: 8). αὐτὸς ἀποδώσει 6: 4 t.r.—Mk 1: 8; 14: 15 al. Freq. the emphasis is scarcely felt: Mt 14: 2; Lk 4: 15; 22: 23; J 6: 24; Ac 22: 19 (cf. Gen 12: 12; Tob 6: 11 BA; Sir 49: 7; Vett. Val. 113, 16.—JWackernagel, Syntax II² '28, 86).—Perh. the development of αὐ. in the direction of οὗτος (which it practically replaces in Mod. Gk.) is beginning to have some influence in the NT (Pla., Phaedr. 229ε αὐτά=this; X., An. 4, 7, 7 αὐτό; Dio Chrys. 3, 37; 15[32], 10 αὐτοί; Aelian, N.A. 6, 10; Mél. de la fac. orient. . .Beyrouth 1, '06, 149 no. 18 εἰς αὐτὸ ἐγεννή-θης=for this [purpose] you were born; Schmid IV 69; 616 αὐτός=οὗτος; Synes., Ep. 3 p. 159ᴀ; 4 p. 165ᴀ; Agathias [VI AD], Hist. 1, 3 p. 144, 17 LDindorf [1871]) καὶ αὐτὸς ἦν Σαμαρίτης Lk 17: 16 (cf. 3: 23; 19: 2 and h above). Yet here αὐτός could have the mng. *alone* (examples of this from Hom. on in many writers in WSchulze, Quaestiones epicae 1892, p. 250, 3) *he alone was a Samaritan.*

3. The oblique cases of αὐ. very oft. (in a fashion customary since Hom.) take the place of the 3rd. pers. personal pron.; in partic. the gen. case replaces the missing possessive pron.

a. w. ref. to a preceding noun διαφέρετε αὐτῶν Mt 6: 26; καταβάντος αὐτοῦ 8: 1; ἀπεκάλυψας αὐτά 11: 25.—26: 43f; Mk 1: 10; 4: 33ff; 12: 19; Lk 1: 22; 4: 41. The gen. is sometimes put first for no special reason (Esth 1: 1e) αὐτοῦ τὰ σημεῖα J 2: 23, cf. 3: 19, 21, 33; 4: 47; 12: 40. αὐτῶν τὴν συνείδησιν 1 Cor 8: 12. Sim. Lk 1: 36 αὐτῇ τῇ καλουμένῃ στείρα w. *her who was called barren.* Forms of αὐ. are sometimes used inexactly in a series, referring to difft. pers.: φέρουσιν αὐτῷ (Jesus) τυφλόν, καὶ παρακαλοῦσιν αὐτὸν (Jesus) ἵνα αὐτοῦ (i.e., τοῦ τυφλοῦ) ἅψηται Mk 8: 22.

b. w. ref. to a noun to be supplied fr. the context: ἐν ταῖς συναγωγαῖς αὐτῶν (i.e. τ. Γαλιλαίων) Mt 4: 23. ἐν ταῖς πόλεσιν αὐτῶν 11: 1. ἐκήρυσσεν αὐτοῖς (i.e., the inhabitants) Ac 8: 5. παρακαλέσας αὐτούς 20: 2. ἀποταξάμενος αὐτοῖς 2 Cor 2: 13. τὰ γινόμενα ὑπ᾿ αὐτῶν Eph 5: 12. ἐδημηγόρει πρὸς αὐτούς Ac 12: 21. τὸν φόβον αὐτῶν 1 Pt 3: 14 (cf. 13 and s. Is 8: 12). Mt 12: 9 (cf. 2); Lk 2: 22; 18: 15; 19: 9; 23: 51; J 8: 44; 20: 15; Ac 4: 5; Ro 2: 26; Hb 8: 9.

c. not infreq. used w. a verb, even though a noun in the case belonging to the verb has already preceded it (cf. Dio Chrys. 6, 23; 78[29], 20; Epict. 3, 1, 22; POxy. 299 [I AD] Λάμπωνι ἔδωκα αὐτῷ δραχμὰς ἤ; FKälker, Quaest. de Eloc. Polyb. 1880, 274) τοῖς καθημένοις ἐν σκιᾷ θανάτου φῶς ἀνέτειλεν αὐτοῖς Mt 4: 16.—5: 40; 9: 28; 26: 71; J 15: 2; 18: 11; Js 4: 17; Rv 2: 7, 17; 6: 4 al.

d. used pleonastically after a relative, as somet. in class. Gk. (Bl-D. §297; Rob. 683), freq. in the LXX fr. Gen 1: 11 (οὗ τὸ σπέρμα αὐτοῦ ἐν αὐτῷ) on (Helbing p. iv; Thackeray 46), and quotable elsewh. in the Koine (Callim., Epigr. 43 [42], 3 ὧν . . . αὐτῶν; Peripl. Eryth. c. 35; POxy. 117 ἐξ ὧν δώσεις τοῖς παιδίοις σου ἓν ἐξ αὐτῶν): οὗ τὸ πτύον ἐν τῇ χειρὶ αὐτοῦ Mt 3: 12; Lk 3: 17. οὗ οὐκ εἰμὶ ἱκανὸς . . . τῶν ὑποδημάτων αὐτοῦ Mk 1: 7. ἧς εἶχεν τὸ θυγάτριον αὐτῆς 7: 25. πᾶν ὃ δέδωκεν . . . ἀναστήσω αὐτό J 6: 39; Ac 15: 17. ἣν οὐδεὶς δύναται κλεῖσαι αὐτήν Rv 3: 8. οἷς ἐδόθη αὐτοῖς 7: 2, cf. 13: 12. οὗ ἡ πνοὴ αὐτοῦ 1 Cl 21: 9.

e. in a constr. not objectionable in class. Gk. (Bl-D. §297; Rob. 724), continuing a relative clause: ἐξ οὗ τὰ πάντα καὶ ἡμεῖς εἰς αὐτόν 1 Cor 8: 6; οἷς τὸ κρίμα . . . καὶ ἡ ἀπώλεια αὐτῶν (for καὶ ὧν ἡ ἀπώλεια) 2 Pt 2: 3.

f. w. a change—α. of pers. Lk 1: 45; Rv 18: 24.

β. of number and gender ἔφυγον—αὐτούς Mt 28: 19. τοῦ παιδίου . . . αὐτῇ Mk 5: 41. φῶς . . . αὐτόν J 1: 10. λαόν—αὐτῶν Mt 1: 21.—14: 14; Mk 6: 45f; 2 Cor 5: 19.

4. ὁ αὐτός, ἡ αὐτή, τὸ αὐτό *the same* (Hom.+).

a. w. a noun τὸν αὐ. λόγον Mt 26: 44; Mk 14: 39; τὸ αὐ. φύραμα Ro 9: 21; cf. Lk 23: 40; 1 Cor 1: 10; 10: 3f; 12: 4ff; 15: 39; Phil 1: 30.

b. without a noun τὸ (τὰ) αὐ. ποιεῖν (Jos., Ant. 5, 129; 9, 271) Mt 5: 46; Lk 6: 33; Eph 6: 9. τὰ αὐτὰ πράσσειν Ro 2: 1. τὸ αὐ. λέγειν *agree* (not only in words; s. on λέγω I 1a) 1 Cor 1: 10. ἀπαγγέλλειν τὰ αὐτά Ac 15: 27. τὸ αὐτό as adv. *in the same way* (X., Mem. 3, 8, 5) Mt 27: 44; 18: 9 D.—ἐπὶ τὸ αὐτό (Hesychius: ὁμοῦ, ἐπὶ τὸν αὐ. τόπον; Iambl., Vi. Pyth. 30, 167; Dit., Syll.³ 736, 66 [92 BC]; BGU 762, 9 [II AD] ἀπὸ τῶν ἐπὶ τὸ αὐ. καμήλων ἓ of the five camels taken together; PTebt. 14, 20; 319, 9 al.; 2 Km 2: 13; Ps 2: 2; 3 Macc 3: 1; Sus 14 Theod.) of place *at the same place, together* (En. 100, 2; Jos., Bell. 2, 346; s. συνέρχομαι 1a) Mt 22: 34; 1 Cor 11: 20; 14: 23; B 4: 10; IEph 5: 3; εἶναι ἐπὶ τὸ αὐ. (Test. Napht. 6: 6) Lk 17: 35; Ac 1: 15; 2: 1; προστιθέναι ἐπὶ τὸ αὐ. *add to the total* Ac 2: 47 (see M-M.).—MWilcox, The Semitisms of Ac, '65, 93–100 (Qumran).—κατὰ τὸ αὐτό *together* in the sense *in each other's company* (PEleph. 1, 5 εἶναι δὲ ἡμᾶς κατὰ ταυτό; 3 Km 3: 18) and also *at the same time* (Aelian, V.H. 14, 8 δύο εἰκόνας εἰργάσατο Πολύκλειτος κατὰ τ. αὐ.) Ac 14: 1; also poss. is *in the same way* (ENestle, Acts 14: 1: ET 24, '13, 187f), as prob. Hs 8, 7, 1 (but s. Pap. Codex of Hs 2–9 ed. CBonner '34, 105, 17, who restores κατ᾿ αὐτούς.—In combinations ἓν καὶ τὸ αὐ. (also class.; exx. in GDKypke, Observ. II 1755, 220; Diod. S. 3, 63, 2 εἷς καὶ ὁ αὐτός) *one and the same thing* 1 Cor 11: 5; cf. 12: 11 (Diod. S. 22, 6, 3 μίαν καὶ τὴν αὐτὴν ἀπόκρισιν; Epict. 1, 19, 15 μία καὶ ἡ αὐ. ἀρχή). W. gen. foll. τὰ αὐτὰ τῶν παθημάτων *the same sufferings as* 1 Pt 5: 9. Without comparison: ὁ αὐτός (Thu. 2, 61, 2; Plut., Caesar 45, 7,

Brutus 13, 1) εἰ *thou art the same* Hb 1: 12 (Ps 101: 28); cf. 13: 8.

On the variation betw. αὐτοῦ and αὑτοῦ, αὐτῶν and αὑτῶν in the mss., s. ἑαυτοῦ, beg.—WMichaelis, D. unbetonte καὶ αὐτός bei Lukas: Studia Theologica 4, '51, 86–93—MBlack, An Aramaic Approach³, '67, 96–100. M-M.

αὐτοσώρας adv. *at the same time* (cf. HUsener, NGG 1892, 45; HDiels, Parmenides' Lehrgedicht 1897, 95) GP 5: 20.*

αὐτοῦ adv. of place (Hom.+; Epict. 4, 4, 14; Vett. Val. 264, 12; Dit., Syll.³167, 37; 273, 20; 1024, 26; pap. [Mayser 457; PSI 374, 14]; LXX; Jos., Ant. 8, 14, Vi. 116) *here* καθίσατε αὐ. (Gen 22: 5) Mt 26: 36; Mk 6: 33 v.l.; Lk 9: 27; *there* Ac 15: 34 v.l.; 18: 19; 21: 4.*

αὐτόφωρος, ον (Soph.+; Sym. Job 34: 11) *(caught) in the act* in the expr. ἐπ' αὐτοφώρῳ (since Hdt. 6, 72; POsl. 21, 9 [71 AD]; BGU 372 II, 11 [II AD]; Philo, Spec. Leg. 3, 52; Jos., Ant. 15, 48; 16, 213) first of a thief (φώρ=Lat. fur), then also of other evildoers (Plut., Eumen. 2, 2 and oft.; Sext. Emp., Rhet. 65), esp. adulterers (X., Symp. 3, 13; Aelian, N.A. 11, 15: μοιχευομένην γυναῖκα ἐπ' αὐ. καταλαβών; Achilles Tat. 5, 19, 6) J 8: 4. M-M.*

αὐτόχειρ, ρος (trag.+; Isocr.; Pla., Leg. p. 824A; Epict. 4, 9, 12; Herodian 7, 2, 8; Vett. Val., Ind.; Dit., Syll.³ 709, 42; Sb 6754, 22; Jos., Bell. 7, 393, Ant. 13, 363) w. *one's own hand* ῥίπτειν Ac 27: 19. M-M.*

αὐχέω (Aeschyl., Hdt.+; Vett. Val. 241, 9; inscr.) *boast* w. acc. (Ael. Aristid. 13 p. 164 D.; Epigr. Gr. 567, 3; 822, 5; Jos., C. Ap. 1, 22, Vi. 340) μεγάλα αὐχεῖ *boasts of great things* Js 3: 5 (cf. Epigr. Gr. 489, 1 in a grave-inscription ὃν μεγάλ' αὐχήσασα πατρὶς Θήβη). S. also μεγαλαυχέω. M-M.*

αὐχμηρός, ά, όν (Soph., Hippocr.+) *dry, dirty, dark* (for the latter mng. Aristot., De Color. 3 τὸ λαμπρὸν ἢ στίλβον...ἢ τοὐναντίον αὐχμηρὸν καὶ ἀλαμπές; Hesychius αὐ. σκοτῶδες; Suidas αὐ. στυγνὸν ἢ σκοτεινόν; Epigr. Gr. 431, 3) of a place (Pla., Leg. 761B τόποι) 2 Pt 1: 19. τόπος αὐχμηρότατος AP 21. M-M. and suppl.*

ἀφαιρέω 2 fut. ἀφελῶ (Bl-D. §74, 3); 2 aor. ἀφεῖλον, inf. ἀφελεῖν; 2 aor. mid. ἀφειλόμην; pf. pass. ἀφῄρημαι; 1 aor. ἀφῃρέθην; 1 fut. ἀφαιρεθήσομαι. (Hom.+; inscr., pap., LXX, Ep. Arist.; Philo, Abr. 8 al.; Joseph.; Test. 12 Patr.).

1. act. *take away* τὶ someth. τὸ ἔριον B 7: 8; *cut off* (Parthenius 8, 9 τ. κεφαλήν) τὸ ὠτίον *the ear* (cf. Ezk 23: 25) Mt 26: 51; Mk 14: 47; Lk 22: 50. ὄνειδος Lk 1: 25 (cf. Gen 30: 23). ἁμαρτίας Hb 10: 4 (cf. Sir 47: 11). τὶ ἀπό τινος (Theophr., Char. 2, 3; Num 21: 7; Josh 5: 9; 1 Esdr 4: 30; Jer 11: 15) *take away someth. fr. someone or someth.* τὰς πονηρίας ἀπὸ τ. ψυχῶν 1 Cl 8: 4 (Is 1: 16). ἐὰν ἀφέλῃς ἀπὸ σοῦ σύνδεσμον καὶ χειροτονίαν καὶ ῥῆμα γογγυσμοῦ *if you put away fr. you bonds and scorn and the complaining word* B 3: 5 (Is 58: 9). τὸ μέρος αὐτοῦ ἀπὸ τοῦ ξύλου τῆς ζωῆς *take away or cut off his share in the tree of life* Rv 22: 19b (on the ἐκ τῆς πόλεως foll. cf. Is 22: 19). W. omission of the obj., to be supplied fr. context (cf. Num 11: 17) ἀπὸ τ. λόγων *take away anything fr. the words* 22: 19a (cf. Diod. S. 12, 75, 4 ἀφ. ἀπὸ τῶν συνθηκῶν=take something away from the agreements; Artem. 2, 70 p. 167, 25 a request to the readers of the βιβλία: μήτε προσθεῖναι μήτε τι τῶν ὄντων ἀφελεῖν; Ael. Aristid. 30, 20 K.=10 p. 121 D.; En. 104, 11; Jos., C.

Ap. 1, 42) ἀ. ἀπὸ τοῦ πόνου τῆς ψυχῆς *take away some of the torment of his soul* 1 Cl 16: 12 (Is 53: 10). Abs. (opp. προστιθέναι as Socrat., Ep. 28, 13) B 19: 11; D 4: 13.

2. pass. *be taken away, robbed* νοσσιᾶς ἀφῃρημένης *when their nest is robbed* B 11: 3 (cf. Is 16: 2; the Funk text reads -μένοι instead of -μένης, giving the sense *when they are taken from the nest*: RAKraft ad loc.). Of sins *be taken away* Hs 9, 28, 3. W. gen. of the pers. *deprived of* someth. ἥτις οὐκ ἀφαιρεθήσεται αὐτῆς *which shall not be taken away fr. her* Lk 10: 42.

3. mid. as act. *take away* τὶ ἀπό τινος (Aristoph., Vesp. 883; Ezk 26: 16) *someth. fr. someone* τ. οἰκονομίαν Lk 16: 3. W. acc. of the thing (Ep. Arist. 244; Jos., Ant. 15, 39) τὰς ἁμαρτίας Ro 11: 27 (Is 27: 9). M-M.*

ἀφανής, ές (Aeschyl., Hdt.+; inscr., pap., LXX, Philo, Jos., Ant. 1, 333; 20, 172 al.) *invisible, hidden* Hb 4: 13; Gosp. fgm. POxy. 1081 (Kl. Texte 8³, p. 25, 6). M-M.*

ἀφανίζω 1 aor. pass. ἠφανίσθην (Soph., Hdt.+; inscr., pap., LXX, En., Philo, Joseph., Test. 12 Patr.) *render invisible* or *unrecognizable* of one's face (opp. φαίνομαι in a play on words as Js 4: 14; Aristot., Hist. Anim. 6, 7, 11; Ps.-Aristot., De Mundo 6, 22) by covering the head (cf. Jer 14: 4; 2 Km 15: 30; Esth 6: 12) or neglect of cleanliness (cf. POxy. 294, 15 [22 AD]) Mt 6: 16 (*disfigure* is also poss.; cf. PAmh. 2, 3). Of treasures *destroy, ruin* (X., An. 3, 2, 11; Epigr. Gr. 531, 2; PRyl. 152, 14; POxy. 1220, 20; PLond. 413, 14f [the 3 last passages of destruction by animals]; LXX) Mt 6: 19f.—Pass. *perish* (Diod. S. 15, 48, 3 [people and cities because of an earthquake]; Philostrat., Vi. Apoll. 1, 36 p. 38, 20 τὸ γένος αὐτῶν; Jos., Ant. 1, 76) Ac 13: 41 (Hab 1: 5); *disappear* (Antig. Car. 12; Artem. 2, 36 p. 134, 26; Eunap. p. 63; Philo, Deus Imm. 123, Virt. 164; Jos., Ant. 9, 28) of smoke Js 4: 14. Of the earth in a holocaust 2 Pt 3: 10 v.l. Fig., of the bond of wickedness IEph 19: 3. Of honey *be spoiled* Hm 5, 1, 5. M-M.*

ἀφανισμός, οῦ, ὁ *disappearance, destruction* (freq. in this sense Polyb.+; Diod. S. 15, 48, 1; Herm. Wr. p. 364 Sc.; LXX; Jos., Ant. 1, 70) ἐγγὺς ἀφανισμοῦ *is near destruction* Hb 8: 13. M-M.*

ἄφαντος, ον (Hom.+, chiefly in poets, then also in prose) *invisible* ἄ. γίνεσθαι (Diod. S. 4, 65, 9 ἐμπεσὼν εἰς τὸ χάσμα...ἄφ. ἐγένετο; Plut., Mor. 409F; Act. Thom. 77 ἄφαντοι γεγόνασιν οἱ δαίμονες, 13 p. 119, 2 v.l.) *vanish* Lk 24: 31 (on ἀπό τινος *fr. someone*—as Pel.-Leg. 6, 24—s. JPsichari, Essai sur le Grec de la LXX: Rev. des Études juives 55, '08, 161–208, esp. 204ff). M-M.*

ἀφεδρών, ῶνος, ὁ *latrine* (Dit., Or. 483, 220f [prechristian] τ. δημοσίων ἀφεδρώνων καὶ. τ. ἐξ αὐτῶν ὑπονόμων; Geopon. 6, 2, 8; Anecd. Gr. p. 469, 23; Etym. Gud. 240, 14) εἰς ἀ. ἐκβάλλεται *passes into the latrine* Mt 15: 17; Mk 7: 19. M-M.*

ἀφεθήσομαι s. ἀφίημι.

ἀφειδία, ας, ἡ (Ps.-Pla., Def. 412D; Plut., Mor. 762D; Nägeli 52) *severe* (lit. *unsparing*) *treatment* σώματος *of the body* (=asceticism) Col 2: 23 (ἀφειδεῖν τοῦ σώματος also in sense *harden* [Lucian, Anach. 24]). M-M.*

ἀφεῖλον, ἀφελεῖν s. ἀφαιρέω.

ἀφεῖναι s. ἀφίημι.

ἀφελότης, ητος, ἡ (Dio Chrys.; Vett. Val. 240, 15; 153, 30) *simplicity* of heart Ac 2: 46. M-M.*

ἀφελπίζω s. ἀπελπίζω.

ἀφελῶ s. ἀφαιρέω.

ἄφεσις, έσεως, ἡ (Pla.+; inscr., pap., LXX, En., Philo, Joseph.).
1. *release* fr. captivity (Polyb. 1, 79, 12; Dit., Syll.³ 374, 21; PGrenf. I 64, 5; 1 Esdr 4, 62; Philo, Mut. Nom. 228 [after Lev 25: 10]; Jos., Ant. 12, 40; 17, 185) Lk 4: 18ab (Is 61: 1; 58: 6); B 3: 3 (Is 58: 6); 14: 9 (Is 61: 1).
2. *pardon, cancellation* of an obligation, a punishment, or guilt (Pla., Leg. 9, 869ᴅ φόνου; Diod. S. 20, 44, 6 ἐγκλημάτων; Dionys. Hal. 8, 50 al.; En. 13, 4; 6; Philo, Mos. 2, 147 ἀ. ἀμαρτημάτων, Spec. Leg. 1, 215; 237; Jos., Bell. 1, 481; exx. fr. inscr. and pap. in Nägeli 56. Cf. also Dt 15: 3; Jdth 11: 14; 1 Macc 10: 34; 13: 34. For history of the word Dssm., B 94-7 [BS 98ff]) ἀμαρτιῶν *forgiveness of sins* i.e. cancellation of the guilt of sin Mt 26: 28; Mk 1: 4; Lk 1: 77; 3: 3; 24: 47; Ac 2: 38; 5: 31 (δοῦναι ἄφεσιν as Diod. S. 20, 54, 2); 10: 43 (λαβεῖν); 13: 38; 26: 18; Col 1: 14; B 5: 1; 6: 11; 8: 3; 11: 1; 16: 8; Hm 4, 3, 1ff. For this ἀ. τ. παραπτωμάτων Eph 1: 7; τοῖς παραπτώμασιν ἀ. Hm 4, 4, 4; ἀ. abs. in same sense Mk 3: 29; Hb 9: 22; 10: 18. αἰτεῖσθαι ἄφεσίν τινι *ask forgiveness for someone* 1 Cl 53: 5.—EBRedlich, The Forgiveness of Sins '37; VTaylor, Forgiveness and Reconciliation (in the NT) '41. M-M. and suppl.*

ἀφέωνται s. ἀφίημι.

ἀφή, ῆς, ἡ (Hdt.+; Dit., Syll.³ 1170, 11; LXX; Ep. Arist.; Philo; cf. Nägeli 18; on its use as medic. t.t. s. Lghtf. on Col 2: 19 and JARobinson on Eph 4: 16) *ligament*, lit. 'joint, connection', Eph 4: 16, Col 2: 19. CBruston, Rev. des Ét. grecques 24, '11, 77ff. M-M.*

ἀφῆκα s. ἀφίημι.

ἀφήκω fut. ἀφήξω (Pla., Rep. 7 p. 530ᴇ; Antipho: Anecd. Gr. p. 470 s.v. ἀφήκοντος) *go away* (Cass. Dio 41, 8; Sb 7250, 5) ποῦ ἀφήξω; *where shall I go?* 1 Cl 28: 3.*

ἀφθαρσία, ας, ἡ *incorruptibility, immortality* ('higher Koine' [Nägeli 41, 1; 31]: Epicurus 60, 3 [PLinde, Epicuri Vocab. '06, 43]; Chrysipp.; Strabo; Plut., Aristid. 6, 3, Mor. 881ʙ al.; Herm. Wr. 12, 14; Wsd 2: 23; 6: 19; 4 Macc 9: 22; 17: 12; Philo, Aet. M. 27 ἀ. τ. κόσμου; Gosp. fgm. POxy. 1081, 14ff [Kl. T. 8³ p. 25, 17 and 20]) 1 Cor 15: 42, 50, 53f; IPol 2: 3. As a quality of the future life (w. ζωή) 2 Ti 1: 10; 2 Cl 14: 5; (w. δόξα, τιμή) ἀ. ζητεῖν Ro 2: 7; ἀ. προσδέχεσθαι Dg 6: 8; πνεῖν ἀφθαρσίαν IEph 17: 1; μεταλαμβάνειν ἀ. 2 Cl 14: 5; ἀρχηγὸς τῆς ἀ. (of Christ) 20: 5; ἀγὼν τῆς ἀ. 7: 5; ἀπάρτισμα ἀ. *the consummation of immortality* (of the gosp.) IPhld 9: 2; διδαχὴ ἀ. *teaching that assures immort.* IMg 6: 2; ὁ τῆς ἀ. στέφανος *the crown which is immortality* MPol 17: 1; 19: 2; ἐν ἀ. πνεύματος ἁγίου 14: 2.—The mng. of ἀ. in Eph 6: 24 is no different; it refers either to those who love the Lord, and as such are now partakers of the future life, or to the Lord himself, who reigns in immortal glory. Its presence in Tit 2: 7 t.r. is prob. due to a misunderstanding of the rare word ἀφθορία. M-M.*

ἄφθαρτος, ον *imperishable, incorruptible, immortal* ('higher Koine' [Nägeli 41, 1; 31]: Philochorus [IV/III ʙᴄ] no. 328 fgm. 188b Jac.; Aristot.; Epicurus; Diod. S.; Dionys. Hal.; Cornutus 1 p. 2, 8; Lucian; Philostrat., Dial. p. 259, 7 K.; Sallust. p. 12, 24; 30, 7; CIG 4240d; Dit., Or. 569, 24; PGM 4, 497; 519; 13, 912; Gosp. fgm. POxy. 1081, 19 [KL. T. 8³ p. 25]; Wsd 12: 1; 18: 4) of God (Diod. S. 6, 2, 2 of gods: ἀΐδιοι and ἄφθαρτοι; Zoroaster in Philo of Bybl. [Euseb., Pr. Ev. 1, 10, 52]; Antipater of Tarsus

[150 ʙᴄ] in Plut., Stoicor. Repugn. 38 p. 1105ꜰ; Herm. Wr. 11, 3; PGM 4, 559 θεοῦ ζῶντος ἀφθάρτου; Sib. Or., fgm. 3, 17; Philo, Sacr. Abel. 95, Mos. 2, 171; Jos., Ant. 3, 88; 10, 278) Ro 1: 23; 1 Ti 1: 17; PK 2; of Christ Dg 9: 2. Of the resurrected body 1 Cor 15: 52. ναός B 16: 9. στέφανος 1 Cor 9: 25; κληρονομία 1 Pt 1: 4; σπορά vs. 23; short ending of Mk; ἀγάπη ἄ. *an imperishable love-feast* IRo 7: 3; ἀγὼν ἄ. 2 Cl 7: 3; ἀγαθὰ ἄ. (Philo, Deus Imm. 151) 6: 6; καρπὸς ἄ. ITr 11: 2; φυτά (Philo, Sacr. Abel. 97) AP 15.—Subst. τὸ ἄ. (Dit., Syll.³ 798, 10 [37 ᴀᴅ]) B 19: 8; ἐν τῷ ἀ. τοῦ πραέως πνεύματος w. *the imperishable quality of a gentle spirit* (s. πνεῦμα 3c) 1 Pt 3: 4. M-M.*

ἀφθονία, ας, ἡ (Pind.+; POslo 78, 16 [136 ᴀᴅ= 'abundance']; Philo, Mos. 1, 6; Jos., Bell. 3, 505, Ant. 12, 133; Ode of Solomon 11, 6) *freedom fr. envy*, hence *willingness* (so Pla., Prot. 327ʙ) Tit 2: 7 v.l.*

ἀφθορία, ας, ἡ *soundness*, lit. incorruption (corresp. to ἄφθορος Diod. S. 4, 7, 3; Artem. 5, 95; Phalaris, Ep. 70; BGU 1106, 11; 1107, 7; PGM 5, 376; 7, 544; Esth 2: 2) of pure doctrine Tit 2: 7. M-M.*

ἀφίδω s. ἀφοράω.

ἀφιερόω 1 aor. ἀφιέρωσα (pass. in Aeschyl., Eumen. 451; Jos., Ant. 11, 148) in H.Gk. relig. t.t. *consecrate* (Diod. S. 1, 90, 4; Plut.; Philo Bybl. [c. 100 ᴀᴅ] in Euseb., Pr. Ev. 1, 9, 29; Dit., Or., Ind., al. in the inscriptions; 4 Macc 13: 13; Philo Alex.; Jos., Ant. 15, 364) ἀφιέρωσαν αὐτὸν (sc. τὸν θεόν) ἐν τῷ ναῷ *they have consecrated him by the temple* instead of conversely basing the consecration of the temple on God B 16: 2.*

ἀφίημι (Hom.+; inscr., pap., LXX, Philo, Joseph., Test. 12 Patr.) pres. act. ind. 2 sg. ἀφεῖς (Rob. 315; W-S. §14, 16; M-M.), 1 pl. ἀφίομεν (ἀφίεμεν v.l.) Lk 11: 4, 3 pl. ἀφίουσιν Rv 11: 9; impf. 3 sg. ἤφιε (Bl-D. §69, 1); fut. ἀφήσω; 1 aor. ἀφῆκα, 2 sg. ἀφῆκας (ἀφῆκες Rv 2: 4 W-H.; Bl-D. §83, 2); 2 aor. imper. ἄφες (as ᴅᴇᴎ in rabb.), ἄφετε; subj. ἀφῶ, 2 pl. ἀφῆτε; inf. ἀφεῖναι Mt 23: 23; Lk 5: 21; ptc. ἀφείς. Pass. pres. ἀφίεμαι, 3 pl. ἀφίονται Mt 9: 2ᴅ; fut. ἀφεθήσομαι; 1 aor. ἀφέθην; pf. 3 pl. ἀφέωνται Lk 5: 20, 23; J 20: 23; 1 J 2: 12 (Bl-D. §97, 3).
1. *let go, send away*—a. lit.—α. w. pers. obj. (X., Cyr. 1, 2, 8; Polyb. 33, 1, 6; Tob 10: 5; Sir 27: 19; Jos., Ant. 16, 135 τ. ἐκκλησίαν) of crowds Mt 13: 36; Mk 4: 36; 8: 13 (mng. 3a is also poss.).
β. w. impers. obj. τὸ πνεῦμα *give up one's spirit* Mt 27: 50 (cf. ἀ. τ. ψυχήν Hdt. 4, 190 and oft. in Gk. lit.; Gen 35: 18; 1 Esdr 4: 21; Jos., Ant. 1, 218; 14, 369 al.). φωνὴν μεγάλην *utter a loud cry* Mk 15: 37 (φων. ἀ. Hdt.+; Epict. 2, 22, 12 al.; Gen 45: 2; Philo, Sacr. Abel. 34; Jos., Bell. 4, 170, Ant. 8, 325, Vi. 158).
b. in a legal sense *divorce* γυναῖκα (Hdt. 5, 39) 1 Cor 7: 11ff.
2. *cancel, remit, pardon* τὸ δάνειον *the loan* Mt 18: 27 (Dit., Or. 90, 12; PGrenf. I 26, 9; Dt 15: 2). ὀφειλὴν a *debt* vs. 32 (cf. 1 Macc 15: 8 πᾶν ὀφείλημα βασιλικὸν ἀ.). Also of remission of the guilt (debt) of sin (Hdt. 6, 30 ἀπῆκέ τ' ἂν αὐτῷ τὴν αἰτίην; 8, 140, 2; Lysias 20, 34 ἀφιέντας τ. τῶν πατέρων ἁμαρτίας; Herodas 5, 26 ἄφες μοι τὴν ἁμαρτίην ταύτην; 38, 72f; 1 Macc 13: 39.—In another construction Diod. S. 9, 31, 4 Κῦρος αὐτὸν ἀφίησι τῶν ἀμαρτημάτων = absolves him of his misdeeds), in OT and NT predom. in relig. sense of divine forgiveness. W. dat. of the pers. and acc. of the thing: ὀφειλήματα *remit, forgive debts* (Appian, Ital. 9 §1 ἠφίει τοῖς ἑαυτοῦ χρήσταις τὰ ὀφλήματα) Mt 6: 12a; cf. b (s. Sir 28: 2 and

ὡς III 1b; FFensham, The Legal Background of Mt 6: 12, Nov Test 4, '60, 1f [Deut 15: 2 LXX]; on the text FCBurkitt, 'As we have forgiven' Mt 6: 12: JTS 33, '32, 253–5); *forgive* ἁμαρτίας (Ex 32: 32; Num 14: 19; Job 42: 10 al.; Jos., Ant. 6, 92) Lk 11: 4; 1 J 1: 9. παραπτώματα Mt 6: 14f; Mk 11: 25(26). Pass. (Lev 4: 20; 19: 22; Is 22: 14; 33: 24 al.) ἁμαρτίαι Lk 5: 20, 23; 7: 47b; 1 J 2: 12; 1 Cl 50: 5; Hv 2, 2, 4; s 7: 4; PK 3 p. 15, 12; ἁμαρτήματα Mk 3: 28 (cf. GDalman, Jesus-Jeshua [Eng. tr. PLevertoff '29], 195–97; JGWilliams, NTS 12, '65, 75–77); PK 3 p. 15, 27; cf. Mt 12: 31f. W. dat. of pers. only Mt 18: 21, 35; Lk 17: 3f; 23: 34 (ELohse, Märtyrer u. Gottesknecht, Exkurs: Lk 23: 34, Göttingen '55). Pass. (Lev 4: 26, 31, 35; Num 15: 25f al.) Lk 12: 10; Js 5: 15.—J 20: 23b (s. JRMantey, JBL 58, '39, 243–9 and HJCadbury ibid. 251–4). W. impers. obj. only Mt 9: 6; Mk 2: 7, 10; Lk 5: 21, 24; 7: 49; J 20: 23. Pass. Mt 9: 2, 5, cf. 4 Q Hab, 4; Mk 2: 5, 9 (cf. HBranscomb, JBL 53, '34, 53–60); Lk 7: 47f. ἀνομίαι Ro 4: 7; 1 Cl 50: 6 (both Ps 31: 1). Quite abs. ἀφίετε 1 Cl 13: 2.

3. *leave*—a. lit., w. pers. obj. (PGrenf. I 1, 16; BGU 814, 16; 18) Mt 4: 11; 8: 15; 26: 44; Mk 1: 20, 31; 12: 12; Lk 4: 39; 9: 42D; *abandon* (Soph., Phil. 486; Hyperid. 5, 32; X., Hell. 6, 4, 5) Mt 26: 56; Mk 14: 50.—W. impers. obj. (PFay. 112, 13; Jer 12: 7; Eccl 10: 4; 1 Esdr 4: 50) J 10: 12; *the house* Mk 13: 34; cf. Mt 23: 38; Lk 13: 35 (Diod. S. 17, 41, 7: Apollo appears and explains that he would leave Tyre, which is doomed to destruction); *Judaea* J 4: 3 (Jos., Ant. 2, 335 τ. Αἴγυπτον); *the way* Hv 3, 7, 1; *everything* Mt 19: 27, 29; Mk 10, 28f; Lk 5: 11; 18: 28f.—*Leave standing* or *lying* (without concerning oneself further about it as, in a way, Diod. S. 5, 35, 3 a fire without putting it out) αὐτόν Mt 22: 22; τὰ δίκτυα 4: 20; Mk 1: 18; ἐκεῖ τὸ δῶρον Mt 5: 24; cf. 18: 12; J 4: 28; ἡμιθανῆ *half dead* Lk 10: 30 (cf. Jdth 6: 13).—*Leave (behind)* w. pers. obj. (2 Km 15: 16; 3 Km 19: 3; Tob 11: 2) as orphans J 14: 18 (Epict. 3, 24, 14; Jos., Ant. 12, 387). τινὰ μόνον 8: 29; 16: 32. W. acc. only Mk 12: 19ff; τινί τινα Mt 22: 25.—τινί τι ἀ. *let someone have someth.* (cf. Jos., Ant. 7, 274 τ. υἱὸν ἄφες μοι) Mt 5: 40; *leave (over, remaining)* (Da 4: 15) Hb 2: 8; *leave, give* (Eccl 2: 18; Ps 16: 14; cf. Diod. S. 25, 16 [Dindorf] τὸν πόλεμον ἀφίημι=I leave [you] war) εἰρήνην J 14: 27. Pass. *be left, remain* (Da 4: 26) οὐ μὴ ἀφεθῇ λίθος ἐπὶ λίθον *not a stone will be left on another* Mt 24: 2; Mk 13: 2; Lk 21: 6.

b. fig. *give up, abandon* (Aeschyl., Prom. 317 ὀργήν; Arrian, Anab. 1, 10, 6; Jos., Ant. 9, 264 ἀ. τ. ἄρτι βίον) τὴν πρώτην ἀγάπην Rv 2: 4; τ. φυσικὴν χρῆσιν Ro 1: 27; *leave (behind)* to go on to someth. else (in orators; Plut., Mor. 793A; Epict. 4, 1, 15 al.) τὸν τῆς ἀρχῆς τοῦ Χρ. λόγον Hb 6: 1; *neglect* (Diod. S. 1, 39, 11; POxy. 1067, 5) also *omit* (Diod. S. 8, 12, 11) τὰ βαρύτερα τοῦ νόμου *what is more important in the law* Mt 23: 23; τὴν ἐντολήν Mk 7: 8 (Hyperid. 5, 22 νόμον).

4. *let, let go, tolerate* w. acc. (Arrian, Anab. 1, 25, 2; Himerius, Or. [Ecl.] 4, 1; 4 Km 4: 27) Mt 15: 14; Mk 5: 19; 11: 6; 14: 6; Lk 13: 8; Ac 5: 38. ἀφεῖς τ. γυναῖκα Ἰεζάβελ *you tolerate the woman Jezebel* Rv 2: 20. ἐὰν ἀφῶμεν αὐτὸν οὕτως *if we let him go on like this* (i.e., doing miracles) J 11: 48. *Allow, let, permit, leave* w. double acc. οὐκ ἀμάρτυρον αὐτὸν ἀφῆκεν *he has not left himself without a witness* Ac 14: 17 (cf. Soph., Oed. Col. 1279 ἀ. τινα ἄτιμον; PFay. 112, 13; POxy. 494, 5 ἐλεύθερα ἀφίημι δοῦλά μου σώματα; 1 Macc 1: 48). W. acc. and inf. (BGU 23, 7; POxy. 121, 15; Ex 12: 23; Num 22: 13) Mt 8: 22; 13: 30; 19: 14; 23: 13; Mk 1: 34; 7: 12, 27; 10: 14; Lk 8: 51; 9: 60; 12: 39; 18: 16; J 11: 44; 18: 8; Rv

11: 9; Hv 1, 3, 1; 3, 1, 8; s 9, 11, 6. W. ἵνα foll. Mk 11: 16. —The imperatives ἄφες, ἄφετε are used w. the subjunctive esp. in the first pers. (this is the source of Mod. Gk. ἄς; Bl-D. §364, 1 and 2; Rob. 931f) ἄφες ἐκβάλω τὸ κάρφος *let me take out the speck* Mt 7: 4; Lk 6: 42 (cf. Epict. 4, 1, 132 ἄφες σκέψωμαι; POxy. 413, 184 [II 1D] ἄφες ἐγὼ αὐτὸν θρηνήσω). ἄφες (ἄφετε) ἴδωμεν *let us see* Mt 27: 49; Mk 15: 36 (cf. Epict. 3, 12, 15 ἄφες ἴδω). It is also used w. the third pers. (Epict. 1, 15, 7 ἄφες ἀνθήσῃ) and w. ἵνα (Epict. 4, 13, 19 ἄφες οὖν, ἵνα κἀγὼ ταὐτὰ ὑπολάβω), so that ἄφες αὐτήν, ἵνα τηρήσῃ αὐτό J 12: 7 is prob. to be transl. *let her keep it* (Mlt. 175f). The second pers. is rare ἄφες ἴδῃς Hs 8, 1, 4 acc. to PMich. Abs. *let it be so, let it go* (Charito 4, 3, 6) Mt 3: 15; GEb 3 (w. ὅτι foll.= 'for'). M-M. B. 768; 839; 1174.

ἀφικνέομαι 2 aor. ἀφικόμην (Hom.+; inscr., pap., LXX; En. 98, 4; Ep. Arist. 175; Joseph.) *reach* of a report εἴς τινα *someone* ἡ ὑπακοὴ εἰς πάντας ἀφίκετο *the report of your obedience has reached* (become known to) *everyone* Ro 16: 19 (cf. Aristot., Eth. Nic. 1097a, 24 ὁ λόγος εἰς ταὐτὸν ἀφ.; Sir 47: 16; Jos., Ant. 17, 155; 19, 127 εἰς τὸ θέατρον ἀφίκετο ὁ λόγος). M-M. B. 703.*

ἀφιλάγαθος, ον *not loving the good* in a list of vices 2 Ti 3: 3 (so far the word is found only here, but cf. POxy. 33 II, 13 [II AD] ἀφιλοκαγαθία, 11 φιλάγαθος and s. Nägeli 52). M-M.*

ἀφιλάργυρος, ον (Diod. S. 9, 11, 2; Diog. L. 4, 38; Inschr. v. Priene 137, 5 [II BC]; Dit., Syll.³ 708, 17 [II BC]; 732, 25 [36/5 BC]; POxy. 33 II, 11 [II AD]; other ref. in Nägeli 31) *not loving money, not greedy* 1 Ti 3: 3 (in instructions for midwives in Soranus p. 5, 27 and for generals in Onosander [I AD] 1, 1; 2; 4; 8 AKoechly [1860] w. σώφρων and νήπτης [=νηφάλιος]); Hb 13: 5; D 15: 1; Pol 5: 2. M-M.*

ἀφιλοξενία, ας, ἡ *inhospitality* (Sib. Or. 8, 304) 1 Cl 35: 5.*

ἄφιξις, εως, ἡ (s. ἀφικνέομαι, hence—Hdt.+—usu. 'arrival'; so also Lysimachus [200 BC] no. 382 fgm. 6 Jac.; Diod. S. 8, 19, 2; pap.; 3 Macc 7: 18; Ep. Arist. 173; Jos., Ant. 20, 51, Vi. 104) *departure* (so surely Demosth., Ep. 1, 2; 3, 39 ἄ. οἴκαδε; Ael. Aristid. 48, 7 K.=24 p. 467 D.; Jos., Ant. 2, 18; 4, 315; 7, 247; other pass. in Gk. lit. are ambiguous) Ac 20: 29—JWackernagel, Glotta 14, '25, 59. M-M.*

ἀφίστημι 1 aor. ἀπέστησα; 2 aor. ἀπέστην, imperative ἀπόστα Hm 6, 2, 6; pres. mid. ἀφίσταμαι, imper. ἀφίστασο; fut. ἀποστήσομαι. (Hom.+; inscr., pap., LXX, En., Ep. Arist., Joseph., Test. 12 Patr.)
1. trans. *cause to revolt, mislead* (Hdt. 1, 76+; Dt 7: 4; Jos., Ant. 8, 198; 20, 102 τ. λαόν) λαὸν ὀπίσω αὐτοῦ *the people, so that they followed him* Ac 5: 37.
2. intrans. (mid. forms, and 2 aor., pf., and plupf. act.) —a. *go away, withdraw* τινός (Hdt. 3, 15; Epict. 2, 13, 26; 4, 5, 28; BGU 159, 4; Sir 38: 12; En. 14, 23; Jos., Ant. 1, 14) Lk 2: 37. ἀπό τινος (PGM 4, 1244; Sir 23: 11f; Jdth 13: 19; 1 Macc 6: 10, 36) Lk 1: 38D; 13: 27 (Ps 6: 9); 24: 51D; Ac 12: 10; 19: 9; Hs 9, 15, 6. ἐκ τοῦ τόπου Hm 5, 1, 3. Abs. (Aesop, Fab. 194 H.) s 8, 8, 2. *Desert* ἀπό τινος *someone* (as Appian, Iber. 34 §137; cf. Jer 6: 8) Ac 15: 38.—*Fall away* (Hdt.+), *become apostate* abs. (Appian, Iber. 38 §156 ἀφίστατο=he revolted; Jer 3: 14; Da 9: 9 Theod.; 1 Macc 11: 43; En. 5, 4) Lk 8: 13. ἀπό τινος (X., Cyr. 5, 4, 1; Polyb. 1, 16, 3; oft. LXX, mostly of falling

away fr. God) Hb 3: 12; Hv 2, 3, 2; s 8, 8, 5; 8, 9, 1 and 3; 8, 10, 3; τινός (Polyb. 14, 12, 3; Herodian 6, 2, 7; Wsd 3: 10; Jos., Vi. 158) Hv 3, 7, 2; 1 Ti 4: 1.

b. *keep away* (Diod. S. 11, 50, 7; Jos., Vi. 261) ἀπό τινος (UPZ 196 I, 15 [119 bc]) Lk 4: 13; Ac 5: 38; 2 Cor 12: 8; cf. Ac 22: 29; Hs 7: 2. Fig. of moral conduct (Sir 7: 2; 35: 3 ἀποστῆναι ἀπὸ πονηρίας; Tob 4: 21 BA) *abstain* 2 Ti 2: 19; Hs 6, 1, 4.

c. fig. *depart, withdraw* affliction Hs 7: 7; life s 8, 6, 4; understanding s 9, 22, 2; righteousness and peace 1 Cl 3: 4; wickedness Hv 3, 6, 1. Cf. m 10, 2, 5 of the Holy Spirit. Of an evil spirit m 5, 2, 7; 6, 2, 6f. M-M.*

ἄφνω adv. (Aeschyl., Thu.+; pap., LXX; Jos., Vi. 126) *suddenly* Ac 2: 2; 16: 26; 1 Cl 57: 4; AP 4: 11.—*Immediately, at once* (Diod. S. 14, 104, 2) Ac 28: 6.*

ἀφοβία, ας, ἡ lit. 'fearlessness' (Pla.+; Epict.; Ep. Arist. 243), but also *lack of reverence* (Pr 15: 16; Ps.-Clem., Hom. 1, 18) ἀ. θεοῦ B 20: 1; D 5: 1 (Funk).*

ἀφόβως adv. (X.+; PTebt. 24, 74 [II bc]; Pr 1: 33; Wsd 17: 4 v.l.; Philo, Migr. Abr. 169; Jos., Ant. 7, 322).
1. *without fear, fearlessly* Lk 1: 74; Phil 1: 14; 1 Cl 57: 7; *without cause to be afraid* (Horapollo 2, 72) 1 Cor 16: 10. In Jd 12 ἀ. is either *boldly* or
2. *without reverence, shamelessly* (s. ἀφοβία). M-M.*

ἀφόδευσις, εως, ἡ (Erotian [I ad] s.v. ἀπόπατοι ed. ENachmanson '18; cf. also schol. on Nicander, Ther. 933) *anus* (cf. Tob 2: 10) of hares: πλεονεκτεῖν τὴν ἀ. *grows a new anus* B 10: 6 (cf. Pliny, Nat. Hist. 8, 81, 218 Archelaus auctor est, quot sint corporis cavernae ad excrementa lepori, totidem annos esse aetatis; Aelian, N.A. 2, 12; Varro, De Re Rust. 3, 12).*

ἀφομοιόω (X., Pla.+) *make like* or *similar* poss. *become like* (Herm. Wr. 454, 17 Sc.), in past tenses *be like, resemble* (Diod. S. 1, 86, 3; Aesop, Fab. 88 P.=137 H.: Ἑρμῆς ἀφομοιωθεὶς ἀνθρώπῳ; EpJer 4; 62; 70) ἀφωμοιωμένος τῷ υἱῷ τοῦ θεοῦ Hb 7: 3.*

ἀφοράω 2 aor. ἀπεῖδον, subj. ἀφίδω, also ἀπίδω v.l. (Bl-D. §14 w. app.) (Hdt., Pla.+; pap.; Philo, Omn. Prob. Lib. 28, Aet. M. 4).
1. *look away, fix one's eyes* trustingly εἴς τινα to or *on someone* (Epict. 2, 19, 29 εἰς τὸν θεόν; 3, 26, 11 al.; Herm. Wr. 7, 2a; 4 Macc 17: 10; Jos., Bell. 2, 410) εἰς τὸν τῆς πίστεως ἀρχηγόν Hb 12: 2.
2. *see* (Jon 4: 5) ὡς ἂν ἀφίδω τὰ περὶ ἐμέ *as soon as I see how things go w. me* Phil 2: 23. M-M.*

ἀφορίζω impf. ἀφώριζον; fut. ἀφορίσω Mt 25: 32—Attic ἀφοριῶ 13: 49; 1 aor. ἀφώρισα; pf. pass. ptc. ἀφωρισμένος; 1 aor. pass. imper. ἀφορίσθητε (Soph., Pla.+; inscr., pap., LXX; Jos., Bell. 2, 488).
1. *separate, take away* Ac 19: 9. τινὰ ἀπό τινος (Is 56: 3; Sir 47: 2) Mt 25: 32 (cf. Diod. S. 5, 79, 2 Rhadamanthys was appointed judge in Hades to διακρίνειν τοὺς εὐσεβεῖς καὶ τοὺς πονηρούς). τινὰ ἐκ μέσου τινῶν *take out* 13: 49. *Exclude, excommunicate* Lk 6: 22. ἑαυτόν (Is 45: 24) *separate oneself, hold aloof* Gal 2: 12. Pass., w. middle mng. *be separate* 2 Cor 6: 17 (Is 52: 11).
2. *set apart, appoint* (Nägeli 35) τινά Gal 1: 15 (no purpose mentioned; JWDoeve, Paulus d. Pharisäer u. Gal 1: 13-15, Nov Test 6, '63, 170-181). W. the purpose given εἴς τι (POxy. 37, 9; 4 Macc 3: 20) εἰς εὐαγγέλιον *to preach the gospel* Ro 1: 1. ἀ. εἰς τὸ ἔργον Ac 13: 2. M-M.*

ἀφορμάω (Hom.+; in act. trag., X.+) *start, set out* εἰς τοὔπισω *start back again, return* 1 Cl 25: 4.*

ἀφορμή, ῆς, ἡ lit. the starting-point or base of operations for an expedition, then gener. the resources needed to carry through an undertaking (e.g. even commercial capital), in our lit. *occasion, pretext, opportunity* for someth., a meaning found in Attic Gk. and quite common in the Koine (Nägeli 15) ἐκκόπτειν τὴν ἀ. τῶν θελόντων ἀ. *cut off the pretext of those who wish a pretext* 2 Cor 11: 12; ἀ. διδόναι τινί (Polyb. 28, 6, 7 μὴ διδόναι τ. ἐχθροῖς ἀφορμὴν εἰς διαβολήν; Pr 9: 9; Philo, Leg. ad Gai. 200; cf. Diod. S. 1, 83; 3 Macc 3: 2) *give someone an occasion* 1 Ti 5: 14; *excuse* Hm 4, 3, 3; τινός *for someth.* 2 Cor 5: 12 (for the gen. cf. Epict. 1, 8, 6; 1, 9, 20; Dio Chrys. 16[33], 38; Jos., Bell. 7, 441, Ant. 5, 57). Pl. (Polyb., Epict., Vett. Val.; Inschr. v. Priene 105, 12; Joseph.) ἀφορμὰς διδόναι τινί, ἵνα ITr 8: 2; Hm 4, 1, 11; ἀ. λαμβάνειν (a favorite expr.; e.g. in Polyb.; Dionys. Hal.; Philo, In Flacc. 47) *grasp an opportunity* Ro 7: 8, 11; w. gen. of the one who gives the opportunity Lk 11: 54D (we scarcely have here the expr. ἀ. ζητεῖν, as POxy. 34 III, 13 ἀ. ζητοῦντες ἁμαρτημάτων). W. εἴς τι for someth. (Appian, Bell. Civ. 5, 53 §222 ἔχειν ἀφορμήν ἔς τι; Philo) 2 Cl 16: 1; εἰς ἀ. τῇ σαρκί *to give the flesh an opportunity* (to become active) Gal 5: 13. M-M.*

ἄφραστος, ον (Hom. Hymns+; Aeschyl.) *too wonderful for words* (so in later prose; Eunap. 45; Test. Levi 8: 15 v.l.; PGM 3, 592 ἄ. ὄνομα) ἔννοια *plan* Dg 8: 9.*

ἀφρίζω (Soph., El. 719; Diod. S. 3, 10, 5; Athen. 11, 43 p. 472a) *foam at the mouth* of a sick person in a frenzy Mk 9: 18, 20.*

ἀφροντιστέω (X., Pla.+; Diod. S. 5, 32, 7; Philostrat., Vi. Apoll. 1, 38 p. 41, 1; PReinach 57, 11) *be careless, unconcerned* Dg 8: 10.*

ἀφρόνως adv. of ἄφρων (Soph., Aj. 766; Diod. S. 16, 70, 2; Artem. 1, 50 p. 46, 21; Gen 31: 28) *foolishly* ἀποκρίνεσθαι Hv 5: 4.*

ἀφρός, οῦ, ὁ (Hom.+; PGM 4, 942; 3204; medical use in Hobart 17f) *foam* appearing at the mouth in epileptic seizures (Jos., Ant. 6, 245) μετὰ ἀφροῦ *so that he foams* Lk 9: 39. M-M.*

ἀφροσύνη, ης, ἡ (Hom+; Artem. 2, 37 p. 141, 15; LXX; Philo; Jos., Ant. 17, 277, Vi. 323; Test. 12 Patr.; Sib. Or. 4, 38) *foolishness, lack of sense*, moral and intellectual Mk 7: 22; 2 Cor 11: 1, 17, 21; 1 Cl 13: 1; 47: 7; Hm 5, 2, 4; s 6, 5, 2f; 9, 15, 3; 9, 22, 2f; Dg 3: 3; 4: 5.*

ἄφρων, ον, gen. ονος (Hom.+; PFay. 124, 12; LXX; Philo; Jos., Bell. 1, 630; 2, 303) *foolish, ignorant* (opp. φρόνιμος as Dio Chrys. 73[23], 3; Pr 11: 29; Philo, Poster. Cai. 32) 2 Cor 11: 19; 1 Cl 3: 3; (w. ἀνόητος) 21: 5; (w. ἀσύνετος as Ps 91: 7) 39: 1.—Lk 11: 40; 12: 20; Ro 2: 20; 1 Cor 15: 36; 2 Cor 11: 16; 12: 6, 11; Eph 5: 17; 1 Pt 2: 15; 1 Cl 39: 7f (Job 5: 2f); ITr 8: 2; Hm 4, 2, 1; 5, 2, 2 (Funk and L.); 4; 6, 2, 4; 11: 4; 12, 4, 2; s 1: 3; 6, 4, 3; 6, 5, 2; 9, 14, 4; 9, 22, 2. M-M.*

ἀφύλακτος, ον (Aeschyl., Hdt.+; Sb 6002, 15 [II bc]; Jos., Ant. 14, 169; cf. Ezk 7: 22; 23: 39A) *without guarding* (them) of idols kept in temples open to the public Dg 2: 7 (v.l. ἀφυλάκτως).*

ἀφυπνόω 1 aor. ἀφύπνωσα *fall asleep* (in this mng. in Heliod. 9, 12; schol. on Pind., Pyth. 1, 10b, Isth. 4, 33c;

Achmes 174, 16; Act. Andr. et Matthiae 16 p. 84, 7 and 8 Bonnet; Paulus Aegineta [VII AD] 1, 98; cf. Lobeck, Phryn. p. 224) Lk 8: 23; Hv 1, 1, 3. M-M.*

ἀφυστερέω pf. pass. ptc. ἀφυστερημένος (Polyb.+; pap., LXX) only trans. (cf. 2 Esdr 19: 20 [Neh 9: 20] withhold μισθός Js 5: 4 (ἀπεστερημένος t.r.). M-M.*

ἀφῶμεν s. ἀφίημι.

ἄφωνος, ον (Aeschyl., Pind., Hdt.+; Dit., Syll.³ 1168, 41; PGM 1, 117; Wsd 4: 19; 2 Macc 3: 29; Philo; Jos., Ant. 6, 337; 12, 413).
1. *silent, dumb* of idols 1 Cor 12: 2 (cf. Epigr. Gr. 402, 1). Of an animal (Timaeus Hist. [IV-III BC] no. 566 fgm. 43a Jac.; Strabo 6, 1, 9 p. 260) Ac 8: 32; 1 Cl 16: 7; B 5: 2 (all 3 Is 53: 7).
2. *incapable of speech*, of human speech 2 Pt 2: 16; *incapable of conveying meaning*, as a language normally does τοσαῦτα... γένη φωνῶν εἰσιν ἐν κόσμῳ καὶ οὐδὲν ἄφωνον 1 Cor 14: 10. M-M. B. 321.*

Ἀχάζ, ὁ indecl. (אָחָז) (in Joseph. Ἄχαζος, ου [Ant. 9, 247]) *Ahaz*, a king of Judah (1 Ch 3: 13; cf. 4 Km 16: 1ff; 2 Ch 28: 16ff; Is 1: 1; 7: 1ff); in genealogy of Jesus Mt 1: 9; Lk 3: 23ff D (here Ἀχάς, as also the v.l. in Mt.).*

Ἀχαΐα, ας, ἡ (Hdt.+; Joseph.) *Achaia* in NT the Rom. province created 146 BC, including the most important parts of Greece, i.e. Attica, Boeotia (perh. Epirus) and the Peloponnesus (Mommsen, Röm. Gesch. V 233ff) Ac 18: 2D, 12, 27; 19: 21; 2 Cor 1: 1; 11: 10; 1 Th 1: 7f. The country for its inhabitants, esp. the Christians living in it Ro 15: 26; 16: 5 t.r.; 1 Cor 16: 15; 2 Cor 9: 2.—JMarquardt, Röm. Staatsverw. I² 1881, 321ff; Brandis, Achaja 2: Pauly-W. I I 1894, 190-8; JWeiss, RE VII 160ff; Ramsay, Bearing 404f; Hahn, index.*

Ἀχαϊκός, οῦ, ὁ (CIG 1296; 3376; CIA III 1030, 34; 1138, 15 al.) *Achaicus* a Christian at Corinth 1 Cor 16: 17; 16: 15 v.l.; subscr.*

ἀχαριστέω (in lit. and inscr.; Jos., Bell. 2, 400) *be ungrateful* (Antipho Soph. 54; X., Mem. 2, 2, 2 et al.) τινί *toward someone* (Plut., Phoc. 36, 5; Vi. Philonid. p. 13 Crönert) τῷ θεῷ PK 2 p. 14, 21.*

ἀχάριστος, ον (Hom.+) *ungrateful* (so since Hdt. 1, 90; Epict. 2, 23, 5; IG XIV 2012; Wsd 16: 29; Sir 29: 16; 4 Macc 9: 10; Philo, De Jos. 99; Jos., Ant. 13, 388, Vi. 172) Lk 6: 35 (w. πονηρός as Celsus 6, 53; Jos., Ant. 6, 305) 2 Ti 3: 2. M-M.*

Ἀχάς s. Ἀχάζ.

ἀχειροποίητος, ον (Ps.-Callisth. p. 38, 18.—χειροποίη-τος freq. Hdt.+; cf. Nägeli 52) *not made by* (human) *hand*, hence *spiritual* of circumcision Col 2: 11. Of the temple Mk 14: 58. Of the heavenly body 2 Cor 5: 1. M-M.*

Ἀχελδαμάχ s. Ἀκελδαμάχ.

ἀχθῆναι, ἀχθήσεσθαι s. ἄγω.

Ἀχίμ, ὁ indecl. *Achim* in genealogy of Jesus Mt 1: 14.*

ἀχλύς, ύος, ἡ (Hom.+; in prose Hippocr.+; Polyb. 34, 11, 15; Aq. Ezk 12: 7; Sym. Job 3: 5; Philo, Cher. 61; Jos., Ant. 9, 56) *mistiness.*
1. lit. (w. σκότος as Dio Chrys. 11[12], 36; Philo, Deus Imm. 130) of darkening of the eyes in a man who is being blinded Ac 13: 11 (schol. on Apollon. Rhod. 2, 259b, also medic. t.t.: Galen, Medicus 16 [XIV 774 K.]; further exx. in Hobart 44f).

2. fig., of mistiness in the eyes of the mind (Heraclit. Sto. 33 p. 48, 14; Plut., Mor. 42c διάνοια ἀχλύος γέμουσα; Himerius, Or. 35 [=Or. 34, 3] p. 146, 20 Colonna ἡ ἀχλὺς τῆς ψυχῆς) 2 Cl 1: 6.*

ἀχρεῖος, ον (Hom.+; pap., LXX; Jos., Vi. 50; 117) *useless, worthless* of slaves (Ps.-Pla., Alcib. 1, 17 p. 122B τῶν οἰκετῶν τὸν ἀχρειότατον; Achilles Tat. 5, 17, 8; PPar. 68, 54 ἀ. δούλους) Mt 25: 30.—Lk 17: 10 the adj., in this sense at least, can be dispensed with (Zahn) and hence is omitted by many (e.g. FBlass; AMerx; Wlh.; JWeiss, APott, D. Text des NTs.² '19, 103; JMoffatt, NT), following the Sin. Syr. But since ἀ. can also mean more gener. *unworthy, miserable* (2 Km 6: 22; Sym., Theod. Is 33: 9; Ezk 17: 6), as well as simply *worthless* without moral connotation (Arrian, Anab. 1, 24, 3; 2, 7, 3), there is no decisive reason for rejecting a reading so well attested as this (so BWeiss; HHoltzmann; Jülicher, Gleichn. 21; EKlostermann; ERiggenbach, NKZ 34, '23, 442f; Schlatter; Rengstorf; FHauck; RSV). M-M.*

ἀχρειόω (also ἀχρεόω Dit., Syll.³ 569, 31; cf. Bl-D. §30, 2) pf. pass. ptc. ἠχρειωμένος; 1 aor. pass. ἠχρεώθην (Philo Mech. 60, 16; Polyb. 3, 64, 8 al.; Vett. Val. 290, 1; Dit., Or. 573, 16: LXX) *make useless.*
1. lit., pass., of damaged sticks Hs 8, 3, 4.—2. fig., pass. *become depraved, worthless* of pers. Ro 3: 12 (Ps 13: 3; 52: 4). M-M.*

ἄχρηστος, ον (Theognis+; Hdt., inscr., pap., LXX, Ep. Arist.; Jos., Bell. 1, 172; Sib. Or. 4, 94) *useless, worthless,* perh. forming a contrast to the name Onesimus; in any case, in a play on words w. εὔχρηστος (as Hv 3, 6, 7; cf. s 9, 26, 4; Jos., Ant. 12, 61) Phlm 11 τόν ποτέ σοι ἄ. *who was once useless to you* (ἄ. τινι as Ep. Arist. 164; ἄ. of a slave Epict. 1, 19, 19 and 22; cf. word-play, χρήσιμον ἐξ ἀχρήστου Pla., Rep. 411B). W. περισσός Dg 4: 2.—Hv 3, 6, 2; s 9, 26, 4; ὀξυχολία ἄ. ἐστιν *ill-temper leads to no good* m 5, 1, 6. M-M.*

ἄχρι this form, which is Attic (Phryn. 14; Moeris 32; Meisterhans³-Schw. 219, 39) is found in NT almost exclusively; the H.Gk. ἄχρις [Dit., Syll.³ 958, 37] occurs only Gal 3: 19 (throughout the ms. tradition) and Hb 3: 13 (predom.), both times before vowels. On the Apostol. Fathers cf. Reinhold 37. On the whole, Bl-D. §21; Mayser 243f; Crönert 144, 3). Hom.+; inscr., pap., LXX, Philo, Joseph.
1. improper prep. w. gen. (Bl-D. §216, 3)—a. of time *until* (2 Macc 14: 15) ἄ. ἧς ἡμέρας *until the day when* Mt 24: 38; Lk 1: 20; 17: 27; Ac 1: 2, 22 v.l.; ἄ. τῆς ἡμέρας ταύτης (BSChilds, JBL 82, '63, 279-92: OT background) 2: 29; 23: 1; 26: 22; ἄ. καιροῦ *for a while* Lk 4: 13 (ἄ. χρόνου ibid. D); Ac 13: 11. ἄ. χρόνων ἀποκαταστάσεως 3: 21. ἄ. αὐγῆς *until sunrise* Ac 20: 11 (cf. Jos., Ant. 6, 215 ἄχρι τῆς ἕω); ἄ. τοῦ δεῦρο (Plut., Anton. 34, 9 [without art.]; Jos., Ant. 10, 265) *until now* Ro 1: 13; ἄ. τοῦ νῦν (Timostratus [II BC] 1; cf. Lucian, Tim. 39; Plut., Rom. 15, 3; Philo, Abr. 182) 8: 22; Phil 1: 5.—1 Cor 4: 11; 2 Cor 3: 14; Gal 4: 2; Phil 1: 6; ἄ. τέλους (Plut., Demosth. 13, 2, Fab. Max. 16, 8) *to the end* Hb 6: 11; Rv 2: 26; ἄ. ἡμερῶν πέντε *within five days* Ac 20: 6; ἄ. νόμου *until the time when,* or better, *before the law was given* Ro 5: 13 (cf. Jos., Ant. 4, 248 ἄ. νομίμων γάμων=until the time of the lawful marriage. Cf. Mt 13: 30 v.l.
b. of place *as far as* (Dit., Syll.³ 937; Judg 11: 33B) short ending of Mk; ἦλθεν ἄ. ἐμοῦ *it came to where I was* Ac 11: 5; cf. 13: 6; 20: 4 t.r.; 28: 15; ἄ. τούτου τοῦ λόγου *as far as this word* 22: 22; ἄ. καὶ ὑμῶν 2 Cor 10: 13f; ἄ. μερισμοῦ *as far as the separation* Hb 4: 12; cf. Rv 14: 20; 18: 5.

c. fig., of manner (Dit., Syll.³ 1109, 84 ἄ. πληγῶν ἔρχεσθαι; Simplicius in Epict. p. 29, 7 ἄ. θανάτου σχεδόν of the lashings by the Spartans) διώκειν ἄ. θανάτου *persecute to the death* Ac 22: 4; πιστὸς ἄ. θανάτου *faithful unto death* Rv 2: 10; cf. 12: 11 (s. Sib. Or. 2, 47). ἄ. τῆς ἀγνοίας *as long as he does not know* Hm 4, 1, 5.

2. conjunction (Bl-D. §383; 455, 3; Rob. 974)—**a.** w. rel. ἄχρι οὗ (=ἄχρι χρόνου ῷ) *until the time when* w. past indic. (X., Hell. 6, 4, 37 ἄχρι οὗ ὅδε ὁ λόγος ἐγράφετο; Jos., Ant. 11, 111) ἄ. οὗ ἀνέστη Ac 7: 18; ἄ. οὗ ἡμέρα ἤμελλεν γίνεσθαι *until the day began to dawn* 27: 33. W. aor. subj. (Hdt. 1, 117; Dit., Syll.³ 799, 26; POxy. 104, 18; 507, 30; BGU 19 I, 5; Job 32: 11) Lk 21: 24; Ro 11: 25; 1 Cor 11: 26; 15: 25; w. ἄν: ἄχρι οὗ ἄν (Hippocr., περὶ συρίγγων 3) Gal 3: 19 v.l.; Rv 2: 25.—*as long as* (X., Cyr. 5, 4, 16; Plut., Mor. 601ε; cf. 2 Macc 14: 10) ἄ. οὗ τὸ σήμερον καλεῖται *as long as it is still called 'today'* Hb 3: 13.

b. without rel., used w. aor. subj. *until* (POxy. 491, 8; 1215) Rv 7: 3; 15: 8; 17: 17 v.l.; 20: 3, 5. W. ἄν and aor. subj. (X., An. 2, 3, 2; Dit., Syll.³ 972, 26f; BGU 419, 11; 830, 13 ἄ. ἄν σοι ἔλθω; PGM 5, 58; Jos., Ant. 12, 152) Gal 3: 19. W. fut. ind. (Sib. Or. 1, 273) Rv 17: 17. —LRydbeck, Fachprosa, '67, 144–53. M-M.*

ἄχρονος, ον *timeless*=*eternal* (Plut., Mor. 393ᴀ; Philo, Sacr. Abel. 76) of God (Proclus, Theol. 124 p. 110, 26) IPol 3: 2 (Martyr. Carpi 16 vGebhardt ὁ θεὸς ἡμῶν ἄ. ὤν).*

ἄχυρον, ου, τό (Hdt.+ in pl. and sing.; inscr., pap., LXX; Jos., Bell. 3, 223, Ant. 2, 289; Sib. Or. 3, 791) *chaff* Mt 3: 12; Lk 3: 17. On the burning of ἄ. cf. Ostraka II 1168 ἄ. εἰς τὰς καμείνους. For heating bath water BGU 760, 9 (II AD). M-M.*

ἀχώρητος, ον (Hesychius) *uncontained* of God Hm 1: 1; PK 2 p. 13, 24; of the name of God's Son *incomprehensible* Hs 9, 14, 5.*

ἀχώριστος, ον (X., Pla.+) *inseparable* w. gen. foll. (Cor-

nutus 14 p. 15, 14; Philo, Gig. 48) ἀ. θεοῦ Ἰ.Χ. *inseparable fr. our God Jesus Christ* ITr 7: 1 (cf. Herm. Wr. 2, 16 τὸ ἀγαθὸν ἀ. τοῦ θεοῦ; Sextus 423; Jos., Ant. 9, 273).*

ἀψευδής, ές (Hes., Hdt.+; BGU 432 II, 2; Wsd 7: 17; Philo) *free fr. all deceit, truthful, trustworthy* in our lit. only of God (cf. Archilochus [VII ʙᴄ] 84 Diehl²; Eur., Or. 364 ἀψευδὴς θεός; Pla., Rep. 2 p. 382ᴇ; Orph. Hymns 168 Kern [of Zeus]; PGM 7, 571; Philo, Ebr. 139) Tit 1: 2, (w. ἀληθινός) MPol 14: 2 and of Christ, who is called IRo 8: 2 τὸ ἀ. στόμα ἐν ῷ ὁ πατὴρ ἐλάλησεν ἀληθῶς (cf. Aeschyl. in Pla., Rep. 2 p. 383ʙ τὸ Φοίβου θεῖον ἀψευδὲς στόμα). M-M.*

ἄψευστος, ον (Crinagoras no. 21, 5; Plut., Artax. 28, 2; Sb 1070; PGM 13, 788; Philo, fgm. 51 Harris 1886) *free fr. lies, truthful* of πνεῦμα (Sib. Or. 3, 701) Hm 3: 2.*

ἀψηλάφητος, ον (Polyb. 8, 19, 5; schol. in Pind., Ol. 6, 87; Cat. Cod. Astr. VIII 1 p. 188, 24) *not capable of being touched, impalpable* of God IPol 3: 2.*

ἀψίνθιον, ου, τό (Hippocr.+; X., An. 1, 5, 1; Aq. Pr 5: 4; Jer 9: 15; 23: 15; so in rabb.) and **ἄψινθος, ου, ἡ** (Aretaeus [II ᴀᴅ], χρονίων νούσων θερ. 1, 13 Hude) *wormwood*, containing a very bitter substance. τὸ ἐλάχιστον ἀ. *a very little bit of wormwood* Hm 5, 1, 5. Water changed to wormw. Rv 8: 11b. As name of a star, and (prob. because of ὁ ἀστήρ) masc. ὁ Ἄψινθος ibid. a (s. Boll 41f).*

ἄψυχος, ον (since Archilochus [VII ʙᴄ] 104 Diehl²; Simonides 116 D.; PGM 7, 441; Philo) *inanimate, lifeless* of musical instruments (Eur., Ion 881; Plut., Mor. 9c) 1 Cor 14: 7; of idols (Wsd 13: 17; 14: 29.—Of statues of the gods: Heraclitus in Celsus 1, 5; Timaeus Hist. 127 [CMüller, Fgm. I p. 224]; Philo, Congr. Erud. Grat. 48) Dg 2: 4. M-M.*

ἄωρος, ον *untimely*=*too early* (Aeschyl., Hdt.+; grave inscr. ZNW 22, '23, 281 nos. 5, 6, 7 et al.; PGM 4, 2877; 5, 332; LXX; Jos., Bell. 4, 502) of children οἵτινες ἄ. ἐτίκτοντο *who were born prematurely* AP 11: 26.*

B

β΄ as numeral=*two* (δύο: Jos., C. Ap. 1, 157) Hs 8, 9, 1; =*second* (δευτέρα), i.e. ἐπιστολή (in the superscriptions of 2 Cor; 2 Th; 2 Ti; 2 Pt; 2 J; 2 Cl, and in the subscriptions of 2 Th; 2 Ti; 2 J), or ὅρασις (in the superscr. of Hv 2), or ἐντολή (in the superscr. of Hm 2).*

Βάαλ, ὁ indecl. (בַּעַל lord) (Jos., Ant. 9, 135f; 138 ὁ Βάαλ) *Baal*, a divinity worshipped by the Semites gener., bitterly opposed by Elijah and later Hebr. prophets, κάμπτειν γόνυ τῇ Β. *bow the knee before B.* Ro 11: 4 (3 Km 19: 18 τῷ Β.). The fem. art. (4 Km 21: 3; Jer 2: 8; 12: 16 al.) may be due to the Hebr. custom of substituting αἰσχύνη (בֹּשֶׁת) for the names of foreign gods; s. ADillmann, Mon.-Ber. d. Berl. Akad. 1881, 601–20; Mlt.-H. 152; Rob. 254. M-M.*

Βαβυλών, ῶνος, ἡ (Alcaeus Lyr. [VII/VI ʙᴄ] 82, 10 D.; Aeschyl., Pers. 52 et al.; LXX; Philo; Joseph.; Sib. Or.—בָּבֶל Gen 11: 9; Babyl. *Bâbilu* or *Bâbili*, which the Babylonians interpreted to mean 'gate of the gods') *Babylon*, capital of Babylonia (Diod. S. 19, 100, 7 Βαβυλῶνα τὴν πόλιν); used also for the country (Bar 1: 1, 4, 9, 11 al.;

1 Esdr 1: 53; 2: 11; 4: 44 al.); so μετοικεσία Βαβυλῶνος *deportation to Babylonia* (Bl-D. §166) Mt 1: 11f, 17; cf. Ac 7: 43 (cf. Ps.-Callisth. 3, 33, 15 ἐπάνω τῆς Βαβυλωνίας). —In late Judaism Rome began to take on the name and many of the characteristics of Babylon as a world-power hostile to God, denounced by the prophets (Apc. Bar. 67, 7; Sib. Or. 5, 143; 159; Billerb. III 816). So also 1 Pt 5: 13 (s. the v.l. and cf. C-HHunzinger, H-WHertzberg-Festschr., '65, 67–77 [Bab., Ro and 1 Pt].—GTManley, Evang. Quart. 16, '44, 138–46, foll. others, thinks of the Bab. in Egypt [Diod. S. 1, 56, 3; Strabo 17, 1, 30; Jos., Ant. 2, 315]. The Bab. in Mesopotamia is also suggested by some, but at the time of Diod. S. [2, 9, 9], i.e., I ʙᴄ, it was almost entirely uninhabited). The same interpr. is preferred by most for Rv (otherwise GAvan den Bergh van Eysinga, NThT 16, '27, 33ff; JOman, Book of Rv '23, 29 al.; JSickenberger, BZ 17, '26, 270–82; Lohmeyer), where B. is always called *the Great* (cf. Da 4: 30; Jos., Ant. 8, 153; Alcaeus, loc. cit., spoke of Βαβυλῶνος ἵρας=holy Babylon) Rv 16: 19; 17: 5; 18: 10, 21; ἔπεσεν, ἔπεσεν Β. 14: 8; 18: 2 (cf. Is 21: 9; Jer 28: 8). M-M.*

βαδίζω *walk,* found X.+; inscr., pap., LXX; En. 106, 7; Jos., Ant. 1, 244; 12, 346. Fig. (Galen: CMG V 4, 1, 1 p. 23, 12 β. ἐπὶ σωφροσύνην δι' ἐγκρατείας; Sib. Or., fgm. 1, 23; Proverb. Aesopi 121 P.: β. τῶν νόμων ἐνώπιον; Psellus p. 213, 26) of human conduct, as (w. πορεύεσθαι, πολιτεύεσθαι) β. κατὰ τὰς ἐπιθυμίας 1 Cl 3: 4. M-M.*

βαθέως s. βαθύς, end.

βαθμός, οῦ, ὁ *step* (Soph.; Hellenist. writers [Nägeli 26], LXX; Jos., Bell. 5, 206, Ant. 8, 140 in concrete mng., as Ac 12: 10D); fig. (Dio Chrys. 24[41], 6; Philo, Aet. M. 58) *grade* (Jos., Bell. 4, 171 οἱ τῶν τολμημάτων βαθμοί), *rank* (cf. IG II 243, 16 τοῖς τᾶς ἀξίας βασμοῖς ἀνελόγησε he kept up to the degrees of his rank): β. ἑαυτῷ καλὸν περιποιεῖσθαι *win a good standing* (or *rank) for oneself* 1 Ti 3: 13. Perh. a t.t. of the mysteries underlies the last ref. (a 'step' in the soul's journey heavenward; cf. Herm. Wr. 13, 9 ὁ βαθμὸς οὗτος, ὦ τέκνον, δικαιοσύνης ἐστὶν ἕδρασμα. Furthermore, philosophy seems also to have used β. to denote the gradual attainment of wisdom (cf. OImmisch, Philol. n.F. 17, '04, p. 33, 1).—On the form of the word s. RSchöll, Sitzungsb. d. bayr. Ak. d. Wiss. 1893 II 500. M-M.*

βάθος, ους, τό (Aeschyl., Hdt.+; inscr., pap., LXX, Philo, Joseph.) *depth.*

1. lit. (w. ὕψος Is 7: 11; Herm. Wr. 11, 20b) Dg 7: 2; (w. the other dimensions; s. Aristot., Phys. 209a, 5; Dio Chrys. 76[26], 6; Plut., Mor. 937F; Dit., Syll.³ 973, 6ff μῆκος, πλάτος, β. [of a ditch]; Philo, Decal. 25; Jos., Ant. 1, 77) Eph 3: 18 (cf. the magic formula γενέσθω φῶς πλάτος βάθος μῆκος ὕψος αὐγή PGM 4, 970 and 978; 12, 158). Of soil Mt 13: 5; Mk 4: 5 (Jos., Ant. 8, 63 τῆς γῆς β.; Theophr., Hist. Pl. 6, 5, 4 χώρας βάθος; BGU 1122, 16 of plants ἔχον τὸ καθῆκον β.). Of the depths of the sea B 10: 10 (cf. schol. on Apollon. Rhod. 1, 461; 4, 865f; Ps 68: 3; Am 9: 3; Mi 7: 19 al. LXX). Of deep water Lk 5: 4. Of sunken eyes Papias 3. ὕψωμα καὶ βάθος Ro 8: 39, since they are said to be creatures and the context speaks apparently only of supernatural forces, are prob. astral spirits; they are both astronomical t.t., and β. means the celestial space below the horizon fr. which the stars arise (PGM 4, 575 ἀστὴρ ἐκ τ. βάθους ἀναλάμπων).

2. fig. ἡ κατὰ βάθους πτωχεία αὐτῶν *their poverty reaching down into the depths* (Strabo 9, 3, 5 ἄντρον κοῖλον κατὰ βάθους)=*extreme poverty* 2 Cor 8: 2; β. πλούτου (Soph., Aj. 130; cf. Jos., Ant. 1, 271 τὸ τῆς τριχὸς βάθος; Pr 18: 3; Aelian, V.H. 3, 18 πλοῦτος βαθύς; Norden, Agn. Th. 243, 3) *depth* (i.e. inexhaustibility) *of the wealth* Ro 11: 33; τὰ β. τῆς θείας γνώσεως *depths of divine knowledge* 1 Cl 40: 1 (Philo, Poster. Cai. 130 β. τῆς ἐπιστήμης); τὰ β. τοῦ θεοῦ *the depths of God* 1 Cor 2: 10, τὰ βάθη τοῦ σατανᾶ Rv 2: 24 v.l. (cf. Jdth 8: 14 βάθος καρδίας ἀνθρώπου; Eunap. 113 β. τῆς ψυχῆς). M-M.*

βαθύνω (Hom.+; LXX; Jos., Bell. 1, 405) *make deep* (Jos., Bell. 5, 130) and intrans. *go down deep* (Proclus, In Rem Publ. II p. 347, 2 Kroll; Philo, Post. Cai. 118 ὁ τῆς διανοίας ὀφθαλμὸς εἴσω προελθὼν καὶ βαθύνας τὰ ἐν αὐτοῖς σπλάγχνοις ἐγκεκρυμμένα κατεῖδε); both are poss., though the latter is preferable ἔσκαψεν καὶ ἐβάθυνεν Lk 6: 48. M-M.*

βαθύς, εῖα, ύ (Hom.+; inscr., pap., LXX) *deep.*

1. lit. (En. 24, 2; Ep. Arist. 118; Jos., Ant. 10, 170) of a well (Pythag., Ep. 3, 3 and Charito 8, 1, 10 φρέαρ β.) J 4: 11.

2. fig. τὰ βαθέα τοῦ σατανᾶ *the* (hidden) *depths of*

Satan Rv 2: 24 (cf. Da 2: 22 and s. βαθός 2). Of sleep (Theocr. 8, 65; Lucian et al.; Jos., Ant. 5, 148; Sir 22: 9; 3 Macc 5: 12) Ac 20: 9. Of peace (Lucian, Tox. 36; Herodian 4, 10, 1; 7, 9, 5; 4 Macc 3: 20; Philo, Somn. 2, 229; Sib. Or. 12, 87) 1 Cl 2: 2. ὄρθρου βαθέως (Aristoph., Vesp. 216; Pla., Crito 43A, Prot. 310A ἔτι βαθέος ὄρθρου; Phlegon: 257 fgm. 36, 1, 9 Jac.; Philo, Mut. Nom. 162, Mos. 1, 179, Spec. Leg. 1, 276; PLeipz. 40 II, 10) *early in the morning* Lk 24: 1 (β. is to be taken, not as an adv., but as gen. of βαθύς, like πραέως [πραέος] 1 Pt 3: 4. Cf. W-S. §9, 5; Rob. 495; Bl-D. §46, 3). M-M.*

βάϊον, ου, τό (Egypt. word, Coptic 'bai'.—The accents βάϊον and βάϊς are preferred by PKatz, ThLZ '36, 284 and Bl-D. §6) *palm branch* (1 Macc 13: 51; Sym. SSol 7: 8; PFlor. 37, 3; CWessely, Stud. z. Paläogr. u. Pap.-kunde 22, '22, no. 157 [II AD]; cf. PTebt. II p. 69. The pap. prefer the form βάϊς (but see Bl-D. §6), found also in Chaeremon Alex. in Porphyr., Abst. 4, 7.—Loanw. in rabb.) τὰ β. τῶν φοινίκων *the palm branches* J 12: 13 (where τῶν φ. is not really needed; but Test. Napht. 5: 4 βάϊα φοινίκων and PLeid. 13, 6, 7 [I AD] βάϊα φοινί[κων]). WRFarmer, JTS 3, '52, 62-6. M-M.*

Βαλαάμ, ὁ indecl. (בִּלְעָם) *Balaam,* a sorcerer (Num 22-4; 31: 16; Dt 23: 5f; Josh 13: 22; 24: 9; Mi 6: 5; Philo, Mos. 1, 264ff, Migr. Abr. 113-15; Jos., Ant. [Βάλαμος, ου] 4, 104; 107-9; 111; 126; 157; Pirqe Aboth 5, 19). Hence, a typical deceiver and false prophet Rv 2: 14; Jd 11 (βαλαακ 𝔓⁷²); 2 Pt 2: 15.*

Βαλάκ, ὁ indecl. (בָּלָק) (LXX; Philo, Conf. Ling. 65.—In Joseph. Βάλακος, ου [Ant. 4, 107]) *Balak,* a Moabite king (Num 22: 2ff; 23: 7; 24: 10; Josh 24: 9; Mi 6: 5), involved w. Balaam (s. above) Rv 2: 14.—Jd 11 𝔓⁷².*

βαλανεῖον, ου, τό (Aristoph.+; inscr., pap., loanw. in rabb.) *bathhouse* MPol 13: 1.*

βαλλάντιον, ου, τό (also βαλάντιον; cf. Bl-D. §11, 2; Rob. 213; W-S. §5, 26a note 51; Helbing 15f. Found since Ps.-Simonides 157 Diehl; Epicharmus [V BC] no. 10 p. 95: Com. Gr. Fgm. I 1, 1899 Kaibel; Philo, De Jos. 180) 207; LXX) *money-bag, purse* Plut., Mor 62B; 802D; Herodian 5, 4, 3 β-α χρημάτων μεστά) Lk 10: 4; 12: 33; 22: 35f. B. 776.*

βάλλω fut. βαλῶ; 2 aor. ἔβαλον, 3 pl. ἔβαλον Lk 23: 34 (Ps 21: 19; Ac 16: 23 and ἔβαλαν Ac 16: 37 (Bl-D. §81, 3; Mlt.-H. 208); pf. βέβληκα; 1 fut. pass. βληθήσομαι; 1 aor. ἐβλήθην; pf. βέβλημαι; plpf. ἐβεβλήμην (Hom.+; inscr., pap., LXX, Philo, Joseph.).

1. *throw*—a. w. simple obj. *scatter seed on the ground* (Diod. S. 1, 36, 4; Ps 125: 6 v.l. [ARahlfs, Psalmi cum Odis '31]; Third Corinthians 3: 26) Mk 4: 26; 1 Cl 24: 5; εἰς κῆπον Lk 13: 19; *cast lots* (Ps 21: 19; 1 Ch 25: 8 al.; Jos., Ant. 6, 61) Mt 27: 35; Mk 15: 24; Lk 23: 34; J 19: 24; B 6: 6.

b. *throw* τινί τι Mt 15: 26; Mk 7: 27. τὶ ἔμπροσθεν τινος Mt 7: 6 (β.=*throw* something before animals: Aesop, Fab. 158 P.). τὶ ἀπό τινος *throw someth. away* (fr. someone) Mt 5: 29f; 18: 8f (Teles p. 60, 2 ἀποβάλλω of the eye). τὶ ἔκ τινος: ὕδωρ ἐκ τοῦ στόματος ὀπίσω τινός *pour water out of the mouth after someone* Rv 12: 15f; β. ἔξω=ἐκβάλλειν *throw out* 2 Cl 7: 4; of worthless salt Mt 5: 13; Lk 14: 35; of bad fish *throw away* Mt 13: 48 (cf. Κυπρ. I p. 44 no. 43 κόπρια βάλλειν probably=*throw refuse away*). Fig. *love drives out fear* 1 J 4: 18. ἐβλήθη ἔξω *he is* (the aor. emphasizes the certainty of the result, and is gnomic [Bl-D. §333; Rob. 836f; cf. Hdb. ad loc.])

thrown away, i.e. expelled fr. the fellowship J 15: 6. τὶ ἐπί τινα: *throw stones at somebody* J 8: 7, 59 (cf. Sir 22: 20; 27: 25; Jos., Vi. 303); *dust on one's head* Rv 18: 19. τὶ εἰς τι *dust into the air* Ac 22: 23 (D εἰς τ. οὐρανόν *toward the sky*); *cast, throw* nets into the lake Mt 4: 18; J 21: 6; cf. vs. 7; a *fishhook* Mt 17: 27 (cf. Is 19: 8). Pass., into the sea, lake Mt 13: 47; Mk 9: 42; βλήθητι εἰς τὴν θάλασσαν *throw yourself into the sea* Mt 21: 21; Mk 11: 23; *throw* into the fire (Jos., Ant. 10, 95; 215) Mt 3: 10; Mk 9: 22; Lk 3: 9; J 15: 6; into Gehenna Mt 5: 29; 18: 9b; 2 Cl 5: 4; into the stove Mt 6: 30; 13: 42, 50 (cf. Da 3: 21); Lk 12: 28; 2 Cl 8: 2.—Rv 8: 7f; 12: 4, 9 (schol. on Apollon. Rhod. 4, 57; 28 p. 264, 18 of throwing out of heaven ἐκβληθέντα κατελθεῖν εἰς Ἅιδου), 13; 14: 19; 18: 21; 19: 20; 20: 3, 10, 14f; *drive out* into the desert B 7: 8; *throw* into prison Mt 18: 30; Rv 2: 10 (Epict. 1, 1, 24; 1, 12, 23; 1, 29, 6 al.; PTebt. 567 [53/4 AD]). Pass. *be thrown* into the lions' den 1 Cl 45: 6 (cf. Da 6: 25 Theod. v.l.; Bel 31 Theod. v.l.).—*Throw on a sickbed* Rv 2: 22. Pass. βεβλημένος *lying* (Jos., Bell. 1, 629) ἐπὶ κλίνης β. Mt 9: 2; cf. Mk 7: 30. Pass. abs. (Conon [I BC/I AD] 26 fgm. 1, 17 Jac. βαλλομένη θνήσκει) *lie on a sickbed* (cf. Babrius 103, 4 κάμνων ἐβέβλητο) Mt 8: 6, 14. ἐβέβλητο πρὸς τὸν πυλῶνα *he lay before the door* Lk 16: 20 (ἐβέβλητο as Aesop 284 Halm; Jos., Ant. 9, 209; Field, Notes 70). β. ἑαυτὸν κάτω *throw oneself down* Mt 4: 6; Lk 4: 9 (cf. schol. on Apollon. Rhod. 4, 1212–14a εἰς τὸν κρημνὸν ἑαυτὸν ἔβαλεν; Jos., Bell. 4, 28).—Fig. εἰς ἀθυμίαν β. τινά *plunge someone into despondency* 1 Cl 46: 9.

c. *let fall* of a tree dropping its fruit Rv 6: 13; *throw down* 18: 21a, to destruction ibid. b.

2. *put, place, lay, bring*—a. w. simple obj. κόπρια β. *put manure on* Lk 13: 8 (POxy. 934, 9 μὴ οὖν ἀμελήσῃς τοῦ βαλεῖν τὴν κόπρον).

b. w. indication of the place to which τὶ εἰς τι: *put money into the temple treasury* Mk 12: 41ff; Lk 21: 1, 4, so that here β. can almost mean *offer up* as a sacrifice Mk 12: 44; Lk 21: 3f; τὰ βαλλόμενα contributions (s. γλωσσόκομον and cf. 2 Ch 24: 10) J 12: 6; *put the finger into the ear* when healing Mk 7: 33; otherw. J 20: 25, 27; *put a sword into the scabbard* 18: 11; *place bits into the mouths* Js 3: 3; εἰς τὴν κολυμβήθραν *take into the pool* J 5: 7; cf. GOxy l. 33f; β. εἰς τὴν καρδίαν *put into the heart* J 13: 2 (cf. Od. 1, 201; 14, 269; Pind., Ol. 13 l. 21 Schröder¹ πολλὰ ἐν καρδίαις ἔβαλεν; schol. on Pind., Pyth. 4, 133; Plut., Timol. 3, 2; Herm. Wr. 6, 4 θεῷ τῷ εἰς νοῦν μοι βαλόντι). Of liquids: *pour* (Epict. 4, 13, 12; PLond. 1177, 46 [113 AD]; Judg 6: 19B) wine into skins Mt 9: 17; Lk 5: 37f; water into a basin (Vi. Aesopi I c. 10 p. 252, 2 βάλε ὕδωρ εἰς τ. λεκάνην; PGM 4, 224; 7, 320 βαλὼν εἰς αὐτὸ [the basin] ὕδωρ) J 13: 5; wormwood in honey Hm 5, 1, 5; *pour* ointment on the body Mt 26: 12; βάρος ἐπὶ τινα *put a burden on some one* Rv 2: 24; δρέπανον ἐπὶ τὴν γῆν *swing the sickle on the earth* as on a harvest field Rv 14: 19; εἰρήνην, μάχαιραν ἐπὶ τὴν γῆν *bring peace, the sword on earth* Mt 10: 34 (Jos., Ant. 1, 98 ὀργὴν ἐπὶ τὴν γῆν βαλεῖν). Cf. β. τὰς χεῖρας *lay hands* ἐπί τινα *on someone* violently J 7: 44 𝔓⁷⁵. τὶ ἐνώπιόν τινος· σκάνδαλον *place a stumbling-block* Rv 2: 14; *lay down* crowns (wreaths) before the throne 4: 10. τὶ τινι (Quint. Smyrn. 12, 250) *deposit money w. the bankers* (to earn interest; cf. Aristoxenus, fgm. 59 τὸ βαλλόμενον κέρμα. Likewise Diog. L. 2, 20) Mt 25: 27.

c. ῥίζας β. *send forth roots, take root* like a tree, fig. (Polemo, Decl. 2, 54 ὦ ῥίζας ἐξ ἀρετῆς βαλλόμενος) 1 Cl 39: 8 (Job 5: 3).

3. intrans. (Hom.; Epict. 2, 20, 10; 4, 10, 29; POsl. 45, 2; En. 18, 6. Cf. Rdm.² 23; 28f; Rob. 799; JMStahl, RhM

66, '11, 626ff) ἔβαλεν ἄνεμος *a storm rushed down* Ac 27: 14. M-M. B. 673.

βάναυσος, ον (Soph., Pla.+) *base, vulgar* οὐδὲν βάναυσον ἐν ἀγάπῃ *there is nothing vulgar in love* 1 Cl 49: 5.*

βαπτίζω fut. βαπτίσω; 1 aor. ἐβάπτισα, mid. ἐβαπτισάμην; impf. pass. ἐβαπτιζόμην; pf. ptc. βεβαπτισμένος; 1 aor. ἐβαπτίσθην; 1 fut. βαπτισθήσομαι (Hippocr., Pla., esp. Polyb.+; UPZ 70, 13 [152/1 BC]; PGM 5, 69; LXX; Philo; Joseph.; Sib. Or. 5, 478) *dip, immerse*, mid. *dip oneself, wash* (in non-Christian lit. also 'plunge, sink, drench, overwhelm'; fig. 'soak' Pla., Symp. 176B, etc.), in our lit. only in ritual sense (as Plut.; Herm. Wr. [s. 2a below]; PGM 4, 44; 7, 441 λουσάμενος κ. βαπτισάμενος; 4 Km 5: 14; Sir 34: 25; Jdth 12: 7).

1. of Jewish ritual washings Mk 7: 4 v.l.; Lk 11: 38; GOxy 15.—WBrandt, Jüd. Reinheitslehre u. ihre Beschreibg. in den Ev. '10; ABüchler, The Law of Purification in Mk 7: 1–23: ET 21, '10, 34–40; JDöller, D. Reinheits- u. Speisegesetze d. ATs '17; JoachJeremias, ThZ 5, '49, 418–28. See IQS 5, 8–23; 2, 25–3, 12; 4, 20–22.

2. in special sense *baptize*—a. of John the Baptist, abs. J 1: 25, 28; 10: 40; hence John is called ὁ βαπτίζων Mk 1: 4; 6: 14, 24 (Gdspd, Probs. 50–2).—Pass. Mt 3: 16; ISm 1: 1; oft. *have oneself baptized* Mt 3: 13f; Lk 3: 7, 12; J 3: 23b; GEb 3; IEph 18: 2 al.—ὕδατι w. *water* Mk 1: 8a; Lk 3: 16a; Ac 1: 5a; 11: 16a; ἐν ὕδατι J 1: 26, 31, 33; ἐν τῷ Ἰορδ. (4 Km 5: 14) Mt 3: 6; Mk 1: 5; εἰς τὸν Ἰορδ. (cf. Plu., De Superst. 166A βάπτισον σεαυτὸν εἰς θάλασσαν; Herm. Wr. 4, 4 βάπτισον σεαυτὸν εἰς τὸν κρατῆρα) Mk 1: 9.—W. the external element and purpose given ἐν ὕδατι εἰς μετάνοιαν Mt 3: 11a (ABOliver, is β. used w. ἐν and the Instrumental?: Rev. and Expos. 35, '38, 190–7).—βαπτίζεσθαι τὸ βάπτισμα Ἰωάννου *undergo John's baptism* Lk 7: 29. εἰς τί ἐβαπτίσθητε; Ac 19: 3 *means*, as the answer shows, *in reference to what (baptism) were you baptized?*, i.e., what kind of baptism did you receive? Or, w. ref. to vs. 5, *in whose name?* (s. 2bβ below). β. βάπτισμα μετανοίας *administer a repentance baptism* vs. 4; GEb 1.—Cf. the lit. on Ἰωάν(ν)ης 1, and on the baptism of Jesus by John: JBornemann, D. Taufe Christi durch Joh. 1896; HUsener, D. Weihnachtsfest² '11; DVölter, D. Taufe Jesu durch Joh.: NThT 6, '17, 53–76; WEBundy, The Meaning of Jesus' Baptism: Journ. of Rel. 7, '27, 56–75; MWJacobus, Zur Taufe Jesu bei Mt 3: 14, 15: NKZ 40, '29, 44–53; Selma Hirsch, Taufe, Versuchung u. Verklärung Jesu '32; DPlooij, The Baptism of Jesus: RHarris-Festschr. (Amicitiae Corolla) '33, 229–52; JKosnetter, D. Taufe Jesu '36; HHRowley, TWManson memorial vol., ed. Higgins '59, 218–29 [Qumran]; JSchneider, Der historische Jesus u. d. kerygmatische Christus '61, 530–42; HKraft, ThZ 17, '61, 399–412 [Joel]; FLentzen-Dies, D. Taufe Jesu nach den Synoptikern, '70. More ref. s.v. περιστερά.

b. of Christian baptism—a. performed by Jesus' disciples J 3: 22, 26; 4: 1, cf. 2. As the Christian sacrament of initiation after Jesus' death Ac 2: 41; 8: 12f, 36, 38; 16: 33; 22: 16; 1 Cor 1: 14–17; D 7 (where baptism by pouring is allowed in cases of necessity); ISm 8: 2.

β. β. τινὰ εἰς (τὸ) ὄνομά τινος (s. ὄνομα I 4cβ) *baptize in* or *w. respect to the name of someone*: (τοῦ) κυρίου Ac 8: 16; 19: 5; D 9: 5; Hv 3, 7, 3. Cf. 1 Cor 1: 13, 15. εἰς τ. ὄν. τ. πατρὸς καὶ τ. υἱοῦ καὶ τ. ἁγίου πνεύματος Mt 28: 19 (on the original form of the baptismal formula see FC Conybeare, ZNW 2, '01, 275–88; ERiggenbach, BFChTh VII 1, '03; VIII 4, '04; HHoltzmann, Ntl. Theologie² I '11, 449f; OMoe: RSeeberg Festschr. '29, I 179–96; GOngaro, Biblica 19, '38, 267–79; GBraumann, Vorpaulinische christl. Taufverkündigung bei Paulus '62); D 7: 1, 3. Likew. ἐν τῷ ὀν. Ἰ. Χριστοῦ Ac 2: 38 v.l.; 10: 48; ἐπὶ τῷ ὀν. Ἰ. Χρ. Ἀc 2: 38 text; more briefly εἰς Χριστόν Gal 3: 27; Ro 6: 3a. To be baptized εἰς Χρ. is for Paul a sharing in Christ's death εἰς τὸν θάνατον αὐτοῦ ἐβαπτίσθημεν vs. 3b (s. Ltzm. ad loc.; HSchlier, Ev. Theol. '38, 335–47; GWagner, D. rel-geschichtliche Problem von Rö 6: 1–11, '62, Eng. tr. Pauline Bapt. and the Pagan Mysteries, by JPSmith, '67; RSchnackenburg, Baptism in the Thought of St. Paul '64, Eng. tr. of D. Heilsgeschehen b. d. Taufe nach dem Ap. Paulus '50). The effect of baptism is to bring all those baptized εἰς ἓν σῶμα 1 Cor 12: 13.

γ. w. the purpose given εἰς ἄφεσιν τ. ἁμαρτιῶν Ac 2: 38 (IScheftelowitz, D. Sündentilgung durch Wasser: ARW 17, '14, 353–412).—Diod. S. 5, 49, 6: the pagans believe that by being received into the mysteries by the rites [τελεται] they become more devout, more just, and better in every way.—ὑπὲρ τ. νεκρῶν 1 Cor 15: 29a, cf. b, is obscure; it has been interpr. (1) locally, over (the graves of) the dead; (2) on account of the dead, infl. by their good ex.; (3) for the benefit of the dead, in var. mngs. See comm. and HPreisker, ZNW 23, '24, 298–304; JZingerle, Heiliges Recht: Jahresh. d. Öst. Arch. Inst. 23, '26; Rtzst., Taufe 43f; AMarmorstein, ZNW 30, '31, 277–85; AB Oliver, Rev. and Exp. 34, '37, 48–53; three articles: Kirchenblatt 98, '42 and six: ET 54, '43; 55, '44; MRaeder, ZNW 46, '56, 258–60; BMFoschini, 5 articles: CBQ 12, '50 and 13, '51.—On the substitution of a ceremony by another person cf. Diod. S. 4, 24, 5: the boys who do not perform the customary sacrifices lose their voices and become as dead persons in the sacred precinct. When someone takes a vow to make the sacrifice for them, their trouble disappears at once.

3. in fig. sense though related to the idea of Christian baptism.

a. typologically of Israel's passage through the Red Sea εἰς τὸν Μωϋσῆν ἐβαπτίσαντο (v.l. ἐβαπτίσθησαν) 1 Cor 10: 2.

b. β. τινὰ (ἐν) πνεύματι ἁγίῳ Mk 1· 8 (v.l.+ἐν); J 1: 33; Ac 1: 5b; 11: 16b. Cf. 1 Cor 12: 13; ἐν πν. ἀγ. καὶ πυρί Mt 3: 11b; Lk 3: 16b (JDunn, Nov T 14, '72, 81–92). —On baptism w. fire: REisler, Orphisch-dionysische Mysterienged. in d. christl. Antike: Vortr. d. Bibl. Warburg II 2, '25, 139ff; C-MEdsman, Le baptême de feu (Acta Sem. Neot. Upsal. 9) '40.—JATRobinson, The Baptism of John and Qumran, HTR 50, '57, 175–91; cf. IQS 4, 20f.

c. of martyrdom (cf. the fig. uses in UPZ 70, 13 [152/1 BC]; Diod. S. 1, 73, 6; Plut., Galba 21, 3 ὀφλήμασι βεβ. 'overwhelmed by debts'; Charito 2, 4, 4, βαπτιζόμενος ὑπὸ τ. ἐπιθυμίας; Vi. Aesopi I c. 21 p. 278, 4 λύπῃ βαπτιζόμενος; Achilles Tat. 3, 10, 1 πλήθει βαπτισθῆναι κακῶν; Herm. Wr. 4, 4 ἐβαπτίσαντο τοῦ νοός; Is 21: 4; Jos., Bell. 4, 137 ἐβάπτισεν τ. πόλιν 'he overwhelmed the city w. misery') δύνασθε τὸ βάπτισμα ὃ ἐγὼ βαπτίζομαι βαπτισθῆναι; Mk 10: 38; cf. vs. 39; Mt 20: 22 v.l.; Lk 12: 50 (GDelling, Novum Testamentum 2, '57, 92–115).—PAlthaus, Senior, D. Heilsbedeutung d. Taufe im NT 1897; WHeitmüller, Im Namen Jesu '03, Taufe u. Abendmahl b. Paulus '03, Taufe u. Ab. im Urchristentum '11; FRendtorff, D. Taufe im Urchristentum '05; HWindisch, Taufe u. Sünde im ältesten Christentum '08; ASeeberg, D. Taufe im NT² '13; AvStromberg, Studien zu Theorie u. Praxis der Taufe '13; GottfrKittel, D. Wirkungen d. chr. Wassertaufe nach d. NT: StKr 87, '14, 25ff; WKoch, D. Taufe im NT³ '21; JLeipoldt, D. urchr. Taufe im Lichte der Relgesch. '28; RReitzenstein, D.

Vorgesch. d. christl. Taufe '29 (against him HHSchaeder, Gnomon 5, '29, 353–70, answered by Rtzst., ARW 27, '29, 241–77); FJDölger, Antike u. Christentum I '29, II '30; HvSoden, Sakrament u. Ethik bei Pls: ROtto-Festschr. '31, 1, 1–40; MSEnslin, Crozer Quarterly 8, '31, 47–67; BWBacon, ATR 13, '31, 155–74; CRBowen: RJHutcheon, Studies in NT, '36, 30–48; GBornkamm, ThBl 17, '38, 42–52; 18, '39, 233–42; HSchlier, Ev. Theol. '38, 335–47 (Ro 6); EBruston, La notion bibl. du baptême: Études théol. et relig. '38, 67–93; 135–50; HGMarsh, The Origin and Signif. of the NT Baptism '41; KBarth, D. kirchl. Lehre v.d. Taufe² '43 (Eng. tr., The Teaching of the Church Regarding Baptism, EAPayne '48); FCGrant, ATR 27, '45, 253–63; HSchlier, D. kirchl. Lehre v.d. Taufe: ThLZ 72, '47, 321–6; OCullmann, Baptism in the NT (tr. JKSReid) '50; MBarth, D. Taufe ein Sakrament? '51; RBultmann, Theology of the NT, tr. KGrobel '51, I, 133–44; JSchneider, D. Taufe im NT '52; DMStanley, Theological Studies 18, '57, 169–215; EFascher, Taufe: Pauly-W. 2. Reihe IV 2501–18 ('32); AOepke, TW I '33, 527–44; GRBeasley-Murray, Baptism in the NT '62; HBraun, Qumran u. d. NT II '66, 1–29; OBetz, D. Proselytentaufe der Qumransekte u. d. NT, Revue de Qumran 1, '58, 213–34; JYsebaert, Gk. Baptismal Terminology, '62. S. τέκνον 1aa. M-M. B. 1482.

βάπτισμα, ατος, τό (found only in Christian writers) baptism.

1. of John's baptism Mt 3: 7; 21: 25; Mk 11: 30; Lk 7: 29; 20: 4; Ac 1: 22; 10: 37; 18: 25; 19: 3; β. μετανοίας Ac 13: 24; 19: 4; GEb 1; β. μετανοίας εἰς ἄφεσιν ἁμαρτιῶν a baptism of repentance for forgiveness of sins Mk 1: 4; Lk 3: 3.

2. of Christian baptism β. φέρον ἄφεσιν ἁμαρτιῶν B 11: 1; β. εἰς τὸν θάνατον Ro 6: 4 (s. βαπτίζω 2bβ). ἓν β. Eph 4: 5. The person baptized is, as it were, buried w. Christ Col 2: 12; 1 Pt 3: 21 (s. ἀντίτυπος). Compared to a soldier's weapons IPol 6: 2. τηρεῖν τὸ β. ἁγνὸν καὶ ἀμίαντον 2 Cl 6: 9. Ritual directions D 7: 1, 4.

3. baptism fig., of martyrdom Mk 10: 38f; Lk 12: 50; Mt 20: 22f v.l. (s. GDelling, Novum Test. 2, '58, 92–115, and βαπτίζω 3c). M-M.*

βαπτισμός, οῦ, ὁ dipping (Antyllus the physician [II AD] in Oribasius 10, 3, 9), washing of dishes Mk 7: 4, 8 t.r. Of ritual washings (Jos., Ant. 18, 117 of John's baptism) Hb 9: 10. βαπτισμῶν διδαχή teaching about baptisms 6: 2; Col 2: 12 v.l. M-M.*

βαπτιστής, οῦ, ὁ Baptist, Baptizer, surname of John Mt 3: 1; 11: 11f; 14: 2, 8; 16: 14; 17: 13; Mk 6: 25 (in vs. 24 ὁ βαπτίζων); 8: 28; Lk 7: 20, 33; 9: 19 (found only in Christian writers, except for Jos., Ant. 18, 116, where it refers to J. Bapt. But cf. Epict. 2, 9, 21 ἡμεῖς παραβαπτισταί).*

βάπτω fut. βάψω; 1 aor. ἔβαψα; pf. pass. ptc. βεβαμμένος (this form Epict. 2, 9, 20 of the experience [τὸ πάθος] that causes a Ἕλλην to become a Ἰουδαῖος].

1. dip, dip in τὶ someth. J 13: 26, ἐμβάπτω 𝔓⁶⁶ et al. (cf. Ruth 2: 14); ἄκρον τοῦ δακτύλου ὕδατος the tip of the finger in water (on the gen. ὕδατος cf. Bl-D. §172 app.; Arat., Phaenomena 651 βάπτων ὠκεανοῖο; 858 Maass) Lk 16: 24. The dat. may also be used (ἔβαψεν τῷ ὕδατι 4 Km 8: 15 v.l.) ibid. v.l.; ἱμάτιον βεβαμμένον αἵματι Rv 19: 13 (the text is quite uncertain; v.l. ῥεραντισμένον, περιρεραμμένον, ἐρραμμένον s. ῥαντίζω, περιρραίνω, ῥαίνω) a garment dipped in blood (but s. 2 below).

2. *dip into dye* (Ev. Thomae Graec. A 8 p. 148 note, Tischendorf² 1876), *dye* (Hdt. 7, 67 εἵματα βεβαμμένα; POxy. 736, 6 [I AD]; Jos., Bell. 4, 563, Ant. 3, 102); in this case Rv 19: 13 means *a garment dyed in blood* (s. JAScott, Class. Journal 16, '20, 53f for exx. of *β.* = 'stain' w. blood fr. Batrachom. 220 and Lucian, Ver. Hist. 18 [2, 38 Teub.]). M-M. B. 415.*

Βαρ s. Βαριωνᾶ.

Βαραββᾶς, ᾶ, ὁ (בַּר אַבָּא) a freq. (e.g. Suppl. Epigr. Gr. VII 489) name, *Barabbas*= son of Abba (Billerb. I 1031).

1. Mt. 27: 16f, 20f, 26; Mk 15: 7, 11, 15; Lk 23: 18; J 18: 40. In GH (18), acc. to Jerome, the name was rendered in Lat. filius magistri eorum (=בַּר רַבָּן). Origen, In Mt Comm. Ser. 121 (ed. EKlostermann '33, 255-7) found the name written in full in old mss. as Ἰησοῦς ὁ Β., and this v.l. occurs Mt 27: 16f.—WBrandt, Ev. Geschichte 1893, 94ff; JMerkel, ZNW 6, '05, 293ff. LCouchoud and RStahl, Jesus B.: Hibbert Journ. 25, '27, 26-42; ADeissmann, Mysterium Christi '31, 32-6; HARigg, Jr., Barabbas: JBL 64, '45, 417-56 (many ref.; against him MHengel, D. Zeloten '61, 348); JBlinzler, D. Prozess Jesu³ '60, 220-35.

2. the rdg. of D in Ac 15: 22 for Βαρσαββᾶς, q.v. 2.*

Βαράκ, ὁ indecl. (בָּרָק; in Jos. Βάρακος, ου [Ant. 5, 203]) *Barak*, an Israelite general (Judg 4f), mentioned w. other heroes Hb 11: 32.*

Βαραχίας, ου, ὁ (בֶּרֶכְיָה; also Jos., Ant. 9, 250) *Barachiah*, name of the father of a certain Zechariah (Gk. Zacharias), who was killed in the temple (s. Ζαχαρίας 2) Mt 23: 35; Lk 11: 51 v.l. Acc. to GH 13 this Zechariah was the son of Jehoiada, not of B., and so identified w. the Zech. who was stoned to death in the temple court, 2 Ch 24: 20ff. Zech., the son of Berechiah, is the well-known prophet (Zech 1:1), who seems elsewh. to have been confused w. the murdered Z. (Pesikta R. Kahana 15). If the ref. in the gospels is to a biblical pers., the Zech. of 2 Ch (the last book in the Hebrew canon; Billerb. I 943; IV 422) must be meant. 'Son of Barachiah' Mt 23: 35 has been considered the gloss of a copyist. The view has been expressed, too, that Jehoiada was not the father, but the grandfather of the ill-fated Z. But since this Z. was not the last prophet or just person to be killed, some scholars hold that the allusion is to Zacharias, son of Baruch, whom the Zealots killed 67/8 AD (Jos., Bell. 4, 334ff). Cf. EbNestle, ZNW 6, '05, 198-200; Wlh., Einl. 118-23; JChapman, JTS 13, '12, 398-410; Rtzst., Herr der Grösse 34ff; JSKennard, Jr., ATR 29, '47, 173-9.*

βάρβαρος, ον (Aeschyl., Hdt.+; inscr., pap., LXX; Ep. Arist. 122; Philo, Joseph.; Sib. Or. 3, 638; 5, 132; loanw. in rabb. [Dalman, Gram.² 183, 185]).

1. *speaking a foreign language, a strange*, i.e. *unintelligible tongue* adj. or noun 1 Cor 14: 11 (cf. Hdt. 2, 158; Aristoph., Av. 199 and its scholia [Ltzm. on 1 Cor 14: 11]; Ovid, Tristia 5, 10, 37 barbarus hic ego sum, quia non intellegor ulli; Ps 113: 1).

2. *not Greek, foreign, barbarous*—a. adj. πόλεις Ἑλληνίδας κ. βαρβάρους Dg 5: 4.

b. subst. *a person not Greek, foreigner, barbarian*, contrasted w. Greeks (Amelius [III AD] calls the writer of John's gospel a *β.*: Eus., Pr. Ev. 11, 19, 1) Ἕλληνες κ. βάρβαροι Ro 1: 14 (cf. Ps.-Eur., Rhes. 404; Pla., Theaet. 175A; Charito 6, 3, 7; Dit., Syll.³ 360, 12; 27; 867, 32, Or. 765, 16ff; Hymn to Isis [WPeek, D. Isishymnos v. Andros '30] p. 124, 31= 125, 27; Philo, Abr. 267; Jos., Ant. 4, 12;

8, 284 al.—The Romans refused to be classified as *β.*: Jüthner ["Ελλην 1] p. 62; MPohlenz, Stoa II '49, 139); cf. Col 3: 11 (44th Ep. of Apollonius of Tyana [Philostrat. I 354, 25]: there is no difference betw. men εἴτε βάρβαρος εἴτε καὶ Ἕλλην.—ThHermann, ThBl 9, '30, 106f). Of the inhabitants of Malta, without derogatory conn. Ac 28: 2, 4.—AEichhorn, Βάρβαρος quid significaverit, Diss. Leipz. '04; HWerner, Barbarus: NJKlA 41, '18, 389-408; HWindisch, TW I 544-51. S. Ἕλλην 1. M-M.*

βαρέω 1 aor. ἐβάρησα; pass., pres. ptc. βαρούμενος, imper. βαρείσθω; 1 aor. ἐβαρήθην; pf. ptc. βεβαρημένος (Hom.+; inscr., pap.; quite rare LXX; Jos., Ant. 15, 55; Sib. Or. fgm. 3, 39; cf. Anz 266-8; Nägeli 26) *weigh down, burden*; only fig.: of heavy eyelids ὀφθαλμοὶ βεβαρημένοι (Philo, Ebr. 131 βεβαρημένος τ. ὀφθαλμούς) Mt 26: 43; Mk 14: 40 v.l. W. ὕπνῳ (Anth. Pal. 3, 22, 17; 4, 8, 12; 7, 290) *heavy w. sleep* Lk 9: 32. Of hearts that become heavy, i.e. lose their sensitiveness (cf. Ex 7: 14) in drunkenness (*β.* οἴνῳ is a common expr. Hom.+) Lk 21: 34. ἐβάρησά τινα ἐν μικρῷ ἢ ἐν μεγάλῳ *I was a burden to anyone in matters small or great* IPhld 6: 3. Of misfortune or injustice (cf. POxy. 525, 3 [II AD] καθ’ ἑκάστην ἡμέραν βαροῦμαι δι’ αὐτόν; Dit., Syll.³ 888, 85; 904, 4) καθ’ ὑπερβολὴν ὑπὲρ δύναμιν ἐβαρήθημεν *we were burdened altogether beyond our strength* 2 Cor 1: 8 (cf. PTebt. 23, 5 [II BC] καθ’ ὑπερβολὴν βεβαρυμμένοι). Abs. βαρούμενοι *oppressed* 5: 4 (Epict. 1, 25, 17). Of financial burdens (Cass. Dio 46, 32; Dit., Or. 595, 15 [174 AD] ἵνα μὴ τὴν πόλιν βαρῶμεν) μὴ βαρείσθω ἡ ἐκκλησία *the church is not to be burdened* 1 Ti 5: 16. M-M.*

βαρέως adv. of βαρύς (Hdt.+; Sb 6263, 26; UPZ 59, 28 [168 BC]; LXX; Jos., Ant. 20, 60; 94) *with difficulty* ἀκούειν *be hard of hearing* (X., An. 2, 1, 9 β. ἀκούειν means 'hear with anger') Mt 13: 15; Ac 28: 27 (both Is 6: 10).*

Βαρθολομαῖος, ου, ὁ (בַּר תַּלְמַי; cf. 2 Km 3: 3; 13: 37; Joseph. Index Niese Θολεμαῖος and Θολομαῖος; Preisigke, Namenbuch) *Bartholomew*, name of one of the 12 apostles Mt 10: 3; Mk 3: 18; Lk 6: 14; Ac 1: 13. Often identified w. Nathanael q.v.; s. UHolzmeister, Biblica 21, '40, 28-39.*

Βαριησοῦς, οῦ, ὁ (בַּר יֵשׁוּעַ) *Bar-Jesus*, name of a false prophet (cf. Ἐλύμας, and ref. there) Ac 13: 6. MWilcox, The Semitisms of Ac, '65, 89.*

Βαριωνᾶ or **Βαριωνᾶς, ᾶ, ὁ** (בַּר יוֹנָה) *Bar-Jona* (=son of Jonah; cf. Jon 1: 1; 4 Km 14: 25) surname of the apostle Simon (Peter) Mt 16: 17. GH 9 has υἱὲ Ἰωάννου= בַּר יוֹחָנָן, which agrees w. J 1: 42 (cf. 21: 15-17). Cf. Dalman, Gramm.² 179, 5; HHirschberg, JBL 61, '42, 171-91, opposed by RMarcus ibid. 281; MHengel, Die Zeloten '61, 55-57.*

Βαρναβᾶς, ᾶ, ὁ (ברנבו?) Suppl. Epigr. Gr. VII 381, 5.—Cf. Dssm., B 175ff, NB 16 [BS 187ff, 307ff], ZNW 7, '06, 91f; Dalman, Worte 32, Gram.² 178, 4; HJCadbury: RHarris-Festschr. [Amicitiae Corolla] '33, 47f, JBL 52, '33, 59) *Barnabas*, a Levite fr. Cyprus, whose real name was Joseph (Ac 4: 36), associated w. Paul until the strife described in Ac 15: 36-40; cf. Gal 2: 13, but also Col 4: 10; Ac 9: 27; 11: 22, 30; 12: 25; chapters 13-15; 1 Cor 9: 6; Gal 2: 1, 9; 2 Cor subsc.; B subsc. In Ac 4: 36 his name is translated υἱὸς παρακλήσεως *son of consolation*, but it is not quite clear how this rendering is derived.—ROPTaylor, ChQR 136, '43, 59-79. M-M.*

βάρος, ους, τό (trag., Hdt.+; inscr., pap., LXX [rare]; Ep. Arist. 93; Philo, Joseph.) *weight, burden*, only fig.

1. *burden* (Diod. S. 13, 81, 3 τοῦ πολέμου; Jos., Bell. 1, 461; 4, 616) of the day's work βαστάζειν τὸ β. τῆς ἡμέρας Mt 20: 12 (cf. Babrius 111, 20 βάρος διπλοῦν βαστάσας). Of temptations ἀλλήλων τὰ β. βαστάζετε Gal 6: 2. ἀναδέχεσθαι τὸ β. τοῦ πλησίον Dg 10: 6. Of the burden of a law (Polyb. 1, 31, 5 τὸ β. τῶν ἐπιταγμάτων) βάλλειν β. ἐπί τινα *impose a burden on someone* Rv 2: 24. For this ἐπιτιθέναι τινὶ β. (X., Oec. 17, 9; Dionys. Hal. 4, 10 ἅπαν ἐπιθεὶς τ. β. τοῖς πλουσίοις) PGiess. 19, 18) Ac 15: 28; β. ἄστατον *an unweighed burden* UGosp l. 62.

2. *weight* of influence which someone enjoys or claims (Polyb. 4, 32, 7 πρὸς τὸ β. τὸ Λακεδαιμονίων; Diod. S. 4, 61; Plut., Per. 37, 1) ἐν β. εἶναι *wield authority, insist on one's importance* 1 Th 2:7.

3. *fulness* (β. πλούτου Eur., El. 1287, Iph. Taur. 416; Plut., Alex. M. 48, 3; cf. 3 Macc 5: 47) αἰώνιον β. δόξης *an everlasting fulness of glory* 2 Cor 4: 17 (cf. Rtzst., Mysterienrel.³ 355). M-M.*

Βαρσα(β)βᾶς, ᾶ, ὁ בַּר שָׁבָא or בַּר סָאבָא) *Barsabbas* (Diod. S. 32, 15, 7 this is the name of a king of the Thracians, but with only one β.; PBenoit et al., Discoveries in the Judean Desert, II, '61, 25, 5 [133 AD]).

1. patronymic of a certain Joseph, surnamed Justus, a member of the first church Ac 1: 23.

2. patronymic of a certain Judas who, with Silas, was appointed by the Jerusalem apostles as a companion of Paul and Barnabas when they returned to Antioch fr. the Apostolic Council Ac 15: 22. (On the name and the spelling s. Dalman, Gramm.² 180; Cadbury, Harris-Festschr. [s. Βαρναβᾶς] 48–50.) M-M.*

Βαρτιμαῖος, ου, ὁ בַּר טִמַי, s. Billerb. II 25) *Bartimaeus*, name of a blind man Mk 10: 46, where ὁ υἱὸς Τιμαίου explains Βαρτιμαῖος. Timai (cf. LXX; Jos., C. Ap. 1, 16; 221) may be an abbreviation, perh. of Timotheus (Wlh. ad loc.).—EbNestle, Marginalien u. Materialien 1893, 83–92: D. blinde Bettler B., Mk 10: 46.*

βαρύνω 1 aor. ἐβάρυνα (Hom.+; Dit., Or. 669, 5; 18; PTebt. 23, 5 [c. 115 BC]; POxy. 298, 26; LXX; En. 103, 11; Philo, Exs. 154; Jos., Bell. 4, 171, Ant. 6, 32; Sib. Or. 3, 462) *weigh down, burden* τ. δίκαιον Ac 3: 14D; β. δεσμοῖς *weigh down w. chains* 2 Cl 20: 4.—Ac 28: 27 v.l.; 2 Cor 5: 4 v.l. M-M.*

βαρύς, εῖα, ύ (Hom.+; LXX, Philo, Joseph.) *heavy.*

1. lit. φορτία βαρέα (cf. Ps 37: 5) *heavy burdens* fig. (Procop. Soph., Ep. 141 β. φορτίον; cf. Jos., Ant. 19, 362) of the law Mt 23: 4; of sleep Ac 20: 9D.

2. fig.—a. *burdensome, difficult to fulfill* of regulations, demands (Polyb. 1, 31, 7; Philo, Mos. 1, 37) αἱ ἐντολαὶ αὐτοῦ β. οὐκ εἰσίν 1 J 5: 3 (cf. Philo, Spec. Leg. 1, 299 αἰτεῖται ὁ θεὸς οὐδὲν βαρύ. ἐπιστολαὶ *severe* 2 Cor 10: 10 (w. ἰσχυρός, q.v. 2).

b. *weighty, important* (Herodian 2, 14, 3) τὰ βαρύτερα τοῦ νόμου *the more important provisions of the law* Mt 23: 23; αἰτιώματα Ac 25: 7 (cf. Synes., Ep. 69 p. 217D ἁμαρτίαι β.).

c. *burdensome, troublesome* (Dio Chrys. 26[43], 7 οὐδὲν οὐδενὶ βαρύς εἰμι; Appian, Samn. 5 β. εἶναί τινι; Wsd 2: 14; 17: 20) β. γίνεσθαί τινι *become a burden to someone* IRo 4: 2.

d. *fierce, cruel, savage* (Il. 1, 89; X., Ages. 11, 12 ἀνταγωνιστὴς β.; 3 Macc 6: 5; Philo, Agr. 120 β. ἐχθροί; Jos., Ant. 15, 354) λύκοι β. Ac 20: 29. M-M. B. 1072.*

βαρύτιμος, ον *very expensive, very precious* (in this sense Strabo 17, 1, 13; Cyranides p. 12, 9) of ointments (Perpl. Eryth. c. 49 μύρον οὐ β.) Mt 26: 7 (cf. πολύτιμος).*

βασανίζω impf. ἐβασάνιζον; 1 aor. ἐβασάνισα; pass., 1 aor. ἐβασανίσθην; 1 fut. βασανισθήσομαι (Pre-Socr.+, Hdt., Aristoph.; Suppl. Epigr. Gr. VIII 246, 8; pap.; LXX, 20 times 4 Macc; Philo) *torture, torment.*

1. lit. of torture in judicial examination (Thu. 8, 92, 2; Charito 4, 3, 2; POxy. 903, 10; 2 Macc 7: 13; 4 Macc 6: 5 al.; Jos., Ant. 2, 105; 16, 232) MPol 2: 2; used on slaves (Antipho 2, 4, 8; POxy. 903, 10) 6: 1.

2. fig., of any severe distress—a. mostly physical: in diseases (Lucian, Soloec. 6; Jos., Ant. 9, 101; 12, 413) Mt 8: 6. Of birth-pangs (Anth. Pal. 9, 311 βάσανος has this mng.) Rv 12: 2. ἦλθες βασανίσαι ἡμᾶς; Mt 8: 29; cf. Mk 5: 7; Lk 8: 28; Rv 11: 10.—9: 5; 14: 10; 20: 10; GP 4: 14; Hv 3, 7, 6; s 6, 4, 1f.

b. essentially mental IEph 8: 1; ἑαυτόν *torment oneself* Hs 9, 9, 3 (Epict. 2, 22, 35; Philo, Deus Imm. 102). For this τὴν ἑαυτοῦ ψυχήν (Test. Ash. 6: 5 ἡ ψυχὴ βασανίζεται) m 4, 2, 2 (w. ταπεινοῦν); ψυχὴν δικαίαν ἀνόμοις ἔργοις ἐβασάνιζεν (Lot) *felt his righteous soul tormented by the lawless deeds* (of the Sodomites) 2 Pt 2: 8 (cf. Harnack, Beitr. VII '16, 105f).

3. gener. *harass* (Maximus Tyr. 11, 2a βασανίζειν τὸν χρυσὸν ἐν πυρί=torture the gold with fire [in the smelting process]) πλοῖον βασανιζόμενον ὑπὸ τῶν κυμάτων *a boat harassed by the waves* Mt 14: 24; cf. Mk 6: 48, unless it be preferable to transl. here: *they were straining at the oars.* M-M.**

βασανισμός, οῦ, ὁ (Alexis in Athen. 1, 56 p. 30F; 4 Macc 9: 6; 11: 2).

1. act. *tormenting, torture* Rv 9: 5b.—2. pass. the condition of those tortured, *torment* vs. 5a; 14: 11; 18: 10, 15; (w. πένθος) vs. 7.*

βασανιστής, οῦ, ὁ (Antipho+; Demosth. 37, 40; Plut., Mor. 498D; Philo, Spec. Leg. 4, 82, Omn. Prob. Lib. 108, In Flacc. 96) *torturer, jailer* Mt 18: 34 (Suppl. Epigr. Gr. VIII 246, 8 [II AD] uses βασανίζω of the treatment of a debtor fr. whom everything possible is to be exacted); MPol 2: 3; ἄγγελοι β. *avenging angels* AP 8: 23.*

βάσανος, ου, ἡ (Theognis, Pind.+, orig. 'touchstone, test'; inscr., pap., LXX, En., Philo; Jos., Ant. 12, 255; 13, 241).

1. *torture, torment* (Herodas 2, 88 and Diod. S. 15, 58, 2 of torture ordered by a court; Dit., Syll.³ 780, 12; PLille 29 I, 22; LXX, esp. oft. 4 Macc; Philo, De Jos. 86; Jos., Bell. 1, 635; Ant. 16, 245) MPol 2: 3, 4; GOxy 7. Of the tortures of hell (cf. Wsd 3: 1; 4 Macc 13: 15) 2 Cl 17: 7b; ὑπάρχειν ἐν β. *be in torment* Lk 16: 23. Of hell τόπος τῆς β. *place of torment* vs. 28. Cf. 2 Cl 10: 4.

2. gener. *severe pain, torment* (w. νόσοι; cf. Sext. Emp., Eth. 153; 1 Macc 9, 56; Philo, Abr. 96) Mt 4: 24.—Hv 3, 7, 6; s 6, 3, 4; 6, 4, 3f; 6, 5, 1; 3; 7; Papias 3. Of persecutions of the Christians 1 Cl 6: 1; 2 Cl 17: 7a. M-M. B. 1115.*

βασιλεία, ας, ἡ (Hdt.+; inscr., pap., LXX, Ep. Arist., Philo, Joseph., Test. 12 Patr.).

1. *kingship, royal power, royal rule, kingdom* (1 Km 15: 28; 20: 31; Sir 10: 8; Jdth 1: 1; Esth 3: 6; 1 Macc 1: 16 al. LXX) λαβεῖν ἑαυτῷ βασιλείαν *obtain royal power* (*for oneself*) Lk 19: 12, 15; without dat. Rv 17: 12 (cf. Jos., Ant. 13, 220); δοῦναί τινι τὴν β. vs. 17; ἔχειν β. ἐπὶ τινων vs. 18; ἐποίησεν ἡμᾶς βασιλείαν *he made us a kingdom* 1: 6; cf. 5: 10; *royal rule* Lk 1: 33; 22: 29; 23: 42 v.l. (ἐν τῇ β. σου *in your royal power*); Ac 1: 6; Hb 1: 8 (Ps 44: 7); 1 Cor 15: 24 (παραδιδόναι as Diod. S. 1, 43, 6); B 4: 4 (Da 7: 24). Ps 95: 10 (in Justin, Ap. I 41, 4, Dial. 73: ὁ κύριος ἐβασίλευσεν ἀπὸ τ. ξύλου) is the basis for β.

'Ιησοῦ ἐπὶ ξύλου *the rule of Jesus on the cross* B 8: 5 (s. Windisch, Hdb. ad loc.).—Hb 11: 33; 1 Cl 61: 1.

2. *kingdom*, i.e., the territory ruled over by a king (Diod. S. 4, 68, 4; Appian, Mithrid. 105 §496 ἡ βασ. ὅλη=the whole kingdom; Dit., Or. 383, 25 [I вс]; Ps 67: 33; 134: 11; Bar 2: 4; Tob 1: 21; 1 Macc 1: 6; 3: 27; 2 Macc 9: 25; 3 Macc 6: 24 al. LXX) Mt 4: 8; 12: 25f; 24: 7; Mk 3: 24; 6: 23 (Socrat., Ep. 1, 10 τ. βασιλείας μέρος διδόναι); 13: 8; Lk 11: 17f; 21: 10; αἱ β. τοῦ αἰῶνος τούτου IRo 6: 1. In the account of the temptation Mt 4: 8; Lk 4: 5 (in a manner very different from Jesus, Alexander [Diod. S. 17, 51, 2] asks his father, Zeus Ammon, for τὴν ἀπάσης τῆς γῆς ἀρχήν and finds a hearing).

3. esp. *the royal reign* or *kingdom* of God, a chiefly eschatological concept, beginning to appear in the prophets, elaborated in apocalyptic passages (Mi 4: 7f; Ps 102: 19; 144: 11-13; Wsd 6: 4; 10: 10; Da 3: 54; 4: 3 al.—Diod. S. 5, 71, 1 Zeus takes over the βασιλεία from Cronus; Sextus 311 κοινωνεῖ βασιλείας θεοῦ σοφὸς ἀνήρ) and taught by Jesus. The expressions vary; β. τοῦ θεοῦ and τῶν οὐρανῶν have essentially the same mng., since the Jews used οὐρανός (-οι) as well as other circumlocutions for θεός (cf. Mt 19: 23f; s. Bousset, Rel.³ 314f); the latter term may also emphasize the heavenly origin and nature of the kgdm.—Dalman, Worte 75-119; JWeiss, D. Predigt Jesu v. Reiche Gottes² '00, 1-35; ESellin, D. isr.-jüd. Heilands-erwartung 1909, D. alt. Prophetismus '12, 136ff; BDuhm, D. kommende RG '10; SMowinckel, Psalmenstudien II '22, 146ff; LDürr, Ursprung u. Ausbau d. isr. Heilands-erwartung '25; Bousset, Rel.³ '26, 213ff; AvGall, Βασιλεία τ. θεοῦ '26; JCWissing, Het begrip van het Koningrijk Gods, Diss., Leiden '27; HGressmann, Der Messias '29; MBuber, Königtum Gottes '32; PVolz, D. Eschatologie der jüd. Gemeinde im ntl. Zeitalter '34; Ltzm., D. Weltheiland '09; TWManson, The Teaching of Jesus '55, 116-284; SAalen, NTS 8, '61/'62, 215-40 ('house' or 'community' of God); GELadd, JBL 81, '62, 230-38 ('realm'); FNötscher, Vom A. zum NT '62, 226-30 (ethical).

a. β. τῶν οὐρανῶν only in Mt: 3: 2; 4: 17; 5: 3, 10, 19f and oft.

b. β. τοῦ θεοῦ Mt 6: 33 v.l.; 12: 28; 21: 31, 43; Mk 1: 15; 4: 11, 26, 30 and oft.; Lk 4: 43; 6: 20; 7: 28; 8: 1 and very oft.; Ac 1: 3; 8: 12; 14: 22; 19: 8; 28: 23, 31; J 3: 3, 5; Ro 14: 17 (defined as δικαιοσύνη, εἰρήνη, χαρά); 1 Cor 4: 20 al.; LJ 1: 2; Dg 9: 1; B 21: 1; Pol 2: 3; β. θεοῦ 1 Cor 6: 10, cf. 9; 15: 50; Gal 5: 21; Pol 5: 3; β. τοῦ Χριστοῦ καὶ θεοῦ Eph 5: 5; τοῦ Χριστοῦ 1 Cl 50: 3.

c. β. τοῦ πατρός Mt 13: 43; 26: 29.

d. β. αὐτοῦ (=τοῦ υἱοῦ τοῦ ἀνθρώπου) Mt 13: 41; cf. Col 1: 13.

e. β. τοῦ πατρὸς ἡμῶν Δαυίδ Mk 11: 10, since the Davidic kgdm. is to be reestablished under the Son of David, the Messiah (cf. Is 9: 5f; Jer 23: 5f).

f. ἡ β. τοῦ κυρίου B 4: 13; ἡ β. αὐτοῦ (=κυρίου) ἡ ἐπουράνιος 2 Ti 4: 18; Epil Mosq 4; ἡ οὐράνιος β. MPol 22: 3; ἡ ἐν οὐρανῷ β. Dg 10: 2.

g. αἰώνιος β. τοῦ κυρίου (cf. Da 4: 3 and CIG II 2715a, b ἐπὶ τῆς τῶν κυρίων 'Ρωμαίων αἰωνίου ἀρχῆς, Dssm., B 277f) 2 Pt 1: 11; cf. MPol 20: 2.—The greatest blessings conceivable are found in the β. Mt 13: 44f. The foll. expr. refer to obtaining it: ἅψασθαι τῆς β. B 7: 11; δέχεσθαι Mk 10: 15; διδόναι Lk 12: 32; εἰσέρχεσθαι εἰς τὴν β. Mt 5: 20; 7: 21; 18: 3; 19: 23; Mk 10: 23ff; Lk 24: 26 𝔓⁷⁵ (first hand); J 3: 5; Ac 14: 22; Hs 9, 12, 3f (HWindisch, D. Sprüche v. Eingehen in d. Reich Gs: ZNW 27, '28, 163-92); εἰσήκειν εἰς τὴν β. 2 Cl 11: 7; ἔρχεσθαι εἰς τὴν β. 9: 6; ἑτοιμάζειν Mt 25: 34; εὔθετον εἶναι τῇ β. Lk 9:

62; εὑρεθῆναι εἰς τὴν β. Hs 9, 13, 2; ζητεῖν Mt 6: 33; Lk 12: 31; καταξιοῦσθαι τῆς β. 2 Th 1: 5; κατοικεῖν ἐν τῇ β. Hs 9, 29, 2; κληρονομεῖν Mt 25: 34; 1 Cor 6: 9f; 15: 50; IPhld 3: 3; cf. κληρονόμος τῆς β. Js 2: 5; μαθητεύεσθαι τῇ β. Mt 13: 52; μεθιστάναι εἰς τὴν β. Col 1: 13; φθάνει ἡ β. ἐπί τινα Lk 11: 20. The phrase ὁρᾶν τὴν β. *see the kgdm.* occurs Mk 9: 1; Lk 9: 27; J 3: 3; Hs 9, 15, 3. The mysteries of the kgdm. can be revealed to those for whom they are intended Mt 13: 11; Mk 4: 11; διαγγέλλειν Lk 9: 60; διαμαρτυρεῖσθαι Ac 28: 23; κηρύσσειν καὶ εὐαγγελίζεσθαι Lk 8: 1; sim. 16: 16; cf. κηρύσσειν τὸ εὐαγγέλιον τῆς β. Mt 4: 23; 9: 35; 24: 14; κηρύσσειν τὴν β. Lk 9: 2; Ac 28: 31; λαλεῖν περὶ τῆς β. Lk 9: 11. Keep fr. entering: κλείειν Mt 23: 13; cf. κλεῖδες τῆς β. 16: 19 (s. κλεῖς 1); αἴρειν ἀπό τινος 21: 43.—Spoken of as present Mt 12: 28; Lk 11: 20, perh. also 17: 20f (see s.v. ἐντός). Viewed as future, but close at hand ἤγγικεν ἡ β. Mt 3: 2; 10: 7; Mk 1: 15; Lk 10: 9, 11; ἐγγύς ἐστιν Lk 21: 31; ἔρχεται Mt 6: 10; Mk 11: 10; Lk 11: 2; 17: 20; μέλλει ἀναφαίνεσθαι 19: 11; προσδέχεσθαι τὴν β. Mk 15: 43; ἐκδέχεσθαι τὴν β. 2 Cl 12: 1; μέλλει ἔρχεσθαι 1 Cl 42: 3; ἡ μέλλουσα β. 2 Cl 5: 5; ἥξει ἡ β. 12: 2. Conceived of as a banquet (Billerb. IV 1154ff): ἀνακλιθῆναι ἐν τῇ β. Mt 8: 11; sim. 26: 29; Mk 14: 25; Lk 13: 28f; 22: 16, 18, 30; cf. the parables 14: 15ff; Mt 22: 2ff. Participants in it are called υἱοὶ τῆς β. Mt 8: 12 (of mere external connection); 13: 38. Prerequisite for participation is μετάνοια Mt 4: 17; Mk 1: 15; the willingness to become like children Mt 18: 3f; 19: 14; Mk 10: 14f; Lk 18: 16f. Only righteousness will inherit the β. Mt 5: 20. Degrees and grades 5: 19; 18: 1, 4. The rich have scant prospects of entering 19: 23f; Mk 10: 23-5; Lk 18: 24f (cf. vs. 29), the servants of sin none at all Mt 13: 24ff, 36ff, 47ff.—Paul, too regards the β. as an ethical reality bestowing righteousness, peace (w. God) and joy Ro 14: 17. It manifests itself in deeds, not in words 1 Cor 4: 20. Sinful men will not inherit it 6: 9f; Gal 5: 21; Eph 5: 5 (cf. 2 Cl 9: 6); the latter passages show that for Paul the kgdm. is essentially future. Cf. also 2 Ti 4: 1. Flesh and blood will not inherit it; spiritual bodies are required for entrance 1 Cor 15: 50 (JoachJeremias, NTS 2, '56, 151-59). God himself calls men into it 1 Th 2: 12.—HJWesterink, Het Koninkrijk Gods bij Pls '37.—The most important lit. to 1931 in PFeine, Theol. d. NTs' '36, 73. Additional recent lit.: GGloege, Reich Gs u. Kirche im NT '29; RFrick, D. Gesch. des R.-Gs-Gedankens in d. alten Kirche '29; EFScott, The Kgdm. of God in the NT '31; H-DWendland, Reichsidee u. Gottesreich '34; ROtto, Reich Gottes u. Menschensohn '34 (Eng. tr., The Kgdm. of God and the Son of Man, tr. Filson and Woolf, '43 and '51); TW I 562-95; WGKümmel, D. Eschatologie der Evangelien '36, Verheissg. u. Erfüllg. '45, ²'53; JHéring, Le Royaume de Dieu et sa Venue (Jesus, Paul) '38, ²'59; JTheissing, D. Lehre Jesu v. d. ew. Seligkeit '40; FCGrant, The Gospel of the Kgdm. '40; JWellhagen, Anden och Riket '41 (Lk); WMichaelis, D. Herr verzieht nicht d. Verheissung '42; RLiechtenhan, D. Kommen des RGs nach dem NT '44; GAFKnight, From Moses to Paul, '49, 173-87; WArndt, CTM 21, '50, 8-29; JBright, The Kgdm. of God: The Biblical Concept and its Mng. for the Church '53; RSchnackenburg, Gottes Herrschaft u. Reich, ⁴'65, tr. JMurray, ²'68; ELadd, Jesus and the Kgdm., '64; NPerrin, The Kgdm. of God in the Teaching of Jesus, '66.—OT background: WSchmidt, Königtum Gottes in Ugarit u. Israel, '61; KHBernhardt, D. Problem der altorientalischen Königs-Ideologie im AT, Vetus Test. suppl. 8, '61.—Patristics: GWHLampe, JTS 49, '48, 58-73. M-M.

βασίλειος, ον (Hom.+; LXX) *royal* (oracular saying in Diod. S. 7, 17 κράτος βασίλειον) β. ἱεράτευμα 1 Pt 2: 9 (Ex 19: 6; 23: 22; but s. JHElliott, The Elect and the Holy, '66, 149–54). Used as a noun the pl. τὰ β. (since Hdt. 1, 30, also Dit., Syll.³ 495, 45; PGM 2, 181; 4, 1061; Esth 1: 9; Philo, In Flacc. 92; Jos., Ant. 13, 138) and more rarely the sg. τὸ β. (X., Cyr. 2, 4, 3; Pr 18: 19; Philo, Sobr. 66; Jos., Ant. 6, 251) means *the (royal) palace* Lk 7: 25.—In 2 Cl τὸ β.=ἡ βασιλεία (cf. Test. Jud. 17: 6, 22f; Sib. Or. 3, 159; Gaius in Euseb., H. E. 3, 28, 2.—Polyaenus 8, 55 uses the pl. τὰ βασίλεια=ἡ βασιλεία: εἰσέρχεσθαι εἰς τὸ β. τοῦ θεοῦ 6: 9; ὁρᾶν τὸ β. τοῦ κόσμου 17: 5. M-M.*

βασιλεύς, έως, ὁ (Hom.+; inscr., pap., LXX, En., Ep. Arist., Philo, Joseph., Test. 12 Patr., loanw. in rabb.) *king.*

1. gener. ποιεῖν τινα β. *make someone king* J 6: 15. βασιλεῖς τῆς γῆς *earthly kings* Mt 17: 25; Rv 1: 5; 6: 15 (Ps 2: 2; 88: 28) al.; Ac 4: 26 (Ps 2: 2); β. τῶν ἐθνῶν Lk 22: 25; (w. ἡγεμόνες) Mt 10: 18; Mk 13: 9; Lk 21: 12. Of kings gener. (w. προφῆται; 2 Macc 2: 13; Boll 139) Lk 10: 24. Of Pharaoh Ac 7: 10; David Mt 1: 6; Ac 13: 22; Herod I (Jos., Ant. 14, 382; 385; Dit., Or. 414; 415; 416; 417) Mt 2: 1, 3; Lk 1: 5; Herod Antipas (not really a king [Jos., Ant. 17, 188; Dit., Or. 416; 417], but occasionally given that title: Cicero, Verr. 4, 27) Mt 14: 9; Mk 6: 14; GP 1: 2; Herod Agrippa I (Jos., Ant. 18, 237; 19, 274; Dit., Or. 418; 419; 428) Ac 12: 1; Agrippa II (Jos., Bell. 2, 223; Dit., Or. 419; 423; 425; 426) 25: 13, 24, 26; Aretas, king of the Nabataeans 2 Cor 11: 32; Melchizedek, king of Salem Hb 7: 1f (Gen 14: 18). Of the Rom. emperor (Appian, Iber. 102 §444, Bell. Civ. 2, 86 §362 'Ρωμαίων βασ. 'Αδριανός al.; Herodian 2, 4, 4; IG III 12, 15 and 17; CIG II 2721, 11; POxy. 33 II, 6; 35 verso, 1; BGU 588, 10; PGM 4, 2448 'Αδριανὸς βασ.; 2452; Jos., Bell. 3, 351; 4, 596; 5, 563, Vi. 34; Magie 62) 1 Ti 2: 2 (the pl. is generic as Appian, Prooem. c. 15 §62; Jos., Ant. 2, 71) UGospl. 48 (s. LBiehl, D. liturg. Gebet für Kaiser u. Reich '37) 1 Pt 2: 13, 17 (s. Pr 24: 21 and esp. Vi. Aesopi I c. 26 p. 288, 17: τέκνον, πρὸ πάντων σέβου τὸ θεῖον, τὸν βασιλέα δὲ τίμα); Rv 17: 9; 1 Cl 37: 3.

2. Fig. of the possessor of the highest power (Ael. Aristid. 46 p. 285 D.: β. Θεμιστοκλῆς) esp.

a. of the Messianic king β. τῶν Ἰουδαίων (so Alex. Jannaeus: Jos., Ant. 14, 36; Herod 16, 311; Aristobulus: Diod. S. 40, 2) Mt 2: 2; 27: 11, 29, 37; Mk 15: 2, 9, 12, 18, 26; Lk 23: 3, 37f; J 18: 33 al.; β. (τοῦ) Ἰσραήλ Mt 27: 42; Mk 15: 32; J 1: 49; 12: 13; GP 3: 7; 4: 11. Hence of Jesus as king of the Christians MPol 9: 3; 17: 3. He is also the κύριος referred to D 14: 3, which quotes β. μέγας fr. Mal 1: 14. Cf. Mt 21: 5 (Zech 9: 9); 25: 34, 40; J 18: 37 (for the judge's question: βασιλεὺς εἶ σύ; cf. Martyr. Carpi etc. 24 OvGebh. '02: βουλευτὴς εἶ; β. βασιλέων (as 2 Macc 13: 4; Philo, Spec. Leg. 1: 18, Decal. 41; cf. PGM 13, 605.—Of Zeus: Dio Chrys. 2, 75) Rv 17: 14; 19: 16—this title is still current for kings in the early Christian era (Dssm., LO 310f [LAE 367f]; Diod. S. 1, 47, 4 an ancient royal inscr. βασ. βασιλέων; 1, 55, 7 β. βασιλέων καὶ δεσπότης δεσποτῶν Σεσόωσις; Memnon [I BC/I AD] no. 434 fgm. 1, 31, 3 Jac. βασ. βασ. of Tigranes; Appian, Bell. Civ. 2, 67 §278; Ezk 26: 7; Da 2: 37; 2 Esdr [Ezra] 7: 12) and purposely reserved by the Christians for their Lord, in strong contrast to earthly kings (cf. Pass. Scilit. 6 p. 24 vGebh.).—B 11: 5 (Is 33: 17).

b. of God (Plut., Mor. 383A: ἡγεμών ἐστι κ. βασιλεὺς ὁ θεός of the human souls who have entered eternal bliss) μέγας β. (Suppl. Epigr. Gr. VIII 32 [III AD] of Zeus; Tob 13: 16; Philo, Migr. Abr. 146 al.; Sib. Or. 3, 499; 616; of human kings since Hdt. 1, 188; Jdth 2: 5; 3: 2; Ep. Arist.;

Philo) Mt 5: 35 (cf. Ps 47: 3); Hv 3, 9, 8; β. τῶν ἐθνῶν (Jer 10: 7; s. ed. HBSwete v.l.) Rv 15: 3; β. τῶν αἰώνων (Tob 13: 7, 11; En. 9: 4; cf. Ps 144: 13; Ex 15: 18; Jos., Ant. 1, 272 δέσποτα παντὸς αἰῶνος, also 14: 24 β. τῶν ὅλων [β. τῶν ὅλων is also a designation of the god Uranus in Diod. S. 3, 56, 5]; PGM 12, 247 αἰώνων βασιλεῦ καὶ κύριε) 1 Ti 1: 17; Rv 15: 3 v.l.; ἐπουράνιος β. τῶν αἰ. 1 Cl 61: 2; β. τῶν βασιλευόντων 1 Ti 6: 15 (as 3 Macc 5: 35; Pel.-Leg. 21, 8; 24, 21). WGrafBaudissin, Kyrios III '29, 70-6.

c. of a king of spirits in the underworld, Abaddon Rv 9: 11.—WSchubart, Das hell. Königsideal nach Inschr. u. Pap., APF 12, '37, 1-26.—M-M. B. 1321; 1324.

βασιλεύω fut. βασιλεύσω; 1 aor. ἐβασίλευσα (Hom.+; inscr., pap., LXX, Ep. Arist., Philo, Joseph., Test. 12 Patr.).

1. *be king, rule* (Bl-D. §177; 233, 2; 234, 5; Rob. 801; 833; 902).—a. of temporal princes τινός *over (of) someth.* (1 Esdr 1: 37; 6: 16; 1 Macc 1: 16; 11: 9 al.) τῆς Ἰουδαίας Mt 2: 22 of Archelaus, who was called king without having the official title (Jos., Vi. 5 βασιλεύοντος 'Αρχελάου, Ant. 17, 188ff; 317ff; 18, 93 βασιλεὺς 'A.); τῶν περάτων τῆς γῆς IRo 6: 1; ἐπί τινα (Gen 37: 8; 1 Km 8: 9; 12: 1 al.) Lk 19: 14, 27.—βασιλεῖαι βασιλεύσουσιν ἐπὶ τ. γῆς *kingdoms (reigns) will reign on (the) earth* (cf. ἐπί 1 1) B 4: 4. On βασιλεὺς τ. βασιλευόντων 1 Ti 6: 15 s. βασιλεύς 2b.

b. of God and those closely united w. him—a. God (Ps.-Phoc. 111) Rv 11: 17; 19: 6 (s. 2 below for both pass.).—β. Christ Lk 1: 33; 1 Cor 15: 25; εἰς τ. αἰῶνας MPol 21.

γ. God and Christ together: their βασιλεία ... βασιλεύσει (s. 1a above: B 4: 4) εἰς τ. αἰῶνας τ. αἰώνων (cf. Ps 9: 37) Rv 11: 15.

δ. saints, who have been called to rule w. God Ro 5: 17b; Rv 5: 10 (ἐπὶ τ. γῆς, as 1a above); 20: 4, 6; 22: 5 (cf. Da 7: 27).

c. fig. death Ro 5: 14 (ἐπί τινα), 17a; sin vs. 21a; grace vs. 21b; sinful lust 6: 12.

2. *become king, obtain royal power,* so esp. in aor. (Hdt. 1, 130; Thu. 2, 99, 3; Polyb. 5, 40, 6; 4 Km 14: 29; 15: 1, 7, 10; 1 Macc 1: 10 al.) Rv 11: 17; 19: 6 (for both s. 1ba above); GH 27a, b; LJ 2: 2. χωρὶς ἡμῶν ἐβασιλεύσατε *without us you have become kings* 1 Cor 4: 8 (Appian, Basil. 1a §5 β. has the sense 'seize the rule'). M-M.*

βασιλικός, ή, όν (Aeschyl., Hdt.+; inscr., pap., LXX, Ep. Arist., Philo, Joseph.) *royal* of a king's official robe (Lind. Tempelchronik C 89 τὰν βασιλικὰν στολάν; Esth 8: 15) ἐσθὴς β. *royal robe* (Diod. S. 17, 47, 4 β. ἐσθ.; 17, 116, 2 and 3) Ac 12: 21 (described Jos., Ant. 19, 344). νόμος β. *royal law,* so called prob. not because of its transcending significance (somewhat in the sense of Ps.-Pla., Minos 317c τὸ μὲν ὀρθὸν νόμος ἐστὶ βασιλικός; Epict. 4, 6, 20; Philo, Post. Cai. 101; 102; 4 Macc 14: 2), but because it is given by the king (of the kingdom of God) Js 2: 8 (cf. Dit., Or. 483, 1 ὁ βασ. νόμος; BGU 820, 2; 1074, 15; 1 Esdr 8: 24; 2 Macc 3: 13). χώρα β. (Dit., Or. 221, 41; 68) *the king's country* Ac 12: 20.—The β. J 4: 46, 49 could be a relative of the royal (Herodian) family (Lucian, Dial. Deor. 20, 1; Ps.-Lucian, De Salt. 8; Plut., Mor. 546E). More prob. the ref. is to a royal official; ref. in Hdb. ad loc. Appian, Mithrid. 80 §358 οἱ βασιλικοί are the soldiers of King Mithridates. M-M.*

βασιλίσκος, ου, ὁ (Polyb. 3, 44, 5; Plut., Mor. 1D; Athen. 13, 20 p. 566B; Dit., Or. 200, 18; POxy. 1566, 9) dim. of βασιλεύς *petty king,* v.l. in J 4: 46 and 49.*

βασίλισσα, ης, ἡ (for Attic βασιλίς and βασίλεια [Phryn. p. 225 L.; Moeris 192], first in Alcaeus Comicus [V/IV BC] 6 and X., Oec. 9, 15, later freq., incl. inscr. [Dit., Ind.; Meisterhans³-Schw. 101, 5; ESchweizer, Gramm. d. pergam. Inschr. 1898, 140; ENachmanson, Laute u. Formen d. magnet. Inschr. '03, 121]; pap. [Mayser 214; 222; 255]; APF 2, '03, 541; 6, '20, 453; LXX; Ep. Arist. 41; Philo, Congr. Erud. Gr. 45; Jos., Bell. 1, 76, Ant. 11, 190 al.) queen Mt 12: 42; Lk 11: 31; Ac 8: 27; Rv 18: 7. M-M.*

βάσις, εως, ἡ (Aeschyl.+; inscr.; pap. [PGM 7, 517]; LXX, Ep. Arist., Philo, Joseph.; Sib. Or. 5, 54; loanw. in rabb.) the (human) foot (so since Pla., Tim. 92A; medical use in Hobart 34f; Philo, Op. M. 118 διτταὶ χεῖρες διτταὶ βάσεις, Post. Cai. 3; Jos., Ant. 7, 113; 303 [w. χεῖρες]; Wsd 13: 18) αἱ β. Ac 3: 7. M-M.*

βασκαίνω 1 aor. ἐβάσκανα, Bl-D. §72 (Aristot.+; LXX).
    1. bewitch, as with the 'evil eye' τινά someone (Aristot., Probl. 34, 20 p. 926b, 24 με; Diod. S. 4, 6, 4; Alex. Aphr., Probl. 2, 53 παῖδας; Dt 28: 56) Gal 3: 1 (one can ward off β. by spitting 3 times: Theocr. 6, 39; s. ἐκπτύω Gal 4: 14).
    2. envy (Demosth. 20, 24; Theocr. 5, 13; Jos., Vi. 425, C. Ap. 1, 72) τινά somebody (Demosth. 8, 19; Dt 28: 54, 56; Sir 14: 6, 8) IRo 3: 1. M-M. B. 1495 (Lat. fascinum).*

βασκανία, ας, ἡ (Pla., Demosth.+) envy (Dio Chrys. 28[45], 5; Vi. Aesopi W c. 16; 4 Macc 1: 26; 2: 15; Philo; Jos., Ant. 3, 268) IRo 7: 2.*

βάσκανος, ου, ὁ (both noun and adj. Demosth.+; Philo, In Flacc. 29; Jos., Ant. 6, 59; Test. Iss. 3: 3) the envious one (as noun e.g. Demosth. 18, 132; Menand., Per. 279; on a clay figure Sb 6295; Vett. Val. 2, 2; 358, 5; Sir 18: 18; 37: 11; Jos., Bell. 1, 208) w. ἀντίζηλος, πονηρός MPol 17: 1.*

Βάσσος, ου, ὁ Bassus, a presbyter in Magnesia IMg 2. The name is not rare in W. Asia Minor (CIG 3112; 3148; 3151; 3493; Inschr. v. Perg. 361; 362 and oft.) and found specif. in Magnesia (Inschr. 122g, 5 Kern; coins ibid. p. xxiv).*

βαστάζω fut. βαστάσω; 1 aor. ἐβάστασα (Hom.+; pap., LXX, En., Joseph.).
    1. take up (Jos., Ant. 7, 284 β. τ. μάχαιραν ἀπὸ τ. γῆς) stones J 10: 31.
    2. carry, bear—a. lit., a burden Hs 9, 2, 4; a jar of water Mk 14: 13; Lk 22: 10; a coffin 7: 14, cf. 1 Cl 25: 3; stones Hs 9, 4f; 9, 4, 1; 3; 9, 6, 7; support: πύργον 9, 4, 2; κόσμον 9, 14, 5; heaven Hs 9, 2, 5.—The cross J 19: 17 (Charito 4, 2, 7; 4, 3, 10 σταυρὸν ἐβάστασα); φάρμακα εἰς τὰς πυξίδας β. carry drugs in boxes Hv 3, 9, 7; of animals used for riding Rv 17: 7 (cf. Epict. 2, 8, 7). Pass. Hv 3, 8, 2; of persons who are carried Ac 3: 2; 21: 35.—Esp. of pregnant women: ἡ κοιλία ἡ βαστάσασά σε Lk 11: 27.—10: 4; Ro 11: 18; B 7: 14.
    b. fig.—α. of anything burdensome (4 Km 18: 14; Sir 6: 25): a cross (following Jesus in his suffering) Lk 14: 27.—Ac 15: 10; D 6: 2; ἀλλήλων τὰ βάρη βαστάζετε Gal 6: 2; cf. vs. 5.
    β. bear, endure (Epict. 1, 3, 2, Ench. 29, 5; Aesop, Fab. 391 P. misfortune and trouble; PBrem. 9, 9 [Wilcken, Chrest. 415, l. 2] οὐ βαστάζουσι τοσοῦτο τέλεσμα; Job 21: 3 v.l.) the burden and heat of the day Mt 20: 12; κακούς Rv 2: 2; ζυγόν D 6: 3; δύνασθαι β. be able to bear words, of divine mysteries J 16: 12; Hv 1, 3, 3; bear patiently, put up with: weaknesses Ro 15: 1; cf. IPol 1: 2; evil Rv 2: 3; κρίμα bear one's judgment= have to pay the penalty Gal 5: 10.

c. carry, bear, weakened in mng., without the idea of a burden: marks Gal 6: 17 (cf. Dssm. B 265ff [BS 352ff]); β. τὸ ὄνομά μου ἐνώπιον ἐθνῶν Ac 9: 15 (cf. POxy. 1242 I, 17, where Alexandrian pagans and Jews appear before Trajan ἕκαστοι βαστάζοντες τ. ἰδίους θεούς); Hs 8, 10, 3; 9, 28, 5.
    3. carry away, remove (PFay. 122, 6 [c. 100 AD]; Bel 36 Theod.).
    a. a corpse (Jos., Ant. 3, 210; 7, 287) J 20: 15. Of sandals remove Mt 3: 11 (cf. PGM 4, 1058 βαστάξας τὸ στεφάνιον ἀπὸ τ. κεφαλῆς; NKrieger, Barfuss Busse Tun, Nov Test 1, '56, 227f). Of disease remove (Galen, De Compos. Medic. Per. Gen. 2, 14, citing a 1st cent. physician, ψώρας τε θεραπεύει καὶ ὑπώπια βαστάζει) Mt 8: 17; IPol 1: 3.
    b. take surreptitiously, pilfer, steal (Polyb. 32, 15, 4; Diog. L. 4, 59; Jos., Ant. 1, 316; 7, 393; PTebt. 330, 7; BGU 46, 10; 157, 8; PFay. 108, 16; POxy. 69, 4) J 12: 6. LRydbeck, Fachprosa, '67, 154-66. M-M. and suppl. B. 707.*

βάτος, ου, ἡ (acc. to Moeris 99 the fem. is Hellenistic, and ὁ βάτος, as in Mk 12: 26, Ex 3: 2-4 [Thackeray 145] and Philo, Mos. 1, 67 is Attic, but Thackeray, PKatz in ZNW 46, '55, 136 with note 8a, and Bl-D.-Funk 49, 1 show that the reverse is true.—Hom.+; Epigr. Gr. 546, 6; 548, 2; LXX) the thorn-bush, of the bush in which Moses saw the vision of God (Ex 3: 2-4; cf. Dt 33: 16; Jos., Ant. 2, 266) Mk 12: 26; ἐπὶ τ. βάτου in the passage about the thorn-bush Lk 20: 37 (ἡ); Ac 7: 30, 35 (ἡ); 1 Cl 17: 5 (ἡ). Symbol of unfruitfulness Lk 6: 44 (cf. Job 31: 40). M-M.*

βάτος, ου, ὁ bath (בַּת; cf. 2 Esdr [Ezra] 7: 22; En. 10, 19) a Hebr. liquid measure, acc. to Jos., Ant. 8, 57= 72 sextarii, or betw. 8 and 9 gals. (FHultsch, Griech. u. röm. Metrologie² 1882, 488: 36, 371; OViedebannt, Forschungen z. Metrologie d. Altertums '17, 127ff: 32, 61) Lk 16: 6. M-M.*

βάτραχος, ου, ὁ (Batr., Hdt.+; PGM 36, 324; 326; LXX; Philo; Jos., Ant. 2, 296) frog. As the form in which unclean spirits appeared Rv 16: 13 (Artem. 2, 15 βάτραχοι ἄνδρας γόητας προσαγορεύουσι).—FXSteinmetzer, D. Froschsymbol in Offb. 16: BZ 10, '12, 252-60. M-M.*

βατταλογέω (βαττολογέω v.l.; s. Rdm. 44; Mlt.-H. 272) 1 aor. subj. βατταλογήσω babble, speak without thinking (explained by πολυλογία) Mt 6: 7; Lk 11: 2 D. Except for writers dependent on the NT the word has been found only in Vi. Aesopi W c. 109, where Perry notes the v.l. βατολογέω for βαττολογέω (it is missing in the corresp. place ed. Eberhard I c. 26 p. 289, 9. But Vi. Aesopi I c. 50 P. has the substantive βαττολογία=foolish talk, though in a different context), and in Simplicius (c. 530 AD), Comm. in Epict. p. 91, 23 in the spelling βαττολογέω= 'prate'. It is perh. a hybrid form, rendering Aram. אמר בטלא='talk idly' (Bl-D. §40 app.). Differently FBussby, ET 76, '64, 26. M-M.*

βδέλυγμα, ατος, τό (Aesop, Fab. 452 P. τοσοῦτον βδέλυγμα, τοσοῦτον μίασμα; oft. LXX; Test. Reub. 3: 12; Suidas.—βδελυγμία as early as Cratinus: Phryn., Praep. Soph. p. 54, 4 Borries ['11]; X., Mem. 3, 11, 13) abomination, detestable thing.
    1. lit., anything that must not be brought before God because it arouses his wrath B 2: 5 (Is 1: 13). β. ἐνώπιον τοῦ θεοῦ detestable in the sight of God (cf. Pr 11: 1) Lk 16: 15.
    2. as in the OT (e.g. Dt 29: 16; 3 Km 11: 6, 33; 4 Km 23:

13; 2 Ch 28: 3) of everything connected w. idolatry: (w. ἀκάθαρτα; cf. Pr 17: 15) Rv 17: 4f. ποιεῖν β. καὶ ψεῦδος *practice abomination and deceit* 21: 27.

3. The expr. τὸ β. τῆς ἐρημώσεως Mt 24: 15; Mk 13: 14 (τὸ β. ἑστηκότα is a 'constructio ad sensum' [cf. ἑστός Mt 24: 15], as Appian, Bell. Civ. 4, 48 §205 τὸ γύναιον ... φέρουσα) is taken fr. Da (9: 27; 11: 31; 12: 11), whence 1 Macc (1: 54) had also taken it; β. τ. ἐρ. (cf. the similar gen. β. ἀνομίας Sir 49: 2) is prob. *the detestable thing causing the desolation of the holy place*; some interpret it as denoting the Antichrist.—GHölscher, ThBl 12, '33, 193ff; ELohmeyer, Mk 275ff; Dodd 23 and Journal of Roman Studies 37, '47, 47ff; FBusch, Z. Verständnis d. synopt. Eschatologie: Mk 13 neu untersucht '38; WGKümmel, Verheissung ²'53; RPesch, Naherwartungen: Tradition u. Redaktion in Mk 13 (Diss. Freiburg im Br.) '68; GRBeasley-Murray, A Commentary on Mk 13, '57, 59–72. For Mk 13 see also s.v. σημεῖον. M-M.*

βδελυκτός, ή, όν (Aretaeus p. 84, 21; schol. on Lucian p. 81, 25 Rabe; Syntipas p. 126, 8; Hesychius; 2 Macc 1: 27; Philo, Spec. Leg. 1, 323) *abominable, detestable.*
1. of pers. (w. ἀπειθής) Tit 1: 16 (cf. Pr 17: 15; Sir 41: 5 v.l.).—2. impers. (Test. Gad 3: 2) of divisions 1 Cl 2: 6; of lusts and pride 30: 1.*

βδελύσσομαι (Hippocr., Aristoph.+ [Nägeli 15; Anz 305]; Maspéro 353, 16; LXX; Pel.-Leg. p. 9, 9) *abhor, detest* τὶ *someth.* (cf. Phalaris, Ep. 141, 2; Eratosth. p. 17, 10; Polyb. 33, 18, 10; Jos., Bell. 6, 172, Ant. 14, 45; Gen 26: 29; Lev 11: 11, 13 al.; CPJ I 141, 9 of hatred for Jews): idols Ro 2: 22. The perf. pass. ptc. ἐβδελυγμένος (cf. Lev 18: 30; Pr 8: 7; Job 15: 16; 3 Macc 6: 9)=βδελυκτός (w. δειλός, ἄπιστος) *abominable* Rv 21: 8. M-M.*

βέβαιος, α, ον (Aeschyl., Hdt.+; inscr., pap., rare in LXX, freq. in Philo; Jos., Ant. 13, 187; 14, 398) *firm, permanent.*
1. lit. of a root *strong* ῥίζα τῆς πίστεως Pol 1: 2. Of an anchor (w. ἀσφαλής) *secure* Hb 6: 19.
2. fig. *reliable, dependable, certain* of πίστις (Appian, Liby. 64 §284 πίστις ἐστὶ βέβαιος; Diod. S. 2, 29, 4 πιστεύοντες βεβαιότερον=believe quite firmly [in relig. sense]; Simplicius in Epict. p. 110, 37 πίστις βεβαία=firm faith in the immortality of the soul on the basis of a declaration by a μάντις; Esth 3: 13c; 3 Macc 5: 31) 1 Cl 1: 2; of hope (cf. Dionys. Hal. 6, 51; Plut., Ant. 3, 7; 4 Macc 17: 4) 2 Cor 1: 7; promise Ro 4: 16; confidence Hb 3: 6. Of the eucharist *dependable* in its effect, or *valid* ISm 8: 1. Of love *steadfast* MPol 1: 2. ἀρχὴν τῆς ὑποστάσεως βεβαίαν κατέχειν *hold firm the original confidence* Hb 3: 14. ὁ λόγος ἐγένετο βέβαιος (on λόγος β. cf. Pla., Phaedo 90c λόγος β. καὶ ἀληθής) *the word was valid* 2: 2 (β. of the Mosaic law as Philo, Mos. 2, 14). ἔχομεν βεβαιότερον (for superl.; cf. Stob., Flor. IV 625, 2 βεβαιοτέραν ἔχε τ. φιλίαν πρὸς τ. γονεῖς) τὸν προφητικὸν λόγον *we possess the prophetic word as something altogether reliable* 2 Pt 1: 19 (on β. ἔχειν cf. Thu. 1, 32; Appian, Bell. Civ. 5, 19 §78 ἔχειν τι βέβαιον=have a firm hold on something; UPZ 162 II, 10 [117 BC]). Of a last will and testament *valid* (legal t.t., cf. JBehm, Διαθήκη '12, p. 87, 4) Hb 9: 17. βεβαίαν τὴν κλῆσιν ποιεῖσθαι *confirm the call* i.e., so that it does not lapse (cf. Ael. Aristid. 13 p. 250 D.; βεβ. ἐλευθερία) 2 Pt 1: 10; (w. ἰσχυρός, τεθεμελιωμένος) Hv 3, 4, 3; β. εἶναι *stand firm* IRo 3: 1; (w. ἀσφαλής) ISm 8: 2. ἐπὶ τὸν τῆς πίστεως βέβαιον δρόμον καταντῆσαι *in steadfastness finish the course of faith* 1 Cl 6: 2. Of the church *well-established, dependable* (Appian, Iber. 37 §150 ἀνὴρ β., Bell. Civ. 2, 13 §47 a servant) 47: 6. M-M. B. 1237.*

βεβαιόω fut. βεβαιώσω; 1 aor. ἐβεβαίωσα, pass. ἐβεβαιώθην (Thu.+; inscr., pap., rare in LXX; Philo, Op. M. 99; Jos., Ant. 1, 273; 17, 42; 20, 28) *make firm, establish* w. acc.
1. of things τὸν λόγον *confirm the preaching* Mk 16: 20 (Ael. Aristid. 25, 64 K.=43 p. 821 D., τὸν λόγον; Sextus 177 τ. λόγους. Cf. Epict. 2, 18, 32 τότε βεβαιώσεις τὸ τοῦ Ἡσιόδου ὅτι ἀληθές ἐστιν). τὰς ἐπαγγελίας *prove the promises reliable, fulfill* (them) Ro 15: 8 (cf. Polyb. 3, 111, 10 βεβαιώσειν ἡμῖν πέπεισμαι τὰς ἐπαγγελίας; Diod. S. 1, 5, 3; Inschr. v. Priene 123, 9 ἐβεβαίωσεν τὴν ἐπαγγελίαν). Of faith ταῦτα πάντα βεβαιοῖ 1 Cl 22: 1.—Pass. τὸ μαρτύριον τοῦ Χριστοῦ ἐβεβαιώθη ἐν ὑμῖν *the testimony of Christ was confirmed in you* 1 Cor 1: 6. (ἡ σωτηρία) εἰς ἡμᾶς ἐβεβαιώθη *the saving message was guaranteed to us* Hb 2: 3 (cf. Ael. Aristid. 46 p. 288 D.: σωτηρίαν β. τινί; POxy. 1119, 17; β. is also legal t.t. to designate properly guaranteed security: PFay. 92, 19; POxy. 899; 1036; cf. Dssm., B 100ff [BS 104ff]). Of hearts: *make firm, strengthen* Hb 13: 9.
2. of pers. (cf. Ps 40: 13; 118: 28) *establish, strengthen* ὁ βεβαιῶν ἡμᾶς εἰς Χριστόν *he who strengthens us in Christ*=makes us faithful disciples 2 Cor 1: 21 (EDinkler, OCullmann-Festschr., '62, 177–80: baptismal terminology). ὃς καὶ βεβαιώσει ὑμᾶς ἀνεγκλήτους *who will strengthen you, so that you are blameless* 1 Cor 1: 8. Pass. *be confirmed* in faith Col 2: 7; in the doctrines IMg 13: 1. M-M.*

βεβαίως adv. (Aeschyl., Thu.+; Lev 25: 30; 3 Macc 5: 42; Philo; Jos., C. Ap. 2, 221) *surely, certainly* (w. ἀληθῶς) πράττεσθαι IMg 11; (w. ἀκριβῶς; cf. Jos., C. Ap. 1, 15) *dependably* (PGM 7, 710; 836) διδάσκειν Pol 3: 2. συναθροίζεσθαι *hold meetings in definite order* i.e., regularly IMg 4.*

βεβαίωσις, εως, ἡ (Thu.+; pap., LXX, Philo) *confirmation*: τοῦ εὐαγγελίου *confirmation, establishment of the gospel* Phil 1: 7; εἰς β. ὁ ὅρκος *an oath serves as confirmation* (Philo, Abr. 273 ἡ δι' ὅρκου β.) Hb 6: 16. The last passage esp. reminds us that β. is a legal t.t. for *guaranteeing, furnishing security* (PPar. 62 II, 8 [II BC] εἰς τ. βεβαίωσιν. Cf. Lev 25: 23; Wsd 6: 18). Dssm., B 100ff [BS 104ff]; NB 56 [BS 230]; LMitteis, Grundzüge d. Pap.-Kunde '12, 188ff; Preisigke, Fachwörter. M-M.*

βεβαιωσύνη, ης, ἡ *confirming, strengthening* στηρίζειν ἐν β. *establish through strengthening* IPhld inscr.*

βεβαμμένος s. βάπτω.

βέβηλος, ον (Aeschyl., Thu.+; Dit., Syll.³ 22, 25; LXX; Philo; Joseph.) *accessible to everyone, profane, unhallowed,* in NT not in a ritualistic sense (Polyaenus 5, 2, 19 ['profane' in contrast to the temple vessels]; LXX; Philo, Mos. 2, 158, Leg. All. 1, 62; Jos., Bell. 6, 271, Ant. 15, 90), but as an ethical and relig. term.
1. of things οἱ β. καὶ γραώδεις μῦθοι *worldly old wives' tales* 1 Ti 4: 7. κενοφωνίαι *profane and empty talk* (cf. 3 Macc 4: 16) 6: 20; 2 Ti 2: 16.
2. of pers. (Ael. Aristid. 17, 18 K.=15 p. 380 D.; 3 Macc 2: 14 al.) *godless* (w. ἀνόσιος, as 3 Macc 2: 2) 1 Ti 1: 9; *irreligious* (w. πόρνος; cf. Philo, Spec. Leg. 1, 102) Hb 12: 16. M-M.*

βεβηλόω 1 aor. ἐβεβήλωσα (Heliod. 2, 25; 10, 36; oft. LXX; Test. 12 Patr.; Hesychius; Suidas) *desecrate, profane* the Sabbath (2 Esdr 23 [Neh 13]: 17; Ezk 20: 13; 1 Macc 1: 43, 45 al. Opp. φυλάσσειν τ. σαββ. Is 56: 2) Mt 12: 5; the sanctuary (Ezk 28: 18; 2 Macc 8: 2) Ac 24: 6; God's name (Lev 18: 21; 21: 6 al.) Hs 8, 6, 2.*

βέβληκα s. βάλλω.

βέβρωκα s. βιβρώσκω.

Βεεζεβούλ, ὁ indecl. (v.l. Βεελζεβούβ and Βεελζεβούλ W-S. §5, 31, cf. 27 n. 56) *Beelzebub*, orig. a Philistine deity; the name זְבוּב בַּעַל means *Baal* (lord) *of flies* (4 Km 1: 2, 6; Sym. transcribes Βεελζεβούβ; Vulgate Beelzebub). Whether זְבוּל בַּעַל (= lord of filth?) represents an intentional change or merely careless pronunciation cannot be determined w. certainty. For various other derivations from Ugaritic and various periods of Hebrew, including the Dead Sea Scrolls, see THGaster, Interpreter's Dict. of the Bible, '62, s.v. 'Beelzebul'. In NT B. is prince of the demons (ἄρχων τῶν δαιμονίων Mt 12: 24; Lk 11: 15). Β. ἔχειν *be possessed by the devil himself* Mk 3: 22. Jesus is called B. by his enemies Mt 10: 25; his exorcisms are ascribed to the help of B. Mt 12: 24ff; Lk 11: 15, 18f.—WGrafBaudissin, RE II 514ff; EKautzsch, Gramm. d. bibl. Aram. 1884, 9; PJensen, D. Gilgameschepos I '06, 644; WEMAitken, Beelzebul: JBL 31, '12, 34–53; HBauer, D. Gottheiten von Ras Schamra: ZAW 51, '33, 89; LGaston, Beelzebul, ThZ 18, '62, 247–55.*

Βελιάρ, ὁ indecl. *Belial* (also Βελιάλ = בְּלִיַעַל 'worthlessness'; on the interchange of λ and ρ s. W-S. §5, 27a) name for the devil (e.g. Test. Reub. 2; 4; 6; Jubil. 15, 33; Damaskusschrift 6, 9 al. [ed. LRost=Kl. T. 167, '33]). The Antichrist, too, is given this name (Test. Dan 5; Sib. Or. 2, 167; 3, 63; 73; Ascension of Is 4, 2). Both mngs. are poss. 2 Cor 6: 15 (cf. the 'either-or' Test. Napht. 2).—WBousset, D. Antichrist 1895, 86f; 99ff, Rel.³ 528a (index); WGrafBaudissin, RE II 548f; MFriedlaender, D. Antichrist '01, 118ff; RHCharles, Rev. of St. John '20 II 76ff. On B. in the OT: PJoüon, Biblica 5, '24, 178–83; JEHogg, Am. Journ. of Sem. Lang. 44, '28, 56–61.— HWHuppenbauer, ThZ 15, '59, 81–89 (Qumran texts); DWThomas in RPCasey memorial vol. '63, 11–19; Pvon der Osten-Sacken, Gott u. Belial, '69.*

βελόνη, ης, ἡ (Aristoph.+; Batr. 130; Memnon [I BC/I AD] no. 434 fgm. 1, 4, 7 Jac.; Maximus Tyr. 29, 4a; PGM 7, 442; 36, 237; cf. HJCadbury, JBL 52, '33, 59f) *needle* τρῆμα β. *eye of a needle* Lk 18: 25. There is no good evidence that this is fig. language for a narrow gate; s. HDB s.v. 'needle's eye', and Exp., 1st ser. 3, 1876, 373–9. M-M. B. 412.*

βέλος, ους, τό (Hom.+; inscr., pap., LXX; Jos., Bell. 4, 424f, Ant. 13, 95; Sib. Or. 3, 730; loanw. in rabb.) *arrow* βέλη πεπυρωμένα *flaming arrows* Eph 6: 16 (cf. Ps.-Apollod. 2, 5, 2, 2 De Hercule βάλλων βέλεσι πεπυρωμένοις; Jos., Ant. 1, 203; Ps.-Scylax, Peripl. 95 p. 40 Fabr.: Αἰθίοπες χρῶνται βέλεσι πεπυρακτωμένοις). M-M. B. 1389.*

βελτιόω (Plut., Mor. 85c; Dit., Syll.³ 888, 5; PLond. 1044, 22 al.; pap.; Philo, Det. Pot. Ins. 56, Sacr. Abel. 42) *improve*, pass. *become better* of the soul (cf. Philo, Dec. 17) Dg 6: 9.*

βελτίων, ον (Soph., Thu.+; inscr., pap., LXX, Philo [Leiseg. on ἀγαθός p. 50]) comp. of ἀγαθός *better* ὁδός Hv 3, 7, 1; βελτίω ποιεῖν *make better* (Jer 33: 13; 42: 15) 1 Cl 19: 1. βελτίω γενέσθαι (Cebes 33, 4; 5) Dg 1. W. gen. foll. β. τινός *better than someone* (Is 17: 3; Sir 30: 16; Jos., Ant. 18, 268) Hv 3, 4, 3.—Neut. βέλτιόν ἐστιν w. inf. foll. (POxy. 1148, 2; Num 14: 3) 2 Cl 6: 6; Hs 1: 9. As adv. βέλτιον γινώσκειν *know very well* (Bl-D. §244; Rob. 665) 2 Ti 1: 18; cf. Ac 10: 28 D. M-M.*

Βενιαμ(ε)ίν, ὁ indecl. (בִּנְיָמִין.—LXX; Philo; Test. 12

Patr. On spelling Bl-D. §38 app.—In Joseph. Βενιαμ(ε)ίς, gen. εῖ [Ant. 2, 122]) *Benjamin*, Jewish tribe (K-DSchunck, Benjamin. Untersuchungen zur Entstehung u. Gesch. eines israel. Stammes '63) Ac 13: 21; Ro 11: 1; Phil 3: 5; Rv 7: 8.*

Βερνίκη, ης, ἡ (colloq. abbreviation CIA III 2618; PPetr. III 1 II, 7; PTebt. 407, 14 for Βερενίκη Polyaenus 8, 50; Dit., Or. 263, 1 and 2; 717, 6; Sb 307; 438; s. also Preisigke, Namenbuch) *Bernice*, daughter of Agrippa I and sister of Agrippa II, b. 28, d. after 79 AD. She lived in marital relations w. various men, incl. her brother Agrippa. Both visited Festus in Caesarea Ac 25: 13, 23; 26: 30. Chief sources: Joseph., Index Niese; Tacit., Hist. 2, 2; 81; Sueton., Tit. 7; Juvenal, Sat. 6, 156–60; Dit., Or. 428.— Schürer I⁴ 559; 564; 589–97; 601; 723; Wilcken, Pauly-W. III 287ff; MWahl, De Regina Berenice 1893. M-M.*

Βέροια, ας, ἡ (Thu. 1, 61, 4; Ptolem. 3, 12, 36; Strabo 7, fgm. 26 p. 330; Ps.-Lucian, Asin. 34; inscr.) *Beroea*, very old city in Macedonia on the river Astraeus in the province of Emathia at the foot of Mt. Bermius. Paul preached there on his journey fr. Thessalonica to Achaia Ac 17: 10, 13.—HKiepert, Lehrb. d. alten Geogr. 1878, §278; JWeiss, RE XII 41, 5ff.*

Βεροιαῖος, α, ον *from Beroea*, subst. *the Beroean* (Dit., Syll.³ 636, 6f; ²848, 2) of Sopater, a companion of Paul Ac 20: 4.*

Βεώρ, ὁ indecl. (בְּעוֹר) *Beor*, father of Balaam (Num 22: 5; 31: 8; Dt 23: 5) 2 Pt 2: 15 (v.l. Βοσόρ; cf. BWeiss, TU VIII 3, 1892, 74).*

Βηθαβαρά, ἡ (Origen declines it) *Bethabara*; Orig. (Comm. in Io. VI 40, 204 Pr.) prefers this reading in J 1: 28, though attested by fewer witnesses (KΨ 33; Syr., Sin. Cur.), to Βηθανία, found in Heracleon and most contemporary mss.; he could find no place called Bethany along the Jordan. S. Βηθανία 2.*

Βηθανία, ας, ἡ also indecl. Βηθανιά as v.l. Mt 21: 17; Mk 11: 1; Lk 19: 29 (acc. to the Onomastica בֵּית עֲנָיָה) *Bethany*.
1. village on the Mt. of Olives, 15 stades=2.775 km. or nearly 2 mi. fr. Jerusalem. Acc. to J 11: 1, 18; 12: 1 home of Mary, Martha, and Lazarus; acc. to Mt 26: 6; Mk 14: 3 home of Simon the leper. Last station on the pilgrim road fr. Jericho to Jerusalem Mk 11: 1; Lk 19: 29, used by Jesus for lodging Mt 21: 17; Mk 11: 11f. Cf. 8: 22 v.l. Place of the ascension Lk 24: 50.—HVincent, RB n.s. 11, '14, 438ff; CKopp, Holy Places of the Gospels, '63, 278–81.
2. place on the east side of the Jordan where John baptized J 1: 28.—FFenner, D. Ortslage v. Bethanien '06; ThZahn, NKZ 18, '07, 265–94; ESchwartz, NGG '08, 520f; Dalman, Orte' Index; KErbes, D. Tauforte des Joh. nebst d. Salem des Melchisedek: Theol. Arb. aus d. Rhein. wiss. Predigerverein, n.F. 24, '28, 71–106; DBuzy, Rech de Sc rel 21, '31, 444–62; PParker, JBL 74, '55, 257–61; Kopp (s. above), 113–29. On the rdg. Βηθαβαρά s. that word.*

Βηθαραβά error for Βηθαβαρά, q.v.

Βηθεσδά, ἡ indecl. (חִסְדָּא בֵּית house of mercy?) *Bethesda*, name of a pool in Jerusalem J 5: 2 v.l. The newer editions have Βηθζαθά (q.v.) in the text; another v.l. is Βηθσαϊδά. Cf. W-S. §5, 27g; Hdb. ad loc.—S. HVincent: Vincent-Abel, Jérusalem II, '26, Sect. XXVIII Sainte Anne et ses sanctuaires; JoachJeremias, ZNW 31, '32, 308–12, Die Wiederentdeckung von Bethesda '49 (the double pool of St. Anna), Eng. transl., The Rediscovery of Bethesda '66; CPronobis, Bethesda z. Zt. Jesu: ThQ 114,

'33, 181–207. Perh. בֵּית אֶשְׁדָּה 'place of outpouring', cf. the dual form in 3 Q 15, 11, 12, JTMilik, Discoveries in the Judaean Desert of Jordan III, '62, 271f, 297; EJVardaman, Bibl. Translator 14, '63, 27-29; DJWieand, NTS 12, '66, 392-404.*

Βηθζαθά, ἡ indecl. *Bethzatha* J 5: 2, in the text, foll. א L Old Lat.; Euseb., Onom. 58, 21 (D Βελζεθα); s. Βηθεσδά. Acc. to 1 Macc 7: 19 and Jos., Bell. 2, 328; 530; 5, 149; 151; 246 Bethz. is the name of the northern extension of the city, which may give a hint as to the location of the pool.—HVincent and FMAbel, Jérusalem I '12, 685ff; GDalman, Jerus. u. s. Gelände '30. On the name s. FCBurkitt. The Syriac Forms of NT Proper Names '12, 20f.*

Βηθλέεμ, ἡ indecl. (בֵּית לֶחֶם house of bread; LXX; Test. Reub. 3: 13. In Joseph. Βήθλεμα, Βηθλέεμα [Ant. 5, 323], ων [5, 136] and Βηθλ[ε]έμη, ης [7, 312]) *Bethlehem,* a town in Judaea, 7 km. or c. 4½ mi. south of Jerusalem, the home of David (1 Km 17: 12; 20: 6=Jos., Ant. 6, 227), hence the birthplace of the Messiah: Mt 2: 1, 5f (Mi 5: 1), 8, 16; Lk 2: 4, 15; J 7: 42. Cf. Baedeker⁷ '10, 94ff; ThZahn, D. Geburtsstätte in Gesch., Sage u. bildender Kunst: NKZ 32, '21, 669ff; Dalman, Orte³ 1ff; WFoerster, ZDPV 57, '34, 1-7; CKopp, Holy Places of the Gospels, '63, 1-47.*

Βηθσαϊδά(ν), ἡ indecl. (בֵּית צֵידָא) *Bethsaida.*

1. place north of Lake Gennesaret (Jos., Ant. 18, 28), east of the Jordan, near where it empties into the lake. Acc. to J 1: 44; 12: 21 home of Philip, Andrew, and Peter. Mt 11: 21; Mk 6: 45; 8: 22; Lk 9: 10; 10: 13 (Βηθσαϊδά 𝔓⁷⁵). To distinguish it from another B. located farther west, B. τῆς Γαλιλαίας (J 12: 21), is a problem not yet solved.—Schürer II⁴ 208f (sources and lit.). Dalman, Orte³ 173ff; CCMcCown, The Problem of the Site of Beths.: Journ. of the Palest. Orient. Soc. 10, '30, 32-58; LVaganay, Mk 6: 45: RB 49, '40, 5-32; PVannutelli, Synoptica '40 III-VIII. CKopp, Dominican Studies 3, '50, 11-40. S. on Καφαρναούμ.—2. J 5: 2 𝔓⁷⁵ et al. (s. Βηθεσδά).*

Βηθφαγή, ἡ indecl. (בֵּית פַּגֵּי house of unripe figs; in Talmud a place בית פאני near Jerusalem: Dalman, Gramm.² 191) *Bethphage,* place on Mt. of Olives (Euseb., Onomast. 58 Kl.) Mt 21: 1; Mk 11: 1; Lk 19: 29.—Billerb. I 839f; Dalman, Orte³ 244ff; ILöw, Bethphagé: Rev. des Études juives 62, '11, 232-5; CKopp, Holy Places of the Gospels, '63, 267-77.*

βῆμα, ατος, τό (Hom. Hymns, Pind.+; inscr., pap., LXX, Joseph.).—**1.** *step, stride* οὐδὲ β. ποδός *not even a foot of ground* Ac 7: 5 (cf. Dt 2: 5).

2. *tribunal* (Thu. 2, 34, 8; Epict. 4, 10, 21; Jos., Bell. 2, 172; 2 Esdr 18 [Neh 8]: 4; 2 Macc 13: 26), esp. *judicial bench* (Isocr., Ep. 8, 7; Ps.-Demosth. 48, 31; POxy. 237 V, 13; PTebt. 316, 11; PAmh. 80, 7 al. S. καθίζω 2aα and cf. Reisch in Pauly-W. III 264; Preisigke, Fachwörter) Mt 27: 19; J 19: 13; Ac 18: 12, 16f; 25: 6, 10, 17; also the judgment seat of God (Sib. Or. 2, 218) and Christ Ro 14: 10 (text and v.l.); 2 Cor 5: 10; Pol 6: 2.—Ac 12: 21, 23 D of the throne-like *speaker's platform* (Appian, Liby. 115 §546; Arrian, Anab. 7, 8, 3; 7, 11, 1; Jos., Ant. 4, 209; 7, 370) of Herod Agrippa I. In mng. 2 בֵּימָה is a loanw. in rabb. M-M.*

βήρυλλος, ου, ὁ, ἡ (Strabo 16, 4, 20; Dionys. Periegeta [II AD] 1012; PHolm. 8, 10; Tob 13: 17 BA; Jos., Bell. 5, 234, Ant. 3, 168.—βηρύλλιον Ex 28: 20 al.; Ezk 28: 13) *beryl,* precious stone of sea-green color (Cyranides p. 12, 9

λευκὸς λίθος) Rv 21: 20 (cf. Plin., H.N. 37, 20; 38, 5).—Lit. on ἀμέθυστος.*

βία, ας, ἡ (Hom.+; inscr., pap., LXX; Ep. Arist. 148; Philo, Joseph.; loanw. in rabb.).

1. *force, violence*—**a.** of natural forces (Dio Chrys. 17[34], 33 β. τῆς θαλάττης; PPetr. II 37 IIa, 6 ἡ βία τοῦ ὕδατος; Wsd 4: 4 ὑπὸ βίας ἀνέμων) ὑπὸ τῆς β. (τῶν κυμάτων: explanatory addition of v.l.) Ac 27: 41.

b. of the force of a mob pressing forward διὰ τὴν β. τοῦ ὄχλου 21: 35.

2. *the use of force* (Jos., Vi. 303) μετὰ βίας (Isocr. 10, 59; Plut., Mor. 96D; Dit., Syll.³ 705, 41; 780, 33; PTebt. 5, 57; Ex 1: 14; Test. Jos. 8: 2) Ac 5: 26; cf. 24: 7 t.r.; *compulsion:* β. οὐ πρόσεστι τῷ θεῷ (s. πρόσειμι I) Dg 7: 4. M-M.*

βιάζω (Hom.+; inscr., pap., LXX, En., Philo, Joseph.; Test. Reub. 5: 4) nearly always as a mid. dep. βιάζομαι *apply force.*

1. trans. *inflict violence on* w. acc. (Herodas 2, 71; Menand., Dyscolus 253; 271; Appian, Bell. Civ. 5, 35 §139; PAmh. 35, 17 [213 BC] βιασάμενος αὐτούς; PGiess. 19, 13; LGötzeler, Quaestiones in Appiani et Polybii dicendi genus 1890, 63; Esth 7: 8; En. 103, 14; 104, 3) lit. τοὺς ὑποδεεστέρους *the poor people* Dg 10: 5.

2. intr.—**a.** *use force, violence* (X., Mem. 3, 9, 10; Diod. S. 4, 12, 5 οἱ βιαζόμενοι=the ones who use force, the intruders; Plut., Mor. 203c; Epict. 3, 24, 69; 4, 8, 40; Lucian, Necyom. 20, Hermot. 22; Dit., Syll.³ 1142, 8 [Dssm., NB 85f (BS 258)]; 888, 24; 1243, 4f; PTebt. 6, 31; PFlor. 382, 54; Dt 22: 25, 28; Philo, Mos. 1, 215; Jos., Bell. 3, 493; 518) οὐ βιαζόμενος *without using force* Dg 7: 4.

b. also in a good sense=*try hard* (to enter) (Epict. 4, 7, 20f; this sense is debatable in this passage; see FWDanker, JBL 77, '58, 234-36).—**c.** *force a way for oneself* Demosth. 55, 17; Appian, Hann. 24 §106).

d. w. εἴς τι *enter forcibly into someth.* (Thu. 1, 63, 1; 7, 69, 4; Polyb. 1, 74, 5; Plut., Otho 12, 10; Philo, Mos. 1, 108 εἰς τἀντὸς βιάζεται; Jos., Bell. 3, 423) πᾶς εἰς τὴν βασιλείαν βιάζεται *everyone enters* (or *tries to enter) the kingdom* w. violence Lk 16: 16. If, however, βιάζεται is to be understood as a passive, as POxy. II, 294, 16 (22 AD), or in the same sense as the mid. in Gen 33: 11; Judg 13: 15, the sense would be *invite urgently,* of the 'genteel constraint imposed on a reluctant guest' (so vHoffmann et al.; cf. FDibelius [s. 1b below]). Cf. the sense of Lk 14:23 and s. FWDanker, JBL 77, '58, 231-43.—The mng. of the parallel pass. Mt 11: 12 ἡ βασιλεία τ. οὐρανῶν βιάζεται is equally not clear. There are these two possibilities:

1. trans. pass.—**a.** in a bad sense *be violently treated, be oppressed* (so the pass. e.g. Thu. 1, 77, 4; Paus. 2, 1, 5 τὰ θεῖα βιάσασθαι; POxy. 294, 16 [22 AD]; Sir 31: 21.—GSchrenk, TW I 608ff; RSV text) *the kingdom suffers violence.*

α. through hindrances raised against it (βιάζομαι=hinder, check: Synes., Provid. 1, 1 p. 89c of the evil man's power, which strives εἴ πη τὸν θεῖον νόμον βιάσαιτο=(to see) whether it could perhaps 'hinder' the divine law; Jos., Ant. 1, 261) It., Vulg., Syr. Sin. and Cur.; Dalman, Worte 113-16; ALoisy; ASchlatter; MDibelius, Joh. d. T. '11, 26ff: hostile spirits.

β. through the efforts of unauthorized persons to compel its coming BWeiss; JWeiss, D. Predigt Jesu vom R. Gottes² '00, 192ff; Wlh.; HWindisch, D. mess. Krieg '09, 35f; HScholander, ZNW 13, '12, 172-5.

γ. βιά. can also mean *occupy* (a territory) *by force* (Appian, Bell. Civ. 3, 24 §91).

βιάζω—βίος

b. in a good sense= *is sought w. burning zeal* HHoltzmann; FDibelius, StKr 86, '13, 285-8; Schniewind.
2. intr. *makes its way w. triumphant force* FCBaur; ThZahn; AHarnack, SAB '07, 947-57; WBrandt, ZNW 11, '10, 247f; ROtto, Reich Gottes u. Menschensohn '34, 84-8; RSV mg.—EGraesser, D. Problem der Parusieverzögerung, ZNW Beih. 22, '57, 180ff. M-M. and suppl.*

βίαιος, α, ον (Hom.+; inscr., pap., LXX, Philo; Jos., Ant. 14, 43) *violent, forcible.*
1. lit. συναλλάγματα *forcibly exacted agreements* B 3: 3 (Is 58: 6).
2. fig. *violent, strong* of a wind Ac 2: 2 (Aristot., Meteor. 370b, 9; Polyb. 21, 31, 6 ἄνεμος; Diod. S. 17, 106, 6 βιαίου πνεύματος φερομένου; Paus. 10, 17, 11 νότος; Ex 14: 21; Ps 47: 8 πνεῦμα; Philo, Somn. 2, 166 πν.; Jos., Bell. 3, 422 πν.). M-M. and suppl.*

βιαστής, οῦ, ὁ (Aretaeus 4, 12, 12; Eustathius Macrembolita [c. 900 AD] 5, 3, 5 IHilberg [1876]; Philo, Agric. 89 v.l., all three in a bad sense) *violent, impetuous man* Mt 11: 12 (s. βιάζω).*

βιβλαρίδιον, ου, τό dim. of βίβλος (Galen XVI p. 5 K. has βιβλιαρίδιον) *little book* Rv 10: 2, vs. 8 v.l., 9f (cf. Artem. 2, 45 p. 149, 6: ἐσθίειν βιβλία in a dream . . . θάνατον σύντομον προαγορεύει; Hv 2, 1, 3. Of a letter 2, 4, 3. The v.l. βιβλιδάριον (Aristoph. acc. to Pollux 7, 210; Agatharchides [II BC] c. 111 [CMüller, Geographi Gr. Min. I 1855 p. 194]; Cat. Cod. Astr. VIII 3, p. 92, 9) in Rv and Hermas; s. BZ 6, '08, 171.*

βιβλιδάριον s. βιβλαρίδιον.

βιβλίδιον, ου, τό (Demosth. et al., inscr., pap.) dim. of βιβλίον *small book, document,* esp. a petition (Plut., Cim. 12, 4, Caesar 65, 1; BGU 432 II, 3f; POxy. 1032, 4; PTebt. 293, 8, cf. Wilcken, Grundz. XXXI 2; Preisigke, Fachwörter 40) Hv 2, 1, 3f; 2, 4, 1. Of a letter (Polyaenus 7, 33, 1) IEph 20: 1. M-M. s.v. βιβλίον.*

βιβλίον, ου, τό (Hdt., Aristoph.+; inscr., pap., LXX, Philo; Jos., Ant. 10, 218, Vi. 418 βιβλία ἱερά; cf. Preisigke, Fachwörter).
1. *book, scroll* Rv 6: 14 (Is 34: 4); 20: 12; of the scroll of the Law (Synes., Ep. 4 p. 162B and prob. as early as Diod. S. 34+35 fgm. 1, 3 [Hecataeus of Abdera—III BC?] of a stone figure of Moses μετὰ χεῖρας ἔχον βιβλίον) Gal 3: 10 (Vi. Aesopi Ic. 81 τὸ βιβλίον τοῦ τῆς πόλεως νόμου); Hb 9: 19 (Ex 24: 7); of the scroll of a prophet Lk 4: 17, 20; B 12: 9 (Ex 17: 14), cf. Hb 10: 7 (Ps 39: 8); of John's gospel J 20: 30 (Plut., Mor. 189D ταῦτα ἐν τοῖς βιβλίοις γέγραπται); cf. 21: 25. W. μεμβράναι 2 Ti 4: 13. Esp. of apocal. books Rv 1: 11; 5: 1ff (ERussell, Bibliotheca Sacra 115, '58, 258-64 [mancipatio];—σφραγίς 1.—Diod. S. 14, 55, 1 βιβλίον ἐπεσφραγισμένον . . . ἀνοίγειν καὶ ποιεῖν τὰ γεγραμμένα); 10: 8; 22: 7, 9f, 18f; Hv 1, 2, 2; 2, 4, 2. Of holy writings gener. τὰ β. (w. ἀπόστολοι) 2 Cl 14: 2 (cf. AvHarnack, Zentralbl. f. Bibliothekswesen 45, '28, 337-42). Cf. Papias 2: 4. β. τῆς ζωῆς *book of life* Rv 13: 8; 17: 8; 20: 12; 21: 27 (s. βίβλος 2).
2. *document* (Demosth., Ep. 1, 3; Appian, Iber. 41 §167 β. ἐσφραγισμένα; Polyaenus 7, 19 [of an ἐπιστολή]; Jos., C. Ap. 1, 101; later pap.: APF 5, 263; Wilcken, Chrest. 42, 8 [314 AD]) β. ἀποστασίου *certificate of divorce* (Dt 24: 1, 3) which, acc. to the law, a Jew had to give his wife when he dismissed her Mt 19: 7; Mk 10: 4.—S. ἀπολύω 2a.—CCMcCown, Codex and Roll in the NT: HTR 34, '41, 219-50. M-M. and suppl.*

βίβλος, ου, ἡ (Aeschyl., Hdt.+; inscr., pap., LXX; En. 104, 12; Ep. Arist.; Philo, Joseph., Test. 12 Patr.; cf. Preisigke, Fachwörter) *book, later esp. sacred, venerable book* (Pla., Rep. 364E; Lucian, Philops. 12, M. Peregr. 11; Ps.-Lucian, Amor. 44; Celsus 1, 16; PPar. 19, 1; POxy. 470, 24; PGM 3, 424 ἱερὰ βίβλος, 13, 15 Ἑρμῆς ἐν ἑαυτοῦ ἱερᾷ β., lines 131, 342 al.; Ep. Arist. 316; Sib. Or. 3, 425).
1. of a single writing β. Μωϋσέως (1 Esdr 5: 48; 7: 6, 9) Mk 12: 26; β. λόγων (cf. Tob 1: 1) Ἡσαΐου Lk 3: 4; β. ψαλμῶν (subscription of Psalter in Sahidic version: ARahlfs, Psalmi cum Odis '31, 340) 20: 42; Ac 1: 20. Gener. β. τῶν προφητῶν 7: 42.—Pl. PK 4 p. 15, 30; β. ἱεραί (Diod. S.1, 70, 9; 34+35 fgm. 1, 4 [in the latter passage of the sacred scriptures of the Jews]; Ael. Aristid. 45, 29 K.=8 p. 95 D.; Dit., Or. 56, 70; 2 Macc 8: 23; Philo; Jos., Ant. 2, 347; 3, 81; 105.—Sg. in PGM s. above) 1 Cl 43: 1. Of books of magic (Ps.-Phoc. 149; PGM 13, 739; cf. Field, Notes 129.—So βιβλία in Celsus 6, 40) Ac 19: 19 (cf. Dssm., Baudissin—Festschr. '17, 121-4). β. γενέσεως Ἰησοῦ X. Mt 1: 1 s. γένεσις 3 and Gdspd., Probs. 9f.—EKrentz, The Extent of Matthew's Prologue, JBL 83, '64, 409-14.
2. esp. β. τῆς ζωῆς *book of life* Phil 4: 3; Rv 3: 5 (cf. Ex 32: 32f); 13: 8 v.l.; 20: 15. Pl. Hv 1, 3, 2. More exactly β. ζώντων 1 Cl 53: 4; Hs 2: 9; judgment will be rendered on the basis of books. Cf. Bousset, Rel.³ 258; BMeissner, Babylonien u. Assyrien II '25, 124ff; LRuhl, De Mortuorum Judicio '03, 68, 101ff; WSattler, ZNW 21, '22, 43-53; LKoep, D. himmlische Buch in Antike u. Christentum, '52. M-M.*

βιβρώσκω pf. βέβρωκα, pass. ptc. βεβρωμένος; 1 aor. pass. ἐβρώθην (Hom.+; pap., LXX; Jos., Bell. 6, 210, Ant. 17, 345) *eat* οἱ βεβρωκότες *those who had eaten* J 6: 13 (thus Aristot. 629b, 9; Polyb. 3, 72, 6). ἐβρώθη ἡ δίαιτα (their) abode was consumed 1 Cl 39: 8 (Job 5: 3). Of sticks *be eaten, gnawed* (Diosc. 3, 9 W. ῥίζα βεβρ.) Hs 8, 1, 6f; 8, 4, 6; 8, 5, 2ff; 8, 6, 4. M-M. B. 327.*

Βιθυνία, ας, ἡ (X.+; inscr.; Philo, Leg. ad Gai. 281; Joseph.) *Bithynia,* province in northern Asia Minor Ac 16: 7; 1 Pt 1: 1; JWeiss, RE X 553f (lit.).*

βίος, ου, ὁ (Hom.+; inscr., pap., LXX, Ep. Arist., Philo, Joseph.) *life in its appearance and manifestations.*
1. of earthly *life* in its functions and its duration (pap., LXX) 2 Cl 1: 6. χρόνος τοῦ βίου *time of life* 1 Pt 4: 3 t.r. εἰσέρχεσθαι εἰς τὸν β. *enter life* Dg 1 (cf. Himerius, Or. [Ecl.] 2, 14 ἔξειμι τοῦ βίου). ἀποτάσσεσθαι τῷ βίῳ *bid farewell to life* IPhld 11: 1; ὁ νῦν β. *the present life* (Ael. Aristid. 30, 20 K.=10 p. 121 D.) 2 Cl 20: 2 and its ἡδοναί *pleasures* (cf. Jos., Ant. 4, 143) Lk 8: 14; IRo 7: 3. Contrasted w. it is a μέλλων β. (Diod. S. 8, 15, 1; Maximus Tyr. 41, 5f) 2 Cl 20: 2 or ἄλλος β. (Sallust. 18 p. 34, 10 ἕτερος β., which brings punishment; Jos., C. Ap. 2, 218 β. ἀμείνων) IEph 9: 2 (ὅλον is cj. without ms. support). αἱ τ. βίου πραγματεῖαι *the affairs of everyday life* 2 Ti 2: 4; ἡσύχιον β. διάγειν 1 Ti 2: 2 (cf. PSI 541 ἵνα εὐσχημονῶν κ. ἀνέγκλητος . . . τὸν βίον ἔχω).
2. of *manner of life, conduct* (Himerius, Or. 41 [=Or. 7], 1 ἥμερος β.; IG VII 396, 15 διενέγκας σεμνόν τε καὶ ἡσύχιον βίον παρ' ὅλον τὸν τῆς ζωῆς αὐτοῦ χρόνον; BGU 372 II, 2 ἀνδράσι πονηρὸν καὶ λῃστρικὸν βίον ποιουμένοις; Wsd 4: 9; 5: 4; 4 Macc 1: 15; 7: 7; 8: 8 Ἑλληνικὸς β.) ἄνομος β. MPol 3. Opp. ἐνάρετος β. 1 Cl 62: 1; β. παράσημον ἀσκεῖν *lead a peculiar life* Dg 5: 2. Pl. of the way of life of several pers. (Diod. S. 3, 34, 8; 3, 35, 1; Strabo 3, 3, 7; Jos., Vi. 256b) 5: 10.

3. (Hes.+; Hdt., X.) *means of subsistence* (UPZ 14, 32 [158 BC]; Pr 31: 14) Dg 5: 4. Specif. *property* (Eur., Suppl. 861 in Diog. L. 7, 22; Diod. S. 12, 40, 3; Vett. Val. Index; Dit., Syll.³ 708, 33; 762, 40; PCairo Preisigke '11, 2, 13; PGM 13, 636 αὔξησόν μου τὸν βίον ἐν πολλοῖς ἀγαθοῖς; SSol 8: 7; 2 Esdr [Ezra] 7: 26; Jos., Ant. 1, 326) Mk 12: 44; Lk 8: 43 v.l.; 15: 12, 30; 21: 4 (Julian, Anth. Pal. 6, 25, 5f: the insignificant gift of poor Cinyres to the nymphs was his ὅλος βίος); β. τοῦ κόσμου *worldly goods* 1 J 3: 17. ἀλαζονεία τοῦ β. 2: 16. M-M. B. 285; 769.*

βιόω 1 aor. inf. βιῶσαι (Bl-D. §75; the form βιῶσαι as early as Aristot., Eth. Nic. 9, 8, 9, also Dionys. Hal. 3, 37, 1; Ps.-Lucian, Macrob. 8; Herm. Wr. 3, 4; Jos., Ant. 1, 152 v.l.) (Hom.+; inscr., pap., LXX; Ep. Arist. 32; 39; Jos., C. Ap. 2, 151) *live* τόν ἐπίλοιπον ἐν σαρκὶ χρόνον *the remaining time in the flesh* 1 Pt 4: 2 (cf. Job 29: 18; 𝔓⁷² reads σῶσαι in 1 Pt 4: 2). M-M.*

Βίτων, ωνος, ὁ (Diod. S. 14, 53, 6) *Bito*, a Roman whose praenomen was Valerius, w. others the bearer of 1 Cl; cf. 65: 1.*

βίωσις, εως, ἡ (Sir Prol. 1. 14; Jew. inscr. in Ramsay, Phrygia II 650 ἐνάρετος β.) *manner of life* Ac 26: 4. M-M.*

βιωτικός, ή, όν (since Aristot., Hist. An. 9, 17 [Lobeck on Phryn. 355]; pap.) *belonging to (daily) life* (so Polyb.+; cf. χρεία β. 'necessities of daily life' Polyb. 4, 73, 8; Diod. S. 2. 29, 5; Philo Bybl. [100 AD] in Euseb., Pr. Ev. 1, 9, 29; Artem. 1, 31; Philo Alex., Mos. 2, 158) μέριμναι β. Lk 21: 34; β. πράξεις Hv 1, 3, 1; β. πράγματα Hv 3, 11, 3; m 5, 2, 2; βάσανοι β. *tortures that befall one during his earthly life* s 6, 3, 4; β. κριτήρια 1 Cor 6: 4 (s. κριτήριον); cf. vs. 3 βιωτικά *ordinary matters* (τά β. in a somewhat different sense Epict. 1, 26, 3; 7; Vett. Val. 286, 14; PRyl. 125, 11; Philo, Omn. Prob. Liber 49; Field, Notes 171). Cf. ERohde, Z. griech. Roman (Kleine Schriften II) '01, 38f; Philostrat., Vi. Soph. 1, 25, 3 mentions quarrels in daily life which, in contrast to grave offenses, are not to be brought to court, but settled at home. M-M.*

βλαβερός, ά, όν (Hom. Hymns, Hes.+; Epict.; Dit., Syll.³ 454, 14; Pr 10: 26; Ep. Arist. 192) *harmful* (w. ἀνόητος) ἐπιθυμίαι 1 Ti 6: 9 (X., Mem. 1, 3, 11 β. ἡδοναί; ἀσυγκρασία β. *harmful lack of community spirit* Hv 3, 9, 4. τρυφαί Hs 6, 5, 5ff. W. dat. of pers. (X., Mem. 1, 5, 3) Hm 6, 1, 3. M-M.*

βλάβη, ης, ἡ (trag., Thu.+; inscr., pap.; Wsd 11: 19; Ep. Arist.; Jos., Ant. 12, 144; 17, 39) *harm* βλάβην οὐ τὴν τυχοῦσαν ... ὑποίσομεν *we shall suffer no ordinary* (=insignificant) *harm* 1 Cl 14: 2. βλάβην παρατιθέναι τινί *cause harm to someone* ITr 5: 1.*

βλάπτω 1 aor. ἔβλαψα, subj. βλάψω; 1 aor. pass. inf. βλαφθῆναι 1 Cl 1: 1 (Hom.+; inscr., pap., LXX, Ep. Arist.; Philo, Aet. M. 37; Joseph.) *harm, injure* τινά *someone* (4 Macc 9: 7; Ep. Arist. 232; Jos., Ant. 14, 355) MPol 10: 2. οὐ μὴ αὐτοὺς βλάψῃ *it will not hurt them* Mk 16: 18. τί *someth.* (Dit., Syll.³ 360, 28; 839, 15; Pr 25: 20a) πνεῦμα 2 Cl 20:4; τὴν σάρκα Hv 3, 10, 7.—W. double acc. (Appian, Hann. 28 §119, Mithrid. 15 §51, Bell. Civ. 2, 131 §550; Jos., Ant. 8, 241) μηδὲν βλάψαν αὐτόν *without doing him any harm* Lk 4: 35. Pass. *be harmed* (Jos., Ant. 3, 193) 1 Cl 1: 1 (here, however, the Gk. tradition has the verb βλασφημέω, q.v. 2bε). M-M. B. 760.*

βλαστάνω (also βλαστάω schol. on Pind., Pyth. 4, 113a; Mk 4: 27; Hs 4: 1f; cf. Bl-D. §101; Rob. 1213. Both forms

in LXX) 1 aor. ἐβλάστησα (Aelian, N.A. 9, 37) *sprout, put forth.*

1. trans. (Hippocr.+; CMG I 1 p. 84, 21; Apollon. Rhod. 1, 1131; Gen 1: 11; Sir 24: 17; Ep. Arist. 230) *produce* ἡ γῆ ἐβλάστησεν τὸν καρπὸν αὐτῆς Js 5: 18 (Philo, Op. M. 47 ἐβλάστησε ἡ γῆ).

2. intr. (Pind.+; Jos., Ant. 3, 176; 17, 215; Jo 2: 22; Sir 39: 13) *bud, sprout* of wheat Mt 13: 26; of seed (Philo, Leg. All. 3, 170 σπαρὲν βλαστάνειν) Mk 4: 27. Of Aaron's sprouting rod Hb 9: 4; cf. 1 Cl 43: 4f (s. Num 17: 23). Of budding trees (opp. ξηρά) Hs 4: 1f. M-M.*

βλαστός, οῦ, ὁ (Hdt.+; pap., LXX; Philo, Op. M. 41) *bud, sprout* of a vine (Strabo 7, 5, 8) βλαστὸς γίνεται *it begins to bud* 1 Cl 23: 4=2 Cl 11: 3. Of the edible shoots (or fruits) of a shrub B 7: 8.*

Βλάστος, ου, ὁ *Blastus* (common name: IG XII 4, 274; 5, 1016; CIA 3052f; CIL VIII 5549f; IX 4547; 5880 al.; BGU 37, 3 [50 AD]), chamberlain of Herod Agrippa I Ac 12: 20. M-M.*

βλασφημέω, impf. ἐβλασφήμουν; 1 aor. ἐβλασφήμησα; 1 aor. pass. ἐβλασφημήθην; 1 fut. βλασφημηθήσομαι (Pla.+; PSI 298, 14; LXX, Philo, Joseph.).

1. in relation to men *injure the reputation of, revile, defame* (Isocr. 10, 45 w. λοιδορεῖν) τινά *someone* (Socrat., Ep. 22, 2; Chio, Ep. 7, 1 ἡμᾶς) μηδένα (Philo, Spec. Leg. 4, 197; Jos., Vi. 232) Tit 3: 2. Pass. Ro 3: 8; 1 Cor 4: 13 v.l.; 10: 30 (ὑπὲρ οὗ=ὑπ. τούτου ὑπ. οὗ); Dg 5: 14. Abs. Ac 13: 45; 18: 6.

2. in relation to a divine being, *blaspheme*—**a.** of heathen gods (Ps.-Pla., Alc. II p. 149c; Diod. S. 2, 21, 7; Philo, Spec. Leg. 1, 53; Jos., Ant. 4, 207; s. bδ below and at the very end of the art.) τὴν θεὸν ἡμῶν Ac 19: 37.

b. of the true God and what pertains to him—**α.** God himself (4 Km 19: 4) τὸν θεόν (cf. Philo, Fuga 84b; Jos., Ant. 4, 202; 6, 183) Rv 16: 11, 21. Abs. (2 Macc 10: 34; 12: 14) Mt 9: 3; 26: 65 (JSKennard, Jr., ZNW 53, '62, 25-51); Mk 2: 7; J 10: 36; Ac 26: 11; 1 Ti 1: 20; 1 Pt 4: 4 (the last 3 passages may be interpr. as not referring exclusively to God). βλασφημίαι, ὅσα ἐὰν βλασφημήσωσιν *whatever blasphemies they utter* Mk 3: 28 (cf. Pla., Leg. 7, p. 800c βλ. βλασφημίαν; Tob 1: 18 S).

β. God's name Ro 2: 24; 2 Cl 13: 2a; ITr 8: 2b (all three Is 52: 5); 1 Ti 6: 1; Rv 13: 6; 16: 9; 2 Cl 13: 1, 2b (quot. of unknown orig.), 4; εἰς τὸ ὄν. τ. θεοῦ Hs 6, 2, 3.

γ. God's Spirit εἰς τὸ πνεῦμα τὸ ἅγιον Mk 3: 29; Lk 12: 10. On blaspheming the Holy Spirit cf. WWeber, ZWTh 52, '10, 320-41; HWindisch, Jesus u. d. Geist in der syn. Überlieferung: Stud. in Early Christianity (Porter-Bacon Festschr.) '28, 218ff; EBuonaiuti, Ricerche Religiose 6, '30, 481-91; OEEvans, ET 68, '57, 240-44; GFitzer, ThZ 13, '57, 161-82; JGWilliams, NTS 12, '65, 75-77; CColpe, JoachJeremias-Festschr., '70, 63-79.

δ. Christ Mt 27: 39; Mk 15: 29; Lk 23: 39; ἕτερα πολλὰ β. 22: 65 (cf. Vett. Val. 67, 20 πολλὰ βλασφημήσει θεούς); τὸν κύριον Hs 8, 6, 4; 8, 8, 2; 9, 19, 3; ISm 5: 2; εἰς τ. κύριον Hv 2, 2, 2; s 6, 2, 4; τὸν βασιλέα μου MPol 9: 3.—The name of Christ Js 2: 7.

ε. things which constitute the significant possessions of Christians τὴν ὁδὸν τ. δικαιοσύνης AP 7: 22; cf. 2 Pt 2: 2. Here and elsewh. pass. ὁ λόγος τ. θεοῦ Tit 2: 5; ὑμῶν τὸ ἀγαθόν Ro 14: 16; τὸ ἐν θεῷ πλῆθος ITr 8: 2a; τὸ ὄνομα ὑμῶν μεγάλως β. 1 Cl 1: 1 (s. βλάπτω); cf.

c. angels δόξας βλ. 2 Pt 2: 10; Jd 8. Angels are also meant in ὅσα οὐκ οἴδασιν β. Jd 10 and ἐν οἷς ἀγνοοῦσιν β. *blaspheming where they have no knowledge* 2 Pt 2: 12 (Bl-D. §152, 1 app.; Rob. 473). S. δόξα 4.—In our lit. β. is used w. the acc. of the pers. or thing (Plut.; Appian [Nägeli 44]; Vett. Val. [s. 2bδ above]; Philo [s. above 1, 2a and bα]; Joseph. [s. above 1, 2a and bα]; 4 Km 19: 22) or w. εἰς and acc. (Demosth. 51, 3; Philo, Mos. 2, 206; Jos., Bell. 2, 406. Specif. εἰς θεούς and sim., Pla., Rep. 2 p. 381ε; Vett. Val. 44, 4; 58, 12; Philo, Fuga 84a; Jos., Ant. 8, 392; Da 3: 96; Bel 8 Theod.). M-M. s.v. -os.*

βλασφημία, ας, ἡ (Eur., Democr., Pla.+; LXX, Joseph., loanw. in rabb.) *slander, defamation, blasphemy.*
1. gener., w. other vices Mk 7: 22; Eph 4: 31; Col 3: 8; πᾶσα β. *all abusive speech* Hm 8: 3; cf. Mt 12: 31a. Pl. (Jos., Vi. 245) Mt 15: 19; 1 Ti 6: 4.
2. specif.—**a.** of evil speech which does not (directly) refer to God.
α. against men (Cleanthes [IV-III BC] in Diog. L. 7, 17, 3; Polyb. 11, 5, 8; Jos., Ant. 3, 307, Vi. 260) β. ἔκ τινος *slander of* (i.e. emanating from) *someone* Rv 2: 9; cf. IEph 10: 2.
β. against the devil κρίσιν βλασφημίας *a reviling judgment* Jd 9 (but cf. Field, Notes 243).
b. against God and what belongs to him (Menand., fgm. 715 Kock ἡ εἰς τὸ θεῖον β.; Ezk 35: 12; 1 Macc 2: 6; 2 Macc 8: 4; 10: 35; 15: 24; Philo, Leg. ad Gai. 368) Mt 26: 65 (OLinton, NTS 7, '61, 258-62); Mk 2: 7 t.r.; 14: 64; Lk 5: 21 (pl.); J 10: 33; Rv 13: 5 (pl.); 2 Cl 13: 3; D 3: 6; β. πρὸς τὸν θεόν (Iambl., Vi. Pyth. 32, 216) Rv 13: 6. βλασφημίας ἐπιφέρεσθαι τῷ ὀνόματι κυρίου 1 Cl 47: 7; β., ὅσα ἐὰν βλασφημήσωσιν Mk 3: 28, s. βλασφημέω 2bα; ἡ τοῦ πνεύματος (obj. gen.) β. Mt 12: 31b, s. βλασφημέω 2bγ. ὀνόματα βλασφημίας (gen. of qual.) Rv 13: 1; 17: 3. ῥήματα βλασφημίας Ac 6: 11 v.l.*

βλάσφημος, ον (Demosth.+; Plut., Herodian; in LXX its mng. is almost always relig.) *slanderous, blasphemous* ῥήματα *scurrilous words* Ac 6: 11, 13 t.r.; cf. Rv 13: 5 v.l. (Dio Chrys. 3, 53 τὶ βλάσφημον περὶ τῶν θεῶν; Herodian 7, 8, 9 βλάσφημα πολλὰ εἰπὼν εἰς τὴν 'Ρώμην καὶ τὴν σύγκλητον; Philo, De Ios. 247; Jos., Vi. 158; 320). β. κρίσιν φέρειν *pronounce a defaming judgment* 2 Pt 2: 11. Of pers.: *blasphemer* (Wsd 1: 6; Sir 3: 16; 2 Macc 9: 28; 10: 36) 1 Ti 1: 13; 2 Ti 3: 2; Hs 9, 18, 3; w. προδόται 9, 19, 3; β. εἰς τὸν κύριον 9, 19, 1. M-M.*

βλέμμα, ατος, τό *glance, look* (Eur.+; Demosth.; Epict. 4, 1, 145; 4, 8, 17; Lucian, Dial. Mar. 15: 2; POxy. 471, 60; Philo, Conf. Lingu. 11; Test. Reub. 5: 3) βλέμματι κ. ἀκοῇ *by what he saw and heard* 2 Pt 2: 8; περίπικρον β. *a very bitter look* Hs 6, 2, 5. (Maximus Tyr. 14, 1c β. ἰταμόν). M-M.*

βλέπω fut. βλέψω, 1 aor. ἔβλεψα (Pind.+; inscr., pap., LXX; En. 98, 7; Ep. Arist., Philo, Joseph., Test. 12 Patr. On the use of βλέπω and ὁράω s. Reinhold 97ff. Esp. oft. in Hermas [70 times]) *see, look (at).*
1. lit. of the activity of the eyes—**a.** w. acc of what is seen: *beam, splinter* Mt 7: 3; Lk 6: 41f.—Mt 11: 4; 13: 16f; 24: 2; Mk 8: 23f; Lk 10: 23f; Ac 2: 33; 9: 8f; Rv 1: 11f; 5: 3f; 22: 8. Large buildings Mk 13: 2 (Choliamb. in Ps.-Callisth. 1, 46a, 8 lines 4, 8, 19: ὁρᾷς τὰ τείχη ταῦθ'; . . . τὰ θεμέλια ταῦτα . . . ὁρᾷς ἐκείνους τοὺς οἴκους;); a woman Lk 7: 44; light (Artem. 5, 20 τὸ φῶς ἔβλεπεν) 5, 77; 8: 16, cf. 11: 33; Jesus J 1: 29; B 5: 10; signs Ac 8: 6; B 4: 14; a vision Ac 12: 9; nakedness Rv 16: 15; the beast 17: 8; smoke 18: 9. *Seeing* contrasted w. hoping Ro 8: 24f. Of angels βλέπουσι τὸ πρόσωπον τοῦ πατρός (expr. fr. oriental court life=have access constantly, 2 Km 14: 24; cf. 4 Km 25: 19) Mt 18: 10 (s. πρόσωπον 1b). Pass. πάντων βλεπομένων *since everything is seen* 1 Cl 28: 1.

W. acc. and ptc. instead of a dependent clause (Dit., Syll.³ 1104, 42; UPZ 68, 6 [152 BC] βλέπω Μενέδημον κατατρέχοντά με=that M. runs after me; 1 Macc 12: 29; Jos., Ant. 20, 219); τὸν ὄχλον συνθλίβοντά σε *that the crowd is pressing around you* Mk 5: 31. τὸν λίθον ἠρμένον *that the stone was taken away* J 20: 1; cf. Mt 15: 31; Lk 24: 12; J 20: 5; 21: 9. τὸν πατέρα ποιοῦντα 5: 19; sim. 21: 20; Ac 4: 14; Hb 2: 9. ὑπὲρ ὃ βλέπει με *beyond what he sees in me* 2 Cor 12: 6.
b. abs.: Ro 11: 10 (Ps 68: 24); Rv 9: 20. τὰ βλεπόμενα (Ael. Aristid. 46 p. 406 D.; Wsd 13: 7; 17: 6) *what can be seen* 2 Cor 4: 18.—*Look on* (Jos., Bell. 1, 596, Ant. 3, 95 βλεπόντων αὐτῶν while they looked on, before their eyes) Ac 1: 9; 1 Cl 25: 4.
c. w. prep. phrase: ἐν τῷ κρυπτῷ *who sees in secret* Mt 6: 4, 6; cf. vs. 18 (s. 4 Macc 15: 18). δι' ἐσόπτρου ἐν αἰνίγματι 1 Cor 13: 12.
d. βλέπων βλέπω *see w. open eyes* Mt 13: 14 (Is 6: 9). βλέπων οὐ βλέπει *though he looks he does not see* 13: 13; Lk 8: 10 (cf. Aeschyl., Prom. 447f; Ps.-Demosth. 25, 89; Polyb. 12, 24, 6; Lucian, Dial. Marin. 4, 3).
2. *be able to see,* in contrast to being blind (trag.; Antipho 4, 4, 2; X., Mem. 1, 3, 4; Aelian, V.H. 6, 12; Dit., Syll.³ 1168, 78 the blind man βλέπων ἀμφοῖν ἐξῆλθε; POxy. 39, 9 [52 AD] ὀλίγον βλέπων=of weak sight; Ex 4: 11; 23: 8; 1 Km 3: 2 al.) Lk 7: 21; ὀφθαλμοὶ τοῦ μὴ β. (Ps 68: 24, cf. 9: 32; Sus 9; Bl-D. §400, 2) *eyes unable to see* Ro 11: 8 (Dt 29: 3).—Mt 12: 22; 15: 31; J 9: 7, 15, 25; Ac 9: 9; Rv 3: 18; Hs 6, 2, 1. Fig. of spiritual sight (Diog. L. 6, 53 with reference to Pla.: βλ. with the eyes of the νοῦς) J 9: 39.
3. *look at, regard:* εἰς w. acc. (Anaxandrides Com. [IV BC] 34, 9 K. εἰς τοὺς καλούς; Ael. Aristid. 28, 126 K.=49 p. 531f D.; Aelian, V.H. 14, 42; Herodian 3, 11, 3; Jdth 9: 9; Pr 16: 25; Sir 40: 29; 4 Macc 15: 18) Lk 9: 62; J 13: 22; Ac 1: 11 (Ps.-Apollod., Epit. 5, 22 and PGM 13, 833 εἰς τ. οὐρανὸν β.); 3: 4. W. acc. *look at a woman* (cf. Synes., Calv. 23 p. 86B ὅστις ἀδίκοις ὀφθαλμοῖς ὁρᾷ τὴν τοῦ γείτονος) Mt 5: 28; *see magic rites* D 3: 4; βιβλίον *look into a book* Rv 5: 3f.
4. of mental functions: *direct one's attention to someth., consider, note* (Jos., Bell. 7, 351, Ant. 20, 57).
a. abs. βλέπετε *take care* Mk 13: 33.—**b.** w. acc. (2 Ch 10: 16) 1 Cor 1: 26; 10: 18; Col 2: 5; 4: 17. βλέπων τ. ἐντολήν w. *regard to the commandment* B 10: 11a.
c. w. indir. question foll. Mk 4: 24; Lk 8: 18; 1 Cor 3: 10; Eph 5: 15; 1 Cl 56: 16; B 10: 11b.—**d.** w. ἵνα foll. 1 Cor 16: 10.
5. *notice, mark someth.:* w. acc. 2 Cor 10: 7 (imper.). W. εἰς τι (Polyb. 3, 64, 10 εἰς τ. παρουσίαν) εἰς πρόσωπον β. *look at someone's face=regard someone's opinion* Mt 22: 16; Mk 12: 14.
6. *watch, look to, beware of:* Mk 13: 9; Phil 3: 2 (GD Kilpatrick, PKahle memorial vol. '68, 146-48: *look at, consider*); 2 J 8. Followed by μή, μήποτε, μήπως and aor. subj. (Pythag., Ep. 4, 1; Epict. 2, 11, 22; 3, 20, 16; PLond. 964, 9 βλέπε μὴ ἐπιλάθῃ οὐδέν; PLeipz. 106, 17 [I BC]) *see to it, take care* Mt 24: 4; Mk 13: 5; Lk 21: 8; Ac 13: 40; 1 Cor 8: 9; 10: 12; Gal 5: 15; Hb 12: 25, or fut. indic. Col 2: 8. W. ἀπό τινος (BGU 1079, 24 [41 AD] βλέπε σατὸν [=σαυτὸν] ἀπὸ τῶν 'Ιουδαίων; APF 4, '08, 568) *beware of* the leaven of the Pharisees Mk 8: 15; of the scribes 12: 38.
7. in a very general sense *perceive, feel.*—**a.** by the senses: a strong wind Mt 14: 30.
b. of mental perception *discover, find* a law Ro 7: 23 (cf. PFay. 111, 16 ἐὰν βλέπῃς τὴν τιμὴν [price] παντὸς ἀγόρασον). W. acc. and ptc. 2 Cl 20: 1; B 1: 3. W. ὅτι foll.

143

(BGU 815, 4; Ep. Arist. 113) 2 Cor 7: 8; Hb 3: 19; Js 2: 22.

8. to designate geographical direction (rather freq. and w. var. preps.; w. κατά and acc. Ezk 11: 1; 40: 6 al.) Ac 27: 12 (s. λίψ and cf. Field, Notes 144).—FHahn, Sehen u. Glauben im J: OCullmann-Festschr., '72, 125–41. M-M. B. 1042.

βλέφαρον, ου, τό (Hom.+; pap., LXX; Third Corinthians 3: 30) usu. pl. *eyelids* Papias 3.*

βληθήσομαι s. **βάλλω**.

βλητέος, α, ον the only verbal adj. in -τέος in NT (Bl-D. §65, 3; Rob. 157), fr. βάλλω *must be put* (s. βάλλω 2b) Lk 5: 38; cf. Mk 2: 22 v.l.—JViteau, Revue de Philol. n.s. 18, 1894, 38.*

βληχρός, ά, όν (Pind.+; Diod. S., Plut.) *feeble* of prayer (w. μικρός) Hs 2: 5. Of pers. (w. ἀργός) πρός τι *too weak for someth.* 5, 4, 3.*

Βοανηργές (var. other spellings are found in the mss., e.g. Βοανεργές) Aram. words *Boanerges*=Hebr. בְּנֵי רְגֶשׁ Mk 3: 17, transl. υἱοὶ βροντῆς *sons of thunder* (cf. Diod. S. 8, 11, 2 of a house that had been struck by lightning: ὀνομάζεται Ἐμβρονταῖον=House of Thunder); surname given by Jesus to the sons of Zebedee (s. Lk 9: 54). Cf. EKautzsch, Gramm. d. Bibl. Aram. 1884, 9; Dalman, Gramm.[2] 144, Worte 33; 39, 4, Jesus 11; RHarris, Exp. 7. Ser III '07, 146–52, ET 36, '25, 139; JBoehmer, StKr 85, '12, 458–64; EPreuschen, ZNW 18, '18, 141–4 (cf. Fischer, ibid. 23, '24, 310f); FSchulthess, D. Problem d. Sprache Jesu '17, 52f, ZNW 21, '22, 243–7; GBardy, Rech de Sc rel 15, '25, 167f; 18, '28, 344; PJoüon, ibid. 438ff; AFridrichsen, Symb. Osl. 13, '34, 40: 'thunderstrokes'; JAMontgomery, JBL 56, '37, 51f. Bl-D §162, 6 App. (The difficulty pertaining to the vowels of Boa is not yet solved; cf. ThNöldeke, GGA 1884, 1022f. Nor is it certain that rges=רְגֵשׁ; Kautzsch points to רְגֵז *wrath*, which would make the word mean *the hot-tempered*. Wlh.[2] ad loc. draws attention to the name Ragasbal. Schulthess first cj. benē reḥēm=fratres uterini, *full brothers,* then benē regeš=partisans, adherents.—Pairs of brothers or sisters known by a special name: WBauer's introd., p. xxv of this book.)*

βοάω impf. ἐβόων Ac 21: 34 t.r.; fut. βοήσω; 1 aor. ἐβόησα, imper. βόησον (Hom.+; inscr., pap., LXX; Philo, Op. M. 79; Joseph.; Sib. Or. 3, 313; 724) *call, shout, cry out,* oft. w. φωνῇ μεγάλῃ (Phlegon: 257 fgm. 36, 1, 1 Jac.; Plut., Coriol. 25, 3; Gen 39: 14; 1 Macc 3: 54; 13: 45 al. LXX; Sus 46 and Bel 18 Theod.).
1. abs. ῥῆξον κ. βόησον *break forth and shout* Gal 4: 27; 2 Cl 2: 1f (both Is 54: 1).
2. of solemn proclamation (Menand. Com. in Diog. L. 6, 83 τὰ βοώμενα of solemn declarations; Aelian, V.H. 3, 42 ἡ τραγῳδία βοᾷ; Sib. Or. 3, 212) φωνὴ βοῶντος (φωνή 2e) Mt 3: 3; Mk 1: 3; Lk 3: 4; J 1: 23; B 9: 3 (all Is 40: 3). Of the shouts of excited crowds (Jos., Ant. 13, 376; cf. X., An. 4, 3, 22) Ac 17: 6; 25: 24; MPol 12: 2.
3. of cries of anguish or for help: Jesus on the cross Mt 27: 46 v.l.; Mk 15: 34; evil spirits when leaving a person Ac 8: 7 (in these three pass. β. φωνῇ μεγάλῃ); sick people Lk 9: 38; 18: 38 (ἐβόησεν λέγων as Diog. L. 6, 44 ἐβόα λέγων; Ps.-Callisth. 1, 25, 1; 1 Km 5: 10; Jdth 6: 18).
4. of prayer as calling on God (Ael. Aristid. 48, 54 K.= 24 p. 479 D.; β. τὸν θεόν) abs. B 3: 5 (Is 58: 9). W. dat. foll. (Sus 60 Theod. v.l. ἐβόησαν τ. θεῷ) Lk 18: 7. W. πρός and acc. (Num 12: 13) ἐξ ἑνὸς στόματος β. πρὸς αὐτόν 1 Cl 34: 7. M-M. B. 1250.*

Βόες, ὁ (ℵ B POxy. 2; v.l. Βόος, Βόοζ; Bl-D. §39, 4;

ARahlfs, Studie über d. griech. Text d. Buches Ruth '22, 73) indecl. (in Jos., Ant. 5, 323ff Βοώζης [Ant. 5, 323] or Βόαζος, ου [Ant. 5, 326]) *Boaz* (בֹּעַז), in the genealogy of Jesus Mt 1: 5. Cf. 1 Ch 2: 11f; Ruth 4: 21 and s. Βόος.*

βοή, ῆς, ἡ (Hom.+; pap., LXX; pl. 2 Macc 4: 22; Jos., Bell. 4, 306; 310) *cry, shout* pl. Js 5: 4 (cf. Jos., Ant. 8, 339 μεγάλῃ βοῇ καλεῖν τ. θεούς).*

βοήθεια, ας, ἡ (Thu.+; inscr., pap., LXX) *help* εὔκαιρος β. *timely help* Hb 4: 16 (cf. Dit., Or. 762, 4 ὁ δῆμος ὁ τῶν Κιβυρατῶν τῷ δήμῳ τῷ Ῥωμαίων βοηθείτω κατὰ τὸ εὔκαιρον, Syll.[3] 693, 12.—Of divine help: Diod. S. 3, 40, 7 τῶν θεῶν β.; Ael. Aristid. 31 p. 600 D.: παρὰ τ. θεῶν; Ps 19: 3; 34: 2; Jos., Ant. 13, 65, Vi. 290). Pl. concr. (*makeshift) aids, helps* (Diod. S. 3, 8, 5) βοηθείαις ἐχρῶντο prob. a nautical t.t. (cf. Philo, De Ios. 33 κυβερνήτης ταῖς τῶν πνευμάτων μεταβολαῖς συμμεταβάλλει τὰς πρὸς εὔπλοιαν βοηθείας. Cf. Diod. S., 3, 40, 5 βοηθέω of the bringing of aid for a ship in danger) *they used supports* (perh. cables) Ac 27: 17. See lit. s.v. ὑποζώννυμι and EHaenchen, Comm. '56 ad loc. M-M.*

βοηθέω 1 aor. ἐβοήθησα, imper. βοήθησον (Aeschyl., Hdt.+; inscr., pap., LXX, Joseph.; Sib. Or. 3, 242).
1. *furnish aid* βοηθεῖτε *help!* (Aristoph., Vesp. 433 ὦ Μίδα καὶ Φρὺξ βοηθεῖτε δεῦρο) Ac 21: 28.
2. *help, come to the aid of* τινι someone Mt 15: 25; Mk 9: 22; Ac 16: 9 (cf. Epict. 2, 15, 15 νοσῶ, κύριε· βοήθησόν μοι; Josh 10: 6; Jos., Bell. 1, 56); Hb 2: 18; Rv 12: 16; 1 Cl 39: 5 (Job 4: 20); 2 Cl 8: 2; IRo 7: 1; D 12: 2. βοήθει μου τῇ ἀπιστίᾳ *help my lack of faith,* or=μοι ἀπιστοῦντι Mk 9: 24.—God as helper (Sb 158 ὁ θεὸς αὐτῷ ἐβοήθησε; PGM 13, 289 βοήθησον ἐν ἀνάγκαις; EPeterson, Εἷς θεός '26, 3f; 309 al.) 2 Cor 6: 2 (Is 49: 8). M-M. B. 1353.*

βοηθός, όν (Hdt.+; LXX) *helpful;* subst. *helper* (Hdt. et al., inscr., pap., ostraca, LXX; Jos., Bell. 1, 317, Ant. 13, 276; 358) of Christ β. τῆς ἀσθενείας ἡμῶν *who aids our weakness* 1 Cl 36: 1. Of God (Herodian 3, 6, 7; UPZ 52, 8 [162 BC] Sarap.; PLond. 410, 8 μετὰ τὸν θεὸν οὐδένα ἔχομεν βοηθόν; POxy. 1381, 83; LXX; Philo; Jos., Ant. 2, 274; Jew. inscr.: Wadd. 2451) Hb 13: 6 (Ps 117: 7). τῶν κινδυνευόντων *helper of those in danger* 1 Cl 59: 3; cf. vs. 4.—βοηθοί auxiliaries B 2: 2. M-M.*

βόησον s. **βοάω**.

βόθρος, ου, ὁ (Hom.+; Paus. 9, 39, 6; Philostrat., Her. 18, 3 p. 195, 16; LXX; Jos., Ant. 9, 35; Test. Reub. 2: 9; Moeris 105 βόθρος ἀττικόν· βόθυνος κοινόν; X. has both forms [Schmid IV 282]) *pit, cistern* Mt 15: 14 D; B 11: 2.*

βόθυνος, ου, ὁ (since Cratinus 210; X., Oec. 19, 3; Clidemus [350 BC] no. 323 fgm. 14 Jac.; PHal. 1, 97 [III BC]; BGU 1122, 17 [14 BC]; LXX; cf. Is 24: 18; 47: 11. S. βόθρος) *pit* Mt 12: 11; 15: 14; Lk 6: 39 (εἰς βόθ. ἐμπ. as Jer 31: 44; on this topic cf. Philo, Virt. 7). M-M.*

βολή, ῆς, ἡ (Hom.+; LXX) *a throw* ὡσεὶ λίθου βολήν *about a stone's throw* (Test. Gad 1: 3) Lk 22: 41 (Thu. 5, 65, 2 μέχρι λίθου βολῆς ἐχώρησαν; Herodian 2, 6, 13; 7, 12, 5; cf. Gen 21: 16; Jos., Ant. 20, 213).*

βολίζω 1 aor. ἐβόλισα *take soundings, heave the lead* (βολίς) Ac 27: 28 (found elsewh. only in Geoponica 6, 17 [pass.='sink'] and Eustathius on Homer 563, 30; 731, 46). LCasson, Ships and Seamanship in the Anc. World, '71, 246, n. 85. M-M.*

βολίς, ίδος, ἡ *missile, arrow, javelin* (Plut., Demetr. 3, 2; Hesych.; Suidas) Hb 12: 20 t.r. (Ex 19: 13).*

144

Βόος, ὁ indecl. (v.l. Βόοζ) *Boaz,* in the genealogy of Jesus Lk 3: 32; s. Βόες.*

βορά, ᾶς, ἡ (Aeschyl., Hdt.+; LXX; cf. Job 38: 39; 3 Macc 6: 7; En. 25, 5; Maspéro 141, 14 κυνὸς β.) *food* (of wild beasts) ἄφετέ με θηρίων εἶναι βοράν IRo 4: 1 (Eur., Phoen. 1603 θηρσὶν ἄθλιον βορ.; Jos., Bell. 4, 324 β. θηρίων).*

βόρβορος, ου, ὁ (Aeschyl., Pla., al.; Jer 45: 6; Jos., Ant. 10, 121) *mud, mire, filth, slime.*
1. of boiling mire in hell AP 8: 23; 9: 24; 16: 31 (cf. Diogenes the Cynic [IV BC] in Diog. L. 6, 39: the wicked are tormented in the next world ἐν τῷ βορβόρῳ; Act. Thom. 56; Martyr. Matthaei 3 Bonnet).
2. of the mud in which swine wallow ὗς λουσαμένη εἰς κυλισμὸν βορβόρου 2 Pt 2: 22. This is usu. taken to mean *a sow, after she has washed herself,* (turns) *to wallowing in the mire* (the ptc. is mid., Mlt. 155f; 238f; s. JRHarris, The Story of Aḥikar 1898, lxvii, also in Charles, APOT II, 772; RSmend, Alter u. Herkunft d. Achikar-Romans '08, 75). But the idea was also current that swine preferred to bathe in mud or slime (Sext. Emp., Pyrrhon. Hypot. I 56 σύες τε ἥδιον βορβόρῳ λούονται . . . ἢ ὕδατι . . . καθαρῷ; cf. Clem. Alex., Protr. 92, 4; Aristot., Hist. An. 8, 6 p. 595a, 31; Galen, Protr. 13, p. 42, 22 John); the transl. might then be *a sow, having* (once) *bathed herself* (in mud), (returns) *to wallowing in the mire* (CBigg, ICC, '01 ad loc.), or *a sow that washes herself by wallowing in the mire* (M-M. s.v. λούω); cf. PWendland, Ein Wort des Heraklit im NT: SAB 1898, 788–96. On swine wallowing in mud, lit. and fig., see Semonides 7, 2ff Diehl²; Heraclitus, fgm. 37; Epict. 4, 11, 29 [cf. 31]; Plut., Mor. 129A; Ael. Aristid. 33, 31 K.=51 p. 582 D.; Philo, Spec. Leg. 1, 148, Agr. 144. M-M.*

βορρᾶς, ᾶ, ὁ (this colloq. form, interchangeable even in class. writers w. βορέας [Kühner-Bl. I 386], is predom. in pap. [Mayser 252; cf. 221] and LXX; it is found En. 32, 1; Jos., Bell. 5, 144, and in inscr. [Dit., Or. 176, 8; 178, 10], and is the only form used by Koine writers like Vett. Val.; cf. Bl-D. §34, 3; 45; Rdm.² 59; Rob. 254) *the north* ἀπὸ βορρᾶ *on the north* Rv 21: 13 (ἀπό II 1); ἀπὸ β. καὶ νότου *from north and south* Lk 13: 29 (on the absence of the art. s. Bl-D. §253, 5 app.; Rob. 793ff). W. the three other points of the compass 1 Cl 10: 4 (Gen 13: 14). M-M. B. 872.*

βόσκω (Hom.+; inscr., pap., LXX; Philo distinguishes betw. β. and ποιμαίνω, Det. Pot. Ins. 25).
1. act. of herdsmen *feed, tend* (Jos., Ant. 6, 254) lambs J 21: 15 (on the fig. use cf. 3 Km 12: 16 νῦν βόσκε τὸν οἶκόν σου, Δαυίδ; Abercius inscr. 4 β. πρόβ.). Sheep vs. 17; Hs 6, 1, 6. Swine Lk 15: 15. ὁ βόσκων *herdsman* (cf. Aristot. 540a, 18; Jer 38: 10) Mt 8: 33; Mk 5: 14; Lk 8: 34.
2. pass. of livestock *graze, feed* (Is 5: 17; 11: 7; Jos., Bell. 6, 153; Sib. Or. 3, 789) ἀγέλη βοσκομένη Mt 8: 30; Mk 5: 11; Lk 8: 32. πρόβατα βοσκόμενα (PTebt. 298, 53) Hs 6, 2, 4, cf. 7; sim. 9, 1, 8. M-M. B. 146.*

Βοσόρ, ὁ indecl. *Bosor* 2 Pt 2: 15 v.l.; s. Βεώρ.*

βοτάνη, ης, ἡ (fr. βόσκω. Hom.+; pap., LXX; En. 7, 1; Philo) *fodder, herb, plant.*
1. lit. Hs 9, 1, 5ff; 9, 21, 1; 3; 9, 22, 1; 9, 23, 1; 9, 24, 1; β. εὔθετος *useful vegetation* Hb 6: 7; πᾶσαν φάγε β. *eat every plant* GEg 1; s. also under 2, ITr 6: 1.—Esp. of weeds Hm 10, 1, 5; s 5, 2, 3ff; 5, 4, 1; 5, 5, 3; 9, 26, 4.
2. fig., of evil persons (foll. Mt 13: 24ff) β. τοῦ διαβόλου *a plant of the devil* IEph 10: 3; ἀπέχεσθαι κακῶν

βοτανῶν IPhld 3: 1. Of false teachings ἀλλοτρίας βοτάνης ἀπέχεσθαι ITr 6: 1. M-M. B. 521.*

βότρυς, υος, ὁ (Hom.+; Epict. 1, 15, 7; BGU 1118, 14 [22 BC]; PLeipz. 30, 4; LXX; En. 32, 4; Ep. Arist. 63; 70; 75; Jos., Ant. 12, 68; 75) *bunch of grapes* Rv 14: 18 (Ps.-Callisth. 3, 21, 2 βότρυες σταφυλῆς). The word is also found in the Phrygian Papias of Hierapolis, in a passage in which he speaks of the enormous size of the grapes in the new aeon (in the Lat. transl. in Irenaeus 5, 33, 3 as 'botrus'). On this see Stephan. Byz. s.v. Εὐκαρπία: Metrophanes says that in the district of Εὐκαρπία in Phrygia Minor the grapes were said to be so large that one bunch of them caused a wagon to break down in the middle. M-M. B. 378.*

βουλευτής, οῦ, ὁ (Hom.+; Job 3: 14; 12: 17) *member of a council,* an advisory or legislative body (inscr., pap., loanw. in rabb.); of Joseph of Arimathaea: member of the Sanhedrin (Jos., Bell. 2, 405 οἱ ἄρχοντες καὶ βουλευταί) Mk 15: 43; Lk 23: 50. M-M.*

βουλεύω, in our lit. only mid. βουλεύομαι; impf. ἐβουλευόμην; fut. βουλεύσομαι (Lk 14: 31); 1 aor. ἐβουλευσάμην; pf. βεβούλευμαι (B 6: 7). (Hom.+; inscr., pap., LXX; Ep. Arist., Philo, Joseph., Test. 12 Patr.).
1. *deliberate* (w. oneself) w. indir. question foll. (Jos., Ant. 1, 339) εἰ Lk 14: 31 (cf. X., Mem. 3, 6, 8); *consider* τὶ *someth.* (Appian, Hann. 54 §227 β. ἀπόστασιν=consider a revolt) Hv 1, 1, 2 and 8; s 9, 28, 5.
2. *resolve, decide* w. acc. ἄ (Jdth 9: 6; 12: 4) 2 Cor 1: 17; βουλὴν πονηράν B 6: 7 (Is 3: 9). W. inf. foll. (PTebt. 58, 28; PFay. 116, 9; 2 Ch 30: 23; Wsd 18: 5; 1 Macc 8: 9; Jos., C. Ap. 2, 296 v.l.) Ac 5: 33 v.l.; 15: 37 t.r.; 27: 39. W. ἵνα foll. (Bl-D. §392, 1a) J 11: 53 (EBammel, CFD Moule-Festschr., '70, 11–40); 12: 10. M-M.*

βουλή, ῆς, ἡ—1. (Hom.+; inscr., pap., LXX, Ep. Arist., Philo, Joseph., Test. 12 Patr.) *purpose, counsel* 1 Cl 61: 2; Hv 1, 2, 4; s 9, 28, 4f; pl. 9, 28, 8; βουλαὶ τῆς καρδίας *motives of the heart* 1 Cor 4: 5; μεστοὶ ὁσίας βουλῆς *full of holy plans* 1 Cl 2: 3; perh. B 10: 10 (Ps 1: 1), see 3 below.
2. *resolution, decision*—a. of men (Jos., Ant. 2, 23) Lk 23: 51 (w. πρᾶξις as Philo, Poster. Cai. 86).—Ac 5: 38. β. τίθεσθαι (Judg 19: 30; Ps 12: 3) *decide* 27: 12 (w. inf. foll.). στρατιωτῶν β. ἐγένετο (w. ἵνα foll.) vs. 42. βουλὴν βουλεύεσθαι of evil designs (Vi. Aesopi I c. 33 p. 298, 6): βουλεύεσθαι βουλὴν πονηράν *form an evil plot* B 6: 7 (Is 3: 9); λαμβάνειν β. πονηρὰν κατά τινος *plot evil against someone* (however, in Leontius 11 p. 21, 11 λαμβάνει βουλήν τινος= he receives [bad] advice from someone) 19: 3; D 2: 6. Cf. Hs 6, 3, 5.
b. of the divine will (Herm. Wr. 1, 8; 18; 31; oft. LXX; Jos., Ant. 4, 42; Sib. Or. 3, 574.—Dodd 126–32) 1 Cl 57: 4f (Pr 1: 25, 30); Ac 2: 23; 4: 28; 13: 36; 20: 27; Dg 8: 10; ἡ ἔνδοξος β. Hv 1, 3, 4; τὸ ἀμετάθετον τῆς β. αὐτοῦ *the unchangeable nature of his resolve* Hb 6: 17; κατὰ τὴν β. τοῦ θελήματος αὐτοῦ acc. *to the purpose of his will* Eph 1: 11; cf. Ac 19: 1 D; τὴν β. τοῦ θεοῦ ἠθέτησαν εἰς ἑαυτούς *they frustrated the purpose of God for themselves* Lk 7: 30. οὐδὲν λέληθεν τὴν β. αὐτοῦ *nothing is hidden from his directing counsel* 1 Cl 27: 6.
3. *council meeting* (Hom.+; Diod. S. 14, 4, 5; Philo; Jos., Bell. 2, 641 al.; loanw. in rabb.) B 11: 7 (Ps 1: 5); perh. B 10: 10 (Ps 1: 1, see 1 above). M-M.*

βούλημα, ατος, τό (Aristoph., Pla.+; Epict.; Dit., Syll.³ 799, 12; pap., LXX, Ep. Arist., Philo; Jos., Ant. 1, 278) *intention* τὸ ἀκέραιον αὐτῶν β. *their pure purpose* 1 Cl 21: 7; τὸ β. τῶν ἐθνῶν *what the Gentiles desire to do* 1 Pt

145

4: 3 (v.l. θέλημα); κωλύειν τινὰ τοῦ β. *hinder someone in his intention* Ac 27: 43. Of God's *will* (Cornutus 16 p. 22, 2 β. τῶν θεῶν; Philo, Mos. 1, 287 τοῦ θεοῦ β.; Jos., Ant. 2, 304) Ro 9: 19; 1 Cl 23: 5; 33: 3. τὸ παντοκρατορικὸν β. αὐτοῦ 8: 5; τὸ μακρόθυμον αὐτοῦ β. 19: 3. M-M.*

βούλησις, εως, ἡ (Eur., Thu. +; Epict., inscr.; PTebt. 43, 35; Jos., C. Ap. 1, 45) *will*: of God's *will* (Ephorus [IV BC]: 70 fgm. 31b Jac.; Diod. S. 17, 66, 7; Phlegon: 257 fgm. 36, 1, 1; 36, 1, 4; 36, 1, 7 Jac.; Parthenius 4, 5; 15, 4 β. θεῶν; Dit., Or. 458, 15; 669, 17; PAmh. 144, 11; POxy. 130, 11; Ep. Arist. 234; Philo, Rer. Div. Her. 246; Jos., Ant. 2, 232; Eupolemus in Euseb., Praep. Ev. 9, 30, 2) 1 Cl 42: 4; ἡ ἔνδοξος β. αὐτοῦ 9: 1; ἡ ἄμωμος β. αὐτοῦ 35: 5; ἡ ὑπέρτατος αὐτοῦ β. 40: 3; παρὰ τὸ καθῆκον τῆς βουλήσεως αὐτοῦ *contrary to what conforms to his will* 41: 3.*

βούλομαι 2 sg. βούλει (Bl-D. §27; Mayser 328) beside Att. βούλῃ (Lk 22: 42 v.l.; Hs 9, 11, 9 v.l.); impf. ἐβουλόμην (on the augment s. Bl-D. §66, 3 w. app.; Rob. 368; W-S. §12, 3), also ἠβούλετο (Hs 5, 6, 5); 1 aor. ἐβουλήθην (ἠβουλήθην 2 J 12 v.l.) (Hom. +; inscr., pap., LXX, En., Ep. Arist., Philo, Joseph., Test. 12 Patr.) *wish, be willing* (no longer difft. in mng. fr. θέλω: Bl-D. §101 s.v. θέλειν, but cf. Epict. 1, 12, 13; cf. RRödiger, Glotta 8, '17, 1ff; WFox, Berl. phil. Wochenschr. 37, '17, 597ff; 633ff; FZucker, Gnomon 9, '33, 191-201; GSchrenk, TW I 628-31; AWifstrand, D. griech. Verba für wollen: Eranos 40, '42, 16-36).
1. of the pers. desiring someth.: *wish, want, desire* w. inf. foll. (Jos., Ant. 5, 280) ἐβουλόμην ἀκοῦσαι *I should like to hear* Ac 25: 22 (Bl-D. §359, 2; Rob. 1055f; cf. Dionys. Hal., De Dem. 42 p. 1087 ἐβουλόμην ἔτι πλείω παρασχέσθαι παραδείγματα. ὃν ἐβουλόμην πρὸς ἐμαυτὸν κατέχειν (on the analogy of θέλω w. inf.=opt. w. ἄν) *whom I would have been glad to keep with me* Phlm 13. οἱ βουλόμενοι πλουτεῖν *those who desire to be rich* 1 Ti 6: 9.—Js 4: 4. W. a thing as obj. in the acc. Hm 12, 5, 4; s 5, 6, 5; 6, 5, 3; β. τὸν θάνατον τοῦ ἁμαρτωλοῦ *desire the death of the sinner* 1 Cl 8: 2 (Ezk 33: 11); β. εἰρήνην *wish for peace* 15: 1; αἷμα ταύρων ... οὐ βούλομαι *I do not desire* B 2: 5 (Is 1: 11); νηστείαν β. Hs 5, 1, 4; ὅσον ἂν βούλωνται *as much as they wished* MPol 7: 2; ὃ βούλει *what(ever) you wish* MPol 11: 2; Hm 12, 5, 1; οὐκ ἐβουλήθη *he did not wish* (to do so) MPol 7: 1.
2. of decisions of the will after previous deliberation—a. of human beings—α. w. acc. τοῦτο β. 2 Cor 1: 17.
β. w. aor. inf. foll. Mt 1: 19; Mk 15: 15; Ac 5: 28, 33; 12: 4; 15: 37; 17: 20; 18: 27; 19: 30; 22: 30; 23: 28; 27: 43; 28: 18; 2 Cor 1: 15; 1 Cl 7: 5; IRo 7: 1; GP 1: 1.
γ. w. pres. inf. foll. Ac 18: 15; Dg 10: 5; εἰ βούλοιτο πορεύεσθαι *whether he was willing to go* 25: 20; β. φιλοπονεῖν 2 Cl 19: 1; β. πιστεύειν Dg 9: 6; β. πείθειν MPol 3: 1; β. μένειν 5: 1.
δ. foll. by acc. and inf. (Jos., Ant. 14, 233 βούλομαι ὑμᾶς εἰδέναι; 246) γινώσκειν ὑμᾶς βούλομαι *I want you to know* Phil 1: 12.—1 Ti 2: 8; 5: 14; Tit 3: 8; Jd 5; 1 Cl 39: 1.
ε. w. aor. subj. foll., in which case β.introduces a deliberative question βούλεσθε ἀπολύσω ὑμῖν; *shall I release to you?* J 18: 39 (Bl-D. §366, 3; Rob. 935).
ζ. w. omission of the inf. which is to be supplied fr. the context ὅπου ἡ ὁρμή ... βούλεται (sc. μετάγειν) Js 3: 4. τοὺς βουλομένους (sc. ἐπιδέχεσθαι) κωλύει 3 J 10. οὐκ ἐβουλήθην (sc. γράφειν) 2 J 12.—1 Cl 54: 2; Dg 11: 7. καθὼς βούλεται *as he* (*it*) *wills* Hm 5, 1, 3; cf. 11: 2, 9; 12, 1, 1; 12, 2, 5; s 6, 5, 2; 9, 11, 9; Dg 9: 1. εἴ τι βούλει (sc. εἰπεῖν) Hs 5, 5, 5.

b. of God, though θέλω is more common, cf. BLGildersleeve, Pindar, 1885, p. 245 (Dio Chrys. 28[45], 15 βουλομένων θεῶν; Ael. Aristid. 50, 1 K. = 26 p. 502 D.; BGU 248, 11 [I AD] θεῶν δὲ βουλομένων; 249, 13; Herm. Wr. 13, 21; LXX; Jos., Ant. 9, 189) abs. Lk 22: 42. ἃ βούλομαι 2 Cl 13: 2 Funk. βουληθεὶς ἀπεκύησεν ἡμᾶς λόγῳ ἀληθείας acc. *to his will he brought us into being through the word of truth* Js 1: 18. W. aor. inf. foll. Hb 6: 17; 1 Cl 16: 10, 12 (Is 53: 10). Foll. by acc. w. inf. 2 Pt 3: 9; 1 Cl 8: 5.—Of Jesus Mt 11: 27; Lk 10: 22.—Of the Holy Spirit 1 Cor 12: 11. M-M. B. 1160.*

βουνός, οῦ, ὁ (found first in Aeschyl., Suppl. 109, prob. of Doric origin [Mayser p. 8; Bl-D. §126, 1ba; Rob. 111], occurring more freq. since Polyb. [3, 83, 1 and 3 and 4; 5, 22, 1f] in lit., inscr., pap., LXX; En. 1, 6; Philo, Poster. Cai. 57; Jos., Bell. 2, 619, Ant. 6, 156; Sib. Or. 3, 680) *hill* Lk 3: 5 (Is 40: 4); 23: 30 (w. ὄρη, Hos 10: 8; in sg. Strabo 3, 2, 9): Hv 1, 3, 4. M-M. B. 24.*

Βοῦρρος, ου, ὁ *Burrus* (both Gk. and Lat. forms of the name are well attested; cf. Hdb. on IEph 2: 1), a deacon in Ephesus, termed σύνδουλος by Ignat., IEph 2: 1.—IPhld 11: 2; ISm 12: 1.*

βοῦς, βοός acc. pl. βόας J 2: 14 (as Il. 5, 556; Arrian, Ind. 7, 7; Polyaenus 6, 52; Aelian, V.H. 12, 44; POxy. 729, 16; Gen 18: 7 al.) *head of cattle* (Hom. +; inscr., pap., LXX, Philo, Aet. M. 23; Joseph.) ὁ *ox*, ἡ *cow* Lk 13: 15; 14: 5. W. πρόβατα (Gen 13: 5; 33: 13 al.) J 2: 14f; D 13: 3; ζεῦγος β. (Jos., Ant. 12, 192) Lk 14: 19. Used in threshing 1 Cor 9: 9; 1 Ti 5: 18 (both Dt 25: 4; cf. Philo, Virt. 145; Jos., Ant. 4, 233. Cf. Pherecrates Com. [V BC] 65 ὑποζυγίοις ἀλοᾶν). M-M. B. 152.*

βραβεῖον, ου, τό (Menand., Monost. [IV p. 359 Meineke]; Ps.-Oppian, Cyn. 4, 197; Vett. Val. 174, 21; 288, 8; Inschr. v. Priene 118, 3 [I BC]; CIG 3674, 15 al.; [Nägeli 37, 3]; PGM 4, 664 *prize* in a contest. ἆθλον and νικητήριον are more common in Gk. lit.
1. lit. 1 Cor 9: 24.—2. fig. (cf. Herm. Wr. 18, 10; Gk. Apocalypse of Baruch 12 James; Philo, Praem. 6; Sib. Or. 2, 149) of the award of victory of the Christians β. τῆς ἄνω κλήσεως *the prize that is the object of* (and can only be attained in connection with) *the upward call* Phil 3: 14; (w. στέφανος) β. ἀναντίρρητον *incontestable prize* MPol 17: 1.
3. gener. *reward* ὑπομονῆς β. *reward for endurance* 1 Cl 5: 5 (cf. Menand., loc. cit. β. ἀρετῆς). M-M.*

βραβεύω *award prizes* in contests, then gener. *be judge, decide, control, rule* (Eur. +; Polyb. 2, 35, 3; Diod. S. 14, 65, 3; Plut., Lycurg. 30, 2, Pomp. 55, 6, Brut. 40, 8 al.; Herm. Wr. 18, 16; Inscr. gr. 163, 11; Dit., Syll.³ 685, 32 [139 BC]; UPZ 20, 22 [163 BC]; 110, 70; 161 [164 BC]; Wsd 10: 12; Philo, Mos. 1, 163 al.; Jos., Bell. 5, 503; 6, 143 al.) abs. ἡ εἰρήνη τοῦ X. βραβευέτω ἐν ταῖς καρδίαις ὑμῶν *let the peace of Christ rule in your hearts* Col 3: 15. M-M.*

βραδέως adv. of βραδύς (Thu. +; Epict. 1, 18, 19; PFay. 97, 37; POxy. 1088, 50; 2 Macc 14: 17; Jos., Bell. 3, 274) *slowly* β. ἐγένετο *it took a long time* Hs 9, 6, 8.*

βραδύγλωσσος, ον (Vi. Aesopi W c. 1 and 2; in c. 3 this is explained thus: λαλεῖν μὴ δυνάμενος διὰ τὸ τῆς γλώσσης βραδύ; Leontius 40 p. 79, 2; Cat. Cod. Astr. II 167.—Ps.-Lucian, Philopatris 13 the word refers to Moses as the author of the creation story. This is plainly influenced by the Bible) *slow of tongue* of Moses 1 Cl 17: 5 (Ex 4: 10).*

βραδύνω intr. (Aeschyl.+; Dit., Or. 515, 53: PFlor. 278 II, 11; POxy. 118, 37; Gen 43: 10; Dt 7: 10; Jos., Bell. 5, 566, Vi. 89) *hesitate, delay* 1 Ti 3: 15; Hs 9, 19, 2. τί βραδύνεις; *why do you delay?* MPol 11: 2; *hold back* τινός *from someth.* (Bl-D. §180, 5; Rob. 518) *in hesitation*: τῆς ἐπαγγελίας *from* (fulfilment of) *the promise* (poss.: *the Lord of the promise does not delay*) 2 Pt 3: 9. M-M.*

βραδυπλοέω (Artem. 4, 30; Anecd. Gr. p. 225, 15) *sail slowly* Ac 27: 7. M-M.*

βραδύς, εῖα, ύ (Hom.+; Dit., Syll.³ 502, 12) *slow,* opp. ταχύς (Ps.-Isocr., ad Demon. 34; Aristot., Eth. Nicom. 6, 10 p. 1142b; Philo, Conf. Lingu. 48) εἰς τὸ λαλῆσαι *slow to speak* Js 1: 19 (Bl-D. §402, 2; Rob. 658; βραδὺ φθέγγεσθαι is praised Dio Chrys. 15[32], 2); βρ. εἰς ὀργήν ibid. (cf. Dionys. Soph., Ep. 9 β. εἰς ἐπιστολήν; Jos., Ant. 15, 107 βραδὺς εἰς τ. ἀποδόσεις.—Menand., Monost. 60 πρὸς ὀργὴν β.). Fig., of mental and spiritual slowness (Il. 10, 226+; Polyb. 4, 8, 7; Dion. Hal., Orat. Vet. 2 p. 448; Sext. Emp., Math. 7, 325 w. ἀσύνετος) β. τῇ καρδίᾳ *slow of heart*= 'dull', w. inf. foll. (as Thu. 3, 38, 6 προνοῆσαι β.) τοῦ πιστεύειν *too dull to believe* (Bl-D. §400, 8) Lk 24: 25. Comp. βραδύτερος (Thu. 4, 8, 1; Theocr. 29, 30; Chio, Ep. 3, 2; Mayser 297): αἴτημα β. λαμβάνειν *receive* (the answer to) *a petition rather slowly* Hm 9: 7; β. μετανοεῖν *be slower in repentance* s 8, 7, 3; 8, 8, 3. βράδιον (Hes., Op. 528; Dit., Or. 502, 17) *rather tardy* 1 Cl 1: 1. M-M.*

βραδύτης, ητος (on accent cf. JWackernagel, NGG '09, 58ff; ESchwyzer, Griech. Gramm. I '39, 382), ἡ (Hom.+; Plut., Mor. 549; Appian, Bell. Civ. 4 p. 1052, 16 Mendelssohn; Vett. Val. 289, 24; Sb 7741, 12 [II AD]; Philo, Op. M. 156; Jos., Ant. 7, 74; 13, 47) *slowness* ὥς τινες βραδύτητα ἡγοῦνται *as some count slowness* 2 Pt 3: 9. M-M.*

βραχίων, ονος, ὁ (Hom.+; inscr., pap., LXX, Philo, Joseph.) *arm,* anthropomorphic symbol of God's power (Ex 15: 16; Is 51: 5; 52: 10; Ps 70: 18; 76: 16;—Eur., Suppl. 738; Philo, Spec. Leg. 1, 145 β. ἰσχύος κ. ἀνδρείας σύμβολον): ἐν β. αὐτοῦ *with his arm* Lk 1: 51 (Ps 88: 11); β. κυρίου (PsSol 13: 2) J 12: 38; 1 Cl 16: 3 (both Is 53: 1f). μετὰ βραχίονος ὑψηλοῦ *with uplifted arm* (Ex 6: 1; 32: 11; Dt 3: 24 al.) Ac 13: 17; cf. 1 Cl 60: 3. M-M. B. 237.*

βραχύς, εῖα, ύ (Pind., Hdt.+; pap., LXX, Ep. Arist., Philo, Joseph., Test. 12 Patr.) *short, little.*
1. of space: βραχύ (so Thu. 1, 63, 2; 2 Km 16: 1) διαστήσαντες *a little farther on* Ac 27: 28.
2. of time: β. (τι) *for a short time* (Ael. Aristid. 13 p. 276 D.) 5: 34; Hb 2: 7 (quotes Ps 8: 6, which is usu. regarded as referring to rank; in Is 57: 17 β. τι denotes time), 9; μετὰ β. *a little later* Lk 22: 58.
3. of quantity (1 Km 14: 29, 43; Jos., Bell. 1, 597, Ant. 9, 48 ἔλαιον βραχύ): *a small amount* β. τι *a little* J 6: 7 (cf. Thu. 2, 99, 5). διὰ βραχέων *in a few words, briefly* Hb 13: 22 (cf., besides the exx. in FBleek ad loc., Ocellus Luc. c. 35; Ptolem., Apotel. 1, 1, 3; Lucian, Toxaris 56; Ps.-Lucian, Charid. 22; Ael Aristid. 13 p. 183 D.; Achilles Tat. 7, 9, 3; PStrassb. 41, 8 διὰ βραχέων σε διδάξω; Ep. Arist. 128; Jos., Bell. 4, 338). LPTrudinger, JTS 23, '72, 128-30.—1 Pt 5: 12 𝔓⁷². M-M. B. 883.*

βρέφος, ους, τό—1. *unborn child, embryo* (Il. 23, 266; Plut., Mor. 1052F; Diosc. 5, 74; Dit., Syll.³ 1267, 23; PGM 8, 1 ἐλθέ μοι κύριε Ἑρμῆ ὡς τὰ βρέφη εἰς τ. κοιλίας τ. γυναικῶν; PFlor. 93, 21 τὸ ἐν γαστρὶ βρέφος; Sir 19: 11; Ps.-Phoc. 184; Jos., Ant. 20, 18; s. ἐξαμβλόω) Lk 1: 41, 44.

2. *baby, infant* (Pind.+; BGU 1104, 24, POxy. 1069, 22 al.; 1 Macc 1: 61; 2 Macc 6: 10; 4 Macc 4: 25; Philo; Jos., Bell. 6, 205) Lk 2: 12, 16 (Diod. S. 2, 4, 5 herdsmen find a divine child, Semiramis [εὑρεῖν τὸ βρέφος]; of Plato as infant s. παρίστημι 1ba); 18: 15; Ac 7: 19; νήπια β. (Dio Chrys. 10[11], 29; En. 99, 5 [restored]) Hs 9, 29, 1; cf. 3; ἀπὸ βρέφους *from childhood* 2 Ti 3: 15 (Ptolem., Apotel. 2, 3, 40; Philo, Spec. Leg. 2, 33; more freq. ἐκ β.: Philo, Somn. 1, 192; Anth. Pal. 9, 567). Fig. 1 Pt 2: 2. M-M. B. 92.*

βρέχω 1 aor. ἔβρεξα (Pind., Hdt.+; pap., LXX).
1. *to wet* (Bl-D. §309, 2) τινί *with something* (schol. on Apollon. Rhod. 2, 819) τοῖς δάκρυσιν τοὺς πόδας *the feet with tears* Lk 7: 38, 44 (cf. Ps 6: 7; IG XIV 1422 δακρύοισιν ἔβρεξαν ὅλον τάφον). Without obj. ἵνα μὴ ὑετὸς βρέχῃ *that no rain may fall* Rv 11: 6 (τ. ἡμ. is acc. of duration of time; Bl-D. §161, 2; Rob. 469ff).
2. *send rain* (Phryn. 291 L.; Polyb. 16, 12, 3).
a. pers. (Bl-D. §129) of God (Gen 2: 5 ἐπὶ τὴν γῆν; s. Philo, Leg. All. 1, 25; 26; 29; POxy. 1482, 6 [II AD] ὁ Ζεὺς ἔβρεχε.—Proverbially of Zeus, who sometimes lets the sun shine and sometimes sends rain: Theognis 25; Theocritus 4, 43; Liban., Declam. 1, 78 t. V p. 57, 1 F.) βρέχει he *causes it to rain* Mt 5: 45; GNaass 2. So also prob. ἔβρεξεν πῦρ καὶ θεῖον (fr. Gen 19: 24 where κύριος is the subj.; cf. Ezk 38: 22; PGM 36, 301; Sib. Or. 5, 508) Lk 17: 29. But here the foll. transl. is also conceivable.
b. impers. βρέχει *it rains* (so since the comic poet Teleclides [V BC]; Epict. 1, 6, 26; Sib. Or. 5, 377) Js 5: 17. M-M.*

βριμάομαι (Aristoph.+) *be indignant* J 11: 33 𝔓⁷⁵ for ἐμβρ., q.v.*

βροντή, ῆς, ἡ (Hom.+; PGM 36, 356; LXX; En. 17, 3; Jos., Ant. 2, 343; Sib. Or. 5, 303) *thunder* βροντὴν γεγονέναι J 12: 29 (speech that is loud and energetic [Philostrat., Vi. Ap. 7, 28, 3 Polyphemus; Diog. L. 2, 36 Xanthippe] or that makes extravagant demands [Herodas 7, 66] is compared to thunder). φωνὴ βροντῆς *crash of thunder* Rv 6: 1; 14: 2; 19: 6 (cf. Ps 76: 19; 103: 7; Sir 43: 17; CBezold-FBoll, Reflexe astral. Keilinschriften bei griech. Schriftstellern [SA Heidelb. '11, 7. Abt.] 21, 1). φωναὶ καὶ βρονταί (s. φωνή 1, end) 4: 5; 8: 5; 11: 19; 16: 18. The 7 thunders which speak 10: 3f are thought by some to be the thunders of the 7 planetary spheres (Boll, Offb. 22). On υἱοὶ βροντῆς Mk 3: 17 cf. Βοανηργές and Appian, Syr. 62 §330 Πτολεμαίῳ Κεραυνὸς ἐπίκλησις. M-M. B. 58.*

βροτός, ή, όν *mortal,* subst. ὁ β. *mortal man* (Hom.+, LXX) 1 Cl 39: 4 (Job 4: 17).*

βροχή, ῆς, ἡ (Phryn. 291 L.; pap. since III BC have it = 'irrigation' [Mayser 421; POxy. 280, 5, 593]) *rain* (Democrit. 14, 8; Ps 67: 10; 104: 32; Philo, Leg. All. 1, 26; Sib. Or., fgm. 1, 32 and in Mod. Gk. [HAKennedy, Sources of NT Gk. 1895, 153; Thumb 226]) of a torrential rain Mt 7: 25, 27. M-M. B. 68.*

βρόχος, ου, ὁ (Hom.+; POxy. 51, 16; LXX) *noose* βρόχον ἐπιβάλλειν τινί *put* or *throw a noose on someone* to catch or restrain him (an expr. fr. war or hunting [β. περιβάλλειν τινί: Arrian, Cyneg. 23, 4; 24, 3; Philo, Mos. 2, 252; Jos., Bell. 7, 250]); only fig. 1 Cor 7: 35. M-M.*

βρυγμός, οῦ, ὁ (Eupolis [V BC] 347; Hippocr., περὶ διαίτης 3, 84) *gnashing* of teeth striking together (Galen, Glossar. Hippocr. XIX p. 90 K. βρυγμός· ὁ ἀπὸ τ. ὀδόντων συγκρουομένων ψόφος; s. also Erotian [I AD],

147

Vocum Hippocraticarum Coll. ed. ENachmanson '18 p. 28, 9; 29, 4; Anecd. Gr. 30, 28; Hesychius; Suidas.—Pr 19: 12; Sir 51: 3), ὁ β. τῶν ὀδόντων *chattering* or *gnashing of the teeth* Mt 8: 12; 13: 42, 50; 22: 13; 24: 51; 25: 30; Lk 13: 28 (always w. κλαυθμός).—Chattering of teeth because of cold: Sallust. c. 19 p. 34, 22 the souls are being punished in τόποι ψυχροί. Cf. Plut., Mor. 567c; Apoc. of Paul 42 (MRJames, Apocryphal NT '24, 547).—Grinding of teeth because of pain: Quint. Smyrn. 11, 206. M-M.*

βρύχω impf. ἔβρυχον *gnash* a sign of violent rage (Theodor. Prodr. 5, 49 H.) τοὺς ὀδόντας ἐπ᾽ αὐτόν they *gnashed their teeth against him* Ac 7: 54 (cf. Lex. Vind. p. 34, 5 βρύχει τ. ὀδόντας ἄνθρωπος, βρυχᾶται δὲ λέων; Job 16: 9; Ps 34: 16; 36: 12; Sib. Or. 2, 203; Hippocr., Mul. 1, 2, Epid. 5, 86 and other medical wr. [Hobart 208] of chattering of the teeth in chills and fevers).*

βρύω (Hom.+; usu. intr. as Jos., Ant. 13, 66; Sib. Or. 6, 8) trans. (as Aelian, fgm. 25 p. 197, 20 Herch.; Himerius, Or. 1, 19; Anacreont. 44, 2 Χάριτες ῥόδα βρύουσιν; Justin, Dial. 114, 4; Ps.-Clement, Hom. 2, 45) *pour forth* Js 3: 11. M-M.*

βρῶμα, ατος, τό (Thu., X.+; pap., LXX; Jos., Ant. 3, 29 and 30; 17, 62; Test. Reub. 2, 7 βρῶσις βρωμάτων) *food.*
1. lit. Ro 14: 15a b, 20; 1 Cor 8: 8, 13; GEb 2b. Pl. (Hippocr.+; oft. LXX; En 98, 2) Lk 3: 11; 9: 13; 1 Cor 6: 13a b; 1 Ti 4: 3; Hb 13: 9; B 10: 9; PK 2 p. 14, 20.—Esp. *solid food* (opp. γάλα) 1 Cor 3: 2 (fig.). Pl. (w. ποτά, as 2 Esdr [Ezra] 3: 7) ITr 2: 3; (w. πόματα, as Plato, Leg. 11 p. 932A; Epict., Ench. 33, 2; Test. Reub. 2: 7) Hb 9: 10.—The mng. 'filth', 'stench', as in Mod. Gk. (Rdm.² 12) is most unlikely for Mt 14: 15, Mk 7: 19 (Bl-D. §126, 3, app.).—Of manna: τὸ πνευματικὸν β. 1 Cor 10: 3.
2. fig.: doing the will of God is Jesus' food J 4: 34; cf. Soph., El. 363.—JBehm, TW I 640-3. M-M. B. 329.*

βρώσιμος, ον (Aeschyl., Prom. 479; Antiatt. [Anecd. Gr. 84, 25]; Dit., Syll.³ 624, 38; PSI 306, 7; PGM 10, 1; Lev 19: 23; Ezk 47: 12; 2 Esdr 19 [Neh 9]: 25) *eatable* τί β. *anything to eat* Lk 24: 41. M-M.*

βρῶσις, εως, ἡ (Hom.+; pap., LXX; Ep. Arist. 129; Philo; Joseph.).
1. *eating* (w. πόσις [this combin. since Od. 1, 191; also Diod. S. 1, 45, 2; Plut., Mor. 114c; Da 1: 10; Philo, Mos. 1, 184]) Ro 14: 17; Col 2: 16. W. obj. gen. (as Pla., Rep. 10 p. 619c; Jos., Ant. 1, 334; Test. Reub. 2: 7 βρῶσις βρωμάτων) β. τῶν εἰδωλοθύτων *eating of meat sacrificed to idols* 1 Cor 8: 4; ἄρτος εἰς β. (as Is 55: 10) *bread to eat* 2 Cor 9: 10; ὡς περὶ β. *as if they referred to eating* B 10: 9; ἔχετε τελείως περὶ τῆς β. *you are fully instructed on eating*, i.e. on dietary laws 10: 10; εἰς β. *to eat* PK 2 p. 14, 17.
2. w. σής Mt 6: 19f β. is usu. taken to mean *corrosion, rust* (cf. Galen 6, 422 [pl.]; 12, 879 ed. Kühn 1823 β.= 'decay' of teeth). As a general term for *consuming*, β. may mean another insect as Mal 3: 11 LXX A, where it renders אוכל= 'grasshopper', perh. מַאֲכֹלֶת = *wood worm* (HGressmann, Hdb. ad loc.). Cf. EpJer 10, where a few mss. have βρῶσις instead of βρώματα w. This combin. may argue against the identification of βρῶσις w. ιός in Mt. It is not likely that a hendiadys is present here.
3. *food* (Soph. fgm. 171 [ed. ACPearson '17]; Philostrat., Vi. Apoll. 8, 7 p. 307, 27; PLond. 1223, 9 χόρτον

εἰς βρῶσιν προβάτων; PLeipz. 118, 15; POxy. 1686, 10; Gen 25: 28; Jer 41: 20; 2 Km 19: 43 v.l. βρῶσιν ἐφάγαμεν; Philo, Op. M. 38).
a. lit. Hb 12: 16; D 6: 3; Dg 4: 1.—b. fig. J 4: 32; 6: 27, 55. M-M.*

βρωτός, ή, όν (Archestratus [IV bc], fgm. 28: Corpusc. Poesis Epicae Gr. Ludibundae ed. PBrandt 1888; Porphyr., Abst. 1, 27) verbal adj. of βιβρώσκω *given for food* PK 2 p. 14, 20 (the ref. is to animals given to man for food and honored by him through use in sacrifice, unless β. refers to animals worshipped as gods and means *eatable*).*

βυθίζω 1 aor. pass. ἐβυθίσθην (Soph.+; 2 Macc 12: 4) trans. *sink.*
1. lit., only pass. (Jos., C. Ap. 1, 308) of ships (Polyb. 2, 10, 5; 16, 3, 2; Diod. S. 13, 40, 5; Dio Chrys. 46[63], 3; Epict. 3, 2, 18 βυθιζομένου τοῦ πλοίου) ὥστε βυθίζεσθαι αὐτά (i.e. τὰ πλοῖα) *so that they began to sink* Lk 5: 7. Of pers. *be plunged* εἰς θάλασσαν 1 Cl 51: 5.
2. fig. (cf. Philod., De Morte 33 [DBassi, Pap. Ercolanesi '14]; Alciphr. 1, 16, 1 τὸ νῆφον ἐν ἐμοὶ συνεχῶς ὑπὸ τοῦ πάθους βυθίζεται; Philostrat., Vi. Apoll. 4, 32 p. 151, 17 of the utter ruin of Sparta; Dit., Syll.³ 730, 7 [I bc] καταβυθ.) *plunge* τινά someone εἰς ὄλεθρον καὶ ἀπώλειαν *into ruin and destruction* 1 Ti 6: 9. M-M. B. 679.*

βυθός, οῦ, ὁ (Aeschyl., Hippocr.+; Herm. Wr. 16, 5; POxy. 886, 10; PGM 13, 1072; LXX; Philo; Sib. Or. 3, 481) *depth of the sea* ἐν τῷ β. *adrift at sea* 2 Cor 11: 25. Of deep sea fish ἐν τῷ β. νήχεται *they swim* (only) *in deep water* B 10: 5 (cf. Aelian, N.A. 2, 15; 9, 57). Of water gener.: ἐκ (τοῦ) β. (Sib. Or. 4, 60) Hv 3, 2, 5f; 3, 5, 2; s 9, 3, 3 and 5; 9, 4, 3f; 9, 5, 3; 9, 15, 4; 9, 16, 1 and 5; 9, 17, 3. M-M.*

βυρσεύς, έως, ὁ (Dio Chrys. 38[55], 22; Artem. 4, 56; Inscr. Rom. IV 1216; PFay. 121, 15 [c. 100 AD]; loanw. in rabb.) *tanner*, surname of Simon, a Christian in Joppa Ac 9: 43; 10: 6, 32. M-M.*

βύσσινος, η, ον (Aeschyl., Hdt.+; Plut.; Diod. S. 1, 85, 5; Dit., Or. 90, 17; 29; pap. [BPGrenfell, Revenue Laws of Ptol. Philad. 1896, 103, 1; PEleph. 26, 4; 27a, 11ff; PLond. 1177, 51]; LXX; Ep. Arist. 87; 320; Jos., Ant. 3, 153; Test. 12 Patr.) *made of fine linen* (s. βύσσος), subst. τὸ β. *fine linen, linen garment* (PHolm. 15, 26, PGM 1, 332; 4, 663; Esth 1: 6; Is 3: 23; Da 10: 5; 12: 6f) Rv 18: 12, 16; 19: 8, 14. M-M.*

βύσσος, ου, ἡ (Semit. loanw.= בּוּץ [HLewy, D. sem. Fremdwörter im Griech. 1895, 125]) *fine linen* (Pliny, H.N. 19, 1, [9], 26; Empedocles [V bc] 93; Theocr. 2, 73; Paus. 5, 5, 2; 7, 21, 7; Pollux 7, 17, 75; PGenève 36, 19; PTebt. 313, 20; 598; LXX; Philo, Congr. Erud. Grat. 117; Jos., Ant. 3, 103 al.) for prominent people (Philostrat., Vi. Apoll. 2, 20) πορφύρα καὶ β. (Pr 31: 22; Jos., Ant. 3, 154; cf. Esth 1: 6; Joseph and Aseneth 5, 6 β. χρυσοϋφής) Lk 16: 19; Rv 18: 12 t.r.—PBatiffol, RB n.s. 9, '12, 541-3. M-M.*

βύω 1 aor. ἔβυσα (Hom.+) *stop the ears* (as Lucian, Catapl. 5 β. τὰ ὦτα, Charon 21; Ps 57: 5) IEph 9: 1.*

βωμός, οῦ, ὁ (Hom.+; inscr., pap., LXX, Philo; Jos., Bell. 1, 39, Ant. 1, 157. Loanw. in rabb.; cf. EMaass, ARW 23, '25, 226f) *altar* Ac 17: 23; ὁ τοῦ Ἡλίου β. 1 Cl 25: 4. M-M. B. 1466f.*

Γ

γ′ third letter of the Gk. alphabet, as a numeral=*three* (Jos., C. Ap. 1, 157; cf. Sib. Or. 5: 24) or *third*=τρίτη in the superscr. of 3 J (sc. ἐπιστολή), of Hv 3 (ὅρασις) and Hm 3 (ἐντολή).*

Γαββαθᾶ indecl. (an Aram. word whose mng. is still uncertain. Acc. to Jos., Bell. 5, 51 Γαβάθ Σαούλ is to be rendered λόφος Σαούλου) *Gabbatha*, a locality in Jerusalem which also had the Gk. name Λιθόστρωτον (q.v.) J 19: 13. CCTorrey ZAW 65, '53, 232f holds the word is Latin, viz. gabata='platter' and was adapted to Aramaic; the stone pavement resembled such a dish.*

Γαβριήλ, ὁ indecl. (גַּבְרִיאֵל, man of God) *Gabriel*, name of an archangel (Da 8: 16; 9: 21; En. 9, 1 al.; Wadd. 2068; PGM 1, 302; 3, 149; 535; 4, 1815; 7, 1013; 1017; 36, 309; Bousset, Rel.³ 325-8; Billerb. II 126ff) Lk 1: 19, 26 (for an angel announcing a birth, cf. Judg 13: 2ff, which is peculiarly embellished Jos., Ant. 5, 276-84).*

γάγγραινα, ης, ἡ *gangrene*, *cancer* of spreading ulcers, etc. (medical term since Hippocr.). Fig. (as Plut., Mor. 65D of slanders) 2 Ti 2: 17.*

Γάδ, ὁ indecl. (גָּד) *Gad* (Gen 30: 11; 49: 19; Philo, Somn. 2, 34; Test. 12 Patr.—In Joseph. Γάδας [Ant. 1, 306] or Γάδης [Ant. 2, 182], ου [Ant. 6, 99]) φυλὴ Γ. Rv 7: 5.*

Γαδαρηνός, ή, όν from Gadara, a city in Transjordania; ὁ Γ. *the Gadarene* (Jos., Vi. 42; 44) Mt 8: 28; Mk 5: 1 v.l.; Lk 8: 26 v.l., 37 v.l. Origen held Gadara could not be the name intended in these passages and adopted the rdg. Γεργεσηνῶν (q.v.); cf. his comments In Joannem 6, 6, 41, 208ff Pr. (cf. 10, 19, 113). The rdg. Γερασηνῶν (q.v.) was also known in his time.—Difficulties which similar-sounding names cause in the tradition are old. A scholion on Od. 1, 85 [in Hes., fgm. 70 Rz.] says w. reference to the Homeric νῆσον ἐς Ὠγυγίην that Antimachus [IV BC] calls the island Ὠγυλίη. The scholion goes on to say: διαφέρουσι δὲ οἱ τόποι.—ThZahn, D. Land der Gadarener, Gerasener, Gergesener: NKZ 13, '02, 923-45; GDalman, Pj 7, '11, 20ff, Orte³ '24; OProcksch, Pj 14, '18, 20; DVölter, D. Heilg. d. Besessenen im Lande der Gerasener od. Gadarener od. Gergesener: NThT 9, '20, 285-97.*

Γάζα, ης, ἡ (עַזָּה) *Gaza* (Diod. S. 19, 59, 2; Strabo 16, 2, 21; Arrian, Anab. 2, 26 and elsewhere in the story of Alexander; inscr.; Gen 10: 19 al.; Ep. Arist.; Joseph.; Sib. Or. 3, 345) one of the 5 chief cities of the Philistines, in south-west Palestine; it was touched by the caravan route leading to Egypt Ac 8: 26 (where the added phrase αὕτη ἐστὶν ἔρημος refers to ὁδός).—WJPhythian-Adams, The Problem of 'Deserted' Gaza: PEF '23, 30-6). Schürer II⁴ 110ff; MMeyer, History of the City of Gaza '07; IBenzinger, Pauly-W. VII '10, 880ff; PThomsen, Reallex. der Vorgesch. IV '26, 178ff. M-M.*

γάζα, ης, ἡ (fr. Persian ganuš treasure; found as a loanw. in Gk. since Theophr., H. Pl. 8, 11, 5; Polyb.; Diod. S.; Plut.; Appian, Mithrid. 23 §93; Dit., Or. 54, 21f; LXX, cf. Hebr. גִּזְבָּר treasurer) *the* (royal) *treasury* ὃς ἦν ἐπὶ πάσης τῆς γάζης αὐτῆς *who was her chief treasurer* Ac 8: 27.—HHSchaeder, Iran. Beiträge I '30, 47. M-M*

γαζοφυλάκειον, ου, τό (v.l. γαζοφυλάκιον, preferred by Bl-D. §13) lit. *treasure room, treasury* (Diod. S. 9, 12, 2;

Strabo 7, 6, 1; Dit., Or. 225, 16; Esth 3: 9; 1 Macc 3: 28). In this sense our sources of information on the Jerusalem temple speak of γαζοφ. in the pl. (2 Esdr 22 [Neh 12]: 44; Jos., Bell. 5, 200; 6, 282) and sg. (1 Macc 14: 49; 2 Macc 3: 6, 24, 28, 40; 4: 42; 5: 18; 2 Esdr 23 [Neh 13]: 5, 7; Jos., Ant. 19, 294). It can be taken in this sense J 8: 20 *in* (or *at*) *the treasury*. For Mk 12: 41, 43; Lk 21: 1 the mng. *contribution box* or *receptacle* is certainly preferable. Acc. to Shekalim 6, 5 there were in the temple 13 such receptacles in the form of trumpets.—Billerb. II 37-41. M-M.*

Γάιος, ου, ὁ (found frequently, e.g. Diod. S. 11, 60, 1; 13, 104, 1; 19, 73, 1) *Gaius* name of several Christians about whom little is known.
   1. fr. Derbe Ac 20: 4.—**2.** fr. Macedonia, companion of Paul in Ephesus 19: 29.
   3. fr. Corinth, baptized by Paul 1 Cor 1: 14. Paul lived w. him when he wrote Ro 16: 23. See Gdspd. s.v. Τίτιος.
   4. the man to whom 3 J was addressed (vs. 1).
   5. name of the copyist of the Martyrdom of Polycarp, MPol 22: 2; Epil Mosq 1: 4.—JChapman, JTS 5, '04, 366 identifies 1 and 4, perh. 3. M-M.*

γάλα, γάλακτος, τό (Hom.+; inscr., pap., LXX; Jos., Ant. 5, 207) *milk*.
   1. lit. as food 1 Cor 9: 7; B 6: 17. W. honey as sign of fertility 6: 8, 10, 13 (cf. Ex 3: 8, 17; 13: 5 al.; Lucian, Saturn. 7, Ep. Sat. 1, 20; Himerius, Or. 13, 7 W. ῥεῖν μέλι καὶ γάλα; Dio Chrys. 18[35], 18 Indian rivers, in which milk, wine, honey and oil flow). γάλα τ. γυναικῶν (Hippocr. VIII p. 206 L.) AP, fgm. 2 p. 12, 24, cf. πήγνυμι 1.
   2. fig. (cf. Philo, Agr. 9 ἐπεὶ δὲ νηπίοις μέν ἐστι γάλα τροφή, τελείοις δὲ τὰ ἐκ πυρῶν πέμματα, καὶ ψυχῆς γαλακτώδεις μὲν ἂν εἶεν τροφαὶ κτλ., Omn. Prob. Lib. 160, Migr. Abr. 29 al.; Epict. 2, 16, 39; 3, 24, 9. For Hebraic associations s. FWDanker, ZNW 58, '67, 94f) of elementary Christian instruction 1 Cor 3: 2; Hb 5: 12f. τὸ λογικὸν ἄδολον γ. the pure (*unadulterated*) *spiritual milk* 1 Pt 2: 2 (Sallust. 4 p. 8, 24 of the mysteries: γάλακτος τροφὴ ὥσπερ ἀναγεννωμένων). Cf. HUsener, Milch u. Honig: RhM 57, '02, 177-95= Kleine Schriften IV '14, 398ff; ADieterich, Mithraslit. '03, 171; RPerdelwitz, D. Mysterienrel. u. d. Problem des 1 Pt '11, 56ff; KWyss, D. Milch im Kultus d. Griech. u. Römer '14; FRLehmann, D. Entstehung der sakralen Bedeutung der Milch: ZMR 22, '17, 1-12; 33-45; EGSelwyn, 1 Pt. '46, ad loc. and 308f; HSchlier, TW I 644f. M-M. B. 385.*

Γαλάτης, ου, ὁ (since Demetrius of Byz. [c. 275 BC] who described in 13 books τὴν Γαλατῶν διάβασιν ἐξ Εὐρώπης εἰς Ἀσίαν [Diog. L. 5, 83]; inscr.; 1 Macc 8: 2; 2 Macc 8: 20; Joseph.; Sib. Or.) *a Galatian*, inhabitant of Galatia (so Demetr. of Byz.; Strabo 12, 5, 2 al.; see the foll. entry) Gal 3: 1 (cf. Callim., Hymn. 4, 184 Schn. Γαλάτησι ἄφρονι φύλῳ. In a Hamb. Pap. [III BC] p. 131, 9 Coll. the Galatians are called ἄφρονες); superscription.*

Γαλατία, ας, ἡ (Diocles 125; Appian, Mithr. 17 §60; 65 §272 al.; Cass. Dio 53, 26; inscr.) *Galatia*, a district in Asia Minor, abode of the Celtic Galatians, and a Roman province to which, in addition to the orig. Galatia, Isauria, Cilicia and northern Lycaonia belonged. The exact mng. of G. in the NT, esp. in Paul, is a much disputed question.

Gal 1: 2; 1 Cor 16: 1; 2 Ti 4: 10 (in this pass. some mss. have Γαλλίαν, and even the better attested rdg. Γαλατίαν can be understood as referring to Gaul: Diod. S. 5, 22, 4 al.; Appian, Celts 1 §2 al.; Polyaenus 8, 23, 2; Jos., Ant. 17, 344; other ref. in Zahn, Einl. I 418.—In order to avoid confusion, it was possible to say something like Γαλατία τῆς ἑῴας=eastern [Appian, Bell. Civ. 2, 49 §202] or Γαλάται οἱ ἐν 'Ασίᾳ [Appian, Bell. Civ. 4, 88 §373]); 1 Pt 1: 1. For the NT there are only two possibilities, both of which involve the Galatia in Asia Minor. The view that G. means the district orig. inhabited by the Galatians (North Gal. theory) is favored in recent times by vDobschütz, Jülicher, MDibelius, Feine, Ltzm., JMoffatt, Goguel, Sickenberger, Lagrange, Meinertz, Oepke, E Haenchen (Ac '71, 483, 2), ASteinmann (esp. detailed, D. Leserkreis des Gal. '08), and Mommsen (ZNW 2, '01, 86). Impressive support is given this point of view by Memnon of Asia Minor, a younger contemporary of Paul. For him the Galatians, of whom he speaks again and again (no. 434 fgm. 1, 11ff Jac.), are the people with a well-defined individuality, who came to Asia Minor from Europe. He would never address the Lycaonians as Γαλάται.—The opp. view, that G. means the Rom. province (South Gal. theory), is adopted by Zahn, Ramsay, EMeyer, EDBurton (Gal '21), GSDuncan (Gal '34), esp. VWeber (Des Pls Reiserouten '20). S. also FStähelin, Gesch. d. kleinasiat. Galater² '07; RSyme, Galatia and Pamphylia under Aug.: Klio 27, '34, 122-48; CHWatkins, D. Kampf des Pls um Galatien '13; JHRopes, The Singular Prob. of the Ep. to the Gal. '29; LWeisgerber, Galat. Sprachreste: JGeffcken-Festschr. '31, 151-75. M-M.*

Γαλατικός, ή, όν (Diod. S. 5, 39, 7; Arrian, Anab. 2, 4, 1; Polyaenus 4, 6, 17; inscr.) *Galatian* χώρα *the Galatian country* Ac 16: 6; 18: 23. Here prob. the district, not the Rom. province, is meant; but s. WRamsay, St. P. the Traveler and Rom. Citizen, 1896, 104; 194 (s. Γαλατία).*

γαλῆ, ῆς, ἡ (contr. fr. γαλέη; since Hdt.; found in Batr.) *weasel* PK 2 p. 14, 19; acc. to Lev 11: 29 its flesh was not to be eaten B 10: 8 (on the odd view expressed here cf. Aelian, N.A. 2, 55; 9, 65; Plut., Is. et Osir. 74 p. 380F; Anton. Lib. 29, 3; Ep. Arist. 144; 163; 165; Physiologus 21 p. 253f L.).*

γαλήνη, ης, ἡ (Hom.+; Epict. 2, 18, 30; Sym. Ps 106: 29; loanw. in rabb.) *a calm* on the sea (Diod. S. 3, 21, 1; Appian, Bell. Civ. 4, 115 §480; Lucian, Dial. Mar. 1, 3; 15, 3; fig., Philo; Jos., Bell. 3, 195) Mt 8: 26; Mk 4: 39; Lk 8: 24. M-M.*

Γαλιλαία, ας, ἡ *Galilee* (fr. גָּלִיל *circle, district,* really גְּלִיל הַגּוֹיִם *district of the Gentiles,* Is 8: 23 [9: 1]; Mt 4: 15, Aram. גְּלִילָא; Strabo 16, 2, 34; 40; LXX; Philo, Leg. ad Gai. 326; Joseph.), after the Exile the northern part of Palestine, bounded by Syria, Sidon, Tyre, Ptolemais, Carmel, the plain of Jezreel, and the Jordan (Jos., Bell. 3, 35-40). It was divided into Northern (Upper) and Southern (Lower) Gal. (Jos., Bell. 3, 35; 2, 568; 573, Vi. 187f; Jdth 1: 8; Shebiith 9, 2), and fr. the death of Herod the Great (4 BC) until 39 AD it belonged to the tetrarchy of Herod Antipas. Mentioned w. Samaria Lk 17: 11; Ac 9: 31; w. the Decapolis Mt 4: 25; w. Judaea Lk 5: 17; Ac 9: 31; J 4: 47, 54. Used to specify names of places, well-known or otherwise: Ναζαρὲτ τῆς Γ. Mt 21: 11; Mk 1: 9; Κανᾶ τῆς Γ. J 2: 1, 11; 4: 46; 21: 2; Βηθσαϊδὰ τῆς Γ. 12: 21; θάλασσα τῆς Γ. the Lake (Sea) of Tiberias, or Gennesaret Mt 4: 18; 15: 29; Mk 1: 16; 7: 31; J 6: 1; τὰ μέρη τῆς Γ. the district of Gal. (s. μέρος 1bγ) Mt 2: 22; ἡ

περίχωρος τῆς Γ. the surrounding country of G. Mk 1: 28.—Outside the gospels only Ac 9: 31; 10: 37; 13: 31.—HGuthe, RE VI 336ff, XXIII 496f; VSchwöbel, D. Landesnatur Palästinas I; II '14; CWatzinger, Denkmäler Palästinas II '35; GBertram, ARW 32, '35, 265-81; GSchrenk, Gal. z. Zt. Jesu '41; WAMeeks, Galilee and Judea in the 4th Gosp., JBL 85, '66, 159-69.

Γαλιλαῖος, α, ον (Joseph.) *Galilean, ὁ Γ. the Galilean,* inhabitant of Galilee Mt 26: 69; Ac 2: 7; cf. J 7: 52; recognizable by his dialect Mk 14: 70; Lk 22: 59.—Lk 13: 1f; 23: 6; J 4: 45; Ac 1: 11 (Epict. 4, 7, 6 οἱ Γαλιλαῖοι= the Christians). Surname of the insurrectionist Judas 5: 37.*

Γαλλία 2 Ti 4: 10 v.l., s. Γαλατία.

Γαλλίων, ωνος, ὁ *Gallio* (Prosopogr. Imp. Rom. II p. 237; Tacit., Annal. 15, 73 Junius Gallio, Senecae frater) proconsul of Achaia 51-2, Ac 18: 12, 14, 17.—ADeissmann, Paulus² '25, 203-25 (lit., esp. p. 210f; Paul² '26, 261-86); LHennequin, Dictionnaire de la Bible, Suppl. II '34, 355-73; MGoguel, RHPhr 12, '32, 321-33. M-M.*

Γαμαλιήλ, ὁ indecl. (גַּמְלִיאֵל, Num 1: 10; 2: 20 al., in Joseph. Γαμαλίηλος, ου [Ant. 20, 213]) *Gamaliel.* The NT knows only Rabban G. the Elder, a Pharisee and renowned teacher of the law in Jerusalem Ac 5: 34. Acc. to 22: 3 Paul's teacher.—Schürer II⁴ 429f; WBacher, Jewish Encycl. V '03, 558ff; Billerb. II 636-9; HBöhlig, Der Rat des G. in Ac 5: 38f; StKr 86, '13, 112-20; HSteege, Beth-El 27, '35, 298-304 (on Ac 5: 34); MSEnslin, Paul and G.: Journ. of Rel. 7, '27, 360-75, G's Speech and Caligula's Statue: HTR 37, '44, 341-9.*

γαμετή, ῆς, ἡ (Hes.+; PTebt. 104, 17 [I BC]; POxy. 795, 4; Dit., Syll.³ 921, 110, Or. 206, 9; Jos., Bell. 1, 475, Ant. 1, 209; 4 Macc 2: 11) *wife* 1 Cl 6: 3.*

γαμέω (Hom.+; inscr., pap.; Phryn. 742 L.) impf. ἐγάμουν (Lk 17: 27); 1 aor. ἔγημα (Lk 14: 20), subj. γήμω (1 Cor 7: 28), ptc. γήμας (Mt 22: 25) and ἐγάμησα (Mt 5: 32; Mk 6: 17; 10: 11); 1 aor. pass. ἐγαμήθην (1 Cor 7: 39); perf. act. γεγάμηκα (1 Cor 7: 10). Cf. Bl-D. §101; Rob. 1213; Mlt.-H. 231.

1. *marry,* said of a man (Hom.+ gener.).

a. w. acc. (Hom. et al.; Dit., Or. 391, 8; 392, 11; Audollent, Defix. Tab. 78; Esth 10: 3c; Jos., Ant. 6, 309; 7, 70) a divorced woman Mt 5: 32; Mk 6: 17; Lk 16: 18b; another wife Mt 19: 9; Mk 10: 11; Lk 16: 18a; Hm 4, 1, 6; a wife Lk 14: 20 (the aor. form is exceptional in the NT, and the more usual expr. is λαβεῖν [γυναῖκα] as in ms. D of 14: 20; cf. 20: 28, 29, 31; 1 Cor 7: 28 DG; GDKilpatrick, JTS 18, '67, 139f).

b. abs. (POxy. 1213, 4; PFlor. 332, 24; 2 Macc 14: 25; 4 Macc 16: 9; Jos., C. Ap. 2, 201) *marry, enter matrimony* Mt 19: 10; 22: 25, 30; 24: 38; Mk 12: 25; Lk 17: 27; 20: 34f; 1 Cor 7: 28, 33; Hm 4, 1, 8; IPol 5: 2; Agr 18.

2. *marry* of both sexes (M. Ant. 4, 32; PEleph. 2, 8[285/4 BC]; BGU 717, 16 οἱ γαμοῦντες) 1 Cor 7: 9f, 36; 1 Ti 4: 3; Hm 4, 4, 1f; Dg 5: 6.

3. *marry* of women—a. act.—α. w. acc. (only Eur., Med. 606 ironically) Mk 10: 12 (t.r. γαμηθῇ ἄλλῳ is adapted to more common usage; s. 3c).

β. abs. (Charito 3, 2, 17 'Αφροδίτη γαμεῖ) 1 Cor 7: 28b, 34; 1 Ti 5: 11, 14.

b. mid. (Hom.+), esp. ptc. ἡ γαμουμένη (as POxy. 496, 5; 905, 10) IPol 5: 2.

c. pass. *get married, be married* (X., An. 4, 5, 24; Plut., Romul. 2, 1; Anton. Lib. 16, 2; 20, 7; Ps.-Apollod. 1, 147

Μήδεια γαμηθεῖσα Αἰγεῖ παῖδα γεννᾷ; POxy. 361, 1 [I AD]; 257, 25; 30; PGrenf. II 76, 11 ἀλλ᾽ ἐξεῖναι αὐτῇ γαμηθῆναι ὡς ἂν βούληθῇ; Philo, Spec. Leg. 1, 110; Jos., Ant. 6, 308) Mk 10: 12 t.r. (s. 3aa); 1 Cor 7: 39.—For lit. s. γαμίζω 1 and cf. HPreisker, Christent. u. Ehe in d. ersten drei Jahrh. '27, Ehe u. Charisma b. Pls: ZsystTh 6, '29, 91-5; WMichaelis, Ehe u. Charisma b. Pls: ibid. 5, '28, 426-52; HSchumacher, D. Eheideal d. Ap. Pls '32; EStauffer, TW I 646-55; FBüchsel, D. Ehe im Urchristent.: ThBl 21, '42, 113-28; AOepke, RAC IV, '59, 650-66; AIsaksson, Marriage and Ministry in the New Temple, '65; RSchnackenburg, Schriften zum NT, '71, 414-34. S. also on γυνή 1. M-M. B. 98.*

γαμίζω impf. pass. ἐγαμιζόμην (Apollon. Dysc., Synt. 3, 153 p. 400 Uhlig ἔστι γὰρ τὸ μὲν πρότερον [i.e. γαμῶ] γάμου μεταλαμβάνω, τὸ δὲ γαμίζω γάμου τινὶ μεταδίδωμι. Otherw. the word is found only in Christian writings).
1. act. *give* (a woman) *in marriage* abs. Mt 24: 38; Mk 12: 25 D. Perh. also γ. abs. and w. acc. 1 Cor 7: 38 is to be understood in this sense, of a father who gives his daughter (or a guardian who gives his ward) in marriage (t.r. ἐκγαμίζων). Another view prefers to take γ. here= γαμέω (on this possibility s. Ltzm., Hdb. ad loc.; Bl-D. §101 p. 44 agrees; cf. Mlt.-H. 409f. It is hard to say how far the rule of Apollon., quoted above, applies, since there are so few exx. of γ. On the increasing frequency of formations in -ίζω s. Psaltes p. 325-31. γαμίζω='marry' is also found in Methodius, Sympos. 3, 14 p. 44, 21 Bonwetsch). In the context of vss. 36-8 παρθένος would then mean either a Christian's fiancée (s. ref. to Gdspd. below and RSV), or perh. even his 'spiritual bride', who lived with him as a virgin.—EGrafe, Theol. Arbeiten aus d. Rhein. wiss. Predigerverein n.F. 3, 1899, 57-69; H Achelis, Virgines subintroductae '02; AJülicher, ARW 7, '04, 373-86; PM 22, '18, 97-119; JSickenberger, BZ 3, '05, 44-69; HKoch, ibid. 3, '05, 401-7; FFahnenbruch, ibid. 12, '14, 391-401; AvanVeldhuizen, ThSt 23, '05, 185-202, NThSt 2, '19, 297-309; RSteck, SchThZ 34, '17, 177-89; StSchiwietz, ThGl 19, '27, 1-15; KHolzhey, ibid. 307f; AJuncker, D. Ethik d. Ap. Pls II '19, 191ff; KMüller, D. Forderung d. Ehelosigkeit für d. Getauften in d. alten Kirche '27; HKoch, Quellen z. Gesch. d. Askese '33; Gdspd., Probs. 158f; RKugelman, CBQ 10, '48, 63-71; AOepke, ThLZ 77, '52, 449-52; WGKümmel: Bultmann-Festschr. '54, 275-95; JO'Rourke, CBQ 20, '58, 292-98; RHASebolt, CTM 30, '59, 103-10; 176-89; HBaltensweiler, Die Ehe im NT, '67; HGreeven, NTS 15, '69, 365-88.
2. pass. *be given in marriage, be married* of women Mt 22: 30; Mk 12: 25; Lk 17: 27; 20: 35. M-M.*

γαμίσκω (Aristot., Pol. 7, 14, 4; Stob. et al.)=γαμίζω act. *give in marriage* Mt 24: 38 v.l.; pass., *be given in marriage* of a woman (Aristot., loc. cit.; Heraclides Hist. 64 [Aristot., Fgm. ed. VRose 1886, 383]; PLond. 1708, 98; 168; 177 ἐγαμίσκετο ἀνδρί) Mk 12: 25 t.r.; Lk 20: 34, 35 v.l.*

γάμος, ου, ὁ (Hom.+; inscr., pap., LXX, Philo, Joseph.; sg. and pl. are oft. used interchangeably w. no difference in mng.; cf. Dit., Syll.³ 1106, 102 διδότω ὁ ἱερεὺς εἰς τοὺς γάμους τὰ γέρη τῷ τὸν γάμον ποιοῦντι. Joseph. distinguishes in Ant. 14, 467f betw. γάμος=wedding and γάμοι =wedding celebration. But for 'marriage' he somet. uses the sg. [s. 2 below], somet. the pl. [Ant. 20, 141]; Field, Notes, 16).

1. *wedding celebration*—a. gener., pl. (the pl. is used in this sense as early as the class. poets and Isaeus 8, 18; 20; BGU 892, 10; 13; 909, 3; PGiess. 31, 16; POxy. 111, 2; 927, 2.—Joseph., s. above) γάμους ποιεῖν *give a wedding celebration* Mt 22: 2 (on γ. ποιεῖν cf. Demosth. 30, 21; Menand., fgm. 450 K.; Achilles Tat. 1, 3, 3; Xenophon Eph. 2, 7, 1; Inscr. gr. 1001 II, 19; Tob 6: 13; 8: 19; 1 Macc 9: 37; 10: 58); καλεῖσθαι εἰς τοὺς γ. *be invited to the wedding* (POxy. 1486) vss. 3, 9 (cf. Tob 9: 5S).—Vs. 4 (on the parable Mt 22: 1-14 s. JSickenberger, ByzZ 30, '30, 253-61; VHasler, ThZ 18, '62, 25-35). Sg. [LXX] Mt 22: 8; J 2: 1f; ἔνδυμα γ. *a wedding garment* Mt 22: 11f (cf. Aristoph., Av. 1692 γαμικὴν χλανίδα; Achilles Tat. 2, 11, 2f).

b. *wedding banquet* (Herodas 7, 86; Diod. S. 4, 81, 4) fig., of the joys of the Messianic Kingdom (cf. Is 25: 6; 4 Esdr 2: 38) Rv 19: 7, 9; εἰσέρχεσθαι εἰς τοὺς γ. Mt 25: 10 (pl. as Esth 2: 18; Diog. L. 3, 2 ἐν γάμοις δειπνῶν). γάμοι can also mean *banquet* without ref. to a wedding (Esth 9: 22) Lk 12: 36; 14: 8.

c. fig. *wedding hall* ἐπλήσθη ὁ γάμος (s. νυμφών) ἀνακειμένων *the hall was filled w. guests* Mt 22: 10 t.r.

2. *marriage* (Diod. S. 2, 5, 1; Maximus Tyr. 26, 6a; 26, 9d; Chio, Ep. 10; Herodian 3, 10, 5; POxy. 905, 4 [120 AD] al.; pap., Wsd 14: 24, 26; Jos., Ant. 6, 210, Vi. 4) Hb 13: 4; IPol 5: 2. M-M. B. 98.*

γάρ (Hom.+; inscr., pap., LXX) conjunction used to express cause, inference, continuation, or to explain. Never comes first in its clause; usu. second, but also third (Hb 11: 32), or even fourth (2 Cor 1: 19, as e.g. Menand., Epitr. 217; 499; Lucian, Pisc. 10, Philops. 15).

1. cause or reason: *for*—a. abs. Mk 1: 22; 9: 49; Lk 1: 15; 21: 4; J 2: 25; Ac 2: 25; Ro 1: 9; 1 Cor 11: 5 and oft.—It should be noted that γάρ w. a verb (and nothing else) can form a sentence (Demosth. 21, 28 δίδωσι γάρ; Epicurus in Diog. L. 10, 32 κινεῖ γάρ; Menand., Sam. 321; Alexis Com. 286 Kock παύσει γάρ.; Axionicus Com. [IV BC] 6, 6 K.: Ael. Aristid. 13 p. 273 D.; Maximus Tyr. 10, 8g δύναται γάρ; Lucian, Dial. Mort. 3, 3; Synes., Ep. 4 p. 163D ἠνεχυρίαστο γάρ=for it had been seized as security; Aristaen., Ep. 2, 7; Anna Comn., Alexias 5, 1 vol. I p. 156, 8 R. προπέποτο γάρ; Ps.-Demetrius, Form. Ep. p. 12, 2 as conclusion of a letter ὀφείλω γάρ; Vi. Aesopi I c. 67 as the ending of a story: οὐκ ἔχεις γάρ=you don't have any [understanding, common sense]; Polyaenus 3 the introduction ends with the words: πρόδηλον γάρ. —Cf. also CHKraeling, JBL 44, '25, 357f; RRottley, JTS 27, '26, 407-9; RHLightfoot, Locality and Doctrine in the Gosp. '38, 10ff; CFDMoule, NTS 2, '55/'56, 58f) ἐφοβοῦντο γάρ Mk 16: 8 (s. φοβέω 1a). But unintentional conclusions of this kind are also found (Horapollo 2, 80 οὗτος γάρ. This breaks the connection and the composition is ended).

b. used w. other particles and conjunctions ἰδοὺ γάρ (Jdth 5: 23; 9: 7; 12: 12; 1 Macc 9: 45) Lk 1: 44, 48; 2: 10; 6: 23; 17: 21; Ac 9: 11; 2 Cor 7: 11. καὶ γάρ *for* (=Lat. etenim, Kühner-G. II 338. Cf. Charito 3, 3, 16 καὶ γάρ; 2 Macc 1: 19; 4 Macc 1: 2; 5: 9) Mk 10: 45; Lk 22: 37; J 4: 23; Ac 19: 40; 1 Cor 5: 7; Hb 5: 12; 12: 29; Hs 9, 8, 2; *for also, for even* (ZNW 19, '20, 175f) Mt 8: 9; Lk 6: 32f; 7: 8; 11: 4; J 4: 45; Ro 11: 1; 15: 3; 16: 2; 2 Cor 2: 10. Cf. FWGrosheide, καὶ γάρ in het NT: ThSt 33, '15, 108-10. γὰρ καί *for also, for precisely* 2 Cor 2: 9. τε γάρ *for indeed* (X., Mem. 1, 1, 3) Ro 1: 26; 7: 7; Hb 2: 11. μὲν γάρ, often followed by δέ, ἀλλά (2 Macc 6: 4; 7: 36; 4 Macc 9: 8f, 31f.—3 Macc 2: 15f) Ac 13: 36; 23: 8 v.l.; 28: 22; Ro 2: 25; 2 Cor 9: 1; 11: 4; Hb 7: 18, 20; 12: 10. ὅτι μὲν γάρ—ἀλλά

Ac 4: 16. καὶ γὰρ οὐ 1 Cor 11: 9; οὐ γὰρ Mt 9: 13; 10: 20; Mk 4: 22; 6: 52; Lk 6: 43; J 2: 17, 34; Ac 2: 34; Ro 1: 16; 2: 11, 13, 28; 4: 13; 1 Cor 1: 17; 2 Cor 1: 8, 13; Gal 4: 30 and oft. μὴ γάρ Js 1: 7. οὐδὲ γάρ Lk 20: 36; J 5: 22; 7: 5; 8: 42; Ro 8: 7; Gal 1: 12. οὔτε γάρ—οὔτε (Wsd 12: 13; Sir 30: 19) for neither—nor 1 Th 2: 5.

c. γάρ is somet. repeated. It occurs twice either to introduce several arguments for the same assertion, as (Sir 37: 13f; 38: 1f; Wsd 7: 16f) J 8: 42; 1 Cor 16: 7; 2 Cor 11: 19f; or to have one clause confirm the other, as (Jdth 5: 23; 7: 27; 1 Macc 11: 10) Mt 10: 19f; Lk 8: 29; J 5: 21f, 46; Ac 2: 15; Ro 6: 14; 8: 2f; Hv 5: 3; or to have various assertions of one and the same sentence confirmed one after the other Mt 3: 2f; J 3: 19f (cf. Wsd 1: 5f; EpJer 6; 7). γάρ also occurs three times (Wsd 9: 13-15; 14: 27-9) Mt 16: 25-7; Lk 9: 24-6; Ro 4: 13-15; 2 Cor 3: 9-11; four times Mk 8: 35-8; Ro 1: 16-18; even five times 1 Cor 9: 15-17.

d. the general is confirmed by the specific Mk 7: 10; Lk 12: 52; Ro 7: 2; 1 Cor 12: 8;—the specific by the general Mt 7: 8; 13: 12; 22: 14; Mk 4: 22, 25.

e. Oft. the thought to be supported is not expressed, but must be supplied fr. the context, e.g. (he has truly been born,) for we have seen his star Mt 2: 2. (Let no one refuse,) ὃς γὰρ ἐὰν θέλῃ Mk 8: 35; Lk 9: 24. (Let no disciple fail to testify,) ὃς γὰρ ἐὰν ἐπαισχυνθῇ με Mk 8: 38. This is common; cf. Ac 13: 36; 21: 13; 22: 26; Ro 8: 18; 14: 10; 1 Cor 1: 18; 5: 3; 9: 9, 17; 14: 9; 1 Th 2: 1. Used w. other particles καὶ γάρ Mt 15: 27; 2 Cor 5: 2; 13: 4; Phil 2: 27; 1 Th 3: 4; 4: 10. καὶ γὰρ οὐ 2 Cor 3: 10. μὲν γάρ Ro 2: 25; 1 Cor 5: 3; 11: 7; 2 Cor 9: 1; Hb 7: 18. οὐ γάρ Mt 9: 13; Mk 9: 6; Lk 6: 43f; Ac 4: 20; Ro 8: 15; 2 Cor 1: 13.

f. oft. in questions, where the English idiom leaves the word untransl., adds then, pray, or prefixes what! or why! to the question (Hyperid., fgm. 219; Ael. Aristid. 47, 27 K.=23 p. 452 D.; Jos., Bell. 1, 589, Ant. 9, 92) ποῖον γὰρ κλέος; what credit is there? 1 Pt 2: 20. μὴ γάρ . . . ἔρχεται; what! Is the Messiah to hail fr. Galilee? J 7: 41. μὴ γὰρ οἰκίας οὐκ ἔχετε; what! Have you no houses? 1 Cor 11: 22. ποία γὰρ ἡ ζωὴ ὑμῶν; what, pray, is your life? Js 4: 14 v.l. πῶς γὰρ ἂν δυναίμην; how in the world can I? Ac 8: 31.—Esp. τίς γάρ; τί γάρ; in direct questions: Mt 9: 5; 16: 26; 23: 17, 19 and oft. τί γὰρ κακὸν ἐποίησεν; why, what evil thing has he done? 27: 23; cf. Mk 15: 14; Lk 23: 22. τί γάρ; transitional, what, then, is the situation? Ro 3: 3; what does it matter? Phil 1: 18.

2. explanatory: for, you see (Dionys. Hal., De Isocr. p. 542 Raderm.; Lucian, Dial. Mort. 10, 9 p. 373 κοῦφα γὰρ ὄντα; BGU 830, 20 ἐπεὶ γὰρ καὶ γείτων αὐτοῦ εἰμί=since I am also, as you see, his neighbor; Ps.-Demetr. 153 p. 35, 16 R.; Ps.-Callisth. 3, 2, 2 ἐγὼ γάρ=for I) Mt 12: 40, 50; 23: 3; 24: 38; Mk 7: 3; Lk 9: 14; J 3: 16; 4: 8f; Ro 7: 2; Hb 3: 4; 2 Pt 2: 8.—Short, explanatory parenthetical clauses (Diod. S. 13, 66, 6 ἦν γὰρ ὁ Κλέαρχος χαλεπός) Mt 4: 18; Mk 1: 16; 2: 15; 5: 42; 16: 4; Ro 7: 1; 1 Cor 16: 5.—S. Dana and Mantey 243.

3. inferential: certainly, by all means, so, then. In self-evident conclusions, esp. in exclamations, strong affirmations, etc. (Diogenes the Cynic in Diog. L. 6, 47 παῦσαι γάρ=stop, then) μὴ γὰρ οἰέσθω ὁ ἄνθρωπος ἐκεῖνος let that man by no means believe Js 1: 7; μὴ γάρ τις ὑμῶν πασχέτω by no means let any of you suffer 1 Pt 4: 15; ἀναλογίσασθε γὰρ τὸν . . . ὑπομεμενηκότα by all means consider him who endured Hb 12: 3; οὐ γάρ no, indeed! Ac 16: 37 (Aristoph., Nub. 232, Ran. 58; Pla., Rep. 492c; Lucian, Jupp. Conf. 16). In weakened sense it is somet. resumptive, esp. in long periodic sentences: ηὐδόκησαν

γάρ they decided, then Ro 15: 27. ἐλεύθερος γὰρ ὢν though I am free, then 1 Cor 9: 19 (cf. vs. 1). Sim. 2 Cor 5: 4.

4. expressing continuation or connection (in later Gk. writers, where more recent users of the texts, not finding the causal force they expect, would often prefer to see it replaced by δέ (unnecessarily, since the grammarian Trypho Alex. [I bc], fgm. 54 ed. AvVelsen 1853 shows clearly that γάρ under certain circumstances εἰς οὖν ἐστὶν ἀντὶ τοῦ δέ=is one and the same thing as δέ) Diod. S. 20, 35, 1; Iambl., Vi. Pyth. §1; 120; 158; 197 [LDeubner, Bemerkungen z. Text der Vi. Pyth. des Jambl. '35, 30f]; Arrian, Ind. 33, 1 ἀλλὰ ἔπλωον . . . = but then they sailed . . . ; schol. on Od. 4, 22 p. 174, 10 Dind.; Dit., Syll.³ 1109, 28 [II ad]; Philo, Leg. All. 3, 192; Jos., Bell. 7, 43, Ant. 1, 68): Ro 1: 18; 2: 25 ('indeed', 'to be sure' as Jos., Ant. 11, 8); 4: 3, 9; 5: 7 ('but'); 12: 3; 14: 5; 1 Cor 10: 1 (t.r. δέ); 2 Cor 1: 12; 10: 12; 11: 5 (B δέ); Gal 1: 11 (v.l. δέ); 5: 13; 1 Ti 2: 5.—Confirming (Arrian, Ind. 22, 6 ἀλλὰ ἐκπεριπλῶσαι γὰρ . . . μέγα ἔργον ἐφαίνετο= but to sail seaward seemed indeed a great accomplishment). Especially in replies it confirms what has been asked about (Bl-D. §452, 2) yes, indeed; certainly 1 Th 2: 20; 1 Cor 9: 10. Many questions w. γάρ have both inferential and causal force.—CHBird, Some γάρ clauses in St Mark's Gospel: JTS n.s. 4, 1953, 171-87. M-M.

γαστήρ, τρός, ἡ (Hom.+; inscr., pap., LXX, Jos., Ant. 19, 350; 20, 18 al.).

1. belly—a. lit., inward parts of the body, not subject to human view 1 Cl 21: 2 (cf. Pr 20: 27).

b. fig., glutton (Hes., Theog. 26+) γαστέρες ἀργαί (ἀργός 2) Tit 1: 12.

2. womb συλλαμβάνειν ἐν γαστρί (Gen 25: 21 LXX Sixtina) Lk 1: 31. ἐν γαστρὶ ἔχειν be pregnant (Hdt. 3, 32+; med. wr. since Hippocr. [Hobart 92]; Paus. 4, 33, 3; Artem. 2, 18; 3, 32 al.; PMagd. 4, 6 [III bc]; PFlor. 130, 3; PLond. 1730, 30; LXX; En. 99, 5) Mt 1: 18, 23 (Is 7: 14); 24: 19; Mk 13: 17; Lk 21: 23; 1 Th 5: 3; Rv 12: 2; w. εἰμί B 13: 2 (Gen 25: 23). M-M. B. 253.*

γαυριάω (X.+; Demosth.; Jdth 9: 7) to glory ἐν τῷ πλούτῳ in riches Hv 1, 1, 8.*

γαυρόω (act. in Plut., al.) mostly pass. γαυροῦμαι pride oneself (Eur., Or. 1532; X., Hiero 2, 15; Wsd 6: 2; 3 Macc 3: 11; 6: 5; Philo, Mos. 1, 284) ἐν τῷ πλούτῳ Hv 3, 9, 6 (Ps.-Phoc. 53 γ. ἐνὶ πλούτῳ.—PFlor. 367, 11 πλούτῳ γαυρωθείς).*

γέ (Hom.+; inscr., pap., LXX, Joseph.) enclit. particle, appended to the word it refers to; it serves to emphasize this word, and often cannot be transl., merely influencing the word order.

1. limiting: at least διά γε τὴν ἀναίδειαν at least because of (his) persistence Lk 11: 8. διά γε τὸ παρέχειν μοι κόπον yet because she bothers me 18: 5.

2. intensive: even ὅς γε τοῦ ἰδίου υἱοῦ οὐκ ἐφείσατο who did not spare even his own son Ro 8: 32. ἁμαρτία γέ ἐστιν indeed, it is a sin Hv 1, 1, 8.

3. oft. added to other particles: ἄρα γε (s. ἄρα, ἆρα), ἀλλά γε (s. ἀλλά).

a. εἴ γε if indeed, inasmuch as (Kühner-G. II 177c) Eph 3: 2; 4: 21; Col 1: 23. τοσαῦτα ἐπάθετε εἰκῆ; εἴ γε καὶ εἰκῆ have you experienced so many things in vain? If it really was in vain Gal 3: 4. εἴ γε καὶ ἐνδυσάμενοι οὐ γυμνοὶ εὑρεθησόμεθα inasmuch as we, having put it on, shall not be found naked 2 Cor 5: 3.

b. εἰ δὲ μή γε otherwise (Pla. et al.; Epict. 3, 22, 27;

Jos., Bell. 6, 120, Ant. 17, 113; Inscr. Rom. IV 833; POxy. 1159, 6; Wilcken, Chrest. 167, 25; PGM 4, 2629; Da 3: 15; Bel 8).

a. after affirmative clauses: εἰ δὲ μή γε (sc. προσέχετε), μισθὸν οὐκ ἔχετε *otherwise you have no reward* Mt 6: 1. Cf. Lk 10: 6. Elliptically: κἂν μὲν ποιήσῃ καρπὸν εἰς τὸ μέλλον· εἰ δὲ μή γε, ἐκκόψεις αὐτήν *if in the future it bears fruit* (very well); *otherwise you may cut it down* 13: 9.

β. after a negative statement: οὐδὲ βάλλουσιν οἶνον νέον εἰς ἀσκοὺς παλαιούς. εἰ δὲ μή γε, ῥήγνυνται *new wine is not poured into old skins; otherwise they burst* Mt 9: 17; cf. Lk 5: 36. *No one is to consider me foolish; otherwise at least accept me as a fool* 2 Cor 11: 16.

c. καί γε (without a word between [classical Gk. sometimes inserts a word between καί and γε: e.g., Pla., Phaedo 58D, Pol. 7 p. 531A]: Hippocr., Septim. 9 vol. VII 450 L.; Cornutus p. 40, 12; Περὶ ὕψους 13, 2; Apsines Rhetor [III AD] p. 332, 17 Hammer; LXX) limiting: *at least* Lk 19: 42 v.l. Intensive: *even* (Jos., Ant. 20, 19) Ac 2: 18 (Jo 3: 2 v.l.). καί γε οὐ μακράν *though he is really not far* 17: 27. Cf. Hm 8: 5; 9: 9.—Kühner-G. II 176, b; Bl-D. §439, 2; Rob. 1129.

d. καίτοι γε *and yet; though, of course* (Epict. 3, 24, 90) J 4: 2; Dg 8: 3.—Kühner-G. II 151f; Bl-D. §439, 1; 450, 3; Rob. 1129.

e. μενοῦν γε in NT somet. at the beginning of its clause, contrary to class. usage (Phryn. 342 L.), stating a correction *rather* Lk 11: 28 v.l.; Ro 9: 20; 10: 18; Phil 3: 8.—Bl-D. §450, 4; Hdb. on Ro 9: 20.

f. μήτι γε *not to mention, let alone* 1 Cor 6: 3 (also class.; exx. in Wettstein; PLond. 42, 23; Bl-D. §427, 3).

g. γέ τοι *indeed*, only in the stereotyped transition formula πέρας γέ τοι *and furthermore* B 5: 8; 10: 2; 12: 6; 15: 6, 8; 16: 3.

h. ὄφελόν γε *would that indeed* 1 Cor 4: 8. M-M.

γέγονα, s. γίνομαι.

Γεδεών, ὁ indecl. (גִּדְעוֹן) *Gideon*, an Israelite hero (Judg 6–8; Philo; Jos., Ant. 5, 213ff [in the form Γεδεών, ῶνος]). Named w. other heroes of faith Hb 11: 32.*

γέεννα, ης, ἡ *Gehenna*, Grecized fr. גֵּי(א) הִנֹּם (Josh 15: 8b; 18: 16b; Neh 11: 30) Targum גֵּיהִנָּם (cf. Dalman, Gramm.² 183), really בֶּן־הִנֹּם גֵּי(א) (Josh 15: 8a; 18: 16a; 2 Ch 28: 3; Jer 7: 32; cf. 2 Kings 23: 10, where the K'thibh has the pl.: sons of H.) *Valley of the Sons of Hinnom*, a ravine south of Jerusalem. There, acc. to later Jewish popular belief, the Last Judgment was to take place. In the gospels it is the place of punishment in the next life, *hell*: κρίσις τῆς γ. *condemnation to G.* Mt 23: 33. βάλλεσθαι (εἰς) (τὴν) γ. (cf. Sib. Or. 2, 291) 5: 29; 18: 9; Mk 9: 45, 47; ἐμβαλεῖν εἰς τὴν γ. Lk 12: 5; ἀπελθεῖν εἰς (τὴν) γ. Mt 5: 30; Mk 9: 43; ἀπολέσαι ἐν γ. Mt 10: 28; υἱὸς γ. *a son of hell* 23: 15 (Semitism, cf. υἱὸς 1cd; Bab. Rosh ha-Shana 17b בני גיהנם. Cf. the oracle Hdt. 6, 86, 3: the perjurer is Ὅρκου παῖς. ἔνοχον εἶναι εἰς τὴν γ. (sc. βληθῆναι) 5: 22. As a place of fire γ. (τοῦ) πυρός (PGM 4, 3072 γέεννα πυρός; Sib. Or. 1, 103) *hell of fire* Mt 5: 22; 18: 9; 2 Cl 5: 4. Fig. φλογιζομένη ὑπὸ τῆς γ. *set on fire by hell* Js 3: 6.—GDalman, RE VI 418ff; PVolz, Eschatol. d. jüd. Gem. '34, 327ff; GBeer, D. bibl. Hades: HHoltzmann-Festschr., '02, 1–29; Billerb. IV '28, 1029–1118. M-M. B. 1485.*

Γεθσημανί (גַּת שְׁמָנֵי oil-press; גַּיא שׁ oil valley [Jerome]), indecl. *Gethsemane*, name of an olive orchard on the Mt. of Olives, called a χωρίον Mt 26: 36; Mk 14: 32. On form

and mng. cf. EKautzsch in W-S. §5, 13, a; Dalman, Gramm.² 191, Orte³ 340ff, Jesus 27; GReymann, Pj 5, '09, 87–96; HWTrusen, Geschichte v. G.: ZDPV 33, '10, 50–97; BMeistermann, Gethsémani '20; MDibelius, Gethsemane: Crozer Quart. 12, '35, 254–65; GKuhn, Evang. Theologie 12, '52/'53, 260–85 [Mk 14: 32–41]; CKopp, Holy Places of the Gospels, '63, 335–50; TLescow, ZNW 58, '67, 215–39; RSBarbour, NTS 16, '69/'70, 231–51.*

γείτων, ονος, ὁ and **ἡ** (Hom.+; inscr., pap., LXX; Philo, Aet. M. 144; 148; Joseph.) *neighbor* (w. φίλοι, φίλαι as 3 Macc 3: 10; Jos., Ant. 18, 376; cf. Epict. 1, 12, 20 with ἀδελφός and others in a related series) Lk 15: 6, 9; 14: 12.—J 9: 8. M-M. B. 1349.*

γελάω fut. γελάσω; 1 aor. ἐγέλασα (Hom.+; inscr., pap., LXX, Philo; Jos., Bell. 4, 386 al.) *laugh* Lk 6: 21, 25 (opp. κλαίω as Theognis 1, 1041 παρὰ κλαίοντι γελῶντες= laughing in the presence of one who is weeping; 1217; Porphyr., Vi. Pyth. 35); Hv 1, 1, 8; 1, 2, 3.—KH Rengstorf, TW I 656–60. M-M. B. 1106f.*

γέλως, ωτος, ὁ (Hom.+; pap., LXX, Philo; Jos., Ant. 4, 276; 5, 239) *laughter*, turned to weeping Js 4: 9. M-M.*

γεμίζω 1 aor. ἐγέμισα, pass. ἐγεμίσθην (Aeschyl.+; Thu., inscr., pap., Gen 45: 17; 3 Macc 5: 47; Philo, Op. M. 71; Jos., Ant. 8, 341) *fill*.

1. τί τινος (Aeschyl., Ag. 443; Demosth. 34, 36; Dit., Or. 383, 146; PSI 429, 12 [III BC] τὸ πλοῖον γεμίσαι ξύλων) *an object w. someth.* a sponge w. vinegar Mk 15: 36; jars w. water J 2: 7; jars w. wine Hm 12, 5, 3; baskets w. fragments J 6: 13. Pass. ἐγεμίσθη ὁ ναὸς καπνοῦ *the temple was filled w. smoke* Rv 15: 8.

2. τί ἔκ τινος Lk 15: 16 (v.l. ἀπὸ τῶν κερατίων). Of filling a censer w. fire fr. the altar Rv 8: 5 (PMagd. 11, 14 [221 BC] γεμίσαι τὸ πλοῖον ἐκ τῶν τόπων; 4 Macc 3: 14 v.l. πηγήν, ἐξ αὐτῆς ἐγέμισαν τ. βασιλεῖ τὸ ποτόν).

3. abs. in pass.: of a boat (PMagd. 11 verso περὶ τοῦ γεμισθῆναι τὸ πλοῖον; PSI 429, 12; BGU 1303, 31) (begin to) *be filled* Mk 4: 37. Of a house *be filled* Lk 14: 23. Cf. Rv 10: 10 v.l. M-M.*

γέμω impf. ἔγεμον (Aeschyl., Hdt.+; pap., LXX; Jos., Bell. 3, 530) *be full*.

1. τινός (Thu. 7, 25, 1 al.; LXX, PGM 8, 94 πυρὸς γ.) *of someth.*: of bones of the dead Mt 23: 27; GNaass 6; of sins B 11: 11 (cf. Isocr., Panath. 10, 29 πολλῶν ἁμαρτημάτων γέμοντες); of rapacity and wickedness Lk 11: 39 (cf. Isocr., Areop. 17, 43 πλείστων γ. ἐπιθυμιῶν; Plut., Pomp. 76, 2, Aemil. 31, 4); of cursing and bitterness (cf. Philod., Ira p. 56 W. πικρίας) Ro 3: 14 (Ps 9: 28; 13: 3); of incense Rv 5: 8; of abominations 17: 4; of the seven plagues 21: 9; of God's wrath 15: 7. ζῷα γέμοντα ὀφθαλμῶν *living creatures full of eyes* (of heavily loaded animals, Posidon.: 87 fgm. 2 Jac. ὄνους γέμοντας οἴνου) 4: 6, 8. ὄρος σχισμῶν ὅλον ἔγεμεν *the mountain was all full of cracks* Hs 9, 1, 7; *be full* of mistiness 2 Cl 1: 6. Pregnant context: θεοῦ γ. *be full of God* IMg 14 (cf. Vergil in Seneca Rhet., Suasoria 3, 5 HJMüller: plena deo, of the Sibyl; Lucan 9, 564; Pollux 1, 15 πλήρης θεοῦ).—2. ἔκ τινος of extortion Mt 23: 25.

3. w. acc. of the thing: θηρίον γέμοντα (constr. ad sensum) ὀνόματα βλασφημίας *full of blasphemous names* Rv 17: 3 (cf. AThumb, Hdb. d. neugriech. Volkssprache² '10 §50c; Bl-D. §159, 1 app.; 172; KWolf, Studien z. Sprache d. Malalas II, Diss. München '12, 33). M-M.*

γενεά, ᾶς, ἡ (Hom.+; inscr., pap., LXX, En., Philo, Joseph., Test. 12 Patr., Sib. Or.) *family, descent.*

1. lit., those descended fr. a common ancestor, a *clan* (Pind., Pyth. 10, 42 the Hyperboreans are a ἱερὰ γενεά; Diod. S. 18, 56, 7; Jos., Ant. 17, 220), then *race, kind* gener. This may be the mng. in Lk 16: 8 εἰς τὴν γ. τὴν ἑαυτῶν the children of this age are more prudent *in relation to their own clan* (i.e., people of their own kind) than are the children of light, but see GRBeasley-Murray, A Commentary on Mk 13, '57, 99–102. The meaning *nation* is possible, e.g., in Mt 23: 36; but s. also 2.

2. basically, the sum total of those born at the same time, expanded to include all those living at a given time *generation, contemporaries* (Hom., al.; BGU 1211, 12 [II BC] ἕως γενεῶν τριῶν); Jesus looks upon the whole contemp. generation of Jews as a uniform mass confronting him ἡ γ. αὕτη (cf. Gen 7: 1; Ps 11: 8) Mt 11: 16; 12: 41f; 23: 36; 24: 34; Mk 13: 30; Lk 7: 31; 11: 29–32, 50f; 17: 25; 21: 32 (EGraesser, ZNW Beih. 22, ²'60). S. also 1 above. This generation is characterized as γ. ἄπιστος καὶ διεστραμμένη Mt 17: 17; Mk 9: 19 D; Lk 9: 41; ἄπιστος Mk 9: 19; πονηρά Mt 12: 45; 16: 4 D; Lk 11: 29; πονηρὰ κ. μοιχαλίς Mt 12: 39; 16: 4; μοιχαλὶς καὶ ἁμαρτωλός Mk 8: 38 (JGuillet, Rech de Sc rel 35, '48, 275–81). Their contemporaries appeared to the Christians as γ. σκολιὰ καὶ διεστραμμένη (the latter term as Mt 17: 17; Lk 9: 41, the former also Ac 2: 40; cf. Ps 77: 8) Phil 2: 15 (Dt 32: 5).—Cf. Wsd 3: 19. A more favorable kind of γ. is mentioned in Ps 23: 6; 111: 2; 1 QS 3, 14.—The desert generation Hb 3: 10 (Ps 94: 10). ἰδίᾳ γ. ὑπηρετήσας *after he had served his own generation* Ac 13: 36; γ. ἡμῶν 1 Cl 5: 1; αἱ πρὸ ἡμῶν γ. 19: 1; πρώτη γ. *the first generation* (of Christians) Hs 9, 15, 4 (Paus. 7, 4, 9 τετάρτη γενεᾷ = *in the fourth generation*).

3. *age*, the time of a generation (since Hdt. 2, 142; Dionys. Hal. 3, 15; Gen 50: 23; Ex 13: 18; 20: 5; EpJer 2; Philo, Mos. 1, 7; Jos., Ant. 5, 336; Sib. Or. 3, 108). Here the original sense gradually disappears, and the mng. 'a period of time' remains.

a. *age, generation* Mt 1: 17 (a similar list of numbers in Hellanicus [400 BC] no. 323a, fgm. 22a Jac. ἐννέα γενεαῖς ὕστερον . . . ἐξ γενεαῖς ὕστερον . . . τρισὶ γενεαῖς ὕστερον); Lk 1: 48; 1 Cl 50: 3; ἐν γενεᾷ καὶ γ. (Ps 44: 18; 89: 1) *in one generation after the other* 7: 5.

b. *period of time* gener. εἰς γενεὰς καὶ γενεάς (Ps 48: 12; 88: 2 al.) *to all ages* Lk 1: 50 (v.l. εἰς γενεὰς γενεῶν and εἰς γενεὰν καὶ γενεάν); cf. 1 Cl 61: 3; εἰς πάσας τὰς γ. (Ex 12: 14) *to all generations* Eph 3: 21; ἀπὸ τῶν γ. *from earliest times* Col 1: 26 (for the combination αἰῶνες and γενεαί cf. Tob 1: 4; 8: 5 S; 13: 12; Esth 10: 3k). ἐκ γενεῶν ἀρχαίων *fr. ancient times* Ac 15: 21 (cf. Sir 2: 10); ἀπὸ γενεᾶς εἰς γ. (Ex 17: 16; Ps 9: 27) *fr. generation to g.* Lk 1: 50 v.l.; MPol 21; ἐν πάσαις ταῖς γ. *in all generations* 1 Cl 60: 1; cf. 11: 2; ἑτέραις γ. *at other times* Eph 3: 5 (cf. Jo 1: 3; Ps 47: 14); ἐν ταῖς παρῳχημέναις γ. *in past ages* Ac 14: 16.

4. in the quot. fr. Is 53: 8 τὴν γ. αὐτοῦ τίς διηγήσεται; Ac 8: 33; 1 Cl 16: 8 the mng. of γ. is not clear; *family* or *origin* may be closest.—MMeinertz, 'Dieses Geschlecht' im NT, BZ n.F. 1, '57, 283–89. M-M.*

γενεαλογέω (Hdt.+; Demetr. in Euseb., Pr. Ev. 9, 29, 2; 1 Ch 5: 1) *trace descent* γενεαλογούμενος ἐξ αὐτῶν *having his descent from them* Hb 7: 6.*

γενεαλογία, ας, ἡ (Pla., Crat. 396c; Polyb. 9, 2, 1; Dionys. Hal. 1, 11; Philo, Congr. Erud. Gr. 44; Jos., Ant. 11, 71, C. Ap. 1, 16) *genealogy* 1 Ti 1: 4 (for the combination w. μῦθοι cf. FJacoby, Fgm. der griech. Historiker I [Genealogie u. Mythographie] '23, p. 47f; Polyb.,

loc. cit. περὶ τὰς γενεαλογίας καὶ μύθους; Emperor Julian, Or. 7 p. 205c); Tit 3: 9, since Irenaeus I Praef.; Tertullian, Praescr. Haer. 33, it has oft. been interpr. as referring to Gnostic teachings, esp. groups of Aeons; cf. MDibelius Hdb.² '31 ad loc.—The interpr. which holds that the errors in question have a Jewish background and involve rabbinical speculation begins w. Ambrosiaster and Jerome, and is more or less favored in recent times by GerhKittel, D. γενεαλογίαι d. Past.: ZNW 20, '21, 49–69; JoachJeremias⁴ '47 ad loc. M-M.*

γενέθλιος, ον (Aeschyl.+; inscr., pap.) *pertaining to birth* γ. ἡμέρα *birthday* (Epicurus, fgm. 217 Us.; Plut., Pomp. 79, 5; Lucian, Enc. Dem. 26; Dit., Or. Ind. VIII; Sb 1626; 2 Macc 6: 7; Philo, Mos. 1, 207; Jos., Bell. 7, 37; 39) MPol 18: 2.—τὰ γενέθλια *birthday celebration* (Dit., Or. 56, 5; 90, 46 τὰ γεν. τοῦ βασιλέως. S. also γενέσια) or *birthday* (Diod. S. 34+35 fgm. 14; Lucian, Gall. 9; Porphyr., Vi. Plotini 2 p. 103, 26 and 27 Westerm.) Mk 6: 21 D.*

γενέσθαι s. γίνομαι.

γενέσια, ίων, τά (fr. adj. γενέσιος, ον, cf. Jos., Ant. 12, 196 ἡ γενέσιος ἡμέρα; 215; Dit., Or. 583, 14) *birthday celebration* (= Att. γενέθλια, while γενέσια earlier [Hdt. 4, 26 al.] meant a commemorative celebration on the birthday of a deceased pers.; cf. Phryn. 103f L.; ERohde, Psyche³ I 235) Mt 14: 6; Mk 6: 21 (so Alciphr. 2, 15, 1; 3, 19, 1; PFay. 114, 20; POxy. 736, 56; loanw. in rabb.—On the locative [dat.] of time Mk 6: 21 cf. Zen.-P. 59 332, 1 [248 BC] τοῖς γενεθλίοις; BGU 1, 9 γενεσίοις; 149, 15 γενεθλίοις). Cf. Schürer I⁴ 439, 27; ZNW 2, '01, 48ff; WSchmidt, Geburtstag im Altertum '08; POsl. III p. 49. M-M.*

γένεσις, εως, ἡ (Hom.+; inscr., pap., LXX, Philo, Joseph.).

1. *beginning, origin, descent* (e.g. Diod. S. 17, 51, 3; 17, 108, 3 of Alexander ἡ ἐξ Ἄμμωνος γ.), also *birth* (Diod. S. 2, 5, 1; 4, 39, 2; Inschr. v. Priene 105, 48; Dit., Or. 56, 25; Ostraka II 1601; Gen 40: 20; Hos 2: 5; Eccl 7: 1 v.l.; Jos., Ant. 2, 215; 234) Mt 1: 18 (s. γέννησις.—The superscription here has a counterpart in the subscription of the infancy narrative of Pythagoras in Iambl., Vi. Pyth. 2, 8: περὶ τῆς γενέσεως τοσαῦτο.—Arrian, Anab. answers the question [7, 29, 3] whether Alex. rightly ἐς θεὸν τὴν γένεσιν τὴν αὐτοῦ ἀνέφερεν with the reflection [7, 30, 2] οὐδὲ ἐμοὶ ἔξω τοῦ θείου φῦναι ἂν δοκεῖ ἀνὴρ οὐδενὶ ἄλλῳ ἀνθρώπων ἐοικώς = it seems to me that a man who is different from all other men could not have come into being apart from divinity); Lk 1: 14.

2. *existence* (Pla., Phaedr. 252D τ. πρώτην γένεσιν βιοτεύειν; Ps.-Aristid., Ἀπελλᾷ γενεθλιακός 30, 27 Keil; POxy. 120, 8; PGM 13, 612; Jdth 12: 18; Wsd 7: 5) πρόσωπον τῆς γ. αὐτοῦ *his natural face* Js 1: 23.

3. the expr. βίβλος γενέσεως Mt 1: 1 is fr. the OT: Gen 2: 4; 5: 1; in the former of these two pass. it= *history of the origin* (cf. Diod. S. 1, 10, 3 ἡ γ. τῶν ἀνθρώπων; schol. on Apollon. Rhod. 3, 1–5a . . . δύο ἱστοροῦνται γενέσεις Μουσῶν = there are two accounts given of the origin of the Muses), which would be a fitting heading for Mt 1, while in the latter it= *genealogy*, which describes the contents of Mt 1: 1–17. Zahn ad loc. regards the expr. as constituting the superscription of the whole gospel: *Book of the History.*—JLindblom: Teologiska Studier for EStave '22, 102–9; OEissfeldt, 'Toledot', in Studien zum NT u. zur Patristik '61, 1–8.

4. ὁ τροχὸς τῆς γενέσεως Js 3: 6 was used in the

Orphic mysteries w. the mng. *wheel of human origin* (Simplicius on Aristot., De Caelo 2 p. 377 Heiberg ἐν τῷ τῆς εἰμαρμένης τε καὶ γενέσεως τροχῷ οὗπερ ἀδύνατον ἀπαλλαγῆναι κατὰ τὸν 'Ορφέα, cf. ERohde, Psyche³ II 130f). In Js it seems to have lost its orig. mng. and to signify *course of life* (cf. Anacreontea 32, 7f Preis.: τροχὸς βίοτος).—For lit. s. τροχός. M-M.*

γενετή, ῆς, ἡ *birth* ἐκ γενετῆς *fr. birth* (Hom.+; Lev 25: 47; Esth 4: 17 m; Jos., Ant. 8, 157) of blind pers. J 9: 1 (so also Heraclides, Pol. 30 τυφλὸς ἐκ γ.; Paus. 4, 12, 7; Sext. Emp., Math. 11, 238; Philostrat., Ep. 12 p. 230, 31 μακαρίων τῶν ἐκ γενετῆς τυφλῶν).—KBornhäuser, NKZ 38, '27, 433-7. M-M.*

γένημα, ατος, τό (cf. Bl-D. §11, 2: 34, 3 app.; Rob. 213) *product, fruit, yield* of vegetable produce Lk 12: 18 v.l. (other rdgs. are γεννήματα and τὸν σῖτον); of wine as the *product of the vine* (cf. Is 32: 12 ἀμπέλου γένημα; the pap. speak of οἴνου γένημα [BGU 774, 3; Fay. Ostraca 7] or οἰνικὸν γένημα [BGU 1123, 9; POxy. 729, 36]) Mt 26: 29; Mk 14: 25; Lk 22: 18 (t.r. γεννήματος). τὰ γ. τῆς δικαιοσύνης ὑμῶν (Hos 10: 12) *the harvest of your righteousness* 2 Cor 9: 10 (t.r. γεννήματα). The word is a new formation in H.Gk. from γίνεσθαι and has no affinity w. the class. γέννημα. It is found since III BC in pap. (Dssm. B 105f; NB 12 [BS 110, 184]; Mayser 214; Nägeli 32), inscr. (CIG 4757, 62; Dit., Or. 262, 9), LXX (Thackeray 118), and in writers like Polyb. (1, 71, 1; 1, 79, 6; 3, 87, 1 acc. to the best mss.). M-M.*

γενναῖος, α, ον (Hom.+; Dit., Or. 589, 1; pap., LXX, Philo; Jos., C. Ap. 1, 319; 2, 24 al.) *genuine, noble* epithet of the martyrs (as 4 Macc) 1 Cl 5: 1; MPol 3, 2: 1.τὸ γενναῖον τῆς πίστεως αὐτοῦ κλέος *the genuine fame for his faith* 1 Cl 5: 6. γέρας γενναῖον λαμβάνειν *receive a noble reward* 6: 2 (of inanimate things: Περὶ ὕψους p. 11, 4; 12, 4 V.). As epithet for Christians gener. *brave, able* 54: 1 (cf. 4 Macc 6: 10; PLond. 1353, 13 ναύτας γενναίους). Sim. of the phoenix *strong, powerful* (Menand., fgm. 223, 12 ἀλέκτρυον) 25: 3.—τὸ γενναῖον as substantive (=γενναιότης, as Soph., Oed. Col. 569; Xenophon; Nicol. Dam. 90 fgm. 9; 47, 4 Jac.) τὸ γενναῖον αὐτῶν *their nobility* MPol 2: 2.*

γενναιότης, ητος, ἡ (Eur., Thu.+; 2 Macc 6: 31; 4 Macc 17: 2; Philo; Jos., Ant. 17, 333; 19, 212) *nobility, bravery* εἰς τοσοῦτον γενναιότητος ἐλθεῖν *reach such a degree of noble courage* MPol 2: 2; cf. 3.*

γεννάω, fut. γεννήσω; 1 aor. ἐγέννησα; pf. γεγέννηκα, pass. γεγέννημαι; 1 aor. pass. ἐγεννήθην (Pind., Hdt.+; inscr., pap., LXX, En.; Ep. Arist. 208; Philo, Joseph., Test. 12 Patr.).—Cf. ARahlfs, Genesis '26, 39.
    1. *beget*—a. lit. *become the father of* (oft. LXX, fr. Gen 4: 18 on) Mt 1: 2ff (s. Diod. S. 4, 67, 2-68, 6, the genealogy of the Aeolians: 67, 4 "Αρνη ἐγέννησεν Αἰόλον κ. Βοιωτόν; 67, 7 'Ιππάλκιμος ἐγέννησε Πηνέλεων; 68: 1 Σαλμωνεὺς ἐγέννησε θυγατέρα . . . Τυρώ; 68, 3 Ποσειδῶν ἐγέννησε Πελίαν κ. Νηλέα; 68, 6 Νηλεὺς παῖδας ἐγέννησε δώδεκα. Interchanged with ἐγέννησε are ἐτέκνωσε, ἦν υἱός, παῖδες ἐγένοντο, etc. The continuity is not as rigid or monotonous as in Mt. But in Diod. S. 4, 69, 1-3 ἐγέννησε is repeated six times in a short space, and 4, 75, 4f we have ἐγέννησε four times with the names of fathers and sons); Ac 7: 8, 29; ἐκ w. gen. of the mother (Eur., fgm. 479; Diod. S. 4, 2, 1; 4, 62, 1; Palaeph. 44; PLond. 1730, 10 οἱ ἐξ αὐτῆς γεννηθέντες υἱοί; Tob 1: 9; 2 Esdr [Ezra] 10: 44; Jos, Ant. 12, 189) Mt

1: 3, 5f. Pass. *be begotten* ἐκ τῆς παιδίσκης κατὰ σάρκα w. *the slave-woman, according to the flesh* Gal 4: 23. ὁ κατὰ σάρκα γεννηθείς *he that was begotten in natural fashion* (opp. ὁ κατὰ πνεῦμα) v. 29. τὸ ἐν αὐτῇ γεννηθὲν ἐκ πνεύματός ἐστιν *that which is conceived in her is of the Spirit* Mt 1: 20 (τὸ γεννηθέν of that which is yet unborn: Diod. S. 17, 77, 3). Here the male principle is introduced by ἐκ (Lucian, Dial. Deor. 20, 14 ἐκ κύκνου γεγεννημένη; Phlegon: 257 fgm. 36, 2, 4 Jac.; Ps-Callisth. 1, 30, 3 ἐξ "Αμμωνος ἐγεννήθη; Test. Sim. 2: 2) as J 1: 13 (ἐγεννήθ. 𝔓⁷⁵ et al.); 3: 6. W. ἀπό (En. 15, 8 οἱ γίγαντες οἱ γεννηθέντες ἀπὸ τ. πνευμάτων κ. σαρκός) ἀφ' ἑνὸς ἐγεννήθησαν *they were begotten by one man* Hb 11: 12 v.l. (for ἐγεννήθησαν). ἐκ πορνείας οὐκ ἐγεννήθημεν J 8: 41. ἐν ἁμαρτίαις σὺ ἐγεννήθης ὅλος *you were altogether conceived in sin* 9: 34.—Lk 1: 35 (where mng. 2 is also poss. [as in τὸ γεννώμενον Philo, Plant. 15]. Cf. AFridrichsen, Symb. Osl. 6, '28, 33-6; HAlmqvist, Plut. u. d. NT '46, 60f).
    b. fig. of the infl. exerted by one person on another (Philo, Leg. ad Gai. 58 μᾶλλον αὐτὸν τῶν γονέων γεγέννηκα) of a teacher on pupils ἐν Χ. 'Ι. διὰ τοῦ εὐαγγελίου ὑμᾶς ἐγέννησα *I became your father as Christians through the gospel* 1 Cor 4: 15; Phlm 10 (cf. Ltzm. and JWeiss on 1 Cor 4: 15; ADieterich, Mithraslit. '03, 146ff).—Pass. ἐκ (τοῦ) θεοῦ γεννᾶσθαι J 1: 13; 1 J 2: 29; 3: 9; 4: 7; 5: 1, 4, 18. Also ἄνωθεν γ. J 3: 3. πᾶς ὁ ἀγαπῶν τὸν γεννήσαντα ἀγαπᾷ τὸν γεγεννημένον ἐξ αὐτοῦ *everyone who loves the father* (=God) *loves the child* (=Christ or one's Christian brother) 1 J 5: 1 (on γεννᾶσθαι ἐκ θεοῦ s. Hdb. on J 3: 3 and 1 J 3: 9 and the sources and lit. listed there; s. also on παλιγγενεσία). On γεννᾶσθαι ἐξ ὕδατος κ. πνεύματος J 3: 5 cf. IQS 4, 20-22 and s. YYadin, JBL 74, '55, 40-43. Cf. σήμερον γεγέννηκά σε (Ps 2: 7) 1 Cl 36: 4; GEb 3; Ac 13: 33 (held by some to have been the orig. rdg. Lk 3: 22; s. HUsener, D. Weihnachtsfest² '11, 38ff); Hb 1: 5; 5: 5.
    2. of women: *bear* (Aeschyl., Suppl. 48; X., De Rep. Lac. 1, 3; Lucian, Sacrif. 6; Plut., Mor. p. 3c; Ps.-Callisth. 1, 9, 2 ἐκ θεοῦ γεννήσασα παῖδα=a woman who has borne a child to a god; BGU 132 II, 5; Judg 11: 1 B; Is 66: 9; 4 Macc 10: 2) Lk 1: 13, 57; 23: 29; (w. τίκτειν) J 16: 21. εἰς δουλείαν γεννῶσα *who bears children for slavery* Gal 4: 24. Pass. *be born* πρὶν ἡμᾶς γεννηθῆναι *before we were born* 1 Cl 38: 3. εἰς τὸν κόσμον *come into the world* J 16: 21; Mt 2: 1, 4; 19: 12; 26: 24 (=1 Cl 46: 8); Mk 14: 21 (cf. En. 38, 2); Lk 1: 35 (1a is also poss.; a v.l. adds ἐκ σοῦ, which can be rendered 'that which is born of you' and 'that which is begotten w. you'; ἐκ Μαρίας ἐγεννήθη Third Corinthians 3: 5); J 3: 4; 9: 2, 19f, 32; IEph 18: 2; ITr 11: 2; ἀληθῶς γ. *be truly born* (in opp. to Docetism) 9: 1. γεγεννημένα (v.l. γεγενημένα) εἰς ἅλωσιν 2 Pt 2: 12. εἰς τοῦτο *for this purpose* J 18: 37. διάλεκτος ἐν ᾗ ἐγεννήθημεν *the language in which we were born* i.e., which we have spoken fr. infancy Ac 2: 8. ἐγὼ δὲ καὶ γεγέννημαι *but I was* (actually) *born a Roman citizen* 22: 28.
    3. fig. *bring forth, produce, cause* (class.; Polyb. 1, 67, 2 στάσις ἐγεννᾶτο; Philo, De Jos. 254; Jos., Ant. 6, 144) 2 Ti 2: 23.—γ. καρπόν *produce fruit* ITr 11: 1. M-M. B. 280.

γέννημα, ατος, τό *that which is produced* or *born* (of living creatures), *child, offspring* (Soph., Oed. R. 1167; Pla., Tim. 24D; 69c; Sir 10: 18 γεννήματα γυναικῶν; Philo) γεννήματα ἐχιδνῶν *brood of vipers* (cf. the Syntipas collection of Aesop's Fables 57 p. 549 P. ὄφεως γεννήματα=brood of snakes. Of snakes also schol. on

Nicander, Ther. 8) Mt 3: 7; 12: 34; 23: 33; Lk 3: 7 (sensu malo Dio Chrys. 41[58], 5 ὦ κακὸν γ.). γεννήματα ληνοῦ καὶ ἄλωνος, βοῶν τε καὶ προβάτων D 13: 3 is justifiable because the last two nouns refer to animals. On the other hand, the variant γέννημα, which is found everywhere for γένημα (q.v.), does not merit serious consideration. M-M*

Γεννησαρέτ indecl., ἡ (more correctly Γεννησάρ as 1 Macc 11: 67, Joseph., Talmud, D, It., Syr. Sin. and Cur., Pesh. in Mt and Mk. Cf. RHarris, ET 40, '29, 189f) *Gennesaret*, prob. name of the fertile and (in I AD) thickly populated plain south of Capernaum, now El-Ghuweir (Jos., Bell. 3, 516ff) Mt 14: 34; Mk 6: 53. This was also the name of the large lake adjacent to the plain, λίμνη Γ. (Jos., Bell. 3, 506 λίμνη Γεννησάρ; 1 Macc 11: 67 τὸ ὕδωρ τοῦ Γεννησάρ; Stephan. Byz. s.v. Τιβεριάς: this is a city πρὸς τῇ Γεννεσιρίτιδι λίμνῃ Lk 5: 1, likew. called θάλασσα τῆς Γαλιλαίας (Mt 4: 18; Mk 1: 16), and θάλ. τῆς Τιβεριάδος (J 21: 1).—Dalman, Orte³ 118; Westm. Hist. Atlas 17 etc.; CKopp, Holy Places of the Gospels, '63, 167-203.*

γέννησις, εως, ἡ (Eur., Pla.; Dit., Syll.³ 1109, 130; PLond. 1731, 10; PGM 13, 981; Eccl 7: 1 v.l. ἡμέρα γεννήσεως) *birth* Mt 1: 18 t.r.; Lk 1: 14 t.r.; 1 J 5: 18 v.l.; IMg 11. M-M.*

γεννητός, ή, όν (oft. in Pla.; Diod. S. 1, 6, 3; Dionys. Hal. 5, 29; Lucian, Icarom. 2) *begotten, born* γεννητὸς γυναικός *he that is born of woman*=man (Job 11: 2, 12; 14: 1; 15: 14; 25: 4) 1 Cl 30: 5 (Job 11: 2). Pl. Mt 11: 11; Lk 7: 28. Of Christ γ. καὶ ἀγέννητος *begotten and unbegotten* IEph 7: 2.*

γένος, ους, τό (Hom.+; inscr., pap., LXX, Ep. Arist., Philo, Joseph., Test. 12 Patr.; Sib. Or. 3, 193; loanw. in rabb.) *race, stock.*
1. *descendants* of a common ancestor ἐκ γένους ἀρχιερατικοῦ *of high-priestly descent* (s. Jos., Ant. 15, 40) Ac 4: 6 (PTebt. 291, 36 ἀπέδειξας σεαυτὸν γένους ὄντα ἱερατικοῦ, cf. 293, 14; 18; BGU 82, 7 al. pap.). υἱοὶ γένους Ἀβραάμ 13: 26 (s. Jos., Ant. 5, 113); γ. Δαυίδ Rv 22: 16; IEph 20: 2; ITr 9: 1; ISm 1: 1. τοῦ γὰρ καὶ γένος ἐσμέν *we, too, are descended from him* Ac 17: 28 (quoted fr. Arat., Phaenom. 5; perh. as early as Epimenides [RHarris, Exp. 8th Ser. IV '12, 348-53; ChBruston, Rev. de Théol. et des Quest. rel. 21, '13, 533-5; DAFrøvig, Symbol. Osl. 15/16, '36, 44ff; MZerwick, Verb. Dom. 20, '40, 307-21; EdesPlaces, Ac 17: 28, Biblica 43, '62, 388-95]. Cf. also IG XIV 641; 638 in Norden, Agn. Th. 194 n.; Cleanthes, Hymn to Zeus 4 [Stoic. I 537] ἐκ σοῦ γὰρ γένος ...; Dio Chrys. 80[30], 26 ἀπὸ τ. θεῶν τὸ τῶν ἀνθρώπων γένος; Ep. 44 of Apollonius of Tyana [Philostrat. I 354, 22] γένος ὄντες θεοῦ; Hierocles 25 p. 474, v. 63 of the Carmen Aur.: θεῖον γένος ἐστὶ βροτοῖσιν), cf. vs. 29.—Also of an individual *descendant, scion* (Hom.; Soph., Ant. 1117 Bacchus is Διὸς γ.). Jesus is τὸ γένος Δαυίδ Rv 22: 16 (cf. Epimenides [VI BC] 457 fgm. 3 Jac., the saying of Musaeus: ἐγὼ γένος εἰμι Σελήνης; Quint. Smyrn. 1, 191 σεῖο θεοῦ γένος ἐστι.
2. *family, relatives* (Appian, Bell. Civ. 5, 54 §228; Basil. 1a §1; BGU 1185, 18; Jos., Ant. 17, 22; 18, 127) τὸ γ. Ἰωσήφ Ac 7: 13.
3. *nation, people* (Appian, Bell. Civ. 2, 71 §294 Ἑβραίων γένος; 2, 90 §380 Ἰουδαίων γ., the latter also Diod. S. 34+35 fgm. 1, 1; 40, 3, 8; Maximus Tyr. 23, 7b; Ael. Aristid. 45 p. 108 D.: τῶν Ἑλλήνων γ.; Achilles Tat. 1, 3, 1; 3, 19, 1; Synes., Ep. 121 p. 258B τὸ Ἑβραίων γ.; Test. Levi 5: 6 τὸ γένος Ἰσραήλ; Jos., Bell. 7, 43, Ant.

10, 183 τὸ Ἑβραίων γ.) Ac 7: 19; Gal 1: 14; Phil 3: 5; B 14: 7 (Is 42: 6). Of the Christians: γένος ἐκλεκτόν *a chosen nation* 1 Pt 2: 9 (Is 43: 20; cf. Esth 8: 12t; s. JCFenton, CBQ 9, '47, 141f); καινὸν γ. Dg 1; τρίτῳ γένει *as a third people* (beside pagans and Jews) PK 2 p. 15, 8 (s. Harnack, Mission⁴ I '24, 259-89); γ. τῶν δικαίων MPol 14: 1; 17: 1; Hs 9, 17, 5. θεοφιλὲς θεοσεβὲς γ. τῶν Χριστιανῶν *godly and pious race of the Christians* MPol 3 (Plut., Mor. 567f: the Greeks acc. to the divine verdict are τὸ βέλτιστον κ. θεοφιλέστατον γένος). τῷ γένει w. name of a people to denote nationality (Menand., Per. 9 J.; Plut., Dem. 28, 3; Jos., Ant. 20, 81; BGU 887, 3; 15; 937, 9 δοῦλος γένει Ποντικός; cf. 2 Macc 5: 22; 3 Macc 1: 3) Mk 7: 26; Ac 4: 36; 18: 2, 24. Pregnant constr. κίνδυνοι ἐκ γένους *perils from the people*= my countrymen, the Jews 2 Cor 11: 26.
4. *class, kind* (Ps.-Xenophon, Cyneg. 3, 1 τὰ γένη τῶν κυνῶν; PGiess. 40, 9 παντὸς γένους πολιτευμάτων; Wsd 19: 21; Philo) of plants (BGU 1119, 27 [I BC] ταῦτα γένη 'the same species of plants'; 1120, 34; 1122, 23) Hs 8, 2, 7; of fish (Heniochus Com. 3; Jos., Bell. 3, 508) Mt 13: 47; of demons 17: 21; Mk 9: 29 (Herm. Wr. 13, 2 τοῦτο τὸ γένος οὐ διδάσκεται). γένη γλωσσῶν (γλῶσσα 3) 1 Cor 12: 10, 28; γ. φωνῶν 14: 10. Cf. Hs 9, 1, 8; 9, 19, 1; 9, 24, 1; 9, 30, 3. M-M. B. 85; 1317.*

γεραίρω (Hom.+; 3 Macc 5: 17) *honor* τινά τινι *someone w. someth.* Dg 3: 5 (Aelian, N.A. 7, 44 τῇ θυσίᾳ γεραίρων τὸ θεῖον; cf. Ps.-Phoc. 222; Sib. Or. 5, 407).*

γέρας, ως, τό (Hom.+; inscr., pap., LXX) *prize, reward* in our lit. given by God (Philo, Spec. Leg. 2, 183; Jos., Ant. 1, 14) 1 Cl 6: 2. λαμβάνειν (Dit., Syll.³ 624, 45; 1037) AP fgm. 2, p. 12, 24.*

Γερασηνός, ή, όν *from Gerasa*, a city in Peraea, east of the Jordan; ὁ Γ. *the Gerasene* (s. Joseph. index Niese; Schürer II⁴ 177ff; Dalman, Pj '07-'12; HGuthe, Gerasa [D. Land der Bibel III 1, 2] '19; JStarr, A New Jewish Source for Gerasa: JBL 53, '34, 167-9; CHKraeling, Gerasa '38.—The word is found Stephan. Byz. s.v. Βάργασα and Γέρασα; Inscr. Rom. IV 374, 11). Readings antedating Origen Mt 8: 28 v.l.; Mk 5: 1 (HSahlin, Studia Theolog. 18, '64, 159-72: Gentile emphasis in the pericope); Lk 8: 26, 37 (s. the foll. word and Γαδαρηνός). M-M.*

Γεργεσηνός, ή, όν *from Gergesa*, a town on the eastern shore of the Sea of Galilee; ὁ Γ. *the Gergesene*. Origen (Com. on J., tom. VI, 41) suggests this rdg., though in the form Γεργεσαῖος, for Mt 8: 28; Mk 5: 1; Lk 8: 26, 37 in place of Gerasenes or Gadarenes. He does not say whether his suggestion is supported by mss., but it is now a v.l. in all the above pass.; s. Γαδαρηνός.—RGClapp, JBL 26, '07, 62-83; FCBurkitt, ibid. 128-33.*

Γερμανικός, οῦ, ὁ *Germanicus* name of a martyr in Smyrna MPol 3.*

γερουσία, ας, ἡ (Eur., X.+ cf. Dit., Or. Index VIII; Thieme 16; APF 3, '06, 138 no. 21, 5; LXX; Philo, In Flacc. 76; 80, Leg. ad Gai. 229; Joseph. Of various boards or councils (e.g. the Roman Senate: Diod. S. 14, 113, 7 and 8), some having a sacred character [Dit., Syll.³ 1112, 1 ἔδοξεν τῇ ἱερᾷ γερουσίᾳ τοῦ Σωτῆρος Ἀσκληπιοῦ; the ἱερὰ γερουσία of Eleusis CIA III 702, 2; 10; 1062, 7]) *council of elders*, esp. the Sanhedrin in Jerusalem (Jdth 4: 8; 1 Macc 12: 6; 2 Macc 1: 10 al.; Jos., Ant. 13, 166) Ac 5: 21 (on the juxtaposition of συνέδριον and γερουσία cf. Inscr. Rom. IV 836, 7 τῷ σεμνοτάτῳ συνεδρίῳ γερουσίας).—Schürer II⁴ 237ff. M-M.*

γέρων, οντος, ὁ (Hom.+; inscr., pap., LXX; Jos., Bell. 6, 271) *old man* (Diog. L. 8, 10: acc. to Pythagoras a γ. is between 60 and 80 yrs. old) J 3: 4. M-M. B. 959.*

γεύομαι fut. γεύσομαι, 1 aor. ἐγευσάμην (Hom.+; pap., LXX, Philo, Joseph.).
1. *taste, partake of, enjoy* w. acc. (as early as class. times [Kühner-G. I 356, 2 and predominantly since Aristotle [Poet. 22]. Also Sb 1106 οἱ συμπόσιον γευόμενοι; 1 Km 14: 43; Job 12: 11; 34: 3; Tob 7: 12 BA) *water* J 2: 9. μηδὲν εἰ μὴ ἄρτον καὶ ὕδωρ Hs 5, 3, 7. W. gen. of the thing (Crates, Ep. 14 ἰχθύος κ. οἴνου; Dio Chrys. 2, 47; POxy. 658, 12; 1576, 4 τοῦ οἴνου; 1 Km 14: 24; 2 Km 3: 35 al.): *a meal*= take part in it Lk 14: 24. μηδενός (Jos., Ant. 7, 42) Ac 23: 14; poisonous plants ITr 11: 1. The obj. of the verb is indicated by the context Mt 27: 34; Ac 20: 11. μὴ ἄψῃ μηδὲ γεύσῃ μηδὲ θίγῃς Col 2: 21 (s. ἅπτω 2a). Abs. γεύομαι= *eat* (Appian, Bell. Civ. 2, 98 §407; Sb 1944; Tob 2: 4 BA; Jos., Ant. 6, 119; 338) Ac 10: 10.
2. fig. *come to know someth.* (Hom.+; Pr 31: 18). W. gen. of the thing (Pind., Nem. 6, 24 πόνων; Hdt. 6, 5 ἐλευθερίης; Dio Chrys. 15[32], 72 πολέμου; Ael. Aristid. 28, 60 K.=49 p. 510 D.: ἀλαζονείας; Maximus Tyr. 33, 4c ἡδονῶν): θανάτου (analogous to rabb. טַעַם מִיתָה [Billerb. I 751f; 4 Esdr 6: 26]; Leonidas in Anth. Pal. 7, 662 ἀδελφὸν ἀστόργου γευσάμενον θανάτου; cf. HPRüger, ZNW 59, '68, 113f) Mt 16: 28; Mk 9: 1; Lk 9: 27; J 8: 52; Hb 2: 9; LJ 2: 1 (where θανάτου is supplied by conjecture); *partake of* knowledge 1 Cl 36: 2 (cf. Herm. Wr. 10, 8 γ. ἀθανασίας; Philo, Virt. 188 σοφίας al.; Jos., Bell. 2, 158); *obtain* a gift Hb 6: 4. W. acc. of the thing: a word of God vs. 5. W. ὅτι foll.: γεύσασθαι ὅτι χρηστὸς ὁ κύριος *experience the Lord's kindness* 1 Pt 2: 3 (Ps 33: 9); RPerdelwitz, D. Mysterienrel. u. d. Problem des 1 Pt '11, 65ff.—On the whole word JBehm, TW I 674-6. M-M. B. 1030.*

γεῦσις, εως, ἡ (Democr. 11D; Aristot. et al.; Paradoxogr. Flor. 20; LXX; Philo) *taste* δοὺς ἀπαρχὰς ἡμῖν γεύσεως *he gave us a foretaste* B 1: 7. μέλι ἄγριον, οὗ ἡ γεῦσις ἦν τοῦ μάννα *wild honey which tasted like manna* GEb 2b.*

γεωργέω (Hyperid. 5, 26, X., Pla.+; inscr., pap., LXX, Ep. Arist., Philo; Jos., Ant. 5, 212) *cultivate* βοτάνας ἄστινας οὐ γεωργεῖ Ἰ. Χρ. *plants which Jesus Christ does not cultivate* IPhld 3: 1. Pass. (Jos., Bell. 7, 145 γῆ) δι' οὓς γεωργεῖται (ἡ γῆ) *on whose account the land is tilled* Hb 6: 7. M-M.*

γεώργιον, ου, τό (Philo Mech. 96, 49; Strabo 14, 5, 6; Dionys. Hal.; Theagenes in schol. on Pind., Nem. 3, 21; Dit., Syll.³ 311, 9 [323 BC]; UPZ 110, 48 [164 BC]; PTebt. 72, 370 [114/13 BC]; Gen 26: 14; Pr 6: 7 al.; Philo, Plant. 2) *cultivated land, field* fig. of a Christian congregation as God's field 1 Cor 3: 9.—AFridrichsen, Ackerbau u. Hausbau: StKr Sonderheft '22, 185f; 102; '30, 297ff, Serta Rudbergiana '31, 25f; WStraub, D. Bildersprache des Ap. Pls '37. M-M.*

γεωργός, οῦ, ὁ *one who tills the soil*—1. *farmer* (Hdt., Aristoph.+; inscr., pap., LXX; Ep. Arist. 111; Philo; Jos., Bell. 4, 84) 2 Ti 2: 6 (on association of γ. w. the teacher s. AHenrichs, ZPE 1, '67, 50-53); Js 5: 7.
2. *vine-dresser, tenant farmer* (Pla., Theaet. p. 178D; Aelian, Nat. An. 7, 28; Gen 9: 20) Mt 21: 33ff, 38, 40f; Mk 12: 1f, 7, 9; Lk 20: 9f, 14, 16 (ELohmeyer, ZsystTh 18, '41, 243-59: wicked tenants; BIersel, 'D. Sohn' in den synoptischen Jesusworten² '64, 124-45); J 15: 1 (God as γ. Herm. Wr. 9, 6; 14, 10; PGM 1: 26 ἧκέ μοι ἀγαθὲ

γεωργέ, Ἀγαθὸς Δαίμων). Gdspd., Probs. 111f. 'cultivator'. M-M. B. 487.*

γῆ, γῆς, ἡ (Hom.+; inscr., pap.; very oft. in LXX in all mngs. found in our lit.; En., Ep. Arist., Philo, Joseph., Test. 12 Patr.) *earth.*
1. *soil, earth,* receiving seed Mt 13: 5, 8, 23; Mk 4: 5, 8, 20, 26, 28, 31; J 12: 24; watered by rain Hb 6: 7; yielding fruit (Jos., Ant. 18, 22) Js 5: 7: 1 Cl 20: 4. καταργεῖν τ. γῆν *waste, use up the ground* Lk 13: 7.—Dalman, Arbeit II.
2. *ground* Mt 10: 29 (πίπτειν ἐπὶ τ. γῆν as Jos., Ant. 7, 381); 15: 35; 25: 18, 25 (Artem. 2, 59 οὐ γὰρ ἄνευ τοῦ τὴν γῆν ἀνασκαφῆναι θησαυρὸς εὑρίσκεται); Mk 8: 6; 9: 20; 14: 35; Lk 22: 44; 24: 5; J 8: 6, 8 (writing on it as Ael. Aristid. 50, 21 K.=26 p. 508 D.); Ac 9: 4, 8; GP 6: 21a. οἰκοδομεῖν οἰκίαν ἐπὶ τὴν γῆν χωρὶς θεμελίου *build a house on the ground without any foundation* Lk 6: 49. The earth opens in the service of a divinity in order to swallow something (Quint. Smyrn. 13, 548f, a person) Rv 12: 16.—3. *the bottom* of the sea B 10: 5.
4. *land* (as opp. to sea, as X., An. 1, 1, 7; Dio Chrys. 63[80], 12; Sb 5103, 6 ἐν γῆ κ' ἐν θαλάσσῃ; BGU 27, 5; Jos., Ant. 4, 125; 11, 53) Mk 4: 1; 6: 47; Lk 5: 3, 11; J 6: 21; 21: 8f, 11; Ac 27: 39, 43f. Of a *region, country* Ac 7: 3f (Gen 12: 1); vs. 6 (Gen 15: 13). In a territorial sense (X., An. 1, 3, 4) Israel Mt 2: 20f; Gennesaret 14: 34 t.r.; Midian Ac 7: 29; Judah Mt 2: 6 (where ENestle in his critical apparatus approves the conjecture of Drusius [died 1616], γῆς, accepted by PWSchmiedel, as last indicated in Zürcher Bibel '31, appendix to NT, p. 5); Zebulon and Naphtali 4: 15 (Is 9: 1); Judaea J 3: 22; Canaan Ac 13: 19; Egypt 7: 36, 40; 13: 17; Hb 8: 9 (Jer 38: 32); of the Chaldaeans Ac 7: 4; *native land* vs. 3. The inhabitants included Mt 10: 15; 11: 24. ἡ γῆ abs.= Palestine Mt 27: 45; Mk 15: 33; Lk 4: 25. On κληρονομεῖν τ. γῆν Mt 5: 5; D 3: 7 s. κληρονομέω 2.
5. *earth*—a. in contrast to heaven (Ael. Aristid. 24, 44 K.=44 p. 838 D.: ἐκ θεῶν ἥκειν ἐπὶ γῆν) Mt 5: 18, 35; 6: 10, 19; 16: 19; Lk 2: 14; 21: 25; Col 1: 16; Hb 1: 10 (Ps 101: 26); 11: 13; 2 Pt 3: 5, 10. τὰ ἐπὶ τῆς γῆς *earthly things* (Ocellus Luc. c. 36 γῆ κ. πάντα τὰ ἐπὶ γῆς; Ps.-Aristot., De Mundo 6, 5; Lucian, Vit. Auct. 18) Col 3: 2, 5 (Maximus Tyr. 25, 6b: in contrast to the ἄνω the γῆ is the seat of all earthly weakness and inferiority). Established on the waters Hv 1, 3, 4. Vanishing w. heaven at the end of time 2 Cl 16: 3 and replaced by a new earth 2 Pt 3: 13; Rv 21: 1 (Is 65: 17; 66: 22).
b. as the inhabited globe (Appian, Mithrid. 57 §234 γῆς ἄρξειν ἁπάσης) Lk 21: 35; Ac 10: 12; 11: 6; 17: 26 al. ἕως ἐσχάτου τῆς γῆς *to the remotest parts of the earth* 1: 8. Hence the inhabitants of the earth *men, humankind* Mt 5: 13; 10: 34; Lk 12: 49, 51. ἐπὶ τῆς γῆς *on earth*= among men Lk 18: 8; J 17: 4; Ro 9: 28; Eph 6: 3 (Ex 20: 12; Dt 5: 16); Js 5: 5; Hs 5, 6, 6. ἀπὸ τῆς γῆς *from the earth*= from among men Ac 8: 33 (Is 53: 8); 22: 22; Rv 14: 3. M-M. B. 17.

γηγενής, ές (Soph., Hdt.+; Diod. S. 1, 86, 3; Herm. Wr. 1, 27; Proclus, Hymn. 1, 15; 3, 5; LXX) *earth-born* (parall. θνητός; cf. Philo, Spec. Leg. 2, 124) 1 Cl 39: 2.*

γῆρας (Hom.+; inscr., pap., LXX, Philo; Jos., Ant. 1, 46 al.), ως (thus Jos., Bell. 5, 461, Ant. 6, 32) or ους (so Test. Jud. 15, 4), τό, dat. γήρᾳ or γήρει (1 Ch 29: 28; Ps 91: 15; Da 6: 1 al.; cf. Helbing 42) as in Ionic (Bl-D. §47, 1; Mlt.-H. 140) *old age* ἐν γήρει Lk 1: 36; but ἐν γήρᾳ (as Lk 1: 36 t.r.; Sir 3: 12; 25: 3) 1 Cl 10: 7. ἕως γήρους (Ps 70: 18) *to old age* 63: 3 (cf. Reinhold 51). M-M.*

γηράσκω (Hom.+; PSI 685, 13; POxy. 904, 2; LXX; Philo, Aet. M. 61; Jos., Ant. 19, 170) 1 aor. ἐγήρασα; pf. γεγήρακα (Diod. S. 16, 20, 3; 18, 24, 2; 1 Cl 23: 3) *grow old* J 21: 18; 1 Cl 23: 3. παλαιούμενον καὶ γηράσκον *becoming obsolete and growing old* Hb 8: 13. M-M.*

γίνομαι (in the form γίγνομαι [s. below] Hom.+; as γίν. since Aristot. gener., inscr., pap., LXX, En., Ep. Arist., Philo, Joseph., Test. 12 Patr., Sib. Or.; cf. Kühner-Bl. II p. 391; KBrugmann⁴-AThumb, Griech. Gramm. '13, 126; Mayser p. 165 and lit. there) impf. ἐγινόμην; fut. γενή-σομαι; 2 aor. ἐγενόμην, 3 sg. opt. γένοιτο; the very rare v.l. (Bl-D §81, 3) γενάμενος is also found in Ps.-Callisth. 1, 20, 1; 1, 41, 11; 1 aor. pass. ἐγενήθην (Doric, H.Gk.; Phryn. 108 L.; pap. fr. III BC, Mayser I 2² '38, 157f; Inscr. [ESchweizer, Gramm. d. pergam. Inschr. 1898, 181; ENachmanson, Laute u. Formen d. magn. Inschr. '03, 168; Thieme 13]; LXX), imper. γενηθήτω; pf. γεγένη-μαι (Meisterhans³-Schw.: Att. since 376 BC; Mayser 391) unquestioned only J 2: 9, and γέγονα (Meisterhans³-Schw.: since 464 BC; Mayser 372. On the aoristic use of γέγονα cf. Mlt. 145f; 238; 239; PChantraine, Histoire du parfait grec '27, 233-45), 3 pl. γέγοναν (Ro 16: 7; Rv 21: 6. Cf. KBuresch, Γέγοναν: RhM 46, 1891, 193ff; Mlt. 52 n.), ptc. γεγονώς; plpf. 3 sg. ἐγεγόνει (J 6: 17), without augment γεγόνει (Ac 4: 22; t.r. ἐγεγόνει; Bl-D. §78; Mlt.-H. 190. On the variation γίνομαι and γίγνομαι s. Bl-D. §34, 4 w. app.; Mlt.-H. 108.

I. as a verb w. its own mng. *come to be, become, originate.* Its relation to εἰμί is seen in Epigr. Gr. 595, 5 οὐκ ἤμην καὶ ἐγενόμην=I was not and then I came to be.

1. be born or **begotten—a.** lit., abs. (Dit., Syll.³ 1168, 6; Epict. 2, 17, 8; Wsd 7: 3; Sir 44: 9) J 8: 58; w. ἔκ τινος foll. (Diod. S. 3, 64, 1; Appian, Basil. 5 §1; Parthenius 1, 4; Athen. 13, 37 p. 576c ἐξ ἑταίρας; PPetr. III 2, 20; PFlor. 382, 38 ὁ ἐξ ἐμοῦ γενόμενος υἱός; 1 Esdr 4: 16; Tob 8: 6; Jos., Ant. 2, 216) Ro 1: 3; Gal 4: 4 (cf. IQS 11, 21). Also of plants 1 Cor 15: 37. Of fruits ἔκ τινος *be produced by a tree* Mt 21: 19 (cf. X., Mem. 3, 6, 13 ὁ ἐκ τ. χώρας γιγνόμενος σῖτος.

b. of things *arise, come about,* etc. (Alcaeus 23 Diehl² καὶ κ᾽ οὐδὲν ἐκ δένος γένοιτο=nothing could originate from nothing)—**a.** of events or phenomena in nature (Sir 40: 10; Ex 10: 22; Job 40: 23; Jos., Ant. 9, 36): lightning, thunder (X., An. 3, 1, 11) J 12: 29; Rv 8: 5; 11: 19; calm (on the sea) Mt 8: 26; Mk 4: 39; Lk 8: 24; storm Mk 4: 37; a cloud Lk 9: 34; flood 6: 48; earthquake (Parian Marbles [III BC]: 239B, 24 Jac.) Mt 8: 24; 28: 2; Ac 16: 26; Rv 6: 12; 11: 13; 16: 18; darkness Mt 27: 45; Mk 15: 33; Lk 23: 44; J 6: 17; hail, fire Rv 8: 7.

β. of other occurrences (Arrian, Anab. 4, 4, 3 τὰ ἱερὰ οὐκ ἐγίγνετο= the sacrifice did not turn out [favorably]; 1 Macc 1: 25; 4: 58; 9: 27; 13: 44; Jdth 7: 29; 14: 19 al.): complaining Ac 6: 1; persecution, oppression Mt 13: 21; 24: 21; Mk 4: 17; 13: 19; Ac 11: 19; discussion J 3: 25; Ac 15: 7; tumult Mt 26: 5; 27: 24; a sound Ac 2: 2, 6; weeping 20: 37; clamor 23: 9; Mt 25: 6; famine Lk 4: 25; 15: 14; Ac 11: 28; ὁρμή (q.v.) 14: 5; war Rv 12: 7; sharp contention Ac 15: 39; tear (in a garment) Mt 9: 16; Mk 2: 21; Lk 6: 49; silence (s. σιγή) Ac 21: 40; Rv 8: 1; στάσις (q.v.) Lk 23: 19; Ac 15: 2; 23: 7, 10; concourse 21: 30; confusion 19: 23; shout vs. 34; Rv 11: 15; dispute Lk 22: 24; envy, strife 1 Ti 6: 4.

γ. of the various divisions of a day (Jdth 13: 1; 1 Macc 5: 30; 4 Macc 3: 8 al.) γενομένης ἡμέρας *when day came* (Jos., Ant. 10, 202, Vi. 405) Lk 4: 42; Ac 12: 18; 16: 35; 23: 12; cf. Lk 6: 13; 22: 66; Ac 27: 29, 33, 39. Differently Mk 6: 21 γενομένης ἡμέρας εὐκαίρου *when a convenient*

day arrived. ὀψέ (cf. Gen 29: 25; 1 Km 25: 37) 11: 19. ὀψίας γενομένης Mt 8: 16; 14: 15, 23; 16: 2; 26: 20; 27: 57; Mk 1: 32; 6: 47; 14: 17; 15: 42; cf. J 6: 16. πρωΐας Mt 27: 1; J 21: 4. νύξ Ac 27: 27. ὥρας πολλῆς γενομένης *when it had grown late* Mk 6: 35; cf. 15: 33; Lk 22: 14; Ac 26: 4.

2. be made, created—a. gener. w. διά τινος J 1: 3a (MTeschendorf, D. Schöpfungsged. im NT: StKr 104, '32, 337-72). W. χωρίς τινος vs. 3b (Isisaretal. v. Kyrene 15 Peek [103 AD] Ἐμοῦ δὲ χωρὶς γείνετ᾽ οὐδὲν πώποτε; Cleanthes, Hymn to Zeus 15 [Stoic. I 537] οὐδέ τι γίγνεται ἔργον σοῦ δίχα; note the related style IQH 1, 20; on the syntax of J 1: 3f see BVawter, CBQ 25, '63, 401-6, who favors a full stop after οὐδὲ ἕν). W. ἔκ τινος Hb 11: 3. Of idols διὰ χειρῶν γινόμενοι made w. hands Ac 19: 26 (cf. PRyl. 231, 3 [40 AD] τοὺς ἄρτους γενέσ-θαι). Of miracles: *be done, take place* (Tob 11: 15; Wsd 19: 13 v.l. Swete) Mt 11: 20f, 23; Lk 10: 13; Ac 8: 13. ἐφ᾽ ὃν γεγόνει τὸ σημεῖον τοῦτο *on whom this miracle had been performed* 4: 22. W. mention of the author (cf. 4 Macc 17: 11) 2: 43; 4: 16, 30; 12: 9; 24: 2. διὰ τῶν χειρῶν τινος Mk 6: 2; Ac 14: 3. ὑπό τινος (Herodian 8, 4, 2; Dit., Or. 168, 46 [115 BC] τὰ γεγονότα ὑπὸ τοῦ πατρὸς φιλάνθρωπα; PTurin I 3, 7 [116 BC]; Wsd 9: 2; Jos., Ant. 8, 111; 347) Lk 9: 7 t.r.; 13: 17; 23: 8; Eph 5: 12. Of commands, instructions *be fulfilled, performed* γενηθήτω τὸ θέλημά σου *thy will be done* (Appian, Liby. 90 §423 τὸ πρόσταγμα δεῖ γενέσθαι; Syntipas p. 25, 3 γενέσθω τὸ αἴτημα) Mt 6: 10; 26: 42; Lk 11: 2; cf. 22: 42. γέγονεν ὃ ἐπέταξας *your order has been carried out* 14: 22. γε-νέσθαι τὸ αἴτημα αὐτῶν *that their demand should be granted* 23: 24. Of institutions: *be established,* the Sabbath for the sake of man Mk 2: 27 (Crates, Ep. 24 οὐ γεγόνασιν οἱ ἄνθρωποι τ. ἵππων χάριν, ἀλλ᾽ οἱ ἵπποι τ. ἀνθρώπων).

b. w. mention of the special nature of an undertaking: ἵνα οὕτως γένηται ἐν ἐμοί *in order to have such action taken in my case* 1 Cor 9: 15. ἐν τῷ ξηρῷ τί γένηται; *what will be done when it (the wood) is dry?* Lk 23: 31.

3. happen, take place (Dicaearch., fgm. 102 W.: a campaign 'takes place'; Diod. S. 32 fgm. 9c τὰς εἰς τ. πατέρα γεγενημένας ἁμαρτίας=the misdeeds perpetrated against his father; 2 Macc 1: 32; 13: 17; 3 Macc 1: 11; 4: 12; 5: 17 al.).

a. gener. τοῦτο ὅλον γέγονεν *all this took place* w. ἵνα foll. Mt 1: 22; 26: 56. ἕως ἂν πάντα γένηται *until all has taken place* (=is past) 5: 18. πάντα τὰ γενόμενα *everything that had happened* (cf. Appian, Bell. Civ. 2, 121 §508 τὰ γενόμενα; 1 Esdr 1: 10; Jdth 15: 1; 1 Macc 4: 20; 2 Macc 10: 21; 3 Macc 1: 17) 18: 31; cf. 21: 21; 24: 6, 20, 34; 26: 54; 27: 54; 28: 11; Mk 5: 14. ἴδωμεν τὸ ῥῆμα τοῦτο τὸ γεγονός *let us see this thing that has taken place* Lk 2: 15. θανάτου γενομένου *since a death has occurred,* i.e. *since he has died* Hb 9: 15. τούτου γενομένου *after this had happened* (Jos., Ant. 9, 56; 129) Ac 28: 9. τὸ γεγονός *what had happened* (Diod. S. 12, 49, 4; Appian, Bell. Civ. 2, 18 §496; Jos., Ant. 14, 292) Lk 8: 34.—μὴ γένοιτο *strong negation,* in Paul only after rhet. questions (cf. Epict., Index p. 540E; Lucian, Dial. Deor. 1, 2, Dial. Meret. 13, 4; Achilles Tat. 5, 18, 4; Aristaen., Ep. 1, 27) *by no means, far from it, God forbid,* lit. 'may it not be' (Gdspd., Probs., 88) Lk 20: 16; Ro 3: 4, 6, 31; 6: 2, 15; 7: 7, 13; 9: 14; 11: 1, 11; 1 Cor 6: 15; Gal 2: 17; 3: 21. More completely (the LXX has exx. only of this usage: Gen 44: 17; 3 Km 20: 3 al.; cf. Josh 22: 29; Demosth. 10, 27; Aliciph. 2, 5, 3 al.; Ael. Aristid. 23, 80 K.=42 p. 795 D.; 30 p. 578 D.; 54 p. 679 ὃ μὴ γένοιτο) Gal 6: 14.—τί γέγονεν ὅτι (cf. Eccl 7: 10) *why is it that* J 14: 22.—Of festivals: *be held, take place, come* (X., Hell. 7, 4, 28 τὰ Ὀλύμπια; 4, 5, 1; 4 Km 23: 22f; 2 Macc 6: 7) feast of dedication J 10: 22; passover Mt 26: 2; sabbath Mk 6: 2; wedding J 2: 1.—Abs. imper. (put twice for emphasis as Lucian, Pisc. 1 βάλλε, βάλλε; Philostrat., Ep. 35 λάβε λάβε; Procop. Soph., Ep. 45) γενηθήτω γεννηθήτω *so let it be* as a closing formula 1 Cor 16: 24 G. (cf. Herodas 4, 85, where the sacristan closes his prayer to Asclepius with the words: ὧδε ταῦτ᾽ εἴη=so may it be).

b. w. dat. of the pers. affected:—**a.** w. inf. foll. (1 Macc 13: 5; Jos., Ant. 6, 232) ὅπως μὴ γένηται αὐτῷ χρονοτριβῆσαι *so that he would not have to lose time* Ac 20: 16.

β. w. adv. or adv. phrase added (1 Esdr 6: 33) κατὰ τὴν πίστιν ὑμῶν γενηθήτω ὑμῖν *according to your faith let it be done to you* Mt 9: 29; cf. 8: 13. γένοιτό μοι κατὰ τὸ ῥῆμά σου *may that happen to me which you have spoken* of Lk 1: 38. πῶς ἐγένετο τῷ δαιμονιζομένῳ *what had happened to the demoniac* Mk 5: 16. ἵνα εὖ σοι γένηται *that it may be well w. you* Eph 6: 3 (Dt 5: 16; cf. Epict. 2, 5, 29 εὖ σοι γένοιτο; Aelian, V.H. 9, 36). γενηθήτω σοι ὡς θέλεις *let it be done for you as you desire*, i.e. *your wish is granted* Mt 15: 28.

γ. w. nom. of the thing (1 Macc 4: 25; Sir 51: 17) γίνεταί τινί τι *someth. happens to* or *befalls a person* Mk 9: 21. ἵνα μὴ χεῖρόν σοί τι γένηται *lest someth. worse come upon you* J 5: 14. τί ἐγένετο αὐτῷ *what has happened to him* Ac 7: 40 (Ex 32: 1, 23). τὸ γεγενημένον αὐτῷ Ac 3: 10 D. ἐγίνετο πάσῃ ψυχῇ φόβος *fear came upon everyone* (cf. Tob 11: 18) 2: 43. Freq. γέγονέ ἐμοί τι *someth. has come to me=I have someth.* ἐὰν γένηται τινι ἀνθρώπῳ ἑκατὸν πρόβατα *if a man has a hundred sheep* Mt 18: 12. τοῖς ἔξω ἐν παραβολαῖς τὰ πάντα γίνεται *those outside receive everything in parables* Mk 4: 11. μήποτε γένηται ἀνταπόδομά σοι *that you may receive no repayment* Lk 14: 12; cf. 19: 9; J 15: 7; 1 Cor 4: 5.

c. w. gen. of the pers. (Diod. S. 16, 64, 2 τὸν τῆς Ἑλένης γεγενημένον ὅρμον=the necklace that had belonged to Helen): ἐγένετο ἡ βασιλεία τοῦ κόσμου τοῦ κυρίου ἡμῶν *the kingdom of the world has come into the possession of our Lord* Rv 11: 15.

d. γίνεταί τι ἐπί τινι *someth. happens in the case of* or *to a person* Mk 5: 33 t.r.; ἐν v.l. This can also be expressed w. εἴς τινα Ac 28: 6 or the double nom. τί ἄρα ὁ Πέτρος ἐγένετο *what had become of Peter* 12: 18 (cf. Jos., Vi. 296 οἱ εἴκοσι χρυσοῖ τί γεγόνασιν).

e. w. inf. foll., to emphasize the actual occurrence of the action denoted by the verb: ἐὰν γένηται εὑρεῖν αὐτό *if it comes about that he finds it=if he actually finds it* Mt 18: 13 (cf. PCattaoui V 20 [=Mitteis, Chrest. p. 422] ἐὰν γένηταί με ἀποδημεῖν; PAmh. 135, 10; BGU 970, 5). ἐγένετο αὐτὸν παραπορεύεσθαι *he happened to be passing* Mk 2: 23; cf. Lk 6: 1, 6. ἐγένετο ἀνεῳχθῆναι τὸν οὐρανόν *just then the heaven opened* Lk 3: 21; cf. 16: 22; Ac 4: 5; 9: 3, 32, 37, 43; 11: 26; 14: 1; 16: 16; 19: 1; 21: 1, 5; 22: 6, 17; 27: 44; 28: 8 (UPZ 62, 29 [161 BC] γίνεται γὰρ ἐντραπῆναι).

f. καὶ ἐγένετο (ἐγένετο δέ) periphrastic like וַיְהִי with וְ foll. to indicate the progress of the narrative; it is followed either by a conjunction like ὅτε, ὡς etc., or a gen. abs., or a prepositional constr., and joined to it is a finite verb w. καί (Jdth 5: 22; 10: 1; Sus 19 Theod.; 1 Macc 1: 1; 5: 1; Gen 39: 7, 13, 19; 42: 35) Mt 9: 10; Mk 2: 15 t.r.; Lk 2: 15 v.l.; 5: 1, 12, 17; 8: 1, 22; 14: 1.—Without the second καί (Jdth 2: 4; 12: 10; 13: 12; 1 Macc 6: 8; 7: 2 v.l.; 9: 23; Sus 28 Theod.; Bel 18 Theod.) Mt 7: 28; 11: 1; 13: 53; 19: 1; 26: 1; Mk 1: 9; 4: 4; Lk 1: 8, 23, 41, 59; 2: 1, 6, 46; 6: 12 al. At times it is followed by an inf., cf. Mlt. 16f. The

phrase is usually omitted in translation; older versions transl. *it came to pass.*—Mlt. 16f; MJohannessohn, Das bibl. καὶ ἐγένετο u. s. Geschichte: Zeitschr. f. vergleichende Sprachforschung 53, '26, 161-212; cf. MDibelius, Gnomon 3, '27, 446-50; HPernot, Études sur la langue des Évangiles '27, 189-99; KBeyer, Semitische Syntax im NT, '62, 29-62; JReiling, Bible Translator 16, '65, 153-63.

4. of pers. and things which change their nature, to indicate their entering a new condition: *become something.*

a. w. nouns (Lamellae Aur. Orphicae ed. AOlivieri '15, p. 16, 5 θεὸς ἐγένου ἐξ ἀνθρώπου [IV/III]; Arrian, Anab. 5, 26, 5; Sir 51: 2; 1 Esdr 4: 26; Wsd 8: 2; 4 Macc 16: 6): ὅπως γένησθε υἱοὶ τοῦ πατρὸς ὑμῶν *that you may become sons of your father* Mt 5: 45; fishermen, fig. Mk 1: 17; a traitor Lk 6: 16; friends 23: 12 (s. Jos., Ant. 11, 121); children of God J 1: 12; children of light 12: 36; a Christian Ac 26: 29; the father Ro 4: 18; a fool 1 Cor 3: 18; a spectacle 4: 9; a man 1 Cor 13: 11 (Tob 1: 9); a curse Gal 3: 13. οὐχ ἑαυτὸν ἐδόξασεν γενηθῆναι ἀρχιερέα *he did not exalt himself to be made high priest* Hb 5: 5. W. double nom. (Ps.-Apollod., Epit. 3, 15 δράκων λίθος ἐγένετο; Quint. Smyrn. 12, 507; Bel 28; 4 Macc 18: 7) οἱ λίθοι ἄρτοι γίνονται *the stones turn into bread* Mt 4: 3. ὁ λόγος σὰρξ ἐγένετο J 1: 14 (the reverse PBerl. 13044, col. III, 28ff [UWilcken, SAB '23, 161f] τί ποιῶν ἄν τις γένοιτο θεός;). τὸ ὕδωρ γενήσεται πηγή 4: 14. ἡ περιτομὴ ἀκροβυστία γέγονεν Ro 2: 25. ἐγενόμην ἐγὼ διάκονος *I became a minister* (lit. 'servant') Col 1: 23 (cf. Herodian 2, 6, 8 ἀνὴρ ἔπαρχος γενόμενος).—Also γ. εἴς τι (Menand., Per. 49 J. τὸ κακὸν εἰς ἀγαθὸν γ.; 1 Km 4: 9; Jdth 5: 18; 1 Macc 2: 11, 43; 3: 58 al.): ἐγένετο εἰς δένδρον μέγα *it became a large tree* Lk 13: 19 v.l. εἰς κεφαλὴν γωνίας Mt 21: 42; Mk 12: 10; Lk 20: 17; Ac 4: 11; 1 Pt 2: 7 (all referring to Ps 117: 22); εἰς χαράν *change into joy* J 16: 20. εἰς οὐδέν *come to nothing* Ac 5: 36. εἰς παγίδα Ro 11: 9 (Ps 68: 23); εἰς κενόν γ. *be done in vain* 1 Th 3: 5. εἰς ἄψινθον Rv 8: 11. Also w. γίνεσθαι omitted: εἰς κατάκριμα (sc. ἐγένετο τὸ κρίμα) Ro 5: 18.

b. used w. an adj. to paraphrase the passive (Jdth 11: 11; 1 Esdr 7: 3; 2 Macc 3: 34; Sus 64 Theod.): ἀπαλοὶ γ. *become tender* Mt 24: 32; Mk 13: 28; ἀπειθῆ γ. Ac 26: 19; ἀποσυνάγωγον γ. *be expelled fr. the synagogue* J 12: 42; ἄφαντον γ. *disappear* Lk 24: 31; σκωληκόβρωτον γ. *be eaten by worms* Ac 12: 23; γνωστόν, φανερὸν γ. *become known* Mk 6: 14; Ac 1: 19; 9: 42; 19: 17; 1 Cor 3: 13; 14: 25; Phil 1: 13; δόκιμον γ. *pass the test* Js 1: 12; ἑδραῖον γ. 1 Cor 15: 58; ἔκδηλον γ. 2 Ti 3: 9; ἔξυπνον γ. Ac 16: 27 (1 Esdr 3: 3=Jos., Ant. 11: 34); s. ἐλεύθερος, ἐμφανής, ἔμφοβος, ἐνεργής, ἔντρομος, καθαρός, μέγας, περικρατής, πλήρης, πρηνής, τυφλός, ὑγιής, ὑπήκοος, ὑπόδικος, φανερός 1.

c. to denote change of location *come, go*—**a.** εἴς τι (Hdt. 5, 87 al.; Philo, Op. M. 86; 2 Macc 1: 13): εἰς Ἱεροσόλυμα γ. (Jos., Ant. 10, 42) Ac 20: 16; 21: 17; 25: 15. εἰς τὸν ἀγρόν Hv 3, 1, 4. Of the voice: ἐγένετο εἰς τὰ ὦτά μου *reached my ear* Lk 1: 44. Fig. (cf. Bar 4: 28) of Abraham's blessing εἰς τὰ ἔθνη *come to the Gentiles* Gal 3: 14; cf. 2 Cor 8: 14 (s. περίσσευμα, ὑστέρημα).

β. ἔκ τινος (Job 28: 2): γ. ἐκ μέσου *be removed*, Lat. e medio tolli (cf. Ps.-Aeschin., Ep. 12, 6 ἐκ μέσου γενομένων ἐκείνων; Plut., Timol. 5, 3; Achilles Tat. 2, 27, 2) 2 Th 2: 7 (HWFulford, ET 23, '12, 40f: 'leave the scene'). Of a voice fr. heaven: ἐκ τ. οὐρανῶν γ. *sound forth fr. heaven* (2 Macc 2: 21; cf. Da 4: 31 Theod.) Mk 1: 11; Lk 3: 22; 9: 35; cf. vs. 36.

γ. ἐπί τι: ἐπὶ τὸ μνημεῖον *go to the tomb* Lk 24: 22; ἐπὶ τοὺς ἀναβαθμούς *come up to the steps* Ac 21: 35. Of fear that befalls someone (2 Macc 12: 22) Lk 1: 65; 4: 36; Ac 5: 5. Of ulcers: *break out on someone* Rv 16: 2 (Ex 9: 10f). Of divine commands: *go out to someone* Lk 3: 2. ἐπί is somet. used w. the gen. (Appian, Liby. 93 §440; Alex. Aphr., Mixt. II 2 p. 213, 21) instead of the acc.: γενόμενος ἐπὶ τοῦ τόπου *when he had arrived at the place* 22: 40 (Wilcken, Chrest. 327, 18 ἐπὶ τ. τόπων γινόμενος).—J 6: 21.

δ. w. κατά and gen. of place: τὸ γενόμενον ῥῆμα καθ᾽ ὅλης τῆς Ἰουδαίας *the message that has spread throughout all Judea* Ac 10: 37. W. acc. of place (X., Cyr. 7, 1, 15; Apollon. Paradox. 3 κατὰ τόπους γ.; Jos., Ant. 1, 174; cf. 2 Macc 9: 8): γενόμενος κατὰ τὸν τόπον Lk 10: 32 v.l.; γενόμενοι κατὰ τὴν Κνίδον Ac 27: 7.

ε. w. πρός and acc. of the direction and goal (PLond. 962, 1 γενοῦ πρὸς Ἄταιν τὸν ποιμένα; PFlor. 180, 45) 1 Cor 2: 3; 2 J 12. Of divine instructions *be given to someone* (Gen 15: 1, 4; Jer 1: 2, 11; 13: 8; Ezk 6: 1; Hos 1: 1; cf. ἐπί w. acc.) J 10: 35; Ac 7: 31 v.l.; 10: 13; 13: 32.

ζ. w. σύν and the dat. *join someone* (X., Cyr. 5, 3, 8; 2 Macc 13: 13) Lk 2: 13.

η. w. ἐγγύς (X., An. 1, 8, 8, Cyr. 7, 1, 7; cf. γίν. πλησίον Philo, Mos. 1, 228; Jos., Ant. 4, 40): ἐγγὺς τοῦ πλοίου γίνεσθαι *come close to the boat* J 6: 19. Fig. of the relation of believers to Christ: *come near* Eph 2: 13.

θ. w. ὧδε *come here* J 6: 25; γ. ὁμοθυμαδόν *come together in unanimity* or *reach unanimity* Ac 15: 25.

ι. ἔμπροσθέν τινος γ. J 1: 15, 30 s. on ἔμπροσθεν 2f and ὀπίσω 2b.

II. As a substitute for the forms of εἰμί (ALink, StKr 69, 1896, 420ff).

1. Used w. the nom. (Wsd 16: 3; Jdth 16: 21; Sir 31: 22; 1 Macc 3: 58) γίνεσθε φρόνιμοι *be prudent* Mt 10: 16. ἄκαρπος γίνεται 13: 22; Mk 4: 19.—W. other words: v. 22; 9: 50; Lk 1: 2; 2: 2; 6: 36 and very oft. Freq. the dat. of advantage is added (1 Macc 10: 47; 2 Macc 7: 37; 4 Macc 6: 28; 12: 17): ἀγαπητόν τινι γ. *be dear to someone* 1 Th 2: 8. ἀπρόσκοπον γ. τινι *be inoffensive to someone* 1 Cor 10: 32; γ. τινι μαθητής J 15: 8; μισθαποδότην γ. τινι *be a rewarder of someone* Hb 11: 6; γ. ὁδηγόν τινι Ac 1: 16. Cf. παρηγορία, σημεῖον, τύπος.—τί γίνεταί τινί τι *a thing results in someth. for someone* τὸ ἀγαθὸν ἐμοὶ ἐγ. θάνατος; Ro 7: 13. ἡ ἐξουσία πρόσκομμα τοῖς ἀσθενέσιν 1 Cor 8: 9.—γίνομαι ὡς, ὥσπερ, ὡσεί τις (Ps 21: 15; 31: 9; 87: 5 al.) *be, become, show oneself like* Mt 6: 16; 10: 25; 18: 3; 28: 4; Lk 22: 26, 44; 1 Cor 4: 13; 9: 20f; Gal 4: 12. καθὼς ἐγένετο—οὕτως ἔσται *as it was—so it will be* Lk 17: 26, 28. οὐ χρὴ ταῦτα οὕτως γίνεσθαι *this should not be so* Js 3: 10. ὁσίως καὶ δικαίως καὶ ἀμέμπτως ὑμῖν ἐγενήθημεν *we proved ourselves . . . toward you* 1 Th 2: 10.

2. used w. the gen.—a. gen. of the possessor (Appian, Bell. Civ. 5, 79 §336 a slave γεγένητο Πομπηΐου= had belonged to Pompey) *belong to someone* Lk 20: 14, 33 (Appian, Bell. Civ. 2, 83 §350 γυνὴ Κράσσου γεγενημένη= who had been the wife of [the younger] Crassus). ἐγένετο γνώμης *he decided* Ac 20: 3 (cf. Plut., Phoc. 23, 4 ἐλπίδος μεγάλης γ.; Cass. Dio 61, 14 τ. ἐπιθυμίας γ.; Wilcken, Ostraka I 508; Jos., Bell. 6, 287). Here perh. belongs ἰδίας ἐπιλύσεως οὐ γίνεται *it is not a matter of private interpretation* 2 Pt 1: 20.

b. in statements pertaining to age (Aristoxenus, fgm. 16 γεγονότα [sc. τὸν Πυθαγόραν] ἐτῶν τεσσαράκοντα; Demetr. of Phalerum [IV–III BC], fgm. 153 Wehrli ['49]; Jos., Ant. 10, 50) ἐτῶν δώδεκα Lk 2: 42; cf. 1 Ti 5: 9.

3. w. dat. of the pers. *belong to someone* (PPetr. II 40b, 7 [277 BC]; Ostraka II 1530 [120 BC]) τὸ γινόμενόν

μοι= what belongs to me) of a woman ἀνδρὶ ἑτέρῳ Ro 7: 3f (cf. Ruth 1: 12f; Dt 24: 2).

4. used w. prep. and adv. *be*—a. w. prep. μετά τινος (Josh 2: 19) Ac 9: 19; 20: 18. οἱ μετ᾽ αὐτοῦ γενόμενοι *his intimate friends* Mk 16: 10. πρός τινα *be w. someone* 1 Cor 16: 10. ὑπό τινα *be under the authority of someone* or *someth.* (1 Macc 10: 38) Gal 4: 4. ἔν τινι to designate one's present or future place of residence (X., An. 4, 3, 29; Appian, Bell. Civ. 5, 4 §15 Ἀντώνιος ἐν Ἐφέσῳ γενόμενος; Aelian, V.H. 4, 15; Herodian 2, 2, 5; POxy. 283, 11; 709, 6 ἐν Μένφει γενόμενος; PTebt. 416, 3; BGU 731 II, 6 ἐν οἰκίᾳ μου; Num 11: 35; Judg 17: 4; 1 Ch 14: 17; Jdth 5: 7 al.) Mt 26: 6; Mk 9: 33; Ac 7: 38; 13: 5; 2 Ti 1: 17; Rv 1: 9; sim. of a state of being (Stoic. III 221, 16; Diod. S. 20, 62, 4 ἐν ἀνέσει γ.; Plut., Tit. Flam. 16, 1 ἐν ὀργῇ γ.; Lucian, Tim. 28; PPetr. II 20 III, 12 [252 BC] ἐν ἐπισχέσει γ.; BGU 5 II, 19 ἐν νόσῳ; POxy. 471 IV, 77f; 4 Km 9: 20; 1 Macc 1: 27 v.l.; Sus 8 Theod.; Jos., Bell. 1, 320, Ant. 16, 372) ἐν ἀγωνίᾳ Lk 22: 44. ἐν ἐκστάσει Ac 22: 17. ἐν πνεύματι *under the Spirit's influence* Rv 1: 10; 4: 2. ἐν ὁμοιώματι ἀνθρώπων *be like men* Phil 2: 7. ἐν ἀσθενείᾳ, φόβῳ, τρόμῳ 1 Cor 2: 3. ἐν δόξῃ 2 Cor 3: 7; ἐν ἑαυτῷ γ. *come to one's senses* (Soph., Phil. 950; X., An. 1, 5, 17; Polyb. 1, 49, 8; Charito 3, 9, 11) Ac 12: 11; γ. ἐν Χριστῷ *be a Christian* Ro 16: 7.

b. w. adv.: ἐκεῖ (X., An. 6, 5, 20; 3 Km 8: 8 v.l.; Jos., Ant. 10, 180) Ac 19: 21. κατὰ μόνας Mk 4: 10.

5. *appear* ([Ps.-] Jos., Ant. 18, 63) Mk 1: 4; J 1: 6, hence *exist* (Diod. S. 3, 52, 4 γέγονε γένη γυναικῶν= there have been nations of women; Appian, Maced. 18 §3 τὸ χρυσίον τὸ γιγνόμενον= the gold that was at hand; Bar 3: 26; 2 Macc 10: 24) Ro 11: 5; 1 J 2: 18. ἐγένετο there *lived* Lk 1: 5. ἔν τινι 2 Pt 2: 1. ἐπὶ τῆς γῆς Rv 16: 18 (Da 12: 1 Theod.). M-M. B. 637.

γινώσκω (in the form γιγνώσκω [s. below] since Homer; γιν. in Attic inscr. in Meisterhans³-Schw. from 325 BC, in pap. fr. 277 BC [Mayser 165]; likew. LXX; En.; Ep. Arist.; Philo; Joseph.; Test. 12 Patr.; Sib. Or.) impf. ἐγίνωσκον; fut. γνώσομαι; 2 aor. ἔγνων, imper. γνῶθι, γνώτω, subj. γνῶ (γνοῖ Mk 5: 43; 9: 30; Lk 19: 15; Bl-D. §95, 2 w. app.; Mlt.-H. 83; Rob. 1214), inf. γνῶναι, ptc. γνούς; pf. ἔγνωκα, 3 pl. ἔγνωκαν J 17: 7 (W-S. §13, 15 note 15); plpf. ἐγνώκειν; pf. pass. ἔγνωσμαι; 1 aor. pass. ἐγνώσθην; 1 fut. γνωσθήσομαι. On the spellings γινώσκειν and γιγνώσκειν s. W-S. §5, 31; Bl-D. §34, 4 w. app.; Mlt.-H. 108.

1. *know, come to know*—a. w. acc. of the thing: mysteries (Wsd 2: 22) Mt 13: 11; Mk 4: 11 t.r.; Lk 8: 10; the Master's will 12: 47f; that which brings peace 19: 42; the truth (Jos., Ant. 13, 291) J 8: 32; the times Ac 1: 7; sin Ro 7: 7; love 2 Cor 2: 4; way of righteousness 2 Pt 2: 21 𝔓⁷²; God's glory 1 Cl 61: 1.—Abs. γνόντες (Is 26: 11) *when they had ascertained it* Mk 6: 38; ἐκ μέρους γ. *know fragmentarily, only in part* 1 Cor 13: 9, 12.—W. prep. γ. τι ἔκ τινος (X., Cyr. 1, 6, 45; Jos., Vi. 364) *know a thing by someth.* (Diod. S. 17, 101, 6): a tree by its fruit Mt 12: 33; Lk 6: 44; 1 J 4: 6; γ. τι ἔν τινι (Sir 4: 24; 26: 9) 1 J 4: 2. Also γ. τι κατά τι (Gen 15: 8): κατὰ τί γνώσομαι τοῦτο; *by what (= how) shall I know this?* Lk 1: 18.

b. w. personal obj. (Plut., Mor. 69c ἄνδρα τοιοῦτον οὐκ ἔγνωμεν): God (Ael. Aristid. 52, 2 K.= 28 p. 551 D.: γ. τὸν θεόν; Herm. Wr. 1, 3; 10, 19a; Sallust. 18 p. 34, 9 θεούς; 1 Km 2: 10; 3: 7; 1 Ch 28: 9; 3 Macc 7: 6; Da 11: 32 Theod.; Philo, Ebr. 45) J 14: 7; 17: 3, 25; Ro 1: 21; Gal 4: 9; 1 J 2: 3, 13; 3: 1, 6; 4: 6ff; 5: 20 (for 1 J s. M-EBoismard, RB 56, '49, 365–91); PK 2. Jesus Christ J 14: 7; 17: 3; 2

Cor 5: 16 (*even though we have known Christ* ['contrary to fact' is also poss.=*even if we had known*; cf. Gal 5: 11], *we now no longer know him*; cf. on this pass. κατά II 5bβ; 7a; σάρξ 6); 1 J 2: 3f. τινὰ ἔν τινι *someone by someth.* (Ps 47: 4; Sir 11: 28; Test. Napht. 3: 4) Lk 24: 35.

c. w. ὅτι foll. (BGU 824, 8; Philo, Det. Pot. Ins. 22) Mt 25: 24; J 6: 69; 7: 26; 8: 52; 14: 20, 31; 17: 7f, 25; 19: 4. W. ὅθεν preceding *by this* one knows (EpJer 22) 1 J 2: 18. ἐν τούτῳ (Gen 42: 33; Ex 7: 17; Josh 3: 10 al.) J 13: 35; 1 J 2: 3, 5; 4: 13; 5: 2. W. combination of two constr. ἐν τούτῳ γινώσκομεν ὅτι μένει ἐν ἡμῖν, ἐκ τοῦ πνεύματος *by this we know that he remains in us, namely by the spirit* 3: 24; cf. 4: 13. W. an indir. question foll. (1 Km 14: 38; 25: 17; 2 Km 18: 29; Ps 38: 5): Mt 12: 7; J 7: 51. W. combination of two questions (double interrogative); ἵνα γνοῖ τίς τί διεπραγματεύσατο *that he might know what each one had gained in his dealings* Lk 19: 15.

2. *learn (of)*, *ascertain*, *find out*—a. w. acc. as obj. (1 Km 21: 3; 1 Ch 21: 2; 4 Macc 4: 4) τοῦτο (1 Km 20: 3) Mk 5: 43. τὰ γενόμενα *what has happened* Lk 24: 18. τὸ ἀσφαλές Ac 21: 34; 22: 30. τὰ περὶ ἡμῶν *our situation* Col 4: 8; *your faith* 1 Th 3: 5. Pass. *become known to someone* w. or without the dat. of the pers. who is informed: of secret things Mt 10: 26; Lk 8: 17; 12: 2. Of plots Ac 9: 24 (cf. 1 Macc 6: 3; 7: 3, 30al.).

b. w. ὅτι foll. (PGiess. 11, 4 [118 AD] γεινώσκειν σε θέλω ὅτι; 1 Esdr 2: 17; Ruth 3: 14) J 4: 1; 5: 6; 12: 9; Ac 24: 11 t.r.

c. abs. (1 Km 14: 29; 3 Km 1: 11; Tob 8: 12 al.) μηδεὶς γινωσκέτω *nobody is to know of this* Mt 9: 30. ἵνα τις γνοῖ *that anyone should obtain knowledge of it* Mk 9: 30.—d. γ. ἀπό τινος *ascertain fr. someone* 15: 45.

3. *understand*, *comprehend*—a. w. acc. foll. (Sir 1: 6; 18: 28; Wsd 5: 7 v.l.; 9: 13; Bar 3: 9 al.): the parables Mk 4: 13; what was said Lk 18: 34; (w. ἀναγινώσκειν in a play on words) Ac 8: 30. ταῦτα J 3: 10; 12: 16; what one says J 8: 43; God's wisdom 1 Cor 2: 8; the nature of God vs. 11; the nature of the divine spirit vs. 14; God's ways Hb 3: 10 (Ps 94: 10); τὸν νόμον *know the law* J 7: 49; Ro 7: 1 (here perh.='have the law at one's fingertips', cf. Menand., Sicyonius 138f, τῶν τοὺς νόμους εἰδότων).

b. abs. Mt 24: 39.—c. w. ὅτι foll. (Wsd 10: 12; EpJer 64; 1 Macc 6: 13; 7: 42; 2 Macc 7: 28 al.) Mt 21: 45; 24: 32; Mk 12: 12; 13: 28f; Lk 21: 30f; J 4: 53; 8: 27f; 2 Cor 13: 6; Js 2: 20.—d. w. indir. question foll. (Job 19: 29): J 10: 6; 13: 12, 28.

4. *perceive*, *notice*, *realize*—a. w. acc.: their wickedness Mt 22: 18; γ. δύναμιν ἐξεληλυθυῖαν *that power had gone out* Lk 8: 46 (on the constr. w. the ptc. cf. PHamb. 27, 13 [III BC]; BGU 1078 [I AD] γίνωσκε ἡγεμόνα εἰσεληλυθότα; PPetr II 11, 1; 40; POxy. 1118, 7; Jos., Ant. 17, 342).—b. abs. (Ex 22: 9; 1 Km 26: 12) Mt 16: 8; 26: 10; Mk 7: 24; 8: 17.

c. w. ὅτι foll. (Gen 3: 7; 8: 11; 1 Macc 1: 5 al.): ἔγνω τῷ σώματι ὅτι ἴαται *she felt in her body that she was healed* Mk 5: 29; cf. 15: 10; J 6: 15; 16: 19; Ac 23: 6.

5. euphem. of sex relations (Menand., fgm. 558 Kock; Heraclides Hist. 64 [Aristot., Fgm. ed VRose 1886, 383]; oft. in Plut. and other later authors, and LXX [Anz 306]) w. acc., said of a man (Gen 4: 1, 17; 1 Km 1: 19; Jdth 16: 22) Mt 1: 25; of a woman (Judg 11: 39; 21: 12; Theodor. Prodr. 9, 486 H.) Lk 1: 34 (DHaugg, D. erste bibl. Marienwort '38; FCGrant, JBL 59, '40, 19f; HSahlin, D. Messias u. d. Gottesvolk, '45, 117-20).

6. *have come to know*, *know* (Nägeli 40 w. exx.)—a. w. acc.—α. of the thing (Bar 3: 20, 23; Jdth 8: 29; Bel 35): τὴν ποσότητα 1 Cl 35: 3; hearts (Ps 43: 22) Lk 16: 15;

the will Ro 2: 18; the truth 2 J 1; sin 2 Cor 5: 21; grace 8: 9; πάντα (2 Km 14: 20) 1 J 3: 20. τί 1 Cor 8: 2a. W. object clause preceding: ὃ κατεργάζομαι οὐ γ. *what I am doing I really do not know* Ro 7: 15 (here γ. almost= *desire*, *want*, *decide* [Polyb. 5, 82, 1; Plut., Lycurg. 3, 9 p. 41b ἔγνω φυγεῖν; Appian, Syr. 5 §18; Arrian, Anab. 2, 21, 8; 2, 25, 8; Paradox. Vat. 46 Keller ὅ τι ἂν γνῶσιν αἱ γυναῖκες; Jos., Ant. 1, 195; 14, 352; 16, 331]; mngs. 3 *understand* and 7 *recognize* are also poss.). W. attraction of the relative ἐν ὥρᾳ ᾖ οὐ γ. *at an hour unknown to him* Mt 24: 50; Lk 12: 46. W. acc. and ptc. (on the constr. s. 4a above) τὴν πόλιν νεωκόρον οὖσαν *that the city is guardian of the temple* Ac 19: 35.

β. of the person *know someone* (Tob 5: 2; 7: 4; Is 1: 3) J 1: 48; 2: 24; 10: 14f, 27; Ac 19: 15; 2 Ti 2: 19 (Num 16: 5); LJ 1: 6. W. acc. and ptc. (s. α above, end) Hb 13: 23.

b. w. acc. and inf. (Da 4: 17) Hb 10: 34.—c. w. ὅτι foll. (Sir 23: 19; Bar 2: 30; Tob 3: 14) J 21: 17; Ac 20: 34; Phil 1: 12; Js 1: 3; 2 Pt 1: 20; 3: 3; γ. τοὺς διαλογισμοὺς ὅτι εἰσὶν μάταιοι *he knows that the thoughts are vain* 1 Cor 3: 20 (Ps 93: 11).— Oft. γινώσκετε, ὅτι *you may be quite sure that* Mt 24: 33, 43; Mk 13: 28f; Lk 10: 11; 12: 39; 21: 31; J 15: 18; 1 J 2: 29 (cf. UPZ 62, 32 [161 BC] γίνωσκε σαφῶς ὅτι πρός σε οὐ μὴ ἐπέλθω; 70, 14; 3 Macc 7: 9; Judg 4: 9; Job 36: 5; Pr 24: 12). In τούτῳ ἴστε γινώσκοντες, ὅτι Eph 5: 5 the question is whether the two verbs are to be separated or not. In the latter case one could point to Sym. Jer 49: 22 ἴστε γινώσκοντες and 1 Km 20: 3.

d. w. indir. question (Gen 21: 26; 1 Km 22: 3; Eccl 11: 5; 2 Macc 14: 32): Lk 7: 39; 10: 22; J 2: 25; 11: 57.

e. w. adv. modifier. Ἑλληνιστί *understand Greek* Ac 21: 37 (cf. X., Cyr. 7, 5; 31 ἐπίστασθαι Συριστί).

f. abs. (Gen 4: 9; 18: 21; 4 Km 2: 3; Sir 32: 8) Lk 2: 43. τί ἐγὼ γινώσκω; *how should I know?* Hs 9, 9, 1.

7. *acknowledge*, *recognize* as that which one is or claims to be τινά (Plut., Ages. 3, 1; Jos., Ant. 5, 112) οὐδέποτε ἔγνων ὑμᾶς *I have never recognized you* Mt 7: 23; cf. J 1: 10. ἐὰν γνωσθῇ πλέον τ. ἐπισκόπου *if he receives more recognition than the bishop* IPol 5: 2. Of God as subject *recognize someone as belonging to him, choose*, almost= *elect* (Am 3: 2; Hos 12: 1; Sib. Or. 5, 330) 1 Cor 8: 3; Gal 4: 9. In these pass. the γ. of God directed toward man is conceived of as the basis and condition for man's coming to know God; cf. on them the language of the Pythagoreans in HSchenkl, Wiener Studien 8, 1886 p. 265, no. 9 βούλει γνωσθῆναι θεοῖς· ἀγνοήθητι μάλιστα ἀνθρώποις; p. 277 no. 92 σοφὸς ἄνθρωπος κ. θεὸν σεβόμενος γινώσκεται ὑπὸ τ. θεοῦ; Porphyr., ad Marcellam 13 σοφὸς ἄνθρωπος γινώσκεται ὑπὸ θεοῦ; Herm. Wr. 1, 31 θεός, ὃς γνωσθῆναι βούλεται καὶ γινώσκεται τοῖς ἰδίοις; 10, 15 οὐ γὰρ ἀγνοεῖ τὸν ἄνθρωπον ὁ θεός, ἀλλὰ καὶ πάνυ γνωρίζει καὶ θέλει γνωρίζεσθαι. Cf. Rtzst., Mysterienrel.³ 299f; Ltzm. on 1 Cor 8: 3.—On the whole word: BSnell, D. Ausdrücke für die Begriffe des Wissens in d. vorplatonischen Philosophie '24; EBaumann, ידע u. seine Derivate: ZAW 28, '08, 22ff; 110ff; WBousset, Gnosis: Pauly-W. VII '12, 1503ff; Rtzst., Mysterienrel.³ 66-70; 284-308; PThomson, 'Know' in the NT: Exp. 9th S. III '25, 379-82; AFridrichsen, Gnosis (Paul): ELehmann-Festschr. '27, 85-109; RMPope, Faith and Knowledge in Pauline and Johannine Thought: ET 41, '30, 421-7; RBultmann, TW I '33, 688-715; HJonas, Gnosis u. spätantiker Geist I '34; ²'55; EPrucker, Gnosis Theou '37; JDupont, La Connaissance religieuse dans les Épîtres de Saint Paul, '49; LBouyer, Gnosis: Le Sens orthodoxe de l'expression jusqu'aux pères Alexandrins:

JTS n.s. 4, '53, 188-203; WDDavies, Knowledge in the Dead Sea Scrolls and Mt 11: 25-30: HTR 46, '53, 113-39; WSchmithals, D. Gnosis in Kor. '55, ³'69; MMagnusson, Der Begriff 'Verstehen' [esp. in Paul], '55; RPCasey, Gnosis, Gnosticism and the NT: CHDodd Festschr., '56, 52-80; IdelaPotterie, οἶδα et γινώσκω [4th Gosp.], Biblica 40, '59, 709-25; H-JSchoeps, Urgemeinde, Judenchristentum, Gnosis '56; EKäsemann, Das Wandernde Gottesvolk (Hb)², '57; HJonas, The Gnostic Religion, '58; JDupont, Gnosis, '60; UWilckens, Weisheit u. Torheit (1 Cor 1 and 2) '59; DGeorgi, Die Gegner des Pls im 2 Cor, '64; DMScholer, Nag Hammadi Bibliography, 1948-69, '71. M-M. B. 1209f.

γλεῦκος, ους, τό (Aristot.+; Plut.; Lucian, Philops. 39; Galen XII p. 88, 6 K., XIII p. 45, 18 al.; Athen. 1 p. 31ε; PPetr. II 40(b), 8 [277 bc]; PSI 544, 2; PGrenf. II 24, 12; Job 32: 19; Jos., Ant. 2, 64) *sweet new wine* (schol. on Nicander, Alexiph. 493 γλεῦκος, ὃ λέγεται ἐν συνηθείᾳ μοῦστος) Ac 2: 13. M-M.*

γλυκύς, εῖα, ύ (Hom.+; inscr., pap., LXX) *sweet* of water (Diod. S. 5, 43, 2; Arrian, Anab. 6, 26, 5; Jos., Bell. 3, 50, Ant. 3, 38) Js 3: 11f (opp. πικρός as Hdt. 4, 52; Plut., Mor. 13D; Philo, Rer. Div. Her. 208, Aet. M. 104); of honey Hm 5, 1, 5f. Fig. of a book *be sweet as honey*, i.e. pleasant to read Rv 10: 9f; of blackberries(?) B 7: 8. Fig. of commandments Hm 12, 4, 5; of patience m 5, 1, 6; of an exchange Dg 9: 5.—The superl. freq. of persons to express affection (Menand.; Dit., Or. 383; 526, Syll.³ 889, 20; POxy., 907, 3; 935, 22 τ. γλυκύτατον ἀδελφόν) IMg 6: 1. M-M. B. 1032.*

γλυκύτης, ητος, ἡ (Hdt. al.; Judg 9: 11; Philo) *sweetness* of honey (Jos., Ant. 3, 28) Hm 5, 1, 5. Fig. *tenderness* of God 1 Cl 14: 3 (cf. Wsd 16: 21; Cat. Cod. Astr. VIII 2 p. 156, 21 of Aphrodite).—JZiegler, Dulcedo Dei '37.*

γλυπτός, ή, όν *carved* (Theophr., Lap. 5 al.; LXX) τὸ γ. *carved image* (LXX; loanw. in rabb.) B 12: 6 (Dt 27: 15).*

γλῶσσα, ης, ἡ (Hom.+; inscr., pap., LXX, En., Philo, Joseph., Test. 12 Patr.).
1. *tongue*—a. lit. Lk 16: 24; as an organ of speech (Iambl., Vi. Pyth. 31, 195 χαλεπώτατόν ἐστιν τὸ γλώττης κρατεῖν) Mk 7: 33, 35; (Vi. Aesopi I c. 7: Isis heals the mute Aesop τὸ τραχὺ τῆς γλώττης ἀποτεμοῦσα, τὸ κωλῦον αὐτὸν λαλεῖν) Lk 1: 64; Ro 3: 13 (Ps 5: 10; 13: 3); Js 1: 26; 3: 5f, 8 (Apion in the schol. on Od. 3, 341 κράτιστον τῶν μελῶν ἡ γλῶσσα.—JGeffcken, Kynika usw. '09, 45-53; GAvdBerghvEysinga, NThT 20, '31, 303-20). 1 J 3: 18; διὰ τῆς γ. w. the tongue, i.e., in speaking 1 Cor 14: 9. παύειν τὴν γ. ἀπὸ κακοῦ keep the tongue from (saying) evil things 1 Pt 3: 10; 1 Cl 22: 3 (both Ps 33: 14). Synon. στόμα 35: 8 (Ps 49: 19); Rv 16: 10; 1 Cl 15: 4f (Ps 77: 36; 11: 4f). τὸ ἐπιεικὲς τῆς γ. *moderation of the tongue* 21: 7. μάστιξ γλώσσης *words of reproof* 56: 10 (Job 5: 21). Conceited speech 57: 2 (cf. 3 Macc 2: 17). Of *evil tongues* Hv 2, 2, 3. ἠγαλλιάσατο ἡ γλῶσσά μου *my tongue exulted* (the organ for the pers.) Ac 2: 26; 1 Cl 18: 15 (both Ps 15: 9). τὴν γ. προβάλλειν *put out the tongue, hiss* of a dragon Hv 4, 1, 9.
b. fig., of forked flames Ac 2: 3 (=שֵׁ לִשׁוֹן Is 5: 24; cf. En. 14, 9f).
2. *language* (Hom. al.; PGiess. 99, 9; Philo, Mos. 2, 40; Jos., Ant. 10, 8; 158) Ac 2: 6 D, 11; 2 Cl 17: 4 (Is 66: 18); πᾶσα γ. *every language*= every person, regardless of the language he speaks Ro 14: 11; Phil 2: 11 (Is 45: 23; cf. POxy. 1381, 198: Ἑλληνὶς δὲ πᾶσα γλῶσσα τὴν σὴν λαλήσει ἱστορίαν καὶ πᾶς Ἕλλην ἀνὴρ τὸν τοῦ Φθᾶ

σεβήσεται Ἰμούθην; PGM 12, 187f) IMg 10: 3. As a distinctive feature of nations γ. can be used as a synonym of φυλή, λαός, ἔθνος (Is 66: 18; Da 3: 4, 7 al.; Jdth 3: 8) Rv 5: 9; 7: 9; 10: 11; 11: 9; 13: 7; 14: 6; 17: 15.
3. a special problem is posed by the t.t. γλῶσσαι, γένη γλωσσῶν, ἐν γλώσσῃ(-αις) λαλεῖν 1 Cor 14: 1-27, 39; 12: 10, 28, 30; 13: 1, 8; Ac 10: 46; 19: 6. Always without the article (in 1 Cor 14: 22 αἱ is anaphoric; vs. 9 belongs under mng. 1a). There is no doubt about the thing referred to, namely the broken speech of persons in religious ecstasy. The phenomenon, as found in Hellenistic religion, is described esp. by ERohde (Psyche³ '03, Engl. transl. '25, 289-93) and Reitzenstein; cf. Celsus 7, 8; 9. The origin of the term is less clear. Two explanations are prominent today. The one (Bleek, Heinrici) holds that γλῶσσα here means antiquated, foreign, unintelligible, mysterious utterances (Diod. S. 4, 66, 7 κατὰ γλῶτταν=according to an old expression). The other (Rtzst., Bousset) sees in glossolalia a speaking in marvelous, heavenly languages. On λαλεῖν ἑτέραις γλώσσαις Ac 2: 4 s. ἕτερος 2, end.—γλώσσαις καιναῖς λαλεῖν Mk 16: 17.—On 'speaking in tongues' cf. HGunkel, Die Wirkungen d. hl. Geistes² 1899; HWeinel, D. Wirkungen d. Geistes u. d. Geister im nachap. Zeitalter 1899; ELombard, De la Glossolalie chez les premiers chrétiens '10; EMosiman, Das Zungenreden geschichtl. u. psychol. unters. '11. WReinhard, D. Wirken d. hl. Geistes '18, 120ff; KLSchmidt, Die Pfingsterzählung u. d. Pfingstereignis '19; against him PWSchmiedel, PM 24, '20, 73-86; HGüntert, Von der Sprache der Götter u. Geister '21, 23ff; AMackie, The Gift of Tongues '22; HRust, D. Zungenreden '24; FBüchsel, D. Geist Gottes im NT '26, 242ff; 321ff; GBCutten, Speaking with Tongues '27; JBehm, TW I 719-26; IJMartin, 3rd, Glossolalia in the Apostolic Church: JBL 63, '44, 123-30; JGDavies, Pentecost and Glossolalia: JTS n.s. 3, '52, 228-31; FWBeare, JBL 83, '64, 229-46; SDCurrie, Interpretation 19, '65, 274-94. M-M. B. 230; 1260.*

γλωσσόκομον, ου, τό (H. Gk. for γλωττοκομεῖον, Phryn. 98 L.; cf. Bl-D. §119, 5 app.; Mlt.-H. 272; loanw. in rabb.) orig. a *case* for the mouthpiece or reed of a flute, then gener. *case, container* for anything at all (Inscr. Gr. 1001 VIII, 25; 31 [c. 200 bc]; PGrenf. I 14, 3 [II bc]; PTebt. 414, 21; POxy. 521, 12; PGM 13, 1009; LXX; Jos., Ant. 6, 11); in NT *money-box* (as Plut., Galba 16, 2; PRyl. 127, 25 [29 ad]; 2 Ch 24: 8, 10) J 12: 6; 13: 29. M-M.*

γλωσσώδης, ες (Aesop 248b Halm; Sexti Pyth. Sententiae [JCOrelli, Opuscula Graecorum Sententiosa I 1819 p. 246] 13 γυνὴ γλ. ὥσπερ σάλπιγξ πολεμίων; Ps 139: 12; Sir 8: 3; 9: 18; 25: 20) *talkative, garrulous*, perh. *glib of tongue* B 19: 7.*

γναφεύς, έως, ὁ (Hdt.+; the older spelling was κναφεύς [cf. Kühner-Bl. I 147f; Meisterhans³-Schw. 74, 1]; the form w. γν. as early as an Att. inscr. of IV bc, and gener. in the Ptolemaic pap. [Mayser 170, further ref. there], also Wilcken, Chrest. 315, 8 [88 ad]; LXX. But later κν. reappears, as e.g. Dio Chrys. 55[72], 4; Artem. 4, 33 p. 224, 4; Diog. L. 5, 36; Celsus 3, 55) *bleacher, fuller*, one who cleans woolen cloth Mk 9: 3. M-M.*

γνήσιος, α, ον (Hom.+; inscr., pap., LXX; Ep. Arist.; Philo; Joseph.).
1. lit. of children *born in wedlock, legitimate* (X., Cyr. 8, 5, 19; Dit., Or. 194, 12; PFlor. 79, 21; 294, 12 γνησίων τέκνων; POxy. 1267, 15 υἱός; PLeipz. 28, 17f; cf. PEleph. 1, 3; Sir 7: 18; Philo, Mos. 1, 15 γν. παῖς, Spec. Leg. 4, 203 τέκνα; Jos., Ant. 17, 45 τέκνα); fig., of

spiritual relationship (Herm. Wr. 13, 3 γνήσιος υἱός εἰμι; Eunap. p. 49: pupils as παῖδες γν.) γ. τέκνον ἐν πίστει true child in the faith 1 Ti 1: 2; cf. Tit 1: 4; γν. σύζυγε Phil 4: 3 (cf. BGU 86, 19 γν. φίλος; PLond. 1244, 5; Ep. Arist. 41).

2. *genuine* (of 'genuine' writings: Harpocration s.v. Ἀλκιβιάδης; Galen XV 748 K.; Athen. 4, 25 p. 144ε; 14, 63 p. 650ᴅ) γνησιώτερος λόγος *more reliable teaching* B 9: 9 (Harpocration s.v. ναυτοδίκαι: Lysias says εἰ γνήσιος ὁ λόγος; Philo, Poster. Cai. 102 γν. φιλοσοφία). ἀγάπη 1 Cl 62: 2 (Inscr. Gr. 394, 48 γν. φιλοστοργία). τὸ γ. *genuineness, sincerity* of love 2 Cor 8: 8 (Dit., Or. 339, 7 [c. 120 ʙᴄ] τὸ πρὸς τὴν πατρίδα γνήσιον). M-M.*

γνησίως adv. (Eur.+; inscr., pap., LXX) *sincerely, genuinely* (so PLond. 130, 3; PTebt. 326, 11; 2 Macc 14: 8; 3 Macc 3: 23) μεριμνᾶν Phil 2: 20.*

γνούς, γνόντος s. γινώσκω.

γνόφος, ου, ὁ (later form for the earlier and poetic δνόφος; e.g. Chron. Lind. D, 28; Heraclides Miles. [I ᴀᴅ], fgm. 28 [LCohn 1884]; Ps.-Aristot., De Mundo 2 p. 392b; Lucian, Peregr. 43; Vett. Val. 145, 16; Sib. Or. 5, 378) *darkness* Hb 12: 18 (Dt 4: 11). M-M.*

γνώμη, ης, ἡ (w. var. mngs. since Pind., Pre-Socr., Hdt.; inscr., pap., LXX; Ep. Arist. 234; Philo, Joseph., Test. 12 Patr.).

1. *purpose, intention, mind* 1 Cor 1: 10; Rv 17: 13 (μία γνώμη as Demosth. 10, 59; Plut., Cam. 40, 2; Ael. Aristid. 23, 31 K.=42 p. 778 D.; Dit., Syll.³ 135, 21; Pollux 8, 151 μίαν γ. ἔχειν; Philo, Mos. 1, 235; Jos., Ant. 7, 60; 276; Ἰησοῦ Χ. IEph 3: 2; IPhld inscr. ἡ εἰς θεὸν γ. *mind directed toward God* IRo 7: 1; IPhld 1: 2; ἡ ἐν θεῷ γ. *mind fixed in God* IPol 1: 1; γ. τοῦ θεοῦ *purpose* or *will of God* IEph 3: 2 (here also Christ as τοῦ πατρὸς ἡ γ.—Jos., Ant. 2, 309; 3, 16; 17 τοῦ θεοῦ γν. is clearly *God's will*. Likew. Isisaretal. fr. Cymae 40 p. 124 Peek; Dit., Or. 383, 110 [I ʙᴄ]); IRo 8: 3; ISm 6: 2; IPol 8: 1; ἡ τ. ἐπισκόπου γ. IEph 4: 1; γ. ἀγαθή *good will* B 21: 2 (cf. Dit., Syll.³ 75, 28).—γ. ὀρθή IEph 1: 1 (Lghtf.); γ. ἀλλοτρία IPhld 3: 3.

2. *opinion, judgment* (Dio Chrys. 55[72], 12 ἑπτὰ σοφῶν τ. γνώμας; Sir 6: 23; 2 Macc 14: 20; 4 Macc 9: 27; Jos., Ant. 13, 416) Ac 4: 18 D; κατὰ τὴν ἐμὴν γ. *in my judgment* 1 Cor 7: 40 (κατὰ τ. γ. as PPetr. II 11 I, 1; Wsd 7: 15); γ. διδόναι *express a judgment, give an opinion* (Diod. S. 20, 16, 1 τ. ἐναντίαν δοὺς γνώμην) 1 Cor 7: 25; 2 Cor 8: 10.—Hs 5, 2, 8.

3. *previous knowledge, consent* (Appian, Bell. Civ. 4, 96 §403 γν. δημοκρατικῆς διανοίας=agreement with or preference for republican government; Jos., Ant. 18, 336) χωρὶς τῆς σῆς γ. *without your consent* Phlm 14; also ἄνευ γνώμης σου IPol 4: 1 (exx. fr. Hellenistic times for both in Nägeli 33; also Isisaretal. [δοξάζω 2]). μετὰ γνώμης τινός w. *someone's consent* IPol 5: 2.

4. *decision, declaration* (Herodas 2, 86 γνώμη δικαίη of judges; Inschr. v. Priene 105, 31 [9 ʙᴄ] γνώμη τοῦ ἀρχιερέως; POxy. 54, 12; PFay. 20, 4) γ. ἀγαθή *favorable decision* 1 Cl 8: 2; cf. B 2: 9; Rv 17: 17. *Resolve, decision* (Thu. 1, 53, 2; 2, 86, 5 γ. ἔχοντες μὴ ἐκπλεῖν; POxy. 1280, 5 ἑκουσίᾳ καὶ αὐθαιρέτῳ γνώμῃ; Philo, In Flacc. 145, Spec. Leg. 2, 88 al.; Jos., Ant. 10, 253) Ac 20: 3 (γίνομαι II 2a). θλιβέντες τῇ γνώμῃ αὐτοῦ *oppressed by his design* IPhld 6: 2 (γνώμη as instrumental dat. in Pind., Nem. 10, 89). M-M. B. 1240.*

γνωρίζω fut. γνωρίσω (γνωριῶ [POxy. 1024, 18] Col 4: 9 Tdf.); 1 aor. ἐγνώρισα, mid. ἐγνωρισάμην; 1 aor. pass.

ἐγνωρίσθην; 1 fut. γνωρισθήσομαι (Aeschyl.+; pap., LXX, Philo, Joseph., Test. 12 Patr.).

1. *make known, reveal* Aeschyl., Prom. 487; Diod. S. 1, 6, 2; 1, 9, 2; 10, 3, 1; Plut., Fab. Max. 21, 3, Cato Maj. 1, 2 al.; LXX; Jos., Ant. 8, 102) γ. τι Ro 9: 22f; Eph 6: 19; τί τινι Lk 2: 15; Hs 9, 5, 4; the ways of life Ac 2: 28 (Ps 15: 11); sins Hv 2, 1, 2; words v 2, 2, 3f; the past and the future B 1: 7; cf. 5: 3. πάντα Eph 6: 21; Col 4: 7, 9; J 15: 15; the name 17: 26.—2 Cor 8: 1; 2 Pt 1: 16. Pass. Eph 3: 5, 10; Hv 2, 4, 2. τινὶ τὸ μυστήριον Eph 1: 9; pass. 3: 3. περὶ τινος Lk 2: 17. W. ὅτι foll. 1 Cor 12: 3; τινί τι, ὅτι Gal 1: 11. W. indir. quest. foll. Col 1: 27; Hv 4, 3, 1; m 8: 2; s 2: 5; 8, 3, 1. W. attraction of the relat. D 9: 2f; 10: 2. Abs. Hm 12, 1, 3. Pass. γνωριζέσθω πρὸς τ. θεόν let (your requests) *be made known to God* Phil 4: 6. γνωρίζεσθαι εἰς πάντα τὰ ἔθνη *be made known among all the nations* Ro 16: 26. Reflexive ἐγνωρίσθη Ἰωσὴφ τοῖς ἀδελφοῖς *J. made himself known to his brothers* Ac 7: 13 (v.l. ἀνεγν. Gen 45: 1; cf. Ruth 3: 3).—1 Cor 15: 1, where apparently the discussion deals with someth. already known, γ. is nevertheless correctly used because of the doctrinal instruction, which evidently introduces someth. new.

2. *know* (Dio Chrys. 4, 33; Plut., Coriol, 23, 4; Herodian 2, 1, 10; Achilles Tat. 7, 14, 1; 3; Herm. Wr. 10, 15; POxy. 705, 39; 1024, 18; 1643, 8. Λόγος τέλειος: PGM 3, 602ff; Pr 3: 6; 15: 10; Job 4: 16 Sym. ἐγνώρισα=LXX ἐπέγνων; Philo, De Jos. 165, Conf. Ling. 183; Jos., Ant. 2, 97, Vi. 420) w. indir. question foll.: τί αἱρήσομαι οὐ γ. *which I shall choose I do not know* Phil 1: 22. Abs. (w. ἰδεῖν) Dg 8: 5. M-M.*

γνώριμος, ον (Pla.+; Dit., Or. 90, 53 [196 ʙᴄ]; Zen.-P. 59 225, 4 [253 ʙᴄ]; LXX) *acquainted with* w. dat. of the pers. (Pla., 7th Epistle p. 324ᴅ γνώριμοι ἐμοί; Ruth 2: 1; 4 Macc 5: 4) J 18: 16 v.l.*

γνῶσις, εως, ἡ (Pre-Socr., Thu.+; Herm. Wr.; inscr., pap., LXX, Philo; Jos., Ant. 8, 171, Vi. 239 al.; Test. 12 Patr.).

1. *knowledge* as an attribute of God Ro 11: 33 and of man 1 Cor 8: 1, 7, 11; κλεὶς τῆς γ. *key to knowledge* Lk 11: 52; μόρφωσις τῆς γ. *embodiment of knowledge* in the law Ro 2: 20 (on γνῶσις among the Hellenistic Jews cf. WBousset, NGG '15, 466ff); the *meaning* of a piece of writing Hv 2, 2, 1; ἀναγγέλλειν γ. *impart knowledge* 1 Cl 27: 7 (Ps 18: 3).

2. specif. of Christian *knowledge:* γ. τοῦ θεοῦ (obj. gen. as Wsd 2: 13; 14: 22; Philo, Deus Imm. 143) 2 Cor 10: 5; IEph 17: 2. πρὸς αὐτόν 2 Cl 3: 1; γ. σωτηρίας Lk 1: 77; ὁδοῦ δικαιοσύνης B 5: 4; γ. δογμάτων 10: 1. τῶν δικαιωμάτων θεοῦ 21: 5 (cf. Musonius p. 34, 9 γνῶσις δικαιοσύνης; 92, 10). In B γν. is also specif. understanding of the Scriptures: 6: 9; 9: 8. Mentioned w. other significant Christian concepts 2 Cor 6: 6; 2 Pt 1: 5ff (w. εὐσέβεια also Herm. Wr. 1, 27; 9, 4a); 3: 18; D 10: 2; B 2: 3; κατὰ γ. *in accordance w. Christian knowledge* 1 Pt 3: 7 (BReicke, Bultmann-Festschr., '54, 296–304: *with understanding*); γ. ἐξειπεῖν *utter profound Christian knowl.* 1 Cl 48: 5; φωτισμὸς τῆς γ. *enlightening of the knowl.* 2 Cor 4: 6. Given by God B 19: 1 and hence sharing in the heavenly fragrance (s. ὀσμή) 2 Cor 2: 14. τελεία καὶ ἀσφαλής 1 Cl 1: 2. ἀθάνατος 36: 2. θεία 40: 1; τὸ τέλειον τῆς γ. *perfection of knowledge* B 13: 7; cf. 1: 5. W. διδαχή 18: 1; λόγος (on this combination cf. the Λόγος τέλειος in PMimaut: PGM 3, 591–609) 1 Cor 1: 5 (on πᾶσα γ. cf. Sir 21: 14); 2 Cor 11: 6; w. σοφία Col 2: 3 (cf. Eccl 1: 17; 2: 26 al.). Although here γ. and σοφία are almost synonymous, Paul distinguishes betw. them 1 Cor

12: 8; he places γ. betw. ἀποκάλυψις and προφητεία 14: 6, and beside μυστήρια 13: 2, and thus invests the term w. the significance of supernatural mystical knowledge—a mng. which the word has in H.Gk., esp. in the mystery cults. Although the text has the sg. 1 Cor 13: 8, the pl. γνώσεις (Lucian, Apol. 12) is fairly well attested as a v.l. Paul had seen Christ the God-man, and the γν. Χριστοῦ Ἰησοῦ *personal acquaintance w. Christ Jesus* (Latyschev, Inscr. Orae Sept. Ponti Eux. I 47, 6f ἡ τ. Σεβαστῶν γν.=personal acquaintance w. the Augusti [Augustus and Tiberius]; Dssm., LO 324, 7 [LAE 383, 8]) was a matter of inestimable value for him Phil 3: 8. Cf. the experience of the devotees in the mystery religions, in which mystical knowledge was intensified and issued in what was called a divine vision (Λόγος τέλ.=PGM 3, 591ff [a slightly different restoration of the text is given in Rtzt., Mysterienrel.[3] 285–7 and Herm. Wr. 374–7 Scott] χάριν σοι οἴδαμεν, . . . ἄφραστον ὄνομα τετιμημένον τῇ τ. θεοῦ προσηγορίᾳ . . . , χαρισάμενος ἡμῖν νοῦν, λόγον, γνῶσιν . . . χαίρομεν, ὅτι σεαυτὸν ἡμῖν ἔδειξας, χαίρομεν ὅτι ἐν πλάσμασιν ἡμᾶς ὄντας ἀπεθέωσας τῇ σεαυτοῦ γνώσει; Plut., Is. et Osir. 352A ὧν τέλος ἐστὶν ἡ τοῦ πρώτου καὶ κυρίου καὶ νοητοῦ γνῶσις).—For lit. s. γινώσκω, end.

3. of the heretical *Gnosis* (Gnosticism): ἀντιθέσεις τῆς ψευδωνύμου γνώσεως *the antitheses* (or *contradictions*) *of knowledge* (*Gnosis*) *falsely so called* 1 Ti 6: 20 (cf. the title of Irenaeus' chief work, and Marcion's 'Antitheses'; on the latter s. WBauer, Rechtgläubigkeit u. Ketzerei '34, 229; MRist, Journal of Rel. 22, '42, 39ff; JKnox, Marcion and the NT '42, 73–6; MDibelius-HConzelmann, The Pastoral Epistles, Eng. tr. '72, 92). M-M.

γνώστης, ου, ὁ (Plut., Flam. 4, 3; PLeipz. 106, 10; 1 Km 28: 3; Sib. Or. fgm. 1, 4) *one acquainted* (with), *expert* (in) (so the pap. in the Berlin Library in Dssm. LO 313f [LAE 371]=Sb 421, if rightly restored; LXX) τῶν ἐθῶν Ac 26: 3. M-M.*

γνωστός, ή, όν (Aeschyl.+; Pla., X.; Dit., Syll.[3] 800, 34; LXX).
1. *known* (the usual mng. in LXX)—a. of things: a *remarkable* miracle Ac 4: 16. γνωστόν ἐστί τινι *it is known to someone* 2: 14; εἰς τὸ γ. εἶναι πᾶσιν *that it might be known to all* 1 Cl 11: 2. W. ὅτι foll. (En. 98, 12) Ac 4: 10; 13: 38; 28: 28 (MWilcox, The Semitisms of Ac, '65, 90f). περὶ τῆς αἱρέσεως ταύτης γ. ἡμῖν ἐστιν *concerning this sect it is known to us* 28: 22. γνωστόν τινι ποιεῖν τι *make someth. known to someone* Hs 5, 5, 1. γνωστὸν γίνεσθαί τινι *become known to someone* Ac 1: 19; 19: 17. Abs. 9: 42.—κύριος (ὁ) ποιῶν ταῦτα γ. ἀπ' αἰῶνος *the Lord who makes this known from of old* 15: 17f.
b. of pers.: γ. w. gen. or dat., subst. *acquaintance, friend, intimate* (4 Km 10: 11; 2 Esdr 15: 10 [Neh 5: 10]; Ps 30: 12; 54: 14) J 18: 15f. Pl. (Sib. Or. 1, 76) Lk 2: 44; 23: 49.
2. *capable of being known, intelligible* (Pla.; Epict. 2, 20, 4; Gen 2: 9; also prob. Sir 21: 7) γνωστὰ αὐτῷ γίνονται τὰ ῥήματα *the words become intelligible to him* Hs 5, 4, 3; τὸ γ. (PAmh. 145, 9): τὸ γνωστὸν τοῦ θεοῦ *what can be known about God* or *God, to the extent that he can be known* (cf. Philo, Leg. All. 1, 60f) Ro 1: 19 (s. POSchjött, ZNW 4, '03, 75–8; AKlöpper, ZWTh 47, '04, 169–80; HDaxer, Ro 1: 18–2: 10, Diss. Rostock '14, 4ff; AFridrichsen, ZNW 17, '16, 159–68). M-M.*

γογγύζω impf. ἐγόγγυζον; fut. γογγύσω (Sir 10: 25; D 4: 7); 1 aor. ἐγόγγυσα (acc. to Phryn. 358 Lob. γ. and

γογγυσμός are Ionic [denied by WSchmid, GGA 1895, 33f; defended by Thumb 215; PMelcher, De Sermone Epict., Diss. Halle '05, 61], in the pap. since 241/39 BC [Nägeli 27], in lit. M. Ant. 2, 3, 3 al.; Lucian, Ocyp. 45; Epict., LXX).
1. *grumble, murmur* as a sign of displeasure (M. Ant. 2, 3, 3; PPetr. II 9[3], 9; III 43, 3, 20) κατά τινος (Ex 16: 7 A) *against someone* Mt 20: 11. περί τινος *speak complainingly about someone* (Num 14: 27) J 6: 41; but περὶ αὐτοῦ can also be construed as a neuter=*about it*, as περὶ τούτου vs. 61. πρός τινα (Ex 17: 3) *against someone* Lk 5: 30. μετ' ἀλλήλων *among yourselves* J 6: 43. Abs. (Jdth 5: 22; Sir 10: 25) 1 Cor 10: 10 (Num 14: 2, 36); GP 8: 28; D 4: 7; B 19: 11.
2. *speak secretly, whisper* τὶ περί τινος J 7: 32.—KHRengstorf, TW I 727–37. M-M.*

γογγυσμός, οῦ, ὁ (s. on γογγύζω; γογγυσμός since Anaxandrides Com. [IV BC] fgm. 31; M. Ant. 9, 37, 1; Cat. Cod. Astr. VII 139, 11; Maspéro 159, 27; LXX).
1. *complaint, displeasure*, expressed in murmuring: ἐγένετο γ. τινος πρός τινα *complaints arose fr. someone against someone* Ac 6: 1. χωρὶς γογγυσμῶν *without complaining* Phil 2: 14; cf. 1 Pt 4: 9. ῥήμα γογγυσμοῦ *grumbling speech* B 3: 5 (Is 58: 9).
2. *secret talk, whispering* γ. περὶ αὐτοῦ ἦν πολύς *there was much secret discussion about him* J 7: 12.—Field, Notes 92. M-M.*

γόγγυσος, ον (Pr 16: 28 Theod.; Herodian Gr. 1, 213, 19) *complaining*; subst. *grumbler* D 3: 6.*

γογγυστής, οῦ, ὁ (Sym. Pr 26: 22; Theod. Pr 26: 20) *grumbler* γογγυσταὶ μεμψίμοιροι *grumblers complaining about their fate* Jd 16.*

γόης, ητος, ὁ *sorcerer, juggler* (so Eur., Hdt.+; Diod. S. 5, 55, 3; 5, 64, 4; Plut., Orac. 407c; Lucian, Piscat. 25; Jos., C. Ap. 2, 145; 161; POxy. 1011, 64.—Nägeli 14); in our lit. more in the sense *swindler, cheat* (Dio Chrys. 15[32], 11; Ael. Aristid. 28, 11 K.=49 p. 494 D.; Philo, Spec. Leg. 1, 315, Rer. Div. Her. 302; Jos., Bell. 4, 85, Ant. 20, 97; Apollonaretal., Berl. Gr. Pap. 11517 [II AD]: Her 55, '20, 188–95 l. 45 in the eyes of his opponent the prophet of Apollo is a 'hungry γόης') 2 Ti 3: 13. πλάνη τῶν γοήτων Dg 8: 4.—THopfner in Pauly-W. XIV '28, 373ff; FPfister, ibid. Suppl. IV '24, 324ff. M-M. B. 1495.*

Γολγοθᾶ, ἡ acc. Γολγοθᾶν Mk 15: 22 (אֲגֻלְגָּל ? unusual formation fr. Aram. אֲגֻלְגָּלְתָּא=Hebr. גֻּלְגֹּלֶת *skull*; cf. Wlh. on Mk 15: 22; Dalman, Gramm.[2] 166) *Golgotha* translated κρανίου τόπος *place of a skull*; name of an eminence near Jerusalem, used as a place of execution Mt 27: 33; Mk 15: 22; J 19: 17.—Dalman, Pj 9, '13, 98ff; 16, '20, 11ff, Orte[3] 364ff; JBoehmer, ZAW 34, '14, 300ff, Studierstube 11, '19, Suppl. 1ff; 21, '29, 128–35; JHerrmann, StKr 88, '16, 381ff; CSachsse, ZNW 19, '20, 29–34; FLeNBower, ChQR 91, '20, 106–38 (lit.); Wandel, StKr 94, '22, 132–61; JoachJeremias, Golgotha '26; Vincent-Abel, Jérusalem II '26, 92ff; CKopp, Holy Places of the Gospels, '63, 374–88.*

Γόμορρα (עֲמֹרָה), ων, τά and ας, ἡ (cf. Bl-D. §57; Mlt.-H. 109; Thackeray 168, 3) *Gomorrah*, name of a ruined city which lay in the depression now occupied by the Dead Sea; example of terrible divine punishment (Gen 19: 24ff) Mt 10: 15; Mk 6: 11 t.r.; Ro 9: 29 (Is 1: 9); 2 Pt 2: 6; Jd 7 (Γόμορα 𝔓[72] in the 2 last passages). M-M.*

γόμος, ου, ὁ *load, freight* (Aeschyl., Hdt.+; Ex 23: 5; 4

164

Km 5: 17) *cargo* of a ship (Dit., Or. 209 note 3; POxy. 63, 6; 708, 3; 16) Ac 21: 3. W. gen. of the owner Rv 18: 11. W. gen. of content (Bl-D. §167; Rob. 499; Ostraka II 1010, 5; 1258 γόμος ἀχύρου) γ. χρυσοῦ *a cargo of gold* vs. 12. M-M.*

[γονεύς, έως, ὁ] in our lit. only pl. οἱ γονεῖς, έων acc. τοὺς γονεῖς (as Hyperid. 3, 6; Anton. Lib. 30, 3; Dit., Or. 731, 1 [c. 200 BC], Syll.³ 796B, 13 [c. 40 AD]; pap. [Mayser I 2² '38, p. 30]; Pr 29: 15; 4 Macc 2: 10; Jos., Ant. 3, 92; Test. Levi 13: 4) *parents* (since Hom. Hymns and Hes.; inscr., pap., LXX, Ep. Arist., Philo, Joseph.) Mt 10: 21; Mk 13: 12 (Petosiris, fgm. 8 line 8: when the sun presents a certain appearance, there will be στάσεις πατράσι πρὸς παῖδας καὶ τὸ ἀνάπαλιν as well as many other calamities [πόλεμοι, θόρυβοι etc.]); Lk 2: 27, 41, 43; 8: 56; 18: 29; 21: 16; J 9: 2f, 18, 20, 22f; Ro 1: 30; 2 Cor 12: 14; Eph 6: 1; Col 3: 20; 2 Ti 3: 2; Tit 1: 11 v.l.; Hv 1, 3, 1; 2, 2, 2. M-M. B. 104.*

γόνυ, ατος, τό (Hom.+; inscr., pap., LXX; Jos., Ant. 17, 94; 19, 234 al.) *knee* τὰ παραλελυμένα γ. *the weakened knees* Hb 12: 12 (Is 35: 3.—Laud. Therap. 20 παραλύσεις γονάτων). τιθέναι τὰ γ. (Latinism: ponere genua; Bl-D. §5, 3b) *bend the knee* as a sign of respect for superiors (w. προσκυνεῖν) Mk 15: 19. Sim. προσπίπτειν τοῖς γ. τινος (s. προσπίπτω 1) Lk 5: 8. τιθέναι τὰ γ. as a posture in prayer (w. προσεύχεσθαι) Lk 22: 41; Ac 9: 40; 20: 36; 21: 5; Hv 1, 1, 3; 2, 1, 2; 3, 1, 5; cf. Ac 7: 60. Also κάμπτειν τὰ γ. (1 Ch 29: 20; 1 Esdr 8: 70 al.) w. πρός τινα *before someone* Eph 3: 14. W. dat. τῇ Βάαλ *bow the knee before Baal* Ro 11: 4 (cf. 3 Km 19: 18).—Intr. (like Is 45: 23) ἐμοὶ κάμψει πᾶν γόνυ *every knee shall bow to me* 14: 11. Sim. Phil 2: 10.—Fig. κάμπτειν τὰ γ. τῆς καρδίας *bow the knees of the heart* (cf. Prayer of Manasseh [=Ode 12] 11) 1 Cl 57: 1. M-M. B. 243.*

γονυπετέω 1 aor. ptc. γονυπετήσας (Polyb. 15, 29, 9; 32, 25, 7; Heliod. 9, 11; Maspéro 2 III, 20; Hesychius: παρακαλεῖ) *kneel down* τινά *before someone in petition* (cf. Tacitus, Annals 11, 30; 12, 18) Mt 17: 14; Mk 10: 17. Abs. (Cornutus 12 p. 12, 7) Mk 1: 40; *fall on one's knees* ἔμπροσθέν τινος Mt 27: 29.*

γοργός, ή, όν (trag.+; inscr., pap., Lucian) *vigorous, strenuous* 1 Cl 48: 5 (Lightfoot) as quoted in Clem. Alex., Strom. 1, 38, 8; 6, 65, 3; v.l. in Funk.*

γοῦν (γε+οὖν) particle *hence, then* in later usage (Hyperid. 5, 2; Aeneas Tact. 154, 2 and numerous others in many places, e.g. Jos., Ant. 15, 153; 16, 22)=οὖν Hs 8, 8, 2; MPol 17: 2; 16: 1 v.l. (Funk).*

γράμμα, ατος, τό (Aeschyl., Hdt.+; inscr., pap., LXX, Ep. Arist., Philo, Joseph.).
1. *letter* of the alphabet (Ps.-Aristot., Mirabilia 133 ἐπιγραφὴ ἀρχαίοις γράμμασιν an inscription in old-fashioned letters; Diod. S. 2, 13, 2 a rock-cut inscription Συρίοις γράμμασιν; Procop. Soph., Ep. 28; Lev 19: 28; Jos., Bell. 5, 235, Ant. 3, 178) Lk 23: 38 t.r. (UPZ 108, 30 [99 BC] official placard in Gk. and Egypt. script. Naturally script and language coincide, as plainly in Diod. S. 19, 23, 3 ἡ ἐπιστολὴ Συρίοις γεγραμμένη γράμμασιν=the letter was written in the Syrian language); 2 Cor 3: 7; Gal 6: 11 (cf. Plut., Cato Maj. 20, 7 συγγράψαι ἰδίᾳ χειρὶ κ. μεγάλοις γράμμασιν; PHib. 29, 9 [265 BC]). Letter as a numeral B 9: 7f. μεταγράφεσθαι πρὸς γ. *copy letter for letter* Hv 2, 1, 4. δι' ὀλίγων γραμμάτων *in a few lines* IRo 8: 2; IPol 7: 3.
2. *a document, piece of writing*, mostly in pl., even of

single copies (Appian, Hann. 52 §221 al.; Polyaenus 7, 7; 7, 19; Alciphr. 4, 15; 4, 16, 1; 1 Esdr 3: 9, 13f; Esth 8: 5, 10 al.; Jos., Ant. 7, 137; 8, 50 al.).
a. *letter, epistle* (since Hdt. 5, 14; PGrenf. I 30, 5 [103 BC]; PAmh. 143, 10; 1 Macc 5: 10; Ep. Arist. 43.—γράμματα of a single letter: Diod. S. 13, 93, 1; Dialekt-Inschr. 4566, 10 [Laconia]; Sb 7995; 7997) Ac 28: 21; Pol 13: 1.—
b. *a promissory note* (Jos., Ant. 18, 156; PTebt. 397, 17; cf. βιβλίον in Rv 5: 1 and see ORoller, ZNW 36, '37, 98–113) Lk 16: 6f.
c. *writing, book* (Ael. Aristid. 46, 41 K.=3 p. 46 D.: ἀσεβῆ γράμματα; Arrian, Peripl. 19, 4 ἐν πολλοῖς γράμμασιν; Biogr. p. 29 δύο γράμματα; Esth 6: 1) of the books of Moses J 5: 47. Of the OT gener. ἱερὰ γράμματα (in the same sense τὰ ἱερ. γ.: Philo, Mos. 2, 290; 292, Praem. 79, Leg. ad Gai. 195; Jos., Ant. 1, 13; 10, 210, C. Ap. 1, 54. Cf. Dit., Or. 56, 36 [339 BC] τῇ ἡμέρᾳ, ἐν ᾗ ἐπιτέλλει τὸ ἄστρον τὸ τῆς Ἴσιος, ἣ νομίζεται διὰ τῶν ἱερῶν γραμμάτων νέον ἔτος εἶναι, and the description of imperial letters as ἱερὰ or θεῖα γράμματα in Dssm., LO 321f [LAE 380]) 2 Ti 3: 15 (because of the technical character of the expression no article is needed; cf. Philo, Rer. Div. Her. 106 ἐν ἱεραῖς γραφαῖς; 159, Poster. Cai. 158; Ro 1: 2; 16: 26; 2 Pt 1: 20).—Of the literally correct form of the law Ro 2: 27. Opp. spirit (cf. Pla., Gorg. p. 484A.—Heraclitus, Ep. 9, 2 opp. γρ.—θεός. Archytas [IV BC] in Stob., Ecl. 4, 135 ed. Hense vol. IV p. 82, 20: νόμος ὁ μὲν ἔμψυχος βασιλεύς, ὁ δὲ ἄψυχος γράμμα=the law, if it is alive, is indeed king; if, however, it is lifeless, it is nothing but a letter.—Romualdus, Stud. Cath. 17, '41, 18–32) 2: 29; 7: 6; 2 Cor 3: 6 (BSchneider, CBQ 15, '53, 163–207).
3. The mng. of γράμματα J 7: 15 is connected w. 1 above; γρ. without the article used w. a verb like ἐπίστασθαι, εἰδέναι means *elementary knowledge*, esp. reading and writing (X., Mem. 4, 2, 20; Dio Chrys. 9[10], 28; Dit., Syll.³ 844, 6. Very oft. in pap.: Oxy. 264, 19; 275, 43; 485, 48; Fay. 24, 21; 91, 45; Genève 8, 31; 9, 27. Is 29: 12; Da 1: 4; Jos., Ant. 12, 209; cf. ἀγράμματος). On the other hand, τὰ γ.. can also mean *higher learning* (X., Cyr. 1, 2, 6; Pla., Apol. 26D; Aristoxenus, fgm. 31 p. 16, 29: Pythagoras γράμματα ἐν Κορίνθῳ ἐδίδασκε; Sext. Emp., Gramm. 1, 2, 48 γραμμάτων ἔμπειρον . . . , τουτέστιν οὔ τ. στοιχείων, ἀλλὰ τ. συγγραμμάτων; PLond. 43, 2 [II BC]; Da 1: 4; Ep. Arist. 121; Test. Reub. 4: 1, Levi 13: 2) Ac 26: 24.—Field, Notes 92f; Gdspd., Probs. 102–4. M-M. B. 1285; 1286.*

γραμματεύς, έως, ὁ (Thu., X.+; inscr., pap., LXX, En.; Philo, In Flacc. 3; Jos., C. Ap. 1, 290; Nägeli 35).
1. *secretary, clerk*, title of a high official in Ephesus (32nd letter of Apollonius of Tyana [Philostrat. I 352, 7] Ἐφεσίων γρ.; Inscr. of the Brit. Mus. III 2 nos. 482; 500; 528; Dit., Or. 493, 11; FImhoof-Blumer, Kleinas. Münzen '01, p. 55 nos. 46; 47 al. Cf. Schulthess in Pauly-W. VII 2, 1747ff) Ac 19: 35.
2. Among the Jews of the NT era, a term for *experts in the law, scholars versed in the law, scribes*; mentioned together w. the high priests (s. ἀρχιερεύς), w. whom and the elders (oft. referred to in the same context) their representatives formed the Sanhedrin Mt 2: 4; 16: 21; 20: 18; 21: 15; 27: 41; Mk 8: 31; 10: 33; 11: 18, 27; 14: 1, 43, 53; 15: 1, 31; GP 8: 31 al. W. the Pharisees Mt 5: 20; 12: 38; 15: 1; 23: 2, 13ff; Mk 2: 16; 7: 1, 5; Ac 23: 9. W. σοφός: ποῦ γρ.; *where is the expert in the law?* 1 Cor 1: 20.—Schürer II⁴ 372–447; Billerb. I 79–82; 691–5; II 647–61; JoachJeremias, Jerusalem z. Zt. Jesu II A '24, 27–32; B 1, '29, 101–14; 122–7; GDKilpatrick, JTS 1, '50, 56–60.

3. Christian γρ. (cf. Lucian, M. Peregr. 11: Χριστια-νῶν γραμματεῖς in Palestine) are mentioned in Mt 13: 52 (Jülicher, Gleichn. 128-33) and most prob. 23: 34 (JHoh, D. christl. γρ.: BZ 17, '26, 256-69). M-M.

Γραπτή, ῆς, ἡ (Jos., Bell. 4, 567; Mélanges de la Faculté Orientale de l'Université de Beyrouth VII ['14-'21] p. 4 no. 3 Μειδύλος Γραπτῆ; Epigr. Gr. 517d; Monum. Asiae Min. Antiqua III '31, no. 794) *Grapte,* name of a Christian woman Hv 2, 4, 3.*

γραπτός, ή, όν (Eur.+; inscr., pap.) *written* (so Gorgias, Palamedes 30 [V bc]; PPetr. III 21g, 38; PAmh. 78, 17; cf. Ep. Arist. 56; LXX) τὸ ἔργον τ. νόμου γραπτὸν ἐν τ. καρδίαις Ro 2: 15 (cf. IQH 18, 27f 'write on the heart.' Similarly Plut., Mor. 780c; Test. Jud. 20: 3 v.l.). M-M.*

γραφεῖον, ου, τό (Aristot. et al.; inscr., pap.) properly a pencil or other writing instrument, then also *the thing written, writing.* In ecclesiast. usage the pl. somet. designated the third part of the Hebr. canon, also called ἀγιόγραφα. 1 Cl 28: 2 may be an early example of this usage (cf. Knopf, Hdb. ad loc.).*

γραφή, ῆς, ἡ (trag., Hdt.+; inscr., pap., LXX, En., Ep. Arist., Philo, Joseph., Test. 12 Patr.) *writing*—**1.** of a little book (γ.=piece of writing: Diod. S. 1, 91, 3 price-list; Maximus Tyr. 16, 1b indictment; Dialekt-Inschr. 4689, 49 and 58 [Messenia]; PHib. 78, 18; 1 Ch 28: 19; 1 Macc 14: 27) Hv 2, 2, 1.

2. in the NT exclusively w. a sacred mng., of Holy Scripture.—**a.** ἡ γ. the individual *Scripture passage* (4 Macc 18: 14; Philo, Rer. Div. Her. 266.—S. also Test. Napht. 5: 8 γραφὴ ἀγία of a written word of a divine sort outside the Bible) Mk 12: 10; 15: 28 v.l.; Lk 4: 21; J 13: 18; 19: 24, 36f; Ac 1: 16; 8: 35; Ro 11: 2; 2 Ti 3: 16; Js 2: 8, 23; 1 Cl 23: 5.

b. Scripture as a whole—**a.** the pl. αἱ γραφαί designates collectively all the parts of Scripture: *the scriptures* (Philo, Fug. 4, Spec. Leg. 1, 214 αἱ ἱεραὶ γ., Rer. Div. Her. 106; 159; Jos., C. Ap. 2, 45 τ. τῶν ἱερῶν γραφῶν βίβλοις) Mt 21: 42; 22: 29; 26: 54; Mk 12: 24; 14: 49; Lk 24: 27, 32, 45; J 5: 39; Ac 17: 2, 11; 18: 24, 28; Ro 15: 4; 2 Pt 3: 16; PK 2 p. 15, 4; αἱ γρ. τῶν προφητῶν *the writings of the prophets* Mt 26: 56; αἱ ἱεραὶ γ. 1 Cl 45: 2; 53: 1 (s. Philo and Joseph. above); γ. ἅγιαι Ro 1: 2; προφητικαί 16: 26 (on the omission of the article in both pass. fr. Ro and 2 Pt 1: 20 s. γράμμα 2c).

β. the sg. as designation of Scripture as a whole (Philo, Mos. 2, 84; Ep. Arist. 155; 168; cf. 1 Ch 15: 15; 2 Ch 30: 5, 18) Ac 8: 32; J 20: 9; 2 Pt 1: 20 (s. ba above); εἶπεν ἡ γ. J 7: 38, 42; λέγει ἡ γ. Ro 4: 3; 9: 17; 10: 11; Gal 4: 30; 1 Ti 5: 18; Js 4: 5; 1 Cl 23: 3; 34: 6; 35: 7; 42: 5; 2 Cl 2: 4; 6: 8; 14: 1f; B 4: 7, 11; 5: 4; 6: 12; 13: 2, also 16: 5 in a quot. fr. En. 89, 56ff; περιέχει ἐν γ. 1 Pt 2: 6; πεπλήρωται, ἐπληρώθη ἡ γ. J 17: 12; cf. 19: 28; πιστεύειν τῇ γ. J 2: 22; οὐ δύναται λυθῆναι ἡ γ. *scripture cannot be set aside* 10: 35. W. Scripture personified: προϊδοῦσα ἡ γ. *scripture foresaw* Gal 3: 8. συνέκλεισεν ὑπὸ ἁμαρτίαν vs. 22.—κατὰ τὴν γ. (w. ref. to a contract PRainer 224, 6 [Dssm., NB 78=BS 112f]; PAmh. 43, 13; 2 Ch 30: 5; 35: 4; 1 Esdr 1: 4) Js 2: 8; κατὰ τὰς γ. (BGU 136, 10 κατὰ γ. w. ref. to the laws) *according to* (the prophecy of) *the holy scriptures* 1 Cor 15: 3f. ἄτερ γραφῆς *without scriptural proof* PK 4 p. 16, 6.—JHänel, D. Schriftbegriff Jesu '19, 13ff; Harnack, D. AT in d. paul. Briefen u. in d. paul. Gemeinden: SAB '28, 124-41; OMichel, Pls u. s. Bibel '29. S. νόμος, end.—Scripture is often quoted by the authors of our lit. with as little care for

literal accuracy as e.g. Maximus Tyr. uses in quoting 'the ancients' (KDürr, Philol. Suppl. VIII '00, 150f). On the other hand, the close acquaintance of Christians with Scripture has its parallels in the familiarity of the Greeks with Homer. Heraclit. Sto. I p. 2 l. 3ff: ἐκ πρώτης ἡλικίας the child is trained on Homer. To the end of his life he occupies himself with Homer's works. M-M.*

γράφω fut. γράψω; impf. ἔγραφον; 1 aor. ἔγραψα; pf. γέγραφα; pf. pass. γέγραμμαι; 2 aor. pass. ἐγράφην (Hom.+; from Pind., Hdt., and in inscr., pap., LXX, En., Ep. Arist., Philo, Joseph., usu. in the mng.:) *write.*

1. of the mechanical activity involved in writing (X., Mem. 4, 2, 20; Demosth. 9, 41) πηλίκοις γράμμασιν ἔγραψα Gal 6: 11 (ἔγραψα as epistolary aorist, as Ps.-Callisth. 2, 19, 2, at the beginning of a letter ἔγραψα σοι=I am writing to you). οὕτως γράφω this is my *handwriting* of one's own signature 2 Th 3: 17; cf. Phlm 19 (on the conclusion of a letter in one's own hand ORoller, D. Formular d. paul. Briefe '33).—J 8: 6 v.l., 8.

2. w. ref. to the content—**a.** *write* w. λέγων foll. (4 Km 10: 6; Da 6: 26; 1 Macc 8: 31; 11: 57.—EKieckers, IndogF 35, '15, 34ff) ἔγραψεν λέγων· Ἰωάννης ἐστὶν ὄνομα αὐτοῦ *he wrote, 'His name is John'* Lk 1: 63. μὴ γράφε· ὁ βασιλεύς J 19: 21. γράψον· μακάριοι Rv 14: 13. ὃ γέγραφα, γέγραφα *what I have written I have written* i.e., it will not be changed (on the pf. cf. the expr. taken over fr. the Romans κέκρικα=I have decided once for all Epict. 2, 15, 5. For the repetition of the same form of the pf. s. Gen 43: 14; for the repetition of the word γρ. see Aeschrio Iamb. [IV bc] 6 [Diehl III, VIII 6] ἔγραψεν ὅσσ' ἔγραψ'.) J 19: 22. τὶ ἐπί τι (Dt 4: 13; 6: 9; 10: 2; Pr 3: 3 v.l.) Rv 2: 17; 19: 16. τὶ ἐπί τινα 3: 12. ἐπί τινος (Ex 34: 1; 36: 37; Da 5: 5) 14: 1.

b. *write down, record:* a vision Rv 1: 19; commandments, parables Hv 5: 5f. ταῦτα πάντα v 5: 8. εἰς βιβλίον (Tob 12: 20) Rv 1: 11. Pass. ἐν τ. βιβλίω J 20: 30; of the book of life ἐν τῷ β. (τῇ β.), ἐπὶ τὸ β. Rv 13: 8; 17: 8; 20: 15; 21: 27; cf. 20: 12; 22: 18f (s. Ep. Arist. 311).

c. γέγραπται (abundantly attested as a legal expr.: Dssm., B 109f, NB 77f [BS 112ff, 249f]; Thieme 22. Cf. also 2 Esdr 20: 35, 37 [Neh 10: 34, 36]; Job 42: 17a; Jos., Vi. 342) is a formula introducing quotations fr. the OT (cf. Jos., C. Ap. 1, 154) Mt 4: 4, 6f, 10; 21: 13; Mk 11: 17; 14: 27; Lk 4: 8; 19: 46. ὡς γέγραπται (Dit., Syll³ 45, 44; Inschr. d. Asklepieion von Kos A, 14 ed. RHerzog, ARW 10, '07, 401) Mk 7: 6. καθὼς γέγραπται (Dit., Syll³. 736, 44 [92 bc]; PRainer 154, 11; cf. 1 Esdr 3: 9; Da 9: 13 Theod.; 2 Ch 23: 18) Ac 15: 15; Ro 1: 17; 2: 24; 3: 10; 4: 17; 8: 36; 9: 33; 1 Cl 48: 2 al. οὕτως γέγραπται 1 Cl 17: 3. καθάπερ γέγραπται (PCauer, Delectus Inscr.² 1883, 457, 50f [III bc]; Inschr. v. Perg. 251, 35 [II bc]; PRev. 29, 9 [258 bc] καθάπερ ἐν τ. νόμῳ γέγρ.) Ro 3: 4; 9: 13; 10: 15; 11: 8. γέγραπται γάρ 12: 19; 14: 11; 1 Cor 1: 19; 1 Cl 36: 3; 39: 3; 46: 2; 50: 4, 6. γεγραμμένον ἐστίν J 2: 17; 6: 31, 45; 10: 34 (γεγραμμένον ἐν τῷ νόμῳ as 2 Esdr 18 [Neh 8]: 14. Cf. Inschr. d. Asklepieion [s. above] l. 9 τὰ γεγραμμένα ἐν τοῖς ἱεροῖς νόμοις); 12: 14. ὁ λόγος ὁ γεγραμμένος (cf. 4 Km 23: 24; 1 Ch 29: 29; 2 Ch 16: 11) 1 Cor 15: 54. κατὰ τὸ γ. (Dit., Syll³ 438, 13; 84; 955, 22; 1016, 6 al.; 2 Esdr [Ezra] 3: 4; 18 [Neh 8]: 15; cf. 1 Esdr 1: 12; Bar 2: 2) 2 Cor 4: 13. ἐγράφη Ro 4: 23; 1 Cor 9: 10; 10: 11. W. a specif. ref. (4 Km 14: 6; 2 Ch 23: 18; 1 Esdr 1: 12; Da 9: 13. Cf. Diod. S. 19, 30 ὡς γέγραπται ἐν τῷ περὶ διαδοχῆς βασιλέων=in the book of the succession of kings; Philod., Περὶ εὐσεβ. p. 61 Gomp. ἐν τοῖς ἀναφερομένοις εἰς Μουσαῖον γέγραπται; Ael. Aristid. 33 p. 618 D.: γέγραπται γὰρ ἐν αὐτῇ [a peace treaty]; 34 p. 654): in the book of Psalms Ac 1: 20; in the second Psalm 13: 33; in the book of the prophets 7: 42; in Isaiah Mk 1: 2 (cf. 2 Ch 32: 32); in the Decalogue B 15: 1. Also of non-canonical apocalypses: (Diod. S. 34+35, fgm. 33, 2 ἐν τοῖς τῆς Σιβύλλης χρησμοῖς εὑρέθη γεγραμμένον ὅτι κτλ.): Eldad and Modat Hv 2, 3, 4; Enoch B 4: 3, cf. 16: 6. Of words of our Lord 4: 14; 14: 6 (JAFitzmyer, NTS 7, '60/'61 297–333).—W. acc. of the pers. or thing (Bar 1: 1; Tob 7: 13 S; 1 Esdr 2: 25 al.): *write about someone or someth.* ὃν ἔγραψεν Μωϋσῆς *about whom Moses wrote* J 1: 45; of righteousness Ro 10: 5 t.r. Also περί τινος (Diod. S. 2, 36, 3; 14, 96, 3; 1 Esdr 2: 17; Esth 1: 1p; 1 Macc 11: 31) Mt 26: 24; Mk 14: 21; J 5: 46; Ac 13: 29 (on ἐτέλεσαν τὰ γεγραμμένα cf. Diod. S. 14, 55, 1 ποιεῖν τὰ γεγρ.). ἐπί τινα w. *reference to someone* Mk 9: 12f; ἐπί τινι J 12: 16. τὰ γεγραμμένα διὰ τ. προφητῶν τῷ υἱῷ τ. ἀνθρώπου Lk 18: 31 (on διὰ τ. π. cf. Esth 8: 10 [=ὑπό 9: 1]; the dat. designating the pers. written *about* is made easier to understand by ref. to 3 Macc 6: 41; 1 Esdr 4: 47). W. ὅτι foll. (cf. X., An. 2, 3, 1) Mk 12: 19; Ro 4: 23; 1 Cor 9: 10.—On μὴ ὑπὲρ ἃ γέγραπται 1 Cor 4: 6 s. ὑπέρ 2.

d. *write (to) someone* τινί (Plut., Pomp. 29, 3; pap.; 1 Macc 12: 22; 2 Macc 2: 16; Da 6: 26; Jos., Ant. 12, 16) Ro 15: 15; 2 Cor 2: 4, 9 t.r.; 7: 12; Phlm 21; 2 Pt 3: 15; 1 J 2: 12ff. δι' ὀλίγων *a few lines, briefly* 1 Pt 5: 12. διὰ μέλανος καὶ καλάμου w. *pen and ink* 3 J 13. The content of the writing is quoted: Rv 2: 1, 8, 12, 18; 3: 1, 7, 14; *write someth. to someone* τινί τι (Plut., Cic. 37, 1; 1 Macc: 10: 24; 11: 29; 13: 35) 1 Cor 14: 37; 2 Cor 1: 13; Gal 1: 20; 3 J 9. τινί τι περί τινος (1 Macc 11: 31) Ac 25: 26; 1 J 2: 26. τινὶ περί τινος (1 Macc 12: 22; Jos., Vi. 62) 2 Cor 9: 1; 1 Th 4: 9; 5: 1; Jd 3. περὶ δὲ ὧν ἐγράψατε (μοι v.l.) *as to the matters about which you wrote (me)* 1 Cor 7: 1 (Pla., Ep. 13 p. 361A περὶ δὲ ὧν ἐπέστειλές μοι; Socrat., Ep. 7, 1 ὑπὲρ ὧν γράφεις); γ. τινί *give someone directions in writing* w. inf. foll. Ac 18: 27; also w. ὅπως ibid. D.—γ. διά τινος signifies either that the person referred to in the διά-phrase participated in writing the document (Dionys. of Cor. in Euseb., H.E. 4, 23, 11) as perh. 1 Pt 5: 12, or that this person is its bearer IRo 10: 1; IPhld 11: 2; ISm 12: 1; Pol 14. The latter mng. obtains in διὰ χειρός τινος Ac 15: 23.

3. *cover w. writing* βιβλίον γεγραμμένον ἔσωθεν καὶ ὄπισθεν *a scroll covered w. writing inside and on the back* Rv 5: 1 (s. Ezk 2: 10).

4. of literary composition: *compose, write* βιβλίον (Jer 39: 25, 44; Mal 3: 16; 2 Ch 32: 17) Mk 10: 4 (Dt 24: 1, 3); J 21: 25b; δύο βιβλαρίδια Hv 2, 4, 3. τίτλον J 19: 19. ἐπιστολήν (Dit., Syll.³ 679, 19; 1 Macc 13: 35; 2 Macc 9: 18; 3 Macc 3: 11; 6: 41) Ac 23: 25 (cf. 3 Macc 3: 30); 2 Pt 3: 1. In a wider sense: ἐντολήν (4 Km 17: 37) *give a written commandment, fix a comm. in writing* Mk 10: 5; 1 J 2: 7f; 2 J 5.—FRMHitchcock, The Use of γράφειν: JTS 31, '30, 271–5; GSchrenk, TW I 742–73 (γράφω and derivatives). M-M. and suppl. B. 1283.

γραώδης, ες (Chrysipp.: Stoic. II 255; Strabo 1, 2, 3 γρ. μυθολογία; Cleomedes 2, 1 p. 162, 14 HZiegler μυθαρίω γραώδει πιστεύσας; Galen; Heliod.; on the Lat. anicula, cf. ASPease, Ciceronis De Natura Deorum, '55, I, 341 n.) *characteristic of old women* 1 Ti 4: 7.*

γρηγορέω (on this new formation in H.Gk. fr. ἐγρήγορα, the pf. of ἐγείρω [Herm. Wr.; Achilles Tat. 4, 17, 3; Cyril of Scyth. p. 80, 19; Phryn. 118 L.], found also LXX; Jos., Ant. 11, 47; Test. Benj. 10: 1 [Thackeray 263; Helbing 82; 84] s. Bl-D. §73; Nägeli 44; Mlt.-H. 386) 1 aor. ἐγρηγόρησα *be* or *keep awake.*

1. lit. (Herm. Wr. 11, 21b; 1 Macc 12: 27; 2 Esdr 17 [Neh 7]: 3) Mt 24: 43; 26: 38, 40; Mk 13: 34; 14: 34, 37; Lk 12: 37, 39 v.l.

2. fig. (Bar 2: 9 al.) *be on the alert, be watchful* (cf. our *keep one's eyes open*) Mt 24: 42; 25: 13; 26: 41; Mk 13: 35, 37; 14: 38; Ac 20: 31; 1 Cor 16: 13; 1 Th 5: 6; 1 Pt 5: 8; Rv 3: 2f; 16: 15; IPol 1: 3. ὑπὲρ τῆς ζωῆς *be vigilant for your life* D 16: 1. Of relig. alertness γρηγοροῦντες ἐν αὐτῇ (= προσευχῇ) *be wide awake about it* Col 4: 2; γ. and καθεύδω, fig. for *be alive* and *be dead* 1 Th 5: 10. M-M.*

γρόνθος, ου, ὁ *fist* (Moeris p. 323 πύξ Ἀττικῶς, γρ. Ἑλληνικῶς; schol. on Il. 219; PAmh. 141, 10 [IV AD]; Aq. Ex 21: 18, Judg 3: 16, Is 58: 4) γ. ἀντὶ γρόνθου *blow for blow* Pol 2: 2.*

γρύζω 1 aor. ἔγρυξα, inf. γρύξαι (Aristoph.; Herodas 3, 37; 85; Dio Chrys. 13[7], 26; Ael. Aristid. 35 p. 676 D. al.; Ex 11: 7; Josh 10: 21; Jdth 11: 19) *mutter, complain* (w. στενάζειν, as Euseb., H.E. 5, 1, 51) MPol 2: 2.*

γυμνάζω pf. pass. ptc. γεγυμνασμένος (Aeschyl.+; inscr., pap.; 2 Macc 10: 15; Philo; Joseph.; Sib. Or. 3, 230) lit. *exercise naked, train,* also fig., of mental and spiritual powers (Isocr., Ad Nicocl. 10; Ps.-Isocr., Ad Demonicum 21 γύμναζε σεαυτὸν πόνοις ἑκουσίοις; Epict.; Dit., Syll.³ 578, 28) τινί *in* or *by someth.* (Ps.-Isocr. [s. above]; Philo, De Jos. 26; Jos., Ant. 3, 15) τῷ νῦν βίῳ *train oneself by the present life* (w. ἀθλέω) 2 Cl 20: 2. Also διά τινος (Philo, Sacrif. Abel. 78) Hb 12: 11; γ. (τινὰ) πρός τι (Epict. 2, 18, 27; 3, 12, 7 al.; Philo, Mos. 1, 48) 5: 14. γύμναζε σεαυτὸν πρὸς εὐσέβειαν 1 Ti 4: 7. καρδία γεγυμνασμένη πλεονεξίας *a heart trained in greed* 2 Pt 2: 14 (cf. Philostrat., Her. 2: 15 θαλάττης οὔπω γεγ.). M-M. and suppl.*

γυμνασία, ας, ἡ (since Pla., Leg. 648c; Dit., Syll.³ 1073, 19; 4 Macc 11: 20) *training* ἡ σωματικὴ γ. *of the body* 1 Ti 4: 8. M-M.*

γυμνητεύω s. γυμνιτεύω.—Dio Chrys. 75[25], 3 and Cass. Dio 47, 34, 2 have γυμνητεύω; likew. Plut., Aem. 16, 8 Z. w. v.l. γυμνιτεύω. The same sentence that contains γυμνητεύω in HSchenkl, Pythagoreerspr. 17 (Wien. Stud. 8, 1886 p. 266) and Porphyr., Ad Marcellam 33 N., has the spelling γυμνιτεύω in Demophilus, Sent. 8 (JCOrelli, Opuscula Gr. Vet. Sententiosa I 1819 p. 38). Bl-D. §24; Mlt-H. 72; 399.

γυμνιτεύω (γυμνητεύω t.r.) *be poorly clothed* (so Dio Chrys. 75[25], 3) 1 Cor 4: 11.*

γυμνός, ή, όν (Hom.+; inscr., pap., LXX, Philo, Joseph.).

1. *naked, stripped, bare* (PFay. 12, 20; Gen 2: 25; 3: 7, 10f al.; Job 1: 21) Mk 14: 52 (Appian, Bell. Civ. 5, 140 §582 γυμνοί...ἔφευγον; Test. Jos. 8: 3 ἔφυγον γυμνός); Ac 19: 16 (cf. Philo, In Flaccum 36); Rv 3: 17; 16: 15; 17: 16. περιβεβλημένος σινδόνα ἐπὶ γυμνοῦ *who wore a linen garment over his naked body* Mk 14: 51 (on the subst. τὸ γυμνόν = the naked body cf. Lucian, Nav. 33 τὰ γυμνά). πόδες (Euphorio [III BC] 53, 1 Coll.; Jos., Ant. 8, 362) Hs 9, 20, 3.

2. *without an outer garment,* without which a decent person did not appear in public (so Hes., Op. 391, oft. in Attic wr.; PMagd. 6, 7 [III BC]; 1 Km 19: 24; Is 20: 2) J 21: 7 (Dio Chrys. 55[72], 1 the ναύτης wears only an under-garment while at work).

3. *poorly dressed* (Demosth. 21, 216; BGU 846, 9;

PBrem. 63, 30; Job 31: 19; Tob 1: 17; 4: 16) Mt 25: 36, 38, 43f; Js 2: 15; B 3: 3 (Is 58: 7).

4. *uncovered, bare* (cf. Diod. S. 1, 76, 2; Themistocl., Ep. 16 p. 756 H. γ. ἀλήθεια; Lucian, Tox. 42, Anachars. 19 ὡς γυμνὰ τὰ γεγενημένα οἱ Ἀρεοπαγῖται βλέποιεν; Heliod., Aeth. 10, 29 w. ἀπαρακάλυπτος; Job 26: 6; Philo, Migr. Abr. 192; Jos., Ant. 6, 286) Hb 4: 13. Fig. of the soul, whose covering is the body: *naked* 2 Cor 5: 3 (cf. Pla., Cratyl. 20 p. 403Β ἡ ψυχὴ γυμνὴ τοῦ σώματος, also Gorg. 523CE; 524F; Aelian, Hist. An. 11, 39. Artem. 4, 30 p. 221, 10f the σῶμα is the ἱμάτιον of the ψυχή; 5, 40; M. Ant. 12, 2 of the divine element in man, 'which the god sees without any covering'.—Of the νοῦς: Herm. Wr. 10, 17). S. on this EKühl, Über 2 Cor 5: 1–10, '04; JThUbbink, Het eeuwige leven bij Pls, Groningen Diss. '17, 14ff; WMundle, D. Problem d. Zwischenzustandes . . . 2 Cor 5: 1–10: Jülicher-Festschr. '27, 93–109; LBrun, ZNW 28, '29, 207–29; Guntermann (ἀνάστασις, end); RBultmann, Exeg. Probl. des 2 Kor: Symb. Bibl. Ups. 9, '47, 1–12; JNSevenster, Studia Paulina (JdeZwaan Festschr.) '53, 202–14; EEEllis, NTS 6, '60, 211–24. γ. κόκκος *a naked kernel* 1 Cor 15: 37, where an adj. is applied to the grain of wheat, when it properly belongs to the bodiless soul which is compared to it; cf. 1 Cl 24: 5. M-M. B. 324f. *

γυμνότης, ητος, ἡ (M. Ant. 11, 27; Philo, Leg. All. 2, 59; Dt 28: 48).

1. *nakedness* (Cornutus 30 p. 59, 18) αἰσχύνη τῆς γ. *disgraceful nakedness* Rv 3: 18.—2. *destitution, lack of sufficient clothing* (Ps.-Dionys. Hal. De Arte Rhet. 10, 6; Dt 28: 48: ἐν λιμῷ κ. ἐν δίψει κ. ἐν γ.; Test. Zeb. 7: 1) Ro 8: 35; 2 Cor 11: 27.*

γυμνόω pf. pass. γεγύμνωμαι (Hom.+; Herm. Wr. 1, 26a; POxy. 903, 7; PLeipz. 37, 18; Sb 4317, 25; LXX; Jos., Ant. 12, 212) *strip, lay bare*; pass. *be made naked* Dg 12: 3.*

γυναικάριον, ου τό (Diocles Com. [V BC] 11; M. Ant. 5, 11; Epict. index Sch.; Phryn. p. 180 L.) dim. of γυνή, lit. *little woman*, but w. derogatory connot., *idle, silly woman* pl. 2 Ti 3: 6.*

γυναικεῖος, α, ον (Hom.+; inscr., pap., LXX, Philo; Jos., Ant. 13, 108) *feminine* σκεῦος γ. periphrasis for *woman, wife* (σκεῦος 2), ἀσθενεστέρῳ σκ. τῷ γυν. 1 Pt 3: 7 (POxy. 261, 12 διὰ γυναικείαν ἀσθένειαν). M-M.*

γυνή, αικός, ἡ (Hom.+; inscr., pap., LXX, En., Ep. Arist., Philo, Joseph., Test. 12 Patr., loanw. in rabb.) *woman.*

1. *of any adult female* (virgins are included, e.g., Eur., Or. 309 of Electra) Mt 9: 20; 13: 33; 27: 55; Lk 1: 42 (cf. Semonides of Amorgos, fgm. 7, 88f Diehl[2] ἀριπρεπὴς μὲν ἐν γυναιξὶ γίγνεται πάσῃσι); 8: 2f (cf. Appian, Bell. Civ. 1, 63 §282 γύναια πολλὰ πολυχρήματα assist Marius); 13: 11; 1 Cor 14: 34f; 1 Ti 2: 11f (Democr., fgm. 110 γυνὴ μὴ ἀσκείτω λόγον· δεινὸν γάρ; Ael. Aristid. 45 p. 41 D.: ὁ ἀνὴρ λεγέτω, γυνὴ δὲ οἷς ἂν ἀκούσῃ χαιρέτω.—NGeurts, Het Huwelijk bij de Griekse en Romeinse Moralisten '28; PTischleder, Wesen u. Stellg. d. Frau nach d. Lehre des hl. Pls '23; HWindisch, Christl. Welt 44, '30, 411–25; 837–40; GDelling, Pls' Stellg. z. Frau u. Ehe '31, cf. OMichel, StKr 105, '33, 215–25; PKetter, Christ and Womankind, tr. IMcHugh, '52; KH Rengstorf, Mann u. Frau im Urchristentum, '54; EKähler, Die Frau in d. paulinischen Briefen, '60. Cf. the lit. on

γαμέω, end, and on σιγάω); Hv 1, 1, 4; 3, 8, 2. Opp. ἀνήρ (Diog. L. 1, 33; 1 Esdr 9: 41) Ac 5: 14; 8: 3; 1 Cor 11: 3, 5ff (on vs. 11 cf. Philosophenspr. p. 491, 73 οὔτε γυνὴ χωρὶς ἀνδρὸς οὔτε . . . ; on vs. 12b cf. 1 Esdr 4: 15f); 1 Cl 6: 1f; 55: 2f; γ. πρεσβῦτις *a lady advanced in years* Hv 1, 2, 2.—The voc. (ὦ) γύναι is by no means a disrespectful form of address (Il. 3, 204; Od. 19, 221; Soph., Oed. R. 655; Charito 3, 2, 1; 5, 9, 3; Cass. Dio 51, 12, 5: Augustus to Cleopatra; Jdth 11: 1; Jos., Ant. 1, 252; 17, 74.—Only rarely is there a tone of disrespect in ὦ γύναι, as, e.g., Quint. Smyrn. 1, 575) Mt 15: 28; Lk 22: 57; J 2: 4 (Gdspd, Probs. 98–101); 19: 26 (cf. GDalman, Jesus-Jeshua [Eng. tr. PLevertoff] '29, 201–3); 20: 13, 15; Hv 1, 1, 7. Cf. JWackernagel, Über einige antike Anredeformen '12, 25f.—σὺν γυναιξὶ κ. τέκνοις (Dio Chrys. 20[37], 33; Dit., Syll.[3] 695, 20; 1 Macc 5: 23; Jos., Vi. 99) Ac 21: 5. σὺν γυναιξὶν 1: 14 (Diog. L. 3, 46: after the death of Plato, his μαθηταί are listed by name, and the list closes: σὺν οἷς καὶ γυναῖκες δύο, who are also named).

2. *wife* (Hom.+; Jos., Ant. 18, 148, C. Ap. 2, 201) Mt 5: 28, 31f; 14: 3; 18: 25; Lk 1: 5, 13, 18, 24; 1 Cor 7: 2ff; 9: 5; Eph 5: 22ff; Col 3: 18f; 1 Cl 1: 3; 11: 2; 21: 6; ISm 13: 1; Pol 4: 2; Hv 1, 1, 2; m 4, 1, 1; 4ff, and oft. Those who understand 1 Ti 3: 2, 12; Tit 1: 16 as inclining toward celibacy may compare Ramsay, Phryg. I 1 p. 151 no. 46: Apellas the priest makes himself liable to punishment by the god because he wishes to remain μετὰ γυναικός.—Of widows γ. χήρα Lk 4: 26 (3 Km 17: 9=Jos., Ant. 8, 320). γυνὴ τοῦ πατρός *father's wife* (Lev 18: 8, 11. Of a stepmother UPZ 189, 6 [112/11 BC]), who need not necessarily have been regularly married to the man in question 1 Cor 5: 1 (for the idea s. Ps.-Phoc. 179–81).

3. From the context the mng. *bride* may be poss. (Gen 29: 21; Dt 22: 24) δείξω σοι τὴν νύμφην τὴν γυναῖκα τ. ἀρνίου Rv 21: 9; cf. 19: 7; Mt 1: 20, 24; Lk 2: 5 v.l. Perh. J 8: 3f.

4. On the woman in heaven Rv 12: 1–17 cf. IQH 3: 7–12, also Boll 98–124 and against him JFreundorfer, D. Apk. des Ap. Joh. '29. Cf. also PPrigent, Apocalypse 12: Histoire de l' exégèse, '59.—On the whole word AOepke, TW 1 776–90. M-M. B. 82; 96.

Γώγ, ὁ, indecl. (גּוֹג) *Gog* symbol. name beside Magog (Ezk 38 and 39; cf. Sib. Or. 3, 319; 512), to designate the enemy to be conquered by the Messiah Rv 20: 8.—Bousset, ZKG 20, '00, 113–31, Rel.[3] 219f; JKlausner, D. Mess. Vorstellungen des jüd. Volkes im Zeitalter d. Tannaiten '04, 99ff; JBoehmer, Wer ist G. von Magog? ZWTh 40, 1897, 321–55; Billerb. III 831–40; KGKuhn, TW I 790–2.*

γωνία, ας, ἡ (Hdt.+; inscr., pap., LXX; En. 18, 2; Ep. Arist. 61; Philo, Joseph., loanw. in rabb.) *corner* τῶν πλατειῶν *street corners* Mt 6: 5. κεφαλὴ γωνίας (Ps 117: 22) *corner-stone* or *keystone* (s. κεφαλή 2b) Mt 21: 42; Mk 12: 10; Lk 20: 17; Ac 4: 11; 1 Pt 2: 7; B 6: 4. αἱ τέσσαρες γωνίαι τῆς γῆς *the four corners of the earth* Rv 7: 1; 20: 8 (X., De Rep. Lac. 12, 1; Test. Ash. 7: 2; PGM 8, 8 ἐν ταῖς δ' γωνίαις τ. οὐρανοῦ). Of the corners of a stone Hs 9, 4, 1; of a structure (Jos., Bell. 3, 243) s 9, 2, 3; 9, 15, 1.—Of a hidden place (Pla., Gorg. 485D βίον βιῶναι ἐν γωνίᾳ; Epict. 2, 12, 17; Celsus 6, 78; Sus 38 Theod.) Ac 26: 26. Of false prophets: κατὰ γωνίαν προφητεύειν *prophesy in a corner* Hm 11: 13. M-M. B. 900.*

Δ

δ΄ as numeral=*four* (τέσσαρες: Jos., C. Ap. 1, 158; cf. Sib. Or. 5, 40) Hs 9, 2, 3; 9, 10, 7; 9, 15, 3;=*fourth* (τετάρτη) in the titles Hv 4; m 4.*

Δαβίδ s. Δαυίδ.

Δαθάν, ὁ indecl. (דָּתָן) (LXX.—In Joseph. Δαθάμης, ου [Ant. 4, 19]) *Dathan* 1 Cl 4: 12; s. Ἀβ(ε)ιρών.*

δαιμονίζομαι 1 aor. pass. ptc. δαιμονισθείς (Mk 5: 18; Lk 8: 36) *be possessed by a demon* (s. δαιμόνιον and δαίμων). The word is known since Soph., but found in this sense in the comic wr. Philemo 191; Plut., Mor. 706D; Cat. Cod. Astr. XI 2 p. 119, 20; Aq. Ps 90: 6. Of a girl κακῶς δαιμονίζεται *is cruelly tormented by a demon* Mt 15: 22. Elsewh. only as a ptc. ὁ δαιμονιζόμενος *demoniac* (Thrasyllus [I AD] in Ps.-Plut., Fluv. C. 16; Cyranides p. 69, 17; Jos., Ant. 8, 47; PGM 13, 242; 4, 3009 acc. to ADieterich, Abraxas 1891, 138—Preisendanz has δαιμονιαζομένος) Mt 4: 24; 8: 16, 28, 33; 9: 32; 12: 22; Mk 1: 32; 5: 15f; Lk 8: 35 D; J 10: 21; Ac 19: 14 D. Also δαιμονισθείς s. above.—JWeiss, RE IV 410-19. M-M.*

δαιμονικός, ή, όν (Plut.; Physiogn. I 345, 8; 12; Cat. Cod. Astr. X 112, 10; Proclus on Pla., Cratyl. p. 93, 9 Pasqu.; Athenagoras, Suppl. 25; Clem. Alex., Strom. 6, 12, 98) *ghost-like* w. ἀσώματος of false teachers ISm 2; both adjectives are chosen because of the saying in 3: 2.*

δαιμόνιον, ου, τό (substant. neut. of the adj. δαιμόνιος [s. 2 below δαιμόνιον πνεῦμα], quotable since Homer; Dit., Or. 383, 175; Herm. Wr. 10, 19; Ps.-Phoc. 101; Philo; Jos., Bell. 1, 373; 6, 429).
1. *a deity, divinity* (Eur., Bacch. 894; Hdt. 5, 87; Pla., Apol. 26B; X., Mem. 1, 1, 1 καινὰ δαιμόνια εἰσφέρειν. Sg., Dit., Syll.³ 545, 14; 601, 15; UPZ 144, 43; 50 [164 BC]; Vett. Val. 355, 15; Philo, Mos. 1, 276; Jos., Bell. 1, 69) ξένων δ. καταγγελεύς *a preacher of strange divinities* Ac 17: 18.
2. *demon, evil spirit*, of independent beings who occupy a position somewhere between the human and the divine (Pla., Symp. 23 p. 202E πᾶν τὸ δαιμόνιον μεταξύ ἐστι θεοῦ τε καὶ θνητοῦ; Chrysipp. [Stoic. II 338] δ. φαῦλα; Plut., Dio 2, 3 φαῦλ. δ., Mor. 267Ff; Ps.-Lucian, Asinus 24 p. 592 οὐδὲ τὰ δ. δέδοικας; Vett. Val. 67, 5; 99, 7; Herm. Wr. 9, 3; PGM 4, 3081; 5, 120; 165; 170; LXX; En. 19, 1. Also δαιμόνιον πνεῦμα: lead tablet fr. Hadrumetum [Dssm., B 26, 35 (BS 271ff)]; PGM 4, 3038; 3065; 3075) who are said to enter into persons and cause illness, esp. of the mental variety (Jos., Bell. 7, 185, Ant. 6, 166ff; 211; 214; 8, 45ff): δ. εἰσέρχεται εἴς τινα Lk 8: 30; δ. ἔχειν Mt 11: 18; Lk 7: 33; 8: 27; J 7: 20; 8: 48f, 52; 10: 20. Hence the healing of a sick person is described as the driving out of demons ἐκβάλλειν (τ.) δ. (Jos., Ant. 6, 211) Mt 7: 22; 9: 34; 10: 8; Mk 1: 34, 39; 16: 9; Lk 9: 49; 11: 14f, 18ff; 13: 32 and oft. Pass. Mt 9: 33. ἐξέρχεται τὸ δ. (s. ἐξέρχομαι 1aδ.—Thrasyllus [I AD] in Ps.-Plut., Fluv. 16 ἀπέρχεται τὸ δαιμόνιον) 17: 18; Mk 7: 29f; Lk 4: 41; 8: 2, 33, 35, 38. They live in deserted places 8: 29, hence a ruined city is a *habitation of demons* Rv 18: 2 (cf. Is 13: 21; 34: 14; Bar 4: 35). Their ruler is Beelzebub (q.v.) Mt 12: 24, 27; Lk 11: 15, 18f. False doctrine is διδασκαλίαι δαιμονίων (subj. gen.) 1 Ti 4: 1. The ability of demons to work miracles is variously described J 10: 21 and Rv 16: 14. They are objects of worship 9: 20, specif. of idolatry (Dt 32: 17; Bar 4: 7; cf. Ps 95: 5; Sib. Or. fgm. 1: 22. Likew.

Persians and Babylonians: Cumont³ 305, 97) 1 Cor 10: 20f; B 16: 7. On Js 2: 19 cf. φρίσσω.—Of the evil spirit of slander Hm 2: 3; of vengeance s 9, 23, 5; of arrogance s 9, 22, 3.—The δ. can appear without a tangible body, and then acts as a *ghost* ISm 3: 2.—JGeffcken, Zwei griech. Apologeten '07, 216ff; JTambornino, De Antiquorum Daemonismo '09; RWünsch, D. Geisterbannung im Altertum: Festschr. Univ. Breslau '11, 9-32; WBousset, Z. Dämonologie d. späteren Antike: ARW 18, '15, 134-72; FAndres, Daimon: Pauly-W. Suppl. III '18, 267-322; MPohlenz, Stoa '49 [index].—HDuhm, D. bösen Geister im AT '04; GABarton, Enc. of Rel. and Eth. IV '11, 594-601; AJirku, D. Dämonen u. ihre Abwehr im AT '12; ALods, Marti-Festschr. '25, 181-93; HKaupel, D. Dämonen im AT '30; Bousset, Rel.³ '26, 331ff; Billerb. IV '28, 501-35; TCanaan, M.D., Dämonenglaube im Lande der Bibel '29; WFoerster, TW II 1-20.—WMAlexander, Demonic Possession in the NT '02; JSmit, De Daemonicis in Hist. Evang. '13; RBultmann, Gesch. d. syn. Tradition² '31, 223ff; HEberlein, NKZ 42, '31, 499-509; 562-72; FFenner, D. Krankheit im NT '30; ATitius, NBonwetsch-Festschr. '18, 25-47; GSulzer, D. Besessenheitsheilungen Jesu '21; HSeng, D. Heilungen Jesu in med. Beleuchtung² '26; WWrede, Z. Messiaserkenntnis d. Dämonen bei Mk: ZNW 5, '04, 169-77; OBauernfeind, D. Worte d. Dämonen im Mk-Ev. '28; AFridrichsen, Theology 21, '31, 122-35; SVMcCasland, By the Finger of God '51; SEitrem, Some Notes on the Demonology in the NT: Symbolae Osloenses, suppl. 12, '50, 1-60; JKallas, The Satanward View (Paul), '66; GMTillesse, Le Secret Messianique dans Mk, '68, 75-111. S. also the lit. s.v. ἄγγελος. M-M. B. 1488.

δαιμονιώδης, ες (PMich. 149 [II AD] VI, 33; VII, 11; VIII 8 and 13; Proclus on Pla., Tim. I p. 113, 21 Diehl; Syntipas p. 13, 22; schol. on Aristoph., Ran. 295; Leontios 8 p. 16, 13; Etym. Mag. p. 336, 38 φάντασμα δαιμονιῶδες ὑπὸ τῆς Ἑκάτης πεμπόμενον; Sym. Ps 90: 6) *demonic* in origin Js 3: 15.*

δαίμων, ονος, ὁ (Hom.+ in the sense 'a divinity'; Herm. Wr., inscr., pap., Philo, Joseph., Sib. Or.) means *demon, evil spirit*, in the only place where it is found in the NT text (so Charito 6, 2, 9 δ. κακός; Epict. 1, 22, 16; Appian, Bell. Civ. 4, 86 §366; Alex. Aphr., Probl. 2, 46; Iambl., Myst. 3, 31, 15 πονηρ.; Himerius, Or. 8 [23], 13 [here the πονηρὸς δ. of the disease strangles his victim with the βρόχος]; Sextus 604; Synes., Ep. 79 p. 227D; Eutecnius 2 p. 30, 13 [of a harpy]; PGM 4, 1227 [ἐκβάλλειν]; 2516 [πονηρός]; 3017; 5, 131; POxy. 1380, 164; BGU 954, 9; Is 65: 11; Philo, Gig. 16b; Jos., Bell. 1, 628, Ant. 8, 45, Vi. 402; Test. Jud. 23: 1. Cf. δαιμόνιον 2) Mt 8: 31. In the t.r. also Mk 5: 12; Lk 8: 29; Rv 16: 14; 18: 2.—ECEOwen, Δαίμων and Cognate Words: JTS 32, '31, 133-53. M-M.*

δαίρω in case this word has an independent existence and is not, as PKatz thinks, to be rejected as an itacistic spelling of δέρω, it means *beat (severely)* Hs 6, 2, 7; cf. δέρω.*

δάκνω 1 aor. pass. ἐδήχθην, subj. δηχθῶ (Hom.+; LXX) *bite*—1. lit. of snakes B 12: 5. Pass. (Diog. L. 5, 78 ὑπ᾽ ἀσπίδος δηχθείς) vs. 7 (cf. Num 21: 6ff).
2. fig. (Hdt. 7, 16, 1; X., Cyr. 4, 3, 3; Epict. 2, 22, 28 δάκνειν ἀλλήλους καὶ λοιδορεῖσθαι; Appian, Syr. 10 §40

=offend, nettle; Hab 2: 7; Philo, Leg. All. 2, 8) w. κατεσθίειν (q.v.) Gal 5: 15. M-M. B. 266f.*

δάκρυον, ου, τό (Hom.+; PPetr. II 1, 4; BGU 1141, 27f; LXX) dat. pl. δάκρυσιν (Lk 7: 38, 44; LXX; Jos., Ant. 1, 275, Vi. 138. Remnant of the poet. δάκρυ: Bl-D. §52) *tear* Rv 7: 17; 21: 4 (both Is 25: 8). Elsewh. pl. (Polyb. 2, 56, 6; 7; Philo) Lk 7: 38, 44 (Theodor. Prodr. 9, 275 H.: bathing feet w. tears). The pl.=*weeping* 2 Ti 1: 4. μετὰ δακρύων (Nicol. Dam.: 90 fgm. 68, 3; fgm. 130, 17 p. 399, 14 Jac.; Diod. S. 34+35, 11 and 34+35 fgm. 26; Lucian, Ver. Hist. 1, 21; Jos., Bell. 5, 420, Vi. 420; Test. Zeb. 1: 7; 2: 1) Mk 9: 24 v.l.; Ac 20: 19, 31; Hb 5: 7; 12: 17; διὰ πολλῶν δ. 2 Cor 2: 4 (διά III 1c. On the 'letter written w. many tears' cf. Synes., Ep. 140 p. 276c τί ταῖς ἐπιστολαῖς τῶν δακρύων ἐγχεῖς: why do you moisten your letters with tears?). M-M. B. 1130.*

δακρύω 1 aor. ἐδάκρυσα (Hom.+; Sb 373; 6178, 2; LXX; Jos., Ant. 9, 9, Vi. 210) *weep*: ἐδάκρυσεν ὁ Ἰησοῦς *Jesus burst into tears* J 11: 35 (as Diod. S. 17, 66, 4; 27, 6, 1; Appian, Samn. 4 §13 ὁ πρεσβύτης ἐδάκρυσε). M-M.*

δακτύλιος, ου, ὁ (Sappho, Hdt.+; inscr., pap., LXX, Philo, Joseph.) a *ring* Lk 15: 22; used to seal someth. (Diod. S. 16, 52, 6; Appian, Hann. c. 50 and 51; Diog. L. 4, 59; 7, 45; Esth 8: 8, 10; Da 6: 18 al.; Jos., Bell. 1, 667; 2, 24) 1 Cl 43: 2. M-M. B. 443.*

δάκτυλος, ου, ὁ (Hdt.+; Batr.; inscr., pap., LXX, Ep. Arist., Philo, Joseph.) *finger* J 20: 25, 27; Mk 7: 33; *move w. the finger* of the slightest movement (Simplicius in Epict. p. 53, 25 ἄκρῳ δακτύλῳ=very lightly indeed 'acc. to the proverb') Mt 23: 4; Lk 11: 46; ἄκρον τοῦ δ. (cf. 4 Macc 10: 7; Jos., Ant. 11, 234 ἄκροις τ. δακτύλοις) *tip of the finger* Lk 16: 24; write w. the finger (cf. Ex 31: 18; Dt 9: 10) J 8: 6, 8 v.l.—*The finger of God*=God's power (Ex 8: 15 [BCouroyer, Le 'Doigt de Dieu', RB 63, '56, 481–95]; Philo, Mos. 1, 112; PGM II p. 209 no. 1 κατὰ τοῦ δ. τοῦ θεοῦ) Lk 11: 20; in another sense γεγραμμένας τῷ δ. τῆς χειρὸς τοῦ κυρίου *written w. the Lord's own hand* B 4: 7; 14: 2 (Ex 31: 18).—ILöw, D. Finger in Lit. u. Folklore der Juden: Gedenkbuch z. Erinnerung an D. Kaufmann 1900, 61–85. M-M. B. 239f.*

Δαλμανουθά, ἡ indecl. *Dalmanutha*, a place of uncertain location near Lake Gennesaret, perh. another name for Magdala, which also has many variants in the tradition (Dalman, Gramm.¹ 133; on this MRossi, Rivista storico-critica delle Scienze Teolog. 5, '09, 345–50) Mk 8: 10. The derivation of the name is as uncertain as the location. —EbNestle, Philologica sacra 1896, 17; Dalman, Worte 52f; OProcksch, Pj 14, '18, 16f; JSickenberger, ZDPV 57, '34, 281–5; BHjerl-Hansen, Dalmanoutha: RB 53, '46, 372–84.*

Δαλματία, ας, ἡ *Dalmatia*, southern Illyricum, across the Adriatic fr. S. Italy (Mommsen, Röm. Gesch. V 19f; 183ff; Stephan. Byz. s.v. Ἴσσα: κατὰ Δαλματίαν καὶ Ἰλλυρίαν; Phlegon: 257 fgm. 36, 12 Jac.; Jos., Bell. 2, 369; CIL III 1 p. 271; 279ff; HKrahe, D. alten balkanillyr. geogr. Namen, Diss. Heidelb. '25) 2 Ti 4: 10. On the v.l. Δελματίαν cf. Bl-D. §41, 1 and M-M.*

δαμάζω 1 aor. ἐδάμασα; pf. pass. 3 sg. δεδάμασται (Hom.+; Da 2: 40) *subdue*.
1. lit., a demoniac Mk 5: 4. Of animals *subdue, tame* Js 3: 7 (Field, Notes, 237f)—2. fig. *tame, control* (Jos., Ant. 3, 86 τὸ φρόνημα) the tongue vs. 8. M-M. and suppl.*

δάμαλις, εως, ἡ (Aeschyl.+; Dit., Syll.³ 1026, 5; 22; LXX; Philo; Jos., Ant. 1, 184) *heifer, young cow*. Of the red heifer (Num 19; Jos., Ant. 4, 80 [here the gen. is δαμάλιδος]) Hb 9: 13; B 8: 1. M-M.*

Δάμαρις, ιδος, ἡ *Damaris* name of an Athenian woman converted by Paul Ac 17: 34. Since this form is found nowhere else as a woman's name, some, as early as HGrotius, have suggested that it be replaced by the rather common name Damalis, q.v. (so h). Hdb. ad loc. M-M.*

Δαμᾶς, ᾶ, ὁ *Damas*, bishop of Magnesia IMg 2. The name is not infreq. in the inscr., and is esp. well attested for western Asia Minor (CIG 2562; 2869; 2880; 2507), specif. for Magnesia by Inschr. v. Magnesia 321; 287. Cf. Δημᾶς.*

Δαμασκηνός, ή, όν *from Damascus* ὁ Δ. *the Damascene* (Strabo; Athen.; Geopon.; Joseph.) 2 Cor 11: 32.*

Δαμασκός, οῦ, ἡ (דַּמֶּשֶׂק Gen 14: 15 al.) *Damascus* (Diod. S. 40 fgm. 2 [Exc. Vat. p. 128] Δ. τῆς Συρίας; Nicol. Dam. in Jos., Ant. 7, 101; Strabo; Joseph.), capital of Coelesyria w. a large Jewish population (Jos., Bell. 2, 561; 7, 368). The city belonged to the Seleucids, the Nabataeans, and finally to the Romans (Schürer II⁴ 150ff) Ac 9: 2ff; 22: 5f, 10f; 26: 12, 20; 2 Cor 11: 32; Gal 1: 17.— HvKiesling, Damaskus, Altes u. Neues 'aus Syrien '19; CWatzinger u. KWulzinger, Damaskus '21; IBenzinger, Pauly-W. IV '01, 2042–8; LJalabert, Dict. d'Arch. IV 119ff; JSauvaget, Esquisse d'une histoire de la ville de Damas '35. On the political situation reflected in 2 Cor 11: 32 s. ESchwartz, NGG '06, 367f; '07, 275; Schürer I⁴ 737; II⁴ 108; 153f; Zahn, NKZ 15, '04, 34; UKahrstedt, Syr. Territorien in hellenist. Zeit '26.—S. Ἀρέτας.*

Δάν, ὁ indecl. (דָּן) (LXX; En. 13, 7; Test. 12 Patr.; Philo Joseph. The latter has both Δάν [Ant. 1, 305] and Δάνος, ου [2, 181]) *Dan*, name of an Israelite tribe (Gen 30: 6; 49: 16) Rv 7: 5 v.l. for Γάδ.*

Δαναΐδες, ων, αἱ *the Danaids*, daughters of Danaus, who were punished in the underworld 1 Cl 6: 2 (s. RKnopf, Hdb. ad loc. The rdg. Δαναΐδες κ. Δίρκαι, found in all mss., is also defended by APlummer, ET 26, '15, 560–2).*

δαν(ε)ίζω 1 aor. ἐδάνισα, mid. ἐδανισάμην (on the spelling s. Bl-D. §23; Mlt.-H. 77).
1. act. *lend* (*money*) (Aristoph.+; X., Pla., inscr., pap., LXX; Jos., Ant. 4, 266) Lk 6: 34a, b, 35; at excessive interest AP 16: 31.
2. mid. *borrow* (*money*) (Aristoph., X.+; inscr., pap.; 2 Esdr 15 [Neh 5]: 4; Ps 36: 21; Jos., Ant. 16, 296) ἀπό τινος (Pla., Tim. 42ε; Philo, Rer. Div. Her. 282) Mt 5: 42. M-M. B. 792f.*

δάν(ε)ιον, ου, τό (since Demosth. 34, 12, Aristot.; inscr., pap., Dt 15: 8, 10; 24: 11; 4 Macc 2: 8; Philo; Jos., Ant. 3, 282; 14, 370) *loan* ἀφιέναι τὸ δ. *cancel the loan* Mt 18: 27. M-M.*

δαν(ε)ιστής, οῦ, ὁ (since Demosth.; Plut., Sol. 13, 5, Mor. 830D; inscr., pap.; 4 Km 4: 1; Ps 108: 11; Sir 29: 28; Philo; Jos., Ant. 18, 147 al.; loanw. in rabb.) *money-lender, creditor* Lk 7: 41 (opp. χρεοφειλέτης as Pr 29: 13). M-M.*

Δανιήλ, ὁ indecl. (דָּנִיֵּאל) (LXX; En. 6, 7; Sib. Or. 2, 247.—Ep. Arist. 49 and Joseph. have Δανίηλος, ου [Ant. 10, 193], likew. Mt 24: 15 D) *Daniel*, the prophet Mt 24: 15; Mk 13: 14 t.r.; 1 Cl 45: 6; 2 Cl 6: 8; B 4: 5.*

δαπανάω fut. δαπανήσω; 1 aor. ἐδαπάνησα, imper. δαπάνησον (Hdt., Thu.+; inscr., pap., LXX, Ep. Arist., Philo, Joseph.) *spend, spend freely.*

1. lit., w. acc. as obj. *property* Mk 5: 26 (cf. 1 Macc 14: 32; Jos., Ant. 15, 303). τὶ εἴς τι (Diod. S. 11, 72, 2; Appian, Bell. Civ. 3, 32 §126; Artem. 1, 31 p. 33, 11f; Sb 8331, 17 [98 AD] πολλὰ δαπανήσας ἰς τὸ ἱερόν; Dit., Or. 59, 15; Bel 6 LXX, 3 Theod.; Jos., Ant. 4, 277) *spend someth. for* or *on someth.* Hs 1: 8; also ἔν τινι (BGU 149, 5 ἐν πυρῷ κατ' ἔτος δαπανᾶται τὰ ὑπογεγραμμένα) ἐν ταῖς ἡδοναῖς ὑμῶν *on your pleasures* Js 4: 3. ἐπί τινι *spend* (money) *on someone*= pay his expenses Ac 21: 24; cf. ὑπέρ τινος 2 Cor 12: 15 (cf. ZNW 18, '18, 201).—W. the connotation of wastefulness (Hesychius; Suidas δαπ.: οὐ τὸ ἁπλῶς ἀναλίσκειν, ἀλλὰ τὸ λαμπρῶς ζῆν καὶ σπαθᾶν καὶ δαπανᾶν τὴν οὐσίαν): πάντα *spend* or *waste everything* Lk 15: 14 (though the neutral sense *use everything up* is also poss.). Cf. also Js 4: 3 above.

2. fig. *wear out, exhaust, destroy* (Jos., Bell. 3, 74) τοὺς ἀνθρώπους Hm 12, 1, 2; pass. ibid., also αἱ δεδαπανημέναι καρδίαι τ. θανάτῳ *the hearts worn out unto death* B 14: 5 (Cat. Cod. Astr. VIII 3 p. 135, 19 ὑπὸ τ. λύπης ἐδαπανώμην).—Of fire (Dio Chrys. 4, 32; 2 Macc 1: 23; 2: 10; Philo, Exsecr. 153; Jos., Ant. 4, 192; Sib. Or. 2, 197) πυρί σε ποιῶ δαπανηθῆναι *I will cause you to be consumed by fire* MPol 11: 2; cf. 16: 1. M-M.*

δαπάνη, ης, ἡ (Hes., Pind., Hdt.+; inscr., pap., LXX, Ep. Arist.; Jos., Bell. 1, 605, Ant. 12, 200) *cost, expense* ψηφίζειν τὴν δ. *calculate the cost* Lk 14: 28. συμψηφίζειν τὴν ποσότητα τῆς δ. *estimate the amount of the expense* Hs 5, 3, 7. M-M. B. 805.*

δασύπους, οδος, ὁ (Cratinus 400; Aristot., Hist. An. 511a, 31; Eutecnius 2 p. 22, 22; Test. Ash. 2: 9) *hare*, whose flesh was forbidden to the Jews B 10: 6 (Dt 14: 7; cf. Lev 11: 5; Test. Ash. 2: 9).*

Δαυίδ, ὁ indecl. (Δαυείδ is another spelling, in late mss. also Δαβίδ, cf. Bl-D.-Funk §38; 39, 1; Mlt.-H. 110; on the abbrev. Δ δ̄ s. LTraube, Nomina Sacra '07) *David* (דָּוִד) (LXX; Sib. Or.; Eupolemus the Jew [IIbc] in Euseb., Pr. Ev. 30, 5 and 7f [Δαβίδ]; Philo, Conf. Lingu. 149 [Δαβίδ].—In Joseph. Δαυίδης, ου [Ant. 6, 199; also 7, 101 in a quot. fr. Nicol. Dam.] or Δαβίδης), king of Israel, in genealogy of Jesus Mt 1: 6, 17; Lk 3: 31. Acc to Mt 1: 20; Lk 1: 27; 2: 4 Joseph was of Davidic descent. Jesus is called υἱὸς Δ. Mt 9: 27; 12: 23; 15: 22; 20: 30f; 21: 9, 15; Mk 10: 47f; 12: 35; Lk 18: 38f; 20: 41; B 12: 10; ἐκ σπέρματος Δ. J 7: 42 (s. below); Ro 1: 3; 2 Ti 2: 8; IEph 18: 2; IRo 7: 3 (Third Corinthians 3: 5); ἐκ γένους Δ. IEph 20: 2; ITr 9: 1; ISm 1: 1.—David eating showbread (1 Km 21: 1-6) Mt 12: 3; Mk 2: 25; Lk 6: 3. His wars 1 Cl 4: 13. His grave Ac 2: 29 (cf. Jos., Bell. 1, 61; Ant. 16, 179). As singer of psalms (inspired Mt 22: 43; Mk 12: 36; Ac 1: 16; 4: 25, prophesying B 12: 10) Mk 12: 36f; Lk 20: 42, 44; Ac 2: 25; Ro 4: 6; 11: 9; B 10: 10 and oft. Ancestor of the Messiah Mt 22: 42. The Messianic Kgdm. described as kgdm. of David Mk 11: 10; his polit. kgdm. the fallen tabernacle of David Ac 15: 16 (Am 9: 11). The Messiah has the key, i.e. sovereignty, of David Rv 3: 7 (Is 22: 22 v.l.). Bethlehem is the city of David Lk 2: 4, 11; J 7: 42. On ἡ ῥίζα Δ. Rv 5: 5; 22: 16 cf. ῥίζα 2. On λίμνη τοῦ Δ. GOxy 25 cf. λίμνη 2.—Described as μεμαρτυρημένος 1 Cl 18: 1; ἐκλεκτός 52: 2.—The mng. of ἄμπελος Δ. in the eucharistic prayer D 9: 2 is debated (s. ἄμπελος 2).

Δάφνος, ου, ὁ *Daphnus*, a Christian in Smyrna ISm 13: 2. (A Christian by this name: Third Corinthians 1: 1). On the name s. Hdb. ad loc.*

δέ (Hom.+; inscr., pap., LXX) one of the most commonly used Gk. particles, used to connect one clause w. another when it is felt that there is some contrast betw. them, though the contrast is oft. scarcely discernible. Most common translations: *but*, when a contrast is clearly implied; *and*, when a simple connective is desired, without contrast; freq. it cannot be translated at all.

1. to emphasize a contrast—a. gener. Mt 6: 1, 6, 15, 17; 8: 20; 9: 17; 23: 25; Mk 2: 21f; Lk 5: 36f; 10: 6; 12: 9f; 13: 9; 1 Cor 2: 15 and oft.

b. for the correlative use μέν—δέ see μέν.

c. in lists of similar things, to bring about a clearer separation betw. the things listed Mt 1: 2-16; 2 Pt 1: 5-8; relating one teaching to another Mt 5: 31; 6: 16; Ro 14: 1; 1 Cor 7: 1; 8: 1; 12: 1; 15: 1; 16: 1.

d. after a negative *rather* (Wsd 2: 11; 4: 9; 7: 6 al.; 2 Macc 4: 5; 5: 6 al.; 3 Macc 2: 24; 3: 15) Mt 6: 33; Lk 10: 20; Ac 12: 9, 14; Ro 3: 4; Eph 4: 15; Hb 4: 13, 15; 6: 12; 9: 1 al.; strengthened δὲ μᾶλλον 12: 13; Mt 10: 6, 28.

e. introducing an apodosis after a hypothetical or temporal protasis, and contrasting it with the protasis (Kühner-G. II 275f; Epict. 1, 4, 32; 1 Macc 14: 29; 2 Macc 1: 34; Act. Thom. 98) Ac 11: 17 t.r.; 2 Pt 1: 5 (for the protasis vs. 3f); Col 1: 22 (where the participial constr. vs. 21 represents the protasis; Ep. Arist. 175; 315).

2. very freq. as a transitional particle pure and simple, without any contrast intended *now, then* Mt 1: 18, 24; 2: 19; 3: 1; 8: 30; Mk 5: 11; 7: 24; 16: 9; Lk 3: 21; 12: 2, 11, 13, 15f, 50; 13: 1, 6, 10; 15: 1, 11 al.; Ac 4: 5; 6: 1, 8; 9: 10; 12: 10, 17, 20; 23: 10; 24: 17; Ro 8: 28; 1 Cor 16: 12, 17; 2 Cor 4: 7; 8: 1; Gal 3: 23. Esp. to insert an explanation *that is* (Aeschyl., Choeph. 190) Ro 3: 22; 9: 30; 1 Cor 10: 11; 15: 56; Eph 5: 32; Phil 2: 8. So in parentheses (Thu. 1, 26, 5 ἔστι δὲ ἰσθμὸς τὸ χωρίον) ἦσαν δὲ ἡμέραι τῶν ἀζύμων Ac 12: 3.

3. resuming a discourse that has been interrupted Mt 3: 4; Lk 4: 1; Ro 5: 8; 2 Cor 10: 2.

4. used w. other particles—a. δὲ καί *but also, but even* (2 Macc 12: 13; 15: 19; Ep. Arist. 40 al.) Mt 3: 10 t.r.; 10: 30; 18: 17; Mk 14: 31; Lk 11: 18; 16: 22; J 2: 2; 3: 23; 18: 2, 5; Ac 22: 28; 1 Cor 15: 15.—ἔτι δὲ καί *and* (*even*) (EpJer 40; 2 Macc 10: 7; Ep. Arist. 35; 151) Lk 14: 26 v.l.; Ac 2: 26 (Ps 15: 9).

b. καί . . . δέ *and also, but also* (Kühner-G. II 253; Wsd 7: 3; 11: 20; 1 Esdr 1: 47; 1 Macc 12: 23; 2 Macc 11: 12; 4 Macc 2: 9; Ep. Arist. index) Mt 10: 18; 16: 18; J 6: 51; 8: 16f; 15: 27; Ac 3: 24; 22: 29; 1 Ti 3: 10; 2 Ti 3: 12; 1 J 1: 3. Cf. Hatch 141f.—Usually δέ comes second in its clause, somet. third (Lucian, Tim. 48, Dial. Mar. 4, 2; Alex. Aphr., Fat. 36, II 2 p. 208, 20; 209, 6) Mt 10: 11; 18: 25; Mk 4: 34; Lk 10: 31; Ac 17: 6; 28: 6 al., occasionally fourth (Menand., Epitr. 64; 309; Archimed. II 150, 10 Heib.; Lucian, Adv. Ind. 19 p. 114; PHib. 54, 20 [245 BC]; Wsd 16: 8; 1 Macc 8: 27) Mt 10: 18; J 6: 51; 8: 16; 1 Cor 4: 18; 1 J 1: 3, or even fifth (Lucian, Apol. 12 p. 722; Alex. Aphr., An. II 1 p. 34, 8; 57, 15; 1 Esdr 1: 22; 4 Macc 2: 9) J 8: 17; 1 J 2: 2; IEph 4: 2.—Epict. index p. 542 Sch.; HGMeecham, The Letter of Aristeas '35, 136; 154f.

δεδώκει s. δίδωμι.

δέησις, εως, ἡ (Lysias, Pla.+; Diod. S., Plut., inscr., pap., LXX, Nägeli 40) *entreaty*; in our lit., as almost always LXX (but not 1 Macc 11: 49), exclusively addressed to God, *prayer* (so Plut., Coriol. 30, 2; Ps.-Lucian, Amor. 19; PPar. 69 II, 11; PPetr. II 19 [1a] 2 [s. below]; Jos., C. Ap. 2, 197) Lk 1: 13; 2: 37; Phil 1: 19; 2 Ti 1: 3; 1 Pt 3: 12; 1 Cl 22: 6 (last two both Ps 33: 16); Pol 7: 2. W. ἱκεσία

(Dit., Or. 569, 11; PPetr. II 19 [1a] 2 μετὰ δεήσεως καὶ ἱκετείας οὕνεκα τοῦ θεοῦ) 1 Cl 59: 2. W. προσευχή, the more general term, to denote a more specif. supplication (3 Km 8: 45; 2 Ch 6: 29; cf. Alex. Aphr., An. Mant. II 1 p. 186, 3 εὐχαὶ καὶ δεήσεις) Ac 1: 14 v.l.; Eph 6: 18; Phil 4: 6; 1 Ti 2: 1; 5: 5; IMg 7: 1. W. προσκαρτέρησις Eph 6: 18; w. ἱκετηρία Hb 5: 7; δ. ποιεῖσθαι pray (PPar. 69 II, 11 ἔνθα σπονδάς τε καὶ δεήσεις ποιησάμενος; BGU 180, 17; PHermopol. 6, 1; 3 Macc 2: 1; cf. Jos., Bell. 7, 107) Lk 5: 33; Phil 1: 4; 1 Ti 2: 1. ἀναφέρειν δέησιν offer prayer (to God) B 12: 7. ἐν δεήσει in or with (your) prayer Hv 3, 10, 7. W. addition of the object ὑπέρ τινος Ro 10: 1; 2 Cor 1: 11; 9: 14; Phil 1: 4; 1 Ti 2: 1f. περί τινος (En. 13, 6) Eph 6: 18; πολὺ ἰσχύει δ. Js 5: 16. M-M.*

δεῖ inf. (τὸ) δεῖν Lk 18: 1; Ac 25: 24; Third Corinthians 1: 9, subj. δέῃ, impf. ἔδει (Bl-D. §358, 1; Rob. 885f) impers. verb (Hom+; inscr., pap., LXX, Ep. Arist., Joseph.) it is necessary, one must or has to, denoting compulsion of any kind.
1. of divine destiny or unavoidable fate (since Hdt. [8, 53 ἔδεε κατὰ τὸ θεοπρόπιον]; Appian, Liby. 122 §578 ἀλῶναι ἔδει Καρχηδόνα=it was necessary that Carthage be captured; Da 2: 28f, 45 Theod.; Wsd 16: 4) Mt 17: 10; 24: 6 (δεῖ γενέσθαι as Jos., Ant. 10, 142); 26: 54; Mk 9: 11; 13: 7, 10, Lk 4: 43; 21: 9; J 3: 14, 30; 9: 4; 10: 16; 20: 9; Ac 1: 16; 3: 21; 4: 12; Ro 1: 27; 1 Cor 15: 53; 2 Cor 5: 10; Rv 1: 1; 4: 1; 22: 6; 2 Cl 2: 5.
2. of the compulsion of duty (Wsd 12: 19; 16: 28; EpJer 5; Tob 12: 1): one ought or should οὐκ ἔδει σε ἐλεῆσαι; should you not have had mercy? Mt 18: 33.—Lk 2: 49; 15: 32; 18: 1; Ac 5: 29; 1 Th 4: 1; Tit 1: 11; 1 Cl 62: 2.
3. of the compulsion of law or custom: ᾗ ἔδει θύεσθαι τὸ πάσχα when the paschal lamb had to be sacrificed Lk 22: 7.—Mt 23: 23; Lk 11: 42; 13: 14; J 4: 20, 24; Ac 15: 5; 18: 21 t.r. Of the compulsion of Roman law 25: 10.
4. of an inner necessity, growing out of a given situation Mt 26: 35 (Jos., Ant. 6, 108 κἂν ἀποθανεῖν δέῃ; PFay. 109, 5 ἐάν σε δῇ [=δέῃ] τὸ εἱμάτιόν σου θεῖναι ἐνέχυρον); Mk 14: 31; J 4: 4; Ac 14: 22; 27: 21; 2 Cor 11: 30.
5. of the compulsion caused by the necessity of attaining a certain result Lk 12: 12; 19: 5; Ac 9: 6; 1 Cor 11: 19; 2 Cl 1: 1; B 4: 1; IEph 7: 1. τὰ δέοντα (PPetr. II 11(1), 6; BGU 251, 5 and oft. pap.; Pr 30: 8; 2 Macc 13: 20) the needs Hs 2, 5, 8.
6. of the compulsion of what is fitting (Epict. 2, 22, 20 φίλος ἔσομαι οἷος δεῖ; 3, 23, 21 ὡς δεῖ; 2 Macc 6: 20; 4 Macc 7: 8) 2 Ti 2: 6, 24. καθὸ δεῖ as is proper Ro 8: 26.—δέον ἐστίν it is necessary, one must (Polyb.; POxy. 727, 19f; 1061, 13; BGU 981 II, 6; Sir. Prol. l. 3; 1 Macc 12: 11; Ep. Arist.) Ac 19: 36; 1 Pt 1: 6 𝔓72 et al.; 1 Cl 34: 2; without ἐστίν (POxy. 899, 40; Ep. Arist. 227; 242; Philo, Aet. M. 107; Jos., Bell. 2, 296) ITr 2: 3; Pol 5: 3. εἰ δέον if it must be 1 Pt 1:6.—On the constr. of δεῖ, note that as a rule the acc. and inf. follow it (Jos., C. Ap. 2, 254; Lucian, Charon 13, Pisc. 17; Bl-D. §408), occasionally the inf. alone Mt 23: 23 (Jos., C. Ap. 1, 53a.—Bl-D. §407); 26: 54; Ac 5: 29.—To convey the idea that someth. should not happen, δεῖ is used w. a negative Lk 13: 16; Ac 25: 24; 2 Ti 2: 24; Tit 1: 11 (ἃ μὴ δεῖ what is not proper [also Ael. Aristid. 54 p. 687 D.] is prob. a mixture of τὰ μὴ δέοντα 1 Ti 5: 13 and ἃ οὐ δεῖ [Job 19: 4]; cf. Bl-D. §428, 4; Rob. 1169); 2 Cl 1: 1.—In τί με δεῖ ποιεῖν; what shall I do? Ac 16: 30, δ. stands for the deliberative subj. (Bl-D. §366, 4).—The impf. ἔδει is used to denote:
a. that something that happened should by all means have happened (Jos., Bell. 4, 232) had to Lk 15: 32; 22: 7; 24: 26; J 4: 4; Ac 1: 16; 17: 3.

b. that someth. that did not take place really should have happened: should have, ought to have Mt 18: 33; 23: 23; Ac 24: 19; (οὓς ἔδει with inf.: Isocr. 3, 40 p. 35A; Lysias 14, 29 p. 142, 23; Lucian, Philops. 21 p. 49) 27: 21; 2 Cor 2: 3. Cf. Bl-D. §358.—EFascher, Theol. Beobachtungen zu δεῖ im AT: ZNW 45, '54, 244–52; Theol. Beobachtungen zu δεῖ: RBultmann-Festschr., '54, 228–54. M-M. B. 640f.

δεῖγμα, ατος, τό (Eur., X., Pla.+; inscr., pap., Philo, Joseph., loanw. in rabb.).
1. proof τινός of someth. (Eur., Supp. 354; Menand., Georg. fgm. 3, 4 J.; Cass. Dio 55, 7, 4; Jos., Ant. 8, 34) Dg 4: 5; 7: 9.
2. example παρέχειν (Dionys. Hal., Rhet. 6, 5 p. 282, 19 R. τ. ἀρετῆς; Philostrat., Vi. Apoll. 6, 12 p. 224, 23) give an example 3: 3; προκεῖσθαι δ. stand as an ex. Jd 7 (sample EKLee, NTS 8, '61/'62, 167). Cf. εἰς τὸ δεῖγμα 2 Pt 2: 6 𝔓72. M-M.*

δειγματίζω 1 aor. ἐδειγμάτισα (PTebt. 576 [I bc]; PSI 442, 18; Ascens. Is. in PAmh. 1 VIII, 21; Acta Petri et Pauli 33. Exx. of the noun δειγματισμός in Mayser 436; also BGU 246, 5, where δ.=public disgrace) expose, make an example of, disgrace τινά someone (schol. on Eur., Hippol. 426) a woman Mt 1: 19 (on the public disgrace of an adulteress cf. Heraclides [IV bc], Polit. 14 FGSchneidewin 1847; Nicol. Dam.: 90 fgm. 1031 Jac. [Pisidians]; Plut., Mor. 291Ef; Dio Chrys. 47[64] 3 mentions a Cyprian law, according to which an adulteress had to cut her hair and was subjected to contempt by the community; Aelian, V.H. 11, 6; Hermogenes p. 90, 2 HRabe '13; among the Jews such a woman was threatened w. more serious perils: cf. J 8: 3ff [Hdb. ad loc.]; Protev. Jac. 14, 1); mock, expose Col 2: 15. M-M.*

δείκνυμι fut. δείξω; 1 aor. ἔδειξα, imper. δεῖξον; pf. δέδειχα (B 13: 3); 1 aor. pass. ptc. δειχθείς (Hb 8: 5; Dg 11: 2) (Hom.+; inscr., pap., LXX; En. 13, 2; Philo, Joseph., Test. 12 Patr. The alternate form δεικνύω, as old as Hdt., also Ps.-Aeschin., Ep. 12, 6; Bl-D. §92; Rob. 311) show.
1. point out, show, make known τινί τι or τινα someth. or someone to someone.
a. lit., kingdoms Mt 4: 8; Lk 4: 5. δεῖξον σεαυτὸν τῷ ἱερεῖ (cf. Lev 13: 49) Mt 8: 4; Mk 1: 44; Lk 5: 14; mountains 1 Cl 10: 7; trees Hs 3: 1; a hall Mk 14: 15; Lk 22: 12. ἃ δεῖ σε ἰδεῖν Hv 3, 1, 2; denarius Lk 20: 24; a pattern Hb 8: 5 (Ex 25: 40); hands and feet Lk 24: 40 v.l.; hands J 20: 20; good works 10: 32; land Ac 7: 3 (Gen 12: 1 LXX). σημεῖον (EpJer 66; Jos., Bell. 2, 259, Ant. 18, 211) J 2: 18.—Of apocalyptic visions (Zech 3: 1) Rv 1: 1; 4: 1; 17: 1; 21: 9f; 22: 1, 6, 8. The Father J 14: 8f (Nicol. Dam. 90 fgm. 3 p. 331, 13 Jac. ὁ Ἀρβάκης ἐδεήθη αὐτοῦ, δεῖξαι οἱ τὸν βασιλέα. σφόδρα γὰρ ἐπιθυμεῖν τὸν δεσπότην ὅστις εἴη θεάσασθαι). Of divine revelation (Hermes: Stob. I 386, 22 W.=458, 20 Sc.; PGM 3, 599) J 5: 20. Of the Parousia to come 1 Ti 6: 15.—1 Cl 5: 5; B 5: 9.
b. fig., a way (1 Km 12: 23; Mi 4: 2) 1 Cor 12: 31; the salvation of God 1 Cl 35: 12 (Ps 49: 23).
2. explain, prove (Ps.-Callisth. 3, 22, 10 ἄρτι δέ σοι δείξω=I will soon prove [it] to you) τὶ someth. Js 2: 18a; 5: 6. τινί τι 1 Cl 26: 1. W. ὅτι foll. B 7: 5; τινί w. ὅτι foll. (3 Macc 6: 15) Mt 16: 21; τινί w. inf. foll. Ac 10: 28. τὶ ἔκ τινος (Alex. Aphr., Quaest. 3, 3 II 2 p. 83, 10) Js 2: 18b; 3: 13. W. double acc. τὸν σωτῆρα δείξας δυνατόν he has revealed the Savior as powerful Dg 9: 6.—JGonda, Δείκνυμι '29. M-M. B. 1045.**

δειλαίνω act the coward (Aristot.+); mid. be cowardly, fearful (Ps.-Lucian, Ocypus 153; PTebt. 58, 27 [111 bc]; 1

Macc 5: 41) IRo 5: 2. μηδὲν δειλαινόμενος *without fearing* Hs 9, 1, 3.*

δειλία, ας, ἡ (Soph., Hdt.+; BGU 372 I, 26; PGiess. 40 II, 11; Herm. Wr. p. 444, 3 Sc.; LXX; Philo; Jos., Vi. 172, C. Ap. 2, 148) *cowardice* πνεῦμα δειλίας *spirit of cowardice* 2 Ti 1: 7; διὰ τὴν δ. *through cowardice* Hs 9, 21, 3; *timidity* MPol 3. M-M.*

δειλιάω 1 aor. ἐδειλίασα (Diod. S. 20, 78, 1 IFischer v.l.; PPar. 68c, 4; LXX; Test. Sim. 2: 3; Pel.-Leg. 12, 12) *be cowardly, timid* (w. ταράσσεσθαι as Is 13: 7f) J 14: 27; before wild beasts MPol 4. M-M.*

δειλινός, ή, όν (Diocles 141 p. 180, 12; Strabo; Plut.; Lucian; pap.; LXX) *in the afternoon* τὸ δειλινόν as adv. *toward evening* (Menand., Kon. 7 J.; Lucian, Lex. 2; Gen 3: 8) Ac 3: 1 D.*

δειλός, ή, όν (Hom.+; LXX; Philo; Jos., Bell. 3, 365, Ant. 6, 215) *cowardly, timid* (w. ἄπιστος et al.) Rv 21: 8; of those of little faith (Dio Chrys. 47[64], 11 τί δέδοικας, ὦ δειλέ;) Mt 8: 26; Mk 4: 40; Hs 9, 28, 4. M-M.*

δεῖνα, ὁ, ἡ, τό (Thu., Aristoph.+; pap., Aq., Sym.) *so-and-so,* of a pers. or thing one cannot or does not wish to name, in our lit. only masc. *a certain, man, somebody* Mt 26: 18. M-M.*

δεινός, ή, όν (Hom.+; Dit., Syll.³ 983, 7; BGU 163, 9; LXX; Philo; Joseph.; cf. Nägeli 56) *fearful, terrible* of punishments 2 Cl 17: 7; MPol 2: 4; Hs 6, 3, 3; of tortures (Ael. Aristid. 49, 16 K.=25 p. 492 D.) 1 Cl 6: 2; δ. ῥήματα *threatening words* MPol 8: 3. Superl. δεινότατος (Philo) of grief *very bad* Hm 10, 1, 2. Subst. τὸ δεινόν= danger (of death) (Diod. S. 19, 83, 5; Appian, Bell. Civ. 5, 90 §378; Philo; Jos., Ant. 1, 164) ἄλλα δεινά *other afflictions* ending of Mk in the Freer ms. 8.—LVoit, Δεινότης '34; ESchlesinger, Δεινότης: Philol. 91, '37, 59-66.*

δεινῶς adv. (Hdt.+; Aelian [oft.]; inscr., pap., LXX; Jos., Ant. 2, 304; 3, 1) *fearfully, terribly* βασανιζόμενος *tortured* Mt 8: 6 (BGU 595, 14 ὁ υἱός μου ἀσθενεῖ δεινῶς; Dit., Syll.³ 1168, 114); καταφθαρῆναι δ. *become terribly corrupt* Hv 1, 3, 1; δ. ἐνέχειν *act in a very hostile manner* Lk 11: 53. δαπανᾶσθαι *be terribly destroyed* Hm 12, 1, 2. M-M.*

δειπνέω fut. δειπνήσω; 1 aor. ἐδείπνησα (Hom.+; inscr., pap., LXX; Ep. Arist. 180; Jos., Ant. 1, 252) *eat, dine* Lk 17: 8; 22: 20; 1 Cor 11: 25 (of the Passover Jos., Ant. 2, 312) of a pagan cult meal POxy. 110; 523.—μετὰ τὸ δειπνῆσαι as Plut., Mor. 645D) Rv 3: 20; addition to Mt 20: 28 D=Agr 22; Hs 9, 11, 8a; the continuation in ibid. b uses it fig. δ. ῥήματα κυρίου. M-M.*

δειπνοκλήτωρ, ορος, ὁ (Athen. 4, 70 p. 171B=ἐλεάτρος; Hesychius; Mich. Glykas 337, 5 IBekker [1836]) one who καλεῖ to the δεῖπνον, *host;* addition to Mt 20: 28 D=Agr 22. Cf. EbNestle, ZNW 7, '06, 362ff; HJVogels, BZ 12, '14, 384f.*

δεῖπνον, ου, τό (Hom.+; inscr., pap., LXX; Ep. Arist. 217; Jos., Ant. 1, 269; 270; Test. 12 Patr.).
1. *dinner, supper,* the main *meal* (toward) evening.— Polyaenus, Exc. 3, 8, opp. ἀριστᾶν) Lk 14: 12; J 13: 4; 21: 20; Hs 5, 5, 3. περὶ δείπνου ὥραν (cf. POxy. 110 δειπνῆσαι... ἀπὸ ὥρας θ') MPol 7: 1; cf. Lk 14: 17; κυριακὸν δ. *the Lord's Supper* 1 Cor 11: 20 (exx. of δ.=a cult meal in JBehm, TW II 34f; Biogr. p. 92 at the sacrifice

a priest calls out: Πίνδαρος ἴτω ἐπὶ τὸ δεῖπνον τοῦ θεοῦ). On τὸ ἴδιον δεῖπνον προλαμβάνει vs. 21 cf. ἴδιος 1aβ and προλαμβάνω 2a. Cf. ESchweizer, D. Herrenmahl im NT. Ein Forschungsbericht: ThLZ 79, '54, 577-92.
2. *(formal) dinner, banquet* Mt 23: 6; Mk 12: 39; Lk 11: 43 D; 14: 17, 24; 20: 46; 1 Cor 10: 27 D; Rv 19: 9. δεῖπνον μέγα (Vi. Aesopi W c. 77 ἐπὶ μέγα δεῖπνον ἐκάλει τινά) Lk 14: 16; Rv 19: 17. ποιεῖν δ. *give a dinner* (PMMeyer, Griech. Texte aus Äg. ['16] 20, 34 δεῖπνον ἐπόει μοι; PGM 1, 106; Da 5: 1 Theod.) Mk 6: 21; Lk 14: 12, 16; J 12: 2; Hs 5, 2, 9. δείπνου γινομένου *when a dinner was being held* J 13: 2 (Athen. 4, 8 p. 132c πότερον ἐν ἄστει γίνεται βελτίω δεῖπνα ἢ ἐν Χαλκίδι;).—Billerb. IV 611-39. M-M. B. 352; 354.*

δεῖπνος, ου, ὁ (Diod. S. 4, 3 v.l.; schol. on Aristoph., Pax 564; Ursing 23) for δεῖπνον only as v.l. Lk 14: 16; Rv 19: 9, 17.—Bl-D. §49, 2; Mlt.-H. 123.*

δεισιδαιμονία, ας, ἡ—1. in a good sense *fear of* or *reverence for the divinity* (Polyb. 6, 56, 7; Diod. S. 1, 70; 11, 89; Dio Chrys. 44[61], 9; Jos., Bell. 2, 174, Ant. 10, 42).
2. in an unfavorable sense *superstition* (Theophr., Char. 16; Polyb. 12, 24, 5; Plut., Sol. 12, 4, Alex. 75, 1, Mor. 66c, cf. his work Περὶ τῆς δεισιδαιμονίας; M. Ant. 6, 30; Agatharchides in Jos., Ant. 12, 5f, C. Ap. 1, 208; Herm. Wr. 9, 9; Philo, Spec. Leg. 4, 147; Jos., Ant. 15, 277) Dg 1; 4: 1.
3. in an objective sense *religion* (Dit., Or. 455, 11; Jos., Ant. 14, 228; 19, 290: the Jews were forbidden by Claudius τὰς τ. ἄλλων ἐθνῶν δεισιδαιμονίας ἐξουθενίζειν) ζητήματα περὶ τῆς ἰδίας δεισιδαιμονίας εἶχον *they had some points of dispute about their religion* Ac 25: 19.— HBolkestein, Theophrastos' Charakter der Δεισιδαιμονία als religionsgesch. Urkunde '29; PJKoets, Δεισιδαιμονία, Diss. Utrecht '29; SEitrem, Symb. Osl. 31, '55, 155-69. M-M. B. 1492f.*

δεισιδαίμων, ον, gen. ονος can, like δεισιδαιμονία, be used in a bad sense *superstitious* (cf. Maximus Tyr. 14, 6f; Philo, Cher. 42; cf. Field, Notes 125-7), but in the laudatory introduction of Paul's speech before the Areopagus Ac 17: 22 it must mean *religious* (so X., Cyr. 3, 3, 58, Ages. 11, 8; Aristot., Pol. 5, 11 p. 1315a, 1; Epigr. Gr. 607, 3 πᾶσι φίλος θνητοῖς εἴς τ' ἀθανάτους δεισιδαίμων) comp. for superl. (as Diog. L. 2, 132): δεισιδαιμονεστέρους ὑμᾶς θεωρῶ *I perceive that you are very religious people* Ac 17: 22 (the Athenians as the εὐσεβέστατοι τ. Ἑλλήνων: Jos., C. Ap. 2, 130. Cf. Paus. Attic. 24, 3 Ἀθηναίοις περισσότερόν τι ἢ τοῖς ἄλλοις ἐς τὰ θεῖά ἐστι σπουδῆς). M-M.*

δέκα indecl. *ten* (Hom.+; inscr., pap., LXX, Ep. Arist., Philo, Joseph., Test. 12 Patr.; Sib. Or. 5, 12; loanw. in rabb.—Jos., Bell. 2, 146 as a round number) Mt 20: 24; 25: 1, 28; Mk 10: 41; Lk 15: 8; 17: 12, 17; δέκα ἀπόστολοι Ac 2: 14 D; θλῖψιν ἡμερῶν δ. Rv 2: 10 (ten days as a relatively short period of time as Gen 24: 55; Da 1: 12, 14); horns 12: 3; 17: 3, 7, 12, 16 (Da 7: 7, 20, 24); soldiers IRo 5: 1; kingdoms B 4: 4f (Da 7: 24, 7); cf. Rv 17: 12; δ. λόγοι *the Ten Commandments* (Ex 34: 28; Dt 10: 4) B 15: 1.—δεκαδύο (inscr. in Meisterhans³-Schw. p. 159; ESchweizer, Gramm. d. perg. Inschr. '08, 164; ENachmanson, Laute u. Formen d. magn. Inschr. '03, 147; pap. in Mayser 316; Polyb., Plut., Ep. Arist., Joseph., LXX) *twelve* Ac 19: 7 t.r.; 24: 11 t.r.; B 8: 3; GEb 5.—For δεκαέξ or δέκα ἕξ (inscr., pap., LXX, Strabo) *sixteen* Rv 13: 18 C see M-M. and L-S-J. lex.—δεκαοκτώ (Inschr. in

Meisterhans³-Schw. and Schweizer; Cleonides [II AD], Introductio Harmonica 2; pap., LXX; Jos., C. Ap. 1, 230; Test. Judah 9: 2) *eighteen* Lk 13: 4, 11 (16 δ. καὶ ὀκτώ, cf. Thackeray 188); B 9: 8 (Jos., Ant. 1, 178).—δεκαπέντε (inscr. in Meisterhans³-Schw.; pap. in Mayser 316; Polyb., Diod. S., Plut., Joseph., LXX) *fifteen* J 11: 18; Ac 27: 5 v.l., 28; Gal 1: 18 (ἡμ. δεκ. means *two weeks* as Appian, Liby. 108 §507 [πεντεκαίδεκα ἡμ.]; Jos., Ant. 13, 427; Berosus in Jos., C. Ap. 1, 140; Dit., Or. 210, 7 [247/8]).—δεκατέσσαρες (inscr. in Schweizer; Dit., Or. 672, 13; pap. in Mayser 316; Polyb., Diod. S., Strabo, Plut., Joseph., LXX) *fourteen* Mt 1: 17 (on the numerical difficulties here s. HSchöllig, ZNW 59, '68, 261-8); 2 Cor 12: 2; Gal 2: 1 (LDieu, Quatorze ans ou quatre ans?: Ephem. théol. Lov. 14, '37, 308-17). M-M.

δεκαδύο, δεκαέξ, δεκαοκτώ, δεκαπέντε s. δέκα. M-M.

Δεκάπολις, εως, ἡ (Jos., Bell. 3, 446; Inscr. Rom. III 1057, 5) *Decapolis*, name of a league orig. consisting of ten cities (αἱ δέκα πόλεις: Jos., Vi. 341f), whose region (except for Scythopolis) lay east of the Jordan. Damascus marked the boundary to the north, Philadelphia to the south. Mt 4: 25; Mk 5: 20; 7: 31.—Schürer II⁴ 148-93; on the pagan cults II 37-41. M-M.*

δεκατέσσαρες s. δέκα. M-M.

δέκατος, η, ον (Hom.+; inscr., pap., LXX, Ep. Arist., Philo, Joseph., Test. 12 Patr.) *tenth*.
   1. as an ordinal number Rv 21: 20; ὅρος Hs 9, 1, 9; 9, 27, 1; hour (prob.=4 p.m.; 3 Macc 5: 14) J 1: 39; Ac 19: 9 D.
   2. as subst.—a. τὸ δ. *a tenth* (*part*) (Appian, Ital. 8 §2; Lucian, Cronosol. 14; Ex 16: 36; Lev 5: 11 al.; Philo, Congr. Erud. Gr. 102) Rv 11: 13.
   b. ἡ δεκάτη *tenth, tithe* (Simonides 106b Diehl; Hdt. 2, 135; 4, 152) of the booty (Maximus Tyr. 24, 5b [for the gods from the spoils of war]) Hb 7: 2, 4 (Gen 14: 20). Of the gift of a tithe prescribed by the Jewish law (LXX; Ps.-Hecataeus in Jos., C. Ap. 1, 188; Philo, Congr. Erud. Gr. 98 al.; Joseph.; cf. on sim. sacred gifts Diod. S. 20, 14, 2; IG XI 1243 [III/II BC]; PHib. 115, 1 [c. 250 BC] μόσχων δεκάτης; PTebt. 307, 8; Ostraka I 348f) pl. (as Lysias 20, 24; 2 Esdr 22 [Neh 12]: 44; 1 Macc 3: 49; 10: 31; 11: 35; Jos., Ant. 14, 203) Hb 7: 8f (δέκ. λαμβάνειν as Diod. S. 5, 42, 1; Ps.-Lucian, Salt. 21). M-M.*

δεκατόω pf. δεδεκάτωκα, pass. δεδεκάτωμαι (2 Esdr 20 [Neh 10]: 38; Dositheus 77, 7; Suidas in conjunction w. Hb 7: 9) *collect, receive tithes* τινά fr. someone Hb 7: 6. Pass. *pay tithes* vs. 9. M-M.*

δεκτός, ή, όν (Alciphr. 3, 34, 4; Iambl., Protr. 21, 19 p. 117, 27 Pistelli; LXX; verbal adj. of δέχομαι) *acceptable, welcome* (Hesychius: δεκτόν· εὐπρόσδεκτον) of prophets Lk 4: 24; LJ 1: 6, only here of human recognition, elsewh. always of acceptance by God: Sabbaths B 15: 8. W. dat. Ac 10: 35; Hs 5, 1, 3; 5. Also παρά τινι (Pr 12: 22; 15: 8, 28) s 2: 7. Sacrifices (w. εὐάρεστος) Phil 4: 18; MPol 14: 1; Hs 5, 3, 8 (cf. Sir 35: 6; Herm. Wr. 13, 21; Dit., Syll.³ 1042, 8f ἀπρόσδεκτος ἡ θυσία παρὰ τ. θεοῦ; fasting B 3: 2 (Is 58: 5). Of time *favorable* 2 Cor 6: 2 (Is 49: 8); year Lk 4: 19; B 14: 9 (both Is 61: 2). M-M.*

δελεάζω *lure* (δέλεαρ bait: Pla., Tim 69D ἡδονὴν μέγιστον κακοῦ δέλεαρ), *entice* (in fig. sense since Isocr. and X.; Jos., Bell. 5, 120) w. ἐξέλκεσθαι Js 1: 14 (cf. M. Ant. 2, 12 τὰ ἡδονῇ δελεάζοντα; Philo, Omn. Prob. Lib. 159 πρὸς ἐπιθυμίας ἐλαύνεται ἢ ὑφ᾽ ἡδονῆς δελεάζεται, Agr. 103.—Cf. schol. on Nicander, Ther. 793

δελεάζοντες τοὺς ἰχθῦς. Since ἐξέλκω is likewise a t.t. of fisherman's speech [e.g., Od. 5, 432], a figurative understanding might be possible: 'drawn out and enticed by his own desire'). Souls 2 Pt 2: 14, 18.*

δένδρον, ου, τό (Hdt.+ [in Hom. δένδρεον]; inscr., pap., LXX, En., Philo, Joseph.) *tree* Mt 3: 10 (ELohmeyer, V. Baum u. Frucht: ZsystTh 9, '32, 377-9); Rv 7: 1, 3; 8: 7; 9: 4. The sound tree and the rotten tree fig. of good and bad people (Paroem. Gr.: Diogenian. 5, 15 ἐκ τ. καρποῦ τὸ δένδρον) Mt 7: 17ff; 12: 33; Lk 6: 43f; IEph 14: 2; δ. ὡραῖον B 11: 10; (εἰς) δ. γίνεσθαι *become a tree* Lk 13: 19; Mt 13: 32. ὡς δένδρα ὁρῶ *like trees* Mk 8: 24 (cf. Dit., Syll.³ 1168, 121). Used by Hermas in various figures s 2: 2; 4: 1ff; 8, 1, 3f al. M-M. B. 49.

δεξιοβόλος (not found elsewh.; but ἀδεξιοβόλος is found in Ps.-Callisth. 1, 24, 10 in ms. A) Ac 23: 23 v.l. (s. δεξιολάβος).*

δεξιολάβος, ου, ὁ Ac 23: 23 (ms. A has δεξιοβόλος), a word of uncertain mng., military t.t., acc. to Joannes Lydus (in Constantinus Porphyrog., De Themat. 1, 5) and Theophyl. Sim., Hist. 4, 1 a light-armed soldier, perh. *bowman* or *slinger*; acc. to a scholion on ChFMatthaei p. 342 *body-guard*. Acc. to EEgli, ZWTh 17, 1884, 20ff δεξιόλαβος *left-handed* (?). *Spearman* Gdspd., RSV.—GDKilpatrick, JTS 14, '63, 393f. W-S. §6, 4; Mlt.-H. 272f. M-M.*

δεξιός, ά, όν (Hom.+; inscr., pap., LXX, Philo, Joseph.) *right* as opposed to left.
   1. used w. a noun χείρ (Hippocr., Epid. 2, 8) Mt 5: 30; Lk 6: 6; Ac 3: 7; Rv 1: 16f; 10: 5 (Dt 32: 40); 13: 16; shoulder Hs 9, 2, 4; eye (Hippocr., Epid. 3, 1, 3 ed. Kühlewein I 218, 19) Mt 5: 29 (the right eye is esp. valuable because its loss is a handicap to the warrior: Jos. Ant. 6, 69-71; here 71 also the thought: it is better to lose the right eye than ἀπολωλέναι in possession of all one's members); cheek vs. 39; D 1: 4; ear (s. on οὖς 1) Lk 22: 50; J 18: 10; foot (Artem. 2, 51; 5, 70) Rv 10: 2. ὅπλα δ. καὶ ἀριστερά *weapons for the right side and the left side* 2 Cor 6: 7 (sword and shield, offense and defense). τὰ δ. μέρη *the right side* (as the lucky side as Artem. 5, 92; Quint. Smyrn. 12, 58) J 21: 6; Hv 3, 1, 9; 3, 2, 1; σύνεσις δ., ἀριστερά *understanding of what is true and what is false* D 12: 1.
   2. abs.—a. ἡ δ. (sc. χείρ) *the right hand* (Hom.+; LXX; Jos., Ant. 17, 184) Mt 6: 3; 27: 29; Rv 1: 17, 20; 2: 1; 5: 1, 7; 1 Cl 28: 3 (Ps 138: 10); B 12: 11 (Is 45: 1). δ. διδόναι *give the right hand* as a sign of friendship and trust (X., An. 1, 6, 6; 2, 5, 3; Diod. S. 13, 43, 4; Appian, Liby. 64 §284; 1 and 2 Macc; Jos., Ant. 18, 326; 328.—Dssm., NB 78f [BS 251]; Nägeli 24) Gal 2: 9 (KGrayston, BRigaux-Festschr., '70, 485: 'came to terms'). ἐπιτιθέναι τὴν δ. ἐπὶ τ. κεφαλήν τινος *lay one's right hand on someone's head* B 13: 5 (Gen 48: 17). ἐν δεξιᾷ *at the right* (Arrian, Anab. 6, 2, 2); ἐν δ. τινος *at someone's right* God's (Ael. Aristid. 37, 6 K.=2 p. 15 D., w. allusion to Pind., calls Athena δεξιὰν κατὰ χεῖρα τοῦ πατρὸς [Zeus] καθεζομένη.—Pind., Nem. 11, 2 names Hera as the ὁμόθρονος of Zeus) Ro 8: 34; Eph 1: 20; Col 3: 1; Hb 10: 12; 1 Pt 3: 22. τῆς μεγαλωσύνης Hb 1: 3; τοῦ θρόνου 8: 1; 12: 2.—The right hand fig. for power (of God: PsSol 13, 1; Jos., Bell. 1, 378) τῇ δεξιᾷ of God (as Is 63: 12) *by* or *with his right hand* (cf. Maximus Tyr. 4, 8a) Ac 2: 33; 5: 31 (BWeiss; Zahn; HHoltzmann; Felten; Beyer; Steinmann; Moffatt Ac 2: 33); it may also be dat. of place (Bl-D. §199; Rob. 526; 543) *at* or *to his right hand* (Weizsäcker;

Wendt; Knopf; Belser; Hoennicke; OHoltzmann; RSV; Moffatt Ac 5: 31).

b. τὰ δ. (sc. μέρη; s. 1 above) *the right side* (X., An. 1, 8, 4). ἐκ δεξιῶν *on the right* (X., Cyr. 8, 5, 15 al.; oft. pap. [Mayser 226]; LXX; Jos., Ant. 4, 305) w. gen. (Tob 1: 2; Zech 4: 3; Sir 12: 12 al.) Mt 25: 33f (cf. Plut., Mor. 192F ἐκέλευσε τοὺς μὲν ἐπὶ δεξιᾷ τοῦ βήματος θεῖναι, τοὺς δ' ἐπ' ἀριστερᾷ ... τ. βελτίονας ... τοὺς χείρονας); Mk 15: 27; Lk 1: 11; Pol 2: 1; abs. (1 Esdr 9: 43; Ex 14: 22, 29; 3 Km 7: 25, 35 al.) Mt 27: 38; Lk 23: 33; B 11: 10; Hv 3, 2, 1f; 4. Also ἐν τοῖς δ. Mk 16: 5 or δεξιά (s. εὐώνυμος, end) Hs 9, 12, 8. καθίσαι ἐκ δ. τινος *sit at someone's right,* i.e., at the place of honor (3 Km 2: 19; Jos., Ant. 8, 7) of the Messiah Mt 20: 21, 23; Mk 10: 37, 40; of God Mt 22: 44 (Ps 109: 1); 26: 64; Mk 12: 36 (Ps 109: 1); 14: 62; 16: 19; Lk 20: 42 (Ps 109: 1); 22: 69; Ac 2: 34; Hb 1: 13; 1 Cl 36: 5; B 12: 10 (the last 4 Ps 109: 1); *stand on the right* as the place of honor (Ps 44: 10) Ac 7: 55f; Hs 9, 6, 2. ἐκ δεξιῶν τινος εἶναι *stand at someone's side* Ac 2: 25 (Ps 15: 8).—AGornatowski, Rechts u. Links im ant. Abergl., Diss. Breslau '36; J Daniélou, TU 73, '59, 689–98. M.-M. B. 865.*

δέομαι pass. dep. 1 aor. ἐδεήθην, imper. δεήθητι, pl. δεήθητε; impf. 3 sg. ἐδεῖτο Lk 8: 38 (Tdf. has the Ion. form ἐδέετο; cf. Bl-D. §89; Helbing 110; Thackeray 243) (in var. mngs. Hdt.+; inscr., pap., LXX) in our lit. only w. the mng. *ask,* which predominates also in LXX and En. (Jos., Vi. 310 al.), w. gen. of the pers.

1. w. inf. foll. (X., Cyr. 1, 5, 4; Herodian 2, 11, 9; Jdth 12: 8; 3 Macc 1: 16; 5: 25) Lk 8: 38; 9: 38; Ac 26: 3.

2. w. acc. of the thing (X., Cyr. 1, 4, 2; Pla., Apol. 17c; 1 Esdr 8: 53 v.l.) δεόμενοι ἡμῶν τὴν χάριν *begging us for the favor* 2 Cor 8: 4. Without gen. of the pers. δέομαι τὸ μὴ παρὼν θαρρῆσαι *I ask that when I am present I need not show boldness* 10: 2.

3. w. direct discourse foll., (*I*) *beg* (*of you*), or even *please* (Gen 19: 18; 44: 18) δέομαί σου, ἐπίτρεψόν μοι *please allow me* Ac 21: 39; 8: 34; Lk 8: 28; Gal 4: 12. W. λέγων added Lk 5: 12. Without gen. of the pers., but w. ὑπὲρ Χριστοῦ (s. ὑπέρ 1aδ) added 2 Cor 5: 20.

4. w. ἵνα foll. (Sir 37: 15; 38: 14; 1 Esdr 4: 46; Jos., Ant. 12, 121) Lk 9: 40; 11: 37 D; B 12: 7; Pol 6: 2; Hv 3, 1, 2; s 5, 4, 1.—Esp. of prayer (w. αἰτεῖσθαι) 1 Cl 50: 2. W. gen. (Epict. 2, 7, 12) τοῦ θεοῦ Ac 10: 2; and εἰ ἄρα foll. 8: 22, ὅπως (cf. Ael. Aristid. 35, 28 K.=9 p. 108 D.; Aesop, Fab. 63 P.=117 H.; ἐδεήθη αὐτῶν ὅπως; Jos., Ant. 9, 9) Mt 9: 38; Lk 10: 2; δ. πρὸς τὸν κύριον (Ps 29: 9; Is 37: 4) w. ὑπέρ τινος and ὅπως foll. Ac 8: 24. W. περί τινος Jdth 8: 31; Sir 21: 1; 28: 4; Da 4: 27; Jos., Ant. 10, 203) Lk 22: 32; B 13: 2 (Gen 25: 21). Without gen. (Tob 3: 11; 3 Macc 1: 24; 2: 10; 5: 7) Ac 4: 31; w. εἰς and inf. foll. 1 Th 3: 10; w. ἵνα foll. Lk 21: 36; δ. ἐπὶ τῶν προσευχῶν *ask in prayer* w. εἴ πως foll. Ro 1: 10. Abs. οἱ δεόμενοι *those who pray* (Lucian, Tim. 5; 8; Wsd 16: 25) 1 Cl 59: 4. M.-M.*

δέον s. δεῖ 6.

δέος, ους, τό (Hom.+; Polemo Soph. 1, 41 p. 14, 21; Epict. 2, 23, 38; Lucian, Necyom. 10, Dial. Deor. 2, 1; 2 Macc; Jos., Ant. 12, 246; 16, 235) *fear, awe* (w. εὐλάβεια) Hb 12: 28.—1 Cl 2: 4 v.l. (Lghtf.) for ἔλεος. M.-M. B. 1153.*

δεπόσιτα, ων, τά *deposits,* Lat. loanw. 'deposita'; military t.t. When gifts of money were given the army on special occasions, the individual soldier received only half of what was due him; the rest was deposited to his credit in the regimental treasury (Lat. apud signa), and he received it (as ἄκκεπτα, q.v.) if and when he was honorably discharged (Sueton., Domit. 7; Vegetius, De Re Milit. 2, 20; PFay. 105 [c. 180 AD]; Geneva Lat. pap. in JNicole and ChMorel, Archives militaires du 1ᵉʳ siècle 1900, and the lit. on it, e.g. Mommsen, Her 35, '00, 443ff; HBlümner NJklA 5, '00, 432ff; AvPremerstein, Klio 3, '03, 1ff; here a ref. to an unedited Berlin pap. no. 6866 of c. 180 AD and further lit.) IPol 6: 2.*

Δερβαῖος, α, ον *from Derbe* (q.v.), ὁ Δ. (Stephan. Byz. s.v. Ἄβαι) of Gaius Ac 20: 4. The difficulty caused by the fact that a certain Gaius is called a Macedonian 19: 29 is prob. the reason for the v.l. Δουβ[ή]ριος in D (of a Maced. city); K and SLake, JBL 53, '34, 44f.*

Δέρβη, ης, ἡ *Derbe,* a city in Lycaonia, in the Roman province of Galatia (Strabo 12, 6, 3; Ptolemaeus 5, 6, 71) Ac 14: 6, 20; 16: 1.—JWeiss, RE X 560, 43ff; WMRamsay, The Cities of St. Paul '07. Cf. EHaenchen, AG '56 p. 46 note. Definitely located at Kerti Hüyük: IDB '62 s.v. Derbe; GOgg, NTS 9, '63, 367–70.*

δέρμα, ατος, τό (Hom.+; inscr., pap., LXX, Philo; Jos., Ant. 1, 270) *skin* αἴγειον *goatskin* (Zen.-P. 11, 8=Sb 6717 [257 BC]; PFay. 107, 2 δέρματα αἴγεια) Hb 11: 37; 1 Cl 17: 1; δ. αἴ. λευκόν Hv 5: 1; s 6, 2, 5. M.-M. B. 200.*

δερμάτινος, η, ον (Hom.+; Dit., Syll.³ 736, 23; PTebt. 112; BGU 814, 10; LXX; Philo) (*made of*) *leather* ζώνη *belt* (4 Km 1: 8; Jos., Ant. 9, 22) Mt 3: 4; Mk 1: 6; GEb 2. M.-M. B. 407.*

δέρρις, εως, ἡ (Thu. 2, 75, 5 al.; Dit., Syll.³ 736, 55 [92 BC]; Sb 6801, 26 [246/5 BC; Zen.-P.]; LXX, esp. Zech 13: 4) *skin,* of John the Baptist ἐν δεδυμένος δέρριν καμήλου (δ. as clothing: Eupolis Com. [V BC] 328) Mk 1: 6 D (cf. a: pellem). EbNestle⁴-EvDobschütz, Einführung in d. Griech. NT '23, 7.*

δέρω 1 aor. ἔδειρα; (2 aor. pass. ἐδάρην); 2 fut. pass. δαρήσομαι (Hom.+; LXX) lit. 'flay, skin'; in our lit. only fig. *beat* (so since Aristoph., Ran. 618; Epict. 3, 19, 5; 3, 22, 54f al.; Dit., Syll.³ 1109, 91; POxy. 653 (b); not LXX) τινά Mt 21: 35; Mk 12: 3, 5; Lk 20: 10f; 22: 63; J 18: 23; Ac 5: 40; 16: 37; 22: 19. Pass. Mk 13: 9 (FWDanker, NovT 10, '68, 162f). τινὰ εἰς πρόσωπον *strike someone in the face* 2 Cor 11: 20. δαρήσεται πολλάς, ὀλίγας (Aristoph., Nub. 968 τυπτόμενος πολλάς, to which a scholiast adds πληγὰς δηλονότι. X., An. 5, 8, 12 ὀλίγας παίειν; s. πληγή 1) *he will receive many, few blows* Lk 12: 47f; ἀέρα δ. *beat the air* of unskilful boxers, who miss their mark 1 Cor 9: 26 (schol. on Lucian, p. 93, 16 Rabe πύκται . . . μὴ . . . πρὸς ἀέρα δέρειν).— Abs. δέρεσθαι καὶ νικᾶν *stand punishment and yet win* IPol 3: 1.—S. also δαίρω. M.-M. B. 553; 567.*

δεσέρτωρ, ορος, ὁ (Lat., loanw. desertor, also in Basilius Magn., Ep. 258; Migne, S. Gr. 32, 997c) *deserter,* military term IPol 6: 2.*

δεσμεύω impf. pass ἐδεσμευόμην—**a.** *bind* (Eur.; X.; Pla., Leg. 7 p. 808D; Epict. 4, 1, 127; PGM 4, 1246: 5, 320; Judg 16: 11 B; cf. 3 Macc 5: 5; Jos., Ant. 14, 348) τινά Lk 8: 29 (cf. Third Corinthians 3: 11); Ac 22: 4.

2. *tie up* in a bundle (Hes.; Polyb.; PLond. 131 recto, 426; 437; PFlor. 322, 31; Gen 37: 7; Jdth 8: 3; Am 2: 8) φορτίον *tie up a burden, load* Mt 23: 4 (Cicero, Tusc. Disp. II, 4, 11). M.-M.*

δεσμέω (Aristot., De Plant. 1, 2 p. 817b, 21; Heliod. 8, 9; Jos., Bell. 1, 71 al.) Lk 8: 29 t.r. for δεσμεύω, q.v.*

δέσμη (Lobeck, Paralipomena Gramm. Graec. 1837, 396, or δεσμή as the gramm. Herodian I 324, 10; II 426, 6 [Lentz] would accent it) ης, ἡ bundle (since Demosth. and Theophr., Hist. Pl. 9, 17, 1; Diod. S. 19, 99, 2 δέσμη καλάμων; Dionys. Hal. 3, 61, 2; pap. [Mayser 285; 435]; Ex 12: 22) δῆσαι εἰς δέσμας tie up in bundles Mt 13: 30. M-M.*

δέσμιος, ου, ὁ prisoner (so trag.; Polyb. 15, 33, 6; 33, 10, 3; Diod. S. 18, 66, 3; PTebt. 22, 18 [112 BC]; POxy. 580; PGM 4, 187; LXX; Jos., Ant. 13, 203; 17, 145.—Nägeli 26) Mt 27: 15f; Mk 15: 6. Of Christians and others in prison Ac 16: 25, 27; 23: 18; 25: 14, 27; 28: 16 v.l., 17; Hb 10: 34; 13: 3; 1 Cl 59: 4. Paul calls himself δ. (τοῦ) Χριστοῦ Ἰησοῦ Phlm 1, 9; Eph 3: 1; cf. 2 Ti 1: 8. Also δ. ἐν κυρίῳ Eph 4: 1. S. on this Rtzst., Mysterienrel.³ 196ff; 214; UWilcken, UPZ I 52–77. M-M.*

δεσμός, οῦ, ὁ (pl. δεσμά [Diod. S. 14, 103, 3; Nicander, Ther. 317; 728; Jos., Bell. 4, 143, Ant. 2, 60; only late in pap. (Mayser 285); PGM 36, 143; 57, 5] Lk 8: 29; Ac 16: 26; 20: 23; 1 Cl 5: 6; 55: 2; IEph 11: 2; ITr 12: 2; ISm 10: 2; IPol. 2: 3; δεσμοί [Nicander, Ther. 479; Polyaenus 2, 31, 3; Dit., Syll.² 588, 6] Phil 1: 13. Both forms also in Attic inscr. [Meisterhans³-Schw. 143, 3] and LXX [Thackeray 154]; Philo [Somn. 1, 181 -ά, Sacr. Abel. 81 -οί].—Bl-D. §49, 3 w. app.; W-S. §8, 12; Crönert 175, 3; Reinhold 54; Mlt.-H. 121f) bond, fetter (Hom.+).
1. lit., of the bond or hindrance which prevents mutes Mk 7: 35 or crippled persons Lk 13: 16 from using their members (s. Dssm., LO 258ff [LAE 306ff], and cf. Dit., Syll.³ 1169, 43). Pl. bonds, fetters Lk 8: 29; Ac 16: 26; 20: 23; 22: 30 t.r.; 23: 29; 26: 29, 31; Jd 6; δ. φορεῖν be in bonds (= δεσμοφορέω) 1 Cl 5: 6; παραδιδόναι εἰς δ. give over to bondage 55: 2; τὰ δ. περιφέρειν IEph 11: 2; cf. IMg 1: 2. πεῖραν λαμβάνειν δεσμῶν (cf. Vett. Val. 68, 17 δεσμῶν πεῖραν λαμβάνοντες) become acquainted w. bonds Hb 11: 36. On B 14: 7 (Is 42: 7) cf. πεδάω.—Oft. simply imprisonment, prison (Diod. S. 14, 103, 3; Lucian, Tox. 29; Jos., Ant. 13, 294; 302, Vi. 241) Phil 1: 7, 13f; 17; Col 4: 18; Phlm 10. μέχρι δεσμῶν 2 Ti 2: 9. ἐν τοῖς δ. τοῦ εὐαγγελίου in imprisonment for the gospel Phlm 13; cf. ISm 11: 1; Pol 1: 1.
2. fig. (Timagenes [I BC] in Jos., Ant. 13, 319; Herm. Wr. 7, 2b φθορᾶς δ.; Ep. Arist. 265 εὐνοίας δ.) IPhld 8: 1; 2 Cl 20: 4; δ. τῆς ἀγάπης bond of the love 1 Cl 49: 2 (Theodor. Prodr. 5, 245 H.; τὰ δεσμὰ τῆς ἀγάπης). δ. κακίας IEph 19: 3. M-M.*

δεσμοφύλαξ, ακος, ὁ (Lucian, Tox. 30; Artem. 3, 60; Vett. Val. 68, 26; Cass. Dio 76, 10, 3; pap. since III BC [Mayser 467], also BGU 1138, 12ff; Jos., Ant. 2, 61; ἀρχιδεσμοφύλαξ Gen 39: 21–3; 41: 10 v.l.) jailer, keeper of the prison Ac 16: 23, 27, 36. M-M.*

δεσμωτήριον, ου, τό (Hdt., Thu.+; PLille 7, 14; BGU 1024 IV, 10; 29; LXX; En.; Philo; Jos., Bell. 4, 385, C. Ap. 2, 247) prison, jail Mt 11: 2; Ac 5: 21, 23; 16: 26; παραδοθῆναι εἰς δ. be thrown into prison Hs 9, 28, 7. M-M.*

δεσμώτης, ου, ὁ (Aeschyl., Hdt.+; PPetr. II 13(3), 9; LXX; Jos., Ant. 2, 61; 18, 193; Sib. Or. 11, 29) prisoner Ac 27: 1, 42. M-M.*

δεσπόζω (Hom. Hymns, Hdt.+; Polyb.; Lucian; Philostrat.; pap., cf. Mayser 33; Herm. Wr. p. 476, 33 Sc.; LXX; Philo, Op. M. 148; Jos., Bell. 4, 575, Ant. 2, 52 al.) be lord or master τινός of someth. (Lucian, Catapl. 2; Ps.-Callisth. 3, 33, 19 τῷ πάντων δεσπόζοντι μεγάλῳ

Σεράπιδι; Philostrat., Vi. Apoll. 1, 13 p. 13, 14) τῆς κτίσεως πάσης of all creation Hv 3, 4, 1.*

δεσπότης, ου, ὁ voc. δέσποτα (since Sappho 97, 8 D., Pind., Hdt.; inscr., pap., LXX) lord, master, owner of a vessel 2 Ti 2: 21; of honey Hm 5, 1, 5; of slaves (Pla., Parm. 133D, Leg. 757A al.; Paroem. Gr.: Zenob. [Hadrian] 2, 81 τ. ἰδίους δεσπότας) 1 Ti 6: 1f; Tit 2: 9; Phlm subsc.; 1 Pt 2: 18; Hs 5, 2, 2; a city Hs 1: 6.—Esp. of God (Eur., Hipp. 88; X., An. 3, 2, 13; Pla., Euthyd. 302D and oft. in Gk. writers. e.g. Herm. Wr. 11, 1c; 1b; Dit., Or. 619, 3; UPZ 1, 1 [IV BC]; PGM 36, 227 δέσποτα; LXX; Artapanus in Euseb., Pr. Ev. 9, 27, 22; Ezek. Trag. ibid. 9, 29, 11; Philo, Rer. Div. Her. 22ff [PKatz, Philo's Bible, '50, 59f]; Jos., Bell. 7, 323, Ant. 8, 111; 18, 23) Lk 2: 29; Ac 4: 24; Rv 6: 10; 1 Cl 7: 5; 9: 4; 11: 1; 24: 1, 5; 36: 2, 4; 40: 1 al.; B 1: 7; 4: 3; Dg 8: 7; Hv 2, 2, 4f; s 1: 9; δ. ἁπάντων (cf. Job 5: 8; Wsd. 6: 7; 8: 3; Sir 36: 1; Test. Jos. 1: 5; Herm. Wr. 5, 4; PGM 3, 590; 4, 1162; 12, 250; Jos., Ant. 1, 72 δ. τῶν ὅλων) 1 Cl 8: 2; 20: 11; 33: 2; 52: 1. Of Christ Lk 13: 25 𝔓⁷⁵; 2 Pt 2: 1; Jd 4 (δεσπ. and κύριος as Jos., Ant. 20, 90).—KHRengstorf, TW II 43–8 (lit.). M-M. B. 1330.**

δεῦρο adv. (Hom.+; inscr., pap., LXX; Jos., Ant. 1, 281; 290).
1. of place come, come here w. imper. foll. (Hom.+; Lucian, Catapl. 24 δεῦρο προσίτω; Gen 24: 31; 2 Km 13: 11; 3 Km 1: 13 al.) δ. ἀκολούθει μοι come! follow me Mt 19: 21; Mk 10: 21; Lk 18: 22. Foll. by 1 pers. aor. subj. (Eur., Bacch. 341; Gen 31: 44; 37: 13; 4 Km 14: 8 al. Cf. Bl-D. §364, 1; Rob. 931f): Ac 7: 34 (Ex 3: 10); Rv 17: 1; 21: 9.—Abs. (Pla., Theaet. 144D: Θεαίτητε, δεῦρο παρὰ Σωκράτη) δεῦρο εἰς τ. γῆν come into the country Ac 7: 3 (Gen 12: 1 v.l., influenced by Ac 7: 3 [ARahlfs, Genesis '26], cf. MWilcox, The Semitisms of Ac, '65, 26f; also 3 Km 1: 53; 1 Macc 12: 45). δεῦρο also stands for come (s. the variants δεῦρο B and ἐλθέ A in Judg 18: 19 and cf. Num 10: 29; 1 Km 17: 44; 4 Km 10: 16; Od. 8, 292; Theognis 1, 1041; Hipponax [VI BC] 4 Diehl²; Pla., Rep. 5, p. 477D; Charito 3, 7, 4 Χαιρέα, δεῦρο; Aristaen., Ep. 2, 7 p. 163 H.; PGM 12, 238 δεῦρό μοι; 13, 268) in δεῦρο ἔξω come out (Menand., Epitr. 520 J.) J 11: 43; δ. πρὸς τὸν πατέρα IRo 7: 2.
2. of time until now (μέχρι τοῦ δεῦρο: Thu. 3, 64, 3; Dit., Syll.³ 821E, 2; 3; PLond. 358, 16; PStrassb. 56, 12; 73, 16; Jos., Ant. 11, 93) ἄχρι τοῦ δ. thus far Ro 1: 13 (Sext. Emp., Math. 8, 401 ἄχρι δ.; PLond. 409, 26 ἄχρεις δεῦρο). M-M.*

δεῦτε adv. (serves as pl. of δεῦρο) come! come on! mostly as hortatory particle w. pl. (Hom.+; Sb 7247, 29; LXX).
1. w. imper. or aor. subj. foll. (imper.: Josh 10: 4; 4 Km 6: 13; Ps 65: 16 and oft.; Jos., Ant. 6, 111; aor. subj.: Gen 11: 3f; 37: 27; Ps 94: 6 al.; En. 6, 2) δ. ἴδετε Mt 28: 6; J 4: 29; δ. ἀριστήσατε come! eat 21: 12; δ. συνάχθητε come! gather Rv 19: 17; δ. ἀκούσατε 1 Cl 22: 1 (Ps 33: 12); δ. ἀποκτείνωμεν αὐτόν come on, let us kill him Mt 21: 38; Mk 12: 7; Lk 20: 14 t.r.; δ. καὶ διελεγχθῶμεν come and let us reason together 1 Cl 8: 4 (Is 1: 18).
2. abs. (Aesop, Fab. 353 H.; LXX) w. ὀπίσω τινός: δ. ὀπίσω μου follow me (4 Km 6: 19) Mt 4: 19; Mk 1: 17. W. εἰς τι: come to the wedding Mt 22: 4; come to a lonely place Mk 6: 31. W. πρός τινα: δ. πρός με come to me Mt 11: 28 (AFridrichsen, E. Unbeachtete Parallele [Epict. 4, 8, 28] in Wikenhauser-Festschr., '53, 83–85); δ. οἱ εὐλογημένοι τοῦ πατρός μου come, you whom my Father has blessed 25: 34. M-M. s.v. δεῦρο.*

δευτεραῖος, αία, ον (Hdt.; X., Cyr. 5, 2, 2; Diod. S. 13, 39, 1; Jos., Ant. 1, 178; Dit., Syll.³ 982, 6f; Zen.-P. 59 736, 39 [III BC]) *on the second day* δευτεραῖοι ἤλθομεν *we came on the second day* Ac 28: 13 (Bl-D. §243; Rob. 298).*

Δευτερονόμιον, ου, τό *Deuteronomy* title in the LXX for the last book of the Pentateuch B 10: 2.—Ramsay, ET 26, '15, 170, where the word is quoted from a Phrygian gravestone 248/9 AD. M-M.*

δευτερόπρωτος, ον a word of doubtful mng., only in the phrase ἐν σαββάτῳ δ. Lk 6: 1 (acc. to mss. ACD), where more recent editions (except Tdf.), following most mss., omit the word or put it in brackets (vSoden). Even many ancient interpreters, understandably, could make nothing of it (Hieron. [Jerome], Ep. 52, 8, 2), and it may owe its origin solely to a scribal error. It might correspond (but cf. M-M.) to δευτερέσχατος (= next to the last) and mean *first but one* (cf. Epiphan., Haer. 30, 32; 51, 31 δευτερό-πρωτον = δεύτερον σάββατον μετὰ τὸ πρῶτον; Eustratius, Life of Eutychius [Migne, S. Gr. 86, 2381] ἡ δευτερο-πρώτη κυριακή = the first Sunday after Easter Sunday), reckoned from Passover.—CTrossen, ThGl 6, '14, 466–75, esp. 470f; HHMeulenbelt, Lk 6: 1: NThSt 5, '22, 140–2; ASchlatter, D. Ev. des Lk '31, 67f; Gdspd., Probs. 83–5; JMBover, Estudios Ecclesiasticos 7, '28, 97–106; J-P Audet, Jésus et le 'Calendrier sacerdotal ancien', Sciences Ecclésiastiques (Montreal) 10, '58, 361–83. M-M.*

δεύτερος, α, ον (Hom.+; inscr., pap., LXX, Joseph., Test. 12 Patr.) *second.*
1. purely numerical Mt 22: 26; J 4: 54 (a similar close in Appian, Bell. Civ. 1, 33 §150 τρίτον τόδε ἔργον ἦν); D 2: 1.—2. of that which follows in time: Hb 8: 7; 10: 9; Rv 2: 11; 11: 14; 20: 14; 21: 8; 2 Cor 1: 15; Tit 3: 10; ὥρα δ. Hs 9, 11, 7 (cf. Jos., Vi. 220); φυλακὴ δ. *second watch in the night* (Arrian, Anab. 6, 25, 5; Jos., Bell. 5, 510) Lk 12: 38. δευτέρα (sc. ἡμέρα) *on the second* (day of the month) MPol 21.
3. of a series: Mt 22: 39; Mk 12: 31; Lk 19: 18; 1 Cor 15: 47; 2 Pt 3: 1; Rv 4: 7; 6: 3; 16: 3; 21: 19. δευτέρα (sc. ἐπιστολή) in the subscr. of 2 Th and 2 Ti.
4. of place: the second sentinel's post Ac 12: 10; the second curtain Hb 9: 3; cf. vs. 7.—Neut. δεύτερον, τὸ δεύτερον used as adv. *for the second time* (class.; Appian to Fronto [I p. 537f Viereck-R.] §6; Dit., Or. 82, 5 [III BC]; Gen 22: 15; Jer 40: 1; Jos., Bell. 1, 25, Vi. 389) δ. εἰσελθεῖν J 3: 4; παρὼν τὸ δ. 2 Cor 13: 2; τὸ δ. ἀπώλεσεν *the second time he destroyed* Jd 5; δ. εἴρηκαν *they said for the second time* Rv 19: 3. Also ἐκ δευτέρου (Diosc. 5, 41; PTebt. 297, 19; PHolm. 1, 32; Jon 3: 1; Jer 1: 13; 1 Macc 9: 1; Jos., Ant. 6, 94) Mk 14: 72; J 9: 24; Ac 11: 9; Hb 9: 28; 2 Ti subscr.; making πάλιν more definite (Heraclit. Sto. 32 p. 48, 8 ἐκ δευτέρου πάλιν) Mt 26: 42; Ac 10: 15; also πάλιν δεύτερον (cf. Herodas 5, 47) J 21: 16; ἐν τῷ δ. *the second time* Ac 7: 13. In enumerations *secondly* (PTebt. 56, 10 [II BC] εὐχαριστῆσαι πρῶτον μὲν τοῖς θεοῖς δεύτερον δὲ σῶσαι ψυχάς; Sir 23: 23; 2 Macc 14: 8) 1 Cor 12: 28; D 1: 2; Hm 10, 3, 2. M-M.

δέχομαι 1 aor. ἐδεξάμην, pass. ἐδέχθην; pf. δέδεγμαι (Hom.+; inscr., pap., LXX, Philo, Joseph., Test. 12 Patr.; Sib. Or. 3, 351).
1. *take, receive* lit. τινά *someone* 1 Cl 28: 2; 54: 3; IEph 6: 1; IPhld 11: 1. εἰς τὰς ἀγκάλας *take someone up in one's arms* Lk 2: 28; one's spirit Ac 7: 59. Of letters *receive* (Procop. Soph., Ep. 20; PFlor. 154, 2) 22: 5; cf. 28: 21 (Jos., Ant. 13, 259). λόγια Ac 7: 38. εὐαγγέλιον 2 Cor 11:

4. τὰ παρ' ὑμῶν *the things*, i.e. *gifts, from you* Phil 4 : 18. Esp. of hospitality τινὰ εἰς τ. οἶκον *receive someone into one's house* Lk 16: 4, cf. vs. 9 (Epict. 3, 26, 25; X., An. 5, 5, 20). Gener. *receive* as a guest, *welcome* Mt 10: 14, 40f; Mk 6: 11; Lk 9: 5, 11 t.r., 53; 10: 8, 10; J 4: 45; Col 4: 10; Hb 11: 31; D 11: 1f, 4; 12: 1. τὰ μιμήματα τῆς ἀληθοῦς ἀγάπης Pol 1: 1. Of receiving children Mt 18: 5; Mk 9: 37; Lk 9: 48. W. adv. ἀσμένως *receive gladly* (Aelian, V. H. 12, 18; Herodian 7, 5, 2; Jos., Ant. 12, 382; cf. 18, 101) Ac 21: 17 t.r. μετὰ φόβου καὶ τρόμου *with fear and trembling* 2 Cor 7: 15; *as an angel of God* Gal 4: 14. τινὰ εἰς ὄνομά τινος IRo 9: 3 (s. ὄνομα I 4cβ). ὃν δεῖ οὐρανὸν (subj.) δέξασθαι *whom the heaven must receive* Ac 3: 21 (cf. Pla., Theaet. 177A τελευτήσαντας αὐτοὺς ὁ τῶν κακῶν καθαρὸς τόπος οὐ δέξεται).
2. *take in hand, grasp* lit. τί someth. (2 Ch 29: 22) τὰ γράμματα *the note* Lk 16: 6f; a cup 22: 17; a helmet Eph 6: 17.
3. *put up with, tolerate* someone or someth. (Gen 50: 17; Jdth 11: 5; Sir 2: 4).
a. of pers. ὡς ἄφρονα 2 Cor 11: 16.
b. of things *approve, accept* (Appian, Bell. Civ. 5, 66 §277) Mt 11: 14. τὰ τοῦ πνεύματος *what comes fr. the Spirit* 1 Cor 2: 14 (Herm. Wr. 4, 4 τ. νοῦν); τὴν παράκλησιν *request, appeal* 2 Cor 8: 17 (of a request also Chio, Ep. 8); love for the truth 2 Th 2: 10; τὸν λόγον (since Eur. and Thu. 4, 16, 1; Polyb. 1, 43, 4; Diod. S. 4, 52, 1; Pr 4: 10; Zech 1: 6; Jos., Ant. 18, 101) *teaching* Lk 8: 13; Ac 8: 14; 11: 1; 13: 48 D; 17: 11; 1 Th 1: 6; 2: 13; Js 1: 21; the Kgdm. of God Mk 10: 15; Lk 18: 17; grace, favor (Plut., Themist. 28, 3 δέξασθαι χάριν) 2 Cor 6: 1; δ. συμβουλήν *accept advice* 1 Cl 58: 2. M-M.*

δέω 1 aor. ἔδησα, subj. δήσω; pf. ptc. δεδεκώς Ac 22: 29; pf. pass. δέδεμαι; 1 aor. pass. inf. δεθῆναι 21: 33 (Hom.+; inscr., pap., LXX, En., Philo; Jos., Bell. 1, 71, Ant. 13, 320 al.).
1. *bind, tie*—a. τὶ someth. 1 Cl 43: 2; τὶ εἴς τι (Ezk 37: 17): tie weeds in bundles Mt 13: 30. τί τινι (cf. Ezk 27: 24): τοὺς πόδας κειρίαις J 11: 44. ἔδησαν (τὸ σῶμα) ὀθονίοις μετὰ τῶν ἀρωμάτων *they bound (the corpse) in linen cloths with spices* 19: 40.
b. of actual binding and imprisonment δ. τινὰ ἀλύσεσι (cf. Lucian, Necyom. 11; Wsd. 17: 16) *bind someone w. chains* of a demoniac Mk 5: 3f; of prisoners Ac 12: 6; 21: 33. Also simply δ. τινά (Judg 16: 5, 7f) Mt 12: 29 (cf. Test. Levi 18, 12); 14: 3; 27: 2; Mk 3: 27; 15: 1; J 18: 12; Ac 9: 14; 21: 13; 22: 29; B 6: 7 (Is 3: 10). (τοὺς) πόδας καὶ (τὰς) χεῖρας *bind hand and foot* (the acc. as Jos., Ant. 19, 294) Mt 22: 13; Ac 21: 11; δ. τινὰ ἐν φυλακῇ *bind someone (and put him) in prison* (4 Km 17: 4) Mk 6: 17. Pass. (Biogr. p. 238) δέδεμαι *be bound*, i.e., *a prisoner* 15: 7. κατέλιπε δεδεμένον *leave behind as a prisoner* Ac 24: 27 (δεδεμένος = in prison, as Diog. L. 2, 24 of Socrates); ἀπέστειλεν δ. J 18: 24. Cf. Col 4: 3; IEph 1: 2 al. in Ignatius. δέδεμαι ἐν τῷ ὀνόματι *be a prisoner because of the name* (= being a Christian) IEph 3: 1. Also δ. ἐν Ἰησοῦ Χριστῷ ITr 1: 1; IRo 1: 1. δεδεμένον ἄγειν τινὰ *bring someone as prisoner* (Jos., Bell. 7, 449) Ac 9: 2, 21; 22: 5; cf. IRo 4: 3. Pass. δ. ἀπάγεσθαι IEph 21: 2; δ. θεοπρεπεστάτοις δεσμοῖς *bound w. chains that are radiant w. divine splendor* ISm 11: 1; δ. ἢ λελυμένος *a prisoner or one (recently) freed* 6: 2.—Fig. ὁ λόγος τ. θεοῦ οὐ δέδεται *God's message cannot be imprisoned* (though the preacher can) 2 Ti 2: 9.—A metaphorical use explains the expr. ἣν ἔδησεν ὁ σατανᾶς *whom Satan had bound* of a deformed woman Lk 13: 16 (cf. Dit., Syll.³ 1175, 14ff; 32ff Ἀριστὼ ἐγὼ ἔλαβον καὶ ἔδησα τὰς χεῖρας καὶ

τοὺς πόδας καὶ τὴν γλῶσσαν καὶ τὴν ψυχήν). For another supernatural binding cf. δεδεμένος τῷ πνεύματι *bound by the Spirit* Ac 20: 22 (similar fig. usage, perh., in Apollon. Rhod. 4, 880 ἀμηχανίη δῆσεν φρένας=perplexity bound his mind).—On the binding of the dragon Rv 20: 2 cf. JKroll, Gott u. Hölle '32, esp. 316ff; Tob 8: 3; Test. Levi 18: 12.

2. *tie* to someth.: an animal (4 Km 7: 10) Mt 21: 2; Mk 11: 2, 4 (πρὸς θύραν); Lk 19: 30; angels Rv 9: 14. δ. δέκα λεοπάρδοις *tied to ten leopards* (on the language: Soph., Aj. 240 κίονι δήσας=πρὸς κίονα 108; on the content: Jos., Ant. 18, 196) IRo 5: 1.—*Fasten* a linen cloth at its four corners Ac 10: 11 t.r.

3. of binding by law and duty, w. dat. of the pers. *to someone*: of a wife to her husband Ro 7: 2; of a husband to his wife 1 Cor 7: 27 (for the form cf. Posidippus [III BC]: Anth. Pal. 9, 359, 5 ἔχεις γάμον; οὐκ ἀμέριμνος ἔσσεαι· οὐ γαμέεις; ζῇς ἔτ' ἐρημότερος). Abs. vs. 39 (cf. Achilles Tat. 1, 11, 2 v.l. ἄλλῃ δέδεμαι παρθένῳ; Iambl., Vi. Pyth. 11, 56 (τὴν μὲν ἄγαμον . . . τὴν δὲ πρὸς ἄνδρα δεδεμένην); τοῖς λαϊκοῖς προστάγμασιν *be bound by the rules for the laity* 1 Cl 40: 5.

4. The combination δ. καὶ λύειν (Ael. Aristid. 40, 7 K.=5 p. 55 D. of Prometheus: ὅσα δήσειεν ὁ Ζεύς, ταῦτ' ἐξὸν Ἡρακλεῖ λῦσαι; 41, 7 K.; Teleclides Com. [V BC] fgm. 42 K. δέω—ἀναλύω) is found Mt 16: 19; 18: 18. On the meaning δέω has here cf. J 20: 22f (cf. IQH 13, 10). Another interpretation starts fr. the Jewish viewpoint. Aram. אֲסַר and שְׁרָא are academic language for the decision of the rabbis as to what was to be regarded as 'bound' (אֲסִיר), i.e. forbidden, or 'loosed' (שְׁרֵי) i.e. permitted; cf. Dalman, Worte 175ff; Billerb. I 738-47. Binding and loosing in magical practice are emphasized by WKöhler, ARW 8, '05, 236ff; ADell, ZNW 15, '14, 38ff. Cf. also VBrander, Der Katholik 94, '14, 116ff; KAdam, Gesammelte Aufsätze '36, 17-52; JRMantey, JBL 58, '39, 243-9; HJCadbury, ibid. 251-4 (both on J 20: 23; Mt 16: 19; 18: 18). M-M. B. 545. **

δή (Hom.+; pap., LXX) particle; never stands first in its clause.

1. denoting that a statement is definitely established *indeed* B 6: 11. ὃς δὴ καρποφορεῖ *who indeed bears fruit* Mt 13: 23 (relat. w. δή as Ep. Arist. 4; 125; Jos., Ant. 17, 19). Cf. Eur. Alc. 233 for deictic force.

2. w. exhortations or commands, to give them greater urgency, *now, then, therefore* (En. 104, 2; Jos., Vi. 209) διέλθωμεν δή *now let us go* Lk 2: 15. δοξάσατε δὴ τὸν θεόν *therefore glorify God* 1 Cor 6: 20. σύνετε δή *understand then* 1 Cl 35: 11. ἄγε δή *come then* (Lucian, Pisc. 21) Dg 2: 1. ἐπιστρέψαντες δὴ ἐπισκεψώμεθα Ac 15: 36; 6: 3 v.l.; 13: 2.—D 1: 6; Dg 1: 1 Funk.

3. w. expr. denoting time ἐκ γὰρ δὴ πολλῶν χρόνων *for (already) many years ago* 1 Cl 42: 5. M-M.*

δηλαδή (trag.+) adv. *clearly, plainly* Papias 4.*

δηλαυγῶς adv. lit. *shining clearly*, then *quite clearly* (Hesychius: δηλαυγῶς· ἄγαν φανερῶς; Democr. [JA Fabricius, Biblioth. Gr. IV p. 333] δηλαυγέσι τεκμηρίοις; PGM 4, 775; 1033; see on this WCrönert, Stud. z. Paläogr. u. Papyruskunde 4, '05, 101) Mk 8: 25 v.l. (s. τηλαυγῶς). The adv. of the comp. δηλαυγέστερον Hs 6, 5, 1 acc. to a Pap. Cod. . . . of Hermas ed. CBonner '34, p. 73 (s. τηλαυγής). M-M.*

δηλονότι=δῆλον ὅτι IEph 6: 1 v.l. Funk.*

δῆλος, η, ον (Hom.+; pap., LXX, Philo, Joseph.) *clear, plain, evident* δ. τινα ποιεῖν *reveal someone* Mt 26: 73

(v.l. ὁμοιάζει); δ. εἶναι ἔν τινι *reveal itself in someth.* 2 Cl 12: 4.—δῆλον (sc. ἐστίν) w. ὅτι foll. *it is clear that* (Herm. Wr. 11, 11; Philo, Aet. M. 75; 129 [w. ἐστί 93]) 1 Cor 15: 27; Gal 3: 11; 1 Ti 6: 7 t.r.; IEph 6: 1 (cf. Thu. 3, 38, 2; X., An. 1, 3, 9; Hero Alex. III p. 314, 11; POxy. 1101, 12; PFlor. 36, 28; 4 Macc 2: 7; Philo, Op. M. 25; Jos., C. Ap. 1, 277; 2, 13). Cf. 2 Cl 14: 2 v.l. Funk. M-M. B. 1233.*

δηλόω fut. δηλώσω; 1 aor. ἐδήλωσα, imper. δήλωσον; 1 aor. pass. ἐδηλώθην; pf. δεδήλωμαι (Aeschyl., Hdt.+; pap., LXX, En.; Aristobulus in Euseb., Pr. Ev. 13, 12, 12; Ep. Arist.; Philo, Aet. M. 3; 150; Jos., C. Ap. 1, 286 al.; Test. 12 Patr.) *reveal, make clear, show* τὶ *someth.* Secrets 1 Cl 18: 6 (Ps 50: 8); future things (Polyaenus 5, 12, 1 νίκην οἱ θεοὶ δηλοῦσιν ἡμῖν; Sib. Or. 3, 819) 1 Cor 3: 13; PK 3 p. 15, 21; cf. Hv 3, 12, 3 (PGM 13, 614 δῆλόν μοι πάντα, addressed to an angel). Preceded by a ὅτι-clause and w. ὡς λέγει foll. Lk 20: 37 D. τινί 2 Pt 1: 14. τινί τι: *explain a parable* Hs 5, 4, 1; pass. 5, 4, 2; 5. σοι δηλώσω *I will explain to you* m 4, 3, 3; *indicate* τινά *someone* B 9: 8; τὶ *someth.* τὸ ἔτι ἅπαξ δηλοῖ τὴν μετάθεσιν *the phrase 'once again' indicates the removal* Hb 12: 27. ἡμέρα καὶ νὺξ ἀνάστασιν ἡμῖν δηλοῦσιν *day and night point out a resurrection to us* 1 Cl 24: 3. Also εἴς τι 1 Pt 1: 11; *give information* τινὶ περί τινος w. ὅτι foll. 1 Cor 1: 11 (cf. PGrenf. II 73, 18). τινί B 17: 1. τινί τι *to someone about someth.* (Jos., C. Ap. 1, 101) Col 1: 8; Hs 6, 4, 1; 3. W. acc. and inf. foll. Hb 9: 8; *notify* w. acc. and ptc. foll. (Lucian, Dial. Deor. 7, 1) οἷς δηλώσατε ἐγγύς με ὄντα *notify them that I am nearby* IRo 10: 2; *report* (Diod. S. 15, 25, 3) τινί *to someone* ITr 1: 1; IPol 7: 1; *set forth* MPol 22: 3. M-M.**

Δημᾶς, ᾶ, ὁ *Demas* (short form of Δημήτριος? Bl-D. §125, 1 or Δημάρατος? Cf. Δαμᾶς above and s. Vi. Aesopi I c. 33 p. 299, 6 Eberh.; Dit., Syll.³ 585, 202 Δημᾶς Καλλικράτεος; Sb. 8066, 95 [inscr. 78 BC]; grave-inscription 1: ZNW 22, '23, 280; PLond. 929, 38; BGU 10, 12; 715 II, 13) a companion of Paul Phlm 24; Col 4: 14; 2 Ti 4: 10. M-M.*

δημηγορέω impf. ἐδημηγόρουν (Aristoph., Lysias+; Pr 30: 31; 4 Macc 5: 15; Jos., Bell. 2, 619, Vi. 92) *deliver a public address* πρός τινα Ac 12: 21.*

Δημήτριος, ου, ὁ (occurs freq.: Dit., Syll., Or. ind.; LXX; Joseph.) *Demetrius.*

1. a Christian 3 J 12.—2. a silversmith in Ephesus, leader of a demonstration against Paul Ac 19: 24, 38. JChapman, JTS 5, '04, 364ff identifies 1 w. Δημᾶς; VBartlet, ibid. 6, '05, 208f, 215 identifies the two Demtr. of the NT. S. ABludau, D. Aufstand d. Silberschmieds Dem. Ac 19: 23-40: Der Katholik 86, '06, 81-92; 201-13; 258-72. M-M.*

δημιουργέω 1 aor. ἐδημιούργησα, pass. ἐδημιουργήθην (Pla.+; Herm. Wr. 1, 13; 4, 1; 5, 11; LXX; Philo; Jos., Ant. 8, 88) *create* of God's creative activity (Dio Chrys. 11[12], 83; Ael. Aristid. 45 p. 126 D.; Charito 3, 3, 16; Herm. Wr. 4, 1a; Philo, Op. M. 16) 1 Cl 20: 10; 38: 3. καιρὸν δ. *create a period* Dg 9: 1.*

δημιουργία, ας, ἡ (Pla.+; Herm. Wr. 10, 18; inscr.; Philo, Ebr. 85; Jos., Ant. 12, 42) *creative act* ὦ τῆς ἀνεξιχνιάστου δημιουργίας O, *the unfathomable act of creativity* (that is revealed in redemption) Dg 9: 5. κατὰ τὴν δ. αὐτοῦ *in accordance w. his creative activity* 1 Cl 20: 6.*

δημιουργός, οῦ, ὁ (Hom.+; inscr.; 2 Macc 4: 1; Philo, Joseph.) *craftsman, maker, creator*, also of divine activity (so e.g. Pla., Tim. 28A and C; 29A; 31A al., Rep. 7 p. 530A; X., Mem. 1, 4, 7; 9; Epict. 2, 8, 21; Maximus Tyr. 41, 4d ὕλην ὑποβεβλημένην δημιουργῷ ἀγαθῷ; Philostrat., Vi. Apoll. 8, 7 p. 312, 26; Herm. Wr. 1, 9-11; Damascius, De Principiis §270, II 137 Ruelle; Philo, Op. M. 10, Mut. Nom. 29; Jos., Ant. 1, 155; 272; 7, 380. On the Gnostics s. AHilgenfeld, Ketzergeschichte 1884 index under Demiurg), as in our lit. throughout: (w. τεχνίτης; cf. Lucian, Icar. 8; Philo, Mut. Nom. 29-31) Hb 11: 10; Dg 7: 2; (w. δεσπότης) ὁ μέγας δ. 1 Cl 20: 11; cf. 33: 2; Dg 8: 7; ὁ δ. τῶν ἁπάντων (Ael. Aristid. 37, 2 K. = 2 p. 13 D.; Herm. Wr. 9, 5 θεός, πάντων δημιουργὸς ὤν; Philostrat., Vi. Soph. 2, 5, 11) 1 Cl 26: 1; 59: 2; (w. πατήρ; cf. Hierocles 1, p. 417; Herm. Wr. 5, 11) 35: 3.—Harnack, SAB '09, 60, 1; ThSchermann, TU 34, 2b, '09, 23; FPfister, SAHeidelb. '14 no. 11, 9; Dodd 136-44 al. CMAvdOudenrijn, Demiourgos: Diss. Utr. '51; WTheiler, RAC III '56, 694-711 (lit.); HFWeiss, Untersuchungen z. Kosmologie, TU 97, '66, 44-52. M-M.*

δῆμος, ου, ὁ (Hom.+; inscr., pap., LXX; Jos., Ant. 12, 120; 123; 14, 24; Sib. Or. 5, 419; loanw. in rabb.) *people, populace, crowd* gathered for any purpose Ac 12: 22; πεῖσον τὸν δ. *try to convince the crowd* (so that it will intercede for you) MPol 10: 2. Specif. *popular assembly* for the transaction of public business: προάγειν εἰς τὸν δ. Ac 17: 5; εἰσελθεῖν εἰς τὸν δ. *go into the assembly* 19: 30; ἀπολογεῖσθαι τῷ δ. *make a defense before the assembly* vs. 33, though it is poss. that *crowd* is the meaning in all pass. in Ac (cf. in the Inscr. fr. Ephesus ed. ELHicks 1890 the common expr. δεδόχθαι or ἔδοξεν τῷ δήμῳ, and esp. M-M.).*

δημόσιος, ία, ιον (Hdt., Aristoph.+; inscr., pap.; Ep. Arist. 81; Jos., Bell. 5, 518 al.; Test. Judah 23: 2; loanw. in rabb.) *public.*
1. = belonging to the state ἐν τηρήσει δ. *in the public prison* Ac 5: 18. ὁδὸς *a public road* (oft. pap.) Hv 4, 1, 2.
2. = in the open δημοσίᾳ as adv. *publicly* (Epict. 3, 4, 1; 3, 22, 2; Vett. Val. 71, 22; Dit., Syll.³ 1173, 9; 13; 18; BGU 1086 II, 3; 2 Macc 6: 10; 3 Macc 2: 27; 4: 7; Jos., Bell. 2, 455) Ac 16: 37 (cf. Dit., Syll.² 680, 3 μαστιγοῦσθαι δημοσίᾳ); 18: 28; 20: 20. M-M.*

δηνάριον, ου, τό (Lat. denarius as δηνάριον first in two inscr. fr. Acraephiae of the time of Sulla [Inscr. Gr. Sept. 4147f]. Exx. fr. later times in Hahn 271 word-index; Dit., Or. ind. VIII; loanw. in rabb.) *denarius,* a Roman silver coin worth normally about 18 cents; the debasement of the coinage under Nero reduced it in value to about eight cents; it was a workman's average daily wage Mt 18: 28; 20: 2, 9f, 13; 22: 19; Mk 6: 37; 12: 15; 14: 5; Lk 7: 41; 10: 35; 20: 24; J 6: 7; 12: 5; Rv 6: 6. τὸ ἀνὰ δηνάριον *a denarius each,* like the others before them Mt 20: 10 (Bl-D. §266, 2).—Hultsch, Pauly-W. V 202ff.—Other ref. s.v. ἀργύριον, end. M-M.*

δήποτε adv. (Hom+; PLond. 904, 22; PTebt. 381, 14; LXX) *at any time;* w. relative *whatever* J 5: 4 v.l.; τί δ. *just why* (Maximus Tyr. 1, 5a; Lucian, Jupp. Conf. 16; Jos., Ant. 11, 89) Dg 1. M-M.*

δήπου adv. (Hom.+; Jos., C. Ap. 1, 127) *of course, surely* Hb 2: 16 (Bl-D. §441, 3; Rob. 302).*

Δία, Διός see Ζεύς.

διά prep. w. gen. and acc. (Hom.+; inscr., pap., LXX, Ep. Arist., Philo, Joseph., Test. 12 Patr.) (for lit. s. ἀνά, beg.) *through.*

A. w. gen.—**I.** of place: *through*—1. w. verbs of going διέρχεσθαι διὰ πάντων (sc. τόπων, Ep. Arist. 132) *go through all the places* Ac 9: 32; cf. Mt 12: 43; Lk 11: 24. ἀπελεύσομαι δι' ὑμῶν εἰς *I will go through your city on the way to* Ro 15: 28; cf. 2 Cor. 1: 16. διαβαίνειν Hb 11: 29. διαπορεύεσθαι διὰ σπορίμων Lk 6: 1. εἰσέρχεσθαι διὰ τῆς πύλης (Jos., Ant. 13, 229) Mt 7: 13a; τ. θύρας J 10: 1f; cf. vs. 9. παρέρχεσθαι διὰ τ. ὁδοῦ *pass by along the road* Mt 8: 28; cf. 7: 13b. παραπορεύεσθαι Mk 2: 23; 9: 30. περιπατεῖν διὰ τοῦ φωτός *walk about through* or *in the light* Rv 21: 24. ὑποστρέφειν διὰ Μακεδονίας *return through M.* Ac 20: 3.—Ἰησ. ὁ ἐλθὼν δι' ὕδατος καὶ αἵματος 1 J 5: 6 first of all refers quite literally to Jesus' passing *through* water at his baptism and *through* blood at his death (on the expression 'come through blood' in this sense cf. Eur., Phoen. 20 in Alex. Aphr., Fat. 31 II 2 p. 202, 10: the oracle to Laius the father of Oedipus, concerning the bloody downfall of his house: πᾶς σὸς οἶκος βήσεται δι' αἵματος). But, as a secondary mng., sense III 1c may also apply: Jesus comes *with* the water of baptism and *with* the blood of redemption for his own.—AKlöpper, 1 J 5: 6-12: ZWTh 43, '00, 378-400.—The ῥῆμα ἐκπορευόμενον διὰ στόματος θεοῦ Mt 4: 4 (Dt 8: 3) is simply the *word that proceeds out of the mouth of God* (cf. Theognis 1, 18 Diehl² τοῦτ' ἔπος ἀθανάτων ἦλθε διὰ στομάτων; Pittacus in Diog. L. 1, 78 διὰ στόματος λαλεῖ; Chrysippus in Diog. L. 7, 187 εἴ τι λαλεῖς, τοῦτο διὰ τοῦ στόματός σου διέρχεται; Test. Iss. 7: 4 ψεῦδος οὐκ ἀνῆλθε διὰ τ. χειλέων μου. Cf. also δέχεσθαι διὰ τῶν χειρῶν τινος Gen 33: 10 beside δέχ. ἐκ τ. χειρ. τινος Ex 32: 4).

2. w. other verbs that include motion: οὗ ὁ ἔπαινος διὰ πασῶν τ. ἐκκλησιῶν (sc. ἀγγέλλεται) *throughout all the churches* 2 Cor 8: 18. διαφέρεσθαι διὰ (א Α κατά) τῆς χώρας *be spread through the whole region* Ac 13: 49. διὰ τ. κεράμων καθῆκαν αὐτόν *they let him down through the tile roof* Lk 5: 19. διὰ τοῦ τείχους καθῆκαν *through an opening in the wall* (Jos., Ant. 5, 15) Ac 9: 25; cf. 2 Cor 11: 33. (σωθήσεται) ὡς διὰ πυρός *as if he had come through fire* 1 Cor 3: 15. διασῴζεσθαι δι' ὕδατος *be brought safely through the water* 1 Pt 3: 20.— δι' ὅλου J 19: 23 s. ὅλος 4.

II. of time:—1. to denote extent—a. in the case of extension over a whole period of time, to its very end *through, during* διὰ παντός (sc. χρόνου; Tdf. writes διαπαντός) *always, continually, constantly* (Hdt. 1, 122; Thu. 1, 38, 1; Vett. Valens 220, 1; 16; PLond. 42, 6; BGU 1078, 2; PGM 7, 235; LXX; Ep. Arist. ind.; Jos., Ant. 3, 281; Sib. Or. fgm. 1, 17) Mt 18: 10; Mk 5: 5; Lk 24: 53; Ac 2: 25 (Ps 15: 8); 10: 2; 24: 16; Ro 11: 10 (Ps 68: 24); 2 Th 3: 16; Hb 9: 6; 13: 15; Hm 5, 2, 3; s 9, 27, 3. διὰ νυκτός *during the night* (νύξ 1b) Ac 23: 31. δι' ὅλης νυκτός *the whole night through* Lk 5: 5 (X., An. 4, 2, 4; Diod. S. 3, 12, 3 δι' ὅλης τῆς νυκτός; PGM 4, 3151; Jos., Ant. 6, 37; cf. δι' ἡμέρας *all through the day:* Inschr. v. Priene 112, 61; 99; 1 Macc 12: 27; 4 Macc 3: 7). δι' ἡμερῶν τεσσεράκοντα Ac 1: 3 means either *for forty days* (Philo, Vi. Cont. 35 δι' ἐξ ἡμερῶν. So AFridrichsen, ThBl 6, '27, 337-41; MSEnslin, JBL 47, '28, 60-73; Beyer) or (s.b below) *now and then in the course of 40 days* (Bl-D. §223, 1 app.; Rob. 581; WMichaelis, ThBl 4, '25, 102f; Bauernfeind). διὰ παντὸς τοῦ ζῆν *throughout the lifetime* Hb 2: 15 (cf. διὰ παντὸς τοῦ βίου: X., Mem. 1, 2, 61; Pla., Phileb. 39E; Dionys. Hal. 2, 21; δι' ὅλου τοῦ ζῆν Ep. Arist. 130; 141; 168).
b. in the case of a period of time within which someth. occurs *during, at* (PTebt. 48, 10) διὰ νυκτός *at night, during the night* (Palaeph. 1, 10; PRyl. 138, 15 κατέλαβα τοῦτον διὰ νυκτός; Jos., Bell. 1, 229. S. νύξ 1b, end) Ac

5: 19; 16: 9; 17: 10. διὰ τῆς ἡμέρας *during the day* Lk 9: 37 D (Antig. Car. 128 διὰ πέμπτης ἡμέρας= *on the fifth day*). διὰ τριῶν ἡμερῶν *within three days* Mt 26: 61; Mk 14: 58.

2. to denote an interval *after* (Hdt. 6, 118 δι' ἐτέων εἴκοσι; Thu. 2, 94, 3; X., Mem. 2, 8, 1; Diod. S. 5, 28, 6 of transmigration of souls: δι' ἐτῶν ὡρισμένων [= *after the passing of a certain number of years*] πάλιν βιοῦν; Dit., Or. 56, 38; 4 Macc 13: 21; Jos., Ant. 4, 209): δι' ἐτῶν πλειόνων *after several years* Ac 24: 17. διὰ δεκατεσσάρων (q.v.) ἐτῶν *after 14 years* Gal 2: 1. δι' ἡμερῶν *several days afterward* Mk 2: 1. διὰ ἱκανοῦ χρόνου Ac 11: 2 D (X., Cyr. 1, 4, 28 διὰ χρόνου).

III. of means, instrument, agency: *by means of, through, with.*

1. w. gen. of the thing:—**a.** to denote means or instrument γράφειν διὰ χάρτου καὶ μέλανος *write w. paper and ink* 2 J 12; cf. 3 J 13 (Plut., Sol. 17, 3). διὰ πυρὸς δοκιμάζειν *test by fire* 1 Pt 1: 7. διὰ χρημάτων κτᾶσθαι Ac 8: 20. Hebraistically in expr. denoting activity διὰ χειρῶν τινος (LXX) Mk 6: 2; Ac 5: 12; 14: 3; 19: 11. Differently γράφειν διὰ χειρός τινος *write through the agency of someone* 15: 23; cf. 11: 30. εἰπεῖν διὰ στόματός τινος *by the mouth of someone* (where mng. I 1 is influential) 1: 16; 3: 18, 21; 4: 25. εὔσημον λόγον διδόναι διὰ τῆς γλώσσης *utter intelligible speech with the tongue* 1 Cor 14: 9. διὰ τοῦ νοὸς λαλεῖν *speak, using one's reason* (=consciously; opp., ecstatic speech) vs. 19 t.r. Of the work of Christ: περιποιεῖσθαι διὰ τοῦ αἵματος *obtain through his blood* Ac 20: 28; cf. Eph 1: 7; Col 1: 20. Also διὰ τοῦ θανάτου Ro 5: 10; Col 1: 22; Hb 2: 14; διὰ τοῦ σώματος Ro 7: 4; διὰ τοῦ σταυροῦ Eph 2: 16; διὰ τῆς θυσίας Hb 9: 26; διὰ τῆς προσφορᾶς τοῦ σώματος Ἰησοῦ *through the offering of the body of Jesus* 10: 10; διὰ παθημάτων 2: 10.

b. to denote manner, esp. w. verbs of saying: ἀπαγγέλλειν διὰ λόγου *by word of mouth* Ac 15: 27; cf. 2 Th 2: 15. δι' ἐπιστολῶν *by letter* (POxy. 1066, 9; 1070, 15 πολλάκις σοι γράψας διὰ ἐπιστολῶν πολλῶν) 1 Cor 10: 11; cf. 2 Th 2: 2, 15. διὰ λόγου πολλοῦ *w. many words* Ac 15: 32. δι' ὁράματος εἰπεῖν *in a vision* 18: 9. διὰ παραβολῆς *in a figurative way, in a parable* Lk 8: 4. διὰ προσευχῆς καὶ δεήσεως προσεύχεσθαι *call on* (*God*) *w. prayer and supplication* Eph 6: 18. διὰ βραχέων ἐπιστέλλειν *write briefly* Hb 13: 22 (cf. 1 Pt 5: 12 Þ⁷²; Isocr. 14, 3; Lucian, Tox. 56; Ep. Arist. 128). Also δι' ὀλίγων γράφειν 1 Pt 5: 12 (Pla., Phileb. 31D; UPZ 42, 9 [162 BC]; 2 Macc 6: 17).

c. closely related is the use denoting attendant circumstance (Kühner-G. I 482f; X., Cyr. 4, 6, 6 διὰ πένθους τὸ γῆρας διάγων; PTebt. 35, 9 [111 BC] διὰ τῆς γνώμης τινός=*with someone's consent*; Jos., Bell. 4, 105) σὲ τὸν διὰ γράμματος καὶ περιτομῆς παραβάτην νόμου *you who,* (though provided) *with the written code and circumcision, are a transgressor of the law* Ro 2: 27. δι' ὑπομονῆς 8: 25. διὰ προσκόμματος *eat with offense* (to the scruples of another) 14: 20. δι' ἀκροβυστίας *in a state of being uncircumcised* 4: 11. διὰ πολλῶν δακρύων *with many tears* 2 Cor 2: 4.—Here prob. belongs διὰ τῆς τεκνογονίας 1 Ti 2: 15. On 1 J 5: 6 s. A I 1 above.

d. to denote the efficient cause: διὰ νόμου ἐπίγνωσις ἁμαρτίας (*only*) *recognition of sin comes through the law* Ro 3: 20; cf. 4: 13. τὰ παθήματα τὰ διὰ τοῦ νόμου *passions aroused by the law* 7: 5. διὰ νόμου πίστεως *by the law of faith* 3: 27; Gal 2: 19. ἀφορμὴν λαμβάνειν διὰ τῆς ἐντολῆς Ro 7: 8, 11; cf. 13. διὰ τ. εὐ. ὑμᾶς ἐγέννησα (spiritual parenthood) 1 Cor 4: 15. διὰ τῆς σοφίας *with its*

wisdom 1 Cor 1: 21. Opp. διὰ τῆς μωρίας τοῦ κηρύγματος *through the foolishness of preaching*=*foolish preaching* ibid. διὰ τῆς Λευιτικῆς ἱερωσύνης Hb 7: 11. Freq. διὰ (τῆς) πίστεως Ro 1: 12; 3: 22, 25, 30f; Gal 2: 16; 3: 14, 26; Eph 2: 8; 3: 12, 17 al. πίστις δι' ἀγάπης ἐνεργουμένη *faith which works through* (= expresses itself in) *deeds of love* Gal 5: 6. διὰ θελήματος θεοῦ *if God is willing* Ro 15: 32; *by the will of God* 1 Cor 1: 1; 2 Cor 1: 1; 8: 5; Eph 1: 1; Col 1: 1; 2 Ti 1: 1.

e. denoting the occasion διὰ τῆς χάριτος *by virtue of the grace* Ro 12: 3; Gal 1: 15.—3: 18; 4: 23; Phlm 22. διὰ δόξης καὶ ἀρετῆς *in consequence of his glory and excellence* 2 Pt 1: 3 t.r.

f. in urgent requests διὰ τῶν οἰκτιρμῶν τοῦ θεοῦ *by the mercy of God* Ro 12: 1; cf. 15: 30; 1 Cor 1: 10; 2 Cor 10: 1.

2. w. gen. of the pers.—**a.** denoting the personal agent or intermediary *through* (*the agency of*), *by* (X., An. 2, 3, 17 δι' ἑρμηνέως λέγειν; Menand., fgm. 245, 1 δι' ἀνθρώπου σῴζειν; Achilles Tat. 7, 1, 3 δι' ἐκείνου μαθεῖν; PMerton 5, 8 γεωμετρηθῆναι δι' αὐτοῦ) ῥηθὲν διὰ τοῦ προφήτου Mt 1: 22; 2: 15, 23; 4: 14 and oft. γεγραμμένα διὰ τῶν προφητῶν Lk 18: 31; cf. Ac 2: 22; 10: 36; 15: 12 al. δι' ἀνθρώπου *by human agency* Gal 1: 1. διὰ Μωϋσέως *through Moses* (Jos., Ant. 7, 338) J 1: 17; *under Moses' leadership* Hb 3: 16. δι' ἀγγέλων *by means of angels* (Jos., Ant. 15, 136) Gal 3: 19; Hb 2: 2. πέμψας διὰ τ. μαθητῶν εἶπεν *sent and said through his disciples* Mt 11: 2f. Cf. the short ending of Mk. γράφειν διά τινος of the bearer IRo 10: 1; IPhld 11: 2; ISm 12: 1 (cf. BGU 1029, 4 [41 AD]), but also of pers. who had a greater or smaller part in drawing up the document in question (Dionys. of Cor. in Euseb., H.E. 4, 23, 11) perh. 1 Pt 5: 12. In this case διά comes close to the mng. *represented by* (LWenger, D. Stellvertretung im Rechte d. Pap. '06, 9ff; Dssm., LO 98 [LAE 123f]). So also κρίνει ὁ θεὸς διὰ Χρ. Ἰ. *God judges, represented by Christ Jesus* Ro 2: 16. Christ as intermediary in the creation of the world J 1: 3, 10; 1 Cor 8: 6; Col 1: 16.—εὐχαριστεῖν τ. θεῷ διὰ Ἰ. Χρ. *thank God through Jesus Christ* Ro 1: 8; 7: 25; Col 3: 17.—Occasionally the mediation becomes actual presence (references for this usage in BKeil, Anonymus Argentinensis '02, p. 192, 1; 306 note) διὰ πολλῶν μαρτύρων *in the presence of many witnesses* 2 Ti 2: 2 (Simplicius in Epict. p. 114, 31 διὰ θεοῦ μέσου=*in the presence of God as mediator*; Philo, Leg. ad Gai. 187 τὸ διὰ μαρτύρων κλαίειν=*weeping in the presence of witnesses*).

b. of the originator of an action (class.; pap.; LXX; Ep. Arist.)—**a.** of men (PSI 354, 6 [254 BC] τὸν χόρτον τὸν συνηγμένον δι' ἡμῶν=*by us*; 500, 5; 527, 11; 1 Esdr 6: 13; 2 Macc 6: 21; 4 Macc 1: 11) 2 Cor 1: 11, where διὰ πολλῶν resumes ἐκ πολλῶν προσώπων.

β. of God (Aeschyl., Ag. 1448; Pla., Symp. 186E ἡ ἰατρικὴ πᾶσα διὰ τ. θεοῦ τούτου [Asclepius] κυβερνᾶται; Ael. Aristid., Sarap. [Or. 8 Dind.= 45 Keil] 14 K. πάντα γὰρ πανταχοῦ διὰ σοῦ τε καὶ διὰ σὲ ἡμῖν γίγνεται; Zosimus in MBerthelot, Les Alchimistes grecs 1888, 143 and a magic ring in Berthelot op. cit. Introd. 133; Ep. Arist. 313) 1 Cor 1: 9; Ro 11: 36 (cf. Norden, Agn. Th. 240ff; 347f); Hb 2: 10b (s. B II 1 below).

γ. of Christ Ro 1: 5; 5: 9, 17f, 21; 8: 37; 2 Cor 1: 20 and oft. (ASchettler, D. paulin. Formel 'durch Christus' '07; GJAJonker, De paulin. formule 'door Christus': ThSt 27, '09, 173-208).

δ. of the Holy Spirit Ac 11: 28; 21: 4; Ro 5: 5.

IV. At times διά w. gen. seems to have causal mng. (Radermacher² 142; POxy. 299, 2 [I AD] ἔδωκα αὐτῷ διὰ σοῦ=*because of you*; Achilles Tat. 3, 4, 5 διὰ τούτων=

for this reason) διὰ τῆς σαρκός *because of the resistance of the flesh* Ro 8: 3. —2 Cor 9: 13; 1 J 2: 12.—On the use of διά w. gen. in Ro s. Schlaeger, La critique radicale de l'épître aux Rom.: Congr. d'Hist. du Christ. II 111f.

B. w. acc.—**I.** of place *through* (class. only in poetry; Hellenistic prose since Dionys. Hal. [JKäser, D. Präpositionen b. Dionys. Hal., Diss. Erlangen '15, 54]; Wadd. no. 1866b τὸν πάτρωνα διὰ πάντα of the governor of a whole province) διήρχετο διὰ μέσον Σαμαρείας καὶ Γαλιλαίας Lk 17: 11 (cf. Sib. Or. 3, 316 ῥομφαία διελεύσεται διὰ μέσον σεῖο).

II. to indicate the reason—**1.** the reason why someth. happens, results, exists: *because of, for the sake of* (do something for the sake of a divinity: UPZ 62, 2 [161 BC] διὰ τὸν Σάραπιν) hated because of the name Mt 10: 22; persecution arises because of the teaching 13: 21; because of unbelief vs. 58; because of a tradition 15: 3; διὰ τὸν ἄνθρωπον *for the sake of man* Mk 2: 27; because of Herodias Mk 6: 17; because of the crowd Lk 5: 19; 8: 19 and oft.; because of the Jews Ac 16: 3. διὰ τὸν θόρυβον 21: 34; because of the rain 28: 2. Juristically to indicate guilt: imprisoned *for insurrection and murder* Lk 23: 25. δι᾽ ὑμᾶς *on your account*= through your fault Ro 2: 24 (Is 52: 5). διὰ τὴν πάρεσιν *because of the passing over* 3: 25 (but s. WGKümmel, ZThK 49, '52, 164). διὰ τὰ παραπτώματα 4: 25 (cf. Is 53: 5). διὰ τὴν χάριν *on the basis of the grace* 15: 15. δι᾽ ἀσθένειαν τῆς σαρκός *because of a physical ailment* (cf. POxy. 726 [II AD] οὐ δυνάμενος δι᾽ ἀσθένειαν πλεῦσαι. Cf. ἀσθένεια 1a) Gal 4: 13. διὰ τὸ θέλημά σου *by thy will* Rv 4: 11. διὰ τὸν χρόνον *according to the time*=by this time Hb 5: 12 (Aelian, V.H. 3, 37 δ. τὸν χρ.=because of the particular time-situation).—W. words denoting emotions *out of* (Diod. S. 5, 59, 8 διὰ τὴν λύπην; 18, 25, 1 διὰ τὴν προπέτειαν=out of rashness; Appian, Celt. 1 §9 δι᾽ ἐλπίδα; 2 Macc 5: 21; 7: 20; 9: 8; 3 Macc 5: 32, 41; Tob 8: 7): διὰ φθόνον *out of envy* Mt 27: 18; Phil 1: 15. διὰ σπλάγχνα ἐλέους *out of tender mercy* Lk 1: 78. διὰ τ. φόβον τινός *out of fear of someone* J 7: 13. διὰ τὴν πολλὴν ἀγάπην *out of the great love* Eph 2: 4. διὰ τ. πλεονεξίαν *in their greediness* B 10: 4.—Of God as the ultimate goal or purpose of life, whereas διά w. gen. (s. A III 2bβ above) represents him as Creator, Hb 2: 10a (cf. Norden, op. cit.; PGM 13, 76 διὰ σὲ συνέστηκεν . . . ἡ γῆ); PK 2.

2. in direct questions διὰ τί; *why?* (Hyperid. 3, 17; Dio Chrys. 20[37], 28; Ael. Aristid. 31 p. 597 D.; oft. LXX) mostly in an interrogative clause Mt 9: 11, 14; 13: 10; 15: 2f; 17: 19; 21: 25; Mk 2: 18; 11: 31; Lk 5: 30; 19: 23, 31; 20: 5; 24: 38; J 7: 45; 8: 43, 46; 12: 5; 13: 37; Ac 5: 3; 1 Cor 6: 7; Rv 17: 7. Only as διὰ τί; (Hyperid. 3, 23) Ro 9: 32; 2 Cor 11: 11. Also διατί; B 8: 4, 6; Hm 2: 5; s 5, 5, 5. Kvan Leeuwen Boomkamp, Τι et Διατι dans les évangiles: Rev. des Études grecques 39, '26, 327–31.—In real and supposed answers and inferences διὰ τοῦτο *therefore* (X., An. 1, 7, 3; 7, 19; oft. LXX) Mt 6: 25; 12: 27, 31; 13: 13, 52; 14: 2; 18: 23; 21: 43; 23: 13 v.l.; 24: 44; Mk 11: 24; 12: 24; Lk 11: 19 al. Also διὰ ταῦτα (Epict.) Eph 5: 6. διὰ τοῦτο ὅτι *for this reason, (namely) that* J 5: 16, 18; 8: 47; 10: 17; 12: 18, 39; 15: 19; 1 J 3: 1. διὰ τοῦτο ἵνα *for this reason, (in order) that* (Lucian, Abdic. 1) J 1: 31; 2 Cor 13: 10; 1 Ti 1: 16; Phlm 15. Also διὰ τοῦτο ὅπως Hb 9: 15.

3. διά foll. by inf. or acc. w. inf., representing a causal clause (Gen 39: 9; Dt 1: 36; 1 Macc 6: 53) διὰ τὸ μὴ ἔχειν βάθος *because it had no depth* Mt 13: 5f; Mk 4: 5f (διὰ τὸ μή w. inf.: X., Mem. 1, 3, 5; Hero Alex. I p. 348, 7; III 274, 19; Lucian, Hermot. 31); *because lawlessness in-*

creases Mt 24: 12; διὰ τὸ εἶναι αὐτὸν ἐξ οἴκου Δ. Lk 2: 4; *because it was built well* 6: 48 al. διὰ τὸ λέγεσθαι ὑπό τινων *because it was said by some* Lk 9: 7 (for the constr. cf. Herodian 7, 12, 7 διὰ τὸ τὰς ἐξόδους ὑπὸ τ. πυρὸς προκατειλῆφθαι).

4. instead of διά w. gen. to denote the efficient cause we may have διά

a. w. acc. of the thing (schol. on Pind., Nem. 4, 79a; 2 Macc 12: 11; Ep. Arist. 77) διὰ τὸ αἷμα *by the blood* Rv 12: 11. διὰ τὰ σημεῖα *by the miracles* 13: 14.

b. w. acc. of the pers. (Aristoph., Plut. 468; Dionys. Hal. 8, 33, 3 p. 1579 μέγας διὰ τ. θεοὺς ἐγενόμην; Plut., Alex. 8, 4; Ael. Aristid. 24, 1 K.=44 p. 824 D.: δι᾽ οὓς [=θεούς] ἐσώθην; Dit., Syll.³ 1122, Or. 458, 40; PGM 13, 579 διῳκονομήθη τ. πάντα διὰ σέ; Ep. Arist. 292; Sir 15: 11; 3 Macc 6: 36; other exx. in SEitrem and AFridrichsen, E. christl. Amulett auf Pap. '21, 24). ζῶ διὰ τὸν πατέρα J 6: 57. διὰ τὸν ὑποτάξαντα *by the one who subjected it* Ro 8: 20. M-M.

διαβαίνω 2 aor. διέβην, ptc. διαβάς (Hom.+; inscr., pap., LXX; En. 32, 2; Joseph.) *go through, cross* w. acc. τὴν ἐρυθρὰν θάλασσαν *the Red Sea* Hb 11: 29 (Anonym. Alex. Hist. [II BC]: 151 fgm. 1, 2 Jac.: Alex. the Great experiences the same miracle at the Pamphylian Sea. Before him ἐσπάσθη τὸ πέλαγος which leaves τὸν χερσωθέντα τόπον free. ἄνεμοι ἀντέσχον τῷ πελάγει, until Alex. and his men διέβησαν.—Ps.-Apollod. 1, 4, 3, 1 διαβ. τὴν θάλασσαν by Poseidon's favor); *cross a river,* w. acc. (Hdt. 1, 75 al.; Gen 31: 21 and oft.; Jos., Ant. 7, 128; Sib. Or. 4, 139) Hv 1, 1, 3; *come over* εἰς Μακεδονίαν Ac 16: 9 (Memnon [I BC/I AD]: no. 434 fgm. 1, 8, 1 Jac. εἰς τὴν Μακεδονίαν διαβαίνειν; PLille 6, 3; PFay. 110, 15 διάβα εἰς Διονυσιάδα; Num 32: 7 al.; Jos., Bell. 7, 21); over a chasm πρός τινα Lk 16: 26 (cf. 1 Macc 5: 40; Jos., Ant. 12, 103). M-M.*

διαβάλλω 1 aor. pass. διεβλήθην (trag., Hdt.+; pap., LXX, Joseph.) *bring charges* w. hostile intent, either falsely and slanderously (BGU 1040, 22; POxy. 900, 13; 4 Macc 4: 1; Jos., Ant. 7, 267) or justly (Hdt. 8, 22, 3; Thu. 3, 4, 4; Aristoph., Thesm. 1169; Philostratus, Ep. 37; PTebt. 23, 4; Da 3: 8; 2 Macc 3: 11; Jos., Ant. 12, 176) διεβλήθη αὐτῷ ὡς διασκορπίζων *charges were brought to him that he was squandering* Lk 16: 1 (dat. as Hdt. 5, 35; Pla., Rep. 8, 566B al.; ὡς w. ptc. as X., Hell. 2, 3, 23; Pla., Epist. 7, 334A). M-M.*

διαβεβαιόομαι (since Demosth. 17, 30; oft. in H. Gk. writers; PRainer 18, 29; BGU 19, 7; PLond. 1131 I, 21; Ep. Arist. 99) mid. dep. *speak confidently, insist* περί τινος (Polyb. 12, 12, 6; Plut., Fab. 14, 4; Sext. Emp., Pyrrh. 1, 191; Jos., C. Ap. 2, 14) *concerning* or *on someth.* 1 Ti 1: 7; Tit 3: 8; *confirm* Papias 2: 3. M-M.*

διάβημα, ατος, τό (Damascius, De Princ. 423 Ruelle; LXX; Hesychius) *step* κατευθύνειν τὰ δ. τινος *guide someone's steps* 1 Cl 60: 2 (cf. Ps 36: 23; 39: 3).*

διαβλέπω fut. διαβλέψω; 1 aor. διέβλεψα (Pla.+; PLond. 418, 19)—**1.** lit. *look intently,* or *open one's eyes (wide)* (Plut., Mor. 973F; cf. HAlmqvist, Plut. u. d. NT '46, 55f) Mk 8: 25 (ERoos, Eranos 51, '53, 155–57).

2. *see clearly* w. inf. foll. Mt 7: 5; Lk 6: 42; LJ 1: 1.*

διαβόητος, ον (Plut.; Dio Chrys.; Lucian, Alex. 4; Xenophon Eph. 1, 7, 3 al.; Dit., Syll.³ 888, 28) *renowned* of the church at Ephesus IEph 8: 1 (for the dat. τ. αἰῶσιν cf. Xenophon Eph. 1, 2, 7 δ. τοῖς θεωμένοις ἅπασιν; for the content s. the entry αἰών, end).*

διαβολή, ῆς, ἡ (Epicharmus, Hdt. +; PSI 441, 19 [III BC]; LXX; Ep. Arist.; Jos., Ant. 6, 285; 286, Vi. 80; Test. Jos. 1, 7) *slander* (w. καταλαλιά) Pol 4: 3.*

διάβολος, ον—1. adj. (since Aristoph.; Thuc. 6, 15, 2; Herm. Wr. 13, 13b; 22b; Philo, Sacr. Abel. 32 p. 215, 6) *slanderous* Pol 5: 2. γυναῖκες 1 Ti 3: 11. πρεσβύτιδες Tit 2: 3.—2 Ti 3: 3.

2. subst. ὁ δ. (since X., Ages. 11, 5; Athen. 11 p. 508E; Esth 7: 4; 8: 1) *the slanderer;* specif. *the devil,* already current in the LXX as transl. of שָׂטָן (Job 2: 1; Zech 3: 1f; 1 Ch 21: 1; cf. Wsd 2: 24; Test. Napht. 8: 4, 6) Mt 4: 1, 5, 8, 11; 13: 39; 25: 41; Lk 4: 2f, 6, 13; 8: 12; J 13: 2; Eph 4: 27; 6: 11; Hb 2: 14; Js 4: 7. παγὶς τοῦ διαβόλου *devil's trap* 1 Ti 3: 7; 2 Ti 2: 26 (cf. IScheftelowitz, Das Schlingen-u. Netzmotiv '12, 11). ὁ ἀντίδικος ὑμῶν διάβολος *your adversary, the devil* 1 Pt 5: 8; τοῦ δ. *botany weed of the devil* IEph 10: 3; ἐνέδραι τοῦ δ. *the devil's ambuscades* ITr 8: 1; cf. MPol 3. Of tortures inflicted by the devil IRo 5: 3. τῷ δ. λατρεύειν *serve the devil* ISm 9: 1; ὄργανα τοῦ δ. *tools of the devil* (of non-Christians) 2 Cl 18: 2; πολυπλοκία τοῦ δ. *the devil's cunning* Hm 4, 3, 4; tempting to sin m 4, 3, 6; dwells in anger m 5, 1, 3; ἔργα τοῦ δ. m 7: 3; doubt described as the devil's daughter m 9: 9; likew. evil desire m 12, 2, 2. The πνεῦμα of the devil is mentioned m 11: 3; it is a πνεῦμα ἐπίγειον m 11: 17; ἐντολαὶ τοῦ δ. m 12, 4, 6; ἀντιπαλαίειν τῷ δ. s 8, 3, 6.—The wicked are υἱοὶ δ. Ac 13: 10; τέκνα τοῦ δ. 1 J 3: 10; they are descended ἐκ τοῦ δ. vs. 8; the devil is their father J 8: 44. On the designation of Judas as δ. 6: 70, cf. 13: 2, 27.—Lit. under δαιμόνιον, end, and ἄγγελος, end. WFoerster, TW II 69–80. BNoack, Satanas u. Soteria '48, 55f. B. 1487.

διαγγέλλω 2 aor. pass. διηγγέλην, subj. διαγγελῶ (Pind., Thu. +; PSI 329, 4; 559, 5; LXX, Philo, Joseph.).
1. *proclaim far and wide* (Demosth. 12, 16; Jos., Vi. 98) the Kgdm. of God Lk 9: 60. τὸ ὄνομα τοῦ θεοῦ Ro 9: 17 (Ex 9: 16). Cf. Mk 5: 19 v.l.
2. *give notice of* (X., An. 1, 6, 2; Jos., Ant. 7, 201) completion of the days of purification Ac 21: 26. Of the church δ. καιρούς *announce seasons* (fulfillment of prophecies) Dg 11: 5.*

διάγε s. γέ 1.

διαγίνομαι 2 aor. διεγενόμην pass, *elapse* of time (Lysias, Or. 1, 15 χρόνου μεταξὺ διαγενομένου; X., Isaeus et al.; Joseph., s. below; PStrassb. 41, 42 πολὺς χρόνος διαγέγονεν [250 AD]; POxy. 68, 18; PLond. 1676, 40; s. διά A II 2; LXX has the word only 2 Macc 11: 26 in another mng.) διαγενομένου τοῦ σαββάτου *when the Sabbath was over* Mk 16: 1. ἡμερῶν διαγενομένων τινῶν *several days afterward* Ac 25: 13 (cf. Jos., Ant. 7, 394). ἱκανοῦ χρόνου διαγενομένου *since* or *when considerable time had passed* 27: 9.*

διαγινώσκω fut. διαγνώσομαι (Hom. +; inscr., pap., LXX, Philo; Jos., Ant. 4, 121; 6, 205) *decide, determine,* legal t.t. (Aeschyl., Antiphon et al.; Dionys. Hal. 2, 14; Grenfell, Rev. Laws of Ptol. Phil. 1896, 14, 1; PTebt. 55, 2; PAmh. 29, 18; POxy. 1032, 53; 1117, 3 al.; Philo, Agr. 116) ἀκριβέστερον τὰ περὶ αὐτοῦ *to determine his case by thorough investigation* Ac 23: 15. τὰ καθ' ὑμᾶς *decide your case* 24: 22. M-M.*

διαγνωρίζω 1 aor. διεγνώρισα (Philo, Det. Pot. Insid. 97) *give an exact report* περὶ τινος Lk 2: 17 v.l. (for ἐγνώρισαν).*

διάγνωσις, εως, ἡ (as legal term e.g. Pla., Leg. 9, 865c; Wsd 3: 18; Jos., Ant. 8, 133; 15, 358; loanw. in rabb.) *decision* (PHib. 93, 10 [c. 250 BC] ἡ δ. περὶ αὐτοῦ ἔστω πρὸς βασιλικά; PLond. 358, 17) τηρεῖσθαι εἰς τὴν τοῦ Σεβαστοῦ δ. *to be kept in custody for the Emperor's decision* (cognitio) Ac 25: 21 (IG XIV 1072 ἐπὶ διαγνώσεων τοῦ Σεβαστοῦ; Jos., Bell. 2, 17). M-M.*

διαγογγύζω (LXX) imp. διεγόγγυζον *complain, grumble* (aloud) w. λέγων foll. Lk 15: 2; 19: 7.*

διαγρηγορέω 1 aor. διεγρηγόρησα *keep awake* (Herodian 3, 4, 4; Niceph. Gregoras, Hist. Byz. p. 205F; 571A); for διαγρηγορήσαντες εἶδαν Lk 9: 32 this would give the mng. *since they had kept awake, they saw.* But acc. to Niceph., op. cit. 205F δ. can also mean *awake fully* (δόξαν ἀπεβαλόμην ὥσπερ οἱ διαγρηγορήσαντες τὰ ἐν τοῖς ὕπνοις ὀνείρατα); in this case: *when they were fully awake, they saw.* M-M.*

διάγω with or without the acc. βίον very common in Gk. writers (cf. also 2 Macc 12: 38; 3 Macc 4: 8; Jos., C. Ap. 2, 229) in the sense *spend one's life, live.* ἐν τρυφῇ Lk 7: 25 v.l. ἐν κακίᾳ Tit 3: 3. ἐν Χριστῷ ITr 2: 2 (cf. Pla., Phaedr. p. 259D ἐν φιλοσοφίᾳ; Plut., Timol. 3, 1 ἐν εἰρήνῃ διάγοντες; Test. Jos. 9: 3 ἐν σωφροσύνῃ; gravestone: Sb 6648, 4 ἐν σκοτίᾳ); ἤρεμον καὶ ἡσύχιον βίον *lead a peaceful and quiet life* 1 Ti 2: 2. M-M.*

διαδέχομαι 1 aor. διεδεξάμην (Hdt. +) *receive* (*in turn*) fr. a former owner, succeed to (Polyb. 9, 28, 8 al.; Dit., Syll.³ 495, 6; 700, 32, Or. 335, 132; 210, 2 τὴν ἀρχιερωσύνην; PTebt. 489; PHamb. 27, 14; POxy. 495, 11; 13; 4 Macc 4: 15; Philo, Mos. 1, 207; Jos., Ant. 7, 337) τὴν λειτουργίαν *ministry* 1 Cl 44: 2. Abs. (as Hdt. 8, 142; s. Field, Notes 116) *in turn* Ac 7: 45. M-M.*

διάδημα, ατος, τό (since X., Cyr. 8, 3, 13; Epict. 1, 24, 17; 4, 8, 30; Dit., Or. 248, 17; 383, 103; pap.; LXX) *diadem, fillet,* properly the sign of royalty among the Persians, a blue band trimmed with white, on the tiara, hence a symbol of royalty gener., *crown* (Diod. S. 4, 4, 4; Lucian, Pisc. 35 βασιλείας γνώρισμα; Ezek. Trag. in Euseb., Praep. Ev. 9, 29, 5; Philo, Fuga 111; Jos., Bell. 1, 70, Ant. 12, 389; Test. Jud. 12: 4) Rv 12: 3; 13: 1; 19: 12 (divinities w. diadems: PGM 4, 521; 675; 2840); Pol 1: 1.*

διαδίδωμι 1 aor. διέδωκα; 2 aor. imper. διάδος; impf. pass. 3 sg. διεδίδετο (s. on this form Bl-D. §94, 1; Mlt-H. 206) *distribute, give* (so Thu. +; X., Cyr. 1, 3, 7; Dit., Syll.³ 374, 12; POxy. 1115, 6; 1194, 17; PLeipz. 35, 10; LXX) τὰ σκῦλα *the spoils* Lk 11: 22. τὸ σιτομέτριον 12: 42 v.l. τί τινι (Thu. 4, 38, 4; Jos., Ant. 7, 86) 18: 22; Rv 17: 13 t.r.; τὰ λοιπὰ τοῖς συνδούλοις *the rest to his fellow slaves* Hs 5, 2, 9. τινί *to someone* J 6: 11. Pass. Ac 4: 35. M-M.*

διάδοχος, ου, ὁ *successor* (Aeschyl. +; Hdt. 5, 26; inscr., pap.; Sir 46: 1; 48: 8; Philo; Jos., Ant. 1, 228 al.) λαμβάνειν δ. *receive as successor* Ac 24: 27 (cf. Jos., Ant. 20, 182). M-M.*

διαζώννυμι 1 aor. διέζωσα, mid. διεζωσάμην; pf. pass. ptc. διεζωσμένος (Thu. +; IG II 763B, 16 et al. in inscr.; Ezk 23: 15 A; Philo, Op. M. 112) *tie around* δ. ἑαυτόν *tie* (a towel) *around oneself* J 13: 4. ἦν διεζωσμένος *he had tied around himself* vs. 5. Mid. τὸν ἐπενδύτην *tie around oneself* (i.e. *put on*) *an outer garment* 21: 7 (Lucian, Somn. 6 ἐσθῆτα, Anach. 6 al.; Jos., Ant. 7, 283 διεζωσμένος μάχαιραν). M-M.*

διαθήκη, ης, ἡ (Democr., Aristoph.+; inscr., pap., LXX, En., Philo, Joseph.).

1. *last will and testament* (so exclusively in Hellenistic times, Eger 99 note; exx. e.g. in Riggenbach 292ff; Behm 10, 1; 2; Philo, Joseph., Test. 12 Patr.; loanw. in rabb.) Hb 9: 16f; δ. κεκυρωμένη *a will that has been ratified* Gal 3: 15; cf. 17, where δ. shades into mng. 2 (s. κυρόω 1, προκυρόω); s. also EBammel, below, and JSwetnam, CBQ 27, '65, 373-90.

2. As a transl. of בְּרִית in LXX δ. loses the sense of 'will, testament' insofar as a δ. decreed by God cannot require the death of the testator to make it operative. Nevertheless, another essential characteristic of a testament is retained, namely that it is the declaration of one person's will, not the result of an agreement betw. two parties, like a compact or a contract. This is without doubt one of the main reasons why the LXX rendered בְּרִית by δ. In the 'covenants' of God, it was God alone who set the conditions; hence *covenant* (s. Murray, New [Oxford] Engl. Dict. s.v. 'covenant' sb. 7) can be used to trans. δ. only when this is kept in mind. So δ. acquires a mng. in LXX which cannot be paralleled w. certainty in extra-Biblical sources, namely 'decree', 'declaration of purpose', 'set of regulations', etc. Our lit., which is very strongly influenced by LXX in this area, seems as a rule to have understood the word in these senses. God has issued a *declaration of his will* Ro 11: 27 (Is 59: 21); 1 Cl 15: 4 (Ps 77: 37); 35: 7 (Ps 49: 16), which he bears in mind (cf. Ps 104: 8f al.) Lk 1: 72; it goes back to the days of the fathers Ac 3: 25. He also issued an *ordinance* (of circumcision) 7: 8 (cf. Gen 17: 10ff). Since he has made known his holy will on more than one occasion, one may speak of διαθῆκαι *decrees, assurances* (cf. διαθῆκαι πατέρων Wsd 18: 22; 2 Macc 8: 15.— But the pl. is also used for a single testament: Diog. L. 4, 44; 5, 16. In quoting or referring to Theophr. sometimes the sing. [Diog. L. 5, 52; 56] is used, sometimes the pl. [5, 51; 57]) Ro 9: 4; Eph 2: 12. Much emphasis is laid on the δ. καινή, mentioned as early as Jer 31: 31 [LXX 38: 31], which God has planned for the future (Hb 8: 8-10; 10: 16). God's *decree* or *covenant* directed toward the Christians is a καινὴ δ. Lk 22: 20; 1 Cor 11: 25; 2 Cor 3: 6; Hb 8: 8; 9: 15a; PK 2 p. 15, 5, or δ. νέα Hb 12: 24; PK 2 p. 15, 6 which, as a δ. αἰώνιος (cf. Jer 39: 40; En. 98, 2) Hb 13: 20, far excels 7: 22; 8: 6 the παλαιὰ δ. 2 Cor 3: 14, or πρώτη δ. Hb 9: 15b, with which it is contrasted. Both are mentioned Gal 4: 24; B 4: 6ff (Ex 34: 28; 31: 18). Blood was shed when the old covenant was proclaimed at Sinai Hb 9: 20 (Ex 24: 8); the same is true of the new covenant Hb 10: 29. τὸ αἷμά μου τ. διαθήκης Mt 26: 28; Mk 14: 24 (ELohse, Märtyrer u. Gottesknecht², '63, 122-29) is prob. to be understood in connection w. this blood (cf. WWrede, ZNW 1, '00, 69-74; THRobinson, My Blood of the Covenant: KMarti-Festschr. '25, 232-7; for a critique of this view s. GWalther, Jesus, D. Passalamm des Neuen Bundes, '50, 22-27 and JoachJeremias ThLZ, '51, 547. For Syriac background JAEmerton, JTS 13, '62, 111-17).— The v.l. Lk 22: 29 may be derived from Jer 39: 40 or Is 55: 3 LXX.—δ. may also be transl. *decree* in the Epistle of Barnabas (4: 6ff; 6: 19; 9: 6; 13: 1, 6; 14: 1ff δ. δοῦναί τινι); the freq. occurrence of the idea of inheritance, however (6: 19; 13: 1, 6; 14: 4f), makes it likely that the 'decree' is to be thought of as part of a will.

3. The mng. *compact, contract* seems to be established for class. times (FNorton, A Lexicographical and Historical Study of Διαθήκη, Chicago '08, 31ff; EBruck, D. Schenkung auf d. Todesfall im griech. u. röm. Recht I '09, 115ff; JWackernagel, D. Kultur d. Gegenw. I 8² '07, 309).

It remains doubtful whether this mng. has influenced our lit. here and there. It is also uncertain just how such fixed expr. as ἡ κιβωτὸς τ. διαθήκης (Ex 31: 7; 39: 14 al.) Hb 9: 4; Rv 11: 19 or αἱ πλάκες τ. διαθ. (Ex 34: 28; Dt 9: 9, 11) Hb 9: 4 were understood by Christian authors. At least for the first expr. it is prob well to retain the stereotyped transl. *ark of the covenant.*—ERiggenbach, D. Begriff d. Διαθήκη im Hb: Theol. Stud. f. ThZahn '08, 289ff, Hb² '22, 205ff al.; ACarr, Covenant or Testament?: Exp. 7th Ser. VII '09, 347ff; JBehm, D. Begriff Δ. im NT '12; ELohmeyer, Diatheke '13; WDFerguson, Legal Terms Common to the Macedonian Inscr. and the NT, Chicago, '13, 42ff; HAAKennedy, Exp. 8th Ser. X '15, 385ff; GVos, Hebrews, the Epistle of the Diatheke: PTR 13, '15, 587-632; 14, '16, 1-61; OEger, ZNW 18, '18, 84-108; EDBurton, ICC Gal '21, 496-505; LGdaFonseca, Διαθήκη—foedus an testamentum?: Biblica 8, '27; 9, '28; EBammel, Gottes διαθήκη (Gal 3: 15-17) u. d. jüd. Rechtsdenken, NTS 6, '60, 313-19; NDow, A Select Bibliography on the Concept of Covenant, Austin Seminary Bulletin 78, 6, '63; CRoetzel, Biblica 51, '70, 377-90 (Ro 9: 4); DJMcCarthy, Berit and Covenant (Deut.), '72, 65-85; JBehm and GQuell, TW II 105-37. M-M.*

διαθρύπτω (Hom.+) *break* τινί τι bread for the hungry B 3: 3 (Is 58: 7).*

διαίρεσις, εως, ἡ—1. *apportionment, division* (Hdt.+; inscr., pap.; Jdth 9: 4; Sir 14: 15; Philo) διαιρέσεις χαρισμάτων *allotments of spiritual gifts* 1 Cor 12: 4; cf. vss. 5, 6 (this interpr. is supported by vs. 11 διαιροῦν ἑκάστῳ καθὼς βούλεται. But *difference, variety* is also poss. [Pla., Soph. 267B τίνα διαίρεσιν ἀγνωσίας τε καὶ γνώσεως θήσομεν; Lucian, Hermot. 52; Epict. 2, 6, 24]).

2. *tearing apart* of the body in certain kinds of torture and execution IRo 5: 3 (cf. Artem. 1, 67 p. 62, 7 διαιρέσεις ὑπὸ σιδήρου; Philo, Agr. 129 ἄνευ τομῆς κ. διαιρέσεως). M-M.*

διαιρέω 2 aor. διεῖλον, subj. διέλω (Hom.+; inscr., pap., LXX) *distribute, divide* (Jos., Ant. 5, 88 τὶ) τινί τι *someth. to someone* (X., Cyr. 4, 5, 51, Hell. 3, 2, 10; PLond. 880, 11 [113 BC] διειρῆσθαι τὰ ὑπάρχοντα αὐτῷ ἔγγαια τοῖς ἑαυτοῦ υἱοῖς; Josh 18: 5; Jdth 16: 24; 1 Macc 1: 6) διεῖλεν αὐτοῖς τὸν βίον *he divided his property between them* Lk 15: 12; *apportion someth. to someone* (Inscr. Gr. 1001 VI, 18 ὁ ἀρτυτὴρ διελεῖ τὰ ἱερὰ τοῖς παροῦσι) 1 Cor 12: 11. Abs. ἐὰν ὀρθῶς μὴ διέλῃς *if you did not divide* (the sacrifice) *rightly* 1 Cl 4: 4 (Gen 4: 7). M-M.*

δίαιτα, ης, ἡ (Pind., Hdt.+; LXX; Jos., Bell. 2, 151, C. Ap. 2, 240 [=way of life]) *food, diet* Dg 5: 4; *habitation, dwelling-place* (Diod. S. 3, 30, 2; Ps.-Aristot., De Mundo 6 p. 398b, 32; Plut., Mor. 515E; Dit., Or. 383, 27 [I BC]; Jos., Ant. 15, 331. So as loanw. in rabb.) 1 Cl 39: 8 (Job 5: 3). δ. τῆς σκηνῆς σου οὐ μὴ ἁμάρτῃ *the dwelling-place of your tent shall not suffer want* 56: 13 (Job 5: 24).*

διακαθαίρω 1 aor. inf. διακαθᾶραι (Aristoph., Pla.+; Bull. de corr. hell. 27, '03, p. 73 l. 79) *clean out* τὶ a threshing-floor Lk 3: 17 (Alciphr. 2, 23, 1 ἄρτι μοι τὴν ἄλω διακαθήραντι). M-M.*

διακαθαρίζω fut. διακαθαριῶ (not found elsewh.) *clean out* τὶ someth. Mt 3: 12; Lk 3: 17 v.l.*

διακατελέγχομαι impf. διακατηλεγχόμην (not found elsewh.) *refute completely* τινί: τοῖς Ἰουδαίοις Ac 18: 28.*

διακελεύω (the mid. since Hdt., the act. only in Philostrat., Vi. Apollon. 1, 31 v.l. and in Suidas) *order* τινί w. inf. foll. J 8: 5 v.l.*

διακονέω impf. διηκόνουν; fut. διακονήσω; 1 aor. διηκόνησα, pass. διηκονήθην; for augm. s. Bl-D. §69, 4 app.; Mlt.-H. 192 (Soph., Hdt.+; rare in inscr., pap.; never in LXX, but in Philo, Joseph.).

1. *wait on someone* (τινί) *at table* (Menand., fgm. 272; Pyrgion [Hellenistic times] no. 467 fgm. 1 Jac. [a communal meal in Crete]; Diod. S. 4, 36, 2; 5, 28, 4; Philo, Vi. Cont. 70; Jos., Ant. 11, 163; 166) Lk 12: 37; 17: 8. Abs. 10: 40; J 12: 2. ὁ διακονῶν *the waiter* Lk 22: 26f.

2. *serve* gener., of services of any kind τινί *someone* (Demosth. 9, 43; UPZ 18, 23 [163 BC]; Sb 4947, 2 διακόνησόν μοι) Mt 4: 11; 8: 15; Mk 1: 13, 31; Lk 4: 39. διακονοῦσαι αὐτῷ *waiting on him* Mt 27: 55; cf. Mk 15: 41. διακόνει μοι *serve me* Hs 8, 4, 1, cf. 2; J 12: 26; Ac 19: 22; Phlm 13. W. dat. of the pers. and acc. of the thing οὐχ ἑαυτοῖς διηκόνουν αὐτά *they were not serving themselves in the things* 1 Pt 1: 12 (for a service consisting in the delivery of a message, cf. Jos., Ant. 6, 298). Also εἰς ἑαυτοὺς αὐτὸ δ. *serve one another w. it* 1 Pt 4: 10. W. acc. of the thing ὅσα διηκόνησεν *what services he rendered* 2 Ti 1: 18; cf. Hs 2: 10. Abs. (POxy. 275, 10 [I AD]) 1 Pt 4: 11. Pass. (Jos., Ant. 10, 242) οὐκ ἦλθεν διακονηθῆναι ἀλλὰ διακονῆσαι *he came not to be served, but to serve* Mt 20: 28; Mk 10: 45; ἁπλῶς δ. *complete a service in simplicity of heart* Hm 2: 6. χάρις διακονουμένη ὑφ' ἡμῶν *work of love that we are carrying on* 2 Cor 8: 19; cf. vs. 20.

3. *care for, take care of* w. dat. of the thing τραπέζαις *look after the tables* Ac 6: 2 (perh. *accounts* s. τράπεζα 3 and 4).—Fig. ἐπιστολὴ Χριστοῦ διακονηθεῖσα ὑφ' ἡμῶν *a letter of Christ, cared for* (i.e. written or delivered) *by us* 2 Cor 3: 3.

4. *help, support someone* w. dat. πότε οὐ διηκονήσαμέν σοι; *when did we not help you?* Mt 25: 44. ἐκ τῶν ὑπαρχόντων *helped to support them w. their means* Lk 8: 3; the saints Ro 15: 25 (JJO'Rourke, CBQ 29, '67, 116-18); Hb 6: 10.

5. of the ecclesiastical office *serve as deacon* 1 Ti 3: 10; καλῶς δ. vs. 13. ἀγνῶς καὶ σεμνῶς Hv 3, 5, 1. Opp. κακῶς s 9, 26, 2. (Of holy service at the altar Jos., Ant. 3, 155. Cf. PGM 36, 304; 335 παρὰ θεοῖς δ.).—WBrandt, Dienst u. Dienen im NT '31; EdSchweizer, D. Leben des Herrn u. d. Gemeinde u. ihren Diensten '46; PHBoulton, Διακονέω *and its Cognates in the 4 Gospels*, TU 73, '59, 415-22. M-M.*

διακονία, ας, ἡ (Thu.+; IG XII 5, 600, 14 [III BC]; 1 Macc 11: 58; Esth 6: 3, 5 [both v.l.]; Joseph.).

1. *service* πνεύματα εἰς δ. ἀποστελλόμενα *spirits sent out for service* Hb 1: 14. πρὸς τὸν καταρτισμὸν τ. ἁγίων εἰς ἔργον διακονίας *to prepare the saints for practical service* Eph 4: 12; δ. τοῦ λόγου Ac 6: 4; ἡ ὑμῶν δ. *service to you* 2 Cor 11: 8.—1 Cor 16: 15; 2 Ti 4: 11; Rv 2: 19.

2. specif. the *service* necessary for preparation of a meal (s. Plut., Philopoem. 2, 3; Jos., Ant. 2, 65; 11, 163 διακονεῖν τινι τὴν ἐπὶ τοῦ πότου διακονίαν) περιεσπᾶτο περὶ πολλὴν δ. *she was distracted w. many preparations* Lk 10: 40.

3. esp. of the *service, office* of the prophets and apostles 1 Ti 1: 12; κλῆρος τῆς δ. Ac 1: 17; τόπος τῆς δ. vs. 25. Of the service of the Levites 1 Cl 40: 5; the *office of a bishop* IPhld 1: 1; 10: 2; ISm 12: 1; Hs 9, 27, 2; δ. λαμβάνειν

receive a ministry Ac 20: 24. διαιρέσεις διακονιῶν 1 Cor 12: 5; δ. τοῦ θανάτου *ministry of death* of the OT law 2 Cor 3: 7. Also δ. τῆς κατακρίσεως *min. of condemnation* vs. 9. Opp. δ. τῆς δικαιοσύνης *min. of righteousness* ibid.; δ. τοῦ πνεύματος *min. of the Spirit* vs. 8 of NT religion; cf. Ac 21: 19; Ro 11: 13; 2 Cor 4: 1; 6: 3; Col 4: 17; 2 Ti 4: 5; δ. τῆς καταλλαγῆς *ministry of reconciliation* 2 Cor 5: 18; τὴν δ. τελέσαι *perform a service* Hm 2: 6; 12, 3, 3; s 1: 9; 2: 7.

4. *aid, support, distribution* (Arrian, Peripl. 3, 1 εἰς διακονίαν=for support), esp. of alms and charitable giving (Act. Thom. 59 χρήματα πολλὰ εἰς διακονίαν τῶν χηρῶν) Ac 6: 1. εἰς δ. πέμψαι τί τινι *send someone someth. for the support* 11: 29; cf. 12: 25. δ. τῆς λειτουργίας *kind contribution* 2 Cor 9: 12; cf. 13. ἡ δ. ἡ εἰς Ἱερουσαλήμ *the contribution meant for Jer.* Ro 15: 31; cf. 2 Cor 8: 4; 9: 1.—On the 'collection': ELombard, RThPh 35, '02, 113-39; 262-81; MGoguel, RHPhr 4, '25, 301-18; KFNickle, The Collection, '66.

5. of the *office of a deacon* Ro 12: 7 (Ltzm., ZWTh 55, '13, 110); IMg 6: 1; IPhld 10: 2; Hs 9, 26, 2.—PJEAbbing, Diakonia, Diss. Utrecht '50; BReicke, Diakonie, Festfreude u. Zelos usw. '51, 19-164. M-M.*

διάκονος, ου, ὁ, ἡ (trag., Hdt.+; inscr., pap., LXX, Philo, Joseph.).

1. masc.—a. *servant* of someone Mt 20: 26; 23: 11; Mk 10: 43; of all 9: 35; Pol 5: 2. Of waiters at table (X., Mem. 1, 5, 2; Polyb. 31, 4, 5; Lucian, Merc. Cond. 26; Athen. 7, 291A; 10, 420E; Jos., Ant. 6, 52) J 2: 5, 9. Of a king's servants Mt 22: 13. Of apostles and other prominent Christians: *servant of the gospel* Col 1: 23; Eph 3: 7; of the church Col 1: 25; δ. καινῆς διαθήκης 2 Cor 3: 6; θεοῦ δ. (Epict. 3, 24, 65 Diogenes as τοῦ Διὸς διάκονος; Achilles Tat. 3, 18, 5 δ. θεῶν; cf. Philo, De Jos. 241; Jos., Bell. 3, 354) 6: 4; 1 Th 3: 2 (cf. 1 Cor 3: 5); Tit 1: 9 v.l. b; Hs 9, 15, 4; δ. Χριστοῦ 2 Cor 11: 23; Col 1: 7; 1 Ti 4: 6; δ. δικαιοσύνης (opp. δ. τοῦ σατανᾶ) 2 Cor 11: 15. Of Jesus' adherents gener.: his servants J 12: 26 (Jos., Ant. 8, 354 Elisha is Ἠλίου καὶ μαθητὴς καὶ δ.).

b. gener. *helper* δ. τοῦ θεοῦ ἐν τ. εὐαγγελίῳ *God's helper in the gospel* 1 Th 3: 2 v.l. (for συνεργός) cf. 1 Ti 4: 6; δ. ἐν κυρίῳ Eph 6: 21; Col 4: 7; δ. περιτομῆς *for the circumcision*=for the Jews, of Christ Ro 15: 8; ἁμαρτίας δ. *one who encourages sin* Gal 2: 17.

c. *deacon* as an official of the church (δ. as holder of a religious office outside Christianity: Inschr. v. Magn. 109 [c. 100 BC] IG IV 474, 12; 824, 6; IX 486, 18; CIG II 1800; 3037, II add. 1793b; Thieme 17f; Mitteilungen d. K. Deutsch. Archäol. Instit. Athen. part 27, '02, p. 330 no. 8) Phil 1: 1 (EBest, Bishops and Deacons, TU 102, '68, 371-76); 1 Ti 3: 8, 12; Tit 1: 9 v.l. a; Phlm subscr. v.l.; 1 Cl 42: 4f; Hv 3, 5, 1; s 9, 26, 2; IEph 2: 1; IMg 2; 6: 1; 13: 1; ITr 2: 3; 3: 1; 7: 2; IPhld inscr.; 4; 7: 1; 10: 1f; 11: 1; ISm 8: 1; 10: 1; 12: 2; IPol 6: 1; Pol 5: 3; D 15: 1.—Harnack, D. Lehre d. Zwölf Apostel: TU II 1; 2, 1884, 140ff, Entstehung u. Entwicklung d. Kirchenverfassung '10, 40ff; FJAHort, The Christian Ecclesia 1898, 202-8; Ltzm., ZWTh 55, '13, 106-13=Kleine Schriften I, '58, 148-53; HLauerer, D. 'Diakonie' im NT: NKZ 42, '31, 315-26. Further lit. s.v. ἐπίσκοπος and πρεσβύτερος.

2. fem. (Heraclit. Sto. 28 p. 43, 15; Epict. 2, 23, 8; 3, 7, 28; Jos., Ant. 1, 298)—a. *helper, agent* ἡ ἐξουσία *the governmental authorities* Ro 13: 4.

b. *deaconess* (ministra: Pliny, Ep. 10, 96, 8. Cf. CIG II 3037 διάκονος Τύχη; ἡ δ. Marcus Diaconus, Vi. Porphyr. p. 81, 6; Mitt. Ath. [s. 1c above] 14, 1889, p. 210; Pel.-Leg. 11, 18) Phoebe as διάκονος Ro 16: 1; subscr. v.l.

For the idea cf. Hv 2, 4, 3; hence Hs 9, 26, 2 may include women. Further lit. s.v. χήρα 2.—On the whole word s. HWBeyer, TW II 81–93. M-M. B. 1334.*

διακόσιοι, αι, α (Hom.+; pap., LXX; Jos., Vi. 90; 115; Test. 12 Patr.) *two hundred* Mk 6: 37; J 6: 7; 21: 8 al.

διακοσμέω (Hom.+; 2 Macc) *set in order, regulate* τὶ (Jos., Ant. 6, 31) the heavens (Philo, Op. M. 53) 1 Cl 33: 3 (as a cosmolog. expr. as early as the Ionic nature philosophers, later esp. in Stoic wr.; cf. Knopf, Hdb. ad loc.).*

διακόσμησις, εως, ἡ (Pla.+; Stoic term) *regulation, orderly arrangement* Papias 4.*

διακούω fut. διακούσομαι (X.+) as legal t.t. *give someone (τινός) a hearing* Ac 23: 35 (so Polyb.; Plut.; Cass. Dio 36, 53[36]; Inschr. v. Magn. 93a, 10; 105, 1 al. in inscr.; BGU 168, 28; PFay. 119, 12 et al. in pap.; Dt 1: 16; Job 9: 33; Jos., Bell. 2, 242). M-M.*

διακρίνω impf. mid. διεκρινόμην; 1 aor. pass. διεκρίθην (Hom.+; inscr., pap., LXX, Ep. Arist., Philo, Joseph.).
1. act.—a. *separate, arrange* τὶ *someth.* (Jos., Ant. 11, 56) πάντα κατὰ τάξιν Dg 8: 7.
b. *make a distinction, differentiate* (PGM 5, 103 σὺ διέκρινας τὸ δίκαιον καὶ τὸ ἄδικον; 4 Macc 1: 14; Jos., Bell. 1, 27) μεταξὺ ἡμῶν τε καὶ αὐτῶν *betw. us and them* Ac 15: 9. τίς σε διακρίνει; *who concedes you any superiority?* 1 Cor 4: 7 (Appian, Bell. Civ. 5, 54 §228 δ. τινά=concede superiority to someone, beside ἐπιλέγεσθαί τινα=select someone; cf. Philo, Op. M. 137 διακρίνας ἐξ ἁπάσης τὸ βέλτιστον). μηθὲν διακρίνων τίνι δῷ *without distinguishing to whom he should give* Hm 2: 6; cf. Ac 11: 12.—Pass. διακρίνεσθαί τινος *be differentiated fr. someone* Dg 5: 1.
c. *judge*—a. *pass judgment (on)* w. acc. ἑαυτόν *on oneself* IEph 5: 3 (mng. 1a is also poss.); προφήτην D 11: 7; abs. 1 Cor 14: 29.
β. *judge correctly* (Job 12: 11; 23: 10) the appearance of the sky Mt 16: 3; oneself 1 Cor 11: 31; *recognize* τὸ σῶμα vs. 29.—γ. *deliberate* Hv 1, 2, 2; περί τινος s 2: 1.
d. legal t.t. *render a decision* (X., Hell. 5, 2, 10; Appian, Bell. Civ. 5, 76 §324 δίκαι διεκρίνοντο; Dit., Syll.³ 545, 18, Or. 43, 4; 11; Ep. Arist. 110) ἀνὰ μέσον τινός *betw. pers.* (as Ezk 34: 17, 20) 1 Cor 6: 5. Cf. EvDobschütz, StKr 91, '18, 410–21 and ἀνά 1b, μέσος 2.
2. mid., w. pass. aor. (Bl-D. §78)—a. *take issue, dispute* πρός τινα w. *someone* (Hdt. 9, 58; Ezk 20: 35f; Jo 4: 2) Ac 11: 2; τινί w. *someone* (Polyb. 2, 22, 11) Jd 9.
b. *be at odds w. oneself, doubt, waver* (this mng. appears first in NT. With no dependence on the NT, e.g., Cyril of Scyth. p. 52, 17; 80, 10; 174, 7) Mt 21: 21; Mk 11: 23; Ro 4: 20; 14: 23; Jd 22. ἐν ἑαυτῷ *in one's own mind* Lk 11: 38 D; Js 2: 4. μηδὲν διακρινόμενος *without any doubting* Js 1: 6; *hesitate* Ac 10: 20. M-M.*

διάκρισις, εως, ἡ (Pre-Socr., X.+; pap.; LXX only Job 37: 16; Ep. Arist.; Philo).
1. *distinguishing, differentiation* of good and evil Hb 5: 14 (Sext. Emp., Hyp. Pyrrh. 3, 168 διάκρισις τῶν τε καλῶν καὶ κακῶν). πνευμάτων *ability to distinguish betw. spirits* 1 Cor 12: 10 (cf. Pla., Leg. 11, 937B ψευδομαρτυριῶν; Diod. S. 17, 10, 5 ἡ τῶν σημείων διάκρισις =critical examination of the miraculous signs. ELerle, Diakrisis Pneumaton, Diss. Hdlbg. '46). σοφὸς ἐν διακρίσει λόγων *skillful in the interpretation of discourse* 1 Cl 48: 5.
2. *quarrel* (Polyb. 18, 28, 3; Dio Chrys. 21[38], 21) Ac 4: 32 D. προσλαμβάνεσθαι μὴ εἰς δ. διαλογισμῶν *wel-*

come, but not for the purpose of getting into quarrels about opinions Ro 14: 1. M-M.*

διακυβερνάω (Pla.+; UPZ 59, 15 [168 BC]; LXX) *govern* of Michael, the guardian angel of Christians Hs 8, 3, 3.*

διακωλύω impf. διεκώλυον (Soph., Hdt.+; Dit., Syll.³ 685, 81; PTebt. 72, 363; BGU 1187, 11; Jos., Bell. 2, 287, Ant. 11, 29) *prevent* διεκώλυεν αὐτόν *he tried to prevent him* (cf. Jdth 12: 7; the imperf. tense as Hierocles 11 p. 442 τῷ κωλύοντι τὴν πονηρίαν θεῷ=to the god who is endeavoring to prevent the injustice [the present participle takes over the function of the imperfect]) Mt 3: 14. M-M.*

διαλαλέω (Eur.+; POxy. 1417, 24; Sym. Ps 50: 16 al.) *discuss* (Appian, Bell. Civ. 2, 20 §72; Jos., Bell. 4, 601) διελάλουν πρὸς ἀλλήλους (πρός as Polyb. 22, 9, 6; Diod. S. 36, 3, 3) *they discussed w. each other* Lk 6: 11. Pass. διελαλεῖτο πάντα τὰ ῥήματα ταῦτα *all these things were talked about* 1: 65 (cf. Polyb. 1, 85, 2; Sb 7033, 18). M-M.*

διαλέγομαι impf. διελεγόμην; 1 aor. διελεξάμην (Hom.; Polyaenus 3, 9, 40; 7, 27, 2) Ac 17: 2; 18: 19, pass. διελέχθην (Att.) Mk 9: 34 (Hom.+; inscr., pap., LXX, Ep. Arist., Philo, Joseph.).
1. *discuss, conduct a discussion* (freq. in Attic wr., also PPetr. III 43[3], 15 [240 BC]; BGU 1080, 11) of lectures which were likely to end in disputations Ac 18: 4; 19: 8f; 20: 9. περί τινος (Ps.-Callisth. 3, 32, 2) 24: 25. τινί w. *someone* (1 Esdr 8: 45; 2 Macc 11: 20; Ep. Arist. 40) 17: 2, 17; 18: 19; 20: 7. πρός τινα (Ex 6: 27; Ps.-Callisth., loc. cit.; Jos., Ant. 7, 278) Ac 24: 12. *Converse* τινί w. *someone* MPol 7: 2.—Of controversies πρός τινα *with someone* (Judg 8: 1 B) Mk 9: 34. περί τινος *about someth.* (cf. Pla., Ap. p. 19D; Plut., Pomp. 4, 4; PFlor. 132, 3) Jd 9.
2. also simply *speak, preach* (X., Mem. 1, 6, 1; 2, 10, 1; Isocr., Phil. 109; Epict. 1, 17, 4; 2, 8, 12; PSI 401, 4 [III BC]; LXX; Philo; Joseph.; ELHicks, CIR 1, 1887, 45); δ. may have in mind many of the above pass. (e.g. Ac 18: 4), clearly so Hb 12: 5 (δ. of a Scripture pass. also Philo, Leg. All. 3, 118).—GDKilpatrick, JTS 11, '60, 338–40. M-M.*

διαλείπω 2 aor. διέλιπον (Hom.+; inscr., pap., LXX, Ep. Arist., Joseph.) *stop, cease* w. neg. and w. ptc. foll. οὐ διέλειπεν καταφιλοῦσα *she has not stopped kissing* (X., Apol. 16 οὐ πώποτε διέλειπον ζητῶν al.; UPZ 47, 22 [II BC]; POxy. 281, 16; BGU 747 I, 7 οὐ διέλιπον παραινῶν; PGiess. 14, 4f al.; Jer 17: 8; Ep. Arist. 274; Jos., Ant. 8, 302; 11, 119) Lk 7: 45. Also *constantly* μὴ διαλίπῃς νουθετῶν *admonish constantly* Hv 1, 3, 2. μὴ διαλίπῃς λαλῶν 4, 3, 6. μὴ δ. αἰτούμενος m 9: 8. M-M. B. 981.*

διάλεκτος, ου, ἡ (Aristoph., Hippocr.+) *language* of a nation or a region (so Aristot., Probl. 10, 38 p. 895a, 6 τοῦ ἀνθρώπου μία φωνή, ἀλλὰ διάλεκτοι πολλαί; Polyb. 1, 80, 6; 3, 22, 3; 39, 1, 3; Diod. S. 1, 37, 9; Plut., Mor. 185E Περσικὴ δ.; Dit., Syll.³ 1267, 30; PGM 13, 139; 444; 699; Esth 9: 26; Da 1: 4; Philo, Mos. 2, 38, Jos., C. Ap. 1, 180 al.—AThumb, Hdb. d. griech. Dialekte '09, 22f; RMunz, Über γλῶττα u. διάλεκτος: Glotta 11, '21, 85–94) Ac 1: 19; 2: 6, 8; 21: 40; 22: 2; 26: 14; Dg 5: 2; Papias 2: 16. M-M. B. 1261.*

διαλιμπάνω impf. διελίμπανον (Galen XVII 1 p. 220 K.—By-form of διαλείπω) *stop, cease* w. ptc. (Tob 10: 7 οὐ διελίμπανεν θρηνοῦσα) ὃς πολλὰ κλαίων οὐ διελίμπανεν *who could not cease shedding many tears* Ac 8: 24 D. Cf. 17: 13 D. M-M.*

διαλλάσσομαι 2 aor. pass. διηλλάγην, imper. διαλλάγηθι *become reconciled* τινί *to someone* (Aeschyl.+; Thu. 8, 70, 2; BGU 846, 10; PGiess. 17, 13f; 1 Km 29: 4; 1 Esdr 4: 31; Jos., Ant. 16, 125; 335) Mt 5: 24. Abs. D 14: 2. M-M.*

διαλογίζομαι mid. dep.; impf. διελογιζόμην (Democr., X., Pla.+; inscr., pap., LXX).
   1. *consider, ponder, reason* (Ep. Arist. 256) τί ἐν ἑαυτῷ *someth. in one's own mind* (Philo, Spec. Leg. 1, 213) Hs 9, 2, 6. ἐν ἑαυτοῖς Mt 16: 7f; 21: 25; Mk 2: 8; Lk 12: 17. Also ἐν τῇ καρδίᾳ Hv 1, 1, 2. ἐν ταῖς καρδίαις Mk 2: 6, 8; Lk 5: 22; Hv 3, 4, 3. ἐν τ. καρδίαις περί τινος Lk 3: 15. παρ' ἑαυτοῖς Mt 21: 25 v.l. πρὸς ἑαυτούς (Pla., Soph. 231c πρὸς ἡμᾶς αὐτοὺς διαλογισώμεθα; Diod. S. 20, 12, 5 διελογίζετο πρὸς αὐτόν) Mk 11: 31. W. indirect quest. foll. Hv 3, 4, 3; Lk 1: 29. Abs. 5: 21; Hv 3, 1, 9; 4, 1, 4. δ. ταῦτα *harbor these thoughts* m 9: 2 (cf. Ps 76: 6).
   2. *consider and discuss, argue* (X., Mem. 3, 5, 1; Ps 139: 9) πρός τινα w. *someone* Mk 8: 16; perh. 11: 31 (s. 1); Lk 20: 14. W. ὅτι foll. Mk 8: 17. Abs. 9: 33. M-M.*

διαλογισμός, οῦ, ὁ (since Demosth. 36, 23; Polyb., Epict., Plut., inscr., pap., LXX).
   1. *thought, opinion, reasoning, design* (Ps.-Pla., Axioch. 367A φροντίδες καὶ διαλογισμοί; mostly LXX; Ep. Arist. 216; Jos., Bell. 1, 320; Test. Jud. 14: 3) Lk 2: 35; 5: 22; 6: 8; 9: 47; Ro 14: 1 (διάκρισις 2). Of the heathen ἐματαιώθησαν ἐν τοῖς δ. αὐτῶν Ro 1: 21. διαλογισμοὺς ποιεῖσθαι *devise plans* (Zen.-P. 60, 40=Sb 6766 [243/2 bc]) 1 Cl 21: 3. The thoughts of the wise men of this world are known to God 1 Cor 3: 20 (Ps 93: 11); *evil machinations* Mt 15: 19; Mk 7: 21. κριταὶ δ. *ponhrῶn judges w. evil thoughts* Js 2: 4 (but here δ. can also be the legal t.t. *decision* [BGU 19 I, 13; 226, 22; PTebt. 27: 35—113 bc]: *judges who give corrupt decisions*).
   2. *doubt, dispute, argument* δ. ἀναβαίνουσιν *doubts arise* Lk 24: 38; εἰσῆλθεν δ. *an argument arose* 9: 46; χωρὶς δ. *without dispute* Phil 2: 14; 1 Ti 2: 8. M-M.*

διάλυσις, εως, ἡ (Eur., Thu.+; POxy. 104, 20; 1034; 2 Esdr 11 [Neh 1]: 7; Philo; Jos., C. Ap. 2, 276) *dissolution, decay* (cf. Philod., Περὶ θεῶν 3, 6 [ed. HDiels, ABA 1916; 1917] the antithesis διάλ. and γένεσις; Diod. S. 3, 29, 7 διάλυσις τ. σώματος; Herm. Wr. 8, 1a δ. σώματος; 4; Philo, Aet. M. 28) of a seed 1 Cl 24: 5.*

διαλύω 1 aor. pass. διελύθην (Eur., Hdt.+; inscr., pap., LXX, Philo, Joseph.) *break up, dissolve.*
   1. lit. of a seed, pass. *decay* 1 Cl 24: 5. Of a ship's stern Ac 27: 41 v.l.
   2. fig. (Philo, Aet. M. 36 δεσμόν) δ. στραγγαλιάς *loose the entanglements* B 3: 3 (Is 58: 6); *destroy, put an end to* (UPZ 19, 21 [163 bc] τῷ λιμῷ διαλυθῆναι; 11, 27 [160 bc]; Jos., Ant. 14, 284) τὶ *someth.* (Dit., Syll.³ 1268 II, 22 [III bc] ἔχθραν) λογισμοὺς ἐθνῶν 1 Cl 59: 3. Of a crowd *disperse* (Hdt. 8, 11 al.). Pass. (Appian, Iber. 42 §172 διελύθησαν [people] *were scattered*; BGU 1012, 12 [II bc] διαλυθῆναι αὐτά sc. τὰ πρόβατα; Jos., Ant. 20, 124) Ac 5: 36 (Appian, Mithrid. 19 §75 διελύθησαν of military forces; likewise 90 §412). M-M.*

διαμαρτάνω 2 aor. διήμαρτον (Thu.+; Diod. S. 5, 76, 4 διαμ. τῆς ἀληθείας=transgress against the truth; PSI 383, 11; 441, 5 [III bc]; POxy. 473, 6; Num 15: 22; Philo; Jos., Bell. 1, 214, Ant. 13, 331 al.) *miss the mark badly, be quite wrong* Dg 3: 2; sin 1 Cl 40: 4; Hm 4, 1, 2; οὐδέν *in no respect* Hs 4: 5. οὐδέποτε m 4, 1, 1 (Manetho in Jos., C. Ap. 1, 287 οὐ πολὺ διημάρτανεν).*

διαμαρτύρομαι 1 aor. διεμαρτυράμην (X., Pla.+; pap., LXX).
   1. *charge, warn, adjure* (X., Cyr. 7, 1, 17; Polyb. 3, 110, 4; Diod. S. 18, 62, 2; Plut., Cim. 16, 9; Jos., Ant. 6, 39 al.; Ex 19: 10, 21; 1 Km 8: 9; 2 Ch 24: 19 al.) w. dat. of the pers. addressed δ. αὐτοῖς Lk 16: 28 (w. ἵνα μή foll.). W. ἐνώπιον τ. θεοῦ 1 Ti 5: 21 (ἵνα); 2 Ti 2: 14 (μή w. inf. as Polyb. 1, 33, 5; Plut., Crass. 16, 6). W. two constr. mixed: δ. ἐνώπιον θεοῦ καὶ Ἰ. Χ. καὶ τὴν ἐπιφάνειαν αὐτοῦ *I charge you before God and J. Chr., and by his appearing* 2 Ti 4: 1.
   2. *testify (of), bear witness (to)* solemnly (orig. under oath) (X., Hell. 3, 2, 13) τινί τι (Ezk 16: 2 διαμάρτυραι τῇ Ἰερουσαλὴμ τὰς ἀνομίας αὐτῆς.—En. 104, 11 διαμαρτυρέομαί τινί τι; cf. Jos., Ant. 9, 167) of repentance to Jews and Gentiles Ac 20: 21. τὶ *the gospel* vs. 24; *God's kingdom* 28: 23; *my cause in Jerusalem* 23: 11. Abs. 2: 40; 8: 25; 1 Th 4: 6. W. λέγων foll. Ac 20: 23; Hb 2: 6. W. ὅτι foll. (PSI 422, 7 [III bc]) Ac 10: 42. W. acc. and inf. foll. Ac 18: 5. M-M.*

διαμάχομαι impf. διεμαχόμην (Eur., Hdt., Thu.+; Sir; Jos., Bell. 2, 55, Ant. 14, 475) *contend sharply* Ac 23: 9.*

διαμένω impf. διέμενον; 1 aor. διέμεινα; pf. διαμεμένηκα (Pre-Socr., X., Pla.+; inscr., pap., LXX; En. 23, 2; Ep. Arist.; Philo; Jos., Ant. 14, 266; 20, 225) *remain* διέμενεν κωφός *he remained mute* Lk 1: 22 (cf. Dit., Syll.³ 385, 8; Ep. Arist. 204 πλούσιος δ.) δ. πρός τινα *remain continually w. someone* Gal 2: 5; cf. Ac 10: 48 D; δ. μετά τινος *stand by someone* (Sir 12: 15) Lk 22: 28; μετὰ νηπιότητος δ. ἔν τινι *remain with innocence in someth.* Hs 9, 29, 2. ἔν τινι (PTebt. 27, 40) *remain somewhere permanently* Hs 9, 28, 5; *continue in someth.* (Pla., Prot. 344B; 3 Macc 3: 11) ITr 12: 2; IPol 8: 3; Hs 9, 29, 1. Abs. *remain, continue* (Dio Chrys. 57[74], 21; LXX; Ep. Arist. 226; 258; 259) Pol 1: 2. Opp. ἀπολέσθαι Hb 1: 11 (Ps 101: 27). πάντα οὕτως δ. *everything remains as it was* 2 Pt 3: 4. διαμείνατε τοιοῦτοι *remain as you are* (Epict. 2, 16, 4) Hs 9, 24, 4; cf. Hs 9, 29, 3. διαμενοῦσι λαμπροί *they will remain bright* s 9, 30, 2. M-M.*

διαμερίζω impf. διεμέριζον; 1 aor. διεμέρισα, mid. διεμερισάμην, pass. διεμερίσθην; pf. pass. διαμεμερισμένος (Pla.+; pap., LXX; Ep. Arist. 183; Joseph.).
   1. *divide, separate*—a. lit. (Pla., Leg. 8, 849D; Gen 10: 25) διαμεριζόμεναι γλῶσσαι ὡσεὶ πυρός *divided tongues, as if of fire* Ac 2: 3; the nations 1 Cl 29: 2 (Dt 32: 8).
   b. *distribute* (Pla., Polit. 289C; LXX) εἴς τινα *share with someone* Lk 22: 17 (Appian, Bell. Civ. 1, 96 §448 ἐς τούσδε διεμέριζεν; PLond. 982, 4 διεμερίσαμεν εἰς ἑαυτούς). τί τινι (2 Km 6: 19; Ezk 47: 21) Ac 2: 45.—Mid. *divide among themselves* (Jos., Bell. 5, 440) clothes (cf. Artem. 2, 53 γυμνοὶ σταυροῦνται) Mt 27: 35; Mk 15: 24; Lk 23: 34; J 19: 24; GP 4: 12 (all after Ps 21: 19).
   2. fig. *divide*, only pass. *be divided* (Lucian, Gall. 22 πρὸς τοσαύτας φροντίδας διαμεριζόμενος) ἐπί τινα *against someone* Lk 11: 17f; 12: 53; also ἐπί τινι 12: 52f.*

διαμερισμός, οῦ, ὁ (=division Pla.+; POxy. 12 VI, 17; LXX; Jos., Ant. 10, 274) *dissension, disunity* (opp. εἰρήνη) Lk 12: 51.*

διανέμω 1 aor. pass. διενεμήθην (Pind.+; inscr., pap.; Philo, Aet. M. 147; Joseph.) *distribute* (so Aristoph., X.+; Dit., Or. 493, 31, Syll.³ 604, 9; Dt 29: 25; Jos., Bell. 1, 308, Ant. 20, 101) εἰς τὸν λαόν *spread* (a report) *among the people* Ac 4: 17. M-M.*

διανεύω, *nod, beckon* (Diod. S. 3, 18, 6; 17, 37, 5; Lucian, Icarom. 15; Ps 34: 19; Sir 27: 22) τινὶ *to someone* (Alexis Com. [IV BC] no. 261, 12, vol. II p. 392 Kock; Lucian, Ver. Hist. 2, 25) ἦν διανεύων αὐτοῖς *he kept nodding to them* Lk 1: 22.*

διανοέομαι (Hdt.+; Nicol. Dam.: 90 fgm. 13 p. 339, 24 Jac.; pap.; Herm. Wr. 1, 7; LXX; Philo; Jos., Vi. 245) *consider* GP 11: 44; Hs 1: 2 Lghtf.*

διανόημα, ατος, τό (X., Pla.+; pap., LXX) *thought* εἰδὼς τὰ δ. *he knew their thoughts* Lk 11: 17.—3: 16 D.*

διάνοια, ας, ἡ (quite common since Aeschyl., Hdt.; Epict., inscr., pap., Ep. Arist., Philo, Joseph., Test. 12 Patr.; LXX, here nearly always for בֵל, לֵבָב).
   1. *understanding, intelligence, mind* as the organ of νοεῖν (Sib. Or. 3, 421) Hm 10, 1, 5. κατὰ διάνοιαν 1 Cl 19: 3. Described as the seat of the λογισμοί Dg 2: 1; as the organ of ζωή, πίστις, ἐγκράτεια 1 Cl 35: 2. Darkened Eph 4: 18; 1 Cl 36: 2; 2 Cl 19: 2; hence πηρὸς τῇ δ. *maimed* or *blind in the understanding* 2 Cl 1: 6 (cf. Ex 36: 1 σοφὸς τῇ δ.; Job 9: 4). In contrast, fixed on God (Philochorus [IV/III BC]: no. 328 fgm. 188b Jac. of the hymn to the goddess) 1 Cl 35: 5. *Insight* 1 J 5: 20. Of moral understanding Hb 8: 10; 10: 16 (both Jer 38: 33 LXX); Hm 5, 2, 7; 11: 1. W. *heart* and *soul* and *mind* (s. Fluchtaf. 1, 10) Mt 22: 37; Mk 12: 30 (ἐξ ὅλης τ. διανοίας Epict. 2, 2, 13); Lk 10: 27 (Dt 6: 5 v.l.); cf. 2 Cl 3: 4. On τετρωμένοι κατὰ διάνοιαν GP 7: 26 s. τιτρώσκω.
   2. *mind* as a kind of thinking, *disposition, thought* (Jos., Ant. 2, 19) εἰλικρινὴς δ. 2 Pt 3: 1; καθαρὰ δ. 1 Cl 21: 8; ἁπλῆ δ. 23: 1; ἄμωμος δ. ITr 1: 1; ὑπερήφανος διανοίᾳ καρδίας αὐτοῦ (1 Ch 29: 18; Bar 1: 22) *proud in the thoughts of his heart* Lk 1: 51; ἐχθρὸς τῇ δ. *hostile in attitude* Col 1: 21; ἀπερισπάστῳ δ. w. *undisturbed mind* IEph 20: 2. The mind becomes discouraged Hv 3, 11, 3; disturbed 2 Cl 20: 1; corrupted away fr. the Lord Hs 4: 7. Fig. *gird up the loins of the mind* 1 Pt 1: 13.
   3. *purpose, plan* (Jos., Vi. 158) UGosp 50f. So prob. in 1 Cl 33: 4, if κατὰ διάνοιαν (lacking in Lat., Syr., and Coptic transl.) is orig.: *in accordance with plan.*
   4. in an unfavorable sense *imagination, conceit* 1 Cl 39: 1.—5. Pl. *senses, impulses* in a bad sense (Num 15: 39) Eph 2: 3. M-M. B. 1240.*

διανοίγω 1 aor. διήνοιξα, pass. διηνοίχθην (since Pla., Lys. p. 210A; LXX).
   1. *open*—**a.** lit. πᾶν ἄρσεν διανοῖγον μήτραν *every first-born male* Lk 2: 23 (Ex 13: 2 al.); the heavens Ac 7: 56.
   b. fig., the ears (Lucian, Charon 21) Mk 7: 34f t.r.; eyes (=make understanding possible, as Gen 3: 5, 7; 4 Km 6: 17) Lk 24: 31; the heart (=enable someone to perceive, as 2 Macc 1: 4; Themist., Orat. 2 De Constantio Imp. p. 29 Harduin διανοίγεταί μου ἡ καρδία κ. διαυγεστέρα γίνεται ἡ ψυχή) Ac 16: 14; the mind Lk 24: 45 (cf. Hos 2: 17).
   2. *explain, interpret* (Aeneas Gaz. [V/VI AD], Theophr. p. 5B Boiss. δ. τὰ τῶν παλαιῶν ἀπόρρητα) the Scriptures Lk 24: 32. Abs. (τὰς γραφάς is to be supplied fr. what precedes) Ac 17: 3.*

διανυκτερεύω *spend the whole night* (intrans. Diod. S. 13, 62, 1; 13, 84, 5; Plut., Mor. 950B; M. Ant. 7, 66; Herodian 1, 16, 4 al.; Job 2: 9c; Philo, Aet. M. 4, In Flacc. 36; Jos., Bell. 3, 418, Ant. 6, 311) ἐν τῇ προσευχῇ Lk 6: 12 (Appian, Bell. Civ. 3, 71, §294 διενυκτέρευσεν ἐν τοῖς ὅπλοις). M-M.*

διανύω 1 aor. διήνυσα (Hom.+)—1. *complete* w. acc.

(Hom. Hymns+; Vett. Val. 81, 27; 109, 4; 330, 9; POxy. 1469, 4; Jos., Bell. 5, 51, Ant. 10, 36) τὸν πλοῦν *the voyage* (Achilles Tat. 5, 17, 1) Ac 21: 7; but *continue* is also possible here (as Xenophon Eph. 3, 2, 12 διενύετο εὐτυχῶς ὁ πλοῦς [Erotici, ed. RHercher, vol. 1, p. 361, 29f]; 1, 11, 2 τ. πλοῦν; 5, 1, 1; 5, 10, 3; 5, 11, 1. S. Field, Notes 134f; Beginn. vol. 4 ad loc. Cf. also Eur., Or. 1663). Either mng. is poss. for δρόμον δ. 1 Cl 20: 2.
   2. intr. *arrive* (*at*), *travel* (*to*) (Polyb. 3, 53, 9; Diod. S. 17, 39, 1 εἰς Βαβυλῶνα; 2 Macc 12: 17, both w. εἰς) 1 Cl 25: 3. M-M.*

διαπαντός s. διά A II 1a.

διαπαρατριβή, ῆς, ἡ (heightened form of παρατριβή 'irritation, friction' Polyb. 2, 36, 5 et al.) *mutual* or *constant irritation* pl. 1 Ti 6: 5 (t.r. παραδιατριβαί).*

διαπέμπω 1 aor. διέπεμψα (Hdt.+; pap.) *send on* ἐπιστολήν (Thu. 1, 129) MPol 20: 1.*

διαπεράω 1 aor. διεπέρασα (Eur., X.+; PFlor. 247, 8; Joseph.) *cross* (*over*) abs. (Jos., Bell. 1, 613) Mt 9: 1; 14: 34. W. the destination given (Jos., Vi. 153) Mk 5: 21 (cf. Dt 30: 13 δ. εἰς τὸ πέραν; PGM 13, 287); 6: 53; Φοινίκην *to Ph.* Ac 21: 2 (Aristot., fgm. 485 Rose εἰς Ἰταλίαν). Point of departure and goal ἐκεῖθεν πρὸς ἡμᾶς δ. Lk 16: 26. M-M.*

διαπλέω 1 aor. διέπλευσα (Thu., Aristoph.+; Dit., Syll.³ 633, 100; PSI 435, 5 [III BC]; Jos., Bell. 2, 103, Ant. 15, 46) *sail through* τὸ πέλαγος *the sea* (Plut., Mor. 206D; Epigr. Gr. 642, 13 πέλαγος διέπλευσε) Ac 27: 5. M-M.*

διαπονέομαι impf. διεπονούμην; 1 aor. pass. ptc. διαπονηθείς (Aeschyl.+; Eccl 10: 9; Philo; Jos., Ant. 8, 165) *be* (*greatly*) *disturbed, annoyed* (so POxy. 743, 22 [2 BC] ἐγὼ ὅλος διαπονοῦμαι; Aq. Gen 6: 6; 1 Km 20: 30) Mk 14: 4 D; Ac 4: 2; 16: 18. M-M.*

διαπορεύομαι impf. διεπορευόμην (Hdt.+; pap., LXX; Ep. Arist. 322) *go, walk through* διά τινος (En. 100, 3) someth. a gate Hs 9, 3, 4; διὰ (τῶν) σπορίμων Mk 2: 23 v.l.; Lk 6: 1; *pass through* (w. acc. of the place X., An. 2, 5, 18; schol. on Apollon. Rhod. 2, 168a; Job 2: 2; Jos., Ant. 5, 67) τὰς πόλεις Ac 16: 4. κατὰ πόλεις Lk 13: 22. διαπορευόμενος *on the way, in passing* (X., An. 2, 2, 11) Ro 15: 24; *go by* Lk 18: 36. M-M.*

διαπορέω impf. διηπόρουν (Pla.+; Hellenistic wr.; pap.; Sym. Ps 76: 5; Da 2: 1; Philo, Leg. All. 1, 85; Jos., Ant. 1, 18) *be greatly perplexed, at a loss* Lk 9: 7. ἐν ἑαυτῷ *in one's own mind* Ac 10: 17. περί τινος *about someth.* (Polyb. 4, 20, 2; Zen.-P. 59 078, 5 [257 BC]) 5: 24 (the constr. δ. περί τινος τί . . . as Jos., Ant. 11, 289). ἐπί τινι (Polyb. 4, 71, 5) *about someth.* Hs 9, 2, 5.—Mid. abs. in the same sense Lk 24: 4 t.r.; Ac 2: 12; Hs 9, 2, 6.*

διαπραγματεύομαι mid. dep., 1 aor. διεπραγματευσάμην (Pla., Phaedo 77D; 95E=examine thoroughly) *gain by trading, earn* (Dionys. Hal. 3, 72; POxy. 1982, 16) τίς τί διεπραγματεύσατο *what each one had gained by trading* Lk 19: 15. M-M.*

διαπρίω impf. pass. διεπριόμην lit. 'saw through' (so Aristoph., Hippocr.+; Diod. S. 4, 76, 5; Dit., Syll.² 587, 160; 304; 1 Ch 20: 3). Pass., fig. *cut to the quick, infuriate* Ac 5: 33. ταῖς καρδίαις *inwardly* 7: 54. M-M.*

διαρθρόω (Hippocr.+) *render capable of articulate speech* (Lucian, Enc. Dem 14 τ. γλῶτταν; Plut., Dem. 11: 1) pass. (Alex. Aphr., An. Mant. II 1 p. 153, 2 διηρθρωμένως λέγει) Lk 1: 64 v.l.*

διαρπάζω (Hom.+; PLond. 35, 21 [161 BC]; LXX) *plunder thoroughly* τὶ *someth.* (Hdt. 1, 88 πόλιν; Diod. S. 12, 76, 5; Appian, Iber. 52 §220; Gen 34: 27; Jos., Ant. 7, 77) a house (Zech 14: 2; Da 2: 5 Theod.; Jos., Bell. 4, 314) Mt 12: 29; Mk 3: 27b; *rob* τὶ *someth.* (Hdt.+) Mk 3: 27a (cf. Inscr. Rom. IV 1029, 18, restored thus: διαρπασάν[των] δὲ καὶ τὰ [σκεύη τῶν σ]ωμάτων=slaves); *steal* ζωήν τινος *someone's livelihood* Hs 9, 26, 2. Of pers. *snatch away, abduct* or *take captive* (Diod. S. 13, 19, 2) τινά someone IRo 7: 1.—Mt 12: 30 v.l. M-M.*

δια(ρ)ρήγνυμι and **διαρήσσω** (Ion.; Bl-D. §101 s.v. ῥήγνυμι; Rob. 1219 s.v. ῥήσσω) 1 aor. διέ(ρ)ρηξα; 2 aor. pass. διε(ρ)ράγη GP 5: 20 (Hom.+; LXX) *tear.*
1. lit. τὶ *someth.*: *a garment* (as a sign of grief Gen 37: 29; Jdth 14: 19; Esth 4: 1 al.; Philippides Com. [IV/III BC] 25, 5 vol. III p. 308 K.; Phlegon of Tralles [Hadr.]: 257 fgm. 36 I 5, Jac.; PLeipz 37, 19 τὴν ἐπικειμένην αὐτοῦ ἐσθῆτα διαρήξαντες; Philo, De Jos. 217; Jos., Bell. 2, 322; Test. Jos. 5: 2.—S. on ἀλαλάζω) Mt 26: 65; Mk 14: 63; Ac 14: 14. Of chains and fetters *break* (Charito 4, 3, 3; Ps.-Apollod. 2, 5, 11, 117; PGM 12, 278; 57, 4; Ps 2: 3; 106: 14; Na 1: 13; Jer 5: 5; Jos., Ant. 5, 300) Lk 8: 29 (spelled διαρήσσων as PGM 4, 1022).—Pass. intr. *tear, burst* (Hero Alex. I p. 18, 21 διαρραγήσεται τὸ τεῖχος; 264, 20; Aesop, Fab. 135 P.=218 H.; 139 P.=239 H.; Lucian, Hist. 20; PGM 36, 263 πέτραι; Bel 27) of nets Lk 5: 6; of the temple curtain GP 5: 20.
2. fig. *shatter, destroy* τὶ *someth.* ἰσχὺν βασιλέων B 12: 11 (Is 45: 1).*

διασαφέω 1 aor. διεσάφησα—1. *explain,* lit. 'make clear' (Eur., Phoen. 398; Pla., Leg. 6, 754A; Polyb. 2, 1, 1; 3, 52, 5; Lucian, M. Peregr. 11; Da 2: 6; Ep. Arist. 171; Jos., Ant. 2, 12; PYale 41, 9) τινί τι: *a parable to someone* Mt 13: 36 (cf. Jos., Ant. 5, 293).
2. *tell plainly, in detail, report* (Polyb. 1, 46, 4; 2, 27, 3; Vett. Val. index; inscr.; PEleph. 18, 3; UPZ 59, 7; 64, 10 al.; 1 Macc 12: 8; 2 Macc 1: 18; 2: 9; 11: 18; Ep. Arist. 51; 297; Jos., Ant. 18, 199; Vi. 374) what had happened Mt 18: 31.—Ac 10: 25 D. M-M.*

διασείω 1 aor. διέσεισα (Hdt.+; Philo, Leg. All. 2, 99; Jos., Bell. 3, 221 al.) *extort money by violence* (lit. 'shake violently'; cf. our slang 'shake down') legal t.t. (UPZ 162 VIII, 13 [117 BC]; 192, 7; 193, 8; POxy. 240, 5 [37 AD] διασεσεισμένῳ ὑπὸ στρατιώτου; 284, 5 [50 AD]; PTebt. 43, 26 [118 BC] συκοφαντηθῶμεν διασεσεισμένοι; 3 Macc 7: 21) w. acc. (UPZ 161, 37 [119 BC]; PAmh. 81, 6) μηδένα *from no one* Lk 3: 14. M-M.*

διασκορπίζω 1 aor. διεσκόρπισα, pass. διεσκορπίσθην; 1 fut. pass. διασκορπισθήσομαι (Polyb. 1, 47, 4; 27, 2, 10; Aelian, V.H. 13, 46; BGU 1049, 7; oft. LXX; Joseph. [s. below]; Test. 12 Patr.) *scatter, disperse* of a flock Mt 26: 31; Mk 14: 27 (both Zech 13: 7 v.l.); God's children J 11: 52; the proud (as Num 10: 34; Ps 67: 2; 88: 11) Lk 1: 51; on the field of battle (Jos., Ant. 8, 404) Ac 5: 37; of the component parts of the bread of the Lord's Supper D 9: 4. Of seed *scatter,* unless it could be taken to mean *winnow* (cf. Ezk 5: 2 δ. τῷ πνεύματι; s. L-S-J lexicon) Mt 25: 24, 26. Of property *waste, squander* Lk 15: 13; 16: 1. M-M.*

διασπαράσσω 1 aor. διεσπάραξα (Aeschyl.+; Parthenius 10, 3 [of dogs]) *tear in pieces* of wolves (Aesop, Fab. 165 H.: the wolf tears the sheep) τὰ ἀρνία 2 Cl 5: 3.*

διασπάω 1 aor. pass. διεσπάσθην; pf. pass. inf. διεσπάσθαι (Eur., Hdt.+; Dit., Syll.³ 364, 11 [III BC]; pap., LXX; Jos., Ant. 6, 186) *tear apart, tear up* of a demoniac: chains (cf. Jer 2: 20) Mk 5: 4; a document B 3: 3 (Is 58: 6); of an angry mob μὴ διασπασθῇ ὁ Παῦλος ὑπ' αὐτῶν that *Paul would be torn in pieces by them* Ac 23: 10 (Dio Chrys. 26[43], 6 ὑπὸ τῶν συγγενῶν διασπασθῆναι; Appian, Bell. Civ. 2, 147 §613; Biogr. p. 444 Ὑπατία διεσπάσθη ὑπὸ τῶν Ἀλεξανδρέων, cf. Hdt. 3, 13; Lucian, Phal. 1, 4). Fig. (w. διέλκειν) *tear apart* the members of Christ, i.e. the churches 1 Cl 46: 7 (cf. Dio Chrys. 28[45], 8 εἰς μέρη δ. τὴν πόλιν; Ael. Aristid. 24, 39 K.=44 p. 836 D.: τὸ σῶμα τ. πόλεως; Iambl., Vi. Pyth. 33, 240 τὸν ἐν ἑαυτοῖς θεόν). M-M.*

διασπείρω 2 aor. pass. διεσπάρην (Soph., Hdt.; PLond. 259, 73; LXX) *scatter* τινὰ someone υἱοὺς Ἀδάμ 1 Cl 29: 2 (Dt 32: 8). Pass. of churches (cf. Lucian, Tox. 33; Iambl., Vi. Pyth. 35, 253; Jos., Ant. 7, 244; 12, 278) Ac 8: 1, 4; 11: 19. M-M.*

διασπορά, ᾶς, ἡ *dispersion* (Philo, Praem. 115; Plut., Mor. 1105A) LXX of dispersion of the Jews among the Gentiles (Dt 28: 25; 30: 4; Jer 41: 17).
1. of those who are dispersed (Is 49: 6; Ps 146: 2; 2 Macc 1: 27; PsSol 8: 28) ἡ δ. τῶν Ἑλλήνων those who are *dispersed among the Gentiles* J 7: 35.—Schürer III⁴ 1ff; JJuster, Les Juifs dans l'Empire romain '14; ACausse, Les Dispersés d'Israël '29; GRosen, Juden u. Phönizier '29; KGKuhn, D. inneren Gründe d. jüd. Ausbreitung: Deutsche Theologie 2, '35, 9–17; HPreisker, Ntl. Zeitgesch. '37, 290–3 (lit.); JATRobinson, NTS 6, '60, 117–31 (4th Gosp.).
2. the place in which the dispersed are found (Jdth 5: 19; Test. Ash. 7: 2). Fig., of Christians who live in dispersion in the world, far fr. their heavenly home αἱ δώδεκα φυλαὶ αἱ ἐν τῇ δ. Js 1: 1. παρεπίδημοι διασποράς 1 Pt 1: 1.—KLSchmidt, TW II 98–104.*

διάσταλμα, ατος, τό (BGU 913, 9 [III AD]) *distinguishing* δ. ῥήματος *special meaning of the teaching* B 10: 11.—PhHaeuser, D. Barnabasbr. '12, 64f.*

διαστέλλω (Pla.+; PLond. 45, 21; LXX; Philo, Mos. 2, 237; Jos., Bell. 5, 62) in our lit. only mid.; impf. διεστελλόμην; 1 aor. διεστειλάμην *order, give orders* (Pla., Rep. 7, 535B; Polyb. 3, 23, 5; Ezk 3: 18f; Jdth 11: 12 al.; Ep. Arist. 131) w. dat. of the pers. (UPZ 42, 23 [162 BC]; 110, 211 [164 BC]; Sb 5675, 3; POxy. 86, 10) Mk 7: 36b; 8: 15; Ac 15: 24. W. dat. of the pers. and ἵνα foll. Mt 16: 20 v.l.; Mk 7: 36a; 9: 9. διεστείλατο αὐτοῖς πολλά he *gave them strict orders* 5: 43. Pass. τὸ διαστελλόμενον *the command* Hb 12: 20 (cf. 2 Macc 14: 28 τὰ διεσταλμένα).—Anz 326f. M-M.*

διάστημα, ατος, τό (Pla.+; pap., LXX, Ep. Arist., Philo, Joseph.—D in Ac 5: 7 spells it διάστεμα [Bl-D. §109, 3 app.]) *interval* ἐγένετο ὡς ὡρῶν τριῶν δ. *after an interval of about three hours* Ac 5: 7 (cf. Aristot. 800b, 5; Polyb. 9, 1, 1 τετραετὲς δ.; Philo; PPar. 1, 381; PGiess. 40 II, 15 μετὰ τὸ πληρωθῆναι τὸ τοῦ χρόνου διάστημα); δ. ποιεῖν (Gen 32: 17) *leave an interval* B 9: 8. M-M.*

διαστολή, ῆς, ἡ (since Anaximander 23; inscr., pap., LXX, Ep. Arist., Philo) *difference, distinction* (so Chrysipp.: Stoic. II 158; Philod., De Pietate 123G; Ex 8: 19 δώσω δ.; Philo, Mos. 2, 158) Ro 3: 22; δ. Ἰουδαίου τε καὶ Ἕλληνος *distinction betw. a Jew and a Gentile* 10: 12. ἐὰν διαστολὴν τοῖς φθόγγοις μὴ δῷ *if they* (musical instruments) *make no clear distinction in their tones* 1 Cor 14: 7. M-M.*

διαστρέφω 1 aor. διέστρεψα; pf. pass. ptc. διεστραμ-μένος (Aeschyl., Hippocr.+; LXX, En., Test. 12 Patr.; Sib. Or. 3, 106).

1. *make crooked, pervert—a.* lit. (Philosophenspr. p. 489, 37 δ. of objects that turn out as failures in the hands of a clumsy workman, and whose shape is therefore distorted) of a vessel on the potter's wheel: *become misshapen* 2 Cl 8: 2.

b. fig. (Demosth. 18, 140 τἀληθές; Dio Chrys. 59[76], 4; En. 99, 2): τὰς ὁδοὺς τοῦ κυρίου τ. εὐθείας *make crooked the straight ways of the Lord* Ac 13: 10 (cf. Pr 10: 9; 11: 20); μετὰ στρεβλοῦ δ. *w. a perverse man you will deal perversely* 1 Cl 46: 3 (Ps 17: 27). διεστραμμένος *perverted* in the moral sense, *depraved* (Dio Chrys. 67[17], 22; Sent. Aesopi 33 p. 255 P. ψυχῆς διεστραμμένης) γενεά w. ἄπιστος Mt 17: 17; Lk 9: 41; Phil 2: 15 (Dt 32: 5; cf. Pr 6: 14; Epict. 3, 6, 8 οἱ μὴ παντάπασιν διεστραμμένοι τῶν ἀνθρώπων; 1, 29, 3). λαλεῖν διεστραμμένα *teach perversions* (of the truth) Ac 20: 30 (cf. Alciphr. 4, 17, 2 διεστραμμένοι κανόνες).

2. *mislead* τινά *someone* 1 Cl 46: 8; 47: 5. τὸ ἔθνος Lk 23: 2 (cf. Polyb. 5, 41, 1; 8, 24, 3; 3 Km 18: 17f). πολλούς 1 Cl 46: 9; *turn away* τινὰ ἀπό τινος (Ex 5: 4) Ac 13: 8. M-M.*

διασῴζω (on the orthography s. Bl-D. §26 app.; Mlt.-H. 84; Mayser 134) 1 aor. διέσωσα, pass. διεσώθην (Eur., Hdt.+; inscr., pap., LXX, En.; Ep. Arist. 45; Joseph.) *bring safely through,* also *save, rescue* without special feeling for the mng. of διά (X., Mem. 2, 10, 2; PGM 4, 1936; 8, 32; En. 100, 6; Philo, Aet. M. 35) act. and pass. δι' ὕδατος (s. διά A I 2) 1 Pt 3: 20; cf. 1 Cl 9: 4 (Jos., C. Ap. 1, 130 περὶ τῆς λάρνακος, ἐν ᾗ Νῶχος διεσώθη, Ant. 1, 78). 1 Pt 3: 20 has a phrase w. εἰς in connection w. δ. (like Lucian, Ver. Hist. 2, 35). ἐκ τῆς θαλάσσης *fr. the shipwreck* Ac 28: 4 (PVat. A 6=Witkowski p. 65: δια-σεσῶσθαι ἐκ μεγάλων κινδύνων; Dit., Syll.³ 528, 10); cf. vs. 1. ἐπὶ τὴν γῆν *bring safely to land* 27: 44. ἵνα τὸν Παῦλον διασώσωσι πρὸς Φήλικα *that they might bring Paul safely to Felix* 23: 24 (δ. πρός τινα as Jos., Ant. 5, 15); *save* fr. danger (Jon 1: 6) 27: 43; 1 Cl 12: 5f. Pass. *escape death* (EpJer 54; Jos., Ant. 9, 141) MPol 8: 2. Of sick persons *be cured* Mt 14: 36; also act. Lk 7: 3. M-M.*

διαταγή, ῆς, ἡ *ordinance, direction* (Vett. Val. 342, 7; 355, 18; Ps.-Callisthenes 1, 33; inscr.; pap. [s. Nägeli 38; Dssm., LO 70f [LAE 86ff]; Inscr. Rom. IV 661, 17; 734, 12; PFay. 133, 4]; 2 Esdr [Ezra] 4: 11) of God Ro 13: 2; 1 Cl 20: 3. ἐλάβετε τὸν νόμον εἰς διαταγὰς ἀγγέλων *you received the law by* [εἰς 9b] *directions of angels* (i.e., by God's directing angels [to transmit it]) Ac 7: 53 (cf. Gal 3: 19; Hb 2: 2; LXX Dt 33: 2; Philo, Somn. 1, 141ff; Jos., Ant. 15, 136 and s. Ltzm., Hdb. on Gal 3: 19). M-M.*

διάταγμα, ατος, τό *edict, command* (Philod., Rhet. II 289 Sudh.; Diod. S. 18, 64, 5; Plut., Marcell. 24, 13; Epict. 1, 25, 4; inscr., pap., LXX; Philo, Sacr. Abel. 88 al.; Joseph.; loanw. in rabb.) of the king (so PGiess. 40 II, 8 of Caracalla; 2 Esdr [Ezra] 7: 11; Esth 3: 13d; Jos., Ant. 11, 215; 19, 292; Preisigke, Fachwörter) Hb 11: 23. διατάγματα τ. ἀποστόλων ITr 7:1. M-M.*

διάταξις, εως, ἡ (since Hdt. 9, 26) *command* (Polyb., Plut., inscr., pap., LXX, Philo; loanw. in rabb.) of God (cf. PRain. 20, 15; Dit., Syll.³ 876, 5; Ep. Arist. 192) 1 Cl 33: 3.*

διαταράσσω 1 aor. pass. διεταράχθην (X., Pla.+; Polyb. 11, 1, 9; Diod. S. 18, 7, 6 [pass.]; Jos., Ant. 2, 120, Vi. 281 [pass.]; Sym. 3 Km 21: 43) *confuse, perplex* (greatly) ἐπὶ τῷ λόγῳ διεταράχθη *she was greatly perplexed at the saying* Lk 1: 29.*

διατάσσω 1 aor. διέταξα; fut. mid. διατάξομαι; 1 aor. mid. διεταξάμην; 1 aor. pass. διετάχθην, ptc. διατα-χθείς; 2 aor. ptc. διαταγείς; pf. pass. ptc. διατεταγμέ-νος (Hes., Hdt.+; inscr., pap., LXX, Ep. Arist., Philo, Joseph.) *order, direct, command* (Jos., Ant. 4, 308; 15, 113) w. dat. of the pers. Mt 11: 1; 1 Cor 9: 14; 16: 1; 1 Cl 20: 6. W. inf. foll. (Jos., Ant. 4, 205) Lk 8: 55; Ac 18: 2. Pass. Dg 7: 2. τὰ διατασσόμενα *orders* 1 Cl 37: 2. Also τὸ διατεταγμένον *order* (Ep. Arist. 92; POxy. 105, 7 τὰ ὑπ' ἐμοῦ διατεταγμένα) Lk 3: 13. κατὰ τὸ δ. αὐτοῖς *in accordance w. their orders* (POxy. 718, 25 κατὰ τὰ διατεταγμένα) Ac 23: 31; cf. 1 Cl 43: 1. τὰ διαταχθέντα *what was ordered* Lk 17: 9, cf. 10; (ὁ νόμος; so Hes., Op. 274) διαταγεὶς δι' ἀγγέλων *ordered through angels* Gal 3: 19 (s. διαταγή, end).—Mid. (in same sense Pla.+; Dit., Syll.³ 709, 26, Or. 331, 53; Philo) *order, command* w. dat. of the pers. Tit 1: 5; IEph 3: 1; ITr 3: 3; IRo 4: 3. W. dat. of the pers. and inf. foll. Ac 24: 23; Hv 3, 1, 4. Abs. οὕτως ἐν τ. ἐκκλησίαις πάσαις δ. *I make this rule in all the churches* 1 Cor 7: 17. καθὼς διετάξατο *just as he directed* Ac 7: 44. W. acc. of the thing τὰ λοιπά 1 Cor 11: 34. οὕτως διατεταγμένος ἦν *he had arranged it so* Ac 20: 13. M-M.*

διατελέω intr. *continue, remain* w. ptc. or adj. to denote the state in which one remains (Hdt.+; Thu. 1, 34, 3 ἀσφαλέστατος διατελεῖ; Diod. S. 11, 49, 4 καλῶς πολιτευόμενοι διετέλεσαν; PHib. 35, 5; UPZ 59, 4 [168 BC]; BGU 287, 7 ἀεὶ θύων τοῖς θεοῖς διετέλεσα; 2 Macc 5: 27; Dt 9: 7; Ep. Arist. 187; Philo, Aet. M. 19; 93; Jos., Ant. 15, 263, Vi. 423) ἄσιτοι διατελεῖτε *you have been continually without food* Ac 27: 33 (Aristotle in Apollon. Paradox. 25 ἄποτος διετέλεσεν). M-M.*

διατηρέω impf. διετήρουν (Pla.+; inscr., pap., LXX, Ep. Arist.; Philo, Aet. M. 35; Jos., Ant. 6, 101; 10, 42) *keep* τὰ ῥήματα ἐν τῇ καρδίᾳ *treasure the words in the heart* Lk 2: 51=συνετήρει 2: 19 (cf. Gen 37: 11; Da 7: 28 Theod. v.l.); δ. ἑαυτὸν ἔκ τινος *keep oneself free fr. someth.* Ac 15: 29 (cf. Pr 21: 23; Test. Dan 6: 8 ἑαυτοὺς ἀπό). βουλὴν *keep counsel* Dg 8: 10 (cf. Diod. S. 4, 16, 3 ὅρκον διετήρησε; Ep. Arist. 206 τ. ἀλήθειαν; Jos., C. Ap. 1, 210). M-M.*

διατί s. διά B II 2.

διατίθημι (Hdt.+) in our lit. only mid. διατίθεμαι (X.+; inscr., pap., LXX, Joseph.; Sib. Or. 3, 498) fut. δια-θήσομαι; 2 aor. διεθέμην, ptc. διαθέμενος.

1. *decree, ordain* (Ps 104: 9; 2 Ch 7: 18) τὶ *someth.* (Appian, Bell. Civ. 4, 95 §401 τοιαῦτα= this sort of thing) τὰ δικαιώματά μου *my ordinances* B 10: 2.—διαθήκην (q.v. 2) δ. *issue a decree* (LXX; the same expr.='conclude an agreement' in Aristoph., Av. 439f) τινί *to* or *for someone* Hb 8: 10; PK 2 p. 15, 5; 6; 7 (both Jer 38[31]: 31-3). ἐν ἡμῖν *among us* B 14: 5. πρός τινα *to someone* (Ex 24: 8; Dt 4: 23; Josh 9: 15) Ac 3: 25; Hb 10: 16.

2. *assign, confer* τὶ *someth.* (X., Cyr. 5, 2, 7 τ. θυγατέρα; Andoc. 4, 30; Diog. L. 1, 69) w. dat. of the pers. favored διέθετό μοι ὁ πατήρ βασιλείαν Lk 22: 29 (cf. 2 Km 5: 3; in sense, 3, Jos., Ant. 13, 407 τ. βασιλείαν διέθετο).

3. extremely oft. *dispose of property by a will, make a will* (Pla., Isaeus+; PEleph. 2, 2; POxy. 104, 4; 105, 2; 489, 3; PLeipz. 29, 8 al.; Jos., Ant. 13, 407; Test. 12 Patr.): ὁ διαθέμενος *the testator* (Isaeus+; BGU 448, 24;

POxy. 99, 9; 15; Dit., Or. 509, 6; 16; cf. JBehm, Διαθήκη im NT '12, 8; 87, 6) Hb 9: 16f. M-M.*

διατρίβω impf. διέτριβον; 1 aor. διέτριψα, ptc. διατρίψας (Hom.+; inscr., pap., LXX; Ep. Arist. 283; Joseph.) lit. 'rub through, wear away'; fig. *spend* (Hdt.+, but even Il. 19, 150 is sim.) w. acc. τὸν χρόνον (Lysias 3, 11; BGU 1140, 4 [5 BC] διατρείψας ἐνταῦθα τὸν πάντα χρόνον; Jos., Ant. 6, 297) Ac 14: 3, 28. ἡμέρας τινὰς (X., Hell. 6, 5, 49; cf. Lev 14: 8) 16: 12; cf. 20: 6; 25: 6, 14. Abs. *stay, remain* μετά τινος *with someone* (Pla., Apol. 33B, Phaed. 49A al.) J 3: 22; 11: 54 v.l.; MPol 5: 1.— Ac 12: 19; 14: 19 v.l. W. the place given ἐν Ἀντιοχείᾳ 15: 35; cf. 14: 7 D (PHal. 1, 182 ἐν Ἀπόλλωνος πόλει δ.; Sb 1002, 9; 2 Macc 14: 23; Jdth 10: 2; Jos., Bell. 1, 387). ἐπὶ γῆς *on earth* Dg 5: 9 (Alciphr. 2, 22, 2 ἐπὶ Κεραμεικοῦ; POxy. 2756 [78/79 AD], 8 and 9 ἐπὶ Ἀλεξανδρίας). ἐκεῖ (Jos., Ant. 8, 267) Ac 25: 14. M-M. B. 569.*

διατροφή, ῆς, ἡ *support, sustenance* (X., Vect. 4, 49; Diod. S. 19, 32, 2; Plut.; PTebt. 52, 16 [114 BC]; POxy. 275, 19; 494, 16 al.; 1 Macc 6: 49; Jos., Ant. 2, 88; 4, 231) pl. in same sense *means of subsistence, food* (with ἔχειν as Epict., Ench. 12, 1) 1 Ti 6: 8. M-M.*

διαυγάζω 1 aor. διηύγασα (Philo Bybl. in Euseb., Pr. Ev. 1, 10, 50; Plut., Mor. 893E; Dionys. Periegetes [II AD] 1120 ed. GBernhardy [1828]; PLond. 130, 70; PGM 4, 991; 13, 165; Aq. Job 25: 5; Jos., Ant. 5, 349 [pass.=a light dawned on him]).
1. *shine through* (Philo Mech. 57, 27) 2 Cor 4: 4 v.l.—2. *dawn, break* ἕως οὖ ἡμέρα διαυγάσῃ *until the day dawns* 2 Pt 1: 19 (cf. Polyb. 3, 104, 5 ἅμα τῷ διαυγάζειν; Passio Andreae 8 p. 18, 30 B.). JBoehmer, ZNW 22, '23, 228-33. M-M.*

διαυγής, ές (Pre-Socr.+; PGM 4, 497; Aq. Pr 16: 2; Philo; Jos., Ant. 3, 37 ὕδωρ; 17, 169) *transparent, pure* ὕαλος Rv 21: 21 (s. διαφανής).*

διαφανής, ές (Soph., Hdt.+) *transparent* (so Aristoph., Hippocr.+; Achilles Tat. 4, 18, 4 ὕαλος διαφανής; Dit., Syll.³ 736, 16; 21; Ex 30: 34; Philo, Leg. ad Gai. 364) Rv 21: 21 t.r. (for διαυγής). M-M.*

διαφέρω 1 aor. διήνεγκα; impf. mid. διεφερόμην (Hom. Hymns, Pind.+; inscr., pap., LXX, Ep. Arist., Philo, Joseph.).
1. trans.—**a.** *carry through* (cf. 1 Esdr 5: 53) σκεῦος διὰ τοῦ ἱεροῦ *a vessel (through) the temple* Mk 11: 16 (perh. in ref. to taking a shortcut; cf. Mishnah, Berakoth 9, 5). Stones through a gate Hs 9, 4, 5; 9, 15, 5; 9, 4, 1 v.l.
b. *spread* of a teaching (Lucian, Dial. Deor. 24, 1 ἀγγελίας δ.; Plut., Mor. 163D φήμη διαφέρεται) Ac 13: 49.
c. *drive* or *carry about, drift* of a ship (Philo, Migr. Abr. 148 σκάφος ὑπ' ἐναντίων πνευμάτων διαφερόμενον. Strabo 3, 2, 7; Lucian, Hermot. 28; Plut., Mor. 552c, Galba 26, 5 al.) 27: 27.
2. intr.—**a.** *differ, be different* τινός *fr. someone or someth.* οὐδέν *in no respect, not at all* (Pla., Apol. 35B οὗτοι γυναικῶν οὐδὲν διαφέρουσι; Epict. 1, 5, 6; 2, 19, 6 al.; cf. Jos., Ant. 2, 153) οὐδὲν δ. δούλου Gal 4: 1.—Dg 3: 5.—δ. τινὸς ἔν τινι (Pla., Pol. 568A; Demosth. 18, 189) *differ fr. someth.* w. *respect to someth.* 1 Cor 15: 41.
b. differ to one's advantage fr. someone or someth.= *be worth more than, be superior to* τινός (class.; Dio Chrys. 27[44], 10; POxy. 1061, 12 [22 BC] διαφέρετε τοῦ Πτολεμαίου ἐμπειρίᾳ; 3 Macc 6: 26; Jos., Ant. 4, 97; 8, 42; 20, 189) Mt 6: 26; 10: 31; 12: 12; Lk 12: 7, 24. Abs.

τὰ διαφέροντα *the things that really matter* (Ps.-Pla., Eryx. 6 p. 394E.—Opp. τὰ ἀδιάφορα) Ro 2: 18; Phil 1: 10 (cf. Plut., Mor. 43E; 73A ὑπὲρ μεγάλων καὶ σφόδρα διαφερόντων al. [PWendland, Philol. 57, 1897, 115]; Wadd. 410, 2 τὰ δ. αὐτοῖς=what is important for them).
c. impers. οὐδέν μοι διαφέρει *it makes no difference to me* (Pla., Prot. 316B al.; Demosth. 9, 50; Polyb. 3, 21, 9; Dionys. Hal., De Lys. 25; Aelian, V.H. 1, 25 al.; POxy. 1348) Gal 2: 6. M-M.*

διαφεύγω 2 aor. διέφυγον *escape* (Hdt.+; Dit., Syll.³ 709, 25; 35; 731, 15; PTebt. 44, 28 [114 BC]; Josh 8: 22; Pr 19: 5; 2 Macc 7: 31; Philo, Spec. Leg. 1, 36; Jos., Bell. 2, 441 al.) Ac 27: 42; IMg 1: 3. M-M.*

διαφημίζω 1 aor. διεφήμισα, pass. διεφημίσθην *make known* by word of mouth, *spread the news about* (Arat., Phaen. 221; Dionys. Hal. 11, 46; Palaeph. p. 21, 12; Vett. Val. index; Jos., Bell. 2, 594; 6, 116) τινά Mt 9: 31. τὸν λόγον (cf. Jos., Bell. 1, 651) *spread widely, disseminate* Mk 1: 45; pass. Mt 28: 15. M-M.*

διαφθείρω pf. pass. ptc. διεφθαρμένος; 2 aor. pass. διεφθάρην (Hom.+; inscr., pap., LXX, Philo, Joseph., Test. 12 Patr.).
1. *spoil, destroy* of rust eating into iron Dg 2: 2; of moths (Philo, Abr. 11), that eat clothes Lk 12: 33.—IMg 10: 2 (fig.); *destroy* persons and nations (Aristot. p. 1323a, 31; Diod. S. 5, 54, 3; 12, 68, 2; Plut., Demosth. 28, 4; LXX; Jos., Ant. 2, 26; 11, 211) Rv 11: 18a; Hv 4, 2, 3; s 9, 1, 9; 9, 26, 1; 7. Pass. *be destroyed* of the outer man 2 Cor 4: 16 (cf. Ps.-Pla., Alcib. 1 p. 135A διαφθαρῆναι τ. σῶμα; Lucian, Dial. Deor. 13, 2; Philo, Decal. 124).—Hv 2, 3, 3. Of ships (Diod. S. 11, 19, 3; 13, 13, 4; schol. on Apollon. Rhod. 2, 1111-12b διαφθαρείσης τῆς νεώς) Rv 8: 9; a kingdom IEph 19: 3. Of the bodies of starving persons *waste away* (Appian, Bell. Civ. 2, 66 §274 λιμῷ διαφθαρῆναι; POxy. 938, 4; Philo, Leg. ad Gai. 124) Hv 3, 9, 3.
2. *ruin* in the moral sense (Diod. S. 16, 54, 4 τὰ ἤθη τ. ἀνθρώπων; Dio Chrys. 26[43], 10 τοὺς νέους; Jos., C. Ap. 2, 264): the earth (i.e., its people) Rv 11: 18b; 19: 2 v.l.; δ. τὴν εἰς θεὸν γνώμην IRo 7: 1. διεφθαρμένοι ἄνθρωποι τὸν νοῦν 1 Ti 6: 5. Of the mind pass. *be corrupted* Hs 4: 7 (cf. Pla., Leg. 10, 888A and Jos., Ant. 9, 222 δ. τὴν διάνοιαν; Aeschyl., Ag. 932 and Dionys. Hal. 5, 21 τ. γνώμην; Dio Chrys. 60+61[77+78], 45 ψυχὴ διεφθαρμένη). M-M. B. 762.*

διαφθορά, ᾶς, ἡ (Aeschyl., Hdt.+; LXX, Philo; Jos., C. Ap. 2, 259) *destruction, corruption* of the body ἰδεῖν δ. (εἶδον 5) Ac 2: 27, 31; 13: 35ff (all Ps 15: 10; s. JRegula, PM 15, '11, 230-3; REMurphy, Šaḥat in the Qumran Lit., Biblica 39, '58, 61-66); ὑποστρέφειν εἰς δ. *return to decay* (i.e., prob. the realm of the dead) vs. 34 (cf. ἐλθεῖν εἰς δ. Job 33: 28; καταβαίνειν εἰς δ. Ps 29: 10).*

διαφορά, ᾶς, ἡ *difference* (Thu. et al.; UPZ 110, 96 [164 BC]; Sir Prol., l. 26; 1 Macc 3: 18; Wsd 7: 20) δ. πολλή *a great difference* (Jos., Vi. 2; cf. Philo, Op. M. 134) B 18: 1; D 1: 1. μεταξύ τινος καὶ ἄλλου *betw. someone and another* MPol 16: 1. M-M. s.v. διάφορος.*

διάφορος, ον—1. *different* (so Hdt.+; POxy. 1033, 88; PGrenf. II 92, 8; Da 7: 7 Theod.; Jos., Ant. 1, 166; Test. 12 Patr.) χαρίσματα *spiritual gifts* Ro 12: 6. βαπτισμοί *washings* Hb 9: 10.
2. *outstanding, excellent* (since Antiphanes Com. 175, 3; Diod. S. 2, 57; Sb 1005; Ep. Arist. 97; Jos., Bell. 5, 161; the rare comparative διαφορώτερος also Sext. Emp., Phys. 1, 218) διαφορώτερον ὄνομα *a more excellent name*

Hb 1: 4 (=1 Cl 36: 2). διαφορώτεραι λειτουργίαι 8: 6. M-M.*

διαφυλάσσω 1 aor. διεφύλαξα (Hdt.+; inscr., pap.; a special favorite of the magical lit. [SEitrem and AFridrichsen, E. chr. Amulett '21, 6; 25]; Ep. Arist. 272; Philo, Aet. M. 36; 74; Jos., Ant. 11, 155 al.—In LXX esp. of God's care, as PGiess. 17, 7; BGU 1081, 4 εὔχομαι τοῖς θεοῖς ὑπέρ σου, ἵνα σε διαφυλάξουσι; 984, 27 al.; PGM 4, 2516; 13, 633) *guard, protect* τινά someone of God 1 Cl 59: 2; of angels Lk 4: 10 (Ps 90: 11). M-M.*

διαχειρίζω 1 aor. mid. διεχειρισάμην (Andoc., Lysias +); in our lit. only mid. in the mng. *lay violent hands on, kill, murder* (Polyb. 8, 23, 8; Diod. S. 18, 46; Plut., Mor. 220B; Herodian 3, 12, 1; Jos., Bell. 1, 113, Ant. 15, 173 al.; Third Corinthians 3: 11) τινά *someone* Ac 5: 30. Cf. 26: 21. M-M.*

διαχλευάζω (Demosth. 50, 49; Polyb. 18, 4, 4; Ps.-Pla., Axioch. p. 364B; Jos., Bell. 2, 281, Ant. 15, 220) *deride* abs. *mock* Ac 2: 13.*

διαχωρίζω (Aristoph.+, X., Pla.; pap., LXX, Philo, Joseph.) *separate* τὶ ἀπό τινος someth. fr. someth. 1 Cl 33: 3 (cf. Gen 1: 4, 6f; Jos., Bell. 1, 535; Test. Jos. 13: 6). Pass. *be separated, part, go away* (Diod. S. 4, 53, 4; Jos., Ant. 15, 259) ἀπό τινος (PGM 12, 459 ποίησον τὸν δεῖνα διαχωρισθῆναι ἀπὸ τοῦ δεῖνος; Herm. Wr. 1, 11b; Gen 13: 9, 11; Sus 13 Theod.) Lk 9: 33; 1 Cl 10: 4 (Gen 13: 14). M-M.*

διγαμία, ας, ἡ *second marriage* (Cat. Cod. Astr. XII 174, 10) Tit 1: 9 v.l. (s. δίγαμος).*

δίγαμος, ον—1. *married to two people* at the same time (Manetho 5, 291).

2. *married for the second time* (Stesichorus [VII/VI BC] 17 Diehl [on this schol., Eur., Or. 249] δ. w. τρίγαμος of women who leave their husbands and marry a second or third time. Eccl. writers [Hippolytus, Elench. 9, 12, 22 Wendl. al.] use it of a normal second marriage; δίγ. in this sense Leontius 13 p. 26, 10; τρίγαμος γυνή= married for the third time also Theocr. 12, 5. Normal marriage is also kept in mind in Ptolem., Apotel. 4, 5, 1; 2: ἄγαμος= unmarried, μονόγαμος= married once, πολύγαμος [also 4, 5, 4] married several times) Tit 1: 9 v.l.*

διγλωσσία, ας, ἡ *being double-tongued* D 2: 4; B 19: 7 v.l.*

δίγλωσσος, ον (as 'bilingual' since Thu. 8, 85, 2; also Diod. S. 17, 68, 5; schol. on Pla. 600A) *double-tongued, deceitful* (of snakes schol. on Nicander, Ther. 371 οἵτινες δύο γλώσσας ἔχουσιν. Also of persons: Pr 11: 13; Sir 5: 9, 14f; 28: 13; Philo, Sacr. Abel. 32 p. 215, 12; Sib. Or. 3, 37.—Theognis 1, 91 likew. speaks of one ὅς μιῇ γλώσσῃ δίχ' ἔχει νόον) D 2: 4; B 19: 7 v.l.*

διγνώμων, ον (schol. on Eur., Or. 633; Simplicius in Epict. p. 134, 53) *double-minded, fickle* D 2: 4; B 19: 7.*

διδακτικός, ή, όν *skilful in teaching* (Philod., Rhet II p. 22, 10 Sudh.; Philo, Praem. 27, Congr. 35) 1 Ti 3: 2; 2 Ti 2: 24. M-M.*

διδακτός, ή, όν (Pind., X., Pla.+=teachable; so also Ep. Arist. 236; Philo) *taught*.

1. of pers. *instructed* (1 Macc 4: 7) διδακτοὶ θεοῦ *taught by God* J 6: 45 (Is 54: 13; cf. PsSol 17: 32 βασιλεὺς δίκαιος διδακτὸς ὑπὸ θεοῦ; Socrat., Ep. 1, 10 προηγόρευσα . . . διδάσκοντος τ. θεοῦ).

2. *imparted, taught* (Jos., Bell. 6, 38) w. gen. (Soph., El. 344 νουθετήματα κείνης διδακτά taught by her) ἐν διδακτοῖς ἀνθρωπίνης σοφίας λόγοις *in words imparted by human wisdom,* opp. ἐν δ. πνεύματος *in that which is imparted by the Spirit* to someone 1 Cor 2: 13. M-M.*

διδασκαλία, ας, ἡ (Pind.+; inscr., pap., LXX).

1. act., *the act of teaching, instruction* (X., Oec. 19, 15 ἆρα ἡ ἐρώτησις δ. ἐστίν; Epict. 2, 14, 1; Dit., Syll.³ 672, 4 [II BC] ὑπὲρ τᾶς τῶν παίδων διδασκαλίας al.; POxy. 1101, 4; Sir 39: 8; Philo; Jos., Ant. 3, 5; 13, 311) Ro 12: 7. Of Timothy 1 Ti 4: 13, 16; εἰς δ. ἐγράφη *was written for instruction* Ro 15: 4; ὠφέλιμος πρὸς δ. *useful for instr.* 2 Ti 3: 16 (perh. a rabbinic-type expr., לְלַמֵּד, cf. Sanh. 73a, underlies the usage of δ. with a prep. in these two passages). πρὸς τ. χρείας *as the needs required* Papias 2: 15.

2. pass., *of that which is taught, teaching* (cf. X., Cyr. 8, 7, 24 παρὰ τῶν προγεγενημένων μανθάνετε. αὕτη γὰρ ἀρίστη δ.; Sir 24: 33; Pr 2: 17; ancient Christian prayer [CSchmidt: Heinrici-Festschr. '14 p. 71, 26] δ. τῶν εὐαγγελίων) w. ἐντάλματα ἀνθρώπων (after Is 29: 13) Mt 15: 9; Mk 7: 7; Col 2: 22; δ. δαιμονίων 1 Ti 4: 1; κακὴ δ. IEph 16: 2; δυσωδία τῆς δ. 17: 1.—Eph 4: 14. Freq. of the teachings of eccl. Christianity: δ. τοῦ σωτῆρος ἡμῶν θεοῦ Tit 2: 10 (on the gen. cf. En. 10, 8 ἡ δ. 'Αζαήλ); δ. ὑγιαίνουσα 1 Ti 1: 10; 2 Ti 4: 3; Tit 1: 9; 2: 1; καλὴ δ. 1 Ti 4: 6; ἡ κατ' εὐσέβειαν δ. *godly teaching* 6: 3. W. no modifiers w. λόγος 5: 17; 6: 1; 2 Ti 3: 10; Tit 2: 7. M-M.*

διδάσκαλος, ου, ὁ (Hom. Hymns, Aeschyl.+; inscr., pap., Esth 6: 1; 2 Macc 1: 10; Philo; Jos., Ant. 13, 115, Vi. 274) *teacher* (*master* in the British sense of *teacher*) δ. ἐθνῶν Dg 11: 1; πέποιθας σεαυτὸν εἶναι δ. νηπίων *you are sure that you are* (i.e. can be) *a teacher of the young* Ro 2: 19f. ὀφείλοντες εἶναι διδάσκαλοι *although you ought to be teachers* Hb 5: 12. W. μαθητής (Epict. 4, 6, 11; Jos., Ant. 17, 334) Mt 10: 24f; Lk 6: 40; IMg 9: 2. Used in addressing Jesus (corresp. to the title רַבִּי rabbi) Mt 8: 19; 12: 38; 19: 16; 22: 16, 24, 36; Mk 4: 38; 9: 17, 38; 10: 17, 20, 35; 12: 14, 19, 32; 13: 1; Lk 7: 40; 9: 38 al.; IEph 15: 1; IMg 9: 2f. W. other titles Dg 9: 6. He is called βασιλεὺς καὶ δ. MPol 17: 3. 'Ραββί w. translation J 1: 38, also 'Ραββουνί 20: 16. W. the art. (= רַבָּא) Mt 9: 11; 17: 24; 26: 18; Mk 5: 35; 14: 14; Lk 22: 11; J 11: 28 (Philo, Leg. ad Gai. 53 πάρεστιν ὁ δ.). ὁ δ. καὶ ὁ κύριος (= מָר) as a title of respect 13: 13f. Used of John the Baptist Lk 3: 12. Of Jewish learned men Lk 2: 46; J 3: 10 (Petosiris, fgm. 36 b l. 13 ὁ διδάσκαλος λέγει=the [well-known] teacher says; sim. Mk 14: 14 and par.).—As an official of the Christian church Ac 13: 1; 1 Cor 12: 28f; Eph 4: 11; 2 Ti 1: 11; Js 3: 1 (ThabOrbiso, Verb. Dom. 21, '41, 169–82); D 15: 1f; paid 13: 2. Cf. Hv 3, 5, 1; m 4, 3, 1; s 9, 15, 4; 9, 16, 5; 9, 25, 2; B 1: 8; 4: 9. HGreeven, ZNW 44, '52/'53, 16–31. Of Polycarp δ. ἀποστολικὸς καὶ προφητικός MPol 16: 2; δ. ἐπίσημος 19: 1; ὁ τῆς 'Ασίας δ. 12: 2. Of heretical teachers δ. πονηρίας Hs 9, 19, 2. υἱὸς διδασκάλου as transl. of Barabbas (q.v.) GH 18 (Kl. T. 8³ p. 10, l. 9ff app.).—EReisch in Pauly-W. V '05, 401ff; Dalman, Worte 272ff; Schürer II⁴ 372ff; 491ff; GFMoore, Judaism I '27, 308ff.—AHarnack, Lehre d. Zwölf Ap.: TU II 1; 2, 1884, 93ff., Mission I⁴ '23, 345ff; CHDodd, Jesus as Teacher and Prophet: Mysterium Christi '30, 53–66; KHRengstorf, TW II 138–68; FVFilson, JBL 60, '41, 317–28; EFascher, ThLZ 79, '54, 325–42; HBraun, Qumran u. d. NT II, '66, 54–74 (Jesus and the Teacher of Righteousness). M-M.

διδάσκω impf. ἐδίδασκον; fut. διδάξω; 1 aor. ἐδίδαξα, pass. ἐδιδάχθην (Hom.+; inscr., pap., LXX; Ep. Arist. 131; Philo, Joseph., Test. 12 Patr.) *teach*.

1. abs. Mt 4: 23; Mk 1: 21; J 7: 14; 1 Cor 4: 17; 1 Ti 4: 11; 6: 2; IEph 15: 1; Pol 2: 3. Of the activity of the Christian διδάσκαλοι Hv 3, 5, 1. ἐποίησαν ὡς ἐδιδάχθησαν *they did as they were told* Mt 28: 15.

2. used—a. w. acc. of the pers. *teach someone* (Dit., Syll.³ 593, 15; PLond. 43, 6 παιδάρια) Hb 8: 11 (Jer 38[31]: 34); Mt 5: 2; Mk 9: 31; Lk 4: 31; J 7: 35 al.; Israel B 5: 8.

b. w. acc. of the thing (X., Cyr. 1, 6, 20; Dit., Syll.³ 578, 34 τὰ μουσικά; Jos., Ant. 9, 4) Mt 15: 9 (Is 29: 13); 22: 16; Ac 18: 11, 25; φόβον θεοῦ B 19: 5 (cf. Ps 33: 12) τὸν περὶ ἀληθείας λόγον Pol 3: 2; Ac 15: 35 (Herm. Wr. 1, 29 τ. λόγους διδάσκων, πῶς σωθήσονται); τ. εὐαγγέλιον MPol 4.

c. w. acc. of the pers. and the thing *teach someone someth.* (X., Mem. 1, 2, 10, Cyr. 1, 6, 28; Sallust. 3 p. 12; Dit., Syll.³ 450, 5f; δ. τοὺς παῖδας τὸν ὕμνον; Philo, Rer. Div. Her. 39; Jos., Ant. 8, 395) ὑμᾶς διδάξει πάντα *he will instruct you in everything* J 14: 26.—Mk 4: 2; Ac 21: 21; Hb 5: 12. Pass. διδάσκομαί τι (Solon 22, 7 Diehl²; Dit., Or. 383, 165 διδασκόμενοι τὰς τέχνας; Philo, Mut. Nom. 5) Gal 1: 12. παραδόσεις ἃς ἐδιδάχθητε *traditions in which you have been instructed* 2 Th 2: 15.—Also τινὰ περί τινος (Dit., Or. 484, 5; PStrassb. 41, 8; Jos., Ant. 2, 254) 1 J 2: 27.

d. w. dat. of the pers. (Plut., Marcell. 12, 4; Aesop 210c, 8 Chambry v.l.) and inf. foll. ἐδίδασκεν τῷ Βαλὰκ βαλεῖν Rv 2: 14.

e. w. acc. of the pers. and inf. foll. (Dit., Syll.³ 662, 12 δ. τοὺς παῖδας ᾄδειν; Philo, Omn. Prob. Lib. 144) Mt 28: 20; Lk 11: 1; Pol 4: 1. W. ὅτι instead of the inf. (Diod. S. 11, 12, 5; 18, 10, 3; Aelian, V.H. 3, 16; Philo, Mut. Nom. 18, Fuga 55) 1 Cor 11: 14, also recitative ὅτι Mk 8: 31; Ac 15: 1.

f. w. other verbs δ. καὶ κηρύσσειν Mt 11: 1; κ. εὐαγγελίζεσθαι Ac 15: 35; κ. νουθετεῖν Col 3: 16; κ. παρακαλεῖν 1 Ti 6: 2; παραγγέλλειν κ. δ. 4: 11.—GBjörck, HN ΔΙΔΑΣΚΩΝ, D. periphrastischen Konstruktionen im Griechischen '40. M-M. B. 1222f.

διδαχή, ῆς, ἡ (Hdt.+; BGU 140, 16 [II AD]; once in LXX; Ep. Arist.; Philo; Joseph.).

1. act. *teaching* as an activity, *instruction* (Hdt. 3, 134, 2; Pla., Phaedr. 275A; Ps 59: 1; Jerus. inscr.: Suppl. Epigr. Gr. VIII 170, 5 [before 70 AD] δ. ἐντολῶν; Philo, Spec. Leg. 2, 3; Jos., Ant. 17, 159) λαλεῖν (ἐν) δ. *speak in the form of teaching* 1 Cor 14: 6; ἐν πάσῃ δ. *in every kind of instruction* 2 Ti 4: 2. Of Jesus' teaching activity Mk 4: 2; 12: 38.

2. pass. *teaching*, of what is taught (Ep. Arist. 207; 294) by the Pharisees and Sadducees Mt 16: 12; by Jesus J 7: 16f; 18: 19; the apostles Ac 2: 42.—Ac 5: 28; 13: 12; Ro 16: 17; 1 Cor 14: 26; 2 J 9f; Rv 2: 24; D inscr.; 1: 3; 2: 1; 6: 1; 11: 2; B 9: 9; 16: 9; 18: 1. κατὰ τ. διδαχήν *in accordance w. the teaching* Tit 1: 9; βαπτισμῶν δ. *teaching about baptisms* Hb 6: 2. τύπος διδαχῆς *pattern of teaching* (of Christianity) Ro 6: 17 (GAJRoss, Exp. 7th Series V '08, 469-75; CLattey, JTS 29, '28, 381-4; 30, '29, 397-9; JMoffatt, JBL 48, '29, 233-8; FCBurkitt, JTS 30, '29, 190f.—Cf. also παραδίδωμι 1b, end, and τύπος 4); δ. καινή Mk 1: 27 (cf. the apocryphal gosp. POxy. 1224 [Kl. Texte 8¹, p. 26, 19ff] ποίαν σέ φασιν διδαχὴν καινὴν διδάσκειν, ἢ τί βάπτισμα καινὸν κηρύσσειν;); Ac 17: 19; δ. ἀφθαρσίας *teaching that assures immortality* IMg 6: 2. Of false teachings Rv 2: 14f; Hb 13: 9; κακὴ δ. IEph

9: 1; δ. ξέναι, μωραί Hs 8, 6, 5. The teaching of the angel of wickedness m 6, 2, 7.

3. Either mng. is poss. Mt 7: 28; 22: 33; Mk 1: 22; 11: 18; Lk 4: 32.—CHDodd, TWManson memorial vol., '59, 106-18 ('catechetical' instr. in the early church). M-M.*

δίδραχμον, ου, τό (the adj. δίδραχμος since Thu.; the noun τὸ δ. in Aristot., Ἀθην. πολ. 10, 7; Pollux; Galen; Cass. Dio 66, 7; IG ed. minor I '24, 79; PTebt. 404, 12; LXX; Philo, Rer. Div. Her. 186f; Jos., Ant. 18, 312) *a double drachma, two-drachma piece,* a coin worth two Attic drachmas, normally worth about 36 cents in our money; it was about equal to a half shekel among the Jews, and was the sum required of each person annually as the temple tax Mt 17: 24 (a διδραχμία as a gift for the temple of the god Suchos: Wilcken, Chrest. 289, 9 [125 BC]; BGU 748 [I AD]).—Schürer II⁴ 314f; Wilcken, Chrest. p. 85f; Dssm., LO 229. On the pl. in Mt 17: 24, s. MBlack, BRigaux-Festschr. '70, 60-62. S. also on ἀργύριον, end. M-M.*

Δίδυμος, ου, ὁ *Didymus* (as a name e.g. Dit., Or. 519, 8; 736, 27; POxy. 243; 251; 255; 263 al.; PFay. 16), lit. *twin,* Greek name of the apostle Thomas (אָמֹות=twin) J 11: 16; 20: 24; 21: 2. M-M.*

δίδωμι (Hom.+; inscr., pap., LXX, En., Ep. Arist., Philo, Joseph., Test. 12 Patr., Sib. Or.) by-form διδῶ (Bl-D. §94, 1 w. app.; Rob. 311f) Rv 3: 9 (δίδω Tregelles, δίδωμι t.r.), 3 pl. διδόασι; impf. 3 sg. ἐδίδου, 3 pl ἐδίδουν, ἐδίδοσαν J 19: 3; fut. δώσω; 1 aor. ἔδωκα, subj. δώσῃ J 17: 2; Rv 8: 3 t.r. (on this Bl-D. §95, 1 w. app.; Rob. 308f), δώσωμεν Mk 6: 37 v.l., δώσωσιν Rv 4: 9 v.l.; pf. δέδωκα; plpf. ἐδεδώκειν (and without augm. δεδώκειν Mk 14: 44; Lk 19: 15; J 11: 57); 2 aor. subj. 2 sg. δῷς cf. Mt 5: 26, 3 sg. δῷ (δώῃ J 15: 16 v.l.; Eph 1: 17; 2 Ti 2: 25: in all these cases read δώῃ subj., not δῴη opt., s. below, δοῖ Mk 8: 37; Bl-D. §95, 2 w. app.; Mlt. 55; Rdm.² 97f and Glotta 7, '16, 21ff), pl. δῶμεν, δῶτε, δῶσιν; 2 aor. opt. 3 sg. Hellenist. δῴη for δοίη Ro 15: 5; 2 Th 3: 16; 2 Ti 1: 16, 18 (on Eph 1: 17; 2 Ti 2: 25 s. above); 2 aor. imper. δός, δότε, inf. δοῦναι, ptc. δούς; pf. pass. δέδομαι; 1 aor. pass. ἐδόθην; 1 fut. δοθήσομαι (W-S. §14, 8ff).

1. *give*—a. lit. τινί τι someth. to someone ταῦτά σοι πάντα δώσω Mt 4: 9. τὸ ἅγιον τοῖς κυσίν 7: 6 (Ps.-Lucian, Asin. 33 τὰ ἔγκατα τοῖς κυσὶ δότε).—vs. 11; 14: 7 and oft. τινὶ ἔκ τινος *give someone some* (of a substance: Tob 4: 16; Ezk 48: 12) Mt 25: 8. Of bread Mk 2: 26; Lk 6: 4. Of sacrifices θυσίαν δ. *bring an offering* 2: 24 (cf. Jos., Ant. 7, 196 θυσίαν ἀποδοῦναι τ. θεῷ). δόξαν δ. θεῷ *give God the glory,* i.e. *praise, honor, thanks* (Josh 7: 19; Ps 67: 35; 1 Esdr 9: 8; 2 Ch 30: 8 and oft.) Lk 17: 18; J 9: 24; Ac 12: 23 al. δόξαν καὶ τιμήν (2 Ch 32: 33) *give glory and honor* Rv 4: 9. Abs. μακάριόν ἐστιν μᾶλλον διδόναι ἢ λαμβάνειν *it is more blessed to give than to receive* Ac 20: 35 (Theophyl. Sim., Ep. 42 τὸ διδόναι ἢ τὸ λαβεῖν οἰκειότερον); cf. 1 Cl 2: 1; Hm 2: 4ff (the contrast δίδωμι—λαμβάνω is frequently found: Epicharmus, fgm. 273 Kaibel; Com. Fgm. Adesp. 108, 4 K.; Maximus Tyr. 32, 10c ὀλίγα δούς, μεγάλα ἔλαβες; Sir 14: 16).—On the logion Ac 20: 35 cf. JoachJeremias, Unbekannte Jesusworte '51, 73ff, Eng. transl., Unknown Sayings of Jesus, '57, 77-81: *giving is blessed, not receiving*; EHaenchen on Ac 20: 35; Plut., Mor. 173D). S. μᾶλλον 3c. *Give to the poor* Mt 19: 21 (HvonCampenhausen, Tradition u. Leben '60, 114-56).

b. *give* in the sense *grant, bestow, impart* (Philo, Leg. All. 3, 106 δ. χρόνον εἰς μετάνοιαν).

α. in many expr. in which the transl. is determined by

the noun object: ἀφορμήν δ. *give an occasion* (for someth.) 2 Cor 5: 12; Hm 4, 1, 11; μαρτυρίαν δ. *give testimony* 1 Cl 30: 7; γνώμην δ. *give an opinion* 1 Cor 7: 25; 2 Cor 8: 10; ἐγκοπήν δ. *cause a hindrance* 1 Cor 9: 12; ἐντολήν δ. *command, order* J 11: 57; 12: 49; 1 J 3: 23; ἐντολήν καινήν δ. *give a new commandment* J 13: 34. εὔσημον λόγον δ. *speak plainly or intelligibly* 1 Cor 14: 9; παραγγελίαν δ. *give an instruction* 1 Th 4: 2; περιτομήν δ. *institute circumcision* B 9: 7; προσκοπήν δ. *put an obstacle in* (someone's) way 2 Cor 6: 3; ῥάπισμα δ. τινί *slap someone* J 18: 22; 19: 3; σημεῖον δ. *give a sign* Mt 26: 48; τόπον δ. τινί *make room for someone* (Plut., Gai. Gracch. 13, 3) Lk 14: 9, fig. *leave room for* Ro 12: 19 (cf. τόπος 2c); Eph 4: 27; ὑπόδειγμα δ. *give an example* J 13: 15; φίλημα δ. τινί *give someone a kiss* Lk 7: 45; *draw or cast lots* Ac 1: 26.

β. esp. oft. of God (Hom.+) and Christ: *give, grant, impose* (of punishments etc.), *send,* of gifts, peace τινί τι Eph 4: 8; 1 Cl 60: 4; τινί τινος *give someone some of a thing* Rv 2: 17. Also τινί ἐκ τινος 1 J 4: 13. τί εἴς τινα 1 Th 4: 8 (Ezk 37: 14); εἰς τὰς καρδίας *put into the hearts* Rv 17: 17 (cf. X., Cyr. 8, 2, 20 δ. τινί τι εἰς ψυχήν). Also ἐν τ. καρδίαις δ. (cf. ἐν 1 6) 2 Cor 1: 22; 8: 16 (cf. Ezk 36: 27). εἰς τὴν διάνοιαν Hb 8: 10 (Jer 38[31]: 33); ἐπὶ καρδίας Hb 10: 16 (δ. ἐπί w. acc. as Jer 6: 21 and s. Jer 38[31]: 33 ἐπὶ καρδίας αὐτῶν γράψω). W. ἵνα foll. *grant that* Mk 10: 37.—The pass. occurs very oft in this sense (Plut., Mor. 265D; 277E) Lk 8: 10; Rv 6: 4; 7: 2; 13: 7, 14f and oft. ἐκδίκησιν διδόναι τινί *inflict punishment on someone* 2 Th 1: 8; βασανισμὸν καὶ πένθος δ. τινί *send torment and grief upon someone* Rv 18: 7; χάριν δ. (Jos., Bell. 7, 325) Js 4: 6; 1 Pt 5: 5 (both Pr 3: 34); ἐξουσίαν δ. *grant someone the power or authority, give someone the right,* etc. (cf. Jos., Ant. 2, 90, Vi. 71) Mt 9: 8; 28: 18; 2 Cor 13: 10; Rv 9: 3; 1 Cl 61: 1. W. gen. foll. *over someone* Mt 10: 1; Mk 6: 7; J 17: 2; τοῦ πατεῖν ἐπάνω τινός *tread on someth.* Lk 10: 19. Simple δ. w. inf. is often used in a sim. sense (Appian, Liby. 19 §78 ἦν [=ἐάν] ὁ θεὸς δῷ ἐπικρατῆσαι; 106 §499) δέδοται *it is given, granted* to someone γνῶναι τὰ μυστήρια *to know the secrets* Mt 13: 11; cf. ἡ δοθεῖσα αὐτῷ γνῶσις B 9: 8. ἔδωκεν ζωὴν ἔχειν *he has granted* (the privilege) of *having life* J 5: 26. μετὰ παρρησίας λαλεῖν *to speak courageously* Ac 4: 29 and oft. Rather freq. the inf. is to be supplied fr. the context (Himerius, Or. 38 [4], 8 εἰ θεὸς διδοίη =if God permits) οἷς δέδοται sc. χωρεῖν Mt 19: 11. ἦν δεδομένον σοι sc. ἐξουσίαν ἔχειν J 19: 11. W. acc. and inf. foll. (Appian, Mithrid. 11, §37; Heliodorus 5, 12, 2 δώσεις με πιστεύειν) οὐδὲ δώσεις τὸν ὅσιόν σου ἰδεῖν διαφθοράν *thou wilt not permit thy Holy One to see corruption* Ac 2: 27; 13: 35 (both Ps 15: 10). ἔδωκεν αὐτὸν ἐμφανῆ γενέσθαι *granted that he should be plainly seen* 10: 40. Pregnant constr.: *grant, order* (Diod. S. 9, 12, 2 διδ. λαβεῖν =permit to; 19, 85, 3 τί =someth.; Appian, Bell. Civ. 4, 125 §524 ὁ καιρὸς ἐδίδου =the opportunity permitted; Biogr. p. 130 ἐδίδου θάπτειν τ. ἄνδρα) ἐδόθη αὐτοῖς ἵνα μὴ ἀποκτείνωσιν *orders were give them not to kill* Rv 9: 5; cf. 19: 8.

γ. fig. ὑετὸν δ. (3 Km 17: 14; Job 5: 10; Zech 10: 1) *yield rain* Js 5: 18; *send rain* Ac 14: 17. τέρατα *cause wonders to appear* Ac 2: 19 (Jo 3: 3). Of heavenly bodies φέγγος δ. *give light, shine* Mt 24: 29; Mk 13: 24 (cf. Is 13: 10). Of a musical instrument φωνὴν δ. (cf. Ps 17: 14; 103: 12; Jdth 14: 9; Pind., Nem. 5, 93) *produce a sound* 1 Cor 14: 7f.

2. *give, give out, hand over* τινί τι a certificate of divorce to one's wife Mt 5: 31 (Dt 24: 1); *pay out* a portion of one's property Lk 15: 12; bread to the disciples Mt 14:

19; 15: 36; Mk 6: 41; 8: 6; Lk 22: 19; J 21: 13. χεῖρα *hold out one's hand* (to someone) Ac 9: 41 (cf. 1 Macc 6: 58; 2 Macc 12: 11; Jos., Bell. 6, 318). The dat. or acc. is somet. to be supplied fr. the context Mt 19: 7; 26: 26f; Mk 14: 22f; Lk 11: 7f; δ. δακτύλιον εἰς τὴν χεῖρα *put a ring on the finger* Lk 15: 22 (cf. Esth 3: 10—δίδωμί τι εἰς τ. χεῖρα also Aristoph., Nub. 506; Herodas 3, 70). W. inf. foll. δ. τινί φαγεῖν *give someone someth. to eat* Mt 14: 16; 25: 35, 42; Mk 5: 43; 6: 37; J 6: 31 al. (cf. Gen 28: 20; Ex 16: 8, 15; Lev 10: 17); *someth. to drink* Mt 27: 34; Mk 15: 23; J 4: 7; Rv 16: 6 (Hdt. 4, 172, 4; Aristoph., Pax 49; PGM 13, 320 δὸς πιεῖν; Jos., Ant. 2, 64).

3. *entrust* τινί τι *someth. to someone* money Mt 25: 15; Lk 19: 13, 15; the keys of the kgdm. Mt 16: 19; perh. Lk 12: 48. W. εἰς τὰς χεῖρας added J 13: 3 (cf. Gen 39: 8; Is 22: 21; 29: 12 al.) or ἐν τῇ χειρὶ τινος 3: 35 (cf. Jdth 9: 9; Da 1: 2; 7: 25 Theod.; 1 Macc 2: 7). Of spiritual things J 17: 8, 14; Ac 7: 38.—τινά τινι *entrust someone to another's care* J 6: 37, 39; 17: 6, 9, 12, 24; Hb 2: 13 (Is 8: 18).

4. *give back, yield* ἡ θάλασσα τ. νεκρούς *the sea gave back its dead* Rv 20: 13; of a field and its crops καρπὸν δ. *yield fruit* (Ps 1: 3) Mt 13: 8; Mk 4: 7f; of wages: *pay, give* τινί τι Mt 20: 4; 26: 15; 28: 12; Mk 14: 11; Lk 22: 5; Rv 11: 18. Fig. *repay* someone (Mélanges Nicole '05, p. 246 λίθῳ δέδωκεν τῷ υἱῷ μου; Ps 27: 4) Rv 2: 23. Of taxes, tribute, rent, etc. τινὶ ἀπὸ τινος *pay rent of someth.* Lk 20: 10 (cf. 1 Esdr 6: 28). τί *pay* (up), *give someth.* Mt 16: 26; 27: 10; Mk 8: 37; δ. κῆνσον, φόρον Καίσαρι *pay tax to the emperor* (Jos., Bell. 2, 403) Mt 22: 17; Mk 12: 14; Lk 20: 22. Esp. λόγον δ. *render account* (POxy. 1281, 9 [21 AD]; PStrassb. 32, 9 δότω λόγον) Ro 14: 12.

5. equivalent to τιθέναι *put, place* ἀργύριον ἐπὶ τράπεζαν *put money in the bank* Lk 19: 23; *appoint* someone (Num 14: 4) κριτάς *judges* Ac 13: 20; w. double acc. *appoint someone someth.* (PLille 28, 11 [III BC] αὐτοῖς ἐδώκαμεν μεσίτην Δωρίωνα) τοὺς μὲν ἀποστόλους some (to be) *apostles* Eph 4: 11. τινὰ κεφαλήν δ. *make someone head* 1: 22. Also δ. τινὰ εἴς τι B 14: 7 (Is 42: 6).—For ποιεῖν, which is read by some mss., in συμβούλιον δ. *hold a consultation* Mk 3: 6.

6. *give up, sacrifice* τὸ σῶμά μου τὸ ὑπὲρ ὑμῶν διδόμενον *my body, given up for you* Lk 22: 19 (cf. Thu. 2, 43, 2; Libanius, Declam. 24, 23 Förster οἱ ἐν Πύλαις ὑπὲρ ἐλευθερίας τ. Ἑλλήνων δεδωκότες τὰ σώματα); ἑαυτὸν (τὴν ψυχήν) δ. *give oneself up, sacrifice oneself* (ref. in Nägeli 56; 1 Macc 6: 44; 2: 50) w. dat. 2 Cor 8: 5. λύτρον ἀντὶ πολλῶν *give oneself up as a ransom for many* Mt 20: 28; Mk 10: 45 (ἀντί 3). Also ἀντίλυτρον ὑπέρ τινος 1 Ti 2: 6. ὑπέρ τινος *for or because of a person or thing* Gal 1: 4; Tit 2: 14 (on the form of these passages cf. KRomaniuk, NovT 5, '62, 55–76). ἑαυτὸν δ. τῷ θανάτῳ ISm 4: 2; δ. ἑαυτὸν εἰς τὸ θηρίον *face the beast* Hv 4, 1, 8. In another sense *go, venture* (cf. our older 'betake oneself') *somewhere* (Polyb. 5, 14, 9; Diod. S. 5, 59, 4; 14, 81, 2; Jos., Ant. 7, 225; 15, 244) Ac 19: 31.

7. δὸς ἐργασίαν Lk 12: 58 is prob. a Latinism=da operam *take pains, make an effort* (Bl-D. §5, 3b note 3; Rob. 109), which nevertheless penetrated the popular speech (Dit., Or. 441, 109 [senatorial decree 81 BC]; POxy. 742, 11 [colloq. letter 2 BC] δὸς ἐργασίαν; PMich. 203, 7 [Trajan]; PGiess. 11, 16 [118 AD]; PBrem. 5, 8 [117/119 AD]). M.-M. B. 749.

διέβην s. διαβαίνω.

διεγείρω 1 aor. διήγειρα; pass. impf. διηγειρόμην or διεγειρόμην (Bl-D. §67, 2 app.); 1 aor. διηγέρθην (Hippocr.+; UPZ 81, 3, 12 [II BC]; PTebt. 804, 15; PGM 13, 279; LXX) *wake up, arouse* someone who is asleep (Teles p. 18, 3; Polyb. 12, 26, 1; 3 Macc 5: 15; Jos., Ant. 8, 349) Mk 4: 38 t.r.; Lk 8: 24. Pass. *awaken* (Esth 1: 1*l*; Philo, Vi. Cont. 89; Jos., Ant. 2, 82 ἐκ τ. ὕπνου) Mt 1: 24 t.r.; Mk 4: 39; Ac 16: 10 D. Fig. (the pass. of the rekindling of a battle: Quint. Smyrn. 3, 20) of a calm sea: διηγείρετο *was becoming aroused* J 6: 18. Act. fig. *arouse, stir up* w. acc. (2 Macc 7: 21; 15: 10; Jos., Bell. 2, 181 τὰς ἐπιθυμίας; Test. Dan 4: 2 τ. ψυχήν) ἐν ὑπομνήσει *by way of a reminder* 2 Pt 1: 13; 3: 1. M-M.*

διεῖλον s. διαιρέω.

διελέγχω 1 aor. pass. διηλέγχθην (Pla.+; Appian, Bell. Civ. 3, 54 §224; pap.; Philo, Spec. Leg. 1, 64; Jos., C. Ap. 2, 149) *convict, convince.* Pass. διελεγχθῶμεν *let us discuss, reason* 1 Cl 8: 4 (Is 1: 18).*

διέλκω (Pla.+; BGU 1116, 21; 1120, 35 [I BC]) *rend, tear apart* (w. διασπάω) the members of Christ 1 Cl 46: 7.*

διενέγκω s. διαφέρω.

διενθυμέομαι (only in Christian wr.) *ponder* περὶ τοῦ ὀράματος *on the vision* Ac 10: 19.*

διεξέρχομαι 2 aor. διεξῆλθον (Soph., Hdt.+; Dit., Syll. ind.; PStrassb. 92, 12; 15 [III BC]; PLond. 977, 15; LXX; Ep. Arist. 168; Philo, Op. M. 130; Jos., Bell. 7, 393, Ant. 3, 303 al.) *come out* Ac 28: 3 v.l. M-M.*

διέξοδος, ου, ἡ (Hdt.+; Vett. Val. 334, 16; LXX; Ep. Arist. 105; Philo, Joseph.) δ. τῶν ὁδῶν Mt 22: 9 is somet. taken to mean *street-crossing*, but is prob. the place where a street cuts *through* the city boundary and goes *out* into the open country, *outlet* (Diod. S. 17, 12, 5 ἐν ταῖς διεξόδοις καὶ τάφροις=among the street-ends and the graves; Eutecnius 3 p. 35, 33 outlet fr. a fox-hole; Num 34: 4f; Josh 15: 4, 7 al.; Jos., Ant. 12, 346. PMagd. 12, 11f [III BC] of the 'conclusion' of a trial.—On the beggars at street-crossings cf. Lucian, Necyom. 17). Corresp. δ. τῶν ὑδάτων, the point where a stream of water flowing underground suddenly breaks *through* and flows *out* freely, *a spring* (Hesychius Miles. 3, [Fgm. Hist. Gr. IV p. 147 Müller: διέξοδοι of two rivers; 4 Km 2: 21) B 11: 6 (Ps 1: 3). M-M.*

διέπω (Hom.+; inscr., pap.; Wsd 9: 3; 12: 15; Jos., C. Ap. 2, 294; Sib. Or. 3, 360) *conduct, administer* (as Dit., Or. 614, 4; cf. 519, 24) 1 Cl 61: 1f; τὴν ἐπαρχικὴν ἐξουσίαν δ. (s. ἐπαρχικός) Phlm subscr.; τὰ ἐπίγεια *manage earthly things* Dg 7: 2.*

διερμηνεία, ας, ἡ (not found elsewh.) *explanation, interpretation, translation* 1 Cor 12: 10 v.l.*

διερμηνευτής, οῦ, ὁ (does not occur again until the Byz. gramm. Eustath., Ad Il. p. 106, 14; Nägeli 50) *interpreter, translator* of ecstatic speech 1 Cor 14: 28. M-M.*

διερμηνεύω 1 aor. διερμήνευσα (Bl-D. §67, 2 app.).
1. *translate* (Polyb. 3, 22, 3; UPZ 162 V, 4 [117 BC]; 2 Macc 1: 36; Ep. Arist. 15; 308; 310; Philo, Poster. Cai. 1, Deus Imm. 144, Migr. Abr. 12; 73) Ταβιθά, ἣ διερμηνευομένη λέγεται Δορκάς *T. which, translated, means Dorcas* [=gazelle] Ac 9: 36.
2. *explain, interpret* (Philod., Rhet. I 84 S.; PPetr. III 17, 2, 6 [III BC]; Philo, Op. M. 31) τὶ *someth.* ecstatic speech 1 Cor 12: 30; 14: 5, 13, 27 (mng. 1 is also poss. here); the mng. of prophecies Lk 24: 27. Pass., of the holy scriptures Ac 18: 6 D. M-M.*

διέρχομαι impf. διηρχόμην; fut. διελεύσομαι; 2 aor. διῆλθον; pf. ptc. διεληλυθώς Hb 4: 14 (Hom.+; inscr., pap., LXX, Ep. Arist., Philo, Joseph.).
1. *go through*—a. w. acc. of place (Ep. Arist. 301; Jos., Bell. 2, 67) an island Ac 13: 6. τὰ ἀνωτερικὰ μέρη *the interior* 19: 1; regions 20: 2. Of a sword (cf. Il. 20, 263; 23, 876; Jdth 6: 6; 16: 9) δ. τὴν ψυχήν *pierces the soul* Lk 2: 35. Used w. place names (Diod. S. 16, 44, 4 τὴν Συρίαν; Jos., Ant. 14, 40) Jericho 19: 1; Pisidia Ac 14: 24; cf. 15: 3, 41; 16: 6; 18: 23; 19: 21; 1 Cor 16: 5.—τοὺς οὐρανούς *go through the heavens* Hb 4: 14; *pass* a guard Ac 12: 10.
b. w. prep.—a. διά τινος *go through* someth. (Hdt. 6: 31 al.; Philo; Sib. Or. 2, 253) through deserts (cf. Jos., Ant. 15, 200 τὴν ἄνυδρον δ.) Mt 12: 43; Lk 11: 24; through a needle's eye Mt 19: 24 v.l.; Mk 10: 25; Lk 18: 25 v.l.; through a gate Hs 9, 13, 6. διὰ μέσου αὐτῶν *through the midst of them* Lk 4: 30; J 8: 59 t.r.; διὰ μέσον Σαμαρίας καὶ Γαλιλαίας prob. *through the region between Samaria and Galilee* Lk 17: 11; cf. J 4: 4; through all the places Ac 9: 32; through the sea 1 Cor 10: 1; δι' ὑμῶν εἰς Μακεδονίαν *through your city to M.* 2 Cor 1: 16.
β. w. ἐν (Sir 39: 4; 1 Macc 3: 8): ἐν οἷς διῆλθον κηρύσσων *among whom I went about preaching* Ac 20: 25.
c. w. ὁπόθεν Papias 3.—d. abs. ἐκείνης (sc. ὁδοῦ) ἤμελλεν διέρχεσθαι *he was to come through that way* Lk 19: 4. διερχόμενος *as he went through* Ac 8: 40; cf. 10: 38; 17: 23.
2. simply *come, go:* εἴς τινα of death: *to all men* Ro 5: 12. εἴς τι (Jos., Ant. 14, 414) of journeys: *go over* εἰς τὸ πέραν *to the other side* Mk 4: 35; Lk 8: 22; cf. Ac 18: 27. εἰς τὸ πεδίον *go off into the country* 1 Cl 4: 6 (Gen 4: 8). Also ἕως τινός (1 Macc 1: 3): ἕως Βηθλέεμ *to B.* Lk 2: 15; ἕως Φοινίκης Ac 11: 19, 22 t.r.; ἕως ἡμῶν 9: 38. ἐνθάδε *come here* J 4: 16.
3. *go about fr. place to place, spread* δ. κατὰ τὰς κώμας *go about among the villages* Lk 9: 6; δ. ἀπὸ τῆς Πέργης *they went on fr. Perga* Ac 13: 14. Abs. διασπαρέντες διῆλθον *they were scattered and went about fr. place to place* 8: 4. Fig. of a report διήρχετο μᾶλλον ὁ λόγος *spread even farther* Lk 5: 15 (cf. Thu. 6, 46, 5; X., An. 1, 4, 7 διῆλθε λόγος; Jos., Vi. 182).
4. *go through* in one's mind, *review* (Hom. Hymn Ven. 276 δ. τι μετὰ φρεσί al.) τὰς γενεάς 1 Cl 7: 5 (εἰς τ. γ. is read by some mss.). M-M.*

διερωτάω 1 aor. διηρώτησα (X., Pla.+; Cass. Dio 43, 10; 48, 8; Jos., Bell. 1, 234; 653) *find by inquiry* οἰκίαν Ac 10: 17.*

διέστη s. διΐστημι.

διεστραμμένος s. διαστρέφω.

διετής, ές (Hdt.+; inscr., pap.; 2 Macc 10: 3; Jos., Ant. 2, 74) *two years old* ἀπὸ διετοῦς καὶ κατωτέρω *two years old and under* Mt 2: 16 (masc., not neut.; cf. Num 1: 3, 20; 1 Ch 27: 23; 2 Ch 31: 16). M-M.*

διετία, ας, ἡ (Cleomedes [II AD] 1, 3; Inschr. v. Magn. 164, 12; Dit., Syll. and Or. ind.; POxy. 707, 24; BGU 180, 7 al.; Graecus Venetus ed. vGebhardt 1875 Gen 41: 1; 45: 5; Philo, In Flacc. 128.—Joseph. does not have δ., but ἐπταετία [Ant. 1, 302]) *a period of two years* διετίας πληρωθείσης *when two years had elapsed* Ac 24: 27. ἐνέμεινεν δ. ὅλην *he stayed two full years* 28: 30. M-M.*

διευθύνω 1 aor. imper. διεύθυνον (Manetho 4, 90; Lucian, Prom. 19; pap.; Ep. Arist. 188; Philo, Agr. 177) *guide, direct, govern* 1 Cl 20: 8. τὴν βουλὴν κατὰ τὸ καλόν *direct their minds according to what is good* 61: 2;

εὐσεβῶς καὶ δικαίως δ. (sc. τὸν βίον) direct one's life in piety and righteousness 62: 1.*

διηγέομαι fut. διηγήσομαι; 1 aor. διηγησάμην (Heraclitus, Thu.+; pap., LXX, Philo; Jos., C. Ap. 1, 196 al.) tell, relate, describe τὶ someth. Lk 8: 39 (cf. Jos., Vita 60). τὴν γενεὰν αὐτοῦ (γενεά 4) Ac 8: 33; 1 Cl 16: 8 (both Is 53: 8). δόξαν θεοῦ 27: 7 (Ps 18: 2). τὰ δικαιώματα θεοῦ recount God's ordinances 35: 7 (Ps 49: 16). τινί τι (Lucian, Nigr. 3; BGU 846, 14 πάντα σοι διήγηται) someth. to someone Mk 9: 9; Lk 9: 10; Ac 16: 10 D; τινί Mk 5: 16; Dg 11: 2. W. indir. quest. foll. Mk 5: 16; Ac 9: 27; 12: 17; 16: 40 D; περί τινος about someone (Lucian, Dial. Mar. 15, 1) Hb 11: 32. M-M.*

διήγησις, εως, ἡ (Pla.+; PSI 85, 8; LXX; Ep. Arist. 1; 8; 322; Philo; Jos., Ant. 11, 68; Thom. Mag. p. 96, 8 R. διήγησις ὅλον τὸ σύγγραμμα, διήγημα δὲ μέρος τι) narrative, account Lk 1: 1 (of a historical report also Diod. S. 11, 20, 1 ἡ διήγησις ἐπὶ τὰς πράξεις). M-M.*

διηνεκής, ές (Hom.+; inscr., pap., Philo; Jos., Ant. 16, 149) continuous, uninterrupted of time εἰς τὸ δ. forever (Appian, Bell. Civ. 1, 4, §15; IG XII 1, 786, 16; PRyl. 427; Sym. Ps 47: 15) Hb 7: 3; 10: 14; for all time vs. 12; continually (Hippocr., Ep. 17, 44) 10: 1. M-M.*

διηνεκῶς adv. (Aeschyl., Ag. 319 [Hom., Hes. διηνεκέως, Mayser 13, 4]; Dit., Or. 194, 12; 544, 19; BGU 646, 22; PGM 4, 1219; LXX; Philo, Sacr. Abel. 94) continually 1 Cl 24: 1.*

διθάλασσος, ον (Strabo 2, 5, 22; Dionys. Perieget. 156; Sib. Or. 5, 334) with the sea on both sides; the τόπος δ. Ac 27: 41 is prob. a sandbank at some distance fr. the shore, with rather deep water on both sides of it, a reef (Breusing 202). Explained differently by JSmith, The Voyage and Shipwreck of St. Paul⁴ 1880, 143; HBalmer, D. Romfahrt des Ap. Pls '05, 413ff; FBrannigan, ThGl 25, '33, 186. L-S-J 'headland'; NEB 'cross-currents'.*

διϊκνέομαι intr. (Thu.+; Ex 26: 28) pierce, penetrate Hb 4: 12 (Jos., Ant. 13, 96 of missiles; sim. Cornutus 31 p. 63, 22f).*

διΐστημι 1 aor. (διέστησα), ptc. διαστήσας; 2 aor. διέστην, ptc. διαστάς.
1. intr. (2 aor.) go away, part (Hom.+; pap.; 3 Macc 2: 32; Philo, Aet. M. 75; Jos., Ant. 18, 136) ἀπό τινος (Herm. Wr. 14, 5) fr. someone Lk 24: 51. Of time pass διαστάσης ὡσεὶ ὥρας μιᾶς after about an hour had passed Lk 22: 59.
2. trans. (1 aor.—Appian, Iber. 36 §144 διαστῆσαι τὸ πλῆθος=divide the crowd; PGM 13, 476 διέστησεν τὰ πάντα; 4, 1150; Jos., Ant. 13, 305) βραχὺ διαστήσαντες (cf. Hippiatr. I 388, 5) w. τὴν ναῦν supplied ('drive on' like Sir 28: 14) after they had sailed a short distance farther Ac 27: 28. FBlass, Acta Apost. 1895, 279 takes it as=βραχὺ διάστημα ποιήσαντες after a short distance. M-M.*

διϊστορέω (Philod., Rhet. II 150 fgm. 6 S.) examine carefully Ac 17: 23 D (first hand).*

διϊσχυρίζομαι impf. διϊσχυριζόμην insist, maintain firmly (so since Lysias, Isaeus, Pla.; Aelian, Hist. An. 7, 18; Cass. Dio 57, 23; Jos., Ant. 17, 336) Lk 22: 59; Ac 15: 2 D. W. inf. foll. (Jos., Ant. 2, 106) Ac 12: 15.*

δικάζω 1 fut. pass. δικασθήσομαι (Hom.+; Maximus Tyr. 3, 81 δ. θεός; pap.; LXX; Ps.-Phoc. 11; Philo; Jos., C.

Ap. 2, 207; Sib. Or. 4, 183) judge, condemn w. neg. (opp. δίκην τίνειν) Hm 2: 5; Lk 6: 37 𝔓⁷⁵ B. M-M.*

δικαιοκρισία, ας, ἡ (POxy. 71 I, 4; 904, 2; PFlor. 88, 26; Sb 7205, 3; Test. Levi 3: 2; 15: 2; Quinta in Origen's Hexapla Hos 6: 5.—δικαιοκρίτης of God: Sib. Or. 3, 704) righteous judgment Ro 2: 5; 2 Th 1: 5 v.l. M-M.*

δικαιοπραγία, ας, ἡ (Aristot.+; schol. on Pla. 107E; Maspéro 2, 1; 3, 6; Test. Dan 13) righteous action 1 Cl 32: 3.*

δίκαιος, αία, ον (Hom.+; inscr., pap., LXX, En., Ep. Arist., Philo, Joseph., Test. 12 Patr.; loanw. in rabb.).
1. of men upright, just, righteous, like צַדִּיק=conforming to the laws of God and man, and living in accordance w. them.
   a. w. emphasis on the legal aspect: δικαίῳ νόμος οὐ κεῖται the law is not intended for a law-abiding man 1 Ti 1: 9. Of Joseph just, honest, good (Jos., Ant. 15, 106; Diod. S. 33, 5, 6 ἀνδρὸς εὐσεβοῦς κ. δικαίου; Conon [I BC-I AD]: 26 fgm. 1, 17 Jac.; Galen XVIII 1 p. 247 K. ἄνδρες δ.) perh. merciful (cf. δικαιοσύνη 2a) Mt 1: 19 (DHill, ET 76, '65, 133f). Of a bishop (w. σώφρων, ὅσιος) Tit 1: 8. General definition ὁ ποιῶν τὴν δικαιοσύνην δ. ἐστιν he who does what is right, is righteous 1 J 3: 7; cf. Rv 22: 11.—Ro 5: 7.
   b. w. emphasis on the relig. aspect: not violating the sovereignty of God, and keeping his laws: Ro 3: 10 (cf. Eccl 7: 20); δ. παρὰ τῷ θεῷ righteous in the sight of God Ro 2: 13; δ. ἐναντίον τοῦ θεοῦ (Gen 7: 1; Job 32: 2) Lk 1: 6. W. φοβούμενος τὸν θεόν of Cornelius Ac 10: 22. W. εὐλαβής (Pla., Pol. 311 AB ἤθη εὐλαβῆ κ. δίκαια, τὸ δίκαιον κ. εὐλαβές) Lk 2: 25. W. ἀγαθός (Epigr. Gr. 648 p. 264, 10; Jos., Ant. 8, 248; 9, 132 ἀνὴρ ἀγ. κ. δίκ.) 23: 50; ἀθῷος (Sus 53) 1 Cl 46: 4; ὅσιος 2 Cl 15: 3; ταπεινός B 19: 6. Serving God w. a pure heart makes one δ. 2 Cl 11: 1. Hence the δίκαιοι=the just, the righteous in a specif. Jewish-Christian sense Mt 13: 43 (cf. Da 12: 3 Theod.) Lk 1: 17; 1 Pt 3: 12 (Ps 33: 16); Lk 22: 6 (Ps 33: 16); 33: 7; 45: 3f; 48: 3 (Ps 117: 20); 2 Cl 6: 9; 17: 7; 20: 3f; B 11: 7 (Ps 1: 5f); MPol 14: 1; 17: 1; also of those who only appear r. (cf. Pr 21: 2) Mt 23: 28; Lk 20: 20; specifically of Christians Mt 10: 41; Ac 14: 2 D; 1 Pt 4: 18 (Pr 11: 31); Hv 1, 4, 2. W. apostles MPol 19: 2; cf. 1 Cl 5: 2. Esp. of the righteous of the OT: πατέρες δ. 1 Cl 30: 7. W. prophets Mt 13: 17; 23: 29 (perh. teachers: DHill, NTS 11, '64/'65, 296-302). Of Abel Mt 23: 35 (construction with τοῦ αἵματος is not improbable: GDKilpatrick, Bible Translator 16, '65, 119); Hb 11: 4; Enoch 1 Cl 9: 3; Lot 2 Pt 2: 7; John the Baptist (w. ἅγιος) Mk 6: 20; δ. τετελειωμένοι just men made perfect (i.e., who have died) Hb 12: 23. Opp. ἄδικοι (Pr 17: 15; 29: 27) Mt 5: 45; Ac 24: 15; 1 Pt 3: 18; ἁμαρτωλοί (Ps 57: 9) Mt 9: 13; Mk 2: 17; Lk 5: 32; 15: 7; ἁμαρτωλοί and ἀσεβεῖς (Ps 1: 5f) 1 Ti 1: 9; 1 Pt 4: 18 (Pr 11: 31); πονηροί (Pr 11: 15) Mt 13: 49. W. regard to the Last Judgment, the one who stands the test is δ. righteous Mt 25: 37, 46.—Ro 1: 17 (s. [ζάω] 2bβ); Gal 3: 11; Hb 10: 38 (all three Hab 2: 4); Ro 5: 19. Resurrection of the just Lk 14: 14; prayer Js 5: 16.
2. of God (NSRhizos, Καππαδοκικά 1856, p. 113: inscr. fr. Tyana Θεῷ δικαίῳ Μίθρᾳ.—JHMordtmann, Mitt. d. Deutsch. Arch. Inst. in Athen 10, 1885, 11-14 has several exx. of ὅσιος κ. δίκαιος as adj. applied to gods in west Asia Minor.—δικ. of Isis: PRoussel, Les cultes égypt. à Delos '16 p. 276.—Oft. in OT; Jos., Bell. 7, 323, Ant. 11, 55 [w. ἀληθινός]) just, righteous w. ref. to his judgment of men and nations κριτὴς δ. a righteous judge (Ps 7: 12; 2 Macc 12: 6) 2 Ti 4: 8; δ. ἐν τοῖς κρίμασιν 1 Cl

195

27: 1; 60: 1; cf. 56: 5 (Ps 140: 5); πατήρ δ. J 17: 25; cf. Ro 3: 26. W. ὅσιος (Ps 144: 17; Dt 32: 4) Rv 16: 5. W. πιστός 1 J 1: 9.

3. of Jesus who, as the ideal of righteousness in senses 1 and 2, is called simply ὁ δ. (HDechent, D. 'Gerechte'—e. Bezeichnung für d. Messias: StKr 100, '28, 439-43) Ac 7: 52; Mt 27: 19, cf. 24 t.r.; 1 J 2: 1; 3: 7. A restriction of the mng. just results in the excellent sense innocent for Lk 23: 47; cf. αἷμα δ. under 4, and s. GDKilpatrick, JTS 42, '41, 34-6 (against him RPCHanson, Hermathena 60, '42, 74-8); Gdspd., Probs. 90f. W. ἅγιος Ac 3: 14.—Also of angels Hs 6, 3, 2.

4. of things ἔργα 1 J 3: 12; αἷμα δ. (Jo 4: 19; La 4: 13=αἷμα δικαίου Pr 6: 17, where αἱ. δίκαιον is a v.l.) blood of a righteous, or better, an innocent man Mt 23: 35, and esp. 27: 4, where δ. is v.l. for ἀθῷον (cf. on Lk 23: 47 in 3 above); ψυχὴ δ. righteous soul (Pr 10: 3) 2 Pt 2: 8; πνεῦμα δ. righteous spirit Hm 5, 2, 7; ἐντολή (w. ἁγία and ἀγαθή) Ro 7: 12. κρίσις (Dt 16: 18; Is 58: 2; 2 Macc 9: 18; 3 Macc 2: 22; Jos., Ant. 9, 4) J 5: 30; 7: 24; 8: 16 v.l.; 2 Th 1: 5; B 20: 2. Pl. Rv 16: 7; 19: 2. φύσει δικαίᾳ by a righteous nature IEph 1: 1 (Hdb. ad loc.); ὁδὸς δ. (Vi. Aesopi I c. 85 of the 'right way') 2 Cl 5: 7; B 12: 4; pl. Rv 15: 3.

5. The neuter denotes that which is obligatory in view of certain requirements of justice (Dio Chrys. 67[17], 12; Jos., Ant. 15, 376) δ. παρὰ θεῷ it is right in the sight of God 2 Th 1: 6. Also δ. ἐνώπιον τοῦ θεοῦ Ac 4: 19; δ. καὶ ὅσιον it is right and holy 1 Cl 14: 1, pl. Phil 4: 8; δ. ἐστιν it is right Eph 6: 1; w. inf. foll. Phil 1: 7; 1 Cl 21: 4 (cf. Hyperid. 6, 14; PSI 442, 14 [III BC] οὐ δίκαιόν ἐστι οὕτως εἶναι; Sir 10: 23; 2 Macc 9: 12; 4 Macc 6: 34); δ. ἡγοῦμαι I consider it right (Diod. S. 12, 45, 1 δ. ἡγοῦντο) 2 Pt 1: 13; τὸ δ. (Appian, Bell. Civ. 4, 97 §409 τὸ δ.=the just cause; Arrian, Anab. 3, 27, 5; Polyb.; Inschr. v. Magn.; pap.; 2 Macc 4: 34; 10: 12; 3 Macc 2: 25; Ep. Arist.; Jos., Bell. 4, 340 Ant. 16, 158) what is right Lk 12: 57. τὸ δ. παρέχεσθαι give what is right Col 4: 1. ὃ ἐὰν ᾖ δ. δώσω ὑμῖν whatever is right I will give you Mt 20: 4 (Diod. S. 5, 71, 1 τὸ δίκαιον ἀλλήλοις διδόναι; 8, 25, 4). Abstract for concrete (Philipp. [=Demosth. 12] 23 μετὰ τοῦ δ.; Dio Chrys. 52[69], 6 ἄνευ νόμου κ. δικαίου; Ael. Aristid. 46 p. 302 D.) τὸ δίκαιον ὀρθὴν ὁδὸν ἔχει righteousness goes the straight way Hm 6, 1, 2. Pl. (Diod. S. 15, 11, 1; 19, 85, 3; Appian, Samn. 11 §4 al.; Lucian, Dial. Mort. 30, 1; Jos., Ant. 19, 288; Sib. Or. 3, 257) δίκαια βουλεύεσθαι have righteous thoughts Hv 1, 1, 8 (cf. Is 59: 4; 1 Macc 7: 12). M-M. B. 1180.

δικαιοσύνη, ης, ἡ (Theognis, Hdt.+; inscr., pap. [rare in the latter], LXX, En., Ep. Arist., Philo, Joseph., Test. 12 Patr.) denoting the characteristics of the δίκαιος: righteousness, uprightness.

1. uprightness, justice as a characteristic of a judge: δ. κρίσεως ἀρχὴ καὶ τέλος uprightness is the beginning and end of judgment B 1: 6. ἐργάζεσθαι δικαιοσύνην enforce justice Hb 11: 33; ποιεῖν κρίμα καὶ δ. practice justice and uprightness 1 Cl 13: 1 (Jer 9: 23); κρίνειν δ. (Ps 71: 2f; 95: 13; Sir 45: 26) judge justly Ac 17: 31; Rv 19: 11. Cf. the ending of Mk in the Freer ms. l. 5; Ro 9: 28 t.r. (Is 10: 22).

2. in a moral and religious sense: uprightness, righteousness, the characteristic required of men by God (acc. to the Jewish concept: Bousset, Rel.³ 387ff; 379ff; 423. Cf. KHFahlgren, Şedāķā '32.—Diog. L. 3, 79, in a treatment of Plato's views, describes the δικαιοσύνη θεοῦ as a challenge to do good in order to avoid punishment after death. Cf. also 3, 83 [likew. on Plato] δικαιοσύνη περὶ

θεούς or δ. πρὸς τοὺς θεούς=performance of prescribed duties toward the gods).

a. righteousness in the sense of fulfilling the divine statutes Mt 3: 15=ISm 1: 1 κατὰ δ. τὴν ἐν νόμῳ γενόμενος ἄμεμπτος as far as righteousness under the law is concerned, blameless Phil 3: 6. δικ. can also mean the practice of piety originating from this uprightness. So several times in Mt: 5: 20 (cf. JMoffatt, ET 13, '02, 201-6; OOlevieri, Biblica 5, '24, 201-5); 6: 1. W. characteristic restriction of mng. mercy, charitableness (cf. Tob 12: 9) 2 Cor 9: 9 (Ps 111: 9), 10, participation in which belongs, according to Mt 6: 1f (cf. δίκαιος 1: 19: Joseph combines justice and mercy), to the practice of piety (on the development of the word's mng. in this direction s. Bousset, Rel.³ 380).

b. righteousness, uprightness as the compelling motive for the conduct of one's whole life: hunger and thirst for uprightness Mt 5: 6 (cf. 6: 33), perh. God's salvation (see 3 below); 'Kingdom of God', FNötscher, Biblica 31, '50, 237-41=Vom A zum NT, '62, 226-30; ἐπιθυμία τῆς δ. desire for upr. Hm 12, 2, 4; διαλέγεσθαι περὶ δ. speak of upr. Ac 24: 25. Opp. ἀδικία 2 Cl 19: 2; ἀνομία 2 Cor 6: 14; Hb 1: 9 (Ps 44: 8); ἁμαρτία 1 Pt 2: 24. ἐργάζεσθαι δ. (Ps 14: 2) do what is right Ac 10: 35; accomplish righteousness Js 1: 20 (W-S. §30, 7g); Hv 2, 3, 3, perh. 5, 1, 1; 12, 3, 1; 12, 6, 2. Also ἔργον δικαιοσύνης ἐργάζεσθαι 1 Cl 33: 8. Opp. οὐδὲν ἐργάζεσθαι τῇ δ. Hs 5, 1, 4; ποιεῖν (τὴν) δ. (2 Km 8: 15; Ps 105: 3; Is 56: 1; 58: 2; 1 Macc 14: 35 al.) do what is right 1 J 2: 29; 3: 7, 10; Rv 22: 11; 2 Cl 4: 2; 11: 7. Also πράσσειν τὴν δ. 2 Cl 19: 3; διώκειν τὴν δ. (cf. Sir 27: 8 διώκ. τὸ δίκαιον) seek to attain upr. Ro 9: 30; 1 Ti 6: 11; 2 Ti 2: 22; 2 Cl 18: 2; ὁδὸς (τῆς) δ. (ὁδός 2b) Mt 21: 32; 2 Pt 2: 21; B 5: 4; κατορθοῦσθαι τὰς ὁδοὺς ἐν δ. walk uprightly Hv 2, 2, 6. ἀρετὴ δικαιοσύνης virtue of upr. Hm 1 : 2; s 6, 1, 4; πύλη δ. gate of upr. 1 Cl 48: 2 (Ps 117: 19), cf. 4. ἐν οἷς δ. κατοικεῖ (cf. Is 32: 16) in which righteousness dwells 2 Pt 3: 13; παιδεία ἡ ἐν δ. training in uprightness 2 Ti 3: 16; ἔργα τὰ ἐν δ. righteous deeds Tit 3: 5; ἐχθρὸς πάσης δ. enemy of every kind of upr. Ac 13: 10. W. ὁσιότης (Wsd 9: 3): holiness and upr. (as the relig. and moral side of conduct; cf. IQS 1, 5; 8, 2; 11, 9-15; IQH 4, 30f) Lk 1: 75 (λατρεύειν ἐν δ. as Josh 24: 14); Eph 4: 24; 1 Cl 48: 4. W. πίστις (cf. Dit., Or. 438, 8; 1 Macc 14: 35) Pol 9: 2; cf. 2 Pt 1: 1. W. εἰρήνη (Is 39: 8; 48: 18) Ro 14: 17; 1 Cl 3: 4. Cf. Hb 7: 2. W. ἀλήθεια (Is 45: 19; 48: 1) Eph 5: 9; 1 Cl 31: 2; 62: 2. W. ἀγάπη 2 Cl 12: 1. W. ἀγαθωσύνη Eph 5: 9. W. γνῶσις κυρίου (cf. Pr 16: 8) D 11: 2; ὅπλα (τῆς) δ. tools or weapons of upr. Ro 6: 13; 2 Cor 6: 7; Pol 4: 1; θώραξ τῆς δ. (Is 59: 17; Wsd 5: 18) breastplate of upr. Eph 6: 14; διάκονοι δικαιοσύνης servants of upr. 2 Cor 11: 15; Pol 5: 2; καρπὸς δικαιοσύνης (Pr 3: 9; 11: 30; 13: 2) Phil 1: 11; Hb 12: 11; Js 3: 18; Hs 9, 19, 2. ὁ τῆς δ. στέφανος the crown of upr. (w. which the upright are adorned; cf. Rtzst., Mysterienrel.³ 258) 2 Ti 4: 8; cf. ἡ τ. δικαιοσύνης δόξα the glory of upr. ending of Mk in the Freer ms. l. 11f. Described as a characteristic to be taught and learned, because it depends on a knowledge of God's will: κῆρυξ δ. preacher of upr. 2 Pt 2: 5; διδάσκειν δ. teach upr. (of Paul) 1 Cl 5: 7. Pl. (Bl-D. §142; Rob. 408) δικαιοσύναι righteous deeds (Ezk 3: 20; 33: 13; Da 9: 18) 2 Cl 6: 9.—ἐλέγχειν περὶ δικαιοσύνης convict w. regard to uprightness (of Jesus) J 16: 8, 10 (s. WHPHatch, HTR 14, '21, 103-5; HWindisch: Jülicher-Festschr. '27, 119f; HWTribble, Rev. and Expos. 32, '37, 269-80; BLindars, BRigaux-Festschr., '70, 275-85).

3. In specif. Pauline thought the expr. ἡ ἐκ θεοῦ δικ.

Phil 3: 9 or δικ. θεοῦ Ro 1: 17; 3: 21f, 26 (s. Reumann, below); 10: 3; 2 Cor 5: 21 (here abstract for concrete; δ.=δικαιωθέντες), and δικ. alone Ro 5: 21; 9: 30; 1 Cor 1: 30; 2 Cor 3: 9 all mean *the righteousness bestowed by God*; cf. ἡ δωρεὰ τῆς δ. Ro 5: 17, also 1 Cor 1: 30 (cf. IQS 11, 9-15; IQH 4, 30-37). In this area it closely approximates *salvation* (cf. Is 46: 13; 51: 5 and s. NHSnaith, Distinctive Ideas of the OT '46, 207-22, esp. 218-22; EKäsemann, ZThK 58, '61, 367-78 [against him RBultmann, JBL 83, '64, 12-16]). Keeping the law cannot bring about *righteousness* Ro 3: 21; Gal 2: 21; 3: 21, because δ. ἐκ νόμου *uprightness based on the law* Ro 10: 5 (cf. 9: 30f), as ἰδία δ. *one's own* selfmade *upr.* 10: 3 is impossible. This righteousness is to be apprehended by faith Ro 1: 17; 3: 22, 26; 4: 3ff, 13; 9: 30; 10: 4, 6, 10 (cf. Hb 11: 7 ἡ κατὰ πίστιν δ. *righteousness based on faith*; s. Bl-D. §224, 1 w. app.), for which reason faith is 'reckoned as righteousness' (Gen 15: 6; Ps 105: 31; 1 Macc 2: 52) Ro 4: 3, 5f, 9, 11, 22; Gal 3: 6; cf. Js 2: 23 (comm. and AMeyer, D. Rätsel des Jk '30, 86ff); 1 Cl 10: 6. This righteousness obligates the redeemed one to serve God faithfully Ro 6: 13, 16, 18ff and assures him that he will have life Ro 8: 10 that will be fully realized at the end of the age; for the time being it is a matter of hope Gal 5: 5 (cf. Is 51: 5).—Somet. δ. θεοῦ is also an attribute of God (cf. Paradox. Vat. 43 Keller αἰτεῖται παρὰ τ. θεῶν οὐδὲν ἄλλο πλὴν δικαιοσύνης), in which he reveals himself as judge Ro 3: 25 and shows his faithfulness vs. 5.—A Schmitt, Δικαιοσύνη θεοῦ: JGeffcken-Festschr. '31, 111-31; FRHellegers, D. Gerechtigkeit Gottes im Rö., Diss. Tüb. '39; AOepke, ThLZ 78, '53, 257-64.—Dodd 42-59; ADescamps, Studia Hellenistica, '48, 69-92.—Esp. on Paul in more recent times: JHRopes, Righteousness in the OT and in St. Paul: JBL 22, '03, 211ff; RGyllenberg, D. paul. Rechtfertigungslehre u. das AT: Studia Theologica I '35, 35-52; JHGerretsen, Rechtvaardigmaking bij Pls '05; GottfrKittel, StKr 80, '07, 217-33; ETobac, Le problème de la Justification dans S. Paul '08; EVDobschütz, Über d. paul. Rechtfertigungslehre: StKr 85, '12, 38-87; GP Wetter, D. Vergeltungsged. b. Pls '12, 161ff; BFWestcott, St. Paul and Justification '13; WMacholz, StKr 88, '15, 29ff; EDBurton ICC, Gal. '21, 460-74; WMichaelis, Rechtf. aus Glauben b. Pls: Deissmann-Festschr. '27, 116-38; ELohmeyer, Grundlagen d. paul. Theologie '29, 52ff; HBraun, Gerichtsged. u. Rechtfertigungslehre b. Pls. '30, OZänker, Δικαιοσύνη θεοῦ b. Pls: ZsystTh 9, '32, 398-420; FVFilson, St. P.'s Conception of Recompense '31; WGrundmann, ZNW 32, '33, 52-65; H-D Wendland, D. Mitte der paul. Botschaft '35; HJJager, Rechtvaardiging en zekerheid des geloofs (Ro 1: 16f; 3: 21-5: 11) '39; HHofer, D. Rechtfertigungsverk. des Pls nach neuerer Forschg. '40; VTaylor, Forgiveness and Reconciliation '41; RBultmann, Theologie des NT '48, 266-80, Engl. transl. KGrobel '51, I 270-85; SSchulz, ZThK 56, '59, 155-85 (Qumran and Paul); CMüller, FRL 86, '64 (Ro 9-11); JBecker, Das Heil Gottes, '64; PStuhlmacher, Gerechtigkeit Gottes b. Paulus, '65; JReumann, Interpretation 20, '66, 432-52 (Ro 3: 21-31); HBraun, Qumran II, '66, 165-80; JAZiesler, The Mng. of Righteousness in Paul, '72.—CMPerella, De justification sec. Hb: Biblica 14, '33, 1-21; 150-69. S. also the lit. on πίστις and ἀμαρτία.

4. Since δ. constitutes the specif. virtue of Christians, the word becomes almost equiv. to Christianity Mt 5: 10; 1 Pt 2: 24; 3: 14; Pol 2: 3; 3: 1; ἐντολὴ δ. *the commandment of upr.* 3: 3; λόγος (τῆς) δ. Hb 5: 13; Pol 9: 1 (but s. also Epict., fgm. Stob. 26; when a man is excited by the

λόγος in meetings, he should give expression to τὰ τῆς δικαιοσύνης λόγια); ῥήματα δ. Hm 8: 9.—ἄγγελος τῆς δ. m 6, 2, 1; 3; 8; 10.—On the whole word s. AKöberle, Rechtfertigung u. Heiligung³ '30; DHill, Greek Words and Hebrew Meanings '67, 82-162; GSchrenk, TW II 194-214. M-M.*

δικαιόω fut. δικαιώσω; 1 aor. ἐδικαίωσα; 1 aor. pass. ἐδικαιώθην, subj. δικαιωθῶ, ptc. δικαιωθείς; 1 fut. pass. δικαιωθήσομαι; pf. pass. δεδικαίωμαι Ro 6: 7; 1 Cor 4: 4, ptc. δεδικαιωμένος Lk 18: 14 (Soph., Hdt. +; pap., LXX; Jos., Ant. 17, 206; Test. 12 Patr.).

1. *show justice, do justice* τινά to someone (Polyb. 3, 31, 9; Cass. Dio 48, 46; 2 Km 15: 4; Ps 81: 3) to one who is just 1 Cl 16: 12 (Is 53: 11); χήραν (χήρᾳ v.l.) 8: 4 (Is 1: 17).

2. *justify, vindicate, treat as just* (Appian, Liby. 17 §70; Gen 44: 16; Sir 10: 29; 13: 22; 23: 11 al.) θέλων δ. ἑαυτόν *wishing to justify himself* Lk 10: 29; δ. ἑαυτὸν ἐνώπιόν τινος *j. oneself before someone* 16: 15 δ. ἑαυτόν (as En. 102, 10; but s. JoachJeremias, ZNW 38, '39, 117f). Of wisdom ἐδικαιώθη ἀπὸ τῶν τέκνων αὐτῆς *is vindicated by her children* (on δικ. ἀπὸ cf. Is 45: 25. S. also Appian, Basil. 8: δικαιόω = consider someth. just or correct) 7: 35; also ἀπὸ τῶν ἔργων αὐτῆς Mt 11: 19 (v.l. τέκνων). On this saying s. DVölter, NThT 8, '19, 22-42; JMBover, Biblica 6, '25, 323-5; 463-65; M-JLagrange, ibid. 461-3. τελῶναι ἐδικαίωσαν τὸν θεόν *tax-collectors acknowledged God's justice* (opp. τὴν βουλὴν τ. θεοῦ ἀθετεῖν) Lk 7: 29 (cf. PsSol 2: 15; 3: 5). δεδικαιωμένος 18: 14. ὁ δικαιούμενός μοι *the one who vindicates himself before (or against) me* B 6: 1 (cf. Is 50: 8).—Dg 5: 14; Hm 5, 1, 7.

3. Paul, who has influenced later wr., uses the word almost exclusively of God's judgment. Esp.

a. of men δικαιοῦσθαι *be acquitted, be pronounced and treated as righteous* and thereby become δίκαιος, receive the divine gift of δικαιοσύνη, as a theological t.t. *be justified* Mt 12: 37; Ac 13: 39; Rv 22: 11 t.r.; Ro 2: 13; 3: 20 (Ps 142: 2), 24, 28; 4: 2; 5: 1, 9; 1 Cor 4: 4; Gal 2: 16f (Ps 142: 2); 3: 11, 24; 5: 4; Tit 3: 7; Phil 3: 12 v.l.; B 4: 10; 15: 7; IPhld 8: 2; Dg 9: 4; (w. ἁγιάζεσθαι) Hv 3, 9, 1. οὐ παρὰ τοῦτο δεδικαίωμαι *I am not justified by this* (after 1 Cor 4: 4) IRo 5: 1. ἵνα δικαιωθῇ σου ἡ σάρξ *that your flesh* (as the sinful part) *may be acquitted* Hs 5, 7, 1; δ. ἔργοις *by* (on the basis of) *works, by what one does* 1 Cl 30: 3; cf. Js 2: 21, 24f (ἔργον 1a and πίστις 2dδ); δι' ἑαυτῶν δ. *by oneself* = as a result of one's own accomplishments 1 Cl 32: 4.

b. of God's activity Ro 3: 26, 30; 4: 5 (on δικαιοῦν τὸν ἀσεβῆ cf. Ex 23: 7; Is 5: 23); 8: 30, 33 (Is 50: 8); Gal 3: 8; Dg 9: 5. For the view (held since Chrysostom) that δ. in these and other pass. means 'make upright' s. Gdspd., Probs. 143-6, JBL 73, '54, 86-91.

c. δικαιόω *make free* or *pure* (Ps 72: 13) and pass. δικαιοῦμαι *be set free, made pure* ἀπό *from* (Sir 26: 29; Test. Sim. 6: 1, both δικ. ἀπὸ [τῆς] ἀμαρτίας) ἀπὸ πάντων ὧν οὐκ ἠδυνήθητε ἐν νόμῳ Μωϋσέως δικαιωθῆναι *from everything fr. which you could not be freed by the law of Moses* Ac 13: 38; cf. vs. 39. ὁ ἀποθανὼν δεδικαίωται ἀπὸ τ. ἀμαρτίας *the one who died is freed fr. sin* Ro 6: 7 (cf. KGKuhn, ZNW 30, '31, 305-10; EKlaar, ibid. 59, '68, 131-4). In the context of 1 Cor 6: 11 ἐδικαιώθητε means *you have become pure.*—In the language of the mystery religions (Rtzst., Mysterienrel.³ 258ff) δικαιοῦσθαι refers to a radical inner change which the initiate experiences (Herm. Wr. 13, 9 χωρὶς γὰρ κρίσεως ἰδὲ πῶς τὴν ἀδικίαν ἐξήλασεν. ἐδικαιώθημεν, ὦ τέκνον, ἀδικίας ἀπούσης) and approaches the sense 'become deified'. Some are inclined to find in 1 Ti 3: 16 a similar use; but see under d.

d. God *is proved to be right* Ro 3: 4; 1 Cl 18: 4 (both Ps 50: 6). Of Christ 1 Ti 3: 16.—Lit. s. on δικαιοσύνη 3 and 4.—HRosman, Iustificare (δικαιοῦν) est verbum causativum: Verbum Domini 21, '41, 144-7; NMWatson, Δικ. in the LXX, JBL 79, '60, 255-66. M-M.*

δικαίωμα, ατος, τό (Thu.+; inscr., pap., LXX).

1. *regulation, requirement, commandment* (so mostly LXX; Philo, Det. Pot. Ins. 68; Jos., Bell. 7, 110, Ant. 17, 108; Cass. Dio 36, 23 of the laws; POxy. 1119, 15 τῶν ἐξαιρέτων τῆς ἡμετέρας πατρίδος δικαιωμάτων) w. ἐντολαί (as Dt 4: 40; cf. 6: 1; 7: 11; Num 36: 13 al.) Lk 1: 6; (w. προστάγματα, as Gen 26: 5) 1 Cl 2: 8; 35: 7 (Ps 49: 16); τὰ δεδομένα δ. the commandments which were given 58: 2 (δικ. διδόναι: Jos., C. Ap. 2, 37); δ. τοῦ νόμου the requirements of the law Ro 2: 26; 8: 4. Esp. of God's requirements: δ. τοῦ θεοῦ Ro 1: 32; B 4: 11; 10: 2 (cf. Dt 4: 1). κυρίου Hm 12, 6, 4. ἐκζητεῖν τὰ δ. κυρίου seek out the Lord's requirements B 2: 1. μανθάνειν 21: 1; γνῶσις τῶν δ. 21: 5. λαλεῖν δ. κυρίου speak of the law of the Lord 10: 11; σοφία τῶν δ. the wisdom revealed in his ordinances 16: 9; δ. λατρείας regulations for worship Hb 9: 1; δ. σαρκός regulations for the body vs. 10.

2. *righteous deed* (Aristot. 1135a, 12f; 1359a, 25; 1373b, 1; 3 Km 3: 28; Bar 2: 19) δι' ἑνὸς δικαιώματος (opp. παράπτωμα) Ro 5: 18.—B 1: 2; Rv 15: 4 (here perh. = 'sentence of condemnation' [cf. Pla., Leg. 9, 864ε; inscr. fr. Asia Minor: PhLeBas, Voyage archéol. II 1853, Explication des inscriptions vol. III p. 22 no. 41 κατὰ τὸ δικαίωμα τὸ κυρωθέν='acc. to the sentence which has become valid']); 19: 8.

3. Ro 5: 16 it is chosen obviously because of the other words in -μα, and is equiv. in mng. to δικαίωσις (on the linguistic possibility cf. Kühner-Bl. II 272: forms in -μα, which express the result of an action.—En. 104, 9 δικαίωμα may stand for δικαιοσύνη [cf. Ezk 18: 21 and v.l.], but the text is corrupt). M-M.*

δικαίως adv. (Hom.+; inscr., pap., LXX, En., Philo; Jos., Ant. 16, 185; Test. 12 Patr.).

1. *justly, in a just manner*—**a.** prop. *judge* (Diod. S. 15, 11, 2 δ. κρίνειν; Sir 35: 18 v.l.) 1 Pt 2: 23; B 19: 11; D 4: 3. Sarcastically GP 3: 7.

b. *uprightly* (w. ὁσίως, ἀμέμπτως) 1 Th 2: 10; (w. ὁσίως) PK 2 p. 15, 2 (Pla., Rep. 1 p. 331α ὁσίως κ. δικαίως; Inschr. v. Priene 46, 12 [I βc]; UPZ 144, 13 [164 βc] τοῖς θεοῖς, πρὸς οὓς ὁσίως ... καὶ δικαίως πολιτευσάμενος; En. 106, 18 δ. κ. ὁσίως; Jos., Ant. 6, 87); ἀναστρέφεσθαι 2 Cl 5: 6; (w. σωφρόνως, εὐσεβῶς) ζῆν Tit 2: 12 (Heraclides, Pol. 39 δ. κ. σωφρόνως βιοῦσι); cf. 1 Cl 51: 2; 62: 1. ἀγαπᾶν love rightly IEph 15: 3. νοεῖν understand rightly B 10: 12. ἐκνήφειν be sober, as you ought 1 Cor 15: 34; δ. ἀναμένειν τινά wait for someone in uprightness IMg 9: 3.

2. *justly, in (all) justice* (X., Symp. 4, 60; Lucian, Dial. Mort. 30, 1 δ. κολασθήσομαι) πάσχειν (Wsd 19: 13; Test. Sim. 4: 3) Hs 6, 3, 6. λέγειν s 1: 4. ἀπολέσθαι B 5: 4; καὶ ἡμεῖς μὲν δ. and we have been justly condemned Lk 23: 41. Opp. οὐ δ. quite unjustly 1 Cl 44: 3.*

δικαίωσις, εως, ἡ *justification, vindication, acquittal* (so Thu.+; Lev 24: 22 and Sym. Ps 34: 23) as a process as well as its result διὰ τὴν δ. Ro 4: 25 (s. DSSharp, ET 39, '28, 87-90). εἰς δ. ζωῆς acquittal that brings life 5: 18.*

δικαστής, οῦ, ὁ (Aeschyl., Hdt.+; inscr., pap., LXX,

Philo; Jos., Bell. 1, 630 [God], Ant. 7, 229 al., C. Ap. 1, 157 [δ. as highest regent in Tyre]) *judge* (w. ἄρχων) Ac 7: 27, 35; 1 Cl 4: 10 (all three Ex 2: 14); Lk 12: 14 t.r. (Diod. S. 4, 33, 4 δ.=arbitrator). M-M.*

δίκη, ης, ἡ (Hom.+; inscr., pap., LXX, Philo, Joseph., loanw. in rabb. Orig.='direction, way', in Hom.=what is right).

1. *penalty, punishment* (Pre-Socr., trag.+; PFay. 21, 24 [II AD] al. pap.; LXX) δίκην τίνειν (trag.; Pla.; Epict. 3, 24, 4; 3, 26, 20; Plut., Mor. 553F; 559D; 561B; 592E; Aelian, V.H. 9, 8; Philo, Spec. Leg. 3, 175, Mos. 1, 245) *pay a penalty, suffer punishment, be punished* τὶ *of* or *with someth.* 2 Th 1: 9; Hm 2: 5; s 9, 19, 3. Also δ. διδόναι (freq. trag.+; Jos., C. Ap. 2, 143, Vi. 343) D 1: 5 (δίκ. διδόναι of divine punishment also Diod. S. 16, 31, 4. But cf. RAKraft, The Didache and Barnabas '65, p. 141 *will be called to account*) and δ. ὑπέχειν (not infreq. since Soph., Oed. Rex 552; also Diog. L. 3, 79; Jos., Ant. 14, 45; 168) Jd 7; δ. αἰτεῖσθαι κατά τινος Ac 25: 15 t.r.

2. *Justice* personified as a goddess Ac 28: 4 (Soph., Ant. 538 ἀλλ' οὐκ ἐάσαι τοῦτο γ' ἡ Δίκη σ', ἐπεὶ κτλ.; Ael. Aristid. 52 p. 606 D.; Arrian, Anab. 4, 9, 7 Δίκη as πάρεδρος of Zeus; Damasc., Vi. Isid. 138; Procop. Soph., Ep. 17; 149; Herm. Wr. p. 420, 1 Sc.; 4 Macc; Philo; Joseph. [TW II 183]).—RHirzel, Themis, Dike u. Verwandtes '07; WJaeger, Paideia '34, 144ff (cf. Eng. tr. '39, vol. 1, 68); SLoenen, Dike '48. M-M. B. 1358.*

δίκτυον, ου, τό (Hom.+; Ps.-X., Cyn. 2, 5; Epict. 2, 1, 8; LXX; Jos., Ant. 9, 92) *net* for catching fish (since Od. 22, 386; also Diod. S. 5, 76, 4; Paus. 2, 30, 3; Lucian, Herm. 65; Alciphr. 1, 14 al.; s. on ἀμφιβάλλω) Mt 4: 20f; Mk 1: 18f; Lk 5: 2, 4ff; J 21: 6, 8, 11 (ἕλκειν τὸ δίκτ.: Theocr., Idyll 1, 40; Vi. Aesopi I c. 26); for catching birds B 5: 4 (Pr 1: 17). M-M.*

δίλογος, ον (Pollux 2, 118, but= 'repeating'. Likew. Diod. S. 20, 37, 1 διλογεῖν τι=say someth. twice; cf. Nägeli 52) *double-tongued*, i.e., *insincere* 1 Ti 3: 8.—Pol 5: 2. M-M.*

διό inferential conjunction (δι' ὅ; cf. Bl-D. §451, 5) (Heraclitus, Thu.+; inscr., pap., LXX) *therefore, for this reason* Mt 27: 8; Mk 5: 33 v.l.; Lk 7: 7; Ac 15: 19; 20: 31; 25: 26; 26: 3; 27: 25, 34; Ro 1: 24; 2: 1; 13: 5 (RBultmann, ThLZ 72, '47, 200 would omit the two last verses as glosses); B 4: 9; 1 Cl 7: 2; 9: 1 al. διὸ καί (Bl-D. §442, 12; 451, 5) *therefore ... also*, denoting that the inference is self-evident (Jos., Ant. 19, 294) Lk 1: 35; Ac 10: 29; 24: 26; Ro 4: 22; 15: 22; 2 Cor 1: 20; 5: 9 al. 𝔓⁷² reads δι' οὗ, w. ref. to Christ 2 Pt 1: 12.—EMolland, Διο: Serta Rudbergiana '31, 43-52. M-M.

Διόγνητος, ου, ὁ (found freq.; Demosth.; Polyb.; M. Ant. 1, 6; inscr., pap.) *Diognetus*, man to whom the Epistle to Diognetus was addressed, Dg 1.*

διοδεύω impf. διώδευον; 1 aor. διώδευσα (Aristot.+; inscr., pap., LXX, Joseph., Sib. Or.).

1. *go, travel through* (Lucian, Dial. Mort. 27, 2; Dit., Or. 613, 3; 665, 22; PAmh. 36, 13) τόπον τινά (cf. Wsd 5: 7; 11: 2) Ac 17: 1.

2. intr. *go about* (Jos., Bell. 2, 340; Jer 2: 6; 1 Macc 12: 32 διωδ. ἐν πάσῃ τῇ χώρᾳ; Sib. Or. 3, 250) κατὰ πόλιν καὶ κώμην fr. one city and village to another Lk 8: 1.—Anz 344. M-M.*

διοίκησις, εως, ἡ *administration, management* (X.+; Dit., Or. 11, 24; 458, 65; pap.; Tob 1: 21; Jos., Bell. 1, 669, Ant. 15, 68; 355 δ. Καίσαρος) of a political body: of

God's rule of the world (Epict. 3, 5, 8; 10; 4, 1, 100 al.; Philo, Spec. Leg. 4, 187; cf. Herm. Wr. 10, 23) τῇ δ. αὐτοῦ *at his direction* 1 Cl 20: 1.—Dg 7: 2.*

Διονύσιος, ου, ὁ (very freq.) *Dionysius,* name of an Athenian (s. Jos., Ant. 14, 149–52), member of the Areopagus, converted by Paul, Ac 17: 34. M-M.*

διόπερ inferential conj. (δι᾽ ὅπερ) (Democr., Thu.+; Diod. S. 4, 33, 6; inscr., pap., LXX; Jos., Ant. 16, 118) *therefore, for this very reason* 1 Cor 8: 13; 10: 14; 14: 13 t.r. M-M.*

διοπετής, ές *fallen from heaven* (of images of the gods Eur., Iph. T. 977; Dionys. Hal. 2, 66; Appian, Mithrid. 53 §213; Herodian 5, 3, 5) τὸ δ. *the image* (of Artemis) *fallen fr. heaven* at Ephesus Ac 19: 35.—EvDobschütz, Christusbilder: TU 18, 1899, 11ff; 41. M-M.*

διόπτρα, ας, ἡ (Euclid, Polyb.+) *optical instrument* Papias 3.*

διορθόω 1 aor. mid. διωρθωσάμην (Pind.+; inscr., pap., LXX; Jos., Ant. 2, 46 al.) *set on the right path* ἐπὶ τὸ ἀγαθὸν δ. *lead to what is good* 1 Cl 21: 6.*

διόρθωμα, ατος, τό (Hippocr., Aristot.+; Inscr. gr. 469, 17; BPGrenfell and JPMahaffy, Revenue Laws of Ptol. Philad. 1896, 57, 1; PPar. 62 I, 7) *reform,* of improvements in internal administration Ac 24: 2 (cf. κατόρθωμα).—SLösch, ThQ 112, '31, 307–12. M-M.*

διόρθωσις, εως, ἡ (Hippocr.+; pap.; Philo, Sacr. Abel. 27; Jos., Bell. 1, 389; 2, 449, Ant. 2, 51) *improvement, reformation, new order* (Pla., Leg. 1 p. 642A; Polyb. 1, 1, 1; PGM 13, 707 πρὸς διόρθωσιν βίου) καιρὸς δ. *the time of the new order* (in contrast to that of the law w. its fleshly stipulations) Hb 9: 10. M-M.*

διορίζω (Aeschyl., Hdt.+; inscr., pap., Herm. Wr. 3, 2a; Philo, Leg. All. 1, 20; Jos., Bell. 2, 503, C. Ap. 2, 250) *set limits to* someth., pass. Dg 7: 2.*

διορύσσω 1 aor. pass. inf. διορυχθῆναι (Hom.+; LXX; Philo, In Flacc. 73) of a thief who *digs through* the (sun-dried brick) wall of a house and gains entrance, *break through, break in* (Aristoph., Plut. 565 κλέπτειν καὶ τοὺς τοίχους διορύττειν; X., Symp. 4, 30; Lucian, Gall. 22; Dit., Or. 483, 118; Job 24: 16.—Joseph. does not have the verb, but Ant. 16, 1 τοιχωρύχος=house-breaker) abs. Mt 6: 19f. W. acc. (PPetr. III 28 verso b, 2 [260 BC] ὅτι διώρυξεν οἰκίαν) pass. 24: 43; Lk 12: 39 *he would not have permitted his house to be broken into.* M-M.*

Διός s. Ζεύς.

Διόσκουροι, ων, οἱ (BGU 248, 13 [I AD]; Mayser 10f; Bl-D. §30, 3; Rob. 199–Ionic form) *the Dioscuri,* Castor and Pollux, twin sons of Zeus and Leda, insignia and also patron deities of an Alexandrian ship Ac 28: 11 (Epict. 2, 18, 29; Ael. Aristid. 43, 26 K.=1 p. 10 D.: Δ. σῴζουσι τοὺς πλέοντας et al.—KJaisle, D. Dioskuren als Retter z. See, Diss. Tüb. '07; EHaenchen, AG, ad loc.). M-M.*

διότι conj. (Hdt.+; inscr., pap., LXX, Joseph.) (Bl-D. §294, 4; 456, 1; Rob. ind.; Meisterhans³-Schw. 252f; Mayser 161; Thackeray 138f; FKälker, Quaest. de Eloc. Polyb. 1880, 243f; 300).

1. *because* (=διὰ τοῦτο ὅτι) in causal clauses Lk 2: 7; 21: 28; Ac 17: 31 t.r.; Ro 8: 21 (but s. 4); 1 Cor 15: 9; Phil 2: 26; 1 Th 2: 8; 4: 6; Hb 11: 5 (Gen 5: 24), 23; Js 4: 3; Dg 6: 5; Hv 3, 5, 4; m 12, 3, 4; s 9, 14, 4.

2. at the beginning of an inferential clause *therefore* (=διὰ τοῦτο) Ac 13: 35; 20: 26.

3. in place of causal ὅτι: *for* Lk 1: 13; Ac 10: 20 t.r.; 18: 10; 22: 18; Ro 1: 19–21; 3: 20; 8: 7; Gal 2: 16 t.r.; 1 Th 2: 18; 1 Pt 1: 16a, b (v.l.), 24 (ὅτι 𝔓⁷²); 2: 6.

4. *that* (Teles p. 46, 4; 47, 12; 48, 11; Antig. Car. 149; 152; Dio Chrys. 21[38], 14; Celsus 2, 49; Dit., Syll.³ 1169, 24; Sb 7638, 8 [257 BC]; UPZ 15, 24 [156 BC] ἐπιγνωσιν διότι=ὅτι; UPZ 16, 15 in a parallel concept of the same petition [ὅτι is v.l. in Ro 8: 21]; Ep. Arist. 151; Jos., Bell. 3, 475, Ant. 15, 142) Ro 8: 21 (s. 1 above). M-M.*

Διοτρέφης, ους, ὁ *Diotrephes* (Thu. 8, 64, 2; Diod. S. 15, 14, 1; Dit., Syll.² 868, 8, Or. 219, 1), a Christian 3 J 9. M-M.*

διπλοκαρδία, ας, ἡ *duplicity,* lit. 'double-heartedness', in a list of vices D 5: 1; B 20: 1.*

διπλοῦς, ῆ, οῦν (Hom.+; inscr., pap., LXX; Philo, Aet. M. 85; Jos., Ant. 4, 249; 13, 239; Test. 12 Patr.; loanw. in rabb.) *double, two-fold* τιμή (POsl. 43, 8 [140/1 AD] ἐκτείσω σοι τὴν τιμὴν διπλῆν) 1 Ti 5: 17 (s. τιμή 2e and PGM 4, 2454, where the emperor διπλᾶ ὀψώνια ἐκέλευσεν δίδοσθαι to the prophet for his services.—Diod. S. 5, 45, 5 τ. ἱερεῦσι μόνοις δίδοται διπλάσιον; 13, 93, 2 διπλοῦς ποιήσειν τοὺς μισθούς). τὰ κτίσματα τοῦ θεοῦ δ. ἐστί *are of two kinds* Hm 8: 1; δ. εἰσιν αἱ ἐνέργειαι m 6, 1, 1; cf. 8: 1. διπλοῦν τὸν καρπὸν ἀποδιδόναι *yield fruit twofold* s 2: 8. τὰ διπλᾶ *double* διπλοῦν τὰ δ. *pay back double* Rv 18: 6a. Neuter διπλοῦν *double* (Dit., Syll.³ 962, 70) κεράσαι ibid. b.—Comp. formed peculiarly as if fr. διπλός: διπλότερος (Appian, Prooem. 10 §40 διπλότερα τούτων; Bl-D. §61, 2; Mlt.-H. 166). Neut. as adv. *twice as much* υἱὸς γεέννης δ. ὑμῶν *twice as bad as you* Mt 23: 15 (Bl-D. §102, 4; Rob. 299; Justin, Dial. 122, says on Mt 23: 15: διπλότερον ὑμῶν βλασφημοῦσιν). M-M.*

διπλόω 1 aor. ἐδίπλωσα (since X., Hell. 6, 5, 19) *to double* τὰ διπλᾶ *pay back double* Rv 18: 6.*

Δίρκη, ης, ἡ *Dirce,* wife of the Theban king Lycus; she was dragged to death by a wild bull. Pl. (with Δίρκαι= people like Dirce cf. Themist. p. 285C . . . Τιμαίους, Δικαιάρχους=men like Timaeus, Dicaearchus; Himerius, Or. [Ecl.] 5, 24 Θησεῖς κ. Κόδροι; schol. on Plato, 169B; Synesius, Baldhead 21 p. 85B) of Christian women who were martyred 1 Cl 6: 2; s. Δαναΐδες (cf. Diod. S. 14, 112, 1 τραγικήν τινα τιμωρίαν λαμβάνειν=receive a punishment of the kind found in tragedy).*

δίς adv. (Hom.+; inscr., pap., LXX; Jos., Vi. 355) *twice* Mk 14: 30, 72; Rv 9: 16 (cf. δισμυρίας). ἅπαξ καὶ δ. (ἅπαξ 1) *once and again=several times* Phil 4: 16; 1 Th 2: 18; 1 Cl 53: 3 (Dt 9: 13). W. gen. foll. (Diod. S. 5, 41, 6 δὶς τοῦ ἐνιαυτοῦ; Jos., Ant. 3, 199) δ. τοῦ σαββάτου *twice in a week* Lk 18: 12; δ. ἀποθνῄσκειν *die twice* Jd 12 (cf. Paroem. Gr.: Apostol. 14, 27 δὶς ἀποθανουμένη ψυχή; the same Plut., Mor. 236D). M-M.*

δισμυριάς, άδος, ἡ *a double myriad,* i.e. 20,000 (also written separately δὶς μυριάς) Rv 9: 16 where the number given is several twenty-thousand times 10,000. An indefinite number of incalculable immensity is indicated (as indefinite as the ἀναρίθμητοι μυριάδες of Theopompus in Περὶ ὕψους 43, 2).*

δισσός, ή, όν (trag., Pla., X.+; PTebt. 27, 53 al. pap.; LXX; Philo, Aet. M. 20; Sib. Or. 1, 327) *double* δ.

ἕξουσιν τὴν κρίσιν they will incur double punishment 2 Cl 10: 5; δ. φόβοι two kinds of fear Hm 7: 4.*

δισσῶς adv. (trag.+; Sir 23: 11; Test. 12 Patr.) doubly κολάζεσθαι be punished doubly Hs 9, 18, 2.*

δισταγμός, οῦ, ὁ (Agatharchides [II bc] 21 CMüller [Geogr. Gr. min. I 1855, p. 120, 8]; Plut., Mor. 214f; schol. on Apollon. Rhod. 3, 539a) doubt εἰς δ. βάλλειν plunge into doubt 1 Cl 46: 9. ἐν δ. γενέσθαι become doubtful Hs 9, 28, 4. B. 1244.*

διστάζω fut. διστάσω; 1 aor. ἐδίστασα (Pla.+; Dit., Or. 315, 66; UPZ 110, 57 [164 bc]; PGiess. 18, 9; BGU 388, 17; Ep. Arist. 53; Jos., Bell. 2, 182).

1. doubt abs. (Diod. S. 20, 15, 3) Mt 14: 31; 28: 17 (IPEllis, NTS 14, '67/'68, 574-80). τῇ ψυχῇ within oneself 1 Cl 23: 3. Also τῇ καρδίᾳ 2 Cl 11: 2. ἐν τῇ καρδίᾳ Hm 9: 5. περί τινος have doubts concerning someth. (Diod. S. 4, 62, 3; 19, 36, 5; Plut., Mor. 62a) 1 Cl 11: 2; Hs 9, 28, 7. W. indirect quest. foll. (Pla., Aristot.; Polyb. 12, 26c, 2) τίνι δῷς consider to whom you should give Hm 2: 4.

2. hesitate in doubt (Diod. S. 10, 4, 4; Dositheus 71, 5) w. inf. foll. δοῦναι D 4: 7; B 19: 11. αἰτεῖσθαι to make a request Hs 5, 4, 3. M-M*

δίστομος, ον (Soph.+; LXX) double-edged of a sword (so Eur., Hel. 983; LXX) μάχαιρα (Judg 3: 16; Pr 5: 4; cf. PGM 13, 92 ἔχε . . . μαχαῖριν ὀλοσίδηρον δίστομον) Hb 4: 12. ῥομφαία (Ps 149: 6; Sir 21: 3) Rv 1: 16; 2: 12; 19: 15 v.l. (w. ὀξεῖα). M-M.*

δισχίλιοι, αι, α (Hdt.+; Abercius Inscr. 21; pap.; LXX; Jos., Bell. 1, 172, Ant. 11, 15; 18 al.) two thousand Mk 5: 13.*

διϋλίζω (in fig. sense in Archytas [c. 360 bc; Stob. III 1, p. 58, 7 H.]. In lit. mng., of wine Plut., Mor. 692d; Diosc. 2, 86; 5, 72; Artem. 4, 48; POxy. 413, 154; Am 6: 6) filter out, strain out (the KJ 'strain at' is widely considered a misprint [so Gdspd., Relig. in Life 12, '42/'43, 205-10 and Probs. '45, 38f], but for the view that it is an archaic usage s. Murray, New [Oxford] Eng. Dict. s.v. 'strain', verb. 14e and esp. 21, and CHopf, Rev. of Engl. Studies 20, '44, 155f) τὸν κώνωπα a gnat fr. a drink Mt 23: 24.*

δίχα adv. (Hom.+; POxy. 237 VIII, 37; PGiess. 66, 3; BGU 908, 22; Sir 47: 21); in our lit. only as improper prep. w. gen. apart from, without (trag., X.+; Philo, Aet. M. 52; 74; Jos., Bell. 1, 346; 6, 95, Ant. 3, 76; 18, 336) δ. πάσης παρεκβάσεως without any divergence at all 1 Cl 20: 3; δ. ἐλλείψεως without interruption vs. 10; cf. 37: 4f; 49: 5; 50: 2; 63: 1.*

διχάζω 1 aor. ἐδίχασα (=divide in two, separate Pla., Pol. 264d; Galen, De Usu Part. II 313, 24 Helmr.; mystery pap. [I ad]: APF 13, '39, 212; Aq. Lev 1: 17; Dt 14: 6) fig. cause a separation, separate (so Maspéro 155, 16 [VI ad] φθόνος πονηρὸς ἐδίχασε ἡμᾶς; Eustath. ad Od. 7, 325 p. 1582, 12) τινὰ κατά τινος turn someone against someone Mt 10: 35. M-M.*

διχηλέω (Aristot. 695a, 18 v.l.; LXX; Ep. Arist. 153; Philo, Spec. Leg. 4, 106) have a divided hoof πᾶν δι-χηλοῦν every animal w. a divided hoof B 10: 11 (Lev 11: 3).*

διχοστασία, ας, ἡ (Solon 3, 37 Diehl²; Bacchylides 11, 67 BSnell ['34]; Hdt. 5, 75; Dionys. Hal. 8, 72, 1; Plut., Mor. 479a; Inscr. Gr. 448, 19; 1 Macc 3: 29; Ps.-Phoc. 151; Sib. Or. 4, 68) dissension (w. ἐριθεῖαι, αἱρέσεις) Gal 5: 20; cf. 1 Cl 46: 5; 51: 1. διχοστασίας ποιεῖν cause dissensions

Ro 16: 17; cf. Hs 8, 7, 5; 8, 10, 2; 1 Cor 3: 3 t.r.; Hv 3, 9, 9; m 2: 3. M-M.*

διχοστατέω 1 aor. ἐδιχοστάτησα (trag.+).—1. disagree γῇ μὴ διχοστατοῦσα without dissent 1 Cl 20: 4. —2. feel doubts, be insecure (Alex. Aphr., Probl., Praef.) Hs 8, 7, 2; 8, 8, 5.*

διχοστάτης, ου, ὁ one who causes dissensions (w. παρά-νομοι) Hs 8, 7, 6.*

διχοτομέω fut. διχοτομήσω (Pre-Socr., Pla.+; Polyb. 6, 28, 2; 10, 15, 5; Plut., Pyrrh. 24, 5; inscr. fr. Lycaonia [JHS 22, '02, 369f]; Ex 29: 17; Jos., Ant. 8, 31) cut in two of the dismemberment of a condemned person Mt 24: 51; Lk 12: 46 (Greek Apocalypse of Baruch 16 [Texts and Stud. V 1, 1897] διχοτομήσατε αὐτοὺς ἐν μαχαίρᾳ. For this idea cf. Od. 18, 339; Hdt. 2, 139; Epict. 3, 22, 3; Sus 55; 59 Theod.; Hb 11: 37). In the context of these two passages the mng. punish w. utmost severity is poss., though no exact linguistic parallels for this mng. have been found. M-M.*

διψάω 3 sing. διψᾷ (Ps.-Pla., Ax. 366a) J 7: 37; Ro 12: 20 (Pr 25: 21); fut. διψήσω; 1 aor. ἐδίψησα (Hom.+; IG XIV 1890, 10f; PGM 36, 112; 148; LXX; Philo; Jos., Bell. 6, 318 al.) thirst.

1. be thirsty, suffer fr. thirst Mt 25: 35, 37, 42, 44; J 4: 13, 15; 19: 28 (cf. GDalman, Jesus-Jeshua [tr. PLevertoff], '29, 207-9); Ro 12: 20 (Pr 25: 21). W. πεινάω to denote the severest privations (Ps 106: 5) 1 Cor 4: 11; Rv 7: 16 (Is 49: 10); ISm 6: 2. Opp. drunkenness LJ 1: 3 (LEWright, JBL 65, '46, 180f). Fig. γῆ διψῶσα thirsty= dry ground 1 Cl 16: 3 (Is 53: 2).

2. fig. of thirst for the water of life J 4: 14; 6: 35; 7: 37; Rv 21: 6; 22: 17 (cf. Is 55: 1).

3. fig. thirst, i.e. long for someth. have a strong desire for someth. (Pla., Rep. 8, p. 562c; Plut., Cato Mai. 11, 5; Philo, Fug. 139 τοὺς διψῶντας κ. πεινῶντας καλο-κάγαθίας; Ps 41: 3; Sir 51: 24) τ. δικαιοσύνην Mt 5: 6 (for the acc. cf. Philipp. Epigr. [I ad] in Anth. App. Planudea book 4= Anth. Pal. 16, 137 Düb. φόνον; Jos., Bell. 1, 628 αἷμα; Cos. and Dam. 10, 64 τ. σωτηρίαν. W. acc. of a pers. Ps 62: 2 v.l. [Psalmi cum Odis ed. ARahlfs '31].—For the idea JMBover, Estudios Eclesiásticos 16, '42, 9-26; FMBraun, Avoir Soif (J 4 and 7), BRigaux Festschr., '70, 247-58.—Absol. POxy. I, 3; JoachJere-mias, Unknown Sayings of Jesus, tr. Fuller, '57, 69f). M-M.*

δίψος, ους, τό (X., al.; Epict.; PTebt. 272, 17; LXX; cf. Thackeray 157; Philo; Jos., Ant. 3, 37; 38; 18, 192. S. also Nägeli 14) thirst (w. λιμός, as Dio Chrys. 7[8], 16; 13[7], 55; Pythag., Ep. 4, 4; Socrat., Ep. 12; Is 5: 13) 2 Cor 11: 27. M-M. B. 333.*

διψυχέω 1 aor. ἐδιψύχησα (not in secular wr. or LXX; not in NT) be undecided, be changeable, doubt (of indecision about accepting Christianity or believing in specif. Christian teachings or hopes, etc.).

1. abs. 1 Cl 23: 2; 2 Cl 11: 5; Hv 2, 2, 7; 4, 1, 4; 7; 4, 2, 4; m 9: 8; s 8, 8, 3; 5; 8, 9, 4; 8, 10, 2. οἱ διψυχοῦντες those who waver Hv 3, 2, 2; m 9: 6. ἔχω τι διψυχῆσαι I am doubtful about someth. Hv 4, 1, 4; cf. 3, 3, 4.

2. w. περί τινος be in doubt about someth. Hs 6, 1, 2. Also ἐπί τινι s 8, 11, 3. μηδὲν ὅλως δ. w. inf. foll. not hesitate at all to . . . m 9: 1. W. indir. quest. foll. doubt whether B 19: 5; D 4: 4. W. ὅτι foll. Hm 9: 7.*

διψυχία, ας, ἡ (neither LXX nor NT.—Hesychius διψυχία· ἀπορία) *indecision, doubt* (in religious matters) Hv 3, 10, 9; m 9: 7, 9ff; w. ἀπιστία 2 Cl 19: 2; w. μαλακίαι Hv 3, 11, 2; w. ὀξυχολία m 10, 1, 1f; 10, 2, 4. αἴρειν τὴν δ. *remove the doubt* m 9: 1; also αἴρειν τὰς δ. v 2, 2, 4; διὰ τὴν δ. m 10, 2, 2; ἀπὸ τῆς δ. *because of doubt* v 3, 7, 1. Called the daughter of the devil m 9: 9.—ABaumeister, Die Ethik des Pastor Hermae, '12, 107-10.*

δίψυχος, ον (not in secular wr. or LXX; the title in Philo, fgm. II 663 Mangey is not fr. Philo's hand.—But Parmenides 6, 5 speaks of δίκρανοι=double-headed people, who stagger helplessly here and there in their thinking) *doubting, hesitating,* lit. *double-minded* Js 4: 8; ἀνὴρ δ. *a doubter* 1 : 8; Hm 9: 6; ὁ δ. m 10, 2, 2; οἱ δ. (w. διστάζοντες) 1 Cl 11: 2; 23: 3; 2 Cl 11: 2.—Hv 3, 4, 3; 4, 2, 6; m 9: 5; 11: 1f, 4; s 8, 7, 1; 9, 21, 1ff. W. ἀπόκενος m 5, 2, 1. κενός m 11: 13. ἀσύνετος m 12, 4, 2. ἄφρων, ταλαίπωρος s 1: 3. βλάσφημος s 9, 18, 3. κατάλαλος s 8, 7, 2.—OJFSeitz, JBL 63, '44, 131-40; 66, '47, 211-19, NTS 4, '57/'58, 327-34 (Hermas and the Thanksgiving Scroll); WIWolverton, ATR 38, '56, 166-75 (Essene Psychology). M-M.*

διωγμίτης, ου, ὁ (Dit., Or. 511, 10, also editor's note 3 w. further exx.) *mounted policeman* MPol 7: 1 (JMarquardt, Röm. Staatsverw. I² 1881, 213).*

διωγμός, οῦ, ὁ (Aeschyl.+; Polyb. 3, 74, 2; Plut.; LXX) *persecution* (only for religious reasons) δ. μέγας *a severe persecution* Ac 8: 1. μετὰ διωγμῶν (D -οῦ; other v.l. -όν) *not without persecutions* Mk 10: 30 (cf. MGoguel, RHPhr 8, '28, 264-77). ἐπεγείρειν δ. ἐπί τινα *stir up a persecution against someone* Ac 13: 50; δ. ὑποφέρειν *suffer persecution* 2 Ti 3: 11. καταπαύειν τ. διωγμόν *bring the persecution to an end* MPol 1: 1. W. θλῖψις Mt 13: 21; Mk 4: 17; 2 Th 1: 4; στενοχωρία 2 Cor 12: 10. W. both Ro 8: 35. W. παθήματα 2 Ti 3: 11. W. ἀκαταστασία 1 Cl 3: 2.*

διώκτης, ου, ὁ (not in secular wr.; Sym. Hos 6: 8) *persecutor* (w. βλάσφημος, ὑβριστής) 1 Ti 1: 13; δ. ἀγαθῶν *persecutor of the good* D 5: 2; B 20: 2. M-M.*

διώκω impf. ἐδίωκον; fut. διώξω (Bl-D. §77); 1 aor. ἐδίωξα, pass. ἐδιώχθην; pf. pass. ptc. δεδιωγμένος (Hom.+; inscr., pap., LXX, En., Philo, Joseph., Test. 12 Patr.).
  1. *hasten, run, press on* (Il. 23, 344; Aeschyl., Sept. 91; X., An. 6, 5, 25; Hg 1: 9; Is 13: 14; Philo, Virt. 30 διώκουσι καὶ ἐπιτρέχουσιν) κατὰ σκοπόν *toward the goal* Phil 3: 14; cf. vs. 12 (on the combination w. καταλαμβάνω cf. Hdt. 9, 58; Lucian, Hermot. 77; Sir 11: 10; La 1: 3 v.l.).
  2. *persecute* (Dit., Or. 532, 25) τινά *someone* (1 Macc 5: 22; En. 99, 14; Jos., Ant. 12, 272) Mt 5: 11f, 44; 10: 23; Lk 11: 49; 21: 12; J 5: 16; 15: 20; Ro 12: 14; 1 Cor 4: 12; 15: 9; Gal 1: 13, 23; 4: 29; Phil 3: 6; Ac 7: 52; 9: 4f; 22: 4, 7f; 26: 11, 14f; Rv 12: 13; D 1: 3; 16: 4; B 20: 2. Pass. (Lucian, Dial. Mar. 9, 1) Mt 5: 10; 2 Cor 4: 9; Gal 5: 11; 6: 12; 2 Ti 3: 12; IMg 8: 2; ITr 9: 1. Of the plots against Joseph 1 Cl 4: 9.
  3. *drive away, drive out* (Od. 18, 409; Hdt. 9, 77 μέχρι Θεσσαλίης, ἐκ τ. γῆς; POxy. 943, 5; BGU 954, 7 ὅπως διώξῃς ἀπ' ἐμοῦ τ. δαίμονα; Cat. Cod. Astr. VIII 2 p. 174, 20) Mt 23: 34 (δ. εἰς τι as Appian, Bell. Civ. 2, 14 §52); 10: 23 v.l.
  4. *run after, pursue*—a. lit. μηδὲ διώξητε *do not run after* (them) Lk 17: 23 (cf. X., Mem. 2, 8, 6; Dit., Syll.³, 1168, 111).
  b. fig. *pursue, strive for, seek after, aspire to* someth.

(Thu. 2, 63, 1 τιμάς; Pla., Gorg. 482ε ἀλήθειαν; Dio Chrys. 60+61 [77+78], 26 πλούτους; Ael. Aristid. 29, 1 K.=40 p. 751 D.; Is 5: 11; Hos 6: 3; Sir 31: 5; Philo, Somn. 1, 199 ἡδονήν δ.; Jos., Ant. 6, 263 τὸ δίκαιον) δικαιοσύνην (Pr 15: 9) *uprightness* Ro 9: 30; 1 Ti 6: 11; 2 Ti 2: 22. νόμον δικαιοσύνης Ro 9: 31 (cf. 2 Esdr [Ezra] 9: 4); hospitality 12: 13; what makes for peace 14: 19; cf. Hb 12: 14; 1 Pt 3: 11 (Ps 33: 15); love 1 Cor 14: 1; virtue (Maximus Tyr. 15, 7c) 2 Cl 10: 1; what is good (Alex. Aphr., An. Mant. II 1 p. 155, 31 δ. τὸ καλόν) 1 Th 5: 15. M-M. B. 700.**

δόγμα, ατος, τό (X., Pla.+; inscr. [Dit., Syll. ind.]; pap., LXX, Philo, Joseph.; Sib. Or. 3, 656 δ. θεοῦ; loanw. in rabb.).
  1. *decree, ordinance, decision, command* (Pla., Rep. 3, 414β; Demosth. 25, 16; Plut., Mor. 742ᴅ; Da 3: 10; 4: 6; 6: 13 Theod. al.) Hb 11: 23 v.l. Of imperial decrees (Jos., Bell. 1, 393; PFay. 20, 22 a δ. of Alex. Severus) ἐξῆλθεν δ. (cf. Da 2: 13 Theod.) παρὰ Καίσαρος Lk 2: 1. ἀπέναντι τῶν δογμάτων Καίσαρος πράττειν *act contrary to the decrees of Caesar* Ac 17: 7. Of the *rules or commandments* of Jesus B 1: 6; IMg 13: 1; of the gospel D 11: 3; of the apostles Ac 16: 4 (cf. the Christian prayer in CSchmidt, GHeinrici-Festschr. '14, p. 71, 24). τριῶν γραμμάτων δόγματα λαμβάνειν *receive instructions from three letters* (of the alphabet) B 9: 7; cf. 10: 1, 9f. Of the Mosaic law (3 Macc 1: 3; Philo, Gig. 52, Leg. All. 1, 54; 55 διατήρησις τ. ἁγίων δογμάτων; Jos., C. Ap. 1, 42) νόμος τῶν ἐντολῶν ἐν δ. *law of commandments consisting in* (single) *ordinances* Eph 2: 15. τὸ καθ' ἡμῶν χειρόγραφον τοῖς δ. *the bond that stood against us, w. its requirements* Col 2: 14.
  2. *doctrine, dogma* (Pla.+; Plut., Mor. 14ε; 779β; 1000ᴅ; Epict. 4, 11, 8; Herodian 1, 2, 4; Philo, Spec. Leg. 1, 269; Jos., Bell. 2, 142) of philosophers δ. ἀνθρώπινον Dg 5: 3. Of false prophets δ. ποικίλα τῆς ἀπωλείας διδάσκειν *teach various doctrines that lead to perdition* AP 1 (cf. Third Corinthians 3: 2; Diod. S. 1, 86, 2 of relig. teaching [about the sacred animals of the Egyptians]). M-M.*

δογματίζω pf. pass. ptc. δεδογματισμένος (=decree, ordain since II ʙᴄ; cf. Nägeli 32; Da 2: 13 al. LXX) pass. *submit to rules and regulations* Col 2: 20. τὰ δεδογματισμένα ὑπό τινος *things decreed by someone* 1 Cl 20: 4; 27: 5 (cf. 3 Macc 4: 11). M-M.*

δοκέω impf. ἐδόκουν; fut. δόξω; 1 aor. ἔδοξα (Hom.+; inscr., pap., LXX, Ep. Arist., Philo, Joseph., Test. 12 Patr.).
  1. trans. *think, believe, suppose, consider* of subjective opinion (Hom.+; pap.; rare LXX).
  a. w. inf. foll., when its subj. is identical w. that of the inf. (X., An. 2, 2, 14; Diod. S. 17, 27, 2 τοὺς δοκοῦντας νενικηκέναι; Pr 28: 24; 4 Macc 13: 14): μὴ δόξητε λέγειν *do not suppose that you are to say* Mt 3: 9. ἐδόκουν πνεῦμα θεωρεῖν *they thought they saw a spirit* Lk 24: 37. ὁ δοκεῖ ἔχειν *what he thinks he has* 8: 18 (cf. Jos., Bell. 3, 319). ὁ δοκῶν πνεῦμα ἔχειν *the one who thinks he has the Spirit* Hm 11: 12; cf. J 5: 39; 16: 2; Ac 27: 13; 1 Cor 7: 40; Phil 3: 4; Js 1: 26; 2 Cl 17: 3; Dg 3: 5; 8: 10; Hm 10, 2, 4.
  b. foll. by the inf. w. a nom. ὅσῳ δοκεῖ μᾶλλον μείζων εἶναι *the greater he thinks he is* (or *seems to be,* s. 2 below) 1 Cl 48: 6. εἴ τις δοκεῖ σοφὸς εἶναι *if anyone thinks that he is wise* 1 Cor 3: 18. εἴ τις δοκεῖ προφήτης εἶναι 14: 37. εἴ τις δοκεῖ φιλόνεικος εἶναι *if anyone is disposed to be contentious* 11: 16.—Gal 6: 3.
  c. foll. by acc. and inf. w. subj. not identical (X., An. 1,

7, 1; PTebt. 413, 6 μὴ δόξῃς με, κυρία, ἠμεληκέναι σου τῶν ἐντολῶν; Gen 38: 15; 2 Macc 7: 16; 3 Macc 5: 5; Jos., Ant. 2, 340) μή τίς με δόξῃ ἄφρονα εἶναι *no one is to consider me foolish* 2 Cor 11: 16. ἃ δοκοῦμεν ἀτιμότερα εἶναι 1 Cor 12: 23.

d. w. ὅτι foll. (Arrian, Alex. An. 4, 28, 2) Mt 6: 7; 26: 53; Mk 6: 49; Lk 12: 51; 13: 2, 4; J 5: 45; 11: 13, 31; 1 Cor 4: 9 t.r.; 2 Cor 12: 19; Js 4: 5; Hv 4, 3, 7; 5: 3.

e. used parenthetically (Bl-D. §465, 2 w. app.; Rob. 434; cf. Anacreontea 35, 15 Preis. πόσον δοκεῖς πονοῦσιν; Aristoph., Acharn. 12; Epict. 2, 19, 7; POxy. 1218, 7 ἡ μήτηρ μου Θαῆσις εἰς ᾿Αντινόου, δοκῶ, ἐπὶ κηδίαν ἀπῆλθεν) πόσῳ δοκεῖτε χείρονος ἀξιωθήσεται τιμωρίας; *how much more severely, do you think, will he be punished?* Hb 10: 29. τί δοκεῖτε ποιήσει; *what, do you think, will he do?* Hs 9, 28, 8; cf. 1 Cor 4: 9. οὔ, δοκῶ *I suppose not* Lk 17: 9 v.l.

f. elliptically (2 Macc 2: 29) ᾗ οὐ δοκεῖτε ὥρᾳ ὁ υἱὸς τ. ἀνθρώπου ἔρχεται *the Son of Man is coming at an hour when you do not think (he will come)* Mt 24: 44; cf. Lk 12: 40. τί δοκεῖτε; *what do you think?* 1 Cl 43: 6; 2 Cl 7: 5. τί δοκεῖς τοὺς κεκλημένους; *what do you think about those who have been called?* Hs 9, 14, 5 (cf. X., An. 5, 7, 26 τούτους τί δοκεῖτε;).

2. intr. *seem* (Hom.+; so mostly LXX—**a.** *have the appearance* w. dat. of the pers. τίς τούτων ... πλησίον δοκεῖ σοι γεγονέναι; *which one of these seems to you to have been a neighbor?* Lk 10: 36. δ. καταγγελεὺς εἶναι *he seems to be a preacher* Ac 17: 18; cf. 1 Cor 12: 22; 2 Cor 10: 9; Hb 12: 11; Dg 8: 10. εἴ τινι μὴ δοκοίη κἂν ταῦτα ἱκανά *if that should seem to anybody to be insufficient* Dg 2: 10. οὐδέν μοι δοκοῦσι διαφέρειν *they seem to me to differ in no way* 3: 5. ἔδοξα ἐμαυτῷ δεῖν πρᾶξαι = Lat. mihi videbar *I was convinced that it was necessary to do* Ac 26: 9 (cf. Aristoph., Vesp. 1265; Demosth. 18, 225 al. in class. and later wr.). τὸ δοκεῖν *in appearance* (only) (Sextus 64; Sb 7696, 55 [250 AD]; Jos., Vi. 75, Ant. 14, 291 v.l. for τῷ δοκεῖν; s. Hdb. on ITr 10) ITr 10; ISm 2; 4: 2. ὁ δοκῶν ἐνθάδε θάνατος *what seems to be death in this world* Dg 10: 7. As an expression serving to moderate a statement Hb 4: 1.

b. *be influential, be recognized as being someth., have a reputation* (cf. Sus 5; 2 Macc 1: 13). οἱ δοκοῦντες (Eur., Hec. 295; Petosiris, fgm. 6 l. 58 οἱ δ. = the prominent dignitaries; Herodian 6, 1, 2; Jos., C. Ap. 1, 67) *the influential men* Gal 2: 2, 6b. A fuller expr. w. the same mng., w. inf. added (X., Cyr. 7, 1, 41; Pla., Gorg. 472A, Euthydem. 303C οἱ δοκοῦντες εἶναί τι; Epict., Ench. 33, 12; Herodian 4, 2, 5; Philo, Mos. 2, 241) vss. 6a, 9 (Pla., Apol. 6 p. 21B οἱ δοκοῦντες σοφοὶ εἶναι). WFoerster, D. δοκοῦντες in Gal 2: ZNW 36, '38, 286–92 (against him, HGreeven, ZNW 44, '52, 41 note 100).—οἱ δοκοῦντες ἄρχειν *those who are reputed to be rulers* Mk 10: 42 (cf. Plut., Arat. 43, 2 ᾧ δουλεύουσιν οἱ δοκοῦντες ἄρχειν).

3. impers. δοκεῖ μοι *it seems to me* (Ael. Aristid. 47 p. 427 D.; ἔμοιγε δοκεῖ; Jos., Ant. 6, 227 δοκεῖ σοι).

a. *I think, believe* (cf. 1 above): τί σοι δοκεῖ; *what do you think?* Mt 17: 25; 22: 17. τί ὑμῖν δοκεῖ 18: 12; 21: 28; 26: 66; J 11: 56. W. περί τινος foll. (Lucian, Dial. Deor. 6, 4) Mt 22: 42. W. acc. and inf. foll. (Ael. Aristid. 46 p. 344 D.) οὐ δοκεῖ σοι τὸ μετανοῆσαι σύνεσιν εἶναι; *do you not think that repentance is understanding?* Hm 4, 2, 2; cf. m 8: 6; 11; 10, 1, 2. τὸ δοκοῦν τινι *someone's discretion* κατὰ τὸ δ. *at their discretion* (Lucian, Tim. 25; cf. Thu. 1, 84, 2 παρὰ τὸ δοκοῦν ἡμῖν) Hb 12: 10.

b. *it seems best to me, I decide* w. inf. foll. (X., An. 1,

10, 17; Diod. S. 18, 55, 2; Appian, Iber. 63 §265; Dit., Syll.³ 1169, 77 [IV BC]; Jos., Ant. 6, 321) Lk 1: 3; Ac 15: 22, 25, 28 (cf. Jos., Ant. 16, 163 ἔδοξέ μοι κ. τῷ ἐμῷ συμβουλίῳ . . . χρῆσθαι; Dio Chrys. 80[30], 8 ἔδοξε τῷ θεῷ); MPol 12: 3. ὡς ἄν σοι δόξῃ *as it may seem best to you* D 13: 7 (Arrian, Cyneg. 3, 4 ὥς μοι δοκεῖ). M-M. B. 1211.

δοκιμάζω fut. δοκιμάσω; 1 aor. ἐδοκίμασα; pf. pass. δεδοκίμασμαι (Hdt., Thu.+; inscr., pap., LXX).

1. *put to the test, examine* (so mostly LXX.—Ep. Arist. 276; Jos., Ant. 1, 233; 3, 15; Test. Ash. 5: 4) w. acc., *test oxen for their usefulness* Lk 14: 19 (Hdt. 2, 38 of the Apis bulls). ἑαυτόν *examine oneself* 1 Cor 11: 28; 2 Cor 13: 5; *one's own work* Gal 6: 4; *the works of God* Hb 3: 9 t.r. (Ps 94: 9); *everything* 1 Th 5: 21; *spirits* 1 J 4: 1; cf. D 12: 1; Hm 11: 7; 1 Cl 42: 4; *heaven and earth* Lk 12: 56; *be convinced* of someone's faithfulness 1 Cl 1: 2; *try to learn* τί ἐστιν εὐάρεστον τῷ κυρίῳ *what is pleasing to the Lord* Eph 5: 10. Of the examination of candidates for the diaconate (acc. to Attic usage: Lysias 16, 3; Pla., Leg. 6, 765c; Attic inscr.) 1 Ti 3: 10. Of God 1 Th 2: 4b (Jer 11: 20; 17: 10; 20: 12; Jos., Ant. 1, 233).—For Ro 2: 18, 12: 2 s. 2b below.

2. w. ref. to the result of the examination—**a.** *prove by testing* of gold (Isocr., Panathen. 14, 39; Dit., Syll.³ 334, 45; Pr 8: 10; Sir 2: 5; Wsd 3: 6) 1 Pt 1: 7; Hv 4, 3, 4; cf. 1 Cor 3: 13 (JGnilka, Ist 1 Cor 3: 10–15 ein Schriftzeugnis für d. Fegefeuer? '55). τὰς ψυχάς AP 3.

b. *accept as proved, approve* (PEleph. 1, 10; POxy. 928, 7 ἵνα ἐὰν δοκιμάσῃς ποιήσῃς; PTebt. 326, 10) w. acc. τί ISm 8: 2. οὓς ἐὰν δοκιμάσητε *whom you consider qualified* 1 Cor 16: 3. ἐδοκιμάσαμεν σπουδαῖον ὄντα *we have tested and found him zealous* 2 Cor 8: 22. τὸ ἀγάπης γνήσιον *prove the genuineness of love* vs. 8. ἐν ᾧ δοκιμάζει *for what he approves* Ro 14: 22. δ. τὰ διαφέροντα *approve* (or *discover* s. under 1) *what is essential* Ro 2: 18; Phil 1: 10. W. inf. (Appian, Iber. 90 §392, Bell. Civ. 2, 114 §475; Jos., Ant. 2, 176, Vi. 161 simply = intend, wish) οὐκ ἐδοκίμασαν τὸν θεὸν ἔχειν ἐν ἐπιγνώσει *they did not see fit to have a true knowledge of God* Ro 1: 28 (WReiss, 'Gott nicht kennen' im AT, ZAW 58, '40/'41, 70–98). W. indir. quest. foll. δ., τί τὸ θέλημα τ. θεοῦ *approve* (or *discover* s. under 1) *what God's will is* 12: 2. Pass. (Prov. Aesopi 171 P. φίλος καὶ ἵππος ἐν ἀνάγκῃ δοκιμάζονται = stand the test; Jos., Ant. 3, 71) δεδοκιμάσμεθα *we have been found worthy* w. inf. foll. 1 Th 2: 4a. δεδοκιμασμένος *tested, approved* of genuine prophets D 11: 11 (Diod. S. 4, 7, 1 δεδοκιμασμένος of the story writer who has a good reputation; cf. Dit., Syll.³ 807, 9; PFay. 106, 23; 2 Macc 4: 3); Ac 2: 22 D. M-M. B. 652. **

δοκιμασία, ας, ἡ (Lysias+; Polyb., Plut., Epict.; Dit., Syll.³ 972, 29; PLeid. X VII 12; 20; IX 12; Sir 6: 21; Jos., Ant. 4, 54) *testing, examination* πειράζειν ἐν δ. *put to the test* Hb 3: 9. πύρωσις τῆς δ. *trial by fire* D 16: 5. M-M. *

δοκιμή, ῆς, ἡ (several mss. of Diosc., Mater. Med. 4, 184 Wellm. II p. 333, 9 note; Achmes 24, 9; Cat. Cod. Astr. X 67, 7; Sym. Ps 67: 31.—Bl-D. §110, 2 app.; Mlt.-H. 352).

1. 'the quality of being approved', hence *character* Ro 5: 4 (as a result of endurance and a prerequisite for hope). γινώσκειν τὴν δ. τινος *put someone to the test* 2 Cor 2: 9; *know someone's character* Phil 2: 22. δ. τῆς διακονίας *the approved character of your service* 2 Cor 9: 13.

2. *test, ordeal* (Sextus 7a δ. πίστεως) ἐν πολλῇ δοκιμῇ θλίψεως *in a great ordeal of affliction* 8: 2; δ. ζητεῖν *desire proof* 13: 3. M-M. *

δοκίμιον, ου, τό (on the spelling s. Mlt.-H. 78; WGrundmann, TW II 259).

1. *testing, means of testing* (Dionys. Hal., Rhet. 11, 1; Herodian 2, 10, 6; Plut., Mor. 230в; Περὶ ὕψους 32, 5 γλῶσσα γεύσεως δοκίμιον; Pr 27: 21) τὸ δ. ὑμῶν τῆς πίστεως κατεργάζεται ὑπομονήν *the testing of your faith* (temptations) *produces endurance* Js 1: 3.

2. neut. sg. of the adj. δοκίμιος *genuine, without alloy* (esp. of metals: BGU 1045 II, 12; 1065, 8; PTebt. 392, 22; cf. Dssm., NB 86ff [BS 259ff]) τὸ δ. ὑμῶν τῆς πίστεως *the genuineness of your faith* (on the usage Bl-D. §263, 2) 1 Pt 1: 7 (δόκιμον 𝔓⁷² et al.; s. δόκιμος). M-M.*

δόκιμος, ον (Pre-Socr., Hdt.+; inscr., pap., LXX, Ep. Arist. 57; Philo, Joseph.) CArbenz, Die Adj. auf -ιμος, Diss. Zürich '33, 38ff.

1. *approved* (by test), *tried and true, genuine* (Alcaeus 119+120+122 Diehl, l. 12 of a man: νῦν τις ἀνὴρ δόκιμος γενέσθω; Test. Jos. 2: 7) Js 1: 12; 2 Cor 10: 18; 13: 7; 2 Ti 2: 15. δ. τραπεζῖται *approved money-changers* (who put genuine money [cf. Epict. 1, 7, 6 δραχμὰς δοκίμους κ. ἀδοκίμους; Socrat., Ep. 6, 12] in circulation) Agr 11. ὁ δ. ἐν Χριστῷ *the approved one in Christ= the tried and true Christian* Ro 16: 10; οἱ δ. 1 Cor 11: 19.

2. *respected, esteemed* (Hdt., al.; Philo, Op. M. 128, De Jos. 201; Jos., C. Ap. 1, 18) δ. τοῖς ἀνθρώποις *among men* Ro 14: 18.—3. *precious* comp. MPol 18: 1. M-M.*

δοκός, οῦ, ἡ (Hom.+; inscr., pap., LXX; Jos., Bell. 3, 214f, Ant. 14, 106; loanw. in rabb.) *beam of wood* Mt 7: 3ff; Lk 6: 41f.—GBKing, HTR 17, '24, 393-404; 26, '33, 73-6; CAWebster, ET 39, '28, 91f; PLHedley, ibid. 427f; SKaatz, Jeschurun 16, '29, 482-4. M-M. B. 599.*

δόλιος, ία, ον (Hom.+; LXX; Jos., Bell. 4, 208, Ant. 1, 335) *deceitful, treacherous;* ἐργάται δ. *dishonest workmen* 2 Cor 11: 13; χείλη δ. *deceitful lips* 1 Cl 15: 5 (Ps 30: 19). W. κατάλαλος: οἱ δ. *treacherous men* (cf. Sir 11: 29) Hs 9, 26, 7. M-M.*

δολιότης, ητος, ἡ (Vett. Val. 2, 3; LXX; Test. 12 Patr.) *deceit, treachery* περιπλέκειν δολιότητα *weave deceit* 1 Cl 35: 8 (Ps 49: 19). W. πονηρία Hs 8, 6, 2.*

δολιόω impf. 3 pl. ἐδολιοῦσαν Bl-D. §84, 3; Mlt.-H. 195 (schol. on Soph., Trach. 412 p. 303 Papag. [1888]; LXX) *deceive* Ro 3: 13 (Ps 5: 10; 13: 3).*

δόλος, ου, ὁ (Hom.+; inscr., pap., LXX; Ep. Arist. 246; Philo; Jos., C. Ap. 2, 200 al.; Test. 12 Patr.; Sib. Or. 3, 191; loanw. in rabb.) *deceit, cunning, treachery* Mk 7: 22 in a list of vices (cf. Herm. Wr. 13, 7b), also Ro 1: 29; D 5: 1; B 20: 1. Pl. 1 Cl 35: 5. ἐν ᾧ δ. οὐκ ἔστιν *in whom there is nothing false* (Theogn. 416 πιστὸν ἑταῖρον, ὅτῳ μή τις ἔνεστι δόλος; LXX) J 1: 47; cf. 1 Pt 2: 22; 1 Cl 16: 10 (both Is 53: 9); 50: 6; Rv 14: 5 t.r. (both Ps 31: 2); Pol 8: 1 (after 1 Pt 2: 22); πλήρης παντὸς δ. *full of every kind of treachery* Ac 13: 10. W. κακία 1 Pt 2: 1 (FW Danker, ZNW 58, '67, 93-95); λαλεῖν δ. *speak deceitfully* 3: 10; 1 Cl 22: 3 (both Ps 33: 14). δόλῳ *by cunning* or *stealth* (Hom.+; Ex 21: 14; Dt 27: 24 al.; Philo, Spec. Leg. 4, 183; Jos., Ant. 10, 164; prayers for vengeance fr. Rheneia: Dit., Syll.³ 1181, 3 and in Dssm., LO 352; 354ff [LAE 423ff]) Mt 26: 4; 2 Cor 12: 16. δόλῳ πονηρῷ w. *wicked cunning* (Dit., Syll.³ 693, 2; 5, cf. 9, Or. 629, 112; BGU 326 II, 3) IEph 7: 1. Also ἐν δ. (Soph., Phil. 102; Wsd 14: 30; 1 Macc 1: 30) Mk 12: 14 v.l.; 14: 1; 1 Th 2: 3. M-M. B. 1171.*

δολόω (Hes., Hdt.+; Vett. Val. 248, 2; Dit., Syll.³ 1168, 102) *falsify, adulterate* (so Diosc. 1, 67; 68 W.; Lucian, Hermot. 59 τὸν οἶνον; PLeid. X V 37; XII 2) 1 Cor 5: 6 D; δ. τὸν λόγον τοῦ θεοῦ 2 Cor 4: 2. M-M.*

δόμα, δόματος, τό (Ps.-Pla., Defin. 415в; Plut.; pap. [Mayser 435]; LXX; Ep. Arist. 224; Philo, Cher. 84) *gift* δ. ἀγαθά *good gifts* (cf. Sir 18: 17) Mt 7: 11; Lk 11: 13. διδόναι δόματά τινι Eph 4: 8 (cf. Ps 67: 19); οὐχ ὅτι ἐπιζητῶ τὸ δ. *not that I desire the gift* Phil 4: 17. M-M.*

δόξα, ης, ἡ (in var. mngs. Hom.+; inscr., pap., LXX, En., Ep. Arist., Philo, Joseph., Test. 12 Patr.).

1. *brightness, splendor, radiance*—a. lit. (PGM 13, 189 τὴν δόξαν τοῦ φωτός, cf. 298ff. On this Rtzst., Mysterienrel.³ 357ff, also 314 δόξα ἐκ τ. πυρός; 315 φῶς κ. δόξαν θείαν [= Cleopatra l. 150]; LXX) οὐκ ἐνέβλεπον ἀπὸ τῆς δ. τοῦ φωτός *I could not see because of the brightness of the light* Ac 22: 11; ὁρᾶν τὴν δ. *see the radiance* Lk 9: 32; cf. vs. 31. Everything in heaven has this radiance: the radiant bodies in the sky 1 Cor 15: 40f (cf. PGM 13, 64 σὺ ἔδωκας ἡλίῳ τὴν δόξαν κ. δύναμιν; 448; Sir 43: 9, 12; 50: 7); cherubim (Sir 49: 8; Ezk 10: 4) Hb 9: 5; angels Lk 2: 9. Esp. God himself (Ex 24: 17; 40: 34; Num 14: 10; Bar 5: 9 τὸ φῶς τῆς δόξης αὐτοῦ; Tob 12: 15; 13: 16 BA; 2 Macc 2: 8; Sib. Or. 5, 427) ὁ θεὸς τῆς δ. (En. 25, 7) Ac 7: 2 (Ps 28: 3), cf. 55; 2 Th 1: 9; 2 Pt 1: 17b; Rv 15: 8; 19: 1; 21: 11, 23. But also of those who appear before God: Moses 2 Cor 3: 7ff; Christians in the next life 1 Cor 15: 43; Col 3: 4. The δόξα τοῦ θεοῦ is bestowed on those who stand in the Judgment Ro 3: 23; 5: 2; Jesus himself has a σῶμα τῆς δ. *radiant, glorious body* Phil 3: 21; cf. 2 Cl 17: 5. Christ is the κύριος τ. δόξης 1 Cor 2: 8 (cf. En. 22, 14; 27, 3; 5; 36, 4; 40, 3 of God; PGM 7, 713 κύριοι δόξης of gods).—The concept has been widened to denote the *glory, majesty, sublimity* of God in general (PGM 4, 1202 ἐφώνησά σου τ. ἀνυπέρβλητον δόξαν) ἀλλάσσειν τὴν δ. τοῦ θεοῦ *exchange the majesty of God* Ro 1: 23; κατενώπιον τῆς δόξης αὐτοῦ Jd 24 (cf. En. 104, 1)= before himself. Christ was raised fr. the dead διὰ τῆς δ. τοῦ πατρός *by the majesty* (here, as in J 2: 11, the concept of *power, might* is also present; cf. Rtzst., Mysterienrel.³ 344; 359 and PGM 4, 1650 δὸς δόξαν καὶ χάριν τῷ φυλακτηρίῳ τούτῳ; Wsd 9: 11 φυλάξει με ἐν τ. δόξῃ; Philo, Spec. Leg. 1, 45.—JPVogel, Het sanscrit woord tejas [= gloedvuur] in de beteekenis van magische Kracht '30) *of the Father* Ro 6: 4. κράτος τῆς δ. *majestic power* Col 1: 11; πλοῦτος τῆς δ. *the wealth of his glory* Ro 9: 23; Eph 1: 18; Col 1: 27; cf. Phil 4: 19. δ. τῆς χάριτος (PGM 4, 1650, s. above) Eph 1: 6; w. τιμή and other ideas (cf. PGM 4, 1616 δὸς δόξαν καὶ τιμὴν κ. χάριν κτλ.) Ro 2: 7, 10; Hb 2: 7 (Ps 8: 6); w. ἀρετή 2 Pt 1: 3 (τῆς ἐπ' ἀρετῇ καὶ δόξῃ διαλήψεως, Inscr. at Aphrodisias II, 14: ZPE 8, '71, 186); ἀπαύγασμα τῆς δ. Hb 1: 3. Doxol. σοῦ ἐστιν ἡ δ. εἰς τ. αἰῶνας, ἀμήν (Ode 12: 15 [Prayer of Manasseh]) Mt 6: 13 t.r.—1 Th 2: 12; 1 Pt 5: 10. Pl. Hv 1, 3, 3. Transferred to Christ: Mt 19: 28; 24: 30; 25: 31; Mk 10: 37; 13: 26; Lk 9: 26; 21: 27; J 1: 14; 2: 11; Js 2: 1 (AMeyer, D. Rätsel d. Js '30, 118ff); B 12: 7.

b. The state of being in the next life is thus described as participation in the radiance or glory—a. w. ref. to Christ: εἰσελθεῖν εἰς τὴν δ. αὐτοῦ *enter into his glory* Lk 24: 26 (βασιλεία 𝔓⁷⁵ first hand); cf. 1 Pt 1: 11 (pl. because of the παθήματα; cf. also Wsd 18: 24; Isocr. 4, 51; POsl. 85, 13 [III AD]); 21. Also of Christ's preëxistence: J 17: 5, 22, 24.

β. w. ref. to his disciples (cf. Da 12: 13; Herm. Wr. 10, 7): Ro 8: 18, 21; 1 Cor 2: 7; 2 Cor 4: 17; 1 Th 2: 12; 2 Ti 2: 10; Hb 2: 10; 1 Pt 5: 1, 4 (στέφανος τ. δόξης; on this expr. cf. Jer 13: 18; Test. Benj. 4: 1); πνεῦμα τῆς δ. w. πν. τοῦ θεοῦ 4: 14. ἵνα πνευματικὴν καὶ ἄφθαρτον τῆς δικαιοσύνης δόξαν κληρονομήσωσιν ending of Mk in the Freer mss. l. 11f (Cleopatra l. 146f ἐνέδυσεν αὐτοὺς θείαν δόξαν πνευματικήν); τόπος τῆς δ.= the life to come 1 Cl 5: 4.

c. *reflection* ἀνὴρ εἰκὼν καὶ δόξα θεοῦ *the man is the image and reflection of God* 1 Cor 11: 7; also γυνὴ δόξα ἀνδρός ibid. (cf. the Jewish inscr. in Lietzmann ad loc.: ἡ δόξα Σωφρονίου Λούκιλλα εὐλογημένη).

2. *magnificence, splendor,* anything that catches the eye (1 Esdr 6: 9; 1 Macc 10: 60, 86; 2 Macc 5: 20): fine clothing (Sir 6: 31; 27: 8; 45: 7; 50: 11) of a king Mt 6: 29; Lk 12: 27; of royal *splendor* gener. (Bar 5: 6; 1 Macc 10: 58; Jos., Ant. 8, 166) Mt 4: 8; Lk 4: 6; Rv 21: 24, 26. Gener. of human splendor of any sort 1 Pt 1: 24 (Is 40: 6).

3. *fame, renown, honor* (Diod. S. 15, 61, 5 abs. δόξα= good reputation; Appian, Bell. Civ. 2, 89 §376 δ. ἀγαθή good reputation, esteem; Polyaenus 8 Procem. δόξα ἀθάνατος=eternal renown; Herm. Wr. 14, 7; Jos., Ant. 4, 14, Vi. 274) J 8: 54; 1 Cl 3: 1; B 19: 3; Hv 1, 1, 8; δ. τοῦ θεοῦ *honor* or *glory with God* Ro 3: 23; 5: 2; cf. 9: 4; δ. ζητεῖν *seek fame* J 5: 44; 7: 18; 8: 50; 1 Th 2: 6; δ. λαμβάνειν (Diog. L. 9, 37 of Democr. οὐκ ἐκ τόπου δόξαν λαβεῖν βουλόμενος) J 5: 41, 44; ὑμεῖς ἡ δ. ἡμῶν *you bring us renown* 1 Th 2: 20; *approval* ἀνθρώπων . . . θεοῦ J 12: 43 (cf. IQH 17, 15; IQS 4, 23).—Jewish liturgy furnishes the pattern for the liturg. formula δ. θεῷ *praise is* (BWeiss; HHoltzmann; Harnack; Zahn; EKlostermann; ASchlatter; Rengstorf) or *be* (Weizsäcker; JWeiss; OHoltzmann) *to God* Lk 2: 14. Cf. 19: 38; Ro 11: 36; Gal 1: 5; 1 Cl 20: 12; 50: 7 al.; εἰς δ. θεοῦ *to the praise of God* 1 Cor 10: 31; 2 Cor 4: 15; Phil 1: 11; 2: 11. Hence the expr. δ. διδόναι τῷ θεῷ *praise God* (Bar 2: 17f; 1 Esdr 9: 8; 4 Macc 1: 12): in thanksgiving Lk 17: 18; Rv 19: 7; as a form of relig. devotion: Ac 12: 23; Rv 11: 13; 14: 7; 16: 9; Ro 4: 20; as an adjuration δὸς δ. τῷ θεῷ *give God the praise* by telling the truth J 9: 24.—GHBoobyer, 'Thanksgiving' and the 'Glory of God' in Paul, Diss. Leipzig '29; LChampion, Benedictions and Doxologies in the Epistles of Paul '35.

4. δόξαι (Diod. S. 15, 58, 1 ἐξουσίαι καὶ δόξαι= offices and honors, also those who held them) of angelic beings (s. Philo, Spec. Leg. 1, 45; PGM 1, 199) *glorious angelic beings* Jd 8; 2 Pt 2: 10 (cf. Ex 15: 11 LXX; Test. Jud. 25: 2 αἱ δυνάμεις τ. δόξης. Also the magical text in Rtzst., Poim. p. 28 [VI 17] χαιρέτωσάν σου αἱ δόξαι εἰς αἰῶνα, κύριε). Cf. JSickenberger, Engels- oder Teufelslästerer? Festschrift zur Jahrhundertfeier d. Univers. Breslau '11, 621ff. However, the mng. *majesties, illustrious persons,* is also poss.—On the whole word Rtzst., Mysterienrel.³ 289; 314f; 344; 355ff; AvGall, D. Herrlichkeit Gottes 1900; IAbrahams, The Glory of God '25.—AHForster, The Mng. of Δόξα in the Greek Bible: ATR 12, '29/'30, 311ff; ECEOwen, Δόξα and Cognate Words: JTS 33, '32, 139-50; 265-79; Christine Mohrmann, Note sur doxa: ADebrunner-Festschr. '54, 321-28; LHBrockington, LXX Background to the NT Use of δ., Studies in the Gospels in memory of RHLightfoot '55, 1-8.—HBöhlig, D. Geisteskultur v. Tarsos '13, 97ff; GPWetter, D. Verherrlichung im Joh.-ev.: Beitr. z. Rel.-wiss. II '15, 32-113, Phos '15; RBLloyd, The Word 'Glory' in the Fourth Gospel: ET 43, '32, 546-8; BBotte, La gloire du Christ dans l'Évangile de S. Jean: Quest. liturgiques 12, '27, 65ff; HLPass, The Glory of the Father; a Study in St John 13-17, '35; WThüsing, Die Erhöhung u. Verherrlichung Jesu im J, '60.—GerhKittel, D. Rel. gesch. u. d. Urchristentum '32, 82ff; JSchneider, Doxa '32; HelmKittel, D. Herrlichkeit Gottes '34; MGreindl, Κλεος, Κυδος, Ευχος, Τιμη, Φατις, Δοξα Diss. Munich '38; AStuiber, RAC IV, 210-16. M-M. B. 1144f.

δοξάζω impf. ἐδόξαζον; fut. δοξάσω; 1 aor. ἐδόξασα, imper. δόξασον; 1 aor. pass. ἐδοξάσθην; pf. pass. δεδόξασμαι J 17: 10 (Xenophanes and trag.+; LXX; Ep. Arist., Philo, Joseph., Test. 12 Patr.).

1. *praise, honor, magnify* (Thu. 3, 45, 4; Polyb. 6, 53, 10 δεδοξασμένοι ἐπ' ἀρετῇ; Dit., Or. 168, 56 [115 BC]; LXX; Ep. Arist.; Jos., Ant. 4, 183) τινά *someone* the Father Mt 5: 16; God (Sib. Or. fgm. 1, 21) 9: 8; 15: 31; Mk 2: 12; Lk 5: 25f; 7: 16; 13: 13; 17: 15; 18: 43; 23: 47; Ac 11: 18; 21: 20; Ro 15: 6, 9; MPol 14: 3; 19: 2; τ. κύριον 20: 1; Hv 3, 4, 2; ἔν τινι *in the person of someone* Gal 1: 24 (FNeugebauer, In Christus, etc. '61, 43); cf. 1 Cor 6: 20; ἐν τῷ ὀνόματι τούτῳ *in this name* (that of a Christian) 1 Pt 4: 16. ἐπί τινι *for, because of someth.* (w. αἰνεῖν) Lk 2: 20 (s. Polyb. above); Ac 4: 21; διά τινος and ἐπί τινι 2 Cor 9: 13. W. εὐχαριστεῖν Ro 1: 21; the name (Nicol. Dam. in Jos., Ant. 1, 160 τοῦ Ἀβράμου ἔτι κ. νῦν τὸ ὄνομα δοξάζεται) of God Hv 2, 1, 2; 3, 4, 3. τὸ ὄνομα *the name,* i.e. God's IPhld 10: 1 (cf. POxy. 924, 13 ἵνα τὸ ὄνομά σου ᾖ διὰ παντὸς δεδοξασμένον; PGM 36, 165). Of Christ IEph 2: 2; ISm 1: 1; Pol 8: 2. τόν σε λυτρωσάμενον ἐκ θανάτου *him who redeemed you fr. death* B 19: 2; *someone's love* IPol 7: 2. Abs.=*praise God* ITr 1: 2. τὴν διακονίαν μου δοξάζω *I magnify my ministry* Ro 11: 13.—δοξάζεται μέλος *a member is honored* 1 Cor 12: 26. δοξασθεὶς μεγάλως *given high honors* 1 Cl 17: 5.

2. *clothe in splendor, glorify,* of the glory that comes in the next life (s. δόξα 1b) Ac 3: 13 (cf. Is 52: 13); Ro 8: 30; B 21: 1; J 7: 39; 12: 16, 23, 28; 13: 31, 32; 17: 1, 5, 10. It is a favorite term in J (s. Thüsing et al. s.v. δόξα, end), in which the whole life of Jesus is depicted as a glorifying of the Son by the Father (J 8: 54; 12: 28; 13: 31; 17: 1, 4; cf. GBCaird, NTS 15, '68/'69, 265-77) and, at the same time, of the Father by the Son (13: 31f; 14: 13; 17: 1). The glorifying of the Son is brought about by the miracles which the Father has him perform 11: 4 (cf. PGM 7, 501ff κυρία Ἴσις, δόξασόν με, ὡς ἐδόξασα τὸ ὄνομα τοῦ υἱοῦ σου Ὥρος; Isisaretalogy fr. Cyme 40 [WPeek, D. Isishymnos '30, 63, 124] spoken by the goddess: οὐδεὶς δοξάζεται ἄνευ τ. ἐμῆς γνώμης), through the working of the Paraclete 16: 14 and through 'his own' 17: 10, who also glorify the Father 15: 8, esp. in martyrdom 21: 19; (on δοξάζεσθαι ἐν J 13: 31f; 14: 13; 15: 8; 17: 10 cf. Diod. S. 12, 36, 2; Sir 48: 4; 1 Macc 2, 64).—2 Cor 3: 10; 2 Th 3: 1; B 6: 16 (Is 49: 5); IPol 8: 1. χαρὰ δεδοξασμένη *joy filled w. glory* 1 Pt 1: 8; Pol 1: 3. οὐχ ἑαυτὸν ἐδόξασεν γενηθῆναι ἀρχιερέα *he did not raise himself to the glory of the high priesthood* Hb 5: 5. Lit., s. δόξα, end, also EGSelwyn, First Ep. of Peter '46, 253-8. M-M.

Δορκάς, άδος, ἡ (Eur., Hdt.+; pap., LXX) *Dorcas,* meaning *gazelle,* as transl. of a name (s. Ταβιθά) Ac 9: 36, 39 (Δορκάς as a name e.g. in Jos., Bell. 4, 145; Lucian, Dial. Meretr. 9; Dit., Syll.² 854, 11; 12; 23; IG VII 942; XIV 646). M-M. Gdspd., Probs. 130.*

δόρυ, ρατος, τό (Hom.+; inscr., LXX; Jos., Bell. 5, 313, Ant. 6, 187; Sib. Or. 4, 63; loanw. in rabb.) *spear* in the description of the righteous man's armor IPol 6: 2. B. 48; 1390.*

δόσις, εως, ἡ—1. *gift* (so since Hom.; Theogn. 444 ἀθανάτων δ.; Sir 18: 15, 16, 18; 20: 14; 26: 14 al.; Ep. Arist. 229 θεοῦ δ.; Philo, Cher. 84; Jos., Ant. 1, 181) Js 1: 17 (Test. Zeb. 1, 3 δ. ἀγαθή of a gift fr. God; HGreeven, ThZ 14, '58, 1-13).

2. *giving* (Antipho, Hdt.; LXX; Ep. Arist. 22; Jos., Ant. 17, 327) Mt 6: 1 v.l. δ. καὶ λήμψις (Epict. 2, 9, 12; Artem. 1, 42 p. 39, 24; Vett. Val. [ind. III]; PTebt. 277, 16; Sir

41: 21; 42: 7) *giving and receiving, debit and credit* Phil 4: 15; cf. Hm 5, 2, 2. M-M.*

δότης, ου, ὁ (Herodian. Gramm. I 60, 26; II 678, 22; Cass. Dio fgm. 66, 2; Etym. Mag. p. 177, 25; 435, 49) *giver* ἱλαρὸς δ. *one who gives cheerfully* 2 Cor 9: 7 (Pr 22: 8a). M-M.*

Δουβέριος Ac 20: 4. For this v.l. of D see s.v. Δερβαῖος.*

δουλαγωγέω (Diod. S. 17, 70, 6; Epict. 3, 24, 76; 4, 7, 17) *enslave, bring into subjection* fig. (Charito 2, 7, 1; Περὶ ὕψους 44, 6; Theophyl. Sim., Ep. 36; Herm. Wr. p. 484, 13 Sc.; Procop. Hist., Aed. 1, 9, 4) the body (w. ὑπωπιάζω) 1 Cor 9: 27. M-M.*

δουλεία, ας, ἡ (Pind.+; Epict., pap., LXX; Philo; Jos., Bell. 7, 255; Test. 12 Patr.) *slavery.*
1. lit. μέχρι δουλείας ἐλθεῖν *come into slavery* of Joseph (Test. Jos. 1: 5; 10: 3) 1 Cl 4: 9; ἑαυτὸν παραδιδόναι εἰς δ. *give oneself up to slavery* 55: 2.
2. fig. (Herm. Wr. 392, 10 Sc.) πνεῦμα δ. *a spirit of slavery* Ro 8: 15. Fear of death leads to slavery Hb 2: 15. Of serving the Mosaic law (cf. Lucian, Abdic. 23 ὑπὸ δουλείαν γενέσθαι νόμου) ζυγῷ δουλείας ἐνέχεσθαι *be held fast in a yoke of slavery* Gal 5: 1; cf. 4: 24; δ. τῆς φθορᾶς Ro 8: 21. Of Christ's life on earth Hs 5, 6, 7. M-M.*

δουλεύω fut. δουλεύσω; 1 aor. ἐδούλευσα; pf. δεδούλευκα J 8: 33, ptc. δεδουλευκώς 2 Cl 17: 7 (Aeschyl., Hdt.+; inscr., pap., LXX, Philo, Joseph., Test. 12 Patr.).
1. of relationship *be a slave, be subjected*—a. lit., of Hagar and Jerusalem Gal 4: 25. τινί *to someone* (Jos., Ant. 4, 115.—C. Ap. 2, 128 the Egyptians claim τὸ μηδενὶ δουλεῦσαι. Likew. in Appian, Bell. Civ. 4, 67 §286 the Rhodians are proud ἕνεκα τύχης ἐς τὸ νῦν ἀδουλώτου; Diod. S. 5, 15, 3 the Iolaës of Sardinia have maintained their freedom ἅπαντα τὸν αἰῶνα ... μέχρι τοῦ νῦν; in 5, 15, 4 even the Carthaginians οὐκ ἠδυνήθησαν [αὐτοὺς] καταδουλώσασθαι) J 8: 33; Ac 7: 7 (Gen 15: 14); Ro 9: 12; B 13: 2 (both Gen 25: 23; cf. Jos., Ant. 1, 275).—
b. fig. Ro 7: 6.
2. of action or conduct *perform the duties of a slave, serve, obey.*
a. lit., w. dat. of the pers. (PHal. 1, 219 [III BC] ὁ Ἀλεξανδρεὺς τῷ Ἀλεξανδρεῖ μὴ δουλευέτω) Mt 6: 24; Lk 16: 13; 2 Cl 6: 1 (on being a slave to more than one master s. Billerb. on Mt 6: 24; Wilcken, Chrest. 203 II, 17; 206, 16ff). τοσαῦτα ἔτη δ. σοι *I have been serving you like a slave for so many years* Lk 15: 29 (cf. Gen 31: 41). Abs. μετ᾿ εὐνοίας δ. *render service w. good will* Eph 6: 7. ἐν καθαρᾷ καρδίᾳ 2 Cl 11: 1; μᾶλλον δ. *serve all the better* 1 Ti 6: 2; πλέον δ. IPol 4: 3.
b. esp. in the expr. δ. τῷ θεῷ *serve God*, where God is thought of as κύριος, and man as δοῦλος (Eur., Or. 418; Ex 23: 33; Philo, Cher. 107, Somn. 2, 100; Jos., Ant. 7, 367; 8, 257; Sib. Or. 3, 740): Mt 6: 24; Lk 16: 13 (on both cf. Sextus 574 οὐκ ἔστιν ἅμα δουλεύειν ἡδονῇ κ. θεῷ); 1 Th 1: 9; 2 Cl 11: 1; 17: 7; Pol 2: 1 (Ps 2: 11); 6: 3; MPol 9: 3; Hm 8: 6; 12, 6, 2; s 4: 2; Dg 2: 5; τῷ Χριστῷ Ro 14: 18; cf. 16: 18; Col 3: 24. τῷ κυρίῳ (Judg 2: 7; 1 Km 7: 4; 12: 20) Ac 20: 19; Ro 12: 11 (t.r. τῷ καιρῷ.—δ. τῷ καιρῷ means 'accommodate oneself to the occasion' [Plut., Arat. 43, 2; Pallad.: Anth. Pal. 9, 441; Procop. Soph., Ep. 113 H. δουλεύειν τῇ χρείᾳ καὶ πείθεσθαι τῷ καιρῷ. The contrast is with πράττεαι ὅσα τις βούλεται, or Herodas 2, 9f: ζῶμεν οὐχ ὡς βουλόμεσθ᾿, ἀλλ᾿ ὡς ἡμέας ὁ καιρὸς ἕλκει], and can have the unfavorable connotation 'be an opportunist'; for this reason it is expressly rejected for this

pass. by Athanas., Origen-Rufinus, and Jerome. S. Ltzm. ad loc.); Hv 4, 2, 5; s 1: 7; 4: 5ff; 6, 3, 6; 8, 6, 2; elements or elemental spirits Gal 4: 9, cf. vs. 8 (in a relig. sense also PGM 13, 72 κύριε, δουλεύω ὑπὸ τὸν σὸν κόσμον τῷ σῷ ἀγγέλῳ).
c. fig. also in other senses: of loving service ἀλλήλοις Gal 5: 13. Be a slave to sin Ro 6: 6; the law 7: 25; desire Hm 12, 2, 5; Tit 3: 3 (X., Mem. 1, 5, 5, Apol. 16; Pla., Phaedr. 238E ἡδονῇ; Polyb. 17, 15, 16; Herodian 1, 17, 22; Philo, Cher. 71; Jos., Ant. 15, 91 δ. ταῖς ἐπιθυμίαις); the virtues Hv 3, 8, 8; m 12, 3, 1; faith m 9: 12; τῇ κοιλίᾳ the belly, i.e. *appetite* (γαστρί X., Mem. 1, 6, 8; Anth. 11, 410, 4) Ro 16: 18. εἰς τὸ εὐαγγέλιον *serve in the gospel* Phil 2: 22. M-M.**

δούλη, ης, ἡ (Hom.+; pap., LXX, Philo; Jos., Ant. 1, 215 al.) *female slave, bondmaid* w. δοῦλοι Ac 2: 18 (cf. Jo 3: 2); IPol 4: 3. As an oriental expr., used by one of humble station in addressing one of a higher rank or the Deity Lk 1: 38, 48 (1 Km 1: 11).*

δοῦλος, η, ον (Soph.+; PGiess. 3, 5 ᾧ πάντα δοῦλα; Ps 118: 91; Wsd 15: 7; Philo; Jos., Ant. 16, 156; Sib. Or. 3, 567) *slavish, servile, subject* τὰ μέλη δ. τῇ ἀκαθαρσίᾳ the members in slavery to impurity Ro 6: 19; τῇ δικαιοσύνῃ ibid.—Subst. τὰ δοῦλα *things subservient* PK 2 (s. ὕπαρξις 1).*

δοῦλος, ου, ὁ (trag., Hdt.+; inscr., pap., LXX, Philo, Joseph., Test. 12 Patr.) *slave* ('servant' for 'slave' is largely confined to Biblical transl. and early American times [s. Murray, New (Oxford) Engl. Dict. s.v. servant, sb., 3a and b]; in normal usage at the present time the two words are carefully distinguished [Gdspd., Probs., 77-9]).
1. lit., in contrast—a. to the master: Mt 8: 9; 10: 24f; 13: 27f; 21: 34ff; 24: 45f, 48, 50; 25: 14, 19, 21, 23, 26, 30; 26: 51 (on δοῦλος of the ἀρχιερεύς s. Jos., Ant. 20, 181); Mk 12: 2, 4; 13: 34; 14: 47; Lk 7: 2f, 8, 10; 12: 37, 43, 45f (Billerb. IV 698-744: D. altjüd. Sklavenwesen; SZucrow, Women, Slaves, etc. in Rabb. Lit. '32; JoachJeremias, Jerusalem IIb '37, 184-8; 217-24).—(Opp. δεσπότης as Diod. S. 15, 8, 2f ὡς δοῦλος δεσπότῃ; Ps.-Lucian, Asin. 5) 1 Ti 6: 1; Tit 2: 9; οἱ δ. in direct address Eph 6: 5; Col 3: 22.—For lit. on Christianity and slavery s. on χράομαι 1a.
b. to a free man (opp. ἐλεύθερος: Pla., Gorg. 57 p. 502D; Dio Chrys. 9[10], 4; Dit., Syll.³ 521, 7 [III BC]; Jos., Ant. 16, 126) 1 Cor 7: 21f (cf. the trimeter: Trag. Fgm. Adesp. 304 N., quot. fr. M. Ant. 11, 30 and Philo, Omn. Prob. Lib. 48, δοῦλος πέφυκας, οὐ μέτεστί σοι λόγου); 12: 13; Gal 3: 28; 4: 1; Eph 6: 8; Col 3: 11; Rv 6: 15; 13: 16; 19: 18; IRo 4: 3. W. παιδίσκη D 4: 10.
c. the house slave in contrast to the son J 8: 35; Gal 4: 7.
d. in contrast to a Christian brother οὐκέτι ὡς δοῦλον, ἀλλὰ ὑπὲρ δοῦλον, ἀδελφὸν ἀγαπητόν Phlm 16.
e. in special uses—a. the apostles are fig. the δοῦλοι of the Christians, i.e., they are unconditionally obligated to serve them 2 Cor 4: 5.
β. Christ, the heavenly κύριος, appears on earth in μορφὴ δούλου the form of a slave (Lucian, Catapl. 13 δοῦλος ἀντὶ τοῦ πάλαι βασιλέως) Phil 2: 7 (lit. on κενόω 1); cf. Hs 5, chap. 2ff (on this MDibelius, Hdb. 564f).
2. acc. to oriental usage, of a king's officials (cf. Dit., Syll.³ 22, 3; Inschr. v. Magn. 115, 4; 1 Km 29: 3; 4 Km 5: 6; Jos., Ant. 2, 70) *minister* Mt 18: 23, 26ff; 22: 3f, 6, 8, 10.—CSpicq, Dieu et L'Homme selon le NT, '61, 55 n. 2.
3. in a wider sense of any kind of dependence δ. ἀνθρώπων *slaves to men* 1 Cor 7: 23. παριστάναι ἑαυτόν τινι δοῦλον Ro 6: 16. Of humble service (opp. πρῶτος) Mt 20: 27; Mk 10: 44; δ. τῆς ἁμαρτίας *slave of sin* J 8: 34; Ro 6: 17, 20. τῆς φθορᾶς *of destruction* 2 Pt 2: 19 (cf. Eur., Hec.

δοῦλος– δρόμος

865 and Plut., Pelop. 3, 1 χρημάτων; Thu. 3, 38, 5; Dio Chrys. 4, 60 τ. δόξης; Athen. 12 p. 531c τῶν ἡδονῶν; 542ᴅ; Aelian, V.H. 2, 41 τοῦ πίνειν; Achilles Tat. 6, 19, 4 τ. ἐπιθυμίας).

4. esp. of the relationship of men to God (δουλεύω 2b) δ. τοῦ θεοῦ *slave of God=subject to God*, owned by him body and soul (Eur., Ion 309 τοῦ θεοῦ καλοῦμαι δοῦλος εἰμί τε; Cass. Dio 63, 5, 2; ChFossey, Inscr. de Syrie: Bull. de corr. hell. 21, 1897, p. 60 [Lucius calls himself the δοῦλος of the Θεὰ Συρία]; PGM 12, 71 δ. τοῦ ὑψ. θεοῦ; 13, 637ff δοῦλος εἰμι σός . . . Σάραπι; 59, 2; 4; LXX; Philo, Rer. Div. Her. 7 al.; Jos., Ant. 11, 90; 101): of Moses (4 Km 18: 12; 2 Esdr 19 [Neh 9]: 14; Ps 104: 26; Jos., Ant. 5, 39) Rv 15: 3. Of Christian prophets 10: 7; 11: 18 (prophets are also called slaves of God in the OT Jer 25: 4; Am 3: 7; Da 9: 6, 10 Theod.). Of the apostles Ac 4: 29; 16: 17 (δ. τοῦ θεοῦ τ. ὑψίστου as Da 3: 93 Theod.); Tit 1: 1. Of God-fearing people gener. (Ps 33: 23; 68: 37 al.) Rv 1: 1; Lk 2: 29; 1 Pt 2: 16; Rv 2: 20; 7: 3; 19: 2, 5; 22: 3, 6; 1 Cl 60: 2; 2 Cl 20: 1; Hv 1, 2, 4; 4, 1, 3; m 3: 4 al. The one who is praying refers to himself as *thy* (God's) *slave* (cf. Ps 26: 9; 2 Ch 6: 23; Da 3: 33, 44) Lk 2: 29; Ac 4: 29 (FJDölger, ΙΧΘΥΣ I '10, 195ff).—Fig., of one's relation to Christ δ. Χριστοῦ, self-designation of Paul Ro 1: 1; Gal 1: 10; Phil 1: 1; cf. Col 4: 12; 2 Ti 2: 24; Js 1: 1; Jd 1; Rv 22: 3; 1 Cor 7: 22; Eph 6: 6.—On δοῦλοι and φίλοι of Christ (for this contrast cf. Philo, Migr. Abr. 45, Sobr. 55; PKatz, Philo's Bible '50, 85ff) J 15: 15, s. φίλος 2aa.—Cf. Dssm., LO 271ff [LAE 323ff]; KHRengstorf, TW II 264-83; GSass, δ. bei Pls: ZNW 40, '41, 24-32 and lit. on χράομαι 1a. M-M. B. 1332.

δουλόω fut. δουλώσω; 1 aor. ἐδούλωσα, pass. ἐδουλώθην; pf. pass. δεδούλωμαι, ptc. δεδουλωμένος (Aeschyl., Hdt. +; LXX, Philo; Jos., Ant. 11, 300; Test. 12 Patr.) *make someone a slave* (δοῦλος), *enslave, subject.*

1. lit., a people Ac 7: 6 (Gen 15: 13). Pass δεδούλωμαί τινι *become a slave to someone*, of one who is defeated in battle 2 Pt 2: 19.

2. fig. (Thu., al.) πᾶσιν ἐμαυτὸν ἐδούλωσα *I have made myself a slave to everyone* 1 Cor 9: 19. Pass. *to be bound (as a slave)* (Menand., Sam. 280 J.; Dio Chrys. 68[18], 12 δεδουλωμένοι τὴν γνώμην) ἐν τοῖς τοιούτοις *in such cases* 1 Cor 7: 15. ὑπὸ τὰ στοιχεῖα τοῦ κόσμου *be enslaved by the elemental spirits* (or: *be subject to rudimentary knowledge*) Gal 4: 3; cf. Dg 2: 10; B 16: 9; *be God's slave* Ro 6: 22; *to righteousness* vs. 18 (cf. Heraclit. Sto. 69 p. 90, 3 δεδουλωμένοι ἡδονῇ; Porphyr., Abst. 1, 42 ἐδουλώθημεν τῷ τοῦ φόβου φρονήματι); of wine Tit 2: 3 (Philostrat., Vi. Apoll. 2, 36 p. 78, 25 δεδουλωμένος ὑπὸ τοῦ οἴνου; Libanius, Epist. 316, 3 Förster δουλεύειν οἴνῳ). M-M.*

δοῦναι, δούς s. δίδωμι.

δοχή, ῆς, ἡ (Eur., Pla. al.=receptacle) *reception, banquet* (so Macho [280 ʙᴄ] in Athen. 8 p. 348ꜰ; Plut., Mor. 1102ʙ; pap., LXX) ποιεῖν δ. *give a banquet* (Gen 21: 8; 26: 30; 1 Esdr 3: 1; Esth 1: 3; Da 5: 1) Lk 5: 29; 14: 13. M-M.*

δράκων, οντος, ὁ (Hom. +; Diod. S. 2, 51, 4; LXX; En. 20, 7 [=seraphim]; Philo; Test. Ash. 7: 3; Sib. Or. 3, 794; loanw. in rabb.; oft. synon. w. ὄφις [PGM 36, 183; 196], Boll 42, 5; 103) *dragon, serpent*, a figurative term for the devil (cf. PGM 4, 994 θεὲ θεῶν . . . κατέχων δράκοντα; 190; Epigr. Gr. 1140b; PsSol 2, 25) Rv 12: 3 (Damasc., Vi. Isid. 67 δράκοντας ἐξαισίους κατὰ μέγεθος ἑπτακεφάλους. Cf. Apollon. Rhod. 4, 127ff the description of the frightful δράκων that guards the golden fleece. Also

the Hydra: acc. to Alcaeus ἐννεακέφαλος, acc. to Simonides, πεντηκοντακέφαλος [schol. on Hesiod, Theogony 313]; Pisander Epic. [VI ʙᴄ] in Paus. 2, 37, 4 al.), 4, 7, 9 (ὁ δ. ὁ μέγας as PGM 4, 2770), 13, 16f; 13: 2, 4, 11 (Arrian, Anab. 3, 3, 5 acc. to Ptolemaeus, son of Lagus: δράκοντας δύο . . . φωνὴν ἱέντας show Alexander the way through the desert); 16: 13; 20: 2.—Lit. on ὄφις 3; also PJoüon, Le Grand Dragon: Rech de Sc rel 17, '27, 444-6; BarbRenz, D. oriental. Schlangendrache '30; J Kroll, Gott u. Hölle '32; WFoerster, D. Bilder in Offb. 12f und 17f: StKr 104, '32, 279-310 (on this RSchütz, ibid. 105, '33, 456-66); TW II 284-6; RLehmann-Nitzsche, D. apokal. Drache Rv 12: Ztschr. f. Ethnologie 65, '33, 193-230; PPrigent, Apoc. 12: Histoire de l' exégèse, in Beitr. zur Gesch. d. bibl. Exegese no. 2, '59. M-M.*

δραμεῖν, -ών s. τρέχω.

δράξ, δρακός, ἡ (Batr. et al.; Herm. Wr. 486, 4 Sc.; LXX; Philo, Somn. 2, 74; Jos., Ant. 3, 251; 8, 322) *the hand spread out* B 16: 2 (Is 40: 12).*

δράσσομαι (Hom. +; Abercius inscr. 14; POxy. 1298, 10; LXX; Jos., Bell. 3, 385, Ant. 14, 425) *catch, seize* (w. acc.: Dionys. Hal. 9, 21, 4; Lev 2: 2; 5: 12; Num 5: 26) τινά *someone* 1 Cor 3: 19. M-M.*

δραχμή, ῆς, ἡ (Hdt.+; inscr., pap., LXX; Ep. Arist. 20; 22; Philo, Spec. Leg. 2, 33; Jos., Bell. 1, 308, Ant. 3, 195; loanw. in rabb.) *drachma*, a Greek silver coin worth normally about 18 or 19 cents Lk 15: 8f (Dio Chrys. 70[20], 5 concern over the loss of just one drachma. Its purchasing power was by no means insignificant; acc. to Demetr. of Phal. [300 ʙᴄ]: 228 fgm. 22 Jac. it was the price of a sheep, or one-fifth the price of an ox. Under specially favorable circumstances it was even possible to buy a whole ox for one drachma, or a slave for four: Appian, Mithrid. 78 §344. On the other hand, the soldiers of Mark Antony look upon a gift of 100 dr. per man as proof of stinginess, acc. to Appian, Bell. Civ. 3, 43 §177; on wages and living costs see ACJohnson, Roman Egypt to Diocletian, in TFrank, An Economic Survey of Ancient Rome II, '59, 301-21).—Lit. on ἀργύριον 2c. M-M.*

δράω 1 aor. ἔδρασα (Hom.+; Dit., Or. 765, 34; POxy. 259, 35; LXX; Ep. Arist. 194; Philo; Jos., Ant. 16, 99, Vi. 357) *do, accomplish* οἱ ταῦτα δράσαντες *the men who have done these things* (cf. Wsd 14: 10; 4 Macc 11: 4; Jos., Ant. 1, 102) 1 Cl 45: 7. B. 537.*

δρέπανον, ου, τό (Hom. +; pap., LXX; Jos., Bell. 3, 225) *sickle* (also a tool for cutting down trees and tree branches: Polyaenus 1, 18) Hs 8, 1, 2; 3; Rv 14: 14ff (cf. here the two Phryg. inscr. in Ramsay, Phrygia II p. 565 no. 466 ἐὰν δέ τις αὐτῶν μὴ φοβηθῇ τούτων τ. καταρῶν τὸ ἀρᾶς δρέπανον εἰσέλθοιτο εἰς τὰς οἰκήσεις αὐτῶν). OT ἀποστέλλειν τὸ δ. (cf. Jo 4: 13) *put in the sickle* Mk 4: 29; cf. Rv 14: 15 (w. θερίζω as Mesomedes 7, 9), cf. ἀποστέλλω 2; 18b (vinedresser's tool as Geopon. 5, 22, 1; Cornutus 27 p. 51, 6). M-M. B. 507.*

δρόμος, ου, ὁ (Hom.+; inscr., pap., LXX, En., Philo, Joseph.; Test. Jud. 2: 3; loanw. in rabb.) *course.*

1. prop. of the *course* of heavenly bodies (Ps.-Pla., Axioch. 370ʙ; Dio Chrys. 19[36], 42; Sext. Emp., Math. 9, 27; M. Ant. 7, 47; Herm. Wr. 4, 8 al.; PGM 12, 251; 13, 575; Jos., Ant. 1, 32) Dg 7: 2. τὸν δ. διανύειν *complete* or *continue their course* 1 Cl 20: 2.—Of a race, fig. (Philo, Leg. All. 3, 48) 2 Ti 4: 7 (s. τελέω 1); of martyrs ἐπὶ τὸν τῆς πίστεως βέβαιον δ. κατήντησαν *they securely reached the goal in the race of faith* 1 Cl 6: 2.

2. fig. of the course of one's life πληροῦν τὸν δ. *complete one's course* Ac 13: 25; τελεῖν *finish* Ac 20: 24. προστιθέναι τῷ δ. *hasten on in your course* IPol 1: 2 (s. JKleist, transl., '46, note ad loc.). M-M.*

δροσίζω 1 aor. pass. ἐδροσίσθην (since Aristoph. [mid.]; 3 Macc 6: 6) *bedew* fig. in a spiritual sense *refresh with dew* IMg 14 (on the fig. use of dew cf. Dt 32: 2; Pr 19: 12; Ode of Solomon 11, 14).*

Δρούσιλλα, ης, ἡ *Drusilla* (also the name of Caligula's sister), youngest daughter of Herod Agrippa I, sister of Agrippa II; betrothed as a child to Antiochus Epiphanes of Commagene (Jos., Ant. 19, 355), but never married to him (Ant. 20, 139); married 53 AD to Azizus of Emesa, but left her husband and married Felix the procurator (Ant. 20, 141ff), to whom she bore a son, Agrippa (20, 143) Ac 24: 24, 27 v.l.—Schürer I⁴ 555; 557; 564; 573 (lit. here, note 25); 577.*

δύναμαι pass. dep.; pres. 2 sg. δύνῃ and δύνασαι; impf. ἠδυνάμην and ἐδυνάμην; fut. δυνήσομαι; 1 aor. ἠδυνήθην (Jos., Ant. 12, 278) and ἠδυνάσθην (Bl-D. §66, 3 w. app.; 79; 93 w. app.; 101 w. app.; Mlt.-H. 188; 206; 234) (Hom.+; inscr., pap., LXX, En., Epist. Arist., Philo, Joseph., Test. 12 Patr.; Sib. Or. 5, 172) *I can, am able.*

1. w. inf. foll.—**a.** pres. inf. οὐδεὶς δύναται δυσὶ κυρίοις δουλεύειν Mt 6: 24; Lk 16: 13.—Mt 9: 15; 19: 12; Mk 2: 7, 19 al. καθὼς ἠδύναντο ἀκούειν Mk 4: 33—perh. here, and surely J 6: 60 the mng. *be able to hear* approaches *like to hear* (cf. Epict. 2, 24, 11); cf. Luke 11: 7. οὐ δυνάμεθα ... μὴ λαλεῖν *we cannot remain silent* τὶ *about someth.* Ac 4: 20. In questions πῶς δύνασθε ἀγαθὰ λαλεῖν; *how can you say good things?* Mt 12: 34. πῶς δύναται σατανᾶς σατανᾶν ἐκβάλλειν; *how can Satan drive out Satan?* Mk 3: 23; cf. J 6: 52; Lk 6: 42.

b. w. aor. inf. δύνασθαι ... εἰσελθεῖν Mk 1: 45.—2: 4; 5: 3; Lk 8: 19; 13: 11; 14: 20 and oft. The impf. ἐδύνατο τοῦτο πραθῆναι *this could have been sold* Mt 26: 9 (Bl-D. §358, 1; cf. Wsd 11: 19f).

c. likew. the impf. w. pf. inf. ἀπολελύσθαι ἐδύνατο *he could have been set free* Ac 26: 32.

2. abs., whereby the inf. can easily be supplied (cf. Eur., Or. 889; Thu. 4, 105, 1; X., An. 4, 5, 11 al.; Sir 43: 30; Bar 1: 6; 1 Macc 6: 3; 9: 9, 60; 4 Macc 14: 17b) Mt 16: 3 (sc. διακρίνειν); 20: 22b; Mk 10: 39 (sc. πιεῖν); 6: 19 (sc. ἀποκτεῖναι); cf. Lk 9: 40; 16: 26; 19: 3; Ac 27: 39; Ro 8: 7. καίπερ δυνάμενος *although he was able to do so* 1 Cl 16: 2. οὔπω γὰρ ἐδύνασθε *you were not yet strong enough* 1 Cor 3: 2. ὑπὲρ ὃ δύνασθε (sc. ἐνεγκεῖν) *beyond your strength* 10: 13.

3. w. acc. foll., w. ποιεῖν to be supplied *be able to do someth.* (Maximus Tyr. 1, 2h τοῦτο δύναται λόγος; PRyl. 77, 38 οὐ γὰρ δύναμαι κοσμητείαν; POxy. 115, 10; 472 II, 22) οὐ δυνάμεθά τι κατὰ τ. ἀληθείας *we can do nothing against the truth* 2 Cor 13: 8; οὐδὲ ἐλάχιστον δ. *not to be able to do even the smallest thing* Lk 12: 26. εἴ τι δύνῃ *if you can do anything* (Vi. Aesopi Ic. 21 p. 279, 11 Eberh.: Αἴσωπε, εἴ τι δύνασαι, λέγε τῇ πόλει) Mk 9: 22 (also perh.: *if you possibly can,* as X., Hell., 7, 5, 15; Heliod. 1, 19, 2; Ael. Aristid. 48, 1 K.=24 p. 465 D.); πλείονα δ. *accomplish more* IPhld 1: 1 (Ammonius, Vi. Aristot. p. 11, 15 πολλὰ δ.). Of God ὁ πάντα δυνάμενος *he who has all power* (Lucian, Nav. 28 δύνανται πάντα οἱ θεοί; Iambl. Vi. Pyth. 28, 148; Philo, Abr. 268) Hm 12, 6, 3; cf. v 4, 2, 6. M-M.

δύναμις, εως, ἡ (Hom.+; inscr., pap., LXX, En., Ep. Arist., Philo, Joseph., Test. 12 Patr.; loanw. in rabb.).

1. *power, might, strength, force* λαμβάνειν δ. *receive power* Ac 1: 8 (cf. Epict. 1, 6, 28; 4, 1, 109); ἰδίᾳ δ. *by one's own power* 3: 12.—Of God's power (Nicol. Dam.: 90 fgm. 66, 33 θεῶν δ.; Diod. S. 1, 20, 6 τοῦ θεοῦ τὴν δύναμιν; 5, 71, 6; 27, 12, 1; 34+35 fgm. 28, 3; Dio Chrys. 11[12], 70, 75; 84; 23[40], 36; Herm. Wr. 14, 9 ὁ θεὸς ..., ᾧ πᾶσα δύναμις τοῦ ποιεῖν πάντα; PGM 4, 641; 7, 582; 12, 250; LXX; Aristobulus in Euseb., Pr. Ev. 13, 12, 4; 7; Ep. Arist.; Jos., Ant. 8, 109; 9, 15; Sib. Or. 3, 72) Mt 22: 29; Ro 1: 16, 20 (Jos., C. Ap. 2, 167 God is known by his δ.); 9: 17 (Ex 9: 16); 1 Cor 1: 18, 24; 1 Cl 11: 2; 33: 3; Dg 7: 9; 9: 1f. In the doxology (1 Ch 29: 11f; on the doxol. in the Lord's Prayer HSchumaker, Cath. World 160, '45, 342-9) Mt 6: 13 t.r.; D 8: 2; 9: 4; 10: 5; Rv 4: 11; 7: 12; 19: 1.—IMg 3: 1; ISm 1: 1; Hv 3, 3, 5; m 5, 2, 1; PK 2. Hence God is actually called δ. Mt 26: 64; Mk 14: 62 (cf. Wsd 1: 3; 5: 23 and Dalman, Worte 164f). Christ possesses a θεία δ. (this expr. in Aristot., Pol. 4[7], 4; PGM 12, 302 al.; cf. θεῖος 1a) 2 Pt 1: 3; cf. 1 Cor 5: 4. Here, as in Hs 9, 26, 8, the power is to be used for punishment. The δ. leaves Christ at his death GP 5: 19 (s. LVaganay, L'Évangile de Pierre '30, 108; 254ff).—*Power of the Holy Spirit* (Jos., Ant. 8, 408) Lk 4: 14; Ac 1: 8; Ro 15: 13, 19; Hm 11: 2, 5. δυνάμει κραταιωθῆναι *be strengthened in power* by the Spirit Eph 3: 16. Therefore the Spirit given the Christian can be called πνεῦμα δυνάμεως 2 Ti 1: 7. The believers are ἐν πάσῃ δ. δυναμούμενοι *equipped w. all power* Col 1: 11; cf. Eph 1: 19; 3: 20 (for Eph 1: 19 cf. IQH 14, 23; 11, 29 al.; for Eph 3: 16, 6: 10 cf. IQH 7, 17 and 19; 12, 35; IQM 10, 5; see KGKuhn, NTS 7, '61, 336); esp. the apostles and other men of God Ac 4: 33; 6: 8.—δ. is also esp. the *power* that works wonders (Suppl. Epigr. Gr. VIII 551, 39 [I BC]; POxy. 1381, 206ff; PGM 4, 2449; 12, 260ff; s. JZingerle, Heiliges Recht '26, 10f; JRöhr, D. okkulte Kraftbegriff im Altertum '23, 14f) Mt 14: 2; Mk 6: 14; Hv 1, 3, 4; perh. also (but s. 4 below) Gal 3: 5; 1 Cor 12: 28f (on the pl. δυνάμεις s. X., Cyr. 8, 8, 14; Herm. Wr. 13, 8 al.; on this ADieterich, E. Mithraslit. '03, 46f). W. ἐξουσία (Dio Chrys. 11[12], 65) Lk 9: 1; ἐν δ. *with power, powerful(ly)* (Synes., Ep. 90 p. 230D τοὺς ἐν δ.) Mk 9: 1; Ro 1: 4; Col 1: 29; 2 Th 1: 11. κατὰ δύναμιν w. gen. (Lucian, Imag. 3) *by the power of* Hb 7: 16. Hebraist.=δυνατός (Judg 3: 29; 20: 46 [ἄνδρες δυνάμεως B=ἄνδρες δυνατοί A]; Wsd 5: 23): τῷ ῥήματι τῆς δ. αὐτοῦ *by his powerful word* 1: 3; μετ' ἀγγέλων δυνάμεως αὐτοῦ w. *his mighty angels* 2 Th 1: 7; μὴ ἔχων δ. *powerless* Hv 3, 11, 2; m 9: 12. ἰσχυρὰν δ. ἔχειν *be very powerful* m 5, 2, 3; cf. m 9: 11; ἐν ποίᾳ δ. *by what power* Ac 4: 7. ὕψος δυνάμεως *pride in* (one's) *power* B 20: 1.—True strength in contrast to mere word or appearance 1 Cor 4: 19f; 1 Th 1: 5. ἔχοντες μόρφωσιν εὐσεβείας, τὴν δὲ δύναμιν αὐτῆς ἠρνημένοι *who have only the outward appearance of religion, and deny its inward power* 2 Ti 3: 5 (cf. Jos., Ant. 13, 409 τὸ ὄνομα τ. βασιλείας εἶχεν, τ. δὲ δύναμιν οἱ Φαρισαῖοι); δ. πίστεως *the power of faith* as over against the word of a profession IEph 14: 2. W. ἰσχύς 2 Pt 2: 11; w. ἐνέργεια Hm 6, 1, 1 (cf. Galen X, 635).—Of the peculiar power inherent in a thing (of the healing power of medicines since Hippocr.; cf. Diod. S. 1, 20, 4; 1, 97, 7; 17, 103, 4; Plut., Mor. 157D al.; Dio Chrys. 25[42], 3; Galen XIII 707 K.) δ. πυρός Hb 11: 34 (Diod. S. 15, 50, 3 δ. τοῦ φωτός=the intensity of the light).

2. *ability, capability* (Pla., Phileb. 58D; Epict. 2, 23, 34; 4 Km 18: 20; Ruth 3: 11; Jos., Ant. 10, 54) κατὰ δύναμιν *according to ability* (Diod. S. 14, 81, 6 v.l.; Dit., Syll.³ 695, 9; 44 [129 BC]; PGM 4, 650; POxy. 1273, 24; BGU 1050, 14; Sir 29: 20; Jos., Ant. 3, 102) 2 Cor 8: 3a; ἑκάστῳ κατὰ τὴν ἰδίαν δ. *to each according to his special capability* (cf. Dit., Syll.³ 695, 55) Mt 25: 15. Opp. *beyond one's ability* ὑπὲρ δύναμιν (Demosth. 18, 193; Appian, Bell. Civ. 2, 1 §3; 2, 13 §49; POxy. 282, 8; Sir 8: 13) 2 Cor 1: 8 or παρὰ δ. (Thu. 3, 54, 4; PPetr. II 3b, 2 [III bc]; POxy. 1418, 3; Jos., Ant. 14, 378) 8: 3b.

3. *meaning* (Pla., Crat. 394β; Polyb. 20, 9, 11; Dionys. Hal. 1, 68; Dio Chrys. 19[36], 19; Cass. Dio 55, 3; Philo, Congr. Erud. Gr. 125) of language 1 Cor 14: 11; of the stones Hv 3, 4, 3; cf. 3, 8, 6f.

4. of the outward expressions of power: *deed of power, miracle, wonder* (Ael. Aristid. 40, 12 K.=5 p. 59 D.: δυνάμεις ἐμφανεῖς; 42, 4 K.=6 p. 64 D. al.; Eutecnius 4 p. 41, 13; POxy. 1381, 42; 90f τ. δυνάμεις ἀπαγγέλλειν; FSteinleitner, D. Beicht '13, nos. 3; 8 al.; Ps 117: 15) w. σημεῖα 2 Th 2: 9; also in pl. Ac 2: 22; 2 Cor 12: 12; Hb 2: 4; in this sense δ. stands mostly in pl. δυνάμεις Mt 7: 22; 11: 20f, 23; 13: 54, 58; Lk 10: 13; 19: 37; 1 Cor 12: 10, 28f; Gal 3: 5 (on the two last pass. s. 1 above); Hb 6: 5. Sg. Mk 6: 5.

5. of the externals of power: *resources* μικρὰν ἔχειν δ. *have few resources* Rv 3: 8. Also *wealth* (X., An. 7, 7, 36, Cyr. 8, 4, 34; Dt 8: 17f) ἐκ τῆς δ. τοῦ στρήνους *fr. the excessive wealth* Rv 18: 3. Esp. of military *forces* (Hdt.+ very oft.; cf. Dit., Or. ind. VIII; LXX; Jos., Ant. 18, 262), even of the heavenly bodies thought of as armies δ. τῶν οὐρανῶν *the armies of heaven* (Is 34: 4 v.l.; 4 Km 17: 16; Da 8: 10 Theod.) Mt 24: 29; Lk 21: 26; cf. Mk 13: 25.

6. *power* as a personal supernatural spirit or angel (Aristot., Met. 4, 12 p. 1019a, 26 daemons δυνάμεις λέγονται; Eth. Epic. col. 9, 16, w. θεοί; Porphyr., Abst. 2, 2 p. 133 Nauck δαίμοσιν ἢ θεοῖς ἤ τισι δυνάμεσιν θῦσαι; Sallust. 15 p. 28, 15 αἱ ἄνω δυνάμεις; Herm. Wr. 1, 26; 13, 15; Synes., Ep. 57 p. 191β; PGM 4, 3051; 4 Macc 5: 13; Philo, Conf. Lingu. 171, Mut. Nom. 59) Ro 8: 38; 1 Cor 15: 24; Eph 1: 21; 1 Pt 3: 22; αἱ δ. τοῦ σατανᾶ IEph 13: 1; θεὸς ἀγγέλων καὶ δ. MPol 14: 1 (cf. the inscr. in FCumont, Étud. syr. '17, p. 321, 5 ὁ θεὸς τ. δυνάμεων).—Desig. of a personal divine being as a power of the most high God (Ael. Aristid. 37, 28 K.=2 p. 27 D.: Athena as δ. τοῦ Διός) οὗτός ἐστιν ἡ δύναμις τοῦ θεοῦ ἡ καλουμένη μεγάλη *this man is what is called the Great Power of God* Ac 8: 10 (cf. inscr. of Saïttaï in Lydia εἷς θεὸς ἐν οὐρανοῖς Μὴν οὐράνιος, μεγάλη δύναμις τοῦ ἀθανάτου θεοῦ: JKeil and AvPremerstein, Zweite Reise in Lydien No. 211=Denkschr. d. Wiener Akad. 54, '11, p. 110; PGM 4, 1275ff. ἐπικαλοῦμαί σε τὴν μεγίστην δύναμιν τὴν ἐν τῷ οὐρανῷ ὑπὸ κυρίου θεοῦ τεταγμένην.—GPWetter, 'D. Sohn Gottes' '16, 8f; WSpiegelberg, Die ägypt. Gottheit der 'Gotteskraft': Ztschr. f. äg. Sprache 57, '22, 145ff; FPreisigke, D. Gotteskraft der frühchristl. Zeit '22).

7. concr., that which gives power (Diod. S. 1, 97, 7 powerful remedy=φάρμακον; cf. ἐξουσία 5) ἡ δύναμις τῆς ἁμαρτίας ὁ νόμος *what gives sin its power is the law* 1 Cor 15: 56. ἔχρισεν αὐτὸν ὁ θεὸς δυνάμει (and so enabled him to work miracles) Ac 10: 38 (Dio Chrys. 66[16], 10 of Jason: χρισάμενος δυνάμει τινί, λαβὼν παρὰ τῆς Μηδείας; Diod. S. 4, 51, 1 τ. τρίχας δυνάμεσί τισι χρίσασα =she anointed her hair with certain magic ointments; 4, 51, 4; 17, 103, 4 ὁ σίδηρος κεχριμένος ἦν φαρμάκου δυνάμει=with a powerful poison).—OSchmitz, D. Begriff δ. bei Pls: ADeissmann-Festschr. '27, 139-67; WGrundmann, D. Begriff d. Kraft in d. ntl. Gedankenwelt '32, TW II 286-318; Dodd 16-20; EFascher, Dynamis Theou: ZThK n. F. 19, '38, 82-108; LBieler, Δύναμις u. ἐξουσία: Wiener Studien 55, '38, 182-90; AHForster, The Mng. of Power for St. Paul, ATR 32, '50, 177-85. M-M.

δυναμόω 1 aor. pass. ἐδυναμώθην (Polemo Soph. 2, 30 p. 26, 11; Porphyr., Sent. 35 p. 29, 6 Mommert, πρὸς Γαῦρον [ABA 1895] 16, 5 p. 57, 8; Herm. Wr. 1, 27 ὑπ' αὐτοῦ [=θεοῦ] δυναμωθείς; Sallust. 16 p. 28, 25; PGM 4, 197; 216; 12, 266; 13, 279; LXX) *strengthen* ἐν πάσῃ δυνάμει δυναμούμενοι *endowed w. all strength* Col 1: 11; δ. ἀπὸ ἀσθενείας *pass fr. weakness to strength* Hb 11: 34 (Eph 6: 10 v.l. δυναμοῦσθε for ἐνδυν. [s. ἐνδυναμόω 2b]. As v.l. also Hv 3, 12, 3 and s 5, 5, 2 Funk). M-M.*

δυνάστης, ου, ὁ (trag., Hdt.+; inscr., pap., LXX).

1. *ruler, sovereign*—a. of God (Soph., Antig. 608 of Zeus; Herm. Wr. 472, 10 Sc.; CWessely, Neue griech. Zauberpap. 1893, 665 τ. δυνάστας μεγάλους θεούς; PGM 4, 180, 265; 988; Sir 46: 5; 2 Macc 12: 15; 15: 3ff al.; 3 Macc 2: 3; Sib. Or. 3, 719) ὁ μακάριος κ. μόνος δ. *the blessed and only Sovereign* 1 Ti 6: 15.

b. of men (Ctesias in Apollon. Paradox. 20; Diod. S. 5, 21, 6 βασιλεῖς καὶ δυνάστας; Appian, Mithr. 102 §472; 108 §516; Lucian, Phal. 2, 1 ἀνὴρ δ.; Philo, Spec. Leg. 1, 142; Jos., Bell. 6, 438, Ant. 14, 36; Test. Jud. 9: 5; Sib. Or. 3, 636) καθαιρεῖν δ. ἀπὸ θρόνων *dethrone rulers* Lk 1: 52 (cf. Job 12: 19).

2. *court official* (Gen 50: 4) fr. the court of the queen of Ethiopia Ac 8: 27. S. on Κανδάκη. M-M.*

δυνατέω (Philod., Περὶ σημ. 11, 8 Gomp.; cf. Bl-D. §108, 2; Mlt.-H. 390) *be strong*—1. lit. 2 Cor 13: 3.—2. *be able, be strong enough* w. aor. inf. foll. Ro 14: 4; 2 Cor 9: 8.*

δυνατός, ή, όν (Pind., Hdt.+; inscr., pap., LXX, Ep. Arist., Philo, Joseph., Test. 12 Patr.; loanw. in rabb.).

1. *powerful, strong, mighty, able*—a. of pers. and their attributes.

a. lit.: of God (Plut., Numa 9, 2; IG XII 8, 74; Keil u. Premerstein, [s. δύναμις 6] no. 224 p. 117; Ps 23: 8; 44: 4, 6; Ps.-Phoc. 54; Ep. Arist. 139) D 10: 4. God as ὁ δ. (Ps 119: 4; Zeph 3: 17) Lk 1: 49. Of angelic beings Hs 9, 4, 1. Of powerful, prominent people (Thu. 1, 89, 3; X., Cyr. 5, 4, 1; Polyb. 9, 23, 4; oft. LXX; Philo, Mos. 1, 49; Jos., Bell. 1, 242 Ἰουδαίων οἱ δυνατοί) Ac 25: 5; 1 Cor 1: 26; Rv 6: 15 t.r. Of pers. gener. δ. εἰμι *I am strong* 2 Cor 12: 10; 13: 9. Of faith Hm 9: 10. Of the spirit 11: 21.

β. fig. δυνατός (εἰμι)=δύναμαι *I am able* or *in a position* Hs 1: 8. W. pres. inf. foll. (X., An. 7, 4, 24; Pla., Ep. 7 p. 340ε; Jos., C. Ap. 1, 187 λέγειν δ.) Tit 1: 9; Hb 11: 19. W. aor. inf. foll. (PEleph. 8, 18; PHib. 78, 15; Num 22: 38; EpJer 40; 63; Da 3: 17) Lk 14: 31; Ac 11: 17; Ro 4: 21; 11: 23; 14: 4 t.r.; 2 Cor 9: 8 t.r.; 2 Ti 1: 12; Js 3: 2; 1 Cl 48: 5; 61: 3; Dg 9: 1. W. ἔν τινι *be strong, capable in someth.*=*distinguish oneself* in it (Ps 23: 8; Sir 21: 7; 47: 5; Jdth 11: 8): in word and deed Lk 24: 19; cf. Ac 7: 22; in the Scriptures=*well-versed* 18: 24; in everything one does Hm 7: 1; οἱ δ. *those who are strong* (*in faith*) Ro 15: 1. W. ἑρμηνεύειν *able to translate* Papias 2: 16.

b. of things (Polyb. 10, 31, 8 προτείχισμα; Zeph 1: 14; Wsd 10: 12; Jos., Ant. 14, 364): ὅπλα δ. πρός τι *weapons powerful enough for someth.* 2 Cor 10: 4. Of commandments Hs 6, 1, 1. Of the created works of God v 1, 1, 3.

2. neut. δυνατόν ἐστι *it is possible* (Pind., Hdt.+; pap.; 2 Macc 3: 6).

a. w. acc. and inf. (Ep. Arist. 230) Ac 2: 24; Dg 9: 4. W. inf. foll. (Horapollo 1, 21 p. 31 μαθεῖν) 9: 6. εἰ δ. *if* (*it is*) *possible* (Ep. Arist. 9; Jos., Ant. 4, 310; 13, 31; Bl-D. §127, 2) Mt 24: 24; Mk 13: 22; Ro 12: 18; Gal 4: 15; more completely εἰ δ. ἐστιν (PPetr. II 11[1], 3; Menand., Epitr. 523 in a prayer εἴπερ ἐστὶ δυνατόν) Mt 26: 39; Mk 14: 35.

b. w. dat. of the pers. (w. or without copula) for someone (Lucian, Icarom. 21 μὴ δυνατόν ἐστί μοι . . . μένειν) 9: 23; 14: 36 (Iambl., Vi. Pyth. 28, 139 τ. θεοῖς πάντα δυνατά; Philo, Virt. 26 πάντα θεῷ δ.); Ac 20: 16; Hs 5, 7, 3 (PGiess. 79 II, 4; Jos., Ant. 3, 189).

c. w. παρά τινι with=for someone Mt 19: 26; Mk 10: 27; Lk 18: 27.

d. τὸ δ.=ἡ δύναμις (Polyb. 1, 55, 4; Appian, Bell. Civ. 5, 45 §191; Ep. Arist. 229, God's power; Ep. Arist. 133) Ro 9: 22. ἐν δυνατῷ εἶναι be in the realm of possibility (Dit., Or. 771, 49) B 17: 1. M-M. B 295f.**

δυνατῶς adv. (Hdt. 7, 11; Inscr. Gr. 1001 VII, 27 [c. 200 BC]; Plut.; Wsd 6: 6) strongly δ. ὁρᾶν see as clearly as possible Hs 9, 1, 3 (cf. Philo, Det. Pot. Ins. 130).*

δύνω 1 aor. ἔδυσα; 2 aor. ἔδυν (Bl-D. §101 p. 45 under δύειν; Mlt.-H. 213; 234) (Hom.+; pap., LXX) go down, set of the sun (Hom.+; Gen 28: 11 al.; En. 100, 2; Jos., Bell. 4, 317, Ant. 8, 415) Mk 1: 32; Lk 4: 40; GP 2: 5. Fig. (cf. Pr 11: 8 v.l.) δῦναι ἀπὸ κόσμου=die IRo 2: 2. M-M. B. 679.*

δύο gen. and acc. δύο, dat. δυσί (as early as Thu. 8, 101, 1 codd., then Aristot.+; Polyaenus 2, 3, 8; 3, 9, 47; pap. in Mayser I² 2, 73; Bl-D. §63, 1; Mlt.-H. 170) (Hom.+; inscr., pap., LXX, Ep. Arist., Philo, Joseph., Test. 12 Patr.; loanw. in rabb.) two.

1. nom.—**a.** used w. subst.: δ. δαιμονιζόμενοι two demoniacs Mt 8: 28; δ. τυφλοί 9: 27; 20: 30; cf. 26: 60; 27: 38 and oft.

b. w. ἐκ foll.: δ. ἐξ ὑμῶν two of you 18: 19; δ. ἐξ αὐτῶν two of them Lk 24: 13; cf. J 1: 35; 21: 2.

c. δ. ἢ τρεῖς two or three used approximately for a small number (Ananius Lyr. [VI BC] in Athen. 3, 37F δύ' ἢ τρεῖς ἀνθρώπους; X., An. 4, 7, 5; Jos., C. Ap. 2, 232) Mt 18: 20; J 2: 6; 1 Cor 14: 29. In the same sense δ. καὶ τρεῖς (Ael. Aristid. 45 p. 4 D.; 11 D.; Polyaenus 6, 1, 2) 2 Cor 13: 1.

d. w. the art. (PGiess. 2 II, 5; 14) Mt 19: 5; Mk 10: 8; 1 Cor 6: 16; Eph 5: 31 (Gen 2: 24).

2. gen. Mt 18: 16 (Dt 19: 15); Lk 12: 6; J 8: 17; Ac 12: 6 al.

3. dat. Mt 6: 24; Mk 16: 12; Lk 16: 13; Ac 12: 6; 21: 33; Hb 10: 28 (Dt 17: 6).

4. acc. Mt 4: 18, 21; 10: 10, 29; 14: 17; 18: 8 and oft.

5. w. prep. εἰς δ. in two (Lucian, Tox. 54; PGM 13, 262; Test. Judah 2: 6) Mt 27: 51a; Mk 15: 38; ἀνὰ δ. two apiece Lk 9: 3; J 2: 6; two by two Lk 10: 1; κατὰ δ. two at a time 1 Cor 14: 27. Also δύο δύο two by two Mk 6: 7 (this way of expressing a distributive number is found also in LXX, Gen 7: 3, 9, 15 and is widely regarded as a Semitism [Wlh., Einl.² '11, 24; JWackernagel, ThLZ 34, '09, 227]. Nevertheless it occurs as early as Aeschyl., Pers. 981; Soph., fgm. 191 Nauck²; POxy. 121 [III AD]; cf. the mixed expr. κατὰ δύο δύο POxy. 886, 19 [III AD], in Mediaeval Gk. [KDieterich, Unters. z. Gesch. d. griech. Sprache 1898, 188], and in Mod. Gk. [JPsichari, Essai sur le Grec de la Septante: Rev. des Ét. juives 55, '08, 161–208, esp. 183ff]. Cf. Dssm., LO 98f [LAE 122f]; Mlt. 21 n. 3; 97; Mlt.-H. 270; 439f; Thumb 128; Bl-D. §248, 1 w. app.; Rdm.² 72). On Mk 6: 7 see JoachJeremias, NT Essays: Studies in Memory of TWManson '59, 136–43. M-M.

δυσβάστακτος, ον (Plut., Mor. 915F; schol. on Pind., Nem. 10, 37b; Philo, Omnis Prob. Lib. 28; Pr 27: 3) hard to bear φορτία burdens Mt 23: 4 t.r.; Lk 11: 46. M-M.*

δύσβατος, ον (Pind., Pla.+; Philo, Ebr. 150; Jos., Ant. 14, 432; Sib. Or. 7, 103) impassable, hard to walk in fig.

(cf. Pind., Nem. 7, 143 ἀμηχανίαι δύσβατοι) of commandments Hm 12, 4, 4.*

δυσεντέριον, ου, τό (H. Gk. form for δυσεντερία [Hdt. +; Jos., Ant. 6, 3]; cf. Phryn. 518 L.; Moeris 129; Etym. Mag. p. 494, 33. S. also Hobart 52f) dysentery, w. fever Ac 28: 8 (t.r. δυσεντερία; pl. forms of both genders as v.l.). M-M.*

δυσερμήνευτος, ον (Diod. S. 2, 52, 5=difficult to describe; Artem. 3, 66; Cat. Cod. Astr. I 114, 26; Philo, Somn. 1, 188) hard to explain πολὺς ὁ λόγος καὶ δ. there is much to be said, and it is hard to explain Hb 5: 11.*

δυσθεράπευτος, ον (since Soph., Aj. 609; Hippocr., περὶ ἰητροῦ 10; Philo, Plant. 32) hard to cure of false Christians IEph 7: 1 (cf. Philo, Deus Imm. 182 δ. . . . τὰ τῆς ψυχῆς ἀρρωστήματα).*

δύσις, εως, ἡ (Aeschyl.+; Heraclitus 120; inscr., pap.; Ps 103: 19) setting (of the sun: Ael. Aristid. 49, 17 K.=25 p. 492 D.; En. 17, 4), west (Jos., Ant. 14, 401; opp. ἀνατολή, as Philo, Cher. 22; cf. Sib. Or. 3, 26) short ending of Mk; IRo 2: 2; 1 Cl 5: 6; τὸ τέρμα τῆς δ. the extreme west 5: 7 (s. τέρμα). M-M. B. 871.*

δύσκολος, ον (Thales, Eur.+; inscr., pap.; Jer 30: 2; Jos., Bell. 6, 36; orig. only of persons, in our lit. always objectively) hard, difficult (X., Oec. 15, 10 ἡ γεωργία δύσκολός ἐστι μαθεῖν; Dit., Or. 339, 54, Syll.³ 409, 33) of commandments Hm 12, 4, 6. δύσκολόν ἐστιν it is hard w. inf. foll. (Dit., Or. 458, 16; Jos., Ant. 6, 43; Philo, Praem. 49 [without copula]) Mk 10: 24; Hs 9, 20, 3. W. dat. of the pers. and inf. foll. it is difficult for someone IRo 1: 2. Abs. ὅπερ δύσκολον (sc. ἐστίν) ISm 4: 1. M-M. B. 651.*

δυσκόλως adv. (Isocr., Pla.+; Vett. Val. 123, 2; POxy. 1294, 10; Jos., Ant. 4, 87) hardly, w. difficulty εἰσέρχεσθαι εἰς τὴν βασιλείαν Mt 19: 23; Mk 10: 23; Hs 9, 20, 2. εἰσπορεύεσθαι Lk 18: 24. ζῆν attain (eternal) life Hm 4, 3, 6; s 9, 23, 3. σῴζεσθαι m 9: 6. ἡμερούσθαι m 12, 1, 2. κολλᾶσθαί τινι s 9, 20, 2. ἀποθανεῖσθαι s 8, 10, 2.*

δυσμαθής, ές slow to learn, hard to teach (so Pla.+; Cebes 35, 2; Philo, Mos. 2, 261) of complacent Christians Hs 9, 22, 1.*

δυσμή, ῆς, ἡ (Aeschyl., Hdt.+; inscr., pap., LXX) going down, setting (of the sun), west, in our lit. and LXX, En., Philo, Jos. (e.g. Ant. 3, 199; 7, 16), Sib. Or. (e.g. 4, 102; 5, 371; 374) exclusively pl., elsewh., nearly so (opp. ἀνατολαί) of east and west (BGU 1049, 8; Ps 106: 3; Test. Jud. 5: 2) Mt 8: 11; Lk 13: 29; ἀπὸ δ. in the west Rv 21: 13 (s. ἀπό II 1). ἐπὶ δυσμῶν in the west (cf. Num 22: 1; 33: 48; Dt 11: 24, 30) Lk 12: 54. Of lightning that flashes across the whole sky ἐξέρχεται ἀπὸ ἀνατολῶν καὶ φαίνεται ἕως δ. it comes fr. the east and shines to the west Mt 24: 27 (cf. 1 Ch 12: 16; Bar 4: 37). M-M. B 871.*

δυσνόητος, ον (Aristot., Plant. 1, 1 p. 816a, 3; Lucian, Alex. 54; Diog. L. 9, 13 δυσνόητόν τε καὶ δυσεξήγητον) hard to understand 2 Pt 3: 16; δ. τινι for someone Hs 9, 14, 4.*

δυσφημέω (trag.; PLond. 1708, 51; 1 Macc 7: 41) slander, defame 1 Cor 4: 13.*

δυσφημία, ας, ἡ (Soph.+; Dionys. Hal. 6, 48; Plut., Mor. 587F; Dit., Syll.³ 799, 15; PLond. 1660, 25; 1677, 16; 1 Macc 7: 38; 3 Macc 2: 26; Jos., Ant. 16, 90) slander, ill repute (opp. εὐφημία; cf. Ael. Aristid., Τέχναι ῥητορικαί 1, 12 Dind. II p. 763 τὸ ἐναντίον τῇ εὐφημίᾳ δυσφημία) 2 Cor 6: 8. M-M.*

δύσχρηστος, ον (Hippocr.; Philo, Sacr. Abel. 32 p. 214, 17) *hard to use, inconvenient* δ. ἡμῖν ἐστιν *he is troublesome to us* B 6: 7 (Is 3: 10).*

δυσωδία, ας, ἡ (Aristot.+; Diod. S. 14, 71, 2; Longus 4, 17, 2; schol. on Nicander, Ther. 308; Suppl. Epigr. Gr. 8, 621; Sym. Is 34: 3; Philo, Mos. 1, 100; 2, 262; Test. Benj. 8: 3) *stench,* then also that which causes the stench, *filth* (Anna Comn., Alex. 13, 10 ed. Reiff. II 205, 10) AP 11, 26. Fig. *filth of false teaching* IEph 17: 1.*

δύω s. δύνω.

δῶ, δώσῃ, κτλ. s. δίδωμι.

δώδεκα indecl. (Hom.+; inscr. [Meisterhans³-Schw. 159]; pap. [Mayser 316]; LXX; Philo; Jos., Vi. 55; 57; Test. 12 Patr.) *twelve* Mt 9: 20; Mk 5: 25, 42; Lk 2: 42 (Plut., Mor. 839Α γίνεσθαι ἐτῶν δώδεκα; on Jesus at 12 yrs. of age s. RBultmann, Gesch. d. syn. Tradition³ '57, 327f.—At the beginning of the story an external parallel in Ps.-Callisth. 1, 14, 1 ὁ δὲ Ἀλέξανδρος ηὔξανε τῇ ἡλικίᾳ, καὶ γενόμενος δωδεκαέτης μετὰ τοῦ πατρός . . .) al.; οἱ δ. the twelve (sc. μαθηταί.—οἱ δ. is to be expanded differently e.g. Lucian, Jupp. Trag. 26 [12 Olympian deities]; Jos., Vi. 56; Ps.-Clem., Hom. 6, 14) 1 Cor 15: 5 (the separation of Judas the betrayer, for which the v.l. ἕνδεκα would make allowance, does not make it impossible to use the fixed expression 'the 12'. X., Hell. 2, 4, 23 still speaks of οἱ τριάκοντα, despite the fact that acc. to 2, 4, 19 Critias and Hippomachus have already been put to death); cf. Mt 10: 1f, 5; 11: 1; 20: 17; 26: 14 al.—1 Clem 43: 2; Hm 12, 3, 2; s 8, 17, 1f al.—Lit. s. on ἀπόστολος and ἐκκλησία, end; KHRengstorf, TW II 321-8.

δωδεκάσκηπτρον, ου, τό *scepter of the twelve tribes* (of Israel) 1 Cl 31: 4 (Knopf, Hdb. ad loc.).*

δωδέκατος, η, ον (Hom.+; inscr., pap. [Mayser 318]; LXX; Ep. Arist. 50) *twelfth* Rv 21: 20; MPol 19: 1; Hs 9, 1, 10; 9, 29, 1. M-M.*

δωδεκάφυλον, ου, τό (the adj. δωδεκάφυλος Sib. Or. 3, 249; δεκάφυλος, τετράφυλος Hdt. 5, 66; Sib. Or. 2, 171) *the twelve tribes* Ac 26: 7; δ. τοῦ Ἰσραήλ 1 Cl 55: 6. M-M.*

δῶμα, ατος, τό (='house' and 'room' since Hom.) *roof, housetop* (Babrius 5, 5; POxy. 475, 22 [II AD]; 1641, 5; PTebt. 241 verso; PGM 1, 56; 75; 4, 2469; 2712; LXX). Proverbially κηρύσσειν ἐπὶ τῶν δ. *proclaim on the housetops*=quite publicly Mt 10: 27; Lk 12: 3 (cf. 2 Km 16: 22 ἐπὶ τὸ δῶμα . . . κατ' ὀφθαλμοὺς παντὸς Ἰσραήλ); ἀναβαίνειν ἐπὶ τὸ δ. *go up to the roof* Lk 5: 19; Ac 10: 9. ὁ ἐπὶ τοῦ δώματος *the one who happens to be on the housetop* Mt 24: 17; Mk 13: 15; Lk 17: 31 (ἐπὶ τοῦ δ. as Jos., Ant. 6, 49). Cf. RMeister, SAB '11, 7, 633; Ltzm., ZNW 20, '21, 172. M-M.*

δωμάτιον, ου, τό (Aristoph., Pla.+; PGM 1, 70; Jos., Bell. 2, 610, C. Ap. 2, 246, Ant. 5, 191) dim. of δῶμα *room* δ. ὑπερῷον *a little room upstairs* MPol 7: 1. B. 464.*

δωρεά, ᾶς, ἡ (Aeschyl., Hdt.; inscr., pap., LXX, Philo, Joseph., loanw. in rabb.) *gift, bounty* of God (Pla., Leg. 2 p. 672Α; Diod. S. 3, 47, 3; Athen. 15, 48 p. 693D τὴν τοῦ θεοῦ δωρεάν; Herm. Wr. 4, 5; Philo, Poster. Cai. 81 δωρεαί . . . τ. θεοῦ καλαὶ πᾶσαι; Jos., Ant. 3, 223) J 4: 10; Ac 8: 20. Pl. 1 Cl 19: 2; 23: 2; 32: 1; 35: 4; δ. διδόναι (Aeschyl., Hdt.+; Dit., Syll.³ 1118, 3) Ac 11: 17. ἀντι-

λέγειν τῇ δ. τοῦ θεοῦ *oppose the gift of God* ISm 7: 1. W. χάρις (Demosth. 21, 172; Polyb. 1, 31, 6; Diod. S. 3, 73, 6; Philo, Rer. Div. Her. 26; Jos., Ant. 5, 54 θεοῦ χ. καὶ δ.) Ro 5: 17; MPol 20: 2; τῆς δ. πνευματικῆς χάριν λαμβάνειν *receive the favor of the spiritual gift* B 1: 2; ἡ δ. ἐν χάριτι *the gift given in grace* Ro 5: 15; ἐπὶ τῇ ἀνεκδιηγήτῳ δ. *for the indescribable gift* 2 Cor 9: 15; δ. ἐπουράνιος *the heavenly gift* Hb 6: 4. W. gen. δ. τοῦ πνεύματος *receive the Spirit as a gift* Ac 2: 38; cf. 10: 45. ἡ ἔμφυτος δ. τῆς διδαχῆς B 9: 9; δ. δικαιοσύνης *the gift of righteousness* Ro 5: 17; δ. τῆς χάριτος *the gift of grace* Eph 3: 7. κατὰ τὸ μέτρον τῆς δ. τοῦ Χριστοῦ acc. *to the measure that Christ has given* 4: 7.—DGDunn, ET 81, '69/'70, 349-51. M-M.*

δωρεάν acc. of δωρεά used as adv. (since Hdt. 5, 23 [δωρεήν]; inscr., pap., LXX, Joseph.).

1. *as a gift, without payment, gratis* (so, in addition to the ref. in Nägeli 35f, Dialekt-Inschr. 2569, 4 [Delphi]; PTebt. 118; PSI 400, 16; Gen 29: 15; Ex 21: 11 δωρεὰν ἄνευ ἀργυρίου al.) δ. λαμβάνειν (Jos., Vi. 425), διδόναι (Bell. 1, 274, Vi. 38) *receive, give without payment* Mt 10: 8 (Sextus 242); cf. Rv 21: 6; 22: 17; δ. εὐαγγελίσασθαι 2 Cor 11: 7. δικαιούμενοι δ. *justified, declared upright, as a gift* Ro 3: 24. οὐδὲ δ. ἄρτον ἐφάγομεν παρά τινος *we have not eaten bread with* (or *from*) *anyone without paying for it* 2 Th 3: 8.

2. *undeservedly, without reason* ἐμίσησάν με δ. *they have hated me without reason* J 15: 25 (Ps 34: 19; cf. 118: 161; 1 Km 19: 5).

3. *in vain, to no purpose* (Job 1: 9; Ps 34: 7) δ. ἀποθνήσκειν Gal 2: 21; ITr 10. M-M. s.v. δωρεά.*

δωρέομαι 1 aor. ἐδωρησάμην; pf. δεδώρημαι, ptc. δεδωρημένος (the act. disappeared in class. times; the mid. is found Hom.+; inscr., pap., LXX, Philo; Jos., Ant. 1, 165, C. Ap. 2, 45) *give, present, bestow* τινί τι *someth. to (on) someone* (Aeschyl., Hdt.+; Dit., Or. 90, 31; 517, 7; POxy. 1153, 15 [I AD]; Fluchtaf. 4, 30) τὸ πτῶμα τῷ Ἰωσήφ *the body to Joseph* Mk 15: 45. τ. θείας δυνάμεως δεδωρημένης *since the divine power has bestowed* 2 Pt 1: 3. Hence in vs. 4 prob. mid., not pass. (of a divine gift Ael. Aristid. 13 p. 297 D.).—Dg 11: 5. M-M.*

δώρημα, ατος, τό (Aeschyl., Hdt.+; IG IV² 128, 53 [c. 280 BC] δ. of Asclepius; Epigr. Gr. 1039, 13; Sir 34: 18; Ezek. Trag. in Euseb., Pr. Ev. 9, 28 θεοῦ δ.; Philo, Somn. 1, 103 δ. παρὰ θεοῦ) *gift, present* δ. τέλειον *a perfect gift* Js 1: 17 (Philo, Abr. 54 δ. τελ.; Ep. Arist. 276 θεοῦ δ. καλόν; Jos., Ant. 4, 318 δ. κάλλιστον; PSI 29, 33 τἀγαθὰ δορήματα); οὐχ ὡς δι' ἑνὸς ἁμαρτήσαντος τὸ δ. *the gift* (of grace) *is not like the effects of one man's sin* Ro 5: 16; ἐκ τῶν ἰδίων δ. *from the gifts that one has himself received* Hm 2: 4. δ. τοῦ κυρίου s 2: 7. M-M.*

δῶρον, ου, τό (Hom.+; inscr., pap., LXX; En. 100, 12; Ep. Arist., Philo; Jos., C. Ap. 2, 207.—Philostrat., Vi. Soph. 2, 10, 7 distinguishes betw. δωρεά and δῶρον) *gift, present.*

1. gener. προσφέρειν δ. *bring gifts* (cf. Gen 43: 26) Mt 2: 11. δῶρα πέμπειν ἀλλήλοις *send gifts to each other* Rv 11: 10. Of God's gifts (Hom.+; Sotades Lyr. [III BC] 9, 7 p. 242 Coll.; Strabo 16, 2, 35; Herm. Wr. 10, 9; Ep. Arist. 231; 272; Philo, Congr. Erud. Gr. 38) 1 Cl 35: 1; w. ἐπαγγελίαι Hv 3, 2, 1; καὶ τοῦτο οὐκ ἐξ ὑμῶν, θεοῦ τὸ δ. *and you have not done this of your own strength; it is a gift of God* Eph 2: 8.

2. esp. of sacrificial *gifts* and *offerings* (Pla., Euthyphr. 15Α; Dit., Syll.³ 1141; 1154 Διὶ δ., Or. 407, 4) Hb 11: 4; 1

210

Cl 4: 2 (Gen 4: 4); εἰς τὰ δ. βάλλειν *put into the offering(-chest)* Lk 21: 4; cf. vs. 1. προσφέρειν τὸ δ. *bring his offering* (Lev 1: 2, 14; 2: 1, 4 and oft.; Test. Iss. 5: 3) Mt 5: 23f; 8: 4; Hb 5: 1; 8: 3f; 9: 9 (w. θυσίαι as Lev 21: 6; cf. Ep. Arist. 234); cf. 1 Cl 44: 4. ἀφιέναι τὸ δ. *leave one's offering* Mt 5: 24; δ. as transl. of קָרְבָּן (Jos., Ant. 4, 73,

C. Ap. 1, 167) Mk 7: 11; cf. Mt 15: 5; ἁγιάζειν τὸ δ. *sanctify the offering* 23: 19; cf. vs. 18. M-M.*

δωροφορία, ας, ἡ (Alciphr. 1, 6; Pollux 4, 47; Bl-D. §119, 1) *the bringing of a gift* of a collection Ro 15: 31 v.l. for διακονία. M-M.*

E

ε′ as numeral=*5* or *fifth* (πέμπτη); Ac 19: 9 D and Hv 5; m 5 in titles (Apollon. Paradox. 46 Θεόφραστος ἐν τῇ ε′ τῶν φυτικῶν αἰτιῶν φησιν).*

ἔα (Aeschyl. + in Attic poets; rare in prose: Pla., Prot. 314D; Epict. 2, 24, 22; 3, 20, 5; an exclam. of surprise or displeasure) *ah!, ha!* Mk 1: 24 t.r.; Lk 4: 34; 1 Cl 39: 5. Some connection w. ἔα, imper. of ἐάω, *let alone!* seems very likely in 1 Cl, and poss. in Mk and Lk (cf. Vulg. and RSV mg., Lk 4: 34). S. ἐάω 2.*

ἐάν (Hom. +; inscr., pap., LXX).—I. Conjunction (Bl-D. §31, 1; 107; 371, 4; 372, 1a; 373; Mlt. and Rob., indices) *if* (only rarely [1 Cor 6: 4; 11: 14, as e.g. Lucian, Vit. Auct. 11 καὶ ἰδιώτης γὰρ ἐὰν ᾖς] anywhere else than at the beg. of the subordinate clause).

1. used w. the subjunctive to denote 'what is expected to occur, under certain circumstances, from a given standpoint in the present, either general or specific'. (Bl-D. §371, 4; Mlt.-Turner 114f.)

a. w. pres. subj., and pres. in apodosis: ἐὰν θέλῃς δύνασαί με καθαρίσαι Mt 8: 2; Mk 1: 40; Lk 5: 12. ἐὰν ἀγαθοποιῆτε, ποία ὑμῖν χάρις ἐστίν; 6: 33. ἐὰν μαρτυρῶ, ἡ μαρτυρία μου οὐκ ἔστιν ἀληθής J 5: 31; cf. 8: 16; 15: 14. περιτομὴ ὠφελεῖ ἐὰν νόμον πράσσῃς Ro 2: 25; cf. 13: 4; 14: 8; 1 Cor 13: 1ff al. W. pres. subj., and aorist in apodosis: ἐὰν ὁ πούς σου σκανδαλίζῃ σε, ἀπόκοψον Mk 9: 45; cf. vs. 47; w. fut. in apod.: ἐὰν ᾖ . . . ἐπαναπαήσεται Lk 10: 6; ἐὰν ὁδηγῇ, πεσοῦνται Mt 15: 14.

b. mostly w. the aor. subj., and pres. in apodosis: ἐὰν ἀγαπήσητε, τίνα μισθὸν ἔχετε; 5: 46, cf. 47; 18: 15ff. ἐὰν μερισθῇ, οὐ δύναται σταθῆναι Mk 3: 24. ἐὰν γαμήσῃ, μοιχᾶται 10: 12. ἐὰν ἀπολέσῃ, οὐχὶ ἅπτει; Lk 15: 8. ἐὰν μείνητε, μαθηταί μού ἐστε J 8: 31; cf. 19: 12. ἐὰν χωρισθῇ, μενέτω 1 Cor 7: 11; cf. vs. 39. ἐὰν φάγωμεν, περισσεύομεν 8: 8. W. aor. subj., and aor. in apodosis ἐὰν εἴπωσιν, μὴ ἐξέλθητε Mt 24: 26. ἐὰν ἁμάρτῃ, ἐπιτίμησον . . . ἐὰν μετανοήσῃ, ἄφες Lk 17: 3; ἐὰν εἴπω, οὐ μὴ πιστεύσητε 22: 67; cf. vs. 68. W. aor. subj., and fut. in apod.: ἐὰν ἀφῆτε, ἀφήσει καὶ ὑμῖν Mt 6: 14. ἐὰν ἅψωμαι, σωθήσομαι 9: 21. ἐὰν ἐμπέσῃ, οὐχὶ κρατήσει; 12: 11; cf. 24: 48, 50; 28: 14; Mk 8: 3; Lk 4: 7; 14: 34; J 15: 10 al.

c. w. pres. and aor. subj. at the same time: ἐὰν δὲ καὶ ἀθλῇ τις (*is an athlete* by profession), οὐ στεφανοῦται, ἐὰν μὴ νομίμως ἀθλήσῃ (*competes acc. to the rules,* single or repeated action) 2 Ti 2: 5.—1 Cor 14: 23: ἐὰν συνέλθῃ (antecedent action) καὶ λαλῶσιν (repeated and lasting), εἰσέλθωσιν δέ (once); cf. vs. 24. ἐὰν ἔχητε πίστιν καὶ μὴ διακριθῆτε Mt 21: 21.

d. At times the mng. of ἐάν approaches closely that of ὅταν *whenever,* or of *when* (Is 24: 13; Am 7: 2; Tob 6: 17 BA ἐὰν εἰσέλθῃς, cf. S ὅταν εἰσ.; 4: 3 BA) 1 J 2: 28 (t.r. ὅταν); J 12: 32; 14: 3; Hb 3: 7 (Ps 94: 7).

2. used w. the indic. (exx. in Dssm., NB 29f [BS 201f]; Bl-D. §372, 1a; Mlt. 168; Mlt.-Turner 115f; Rdm.² 200; Rob. 1009f).

a. w. fut. ind., in the same mng. (CIG II 2485 ἐὰν θελήσει; pap.; Test. Reub. 4, 11; Bl-D. §373, 2 w. app.): ἐὰν οὗτοι σιωπήσουσιν, οἱ λίθοι κράξουσιν Lk 19: 40 (D σιγήσουσιν, t.r. σιωπήσωσιν). ἐὰν μή τις ὁδηγήσει με Ac 8: 31 (t.r. ὁδηγήσῃ). ἐὰν μετανοήσουσιν Hv 1, 3, 2; ἐὰν προσθήσω m 4, 3, 7; ἐὰν ἔσῃ m 5, 1, 2.

b. w. pres. ind. (Ocellus [II bc] 5 Harder ['26]; Cyril of Scyth. p. 145, 5 ἐὰν ἔστιν; CIG II 2485 ἐὰν βούλονται; Test. Jud. 15: 1) ἐὰν στήκετε ἐν κυρίῳ 1 Th 3: 8 (t.r. στήκητε); IMg 5: 2; Hv 3, 12, 3; ἐὰν οἴδαμεν 1 J 5: 15.

c. w. aor. ind. In Mt 15: 5=Mk 7: 11 the Nestle-Aland text accents ὠφελήθης instead of ὠφεληθῇς, thus giving us an example of ἐάν w. aor. ind., strongly supported by Bl-D. §360, 1. This constr. is rare but occasionally found in the late κοινή (Rob. 1009).

3. w. other particles:—a. ἐὰν καί *even if* Gal 6: 1; likew. ἐὰν δὲ καί (POxy. 472 II, 7) *but if* 1 Cor 7: 11, 28; 2 Ti 2: 5. ἐὰν δὲ καὶ παρακούσῃ *but if he refuses to listen* Mt 18: 17.

b. ἐὰν μή *if not, unless* w. pres. subj. ἐὰν δὲ μὴ ᾖ ἀξία Mt 10: 13; cf. Lk 13: 3; J 3: 2f, 5, 27. Mostly w. aor. subj. ἐὰν μὴ περισσεύσῃ Mt 5: 20; 6: 15; 12: 29; 18: 3; 21: 21; Mk 3: 27; 4: 22 (cf. KBeyer, Semitische Syntax im NT, '62, 131); J 4: 48; 6: 44; 7: 51; Ro 10: 15; 1 Cor 9: 16; 14: 6. W. fut. ἐὰν μὴ μετανοήσουσιν Rv 2: 22.

c. ἐάνπερ *if indeed, if only, supposing that* 'referring to still another condition (fact)' (Bl-D. §454, 2) w. pres. subj. (Pla., Ap. 12 p. 25B; X., Cyr. 4, 6, 8; PFay. 124, 9) Hb 6: 3; IRo 1: 1 and aor. (Plut., Lyc. 3, 2; BGU 1141, 30) 1: 2; IPol 7: 1; Hb 3: 14 (vs. 6 t.r.).

d. ἐάν τε . . . ἐάν τε *whether . . . or whether* (X., Cyr. 3, 3, 17, Mem. 2, 4, 6; Ael. Aristid. 53 p. 622 D.; Maximus Tyr. 1, 9a) Ro 14: 8.

II. freq. in place of ἄν (q.v.) after relatives (so Lysias 24, 18 Thalh. v.l. acc. to mss.; pap. since 246 bc [Mayser 152f]; LXX [Thackeray 67].—Dssm., NB 29f [BS 201f]; Mlt. 42f; Bl-D. §107 w. app.; Rdm.² 203f; Crönert 130f; Rob. 190f) ὃς ἐάν=ὃς ἄν (PTebt. 107, 8 [II bc]; Gen 15: 14) Mt 5: 19, 32. ὅπου ἐάν=ὅπου ἄν 8: 19. ὁσάκις ἐάν=ὁσάκις ἄν Rv 11: 6. οὗ ἐάν=οὗ ἄν 1 Cor 16: 6.—LRydbeck, Fachprosa, '67, 119–44. M-M.

ἐάνπερ s. ἐάν I 3c.

ἐαρινός, ή, όν (Hom. +; Diod. S. 5, 41, 6; inscr., pap.; Philo, Mos. 2, 186 al.) *of spring* καιροὶ ἐ. *seasons of spring* (as Philo, Op. M. 153 ἐαριναὶ ὧραι) 1 Cl 20: 9.*

ἑαυτοῦ, ῆς, οῦ pl. ἑαυτῶν reflexive pron. (Hom. +; inscr., pap., LXX). The contract forms αὑτοῦ and αὑτῶν are deleted in the newer editions and replaced by the uncontracted forms or by αὐτοῦ, αὐτῶν (W-S. §22, 16; Bl-D. §64, 1 w. app.; Mayser 305; Rob. 226; Mlt.-Turner 190).

1. of the third pers. sg. and pl., to indicate identity w. the pers. speaking or acting ταπεινοῦν ἑαυτόν *humble oneself* Mt 18: 4; 23: 12. Opp. ὑψοῦν ἑ. *exalt oneself* 23: 12. ἀπαρνεῖσθαι ἑ. *deny oneself* 16: 24; Mk 8: 34;

εὐνουχίζειν ἑ. *make a eunuch of oneself* Mt 19: 12; σῴζειν ἑ. (Jos., Ant. 10, 137) 27: 42; κατακόπτειν ἑ. *beat oneself* Mk 5: 5 et al. ἀγοράζειν τι ἑαυτῷ *buy someth. for oneself* Mt 14: 15; Mk 6: 36, but see below. W. the middle (cf. X., Mem. 1, 6, 13 ποιεῖσθαι ἑαυτῷ φίλον; Sir 37: 8): διεμερίσαντο ἑαυτοῖς *they divided among them* J 19: 24 (Ps 21: 19).—The simple dat. may also be used to emphasize the subject as agent (Hdt. 1, 32; Strabo 2, 1, 35; POxy. 2351, 49; Ps 26: 12; SSol 1: 8) βαστάζων ἑαυτῷ τὸν σταυρόν *bearing the cross without help* J 19: 17; ἑαυτοῖς κρίμα λήμψονται *they themselves will be responsible for the judgment they are to receive* Ro 13: 2; οὐκ ἐπαινοῦμεν τοὺς προσιόντας ἑαυτοῖς *we do not commend those who take the initiative in advancing themselves* MPol 4 (Funk); cf. στρῶσον σεαυτῷ *make your own bed* Ac 9: 34. This may be the place for Mk 6: 36; Mt 14: 15.— LRydbeck, Fachprosa '67, 51–61.—Used esp. w. prep.

a. ἀφ᾽ ἑαυτοῦ (ἀπό V 5): ποιεῖν τι *do someth. of one's own accord* J 5: 19. λαλεῖν *speak on one's own authority* (Diod. S. 12, 66, 2 ἐκήρυξέ τις ἀφ᾽ ἑαυτοῦ, i.e., without orders from a higher authority) 7: 18; 16: 13; λέγειν 11: 51; 18: 34 (M. Ant. 11, 19 τοῦτο οὐκ ἀπὸ σαυτοῦ μέλλεις λέγειν). καρπὸν φέρειν *bear fruit by itself* 15: 4. ἱκανὸν εἶναι *be competent by oneself* 2 Cor 3: 5 (ἀφ᾽ ἑαυτῶν interchanging w. ἐξ ἑαυτῶν. S. also 1e). γινώσκειν *know by oneself* Lk 21: 30. κρίνειν *judge for oneself* 12: 57.

b. δι᾽ ἑαυτοῦ (POxy. 273, 21; PTebt. 72, 197): κοινὸς δι᾽ ἑαυτοῦ *unclean in itself* Ro 14: 14 (EpJer 26).

c. ἐν ἑαυτῷ *to or in oneself*, mostly w. verbs of speaking, in contrast to audible utterance; s. διαλογίζομαι 1, εἶπον 5, λέγω 6; otherw. ἔχειν τι ἐν ἑαυτῷ *have someth. in oneself* (cf. Jdth 10: 19; Jos., Ant. 8, 171) J 5: 26, 42; 6: 53; 17: 13; 2 Cor 1: 9. Gener., of what takes place in the inner consciousness διαπορεῖν Ac 10: 17. Esp. γίνεσθαι ἐν ἑαυτῷ *come to one's senses* 12: 11 (X., An. 1, 5, 17 ὁ Κλέαρχος ἐν ἑαυτῷ ἐγένετο; Polyb. 1, 49, 8). For this

d. εἰς ἑαυτὸν ἔρχεσθαι *come to one's senses* Lk 15: 17 (Diod. S. 13, 95, 2; Epict. 3, 1, 15).

e. ἐξ ἑαυτῶν (Soph., El. 343 ἐκ σαυτῆς; Theophr. in Ps.-Demetr. c. 222 ἐξ αὐτοῦ) *of (our) own strength* 2 Cor 3: 5.

f. καθ᾽ ἑαυτόν *by oneself* (X., Mem. 3, 5, 4; Plut., Anton. 54, 1; 2; 2 Macc 13: 13) μένειν *live by oneself* (in a private house) Ac 28: 16. πίστις νεκρά ἐστιν καθ᾽ ἑαυτήν *faith (when it remains) by itself is dead* Js 2: 17 (Diog. L. 1, 64 from a letter of Solon: religion and lawgivers can do nothing καθ᾽ ἑαυτά=if they are dependent on themselves alone).—βασιλεία μερισθεῖσα καθ᾽ ἑαυτῆς *a kingdom that is divided against itself* Mt 12: 25.—μεθ᾽ ἑαυτοῦ, μεθ᾽ ἑαυτῶν *with oneself, themselves* (cf. 1 Km 9: 3; 24: 3 ἔλαβεν μεθ᾽ ἑ.) Mt 12: 45; 25: 3.

g. παρ᾽ ἑαυτῷ τιθέναι τι *put someth. aside* 1 Cor 16: 2 (X., Mem. 3, 13, 3; cf. Jos., Ant. 9, 68 οἴκαδε παρ᾽ αὐτῷ).

h. τὰ περὶ ἑαυτοῦ *the passages concerning himself* Lk 24: 27.

i. πρὸς ἑαυτὸν προσεύχεσθαι *pray to oneself* (=silently) 18: 11 (cf. Aristaen., Ep. 1, 6; 2 Macc 11: 13; Jos., Ant. 11, 210; Vi. Aesopi I c. 9 πρὸς ἑαυτὸν εἶπεν; 38). ἀπέρχεσθαι πρὸς αὐτούς (v.l. ἑαυτούς) *go home* J 20: 10, cf. Lk 24: 12 t.r. (cf. Polyb. 5, 93, 1; Num 24: 25; Jos., Ant. 8, 124; but s. MBlack, An Aramaic Approach³, '67, 102f).

2. for the first and second pers. pl. (gener. H.Gk.; cf. FKälker, Quaest. de elocut. Polyb. 1880, 277; Mlt. 87; Bl-D. §64, 1; Mayser 303, w. further lit. in note 3; Rob. 689f) ἑαυτούς=ἡμᾶς αὐτούς (Themistocl., Ep. 15; Jos., Bell. 5, 536) 1 Cor 11: 31. ἐν ἑαυτοῖς=ἐν ἡμῖν αὐτοῖς Ro 8: 23; 2 Cor 1: 9. δι᾽ ἑαυτῶν=δι᾽ ἡμῶν αὐ. 1 Cl 32: 4;

ἑαυτοῖς=ὑμῖν αὐτοῖς (cf. Jos., Ant. 4, 190; 8, 277) Mt 23: 31; 1 Cl 47: 7.—This replacement of the first and second pers. by the third is very much less common in the sg. (Ps.-Pla., Alcib. 2, 143c; Dio Chrys. 30[47], 6 σὺ . . . αὐτόν; Aelian, V.H. 1, 21; Galen, Protr. 10 p. 30, 10 John; Syntipas p. 115, 10 μεθ᾽ ἑαυτοῦ=with me; Transjord. inscr.: NGG Phil.-hist. Kl. Fachgr. V n.F. I 1 '36, p. 3, 1; other exx. in Mlt. 87, n. 2; Mayser 304; KHauser, Gramm. der griech. Inschr. Lykiens, Zürich Diss. '16, 100), and can hardly be established w. certainty for the NT gener.; cf. J 18: 34; Ro 13: 9 t.r.; but ISm 4: 2; Hv 4, 1, 5; s 2: 1; 9, 2, 5.

3. for the reciprocal pron. ἀλλήλων, ἀλλήλοις, ἀλλήλους (even in class. auth., Kühner-G. I 573; pap. in Mayser 304; LXX.— W-S. §22, 13; Bl-D. §287 w. app.; Rob. 690) *each other, one another* λέγοντες πρὸς ἑαυτούς *as they said to each other* Mk 10: 26; cf. J 12: 19 (πρὸς ἑ. as Antig. Car. 39 μάχεσθαι πρὸς αὐτούς; Lucian, Philops. 29, Ver. Hist. 1, 35). χαρίζεσθαι ἑαυτοῖς *forgive one another* Eph 4: 32; Col 3: 13. νουθετεῖν ἑαυτούς *admonish one another* vs. 16. εἰρηνεύειν ἐν ἑαυτοῖς *live in peace w. one another* 1 Th 5: 13; τὴν εἰς ἑαυτοὺς ἀγάπην 1 Pt 4: 9.

4. in place of the possessive pron. *his, her* (Mayser 304f; Mlt. 87f) Mt 8: 22; 21: 8; 25: 1; Lk 2: 39; 9: 60; 11: 21; 12: 36 al. M-M.

ἐάω impf. εἴων; fut. ἐάσω; 1 aor. εἴασα, imper. ἔασον, opt. 3 sg. ἐάσαι 1 Cl 33: 1; 1 aor. pass. inf. ἐαθῆναι (Hom.+; inscr., pap., LXX, Ep. Arist., Philo; Jos., Ant. 2, 31; Test 12 Patr.) *let*.

1. *let, permit* w. acc. and inf. (Lucian, Dial. Mort. 13, 5) εἴασεν πάντα τὰ ἔθνη πορεύεσθαι *he let all the nations go* Ac 14: 16.—23: 32; 27: 32; 28: 4; 1 Cl 38: 2; 53: 3 (Ex 32: 10); 55: 4; Dg 9: 1. W. neg. οὐκ ἐᾶν *not permit, prevent* (Appian, Bell. Civ. 5, 92 §384; PSI 380, 1 [249 BC]; 402, 11; 602, 10; Job 9: 18; 1 Macc 12: 40; 15: 14; 2 Macc 12: 2) Mt 24: 43; Lk 4: 41 (w. pres. inf. as Polyaenus 7, 21, 5 and 6); 1 Cor 10: 13; ending of Mk in the Freer ms. 3; 1 Cl 33: 1; IEph 3: 2; 9: 1; Hv 3, 1, 9. W. ἵνα instead of the inf. v 2, 3, 1. W. omission of the inf. (Soph., Ant. 538; POxy. 1293, 21) οὐκ εἴασεν αὐτοὺς τὸ πνεῦμα Ἰησοῦ (sc. πορευθῆναι) *the Spirit of Jesus prevented them* (fr. going) Ac 16: 7. οὐκ εἴων αὐτὸν (sc. εἰσελθεῖν) οἱ μαθηταί 19: 30.

2. *let go, leave alone* (Demosth. 9, 26, Ael. Aristid. 34, 42 K.= 50 p. 562 D.; ἐῶ τὰ ἄλλα; PFay. 122, 6; PTebt. 319, 24; Jos., C. Ap. 2, 118) τὶ *someth.* στρεβλὴν (sc. ὁδόν) *avoid the crooked way* Hm 6, 1, 2. W. relative as obj. s 9, 2, 7;=ἀφιέναι τινά *let someone go* (Maximus Tyr. 8, 5g; 6h) Ac 5: 38 t.r.; Rv 2: 20 t.r.; *leave someone to herself* Hv 2, 3, 1. Abs. ἐᾶτε ἕως τούτου *stop! No more of this!* Lk 22: 51 (cf. Il. 21, 221 ἔασον; s. ABBruce, Expos. Gk. Test. 1897, ad loc.). ἔα δέ *let alone, not to speak of, much more et al.* now s 1 Cl 39: 5, but s. also ἔα (Job 4: 19 v.l., 15, 16. Cf. PKatz, JTS 47, '46, 168f).

3. perh. nautical t.t. ἐᾶν τὰς ἀγκύρας εἰς τὴν θάλασσαν *leave the anchors in the sea* Ac 27: 40. M-M.*

ἑβδομάς, άδος, ἡ *week* (Hippocr., Aphorism. 2, 24; Jo. Lydus, De Mens. 2, 4 p. 21 Wünsch al.; LXX; Philo; Test. Levi 16: 1.—In Jos.=sabbath: Bell. 2, 147; 4, 99, C. Ap. 2, 175) B 16: 6 (quot. of uncertain origin; s. Windisch, Hdb. ad loc.). B. 1005.*

ἑβδομήκοντα indecl. (Hdt.+; pap., LXX, Ep. Arist., Philo, Joseph., Test. 12 Patr.) *seventy* Lk 10: 1, 17 (οἱ ἑβδ. w. someth. to be supplied as Plut., Mor. 345D; Jos., Vi. 56b; 58); Ac 23: 23. ἑ. δύο *seventy-two* (Antig. Car. 111, the 72 children of Heracles; Plut., Mor. 356B: the 72 fellow-conspirators of Typho) Lk 10: 1 v.l.; 17 v.l. (BM Metzger, NTS 5, '59, 299-306; SJellicoe, ibid. 6, '60, 319-21). ἑ. πέντε seventy-five Ac 7: 14. ἑ. ἕξ seventy-six 27: 37. M-M.*

ἑβδομηκοντάκις seventy times ἑβ. ἑπτά may be short for ἑβ. ἑπτάκις seventy times seven times (cf. PGM 1, 143 ἑπτάκις ἑπτά seven times seven), but is more likely seventy-seven times (as Gen 4: 24; cf. Test. Benj. 7: 4) Mt 18: 22 (Mlt. 98, but cf. Mlt.-H. 175; Bl-D. §248, 2; Gdspd., Probs. 29-31. In Polyaenus 8, 33; Plut., Mor. 245D the number 7777 is found, denoting an immeasurable throng). M-M.*

ἕβδομος, η, ον (Hom.+; pap., LXX, Ep. Arist., Philo; Jos., C. Ap. 1, 159; Test. 12 Patr.) the seventh Jd 14; Rv 8: 1; 10: 7; 11: 15; 16: 17; 21: 20; hour (Polyaenus 8, 16, 1 ὥρα ἑβ.) J 4: 52; day Ac 21: 27 D; Hb 4: 4b; B 15: 3, 5 (the last 3 times Gen 2: 2). ἡ ἑβδόμη (sc. ἡμέρα; cf. Antig. Car. c. 140; Dialekt-Inschr. 4705, 8 [Thera] ἑπάγεσθαι τὰν ἑβδόμαν of the celebration 'of the seventh'; Bar 1: 2; Ezk 30: 20; Philo, Vit. Cont. 30; 32) Hb 4: 4a.**

ἐβεβλήκει, ἐβέβλητο s. βάλλω.

Ἔβερ, ὁ indecl. Eber (Gen 10: 24f.—In Joseph. Ἔβερος, ου [Ant. 1, 147]), in the genealogy of Jesus Lk 3: 35.*

ἐβλήθην s. βάλλω.

Ἑβραϊκός, ή, όν (Philo; Jos., Ant. 1, 5; PGM 4, 3085; cf. Fluchtaf. 1, 12; 15) Hebrew γράμμασιν Ἑ. with Η. letters (Ep. Arist. 3; 30), which takes for granted that the language was also Hebrew (Jos., Ant. 1, 5; 12, 48) Lk 23: 38 t.r.; cf. Kleine Texte 8³, p. 9, 27.*

Ἑβραῖος, ου, ὁ (W-H. Ἑβ.; cf. their Introd.² §408; Bl-D. §39, 3) Hebrew (Paus. 1, 5, 5; Appian, Bell. Civ. 2, 71; Plut.; Porphyr., Vi. Pyth. 11; Sallust. 9 p. 18, 17; Damasc., Vi. Isidori 56 ὁ Ἑβραίων θεός; 141; PGM 4, 3019, corresp. to what the Jews oft. called themselves; LXX; the poet Ezekiel; Philo; Joseph.; Sib. Or.; Test. Jos. 12, 2; 3; inscr. [exx. in Schürer III⁴ 83, 29]; συναγωγὴ Ἑβραίων s. on συναγωγή 2; MDibelius, Hdb.² on Phil 3: 5 exc.).
   1. as a national name for Jews in contrast to Gentiles (in this sense Euseb. applies the term Ἑβρ. to such Jews as Philo [H.E. 2, 4, 2] and Aristobulus [Praep. Evang. 8, 8, 34] who spoke Gk. and were Gk. scholars; s. the Jew. grave inscr. in Rome and Lydia: Ltzm., Hdb.³ on 2 Cor 11: 22 exc.; Monum. As. Min. Ant. III '31 no. 32) 2 Cor 11: 22; Phil 3: 5. The word prob. has this mng. in the title πρὸς Ἑβρ. of Hb, as well as in the name of the old orig. Gk. GH in Clem. Alex. and Origen (Kl. T. 8³, p. 7, 2; 12; note on l. 8; cf. p. 5, 9f; 18; 22; 11, 25f) τὸ καθ᾽ Ἑβραίους εὐαγγέλιον.
   2. as a name for the Aramaic-speaking Jews in contrast to those who spoke Gk. (Ἑλληνισταί, q.v., and cf. GPWetter, ARW 21, '22, 410ff) Ac 6: 1 (Philo, Conf. Ling. 129, makes a difference betw. Ἑβρ. and ἡμεῖς, who speak Gk. [Congr. Erud. Grat. 43f]).—S. on Ἰσραήλ, end. HKosmala, Hebräer-Essener-Christen '59. M-M.*

Ἑβραΐς, ΐδος, ἡ (fem. of Ἑβραῖος, Jos., Ant. 2, 225f and of Ἑβραϊκός, Kühner-Bl. II 274, 1) ἡ Ἑ. διάλεκτος (cf. Ἑβ. φωνή 4 Macc 12: 7; 16: 15) the Hebr. language Ac 21: 40; 22: 2; 26: 14; Papias 2: 16, i.e., the Aramaic spoken at that time in Palestine.—Zahn. Einl.³ I 18f; Dalman, Jesus 6ff (Eng.transl. 7ff). But PNepper-Christensen, Das Matthäusevangelium '58, 101-35 and JM

Grintz, JBL 79, '60, 32-47 hold that some form of Hebrew was commonly spoken.*

Ἑβραϊστί adv. (Sir., Praef., l. 22; Jos., Ant. 10, 8; PGM 5, 475; 13, 81; 150 ἀβραιστί) in Hebrew or Aramaic (s. on Ἑβραῖς) J 5: 2; 19: 13, 17, 20; 20: 16; Rv 9: 11; 16: 16. M-M.*

ἐγγεννάω (Polyb. 6, 55, 4; Cornutus 20 p. 37, 12; Plut., Mor. 132E; Herm. Wr. 10, 15b; Sir 22: 4 v.l.) generate in someth.; pass. be generated of a worm in the flesh of the dead phoenix 1 Cl 25: 3.*

ἐγγίζω Att. fut. ἐγγιῶ; 1 aor. ἤγγισα; pf. ἤγγικα; in our lit. only intr. approach, come near (so in Aristot., Polyb., Diod. S., Epict. et al., pap., LXX, En., Philo, Joseph., Test. 12 Patr.; cf. Nägeli 36; Anz 344f; KW Clark, JBL 59, '40, 367-74).
   1. w. dat. of the pers. (Gen 27: 21) or thing (Polyb. 18, 4, 1; Ex 32: 19; Jos., Bell. 5, 408 τ. πόλει) τῷ παιδί B 6: 1 (Is 50: 8); τῇ πύλῃ τῆς πόλεως the city gate Lk 7: 12; the house 15: 25; Damascus Ac 9: 3; 22: 6; cf. 10: 9; the grave GP 9: 36.—Jesus Lk 15: 1; 22: 47. τῷ θεῷ draw near to God (Philo, Leg. All. 2, 57, Deus Imm. 161; Theodor. Prodr. 7, 475 H. θεοῖς ἐγγ.) of priestly service (Ex 19: 22; 34: 30; Lev 10: 3 al.), fig. of the spiritual service of Christians Hb 7: 19; Js 4: 8; Mt 15: 8 t.r. (cf. Jdth 8: 27; Ps 148: 14; Is 29: 13 al.).
   2. w. εἰς, only with indications of place (Tob 11: 1; En. 14, 10): Jerusalem Mt 21: 1; Mk 11: 1.—Lk 18: 35; 19: 29. εἰς τὴν κώμην to the village 24: 28; εἰς συναγωγήν Hm 11: 13.— W. πρός and dat. to show place (Pr 5: 8) Lk 19: 37.
   3. w. ἐπί τινα Lk 10: 9 (cf. Ps 26: 2; 68: 4 v.l.).
   4. μέχρι θανάτου ἐ. come close to dying Phil 2: 30 (cf. Job 33: 22; Sir 51: 6 ἤγγισεν ἕως θανάτου). PKatz, ThZ 5, '49, 7; ADebrunner, Mus. Helvet. 11, '54, 58f.
   5. abs.—a. of pers. approaching in space (Gen 18: 23; 27: 27) Ac 23: 15; ἤγγικεν ὁ παραδιδούς με my betrayer is near Mt 26: 46; Mk 14: 42; a thief Lk 12: 33; the tribune Ac 21: 33; the blind man Lk 18: 40; Jesus 19: 41; 24: 15.
   b. of approaching in time (POxy. 1202, 8; w. dat., Epict. 3, 10, 14). W. indications of time (KWClark, JBL 59, '40, 367-83) the hour Mt 26: 45; the day (Ezk 7: 4; 12: 23) Ro 13: 12; Hb 10: 25; ὁ καιρός (La 4: 18; 1 Macc 9: 10) Lk 21: 8; cf. Mt 21: 34; ὁ χρόνος Ac 7: 17; the Passover Lk 22: 1; the end 1 Pt 4: 7; the final stumbling-block B 4: 3; cf. ending of Mk in the Freer ms. 8; the judgment GP 7: 25; destruction of the temple Lk 21: 20; redemption vs. 28. Esp. of the approaching Kingdom of God: ἤγγικεν ἡ βασιλεία τῶν οὐρανῶν (or τοῦ θεοῦ) Mt 3: 2; 4: 17; 10: 7; Mk 1: 15; Lk 10: 9, 11 (WRHutton, ET 64, '52/'53, 89-91: has come for the Lk passages). Of the Lord's return Js 5: 8. —On 'realized eschatology' s. CHDodd, Parables of the Kgdm².'36, 44-51, ET 48, '36/'37, 138-42; JYCampbell, ET 48, '36/'37, 91-94; RHFuller, The Mission and Achievement of Jesus '54, 20-25; RFBerkey, JBL 82, '63, 177-87; MBlack, An Aramaic Approach³, '67, 208-11. M-M.*

ἔγγιστα superl. of the adv. ἐγγύς, q.v., beg., 1c, 2b.

ἔγγραφος, ον (Polyb.; Dio Chrys. 59[76], 2 ἔ. νόμος; Plut.; Lucian; inscr.; POxy. 70, 4, al. in pap.) enrolled ἔ. γίνεσθαι 1 Cl 45: 8; recorded Hs 5, 3, 8.*

ἐγγράφω 1 aor. ἐνέγραψα; pf. pass. ἐγγέγραμμαι; 2 fut. pass. ἐγγραφήσομαι (Aeschyl., Hdt.+; inscr., pap., LXX, En., Philo, Joseph.) write in, record.
   1. lit. (Jos., Vi. 261) ἐγγράφειν εἰς τ. ἀριθμόν enroll

among the number Hs 9, 24, 4; cf. s 5, 3, 2 (Ps.-Pla., Axioch. 5 p. 336ε εἰς τ. ἐφήβους; Appian, Maced. 4 §2; Dit., Syll.³ 736, 163 ἐ. εἰς τοὺς πολεμάρχους; 858, 10). τὰ ὀνόματα ἐγγέγραπται ἐν τοῖς οὐρανοῖς the names are recorded in heaven Lk 10: 20; cf. ISm 5: 3. ἐγγραφήσονται εἰς τὰς βίβλους τῆς ζωῆς they will be inscribed in the books of life Hv 1, 3, 2; cf. m 8: 6 (Lucian, Philops. 38; Dit., Syll.³ 921, 97 ἐ. εἰς τὸ γραμματεῖον).

2. fig. write in (cf. schol. on Pla. 504ᴅ ἐ. ἐν τῷ πίνακι; Dit., Syll.³ 966, 38 ἐ. ἐν ταῖς στήλαις): ἐπιστολὴ ἐγγεγραμμένη ἐν ταῖς καρδίαις ἡμῶν a letter, written in our hearts 2 Cor 3: 2 (cf. Plut., Mor. 779ʙ; En. 103, 3; Jos., Ant. 4, 210 νόμους ... ταῖς ψυχαῖς ἐγγραφέντας); in the continuation vs. 3 ἐγγεγραμμένη οὐ μέλανι, ἀλλὰ πνεύματι θεοῦ, ἐγγρ. is surely a synonym of γράφω (as PLond. 358, 15 [c. 150 ᴀᴅ]; Herm. Wr. 13, 15; Nägeli 48) written not w. ink. but w. the Spirit of God. M-M.*

ἔγγυος, ον as adj. under good security, as noun ὁ ἐ. guarantee (X.+; inscr., pap.; Sir 29: 15f. Linguist. exx. and discussion of the subj. in JPartsch, Griech. Bürgschaftsrecht I '09, 105ff; 228ff; 281ff; LMitteis, Grundzüge d. Pap.-kunde '12, 264ff; JBehm, D. Begriff διαθήκη '12, 77; ELohmeyer, Diatheke '13, p. 145) κρείττονος διαθήκης ἔ. guar. of a better covenant Hb 7: 22. M-M.*

ἐγγύς adv. (Hom.+; pap., LXX); comp. ἐγγύτερον (X. et al.; Jos., Ant. 19, 217 [cf. C. Ap. 2, 224 ἐγγίω]); superl. ἔγγιστα (Antipho, Hippocr. et al.; inscr. [Bull. corr. hell. 18, 1894, p. 324 no. 2, 26; Dit., Or.]; BGU 69, 8; 759, 9; LXX; Joseph. [always, e.g. Bell. 1, 289, Ant. 4, 254]).

1. of space near, close to—a. w. gen. foll. (Hom.+; also Joseph. as a rule [Schmidt 379f]; Test. Dan 6: 11) ἐ. τοῦ Σαλίμ J 3: 23; ἐ. Ἰερουσαλήμ Lk 19: 11; J 11: 18; Ac 1: 12; ἐ. τῆς πόλεως J 19: 20; ἐ. τοῦ τόπου 6: 23; ἐ. τῆς ἐρήμου 11: 54; ἐ. ὑδάτων Hv 3, 2, 9; 3, 7, 3. W. gen. of the pers. Hs 8, 6, 5; 9, 6, 2; AP 20: 34.

b. w. dat. foll. (Il. 22, 453; X., Cyr. 2, 3, 2; al. in later writers as Polyb. 21, 28, 8; Dionys. Hal. 6, 52. Cf. Kühner-G. I 408; JObrecht, D. echte u. soziative Dativ bei Pausanias, Zürich Diss. '19, 14; Ps 33: 19; 144: 18; Jos., Ant. 1, 335; 7, 218) Ac 9: 38; 27: 8.

c. abs. ἐ. εἶναι be close by J 19: 42; IRo 10: 2; αἱ ἐγγὺς κῶμαι the neighboring villages Mk 1: 38 D (Appian, Iber. 42 §174 οἱ ἐγγὺς βάρβαροι; likew. Appian, Syr. 42 §220). αἱ ἔγγιστα ἐκκλησίαι the closest churches IPhld 10: 2; cf. Mk 6: 36 D οἱ ἔγγιστα ἀγροί (Dionys. Hal. 1, 22, 1 ἡ ἔγγιστα νῆσος; Ps.-Callisth. 2, 11, 6).

d. ἐ. γίνεσθαι come near (opp. μακρὰν εἶναι) Eph 2: 13. W. gen. (Vett. Val. 196, 28f) 2 Cl 18: 2; ἐ. τοῦ πλοίου γίνεσθαι J 6: 19; ἐ. ἔρχεσθαι (Theophanes [IX ᴀᴅ], Chron. 389, 12f de Boor ἐγγὺς σου ἐλθεῖν=come to you; BGU 814, 30f [III ᴀᴅ]) Hv 4, 1, 9 (JoachJeremias, Unknown Sayings of Jesus, '57, 85f quotes POxy. 1224, fgm. 2 recto 1, 4f ἐγγὺς ὑμῶν γ]ενήσεται).

2. of time near—a. of the future: καιρός Mt 26: 18; Rv 1: 3; 22: 10. Of summer (Herodas 3, 45 ὁ χειμὼν [winter] ἐγγύς) Mt 24: 32; Mk 13: 28; Lk 21: 30. Of a festival J 2: 13; 6: 4; 7: 2; 11: 55. Of the Kingdom Lk 21: 31. Of the Parousia Phil 4: 5; 1 Cl 21: 3. Of death Hs 8, 9, 4. ἐγγύτερον ἡμῶν ἡ σωτηρία, ἤ ... our salvation is nearer than ... Ro 13: 11. Abs. soon ἐ. τὸ ἔργον τελεσθήσεται will soon be completed Hs 9, 10, 2.

b. of the past ἔγγιστα a very short time ago 1 Cl 5: 1.

3. fig. (Vi. Aesopi I c. 6 p. 241, 7 ἐγγὺς ἡ γνώμη=his purpose is obvious) ἐ. σου τὸ ῥῆμά ἐστιν the word is close to you, explained by what follows: in your mouth and your

heart Ro 10: 8 (Dt 30: 14); κατάρας ἐ. close to being cursed=under a curse Hb 6: 8 (cf. Ael. Aristid. 26, 53 K.=14 p. 343 D.: ἀμήχανον καὶ κατάρας ἐγγύς); ἐ. ἀφανισμοῦ ready to disappear altogether 8: 13; οἱ ἐ. (opp. οἱ μακράν as Is 57: 19; Esth 9: 20; Da 9: 7 Theod.; Test. Napht. 4, 5) those who are near Eph 2: 17; ἐ. (εἶναι) be near of God Hv 2, 3, 4 (cf. Dio Chrys. 14[31], 87 τινὲς σφόδρα ἐγγὺς παρεστῶτες τοῖς θεοῖς); πάντα ἐ. αὐτῷ ἐστιν everything is near him (i.e., God) 1 Cl 27: 3; cf. IEph 15: 3; ἐ. μαχαίρας close to the sword (martyrdom) is close to God ISm 4: 2 (cf. Paroem. Gr. II p. 228, Aesop 7 ὁ ἐγγὺς Διός, ἐγγὺς κεραυνοῦ; Pla., Philebus 16ᴄ ἐγγυτέρω θεοῦ; X., Mem. 1, 6, 10; Pythag., Ep. 2; Crates, Ep. 11 ἐγγυτάτω θεοῦ; Lucian, Cyn. 12 οἱ ἔγγιστα θεοῖς; Wsd 6: 19). Agr 3 s.v. πῦρ 2; ἐ. ἐπὶ θύραις at (your) very door Mt 24: 33; Mk 13: 29. M-M. B. 867.**

ἐγεγόνει s. γίνομαι.

ἐγείρω fut. ἐγερῶ; 1 aor. ἤγειρα; pres. pass. ἐγείρομαι, imper. 2nd. sg. ἐγείρου, pl. ἐγείρεσθε; pf. pass. ἐγήγερμαι; 1 aor. ἠγέρθην; 1 fut. ἐγερθήσομαι (Bl-D. §101 and 73 app.; Rob. 1215) (Hom.+; inscr., pap., LXX, En., Philo, Joseph., Test. 12 Patr.).

1. active—a. trans. wake, rouse.

a. lit., of sleeping persons Mt 8: 25; Ac 12: 7.

β. fig. raise, help to rise of a pers. sitting down Ac 3: 7. Lying down Mk 1: 31; 9: 27. Stretched out Ac 10: 26. Fallen Mt 12: 11; 1 Cl 59: 4; Hv 3, 2, 4. Esp. of the sick raise up=restore to health Js 5: 15. Of the dead raise (Apollodor. [II ʙᴄ]: 244 fgm. 138a Jac., of Asclepius. Also schol. on Lucian p. 55, 23 Rabe; Sir 48: 5 ὁ ἐγείρας νεκρὸν ἐκ θανάτου; PGM 4, 195) Mt 10: 8; J 5: 21; Ac 26: 8. Of the raising of Jesus Ac 5: 30; 10: 40; 13: 37; 1 Cor 6: 14; 15: 15ff; 2 Cor 4: 14. More fully ἐ. τινὰ ἐκ νεκρῶν (mostly of Jesus' resurr.) J 12: 1, 9, 17; Ac 3: 15; 4: 10; 13: 30; Ro 4: 24; 8: 11; 10: 9; Gal 1: 1; Eph 1: 20; Col 2: 12; 1 Th 1: 10; Hb 11: 19; 1 Pt 1: 21; IMg 9: 3; Pol 2: 1f. ἀπὸ νεκρῶν ITr 9: 2. Of the raising of Christ's flesh ISm 7: 1.

γ. lift up ἔγειρον τ. λίθον lift up the stone, push the stone aside (Seleucus of Alex. [I ᴀᴅ]: no. 341 fgm. 4 Jac. in play, not at work) LJ 1: 5; LEWright, JBL 65, '46, 182; JoachJeremias, Unknown Sayings of Jesus, '57, 95–98; AFWalls, Vigiliae Christianae 16, '62, 71–6.—Raise κονιορτόν (Polyaenus 4, 19; 7, 44, 1) Hv 4, 1, 5 (Jos. Bell. 5, 471 speaks in the pass. of the dust that 'is raised').

δ. raise up, erect, restore of buildings (Dio Chrys. 11[12], 18; Aelian, N. A. 11, 10; Herodian 3, 15, 3; 8, 2, 5; Lucian, Pseudomant. 19; Anth. Pal. 9, 696; Dit., Or. 677, 3; 1 Esdr 5: 43; Sir 49: 13) the temple (ναόν: Appian, Bell. Civ. 1, 26 §120; Lucian, Sacr. 11; Jos., Ant. 15, 391; 20, 228) J 2: 19f. Sim. κέρας σωτηρίας a horn of salvation Lk 1: 69.

ε. fig. raise up, bring into being (Judg 2: 16, 18 ἤγειρε αὐτοῖς κύριος κριτάς; 3: 9, 15 σωτῆρα; Pr 10: 12; Jos., Ant. 8, 199) τέκνα τινί Mt 3: 9; Lk 3: 8. ἤγειρεν τὸν Δαυὶδ αὐτοῖς εἰς βασιλέα he gave them David as (their) king Ac 13: 22 (cf. Jos., Ant. 19, 295). W. double acc. and dat. of advantage vs. 23 v.l.; τὶ someth. (Theognis 1, 549 πόλεμον ἐγ.; Appian, Hann. 41 §177 θόρυβον; Nicol. Dam.: 90 fgm. 50 Jac. μάχην) cause θλῖψιν Phil 1: 17 (Lucian, Syr. Dea 18 πένθος τινί).

b. intr., only in imper., used as a formula: ἔγειρε get up!, come! (Eur., Iph. A. 624; Aristoph., Ran. 340; Aesop-mss. [Ursing 80]) Mt 9: 5f; Mk 2: 9 (v.l. ἐγείρου), 11; 3: 3; 10: 49; Lk 5: 23f; 6: 8; J 5: 8; Rv 11: 1. Awakening of the 'dead' (with καθεύδειν and ἐγείρειν associated in figurative use, as in Plut., Mor. 462) in Mk 5:41; Lk 8: 54 (v.l. ἐγείρου); Eph 5: 14 (MDibelius, Hdb. ad loc., but without Gnostic motif acc. to KGKuhn, NTS 7, '60/'61, 341–46; cf. PsSol 16: 1–4) parallels the usage in passages cited in 1a, b above and 2 b, c below.

2. *Passive intr.—a.* *wake up, awaken* fr. sleep PStrassb. 100, 15 [II BC] ἐγερθεὶς ἐκάλουν βοηθούς) Mt 1: 24; 25: 7; Mk 4: 27; J 11: 12 𝔓⁷⁵. Fig. ἐξ ὕπνου ἐγερθῆναι *awaken fr. sleep* (i.e., thoughtless indolence) Ro 13: 11 (cf. Epict. 2, 20, 15 ἐ. ἐκ τῶν ὕπνων, fr. the sleep of carelessness).

b. *rise, get up* of those who have awakened Mt 2: 13f, 20f; 8: 26; Lk 11: 8; who were sitting down (Ep. Arist. 94) Mt 9: 19; Lk 13: 25; J 11: 29; Hv 1, 4, 1; kneeling 2, 1, 3; of the sick Mt 8: 15; 9: 7; of those called back to life (cf. 4 Km 4: 31) Mt 9: 25; Lk 7: 14. ἐκ τοῦ δείπνου *rise from the table* J 13: 4; of one who has fallen Ac 9: 8 (on ἀπὸ τ. γῆς cf. 2 Km 12: 17; Ps 112: 7).

c. *be raised, rise* (Is 26: 19; cf. 4 Km 4: 31) of one who has died Lk 16: 30 v.l. (𝔓⁷⁵); but esp. of Christ ἐκ νεκρῶν Mk 6: 14; Lk 9: 7; J 2: 22; 21: 14; Ro 6: 4, 9; 8: 34; 1 Cor 15: 12, 20; 2 Ti 2: 8. For this ἀπὸ τῶν νεκρῶν Mt 14: 2; 27: 64; 28: 7; ITr 9: 2. Abs. Mt 11: 5; 16: 21; 17: 23; 26: 32; 27: 52; 28: 6; Mk 6: 16; 12: 26; 14: 28 al.—For lit., s. on ἀνάστασις 2, end.

d. *rise in arms,* of nations (Jer 6: 22 v.l.) ἐ. ἐπί τινα *against someone* one nation against another Mt 24: 7; Mk 13: 8; Lk 21: 10 (for ἐπί τινα cf. Appian, Liby. 68 §307; Jer 27: 9; Jos., Ant. 8, 199).

e. *appear* of prophets Mt 11: 11; Lk 7: 16; J 7: 52; of false prophets Mt 24: 11, 24; Mk 13: 22. Of accusers in court (w. ἐν τῇ κρίσει; cf. ἀνίστημι 2c) Mt 12: 42; Lk 11: 31 (on omission of ἐν τῇ κρίσει in ms. D, see MBlack, An Aramaic Approach³, '67, 134).

f. imper. ἐγείρου *get up!* Mk 2: 9 v.l.; Lk 8: 54 v.l.; ἐγείρεσθε, ἄγωμεν *get up! let us be going* Mt 26: 46; Mk 14: 42; J 14: 31. M-M. B. 271; 670.

ἔγερσις, εως, ἡ (Pre-Socr.+; LXX; Ep. Arist. 160) *resurrection,* lit. 'awakening' of a dead person (so Menander of Ephesus in Jos., Ant. 8, 146=C. Ap. 1, 119; PGM 13, 277 ἔγερσις σώματος νεκροῦ) of Jesus Mt 27: 53; PK 4 p. 15, 35. M-M.*

ἐγκάθετος, ον (Hyperid., fgm. 56; Demosth., Ep. 3, 34; Polyb. 3, 15, 1; Ps.-Pla., Axioch. 368E; Jos., Bell. 2, 27; 6, 286; Job 31: 9) *hired to lie in wait;* subst. ἐγκάθετοι *spies* Lk 20: 20.*

ἐγκάθημαι (Aristoph., X.+; Herm. Wr. 16, 14; LXX) *lie couched* εἴς τι (Judg 2: 2) *in someth.* fig., of grief in the heart Hm 10, 3, 3 (Polyb. 2, 23, 7 ἐγκαθημένου τ. ψυχαῖς τοῦ φόβου).*

ἐγκαίνια, ίων, τά (Bl-D. §141, 3; 2 Esdr [Ezra] 6: 16f; 22[Neh 12]; 27; Da 3: 2 Theod.; Philo, Congr. Erud. Gr. 114) *the festival of Rededication* J 10: 22, known also as Hanukkah and the Feast of Lights, beg. the 25th of Chislev (roughly=November-December) to commemorate the purification and rededication of the temple by Judas Maccabaeus on that date in 165 BC. Cf. 1 Macc 4: 36–9 (56 ὁ ἐγκαινισμὸς τ. θυσιαστηρίου; vss. 36, 54; 5: 1 ἐγκαινίζειν). 2 Macc 10: 1–8; Jos., Ant. 12, 316ff; Schürer I⁴ 208f w. lit.; ThSchärf, D. gottesdienstl. Jahr d. Juden '02, 92–6; Billerb. II 539–41.*

ἐγκαινίζω 1 aor. ἐνεκαίνισα; pf. pass. ἐγκεκαίνισμαι (Pollux 1, 11; LXX; perh. UPZ 185 II, 6 [II BC], where it is restored; Ode of Solomon 11, 11).

1. *renew* (1 Km 11: 14) πνεῦμα ἐ. a spirit 1 Cl 18: 10 (Ps 50: 12); ἐ. ὁδόν *open a way* Hb 10: 20.

2. *inaugurate, dedicate* w. solemn rites (IG XII 5, 712, 58; Dt 20: 5; 3 Km 8: 63; 2 Ch 7: 5) of a covenant Hb 9: 18. M-M. s.v. ἐν-.*

ἐγκακέω 1 aor. ἐνεκάκησα (Polyb. 4, 19, 10; BGU 1043, 3; Sym., Gen 27: 46; Num 21: 5; Is 7: 16; Theod. Pr 3: 11).—**1.** *become weary, tired* w. ptc. foll. (Bl-D. §414, 2) 2 Th 3: 13; cf. Gal 6: 9. Abs. Lk 18: 1.—**2.** *lose heart, despair* 2 Cor 4: 1, 16; Eph 3: 13; *be afraid,* of women in child-birth 2 Cl 2: 2. (In all NT pass. t.r. has ἐκκακέω, q.v.). M-M. s.v. ἐν-.*

ἐγκαλέω imper. 3 pl. ἐγκαλείτωσαν; impf. ἐνεκάλουν; fut. ἐγκαλέσω (Soph., X., Pla.+; inscr., pap., LXX, Joseph.). Legal t.t. *accuse, bring charges against* τινί (class.; PEleph. 1, 7; Sir 46: 19; Wsd 12: 12; Jos., C. Ap. 2, 138) *someone* Ac 19: 38 (ἐ. ἀλλήλοις as PHib. 96 [s. below]; Jos., Ant. 3, 213); 23: 28; for this, ἐ. κατά τινος Ro 8: 33. Pass. *περί τινος because of someth.* (the act. Diod. S. 11, 83, 3; UPZ 63, 9 [158 BC]; PHamb. 25, 3; Jos., Ant. 12, 172) περὶ ζητημάτων τοῦ νόμου *because of questions concerning the law* Ac 23: 29; *because of a hope* 26: 7. τινός *because of someth.* (non-class.; Plut., Aristid. 10, 7; Cass. Dio 58, 4 ἀσεβείας ἐς τὸν Τιβέριον ἐγκληθείς; Jos., Ant. 5, 56) ἐ. στάσεως 19: 40; περὶ πάντων ὧν ἐγκαλοῦμαι *on all the charges made against me* 26: 2 (PHib. 96, 6; 22 [259 BC] περὶ ὧν ἐνεκάλεσαν ἀλλήλοις). M-M. B. 1439.*

ἐγκάρδια, ίων, τά from the adj. ἐγκάρδιος, ον *found in the heart* (Democr.+; Philo, Spec. Leg. 1, 6) *what is in the heart* 2 Cl 9: 9 (cf. Philod., παρρ. fgm. 28, 6 p. 14 Ol. τάγκ. τις ἐρεῖ; Syntipas p. 10, 1). But the correct rdg. is perh. τὰ ἐν καρδίᾳ (2 Ch 32: 31; Dt 8: 2; 1 Km 9: 19 al.).*

ἔγκαρπος, ον (Soph., Pla.+; PTebt. 815, 6; 55 [III BC]; Jer 38: 12) *fruitful* fig. (Ael. Aristid. 46 p. 404 D.: λόγος ἔ.; Maximus Tyr. 34, 4b βίος) ἀνάλυσις a *fruitful departure* 1 Cl 44: 5; μνεία 56: 1.*

ἔγκατα, άτων, τά (Hom.+; Theocr. 22, 202; Pollux 6, 51) *inmost parts* 1 Cl 18: 10 (Ps 50: 12).*

ἐγκατάλειμμα, ατος, τό (Aristot., fgm. 13 Rose; PPetr. II 4[11], 2 [255/4 BC]; LXX; Test. Sim. 6: 3) *something left* as a *remnant* or *posterity* 1 Cl 14: 5 (Ps 36: 37).*

ἐγκαταλείπω impf. ἐγκατέλειπον; fut. ἐγκαταλείψω; 2 aor. ἐγκατέλιπον, subj. ἐγκαταλίπω; perf. pass. inf. ἐγκαταλελεῖφθαι; 1 aor. pass. ἐγκατελείφθην; 1 fut. ἐγκαταλειφθήσομαι (Hes., Hdt.+; inscr., pap., LXX; En. 99, 5; Joseph.).

1. *leave behind* Ro 9: 29 (Is 1: 9.—Cf. Lucian, Dial. Deor. 25, 1 εἰ μὴ ἐγὼ . . . , οὐδὲ λείψανον ἀνθρώπων ἐπέμεινεν ἄν).

2. *forsake, abandon, desert* (Socrat., Ep. 14, 10 of the soul aband. the body; Dit., Syll.³ 364, 89; 97; 495, 135 [III BC]; UPZ 71, 8 [152 BC]; POxy. 281, 21; PTebt. 27, 16; LXX) τινά *someone* (X., Cyr. 8, 8, 4; Polyb. 3, 40, 7; Appian, Mithrid. 105 §493 desert one who is in danger; Jos., Vi. 205) 2 Ti 4: 10, 16; assembling Hb 10: 25 (*do or carry on someth. in a negligent manner* is also poss. Diod. S. 15, 9, 1 τὴν πολιορκίαν; Wilcken, Chrest. 72, 8ff μηδένα δὲ τῶν ἱερέων ἢ ἱερωμένων ἐγκαταλελοιπέναι τὰς θρησκείας. Of feeling or being forsaken by God (Test. Jos. 2: 4) Mt 27: 46; Mk 15: 34 (both Ps 21: 2; cf. Billerb. II 574–80; GDalman, Jesus-Jeshua [tr. PLevertoff] '29, 204–7; WHasenzahl, D. Gottverlassenh. des Christus . . . u. d. christolog. Verständnis des griech. Psalters '37; FWDanker, ZNW 61, '70, 48–69 [lit.]); 2 Cor 4: 9; Hb 13: 5 (Josh 1: 5; Dt 31: 6, 8; 1 Ch 28: 20); B 4: 14;

Hm 9: 2 (as Dt 31: 6, 8); s 2: 9; 1 Cl 11: 1; *abandon* the fountain of life B 11: 2 (Jer 2: 13); God's commandments D 4: 13; B 19: 2; ἐ. τὴν ἀγάπην *forsake love* 1 Cl 33: 1 (Dio Chrys. 57[74], 8 τ. φιλίαν; Jos., Ant. 2, 40 τ. ἀρετήν).

3. *leave* (Menand., Epitr. 550 τούτοις μή μ' ἐγκαταλίπῃς), *allow to remain* (cf. Demosth. 57, 58) τὴν ψυχὴν εἰς ᾅδην *the soul in Hades* Ac 2: 27 (Ps 15: 10), 31 (for ἐ. τινὰ εἰς cf. PsSol 2: 7). M-M.*

ἐγκαταστηρίζω 1 aor. ἐγκατεστήριξα (Cornutus 6 p. 7, 14) *establish* τί τινι the Logos in the hearts Dg 7: 2.*

ἐγκατασφραγίζω 1 aor. pass. ἐγκατεσφραγίσθην *seal* τί εἴς τι the covenant in the hearts B 4: 8 (cf. FJDölger, Sphragis '11, 108f; AvStromberg, Taufe [s. βαπτίζω, end] '13, 87).*

ἐγκατοικέω (Eur.; Hdt. 4, 204; Lycophron v. 1204; Polyb. 18, 26, 13; Jos., C. Ap. 1, 296) *live, dwell* ἐν αὐτοῖς *among them* 2 Pt 2: 8. Fig. of love ἐν ὑμῖν B 1: 4.*

ἐγκαυχάομαι (Aesop., Fab. 230 Halm; schol. to Lucian p. 166, 18 Rabe; Ps 51: 3; 73: 4; 96: 7; 105: 47; Test. Jud. 13: 3) *boast* ἔν τινι (so in all the Ps-passages above) *of someone* 2 Th 1: 4. ἐν ἀλαζονείᾳ *in arrogance* 1 Cl 21: 5. M-M. s.v. ἐν-.*

ἔγκειμαι (Hes.+; Hdt., inscr., pap., LXX, Joseph.) *insist, warn urgently* (so Herodas 5, 3; Plut., Fab. Max. 9, 2; Lucian, Demon. 12; Jos., Vi. 19, Ant. 15, 31) MPol 9: 3.— ITr 12: 3 v.l. Funk (for περίκειμαι).*

ἐγκεντρίζω 1 aor. ἐνεκέντρισα, pass. ἐνεκεντρίσθην; 1 fut. pass. ἐγκεντρισθήσομαι *graft* of trees (so Aristot., De Plant. 6 p. 820b, 34 al.; Theophr., Hist. Pl. 2, 2, 5; M. Ant. 11, 8, 6. W. the mng. 'sting' Wsd 16: 11) εἴς τι *on* someth. Ro 11: 24. For this, τινί vs. 24. Abs. vss. 19, 23. ἐ. ἐν αὐτοῖς *graft in among them* vs. 17. M-M. s.v. ἐν-.*

ἐγκεράννυμι perf. pass. ptc. ἐγκεκραμένος (Hom.+; Ps.-Lucian, Amor. 32) *mix*, pass. *be united* τινί w. someone IEph 5: 1.*

ἐγκλείω perf. pass. ἐγκέκλεισμαι (Soph., Hdt.+; pap.; Ezk 3: 24; 2 Macc 5: 8) *lock up, shut up, enclose* τινά τινι Dg 2: 7; 6: 7; 7: 2. For this τινὰ ἔν τινι (Jos., Ant. 8, 255; 13, 221) Lk 3: 20 D; *keep within bounds* 1 Cl 33: 3.*

ἔγκλημα, τος, τό (Soph., Thu.+; inscr., pap., Joseph.) *charge, accusation.*

1. legal t.t. (Appian, Bell. Civ. 1, 96 §446; Jos., Bell. 7, 450) ἀπολογία περὶ τοῦ ἐ. *defense against the accusation* Ac 25: 16; ἐ. ἄξιον θανάτου ἢ δεσμῶν *a charge deserving death or imprisonment* 23: 29.

2. gener. *reproach* (Diod. S. 20, 33, 7; Heraclit. Sto. 21 p. 31, 13; 25 p. 39, 15; Ael. Aristid. 47, 67 K.=23 p. 462 D.; Jos., Ant. 2, 120; C. Ap. 2, 182) φυλάσσεσθαι τὰ ἐ. *guard against reproaches* ITr 2: 3.—Ac 23: 24 v.l. M-M.*

ἐγκομβόομαι 1 aor. ἐνεκομβωσάμην *put* or *tie* someth. *on oneself* (Apollod. of Carystus [IV BC] ἐ. τὴν ἐπωμίδα [tunic]: Com. Att. fgm. Kock III 281 no. 4; cf. ἐγκόμβωμα=any garment which is tied on) ἀλλήλοις τ. ταπεινοφροσύνην ἐγκομβώσασθε *in your relations w. each other clothe yourselves w. humility* 1 Pt 5: 5 (EGSelwyn, 1 Pt, '46 ad loc.). M-M.*

ἐγκοπή, ῆς, ἡ *hindrance* (so Heraclitus 131; Diod. S. 1, 32, 8; Dionys. Hal., Comp. Verb. 22; Περὶ ὕψους 41, 3; Vett. Val. Index) ἐγκοπὴν (v.l. ἐκκοπὴν) διδόναι τινί *cause a hindrance to someth.* 1 Cor 9: 12.*

ἐγκόπτω 1 aor. ἐνέκοψα; impf. pass. ἐνεκοπτόμην (Hippocr. et al., inscr., pap.; Jos., Bell. 1, 629; 6, 111) *hinder, thwart* (so Hesychius: ἐμποδίζω, διακωλύω; Polyb. 23, 1, 12; M. Ant. 11, 1, 2; PAlex, 4, 3 [=Witkowski p. 51 and Sb 4305]) in NT w. the acc. (Bl-D. §152, 4 app.) τίς ὑμᾶς ἐνέκοψεν; foll. by inf. w. μή as neg. (Bl-D. §429; Rob. 1094) *who hindered you?* Gal 5: 7; cf. 1 Th 2: 18. εἰς τὸ μὴ ἐγκόπτεσθαι τὰς προσευχὰς ὑμῶν *in order that your prayers may not be hindered* 1 Pt 3: 7. ἐνεκοπτόμην τὰ πολλά w. gen. of the inf. foll. (Bl-D. §400, 4) *I have so often been prevented* Ro 15: 22.—ἵνα μὴ ἐπὶ πλεῖόν σε ἐγκόπτω Ac 24: 4 is understood by Syr. and Armen. versions to mean *in order not to weary you any further;* cf. ἔγκοπος *weary* Diog. L. 4, 50; LXX; and ἔγκοπον ποιεῖν *to weary* Job 19: 2; Is 43: 23. But *delay, detain* is also poss.—GStählin, TW III 855-7. M-M. B. 1355.*

ἐγκράτεια, είας, ἡ (X., Pla.+; Diod. S. 10, 5, 2; Epict. 2, 20, 13; Vett. Val. Index; Herm. Wr. 13, 9; PFay. 20, 21; Sir 18: 29 (v.l.); 4 Macc 5: 34; Ep. Arist. 278; Philo; Essenes in Jos., Bell. 2, 120; 138, and a prophet Ant. 8, 235; Test. 12 Patr.) *self-control* (esp. w. ref. to matters of sex; cf. Simplicius in Epict. p. 117, 18; 123, 14; Test. Napht. 8: 8) 2 Cl 15: 1. In a list of virtues Gal 5: 23. W. other virtues (Lucian, Demosth. Enc. 40; PFay. very oft.) 1 Cl 35: 2; 62: 2; 64; w. δικαιοσύνη Ac 24: 25; w. γνῶσις and ὑπομονή 2 Pt 1: 6; w. μακροθυμία B 2: 2; w. ἁπλότης Hv 2, 3, 2; w. πίστις and φόβος m 6, 1, 1. ἀγαπᾶν ἐν πάσῃ ἐ. *in all chastity* Pol 4: 2; ἐ. διπλῆ Hm 8: 1. Personified as a virtue v 3, 8, 4; 7; s 9, 15, 2. Bestowed by God 1 Cl 38: 2.—WGrundmann, TW II 338-40. M-M.*

ἐγκρατεύομαι (Pythag.; Aristot., Eth. Eud. 2, 7 p. 1223b, 13 and later writers; Gen 43: 31) mid. dep. *control oneself, abstain* fr. someth. ἀπὸ παντὸς πονηροῦ πράγματος *from every evil deed* Hs 5, 1, 5; cf. m 8: 1ff, where ἐ. takes the acc., gen. (Sir 19: 6 v.l.), ἀπό, ἐπί, and the inf. after it (Bl-D. §154). Esp. of sexual continence 1 Cor 7: 9; 1 Cl 30: 3. As a consequence of the fear of God Hm 1: 2. W. acc. of content (Abel §43f, 4) πάντα ἐ. *exercise self-control in all respects* of athletes 1 Cor 9: 25.—LBouvet, L'ascèse dans S. Paul, Diss. Lyon '36; MHansen, Het ascetisme en Pl's verkondiging van het nieuwe leven '38. M-M.*

ἐγκρατής, ές (Pre-Socr.+; trag., Hdt., inscr., pap., LXX, Jos., Vi. 396) *self-controlled, disciplined* abs. (as Ps.-Pla., Def. 415D; Aristot., Eth. Nic. 7, 4 p. 1146b, 10ff; Wsd 8: 21; Sir 26: 15; Philo, de Jos. 54) w. δίκαιος and ὅσιος Tit 1: 8; cf. 2 Cl 4: 3; Pol 5: 2. As an epithet: Ἑρμᾶς ὁ ἐ. Hv 1, 2, 4. M-M.*

ἐγκρίνω 1 aor. ἐνέκρινα, inf. ἐγκρῖναι (Eur.+; Pla., X.; CIG II 2715a, 11 ἐ. εἰς τοὺς ἐφήβους; IG VII 29, 6; Ep. Arist. 228; Jos., Bell. 2, 138) *to class* τινά τινι someone w. someone (Synes., Ep. 105 p. 250c) 2 Cor 10: 12 (in a play on words w. συγκρῖναι *compare*). M-M. s.v. ἐν-.*

ἐγκρίς, ίδος, ἡ (Stesichorus [VII/VI BC] 2; Pherecrates [V BC] 83; LXX) *pancake, fritter* ἐ. ἐν ἐλαίῳ (cf. Athen. 14 p. 645E ἐγκρίδες πεμμάτιον ἑψόμενον ἐν ἐλαίῳ κ. μετὰ τοῦτο μελιττούμενον; Num 11: 8; Ex 16: 31; Philo, Det. Pot. Insid. 118) *a pancake baked in oil* of the food of John the Baptist (for ἀκρίδες) GEb 2.*

ἐγκρύπτω 1 aor. ἐνέκρυψα (Hom.+; LXX; Jos., Ant. 9, 142) *hide* τί εἴς τι (Ps.-Apollod., Bibl. 1, 5, 1, 4 εἰς πῦρ) *put someth. into someth.* (Ps.-Lucian, Asin. 31; PMich. 154 I 23) Mt 13: 33; Lk 13: 21 𝔓⁷⁵ et al.*

ἔγκυος, ον (Hdt.+; Dit., Syll.³ 1168, 12; 14; 17; BGU

1104, 21; POxy. 267, 20; 1273, 33; Sir 42: 10; Philo, Spec. Leg. 3, 108; Jos., Ant. 4, 278, C. Ap. 2, 245) *pregnant* Lk 2: 5. M-M. s.v. ἐν -. B. 283.*

ἐγκύπτω perf. ἐγκέκυφα (Hdt.+; LXX) *look closely* εἴς τι *into someth.* (Hdt. 7, 152; Bel 40) εἰς ἐπιστολάς Pol 3: 2 (of looking at a piece of lit. PLond. 1356, 35; 1359, 4). Fig. *gain an insight into, study* someth. (Ep. Arist. 140): divine knowledge 1 Cl 40: 1; holy scriptures 45: 2; oracles of God 53: 1; cf. 62: 3.*

ἔγνωκα, ἔγνων, ἔγνωσμαι s. γινώσκω.

ἐγχρίω 1 aor. ἐνέχρισα, inf. ἐγχρῖσαι (v.l. ἔγχρισαι aor. mid. imper.) *rub on* (so Duris [IV/III BC] et al.; LXX) τί *someth.* (on) the eyes (PGM 7, 336 ἔνχριε [anoint] τοὺς ὀφθαλμούς σου; 5, 64; Jer 4: 30; cf. Tob 6: 9; 11: 8) Rv 3: 18. M-M.*

ἐγχώριος, ον (Pind., Hdt.+; pap., LXX; Jos., C. Ap. 1, 314) *belonging to the country* ἔθη local *customs* Dg 5: 4.*

ἐγώ (Hom.+; inscr., pap., LXX, En., Ep. Arist., Philo, Joseph.) pers. pron. of the first pers. ἐμοῦ (μου), ἐμοί (μοι), ἐμέ (με); pl. ἡμεῖς, ἡμῶν, ἡμῖν, ἡμᾶς: *I*, used w. a verb to emphasize the pers.: ἐγὼ ἀποστέλλω Mt 10: 16; ἐγὼ λέγω 21: 27; ἐγὼ ἐπιτάσσω σοι Mk 9: 25; ἐγὼ καταλύσω 14: 58. Esp. in the antitheses of the Sermon on the Mount Mt 5: 22-44 (cf. ELohse, JoachJeremias-Festschr., '70, 189-203 [rabb.]). ἐγώ εἰμι *it is I* (in contrast to others) Mt 14: 27; Lk 24: 39; J 6: 20; *I am the man* 9: 9; w. strong emphasis: *I am he* (i.e., the Messiah) Mk 13: 6; Lk 21: 8; J 8: 24, 28. For the solemn I-style in J, esp. 10: 7-14, cf. the Isis inscr. in Diod. S. 1, 27, 4; IG XII, V 1 no. 14; PGM 5, 145ff (all three in Dssm., LO 109-12 [LAE 134ff]; further material there 109, 3 and in Hdb., excur. on J 8: 12. S. WPeek, D. Isishymnos v. Andros '30; GPWetter, 'Ich bin es': StKr 88, '15, 224-38; KZickendraht, ibid. 94, '22, 162-8; ESchweizer, Ego Eimi '39; WManson, JTS 48, '47, 137-45; HSahlin, Zur Typologie des Joh-evangeliums '50, 63-71; Bultmann 167, 2; GMacRae, CFDMoule-Festschr., '70, 122-34 [Gnostics]). —ἰδοὺ ἐγώ (oft. LXX; cf. PKatz, Philo's Bible '50, 75ff) Mt 23: 34; 28: 20; Mk 1: 2 v.l. (Mal 3: 1); Lk 24: 49. ἰδοὺ ἐγώ, κύριε *here I am, Lord* Ac 9: 10 (cf. Gen 22: 1; 27: 1 al.).—ἐγώ *I* (will), or *yes* (Judg 13: 11; cf. Epict. 2, 12, 18 ἔγωγε) Mt 21: 29.—In the gospel mss. ἐ. is also found without special emphasis, either as a Hebraism, Mk 12: 26 (Ex 3: 6); J 10: 34 (Ps 81: 6), or as a copyist's addition (Bl-D. §277, 2 app.).—On the interchange of pl. and sg. (cf. Apollon. Rhod. 3, 784 ἄμμι [=ἡμῖν], on which the scholion reads: ἀντὶ ἐνικοῦ [=singular] τοῦ ἐμοὶ κεῖται τὸ ἄμμι; 3, 1111; Appian, Bell. Civ. 3, 18 §67 ἡμῖν=to me. Likew. 3, 48 §196 ἡμῖν in the words of Octavian; 3, 38 §152 μετεβάλομεν=I; Jos., Ant. 2, 68) s. Mlt. 86f, esp. in Paul, s. Bl-D. §280; Rob. 406f; KDick, D. schriftstellerische Pl. b. Pls. '00; EHAskwith, Exp. 8th Ser. I '11, 149-59; EvDobschütz, Wir u. Ich b. Pls: ZsystTh 10, '33, 251-77; WFLofthouse, ET 64, '52f, 241-5; ADRogers, ibid. 77, '66, 339f. For J, s. AvHarnack, Das 'Wir' in den joh. Schriften: SAB '23, 96-113.—FSlotty, Der sog. Pl. modestiae: IndogF 44, '27, 155-90; UHolzmeister, De 'plurali categoriae' in NT a Patribus adhibito: Biblica 14, '33, 68-95.—In the oblique cases the longer forms ἐμοῦ, ἐμοί, ἐμέ are used as a rule where the main emphasis lies on the pron. ὁ ἀκούων ὑμῶν, ἐμοῦ ἀκούει Lk 10: 16; τῆς πίστεως ὑμῶν τε καὶ ἐμοῦ Ro 1: 12 al., where the emphasis is suggested by the position of the pron. The enclit. forms occur where the main emphasis lies on the noun or verb οὐκ ἔστιν μου ἄξιος Mt 10: 37; τίς μου

ἥψατο; Mk 5: 31; ἀπαγγείλατέ μοι Mt 2: 8 and oft. With prep. (Mayser 302f) the enclit. forms are used only in the case of ἔμπροσθεν and ὀπίσω, somet. ἐνώπιον (Ac 10: 30; but cf. Lk 4: 7 ἐ. ἐμοῦ), as well as w. πρός w. acc. after verbs of motion (δεῦτε πρός με Mt 11: 28; cf. 3: 14; ἐρχέσθω πρός με J 7: 37; ἀπεσταλμένοι πρός με Ac 11: 11 al.). Only the enclit. forms are used as substitutes for the possessive adj. ὁ λαός μου *my people* Mt 2: 6; μενεῖτε ἐν τῇ ἀγάπῃ μου *you will remain in my love*, i.e., make it possible for me to continue to love you J 15: 10. μου stands as objective gen. μιμηταί μου γίνεσθε *become imitators of me* 1 Cor 4: 16.—The expr. τί ἐμοὶ καὶ σοί; is Hebraistic (= מַה־לִּי וָלָךְ), but it also made its way into colloq. Gk. (cf. Epict. 1, 22, 15; 1, 27, 13; 2, 19, 19; 1, 1, 16; ESchwartz, GGN '08, p. 511, 3; DCHesseling: Donum natalicium Schrijnen '29, 665-8; FCBurkitt, JTS 13, '12, 594f; CLattey, ibid. 20, '19, 335f); it may be rendered *what have I to do w. you? what have we in common? leave me alone! never mind!* It serves to refuse a request or invitation (2 Km 16: 10; 19: 23; 4 Km 3: 13) J 2: 4 (cf. PGächter, ZkTh 55, '31, 351-402. Differently JDMDerrett, Law in the NT, '70, 238-42.—Apparent indifference toward close relatives compared with the things of God, as Epict. 3, 3, 5 οὐδέν ἐμοὶ καὶ τῷ πατρί, ἀλλὰ τῷ ἀγαθῷ) and as a protest against hostile measures (Judg 11: 12; 3 Km 17: 18; 2 Ch 35: 21; 1 Esdr 1: 24) Mk 5: 7; Lk 8: 28; likew. τί ἡμῖν κ. σοί; (s. τίς 1bε) Mt 8: 29; Mk 1: 24; Lk 4: 34 (cf. OBauernfeind, D. Worte d. Dämonen im Mk '27).—On the 'I' Ro 7: 7ff cf. WGKümmel, Rö 7 u. d. Bekehrung des Pls '29; RBultmann: Imago Dei '32, 53-62. —On the whole word, EStauffer, TW II 341-60. M-M.

ἐδαφίζω Att. fut. ἐδαφιῶ (Aristot.+; inscr., LXX) *dash to the ground* (Ps 136: 9; Hos 10: 14; 14: 1 al.) and of a city *raze to the ground* (Is 3: 26) both mngs. at once Lk 19: 44. M-M.*

ἔδαφος, ους, τό (Hom.+; inscr., pap., LXX, En., Ep. Arist.; Philo, Aet. M. 129; Test. Levi 16, 4; Joseph.; Sib. Or. 3, 503) *ground* πίπτειν εἰς τὸ ἔ. (4 Macc 6: 7; cf. Jos., Ant. 8, 119; BGU 1253, 5 ῥίψαντες ἐπὶ τὸ ἔ.) *fall to the ground* Ac 22: 7. M-M. B. 17f; 471.*

ἔδεσμα, ατος, τό (Pla. et al.; Jos., Ant. 1, 43) *food* in our lit. only pl. (as Batr. 31; X., Hiero 1, 23; Dit., Or. 665, 59; LXX; Test. 12 Patr.) Hm 5, 2, 2; 6, 2, 5; 8: 3; 12, 2, 1; s 5, 2, 9ff; 5, 3, 7; 5, 5, 3. μὴ ἔχειν ἐδέσματα *have nothing to eat* v 3, 9, 3.*

ἔδομαι s. ἐσθίω.

ἑδράζω 1 aor. ἥδρασα; perf. pass. ptc. ἡδρασμένος (Simias Rhod. [III BC] 20, 1 p. 72 HFränkel; Dionys. Hal., Comp. Verb. 6; Heliod. 9, 25; Anth. Pal. 15, 24, 1; Herm. Wr. 5, 4; LXX) *establish, fix, settle*; fig. ἐ. ἐπὶ τὸν τοῦ βουλήματος θεμέλιον *fix* (someth.) *upon the foundation of his will* 1 Cl 33: 3; τὰ γενόμενα ἐ. *establish what exists* 60: 1. Pass. (Callixenus [III BC] in Athen. 5 p. 204D; Dio Chrys. 1, 78 ἡδρασμένος) ἐν ὁμονοίᾳ θεοῦ *established in godly harmony* IPhil. inscr.; ἐν ἀγάπῃ ISm 1: 1; πίστει *in faith* 13: 2; γνώμῃ ἡ. ὡς ἐπὶ πέτραν *attitude founded as if upon a rock* IPol 1: 1 (cf. Sir 22: 17).*

ἑδραῖος, (αία,) αῖον *firm, steadfast* (so Eur., Pla.; Vett. Val. 9, 15; PStrassb. 40, 24; Sym.) ἐ. γίνεσθαι *be firm* 1 Cor 15: 58; ἑστηκέναι ἐ. *stand firm* (Herm. Wr. 2, 7) 7: 37; cf. IPol 3: 1. W. τεθεμελιωμένος Col 1: 23; ἐ. τῇ πίστει *steadfast in the faith* 1 Pt 5: 9 𝔓⁷²; IEph 10: 2. M-M.*

ἑδραίωμα, ατος, τό (only in Christian wr.) *foundation*, perh. *mainstay*, fig. ἑ. τῆς ἀληθείας 1 Ti 3: 15. M-M.*

ἔδραμον s. τρέχω.

Ἐζεκίας, ου, ὁ *Hezekiah*, in the genealogy of Jesus Mt 1: 9f (1 Ch 3: 13; 4 Km 18: 1ff; 20: 1ff; Is 1: 1; 38: 1ff; Joseph.); Lk 3: 23ff D (here the gen. is Ἐζεκία).*

ἔζην s. ζάω.

ἐθελο-. Compounds with ἐθελο- can mean:

1. to be or do someth. designedly or on purpose (ἐθελο-δουλεία, -έω, -ος; ἐθελοκακέω; ἐθελουργία, -έω etc.).

2. to wish to be or do someth. that a person is not or cannot do, so that it remains a wish and nothing more (ἐθελοπρόξενος Thu. 3, 70, 3=represent oneself as a πρόξ. and wish to regulate other people's affairs without the proper authority.—ἐθελοφιλόσοφος Etym. Magn. p. 722, 17=one who wants to be a phil. but is not.—ἐθελο-κωφέω=be unwilling to hear, pretend to be deaf). The second mng. is of value for our lit.; s. the following two entries.

ἐθελοδιδάσκαλος, ου, ὁ *a volunteer teacher* in contrast to one authorized by the church Hs 9, 22, 2.*

ἐθελοθρησκία, ας, ἡ (Hesychius; Suidas ἐθελοθρησκεῖ: ἰδίῳ θελήματι σέβει τὸ δοκοῦν=by his own volition he worships what seems best; JFSchleusner, Nov. Lexicon in NT, 1829 s.v.—A Christian formation; Nägeli 51) *self-made religion*, perh. *would-be religion* Col 2: 23. (Bl-D. §118, 2; Mlt.-H. 290; BReicke, Studia Theologica 6, '52, 45f). M-M.*

ἐθέλω Dg 10: 6 s. θέλω.

ἐθέμην, ἔθηκα s. τίθημι.

ἐθίζω perf. pass. ptc. εἰθισμένος (Eur., Thu.+; inscr., pap., LXX; Philo, e.g. Mos. 2, 205; Jos., Ant. 11, 16, C. Ap. 1, 225) *accustom* κατὰ τὸ εἰθισμένον τοῦ νόμου *acc. to the custom of* (i.e., required by) *the law* Lk 2: 27 (BGU 1073, 12 κατὰ τὰ εἰθισμένα). M-M.*

ἐθνάρχης, ου, ὁ *ethnarch*, a title used w. var. mngs. (Strabo 17, 1, 13; Ps.-Lucian, Macrob. 17; Dit., Or. 616= στρατηγὸς νομάδων; epitaph in Dschize: ZDPV 20, 1897, 135; coins [Ztschr. f. Numismatik 35, '03, 197ff]; 1 Macc 14: 47; 15: 1, 2; Jos., Bell. 2, 93, Ant. 14, 117; 19, 283. Cf. Philo, Rer. Div. Her. 279) *head of an ethnic community* or *minority, governor* 2 Cor 11: 32.—ESchürer, StKr 72, 1899, 95ff, Gesch. II⁴ 108, 51; ThZahn, NKZ 15, '04, 34ff; ESchwartz, GGN '06, 367f; JStarcky, Dict. de la Bible, Suppl. VII '66, 915f. S. also s.v. Ἀρέτας. M-M.*

ἐθνικός, ή, όν (since Polyb. 30, 13, 6; BGU 1764, 13 [I BC] =national; Philo, Mos. 1, 69; 188=national; so also Jos., Ant. 12, 36) in Christian usage (a Christian source in Epigr. Gr. 430, 6 [III/IV AD] ἐθνικῇ ἐν σοφίᾳ=in pagan learning) *Gentile, heathen* φιλίαι ἐθνικαί *friendships w. heathen* Hm 10, 1, 4. In the NT only as subst. ὁ ἐθνικός *the Gentile* in contrast to the Jew Mt 5: 47; 6: 7; 3 J 7. W. τελώνης Mt 18: 17. M-M.*

ἐθνικῶς adv. (Apollon. Dysc., Synt. p. 190, 5 Bekker; Diog. L. 7, 56 ἐθνικῶς τε καὶ ἑλληνικῶς) in Christian usage *like the heathen* ζῆν *live*, in contrast to the Jewish way of life Gal 2: 14.*

ἔθνος, ους, τό (Hom.+; inscr., pap., LXX, Ep. Arist., Philo, Joseph., Test. 12 Patr.).

1. *nation, people* τὸ ἔ. τῆς Σαμαρείας *the Samaritan people* Ac 8: 9 (cf. Jos., Ant. 18, 85). τῶν Ἰουδαίων 10: 22 (Polyb. in Jos., Ant. 12, 135; Agatharchides in Jos., Ant. 12, 6; Diod. S. 34+35 fgm. 1, 2 τὸ τῶν Ἰουδαίων ἔθνος; Philo, Decal. 96 al.); δώδεκα ἔ. Hs 9, 17, 2.—B 13: 2 (Gen 25: 23); ἔθνη ἑπτὰ ἐν γῇ Χανάαν *seven nations in Canaan* Ac 13: 19 (Dt 7: 1). The people in contrast to kings 9: 15. ἔθνος ἐπὶ ἔθνος *one nation against another* Mt 24: 7; Mk 13: 8; Lk 21: 10 (cf. 2 Ch 15: 6); πάντα τὰ ἔ. (Appian, Bell. Civ. 2, 106 §440 ἐν ἔθνεσιν ἅπασι; Jos., Ant. 11, 215 ἅπαντα τὰ ἔ.) Mt 24: 14; 28: 19; Mk 11: 17 (Is 56: 7); 13: 10. More specif. πάντα τὰ ἔ. τοῦ κόσμου Lk 12: 30; cf. 1 Cl 59: 4; 2 Cl 13: 2. πᾶν ἔθνος ἀνθρώπων *every nation of mankind* Ac 17: 26. ἄρχοντες ἐθνῶν Mt 20: 25. For this οἱ δοκοῦντες ἄρχειν τῶν ἐ. Mk 10: 42; οἱ βασιλεῖς τῶν ἐ. Lk 22: 25.

2. (τὰ) ἔθνη (corresp. to Heb. גּוֹיִם in LXX; usu. in Gk. for foreigners, also: Aristot., Pol. 1324b, 10 [opp. Ἕλλη-νες]; Ael. Aristid. 45, p. 3 Dind.; Cass. Dio 36, 41; Ps.-Callisth. 2, 7, 4 [opp. ἡ Ἑλλάς]; CIA II 445-8 [c. 150 BC]; Dit., Syll.³ 760, 3; PStrassb. 22, 19; PFay. 20, 11; this is an expression favored by Appian in Rome for the foreign peoples in contrast to the Italians: Bell. Civ. 2, 26 §99; 2, 28 §107; 3, 35 §140; 4, 57 §246 and oft.; cf. Nägeli 46) *heathen, pagans, Gentiles*, w. ἡγεμόνες κ. βασιλεῖς Mt 10: 18. Named w. the Jews (Jos., Ant. 13, 196; cf. Sib. Or. 3, 663) Ac 14: 5; 21: 21; 26: 17; Ro 3: 29; 9: 24; 15: 10 (Dt 32: 43); ISm 1: 2. They, too, are to share in salvation Ac 11: 1, 18; 14: 27; 15: 3, 7 (MKiddle, The Admission of the Gentiles in Lk and Ac: JTS 36, '35, 160-73; JoachJere-mias, Jesu Verheissung für die Völker '56 [lit.], Eng. transl. Jesus' Promise to the Nations '58). But s. Mt 10: 5f and cf. MornaDHooker, ET 82, '71, 361-65. Contrasted w. Christians Hs 1: 10. Of Gentile Christian churches: πᾶσαι αἱ ἐκκλησίαι τῶν ἐθνῶν Ro 16: 4, and their members: μετὰ τῶν ἐθνῶν συνήσθιεν *it was his custom to eat w. Gentile Christians* Gal 2: 12; cf. vs. 14. ὑπὲρ ὑμῶν τῶν ἐθνῶν *for you Gentile Christians* Eph 3: 1. Somet. the word has the connotation of relig. and moral inferiority which was taken for granted by the Jews Mt 6: 32 (cf. Gdspd., Probs., 26f); Lk 12: 30; Hm 4, 1, 9; ἔ. καὶ ἁμαρτωλοί s 4: 4 al. Pagans as subjects of conversion 2 Cl 13: 3. Prejudiced against the Christians ITr 8: 2; ἄνομα ἔ. *lawless heathen* MPol 9: 2. Contrasted w. the δίκαιοι (w. ἀποστάται) Hv 1, 4, 2; cf. 2, 2, 5.—KLSchmidt, TW II 362-70. M-M. B. 1315; 1489.

ἔθος, ους, τό (trag.+; inscr., pap., LXX; En. 106, 14; Ep. Arist., Philo, Joseph.).

1. *habit, usage* καθὼς ἔ. τισίν (Ep. Arist. 311; Jos., Ant. 20, 28) *as the habit of some people is* Hb 10: 25; cf. J 19: 40; Ac 25: 16. ἔθος ἔχειν *be accustomed* w. inf. foll. 19: 14 D. ἐπορεύθη κατὰ τὸ ἔ. *he went, as usual* Lk 22: 39 (cf. Lucian, Alex. 54; POxy. 370; PLond. 171b, 19; Bel 15 Theod.). ὡς ἔθος αὐτοῖς λέγειν (cf. 1 Macc 10: 89; 2 Macc 13: 4; PFay. 125, 5 ὡς ἔθος ἐστί σοι) *as they are accustomed to say* MPol 9: 2; cf. 13: 1; 18: 1.

2. *custom, law* τὰ ἔ. τὰ πατρῷα *the customs of the fathers* Ac 28: 17 (Dit., Syll.³ 1073, 20f κατὰ τὸ πάτριον ἔθος; Jos., Bell. 7, 424; 4 Macc 18: 5). τὰ ἔ. ἃ παρέδωκεν ἡμῖν Μωϋσῆς *the customs that Moses handed down* 6: 14; cf. 15: 1 (on the dat. τῷ ἔθει cf. PHolm. 2, 18 τῆδε τάξει =acc. to this recipe); 16: 21 (ἤθη v.l.); τοῖς ἔ. περιπατεῖν *live acc. to the laws* 21: 21; τὰ κατὰ Ἰουδαίους ἔ. *customs of the Jews* (cf. Jos., Ant. 15, 286) 26: 3 (ἤθη v.l.); κατὰ τὸ ἔ. τῆς ἱερατείας *as the custom is in the priestly office* Lk 1: 9; κατὰ τὸ ἔ. τῆς ἑορτῆς *acc. to the custom (prevailing) at the festival* 2: 42 (on κατὰ τὸ ἔ. cf. pap. in Dssm., NB

79 [BS 251f]; inscr. in Dit., Syll., Index). τὰ ἐγχώρια ἔθη *the customs of the country* Dg 5: 4; w. country and language 5: 1. M-M. B. 1358.*

ἔθρεψα s. τρέφω.

ἔθω s. εἴωθα.

εἰ (Hom.+; inscr., pap., LXX, Ep. Arist., Philo, Joseph.).
I. conditional particle *if* (Bl-D. §371f, neg. §428, 1; 2; Rob., indexes).
1. w. the indic.—a. in all tenses, to express a condition thought of as real or to denote assumptions relating to what has already happened εἰ υἱὸς εἶ τοῦ θεοῦ *if you really are the Son of God* Mt 4: 3; 5: 29f; 6: 23; 8: 31; Ac 5: 39. εἰ σὺ Ἰουδαῖος ἐπονομάζῃ *if you call yourself a Jew* Ro 2: 17. εἰ κατακαυχᾶσαι, οὐ σὺ βαστάζεις *if you do boast, (remember) you do not support* 11: 18 and very oft. In Paul the verb is freq. missing, and is to be supplied fr. the context: εἰ Χριστὸς ἐν ὑμῖν (sc. ἐστιν), τὸ μὲν σῶμα νεκρόν (sc. ἐστιν) 8: 10. εἰ τέκνα (sc. ἐστέ) *if you are children, then* . . . vs. 17, εἰ χάριτι (γέγονεν), οὐκέτι ἐξ ἔργων 11: 6 al. The negative in clauses where the reality of the condition is taken for granted is οὐ (class. μή): εἰ οὐ δύναται τοῦτο παρελθεῖν Mt 26: 42. εἰ δὲ ὑμεῖς οὐκ ἀφίετε Mk 11: 26 v.l. εἰ πιστοὶ οὐκ ἐγένεσθε Lk 16: 11f; εἰ οὐκ ἀκούουσιν vs. 31. εἰ οὐ φοβοῦμαι Lk 18: 4; cf. J 5: 47; 10: 37; Ro 8: 9; 11: 21; 1 Cor 7: 9; 9: 2; 11: 6; 15: 13ff, 29, 32; 16: 22 al. εἰ is rarely found w. the future εἰ πάντες σκανδαλισθήσονται Mt 26: 33; Mk 14: 29. εἰ ἀρνησόμεθα 2 Ti 2: 12. εἰ ὑπομενεῖτε 1 Pt 2: 20. εἰ καὶ οὐ δώσει (class. ἐὰν καὶ μὴ δῷ Bl-D. §372, 3; Rob. 1012) Lk 11: 8. W. aor., when the events are regarded as having taken place Mt 24: 22; Mk 3: 26; 13: 20.
b. w. the pres., impf., aor., or plpf. indic. to express an unreal (contrary to fact) condition (Bl-D. §360, 372; Rob. 1012ff). ἄν is usu. found in the apodosis (regularly in class.) εἰ ἐν Τύρῳ καὶ Σιδῶνι ἐγένοντο αἱ δυνάμεις, πάλαι ἂν μετενόησαν *if the wonders had been done in T. and S., they would have repented long ago* Mt 11: 21. εἰ ἤμεθα ἐν ταῖς ἡμέραις τῶν πατέρων ἡμῶν *if we had lived in the days of our fathers* 23: 30. εἰ ᾔδει ὁ οἰκοδεσπότης *if the master of the house had known* 24: 43. εἰ ἦν προφήτης, ἐγίνωσκεν ἄν *if he were a prophet, he would know* Lk 7: 39 and oft. The pres. indic. εἰ ἔχετε (v.l. εἴχετε) πίστιν . . . ἐλέγετε ἄν *if you had faith . . . you would say* Lk 17: 6. Somet. ἄν is lacking in the apodosis (Polyaenus 2, 3, 5 εἰ ἐπεποιήκειμεν . . . νῦν ἐχρῆν=if we had done . . . it would have been necessary; PReinach 7 [II вc]; POxy. 526; 530; PMelcher, De sermone Epict., Diss. Halle '05, 75; Mlt. 200f) εἰ μὴ ἦν οὗτος παρὰ θεοῦ, οὐκ ἠδύνατο *if this man were not from God, he would not have been able to* . . . J 9: 33. εἰ μὴ ἦλθον, ἁμαρτίαν οὐκ εἴχοσαν *if I had not come, they would not have sin* 15: 22; cf. vs. 24. W. the apodosis placed first Mk 9: 42 (v.l. περιέκειτο), Lk 17: 2; J 19: 11.
2. εἰ w. subj., as καὶ εἴ τις θελήσῃ Rv 11: 5, is unusual, perh. a textual error; Bl-D. §372, 3 app. conjectures κἄν for καὶ εἰ. But εἰ w. subj. is found in the older poets and Hdt. (Kühner-G. II 474), in Aristoph., Equ. 698 et al., in var. dialects (EHermann, Griech. Forschungen I '12, 277f) and in later times (e.g. Epict., Vett. Val., Lucian [ed. CJacobitz, Index graec. 473a]; Philostrat., Vi. Apoll. p. 84, 28; 197, 9; inscr. [Rdm.² 199]; PRyl. 234, 12; POxy. 496, 11; Dt 8: 5); Bl-D. §372, 3; Mlt. 187; Reinhold 107; OSchulthess, AKaegi-Festschr. '19, 161f.
3. εἰ w. the optative is rare: εἰ καὶ πάσχοιτε . . . μακάριοι *even if you should suffer, . . . you would be blessed*

1 Pt 3: 14. εἰ θέλοι τὸ θέλημα τοῦ θεοῦ *if it should be God's will* vs. 17. εἴ τι ἔχοιεν (sc. κατηγορεῖν) πρὸς ἐμέ *if they should have any charges to bring against me* Ac 24: 19. εἰ δυνατὸν εἴη (Jos., Ant. 12, 12) *if it should be possible* 20: 16 (but cf. Bl-D. §385, 2). εἰ τύχοι is used as a formula (oft. in secular wr., incl. Philo; cf. KReik, D. Opt. bei Polyb. u. Philo '07, 154) *it may be, for example, perhaps* 1 Cor 15: 37; used to tone down an assertion which may be too bold 14: 10 (Lucian, Icarom. 6 καὶ πολλάκις, εἰ τύχοι, μηδὲ ὁπόσοι στάδιοι Μεγαρόθεν Ἀθήναζέ εἰσιν, ἀκριβῶς ἐπιστάμενοι).
II. After verbs of emotion *that* (Kühner-G. II 369, 8; Rob. 965. Cf. Appian, Bell. Civ. 5, 67 §283 ἀγανακτέω εἰ=be exasperated that; Sir 23: 14 θελήσεις εἰ μὴ ἐγεν-νήθης; 2 Macc 14: 28; 4 Macc 2: 1; 4: 7. S. on θαυμάζω 1a γ) ἐθαύμασεν εἰ ἤδη τέθνηκεν *he was surprised that he was already dead* Mk 15: 44a. μὴ θαυμάζετε εἰ μισεῖ ὑμᾶς ὁ κόσμος *do not wonder that the world hates you* 1 J 3: 13. Sim. also (Procop. Soph., Ep. 123 χάριν ἔχειν εἰ=that) μαρτυρόμενος . . . εἰ παθητὸς ὁ Χριστός *testifying . . . that the Christ was to suffer* Ac 26: 23.—οὐ μέγα εἰ *it is not surprising that* 2 Cor 11: 15 (cf. Aeschines, In Ctes. 94 ἐστὶ δεινὸν εἰ; Diod. S. 23, 15, 5, παράδοξον . . . εἰ=incredible . . . that; ibid. θαυμαστὸν εἰ; Gen 45: 28 μέγα μοί ἐστιν εἰ).—*That* is also poss. after verbs of knowing or not knowing, e.g., J 9: 25; Ac 19: 2; 1 Cor 1: 16; 7: 16; so CBurchard, ZNW 52, '61, 73-82.
III. In causal clauses, when an actual case is taken as a supposition, where we also can use *if* instead of *since:* εἰ τὸν χόρτον . . . ὁ θεὸς οὕτως ἀμφιέννυσιν *if God so clothes the grass* Mt 6: 30; Lk 12: 28; cf. Mt 7: 11; Lk 11: 13; J 7: 23; 10: 35; 13: 14, 17, 32; Ac 4: 9; 11: 17; Ro 6: 8; 15: 27; Col 2: 20; Hb 7: 15; 1 Pt 1: 17; 1 J 4: 11.
IV. In aposiopesis (Bl-D. §482; Rob. 1203) εἰ ἔγνως *if you only knew* Lk 19: 42. εἰ βούλει παρενέγκαι *if you would only let (this) pass* 22: 42 v.l. (cf. the letter fr. IV вc in Dssm., LO 120, note 5 [LAE 149]).—Hebraistic in oaths, like אִם: *may this or that happen to me, if*—(cf. 2 Km 3: 25; GWBuchanan, HTR 58, '65, 319-24); this amounts to a strong negation *certainly not* (cf. Ps 7: 4f; Gen 14: 23) ἀμὴν λέγω ὑμῖν εἰ δοθήσεται *truly, I tell you, it will not be given* Mk 8: 12 (NDColeman, JTS 28, '27, 159-67 interprets this as strongly positive; against him FCBurkitt, ibid. 274-76). εἰ εἰσελεύσονται *they shall certainly not enter* Hb 3: 11; 4: 3, 5 (all 3 Ps 94: 11); Bl-D. §372, 4; 454, 5; Mlt.-H. 468f; Rob. 94; 1024.
V. Interrogative particle—1. (not class., Bl-D. §440, 3 w. app.; Rob. 916) w. direct questions (Gen 17: 17; 44: 19; Am 3: 3-6; 6: 12): εἰ ἔξεστιν; *is it permitted?* Mt 12: 10; 19: 3; Mk 10: 2; Ac 21: 37; 22: 25. εἰ ὀλίγοι οἱ σωζόμενοι; *are there only a few who will be saved?* Lk 13: 23; cf. 22: 49; Ac 1: 6; 7: 1; 19: 2.
2. freq. in indir. questions *whether* (Hom.+)—a. w. pres. indic. (Gen 27: 21; 42: 16; Jos., Ant. 10, 259; 16, 225) εἴπῃς εἰ σὺ εἶ ὁ Χριστός *whether you are the Christ* Mt 26: 63. ἴδωμεν εἰ ἔρχεται Mt 27: 49; Mk 15: 36 (Lucian, Dial. Mort. 20, 3 φέρ' ἴδω εἰ=let me see whether, De Merc. Cond. 6); cf. Lk 14: 31; 2 Cor 13: 5; 1 J 4: 1.—W. the fut. indic. (4 Km 1: 2; Job 5: 1) εἰ θεραπεύσει αὐτόν *whether he would heal him* Mk 3: 2 (v.l. θεραπεύει); Lk 6: 7 t.r.; εἰ σώσεις *whether you will save* 1 Cor 7: 16.—W. the aor. indic. (Esth 4: 14) εἰ πάλαι ἀπέθανεν *whether he had already died* Mk 15: 44b.
b. w. subj. διώκω εἰ καταλάβω *I press on (to see) whether I can capture* Phil 3: 12 (Bl-D. §368; 375; Rob. 1017).
c. w. opt. (X., An. 1, 8, 15; 2, 1, 15; 4 Macc 9: 27; 11: 13) ἀνακρίνοντες . . . εἰ ἔχοι ταῦτα *examining* . . .

to see whether this was really so Ac 17: 11. εἰ βούλοιτο πορεύεσθαι 25: 20; cf. 17: 27.

VI. Combined w. other particles, w. the other particles foll.:—**1.** εἰ ἄρα s. ἄρα 2.—εἴ γε s. γέ 3a.

2. εἰ δὲ καί but if, and if Lk 11: 18; 1 Cor 4: 7; and even if 2 Cor 4: 3; 11: 6.

3. εἰ δὲ μή if not, otherwise—**a.** after affirmat. clauses, w. the aor. ind. and ἄν in the apodosis J 14: 2; or pres. ind. (Demosth., Prooem. 29, 3) and fut. (Gen 30: 1; Bel 29 Theod.; PLond. 1912 [letter of Claudius, 41 AD], 98) Rv 2: 5, 16; or pres. imper. J 14: 11.

b. after negat. clauses, otherwise (X., An. 7, 1, 8; Diod. S. 3, 47, 4; Dio Chrys. 10[11], 100; Lebas-Wadd., Asia Min. 1651 μὴ ἀδικεῖν . . . , εἰ δὲ μή; UPZ 196 I, 33 [119 BC]; Job 32: 22) Mk 2: 21f.

4. εἰ καί even if, even though, although Lk 11: 8; 18: 4; 1 Cor 7: 21; 2 Cor 4: 16; 7: 8; 12: 11; Phil 2: 17; Col 2: 5; Hb 6: 9.

5. εἰ μὲν γάρ for if Ac 25: 11 t.r.; 2 Cor 11: 4; Hb 8: 4 t.r.

6. εἰ μὲν οὖν if, then Hb 7: 11. W. εἰ δέ foll. (X., Cyr. 8, 7, 22; Ael. Aristid. 28, 156 K.=49 p. 542 D.) Ac 19: 38.

7. εἰ μέντοι if, however Js 2: 8.—**8.** εἰ μή after negatives —**a.** except, if not, mostly without a verb depending on εἰ μή (X., An. 2, 1, 12) Mt 11: 27; 12: 24; 16: 4; J 3: 13; Ro 7: 7; Gal 1: 19 (HKoch, Z. Jakobusfrage Gal 1: 19: ZNW 33, '34, 204–9); but also with a verb (Jos., Ant. 8, 316) Mt 5: 13; Mk 6: 5; Ac 12: 25 v.l.

b. but (Dit., Or. 201, 20 οὐκ ἀφῶ αὐτοὺς καθεσθῆναι εἰς τὴν σκιάν, εἰ μὴ ὑπὸ ἡλίου ἔξω; in note 33 Dit. gives exx. fr. Aristoph. for this use) without a verb Mt 12: 4; w. a verb (Theodr. Prodr. 7, 426 H.) Gal 1: 7, but s. ἄλλος 1eβ. For ἐκτὸς εἰ μή s. ἐκτός 1.

9. εἰ μήτι unless indeed, unless perhaps (Ael. Aristid. 46 p. 198 D.; Jos., Ant. 4, 280) Lk 9: 13; 2 Cor 13: 5; w. ἄν (Ps.-Clem., Hom. 16, 4) 1 Cor 7: 5 (cf. Dssm., NB 32, 1 [BS 204n.]; Bl-D. §376; Mlt. 169; 239; Reinhold 35; JTrunk, De Basilio Magno sermonis Attic. imitatore '11, 56; JWackernagel, Antike Anredeformen '12, 27f).

10. εἰ οὖν if, therefore Mt 6: 23; Lk 11: 36; 12: 26; J 13: 14; 18: 8; Col 3: 1; Phlm 17.

11. εἴπερ if indeed, if after all, since (X., An. 1, 7, 9; Menand., Epitr. 523; PHal. 7, 6; UPZ 59, 29 [168 BC]; Jdth 6: 9) Ro 3: 30; 8: 9, 17; 2 Th 1: 6.—if indeed, provided that εἴπερ ἄρα (ἄρα 1) 1 Cor 15: 15. καὶ γὰρ εἴπερ for even if (cf. Od. 1, 167; Bl-D. §454, 2) 1 Cor 8: 5.

12. εἴ πως (the spelling εἴπως is also correct; Bl-D. §12 app.) if perhaps, if somehow.

a. w. opt. (X., An. 2, 5, 2; 4, 1, 21; POxy. 939, 15) εἴ πως δύναιντο παραχειμάσαι if somehow they could spend the winter Ac 27: 12.

b. w. fut. indic. (3 Km 21: 31; 4 Km 19: 4; Jer 28: 8) εἴ πως εὐοδωθήσομαι whether, perhaps, I shall succeed Ro 1: 10; cf. 11: 14; Phil 3: 11.

13. εἴτε—εἴτε (class.; inscr. since 416 BC Meisterhans'-Schw.; pap. [Mayser II 3, 159]; LXX; Jos., Ant. 16, 33; 37; Bl-D. §446; 454, 3; Rob. index) if—if, whether—or.

a. w. a verb in pres. indic. (Herm. Wr. 12, 22 three times) 1 Cor 12: 26; 2 Cor 1: 6; or pres. subj. 1 Th 5: 10.

b. w. no verb Ro 12: 6–8; 1 Cor 3: 22; 8: 5; 2 Cor 5: 10 al. εἴτε only once 1 Cor 14: 27.

VII. Used w. the indef. pron. εἴ τις, εἴ τι everyone who or whoever; everything that or whatever Mt 16: 24; 18: 28; Mk 4: 23; 9: 35; Lk 9: 23; 14: 26; 1 Ti 3: 1, 5; 5: 4, 8, 16 al. Cf. 1 Cor 12: 31 v.l. (ADebrunner, Coniect. Neot. XI, '47, 37). W. subj. εἴ τις θελήσῃ Rv 11: 5 s. above I 2. M-M.

εἰ μήν, more correctly ἦ μήν (Bl-D. §24; Rob. 1150) for class. ἦ μήν (which is found also Jos., Ant. 13, 76; 17, 42), in Hellenistic-Roman times (Dit., Syll.³ 993, 20 [III BC]; 736, 27 [92 BC]; IG IV 840, 15 [EHermann, Gr. Forschungen I '12, 312]; pap. since 112 BC [Mayser 78]; LXX e.g. Ezk 33: 27; 34: 8 al.; Num 14: 28; Jdth 1: 12; Bar 2: 29 [Thackeray 83]) formula used in oaths surely, certainly Hb 6: 14 (Gen 22: 17).—Dssm., NB 33ff [BS 205ff]. M-M.*

εἶα, εἶασα s. ἐάω.

εἰδέα, ας, ἡ (Artem. 2, 44 φαίνονται οἱ θεοὶ ἐν ἀνθρώπων ἰδέᾳ [v.l. εἰδέᾳ] τε καὶ μορφῇ; PGenève 16, 17; EpJer 62; Philo, Spec. Leg. 4, 113 with v.l.) appearance (though face is also poss., cf. Diod. S. 3, 8 of Ethiopians ταῖς ἰδέαις σιμοί; Da 1: 15 Theod.; perh. Plut., Flamin. 1; Field, Notes 22) Mt 28: 3 (incorrect spelling [Bl-D. §23 app.]; cf. ἰδέα). M-M.*

εἰδέναι s. οἶδα.

εἶδον (Hom.+; inscr., pap., LXX; Ep. Arist. 176; Philo, Joseph., Test. 12 Patr.) used as the 2 aor. of ὁράω: the mixed form εἶδα Rv 17: 3, 6 (both as v.l.), fr. 1 and 2 aor., somet. occurs instead of εἶδον (Bl-D. §81, 3 w. app.; Rob. 337–9), also εἴδαμεν Mk 2: 12; Ac 4: 20, εἴδατε as v.l. Lk 7: 22; J 6: 26, εἶδαν Mt 13: 17; Mk 6: 33 D; Lk 10: 24 al. (wherever εἶδον is not the main rdg., it is v.l.). Beside it, is freq. found in mss. the phonetic spelling (Bl-D. §23) ἴδον Rv 4: 1; 6: 1ff, ἴδεν Lk 5: 2; Rv 1: 2, ἴδετε Phil 1: 30 (all as v.l.); subj. ἴδω; imper. ἴδε (Moeris p. 193 ἰδέ ἀττικῶς· ἴδε ἑλληνικῶς. Bl-D. §13; 101 p. 47 [ὁρᾶν]; Rob. 1215 [εἰδέω]; cf. PRyl. 239, 21; LXX); inf. ἰδεῖν; ptc. ἰδών. see.

1. lit. of perception by sight see, perceive.

a. w. acc. τινά, τί someone, someth. a star Mt 2: 2; cf. 9f; a child vs. 11; the Spirit of God as a dove 3: 16; a light 4: 16 (Is 9: 2); two brothers vss. 18, 21 and oft. W. ἀκούειν (Lucian, Hist. 29) Lk 7: 22; Ac 22: 14; 1 Cor 2: 9; Phil 1: 27, 30; 4: 9; Js 5: 11. Contrasted w. πιστεύειν J 20: 29 (cf. 2 Cor 5: 7); look at someone Mk 8: 33; J 21: 21; at someth. critically Lk 14: 18.—Also of visions which one sees (Sir 49: 8): εἶδον κ. ἰδοὺ θύρα ἠνεῳγμένη ἐν τ. οὐρανῷ . . . κ. θρόνος . . . κ. ἐπὶ τὸν θρόνον καθήμενος . . . Rv 4: 1f (Test. Levi 5: 1 ἤνοιξέ μοι ὁ ἄγγελος τ. πύλας τοῦ οὐρανοῦ κ. εἶδον τὸν ὕψιστον ἐπὶ θρόνον καθήμενον). ἰδεῖν ὅραμα Ac 10: 17; 11: 5; 16: 10. ἐν ὁράματι in a vision 9: 12 t.r.; 10: 3; cf. ἐν τῇ ὁράσει Rv 9: 17. ἰδεῖν τοῖς ὀφθαλμοῖς see w. one's own eyes Mt 13: 15; J 12: 40; Ac 28: 27 (all 3 Is 6: 10). The combination ἰδὼν εἶδον I have surely seen 7: 34 (Ex 3: 7) is Hebraistic (רָאֹה רָאָה; but cf. Lucian, Dial. Mor. 4, 3 Jacobitz). The ptc. with and without acc. freq. serves to continue a narrative Mt 2: 10; 5: 1; 8: 34; Mk 5: 22; 9: 20; Lk 2: 48 and oft. The acc. is to be supplied Mt 9: 8, 11; 21: 20; Mk 10: 14; Lk 1: 12; 2: 17; Ac 3: 12 and oft.

b. w. acc. and a ptc. (Lucian, Philops. 13 εἶδον πετόμενον τὸν ξένον) ἰδὼν πολλοὺς ἐρχομένους when he saw many coming Mt 3: 7. εἶδεν τὴν πενθερὰν αὐτοῦ βεβλημένην he saw his mother-in-law lying 8: 14; cf. 9: 9; 16: 28; Ac 28: 4 (cf. Jos., Ant. 7, 241); B 7: 10; Hm 5, 2, 2 and oft.

c. w. indir. question foll.: ἰδεῖν τὸν Ἰησοῦν τίς ἐστιν to see who Jesus was Lk 19: 3; ἰ. τί ἐστιν τὸ γεγονός what had happened Mk 5: 14. ἴδωμεν εἰ ἔρχεται Ἠλίας let us see whether Elijah will come 15: 36 (s. εἰ V 2a). ἴδωμεν τί καλόν 1 Cl 7: 3. ἴδετε πηλίκοις ὑμῖν γράμμασιν ἔγραψα notice with what large letters I write to you Gal 6: 11.—**d.** w. ὅτι foll. Mk 2: 16; 9: 25; J 6: 24; 11: 31; Rv 12: 13.

e. the formulas ἔρχου καὶ ἴδε come and see J 1: 46; 11:

34; cf. 1: 39 and ὑπάγετε ἴδετε Mk 6: 38, borrowed fr. Jewish usage (cf. δεῦρο καὶ ἴδε, δεῦτε ἴδετε 4 Km 6: 13; 7: 14; 10: 16; Ps 45: 9; 65: 5; ἐξέλθατε καὶ ἴδετε SSol 3: 11), direct attention to a particular object.

2. *feel, become aware of* of sense perception of any kind (Alexis Com. 222, 4 ὀσμήν; Diod. S. 1, 39, 6 the blowing of the wind; Oenomaus in Euseb., Pr. Ev. 5, 28, 2 τὴν θείαν φωνήν; Aristaen., Ep. 2, 7 ὄψει τὸ πήδημα [the beating of the heart]; Ezk 3: 13 εἶδον φωνήν) σεισμόν Mt 27: 54.

3. gener. *see, notice, note* (Philo, Abr. 191) *faith* 9: 2; *thoughts* Lk 9: 47 v.l.; *God's kindness* Ro 11: 22. W. ὅτι foll. Mt 27: 3, 24; Ac 12: 3; Gal 2: 7, 14.

4. *consider* someth., w. indir. question foll. (X., Symp. 2, 15) ἴδετε ποταπὴν ἀγάπην δέδωκεν *consider the great love that God has shown* 1 J 3: 1. W. περί τινος: περί τ. λόγου τούτου *deliberate concerning this matter* Ac 15: 6.

5. *see someth.=experience someth.* (Ps 26: 13); *good days* 1 Pt 3: 10 (Ps 33: 13; τ. βασιλείαν J 3: 3. θάνατον *see death=die* Lk 2: 26; Hb 11: 5 (cf. Ps 88: 49; Anth. Pal. 6, 230 ἰδεῖν Ἀίδην); *grief* Rv 18: 7 (cf. 1 Macc 13: 3 τὰς στενοχωρίας; Eccl 6: 6 ἀγαθωσύνην); τὴν διαφθοράν *experience decay=decay* Ac 2: 27, 31; 13: 35-7 (all Ps 15: 10); τ. ἡμέραν (Soph., Oed. R. 831; Aristoph., Pax 345; Polyb. 10, 4, 7; 32, 10, 9; Ael. Aristid. 32 p. 601 D.; Lam 2: 16; Jos., Ant.6, 305): τὴν ἡμέραν τ. ἐμήν J 8: 56; μίαν τῶν ἡμερῶν Lk 17: 22.

6. *look after, visit* (X., An. 2, 4, 15; Appian, Bell. Civ. 4, 19 §73 visit a country place; 5, 62 §266 visit or look after a sick woman) Lk 8: 20; Ac 16: 40; 1 Cor 16: 7. τὸ πρόσωπόν τινος (Lucian, Dial. Deor. 24, 2) *visit someone* 1 Th 2: 17; 3: 10; *come* or *learn to know* someone (Epict. 3, 9, 14 Ἐπίκτητον ἰδεῖν) Lk 9: 9; 23: 8; J 12: 21; Ro 1: 11; w. προσλαλῆσαι Ac 28: 20. M-M. B. 1041.

εἶδος, ους, τό (Hom.+; inscr., pap., LXX.—CRitter, Neue Unters. über Plato '09, 228-320).

1. *form, outward appearance* (X., Cyr. 1, 2, 1; Pla., Symp. 210B; Philostrat., Ep. 51; Gen 41: 2-4; Ezk 1: 26; Philo; Jos., Ant. 6, 296; Test. Sim. 5: 1) σωματικῷ εἴδει *in bodily form* Lk 3: 22; cf. GEb 3. τὸ εἶδος τοῦ προσώπου αὐτοῦ *the appearance of his face* Lk 9: 29. Of God (cf. Ex 24: 17) εἶδος αὐτοῦ (w. φωνή) J 5: 37. Of the form of heathen gods Dg 2: 1. οὐκ ἔχειν εἶδος *have no comeliness* 1 Cl 16: 3 (Is 53: 2). τὸ πῦρ καμάρας εἶδος ποιῆσαν *formed the shape of a vaulted room* MPol 15: 2.

2. *kind* (X., Pla.+; PTebt. 58, 10f [111 BC]; PFay. 34, 6; POxy. 905, 6; Sir 23: 16; 25: 2; Philo; Jos., Ant. 10, 37 πᾶν εἶδος πονηρίας) ἀπὸ παντὸς εἴδους πονηροῦ *fr. every kind of evil* 1 Th 5: 22 (JoachJeremias, Unknown Sayings of Jesus, '57, 92 [money-changing?]).

3. active *seeing, sight* (Num 12: 8; Ps.-Clem., Hom. 17, 18 στόμα κατὰ στόμα, ἐν εἴδει καὶ οὐ δι' ὁραμάτων καὶ ἐνυπνίων. So also the interpr. of 2 Cor 5: 7 in Severian of Gabala [Pauluskomm. aus d. griech. Kirche ed. KStaab '33, 291] and in Theodoret III 314 Noesselt) διὰ πίστεως, οὐ διὰ εἴδους *by faith, not by sight* 2 Cor 5: 7 (the same contrast betw. πιστεύειν and ἰδεῖν [s. εἶδον 1a] also J 20: 29). M-M. B. 874.*

εἰδωλεῖον, ου, τό (on the spelling εἰδώλιον cf. Bl-D. §13; 111, 5; PKatz, ThLZ '36, 283; Rob. 154) *an idol's temple* 1 Cor 8: 10 (cf. 1 Esdr 2: 7; Bel 10; 1 Macc 10: 83). M-M.*

εἰδωλόθυτος, ον (4 Macc 5: 2) only subst. τὸ εἰδωλόθυτον *meat offered to an idol*, an expr. which (cf. εἴδωλον 2) was possible only among Jews (Ps.-Phoc. 31) and Christians. The pagan said ἱερόθυτον (q.v.). It refers to sacrificial

meat, part of which was burned on the altar, part was eaten at a solemn meal in the temple, and part was sold in the market (so Artem. 5, 2) for home use. Fr. the Jewish viewpoint it was unclean and therefore forbidden. Ac 15: 29 (for lit., s. on πνικτός); 21: 25; 1 Cor 8: 1, 4, 7, 10; 10: 19, 28 t.r.; Rv 2: 14, 20; D 6: 3.—MRauer, D. 'Schwachen' in Korinth u. Rom '23, 40-52; HvSoden, Sakrament u. Ethik b. Pls: Marburger Theol. Stud. 1, '31, 1ff.*

εἰδωλολατρέω (Test. Levi 17: 11) *be* or *become an idolater* of Christians who consult oracles Hm 11: 4, or become apostate under persecution s 9, 21, 3.*

εἰδωλολάτρης, ου, ὁ (Sib. Or. 3, 38) *idolater* 1 Cor 5: 10; Rv 21: 8; 22: 15. Of those who are covetous, etc. (s. εἰδωλολατρία) Eph 5: 5; cf. 1 Cor 5: 11. W. πόρνοι, μοιχοί 6: 9; εἰ. γίνεσθαι *take part in idol-worship* 10: 7. Of Christians who consult false prophets Hm 11: 4. M-M.*

εἰδωλολατρία, ας, ἡ (Test. Jud. 19: 1) *idolatry* D 3: 4. In a catalogue of vices Gal 5: 20; B 20: 1; D 5: 1. Of greed Col 3: 5 (cf. Eph 5: 5; Pol 11: 2 and s. HWeinel, D. Wirkungen des Geistes u. der Geister 1899, 14f). The unregenerate heart is πλήρης εἰδωλολατρίας *full of idolatry* B 16: 7; φεύγειν ἀπὸ τῆς εἰ. 1 Cor 10: 14. Pl. πορεύεσθαι ἐν ἀθεμίτοις εἰ. *walk in unlawful id.*, i.e., commit unlawful deeds connected w. idolatry 1 Pt 4: 3. M-M.*

εἴδωλον, ου, τό (Hom.+ in secular Gk.: form, image, shadow, phantom).

1. *image, idol* (Is 30: 22; 2 Ch 23: 17; Tob 14: 6; EpJer 72; cf. Polyb. 30, 25, 13 θεῶν ἢ δαιμόνων εἴδωλα; Vett. Val. 67: 5; 113, 17; Cat. Cod. Astr. VII p. 176, 22; Dit., Or. 201, 8); sacrifices made to it (Nicol. Dam.: 90 fgm. 13, 23 p. 407, 31 Jac. πρὸς τῷ εἰδώλῳ ἀποσφάττεσθαι; Num 25: 2; 1 Macc 1: 43) Ac 7: 41; gold and silver (Ps 113: 12) Rv 9: 20. εἴδωλα ἄφωνα *idols that cannot speak* 1 Cor 12: 2 (cf. Hab 2: 18; 3 Macc 4: 16.—Even the pagan knows that the images of the gods are lifeless: Artem. 4, 36 ταῦτα οὐ ζῇ).

2. *false god, idol* (oft. LXX, also Philo; Jos., Ant. 9, 273; 10, 50; Test. Reub. 4: 6) βδελύσσεσθαι τὰ εἰ. *abhor idols* Ro 2: 22; cf. B 4: 8; . . . ὅτι εἰ. τί ἐστιν; (do I mean to say) *that an idol is anything?* 1 Cor 10: 19. Contrasted w. the temple of God, i.e., the church 2 Cor 6: 16. Contrasted w. God 1 Th 1: 9. φυλάσσειν ἑαυτὸν ἀπὸ τῶν εἰ. *keep oneself fr. idols* 1 J 5: 21; cf. Ac 15: 20. ἀπὸ τῶν εἰ. ἀποσπᾶν *tear away fr. idols* 2 Cl 17: 1; οὐδὲν εἰ. ἐν κόσμῳ *there is no such thing as an idol in the world* (i.e., an i. has no real existence) 1 Cor 8: 4. τῇ συνειδήσει (v.l. συνηθείᾳ) *because of their consciousness, up to now, that this is an idol* vs. 7; ἱερεῖς τῶν εἰ. *priests of the idols* B 9: 6. M-M. B. 1491.*

εἰδώς, υἷα, ός s. οἶδα.

εἰκάζω 1 aor. opt. εἰκάσαιμι *suppose, imagine* (so Aeschyl., Hdt.+; Wsd; En. 21, 7; Ep. Arist. 105; Philo, Fuga 179; Jos., Ant. 17, 136, Vi. 148) Dg 2: 3; 7: 2.*

εἰκαιότης, ητος, ἡ (Philod.; Diog. L. 7, 48; Philo, Det. Pot. Ins. 10 et al.; Aq. Pr 30: 8) *silliness, thoughtlessness* w. ἀπάτη Dg 4: 6.*

εἰκῆ adv. (Aeschyl.+; inscr.; Pr 28: 25; for the spelling εἰκῇ s. Bl-D. §26 app.; Rob. 295f).

1. *without cause* (Artem. 2, 60; UPZ 106, 15 [99 BC]; 108, 24) Mt 5: 22 t.r. (PWernberg-Møller, NTS 3, '56/'57,

71-73); εἰ. φυσιούμενος *puffed up without cause* Col 2: 18.

2. *in vain, to no avail* (Lucian, Anach. 19) πάσχειν *experience* Gal 3: 4. κοπιᾶζειν *work* 4: 11.

3. *to no purpose* (Lucian, Jupp. Trag. 36; Ep. Arist. 161; 168) of the government τὴν μάχαιραν φορεῖν *carry the sword to no purpose* Ro 13: 4.

4. *without due consideration, in a haphazard manner* (Heraclitus, fgm. 47 Diels; Epict. 1, 28, 28; 1, 6, 7; Arrian, Anab. 6, 3, 2; Apollon. Dysc.: Gramm. Gr. II 2 p. 215, 1 U.; Sb 5675, 12 [II вс]; PLeipz. 104, 29 [I вс]; Pr 28: 25; Ep. Arist. 51; 162; Jos., C. Ap. 2, 234) w. ἀτάκτως *thoughtlessly* (perh. *at random) and in disorder* 1 Cl 40: 2. πιστεῦσαι 1 Cor 15: 2 (here mng. 3 is also poss.). M-M.*

εἰκός neut. of the ptc. of ἔοικα (trag., Hdt.+; BGU 1208, 18 [27/26 вс]; Ep. Arist. 223; Philo; Jos., Bell. 6, 52 al.) *probable, reasonable* Dg 3: 3.*

εἴκοσι indecl. (Hom.+; inscr., pap., LXX, Ep. Arist.; Jos., Vi. 118 al.; Test. 12 Patr.) *twenty* Lk 14: 31; Ac 1: 15; 27: 28; Hv 4, 1, 1; μόγις εἰ. ἐκύλιον Lk 23: 53 D (cf. Jos., Bell. 6, 293 μόλις ὑπ' ἀνθρώπων εἰ.); εἰ. τρεῖς (cf. Bl-D. §63, 2 app.) *twenty-three* 1 Cor 10: 8; εἰ. τέσσαρες (Test. Jos. 15: 1) Rv 4: 4, 10; 5: 8; 11: 16; 19: 4; εἰ. πέντε J 6: 19; Hs 9, 4, 3; 9, 5, 4; 9, 15, 4. M-M.*

εἰκοσιτρεῖς 1 Cor 10: 8; better written as two words εἴκοσι (q.v.) τρεῖς.*

εἰκτικῶς adv. (Philod., Περὶ σημ. 18 Gomp.; Maximus Tyr. 7, 3b) *readily yielding* 1 Cl 37: 2 (restored by conjecture: s. the text-crit. note of Bihlmeyer ad loc.).*

εἴκω 1 aor. εἶξα, inf. εἶξαι (Hom.+; Epict., pap.; Wsd 18: 25; 4 Macc 1: 6; Jos., Ant. 1, 115 τ. θεῷ; 2, 304; 4, 143 τ. ἐπιθυμίαις) *yield* (Pind., Isth. 1, 6; Diog. L. 2, 143) τινί *to someone* (Appian, Hann. 19 §84, Bell. Civ. 1, 1 §1 ἀλλήλοις) οἷς οὐδὲ πρὸς ὥραν εἴξαμεν *to whom we did not yield even for a moment* Gal 2: 5 (ὥρα 2aβ). ἡμῖν 1 Cl 56: 1.*

εἰκών, όνος, ἡ (Aeschyl., Hdt.+; inscr., pap., LXX, En., Ep. Arist. 135; Philo; Jos., Ant. 15, 277; Test. 12 Patr.; Sib. Or. 3, 8; loanw. in rabb.)

1. *image, likeness*—**a.** lit. of the emperor's head on a coin (so Artem. 4, 31; of the emperor's image Jos., Bell. 2, 169; 194, Ant. 19, 185) Mt 22: 20; Mk 12: 16; Lk 20: 24. Of an image of a god (Diod. S. 2, 8, 7 [Zeus]; Appian, Mithrid. 117 §575 θεῶν εἰκόνες; Lucian, Sacr. 11; 2 Ch 33: 7; Is 40: 19) Rv 13: 14f; 14: 9, 11; 15: 2; 16: 2; 19: 20; 20: 4.

b. fig. εἰκὼν τοῦ θεοῦ of a man (cf. Wilcken, Chrest. 109, 11 [III вс] Philopator as εἰκὼν τοῦ Διός; Rosetta Stone=Dit., Or. 90, 3 [196 вс] Ptolemy V as εἰκὼν ζῶσα τοῦ Διός, cf. APF 1, '01, 483, 11; Plut., Themist. 27, 4; Lucian, Pro Imag. 28 εἰκόνα θεοῦ τ. ἄνθρωπον εἶναι; Diog. L. 6, 51 τ. ἀγαθοὺς ἄνδρας θεῶν εἰκόνας εἶναι; Sextus 190; Herm. Wr. 1, 12 al.; Apuleius as image of God, Rtzst., Mysterienrel.³ 43; JHehn, Zum Terminus 'Bild Gottes': ESachau-Festschr. '15, 36–52) 1 Cor 11: 7 (on the gradation here cf. Herm. Wr. 11, 15a); of Christ (Helios as εἰκών of deity: Pla., Rep. 6 p. 509; Proclus, Hymni 1, 33f [Orphica p. 277 Abel]; Herm. Wr. 11, 15; Stob. I 293, 21=454, 1ff Sc.; Hierocles 1 p. 418: the rest of the gods are εἰκόνες of the primeval god.—The Logos: Philo, Conf. Ling. 97; 147. Wisdom: Wsd 7: 26) 2 Cor 4: 4; Col 1: 15 (EPreuschen, ZNW 18, '18, 243).—εἰ. τοῦ χοϊκοῦ, τοῦ ἐπουρανίου *image of the earthly, heavenly* (man) 1 Cor 15: 49. (S. SVMcCasland, The Image of God

Acc. to Paul: JBL 69, '50, 85–100). The image corresponds to its original (cf. ὁμοίωμα 2 and 3; Doxopatres [XI AD]: Rhet. Gr. II 160, 1 εἰ. καὶ ὁμοίωμα διαφέρει).

2. *form, appearance* (Istros [III вс]: no. 334 fgm. 53 Jac. ἀνθρωποειδὴς εἰκών=a human figure; Artem. 1, 35 p. 36, 5 τὸ πρόσωπον κ. τὴν εἰκόνα=the face and the form; Ps.-Callisth. 2, 27; Hierocles 20 p. 465: to his followers Pythagoras has θείαν εἰκόνα=the appearance of a god; Kleopatra l. 154 ἐτελειώθη ἡ εἰκὼν σώματι κ. ψυχῇ κ. πνεύματι; Herm. Wr. 1, 12 of the first man, the son of the πατὴρ πάντων: τὴν τοῦ πατρὸς εἰκόνα ἔχων; 5, 6; En. 106, 10) ὁμοίωμα εἰκόνος φθαρτοῦ ἀνθρώπου *the likeness of the form of mortal man* Ro 1: 23 (MD Hooker, NTS 6, '60, 297–306). συμμόρφους τῆς εἰ. τοῦ υἱοῦ *conformed to the appearance of his Son* 8: 29; cf. 2 Cor 3: 18; εἰ. τ. πραγμάτων *form of things* in contrast to their σκιά Hb 10: 1.—The infl. of Gen 1: 26f is very strong (κατ' εἰκόνα θεοῦ; Test. Napht. 2: 5. Cf. AStruker, D. Gottesebenbildlichkeit d. Menschen in d. christl. Lit. d. zwei erst. Jahrh. '13). Man made by God ἐκ τῆς ἰδίας εἰ. *in his own form* Dg 10: 2; cf. τῆς ἑαυτοῦ εἰ. χαρακτήρ 1 Cl 33: 4; cf. vs. 5; B 5: 5; 6: 12. Gen 1: 27 also infl. Col 3: 10: the new man is made new κατ' εἰκόνα τοῦ κτίσαντος αὐτόν. (Philo, Leg. All. 3, 96, in Platonic fashion, expresses the thought that first of all an image proceeded fr. God, which, in turn, served as a model for man; against this view s. FWEltester, Eikon im NT, '58, 157).—JM Bover, 'Imaginis' notio apud B. Paulum: Biblica 4, '23, 174–9; TW II 378–93; HWillms, Εἰκών I '35; EGSelwyn, Image, Fact and Faith: NTS 1, '55, 235–47; GBLadner, RAC IV, '59, 771–86; JJervell, Imago Dei (Genesis, late Judaism, Gnosis, NT) FRL no. 58, '60; KPrümm, Verbum Domini 40, '62, 232–57 (Paul); ELarsson, Christus als Vorbild, '62. M-M.*

εἰλέω 1 aor. εἴλησα 4 Km 2: 8 (Hippocr.: CMG I 1 p. 97, 14 et al.; Lycophron v. 1202 ἐν σπαργάνοις εἰλημένον; Hesychius) *wrap τινί in someth.* (cf. Is 11: 5) GP 6: 24 acc. to the mss. (s. ἐνειλέω; the same variation in Herodian 2, 1, 1 with v.l.).*

εἴληφα, εἴλημμαι s. λαμβάνω.

εἰλικρίνεια, ας, ἡ (also εἰλικρινία s. W-S. §5, 13c; Mlt.-H. 100; 348. Pre-Socr.+; POxy. 1252 verso II, 38; Wsd 7: 25 v.l.) *sincerity, purity of motive* w. ἀλήθεια 1 Cor 5: 8. ἐξ εἰλικρινείας *out of pure motives* 2 Cor 2: 17; (w. ἁγιότης) ἐν εἰ. τοῦ θεοῦ *in godly sincerity* 1: 12. M-M.*

εἰλικρινής, ές, gen. οὖς (X., Pla.+; pap.; Wsd 7: 25; Philo; Jos., Ant. 19, 321) *unmixed,* then *pure* in moral sense (so Pla., Phaedo 66A εἰλικρινεῖ τῇ διανοίᾳ χρώμενος; 81c ψυχὴ εἰλ.; Ael. Aristid. 13 p. 158 D.; Dit., Or. 227, 12; 763, 40; Test. Benj. 6: 5), *sincere* w. ἀπρόσκοπος Phil 1: 10. W. ἀκέραιος 1 Cl 2: 5; εἰ. διάνοια *pure mind* (s. Plato above) 2 Pt 3: 1; καρδία 2 Cl 9: 8. M-M.*

εἰλικρινῶς adv. (Pla.+; Epict. 4, 2, 6; Dit., Or. 441, 5; Inscr. gr. 394, 48; Philo) *sincerely, candidly* κατανοεῖν *consider* 1 Cl 32: 1.*

εἰλίσσω s. ἑλίσσω.

εἰλόμην s. αἱρέω.

εἰμί (Hom.+; inscr., pap., LXX, En., Ep. Arist., Philo, Joseph., Test. 12 Patr.) imper. ἴσθι, ἔστω—also colloq. ἤτω (BGU 276, 24; 419, 13; POxy 533, 9; Ps 103: 31; 1 Macc 10: 31) 1 Cor 16: 22; Js 5: 12; 1 Cl 48: 5; Hv 3, 3, 4;—3 pers. pl. ἔστωσαν (inscr. since 200 вс Meisterhans³-Schw. 191; PPetr. III 2, 22 [237 вс]) Lk 12: 35; 1 Ti 3: 12.

Inf. εἶναι. Impf. 1 pers. only mid. ἤμην Jos., Bell. 1, 389; 631; s. further below); ἦν only Ac 20: 18 D, 2 pers. ἦσθα (Jos., Ant. 6, 104) Mt 26: 69; Mk 14: 67 and ἦς (Lobeck, Phryn. 149; Jos., Ant. 17, 110 al.; Sb 6262, 16 [III AD]) Mt 25: 21, 23 al., 3 pers. ἦν, 1 pers. pl. ἦμεν. Beside this the mid. form ἤμην (pap. since III BC; Job 29: 16; Tob 12: 13 BA), s. above, gives the pl. ἤμεθα (pap. since III BC; Bar 1: 19) Mt 23: 30; Ac 27: 37; Eph 2: 3. Fut. ἔσομαι. (Mlt.-H. 201-3; Rob. index; Bl-D. §98; Rdm.² 99; 101f; Helbing 108f; Reinhold 86f).

I. as predicate to be—1. be, exist of God (Epicurus in Diog. L. 10, 123 θεοί εἰσιν; Zaleucus in Diod. S. 12, 20, 2 θεοὺς εἶναι; Wsd 12: 13) ἔστιν ὁ θεός God exists Hb 11: 6; cf. 1 Cor 8: 5. ὁ ὢν καὶ ὁ ἦν (thou) who art and wast (cf. Sib. Or. 3, 16; PMich. 155, 3 [II AD] ὁ ὢν θεὸς ὁ Ἰάω κύριος παντοκράτωρ=the god who exists . . .) Rv 11: 17; 16: 5. ὁ ὢν καὶ ὁ ἦν καὶ ὁ ἐρχόμενος, where ἦν is treated as a ptc. (for the incorrect use of ἦν cf. Simonides 74 D.: ἦν ἑκατὸν φιάλαι) 1: 4; 4: 8 (cf. Ex 3: 14; Wsd 13: 1; Paus. 10, 12, 10 Ζεὺς ἦν, Ζ. ἔστι, Ζ. ἔσσεται; cf. Theosophien 18. S. OWeinreich, ARW 19, '19, 178f). ἐγώ εἰμι (inscr. in the Athena-Isis temple of Saïs in Plut., Is. et Os. 9 p. 354C: ἐγώ εἰμι πᾶν τὸ γεγονὸς κ. ὄν κ. ἐσόμενον) Rv 1: 8 (cf. ἐγώ, beg.). ὁ ὤν, . . . θεός Ro 9: 5 is classed here and taken to mean Christ by JWordsworth ad loc. and HJWarner, JTS 48, '47, 203f. Of the λόγος: ἐν ἀρχῆ ἦν ὁ λ. J 1: 1 (for ἦν cf. Herm. Wr. 1, 4; 3, 1b ἦν σκότος, p. 422, 23 Sc. γέγονεν ἡ ὕλη καὶ ἦν). Of Christ πρὶν Ἀβραὰμ γενέσθαι, ἐγὼ εἰμί before Abraham was born, I am 8: 58 (on the pres. εἰμί cf. Parmenides 8, 5: of the Eternal we cannot say ἦν οὐδ' ἔσται, only ἔστιν; Ammonius Hermiae [Comm. in Aristotle IV 5 ed. ABusse 1897] c. 6 p. 172: in Timaeus we read that we must not say of the gods τὸ ἦν ἢ τὸ ἔσται μεταβολῆς τινος ὄντα σημαντικά, μόνον δὲ τὸ ἐστί; Ps 89: 2). Of the world πρὸ τοῦ τὸν κόσμον εἶναι before the world existed 17: 5. Of the beast ἦν καὶ οὐκ ἔστιν Rv 17: 8. τὸ μὴ ὄν that which does not exist, the unreal (Sallust. 17 p. 32, 7 and 9; Philo, Aet. M. 5; 82) Hm 1: 1. τὰ ὄντα that which exists contrasted w. τὰ μὴ ὄντα Ro 4: 17; cf. 1 Cor 1: 28; 2 Cl 1: 8. Of God κτίσας ἐκ τοῦ μὴ ὄντος τὰ ὄντα what is out of what is not Hv 1, 1, 6 (on the contrast τὰ ὄντα and τὰ μὴ ὄντα cf. Ps.-Arist. on Xenophanes.⁵ 21 A, 28; Artem. 1, 51 p. 49, 19 τὰ μὴ ὄντα ὡς ὄντα; Ocellus Luc. c. 12; Sallust. 17 p. 30, 28-32, 12; Philo, Op. M. 81; PGM 4, 3077f ποιήσαντα τὰ πάντα ἐξ ὧν οὐκ ὄντων εἰς τὸ εἶναι; 13, 272f τὸν ἐκ μὴ ὄντων εἶναι ποιήσαντα καὶ ἐξ ὄντων μὴ εἶναι).—Freq. used to introduce parables and stories (once) there was: ἄνθρωπός τις ἦν πλούσιος there was (once) a rich man Lk 16: 1, 19. ἦν ἄνθρωπος ἐκ τ. Φαρισαίων there was a man among the Pharisees J 3: 1.—There is, there are ὥσπερ εἰσὶν θεοὶ πολλοί as there are many gods 1 Cor 8: 5. διαιρέσεις χαρισμάτων εἰσὶν there are various kinds of spiritual gifts 12: 4ff; 1 J 5: 16 al. Neg. οὐκ ἔστι there is (are) not, no (Ps 52: 2; Simplicius in Epict. p. 95, 42 as a quot. from 'the tragedy' οὐκ εἰσὶν θεοί δίκαιος there is no righteous man Ro 3: 10 (Eccl 7: 20). ἀνάστασις νεκρῶν οὐκ ἔστιν there is no resurr. of the dead 1 Cor 15: 12; cf. Mt 22: 23; Ac 23: 8 (cf. 2 Macc 7: 14). εἰσὶν οἵ, or οἵτινες there are people who (class., LXX.—In an incorrect combination of sing. and pl.: Arrian, Ind. 24, 9 ἔστι δὲ οἱ διέφυγον=but there are some who escaped) Mt 16: 28; 19: 12; Mk 9: 1; Lk 9: 27; J 6: 64; Ac 11: 20. Neg. οὐδείς ἐστιν ὅς there is no one who Mk 9: 39; 10: 29; Lk 1: 61; 18: 29. As a question τίς ἐστιν ὅς; who is there that? Mt 12: 11.

2. to denote temporal existence live (class.; Philo, De Jos. 17; Jos., Ant. 7, 254) εἰ ἤμεθα ἐν ταῖς ἡμέραις τῶν πατέρων ἡμῶν if we had lived in the days of our fathers Mt 23: 30. ὅτι οὐκ εἰσὶν because they were no more 2: 18 (Jer 38: 15).

3. to denote a sojourn stay, reside ἴσθι ἐκεῖ stay there Mt 2: 13, cf. vs. 15. ἐπ' ἐρήμοις τόποις in lonely places Mk 1: 45. ἦν παρὰ τὴν θάλασσαν he stayed by the lakeside 5: 21.

4. of phenomena, events, etc. take place, occur (class.; LXX) ἔσται θόρυβος τοῦ λαοῦ a popular uprising Mk 14: 2. γογγυσμὸς ἦν there was (much) muttering J 7: 12. σχίσμα there was a division 9: 16; 1 Cor 1: 10; 12: 25. ἔριδες . . . εἰσὶν quarrels are going on 1: 11. δεῖ αἱρέσεις εἶναι 11: 19. θάνατος, πένθος, κραυγή, πόνος ἔσται Rv 21: 4. ἔσονται λιμοὶ κ. σεισμοί Mt 24: 7. Hence τὸ ἐσόμενον what was going to happen (Sir 48: 25) Lk 22: 49. πότε ταῦτα ἔσται; when will this happen? Mt 24: 3. πῶς ἔσται τοῦτο; how can this be? Lk 1: 34. Hebraistically (הָיָה; cf. KBeyer, Semitische Syntax im NT, '62, 63-65) καὶ ἔσται w. fut. of another verb foll. and it will come about that Ac 2: 17 (Jo 3: 1); 3: 23 (w. δέ); Ro 9: 26 (Hos 2: 1).—W. dat. ἐστί τινι happen, be granted, come, to someone (X., An. 2, 1, 10; Jos., Ant. 11, 255) Mt 16: 22; Mk 11: 24; Lk 2: 10.

5. w. indications of time, etc. (X., Hell. 4, 5, 1, An. 4, 3, 8; Sus 13 Theod.; 1 Macc 6: 49; 2 Macc 8: 26; Jos., Ant. 6, 235 νουμηνία δ' ἦν; 11, 251): ἦν ὥρα ἕκτη it was the sixth hour (=12 o'clock acc. to Jewish reckoning) Lk 23: 44; J 4: 6; 19: 14.—Mk 15: 25; J 1: 39. ἦν ἑσπέρα ἤδη it was already evening Ac 4: 3. πρωΐ J 18: 28. ἦν παρασκευή Mk 15: 42. ἦν ἑορτὴ τῶν Ἰουδαίων J 5: 1. σάββατόν ἐστιν vs. 10 et al. Short clauses (as Polyaenus 4, 9, 2 νὺξ ἦν. 7, 44, 2 πόλεμος ἦν. Exc. 36, 8 ἦν ἀρίστου ὥρα. Jos., Ant. 19, 248 ἔτι δὲ νὺξ ἦν.) χειμὼν ἦν. J 10: 22; night (Jos., Bell. 4, 64) 13: 30; cold 18: 18; hot Lk 12: 55.

6. be present, available, provided πολλοῦ ὄχλου ὄντος since a large crowd was present Mk 8: 1. ὄντων τῶν προσφερόντων those are provided who offer Hb 8: 4. οὔπω ἦν πνεῦμα the Spirit had not yet come J 7: 39. ἀκούσας ὄντα σιτία when he heard that the grain was available Ac 7: 12.

7. ἔστιν w. inf. foll. it is possible (Περὶ ὕψους 6; Diog. L. 1, 110 ἔστιν εὑρεῖν=it is possible to find); neg. οὐκ ἔστιν νῦν λέγειν it is not possible to speak at this time Hb 9: 5. οὐκ ἔστιν φαγεῖν it is impossible to eat 1 Cor 11: 20 (so Hom. +; UPZ 70, 23 [153/1 BC] οὐκ ἔστι ἀνακύψαι με πώποτε. . .ὑπὸ τῆς αἰσχύνης; 4 Macc 13: 5; Wsd 5: 10; Sir 14: 16; 18: 6; EpJer 49 al.; Ep. Arist. 163; Jos., Ant. 2, 335).

II. As a copula, uniting subject and predicate. On absence of the copula, Mlt.-Turner 294-310.

1. gener. πραΰς εἰμι I am gentle Mt 11: 29. ἐγώ εἰμι Γαβριήλ Lk 1: 19. σὺ εἶ ὁ υἱὸς τοῦ θεοῦ Mk 3: 11; J 1: 49 and very oft.—The pred. can be supplied fr. the context: καὶ ἐσμέν and we are (really God's children) 1 J 3: 1 (Eur., Ion 309 τ. θεοῦ καλοῦμαι δοῦλος εἰμί τε. Dio Chrys. 14[31], 58 θεοφιλεῖς οἱ χρηστοί λέγονται καὶ εἰσίν; Epict. 2, 16, 44 Ἡρακλῆς ἐπιστεύθη Διὸς υἱὸς εἶναι καὶ ἦν.).

2. to describe a special relation betw. the subject and a predicate noun ἡμεῖς ναὸς θεοῦ ἐσμεν ζῶντος we are a temple of the living God 2 Cor 6: 16. ἡ ἐπιστολὴ ὑμεῖς ἐστε you are our letter (of recommendation) 3: 2. σφραγίς μου τῆς ἀποστολῆς ὑμεῖς ἐστε you are the seal of my apostleship 1 Cor 9: 2 and oft.

3. explanatory: is a representation of, is the equivalent of. εἰμί here, too, serves as copula; we usually translate mean, so in the formula τοῦτ' ἔστιν this or that means, that is to say (Epict., Ench. 33, 10; Arrian, Tact. 29, 3;

Dit., Syll.³ 880, 50; PFlor. 157, 4; PSI 298, 9; PMerton 91, 9; Jos., C. Ap. 2, 16) Mt 27: 46; Mk 7: 2; Ac 1: 19; 19: 4; Ro 7: 18; 9: 8; 10: 6, 8; Phlm 12; Hb 7: 5 al.; in the sense *that is* (*when translated*) (Polyaenus 8, 14, 1 Μάξιμος ἀνηγορεύθη· τοῦτο δ' ἂν εἴη Μέγιστον) Mt 27: 46; Ac 1: 19. So also w. relative pron.: ὅ ἐστιν Mk 3: 17; 7: 11, 34; Hb 7: 2. After verbs of asking, recognizing, knowing and not knowing (Antiphanes Com. 231, 1f τὸ ζῆν τί ἐστι;) μάθετε τί ἐστιν *learn what* (*this*) *means* Mt 9: 13. εἰ ἐγνώκειτε τί ἐστιν 12: 7; cf. Mk 1: 27; 9: 10; Lk 20: 17; J 16: 17f; Eph 4: 9. W. an indir. question (Stephan. Byz. s.v. Ἀγύλλα: τὶς ἠρώτα τί ἂν εἴη τὸ ὄνομα) τί ἂν εἴη ταῦτα Lk 15: 26; τί εἴη τοῦτο 18: 36. τίνα θέλει ταῦτα εἶναι *what this means* Ac 17: 20 and sim.—Esp. in interpr. of the parables (Artem. I, 51 p. 48, 26 ἄρουρα οὐδὲν ἄλλο ἐστὶν ἢ γυνή=*field means nothing else than woman*) ὁ ἀγρός ἐστιν ὁ κόσμος *the field means the world* Mt 13: 38; cf. vss. 19f, 22f; Mk 4: 15f, 18, 20; Lk 8: 11ff (cf. Gen 41: 26f; Ezk 37: 11). On τοῦτό ἐστιν τὸ σῶμά μου Mt 26: 26; Mk 14: 22; Lk 22: 19 and its various interpretations, see the lit. s.v. εὐχαριστία. Cf. Hipponax (VI bc) 45 Diehl αὕτη ἐστι συμφορά=*this means misfortune.*

4. Very commonly the simple tense forms are replaced by the periphrasis εἶναι and the ptc. (Bl-D. §352–5 w. app.; Mlt. 225–7; 249; Mlt.-H. 451f; Rdm.² 102; 105; 205; Kühner-G. I 38ff; Rob. 374–6; 1119f; very oft. LXX).

a. (as in class. usage) w. the pf. ptc. to express the pf., plpf. and fut. pf. act. and pass. (cf. Mayser 329; 377) ἦσαν ἐληλυθότες *they had come* Lk 5: 17. ἦν αὐτῶν ἡ καρδία πεπωρωμένη *their hearts were hardened* Mk 6: 52. ἠλπικότες ἐσμέν *we have set our hope* 1 Cor 15: 19. ὁ καιρὸς συνεσταλμένος ἐστιν *the time has become short* 7: 29. ἦν ἐστώς (En. 12, 3) *he was standing* (more exactly *he took his stand*) Lk 5: 1.

b. w. pres. ptc.—**α.** to express the pres. ἐστὶν προσαναπληροῦσα τὰ ὑστερήματα *supplies the wants* 2 Cor 9: 12.

β. impf. or aor. ἦν καθεύδων *he was sleeping* Mk 4: 38. ἦσαν ἀναβαίνοντες . . . ἦν προάγων 10: 32; cf. Lk 1: 22; 5: 17; 11: 14 al.

γ. fut. ἔση σιωπῶν *you will be silent* Lk 1: 20; cf. 5: 10; Mt 24: 9; Mk 13: 13; Lk 21: 17, 24 al.; 2 Cl 17: 7 Bihlm.

δ. ἦν τὸ φῶς . . . ἐρχόμενον εἰς τ. κόσμον *the light came* (*was coming*) *into the world* J 1: 9 is a timeless dogmatic saying.

c. w. aor. ptc. as plpf. (Aelian, N.A. 7, 11; Hippiatr. 34, 14 vol. 1 p. 185, 3 ἦν σκευάσας; Wadd. 2070b ἦν κτίσας. Act. Thom. 16; 27.—JVogeser, Z. Sprache d. griech. Heiligenlegenden, Diss. Munich '07, 14; JWittmann, Sprachl. Untersuchungen zu Cosmas Indicopleustes, Munich Diss. '13, 20; StBPsaltes, Gramm. d. byzant. Chroniken '13, 230; Björck [διδάσκω, end] 75; Bl-D. §355 w. app.). ἦν βληθείς *had been thrown* Lk 23: 19; J 18: 30א*.—GP 6: 23; 12: 51.

d. Notice esp. the impersonals δέον ἐστίν *it is necessary* (class.; POxy. 727, 19; Sir praef. l. 3; 1 Macc 12: 11 δέον ἐστὶν καὶ πρέπον) Ac 19: 36; 1 Cl 34: 2; 1 Pt 1: 6 t.r.; πρέπον ἐστίν *it is fitting* (class.; POxy. 120, 24; 3 Macc 7: 13) Mt 3: 15; 1 Cor 11: 13.

e. In many cases the usage w. the ptc. serves to emphasize the duration of an action or condition (BGU 183, 25 ἐφ' ὃν χρόνον ζῶσα ἦ Σαταβοῦς) ἦν διδάσκων *he customarily taught* Mk 1: 22; Lk 4: 31; 19: 47. ἦν θέλων *he cherished the wish* 23: 8. ἦσαν νηστεύοντες *they were keeping the fast* Mk 2: 18. ἦσαν συλλαλοῦντες *they were conversing for a while* 9: 4. ἦν προσδεχόμενος *he was waiting for* (the kgdm.) 15: 43. ἦν συγκύπτουσα *she was bent over* Lk 13: 11.

f. to emphasize the adjectival idea inherent in the ptc. rather than the concept of action expressed by the finite verb ζῶν εἰμι *I am alive* Rv 1: 18. ἦν ὑποτασσόμενος *he was obedient* Lk 2: 51. ἦν ἔχων κτήματα πολλά *he was very rich* Mt 19: 22; Mk 10: 22. ἴσθι ἐξουσίαν ἔχων *you shall have authority* Lk 19: 17 (Lucian, Tim. 35 ἴσθι εὐδαιμονῶν). ἦν καταλλάσσων *he was reconciling* 2 Cor 5: 19.

5. the formula ἐγώ εἰμι is oft. used in the gospels (corresp. to Hebr. אני הוא Dt 32: 39; Is 43: 10), in such a way that the predicate must be understood fr. the context: Mt 14: 27; Mk 6: 50; 13: 6; 14: 62; Lk 22: 70; J 4: 26; 6: 20; 8: 24, 28; 13: 19; 18: 5f and oft.; s. on ἐγώ.—In a question μήτι ἐγώ εἰμι; *surely it is not I?* Mt 26: 22, 25.

6. used w. a pron.:—**a.** w. demonstr. pron. τὰ ὀνόματά ἐστιν ταῦτα Mt 10: 2. αὕτη ἐστὶν ἡ μαρτυρία J 1: 19. W. inf. foll. θρησκεία αὕτη ἐστίν, ἐπισκέπτεσθαι Js 1: 27. W. ὅτι foll. αὕτη ἐστὶν ἡ κρίσις, ὅτι τὸ φῶς ἐλήλυθεν J 3: 19; cf. 21: 24; 1 J 1: 5; 3: 11; 5: 11. W. ἵνα foll. τοῦτό ἐστιν τὸ ἔργον, ἵνα πιστεύητε J 6: 29; cf. vs. 39f; 15: 12; 17: 3; 1 J 3: 11, 23; 5: 3. W. τηλικοῦτος: τὰ πλοῖα, τηλικαῦτα ὄντα *though they are so large* Js 3: 4. W. τοσοῦτος: τοσούτων ὄντων *although there were so many* J 21: 11. W. τοιοῦτος: τοιοῦτος ὢν Phlm 9.

b. w. indef. pron. εἰδωλόθυτόν τί ἐστιν *meat offered to idols means anything* 1 Cor 10: 19. Esp. εἰμί τι *I mean someth.* of pers. 1 Cor 3: 7; Gal 2: 6; 6: 3; and of things vs. 15. εἰμί τις Ac 5: 36.

c. w. interrog. pron. ὑμεῖς τίνα με λέγετε εἶναι; *who do you say I am?* Mt 16: 15; cf. 21: 10; Mk 1: 24; 4: 41; 8: 27, 29; Lk 4: 34 al.; σὺ τίς εἶ; J 1: 19; 8: 25; 21: 12 al.; σὺ τίς εἶ ὁ κρίνων; (Pla., Gorg. 452b; Strabo 6, 2, 4 σὺ τίς εἶ ὁ τὸν Ὅμηρον ψέγων ὡς μυθογράφον;) Ro 14: 4; ἐγὼ τίς ἤμην; (cf. Ex 3: 11) Ac 11: 17. W. πόσος: πόσος χρόνος ἐστίν; *how long a time?* Mk 9: 21. W. ποταπός *of what sort* Lk 1: 29.

d. w. relative pron. οἷος 2 Cor 10: 11; ὁποῖος Ac 26: 29; 1 Cor 3: 13; Gal 2: 6; ὅς Rv 1: 19; ὅστις Gal 5: 10, 19.

e. w. possess. pron. ὑμετέρα ἐστὶν ἡ βασιλεία Lk 6: 20. οὐκ ἔστιν ἐμὸν δοῦναι Mk 10: 40.

7. w. numerals ἦσαν οἱ φαγόντες πεντακισχίλιοι ἄνδρες 6: 44 (cf. Polyaenus 7, 25 ἦσαν οἱ πεσόντες ἀνδρῶν μυριάδες δέκα); cf. Ac 19: 7; 23: 13. Λάζαρος εἷς ἦν ἐκ τῶν ἀνακειμένων *L. was one of those at the table* J 12: 2; cf. Gal 3: 20; Js 2: 19. τῶν πιστευσάντων ἦν καρδία καὶ ψυχὴ μία Ac 4: 32. εἷς εἶναι *be one and the same* Gal 3: 28. ἓν εἶναι *be one* J 10: 30; 17: 11, 21ff; 1 Cor 3: 8.

8. the ptc. ὤν, οὖσα, ὄν used w. a noun or adj. may function as an if-, since-, or although-clause πονηροὶ ὄντες Mt 7: 11; 12: 34.—Lk 20: 36; J 3: 4; 4: 9; Ac 16: 21; Ro 5: 10; 1 Cor 8: 7; Gal 2: 3 al.

9. used w. an adverb—**a.** w. adv. of time or place ἐγγύς *be near* Mt 26: 18; Mk 13: 28. ἐγγύς τινος *be near someone* J 11: 18; 19: 20; Ro 10: 8 (Dt 30: 14). ἐγγύς τινι Ac 9: 38; 27: 8. μακράν *be far* Mk 12: 34; J 21: 8; Eph 2: 13. For this πόρρω Lk 14: 32. ἐπάνω τινός *be over someone* J 3: 31. χωρὶς τινος *without someth.* Hb 12: 8. ἐνθάδε Ac 16: 28. ἔσω J 20: 26. ἀπέναντί τινος Ro 3: 18 (Ps 35: 2). ἐντός τινος Lk 17: 21; ἐκτός τινος 1 Cor 6: 18; ἔμπροσθέν τινος Lk 14: 2. ἔναντί τινος Ac 8: 21; ἐνώπιόν τινος Lk 14: 10; Ac 4: 19; 1 Pt 3: 4; Rv 7: 15; ἀντίπερά τινος Lk 8: 26; ὁμοῦ J 21: 2; οὗ Mt 2: 9; ὅπου Mk 2: 4; 5: 40. ὧδε Mt 17: 4; Mk 9: 5; Lk 9: 33. Also w. fut. mng. ESchwartz, GGN '08, 161 n.; on the fut. use of the pres. cf. POxy. 531, 22 [II ad] ἔστι δὲ τοῦ Τῦβι μηνὸς σοὶ ὃ θέλεις) ὅπου εἰμί J 7: 34, 36; 12: 26; 14: 3; 17: 24.

b. w. adv. of quality: οὕτως εἶναι *be so* preceded by

ὥσπερ, καθώς or followed by ὡς, ὥσπερ Mt 13: 40; 24: 27, 37, 39; Mk 4: 26; Lk 17: 26. W. dat. of pers. οὕτως ἔσται ὁ υἱὸς τ. ἀ. τῇ γενεᾷ ταύτῃ so the Son of Man will be for this generation 11: 30. εἰμὶ ὥσπερ, ὡς I am like Mt 6: 5; Lk 18: 11. W. dat. ἔστω σοι ὥσπερ τελώνης he shall be to you as a tax-collector Mt 18: 17. εἰμὶ ὥς τις I am like someone of outward and inward similarity 28: 3; Lk 6: 40; 11: 44; 22: 27 al. καθὼς εἰμί as I am Ac 22: 3; 1 J 3: 2, 7; 4: 17. ἀνεκτότερον ἔσται it will be more tolerable τινί for someone Lk 10: 12, 14. τὰ σπλάγχνα αὐτοῦ περισσοτέρως εἰς ὑμᾶς his heart is inclined toward you even more 2 Cor 7: 15.

III. Used w. prepositions.—1. εἶναι ἀπό τινος be or come from a certain place (X., An. 2, 4, 13) J 1: 44.

2. εἴς τινα be directed, inclined toward someone Ac 23: 30; 2 Cor 7: 15; 1 Pt 1: 21. εἰς τ. κοίτην be in bed Lk 11: 7. εἰς τὸν κόλπον J 1: 18. Also become someth. εἰς χολὴν πικρίας εἶναι become bitter gall Ac 8: 23. εἰς σάρκα μίαν Mt 19: 5; Mk 10: 8; 1 Cor 6: 16; Eph 5: 31 (all Gen 2: 24. Cf. Syntipas p. 42, 24 οὐκ ἔτι ἔσομαι μετὰ σοῦ εἰς γυναῖκα); τὰ σκολιὰ εἰς εὐθείας Lk 3: 5 (Is 40: 4); εἰς πατέρα 2 Cor 6: 18; Hb 1: 5 (2 Km 7: 14; 1 Ch 22: 10; 28: 6); εἰς τὸ ἕν 1 J 5: 8. Serve as someth. (Inschr. v. Priene 50, 39 [c. II BC] εἶναι εἰς φυλακὴν τ. πόλεως; Aesop., Fab. 26, 3 l. 5 Chambry εἰς ὠφέλειαν; Gen 9: 13; s. also εἰς 4d) 1 Cor 14: 22; Col 2: 22; Js 5: 3. ἐμοὶ εἰς ἐλάχιστόν ἐστιν (telescoped fr. ἐλάχ. ἐστιν and εἰς ἐλάχ. γίνεται, of which there are many exx. in WSchmid, Atticismus 1887-97, I 398; II 161, 237; III 281; IV 455) it is of little or no importance to me 1 Cor 4: 3.

3. ἔκ τινος belong to someth. or someone 1 Cor 12: 15f; Mt 26: 73; Mk 14: 69f; Lk 22: 58 and oft. (cf. X., Mem. 3, 6, 17; oft. LXX). ἐκ τοῦ ἀριθμοῦ τῶν δώδεκα belong to the twelve 22: 3. Of origin come from somewhere 23: 7; J 1: 46; 3: 31; 1 Cor 11: 8 al. ὅς ἐστιν ἐξ ὑμῶν who is a fellow-countryman of yours Col 4: 9. ἐξ οὐρανοῦ, ἐξ ἀνθρώπων be of heavenly (divine), human descent Mt 21: 25; Mk 11: 30; Lk 20: 4. Be generated by (cf. Sb 8141, 21f [inscr. I BC] οὐδ' ἐκ βροτοῦ ἦεν ἄνακτος, ἀλλὰ θεοῦ μεγάλου ἔκγονος; En. 106, 6) Mt 1: 20. Esp. in Johannine usage ἐκ τοῦ διαβόλου εἶναι originate from the devil J 8: 44; 1 J 3: 8. ἐκ τοῦ πονηροῦ 3: 12; ἐκ τοῦ κόσμου J 15: 19; 17: 14, 16; 1 J 4: 5. ἐκ τῆς ἀληθείας εἶναι 2: 21; J 18: 37 etc. To denote a close relationship ἐξ ἔργων νόμου εἶναι found one's religion on keeping the law Gal 3: 10. ὁ νόμος οὐκ ἔστιν ἐκ πίστεως the law has nothing to do with faith vs. 12.

4. ἔν τινι of place ἐν τοῖς τ. πατρός μου in my father's house Lk 2: 49 (cf. Jos., Ant. 16, 302 καταγωγὴ ἐν τοῖς Ἀντιπάτρου). ἐν τῇ ὁδῷ on the way Mk 10: 32. ἐν τῇ ἐρήμῳ Mt 24: 26. ἐν ἀγρῷ Lk 15: 25. ἐν δεξιᾷ τ. θεοῦ at God's right hand Ro 8: 34; in heaven Eph 6: 9. Fig., live in the light 1 J 2: 9; cf. vs. 11; 1 Th 5: 4; in the flesh Ro 7: 5; 8: 8. ἐν οἷς εἰμι in the situation in which I find myself Phil 4: 11 (X., Hell. 4, 2, 1; Diod. S. 12, 63, 5; 12, 66, 4; Appian, Hann. 55 §228 ἐν τούτοις ἦν=he was in this situation; Jos., Ant. 7, 232 ἐν τούτοις ἦσαν=found themselves in this sit.). Of states of being: ἐν δόξῃ 2 Cor 3: 8; ἐν εἰρήνῃ Lk 11: 21; ἐν ἔχθρᾳ at enmity 23: 12; ἐν κρίματι under condemnation vs. 40. ἐν ῥύσει αἵματος suffer from hemorrhages Mk 5: 25; Lk 8: 43 (cf. Soph., Aj. 271 ἦν ἐν τῇ νόσῳ). Periphrastically for an adj. ἐν ἐξουσίᾳ authoritative Lk 4: 32. ἐν βάρει important 1 Th 2: 7. ἐν τῇ πίστει true believers, believing 2 Cor 13: 5. ἐν ἑορτῇ be at the festival=take part in it Lk 2: 23. ἐν τούτοις ἴσθι devote yourself to these things 1 Ti 4: 15 (cf. X., Hell. 4, 8, 7 ἐν τοιούτοις ὄντες=occupied w. such things; Jos., Ant. 2, 346 ἐν ὕμνοις ἦσαν=they occupied themselves w. the singing of hymns). Of characteristics, emotions, etc. ἔν τινί ἐστιν, e.g. ἀδικία J 7: 18; ἄγνοια Eph 4: 18; ἀλήθεια J 8: 44; 2 Cor 11: 10 (cf. 1 Macc 7: 18); ἁμαρτία 1 J 3: 5. Also of God, who is among his people 1 Cor 14: 25 (Is 45: 14; Jer 14: 9). Of the spirit J 14: 17. Of special interest is the expr. ἐν τῷ θεῷ εἶναι of humankind: have its basis of existence in God Ac 17: 28; of Christians 1 J 2: 5; 5: 20 (cf. Norden, Agn. Th. 23, 1). Equiv. to ἔκ τινος εἶναι be among Mt 27: 56; cf. Mk 15: 40; Ro 1: 6.—ἔν τινι rest upon, arise from someth. (Aristotle p. 1323b, 1 ἐν ἀρετῇ; Sir 9: 16) Ac 4: 12; 1 Cor 2: 5; Eph 5: 18.

5. w. ἐπί—a. w. gen. be on someth. of place, on the roof Lk 17: 31.—J 20: 7 (cf. 1 Macc 1: 59). Also fig., of one who is over πάντων (1 Macc 10: 69; Jdth 14: 13 ὁ ὢν ἐπὶ πάντων τῶν αὐτοῦ) Ro 9: 5.

b. w. dat. be at someth. the door Mt 24: 33; Mk 13: 29.

c. w. acc. be on someone: grace Lk 2: 40; Ac 4: 33; spirit (Is 61: 1); Lk 2: 25. εἶναι ἐπὶ τὸ αὐτό be in the same place, together (Gen 29: 2 v.l.) Ac 1: 15; 2: 1, 44 v.l.; 1 Cor 7: 5.

6. w. κατά—a. w. gen. be against someone (Sir 6: 12) Mt 12: 30; Mk 9: 40; Lk 9: 50; Gal 5: 23.

b. w. acc. live in accordance with (Sir 28: 10; 43: 8; 2 Macc 9: 20) κατὰ σάρκα, πνεῦμα Ro 8: 5. οὐκ ἔστιν κατὰ ἄνθρωπον not human (in origin) Gal 1: 11.—εἶναι κατὰ τὴν Ἰουδαίαν be in Judaea Ac 11: 1; 13: 1.

7. w. μετά and gen. be with someone (Judg 14: 11) Mt 17: 17; Mk 3: 14; 5: 18; J 3: 26; 12: 17. Also be with in the sense be favorable to, in league with (Ex 23: 2) Mt 12: 30; Lk 11: 23. Of God, who is with someone (Gen 21: 20; Judg 6: 13 al.; Philo, Det. Pot. Ins. 4; Jos., Ant. 6, 181; 15, 138) Lk 1: 66; J 3: 2; 8: 29; Ac 10: 38 al.

8. w. παρά—a. and gen. come from someone (X., An. 2, 4, 15) fr. God J 6: 46; 7: 29.

b. w. dat. be with, among persons Mt 22: 25; Ac 10: 6. W. neg. be strange to someone, there is no . . . in someone Ro 2: 11; 9: 14; Eph 6: 9.

c. w. acc. παρὰ τὴν θάλασσαν by the sea- (or lake-) shore Mk 5: 21; Ac 10: 6.

9. w. πρός τινα or τι be close to someth. Mk 4: 1. πρὸς ἑσπέραν ἐστίν it is toward evening Lk 24: 29; be with someone Mt 13: 56; Mk 6: 3. I am to be compared w. IMg 12.

10. w. σύν τινι be with someone (Jos., Ant. 7, 181) Lk 22: 56; 24: 44; Ac 13: 7. Accompany, associate w. someone Lk 8: 38; Ac 4: 13; 22: 9; take sides with someone (X., Cyr. 5, 4, 37; 7, 5, 77; Jos., Ant. 11, 259 [of God]) Ac 14: 4.

11. w. ὑπέρ—a. and gen. be for someone Mk 9: 40; Lk 9: 50.—b. w. acc. be over=more than someone (Sir 25: 10; 30: 16) Lk 6: 40.

12. w. ὑπό τι or τινα of place be under someth. J 1: 48; 1 Cor 10: 1. Fig. be under (the power of) someth. Ro 3: 9; 6: 14f; Gal 3: 10, 25.

IV. εἰμί w. gen.—1. to denote the possessor Mt 5: 3, 10; 19: 14; Mk 12: 7; Lk 18: 16; 1 Cor 6: 19. Esp. of God. who owns the Christian Ac 27: 23; 1 Cor 3: 23; 2 Ti 2: 19 (Num 16: 5).

2. to denote the fact of belonging to something or someone (X., Hell. 2, 4, 36; Iambl., Vi. Pyth. 33, 230 τῶν Πυθαγορείων) οἱ τῆς ὁδοῦ ὄντες those who belong to the Way Ac 9: 2. εἰμὶ Παύλου I belong to Paul 1 Cor 1: 12; 3: 4; cf. Ro 8: 9; 2 Cor 10: 7; 1 Ti 1: 20; Ac 23: 6. ἡμέρας εἶναι belong to the day 1 Th 5: 8, cf. vs. 5.

3. to denote function (X., An. 2, 1, 4) οὐχ ὑμῶν ἐστιν it is no concern of yours Ac 1: 7.

4. to denote a quality παιδεία οὐ δοκεῖ χαρᾶς εἶναι discipline does not seem to be (partake of) joy Hb 12: 11.—10: 39.—5. to denote origin 2 Cor 4: 7.

6. to denote age (POxy. 275, 9 [66 AD] οὐδέπω ὄντα τῶν ἐτῶν; Tob 14: 11) Mk 5: 42; Lk 3: 23; Ac 4: 22.

V. An extraordinary use of the pres. ptc. is found Ac 13: 1 ἡ οὖσα ἐκκλησία the church there (cf. Ps.-Pla., Eryx. 6 p. 394c οἱ ὄντες ἄνθρωποι=the people with whom he has to deal; PLond. 1168, 5 ἐπὶ ταῖς οὔσαις γειτνίαις; PGenève 49; PSI 229, 11 τοῦ ὄντος μηνός of the current month). αἱ οὖσαι (sc. ἐξουσίαι) those that exist Ro 13: 1 (cf. UPZ 180a I, 4 [113 bc] ἐφ᾽ ἱερέων καὶ ἱερειῶν τῶν ὄντων καὶ οὐσῶν). LCMcGaughy, Toward a Descriptive Analysis of EINAI as a Linking Verb in the Gk. NT, Diss. Vanderbilt, ’70. Mlt. 228. M-M. B. 635.

εἶμι (Hom.+ in pres. w. pres. mng. 'I go') in Att. used as fut. of ἔρχομαι=I shall go (rare in H. Gk.) J 7: 34 v.l., cf. 36; 12: 26; 14: 3; 17: 24 where εἰμί may also be read as εἶμι. (Bl-D. §99, 1).*

εἵνεκεν prep. w. gen. (Pind.+; inscr. [OBenndorf and GNiemann, Reisen im s.-w. Kleinasien I 1884, 109]; Sb 1568; PGiess. 40 II, 21; PGM 5, 385; LXX) on account of Lk 4: 18 (Is 61: 1); Ac 28: 20; 2 Cor 3: 10; s. ἕνεκα.

εἴπερ s. εἰ VI 11.

εἶπον (Hom.+; inscr., pap., LXX, En., Ep. Arist., Philo, Joseph., Test. 12 Patr.) used as 2 aor. of λέγω 'say' (Bl-D. §101, p. 46); subj. εἴπω, imper. εἰπόν; inf. εἰπεῖν, ptc. εἰπών. Somet. takes 1 aor. endings (Meisterhans³-Schw. 184, 6; ESchweizer, Gramm. d. perg. Inschr. 182; Mayser 331; Ep. Arist. ind.) εἶπα, εἶπας, εἶπαν; imper. εἰπόν Mk 13: 4; Lk 22: 67; Ac 28: 26 (on the accent cf. W-S. §6, 7d; Mlt.-H. 58. But, on the other hand, εἶπον acc. to PKatz, ThLZ 61, ’36, 284 and Bl-D. §81, 1), εἰπάτω, εἰπά-τωσαν; ptc. εἴπας Ac 7: 37, fem. εἴπασα Hv 3, 2, 3; 4, 3, 7. Fut. ἐρῶ; pf. εἴρηκα, 3 pl. εἰρήκασιν and εἴρηκαν (Rv 19: 3), inf. εἰρηκέναι; plpf. εἰρήκειν; 1 aor. pass. ἐρ-ρέθην, ptc. ῥηθείς; pf. pass. εἴρηται, ptc. εἰρημένος (Bl-D. §70, 1; 81, 1 w. app.; 101 p. 46; W-S. §13, 13; Rob. index) say, speak.

1. w. acc. τὸν λόγον Mt 26: 44. ὅσα Lk 12: 3. τί vs. 11; a parable tell (Artem. 4, 80 Μενεκράτης εἶπεν ὄνειρον) 19: 11; the truth 2 Cor 12: 6 and oft. τοῦτο ἀληθές this as someth. true=this truly J 4: 18. τί εἴπω; what shall I say? J 12: 27. As a rhetor. transition formula τί ἐροῦμεν; what shall we say or conclude? what then? Ro 3: 5; 6: 1; 7: 7; 9: 14, 30. λόγον εἴς τινα say someth. against someone Lk 12: 10. For this κατά τινος Mt 5: 11; 12: 32. τί τινι say someth. to someone Gal 3: 16. ἔχω σοί τι εἰπεῖν I have someth. to say to you (cf. Lucian, Tim. 20; Lk 7: 40. τί εἴπω ὑμῖν; what shall I say to you? 1 Cor 11: 22. τί πρὸς τινα say someth. to someone (Pla., Prot. 345c; Herodas 2, 84; Philostrat., Vi. Apoll. 6, 20, 6; Ex 23: 13; Jos., Vi. 205) a parable Lk 12: 16; speak w. reference to someone Mk 12: 12; Lk 20: 19. Also πρὸς ταῦτα to this Ro 8: 31. τί περὶ τινος say someth. about someone or someth. (X., Vect. 4, 13) J 7: 39; 10: 41. εἰρήκει περὶ τοῦ θανάτου he had referred to death 11: 13. W. acc. of the pers. ὃν εἶπον of whom I said J 1: 15. ὁ ῥηθείς the one who was mentioned Mt 3: 3. εἰπεῖν τινα καλῶς speak well of someone Lk 6: 26. κακῶς speak ill of someone Ac 23: 5 (Ex 22: 27). W. omission of the nearer obj., which is supplied fr. the context Lk 22: 67; J 9: 27 al. As an answer σὺ εἴπας sc. αὐτό you have said it is evasive or even a denial (as schol. on Pla. 112E Socrates says: σὺ ταῦτα εἴπες, οὐκ ἐγώ. S. also the refusal to give a clearly affirmative answer in Const. Apost. 15, 14, 4 οὐκ εἶπεν ὁ κύριος ‘ναί’, ἀλλ᾽ ὅτι ‘σὺ εἶπας’.—λέγω II 1e, end) Mt 26: 25, 64.—W. indication of the pers., to whom someth. is said: in the dat. Mt 5: 22; 8: 10, 13, 19, 21 and oft. τινὶ περὶ τινος tell someone about someth. 17: 13; J 18: 34. Also πρός τινα

for the dat. (Lucian, Dial. Mort. 1; Jos., Ant. 11, 210) Mk 12: 7; Lk 1: 13, 34, 61 and very oft.

2. abs. say, speak—**a.** modified by an adv. ὁμοίως Mt 26: 35. ὡσαύτως 21: 30; or an adv. expr. ἐν παραβολαῖς in parables=parabolically 22: 1. διὰ παραβολῆς using a parable Lk 8: 4. εἰπὲ λόγῳ say the word 7: 7; Mt 8: 8.

b. w. direct discourse foll.: Mt 2: 8; 9: 22; 12: 24, 49; 14: 29; 15: 16, 32; 17: 17 and very oft. οὐδὲ ἐροῦσιν=nor will they be able to say Lk 17: 21 (cf. Herodas 4, 73 οὐδ᾽ ἐρεῖς, with direct discourse foll. as in Lk).—As a formula introducing an objection (Diod. S. 13, 21, 5 ἐροῦσί τινες ἴσως; Dio Chrys. 14[31], 47 ἴσως οὖν ἐρεῖ τις) ἀλλὰ ἐρεῖ τις (X., Cyr. 4, 3, 10; Appian, Bell. Civ. 3, 16 §59 ἀλλὰ . . . ἐρεῖ τις; Ps.-Clem., Hom. 9, 16 p. 98, 1; 5 Lag.) 1 Cor 15: 35; Js 2: 18. ἐρεῖς οὖν Ro 11: 19; w. μοι added 9: 19.

c. w. ὅτι foll. (Diod. S. 12, 16, 5; 12, 74, 3; Jos., Vi. 205) Mt 28: 7, 13; J 7: 42; 8: 55; 16: 15; 1 J 1: 6, 8, 10; 1 Cor 1: 15; 14: 23 al.—**d.** w. acc. and inf. foll. Ro 4: 1 (text uncertain).

3. Various modifications in mng. result from the context.

a. in answer to a question (Ps.-Pla., De Virt. 2 p. 376D οὐκ ἔχω εἰπεῖν=I cannot answer that; Ps.-Pla., Eryx. 21 p. 401D ἔχειν εἰπεῖν=be able to answer) Mt 15: 34; 16: 14; 26: 18 al. On its use w. ἀποκρίνεσθαι, freq. in the historical books to denote transition, s. ἀποκρ. 2. Also without a preceding question in conversation Mt 14: 18; 15: 27; Mk 9: 39; Lk 1: 38 and oft.

b. with questions w. direct discourse foll. (Epict. 3, 23, 18a=ask; Zech 1: 9a) Mt 9: 4; 17: 19, 24; 18: 21; 20: 32; 26: 15 al. W. dat. of pers. Mt 13: 10, 27.

c. w. commands (Ex 19: 8b; 2 Ch 24: 8; w. inf. foll.: Ex 35: 1b; Wsd 9: 8; Epict. 1, 14, 3 ὅταν [ὁ θεὸς] εἴπῃ τοῖς φυτοῖς ἀνθεῖν, ἀνθεῖ; Abercius inscr. 17) and requests: εἶπεν δοθῆναι αὐτῇ φαγεῖν he ordered that she be given someth. to eat Mk 5: 43. εἶπεν καὶ ταῦτα παρατιθέναι he told them to place this also before (the people) 8: 7. W. ἵνα foll. Mt 4: 3; Mk 9: 18; Lk 4: 3.

d. call w. double acc. (Maximus Tyr. 14, 5c κόλακα τὸν Ὀδυσσέα; Diog. L. 6, 40 Diogenes the Cynic is called a 'dog'; Sib. Or. 4, 140) ἐκείνους εἶπεν θεούς J 10: 35. ὑμᾶς εἴρηκα φίλους 15: 15 (cf. Od. 19, 334; X., Apol. 15; Lucian, Tim. 20).

e. foretell (Dt 1: 21; 19: 8; Is 41: 22 τὰ ἐπερχόμενα εἴπατε ἡμῖν; Jos., Ant. 8, 273 καθὼς εἶπεν ὁ προφήτης) Mt 28: 6; Mk 14: 16; Lk 22: 13; J 14: 28; 16: 4.

f. conclude, as in the transitional formula τί ἐροῦμεν; what conclusion are we to draw? Ro 3: 5; 6: 1; 9: 14, 30; on Ro 4: 1 s. FWDanker, FWGingrich-Festschr. ’72, 103f.

4. regularly used w. quotations: Tit 1: 12; usually fr. the OT ἐρρέθη Ro 9: 12; καθὼς εἴρηκεν Hb 4: 3. τὸ ῥηθὲν ὑπὸ κυρίου διὰ τοῦ προφήτου Mt 1: 22. ὑπὸ τ. θεοῦ 22: 31. διὰ τοῦ προφήτου Ac 2: 16; cf. Mt 2: 17, 23; 4: 14; 8: 17; 12: 17; 13: 35; 24: 15 al. τὸ εἰρημένον what is written Lk 2: 24; Ac 13: 40; Ro 4: 18.—EHowind, De ratione citandi in Ciceronis Plutarchi Senecae Novi Testamenti scriptis obvia, Diss. Marburg ’21.

5. Corresp. to אָמַר בְּלִבּוֹ the expr. εἰπεῖν ἐν ἑαυτῷ (Esth 6: 6; Tob 4: 2 BA; S has ἐν τῇ καρδίᾳ αὐτοῦ [s. below]) means say to oneself or quietly, think (to oneself) Mt 9: 3; Lk 7: 39; 16: 3; 18: 4. For this ἐν τῇ καρδίᾳ αὐτοῦ (Dt 8: 17; 9: 4; Ps 9: 27; 13: 1; s. above) Lk 12: 45; Ro 10: 6. M-M. B. 1253f.

εἴπως s. εἰ VI 12.

εἰργασάμην etc. s. ἐργάζομαι.

εἴρηκα s. εἶπον.

Εἰρηναῖος, ου, ὁ (inscr., pap.; Jos., Bell. 2, 21) *Irenaeus,* bishop of Lyons MPol 22: 2; Epil Mosq 1ff.*

εἰρήναρχος, ου, ὁ (Inschr. v. Milet: Ergebnisse I 7, '24, no. 263, 7; Inscr. Rom. IV 1543; POxy. 1507, 1; 1662, 19) *chief of police, police captain,* a magistrate of imperial times MPol 6: 2; 8: 2.—Lghtf. ad loc.; WLiebenam, Städteverwaltung im röm. Kaiserreich '00, 358.*

εἰρηνεύω fut. εἰρηνεύσω 1 Cl 56: 12f; 1 aor. inf. εἰρηνεῦσαι 63: 4.
1. trans. (Cass. Dio 77, 12; 1 Macc 6, 60) *reconcile* τινά (cf. Polyb. 5, 8, 7) those who are quarreling B 19: 12; D 4: 3.
2. intr. (Pla., Theaet. 180β; Cass. Dio 42: 15; inscr. fr. Halicarnassus [Hdb. I 2³, '12, 410] εἰρηνεύουσι γῆ καὶ θάλαττα; LXX).
a. *live in peace, be at peace* (Inschr. d. Brit. Mus. 894; 2 Ch 14: 5; Job 3: 26; 2 Macc 12: 4) τινί w. *someone* (Job 5: 23; Sir 6: 6) 1 Cl 56: 12. Of the church, which is enjoying peace IPhld 10: 1; cf. ISm 11: 2; IPol 7: 1. ἐν σαρκὶ καὶ πνεύματι *be at peace outwardly and inwardly* ITr inscr.; εἰρηνεῦσαι *attain peace* 1 Cl 63: 4.
b. *keep the peace* abs. (Appian, Liby. 67 §303, Syr. 4 §15, Bell. Civ. 5, 22 §88; Test. Gad 6: 6) 2 Cor 13: 11. δαιμόνιον μηδέποτε εἰρηνεῦον *an evil spirit that never keeps the peace* Hm 2: 3. εἰρηνεύετε ἐν ἀλλήλοις *keep the peace among yourselves* Mk 9: 50 (AvanVeldhuizen, Zout en Vrede: NThSt 15, '32, 252–9). For this ἐν ἑαυτοῖς 1 Th 5: 13; Hv 3, 6, 3; 3, 9, 2 and 10; 3, 12, 3; s 8, 7, 2. μετά τινος *with someone* (3 Km 22: 45; Test. Benj. 5: 1) Ro 12: 18; 1 Cl 54: 2. οἱ εἰρηνεύοντες *those who are peaceable* (Sir 28: 9, 13) 15: 1. M-M.*

εἰρήνη, ης, ἡ (Hom.; inscr., pap., LXX, Ep. Arist., Philo, Joseph., Test. 12 Patr., loanw. in rabb.).
1. *peace*—a. lit., opp. πόλεμος IEph 13: 2. ἐρωτᾷ τὰ πρὸς εἰρήνην *asks for terms of peace* Lk 14: 32 (cf. Test. Jud. 9: 7 αἰτοῦσιν ἡμᾶς τὰ πρὸς εἰρήνην; Anna Comn., Alex. 8, 5 ed. R. II 12, 17 τὰ περὶ εἰρήνης ἐρωτῶντες.— It is also poss. to transl. *inquires about his health* like ἐρωτ. [τὰ] εἰς εἰρήνην=שָׁאַל לְשָׁלוֹם 2 Km 8: 10; 11: 7; cf. HStJThackeray, JTS 14, '13, 389–99; RHelbing, D. Kasussyntax d. Verba b. d. LXX '28, 40); ἐν εἰ. εἶναι *be in peace, out of danger* Lk 11: 21. λαμβάνειν τὴν εἰ. ἐκ τινος *take peace away fr. someth.*=plunge it into a state of war Rv 6: 4.—Ac 24: 2. Of those who are fighting αἰτεῖσθαι εἰ. *ask for peace* (Anonym. Alex.-gesch. [II вс]: 151 fgm. 1, 5 Jac.) Ac 12: 20.
b. fig. *peace, harmony* w. ὁμόνοια (Chrysipp.: Stoic. II 1076; Dio Chrys. 21[38], 14; 22[39], 2; Dit., Syll.³ 685, 13 [139 вс]; Jos., Ant. 4, 50) 1 Cl 60: 4; 61: 1; 63: 2. Opp. ὀργή D 15: 3; opp. μάχαιρα Mt 10: 34; cf. Lk 12: 51. συναλλάσσειν εἰς εἰ. *pacify* Ac 7: 26; σύνδεσμος τῆς εἰ. Eph 4: 3. βασιλεὺς εἰρήνης *king of peace* (as transl. of Salem; cf. Philo, Leg. All. 3, 79) Hb 7: 2. Of the church εἰ. ἔχειν *have peace, rest* (fr. persecution, as Ac 14: 2 v.l.; Diod. S. 11, 72, 1; cf. Jos., Bell. 2, 401) Ac 9: 31; εἰ. βαθεῖα (s. βαθύς 2) 1 Cl 2: 2. ὁδὸς εἰρήνης *the way of peace,* that leads to peace Ro 3: 17 (Ps 13: 3; Is 59: 8); Lk 1: 79. μετ' εἰρήνης *peaceably* (Diod. S. 3, 18, 7; Vi. Aesopi W c. 97 μετ' εἰρήνης ζῆν; EpJer 2; 1 Esdr 5: 2; 1 Macc 12: 4, 52 al.; Jos., Ant. 1, 179; 8, 405) Hb 11: 31; ποιεῖν εἰ. *make peace* (Hermocles [IV/III вс] p. 174, 21 Coll.=Athen. 6 p. 253ε) Eph 2: 15; οἱ ποιοῦντες εἰ. *those who make peace* Js 3: 18. βούλεσθαι εἰ. (Pr 12: 20) *wish for peace* 1 Cl 15: 1. διώκειν *strive toward peace* (w.

δικαιοσύνη, πίστις, ἀγάπη) 2 Ti 2: 22; Gal 5: 22; εἰ. διώκειν μετὰ πάντων *strive to be at peace w. everyone* Hb 12: 14 (cf. Epict. 4, 5, 24 εἰ. ἄγεις πρὸς πάντας). τὰ τῆς εἰ. διώκειν *strive after peace* Ro 14: 19; ζητεῖν εἰ. 1 Pt 3: 11 (Ps 33: 15); τὰ πρὸς εἰ. *what makes for peace* Lk 19: 42. W. ἀσφάλεια 1 Th 5: 3; ἀπέστη ἡ εἰ. *peace has disappeared* 1 Cl 3: 4; εἰ. ἔχειν ἐν ἑαυτοῖς *have peace within one's group* Hv 3, 5, 1.
c. *order* opp. ἀκαταστασία 1 Cor 14: 33; cf. 7: 15, and 1 Cl 20: 1, 9ff.
2. corresp. to Hebr. שָׁלוֹם *welfare, health* (WCaspari, Vorstellung u. Wort 'Friede' im AT '10, esp. p. 128ff) in a farewell greeting: ὑπάγειν ἐν εἰ. *go in peace,* approx. equiv. to 'keep well' Js 2: 16. For this πορεύεσθαι ἐν εἰ. (Judg 18: 6 B; 2 Km 3: 21) Ac 16: 36; ὑπάγειν εἰς εἰρήνην Mk 5: 34; πορεύεσθαι εἰς εἰ. (1 Km 1: 17; 20: 42; 29: 7; Jdth 8: 35) Lk 7: 50; 8: 48. προπέμπειν τινὰ ἐν εἰ. *send someone on his way in peace* 1 Cor 16: 11 (cf. Vi. Aesopi I c. 32 p. 297, 1 ἐν εἰρήνῃ ἀπέστειλεν [αὐτόν]. ἀπολύειν τινὰ μετὰ εἰρήνης *send someone away w. a greeting of peace* Ac 15: 33 (cf. Gen 26: 29; Jos., Ant. 1, 179). In the formula of greeting εἰ. ὑμῖν=שָׁלוֹם לָכֶם (cf. Judg 6: 23; 19: 20; Da 10: 19 Theod.; Tob 12: 17) Lk 24: 36 𝔓⁷⁵ et al.; J 20: 19, 21, 26. εἰρήνη τῷ οἴκῳ τούτῳ *peace to this house* Lk 10: 5; cf. vs. 6; Mt 10: 12 v.l., 13 (on εἰ. ἐπί w. acc. cf. Is 9: 7; Ps 84: 9).—A new and characteristic development is the combination of the Greek epistolary greeting χαίρειν with a Hebrew expression in the Pauline and post-Pauline letters χάρις καὶ εἰρήνη (s. χάρις 2c) Ro 1: 7; 1 Cor 1: 3; 2 Cor 1: 2; Gal 1: 3; Eph 1: 2; Col 1: 2; 1 Th 1: 1; 2 Th 1: 2; Tit 1: 4; Phlm 3; Rv 1: 4. (χάρις, ἔλεος, εἰρήνη) 1 Ti 1: 2; 2 Ti 1: 2; 2 J 3. (χάρις καὶ εἰ.—or w. ἔλεος—πληθυνθείη, cf. Da 4: 1; 4: 37c LXX; 6: 26 Theod.) 1 Pt 1: 2; 2 Pt 1: 2; Jd 2; 1 Cl inscr.; Pol inscr.; MPol inscr.; cf. Gal 6: 16; Eph 6: 23; 2 Th 3: 16; 1 Pt 5: 14; 3 J 15; ISm 12: 2; B 1: 1 (χαίρετε ἐν εἰ.); mng. 3 also is felt in this expr. to a degree.
3. Since, acc. to the prophets, peace will be an essential characteristic of the messianic kgdm. (εἰ. as summum bonum: Seneca, Ep. 66, 5), Christian thought also freq. regards εἰ. as nearly synonymous w. messianic salvation εὐαγγελίζεσθαι εἰ. *proclaim peace,* i.e., messian. salvation (Is 52: 7) Ac 10: 36; Ro 10: 15 t.r.; Eph 2: 17; τὸ εὐαγγέλιον τῆς εἰ. 6: 15; ἔχειν ἐν Χριστῷ εἰ. J 16: 33; ἔχειν εἰ. πρὸς τὸν θεόν *have peace w. God* Ro 5: 1 (on εἰ. πρός τινα cf. Pla., Rep. 5, 465β; X., Hiero 2, 11; Diod. S. 21, 12; Epict. 4, 5, 24; Jos., Ant. 8, 396). ἀφιέναι εἰ. *leave peace* τινί J 14: 27. Hence εἰ. τοῦ Χριστοῦ *the peace brought by Christ* Col 3: 15; εἰ. τοῦ θεοῦ Phil 4: 7; ὁ θεὸς τῆς εἰ. (Test. Dan 5: 2) Ro 15: 33; 16: 20; 2 Cor 13: 11; Phil 4: 9; 1 Th 5: 23; Hb 13: 20; ὁ κύριος τῆς εἰ. 2 Th 3: 16; αὐτός (i.e. ὁ Χριστός) ἐστιν ἡ εἰρήνη ἡμῶν Eph 2: 14 (cf. POxy. 41, 27, where an official is called εἰρήνη πόλεως.—FDCoggan, ET 53, '42, 242 [peace-offering]; but cf. NHSnaith, ibid. 325f). ἐπαναδράμωμεν ἐπὶ τὸν τῆς εἰ. σκοπόν *let us run toward the goal of peace* 1 Cl 19: 2.—2 Pt 3: 14. (w. ζωή) Ro 8: 6; (w. δόξα and τιμή) 2: 10; (w. δικαιοσύνη and χαρά.—W. χαρά En. 5, 9; Philo, Leg. All. 1, 45) Ro 14: 17; 15: 13. Also Lk 2: 29 and the angelic greeting ἐπὶ γῆς εἰ. *peace on earth* 2: 14 are prob. to be classed here; cf. 19: 38.—On peace as a gift of God cf. Epict. 3, 13, 12 εἰρήνη ὑπὸ τοῦ θεοῦ κεκηρυγμένη διὰ τοῦ λόγου [=philosophy]; Oenomaus in Euseb., Pr. Ev. 5, 26, 5: it is the task of the gods to establish and to promote εἰρήνη and φιλία.—HFuchs, Augustin u. d. antike Friedensgedanke '26, 39–43; 167–223; GvRad and WFoerster, TW II 398–418; WNestle, D. Friedensgedanke in d.

227

εἰρήνη – εἰς

antiken Welt: Philol. Suppl. 31, '38; WSvanLeeuwen, Eirene in het NT '40; on the word's history, KBrugmann and BKeil, Εἰρήνη: Ber. d. Sächs. Ges. d. Wiss. 68, '16 nos. 3 and 4; GKöstner, Εἰρήνη in d. Briefen des hl. Apostels, Diss. Rome, '58, WEisenbeis, D. Wurzel שלם im AT, Beih. ZAW 113, '69. M-M. B. 1376. **

εἰρηνικός, ή, όν (X., Pla.+; POxy. 1033, 5; LXX; Ep. Arist. 273; Philo, Spec. Leg. 1, 224 al.; Test. Gad 6: 2) peaceable, peaceful ἄνθρωπος εἰ. 1 Cl 14: 5 (Ps 36: 37). Of Christian σοφία Js 3: 17. καρπὸν εἰ. ἀποδιδόναι yield peaceful fruit Hb 12: 11. M-M.*

εἰρηνοποιέω 1 aor. εἰρηνοποίησα (LXX Pr 10: 10; Aq., Sym., Theod. Is 27: 5; Cat. Cod. Astr. II 203; mid., Hermes in Stob. p. 498, 10 Sc.) make peace Col 1: 20.*

εἰρηνοποιός, όν (X., Hell. 6, 3, 4; Cornutus 16 p. 23, 2; Cass. Dio 44, 49, 2; 72, 15, 5 εἰρ. τ. οἰκουμένης; Plut., Mor. 279B; Pollux 152; PSI 1036, 28 [192 AD]; Philo, Spec. Leg. 2, 192) making peace; subst. ὁ εἰ. the peace-maker Mt 5: 9 (HWindisch, Friedensbringer—Gottessöhne: ZNW 24, '25, 240-60).*

εἰρωνεία, ας, ἡ (Pla.+; 2 Macc 13: 3) pretense τῆς νηστείας hypocritical fasting Dg 4: 1.*

εἰς prep. w. acc. (Hom.+; LXX, En., Ep. Arist., Philo, Joseph., Test. 12 Patr. S. the lit. under ἀνά, beg., also ATheimer, Die Präp. εἰς, ἐν, ἐκ im NT: Progr. z. 24. u. 29. Jahresbericht des niederösterr. Landes-Real- u. Obergymnasiums Horn 1896; '01; AOepke, TW II 418-32), indicating motion into a thing or into its immediate vicinity.

1. of place into, in, toward, to—a. into, toward, to a. after verbs of going, or those that include motion toward a place; so after ἄγω, ἀκολουθέω, ἀναβαίνω, ἀνάγω, ἀναχωρέω, ἀνέρχομαι, ἄπειμι, ἀπέρχομαι, ἀποδημέω, ἀποπλέω, γίνομαι δεῦρο, διαβαίνω, διαπεράω, διασῴζω, διέρχομαι, διώκω, εἰσάγω, εἴσειμι, εἰσέρχομαι, εἰσπορεύομαι, ἐκπηδάω, ἐκπλέω, ἐκπορεύομαι, ἐμβαίνω, ἐνδύνω, ἐξέρχομαι, ἐπανάγω, ἐπιβαίνω, ἐπιστρέφω, ἔρχομαι (cf. Gdspd., Probs., 56f), εὐθυδρομέω, ἥκω, καθίζω, καταβαίνω (cf. Gdspd., Probs. 52-4), κατάγομαι, καταντάω, καταπλέω, καταφεύγω, κατέρχομαι, μεταβαίνω, ὁρμάω, παραβάλλω, παραγίνομαι, πέτομαι, πλέω, πορείαν ποιοῦμαι, πορεύομαι, προάγω, συμβάλλω, συνάγομαι, συναναβαίνω, συνέρχομαι, ὑπάγω, ὑποστρέφω, ὑποχωρέω, φεύγω, χωρέω; see these entries. Hence w. nouns that denote an accessible place εἰς τὴν πόλιν into the city Mt 26: 18 al.; εἰς τὸν οἶκον into the house 9: 7; synagogue Ac 17: 10; boat Mt 8: 23; J 6: 17; world J 1: 9; heaven Lk 2: 15; abyss 8: 31. φεύγειν εἰς τὰ ὄρη Mk 13: 14; εἰς τ. ναόν 2 Th 2: 4; εἰς (τὸ) μέσον (Sir 27: 12; cf. 48: 17): ἔστη εἰς τὸ μέσον (X., Cyr. 4, 1, 1), he (came and) stood among them J 20: 19, 26; cf. Mk 14: 60; Lk 6: 8, also ἔγειρε εἰς τὸ μ. get up and come here Mk 3: 3. W. names of places and countries to Spain Ro 15: 24, 28. εἰς Ἱερουσαλήμ vs. 25 al. Also on, in εἰς (τὰς) ὁδούς Lk 14: 23; Mt 10: 5, 10; Mk 6: 8; 10: 17. εἰς ἀγρόν 16: 12. W. another mng. ἀναβαίνει εἰς τὸ ὄρος 3: 13; Mt 15: 29.

β. after verbs of sending, moving, etc., which result in movement or include a movement of the body to, into, among; so after ἀπολύω, ἀποστέλλω, βάλλω, βαπτίζω, δίδωμι, ἐγκεντρίζω, ἐκβάλλω, ἐκπέμπω, ἐκχέω, ἐμβάπτω, ἐξαποστέλλω, καθίημι, μεταπέμπομαι, παρακύπτω, πέμπω, χαλάω; s. these entries. ἐμπίπτειν εἰς τοὺς λῃστάς fall among robbers Lk 10: 36. εἰς τὰς ἀκάνθας among the thorns Mk 4: 7; εἰς τ. λαόν Ac 4: 17 et al., where the transl. depends on the verb in question.

γ. δέχεσθαι εἰς τὰς ἀγκάλας take in (into) one's arms Lk 2: 28 (cf. Jos., Ant. 8, 28).

b. in the vicinity of, near, to (Jos., Vi. 115 εἰς τ. κώμην) εἰς (τὴν) θάλασσαν Mk 7: 31; 3: 7 v.l.; Mt 17: 27. εἰς πόλιν (Hdt. 2, 169; 4, 200; Diod. S. 15, 32, 2 παραγενόμενος εἰς πόλιν) J 4: 5 (cf. vs. 28). εἰς τὸ μνημεῖον 11: 31, 38; 20: 1, 3f (cf. vs. 6). ἐγγίζειν εἰς (Tob 11: 1) Mt 21: 1; Mk 11: 1; Lk 18: 35; 19: 29. εἰς τοὺς φραγμοὺς to the hedges 14: 23. κλίνειν τὸ πρόσωπον εἰς τ. γῆν toward the ground 24: 5.

c. when the nearness becomes actual contact, on, in: of striking (PRyl. 145, 13 [38 AD] ἔδωκεν πληγὰς πλείους εἰς πᾶν μέρος τοῦ σώματος; cf. PTebt. 39, 32) τύπτειν εἰς τ. κεφαλήν on the head Mt 27: 30 (cf. Arrian, Anab. 2, 26, 4 ἐμβάλλειν εἰς τ. κεφαλήν). ῥαπίζειν εἰς τὴν σιαγόνα on the cheek 5: 39.—εἰς τ. ὄμματα Mk 8: 23; εἰς τ. ὁδόν 11: 8; ἀναπίπτειν εἰς τ. ἔσχατον τόπον sit in the lowest place Lk 14: 10; cf. vs. 8. εἰς τὴν χεῖρα, τοὺς πόδας on his hand, his feet Lk 15: 22.

d. It can also denote simply direction toward someth. a. w. verbs of looking (fr. Od. 10, 37; Il. 3, 364; LXX) ἀναβλέπειν εἴς τι look up toward someth. (2 Macc 7: 28; Sus 35 Theod.) Mk 6: 41; Lk 9: 16; Ac 22: 13; cf. ἀτενίζω, βλέπω, ἐμβλέπω.—ἐπαίρειν τοὺς ὀφθαλμοὺς εἴς τινα raise one's eyes toward someone Lk 6: 20.

β. after verbs of saying, teaching, proclaiming, preaching, etc. (trag.; Hdt. 8: 26; Thu. 1, 72, 2; 5, 45, 1 and many later wr., incl. LXX) λαλεῖν εἰς τ. κόσμον say to the world J 8: 26. τὸ εὐαγγέλιον εἰς ὅλον τ. κόσμον the gospel in the whole world Mk 14: 9. εἰς πάντα τὰ ἔθνη 13: 10; Lk 24: 47. εἰς ὑμᾶς 1 Th 2: 9. εὐαγγελίζεσθαι εἴς τινα 2 Cor 10: 16; 1 Pt 1: 25; γνωρίζειν Ro 16: 26. ἀπαγγέλλειν τι εἴς τινα Mk 5: 14; Lk 8: 34. διαμαρτύρεσθαι εἰς Ἰερουσαλήμ, μαρτυρεῖν εἰς Ῥώμην bear witness in Jerusalem, Rome Ac 23: 11. In these and similar cases εἰς approaches ἐν in mng.; s. 9 below.

γ. The same is true of βαπτίζεσθαι εἰς τὸν Ἰορδάνην Mk 1: 9 and νίπτεσθαι εἰς τὴν κολυμβήθραν J 9: 7; these expr. look like exx. of the interchange of εἰς and ἐν, but were orig. formed on the analogy of X., Cyr. 1, 3, 5 ἀποκαθαίρει τὴν χεῖρα εἰς τὰ χειρόμακτρα=lit. 'into the towels'; cf. Epict. 3, 22, 71 ἵν' αὐτὸ (sc. τὸ παιδίον) λούσῃ εἰς σκάφην; Alciphr., Ep. 3, 7, 1; Athen. 10 p. 438E.

2. of time—a. w. indication of the time a. up to which someth. continues εἰς τέλος to the end (Epict. 1, 7, 17) Mt 10: 22; 24: 13; Mk 13: 13. εἰς ἐκείνην τὴν ἡμέραν until that day 2 Ti 1: 12. εἰς ἡμέραν Χριστοῦ Phil 1: 10. εἰς Χριστόν until the coming of the Messiah Gal 3: 24.

β. for or on which someth. happens μεριμνᾶν εἰς τὴν αὔριον be anxious for tomorrow Mt 6: 34; cf. Hs 6, 5, 3; εἰς τὸ μέλλον for the future 1 Ti 6: 19. εἰς τὸ μεταξὺ σάββατον on the next Sabbath Ac 13: 42. εἰς ἡμέραν (UPZ 66, 5 [153 BC]) for the day Phil 2: 16; cf. Eph 4: 30; Rv 9: 15.

γ. at which someth. takes place (Appian, Mithrid. 74 §321 ἐς ἑσπέραν=in the evening; Epict. 4, 10, 31 αὔριον ἢ εἰς τὴν τρίτην; En. 1, 1 οἵτινες ἔσονται εἰς ἡμέραν ἀνάγκης) εἰς τὸν καιρὸν αὐτῶν in their time Lk 1: 20; εἰς τὸ μέλλον in the future 13: 9. εἰς τέλος in the end, finally (Hdt. 3, 40; Gen 46: 4; Ps.-Clem., Hom. 18, 2) Lk 18: 5 (Bl-D. §207, 3 app. prefers mng. 3 and ὑπωπιάζω 2; s. also Mlt.-Turner 266). εἰς τὸ πάλιν=πάλιν 2 Cor 13: 2; cf. WSchmid I 167; II 129; III 282; IV 455; 625.

b. to indicate duration of time for, throughout (Nicol. Dam.: 90 fgm. 4 p. 332, 16 Jac. εἰς νύκτα; Arrian, Anab. 4, 30, 1 ἐς τρεῖς ἡμέρας) εἰς ἔτη πολλά for many years Lk

12: 19. εἰς τὸν αἰῶνα, εἰς τοὺς αἰῶνας (αἰών 1b) *forever* Mt 21: 19; Mk 3: 29; 11: 14; Lk 1: 33; J 8: 35 and oft. εἰς ἡμέραν αἰῶνος *to the day of eternity* 2 Pt 3: 18. εἰς γενεὰς καὶ γενεάς *for generation after generation* Lk 1: 50. εἰς τὸ διηνεκές *forever* Hb 7: 3; 10: 1, 12, 14 (cf. Thu. 2, 64, 3 ἐς ἀΐδιον).

3. In addition to place and time, it can be used to indicate degree: εἰς τέλος *completely, fully, absolutely* (s. on τέλος 1dγ) 1 Th 2: 16; B 4: 6; 19: 11; Hv 3, 7, 2; m 12, 2, 3; s 8, 6, 4; 8, 8, 5; 8, 9, 3.—J 13: 1 combines in εἰς τέλος the mngs. *to the end* (s. 2aα above) and *to the uttermost* (cf. Appian, Mithrid. 58 §239 ἡμῶν ἀμυναμένων ἤδη καὶ ἀμυνουμένων ἐς τέλος=we have defended ourselves up to now and will defend ourselves ἐς τέλος). εἰς τὰ ἄμετρα 2 Cor 10: 13, 15 (cf. PVat. A 12=Witkowski p. 65 [168 BC] εἰς τὰ ἔσχατα). εἰς περισσείαν 10: 15. εἰς ὑπερβολήν (Eur., Hipp. 939; Aeschin., F. Leg. 4) 4: 17. εἰς τὸ παντελές (q.v.) Lk 13: 11; Hb 7: 25.

4. to indicate the goal.—**a.** when it is a state of being, w. verbs of going, coming, leading, etc., used in a fig. sense: ἀπέρχεσθαι εἰς κόλασιν αἰώνιον Mt 25: 46 (cf. Sir 41: 10). εἰσφέρειν εἰς πειρασμόν 6: 13. πορεύεσθαι εἰς θάνατον Lk 22: 33. ὑπάγειν εἰς ἀπώλειαν Rv 17: 8, 11. βάλλειν εἰς θλῖψιν 2: 22. παραδιδόναι εἰς θλῖψιν Mt 24: 9; cf. 2 Cor 4: 11; Lk 24: 20. συγκλείειν εἰς ἀπείθειαν Ro 11: 32. ἐμπίπτειν εἰς κρίμα 1 Ti 3: 6f; cf. 6: 9. μετατίθεσθαι εἰς *turn away to* Gal 1: 6. ἄγειν εἰς μετάνοιαν Ro 2: 4; cf. Hb 2: 10. αἰχμαλωτίζειν εἰς ὑπακοήν 2 Cor 10: 5. ἀνακαινίζειν εἰς μετάνοιαν Hb 6: 6; cf. 2: 10. Sim. ἀπάγω, ἀποβαίνω, εἰσέρχομαι, εἰσφέρω, ἐκβάλλω, ἐλευθερόω, ἐπιστρέφω, κατευθύνω, μεταβαίνω, ὁδηγέω et al.; s. these entries.

b. w. verbs of changing: στρέφειν (Esth 4: 17h; 1 Macc 1: 39), μεταστρέφειν (Sir 11: 31; 1 Macc 9: 41; 3 Macc 6: 22) τι εἰς τι Rv 11: 6; Ac 2: 20 (Jo 3: 4); Js 4: 9. μεταλλάσσειν Ro 1: 26. μετασχηματίζεσθαι (q.v.) 2 Cor 11: 13f.

c. in hostile or friendly sense (Thu. 1, 38; 66; 130; X., Cyr. 1, 3, 5; Paus. 7, 9, 3; 7, 10, 2; Aelian, V.H. 11, 10).

α. in a hostile sense (Arrian, Anab. 1, 1, 4; PEleph. 1, 9 [311/10 BC] κακοτεχνεῖν εἰς Δημητρίαν; UPZ 170B, 47 [127 BC]): ἁμαρτάνειν εἴς τινα (Herodian 7, 9, 11; EpJer 12; Jdth 5: 20; 11: 10) *sin against someone* Lk 15: 18, 21. βλασφημεῖν εἴς τινα (Bel 8 Theod.) *blaspheme against someone* Mk 3: 29; Lk 12: 10; 22: 65; θαρρεῖν εἴς τινα 2 Cor 10: 1. ψεύδεσθαι εἴς τινα (Sus 55; 59 Theod.) Col 3: 9. Also w. nouns and adj. (Paus. 7, 8, 4; PFay. 12, 7 [c. 103 BC] ἀδικήματα εἴς με) Ac 6: 11; 23: 30; Ro 8: 7.

β. in a friendly sense: μακροθυμεῖν 2 Pt 3: 9. τὸ αὐτὸ φρονεῖν Ro 12: 16. So also πιστεύειν εἴς τινα *trust or believe in someone* Mt 18: 6; Mk 9: 42 and oft. (s. πιστεύω). Also w. nouns (Dit., Or. 49, 10 [III BC] φιλοτιμία εἰς; 51, 4; UPZ 22, 17 [162 BC]; 39, 5 εἰς τὸ θεῖον εὐσέβεια; 2 Macc 9: 26 εὔνοια) ἀγάπη Ro 5: 8; 2 Cor 2: 4, 8; Col 1: 4; 1 Th 3: 12. διακονία Ro 15: 31 (cf. the v.l. Ac 12: 25 and s. JDupont, Novum Testamentum 1, '56, 275-303); 2 Cor 8: 4. ἐλπίς (2 Macc 9: 20; Synes., Ep. 104 p. 246A εἰς τὸν κομήτην ἐ.) Ac 24: 15. κοινωνία Phil 1: 5. πεποίθησις 2 Cor 8: 22. μέγεθος Eph 1: 19. πίστις (Jos., Ant. 16, 48; 18, 334) Ac 20: 21; 24: 24; 26: 18; Col 2: 5; and adj. φιλόξενος 1 Pt 4: 9. χρηστός Eph 4: 32.

d. w. the vocation, use, or end indicated *for, as*: αἱρέομαι εἴς τι 2 Th 2: 13. ἀφορίζω Ro 1: 1; Ac 13: 2. προγράφω Ro 15: 4; Jd 4. ἀποστέλλω Hb 1: 14. πέμπω Phil 4: 16; 1 Th 3: 2. ποιῶ τι εἰς 1 Cor 10: 31; 11: 24. Cf. under κεῖμαι, προορίζω, τάσσω, τίθημι.—εἰμί εἴς τι *serve as someth.* (s. εἰμί III 2; also inscr. 134, 33ff fr. the

Delphinion at Miletus [I AD] 1914; s. Dssm., LO 97, 1 [LAE 123]) 1 Cor 14: 22; for destruction Col 2: 22; as a testimony Js 5: 3. Used w. a noun σκεῦος εἰς τιμήν, ἀτιμίαν *a vessel meant for honorable, dishonorable use* Ro 9: 21; cf. vs. 22f; 2 Ti 2: 20f; φύλλα τοῦ ξύλου εἰς θεραπείαν Rv 22: 2. φῶς εἰς ἀποκάλυψιν *a light serving as a revelation* Lk 2: 32. θεράπων εἰς μαρτύριον τῶν λαληθησομένων *a servant to bear witness to what would be said* Hb 3: 5. W. acc. of the pers. ἡ εἰς ὑμᾶς χάρις *the grace meant for you* 1 Pt 1: 10. διδόναι εἰς τι *pay out for someth.*, *money for a field* Mt 27: 10.

e. the result of an action or condition *into, to, so that*: αὐξάνειν εἰς ναόν *grow into a temple* Eph 2: 21. πληροῦσθαι εἴς τι 3: 19. λυπηθῆναι εἰς μετάνοιαν *be grieved so that repentance takes place* 2 Cor 7: 9. Of prayer ἀναβαίνειν εἰς μνημόσυνον Ac 10: 4. ὁμολογεῖν εἰς σωτηρίαν *confess to salvation=so as to receive salvation* Ro 10: 10; cf. 1: 16; 1 Pt 2: 2; εἰς ἔπαινον κτλ. *to praise* etc. 1 Pt 1: 7; εἰς βοήθειαν (1 Ch 12: 17; Jdth 6: 21) Hb 4: 16; cf. 10: 39; Rv 13: 3; Ro 6: 16; 8: 15; 13: 4, 14; 1 Cor 11: 34; 2 Cor 2: 16 al.; εἰς κενόν (s. κενός 2aβ) 2 Cor 6: 1; Gal 2: 2; Phil 2: 16; 1 Th 3: 5. σχίζειν εἰς δύο *tear in two* Mt 27: 51; Mk 15: 38. Cf. GP 5: 20 (cf. Polyb. 2, 16, 11; Lucian, Lapith. 44, Toxar. 54; 1 Km 15: 29; Tob 5: 3 S; 1 Macc 9: 11). W. subst. inf. foll. *so that* Ro 1: 20; 3: 26; 4: 18; 6: 12; 7: 4; 1 Th 3: 13; 2 Th 2: 10f; Hb 11: 3 al.

f. to denote purpose *in order to, to* (Appian, Liby. 101 §476 ἐς ἔκπληξιν=in order to frighten) εἰς ἄγραν *in order to catch someth.* Lk 5: 4. εἰς ἀπάντησιν, συνάντησιν, ὑπάντησίν τινι (q.v.) *to meet someone, toward someone* Mt 8: 34; 25: 1; J 12: 13. εἰς μαρτύριον αὐτοῖς *as a witness*, i.e. *proof, to them* Mt 8: 4; 10: 18; 24: 14 al. εἰς ἄφεσιν ἁμαρτιῶν *for forgiveness of sins, so that sins might be forgiven* Mt 26: 28; cf. Mk 1: 4; Lk 3: 3; Ac 2: 38. εἰς μνημόσυνόν τινος *in memory of someone* Mt 26: 13; Mk 14: 9; cf. Lk 22: 19 al.; εἰς ὅ *for which purpose* (Hdt. 2, 103) Col 1: 29; otherw. 2 Th 1: 11 *with this in view*; εἰς τί *why?* (Wsd 4: 17; Sir 39: 16, 21) Mt 14: 31; Mk 14: 4; 15: 34; Hm 2: 5; D 1: 5. εἰς τοῦτο *for this reason or purpose* Mk 1: 38; J 18: 37; Ac 9: 21; 26: 16; Ro 9: 17; 14: 9; 2 Cor 2: 9; 1 J 3: 8; Hs 1: 9. εἰς αὐτὸ τοῦτο *for this very reason* 2 Cor 5: 5; Eph 6: 22; Col 4: 8. W. subst. inf. foll. (X., Ages. 9, 3, Mem. 3, 6, 2) *in order to* (oft. LXX; neg. μή *in order not to*; s. Bl-D. §402, 2) Mt 20: 19; 26: 2; 27: 31; Mk 14: 55 and oft. εἰς ὁδόν *for the journey* 6: 8.

g. As in Mod. Gk., it is used for the dat., the dat. of advantage, but also=*for* in general (X., An. 3, 3, 19 τ. ἵππους εἰς ἱππέας κατασκευάσωμεν; Lycurg. c. 85 διεκαρτέρουν εἰς τ. πατρίδα; UPZ 180a I, 7 [113 BC] τὸν εἰς Τάγην οἶκον ᾠκοδομημένον; BGU 37, 4f [50 AD] ξύλα εἰς τοὺς ἐλαιῶνάς μου *wood for my olive orchards*; PLond. 43, 9; PTebt. 5, 77; POxy. 37 I, 9; EpJer 9; Sir 37: 7, cf. 8; Jdth 14: 2; Bel 3 Theod., 22 LXX) εἰς πάντα τ. λαόν Lk 9: 13; cf. 3 J 5. εἰς ἡμᾶς Eph 1: 19; cf. Col 1: 25; 1 Th 4: 10; Ro 10: 12. χρείαν ἔχειν εἰς τ. ἑορτήν J 13: 29; cf. Mk 8: 19f; Gal 2: 8; 1 Th 2: 9; 5: 15 et al.—εἰς is commonly used in speaking of the person *for* whom a payment etc. is made (Dssm., B 113-15; NB 23 [BS 117f; 194f]) 1 Cor 16: 1; 2 Cor 8: 4; 13: 1; Ro 15: 26; Ac 24: 17. εἰς λόγον τινός *in an account for someth.* (POxy. 275, 19; 21 [66 AD]; 496, 10; 530, 15) Phil 4: 15; cf. vs. 17. εἰς Χριστόν Phlm 6 prob. *in honor of Christ* (Tetrast. Iamb. 1, 7, 4 p. 266 εἰς θεούς; Pla., Lysis 205D ᾄδεις εἰς σαυτὸν ἐγκώμιον; Ps.-Pla., Minos 319C; Athen. 15, p. 667C; Synes., Ep. 75 p. 222B).

h. In τὰ εἰς Χριστὸν παθήματα 1 Pt 1: 11 εἰς Χρ. may be construed genitivally (UPZ 180a II, 2 [113 BC] χωρὶς τοῦ εἰς αὐτὴν οἴκου; PTebt 16, 9) or as an expression of the objective in mind, as in 4cβ (for a parallel expr. in a hostile sense cf. Polyb. 1, 7, 12 τῆς εἰς ἐκείνους τιμωρίας; 1, 69, 7; 38, 1[4], 13; s. [s.v. ἀνά, beg.] Kuhring 13; Rudberg 201. S. the handbooks on this pass.).

5. to denote reference to a person or thing *for, to, with respect* or *reference to* (Arrian, Anab. 6, 26, 3 τοῦτο τὸ ἔργον εἰς καρτερίαν ἐπαινῶ 'Αλεξάνδρου=I praise this deed with regard to Alexander's endurance) εὔθετος εἴς τι fit, suitable for someth. Lk 14: 35. For this εὔχρηστος 2 Ti 4: 11. ἠτοιμασμένος ready for 2: 21. εὐκαιρέω εἴς τι Ac 17: 21. ἱκανόω Col 1: 12. ἰσχύω Mt 5: 13. περισσεύω 2 Cor 9: 8. συνεργέω Ro 8: 28. τοῦτο οὐκ εἰς ταύτας τ. ἡμέρας λέγω I say this not with reference to these days Hs 9, 26, 6.—After the verbs ἀπορέομαι, διακρίνομαι, καυ- χάομαι, παρρησίαν ἔχω, s. these entries. After the adj. ἄκαρπος, ἀκέραιος, βραδύς, σοφός, συνεργός, ὑπήκοος, φρόνιμος, s. these entries. W. acc. of the pers. ἀσθενεῖν εἴς τινα be weak toward someone 2 Cor 13: 3. εὐδοκεῖν 2 Pt 1: 17. λέγειν εἴς τινα say w. reference to someone (Diod. S. 11, 50, 4) Ac 2: 25.—On Ro 6: 17 s. παραδίδωμι 1b, end. δέχομαί τινα εἰς ὄνομα τινος Mt 10: 41f; s. ὄνομα II.

6. Other uses of εἰς—a. *at, in the face of* μετανοεῖν εἰς τὸ κήρυγμα repent at the proclamation Mt 12: 41; Lk 11: 32; cf. Ro 4: 20 and perh. Mt 3: 11. JRMantey, JBL 70, '51, 45–8, 309–11 argues for a causal use here *because of the proclam.*, with reff.; against him RMarcus, ibid. 129f; 71, '52, 43f.

b. ὀμνύναι εἴς τι swear by someth. Mt 5: 35 (cf. PGiess. 66, 9 [early II AD] ἐρωτῶ εἰς τὴν τ. θεῶν εὐσέβειαν).

c. W. numbers εἰς is distributive '-fold' (Pind., Olymp. 2, 68; Dialekt-Inschr. p. 884, n. 62, 36 [IV BC]) Mk 4: 8 (otherw. ἐς τετρακοσίους, ἐς ὀγδόηκοντα about 400, about 80: Arrian, Anab. 5, 15, 2; 6, 2, 4; 7, 20, 3).

d. For βαπτίζω εἰς s. βαπτίζω 2bβγ.—e. μένειν εἰς *remain with* (PFay. 111, 12 [95/6 AD]) so perh. J 6: 27.

7. In pregnant constructions: σῴζειν εἰς bring safely into 2 Ti 4: 18 (cf. X., An. 6, 4, 8; Diod. S. 2, 48; Cebes 27; Dit., Syll.³ 521, 26 [III BC], Or. 56, 11; 4 Macc 15: 3). διασῴζειν 1 Pt 3: 20 (cf. Gen 19: 19). μισθοῦσθαι ἐργάτας εἰς τ. ἀμπελῶνα to go into the vineyard Mt 20: 1. ἐλευθεροῦσθαι εἰς be freed and come to Ro 8: 21. ἀποδιδόναι τινὰ εἰς Αἴγυπτον Ac 7: 9 (cf. Gen 37: 28). ἔνοχος εἰς τ. γέενναν Mt 5: 22; cf. 10: 9; Mk 6: 8; J 20: 7.

8. The predicate nom. and the predicate acc. are somet. replaced by εἰς w. acc. under Semitic influence, which has strengthened Gk. tendencies in the same direction:

a. predicate nom.—a. w. γίνεσθαι (PFay. 119 [100 AD] ἵνα μὴ εἰς ψωμίον γένηται; Wsd 14: 11; 1 Macc 1: 36; 10: 70; Jdth 5: 10, 18 al.) Mt 21: 42 (Ps 117: 22). ἐγένετο εἰς δένδρον Lk 13: 19; cf. J 16: 20; Ac 5: 36; Rv 8: 11; 16: 19.

β. w. εἶναι (Bar 2: 23; Jdth 5: 21, 24; Sir 31: 10 al.) Mt 19: 5 (Gen 2: 24); Lk 3: 5 (Is 40: 4); 2 Cor 6: 18; Hb 1: 5; 8: 10 (in the last 3 pass. OT expressions are also reproduced). Not fr. the OT: 1 J 5: 8.

γ. λογίζεσθαι εἰς (Wsd 2: 16; 1 Macc 2: 52) Ro 4: 3 (Gen 15: 6); cf. 2: 26; 9: 8. λ. εἰς οὐθέν (Is 40: 17; Wsd 3: 17; cf. 9: 6) Ac 19: 27.

b. predicate acc. (Heliod. 6, 14, 1 τ. πήραν εἰς καθέ- δραν ποιησαμένη=she used the knapsack as a seat; Vett. Val. 59, 7; 1 Macc 10: 54; 11: 62; Jdth 5: 11 al.) ἐγείρειν τινὰ εἰς βασιλέα Ac 13: 22 (cf. 1 Km 13: 14). ἀνατρέφεσθαί τινα εἰς υἱόν 7: 21 (cf. Ex 2: 10). τέθεικά σε εἰς φῶς ἐθνῶν 13: 47 (cf. Is 49: 6). Cf. Mt 21: 46; 1 Cl 42: 4.—Bl-D. §145 w. app.; 157, 5; Rdm.² 20f; Mlt. 71f; Mlt.-H. 462. MJohannessohn, D. Gebrauch d. Kasus in LXX, Diss. Berlin '10, 4f.

9. εἰς is freq. used where ἐν would be expected (s. 1dβ above; for Markan usage s. JJO'Rourke, JBL 85, '66, 349–51)—a. of place (Hdt. 7, 239; Diod. S. 13, 101, 3; 20, 30, 2; Vett. Valens Index III p. 394b; PTebt. 38, 14 [113 BC] εἰς ὂν ἐνοικεῖ . . . οἶκον; POxy. 294, 6 [22 AD]; 929, 12; BGU 385, 5; 423, 7; Epigr. Gr. 134; LXX. Cf. GNHatzidakis, Einl. in die neugr. Gramm. 1892, 210f; Mlt. 62f, 234f; Rob. 592f; Rdm.² 14; 140; Bl-D. §205; EOldenburger, De Or. Sib. Elocutione, Diss. Rostock '03, 26ff) εἰς τ. κοίτην εἶναι Lk 11: 7. εἰς τὴν οἰκίαν Mk 10: 10. οἱ εἰς τ. οἶκόν μου (ὄντες) Lk 9: 61. οἱ εἰς μακρὰν (ὄντες) Ac 2: 39. καθημένου εἰς τὸ ὄρος Mk 13: 3 (cf. Musonius 43, 18 H. καθῆσθαι εἰς Σινώπην). ὁ εἰς τὸν ἀγρὸν (ὤν) he who is in the field 13: 16. γίνεσθαι εἰς τὴν Καφαρναούμ happen in Capernaum Lk 4: 23. εἰς συν- αγωγὰς δαρήσεσθε you will be beaten in the synagogues Mk 13: 9. εὑρέθη εἰς "Αζωτον he found himself in A. Ac 8: 40 (cf. Esth 1: 5 τοῖς ἔθνεσιν τοῖς εὑρεθεῖσιν εἰς τ. πόλιν; Gen 37: 17 v.l.). ἀποθανεῖν εἰς Ἱερ. Ac 21: 13 (cf. Aelian, V.H. 7, 8 Ἡφαιστίων εἰς Ἐκβάτανα ἀπέθανε). κατοικεῖν εἰς Ἱερ. Ac 2: 5; cf. Mt 2: 23; 4: 13; Ac 7: 4; Hb 11: 9 (cf. Thu. 2, 102, 6; X., An. 1, 2, 24; Num 35: 33). χάριν, εἰς ἣν ἐστήκατε the favor in which you stand 1 Pt 5: 12 v.l. ἔχειν βιβλίον εἰς τὰς χεῖρας have a book in one's hands Hv 1, 2, 2. εἰς ταύτην τὴν πόλιν in this city v 2, 4, 3 al. ὁ ὢν εἰς τ. κόλπον τ. πατρός who rests in the bosom (or on the breast) of the Father J 1: 18 (BGU 845, 20 [II AD] οἱ δοῦλοί σου εἰς τὴν κέλλαν αὐτῶν ἔχουσιν ἐλαίας).

b. fig., instrumental use (Arrian, Anab. 5, 12, 3 ἐς ἀκρίβειαν=with care; Vi. Aesopi I c. 7 νικᾶν εἰς εὐσέ- βειαν πάντα ψόγον=overcome all censure with piety) εἰς διαταγὰς ἀγγέλων Ac 7: 53 (=ἐν διαταγαῖς, Bl-D. §206, 1). Sim. ὕπαγε εἰς εἰρήνην (1 Km 1: 17) Mk 5: 34; Lk 7: 50; 8: 48 (=ἐν εἰρήνῃ). Mlt.-Turner 254f. M-M.

εἷς, μία, ἕν, gen. ἑνός, μιᾶς, ἑνός numeral *one* (Hom.+; LXX, En., Ep. Arist., Philo, Joseph., Test. 12 Patr.).

1. lit.—a. in contrast to more than one—α. adj. μίλιον ἕν Mt 5: 41; cf. 20: 12; 25: 15, 24; Ac 21: 7; 28: 13; 2 Pt 3: 8. Opp. πάντες Ro 5: 12 (εἷς ἄνθρωπος as Hippocr., Ep. 11, 2; SHanson, Unity of the Church in the NT, '46, 65–73 [lit.]).

β. noun, w. partitive gen. (Diod. S. 1, 91, 5 αὐτῶν εἷς; Jos., Vi. 204) Mt 5: 19; 6: 29; 18: 6; Mk 9: 42; Lk 12: 27; 17: 2, 22; 23: 39; J 19: 34 or w. ἐκ (Maximus Tyr. 1, 6 a, b ἐκ πολλῶν εἷς; Lucian, Somn. 9; Jos., Bell. 7, 47) Mt 18: 12; 22: 35; 26: 21; Mk 14: 18; J 1: 40; 6: 8; Ac 11: 28 al. ὁ εἷς τῶν δώδεκα one of the twelve Mk 14: 10 is a peculiar expr. (cf. BGU 1145, 25 [18 BC] ὁ εἷς αὐτῶν Ταυρῖνος; UPZ 161, 50; 54; PTebt. 138; 357, 10).

b. in contrast to the parts, of which a whole is made up (Theophrastus in Apollon. Paradox. 16 τὰ πολλὰ ἓν γίγνεσθαι; Stephan. Byz. s.v. Ὠκεανός: γίγνεται ἐκ δύο εἰς ἕν) ἔσονται οἱ δύο εἰς σάρκα μίαν Mt 19: 5; 1 Cor 6: 16 (both Gen 2: 24). οἱ πολλοὶ ἓν σῶμά ἐσμεν we, though many, form one body Ro 12: 5; cf. 1 Cor 12: 12, 20; Eph 2: 15. πάντες εἷς ἐστε you are all one Gal 3: 28. ἕν εἰσιν 1 Cor 3: 8; cf. J 10: 30; 17: 11, 21–3 (cf. IQS 5, 2). For this εἰς τὸ ἕν 1 J 5: 8 (Appian, Iber. 66 §280 ἐς ἕν=together, as a unity). εἰς ἕν J 11: 52 (cf. IQS 5, 7). ὁ ποιήσας τὰ ἀμφότερα ἕν who has united the two divisions Eph 2: 14.

c. w. negative foll. εἷς . . . οὐ (μή), stronger than οὐδείς (Aristoph., Eccl. 153, Thesm. 549; X., An. 5, 6, 12; Demosth. 30, 33 ἡ γυνὴ μίαν ἡμέραν οὐκ ἐχήρευσεν; Dionys. Hal., Comp. Verb. 18) ἓν ἐξ αὐτῶν οὐ πεσεῖται *not one of them will fall* Mt 10: 29 (Lucian, Herm. 28 ἓν ἐξ ἁπάντων); cf. 5: 18; Mk 8: 14; Lk 11: 46; 12: 6. Rarely the neg. comes first Mt 5: 36.

2. emphatically—**a.** *one and the same* (Pind., Nem. 6, 1 ἓν ἀνδρῶν, ἓν θεῶν γένος. ἐκ μιᾶς δὲ πνέομεν ἀμφότεροι; Dio Chrys. 19[36], 6; Maximus Tyr. 19, 4a; Dit., Or. 338, 59 [I ΒC]; Gen 11: 1; 40: 5; Lev 22: 28; Wsd 7: 6) ἐν ἑνὶ οἴκῳ *in one and the same house* Lk 12: 52 (Diod. S. 14, 43, 1 ἐν ἑνὶ τόπῳ). ἐν ἑνὶ στόματι w. *one voice* Ro 15: 6; τοῦ ἑνὸς ἄρτου *one and the same loaf* 1 Cor 10: 17; εἷς ὁ θεός *one and the same God* (Amphitheos of Heracleia: no. 431 fgm. 1b Jac. Διόνυσος κ. Σαβάζιος εἷς ἐστι θεός) Ro 3: 30; cf. 9: 10; 1 Cor 6: 16f; 12: 9, 13. εἷς κύριος, μία πίστις, ἓν βάπτισμα· εἷς θεός κτλ. (cf. the three genders of εἷς consecutively in Simonides 97 Diehl ἓν πέλαγος, μία ναῦς, εἷς τάφος [of shipwrecked pers.]) Eph 4: 5f (MDibelius, D. Christianisierung e. hellenist. Formel: NJklA 35, '15, 224ff. The repetition of εἷς is like Herm. Wr. 11, 11; Epict. 3, 24, 10ff).—Rv 9: 13; 18: 8; Ac 17: 26. ἐν ἑνὶ πνεύματι, μιᾷ ψυχῇ Phil 1: 27; cf. Ac 4: 32. τὸ ἓν φρονεῖν *be of one mind* Phil 2: 2. συνάγειν εἰς ἕν *unite, bring together* (Pla., Phileb. 23E; Dionys. Hal. 2, 45, 3 συνάξειν εἰς ἓν τὰ ἔθνη; POxy. 1411, 3 τῶν δημοσίων εἰς ἓν συναχθέντων; Jos., Bell. 3, 518) J 11: 52. τὸ ἓν καὶ τὸ αὐτό *one and the same* 1 Cor 12: 11 (cf. Diod. S. 11, 47, 3; Epict. 1, 11, 28; 1, 19, 15); cf. ἓν καὶ αὐτό τινι 11: 5.—εἰς ἕνα τόπον *in a place by itself* (Jos., Ant. 6, 125) J 20: 7.

b. (a) *single, only one* (Diod. S. 16, 11, 2; Appian, Bell. Civ. 2, 44 §180 εἷς ἀνήρ; Maximus Tyr. 11, 6c μαντεῖον ἕν and oft.) λόγον ἕνα Mt 21: 24; Gal 5: 14. ἕνα ἄρτον Mk 8: 14. εἷς ἄρτος 1 Cor 10: 17a (εἷς ἄ. is also the symbol of the unity of the brotherhood among the Pythagoreans: Diog. L. 8, 35; here Diog. L. adds that οἱ βάρβαροι hold the same view ἔτι καὶ νῦν). ἓν ἔργον J 7: 21 (here, following ἕν, καί adds an indication of the greatness of the accomplishment, as Appian, Bell. Civ. 2, 133 §555 ἓν ψῆφον [= a single vote or decree] καί). εἷς ἐστιν ὁ ἀγαθός Mt 19: 17; ποιῆσαι ἕνα προσήλυτον 23: 15; ἕνα εἶχεν υἱὸν ἀγαπητόν *he had an only son, whom he loved dearly* Mk 12: 6 (εἷς υἱ. as Phalaris, Ep. 18). ὁ δὲ θεὸς εἷς ἐστιν Gal 3: 20; cf. Mk 12: 32; 1 Cor 8: 4, 6 (v.l. adds to God the Father and Jesus Christ ἓν πνεῦμα ἅγιον κτλ. Cf. also Maximus Tyr. 11, 5a θεὸς εἷς . . . κ. πατήρ, κ. θεοὶ πολλοί and as early as Xenophanes, fgm. 19 Diehl² εἷς θεὸς ἔν τε θεοῖσι κ. ἀνθρωποῖσι μέγιστος; Js 2: 19; PK 3 p. 15, 20 (Herm. Wr. 11, 11; 14 εἷς ὁ θεός; POxy. 1382, 20 εἷς Ζεὺς Σάραπις; Sb 159, 1 εἷς θεὸς ὁ βοηθῶν ὑμῶν; Philo, Spec. Leg. 1, 67; Jos., Ant. 5, 97 θεός τε εἷς; 8, 343, C. Ap. 2, 193; Sib. Or. 4, 30, fgm. 1, 7. Cf. EPeterson, Εἷς Θεός '26; D. Monotheismus als polit. Problem '35). εἷς ἐστιν ὑμῶν ὁ διδάσκαλος Mt 23: 8; cf. vs. 9. μιᾶς γυναικὸς ἀνήρ *the husband of only one wife* or *a husband married only once* (Ael. Aristid. 46 p. 346 D.: ὑπὲρ μιᾶς γυναικός=for only one woman; μία γυνή is not rare: Diod. S. 17, 72, 6; Hippostratus [III ΒC]: no. 568 fgm. 1 Jac.; Appian, Bell. Civ. 4, 95 §402. That the Egyptian priests of Diod. S. 1, 80, 3 γαμοῦσι μίαν means that they marry only one woman, not, however, that they lead a strictly moral life. In order to designate this the Greeks never use the expression μιᾶς γυναικὸς ἀνήρ or anything like it) 1 Ti 3: 2, 12; Tit 1: 6. Correspondingly ἑνὸς ἀνδρὸς γυνή (Paus. 7, 25, 13 the priestess of the earth-goddess must be a woman who, before she became a priestess, was not πλέον ἢ ἑνὸς ἀνδρὸς ἐς πεῖραν ἀφιγμένη) 1 Ti 5: 9. Abs. 1 Cor 9: 24; 2 Cor 5: 14. μεσίτης ἑνός *an intermediary for one alone* Gal 3: 20; cf.

Js 4: 12. οὐδὲ εἷς *not even a single* (X., Mem. 1, 6, 2, Cyr. 1, 3, 10 et al.; Sir 42: 20; 49: 14 v.l.; 1 Macc 11: 70) Mt 27: 14; Ac 4: 32. Freq. at the end of a sentence or clause (ref. fr. comedy in ESchwartz, NGG '08, p. 534, 3. Also Hermocles [IV–III ΒC] p. 174, 17 Coll.; Dio Chrys. 21[38], 23; Ael. Aristid. 28, 156 K.=49 p. 542 D.; 53 p. 617 D.; Epict. 2, 18, 26, Enchir. 1, 3; Philonides in Stob. 3, 35, 6 ed. Hense III p. 688; Wilcken, Chrest. 59, 5 [39 ΑD]; Bel 18 Theod.; 1 Macc 7: 46) Ro 3: 10. This is a good reason for placing the period after οὐδὲ ἕν J 1: 3 (s. GAvandenBergh van Eysinga, PM 13, '09, 143-50. EHennecke, Congr. d'Hist. du Christ. I '28, 207-19; Md'Asbeck, ibid. 220-8; REisler, Rev. de Philol. 3 sér. 4, '30, 350-71; RSV mg.). οὐκ ἔστιν ἕως ἑνός *there is not even one* Ro 3: 12 (Ps 13: 3).—ἕν *only one thing*: ἔτι ἕν σοι λείπει *you still lack only one thing* (Jos., Bell. 4, 257) Lk 18: 22. ἕν σε ὑστερεῖ *you lack only one thing* Mk 10: 21; cf. Lk 10: 42. ἓν οἶδα *at least this one thing I know* J 9: 25. ἓν τοῦτο *this one thing* (Porphyr., Vi. Plot. 19 p. 112, 30 W.) 2 Pt 3: 8. ἓν δέ is a short interjectional sentence (like Xenophon Eph. 5, 3 τοσοῦτο δέ·) *just one thing!* Phil 3: 13 (AFridrichsen, Con. Neot. 9, '44, 31f). μία εἴσοδος *the only entrance* Hs 9, 12, 6.

c. *alone* (οὐδείς) . . . εἰ μὴ εἷς ὁ θεός Mk 2: 7 (in the parallel Lk 5: 21 μόνος ὁ θεός, cf. Herm. Wr. 11, 11 εἰ μὴ εἷς ὁ θεός . . . εἰ μὴ μόνῳ τῷ θεῷ); 10: 18; 12: 29 (Dt 6: 4); Mt 23: 10; Lk 18: 19.—EFFBishop, ET 49, '38, 363-6.

3. *someone*=class. τις, whereby εἷς can mean exactly the same thing as the indef. art. (Aristoph. + [Av. 1292 εἷς κάπηλος]; Περὶ ὕψους 33, 4 p. 62, 18 V., εἷς ἕτερος; Strabo 5, 3, 2, p. 230c ἐπηγγείλατο ἕνα μύριον ἱππικόν; Syntipas p. 29, 3 μία γαλῆ; Appian, Liby. 117 §554 νυκτὸς μιᾶς=one night; Marc. Diac. 27, 5 Bonn ἐν μιᾷ ἡμέρᾳ=on a certain day; Dit., Syll.³ 1170, 15 [160 ΑD] μιᾷ ἡμέρᾳ; UPZ 162 I, 27 [117 ΒC]; PAmh. 30, 28 [II ΒC] Κονδύλου ἑνὸς τῶν ἁλιέων; BGU 1044, 6; Gen 21: 15; Jdth 14: 6; 1 Esdr 3: 5. Bl-D. §247, 2 w. app.; Mlt. 96f; Rob. 674f; Mlt.-Turner 195f; EBruhn, RhM 49, 1894, 168-71; JWackernagel, Syntax II² '28, 151; MBlack, An Aramaic Approach³, '67, 104-6.)

a. *someone, anyone* Mt 18: 24; 19: 16; Mk 10: 17; εἷς ὀνόματι Κλεοπᾶς Lk 24: 18. Oft. w. partitive gen. foll. (Alexis 220, 5; Diod. S. 20, 107, 5 εἷς τῶν φίλων; Epict. 4, 2, 9; Dio Chrys. 71[21], 15 εἷς τῶν Σπαρτῶν; Jos., Ant. 9, 106) ἕνα τῶν προφητῶν (some) *one of the prophets* Mt 16: 14. ἕνα τ. συνδούλων 18: 28. ἐν μιᾷ τ. πόλεων Lk 5: 12. ἐν μιᾷ τ. ἡμερῶν *on one of the days* vs. 17; cf. 15: 19, 26; 22: 47.

b. as indef. art. (s. 3 above) εἷς γραμματεύς *a scribe* Mt 8: 19. συκῆν μίαν *a fig tree* Mt 21: 19; cf. 26: 69; Mk 12: 42. παιδάριον ἕν J 6: 9 t.r.; ἑνὸς ἀετοῦ Rv 8: 13; cf. 18: 21; 19: 17. εἷς στέφανος AP 10.

c. used w. τὶς (class; Jdth 2: 13) εἷς τις νεανίσκος *a certain young man* Mk 14: 51 v.l. W. partitive gen. foll. (Trypho Alex. [I ΒC] in Athen. 3 p. 78Α ἕνα τινὰ τ. Τιτάνων; Aesop, Fab. 237; 300 H.; Hierocles 27 p. 484; IG XII 5, 445, 12 [III ΒC] ἕνα τινὰ αὐτῶν; Ael. Aristid. 29, 14 K. =40 p. 755 D.: εἷς τις τ. χορευτῶν; εἷς τις τῶν παρεστηκότων *a certain one of the bystanders* vs. 47. For this εἷς τις ἐξ αὐτῶν (Jos., Vi. 290) Lk 22: 50; J 11: 49.

4. perh. Hebraistic (cf. Num 1: 1 ἐν μιᾷ τοῦ μηνὸς τ. δευτέρου; 2 Esdr[Ezra] 10: 17; Esth 1: 1a; Jos., Ant. 1, 29.—But s. also Jo. Lydus, Mens. 3, 4 W. τὴν κεφαλὴν τ. χρόνου οἱ Πυθαγόρειοι οὐχὶ πρώτην ἀλλὰ μίαν ὠνόμασαν; Callim., fgm. 482 Schn. πρὸ μιῆς ὥρης=before the first hour of the day) is its use w. expressions denoting time instead of the ordinal number: *the first* εἷς μίαν σαββάτων *on the first day of the week* Mt 28: 1; cf. Lk 24: 1; Mk 16: 2; J 20: 1, 19; Ac 20: 7. For this κατὰ μίαν σαββάτου 1 Cor 16: 2.—Not Semitic (Hdt. 4, 161 μία, ἄλλη, τρίτη; Ael. Aristid. 36, 40 K.=48 p. 453 D.: ἕν, δεύτερον, τρίτον, τέταρτον) εἰς καὶ δεύτερος *a first and second* Tit 3: 10 (cf. Alciphr., Ep. 1, 9, 2; Galen XII 746 K.: ὕδωρ ὄμβριον ἔγχριε μέχρι μιᾶς καὶ δευτέρας ἡμέρας; Maximus Tyr. 28, 2h μία–δευτέρα; Ep. Arist. 143; Jos., Ant. 11, 150; 16, 350 πεσόντος ἑνός καὶ δευτέρου). S. also ἡ Οὐαὶ ἡ μία Rv 9: 12.—If ἐν τριάκοντα is to be read Mk 4: 8, 20, it is prob. to be considered an Aramaism *thirty-fold* (Bl-D. §248, 3; EKautzsch, Gramm. d. bibl. Aram. 1884 §66, 2; JTHudson, ET 53, '41/'42, 266f).

5. Special combinations: **a.** εἷς–εἷς (class. εἷς μὲν ... εἷς δέ: X., Cyr. 1, 2, 4; Aristot., Rhet. 2, 20 p. 1393a; pap. in Wilcken, Chrest. 50, 11 [III BC] ἐν μὲν ... ἐν δέ, Mitteis, Chrest. 372 V, 14 [II AD] ὁ εἷς ... ὁ εἷς, POxy. 1153, 14 [I AD] εἷς ... καὶ ἕν; 2 Km 12: 1; Sir 34: 23f εἷς ... καὶ εἷς; Esth 10: 3g δύο, ἕνα τῷ λαῷ ... καὶ ἕνα τ. ἔθνεσιν) *(the) one—the other* Mt 20: 21; 24: 40f; 27: 38; J 20: 12; Gal 4: 22; B 7: 6f. εἷς τὸν ἕνα *one another* (=ἀλλήλους) 1 Th 5: 11 (cf. Theocr. 22, 65 εἷς ἑνί).

b. εἷς ... εἷς ... εἷς *one ... another ... a third* Mt 17: 4 (cf. 1 Km 10: 3; 13: 17, 18).

c. εἷς ἕκαστος *every single*, strengthening ἕκαστος, adj. Eph 4: 16. Mostly subst.; s. ἕκαστος 2.

d. ὁ εἷς ... ὁ ἕτερος *the one ... the other* (Aristot., De Rep. Ath. 37, 1; Hyperid. 5, 14f; UPZ 161, 39; 43; 46 [119 BC]; PGenève 48, 6 μίαν μὲν ... τὴν δὲ ἑτέραν; BGU 194, 15f; Esth 5: 1a) Mt 6: 24; Lk 7: 41; 16: 13; 17: 34f; 18: 10 al. For this ὁ εἷς ... ὁ ἄλλος Rv 17: 10.

e. καθ' ἕνα, καθ' ἕν (Hdt., Pla. et al.; 1 Esdr 1: 31; 4 Macc 15: 12, 14; Jos., Bell. 4, 240, Ant. 12, 191) καθ' ἕνα πάντες *all, one by one* 1 Cor 14: 31 (cf. Ps.-Xenophon, Cyn. 6, 14). ὑμεῖς οἱ καθ' ἕνα ἕκαστος *each one of you* Eph 5: 33. καθ' ἕν *one after the other* (hence τὸ καθ' ἕν 'a detailed list': PLille 11, 8 [III BC]; PTebt. 47, 34; 332, 16) J 21: 25. For this καθ' ἕν ἕκαστον (X., Cyr. 1, 6, 22, Ages. 7, 1; Ep. Arist. 143) Ac 21: 19. ἕν καθ' ἕν (Aesop, Fab. 274 P. =Babr. no 184 Cr.; PLeid. IIX 1, 22) *each one* Rv 4: 8. In this pass. the second ἕν could be an undeclined nom. as in εἷς κατὰ εἷς (cf. Lucian, Soloec. 9; 3 Macc 5: 34. Other exx. in W-S. §26, 9; 11 and Wettstein I 627) *one after the other* Mk 14: 19; J 8: 9. τὸ καθ' εἷς opp. οἱ πολλοί *individually* Ro 12: 5. However, κατὰ ἕνα= ἕκαστον Hs 9, 3, 5; 9, 6, 3 (Bl-D. §305). ἀνὰ εἷς ἕκαστος *each one* Rv 21: 21.

f. ἀπὸ μιᾶς s. ἀπό VI (as idiom w. noun to be supplied Wilcken, Chrest. 46, 15 [338 AD] μίαν ἐκ μιᾶς, i.e. ἡμέραν=day after day). M-M. B. 937; 1007f.

εἰσάγω 2 aor. εἰσήγαγον (Hom. +; inscr., pap., LXX, En., Ep. Arist.; Philo, Sacr. Abel. 11 al.; Jos., Bell. 1, 229 al.; Test. 12 Patr.) *bring* or *lead in, into* τινά *someone* J 18: 16; Lk 2: 27. τινὰ εἴς τι *someone into someth.* (X., An. 1, 6, 11; 4 Km 9: 2; Jos., Ant. 1, 38) into a city Ac 9: 8; barracks 21: 37; 22: 24; the arena MPol 6: 2; the house Lk 22: 54; B 3: 3 (Is 58: 7); the temple Ac 21: 28f; cf. B 16: 9; GOxy 8; the Kingdom MPol 20: 2; the world 1 Cl 38: 3; cf. B 6: 16; a tomb GP 6: 24. τὸν πρωτότοκον εἰς τὴν οἰκουμένην *his first-born son into the world* Hb 1: 6. ὧδε Lk 14: 21.—τὶ Ac 7: 45. M-M.*

εἰσακούω fut. εἰσακούσομαι; 1 aor. εἰσήκουσα, pass. εἰσηκούσθην; 1 fut. pass. εἰσακουσθήσομαι (Hom. +; PSI 377, 22; LXX) *listen to.*

1. *obey* (Soph., Thu. et al.; PSI 377, 20; Dt 1: 43; 9: 23; Sir 3: 6; 39: 13) τινός 1 Cor 14: 21; 1 Cl 8: 4 (Is 1: 19f).

2. of God *hear* (oft. LXX)—**a.** w. ref. to the pers. making the request 1 Cl 22: 7 (Ps 33: 18); 57: 5 (Pr 1: 28). Pass. Mt 6: 7; Hb 5: 7 (s. ἀπό V 1).

b. w. ref. to the prayer (Ps 4: 2; Bar 2: 14; Sir 34: 26; Jos., Ant. 1, 190; Test. Levi 4: 2) Lk 1: 13 (cf. Sir 51: 11); Ac 10: 31. M-M.*

εἰσδέχομαι fut. εἰσδέξομαι; 1 aor. ptc. εἰσδεξάμενος (Pind., Hdt. +; inscr., pap., LXX; Ep. Arist. 103) *take in, receive, welcome* 2 Cor 6: 17 (Ezk 20: 34); 1 Cl 12: 3 (cf. Jos., Ant. 14, 285). M-M.*

εἴσειμι inf. εἰσιέναι, ptc. εἰσιών; impf. εἰσῄειν (Hom. +; inscr., pap., LXX, Joseph.) *go in, into* εἴς τι *someth.* (Dit., Syll.[3] 982, 3 εἰς τὸν ναόν; UPZ 162 VIII, 19 [117 BC]; Ex 28: 29; Jos., Bell. 3, 325, Ant. 3, 269 εἰς τὸ ἱερόν): the temple Ac 3: 3; 21: 26; cf. Hb 9: 6; MPol 9: 1. πρός τινα *to someone* (Soph., Phil. 953; X., Cyr. 2, 4, 5; Test. Jos. 3: 6) Ac 21: 18. M-M.*

εἰσέρχομαι fut. εἰσελεύσομαι; 2 aor. εἰσῆλθον (for this εἰσῆλθα, Bl-D. §81, 3; Mlt.-H. 208, Mt 7: 13; Lk 11: 52; imper. εἰσελθάτω Mk 13: 15; pf. ptc. εἰσεληλυθώς Hs 9, 12, 4; 9, 13, 4 (Hom. +; inscr., pap., LXX, En., Ep. Arist., Philo, Joseph., Test. 12 Patr.).

1. *come (in, into), go (in, into), enter.*

a. εἴς τι of a place:—**α.** w. names of cities (Jos., Ant. 9, 122) into Jerusalem Mt 21: 10. εἰς Ἱεροσόλυμα εἰς τὸ ἱερόν *into Jerusalem and into the temple* Mk 11: 11. Caesarea Ac 10: 24; 23: 33. Capernaum Mt 8: 5; Mk 2: 1; Lk 7: 1.

β. of other places: into the sanctuary Hb 9: 12, 24f; temple (Jos., Ant. 3, 319) Lk 1: 9; Rv 15: 8; house Mt 10: 12; 12: 29; Mk 7: 17; Lk 1: 40; 8: 41; Ac 11: 12; 16: 15; 21: 8; synagogue Mk 1: 21; 3: 1; Lk 4: 16; 6: 6; Ac 14: 1; 18: 19; cf. Js 2: 2; city Mt 10: 11; 27: 53; Mk 1: 45; Lk 10: 8; 22: 10; Ac 9: 6; 14: 20 al.; village Mk 8: 26; Lk 9: 52; 17: 12; barracks Ac 23: 16; praetorium J 18: 28; 19: 9; cf. Ac 25: 23; Mt 6: 6; J 18: 1; Mk 16: 5; J 20: 6; 10: 1; Mt 24: 38; Lk 17: 27; 1 Cl 9: 4. εἰς τ. νεφέλην Lk 9: 34 (cf. Ex 24: 18).

γ. gener. εἰς τὸν κόσμον *come into the world* (Philo, Op. M. 78) in var. mngs.: of first appearance, of sin and death Ro 5: 12; 1 Cl 3: 4 (cf. Wsd 2: 24); of birth (M. Ant. 6, 56) 1 Cl 38: 3; of the incarnation of Christ Hb 10: 5.

δ. Freq. the 'place to which' is not mentioned, but can be inferred fr. the context (Tob 5: 9; 8: 13; Jdth 14: 14; 1 Macc 7: 36; 2 Macc 1: 15 al.; PTebt. 418, 6ff): εἰσελθὼν διήρχετο τὴν Ἱεριχὼ *he entered Jericho and was passing through it* Lk 19: 1. καὶ ὅτε εἰσῆλθον (sc. εἰς τ. οἶκον) *and when they had entered* Ac 1: 13. μὴ εἰσελθάτω (sc. εἰς τὴν οἰκίαν) Mk 13: 15, also εἰσελθών Mt 9: 25; cf. Ac 5: 7, 10; 10: 25; 1 Cor 14: 23f. But the idea of destination can be so unimportant that εἰ. comes to mean simply *come, go* Lk 18: 25a; cf. Mt 19: 24 (s. 1f below).

b. εἴς τινα—**a.** *come* or *go in among* εἰς τὸν δῆμον *the crowd* Ac 19: 30. εἰς ὑμᾶς 20: 29.

β. *enter into someone* (Wsd 1: 4 of wisdom; Jos., Ant. 4, 121 of the divine spirit entering into prophets) esp. of demons, which take possession of someone's body as their dwelling Mk 9: 25; Lk 8: 30 (Lucian, Philops. 16: the exorcist asks the demoniacs ὅθεν [οἱ δαίμονες] εἰσεληλύθασιν εἰς τὸ σῶμα). Of demons: into the swine Mk 5: 12f; Lk 8: 32f. Of Satan: into Judas 22: 3; J 13: 27; into a person Hm 12, 5, 4. For this εἰ. ἔν τινι (s. ἐν I 6) εἰσῆλθεν ἐν αὐτοῖς Rv 11: 11; cf. Lk 9: 46; 1 Cl 48: 2 (Ps 117: 19).

c. πρός τινα *come* or *go to someone* (X., Mem. 3, 10, 1; Cebes, Tab. 29; Jos., Ant. 8, 235; Gen 16: 4; Ps 50: 2;

Jdth 12: 13; 15: 9) Mk 15: 43; Ac 10: 3; 11: 3; 16: 40; Rv 3: 20; 1 Cl 12: 4.

d. ἐπί τινα *come to someone* (cf. Ezk 44: 25) ἐν παντὶ χρόνῳ ᾧ εἰσῆλθεν καὶ ἐξῆλθεν ἐφ' ἡμᾶς *went in and out among us=associated with us* Ac 1: 21 (on εἰ. καὶ ἐξέρχ. cf. Eur., Phoen. 536 ἐς οἴκους εἰσῆλθε κ. ἐξῆλθ'; Num 27: 17; 2 Ch 1: 10; J 10: 9).

e. w. indication of the place from which, εἰ. ἔκ τινος: ἐξ ἀγροῦ *come in from the field* Lk 17: 7 (cf. PEleph. 13, 6 [223/2 BC] οὔπω εἰσελήλυθεν ἐξ ἀγροῦ; Gen 30: 16).

f. w. indication of the place through which διά τινος (2 Ch 23: 20; Jo 2: 9; Jer 17: 25; Jos., Ant. 13, 229 εἰ. δι' ἄλλης πύλης) Mt 7: 13; 19: 24; Lk 13: 24; 18: 25a; J 10: 1, 2 (ἐρχόμενος ℜ[75]), 9.

g. w. ὑπὸ τὴν στέγην *under the roof,* i.e., *enter* the house (Gen 19: 8 v.l.) Mt 8: 8; Lk 7: 6.

h. w. adv. εἰ. ἔσω *go inside* (2 Ch 29: 18; Bel 19 Theod.) Mt 26: 58. ὧδε *come in here* (Zech 7: 3; Ezk 40: 4) 22: 12. ὅπου ἐὰν εἰσέλθῃ *wherever he goes in* Mk 14: 14; Hb 6: 20.

2. fig.—**a.** of pers.: *come into someth. = share in someth., come to enjoy someth.* (Jos., C. Ap. 2, 123 εἰς τοὺς ἡμετέρους νόμους) εἰς τὴν βασιλείαν τ. θεοῦ (τ. οὐρανῶν) Mt 5: 20; 7: 21; 19: 24; Mk 9: 47; 10: 15, 23ff; Lk 18: 17, 25; J 3: 5; 2 Cl 6: 9 al. (cf. Da 11: 9). For this εἰς τὴν ζωήν *enter into eternal life*=attain it Mt 18: 8f; 19: 17; Mk 9: 43, 45. HWindisch, D. Sprüche v. Eingehen in d. Reich Gs.: ZNW 27, '28, 163–92.—εἰς τὴν κατάπαυσιν *enter into rest* Hb 3: 11, 18; 4: 1, 3, 5f, 10f (all Ps 94: 11). Of Christ εἰ. εἰς τ. δόξαν αὐτοῦ *into his glory* Lk 24: 26. Of temptations εἰ. εἰς πειρασμόν *come into temptation* Mt 26: 41; Lk 22: 40, 46; εἰς χαράν Mt 25: 21, 23; Pol 1: 3. εἰς τὸν κόπον τινός *enter into someone's labor,* i.e., enjoy the fruit of his labor J 4: 38 (cf. Pr 23: 10).—W. this usage, too (s. 1aδ above) the goal need not be mentioned, but can be implied Mt 7: 13; 23: 13; Lk 11: 52 (cf. 3 Macc 1: 12); Ro 11: 25.

b. of things *go (in), come (in)* of food: into the mouth (Ezk 4: 14; Da 10: 3) Mt 15: 11 (cf. Sextus 110); Ac 11: 8. Of thoughts: εἰσῆλθεν δὲ διαλογισμὸς ἐν αὐτοῖς *an argument arose among them* Lk 9: 46. εἰς τὰ ὦτά τινος *come to someone's ears* (Ps 17: 7) Js 5: 4; *reach into* Hb 6: 19. M-M.

εἰσῄει s. εἴσειμι.

εἰσήκω fut. εἰσήξω (Aeschyl. +; Sb 631d) *enter* the kgdm. of God 2 Cl 11: 7. *

εἰσκαλέομαι 1 aor. εἰσεκαλεσάμην in our lit. only mid. (so Hippocr., Progn. 1; Polyb. 21, 22, 2; PPetr. II 12(3), 10 [214 BC]; III 29(h), 5.—Pass., Jos., Vi. 221, act., Ant. 11, 252) *invite in* τινά someone Ac 10: 23. M-M. *

εἴσοδος, ου, ἡ (Hom. +; inscr., pap., LXX)—**1.** (*a way of*) *entering, entrance, access* (Hdt. 1, 118; X., Hell. 4, 4, 7; Ep. Arist. 120; Philo, Deus Imm. 132; Jos., Bell. 5, 346; 1 Km 29: 6; Ps 120: 8) τῶν ἁγίων (in)*to the sanctuary* Hb 10: 19. For this, εἰς τὴν αἰώνιον βασιλείαν 2 Pt 1: 11. Abs. πρὸ προσώπου τῆς εἰσόδου αὐτοῦ *before his coming* Ac 13: 24. Fig. εἴσοδον ἔχειν πρός τινα *find entrance* (=*welcome*) w. *someone* 1 Th 1: 9; cf. 2: 1 (cf. the Lat. pap. POxy. 32, 14 [II AD] ideo peto a te ut habeat introitum at (sic!) te; Dssm., LO 164 and M-M. s.v.; M. Ant. 5, 19 τὰ πράγματα ... οὐδ᾽ ἔχει εἴσοδον πρὸς ψυχήν); but εἰ. can also mean *visit* (Eur., Andr. 930, 952) here.

2. *entrance,* place of entering (fr. Od. 10, 90; Herm. Wr. 1, 22. So mostly inscr., pap.; Judg 1: 24f; 4 Km 23: 11; Jos., Bell. 5, 220, Ant. 15, 347) of Christ μία εἴσοδός

ἐστι πρὸς τὸν κύριον (this) *is the only entrance to the Lord* Hs 9, 12, 6 (εἴσ. πρός w. acc. as Philo, Fuga 183). M-M. *

εἰσπηδάω 1 aor. εἰσεπήδησα (since Hdt. 4, 132; Dit., Syll.[3] 372, 9; POxy. 37 I, 16; 1120, 14; Am 5: 19; Jos., Ant. 5, 46 al.) *leap in, rush in* abs. (Menand., Sam. 219; Herodian 7, 5, 3; PTebt. 304, 10 [167/8 AD]; Sus 26 Theod.) Ac 16: 29. W. εἰς (X., An. 1, 5, 8; PHal. 1, 169 [III BC]) 14: 14 v.l. M-M. *

εἰσπορεύομαι impf. εἰσεπορευόμην in our lit. only mid. *go (in).*

1. lit. w. εἴς τι *into someth.* foll. (Cebes 4, 2; Gen 23: 10; Ex 1: 1 al.) εἰς Καφαρναούμ *come to Capernaum* Mk 1: 21; into villages 6: 56; cf. 11: 2; the temple (cf. Ex 28: 30; 30: 20f) Ac 3: 2; a house Lk 22: 10; Ac 18: 4 D; εἰς τ. βασιλείαν τ. θεοῦ Lk 18: 24 (s. εἰσέρχομαι 2a). W. attraction of the relative ἐν ᾗ εἰσπορευόμενοι εὑρήσετε *in which, when you enter, you will find* 19: 30. W. the 'place where' expr. by a clause: εἰσπορεύεται ὅπου ἦν τὸ παιδίον *he went in where the child was* Mk 5: 40. κατὰ τοὺς οἴκους εἰσπορευόμενος *going into one house after the other* Ac 8: 3. W. πρός τινα foll. (Cebes 29, 3; Dit., Syll.[2] 491, 17; POxy. 717, 7 [I BC]; Gen 44: 30; Esth 2: 13f; Da 11: 16 Theod.) *come to someone* 28: 30. Abs. οἱ εἰσπορευόμενοι (cf. Zech 8: 10) *those who enter* Lk 8: 16; 11: 33. ἦν μετ' αὐτῶν εἰσπορευόμενος καὶ ἐκπορευόμενος εἰς Ἰερουσαλήμ *he went in and out among them at Jerusalem* Ac 9: 28 (cf. Tob 5: 18). Of the devil, who enters a pers. and takes possession of him Hm 12, 5, 4. Of foods εἰ. εἰς τὸ στόμα *go into the mouth* Mt 15: 17; into a person Mk 7: 15, 18f.

2. fig. *come in, enter* εἴς τινα *someone:* grief Hm 10, 2, 2f. Abs. of desires Mk 4: 19. M-M. *

εἰστήκει s. ἵστημι.

εἰστρέχω 2 aor. εἰσέδραμον, ptc. εἰσδραμών (since Thu. 4, 67, 5; 111, 1; Jos., Ant. 7, 359 al.; 2 Macc 5: 26) *run in* Ac 12: 14. *

εἰσφέρω aor. εἰσήνεγκα and εἰσήνεγκον Bl-D. §81, 2 w. app.; Mlt.-H. 263 (Hom. +; inscr., pap., LXX; En. 14, 8; Philo; Jos., Ant. 3, 194 al.) *bring in, carry in.*

1. lit. τινά: μὴ εὑρόντες ποίας (sc. ὁδοῦ) εἰσενέγκωσιν αὐτόν (i.e., εἰς τ. οἶκον) *since they found no way to bring him in* Lk 5: 19; cf. vs. 18. οὐδὲν εἰσηνέγκαμεν εἰς τ. κόσμον *we have brought nothing into the world* (Philo, Spec. Leg. 1, 294f τὸν μηδὲν εἰς τ. κόσμον εἰσενηνοχότα; cf. Cicero, Tusc. 1, 38[91]) 1 Ti 6: 7; Pol 4: 1. Pass. τὸ αἷμα εἰσφέρεται ... εἰς τὰ ἅγια *the blood is brought into the sanctuary* Hb 13: 11 (cf. Lev 4: 5; 16: 27 [Pass.]). Also forcefully *drag in* (PAmh. 77, 22 [139 AD]) Lk 12: 11.

2. fig. εἰ. τινὰ εἰς πειρασμόν *bring* or *lead someone into temptation* Mt 6: 13; Lk 11: 4; D 8: 2; Pol 7: 2. τὶ εἰς τὰς ἀκοάς τινος *bring someth. to someone's ears* Ac 17: 20 (cf. Soph., Aj. 149 εἰς ὦτα φέρει πάντων Ὀδυσσεύς); *introduce* ξένας διδαχάς *strange doctrines* Hs 8, 6, 5 (cf. POxy. 123, 13 συνείδησιν εἰσήνεγκαν=they sent a report; also X., Mem. 1, 1, 2 καινὰ δαιμόνια εἰσφέρειν). M-M. *

εἶτα adv. (Soph., Thu. +; inscr., pap., LXX; En. 97, 6; Ep. Arist.; Joseph.; Test. Napht. 2: 8; Sib. Or. 5, 474; loanw. in rabb.).

1. temporal *then, next* (placed first) εἶτα γενομένης θλίψεως *then when oppression comes* Mk 4: 17; cf. 8: 25; Lk 8: 12; J 13: 5; 19: 27; 20: 27; 1 Cor 15: 24; Js 1: 15;

1 Cl 25: 3; 56: 13; B 8: 2; 12: 2; 13: 2; Hv 3, 7, 3 al.; GP 11: 47. In enumerations: πρῶτον . . . εἶτα (X., An. 1, 3, 2; Philo Mech. 71, 26f; Epict. 1, 15, 7; 1, 26, 3 al.; BGU 665, 10 [I AD]; Ep. Arist. 77; Jos., Ant. 15, 149) *first . . . then* 1 Ti 2: 13; 3: 10; 1 Cor 12: 28 t.r.; 1 Cl 23: 4; 2 Cl 11: 3; B 6: 17. ἔπειτα . . . εἶτα *after that . . . then* (Galen XIII 740 K.) 1 Cor 15: 7; for this εἶτα . . . ἔπειτα (Galen XIII 743 K.) vs. 5f. Since in enumerations εἰ. oft. serves to put things in juxtaposition without reference to chronological sequence, it becomes in general

2. a transition-word *furthermore, then, next* (Wsd 14: 22) B 6: 3; 11: 10; Dg 11: 6, introducing a new argument in a demonstration Hb 12: 9.—The Ionic-Hellenistic form εἶτεν (Phryn. 124 L.; Dit., Syll.³ 972, 150 [175–171 BC]; 736, 30f [92 BC]; PGM 13, 400; Mayser 14; cf. Bl-D. §35, 3 w. app.; Rob. 119; 160) is found Mk 4: 28, where t.r. has εἶτα . . . εἶτα. M-M.**

εἶτε s. εἰ VI 13.

εἶτεν s. εἶτα, end. M-M.

εἴωθα pf. of an obsolete pres. ἔθω; plpf. εἰώθειν, *be accustomed* (so Hom.+; pap., LXX, Philo; Jos., Ant. 11, 37) Mt 27: 15; Mk 10: 1; B 7: 8; IEph 7: 1. ὡς εἰώθειν *as I have been accustomed to do* Hs 5, 1, 2. ἃ εἰώθεσαν ποιεῖν αἱ γυναῖκες GP 12: 50. τὸ εἰωθός (Jos., Ant. 17, 150): κατὰ τὸ εἰωθὸς αὐτῷ *according to his custom* Lk 4: 16. κατὰ τὸ εἰ. τῷ Παύλῳ *as Paul's custom was* Ac 17: 2 (cf. PSI 488, 19 [258 BC] κατὰ τὸ εἰωθός; Num 24: 1; Sus 13). M-M.*

εἴων s. ἐάω.

ἐκ, before vowels ἐξ, prep. w. gen. (Hom.+; LXX, En., Ep. Arist., Philo, Joseph., Test. 12 Patr.; s. lit. s.v. ἀνά and εἰς, beg.) *from, out of, away from.*
1. to denote separation.—a. to introduce the place fr. which the separation takes place. Hence esp. w. verbs of motion ἀναβαίνω, ἀναλύω, ἀνίστημι, ἐγείρομαι, εἰσέρχομαι, ἐκβάλλω, ἐκπορεύομαι, ἐξέρχομαι, ἔρχομαι, ἥκω, καταβαίνω, μεταβαίνω, ῥύομαι, συνάγω, φεύγω; see these entries. καλεῖν ἐξ Αἰγύπτου Mt 2: 15 (Hos 11: 1); ἐκ σκότους 1 Pt 2: 9. αἴρειν ἐκ τ. κόσμου J 17: 15. ἐξαλείφειν ἐκ τῆς βίβλου Rv 3: 5 (Ex 32: 32f; Ps 68: 29). ἀποκυλίειν τ. λίθον ἐκ τ. θύρας Mk 16: 3; J 20: 1; Rv 6: 14; σῴζειν ἐκ γῆς Αἰγ. Jd 5; διασῴζειν ἐκ τ. θαλάσσης Ac 28: 4. παραγίνεσθαι ἐξ ὁδοῦ *arrive on a journey* (lit. from, i.e. interrupting a journey) Lk 11: 6; fig. ἐπιστρέφειν ἐξ ὁδοῦ *bring back fr. the way* Js 5: 20; cf. 2 Pt 2: 21. ἐκ τῆς χειρός τινος (Hebraistically, מִיַּד, oft. LXX; cf. Bl-D. §217, 2; Rob. 649) *from someone's power* ἐξέρχεσθαι J 10: 39; ἁρπάζειν 10: 28f (cf. Plut., Ages. 34, 6 ἐκ τῶν χειρῶν τῶν Ἐπαμινώνδου τ. πόλιν ἐξαρπάσας); ἐξαιρεῖσθαι Ac 12: 11 (cf. Aeschin. 3, 256 ἐκ τ. χειρῶν ἐξελέσθαι τῶν Φιλίππου; Sir 4: 9; Bar 4: 18, 21 al.); ῥύεσθαι Lk 1: 74; cf. vs. 71 (Ps 105: 10; Wsd 2: 18).—After πίνειν, of the object fr. which one drinks (X., Cyr. 5, 3, 3): ἐκ τ. ποτηρίου Mt 26: 27; Mk 14: 23; 1 Cor 11: 28; cf. 10: 4; J 4: 12. Sim. φαγεῖν ἐκ τ. θυσιαστηρίου Hb 13: 10.

b. w. a group or company fr. which the separation takes place (Hyperid. 6, 17 and Lucian, Cyn. 13 ἐξ ἀνθρώπων) ἐξολεθρεύειν ἐκ τοῦ λαοῦ Ac 3: 23 (Ex 30: 33; Lev 23: 29). συμβιβάζειν ἐκ τ. ὄχλου 19: 33; ἐκλέγειν ἐκ τ. κόσμου J 15: 19; cf. Mt 13: 41, 47; Ac 1: 24; 15: 22; Ro 9: 24. For ἐκ freq. ἐκ μέσου Mt 13: 49; Ac 17: 33; 23: 10; 1 Cor 5: 2; 2 Cor 6: 17 (cf. Ex 31: 14).—ἀνιστάναι τινὰ ἐκ τινος Ac 3: 22 (Dt 18: 15); ἐκ νεκρῶν 17: 31. ἐγείρειν τινὰ ἐκ νεκρῶν J 12: 1, 9, 17; Ac 3: 15; 4: 10; 13: 30; Hb 11: 19.

ἀνίστασθαι ἐκ νεκρῶν Ac 10: 41; 17: 3; ἀνάστασις ἐκ νεκρ. Lk 20: 35; 1 Pt 1: 3; cf. Ro 10: 7.

c. of situations and circumstances out of which someone is brought, *from:* ἐξαγοράζειν ἔκ τινος *redeem fr. someth.* Gal 3: 13. For this λυτροῦν (cf. Sir 51: 2) 1 Pt 1: 18; σῴζειν ἔκ τινος *save fr. someth.* J 12: 27; Hb 5: 7; Js 5: 20 (Od. 4, 753; MLetronne, Recueil des Inscr. 1842/8, 190; 198 σωθεὶς ἐκ; Dit., Syll.³ 1130, 1f; PVat. A, 7 [168 BC]=Witkowski p. 65 διασεσῶσθαι ἐκ μεγάλων κινδύνων; Sir 51: 11; Ep Jer 49). ἐξαιρεῖσθαι Ac 7: 10 (cf. Wsd 10: 1; Sir 29: 12). τηρεῖν ἔκ τινος *keep from someth.* Rv 3: 10; μεταβαίνειν ἔκ τινος εἴς τι J 5: 24; 1 J 3: 14; μετανοεῖν ἔκ τινος *repent and turn away fr. someth.* Rv 2: 21f; 9: 20f; 16: 11. ἀναπαύεσθαι ἐκ τ. κόπων *rest fr. one's labors* 14: 13. ἐγείρεσθαι ἐξ ὕπνου *wake fr. sleep* (Epict. 2, 20, 15; Sir 22: 9) Ro 13: 11. ζωὴ ἐκ νεκρῶν 11: 15. ζῶντες ἐκ νεκρῶν *men who have risen fr. death to life* 6: 13 (cf. Soph., Oed. R. 454; X., An. 7, 7, 28; Demosth. 18, 131 ἐλεύθερος ἐκ δούλου καὶ πλούσιος ἐκ πτωχοῦ γεγονώς; Palaeph. 3, 2).

d. of pers. and things with whom a connection is severed or is to remain severed: τηρεῖν αὐτοὺς ἐκ τοῦ πονηροῦ *keep them fr. the evil one* J 17: 15; cf. Ac 15: 29. Pregnant constr.: ἀνανήφειν ἐκ τῆς τοῦ διαβόλου παγίδος 2 Ti 2: 26. νικᾶν ἔκ τινος *free oneself from . . . by victory* Rv 15: 2. ἐλεύθερος ἐκ 1 Cor 9: 19 (cf. Eur., Herc. Fur. 1010 ἐλευθεροῦντες ἐκ δρασμῶν πόδα).

2. to denote the direction fr. which someth. comes καταβαίνειν ἐκ τοῦ ὄρους (Il. 13, 17; X., An. 7, 4, 12; Ex 19: 14; 32: 1 al.) Mt 17: 9. θρὶξ ἐκ τῆς κεφαλῆς ὑμῶν οὐ μὴ ἀπόληται Lk 21: 18. ἐκπίπτειν ἐκ τ. χειρῶν Ac 12: 7. διδάσκειν ἐκ τοῦ πλοίου Lk 5: 3. ἐκ τῆς πρύμνης ῥίψαντες τὰς ἀγκύρας Ac 27: 29. κρέμασθαι ἔκ τινος (Hom.+; 1 Macc 1: 61; 2 Macc 6: 10; Jos., Ant. 14, 107) 28: 4. ἐκ ῥιζῶν *to* (lit. from) *its roots* (Job 28: 9; 31: 12) Mk 11: 20; B 12: 9.—Since the Greek feeling concerning the relation betw. things in this case differed fr. ours, ἐκ could answer the question 'where?' (cf. Soph., Phil. 20; Synes., Ep. 131 p. 267A ἐκ τῆς ἑτέρας μερίδος=on the other side; BGU 975, 11; 15 [45 AD]; PGM 36, 239; LXX) ἐκ δεξιῶν *at (on) the right* (δεξιός 2b) Mt 20: 21, 23; 22: 44 (Ps 109: 1); 25: 33; Lk 1: 11; Ac 2: 25 (Ps 15: 8), 34 (Ps 109: 1); 7: 55f; B 11: 10. ἐξ ἐναντίας *opposite* Mk 15: 39 (Hdt. 8, 6; Thu. 4, 33, 1; Wilcken, Chrest. 461, 6; Sir 37: 9; Wsd 4: 20 al.); ὁ ἐξ ἐναντίας *the opponent* (Sext. Emp., Adv. Phys. 1, 66; 2, 69, Adv. Eth. 1, 25; Bias in Diog. L. 1, 84) Tit 2: 8.

3. to denote origin, cause, motive, reason—a. in expr. which have to do w. begetting and birth *from, of, by:* ἐκ introduces the role of the male (Ps.-Callisth. 1, 9 ἐκ θεοῦ ἔστι; Dit., Syll.³ 1163, 3; 1169, 63, Or. 383, 3; 5 [I BC]) ἐν γαστρὶ ἔχειν ἔκ τινος Mt 1: 18. κοίτην ἔχειν ἔκ τινος Ro 9: 10; also of the female (Dit., Syll.³ 1160, 3; PEleph. 1, 9 [311/10 BC] τεκνοποιεῖσθαι ἐξ ἄλλης γυναικός; PFay. 28, 9 γεννᾶσθαι ἐκ; Jos., Ant. 1, 191) γεννᾶν τινα ἐκ *beget someone by* (a woman; s. γεννάω 1a) Mt 1: 3, 5 etc. γίνεσθαι ἐκ γυναικός (Jos., Ant. 11, 152) Gal 4: 4; cf. vs. 22f.—γεννᾶσθαι ἐξ αἱμάτων κτλ. J 1: 13; ἐκ τ. σαρκός 3: 6; ἐκ πορνείας 8: 41. ἐγείρειν τινὶ τέκνα ἐκ Mt 3: 9; Lk 3: 8. (τίς) ἐκ καρποῦ τ. ὀσφύος αὐτοῦ Ac 2: 30 (Ps 131: 11). γεννᾶσθαι ἐκ τ. θεοῦ J 1: 13; 1 J 3: 9; 4: 7; 5: 1, 4, 18; ἐκ τ. πνεύματος J 3: 6 (opp. ἐκ τ. σαρκός). εἶναι ἐκ τοῦ θεοῦ (Menand., Sam. 257) J 8: 47; 1 J 4: 4, 6; 5: 19; opp. εἶναι ἐκ τ. διαβόλου J 8: 44; 1 J 3: 8 (cf. Dit., Or. 90, 10 of Ptolemaeus Epiphanes ὑπάρχων θεὸς ἐκ θεοῦ κ. θεᾶς).

b. to denote origin as to family, race, city, people, district, etc.: ἐκ Ναζαρέτ J 1: 46. ἐκ πόλεως vs. 44. ἐξ οἴκου Lk 1: 27; 2: 4. ἐκ γένους (Jos., Ant. 11, 136) Phil 3: 5; Ac 4: 6. ἐκ φυλῆς (Jos., Ant. 6, 45; 49) Lk 2: 36; Ac 13: 21; Ro 11: 1. Ἑβρ. ἐξ Ἑβραίων a Hebrew, the son of Hebrews Phil 3: 5 (Gdspd., Probs. 175f). ἐκ σπέρματός τινος J 7: 42; Ro 1: 3; 11: 1. ἐξ ἐθνῶν ἁμαρτωλοί Gal 2: 15; cf. Lk 23: 7; Ac 23: 34. ἐκ τ. γῆς J 3: 31. For this ἐκ τῶν κάτω J 8: 23 (opp. ἐκ τ. ἄνω). ἐκ (τούτου) τ. κόσμου 15: 19; 17: 14; 1 J 2: 16; 4: 5. ἐξ οὐρανοῦ ἢ ἐξ ἀνθρώπων Mt 21: 25; Mk 11: 30.

c. to denote origin of another kind (Maximus Tyr. 13, 3f φῶς ἐκ πυρός) καπνὸς ἐκ τ. δόξης τ. θεοῦ Rv 15: 8 (cf. EpJer 20 καπνὸς ἐκ τ. οἰκίας). ἡ σωτηρία ἐκ τ. Ἰουδαίων ἐστίν J 4: 22. εἶναι ἔκ τινος come, be descended from someone or someth. (Jos., Ant. 7, 209) Mt 5: 37; J 7: 17, 22; 1 J 2: 16, 21; εἶναι is oft. to be supplied Ro 2: 29; 11: 36; 1 Cor 8: 6 (Plut., Mor. 1001c); 11: 12; Gal 5: 8. ἔργα ἐκ τοῦ πατρός J 10: 32. οἰκοδομὴ ἐκ θεοῦ 2 Cor 5: 1; χάρισμα 1 Cor 7: 7; δικαιοσύνη Phil 3: 9. φωνὴ ἐκ τ. στόματος αὐτοῦ Ac 22: 14. Here belongs the constr. w. ἐκ for the subj. gen., as in ἡ ἐξ ὑμῶν (v.l.) ἀγάπη 2 Cor 8: 7; ὁ ἐξ ὑμῶν ζῆλος 9: 2 v.l.; Rv 2: 9 (cf. Vett. Val. 51, 16; CIG II 3459, 11 τῇ ἐξ ἑαυτῆς κοσμιότητι; pap. [Rossberg —ἀνά, beg.—p. 14f]; 1 Macc 11: 33 χάριν τῆς ἐξ αὐτῶν εὐνοίας; 2 Macc 6: 26). ἐγένετο ζήτησις ἐκ τ. μαθητῶν Ἰωάννου there arose a discussion on the part of John's disciples J 3: 25 (Dionys. Hal. 8, 89, 4 ζήτησις πολλὴ ἐκ πάντων ἐγένετο; Appian, Bell. Civ. 2, 24 §91 σφαγή τις ἐκ τῶν στρατιωτῶν ἐγένετο).

d. subst.: οἱ ἐξ Ἰσραήλ the Israelites Ro 9: 6. οἱ ἐξ ἐριθείας selfish, factious people 2: 8. οἱ ἐκ νόμου partisans of the law 4: 14; cf. vs. 16. οἱ ἐκ πίστεως those who have faith Gal 3: 7, 9; cf. Ro 3: 26; 4: 16. οἱ ἐκ περιτομῆς the circumcision party Ac 11: 2; Ro 4: 12; Gal 2: 12. οἱ ἐκ τῆς περιτομῆς Tit 1: 10. For this οἱ ὄντες ἐκ περιτομῆς Col 4: 11. οἱ ἐκ τ. συναγωγῆς members of the synagogue Ac 6: 9. οἱ ἐκ τῶν Ἀριστοβούλου Ro 16: 10f. οἱ ἐκ τῆς Καίσαρος οἰκίας Phil 4: 22 (s. Καῖσαρ and οἰκία 3). In these cases the idea of belonging often completely overshadows that of origin.

e. of the effective cause by, because of (cf. the 'perfectivizing' force of ἐκ and other prepositions in compounds, e.g. Mt 4: 7; Mk 9: 15. Bl-D. §318, 5)—α. personal in nature (originator.—X., An. 1, 1, 6; Diod. S. 19, 1, 4 [saying of Solon]; Arrian, Anab. 3, 1, 2; 4, 13, 6 of an inspired woman κατεχομένη ἐκ τοῦ θείου; Achilles Tat. 5, 27, 2; Sib. Or. 3, 395; Nicetas Eugen. 7, 85 H. ἐκ θεῶν σεσωσμένη; Ps.-Clem., Hom. p. 7, 19 Lag. τὸν ἐκ θεοῦ σοι ἀποδιδόμενον μισθόν): ὠφελεῖσθαι ἔκ τινος Mt 15: 5; Mk 7: 11. ζημιοῦσθαι 2 Cor 7: 9. λυπεῖσθαι 2: 2. εὐχαριστεῖσθαι 1: 11. ἀδικεῖσθαι Rv 2: 11. ἐξ ἐμαυτοῦ οὐκ ἐλάλησα J 12: 49 (cf. Soph., El. 344 οὐδὲν ἐξ σαυτῆς λέγεις).

β. impersonal in nature (Arrian, Anab. 3, 21, 10 ἀποθνήσκειν ἐκ τ. τραυμάτων; 6, 25, 4; POxy. 486, 32 τὰ ἐμὰ ἐκ τ. ἀναβάσεως τ. Νίλου ἀπολωλέναι): ἀποθανεῖν ἐκ τ. ὑδάτων Rv 8: 11. πυροῦσθαι 3: 18. σκοτοῦσθαι 9: 2. φωτίζεσθαι 18: 1. κεκοπιακώς ἐκ τῆς ὁδοιπορίας J 4: 6 (Aelian, V.H. 3, 23 ἐκ τοῦ πότου ἐκάθευδεν).

f. of the reason which is a presupposition for someth.: by reason of, as a result of, because of (X., An. 2, 5, 5; Appian, Bell. Civ. 1, 42 §185 ἐκ προδοσίας; POxy. 486, 28 ἐκ τῆς ἐπιστολῆς; numerous examples in Mayser II 2 p. 388; Philo, De Jos. 184 ἐκ διαβολῆς; Jos., Vi. 430): δικαιοῦσθαι ἔκ τινος Ro 4: 2; Gal 2: 16; 3: 24; cf. Ro 3: 20, 30 (cf. εἴ τις ἐκ γένους [δίκαι]ός ἐστι=has the right of citizenship by descent: letter of MAurelius 34, ZPE 8, '71, 170). οὐκ . . . ἡ ζωὴ αὐτοῦ ἐστιν ἐκ τῶν ὑπαρχόντων αὐτῷ he does not live because of his possessions

Lk 12: 15. ἐκ ταύτης τ. ἐργασίας Ac 19: 25. ἐξ ἔργων λαβεῖν τὸ πνεῦμα Gal 3: 2, 5; cf. Ro 11: 6. ἐξ ἀναστάσεως λαβεῖν τ. νεκρούς Hb 11: 35. ἐσταυρώθη ἐξ ἀσθενείας 2 Cor 13: 4. τὸ ἐξ ὑμῶν as far as it depends on you Ro 12: 18.—ἐκ τοῦ πόνου in anguish Rv 16: 10; cf. vs. 11; 8: 13.—ἐκ τούτου for this reason, therefore (Dit., Syll.³ 1168, 47; 1169, 18; 44; 62f; BGU 423, 17) J 6: 66; 19: 12.—Sim. ἐκ can introduce the means which one uses for a definite purpose, with, by means of (Polyaenus 3, 9, 62 ἐξ ἱμάντος=by means of a thong) ἐκ τοῦ μαμωνᾶ Lk 16: 9 (X., An. 6, 4, 9; PTebt. 5, 80 [118 BC] ἐκ τ. ἱερῶν προσόδων; Jos., Vi. 142 ἐκ τ. χρημάτων); cf. 8: 3.

g. of the source, fr. which someth. flows:—α. λαλεῖν ἐκ τ. ἰδίων J 8: 44. ἐκ τοῦ περισσεύματος τ. καρδίας Mt 12: 34. τὰ ἐκ τ. ἱεροῦ the food from the temple 1 Cor 9: 13. ἐκ τ. εὐαγγελίου ζῆν get one's living by preaching the gospel vs. 14.

β. information, insight, etc. (X., An. 7, 7, 43 ἐκ τῶν ἔργων κατέμαθες) κατηχεῖσθαι ἐκ Ro 2: 18. ἀκούειν ἐκ J 12: 34. γινώσκειν Mt 12: 33; Lk 6: 44; 1 J 3: 24; 4: 6. ἐποπτεύειν 1 Pt 2: 12. δεικνύναι Js 2: 18.

γ. of the inner life, etc., fr. which someth. proceeds (since Il. 9, 486): ἐκ καρδίας Ro 6: 17; 1 Pt 1: 22 (cf. Theocr. 29, 4; M. Ant. 3, 3). ἐκ ψυχῆς Eph 6: 6; Col 3: 23 (X., An. 7, 7, 43; Oec. 10, 4; Jos., Ant. 17, 177; 1 Macc 8: 27). ἐκ καθαρᾶς καρδίας 1 Ti 1: 5; 2 Ti 2: 22. ἐξ ὅλης τ. καρδίας σου καὶ ἐξ ὅλης τ. ψυχῆς σου καὶ ἐξ ὅλης τ. διανοίας σου καὶ ἐξ ὅλης τ. ἰσχύος σου Mk 12: 30; cf. also Lk 10: 27 (Dt 6: 5; cf. Wsd 8: 21; 4 Macc 7: 18; Epict. 2, 23, 42 ἐξ ὅλης ψυχῆς). ἐκ πίστεως Ro 14: 23; cf. 2 Cor 2: 17. Also of circumstances which accompany an action without necessarily being the source of it: γράφειν ἐκ πολλῆς θλίψεως write out of great affliction 2 Cor 2: 4.

h. of the material out of which someth. is made (Hdt. 1, 194; Pla., Rep. 10 p. 616c; Dit., Or. 194, 28 [42 BC] a statue ἐκ σκληροῦ λίθου; PMagd. 42, 5 [221 BC]; POxy. 707, 28; PGM 13, 659; Wsd 15: 8; 1 Macc 10: 11; Jdth 1: 2) of, from στέφανος ἐξ ἀκανθῶν Mt 27: 29; J 19: 2; cf. 2: 15; 9: 6; Ro 9: 21; 1 Cor 15: 47; Rv 18: 12; 21: 21; perh. also 1 Cor 11: 12 ἡ γυνὴ ἐκ τοῦ ἀνδρός.

i. of the underlying rule or principle according to, in accordance with (class. [Kühner-G. I 461g], also Dit., Or. 48, 12 [III BC] ἐκ τ. νόμων; PEleph. 1, 12 [312/11 BC] ἐκ δίκης; PPetr. III 26, 9 ἐκ κρίσεως; LXX, e.g. 1 Macc 8: 30; Jos., Ant. 6, 296 ἐκ κυνικῆς ἀσκήσεως πεποιημένος τὸν βίον) ἐκ τ. λόγων Mt 12: 37 (cf. Wsd 2: 20). ἐκ τ. στόματός σου κρινῶ σε by what you have said Lk 19: 22 (cf. Sus 61 Theod.; X., Cyr. 2, 2, 21 ἐκ τ. ἔργων κρίνεσθαι). Rv 20: 12. ἐκ τ. καλοῦντος Ro 9: 12. ἐκ τ. ἔχειν in accordance w. your ability 2 Cor 8: 11. ἐξ ἰσότητος on the basis of equality vs. 13.

4. It is also used in periphrasis—a. for the partitive gen. (Bl-D. §164, 1 and 2; 169; Rob. 599; 1379).

α. after words denoting number εἷς, μία, ἕν (Hdt. 2, 46, 2 ἐκ τούτων εἷς; POxy. 117, 15 [II/III AD] δύο . . . ἐξ ὧν . . . ἓν ἐξ αὐτῶν; Tob 12: 15 BA; Sir 32: 1; Jos., Bell. 7, 47) Mt 10: 29; 18: 12; 22: 35; 27: 48; Mk 9: 17 and oft.; εἷς τις J 11: 49; δύο Mk 16: 12; Lk 24: 13; J 1: 35; 21: 2. πέντε Mt 25: 2. πολλοί (1 Macc 5: 26; 9: 69) J 6: 60; 7: 31; 11: 19, 45. οἱ πλείονες 1 Cor 15: 6. οὐδείς (Epict. 1, 29, 37; 1 Macc 5: 54; 4 Macc 14: 4) J 7: 19; 16: 5. χιλιάδες ἐκ πάσης φυλῆς Rv 7: 4.

β. after the indef. pron. (Plut., Galba 27, 2; Herodian 5, 3, 9; 3 Macc 2: 30; Jos., Vi. 279) Lk 11: 15; J 6: 64; 7: 25, 44, 48; 9: 16; 11: 37, 46 al. Also after the interrog. pron. Mt 6: 27; 21: 31; Lk 11: 5; 12: 25; 14: 28 al.

γ. the partitive w. ἐκ as subj. (2 Km 11: 17) εἶπαν ἐκ τ. μαθητῶν αὐτοῦ J 16: 17.—Rv 11: 9. As obj., pl. Mt 23:

34; Lk 11: 49; 21: 16; 2 J 4 (cf. Sir 33: 12; Jdth 7: 18; 10: 17 al.).

δ. used w. εἶναι *belong to someone* or *someth.* (Jos., Ant. 12, 399) καὶ σὺ ἐξ αὐτῶν εἶ *you also belong to them* Mt 26: 73; cf. Mk 14: 69f; Lk 22: 58; J 7: 50; 10: 26; Ac 21: 8; cf. 2 Cl 18: 1. οὐκ εἰμὶ ἐκ τ. σώματος *I do not belong to the body* 1 Cor 12: 15f; cf. 2 Cl 14: 1.

ε. after verbs of supplying, receiving, consuming: ἐσθίειν ἔκ τινος (Tob 1: 10; Sir 11: 19; Jdth 12: 2) 1 Cor 9: 7; 11: 28; J 6: 26, 50f; Rv 2: 7. πίνειν Mt 26: 29; Mk 14: 25; J 4: 13f; Rv 14: 10; χορτάζειν ἔκ τινος *gorge w. someth.* 19: 21; μετέχειν 1 Cor 10: 17; λαμβάνειν (1 Esdr 6: 31; Wsd 15: 8) J 1: 16; Rv 18: 4; Hs 9, 24, 4. διδόναι (Tob 4: 16; Ezk 16: 17) Mt 25: 8; 1 J 4: 13. διαδιδόναι (Tob 4: 16 A) J 6: 11.

ζ. after verbs of filling: ἐπληρώθη ἐκ τῆς ὀσμῆς *was filled w. the fragrance* 12: 3. γεμίζειν τ. κοιλίαν ἔκ τινος *fill the belly w. someth.* Lk 15: 16; cf. Rv 8: 5. γέμειν ἐξ ἁρπαγῆς *be full of greed* Mt 23: 25.

b. in periphrasis for the gen. of price or value *for* (Palaeph. 45; PFay. 111, 16 [95/6 AD]; 119, 5; 131, 5; PLond. 277, 9 [33 AD]; Jos., Ant. 14, 34) ἀγοράζειν τι ἔκ τινος Mt 27: 7 (POxy. 745, 2 [c. 1 AD] τ. οἶνον ἠγόρασας ἐκ δραχμῶν ἐξ; EpJer 24); cf. Ac 1: 18; Mt 20: 2.

5. of time—**a.** of the time when someth. begins *from*, *from—on*, *for*, etc. ἐκ κοιλίας μητρός *from birth* (Ps 21: 11; 70: 6; Is 49: 1) Mt 19: 12 al.; also ἐκ γενετῆς J 9: 1 (since Od. 18, 6; Il. 24, 535; s. also γενετή). ἐκ νεότητος (since Il. 14, 86; Ps 70: 5; Sir 7: 23; Wsd 8: 2; 1 Macc 2: 66) Mk 10: 20; Lk 18: 21. ἐξ ἱκανῶν χρόνων *for a long time* 23: 8. ἐκ πολλῶν χρόνων *a long time before* 1 Cl 42: 5 (cf. ἐκ πολλοῦ Thu. 1, 68, 3; 2, 88, 2; ἐξ ὀλίγων ἡμερῶν Lysias, Epitaph. 1). ἐκ γενεῶν ἀρχαίων Ac 15: 21 (cf. X., Hell. 6, 1, 4 ἐκ πάντων προγόνων). ἐκ τ. αἰῶνος *since the world began* J 9: 32 (cf. ἐξ αἰῶνος Sext. Emp., Adv. Phys. 1, 76; Diod. S. 4, 83, 3; Aelian, V.H. 6, 13; 12, 64; Dit., Or. 669, 61; Sir 1: 4; 1 Esdr 2: 17, 21; Jos., Bell. 5, 442). ἐξ ἐτῶν ὀκτώ *for eight years* Ac 9: 33; cf. 24: 10. ἐξ ἀρχῆς (PTebt. 40, 20 [117 BC]; Sir 15: 14; 39: 32; Jos., C. Ap. 1, 225) J 6: 64. ἐκ παιδιόθεν *fr. childhood* Mk 9: 21 (s. παιδιόθεν. On the use of ἐκ w. an adv. cf. ἐκ τότε POxy. 486 [II AD]; ἐκ πρωίθεν 1 Macc 10: 80).

b. of sequence of time—**a.** ἡμέραν ἐξ ἡμέρας *day after day* 2 Pt 2: 8; 2 Cl 11: 2 (cf. Ps.-Eur., Rhes. 445; Theocr. 18, 35; Gen 39: 10; Num 30: 15; Sir 5: 7; Esth 3: 7; En. 98, 8).

β. ἐκ δευτέρου *for the second time, again*, s. δεύτερος 4. ἐκ τρίτου Mt 26: 44 (cf. PHolm. 1, 32 ἐκ τετάρτου).

6. various uses—**a.** blending of constructions, cf. Rob. 599f; ἐκ for ἐν (class.; cf. Kühner-G. I 546f; LXX, e.g. Sus 26 Theod.; 1 Macc 11: 41; 13: 21; Jdth 15: 5) ὁ πατὴρ ὁ ἐξ οὐρανοῦ δώσει Lk 11: 13. μὴ καταβάτω ἆραι τὰ ἐκ τῆς οἰκίας αὐτοῦ Mt 24: 17. τὴν ἐκ Λαοδικείας (ἐπιστολὴν) ἵνα καὶ ὑμεῖς ἀναγνῶτε Col 4: 16.

b. like the O.T. usage of מִן: ἔκρινεν ὁ θεὸς τὸ κρίμα ὑμῶν ἐξ αὐτῆς *God has pronounced judgment for you against her* Rv 18: 20 (cf. Ps 118: 84; Is 1: 24; En. 100, 4; 104, 3). ἐξεδίκησεν τὸ αἷμα τ. δούλων αὐτοῦ ἐκ χειρὸς αὐτῆς 19: 2, cf. 6: 10 (both 4 Km 9: 7).

c. adv. expressions: ἐξ ἀνάγκης (ἀνάγκη 1). ἐκ συμφώνου *by mutual consent* (BGU 446, 13; PRainer 11, 14 et al. in pap.; cf. Dssm., NB 82f [BS 225]) 1 Cor 7: 5. ἐκ λύπης *reluctantly* 2 Cor 9: 7. ἐκ περισσοῦ *extremely* (Dio Chrys. 14[31], 64; Lucian, Pro Merc. Cond. 13; Da 3: 22 Theod.) Mk 6: 51. ἐκ μέτρου *by measure=sparingly* J 3: 34. ἐκ μέρους *part by part=as far as the parts are concerned, individually*, 1 Cor 12: 27 (distributive; cf.

PHolm. 1, 7 ἐκ δραχμῶν ϛ'=6 dr. each); mostly in contrast to 'complete', *only in part* 13: 9 (BGU 538, 35; 574, 10; 887, 6; 17 al. in pap.; Ep. Arist. 102). ἐξ ὀνόματος *individually, personally, by name* IEph 20: 2; IPol 4: 2; 8: 2.

d. ἐκ—εἰς w. the same word repeated gives it special emphasis (Plut., Galba 14, 2 ἐκ προδοσίας εἰς προδοσίαν; Ps 83: 8) ἐκ πίστεως εἰς πίστιν Ro 1: 17.—2 Cor 2: 16 (twice).—The result and goal are thus indicated Ro 11: 36; 1 Cor 8: 6; Col 1: 16. AFridrichsen, Con. Neot. 12, '48, 54. M-M.

ἕκαστος, η, ον (Hom.+; inscr., pap., LXX, Ep. Arist., Philo, Joseph., Test. 12 Patr.) *each, every*.

1. adj. ἕκαστον δένδρον *every tree* (perh. *both kinds of trees*, good and bad, w. ἕκαστος=ἑκάτερος, as in late H.Gk.; s. HSahlin, Zwei Lukas-Stellen, '45, 5 w. ref. there; L-S-J s.v. ἕκαστος IV) Lk 6: 44. ἑκάστῳ στρατιώτῃ J 19: 23. καθ' ἑκάστην ἡμέραν *every day* (Thu. 6, 63, 2; X., Mem. 4, 2, 12 et al.; PAmh. 136, 7 et al. in pap.; Ex 5: 8; Esth 2: 11; 3: 4 al.) Hb 3: 13; B 19: 10. κατὰ μῆνα ἕκαστον (Lucian, Nav. 24; BGU 86, 36 et al. in pap.) Rv 22: 2, but ἕκ. may refer to ξύλον.

2. subst. *each one, every one* Mt 16: 27; J 6: 7; Ac 4: 35; Ro 2: 6; 12: 3. W. partitive gen. foll. Lk 13: 15; Ac 2: 38; Ro 14: 12; 1 Cor 15: 38; 16: 2; 1 Cl 24: 5; 41: 1; B 2: 8. Followed by ἴδιος (1 Esdr 5: 8; Job 2: 11; 3 Macc 5: 21, 34): ἑκάστῳ κατὰ τὴν ἰδίαν δύναμιν Mt 25: 15. Cf. Lk 6: 44; Ac 2: 8; Ro 14: 5 al.—ἕ. *every one* (has or does someth., but one does one thing, another someth. else) 1 Cor 1: 12; 14: 26.—Strengthened εἷς ἕκαστος *every single one* (Hdt. 6, 128; Thu. 1, 77, 6; 2, 60, 4 et al.; PTebt. 397, 1; 4 Macc 13: 13; 15: 19; Jos., Ant. 19, 305) Mt 26: 22; Ac 2: 6; 20: 31; Dg 8: 3; Hs 8, 1, 5; 8, 11, 2 al. W. part. gen. foll. (X., An. 6, 6, 12; Ptolem., Apotel. 1, 2, 11 εἷς ἕκαστος τῶν ἀνθρώπων; 4 Macc 8: 5, 9; 13: 18; 16: 24) Lk 4: 40; 16: 5; Ac 2: 3; 17: 27; 21: 26; 1 Cor 12: 18; Eph 4: 7; 1 Th 2: 11; 2 Th 1: 3. ἀνὰ εἷς ἕκαστος *every single one* (ἀνά 2) Rv 21: 21. καθ' ἓν ἕκαστον *one after the other= in detail* (Hyperid. 3, 14; Dionys. Hal., Comp. 3; 23; PHal. 1, 223 [III BC]) Ac 21: 19; 1 Cl 32: 1. For this καθ' ἕκαστα (PGdspd. 15, 14) B 1: 7.—The sg. is used w. pron. or verbs in the pl. (Hom.+; LXX; Jos., Bell. 6, 19) ὑμῖν ἑκάστῳ Rv 2: 23; cf. 6: 11. ἵνα σκορπισθῆτε ἕκαστος J 16: 32; cf. Mt 18: 35; Lk 2: 3 (Appian, Liby. 39 §164 ἀνεζεύγνυον ἑκάτερος ἐς τὸ αὑτοῦ στρατόπεδον); Ac 11: 29; Eph 4: 25; Hb 8: 11 (Jer 38: 34); Rv 5: 8; 20: 13. The pl. ἕκαστοι is extremely rare (Polyb. 1, 12, 9; Diod. S. 14, 5, 4; Phlegon: 257 fgm. 36, 3, 14 Jac.; Lucian, Herm. 68; UPZ 110, 47; 53; 152 [164 BC]) Phil 2: 4; Rv 6: 11 t.r. M-M.

ἑκάστοτε adv. of time (Pre-Socr., Hdt.+; Dit., Syll.³ 107, 44; 45; 114, 20; 578, 60; PAmh. 78, 4; PFlor. 367, 20) *at any time, always* 2 Pt 1: 15. M-M.*

ἑκάτερος, α, ον (Pind.+; pap., LXX; En. 24, 2; Ep. Arist.; Philo, Sacr. Abel. 138; Jos., Ant. 12, 239; Test. 12 Patr.) *each of two, both* Dg 12: 4; Agr 2.*

ἑκατόν indecl. (Hom.+; inscr., pap., LXX, Ep. Arist., Philo, Test. 12 Patr.—Jos., Bell. 2, 145 as round number) *one hundred* Mt 13: 8, 23; 18: 12, 28; Lk 15: 4; 16: 6f; 24: 13 v.l. (ἑκ. ἑξήκοντα) J 19: 39; 21: 11; Ac 1: 15; Rv 7: 4; 14: 1, 3; 21: 17; Hv 4, 1, 6 (Lghtf.).—Mk 4: 8, 20 ἐν ἑ. is prob. the correct rdg. (εἷς 4); κατὰ ἑ. *by hundreds* 6: 40. M-M.*

ἑκατονταετής, ές (so rightly L., W-H. [cf. Bl-D. §13;

Lob., Phryn. p. 406f]; mostly [also by N.] accented έκατονταέτης) *a hundred years old* (since Pind., Pyth. 4, 502; Gen 17: 17; Philo, Mut. Nom. 1) ἐ. που ὑπάρχων *about 100 yrs. old* Ro 4: 19.*

έκατονταπλασίων, ον *a hundred fold* (X., Oec. 2, 3; 2 Km 24: 3.—Neut. pl. as adv. Strabo 3, 1, 5) Lk 8: 8. έκατονταπλασίονα λαμβάνειν (Georg. Mon. 678, 60 de Boor [1892] ἔλαβον τὸ χρέος έκατονταπλασίονα) Mt 19: 29 t.r.; Mk 10: 30; Lk 18: 30 v.l. (cf. JLebreton, Rech de Sc rel 20, '30, 42-4).*

έκατοντάρχης, ου, ὁ (Aeschyl. in Athen. 1 p. 11 D.; Hdt. 7, 81 et al.; Dionys. Hal.; Plut.; Vett. Val. p. 78, 26; Herodian 5, 4, 7; Dit., Or. 665, 23 [49 AD]; PRyl. 141, 2 [37 AD]; 4 Km 11: 10, 15; cf. Thackeray 156; Jos., Bell. 2, 63) *centurion, captain* Mt 8: 13; Lk 7: 6; 23: 47; Ac 10: 1, 22; 21: 32; 22: 26; 24: 23; 27: 1, 6, 11, 31, 43. For this έκατόνταρχος (X., Cyr. 5, 3, 41; Plut., Lucull. 35, 2; Herodian 5, 4, 12; Sb 599; PReinach 26, 4; 30, 2; LXX; Philo, Mos. 1, 317; Jos., Bell. 3, 124, Ant. 17, 282.—Both forms in the same pass.: Jos., Ant. 14, 69) Mt 8: 5, 8; 27: 54 (in all these pass. έκατοντάρχης is v.l.); Ac 22: 25; 28: 16 v.l.; 1 Cl 37: 3.—Lk 7: 2 can be either form, as well as the gen. pl. Ac 23: 17, 23, since the placing of the accents in the editions is not definitive (Mayser 256f).— Schürer I⁴ 458-66 [lit.]; CCichorius, Cohors: Pauly-W. IV '01, 231-56; AvDomaszewski, D. Rangordnung d. röm. Heeres '08; ABludau, D. Militärverhältnisse in Cäsarea im apost. Zeitalter: Theol.-prakt. Monatsschr. 17, '06, 136-43; FLundgreen, D. paläst. Heerwesen in d. ntl. Zeit: Pj 17, '21, 46-63; TRSBroughton, The Rom. Army: Beginnings I 5, '33, 427-41; GZuntz, The Centurion of Capernaum, etc.: JTS 46, '45, 183-90. M-M.*

έκατόνταρχος s. έκατοντάρχης.

έκβαίνω 2 aor. ἐξέβην (Hom.+; pap., LXX, Ep. Arist., Philo) *go out, come from* w. ἀπό (PGenève 54, 25 ἀπὸ τ. κώμης; Sir 38: 18) Hb 11: 15. M-M.*

έκβάλλω fut. ἐκβαλῶ; 2 aor. ἐξέβαλον; plpf. ἐκβεβλήκειν Mk 16: 9; 1 aor. pass. ἐξεβλήθην; 1 fut. ἐκβληθήσομαι (Hom.+; inscr., pap., LXX, En., Philo, Joseph.).
1. *drive out, expel,* lit. *throw out* more or less forcibly τινά (Dit., Syll.³ 1109, 95; PTebt. 105, 31; Gen 3: 24 al.; Jos., Bell. 1, 31, Ant. 1, 58) Mt 21: 12 (Charito 3, 2, 12 πάντας ἐκβ. fr. the temple of Aphrodite; Lysimachus in Jos., C. Ap. 1, 306 God demands that the Eg. king ἐκβάλλειν ἐκ τῶν ἱερῶν those who are unclean; CRoth, Cleansing of the Temple and Zech 14: 21, NovTest. 4, '60, 174-81); Mk 1: 12 is perh. to be understood in this sense, cf. Gen 3: 24 and see 2 below; 11: 15; Lk 19: 45; 20: 12. Pass. Mt 9: 25; Hs 1: 4; 9, 14, 2. τινὰ or τὶ ἐκ τινος (Dio Chrys. 49[66], 3; Dit., Syll.³ 317, 12; PLond. 887, 6 [III BC]; PMagd. 12, 11; Ex 6: 1; Num 22: 6 al.; Philo, Cher. 10) J 2: 15. ἀπό τινος (Ex 23: 31; Num 22: 11; 2 Ch 11: 16; Philo, Det. Pot. Ins. 163; Jos., Ant. 13, 352) Ac 13: 50; Hs 8, 7, 5. ἔξω τινός *out of someth.* (Lev 14: 40; 1 Macc 13: 47 v.l.): a vineyard Mt 21: 39; Mk 12: 8; Lk 20: 15; a city (Hyperid. 5: 31) Lk 4: 29; Ac 7: 58; cf. Hs 1: 6; ἐ. ἔξω (without amplification a 2 Ch 29: 16) J 6: 37; 9: 34f (s. below); Ac 9: 40. Pass. Lk 13: 28; J 12: 31 (βάλλω 𝔓⁶⁶ et al.). W. the destination given ἐ. εἰς τι *drive someone out into someth.* (Dt 29: 27; 2 Ch 29: 16; Jer 22: 28): into the darkness outside (cf. En. 10, 4) Mt 8: 12; 22: 13; 25: 30.—Mid., throw someth. overboard to save oneself Ac 27: 38 (the act. in this sense Diod. S. 3, 40, 5; Jos., Bell. 1,

280).—Fig. λόγους ἐ. εἰς τὰ ὀπίσω *cast words behind oneself*= pay no attention to them 1 Cl 35: 8 (Ps 49: 17); ἐ. τὸ ὄνομα *disdain, spurn the name* Lk 6: 22 (cf. Pla., Crito p. 46B, Rep. 2 p. 377C; Soph., Oed. Col. 636; 646); differently, Wlh. ad loc.; cf. Black, An Aramaic Approach³, '67, 135f, w. special ref. to Dt 22: 14, 19.—Used esp. of the expulsion of demons who have taken possession of a pers. (Jos., Ant. 6, 211; PGM 4, 1227 πρᾶξις γενναία ἐκβάλλουσα δαίμονας; 1253) Mt 9: 34; 10: 1, 8; 12: 26; 17: 19; Mk 1: 34, 39, 43; 3: 15, 23; 6: 13; 7: 26 (ἔκ τινος); 9: 18, 28; 16: 9 (παρά τινος); Lk 9: 40; 11: 14; 13: 32. W. the means given (Lucian-Epigr. in Anth. Pal. 11, 427 δαίμονα ἐ. δυνάμει) τῷ σῷ ὀνόματι *by your name* Mt 7: 22. λόγῳ *with a word* 8: 16. For this ἔν τινι *by someone* or *someth.* by the ruler of the demons 9: 34; Mk 3: 22; by Beelzebub Mt 12: 24, 27; Lk 11: 15, 18f; by the name of Jesus Mk 9: 38; 16: 17; Lk 9: 49; by the finger of God Lk 11: 20; cf. vs. 19.—*Expel someone fr. a group, repudiate someone* a servant girl Gal 4: 30 (Gen 21: 10); a wife (Demosth. 59, 63; 83; Diod. S. 12, 18, 1; BGU 1050, 15; PGiess. 2, 23; Lev 21: 7; Pr 18: 22a; Sir 7: 26; Jos., Ant. 16, 215; 17, 78) Agr 18; ἐκ τ. ἐκκλησίας ἐ. 3 J 10 (cf. POxy. 104, 17; Jos., Bell. 2, 143). The verses J 9: 34f, referred to above, prob. belong here too, since the Johannine love of multiple meaning has combined the mngs. *drive out of the audience-room* and *expel from the synagogue.*
2. without the connotation of force: *send out* (PRyl. 80, 1 [I AD] ἐκβάλετε . . . ὑδροφύλακας; 1 Macc 12: 27) workers Mt 9: 38; Lk 10: 2 (cf. PMich. 618, 15f [II AD]); *send away* Js 2: 25; *release* Ac 16: 37; *lead out* (Μαρτύριον τῆς ἀγ. Αἰκατερίνας 18 p. 17 Viteau: ἐκέλευσεν ὁ βασ. ἐκβληθῆναι αὐτὴν ἐκ τ. φυλακῆς; Theophanes, Chron. 388, 28 de Boor) Mk 1: 12 (but see 1 above); *bring out of* sheep J 10: 4 (cf. Hs 6, 2, 6; Longus 3, 33, 2 προσέβαλλε ταῖς μητράσι τοὺς ἄρνας; BGU 597, 4 ἵνα βάλῃ τὸν μόσχον πρὸ τ. προβάτων).
3. *take out, remove* fr. someth. (1 Macc 13: 48) a beam or splinter ἐκ τ. ὀφθαλμοῦ Mt 7: 4f; Lk 6: 42 (cf. Aesop. p. 28 Ursing ἐκβάλλεις ἄκανθα[ν] ἐκ ποδῶν μου); *bring out τὶ someth.* (Horapollo 2, 105) ἐκ τοῦ ἀγαθοῦ θησαυροῦ ἐ. τὰ ἀγαθά *out of the good treasure* (=the tr. of the good) *that which is good* Mt 12: 35; 13: 52; *take out* a sum of money Lk 10: 35. Of an eye, tear *out* and *throw away* Mk 9: 47 (Syntipas p. 101, 2; cf. La 3: 16 ἐ. ὀδόντας). Of indigestible material in the body (Ps.-Plut., Hom. 205; schol. on Nicander, Alexiph. 485; cf. Ps.-Aristot., Mirabilia 6 οἱ κυνηγοὶ εἰς ἀγγεῖον αὐτὴν [=τὴν τοῦ ἀνθρώπου κόπρον] ἐμβάλοντες=the hunters let their excrement fall into a pot.—ἐκβ. τι=let someth. fall Diog. L. 6, 35) *evacuate* Mt 15: 17.—Two unusual uses: τὴν αὐλὴν τὴν ἔξωθεν τοῦ ναοῦ ἔκβαλε ἔξωθεν *leave out* (of consideration) *the outer court of the temple* Rv 11: 2 (Epicurus in Diog. L. 10, 147 ἐκβ. τι=disregard someth.; M. Ant. 12, 25 βάλε ἔξω τὴν ὑπόληψιν=do not concern yourself about . . . ; Mitteis, Chrest. 372 VI, 23 [II AD] τὸ ἀναγνωσθὲν δάνειον ἐκβάλλω=I pass over, omit. On the belief of the Jews that the temple could be saved, while the beleagured city was ruined, cf. Jos., Bell. 5, 459); ἐκ. εἰς νῖκος τὴν κρίσιν *lead justice on to victory* Mt 12: 20 (s. κρίσις 3). M-M. B. 713.

ἔκβασις, εως, ἡ (Hom.+; pap., LXX; Jos., Ant. 1, 91) *a way out, end* (Menand., fgm. 696 Kock III 200 τ. κακοῦ; Polyb. 3, 7, 2; Epict. 2, 7, 9, Ench. 32, 3; Vett. Val. 180, 14f ἡ ἔκβασις τ. πραγμάτων; cf. 186, 24; PFlor. 74, 16 τ. ἑορτῆς) 1 Cor 10: 13 (cf. WWGauld, ET 52, '40/'41,

237

337–40). ἐ. τῆς ἀναστροφῆς Hb 13: 7 can mean the end of one's life (cf. Marinus, Vi. Procli 26 ἐ. τοῦ βίου; Wsd 2: 17), but can also prob. be understood as (successful) outcome, result of one's way of life (cf. PRyl. 122, 5 [II AD]=produce [τῶν ἐδαφῶν]; Wsd 11: 14). M-M.*

ἐκβλαστάνω 1 aor. ἐξεβλάστησα (Hippocr., Alim. 6 ed. Litt. IX p. 100; Lucian, Ver. Hist. 2, 41) sprout up (so lit., Theophr., Caus. Pl. 1, 3, 5 FWimmer [1866] ἐκβλαστάνει; 3, 23, 1; Num 17: 20; Job 38: 27) Mk 4: 5 v.l.*

ἐκβολή, ῆς, ἡ (Aeschyl.+; pap., LXX; Jos., Ant. 17, 86, C. Ap. 1, 294 al.) nautical t.t. jettisoning, lit. 'throwing out' of a ship's cargo to save the vessel in a storm (cf. Aeschyl., Sept. 769; Aristot., Eth. Nic. 3, 1, 5 p. 1110a, 9; Lucian, De Mer. Cond. 1): ἐκβολὴν ποιεῖσθαι jettison (Pollux 1, 99; Jon 1: 5) Ac 27: 18. M-M.*

ἔκβολος, ον (Eur.+; Jdth 11: 11) rejected, excluded ἔσονται ἔκβολοι they will be excluded Hv 3, 5, 5.*

ἐκγαμίζω (Rhet. Gr. IV 247, 14.—Eustath. in Il. 9, 384 p. 758, 54 ἐγγαμίζειν οἱ ὕστερον λέγουσιν) marry, give in marriage, as v.l. in Mt 24: 38 and 1 Cor 7: 38 (here twice). Pass. be married, be given in marriage Mt 22: 30; Lk 17: 27; 20: 35, everywhere as v.l. The newer editions have γαμίζω (q.v. 1). M-M.*

ἔκγονος, ον usu. subst. ὁ, ἡ ἔκγονος (Hom.+; inscr., pap.; cf. Mayser 228) τὰ ἔκγονα gener. descendants (Diod. S. 4, 82, 4; Diog. L. 3, 81; LXX, Philo; Jos., Ant. 11, 2; 111) or spec. grandchildren (Hesychius τέκνα τέκνων; Dit., Or. 740 [I BC] τ. τέκνων καὶ τ. ἐκγόνων; Dio Chrys. 21[38], 21; Charito 2, 9, 2; Herm. Wr. 10, 14b). The ancient versions understand it in the latter sense 1 Ti 5: 4. M-M. B. 112; 121.*

ἐκδαπανάω 1 fut. pass. ἐκδαπανηθήσομαι spend, exhaust (Polyb. 24, 7, 4 τὰς προσόδους; Jos., Ant. 15, 117 τὰς προθυμίας; Galen, cf. Nägeli 33) fig. in pass. be spent of the sacrifice of one's own life ὑπέρ τινος for someone 2 Cor 12: 15 (ZNW 18, '18, 201).*

ἐκδέχομαι impf. ἐξεδεχόμην (Hom.+; pap., LXX; Ep. Arist. 205; Philo, Op. M. 34; Joseph.) expect, wait (this mng. Soph.+; pap.) τινά (for) someone (Soph., Philoct. 123; Polyb. 3, 45, 6; BGU 892, 6 ἐκδεχόμενός σε) Ac 17: 16; 1 Cor 11: 33; 16: 11. τὶ (for) someth. (Plut., Mar. 17, 1; Ps.-Apollod. 1, 9, 27, 3; POxy. 724, 12; 939, 27; PFlor. 332, 5 σου τὴν παρουσίαν; Jos., Ant. 11, 328; Test. Gad 7: 4) the movement of the water J 5: 3 v.l.; the kgdm. of God 2 Cl 12: 1 (Lucian, Nav. 28 ἐ. τὴν βασιλείαν); τ. ἅγιον αἰῶνα B 10: 11; fruit Js 5: 7; 2 Cl 20: 3; the heavenly city Hb 11: 10. Foll. by ἕως wait until (Dionys. Hal. 6, 67 ἕως ἂν γένηταί τι) Hb 10: 13. W. acc. and ἕως foll. ἐκδέξομαι αὐτὸν ἕως ὀψέ I will wait for him until evening Hs 9, 11, 2. ἔκδεξαί με ὧδε, ἕως wait here for me, until Hs 9, 10, 5. M-M.*

ἔκδηλος, ον quite evident, plain (Hom.+; Demosth. 24, 10; Vett. Val. 92, 10; Dit., Syll.³ 695, 63 [II BC], Or. 665, 13 [49 AD]; PHermopol. 6, 3; 3 Macc 3: 19; 6: 5; Ep. Arist. 85; Philo; Joseph.; Third Corinthians 1: 16) 2 Ti 3: 9. M-M.*

ἐκδημέω 1 aor. inf. ἐκδημῆσαι—1. leave one's country, take a long journey (Soph., Oed. R. 114; Hdt. 1, 30; Pla., Leg. 12 p. 952D; Epict. 1, 4, 22; BGU 1197, 7 [4 BC]; PTebt. 316, 20; POxy. 59, 16; Jos., Ant. 9, 88) fig. (cf. ἐκδημία of death Anth. Pal. 3, 5) ἐκ τοῦ σώματος leave, get away fr., the body 2 Cor 5: 8 (lit. on γυμνός 4).

2. be in a strange land (opp. ἐνδημέω, as Philo, Spec. Leg. 4, 142) fig. be away abs. vs. 9 (cf. Pla., Leg. 9 p. 864E ἐκδημῶν abs.=living in exile); w. ἀπὸ τ. κυρίου vs. 6. M-M.*

ἐκδίδωμι (Hom.+; inscr., pap., LXX, Philo, Joseph.) in our lit. only mid.; fut. ἐκδώσομαι; 2 aor. ἐξεδόμην, 3 pers. ἐξέδετο (on this form cf. Bl-D. §94, 1; Mlt.-H. 212; it is also found (PSI 288, 8 [II AD] let out for hire, lease (so class., the act., Pla., Leg. 7 p. 806D, mid. Polyb. 6, 17, 2; of hiring out a son as apprentice POxy. 275, 6 [66 AD]; PTebt. 385, 3) τὶ a vineyard Mt 21: 33, 41; Mk 12: 1; Lk 20: 9. M-M. B. 810.*

ἐκδιηγέομαι tell (in detail) (Aristot., Rhet. 23 p. 1434b, 4; Galen; LXX; Philo, Mos. 1, 235; Jos., Bell. 5, 567, Ant. 5, 279) τὶ someth. Ac 15: 3. Abs. w. dat. of the pers. 13: 41 (Hab 1: 5).*

ἐκδικέω fut. ἐκδικήσω; 1 aor. ἐξεδίκησα, imper. ἐκδίκησον (Diod. S., Plut., Herodian, inscr., pap., LXX; En. 20, 4; Philo, Joseph.; s. Anz 364).

1. avenge someone, procure justice for someone (Plut., Ag. et Cleom. 5, 5; PAmh. 134, 10; PStrassb. 41, 9; 1 Macc 6: 22; Jos., Ant. 6, 303) τινά Lk 18: 5. ἑαυτόν take one's revenge Ro 12: 19 (cf. POxy. 937, 7 ἐκδικήσω ἐμαυτόν). ἐ. με ἀπὸ τ. ἀντιδίκου μου see to it that I get justice against my opponent Lk 18: 3 (cf. Test. Levi 2: 2). —On the parable, GDelling, ZNW 53, '62, 1–25= Studien zum NT, '70, 203–25.

2. take vengeance for someth., punish someth. τὶ (Ctesias, fgm. 37 φόνον; Plut., Ant. 67, 2 τ. τοῦ πατρὸς θάνατον; Herodian 2, 6, 9; Jos., Ant. 9, 171) 2 Cor 10: 6. τὸ αἷμα (Dt 32: 43; 4 Km 9: 7; prayers for vengeance fr. Rheneia: Dssm., LO⁴ 353f, 359 [LAE 424f, 431f]; cf. Dit., Syll.³ 1181, 11), w. the pers. on whom vengeance is taken, or who is punished, designated by ἐκ (Num 31: 2; 1 Km 24: 13; Vis. Pauli 40) Rv 6: 10, or ἐκ χειρός τινος (4 Km 9: 7) 19: 2.

3. ἐ. τὸν τόπον do justice to one's official position IPol 1: 2 (cf. Cornelius in Euseb., H.E. 6, 43, 9 and 11; Origen, In Mt. t. 12, 14 p. 98, 28ff ed. EKlostermann '35: οἱ τ. τόπον τῆς ἐπισκοπῆς ἐκδικοῦντες χρῶνται τῷ ῥητῷ ὡς Πέτρος). M-M.*

ἐκδίκησις, εως, ἡ vengeance, punishment (Polyb. 3, 8, 10 ἐ. ποιεῖσθαι; Dit., Syll.³ 563, 15 [III BC]; LXX, En., Philo, Test. 12 Patr.) abs. punishment (of Paul's opponent) 2 Cor 7: 11. ἐμοὶ ἐκδίκησις vengeance belongs to me Ro 12: 19; Hb 10: 30. Of the Last Judgment ἡμέραι ἐκδικήσεως Lk 21: 22 (cf. Dt 32: 35; En. 25, 4; Philo, Leg. All. 3, 106). W. gen. of the pers. being punished (Ezk 9: 1; Jdth 8: 35; 9: 2 εἰς ἐ. ἀλλογενῶν) εἰς ἐ. κακοποιῶν for pun. of the evil-doers 1 Pt 2: 14. ἐ. ποιεῖν see to it that justice is done, w. gen. of the person for whom it is done (Num 31: 2; 1 Macc 2: 67) Lk 18: 7f; also w. the dat. of the pers. for whom it is done (Judg 11: 36; Test. of Solomon 22, 4 ed. McCown '22) Ac 7: 24. W. the dat. to denote the pers. being punished διδόναι ἐκδίκησίν τινι 2 Th 1: 8 (cf. Sir 12: 6 τ. ἀσεβέσιν ἀποδώσει ἐ.).—GSchrenk, TW II 440ff. M-M.*

ἔκδικος, ον (trag.+; inscr., pap., LXX; Sib. Or. 3, 365) avenging, subst. the avenger, the one who punishes (Plut., Mor. p. 509F; Herodian 2, 14, 3; 7, 4, 5; Sir 30: 6; Wsd 12: 12; 4 Macc 15: 29) of God (Appian, Bell. Civ. 2, 85 §360; Jos., Bell. 5, 377) ἐ. περὶ πάντων τούτων 1 Th 4: 6. Of the authorities: ἐ. εἰς ὀργὴν τῷ τὸ κακὸν πράσσοντι an avenger who brings (God's) wrath upon the evil-doer Ro 13: 4. M-M.*

ἐκδιώκω fut. ἐκδιώξω; 1 aor. ptc. ἐκδιώξας (since Thu. 1, 24, 5; pap., LXX=drive away; likew. En. 23, 4; Jos., C. Ap. 1, 292; Test. Jud. 18: 4) *persecute severely* (so perh. Demosth. 32, 5; certainly BGU 836, 5; Ps 118: 157; Sir 30: 19) τινά *someone* 1 Th 2: 15. Cf. Lk 11: 49 v.l. M-M.*

ἔκδοτος, ον (since Hdt. 3, 1; Polyb.; Palaeph. 41, 2; Vett. Val.; PGrenf. I 1 [1], 7 [II вc]; Jos., Ant. 6, 316 al.; Sym.; Theod.) *given up, delivered up* Ac 2: 23. ἑαυτὸν ἔ. δέδωκα τῷ θανάτῳ *I have delivered myself up to death* ISm 4: 2 (διδόναι τινὰ ἔ. as Demosth. 23, 85; Polyb. 20, 10, 5; 28, 4, 11; Dit., Syll.³ 372, 13 [III вc]; Bel 22 Theod.; cf. Vett. Val. 106, 24; 220, 16). M-M.*

ἐκδοχή, ῆς, ἡ (Aeschyl.+; Philo) found nowhere else (except Hesychius: ἐκδοχή· προσδοκία) in the mng. which it must have in its only occurrence in OT and our lit.: *expectation* φοβερὰ ἐ. τῆς κρίσεως *a fearful ex. of judgment* Hb 10: 27. M-M.*

ἐκδύω 1 aor. ἐξέδυσα, mid. ἐξεδυσάμην (Hom.+; inscr., pap., LXX, Philo) *strip, take off.*
1. act., lit., w. acc. of the pers. (Dit., Syll.³ 1169, 47 [IV вc]; PMagd. 6, 13 [221 вc]; 1 Ch 10: 9; Hos 2: 5) Mt 27: 28; Lk 10: 30. W. acc. of the pers. and the thing (Gen 37: 23; Test. Jud. 3: 5; Test. Zeb. 4: 10) Mt 27: 31; Mk 15: 20. Fig. strip someone= *plunder* B 10: 4.
2. mid., *strip, undress (oneself)* abs., lit. (as X., Hell. 3, 4, 19 et al.; Is 32: 11) Gosp.-fgm.= POxy. 655 (Kl. T. 8³, p. 23) Ib, 23. Fig., of the body as a garment (Artem. 5, 40 ἐκ τῶν σαρκῶν ἐκδύνειν) οὐ θέλομεν ἐκδύσασθαι *we do not want to strip ourselves* 2 Cor 5: 4; cf. vs. 3 v.l.—Lit. on γυμνός 4. M-M.*

ἐκεῖ adv. of place (Aeschyl.+; inscr., pap., LXX; En. 103, 7; Joseph., Test. 12 Patr.).
1. *there, in that place* Mt 2: 13, 15; 5: 24; 8: 12; 12: 45 and oft. Somet. more definitely ἐκεῖ πρὸς τῷ ὄρει Mk 5: 11. W. the art. οἱ ἐκεῖ *those who were there* (X., Hell. 1, 6, 4; Celsus 2, 43; PRyl. 239, 9 [III AD] ἐπίμινον τοῖς ἐκεῖ; Jos., Ant. 1, 243; 9, 114) Mt 26: 71. Corresp. to the relatives οὗ, ὅπου . . . ἐκεῖ *where . . . there* (Epict. 4, 4, 15; Jos., C. Ap. 1, 32) Mt 6: 21; 18: 20; Mk 6: 10; Lk 12: 34. Pleonastic after ὅπου (Bl-D. §297; cf. Gen 13: 4; Ex 20: 24) Rv 12: 6, 14.—ISm 8: 2.
2. *there, to that place*=ἐκεῖσε 1 (since Hdt. 1, 209; Thu. 3, 71, 2; Epict. 1, 27, 18; Griech. Texte aus Aegypt., ed. PMMeyer ['16] 20, 46 ἐκεῖ πέμπω τ. ἐπιστολάς; PFlor. 125, 7; 133, 9; Gen 19: 22; 2 Km 2: 2; Tob 7: 16 al.; Jos., Ant. 18, 327; 20, 212) ἐκεῖ ἀπέρχεσθαι *go there* (thither) Mt 2: 22; cf. 26: 36. βάλλειν Lk 21: 2. ἔρχεσθαι (Hdt. 1, 121; Jos., Ant. 6, 83) J 18: 3. προπέμπεσθαι Ro 15: 24. συνάγεσθαι Mt 24: 28; J 18: 2. συντρέχειν Mk 6: 33. ὑπάγειν J 11: 8. μετάβα ἔνθεν ἐκεῖ *move from here to there* Mt 17: 20.—Hv 3, 1, 3. M-M.

ἐκεῖθεν adv. of place (trag., Thu.+; pap., LXX, En.; Jos., Bell. 7, 96; Ant. 8, 303) *from there* Mt 4: 21; 5: 26; 9: 9, 27; 11: 1; 12: 9, 15; 13: 53; 14: 13 al. οἱ ἐ. (Thu. 1, 62, 4) Lk 16: 26 v.l.; D 1: 5. M-M.

ἐκεῖνος, η, ο demonstr. pron. (Hom.+; inscr., pap., LXX, En., Ep. Arist., Joseph.) *that person* or *thing, that.*
1. abs.—a. denoting the remoter object; opp. οὗτος Lk 18: 14. τοῦτο ἢ ἐκεῖνο *this or that* Js 4: 15. ἡμῖν . . . ἐκεῖνοις Mt 13: 11; Mk 4: 11; cf. 2 Cor 8: 14. ἐκεῖνον . . . ἐμέ J 3: 30. ἐκεῖνοι . . . ἡμεῖς 1 Cor 9: 25; Hb 12: 25; 1 J 4: 17. ἄλλοι . . . ἐκεῖνος J 9: 9. Opp. a certain pers.: Jesus Mk 16: 19f; the Jews J 2: 20f et al.

b. referring back to and resuming a word immediately preceding, oft. weakened to *he, she, it* (X., An. 4, 3, 20) Mk 16: 10f. Esp. oft. so in J: 5: 37; 8: 44; 10: 6; 11: 29; 12: 48; 14: 21, 26; 16: 14 al. Hence 19: 35 perh. the eyewitness (just mentioned) is meant, who then, to be sure, would be vouching for his own credibility and love of the truth (s. 1c and e).—Interchanging w. αὐτός (cf. Thu. 1, 32, 5; X., Cyr. 4, 5, 20; Lysias 14, 28; Kühner-G. I 649) ἐζωγρημένοι ὑπ' αὐτοῦ εἰς τὸ ἐκείνου θέλημα *under the spell of his will* 2 Ti 2: 26. Used to produce greater emphasis: ἐκεῖνον λαβών *take that one* Mt 17: 27; cf. J 5: 43. τῇ ἐκείνου χάριτι *by his grace* Tit 3: 7. Pleonastic after a participial subj. (X., Cyr. 6, 2, 33 ὁ γὰρ λόγχην ἀκονῶν, ἐκεῖνος καὶ σὴν ψυχὴν οὐ παρακονᾷ) τὸ ἐκπορευόμενον ἐκεῖνο κοινοῖ Mk 7: 20. ὁ πέμψας ἐκεῖνος J 1: 33. ὁ ποιήσας με ὑγιῆ ἐκεῖνος 5: 11. ὁ λαλῶν ἐκεῖνός ἐστιν 9: 37. (αὐτός 𝔓⁶⁶ Lat.). ὁ εἰσερχόμενος ἐκεῖνος κλέπτης ἐστιν 10: 1. τῷ λογιζομένῳ . . . ἐκείνῳ κοινόν Ro 14: 14 al.

c. w. ref. to well-known or notorious personalities Kühner-G. I 650; Arrian, Periplus 1, 1 ὁ Ξενοφῶν ἐκεῖνος) Jesus: J 7: 11; 9: 12, 28; 1 J 2: 6; 3: 3, 5, 7, 16; 4: 17. Many scholars also refer the ἐκ. J 19: 35 to Jesus (Erasmus; Zahn; ESchwartz, NGG '07, 361; Bultmann; Lagrange.—Acc. to Iambl., Vi. Pyth. 35, 255 [also Aristoxenus, fgm. 33 p. 17, 3 οἱ Πυθαγόρειοι παρ' ἐκείνου μαθόντες] the Pythagoreans called their master after his death simply ἐκεῖνος.—Yet how much more clearly this idea might have been conveyed by simply using ὁ κύριος!); s. 1b and e, and cf. FBlass, StKr 75, '02, 128–33.—W. an unfavorable connotation (Themistocl., Ep. 16 p. 755, 14; 27; Lucian, M. Peregr. 13 of Jesus; Julian, Letter 60 p. 379A of the Christians) of the Jews B 2: 9; 3: 6; 4: 6; 8: 7 al.

d. w. relative foll: ἐκεῖνός ἐστιν ᾧ ἐγὼ βάψω J 13: 26. ἐκεῖνον . . . ὑπὲρ οὗ Ro 14: 15. ἐκείνης ἀφ' ἧς Hb 11: 15. W. ὅτι foll. (Ael. Aristid. 39 p. 747 D.) Mt 24: 43.

e. In indirect discourse the speaker refers to himself as ἐκ. (Isaeus 8, 22a; Polyb. 3, 44, 10; 12, 16, 5). Is it possible to see in this an indication that the narrator of the 4th Gospel, who could no more use the I-form than could the speaker in indirect discourse, is designating himself by ἐκ. 19: 35, and by what he says is seeking to corroborate the statement of another? S. also 1b and c.

2. used w. nouns—a. to differentiate pers. or things already named, fr. others: τῇ οἰκίᾳ ἐκείνῃ *that* (particular) *house* Mt 7: 25; cf. vs. 27. τῇ πόλει ἐκείνῃ *that city* (just mentioned) 10: 15; 18: 32; Mk 3: 24f; Lk 6: 48f; J 18: 15; Ac 1: 19; 3: 23 (Dt 18: 19); 8: 8; 14: 21; 16: 3 and oft.

b. of time—α. of the past, when the time cannot (or is not to) be given w. exactness: ἐν τ. ἡμέραις ἐκείναις *in those days* (Ex 2: 11; Judg 18: 1; 1 Km 28: 1; Jdth 1: 5) Mt 3: 1, cf. 24: 38; Mk 1: 9; 8: 1; Lk 2: 1. Of a definite period (1 Macc 1: 11; 9: 24; 11: 20) Lk 4: 2; 9: 36.

β. of the future (ἐκείνη ἡ ἡμέρα Plut., Gai. Marc. 35, 6; Epict. 3, 17, 4; Ael. Aristid. 19, 8 K.=41 p. 765 D.) ἐν ἐκ. τ. ἡμέραις Mt 24: 19; Ac 2: 18 (Jo 3: 2); Rv 9: 6. Also in sg. ἐν ἐκείνῃ τ. ἡμέρᾳ (Jdth 11: 15) Lk 17: 31; J 16: 23, 26; esp. of the Judgment Day Mt 7: 22; Lk 6: 23; 10: 12; 2 Th 1: 10; 2 Ti 1: 12, 18. ὁ αἰὼν ἐ. (opp. αἰὼν οὗτος) *the age to come* Lk 20: 35 (s. αἰών 2b).

γ. of a period ascertainable fr. the context Mt 13: 1; Mk 4: 35; J 1: 39 (Jos., Ant. 7, 134 μεῖναι τὴν ἡμέραν ἐκείνην) al. ἀπ' ἐκείνης τ. ἡμέρας (Jos., Bell. 4, 318, Ant. 7, 382) Mt 22: 46. κατὰ τὸν καιρὸν ἐ. *at that time* Ac 19: 23. κατ' ἐ. τὸν καιρόν (Jos., Ant. 1, 171 al.) 12: 1. ἐν ἐ. τῇ ὥρᾳ Rv 11: 13.

3. adverbial gen. ἐκείνης (sc. τῆς ὁδοῦ) *there* Lk 19: 4.

Cf. Bl-D. §186, 1; Rob. 494.—WHavers, IndogF 19, '06, 83ff. M-M.

ἐκεῖσε adv. of place (Aeschyl., Hdt.+; inscr., pap.).

1. *there, to that place* (class.) κἀκεῖσε=καὶ ἐκεῖσε: ὧδε κ. *here and there* (hither and thither) Plut., Mor. 34A; Lucian, Hermotim. 1; Polyaenus, Exc. 57, 5) Hm 5, 2, 7; s 6, 1, 6; 6, 2, 7; 9, 3, 1.

2. *by exchange of concept*=ἐκεῖ 1 *there, at that place* (Hippocr.+; Chrysipp.: Stoic. II 244; Polyb. 5, 51, 3; POxy. 60, 9; 1204, 6; PSI 162, 11; Job 39: 29; Jos., Ant. 3, 40; 8, 350) Ac 21: 3; τοὺς ἐ. ὄντας 22: 5 (Bl-D. §103 w. app.). M-M.*

ἐκζητέω fut. ἐκζητήσω; 1 aor. ἐξεζήτησα; 1 aor. pass. ἐξεζητήθην; 1 fut. ἐκζητηθήσομαι (Ael. Aristid. 38 p. 726 D.; inscr., pap., LXX; En. 104, 7).

1. *seek out, search for* w. acc. of pers. or thing sought (POxy. 1465, 11 [I BC] τοὺς αἰτίους; LXX; Ep. Arist. 24) τὶ (Aelian, N.A. 15, 1 p. 356, 24; Test. Ash. 5: 4) Hb 12: 17; B 21: 8. ἐκζ. τὰ δυνάμενα ἡμᾶς σῴζειν *seek out the things that can save us* 4: 1. κρίσιν *search for justice* 1 Cl 8: 4 (Is 1: 17). τὰ εὐάρεστα 35: 5. τὰ δικαιώματα κυρίου B 2: 1. τόπον 1 Cl 14: 5 (Ps 36: 36). τὰ πρόσωπα τῶν ἁγίων *seek the faces of the saints* i.e. associate w. them, attend their meetings D 4: 2; B 19: 10. τινά: ἐ. τὸν κύριον *seek the Lord* to serve him (Ps 33: 5; 68: 33; Dt 4: 29 al.) Ac 15: 17 (Am 9: 12); cf. Ro 3: 11 (Ps 13: 2; 52: 3); Hb 11: 6; 1 Cl 13: 1.—περί τινος *seek for someth.* 1 Pt 1: 10 (w. ἐξεραυνάω as 1 Macc 9: 26 A). Foll. by an indirect question instead of an obj. B 10: 4; 21: 6. Abs. (BGU 1141, 41 [14 BC]; Inscr. Rom. IV 834, 5) ἐ. ἐπιμελῶς *search carefully* Hv 3, 3, 5.

2. *desire, seek to get* (1 Macc 7: 12) ἐ. τι ἐκ τ. χειρῶν τινος B 2: 5 (Is 1: 12).—3. *seek out, visit* τινά: τοὺς πεινῶντας Hv 3, 9, 5.

4. *charge with, require of* τὸ αἷμα (Gen 9: 5; 42: 22; 2 Km 4: 11; Ezk 3: 18; Jo 4: 21 v.l.) ἀπό τινος Lk 11: 50f; Pol 2: 1. M-M.*

ἐκζήτησις, εως, ἡ (only in Christian wr.) *useless speculation* 1 Ti 1: 4 (v.l. ζητήσεις).*

ἐκθαμβέω 1 aor. pass. ἐξεθαμβήθην (Orph., Arg. 1217; PGrenf. I 53, 18 [IV AD]; Sir 30: 9), in our lit. only in Mk and only pass. *be amazed* (Galen XVI 493 K.) Mk 9: 15; *be alarmed* 16: 5f; *be distressed* w. ἀδημονεῖν 14: 33. M-M.*

ἔκθαμβος, ον *utterly astonished* (so Polyb. 20, 10, 9; Audollent, Defix. Tab. 271, 20 [III AD]; 1 Km 4: 13 Sym. But=terrible Da 7: 7 Theod.) Ac 3: 11. ἔκθαμβον γενέσθαι πρός τινα *be greatly astonished at someone* AP 4: 11. Abs. ἐ. γενέσθαι Hv 3, 1, 5. M-M.*

ἐκθαυμάζω impf. ἐξεθαύμαζον (Dionys. Hal., Thu. Jud. 34 et al.; LXX; Ep. Arist. 312; Philo, Somn. 2, 70) *wonder greatly* (in the sense of grudging admiration) ἐπί τινι at someone Mk 12: 17 (cf. Sir 27: 23 ἐπί τινος). M-M.*

ἔκθετος, ον (Eur., Andr. 70; Vett. Val. 106, 14; Sb 5252, 19 [I AD]) *exposed, abandoned* of infants (Manetho, Apot. 6, 52) βρέφη Ac 7: 19. M-M.*

ἐκκαθαίρω 1 aor. ἐξεκάθαρα (Hom.+; inscr.; Zen.-P. 59 729, 10 [III BC]; LXX, Philo; Jos., Ant. 3, 227) *clean out, cleanse.*

1. w. acc. of what is removed as unclean (Pla., Euth. p. 3A; Aristot., Hist. An. 9, 40 et al.; Philo, Mos. 1, 303) ἐ. τὴν παλαιὰν ζύμην *clean out the old yeast* 1 Cor 5: 7.

2. w. acc. of what is cleansed (Hom.+; Philostrat., Vi.

Apoll. 5, 7 p. 169, 32; Dit., Or. 483, 158; Jos., Bell. 4, 323) fig. (Plut., Mor. 64F λογισμόν; Epict. 2, 23, 40; Vett. Val. 242, 15) ἑαυτὸν ἐ. *cleanse oneself* ἀπό τινος (Epict. 2, 21, 15) 2 Ti 2: 21. M-M.*

ἐκκαίω 1 aor. ἐξέκαυσα, pass. ἐξεκαύθην (Hdt.+; LXX; Sib. Or. 4, 178) *kindle*; fig. (Jos., Vi. 134 αὐτούς) στάσιν *a schism* (Diod. S. 20, 33, 7 στάσιν ἐξέκαυσαν) 1 Cl 1: 1 (cf. Polyb. 2, 1, 3 πόλεμον; Diod. S. 15, 92, 3; Sir 28: 8).—Pass. *be inflamed* with sensual desire (Charito 5, 9, 9; Longus 3, 13, 3) ἐξεκαύθησαν εἰς ἀλλήλους *toward each other* Ro 1: 27 (Alciphr. 3, 31, 1 ἐξεκαύθην εἰς ἔρωτα. Cf. Plut., Tib. Gracch. 13, 4, Alex. 31, 3; Sir 16: 6 al.; Jos., Vi. 263). M-M.*

ἐκκακέω 1 aor. ἐξεκάκησα (Vett. Val. 201, 15; Herm. Wr. 484, 3 Sc.; Hesychius; Sym. Jer 18: 12; Philo, Conf. Lingu. 51 codd.) *lose heart* (w. διψυχέω.—Astrampsychus p. 31 Dec. 61, 3) Hm 9: 8 (v.l. in Lk 18: 1; 2 Cor 4: 1, 16; Gal 6: 9; Eph 3: 13; 2 Th 3: 13 for ἐγκακέω q.v.).*

ἐκκεντέω 1 aor. ἐξεκέντησα (Aristot.+) *pierce* (so Polyb. 5, 56, 12; Polyaenus 5, 3, 8; LXX) τινά *someone* (=kill him: Num 22: 29; 2 Macc 12: 6) Rv 1: 7. ὄψονται εἰς ὃν ἐξεκέντησαν *they will look at him whom they have pierced* J 19: 37; cf. Dssm., Heidelb. Pap.-Sammlung I '05, 66ff; ARahlfs, ZNW 20, '21, 182ff.*

ἐκκλάω 1 aor. pass. ἐξεκλάσθην (since Pla., Rep. 10 p. 611D; Paus. 8, 40, 2; Lev 1: 17) *break off* (PTebt. 802, 12; 19 [135 BC]) of branches Ro 11: 17, 19, 20.*

ἐκκλείω 1 aor. ἐξέκλεισα, inf. ἐκκλεῖσαι; pass. ἐξεκλείσθην; 1 fut. ἐκκλεισθήσομαι (Eur., Hdt.+; pap.; LXX rarely as v.l.) *shut out, exclude.*

1. lit. τινά *someone* in the sense of withdrawal of fellowship (Hdt. 1, 144 et al.; PMagd. 10, 6 [III BC]) Gal 4: 17 (s. MHitchcock, JTS 40, '39, 149–51). Pass. ἐ. ἀπὸ πόλεως *be excluded fr. one's home city* Hs 1: 5. ἔξω τῆς θύρας τοῦ πύργου *be shut outside the door of the tower* v 3, 9, 6 (cf. Jos., Vi. 294).

2. fig. *exclude someth.*=make it impossible (Polyb. 17, 8, 2; Diod. S. 3, 16; Lucian, Pseudolog. 11; PMagd. 12, 4 [III BC]) of boasting ἐξεκλείσθη *it is eliminated* Ro 3: 27. M-M.*

ἐκκλησία, ας, ἡ (Eur., Hdt.+; Dit., Syll. and Or., Index; Magie, Ind.; LXX; Philo; Joseph.

1. *assembly*, as a regularly summoned political body (Jos., Ant. 12, 164; 19, 332, Vi. 268) Ac 19: 39 (on the ἐκκλ. in Ephesus cf. CIG III 325; Anc. Inscr. of Brit. Mus. III 481, 340; on the ἐκκλ. in the theater there cf. the last-named inscr. l. 395; Forschungen in Ephesos II '12 p. 147ff=Dit., Or. 480, 9). CGBrandis, Ἐκκλησία: Pauly-W. V 2, '05, 2163–200.

2. *assemblage, gathering, meeting* gener. (1 Km 19: 20; 1 Macc 3: 13; Sir 26: 5) Ac 19: 32, 40.

3. the *congregation* of the Israelites, esp. when gathered for religious purposes (Dt 31: 30; Judg 20: 2; 1 Km 17: 47; 3 Km 8: 14; Philo; Jos., Ant. 4, 309; Diod. S. 40, 3, 6) Hb 2: 12 (Ps 21: 23), e.g. to hear the law (Dt 4: 10; 9: 10; 18: 16) Ac 7: 38.

4. of the Christian *church* or *congregation* (but also, e.g., of the community of Pythagoras [Hermippus in Diog. L. 8, 41] As a matter of fact, in Himerius, Or. 39 [Or. 5], 5 Orpheus forms for himself τὴν ἐκκλησίαν, a group of wild animals, who listen to him, in the Thracian mountains where there are no people)—a. *a church meeting:* συνερχομένων ὑμῶν ἐν ἐ. *when you come together in church* 1 Cor 11: 18; cf. 14: 4f, 19, 28, 35; pl. vs. 34. ἐν ἐ.

ἐξομολογεῖσθαι τὰ παραπτώματα *confess one's sins in church* D 4: 14; cf. 3 J 6 (JYCampbell, JTS 49, '48, 130-42; for the Johannines s. ESchweizer below).

b. *the church* or *congregation* as the totality of Christians living in one place: Mt 18: 17; Ac 5: 11; 8: 3; 1 Cor 4: 17; Phil 4: 15; 1 Cl 44: 3; Hv 2, 4, 3; cf. Ac 15: 22. More definitely the church at Jerusalem Ac 8: 1; 11: 22; Cenchreae Ro 16: 1; Corinth 1 Cor 1: 2; 2 Cor 1: 1; 1 Cl inscr.; 47: 6; Thessalonica 1 Th 1: 1; 2 Th 1: 1; Colossae Phlm subscr. v.l. Likew. w. other names: Rv 2: 1, 8, 12, 18; 3: 1, 7, 14; IEph inscr.; 8: 1; IMg inscr.; ITr inscr.; 13: 1; IRo 9: 1; IPhld inscr.; 10: 1; ISm 11: 1; Pol inscr. Plural: Ac 15: 41; 16: 5; Ro 16: 16; 1 Cor 7: 17; 2 Cor 8: 18f, 23f and oft. The churches in Judaea Gal 1: 22; 1 Th 2: 14; Galatia Gal 1: 2; 1 Cor 16: 1; Asia 16: 19; Rv 1: 4; Macedonia 2 Cor 8: 1. κατ' ἐκκλησίαν *in each individual church* Ac 14: 23 (cf. Dit., Or. 480, 9 [s. 1 above]: ἵνα τιθῆνται κατ' ἐκκλησίαν in order that they [the statues] might be erected in each indiv. ἐ.). On κατὰ τ. οὖσαν ἐ. Ac 13: 1 cf. εἰμί V, beg.

c. of house-churches Πρίσκαν καὶ 'Ακύλαν . . . καὶ τὴν κατ' οἶκον αὐτῶν ἐ. Ro 16: 5; cf. 1 Cor 16: 19. Νύμφαν καὶ τὴν κατ' οἶκον αὐτῆς ἐ. Col 4: 15; ἡ κατ' οἶκόν σου ἐ. Phlm 2.—FVFilson, JBL 58, '39, 105-12.

d. *the church* universal, to which all believers belong: Mt 16: 18 (OBetz, ZNW 48, '57, 49-77: Qumran parallels; cf. HBraun, Qumran I, '66, 30-37); Ac 9: 31; 1 Cor 6: 4; 12: 28; Eph 1: 22; 3: 10, 21; 5: 23ff, 27, 29, 32 (HSchlier, Christus u. d. Kirche im Eph '30; also ThBl 6, '27, 12-17); Col 1: 18, 24; Phil 3: 6; 1 Ti 5: 16 or under b above (s. βαρέω, end); B 7: 11; Hv 2, 2, 6; 2, 4, 1 (with the depiction of the church as an elderly lady fig. Ps.-Demetr. c. 265 where Hellas, the fatherland, is represented as λαβοῦσα γυναικὸς σχῆμα); 3, 3, 3; IEph 5: 1f and oft.

e. The local as well as the universal church is more specif. called ἐ. τοῦ θεοῦ or ἐ. τ. Χριστοῦ. This is essentially Pauline usage, and it serves to give the current Gk. term its Christian coloring and thereby its special mng.:

α. ἐ. τοῦ θεοῦ 1 Cor 1: 2; 10: 32; 11: 16, 22; 15: 9; 2 Cor 1: 1; Gal 1: 13; 1 Th 2: 14; 2 Th 1: 4; 1 Ti 3: 5, 15; Ac 20: 28; ITr 2: 3; 12: 1; IPhld 10: 1; ISm inscr. al.

β. ἐ. τοῦ Χριστοῦ Ro 16: 16.—**γ.** both together ἐ. ἐν θεῷ πατρὶ καὶ κυρίῳ 'Ιησοῦ Χριστῷ 1 Th 1: 1.

δ. other specif. designations: ἐ. τῶν ἀγίων 1 Cor 14: 33; ἐ. τῶν ἐθνῶν Ro 16: 4; ἡ ἐ. ἡ πρώτη ἡ πνευματική *the first, spiritual church* (conceived of as pre-existent) 2 Cl 14: 1; ἐ. ζῶσα *the living church* the body of Christ vs. 2; ἡ ἀγία ἐ. Hv 1, 1, 6; 1, 3, 4; ἡ καθολικὴ ἐ. ISm 8: 2; ἡ ἀγία καὶ καθολικὴ ἐ. MPol inscr.; ἡ κατὰ τὴν οἰκουμένην καθολικὴ ἐ. 8: 1; 19: 2; ἐν σῶμα τῆς ἐ. ISm 1: 2.—The literature before '32 is given in OLinton, D. Problem der Urkirche in d. neueren Forschung (cf. 138-46) '32 and AMedebielle, Dict. de la Bible, Suppl. II '34, 487-691. Esp. important: EDBurton, Gal (ICC) '21, 417-20; KHoll, D. Kirchenbegriff des Pls usw.: SAB '21, 920-47=Ges. Aufs. II '28, 44ff; FKattenbusch, D. Vorzugsstellung d. Petrus u. d. Charakter d. Urgemeinde zu Jerusalem: KMüller-Festschr. '22, 322-51; KLSchmidt, D. Kirche des Urchristentums: Dssm.-Festschr. '27, 259-319, TW III 502-39. Fr. more recent times: EPeterson, D. Kirche aus Juden u. Heiden '33; KLSchmidt, D. Polis in Kirche u. Welt '39; WBieder, Ekkl. u. Polis im NT u. in d. alten Kirche '41; OMichel, D. Zeugnis des NTs v. d. Gemeinde '41; NADahl, D. Volk Gottes '41; RNFlew, Jesus and His Church², '43; GJohnston, The Doctrine of the Church in the NT '43; WGKümmel, Kirchenbegriff u. Geschichtsbewusstsein in d. Urg. u. b. Jesus '43; LCer-

faux, The Church in the Theol. of St. Paul, tr. GWebb and AWalker, '59; Doris Faulhaber, D. Johev. u. d. Kirche '38; AFridrichsen, Kyrkan i 4. ev.: Sv. Teol. Kv. 16, '40, 227-42; ESchweizer, NT Essays (Manson memorial vol.) '59, 230-45; EWolf, Ecclesia Pressa—eccl. militans: ThLZ 72, '47, 223-32; SHanson, Unity of the Church in the NT '46; HvCampenhausen, Kirchl. Amt u. geistl. Vollmacht in den ersten 3 Jahrh. '53; EKäsemann, Sätze hlg. Rechtes im NT, NTS 1, '55, 248-60; ARGeorge, ET 58, '46/'47, 312-16; in ATR: JBBernardin 21, '39, 153-70; BSEaston 22, '40, 157-68; SCWalke 32, '50, 39-53 (Apost. Fath.); JLMurphy, American Ecclesiastical Review 140, '59, 250-59; 325-32; PSMinear, Images of the Church in the NT, '60; BMMetzger, Theology Today 19, '62, 369-80; ESchweizer, Church Order in the NT, tr. FClarke '61; RSchnackenburg, The Church in the NT, tr. WJO'Hara '65; LCerfaux, JBL 85, '66, 250-51. S. also ἐπίσκοπος 2, end, and Πέτρος; πέτρα 1. M-M. B. 1476f.

ἐκκλησιαστικός, ή, όν (Demosth. +) *pertaining to the church* (Cat. Cod. Astr. VII 216) ὁ ἐ. κανὼν καὶ καθολικός *the generally accepted rule of the church* Epil Mosq 1 (fr. Irenaeus 3, 3, 4).*

ἐκκλίνω 1 aor. ἐξέκλινα (Thu.+; inscr., pap., LXX; Jos., Ant. 13, 14; Anz 319; Test. 12 Patr.) intr. (Bl-D. §308) *turn away* (Polyaenus 3, 10, 12) ἀπό τινος *fr. someone* or *someth.*, fr. evil 1 Pt 3: 11; 1 Cl 22: 4 (both Ps 33: 15). Pers. ἀπ' αὐτῶν (Thu. 5, 73, 3; Sir 7: 2; 22: 13; 1 Macc 6: 47) Ro 16: 17. W. acc. (Polyb. 1, 34, 4; Aelian, V.H. 4, 28) τινά (Appian, Bell. Civ. 4, 129 §542 τὸν ἐχθρόν; Jos., Vi. 304) *shun, avoid someone* IEph 7: 1. Abs. *turn aside* fr. the way (Socrat., Ep. 1, 9; Appian, Bell. Civ. 5, 16 §66; M. Ant. 8, 50, 1 ἔκκλινον=turn aside!) Ro 3: 12 (Ps 13: 3; 52: 4). M-M.*

ἐκκολάπτω pf. pass. ptc. ἐκκεκολαμμένος (inscr.: Sb 7259, 34 [95/4 BC]) (Thu.+ [1, 132, 3]; Dit., Syll.³ 543, 27; 1047, 44; Ex 36: 13) *chisel out* λίθος ὡς ἐκ πέτρας ἐ. *a stone seemingly chiseled out of the rock* Hs 9, 9, 7.*

ἐκκόλαψις, εως, ἡ (Aristot., Hist. An. 561b, 29) *chiseling out* an opening for a door Hs 9, 2, 2.*

ἐκκολυμβάω 1 aor. ἐξεκολύμβησα (Eur., Hel. 1609; Diod. S. 20, 86, 4; 88, 6; Dionys. Hal. 5, 24) *swim away* (Anticleides [III BC]: 140 fgm. 4 Jac.; Diod. S. 14, 73, 4) Ac 27: 42.*

ἐκκομίζω impf. pass. ἐξεκομιζόμην (Hdt. +; inscr., pap., Joseph.) *carry out* of a corpse being taken to a burial-place outside the town (Polyb. 35, 6, 2; Plut., Agis 21, 1; Herodian 2, 1, 2; BGU 326 II, 1 [II AD]; Philo, Mos. 1, 100; Jos., Bell. 5, 567) Lk 7: 12. M-M.*

ἐκκοπή, ῆς, ἡ s. ἐγκοπή.

ἐκκόπτω fut. ἐκκόψω; 1 aor. ἐξέκοψα, imper. ἔκκοψον; 2 aor. pass. ἐξεκόπην; 2 fut. ἐκκοπήσομαι Ro 11: 22 (Hdt.+; inscr., pap., LXX, Joseph., Sib. Or.) *cut off* or *down*.

1. lit., of a tree *cut down* (Hdt. 9, 97; Dit., Syll.³ 966, 34; 41; PFay. 113, 10; Dt 20: 19f; En. 26, 1; Jos., Ant. 10, 52) Mt 3: 10; 7: 19; Lk 3: 9 (Harpocration s.v. ὀξυθυμία: ἐκκόπτοντες . . . καίουσι useless trees); 13: 7, 9. Of a branch *cut off* Ro 11: 24, cf. vs. 22; of a hand Mt 5: 30; 18: 8 (cf. Aeschines 1, 172 τοὺς ὀφθαλμούς; Maximus Tyr. 32, 10g; Syntipas p. 107, 2 γλῶτταν; Jos., Ant. 10, 140 τ. ὀφθαλμούς). Of a door, *hew out* of rock Hs 9, 2, 2 (cf. Sib. Or. 5, 218 ἐ. πέτρην).

2. fig., of pers.: *exterminate* (Hdt. 4, 110; Lucian,

Jupp. Trag. 21; Jos., Vi. 193) ἐκ ριζῶν *root and branch* B 12: 9. Of things (Epict. 2, 22, 34; Vett. Val. 268, 6; Herm. Wr. 1, 22; Dit., Or. 669, 64; Sb 4284, 8 τὰ βίαια καὶ ἄνομα; Job 19: 10; 4 Macc 3: 2, 3, 4) τὴν ἀθέμιτον ὀργήν *root out the lawless anger* 1 Cl 63: 2. τὴν ἀφορμὴν *remove the occasion* 2 Cor 11: 12 (cf. ἀφορμή).—GStählin, TW III 857-60. M-M. p. xxxii.*

ἐκκρεμάννυμι impf. mid. ἐξεκρεμάμην (colloq. form ἐξεκρεμόμην, 3 pers. ἐξεκρέμετο Bl-D. §93 w. app.; Mlt.-H. 206).
   1. act. (Jos., Bell. 7, 429) *hang out* τὶ ἔκ τινος *someth. fr. someth.* (Aristoph., Eq. 1363) lit. 1 Cl 12: 7.
   2. mid. (Eur., Thu.+; Gen 44: 30) *hang on* (Jos., Bell. 5, 433) fig. (Philo, Abr. 170) ὁ λαὸς ἐξεκρέματο αὐτοῦ ἀκούων *the people hung upon his words* Lk 19: 48 (cf. Eunap., Vi. Soph. p. 29 τῆς φωνῆς ἐξεκρέμαντο κ. τῶν λόγων).*

ἐκλαλέω 1 aor. ἐξελάλησα (Eur.; Demosth.; Jdth 11: 9; Philo, Mos. 1, 283, Vi. Cont. 26; Jos., Ant. 16, 375) *tell* τινί *someone* (Ps.-Apollod., Epit. 2, 1; Philo, Sacr. Abel. 60) w. ὅτι foll. Ac 23: 22.*

ἐκλάμπω fut. ἐκλάμψω; 1 aor. ἐξέλαμψα (Aeschyl., Hdt.+; Herm. Wr. 10: 4b; PLond. 130, 95; LXX; Philo) *shine (out)* of the sun (X., Hell. 1, 1, 16; Diod. S. 3, 48, 2; Lucian, Ver. Hist. 1, 6; Sir 50: 7; Jos., Ant. 9, 225) μικρὸν ἐξέλαμψεν Hv 4, 1, 6. Of the sun also Mt 13: 43, where its radiance is compared w. that of the righteous (cf. Da 12: 3 Theod.; EpJer 66 v.l.; of a face of a beautiful woman: Charito 5, 3, 9). Of a flame *blaze up* (Diod. S. 1, 57, 7 τοῦ πυρὸς ἐκλάμψαντος; Appian, Syr. 56 §284; Jos., Ant. 4, 55) MPol 15: 1. M-M.*

ἐκλανθάνομαι pf. ἐκλέλησμαι (Hom.+; Philo, Leg. All. 3, 92) *forget (altogether)* τινός (Polyb. 5, 48, 6; POxy. 1203, 8 [I AD]; Sym. Ps 12: 2; Philo, De Jos. 99; Jos., Ant. 4, 53; 7, 318) τῆς παρακλήσεως Hb 12: 5. M-M.*

ἐκλέγομαι impf. ἐξελεγόμην; 1 aor. ἐξελεξάμην; pf. pass. ἐκλέλεγμαι, ptc. ἐκλελεγμένος Lk 9: 35 (Hdt.+; inscr., pap., LXX, Ep. Arist., Joseph., Test. 12 Patr.; the act. does not occur in our lit.) *choose, select* (for oneself) τινά (τὶ) *someone* (*someth.*).
   1. w. indication of that from which the selection is made τινὰ ἔκ τινος (Isocr. 9, 58; 2 Km 24: 12; 2 Ch 33: 7; Sir 45: 4) *choose someone fr. among a number* πάντων 1 Cl 59: 3; of two Ac 1: 24. ὑμᾶς ἐκ τοῦ κόσμου J 15: 19. ἐξ αὐτῶν Hs 9, 9, 3. ἐκλεξαμένους ἄνδρας ἐξ αὐτῶν πέμψαι *to choose men fr. among them and to send them* Ac 15: 22, 25. For this τινὰ ἀπό τινος (Dt 14: 2; Sir 45: 16): ἀπ᾽ αὐτῶν δώδεκα *twelve of them* Lk 6: 13.
   2. w. simple acc. *choose someone* (*someth.*) *for oneself* —a. w. acc. of the pers. (Jo 2: 16; Bar 3: 27; 1 Macc 10: 32; Jos., Ant. 7, 372 God chooses Solomon): Mk 13: 20; J 13: 18; 15: 16; GEb 2 (ll. 18, 21). Jesus 1 Cl 64. The twelve J 6: 70; PK 3 p. 15, 17. The apostles Ac 1: 2; B 5: 9. Stephen Ac 6: 5. A faithful slave Hs 5, 2, 2. Of God: the fathers (as his own) Ac 13: 17 (oft. LXX, cf. Dt 4: 37; 10: 15).
   b. w. acc. of the thing (X., Mem. 1, 6, 14; Pla., Leg. 2 p. 670D, Tim. p. 24c; Demosth. 18, 261 et al.; PMagd. 29, 4 [III BC] τ. βέλτιστον τόπον; Is 40: 20; 1 Macc 7: 37; 2 Ch 35: 19d; Jos., Bell. 2, 149 τόπους): B 21: 1; the good part Lk 10: 42; places of honor 14: 7; a good place Hv 3, 1, 3; a fast B 3: 1, 3 (Is 58: 5f).
   3. w. indication of the purpose for which the choice is made:—a. εἴς τι *for someth.* (Ps 32: 12) eternal life Hv 4, 3, 5. εἰς τὸ ἱερατεύειν *to be priest* 1 Cl 43: 4.

   b. w. ἵνα foll. 1 Cor 1: 27f.—c. w. inf. foll. (1 Ch 15: 2; 28: 5; 1 Esdr 5: 1) ἐξελέξατο ἡμᾶς εἶναι ἡμᾶς ἁγίους *he has chosen us that we might be holy* Eph 1: 4. Without obj. ἐν ὑμῖν ἐξελέξατο ὁ θεὸς διὰ τοῦ στόματός μου ἀκοῦσαι *in your presence God chose that (they) were to hear through my mouth* Ac 15: 7. W. ellipsis of the inf. ἐξελέξατο τοὺς πτωχοὺς (sc. εἶναι) πλουσίους *he chose the poor that they might be rich* Js 2: 5.
   4. abs.: ἐκλελεγμένος *chosen* of Jesus, as Son of God Lk 9: 35 (ἀγαπητός is found in the parallels Mt 17: 5; Mk 9: 7, and in Lk as v.l.; it=ἐκλελεγμένος also Vett. Val. 17, 2). Of the Christians 1 Cl 50: 7; cf. Pol 1: 1. Of the church IEph inscr.
   5. ἐξ ἀκανθῶν ἐκλέγονται σῦκα Lk 6: 44 D; s. συλλέγω.—HHRowley, The Biblical Doctrine of Election, '50; GQuell and GSchrenk, TW IV 147-97 ἐκλέγεσθαι, ἐκλογή, ἐκλεκτός. M-M.*

ἐκλείπω fut. ἐκλείψω; 2 aor. ἐξέλιπον. In our lit. only intr. (so trag., Thu., et al.; inscr., pap., LXX; En. 100, 5; Joseph.; Test. 12 Patr.) *fail, die out* (Plut., Lycurgus 31, 8 of a race) of faith Lk 22: 32; of years *come to an end* Hb 1: 12 (Ps 101: 28); of money *give out* (X., Hell. 1, 5, 3; PSI 495, 16[258 BC] ἡμῖν τὸ ἐφόδιον ἐγλέλοιπεν =our travel-money is all gone; 1 Macc 3: 29) Lk 16: 9 (v.l. ὅταν ἐκλίπητε *when you die*; for this mng. of ἐκλ. cf. Pla., Leg. 6 p. 759E; 9 p. 856E; X., Cyr. 8, 7, 26; Arrian, Anab. 6, 10, 2; POxy. 497, 15 [II AD]; Gen 49: 33; Ps 17: 38; Tob 14: 11; Wsd 5: 13; Jos., Bell. 4, 68, Ant. 2, 184; Test. Reub. 1: 4). Of one's appearance εἶδος ἐκλεῖπον παρὰ τὸ εἶδος τ. ἀνθρώπων *an appearance inferior to that of men* 1 Cl 16: 3 (cf. Is 53: 3). Of the sun *grow dark*, perh. *be eclipsed* (Thu. 2, 28; 7, 50, 4; X., Hell. 1, 6, 1; Marm. Par. [III BC]: 239B, 16 Jac.; Dio Chrys. 57[74], 28; Plut., Pelop. 31, 3; Sir 17: 31; Philo, Mos. 2, 271) Lk 23: 45 (JFSawyer, JTS 23, '72, 124-8). M-M.*

ἐκλεκτός, ή, όν (since Pla., Leg. 12 p. 946D; inscr., pap., LXX, En., Philo; Jos., Ant. 7, 59; Test. 12 Patr.; Sib. Or.).
   1. *chosen, select*—a. gener. of angels 1 Ti 5: 21 (after En. 39, 1). Of the Messiah ὁ ἐ. τοῦ θεοῦ (cf. En. 39, 6f; 40, 5; 45, 3-5; 49, 2-4 al.) Lk 23: 35 (cf. 9: 35); J 1: 34 v.l. (AvHarnack, SAB '15, 552-6=Studien I '31, 127-32). Of David 1 Cl 52: 2 (Ps 88: 20; cf. Sir 47: 22).
   b. esp. of those whom God has chosen fr. the generality of mankind and drawn to himself Mt 20: 16 v.l.; 22: 14 (KStendahl, The Called and the Chosen: The Root of the Vine, ed. AFridrichsen '53, 63-80). Hence of the Christians in particular (as in the OT of the Israelites 1 Ch 16: 13; Ps 88: 4; 104: 6, 43; Is 65: 9, 15, 23 al.—PAltmann, Erwählungstheol. u. Universalismus im AT, Beih. 92, ZAW, '64) *chosen* 24: 22, 24, 31; Mk 13: 20, 22, 27; 1 Pt 1: 1; 2 Ti 2: 10; 1 Cl 6: 1; 58: 2; Hv 2, 4, 2. ἐ. τοῦ θεοῦ (cf. En. 1, 8) Lk 18: 7 (cf. IQS 8, 6; IQH 2, 13); Ro 8: 33 (cf. the Qumran passages just cited); Col 3: 12; Tit 1: 1; 1 Cl 1: 1; 2: 4; 46: 3f, 8; 49: 5; 59: 2; 2 Cl 14: 5; Hv 1, 3, 4; 2, 1, 3; 2, 2, 5 al. W. κλητοί and πιστοί (Sib. Or. 3, 69 w. πιστοί) Rv 17: 14. γένος ἐκλεκτόν 1 Pt 2: 9 (Is 43: 20). Of a church 2 J 1, 13 (w. personification of the church); ITr inscr. Opp. ἄπιστοι MPol 16: 1; ἄγιοι ἐ. 22: 1.
   2. Since the best is usually chosen, *choice, excellent* (PReinach 43, 9; BGU 603, 18; 38; Ps 17: 27; Sir 24: 15; Bar 3: 30; Wsd 3: 14) ἀνὴρ ἐ. (Ep. Arist. 13; Sib. Or. 3, 521) IPhld 11: 1. Perh. Ro 16: 13 ὁ ἐ. ἐν κυρίῳ *the outstanding Christian*. Of a stone *choice* (Strabo 1, 3, 18 after Ibycus [fgm. 21 Diehl] λίθος, ὃν καλεῖ ἐκλεκτόν; En. 8, 1) 1 Pt 2: 4, 6 (Is 28: 16). M-M.**

ἐκλελεγμένος s. ἐκλέγομαι.

ἐκλέλησμαι s. ἐκλανθάνομαι.

ἐκλήθην s. καλέω.

ἐκλιπαρέω 1 aor. ἐξελιπάρησα (Strabo et al.; Apollon. Paradox. 3; Philostrat., Vi. Apoll. 4, 1 p. 125, 17; Philo, In Flacc. 31; Jos., Ant. 5, 260) *beg, entreat* πολλά *earnestly* (Diog. L. 4, 7) MPol 4.*

ἐκλογή, ῆς, ἡ—1. act. *selection, election* as t.t., *choosing* (Pla., Rep. 3 p. 414A; PTebt. 5, 166 [118 BC]; POxy. 496, 15; BGU 1158, 13; PsSol 9: 4; Ep. Arist. 33; Jos., Bell. 2, 165, Ant. 8, 24) σκεῦος ἐκλογῆς (Hebraistic=σ. ἐκλεκτόν) *a chosen instrument* Ac 9: 15. Esp. of God's selection of Christians 2 Pt 1: 10; 1 Th 1: 4. κατ' ἐκλογήν (Polyb. 6, 10, 9; Alciphr. 2, 36, 1. The expression is capable of various interpretations, either='by choice' as Apollon. Rhod. 2, 16b or adjectivally, as Diod. S. 13, 72, 4 ὁπλῖται κατ' ἐκλογήν=picked, select hoplites): κατ' ἐκλογὴν χάριτος acc. to selection by grace=selected by grace Ro 11: 5. ἡ κατ' ἐ. πρόθεσις τ. θεοῦ *the purpose of God which operates by selection* 9: 11. κατὰ τὴν ἐ. ἀγαπητοί as far as (*their*) *selection* or *election* (*by God*) *is concerned, beloved* 11: 28. μαρτύριον ἐκλογῆς Dg 4: 4. ἐκλογὰς ποιεῖν ἀπό τινων *make a selection from among some people* MPol 20: 1 (cf. Antig. Car. 26 ποιεῖσθαι τ. ἐκλογήν ἔκ τινος=make a selection from).

2. pass. *that which is chosen* or *selected* (Polyb. 1, 47, 9 ἡ ἐ. τῶν ἀνδρῶν; Athen. 14 p. 663c; Phryn. 1; Philo, Spec. Leg. 4, 157) of pers. *those selected* (ἐκλογή collect.) Ro 11: 7; 1 Cl 29: 1.—AvHarnack, TU 42, 4, '18 app.: Z. Terminologie der Wiedergeburt usw. M-M.*

ἐκλύω 1 aor. pass. ἐξελύθην; 1 fut. ἐκλυθήσομαι (Hom. +; pap., LXX). In our lit. only pass. *become weary* or *slack, give out* (so Hippocr., X.+; Epict. 2, 19, 20; Phlegon: 257 fgm. 36, 1 and 2 Jac.; Vett. Val. 18, 23; 126, 28; LXX; Philo, Virt. 88; Jos., Ant. 5, 134; 13, 233): fr. hunger (Diod. S. 19, 49, 2; 2 Km 16: 2; 17: 29; La 2: 19; 1 Macc 3: 17) Mt 15: 32; Mk 8: 3. Of the waist *be ungirded* D 16: 1. θερίσομεν μὴ ἐκλυόμενοι *we will reap if we do not give out* Gal 6: 9; *lose courage* (Dt 20: 3; 1 Macc 9: 8) μηδὲ ἐκλύου *do not lose heart* Hb 12: 5 (Pr 3: 11); fully ἐ. ταῖς ψυχαῖς (Polyb. 20, 4, 7; 29, 17, 4; cf. Diod. S. 20, 1, 4) vs. 3. M-M.*

ἐκμάσσω impf. ἐξέμασσον; 1 aor. ἐξέμαξα (trag., PreSocr.+; Epict. 1, 19, 49; inscr.; Sir 12: 11; EpJer 11, 23) *wipe* τί τινι *someth.* w. *someth.* (Plut., Artax. 19, 5; Artem. 5, 4) feet with one's hair Lk 7: 38, 44; J 11: 2; 12: 3; of feet, with a towel *dry* 13: 5. M-M.*

ἐκμυκτηρίζω impf. ἐξεμυκτήριζον (LXX; Test. Jos. 2: 3) *ridicule, sneer,* lit. 'turn up the nose' τινά (*at*) *someone* (Ps 2: 4; 34: 16) Lk 16: 14; 1 Cl 16: 16 (Ps 21: 8). Abs. Lk 23: 35.*

ἐκνεύω 1 aor. ἐξένευσα (Eur., X.+) *turn* (4 Km 2: 24; 23: 16; 3 Macc 3: 22), *turn aside, withdraw* (Plut., Mor. 577B; Philo, Mos. 2, 251; Jos., Ant. 7, 83; 9, 120; Justin, Dial. 9, 3=ὑποχωρέω) J 5: 13 (cf. BGU 1189, 7 [I BC] ἐκνεύειν τὴν ἐμφανείαν=make oneself invisible). M-M.*

ἐκνήφω 1 aor. ἐξένηψα *become sober* (Lynceus in Athen. 4, 5 p. 130B; LXX) fig. *come to one's senses* (Plut., Demosth. 20, 3; Aretaeus p. 41, 10; Sib. Or. fgm. 3, 41) ἐκνήψατε δικαίως 1 Cor 15: 34. M-M.*

ἐκούσιος, ία, ιον (Soph., Thu.+; inscr., pap., LXX, Philo) *voluntary, as a volunteer* κατὰ ἐκούσιον (opp. κατὰ ἀνάγκην) *of one's own free will* Phlm 14 (Num 15: 3 καθ' ἑκούσιον; Thu. 8, 27, 3 καθ' ἑκουσίαν [sc. γνώμην]; as opposed to legal compulsion, cf. Plut., Mor. 446E). Of apostates MPol 4. M-M.*

ἑκουσίως adv. (Eur., Thu.+; inscr., pap., LXX, Philo; Test. Dan 4: 6; Sib. Or. 11, 78) *willingly* ποιμαίνειν (opp. ἀναγκαστῶς) 1 Pt 5: 2; *without compulsion,* i.e. *deliberately, intentionally* ἁμαρτάνειν (Ps.-Demetr., Form. Ep. p. 5, 17) Hb 10: 26. M-M.*

ἔκπαλαι adv. (Plut., Themist. 30, 1, Aristid. 17, 2; Arrian, Exp. Alex. 1, 9, 8 Roos; Dit., Or. 584, 5 [II AD]; POxy. 938, 3; Philo, Agr. 152; Jos., Bell. 7, 159, Ant. 16, 244; Lobeck, Phryn. p. 45ff) *for a long time, long ago* 2 Pt 2: 3; 3: 5. M-M.*

ἐκπειράζω fut. ἐκπειράσω; 1 aor. ἐξεπείρασα (LXX; as quot. fr. Dt 8: 2 in Philo, Congr. Erud. Grat. 170) *put to the test, try, tempt* τινά *someone* the Lord God Mt 4: 7; Lk 4: 12 (both Dt 6: 16); 1 Cor 10: 9. Jesus Lk 10: 25; Hv 5: 3. Pass. ἐκπειρασθεὶς ὑπό τ. διαβόλου *tempted by the devil* Hm 4, 3, 6; cf. 12, 5, 4.*

ἐκπέμπω 1 aor. ἐξέπεμψα; 1 aor. pass. ἐξεπέμφθην, ptc. ἐκπεμφθείς (Hom.+; inscr., pap., LXX; Philo, Op. M. 58) *send out* (Jos., Ant. 2, 11) spies 1 Cl 12: 2. ἐκπεμφθέντες ὑπὸ τοῦ ἁγίου πνεύματος *sent out by the Holy Spirit* Ac 13: 4. Of Christ ἀπό τ. θεοῦ ἐκπεμφθήναι 1 Cl 42: 1; *send away* (Jos., Ant. 1, 216, Vi. 332 εἰς τὰ Ἱερ.) εἰς Βέροιαν Ac 17: 10. M-M.*

ἐκπέπτωκα s. ἐκπίπτω.

ἐκπερισσῶς adv. *excessively* ἐ. λαλεῖν *say with great emphasis* Mk 14: 31 (PJoüon, Rech de Sc rel 29, '39, 240f).*

ἐκπεσεῖν s. ἐκπίπτω.

ἐκπετάννυμι 1 aor. ἐξεπέτασα; plpf. ἐκπεπετάκειν (Eur.+; Polyb., Plut., Lucian; Epigr. Gr. 779, 2; LXX; En. 14, 8; Jos., Ant. 3, 128.—Anz 286) *spread* or *hold out* τὰς χεῖρας *the hands* in an imploring gesture Ro 10: 21; B 12: 4 (both Is 65: 2); Hs 9, 3, 2. M-M.*

ἐκπέτασις, εως, ἡ (Plut., Mor. 564B) *spreading out, opening* σημεῖον ἐκπετάσεως ἐν οὐρανῷ *a sign,* (consisting of) *an opening in the heaven* D 16: 6. (EStommel, Röm. Quartalschrift 48, '53, 21–42).*

ἐκπηδάω 1 aor. ἐξεπήδησα (Soph., Hdt.+; pap., LXX) —1. *rush* (lit. 'leap') *out* (so Menand., Per. 277; UPZ 170B, 28 [127/6 BC]) εἰς τὸν ὄχλον *into the crowd* Ac 14: 14 (cf. Jdth 14: 17 ἐξεπήδησεν εἰς τ. λαόν; Jos., Ant. 6, 191).

2. *start up, get up quickly* (X., Cyr. 1, 4, 8; Appian, Bell Civ. 2, 36 §142; Polyaenus 8, 2; Wilcken, Chrest. 1 II, 13 [c. 246 BC]; Jos., Ant. 8, 273) Ac 10: 25 D. M-M.*

ἐκπίπτω 1 aor. ἐξέπεσα (Bl-D. §81, 3 w. app.; Mlt.-H. 208); 2 aor. ἐξέπεσον; pf. ἐκπέπτωκα (Hom.+; inscr., pap., LXX, Ep. Arist., Philo, Joseph.) *fall off* or *from.*

1. lit., of withered flowers that fall to the ground (but ἐ. also means 'fall'=perish: X., Hell. 1, 1, 32; Lucian, De Merc. Cond. 42, end) Js 1: 11; 1 Pt 1: 24 (both Is 40: 7). ἔκ τινος *from something* (Is 6: 13 v.l.; 14: 12) chains from the hands Ac 12: 7. εἴασαν αὐτὴν ἐκπεσεῖν *they let it* (the boat) *fall* 27: 32, but s. 2 below.

2. nautical t.t. *drift off course, run aground* εἴς τι *on someth.* (Eur., Hel. 409 εἰς γῆν; Thu. 2, 92, 3; Diod. S. 2, 60, 1) on the Syrtis 27: 17; on an island vs. 26. κατὰ

τραχεῖς τόπους *the rocks* vs. 29. Abs. perh. vs. 32, s. 1 above.

3. fig.—a. *lose* (Hdt. 3, 14; Thu. 8, 81, 2) τινός someth. (Plut., Tib. Gracch. 21, 7; Dit., Or. 521, 2; PTebt. 50, 14; Philo, Leg. All. 3, 183; Jos., Ant. 7, 203 βασιλείας) grace, favor Gal 5: 4; one's own stability 2 Pt 3: 17.

b. *fail, weaken* (Pla., Ep. 2 p. 314β; Diod. S. 14, 109, 5; Plut., Mor. p. 9β; Sir 34: 7) of God's word Ro 9: 6 (on the probability of commercial metaphor, FWDanker, FW Gingrich-Festschr., '72, 107). Of love 1 Cor 13: 8 v.l. (acc. to AHarnack, SAB '11, p. 148, 1, original). M-M.*

ἐκπλέκω 1 aor. ἐξέπλεξα (BGU 665, 5 [I AD]; PTebt. 315, 21; 29 [II AD]; POxy. 1490, 6) *disentangle (oneself)* ὥστε ἀπὸ τ. ἀκανθῶν . . . μὴ δύνασθαι ἐκπλέξαι τὰ πρόβατα so that the sheep could not disentangle themselves fr. the thorn-bushes Hs 6, 2, 6 (cf. Artem. 4, 57 ἄκανθαι . . . τὰς ἐμπλοκάς).*

ἐκπλέω 1 aor. ἐξέπλευσα (Soph., Hdt.+; Dit., Syll.³ 454, 13 [III BC], Or. 69, 5; PSI 444, 1 [III BC]; POxy. 1271, 3; Jos., Ant. 18, 247 al.) *sail away* εἴς τι to a place (X., Hell. 4, 8, 32; Diod. S. 14, 99, 4; Jos., Bell. 1, 481) Ac 15: 39; 18: 18. ἀπό τινος fr. a place 20: 6. M-M.*

ἔκπληκτος, ον act. *shocking, frightful* (so Hero I 338, 5; 342, 4; Lucian, Herm. 18; Orph. Hymn. 39, 10) βουλή (w. πονηρά) Hv 1, 2, 4.*

ἐκπληρόω pf. ἐκπεπλήρωκα (trag., Hdt.+; inscr., pap., LXX, Philo; Jos., Ant. 19, 193) *fulfill* of promises Ac 13: 33 (cf. Hdt. 8, 144; Polyb. 1, 67, 1 τ. ἐλπίδας καὶ τ. ἐπαγγελίας; Ael. Aristid. 51, 46 K.=27 p. 545 D.: ἐνύπνιον; PTebt. 10, 7; 48, 12; 3 Macc 1: 2, 22); *bring to completion* (Hdt. 8, 82; PRyl. 66, 8; 2 Macc 8: 10) ἐ. τὰς ἡμέρας τῶν ἁμαρτιῶν fill up the days of the sins, i.e., in this pass. *atone fully* for them Hv 3, 7, 6 (with ἐ. τὰς ἡμέρας cf. Diod. S. 2, 57, 5 τὸν χρόνον ἐκπληρώσαντες). M-M.*

ἐκπλήρωσις, εως, ἡ (Dionys. Hal. 6, 86; Epict. 4, 1, 175; BGU 1825, 23 [I BC]; 2 Macc 6: 14; Philo, Op. M. 146, Leg. All. 3, 34; 145) *completion* διαγγέλλων τὴν ἐ. τῶν ἡμερῶν τοῦ ἁγνισμοῦ *giving notice that the days of purification would be completed* Ac 21: 26 (cf. Strabo 17, 1, 46 ἐκπλ. τ. ἐνιαυτοῦ).*

ἐκπλήσσω Att. ἐκπλήττω MPol 7: 2; 1 aor. ἐξέπληξα; in NT (and LXX) only in pass.—impf. ἐξεπλησσόμην; 2 aor. ἐξεπλάγην (Hom.+; LXX).
1. act. *amaze, astound, overwhelm* (lit. strike out of one's senses) τινά someone (Appian, Mithrid. 116 §566; Ammonius Hermiae in Aristotle, Lib. De Interpr. p. 66, 6 Busse τὸν ἀκροατήν; Jos., Bell. 7, 419) B 1: 3.
2. pass. *be amazed, overwhelmed* w. fright (Dio Chrys. 80[30], 12) Mt 19: 25; Mk 10: 26; or *wonder* (Dio Chrys. 71[21], 14; Dit., Syll.³ 1168, 46 [IV BC]; Jos., Ant. 8, 168; 17, 110; 142) Mt 13: 54; Mk 6: 2; 7: 37; Lk 2: 48 (perh. joy); MPol 7: 2. W. the reason given: ἐπί τινι at someth. or someone (X., Cyr. 1, 4, 27 ἐπὶ τῷ κάλλει; Dio Chrys. 29[46], 1; Aelian, V. H. 12, 41) Mt 7: 28; 22: 33; Mk 1: 22; 11: 18; Lk 4: 32; 9: 43; Ac 13: 12; B 7: 10; 16: 10. M-M.*

ἐκπνέω 1 aor. ἐξέπνευσα *breathe out* (the life or the soul), *expire,* euphem. for *die* Mk 15: 37, 39; Lk 23: 46 (without obj. since Soph., Aj. 1026; Plut., Mor. 597F; M. Ant. 4, 33, 2; Jos., Ant. 12, 357. W. βίον or ψυχήν since Aeschyl.).*

ἐκπορεύομαι impf. ἐξεπορευόμην; fut. ἐκπορεύσομαι (mid. since X.; inscr., pap., LXX, En.) *go out.*

1. lit.—a. abs. (BGU 1078, 4 [39 AD]) *go away* Ac 3: 11 D. ὄχλοι ἐκπορευόμενοι *crowds* or *people that came out* Lk 3: 7; *go out* Ac 25: 4. εἰσπορεύεσθαι καὶ ἐ. *go in and out* 9: 28 (cf. Dt 31: 2; Tob 5: 18; 1 Macc 3: 45). Esp. of demons *come out* Mt 17: 21; Ac 19: 12.
b. w. indication of the place fr. which: ἐκ τινος (Polyb. 6, 58, 4; Mi 1: 3; Ezk 47: 12 al.) *out of the sanctuary* Mk 13: 1. ἐκ γῆς Αἰγύπτου B 2: 7 (cf. Dt 25: 17). Of a bride *come out of the bridal chamber* Hv 4, 2, 1. ἔξω τῆς πόλεως *outside the city* Mk 11: 19. ἀπό τινος (Jer 5: 6; Sir 42: 13) from Jericho Mt 20: 29; Mk 10: 46. ἐκεῖθεν 6: 11 (cf. 2 Km 16: 5). παρά τινος *proceed from someone* (Ezk 33: 30) of the Spirit ὁ παρὰ τοῦ πατρὸς ἐκπορεύεται J 15: 26.
c. w. the goal indicated: εἴς τι (X., An. 5, 6, 33; Jer 6: 25; Ezk 44: 19) εἰς ὁδὸν *set out on a journey* Mk 10: 17. εἰς ἀφεδρῶνα 7: 19 (s. ἀφεδρών). ἐ. εἰς ἀνάστασιν ζωῆς *come out* (of the graves) *to a resurrection that brings life* J 5: 29. ἐπί τινα *to someone* (cf. Zech 6: 6, 8) Rv 16: 14. πρός τινα *to someone* (Judg 9: 33; Is 36: 16) Mt 3: 5; Mk 1: 5.
2. fig. *come* or *go out, proceed* of words and thoughts τὸ ἐκπορευόμενον ἐκ τοῦ στόματος *what comes out of the mouth* (cf. Pr 3: 16a) Mt 15: 11, cf. vs. 18; Lk 4: 22; Eph 4: 29. For this τὰ ἐκ τοῦ ἀνθρώπου ἐκπορευόμενα *what comes out of a man* Mk 7: 15, cf. vs. 20. ἔσωθεν ἐκ τ. καρδίας vs. 21, cf. vs. 23. ῥῆμα ἐκπορευόμενον διὰ στόματος θεοῦ (διὰ AI 1) Mt 4: 4 (Dt 8: 3). Of truth ἐ. ἐκ τοῦ στόματος Hm 3: 1. Of fire, lightning, etc. (Job 41: 12): lightning (Ezk 1: 13) Rv 4: 5; fire 9: 17f; 11: 5; fiery locusts Hv 4, 1, 6. Of streams of water *flow out* Ezk 47: 1, 8, 12) ἐκ τ. θρόνου τ. θεοῦ Rv 22: 1. Of a sword *project* ἐκ τ. στόματος 1: 16; 19: 15; ἐ. ἦχος περὶ αὐτοῦ εἰς πάντα τόπον *reports of him spread into every place* Lk 4: 37. M-M.*

ἐκπορνεύω 1 aor. ἐξεπόρνευσα (Poll. 6, 30; Test. Dan 5: 5; LXX) *indulge in immorality* Jd 7.*

ἐκπρεπής, ές (Hom.+; LXX) *remarkable, outstanding* Hv 1, 1, 3. Superlative (Aesop, Fab. 349 P.=Babr. 114 Cr.) κάλλει ἐκπρεπεστάτη *remarkable for beauty* (a woman; cf. Parthenius 29: 1; Philo, Congr. Erud. Gr. 124; Jos., Ant 3, 78) 3, 10, 5.*

ἐκπτύω 1 aor. ἐξέπτυσα (Hom.+; Plut., Mor. p. 328c; Epict. 3, 12, 17) lit. *spit (out)* as a sign of disdain (s. ἐξουθενέω 2) or to ward off evil spirits (s. βασκαίνω 1 and Theocr. 6, 39; 20, 11; Lucian, Navig. 15, Pro Merc. Cond. 6; Theophr., Char. 16, 14 μαινόμενον ἰδὼν ἢ ἐπίληπτον φρίξας εἰς κόλπον πτύσαι), hence *disdain* Gal 4: 14 (ἐ. is omitted by 𝔓⁴⁶).—Ltzm. ad loc.; SSeligmann, D. böse Blick I '10, 293–8. S. also πτύσμα. M-M.*

ἐκπυρόω 1 fut. pass. ἐκπυρωθήσομαι (Eur.+; Cornutus 17 p. 27, 10; 2 Macc 7: 3f) *set on fire, destroy by fire* of the end of the world (Heraclitus, fgm. 31 γῆ κ. οὐρανὸς πάλιν ἐκπυροῦται; Vorsokr. I 141, 21; 146, 18; Stoics since Zeno: Stoic. I p. 27, 15; 114, 36; II 182, 16; Plut., Mor. 1067A; MPohlenz, Stoa '49 I p. 486 index: ἐκπύρωσις) 2 Pt 3: 10 as conjectured by FOlivier, RThPh '20, 237ff; Religio 11, '35, 481–9.*

ἐκριζόω 1 aor. ἐξερίζωσα, pass. ἐξεριζώθην; 1 fut. ἐκριζωθήσεται (Aesop 179 Halm; Babrius 36, 8; Geopon. 3, 5, 8; Dit., Syll.³ 889, 9f; 1239, 16f; Maspéro 87, 9; LXX; Test. Ash. 1: 7; 4: 2; Sib. Or., fgm. 3, 21) *uproot, pull out by the roots.*
1. lit. (Wsd 4: 4; Test. of Solomon D 6, 1 McCown '22) grain w. weeds Mt 13: 29.—15: 13. Of a tree (Dit., Syll.³

244

889, 9; Da 4: 14, 26) ἐκριζώθητι *be uprooted* Lk 17: 6. δένδρα ἐκριζωθέντα *uprooted trees* Jd 12. **2.** fig. *utterly destroy* (Dit., Syll.³ 1239, 16; Sir 3: 9; Zeph 2: 4 al.) a people 1 Cl 6: 4. Of doubt: πολλοὺς ἐκριζοῖ ἀπὸ τῆς πίστεως *it uproots many fr. the faith* Hm 9: 9. M-M.*

ἐκρίπτω 2 aor. pass. ἐξερίφην (trag.+; PLond. 106, 13; LXX) *hurl* or *drive away*—**1.** lit. of chaff blown by the wind B 11: 7 (Ps 1: 4).—**2.** fig. ἐκριφῆναι ἐκ τῆς ἐλπίδος *be driven out fr. the hope* 1 Cl 57: 2 (cf. Pr 5: 23).*

ἔκρυσις, εως, ἡ (Hippocr., Aristot., inscr.) *outflow, efflux* Papias 3.*

ἔκστασις, εως, ἡ (Hippocr.+; inscr., pap., LXX, Philo; Jos., Ant. 17, 247; Test. 12 Patr.). **1.** *distraction, confusion, astonishment, terror,* lit. being beside oneself (Menand., fgm. 149 Kock πάντα δὲ τὰ μηδὲ προσδοκῶμεν' ἔκστασιν φέρει; Περὶ ὕψους 1, 4; Dit., Syll.³ 1240, 14; 1 Km 11: 7; 2 Ch 14: 13; Ps 30: 23) ἐξέστησαν μεγάλῃ ἐκστάσει *they were quite beside themselves w. amazement* Mk 5: 42 (cf. Gen 27: 33; Ezk 26: 16; 27: 35 al.). ἐ. ἔλαβεν ἅπαντας Lk 5: 26. W. τρόμος Mk 16: 8. W. θάμβος Ac 3: 10. **2.** *trance, ecstasy* a state of being brought about by God, in which consciousness is wholly or partially suspended (Galen XIX 462 K. ἐ. ἐστιν ὀλιγοχρόνιος μανία; Philo, Rer. Div. Her. 257; 258; 264; 265 [after Gen 2: 21; 15: 12], Vi. Cont. 40; Plotinus 6, 9, 11; PGM 4, 737) γενέσθαι ἐν ἐκστάσει *fall into a trance* Ac 22: 17; ἐγένετο ἐπ' αὐτὸν ἐ. *a trance came over him* 10: 10. For this t.r. has ἐπέπεσεν ἐπ' αὐ. ἐ. Cf. 11: 5.—ERohde, Psyche³ II 18ff; WRInge, Ecstasy: Enc. of Rel. and Eth. V 157-9; AOepke, TW II 447-57 (lit.). M-M. B. 1094.*

ἐκστρέφω pf. pass. ἐξέστραμμαι (Hom.+; LXX) *turn aside, pervert* τινά someone (Aristoph., Nub. 554 ἐκστρέψας τοὺς ἱππέας Hs 8, 6, 5. Pass. ἐξέστραπται ὁ τοιοῦτος *such a man is perverted* Tit 3: 11 (cf. Dt 32: 20).*

ἐκσφενδονάω 1 aor. ἐξεσφενδόνησα (Suidas) *hurl away* (lit. w. a sling) fig. τινὰ ἀπό τινος *someone fr. someth.* B 2: 10.*

ἐκσῴζω 1 aor. ἐξέσωσα (Aeschyl., Hdt.+) *bring safely* ἐκσῶσαι, v.l. for ἐξῶσαι, because of similarity of sound (s. ἐξωθέω) Ac 27: 39.*

ἐκταράσσω (Isocr.+; pap., LXX) *agitate, throw into confusion* τινά someone Ac 15: 24 D; τὴν πόλιν 16: 20 (cf. Plut., Coriol. 19, 2. Oft. Cass. Dio; PGenève 1, 12; Jos., Bell. 7, 41, Ant. 17, 253). M-M.*

ἐκτείνω fut. ἐκτενῶ; 1 aor. ἐξέτεινα (Aeschyl., Hdt.+; inscr., LXX, Philo; Jos., Ant. 11, 239 ἐπί τι; Test. 12 Patr.) *stretch out.* **1.** lit. ἐ. ἑαυτό *stretch itself out* Hv 4, 1, 9. Of nets *spread out* B 5: 4 (Pr 1: 17). ἀγκύρας ἐκτείνειν Ac 27: 30 s. ἄγκυρα.—Esp. in the expr. ἐ. τὴν χεῖρα (τὰς χεῖρας) *hold out* or *extend the hand(s)* (class.; Diod. S. 13, 15, 1; oft. LXX; Jos., Ant. 8, 233, cf. 13, 14) of a man w. a disabled hand: Mt 12: 13; Mk 3: 5; Lk 6: 10. To grasp someth. (Gen 22: 10 al.) Mt 26: 51; D 4: 5; B 19: 9. To take hold of someone Mt 14: 31. To heal someone (by touch; cf. OWeinreich, Antike Heilungswunder '09, 15ff; 51ff; JBehm, D. Handauflegung '11, 102ff) Mt 8: 3; Mk 1: 41; Lk 5: 13. W. εἰς to indicate purpose Ac 4: 30. ἐ. τὴν χεῖρα ἐπί τινα *lay a hand on someone* (Diog. L. 6, 29 τὰς χεῖρας ἐπὶ τοὺς φίλους ἐ.) w. hostile intent (Jer 6: 12; 1 Macc 6: 25; 12: 42; 2 Macc 15: 32; cf. Jos., Ant. 7, 327) Lk 22: 53.

To point at someone Mt 12: 49. As a gesture in prayer (1 Esdr 8: 70; 4 Macc 4: 11; Agatharchides in Jos., C. Ap. 1, 209—Earlier writers would have said ἀνατείνω τὰς χεῖρας: Pind., Ol. 7, 65; [Ps.-]Plut., Mor. 774в) 1 Cl 2: 3; B 12: 2. Gesture of a speaker Ac 26: 1 (cf. Quintilian 9, 3, 84ff; Apuleius, Metam. 2, 21; KSittl, D. Gebärden d. Griechen u. Römer 1890, 350ff). Of one who is crucified (Epict. 3, 26, 22 ἐκτείνας σεαυτὸν ὡς οἱ ἐσταυρωμένοι; Jos., Ant. 19, 94) J 21: 18; B 12: 2. **2.** fig. *draw out at length* λόγους ἐ. (Pla., Leg. 10 p. 887Α ὁ λόγος ἐκταθείς, others sim.) *speak at length* 1 Cl 57: 4 (Pr 1: 24). M-M.*

ἐκτελέω 1 aor. ἐξετέλεσα (Hom.+; inscr., pap., LXX; Jos., Bell. 2, 313; 7, 395) *finish, bring to completion* of a building Lk 14: 29f (cf. 2 Ch 4: 5).—Hm 12, 3, 3 v.l (for τελῶ). M-M.*

ἐκτένεια, ας, ἡ (late word [Phryn. p. 311 Lob.]; Molpis in Athen. 4 p. 141ε; oft. in inscr. [s. Thieme; Rouffiac]; PPetr. III 144 IV, 17 [III вc]; Wilcken, Chrest. 1 IV, 17; LXX; Jos., Ant. 7, 231) *perseverance, earnestness* ἐν ἐ. *earnestly* (=ἐκτενῶς) Ac 12: 5 D; 26: 7 (cf. Jdth 4: 9). For this μετὰ ἐκτενείας 1 Cl 33: 1; μετὰ πάσης ἐκτενείας 37: 1 (Inscr. Rom IV 984, 6 μετὰ πάσης ἐ. καὶ λαμπρότητος; 2 Macc 14: 38).—IMg 14 v.l. Funk. M-M.*

ἐκτενής, ές (Aeschyl.; Polyb. 22, 5, 4; inscr. [s. on ἐκτένεια]; PTebt. 24, 45; 3 Macc 3: 10; 5: 29; Philo) comp. ἐκτενέστερος (Inscr. Rom. IV 293 II, 38) *eager, earnest,* lit. 'strained' Ac 12: 5 t.r. ἐκτενῆ τὴν δέησιν ποιεῖσθαι *make earnest supplication* 1 Cl 59: 2 (UPZ 110, 46 [164 вc] τὴν ἐκτενεστάτην ποιήσασθαι πρόνοιαν). τὴν ἀγάπην ἐκτενῆ ἔχειν *keep love constant* 1 Pt 4: 8. μετ' ἐκτενοῦς ἐπιεικείας w. *constant gentleness* 1 Cl 58: 2; 62: 2. M-M.*

ἐκτενῶς adv. (Aristot. et al.; Polyb. 31, 14, 12; Diod. S. 2, 24, 3; M. Ant. 1, 4; Vett. Val. p. 187, 5; inscr. [s. ἐκτένεια]; LXX; Jos., Ant. 6, 341) *eagerly, fervently, constantly* ἀγαπᾶν 1 Pt 1: 22. Of prayer (as always in LXX: Jon 3: 8; 3 Macc 5: 9 al.) προσευχὴ ἐ. γινομένη Ac 12: 5. βοᾶν πρὸς τὸν θεὸν ἐ. 1 Cl 34: 7.—Neut. of the comp. of ἐκτενής as adv. ἐκτενέστερον (Agatharch. in Athen. 12 p. 527c; Dit., Syll.³ 695, 66): ἐ. προσεύχεσθαι prob. elative *very fervently* Lk 22: 44. M-M.*

ἐκτίθημι impf. mid. ἐξετιθέμην; 1 aor. pass. ἐξετέθην; not in act. in our lit. (Hom.+; inscr., pap., LXX, Ep. Arist., Philo, Joseph.). **1.** *expose, abandon* (Jos., C. Ap. 1, 308) of children (so act. and mid. since Hdt. 1, 112; Diod. S. 2, 4, 3 παιδίον; 3, 58, 1; 4, 64, 1 τὸ βρέφος; Aelian, V. H. 2, 7; Lucian, De Sacrif. 5; BGU 1104, 24 [8 вc] τὸ βρέφος ἐκτίθεσθαι; Wsd 18: 5) Ac 7: 21 (of Moses also Philo, Mos. 1, 12); AP fgm. 3, p. 12, 37 (εἰς θάνατον indicates the normal result of the exposure); cf. fgm. 1, p. 12, 12. **2.** fig. *explain, set forth* (Aristot. et al.; Diod. S. 12, 18, 4; Athen. 7 p. 278d; PHib. 27, 24 τὴν ἀλήθειαν; 2 Macc 11: 36; Ep. Arist. 1: 161; Jos., Ant. 1, 214) τί τινι *someth. to someone* (PMMeyer, Griech. Texte aus Aegypt. '16 no. 1, 13 [II вc] ᾧ καὶ τὰ καθ' ἑαυτοὺς ἐκτεθειμένων ἡμῶν; Jos., Ant. 2, 11) Ac 18: 26; 28: 23. τινί w. λέγων foll. 11: 4. M-M.*

ἐκτίλλω impf. ἐξέτιλλον; 1 aor. ἐξέτιλα (since Anacr. 54, 9 Diehl²; BGU 1818, 15 [I вc]; LXX) *pull out* τί (Aristot. 603b, 22 τρίχας; Aëtius 160, 19) sticks Hs 8, 4, 3; weeds (Antig. Car. 34) s 5, 2, 4f; 5, 4, 1; 5, 5, 3.*

ἐκτινάσσω 1 aor. ἐξετίναξα, mid. ἐξετιναξάμην (Hom. +; pap., LXX; Sib. Or. 5, 152).

1. *shake off* τὶ (Is 52: 2 τὸν χοῦν) τὸν κονιορτὸν τῶν ποδῶν *the dust that clings to one's feet* (AMerx, D. vier kanon. Ev. II 1, '02, 178f takes the words to mean the dust which is raised by the feet and settles in the clothes) Mt 10: 14; cf. Mk 6: 11; Lk 9: 5 D. For this the mid. ἐκτινάσσεσθαι τὸν κονιορτὸν ἐπί τινα Ac 13: 51, a symbolic act denoting the breaking off of all association (differently EBöklen, Deutsch. Pfarrerbl. 35, '31, 466ff).

2. *shake out* clothes Ac 18: 6 (here mid., but act. e.g. BGU 827, 22 ἐκτίνασσε τὰ ἱμάτια; Sb 7992, 17.—UPZ 6, 10f, ἐκτινάσσειν is a gesture protesting innocence; cf. GGA '26, 49). M-M.*

ἐκτιτρώσκω 1 aor. ἐξέτρωσα (Hdt. 3, 32; PGdspd. 15, 15; Sym. Job 21: 10) *cause an abortion* AP 11: 26.*

ἕκτος, η, ον (Hom.+; pap., LXX, Ep. Arist., Philo, Joseph., Test. 12 Patr.) *sixth* Hs 9, 1, 7; 9, 23, 1; month Lk 1: 26, 36; seal Rv 6: 12; cf. 9: 13f; 16: 12; 21: 20; hour (=12 o'clock if Jewish reckoning is employed; Jos., Vi. 279) Mt 20: 5; 27: 45; Mk 15: 33; Lk 23: 44; J 4: 6; 19: 14; Ac 10: 9. M-M.*

ἐκτός adv. (Hom.+; inscr., pap., LXX, Ep. Arist., Philo; Jos., Ant. 14, 471) *outside.*

1. τὸ ἐκτός (sc. μέρος) *the outside* Mt 23: 26 (cf. PTebt. 316, 95 [99 AD] ἐν τῷ ἐ.; Sir Prol. l. 5 οἱ ἐ.; Lucian, Vit. Auct. 26u; Proclus on Pla., Cratyl. p. 23, 12 P. τὰ ἐ.). —ἐκτὸς εἰ μή *unless, except* (post-class., in Dio Chrys., Plut., Lucian [Nägeli 33]; Vett. Val. Ind. III; Le Bas-Waddington, Inscript. III 2 no. 1499; CIG 2825; Lyc. Inscr.: JHS 34, '14, p. 31 no. 44, 6; Bl-D. §376; Rob. 640) 1 Cor 14: 5; 15: 2; 1 Ti 5: 19.

2. as improper prep. w. gen. (s. ἀνά, beg.).—**a.** *outside* (Parthenius 9, 4 ἐκτὸς ἐγένετο αὐτοῦ=he was beside himself) ἐ. τοῦ σώματος *outside the body* 2 Cor 12: 2. Of sin, apart from fornication ἐ. τοῦ σώματος ἐστιν *remains outside the body*, since immorality pollutes the body itself 1 Cor 6: 18. ταῦτα τῆς ἐκείνου μεγαλειότητος *these things lie outside the divine majesty* Dg 10: 5. ποιεῖν τι ἐ. τῆς ἐντολῆς τ. θεοῦ *do someth.* (good) *apart fr. God's commandment*, i.e., beyond what he commands Hs 5, 3, 3. *Outside* the altar ITr 7: 2 Funk.

b. *except* οὐδὲν ἐ. ὧν *nothing except what* (cf. 1 Ch 29: 3; 2 Ch 17: 19; Test. Napht. 6: 2) Ac 26: 22; ἐ. τοῦ ὑποτάξαντος *except him that subjected* 1 Cor 15: 27. M-M.*

ἐκτρέπω 2 aor. pass. ἐξετράπην; 2 fut. ἐκτραπήσομαι (trag., Hdt.+; PRyl. 133, 22 [I AD]; Am 5: 8). In our lit., as it seems, only pass. with mid. sense *turn, turn away* (Hdt.+) w. that to which one turns indicated by εἰς (Diod. S. 16, 12, 3; 17, 108, 4 εἰς ὕβρεις; Epict. 1, 6, 42; Philo, Spec. Leg. 2, 23; Jos., Ant. 8, 251 εἰς ἀσεβεῖς ἐξετράπη πράξεις) 1 Ti 1: 6. ἐπὶ τοὺς μύθους 2 Ti 4: 4 (cf. Pla., Soph. 222A: ἀπὸ–ἐπί; Galen XI 792 K. Πάμφιλος εἰς μύθους γραῶν ἐξετράπετο; ἐξετράπην τῶν ματαίων ἐπὶ τὸν ὕψιστον θεόν Ode of Solomon 11, 9). ὀπίσω τοῦ Σατανᾶ *to follow Satan* 1 Ti 5: 15. W. acc. *turn away from* or *avoid* someth. (Demosth. 19, 225; Polyb. 35, 4, 14; Musonius p. 26, 4 H.; inscr. of the Epicurean Diogenes of Oenoanda [RhM 47, 1892, 41ff] col. 29, 7 ἐ. δεῖ τοὺς σοφιστικοὺς λόγους; Jos., Ant. 4, 290) 6: 20. W. gen. (Ps.-Aristot., Mirabilia 137 ἐκτρέπεσθαι τῆς ὁδοῦ; Lucian, Dial. Deor. 25, 2; Jos., Ant. 6, 34 τῶν τοῦ πατρὸς ἐπιτηδευμάτων ἐκτραπόμενοι) τῆς ἐλπίδος *let oneself be turned aside* IMg 11. ἵνα μὴ τὸ χωλὸν ἐκτραπῇ Hb 12: 13 is difficult. In line w. the previous mngs. one possibility is: *turn from the way* (abs. as X., An. 4, 5, 15). But ἐ. is oft. taken here, because of the context, as a medical t.t. *be*

dislocated (Hippocr., κατ' ἰητρ. 14 Kühlewein; Diosc., Mat. Med. 2, 15 W.; Hippiatr. 26, 6 p. 126, 24 ἐὰν ἵππος ὦμον ἐκτραπῇ) *in order that what is lame may not be dislocated.* Linguistically another possibility is: *that what is lame might not be avoided* (Lucian, Pseudolog. 17 ἡμεῖς τοὺς χωλοὺς ἐκτρεπόμεθα=we go out of the lame men's way). M-M.*

ἐκτρέφω 1 aor. ἐξέθρεψα (trag., Hdt.+; inscr., pap., LXX; Jos., C. Ap. 2, 139).

1. *nourish* w. acc. (Plut., Lycurg. 16, 4; PRyl. 178, 14 [I AD]; Gen 47: 17) w. θάλπειν *nourish and cherish* (Vi. Aesopi Ic 9 p. 250, 13 τρέφει κ. θάλπει) Eph 5: 29.

2. *rear, bring up* τινά of children (X., An. 7, 2, 32; Polyb. 6, 6, 2; Epict. 2, 22, 10; Dit., Syll.³ 709, 34; oft. LXX) Eph 6: 4; Hv 3, 9, 1. M-M.*

ἐκτρίβω (Soph., Hdt.+; Sb 6796, 194; LXX)—**1.** *wear out* (lit. by rubbing), *drive out* (Pap. of Cornell Univ. ['26] 1, 194 [III BC]) τὶ the Holy Spirit Hm 10, 1, 2f; 10, 2, 1f (Appian, Bell. Civ. 2, 98 §409 τὸ πνεῦμα [=breath] ἐκτρῖψαι).

2. *ruin, destroy* (Hdt.; Plut., Mor. 529c; Ael. Aristid. 19, 1 K.=41 p. 762 D.; oft. LXX) τινά *someone* Hs 6, 1, 4. τ. ψυχάς 6, 2, 1.*

ἔκτρομος, ον *trembling* (inscr. fr. Hadrumetum in Dssm. B p. 29 l. 26 [BS 273ff]; cf. p. 44=Fluchtaf. no. 5, 26; PGM 4, 3076 [LAE 254]) in our lit. only as v.l. ἔκφοβος εἰμι καὶ ἔ. *I am full of fear and trembling* Hb 12: 21 (for ἔντρομος). M-M.*

ἔκτρωμα, ατος, τό (Aristot., De Gen. An. 4, 5, 4 p. 773b, 18; PTebt. 800, 30 [142 BC], here in the sense 'premature birth'; Num 12: 12; Job 3: 16; Eccl 6: 3; Philo, Leg. All. 1, 76; Phryn. p. 208f Lob.) *untimely birth, miscarriage.* So Paul calls himself, perh. taking up an insult (ἔ. as a term of contempt in Tzetzes [XII AD], Hist. Var. 5, 515 Kiessl.) hurled at him by his opponents 1 Cor 15: 8; imitated IRo 9: 2. ESchwartz, NGG '07, 276 refers to Euseb., H.E. 5, 1, 45. Cf. AvHarnack, SAB '22, p. 72, 3; AFridrichsen, Paulus abortivus: Symb. Philol. f. OADanielsson '32, 78–85; JMunck, NT Essays: memorial vol. for TWManson, '59, 180–93; JSchneider, TW II 463–5.—Acc. to G Björck, Con. Neot. 3, '39, 3–8 'monster', 'horrible thing'. M-M.*

ἐκτυπόω 1 aor. pass. ἐξετυπώθην (Pla., X.+; LXX; Ep. Arist. 98; Philo, Somn. 2, 191) *to shape* after a model εἰς τ. μορφὴν τούτων ἐκτυπωθῆναι *be shaped in their form* Dg 2: 3 (Cos. and Dam. 13, 23 ἐν ᾧ ἐκτυποῦνται σχήματι).*

ἐκφέρω fut. ἐξοίσω; 1 aor. ἐξήνεγκα (Hom.+; inscr., pap., LXX, Ep. Arist.; Philo, Op. M. 164; Joseph.).

1. lit. *carry* or *bring out* τὶ (opp. εἰσφέρω) 1 Ti 6: 7, sim. Pol 4: 1; a corpse for burial (Il. 24, 786 and oft. in later auth. as Epict. 2, 22, 10; Jos., Ant. 15, 46) Ac 5: 6, 9f; στολήν (cf. 4 Km 10: 22; also X., Cyr. 5, 2, 7; Herodian 2, 1, 2) Lk 15: 22 (v.l. ἐνέγκατε 𝔓⁷⁵ et al.); sick people into the streets Ac 5: 15.

2. *lead* (*out*) or *send* (*out*) with ἔξω (Leontios 13 p. 27, 8) ἔξω τ. κώμης Mk 8: 23.—**3.** fig. *produce* of everything that nature causes to grow: plants and their products (Hdt. 1, 193; X., Oec. 16, 5; Polyb. 36, 16, 8; Plut., Mor. p. 2E; 937D; Epict. 4, 8, 36; Gen 1: 12; Hg 1: 11; SSol 2: 13) fruit 1 Cl 24: 5; thorns and thistles Hb 6: 8; even κέρατα ἐ. *grow horns* 1 Cl 52: 2 (Ps 68: 32). M-M.*

ἐκφεύγω fut. ἐκφεύξομαι; 2 aor. ἐξέφυγον; 2 pf. ἐκπέφευγα (Hom.+; pap., LXX).

1. *run away, seek safety in flight* (2 Km 17: 2 A) ἐκ τ. οἴκου Ac 19: 16.

2. *escape*—**a.** abs. (Hdt. 5, 95, 1 φεύγων ἐκφεύγει=he escapes by flight; Lucian, Alex. 28; Jos., Bell. 1, 65, Ant. 2, 341) lit. Ac 16: 27; fig. (Sir 16: 13) 1 Th 5: 3; Hb 2: 3; 12: 25.

b. w. acc. of that which one escapes—**a.** lit., a monster (Artem. 4 p. 200, 25 θηρίον ἐ.) Hv 4, 2, 3.

β. fig. (Diod. S. 5, 59, 2 τὸ μύσος ἐ.; 17, 112, 3 τὸν κίνδυνον; Ael. Aristid. 34 p. 656 D.: τὴν αἰσχύνην; Ep. Arist. 268; Philo, Leg. All. 3, 93 λήθην) tribulations Lk 21: 36; Hv 4, 2, 4b; 5; judgment (2 Macc 7: 35; cf. PRyl. 28, 164ff ἐν κρίσει βαρηθεὶς ἔσται καὶ ἐκφεύξεται) Ro 2: 3. τὰς χεῖρας τινος (Phalaris, Ep. 92; Sus 22; Tob 13: 2) 2 Cor 11: 33. τὸ ἀποθανεῖν (Pla., Apol. 39A) ITr 2: 1.

c. καλῶς ἐξέφυγες you have made good your escape or you deserved to escape Hv 4, 2, 4a.

3. *shun, avoid* τὶ (Epict. 4, 5, 2 Σωκράτης πανταχοῦ ἐξέφυγεν μάχην; Diog. L. 10, 117; Philo, Leg. All. 3, 236 κακίαν) the world Hv 4, 3, 4. M-M.*

ἐκφοβέω (trag., Thu.+; PLond. 342, 9; Sb 4284, 10 ἐκφοβῶν ἡμᾶς; LXX; En.; Jos., Bell. 1, 492, Ant. 2, 82) *frighten, terrify* τινὰ διά τινος someone w. someth. 2 Cor 10: 9. M-M.*

ἔκφοβος, ον *terrified* (Aristot., Physiogn. 6 p. 812b, 29; Plut., Fab. 6, 8) ἔκφοβοι ἐγένοντο they became terrified Mk 9: 6; w. ἔντρομος Hb 12: 21 (cf. Dt 9: 19).*

ἔκφρικτος, ον *frightening, enough to make one tremble* (opp. ἥμερος) of words Hv 1, 3, 3.*

ἐκφύω (Hom.+; Sym. Ps 103: 14; Philo; Joseph.) trans. *put forth*, lit. 'cause to grow' (cf. Jos., Ant. 10, 270) τὰ φύλλα (the branch) *puts forth leaves* (ἐκφύῃ pres. subj.) Mt 24: 32; Mk 13: 28 (cf. Artem. 5, 63; 65; Ep. Arist. 70; Philo, Sacr. Abel. 25; Ps.-Clem., Hom. 2, 45; 19, 14). The accentuation ἐκφυῇ (Bl-D. §76, 2; W-S. §13, 11; Mlt.-H. 264), which is freq. preferred but certainly to be rejected, would make the form a 2 aor. pass. subj., give it intrans. mng., and make τὰ φύλλα the subj.: *the leaves sprout* (cf. Jos., Ant. 2, 83). M-M.*

ἐκφωνέω (Dionys. Hal., Comp. Verb. 14 et al.; pap.) *cry out* (so Plut., Caes. 66, 8; Philo, De Jos. 51) Lk 16: 24 v.l.*

ἐκχέω (Hom.+; inscr., pap., LXX, En., Philo, Joseph., Test. 12 Patr.) fut. ἐκχεῶ; 1 aor. ἐξέχεα. Beside it the H.Gk. form ἐκχύν(ν)ω (W-S. §15; Bl-D. §73 w. app.; 74, 2; 101; Mlt.-H. 195; 215; 265) pf. pass. ἐκκέχυμαι; 1 aor. ἐξεχύθην; 1 fut. ἐκχυθήσομαι, *pour out*.

1. lit., of liquids: water D 7: 3; αἷμα ἐ. *shed blood=commit a murder* (αἷμα 2a) Ac 22: 20; Ro 3: 15 (Is 59: 7; Ps 13: 3); Rv 16: 6. αἷμα ἐκχυννόμενον (Jos., Ant. 19, 94 αἷμα πολὺ ἐκκεχυμένον) Mt 23: 35; cf. Lk 11: 50. In the cultic sense *pour out* (cf. Lev 4: 7), esp. of Jesus' death 1 Cl 7: 4. αἷμα ἐ. περὶ πολλῶν εἰς ἄφεσιν ἁμαρτιῶν *blood shed for* (the benefit of) *many, for the forgiveness of sins* Mt 26: 28 (w. purpose indicated by εἰς like Lucian, Tim. 5 εἰς εὐεργεσίαν; αἷ. ἐ. ὑπὲρ πολλῶν Mk 14: 24; cf. Lk 22: 20. Wine ἐκχεῖται *is spilled* (*out*) (cf. Gen 38: 9) Mt 9: 17; cf. Lk 5: 37; ἐ. φιάλην, as we say, *pour out a bowl* (i.e., its contents) Rv 16: 1ff, 8, 10, 12, 17. Of solid objects (Lev 4: 12) ἐξεχύθη πάντα τὰ σπλάγχνα *all his bowels poured out* Ac 1: 18 (cf. Quint. Smyrn. 8, 302 ἔγκατα πάντ' ἐχύθησαν; 9, 190; 2 Km 20: 10; Jos., Bell. 7, 453; Act. Thom. 33). Of coins *scatter* on the ground J 2: 15.

2. fig. (cf. Lycophron 110 πόθον; Ps.-Demetr., Eloc. 134 τοῦ λόγου τὴν χάριν; Aelian, N. An. 7, 23 θυμόν;

Philo, Spec. Leg. 1, 37 of light; Jos., Ant. 6, 271 φόνον) of the Holy Spirit which acc. to Joel's prophecy, is to pour down on men like rain (Jo 2: 23; cf. 1QS 4, 21): *pour out* Ac 2: 33. ἐπί τινα (after Jo 3: 1) 2: 17f; 10: 45; Tit 3: 6; B 1: 3; 1 Cl 46: 6. The Holy Spirit has perh. brought the idea of outpouring into Ro 5: 5 ἡ ἀγάπη τ. θεοῦ ἐκκέχυται ἐν ταῖς καρδίαις ἡμῶν διὰ πνεύματος ἁγίου τοῦ δοθέντος ἡμῖν. But gener., whatever comes from above is connected w. this verb (Ps 44: 3 χάρις; Sir 18: 11 ἔλεος; Hos 5: 10 ἐπ' αὐτοὺς ἐκχεῶ ὡς ὕδωρ τὸ ὅρμημά μου; Philo, Aet. M. 147 ἄνωθεν ἐ.; Test. Levi 18: 5).

3. pass. *give up* or *abandon oneself* (Polyb. 31, 25, 4 εἰς ἑταίρας; Plut., Anton. 21, 1; Philo, Op. M. 80; Test. Reub. 1: 6) w. dat. (Alciphr. 3, 34, 1 τῷ γέλωτι) τῇ πλάνῃ τ. Βαλαάμ Jd 11; λίαν ἐ. ἀγαπῶν ὑμᾶς I am wholly consumed by love for you IPhld 5: 1. M-M.*

ἐκχύν(ν)ω s. ἐκχέω.

ἔκχυσις, εως, ἡ (Aristot. et al.; PTebt. 86, 9 [II BC]; PLond. 1177, 84; LXX; En. 17, 7) *outpouring* of the Holy Spirit 1 Cl 2: 2 (w. ἐπί τινα as 3 Km 18: 28).*

ἐκχωρέω 1 aor. ἐξεχώρησα (Soph., Hdt.+; inscr., pap., LXX) *go out, go away, depart* abs. (PLond. 106, 16 [III BC]; Jos., Bell. 1, 137) Lk 21: 21; 1 Cl 54: 2. W. gen. foll. (PMagd. 20, 7 [221 BC] τῆς οἰκίας) τῆς γῆς (Diod. S. 5, 15, 4; Jos., Ant. 1, 74) 31: 4. ἰδίων πόλεων 55: 1. For this ἔκ τινος (PAmh. 30, 42 [II BC] ἐκ τ. οἰκίας) ἐκ τῆς χώρας (as Dit., Syll.³ 679, 53) Hs 1: 4. M-M.*

ἐκψύχω 1 aor. ἐξέψυξα (since Hippocr., Morb. 1, 5, medical term [Hobart 37]; Herodas 4, 29; Ezk 21: 12) *breathe one's last, die* (Babrius 115, 11; Judg 4: 21 A) Ac 5: 5, 10; 12: 23. M-M.*

ἑκών, οῦσα, όν (Hom.+; inscr., pap., LXX, Philo; Jos., Vi. 347; 351) *willing(ly), glad(ly)* Dg 2: 9; IRo 4: 1. Opp. force 5: 2; MPol 4: 1; *of one's own free will* (cf. Epict. 3, 5, 9; 4, 3, 9; Lucian, Herm. 77; Dit., Syll.³ 1176, 4) ἐ. τοῦτο πράσσω 1 Cor 9: 17. ὑπετάγη οὐχ ἑκοῦσα *it was subjected against its own will* (v.l. οὐ θέλουσα) Ro 8: 20 (cf. Philo, Ebr. 122). M-M.*

ἔλαθον s. λανθάνω.

ἐλαία, ας, ἡ—**1.** *olive tree* (Hom.+; inscr., pap., LXX, Ep. Arist.; Philo, Aet. M. 63; Joseph.) Ro 11: 17, 24; pl. Rv 11: 4 (cf. Zech 4: 3, 11). τὸ ὅρος τῶν ἐλαιῶν (Zech 14: 4; cf. Jos., Bell. 2, 262, Ant. 20, 169) *the Mount of Olives* east of Jerusalem (Dalman, Orte³ 277ff) Mt 21: 1; 24: 3; 26: 30; Mk 11: 1; 13: 3; 14: 26; Lk 19: 37; 22: 39; J 8: 1. For Lk 19: 29; 21: 37 s. ἐλαιών.

2. *olive*, the fruit of the olive tree (Aristoph., Pla.+; Diosc.; Plut.; PHib. 49, 8 [257 BC]; PFay. 130, 16; POxy. 1494, 16) Js 3: 12.—Lit., s. ἀγριέλαιος. M-M. B. 380.*

ἔλαιον, ου, τό (Hom.+; inscr., pap., LXX; Ep. Arist. 92; Philo; Jos., Vi. 74 al.; Test. 12 Patr.) *olive oil*.

1. gener. Lk 16: 6. W. wine and flour (cf. Dt 7: 13; 11: 14; 28: 51; 2 Ch 31: 5; Ezk 16: 19 al.) Rv 18: 13. W. wine Hm 11: 15; D 13: 6. For lamps Mt 25: 3f, 8. As a means of treating wounds (Is 1: 6) Lk 10: 34 (used w. wine, as e.g. Theophr., Hist. Pl. 9, 12 ἐν οἴνῳ καὶ ἐλαίῳ; Hobart 28f) and otherw. for healing Mk 6: 13; Js 5: 14 (s. on ἀλείφω 1 and cf. Dit., Syll.³ 1170, 27.—Artem. 4, 82 a seemingly dead man is brought back to life by being anointed with warm oil).

2. esp. *oil* used for anointing (Posidon.: 87 fgm. 10 Jac.; Jos., Bell. 5, 565) Lk 7: 46 (cf. 4 Km 9: 6; Ps 22: 5). Fig. ἔχρισέν σε ὁ θεὸς ἔ. ἀγαλλιάσεως God anointed you w.

the oil of gladness Hb 1: 9 (Ps 44: 8). ἔ. ἀμαρτωλῶν oil of sinners 1 Cl 56: 5 (Ps 140: 5).

3. the effect for the cause: olive orchard τὸ ἔ. καὶ τὸν οἶνον μὴ ἀδικήσῃς do not harm the olive orchard and the vineyard Rv 6: 6 (cf. SReinach, Revue Archéol. 3 s. 39, '01, 350-74; JMoffatt, Exp. 7th Ser. VI '08, 359-69; SKrauss, ZNW 10, '09, 81-9; AvHarnack, Erforschtes u. Erlebtes '24, 53ff).—On the whole word HSchlier, TW II 468-70; Dalman under ἄρτος 1a. M-M. B. 380.*

ἐλαιών, ῶνος, ὁ olive grove, olive orchard (oft. in pap. since III BC [Dssm., NB 36ff=BS 208ff; BOlsson, Aegyptus 13, '33, 327ff]; Strabo 16, 4, 14; LXX; Philo, Spec. Leg. 2, 105). This word, which has become a proper name, is surely to be read Ac 1: 12 ἀπὸ ὄρους τ. καλουμένου ἐλαιῶνος from the hill called 'The Olive Grove'=the Mount of Olives s. ἐλαία (cf. Jos., Ant. 7, 202 διὰ τοῦ Ἐλαιῶνος ὄρους; PLond. 214, 10 εἰς ἀμπελικὸν χωρίον καλούμενον Ἐλαιῶνα; Test. Napht. 5: 1 ἐν τῷ ὄρει τοῦ Ἐλαιῶνος). Therefore it is also to be read Lk 19: 29; 21: 37, although the accentuation ἐλαιῶν cannot be ruled out absolutely (Bl-D. §143 app.; Mlt. 49; 235; Rob. 154 n. 2; 267). The name Olivet is fr. Lat. olivetum=olive grove.— WSchmauch, Der Oelberg: ThLZ 77, '52, 391-6; JB Curtis, Hebrew Union College Annual 28, '57, 137-80. M-M.*

Ἐλαμίτης, ου, ὁ (this form also Is 21: 2 for the usual Ἐλυμαῖος; for the correct spelling Αἰλαμῖται, as cod. B, cf. Bl-D. §38) an Elamite, inhabitant of Elam, a district north of the Persian Gulf, east of the lower Tigris valley Ac 2: 9.*

ἐλάσσων, ἔλασσον (Hom+; inscr., pap., LXX [Thackeray 121, 2; 122]; Att. ἐλάττων Hb 7: 7; 1 Ti 5: 9; Hv 3, 7, 6; s 9, 28, 4. Cf. Bl-D. §34, 1; Mlt.-H. 107) used as comp. of μικρός smaller in age=younger (opp. μείζων) Ro 9: 12; B 13: 2 (both Gen 25: 23), 5; inferior (cf. PRyl. 77, 39) J 2: 10; Hs 9, 28, 4; τόπος ἐ. an inferior place Hv 3, 7, 6. Opp. κρεῖττον Hb 7: 7 (the neut. sg. for more than one pers. as Περὶ ὕψους p. 56, 13 Vahlen τὸ θνητόν; Plut., Mor. 160D τὸ παρόν=οἱ παρόντες); opp. μεῖζον (Ael. Aristid. 29 p. 561 D.; Jos., Ant. 15, 226) Mt 20: 28 D=Agr 22; οὐκ ἐ. w. gen. foll. not less than (2 Macc 5: 5) Hs 2: 4; 9, 11, 7. Adv. ἔλαττον less ἔ. ἐτῶν ἑξήκοντα less than 60 years 1 Ti 5: 9 (cf. Pla., Ep. 2 p. 314B οὐκ ἐλάττω τριάκοντα ἐτῶν; Kühner-G. II 311f). M-M.*

ἐλαττονέω 1 aor. ἠλαττόνησα (Aristot., Plant. 2, 3 p. 825a, 23; BGU 1195, 19; LXX) have less or too little abs. (PMagd. 26, 12 [217 BC]) 2 Cor 8: 15 (Ex 16: 18). M-M.*

ἐλαττόω 1 aor. ἠλάττωσα; pf. pass. ptc. ἠλαττωμένος (Thu.+; inscr., pap., LXX, Ep. Arist., Philo, Joseph.).

1. make lower, inferior (Jos., C. Ap. 2, 202) τινά someone, παρά w. acc. shows the pers. or thing in comparison w. whom, or w. what, the subj. is made inferior (PTebt. 19, 11 [114 BC] σὺ δὲ ὀρθῶς ποιήσεις τὸ προσάγγελμα μὴ ἐλαττώσας παρὰ τὸ πρῶτον) Hb 2: 7, 9 (both Ps 8: 6).

2. pass. (as predom.)—a. be worse off or in need (1 Km 2: 5; 21: 15; 2 Km 3: 29; Ps 33: 11 al.) 2 Cor 12: 13 v.l.; Dg 10: 6.

b. intr. diminish (Peripl. Eryth. c. 45; Philo, Leg. All. 2, 3, Virt. 46, Gig. 27, Aet. M. 65; 120; Jos., Ant. 7, 31. Of persons: Thu. 4, 59, 2; Dit., Or. 139, 10 [II BC]; PTebt. 382, 13 [I BC]) J 3: 30 (opp. αὐξάνω, q.v. Perh. the diminution of light is spec. in mind here: Cass. Dio 45, 17: τὸ φῶς τοῦ ἡλίου ἐλαττοῦσθαί τε καὶ σβέννυσθαι ἐδόκει). M-M.*

ἐλάττωμα, ατος, τό (Polyb., Dionys. Hal., Diod. S. 11, 62, 2; 12, 4, 4; Vett. Val. 265, 5; Philostrat., Vi. Apoll. 8, 7 p. 310, 31; inscr.; PTebt. 97, 1 [118 BC]; BGU 1060, 26; LXX; Jos., C. Ap. 1, 256) defect Hs 9, 9, 6.*

ἐλάττων s. ἐλάσσων.

ἐλαύνω pf. ἐλήλακα; impf. pass. ἠλαυνόμην (Hom.+; inscr., pap., LXX; Philo, Fuga 85; Joseph.) drive of the wind (Jos., Bell. 7, 317, Ant. 5, 205), which drives clouds 2 Pt 2: 17 or ships Js 3: 4 (Aristaen., Ep. 2, 11; Sb 997 καταπλέων ὑπὸ χειμῶνος ἐλασθείς; 998). Cf. Jd 23 as a cj. of Wohlenberg in N. Of a demon who drives a demoniac (cf. Appian, Macedon. 18 §2 αὐτὸν ἐλαύνοντος θεοῦ=since a god drove him on) w. εἰς Lk 8: 29. Abs. either intr. advance, make progress (Apollon. Rhod. 3, 1238; Polyaenus 3, 10, 17; Aesop, Fab. 21 P.; Is 33: 21 οὐδὲ πορεύσεται πλοῖον ἐλαῦνον) or trans. row (Od. 3, 157; Ps.-Demosth. 50, 53 ἄσιτοι δὲ οὐκ ἂν ἐδύναντο ἐλαύνειν; Isocr., Areop. 20) Mk 6: 48; J 6: 19. M-M. B. 713; 715.*

ἐλαφρία, ας, ἡ (Aretaeus p. 162, 10; Hesychius) vacillation, levity τῇ ἐ. χρᾶσθαι be vacillating, fickle 2 Cor 1: 17.*

ἐλαφρός, ά, όν (Hom.+; inscr., pap., LXX) comp. ἐλαφρότερος (Crinagoras no. 47, 6; Philo, Leg. All. 1, 42; Jos., Ant. 2, 61).

1. light in weight (Hom.+; Lucian, De Merc. Cond. 13 φέρειν τὸν ζυγὸν ἐλαφρόν; PGiess. 47, 7): a burden Mt 11: 30. Fig. easy to bear, insignificant (Hdt. 7, 38; Plut.; Ex 18: 26) τὸ ἐ. τῆς θλίψεως the insignificant affliction 2 Cor 4: 17.

2. quick, nimble (Hom.+). Of ill temper (Crinagoras loc. cit. of the θυμός) impetuous Hm 5, 2, 4.

3. frivolous, fickle, vacillating (Polyb. 6, 56, 11) Hm 11: 6; 12, 4, 5.—Comp. adv. ἐλαφροτέρως more lightly θλίβειν τινά Hs 7: 6. M-M. B. 1073.*

ἔλαχε s. λαγχάνω.

ἐλάχιστος, ίστη, ον (since Hom. Hymns, Merc. 573 and Hdt.; inscr., pap., LXX) used as superl. of μικρός. From it a colloq. comp. ἐλαχιστότερος is formed (Bl-D. §61, 2; Mlt. 236).

1. in our lit. only rarely as a true superl. (Jos., Bell. 6, 198) smallest, least (PTebt. 24, 67 [117 BC]; Josh 6: 26) ὁ ἐ. τῶν ἀποστόλων the least of the apostles 1 Cor 15: 9.

2. mostly elative (Bl-D. §60, 2; Mlt. 236)—a. very small, quite unimportant, insignificant etc. (Jos., Bell. 6, 330 ἐλ. μέρος) Js 3: 4; ἐ. κοκκάριον a very small grain Hm 11: 20, cf. 21. Of commandments unimportant Mt 5: 19a (FDibelius, ZNW 11, '10, 188-90; GDalman, Jesus-Jeshua '29, 62-65 [Eng. transl. PLevertoff]). Of animals the smallest 1 Cl 20: 10. Of parts of the body 37: 5; ἐ. ἐξαμαρτεῖν sin a little Hs 8, 10, 1; κριτήρια ἐ. trivial cases 1 Cor 6: 2; οὐδαμῶς ἐ. εἶ ἐν τ. ἡγεμόσιν Ἰούδα you are by no means least among the leaders of Judah Mt 2: 6. Of pers. unimportant (Dit., Syll.³ 888, 58) Mt 5: 19b; 25: 40, 45 (WBrandt, D. geringsten Brüder: Jahrb. d. Theol. Schule Bethel 8, '37, 1ff); τὸ ἐ. ἀψίνθιον the very little wormwood Hm 5, 1, 5. ἐλάχιστον a very little thing Lk 12: 26; (opp. τὸ πολύ) 16: 10; 19: 17; 2 Cl 8: 5 (on ἐν ἐλ. cf. PCattaoui V 23 in Mitteis, Chrest. p. 422). ἐμοὶ εἰς ἐ. ἐστιν 1 Cor 4: 3 (s. εἰμί III 2); ἐ. τῶν ῥάβδων a very small part of the sticks Hs 8, 1, 14f; 8, 5, 5f; 10, 1, 3.

b. w. ref. to number very few Hs 9, 8, 7.—Neut. as adv. (Polyaenus 8, 7, 2) ἐ. βασανίζεσθαι be tortured (punished) a very short time here=for too short a time Hs 6, 4,

2; 4.—Comp. ἐμοὶ τῷ ἐλαχιστοτέρῳ *to me, the very least* Eph 3: 8 (s. 1 above: 1 Cor 15: 9). M-M.*

Ἐλδάδ, ὁ indecl. *Eldad,* a Hebrew prophet who, w. Modad, prophesied in camp during the journey through the desert (Num 11: 26-9: Ἐλδὰδ καὶ Μωδάδ 27). Ἐ. καὶ Μ. is the title of a lost apocalyptic book, which is quoted as an authority Hv 2, 3, 4.—Schürer III⁴ 360f.*

Ἐλεάζαρ, ὁ indecl. (Ex 6: 23 al.; Philo, Somn. 2, 186.— Ep. Arist.; Joseph.: Ἐλεάζαρος, ου [Ant. 4, 152]) *Eleazar,* in the genealogy of Jesus Mt 1: 15; Lk 3: 23ff D.*

ἐλεάω (Pr 21: 26; 4 Macc 9: 3) the forms which grammatically belong to such a present have arisen from a mixture of the inflectional types -άω and -εῖν (Bl-D. §90; Mlt.-H. 195ff) *have mercy on* of men: ἐλεᾶτε Jd 22; 23 (both w. ἐλέγχετε as v.l.); 1 Cl 13: 2; Pol 2: 3; cf. B 20: 2. Of God: ἐλεῶντος θεοῦ Ro 9: 16.*

ἐλεγμός, οῦ, ὁ (LXX w. var. mngs.) *conviction* of a sinner (Num 5: 18ff), also *reproof* (Sir 21: 6; 32: 17; 48: 7) and *punishment* (4 Km 19: 3; Jdth 2: 10; 1 Macc 2: 49) w. διδασκαλία and ἐπανόρθωσις 2 Ti 3: 16 (v.l. ἔλεγχον).*

ἔλεγξις, εως, ἡ (Philod., Rhet. I p. 134, 8 Sudh.; Philostrat., V. Apoll. 2, 22; Job 21: 4; 23: 2; En. 14, 1; Protev. Jac. 16, 1; Hesychius) *conviction, rebuke, reproof* ἔ. ἔσχεν ἰδίας παρανομίας *he received a rebuke for his transgression* 2 Pt 2: 16. M-M.*

ἔλεγχος, ου, ὁ (Pind., Pre-Socr.+; pap., LXX, Philo, Joseph.).
1. *proof, proving* (Pla., Gorg. 471E; Demosth. 44, 15 τὸ πρᾶγμα τὸν ἔλεγχον δώσει; Epict. 3, 10, 11; POxy. 237 VIII, 17; PStrassb. 41, 6 ὁ ἔλ. δεικνύσει; Job 23: 7, cf. vs. 4; Philo, Praem. 4 ἔ. τ. ἀληθείας; Jos., Bell. 1, 626; 628, C. Ap. 2, 17) hence perh. *inner conviction* ἔ. πραγμάτων οὐ βλεπομένων *a proving of* (or *conviction about*) *unseen things* Hb 11: 1.
2. *conviction* of a sinner (BGU 1138, 13 [19/18 BC]; Epigr. Gr. 814) σύ μου ἔ. εἶ *will you convict me?* (also poss.: *complaint* [Hab 2: 1] *will you bring a complaint against me?*) Hv 1, 1, 6.
3. *reproof, censure, correction* (Job 6: 26; 13: 6; Wsd 2: 14; Philo, Rer. Div. Her. 76) 1 Cl 57: 4f (Pr 1: 25, 30); 2 Ti 3: 16 v.l. M-M.*

ἐλέγχω fut. ἐλέγξω; 1 aor. imper. ἔλεγξον, inf. ἐλέγξαι; pass. ἠλέγχθην (Hom.+; inscr., pap., LXX, Philo, Joseph., Test. 12 Patr.; Sib. Or. 4, 21).
1. *bring to light, expose, set forth* (Aristoph., Eccl. 485; Herodian 3, 12, 4; PHib. 55, 3 [250 BC] τὸν ποιμένα τ. ἐλέγξοντα περὶ ὧν μοι εἶπας) Eph 5: 11, 13; Dg 2: 8. τὰ κρυπτά (Artem. 1, 68) IPhld 7: 1. ταῦτα ἔλεγχε *declare this* Tit 2: 15; τ. ἁμαρτίας τινὸς πρὸς τὸν κύριον *expose someone's sins before the Lord* Hv 1, 1, 5 (Jos., Vi. 339 τὰς πονηρίας ἐ.); *demonstrate, prove* (POxy. 237 VIII, 40; Wsd 2: 11) τὶ Dg 9: 6; *disprove* 2: 9.
2. *convict* or *convince* someone of someth., *point someth. out to someone* (PAmh. 33, 34 [157 BC]; BGU 1138, 13 [19/18 BC]; POxy. 1032, 30; PStrassb. 41, 31; Jos., Ant. 4, 219; Sib. Or. 5, 34) τινά Tit 1: 9, 13; Jd 22: v.l. (COsburn, ZNW 63, '72, 139-44 [text]); 23 v.l.; περί w. gen. introduces the thing of which one is convicted or convinced (Aristoph., Plut. 574; Jos., C. Ap. 2, 5; PLeipz. 43, 11 μάρτυρας τοὺς ἐλέγχοντας θαῆσιν περὶ ἀφαιρέσεως ἐκ βιβλίων χρειστιακῶν) J 8: 46; 16: 8 (s. δικαιοσύνη 2, end); Jd 15 (En. 1, 9). Pass. ἐ. ὑπό τινος Ac 6: 10 D; 1 Cor 14: 24; ὑπό τ. συνειδήσεως ἐλεγχόμενοι J 8: 9 v.l. (cf. Philo, De Jos. 48 ὑπὸ τοῦ συνειδότος ἐλεγχόμε-

νος, Spec. Leg. 3, 54 al.); ἀπὸ τῆς ὀσμῆς ἐλέγχεσθαι *be convicted* (perh. *tested*) *by the odor* IMg 10: 2. ἐλεγχόμενοι ὡς παραβάται *convicted as transgressors* Js 2: 9.
3. *reprove, correct* (Aelian, V.H. 13, 25; Sir 20: 2; 31: 31; Pr 9: 7f al.) 2 Ti 4: 2; τινά 1 Ti 5: 20; D 2: 7. W. the connotation of refuting (Diod. S. 13, 90, 4; Appian, Bell. Civ. 5, 28, end; PGM 4, 2620) πᾶσαν αἵρεσιν Epil Mosq 1.—τινὰ περί τινος Lk 3: 19. τινὰ ἐπί τινι B 19: 4. ἔλεγξον αὐτὸν μεταξὺ σοῦ καὶ αὐτοῦ μόνου *show him his fault while you are alone w. him* Mt 18: 15 (cf. CD 9, 6-8 and s. Lev 19: 17).
4. heightened, *punish, discipline* (Wsd 1: 8; 12: 2; Job 5: 17 al.) Hb 12: 5 (Pr 3: 11); (w. παιδεύειν, as Sir 18: 13) Rv 3: 19.—FBüchsel, TW II 470-4; LJLutkemeyer, CBQ 8, '46, 221-3. M-M. B. 1442.**

ἐλεεινός, ή, όν (Hom.+; Diod. S. 13, 28, 3; Dio Chrys. 33[50], 3; 4; Ael. Aristid. 34, 47 K.=50 p. 564 D.; Philostrat., Imag. 1, 4 p. 300, 6; POxy. 130, 3; 131, 2; Jos., Ant. 4, 133, Vi. 138 for Att. ἐλεινός.—Bl-D. §31, 3; Rob. 204) *miserable, pitiable* (w. ταλαίπωρος) Rv 3: 17. Comp. ἐλεεινότεροι πάντων ἀνθρώπων as superl. (cf. Bl-D. §60; Mlt. 78f) *most miserable of all men* 1 Cor 15: 19. M-M.*

ἐλεέω fut. ἐλεήσω; 1 aor. ἠλέησα, imper. ἐλέησον; 1 aor. pass. ἠλεήθην; 1 fut. ἐλεηθήσομαι; pf. pass. ptc. ἠλεημένος (Hom.+; inscr., pap., LXX, Philo, Joseph., Test. 12 Patr.) *have mercy* or *pity* τινά *on someone* (Diod. S. 12, 30, 4; 20, 4, 6 τοὺς πολίτας; Zen.-P. 59 145, 12 [256 BC]; UPZ 78, 24 [159 BC]; PFay. 106, 16 [II AD] ἀξιῶ σε ἐλεῆσαί με; PFlor. 378, 3; Philo) Hv 1, 3, 2. τὸν σύνδουλον Mt 18: 33. Abs. *feel pity* MPol 2: 2. Esp. *be merciful, show mercy to someone, help someone* (out of pity) Mt 9: 27; 15: 22; 17: 15; 20: 30f (on κύριε ἐλέησον cf. Epict. 2, 7, 12 [ThZahn, D. Stoiker Epikt. u. s. Verh. z. Christentum² 1895, 46f; FJDölger, Sol salutis '20, 62f]; Ps 6: 3; 9: 14 al.; EPeterson, Εἷς θεός '26, 164-7; Achilles Tat. 3, 5, 4 ἐλέησον δέσποτα Πόσειδον; Jos., Ant. 9, 64 δέσποτα ἐλέησον); Mk 10: 47f; Lk 16: 24; 17: 13; 18: 38f; D 2: 7; *do acts of mercy* Ro 12: 8; τινά *to someone* (Charito 1, 9, 5; Celsus 2, 71) AP 15: 30; B 20: 2; D 5: 2. Of God's mercy (Epici p. 20: Cypria fgm. 1, 3 Ζεὺς ἐλέησε; Hes., Astron. fgm. 182 Rz.; Ἥφαιστος; Phanodemus [IV BC]: no. 325 fgm. 14b Jac.: Artemis; Menand., Epitr. 490 θεῶν τις ὑμᾶς ἠλέησε; Diod. S. 24, 12, 2 δαιμονίου ἐλεήσαντος; UPZ 78, 24 [159 BC] of Isis, θεὰ θεῶν: ἐλέησον τὰς διδύμας; Jos., Ant. 11, 1; Sib. Or. 3, 628); Mk 5: 19; Phil 2: 27; Ro 9: 15 (Ex 33: 19), 16, 18; 11: 32; 1 Cl 18: 2 (Ps 50: 3); 59: 4; 2 Cl 1: 7; B 3: 5 (on the acc. of the thing cf. Diod. S. 18, 25, 2). Pass. *find* or *be shown mercy* (Appian, Hann. 28 §119 ἐλεεῖσθαι ὑπό τινος, Bell. Civ. 4, 13 §52) Mt 5: 7; Ro 11: 30f; 1 Ti 1: 13, 16; IEph 12: 1; 1 Cl 56: 16. οἱ οὐκ ἠλεημένοι νῦν δὲ ἐλεηθέντες *who once had not found mercy, but now have found it* 1 Pt 2: 10. Of a church ἠλεημένη *which has found mercy* (cf. Hos 1: 6) IRo inscr.; IPhld inscr.; ISm inscr.; *receive as a gracious gift, be favored with* ἠλεημένος ὑπὸ κυρίου πιστός εἶναι (Herm. Wr. 13, 7 ἐλεηθεὶς ὑπὸ τ. θεοῦ) 1 Cor 7: 25; cf. 2 Cor 4: 1; IRo 9: 2; IPhld 5: 1.—RBultmann, TW II 474-83. M-M.**

ἐλεημοσύνη, ης, ἡ (Callim. 4, 152 w. mng. 'pity'; P Genève 51, 26; LXX) *kind deed,* then specif. *alms, charitable giving* so Diog. L. 5, 17; Da 4: 27; Tob; Sir; Sib. Or. 2, 80) Mt 6: 4; D 15: 4. ποιεῖν ἐ. *give alms* (Tob 1: 3, 16; 4: 7f; Sir 7: 10) Mt 6: 2f; Ac 9: 36 (Joach Jeremias, ZNW 44, '53, 103f); 10: 2; 24: 17; διδόναι ἐ. (Diog. L., loc. cit. πονηρῷ ἀνθρώπῳ ἐλεημοσύνην ἔδωκεν) Lk 11: 41 (cf. Black, Aramaic Approach, 2); 12: 33; αἰτεῖν ἐ. ask for alms Ac 3: 2; λαμβάνειν vs. 3; πρὸς τὴν ἐ. καθήμενος (the one who) sat begging vs. 10. Alms ascend to God Ac 10: 4; they are remembered before God vs. 31; cf. 2 Cl 16: 4. ἱδρωσάτω ἡ ἐ. εἰς τὰς χεῖράς σου let your alms sweat in your hands, i.e., do not give them hastily D 1: 6 (cf. Sib. Or. 2, 79f).—Billerb. IV 536–58: D. altjüd. Privatwohltätigkeit; HBolkestein, Wohltätigkeit u. Armenpflege im vorchristl. Altertum '39; Dodd 59–62. M-M.*

ἐλεήμων, ον gen. -ονος (Hom.+; Epict. 2, 21, 3; 5; 6; LXX) merciful, sympathetic of God (so predom. LXX; Ep. Arist. 208; Test. Jud. 19: 3; Philo, Somn. 1, 93.—Sb 8266, 19 [261/60 BC] of the god Amenophis; Apollod. [II BC]: 244 fgm. 121 Jac. of Leto; Isishymn. v. And. 128; of Isis: Suppl. Epigr. Gr. VIII 550, 34 [I BC]) w. οἰκτίρμων (as Ex 34: 6 al. LXX) 1 Cl 60: 1. Of Christ (PGM 13, 290) Hb 2: 17. Of men (Epict. [s. above]; Ptolem., Apotel. 3, 14, 33; Herm. Wr. 1, 22; Ps 111: 4; Pr 11: 17; 20: 6; Jos., Ant. 10, 41; Test. Sim. 4: 4) Mt 5: 7; 2 Cl 4: 3; D 3: 8. εἰς πάντας toward everyone Pol 6: 1. M-M.*

ἔλεος, ους, τό (Hom.+, but in secular Gk. almost always ὁ ἔλεος; so in Diod. S. 12, 18, 4; Herm. Wr. 13, 3; Dit., Syll.³ 814, 21 [67 AD]; PMagd. 18, 6 [III BC]; En. 12, 6; Ep. Arist. 208; Philo; Jos., Bell. 1, 560, Ant. 4, 239 ἐξ ἐλέου; POxy. 2754, 5 [111 AD].—Neut., Polyb. 1, 88, 2 and Diod. S. 3, 18, 5 (v.l. in latter pass.); Herm. Wr. 13, 8a; gravestone: Sb 6650, 4; pap.; also predom. in LXX [Thackeray 158; Helbing 47]; En. 5, 6; 27, 4; Test. 12 Patr. and always in our lit. [Bl-D. §51, 2 w. app.; Mlt. 60. For the Apost. Fathers cf. Reinhold 54]; the masc. appears now and then as v.l.: Mt 9: 13; 12: 7; 23: 23; Tit 3: 5; Hb 4: 16) mercy, compassion, pity, clemency.
1. of men toward men Mt 9: 13; 12: 7 (both Hos 6: 6); 23: 23; Js 3: 17; ποιεῖν ἐ. show mercy, do good (Gen 24: 44, 49; 1 Km 15: 6 al.) Js 2: 13, μετά τινος to someone (Judg 1: 24; 8: 35; 1 Km 20: 8 al.) Lk 10: 37.
2. of God toward men (Timocles Com. [IV BC] 31 τοῖς τεθνεῶσιν ἔλεος ἐπιεικὴς θεός; LXX).
a. gener. Lk 1: 50 (cf. Ps 102: 17), 54 (cf. Ps 97: 3); (w. εἰρήνη as En. 5, 5) Gal 6: 16; B 15: 2; Hv 3, 9, 8; s 4: 2. ἔλεος κυκλώσει τινά mercy will surround someone (for protection) 1 Cl 22: 8 (Ps 31: 10). In greetings (w. εἰρήνη; cf. Tob 7: 12 S) Pol inscr.; (w. χάρις [cf. Wsd 3: 9; 4: 15], εἰρήνη) 1 Ti 1: 2; 2 Ti 1: 2; 2 J 3; cf. ISm 12: 2; w. εἰρήνη, ἀγάπη Jd 2; MPol inscr.; ἐν παντὶ ἐ. IPhld. inscr. Hebraistic: ἐμεγάλυνεν κύριος τὸ ἔ. αὐτοῦ μετ' αὐτῆς the Lord had showed great mercy to her Lk 1: 58. ἔχειν ἐ. find mercy Hv 2, 2, 3. Cf. also 1 Cl 9: 1; 28: 1; 50: 2; 56: 5 (Ps 140: 5); ITr 12: 3.
b. esp. the mercy shown by God in Christ to men Ro 15: 9; Tit 3: 5; Hv 3, 9, 1. πλούσιος ἐν ἐλέει rich in mercy Eph 2: 4. κατὰ τὸ πολὺ αὐτοῦ ἔ. acc. to his great mercy 1 Pt 1: 3 (cf. Ps 50: 3; 24: 7.—κατ' ἔλεον of Zeus: Lucian, Dial. Deor. 13, 1; of Hera: Παραδοξογράφοι ed. AWestermann ibid. p. 222, 7; of Athena ibid. 227, 17 and 19); cf. 1 Cl 18: 2 (Ps 50: 3); λαμβάνειν ἔ. receive mercy Hb 4: 16; ποιεῖν ἔ. μετά τινος show mercy to someone Lk 1: 72. σπλάγχνα ἐλέους merciful heart vs. 78. διδόναι ἔ. 2 Ti 1: 16. εὑρίσκειν ἔ. 1: 18. σκεύη ἐλέους vessels of mercy (opp. σκεύη ὀργῆς; s. σκεῦος 2) Ro 9: 23. τῷ ὑμετέρῳ ἐλέει because of the mercy shown to you (dat. of cause; s. ἀπιστία 2b) 11: 31.
3. of Christ toward men τὸ ἔλεος τοῦ κυρίου ἡμῶν Ἰησοῦ Χριστοῦ Jd 21.—AKlocker, Wortgeschichte von ἔλεος u. οἶκτος, etc., Diss. Innsbruck, '53; NGlueck, Das Wort Ḥesed im AT, Beih. ZAW, '61.—Cf. ἐλεέω, end. M-M.**

ἐλευθερία, ας, ἡ (Pind., Hdt.+; inscr., pap., LXX, Philo, Joseph.) freedom, liberty (opp. δουλεία: Jos., Bell. 7, 255) 2 Pt 2: 19; IPol 4: 3; Hs 5, 2, 7. Esp. of the freedom which stands in contrast to the constraint of the Mosaic law, looked upon as slavery Gal 2: 4; 5: 1 (τῇ ἐ. dat. of advantage for the freedom. KHRengstorf, ThLZ 76, '51, 659–62). Over against this serfdom Christianity regards itself as a νόμος τ. ἐλευθερίας Js 1: 25 (FNötscher, Vom AT zum NT, '62, 80–122 [Qumran]); 2: 12 (on both Js-passages cf. EStauffer, ThLZ 77, '52, 527–32).—In gener. of the liberty of a Christian (cf. Philo, Conf. Lingu. 94, Migr. Abr. 25, Rer. Div. Her. 124; 273; 275) 1 Cor 10: 29; 2 Cor 3: 17. ἐπ' ἐλευθερίᾳ καλεῖσθαι be called for freedom (=to be free; cf. Plut., Sulla 9, 14; Dit., Syll.² 845, 4; 8; BGU 1141, 24 [14 BC].—Lucian, Sat. 9 ἐπὶ τῇ ἐλευθερίᾳ ζῶμεν) Gal 5: 13a. This freedom must not degenerate into license vs. 13b; 1 Pt 2: 16. In contrast to the slavery of corruption stands the ἐ. τῆς δόξης τῶν τέκνων τοῦ θεοῦ the glorious freedom of God's children Ro 8: 21.—JWeiss, D. christl. Freih. nach der Verkünd. des Ap. Pls '02; ABonhöffer, Epiktet u. d. NT '11, 164; RBultmann, ZNW 13, '12, 97ff; 177ff; esp. 100ff, Theol. des NT '48, 326–48, Theology of the NT, tr. KGrobel '51, I 330–45; OSchmitz, D. Freiheitsged. b. Epikt. u. d. Freiheitszeugnis d. Pls '23; Mich. Müller, Freiheit: ZNW 25, '26, 177–236; KDeissner, Autorität u. Freiheit im ältesten Christentum '31; WBrandt, Freiheit im NT '32; EGGulin, D. Freiheit in d. Verk. d. Pls.: ZsystTh 18, '41, 458–81; EFuchs, D. Freiheit des Glaubens [Ro 5–8] '49; HWedell, Idea of Freedom in ... Paul: ATR 22, '50, 204–16; ANWilder, Eleutheria in the NT, Ecumenical Review (Geneva) 13, '61, 409–20; KNiederwimmer, D. Begriff d. Freiheit im NT, '66; DNestle, Eleutheria, I Die Griechen, '67; HSchlier, TW II 484–500. M-M.*

ἐλεύθερος, έρα, ον (Hom.+; inscr., pap., LXX, Philo, Joseph., Test. 12 Patr.) free in our lit. used as adj. and subst.
1. of political and social freedom (Jos., C. Ap. 2, 134. Cf. the pride of the Indians in freedom: Arrian, Ind. 10, 8 πάντας Ἰνδοὺς εἶναι ἐλευθέρους, οὐδὲ τινα δοῦλον εἶναι Ἰνδόν) J 8: 33; (opp. slave) 1 Cor 7: 21; 12: 13; Gal 3: 28 (cf. the temple law fr. Philadelphia [I BC]; Dit., Syll.³ 985 πρόσοδον ... ἀνδράσι κ. γυναιξίν, ἐλευθέροις κ. οἰκέταις; 67th letter of Apollonius of Tyana [Philostrat. I 363, 31]: the temple of Artemis at Eph. is open to all, Ἕλλησι, βαρβάροις, ἐλευθέροις, δούλοις); 4: 22f; 30f (oft. in marriage contracts since PEleph. 1, 4 [311 BC]); Eph 6: 8; Col 3: 11; Rv 6: 15; 13: 16; 19: 18; Hs 5, 2, 2. Paradox: the free man a slave of Christ 1 Cor 7: 22, which infl. IRo 4: 3.
2. independent, not bound οὐκ εἰμὶ ἐ.; (cf. Epict. 3, 22, 48) 1 Cor 9: 1; free fr. the tax Mt 17: 26; ἐ. τῇ δικαιοσύνῃ independent as far as righteousness is concerned Ro 6: 20; ἐ. ἀπό τινος (Pla., Leg. 8 p. 832D; X., Cyr. 3, 2, 23; Jos., Ant. 5, 34): ἐ. ἀπὸ τ. νόμου no longer bound by the law which joined her to her husband (cf. Dt 21: 14) Ro 7: 3; ἐ ἔκ τινος independent of someone 1 Cor 9: 19 (cf. Eur., Herc. Fur. 1010). W. inf. ἐ. ἐστὶν ... γαμηθῆναι 7: 39.
3. in the relig. and moral sense (Ps.-Dicaearch. p. 146 F. τοῖς τρόποις ὄντες ἐλεύθεροι=free men, judging by their customs) 1 Pt 2: 16. Of the freedom of the heavenly Jerusalem, representing Christianity in contrast to Judaism Gal 4: 26. Of the true freedom of one set free by Christ J 8: 36. M-M. B. 1336.*

ἐλευθερόω fut. ἐλευθερώσω; 1 aor. ἠλευθέρωσα; 1 aor. pass. ἠλευθερώθην; 1 fut. ἐλευθερωθήσομαι (Aeschyl., Hdt.+; inscr., pap., LXX, Ep. Arist., Philo; Jos., Ant. 14, 357) free, set free.

1. lit. (Appian, Hann. 27 §116) ἀπὸ τ. κοινοῦ ἐλευ-θεροῦσθαι (of slaves) *be freed at the church's expense* IPol 4: 3.
2. elsewh. in our lit. only w. ref. to relig. and moral matters (Epict. 4, 7, 17 ἠλευθέρωμαι ὑπὸ τοῦ θεοῦ . . . , οὐκέτι οὐδεὶς δουλαγωγῆσαί με δύναται; Maximus Tyr. 36, 5a ἄνδρα ἐλευθερωθέντα ὑπὸ τοῦ Διός; Third Corinthians 3: 6, 18), τινά *someone* J 8: 32, 36; ἀπὸ τ. ἀμαρτίας *fr. sin* Ro 6: 18, 22. ἀπὸ τ. νόμου τ. ἀμαρτίας 8: 2; ἀπὸ τ. δουλείας τ. φθορᾶς Ro 8: 21. τῇ ἐλευθερίᾳ *for freedom* (fr. the Mosaic law) Gal 5: 1.—JEFrame, Paul's Idea of Deliverance: JBL 49, '30, 1–12. M-M.*

ἔλευσις, εως, ἡ (Dionys. Hal. 3, 59, 1 ed. JJReiske 1774 [ed. CJacoby 1885ff has ἔλασις]; Cornutus 28 p. 54, 11; Cass. Dio 8, 10, 7; Syntipas p. 23, 28; Cat. Cod. Astr. XII 157, 1; Hesychius; Etym. Gud. 454, 9) *coming, advent* of the first coming of Christ: ἔ. τοῦ δικαίου Ac 7: 52; ἔ. τοῦ κυρίου ἡμῶν Pol 6: 3; ἡ ἔ. τοῦ Χριστοῦ 1 Cl 17: 1.—Of the second advent of Christ (Act. Thom. 28) Lk 21: 7 D; 23: 42 D (in Irenaeus 1, 10 of both).—GDKilpatrick, JTS 46, '45, 136–45.*

ἐλεύσομαι s. ἔρχομαι.

ἐλεφάντινος, η, ον (Alcaeus+; Epict. 2, 19, 26; Dit., Syll.² 586; LXX, Joseph.) *made of ivory* σκεῦος *articles made of ivory* Rv 18: 12. Of a couch (cf. Appian, Liby. 32 §137=a chair for a king, Bell. Civ. 2, 106 §442; Jos., Bell. 7, 126.—Ant. 8, 140 Solomon's ivory throne) Hv 3, 1, 4. M-M.*

ἐλήλακα s. ἐλαύνω.

ἐλήλυθα s. ἔρχομαι.

ἐλθεῖν s. ἔρχομαι.

Ἐλιακίμ, ὁ indecl. (אֶלְיָקִים) *Eliakim* (cf. 4 Km 18: 18; 23: 34 al.—In Jos., Ant. 10, 82 Ἐλιάκ[ε]ιμος), in the genealogy of Jesus Mt 1: 13; Lk 3: 30, also 3: 23ff D.*

ἔλιγμα, ατος, τό (Soranus 155, 5; Athen.; Hesychius) *package, roll* σμύρνης καὶ ἀλόης J 19: 39 v.l., certainly false (for μίγμα).—S. GRudberg, Eranos 15, '15, 67.*

Ἐλιέζερ, ὁ indecl. (אֱלִיעֶזֶר) *Eliezer* (cf. Gen 15: 2; Ex 18: 4 al.; Philo), in the genealogy of Jesus Lk 3: 29.*

Ἐλιούδ, ὁ indecl. *Eliud,* in the genealogy of Jesus Mt 1: 14f; Lk 3: 23ff D.*

Ἐλισάβετ, ἡ indecl. (אֱלִישֶׁבַע; cf. EKönig, ET 21, '10, 185–7; LKöhler, AKaegi-Festschr. '19, 186.—Suppl. Epigr. Gr. VIII 202 [I BC/I AD, ossuary fr. Jerus.] Ἐλισά-βη) *Elizabeth* (cf. Ex 6: 23; Philo, Poster. Cai. 76), wife of Zacharias the priest, mother of John the Baptist Lk 1: 5, 7, 13, 24, 36, 40f, 57; GEb 1. According to a few witnesses also Lk 1: 46 (on this s. Harnack, SAB '00, 538ff=Studien I '31, 62ff; Zahn, Lk Exkurs III p. 745ff [older lit. here]; ENorden, D. Geburt d. Kindes '24, 76ff; RHarris, ET 41, '30, 266f; 42, '31, 188–90). Acc. to vs. 36 Mary, the mother of Jesus, was related to her.*

Ἐλισαιέ, ὁ indecl. (3 Km 19: 16f, 19; 4 Km 2–8; Sir 48: 12) 1 Cl 17: 1 and

Ἐλισαῖος, ου, ὁ (Ep. Arist. 47 al. and Jos., Ant. 8, 352–4; 9, 28 have Ἐλισαῖος) Lk 4: 27 *Elisha* (אֱלִישָׁע), the Hebrew prophet.*

ἐλίσσω fut. ἐλίξω, pass. ἐλιχθήσομαι (Hom.+; predom. poet., but also Philo Mech. 76, 8; Lucian.—Isishymn. v. And. 172; pap., LXX) *roll up* τὶ *someth.* ὡσεὶ περιβόλαιον ἐλίξεις αὐτούς *thou wilt roll them up like a*

cloak Hb 1: 12 (Ps 101: 27 v.l.). Of the heaven (cf. Suppl. Epigr. Gr. VII 14, 8 [I AD] Hymn to Apollo: οὐρανὸν διελίσσει; PGM 12, 241 ἡ γῆ ἐλίσσεται) ὡς βιβλίον ἐλισσόμενον *like a scroll that is rolled up* (Aeneas Tact. 1553 ἐλ. τὸ βιβλίον; Vit. Hes. p. 48, 8; PGM 36, 234 of rolling up an inscribed lead tablet) Rv 6: 14; cf. ἑλιχθή-σεται ὡς βιβλίον AP fgm. 5, p. 13, 10 (Is 34: 4). M-M.*

ἕλκος, ους, τό (Hom.+) *sore, abscess, ulcer* (so Thu., Theophr., Polyb., also Dit., Syll.³ 1168, 114; 1169, 38; LXX), also *wound* (Antig. Car. 36) Lk 16: 21; ἕ. κακὸν καὶ πονηρόν (cf. Dt 28: 35; Job 2: 7) *a foul and angry sore* Rv 16: 2. ἐβλασφήμησαν ἐκ τῶν ἑ. αὐτῶν *they blasphemed because of their sores* vs. 11. M-M. B. 304.*

ἑλκόω (trag.+, esp. in medical wr. [Hippocr.: CMG I 1 p. 49, 23; Galen: CMG V 4, 1, 1 p. 80, 13; Hobart 31f], also Aristeas Hist. in Euseb., Pr. Ev. 9, 25, 3) *cause sores, ulcers* pf. pass. ptc. εἱλκωμένος (on the reduplication s. Bl-D. §68; Rob. 364) *covered w. sores* (X., De Re Equ. 1, 4; 5, 1; Plut., Phoc. 2, 3; Artem. 1, 23; 28; 41) Lk 16: 20.*

ἑλκύω s. ἕλκω fut. and aor.

ἕλκω impf. εἷλκον; fut. ἑλκύσω; 1 aor. εἵλκυσα; for the forms w. -υ- s. Mlt.-H. 236; Bl-D. §101 p. 45 (Hom.+; inscr., pap., LXX, Joseph.) *drag, draw.*

1. trans.—a. lit. τὶ *someth.* a sword (Soph., Ant. 1233; Libanius, Or. 13 p. 73, 5 F. ξίφος) J 18: 10; *haul a net* 21: 6, 11; τινά (Diod. S. 34+35 fgm. 2, 14 τινὰ εἰς; Achilles Tat. 7, 15, 4 εἱλκόν με εἰς τὸ δεσμωτήριον; Jos., Bell. 1, 591 τινὰ εἰς.—Also Clearchus, fgm. 73; Diod. S. 14, 5, 3 ἕ. τινὰ ἐπὶ τὸν θάνατον) ἔξω τ. ἱεροῦ *drag someone out of the temple* Ac 21: 30; εἰς τ. ἀγορὰν ἐπὶ τ. ἄρχοντας 16: 19; εἰς κριτήρια *hale into court* Js 2: 6 (Herodas 5, 59 ἕ. τινὰ εἰς τὰς ἀνάγκας=to punishment). οἱ ἕλκοντες ἡμᾶς LJ 2: 3 is expanded by Dssm. w. εἰς τὰ κριτήρια; differently by others. Actually nothing need be supplied, since ἕ. τινά means *pull* or *tug someone back and forth, mistreat someone* (Libanius, Or. 58 p. 183, 20 F. ἕλκων κάπηλον; cf. Jos., Bell. 1, 338: εἷλκεν τοὺς ἔνδοθεν). Of stones ἐκ τοῦ βυθοῦ ἐλκομένων *which were dragged out of the deep* Hv 3, 2, 6; 3, 5, 2.

b. fig. of the pull on man's inner life (Pla., Phaedr. 238A; Aelian, Nat. An. 4, 13; Porphyr., Marc. 16 μόνη ἡ ἀρετὴ τ. ψυχὴν ἄνω ἕλκει καὶ πρὸς τὸ συγγενές; Jer 38: 3; SSol 1: 4; 4 Macc 14: 13; 15: 11; Jos., Ant. 15, 27) *draw, attract* J 6: 44. ἕλκ. πρός with acc. (Hierocles 25 p. 477 it is said of God ἑλκύσαι πρὸς τὴν ἀλήθειαν τοὺς ἀνθρώπους): πρὸς ἐμαυτόν 12: 32.

2. intr. *flow along* of a river ἦν ποταμὸς ἕλκων ἐκ δεξιῶν *a river flowed along on the right* B 11: 10 (cf. Da 7: 10 Theod.). M-M. B. 571.*

Ἑλλάς, άδος, ἡ *Greece* (Hes.+; inscr., 1 Macc 8: 9; Philo; Joseph.; Sib. Or.); in popular usage it could also designate the Rom. province officially known as Achaia (s. Ἀχαία; Paus. 7, 16) Ac 20: 2. M-M.*

ἐλλείπω (Hom. Hymns, trag.+; inscr., pap., En. 23, 2; Ep. Arist.; Philo; Jos., Ant. 17, 110, C. Ap. 2, 206) *leave off* ἀπό τινος *fr. someth.* (=perh. *leave out of consideration*) B 4: 9. μὴ ἐλλείπητε μηδενὶ ἑαυτῶν *do not fail, as far as you are concerned, in any respect* 21: 8. Abs. μὴ ἐλλείπητε *do not fail* 21: 2.*

ἔλλειψις, εως, ἡ (since Democr. 102 and Pla.; Philo) *failing* δίχα ἐλλείψεως *without failing* 1 Cl 20: 10.*

Ἕλλην, ηνος, ὁ *a Greek* (so Hdt.+)—1. a man of Greek language and culture (opp. βάρβαρος, like Thu. 1, 1, 2 et al.; Philo, Ebr. 193 al.; Jos., Ant. 4, 12 al.—UWilcken,

Hellenen u. Barbaren: NJklA 17, '06, 457-71; JJüthner, Hell. u. Bar. '23; HRiesenfeld, Con. Neot. 9, '44, 1ff) Ro 1: 14.

2. in the broader sense, all persons who came under the influence of Greek, i.e. pagan, culture.

a. *Gentile, pagan, heathen* (2 Macc 4: 36; 11: 2; 3 Macc 3: 8; 4 Macc 18: 20; Sib. Or. 5, 265; Phot., Bibl. 62, 8: 219 Jac. την θρησκείαν "Ελλην) J 7: 35; Ac 9: 29 v.l. (for 'Ελληνιστάς); 11: 20 (v.l. 'Ελληνιστάς); 16: 1, 3; 21: 28; 1 Cor 1: 22; Gal 2: 3; PK 2 p. 14, 1; 7; p. 15, 7; Dg 1; 3: 3; 5: 17. The expr. 'Ιουδαῖοι καὶ "Ελληνες, which clearly indicates Israel's advantages fr. the Jewish standpoint, embraces the whole human race Ac 14: 1; 18: 4; 19: 10, 17; 20: 21; Ro 1: 16; 2: 9f; 3: 9; 10: 12; 1 Cor 1: 24; 10: 32; 12: 13; Gal 3: 28; Col 3: 11 (Wilcken, Chrest. 55, 6 [III BC] παρὰ τῶν 'Ιουδαίων καὶ τῶν 'Ελλήνων does not mean to indicate that the Jews have any special privilege [despite the fact that 'I. comes before 'E.]. Here the expression is used in a pagan source. Cf. also Epict. 2, 9, 19 τί ὑποκρί-νῃ 'Ιουδαῖον ὢν "Ελλην=why do you play the part of a Jew, when you are actually a Greek?).

b. used of proselytes (cf. Jos., Bell. 7, 45) J 12: 20. οἱ σεβόμενοι "Ελληνες *God-fearing Gentiles* Ac 17: 4.—L Weniger, Jesus u. d. Griechen: NJklA 41, '18, 477-80; JLeipoldt, Jesu Verh. zu Griech. u. Juden '41. On the whole word-group: HWindisch, TW II 501-14. M-M., and esp. B. 1489.*

'Ελληνικός, ή, όν (Aeschyl., Hdt. +; inscr.; PWien Bosw. 7, 17; LXX; Ep. Arist. 38; Philo; Jos., Ant. 12, 240; 263) *Greek* Lk 23: 38 t.r.; ἐν τῇ 'Ε. (sc. γλώσσῃ) *in the Greek language* Rv 9: 11.*

'Ελληνίς, ίδος, ἡ (trag., Thu. +; inscr.; PGiess. 36, 10; 2 Macc 6: 8).

1. as adj.—**a.** *Greek* (opp. βάρβαρος) πόλις (Nicol. Dam.: 90 fgm. 136, 10 Jac.; Ael. Aristid. 24, 29 K.=44 p. 833 D.; Jos., Ant. 17, 320; 18, 377 al.) Dg 5: 4.—**b.** *Gentile* (cf. "Ελλην 2a) γυνή Ac 17: 12.

2. as subst. ἡ 'Ε. *Gentile woman* Mk 7: 26.—S. Συρο-φοινίκισσα and Χαναναῖος. M-M.*

'Ελληνιστής, οῦ, ὁ *a Hellenist,* a Greek-speaking Jew in contrast to one speaking a Semitic lang. (Chrysost., Hom. 14 on Ac 6: 1 and Hom. 21 on Ac 9: 29 ed. Montf. IX 111; 169) Ac 6: 1; 9: 29; 11: 20 v.l.—Zahn, Einl. I 41; 51; GPWetter, ARW 21, '22, 410ff; HJCadbury: Beginn. I 5, '33, 59-74; ECBlackman, ET 48, '37, 524f; CFDMoule, ET 70, '58/'59, 100-102; MSimon, St. Stephen and the Hellenists in the Primitive Church, '58.*

'Ελληνιστί adv. (X., An. 7, 6, 8; pap. [Mayser 457; PGiess. 36, 6]; Philo; Joseph.; loanw. in rabb.) *in the Greek language* (w. 'Εβραϊστί, 'Ρωμαϊστί; cf. Jos., Ant. 14, 191) J 19: 20. 'Ε. γινώσκειν *understand Greek* Ac 21: 37. Schürer III⁴ 140f.*

ἐλλογέω (this is the regular form [cf. Nägeli 48: exx. fr. inscr., pap.]; formations like ἐλλόγα Phlm 18 and ἐλ-λογᾶται Ro 5: 13 v.l. arose through confusion of the inflectional types -εῖν and -ᾶν [Bl-D. §90 w. app.; Mlt.-H. 196; 198; 307]) commercial t.t. *charge to someone's* (τινί) *account* (PRyl. 243, 11 [II AD]; BGU 140, 31f; PStrassb. 32 10 ἵνα οὕτως αὐτῷ ἐλλογηθῇ) Phlm 18. Sin οὐκ ἐλλο-γεῖται Ro 5: 13. M-M.*

ἐλλόγιμος, ον (Hdt. +) *to be taken into account,* hence —**1.** *included* ἐντεταγμένος καὶ ἐ. εἰς τ. ἀριθμὸν τῶν σωζομένων *enrolled and included in the number of those who are saved* 1 Cl 58: 2. μικροὶ καὶ ἐλλόγιμοι *small, but included* 57: 2.

2. *reputable, eminent* (Dit., Syll.³ 803, 8, Or. 56, 9; Philo, Mos. 1, 266) ἄνδρες ἐ. (Philostrat., Vi. Apoll. p. 50, 31; Herm. Wr. 12, 6; Celsus 1, 21) 44: 3. Superl. ἐλλογι-μώτατος *distinguished* ἄνδρες (in sg. Philostrat., Vi. Apoll. p. 106, 32; 112, 26) 62: 3.*

'Ελμαδάμ and v.l. 'Ελμωδάμ, ὁ indecl. *Elmadam,* in the genealogy of Jesus Lk 3: 28.*

ἑλόμενος s. αἱρέω.

ἐλπίζω Att. fut. ἐλπιῶ; 1 aor. ἤλπισα; pf. ἤλπικα (trag., Hdt. +; inscr., pap., LXX, En., Philo, Joseph.) *hope, hope for* (also *expect, foresee, fear,* e.g., punishment: Diod. S. 13, 43, 1; contempt: Chio, Ep. 9; sorrow: Procop. Soph., Ep. 140; a misfortune: Lucian, Dial. Deor. 25, 1, Gall. 25, end).

1. abs. (Philo, Det. Pot. Ins. 138 τὸ ἐλπίζειν) 2 Cor 8: 5; B 12: 7; pres. pass. ptc. ἐλπιζόμενα *what we hope for* (Polyaenus 3, 9, 11 τὰ ἐλπιζόμενα) Hb 11: 1.

2. w. indication of what is hoped for: in acc. (Is 38: 18; Wsd 2: 22) πάντα 1 Cor 13: 7. ὃ βλέπει τις Ro 8: 24; cf. vs. 25. W. aor. inf. foll. (Thu. 2, 80, 1; Agathias Hist. 3, 5 p. 243f LDind.; Philo, Migr. Abr. 195) παρ' ὧν ἐλπίζετε λαβεῖν *from whom you expect to receive again* Lk 6: 34; cf. 2 Cl 1: 2; Ro 15: 24; 1 Cor 16: 7; Phil 2: 19, 23; 1 Ti 3: 14; 2 J 12; 3 J 14; B 1: 3; Hs 8, 9, 4. W. perf. inf. 2 Cor 5: 11; B 17: 1. W. ὅτι foll. (Polyb. 3, 63, 7; Arrian, Alex. An. 1, 4, 7; POxy. 1672, 7 [c. 40 AD]; Philo, Leg. All. 3, 85) Lk 24: 21; Ac 24: 26; 2 Cor 1: 13; 13: 6; Phlm 22; Hs 8, 2, 9. W. acc. and pres. inf. Hm 12, 6, 4. W. the connotation of desire (Appian, Bell. Civ. 2, 1 §3 ἐ. περὶ ἀπάντων) ἤλπιζέν τι σημεῖον ἰδεῖν *he hoped to see a sign* Lk 23: 8. ἐλπίζει καταντῆσαι *hopes to attain* Ac 26: 7.

3. w. indication of the pers. or thing on whom (which) the hope is based *put one's hope in someone or someth.*: τινί *in someth.* (Thu. 3, 97, 2 τῇ τύχῃ) τῷ ὀνόματι Mt 12: 21; εἴς τι (Is 51: 5; Sir 2: 9): εἰς τ. οἰκοδομήν *put one's hope in the building* (the temple) B 16: 1. εἴς τινα *in someone* (Herodian 7, 10, 1; cf. Ps 118: 114): Moses J 5: 45. εἰς θεόν (Ps 144: 15; PIand. 11, 2; Sib. Or. 5, 284; cf. Jos., Bell. 6, 99) 1 Pt 3: 5. εἰς Χριστόν IPhld 11: 2; cf. 5: 2; εἴς τινα w. ὅτι foll. 2 Cor 1: 10. For this, ἔν τινι (Ps 55: 5 v.l.; Judg 9: 26 B; 4 Km 18: 5) 1 Cor 15: 19. For this ἐπί τινα: ἐπὶ τ. θεόν (Ps 41: 6, 12 al.; Philo) 1 Ti 5: 5; cf. 1 Cl 11: 1; 12: 7; B 6: 3; 19: 7; Hm 12, 5, 2. ἐπὶ κύριον 1 Cl 16: 16 (Ps 21: 9); 22: 8 (Ps 31: 10). ἐπὶ 'Ιησοῦν B 6: 9; 8: 5. ἐπί τι (Ps 51: 10; Synes., Ep. 58 p. 202D ἐπὶ τὴν ἐκκλησίαν ἤλπισε): ἐπὶ τὴν χάριν 1 Pt 1: 13. ἐπὶ τὸ ὄνομα θεοῦ 1 Cl 59: 3; B 16: 8. ἐπὶ τὸν σταυρόν 11: 8. For this, ἐπί τινι (pers.: Ps 7: 2; 15: 1 al.; thing: Appian, Maced. 9 §7 ἐπὶ τῷδε=on this account; Ps 12: 6; Is 26: 8; 42: 4) 1 Ti 4: 10; 6: 17; Ro 15: 12 (Is 11: 10); B 12: 2f. M-M.**

ἐλπίς, ίδος, ἡ (Hom. +; inscr., pap., LXX, En., Ep. Arist., Philo, Joseph., Test. 12 Patr.; loanw. in rabb.) *hope.*

1. gener. *hope, expectation, prospect* ἐπ' ἐλπίδι (for the spelling s. 2a below; Ro 8: 20) *in hope* (Ps.-Pla., Alc. 1 p. 105A ἐπὶ τίνι ἐλπίδι ζῇς; Eur., Herc. Fur. 804; X., Mem. 2, 1, 18; Diod. S. 13, 21, 7; Jos., Ant. 4, 36) 1 Cor 9: 10a. παρ' ἐλπίδα *contrary to* (all human) *expectation* (Aeneas Tact. 1020; Lycophron v. 535; Dionys. Hal. 6, 25; Philo, Mos. 1, 250; Jos., Bell. 3, 183, Vi. 380) Ro 4: 18. W. objective gen. (Diod. S. 16, 55, 4 τῆς εὐεργεσίας ἐλπίς; Appian, Celt. 1 §9 ἐλπὶς ἀναβιώσεως; Jos., Vi. 325 ἐ. κέρδους) ἐλπὶς τ. ἐργασίας *hope of gain* Ac 16: 19; μετανοίας Hs 6, 2, 4; 8, 7, 2; 8, 10, 2. W. gen. of the inf. (Dositheus 19, 6 ἐ. τοῦ δύνασθαι) τοῦ σώζεσθαι Ac 27:

20; τοῦ μετέχειν 1 Cor 9: 10b. ἐλπίδα ἔχειν (oft. in secular wr. and LXX) w. gen. of the inf. τοῦ μετανοῆσαι Hs 8, 6, 5; τῇ ἐ. ἐσώθημεν we are saved (or possess salvation) only in expectation (not yet in reality) Ro 8: 24 (Diod. S. 20, 40, 1 περιεβάλετο ταῖς ἐλπίσι μείζονα δυναστείαν=he was in hope of gaining control over a larger realm). ἡ ἐ. ἡμῶν βεβαία ὑπὲρ ὑμῶν our hope for you is secure (Paul hopes that the Cor. will hold out under oppression in the future as they have in the past) 2 Cor 1: 7.

2. esp. hope pertaining to supernatural beings and supernatural things, spoken of in God's promises.

a. without specif. ref. to the Christian hope ἐπ᾽ ἐλπίδι (for the spelling ἐφ᾽ ἐλπίδι s. Bl-D. §14 w. app.; Rob. 224 and cf. an inscr. fr. Asia Minor in Papers of the Amer. School of Classical Studies at Athens II, 1888, p. 89 l. 15 ἐπ᾽ ἐλπίδι and l. 26 ἐφ᾽ ἐλπίδος) in (the) hope (Diod. S. 13, 21, 7 ἐπ᾽ ἐλπίδι [σωτηρίας]) Ro 8: 20 (cf. Bl-D. §235, 2); cf. Tit 1: 2. ἐπ᾽ ἐλπίδι ἐπίστευσεν in hope he believed (in God) Ro 4: 18. The ἐπ᾽ ἐ. of Ac 2: 26 could also be understood in this way. But it is also poss. that in this quot. fr. Ps 15: 9 the OT mng. in safety (Judg 18: 7 B, 27 B; Hos 2: 20; Pr 1: 33) is correct, as 1 Cl 57: 7 (Pr 1: 33). Of the Jewish messianic hope Ac 23: 6 (ἐ. καὶ ἀνάστασις for ἐ. τῆς ἀν. [obj. gen] like 2 Macc 3: 29 ἐ. καὶ σωτηρία); 26: 6; 28: 20.

b. of Christian hope: abs. Ro 5: 4f; 12: 12; 15: 13; 1 Cor 13: 13 (on the triad: faith, hope, love s. on ἀγάπη I 1a); Hb 3: 6; 6: 11; 10: 23; 1 Pt 3: 15; ἐ. ἀγαθή (Pla., Phaedo 67c; X., Mem. 2, 1, 18 et al.; FCumont, Lux Perpetua '49 p. 401-5 with numerous reff., including some from the mystery religions [IG V 2 p. 63: 64/61 bc]) 2 Th 2: 16 (POtzen, ZNW 49, '58, 283-85); ἐ. κρείττων Hb 7: 19; ἐ. ζῶσα 1 Pt 1: 3. W. subj. gen. Phil 1: 20; ἐ. τῶν ἐκλεκτῶν 1 Cl 58: 2. W. obj. gen., which designates the obj. of the hope (Ps.-Callisth. 1, 18, 1 ἱλαρὸς ἐπὶ τῇ τοῦ τέκνου ἐλπίδι=glad because of the hope for the son) ἐπ᾽ ἐ. τῆς ἐπαγγελίας because of hope in the promise Ac 26: 6, cf. vs. 7; ἐ. ζωῆς αἰωνίου Tit 1: 2; 3: 7; cf. B 1: 4, 6; Hs 9, 26, 2; ἐ. τῆς δόξης τ. θεοῦ Ro 5: 2; cf. Col 1: 27; ἐ. σωτηρίας (cf. Aeneas Tact. l. 14; Lucian, Abdic. 31; Philo, Leg. ad Gai. 329; Jos., Bell. 3, 194) 1 Th 5: 8. ἐλπίδα δικαιοσύνης ἀπεκδεχόμεθα Gal 5: 5 is also obj. gen., since it is a blending of the two expressions 'we await righteousness' and 'we have hope of righteousness' (cf. Job 2: 9a προσδεχόμενος τὴν ἐλπίδα τῆς σωτηρίας μου); ἐ. τοῦ κυρίου ἡμῶν 1 Th 1: 3 prob. belongs here also: hope in our Lord. —The gen. can also give the basis for the hope: ἐ. τοῦ εὐαγγελίου hope that is based on the gospel Col 1: 23; ἐ. τῆς κλήσεως the hope that is given w. the calling Eph 1: 18; 4: 4; ἐ. τῆς πίστεως hope that faith affords B 4: 8; ὁ θεὸς τῆς ἐ. Ro 15: 13; ἐ. εἰς (Plut., Galba 19, 6; Achilles Tat. 6, 17, 5): ἐ. εἰς θεόν hope in God 1 Pt 1: 21; εἰς τ. Ἰησοῦν B 11: 11; ἐ. ἐν (αὐτῷ): Diod. S. 17, 26, 2): ἐν τῷ ὀνόματι αὐτοῦ Mt 12: 21 D, t.r.; ἐπὶ λίθον ἡ ἐ.; is (our) hope based on a stone? (w. ref. to Is 28: 16) B 6: 3. ἔχειν ἐλπίδα Ro 15: 4; 2 Cor 3: 12; ἐ. μὴ ἔχοντες (Diod. S. 21, 12, 1 μηδεμίαν ἔχειν ἐλπίδα σωτηρίας) Eph 2: 12; 1 Th 4: 13; Hv 3, 11, 3; s 9, 14, 3; οὐκ ἔχουσιν ἐλπίδα (Wsd 3: 18) Hv 1, 1, 9. W. ἐπί τινι in someone 1 J 3: 3 (cf. Appian, Bell. Civ. 3, 86 §354 ἐφ᾽ ἑνί; Lucian, Somn. 2; Ps 61: 8; Is 26: 3f); likew. εἴς τινα (Thu. 3, 14, 1.—Appian, Liby. 51 §223 ἐλπίδα τῆς σωτηρίας ἔχειν ἔν τινι=place a hope of safety in someone) Ac 24: 15; πρός τινα ibid. v.l. The obj. of the hope follows in the aor. inf. 2 Cor 10: 15; in the acc. w. inf. Ac 24: 15; w. ὅτι Ro 8: 20 v.l.; Phil 1: 20; w. διότι (q.v. 4) Ro 8: 20.

3. the one in whom one places his hope can be called

ἐλπίς (object of) hope (Thu. 3, 57, 4 ὑμεῖς, ὦ Λακεδαιμόνιοι, ἡ μόνη ἐλπίς; Plut., Mor. 169c; Oenom. in Eus., Pr. Ev. 5, 23, 5: in the Persian Wars, for the Athenians there was σωτηρίας ἐλπὶς μόνος ὁ θεός; IG III 1311; Jer 17: 7) of a church 1 Th 2: 19; of Christ, our hope 1 Ti 1: 1; cf. Col 1: 27; IEph 21: 2; IPhld 11: 2; IMg 11; ITr inscr.; 2: 2; Pol 8: 1.

4. hope, something hoped for (Vi. Aesopi I c. 8 ἀπὸ θεῶν λήμψεσθαι ἐλπίδας) ἐ. βλεπομένη οὐκ ἔστιν ἐ. a thing hoped for, when it is seen, is no longer hoped for Ro 8: 24. διὰ τ. ἐλπίδα τὴν ἀποκειμένην ὑμῖν ἐν τ. οὐρανοῖς because of what you hope for, which is stored up for you in the heavens Col 1: 5; προσδεχόμενοι τ. μακαρίαν ἐ. waiting for the blessed hope Tit 2: 13 (cf. 2 Macc 7: 14 τὰς ὑπὸ τοῦ θεοῦ προσδοκᾶν ἐλπίδας and Aristotle, Nicom. Ethics 1, 9, 10 οἱ δὲ λεγόμενοι διὰ τὴν ἐλπίδα μακαρίζονται); ἡ προκειμένη ἐ. Hb 6: 18.— PVolz, D. Eschatol. der jüd. Gemeinde '34, 91ff; JdeGuibert, Sur l'emploi d'ἐλπίς et ses synonymes dans le NT: Rech de Sc rel 4, '13, 565-96; APott, D. Hoffen im NT '15; TSLiefeld, Lutheran Quarterly 6, '54, 30-41; WGrossouw, l'espérance dans le NT: RB 61, '54, 508-32; RBultmann and KHRengstorf, TW II 515-31. M-M. B. 1164. **

Ἐλύμας, α, ὁ Elymas (in Diod. S. as name of a Libyan king) a magician of Cyprus Ac 13: 8, who was also called Barjesus acc. to vs. 6. Ac obviously considers the two names to be linguistically equiv. to each other; it is hardly correct to assume, w. some, that vs. 8 means to say that the word Elymas=μάγος. Those (e.g. Wendt) who hold this opinion think of the Arab. verb 'alima=recognize, gain insight into someth., whence 'alîm=magician, one who tries to see into the future. Dalman (Gramm.² 162) finds in Ἐ. Ἐλυμαῖος=Ἐλαμίτης; Grimme interprets it as 'astrologer', Burkitt as ὁ λοιμός pestilence (s. λοιμός II), Harris, Zahn, Clemen and Wlh. prefer the rdg. Ἕτοιμας, from D, and identify the magician w. the sorcerer Ἄτομος in Jos., Ant. 20, 142. Cf. RHarris, Exp. '02, I 189ff; FCBurkitt, JTS 4, '03, 127ff; CClemen, Paulus '04, I 222f; ThZahn, NKZ 15, '04, 195ff, D. Urausgabe der AG des Luk. '16, 149f; 350ff; HGrimme, OLZ 12, '09, 207ff; Wlh., Kritische Analyse der AG '14, 24; EHaenchen, AG '56 on Ac 13: 8. M-M.*

ἐλωΐ (אֱלָהִי) Aram. for ἠλί my God Mt 27: 46 v.l.; Mk 15: 34. Cf. EKautzsch, Gramm. d. Bibl.-Aram. 1884, 11; Wlh. on Mk; Dalman, Jesus 184-7; FWDanker, ZNW 61, '70, 52f (lit.). M-M.*

ἔμαθον s. μανθάνω.

ἐμαυτοῦ, ῆς reflexive pron. of the first pers. (on the origin and use of this word, found also in inscr., pap., LXX, Jos., Vi. 361, s. Kühner-Bl. I 596ff. Cf. also Bl-D. §283; Rob. 687-90) in gen., dat., acc. myself.

1. as possessive gen. w. a noun τὸ ἐμαυτοῦ σύμφορον my own advantage (opp. τὸ τῶν πολλῶν) 1 Cor 10: 33.

2. w. a verb ἐμφανίσω ἐμαυτόν J 14: 21. οὐδὲ ἐμαυτὸν ἠξίωσα I did not consider myself worthy Lk 7: 7. συγχαίρω ἐμαυτῷ I rejoice with (=congratulate) myself B 1: 3. δοξάσω ἐμαυτόν J 8: 54. ἁγιάζω ἐμαυτόν 17: 19. μετρῶ ἐμαυτόν ITr 4: 1. ἥγημαι ἐμαυτὸν μακάριον Ac 26: 2. ἔδοξα ἐμαυτῷ (Aristoph., Vesp. 1265; Demosth. 18, 225) I once believed vs. 9; σύνοιδα τι ἐμαυτῷ I am aware of someth. 1 Cor 4: 4; cf. B 1: 4. πᾶσιν ἐμαυτὸν ἐδούλωσα I made myself a slave to all 1 Cor 9: 19.

3. freq. used w. prep. ἀπ᾽ ἐμαυτοῦ of my own accord, on my own authority J 5: 30; 7: 17, 28; 8: 28, 42; 14: 10; of my own free will 10: 18. ἐξ ἐμαυτοῦ on my own authority

12: 49. εἰς ἐμαυτόν for εἰς ἐμέ 1 Cor 4: 6. ἐν ἐμαυτῷ to myself Hv 1, 2, 1; 3, 1, 5; 4, 1, 4. περὶ ἐμαυτοῦ J 8: 14, 18; Ac 24: 10. πρὸς ἐμαυτόν J 12: 32; 14: 3; with me (Aristoph., Ran. 53) Phlm 13. ὑπὲρ ἐμαυτοῦ 2 Cor 12: 5. ὑπ' ἐμαυτόν under my authority Mt 8: 9; Lk 7: 8. Referring back to the subj. of the governing clause θέλω πάντας ἀνθρώπους εἶναι ὡς καὶ ἐμαυτόν I wish that everyone were as I am 1 Cor 7: 7. M-M.

ἐμβαίνω 2 aor. ἐνέβην, ptc. ἐμβάς (Hom.+; inscr., pap., LXX, Joseph.) go in, step in a pool (cf. Jos., Ant. 5, 18) J 5: 4. Get into a ship, embark (Ael. Aristid. 46 p. 228 D.; Wilcken, Chrest. 1 II, 18 [III BC] εἰς ναῦς; Jos., Vi. 164; 304) εἰς πλοῖον (X., An. 1, 4, 7; 1 Macc 15: 37) Mt 8: 23; 9: 1; 13: 2; 14: 22; 15: 39; Mk 4: 1; 5: 18; 6: 45; 8: 10 (cf. vs. 13, where εἰς [τὸ] πλοῖον is to be supplied, and is read by D and t.r.—Similar expansion Dio Chrys. 2, 22); Lk 8: 22 (v.l. ἀνέβη 𝔓⁷⁵ et al.), 37; cf. 5: 3; J 6: 17; 21: 3; Ac 21: 6. εἰς τὰ πλοιάρια J 6: 24 (X., An. 1, 3, 17 εἰς τὰ πλοῖα). M-M.*

ἐμβάλλω 2 aor. ἐνέβαλον, inf. ἐμβαλεῖν (Hom.+; inscr., pap., LXX; Ep. Arist. 117; Philo, Joseph., Test. 12 Patr.) throw (in, into) τινά someone εἰς τὴν γέενναν Lk 12: 5 (UPZ 70, 8 [152/1 BC] ἐνβέβληκαν [sc. οἱ θεοί] ὑμᾶς εἰς ὕλην μεγάλην. But ἐ. can also mean send somewhere: PPetr. II 41, 2 [III BC]; BGU 1209, 14 [I BC]; Jos., C. Ap. 1, 257).—Put or set (in, into) (Didymus [I BC/I AD] ed. MSchmidt [1854] p. 258, 58; Leo 1, 10; Dit., Syll.³ 1170, 16 μέλι ἐ. εἰς τὸ γάλα) λίθον εἰς τὰ θεμέλια set a stone into the foundations B 6: 2 (Is 28: 16). καρδίας σαρκίνας 6: 14. Pass. be set εἰς τὸν τόπον in the place Hs 9, 6, 5f. M-M.*

ἐμβαπτίζω (Nicander [II BC] in Athen. 4, 11 p. 133D; Plut., Sulla 21, 8) dip (in, into). Mid. dip for oneself (s. ἐμβάπτω) Mk 14: 20 D.*

ἐμβάπτω 1 aor. ἐνέβαψα (Aristoph., X.+) dip (in, into) τὶ ἔν τινι Mt 26: 23; cf. J 13: 26b 𝔓⁶⁶ et al. Mid. dip for oneself (Aristoph. in Athen. 9 p. 367B) abs. (sc. the hand, or what the hand holds) Mk 14: 20 (cf. Athen. 6 p. 345E).*

ἐμβατεύω (Aeschyl.+; inscr.; pap.; LXX) is found in our lit. only Col 2: 18 ἃ ἑόρακεν ἐμβατεύων, a passage whose interpr. is much disputed. It has the foll. mngs.:
1. set foot upon, enter, visit (since Aeschyl, Pers. 449; Jos., Ant. 2, 265; 1 Macc 12: 25; 13: 20 al.).
2. come into possession of (Eur., Demosth., pap.), even by force (Jos 19: 49, 51).
3. enter into a subj., to investigate it closely, go into detail (2 Macc 2: 30; Philo, Plant. 80 Wendl. v.l.), hence in Col 2: 18 perh. entering at length upon the tale of what he has seen in a vision (ADNock, JBL 52, '33, 132).
4. Three inscr. of Asia Minor [II AD], which refer to the Apollo of Klaros (the wording in question is found in MDibelius, D. Isisweihe bei Apuleius=SAHeidelberg '17, 4 p. 33f; one of these inscr. also in Dit., Or. 530; cf. l. 15), show that ἐ. was a t.t. of the mystery religions. Then perh. who enters (the sanctuary) which he saw (in ecstasy) (cf. also Clemen 340f) or taking his stand on what he has seen in the mysteries (M-M). AFridrichsen, ZNW 21, '22, 135-7 connects the words w. what follows: puffed up without reason by what he saw when he was initiated.— Field, Notes 197f; SEitrem, Studia Theologica 2, '48, 90-4; SLyonnet, Col 2: 18 et les mystères de Apollon Clarien, Biblica 43, '62, 417-35: 'investigate, examine thoroughly.'—HPreisker, TW II 531-3. The conviction that the text must be corrupt led to var. conjectures (their history in RHarris, Sidelights on NT Research '09, 198f). M-M.*

ἐμβιβάζω 1 aor. ἐνεβίβασα (Thu.+; inscr., pap., LXX; Jos., Vi. 168) put in τινὰ εἴς τι someone (into) something εἰς πλοῖον put someone on board ship Ac 27: 6. M-M.*

ἐμβλέπω 1 aor. ἐνέβλεψα (Soph.+; pap., LXX, Philo, Joseph.).
1. look at, fix one's gaze upon τινί (Pla., Rep. 10 p. 608D; Polyb. 15, 28, 3; Sir 42: 12; Jos., Bell. 3, 385; 7, 341) someone Mk 10: 21, 27; 14: 67; Lk 20: 17; 22: 61; J 1: 36, 42; Hv 3, 8, 2 (most of these pass. read: ἐμβλέψας αὐτῷ or αὐτοῖς λέγει or εἶπεν; cf. X., Cyr. 1, 3, 2 ἐμβλέπων αὐτῷ ἔλεγεν; Syntipas p. 106, 10). ἐμβλέπε τοῖς λοιποῖς look at the rest Hs 9, 2, 7. εἴς τι look at someth. (Ps.-Pla., Alc. 1 p. 132E; LXX) Mt 6: 26, if ἐ. is to be taken literally here (s. 2 below); Ac 1: 11 v.l.; MPol 9: 2. Abs. (X., Mem. 3, 11, 10; Herodas 5, 40; Bel 40 Theod.) Mt 19: 26 (cf. Job 2: 10); B 5: 10. Abs. also Ac 22: 11, if the rdg. οὐκ ἐνέβλεπον is tenable. The v.l. οὐδὲν ἔβλεπον has 9: 8 in its favor, as well as the fact that the verbs ἐμβλ. and βλ. are not infreq. interchanged in the mss. (cf. Ac 1: 11; Sir 51: 7), and the observation that ἐμβλ. 22: 11 would have to mean be able to see; the latter mng. cannot be established beyond all doubt by ἐνέβλεπεν τηλαυγῶς ἅπαντα Mk 8: 25, since for this pass. he could see everything plainly is no more likely than he had a clear view of everything (on the acc. cf. Herodas 6, 44; Anth. Pal. 11, 3; Judg 16: 27; Sib. Or. 7, 124).
2. fig. look at in a spiritual sense, consider εἴς τι (PSI 542, 16 [III BC]; UPZ 162 III, 7 [117 BC]; PTebt. 28, 15 [114 BC]; Is 51: 1f; Sir 2: 10 al.) ἐ. τοῖς ὄμμασιν τῆς ψυχῆς εἰς τὸ μακρόθυμον αὐτοῦ βούλημα 1 Cl 19: 3 (Philo, Sobr. 3 τὸ ψυχῆς ὄμμα...ἐμβλέπον). So perh. also Mt 6: 26 (s. 1 above). M-M.*

ἐμβριθής, ές (Hdt.+; BGU 1769, 4 [I BC]; Philo) dignified, serious (Philostrat., Vi. Soph. 2, 14; Damasc., Vi. Isid. 16) ἐμβριθεῖ τῷ προσώπῳ w. a serious face MPol 9: 2 (Himerius, Or. 48 [=Or. 14], 13 πρόσωπον ἐμβριθές).*

ἐμβριμάομαι, also ἐμβριμόομαι Mk 14: 5 v.l.; J 11: 33 v.l., 38 v.l. Cf. Bl-D. §90; Mlt.-H. 198; 201. 1 aor. ἐνεβριμησάμην; pass. ἐνεβριμήθην (Aeschyl.+ in the sense 'snort'. As an expr. of anger and displeasure in Lucian, Necyomant. 20; Ps.-Libanius, Declam. 40 Förster VII p. 336; Aq. Ps 7: 12; Sym. Is 17: 13; cf. LXX La 2: 6 ἐμβριμήματι ὀργῆς) w. dat. of the pers. scold, censure (Da 11: 30) Mk 14: 5; warn sternly 1: 43 (cf. KLake, HTR 16, '23, 197f); Mt 9: 30. ἐν ἑαυτῷ be deeply moved J 11: 38 (ἐβριμήσατο 𝔓⁷⁵); for this τῷ πνεύματι vs. 33 (on the apparent harshness of expression: MBlack, An Aramaic Approach³, '67, 240-43). ἐμβρειμ[ησάμενος] εἶπεν α[ὐτοῖς] he said to them indignantly UGosp 51f=AHuck, Synopse⁹ '36, p. 162 n. (HJCadbury et al., Gospel Parallels '49, p. 145 n.; KAland, Synopsis Quattuor Evangel., '64 p. 345).— CBonner, Traces of Thaumaturgic Technique in the Miracles: HTR 20, '27, 171-81; EBevan, JTS 33, '32, 186-8. M-M.*

ἐμβροχή, ῆς, ἡ fig. as medical t.t. wet application, cold compress (Plut., Mor. p. 42c; Soranus p. 36, 21; Galen: CMG V 9, 1 p. 375, 17; Oribasius, Ecl. 89, 7: CMG VI 2, 2 p. 268, 1) τοὺς παροξυσμοὺς ἐμβροχαῖς παῦε quiet the attacks of fever w. cold compresses IPol 2: 1.*

ἐμέω 1 aor. ἤμεσα (Hom.+; Dit., Syll.³ 1169, 126; Is 19: 14) spit out fig. (Herm. Wr. 7, 1a) τινὰ ἐκ τοῦ στόματος someone from one's mouth like lukewarm water (cf. Test. Ash. 7: 2) Rv 3: 16 (lit. 'vomit'; contrasted w. πτύω=spit out: Artem. 1, 33 p. 35, 8). M-M. B. 265.*

ἐμμαίνομαι *be enraged* τινί *against someone* (Jos., Ant. 17, 174) περισσῶς ἐμμαινόμενος αὐτοῖς *being furiously enraged at them* Ac 26: 11. M-M.*

Ἐμμανουήλ, ὁ indecl. (עִמָּנוּ אֵל Is 7: 14; 8: 8. Greek Christians spell it Ἐμμανουήλ: Recueil des inscriptions grecques chrétiennes d'Egypte, ed. GLefebvre '07, 214; 222; POxy. 1162, 14 [IV AD]; PUps. 8 verso] *Emmanuel.* In a quot. of Is 7: 14 applied to Jesus Mt 1: 23 and defined as μεθ' ἡμῶν ὁ θεός.—HWildberger, Jesaja I, '72, 263 (lit.).*

Ἐμμαοῦς, ἡ *Emmaus,* a village (κώμη) in Judaea 60 stades (6¾ mi., 11½ km.) fr. Jerusalem Lk 24: 13. The site cannot be determined w. certainty. Three are proposed: 1. The old Emmaus of Maccabaean times, not infreq. mentioned by Joseph. (Niese edition, index), later Nicopolis, and now 'Amwâs; so Eusebius-Jerome, Onomastikon p. 90 Kl.; JBoehmer (Studierstube 6, '08, 285-9; ET 20, '09, 186-9; 429); Dalman (Orte³ 240ff); LPirot (Dict. de la Bible, Suppl. II '34, 1049-63); EFFBishop, ET 55, '43/'44, 152f, et al.; CKopp, The Holy Places of the Gospels, transl. RWalls, '63, 396-400. It is located rather far fr. Jerusalem for the 60 stades of vs. 13; but F-MAbel (RB 34, '25, 347-67) prefers to take the v.l. 160 stades as the original.—2. Since the middle ages some have thought of present-day el-Kubêbe (Baedeker, Plummer, Zahn et al., later PViaud, Qoubeibeh Emm. évangélique '30 [against this HVincent, RB 40, '31, 57-91]; AdeGuglielmo, CBQ 3, '41, 293-301).—3. The military colony of Vespasian, about 34 stades west of Jerusalem, called Ἀμμαοῦς in Jos. (Bell. 7, 217, where a v.l. has ἑξήκοντα for τριάκοντα) and presumably identical w. present-day Kalōniye (Buhl 166; 186; Schürer I⁴ 640, 142; Wlh. et al.). Cf. also M-JLagrange, Luc '21, 617ff; HVincent and F-MAbel, Emmaüs, sa Basilique et son Histoire '32.*

ἐμμένω 1 aor. ἐνέμεινα (Aeschyl., Hdt.+; inscr., pap., LXX, En., Philo, Joseph.) *stay* or *remain* (*in*).
   1. of place w. ἐν (Thu. 2, 23, 3; X., An. 4, 7, 16)—a. lit. (PTebt. 230 descr. [II BC] ἐν καπηλείῳ ἐν ἰδίῳ μισθώματι Ac 28: 30.—b. fig. αἱ πονηρίαι αὐτῶν ἐν τ. καρδίαις ἐμμένουσι Hv 3, 6, 3.
   2. *persevere in, stand by* τινί *someth.* (Attic wr., also Diod. S. 15, 19, 4; Plut., Ages. 23, 5; Dit., Syll.³1219, 20 [III BC]; POxy. 138, 36; Sir 11: 21; 1 Macc 10: 26; Philo, Congr. Erud. Gr. 125; Jos., C. Ap. 2, 257) τῇ ἁπλότητι Hv 3, 1, 9; ταῖς πράξεσιν s 8, 7, 3. τῇ πίστει (Jos., Ant. 19, 247, Vi. 34) Ac 14: 22; Hs 8, 9, 1. πᾶσιν τοῖς γεγραμμένοις ἐν τῷ βιβλίῳ *abide by everything written in the book* Gal 3: 10 (Dt 27: 26 underlies this. But the change of [ἐν] πᾶσι τοῖς λόγοις τ. νόμου there into πᾶσιν τ. γεγραμμ. ἐν τ. β. here seems to have been caused by the infl. [prob. unconscious] of a common legal formula of the official style, which uses ἐμμ. followed by the dat. of a ptc., mostly in pl., w. or without ἐν; s. Dssm., NB 76f [BS 248f]; ABerger, D. Strafklauseln in den Pap.-urkunden '11, 3f; OEger, ZNW 18, '18, 94.—The legal formula also influences religious language in Alex. Aphr., Fat. 17, II 2 p. 188, 15 ἐμμένειν τοῖς ὑπὸ τῶν θεῶν προαγορευομένοις). For this ἔν τινι (Thu. 4, 118, 14; Polyb. 3, 70, 4 ἐν τ. πίστει; Sir 6: 20) ἐν τ. διαθήκῃ μου Hb 8: 9 (Jer 38: 32); ἐν τοῖς ἔργοις Hm 4, 1, 9. ἐπί τινι (Is 30: 18 v.l.): ἐφ' οἷς ἐπιστεύσαμεν *remain true to the things we have believed* 2 Cl 15: 3. Abs. (En. 5, 4; Sib. Or. 5, 524) *persevere, stand firm* Hv 2, 2, 7; 2, 3, 2. M-M.*

ἐμμέσω is read by Tdf.⁷, BWeiss Rv 1: 13; 2: 1; 4: 6; 5: 6; 6: 6; 22: 2 for ἐν μέσῳ. M-M.

Ἐμμώρ, ὁ indecl. (חֲמוֹר) (LXX.—Theodot. [II BC] in Euseb., Pr. Ev. 9, 22, 2 and Philo, Migr. Abr. 224 Ἐμώρ.—In Jos., Ant. 1, 337 Ἔμμωρος, ου) *Hamor,* from whose sons (Test. Levi 5: 4; 6: 3), living near Shechem, Abraham bought a burial-place (Josh 24: 32 Aq., Sym., cf. Gen 33: 19; 34: 2) Ac 7: 16.*

ἐμνήσθην s. μιμνήσκομαι.

ἐμός, ἡ, όν possess. pron. (Hom.+; LXX) *my, mine* (Bl-D. §285 w. app.; Rob. 684; 770).
   1. as adj.—a. attrib., often without special emphasis.
   α. for the possess. gen., where μου could be used in nearly all cases Mt 18: 20; J 3: 29; 10: 27; 15: 11; Ro 10: 1. With emphasis τῇ ἐμῇ χειρί w. *my own hand* (cf. PSI 223, 6 ὁλόγραφον χειρὶ ἐμῇ) 1 Cor 16: 21; Gal 6: 11; Col 4: 18; 2 Th 3: 17; Phlm 19. ὁ ἐμὸς καιρός *my time*=the time when I am to be fully revealed J 7: 6, 8. ἡ ἡμέρα ἡ ἐμή 8: 56 and sim.—IRo 7: 2; 9: 3; Hs 5, 3, 3.
   β. for the obj. gen. (Aeschyl., Pers. 700 τὴν ἐμὴν αἰδῶ respect for me; X., Cyr. 3, 1, 28; 8, 3, 32; Antipho 5, 41; Jos., Ant. 1, 100) εἰς τὴν ἐμὴν ἀνάμνησιν *in memory of me* (but s. PSchorlemmer, Die Hochkirche '25, nos. 4; 5; ELohmeyer, JBL 56, '37, 244f) 1 Cor 11: 24f; Lk 22: 19. πίστις ἐμή *faith in me* PK 3 p. 15, 21.
   b. pred. J 7: 16; 14: 24; 16: 15. οὐκ ἔστιν ἐμὸν τοῦτο δοῦναι *it is not for me to give* Mt 20: 23; Mk 10: 40 (Pla., Leg. 2 p. 664B ἐμὸν ἂν εἴη λέγειν; Lucian, Jupp. Conf. 10 οὐκ ἐμὸν τοῦτο; Jos., Ant. 2, 335 σόν ἐστι ἐκπορίζειν).
   2. as noun τὸ ἐμόν *my property* (cf. Jos., Ant. 18, 199) Mt 25: 27; J 16: 14f. For this τὰ ἐμά (cf. Phalaris, Ep. 16; Jos., Ant. 13, 57) Mt 20: 15 (perh. *on my own premises* WHPHatch, ATR 26, '44, 250-3); Lk 15: 31 (Ps.-Callisth. 1, 38, 5 τὰ σὰ ἡμέτερα γενήσ.); J 17: 10.—οἱ ἐμοί (Ael. Aristid. 50, 5 K.=26 p. 503 D.; Sb 1911 [inscr.]; POsl. 25, 10 [217 AD]; Jos., Vi. 291) Rv 13: 14 v.l.—GDKilpatrick, The Poss. Pron. in the NT: JTS 42, '41, 184-6. M-M.

ἐμπαιγμονή, ῆς, ἡ (hapax legomenon) *mocking* ἐλεύσονται ἐν ἐ. ἐμπαῖκται *mockers will come w. their mocking* 2 Pt 3: 3.*

ἐμπαιγμός, οῦ, ὁ (Herodian, Gr. I 166, 7; II 119, 6; PsSol 2, 11) *scorn, mocking* (so Ezk 22: 4; Sir 27: 28; Wsd 12: 25) or *derisive torture* (2 Macc 7: 7, of an esp. painful kind) w. μάστιγες as experienced by the martyrs Hb 11: 36. M-M.*

ἐμπαίζω fut. ἐμπαίξω; 1 aor. ἐνέπαιξα; 1 aor. pass. ἐνεπαίχθην; 1 fut. ἐμπαιχθήσομαι (trag.+; pap., LXX, Anz 288).
   1. *ridicule, make fun of, mock* (in word and deed) τινί *someone* (Hdt. 4, 134; Epict. 1, 4, 10; oft. LXX) Mt 27: 29, 31; Mk 10: 34; 15: 20; Lk 14: 29; 22: 63; 23: 36. Abs. Mt 20: 19; 27: 41; Mk 15: 31; Lk 23: 11. Pass. (2 Macc 7: 10) 18: 32.—For lit. on the mocking of Jesus s. on στέφανος 1.
   2. *deceive, trick, make a fool of* (Anth. Pal. 10, 56, 2 τοῖς ἐμπαιζομένοις ἀνδράσι ταῦτα λέγω. Cf. Vett. Val. p. 16, 14; also prob. Epict. 2, 7, 9; 2, 19, 28; 4, 1, 134; Vi. Aesopi W. c. 129; Jer 10: 15) Mt 2: 16. M-M.*

ἐμπαίκτης, ου, ὁ (Is 3: 4) *mocker* Jd 18; 2 Pt 3: 3.*

ἐμπέμπω *send* (*in*) Lk 19: 14 D.*

ἐμπεπλησμένος s. ἐμπίμπλημι.

ἐμπεριέχω (Aristot., Theophr. et al.; Jos., Ant. 14, 422) *embrace* of God ὁ τὰ πάντα ἐμπεριέχων *he who embraces all things* 1 Cl 28: 4 (Herm. Wr. fgm. 26 p. 542 Sc. of God: πάντα ἐμπεριέχει. Cf. Knopf, Hdb. ad loc.).*

ἐμπεριπατέω (Plut., Lucian, Achilles Tat., pap., LXX, Philo, Joseph.) *walk about, move ἐν αὐτοῖς among them* (w. ἐνοικεῖν) 2 Cor 6: 16 (Lev 26: 12).*

ἐμπερίτομος, ον (in a state of being) *circumcised* B 9: 6 v.l. (found elsewh. only in Ps.-Clem., Hom. p. 4, 22 Lag., and Philostorg., H.E. 3, 4).*

ἐμπί(μ)πλημι alternate form ἐμπι(μ)πλάω Ac 14: 17; impf. pass. 3 sg. ἐνεπίμπλατο MPol 12: 1; 1 aor. ἐνέπλησα; pf. pass. ἐμπέπλησμαι, ptc. ἐμπεπλησμένος; 1 aor. pass. ἐνεπλήσθην; Bl-D. §93; 101, p. 48; Mlt.-H. 205; 384 (Hom.+; inscr., pap., LXX, Philo, Joseph., Test. 12 Patr.).

1. *fill* ὅλην τὴν πέτραν *cover the whole rock* Hs 9, 4, 2 (cf. Ezk 35: 8). Fig. (cf. Himerius, Or. 47 [=Or. 3], 4 μουσικῆς ἐμπ.= fill with song; Is 29: 19; Jer 15: 17; Sir 4: 12) τινά or τί τινος *someone* or *someth. w. someth.* (Pla., 7th Letter p. 351A πάντα κακῶν ἐμπεπλήκασιν; Jos., Ant. 3, 99) Ac 14: 17. Pass. w. gen. (Socrat., Ep. 13, 1; Appian, Bell. Civ. 2, 77 §324 μετανοίας; Heliod. 7, 27, 4 ὀργῆς; Jos., Ant. 5, 146 ὕβρεως) ἐ. θάρσους καὶ χαρᾶς MPol 12: 1 (Diod. S. 20, 8, 6 ἐνέπλησε τὴν δύναμιν θάρσους= he filled the army w. courage). πεινῶντας ἐνέπλησεν ἀγαθῶν (cf. Ps 106: 9 ψυχὴν πεινῶσαν ἐνέπλησεν ἀγαθῶν; Jer 38: 25.—Eutecnius 4 p. 41, 26 of Dionysus: σύμπασαν γῆν ἐμπιπλάντα τ. ἀγαθῶν; Appian, Hann. 60 p. 251 ἄνδρας ἐμπλήσας κακῶν= overwhelm with evils) *he has filled the hungry w. good things* Lk 1: 53 leads over to

2. *satisfy* (Diod. S. 5, 39, 4 ἀπὸ λαχάνων ἐμπίμπλανται; oft. LXX; Jos., Ant. 4, 234 al.) τινά τινος *someone w. someth.* Ac 14: 17; ἐ. τὴν ἑαυτοῦ ψυχήν *satisfy oneself* Hs 5, 3, 7. Abs. (Dio Chrys. 57[74], 11; Appian, Bell. Civ. 2, 64 §268) ὡς ἐνεπλήσθησαν *when they had eaten their fill* J 6: 12. μετὰ τὸ ἐμπλησθῆναι D 10: 1. οἱ ἐμπεπλησμένοι *those who have plenty to eat* Lk 6: 25. Cf. B 3: 5 v.l. (Funk; Is 58: 10).

3. ἐμπλησθῆναί τινος *have one's fill of someth.* in the sense *enjoy someth.* (cf. 'looking one's fill' Od. 11, 451; Socrat., Ep. 27, 5; Sus 32; Philo, Deus Imm. 151) ὑμῶν *your company* Ro 15: 24. M-M.*

ἐμπί(μ)πρημι 1 aor. ἐνέπρησα (Hdt.+; inscr., pap., LXX, Philo, Joseph.) Bl-D. §93; 101 p. 48; Mlt.-H. 207; *set on fire, burn* πόλιν (Dit., Or. 8, 11; Judg 18: 27; 2 Macc 8: 6; Philo, Aet. M. 20; Jos., Bell. 5, 411) Mt 22: 7 (KHRengstorf, D. Stadt der Mörder [Mt 22: 7], Beih. ZNW 26, '60, 106-29). ναόν (Appian, Celt. 6 §2; Jos., Bell. 5, 405) GP 7: 26. W. another mng. Ac 28: 6 v.l.; s. πίμπρημι. M-M.*

ἐμπίπτω fut. ἐμπεσοῦμαι; 2 aor. ἐνέπεσον (Hom.+; inscr., pap., LXX; En. 15, 11; Ep. Arist. 161; Joseph.; Test. 12 Patr.) *fall (in, into).*

1. lit. (Dio Chrys. 57[74], 22 εἰς βόθρον; Jos., Ant. 4, 284 εἰς ὄρυγμα ἐ. βόσκημα) εἰς βόθυνον *into a pit* (Is 24: 18; Jer 31: 44) Mt 12: 11; Lk 6: 39. ἐ. ἐπὶ πῦρ *fall into the fire* Hv 3, 2, 9.

2. *fall (into* or *among)* fig. (Dit., Syll.³ 1170, 3 εἰς νόσους; PTebt. 17, 9 [114 BC] εἰς δαπάνας) εἰς τοὺς λῃστάς *among robbers* (Epict. 3, 13, 3 εἰς λῃστὰς ἐμπ.; Porphyr., Vi. Pyth. 15; cf. Socrat., Ep. 1, 9 εἰς τ. ἱππέας) Lk 10: 36; εἰς τὰ ἄγκιστρα τῆς κενοδοξίας ἐ. *be caught on the fishhooks of false doctrine* IMg 11 (cf. schol. on Pla. 190E ἐμπεσούμεθα εἰς τὸ Πρωταγόρειον δόγμα); ἐ. εἰς χεῖράς τινος *fall into someone's hands* (Charito 8, 3, 7; Alciphr. 3, 36, 1; Sir 38: 15; Sus 23) GP 11: 48; θεοῦ Hb 10: 31 (cf. 2 Km 24: 14; 1 Ch 21: 13; Sir 2: 18; Jos., Ant. 7, 323). εἰς πειρασμόν 1 Ti 6: 9 (cf. Diod. S. 17, 105, 6

ἐνέπεσε εἰς λύπην καὶ φροντίδα; Pr 17: 20 εἰς κακά; 1 Macc 6: 8 εἰς ἀρρωστίαν). εἰς κρίμα τοῦ διαβόλου 3: 6. εἰς ὀνειδισμὸν καὶ παγίδα τοῦ διαβόλου vs. 7 (cf. 6: 9 and Pr 12: 13; Sir 9: 3). εἰς ταύτας τὰς πράξεις τὰς πολλὰς *get into these many activities* Hm 10, 1, 5. εἰς ἐπιθυμίαν Hm 12, 1, 2 (cf. 1 Ti 6: 9.—X., Hell. 7, 5, 6 εἰς ἀθυμίαν; Ael. Aristid. 37 p. 701 D.).

3. abs. *set in, arise* (Pla., Rep. 8 p. 545D στάσις; Epict. 2, 5, 10 χειμὼν ἐμπέπτωκε) ζήλου ἐμπεσόντος περὶ τινος *when jealousy arose about someth.* 1 Cl 43: 2. M-M.*

ἔμπλαστρος, ου, ἡ (Philumen. p. 12, 22; 14, 28 al.; Galen XIII 688; 690 K.; Oribas., Ecl. 89, 4 p. 267, 28; Geopon. 12, 12, 2; Cos. and Dam. 47, 65) *a plaster* used for healing wounds IPol 2: 1.*

ἐμπλέκω pf. pass. ptc. ἐμπεπλεγμένος; 2 aor. pass. ἐνεπλάκην (Aeschyl.+; pap., LXX) *entangle,* in our lit. only pass.

1. lit. of sheep whose wool is caught in thorns Hs 6, 2, 6f (Arrian, Anab. 6, 22, 8 of hares who are caught in thorns; Aesop, Fab. 74 P.= 128 H.).

2. fig. ταῖς τοῦ βίου πραγματείαις *become entangled in civilian pursuits* 2 Ti 2: 4 (cf. Epict. 3, 22, 69; Polyb. 24, 11, 3 τ. Ἑλληνικοῖς πράγμασιν ἐμπλεκόμενος). Of the defilements of the world *be involved in* 2 Pt 2: 20.*

ἐμπλοκή, ῆς, ἡ (Polyb. 18, 18, 11; 15; Plut., Mor. 916D; pap.) *braiding, braid* τριχῶν (fashionable) *braiding of hair* 1 Pt 3: 3 (Nicol. Dam.: 90 fgm. 2 Jac.; Strabo 17, 3, 7 ἐ. κόμης). M-M.*

ἐμπνέω (Hom.+; LXX, Philo; Jos., Bell. 5, 458, Ant. 12, 256).

1. *breathe* fig. ἀπειλῆς καὶ φόνου *he breathed murderous threats* Ac 9: 1 (for its use w. gen. cf. Perictyone in Stob. 4, 28, 19 Ἀραβίης ὀδμῆς ἐμπνέοντα; Josh 10: 40. Cf. Chio, Ep. 3, 3 Ἄρεος πνέω= breathe the lust of war; Theocr. 22, 82 the two opponents φόνον ἀλλήλοισι πνέοντες).

2. *inspire* (Hes., Theogony 31 the Muses ἐνέπνευσαν δέ μ' ἀοιδὴν θέσπιν, ἵνα κτλ.; Plut., Mor. 421B; PGM 2, 84) of prophets ἐμπνεόμενοι ὑπὸ τῆς χάριτος αὐτοῦ IMg 8: 2 (cf. Περὶ ὕψους 16: 2 ἐμπνευσθεὶς ὑπὸ θεοῦ; Lucian, Phal. 2, 12 of the Pythia: ἐμπνεῖται; schol. on Apollon. Rhod. 4, 1381 to 1382; the poet ἐμπέπνευσται by the Muses). M-M.*

ἐμποδίζω 1 aor. ἐνεπόδισα (Soph., Hdt.+; inscr., pap., LXX; Jos., Ant. 19, 226, Vi. 48) *hinder* τινί *someone* Aristot.; Polyb.; Epict. 2, 22, 15; 17; 3, 4, 6) w. inf. foll. ζῆσαι *from living* IRo 6: 2. μηδὲν ἀλλήλοις *without hindering each other* 1 Cl 20: 2. B. 1355.*

ἐμπορεύομαι fut. ἐμπορεύσομαι—1. intr. *carry on business* (since Thu. 7, 13, 2; Dit., Syll.³ 1166; Ezk 27: 13) Js 4: 13.

2. *buy and sell, trade in* (oft. w. acc. as obj., of a thing [Philo, Vi. Cont. 89; Jos., Bell. 1, 514, Ant. 4, 134]; rarely w. acc. of a pers., cf. Achilles Tat. 8, 10, 11; Athen. 13, 25 p. 569F Ἀσπασία ἐνεπορεύετο πλήθη καλῶν γυναικῶν; Pr 3: 14) ὑμᾶς ἐμπορεύσονται *they will exploit you* (cf. vs. 1 τὸν ἀγοράσαντα αὐτοὺς δεσπότην) 2 Pt 2: 3. M-M. B. 819.*

ἐμπορία, ας, ἡ (Hes., Hdt.+; Dit., Syll.³ 185, 32 [IV BC], Or. 629, 164; PTebt. 6, 25 [II BC]; PGiess. 9, 3; LXX; Ep. Arist. 114; Jos., C. Ap. 1, 60; 61; Test. Jos. 11: 5; loanw. in rabb.) *business, trade* Mt 22: 5. ἐμπορίαν ἀσκεῖν engage in business 2 Cl 20: 4 (the verb also governs θεοσέβειαν). M-M.*

ἐμπόριον, ου, τό (Hdt.+; inscr., pap. [Mayser 93, 2]; LXX; Jos., Ant. 9, 17) market οἶκος ἐμπορίου (epexeg. gen.) market-house J 2: 16. M-M.*

ἔμπορος, ου, ὁ (Hom.+) merchant (Thu.+; inscr., pap., LXX; Philo, Op. M. 147; Jos., Ant. 2, 32; 20, 34; Test. Zeb. 4: 6; loanw. in rabb.), actually wholesale dealer in contrast to κάπηλος 'retailer' (for the contrast cf. Pla., Rep. 2 p. 371D) Mt 13: 45; Rv 18: 3, 11, 15, 23. For this pleonast. ἄνθρωπος ἔ. Mt 13: 45 v.l. M-M. B. 821.*

ἔμπροσθεν (Hdt.+; inscr., pap., LXX; Philo, Joseph., Test. 12 Patr.) ἔμπροσθε (Dit., Syll.³ 371, 13 [289/8 BC]; 915, 27) AP 6; orig. adv. of place, then used as prep. (Bl-D. §104, 2; 214, 1; 6; Mlt.-H. 329).
1. adv.—a. in front, ahead (opp. ὄπισθεν, as X., Equ. 1, 3; Polyb. 12, 15, 2; Aelian, V.H. 12, 21; Palaeph. 29, 2; 2 Ch 13: 14; Ezk 2: 10) Rv 4: 6; εἰς τὸ ἔ. toward the front (Diod. S. 11, 18, 5; 19, 26, 10; 19, 83, 2; Jos., C. Ap. 1, 203) προδραμὼν εἰς τὸ ἔ. he ran ahead Lk 19: 4 (where εἰς τὸ ἔ. is pleonast., as Artem. 2, 9 p. 93, 2 προϊέναι εἰς τοὔμπροσθεν; Bl-D. §484; Semitism (?) MBlack, An Aramaic Approach³, '67, 116); τὰ ἔ. (sc. ὄντα; cf. X., An. 6, 3, 14; 1 Macc 13: 27) what lies ahead Phil 3: 13.
b. forward, ahead πορεύεσθαι ἔ. (X., Cyr. 4, 2, 23) Lk 19: 28. αἱ ἔ. ἐκκλησίαι the churches farther on or principal churches (s. JKleist., tr., '46, ad loc. w. note) IPol 8: 1.
2. improper prep. w. gen. (s. on ἀνά, beg.) in front of, before.
a. purely local (X., Cyr. 3, 2, 5; Jos., Bell. 6, 366) Hs 9, 2, 7 (opp. ὄπισω); ἔ. τοῦ ναοῦ before the shrine (Cebes, Tab. 1, 1) 1 Cl 41: 2; ἔ. τοῦ θυσιαστηρίου Mt 5: 24; ἔ. τοῦ βήματος Ac 18: 17; ἔ. τοῦ Ἰησοῦ Lk 5: 19; cf. 14: 2; AP 3: 6; GP 4: 12. γονυπετεῖν ἔ. τινος kneel before someone Mt 27: 29; πίπτειν ἔ. τῶν ποδῶν τινος fall at someone's feet Rv 19: 10; 22: 8; βάλλειν ἔ. τινος Mt 7: 6 (PGM 4, 1229 βάλε ἔ. αὐτοῦ κλῶνας ἐλαίας).
b. before, in the presence of (Gen 45: 5) ὁμολογεῖν and ἀρνεῖσθαι Mt 10: 32f; 26: 70; Lk 12: 8; cf. Gal 2: 14. Esp. of appearing before a judge Mt 27: 11; also before the divine judge 25: 32; Lk 21: 36; 1 Th 2: 19; 3: 13; GP 11: 48; cf. 2 Cor 5: 10. But the judicial element is not decisive in all the pass. in which men stand or come ἔ. τοῦ θεοῦ or ἔ. τ. κυρίου; cf. 1 Th 1: 3; 3: 9; 1 J 3: 19.
c. before, in the sight of (Dit., Syll.³ 1173, 13 [138 AD] the man who was healed ηὐχαρίστησεν ἔμπροσθεν τοῦ δήμου) Mt 5: 16; 6: 1; 17: 2; 23: 13 in the face of; Mk 2: 12; 9: 2; Lk 19: 27; J 12: 37; Ac 10: 4.
d. It is a reverential way of expressing oneself, when one is speaking of an eminent per., and esp. of God, not to connect him directly w. what happens, but to say that it took place 'before him' (cf. Dalman, Worte 171–4): ἐπακοῦσαι ἔ. αὐτοῦ ἔθνη that the nations should obey (before) him B 12: 11 (Is 45: 1). ποιεῖν τὸ πονηρὸν ἔ. τοῦ κυρίου Hm 4, 2, 2 (cf. Judg 2: 11; 3: 12; 4: 1). εὐδοκία ἔ. σου pleasing to thee Mt 11: 26; Lk 10: 21; θέλημα ἔ. τ. πατρὸς ὑμῶν Mt 18: 14.
e. before, ahead of, w. motion implied ἔ. τινος (UPZ 78, 15 [159 BC] ἔμπροσθεν αὐτῶν ἐπορευόμην) J 10: 4; B 11: 4 (Is 45: 2); προπορεύεσθαι ἔ. τινος 3: 4 (Is 58: 8); cf. 4: 12; ἀποστέλλεσθαι ἔ. τινος (Gen 24: 7; 32: 4) J 3: 28; σαλπίζειν ἔ. τινος blow a trumpet before someone Mt 6: 2; τὴν ὁδὸν κατασκευάζειν ἔ. τινος Mt 11: 10; Lk 7: 27.
f. of rank (Pla., Leg. 1 p. 631D; 5 p. 743E; 7 p. 805D; Demosth. 56, 50 εἶναι ἔ. τινος; Gen 48: 20) ἔ. τινος

γίνεσθαι rank before (i.e. higher than) someone J 1: 15, 30 (Plut., Pericl. 11, 1 οἱ ἀριστοκρατικοὶ . . . Περικλέα . . . πρόσθεν ὁρῶντες γεγονότα τῶν πολιτῶν). If ἔ. τινος γ. is to be understood temporally here (as 3 Km 3: 12; 16: 25, 33; 4 Km 18: 5; Eccl 1: 16; 2: 7, 9; Jos., Ant. 1, 109)='be earlier than someone', the foll. ὅτι πρῶτός μου ἦν, which gives the reason for it, would simply result in tautology (but cf. OCullmann, Coniect. Neot. 11, '47, 31 who holds that the ὅτι- clause refers to the absolute time of the Prologue while the preceding words merely give the order in which the ministries of John and Jesus began). S. on ὀπίσω 2b. M-M.*

ἐμπτύω fut. ἐμπτύσω; 1 aor. ἐνέπτυσα; 1 fut. pass. ἐμπτυσθήσομαι (Hdt.+; pap., LXX) spit on or at τινί someone (cf. Aristot. in Aelian, V.H. 1, 15; Nicol. Dam.: 90 fgm. 103g, 2 Jac.; Ps.-Callisth. 1, 18, 9) Mk 10: 34; 14: 65; 15: 19. ταῖς ὄψεσί τινος spit in someone's face GP 3: 9. εἴς τινα Mt 27: 30. εἰς τὸ πρόσωπόν τινος (Herodas 5, 76; Plut., Mor. 189A; PMagd. 24, 7 [218 BC]; Num 12: 14; Test. Zeb. 3: 4) Mt 26: 67. Abs. spit upon of a scapegoat B 7: 8f. Pass. be spit upon (Musonius 10 p. 52 H.) Lk 18: 32. M-M.*

ἐμφανής, ές (Aeschyl.+; inscr., pap., LXX; Philo, Aet. M. 56; Joseph.) visible ἐμφανῆ γενέσθαι become visible (Jos., Ant. 15, 52) τινί to someone (Aelian, V.H. 1, 21) Ac 10: 40 of the resurrected Lord (Ps.-Pla., Alc. 2 p. 141A θεὸς ἐμφανὴς γίγνεται; POxy. 2754, 4 [111 AD] of the emperor); ἐ. ἐγενόμην I have been revealed (i.e. revealed myself) Ro 10: 20 (Is 65: 1). W. the same mng. ἔ. εἶναί τινι (POxy. 260, 11 [59 AD]; cf. Mi 4: 1) Gosp.-fgm. in POxy. 655 (=Kl. Texte 8³, p. 23, 20f).—Gosp.-fgm. in POxy. 1081 (p. 25, 2). M-M.*

ἐμφανίζω fut. ἐμφανίσω; 1 aor. ἐνεφάνισα; 1 aor. pass. ἐνεφανίσθην (Pla., X., et. al.; inscr., pap., LXX, En., Philo, Joseph.) make visible.
1. reveal—a. lit. ἐ. σεαυτόν τινι J 14: 22 (cf. Ex 33: 13, [18] ἐμφάνισόν μοι σεαυτόν). Pass. become visible, appear τινί to someone (Diog. L., Prooem. 7 αὐτοῖς θεοὺς ἐμφανίζεσθαι λέγοντες; Philo, Leg. All. 3, 101; Jos., Bell. 6, 47, Ant. 1, 223; Wsd 17: 4) πολλοῖς Mt 27: 53. σοί Hv 3, 1, 2; cf. 3, 10, 2. τῷ προσώπῳ τοῦ θεοῦ before the face of God (of Christ's appearance before God in heaven) Hb 9: 24.
b. fig., of what transpires within one's soul (cf. Wsd 1: 2; Philo, Leg. All. 3, 27) ἐμφανίσω αὐτῷ ἐμαυτόν I will reveal myself to him J 14: 21.
2. make known, make clear, explain, inform, make a report esp. of an official report to the authorities (as PMagd. 11, 9 [221 BC]; UPZ 42, 18 [162 BC]; PEleph. 8, 3; 2 Macc 11: 29); w. ὅτι foll. (X., Cyr. 8, 1, 26) Hb 11: 14. τινί τι (X., Mem. 4, 3, 4; Diod. S. 14, 11, 2; Esth 2: 22; Jos., Ant. 4, 43) GP 11: 43. τὶ πρός τινα someth. to someone Ac 23: 22; ἐ. τινὶ κατά τινος bring formal charges against someone (Jos., Ant. 10, 166) 24: 1; 25: 2; ἐ. περί τινος concerning someone 25: 15 (cf. PHib. 72, 4 [III BC]; PSI 400, 2; 2 Macc 3: 7; En. 22, 12; Jos., Ant. 14, 226); τινί w. ὅπως foll. 23: 15 (cf. PSI 442, 23 [III BC] ταῦτα δὲ ἐνεφάνισά σοι, ὅπως ἂν μηδείς σε παρακρούηται). M-M.*

ἔμφοβος, ον (= 'terrible' in Soph., Oed. C. 39) afraid, startled, terrified (Theophr., Char., 25, 1; Vett. Val. 59, 7; PGM 13, 871; 1 Macc 13: 2 v.l. [Kappler]; Sir 19: 24) ἔ. γίνεσθαι be afraid, etc. (cf. Aesop 83 H.) Lk 24: 5, 37; Ac 10: 4; 22: 9 t.r.; 24: 25 (s. Field, Notes 139); Rv 11: 13. M-M.*

ἐμφράσσω 1 aor. ἐνέφραξα (Thu.+; POsl. 111, 130; 169 [235 AD]; LXX; Jos., Ant. 9, 36; 12, 346) *stop (up), shut* τὸ στόμα *stop the mouth* (Demosth. 19, 208; Esth 4: 17o; Job 5: 16; Ps 62: 12) of a monster (Da 6: 23 Theod.; cf. Aelian, N.A. 14, 8 p. 345, 7) Hv 4, 2, 4.*

ἐμφύρω pf. pass. ptc. ἐμπεφυρμένος (Aeschyl., fgm. 38 ἵπποι δ᾽ ἐφ᾽ ἵπποις ἐμπεφυρμένοι; Lycophron 1380; Ezk 22: 6 v.l.) *mix up, knead in* ἐμπεφυρμένος τινί *mixed up w. someth.* = *involved* (in earthly pursuits) Hm 10, 1, 4; s 8, 8, 1; 9, 20, 1f. W. the world m 12, 1, 2.*

ἐμφυσάω 1 aor. ἐνεφύσησα (Aristoph., Hippocr.+; POxy. 1088, 25 [I AD]; LXX; Philo) *breathe on* τινί *someone* 1 Cl 39: 6 (Job 4: 21). Abs. (unless αὐτοῖς also belongs to ἐνεφύσ.), for the purpose of transmitting the Spirit J 20: 22 (cf. Gen 2: 7; Wsd 15: 11; Philo, Op. M. 135 ὃ ἐνεφύσησεν, οὐδὲν ἦν ἕτερον ἢ πνεῦμα θεῖον; PGM 12, 138=13, 762 ὃ ἐνεφύσησας πνεῦμα ἀνθρώποις εἰς ζωήν. Stephan. Byz. s.v. Ἰκόνιον: the deluge at the time of Deucalion destroyed everyone [πάντας]. When the earth had dried out, ὁ Ζεὺς ἐκέλευσε τῷ Προμηθεῖ καὶ τῇ Ἀθηνᾷ εἴδωλα διαπλάσαι ἐκ τοῦ πηλοῦ, καὶ προσκαλεσάμενος τοὺς ἀνέμους ἐμφυσῆσαι πᾶσιν ἐκέλευσε καὶ ζῶντα ἀποτελέσαι). M-M.*

ἔμφυτος, ον *implanted* (since Pre-Socr., trag., Hdt.; inscr., pap.; Wsd 12: 10; Ps.-Phoc. 128; Philo; Jos., Bell. 1, 88, Ant. 16, 232, mostly in the sense 'implanted by Nature, inborn') of subsequent implantation (Hdt. 9, 94 αὐτίκα ἔμφυτον μαντικὴν εἶχε) λόγος ἔ. *the word of the gospel implanted* in you Js 1: 21 (cf. WLKnox, JTS 46, '45, 14f). ἡ ἔ. δωρεὰ τῆς διδαχῆς αὐτοῦ *the implanted gift of his teaching* B 9: 9. οὗ τὸ ἔ., τῆς δωρεᾶς πνευματικῆς χάριν, εἰλήφατε *whose implanted blessing, the favor of the spiritual gift, you have received* 1: 2 (the rdg. οὕτως for οὗ τό is prob. preferable; the transl. would then be: *in such a measure you have received the implanted grace of the spiritual gift*; cf. Windisch, Hdb. ad loc.). M-M.*

ἐμφωνέω v.l. for φωνέω Lk 16: 24 D. Cf. also ἐκφωνέω.*

ἐν prep. w. dat. (Hom.+; inscr., pap., LXX, En., Ep. Arist., Philo, Joseph., Test. 12 Patr.). For lit. s. ἀνά and εἰς, beg. For special NT uses s. AOepke, TW II 534–9. The uses of this prep. are so many-sided, and oft. so easily confused, that a strictly systematic treatment is impossible. It must suffice to list the main categories, which will help in establishing the usage in individual cases.

I. of place—1. lit.—a. *in* of the space within which someth. is found: ἐν τῇ πόλει Lk 7: 37. ἐν Βηθλέεμ Mt 2: 1. ἐν τῇ ἐρήμῳ 3: 1. ἐν τῷ ἱερῷ Ac 5: 42. ἐν οἴκῳ 1 Ti 3: 15 and very oft. ἐν τοῖς τοῦ πατρός μου *in my Father's house* Lk 2: 49 and perh. Mt 20: 15 (cf. Jos., Ant. 16, 302, C. Ap. 1, 118 ἐν τοῖς τοῦ Διός; PTebt. 12, 3; POxy. 523, 3; Tob 6: 11 S; Gdspd., Probs. 81–3). ἐν τῇ ἀγορᾷ Mt 20: 3. ἐν (τῷ) οὐρανῷ *in heaven* (Arat., Phaen. 10; Diod. S. 4, 61, 6; Plut., Mor. 359b τὰς ψυχὰς ἐν οὐρανῷ λάμπειν ἄστρα) Ac 2: 19 (Jo 3: 3); Rv 12: 1; IEph 19: 2.

b. *on* ἐν τῷ ὄρει (X., An. 4, 3, 31; Diod. S. 14, 16, 2 λόφος ἐν ᾧ=a hill on which; Jos., Ant. 12, 259) J 4: 20f; Hb 8: 5 (Ex 25: 40). ἐν τῇ ὁδῷ *on the way* Mt 5: 25. ἐν πλαξίν *on tablets* 2 Cor 3: 3. ἐν ταῖς γωνίαις τῶν πλατειῶν *on the street corners* Mt 6: 5.

c. denoting nearness *at, near* (Soph., fgm. 34 N.² ἐν παντὶ λίθῳ=near every stone; Artem. 4, 24 p. 217, 19 ἐν Τύρῳ=near Tyre; Polyaenus 8, 24, 7 ἐν τῇ νησῖδι=near the island; Diog. L. 1, 34; 85; 97 τὰ ἐν ποσίν=what is before one's feet; Jos., Vi. 227 ἐν Χαβ.) ἐν τῷ γαζο-

φυλακείῳ (q.v.) J 8: 20. ἐν τῷ Σιλωάμ *near the pool of Siloam* Lk 13: 4. καθίζειν ἐν τῇ δεξιᾷ τινος *sit at someone's right hand* (cf. 1 Esdr 4: 29) Eph 1: 20; Hb 1: 3; 8: 1.

d. w. quotations and accounts of the subject-matter of literary works: *in* (Ps.-Demetr. c. 226 ὡς ἐν τῷ Εὐθυδήμῳ; Simplicius in Epict. p. 28, 37 ἐν τῷ Φαίδωνι; Ammon. Hermiae in Aristot. De Interpret. c. 9 p. 136, 20 Busse ἐν Τιμαίῳ παρειλήφαμεν=we have received as a tradition; 2 Macc 2: 4; 1 Esdr 1: 40; 5: 48; Sir 50: 27) ἐν τῇ ἐπιστολῇ 1 Cor 5: 9. ἐν τῷ νόμῳ Lk 24: 44; J 1: 45. ἐν τοῖς προφήταις Ac 13: 40. ἐν Ἠλίᾳ *in the story of Elijah* Ro 11: 2. ἐν τῷ Ὡσηέ 9: 25. ἐν Δαυίδ *in the Psalter* (*by David* is also poss.: s. III 1b below) Hb 4: 7. ἐν ἑτέρῳ προφήτῃ *in another prophet* B 6: 14.

e. in reference to spiritual matters φανεροῦσθαι ἐν ταῖς συνειδήσεσι *be made known to* (your) *consciences* 2 Cor 5: 11. ἐν τῇ καρδίᾳ Mt 5: 28; 13: 19 al.

2. to denote the object to which someth. happens or in which someth. shows itself, or by which someth. is recognized: *to, by*, etc. ἵνα οὕτως γένηται ἐν ἐμοί *that this may be done in my case* 1 Cor 9: 15. ἐδόξαζον ἐν ἐμοὶ τὸν θεόν perh. *they glorified God in my case* Gal 1: 24, though *because of me* and *for me* are also possible. ποιεῖν τι ἔν τινι *do someth. to* (*with*) *someone* (Epict., Ench. 33, 12; Ps.-Lucian, Philopatr. 18 μὴ ἑτεροῖόν τι ποιήσῃς ἐν ἐμοί; Gen 40: 14; Jdth 7: 24; 1 Macc 7: 23) Mt 17: 12; Lk 23: 31. ἐργάζεσθαί τι ἔν τινι Mk 14: 6. ἔχειν τι ἔν τινι *have someth. in someone* J 3: 15 (but ἐν αὐτῷ is oft. constr. w. πιστεύων, cf. v.l.); cf. 14: 30 (s. BNoack, Satanas u. Soteria '48, 92). Esp. w. verbs of striking against: προσκόπτω, πταίω, σκανδαλίζομαι; s. these entries.— γινώσκειν ἔν τινι *know* or *recognize by some-one* or *someth.* (class. Sir 4: 24; 11: 28; 26: 9) Lk 24: 35 (perh. *on the occasion of, when*); J 13: 35; 1 J 3: 19. μανθάνειν ἔν τινι *learn by someone* 1 Cor 4: 6. ζητεῖν τι ἔν τινι *require someth. in the case of someone* 4: 2. ὁρᾶν ἔν τινι Phil 1: 30.

3. to denote the presence of a person: *before, in the presence of*, etc. (cf. PPetr. II 4[6], 16 [255/4 BC] δινὸν γάρ ἐστιν ἐν ὄχλῳ ἀτιμάζεσθαι=before a crowd; Od. 2, 194; Eur., Andr. 360; Pla., Leg. 9 p. 879b; Demosth. 24, 207; Polyb. 5, 39, 6; Epict. 3, 22, 8; Appian, Maced. 18 §2 ἐν τοῖς φίλοις=in the presence of his friends; Sir 19: 8; Jdth 6: 2) σοφίαν λαλοῦμεν ἐν τοῖς τελείοις *in the presence of spiritual adults* 1 Cor 2: 6 (Simplicius in Epict. p. 131, 20 λέγειν τὰ θεωρήματα ἐν ἰδιώταις). ἐν τ. ὠσὶν ὑμῶν *in your hearing* Lk 4: 21 (cf. Judg 17: 2; 4 Km 23: 2; Bar 1: 3f), where the words can go just as well w. πεπλήρωται, linguistically, as w. ἡ γραφὴ αὕτη (this passage of scripture read in your hearing). ἐν ὀφθαλμοῖς τινος *in someone's eyes*, i.e. *judgment* (Wsd 3: 2; Sir 8: 16; Jdth 3: 4; 12: 14; 1 Macc 1: 12) Mt 21: 42 (Ps 117: 23). ἔν τινι in the same mng. as early as trag. (Soph., Oed. C. 1213 ἐν ἐμοί=in my judgment, Ant. 925 ἐν θεοῖς καλά; also Pla., Prot. 337b; 343c) ἐν ἐμοί 1 Cor 14: 11; possibly J 3: 21 (s. 5d below) and Jd 1 belong here.—In the 'forensic' sense ἔν τινι can mean *in someone's court* or *forum* (Soph., Ant. 459; Pla., Gorg. 464D, Leg. 11, 916b; Ael. Aristid. 38, 3 K.=7 p. 71 D.; 46 p. 283, 334 D.; Diod. S. 19, 51, 1; Ps.-Heraclit., Ep. 4, 6; but in several of these pass. the mng. does not go significantly beyond 'in the presence of' [s. above]) ἐν ὑμῖν 1 Cor 6: 2 (*by you* is also poss.; s. III 1b below).

4. to denote a rather close relation—a. *among, in* (Hom.+; PTebt. 58, 41 [111 BC]; Sir 16: 6; 31: 9; 1 Macc 4: 58; 5: 2) ἐν τῇ γενεᾷ ταύτῃ *in the generation now living* Mk 8: 38. ἐν τῷ γένει μου *among my people* Gal 1: 14. ἐν

τῷ ὄχλῳ *in the crowd* Mk 5: 30 (cf. Sir 7: 7). ἐν ἀλλήλοις *mutually* (Thu. 1, 24, 4) Ro 1: 12; 15: 5. ἐν τοῖς ἡγεμόσιν (= among the commanding officers: Diod. S. 18, 61, 2; Appian, Bell. Civ. 5, 21 §84) Ἰούδα Mt 2: 6 et al. ἐν ἀνθρώποις *among men* (as Himerius, Or. 48 [14], 11) Lk 2: 14.

b. of clothes: *in, with* (Hdt. 2, 159; X., Mem. 3, 11, 4; Diod. S. 1, 12, 9; Herodian 2, 13, 3; Jdth 10: 3; 1 Macc 6: 35; 2 Macc 3: 33) ἠμφιεσμένον ἐν μαλακοῖς *dressed in soft clothes* Mt 11: 8. περιβάλλεσθαι ἐν ἱματίοις Rv 3: 5; 4: 4. ἔρχεσθαι ἐν ἐνδύμασι προβάτων *come in sheep's clothing* Mt 7: 15. περιπατεῖν ἐν στολαῖς *walk about in long robes* Mk 12: 38; cf. Ac 10: 30; Mt 11: 21; Lk 10: 13. ἐν λευκοῖς *in white* (Artem. 2, 3; 4, 2 ἐν λευκοῖς προϊέναι; Epict. 3, 22, 1) J 20: 12; Hv 4, 2, 1. Prob. corresp. ἐν σαρκί *clothed in flesh* (cf. Diod. S. 1, 12, 9 gods appear ἐν ζῴων μορφαῖς) 1 Ti 3: 16; 1 J 4: 2; 2 J 7. ἐν πάσῃ τῇ δόξῃ αὐτοῦ *in all his glory* Mt 6: 29 (cf. 1 Macc 10: 86). ἐν τ. δόξῃ τοῦ πατρός *clothed in his Father's glory* 16: 27; cf. 25: 31; Mk 8: 38; Lk 9: 31.

c. to introduce the persons who accompany someone, or the things he brings with him, with which he is equipped or burdened: *with.*

α. esp. of a military force (1 Macc 1: 17; 7: 14, 28 al.): ἐν δέκα χιλιάσιν ὑπαντῆσαι *meet, w.* 10,000 *men* Lk 14: 31 (cf. 1 Macc 4: 6, 29 συνήντησεν αὐτοῖς Ἰούδας ἐν δέκα χιλιάσιν ἀνδρῶν). ἦλθεν ἐν μυριάσιν αὐτοῦ Jd 14 (cf. Jdth 16: 3 ἦλθεν ἐν μυριάσι δυνάμεως αὐτοῦ).

β. of things (oft. LXX; PTebt. 41, 5 [c. 119 BC]; 16, 14 [114 BC]; 45, 17 al., where people rush into the village or the house ἐν μαχαίρῃ, ἐν ὅπλοις) ἐν ῥάβδῳ ἔρχεσθαι *come with a stick* (as a means of punishment) 1 Cor 4: 21 (cf. Lucian, Dial. Mort. 23, 3 Ἑρμῆν καθικόμενον ἐν τῇ ῥάβδῳ; Gen 32: 11; 1 Km 17: 43; 1 Ch 11: 23; Dssm., B 115f [BS 120]). ἐν πληρώματι εὐλογίας *with the full blessing* Ro 15: 29. ἐν τῇ βασιλείᾳ αὐτοῦ Mt 16: 28. ἐν αἵματι Hb 9: 25 (cf. Mi 6: 6). ἐν τῷ ὕδατι καὶ ἐν τῷ αἵματι 1 J 5: 6. ἐν πνεύματι καὶ δυνάμει τοῦ Ἠλίου *equipped w. the spirit and power of Elijah* Lk 1: 17. φθάνειν ἐν τῷ εὐαγγελίῳ *come with the preaching of the gospel* 2 Cor 10: 14. μὴ ἐν ζύμῃ παλαιᾷ *not burdened w. old yeast* 1 Cor 5: 8.

d. to denote a state of being (so freq. w. γίνομαι, εἰμί; Attic wr.; PPetr. II 11(1), 8 [III BC] γράφε, ἵνα εἰδῶμεν ἐν οἷς εἶ; 39(g), 16; UPZ 110, 176 [164 BC] et al.; LXX): ὑπάρχων ἐν βασάνοις Lk 16: 23. ἐν τῷ θανάτῳ 1 J 3: 14. ἐν ζωῇ Ro 5: 10. ἐν τοῖς δεσμοῖς Phlm 13. ἐν πειρασμοῖς 1 Pt 1: 6. ἐν ὁμοιώματι σαρκός Ro 8: 3. ἐν πολλῷ ἀγῶνι 1 Th 2: 2. ἐν φθορᾷ *in a state of corruptibility* 1 Cor 15: 42. ἐν ἑτοίμῳ ἔχειν 2 Cor 10: 6 (cf. PEleph. 10, 7 [223/2 BC] τ. λοιπῶν ἐν ἑτοίμῳ ὄντων; PGenève 76, 8; 3 Macc 5: 8) ἐν ἐκστάσει *in a state of trance* Ac 11: 5. Of qualities: ἐν πίστει κ. ἀγάπῃ κ. ἁγιασμῷ 1 Ti 2: 15. ἐν κακίᾳ καὶ φθόνῳ Tit 3: 3. ἐν πανουργίᾳ 2 Cor 4: 2. ἐν εὐσεβείᾳ καὶ σεμνότητι 1 Tim 2: 2. ἐν τῇ ἀνοχῇ τοῦ θεοῦ Ro 3: 26.

5. to indicate a very close connection: a. fig., of pers., to indicate the state of being filled w. or gripped by someth.: *in someone* = in his innermost being ἐν αὐτῷ κατοικεῖ πᾶν τὸ πλήρωμα *in him dwells all the fulness* Col 2: 9. ἐν αὐτῷ ἐκτίσθη τὰ πάντα (prob. to be understood as local, not instrumental, since ἐν αὐ. would otherwise be identical w. δι' αὐ. in the same vs.) *everything was created in him* Col 1: 16 (cf. M. Ant. 4, 23 ἐν σοὶ πάντα; Herm. Wr. 5, 10; AFeuillet, NTS 12, '65, 1–9). ἐν τῷ θεῷ κέκρυπται ἡ ζωὴ ὑμῶν *your life is hid in God* 3: 3; cf. 2: 3. Of sin in man Ro 7: 17f; cf. κατεργάζεσθαι vs. 8. Of Christ who, as a spiritual being, fills people 8: 10; 2 Cor 13: 5, *abides* J 6: 56, *lives* Gal 2: 20, and *takes form* 4: 19 in them. Of the

Divine Word: οὐκ ἔστιν ἐν ἡμῖν 1 J 1: 10; μένειν ἔν τινι J 5: 38; ἐνοικεῖν Col 3: 16. Of the Spirit: οἰκεῖν (ἐνοικεῖν) ἔν τινι Ro 8: 9, 11; 1 Cor 3: 16; 2 Ti 1: 14. Of spiritual gifts 1 Ti 4: 14; 2 Ti 1: 6. Of miraculous powers ἐνεργεῖν ἔν τινι *be at work in someone* Mt 14: 2; Mk 6: 14. The same expr. of God or evil spirits, who somehow work in men: 1 Cor 12: 6; Phil 2: 13; Eph 2: 2 al.

b. esp. to describe certain mental processes, whereby their inward quality is to be emphasized: ἐν ἑαυτῷ *to himself,* i.e. in silence διαλογίζεσθαι Mk 2: 8; Lk 12: 17; διαπορεῖν Ac 10: 17; εἰδέναι J 6: 61; λέγειν Mt 3: 9; 9: 21; Lk 7: 49; εἰπεῖν 7: 39 al.; ἐμβριμᾶσθαι J 11: 38.

c. of the whole, w. which the parts are closely joined: μένειν ἐν τῇ ἀμπέλῳ *remain in the vine* J 15: 4. ἐν ἑνὶ σώματι μέλη πολλὰ ἔχομεν *in one body we have many members* Ro 12: 4. κρέμασθαι ἔν τινι *depend on someth.* Mt 22: 40.

d. esp. in Paul. or Joh. usage, to designate a close personal relation (cf. ἐν τῷ Δαυιδ εἰμί 2 Km 19: 44): of Christ εἶναι, μένειν ἐν τῷ πατρί (ἐν τῷ θεῷ) J 10: 38; 14: 10f; and of Christians 1 J 3: 24; 4: 13, 15f; *be* or *abide in Christ* J 14: 20; 15: 4f; μένειν ἐν τῷ υἱῷ καὶ ἐν τῷ πατρί 1 J 2: 24. ἔργα ἐν θεῷ εἰργασμένα *done in communion with God* J 3: 21 (but s. 3 above).—In Paul the relation of the individual to Christ is very oft. expressed by the formula or formulaic expression (FNeugebauer, NTS 4, '57/'58, 124–38) ἐν Χριστῷ, ἐν κυρίῳ etc., also vice versa ἐν ἐμοὶ Χριστός Gal 2: 20.—Cf. Dssm., D. ntl. Formel 'in Christo Jesu' 1892; EWeber, D. Formel 'in Chr. Jesu' u. d. paul. Christusmystik: NKZ 31, '20, 213ff; LBrun, Zur Formel 'in Chr. Jesus' im Phil: Symbolae Arctoae 1, '22, 19–37; MHansen, Omkring Paulus-Formeln 'i Kristus': Teol. Tidsskr. 4, 10, '29, 135–59; HBöhlig, Ἐν κυρίῳ: GHeinrici-Festschr. '14, 170–5; OSchmitz, D. Christusgemeinschaft d. Pls² '56; AWikenhauser, D. Christusmystik d. Pls² '56; KMittring, Heilswirklichkeit b. Pls; Beitrag z. Verständnis der unio cum Christo in d. Plsbriefen '29; ASchweitzer, D. Mystik d. Ap. Pls '30 (Eng. tr., WMontgomery, The Myst. of Paul the Ap., '31); WSchmauch, In Christus '35; BSEaston, Pastoral Ep. '47, 210f; FBüchsel, 'In Chr.' b. Pls: ZNW 42, '49, 141–58. Also HKorn, D. Nachwirkungen d. Christusmystik d. Pls in den Apost. Vätern, Diss. Berlin '28; EAndrews, Interpretation 6, '52, 162–77; H-LParisius, ZNW 49, '58, 285–88 (10 'forensic' passages); JAAllan, NTS 5, '58/'59, 54–62 (Eph), ibid. 10, '63, 115–21 (pastorals); FNeugebauer, In Christus, etc. '61; MEDahl, The Resurrection of the Body (1 Cor 15) '62, 110–13.—Paul has the most varied expressions for this new life-principle: life in Christ Ro 6: 11, 23; love in Christ 8: 39; grace, which is given in Christ 1 Cor 1: 4; freedom in Chr. Gal 2: 4; blessing in Chr. 3: 14; unity in Chr. vs. 28. στήκειν ἐν κυρίῳ *stand firm in the Lord* Phil 4: 1; εὑρεθῆναι ἐν X. *be found in Christ* 3: 9; εἶναι ἐν X. 1 Cor 1: 30; οἱ ἐν X. Ro 8: 1.—1 Pt 5: 14; κοιμᾶσθαι ἐν X., ἀποθνήσκειν ἐν κυρίῳ 1 Cor 15: 18.—Rv 14: 13; ζῳοποιεῖσθαι 1 Cor 15: 22.—The formula is esp. common w. verbs that denote a conviction, hope, etc. πεποιθέναι Gal 5: 10; Phil 1: 14; 2 Th 3: 4. παρρησίαν ἔχειν Phlm 8. πέπεισμαι Ro 14: 14. ἐλπίζειν Phil 2: 19. καύχησιν ἔχειν Ro 15: 17; 1 Cor 15: 31. τὸ αὐτὸ φρονεῖν Phil 4: 2. ὑπακούειν Eph 6: 1. λαλεῖν 2 Cor 2: 17; 12: 19. ἀλήθειαν λέγειν Ro 9: 1. λέγειν καὶ μαρτύρεσθαι Eph 4: 17. But also apart fr. such verbs, in countless pass. it is used w. verbs and nouns of the most varied sort, often without special emphasis, to indicate the scope within which someth. takes place or has taken place, or to designate someth. as Christian ἁγιάζεσθαι 1 Cor 1: 2, beside ἅγιος ἐν X. Phil 1: 1; ἀσπάζεσθαί τινα 1 Cor

16: 19. δικαιοῦσθαι Gal 2: 17. κοπιᾶν Ro 16: 12. παρακαλεῖν 1 Th 4: 1. προσδέχεσθαί τινα Ro 16: 2; Phil 2: 29. χαίρειν 3: 1; 4: 4, 10. γαμηθῆναι ἐν κυρίῳ *marry in the Lord*=marry a Christian 1 Cor 7: 39. προϊστάμενοι ὑμῶν ἐν κυρίῳ *your Christian leaders (in the church)* 1 Th 5: 12 (but s. προΐστημι 1 and 2).—εὐάρεστος Col 3: 20. νήπιος 1 Cor 3: 1. φρόνιμος 4: 10. παιδαγωγοί vs. 15. ὁδοί vs. 17. Hence used in periphrasis for 'Christian' οἱ ὄντες ἐν κυρίῳ Ro 16: 11; ἄνθρωπος ἐν Χ. 2 Cor 12: 2; αἱ ἐκκλησίαι αἱ ἐν Χ. Gal 1: 22; 1 Th 2: 14; νεκροὶ ἐν Χ. 4: 16; ἐκλεκτός Ro 16: 13. δόκιμος vs. 10. δέσμιος Eph 4: 1. πιστὸς διάκονος 6: 21; ἐν Χ. γεννᾶν τινα *become someone's father in the Christian life* 1 Cor 4: 15. τὸ ἔργον μου ὑμεῖς ἐστε ἐν κυρίῳ 9: 1.—The use of ἐν πνεύματι as a formulaic expression is sim.: ἐν πν. εἶναι *be under the impulsion of the spirit,* i.e., the new self, as opposed to ἐν σαρκί *under the domination of the old self* Ro 8: 9; cf. ἐν νόμῳ 2: 12. λαλεῖν *speak under divine inspiration* 1 Cor 12: 3. ἐγενόμην ἐν πνεύματι *I was in a state of inspiration* Rv 1: 10; 4: 2; opp. ἐν ἑαυτῷ γενόμενος *came to himself* Ac 12: 11 (cf. X., An. 1, 5, 17 et al.).—The expr. ἐν πν. εἶναι is also used to express the idea that someone is under the special infl. of the spirit, even a demonic spirit. Mt 22: 43; Mk 12: 36; Lk 2: 27; 1 Cor 12: 3; Rv 17: 3; 21: 10. ἄνθρωπος ἐν πν. ἀκαθάρτῳ (ὤν) Mk 1: 23 (s. GBjörck, Coniect. NT 7, '42, 1–3).—ἐν τῷ πονηρῷ κεῖσθαι *be in the power of the evil one* 1 J 5: 19. οἱ ἐν νόμῳ *those who are subject to the law* Ro 3: 19. ἐν τῷ Ἀδὰμ ἀποθνῄσκειν *die because of a connection w. Adam* 1 Cor 15: 22.—On the formula ἐν ὀνόματι (Χριστοῦ) s. ὄνομα I 4, esp. cγ.

6. ἐν is somet. used w. verbs of motion where εἰς would normally be expected (Diod. S. 23, 8, 1 Ἄννων ἐπέρασε ἐν Σικελίᾳ; Hero I 142, 7; 182, 4; Paus. 7, 4, 3 διαβάντες ἐν τῇ Σάμῳ; Epict. 1, 11, 32; 2, 20, 33; Aelian, V.H. 4, 18; Vett. Val. 210, 26; 212, 6 al., cf. Index; Pel.-Leg. 1, 4; 5; 2, 1; PPar. 10, 2 [145 BC] ἀνακεχώρηκεν ἐν Ἀλεξανδρείᾳ; POxy. 294, 4; BGU 22, 13; Tob 5: 5 BA; 1 Macc 10: 43 [cf. on the LXX Thackeray 25]): εἰσέρχεσθαι Lk 9: 46; Rv 11: 11; καταβαίνειν J 5: 4 v.l.; ἀπέρχεσθαι (Diod. S. 23, 18, 5) Hs 1: 6. To be understood otherwise: ἐξῆλθεν ὁ λόγος ἐν ὅλῃ τῇ Ἰουδαίᾳ *the word went out=spread in all Judaea* Lk 7: 17; likew. 1 Th 1: 8. The metaphorical expr. ἐπιστρέψαι ἀπειθεῖς ἐν φρονήσει δικαίων *turn the disobedient to the wisdom of the righteous* Lk 1: 17 is unique. S. also δίδωμι, ἵστημι, καλέω, and τίθημι. ἐν μέσῳ *among* somet. answers to the question 'whither' (Bl-D. §215, 3 w. app.) Mt 10: 3; 8: 7.

II. of time—1. to denote a period of time
a. covered by an occurrence or action *in the course of, within* ἐν τρισὶν ἡμέραις (X., Ages. 1, 34; Diod. S. 13, 14, 2; 20, 83, 4; Arrian, Anab. 4, 6, 4 ἐν τρισὶν ἡμέραις; Aelian, V.H. 1, 6; Inschr. v. Priene 9, 29; Dialekt-Inschr. 1222, 4 [Arcadia] ἰν ἀμέραις τρισί; Ep. Arist. 24) Mt 27: 40; J 2: 19f.
b. within which, at a certain point, someth. occurs Mt 2: 1. ἐν ταῖς ἡμέραις ἐκείναις 3: 1. ἐν τῷ ἐξῆς *afterward* Lk 7: 11. ἐν τῷ μεταξύ *meanwhile* (PTebt. 72, 190; PFlor. 36, 5) J 4: 31.
2. to denote the point of time when someth. occurs ἐν ἡμέρᾳ κρίσεως Mt 11: 22. ἐν τῇ ἐσχάτῃ ἡμέρᾳ J 6: 44; 11: 24; cf. 7: 37. ἐν ἐκείνῃ τῇ ὥρᾳ Mt 8: 13; 10: 19; cf. 7: 22. ἐν σαββάτῳ 12: 2; J 7: 23. ἐν τῇ ἡμέρᾳ J 11: 9 (opp. ἐν τῇ νυκτί vs. 10). ἐν τῷ δευτέρῳ *on the second visit* Ac 7: 13. ἐν τῇ παλιγγενεσίᾳ *in the new age* Mt 19: 28. ἐν τῇ παρουσίᾳ 1 Cor 15: 23; 1 Th 2: 19; 3: 13; Phil 2: 12 (here, in contrast to the other pass., there is no reference to the second coming of Christ); 1 J 2: 28. ἐν τῇ ἀναστάσει

in the resurrection Mt 22: 28; Mk 12: 23; Lk 14: 14; 20: 33; J 11: 24. ἐν τῇ ἐσχάτῃ σάλπιγγι *at the last trumpet-call* 1 Cor 15: 52. ἐν τῇ ἀποκαλύψει *when* the Lord *appears* (in the last days) 2 Th 1: 7; 1 Pt 1: 7, 13; 4: 13.
3. to introduce an activity whose time is given *when, while, during* (Diod. S. 23, 12, 1 ἐν τοῖς τοιούτοις=in the case of this kind of behavior) ἐν τῇ προσευχῇ *when* (*you*) *pray* Mt 21: 22. ἐν τῇ στάσει *during the revolt* Mk 15: 7. ἐν τῇ διδαχῇ *in the course of his teaching* Mk 4: 2; 12: 38. ἐν αὐτῷ *in it* (the preaching of the gospel) Eph 6: 20. γρηγοροῦντες ἐν αὐτῇ (τῇ προσευχῇ) *while you are watchful in it* Col 4: 2. Esp. w. the pres. inf. used substantively: ἐν τῷ σπείρειν *while* (*he*) *sowed* Mt 13: 4; Mk 4: 4, ἐν τῷ καθεύδειν τοὺς ἀνθρώπους *while people were asleep* Mt 13: 25, ἐν τῷ κατηγορεῖσθαι αὐτόν 27: 12. W. the aor. inf. the meaning is likewise *when.* Owing to the fundamental significance of the aor. the action in such a construction is not thought of as durative, but merely as punctiliar. Cf. Rob. 1073, disagreeing w. Bl-D. §404. ἐν τῷ γενέσθαι τὴν φωνήν Lk 9: 36. ἐν τῷ ἐπανελθεῖν αὐτόν 19: 15. ἐν τῷ εἰσελθεῖν αὐτούς 9: 34.
III. causal or instrumental—1. introducing the means or instrument, a construction that begins w. Homer, (many examples of instrumental ἐν in Radermacher's edition of Ps.-Demetr., Eloc. p. 100) but whose wide currency in our lit. is partly caused by the infl. of the LXX, and its similarity to the Hebr. constr. w. בְּ (Bl-D. §219 w. app.; Mlt. 104; Mlt.-H. 463f).
a. w. things: κατακαίειν ἐν πυρί Rv 17: 16 (cf. Bar 1: 2; 1 Esdr 1: 52; 1 Macc 5: 5 al.; as early as Il. 24, 38; cf. POxy. 2747, 74; Aelian, Hist. An. 14, 15. Further, the ἐν Rv 17: 16 is not textually certain). ἐν ἅλατι ἁλίζειν, ἀρτύειν Mt 5: 13; Mk 9: 50; Lk 14: 34 (but s. WRHutton, ET 58, '46/'47, 166–8). ἐν τῷ αἵματι λευκαίνειν Rv 7: 14. ἐν αἵματι καθαρίζειν Hb 9: 22. ἐν ῥομφαίᾳ ἀποκτείνειν *kill with the sword* Rv 6: 8 (cf. Lucian, Conscr. Hist. 12 ἐν ἀκοντίῳ φονεύειν; 1 Esdr 1: 50; 1 Macc 2: 9; cf. 3: 3; Jdth 16: 4). ἐν μαχαίρῃ πατάσσειν Lk 22: 49; ἐν μ. ἀπόλλυσθαι *perish by the sword* Mt 26: 52. ποιμαίνειν ἐν ῥάβδῳ σιδηρᾷ Rv 2: 27; 12: 5; 19: 15 (s. ποιμαίνω 2aγ and cf. PGM 36, 109). καταπατεῖν τι ἐν τοῖς ποσίν *tread someth. w. the feet* Mt 7: 6 (cf. Sir 38: 29—ἐν ὀφθαλμοῖσιν ὁρᾶν=see with the eyes: Od. 8, 459; Callinus [VII BC], fgm. 1, 20 Diehl²). ποιεῖν κράτος ἐν βραχίονι *do a mighty deed w. one's arm* Lk 1: 51 (cf. Sir 38: 30); cf. 11: 20. δικαιοῦσθαι ἐν τῷ αἵματι *be justified by the blood* Ro 5: 9. ἐν ἁγιασμῷ πνεύματος 2 Th 2: 13; 1 Pt 1: 2; ἐν τ. παρακλήσει 2 Cor 7: 7. εὐλογεῖν ἐν εὐλογίᾳ Eph 1: 3.—The ἐν which takes the place of the gen. of price is also instrumental ἠγόρασας ἐν τῷ αἵματί σου Rv 5: 9 (cf. 1 Ch 21: 24 ἀγοράζω ἐν ἀργυρίῳ).
b. with pers.: *with the help of* (Diod. S. 19, 46, 4 ἐν τοῖς μετέχουσι τοῦ συνεδρίου=with the help of the members of the council; Philostrat., Vi. Apoll. 7, 9 p. 259, 31 ἐν ἐκείνῳ ἑαλωκότες) ἐν τῷ ἄρχοντι τ. δαιμονίων ἐκβάλλει τὰ δαιμόνια Mt 9: 34. ἐν ἑτερογλώσσοις λαλεῖν 1 Cor 14: 21. κρίνειν τ. οἰκουμένην ἐν ἀνδρί Ac 17: 31 (cf. Dit., Syll.² 850, 8 [173/2 BC] κριθέντω ἐν ἄνδροις τρίοις; Synes., Ep. 91 p. 231B ἐν ἀνδρί; perh. 1 Cor 6: 2 (s. I 3 above); ἀπολύτρωσις ἐν Χρ. *redemption through Christ* Ro 3: 24. Before a substantive inf. (oft. LXX; cf. KHuber, Unters. über den Sprachchar. des griech. Lev., Zürcher Diss. '16, 83): *while, in that* w. pres. inf. (POxy. 743, 35 [2 BC] ἐν τῷ δέ με περισπᾶσθαι οὐκ ἠδυνάσθην συντυχεῖν Ἀπολλωνίῳ) ἐν τῷ τὴν χεῖρα ἐκτείνειν σε *in that thou dost extend thy hand* Ac 4: 30; cf. 3: 26; Hb 8: 13. W. aor. inf. ἐν τῷ ὑποτάξαι αὐτῷ τὰ πάντα Hb 2: 8. Somet. the instrumental and temporal (s. II above) uses

are so intermingled that it is difficult to decide between them Lk 1: 21; βασανιζομένους ἐν τῷ ἐλαύνειν as they rowed or because of the rowing Mk 6: 48.—Hv 1, 1, 8 et al. (Bl-D. §404, 3 w. app.; Rob. 1073).

2. to denote kind and manner, esp. in periphrasis for adverbs (Kühner-G. I 466): ἐν δυνάμει w. power, powerfully Mk 9: 1; Ro 1: 4; Col 1: 29; 2 Th 1: 11; ἐν δικαιοσύνῃ justly Ac 17: 31; Rv 19: 11. ἐν χαρᾷ joyfully Ro 15: 32. ἐν ἐκτενείᾳ earnestly Ac 26: 7. ἐν σπουδῇ zealously Ro 12: 8. ἐν χάριτι graciously Gal 1: 6; 2 Th 2: 16. ἐν (πάσῃ) παρρησίᾳ freely, openly J 7: 4; 16: 29; Phil 1: 20. ἐν πάσῃ ἀσφαλείᾳ Ac 5: 23. ἐν τάχει (PHib. 47, 35 [256 BC]) ἀπόστειλόν σοι ἐν τάχει) Lk 18: 8; Ro 16: 20; Rv 1: 1; 22: 6. ἐν μυστηρίῳ 1 Cor 2: 7 (belongs prob. not to σοφία, but to λαλοῦμεν: in the form of a secret; cf. Polyb. 23, 3, 4; 26, 7, 5; Diod. S. 17, 8, 5 ἐν δωρεαῖς λαβόντες=as gifts; 2 Macc 4: 30 ἐν δωρεᾷ=as a gift; Sir 26: 3; Polyb. 28, 17, 9 λαμβάνειν τι ἐν φερνῇ). Of the norm: ἐν μέτρῳ ἑνὸς ἑκάστου μέρους acc. to the measure of each individual part Eph 4: 16. On 1 Cor 1: 21 s. AJWedderburn, ZNW 64, ’73, 132-34.

3. of the cause or reason (PPar. 28, 13 [c. 160 BC] διαλυόμενοι ἐν τῷ λιμῷ; Ps 30: 11; 1 Macc 16: 3 ἐν τῷ ἐλέει; 2 Macc 7: 29; Sir 33: 17) because of, on account of.

a. gener. ἁγιάζεσθαι ἔν τινι Hb 10: 10; 1 Cor 7: 14. ἐν τ. ἐπιθυμίαις τῶν καρδιῶν Ro 1: 24; perh. ἐν Ἰσαὰκ κληθήσεταί σοι σπέρμα 9: 7; Hb 11: 18 (both Gen 21: 12). ἐν τῇ πολυλογίᾳ αὐτῶν because of their many words Mt 6: 7. ἐν τούτῳ πιστεύομεν this is the reason why we believe J 16: 30; cf. Ac 24: 16; 1 Cor 4: 4; 2 Cor 5: 2. W. attraction ἐν ᾧ=ἐν τούτῳ ὅτι for the reason that= because s. IV 6d below. Sim., of the occasion: ἔφυγεν ἐν τῷ λόγῳ τούτῳ at this statement Ac 7: 29; cf. 8: 6.

b. w. verbs that express feeling or emotion, to denote that toward which the feeling is directed; so: εὐδοκεῖν (εὐδοκία), εὐφραίνεσθαι, καυχᾶσθαι, χαίρειν et al.

IV. Various other uses—1. ἔν τινι as far as—it is concerned.

a. w. adj. πλούσιος ἐν ἐλέει Eph 2: 4; cf. Tit 2: 3; Js 1: 8.—b. w. verbs Hb 13: 21; Js 1: 4.

2. amounting to (BGU 970, 14 [II AD] προσηνέγκαμεν αὐτῷ προοῖκα ἐν δραχμαῖς ἐννακοσίαις) πᾶσαν τὴν συγγένειαν ἐν ψυχαῖς ἑβδομήκοντα πέντε Ac 7: 14.

3. consisting in (BGU 72, 11 [191 AD] ἐξέκοψαν πλεῖστον τόπον ἐν ἀρούραις πέντε) τὸν νόμον τῶν ἐντολῶν ἐν δόγμασιν Eph 2: 15.

4. ἐν w. dat. stands—a. for the ordinary dat. (Diod. S. 3, 51, 4 ἐν ἀψύχῳ ἀδύνατον=it is impossible for a lifeless thing; Ael. Aristid. 49, 15 K.=25 p. 492 D.: ἐν Νηρίτῳ θαυμαστὰ ἐνεδείξατο=[the god] showed wonderful things to N.; 53 p. 629 D.: οὐ γὰρ ἐν τοῖς βελτίστοις εἰσὶ παῖδες, ἐν δὲ πονηροτάτοις οὐκέτι=it is not the case that the very good have children, and the very bad have none [datives of possession]; 54 p. 653 D.: ἐν τ. φαύλοις θετέον=to the bad; EpJer 66 ἐν ἔθνεσιν; Aesop 19, 8; 348a, 5 Chambry v.l.) ἀποκαλύψαι τὸν υἱὸν αὐτοῦ ἐν ἐμοί Gal 1: 16. φανερόν ἐστιν ἐν αὐτοῖς Ro 1: 19 (Aesop 15c, 11 Chambry τ. φανερὸν ἐν πᾶσιν=evident to all). ἐν ἐμοὶ βάρβαρος (corresp. to τῷ λαλοῦντι βάρβ.) 1 Cor 14: 11 (Amphis Com. [IV BC] 21 μάταιός ἐστιν ἐν ἐμοί). δεδομένον ἐν ἀνθρώποις Ac 4: 12. θεῷ—ἐν ἀνθρώποις Lk 2: 14.

b. very rarely for the genitive (Philo Mech. 75, 29 τὸ ἐν τῷ κυλίνδρῳ κοίλασμα; Ep. Arist. 31 ἡ ἐν αὐτοῖς θεωρία=ἡ αὐτῶν θ.; cf. 29) ἡ δωρεὰ ἐν χάριτι the gift of grace Ro 5: 15.

5. The OT is the source of the expr. ὀμνύναι ἔν τινι swear by someone or someth. (oft. LXX) Mt 5: 34ff; 23: 16,

18ff; Rv 10: 6; παραγγέλλομέν σοι ἐν Ἰησοῦ Ac 19: 14 v.l. The usage in ὁμολογεῖν ἔν τινι acknowledge someone Mt 10: 32; Lk 12: 8 (s. ὁμολογέω 4) is Aramaic. ἀλλάσσειν, μεταλλάσσειν τι ἔν τινι exchange someth. for someth. else Ro 1: 23, 25 (cf. Ps 105: 20) is, however, not un-Greek (Soph., Ant. 945 Danaë had to τὸ οὐράνιον φῶς ἀλλάξαι ἐν χαλκοδέτοις αὐλαῖς).

6. ἐν ᾧ is used w. var. mngs.—a. of place wherein Ro 2: 1; 14: 22; 2 Cor 11: 12.

b. of time: while, as long as (Soph., Trach. 929; Plut., Mor. 356c; Pamprepios of Panopolis [V AD] 1, 22 [ed. HGerstinger, SB der Wiener Ak. d. W., vol. 208, 3. 1928]) Mk 2: 19; Lk 5: 34; 24: 44 D; J 5: 7.

c. instrumental: whereby Ro 14: 21.—d. causal: because 8: 3; Hb 2: 18; 6: 17. See III, 3.

e. circumstantially, of the condition(s) under which someth. takes place: ἐν ᾧ καταλαλοῦσιν whereas they slander 1 Pt 2: 12, cf. 3: 16; ἐν ᾧ ξενίζονται in view of your changed attitude they consider it odd 4: 4. ἐν ᾧ in 1 Pt 3: 19 may similarly refer to a changed circumstance, i.e., from death to life (WJDalton, Christ's Proclamation to the Spirits, ’65, esp. 135-42: ‘in this sphere, under this influence’ [of the spirit]). Other possibilities: as far as this is concerned: πνεῦμα· ἐν ᾧ spirit; as which (FZimmermann, APF 11, ’35, 174 ‘meanwhile’ [indessen]; BReicke, The Disobedient Spirits and Christian Baptism, ’46, 108-15: ‘on that occasion’=when he died.—For ἐν ᾧ 1 Pt 2: 12; 3: 16 see also ὅς 2a.).—WRHutton, Considerations for the Translation of ἐν, Bible Translator 9, ’58, 163-70; response by NTurner, ibid. 10, ’59, 113-20.—On ἐν w. article and inf. s. ISoisalon-Soininen, Die Infinitive in der LXX, ’65, 80ff. M-M.

ἐναγκαλίζομαι 1 aor. ptc. ἐναγκαλισάμενος (Meleag. [I BC]: Anth. Pal. 7, 476, 10; Plut., Mor. 492D; Alciphr. 4, 19, 5; IG XII 7, 395, 25 ὧν τέκνα ἐνηνκαλίσατο; Pr 6: 10; 24: 33) take in one's arms τινά someone Mk 9: 36; 10: 16 (Diod. S. 3, 58, 2f: Cybele takes the little children into her arms [ἐναγκ.] and cures them [σῴζω] when they are sick. For this reason she is commonly called ‘the mother of the mountain’ [ὀρεία μήτηρ]). M-M.*

ἐνάλιος, ον (Pind.+; as εἰνάλιος as early as Homer, also Philo, Decal. 54) belonging to the sea (τὰ) ἐνάλια sea creatures Js 3: 7.*

ἐναλλάξ adv. (Pind.+; Dit., Syll.³ 963, 7; 969, 15; PGM 4, 145; Gen 48: 14) in the opposite direction, crosswise, alternately ὑποδεικνύουσα αὐτοῖς ἐ. as she pointed in the wrong direction 1 Cl 12: 4. ποιεῖν τὰς χεῖρας place one's hands crosswise B 13: 5 (Gen 48: 14).*

ἐνάλλομαι leap upon (Soph., Oed. R. 1261; Job 6: 27 [ἐπί τινι]) Ac 19: 16 D.*

ἐνανθρωπέω (Heliod. 2, 31, 1 ψυχὴ ἐνανθρωπήσασα; Etym. Gud. 467, 2) take on human form 1 J 4: 17 v.l.*

ἔναντι adv. used as improper prep. w. gen. (Dit., Syll.³ 646, 52 [170 BC] ἔναντι Γαΐου; POxy. 495, 5 [181/9 AD]; oft. LXX; JWackernagel, Hellenistica ’07, 1ff).

1. lit. opposite, before ἔ. τοῦ θεοῦ before God, i.e., in the temple (Ex 28: 29) Lk 1: 8.—2. fig. in the eyes, in the judgment ἔν. τοῦ θεοῦ Ac 8: 21; 1 Cl 39: 4 (Job 4: 17 v.l.); ἔ. Φαραώ Ac 7: 10 v.l. M-M.*

ἐναντίον neut. of ἐναντίος—1. improper prep. w. gen. (Hom.+; inscr., pap., LXX, En., Jos., Ant. 16, 344).

a. before ἐ. τοῦ θεοῦ before God 2 Cl 11: 7; ἐ. τοῦ λαοῦ in the presence of the people (Ex 19: 11) Lk 20: 26; ἐ. πάντων Mk 2: 12 t.r.; ἐ. τοῦ κείραντος before the shearer

ἐναντίον — ἐνδέχομαι

Ac 8: 32; 1 Cl 16: 7; B 5: 2 (all three Is 53: 7). ἀναγγέλλειν ἐ. τινός proclaim before someone 1 Cl 16: 3 (Is 53: 2).

b. *in the sight* or *judgment* (*of*) (cf. Gen 10: 9; Sir 39: 20; 1 Macc 3: 18) δίκαιος ἐ. τοῦ θεοῦ Lk 1: 6; δυνατὸς ἐ. τοῦ θεοῦ 24: 19. ἔδωκεν αὐτῷ χάριν καὶ σοφίαν ἐ. Φαραώ Ac 7: 10 (Gen 39: 21).

2. *adv. w. art.* τοὐναντίον *on the other hand* (X., Pla. et al.; 3 Macc 3: 22; Philo, Op. M. 2; Jos., Ant. 1, 270; 18, 24) 2 Cor 2: 7; Gal 2: 7; 1 Pt 3: 9; MPol 12: 1. M-M s.v. ἐναντίος.*

ἐναντιόομαι (Aeschyl.+; inscr., pap., LXX; Ep. Arist. 254; Manetho in Jos., C. Ap. 1, 240; Jos., Ant. 14, 309) *oppose* (*oneself*) w. dat. (Diod. S. 16, 74, 2; UPZ 144, 22 [164 bc]; BGU 970, 12 [II ad] τοῖς διατεταγμένοις) Ac 13: 45 v.l.; τῷ θελήματι θεοῦ *the will of God* 1 Cl 61: 1 (cf. PGM 12, 262).*

ἐναντίος, α, ον (Hom.+; inscr., pap., LXX, Ep. Arist., Philo, Joseph.)—1. *opposite, against, contrary* of the wind (X., An. 4, 5, 3; Dio Chrys. 17 [34], 19; Jos., Bell. 3, 421) Mt 14: 24; Mk 6: 48; Ac 27: 4.

2. *opposed, contrary* τινί *to someone* (Pr 14: 7) Ἰουδαίων . . . πᾶσιν ἀνθρώποις ἐναντίων *who are hostile to all men* 1 Th 2: 15. ἐναντίον εἶναί τινι *be opposed, hostile to someone* τῷ θεῷ B 16: 7; ISm 6: 2. ἐναντίον ποιεῖν τί τινι (PSI 282, 13 [183 ad] μηδὲ ποιῆσαι ἐναντίον τι τῇ αὐτῇ ὑπογραφῇ; Jos., Ant. 2, 43; 5, 169) Ac 28: 17. ἐναντία πράσσειν πρὸς τὸ ὄνομά τινος 26: 9 (ἐν. πράσσειν as Jos., Ant. 18, 279; 19, 305).—τὰ ἐναντία *the opposite*, ἀπολαμβάνειν τὰ ἐναντία παρά τινος *receive the opposite fr. someone* Hv 5: 7 (cf. POxy. 1258, 10f [45 ad] εὐορκοῦντι μέν μοι εὖ εἴη, ἐπιορκοῦντι δὲ τὰ ἐναντία. Likew. Dit., Syll.³ 914, 45; 921, 113; Jos., C. Ap. 2, 37).

3. ἐξ ἐναντίας (class., oft. LXX; Bl-D. §241, 1)—a. corresp. to 1 ἐξ ἐ. τινός *opposite someone* παρεστηκέναι Mk 15: 39 (cf. Sir 37: 9).

b. corresp. to 2 ὁ ἐξ ἐ. *the opponent* Tit 2: 8 (cf. Sext. Emp., Phys. 1, 66 οἱ ἐξ ἐ.; 2, 69, Eth. 1, 25; Diog. L. 1, 84; Wilcken, Chrest. 461, 1 πρὸς τὸν ἐξ ἐναντίας; Philo, Aet. M. 7). M-M.*

ἐναργής, ές (Hom.+; inscr., pap., Ep. Arist., Philo; Jos., Ant. 14, 266, C. Ap. 2, 190) *clear, evident, visible* Hb 4: 12 B (in the text, ἐνεργής). For the ἐνεργής of the Gk. text in 1 Cor 16: 9 and Phlm 6 some Lat. mss. have 'evidens' or 'manifesta'. B. 1233.*

ἐνάρετος, ον (favorite word of the Stoics [cf. Phryn. 328f L.]; Chrysipp.: Stoic. III 72; 4 Macc 11: 5; Philo, Deus Imm. 11; Jos., Bell. 6, 89; Dit., Or. 485, 2; 505, 8) *virtuous* βίος 1 Cl 62: 1. Perh. subst. ἐνάρετον κ. τέλειον (τέλειος 1 aβ) IPhld 1: 2.*

ἐνάρχομαι 1 aor. ἐνηρξάμην (since Eur., who uses it as a sacrificial t.t., construed w. acc.) *begin, make a beginning* (so, without further connotation, in later wr., Polyb. et al.; PTebt. 24, 34; 36 [117 bc]; LXX; Ep. Arist. 129) τὶ someth. (opp. ἐπιτελεῖν, ἐπιτελεῖσθαι) ἐν ὑμῖν ἔργον ἀγαθόν Phil 1: 6. Abs. (Sb 4369b, 23 [III bc]) ἐναρξάμενοι πνεύματι *you who have made a beginning* (in your Christian life) *in the Spirit* Gal 3: 3. M-M.*

ἔνατος, η, ον (Hom.+; inscr., pap., LXX, Ep. Arist.; Jos., Ant. 14, 148; for the spelling Bl-D. §11, 2; Rob. 213) *ninth* Rv 21: 20; Hs 9, 1, 9; 9, 26, 1. ὥρα (=3 p.m.) Mt 20: 5; 27: 45f; Mk 15: 33f; Lk 23: 44; Ac 10: 3, 30; GP 6: 22. As a time for prayer Ac 3: 1 (cf. Elbogen² 98; Billerb. II 696-702 and προσεύχομαι, end). M-M.*

ἐναφίημι (Hdt.+; pap.; Ezk 21: 22; Jos., Bell. 6, 336) *let, permit* Mk 7: 12 D.*

ἐνγ- s. ἐγγ.

ἐνδεής, ές (Soph., Hdt.+; inscr., pap., LXX, Philo; Jos., Ant. 17, 175 al.) *poor, impoverished* lit. Ac 4: 34; *poorly instructed* Hv 3, 1, 2. Comp. ἐνδεέστερος: ἐνδεέστερον γίνεσθαί τινος *become needier than someone* perh.= *more humble* m 8: 10. Likew. ἑαυτὸν ἐ. ποιεῖν τινος 11: 8. M-M.*

ἔνδειγμα, ατος, τό (Pla., Critias p. 110b; Demosth. 19, 256) *evidence, plain indication* ἔ. τῆς δικαίας κρίσεως τ. θεοῦ *of God's righteous judgment* 2 Th 1: 5.*

ἐνδείκνυμι 1 aor. ἐνεδειξάμην in our lit. only in mid. (Hom.+; inscr., pap., LXX, Ep. Arist., Philo; Jos., Bell. 2, 109, Ant. 19, 33 al.).

1. *show, demonstrate* τὶ someth. (X., An. 6, 1, 19 εὔνοιαν; Wsd 12: 17) τὴν ὀργήν Ro 9: 22. πᾶσαν πίστιν ἀγαθήν Tit 2: 10; cf. 3: 2. Hb 6: 11; 1 Cl 21: 7. τὶ εἴς τινα or εἴς τι *show someth. toward someone* or *someth.* οἱ εἰς τὰ κωφὰ τὴν αὐτὴν ἐνδεικνύμενοι φιλοτιμίαν those who show the same respect to speechless (idols) Dg 3: 5. ἀγάπην εἰς τὸ ὄνομα αὐτοῦ *show love for his name* (ἧς for ἥν by attraction) Hb 6: 10. τὴν ἔνδειξιν ἐνδείκνυσθαι (as Pla., Leg. 12 p. 966b) εἴς τινα *give proof to someone* 2 Cor 8: 24. *Appoint, designate* Lk 10: 1 𝔓⁷⁵. Used w. double acc. (Jos. Bell. 2, 109) ἐ. τὸ ἔργον τοῦ νόμου γραπτόν *show that what the law demands is written* Ro 2: 15; cf. Dg 5: 4. τὶ ἔν τινι *show someth. in someone* Ro 9: 17 (Ex 9: 16); cf. 1 Ti 1: 16; *someth. in* or *by someth.* τὴν σοφίαν ἐν ἔργοις ἀγαθοῖς 1 Cl 38: 2. τὸ πλοῦτος τ. χάριτος ἐν χρηστότητι Eph 2: 7.

2. τί τινι *do someth. to someone* (Vett. Val. 200, 19; Gen 50: 17; 2 Macc 13: 9; Test. Zeb. 3: 8 ἐνεδείξαντο αὐτῷ κακά) πολλά μοι κακὰ ἐνεδείξατο *he did me a great deal of harm* 2 Ti 4: 14. M-M.*

ἔνδειξις, εως, ἡ (Pla.+; Philo; Jos., Ant. 19, 133).— 1. *sign, omen* ἐστιν αὐτοῖς ἔ. ἀπωλείας *a sign of destruction for them* Phil 1: 28.

2. *proof* (Polyb. 3, 38, 5) εἰς ἔνδειξιν τινος (Philo, Op. M. 45; 87) Ro 3: 25; for this πρὸς τὴν ἔ. τινος (Plut., Pericl. 31, 1) vs. 26; ἔ. ἐνδείκνυσθαι 2 Cor 8: 24 (ἐνδείκνυμι 1). WGKümmel, πάρεσις und ἔνδειξις, ZThK 49, '52, 154-67 favors 'demonstration' for the above passages. M-M.*

ἕνδεκα indecl. (Hom.+; pap., LXX) *eleven* οἱ ἕ. μαθηταί *the eleven disciples* (without Judas) Mt 28: 16. ἀπόστολοι Ac 1: 26. For this οἱ ἕ. (already established as the name of a board in Athens: Lysias 10, 10; Antipho 5, 70; X.; Pla.; Alciphr. 2, 19, 2) Mk 16: 14; Lk 24: 9, 33; Ac 2: 14; 1 Cor 15: 5 v.l. M-M.*

ἑνδέκατος, η, ον (Hom.+; POsl. 141, 2 [50 ad] al.; LXX; Ep. Arist.; Jos., Ant. 14, 150) *eleventh* Rv 21: 20; Hs 9, 1, 10; 9, 28, 1. περὶ τὴν ἐ. ὥραν *at the eleventh hour* (=5 p.m.) Mt 20: 9 (cf. Sb 19, 10 [25 ad] ὥρᾳ [sic] ἐνδεκάτῃ τ. ἡμέρας). Without ὥρα (like our *at 5*) vs. 6. M-M.*

ἐνδελεχισμός, οῦ, ὁ (Philumen. the physician in Oribasius 45, 29, 21; LXX; Jos., Bell. 6. 94, Ant. 11, 77) *continuity* θυσίαι ἐνδελεχισμοῦ *perpetual sacrifices* (תָּמִיד) 1 Cl 41: 2, i.e., the daily burnt offerings; cf. Ex 29: 38f; Num 28: 3ff.—Schürer II⁴ 345ff; OHoltzmann, Tamid (=Mishna V 9) '28.*

ἐνδέχομαι ('receive', trag., Hdt.+) in our lit. only impers. ἐνδέχεται *it is possible* (Thu.+; PPetr. II 45 III, 8 [246

262

BC]; PGiess. 48, 6; POxy. 237 VIII, 31; cf. 2 Macc 11: 18; Jos., Ant. 9, 210) ὃ ἐὰν ἐνδέχηται *whatever is possible* or *permitted* Hv 3, 3, 4 (Philo, Sacr. Abel. 31 ὅσα ἂν ἐνδέχηται). W. acc. and inf. foll. (Artem. 4, 47 p. 228, 24; Phlegon: 257 fgm. 36, 2, 4 Jac. οὐκ ἐνδέχεται with acc. and inf.; Philo, Cher. 51) οὐκ ἐνδέχεται *it is impossible that* Lk 13: 33; Hm 11: 12. M-M.*

I. **ἐνδέω** fut. ἐνδήσω (Hom.+; LXX, Philo; Jos., Ant. 4, 123; 12, 194) *bind in* or *on* lit. to 'leopards' (=soldiers) IRo 5: 1 Funk; fig. *entangle, involve* ἑαυτόν *oneself* τινί: οὐ μικρῷ κινδύνῳ *in no little danger* 1 Cl 59: 1.*

II. **ἐνδέω** fut. ἐνδεήσω (Eur., Hdt.+) in our lit. only mid. (X., Pla.+; LXX) *be in want* (PAmh. 81, 14 εἰς τὸ μηδὲν ἐνδεῖσθαι) ὁ ἐνδεόμενος *the needy one* D 4: 8; 5: 2; B 20: 2.*

ἐνδημέω 1 aor. ἐνεδήμησα (Lysias 9, 5; Plut., Gen. Socr. 6 p. 578E; inscr., pap.; Jos., Ant. 3, 262) *be at home*, in our lit. only fig. (Charito 6, 3, 2 the god Eros ἐνδεδήμηκεν εἰς τ. ἐμὴν ψυχήν) ἐ. ἐν τῷ σώματι *be at home in the body* = phys. life 2 Cor 5: 6; ἐ. πρὸς τὸν κύριον *be at home w. the Lord* of the after-life in heaven after departure fr. the body vs. 8. Abs. in the same sense (opp. ἐκδημεῖν or ἀποδημεῖν, q.v., as vss. 6 and 8) vs. 9.—RBerry, Scottish Journ. of Theol. 14, '61, 60–76.—S. γυμνός 4. M-M.*

ἐνδιδύσκω impf. mid. ἐνεδιδυσκόμην (Delph. inscr. in Dit., Syll.² 857, 13 [156/1 BC]; pap.; LXX; Jos., Bell. 7, 29) *dress, put on* τινά τι (2 Km 1: 24) αὐτὸν πορφύραν *dress him in a purple garment* Mk 15: 17. Mid. *dress oneself* τὶ *in someth.* (Jdth 9: 1 v.l.; 10: 3 v.l.) Lk 8: 27 v.l.; 16: 19. Fig. (Kleopatra 146f ἐξήνεγκεν αὐτοὺς . . . ἐκ θανάτου εἰς ζωὴν κ. ἐνέδυσεν αὐτοὺς θείαν δόξαν πνευματικήν, ἣν οὐκ ἐνεδιδύσκοντο τὸ πρίν) τὰ πνεύματα ταῦτα Hs 9, 13, 5 (cf. also ἐνδύσασθαι Χριστόν). M-M.*

ἔνδικος, ον (Pind.+; Gortynian Law-code [Inscr. Gr. 1333—V BC]; Philo) *based on what is right*, hence *just, deserved* ὧν τὸ κρίμα ἔνδικόν ἐστιν *their condemnation is deserved* Ro 3: 8. μισθαποδοσία *a just penalty* Hb 2: 2. M-M.*

ἔνδοθεν adv. (Hom.+; LXX; Philo, Det. Pot. Ins. 127; Jos., Ant. 11, 108; Sib. Or. 5, 232) *inside, within* GOxy 39 (the contrast here 35; 39 as Appian, Hann. 32 §134 ἔνδοθεν—τὰ ἐκτός).*

ἐνδόμησις rdg. of the t.r. for ἐνδώμησις, q.v. M-M.

ἐνδοξάζομαι 1 aor. pass. ἐνεδοξάσθην *be glorified, honored* (LXX; Test. Sim. 6: 5; PGM 13, 448 διά σε ἐνεδοξάσθη) of the name of the Lord Jesus 2 Th 1: 12. ἐν τοῖς ἁγίοις αὐτοῦ *among his saints* vs. 10. M-M.*

ἔνδοξος, ον (Theognis+; X.; Pla.; inscr., pap., LXX, En., Ep. Arist., Philo, Joseph., Test. 12 Patr.).

1. *honored, distinguished, eminent* (Pla., Sophist. 223B; inscr.; LXX; Jos., Bell. 5, 287, Ant. 6, 180) comp. Mt 20: 28 D=Agr 22. Opp. ἄτιμος 1 Cor 4: 10. Opp. ἄδοξος (as Teles p. 52, 3; Philo, Ebr. 195) 1 Cl 3: 3; MPol 8: 1; comp. ἐ. παρὰ τῷ θεῷ *more honorable in the sight of God* Hs 5, 3, 3. ἀνὴρ ἐ. τῇ ὄψει *of distinguished appearance* Hv 5: 1.

2. *glorious, splendid* ἐ. ἄγγελος Hs 7: 1; 9, 1, 3; cf. 9, 7, 1. Of clothing Lk 7: 25 (cf. Herodian 1, 16, 3 τὴν ἔνδοξον πορφύραν περιτίθενται). Of the church, brilliant in purity Eph 5: 27; τὰ ἔ. *splendid deeds* Lk 13: 17 (cf. Ex 34: 10; Job 5: 9; 9: 10; 34: 24; Aeschin. 3, 231 ἔνδοξα κ. λαμπρὰ πράγματα).—Much used in this sense as a favorable epithet: (w. μέγας; Dt 10: 21) πράξεις 1 Cl

19: 2. ἐπαγγελίαι 34: 7; (w. μεγαλοπρεπής; cf. Dit., Or. 513, 11) βούλησις 9: 1. θρησκεία 45: 7; (w. μακάριος) πνεύματα B 1: 2. βουλῇ Hv 1, 3, 4; δύναμις Hm 7: 2. δωρεαί 1 Cl 23: 2. πράγματα Hv 4, 1, 4. Of the holy names (Tob 8: 5 BA; Prayer of Manasseh [= Ode 12] 3; PGM 12, 257) ἔ. ὄνομα 1 Cl 43: 2. μέγα καὶ ἔ. ὄνομα Hv 4, 1, 3. πανάγιον καὶ ἔ. ὄνομα 1 Cl 58: 1; cf. Hv 3, 3, 5. M-M.**

ἐνδόξως adv. (inscr. [e.g. Dit., Syll. index]; pap., LXX; Sib. Or. 2, 153) *gloriously* οἰκοδομεῖσθαι B 16: 6, 8 (cf. Tob 14: 5); ἐ. πάντα ἔχει *all is glorious* Hs 5, 5, 4; 9, 18, 4; τίθησιν ἐ. *he gave it a place of honor* B 12: 6.*

ἔνδυμα, ατος, τό (since V BC [Dit., Syll.³ 1218, 3]; Polyb. 38, 20, 7; Strabo 3, 3, 7; Plut., Sol. 8, 5; Dit., Syll.³ 1179, 7; PFay. 12, 20 [103 BC]; LXX; Philo, Spec. Leg. 1, 85; Jos., Bell. 5, 231, Ant. 3, 153) *garment, clothing*.

1. lit. Mt 6: 25, 28; Lk 12: 23; Gosp.-fgm. in POxy. 655 (Kl. Texte 8³, p. 23; JoachJeremias, Unknown Sayings of Jesus, '57, 86f), Ia 24, b 17; GP 4: 12; τὸ ἐ. αὐτοῦ λευκὸν ὡς χιών Mt 28: 3 (cf. Da 7: 9 Theod.); ἐ. ἀπὸ τριχῶν καμήλου *clothing made of camel's hair* Mt 3: 4; GEb 2; ἐ. γάμου *a wedding robe* Mt 22: 11f (on the lack of a festal robe cf. Lucian, Nigr. 14); τὸ τῆς αἰσχύνης ἔ. *the garment worn for modesty's sake* (Pythagoreans in Diog. L. 8, 43) GEg 2 (cf. Esth 4: 17k ἱμάτια στενοχωρίας).

2. fig. ἐ. προβάτων (cf. Dox. Gr. 573, 21 τὸ ἐκ τῶν προβάτων ἔ.) *sheep's clothing*, disguising a wolf Mt 7: 15.—Hermas is esp. fond of its fig. use (cf. Ode of Solomon 11, 11) ἔχειν ἐ. τῆς ἐπιθυμίας τῆς ἀγαθῆς *clothe oneself in the garment of good desire* m 12, 1, 2. Sim. of Christian virtues as the clothing of the spiritual maidens: ἐνδύειν τὸ ἔ. αὐτῶν s 9, 13, 2; ἀποδύσασθαι τὸ ἔ. *take off the clothing* = renounce the virtues 9, 13, 8; cf. vs. 7. M-M. B. 395.*

ἐνδυναμόω 1 aor. ἐνεδυνάμωσα, pass. ἐνεδυναμώθην; pf. pass. ptc. ἐνδεδυναμωμένος Hs 5, 4, 4 (Judg 6: 34 B; Ps 51: 9 v.l. [ARahlfs, Psalmi cum Odis '31 and Swete]; 1 Ch 12: 19 v.l.; Aq. Gen 7: 20).

1. *strengthen* τινά someone or τὶ someth. (Cat. Cod. Astr. XI 2 p. 166, 22) of God or Christ, who give power (Herm. Wr. 1, 32 ἐνδυνάμωσόν με) Phil 4: 13; 2 Ti 4: 17; Hs 5, 5, 2; 7: 4. Of Christ 1 Ti 1: 12; ISm 4: 2; ἐ. τινὰ ἐν τινι *make someone strong in someth.* Hs 6, 1, 2.

2. pass. *become strong* (Plotinus 4, 9, 5; Achmes 37, 2)—a. of one who is physically weak; so perh. Ac 9: 22 (cf. vs. 19).

b. usu. of relig. and moral strength: ἐ. τῇ πίστει *grow strong in faith* Ro 4: 20. ἐν τῇ πίστει Hv 3, 12, 3. ἐν ταῖς ἐντολαῖς *in keeping the commandments* m 12, 5, 1; cf. 5, 2, 8. ἐν πᾶσι τοῖς δικαιώμασι τοῦ κυρίου Hm 12, 6, 4. ἐν κυρίῳ Eph 6: 10. διὰ τοῦ πνεύματος Hs 9, 1, 2; cf. 9, 13, 7. Of women ἐνδυναμωθεῖσαι διὰ τῆς χάριτος τ. θεοῦ 1 Cl 55: 3. ἐνδυναμοῦ *be strong* ἐν τ. χάριτι 2 Ti 2: 1. Abs. Hm 5, 2, 8. M-M.*

ἐνδύνω (epic, Ionic, poet. form beside ἐνδύω, as early as Hom.; Aelian, V.H. 4, 22; PGM 7, 271; LXX [Helbing 83; 92]) *go (in), enter, creep (in)*.

1. lit. (Antig. Car. 172: slip εἰς τοὺς κόλπους) εἰς τὰς οἰκίας *worm their way into houses* 2 Ti 3: 6.

2. fig. μὴ καθ' ἑαυτοὺς ἐνδύνοντες μονάζετε *do not retire within yourselves and live alone* B 4: 10. M-M.*

ἔνδυσις, εως, ἡ (Pla.+; LXX)—1. *putting on* ἐνδύσεως ἱματίων κόσμος *adornment that consists in putting on robes* 1 Pt 3: 3.

2. *clothing* (Athen. 12 p. 550c; Cass. Dio 78, 3; Job 41: 5; Esth 5: 1a; Ep. Arist. 96) Dg 9: 6. M-M.*

ἐνδύω 1 aor. ἐνέδυσα, mid. ἐνεδυσάμην; pf. ptc. ἐνδεδυμένος (Hom.+; pap., LXX, Philo, Joseph., Test. 12 Patr.).

1. act. *dress, clothe* τινά *someone* (Appian, Bell. Civ. 5, 99 §411; PGiess. 77, 8; Gen 3: 21; Ex 29: 5; Num 20: 26) ἐνδύσατε αὐτόν *dress him* Lk 15: 22. τινά τι *put someth. on someone* (class.; Diod. S. 2, 27, 3; Gen 41: 42; Ex 40: 13; 1 Macc 10: 62 al.): Mt 27: 28 v.l., 31 ἐνέδυσαν αὐτὸν τὰ ἱμάτια αὐτοῦ Mk 15: 20; αὐτὸν ἐ. τὸ ἔνδυμα αὐτῶν *clothe him w. their clothing* Hs 9, 13, 2 (s. ἐνδιδύσκω).

2. mid. *clothe oneself in, put on, wear* τὶ *someth.*
   a. lit. (Philo, Somn. 1, 214) Mt 6: 25; Lk 12: 22; Gosp.-fgm. in POxy. 655 (Kl. Texte 8³, p. 23), Ia 19. ἱμάτιον Lk 8: 27. δύο χιτῶνας Mk 6: 9. ἐσθῆτα βασιλικήν Ac 12: 21. σάκκον B 3: 2 (cf. Ps 34: 13; Jon 3: 5; Jos., Ant. 8, 385; 11, 256). τὰ ὅπλα Ro 13: 12. τὴν πανοπλίαν *put on the whole armor* (Jos., Ant. 13, 309) Eph 6: 11; cf. vs. 14. θώρακα πίστεως 1 Th 5: 8 (cf. Wsd 5: 18 [esp. the rdg. of S]; Is 59: 17; Test. Levi 8: 2 ἐνδύσαι τὸ πέταλον τῆς πίστεως; Jos., Ant. 7, 283 θώρακα ἐνδεδυμένος; on this matter s. MDibelius, Hdb. on Eph 6: 11). ἐνδεδυμένος (POxy. 285, 11 [c. 50 AD] ἐνδεδυμένος χιτῶνα λεινοῦν; 2 Ch 5: 12; Da 10: 5) *clothed* ἔνδυμα *in a garment* (Zeph 1: 8) AP 5: 17. ἔνδυμα γάμου Mt 22: 11. τρίχας καμήλου Mk 1: 6. χιτῶνας Hs 9, 2, 4. βύσσινον *a fine linen garment* Rv 19: 14. ποδήρη *a long robe* 1: 13. λίνον καθαρόν 15: 6.—Abs. 2 Cor 5: 3; here it is uncertain whether an obj. is to be supplied, or whether we might transl.: *when we have dressed ourselves* (cf. Aristot., Anima 1, 3 p. 407b, 23 ψυχὴν . . . ἐνδύεσθαι σῶμα; Herm. Wr. 10, 18). Lit. on γυμνός 4.
   b. fig., very oft., of the taking on of characteristics, virtues, intentions, etc. (LXX; PGM 11a, 19 πάλιν θεὸς ἐνδύσεται τὸ ἑαυτῆς κάλλος ὅπερ ἐξεδύσατο). Esp. in the usage of Hermas, upon which the use of Lat. 'induere' in the same sense has prob. had its infl. (exx. in Wettstein on Lk 24: 49). The mid. sense is not always clearly right; the pass. is somet. better. ἀφθαρσίαν 1 Cor 15: 53f. ἐξ ὕψους δύναμιν *be clothed w. power fr. above* Lk 24: 49; cf. Hs 9, 13, 8 (cf. Ps 92: 1). ἰσχύν (Is 51: 9; 52: 1; Pr 31: 26) Hv 3, 12, 2. σπλάγχνα οἰκτιρμοῦ *compassion* Col 3: 12. ἀκακίαν Hs 9, 29, 3. ἀλήθειαν m 11: 4. ἀρετήν m 1: 2; s 6, 1, 4. ἀφροσύνην s 6, 5, 3. ἐπιθυμίαν m 1; 12, 2, 4. ἱλαρότητα m 10, 3, 1. μακροθυμίαν m 5, 2, 8. πίστιν (Philo, Conf. Lingu. 31) v 4, 1, 8; m 9: 7; s 6, 1, 2. σεμνότητα m 2: 4. ὑπερηφανίαν s 8, 9, 1. ὁμόνοιαν 1 Cl 30: 3. χάριν IPol 1: 2. Note the bold figure τὸν κύριον Ἰησοῦν Χριστὸν ἐ. *clothe oneself in the Lord Jesus Christ* (cf. Dionys. Hal. 11, 5 Ταρκύνιον ἐνδύεσθαι; Ephippus [after 323 BC] in Athen. 12, 53 p. 537E: Alex. the Great liked to put on the ἱερὰς ἐσθῆτας of the gods, and so became Ammon, Artemis, Hermes, Heracles; Artem. 3, 14 θεοῦ σκευὴν ἔχειν καὶ περικεῖσθαι) Ro 13: 14; cf. Gal 3: 27 (s. Apuleius, Metamorph. 11 and cf. MDibelius, Die Isisweihe etc., Botschaft u. Geschichte 2, '56, 30–79). Sim. Hs 9, 24, 2 says τὸ πνεῦμα τὸ ἅγιον ἐ., which expresses the same idea as τὸν καινὸν ἄνθρωπον *put on the new* (i.e. spiritual) *man* Eph 4: 24; Col 3: 10. For the fig. cf. FJDölger, ΙΧΘΥΣ I '10, 116ff; WStraub, D. Bildersprache des Ap. Pls '37. M-M. B. 393.**

ἐνδώμησις, εως, ἡ (used of a bldg. for relig. purposes Dit., Syll.³ 996, 31; found also in an inscr. fr. Tralles: Bull. de corr. hell. 28, '04, 78, 1; 9; Jos., Ant. 15, 335 has ἐνδόμησις in most mss. [one reads ἐνδώμησις] mng. a mole in a harbor) *interior structure*, prob. = *construction*, hence *material*; perh. *foundation* τοῦ τείχους Rv 21: 18. M-M. s.v. -δομ-.*

ἐνεγκ- s. φέρω.

ἐνέδρα, ας, ἡ (Thu.+; Philo, Spec. Leg. 4, 67; Jos., Vi. 216 al.; pap., LXX) *plot, ambush* ἐ. ποιεῖν (Thu. 3, 90, 2 ἐνέδραν πεποιημένοι; Palaeph. 1 p. 4, 16; 4 p. 11, 18) Ac 25: 3; cf. 23: 16 (v.l. τὸ ἔνεδρον); αἱ ἐ. τοῦ διαβόλου ITr 8: 1; cf. IPhld 6: 2. M-M. B. 1417.*

ἐνεδρεύω (Thu.+; inscr., pap., LXX) *lie in wait* τινά *for someone* (Ps.-Demosth. 40, 10; Diod. S. 19, 69, 1; Dit., Syll.³ 730, 19 [I BC]; PReinach 7, 26 [II BC]; Dt 19: 11; Wsd 2: 12; Jos., Bell. 2, 595, Ant. 5, 172) Ac 23: 21. W. inf. foll. (cf. Jos., Ant. 6, 331) *plot* Lk 11: 54. M-M.*

ἔνεδρον, ου, τό (Herodian Gr. I 378, 2;=deceit POxy. 892, 11 [338 AD]. In LXX it has almost driven out the class. ἐνέδρα; cf. Thackeray 156f)=ἐνέδρα (q.v.) Ac 23: 16 v.l. M-M.*

ἐνειλέω 1 aor. ἐνείλησα (Ps.-Aristot., De Mundo 4 p. 396a, 14; Artem. 1, 54 et al.; PTebt. 24, 62 [117 BC]; PRyl. 144, 18 [38 AD]; 1 Km 21: 10) *wrap (up), confine* τινί in *someth.* (Aeneas Tact. 1346; Plut., Brut. 45, 4; Dio Chrys. 73[23], 3 σπαργάνοις; Philostrat., Her. 12, 1 p. 187, 2 βρέφος τῇ λεοντῇ=the child in the lion-skin) lit. τῇ σινδόνι *in the linen cloth* (Diosc. 5, 72 τὶ ὀθονίῳ) Mk 15: 46; GP 6: 24 (so Gebhardt, Blass; s. εἱλέω). ἐνειλημένος τοῖς δεσμοῖς *confined in chains* Pol 1: 1 (s. ἐνελίσσω). M-M.*

ἔνειμι ptc. ἐνών (Hom.+; pap., LXX; Ep. Arist. 285; Joseph.) *be in* 2 Cl 19: 2. τὰ ἐνόντα *what is inside, the contents* (Thu. 4, 57, 3 et al.; PTebt. 414, 20 [II AD] τὸ σφυρίδιν μετὰ τῶν ἐνόντων; Jos., Bell. 6, 183) Lk 11: 41. ἔνεστι impers. *it is possible* (Polyb. 21, 4, 14; 22, 14, 2: ὡς ἔνι μάλιστα=as much as is possible; Phalaris, Ep. 88 ὡς ἐνῆν; Jos., Ant. 1, 244) IRo 4: 1 v.l.; Hs 8, 10, 2 v.l. Shortened to ἔνι, q.v. M-M.*

ἕνεκα (Attic; PLond. 42, 14 [168 BC]; POxy. 533, 25; 1293, 16f [other exx. in Mayser 242]; LXX [Thackeray 135]; Jos., Ant. 3, 107; Ac 26: 21; Mt 19: 5; Lk 6: 22; Ac 19: 32, but unanimously attested only in Ac 26: 21; also Mk 13: 9 v.l.; 2 Cl 1: 2; MPol 17: 3; Hv 1, 3, 1; m 12, 4, 2), **ἕνεκεν** (increasingly prominent fr. III BC on; it is the prevailing form in inscr. [Meisterhans³-Schw. 217; Thieme 8; Hauser 21], pap. [Mayser 241], LXX [Thackeray 82], Ep. Arist., and our lit.), **εἵνεκεν** q.v. (Sb 1568 [II BC]; PGiess. 40 II, 21; PGM 5, 385; inscr. since 161 AD; LXX [Thackeray 82f]; Lk 4: 18 [Is 61: 1]; 18: 29; Ac 28: 20; 2 Cor 3: 10; B 14: 9; Hv 3, 2, 1א), **εἵνεκα** (Ostraka II 1148 [II BC]; En. 101, 2; later exx. in Crönert 114; Hv 3, 1, 9א; Reinhold 39f). Bl-D. §30, 3; 35, 3 w. app.; Mlt.-H. 67f; 329f; Rob. index. Improper prep. w. gen. *because of, on account of, for the sake of* Mt 5: 10f; 10: 18, 39; 16: 25; 19: 29; Mk 8: 35; 10: 29; Lk 6: 22; 9: 24; 18: 29; 21: 12; Ac 28: 20; Ro 8: 36 (Ps 43: 23); 14: 20; 2 Cor 3: 10; 7: 12; 2 Cl 1: 2; ITr 12: 2; IPol 3: 1; Pol 2: 3; MPol 13: 2; 17: 3; Hv 1, 1, 6; 3, 5, 2; m 5, 2, 2; 12, 4, 2; s 1: 5; 9, 28, 5f; D 10: 3; ἔ. τούτου *for this reason* (Lucian, Dial. Deor. 23, 2) Mt 19: 5; Mk 10: 7 (Gen 2: 24); Hv 1, 3, 1. For this ἔ. τούτων Ac 26: 21. Used w. a rel. οὗ εἵ. (Musonius, Ep. 1, 11; Quint. Smyrn. 12, 227; PGiess. 27 [117 AD]) Lk 4: 18 (Is 61: 1); τίνος ἔ.; *why?* (Demosth.; Menand., Epitr. 330 J.; Dio Chrys. 14[31], 84) Ac 19: 32; ἔ. τοῦ w. inf. foll. (Menand., fgm. 425, 2; Am 1: 6; 2: 4; 1 Esdr 8: 21; Jos., Ant. 11, 293) *in order that* ἔ. τοῦ φανερωθῆναι τὴν σπουδὴν ὑμῶν *in order that your zeal might be made known* 2 Cor 7: 12 (Bl-D. §403 w. app.; Rob. 1073). M-M.*

ἐνελίσσω pf. pass. ἐνείλιγμαι (Hdt.+) *wrap* (*up*) τινί *in someth.* (POxy. 1153, 23 [I AD]) in our lit. only as a conjecture by Zahn; ἐνειλιγμένος τοῖς δεσμοῖς *bound in chains* Pol 1: 1 (cf. ἐνειλέω).*

ἐνενήκοντα indecl. (Hom.+; pap., LXX, Philo; Jos., Ant. 18, 365; on spelling cf. Bl-D. §11, 2; Mayser 214) *ninety* Mt 18: 12f; Lk 15: 4, 7. M-M.*

ἐνεός, ά, όν (Pla.+; LXX; Jos., Ant. 4, 276) *speechless* (EpJer 40 ἐνεὸν οὐ δυνάμενον λαλῆσαι) οἱ ἄνδρες εἱστήκεισαν ἐνεοί *the men stood speechless* fr. fright Ac 9: 7 (cf. Apollon. Paradox. 6: Pythagoras ἤκουσε φωνὴν μεγάλην ὑπὲρ ἄνθρωπον "Πυθαγόρα χαῖρε." τοὺς δὲ παρόντας περιδεεῖς γενέσθαι; Quint. Smyrn. 8, 250f: the Trojans ἐθάμβεον when they heard the voice of Ares commanding them, but could not see the form of the god). M-M.*

ἐνέπλησα s. ἐμπίμπλημι.

ἐνέπρησε s. ἐμπίμπρημι.

ἐνέργεια, ας, ἡ (Pre-Socr.+; inscr., pap., LXX, Ep. Arist., Philo).
1. *working, operation, action* so in NT, and always of supernatural beings (cf. Chrysipp.: Stoic. II 115; Diod. S. 15, 48, 1 θεία ἐνέργ.; Ps.-Callisth. 1, 30, 4 τὴν τοῦ θεοῦ ἐ.; Sallust. 3 p. 4, 8; c. 4 p. 4, 27; Dit., Or. 262, 4 [III AD] περὶ τῆς ἐνεργείας θεοῦ Διός; Herm. Wr. 10, 22b; 16, 13 δαίμονος γὰρ οὐσία ἐνέργεια; PGM 3, 290; Wsd 7: 26; 13: 4; 2 Macc 3: 29; 3 Macc 4: 21; 5: 12, 28; Ep. Arist. 266; Aristobulus in Euseb., Pr. Ev. 8, 10, 12 ἐ. τοῦ θεοῦ) ἐ. πλάνης *a deluding influence* 2 Th 2: 11. πίστις τῆς ἐνεργείας τ. θεοῦ *faith in the working of God* Col 2: 12; cf. Ac 4: 24 D; 1 Cor 12: 10 v.l. Mostly in the expr. κατὰ (τὴν) ἐνέργειαν: κ. τ. ἐ. τοῦ κράτους *according to the manifestation of his power* Eph 1: 19 (for the genitival constr. cf. 1QS 11, 19f; 1QH 4, 32); cf. 3: 7; 4: 16; Col 1: 29; κ. τ. ἐ. τοῦ δύνασθαι αὐτόν *through the power that enables him* Phil 3: 21. κατ᾽ ἐνέργειαν τοῦ Σατανᾶ *by the activity of Satan* 2 Th 2: 9.
2. *way of working* τῆς ὀξυχολίας Hm 5, 1, 7; 5, 2, 1. W. δύναμις (Aristotle p. 23a, 10ff; Philo, Rer. Div. Her. 110 al.) 6, 1, 1a. Pl. (Epict. 2, 16, 18; 4, 11, 33; Philo) 6, 1, 1b; 6, 2, 2; 6 v.l. The pl. also v 3, 8, 3, where the word almost comes to have the sense *meaning.* M-M.*

ἐνεργέω 1 aor. ἐνήργησα; pf. ἐνήργηκα (Aristot.+; inscr., pap., LXX, Ep. Arist., Philo, Joseph.).
1. intr. *work, be at work, operate, be effective—*a. act. (Philo Mech. 59, 48; 96, 12; Vett. Val. 226, 2; Herm. Wr. 12, 11a, b; PGiess. 78, 4 [II AD] καλῶς δὲ ποιήσεις καὶ περὶ τὰ λοιπὰ ἐνεργήσασα; Wsd 15: 11; 16: 17; Jos., Ant. 15, 290, Vi. 156) τὸ θέλειν καὶ τὸ ἐ. *the will and the action* Phil 2: 13b. Used w. ἐν and dat. of the pers. (Test. Dan 5: 5 ἐνεργούντων ἐν ὑμῖν τῶν πνευμάτων) αἱ δυνάμεις ἐνεργοῦσιν ἐν αὐτῷ *miraculous powers are at work in him* Mt 14: 2; Mk 6: 14; cf. Eph 2: 2. Of God (Julian 4, 142d ἐνεργεῖν ἐθέλει) ὁ ἐνεργῶν B 2: 1 (s. HWindisch, Hdb. ad loc.). W. dat. of advantage (cf. Pr 31: 12) ὁ ἐνεργήσας Πέτρῳ *the one who was at work for Peter* Gal 2: 8 (the εἰς foll. supplies the goal of the activity, as Ro 7: 5; s. b below).
b. mid., in our lit. always w. impers. subj. (Diod. S. 13, 85, 2 the siege 'went into effect', 'began'; Herm. Wr. 12, 11c τὰ ἀσώματα) τὰ παθήματα ἐνηργεῖτο ἐν τ. μέλεσιν *the passions were at work in our members* Ro 7: 5 (the εἰς foll. introduces the goal; s. a above on Gal 2: 8). ἡ παράκλησις ἡ ἐνεργουμένη ἐν ὑπομονῇ *consolation*

which becomes effective in enduring 2 Cor 1: 6. ὁ θάνατος ἐν ἡμῖν ἐνεργεῖται *death is working in us* 4: 12 (Lucian, Charon 2 ἐνεργεῖν τὰ τοῦ θανάτου ἔργα). Of God's word 1 Th 2: 13. δύναμις ἐνεργουμένη ἐν ἡμῖν *the power that works in us* Eph 3: 20; cf. Col 1: 29. πίστις δι᾽ ἀγάπης ἐνεργουμένη *faith working* (=expressing itself) *through love* Gal 5: 6. τὸ μυστήριον ἐνεργεῖται τῆς ἀνομίας *the mystery of lawlessness is at work* 2 Th 2: 7. δέησις ἐνεργουμένη *effective prayer* Js 5: 16. τὰ ἐνεργούμενα *the forces at work* 1 Cl 60: 1. τὰ καθ᾽ ἕκαστα βλέποντες ἐνεργούμενα *we see how one thing after the other works itself out*= *comes to pass* B 1: 7.—JRoss, ἐνεργεῖσθαι in the NT: Exp. 7 Ser. VII '09, 75–7; JBMayor, ibid. 191f; AEGarvie, ET 55, '43/'44, p. 97. For the view that the passages in b are passive, not mid., s. the art. by Clark below, p. 98ff and ref. there.
2. trans. *work, produce, effect* w. acc. of the thing (Philo Mech. 59, 48; Polyb. 3, 6, 5; Diod. S. 13, 85, 2; POxy. 1567; Pr 21: 6; 31: 12; Jos., Ant. 3, 155; 15, 283) *someth.*: of God ὁ τὰ πάντα ἐνεργῶν Eph 1: 11 (cf. Ep. Arist. 210). Of the Spirit 2: 2. τὶ ἔν τινι *produce someth. in someone* ὁ ἐνεργῶν τὰ πάντα ἐν πᾶσιν 1 Cor 12: 6; cf. 11. ὁ ἐνεργῶν ἐν ὑμῖν τὸ θέλειν *he produces the will in you* Phil 2: 13a. οὐδὲ ἐνεργῆσαι δύναται εἰς αὐτούς *it cannot influence them* Hm 5, 2, 1; δυνάμεις ἐ. Gal 3: 5; ἐνέργειαν ἐ. Eph 1: 20.—GHWhitaker, ET 26, '14/'15, 474–76; KWClark, The Mng. of ἐνεργέω and καταργέω in the NT: JBL 54, '35, 93–101. M-M.*

ἐνέργημα, ατος, τό (since Epicurus p. 4, 10 Us.)—1. *activity* (Polyb. 2, 42, 7; 4, 8, 7; Diod. S. 4, 51, 6; Vett. Val. 264, 13; Ep. Arist. 156; Philo, Det. Pot. Ins. 114; PGM 1, 194; 12, 317) ἐνεργήματα δυνάμεων *activities that call forth miracles* 1 Cor 12: 10. διαιρέσεις ἐνεργημάτων vs. 6.
2. *experience* (Plut., Mor. 899D; Herm. Wr. 1, 22) τὰ συμβαίνοντά σοι ἐνεργήματα *the experiences that befall you* D 3: 10; B 19: 6. M-M.*

ἐνεργής, ές (Aristot.+; Polyb. 11, 23, 2; Plut., Sol. 31, 2; Diosc., Mat. Med. 1, 18; Vett. Val. 276, 11; Herm. Wr. 10, 23; POxy. 1088, 56 [I AD]) *effective, active, powerful* κοινωνία τῆς πίστεως Phlm 6. ὁ λόγος τοῦ θεοῦ Hb 4: 12. Of a door (fig.), the opening of which promises a rich field of labor 1 Cor 16: 9. M-M.*

ἐνερείδω (Hom.+) *thrust in* pf. pass. ἐνήρεισμαι *be thrust in, become fixed* (cf. Plut., Mor. 327B; 344C) ἔρις ἐνήρεισται (gener. accepted conjecture of Zahn for the impossible ἐνείρισται of the mss.) ἐν ὑμῖν *is firmly rooted among you* IEph 8: 1.*

ἐνεστηκώς, ἐνεστώς s. ἐνίστημι.

ἐνευλογέω 1 fut. pass. ἐνευλογηθήσομαι *bless* Ac 3: 25 (Gen 22: 18); Gal 3: 8 (Gen 12: 3 v.l.).*

ἐνέχω impf. ἐνεῖχον (Pind.+; inscr., pap., LXX; Jos., Ant. 16, 214).
1. act. τινί *have a grudge against someone* (ellipt. for χόλον ἐ. τινί: so Hdt. 1, 118; cf. Gen 49: 23; cf. our colloq. 'have it in for someone') Mk 6: 19. Abs. δεινῶς ἐ. *be very hostile* (Weizsäcker) Lk 11: 53.
2. pass., w. dat. *be subject to, be loaded down with* (oft. since Pind., Pyth. 8, 69 and Hdt. 2, 121, 2; PTebt. 5, 5 [118 BC]; BGU 1051, 34 al.; 3 Macc 6: 10; Ep. Arist. 16; Jos., Ant. 18, 179) ζυγῷ δουλείας Gal 5: 1. θλίψεσιν 2 Th 1: 4 v.l.—Field, Notes 28f; 64. M-M.*

ἔνθα adv. (Hom.+; pap., LXX)—1. *there* MPol 18: 2.—

2. relat. *where* (Parthenius 5, 5; 8, 4; Appian, Iber. 89 §387; Jos., Ant. 14, 5, C. Ap. 2, 282) GP 13: 56.*

ἐνθάδε adv., in our lit. only of place (so Hom.+; inscr., pap.).

1. *here, to this place* (3 Macc 6: 25; Jos., Ant. 4, 134) ἔρχεσθαι ἐ. (Herodas 2, 97; Preisigke, Griech. Urkunden zu Kairo '11, no. 48, 6; POxy. 967) J 4: 16; Hs 9, 5, 5. διέρχεσθαι J 4: 15. συνέρχεσθαι Ac 25: 17.

2. *here, in this place* (Lucian, Dial. Mort 20, 3; En. 19, 1; Jos., Bell. 1, 633, Ant. 1, 343) Lk 24: 41; Ac 10: 18; 16: 28; 17: 6; 25: 24; τὰ ἐ. *the things that are here* (POxy. 1154, 10 [I AD] εἰμὶ ξένος τῶν ἐ.; Jos., Ant. 16, 322) 2 Cl 6: 6. ἡ ἐ. ἀπόλαυσις *enjoyment here and now* (Herm. Wr. 6, 3α τὸ ἐ. ἀγαθόν; POxy. 1296, 5 [III AD] οἱ ἐ. θεοί) 10: 3f. ὁ δοκῶν ἐ. θάνατος *what seems to be death here* (on earth) Dg 10: 7. M-M.*

ἔνθεν adv. (Hom.+; LXX)—1. of place *from here* (Jos., Ant. 4, 323) μετάβα ἔ. ἐκεῖ *move fr. this place to that* Mt 17: 20; διαβαίνειν ἔ. Lk 16: 26.

2. of time *from then on* (Apollon. Rhod. 1, 1138; 2, 713; Sib. Or. 1, 387) 2 Cl 13: 3; IEph 19: 3.*

ἔνθεος, ον (trag., X., Pla.+; Dialekt-Inschr. 805d [Boeotia]; PGM 1, 21; 160; 13, 144; Philo; Jos., Bell. 3, 353, Ant. 9, 35; Sib. Or. 3, 295; 5, 263) *inspired by God*, in our lit. only as a rdg. of the Sacra Parallela (KHoll, Fgmte. vornic. Kirchenväter aus den Sacr. Par. 1899, p. 22) on ITr 8: 2 τὸ ἔ. πλῆθος (Lghtf. has it in the text for ἐν θεῷ).*

ἐνθυμέομαι dep.; 1 aor. ἐνεθυμήθην (Aeschyl., Pre-Socr.+; pap., LXX) *reflect (on), consider, think* w. acc. of the thing (Thu. 5, 32, 1; Celsus 7, 18; Sir 16: 20; Bar 3: 31; 4 Macc 8: 27; Philo, Mut. Nom. 240; Jos., Bell. 1, 232, Ant. 11, 155) ταῦτα Mt 1: 20. πονηρὰ (Wsd 3: 14) ἐν ταῖς καρδίαις *think evil in your hearts* 9: 4. περί τινος (Pla., Rep. 10 p. 595A; Isocr. 15, 199, Ep. 9, 8 Blass; Appian, Bell. Civ. 2, 5 §18; Wsd 6: 15) Ac 10: 19 v.l. (s. διενθυμέομαι). M-M.*

ἐνθύμησις, εως, ἡ (since Eur.; Thu. 1, 132, 5; Ps.-Lucian, Salt. 81; Vett. Val. 301, 8; Herm. Wr. 1, 22; PGM 5, 328; BGU 1024 IV, 12; Sym. Job 21: 27; Ezk 11: 21) *thought, reflection, idea* Mt 9: 4; 12: 25; Hm 4, 1, 3. ἡ ἐ. ἀναβαίνει ἐπὶ τὴν καρδίαν *the idea arises in the heart* m 4, 1, 2; 6, 2, 7. χαράγματι τέχνης καὶ ἐνθυμήσεως ἀνθρώπου τὸ θεῖον εἶναι ὅμοιον *that the divine nature is like something fashioned by the skill and thought of man* Ac 17: 29. κριτικὸς ἐνθυμήσεων καὶ ἐννοιῶν *passing judgment on the reflections and thoughts* Hb 4: 12; cf. 1 Cl 21: 9. M-M.*

ἐνί poet. form of ἐν IEph 11: 2.*

ἔνι (for ἔνεστιν [cf. ἔνειμι and Bl-D. §98; Mlt.-H. 306; Rob. s.v. εἰμι p. 313] Hom.+; inscr., pap.; Philo; Sib. Or. 3, 39.—On the LXX cf. PKatz and ADebrunner, Mus. Helv. 11, '54, 57-64) in our lit. only w. a negative οὐκ ἔνι *there is not* or *no* (Vi. Aesopi I c. 17 p. 270, 6) ἐν ὑμῖν οὐδεὶς σοφός; *is there no wise man among you?* 1 Cor 6: 5. Ἰουδαῖος οὐδὲ Ἕλλην *there is neither Jew nor Gentile* Gal 3: 28; Col 3: 11. παρ' ᾧ οὐκ ἔ. παραλλαγή *with whom there is no variation* Js 1: 17. M-M.*

ἐνιαυτός, οῦ, ὁ (Hom.+; inscr., pap., LXX, En., Ep. Arist., Philo; Jos., Ant. 15, 378, C. Ap. 1, 157).

1. *year* Rv 9: 15; ἐ. καὶ μῆνας ἕξ *a year and a half* Ac 18: 11; cf. Js 5: 17 (GerhKittel, Rabbinica '20, 31-5). ἀρχιερεὺς τοῦ ἐ. ἐκείνου *high priest for that year* J 11: 49,

51; 18: 13 (cf. UHolzmeister, ZkTh 44, '20, 306-12.—The supposition that there was a different high priest every year holds good for Asia Minor [Inscr. Brit. Mus. III 498; cf. CGBrandis, Pauly-W. II 475] and for Syria [Lucian, De Syria Dea 42], but not for Jerusalem). ποιεῖν ἐ. *spend a year* Js 4: 13 (cf. Pr 13: 23).—In acc. in answer to the question 'how long?' (Thu.+): ὅλον ἐ. *for a whole year* Ac 11: 26; Hs 6, 4, 4; ὅλον τὸν ἐ. *the whole year through* s 6, 5, 4; ἅπαξ τοῦ ἐ. *once a year* Hb 9: 7 (Ex 30: 10; Lev 16: 34; cf. Philo, Leg. ad Gai. 306). μέχρις ἐνιαυτοῦ *for as long as a year* Hs 6, 5, 3. κατ' ἐνιαυτόν *every year, annually* (Thu. 1, 93, 3 al.; oft. inscr.; UPZ 122, 6 [157 BC] of an annual pilgrimage; LXX; Ep. Arist. 180) Hb 9: 25; 10: 1, 3; B 10: 6. Also παρ' ἐνιαυτόν B 10: 7 (Diod. S. 4, 65, 1; Dit., Syll.³ 193, 14 [IV BC] παρὰ τὸν ἐ. ἕκαστον).

2. more gener. of a period of time (Aristoph., Ran. 347; Pla., Leg. 10 p. 906c; Diod. S. 38+39 fgm. 5: God has ordained eight ages; each one is an ἐνιαυτὸς μέγας; Jos., Ant. 1, 106 ὁ μέγας ἐνιαυτός consists of 600 years), of the age of salvation brought by the Messiah ἐ. κυρίου δεκτός Lk 4: 19; B 14: 9 (both Is 61: 2.—Cf. also Phlegon: 257 fgm. 1, 9 Jac., where Pythia announces the coming of a rather long period of time as φιλόφρων ἐνιαυτός).

3. The mng. of ἐ. in the combination καιροὶ καὶ ἐνιαυτοί Gal 4: 10 is not certain. It could be an allusion to the so-called 'sabbatical years' (Lev 25), but it may also mean certain *days of the year* (Dit., Syll.² 438, 162 [c. 400 BC]), as the New Year festival. GABarton, JBL 23, '14, 118-26. M-M. B. 1012.*

ἐνιδρύω 1 aor. ἐνίδρυσα (Hdt.+; inscr., pap.; Philo, De Prov. in Euseb., Pr. Ev. 8, 14, 63) *place* or *establish in* τινί someone τὸν λόγον ἀνθρώποις Dg 7: 2 (Plut., Mor. 1008A τῇ κεφαλῇ τὸν λογισμόν).*

ἔνιοι, αι, α (Orph., Aristoph., Hdt.+; inscr., pap.; 3 Macc 2: 31; 3: 4; Jos., Ant. 1, 121; 18, 45) *some, several* 1 Cl 44: 6; 2 Cl 19: 2; Dg 5: 3; Papias 2: 15; 4.*

ἐνίοτε adv. (Eur., Hippocr.+; Zen.-P. 59 362, 25 [242 BC]; Sir 37: 14) *sometimes* Mt 17: 15 D et al.; 2 Cl 19: 2 v.l. B. 987.*

ἐνίστημι 2 aor. ἐνέστην, ptc. ἐνστάς; pf. ἐνέστηκα, ptc. ἐνεστηκώς and ἐνεστώς; fut. mid. ἐνστήσομαι (Eur., Hdt.+; inscr., pap., LXX; Philo, Aet. M. 10; Joseph.) in our lit. only intrans.

1. in past tenses *be present, have come* (X.+; Polyb., inscr., pap., LXX) ἐνέστηκεν ἡ ἡμέρα τοῦ κυρίου *the day of the Lord has come* 2 Th 2: 2 (cf. Phlegon: 257 fgm. 36, 6 Jac, ἐνστάσης τῆς ἡμέρας τοῦ γάμου=when the wedding day came; PGM 13, 364 ὅταν ἐνστῇ ἡ ἡμέρα; Jos., Ant. 12, 175 ἐνστάσης τῆς ἡμέρας=when the day came; cf. Gdspd., Probs. 179f; but BBWarfield, Expositor, 3d series 4, 1886, 37 and AOepke, TW II, 540 favor mng. 2 below). ὁ καιρὸς ὁ ἐνεστηκώς (Polyb. 1, 60, 9; 21, 3, 3; Jos., Ant. 16, 162; pap.) *the present time* Hb 9: 9; cf. 1 Cl 55: 1. ὁ αἰὼν ὁ ἐνεστώς *the present age* Gal 1: 4. ἐνεστώς fairly oft. in contrast to μέλλων (Sext. Emp., Phys. 2, 193; Philo, Plant. 114) ἡ ἐ. χάρις IEph 11: 1. ἐνεστῶτα, μέλλοντα Ro 8: 38; 1 Cor 3: 22; B 1: 7; 4: 1; 5: 3.—EDBurton, Gal. ICC, 432f.

2. *impend, be imminent*, w. the connotation of threatening (Hdt., Polyb.; PGM 13, 1049; LXX; Jos., Ant. 4, 209) 2 Ti 3: 1. ἡ ἐ. ἀνάγκη *the impending distress* 1 Cor 7: 26; B 17: 2 (though mng. 1 is also possible in these three passages). M-M.*

ἐνισχύω 1 aor. ἐνίσχυσα, pass. ἐνισχύθην—1. intrans. (Aristot., Theophr., Diod. S. 18, 61, 3, LXX) *grow strong,*

regain one's strength (cf. Epict. 3, 24, 108; Gen 48: 2) ἐνίσχυσεν Ac 9: 19 (v.l. ἐνισχύθη). Cf. 19: 20 D.
  2. trans. (Hippocr. al. [Hobart 81]; 2 Km 22: 40; Sir 50: 4; Jos., Ant. 7, 269) *strengthen* τινά Lk 22: 43; B 14: 7 (Is 42: 6). τὶ *urge someth. insistently* MPol 17: 2. M-M.*

ἐνκ- s. ἐγκ.

ἐννέα indecl. (Hom.+; pap., LXX; Jos., Ant. 1, 85 al.; Test. 12 Patr.) *nine* Mt 18: 12f; Lk 15: 4, 7; IRo 10: 3; οἱ ἐ. *the* (other) *nine* Lk 17: 17 (Bl-D. §306, 5; 480, 1). M-M.*

ἐννεός s. ἐνεός.

ἐννεύω impf. ἐνένευον (Aristoph., fgm. Babyl. 58 Dind.; Lucian, Dial. Mer. 12, 1; Jos., Ant. 8, 97; Pr 6: 13; 10: 10) *nod* or *make signs* τινί *to someone as a signal* Lk 1: 62. ἐ. τινὶ τῇ χειρί *motion to someone w. the hand* Hv 3, 1, 9 (cf. Pr 6: 13; 10: 10 ὀφθαλμῷ).*

ἐννοέω 1 aor. ptc. ἐννοήσας (trag., Hdt.+; pap.; Job 1: 5; Bar 2: 16; Ep. Arist.; Philo; Jos., Ant. 16, 105, C. Ap. 2, 130; Test. 12 Patr.) *have in mind, consider* τὶ *someth.* ἐ. ἔννοιαν *conceive a plan* Dg 8: 9.*

ἔννοια, ας, ἡ *thought, knowledge, insight* (so esp. in the philosophers: Pla., Phaedo 73c; Aristot., Eth. Nicom. 9, 11 p. 1171a, 31f; 10, 10 p. 1179b, 13f; Epict. 2, 11, 2; 3 al.; Plut., Mor. 900a; Diog. L. 3, 79; Herm. Wr. 1, 1; Philo, but also elsewh. i.e., in contexts having nothing to do with philosophy: X., An. 3, 1, 13; Diod. S. 20, 34, 6; PReinach 7, 15 [II bc]; Pr 1: 4; 2: 11 al.; Jos., Bell. 2, 517, Ant. 14, 481; Test. 12 Patr.) κ. ὑμεῖς τ. αὐτὴν ἔννοιαν ὁπλίσασθε *arm yourselves also w. the same insight* 1 Pt 4: 1; ἐννοεῖν ἔ. Dg 8: 9. Pl. (Jos., Ant. 6, 37) w. διαλογισμοί 1 Cl 21: 3. W. ἐνθυμήσεις (Sym., Job 21: 27) Hb 4: 12; 1 Cl 21: 9. W. λογισμοί Pol 4: 3. M-M. B. 1212.*

ἔννομος, ον (Pind., Aeschyl.+; inscr., pap., Sir Prol. l. 14; Philo, Abr. 242, Poster. Cai. 176; Jos., Ant. 19, 302; Sib. Or. 3, 246) *legal, lawful* ἐ. ἐκκλησία Ac 19: 39 could, acc. to the context, mean a legally convened assembly in contrast to a mob. But certain features of the word's usage (Lucian, Deor. Conc. 14; Dit., Syll.³ 672, 37 [II bc] ἐν τᾷ ἐννόμῳ ἐκκλησίᾳ) suggest the interpr. *regular assembly* in contrast to one called for a special occasion.—*Subject to the law, obedient to the law* (Aelian, V.H. 2, 22 v.l.): ἔ. Χριστοῦ *subject to the law of Christ* 1 Cor 9: 21 (Bl-D. §182, 3 app.; Rob. 504.—Proclus on Pla., Crat. p. 93, 5 P., the contrast ἔ. and ἔκνομος). Fr. a purely linguistic point of view it is also poss. to transl. *true to the law, upright* (so ἔ. in Aeschyl., Suppl. 404; Pla., Rep. 4 p. 424e) *acc. to the judgment of Christ.*—CHDodd, Studia Paulina (JdeZwaan Festschr.) '53, 96–110. M-M.*

ἐννόμως adv. (= in accordance w. the law: Lysias 9, 12; 30, 35; Lucian, Symp. 32; Cass. Dio 56, 7, 2; Pr 31: 25) Ro 2: 12 v.l. as substitute for and in the sense of ἐν νόμῳ *subject to* or *in possession of the law* (opp. ἀνόμως, which prob. gave rise to the v.l.).*

ἔννυχος, ον *at night* (Il. 11, 716; Pind., trag., then Aesop, Fab. 110 H.; IG VII 584, 5; Sb 6699 [early Ptolem.]; 3 Macc 5: 5; Sib. Or. 3, 293) acc. neut. pl. as adv. (cf. Soph., Ajax 930 πάννυχα) ἔννυχα (v.l. ἔννυχον) *at night-time* πρωῒ ἔ. λίαν *in the early morning, when it was still quite dark* Mk 1: 35. M-M.*

ἐνοικέω fut. ἐνοικήσω; 1 aor. ἐνῴκησα (Eur., Hdt.+; inscr., pap., LXX; Jos., Bell. 6, 55 ἐ. ψυχὴ σώματι; Sextus 144 διανοίᾳ θεὸς ἐ.) *live, dwell (in)*; in our lit.—except for Lk 13: 4 v.l.—always w. ἔν τινι and of God or of

spiritual things that take up their abode in or among men ἐνοικήσω ἐν αὐτοῖς *I will dwell among them* 2 Cor 6: 16. Of the Holy Spirit, which indwells in men Ro 8: 11; 2 Ti 1: 14. Of the word of Christ Col 3: 16. Of faith 2 Ti 1: 5. Of sin Ro 7: 17 (cf. Test. Sim. 5: 1). M-M.*

ἐνοξίζω 1 aor. ἐνώξισα (hapax legomenon) *become sour* IMg 10: 2.*

ἔνοπλος, ον (trag.+; pap.; PGM 13, 197; Philo, Aet. M. 57; Jos., Bell. 2, 444, Ant. 14, 294) *armed* GH 20b.*

ἐνοπτρίζομαι (Plut., Mor. 696a; Porphyr., Ad Marcellam 13 twice [s. PCorssen, ZNW 19, '20, 2f]; Philo, Migr. Abr. 98) *see (as) in a mirror* τὴν ὄψιν 1 Cl 36: 2. Another possibility is the simple mng. *look at, see* (Hierocles 1 p. 416: 'as it is impossible for an impure eye to contemplate radiant objects, so it is for a soul without virtue τῆς ἀληθείας ἐνοπτρίσασθαι κάλλος').*

ἐνοράω 2 aor. ἐνεῖδον, ptc. ἐνιδών (Hdt., Aristoph.+; Philo, Op. M. 15) *see, perceive* δύναμιν Dg 12: 5.*

ἐνορκίζω (act. CIG IV 9288, 6; IG XII 3, 1238; Monum. As. Min. Ant. III '31, no. 77, 1; 2 Esdr 23 [Neh 13]: 25 v.l.) *adjure, cause someone* (τινά) *to swear* τι *by someth.* w. acc. and inf. foll. ὑμᾶς τὸν κύριον *you by the Lord* 1 Th 5: 27 (Bl-D. §149; 155, 7; 392, 1d; Rob. 484; 1085). M-M.*

ἑνότης, ητος, ἡ (Aristot.+; Epicurus [HUsener, Epicurea 1887 p. 13, 14]; Plut., Mor. 95a; 416e al.; Test. Zeb. 8: 6) *unity* τηρεῖν τὴν ἑ. τοῦ πνεύματος *maintain the unity of the spirit* Eph 4: 3. ἑ. τῆς πίστεως *unity in the faith* vs. 13; σύνδεσμος τῆς ἑ. *bond of unity* Col 3: 14 v.l. SHanson, The Unity of the Church in the NT: Col, Eph, '46, esp. 122, 138f, 158.—Esp. common in Ign.: ἐν ἑ. IEph 4: 2. ἐν ἑ. γίνεσθαι *become a unity* 14: 1. ἐν ἑ. σύμφωνα εἶναι *sound together in unison* 5: 1. ἐν τῇ ἑ. ὑμῶν IPhld 2: 2. ἑ. τῆς ἐκκλησίας 3: 2. Esp. also of the unity of Christians w. God and Christ ἐν ἑ. Ἰησοῦ Χριστοῦ ὄντες 5: 2; ἑ. θεοῦ 8: 1; 9: 1; ISm 12: 2 (here ἐν should be placed before ἑνότητι, Hdb. ad loc.); IPol 8: 3. M-M.*

ἐνοχλέω (Aristoph., Hippocr.+; inscr., pap., LXX) *trouble, annoy* (Memnon [I bc/I ad]: no. 434 fgm. 1, 29, 6 Jac. ἐνοχλεῖσθαι ὑπό τινος; Dio Chrys. 3, 57; POxy. 899, 44; Jos., Vi. 159, Ant. 12, 153) οἱ ἐνοχλούμενοι ἀπὸ πνευμάτων ἀκαθάρτων *those who were troubled by unclean spirits* Lk 6: 18 (cf. Galen XIX p. 171 K.; Lucian, Philops. 31 οἰκία ἐνοχλουμένη ὑπὸ τῶν φασμάτων; Appian, Bell. Civ. 3, 61 §252 τοῦ δαιμονίου ἐνοχλοῦντος=the [evil] divinity causing unrest). Abs. *cause trouble* Hb 12: 15 (Dt 29: 17 v.l.). Cf. PKatz s.v. χολή. M-M.*

ἔνοχος, ον (Pla.+; inscr., pap., LXX; Ep. Arist. 25; Philo; Jos., Ant. 17, 127)=ἐνεχόμενος *caught in.*
  1. *subject to* w. gen. (Sir Prol. l. 13) ἔ. δουλείας *subject to slavery* Hb 2: 15.
  2. mostly as a legal term *liable, answerable, guilty.*
  a. w. dat. to denote the court τ. κρίσει, τ. συνεδρίῳ Mt 5: 21, 22ab (sim. datives are not uncommon in Gk., e.g. X., Mem. 1, 2, 64; OBenndorf, Reisen im südwestl. Kleinasien II 1889, 166 no. 193 ἔνοχος ἔστω πᾶσι θεοῖς; POxy. 275, 32 [66 ad]).
  b. w. gen. (cf. Mlt. 39; Wilcken, APF 1, '01, 170; ENachmanson, Eranos 11, '11, 232).
  a. to denote the punishment θανάτου *deserving of death* (Diod. S. 27, 4, 7; Gen 26: 11) Mt 26: 66; Mk 14: 64. αἰωνίου κρίσεως 3: 29 v.l.

β. to denote the crime (Antipho 6, 46 τοῦ φόνου; Lysias 14, 5; Pla., Leg. 11 p. 914ε τῶν βιαίων; Vett. Val. 117, 10 ἔ. μοιχείας; 2 Macc 13: 6; Philo, Decal. 133) *guilty* αἰωνίου ἁμαρτήματος Mk 3: 29. τῆς ἁμαρτίας τοῦ καταλαλοῦντος *involved in the sin of the slanderer* Hm 2: 2; cf. 4, 1, 5. ἔ. τούτου τοῦ αἵματος s 10, 4, 3 (Gk. Text POxy. 404).

γ. to denote the pers. (or thing) against whom the sin has been committed (Is 54: 17 ἔνοχοί σου *those who wrong you*; cf. Dssm. LO⁴ 91f [LAE 116]) ἔ. τοῦ σώματος καὶ τοῦ αἵματος *sin against the body and the blood* 1 Cor 11: 27; γέγονεν πάντων ἔ. *has sinned against all* (the commandments) Js 2: 10.

c. ἔ. εἰς τ. γέενναν τοῦ πυρός is to be explained as brachylogy *guilty enough to go into the hell of fire* Mt 5: 22c.—RSBagnall, Bull. of the Am. Soc. of Papyrologists 6, '69, 91f. M-M. B. 1445.*

ἐνόω 1 aor. pass. ἡνώθην; pf. pass. ptc. ἡνωμένος (Aristot. +; Sb 2034, 5; 4832, 5; Sym.; Philo, Migr. Abr. 220, Mut. Nom. 200; Jos., Bell. 3, 15) *unite*, in our lit. only pass. Of a church ἡνωμένη *united* IEph inscr. Of prayer ἡ ἡνωμένη ὑμῶν ἐν θεῷ προσευχή *your united prayer in God* IMg 14. Of the Lord ἡνωμένος ὤν 7: 1. Here τῷ πατρί is to be supplied; it actually occurs ISm 3: 3, *united w. the Father*. The dat. is also used elsewh. to indicate that w. which (or whom) the unification takes place (Herm. Wr. 1, 10; Proclus on Pla., Cratyl. p. 59, 23; 83, 27 P.) τῷ ἐπισκόπῳ IMg 6: 2. πάσῃ ἐντολῇ IRo inscr. B. 844.*

ἐνπ- s. ἐμπ.

ἐνσκιρόω pf. pass. ptc. ἐνεσκιρωμένος (X., De Re Equ. 4, 2; Stoic. III p. 102, 38; Theod. Is 27: 1; Etym. Mag. p. 344, 30) *harden, make callous* Hv 3, 9, 8.*

ἐνστερνίζομαι pf. mid. ptc. ἐνεστερνισμένος (late word, found almost always in Christian wr., usu. in mid.; Hesychius; Suidas; Psellus p. 72, 17) *store away in one's heart* ἐπιμελῶς ἐ. ἦτε τοῖς σπλάγχνοις (sc. τ. λόγους) *you had carefully stored away in your heart of hearts* 1 Cl 2: 1.*

ἔνταλμα, ατος, τό (LXX; PLond. 1384, 55 [VIII AD]) *commandment* (w. διδασκαλία) ἐ. ἀνθρώπων Mt 15: 9; Mk 7: 7; Col 2: 22 (all three Is 29: 13); τὰ τοῦ κυρίου ἐ. 2 Cl 17: 3.*

ἐντάσσω pf. pass. ptc. ἐντεταγμένος (X., An. 3, 3, 18; inscr., pap., LXX; Jos., C. Ap. 1, 172) *enroll* εἴς τι *in someth.* εἰς τὸν ἀριθμὸν τῶν σωζομένων 1 Cl 58: 2.*

ἐνταῦθα adv. (Hom. +; inscr., pap., LXX; Jos., Ant. 14, 83) of place *here* GOxy 23.*

ἐνταφιάζω 1 aor. ἐνεταφίασα (Anth. Pal. 11, 125, 5; Plut., Mor. 995c; Dit., Syll.³ 1235, 5 [I AD]; Gen 50: 2; Test. Jud. 26: 3) *prepare for burial, bury* J 19: 40. πρὸς τὸ ἐνταφιάσαι με *to prepare me for burial* Mt 26: 12. M-M.*

ἐνταφιασμός, οῦ, ὁ (schol. on Eur., Phoen. 1654 and on Aristoph., Plut. 1009.—ἐνταφιαστής as early as PPar. 7, 6 [100 BC]; Gen 50: 2) *preparation for burial*, or *burial* itself Mk 14: 8; J 12: 7.—Field, Notes 98. M-M.*

ἐντέλλω (Pind. +) but usu., and in our lit. exclusively, mid. dep. (oft. Hdt. +; inscr., pap., LXX, Joseph., Test. 12 Patr.) fut. ἐντελοῦμαι (Mt 4: 6; Lk 4: 10); 1 aor. ἐνετειλάμην; pf. ἐντέταλμαι (in our lit. only w. act. mng. as Polyb. 17, 2, 1; Herodian 1, 9, 9; Tob 5: 1; 2 Macc 11: 20; Jos., Vi. 318 [plpf.]), 2 sg. ἐντέταλσαι Hm 12, 6,

4; *command, order, give orders* abs. Mt 15: 4 v.l. (w. λέγων foll.); Pol 6: 3; B 7: 3. τινι *to someone* Mt 17: 9; J 14: 31; Ac 1: 2; 13: 47; τί *someth.* (Herodian 1, 9, 10; Sir 48: 22) IRo 3: 1; Hm 12, 6, 4. τινί τι (Hdt. 1, 47; Diogenes of Oenoanda [II AD] fgm. 66 ed. JWilliam '07 φίλοις τάδε ἐντέλλομαι; Jos., Vi. 242) Mt 28: 20; Mk 10: 3; J 15: 14; περί τινος *concerning someth.* (1 Macc 9: 55) Hb 11: 22. τινὶ περί τινος (UPZ 61, 9 [161 BC]; APF 8 p. 212 no. 14, 12; Sir 17: 14; 1 Macc 3: 34) Mt 4: 6; Lk 4: 10 (both Ps 90: 11). W. inf. foll. (Gen 42: 25; 2 Ch 36: 23; Manetho in Jos., C. Ap. 1, 98) Mt 19: 7; J 8: 5; Hm 4, 1, 1. W. gen. of the inf. foll. Lk 4: 10 (Ps 90: 11). W. ὅτι foll. *say emphatically* IRo 4: 1. W. ἵνα foll. (Jos., Ant. 8, 375; 7, 356) Mk 13: 34; J 15: 17.—τ. διαθήκης ἧς (by attraction for ἥν) ἐνετείλατο πρὸς ὑμᾶς ὁ θεός *of the decree which God has ordained for you* Hb 9: 20. M-M.**

ἔντερον, ου, τό (Hom. +, mostly pl., as also Artem. 1, 33 p. 35, 15 [where a distinction is made between ἔντερα and σπλάγχνα]; PGM 4, 2596; 2658; Gen 43: 30; 2 Macc 14: 46) *intestine(s)*, then also *entrails* (so in the sg. Hippocr., π. νουσ. 3, 14 vol. VII 134; Diocles 43 p. 136, 33; Sir 31: 20) φαγεῖν τὸ ἔ. ἄπλυτον μετὰ ὄξους *eat the entrails unwashed, with vinegar* B 7: 4 (quot. of uncertain orig.).*

ἐντεῦθεν adv.—1. of place (Hom. +; inscr., pap., LXX) *from here* (En. 22, 13; Jos., Bell. 6, 299; 7, 22) Lk 4: 9; 13: 31; J 7: 3; 14: 31; 1 Cl 53: 2 (Ex 32: 7). ἄρατε ταῦτα ἐντεῦθεν *take these things away from here* J 2: 16. ἐντεῦθεν καὶ ἐντεῦθεν fr. *here and fr. there=on each side* (cf. Num 22: 24) J 19: 18. For this ἐντεῦθεν κ. ἐκεῖθεν Rv 22: 2; ἡ βασιλεία ἡ ἐμὴ οὐκ ἔστιν ἐ. *my kingdom is not from here=ἐκ. τ. κόσμου τούτου* J 18: 36.

2. to indicate the reason or source (cf. Thu. 1, 5, 1; 1 Esdr 4: 22; Jos., Ant. 4, 225, C. Ap. 2, 182) ἐ., ἐκ τῶν ἡδονῶν fr. *this, namely your passions* Js 4: 1. M-M.*

ἔντευξις, εως, ἡ (Pla. +; inscr., pap.; 2 Macc 4: 8)—1. *petition, request* (Polyb. 5, 35, 4; Diod. S. 16, 55, 3; Plut., Tib. Gracch. 11, 6; Ep. Arist. 252; Jos., Ant. 15, 79; inscr., pap. [Mitteis, Grundzüge 13ff; RLaqueur, Quaestiones epigraph., Diss. Strassb. '04, 8ff; Wilcken, APF 4, '08, 224; Dit., Or. 138 note 10; Dssm., B 117f; 143f (BS 121; 146)]); the letter fr. the church at Rome to the church at Corinth calls itself a *petition, appeal* 1 Cl 63: 2; so does the sermon known as 2 Cl (19: 1).—Since a petition denoted by ἔ. is preferably directed to a king, the word develops the mng.—

2. *prayer* (Plut., Num. 14, 12 ποιεῖσθαι τὰς πρὸς τὸ θεῖον ἐντεύξεις; En. 99, 3), and chiefly—a. *intercessory prayer* (w. προσευχή, the general word for prayer, and εὐχαριστία, a prayer of thanksgiving; cf. Elbogen² 4ff; 73) 1 Ti 2: 1; cf. Hs 2: 5ab; Hs 5, 4, 3.

b. gener. *prayer* Hm 5, 1, 6; 10, 3, 2f; 11: 9, 14; s 2: 5c, 6, 7.

c. It can even approach the mng. *prayer of thanksgiving* 1 Ti 4: 5 (=εὐχαριστία vss. 3, 4).

d. The context requires the mng. *power of intercession* Hm 10, 3, 3 end; Hs 5, 4, 4. M-M.*

ἐντίθημι ptc. ἐντιθείς (Hom. +; Lucian, Alex. 47 ἀλήθειαν; inscr., pap., LXX; Jos., Ant. 11, 239) *put in, implant* τὸ ὄνομα τ. κυρίου Ἰησοῦ Ac 18: 4 D.*

ἔντιμος, ον (Soph. +; inscr., pap., LXX, En.; Jos., Ant. 15, 243).

1. *honored, respected*—a. of rank *distinguished* ἐντιμότερός σου *someone more distinguished than you* (cf. Num 22: 15) Lk 14: 8 (ἔ. at a banquet: Lucian, De Merc. Cond. 26).

b. esp. for one's qualities *esteemed, highly honored* (opp. ἄτιμος) 1 Cl 3: 3; ἐ. ἔχειν τινά *hold someone in esteem* (Pla.; Diod. S.) Phil 2: 29.

2. *valuable, precious* (Ps.-Demosth. 56, 9) of slaves Lk 7: 2; Hs 5, 2, 2. Of stones (Diod. S. 2, 50, 1; Tob 13: 17 BA; cf. Job 28: 10) 1 Pt 2: 4, 6; B 6: 2 (in both cases Is 28: 16). M-M.*

ἐντολή, ῆς, ἡ (Pind., Hdt.+; inscr., pap., LXX, En., Ep. Arist., Philo, Joseph., Test. 12 Patr.) *command(ment), order.*

1. of men—**a.** of official decrees, perh. *writ, warrant* J 11: 57 (ἐντολὰς διδόναι ἵνα, as Dit., Or. 441, 59 [81 BC]).

b. of the commands of other pers. in high position: father (Tob 4: 19) Lk 15: 29. Apostles Ac 17: 15; Col 4: 10. Jewish teachings as ἐντολαὶ ἀνθρώπων Tit 1: 14.

2. of divine authorities (cf. Dit., Syll.³ 888, 51 [238 AD] of imperial decrees: ταῖς θείαις ἐντολαῖς).

a. of the commandments of the OT law—**α.** the sg. takes in all the commandments as *the law* (4 Macc 13: 15; 16: 24) κατὰ τ. ἐντολήν *according to the law* Lk 23: 56; cf. Ro 7: 8ff; Hb 7: 18; 9: 19. κατὰ νόμον ἐντολῆς σαρκίνης *acc. to the norm of a law dependent on the physical life* 7: 16.

β. more freq. the pl. stands for the totality of legal ordinances (Epict. 4, 7, 17 ἔγνωκα τοῦ θεοῦ τὰς ἐντολάς; Suppl. Epigr. Gr. VIII 170, 4) Mt 5: 19; 19: 17; Mk 10: 19; Lk 18: 20.

γ. of single commandments Eph 6: 2; Mt 22: 36, 38 (cf. Ep. Arist. 228 ὁ θεὸς πεποίηταί ἐ. μεγίστην.—HAHunt, The Great Commandment: ET 56, '44, 82f; CBurchard, Das doppelte Liebesgebot, JoachJeremias-Festschr., '70, 39–62), 40; Mk 10: 5; 12: 28, 31; Ro 13: 9; B 7: 3; 9: 5. ὁ νόμος τῶν ἐντολῶν Eph 2: 15.

b. of divine commandments gener. (Julian, Caesares p. 336C: Mithras gave ἐντολαί to his initiates), as they concern men 1 Cor 7: 19; 1 J 3: 22–4 al.; ISm 8: 1. φυλάσσειν *observe* (Jos., Ant. 7, 384) B 4: 11. τηρεῖν Rv 12: 17; 14: 12. κατορθώσασθαι τὰς ἐ. τοῦ κυρίου *preserve the Lord's commandments* Hv 3, 5, 3.

c. of God's commands to Christ J 10: 18 (λαμβάνειν as Jos., Bell. 4, 498); 12: 49f; 14: 31 v.l.; 15: 10b; B 6: 1.

d. of the precepts of Jesus J 13: 34; 14: 15, 21; 15: 10a, 12; 1 Cor 14: 37; 2 Cl 3: 4; 6: 7; 17: 3. Of the commands in the Sermon on the Mount 1 Cl 13: 3. ποιεῖν τὰς ἐντολάς μου 2 Cl 4: 5 (fr. an unknown gospel). ἡ Ἰησοῦ Χριστοῦ 17: 6; IEph 9: 2; cf. Pol 2: 2; IRo inscr.; φυλάσσειν τὰς ἐ. τοῦ κυρίου *observe the Lord's commandments* 2 Cl 8: 4.

e. of the commands of the angel of repentance Hv 5: 5; s 10, 3, 4 (POxy. 404); cf. the title of the second part: ἐντολαί, also m 1: 2; 2: 7 al.

f. the whole Christian religion is thought of as an ἐντολή (a new law) 1 Ti 6: 14; 2 Pt 2: 21. ἡ τ. ἀποστόλων ὑμῶν ἐ. τοῦ κυρίου κ. σωτῆρος *the command of the Lord and Savior (given) through your apostles* 3: 2; cf. ITr 13: 2.—GSchrenk, TW II 542–53. M-M.

ἐντόπιος, ία, ιον (Pla.+; Dionys. Hal. 8, 83; inscr., pap.; the anti-Semite Molon [I BC] in Euseb., Pr. Ev. 9, 19, 2) *local, belonging to a certain place* subst. οἱ ἐ. *the local residents* (Dit., Or. 194, 11 [42 BC]; PLond. 192, 94 [I AD]) Ac 21: 12 (opp. Paul's companions). M-M.*

ἐντός adv. of place (Hom.+; inscr., pap., LXX, Ep. Arist., Philo, Joseph.) in our lit. only as improper prep. w. gen. *inside, within, within the limits of* (Lucian, Dial. Mort. 14, 5; Jos., Bell. 3, 175 τ. πόλεως ἐντός; 7, 26) τοῦ θυσιαστηρίου *within the sanctuary* IEph 5: 2; ITr 7: 2. ἐάν τις τούτων ἐ. ᾖ *if anyone is in their company* (i.e., the

comp. of faith, hope, and love) Pol 3: 3.—In ἡ βασιλεία τοῦ θεοῦ ἐντὸς ὑμῶν ἐστιν Lk 17: 21 (cf. LJ 2: 3=JBL 65, '46, 177, also POxy. 654, 16 and WSchubart, ZNW 20, '21, 215–23), ἐ. ὑμῶν may mean *within you, in your hearts* (cf. Ps 38: 4; 102: 1; 108: 22, all ἐντός μου; Jos., Ant. 5, 107; cf. L-S-J lex. and RSV mg.), though many prefer to transl. *among you, in your midst,* either now or suddenly in the near future (cf. X., Hell. 2, 3, 19 ἐ. τούτων, An. 1, 10, 3 ἐ. αὐτῶν, though the relevance of the X. passages is doubtful—s. Field, Notes 71 and Roberts below; Ps 87: 6 Sym.; cf. Jos., Ant. 6, 315; Arrian, Anab. 5, 22, 4 ἐ. αὐτῶν = in their midst; so RSV text, and s. Noack and Bretscher below). Cf. AWabnitz, Rev. de Théol. et des Quest. rel. 18, '09, 221ff; 289ff; 456ff; ChBruston, ibid. 346ff; BSEaston, AJTh 16, '12, 275–83; KFProost, ThT 48, '14, 246ff; JHéring, Le royaume de Dieu et sa venue '37; PMSAllen, ET 50, '39, 233–5; ASledd, ibid. 235–7; WGKümmel, Verheissung u. Erfüllung '45, 17ff; BNoack, D. Gottesreich bei Lk (17: 20–4) '48; CHRoberts, HTR 41, '48, 1–8, citing Pap. Russischer u. Georgischer Sammlungen III, '30, 1, 9: ἵνα ἐντός μου αὐτὸ εὕρω; HJCadbury, Christ. Century 67, '50, 172f (*within your possession* or *reach*; cf. Tertullian, Adv. Marc. 4, 35), cf. Pol 3: 3 above and JGGriffiths, ET 63, '51f, 30f; HRiesenfeld, Nuntius 2, '49, 11f; AWikgren, ibid. 4, '50, '27f; PM Bretscher, CTM 15, '44, 730–6; 22, '51, 895–907. W. stress on the moral implications, RFrick, Beih. ZNW 6, '28, 6–8, cf. ARüstow, ZNW 51, '60, 197–224.—τὸ ἐ. τοῦ ποτηρίου *the inside of the cup*=what is in the cup (cf. τὰ ἐ. τοῦ οἴκου 1 Macc 4: 48, also schol. on Nicander, Alexiph. 479 τὰ ἐντός=the inside; Is 16: 11) Mt 23: 26. M-M.*

ἐντρέπω 2 aor. pass. ἐνετράπην; 2 fut. pass. ἐντραπήσομαι (Hom.+; pap., LXX, Joseph.).

1. act.—**a.** *make someone (τινά) ashamed* (Diog. L. 2, 29; Aelian, V. Hist. 3, 17; Sext. Emp., Psych. 3, 16) οὐκ ἐντρέπων ὑμᾶς γράφω ταῦτα *I write this not to make you ashamed* 1 Cor 4: 14.—**b.** *respect* τινά 1 Cl 38: 2.

2. mostly pass.—**a.** *be put to shame, be ashamed* (UPZ 62, 29 [161/60 BC]; 70, 4; Ps 34: 26; Is 44: 11) 2 Th 3: 14; Tit 2: 8; IMg 12.

b. w. mid. sense *turn toward someth.* or *someone, have regard for, respect* τινά (Alexis Com. 71 ed. Kock II 320; Polyb. 9, 36, 10; 30, 9, 2; Diod. S. 19, 7, 4 θεούς; Ex 10: 3; Wsd 2: 10; 6: 7; Jos., Bell. 7, 362) τὸν υἱόν μου Mt 21: 37; Mk 12: 6; Lk 20: 13. ἄνθρωπον μὴ ἐντρεπόμενος *who had no respect for man* 18: 2, cf. vs. 4. ὡς ἀδελφήν *respect* someone *as a sister* Hv 1, 1, 7. τὸν κύριον Ἰησοῦν 1 Cl 21: 6. ἀλλήλους IMg 6: 2. τοὺς διακόνους ὡς Ἰησοῦν ITr 3: 1; cf. ISm 8: 1; ITr 3: 2. W. αὐτούς to be supplied fr. the context: ἐντρεπόμεθα Hb 12: 9. M-M.*

ἐντρέφω (Eur.+) *bring up, rear,* then *train in* τινί someth. (Pla., Leg. 7 p. 798A; Epict. 4, 4, 48; Philo, Spec. Leg. 1, 314, Leg. ad Gai. 195 τ. ἱεροῖς γράμμασιν; Jos., Bell. 6, 102, C. Ap. 1, 269) ἐντρεφόμενος τοῖς λόγοις τῆς πίστεως 1 Ti 4: 6. M-M.*

ἔντρομος, ον (Plut., Fab. Max. 3, 1; Meleager [I BC]: Anth. Pal. 5, 204, 8; schol. on Eur., Phoen. 1284–7; LXX) *trembling* Lk 8: 47 D. ἔ. γενόμενος (cf. Soranus p. 68, 7f; Ps 17: 8; 76: 19) *trembling* Ac 7: 32; 16: 29; ἔκφοβος καὶ ἔ. (as 1 Macc 13: 2) *full of fear and trembling* Hb 12: 21. M-M.*

ἐντροπή, ῆς, ἡ—**1.** *shame, humiliation* (Diod. S. 40, 5a; schol. on Apollon. Rhod. 3, 656–63a; Ps 34: 26; 68: 8, 20) πρὸς ἐντροπήν τινι *to put someone to shame* 1 Cor 6: 5; 15: 34.

2. *respect, regard* (so Soph.+; Polyb. 4, 52, 2; Dio Chrys. 29[46], 4; Dit., Or. 323, 7 [II вс]; PGM 5, 17; Jos., Ant. 2, 46; 14, 375) πᾶσαν ἐ. τινι ἀπονέμειν *pay someone all the respect due him* IMg 3: 1. M-M. B. 1141.*

ἐντρυφάω (Eur.+) *revel, carouse* (X., Hell. 4, 1, 30; Diod. S. 19, 71, 3; LXX; Philo, Spec. Leg. 3, 27) ἔν τινι (Is 55: 2 ἐν ἀγαθοῖς, also Cass. Dio 65, 20) ἐν ταῖς ἀπάταις *revel in their lusts* 2 Pt 2: 13 (v.l. ἀγάπαις and ἀγνοίαις). *Delight* ἐντρύφα ἐν αὐτῇ (i.e. ἱλαρότητι) *delight in it* Hm 10, 3, 1. M-M.*

ἐντυγχάνω 2 aor. ἐνέτυχον; 1 aor. subj. mid. ἐντεύξωμαι Hm 10, 2, 5 (cf. the simplex 2 Macc 15: 7) (Soph., Hdt.+; inscr., pap., LXX, En.; Ep. Arist. 174; Philo; Joseph.).

1. *meet, turn to, approach, appeal, petition*—**a.** τινί *approach* or *appeal to someone* (Polyb. 4, 30, 1; Diod. S. 19, 60, 1; Dit., Or. 664, 10; 669, 46; PTebt. 58, 43; Da 6: 13 LXX; Jos., Ant. 16, 170) MPol 17: 2. τινὶ περί τινος (Polyb. 4, 76, 9; PSI 410, 14 [III вс] περὶ ῞Ωρου ἐντυχεῖν ᾽Αμμωνίῳ; PAmh. 142, 10) περὶ οὗ ἅπαν τὸ πλῆθος ἐνέτυχόν μοι *concerning whom all the people appealed to me* Ac 25: 24 (Jos., Ant. 12, 18 περὶ ὧν ἐντυγχάνειν μέλλει τῷ βασιλεῖ; cf. Field, Notes 140). ὑπέρ τινος *plead for someone* (Aelian, V.H. 1, 21; PAmh. 35, 20; PTebt. 183 [II вс]) of intercession by the Holy Spirit κατὰ θεὸν ἐ. ὑπὲρ ἁγίων Ro 8: 27. Of Christ's intercession Ro 8: 34; Hb 7: 25. τινὶ κατά τινος *appeal to someone against a third person* (cf. PGiess. 36, 15 [161 вс] ἐνετύχομεν καθ᾽ ὑμῶν; PAmh. 134, 10; 1 Macc 8: 32; 11: 25) Ro 11: 2; Hm 10, 2, 5.

b. Since petitions are also directed toward God, ἐ. comes to mean *pray* (Maximus Tyr. 10, 1b ἐντυχεῖν θεοῖς; BGU 246, 12 [c. 200 AD] εἰδότες ὅτι νυκτὸς καὶ ἡμέρας ἐντυγχάνω τῷ θεῷ ὑπὲρ ὑμῶν; Wsd 8: 21; 16: 28; En. 9, 3; 10 al.; Philo, Mos. 1, 173) w. dat. of the one being prayed for Hs 2: 6. τῷ θεῷ (w. ἐξομολογεῖσθαι) *to God* m 10, 3, 2. Also πρὸς τὸν κύριον (cf. Plut., Fab. 20, 2) Hs 2: 8. περί τινος *for someone* 1 Cl 56: 1; Pol 4: 3.

2. *read* (Pla.+; Polyb. 1, 3, 10; Plut., Rom. 12, 6; Vett. Val. 358, 25; 2 Macc 2: 25; 15: 39; Philo, Spec. Leg. 4, 161 [a book] ἐντυγχάνειν κ. ἀναγινώσκειν; Jos., Ant. 1, 15; 12, 226) Dg 12: 1.—RLaqueur, Quaestiones Epigr., Diss. Strassb. ᾽04, 15ff. M-M.*

ἐντυλίσσω 1 aor. ἐνετύλιξα; pf. pass. ptc. ἐντετυλιγμένος (Aristoph., Plut. 692, Nub. 987; Epict. 1, 6, 33; Athen. 3, 69 p. 106ε; PSI 1082, 16).

1. *wrap* (*up*) σῶμα σινδόνι *a body in a linen cloth* Lk 23: 53; Mt 27: 59; in the latter pass. ἐν σινδόνι is also well attested (cf. PGM 7, 826 ἐντύλισσε τὰ φύλλα ἐν σουδαρίῳ).—**2.** *fold up* of the σουδάριον J 20: 7. M-M.*

ἐντυπόω (Ps.-Aristot., Mirabilia 155; Ps.-Aristot., De Mundo 6; Cass. Dio; Plut.; Philostrat., Vi. Apoll. 3, 42 p. 117, 13; Ex 36: 37 v.l.; Ep. Arist. 67; Philo, Leg. All. 3, 95 τῇ ψυχῇ; Jos., Bell. 2, 120) *carve, impress* ἐν γράμμασιν ἐντετυπωμένη λίθοις *carved in letters on stone* 2 Cor 3: 7 (Istros [III вс]: no. 334 fgm. 53 Jac. ἐντετύπωται τῷ λίθῳ ἀνθρωποειδὴς εἰκών=a human figure was chiseled in the stone). M-M.*

ἐνυβρίζω 1 aor. ἐνύβρισα (Soph.+; Polyb.; Diod. S.; Epigr. Gr. 195; POxy. 237 VI, 17; Jos., Ant. 20, 117 al.) *insult, outrage* τὶ (Jos., Ant. 1, 47 μου τὴν γνώμην= God's command) τὸ πνεῦμα Hb 10: 29. M-M.*

ἐνυπνιάζομαι fut. ἐνυπνιασθήσομαι (so as dep. Hippocr.+; Plut., Brut. 24, 3; Jo. Lydus, De Ostentis p. 76,

21; Philo, Somn. 2, 105 and always in O and NT) *to dream* ἐνυπνίοις ἐ. *have visions in dreams* Ac 2: 17 (Jo 3: 1). Of false prophets ἐνυπνιαζόμενοι Jd 8.*

ἐνύπνιον, ου, τό (Aeschyl., Hdt.+; Arrian, Alex. An. 2, 18, 1; inscr., pap., LXX, Philo; Jos., C. Ap. 1, 207; 211; Test. 12 Patr.) *a dream* Ac 2: 17 (Jo 3: 1). M-M. B. 269.*

ἐνφ- s. ἐμφ.

ἐνώπιον prop. neut. of ἐνώπιος, used as an improper prep. (s. on ἀνά, beg.) w. gen. (as Dit., Syll.² 843, 7 [Trajan] ἐνώπιον τῶν προγεγραμμένων θεῶν; PCair. Zen. [I ᾽25] 73, 14 [257 вс]; PLond. 35, 6 [161 вс]; PGrenf. I 38, 11; POxy. 658, 9; LXX, En., Test. 12 Patr.), esp. in Lk (22 times), Ac (13 times) and Rv (32 times); 9 times in 1 Cl; not at all in Mt, Mk, 2 Pt, 2 J, Jd; once each in J, 1 J, 3 J, Js, 1 Pt.—*before.*

1. *of place before someone* or *someth.* εἶναι ἐ. τινος Rv 7: 15; usu. εἶναι must be supplied 1: 4; 4: 5f; 8: 3; 9: 13. After 'stand', 'place', 'step', etc. (schol. on Apollon. Rhod. 4, 1043b of suppliants: ὥσπερ ἐνώπιον τῶν θεῶν ἱστάμενοι): στῆναι Ac 10: 30; ἑστηκέναι Rv 7: 9; 8: 2 (RHCharles, ICC Rv ᾽20 ad loc.: *attend upon, be in the service of*); 11: 4; 12: 4; 20: 12; παρεστηκέναι cf. 3 Km 12: 6; Judg 20: 28) Lk 1: 19; Ac 4: 10; ἱστάναι 6: 6; καθῆσθαι Rv 11: 16. θύρα ἠνεῳγμένη ἐ. τινος *a door that stands open before someone* 3: 8. After verbs of motion: τιθέναι Lk 5: 18; βάλλειν Rv 4: 10; ἀναβαίνειν 8: 4; πίπτειν of worshippers or admirers falling down before someone (1 Km 25: 23) 4: 10; 5: 8; cf. 7: 11; προσκυνεῖν (Ps 21: 28, cf. 30) Lk 4: 7; Rv 3: 9; 15: 4. Of a forerunner or herald: after προέρχεσθαι (cf. 2 Ch 1: 10; 1 Km 12: 2ab) Lk 1: 17; προπορεύεσθαι vs. 76. σκάνδαλα βάλλειν ἐ. τινος Rv 2: 14.

2. *in the sight of, in the presence of*—**a.** lit. φαγεῖν ἐ. τινος Lk 24: 43; 13: 26 (cf. 2 Km 11: 13; 3 Km 1: 25). σημεῖα ποιεῖν J 20: 30. ἀνακρίνειν Lk 23: 14; cf. 5: 25; 8: 47; Ac 19: 9, 19; 27: 35; Rv 13: 13; 14: 3, 10; 3 J 6; ἐ. πολλῶν μαρτύρων 1 Ti 6: 12. ἐ. πάντων 5: 20; cf. Lk 11: 53 D; βαπτισθῆναι ἐ. αὐτοῦ 3: 7 D.

b. not literally ἡμεῖς ἐ. τοῦ θεοῦ πάρεσμεν Ac 10: 33. Also after verbs of motion βαστάζειν τὸ ὄνομα ἐ. τ. ἐθνῶν Ac 9: 15. After ἀρνεῖσθαι Lk 12: 9; ὁμολογεῖν Rv 3: 5; κατηγορεῖν 12: 10; καυχᾶσθαι 1 Cor 1: 29; δικαιοῦν ἑαυτόν Lk 16: 15. πίστιν κατὰ σεαυτὸν ἔχε ἐ. τοῦ θεοῦ *keep (your) faith to yourself in the sight of God* (=God, at least, sees it) Ro 14: 22; cf. 2 Cor 4: 2; MPol 14: 1f. Also a favorite expr. in assertions and oaths which call upon God, as the One who sees all: Gal 1: 20; 1 Ti 5: 21; 6: 13; 2 Ti 2: 14; 4: 1.—προορώμην τ. κύριον ἐ. μου Ac 2: 25 (Ps 15: 8).

3. *in the opinion* or *judgment of* ἐ. ἀνθρώπων Ro 12: 17; 2 Cor 8: 21b (cf. Pr 3: 4). As a rule (as ibid. a) of θεός or κύριος; so after τὰ ἀρεστά 1 J 3: 22; βδέλυγμα Lk 16: 15; δίκαιος 1: 6 v.l.; Ac 4: 19; δικαιοσύνη Lk 1: 75; δικαιοῦσθαι Ro 3: 20; εὐάρεστος Hb 13: 21; 1 Cl 60: 2; καλός, ἀπόδεκτος 1 Ti 2: 3; 5: 4; μέγας (4 Km 5: 1) Lk 1: 15; πολυτελής 1 Pt 3: 4; πεπληρωμένος Rv 3: 2. The combinations ἀρεστός and εὐάρεστος ἐ. τινος just mentioned form a transition to combinations in which ἐ. w. gen. stands simply

4. *for the dative:* ἤρεσεν ὁ λόγος ἐ. παντὸς τ. πλήθους Ac 6: 5 (cf. Dt 1: 23 v.l.; 2 Km 3: 36). φανεροῦσθαι ἐ. τοῦ θεοῦ 2 Cor 7: 12; cf. Lk 24: 11; Hb 4: 13.

5. special uses—**a.** *among, before* γίνεται χαρὰ ἐ. τῶν ἀγγέλων Lk 15: 10. ἔσται σοι δόξα ἐ. πάντων 14: 10. εὑρίσκειν χάριν ἐ. τοῦ θεοῦ Ac 7: 46 (cf. Gen 6: 8 v.l. [ARahlfs, Genesis ᾽26, 61] al.). After verbs of remembering and forgetting: μνησθῆναι ἐ. τοῦ θεοῦ Ac 10: 31; Rv 16: 19. ἐπιλελησμένον ἐ. τοῦ θεοῦ Lk 12: 6.

b. in relation to ἁμαρτάνειν ἐ. τινος *sin against someone* Lk 15: 18, 21 (cf. Jdth 5: 17; 1 Km 7: 6; 20: 1). ταπεινώθητε ἐ. κυρίου *humble yourselves before the Lord* Js 4: 10.

c. *by the authority of, on behalf of* Rv 13: 12, 14; 19: 20. Also simply *by* Lk 3: 7 D.—AWikenhauser, Ἐνώπιος-ἐνώπιον-κατενώπιον: BZ 8, '10, 263-70. M-M.**

Ἐνώς, ὁ indecl. (אֱנוֹשׁ) *Enos*, son of Seth (Gen 4: 26; Philo, Det. Pot. Ins. 138f.—In Jos., Ant. 1, 79; 83 Ἄνωσος [v.l. Ἔνωσος], ου), in the genealogy of Jesus Lk 3: 38.*

ἕνωσις, εως, ἡ (Pre-Socr.+; Aristot., Phys. 222a, 20; M. Ant. 6, 38; Herm. Wr. 1, 6; 14, 6 al.; Philo, Leg. All. 1, 8) *union, unity* IMg 13: 2; ITr 11: 2. σαρκὸς καὶ πνεύματος *with flesh and spirit* IMg 1: 2. ἕ. τοῦ αἵματος *unity of his blood* (capable of more than one interpr., but the main thing is the idea of union through the *one* blood) IPhld 4. τὴν ἕ. ἀγαπᾶν 7: 2. τῆς ἑ. φροντίζειν *be intent on unity* IPol 1: 2. ἄνθρωπος εἰς ἕ. κατηρτισμένος *a man made for unity* IPhld 8: 1. τὴν ἕ. ποιεῖσθαι *enter into a union* (in marriage) IPol 5: 2.—ThPreiss, La mystique de l'imitation du Christ et de l'unité chez Ign. d'Ant.: RHPhr 18, '38, 197-241.*

ἐνωτίζομαι 1 aor. ἐνωτισάμην *give ear, pay attention* (Hesychius; Const. Dukas 84, 19 IBekker [1834]) τὶ *to someth.* (Syntipas ̓p. 12, 6 al.; Psellus p. 77, 6; Gen 4: 23; Job 33: 1; Test. Reub. 1: 5, Iss. 1: 1) τὰ ῥήματα Ac 2: 14 (cf. Ps 5: 2). Abs. B 9: 3 (Is 1: 2). M-M.*

Ἐνώχ, ὁ indecl. (חֲנוֹךְ) (LXX; En.; Philo; Test. 12 Patr.—In Jos., Ant. 1, 79; 85; 9, 28 Ἄνωχος [v.l. Ἔνωχος], ου) *Enoch*, son of Jared, father of Methuselah (Gen 5: 18ff). In the genealogy of Jesus Lk 3: 37. As an example of faith and obedience toward God, and therefore translated to heaven (Gen 5: 22, 24; Sir 44: 16; Jos., Ant. 1, 85) Hb 11: 5; 1 Cl 9: 3. Prophetic word fr. Enoch Jd 14f (=En. 1, 9). Here he is called ἕβδομος ἀπὸ Ἀδάμ (cf. Diog. L. 3, 1 Plato is ἕκτος ἀπὸ Σόλωνος in the line of Solon's descendants; Athen. 13 p. 555D says of Socrates' father-in-law Aristides: οὐ τοῦ δικαίου καλουμένου . . . ἀλλὰ τοῦ τρίτου ἀπ' ἐκείνου).—The quot. fr. Enoch in B 4: 3 cannot be identified w. certainty. Enoch is introduced by conjecture 1 Pt 3: 19 (following others by FrSpitta 1890 and JRHarris, Exp. 6th ser. IV '01, 346-9; V '02, 317-20; Moffatt; so Gdspd., Probs. 195-8, JBL 73, '54, 91f, but against it EGSelwyn, 1 Pt, '46, 197f).—HOdeberg, TW II 553-7; PKatz, Gnomon 26, '54, 226; HLudin Jansen, D. Hen. gestalt. E. vergleich. rel. gesch. Untersuchung '39.*

ἐξ prep. s. ἐκ.

ἕξ indecl. (Hom.+; pap., LXX, Ep. Arist., Philo, Joseph., Test. 12 Patr.) *six* Mt 17: 1; Mk 9: 2; Lk 4: 25; 13: 14; J 2: 6, 20 al. πρὸ ἕξ ἡμερῶν τοῦ πάσχα *six days before the Passover* 12: 1.—MPol 9: 3; Hv 3, 2, 5. M-M.

ἐξαγγέλλω 1 aor. ἐξήγγειλα (Hom.+; Philo; Jos., Vi. 357 al.) *proclaim, report* (so Hdt.+; inscr. [Dit., Or. 266, 34, cf. the note]; PGM 5, 294; LXX; Philo, Plant. 128; Test. Jos. 5: 2, 3) short ending of Mk. τὰς ἀρετάς 1 Pt 2: 9. M-M.*

ἐξαγοράζω 1 aor. ἐξηγόρασα.
1. *buy, buy up* τὶ *someth.* (Polyb. 3, 42, 2; Plut., Crass. 2, 5) or *redeem* (lit. 'buy back'), *deliver* τινά *someone* (Diod. S. 15, 7, 1; 36, 2, 2 [but cf. SLyonnet, Biblica 42,

'61, 85-89, Sin, Redemption and Sacrifice, '70, 104-19]) τοὺς ὑπὸ νόμον *those who are subject to the law* Gal 4: 5. The thing from which deliverance is obtained is added with ἐκ: ἡμᾶς ἐκ τῆς κατάρας τοῦ νόμου 3: 13. Dssm., LO 270-8 [LAE 322-34].

2. The mid. ἐξαγοράζεσθαι τ. καιρόν Col 4: 5; Eph 5: 16 cannot be interpr. w. certainty. One possible mng. is *make the most of the time* (which is severely limited because of the proximity of the Parousia as well as for other reasons; but s. also καιρός 2; cf. Plut., Sert. 6, 6 καιρὸν ὠνεῖσθαι); cf. Murray, New [Oxford] Engl. Dict. s.v. redeem 8, 'save (time) fr. being lost'.—RMPope, ET 22, '11, 552-4.—But the earliest occurrence of ἐξαγ. suggests a different sense as the verb is used with the acc. Heraclides [III BC], Reisebilder 1951 §22 p. 82 FPFister: τὸν ἀδικηθέντα ἐξαγοράζειν=buy off the claims of the injured man, satisfy the one who has been wronged. So also the mid. διὰ μιᾶς ὥρας τὴν αἰώνιον κόλασιν ἐξαγοραζόμενοι *with a single hour* (*of torment*) *buying off* (avoiding) *eternal punishment* MPol 2: 3. Is this possibly the way to understand ἐξαγ. in Col 4: 5; Eph 5: 16? The καιρός is συνεσταλμένος and its 'evil' days present wrathful demands (1 Cor 7: 29-32) which must be satisfied.—Some mss. of MPol 2: 3 read ζωήν instead of κόλασιν; in this case ἐ. would mean *purchase* (cf. KLake, transl. ad loc., note 2, also transll. of Kleist and Gdspd.). M-M.*

ἐξάγω 2 aor. ἐξήγαγον (Hom.+; inscr., pap., LXX, Philo; Jos., Ant. 6, 229, Vi 183) *lead out, bring out.*
1. lit. τινά *someone* 1 Cl 10: 6 (Gen 15: 5); 12: 4; (out) of a country Ac 7: 36, 40 (Ex 32: 1); 13: 17 (cf. Dt 4: 37); Hb 8: 9 (Jer 38: 32); 1 Cl 53: 2; B 4: 8; 14: 3 (the last three Ex 32: 7ff; Dt 9: 12); (out) of prison (PTebt. 15, 13 [114 BC]; Gen 40: 14; Ps 141: 8) Ac 5: 19; 12: 17; 16: 37, 39; (out) of the river Hv 1, 1, 2; sheep fr. the fold (Pollux 1, 250; cf. Philo, Agr. 44) J 10: 3. W. indication of the destination: into the desert (Ex 16: 3) Ac 21: 38. W. ἵνα foll. Mk 15: 20. ἕως πρὸς Βηθανίαν *as far as Bethany* Lk 24: 50. ἔξω (τινός) Mk 8: 23 D; Lk 24: 50 v.l. (cf. Gen 15: 5; 19: 17).
2. fig. (Diod. S. 3, 33, 6 ἐξάγειν ἐκ τοῦ ζῆν=remove from life, put to death) ἐ. ἐκ δεσμῶν *free from bonds* B 14: 7 (Is 42: 7). M-M.*

ἐξαίρετος, ον *taken out*—**1.** *separated* (Thu.+) ἔκ τινος *from someth.* ἐκ κακῶν οὐκ ἐ. ἔσονται *they will not be delivered fr. evils* 1 Cl 39: 9 (Job 5: 5).
2. *chosen, excellent, remarkable* (Hom.+; Dit., Or. 503, 9; POxy. 73, 26; Gen 48: 22; Philo, Abr. 7; Jos., Bell. 1, 403, Ant. 12, 22, C. Ap. 2, 128) τὸ εὐαγγέλιον ἐ. τι ἔχει *has someth. distinctive* (cf. Epict. 1, 2, 17; 3, 1, 25; Philo, Leg. All. 3, 86) IPhld 9: 2.*

ἐξαιρέτως adv. (Philo Bybl. [100 AD] in Euseb., Pr. Ev. 1, 9, 29; Plut., Mor. 667F; Epict. 1, 6, 12; Lucian; Herodian; Vett. Val. et al.; Dit., Or. 603, 6; PAmh. 136, 11; BGU 168, 4; PLeipz. 64, 3; Aq. Dt 32: 12; Philo, Plant. 21; Jos., Bell. 2, 125, Ant. 19, 335) *especially* ITr 12: 2; ISm 7: 2; Dg 4: 4.*

ἐξαιρέω 2 aor. ἐξεῖλον, imper. ἔξελε, mid. ἐξειλάμην, inf. ἐξελέσθαι Ac 7: 34 (=Ex 3: 8; cf. Bl-D. §81, 3 app.); fut. ἐξελῶ (Bl-D. §74, 3), mid. ἐξελοῦμαι (Hom.+; inscr., pap., LXX; Jos., Bell. 4, 658, Ant. 14, 40; Test. 12 Patr.).
1. act. *take out, tear out* τὶ *someth.* an eye (Heliod. 2, 16, 1 τ. ὀφθαλμὸν ἐξεῖλε τὸν δεξιόν; Heraclid., Pol. 30; Phalaris, Ep. 147, 3; Plut., Is. et Os. 55 p. 373E) Mt 5: 29;

18: 9 (on the content Jos., Ant. 6, 71). τί τινος someth. fr. someone B 6: 14.

2. mid.—a. set free, deliver, rescue (Aeschyl., Suppl. 924; Polyb. 1, 11, 11; LXX) τινά someone Ac 7: 34; 23: 27; 1 Cl 52: 3 (Ps 49: 15). τινὰ ἔκ τινος someone fr. someth. (Demosth. 18, 90; PPetr. III 36 (a) recto, 21 ἐξελοῦ με ἐκ τῆς ἀνάγκης; Wsd 10: 1; Sir 29: 12; Bar 4: 18, 21 al.) Ac 7: 10; 12: 11 (ἐκ χειρός Ex 18: 4 and oft. in OT. But also Aeschines 3, 256; see on ἐκ 1a); Gal 1: 4; 1 Cl 56: 8 (Job 5: 19). Abs. 1 Cl 39: 9 (Job 5: 4).

b. select, choose out (for oneself) (Od. 14, 232; Hdt. 3, 150; LXX) τινὰ ἔκ τινος (cf. X., An. 2, 5, 20) Ac 26: 17; but in this pass. the mng. deliver, save is also poss., and prob. to be preferred w. HHoltzmann, Wendt, Preuschen, Zahn, Steinmann, Engl. transll., against Overbeck, Knopf, Beyer. M-M.*

ἐξαίρω 1 aor. ἐξῆρα, imper. 2 pl. ἐξάρατε remove, drive away (so Soph.+; PRyl. 133, 19 [33 AD]; PLond. 177, 21; PGM 7, 367; LXX; En. 1, 1; Philo; Jos., C. Ap. 1, 81; Test. 12 Patr.) τὸν πονηρὸν ἐξ ὑμῶν drive out the evil man fr. among you 1 Cor 5: 13 (Dt 24: 7); pass. vs. 2 v.l. ἐξάρωμεν τοῦτο let us put an end to this 1 Cl 48: 1. M-M.*

ἐξαιτέω 1 aor. mid. ἐξῃτησάμην (Soph., Hdt.+; Dit., Syll.³ 326, 29 [IV BC]; BGU 944, 8) in our lit. only mid.

1. ask for, demand τινά someone (X., An. 1, 1, 3; Demosth. 29, 14; Plut., Per. 32, 5; Palaeph. 40 p. 61, 1; Jos., Ant. 16, 277; 18, 369) ὁ σατανᾶς ἐξῃτήσατο ὑμᾶς τοῦ σινιάσαι Satan asked for you, to sift you Lk 22: 31 (cf. Plut., Mor. 417D βίαιοι δαίμονες ἐξαιτούμενοι ψυχὴν ἀνθρωπίνην; Test. Benj. 3: 3); cf. Field, Notes 76, 'obtain by asking'.

2. ask τινά someone (trag.) w. ἵνα foll. MPol 7: 2. M-M.*

ἐξαίφνης adv. (Hom.+; Dit., Or. 56, 48; UPZ 78, 7 [159 BC]; PSI 184, 5; LXX; Jos., Ant. 12, 362) suddenly, unexpectedly Mk 13: 36; Lk 2: 13; 9: 39; Ac 9: 3; 22: 6; 1 Cl 23: 5; IPol 8: 1; Hv 2, 1, 4; 3, 12, 2; s 6, 1, 2. (W-H. ἐξέφνης except for Ac 22: 6; some mss. spell it thus in this pass. also).—S. εὐθέως. M-M.*

ἐξάκις (Pind.+; Sb 1838; LXX) six times 1 Cl 56: 8 (Job 5: 19).*

ἐξακισχίλιοι, αι, α (Hdt. 1, 192; Thu. 2, 13, 3 al.; LXX; Jos., Bell. 4, 115, Ant. 14, 33) six thousand B 15: 4.*

ἐξακολουθέω fut. ἐξακολουθήσω; 1 aor. ἐξηκολούθησα (Epicurus p. 156, 6 Us.; Philo Mech. 58, 5; Polyb.; Dionys. Hal., Comp. Verb. 24; Epict. 1, 22, 16; Plut.; inscr., pap., LXX, Test. 12 Patr., Joseph.) follow, in our lit. only fig. w. dat.

1. obey, follow an authority that may be personal 1 Cl 14: 1 (cf. Leo 20, 12 ἐξ. τινί a pers. authority; Am 2: 4; Test. Zeb. 9: 5, Napht. 3: 3 v.l. πνεύμασι πλάνης) or impersonal: σεσοφισμένοις μύθοις 2 Pt 1: 16 (cf. Jos., Ant. 1, 22 τοῖς μύθοις ἐξακολουθήσαντες). ταῖς ἀσελγείαις 2: 2 (cf. Test. Iss. 6: 2 τοῖς πονηροῖς διαβουλίοις).

2. follow, pursue a way τῇ ὁδῷ τοῦ Βαλαάμ vs. 15 (cf. Is 56: 11 ταῖς ὁδοῖς αὐτῶν ἐξηκολούθησαν). M-M.*

ἐξακοντίζω (Eur., X.+) hurl out as a javelin, fig. (Menand. ?, fgm. 1091 K. γλώσσῃ ματαίους ἐ. λόγους) w. no object expressed, perh. aim (at) or plunge (into) εἰς ἔριν 1 Cl 14: 2.*

ἐξακόσιοι, αι, α (Hdt. 1, 51 al.; pap., LXX; Jos., Vi. 200; 241) six hundred Rv 13: 18; 14: 20; 1 Cl 43: 5.*

ἐξακριβάζομαι (LXX; the act. Jos., Ant. 19, 332) ask or inquire exactly τί about someth. (Num 23: 10) Hm 4, 3, 3. τί παρά τινος of someone about someth. 4, 2, 3.*

ἐξαλείφω 1 aor. ἐξήλειψα, pass. ἐξηλείφθην (Aeschyl., Hdt.+; inscr., pap., LXX).

1. in accordance w. the basic mng.—a. wipe away πᾶν δάκρυον ἐκ τῶν ὀφθαλμῶν Rv 7: 17; 21: 4.

b. wipe out, erase (X., Hell. 2, 3, 51 τινὰ ἐκ τ. καταλόγου; Anaxippus Com. [IV BC] 1, 5 ἐκ τ. βυβλίων; Dit., Syll.³ 921, 19 ἐξαλειψάτω τὸ ὄνομα ὁ ἱερεύς, Or. 218, 129; Ps 68: 29 ἐ. ἐκ βίβλου ζώντων; Jos., Ant. 6, 133 τὸ ὄνομα ἐξ.) τὸ ὄνομα ἐκ τῆς βίβλου τῆς ζωῆς the name fr. the book of life Rv 3: 5; 1 Cl 53: 4 (Ex 32: 32).

2. Certain expr. show the infl. of the transition (s. the graffito in Rdm.² 228[219]) to the more general mng. remove, destroy, obliterate (Philostrat., Vi. Apoll. 8, 7 p. 313, 4; Κυπρ. I p. 58 no. 1; Jos., Ant. 17, 335), in so far as the removal results fr. the blotting out of a written record (cf. Dio Chrys. 14[31], 86; Jos., Ant. 4, 210); they are ἐ. τὸ καθ' ἡμῶν χειρόγραφον Col 2: 14. τὸ ἀνόμημά μου 1 Cl 18: 2 (Ps 50: 3). τὰς ἀνομίας 18: 9 (Ps 50: 11; EDalglish, Ps 51 in the Light of Near East, etc., '62, 86–89 [Semitic background]). τὰς ἁμαρτίας Ac 3: 19 (cf. Ps 108: 14; 3 Macc 2: 19; En. 10, 20). Only the more general sense is pertinent (as Diod. S. 3, 40, 7 ἐ. τὰς ἐλπίδας; Test. Jud. 22: 3) for 1 Cl 53: 3. ἐξαλείψωμεν ἀφ' ἡμῶν τὰ πρότερα ἁμαρτήματα let us remove fr. ourselves our former sins 2 Cl 13: 1 (ἐξ. ἀπό as Gen 7: 23; PsSol 2, 17). Pass. (Lucian, Pro Imag. 26; Jos., Ant. 4, 210) 1 Cl 53: 5; Hs 9, 24, 4. M-M.*

ἐξάλλομαι (Hom.+; LXX)—1. leap out (Hom. et al.; Mi 2: 12 ἐξ ἀνθρώπων) ἐξαλοῦνται ἐκ τ. μνημείων οἱ νεκροί GNaass 6.

2. leap up (so Aristoph., Vesp. 130; X., Cyr. 7, 1, 27; Jos., Bell. 1, 443; Is 55: 12) ἐξαλλόμενος ἔστη Ac 3: 8. Cf. 14: 10 E. M-M.*

ἐξαμαρτάνω 2 aor. ἐξήμαρτον (trag., Hdt.+; LXX, Philo; Jos., Ant. 12, 278; 13, 71) sin ἐ. τι commit a sin (Soph., Phil. 1012; Hdt. 3, 145 al.) Hm 6, 2, 7; ἐλάχιστον ἐ. commit a very little sin s 8, 10, 1 (Lucian, Jupp. Trag. 20 τὰ τοιαῦτα ἐ.).*

ἐξαμβλόω 1 aor. pass. ἐξημβλώθην (Eur.+; Philo, Det. Pot. Ins. 147; Jos., Ant. 4, 278) cause to miscarry τὰ βρέφη τὰ ἐξαμβλωθέντα AP fgm. 2 (Ps.-Apollod. 3, 4, 3 W. βρέφος ἐξαμβλωθέν).*

ἐξανάστασις, εως, ἡ (intr. = 'getting up' in Hippocr.; Polyb. 3, 55, 4 al.) the resurrection ἡ ἐ. ἡ ἐκ νεκρῶν the resurrection fr. the dead Phil 3: 11. M-M.*

ἐξανατέλλω 1 aor. ἐξανέτειλα (intr. in Empedocles [V, BC] 62, 4; Moschus 2, 58; Ps 111: 4) spring up of a quick-growing plant Mt 13: 5; Mk 4: 5.*

ἐξανίστημι fut. ἐξαναστήσω; 1 aor. ἐξανέστησα; 2 aor. ἐξανέστην.

1. trans. (Soph., Hdt.+; LXX; Jos., Ant. 5, 46) raise up, awaken τινά someone 1 Cl 26: 2 (quot. of uncertain orig.; possibly Ps 70: 21f LXX?). τοὺς ἀσθενοῦντας raise up the weak 59: 4. Fig. ἐ. σπέρμα raise up offspring (Gen 19: 32, 34) Mk 12: 19; Lk 20: 28.

2. intr. in mid. and 2 aor. act. (Pind., Hdt.+; Jos., Bell. 2, 279, Ant. 17, 132 al.; LXX) stand up—a. to speak (X., An. 6, 1, 30) Ac 15: 5.—b. rise up (Judg 5: 7 A; En. 15, 12) B 4: 4. M-M.*

ἐξανοίγω (Aristoph.+; Diod. S. 1, 33, 11; Strabo 16, 1, 10) to open (fully) Ac 12: 16 D.*

ἐξαπατάω 1 aor. ἐξηπάτησα (Hom.+; inscr., pap.; Ex 8: 25; Sus 56 Theod.) *deceive, cheat* τινά someone (Jos., Ant. 10, 111) Ro 7: 11; 2 Th 2: 3; IEph 8: 1. Of the serpent's deception of Eve 2 Cor 11: 3; 1 Ti 2: 14, in the former pass. = *lead astray* (Hdt. 2, 114). τὰς καρδίας τῶν ἀκάκων *the hearts of the simple-minded* Ro 16: 18 (Philo, Leg. All. 3, 109 τ. αἴσθησιν). ἑαυτὸν ἐ. *deceive oneself* (Ael. Aristid. 24, 35 K. = 44 p. 835 D.; Lucian, De Merc. Cond. 5, end; Jos., Ant. 13, 89; cf. Epict. 2, 20, 7; 2, 22, 15 μὴ ἐξαπατᾶσθε) 1 Cor 3: 18; τινά τινι ἐ. *deceive someone w. someth.* τῇ ὕλῃ IRo 6: 2. M-M.*

ἐξάπινα adv. (inscr.: Sb 7792, 4; PGiess. 68, 6 [II AD]; Iambl., Protr. 20; Zonaras 7, 25; 10, 37; LXX) *suddenly* Mk 9: 8; *unexpectedly* ἔρχεσθαι Hs 9, 7, 6. S. also εὐθέως M-M.*

ἐξαπλόω pf. pass. ptc. ἐξηπλωμένος *unfold, spread out* (Ps.-Lucian, Philopatris 17; Galen, De Temper. p. 27, 12 Helmr.; Herm. Wr. p. 436, 9 Sc.; Suidas) a linen cloth Hv 3, 1, 4.*

ἐξαπορέω 1 aor. ἐξηπορήθην, in our lit. only pass. dep. ἐξαπορέομαι (this in Diod. S., Plut. et al.; Dit., Syll.³ 495, 12 [III BC]; PEleph. 2, 10 [285/4 BC]) *be in great difficulty, doubt, embarrassment* w. gen. of that in respect to which this occurs (Dionys. Hal. 7, 18 τοῦ ἀργυρίου) τοῦ ζῆν *despair of living* 2 Cor 1: 8. Abs. (Ps 87: 16) ἀπορούμενοι ἀλλ' οὐκ ἐξαπορούμενοι *perplexed, but not despairing* 4: 8. M-M.*

ἐξαποστέλλω fut. ἐξαποστελῶ; 1 aor. ἐξαπέστειλα (since Ep. Phil. in Demosth. 18, 77; inscr., pap., LXX; Ep. Arist. 126; Jos., Ant. 18, 201. Cf. Anz 356f; OGlaser, De ratione, quae intercedit inter sermonem Polybii et eum, qui in titulis saec. III, II, I apparet 1894, 33f).

1. *send out, send away* τινά someone (Polyb. 4, 11, 6)—a. to remove him fr. a place: *send away* or *off* Ac 17: 14 (w. inf. foll. as Ep. Arist. 13). εἰς Ταρσόν (cf. PSI 384, 4 ἐ. αὐτὸν . . . εἰς Φιλαδέλφειαν) 1 Macc 11: 62; 2 Macc 14: 27) 9: 30.

b. *in order to have him fulfill a mission in another place* (Diod. S. 17, 2, 5 τινὰ εἰς; Ps.-Callisth. 3, 26, 5) Ac 7: 12. Βαρναβᾶν ἕως Ἀντιοχείας 11: 22. Of the sending out of the apostles 22: 21. Of higher beings sent by God (cf. Wsd 9: 10): angels (Gen 24: 40; Ps 151: 4) 12: 11; Hs 9, 14, 3; Jesus: ἐξαπέστειλεν ὁ θεὸς τὸν υἱὸν αὐτοῦ (sc. ἐξ οὐρανοῦ, cf. Ps 56: 4) Gal 4: 4. ὁ ἐξαποστείλας ἡμῖν τὸν σωτῆρα 2 Cl 20: 5. Cf. in relation to the mission of Jesus ἡμῖν ὁ λόγος τ. σωτηρίας ταύτης ἐξαπεστάλη Ac 13: 26. S. also the short ending of Mk. Of the Spirit (Ps 103: 30) ἐ. ὁ θεὸς τὸ πνεῦμα τοῦ υἱοῦ αὐτοῦ εἰς τὰς καρδίας ἡμῶν Gal 4: 6. ἐ. τὴν ἐπαγγελίαν τ. πατρός μου ἐφ' ὑμᾶς *I will send the promise of my Father* (= what my Father has promised) *upon* or *to* (PRyl. 127, 22 [29 AD] τοὺς αἰτίους ἐξαποστεῖλαι ἐπὶ σέ) you Lk 24: 49 (v.l. ἀποστέλλω 𝔓⁷⁵ et al.).

2. *send away* (Ps.-Callisth. 3, 26, 6; w. double acc. Polyb. 15, 2, 4) τινὰ κενόν someone *empty-handed* (Gen 31: 42; Job 22: 9) Lk 1: 53; 20: 10f.—Hv 4, 2, 6 v.l. for ἀποστέλλω. M-M.*

ἐξάπτω 1 aor. ἐξῆψα *light, kindle* (so in lit. mng. Tim. Locr. 7 p. 97E; Aeneas Tact. 1698; Hero Alex. I p. 214, 12; Aelian, V.H. 5, 6 τὴν πυράν; PGM 13, 12; Ex 30: 8; 1 Macc 4: 50; Philo, Gig. 25.—Fig. Jos., Vi. 105; 123) τὸ πῦρ (Aristot., Part. An. 2, 9 p. 655a, 15) MPol 15: 1.*

ἐξάρατε, ἐξαρθῇ s. ἐξαίρω.

ἐξαριθμέω 1 aor. ἐξηρίθμησα *count* (so Hdt.+; inscr.,

pap., LXX) τὶ someth. (Lycophron v. 1255) τὴν ἄμμον τῆς γῆς *the sand of the earth* 1 Cl 10: 5a (Gen 13: 16). τοὺς ἀστέρας 10: 6 (Gen 15: 5). Pass. 10: 5b (on the figure cf. Ael. Aristid. 46, 3 K. = 3 p. 30 D.: ἐξαρ. τοὺς χόας τ. θαλάττης).*

ἐξαρτάω pf. pass. ptc. ἐξηρτημένος (Eur.+; Polyb. 18, 1, 4; Hero Alex. I p. 434, 16; POxy. 471, 83 [II AD]).

1. *hang up* τινός *by* someth. (Proclus on Pla., Cratyl. p. 89, 11 Pasqu.) τῶν πλοκάμων *by the braids of their hair* AP 9: 24.

2. pass. (Eur., X.+; pap.; Ex 28: 7) *be attached to, be an adherent of* τινός someone (Eur., Suppl. 735; Plut., Galb. 8, 2, Arat. 42, 1, Gracchi 27, 4 ἐξηρτημένον αὐτοῦ πλῆθος) Mk 3: 21 v.l.*

ἐξαρτίζω 1 aor. ἐξήρτισα; pf. pass. ptc. ἐξηρτισμένος (late; Ex 28: 7 v.l.).

1. *finish, complete* (IG XII [2] 538; POxy. 296, 7 [I AD] of documents; Jos., Ant. 3, 139) ἐ. ἡμᾶς τ. ἡμέρας *our time was up* Ac 21: 5 (cf. Hippocr., Epid. 2, 180 ἀπαρτίζειν τὴν ὀκτάμηνον).

2. *equip, furnish* (Diod. S. 14, 19, 5 Vogel v.l.; Lucian; Arrian; Jos., Ant. 3, 43 v.l.; CIG II 420, 13; Wilcken, Chrest. 176, 10 [I AD]; PAmh. 93, 8; PTebt. 342, 17) πρὸς πᾶν ἔργον ἀγαθὸν ἐξηρτισμένος *for every good deed* 2 Ti 3: 17 (with ἐξηρτισμένος πρός τι cf. Diod. S. 19, 77, 3 ναῦς ἐξηρτισμένας πρὸς τὸν πόλεμον πρὸς τὴν τῶν Ἑλλήνων ἐλευθέρωσιν). M-M.*

ἐξασθενέω fut. ἐξασθενήσω (Hippocr.+; Plut.; Aelian, N.A. 16, 27; Vett. Val. 125, 11; 139, 29; BGU 903, 15; PTebt. 50, 33; Ps 63: 9) in our lit. only fig. (cf. Diod. S. 20, 78, 1 τοῖς λογισμοῖς; Philo; Agatharchides in Jos., C. Ap. 1, 211) *become quite weak* ἐν τῇ ἀγάπῃ IPhld 6: 2 (for the constr. w. ἐν cf. Vett. Val. 59, 13).*

ἐξαστράπτω (Pollux 1, 117; Zosimus the alchemist p. 111 Berthelot; Rhet. Gr. I 640, 31; Tryphiodorus [V AD] v. 103 [ed. Weinberger 1896]; Leontios 44b p. 91, 12; Na 3: 3; Ezk 1: 4, 7) *flash* or *gleam like lightning* fig. of a white garment Lk 9: 29. M-M.*

ἐξαυτῆς (= ἐξ αὐτῆς τ. ὥρας; cf. Philo, Mut. Nom. 142) *at once, immediately, soon thereafter* (since Theognis 231 Diehl v.l.; Cratinus [V BC], fgm. 34 [I 22 Kock]; Polyb.; Jos., Ant. 7, 122; 15, 186. Written as one word PLond. 893, 6 [40 AD]; PRyl. 236, 22; PTebt. 421, 2; POxy. 64, 3) Mk 6: 25; Ac 10: 33; 11: 11; 21: 32; 23: 30; Phil 2: 23; Hv 3, 1, 6. M-M.*

ἐξεγείρω fut. ἐξεγερῶ; 1 aor. ἐξήγειρα (trag., Hdt.+; LXX; Joseph.; Sib. Or. 3, 767).

1. *awaken* fr. sleep (trag.+; Epict. 2, 20, 17; Dit., Syll.³ 1168, 118; Sir 22: 9; 1 Esdr 3: 13) 1 Cl 26: 2 (Ps 3: 6). Pass. *wake up* (Hdt. 1, 34 al.) εὐθὺς ἐξεγερθείς *as soon as he had awakened* (or *risen*) Mk 6: 45 D.

2. *raise* (lit. 'awaken') fr. the dead (cf. Aeschyl., Choëph. 495; Da 12: 2 Theod.; the awakening of the spirits of the dead Fluchtaf. 5, 21 p. 24) 1 Cor 6: 14.

3. *raise up* to a sitting position τινὰ τῆς χειρός someone *by the hand* Hv 3, 1, 7. Pass. *rise up* 3, 12, 2.

4. *cause to appear, bring into being* (Cantharus Com. [V BC], fgm. 1; Zech 11: 16; Jos., Ant. 8, 271) Ro 9: 17. M-M.*

ἐξέδετο s. ἐκδίδωμι.

ἐξείλατο s. ἐξαιρέω.

ἔξειμι fr. εἶμι inf. ἐξιέναι, ptc. ἐξιών; impf. ἐξῄειν (Hom.+; inscr., pap., LXX, Joseph.) *go out, go away* without further indication of place (Herodian 7, 9, 4; Jos., C. Ap. 1, 231) Ac 13: 42; 17: 15; MPol 8: 1. ἔκ τινος (Hdt. 1, 94, 4; Lucian, Eunuch. 6) Ac 13: 42 v.l.; *go on a journey* (Ael. Aristid. 51, 1 K.=27 p. 534 D.) Ac 20: 4 D, 7. ἐπὶ τὴν γῆν *get to land* Ac 27: 43 (cf. PLeipz. 110, 5 ἐ. ἐπὶ τὴν Καπαδοκίαν; Jos., Vi. 289). M-M.*

ἔξειμι fr. εἰμί s. ἔξεστιν.

ἐξεῖπον defective aorist (trag.; Thu. 7, 87, 4 al.; En. 14, 16; Jos., Vi. 204) *express, proclaim* τὶ 1 Cl 49: 3. γνῶσιν 48: 5. ὅσα Dg 11: 8. W. relative clause as obj. 2 Cl 14: 5.*

ἔξελε, ἐξελέσθαι s. ἐξαιρέω.

ἐξελέγχω 1 aor. inf. ἐξελέγξαι (trag.+; Thu. 3, 64, 4; Dit., Syll.³ 417, 8, Or. 669, 58; Zen.-P. 33 [= Sb 6739], 5; PTebt. 25, 14; LXX; Philo; Jos., C. Ap. 1, 105; 2, 138) only Jd 15 as v.l. for ἐλέγξαι *convict*. M-M.*

ἐξελήλυθα s. ἐξέρχομαι.

ἐξελίσσω (Eur.+) *unroll*, of heavenly bodies that τοὺς ἐπιτεταγμένους αὐτοῖς ὁρισμούς *roll on* or *travel through their appointed courses* 1 Cl 20: 3 (Plut., Is. et Os. 42 p. 368A of the σελήνη: τὸν αὐτῆς κύκλον ἐξελίσσει; Heliod. 5, 14, 3).*

ἐξέλκω (Hom.+; LXX) *drag away* ὑπὸ τῆς ἰδίας ἐπιθυμίας ἐξελκόμενος *taken in tow by his own desire(s)* Js 1: 14 (cf. Pla., 7th Letter p. 325B εἶλκεν δέ με ἡ ἐπιθυμία; X., Cyr. 8, 1, 32 ἑλκόμενος ὑπὸ τῶν ἡδονῶν; Aelian, Hist. An. 6, 31 ὑπὸ τ. ἡδονῆς ἑλκόμενοι). M-M.*

ἐξεμπλάριον, ίου, τό (Lat. loanw., 'exemplarium'; occurs in the so-called 'confession inscrs.' fr. Phrygia and Lydia [s. FSteinleitner, D. Beicht '13, 130a, index; Ramsay, Phrygia I 1 p. 151 no. 47, also 46 and 48]; POxy. 1066; Ps.-Methodius, In Ramos Palmarum 2: Migne, S. Gr. XVIII p. 388A. The material in JHS 7, 1887 p. 385ff is doubtful. An inscr. fr. Dionysopolis in Phrygia contains ἔξενπλον [Ramsay, Phrygia I p. 149]) *(living) example, embodiment* τῆς ἀγάπης IEph 2: 1; ITr 3: 2. θεοῦ διακονίας *of God's ministry* ISm 12: 1.*

ἐξενεγκ- s. ἐκφέρω.

ἐξέπεσα s. ἐκπίπτω.

ἐξεπλάγην s. ἐκπλήσσω.

ἐξέραμα, ατος, τό (Diosc., De Venen. 19) *vomit, what has been vomited* of a dog (Philumen. p. 8, 30) 2 Pt 2: 22. M-M.*

ἐξεραυνάω 1 aor. ἐξηραύνησα (H.Gk. substitute for ἐξερευνάω, which is found Soph.+. On the sound-change s. on ἐραυνάω. The compound form also in Polyb.; Plut.; Vett. Val. 267, 5; LXX; PsSol 17, 9; Philo, Plant. 141; Jos., Bell. 4, 654) *inquire carefully* περί τινος *concerning a thing* 1 Pt 1: 10. M-M.*

ἐξερευνάω s. ἐξεραυνάω.

ἐξερίζω 1 aor. ἐξήρισα (Plut., Pomp. 56, 3; Appian, Bell. Civ. 2, 151 §634) *be factious, contentious* ἐξήρισαν εἰς τοσοῦτο θυμοῦ *carried their factiousness to such a pitch of fury* 1 Cl 45: 7.*

ἐξέρχομαι fut. ἐξελεύσομαι; 2 aor. ἐξῆλθον (but ἐξῆλθα J 21: 3 v.l.; Ac 16: 40; 2 Cor 6: 17 [Is 52: 11]; 1 J 2: 19; 3 J 7; Rv 18: 4); pf. ἐξελήλυθα (Hom.+; inscr., pap., LXX; Jos., Bell. 2, 480; Test. 12 Patr.).
1. of living beings, almost always personal in nature—
a. lit. *go out, come out, go away, retire.*

a. of men, w. indication of the place from which (and goal) ἔκ τινος (Hdt. 8, 75; 9, 12) ἐκ τ. μνημείων Mt 8: 28; 27: 53. ἐκ γῆς Χαλδαίων Ac 7: 4; cf. Mk 7: 31; J 4: 30 (ἐκ τ. πόλεως as X., Hell. 6, 5, 16); Ac 22: 18; Hb 3: 16; 1 Cl 10: 2. ἐκ τοῦ πλοίου *get out* Mk 5: 2; cf. Rv 14: 15, 17f.—ἀπό τινος (Heraclitus, Ep. 5, 3; Aesop, Fab. 248b H.; POxy. 472, 1; 528, 7; LXX; Jos., Ant. 12, 407 ἀ. τ. Ἱεροσ.) ἀπὸ Βηθανίας Mk 11: 12; cf. Lk 17: 29; Phil 4: 15. ἀπὸ τ. πόλεως Lk 9: 5; cf. Mt 24: 1; Ac 16: 40. ἀπ᾽ ἐμοῦ *leave me* Lk 5: 8; ἐξ. ἀπὸ τ. ἀνδρός *leave her husband* Mk 10: 12 D.—ἔξω τινός Mt 10: 14 (cf. Jdth 14: 2); foll. by εἰς w. acc. of the place Mt 21: 17; Mk 14: 68; foll. by παρά w. acc. of the pers. Hb 13: 13.—W. gen. alone (Hom.+; Longus 4, 23, 2; POxy. 942, 4) τ. οἰκίας Mt 13: 1.—ἐκεῖθεν 15: 21; Mk 6: 1, 10; Lk 9: 4; J 4: 43. ὅθεν ἐξῆλθον Mt 12: 44; Lk 11: 24b.

β. of men; in such a way that the place fr. which is not expressly named, but can be supplied fr. the context *go away* fr. region or house, *get out (of), disembark (fr.)* a ship, etc. Mt 9: 31f; 12: 14; 14: 14; 18: 28; Mk 1: 35, 45; Lk 4: 42; 5: 27; J 11: 31, 44; 13: 30f; 18: 1, 4; Ac 12: 9f, 17; 16: 3 (*go out*); Hb 11: 8; D 11: 6; ἐ. ἔξω (cf. Gen 39: 12ff) Mt 26: 75; Lk 22: 62; J 19: 4f; Rv 3: 12.

γ. in Johannine usage of Jesus, who comes forth from the Father: ἐκ τοῦ θεοῦ ἐξῆλθον J 8: 42. ἀπὸ θεοῦ ἐξῆλθεν καὶ πρὸς τὸν θεὸν ὑπάγει 13: 3. παρὰ τοῦ πατρὸς ἐξῆλθον 16: 27; cf. 17: 8 (on ἐξ. παρά τινος cf. Num 16: 35). ἐξῆλθον ἐκ τοῦ πατρός 16: 28. ἀπὸ θεοῦ ἐξῆλθες vs. 30.

δ. of spirits that *come* or *go out* of persons (Damasc., Vi. Isid. 56 οὐκ ἐπείθετο τὸ δαιμόνιον τῆς γυναικὸς ἐξελθεῖν; PGM 4, 1243 ἔξελθε, δαῖμον, . . . καὶ ἀπόστηθι ἀπὸ τοῦ δεῖνα) ἔκ τινος Mk 1: 25f; 5: 8; 7: 29; 9: 25; Lk 4: 35 bis, 𝔭⁷⁵ et al.; ἀπό τινος (cf. En. 22, 7) Mt 12: 43; 17: 18; Lk 4: 35, 41; 8: 29, 33, 38; 11: 24; Ac 16: 18. Abs. Mk 5: 13; 7: 30; 9: 26, 29; Lk 4: 36; Ac 8: 7 (text prob. damaged).

ε. of persons, w. indication of the goal εἴς τι (X., Hell. 7, 4, 24 al.) εἰς τὰς ὁδούς *into the streets* Mt 22: 10. εἰς τὸν πυλῶνα 26: 71; cf. Mk 14: 68. εἰς τὴν ἔρημον Mt 11: 7. εἰς τὸ ὄρος τῶν ἐλαιῶν *to the Mount of Olives* 26: 30; Mk 14: 26. εἰς τὴν Γαλιλαίαν J 1: 43. εἰς Μακεδονίαν Ac 16: 10; 2 Cor 2: 13. εἰς τὸν λεγόμενον κρανίου τόπον J 19: 17. εἰς τὸν κόσμον 1 J 4: 1; 2 J 7. εἰς ὑπάντησίν τινι *to meet someone* (Jdth 2: 6 S; cf. ἐ. εἰς ἀπάντησίν τινι 1 Esdr 1: 23; 1 Macc 12: 41 or εἰς συνάντησίν τινι Tob 11: 16 BA; Jdth 2: 6; 1 Macc 3: 11, 16; 10: 2, 86) Mt 8: 34; J 12: 13; also εἰς ὑπάντησίν τινος (cf. εἰς ἀπάντησίν τινος 2 Ch 19: 2; Tob 11: 16 S; 1 Macc 12: 41 v.l. [ed. WKappler '36]; εἰς συνάντησίν τινος 3: 11 v.l. [ed. Kappler]) Mt 25: 1 (EPeterson, ZsystTh 7, '30, 682-702). πρός τινα (1 Macc 9: 29; Tob 11: 10 BA) *to someone* J 18: 29, 38; 2 Cor 8: 17. ἐπί τινα *go out against someone* (PTebt. 283, 9 [I BC] ἐξελήλυθεν ἐπὶ τ. μητέρα μου; Jdth 2: 7) Mt 26: 55; Mk 14: 48. ἐπὶ τ. γῆν *step out on the land* Lk 8: 27.

ζ. of persons, w. the purpose expressed by the inf. Mt 11: 8; 20: 1; Mk 3: 21; 4: 3; Lk 7: 25f; 8: 35; Ac 20: 1; Rv 20: 8; w. gen. of the inf. τοῦ σπείρειν *to sow* Mt 13: 3; Lk 8: 5; by the ptc. Rv 6: 2; 1 Cl 42: 3; w. ἵνα Rv 6: 2.

η. At times the word, used in its proper sense, acquires some special feature fr. the context: οὐ μὴ ἐξέλθῃς ἐκεῖθεν *you will never be released from there* Mt 5: 26; Lk 12: 59; D 1: 5. ἐξελεύσονται εἰς τὸ σκότος *they will have to go out into the darkness* Mt 8: 12 v.l. *(Get up and) go out, get ready* of a servant, to fulfill his mission (Mitteis, Chrest. 89, 36) οἱ ἄγγελοι Mt 13: 49. *Appear, make an* appearance (Aristoph., Av. 512, Ach. 240) ἐξῆλθον οἱ Φ. the Pharisees appeared Mk 8:11 (so LKoehler, ThZ 3, '47, 471; also KLSchmidt and ADebrunner, ibid. 471-3). On εἰσέρχεσθαι καὶ ἐ. J 10:9; Ac 1:21 s. under εἰσέρχομαι 1d.

b. non-literal uses—a. go out, proceed ἐκ τῆς ὀσφύος τινός fr. someone's loins= be descended fr. him (Gen 35: 11; 2 Ch 6:9) Hb 7:5. W. gen. of source Mt 2:6 (Mi 5:1). Leave a congregation 1 J 2:19.

β. ἐξέλθατε ἐκ μέσου αὐτῶν come away from among them 2 Cor 6:17 (Is 52:11).—γ. ἐξῆλθεν ἐκ τ. χειρὸς αὐτῶν he escaped fr. them J 10:39.

δ. ἐ. ἐκ τοῦ κόσμου leave the world as a euphemism for die (so as a Jewish expr. אָזַל מִן עָלְמָא Targ. Koh. 1: 8; cf. Dalman, Worte 141. S. also HKoch, ZNW 21, '22, 137f.—The Greeks say ἐξέρχ. τοῦ σώματος: Iambl., Myst. in Stob. 1, 49, 67 p. 457, 9; Sallust. 19 p. 34, 20; or τοῦ βίου: Himerius, Or. [Ecl.] 2, 14) 1 Cor 5:10; 2 Cl 5:1; 8:3. Also ἀπὸ τ. κ. AP 2:5.

c. of a snake come out Ac 28:3.

2. of things—a. lit. come out, flow out of liquids (Judg 15:19) J 19:34; Rv 14:20.

b. non-literal uses:—a. go out of noise, a message, etc.: a voice rings out Rv 16:17; 19:5. The sound of preaching goes out (cf. Mi 4:2) Ro 10:18 (Ps 18:5); also rumors and reports Mt 9:26; Lk 4:14; 7:17; Mk 1:28; J 21:23; ἡ πίστις τινός the news of someone's faith 1 Th 1:8; cf. B 11:8; 19:4. A decree goes out (Da 2:13 Theod.) Lk 2:1. ἀφ' ὑμῶν ὁ λόγος τ. θεοῦ ἐξῆλθεν; did the word of God (Christian preaching) originate fr. you? 1 Cor 14:36.

β. go out with the source or place of origin given, of the lightning ἐ. ἀπὸ ἀνατολῶν goes out fr. the east Mt 24:27. Of words ἐκ τοῦ αὐτοῦ στόματος ἐ. εὐλογία καὶ κατάρα fr. the same mouth come blessing and cursing Js 3:10. ἐκ τῆς καρδίας ἐ. διαλογισμοὶ πονηροί evil thoughts come Mt 15:19; cf. vs. 18. Of a sword ἐ. ἐκ τ. στόματος came out of the mouth Rv 19:21.

γ. be gone, disappear (Hippocr. of diseases; X., An. 7, 5, 4 of time; Gen 47:18) ἐξῆλθεν ἡ ἐλπὶς τ. ἐργασίας αὐτῶν their hope of gain was gone Ac 16:19; cf. Mk 5:30. M-M.*

ἐξεστακέναι s. ἐξίστημι.

ἔξεστι impersonal verb, 3 sing. of the unused ἔξειμι (Eur., Hdt. +; LXX) it is permitted, it is possible, proper.

1. w. pres. inf. foll. (Lucian, Jud. Voc. 3; Esth 8:12g; 4 Macc 1:12) Mt 12:2, 12; 14:4. W. aor. inf. foll. (X., An. 4, 3, 10) Mt 12:10; 15:26 v.l.; 19:3; 22:17; 27:6; Mk 3:4 (ἔξεστιν—ἤ); 12:14; Lk 6:9; 14:3. Without inf., which is easily supplied fr. the context (cf. PRyl. 77, 43 τοῦτο δὲ οὐκ ἐξῆν) Mk 2:24; Lk 6:2; Ac 8:37 v.l.; 1 Cor 10:23.

2. foll. by dat. of the pers. and pres. inf. (X., Hiero 1, 26; BGU 1127, 20 [18 bc]; PSI 203, 7; Jos., Ant. 13, 252) Mk 6:18; Ac 16:21; 22:25. Foll. by dat. of the pers. and aor. inf. (2 Esdr [Ezra] 4:14; 1 Macc 14:44) Mt 20:15; Mk 10:2; J 5:10; 18:31 (JAllen, Why Pilate?: CFDMoule-Festschr., '70, 78-83); Ac 21:37.—Foll. by dat. of the pers. without the necessity of supplying an inf. (PRyl. 62, 16 πάντα τὰ ἄλλα ἔξεστί μοι) 1 Cor 6:12.

3. foll. by acc. w. inf. (Pla., Pol. p. 290d al.) Mk 2:26; Lk 6:4 (cf. Bl-D §409, 3 app.; Rob. 1084f); 20:22.

4. The ptc. of ἐ. is ἐξόν; by the addition of the copula, which, however, must oft. be understood (Ac 2:29; 2 Cor 12:4, as Isaeus 6, 50; Jos., Ant. 8, 404), it comes to mean the same as ἔξεστιν: ἐ. (ἐστιν) w. pres. inf. foll. ISm 8:2; w. aor. inf. foll. Ac 2:29; foll. by dat. of the pers. and aor. inf. (Esth 4:2; Jos., Ant. 20, 202) Mt 12:4. W. dat., and

inf. to be supplied μὴ εἶναι ἐ. αὐτῷ he had no authority MPol 12:2. M-M. B. 647.*

ἐξετάζω 1 aor. ἐξήτασα (Soph., Thu.+; inscr., pap., LXX; Ep. Arist. 32; Philo, Joseph.; Test. Gad 7:3).

1. scrutinize, examine, inquire (Thu.+; Wsd 6:3; Sir 3: 21) ἀκριβῶς ἐ. (Lucian, Dial. Mort. 30, 3; POxy. 237 VI, 31 τὸ πρᾶγμα ἀκρειβῶς ἐξητασμένον; Dt 19:18; Philo, Somn. 1, 228; Jos., Ant. 3, 70) τὶ someth. (Dionys. Hal., Ep. ad Pomp. 1, 16 τὴν ἀλήθειαν; Dio Chrys. 17[34], 26; Philo, Migr. Abr. 185) Hs 9, 13, 6; περὶ τινος make a careful search for someone Mt 2:8 (on ἐ. περὶ τινος cf. Pla., Leg. 3 p. 685a; PGenève 54, 30; BGU 380, 5; Jos., C. Ap. 2, 237). W. indir. quest. foll. (cf. Thu. 7, 33, 6; Epicrates Com. [IV bc] 11, 17 vol. II p. 287 Kock; Aelian, V.H. 1, 28) Mt 10:11.

2. question, examine τινά someone (Soph., Oed. Col. 211; X., Mem. 1, 2, 36; PGrenf. I 53, 22) J 21:12 (w. dir. quest. foll.). As legal t.t. question judicially, esp. in connection w. torture (Polyb. 15, 27, 7; Herodian 4, 5, 3; 4; Dit., Syll.³ 780, 11 [6 bc]; Dt 19:18; Esth 1:1[o]; Sir 23: 10; Jos., Ant. 18, 183). Pass. Hs 9, 28, 4; w. relative clause foll. περὶ ὧν ἔπραξε D 1:5 (cf. PGM 7, 331 περὶ ὧν σε ἐξετάζω). M-M.*

ἐξετασμός, οῦ, ὁ (Demosth. 18, 16; Diod. S. 11, 3, 7; 9; Plut., Mor. 1068b; IG II² 500, 12; LXX) examination, inquiry of God's judgment (Wsd 4:6) ἐ. ἀσεβεῖς ὀλεῖ a searching inquiry shall destroy the godless 1 Cl 57:7 (Pr 1:32).*

ἐξέφνης s. ἐξαίφνης.

ἐξεχύθην s. ἐκχέω.

ἐξέχω stand out, be prominent (Aristoph. +; Dit., Syll.³ 827 III, 11 [116/17 ad]; LXX; cf. 2 Esdr 13 [Neh 3]: 25, 27 ὁ πύργος ὁ ἐξέχων ἐκ τοῦ οἴκου τ. βασιλέως) of raised places as places of honor οἱ ἐξέχοντες τόποι Agr 22= Mt 20:28 D.*

ἐξηγέομαι mid. dep. 1 aor. ἐξηγησάμην (Hom. +) lit. 'lead,' but never so in our lit.; explain, interpret, tell, report, describe (so Hdt. +; inscr., pap., LXX, Ep. Arist.; Philo, Leg. All. 3, 21; Berosus in Jos., C. Ap. 1, 140) τὶ someth. τὰ ἐν τῇ ὁδῷ their experiences on the way Lk 24: 35. πάντα GP 11:45. τ. δεσμὸν τ. ἀγάπης τ. θεοῦ describe the bond of the love of God 1 Cl 49:2. τί τινι relate someth. to someone (Judg 7:13) Ac 10:8; Hv 4, 2, 5. καθ' ἕν ἕκαστον one by one Ac 21:19. ἐ. καθὼς ὁ θεὸς ἐπεσκέψατο 15:14. ὅσα ἐποίησεν ὁ θεός vs. 12.—Oft. t.t. for the activity of priests and soothsayers who impart information or reveal divine secrets; also used w. ref. to divine beings themselves (Pla., trag., Thu., X.; Wettstein on J 1:18.—Arrian, Anab. 2, 3, 3 of soothsayers: τὰ θεῖα ἐξηγεῖσθαι; 6, 2, 3; Ael. Aristid. 13 p. 219 D.: τὰ μέλλοντα ὥσπερ μάντις ἐξηγεῖτο, 45, 30 K. of the proclamation of the Serapis-miracles; Pollux 8, 124 ἐξηγηταὶ δ' ἐκαλοῦντο οἱ τὰ περὶ τῶν διοσημιῶν καὶ τὰ τῶν ἄλλων ἱερῶν διδάσκοντες; Jos. of the interpr. of the law: Bell. 1, 649; 2, 162, Ant. 18, 81). ἐκεῖνος ἐξηγήσατο he has made known or brought news of (the invisible God) J 1:18 (so also JHMichael, JTS 22, '21, 14-16 against RHarris, The Origin of the Prologue '17, 35; s. Hdb.³ ad loc.; AWPersson, D. Exegeten u. Delphi '18). M-M. B. 1238.*

ἐξήγησις, εως, ἡ—1. narrative, description (Thu. +; Pla., Leg. 1 p. 631a; Polyb. 6, 3, 1; Judg 7:15 B; Sir 21:16) τῆς τελειότητος αὐτῆς οὐκ ἔστιν ἐ. its perfection cannot be fully described 1 Cl 50:1.

2. *explanation, interpretation* (Pla.+; Diod. S. 2, 29, 3; Dionys. Hal., Thu. Jud. 54, 3; Philo, Vi. Cont. 78; Jos., Ant. 11, 192) τοῦ πύργου Hv 3, 7, 4.*

ἐξῄειν impf. of ἔξειμι (1).

ἐξήκοντα indecl. (Hom.+; pap., LXX, Ep. Arist., Philo; Jos., Ant. 11, 18) *sixty* Mt 13: 8, 23; Mk 4: 8, 20; Lk 24: 13 (Strabo 16, 2, 36: 60 stades fr. Jerus.; Jos., Vi. 115 ἀπέχ. ἑ. σταδίους); 1 Ti 5: 9; Rv 11: 3; 12: 6; 13: 18. M-M.*

ἑξῆς adv. (Hom.+; inscr., pap., LXX, Ep. Arist., Philo, Joseph., Test. 12 Patr.)—**1.** *next* in a series, *in the next place* (Dionys. Hal. 1, 71, 2; Philo, Op. M. 131 al.) Dg 3: 1.

2. of time—so always in NT—τῇ ἑ. ἡμέρᾳ (Dit., Syll.³ 1170, 24;² 680, 4; Jos., Ant. 4, 302) *on the next day* Lk 9: 37. Freq. the noun must be supplied τῇ ἑξῆς (Ep. Arist. 262; Jos., Bell. 2, 430; POxy. 1063, 6) Ac 21: 1; 25: 17; 27: 18. W. ἐν τῷ ἑξῆς Lk 7: 11 χρόνῳ is to be supplied (soon) *afterward.* M-M.*

ἐξηχέω pf. pass. ἐξήχημαι (mostly act. intr. 'sound forth': Jo 3: 14; Sir 40: 13; Philo, In Flacc. 39, Rer. Div. Her. 15, Dec. 46) trans. *cause to resound* or *be heard* (Polyb. 30, 4, 7; Philo, Abr. 180) pass. *be caused to sound forth, ring out* (3 Macc 3: 2) ἀφ' ὑμῶν ἐξήχηται ὁ λόγος τοῦ κυρίου *the word of the Lord has sounded forth fr. you* 1 Th 1: 8.*

ἐξιλάσκομαι fut. ἐξιλάσομαι; 1 aor. ἐξιλασάμην *propitiate* τινά *someone* θεόν (of a god as early as the oracle in Hdt. 7, 141 Δία; X., Cyr. 7, 2, 19 'Απόλλωνα; Menand., fgm. no. 544, 6 p. 164 Kock τὸν θεόν; Polyb. 3, 112, 19; Diod. S. 1, 59, 2 θυσίαις τὸ θεῖον; 14, 77, 4 τ. θεούς; 20, 14, 3; Strabo 4, 1, 13; Dio Chrys. 15[32], 77; Ael. Aristid. 46, 3 K.=29 p. 572; Jos., Ant. 6; Ep. Arist. 316; Philo, Poster. Cai. 72 [after Lev 16: 10]; Jos., Bell. 5, 19; Sib. Or. 7, 30.—S. also CIA III 74, 16 ἁμαρτίαν [against Μὴν Τύραννος] ἐξειλάσασθαι='atone for sin') 1 Cl 7: 7; Hv 1, 2, 1.*

ἕξις, εως, ἡ (Pre-Socr.+ in var. mngs.; LXX) in the only place in which it is used in our lit. it seems to mean *exercise, practice* (though the mng. nearest this to be found in the sources is the *skill* acquired through exercise [Pla.+; Polyb. 10, 47, 7; 21, 9, 1; Diod. S. 2, 29, 4; Sir Prol l. 11; Ep. Arist. 121; Philo, Leg. All. 1, 10]) αἰσθητήρια διὰ τὴν ἕ. γεγυμνασμένα *senses that are trained by practice* Hb 5: 14.*

ἐξίστημι, w. the Koine by-form ἐξιστάνω (Bl-D. §93 app.; Mlt.-H. 241) Ac 8: 9 (t.r. ἐξιστῶν fr. ἐξιστάω) 1 aor. ἐξέστησα; 2 aor. ἐξέστην; pf. ἐξέστακα; mid. ἐξίσταμαι; impf. ἐξιστάμην.

1. trans. *change, displace,* then *drive one out of one's senses, confuse, amaze, astound* (so oft. w. the added words τινὰ φρενῶν Eur., Bacch. 850; τινὰ τοῦ φρονεῖν X., Mem. 1, 3, 12; τινὰ ταῖς διανοίαις Polyb. 11, 27, 7, but also w. simple acc.; s. the foll.) τινά *someone* (Musonius p. 35, 12 τὰ ἐξιστάντα τοὺς ἀνθρώπους; Lucian, De Domo 19; Stob., Ecl. III 517, 15 οἶνος ἐξέστησέ με; Josh 10: 10; Judg 4: 15; 2 Km 22: 15 al.; Jos., Bell. 3, 74; Test. Benj. 3: 3) Lk 24: 22. Of a sorcerer τὸ ἔθνος τῆς Σαμαρείας Ac 8: 9, 11.

2. intr. (2 aor. and pf. act.; all of the mid.) *become separated fr. someth., lose someth.,* in our lit. only of spiritual and mental balance.

a. *lose one's mind, be out of one's senses* (so Eur., Isocr.+, mostly [as Jos., Ant. 10, 114] w. τῶν φρενῶν, τοῦ φρονεῖν, or sim. addition. Without such addition e.g.

Aristot., Hist. An. 6, 22 p. 577a, 12 ἐξίσταται καὶ μαίνεται; Test. of Job 39; Menand., Sam. 64 J. ἐξέστηχ' ὅλως; Dio Chrys. 80[30], 6; Is 28: 7; Philo, Ebr. 146) ἔλεγον ὅτι ἐξέστη *they said, 'He has lost his senses'* Mk 3: 21 (cf. Irish Eccl. Record 64, '44, 289–312; 65, '45, 1–5; 6–15; JESteinmueller, CBQ 4, '42, 355–9; HWansbrough, NTS 18, '71/'72, 233–35; lit. also on παρά I 4bβ). Prob. ironical εἴτε ἐξέστημεν . . . εἴτε σωφρονοῦμεν *if we were out of our senses . . . ; if we are in our right mind* 2 Cor 5: 13 (ChBruston, Rev. de Théol. et des Quest. rel. 18, '08; 344ff).

b. in our lit. more freq., in the weakened or attenuated sense *be amazed, be astonished,* of the feeling of astonishment mingled w. fear, caused by events which are miraculous, extraordinary, or difficult to understand (Philippides Com. [IV/III BC] fgm. 27 K. ἐγὼ ἐξέστην ἰδών=I was astounded when I saw [the costly vessels]) Gen 43: 33; Ruth 3: 8; 1 Km 14: 15 al.) MPol 12: 1. ἐξίσταντο πάντες οἱ ὄχλοι (cf. Ex 19: 18; Lev 9: 24) Mt 12: 23; cf. Mk 2: 12. ἐξέστησαν ἐκστάσει μεγάλῃ (cf. Gen 27: 33) *they were utterly astonished* 5: 42. λίαν ἐν ἑαυτοῖς ἐξίσταντο *they were utterly astounded within them* 6: 51.—Lk 8: 56; Ac 2: 7 (w. θαυμάζω), 12 (w. διαποροῦμαι); 8: 13; 9: 21; 10: 45 (w. ὅτι foll.); 12: 16. ἐξίσταντο ἐπὶ τῇ συνέσει αὐτοῦ *they were amazed at his intelligence* Lk 2: 47 (ἐπί τινι as Wsd 5: 2; Hos 3: 5). Of heaven B 11: 2 (Jer 2: 12). M-M.*

ἐξισχύω 1 aor. ἐξίσχυσα (Strabo 17, 1, 3; Vett. Val. 288, 12) *be able, be strong enough, be in a position* w. inf. foll. (Proclus on Pla., Cratyl. p. 65, 19 Pasqu.; POxy. 1120, 7; BGU 275, 11; Sir 7: 6 v.l.; Jos., Bell. 1, 451) Eph 3: 18. M-M.*

ἔξοδος, ου, ἡ *going out, away* (trag.+; inscr., pap., LXX, Philo, Joseph., Test. 12 Patr.).

1. *the Exodus* fr. Egypt (Ps 104: 38; 113: 1; Philo, Mos. 2, 248; Jos., Ant. 5, 72, C. Ap. 223; Test. Sim. 9) Hb 11: 22.

2. euphemistically *departure, death* (Wsd 3: 2; 7: 6; Philo, Virt. 77; Jos., Ant. 4, 189 ἑ. τοῦ ζῆν; Test. Napht. 1: 1. Cf. Epict. 4, 4, 38) μετὰ τὴν ἐμὴν ἕ. *after my death* 2 Pt 1: 15 (cf. the last will and test. of Abraham, bishop of Hermonthis, PLond. 77, 57 κελεύω μετὰ τ. ἐμὴν ἔξοδον τ. βίου). τὴν ἕ., ἣν ἤμελλεν πληροῦν *his departure, which he was to accomplish* Lk 9: 31.

3. *fate, destination* of stones in the apocal. figure Hv 3, 4, 3. M-M.*

ἐξοιδέω 1 aor. inf. ἐξοιδῆσαι (Eur., Polyb.,+) *swell, be swollen up* Papias 3.*

ἐξοίσουσι s. ἐκφέρω.

ἐξολεθρεύω 1 aor. ἐξωλέθρευσα; 1 fut. pass. ἐξολεθρευθήσομαι (Crito [early II AD]: 200 fgm. 2 Jac.; LXX; Sib. Or. 5, 454; 12, 102; 14, 107; Test. 12 Patr.; Pel.-Leg. p. 23, 15; 24, 18; Maspéro 2 III, 28 [VI AD].—As v.l. in Plut., Dio 18, 9 Ziegler, Jos., Ant. 8, 270 N., and Sib. Or. 3, 309 G. On the spelling of the word cf. Bl-D. §32, 1; Thackeray p. 87f; Mlt.-H. 71) *destroy utterly, root out* τινά 1 Cl 53: 3 (Dt 9: 14). τι: πάντα τὰ χείλη τὰ δόλια *all lying lips* 15: 5 (Ps 11: 4). τὶ ἔκ τινος *someth. fr. someth.* 22: 6 (Ps 33: 17). Pass. B 7: 3 (Lev 23: 29). ἐκ τοῦ λαοῦ Ac 3: 23 (Lev 23: 29). ἀπό τινος 1 Cl 14: 4 (Ps 36: 38, but without ἀπό τ. For the combination ἑ. ἀπὸ τ. γῆς cf. 1 Macc 2: 40; Jdth 6: 2). M-M.*

ἐξομοιόω *make just like* or *similar* (Hdt.+; Sextus 381). Pass. *become just like* or *similar, resemble fully* (trag.+;

2 Macc 4: 16; Philo, Aet. M. 44) τινί someone (Epict. 1, 2, 18; 2, 14, 12; Socrat., Ep. 6, 4) τέλεον αὐτοῖς ἐξομοιοῦσθε finally you become quite like them Dg 2: 5.*

ἐξομολογέω 1 aor. ἐξωμολόγησα; fut. mid. ἐξομολογήσομαι (quotable since III BC—PHib. 30, 18 [300–271 BC]; LXX, Philo, Joseph.).
   1. act. promise, consent abs. Lk 22: 6 (the act. is found as rarely [perh. Alex. Aphr., An. Mant. II 1 p. 168, 15] as the pass. [perh. Dit., Syll.³ 685, 95]).
   2. mid.—a. confess, admit (Plut., Eum. 17, 7, Anton. 59, 3 τ. ἀλήθειαν, Stoic. Repugn. 17 p. 1042A; Sus 14; Jos., Bell. 1, 625, Ant. 8, 256) τὶ someth. (POsl. 17, 14 [136 AD] τὸ ἀληθές; Cyranides p. 100, 18 πάντα ὅσα ἔπραξεν) τὰς ἁμαρτίας (Jos., Ant. 8, 129; s. the inscr. in FSteinleitner, D. Beicht '13, p. 40; 48; 49; 53) Mt 3: 6; Mk 1: 5; Js 5: 16 (s. PAlthaus, Zahn-Festgabe '28, 1ff); Hv 1, 1, 3; s 9, 23, 4. τὰς ἀ. τῷ κυρίῳ confess sins to the Lord Hv 3, 1, 5, cf. 6. τὰ παραπτώματα ἐν ἐκκλησίᾳ confess transgressions in the congregation D 4: 14. περὶ τῶν παραπτωμάτων make a confession of transgressions 1 Cl 51: 3. ἐπὶ τ. ἁμαρτίαις for sins B 19: 12. Abs. make a confession of sins Ac 19: 18; 2 Cl 8: 3. W. dat. of the one to whom sins are confessed 1 Cl 52: 1, 2 (w. similarity in form to Ps 7: 18; 117: 19 and sim. Ps passages, but not=praise because of 1 Cl 51: 3 [s. 2c below]).—JSchnitzer, D. Beichte im Lichte d. Religionsgesch.: Ztschr. f. Völkerpsychol. 6, '30, 94–105; RPettazzoni, La confessione dei Peccati II '35.
   b. acknowledge (PHib. 30 s. above; POxy. 1473, 9) w. ὅτι foll. Phil 2: 11 (Is 45: 23; s. below c).—Nägeli 67.
   c. fr. the mng. confess there arose, as Rtzst., Erlösungsmyst. 252 shows, the more general sense praise, of praise directed toward God (so mostly LXX) w. dat. of the one praised (oft. LXX; Philo, Leg. All. 1, 80) σοί (2 Km 22: 50; 1 Ch 29: 13; Ps 85: 12; 117: 28 al.) Mt 11: 25=Lk 10: 21 (s. Norden, Agn. Th. 277ff; JWeiss, GHeinrici-Festschr. '14, 120ff; TArvedson, D. Mysterium Chr. [Mt 11: 25–30] '37; NPWilliams, ET 51, '40, 182–6; 215–20; AMHunter, NTS 8, '62, 241–49); Ro 15: 9 (Ps 17: 50); 1 Cl 26: 2; 61: 3; B 6: 16 (cf. Ps 34: 18). τῷ θεῷ (Tob 14: 7; Philo, Leg. All. 2, 95) Ro 14: 11 (Is 45: 23); Hm 10, 3, 2. τῷ κυρίῳ (fr. Gen 29: 35 on, oft. in LXX) 1 Cl 48: 2 (Ps 117: 19). M-M.*

ἐξομολόγησις, εως, ἡ (Dionys. Hal.; Plut.; Philo, Leg. All. 1, 82; Jos., Bell. 5, 435) praise of God (so LXX) of rich men λίαν μικρὰν ἔχει τὴν ἐ. Hs 2: 5; because of the nearness of ἔντευξις='intercessory prayer' perh. ἐξομ. here acquires the more specialized sense 'prayer of thanksgiving' (s. MDibelius, Hdb. on Hs 2: 5; cf. m 10, 3, 2).*

ἐξόν s. ἔξεστιν 4.

ἐξορκίζω (Demosth.+; inscr., pap.; Jos., Ant. 2, 200; 11, 145, mostly=ἐξορκόω 'cause someone to swear') adjure, charge under oath τινά someone (so POsl. 148, 10 [II/I BC] ἐξορκίζω; Fluchtaf. 4, 1ff [III AD]; PGM 3, 10; 119; 4, 1239 ἐξορκίζω σε δαίμον κατὰ τούτου τ. θεοῦ; 12, 137; BGU 956, 1 [III AD] ἐ. ὑμᾶς κατὰ τ. ἁγίου ὀνόματος; cf. 3 Km 22: 16) ἐ. σε κατὰ τοῦ θεοῦ I adjure you by God Mt 26: 63 (w. ἵνα foll. as Cyranides p. 120, 3). Exorcise an evil spirit Ac 19: 13 v.l., 14 v.l. M-M.*

ἐξορκιστής, οῦ, ὁ an exorcist (so an epigr. of Lucian in Anth. Pal. 11, 427; Ptolem., Apotelesm. 4, 4, 10 Boll-B.), who drives out demons by magical formulas. Of wandering Jewish exorcists Ac 19: 13. For the idea cf. Jos., Ant. 8, 42ff, esp. 45: Solomon as the author of τρόποι ἐξορκώσεων, which drive out demons.—WHeitmüller, 'Im Namen Jesu' '03 index III.*

ἐξορύσσω 1 aor. ἐξώρυξα (Hdt.+; pap., LXX, Philo, Joseph.) dig out, of eyes tear out (so Hdt. 8, 116; Plut., Artax. 14, 10; Lucian, Dial. Deor. 1, 1; Jos., Ant. 6, 71; 1 Km 11: 2; Judg 16: 21 A) Gal 4: 15 (the eye as a precious member: Aeschyl., Sept. 530; Moschus 4, 9; Callim., H. 3, 211; Artem. 1, 25; Heliod. 2, 16, 4 the beloved is ὀφθαλμὸς κ. ψυχὴ κ. πάντα ἐμαυτῆς; Eustath. Macremb. 6, 10 Ζεῦ Πάτερ, μή μου τοὺς ὀφθαλμοὺς ἐκκόψῃς.—JBligh, TU 102, '68, 382f. W. ref. to a roof Mk 2: 4 it prob. means making an opening by digging through the clay of which the roof was made (ABertholet, Kulturgesch. Israels '20, 122; CCMcCown, JBL 58, '39, 213–16), and putting the debris to one side (ἐ. of debris that has been dug out Hdt. 2, 150; 7, 23), so that it does not fall on the heads of those in the house.—S. on στέγη. M-M.*

ἐξουδενέω (so Vi. Aesopi W c. 77b p. 96, 37 P.; BGU 1117, 31 [13 BC]; 2 Cor 10: 10 B) and **ἐξουδενόω** (so Sb 7524, 11 [249 BC]; pap.: APF 11, '35, 125 [II BC]; Syntipas p. 78, 15; schol. on Lucian p. 279, 10 Rabe. The NT mss. vary; on the spelling s. Phryn. p. 182 Lob.; Bl-D. §33 app.; 108, 2 app.; Mlt.-H. 111f; 310; 396. For LXX Thackeray 105) 1 aor. pass. ἐξουδενήθην (ἐξουδενώθην) treat with contempt (4 Km 19: 21) Mk 9: 12; cf. ἐξουθενέω. M-M.*

ἐξουθενέω (Herodian Gr. II 508, 10; Cass. Dio 7, 8, 8; Vi. Aesopi I c. 80 ἐξουθενηθείς; Vi. Aesopi W c. 77b p. 97, 2 P. ἐξουθένησας [beside p. 96, 37 ἐξουθενῆσαι]; schol. on Pla. 483B) and **ἐξουθενόω** (Rhet. Gr. I 623, 27; Mk 9: 12 א; 1 Cl 18: 17=Ps 50; 19. For the spelling s. the ref. s.v. ἐξουδενέω) 1 aor. ἐξουθένησα; pf. pass. ἐξουθένημαι.
   1. despise, disdain τινά someone (Ps.-Callisth. p. 72, 19; schol. on Soph., Ajax 368 p. 36 Papag. [1888]) Lk 18: 9 (Field, Notes 72); Ro 14: 3, 10; 1 Cor 16: 11. τὶ someth. (Jos., Bell. 6, 315. Pass.: Philo, Leg. All. 2, 67) 1 Cl 18: 17 (Ps 50: 19). ἐξουθενημένος despised, of no account οἱ ἐ. (Philo, Mos. 2, 241) 1 Cor 6: 4; τὰ ἐ. 1: 28. Of the speaking ability of the apostle when he appears in person (parall. ἀσθενής): it amounts to nothing 2 Cor 10: 10. The expr. τ. πειρασμὸν ὑμῶν ἐν τ. σαρκί μου οὐκ ἐξουθενήσατε Gal 4: 14 is perh. unclear because of the mixture of two ideas: 'You did not despise me in my physical weakness' and 'You did not yield to the temptation to despise me because of my physical weakness'. S. 2.
   2. reject w. contempt (1 Km 8: 7; PsSol 2: 5; En. 99, 14). So 1 Th 5: 20; Ac 4: 11.—Since at least for διαπτύω τι the mng. 'reject someth.' is well established (Dositheus, Ars Gramm. 68, 10 Tolk.: διέπτυσεν αὐτοῦ τὰς ἱκετείας) and likewise for περιπτύω (Simplicius in Epict. p. 58, 8; 61, 20; 98, 36; 119, 18), it may also be poss. to transl. Gal 4: 14 (s. 1): 'You neither treated me w. contempt nor did you turn away from the temptation that my physical appearance might have become to you.'
   3. treat w. contempt τινά Lk 23: 11; B 7: 9. Pass. Mk 9: 12 v.l. M-M.*

ἐξουθένημα, ατος, τό a despised thing ἐγὼ εἰμι ἐ. λαοῦ I am an object of contempt for the people 1 Cl 16: 15 (Ps 21: 7 v.l. [ARahlfs, Psalmi cum Odis '31 ad loc.]).*

ἐξουσία, ας, ἡ (Soph., Thu.+; inscr., pap., LXX, En., Ep. Arist., Philo, Joseph., Test. 12 Patr.) from ἔξεστιν.
   1. freedom of choice, right to act, decide, or dispose of one's property as one wishes (BGU 1158, 13 [9 BC] legal t.t., esp. in wills: POxy. 272, 13; BGU 183, 25 ἔχειν αὐτὴν τὴν ἐ. τῶν ἰδίων πάντων; PTebt. 319, 21.—Sir 30: 11) ἐξουσίαν ἔχειν have the right 2 Th 3: 9. W. inf. foll. (Teles p. 23, 14; 24, 11; Tob 2: 13 S; 7: 10 S) J 10: 18; 1 Cor 9: 4ff; Hb 13: 10; Rv 13: 5. W. obj. gen. foll. (Epict.

3, 24, 70 τίς οὖν ἔτι ἔχει μου ἐξουσίαν;) εἰ ἄλλοι τῆς ὑμῶν ἐ. μετέχουσι 1 Cor 9: 12. Also ἐ. ἐπὶ τὸ ξύλον τῆς ζωῆς *the right to the tree of life* Rv 22: 14. W. verbs of two constr. ἔχει ἐ. ὁ κεραμεὺς τοῦ πηλοῦ ἐκ τοῦ αὐτοῦ φυράματος *the potter has a right over the clay, to make fr. the same lump* Ro 9: 21. ἐ. ἔχειν περί τινος (4 Macc 4: 5) *be at liberty w. regard to a thing* (opp. ἀνάγκην ἔχειν) 1 Cor 7: 37; cf. 8: 9; ἐ. ἐν τ. εὐαγγελίῳ *a right in the gospel* 9: 18. ἐν τῇ σῇ ἐ. ὑπῆρχεν *was at your disposal* Ac 5: 4 (Esth 4: 17b; Appian, Liby. 52 §226 ἐν ἐ. εἶναι τί τινι= someth. is at someone's disposal, is within one's power).

2. *ability* to do someth., *capability, might, power* (1 Esdr 4: 28, 40; 2 Macc 7: 16) ἡ ἐ. τ. ἵππων ἐν τ. στόματι αὐτῶν ἐστιν Rv 9: 19; cf. vs. 3; 13: 2, 4; 18: 1; Mt 9: 8; Ac 8: 19. W. inf. foll. to indicate the thing that one is able to do (Diod. S. 4, 52, 4 ἀμύνασθαι εἶχεν ἐξουσίαν) ἐκβάλλειν τ. δαιμόνια Mk 3: 15. ἐμβαλεῖν εἰς τ. γέενναν Lk 12: 5; cf. J 1: 12; J 7: 1 v.l.; Rv 9: 10; 11: 6. W. gen. of the inf. foll. τοῦ πατεῖν ἐπάνω ὄφεων Lk 10: 19; ποιεῖν ἐ. *exercise power* Rv 13: 12. ἐ. ἔχειν τινός *have power over someone* (Epict. 4, 12, 8) GP 3: 7; also ἐ. ἔχειν ἐπί τινος Rv 20: 6. Esp. of God's power (Theodor. Prodr. 5, 313 ἡ θεῶν ἐ.; Da 4: 17; Jos., Ant. 5, 109; 18, 214) Lk 12: 5; Ac 1: 7; Jd 25. πάντων τ. ἐξουσίαν *power over all* Hm 4, 1, 11; τέλους ἐ. *power over the end* PK 2. ἐ. ἐπὶ τ. πληγάς *control over the plagues* Rv 16: 9. Also of Satan's power Ac 26: 18; ending of Mk in the Freer ms. l. 8; B 2: 1. The power that comes fr. God can involve supernatural knowledge, and both may be expressed by ἐ. (Herm. Wr. 1, 13; 14; 32). So his hearers conclude fr. Jesus' teaching that he must have ἐ. Mk 1: 22 ('license' L-S-J suppl., '68; against this AWArgyle, ET 80, '68/'69, 343); cf. Mt 7: 29 (Rtzst., Poim. 48, 3, Mysterienrel.³ 302; 363; JStarr, HTR 23, '30, 302-5; HWindisch, Pls. u. Christus '34, 151ff; DDaube, JTS 39, '38, 45-59; HJFlowers, ET 66, '55, 254 ['like a king']; DFHudson, ET 67, '55/'56, 17; JCoutts, JTS 8, '57, 111-18 [Jesus and the 12]). The prep. expr. κατ᾽ ἐξουσίαν *in accordance w. knowledge and power* Mk 1: 27 and ἐν ἐ. Lk 4: 32 belong to this classification; cf. 4: 36. The close relation of ἐ. w. Gnosis and teaching also B 18: 1.—But it is not always possible to draw a hard and fast line betw. this mng. and

3. *authority, absolute power, warrant* (Sextus 36: the πιστός has ἐξ. fr. God) ἐ. καὶ ἐπιτροπή (cf. Ps.-Pla., Defin. p. 415c ἐξουσία, ἐπιτροπὴ νόμου) *authority and commission* Ac 26: 12. ἐν ποίᾳ ἐξουσίᾳ ταῦτα ποιεῖς; *by whose authority are you doing this?* Mt 21: 23, 24, 27; Mk 11: 28, 29, 33; Lk 20: 2, 8. ἐ. διδόναι τινὶ *put someone in charge* (Diod. S. 13, 36, 2; 14, 81, 6; Vi. Aesopi I c. 11; Jos., Ant. 2, 90; 20, 193) Mk 13: 34; PK 2 p. 14, 13. Of apostolic authority 2 Cor 10: 8; 13: 10; ISm 4: 1. Of Jesus' absolute authority Mt 28: 18 (cf. Herm. Wr. 1, 32; Da 7: 14; DMStanley, CBQ 29, '67, 555-73). W. gen. of the one who has authority ἐ. τοῦ Χριστοῦ Rv 12: 10. W. gen. of that over which the authority is exercised (Diod. S. 2, 27, 3; Fluchtaf. 4, 21; Ps 135: 8, 9; Wsd 10: 14; Sir 17: 2; Jos., Vi. 190) ἐ. πνευμάτων ἀκαθάρτων *over the unclean spirits* Mt 10: 1; Mk 6: 7; cf. J 17: 2; Hm 4, 3, 5; PK 2 p. 13, 22. Also ἐπί w. acc. (cf. Sir 33: 20) Lk 9: 1; cf. Rv 6: 8; 13: 7. Likew. ἐπί w. gen. (cf. Da 3: 97) Rv 2: 26; 11: 6b; 14: 18. παρά τινος indicates the source of the authority (s. παρά I 3b) Ac 9: 14; 26: 10 (ἐξ. λαμβάνειν as Diod. S. 11, 42, 6; Vi. Aesopi I c. 11) and κατά τινος the one against whom it is directed (Sb 8316, 6f κύριε Σάραπι δὸς αὐτῷ κατεξουσίαν κατὰ τῶν ἐχθρῶν αὐτοῦ) J 19: 11 (Hv Campenhausen, ThLZ 73, '48, 387-92). W. pres. inf. foll. (cf. X., Mem. 2, 35; 1 Macc 10: 35; 11: 58; Jos., Ant. 4, 247) Mt 9: 6; Mk 2: 10; Lk 5: 24; J 5: 27. W. aor. inf. foll.

(Jdth 8: 15; 1 Esdr 8: 22; 1 Macc 1: 13) 19: 10. Foll. by gen. of the pres. inf. (4 Macc 5: 15) Hm 12, 4, 2.

4. the power exercised by rulers or others in high position by virtue of their office.

a. *ruling power, official power* (Ps.-Pla., Alc. 1 p. 135B al.; LXX; Jos., Bell. 2, 140, Vi. 80) ἐ. ὡς βασιλεύς Rv 17: 12f (Diod. S. 2, 45, 1 βασιλικὴν ἐξ. ἔχειν; 14, 32, 5 ἐξ. λαμβάνειν); ἐ. τοῦ ἡγεμόνος Lk 20: 20; cf. J 19: 10f, s. 3 above. ἐ. ἐπάνω δέκα πόλεων Lk 19: 17. ἄνθρωπος ὑπὸ ἐξουσίαν τασσόμενος *a man under authority* 7: 8 (M Frost, ET 45, '34, 477f); cf. Mt 8: 9; Hs 1: 3.—The power of a particular office (Diod. S. 1, 70, 1; 14, 113, 6 ἡ ὑπατικὴ ἐξουσία; Plut., Mar. 2, 1, Caes. 58, 1) ἐπαρχικὴ ἐ. *the power of prefect* Phlm subscr.

b. the *domain* in which the power is exercised (4 Km 20: 13; Ps 113: 2) Lk 4: 6. ἐκ τ. ἐξουσίας Ἡρῴδου ἐστίν *he comes fr. Herod's jurisdiction* 23: 7. ἐ. τοῦ σκότους *domain of darkness* 22: 53; Col 1: 13 (opp. the βασιλεία of Christ). Hence ἐ. τοῦ ἀέρος simply *domain of the air* Eph 2: 2; s. ἀήρ.

c. the bearers of the authority—**α.** human *authorities, officials, government* (Dionys. Hal. 8, 44; 11, 32; POxy. 261, 15) Lk 12: 11 (here and elsewh. in NT w. ἀρχή, as also in Pla.); Ro 13: 1, 2, 3 (with 13: 1b cf. the 'ancient saying' [s. Hes., Theogony 96 ἐκ δὲ Διὸς βασιλῆες. On this HFränkel, Dichtung u. Philos. des frühen Griechentums '51, p. 141, 5] in Artem. 2, 36 p. 135, 24; 2, 69 p. 161, 17 τὸ κρατοῦν δύναμιν ἔχει θεοῦ= the ruling power has its authority from God; Wsd 6: 3; Jos., Bell. 2, 140 οὐ δίχα θεοῦ περιγενέσθαι τινὶ τὸ ἄρχειν · . . . ἐξουσίαν. For the view that the ἐ. of Ro 13 are spirit powers, as β below, s. OCullmann, Christ and Time [tr. Filson] '50, 191-210); Tit 3: 1.—On this subj. LGaugusch, D. Staatslehre d. Ap. Pls nach Ro 13: ThGl 5, '34, 529-50; JEUitman, Onder Eig. Vaandel 15, '40, 102-21; HvCampenhausen, ABertholet Festschr. '50, 97-113; OCullmann, Zur neuesten Diskussion über die ἐξουσίαι in Rö 13: 1: ThZ 10, '54, 321-36, D. Staat im NT '61² [Eng. transl.: The State in the NT '56, 93-114]; against him AStrobel, ZNW 47, '56, 67-93.—GBCaird, Princip. and Powers '56; RMorgenthaler ThZ 12, '56, 289-304; CD Morrison, The Powers that Be '60; EBarnikol, Rö 13. Der nichtpaulinische Ursprung der absoluten Obrigkeitsbejahung v. Rö 13: 1-7 '61, 65-133; HSchlier, Principalities and Powers in the NT '61 (Eng. transl.). οἱ ἐπ᾽ ἐξουσίαν ἀχθέντες *those who are brought before the authorities* Hs 9, 28, 4.

β. of rulers and functionaries of the spirit world (Test. Levi 3: 8; Test. Solom. 20: 15 CCMcCown ['22]), sg. (w. ἀρχή and δύναμις) 1 Cor 15: 24; Eph 1: 21; Col 2: 10. Pl. (w. ἀρχαί) Eph 3: 10; 6: 12; Col 1: 16; 2: 15; (w. ἄγγελοι, δυνάμεις) 1 Pt 3: 22.

5. Various opinions are held concerning the mng. of 1 Cor 11: 10 ὀφείλει ἡ γυνὴ ἐξουσίαν ἔχειν ἐπὶ τῆς κεφαλῆς διὰ τοὺς ἀγγέλους. Many now understand it as '*a means of exercising power*' (cf. δύναμις 7.—It is abstract for concrete, as βασιλεία [1] in Diod. S. 1, 47, 5: a stone figure ἔχουσα τρεῖς βασιλείας ἐπὶ τῆς κεφαλῆς = that wears three symbols of royal power [diadems] on its head, that is to say, the *veil* (κάλυμμα is v.l. for ἐξ. here; s. critical apparatus in N.) by which women at prayer (when they draw near to the heavenly realm) protect themselves fr. the amorous glances of certain angels. But the veil may also have been simply a symbol of womanly dignity, esp. befitting a Christian woman, esp. in the presence of holy angels (s. Cadbury below).—WWeber, ZWTh 46, '03, 487-99; Dibelius, Geisterwelt 12-23 al.; EFehrle, Die kultische Keuschheit im Altertum '10, 39; RPerdelwitz, StKr 86, '13, 611-13; LBrun, ZNW 14, '13,

298-308; GerhKittel, Rabbinica '20, 17ff; Billerb. III 423-35; KBornhäuser, NKZ 41, '30, 475-88; WFoerster, ZNW 30, '31, 185f; MGinsburger, RHPhr 12, '32, 245-7; OMotta, ET 44, '33, 139-41; CSpicq, RB 48, '39, 557-62; EHBlakeney, ET 55, '44, 138; StLösch, ThQ 127, '47, 216-61; JAFitzmyer, NTS 3, '57, 48-58; HJCadbury, HTR 51, '58, 1f (Qumran parallels); MornaDHooker, NTS 10, '64, 410-16; AIsaksson, Marriage and Ministry in the NT '65, 176-81.—LCerfaux and JTondriau, Un Concurrent du Christianisme: Le Culte des Souverains dans la Civilisation Gr.-Ro. '57. S. on ἄγγελος 2c.—On the whole word WFoerster, TW II 559-71. M-M.**

ἐξουσιάζω 1 fut. pass. ἐξουσιασθήσομαι (Aristot., Eth. Eud. 1, 5 p. 1216a, 2; Dionys. Hal. 9, 44, 6; inscr., pap., LXX) *have the right* or *power for someth.* or *over someone* ὁ ἐξουσιάζων *one who is in authority* (Eccl 10: 4, 5) Lk 22: 25. Specif. *the right* or *power to do with someth. as one sees fit* (IG XIV 79, 4) w. gen. of that over which one has the power (CIG III 4584 θυγατέρα αὐτῶν μὴ ἐξουσιάζειν τοῦ μνήματος) of husband and wife w. ref. to their marital duties ἐ. τοῦ ἰδίου σώματος *have power over her* (*his*) *own body* 1 Cor 7: 4. Paul uses the pass. in a play on words w. ἔξεστιν: οὐκ ἐξουσιασθήσομαι ὑπό τινος *I will not be mastered by anything* 6: 12. M-M.*

ἐξουσιαστικός, ή, όν (Symmachus Eccl. 8, 4; Vett. Val., Iamblichus. -ώτερον Polyb. 5, 26, 3) *authoritative* Mk 1: 27 v.l.*

ἐξοχή, ῆς, ἡ *prominence* (cf. Theod. Job 39: 28; Sym. SSol 2: 14; Jer 13: 4; Jos., Ant. 3, 135; 231), metaph. *excellence, advantage* (Cicero, Ad Att. 4, 15, 7; Vett. Val. 17, 23) κατ' ἐξοχήν *par excellence* (Strabo 1, 2, 10; Philo, Leg. All. 1, 106; Dit., Syll.³ 810, 16 [55 AD], Or. 764, 52 [II BC]) ἄνδρες οἱ κατ' ἐ. τῆς πόλεως *the most prominent men of the city* Ac 25: 23. M-M.*

ἔξοχος, ον (Hom.+ in poetry; in prose in Cornutus 16 p. 20, 21, Plut., Lucian, Herodian and other late wr., incl. Vett. Val. 16, 1) *prominent* (Sib. Or. 5, 284) μάρτυς a *prominent martyr* MPol 19: 1. Superl. (Ps.-Lucian, Asin. 2; Dit., Or. 640, 16; POxy. 1469, 1) τὸ ἐξοχώτατον *the most preëminent thing* 1 Cl 33: 4. M-M.*

ἐξυπνίζω fut. ἐξυπνίσω (Plut., Mor. 979D; 1044D; M. Ant. 6, 31; Judg 16: 14 B, 20 B; 3 Km 3: 15; Test. Levi 8: 18, Judah 25: 4. Hellenist. substitute for ἀφυπνίζω: Phryn. p. 96; 224 L.) *wake up, arouse* τινά someone of sleeping persons (Chrysipp.: Stoic. II 334) τὸν κεντυρίωνα GP 10: 38. Fig. of the dead (Job 14: 12) J 11: 11. M-M.*

ἔξυπνος, ον (PGiess. 19, 4; LXX) *awake, aroused* ἔ. γίνεσθαι (Syntipas p. 58, 5; 117, 2; 1 Esdr 3: 3; Jos., Ant. 11, 34) *awaken* ἔ. γενόμενος (Leontios 8 p. 15, 14; Test. Levi 5: 7) Ac 16: 27. M-M.*

ἔξω adv. of place (Hom.+; inscr., pap., LXX, En., Philo, Joseph., Test. 12 Patr.).
1. used as adv.—a. *outside*—α. w. a verb δεδεμένον πρὸς θύραν ἔ. *tied at the door outside* Mk 11: 4. ἔ. εἶναι (X., An. 2, 6, 3; 7, 2, 29) ἔ. ἐπ' ἐρήμοις τόποις ἦν 1: 45; ἑστάναι ἔ. *stand outside* (Gen 24: 31; Dt 24: 11; Sir 21: 23) Mt 12: 46f; Mk 3: 31 (cf. vs. 32) Lk 8: 20; 13: 25; w. πρός and dat. πρὸς τ. θύρᾳ J 18: 16; πρὸς τ. μνημείῳ ἔ. 20: 11; καθῆσθαι ἔ. Mt 26: 69; προσεύχεσθαι ἔ. *pray outside* Lk 1: 10; ἔ. ἔχειν τι *have someth. free of* uncovered shoulders Hs 9, 2, 4; 9, 5; 5; 9, 13, 8. The verb is to be supplied in pass. like Rv 22: 15.
β. as subst. w. art. οἱ ἔξω *those who are outside* (2 Macc 1: 16; Petosiris, fgm. 6 1. 206=the foreigners; fig. Thu. 5,

14, 3) of those who did not belong to the circle of the disciples Mk 4: 11. Of non-Christians gener. (Iambl., Vi. Pyth. 35, 252 of non-Pythagoreans; Simplicius in Epict. p. 132, 6 those who are not ascetics) 1 Cor 5: 12f; Col 4: 5; 1 Th 4: 12.
γ. as a substitute for an adj. *outer, outside* (Pla., Phaedr. 248A ὁ ἔξω τόπος. The same expr. BGU 1114, 5 [4 BC]; cf. POxy. 903, 20 τὰς ἔξω θύρας). αἱ ἔ. πόλεις the *foreign* (lit. 'outside', i.e. non-Jewish) *cities* Ac 26: 11. ὁ ἐ. ἡμῶν ἄνθρωπος our *outer man* (i.e., the body, as Zosimus 13: Hermet. IV p. 107, 16) 2 Cor 4: 16 (s. ἄνθρωπος 2ca). Differently οἱ ἔ. ἄνθρωποι 2 Cl 13: 1, where the words have the mng. of οἱ ἔξω (s. above β) *those on the outside* (as Lucian, De Merc. Cond. 21); τὸ ἐ. (opp. τὸ ἔσω) the *outside* (Thu. 7, 69, 4) 2 Cl 12: 2, cf. vs. 4 (apocryphal saying of Jesus).
b. *out* (Hom.+) ἐξέρχεσθαι ἔ. *go out(side)* (Jos 2: 19; cf. Ps 40: 7) Mt 26: 75; Lk 22: 62; J 19: 4, 5; Rv 3: 12; ἐξῆλθεν ἔ. εἰς τὸ προαύλιον Mk 14: 68. ἐξῆλθεν ἔ. πρὸς αὐτούς (cf. Gen 24: 29; Judg 19: 25) J 18: 29. ἔ. ποιεῖν τινα *take someone out* Ac 5: 34. ἄγειν J 19: 4, 13. ἐξάγειν (Gen 15: 5; Judg 19: 25) Mk 8: 23 v.l.; Lk 24: 50 v.l.; προάγειν Ac 16: 30. (M. Ant. 12, 25 βάλε ἔξω) Mt 5: 13; 13: 48; Lk 14: 35; J 15: 6; 1 J 4: 18. ἐκβάλλειν (2 Ch 29: 16) Lk 13: 28; J 6: 37; 9: 34f; 12: 31; Ac 9: 40; δεῦρο ἔ. *come out!* J 11: 43 (δεῦρο 1).
2. as improper prep. w. gen.—a. in answer to the question 'where?' *outside* (Thu. 8, 67, 2 al.; Num 35: 5, 27; Jdth 10: 18; 13: 3; Jos., Ant. 13, 91; 101) Lk 13: 33. ἔ. τῆς παρεμβολῆς *outside the camp* Hb 13: 11 (cf. Ex 29: 14 al.); Ac 28: 16 v.l.; ἔ. τ. πύλης Hb 13: 12 (Jos., Bell. 4, 360 ἔ. τῶν πυλῶν).
b. to the question 'whither?' *out* (fr. within), *out of* (Hom.+) ἀπελθεῖν ἔ. τ. συνεδρίου Ac 4: 15. Likew. after ἐξέρχεσθαι (Polyaenus 3, 7, 3; cf. Jos., Ant. 8, 399) Mt 10: 14; 21: 17; Ac 16: 13; Hb 13: 13 (ἐξέρχ. ἔ. τ. παρεμβολῆς as Num 31: 13); ἐκπορεύεσθαι Mk 11: 19; ἀποστέλλειν τινά 5: 10; ἐκφέρειν τινά (Lev 4: 12) Mk 8: 23; βάλλειν τινά 2 Cl 7: 4; ἐκβάλλειν τινά (Lev 14: 40) Mt 21: 39; Mk 12: 8; Lk 4: 29; 20: 15; w. acc. to be supplied, Ac 7: 58; σύρειν τινα 14: 19; ἕλκειν τινά 21: 30; προπέμπειν τινά 21: 5 (on ἕως ἔ. cf. 1 Km 9: 26). M-M.**

ἔξωθεν adv. of place (Aeschyl., Hdt.+; inscr., pap., LXX, Philo, Joseph.).
1. used as adv.—a. *from the outside* (Hierocles 7 p. 430 ἡ ἔ. βία= force from the outside; Judg 12: 9; Jdth 13: 1) τὸ ἔ. εἰσπορευόμενον what goes into (a man) fr. the outside Mk 7: 18.
b. *outside*—α. as contrast to ἔσωθεν (Aeneas Tact. 1331; Diocles 141 p. 178, 13; Gen 6: 14; Ex 25: 11 al.; PGM 5, 307) Mt 23: 27f; 2 Cor 7: 5; Rv 5: 1 v.l. (Plut., Dio 31, 2 μία [sc. ἐπιστολή] δ' ἦν ἐπιγεγραμμένη); IRo 3: 2.
β. as subst. w. art. οἱ ἔ. *those on the outside* i.e. non-Christians 1 Ti 3: 7; Mk 4: 11 v.l. (cf. Hdt. 9, 5; Diod. S. 19, 70, 3; Himerius, Or. [Ecl.] 5, 18; Celsus 3, 14; Jos., Bell. 4, 179, Ant. 15, 316). τὸ ἔ. the *outside* (Dit., Syll.³ 813A, 6; Ezk 41: 17) Mt 23: 25; Lk 11: 39f.
γ. as a substitute for an adj. *having to do w. the outside, external* (Demosth. 18, 9 οἱ ἔ. λόγοι; 4 Macc 6: 34; 18: 2; Jos., Ant. 14, 477) ὁ ἔ. κόσμος *external adornment* 1 Pt 3: 3; ἡ ἔ. ἐπιφάνεια the *outer surface* Papias 3.
c. *outward*, out ἔκβαλε ἔ. *throw out= leave out* (ἐκβάλλω 3) Rv 11: 2b.
2. as improper prep. w. gen. (trag., X.+)—a. *from outside* ἔ. τ. ἀνθρώπου εἰσπορευόμενον εἰς αὐτόν Mk 7: 15.
b. *outside* (Dio Chrys. 17[34], 21; 67[17], 1; PFlor. 50,

99; Ex 26: 35 al.; Jos., Bell. 5, 201, Vi. 118 ἔ. τῆς κώμης; Test. Zeb. 3: 6) ἔ. τῆς πόλεως (Aeneas Tact. 951) Rv 14: 20. ἡ αὐλὴ ἡ ἔ. τοῦ ναοῦ the court outside the temple 11: 2a. οὐθὲν ἔ. ἐστιν τῆς ἀληθείας nothing is apart fr. the truth Hv 3, 4, 3. M-M.*

ἐξωθέω 1 aor. ἐξῶσα (Tdf. has the older form ἐξέωσα Ac 7: 45; so also PSI 41, 16; PFlor. 58, 9) (trag., Hdt.+; pap., LXX; Philo, Poster. Cai. 55; Jos., Bell. 5, 338; 342) push out τινά drive someone out fr. a place, expel (Thu., X., Polyb. et al.) ἀπὸ προσώπου τινός before someone Ac 7: 45. As a seaman's t.t. beach, run ashore (so Thu., X.+) τὸ πλοῖον εἰς τὸν αἰγιαλόν 27: 39. M-M.*

ἐξώτερος, α, ον (Strabo; POxy. 896, 14; LXX) adjectival comparison of the adv. ἔξω (Bl-D. §62; Rob. 298).
1. outside (in contrast to inside or in the middle; cf. 3 Km 6: 29f) ἐξώτεροι τεθήσονται they (the stones) will be placed outside Hs 9, 7, 5; cf. 9, 8, 3; 5; 7. τὰ ἐξώτερα μέρη τ. οἰκοδομῆς the outside of the building 9, 9, 3.
2. as superl. farthest, extreme (Ex 26: 4) τὸ σκότος τὸ ἔ. the darkness farthest out Mt 8: 12; 22: 13; 25: 30. M-M.*

ἔοικα (Hom.+; in the mng. 'seem' also Job 6: 3, 25; Jos., C. Ap. 2, 175) be like, resemble τινί someone or someth. (Hes., fgm. 263 Rz. ποταμῷ ῥέοντι ἐοικώς κλύδωνι θαλάσσης Js 1: 6. ἀνδρί vs. 23. M-M.*

ἑορτάζω (Eur., Hdt.+; Plut., Mor. 378в; Paus. 2, 11, 3; Dit., Or. 493, 25; BGU 646, 6; 11; LXX) celebrate a festival of the Passover (Jos., Ant. 5, 20) as a figure of the Christian life 1 Cor 5: 8 (Philo, Sacr. Abel. 111 ἑορτὴ ψυχῆς ἡ ἐν ἀρεταῖς . . . μόνος ἑορτάζει ὁ σοφός). M-M.*

ἑορτή, ῆς, ἡ (Hom.+; inscr., pap., LXX, Ep. Arist., Philo. Joseph.) festival, feast ἐν μέρει ἑορτῆς with regard to a festival Col 2: 16. More specif. defined ἡ ἑ. τοῦ πάσχα the Passover festival Lk 2: 41; J 13: 1. τὸ πάσχα ἡ ἑ. τῶν Ἰουδαίων 6: 4. ἡ ἑ. τῶν ἀζύμων the festival of unleavened bread Lk 22: 1; cf. GP 2: 5. ἡ ἑ. τῶν Ἰουδαίων ἡ σκηνοπηγία the Jews' feast of Tabernacles or Booths J 7: 2; ἡ ἑ. the festival is shown by the context to be a particular one: Passover Mt 26: 5; Lk 2: 42; J 4: 45; 11: 56; 12: 12, 20 al.; the feast of Tabernacles 7: 8, 10f, 14, 37.—5: 1 the witnesses and editions vary betw. the indefinite ἑ. a festival and ἡ ἑ. the festival (for the attestation and interpr. s. Hdb. ad loc.; JThUbbink, NThSt 5, '22, 131-6). Simply ἑ. of the feast of Tabernacles PK 2 p. 14, 29.—ἐν τ. ἑ. during the festival (Jos., Bell. 2, 89, Ant. 20, 109 ἐν τ. ἑ.) Mt 26: 5; Mk 14: 2; J 4: 45; 7: 11; 12: 20; εἶναι ἐν τ. ἑορτῇ take part in the festival 2: 23 (CBurchard, ZNW 61, '70, 157-88—also Mk 14: 2, Mt 26: 5, J 7: 11). εἰς τ. ἑορτήν for the festival 13: 29 (cf. BGU 596, 7 [84 AD] ὅπως εἰς τ. ἑορτὴν περιστερείδια ἡμεῖν ἀγοράσῃ). ἀναβαίνειν (i.e. to Jerusalem) εἰς τ. ἑ. (Jos., Bell. 1, 73; 6, 300) 4: 45; 11: 56; 12: 12. τ. ἑορτῆς μεσούσης when the festival was half over 7: 14. τ. ἑορτῆς παυσαμένης GP 14: 58. κατὰ ἑορτήν at each (Passover) festival Mt 27: 15; Mk 15: 6; Lk 23: 17 t.r. (should it be limited to the Passover? Any festival at all could be the proper occasion to free a prisoner. Cf. Heliod. 8, 7 p. 227, 6ff Bekker: ἡ δέσποινα . . . τήμερον ἀφήσειν ἐπηγγείλατο [Theagenes], ἑορτὴ τινα πάτριον εὐωχεῖν μέλλουσα). κατὰ τὸ ἔθος τ. ἑορτῆς acc. to the custom of the feast Lk 2: 42. τ. ἑορτὴν ποιεῖν keep the festival (Ael. Aristid. 29, 4 K.=40 p. 752 D.; Vi. Aesopi I c. 123; Ex 23: 16) Ac 18: 21 D. Of a joyous festival (opp. πένθος time of sorrow) Dg 4: 5. M-M.*

ἐπαγγελία, ας, ἡ (Demosth.+; Aristot., Eth. Nic. 10, 1 p. 1164a, 29; inscr., pap., LXX, Philo, Joseph.) announcement, in later Gk. w. the special sense promise, pledge, offer (Polyb. 1, 43, 6; 7, 13, 2; 18, 11, 1 al.; Diod. S. 1, 5, 3; 4, 16, 2; Epict. 1, 4, 3 ἡ ἀρετὴ ταύτην ἔχει τὴν ἐπαγγελίαν εὐδαιμονίαν ποιῆσαι; Inscr. Gr. 473, 10; Inschr. v. Priene 123, 9; 1 Macc 10: 15; Philo, Mut. Nom. 201; Jos., Ant. 5, 307).
1. of men προσδέχεσθαι τὴν ἀπό τινος ἐ. wait for a promise fr. someone Ac 23: 21. Almost=profession IEph 14: 2.
2. as a rule in our lit. of divine promises (Herm. Wr. in Stob. I 387, 15 W.; Jos., Ant. 2, 219; Prayer of Manasseh [=Ode 12] 6; PsSol 12: 6; perh. Ps 55: 9).
a. God's promise sg. Ac 2: 39; Ro 4: 13f, 16; 9: 9 (where λόγος is to be supplied w. the gen. ἐπαγγελίας: this word is a word of promise); Gal 3: 17; 2 Pt 3: 9; 1 Cl 26: 1; 2 Cl 15: 4; B 5: 7; 16: 9. Pl. Ro 9: 4; 2 Cor 7: 1; Gal 3: 16; Hb 7: 6; 8: 6; 11: 17; 1 Cl 27: 1. Prep. phrases: δι' ἐπαγγελίας by or because of a promise Gal 3: 18b; 4: 23; also ἐξ ἐπαγγελίας 3: 18a. ἐν ἐπαγγελίᾳ with promise Eph 6: 2. κατ' ἐπαγγελίαν in accordance w. the promise (PSI 281, 58 κατὰ τ. ἐπαγγελίας αὐτοῦ; 1 Esdr 1: 7) Ac 13: 23; Gal 3: 29; cf. 2 Ti 1: 1.—For var. reasons the gen. is used w. ἐ.: to denote the one fr. whom the promise comes (τ.) θεοῦ Ro 4: 20; 2 Cor 1: 20; Gal 3: 21; 2 Cl 11: 1; 1 Ti 1: 1 v.l.; to denote the thing promised (Jos., Ant. 3, 77 τ. ἀγαθῶν) ἐ. τ. αἰωνίου κληρονομίας Hb 9: 15. τ. ζωῆς 1 Ti 4: 8; τ. παρουσίας 2 Pt 3: 4; to denote the one(s) for whom the promise is intended τ. πατέρων Ro 15: 8 (on βεβαιῶσαι τὰς ἐ. cf. Inschr. v. Priene 123, 9 ἐβεβαίωσεν τ. ἐπαγγελίαν).—On the other hand, τῆς ἐπαγγελίας is oft. added, as a kind of gen. of quality, to indicate the relation of the noun in question to the promise: γῆ τ. ἐ. the promised land Hb 11: 9; τέκνα τ. ἐ. children of the promise, i.e., those born because of the promise Ro 9: 8; Gal 4: 28; πνεῦμα τ. ἐ. Eph 1: 13; διαθῆκαι τ. ἐ. 2: 12. As an obj. gen. in πίστις τῆς ἐ. faith in the promise B 6: 17.—ἐ. w. inf. foll. εἰσελθεῖν to enter Hb 4: 1.—ἐ. γενομένη πρὸς τ. πατέρας a promise made to the fathers Ac 13: 32; also εἰς τ. πατ. 26: 6 (Diod. S. 2, 60, 4 γεγενημένη ἐπ.=a promise given).—Of Christ's promise 2 Cl 5: 5.
b. what was promised (Vi. Aesopi I c. 79; PsSol 12: 6) 1 J 2: 25. W. epexeg. gen. foll. ἡ ἐ. τοῦ πνεύματος what was promised, namely the Spirit Ac 2: 33; Gal 3: 14. Foll. by gen. of the one who promises ἐ. τοῦ πατρός Lk 24: 49; Ac 1: 4; κομίσασθαι τὴν ἐ. Hb 10: 36; 11: 13, 39. λαβεῖν 2 Cl 11: 7; cf. 10: 3f. ἀπολαβεῖν B 15: 7.
c. It is not always poss. to draw a hard and fast line betw. a and b: Ac 7: 17; Gal 3: 22; Eph 3: 6; Hb 6: 12, 15, 17; 11: 9b, 33; 1 Cl 10: 2; 34: 7.—FBaumgärtel, Verheissung: Zur Frage des evang. Verständnisses des AT '52; JSchniewind and GFriedrich, TW II 573-83. M-M.*

ἐπαγγέλλομαι (the act. Hom.+; the mid., which alone occurs in our lit., since Soph., Hdt., Thu.; inscr., pap., LXX, Ep. Arist., Philo, Joseph.) 1 aor. ἐπηγγειλάμην; pf. ἐπήγγελμαι, the latter also w. pass. mng. (cf. Kühner-G. I 120) 2 Macc 4: 27; Gal 3: 19; 1 Cl 35: 4; announce, proclaim.
1. promise, offer—a. of human promises and offers τινί τι promise someth. to someone (PTebt. 58, 32 [111 bc]; 1 Macc 11: 28; 2 Macc 4: 8) ἐλευθερίαν Hs 5, 2, 7; 2 Pt 2: 19. W. dat. and inf. foll. (cf. Polyb. 1, 46, 4; PTebt. 411, 9; 3 Macc 1: 4; Jos., C. Ap. 1, 57). ἐπηγγείλαντο αὐτῷ ἀργύριον δοῦναι they promised to give him money Mk 14: 11.—ὅραμα Hv 3, 2, 3.

b. of God: *promise* (2 Macc 2: 18; 3 Macc 2: 10) τί someth. Ro 4: 21; Tit 1: 2; ITr 11: 2; τινί τι (Sb 7172, 25 [217 BC] ἃ ἐπηγγείλαντο [the gods] αὐτῷ) Hv 5: 7; Dg 10: 2. στέφανον τῆς ζωῆς τοῖς ἀγαπῶσιν Js 1: 12; cf. 2: 5 (ἧς ἐπηγγείλατο w. attraction of the relative=ἣν ἐ.). ἡ ἐπαγγελία, ἣν αὐτὸς ἐ. ἡμῖν *what he himself has promised us* 1 J 2: 25 (ἡ ἐπαγγελία, ἣν ἐπ. τινι as Esth 4: 7. Cf. also Diod. S. 15, 6, 5 ἐπηγγείλατο ἐπαγγελίαν); cf. Ac 7: 17 v.l.; Hv 1, 3, 4; s 1: 7. W. inf. foll. (Jos., Ant. 3, 23) Ac 7: 5; 2 Cl 11: 6; Hv 3, 1, 2. W. ὅτι foll. 1 Cl 32: 2. W. λέγων foll. Hb 12: 26. Abs. the abs. use also PPetr. I 29, 12 [III BC]) *make a promise* τινί Hb 6: 13. God is described as ὁ ἐπαγγειλάμενος 10: 23; 11: 11 (a Phrygian inscr. [Inscr. Rom. IV 766] calls aspirants for a city office, who make all kinds of promises, οἱ ἐπαγγειλάμενοι).— Of faith πάντα ἐπαγγέλλεται Hm 9: 10.—Pass. τὸ σπέρμα, ᾧ ἐπήγγελται *the offspring for whom the promise was intended* Gal 3: 19. ἐπηγγελμέναι δωρεαί *promised gifts* 1 Cl 35: 4.

2. *profess, lay claim to, give oneself out as an expert in* someth. w. acc. (X., Mem. 1, 2, 7 τ. ἀρετήν, Hell. 3, 4, 3 στρατιάν; Diog. L., Prooem. 12 σοφίαν; Lucian, Vit. Auctio 7 τ. ἄσκησιν; Philo, Virt. 54 θεοῦ θεραπείαν) θεοσέβειαν *religion* 1 Ti 2: 10. γνῶσιν 6: 21. πίστιν IEph 14: 2; here also w. inf. foll. (cf. Wsd 2: 13 γνῶσιν ἔχειν θεοῦ) Χριστοῦ εἶναι. M-M.*

ἐπάγγελμα, ατος, τό (Pla., Demosth. al.; Philo; Jos., C. Ap. 1, 24) *announcement, promise* in our lit. only of God's promise.

1. *the promise* itself κατὰ τὸ ἐ. *according to the promise* 2 Pt 3: 13.—2. *the thing promised* (Ael. Aristid. 52 p. 599 D.; Philo, Mut. Nom. 128) τὰ μέγιστα ἐ. ἡμῖν δεδώρηται *he has granted us the very great things he promised* 1: 4.*

ἐπάγω 1 aor. ptc. ἐπάξας (Bl-D. §75 w. app.; Mlt.-H. 226; Rob. 348); 2 aor. ἐπήγαγον (Hom.+; inscr., pap., LXX, Philo, Joseph., Test. 12 Patr.) *bring on*; fig. *bring someth. upon someone*, mostly someth. bad τινί τι (Hes., Op. 240 πῆμά τινι ἐ. al.; Dit., Or. 669, 43 πολλοῖς ἐ. κινδύνους; PRyl. 144, 21 [38 AD] . . . μοι ἐ. αἰτίας; Bar 4: 9, 10, 14, 29; Da 3: 28, 31; Philo, Mos. 1, 96; Jos., Vi. 18; Sib. Or. 7, 154) κατακλυσμὸν κόσμῳ ἐπάξας 2 Pt 2: 5 (cf. Gen 6: 17; 3 Macc 2: 4 of the deluge ἐπαγαγὼν αὐτοῖς ἀμέτρητον ὕδωρ). λύπην τῷ πνεύματι *bring grief upon the spirit* Hm 3: 4. ἑαυτοῖς ταχινὴν ἀπώλειαν *bring swift destruction upon themselves* 2 Pt 2: 1 (cf. ἑαυτοῖς δουλείαν Demosth. 19, 259). Also ἐπί τινά τι (Ex 11: 1; 33: 5; Jer 6: 19; Ezk 28: 7 and oft.) ἐφ᾽ ἡμᾶς τὸ αἷμα τ. ἀνθρώπου τούτου *bring this man's blood upon us* Ac 5: 28 (cf. Judg 9: 24 B ἐπαγαγεῖν τὰ αἵματα αὐτῶν, τοῦ θεῖναι ἐπὶ Ἀβιμελεχ, ὃς ἀπέκτεινεν αὐτούς). ἐ. τισι διωγμὸν κατά τινος *stir up, within a group, a persecution against someone* Ac 14: 2 D. M-M.*

ἐπαγωνίζομαι (Dionys. Hal., Plut et al.; inscr., Philo) *fight, contend*. The dat. dependent on it indicates for the most part either the one against whom one is fighting (Plut., Fab. 23, 2), or the pers. or thing upon whom (which) one depends for support in a fight (Plut., Numa 8, 16 ἑτέροις τεκμηρίοις). τῇ πίστει Jd 3, fr. the context, can only mean *for the faith* (cf. Plut., Mor. 1075D; Inscr. Gr. 394, 19 [I BC] ἐπηγωνίσατο τῇ πρὸς τ. πόλιν εὐνοίᾳ). M-M.*

ἐπαθροίζω *collect besides* or *in addition* pass. (Plut., Anton. 44, 1) τῶν ὄχλων ἐπαθροιζομένων *when the crowds had gathered even more* Lk 11: 29.*

Ἐπαίνετος, ου, ὁ *Epaenetus*, one of the first Christians in Asia Ro 16: 5. For the name s. Diod. S. 19, 79, 2; Dit., Syll.³ 43, 39; 585, 250; 944, 26; 1174, 4. M-M.*

ἐπαινέω fut. ἐπαινέσω; 1 aor. ἐπῄνεσα (Hom.+; inscr., pap., LXX, Ep. Arist., Philo, Joseph., Test. 12 Patr.) *praise* τινά *someone* (Jos., Vi. 232 ἐμέ; 279) 1 Cor 11: 22a; IMg 12; ISm 5: 2; MPol 4. ἑαυτὸν ἐ. *praise oneself* Hs 9, 22, 2. τί *someth.* (Aelian, V.H. 2, 12; Jos., Ant. 14, 293 τ. ἔργον) 1 Cl 33: 6. Abs. 1 Cor 11: 22b, unless ὑμᾶς is to be supplied, cf. ibid. a. W. acc. and ὅτι foll. *praise someone because* or *in that* Lk 16: 8 (s. the lit. on οἰκονόμος 1a; JDMDerrett, NTS 7, '60/'61, 210 n. 3 'sanction'); 1 Cor 11: 2. τοῦτο . . . οὐκ ἐπαινῶ ὅτι *this is someth. I cannot praise* (approve of), namely that 11: 17 (for the mng. 'approve of': Appian, Bell. Civ. 3, 14 §49; Ael. Aristid. 24, 22 K.=44 p. 831 D.; Aelian, fgm. 235 p. 263, 17 τὸ θεῖον οὐκ ἐπῄνει τὰ ὑπὸ τ. βασιλέως πραττόμενα. Oft. Philostrat. [Schmid IV 294]; Jos., Ant. 14, 293. Other exx. in AFridrichsen, Horae Soederblomianae I, 1, '44, 28–32). Pass. ἡ γῆ τοῦ Ἰακὼβ ἐπαινουμένη παρὰ πᾶσαν τὴν γῆν *praised above every land* B 11: 9 (quot. fr. an unknown prophet). Also in relig. usage: *praise God* (Philo) Ro 15: 11 (Ps 116: 1 v.l.). M-M.*

ἔπαινος, ου, ὁ (Pind., Hdt.+; inscr., pap., LXX, Philo; Jos., C. Ap. 2, 4, Vi. 158).

1. *praise, approval, recognition*—a. coming to men—α. from men ἔκ τινος 1 Cl 30: 6; Ro 2: 29; 13: 3. εἰς ἔπαινόν τινος *to give recognition to someone* 1 Pt 2: 14 (WC vanUnnik, NTS 2, '55, 198–202, w. ref. to Diod. S. 15, 1, 1). ὁ ἀδελφός, οὗ ὁ ἐ. ἐν τ. εὐαγγελίῳ διὰ πασῶν τῶν ἐκκλησιῶν *the brother whose fame in the things of the gospel has gone through all the churches* 2 Cor 8: 18.

β. from God (cf. Wsd 15: 19) 1 Cl 30: 6; Ro 2: 29 (AFridrichsen, Symbolae Arctoae 1, '22, 39–49). ὁ ἔ. γενήσεται ἑκάστῳ ἀπὸ τ. θεοῦ 1 Cor 4: 5 (on ἔ. γίνεταί τινι cf. Dit., Syll.³ 304, 24).—εἰς ἔ. καὶ δόξαν (for the combination of the two nouns cf. Inschr. v. Priene 53, 15 [II BC] ἀξίως ἐπαίνου καὶ τιμῶν ποιεῖσθαι τ. κρίσεις; 199, 9 [I BC]; Dio Chrys. 14[31], 111 δόξα κ. ἔ. 1 Ch 16: 27; s. below b) 1 Pt 1: 7.

b. coming to God (cf. Ps 21: 26; 34: 28; Sir 39: 10; concrete 'song of praise' in God's honor: Diod. S. 3, 73, 5; Arrian, Anab. 7, 3, 3 ἔπαινοι θεῶν) εἰς δόξαν καὶ ἐπ. (s. above αβ) θεοῦ Phil 1: 11; cf. Eph 1: 6, 12, 14.

2. *a thing worthy of praise* (Sir 39: 10 ἔ. αὐτοῦ='what is praiseworthy in him; his praiseworthy deeds') Phil 4: 8. M-M. B. 1189.*

ἐπαίρω 1 aor. ἐπῆρα, inf. ἐπᾶραι, ptc. ἐπάρας; pf. ἐπῆρκα J 13: 18 Tdf.; 1 aor. pass. ἐπήρθην (trag., Hdt.+; inscr., pap., LXX, En., Philo, Joseph., Test. 12 Patr.).

1. *lift up, hold up* τί *someth.* ῥάβδον *a staff* (Ex 10: 13) Hv 3, 2, 4. τὸν ἀρτέμωνα Ac 27: 40 s. on ἀρτέμων. Esp. in the expr. ἐ. χεῖρας *lift up, raise the hands* in prayer (Aesop, Fab. 49 P.=83 H.; Horapollo 1, 15 τ. χεῖρας εἰς οὐρανὸν ἐπαίροντα . . . προσευχόμενος τῇ θεῷ; 2 Esdr 18 [Neh 8]: 6; Ps 133: 2; for the idea cf. LvSybel, Christl. Antike I '06, 256; 258; GAppel, De Romanorum Precationibus '09, 194. Cf. also ἐκτείνω 1) 1 Ti 2: 8, or in blessing (Sir 50: 20) Lk 24: 50. ἐ. τὰς κεφαλάς (w. ἀνακύπτειν) *raise (your) heads* (Philo, Op. M. 158; Jos., Bell. 1, 629; cf. ἐ. τὸ πρόσωπον 4 Km 9: 32; αὐχένα Philo, Fug. 107) of men who regain their courage Lk 21: 28. ἐ. τοὺς ὀφθαλμούς (Gen 13: 10; 1 Ch 21: 16 al.) *look up* Mt 17: 8; Lk 16: 23; J 4: 35; 6: 5; εἴς τινα Lk 6: 20; εἰς τὸν οὐρανόν *to heaven* Lk 18: 13 (En. 13, 5 οὐκέτι

δύνανται . . . ἐπᾶραι τ. ὀφθ. εἰς τ. οὐρ. ἀπὸ αἰσχύνης περὶ ὧν ἡμαρτήκεισαν); J 17: 1. ἐ. τὴν πτέρναν *raise one's heel* to tread on someone 13: 18 (ἐπί τινα as 1 Km 20: 33). ἐ. τὴν φωνήν *raise one's voice* (Demosth. 18, 291; Charito 5, 7, 10; Philostrat., Vi. Apollon. 5, 33 p. 190, 21; Judg 2: 4; 9: 7; 2 Km 13: 36) Lk 11: 27; Ac 2: 14; 14: 11; 22: 22.

2. pass.—a. lit. *be taken up* Ac 1: 9. Of the exaltation to heaven of those who endured 1 Cl 45: 8.

b. fig.—α. *rise up, offer resistance, be in opposition* ἐπί τινα or τι *against* or *to someone* or *someth.* (as 2 Esdr [Ezra] 4: 19; 1 Macc 8: 5; 10: 70) ἐπὶ τὸ ποίμνιον 1 Cl 16: 1. κατά τινος: πᾶν ὕψωμα ἐπαιρόμενον κατὰ τ. γνώσεως τ. θεοῦ 2 Cor 10: 5 (ὕψωμα 2).

β. *be presumptuous, put on airs* abs. (Aristoph., Nub. 810; Thu. 4, 18, 4; Aeschin. 87, 24; Sir 11: 4; 32: 1; 1 Macc 2: 63; Jos., Vi. 24) 2 Cor 11: 20; 1 Cl 21: 5. W. ὑπερυψοῦσθαι 14: 5 (Ps 36: 35). W. the dat. to denote the basis for the presumption (Hdt. 9, 49; Thu. 1, 120, 3; X., Cyr. 8, 5, 24; Appian, Bell. Civ. 5, 118 §489 ταῖς ναυσὶν ἐπαιρόμενος=proud of his fleet; Zeph 1: 11; Philo, Mos. 1, 70; Jos., Ant. 9, 193) ἑαυτοὺς βουλόμενοι ἐπαίρεσθαι τ. διανοίαις αὐτῶν *want to put on airs w. their imaginations* 1 Cl 39: 1 (cf. Appian, Liby. 111 §522 ἐπήρθησαν τοῖς φρονήμασι=they became presumptuous in their self-reliance). M-M.*

ἐπαισχύνομαι 1 aor. ἐπαισχύνθην (2 Ti 1: 16); 1 fut. ἐπαισχυνθήσομαι (Aeschyl., Hdt.+; LXX) *be ashamed.*

1. w. acc. of the pers. *of someone* (X., Hell. 4, 1, 34; Lucian, Dem. Enc. 46b) Mk 8: 38; Lk 9: 26. W. acc. of the thing (Pla., Soph. 247c; Diod. S. 1, 83, 4; Job 34: 19) τοὺς λόγους *of the words* Mk 8: 38; Lk 9: 26. τὸ εὐαγγέλιον *of the gospel* Ro 1: 16 (OMichel, GWehrung-Festschr. '40, 36–53). τὸ ὄνομα τοῦ κυρίου Hs 8, 6, 4; 9, 21, 3. τὸ μαρτύριον τοῦ κυρίου ἡμῶν *of witnessing to our Lord* 2 Ti 1: 8. τὴν ἅλυσίν μου *of my chains* vs. 16; cf. ISm 10: 2 (w. ὑπερηφανεῖν).

2. w. ἐπί τινι *of a thing* (Is 1: 29; cf. Aristot., De Rhet. 2, 2) ἐφ' οἷς νῦν ἐπαισχύνεσθε *of which you are now ashamed* Ro 6: 21.

3. w. inf. foll. (Aeschyl., Ag. 1373; Lucian, Dem. Enc. 46a) οὐκ ἐ. ἀδελφοὺς αὐτοὺς καλεῖν *he is not ashamed* (i.e. is not too proud) *to call them brothers* Hb 2: 11; Hs 9, 14, 6. W. acc. of the pers. and inf. Hb 11: 16.

4. abs. (Pla., Rep. 9 p. 573в; Test. Jos. 2: 5) 2 Ti 1: 12.*

ἐπαιτέω (Hom.+ in sense 'ask for more'; pap., LXX) *beg as a mendicant* (so Soph., Oed. Col. 1364; Cat. Cod. Astr. VIII 4 p. 140, 9; Ps 108: 10; Sir 40: 28; Jos., Bell. 2, 295) Lk 16: 3; 18: 35; Mk 10: 46 v.l. M-M.*

ἐπακολουθέω 1 aor. ἐπηκολούθησα (Aristoph., Thu.+; inscr., pap., LXX, Philo, Joseph.) *follow, come after.*

1. lit. τοῖς ἴχνεσιν αὐτοῦ *his footsteps* (Philo, Virt. 64) 1 Pt 2: 21. ἐπηκολούθησάν μοι εἰς λόγον θεοῦ *they followed me in the cause of God* ISm 10: 1 (cf. Philo, Leg. ad Gai. 185). Of the prophets, who followed Moses in time 1 Cl 43: 1.

2. fig. *follow after,* i.e. *devote oneself to* someth., w. dat. (cf. Pla., Rep. 2 p. 370c; Josh 14: 14 τῷ προστάγματι κυρίου; Jos., C. Ap. 1, 6) παντὶ ἔργῳ ἀγαθῷ ἐ. *devote oneself to every good work* 1 Ti 5: 10. In contrast to προάγω: Pol 3: 3; 1 Ti 5: 24.—τὰ ἐπακολουθοῦντα σημεῖα Mk 16: 20 are not only the *following* or *accompanying signs,* but also *authenticating* (for this mng. of ἐ. cf. PTebt. 100, 20f [117/16 вc]; PEleph. 10, 8 [223 вc]; PGenève 22, 1). M-M.*

ἐπακούω fut. ἐπακούσομαι; 1 aor. ἐπήκουσα (Hom.+; inscr., pap., LXX, En., Philo, Joseph., Test. 12 Patr., Sib. Or. 4, 22).

1. *hear, listen to* (Aeschyl., Choëph. 725; Lucian, Tim. 34 τ. εὐχῶν; BGU 1080, 6; PGM 13, 207 μοι; LXX; Jos., Ant. 9, 10) τινός *someone* (Lucian, Pseudol. 23; UPZ 78, 24 [159 вc] Isis, ἐπάκουσόν μου; PGM 3, 497; Gen 17: 20 al.) 1 Cl 8: 3 (quot. of unknown orig.; cf. Is 65: 24); B 3: 5; ἐπήκουσά σου 2 Cor 6: 2 (Is 49: 8; Third Corinthians 3: 30).—OWeinrich, Θεοὶ ἐπήκοοι: Mitt. d. Dtsch. Arch. Inst. Ath. Abt. 37, '12, 1–68.

2. *obey* (Hes., Op. 275; Hdt. 4, 141; Pla., Soph. p. 227c; Vett. Val. 67, 16; Judg 12: 17 A; 1 Macc 10: 38 v.l.) abs. πρέπον ἐστὶν ἐ. κατὰ μηδεμίαν ὑπόκρισιν *it is fitting to be obedient without hypocrisy* IMg 3: 2. ἔμπροσθέν τινος *before someone=obey someone* B 12: 11 (Is 45: 1). M-M.*

ἐπακροάομαι impf. ἐπηκροώμην (Menand., Epitr. 554; Plato Com. [V/IV вc], fgm. 16 al.) *listen to* τινός *someone* (Lucian, Icarom. 1; Philostrat., Vi. Apoll. 4, 36 p. 154, 13; Test. Jos. 8: 5) Ac 16: 25. M-M.*

ἐπάλληλος, ον *following one another in quick succession, rapidly succeeding* (Polyb., Diod. S. Plut. et al.) esp. of misfortunes (Plut., Pomp. 25, 10; Philo, Mos. 2, 263, In Flacc. 121 τὰς συνεχεῖς κ. ἐπαλλήλους κακώσεις; Jos., Bell. 5, 32) ἐ. γενόμεναι συμφοραί 1 Cl 1: 1.*

ἐπάν temporal conj. used w. subj. (X.+; inscr., pap.; Bel 11. As ἐπήν Hom.+) *when, as soon as* w. pres. subj. ἐ. πονηρὸς ᾖ *when it is unsound* Lk 11: 34. W. aor. subj., like the Lat. fut. exact. (Jos., Ant. 8, 302) ἐ. εὕρητε Mt 2: 8. ἐ. νικήσῃ αὐτόν lit. *when he will have overcome him* Lk 11: 22. M-M.*

ἐπάναγκες adv. (Hdt.+; Epict. 2, 20, 1; M. Ant. 1, 16, 8; inscr., pap.; Jos., Ant. 16, 365) *by compulsion, necessarily* τὰ ἐ. *the necessary things* Ac 15: 28. M-M.*

ἐπανάγω 2 aor. ἐπανήγαγον (Hdt.+; inscr., pap., LXX, Ep. Arist.; Jos., Ant. 12, 128; 345) *lead* or *bring up* in our lit. only intrans.

1. *put out to sea, go out* ἠρώτησεν αὐτὸν ἀπὸ τῆς γῆς ἐ. ὀλίγον *he asked him to put out a little way from the land* Lk 5: 3 (trans.='put out' ships and men at sea X., Hell. 6, 2, 28 ἀπὸ τῆς γῆς; 2 Macc 12: 4). εἰς τὸ βάθος *to the deep water* vs. 4.

2. *return* (X., Cyr. 4, 1, 3; Diod. S. 16, 26 al.; 2 Macc 9: 21) εἰς τὴν πόλιν Mt 21: 18. M-M.*

ἐπανακάμπτω 1 aor. ἐπανέκαμψα (Aristot.; Aq., Sym., Theod. Is 35: 10) *return* (Syntipas p. 14, 8 al.) εἰς τὴν πόλιν Hs 1: 2, 5. ἐπὶ τὰς παρθένους *to the virgins* s 9, 14, 1.*

ἐπαναμιμνήσκω 1 aor. pass. ἐπανεμνήσθην *remind someone* (τινά) *of someth. again* (Pla., Leg. 3 p. 688а; Demosth. 6, 35) Ro 15: 15. Pass. *call to mind, remember* someth. *again* τοῦ ῥήματος Hv 4, 1, 7.*

ἐπαναπαύομαι (found in act. in Aelian, N.A. 5, 56 and Judg 16: 26 A; the mid. occurs in Hero Alex. I p. 424, 12; Epict.; Artem.; Herodian 2, 1, 2; Jos., Ant. 8, 84, almost always in LXX and without exception in our lit.) fut. ἐπαναπαύσομαι; 2 aor. pass. ἐπανεπάην D 4: 2; 2 fut. pass. ἐπαναπαήσομαι Lk 10: 6; perf. mid. ἐπαναπέπαυμαι 1 Pt 4: 14 Ɗ⁷² et al.

1. *rest, take one's rest* GH 27; B 4: 13. ἐπί τινα *rest upon someone* ἐπ' αὐτὸν ἡ εἰρήνη ὑμῶν *your peace will rest upon him* Lk 10: 6 (Num 11: 25, 26 ἐπανεπαύσατο τ. πνεῦμα ἐπ' αὐτούς; 4 Km 2: 15; cf. 1 Pt 4: 14 v.l.).

2. *find rest, comfort,* or *support* τινί *in someth.* fig. (Herm. Wr. 9, 10 τῇ πίστει ἐ.) τοῖς λόγοις τ. ἁγίων D 4: 2. In the sense *rely on* (Trypho Gr. 194 [I BC]; Artem. 4, 65; Epict. 1, 9, 9; Mi 3: 11; 1 Macc 8: 11) νόμῳ Ro 2: 17. M-M.*

ἐπανατρέχω 2 aor. ἐπανέδραμον (Philod., De Ira p. 63 W.; Lucian, De Merc. Cond. 36; PLond. 1044, 14; 1727, 46; Jos., Ant. 18, 361) *run, hasten on* ἐπὶ τὸν σκοπόν *toward the goal* 1 Cl 19: 2.*

ἐπανέρχομαι 2 aor. ἐπανῆλθον (Eur., Hdt.+; inscr., pap., LXX) *return* (so Thu., X., Pla.; Dit., Syll.³ 591, 7 [c. 195 BC]; PLond. 904, 23; POxy. 933, 17; PTebt. 333, 10; Pr 3: 28; 2 Macc 4: 36; Jos., Bell. 7, 106, Ant. 1, 91) abs. ἐν τῷ ἐπανέρχεσθαί με *when I return* Lk 10: 35; cf. 19: 15; Hs 8, 2, 9. M-M.*

ἐπανήκω fut. ἐπανήξω *come back again* (since Eur., Iph. A. 1628; Polyb. 6, 58, 3; Dit., Syll.³ 730, 6; PAmh. 50, 5 [II BC]; LXX; Ep. Arist. 8; Jos., Ant. 12, 179; 191) Hs 9, 11, 2.*

ἐπανίστημι *set up,* fut. mid. ἐπαναστήσομαι. Also 2 aor. act. ἐπανέστην *rise up, rise in rebellion* (so since Hdt., Thu., Aristoph.; LXX; Philo, Spec. Leg. 3, 17; Sib. Or. 11, 175) τινί *against someone* (so Hdt., Thu. et al.; Dt 33: 11; Jdth 5: 11; 16: 17; Jos., Bell. 1, 24; 2, 443) ἐπανέστησάν μοι *have risen against me* B 5: 13 (Ps 26: 12). Also ἐπί τινα (LXX) Mt 10: 21; Mk 13: 12 (cf. Mi 7: 6). M-M.*

ἐπανόρθωσις, εως, ἡ *correcting, restoration* (cf. e.g. 1 Esdr 8: 52; 1 Macc 14: 34) transf. *improvement* (Ps.-Pla., Tim. L. p. 104A; Heraclides 3; Plut., Mor. 22A; 46D al.—ἐ. τοῦ βίου: Polyb. 1, 35, 1; Epict. 3, 21, 15 οὕτως ὠφέλιμα γίνεται τὰ μυστήρια . . . , ὅτι ἐπὶ ἐπανορθώσει τ. βίου κατεστάθη πάντα . . . , cf. Ench. 51, 1; Iambl., Vi. Pyth. 6, 30; 21, 96 πρὸς ἐ.; POxy. 78, 29; 237 VIII, 30; Ep. Arist. 130; 283 πρὸς ἐ.; Philo, Ebr. 91 πρὸς ἐ., Conf. Lingu. 182, Leg. All. 1, 85; cf. 2 Macc 2: 22) ὠφέλιμος πρὸς ἐ. *useful for improvement* 2 Ti 3: 16. M-M. B. 751.*

ἐπάνω adv. (Hdt.+; inscr., pap., LXX, En., Joseph.) *above, over.*

1. used as adv. (Gen 7: 20; Bar 2: 5; Jos., C. Ap. 1, 33)—**a.** of place (En. 18, 5) οἱ ἄνθρωποι οἱ περιπατοῦντες ἐ. οὐκ οἴδασιν *the people who walk over (them) know nothing (about them)* Lk 11: 44. τὰ ἐ. (cf. Dit., Syll.³ 972, 74; 82; POxy. 502, 54 τὰ ἐ.=what has been mentioned above) *the upper parts* (PGM 2, 157 τὰ ἐπ. τῆς θύρας) Hs 9, 1, 6.

b. with numbers (colloq. Bl-D. §185; cf. Rob. 666; cf. Lev 27: 7) *more than* ὤφθη ἐ. πεντακοσίοις ἀδελφοῖς *he appeared to more than 500 brethren* 1 Cor 15: 6. πραθῆναι ἐ. δηναρίων τριακοσίων *be sold for more than 300 denarii* Mk 14: 5.

2. as improper prep. w. gen. *over, above, on*—**a.** of place (Dit., Syll.³ 1173, 3 ἐ. τ. βήματος POxy. 485, 8; PFlor. 50, 32; LXX; Jos., Bell. 2, 344, Ant. 6, 274) ἐ. ὄρους *on (the top of) a hill* Mt 5: 14; ἐ. τῆς πύλης Hs 9, 4, 2; ἐ. αὐτῶν Mt 21: 7; cf. 23: 18, 20, 22; 27: 37; 28: 2; Rv 6: 8; 20: 3. ἐ. αὐτῆς prob. *at her head* Lk 4: 39 (perh. also poss.: bending *over her*) πατεῖν ἐ. ὄφεων *tread on snakes* Lk 10: 19 (cf. PGM 13, 282 ἐὰν θέλῃς ἐπάνω κροκοδείλου διαβαίνειν). ἐ. τῶν ὀρέων *over the mountains* D 9: 4. ἐστάθη ἐ. οὗ ἦν τὸ παιδίον *stopped over the place where the child was* Mt 2: 9.

b. fig. (Socrat., Ep. 20 ὢν ἐ. πλούτου) of authority (Da 6: 3 Theod.) *over someth.* ἐξουσία ἐ. δέκα πόλεων Lk 19: 17, cf. 19. ἐ. πάντων ἐστίν *is above all* J 3: 31 (Cebes 26,

3 ἐ. πάντων ἐστί; Jos., Ant. 4, 216 τὸ δίκαιον ἐπάνω πάντων). M-M. and suppl.**

ἐπάξας s. ἐπάγω.

ἐπαοιδός, οῦ, ὁ (Ionic form, dominant in the Koine [Manetho 5, 138; Epict. 3, 24, 10; LXX; Philo, Migr. Abr. 83; Sib. Or. 225] for the Attic ἐπῳδός; cf. Lobeck, Phryn. p. 243) *enchanter* D 3: 4.*

ἐπάραι etc. s. ἐπαίρω.

ἐπάρατος, ον (Thu.+; Cass. Dio; Dit., Syll.³ 799, 23 [38 AD]; Philo; Jos., Ant. 1, 58; 6, 117; 7, 208) *accursed* J 7: 49. On this subject s. Billerb. II 494–519. M-M.*

ἐπαρκέω 1 aor. ἐπήρκεσα (Hom.+; pap.; 1 Macc 8: 26; 11: 35; Jos., Ant. 8, 113) *help, aid* (Hdt.; Aristoph., Plut. 830; X., Mem. 2, 7, 1 τινί *someone* (Hdt.; Aristoph., Plut. 830; X., Mem. 2, 7, 1 ἀλλήλοις ἐ.; Aristot., Eth. Nicom. 4, 2; 8, 14; 16; Polyb. 1, 51, 10; Lucian, Nigr. 26 τ. δεομένοις; Jos., Ant. 1, 247) θλιβομένοις 1 Ti 5: 10. χήραις vs. 16. M-M.*

ἐπαρχεία, ας, ἡ (on the spelling cf. Bl-D. §23; Mlt.-H. 315) *province,* ruled over by a prefect or governor (Polyb. 1, 15, 10; 2, 19, 2 al.; Dit., Or. Index VIII p. 657; POxy. 471, 22; 1410, 3; LXX only as v.l.; Jos., Bell. 5, 520; loanw. in rabb.) Ac 23: 34; 25: 1 v.l. (Mlt.-H. 157). M-M.*

ἐπάρχειος, ον *belonging to an eparch* or *prefect* ἡ ἐπάρχειος (sc. χώρα) *the province* (Dit., Or. 549, 2; IG XIV 911) ἐπιβὰς τῇ ἐ. *after he had arrived in the province* Ac 25: 1 (s. ἐπαρχεία).*

ἐπαρχικός, ή, όν *pertaining to the ἔπαρχος,* q.v. (lit.; inscr., e.g. Dit., Or. 578, 14) ἐπαρχικὴ ἐξουσία (Cass. Dio 75, 14) Phlm subscr. This refers to an office in Rome, that of the 'praefectus urbi', the governor of the capital city.*

ἔπαρχος, ου, ὁ (Aeschyl.+; inscr., pap., LXX; Jos., Ant. 20, 193 al.) *prefect, commanding officer* (s. Hahn 118, 8; MMentz, De Magistratuum Romanorum Graecis Appellationibus, Diss. Jena '04, 46f). w. other military officers 1 Cl 37: 3.*

ἔπαυλις, εως, ἡ (Hdt.+; inscr., pap., LXX) *farm, homestead, residence* (Diod. S. 12, 43, 1; 12, 45, 1; Plut., Vit. p. 170B; 337A; 446B al.; Dit., Syll.³ 364, 13 [III BC]; PTebt. 120, 130; POxy., 248, 28; LXX; Philo, Abr. 139, Spec. Leg. 2, 116, Mos. 1, 330 al.; Jos., Bell. 2, 57 al.) Ac 1: 20 (Ps 68: 26). M-M.*

ἐπαύριον adv. *tomorrow* (Polyb. 8, 15, 6; PLille 15, 2 [242 BC]; PTebt. 119, 17; LXX) in our lit. almost exclusively (as Polyb. 3, 53, 6; PHamb. 27, 4 [III BC] and mostly LXX) τῇ ἐ. (sc. ἡμέρᾳ) *on the next day* Mt 27: 62; Mk 11: 12; J 1: 29, 35, 43; 6: 22; 12: 12; Ac 10: 9, 23f; 14: 20; 20: 7; 21: 8; 22: 30; 23: 32; 25: 6, 23. εἰς τὴν ἐ. (Polyb. 8, 13, 6) *until the next day* Ac 4: 3 D. M-M.*

ἐπαφίημι 2 aor. subj. ἐπαφῶ (X.+; pap., LXX; Jos., Ant. 19, 175) *let loose upon* τινά τινι (Paus. 1, 12, 3 ἐλέφαντάς τινι) τῷ Πολυκάρπῳ λέοντα MPol 12: 2.*

Ἐπαφρᾶς, ᾶ, ὁ (Dialekt-Inschr. 1489, 1 [Locris]; CIG I 268, 37; II 18; 20; 1963; 2248, 4; Dit., Syll.³ 1112, 26; 1243, 34) *Epaphras* (prob. short form of Ἐπαφρόδιτος q.v.; cf. Bl-D. §125, 1; Mlt.-H. 119; 314) a Christian of Colossae Col 4: 12, founder of the church there 1: 7; cf. Phlm 23. M-M.*

ἐπαφρίζω (Moschus 5, 5 intr. 'foam up') trans. *cause to splash up like foam* τι *someth.* fig. κύματα ἐπαφρίζοντα (ἀπαφρ.- 𝔓⁷² et al.) τὰς ἑαυτῶν αἰσχύνας *waves casting up their own shameless deeds like foam* Jd 13.*

'Επαφρόδιτος, ου, ὁ (very common, also in inscr. and pap.; s. also Schürer I⁴ 80, 8) *Epaphroditus,* messenger sent by the Phil. church to Paul Phil 2: 25; 4: 18; subscr. —RHarris, Ep., Scribe and Courier: Exp. 8, 1898, 101– 10. M-M.*

ἐπέβην s. ἐπιβαίνω.

ἐπεγείρω 1 aor. ἐπήγειρα, pass. ἐπηγέρθην (Hom. +; LXX; En. 99, 16; Philo, Mos. 1, 297; Jos., Ant. 8, 371; Sib. Or. 3, 153) *rouse up, awaken.* In our lit. only fig. *arouse, excite, stir up* τὶ someth. (Maximus Tyr. 23, 6b; Jos., Ant. 14, 442 τὸ φρόνημα) τὰς ψυχὰς τ. ἐθνῶν (κατά τινος) Ac 14: 2. ἐ. διωγμὸν ἐπί τινα *stir up a persecution against someone* 13: 50 (Test. Levi 10: 2 ἐπεγ. ἐπ' αὐτὸν κακά). Pass. ἐπεγείρεσθαι ἐπί τινα *be aroused against someone,* also *rise up, revolt against someone* 1 Cl 3: 3 (cf. Dit., Syll.³ 730, 10 [I BC]; Is 19: 2; Jer 29: 7; Mi 5: 4). M-M.*

ἐπεί conj. (Hom. +; inscr., pap., LXX, En., Ep. Arist., Philo, Joseph.).
   1. temporal *when, after* (Diod. S. 3, 35, 1; Ps.-Callisth. 3, 34, 4 ἐπεὶ ἦλθον=when they had come) only as a doubtful rdg. in Lk 7: 1, where more recent editions usu. have ἐπειδή (Bl-D. §455, 1; Rob. 971).
   2. causal *because, since, for* Mt 18: 32; 21: 46; 27: 6; Mk 15: 42; Lk 1: 34; J 13: 29; 19: 31; Ac 13: 46 v.l.; 1 Cor 14: 12; 2 Cor 11: 18; 13: 3; Hb 5: 2, 11; 6: 13; 9: 17; 11: 11; 2 Cl 2: 3; B 6: 2f, 11 al. ἐπεὶ καί *since indeed* (as Appian, Bell. Civ. 5, 71 §302) Or GP 2: 5. ἐ. οὖν *inferential since, then* (X., Mem. 3, 9, 5; Job 35: 7; 4 Macc 4: 26) Hb 2: 14; 4: 6; IMg 2; 5: 1. οὐκ ἐπεί *not that* ITr 8: 1. W. ellipsis *for* (if it were different), *for otherwise* (also class.: Pla., Euthyphro p. 9ʙ; X., Cyr. 2, 2, 31; Aristot., Eth. Nic. 2, 2, 1. Also Plut., Agis 2, 5; Epict., Ench. 33, 9; BGU 530, 30; 4 Macc 1: 33; 2: 7, 19 al.; Bl-D. §456, 3 w. app.; Rob. 1025f) Ro 3: 6; 11: 6, 22; 1 Cor 14: 16; 15: 29; Hb 10: 2 (cf. UPZ 110, 204 [164 BC] ἐπεὶ οὐκ ἂν οὕτως ἀλόγητοι ἦτε='for otherwise you would not be so unreasonable'); IMg 3: 2. ἐ. ἔδει αὐτὸν πολλάκις παθεῖν *for otherwise he would have had to suffer many times* Hb 9: 26. ἐ. ἄρα *for otherwise, you see* 1 Cor 5: 10; 7: 14. M-M.**

ἐπειδή conj. (Hom. +; pap., LXX)—1. temporal *when, after* (Arrian, Anab. 5, 20, 1; Jos., Bell. 1, 231, Ant. 2, 334 al.) Lk 7: 1 (v.l. ἐπεὶ δέ).
   2. causal (Diod. S. 19, 100, 7) *since, since then,* (just) *because* Lk 11: 6; Ac 13: 8 D, 46; 14: 12; 15: 24; 1 Cor 1: 22; 14: 16; Phil 2: 26; 1 Cl 57: 4 (Pr 1: 24); 62: 3; 2 Cl 12: 1; B 7: 5, 9 al. ἐπειδὴ γάρ *for since* (Hero I p. 32, 20; Philo, Aet. M. 121) 1 Cor 1: 21; 15: 21. M-M.**

ἐπειδήπερ conj. (Thu. 6, 18, 3 and other Attic wr.; Aristot., Phys. 8, 5 p. 256b, 25; Dionys. Hal. 2, 72; PFlor. 118, 5; PRyl. 238, 10; PStrassb. 5, 10; Philo, In Flacc. 32, Leg. ad Gai. 164, Vi. Cont. 10; Jos., Bell. 7, 102, Ant. 1, 34; 5, 74) causal *inasmuch as, since* ('w. ref. to a fact already known' Bl-D. §456, 3) Lk 1: 1 (Diod. S. 4, 7, 1: 'since we have referred to the Muses in connection with Dionysus, it is appropriate to recount the main facts about them'; Jos., Bell. 1, 17). M-M.*

ἐπεῖδον 2 aor. of ἐφοράω, imper. ἔπιδε, inf. ἐπιδεῖν (Hom. +; pap., LXX; Jos., Bell. 1, 76, Ant. 2, 346; Sib. Or. 5, 329) *fix one's glance upon, look at, concern oneself*

with (of God's concern w. human things: Aeschyl.; Jos., C. Ap. 2, 181) ἐπί τι (1 Macc 3: 59; 3 Macc 6: 3) Ac 4: 29. ἐπί τινι *look with favor on someone* or *someth.* 1 Cl 4: 2 (Gen 4: 4). W. inf. foll. ἀφελεῖν ὄνειδός μου *to take away my reproach* Lk 1: 25.—HMiddendorf, Gott sieht. Diss. Freiburg '35. M-M.*

ἔπειμι (fr. εἶμι) ptc. ἐπιών, οὖσα, όν; this is the only form used in our lit., nearly always in the fem., and of time τῇ ἐπιούσῃ ἡμέρᾳ *on the next day* (Hdt. +; Jos., C. Ap. 1, 309) Ac 7: 26. Also simply τῇ ἐ. (Polyb. 2, 25, 11; 5, 13, 10; Appian, Mithrid. 99 §458; PPetr. III 56b, 12; Pr 3: 28; 27: 1; Jos., Ant. 3, 30; 4, 64) 16: 11; 20: 15; 21: 18. τῇ ἐπιούσῃ νυκτί *the next night* (Ael. Aristid. 48, 75 K.=24 p. 485 D.) 23: 11. τῷ ἐπιόντι σαββάτῳ 18: 19 D. M-M.*

ἐπείπερ conj. (Aeschyl. +; pap.; Jos., Ant. 18, 296; 19, 268) *since indeed* Ro 3: 30 v.l. M-M.*

ἐπεισαγωγή, ῆς, ἡ (since Thu. 8, 92, 1) *bringing in* (besides), *introduction* (Hippocr., Praec. 7; Dionys. Hal., Veterum Cens. 2, 10; Jos., Ant. 11, 196 ἑτέρας [of an additional wife] ἐ.) γίνεται ἐ. κρείττονος ἐλπίδος *a better hope is introduced* Hb 7: 19. M-M.*

ἐπεισέρχομαι fut. ἐπεισελεύσομαι (Hdt. +; pap.; Philo, Op. M. 119) *rush in suddenly and forcibly* (UPZ 13, 19 [160 BC]; 1 Macc 16: 16; Jos., Ant. 11, 265) ἐπί τινα *upon someone* of the Day of Judgment ἐπὶ πάντας τοὺς καθημένους ἐπὶ πρόσωπον πάσης τῆς γῆς Lk 21: 35. M-M.*

ἔπειτα adv. (Hom. +; inscr., pap., LXX, Philo, Joseph.) *then, thereupon.*
   1. of time Lk 16: 7; Gal 1: 21; Js 4: 14; 2 Cl 11: 4; 13: 3; D 12: 1. Pleonast. ἔ. μετὰ τοῦτο (Pla., Lach. 190D; Sosipater in Athen. 9 p. 378B) J 11: 7 (εἶτα 𝔓⁴⁵ᵛⁱᵈ, 𝔓⁶⁶ D). ἔ. μετὰ τρία ἔτη Gal 1: 18; cf. J 11: 7.
   2. to denote succession in enumerations—a. together w. indications of chronological sequence πρῶτον. . .ἔ. *first . . . then* (X., An. 3, 2, 27; Diod. S. 16, 69, 4; Ael. Aristid. 23, 6 K.=42 p. 769 D.; 4 Macc 6: 3; Jos., Ant. 12, 92) 1 Cor 15: 46; 1 Th 4: 17; Pol 4: 2. πρότερον . . . ἔπειτα Hb 7: 27; ἀπαρχή . . . ἔ. *as first-fruit . . . next* 1 Cor 15: 23. ἔ. . . . . ἔ. *thereupon . . . then* (Ael. Aristid. 48, 38 K.= 24 p. 475 D.) 15: 6f. Cl 15: 5 v.l.
   b. of succession alone: πρῶτον. . .ἔ. (POxy. 1217, 5 πρῶτον μὲν ἀσπαζομένη σε, ἔπειτα εὐχομένη . . . ; Jos., Ant. 20, 13, C. Ap. 1, 104) Hb 7: 2; Js 3: 17. As fourth and fifth member in a list 1 Cor 12: 28. M-M.*

ἐπέκεινα adv. *farther on, beyond* (Hdt. +; LXX w. and without gen.; En.) οἱ ἐ. ἀδελφοὶ *the brothers farther on* MPol 20: 1 (Appian, Hann. 6 §21 τοῖς ἐπέκεινα Κέλτοις; Herodian 4, 15, 3 οἱ ἐ. βάρβαροι). W. gen. (Chares [after 323 BC] in Athen. 13, 35 p. 575B; Arrian, Anab. 5, 5, 3 ἐπ. Καυκάσου; Maximus Tyr. 11, 10e τούτων ἐπ. ἐλθεῖν; Synes., Ep. 148 p. 285B ἐ. Θούλης) Βαβυλῶνος *beyond Babylon* Ac 7: 43 (Am 5: 27).*

ἐπεκλήθην s. ἐπικαλέω.

ἐπεκτείνομαι (as act. in Aristot., Strabo, Vett. Val. 362, 20) in our lit. only mid. (Theophr., H. Pl. 6, 8, 4; Cass. Dio 45, 1, 3; Cos. and Dam. 2, 6) *stretch out, strain* τινί *toward someth.* (Galen, De Usu Part. II 388, 9 Helmr.) τοῖς ἔμπροσθεν *toward the* (goal) *that lies before* (me) Phil 3: 13. M-M.*

ἐπελαθόμην s. ἐπιλανθάνομαι.

ἐπενδύομαι (the act. Hdt. 1, 195; Jos., Ant. 5, 37) in our lit. only mid. *put on* (in addition) (Plut., Pelop. 11, 1; Jos.,

Ant. 3, 159) τὶ someth. of the heavenly, glorious body 2 Cor 5: 2. Abs. vs. 4.—S. on γυμνός 4.*

ἐπενδύτης, ου, ὁ (Soph., fgm. no. 406 Nauck²; Ael. Dion. χ, 11; Pollux 7, 45; 1 Km 18: 4; 2 Km 13: 18) *outer garment, coat* (Suidas: τὸ ἐπάνω ἱμάτιον in contrast to ὑποδύτης, the ἐσώτερον ἱμάτιον) τὸν ἐ. διεζώσατο *put on his outer garment* J 21: 7.*

ἐπεξεργάζομαι (Soph.+) *cause* or *create in addition* ἑαυτοῖς κίνδυνον *danger for yourselves* 1 Cl 47: 7.*

ἐπέρχομαι fut. ἐπελεύσομαι; 2 aor. ἐπῆλθον (3 pl. ἐπῆλθαν Ac 14: 19; Bl-D. §81, 3 w. app.; Mlt.-H. 208) (Hom.+; inscr., pap., LXX; En. 106, 1; Ep. Arist., Joseph., Test. 12 Patr.).
1. *come, come along, appear*—**a.** of place, abs. Agr 22=Mt 20: 28 D. ἀπό τινος (1 Macc 8: 4) ἐπῆλθαν ἀπὸ Ἀντιοχείας Ἰουδαῖοι *Jews came fr. Antioch* Ac 14: 19.
b. of time *come (on), approach*—α. of time itself (Jos., Ant. 6, 305 ἡ ἐπερχομένη ἡμέρα) νύξ 1 Cl 24: 3. ὁ αἰὼν ὁ ἐπερχόμενος *the coming age* Hv 4, 3, 5. ἐν τοῖς αἰῶσι τοῖς ἐπερχομένοις *in the ages to come* Eph 2: 7.
β. of what time brings; in our lit. exclusively of someth. unpleasant κακὰ ἐπερχόμενα 1 Cl 56: 10 (Job 5: 21). ἐπὶ ταῖς ταλαιπωρίαις ὑμῶν ταῖς ἐπερχομέναις *over the miseries that are coming upon you* Js 5: 1. In the same eschatological sense (cf. Is 41: 22f) Hv 3, 9, 5; 4, 1, 1; s 7: 4; 9, 5, 5. τὰ ἐπερχόμενα (cf. Is 41: 4, 22f; Jdth 9: 5) τὰ ἐ. τῇ οἰκουμένῃ *what is coming upon the world* Lk 21: 26.
2. *come over* or *upon*—**a.** of unpleasant happenings, abs. (Horapollo 2, 25 ὁ θάνατος; Pr 27: 12; Jos., Ant. 2, 86) *come about* Ac 13: 40. ἐπί τινα (Gen 42: 21; Wsd 12: 27; EpJer 48; 2 Macc 9: 18) *come upon someone* ὅπως μηδὲν ἐπέλθη ἐπ' ἐμὲ ὧν εἰρήκατε *that none of the things you have spoken of may come upon me* Ac 8: 24.—Hm 5, 1, 3 v.l.
b. of an enemy *attack* (Hom.+; inscr., pap.; 1 Km 30: 23; Jos., Ant. 5, 195; 6, 23) abs. Lk 11: 22 (v.l. ἐλθών 𝔓⁷⁵ et al.).
c. fr. above (Biogr. p. 448 of an inspiration: τοῦτο ἐπελθὸν αὐτῷ πράττειν ἐκ τοῦ θείου) of the Holy Spirit ἐπί τινα 1: 35 (FXSteinmetzer, 'Empfangen v. Hl. Geiste' '38); Ac 1: 8 (cf. Is 32: 15). M-M.*

ἐπερωτάω impf. ἐπηρώτων; fut. ἐπερωτήσω; 1 aor. ἐπηρώτησα; 1 aor. pass. ptc. ἐπερωτηθείς (Hdt., Thu. +; inscr., pap., LXX, Ep. Arist., Joseph.).
1. *ask* (a question)—**a.** gener. τινά Mk 9: 32; 12: 34; Mt 22: 46; Lk 2: 46; 1 Cor 14: 35. τινά τι *someone about someth.* (Aeschines 1, 79) αὐτὸν τὴν παραβολήν *they asked him about the parable* Mk 7: 17; cf. 11: 29; Lk 20: 40; Hm 4, 1, 4. τινὰ περί τινος (Hdt. 1, 32; Demosth. 43, 66; PFlor. 331, 3) Mk 10: 10; J 16: 19 D. W. acc. of the pers. and foll. by a question introduced by λέγων (Test. Jos. 11: 2) Mt 12: 10; 17: 10; 22: 23; Mk 9: 11; 12: 18; Lk 3: 10 al. Foll. by εἰ and a dir. question εἴ τι βλέπεις; *do you see someth.?* Mk 8: 23 or an indirect question (PHib. 72, 15 [241 BC]; Jos., Ant. 12, 163) Mk 10: 2; 15: 44; Lk 6: 9; 23: 6 (ἐρωτάω 𝔓⁷⁵); Ac 5: 8 D. Followed by other questions, direct Mk 5: 9; 7: 5; 9: 16, 28 al. and indirect (X., Hell. 6, 4, 2, Oec. 6, 6) Lk 8: 9; 17: 20; Ac 23: 34; 2 Cl 12: 2. τί ἄρα ἔσται αὐτοῖς *what will happen to them* Hm 11: 2. Abs. LJ 2: 4 (context mutilated).
b. of a judge's questioning in making an investigation Mt 27: 11; Mk 14: 60f; 15: 2, 4; J 9: 23; Ac 5: 27.
c. The usage of the word w. regard to questioning the gods (Hdt. 1, 53, 1 and oft.; Dit., Syll.³ 977, 24; 1160; 1168, 16; Jos., Ant. 6, 123) approaches the mng. in the

LXX: ἐ. τὸν θεόν, τὸν κύριον etc. *inquire after God,* i.e. after the thought, purpose, or will of God Ro 10: 20 (Is 65: 1).
2. *ask for* τινά τι *ask someone for someth.* (Ps 136: 3) αὐτὸν σημεῖον ἐκ τοῦ οὐρανοῦ Mt 16: 1.—HGreeven, TW II 684f. M-M.

ἐπερώτημα, ατος, τό (Hdt.+; inscr., pap.; Da 4: 17 Theod.).
1. *question* (Hdt. 6, 67; Thu. 3, 53, 2; 3, 68, 1; Sir 33: 3 v.l.) ξένον ἐ. *strange question* UGosp. l. 64. λαλεῖ αὐτοῖς κατὰ τὰ ἐ. αὐτῶν *according to their questions* Hm 11: 2.
2. *request, appeal* (ἐπερωτάω 2) συνειδήσεως ἀγαθῆς ἐ. εἰς θεόν *an appeal to God for a clear conscience* 1 Pt 3: 21. But cf. also *a pledge* (s. L-S-J s.v. 3 with pap. ref.) *to God proceeding fr. a clear conscience* (so GCRichards, JTS 32, '31, 77 and EGSelwyn, 1 Pt ad loc.). Cf. also BReicke, The Disobed. Spirits and Christian Baptism '46, 182–6; NClausen-Bagge, Eperotema '41; HGreeven, TW II 685f. M-M.*

ἔπεσα, ἔπεσον s. πίπτω.

ἐπέστην s. ἐφίστημι.

ἐπέχω impf. ἐπεῖχον; 2 aor. ἐπέσχον (Hom.+; inscr., pap., LXX, Ep. Arist.; Philo, Deus Imm. 149; Joseph.; Sib. Or. 3, 317).
1. trans. *hold fast* τινά someone (Test. Jos. 15: 3) Lk 4: 42 D. τὶ someth. (Diod. S. 12, 27, 3 ταραχὴ τ. πόλιν ἐπεῖχε; Plut., Otho 17, 6 τ. πόλιν ἐπεῖχε κλαυθμός; Jos., Bell. 1, 230; Sib. Or. 3, 340) λόγον ζωῆς Phil 2: 16.
2. intr.—**a.** *hold toward, aim at,* fig. of mental processes (Hdt., Thu.) τινί someone (PFay. 112, 11 [99 AD] ἐπέχον τῷ δακτυλιστῇ. W. dat. of the thing Polyb. 3, 43, 2; BGU 827, 21; Sir 34: 2; 2 Macc 9: 25) ἐπεῖχεν αὐτοῖς *he fixed his attention on them* Ac 3: 5. ἔπεχε σεαυτῷ *take pains with yourself* 1 Ti 4: 16. W. indir. quest. foll. ἐπέχων πῶς . . . ἐξελέγοντο *he noticed how . . . they sought out* Lk 14: 7.
b. *stop, stay* (Soph. et al.; PTebt. 12, 8; Gen 8: 10; Philo, De Jos. 96 ἐ. ταύτας [=three days]; Jos., Bell. 6, 354) ἐπέσχεν χρόνον εἰς τὴν Ἀσίαν *he stayed for a while in Asia* Ac 19: 22. M-M.*

ἐπήλυτος, ον (Dionys. Hal. 3, 72; Job 20: 26; Philo, Cher. 120f; Sib. Or. 7, 85) *come lately, come after* ὡς ἐπήλυτοι *as those who have come lately,* or *as followers, imitators* B 3: 6 (so ℵ.—v.l. προσήλυτοι; cf. Bihlmeyer ad loc.).*

ἐπῆρα, ἐπήρθην s. ἐπαίρω.

ἐπηρεάζω (Hdt.+; inscr., pap.; Philo, Mos. 2, 199, De Jos. 71) *threaten, mistreat, abuse* as a rule w. the dat. (as Ael. Aristid. 23, 28 K.=42 p. 777 D.; PFlor. 99, 10 [I/II AD]; Jos., Bell. 1, 13); τινά (Dit., Or. 484, 26 [II AD]): περὶ τῶν ἐπηρεαζόντων ὑμᾶς *for those who mistreat you* (in something they do, as PFay. 123, 7; PLond. 157, 4) Lk 6: 28, cf. Mt 5: 44 v.l. τὴν ἀγαθὴν ἀναστροφήν *revile (your) good conduct* 1 Pt 3: 16. M-M.*

ἐπήρεια, ας, ἡ (Thu.+; Dit., Or. 669, 6; 262, 23f; BGU 340, 21; PRyl. 28, 139; Sym.; Philo, In Flacc. 103; 179; Jos., Ant. 13, 382; 15, 23) *abuse, ill-treatment* ἐ. τοῦ ἄρχοντος τοῦ αἰῶνος τούτου IMg 1: 3 (Lucian, Laps. 1 δαίμονος ἐπήρεια. S. Dssm., LO 398, 7 [LAE 454, 7] ἐπήρ. τ. ἀντικειμένου).*

ἐπί prep. w. gen., dat., or acc.; s. the lit. on ἀνά, beg. (Hom.+; inscr., pap., LXX, En., Ep. Arist., Philo, Joseph., Test. 12 Patr.).

I. with the genitive—1. of place—a. lit.—α. *on, upon,* answering the question 'where?' ἐπὶ (τῆς) γῆς *on (the) earth* Mt 6: 10, 19; 9: 6; 23: 9; Mk 6: 47 al. ἐ. τῆς θαλάσσης *on the sea* (cf. Job 9: 8; Dio Chrys. 10[11], 129 βαδίζειν ἐπὶ τῆς θαλ.; Lucian, Philops. 13 βαδίζειν ἐφ᾽ ὕδατος, V.H. 2, 4; Artem. 3, 16 ἐπὶ τ. θαλάσσης περιπατεῖν; schol. on Nicander, Ther. 15 p. 5, 26ff relying on the testimony of Hesiod: Orion was given a gift [δωρεά] by the gods καὶ ἐπὶ κυμάτων πορεύεσθαι καὶ ἐπὶ τῆς γῆς) Mt 14: 26; Mk 6: 48f; J 6: 19 (w. acc. ᵽ⁷⁵; see III iaa below). ἐ. τῶν νεφελῶν *on the clouds* Mt 24: 30; 26: 64 (Da 7: 13; cf. Philo, Praem. 8). ἐ. κλίνης 9: 2; Lk 17: 34. ἐ. τοῦ δώματος *on the roof* vs. 31; Mt 24: 17; 10: 27. W. verbs: κάθημαι ἐπὶ τινος *sit on someth.* (Job 2: 8) Mt 24: 3; 27: 19; Ac 8: 28; Rv 6: 16; 9: 17. ἑστηκέναι ἐπὶ τινος *stand on someth.* Ac 21: 40; Rv 10: 5, 8. With parts of the body: ἐ. χειρῶν αἴρειν *carry on* (i.e. *with*) *their hands* Mt 4: 6; Lk 4: 11 (both Ps 90: 12). ἐ. κεφαλῆς *on the head* (Hdt. 5, 12) J 20: 7; 1 Cor 11: 10; Rv 12: 1. ἐ. τοῦ μετώπου Rv 7: 3; 9: 4. ἐ. γυμνοῦ *on the naked body* Mk 14: 51.—ἄνδρες εὐχὴν ἔχοντες ἐφ᾽ ἑαυτῶν *men who have an oath over them*=*have taken an oath* Ac 21: 23.

β. *on, upon* answering the question 'whither?'; w. verbs of motion (Appian, Iber. 98 §427 ἀπέπλευσεν ἐπ᾽ οἴκου =*he sailed (toward) home;* PGM 4, 2469 ἀναβὰς ἐπὶ δώματος; Jos., Ant. 4, 91 ἔφευγον ἐπὶ τ. πόλεων) βάλλειν τὸν σπόρον ἐ. τῆς γῆς Mk 4: 26; also σπείρειν vs. 31. πίπτειν (Wsd 18: 23) 9: 20; 14: 35. καθιέναι Ac 10: 11. τιθέναι (Sir 17: 4) Lk 8: 16; J 19: 19; Ac 5: 15. ἔρχεσθαι Hb 6: 7; Rv 3: 10; γίνεσθαι ἐ. *reach, be at* J 6: 21. γενόμενος ἐ. τοῦ τόπου *when he reached the place* Lk 22: 40. καθίζειν *take one's seat* Mt 19: 28; 23: 2; 25: 31; J 19: 13 (ἐπὶ βήματος of Pilate as Jos., Bell. 2, 172). κρεμαννύναι ἐ. ξύλου *hang on a tree* (i.e. cross) (Gen 40: 19) Ac 5: 30; 10: 39; cf. Gal 3: 13 (Dt 21: 23).

γ. *at, near* of immediate proximity to things (Hdt. 7, 115; X., An. 4, 3, 28 al.; LXX) ἐ. τ. θυρῶν *at the gates* (Plut., G. Gracch. 14, 3; PRyl. 127, 9 [29 AD] κοιμωμένου μου ἐπὶ τῆς θύρας; 1 Macc 1: 55) Ac 5: 23. ἐ. τῆς θαλάσσης *near the sea* (Polyb. 1, 44, 4; Ex 14: 2; Dt 1: 40; 1 Macc 14: 34) J 21: 1. ἐ. τῆς ὁδοῦ *by the road* Mt 21: 19. ἐσθίειν ἐ. τῆς τραπέζης τινός *eat at someone's table* Lk 22: 30 (cf. POxy. 99, 14 [55 AD] τράπεζα, ἐφ᾽ ἧς Σαραπίων καὶ μέτοχοι). ἐ. τοῦ (τῆς) βάτου *at the thornbush*= *in the passage about the thornbush* (i.e., Ex 3: 1ff) Mk 12: 26; Lk 20: 37.

δ. *before* w. persons, esp. in the language of lawsuits (Pla., Leg. 12 p. 943D; Isaeus 5, 1 al.; UPZ 71, 15; 16 [152 BC]; POxy. 38, 11; BGU 909, 23; Jos., Vi. 258) ἐ. τοῦ ἡγεμόνος *in the governor's presence* Mt 28: 14. ἐ. ἡγεμόνων καὶ βασιλέων Mk 13: 9. ἐπὶ σου *before you* (the procurator) Ac 23: 30. ἐ. Τερτούλλου Phlm subscr.; στάντος μου ἐ. τοῦ συνεδρίου Ac 24: 20 (cf. Diod. S. 11, 55, 4 ἐπὶ τοῦ κοινοῦ συνεδρίου τ. Ἑλλήνων). κρίνεσθαι ἐ. τῶν ἀδίκων *go to law before the unrighteous* 1 Cor 6: 1. κριθήσεται ἐφ᾽ ὑμῶν *before your tribunal* D 11: 11. μαρτυρεῖν ἐ. Ποντίου Πιλάτου *testify before Pontius Pilate* 1 Ti 6: 13 (s. μαρτυρέω 1d). ἐ. τοῦ βήματος (POxy. 37 I, 3 [43 AD]) ἑστὼς ἐπὶ τοῦ βήματος Καίσαρός εἰμι *I am standing before Caesar's tribunal* Ac 25: 10 (Appian says Prooem. c. 15 §62 of himself: δίκαις ἐν Ῥώμῃ συναγορεύσας ἐπὶ τῶν βασιλέων=I acted as attorney in lawsuits in Rome before the emperors).—Gener. *in someone's presence* (Appian, Syr. 61 §324 ἐφ᾽ ὑμῶν=in your presence) ἐ. Τίτου *before Titus* 2 Cor 7: 14.

b. fig.—α. *over* of power, authority, control of or over someone or someth. (Hdt. 5, 109 al.; BGU 1120, 1 [5 BC] πρωτάρχῳ ἐ. τοῦ κριτηρίου; 287, 1. LXX) βασιλεύειν ἐ.

τινος (Judg 9: 8, 10; 1 Km 8: 7) Rv 5: 10. ἔχειν βασιλείαν ἐ. τῶν βασιλέων 17: 18. ἐξουσίαν ἔχειν ἐ. τινος *have power over someone* 20: 6. διδόναι ἐξουσίαν ἐπὶ τινος 2: 26. καθιστάναι τινὰ ἐπὶ τινος *set someone over, put someone in charge, of someth.* or *someone* (Pla., Rep. 5 p. 460B; Demosth. 18, 118; Gen 39: 4f; 1 Macc 6: 14; 10: 37; 2 Macc 12: 20 al.; Ep. Arist. 281) Mt 24: 45; Lk 12: 42; Ac 6: 3. εἶναι ἐπὶ τινος (Synes., Ep. 79 p. 224D; Tob 1: 22; Jdth 14: 13; 1 Macc 10: 69) ὃς ἦν ἐπὶ πάσης τῆς γάζης αὐτῆς *who was in charge of all her treasure* 8: 27. Of God ὁ ὢν ἐ. πάντων (Apollonius of Tyana [I AD] in Euseb., Pr. Ev. 4, 13) Ro 9: 5; cf. Eph 4: 6. ὁ ἐπὶ τινος w. ὤν to be supplied (Demosth. 18, 247 al.; Diod. S. 13, 47, 6; Plut., Pyrrh. 5, 7, Aemil. Paul. 23, 6; PTebt. 5, 88 [118 BC] ὁ ἐπὶ τ. προσόδων; 1 Macc 6: 28; 2 Macc 3: 7; 3 Macc 6: 30 al.; Ep. Arist. 110; 174) ὁ ἐ. τοῦ κοιτῶνος *the chamberlain* Ac 12: 20.

β. *on the basis of* (Antig. Car. 164 ἐπὶ τῶν οἴνων ἀλλοιοῦσθαι) ἐ. δύο ἢ τριῶν μαρτύρων *on the evidence of two or three witnesses* 1 Ti 5: 19. Sim. in the expr. ἐ. στόματος δύο μαρτύρων (Dt 19: 15) Mt 18: 16; 2 Cor 13: 1. ἐπ᾽ αὐτῆς *on the basis of it* Hb 7: 11. ἐπ᾽ ἀληθείας *based on truth*=*in accordance w. truth, truly* (Demosth. 18, 17 ἐπ᾽ ἀληθείας οὐδεμιᾶς εἰρημένα; POxy. 255, 16 [48 AD]; Tob 8: 7; En. 104, 11) Mk 12: 14, 32; Lk 4: 25; 20: 21; Ac 4: 27. ἐφ᾽ ἑαυτοῦ *based on himself*=*to* or *by himself* (X., An. 2, 4, 10; Demosth. 18, 224 ἐκρίνετο ἐφ᾽ ἑαυτοῦ; Dionys. Hal., Comp. Verb. 16 ἐπὶ σεαυτοῦ. Cf. Kühner-G. I 498e) 2 Cor 10: 7.

γ. to introduce the object which is to be discussed or acted upon λέγειν ἐπὶ τινος *speak of, about someth.* (Pla., Charm. p. 155D, Leg. 2 p. 662D; Isocr. 6, 41; Aelian, V.H. 1, 30; Jer 35: 8; Ep. Arist. 162; 170) Gal 3: 16. *Do someth. on, in the case of* (cf. 1 Esdr 1: 22) σημεῖα ποιεῖν ἐπὶ τῶν ἀσθενούντων *work miracles on the sick* J 6: 2. ἐπὶ τινος δεῖ ἐγκρατεύεσθαι *in the case of some things it is necessary to practice self-control* Hm 8: 1.—On B 13: 6 s. τίθημι I 1bε.

2. of time (Hom. +) *in the time of, under* (kings or other rulers) ἐ. Ἐλισαίου *in the time of Elisha* Lk 4: 27. ἐ. τῆς μετοικεσίας *at the time of the exile* Mt 1: 11. *Under*= *during the rule or administration of* (Hes., Op. 111; Hdt. 6, 98 al.; Dit., Or. 90, 15; PAmh. 43, 2 [173 BC]; UPZ 162 V, 5 [117 BC]; 1 Esdr 2: 12; 1 Macc 13: 42; 2 Macc 15: 22; Jos., Ant. 12, 156 ἐπὶ ἀρχιερέως Ὀ.) ἐ. Ἀβιαθὰρ ἀρχιερέως *under, in the time of, Abiathar the high priest* Mk 2: 26. ἐ. ἀρχιερέως Ἅννα καὶ Καιάφα Lk 3: 2. ἐ. Κλαυδίου Ac 11: 28. ἐ. τῶν πατέρων *in the time of the fathers* 1 Cl 23: 3. ἐπ᾽ ἐσχάτων τῶν ἡμερῶν *in the last days* (Gen 49: 1; Num 24: 14; Mi 4: 1; Jer 37: 24; Da 10: 14) 2 Pt 3: 3; Hs 9, 12, 3; cf. Hb 1: 2. ἐπ᾽ ἐσχάτου τοῦ χρόνου *in the last time* Jd 18. ἐπ᾽ ἐσχάτου τῶν χρόνων *at the end of the times* 1 Pt 1: 20. ἐ. τῶν προσευχῶν μου *when I pray, in my prayers* (cf. PTebt. 58, 31 [111 BC] ἐπὶ τ. διαλόγου 'in the discussion'; 4 Macc 15: 19 ἐπὶ τ. βασάνων 'during the tortures'; Sir 37: 29; 3 Macc 5: 40; Synes., Ep. 121 p. 258C ἐπὶ τῶν κοινῶν ἱερῶν) Ro 1: 10; Eph 1: 16; 1 Th 1: 2; Phlm 4.

II. with the dative—1. of place—a. lit.—α. *on, in, above* answering the question 'where?' (Hom. +; inscr., pap., LXX) ἐ. πίνακι *on a platter* Mt 14: 8, 11; Mk 6: 25, 28. ἀνακλῖναι ἐ. τῷ χλωρῷ χόρτῳ *on the green grass* 6: 39. ἐ. τοῖς κραβάττοις vs. 55. ἐπέκειτο ἐπ᾽ αὐτῷ *lay on it* (*before it* is also poss.) J 11: 38. καθήμενος ἐπὶ τῷ θρόνῳ Rv 4: 9; 5: 13; 7: 10 and oft. ἐφ᾽ ἵπποις λευκοῖς *on white horses* 19: 14. ἐπὶ σανίσιν *on planks* Ac 27: 44. ἐ. τῇ στοᾷ *in the colonnade* 3: 11. τὰ ἐ. τοῖς οὐρανοῖς *what is above* (or *in*) *the heavens* Eph 1: 10. ἐπ᾽ αὐτῷ *above him, at his head* Lk 23: 38 (=Mt 27: 37 ἐπάνω τ. κεφαλῆς αὐτοῦ).

β. *on, upon* answering the question 'whither?' (Hom.+) w. verbs that indicate a direction: οἰκοδομεῖν ἐπί τινι *build upon someth.* Mt 16: 18. ἐποικοδομεῖν Eph 2: 20. ἐπιβάλλειν ἐπίβλημα ἐ. ἱματίῳ παλαιῷ *put a patch on an old garment* Mt 9: 16. ἐπιπίπτειν ἐπί τινι Ac 8: 16. λίθον ἐπ᾽ αὐτῇ βαλέτω J 8: 7 v.l. This passage forms a transition to the next mng.

γ. *against* in a hostile sense (Hom.+; 2 Macc 13: 19; Sir 28: 23 v.l.) Lk 12: 52f; Ac 11: 19.

δ. of immediate proximity *at, near, by* (Hom.+) ἐ. τῇ θύρᾳ (ἐ. θύραις) *at the door* (Hom.+; Wsd 19: 17; Jos., Ant. 17, 90) Mt 24: 33; Mk 13: 29; Ac 5: 9. ἐ. τοῖς πυλῶσιν Rv 21: 12. ἐ. τῇ πηγῇ J 4: 6 (Jos., Ant. 5, 58 ἐπί τινι πηγῇ). ἐ. τῇ προβατικῇ (sc. πύλῃ) *near the sheepgate* 5: 2; cf. Ac 3: 10. ἐ. τῷ ποταμῷ *near the river* (since Il. 7, 133; Jos., Ant. 4, 176 ἐπί τ. Ἰορδάνῳ) Rv 9: 14.—Of pers. (Diod. S. 14, 113, 6) ἐφ᾽ ὑμῖν *among you* 2 Cor 7: 7. Cf. Ac 28: 14 t.r.

b. fig.—**α.** *over* of power, authority, control of or over someone or someth. (X., Cyr. 1, 2, 5; 2, 4, 25 al., An. 4, 1, 13; Demosth. 19, 113; Aeschines 2, 73; Esth 8: 12e) Mt 24: 47; Lk 12: 44.

β. *to, in addition to* (Hom.+; PEleph. 5, 17 [284/3 BC] μηνὸς Τῦβι τρίτῃ ἐπ᾽ εἰκάδι; Tob 2: 14; Sir 3: 27; 5: 5) προσέθηκεν τοῦτο ἐ. πᾶσιν *he added this to everything else* Lk 3: 20 (cf. Lucian, On Funerals, 24). ἐ. τ. παρακλήσει ἡμῶν *in addition to our comfort* 2 Cor 7: 13. λύπη ἐ. λύπῃ *grief upon grief* Phil 2: 27 t.r. (cf. Soph., Oed. C. 544, also Polyb. 1, 57, 1 πληγὴν ἐπὶ πληγῇ; Plut., Mor. 123F; Polyaenus 5, 52 ἐπὶ φόνῳ φόνον; Quint. Smyrn. 5, 602 ἐπὶ πένθει πένθος=sorrow upon sorrow; Sir 26: 15). ἐ. τῇ σῇ εὐχαριστίᾳ *to your prayer of thanks* 1 Cor 14: 16. So perh. also Hb 8: 1. ἐ. πᾶσι τούτοις *to all these* Col 3: 14; Lk 16: 26 v.l. (X., Mem. 1, 2, 25 al.; Sir 37: 15; cf. 1 Macc 10: 42).

γ. of that upon which a state of being, an action, or a result is based (Hom.+) ἐπ᾽ ἄρτῳ ζῆν *live on bread* Mt 4: 4; Lk 4: 4 (both Dt 8: 3. Cf. Ps.-Pla., Alcib. 1 p. 105C; Plut., Mor. 526D; Alciphr. 3, 7, 5; Sib. Or. 4, 154). ἐ. τῷ ῥήματί σου *depending on your word* Lk 5: 5. οὐ συνῆκαν ἐ. τοῖς ἄρτοις *they did not arrive at an understanding (of it) (by reflecting) on the miracle of) the loaves* Mk 6: 52 (cf. Demosth. 18, 121 τί σαυτὸν οὐκ ἐλλεβορίζεις ἐπὶ τούτοις [sc. λόγοις]; =why do you not come to an understanding concerning these words?). ἐ. τῇ πίστει *on the basis of faith* Ac 3: 16; Phil 3: 9. ἐπ᾽ ἐλπίδι *on the basis of hope, supporting itself on hope* Ac 2: 26 (? s. ἐλπίς 2a); Ro 4: 18; 8: 20; 1 Cor 9: 10; Tit 1: 2.—Ac 26: 6 ἐπ᾽ ἐλπίδι gives the basis of the trial at law, as does ἐ. εὐεργεσίᾳ 4: 9. ἀπολύειν τ. γυναῖκα ἐ. πορνείᾳ Mt 19: 9 (cf. Dio Chrys. 26[43], 10 ἀπολύειν ἐπ᾽ ἀργυρίῳ). ἐ. δυσὶν μάρτυσιν *on the basis of the testimony of two witnesses* (cf. Appian, Iber. 79 §343 ἤλεγχον ἐπὶ μάρτυσι) Hb 10: 28 (Dt 17: 6); *on the basis of* 8: 6; 9: 10, 15 (here it may also be taken in the temporal sense; s. 2 below), 17. ἁμαρτάνειν ἐ. τῷ ὁμοιώματι τ. παραβάσεως Ἀδάμ Ro 5: 14 (ὁμοίωμα 1). δαπανᾶν ἐπί τινι *pay the expenses for someone* Ac 21: 24. ἀρκεῖσθαι ἐπί τινι *be content w. someth.* 3 J 10.—W. verbs of believing, hoping, trusting: πεποιθέναι (Wsd 3: 9; Sus 35; 1 Macc 10: 71; 2 Macc 7: 40 and oft.) Lk 11: 22; 18: 9; 2 Cor 1: 9; Hb 2: 13 (2 Km 22: 3). πιστεύειν Lk 24: 25; Ro 9: 33; 10: 11; 1 Pt 2: 6 (the last three Is 28: 16). ἐλπίζειν (2 Macc 2: 18; Sir 34: 7) Ro 15: 12 (Is 11: 10); 1 Ti 4: 10; 6: 17; cf. 1 J 3: 3. παρρησιάζεσθαι Ac 14: 3.— After verbs which express feelings, opinions, etc. *at, because of, from, with* (Hom.+) διαταράσσεσθαι Lk 1:

29. ἐκπλήσσεσθαι Mt 7: 28; Mk 1: 22; Lk 4: 32; Ac 13: 12. ἐξίστασθαι (Jdth 11: 16; Wsd 5: 2 al.) Lk 2: 47. ἐπαισχύνεσθαι (Is 1: 29) Ro 6: 21. εὐφραίνεσθαι (Sir 16: 1; 18: 32; 1 Macc 11: 44) Rv 18: 20. θαμβεῖσθαι Mk 10: 24; cf. Lk 5: 9; Ac 3: 10. θαυμάζειν (Lev 26: 32; Jdth 10: 7 al.; Jos., Ant. 10, 277) Mk 12: 17 t.r. μακροθυμεῖν (Sir 18: 11; 29: 8; 35: 19) Mt 18: 26, 29; Lk 18: 7; Js 5: 7. μετανοεῖν (Plut., Ag. 19, 5; Ps.-Lucian, Salt. 84; Prayer of Manasseh [=Ode 12] 7) 2 Cor 12: 21. ὀδυνᾶσθαι (cf. Tob 6: 15) Ac 20: 38. ὀργίζεσθαι Rv 12: 17. σπλαγχνίζεσθαι Mt 14: 14; Lk 7: 13. συλλυπεῖσθαι Mk 3: 5. στυγνάζειν 10: 22. χαίρειν (PEleph. 13, 3; Jos., Ant. 1, 294; Tob 13: 15; Bar 4: 33) Mt 18: 13; Lk 1: 14; 13: 17; Ro 16: 19 al. χαρὰν καὶ παράκλησιν ἔχειν Phlm 7. χαρὰ ἔσται Lk 15: 7; cf. vs. 10 (Jos., Ant. 6, 116 ἡ ἐπὶ τῇ νίκῃ χαρά). Also w. verbs that denote aroused feelings παραζηλοῦν and παροργίζειν *make jealous* and *angry* at Ro 10: 19 (Dt 32: 21). παρακαλεῖν 1 Th 3: 7a, as well as those verbs that denote an expression of the emotions ἀγαλλιᾶσθαι (cf. Tob 13: 15; Ps 69: 5) Lk 1: 47; Hs 8, 1, 18; 9, 24, 2. καυχᾶσθαι (Diod. S. 16, 70; Sir 30: 2) Ro 5: 2. κοπετὸν ποιεῖν (cf. 3 Macc 4: 3) Ac 8: 2. ὀλολύζειν Js 5: 1. αἰνεῖν (cf. X., An. 3, 1, 45 al.) Lk 2: 20. δοξάζειν (Polyb. 6, 53, 10.—S. also Diod. S. 17, 21, 4 δόξα ἐπὶ ἀνδρείᾳ=fame because of bravery) Ac 4: 21; 2 Cor 9: 13. εὐχαριστεῖν *give thanks for someth.* (s. εὐχαριστέω 2; UPZ 59, 10 [168 BC] ἐπὶ τῷ ἐρρῶσθαί σε τ. θεοῖς εὐχάριστουν) 1 Cor 1: 4; cf. 2 Cor 9: 15; 1 Th 3: 9.—ἐφ᾽ ᾧ=ἐπὶ τούτῳ ὅτι *for this reason that, because* (Diod. S. 19, 98; Appian, Bell. Civ. 1, 112 §520; Ael. Aristid. 53 p. 640 D.; Synes., Ep. 73 p. 221c; Damasc., Vi. Isid. 154; Syntipas p. 12, 9; 127, 8; Thomas Mag. ἐφ᾽ ᾧ ἀντὶ τοῦ διότι. Cf. W-S. §24, 5b and 12f. S. WGKümmel, D. Bild des Menschen im NT '48, 36–40) Ro 5: 12 (SLyonnet, Biblica 36, '55, 436–56 [denies a causal sense here]. On the probability of commercial idiom s. FWDanker, FWGingrich-Festschr. '72, 104f, also Ro 5: 12, Sin under Law, NTS 14, '68, 424–39); 2 Cor 5: 4; Phil 3: 12; *for, indeed* 4: 10.

δ. to introduce the pers. or thing because of which someth. exists or happens *to, with* πράσσειν τι ἐπί τινι *do someth. to someone* Ac 5: 35 (likew. Appian, Bell. Civ. 3, 15 §51; cf. δρᾶν τι ἐ. τινι Hdt. 3, 14; Aelian, N. An. 11, 11); *about* γεγραμμένα ἐπ᾽ αὐτῷ J 12: 16 (cf. Hdt. 1, 66). προφητεύειν ἐ. τινι Rv 10: 11. μαρτυρεῖν *bear witness about* Hb 11: 4; Rv 22: 16.

ε. of purpose, goal, result (Hom., Thu.+; Dit., Syll.³ 888, 5 ἐπὶ τῇ τῶν ἀνθρ. σωτηρίᾳ; PTebt. 44, 6 [114 BC] ὄντος μου ἐπὶ θεραπείᾳ ἐν τῷ Ἰσιείῳ; LXX; Jos., Ant. 5, 101) καλεῖν τινα ἐπί τινι *call someone for someth.* Gal 5: 13 (on ἐπ᾽ ἐλευθερίᾳ cf. Demosth. 23, 124; [59], 32) ἐ. ἀκαθαρσίᾳ *for impurity,* i.e. so that we should be impure 1 Th 4: 7. κτισθέντες ἐ. ἔργοις ἀγαθοῖς *for good deeds* Eph 2: 10. λογομαχεῖν ἐ. καταστροφῇ τῶν ἀκουόντων *for the ruin of those who hear* 2 Ti 2: 14 (cf. Eur., Hipp. 511; X., Mem. 2, 3, 19 ἐπὶ βλάβῃ; Hdt. 1, 68 ἐ. κακῷ ἀνθρώπου; Polyb. 27, 7, 13 and PGM 4, 2440 ἐπ᾽ ἀγαθῷ='for good').

ζ. of manner, corresponding to an adv. (Aeschyl., Suppl. 628 ἐπ᾽ ἀληθείᾳ; UPZ 162 VI, 3 [117 BC] κακοτρόπως καὶ ἐπὶ ῥαδιουργίᾳ; POxy. 237 VI, 21) ὁ σπείρων ἐπ᾽ εὐλογίαις (in contrast to ὁ σπείρων φειδομένως *he who sows sparingly*) *he who sows in blessing* (i.e. generously) 2 Cor 9: 6. ἐπ᾽ εὐλογίαις θερίζειν *reap generously* ibid.

2. of time (Hom.+; PTebt. 5, 66 [118 BC]; PLond. 954, 18; PAmh. 157; LXX) *at, in, at the time of, during* ἐ. τοῖς νῦν χρόνοις *in these present times* 2 Cl 19: 4. ἐ. τῇ πρώτῃ διαθήκη *at the time of the first covenant* Hb 9: 15. ἐ. συντελείᾳ τ. αἰώνων *at the close of the age* 9: 26 (cf. Sir 22: 10 and PLond. 954, 18 ἐ. τέλει τ. χρόνου; POxy. 275, 20 [66 AD] ἐ. συνκλεισμῷ τ. χρόνου). ἐ. τῇ θυσίᾳ *at the time of, together with, the sacrifice* Phil 2: 17. ἐ. πάσῃ τῇ μνείᾳ ὑμῶν *at every remembrance of you* Phil 1: 3. ἐ. παροργισμῷ ὑμῶν *during your wrath,* i.e. *while you are angry* Eph 4: 26. ἐ. πάσῃ τῇ ἀνάγκῃ *in all (our) distress* 1 Th 3: 7b. ἐ. πάσῃ τῇ θλίψει 2 Cor 1: 4. ἐπὶ τούτῳ *in the meanwhile* J 4: 27 (Lucian, Dial. Deor. 17, 2, cf. Philops. 14 p. 41; Syntipas p. 76, 2 ἐφ᾽ ἡμέραις ἑπτά; 74, 6).

3. The formula ἐ. τῷ ὀνόματί τινος, used w. many verbs, prob. means (acc. to WHeitmüller, 'Im Namen Jesu' '03, 13ff) 'in connection with, or by the use of, i.e. naming, or calling out, or calling upon the name' (88): βαπτίζειν Ac 2: 38. δέχεσθαί τινα Mt 18: 5; Mk 9: 37; Lk 9: 48. διδάσκειν Ac 4: 18; 5: 28. δύναμιν ποιεῖν Mk 9: 39. ἐκβάλλειν δαιμόνια Lk 9: 49 v.l. ἔρχεσθαι Mt 24: 5; Mk 13: 6; Lk 21: 8. κηρύσσειν 24: 47. λαλεῖν Ac 4: 17; 5: 40. καλεῖν τινα ἐ. τῷ ὀν. τινος *call someone by using,* i.e. *after, the name of someone* (2 Esdr 17 [Neh 7]: 63) Lk 1: 59.—ὄνομα I 4cε. II.

III. with the accusative.—1. of place—a. lit.—α. *across, over* w. motion implied (Hom.+; LXX) περιπατεῖν, ἐλθεῖν ἐ. τ. θάλασσαν or ἐ. τ. ὕδατα Mt 14: 25, 28f; J 6: 19 𝔓⁷⁵. Of spreading *across the land:* famine Ac 7: 11; 11: 28; darkness Mt 27: 45; Lk 23: 44. ἐ. σταδίους δώδεκα χιλιάδων *across twelve thousand stades* Rv 21: 16 v.l. (Polyaenus 5, 44, 4 ἐπὶ στάδια δέκα); ἐ. πλεῖον *further* (1 Esdr 2: 24; 2 Macc 10: 27) Ac 4: 17.

β. of motion that reaches its goal completely (Hom.+; LXX) *on, upon someone* or *someth.* πέσατε ἐφ᾽ ἡμᾶς Lk 23: 30 (Hos 10: 8). ἔπεσεν ἐ. τὰ πετρώδη Mt 13: 5; cf. Lk 13: 4. ἔρχεσθαι ἐ. τινα *come upon someone* Mt 3: 16; also καταβαίνειν fr. above J 1: 33; cf. Rv 16: 21. ἀναβαίνειν (Jos., Ant. 13, 138) Lk 5: 19. ἐπιβαίνειν Mt 21: 5 (Zech 9: 9).—Ac 2: 3; 9: 4 al.; διασωθῆναι ἐ. τ. γῆν *be brought safely to the land* 27: 44; cf. vs. 43; Lk 8: 27. ἐ. τὸ πλοῖον *to the ship* Ac 20: 13. ἀναπεσεῖν ἐ. τὴν γῆν *lie down or sit down on the ground* Mt 15: 35. τιθέναι τι ἐ. τι *put someth. on someth.* Mt 5: 15; Lk 11: 33; Mk 8: 25 v.l.; likew. ἐπιτιθέναι Mt 23: 4; Mk 8: 25; Lk 15: 5; J 9: 6, 15; Ac 15: 10. ἐπιβάλλειν τ. χεῖρας ἐ. τινα (Gen 22: 12 al.) Mt 26: 50; Lk 21: 12; Ac 5: 18. Mainly after verbs of placing, laying, putting, bringing, etc. *on, to:* ἀναβιβάζω, ἀναφέρω, βάλλω, γράφω, δίδωμι, ἐπιβιβάζω, ἐπιγράφω, ἐποικοδομέω, ἐπιρ(ρ)ίπτω, θεμελιόω, ἵστημι, κατάγω, οἰκοδομέω, σωρεύω; s. these entries. Sim. βρέχειν ἐ. τινα *cause rain to fall upon someone* Mt 5: 45; also τ. ἥλιον ἀνατέλλειν ἐ. τινα *cause the sun to rise so that its rays fall upon someone* ibid. τύπτειν τινὰ ἐ. τὴν σιαγόνα *strike on the cheek* Lk 6: 29. πίπτειν ἐ. (τὸ) πρόσωπον (Jdth 14: 6) *on the face* Mt 17: 6; 26: 39; Lk 5: 12; 17: 16; 1 Cor 14: 25; Rv 7: 11.—*To, upon* w. acc. of the thing πορεύεσθαι ἐ. τὴν ὁδόν *go to the road* Ac 8: 26; cf. 9: 11. ἐ. τὰς διεξόδους Mt 22: 9. ἵνα μὴ πνέῃ ἄνεμος ἐ. πᾶν δένδρον *so that no wind should blow upon any tree* Rv 7: 1.

γ. of motion that comes close to someth. or someone *to, up to, in the neighborhood of, on* ἐ. τὸ μνημεῖον *up to the tomb* Mk 16: 2 t.r.; Lk 24: 1 t.r., 22, 24. ἔρχεσθαι ἐπί τι ὕδωρ *come to some water* Ac 8: 36. ἐ. τὴν πύλην τὴν σιδηρᾶν *to the iron gate* 12: 10. καταβαίνειν ἐ. τὴν θάλασσαν *go down to the sea* J 6: 16. ἐ. τὸν Ἰορδάνην Mt 3: 13. ἀνέπεσεν ἐ. τὸ στῆθος *he leaned back on* (Jesus') *breast* J 21: 20; 13: 25. πίπτειν ἐ. τοὺς πόδας *fall at* (someone's) *feet* Ac 10: 25. ἐ. τ. ἀκάνθας *among the*

thorns Mt 13: 7.—W. acc. of the pers. *to someone* ἐ. τὸν Ἰησοῦν ἐλθόντες *they came to Jesus* J 19: 33; cf. Mt 27: 27; Mk 5: 21. Esp. in the lang. of the law-courts *before* ἐ. ἡγεμόνας καὶ βασιλεῖς ἄγεσθαι *be brought before governors and kings* Mt 10: 18; cf. Lk 21: 12 (cf. BGU 22, 36 [114 AD] ἀξιῶ ἀκθῆναι [=ἀχθῆναι] τ. ἐνκαλουμένους ἐπὶ σὲ πρὸς δέουσαν ἐπέξοδον). ὑπάγεις ἐπ᾽ ἄρχοντα *you are going before the magistrate* Lk 12: 58; cf. Ac 16: 19. ἤγαγον αὐτὸν ἐπὶ τὸν Πιλᾶτον Lk 23: 1. ἐπὶ τοὺς ἀρχιερεῖς Ac 9: 21. ἐ. Καίσαρα πορεύεσθαι *come before the emperor* 25: 12. ἐ. τὰς συναγωγάς Lk 12: 11. ἐ. τὸ βῆμα Ac 18: 12.

δ. of motion that takes a particular direction *to, toward* ἐκτείνας τ. χεῖρα ἐ. τοὺς μαθητάς Mt 12: 49; cf. Lk 22: 53. πορεύεσθαι ἐ. τὸ ἀπολωλός *go after the one that is lost* 15: 4. ἐ. τὴν Ἄσσον *in the direction of Assos* Ac 20: 13. ἐπιστρέφειν ἐ. τι *turn to someth.* 2 Pt 2: 22 (cf. Pr 26: 11). ὡς ἐ. λῃστήν *as if against a robber* Mt 26: 55; Mk 14: 48; Lk 22: 52. This forms a transition to the next mng.

ε. *against* w. hostile intent (Hdt. 1, 71; X., Hell. 3, 4, 20 al.; Jos., Ant. 13, 331; LXX) ὥρμησαν ἐ. αὐτόν Ac 7: 57. ἔρχεσθαι Lk 14: 31. ἐπαναστήσονται τέκνα ἐ. γονεῖς Mt 10: 21; cf. 24: 7; Mk 13: 8, 12. ἐφ᾽ ἑαυτόν *divided against himself* Mt 12: 26; Mk 3: 24f, 26; Lk 11: 17f; cf. J 13: 18 (s. Ps 40: 10); Ac 4: 27; 13: 50 al.

ζ. answering the question 'where?' (Hom.+; LXX) *on, over someth.* καθεύδειν ἐπί τι *sleep on someth.* Mk 4: 38. καθῆσθαι ἐπί τι *sit on someth.* J 12: 15; Rv 4: 4; 6: 2; 11: 16 al.; cf. Lk 21: 35b; κεῖσθαι ἐπί τι *lie upon someth.* 2 Cor 3: 15. κατακεῖσθαι Lk 5: 25. ἑστηκέναι ἐ. τὸν αἰγιαλόν *stand on the shore* Mt 13: 2; cf. Rv 14: 1. σκηνοῦν ἐ. τινα *spread a tent over someone* Rv 7: 15. ἐ. τὴν δεξιάν *at the right hand* 5: 1. λίθος ἐ. λίθον *stone upon stone* Mt 24: 2. ἐπὶ τὸ αὐτό *at the same place, together* (Ps.-X., Respublica Athen. [The Old Oligarch] 2, 2; Pla., Rep. p. 329A; Dit., Syll.³ 736, 66 [92 BC]. In pap.= 'in all': PTebt. 14, 20 [114 BC]; PFay. 102, 6.—2 Km 2: 13) εἶναι ἐ. τὸ αὐτό *be together* Ac 17: 35; Ac 1: 15; 2: 1, 44 v.l. In 1 Cor 7: 5 it is a euphemistic expr. for sexual union. κατοικεῖν ἐπὶ τὸ αὐτό *live in the same place* (Dt 25: 5) Hm 5, 1, 4. Also w. verbs of motion (Sus 14 Theod.) συνέρχεσθαι ἐπὶ τὸ αὐτό *come together to the same place* 1 Cor 11: 20; 14: 23; cf. B 4: 10. συνάγεσθαι (Phlegon of Tralles [Hadr.]: 257 fgm. 36 III 9 Jac.; Jos., Bell. 2, 346) Mt 22: 34; Ac 4: 26 (Ps 2: 2); 1 Cl 34: 7. ἐπὶ τὸ αὐτό μίγνυσθαι *be mixed together* Hm 10, 3, 3. προσετίθει ἐπὶ τὸ αὐτό *added to their number* Ac 2: 47.—*At, by, near someone* or *someth.* καθῆσθαι ἐ. τὸ τελώνιον *sit at the tax-office* Mt 9: 9; Mk 2: 14. ἑστηκέναι ἐ. τὴν θύραν *stand at the door* Rv 3: 20. ἐφ᾽ ὑμᾶς *among you* 2 Th 1: 10; cf. Ac 1: 21.—Of pers., *over whom someth.* is done ὀνομάζειν τὸ ὄνομα Ἰησοῦ ἐπί τινα *speak the name of Jesus over someone* Ac 19: 13. ἐπικαλεῖν τὸ ὄνομά τινος ἐπί τινα (Jer 14: 9; 2 Ch 7: 14; 2 Macc 8: 15) Ac 15: 17 (Am 9: 12); Js 2: 7; Hs 8, 6, 4. προσεύχεσθαι ἐπί τινα *pray over someone* Js 5: 14.

b. fig.—a. *over* of power, rule, control *over someone* or *someth.* (X., Hell. 3, 4, 20 al.; Dionys. Byz. §56 θεῷ ἐπὶ πάντα δύναμις; LXX) βασιλεύειν ἐπί τινα *rule over someone* (Gen 37: 8; Judg 9: 15 B al.) Lk 1: 33; 19: 14, 27; Ro 5: 14. καθιστάναι τινὰ ἐπί τινα *set someone over someone* (X., Cyr. 4, 5, 58) κριτὴν ἐφ᾽ ὑμᾶς *as judge over you* Lk 12: 14; ἡγούμενον ἐπ᾽ Αἴγυπτον Ac 7: 10; cf. Hb 2: 7 v.l. (Ps 8: 7); 3: 6; 10: 21. ἐξουσίαν ἔχειν ἐπί τι Rv 16: 9. ἐξουσίαν διδόναι ἐπί τι (Sir 33: 20) Lk 9: 1; 10: 19; Rv 6: 8; cf. 22: 14. φυλάσσειν φυλακὰς ἐπί τι Lk 2: 8. ὑπεραίρεσθαι ἐπί τινα *exalt oneself above someone* 2 Th

2: 4 (cf. Da 11: 36); but here the mng. *against* is also poss. (s. above aε). πιστὸς ἐ. τι *faithful over someth.* Mt 25: 21, 23.

β. *to* of additions to someth. already present Mt 6: 27; Lk 12: 25; Rv 22: 18a. λύπην ἐ. λύπην *sorrow upon sorrow* Phil 2: 27 (cf. Is 28: 10, 13; Ezk 7: 26; Ps 68: 28).

γ. *on, upon, to, over* of powers, conditions, etc., which come upon someone or under whose influence he finds himself. ἐγένετο ῥῆμα θεοῦ ἐ. Ἰωάννην *the word of God came to John* Lk 3: 2 (cf. Jer 1: 1). Of divine blessings Mt 10: 13; 12: 28; Lk 10: 6; 11: 20; cf. 10: 9; Ac 10: 10. ἵνα ἐπισκηνώσῃ ἐπ' ἐμὲ ἡ δύναμις τ. Χριστοῦ *that the power of Christ may rest upon me* 2 Cor 12: 9. χάρις θεοῦ ἦν ἐπ' αὐτό Lk 2: 40. Various verbs are used of the Holy Spirit in connection w. ἐπί τινα: ἐκχεῖσθαι Ac 2: 17f (Jo 3: 1f); cf. 10: 45; Tit 3: 6. ἐξαποστέλλεσθαι Lk 24: 49. ἐπέρχεσθαι 1: 35; Ac 1: 8. ἐμπίπτειν 10: 44. καταβαίνειν Lk 3: 22; J 1: 33. τίθεσθαι Mt 12: 18 (cf. Is 42: 1). Also εἶναι Lk 2: 25. μένειν J 1: 32f. ἀναπαύεσθαι 1 Pt 4: 14. Of unpleasant or startling experiences Lk 1: 12, 65; 4: 36; Ac 13: 11; 19: 17; Rv 11: 11.—Lk 19: 43; 21: 35, cf. vs. 34; J 18: 4; Eph 5: 6; cf. Rv 3: 3.—Ro 2: 2, 9; 15: 3 (Ps 68: 10). Of the blood of the righteous, that comes *over* or *upon* the murderers Mt 23: 35; 27: 25; Ac 5: 28. Of care, which one casts *on* someone else 1 Pt 5: 7 (Ps 54: 23).

δ. *to, toward* of the goal ἐπιστρέφειν, ἐπιστρέφεσθαι ἐπί τινα *turn to* (Dt 30: 10; 31: 20 al.) Lk 1: 17; Ac 9: 35; 11: 21; 14: 15; 26: 20; Gal 4: 9; 1 Pt 2: 25.

ε. *in, on, for, toward* of feelings, actions, etc. directed toward a pers. or thing: after words that express belief, trust, hope πιστεύειν ἐ. τινα (Wsd 12: 2) Ac 9: 42; 11: 17; 16: 31; 22: 19; Ro 4: 24. πίστις Hb 6: 1. πεποιθέναι (Is 58: 14) Mt 27: 43; 2 Th 3: 4; 2 Cor 2: 3. ἐλπίζειν (1 Ch 5: 20; 2 Ch 13: 18 al.) 1 Pt 1: 13; 1 Ti 5: 5. After words that characterize an emotion or its expression *for* κόπτεσθαι (Zech 12: 10) Rv 1: 7; 18: 9. σπλαγχνίζεσθαι Mt 15: 32; Mk 8: 2; 9: 22; Hm 4, 3, 5; s 9, 24, 2. χρηστός *toward* Lk 6: 35. χρηστότης Ro 11: 22; Eph 2: 7; cf. Ro 9: 23. Esp. also if the feelings or their expressions are of a hostile nature *toward, against* ἀποτομία Ro 11: 22. μαρτύριον Lk 9: 5. μάρτυς ἐ. τ. ἐμὴν ψυχὴν *a witness against my soul* (cf. Dssm., LO 258; 355 [LAE 304; 417]) 2 Cor 1: 23. ἀσχημονεῖν 1 Cor 7: 36. μοιχᾶσθαι Mk 10: 11. τολμᾶν 2 Cor 10: 2. βρύχειν τ. ὀδόντας Ac 7: 54.

ζ. to introduce the person or thing by reason of whom (or which) someth. happens, *on* ὁ ἄνθρωπος ἐφ' ὃν γεγόνει τὸ σημεῖον *the man on whom the miracle had been performed* Ac 4: 22. ἐφ' ὃν λέγεται ταῦτα *the one about whom this was said* Hb 7: 13. γέγραπται ἐπ' αὐτόν Mk 9: 12f. Cf. Ro 4: 9; 1 Ti 1: 18; βάλλειν κλῆρον ἐ. τι *for someth.* Mk 15: 24; J 19: 24 (Ps 21: 19).

η. of purpose, goal, result ἐ. τὸ βάπτισμα *for baptism* = to have themselves baptised Mt 3: 7. ἐ. τὴν θεωρίαν ταύτην *for* (i.e. to see) *this sight* Lk 23: 48 (sim. Hom.+; POxy. 294, 18 [22 AD]; LXX). ἐ. τὸ συμφέρον *to* (*our*) *advantage* Hb 12: 10. ἐ. σφαγήν Ac 8: 32 (Is 53: 7). Cf. Mt 22: 5; ἐ. τ. τελειότητα Hb 6: 1. ἐ. τοῦτο *for this* (X., An. 2, 5, 22; Jos., Ant. 12, 23) Lk 4: 43. ἐφ' ὅ; *for what* (*reason*)? Mt 26: 50 v.l. (s. ὅς 2a and 9b).

2. of time—a. answering the question 'when?' ἐ. τὴν αὔριον *on the next day* (Sb 6011, 14 [I BC]; PRyl. 441 ἐπὶ τὴν ἐπαύριον) Lk 10: 35; Ac 4: 5. ἐ. τὴν ὥραν τ. προσευχῆς *at the hour of prayer* 3: 1 (Polyaenus 8, 17 ἐπὶ ὥραν ὡρισμένην).

b. of extension over a period of time *for, over a period of* (Hom.+; BGU 1058, 9 [13 BC]; POxy. 275, 9; 15 ἐ. τὸν ὅλον χρόνον; PTebt. 381, 19 ἐφ' ὃν χρόνον περίεστιν ἡ

μήτηρ; LXX; Jos., Ant. 11, 2; Test. Judah 3: 4) ἐ. ἔτη τρία *for three years* (Phlegon: 257 fgm. 36, 2, 1 Jac.) Lk 4: 25. ἐ. τρεῖς ἡμέρας *for three days* (Diod. S. 13, 19, 2; Arrian, Anab. 4, 9, 4; Dialekt-Inschr. 4706, 119 [Thera] ἐπ' ἁμέρας τρεῖς) GP 8: 30 al. ἐ. ἡμέρας πλείους *over a period of many days* (Jos., Ant. 4, 277) Ac 13: 31.—16: 18 (ἐπὶ πολλὰς ἡμέρας as Appian, Liby. 29 §124; cf. Diod. S. 3, 16, 4); 17: 2; 19: 8, 10, 34; 27: 20; Hb 11: 30. ἐ. χρόνον *for a while* (cf. Il. 2, 299; Hdt. 9, 22; Apollon. Rhod. 4, 1257; Jos., Vi. 2) Lk 18: 4. ἐ. πλείονα χρόνον (Diod. S. 3, 16, 6; Hero Alex. I p. 344, 17) Ac 18: 20. ἐφ' ὅσον χρόνον *as long as* Ro 7: 1; 1 Cor 7: 39; Gal 4: 1. Also ἐφ' ὅσον *as long as* Mt 9: 15; 2 Pt 1: 13 (for other mngs. of ἐφ' ὅσον s. below under 3). ἐφ' ἱκανόν (sc. χρόνον) *for a considerable time* (Ep. Arist. 109) Ac 20: 11. ἐπὶ πολύ *for a long time, throughout a long period of time* (Thu. 1, 7; 1, 18, 1; 2, 16, 1 al.; Lucian, Toxar. 20; Wsd 18: 20; Sir 49: 13; Jos., Vi. 66) Ac 28: 6. ἐπὶ πλεῖον *the same* (schol. on Pind., Nem. 7, 56b; PLille 3, 16 [III BC]; Jdth 13: 1; Sir prol. l. 7; Jos., Ant. 18, 150) Ac 20: 9; *any longer* (Lucian, Dial. Deor. 5, 3; Appian, Hann. 54 §227; 3 Macc 5: 18; Wsd 8: 12) Ac 24: 4; 1 Cl 55: 1.

3. w. indications of number and measure (Hdt. et. al.; LXX) ἐ. τρίς (CIG 1122, 9; PHolm. 1, 18) *three times* Ac 10: 16; 11: 10. So also ἐπὶ πολύ *more than once* Hm 4, 1, 8. ἐπὶ πολύ (also written ἐπιπολύ) in a different sense *to a great extent, carefully* (Hdt., Thu.+; Lucian, Dial. Deor. 6, 2; 25, 2; 3 Macc 5: 17; Jos., Ant. 17, 107) B 4: 1. ἐπὶ πλεῖον *to a greater extent, further* (Hdt., Thu.+; Diod. S. 11, 60, 5 al.; prob. 2 Macc 12: 36; Test. Gad 7: 2) 2 Ti 3: 9; 1 Cl 18: 3; 2 Cl 50: 4). ἐπὶ τὸ χεῖρον 2 Ti 3: 13. ἐφ' ὅσον *to the degree that, in so far as* (Diod. S. 1, 93, 2; Maximus Tyr. 11, 3c ἐφ' ὅσον δύναται; Hierocles 14 p. 451) Mt 25: 40, 45; B 4: 11; 17: 1; Ro 11: 13. M-M.

ἐπιβαίνω 2 aor. ἐπέβην; pf. ἐπιβέβηκα (Hom.+; inscr., pap., LXX; Philo, Aet. M. 71; Joseph.; Sib. Or. 5, 127).

1. *go up* or *upon, mount, board* ἐπί τι (Hdt. 8, 120; Thu. 1, 111, 2; 7, 69, 4; X., Hell. 3, 4, 1; Dit., Syll.³ 709, 36 [107 BC]; in all these cases the boarding of ships is involved. Gen 24: 61 ἐπὶ τὰς καμήλους. 1 Km 25: 20, 42 ἐπὶ τὴν ὄνον. Jos., Ant. 11, 258 ἐπὶ τ. ἵππον) ἐπὶ ὄνον Mt 21: 5 (Zech 9: 9). πλοίῳ (Thu. 7, 70, 5) Ac 27: 2. Abs. *go on board, embark* (Thu. 7, 62, 2) 21: 1 D, 2.—So perh. also ἐ. εἰς Ἱεροσόλυμα *embark for Jerusalem* (i.e. to the seaport of Caesarea) vs. 4. But this pass. may also belong to

2. *set foot in* (Hom.+) εἰς τ. Ἀσίαν *set foot in Asia* Ac 20: 18 (cf. Diod. S. 14, 84, 1 εἰς τ. Βοιωτίαν; POxy. 1155, 4 [104 AD] ἰς Ἀλεξάνδρειαν; PFlor. 275, 22). W. dat. (Diod. S. 16, 66, 6) τῇ ἐπαρχείῳ *the province* 25: 1 (cf. Dit., Syll.³ 797, 16 [37 AD] ἐπιβὰς τῇ ἐπαρχείᾳ.—So Ac 25: 1 v.l.). M-M.*

ἐπιβάλλω 2 aor. ἐπέβαλον, 3 pl. ἐπέβαλαν Mk 14: 46; Ac 21: 27 (Mlt.-H. 208) (Hom.+; inscr., pap., LXX, Ep. Arist.; Philo, Leg. All. 3, 57 al.; Joseph., Test. 12 Patr.).

1. act. trans.—a. *throw over* τί τινι: βρόχον *a noose* 1 Cor 7: 35. τί ἐπί τι Rv 18: 19 v.l.

b. *lay on, put on* ἱμάτιον τινι (Lev 19: 19.—Od. 14, 520 χλαῖναν) Mk 11: 7; without the dat. 10: 50 v.l. τὴν χεῖρα *lay the hand* (Dt 15: 10) ἐπί τι *on someth.* Lk 9: 62. τὰς χεῖρας *hands* τινι *on someone* violently (Polyb. 3, 2, 8; 3, 5, 5; Lucian, Tim. 4; UPZ 106, 19 [99 BC]; Jos., Bell. 2, 491; Esth 6: 2) Mk 14: 46; Ac 4: 3. Also ἐπί τινα (PLeid. G 19 [II BC], H 26) Mt 26: 50; Lk 20: 19; 21: 12; J 7: 44 (ἔβαλεν 𝔓75 et al.); Ac 5: 18; 21: 27. The sing. τ. χεῖρα in this connection is rare (Aristoph., Nub. 933, Lysistr. 440;

Gen 22: 12) J 7: 30. ἐ. τὰς χεῖρας foll. by inf. of purpose Ac 12: 1 ἐπίβλημα ἐπὶ ἱματίῳ Mt 9: 16; ἐπὶ ἱμάτιον Lk 5: 36.

2. act. intrans.—**a.** *throw oneself* or *beat upon* (Pla., Phaedr. 248A; 1 Macc 4: 2) τὰ κύματα εἰς τὸ πλοῖον Mk 4: 37.

b. The mng. of καὶ ἐπιβαλὼν ἔκλαιεν Mk 14: 72 is in doubt. Theophylactus offers a choice betw. ἐπικαλυψάμενος τ. κεφαλήν (so ASchlatter, Zürcher Bibel '31; Field, Notes 41-3; but in that case τὸ ἱμάτιον could scarcely be omitted) and ἀρξάμενος, which latter sense is supported by the v.l. ἤρξατο κλαίειν in DΘ, as well as by it., syr. sin. ἐ. can actually have the mng. *begin* (PTebt. 50, 12 [112/11 BC] ἐπιβαλὼν συνέχωσεν= 'he set to and dammed up' [Mlt. 131f]; Diogen. Cyn. in Diog. L. 6, 27 ἐπέβαλε τερετίζειν). Acc. to this the transl. would be *and he began to weep* (EKlostermann; OHoltzmann; JSchniewind; CCD; cf. also Bl-D. §308 and app.). Others (BWeiss; HHoltzmann; 20th Cent.; Weymouth; L-S-J) proceed fr. the expressions ἐ. τὸν νοῦν or τὴν διάνοιαν (Diod. S. 20, 43, 6) and fr. the fact that ἐ. by itself, used w. the dat., can mean *think of* (M. Ant. 10, 30; Plut., Mor. 499E), to the mng. *and he thought of it,* or *when he reflected on it.* Wlh. ad loc. has urged against this view that it is made unnecessary by the preceding ἀνεμνήσθη κτλ. Least probable of all is the equation of ἐπιβαλὼν with ἀποκριθείς (HEwald) on the basis of Polyb. 1, 80, 1; 22, 3, 8; Diod. S. 13, 28, 5 ἐπιβαλὼν ἔφη.

c. *fall to, belong to* τὸ ἐπιβάλλον μέρος *the part that falls* to someone (Diod. S. 14, 17, 5; Dit., Syll.³ 346, 36; 546B, 19; 1106, 80; POxy. 715, 13ff; PFay. 93, 8; cf. Tob 6: 12.—Dssm., NB 57 [BS 230]) Lk 15: 12 (JDMDerrett, Law in the NT '70, 106). Impers. ἐπιβάλλει τινί *someone has opportunity* or *it is proper for someone* (Polyb. 18, 51, 1; Dit., Or. 443, 10; UPZ 110, 10 [164 BC] πᾶσιν ἐπιβάλλει; Tob 3: 17; Jos., Bell. 1, 434, Ant. 19, 6) Pol 1: 1.

3. mid. *throw oneself upon someth., take someth. upon oneself, undertake* w. acc. (Thu. 6, 40, 2; UPZ 41, 26 [161/0 BC] πᾶν ὃ ἂν ἐπιβάλληαθε) πρᾶξιν Hm 10, 2, 2. πολλά s 6, 3, 5. M-M.*

ἐπιβαρέω 1 aor. ἐπεβάρησα *weigh down, burden* (Dionys. Hal. 4, 9; 8, 73; Appian, Bell. Civ. 4, 15 §60; 4, 31 §133; Kyr.-Inschr. l. 8; Dit., Syll.³ 807, 16 [c. 54 AD]; POxy. 1481, 12 [II AD]; POsl. 60, 8) τινά *someone* πρὸς τὸ μὴ ἐπιβαρῆσαί τινα ὑμῶν *that I might not be a burden to any of you* 1 Th 2: 9; 2 Th 3: 8. ἵνα μὴ ἐπιβαρῶ 2 Cor 2: 5 seems to have the mng. 'in order not to heap up too great a burden of words'= *in order not to say too much* (Heinrici; Schmiedel; Ltzm.; H-DWendland), although there are no exx. of it in this mng. Other possibilities are *exaggerate, be too severe with.* M-M.*

ἐπιβιβάζω 1 aor. ἐπεβίβασα *put someone* (τινά) *on* someth., *cause someone to mount* (Thu.+; LXX) *put Jesus* ἐπὶ τ. πῶλον Lk 19: 35 (cf. ET 42, '31, 236f; 288; 381f; 382f; 526f); cf. Ac 23: 24. τινὰ ἐπὶ τὸ ἴδιον κτῆνος *on his own animal* Lk 10: 34 (cf. 3 Km 1: 33; but ἐπιβ. ἐπί can also mean *load upon* [2 Km 6: 3], assuming that the man was unconscious).*

ἐπιβλέπω 1 aor. ἐπέβλεψα (Soph., Pla.+; LXX; Ep. Arist.; Jos., Ant. 12, 58; Test. 12 Patr.) *look at, gaze upon* of God ἐν ταῖς ἀβύσσοις *look into the depths* 1 Cl 59: 3 (cf. Sir 16: 19; Da 3: 55 Theod.); *look at, consider, care about* Js 2: 3. Of God's loving care, that looks upon someone or someth. (LXX; cf. Jos., Ant. 1, 20; PGM 13, 621) ἐπί τινα 1 Cl 13: 4 (Is 66: 2). ἐπί τι: ἐπὶ τὴν

ταπείνωσιν *upon the humble station* Lk 1: 48 (cf. 1 Km 1: 11; 9: 16). Also of Jesus *look at,* i.e. take an interest in ἐπὶ τὸν υἱόν μου Lk 9: 38. M-M.*

ἐπίβλημα, ατος, τό (Plut., Arrian et al.; as a piece of clothing used as a covering as early as Dit., Syll.³ 1218, 4 [c. 420 BC], also Is 3: 22) *a patch* Mt 9: 16; Mk 2: 21; Lk 5: 36. M-M.*

ἐπιβοάω (act. Aeschyl., Thu.+; IG IV² 1, 742, 6 [II/III AD]; 4 Macc 6: 4) *cry out loudly* (Heraclit. Sto. 6 p. 9, 15) of an aroused mob (Jos., Bell. 4, 283 ἐπεβόα πλῆθος, Ant. 11, 57) Ac 25: 24 t.r.; MPol 3; 12: 2f. M-M.*

ἐπιβουλή, ῆς, ἡ (Hdt., Thu.+; UPZ 8, 14 [161 BC]; POxy. 237 VI, 6; 31; LXX, Philo, Joseph.) *a plot* εἴς τινα *against someone* (Jos., Ant. 2, 197; 16, 319) Ac 23: 30. Also τινί 20: 3. ἡ ἐ. αὐτῶν *their plot* 9: 24. Pl. (Epict. 1, 22, 14; 1 Esdr 5: 70; 2 Macc 8: 7 v.l.) ἐν ταῖς ἐ. τῶν Ἰουδαίων *through the plots of the Jews* 20: 19. M-M.*

ἐπιγαμβρεύω *become related by marriage* (schol. on Eur., Orest. 585-604, Phoen. 347; LXX), then *marry as next of kin,* usu. brother-in-law of levirate marriage γυναῖκα Mt 22: 24 (Dt 25: 5 Aq.; cf. Gen 38: 8 v.l. [ARahlfs, Genesis '26, 159]). For the word cf. Anz 378; for the idea KHRengstorf, Jebamot '29. M-M.*

ἐπίγειος, ον (Pla.+; Philo; Jos., Ant. 6, 186; 8, 44) *earthly.*

1. adj., in contrast to the heavenly (Plut., Mor. 566D; M. Ant. 6, 30, 4 ἐ. ζωή; pap.; Test. Jud. 21: 4) σῶμα 1 Cor 15: 40 (opp. ἐπουράνιος; on this contrast s. below 2b and MEDahl, Resurrection of the Body '62, 113–16). Of the body οἰκία ἐ. *earthly dwelling* (cf. Philo, Cher. 101) 2 Cor 5: 1 (EEEllis, Paul and his Recent Interpreters '61, 40–43). W. the connotation of weakness (Lucian, Icarom. 2): σοφία *earthly wisdom*= human philosophy Js 3: 15; cf. εὕρημα ἐ. *an earthly* (i.e. *purely human) discovery* Dg 7: 1. πνεῦμα ἐ. *earthly spirit* of the spirit in false prophets Hm 9: 11; 11: 6, 11f, 14, 17, 19.

2. subst.—**a.** τὰ ἐ. (M. Ant. 7, 48; Philo, Op. M. 101; 113.—Opp. τὰ ἐπουράνια as Herm. Wr. fgm. 26 p. 544, 1 Sc. Cf. Philo, Op. M. 117) *earthly things* J 3: 12 (LBrun, Symb. Osl. 8, '29, 57–77); cf. Pol 2: 1; Dg 7: 2. τὰ ἐ. φρονεῖν *think only of earthly things* Phil 3: 19.

b. οἱ ἐ.: in the expr. πᾶν γόνυ ἐπουρανίων καὶ ἐπιγείων καὶ καταχθονίων Phil 2: 10 the second of the three main concepts (cf. PGM 4, 225f; 3038ff, esp. 3042f πᾶν πνεῦμα δαιμόνιον . . . ἐπουράνιον ἢ ἀέριον εἴτε ἐπίγειον εἴτε ὑπόγειον ἢ καταχθόνιον. 5, 167 πᾶς δαίμων οὐράνιος κ. αἰθέριος κ. ἐπίγειος κ. ὑπόγειος. 12, 67 θεοὶ οὐράνιοι κ. ἐπίγειοι κ. ἀέριοι κ. ἐπιχθόνιοι. 17a, 3 Ἄνουβι, θεὲ ἐπίγειε κ. ὑπόγειε κ. οὐράνιε. Fluchtaf. 4, 11); cf. ITr 9: 1.—IEph 13: 2 it is impossible to say w. certainty from which nom. ἐπιγείων is derived, ἐπίγειοι or ἐπίγεια. M-M.*

ἐπιγελάω fut. ἐπιγελάσομαι (Pla., X.+; LXX) *laugh* τινί *at someth.* (Jos., Bell. 1, 233 ταῖς ἐλπίσιν) ἐ. τῇ ὑμετέρᾳ ἀπωλείᾳ *at your destruction* 1 Cl 57: 4 (Pr 1: 26).*

ἐπιγίνομαι 2 aor. ἐπεγενόμην (Hom.+; inscr., pap., LXX; Philo, Aet. M. 20 al.) of wind *come up* (Thu. 3, 74, 2; 4, 30, 2; Diod. S. 18, 20, 7 ἐπιγενομένου μεγάλου πνεύματος; Jos., Ant. 9, 209) Ac 28: 13. Of the night *come on* (Hdt. 8, 70 al.; Arrian, Anab. 1, 2, 7 νὺξ ἐπιγενομένη; 2, 11, 5; Polyaenus 3, 7, 3 al.; Jos., Ant. 1, 301) 27: 27 v.l. M-M.*

ἐπιγινώσκω fut. ἐπιγνώσομαι; 2 aor. ἐπέγνων; pf. ἐπέγνωκα; 1 aor. pass. ἐπεγνώσθην (Hom.+; Herm. Wr. 9, 4a [θεόν]; inscr., pap., LXX, En., Ep. Arist., Philo, Joseph., Test. 12 Patr.) *know, understand, recognize.*

1. with the preposition making its influence felt—
a. *know exactly, completely, through and through* τὶ someth. (Jos., Ant. 20, 128 τ. ἀλήθειαν) τ. ἀσφάλειαν Lk 1:4. τ. δικαίωμα τ. θεοῦ Ro 1:32. τ. χάριν τ. θεοῦ Col 1:6 (here ἐ. is the second stage after ἀκούειν; cf. IEph 4:2). Abs. 1 Cor 13:12a (opp. γινώσκειν ἐκ μέρους); PK 3 p. 15, 27. Pass. 1 Cor 13:12b; 2 Cor 6:9.
b. *recognize, know again* τινά someone Lk 24:16, 31. τὶ someth. Ac 12:14 (τ. φωνήν τινος as 1 Km 26:17; Judg 18:3). W. acc. of the pers. and ὅτι foll. 3:10; 4:13.
c. *acknowledge, give recognition* τινά (to) someone (Chio, Ep. 6; Ruth 2:10, 19) Mt 17:12 (mng. 1b is also poss.); 1 Cor 16:18.
2. with no emphasis on the prep., essentially=γινώσκειν (X., Hell. 5, 4, 12 cf. with 6, 5, 17; Thu. 1, 132, 5; Dit., Syll.³ 741, 21; 747, 30; PFay. 112, 14; PTebt. 297, 9 al.; Ep. Arist. 246; Sib. Or. 3, 96).
a. *know* abs. Dg 10:3. τινά Mt 11:27 (the parallel Lk 10:22 has the simple verb γιν.), s. on παραδίδωμι 3, end; 14:35; Mk 6:54; Hv 5:3. τὶ Ac 27:39. τὴν ἀλήθειαν 1 Ti 4:3; cf. 1 Cl 32:1; Hs 8, 6, 3; 8, 11, 2. τινὰ ἀπό τινος *someone by someth.* (cf. Sir 19:29) Mt 7:16, 20 (the parallel Lk 6:44 has the simplex). ἐ. μέλη ὄντας *recognize that you are members* IEph 4:2. W. ὅτι foll. Ac 19:34. W. acc. and ὅτι foll. 1 Cor 14:37; 2 Cor 13:5; Hv 5:4. Pass. w. indir. quest. foll. Hs 4:3.
b. *learn, find out* (Jos., Vi. 181) abs. Mk 6:33 (v.l. ἔγνωσαν). W. ὅτι foll. (1 Macc 6:17) Lk 7:37; 23:7; Ac 22:29; 28:1. Also as legal t.t. *ascertain* (2 Macc 14:9) τὶ 23:28; cf. 24:8. W. ὅτι foll. Ac 24:11. W. relative clause foll. 22:24.
c. *notice, perceive, learn of* abs. Ac 9:3; (Field, Notes 117f). τὶ Lk 5:22. τὶ ἐν ἑαυτῷ *perceive someth. (in oneself)* Mk 5:30 (the parallel Lk 8:46 has the simplex). W. ὅτι foll. Lk 1:22. τῷ πνεύματι, ὅτι *perceive (in one's own mind) that* Mk 2:8.
d. *understand, know* τὶ or τινά 2 Cor 1:13f (here the intensifying ἕως τέλους causes ἐ. to equal the simple verb). τὸ ἀληθῶς ζῆν *know the true life* Dg 10:7. σὺ κάλλιον ἐπιγινώσκεις *you know very well* Ac 25:10 (the influence of the adverb causes the compound to sink to the level of the simplex, as PLond. 354, 23 [c. 10 BC] ἐπιγνόντα ἀκρειβῶς ἕκαστα).
e. *learn to know* abs. 2 Pt 2:21b. τὶ someth. (Herodian 2, 1, 10) 2:21a; Hm 6, 2, 6; s 9, 16, 7; PK 4 p. 16, 1. περὶ τινος someone IRo 10:2. M-M.**

ἐπίγνωσις, εως, ἡ (Philo Mech. 59, 2; Polyb. 3, 7, 6; 3, 31, 4; Diod. S. 3, 38, 2; Epict. 2, 20, 21; Plut., Mor. 1145A; Herodian 7, 6, 7; pap. [Mayser 438; PTebt. 28, 11—c. 114 BC]; LXX, Ep. Arist., Philo) *knowledge, recognition* in our lit. limited to relig. and moral things (Hierocles 22 p. 467). W. gen. of the thing known (Diod. S. 3, 56, 5 τῶν ἄστρων ἐ.) δόξης ὀνόματος αὐτοῦ 1 Cl 59:2 (here ἀγνωσία as a contrast to ἐπίγν.). (τῆς) ἀληθείας a *knowledge of the truth* (Epict. 2, 20, 21; Philo, Omn. Pr. L. 74.—MDibelius, Ἐπίγνωσις ἀληθείας: GHeinrici-Festschr. '14, 178–89) 1 Ti 2:4; 2 Ti 2:25; 3:7; Tit 1:1; Hb 10:26 (for the expr. εἰς ἐπίγνωσιν ἔρχεσθαι in 1 Ti 2:4; 2 Ti 3:7 cf. 2 Macc 9:11). ἁμαρτίας *consciousness of sin* Ro 3:20. τοῦ μυστηρίου τ. θεοῦ Col 2:2. τοῦ θελήματος αὐτοῦ 1:9. παντὸς ἀγαθοῦ Phlm 6 (cf. Herm. Wr. 3, 3b ἀγαθῶν ἐ.; Ep. Arist. 139). W. gen. of the pers.

known ἐ. τοῦ θεοῦ *knowledge of God* (Pr 2:5; Hos 4:1; cf. also WLKnox, St. Paul and the Church of the Gentiles '39, 150 n. 1) Col 1:10; 2 Pt 1:2; cf. Eph 1:17; 2 Pt 1:3; Dg 10:1. Also ἡ περὶ σου ἐ. MPol 14:1; ἐ. τοῦ υἱοῦ τοῦ θεοῦ Eph 4:13; cf. 2 Pt 1:8; 2:20. Knowledge of God and Christ 2 Pt 1:2; but legal terminology may be reflected here (=cognitio), cf. PTebt. 28, 11 πρὸς τὸ μὴ ἕκαστα ὑπ' ἐπίγνωσιν ἀχθῆναι [114 BC]; Dit., Syll.³ 826D, 16f. Abs. (cf. Hos 4:6) θεὸν ἔχειν ἐν ἐ. *to recognize God* Ro 1:28; (w. αἴσθησις) Phil 1:9; ἀνακαινούμενος εἰς ἐ. *renewed in knowledge* Col 3:10. κατ' ἐπίγνωσιν *in accordance w. (real) knowledge* Ro 10:2. M-M.*

ἐπιγραφή, ῆς, ἡ (Thu.+; inscr., pap., Philo; Jos., Ant. 15, 272) *inscription, superscription* of the 'titulus' fastened to the cross (cf. Sueton., Calig. 32, Domit. 10; Cass. Dio 54, 3; Euseb., H.E. 5, 1, 44) ἐ. τῆς αἰτίας Mk 15:26. ἦν ἐ. ἐπ' αὐτῷ Lk 23:38. Of the legends on coins Mt 22:20; Mk 12:16; Lk 20:24. M-M.*

ἐπιγράφω fut. ἐπιγράψω; pf. pass. ἐπιγέγραμμαι; plpf. pass. ἐπεγεγράμμην; 2 aor. pass. ἐπεγράφην (Hom.+; inscr., pap., LXX, Philo; Jos., Ant. 4, 213, C. Ap. 1, 46) *write on* or *in.*

1. lit. ὀνόματα ἐπιγεγραμμένα Rv 21:12. ἦν ἡ ἐπιγραφή . . . ἐπιγεγραμμένη *the inscription . . . placed over him* Mk 15:26; cf. GP 4:11 (cf. Ael. Aristid. 50, 46 K.=26 p. 516 D.: ἐπίγραμμα ἐπιγέγραπται). Of a dedicatory inscr. on an altar βωμὸς ἐν ᾦ ἐπεγέγραπτο (for ἐ. ἐν cf. Dit., Syll.³ 89, 24 ἐν τῇ στήλη; 27; ²588, 139; POxy. 886, 16) Ac 17:23 (cf. Dit., Syll.³ 814, 48 . . . βωμόν, ἐπιγράφοντας . . .). ῥάβδους ἐπιγεγραμμένας ἑκάστης φυλῆς κατ' ὄνομα *rods marked w. the name of each tribe* 1 Cl 43:2 (for the constr. ἐ. τί τινος cf. Plut., Mor. 400E; for the idea Num 17:16ff.—Diod. S. 13, 106, 9 a staff with an ἐπιγραφή). *Enroll* εἰς τὰς βίβλους τῶν ζώντων Hs 2:9.
2. fig. *write in* or *on* ἐπί τι (cf. Dit., Syll.³ 957, 68; 82; 1168, 7) ἐπὶ καρδίας Hb 8:10 (Jer 38:33 v.l.; cf. Pr 7:3). ἐπὶ τὴν διάνοιαν 10:16. ἔργω ἐπιγράφεσθαι *to be engaged in a work* (Socrat., Ep. 7, 2 μου εἰπόντος, ὡς οὐκ ἂν . . . ἔργω ἐπιγραφείην ἀδίκως; Appian, Bell. Civ. 1, 70 §323 ἔργοις ἐπιγράφεσθαι=take part in) οὔτε . . . κρείττονι ἔργω ἔχετε ἐπιγραφῆναι *and you can not be engaged in any better work* IRo 2:1. M-M.*

ἔπιδε s. ἐπεῖδον.

ἐπιδείκνυμι fut. ἐπιδείξω; 1 aor. ἐπέδειξα (Pind., Hdt. +; inscr., pap., LXX, Ep. Arist., Philo, Joseph.).

1. *show, point out* τινί τι someth. to someone (Jos., Ant. 10, 31) Mt 22:19; 24:1; MPol 1:1. ἐ. ἑαυτόν τινι *show oneself to someone* Lk 17:14 (Appian, Mithrid. 89 §407 Ἀλέξανδρος αὐτὸν ἐπέδειξεν). ἐ. τινὶ σημεῖον ἐκ. τ. οὐρανοῦ *show someone (=do in someone's presence) a sign from heaven* Mt 16:1. Also the mid. in the same mng. show τ. φυλάρχοις τὰς σφραγῖδας (cf. Dit., Syll.³ 1157, 46f) 1 Cl 43:5. The mid. is found in a special sense Ac 9:39 ἐπιδεικνύμεναι χιτῶνας, where the women *show* the garments *on themselves,* i.e., as they are wearing them (Socrat., Ep. 23, 3 τοιαῦτα ἐπιδεικνύμενοι='show such things on oneself').
2. fig.—a. *represent* (Pla., X., Symp. 3, 3 al.) τὸ ψεῦδός μου ἀληθὲς ἐπέδειξα *my lies I represented as truth* Hm 3:3.
b. *demonstrate, show* (Aristoph., Pla. et al.; Herm. Wr. 4, 7; PGiess. 2 I, 24; LXX, esp. 4 Macc) τὶ someth., *give proof* Hb 6:17. ἐ. ἑαυτόν *reveal oneself* Dg 8:5; cf. vs. 6. τινί w. indir. quest. foll. B 6:13. W. ὅτι foll. (Philo, Agr.

22) 5: 7. W. διά τινος (Jos., C. Ap. 2, 1 διὰ τοῦ βιβλίου) and acc. foll. Ac 18: 28. Likew. the mid. oft. Philo) 1 Cl 24: 1. W. ὅτι foll. MPol 2: 2. M-M.**

ἐπιδέομαι (Hdt.+; LXX; Jos., C. Ap. 2, 192) *need, be in need* τινός (*of*) *a thing* (Alex. Aphr., An. Mant. II 1 p. 163, 1 οὐδενὸς ἐπιδεῖται=needs nothing; UPZ 59, 22 [108 BC] πάντων; Job 6: 22) τῆς προσευχῆς καὶ ἀγάπης IMg 14. Of God οὐ τὰ πάντα ἐπιδέεται PK 2. οἱ ἐπιδεόμενοι *those in need* (Sir 34: 21) Dg 10: 6.*

ἐπιδέχομαι (Hdt.+; inscr., pap., LXX, Ep. Arist., Philo; Jos., Vi. 218).
   1. *receive as a guest* τινά *someone* (Polyb. 21, 18, 3; POxy. 281, 9 [20–50 AD]; 1 Macc 10: 1; 12: 8, 43 al.; Sib. Or. 7, 130) 3 J 10.—*Take along* Ac 15: 40 D.
   2. *accept*=not reject (Polyb. 6, 24, 4; UPZ 110, 161 [164 BC]; 1 Macc 10: 46; Sir 51: 26) τινά *recognize someone's authority* 3 J 9. M-M.*

ἐπιδημέω (Thu.+; inscr., pap., Joseph.)—**1.** *stay in a place as a stranger* or *visitor, be in town* (X., Pla. al.; Jos., Vi. 200 Γαλιλαῖον ἐπιδημοῦντα τοῖς Ἱεροσολύμοις; UPZ 42 I, 4 ἐν Μέμφει. Cf. Wilcken, APF 4, '08, 374; 422) οἱ ἐπιδημοῦντες Ῥωμαῖοι Ac 2: 10. οἱ ἐ. ξένοι 17: 21 (Inschr. v. Priene 108, 286; 111, 187 [I BC] τοὺς ἐπιδεδημηκότας ξένους). ἐν τῇ Ἐφέσῳ ἐπιδημοῦντές τινες Κορίνθιοι *some Corinthians were staying at Ephesus* 18: 27 D.
   2. *return home* (X., Pla.) ὅταν ἐπιδημήσῃς εἰς αὐτήν *when you go home to it* Hs 1: 9. M-M.*

ἐπιδημία, ας, ἡ (X., Pla.+; inscr., pap.; Philo, In Flacc. 33; Jos., Ant. 8, 102; Plut., Mor. 117F) *stay, sojourn* of earthly life ἐ. τῆς σαρκὸς ἐν τῷ κόσμῳ τούτῳ *our stay* (lit. 'the sojourn of our flesh') *in this world* 2 Cl 5: 5.*

ἐπιδιατάσσομαι (only in Christian wr.; cf. OEger, ZNW 18, '18, 92f) legal t.t. *add a codicil* to a will Gal 3: 15.—MConrat, ZNW 5, '04, 215f. M-M.*

ἐπιδίδωμι impf. 3 sing. ἐπεδίδου, 3 pl. ἐπεδίδουν; fut. ἐπιδώσω; 1 aor. ἐπέδωκα. 2 aor. ptc. ἐπιδούς; pf. ἐπιδέδωκα; pf. pass. ptc. ἐπιδεδομένος; 1 aor. pass. ἐπεδόθην (Hom.+; inscr., pap., LXX, Ep. Arist., Philo, Joseph., Test. 12 Patr.).
   1. *give, hand over, deliver* τινί τι someth. to someone (for a meal: Lucian, Symp. 36; Aberciusinschr. 15) a scorpion Lk 11: 12; a stone Mt 7: 9. A snake vs. 10. Cf. Lk 24: 30, 42. Bread vs. 30; cf. J 13: 26 𝔓⁶⁶ et al. A letter Ac 15: 30 (cf. Diod. S. 14, 47, 2; Plut., Alex. 19, 6; PPar. 20, 5; PEleph. 15, 3; Jos., Ant. 15, 170). Abs. *give* Ac 27: 35 v.l.—Hv 3, 2, 5; s 8, 1, 2 and oft. τινὶ τ. χεῖρα Hv 1, 1, 2. Pass. ἐπεδόθη αὐτῷ βιβλίον τοῦ προφήτου Ἡσαΐου *the book of the prophet Isaiah was handed to him* Lk 4: 17 (cf. Jos., Vi. 361 ἐ. τὰ βιβλία).
   2. *give up* or *over, surrender* (Thu. 4, 11, 4; Plut., Mor. 319D; Athen. 12, 29 p. 525E εἰς τρυφήν) ἑαυτόν τινι (Polyaenus 4, 6, 1; Alex. Aphr., Fat. 32, II 2 p. 204, 27; Dit., Or. 730, 7; Jos., Bell. 6, 56, Ant. 4, 42) 1 Cl 14: 2; 2 Cl 9: 7. Abs. ἐπιδόντες ἐφερόμεθα *we gave* (ourselves) *up* (to the wind) *and let ourselves be driven* Ac 27: 15 (cf. Lucian, Hermot. 28 ἐ. ἑαυτὸν τῇ πνεούσῃ). M-M.**

ἐπιδιορθόω (Dialekt-Inschr. 5039, 9 [Crete, II BC]; Themist., Or. 7 p. 113, 14; usu. in Christian wr.). In the only place where it occurs in our lit., both the 1 aor. subj. mid. ἐπιδιορθώσῃ and the 1 aor. subj. act. ἐπιδιορθώσῃς are attested; *set right* or *correct in addition* (to what has already been corrected) τὰ λείποντα *what remains* Tit 1: 5 (cf. Philo, In Flacc. 124 ἡ τῶν λειπομένων ἐπανόρθω-

σις). Simply *correct* is also poss. (Philopon., In Aristot., An. p. 525, 26; 28; 30 Hayduck). M-M.*

ἐπιδύω (w. tmesis Il. 2, 413; otherw. LXX; Philo, Spec. Leg. 3, 152 μὴ ἐπιδυέτω ὁ ἥλιος) *set* (upon) of the sun Eph 4: 26 (Plut., Mor. 488C πρὶν ἢ τὸν ἥλιον δῦναι τὰς δεξιὰς ἐμβαλόντες ἀλλήλοις; s. ἐπί II 2).*

ἐπιείκεια, ας, ἡ (W-H. ἐπιεικία; cf. Mlt.-H. 348) *clemency, gentleness, graciousness* (Thu.; Aristot., Eth. Nic. 5, 14; Ps.-Pla., Def. 412B; Polyb. 1, 14, 4; Herodian 5, 1, 6; inscr., pap., LXX; Philo, Mos. 1, 198; Jos., Ant. 6, 144; 15, 48) IPhld 1: 1. τῇ σῇ ἐ. *with your* (customary) *graciousness* Ac 24: 4. τῇ ἐπιεικείᾳ *by gentleness* IEph 10: 3. W. πραΰτης (Plut., Pericl. 39, 1, Sertor. 25, 6; Appian, Basil. 1 §5; Philo, Op. M. 103) 2 Cor 10: 1; Dg 7: 4; 1 Cl 30: 8; w. μακροθυμία 13: 1; w. ταπεινοφροσύνη 30: 8; 56: 1. μετ' ἐκτενοῦς ἐπιεικείας w. *constant forbearance* 58: 2; 62: 2. ἐν πάσῃ ἐ. θεοῦ ζῶντος w. *all the gentleness of the living God* IPhld 1: 2 (ἐ. as attribute of God, Dio Chrys. 80[30], 19; Wsd 12: 18; Bar 2: 27; Da 3: 42; 2 Macc 2: 22; Ep. Arist. 192; 207).—AvHarnack, 'Sanftmut, Huld u. Demut' in d. alten Kirche: JKaftan-Festschr. '20, 113ff; LHMarshall, Challenge of NT Ethics '47, 305–8; CSpicq, RB 54, '47, 333–9; HPreisker, TW II 585–7. S. πραΰτης, end. M-M.*

ἐπιεικής, ές (Hom.+; inscr., pap. [Mayser 92, 6]; LXX; Ep. Arist.; Philo; Jos., C. Ap. 2, 211. Cf. Mlt.-H. 89; 314; 348) *yielding, gentle, kind* (so Thu.+) w. ἄμαχος 1 Ti 3: 3; Tit 3: 2. W. ἀγαθός perh.=*right-minded* (as Diod. S. 16, 30, 2, while in 16, 32, 2 ἀσεβής is in contrast to ἐπιεικής) 1 Pt 2: 18. W. εἰρηνικός Js 3: 17. W. σώφρων (Hyperid. 6, 5) 1 Cl 1: 2. W. εὔσπλαγχνος 29: 1 (of God, as Ep. Arist. 211).—τὸ ἐπιεικές=ἡ ἐπιείκεια (Thu., Pla. et al.; POxy. 1218, 5; Ep. Arist. 188; Philo, Somn. 295 τὸ τῶν δεσποτῶν ἐ.). τὸ ἐ. ὑμῶν *your forbearing spirit* Phil 4: 5. τὸ ἐ. τῆς γλώσσης αὐτῶν *the gentleness of their tongue* 1 Cl 21: 7.—Neut. of the comp. as adv. (PTebt. 484 [c. 14 AD]; Esth 3: 13b; Jos., Ant. 15, 14) ἐπιεικέστερον λαλεῖν *speak more gently* Hm 12, 4, 2. M-M.*

ἐπιεικία s. ἐπιείκεια.

ἐπιζητέω impf. ἐπεζήτουν; 1 aor. ἐπεζήτησα (Hdt.+; inscr., pap., LXX, Ep. Arist., Philo, Joseph.).
   1. *search for, seek after*—**a.** lit. τινά *someone* (PHamb. 27, 4 [250 BC] αὐτὸν ἐπεζήτουν καὶ οὐχ ηὕρισκον; Jos., Ant. 17, 295) Lk 4: 42; Ac 12: 19.
   b. *inquire, want to know* περὶ τῆς θεότητος *inquire about the Godhead* Hm 10, 1, 4 (w. ἐρευνᾶν). ἐ. τι *want to know someth.* (Philo, Spec. Leg. 1, 46) Ac 19: 39; Hs 6, 4, 1; 9, 16, 1; v 3, 11, 1.
   c. *discuss, debate, dispute* (Aristot., Eth. Nic. 9, 9, 2 p. 1169b, 13 ἐπιζητεῖται πότερον . . . ἤ='it is debated whether . . . or') τὰ ἐπιζητούμενα παρ' ὑμῖν πράγματα *the matters that are in dispute* (or *being discussed*) *among you* 1 Cl 1: 1.
   2. *strive for*—**a.** *wish, wish for* abs. Dg 11: 5. τὶ (Diod. S. 17, 101, 6; Jos., Ant. 6, 149; 14, 407) Mt 6: 32; Lk 12: 30; Ro 11: 7; Phil 4: 17; Hb 11: 14. τὴν μέλλουσαν πόλιν 13: 14 (cf. Is 62: 12). ζωήν Dg 12: 6. W. inf. foll. (Polyb. 3, 57, 7; Diod. S. 19, 8, 4; PTebt. 314, 6) Ac 13: 7; Dg 11: 2. τί ἐπιζητεῖς; *what do you want?* Hs 7: 1.
   b. *demand, desire* (Theophr.+; PLille 7, 6 [III BC]; 1 Macc 7: 13) σημεῖον Mt 12: 39; 16: 4. M-M.*

ἐπιθανάτιος, ον (Dionys. Hal. 7, 35; Bel 31; Etym. Mag. p. 457, 40) *condemned to death* 1 Cor 4: 9.*

ἐπίθες s. ἐπιτίθημι.

ἐπίθεσις, εως, ἡ (Pla., X.+; inscr., pap., LXX, Ep. Arist., Philo; Jos., Ant. 18, 7, Vi. 293) *laying on* (so Plut.) τῶν χειρῶν *the laying on of hands* (Philo, Leg. All. 3, 90, Spec. Leg. 1, 203) Ac 8: 18; 1 Ti 4: 14; 2 Ti 1: 6; Hb 6: 2.—JBehm, D. Handauflegung im Urchristentum '11; HPSmith, AJTh 17, '13, 47ff; JCoppens, L'Imposition des mains et les Rites connexes dans le NT '25; FCabrol, Impos. des mains: Dict. d'Arch. VII, 1, '26, 391ff; NAdler, Taufe u. Handauflegung (AG 8: 14–17) '51; ELohse, D. Ordination im Spätjudentum u. im NT '51; Billerb. II, '56, 647–61; DDaube, The NT and Rabbinic Judaism '56, 244–6; JoachJeremias, ZNW 52, '61, 101–4. M-M.*

ἐπιθυμέω impf. ἐπεθύμουν; fut. ἐπιθυμήσω; 1 aor. ἐπεθύμησα (Aeschyl., Hdt.+; inscr., pap., LXX, En., Ep. Arist., Philo, Joseph., Test. 12 Patr.) *desire, long for* w. gen. of the thing desired (Hdt. 2, 66; X., Mem. 1, 6, 5; Ex 34: 24; Ps 44: 12; Pr 23: 3, 6; Ep. Arist. 223; Jos., Ant. 12, 309) silver, gold, clothing Ac 20: 33; a good work 1 Ti 3: 1; earthly things 2 Cl 5: 6. W. acc. of the thing (Teles p. 42, 12; Diod. S. 37, 29, 2 τὸν πλοῦτον; Tetrast. Iamb. 2, 22, 1 p. 292; Mi 2: 2; Wsd 16: 3; Sir 1: 26; 16: 1; 40: 22; Ep. Arist. 211) τὰ τοῦ πλησίον D 2: 2. τὴν οἰκοδομὴν αὐτοῦ Hs 9, 9, 7. μηδέν IRo 4: 3. W. acc. of the pers. of sexual desire (referring to γυναῖκα; cf. En. 6, 2) αὐτήν (lacking in some witnesses; others have αὐτῆς, which corresponds to X., An. 4, 1, 14; Sus 8; Philo, Spec. Leg. 3, 66) Mt 5: 28; Hv 1, 1, 4 (cf. Ex 20: 17; Dt 5: 21; 4 Macc 2: 5; lead tablet fr. Hadrumetum 44f: Dssm., B 31 [BS 274ff], Fluchtaf. 5 p. 25f μηδεμίαν ἄλλην γυναῖκα μήτε παρθένον ἐπιθυμοῦντα). W. inf. foll. (Soph., Hdt. al.; POxy. 963; Is 58: 2; Sus 15 Theod.; Jos., Bell. 6, 112) Mt 13: 17; Lk 15: 16; 16: 21; 17: 22; 1 Pt 1: 12; Rv 9: 6; 2 Cl 5: 7; Pol 1: 3; MPol 17: 1; 19: 1. Foll. by acc. and inf. Hb 6: 11. Abs. (Is 58: 11; 4 Macc 2: 6) Ro 7: 7 (SLyonnet, OCullmann-Festschr., '62, 157–65); 13: 9 (both Ex 20: 17); 1 Cor 10: 6; Js 4: 2. ἐπιθυμίᾳ ἐπιθυμεῖν *eagerly desire* (Gen 31: 30; cf. Diod. S. 16, 61, 3 νόσῳ νοσεῖν = be very ill) Lk 22: 15; GEb 6; cf. Bl-D. §198, 6; Rob. 531; Mlt.-H. 443f. ἐ. κατά τινος *desire against* or *rise in protest against* someth. Gal 5: 17. M-M. B. 1162.**

ἐπιθυμητής, οῦ, ὁ (Hdt. 7, 6 al.; LXX; Jos., C. Ap. 2, 45) *one who desires,* also in a bad sense (BGU 531 II, 22 [I AD] οὔτε εἰμὶ ἄδικος οὔτε ἀλλοτρίων ἐπιθυμητής [for ἀλλοτρ. ἐπιθυμ. s. Vett. Val. index III p. 397]; Pr 1: 22) κακῶν *desirous of evil* 1 Cor 10: 6 (Num 11: 34). μὴ γίνου ἐ. *do not be lustful* D 3: 3. M-M.*

ἐπιθυμία, ας, ἡ (Pre-Socr., Hdt.+; inscr., pap., LXX, Ep. Arist., Philo, Joseph., Test. 12 Patr.) *desire, longing, craving.*
   1. as a neutral term, as predom. in secular Gk. αἱ περὶ τὰ λοιπὰ ἐ. *desires for other things* Mk 4: 19. ἐ. πράξεων πολλῶν *desire for much business* Hm 6, 2, 5 (but mng. 3 below is also poss.). ἐ. τῆς ψυχῆς *the desire of the soul* Rv 18: 14.
   2. in a good sense (Diod. S. 11, 36, 5 ἐπιθ. τῆς ἐλευθερίας = for freedom; Pr 10: 24 ἐ. δικαίου δεκτή; Jos., C. Ap. 1, 111) ἐπιθυμίαν ἔχειν εἴς τι *have a longing for someth.* Phil 1: 23 (ἐ. ἔχειν as Jos., C. Ap. 1, 255; ἐ. εἰς as Thu. 4, 81, 2). ἐπιθυμίᾳ ἐπιθυμεῖν (Gen 31: 30) *eagerly desire* Lk 22: 15 (s. on ἐπιθυμέω); ἐν πολλῇ ἐ. w. *great longing* 1 Th 2: 17.
   3. in a bad sense as a desire for someth. forbidden (as early as Plato, Phaedo 83B ᾗ τοῦ ὡς ἀληθῶς φιλοσόφου ψυχὴ οὕτως ἀπέχεται τ. ἡδονῶν τε καὶ ἐπιθυμιῶν κτλ.; Polystrat. p. 30; Duris [III BC]: 76 fgm. 15 Jac., then above

all, the Stoics [EZeller, Philos. d. Griechen III 1⁴, '09, 235ff], e.g. Epict. 2, 16, 45; 2, 18, 8f; 3, 9, 21 al.; Maximus Tyr. 24, 4a μέγιστον ἀνθρώπῳ κακὸν ἐπιθυμία; Herm. Wr. 1, 23; 12, 4, also in Stob. p. 444, 10 Sc.; Wsd 4: 12; Sir 23: 5; 4 Macc 1: 22; 3: 2 al.; Philo, Spec. Leg. 4, 93, Leg. All. 2, 8, Vi. Cont. 74; Jos., Bell. 7, 261, Ant. 4, 143) Ro 7: 7f; Js 1: 14f; 2 Pt 1: 4. ἐ. πονηρά (X., Mem. 1, 2, 64) Hv 1, 2, 4; 3, 7, 3; 3, 8, 4; m 8: 5. ἐ. κακή (Pla., Leg. 9 p. 854A; Pr 12: 12; 21: 26) Col 3: 5. Of sexual desire (as early as Alcaeus [acc. to Plut., Mor. 525AB]; lead tablet fr. Hadrumetum 7 in Dssm., B 28 [BS 273ff] and Fluchtaf. no. 5 p. 23; PGM 17a, 9; 21; Sus Theod. 8; 11; 14 al., LXX 32; Jos., Ant. 4, 130; 132) D 3: 3. πάθος ἐπιθυμίας 1 Th 4: 5. κατ' ἐπιθυμίαν (cf. Epict. 3, 15, 7; M. Ant. 2, 10, 1; 2; 3) *in accordance with physical desire alone* IPol 5: 2. πρὸς ἐπιθυμίαν τ. ἀνθρώπων GOxy 38 (Ps.-Pla., Eryx. 21 p. 401E πρὸς τὰς ἐπιθυμίας τοῦ σώματος = to satisfy the desires of the body; cf. 405E: gambling, drunkenness and gluttony are called ἐπιθυμίαι. —In GOxy 38, since the ν in ἐπιθυμίαν is missing and restored, the word might also be ἐπιθυμίας). ἐ. γυναικός (Da 11: 37) Hm 6, 2, 5. Pl. (oft. LXX; Ep. Arist. 256; Philo) w. παθήματα Gal 5: 24. In a list of vices (cf. Philo, Congr. Erud. Grat. 172, Migr. Abr. 60, Vi. Cont. 2) 1 Pt 4: 3; D 5: 1. ἐ. πολλαὶ ἀνόητοι *many foolish desires* 1 Ti 6: 9; νεωτερικαὶ ἐ. *youthful desires* 2 Ti 2: 22; κατὰ τὰς ἰδίας ἐ. *in accordance w. their own desires* 4: 3; αἱ πρότερον ἐν τῇ ἀγνοίᾳ ἐ. *the desires that ruled over you formerly, when you were ignorant* 1 Pt 1: 14.—W. gen.: subjective gen. ἐ. ἀνθρώπων 1 Pt 4: 2; τοῦ πατρὸς ὑμῶν J 8: 44; gen. of quality ἐ. μιασμοῦ *defiling passion* 2 Pt 2: 10. ἐ. τῆς ἀπάτης *deceptive desires* Eph 4: 22. ἐ. τῶν ἀσεβειῶν Jd 18. ἐ. τῆς πονηρίας *evil desire* Hv 1, 1, 8. ἐ. τῆς ἀσελγείας 3, 7, 2; the gen. can also indicate the origin and seat of the desire ἐ. τῶν καρδιῶν *of the hearts* (Sir 5: 2) Ro 1: 24. ἐ. τοῦ θνητοῦ σώματος 6: 12 (Ps.-Pla., Eryx. 21 p. 401E, s. above; Sextus 448 ἐπιθυμίαι τοῦ σώματος). τῆς σαρκός Eph 2: 3; 1 J 2: 16; 2 Pt 2: 18. τῶν ὀφθαλμῶν 1 J 2: 16; to denote someth. to which desire belongs gener. vs. 17; σαρκικαὶ ἐ. 1 Pt 2: 11; D 1: 4; σωματικαὶ ἐ. (4 Macc 1: 32) ibid.; κοσμικαὶ ἐ. *worldly desires* Tit 2: 12; 2 Cl 17: 3; εἰς ἐ. *to arouse desires* Ro 13: 14; ποιεῖν τὰς ἐ. *act in accordance w. the desires* J 8: 44. τελεῖν ἐ. σαρκός *gratify the cravings of the flesh* Gal 5: 16; ὑπακούειν ταῖς ἐ. *obey the desires* Ro 6: 12; δουλεύειν ἐ. *be a slave to the desires* Tit 3: 3; cf. δοῦλος ἐπιθυμίας IPol 4: 3. ἄγεσθαι ἐπιθυμίαις *be led about by desires* 2 Ti 3: 6. πορεύεσθαι κατὰ τὰς ἐ. Jd 16; 18; 2 Pt 3: 3; ἐν ἐπιθυμίαις (Sir 5: 2) 1 Pt 4: 3. ἀναστρέφεσθαι ἐν ταῖς ἐ. Eph 2: 3.—FBüchsel, TW III '36, 168–73; BSEaston, Pastoral Ep. '47, 186f. M-M.**

ἐπιθύω 1 aor. ἐπέθυσα (Aeschyl.+; Dit., Or. 222, 37; 332, 29; pap. [Mayser 33]; LXX; En. 19, 1) *offer a sacrifice* (w. ὀμνύναι) MPol 4; 8: 2; Ac 14: 13 v.l.*

ἐπικαθίζω 1 aor. ἐπεκάθισα (Jos., Ant. 18, 57) intr. *sit* or *sit down (on)* (Plut., Them. 12, 1; Gen 31: 34; 2 Km 13: 29) ἐπάνω τινός *on someth.* Mt 21: 7. The less well attested, certainly false rdg. ἐπεκάθισαν ἐπάνω αὐτόν would give the verb the trans. mng. *set* or *put upon* (Hippocr., Art. 78 τινὰ ἐπί τι, likew. 3 Km 1: 38, 44; Ezk 32: 4). M-M.*

ἐπικαθυπνόω (hapax legomenon) *fall asleep* τινί *over someth.* ταῖς ἁμαρτίαις B 4: 13.*

ἐπικαίω plpf. ἐπεκεκαύκειν (found in tmesis as early as Hom.; Sb 6720, 4) *burn (on the surface), scorch* of the sun (Pla., Ep. 7 p. 340D οἱ τὰ σώματα ὑπὸ τ. ἡλίου ἐπικεκαυμένοι, likew. Dio Chrys. 53[70], 2. Cf. Polyb. 38, 8, 7) abs. *scorch* Hs 9, 1, 6.*

ἐπικαλέω 1 aor. ἐπεκάλεσα; fut. mid. ἐπικαλέσομαι; 1 aor. mid. ἐπεκαλεσάμην; pf. pass. ἐπικέκλημαι, ptc. ἐπικεκλημένος; plpf. 3 sing. ἐπεκέκλητο; 1 aor. pass. ἐπεκλήθην (in tmesis as early as Hom., otherw. Hdt.+; inscr., pap., LXX, Ep. Arist., Joseph., Test. 12 Patr.).

1. act. and pass.—a. *call, call out* (to a divinity, since Hdt. 2, 39; 3, 8) 1 Cl 39: 7 (Job 5: 1).

b. *name, give a name*—a. *give a surname* (X., Pla.+; Dit., Or. 603, 10; PFay. 12, 1; PTebt. 399, 15 al.; 1 Macc 2: 2) τινά τι: τὸν οἰκοδεσπότην Βεεζεβούλ *call the master of the house Beelzebub* Mt 10: 25. Pass. ὁ ἐπικαλούμενος *who is also called* (Socrat., Ep. 21, 3; Diod. S. 3, 84, 1; Diog. L. 4, 18; Jos., Ant. 18, 206 al.) Ac 10: 18; 11: 13; 12: 12. With Συμεὼν ὁ ἐπικαλούμενος Νίγερ Ac 13: 1 D cf. Diod. S. 17, 20, 7 Κλεῖτος ὁ Μέλας ἐπικαλούμενος. Also ὁ ἐπικληθείς (Jos., Bell. 1, 60, Ant. 13, 103; Diog. L. 5, 58 of Strato of Lamps.: φυσικὸς ἐπικληθείς) 4: 36; 12: 25; GEb 2. ὃς ἐπικαλεῖται Ac 10: 5, 32. ὃς ἐπεκλήθη (Jos., Ant. 13, 218; 271) 1: 23. οὐκ ἐπαισχύνεται θεὸς ἐπικαλεῖσθαι *to be called their God* Hb 11: 16.

β. The pass. is used w. ὄνομα, as in the OT, in ἐπικαλεῖται τὸ ὄνομά τινος ἐπί τινα *someone's name is called over someone* to designate the latter as the property of the former (of God's name 2 Km 6: 2; 3 Km 8: 43; Jer 7: 30; 14: 9 and oft.) Ac 15: 17 (Am 9: 12, also 2 Ch 7: 14). τὸ καλὸν ὄνομα τὸ ἐπικληθὲν ἐφ᾽ ὑμᾶς Js 2: 7; cf. Hs 8, 6, 4. Sim. οἱ ἐπικαλούμενοι τ. ὀνόματι αὐτοῦ *those who are called by his name* 9, 14, 3 (cf. Is 43: 7).

2. mid. *call upon* someone for aid—a. legal t.t.—a. τινὰ μάρτυρα *call on someone as a witness* (Pla., Leg. 2 p. 664c) 2 Cor 1: 23 (θεοὺς ἐπικαλεῖσθαι μάρτυρας: Polyb. 11, 6, 4; Heliod. 1, 25, 1; Jos., Ant. 1, 243).

β. *appeal* τινά *to someone* (cf. Plut., Marcell. 2, 7, Tib. Gracch. 16, 1) Καίσαρα *appeal to Caesar* Ac 25: 11f; 26: 32; 28: 19. Also τὸν Σεβαστόν 25: 25. W. inf. foll. τοῦ δὲ Παύλου ἐπικαλεσαμένου τηρηθῆναι αὐτὸν εἰς τὴν τοῦ Σεβαστοῦ διάγνωσιν *when Paul appealed to be held in custody for the Emperor's decision* 25: 21.—ANSherwin-White, Rom. Society and Law in the NT '63, 57-70; AHMJones, Studies in Rom. Gov't. and Law '60, 53ff.

b. of calling on a divinity (ἐ. τοὺς θεούς Hdt.+; X., Cyr. 7, 1, 35; Pla., Tim. 27c; Polyb. 15, 1, 13; Diod. S. 5, 49, 5 calling on the gods by the initiates; Epict. 2, 7, 12; 3, 21, 12 al.; Herm. Wr. 16, 3; Dit., Or. 194, 18 [I BC]; prayers for vengeance fr. Rheneia 1 [Dssm., LO 352ff—LAE 424ff; Dit., Syll.³ 1181]; POxy. 1380, 153 [early II AD]; 886, 10 [III AD]; PGM 3, 8; 43; 4, 1182; 1217; 1345; 13, 138; 270; LXX; Ep. Arist. 17; 193; 226; Jos., Ant. 4, 222 al.) ἐπικαλεῖσθαι τ. κύριον (1 Km 12: 17f; 2 Km 22: 7) Ro 10: 12; 2 Ti 2: 22; 1 Cl 52: 3; 60: 4 (Pr 1: 28); 60: 4. Also ἐπικαλεῖσθαι τὸ ὄνομα κυρίου (Gen 13: 4; 21: 33 and oft.; Jos., Bell. 5, 438; PGM 1, 161; 4, 1209; 1609; 1811; 13, 871) Ac 2: 21 (Jo 3: 5); 9: 14, 21; 22: 16; Ro 10: 13 (Jo 3: 5); 1 Cor 1: 2; 1 Cl 64: 1. Abs. (Ps 4: 2) Ro 10: 14; Ac 7: 59. εἰ πατέρα ἐπικαλεῖσθέ τινα *if you call upon someone as Father* 1 Pt 1: 17 (ⓓ⁷² καλεῖτε, which may be classed under 1ba).—JWTyrer, JTS 25, '24, 139-50; reply by RHConnolly, ibid. 337-68; FNötscher, Epiklese, Biblica 30, '49, 401-4=Vom A zum NT, '62, 221-25. M-M.*

ἐπικάλυμμα, ατος, τό (Aristot.+; LXX) *cover, veil* ἐ. τῆς κακίας *a covering for evil* 1 Pt 2: 16 (Menand., fgm. 90 Kock πλοῦτος δὲ πολλῶν ἐπικάλυμμ᾽ ἐστὶ κακῶν).*

ἐπικαλύπτω 1 aor. pass. ἐπεκαλύφθην (Hes.+; LXX; En. 10, 5; Philo, Leg. All. 2, 58; Jos., Ant. 12, 241) *cover* ὧν ἐπεκαλύφθησαν αἱ ἁμαρτίαι *whose sins are covered* Ro 4: 7; 1 Cl 50: 6 (both Ps 31: 1).*

ἐπικαταλλάσσομαι 2 aor. ἐπικατηλλάγην (hapax legomenon) τινι *be reconciled to someone* 1 Cl 48: 1.*

ἐπικατάρατος, ον (inscr. fr. Euboea Dit., Syll.³ 1240, 2 [II AD] and Halicarnassus CIG 2664 [II/III AD]; Vi. Aesopi I c. 3 ἐπικατάρατε; schol. on Soph., Ant. 867 p. 258 Papag. [1888]; LXX; Philo, Leg. All. 3, 111; 113; En. 102, 3; Dssm., LO 74f [LAE 93f]) *cursed* ἐ. πᾶς ὃς . . . *cursed be every one, who . . .* Gal 3: 10 (Dt 27: 26), 13. (W. παραβάτης τοῦ νόμου; opp. μακάριος) Lk 6: 5 D=Agr 8 (JoachJeremias, Unknown Sayings of Jesus, tr. Fuller, '57, 49-54). ἐ. ὁ εἷς B 7: 7; cf. 9. Of fish who are *cursed* and must live in the depths of the sea 10: 5. M-M.*

ἐπίκειμαι impf. ἐπεκείμην (Hom.+; inscr., pap., LXX, Ep. Arist., Joseph.).

1. lit. *lie upon* ἐπί τινι *someth.* (Paus. 5, 10, 2) of a stone J 11: 38 (JSwetnam, CBQ 28, '66, 155-73). ἐπί τινος *on someth.* (Cass. Dio 67, 16; Herm. Wr. 1, 13b) of the brass serpent B 12: 7. Abs. ὀψάριον ἐπικείμενον *fish lying on it* J 21: 9 (cf. PTebt. 47, 25 [113 BC]; PGrenf. II 57, 9 τ. ἐπικειμένην σποράν; 2 Macc 1: 21).

2. fig.—a. *be on* of the image on a coin IMg 5: 2.—b. *press around, press upon, be urgent* w. dat. of the pers. (X., An. 4, 3, 7; Job 19: 3; 21: 27; Jos., Ant. 6, 334 al.) Lk 5: 1. ἐπέκειντο αἰτούμενοι *they urgently demanded* 23: 23 (cf. Hdt. 5, 104; Jos., Ant. 18, 184 πολλῷ μᾶλλον ἐπέκειτο ἀξιῶν. Also 20, 110).—χειμῶνος ἐπικειμένου *since a storm lay upon us* Ac 27: 20 (cf. Plut., Timol. 28, 7; Wsd 17: 20 v.l.).

c. *be imposed, be incumbent* (Lucian, Calumn. 17 θάνατος; 1 Macc 6: 57) δικαιώματα ἐπικείμενα *regulations imposed* Hb 9: 10. ἀνάγκη μοι ἐπίκειται *necessity is laid upon me* (cf. Il. 6, 459; Sib. Or. 3, 572) 1 Cor 9: 16. ἀγὼν ἡμῖν ἐπίκειται *a conflict confronts us* 1 Cl 7: 1. διακονίαι ἐπίκεινταί τινι *duties are imposed on someone* 40: 5. In a somewhat weakened sense *stand before* (Achilles Tat. 2, 16, 2) ὁ τοκετός μοι ἐπίκειται *the pains of birth* (typical of the tortures to come) *are upon me* IRo 6: 1. τούτοις ἐπίκειται μετάνοια *repentance is open to them* Hs 8, 7, 2. M-M.*

ἐπικέλλω 1 aor. ἐπέκειλα nautical t.t. (Apollon. Rhod. 1, 1362; 2, 352 al.) *bring to shore, run aground* ἐ. τὴν ναῦν (cf. Od. 9, 148) *run the ship aground* Ac 27: 41 (v.l. ἐπώκειλαν). M-M.*

ἐπικερδαίνω (Plut., Flam. 3, 2; Cass. Dio 36, 12) *gain in addition* Mt 25: 20 D; 22 D.*

ἐπικεφάλαιον, ου, τό *poll tax* (Aristot., Oec. 2 p. 1346a, 4; pap.) Mk 12: 14 D (for κῆνσον). M-M.*

Ἐπικούρειος, ου, ὁ (Numenius [s. on στρεβλόω 2] 1, 3 p. 63; Alciphr. 3, 19, 3; Diog. L. 10, 3; 31; Dit., Syll.³ 1227 φιλόσοφος Ἐπικούρειος; Inscr. Rom. IV 997; Jos., Ant. 10, 277; 19, 32. For the spelling W-S. §5, 13e; cf. Philo, Poster. Cai. 2) *an Epicurean*, a follower of Epicurus Ac 17: 18.—RDHicks, Encycl. of Rel. and Eth. V 324-30; WBarclay, ET 72, '60, 78-81; 72, '61, 101-4; 146-9. M-M.*

ἐπικουρία, ας, ἡ (trag., Hdt.+; Diod. S. 1, 90, 2; Appian, Syr. 37 §192 θεῶν ἐ.; Dit., Syll.³ 1015, 24 [III BC]; PFlor. 382, 40; Wsd 13: 18; Philo, Spec. Leg. 1, 298 τοῦ θεοῦ; Jos., Ant. 1, 281 ἡ ἐμὴ [=θεοῦ] ἐπ.; 20, 56) *help* ἐπικουρίας τυχὼν τῆς ἀπὸ θεοῦ *I have had help fr. God* Ac 26: 22 (Jos., Ant. 2, 94 ἐπικουρίας τυγχάνειν). M-M. B. 1354, verb.*

ἐπικράζω (Lucian, Anach. 16; Pollux 5, 85) *shout threats κατά τινος against someone* Ac 16: 39 D. W. direct discourse foll. 28: 19 v.l.*

ἐπικρίνω 1 aor. ἐπέκρινα (Pla.+; inscr., pap., LXX, Philo; Jos., Bell. 6, 416, Ant. 14, 192) *decide, determine* foll. by acc. and inf. (Dit., Syll.³ 1109, 71) ἐπέκρινεν γενέσθαι τὸ αἴτημα αὐτῶν *he decided that their demand should be granted* Lk 23: 24. M-M.*

ἐπιλαμβάνομαι 2 aor. ἐπελαβόμην (in our lit., as well as LXX, only in the mid., which is used since Hdt., also inscr., pap.; Philo, Somn. 2, 68; Jos., Bell. 6, 232).
　1. *take hold of, grasp, catch,* sometimes w. violence, w. gen. foll. (Hdt. 6, 114 al.; LXX) of the pers. (Laud. Therap. 24 ἐπιλαμβάνονται τοῦ ἀνδρός; 2 Km 13: 11; Is 3: 6) Mt 14: 31; Ac 17: 19; 21: 30, 33; of the thing (LXX) τῆς χειρός τινος (cf. Pla., Prot. 335c; Zech 14: 13; Jos., Ant. 9, 180) Mk 8: 23; Ac 23: 19; fig. Hb 8: 9 (Jer 38: 32). Foll. by gen. of the pers. and of the thing by which the person is grasped (X., An. 4, 7, 12 ἐ. αὐτοῦ τῆς ἴτυος; Diod. S. 17, 30, 4; Epict. 1, 29, 23; Bel 36 LXX; Test. Jos. 8: 2) μου τῆς χειρός *me by the hand* Hv 3, 2, 4 (Plut., Mor. 207c ἐπιλαβόμενος αὐτοῦ τῆς χειρός). αὐτοῦ τῆς πήρας *him by the knapsack* s 9, 10, 5. W. acc. of the pers. (cf. Pla., Leg. 6 p. 779c) Lk 9: 47; 23: 26. Freq., where ἐ. seems to govern the acc., that case is actually the object of the finite verb upon which ἐ. depends: Lk 14: 4; Ac 9: 27; 16: 19; 18: 17.
　2. fig.—a. *catch* w. double gen. (cf. 1 above) *someone in someth.* αὐτοῦ λόγου *him in someth. he said* Lk 20: 20; also αὐτοῦ ῥήματος vs. 26.
　b. *take hold of,* in order to make one's own (Hdt. 1, 127; 5, 23; Polyb. 6, 50, 6; 15, 8, 12; Pr 4: 13) τῆς αἰωνίου ζωῆς 1 Ti 6: 12; cf. vs. 19.
　c. *be concerned with, take an interest in; help* is also poss. (schol. on Aeschyl., Pers. 742; Sir 4: 11) ἀγγέλων, σπέρματος 'Αβραάμ Hb 2: 16. This may be the place for the variant readings ἐπιλαβών (but the act. is never used in LXX or NT) and ἐπιλαβόμενος in the apparatus of The Gk. NT, ed. Aland, Black, Metzger, Wikgren '66, for ἐπιβαλών Mk 14: 72, q.v. M-M.*

ἐπιλάμπω 1 aor. ἐπέλαμψα *shine out, shine forth* (Hom. +; inscr.; PGM 3, 135; LXX; Philo).
　1. lit. (Dio Chrys. 71[21], 14) Ac 12: 7 D.—2. fig., of God's mercy ὅταν ἐπιλάμψῃ τὸ ἔλεος τοῦ κυρίου *when the mercy of the Lord will shine forth* Hs 4: 2 (Is 4: 2 of God; Wsd 5: 6 of righteousness; Proclus, Theol. 185 p. 162, 4 τὸ θεῖον φῶς ἄνωθεν ἐπιλάμπον. In the inscr. t.t. for the 'shining forth' of the ruler who is given divine honors: Dit., Syll.³ 814, 34; 900, 26, Or. 669, 7. Likewise POsl. 126, 5 [161 AD]).*

ἐπιλανθάνομαι 2 aor. ἐπελαθόμην; pf. (also w. pass. mng., Kühner-G. I p., 120) ἐπιλέλησμαι (Hom.+; inscr., pap., LXX, Philo, Joseph.).
　1. prop. *forget* w. gen. (class., also LXX, Philo, Joseph.) of the pers. (cf. also PSI 353, 16; Gen 40: 23; Dt 6: 12 al.) 1 Cl 35: 11 (Ps 49: 22); B 10: 3; Hs 6, 4, 2. W. gen. of the thing (Diod. S. 4, 61, 6; Dit., Or. 116, 15; Herm. Wr. 10, 6; Ps 105: 13; 1 Macc 1: 49; 2 Macc 2: 2; Jos., Bell. 6, 107, Ant. 2, 327; 10, 195) Hv 3, 13, 2; s 6, 2, 2. Foll. by acc. of the thing (Hdt. 3, 46 al.; UPZ 61, 10 [161 BC]; PLond. 964; POxy. 744, 12; 1489, 3; LXX) τὰ ὀπίσω *what lies behind*

Phil 3: 13. W. inf. foll. (Hyperid. 2, 8; Aelian, V.H. 3, 31) Mt 16: 5; Mk 8: 14. W. ὅτι foll. (Jos., C. Ap. 1, 230) 1 Cl 46: 7. W. indir. quest. foll. ὁποῖος ἦν *what sort of person he was* Js 1: 24.—Hs 6, 5, 3.
　2. not lit. *neglect, overlook, care nothing about* w. gen. of the thing (Diod. S. 4, 64, 1 ἐπιλαθόμενος τοῦ χρησμοῦ = he disregarded the oracle; Ps 9: 13; 73: 19, 23) τοῦ ἔργου ὑμῶν Hb 6: 10. W. neg. (X., Ages. 2, 13 τοῦ θείου) τῆς φιλοξενίας 13: 2. τῆς εὐποιΐας, κοινωνίας vs. 16. Pass. (cf. Is 23: 16) ἐν ἐξ αὐτῶν οὐκ ἔστιν ἐπιλελησμένον ἐνώπιον τοῦ θεοῦ *not one of them has escaped God's notice* Lk 12: 6. M-M.*

ἐπιλέγω 1 aor. mid. ἐπελεξάμην (Hdt.+; inscr., pap., LXX, Ep. Arist., Joseph.).
　1. act. and pass. *call* or *name (in addition)* (Pla., Leg. 3 p. 700B). Pass. (Jos., Ant. 13, 285 Πτολεμαῖον τὸν Λάθουρον ἐπιλεγόμενον) 'Ραὰβ ἡ ἐπιλεγομένη πόρνη *who is called a harlot* 1 Cl 12: 1 (on the rdg. cf. Knopf, Hdb. ad loc.). κολυμβήθρα ἡ ἐπιλεγομένη Ἑβραϊστὶ Βηθζαθά *is called B. in Hebrew* J 5: 2. Herod MPol 6: 2 Funk.
　2. mid. *choose, select* τινά *someone* Ac 15: 40 (cf. Hdt. 3, 157; Thu. 7, 19, 3; Diod. S. 3, 74, 2; 14, 12, 3; 1 Esdr 9: 16; 1 Macc 12: 45; Ep. Arist. 39; 46; Jos., Ant. 4, 28). M-M.*

ἐπιλείπω fut. ἐπιλείψω (Hdt.+) *leave behind,* hence w. acc. as obj. also w. the mng. *fail* ἐπιλείψει με ὁ χρόνος *time would fail me* Hb 11: 32 (Isocr. 1, 11 ἐπιλίποι δ' ἂν ἡμᾶς ὁ πᾶς χρόνος; 6, 81; 8, 56; Demosth. 18, 296; Dionys. Hal., Comp. Verb. 4; Athen. 5 p. 220F; Philo, Sacr. Abel. 27; Jos., Ant. 8, 323 al.). M-M.*

ἐπιλείχω impf. ἐπέλειχον (Longus, Past. 1, 24, 4 ἐπιλείχω is a conjecture with no support in the tradition) *lick* τὰ ἕλκη *the sores* Lk 16: 21 (cf. 3 Km 22: 38 ἐξέλειξαν οἱ κύνες τὸ αἷμα). M-M.*

ἐπιλελησμένος s. ἐπιλανθάνομαι.

ἐπιλησμονή, ῆς, ἡ (Cratinus Com. [V BC], fgm. 410 K.; inscr.: WDFerguson, The Legal Terms Common to the Macedon. Inscr. and the NT '13, 57; Sir 11: 27) *forgetfulness* ἀκροατὴς ἐπιλησμονῆς *a forgetful hearer* Js 1: 25 (on the constr. s. Mlt.-H. 440; Rob. 496f; cf. Bl-D. §165).*

ἐπίλοιπος, ον (Pind., Hdt.+; inscr., pap., LXX) *left, remaining* τὸν ἐ. χρόνον *the remaining time* (Hdt. 2, 13; Theopomp.: 115 fgm. 287 Jac. al.) 1 Pt 4: 2 (cf. 3 Macc 3: 26; PPetr. II 13, 19, 4 τὸν ἐ. βίον).—Subst. τὰ ἐπίλοιπα *the rest* (Hdt. 4, 154; Da 7: 7, 19 Theod.) Lk 24: 43 v.l. M-M.*

ἐπίλυσις, εως, ἡ (Aeschyl.+ w. var. mngs.; inscr., pap.) *explanation, interpretation* (so Sext. Emp., Pyrrh. 2, 246; Vett. Val. 221, 9; 330, 10; Heliod. 1, 18, 2 ὀνειράτων ἐπίλυσις; Gen 40: 8 Aq.; Philo, Vi. Cont. 75, l. 8 v.l.; Clem. of Alex., Paed. 2, 1, 14) πᾶσα προφητεία ἰδίας ἐπιλύσεως οὐ γίνεται 2 Pt 1: 20 (γίνομαι II 2a and ἴδιος 1aβ.—Ps.-Callisth. 2, 1, 5 Stasagoras complains about the unfavorable interpretation of an omen by the prophetess in these words: σὺ σεαυτῇ ἐπέλυσας τὸ σημεῖον=you gave the omen your own interpretation.—S. also WArndt, CTM 7, '36, 685–91). Of the interpretation of a parable Hs 5, 5, 1; 5, 6, 8; 5, 7, 1; 8, 11, 1; 9, 13, 9; 9, 16, 7. M-M.*

ἐπιλύω impf. ἐπέλυον; 1 fut. pass. ἐπιλυθήσομαι (Pla.+; IG IV² 1, 77, 18; pap.) *set free, release.*
　1. fig. *explain, interpret* (Sext. Emp., Pyrrh. 2, 246;

Vett. Val. 173, 6; Athen. 10 p. 449ε; Aq. Gen 40: 8, 41: 8, 12; Philo, Agr. 16; Jos., Ant. 8, 167 [mid.]) τινί τι someth. to someone parables Mk 4: 34; Hs 5, 3, 1f; 5, 4, 2f; 5, 5, 1; 9, 10, 5; 9, 11, 9.

2. *decide, settle* pass., of a dispute Ac 19: 39. M-M.*

ἐπιμαρτυρέω *bear witness* (Pla., Crat. 397α; Lucian, Alex. 42; Plut., Lys. 22, 9 al.; PLond. 1692a, 19 [VI ad]; Jos., Ant. 7, 349) foll. by acc. and inf. 1 Pt 5: 12. M-M.*

ἐπιμέλεια, ας, ἡ (very common Hdt.+; inscr., pap., LXX, Ep. Arist., Philo, Joseph.) *care, attention* ἐπιμελείας τυχεῖν *be cared for* (Isocr. 6, 154; 7, 37; Athen. 13, 56 p. 589c; POxy. 58, 22 αἱ ταμιακαὶ οὐσίαι τῆς προσηκούσης ἐπιμελείας τεύξονται; Philo, Spec. Leg. 3, 106; Jos., Ant. 2, 236) Ac 27: 3. ἐν πάσῃ ἐ. σαρκικῇ καὶ πνευματικῇ w. *all diligence, both of the body and of the spirit* IPol 1: 2 (cf. Diod. S. 14, 84, 2 ἐπιμέλεια τοῦ σώματος=care for the body). M-M.*

ἐπιμελέομαι pass. dep., fut. ἐπιμελήσομαι; 1 aor. ἐπεμελήθην, imper. ἐπιμελήθητι (Hdt.+; inscr., pap., LXX) *care for, take care of* w. gen. (Hdt.+; Herm. Wr. 10, 22b; Gen 44: 21; Sir 30: 25; Philo; Jos., Ant. 1, 53; 8, 297) τινός *someone* or *someth.* Lk 10: 34f; 1 Ti 3: 5. πίστεως, ἐλπίδος Agr 7. M-M.*

ἐπιμελής, ές *careful, attentive* (so act. in X., Pla., et al.; inscr., pap., Ep. Arist. 93; Philo; Jos., C. Ap. 1, 163) Pol 5: 2.*

ἐπιμελῶς adv. (X., Pla.+; inscr., pap., LXX; Ep. Arist. 81; Philo; Jos., Ant. 12, 318; 17, 12) *carefully, diligently* ζητεῖν *hunt carefully* Lk 15: 8; ἐκζητεῖν ἐ. Hv 3, 3, 5; πυνθάνεσθαι Dg 1. κατανοεῖν *consider, look at carefully* Hs 8, 2, 5; καθαρίζειν ἐ. s 9, 7, 2. ἐνστερνίζεσθαι 1 Cl 2: 1; cf. 1 Cl 40: 2 v.l. Funk; φυλάσσειν ἐ. Dg 7: 1. τελεῖν διακονίαν ἐ. *perform a service carefully* Hm 12, 3, 3. M-M.*

ἐπιμένω impf. ἐπέμενον; fut. ἐπιμενῶ; 1 aor. ἐπέμεινα (Hom.+; inscr., pap.; Ex 12: 39; Joseph.; Test. 12 Patr.) *stay, remain.*

1. lit. ἐν Ἐφέσῳ 1 Cor 16: 8 (cf. PLond. 897, 12 [84 ad] ἐν Ἀλεξανδρείᾳ ἐπιμένειν; PFay. 296). αὐτοῦ *there* Ac 21: 4; cf. 15: 34 v.l. W. the time more definitely given (Jos., Bell. 2, 545 ἔνθα δύο ἡμέρας ἐπ., Vi. 47) ibid.; ἐ. ἡμέρας τινάς *stay there for several days* 10: 48. ἡμέρας πλείους (Jos., Ant. 16, 15) 21: 10. ἡμέρας τρεῖς 28: 12. ἡμέρας ἑπτά vs. 14. ἡμέρας δεκαπέντε Gal 1: 18. ἐ. χρόνον τινά *for some time* 1 Cor 16: 7. πρός τινα *with someone* ibid.; Gal 1: 18. παρά τινι Ac 28: 14. ἐπί τινι (X., An. 7, 2, 1) ibid. v.l. W. dat. (PRyl. 153, 3 [II ad]; 239, 9) ἄσκυλτον ἐ. τῇ πυρᾷ *remain unmoved on the pyre* MPol 13: 3. τῇ σαρκὶ *remain in the body* Phil 1: 24.

2. fig. *continue, persist (in), persevere* w. dat. (X., Oec. 14, 7 τῷ μὴ ἀδικεῖν, Hell. 3, 4, 6; Aelian, V.H. 10, 15; Dit., Syll.³ 1243, 26 ἐ. τῇ αὐθαδίᾳ; POxy. 237 VI, 18 τῇ αὐτῇ ἀπονοίᾳ; PTebt. 424, 4; Jos., Vi. 143; Test. Levi 4: 1 τ. ἀδικίαις) τῇ ἁμαρτίᾳ *in sin* Ro 6: 1. τῇ πίστει Col 1: 23. τῇ ἀπιστίᾳ Ro 11: 23. ταῖς ἡδοναῖς Hs 8, 8, 5; 8, 9, 4. ταῖς πράξεσι s 9, 20, 4; τῇ ἐπιθυμίᾳ 9, 26, 2. αὐτοῖς (w. ref. to ταῦτα, τούτοις vs. 15; cf. Jos., Ant. 8, 190) 1 Ti 4: 16. ἐ. τῇ χρηστότητι *continue in the sphere of* (God's) *goodness* Ro 11: 22. τῇ πορνείᾳ Hm 4, 1, 5; cf. 6. ἐν τῇ ἀληθείᾳ Hv 3, 6, 2. W. ptc. foll. *keep on, persist* (stubbornly) *in doing someth.* (Pla., Meno 93d; Menand., Her. 35 J. ἐπιμένεις τὸ χρέος ἀπεργαζόμενος; Cornutus 17 p. 31, 11; POxy. 237 VI, 18 [186 ad] ἐπιμένει ἐνυβρίζων μοι; 128, 7 ἐ. λέγων) ἐ. κρούων Ac 12: 16.

ἐπέμενον ἐρωτῶντες αὐτόν *they persisted in questioning him* J 8: 7; cf. 2 Cl 10: 5. ἐ. ἕως τέλους λειτουργοῦντες Hs 9, 27, 3. But ἐπιμένοντος πάλιν αὐτοῦ καὶ λέγοντος *when he insisted again and said* MPol 10: 1. Without ptc. in the same mng. 8: 2. Likew. abs. *persist* Hs 6, 5, 7. ἐπιμενόντων τῶν ζητούντων αὐτόν *when those who were looking for him did not give up (the search)* MPol 6: 1. M-M.*

ἐπίμονος, ον (Clearchus, fgm. 24 p. 17, 15; Polyb. 6, 43, 2 ἀκμαί; Plut., Mor. p. 166c κολαστήριον; Dit., Syll.³ 679, 80 [143 bc]; Sym. Dt 28: 59; Philo, Ebr. 21) *lasting* ἡ στάσις *the rebellion continues* 1 Cl 46: 9. ἡ ἐ. κόλασις *continuous torture* MPol 2: 4.*

ἐπινεύω 1 aor. ἐπένευσα (Hom.+; inscr., pap., LXX) *give consent (by a nod)* οὐκ ἐπένευσεν *he did not give his consent* (PRyl. 119, 21 [I ad]; cf. Philo, Migr. Abr. 111; Jos., Vi. 124) Ac 18: 20. M-M.*

ἐπινοέω 1 aor. ἐπενόησα (Hdt., Aristoph.+; inscr., pap., LXX, Ep. Arist., Philo; Jos., Bell. 3, 190, Ant. 17, 37) *notice someth.* undesirable κατά τινος *against someone= in someone* 1 Cl 39: 4 (Job 4: 18). τὶ περί τινος *someth. about someth.* οὐδὲν ἐπινοεῖς περὶ αὐτῶν; *do you not notice anything about them?* Hs 9, 9, 1.—ECE Owen, ἐπινοέω, ἐπίνοια and Allied Words: JTS 35, '34, 368–76.*

ἐπίνοια, ας, ἡ (trag., Pre-Socr., Thu.+; Dit., Syll.³ 902, 5, Or. 580, 7; POxy. 237 VII, 35; 1468, 5; LXX, Ep. Arist., Philo; Jos., Bell. 4, 356, Vi. 223 al.; Test. Jos. 5: 2, 3; Sib. Or. 5, 81) *thought, conception* (Thu. 3, 46, 6 al.; Wsd 6: 16; 9: 14; 2 Macc 12: 45) θνητή ἐ. Dg 7: 1 (cf. Philo, Mut. Nom. 219 ἀνθρωπίνη ἐ.); *inventiveness* (X., Cyr. 2, 3, 19 al.) w. φροντίς 5: 3; *intent* (Aristoph., Thesm. 766; 4 Macc 17: 2) ἡ ἐ. τῆς καρδίας σου *the intent of your heart* Ac 8: 22. M-M.*

ἐπινομή, ῆς, ἡ (found elsewh. only in the mngs. 'spread' of fire, etc. [Plut., Alex. 35, 4; Aelian, N.A. 12, 32], 'pasturage' [pap.], and in medical wr. 'final turns of a bandage') μεταξὺ ἐπινομὴν ἔδωκαν (v.l. δεδώκασιν) 1 Cl 44: 2 prob. *afterward they laid down a rule.* This takes for granted that ἐ. ἐπινομῇ, which is the rdg. of the Codex Alexandr., is derived fr. ἐπινέμω 'distribute', 'allot' (s. Knopf, Hdb. ad loc.; also KLake ad loc., who compares ἐπινομίς, 'supplement, codicil'). The Latin translator (who rendered it 'legem') seems to have read and understood it so. The later Gk. ms. has ἐπιδομήν. The Syriac presupposes ἐπὶ δοκιμῇ; the Coptic is as much at a loss as many modern interpreters admittedly are. Lghtf. proposes ἐπιμονήν. Cf. also RSohm, Kirchenrecht 1892 p. 82, 4.*

ἐπιορκέω fut. ἐπιορκήσω (Hom.+; inscr., pap., LXX, Philo; Test. Ash. 2: 6.—On the spelling ἐφιορκέω s. Bl-D. §14 app.; Mlt.-H. 99; 314f).

1. *swear falsely, perjure oneself* (so mostly).—2. *break one's oath* (Chrysipp.: Stoic. II 63; Herodian 3, 6, 7; Procop. Soph., Ep. 61; 1 Esdr 1: 46). In Mt 5: 33; D 2: 3 both mngs. are poss. M-M.*

ἐπίορκος, ον (Hom.+) of persons (Hes.+; Jos., Vi. 102) *perjured* subst. (Zech 5: 3; Philo, Decal. 88) *perjurer* 1 Ti 1: 10 (w. ψευσταί).*

ἐπιοῦσα, ης, ἡ *the next day* s. ἔπειμι.

ἐπιούσιος, ον according to Origen, De Orat. 27, 7, coined by the evangelists. Grave doubt is cast on the one possible occurrence of ἐ. which is independent of our lit. (Sb 5224,

20), by BMMetzger, How Many Times Does ἐ. Occur Outside the Lord's Prayer? ET 69, '57/'58, 52-4=Historical and Literary Studies, '68, 64-66; it seems likely that Origen was right after all. Found in our lit. only w. ἄρτος in the Lord's Prayer Mt 6: 11; Lk 11: 3; D 8: 2. Variously interpreted: Sin. Syr. (on Lk) and Cur. Syr. אמינא *continual* (DYHadidian, NTS 5, '58/'59, 75-81); Peshitta דסונקנן *for our need*; Itala 'panis quotidianus', 'daily bread'; Jerome 'panis supersubstantialis' (on this JHennig, Theol. Studies 4, '43, 445-54); GH 7, מְחָר=Lat. 'crastinus' *for tomorrow*. Of the more recent interpretations the following are worth mentioning:

1. deriving it fr. ἐπί and οὐσία *necessary for existence*: in agreement w. Origen, Chrysostom, Jerome e.g. Beza, Tholuck, HEwald, Bleek, Weizsäcker, BWeiss, HCremer; Billerb. I 420; ChRogge, Philol. Wochenschr. 47, '27, 1129-35; FHauck, ZNW 33, '34, 199-202; RFWright, CQR 157, '56, 340-45.

2. a substantivizing of ἐπί τὴν οὖσαν sc. ἡμέραν *for the current day, for today* (cf. Thu. 1, 2, 2 τῆς καθ' ἡμέραν ἀναγκαίου τροφῆς; Vi. Aesopi W. c. 110 τὸν καθημερινὸν ζήτει προσλαμβάνειν ἄρτον καὶ εἰς τὴν αὔριον ἀποθησαυρίζε.—Acc. to Artem. 1, 5 p. 12, 26-28 one loaf of bread is the requirement for one day. S. ἐφήμερος.) ADebrunner, Glotta 4, '12, 249-53; 13, '24, 167-71, SchThZ 31, '14, 38-41, Kirchenfreund 59, '25, 446-8, ThBl 8, '29, 212f, Bl-D. §123, 1; 124, Philol. Wochenschr. 51, '31, 1277f (but cf. CGSheward, ET 52 '40/'41, 119f); KBrugmann⁴-AThumb, Griech. Gramm. '13, 675, ESchwyzer II 473, 2.

3. *for the following day* fr. ἡ ἐπιοῦσα sc. ἡμέρα (s. ἔπειμι): Grotius, Wettstein; Lghtf., On a Fresh Revision of the English NT³ 1891, 217-60; Zahn, JWeiss; Harnack, SBA '04, 208; EKlostermann; Mlt.-H. p. 313f; PW Schmiedel, W-S. §16, 3b note 23, SchThZ 30, '13, 204-20; 31, '14, 41-69; 32, '15, 80; 122-33, PM '14, 358-64, Philol. Wochenschr. 48, '28, 1530-6, ThBl. 8, '29, 258f; ADeissmann, Heinrici-Festschr. '14, 115-19, RSeeberg-Festschr. '29, I 299-306, The NT in the Light of Modern Research, '29, 84-6; AFridrichsen, Symb. Osl. 2, '24, 31-41 (GRudberg ibid. 42; 3, '25, 76); 9, '30, 62-8; OHoltzmann, ASteinmann, D. Bergpredigt '26, 104f; FXPölzl-ThInnitzer, Mt⁴ '32, 129f; SKauchtschischwili, Philol. Wochenschr. 50, '30, 1166-8.—FStiebitz, ibid. 47, '27, 889-92, w. ref. to Lat. 'diaria'=the daily ration of food, given out for the next day; someth. like: *give us today our daily portion*—acc. to FJDölger, Ant. u. Chr. 5, '36, 201-10, one loaf of bread (likew. WCrönert, Gnomon 4, '28, p. 89, 1). S. also s.v. σήμερον.

4. deriving it fr. ἐπιέναι—a. on the analogy of τὸ ἐπιόν='the future', *bread for the future*; so Cyrillus of Alex. and Peter of Laodicea; among the moderns, who attach var. mngs. to it, esp. ASeeberg, D. 4te Bitte des V.-U., Rektoratsrede Rostock 1914, Heinrici-Festschr. '14, 109. Cf. LBrun, Harnack-Ehrung '21, 22f.

b. in the mng. 'come to': *give us this day the bread that comes to it*, i.e. *belongs to it*; so KHolzinger, Philol. Wochenschr. 51, '31, 825-30; 857-63; 52, '32, 383f.

c. equal to ἐπιών=*next* acc. to TGShearman, JBL 53, '34, 110-17.

d. The petition is referred to the *coming* Kingdom and its feast by: REisler, ZNW 24, '25, 190-2; JSchousboe, Rev. d'Hist. des relig. 48, '27, 233-7; ASchweitzer, D. Mystik des Ap. Pls '30, 233-5; JoachJeremias, Jesus als Weltvollender '30, 52; ELittmann, ZNW 34, '35, 29.—Cf. also GLoeschcke, D. Vaterunser-Erklärung des Theophilus v. Antioch. '08; GWalther, Untersuchungen z. Gesch. d. griech. Vaterunser-Exegese '14; DVölter, PM

18, '14, 274ff; 19, '15, 20ff, NThT 4, '15, 123ff; ABolliger, SchThZ 30, '13, 276-85; GKuhn, ibid. 31, '14, 33ff; 36, '19, 191ff; EvDobschütz, HTR 7, '14, 293-321; RWimmerer, Glotta 12, '22, 68-82; ECEOwen, JTS 35, '34, 376-80; JHensler, D. Vaterunser '14; JSickenberger, Uns. ausreichendes Brot gib uns heute '23; PFiebig, D. Vaterunser '27, 81-3; GDalman, Worte² '30, 321-34; HHuber, D. Bergpredigt '32; GBonaccorsi, Primi saggi di filologia neotest. I '33, 61-3; 533-9; JHerrmann, D. atl. Urgrund des Vaterunsers: OProcksch-Festchr. '34, 71-98; WFoerster TW II '35, 587-95; MBlack, JTS 42, '41, 186-9, An Aramaic Approach³, '67, 203-7, 299f, n. 3; SMowinckel, Artos epiousios: Norsk Teol. Tidsskr. 40, '42, 247-55; ELohmeyer, D. Vaterunser erkl. '46. M-M. and suppl. *

ἐπιπέτομαι 2 aor. ἐπέπτην, ptc. ἐπιπτάς (Hom. +) *fly upon* ἐπί τι (Pla., Rep. 2 p. 365A; Dio Chrys. 70[20], 12) ἐ. ἐπὶ τὸν τοῦ ἡλίου βωμόν *light on the altar of the sun-god* 1 Cl 25: 4. *

ἐπιπίπτω 2 aor. ἐπέπεσον; pf. ἐπιπέπτωκα (Hdt. +; inscr., pap., LXX; Philo, De Jos. 256; Jos., Ant. 6, 23; 8, 377; Test. 12 Patr.) *fall upon*.

1. lit.—a. *fall upon someth.* ἐπί τι (X., Oec. 18, 7) of a hailstone *on a man's head* Hm 11: 20.

b. *approach someone* (τινί) *impetuously, eagerly* (Syntipas p. 11, 12) ἐπέπεσεν αὐτῷ *he threw himself upon him* Ac 20: 10. ὥστε ἐπιπίπτειν αὐτῷ (w. ἵνα foll.) *so that they pressed about him* (in order that) Mk 3: 10 (cf. Thu. 7, 84, 3 ἀθρόοι ἀναγκαζόμενοι χωρεῖν ἐπέπιπτον ἀλλήλοις). ἐπί τι (Gen 50: 1 B) ἐπὶ τὸν τράχηλόν τινος *fall on someone's neck* (=*embrace someone*) (Gen 45: 14; 50: 1 A [cf. MWilcox, The Semitisms of Ac, '65, 67]; Tob 11: 9, 13) Lk 15: 20; Ac 20: 37. ἐπιπεσὼν ἐπὶ τὸ στῆθος τοῦ Ἰησοῦ *he pressed close to Jesus' breast* J 13: 25 𝔓⁶⁶ et al.

2. fig., of extraordinary events, misfortunes, etc. *come upon* ἐπί τινα *someone*. ὀνειδισμοί *reproaches have fallen upon someone* Ro 15: 3 (Ps 68: 10). φόβος ἐ. ἐπί τινα *fear came upon someone* (Josh 2: 9; Jdth 14: 3; Job 4: 13) Lk 1: 12; Ac 19: 17; cf. Rv 11: 11. φόβ. ἐ. τινί (Da 4: 5; Job 13: 11.—ἐ. τινί also Memnon [I BC/I AD]: no. 434 fgm. 1, 28, 3 Jac.; Synes., Kingship 16 p. 18C δέος ἐπιπεσεῖν ἅπασιν) 1 Cl 12: 5. Abs. ἐπέπεσεν στάσις τῶν Φαρισαίων καὶ Σαδδουκαίων *a quarrel broke out betw. the Ph. and S.* Ac 23: 7 v.l. Of the Holy Spirit, who *comes upon someone* ἐπί τινι 8: 16. ἐπί τινα (cf. Ezk 11: 5) 8: 39 v.l.; 10: 44; 11: 15; 19: 6 D. Of a trance ἔκστασις ἐ. ἐπί τινα (Da 10: 7 Theod.) 10: 10 t.r. M-M. *

ἐπιπλήσσω 1 aor. ἐπέπληξα *strike at, rebuke, reprove* (Hom. +; Pla., Polyb.; BGU 1138, 22 [19 BC]) τινί *someone* (Il. 12, 211; Epict., Ench. 33, 16; Appian, Liby. 65 §291, Bell. Civ. 5, 13 §51; Philo, Leg. All. 2, 46; Jos., Ant. 1, 246; 19, 346) 1 Ti 5: 1. Also τινά ('the tragedy' in Simplicius in Epict. p. 95, 43 ἐπιπλήττουσί με; Lucian, Hermot. 20; UPZ 15, 32 [156 BC]) Mt 12: 15f D (s. Huck⁹ 58). Abs. (X., Oec. 13, 12) Lk 24: 43 D (where ἐπλήσοντι is to be corrected to ἐπιπλήσσοντι). M-M. *

ἐπιποθέω 1 aor. ἐπεπόθησα (Hdt. +; LXX, Philo) *long for, desire* τὶ *someth.* (Pla., Protag. p. 329D; Plut., Agis 6, 2; Lucian, D. Deorum 4, 3; Ps 118: 131, 174) γάλα *milk* 1 Pt 2: 2. τινά *someone* (Hdt. 5, 93; Diod. S. 17, 101, 6; Epict. 3, 24, 53; Sir 25: 21) πάντας ὑμᾶς Phil 1: 8; 2: 26 (v.l. π. ὑ. ἰδεῖν). ὑμᾶς 2 Cor 9: 14. W. inf. foll. (Philo, Abr. 87 ἐ. θεὸν ἀνευρεῖν) τὸ οἰκητήριον ἐπενδύσασθαι 2 Cor 5: 2. ἰδεῖν τινα Ro 1: 11; 1 Th 3: 6; 2 Ti 1: 4. πρὸς φθόνον ἐπιποθεῖ τὸ πνεῦμα Js 4: 5 is difficult; prob. *he*

(God) *yearns jealously over the spirit*; cf. MDibelius ad loc. (w. lit.). AMeyer, D. Rätsel des Jk '30, 258f; ASchlatter, D. Brief d. Jak. '32, 248-53.—CSpicq, RB 64, '57, 184-95. B. 1162*

ἐπιπόθησις, εως, ἡ (Appian, Gall. 5 §2; Aq. Ezk 23: 11; Clem. Alex., Strom. 4, 21, 131; Damascius, De Princ. 38; Etym. Mag. p. 678, 39) *longing* 2 Cor 7: 7, 11.*

ἐπιπόθητος, ον (Appian, Iber. 43 §179) *longed for, desired* ἀδελφοὶ ἀγαπητοὶ καὶ ἐ. Phil 4: 1. εἰρήνη *peace that we desire* 1 Cl 65: 1. ἡ ἐ. ὄψις ὑμῶν *the longed-for sight of you* B 1: 3.*

ἐπιποθία, ας, ἡ (Suidas) *longing, desire* ἐπιποθίαν ἔχων τοῦ ἐλθεῖν *having a desire to come* Ro 15: 23; 2 Cor 7: 11 v.l.*

ἐπιπολύ B 4: 1 s. ἐπί III 3.

ἐπιπορεύομαι *go* or *journey* (*to*) (Ephorus Cumanus [IV BC]: 70 fgm. 5 Jac.; Philo Mech. 90, 19; Polyb. 4, 9, 2; PLille 3, 78 [241 BC]; Wilcken, Chrest. 116, 3; 3 Macc 1: 4; Jos., Ant. 12, 400) πρός τινα *to someone* (Jos., Bell. 2, 481) Lk 8: 4. M-M.*

ἐπιπρέπω (Hom. +) *be becoming, suit, go well with* τινί *someone* or *someth.* (X., Cyr. 7, 5, 83; Lucian, D. Mar. 1, 1 ὁ ὀφθαλμὸς ἐπιπρέπει τῷ προσώπῳ) ἡ κόμη ἐπιπρέπουσα τῷ προσώπῳ *the hair went well with the face* AP 3: 10.*

ἐπι(ρ)ράπτω for the spelling s. W-S. §5, 26b (Galen 18, p. 579 Kühn; Nonnus, Dionys. 9, 3; 42, 315) *sew* (*on*) ἐπί τι *on someth.* a patch on a garment Mk 2: 21. JFSpringer, The Marcan ἐπιράπτει: Exp. VIII 121, '21, 79f.*

ἐπι(ρ)ρίπτω 1 aor. ἐπέριψα; 2 aor. pass. ἐπερρίφην (Hom. +; PTebt. 5, 183; 185; 249 [118 BC]; LXX. On the spelling cf. W-S. §5, 26b) *throw* τὶ ἐπί τι *someth. on someth.* (Kleopatra l. 112; LXX).
1. lit., of clothes, on an animal used for riding Lk 19: 35 (cf. 2 Km 20: 12; 3 Km 19: 19=Jos., Ant. 8, 353). Pass. of a vine ὅταν ἐπιρριφῇ ἐπὶ τὴν πτελέαν *when it is attached to the elm* Hs 2: 3.
2. fig. τ. μέριμναν ἐ. ἐπὶ θεόν *cast one's care upon God* 1 Pt 5: 7 (𝔓⁷²; Ps 54: 23); Hv 3, 11, 3; 4, 2, 4f (in all these pass. Ps 54: 23 is in the background). M-M.*

ἐπιρρώννυμι impf. ἐπερρώννυον (Soph., Hdt. +; PSI 452, 26; 2 Macc 11: 9) *strengthen, encourage* τὴν δειλίαν τινός *strengthen someone, fearful though he may be* MPol 3.*

ἐπισείω 1 aor. ἐπέσεισα (Hom. +; Jos., Bell. 1, 215; 2, 412).
1. *shake at* or *against* τινὶ τὴν χεῖρα *shake one's hand at someone* (in a threatening gesture) MPol 9: 2 (Artem. 5, 92 αὐτῷ χεῖρα ἐπισεῖσαι; Ael. Aristid. 39 p. 747 D.: ὑμῖν τὰ ὅπλα ἐπισείων).—2. *urge on, incite* τοὺς ὄχλους Ac 14: 19 D.*

ἐπίσημος, ον (trag., Hdt. +; inscr., pap., LXX).
1. *splendid, prominent, outstanding* (Hdt., trag. +; pap., LXX, Ep. Arist., Philo; Joseph.) κριὸς ἐ. ἐκ ποιμνίου *a splendid ram fr. the flock* MPol 14: 1. Of men (Diod. S. 5, 83, 1; Jos., Bell. 6, 201; 3 Macc 6: 1) ἐ. ἐν τοῖς ἀποστόλοις *outstanding among the apostles* Ro 16: 7. διδάσκαλος MPol 19: 1.
2. Also in a bad sense: *notorious* (trag. +; Plut., Fab. Max. 14, 2; Jos., Ant. 5, 234) δέσμιος Mt 27: 16. M-M.*

ἐπισήμως adv. (Polyb. 6, 39, 9; Jos., Bell. 6, 92; Sym. Ps 73: 4) *in an outstanding manner* θηριομαχεῖν MPol 3.*

ἐπισιτισμός, οῦ, ὁ *provisions* (so X., An. 7, 1, 9; Polyb. 2, 5, 3; Herodian 6, 7, 1; Dit., Or. 200, 15; Sb 6949, 15; LXX; Jos., Bell. 3, 85) εὑρίσκειν ἐ. *find someth. to eat* Lk 9: 12. M-M.*

ἐπισκέπτομαι mid. dep., fut. ἐπισκέψομαι, 1 aor. ἐπεσκεψάμην (trag., Hdt. +; inscr., pap., LXX; Philo; Jos., Ant. 11, 24; s. Bl-D. §101 p. 48 s.v. σκοπεῖν; Mlt.-H. 258 s.v. -σκέπτομαι).
1. *look at, examine, inspect* (Hdt. 2, 153 al.) w. acc. (Diod. S. 12, 11, 4; Num 1: 3; 1 Km 13: 15; 2 Km 18: 1) Hs 8, 2, 9; 8, 3, 3; 9, 10, 4; 1 Cl 25: 5. Also *look for, select* w. acc. (PPetr. II 37, 2b verso 4 [III BC] ἐπισκεψάμενος ἐν ἀρχῇ ἃ δεῖ γενέσθαι ἔργα) ἄνδρας Ac 6: 3.
2. *go to see, visit* τινά *someone* (Demosth. 9, 12; PLille 6, 5 [III BC] διαβάντος μου . . . ἐπισκέψασθαι τ. ἀδελφήν; Judg 15: 1) ἀδελφούς Ac 7: 23; 15: 36. ἀλλήλους Hv 3, 9, 2. Esp. of visiting the sick (X., Mem. 3, 11, 10; Plut., Mor. 129c; Lucian, Philops. 6; Herodian 4, 2, 4; Sir 7, 35; Jos., Ant. 9, 178) Mt 25: 36, 43; Pol 6: 1. Otherw. also w. the connotation of care: *look after* widows and orphans ἐν τῇ θλίψει αὐτῶν *in their distress* Js 1: 27; cf. Hs 1: 8. ὀρφανοὺς καὶ ὑστερουμένους Hm 8: 10.
3. of God's gracious visitation in bringing salvation (Gen 21: 1; 50: 24f; Ex 3: 16; 4: 31; Sir 46: 14; Jdth 8: 33; En. 25, 3; Test. Levi 16: 5) *visit* Lk 1: 68. ἐπισκέψεται ἡμᾶς ἀνατολὴ ἐξ ὕψους vs. 78; τὸν λαόν 7: 16 (cf. Ruth 1: 6).—Hb 2: 6 (Ps 8: 5); *be concerned about* w. inf. foll. (cf. Bl-D. §392, 3) ὁ θεὸς ἐπεσκέψατο λαβεῖν ἐξ ἐθνῶν λαόν *God concerned himself about winning a people fr. among the Gentiles* Ac 15: 14. M-M.*

ἐπισκευάζομαι 1 aor. ἐπεσκευασάμην (as a rule—Aristoph., Thu. +; inscr., pap., LXX—act. In our lit. only mid. as Jos., Bell. 1, 297) *make preparations* (Thu. 7, 36, 2) Ac 21: 15. M-M.*

ἐπισκηνόω 1 aor. ἐπεσκήνωσα *take up quarters, take up one's abode* w. ἐπί and acc. of the place where one takes up quarters (Polyb. 4, 18, 8 ἐπὶ τὰς οἰκίας) ἵνα ἐπισκηνώσῃ ἐπ' ἐμὲ ἡ δύναμις τ. Χριστοῦ *that the power of Christ may dwell in me* 2 Cor 12: 9 (cf. ἐπισκιάζω, which Philo paraphrases with ἐπισκηνόω). M-M.*

ἐπισκιάζω 1 aor. ἐπεσκίασα (Hdt. +; Philo, Deus Imm. 3 and oft.; LXX).
1. *overshadow, cast a shadow* (Aristot., Gen. An. 5, 1; Theophr., C.Pl. 2, 18, 3) τινί *upon someone* (Theophr., De Sens. 79) ἵνα κἂν ἡ σκιὰ ἐπισκιάσῃ τινὶ αὐτῶν *that at least his shadow might fall on one of them* Ac 5: 15.
2. *cover* (Hdt. 1, 209 τῇ πτέρυγι τὴν Ἀσίην; Aelian, V.H. 3, 3) w. acc. of the pers.; of the cloud that indicates the presence of God (cf. Ex 40: 35; Odes of Solomon 35, 1) Mt 17: 5; Lk 9: 34. W. dat. (Ps 90: 4) Mk 9: 7.
3. as a mysterious expression for that which enabled Mary to give birth to the divine child δύναμις ὑψίστου ἐπισκιάσει σοι Lk 1: 35. Cf. on this passage JHehn, BZ 14, '17, 147-52; AAllgeier, ibid. 338ff, Byz.-Neugriech. Jahrb. 1, '20, 131-41; Histor. Jahrbuch 45, '25, 1ff; HLeisegang, Pneuma hagion '22, 24ff; ENorden, D. Geburt des Kindes '24, 92-9; LRademacher: PKretschmer-Festschr. '26, 163ff; AFridrichsen, Symb. Osl. 6, '28, 33-6; MDibelius, Jungfrauensohn u. Krippenkind: SB der Heidelb. Ak. 1931/32, 4. Abh. '32, 23f; 41; HvBaer, D. Hl. Geist in d. Lkschriften '26, 124ff; KBornhäuser, D. Geburts-u. Kindheitsgesch. Jesu '30, 81ff; StLösch, Deitas Iesu u. antike Apotheose '33, 101. M-M.*

ἐπισκοπέω fut. ἐπισκοπήσω; 1 aor. ἐπεσκόπησα; pf. pass. ptc. ἐπεσκοπημένος (Aeschyl. +; inscr., pap., LXX, Philo; Jos., C. Ap. 2, 284; Test. 12 Patr.).

1. *look at, take care, see to it* w. μή foll. (Philo, Decal. 98) Hb 12: 15.

2. *oversee, care for* (Pla., Rep. 6 p. 506A τὴν πολιτείαν; Dio Chrys. 8[9], 1 of Diogenes the Cynic's mission in life; Wadd. 2309; 2412e; pap. [Witkowski² p. 96]; 2 Ch 34: 12), hence in a distinctively Christian sense of the activity of church officials 1 Pt 5: 2 𝔓⁷² et al., esp. of the bishop: *be a bishop* τινά *over someone* of Jesus, the ideal bishop IRo 9: 1. In a play on words w. ἐπίσκοπος: ἐπισκόπῳ μᾶλλον ἐπισκοπημένῳ ὑπὸ θεοῦ *the bishop, who rather has God over him as bishop* IPol inscr. (ἐπισκοπέω of God: Jos., C. Ap. 2, 160). Abs. *serve as bishop* Hv 3, 5, 1. M-M.*

ἐπισκοπή, ῆς, ἡ (Lucian, Dial. Deor. 20, 6='visit'; Dit., Or. 614, 6 [III AD]='care, charge'; Etym. Gud. 508, 27=πρόνοια; LXX).

1. *a visitation* of demonstrations of divine power mostly in the good sense (so Gen 50: 24f; Ex 3: 16; Wsd 2: 20; 3: 13; Job 10: 12; 29: 4 al.) καιρὸς τῆς ἐ. *the time of your gracious visitation* (Wsd 3: 7) Lk 19: 44. ἐν ἐ. τῆς βασιλείας τοῦ Χριστοῦ *when the kingdom of Christ visits us* 1 Cl 50: 3. ἡμέρα ἐπισκοπῆς 1 Pt 2: 12 is understood in this sense by the majority (e.g. Usteri, BWeiss, Kühl, Knopf, Windisch, FHauck, Vrede). S. also 2 below.—The gracious visitation can manifest itself as *protection, care* (Job 10: 12; Pr 29: 13; 3 Macc 5: 42) ἐν ἑνότητι θεοῦ καὶ ἐπισκοπῇ *in unity w. God and under his protection* IPol 8: 3.

2. *a visitation* of an unpleasant kind (Hesych.=ἐκδίκησις; Jer 10: 15; Sir 16: 18; 23: 24; Wsd 14: 11); ἡμέρα ἐ. (cf. Is 10: 3) 1 Pt 2: 12 is so understood by the minority (e.g. HermvSoden, Bigg, Gdspd.; FWDanker, ZNW 58, '67, 98f, w. ref. to Mal 3: 13–18). S. 1 above.

3. *position* or *office as an overseer* (Num 4: 16) of Judas' position as an apostle τὴν ἐ. λαβέτω ἕτερος *let another take his office* Ac 1: 20 (Ps 108: 8). Esp. *the office of a bishop* (a Christian inscr. of Lycaonia [IV AD] in Ramsay, Phrygia II p. 543) 1 Ti 3: 1 (cf. UHolzmeister, Biblica 12, '31, 41–69; CSpicq, RSphth 29, '40, 316–25); 1 Cl 44: 1, 4. M-M.*

ἐπίσκοπος, ου, ὁ (Hom.+; inscr., pap., LXX, Philo, Joseph.—LPorter, The Word ἐπίσκοπος in Pre-Christian Usage: ATR 21, '39, 103–12) *overseer.*

1. *of God* (so Il. 22, 255; Aeschyl., Sept. 272; Soph., Ant. 1148; Pla., Leg. 4, 717D; Plut., Cam. 5, 6 θεοὶ χρηστῶν ἐπίσκοποι καὶ πονηρῶν ἔργων; Maximus Tyr. 5, 8e ὦ Ζεῦ κ. Ἄπολλον, ἐθῶν ἀνθρωπίνων ἐπίσκοποι; Babrius 11, 4; Herodian 7, 10, 3. Oft. Cornutus, ed. Lang, index; Dit., Syll³ 1240, 21; UPZ 144, 49 [164 BC]; PGM 4, 2721; Job 20: 29; Wsd 1: 6; Philo, Migr. Abr. 115 al.; Sib. Or., fgm. 1, 3) παντὸς πνεύματος κτίστης κ. ἐπίσκοπος *creator and guardian of every spirit* 1 Cl 59: 3.—Of Christ (w. ποιμήν) ἐ. τῶν ψυχῶν *guardian of the souls* 1 Pt 2: 25. The passages IMg 3: 1 θεῷ τῷ πάντων ἐ.; cf. 6: 1 show the transition to the next mng.

2. *of persons who have a definite function or a fixed office within a group* (Aristoph., Av. 1023; IG XII 1, 49, 43ff [II/I BC]; 50, 34ff [I BC]; Wadd. 1989; 1990; 2298; Num 31: 14 al.; PPetr. III 36 (a) verso 16 [III BC]; Jos., Ant. 10, 53; 12, 254), including a religious group (IG XII 1, 731, 8: an ἐ. in the temple of Apollo at Rhodes. S. Dssm., NB 57f [BS 230f]. Cf. also Num 4: 16. On the Cynic-Stoic preacher as ἐπισκοπῶν and ἐπίσκοπος s. ENorden, Jahrbücher f. klass. Philol. Suppl. 19, 1893, 377ff.—Philo, Rer. Div. Her. 30 Moses as ἐ.); *superintendent, guardian, bishop* Ac 20: 28 (RSchnackenburg, Schriften zum NT, '71, 247–67); (w. διάκονοι) Phil 1: 1; D

15: 1; 1 Ti 3: 2; Tit 1: 7 (cf. BSEaston, Pastoral Epistles '47, 173; 177; 227). ἀπόστολοι, ἐ., διδάσκαλοι, διάκονοι Hv 3, 5, 1; (w. φιλόξενοι) s 9, 27, 2. Esp. freq. in Ignatius IEph 1: 3; 2: 1f; 3: 2; 4: 1; 5: 1f and oft.; 2 Ti subscr.: Tim., bishop of the Ephesians; Tit subscr., Titus bishop of the Cretans.—EHatch-AHarnack, D. Gesellschaftsverf. d. christl. Kirchen im Altert. 1883; Harnack, D. Lehre d. 12 Apostel 1884, 88ff, Entstehung u. Entwicklung der Kirchenverfassung u. des Kirchenrechts in d. zwei ersten Jahrh. '10; ELoening, D. Gemeindeverf. d. Urchristent. 1888; CWeizsäcker, D. apost. Zeitalter² 1892, 613ff; RSohm, Kirchenrecht I 1892; JRéville, Les origines de l'épiscopat 1894; HBruders, D. Verf. d. Kirche bis z. J. 175, '04; RKnopf, D. nachapostl. Zeitalter '05, 147ff; PBatiffol-FXSeppelt, Urkirche u. Katholicismus '10, 101ff; OScheel, Z. urchristl. Kirchen- u. Verfassungsproblem: StKr 85, '12, 403–57; HLietzmann, Z. altchr. Verfassungsgesch.: ZWTh 55, '13, 101–6 (=Kleine Schriften I, '58, 144–8); EMetzner, D. Verf. d. Kirche in d. zwei ersten Jahrh. '20; KMüller, Beiträge z. Gesch. d. Verf. in d. alten Kirche: ABA '22, no. 3; HDieckmann, D. Verf. d. Urkirche '23; GvHultum, ThGl 19, '27, 461–88; GHolstein, D. Grundlagen d. evangel. Kirchenrechts '28; JoachJeremias, Jerusalem II B 1, '29, 132ff (against him KGGoetz, ZNW 30, '31, 89–93); BHStreeter, The Primitive Church '29; OLinton, D. Problem d. Urkirche usw. '32 (lit. from 1880); JLebreton et JZeiller, L'Église primitive '34; HBeyer, D. Bischofamt im NT: Deutsche Theologie 1, '34, 201–25, TW II '35, 604–19; HGreeven, Propheten, Lehrer, Vorsteher bei Pls: ZNW 44, '52/'53, 1–43 (lit.); HvCampenhausen, Kirchl. Amt u. geistl. Vollmacht in den ersten 3 Jahrhunderten '53; WMichaelis, Das Ältestenamt der christlichen Gemeinde im Lichte der Hl. Schrift '53; RBultmann, Theol. of the NT (transl. KGrobel) '55, II, 95–111; TWManson, The Church's Ministry '56; FNötscher, Vom Alten zum NT '62, 188–220; DMoody, Interpretation 19, '65, 168–81; HBraun, Qumran u. das NT '66, II 326–42; RGG³ I 335–7 (lit.); JAFitzmyer, PSchubert-Festschr., '66, 256f, n. 41 (lit.). M-M.**

ἐπισκοτέω (Hippocr., Pla.+; Jos., Bell. 5, 343, C. Ap. 1, 214) *darken, obscure.*

1. ἐπισκοτεῖσθαι ὑπὸ πράξεων *be prevented by* (these) *occupations fr. seeing* Hm 10, 1, 4 (cf. Philo, De Jos. 147).

2. *throw a shadow upon, injure* (Menand., fgm. 48 Kock) pass. *be hindered* (Polyb. 2, 39, 12 ἐπισκοτεῖσθαι κ. κωλύεσθαι; Heraclit. Sto. 19 p. 29, 15) of the Spirit μὴ ἐπισκοτούμενον ὑπὸ ἑτέρου πονηροῦ πνεύματος Hm 5, 1, 2 (cf. Diog. L. 5, 76 ἐπεσκοτήθη ὑπὸ τοῦ φθόνου).*

ἐπισπάομαι in our lit. only mid. (which is found Hdt.+; Herm. Wr., inscr., pap., LXX, Philo; Jos., Ant. 14, 424, C. Ap. 2, 31).

1. *draw to oneself* lit. τινί τι an animal MPol 3 (cf. Diod. S. 17, 13, 2 ἐπισπᾶσθαι πληγάς=draw the blows [of the enemies] to oneself [in order to die more quickly]).

2. fig. *bring upon* (Hdt. 7, 72; Polyb. 3, 98, 8; Anth. Pal. 11, 340, 2 ἔχθραν; Dit., Or. 13, 6 τ. κρίσιν; Wsd 1: 12) τί τινι *someth.* (on) *someone* αἰχμαλωτισμὸν ἑαυτοῖς *bring captivity on themselves* Hv 1, 1, 8. ἀσθένειαν τῇ σαρκὶ αὐτῶν v 3, 9, 3. μεγάλην ἁμαρτίαν ἑαυτῷ m 4, 1, 8. ἑαυτῷ λύπην s 9, 2, 6.

3. medical t.t. *pull over the foreskin* (Soranus, Gynaec. 2, 34 p. 79, 1 of the nurse: ἐπισπάσθω τὴν ἀκροποσθίαν) to conceal circumcision 1 Cor 7: 18 (this special use of the word is not found elsewh., not even 4 Macc 5: 2, where ἐπισπᾶσθαι means 'drag up', as 10: 12). For the idea cf. 1 Macc 1: 15; Jos., Ant. 12, 241; rabbinic מָשׁוּךְ Billerb. IV 33f. M-M.*

ἐπισπείρω 1 aor. ἐπέσπειρα (since Pind., Nem. 8, 39; Hdt.) agricultural t.t. *sow afterward* (Theophr., Hist. Pl. 7, 1, 3; 5, 4 al.) τὶ someth. ζιζάνια ἀνὰ μέσον τοῦ σίτου *weeds among the wheat* Mt 13: 25. M-M.*

ἐπισπουδάζω (Lucian, Pisc. 2; PHib. 49, 3 [III BC]; PLille 3, 27; LXX) *be more zealous* περί τινος *for someone*; but the text is prob. corrupt; ἐπί may be repeated from the preceding ἔτι Hs 2: 6 (cf. the sound of the words in POxy. 1172 ἔτι καὶ ἔτι ἐπισπουδάζει and s. MDibelius, Hdb. ad loc.).*

ἐπίσταμαι pass. dep.; impf. ἠπιστάμην Dg 8: 1 (Hom. +; inscr., pap., LXX, En., Philo, Joseph.).
 1. *understand* τὶ someth. (X., Symp. 3, 6; Wsd 8: 8) μηδὲν ἐπιστάμενος *without understanding anything* 1 Ti 6: 4. Abs. (w. οἶδα) w. relative clause foll. σὺ τί λέγεις Mk 14: 68.
 2. *know, be acquainted with* τινά (Aristoph., Equ. 1278 Ἀρίγνωτον; Musonius 3 p. 12, 5H.; Plut., Cic. 44, 5; Lucian, Dial. Mort. 9, 3; PGM 13, 844; Wsd 15: 3; Jos., C. Ap. 1, 175) τὸν Παῦλον Ac 19: 15. τὸν θεόν PK 2 p. 14, 11. τὶ someth. (class., also Lucian, Dial. Deor. 25, 2; PRyl. 243, 6; Num 32: 11; 1 Esdr 8: 23 al.; Jos., C. Ap. 1, 15) Jd 10. πολλά B 1: 4. τὸ βάπτισμα Ἰωάννου Ac 18: 25. τὸ τῆς αὔριον *what will happen tomorrow* Js 4: 14 v.l. τὰς γραφάς 1 Cl 53: 1. περί τινος *know about someth.* (Thu. 6, 60, 1; Pla., Euthyphr. p. 4E) ἐπίσταται περὶ τούτων ὁ βασιλεύς *the king knows about this* Ac 26: 26. W. ὅτι foll. (X., An. 1, 4, 8 al.; Ex 4: 14; Tob 11: 7) Ac 15: 7; 19: 25; 22: 19; 1 Cl 45: 3. Also ὡς (Soph., Aj. 1370; X., Cyr. 2, 3, 22) Ac 10: 28. W. indir. quest. foll.: πῶς ἐγενόμην 20: 18 (cf. PTebt. 408, 3 [3 AD] ἐπιστάμενος πῶς σε φιλῶ). ποῦ ἔρχεται Hb 11: 8. πῶς νοήσω αὐτόν Hm 6, 2, 5. W. acc. and ptc. (X., An. 6, 6, 17; Jos., Vi. 142) ὄντα σε κριτήν *that you have been a judge* Ac 24: 10. πολλοὺς παραδεδωκότας ἑαυτούς 1 Cl 55: 2. M-M. B. 1210.*

ἐπίστασις, εως, ἡ (Soph.+ in var. mngs.; PAmh. 134, 9 al. in pap.; 2 Macc; Ep. Arist.; Philo, Leg. All. 3, 49; Jos., Ant. 16, 395) occurs twice in our lit., both times w. the v.l. ἐπισύστασις (q.v.). For ἐ. ποιεῖν ὄχλου Ac 24: 12 the best mng. is prob. *attack, onset* (cf. 2 Macc 6: 3 AV). For ἡ ἐ. μοι ἡ καθ᾽ ἡμέραν 2 Cor 11: 28 *pressure* is an outstanding possibility: *the daily pressure on me*. Other possibilities: *the attention* or *care daily required of me* (ἐ.=*attention, care*: Aristot., Phys. 196a, 38; Polyb. 2, 2, 2; 11, 2, 4; Diod. S. 29, 32 end; Ep. Arist. 256); *superintendence, oversight* (X., Mem. 1, 5, 2 codd.; s. also L-S-J s.v. II 3) *the burden of oversight, which lies upon me day in and day out*; finally, ἐ. can also mean *stopping, hindrance, delay* (BGU 1832, 16; 1855, 19; Polyb. 8, 28, 13); then: *the hindrances that beset me day by day*. M-M.*

ἐπιστάτης, ου, ὁ (Hom.+; used for var. officials in lit., inscr., pap., LXX; Jos., Ant. 8, 59, C. Ap. 2, 177) in Lk six times in the voc. ἐπιστάτα as a title addressed to Jesus, nearly always by the disciples (the synopt. parallels have διδάσκαλε [cf. Ammonius [100 AD] p. 45 Valck. and Philo, Poster. Cai. 54 ἐπ. κ. διδάσκαλοι], κύριε, ῥαββὶ) *master* (cf. IG XII 1, 43 ἐπιστάταν τῶν παίδων; Inschr. v. Priene 112, 73ff [after 84 BC] ἐ. τῶν ἐφήβων *whose task was* τὰς ψυχὰς πρὸς ἀρετὴν προάγεσθαι; Rouffiac p. 56f.—Diod. S. 3, 72, 1 Aristaeus the tutor of Dionysus and 3, 73, 4 Olympus the tutor of Zeus are both called ἐπιστάτης; 10, 3, 4 Pherecydes is the ἐπ.=teacher of Pythagoras) Lk 5: 5; 8: 24, 45; 9: 33, 49; 17: 13. —OGlombitza, ZNW 49, '58, 275-8. M-M.*

ἐπιστέλλω 1 aor. ἐπέστειλα *inform* or *instruct by letter*, also simply *write* (so Hdt.+; Dit., Syll.³ 837, 14; pap., LXX) w. dat. of the pers. (PFay. 133, 12; Jos., Ant. 4, 13; 14, 52) διὰ βραχέων ἐπέστειλα ὑμῖν *I have written to you briefly* Hb 13: 22 (cf. Herm. Wr. 14, 1 σοι δι᾽ ὀλίγων ἐ.). ἱκανῶς ἐ. τινὶ περί τινος *sufficiently to someone about someth.* 1 Cl 62: 1 (cf. Ps.-Aeschin., Ep. 12, 14; Jos., Ant. 12, 50). περί τινος (cf. UPZ 110, 185 [164 BC]; Jos., Ant. 18, 300) *concerning someone* Ac 21: 25. τινὶ περί τινος (BGU 1081, 5) 1 Cl 47: 3. W. subst. inf. foll. τοῦ ἀπέχεσθαι *to abstain* Ac 15: 20. Abs. 1 Cl 7: 1. M-M.*

ἐπιστῆ, ἐπίστηθι s. ἐφίστημι.

ἐπιστήμη, ης, ἡ (Soph., Thu.+; Epict.; Vett. Val. 211, 18; Herm. Wr. 4, 6; 10, 9 ἐπιστήμη δῶρον τ. θεοῦ; PFay. 106, 22; POxy. 896, 5; LXX, Philo) *understanding, knowledge* (w. σοφία, σύνεσις, γνῶσις [Aeneas Tact. 580 μετὰ ξυνέσεως κ. ἐπ.]) B 2: 3; 21: 5. As a Christian virtue Hv 3, 8, 7 (cf. Cebes 20, 3.—For the relationship between πίστις and ἐπιστήμη s. Simplicius in Epict. p. 110, 35ff τὸ ἀκοῦσαι παρὰ θεοῦ ὅτι ἀθάνατός ἐστιν ἡ ψυχή, πίστιν μὲν ποιεῖ βεβαίαν, οὐ μέντοι ἐπιστήμην. εἰ δέ τις ἀξιοῦται παρὰ θεοῦ καὶ τὰς αἰτίας μανθάνειν...=when someone hears from God [through the mediation of a μάντις] that the soul is immortal, that creates, to be sure, a firm faith, but not knowledge. But when someone is considered worthy by God of learning the causes as well...[then ἐπιστήμη puts in its appearance]). ἔπαινος ἐπιστήμης Phil 4: 8 v.l.*

ἐπιστήμων, ον gen. ονος (Hom.+; Epict. 2, 22, 3; POxy. 1469, 12; LXX, Philo) *expert, learned, understanding* (w. σοφός, as Dt 1: 13; 4: 6; Da 5: 11; Philo, Migr. Abr. 58) Js 3: 13; B 6: 10; (w. συνετός, as Da 6: 4) οἱ ἐνώπιον ἑαυτῶν ἐ. *those who are experts in their own estimation* 4: 11 (Is 5: 21). M-M.*

ἐπιστηρίζω 1 aor. ἐπεστήριξα (Aristot.+; LXX) *strengthen* τινά or τί the brothers Ac 11: 2 D; cf. 18: 23 t.r. Souls Ac 14: 22; churches 15: 41. Abs. vs. 32 (sc. ἀδελφούς).*

ἐπιστολή, ῆς, ἡ *letter, epistle* (so Eur., Thu.+; inscr., pap., LXX; En. 100, 6; Ep. Arist.; Philo; Joseph.; loanw. in rabb.) 2 Cor 7: 8; 2 Th 3: 17; 1 Cl 47: 1; 63: 2; IEph 12: 2; ISm 11: 3; Pol 13: 2b. δι᾽ ἐπιστολῆς (Diod. S. 19, 48, 1; Polyaenus 7, 39; 53rd letter of Apollonius of Tyana [Philostrat. I 358, 9]; Ps.-Demetr., Form. Ep. p. 5, 10; BGU 884, 6; 1046 II, 5) *by a letter* 2 Th 2: 2 (Vi. Aesopi W c. 104 ἐπ. ὡς ἐκ τοῦ Αἰσώπου; Polyaenus 8, 50 of two dead persons ὡς ἔτι ζώντων ἐπιστολή), 15, cf. 3: 14. γράφειν ἐπιστολήν (Philo, Leg. ad Gai. 207) Ac 15: 23 D; 23: 25; Ro 16: 22; ἐν τῇ ἐπ. 1 Cor 5: 9 (ἐν τῇ ἐπ.=᾽in the letter known to you᾽ [s. ὁ II 1aα] as Lind. Tempelchronik B 14 ἐν τᾷ ἐπιστολᾷ; Hyperid. 3, 25 ἐν τ. ἐπιστολαῖς; Pla., 7th Epistle p. 345c ἡ ἐπ.=the letter [known to you]). ταύτην δευτέραν ὑμῖν γράφω ἐ. 2 Pt 3: 1 (cf. BGU 827, 20 ἰδοὺ τρίτην ἐπιστολήν σοι γράφω; PMich. 209, 5 δευτέραν ἐπιστολὴν ἔπεμψά σοι). ἀναδιδόναι τὴν ἐπιστολήν τινι *deliver the letter to someone* Ac 23: 33. Also ἐπιδιδόναι 15: 30. διαπέμπεσθαι *send* MPol 20: 1. διακονεῖν *care for* 2 Cor 3: 3. ἀναγινώσκειν (X., An. 1, 6, 4; 1 Macc 10: 7; Jos., C. Ap. 2, 37) 3: 2; Col 4: 16; 1 Th 5: 27. In all probability the plur. in our lit.—even Ac 9: 2; Pol 3: 2—always means more than one letter, not a single one (as Eur., Iph. A. 111; 314; Thu. 1, 132, 5; 4, 50, 2, also M. J. Brutus, Ep. 1, 1 [fr. Mithridates]; 1 Macc 10: 3, 7; Jos., Ant. 10, 15; 16), δι᾽ ἐπιστολῶν *with letters* 1 Cor 16: 3. Differently δι' ἐπιστολῶν ἀπόντες (do someth.) *by means of letters when we are absent* 2 Cor 10: 11 (cf. UPZ 69, 3 [152 BC] ἀπόντος μου . . . διὰ τοῦ ἐπιστολίου); vs. 9; ἐ. βαρεῖαι καὶ ἰσχυραί *the letters are weighty and powerful* vs. 10. ἔγραψεν ὑμῖν ὡς καὶ ἐν πάσαις ἐ. 2 Pt 3: 16. ἐ. συστατικαί *letters of recommendation* 2 Cor 3: 1 (s. on συστατικός). ἐπιστολὰς πέμπειν (Ps.-Demosth. 11, 17; Diod. S. 17, 23, 6 ἔπεμψεν ἐπιστολάς=letters; Dit., Or. 42, 6; 2 Macc 11: 34) IPol 8: 1; cf. Pol 13: 2a. ἐπιστολὴ πρός τινα *a letter to someone* (2 Esdr 12 [Neh 2]: 7; 2 Macc 11: 27; Jos., C. Ap. 1, 111) Ac 9: 2; 22: 5 (letters empowering someone to arrest people and deliver them to the authorities in the capital city, as PTebt. 315, 29ff [II AD]); 2 Cor 3: 1 (πρὸς ὑμᾶς ἢ ἐξ ὑμῶν).—At the end of a letter 1 Cl 65: 2; 2 Cl 20: 5 Funk; B 21: 9.—GJBahr, Paul and Letter Writing in the First Century, CBQ 28, '66, 465–77. Lit. on χαίρω 2b. M-M. B. 1286.*

ἐπιστομίζω *stop the mouth,* mostly fig. (Aristoph., Equ. 845; Pla., Gorg. 482ε al.; Plut., Mor. 156α; 810ε), *silence* τινά *someone* (Demosth. 7, 33; Libanius, Or. 2 p. 243, 20 F.) οὓς δεῖ ἐπιστομίζειν *who must be silenced* Tit 1: 11. The mng. *bridle, hinder, prevent* (Lucian, Pro Im. 10, Calumn. 12; Philo, Det. Pot. Insid. 23; Jos., Ant. 17, 251) is also poss., esp. ibid. v.l. M-M.*

ἐπιστρέφω fut. ἐπιστρέψω; 1 aor. ἐπέστρεψα; 2 aor. pass. ἐπεστράφην (Hom.+; inscr., pap., LXX, Joseph., Test. 12 Patr.).
1. act.—a. trans. *turn* in a relig.-moral sense (Plut., Mor. p. 21c ἐ. τινὰ πρὸς τὸ καλόν; Jos., Ant. 10, 53) τινὰ or τὶ ἐπί τινα *someone or someth. to someone* (2 Ch 19: 4; Jdth 7: 30) πολλοὺς ἐπὶ κύριον Lk 1: 16. καρδίας πατέρων ἐπὶ τέκνα vs. 17 (cf. Sir 48: 10; cf. Hes., Works and Days, 182). τινὰ ἔκ τινος *turn someone fr. someth.* (cf. Mal 2: 6) Js 5: 20; cf. vs. 19. Of God τοὺς πλανωμένους ἐπίστρεψον *bring back those who have gone astray* 1 Cl 59: 4. Sim. of the presbyters Pol 6: 1. Cf. 2 Cl 17: 2.
b. intr.—a. lit. *turn around, turn back* (X., Hell. 4, 16; Polyb. 1, 47, 8; Aelian, V.H. 1, 6; LXX) abs. Lk 8: 55 (cf. Judg 15: 19); Ac 15: 36; 16: 18; Rv 1: 12b; εἴς τι (Dit., Syll.³ 709, 11 [c. 107 BC]; 2 Km 15: 27; 1 Esdr 5: 8; 1 Macc 5: 68; 3 Macc 7: 8 εἰς τὰ ἴδια ἐ.) Mt 12: 44 (exorcism of evil spirits so that they never return: Jos., Ant. 8, 45; 47 μηκέτ' εἰς αὐτὸν ἐπανήξειν); Lk 2: 39. εἰς τὰ ὀπίσω Mk 13: 16; Lk 17: 31; also ἐ. ὀπίσω Mt 24: 18. ἐπί τι (Dit., Syll.³ 709, 20) 2 Pt 2: 22. ἐπί τινα Lk 10: 6 D. πρός τινα *to someone* Lk 17: 4. W. inf. foll. to denote purpose (Jdth 8: 11 v.l.) βλέπειν Rv 1: 12a (s. φωνή 2a). Also simply *turn* πρὸς τὸ σῶμα Ac 9: 40 (on ἐ. πρός w. acc. cf. Aesop, Fab. 248 H.; 1 Macc 7: 25; 11: 73 v.l.).
β. fig., of a change of mind or of a course of action, for the better or the worse (Ps 77: 41; 2 Esdr 19 [Neh 9]: 28) *turn back, return* Ac 15: 16 D. ἐπί τι *to someth.* Pol 7: 2; Gal 4: 9. ἔκ τινος *from someth.* (cf. 3 Km 13: 26) 2 Pt 2: 21 v.l. Esp. of a change in the sinner's relation with God *turn* (oft. LXX) ἐπί w. acc.: ἐπὶ τὸν κύριον Ac 9: 35; 11: 21. ἐπὶ τὸν θεόν 26: 20. πρὸς κύριον (1 Km 7: 3; Hos 5: 4; 6: 1; Am 4: 6 al. LXX) 2 Cor 3: 16; Hm 12, 6, 2. πρὸς τὸν θεόν 1 Th 1: 9. Here and occasionally elsewh. the thing from which one turns is added, w. ἀπό and the gen. (2 Ch 6: 26; Bar 2: 33 v.l.) Ac 14: 15; perh. 15: 19. ἐ. ἀπὸ σκότους εἰς φῶς καὶ τῆς ἐξουσίας τ. σατανᾶ ἐπὶ θεόν 26: 18. Abs. Mt 13: 15; Mk 4: 12; Ac 28: 27 (all three Is 6: 10); Lk 22: 32 (s. CHPickar, CBQ 4, '42, 137–40); (w. μετανοεῖν) Ac 3: 19.
2. mid., w. aor. pass.—a. lit.—a. *turn around* (Hdt. 3,

156; X., Cyr. 6, 4, 10, Symp. 9, 1 al.; Jos., Ant. 7, 265; 16, 351) ἐπιστραφεὶς ἐν τῷ ὄχλῳ *he turned around in the crowd* Mk 5: 30. ἐπιστραφεὶς καὶ ἰδών 8: 33 (Jos., Bell. 2, 619 ἐπιστραφεὶς κ. θεασάμενος).—J 21: 20.
β. *return* (Eur., Alc. 188; 1 Macc 4: 24) εἰς τὰ ὀπίσω (Lucian, Catapl. 14) Hv 4, 3, 7. Of a greeting, which is to return unused Mt 10: 13.
b. non-literal use *turn (about)* (Ps.-Demosth. 10, 9; Epict. 2, 20, 22 οἱ πολῖται ἡμῶν ἐπιστραφέντες τιμῶσι τὸ θεῖον; Dt 30: 10; Jer 3: 14; Ps 7: 13 al.) ἐ. ἐπί τινα (Is 55: 7) 1 Pt 2: 25. πρός τινα: (Diog. L. 3, 25 all Greeks to Pla.; Synes., Provid. 1, 9 p. 97c πρὸς τὸν θεόν) πρὸς τ. κύριον (Hos 14: 2f; Jo 2: 13 al.) Hm 12, 6, 2. πρός με (Am 4: 8; Jo 2: 12 al.) 1 Cl 8: 3 (scripture quot. of unknown orig.). Abs. *be converted* J 12: 40 t.r.; Hm 12, 4, 6. ἐγγὺς κύριος τοῖς ἐπιστρεφομένοις *the Lord is near to them who turn (to him)* v 2, 3, 4.—ADNock, Conversion. The Old and the New in Religion fr. Alex. the Gr. to Augustine of Hippo '33; EKDietrich, Die Umkehr (Bekehrung u. Busse im AT u. Judentum), '36. M-M.**

ἐπιστροφή, ῆς, ἡ (trag., Thu.+; inscr., pap., LXX, Joseph.) in our lit. only in intrans. sense *turning (toward).*
1. *attention* (Soph.+) ἐ. ποιεῖσθαι *give attention, concern oneself* (Demosth. 12, 1; 19, 306; Appian, Bell. Civ. 4, 35 §148; Inscr. Gr. 543, 3; PPetr. II 19 [2], 2; Jos., Ant. 9, 237) w. περί τινος (Chrysipp.: Stoic. III 187; Dit., Syll.³ 685, 128 [139 BC]) 1 Cl 1: 1.
2. *conversion* (Sir 18: 21; 49: 2; PsSol 16: 11; Jos., Ant. 2, 293; Porphyr., Ad Marcellam 24 μόνη σωτηρία ἡ πρὸς τ. θεὸν ἐπιστροφή; Hierocles, Carm. Aur. 24 p. 473 Mull.; Simplicius in Epict. p. 107, 22 ἡ ἐπὶ τὸ θεῖον ἐπιστροφή) τῶν ἐθνῶν Ac 15: 3. εἶναι εἰς ἐ. τινι *be a means of conversion for someone* B 11: 8.—PAubin, Le problème de la 'conversion' '63. M-M.*

ἐπισυνάγω fut. ἐπισυνάξω; 1 aor. inf. ἐπισυνάξαι Lk 13: 34 beside the 2 aor. inf. ἐπισυναγαγεῖν Mt 23: 37 (W-S. §13, 10; Mlt.-H. 226); perf. pass. ptc. ἐπισυνηγμένος; 1 aor. pass. ἐπισυνήχθην; 1 fut. pass. ἐπισυναχθήσομαι (Polyb.; Plut., Mor. 894α al.; inscr., pap., LXX, En., Ep. Arist., Joseph.) in our lit. always=συνάγω (cf. Lk 17: 37=Mt 24: 28) *gather (together)* τινὰ *someone* (3 Km 18: 20 [συνάγ: Ps 105: 47 al.; Test. Napht. 8: 3) τὰ τέκνα Mt 23: 37a; Lk 13: 34. Of a hen that gathers its brood Mt 23: 37b. τοὺς ἐκλεκτοὺς ἐκ τῶν τεσσάρων ἀνέμων *his chosen people from the four winds* 24: 31; Mk 13: 27. Pass. *be gathered* (Dit., Or. 90, 23, Syll.³ 700, 21 [117 BC]; 2 Ch 20: 26; 1 Esdr 9: 5 al.; En. 22, 3; Philo, Op. M. 38) of birds of prey around a dead body Lk 17: 37. Of a crowd gathering (Jos., Ant. 18, 37) 12: 1. ὅλη ἡ πόλις Mk 1: 33. M-M.*

ἐπισυναγωγή, ῆς, ἡ (scarcely to be differentiated fr. συναγωγή: IG XII 3 suppl. no. 1270, 11f [II BC; cf. Dssm., LO 81; LAE 101ff]; 2 Macc 2: 7).
1. *meeting* of a church ἐγκαταλείπειν τὴν ἐ. ἑαυτῶν *neglect their own meeting(s)* Hb 10: 25.—2. the action of ἐπισυνάγεσθαι: *assembling* ἐπί τινα *with someone* 2 Th 2: 1. M-M.*

ἐπισυντρέχω (hapax legomenon) *run together* of crowds Mk 9: 25. M-M.*

ἐπισυρράπτω for ἐπι(ρ)ράπτω (q.v.) Mk 2: 21 D.*

ἐπισύστασις, εως, ἡ *uprising, disturbance, insurrection* (Sext. Emp., Eth. 127; Berosus in Jos., C. Ap. 1, 149; Dit., Syll.³ 708, 27 [I BC]; Num 17: 5; 26: 9; 1 Esdr 5: 70; Artapanus in Euseb., Pr. Ev. 9, 23, 1) Ac 24: 12 t.r.; the more recent editions read ἐπίστασις. On 2 Cor 11: 28 s. ἐπίστασις. M-M.*

ἐπισφαλής, ές (Hippocr., Pla.+; Diod. S. 13, 77, 2; POxy. 75, 20; Wsd 9, 14; Philo, Praem. 33; Jos., Ant. 5, 52; 139) *unsafe, dangerous* of a voyage in the autumn Ac 27: 9. M-M.*

ἐπισφραγίζω 1 aor. ἐπεσφράγισα (Diod. S. 14, 55, 1 βιβλίον ἐπεσφραγισμένον; pap.; 2 Esdr 20 [Neh 10]: 1; the mid. in Pla. et al.; Philo) *seal, put a seal on* τ. διωγμόν *the persecution*, thereby bringing it to an end, as a letter MPol 1: 1.*

ἐπισχύω impf. ἐπίσχυον (X.+; BGU 1761, 3 [I BC]) intr. *grow strong* (Theophr. et al.; Vett. Val. 48, 6 τῶν δὲ τοιούτων καὶ ὁ λόγος ἐπισχύει πρὸς συμβουλίαν ἢ διδαχήν; 1 Macc 6: 6) ἐπίσχυον λέγοντες *they insisted and said* Lk 23: 5 (MBlack, An Aramaic Approach³, '67, 255 [Old Syriac]). M-M.

ἐπισωρεύω (Epict. 1, 10, 5; Vett. Val. 332, 24; 344, 13 al.; Sym. Job 14: 17; SSol 2: 4) *heap up* fig. διδασκάλους *accumulate a great many teachers* 2 Ti 4: 3. τινί (*in addition*) *to* (Athen. 3 p. 123E) ἐ. ταῖς ἁμαρτίαις ὑμῶν *heap sin upon sin* B 4: 6. M-M.*

ἐπιταγή, ῆς, ἡ (Polyb.+; Diod. S. 1, 70, 1 νόμων ἐπιταγή; inscr.; PFlor. 119, 5; LXX; En.; Ep. Arist.) *command, order, injunction* ἐπιταγὴν ἔχειν *have a command* 1 Cor 7: 25. κατ' ἐπιταγήν *in accordance w. the command = by command* (Dit., Syll.³ 1153; 1171, 3; IG XII 1, 785; JHS 26, '06, p. 28 no. 6 κατ' ἐπ. τ. θεοῦ; PGM 12, 62; 1 Esdr 1: 16; En. 5, 2) Ro 16: 26; 1 Ti 1: 1; Tit 1: 3; Hv 3, 8, 2. But κατ' ἐ. acquires another mng. fr. the context in the expr. κατ' ἐ. λέγειν *say as a command* 1 Cor 7: 6; 2 Cor 8: 8. μετὰ πάσης ἐ. *with all impressiveness* Tit 2: 15. M-M.*

ἐπιτάσσω 1 aor. ἐπέταξα; pf. pass. ptc. ἐπιτεταγμένος (trag., Hdt.+; inscr., pap., LXX, Ep. Arist., Joseph.) *order, command* τινί *someone* (Soph., Ant. 664; X., Cyr. 4, 2, 33; Dit., Syll.³ 83, 33; PTebt. 59, 9; Gen 49: 33; Esth 1: 1q, 8) B 19: 7; D 4: 10. τοῖς πνεύμασι (cf. PGM 12, 316a τῷ θεῷ) Mk 1: 27; Lk 4: 36; cf. Mk 9: 25; the wind and waves (cf. 2 Macc 9: 8) Lk 8: 25. τί τινι (Hdt.; Dit., Syll.³ 748, 25 [71 BC]; Jos., Ant. 1, 172) τινὶ τὸ ἀνῆκον *order someone* (to do) *his duty* Phlm 8. τινί w. pres. inf. (class.) foll. (X., An. 2, 3, 6; 1 Macc 4: 41) Ac 23: 2; Hs 9, 4, 4; w. aor. inf. (X., Cyr. 7, 3, 14; Dit., Syll.³ 683, 37 [140 BC], Or. 443, 2) Mk 6: 39; Lk 8: 31; Hs 9, 5, 1. Foll. by aor. inf. without dat. (class., also oft. LXX) ἐπέταξεν ἐνέγκαι τὴν κεφαλὴν αὐτοῦ *he gave orders to bring his head* Mk 6: 27. Abs. (Thu. 1, 140, 2; POxy. 294, 21 [22 AD] ὡς ἐπέταξεν ὁ ἡγεμών; Esth 8: 8; 1 Macc 10: 81; PGM 12, 316b) Lk 14: 22; B 6: 18.—Pass. ἐξελίσσειν τοὺς ἐπιτεταγμένους αὐτοῖς ὁρισμούς *roll on in their appointed courses* 1 Cl 20: 3. τὰ ἐπιτασσόμενα (Dit., Syll.³ 742, 2; POxy. 275, 11) ὑπὸ τοῦ βασιλέως *the king's commands* 37: 3 (cf. Dit., Syll.³ 748, 18 τὰ ἐπιτασσόμενα ὑπ' αὐτῶν; Herm. Wr. 16, 10b ὑπὸ τ. θεῶν).—Hs 9, 6, 2 v.l. M-M.*

ἐπιτελέω fut. ἐπιτελέσω; 1 aor. ἐπετέλεσα (Hdt.+; inscr., pap., LXX, Ep. Arist., Philo, Joseph.).
1. *end, bring to an end, finish* someth. begun (1 Km 3: 12; 1 Esdr 4: 55; 6: 27) τί someth. Ro 15: 28; Phil 1: 6; 2 Cor 8: 6, 11a. Abs. vs. 11b. So also Gal 3: 3, either as mid.: *you have begun in the Spirit; will you now end in the flesh?* or as pass. *will you be made complete in the flesh?* w. ref. to the Judaizers.

2. *complete, accomplish, perform, bring about* τὶ someth. πάντα (1 Esdr 8: 16) 1 Cl 1: 3; 2: 8; 48: 4. πᾶν ἔργον ἀγαθόν 33: 1 (POsl. 137, 9 [III AD] ἐ. τὰ καθήκοντα ἔργα). τὰ ἀνήκοντα τῇ βουλήσει 35: 5 (PTebt. 294, 11 τὰ τῇ προφητείᾳ προσήκοντα ἐπιτελεῖν). τὰ διατασσόμενα *carry out the commands* (PGM 4, 1539f τ. ἐντολάς) 37: 2f; cf. 40: 1f. τ. λειτουργίαν *perform a service* (Philo, Somn. 1, 214; s. below) 1 Cl 20: 10; Lk 13: 32 v.l. ἁγιωσύνην *bring about sanctification* 2 Cor 7: 1 (cf. Ep. Arist. 133 κακίαν; 166 ἀκαθαρσίαν). τὴν σκηνήν *erect the tent* Hb 8: 5. Esp. of the performance of rituals and ceremonies (Hdt.+; Dit., Syll.³ 1109, 111 ἐ. τὰς λιτουργίας; UPZ 43, 20 [162/1 BC]; 106, 21 [99 BC]; PTebt. 292, 20f; Wilcken, Chrest. 70, 9–11; Ep. Arist. 186; Philo, Ebr. 129; Jos., C. Ap. 2, 118) τ. λατρείας ἐ. *perform the rituals* (Philo, Somn. 1, 214) Hb 9: 6. θυσίας *bring sacrifices* (Hdt. 2, 63; 4, 26; Diod. S. 17, 115, 6; Herodian 1, 5, 2; Dit., Syll. index; Inschr. v. Priene 108, 27; Philo, Somn. 1, 215; Jos., Ant. 4, 123; 9, 273; POxy. 2782, 6–8 [II/III AD]) Dg 3: 5. The pass. in this mng. 1 Cl 40: 3. τὴν ἡμέραν γενέθλιον ἐ. *celebrate the birthday* MPol 18: 2 (Epici p. 18, 3 γάμους ἐπετέλεσεν; Ammonius, Vi. Aristot. p. 11, 23 Westerm. ἑορτὴν ἐ.).—Mid. (=act., as Polyb. 1, 40, 16; 2, 58, 10; Diod. S. 3, 57, 4 πρᾶξιν ἐπιτελέσασθαι) γυναῖκες ἐπετελέσαντο ἀνδρεῖα *women have performed heroic deeds* 1 Cl 55: 3.
3. *fulfill* (Lucian, Charon 6 τ. ὑπόσχεσιν) of a saying of scripture, pass. 1 Cl 3: 1.
4. *lay someth. upon someone, accomplish someth. in the case of someone* τινί τι (Pla., Leg. 10 p. 910D δίκην τινί) pass. τὰ αὐτὰ τῶν παθημάτων τῇ ἀδελφότητι ἐπιτελεῖσθαι *the same sufferings are laid upon the brotherhood* or *are accomplished in the case of the brotherhood* 1 Pt 5: 9. M-M.*

ἐπιτήδειος, εία, ον *necessary, proper*, adj. (Eur., Hdt.+) καιρῷ ἐπιτηδείῳ *at a suitable time* Ac 24: 25 v.l. (καιρὸς ἐ. as Jos., Vi. 125; 176).—Subst. τὰ ἐ. *what is necessary* (Hdt. 2, 174; Thu. 2, 23, 3; inscr., pap., LXX; Jos., Bell. 3, 183, Ant. 2, 326; 12, 376) w. τοῦ σώματος added *what is necessary for the body*, i.e. *for life* Js 2: 16. M-M. B. 644.*

ἐπιτήδευμα, ατος, τό (Thu.+; Diod. S. 3, 70, 7; Epict. 3, 23, 5 al.; Vett. Val. 73, 20; Dit., Syll.³ 703, 15; 721, 12; 42; 766, 5; pap.; LXX; Philo, Op. M. 80; Jos., Ant. 15, 368, C. Ap. 2, 123; 181 in var. mngs.) *pursuit, way of living* (Hippocr., Epid. 1, 23; Menand., Kith., fgm. 4, 2 J. ἐ. τῷ βίῳ; Oenomaus in Euseb., Pr. Ev. 5, 34, 10 θεῖόν τι ἐπ.= a sort of divine way of life) of Christianity Dg 1.*

ἐπιτηδεύω 1 aor. ἐπετήδευσα (Soph., Hdt.+; Diod. S. 1, 70, 2) Epict. 3, 1, 15; 3, 5, 8; BGU 1253, 11 [II BC]; LXX; Jos., Ant. 18, 66, C. Ap. 2, 189) *take care* w. ὡς foll. MPol 17: 1.*

ἐπιτηρέω (Hom. Hymns, Thu.+; inscr. [Sb 8304, 8]; pap.; Jdth 13: 3) *watch carefully, lie in wait* B 10: 4.*

ἐπιτίθημι 3 pl. ἐπιτιθέασιν Mt 23: 4, imper. ἐπιτίθει 1 Ti 5: 22; impf. 3 pl. ἐπετίθεσαν Ac 8: 17; fut. ἐπιθήσω; 1 aor. ἐπέθηκα; 2 aor. ἐπέθην, imper. ἐπίθες, ptc. ἐπιθείς; fut. mid. ἐπιθήσομαι; 2 aor. mid. ἐπεθέμην (Hom.+; inscr., pap., LXX, Philo, Joseph., Test. 12 Patr.).
1. act.—a. *lay* or *put upon*—a. lit. τὶ (which somet. is to be supplied fr. the context; cf. Esth 5: 2) ἐπί τι or τινα (X., Cyr. 7, 3, 14; Dit., Syll.³ 1173, 9; cf. 1169, 4; PSI 442, 13 [III BC]; Gen 22: 9; 42: 26 and oft.) *someth. upon someth.* or *someone* Mt 23: 4; Lk 15: 5; J 9: 6 (most mss.

read ἐπέχρισεν), 15; Ac 15: 10; 28: 3; B 7: 8. χεῖρα
(χεῖρας) ἐπί τινα or τι *lay hand(s) on someone or someth.*
(Dit., Syll.³ 1173, 4; Ex 29: 10; Lev 1: 4; 4: 4 al.—KSud-
hoff, Handanlegg. des Heilgottes: Archiv f. Gesch. d.
Med. 18, '26, 235–50) Mt 9: 18; Mk 8: 25 (v.l. ἔθηκεν);
16: 18; Ac 8: 17; 9: 17. Also τινὶ τὰς χεῖρας (Jos., Ant. 9,
268; 16, 365) Mt 19: 13, 15; Mk 5: 23; 6: 5; 8: 23; Lk
4: 40; 13: 13; Ac 6: 6; 8: 19; 9: 12; 13: 3; 19: 6; 28: 8;
of ordination as an elder 1 Ti 5: 22 (Gdspd., Probs. 181f;
cf. IQ Gen. Apoc. 20, 29); cf. Mk 7: 32; B 13: 5 (Gen 48:
18). S. on ἐπίθεσις.—In other combinations ἐ. τί τινι
(X., Oec. 17, 9; Esth 2: 17; 1 Esdr 4: 30; Jos., Ant. 9, 149
ἐπέθεσαν αὐτῷ τ. στέφανον) Lk 23: 26; J 19: 2. τοὺς
λίθους ἐπετίθουν ἀλλήλαις *they placed the stones on one
another's shoulders* Hs 9, 3, 5.—τὶ ἐπί τινος (Hdt. 1, 121,
4 al.; 1 Km 6: 18; Sus 34) Mt 21: 7; Lk 8: 16 v.l. ἐπέθηκαν
ἐπὶ τ. κεφαλῆς αὐτοῦ *they placed* (the crown of thorns) *on
his head* Mt 27: 29. ἐπάνω τ. κεφαλῆς *put above* (*his*)
head vs. 37.—τῷ μνημείῳ λίθον *a stone at the grave* Lk
23: 53 v.l. (λίθοι) ἐπιτιθέμενοι εἰς τ. οἰκοδομήν *stones
put into the building* Hv 3, 5, 2.
β. fig. ἐ. πληγάς τινι *inflict blows upon someone*
(BGU 759, 13 [II AD] πληγὰς πλείστας ἐπέθηκάν μοι)
Ac 16: 23; cf. Lk 10: 30. Differently ἐπιθήσει ὁ θεὸς ἐπ'
αὐτὸν τ. πληγάς *God will bring upon him the plagues* Rv
22: 18b (cf. δίκην τινί class., also Dt 26: 6; τειμωρίαν
τινί Isisaretal. of Cyme 20; 35 Peek); s. BOlsson, D.
Epilog der Offb. Joh.: ZNW 31, '32, 84–6.—Pass. Ac 15:
28.—ἐ. τινὶ ὄνομα *give a surname to someone* (cf. Hdt. 5,
68 al.; 2 Esdr 19 [Neh 9]: 7) Mk 3: 16f (on the giving of new
names to disciples cf. Diog. L. 5, 38: Theophrastus' name
was Τύρταμος. His teacher, Aristotle μετωνόμασεν and
gave him the name Theophrastus because of his god-like
eloquence). B 12: 8f ἐ. τὸ ἔλεος ἐπί τινα *bestow mercy
upon someone* 15: 2.—b. add ἐπί τι (Hom., al.) ἐπ' αὐτά
Rv 22: 18a.
2. mid.—a. *give τινί τι someth. to someone* (BGU 1208
1, 4 [27 BC]; PRyl. 81, 9 τὴν ὅλου τ. πράγματος ἐξουσίαν
τοῖς κατασπορεῦσι ἐπεθέμην) ἀναγομένοις τὰ πρὸς τὰς
χρείας *when we sailed they gave us what we needed* Ac
28: 10.
b. *set upon, attack* (Jos., Ant. 1, 328) τινί (Hdt.,
Aristoph. et al.; Appian, Liby. 102 §482; PTebt. 15, 11
[114 BC]; PFlor. 332, 7; LXX; Philo, Leg. ad Gai. 371;
Jos., Ant. 4, 96) foll. by subst. inf. of purpose in gen. (Gen
43: 18) οὐδεὶς ἐπιθήσεταί σοι τοῦ κακῶσαί σε *in order to
harm you* Ac 18: 10. M-M.*

ἐπιτιμάω impf. 3 sg. ἐπετίμα, 3 pl. ἐπετίμων; 1 aor.
ἐπετίμησα (Thu., Pla.+; inscr., pap., LXX, En., Philo,
Joseph.).
1. *rebuke, reprove, censure* also *speak seriously, warn* in
order to prevent an action or bring one to an end. Abs.
(Thu. 4, 28, 1; Demosth. 1, 16 al.; Dit., Syll.³ 344, 55 [?];
Sir 11: 7; Jos., Ant. 5, 105) Lk 4: 41; 2 Ti 4: 2. τινί (X.,
Pla.+; Epict. 3, 22, 10 al.; Lucian, Dial. Mort. 1, 8; PMagd.
24, 5 [218 BC]; UPZ 64, 7; Gen 37: 10 al.; Philo, De Jos.
74; Jos., C. Ap. 2, 239) Mt 8: 26; 17: 18; 19: 13; Mk 4: 39
(cf. Ps 105: 9); 8: 32f; 10: 13; Lk 4: 39; 8: 24; 9: 21, 42,
55; 17: 3; 18: 15; 19: 39; 23: 40.—Foll. by ἵνα or ἵνα μή to
introduce that which the censure or warning is to bring
about or prevent Mt 12: 16; 16: 20; 20: 31; Mk 3: 12 (for
πολλὰ ἐπετίμα cf. Ps.-Xenophon, Cyn. 12, 16); 8: 30 (on
Mk 3: 12, 8: 30 s. GABarton, JBL 41, '22, 233–6); 10: 48;
Lk 18: 39. Foll. by λέγων and dir. discourse Mt 16: 22;
Mk 1: 25 v.l.; 9: 25 (for the terminology of exorcism in Mk
s. HCKee, NTS 14, '68, 232–46); Lk 4: 35. In Jd 9 ἐ.
could = *rebuke* as a contrast to blaspheme, avoided by the
archangel. But the next mng. is also poss. here.

2. *punish* (Diod. S. 3, 67, 2 πληγαῖς ἐπιτιμηθείς;
3 Macc 2: 24; En. 98, 5; Jos., Ant. 18, 107).—EStauffer,
TW II 620–3. M-M.*

ἐπιτιμία, ας, ἡ (Demosth.+; Philo.—In Jos., C. Ap. 2,
199 ἐπιτίμιον) *punishment* (so Dit., Or. 669, 43 [I AD];
PLond. 77, 53; Wsd 3: 10) 2 Cor 2: 6. M-M.*

ἐπιτοαυτό s. ἐπί III 1aζ.

ἐπιτρέπω 1 aor. ἐπέτρεψα; 2 aor. pass. ἐπετράπην; pf.
pass. ἐπιτέτραμμαι (Hom.+; inscr., pap., LXX, Joseph.).
1. *allow, permit* (so Pind. et al.) τινί someone w. inf.
foll. (X., An. 1, 2, 19; Hell. 6, 3, 9; Epict. 1, 10, 10;
2, 7, 12; PMagd. 2, 7 [221 BC]; 12, 11; PRyl. 120, 16; Job
32: 14; 4 Macc 4: 18; Jos., Ant. 8, 202) Mt 8: 21; 19: 8;
Mk 10: 4; Lk 8: 32a; 9: 59, 61; Ac 21: 39; 27: 3; 1 Ti
2: 12; Dg 10: 2; IEph 10: 1; IRo 6: 3; Hm 4, 1, 4; D
10: 7; GOxy 12. Without inf. (Pind., Ol. 3, 64; Dit., Syll.³
260, 16; 360, 15; 34): ἐπέτρεψεν αὐτοῖς *he gave them
permission* Mk 5: 13; Lk 8: 32b. ᾧ ἂν αὐτὸς ἐπιτρέψῃ
whomever he permits = *appoints* ISm 8: 1. οὐκ ἐμαυτῷ
ἐπιτρέψας *not on my own initiative* Pol 3: 1. Quite abs.
(Pind., Ol. 6, 36; X., Cyr. 5, 5, 9; Dit., Syll.³ 490, 10; 591,
36) ἐπέτρεψεν ὁ Πιλᾶτος P. *gave his permission* J 19: 38;
cf. Ac 21: 40; MPol 7: 2. Of God (BGU 451, 10 [I/II AD]
θεῶν ἐπιτρεπόντων; 248, 15 [cf. Dssm., NB 80-BS 252];
Jos., Ant. 20, 267 κἂν τὸ θεῖον ἐπιτρέπῃ) 1 Cor 16: 7; Hb
6: 3.—Pass. (Dit., Syll.³ 1073, 44; 52; POxy. 474, 40)
ἐπιτρέπεταί τινι *someone is permitted* w. inf. foll. (Jos.,
Ant. 5, 3) Ac 26: 1; 28: 16; 1 Cor 14: 34. Abs. ἐκείνῳ
ἐπιτέτραπται *it is entrusted to him* = *it is his duty* Hv
2, 4, 3.
2. *order, instruct* (X., An. 6, 5, 11; Arrian, Ind. 23, 5 ἐ.
τινί; Cass. Dio, fgm. 40, 5 Boiss. Cod.; PLond. 1173, 3;
Jos., Vi. 138) w. dat. of the pers. and inf. 1 Cl 1: 3. M-M.
B. 1340.*

ἐπιτροπεύω (Hdt.+; inscr., pap., Philo; Jos., Bell. 7, 9,
Ant. 10, 278) *hold the office of an ἐπίτροπος, be a procurator* (Plut., Mor. 471A; IG XIV 911) τινός *of a country*
(Hdt. 3, 15) ἐπιτροπεύοντος Ποντίου Πιλάτου τῆς Ἰουδαίας *while P.P. was procurator of Judaea* Lk 3: 1 D
(ἡγεμονεύοντος in the text). M-M.*

ἐπιτροπή, ῆς, ἡ (Thu.+; inscr., pap., 2 Macc 13: 14)
permission, a commission, full power (Polyb. 3, 15, 7;
Diod. S. 17, 47, 4; Dionys. Hal. 2, 45; POxy. 743, 32 [2 BC]
περὶ πάντων αὐτῷ τ. ἐπιτροπὴν δέδωκα; Philo, Poster.
Cai. 181; Jos., Ant. 8, 162) μετ' ἐπιτροπῆς (w. ἐξουσία)
Ac 26: 12. M-M.*

ἐπίτροπος, ου, ὁ (Pind., Hdt.+; inscr., pap., LXX, Philo,
Joseph.; loanw. in rabb.).
1. *manager, foreman, steward* (Hdt.+; Philo, Omn.
Prob. Lib. 35; Jos., Ant. 7, 369) Mt 20: 8. So perh. also Lk
8: 3 (cf. Jos., Ant. 18, 194), where, however, the office may
also be of a political nature, and the meaning would be:
2. *governor, procurator* (Hdt.+; Jos., Ant. 15, 406 al.;
cf. Dit., Or. index VIII; Magie 162f; Hahn 118; 224, 2;
Rouffiac 46; Preisigke, Fachw. p. 93).
3. *guardian* (Hdt. 9, 10; Thu. 2, 80, 6; Diod. S. 11, 79,
6; Dit., Syll.³ 364, 53; 1014, 122 al.; POxy. 265, 28; PRyl.
109, 18; 2 Macc 11: 1; 13: 2; 14: 2; Philo, Somn. 1, 107)
Gal 4: 2.—OEger, ZNW 18, '18, 105–8; SBelkin, JBL 54,
'35, 52–5. M-M.*

Ἐπίτροπος, ου, ὁ (very rare; Dit., Syll.³ 957, 34) *Epitropus* IPol 8: 2; s. Hdb. ad loc.*

ἐπιτυγχάνω 2 aor. ἐπέτυχον (Pre-Socr., Hdt.+; inscr.,

pap., LXX, Jos., Ant. 5, 288) *obtain, attain to, reach* w. gen. of what is reached (Aristoph., Plut. 245; Thu. 3, 3, 3; BGU 113, 3; 522, 8; Jos., Ant. 18, 279) of a thing (Appian, Iber. 48 §200 εἰρήνης) Hm 10, 2, 4; 2 Cl 5: 6. τῆς ἐπαγγελίας Hb 6: 15; cf. 11: 33. τοῦ κλήρου ITr 12: 3. χάριτος IRo 1: 2a.—θεοῦ *attain to God*, specif. Ignatian expr., meant to designate martyrdom as a direct way to God: IEph 12: 2; IMg 14; ITr 12: 2; 13: 3; IRo 1: 2; 2: 1; 4: 1; 9: 2; IPol 2: 3; 7: 1; cf. IPhld 5: 1. Also ἐ. Ἰησοῦ Χριστοῦ IRo 5: 3.—W. acc. (X., Hell. 4, 5, 19; 4, 8, 21; 6, 3, 16; UPZ 41, 26 [161/0 BC] πᾶν ἐπιτυγχάνειν) Ro 11: 7. οὐδὲν τ. αἰτημάτων *none of the things requested* Hm 9: 5.—W. inf. foll. (Lucian, Necyom. 6; Jos., Bell. 1, 302) IEph 1: 2; IRo 1: 1. Abs. (Pla., Men. p. 97c; Dit., Syll.³ 736, 79 [92 BC]) Ac 13: 29 D; Js 4: 2; IRo 8: 3. M-M.*

ἐπιφαίνω 1 aor. ἐπέφανα, inf. ἐπιφᾶναι, imper. ἐπίφανον; 2 aor. pass. ἐπεφάνην (Theognis, Hdt.+; inscr., pap., LXX, Philo, Joseph.).
   1. act.—a. trans. *show* ἐπίφανον τὸ πρόσωπόν σου 1 Cl 60: 3 (Ps 79: 4, 8, 20; Da 9: 17 Theod.).
   b. intr. *appear, show itself* (Theocr. 2, 11 of stars; Polyb. 5, 6, 6 of daylight; Dt 33: 2; Ps 117: 27) of sun and stars Ac 27: 20; cf. Lk 1: 79.
   2. pass. *show oneself, make an appearance* (Hdt., Thu. et. al.; LXX) of God (cf. Charito 1, 14, 1 Ἀφροδίτην ἐπιφαίνεσθαι; schol. on Apollon. Rhod. 2, introd. ἐπεφάνη αὐτοῖς ὁ Ἀπόλλων; Dit., Syll.³ 557, 6 ἐπιφαινομένης αὐτοῖς Ἀρτέμιδος; 1168, 26; Sb 6152, 5 [96 BC] Isis; 6153, 6; Gen 35: 7; 2 Macc 3: 30; 3 Macc 6: 9; Philo; Jos., Ant. 5, 277; 8, 240; 268) τοῖς δεομένοις 1 Cl 59: 4. Of God's grace Tit 2: 11; of his love 3: 4. M-M.*

ἐπιφάνεια, ας, ἡ (Pre-Socr.; Polyb. et al.; inscr., LXX, Ep. Arist., Philo, Joseph.) *appearing, appearance*; esp. also the splendid appearance, e.g., of the wealthy city of Babylon (Diod. S. 2, 11, 3). As a relig. t.t. it means a visible manifestation of a hidden divinity, either in the form of a personal appearance, or by some deed of power by which its presence is made known (Dionys. Hal. 2, 68; Diod. S. 1, 25, 3 and 4; 2, 47, 7 [the appearance of Apollo]; in 5, 49, 5 τῶν θεῶν ἐπιφάνεια to help men; Plut., Them. 30; 3; Ael. Aristid. 48, 45 K.=24 p. 477 D.; Polyaenus 2, 31, 4 Διοσκούρων ἐπ.; oft. inscr., and in LXX esp. 2 and 3 Macc.; Aristobul. in Euseb., Pr. Ev. 8, 10, 3; Ep. Arist. 264; Jos., Ant. 1, 255; 2, 339; 3, 310; 9, 60; 18, 75; 286. For material and lit. s. FPfister, Epiphanie: Pauly-W. Suppl. IV '24, 277–323; MDibelius, Hdb. exc. on 2 Ti 1: 10; OCasel, D. Epiphanie im Lichte d. Religionsgesch.: Benedikt. Monatsschr. 4, '22, 13ff; RHerzog, Die Wunderheilungen v. Epidauros '31, 49; BSEaston, Pastoral Epistles '47, 171f; EPax, Ἐπιφάνεια '55; DLührmann, KGKuhn-Festschr., '71). In our lit., except for Papias, only of Christ's appearing on earth.
   1. of Jesus' coming in judgment 1 Ti 6: 14; 2 Ti 4: 1, 8. ἐ. τ. δόξης Tit 2: 13 (for this combination cf. Dit., Or. 763, 19f; Epict. 3, 22, 29). ἐ. τῆς παρουσίας 2 Th 2: 8 is pleonastic, since both words have the same technical sense: *the appearance of his coming*; ἡμέρα τῆς ἐ. *the day of the appearing* 2 Cl 12: 1; 17: 4.
   2. of Jesus' first appearance on the earth 2 Ti 1: 10 (Diod. S. 3, 62, 10 the mythographers speak of two appearances of Dionysus: δευτέραν ἐπιφάνειαν τοῦ θεοῦ παρ' ἀνθρώποις).
   3. *surface* (Democr., Aristot.+) ἔξωθεν Papias 3. M-M.*

ἐπιφανής, ές (Pind., Hdt.+; inscr., pap., LXX, Philo; Jos., Ant. 4, 200 al.) *splendid, glorious, remarkable* of the

day of God's judgment (Mélanges GGlotz '32, 290, 28: inscr. [II BC] ἡμέραι ἐπ.) ἡμέρα κυρίου μεγάλη καὶ ἐ. Ac 2: 20 (Jo 3: 4). M-M.*

ἐπιφαύσκω fut. ἐπιφαύσω (Hesychius=ἀνατέλλω, φαίνω.—mid. Job 41: 10) *arise, appear, shine* (of heavenly bodies Job 25: 5; 31: 26; of the day Cass. Dio 9, 12, 8 and Act. Thom. 34) τινί *for* or *upon someone* (Orph. Hymn. 50, 9 Q. of Bacchus θνητοῖς ἢ ἀθανάτοις ἐπιφαύσκων) of Christ ἐπιφαύσει σοι Eph 5: 14 (v.l. ἐπιψαύσεις τοῦ Χριστοῦ, to be rejected, w. Chrysost.). The origin of the quot. has not been established w. certainty.—Rtzst., Erlösungsmyst. 6; 136; KGKuhn, NTS 7, '61, 334–46 [Qumran]. S. also on ἐπιφώσκω.*

ἐπιφέρω 2 aor. ἐπήνεγκον, inf. ἐπενεγκεῖν (Hom.+; inscr., pap., LXX, Ep. Arist.; Philo, Aet. M. 47 al.; Joseph.).
   1. *bring, give, grant* τινί τι someth. to someone τὴν χάριν 1 Cl 7: 4.
   2. *bring over* or *upon*—a. lit. τὶ ἐπί τινα bring someth. and *put it on someone* Ac 19: 12 t.r.
   b. fig. τί τινι *bring someth. upon someone* or *someth.* (Ep. Arist. 206 αἰσχύνην ἀνθρώποις; Philo, Leg. ad Gai. 133) ἁμαρτίαν 1 Cl 47: 4; Hv 1, 2, 4; m 11: 4. βλασφημίας τῷ ὀνόματι *blasphemies on the name* 1 Cl 47: 7. *Add someth. to someth.* (Aristot., Rhet. 3, 6; Philo, Leg. ad Gai. 125) Phil 1: 17 v.l.
   3. *bring, pronounce* (of a charge, accusation since Hdt. 1, 26, also Polyb. 5, 41, 3; 38, 18, 2; PRainer 232, 11 ψευδεῖς αἰτίας τινὶ ἐ.; Jos., Ant. 2, 130; 4, 248; 11, 117) αἰτίαν Ac 25: 18 v.l. κρίσιν βλασφημίας *pronounce a reviling judgment* Jd 9.
   4. *inflict* (Ep. Arist. 253 θάνατον; Jos., Ant. 2, 296 πληγὴν τ. Αἰγυπτίοις. Cf. also PTebt. 331, 10) τὴν ὀργήν *wrathful punishment* Ro 3: 5. M-M.*

ἐπιφωνέω impf. ἐπεφώνουν (Soph.+; inscr., pap., LXX, Ep. Arist., Philo) *cry out (loudly)* τινί *against someone* (cf. Plut., Alex. 3, 6) Ac 22: 24. ἄλλο τι someth. *different* 21: 34 (s. ἄλλος 1c, end). W. direct discourse foll. (Dit., Or. 595, 35; PRyl. 77, 33; 1 Esdr 9: 47) Lk 23: 21; Ac 12: 22. M-M.*

ἐπιφώσκω (Poëta De Vir. Herb. 25; pap.; mid. Job 41: 10 v.l.) *shine forth, dawn, break*; perh. *draw on* (PLond. 130, 39; PGrenf. II 112, 15 τῇ ἐπιφώσκουσῃ κυριακῇ; Ps.-Clem., Hom. 3, 1 p. 36, 23 Lag.) σάββατον ἐπέφωσκεν *the Sabbath dawned* or *drew on* Lk 23: 54; cf. GP 2: 5. ἐπιφώσκοντος τοῦ σαββάτου GP 9: 34; cf. vs. 35. τῇ ἐπιφωσκούσῃ εἰς μίαν σαββάτων *as the first day of the week dawned* or *drew near* Mt 28: 1. Cf. GFMoore, Journ. of the Amer. Orient. Soc. 26, '05, 323–9; CHTurner, JTS 14, '13, 188–90; FCBurkitt, ibid. 538–46; PGardner-Smith, ibid. 27, '26, 179–81; MBlack, An Aramaic Approach³, '67, 136–38. M-M.*

ἐπιχειρέω impf. ἐπεχείρουν; 1 aor. ἐπεχείρησα (Hom. +; inscr., pap., LXX) *set one's hand to, attempt, try* w. inf. foll. (Hdt., Aristoph. et al.; LXX; Philo; Jos., Ant. 4, 310; 8, 3) ἀνελεῖν αὐτόν Ac 9: 29. ὀνομάζειν ἐπὶ τινα τὸ ὄνομα 19: 13. W. acc. *attempt someth.* (unless νοῆσαι is to be understood w. it) Hs 9, 2, 6. Of literary composition (Hippocr., Περὶ ἀρχαίης ἰητρικῆς prol.: ὁπόσοι μὲν ἐπεχείρησαν περὶ ἰητρικῆς λέγειν ἢ γράφειν; Galen, Foet. Format. prooem.; Thessalus of Trall.: Cat. Cod. Astr. VIII 3 p. 134 πολλῶν ἐπιχειρησάντων . . . παραδοῦναι; Polyb. 2, 37, 4; 3, 1, 4; 12, 28, 2; Diod. S. 4, 1, 2; Jos., Vita 40; 338, C. Ap. 2, 222) ἀνατάξασθαι διήγησιν Lk 1: 1.—HJCadbury, Comm. on the Preface of Luke: Beginn. I 2, '22, 489ff. M-M.*

ἐπιχείρησις, εως, ἡ (Hdt.+; Jos., Ant. 15, 103; 16, 188) *attempt, attack* ἐπί τινα Ac 12: 3 D.*

ἐπιχέω (Hom.+; pap.; LXX; Jos., Ant. 2, 343 al.)—1. *pour over, pour on* τὶ someth. oil and wine (Hippocr., Mul. 2, 133 vol. VIII 296, 15 L.; Hippiatr. I 9, 4) Lk 10: 34.
2. *pour in* (Pla., Rep. 407D; PGM 13, 12; Ep. Arist. 293) τὶ εἴς τι someth. into a vessel Hm 5, 1, 5. M-M.*

ἐπιχορηγέω 1 aor. ἐπεχορήγησα; 1 fut. pass. ἐπιχορηγηθήσομαι.
1. *furnish* or *provide* (*at one's own expense*) (Dionys. Hal. 10, 54) fig. ἐ. τὴν ἀρετήν 2 Pt 1: 5.
2. *give, grant* (Dionys. Hal. 1, 42; Diog. L. 5, 67; Phalaris, Ep. 50; Alex. Aphr., Probl. 1, 81. In marriage contracts ἐ. τὰ δέοντα: BGU 183, 6; POxy. 905, 10; PRainer 27, 12) τί τινι someth. to someone Hs 2: 5, 7. σπέρμα τῷ σπείραντι give seed to the sower 2 Cor 9: 10. ὑμῖν τὸ πνεῦμα he who gives you the Spirit Gal 3: 5. αὐτῷ τ. ἐγκράτειαν 1 Cl 38: 2, end.—Pass. ἐπιχορηγηθήσεται ὑμῖν ἡ εἴσοδος you will be granted an entrance 2 Pt 1: 11. Without an acc. to denote what is given (En. 7, 3), ἐ. comes to mean
3. *support* (Sir 25: 22; s. ἐπιχορηγία) ὁ πλούσιος ἐπιχορηγείτω τῷ πτωχῷ let the rich man support the poor man 1 Cl 38: 2. Pass. ὁ πένης ἐπιχορηγούμενος ὑπὸ τοῦ πλουσίου the poor man, who is supported by the rich Hs 2: 6. πᾶν τὸ σῶμα διὰ τῶν ἀφῶν καὶ συνδέσμων ἐπιχορηγούμενον καὶ συμβιβαζόμενον the whole body supported and held together by sinews and ligaments Col 2: 19 (for the pass. of the simple verb the mng. *be supported, receive help* is well attested [Ps.-X., Respubl. Athen. [the 'Old Oligarch'] 1, 13; Polyb. 3, 75, 3; 4, 77, 2; 9, 44, 1; Sir 44: 6; 3 Macc 6: 40], and in Hs 2: 5 the simplex and the compound are used w. the same value). M-M.*

ἐπιχορηγία, ας, ἡ *support* (Dit., Syll.³ 818, 9 [79 AD]; s. ἐπιχορηγέω 3) τοῦ πνεύματος Phil 1: 19; ἀφὴ τῆς ἐ. *a ligament that serves for support* (cf. Col 2: 19) Eph 4: 16. M-M.*

ἐπιχρίω 1 aor. ἐπέχρισα (Hom.+; Sym. Ezk 13: 10; 22: 28).
1. *spread* or *smear* (*on*) (Soranus p. 75, 7; Galen: CMG V 9, 1 p. 136, 30; Diosc. 3, 25; PLeid. X VII, 36) τὶ ἐπί τι someth. on someth. πηλὸν ἐπὶ τοὺς ὀφθαλμούς J 9: 6 v.l., nevertheless in most mss. (cf. Dit., Syll.³ 1173, 17 in a report of a healing κολλύριον ἐπιχρεῖσαι ἐπὶ τ. ὀφθαλμούς). σφραγῖδας *seals,* i.e. the wax that receives the impression fr. the seal GP 8: 33.
2. *anoint* (Od. 21, 179; Lucian, Hist. Scrib. 62; Galen: CMG V 4, 2 p. 246, 20) ἐ. τοὺς ὀφθαλμούς *anoint the eyes* J 9: 11. M-M.*

ἐπιψαύω fut. ἐπιψαύσω (Hom.+; Diod. S. 3, 28, 3; 17, 20, 6; Hero Alex. I p. 6, 11ff; Heraclit. Sto. 44 p. 66, 12) *touch, grasp, attain to* τινός someone (Arrian, Cyneg. 9, 2 ἀλλήλων) Eph 5: 14 D; s. ἐπιφαύσκω.*

ἔπλησα s. πίμπλημι.

ἐποικοδομέω 1 aor. ἐποικοδόμησα (on the lack of augment s. Mlt.-H. 191); 1 aor. pass. ἐποικοδομήθην (Thu. +; inscr., pap., Philo, Joseph.) *build on someth.* (already built or at hand), *build on to* (X.; Pla., Leg. 5 p. 736E; inscr.; PGiess. 67, 12; Jos., Ant. 12, 253).

1. lit.—a. of a tower ἔμελλε πάλιν ἐποικοδομεῖσθαι *the building of it was to be continued* Hs 9, 5, 1; cf. v 3, 8, 9.
b. in figurative language of the beginnings of a congregation as of a building (w. θεμέλιον τιθέναι; cf. Jos., Ant. 11, 79.—Philo, Somn. 2, 8: θεμέλ. . . . ἄλλα . . . σοφ. ἀρχιτέκτων . . . ἐποικοδομ.) 1 Cor 3: 10; cf. vs. 14. ἐ. ἐπί τι *build upon someth.* (Dit., Or. 483, 117 ἐπὶ τοὺς τοίχους ἐ.) vs. 12. ἐποικοδομηθέντες ἐπὶ τῷ θεμελίῳ τῶν ἀποστόλων *built on the foundation of the apostles* Eph 2: 20 (ἐπί w. dat. as X., An. 3, 4, 11). ὡς λίθοι ζῶντες ἐποικοδομεῖσθε οἶκος πνευματικός *let yourselves be built up into a spiritual house* 1 Pt 2: 5 v.l.
2. in a non-literal sense, as the orig. figure fades (Epict. 2, 15, 8) Ac 20: 32 t.r. ἐποικοδομούμενοι ἐν αὐτῷ *built upon him* (i.e. Christ; the prep. is explained by the preceding ἐρριζωμένοι) Col 2: 7. Clearly non-literal Jd 20 ἐ. (ἀνοικ. 𝔓⁷²) ἑαυτοὺς τῇ πίστει *build each other up on the basis of the faith* (ἐ. w. dat. as Epict. loc. cit.; Philo, Gig. 30, Conf. Lingu. 5). M-M.*

ἐποκέλλω 1 aor. ἐπώκειλα *run aground* (Hdt. 6, 16; 7, 182; Thu. 4, 26, 6; Arrian, Anab. 5, 20, 9 a ship) τὴν ναῦν Ac 27: 41 v.l. (for ἐπέκειλαν).*

ἐπονομάζω (trag., Hdt.+; LXX; Jos., Ant. 17, 14) *call, name* pass. σὺ Ἰουδαῖος ἐπονομάζῃ *you call yourself a Jew* Ro 2: 17 (ἐπι- without special mng. as Maximus Tyr. 39, 4a; 5c; Appian, Basil. 1 §1; Dionys. Byz. §35; Himerius, Or. 48[= Or. 14], 13; Test. Jud. 1: 3). M-M.*

ἐποπτεύω 1 aor. ἐπώπτευσα (Hom.+; Sym. Ps 9: 35; 32: 13; Jos., C. Ap. 2, 294) *observe, see* τὶ someth. (Polyb. 5, 69, 6; 31, 15, 10; Heraclit. Sto. 53 p. 75, 19) τὴν ἀναστροφήν *conduct* 1 Pt 3: 2. Abs. ptc. (ἐκ τ. καλῶν ἔργων *is to be taken* w. δοξάσωσιν: BWeiss, Kühl, HermvSoden, Knopf; differently Wohlenberg, Vrede) ἐποπτεύοντες *when they observe* them (sc. τ. ἔργα) 2: 12. Cf. HGMeecham, ET 65, '53, 93f. M-M.*

ἐπόπτης, ου, ὁ (Pind., Aeschyl.+; inscr., pap., LXX, Ep. Arist.; Jos., C. Ap. 2, 187) *one who watches* or *observes, an overseer.*
1. of God (Pind., Nem. 9, 5 al.; Cornutus 9 p. 9, 20; Dit., Or. 666, 25 [Nero] τ. Ἥλιον ἐ. καὶ σωτῆρα; Sb 1323 of the sun-god θεῷ ὑψίστῳ κ. πάντων ἐπόπτῃ; PGM 12, 237; Esth 5: 1a; 2 Macc 3: 39; 7: 35; 3 Macc 2: 21; Ep. Arist. 16. Also of emperors, e.g. Inschr. v. Perg. 381. Cf. CBurk, De Chionis Epistulis, Diss. Giessen '12, 11) τὸν ἐ. ἀνθρωπίνων ἔργων *the one who oversees* or *watches over the deeds of men* 1 Cl 59: 3 (Diod. S. 16, 49, 5 τοὺς θεοὺς ἐπόπτας τῶν ὅρκων).
2. of men, esp. as t.t. of the mysteries, to designate those who have been initiated into the highest grade of the mysteries (Dit., Syll.³ 42, 50 [c. 460 BC]; 1052, 4 Ῥοδίων ἱεροποιοὶ μύσται κ. ἐπόπται εὐσεβεῖς; 1053, 3; Inscr. Gr. 1141, 1 [II BC]; Plut., Alc. 22, 4; Himerius, Or. [Ecl.] 10, 4; PGM 7, 572) *eyewitness* 2 Pt 1: 16. M-M.*

ἔπος, ους, τό (Hom.+; inscr., pap., LXX) *word* ὡς ἔ. εἰπεῖν (class., also Philo and Jos., Ant. 15, 387) *so to speak, one might almost say;* perh. *to use just the right word* (for both mngs. see the many exx. in FBleek ad loc.; s. also POxy. 67, 14) Hb 7: 9. M-M. B. 1261f.*

ἐπουράνιος, ον (Hom.+; Epigr. Gr. 261, 10; LXX; Philo, Leg. All. 3, 168) *heavenly.*
1. adj.—a. w. reference to heaven, the place where God dwells w. the beings and things that pertain to him; they may actually be there with him, or they may belong there by nature, or come from there, etc.

a. applied to God (Od. 17, 484; Il. 6, 131; Sb 4166 Ζεὺς ἐπουράνιος; Herm. Wr. 434, 9 Sc.; 3 Macc 6: 28; 7: 6; Sib. Or. 4, 51; 135) πατὴρ ἐ. Mt 18: 35 v.l.; δεσπότης ἐ. 1 Cl 61: 2.

β. of Christ ἐ. (ἄνθρωπος) 1 Cor 15: 48f; ἐ. ἀρχιερεὺς Ἰ. Χ. MPol 14: 3.—γ. οἱ ἐ. (ἄνθρωποι) 1 Cor 15: 48; Ἰερουσαλὴμ ἐ. Hb 12: 22 (for the idea s. πόλις 2); βασιλεία ἐ. 2 Ti 4: 18; Epil Mosq 4; MPol 20: 2 v.l. Funk; (πατρὶς) ἐ. Hb 11: 16.—δ. ζωὴ ἐ. 2 Cl 20: 5; κλῆσις ἐ. Hb 3: 1; δωρεὰ ἐ. 6: 4.

b. w. ref. to the heaven in which the sun, moon, and stars are located σώματα ἐ. (opp. ἐπίγεια) celestial bodies 1 Cor 15: 40 (acc. to vs. 41 the sun, moon, and stars are thought of, and are represented fig., as living beings clothed in light; cf. PWendland, D. hellenist.-röm. Kultur² '12, 158).

2. subst.—a. τὰ ἐπουράνια (of things in heaven: Pla., Ap. 19ʙ; Sext. Emp., Astrol. 44).

a. periphrasis for heaven καθίσας ἐν τοῖς ἐ. sitting in heaven Eph 1: 20; cf. 2: 6. ἐξουσίαι ἐν τοῖς ἐ. the powers in heaven of angelic beings 3: 10. Since there is more than one heaven (cf. 2 Cor 12: 2), τὰ ἐ. can be the dwelling-place of evil spirits 6: 12. Even 1: 3 ὁ εὐλογήσας ἐν τοῖς ἐ. is, acc. to the usage of Eph, to be understood locally in heaven (cf. RMPope, ET 23, '12, 365-8).—ATLincoln, NTS 19, '73, 467-83.

β. the heavenly things (Philo, Gig. 62) J 3: 12 (ἐπίγειος 2a).—Hb 8: 5; 9: 23; heavenly goods αἰτεῖν τὰ ἐ. Agr 10; τὰ ἐ. γράψαι write about heavenly things ITr 5: 1. νοεῖν τὰ ἐ. understand the heavenly things 5: 2. τὰ πάντα divided into ἐ. and ἐπίγεια Pol 2: 1; heavenly beings ISm 6: 1.

b. οἱ ἐπουράνιοι (as a designation of the gods Theocr. 25, 5; Moschus 2, 21; Lucian, Dial. Deor. 4, 3) heavenly beings Phil 2: 10 (s. on ἐπίγειος 2b); ITr 9: 1.—IEph 13: 2. M-M.*

ἐπράθην s. πιπράσκω.

ἑπτά indecl. (Hom.+; pap., LXX, Ep. Arist., Philo, Joseph., Test. 12 Patr., loanw. in rabb.) seven in dating an event MPol 21. As a sacred number (WRoscher, D. Sieben- u. Neunzahl in Kultus u. Mythus der Griechen '04; JHGraf, D. Zahl 'Sieben' '17; JHehn, Z. Bed. der Siebenzahl: Marti-Festschr. [=Beih. ZAW 41] '25, 128-36; RGordis, JBL 62, '43, 17-26.—Jos., Bell. 7, 149 παρὰ τ. Ἰουδαίοις ἑβδομάδος ἡ τιμή), perhaps at times determining the choice of a number (Pla., Theaet. 174ᴇ τίς ἑπτὰ πάππους πλουσίους ἔχων; Diod. S. 4, 27, 2 ἑπτὰ θυγατέρας; 4, 61, 3f): seven demons Mt 12: 45; Lk 8: 2; 11: 26; loaves of bread Mt 15: 34, 36f; 16: 10; Mk 8: 5f, 8, 20; brothers Mt 22: 25f, 28; Mk 12: 20, 22f; Lk 20: 29, 31, 33. Seven church officials (PGaechter, Petrus u. seine Zeit '58, 106-35) Ac 6: 3; cf. 21: 8, where οἱ ἑπτά 'the seven', corresp. to οἱ δώδεκα, designates a definite fixed group (οἱ ἑπτά = the seven wise men: Diog. L. 1, 40; 82; = the seven against Thebes: Aeschyl.; Diod. S. 4, 64, 1; 4, 66, 1). Esp. in Rv: seven churches 1: 4, 11; lampstands vs. 12; stars vss. 16, 20; 2: 1; torches 4: 5; seals 6: 1 (cf. GP 8: 33); angels 8: 2, 6; 15: 1, 6f; 21: 9; trumpets 8: 2, 6; thunders 10: 3f; bowls 15: 7; 16: 1; emperors 17: 9; plagues 15: 1, 6; 21: 9. Seven virtues Hv 3, 8, 2 al. On ἑβδομηκοντάκις ἑπτά Mt 18: 22 s. ἑβδομηκοντάκις. KHRengstorf, TW II 623-31. M-M.

ἑπτάκις adv (Pind., Aristoph.+; PGM 4, 1272; 1, 143 [ἑπτάκις ἑπτά]; LXX; Ep. Arist. 177; Philo, Op. M. 91; Jos., Ant. 3, 242) seven times (as a relatively large number, cf. Diod. S. 4, 16, 2: the brave Amazon was victorious

seven times) Lk 17: 4b; 1 Cl 5: 6; ἕως ἐ. as many as seven times Mt 18: 21f; ἐ. τῆς ἡμέρας seven times a day Lk 17: 4a (cf. Lucian, Jupp. Trag. 49 πεντάκις τῆς ἡμ.; Jos., Ant. 3, 199 δὶς τῆς ἡμ.; Horapollo 1, 8 p. 9 τριακοντάκις τῆς ἡ.). M-M.*

ἑπτακισχίλιοι, αι, α (Hdt. et al.; Dialekt-Inschr. IV, 1210, ⁿ3 II, 25 [I ʙᴄ, Sicily]; LXX) seven thousand Ro 11: 4.*

ἑπταπλασίων, ον, gen. ονος (Oribasius, Ecl. 89, 22: CMG VI 2, 2 p. 269, 9; 2 Km 12: 6; Ps 78: 12; Jos., Ant. 1, 77; Acta Phil. 20 p. 11, 1 B.) sevenfold ἑπταπλασίονα (ἀπο)λαμβάνειν receive Lk 18: 30 D.*

ἑπταπλασίως adv. (LXX; the adj. Pla., Ep. 7, 332ᴀ; Eutocius [Archimed., Op. Omn. ed. JLHeiberg III '15] p. 244, 24) sevenfold Hs 6, 4, 2.*

Ἔραστος, ου, ὁ Erastus (the name is found in lit. and inscr.; cf. Dit., Syll.³ 838, 6).

1. a Christian at Corinth, designated as οἰκονόμος τῆς πόλεως city treasurer Ro 16: 23. A Lat. inscr. fr. Corinth, published in the lit. quoted below, mentions an official named Erastus.

2. a companion of Paul Ac 19: 22; 2 Ti 4: 20.—FJde Waele, Erastus: Mededeelingen van het Nederlandsch Hist. Inst. te Rome 9, '29, 40-8; HJCadbury, E. of Cor.: JBL 50, '31, 42-58; WMiller, Who was E.?: Bibliotheca Sacra 88, '31, 342-6. M-M.*

ἐραυνάω later form, in inscr. since the time of Pompey (IG XII 5, 653; 21) and in pap. since 22 ᴀᴅ (POxy. 294, 9f) for the class. ἐρευνάω (Hom.+; Zen.-P. Mich. 84, 12 [III ʙᴄ]; UPZ 5, 10; 6, 9; 27 [both 163 ʙᴄ]; Philo; Jos., Ant. 2, 134 al.).—Bl-D. §30, 4 app.; Mlt.-H. 86; Thumb 176f; ENachmanson, Eranos 11, '11, 239; JWackernagel, ThLZ 33, '08, 37. For the LXX s. Thackeray 79; Helbing 7. Search, examine, investigate τὶ someth. τὰς γραφάς J 5: 39 (HIBell, ZNW 37, '39, 10-13). καρδίας Ro 8: 27. νεφροὺς καὶ καρδίας minds (lit. kidneys) and hearts Rv 2: 23. Of the Spirit πάντα fathoms everything 1 Cor 2: 10 (Horapollo 1, 34 πάντα ἐξερευνᾷ ὁ ἥλιος). πνεῦμα κυρίου λύχνος ἐραυνῶν τ. ταμεῖα τῆς γαστρός a lamp that illuminates the storehouses of the body 1 Cl 21: 2 (Pr 20: 27). περὶ τινος examine someth. B 4: 1; Hm 10, 1, 4; 6. With indir. quest. foll. 1 Pt 1: 11. Abs. ἐραύνησον κ. ἴδε (4 Km 10: 23) J 7: 52.—GDelling, TW II 653f. M-M.*

ἐραυνητής, οῦ, ὁ (this spelling PFay. 104 [III ᴀᴅ]; in the form ἐρευνητής Clearch. in Athen. 6 p. 256ᴀ; Jos., Ant. 17, 110 al., also UPZ 149, 15 [c. 200 ʙᴄ]) searcher, examiner of God ἐ. ἐννοιῶν κ. ἐνθυμήσεων 1 Cl 21: 9.*

ἐράω imper. ἐράτω (Pind., Hdt.+; PSI 406, 36 [III ʙᴄ]; Philo). Also fr. ἔραμαι (Hom.+) 1 aor. pass. ἠράσθην love passionately, also with other than a sensual mng. τινός someth. (Aeschyl., Eum. 852 γῆς; Herm. Wr. 6, 4b; Pr 4: 6; Philo, Spec. Leg. 2, 258 ἀληθείας) τῆς σαρκός IRo 2: 1. Desire, yearn (Il. 9, 64) ἐ. τοῦ ἀποθανεῖν 7: 2. W. inf. foll. (Pind.+) ἀπὸ τοῦ κοινοῦ ἐλευθεροῦσθαι have a burning desire to be freed (fr. slavery) at the expense of the church IPol 4: 3.—BBWarfield, The Terminology of Love in the NT, PTR 16, '18, 1-45; 153-203.*

ἐργάζομαι impf. ἠργαζόμην; 1 aor. ἠργασάμην, εἰργασάμην 2 J 8 Tdf.; pf. ptc. εἰργασμένος (for augment in the aor. cf. Mayser 332; Meisterhans³-Schw. 171; Bl-D. §67, 3; Moulton, CIR 15 '01, p. 35f; Mlt.-H. 189f) (Hom.+; inscr., pap., LXX, En., Ep. Arist., Philo, Joseph., Test. 12 Patr.).

1. intr. *work, be active* (Hes., Hdt. et al.) D 12: 3. ταῖς χερσίν *work w. one's hands* 1 Cor 4: 12 (ἐργ. ἰδίαις χερσίν as Biogr. p. 253; on the depreciation of manual labor cf. Jos., Ant. 17, 333); 1 Th 4: 11. Also διὰ τῶν χειρῶν B 19: 10. νυκτὸς καὶ ἡμέρας *work night and day* 1 Th 2: 9; 2 Th 3: 8. ἐν τῷ ἀμπελῶνι *in the vineyard* Mt 21: 28. τῷ σαββάτῳ *on the Sabbath* Lk 6: 5 D (JoachJeremias, Unknown Sayings of Jesus, tr. Fuller, '57, 49–54). Of a sum of money (five talents) ἐ. ἐν αὐτοῖς *work with them* (Demosth. 36, 44 ἐ. ἐν ἐμπορίῳ καὶ χρήμασιν) Mt 25: 16. Abs. Lk 13: 14; J 9: 4b; Ac 18: 3; 1 Cor 9: 6; 2 Th 3: 10, 12. τῷ ἐργαζομένῳ *to the workman* Ro 4: 4; cf. vs. 5 (ἐργαζόμενοι καλοί, Ode of Solomon 11, 20) and Lk 6: 5 D. Of God and Christ: *work* J 5: 17 (cf. Maximus Tyr. 15, 6e; f: Heracles must work without ceasing, since Zeus his father does the same).

2. trans.—a. *do, accomplish, carry out* w. acc. (Ael. Aristid. 42, 13 K.=6 p. 69 D.: ταῦτα ἐργαζομένου σου τοῦ κυρίου [Asclepius]) ἔργον (X., An. 6, 3, 17 κάλλιστον ἔργον ἐ.; Pla., Polit. 1 p. 346D; Appian, Celt. 18 §2, Bell. Civ. 2, 58 §238 al.; Arrian, Anab. 7, 17, 3; PPetr. II 9[2], 4 [III BC]; Sir 51: 30) Ac 13: 41 (Hab 1: 5); 1 Cl 33: 8. τὰ ἔργα τοῦ θεοῦ *do the work of God* (Num 8: 11) J 6: 28; 9: 4. τὸ ἔργον κυρίου *the Lord's work* 1 Cor 16: 10. ἐ. τι εἴς τινα *do someth. to someone* (Ps.-Demosth. 53, 18); ἔργον καλὸν εἴς τινα *do a fine thing to someone* Mt 26: 10; cf. B 21: 2; 3 J 5. Also ἔν τινι Mk 14: 6. In a different sense (cf. Ex 35: 10): ἔργα ἐν θεῷ εἰργασμένα *deeds performed in God* J 3: 21. ἐ. τὸ ἀγαθόν *do what is good* (cf. Dio Chrys. 16[33], 15; Jos., Ant. 6, 208) Ro 2: 10; Eph 4: 28; Hm 2: 4. Opp. ἐ. πονηρόν (Lucian, Catapl. 24) m 10, 2, 3. ἐ. ἀγαθὸν πρὸς πάντας *do good to all men* Gal 6: 10. κακὸν ἐ. Dio Chrys. 13[7], 33; Palaeph. 1 and 3): κακὸν τῷ πλησίον ἐ. *do wrong to one's neighbor* Ro 13: 10 (cf. Pr 3: 30; Ep. Arist. 273). Gener. *someth.* Col 3: 23; 2 J 8; μηδὲν ἐ. *do no work* 2 Th 3: 11. οὐδὲν τῇ δικαιοσύνῃ *do nothing for righteousness* Hs 5, 1, 4 (Ps.-Aristot., Mirabilia 142 οὐδὲν ἐργ.=accomplish nothing).—Also used with attributes, etc. (in Isocr. w. ἀρετήν, σωφροσύνην; Philo, Gig. 26 τελειότητα) δικαιοσύνην (Ps 14: 2) *do what is right* Ac 10: 35; Hb 11: 33; Hv 2, 2, 7; m 5, 1, 1; s 9, 13, 7. ἐ. δικαιοσύνην θεοῦ *do what is right in God's sight* Js 1: 20 (but s. c below). τὴν ἀνομίαν (Ps 5: 6; 6: 9 al.) Mt 7: 23. ἁμαρτίαν *commit sin* Js 2: 9 (Jos., Ant. 6, 124 τὸ ἁμάρτημα). Of the effect: τί ἐργάζῃ; *what work are you doing?* J 6: 30 (cf. Philo, Leg. All. 3, 83).

b. *practice, perform, officiate at* (τέχνην, etc., X., Pla. et al.) τὰ ἱερά *the temple rites* 1 Cor 9: 13.

c. *bring about, give rise to* (Soph., Ant. 326; Epict., fgm. Stob. 14 πενία λύπην ἐργάζεται) μετάνοιαν 2 Cor 7: 10. ἐ. δικαιοσύνην θεοῦ *bring about the righteousness that will stand before God* (but s. a above) Js 1: 20.

d. *work (on)* τὴν θάλασσαν *work on the sea for a livelihood* (Aristot., Probl. 38, 2 p. 966b, 26; Dionys. Hal. 3, 46; Appian, Liby. 2 §5; 84 §397; Lucian, De Elect. 5) Rv 18: 17 (s. CLindhagen, ΕΡΓΑΖΕΣΘΑΙ, '50: Uppsala Univ. Årsskrift '50, 5, 5–26).

e. ἐ. τὴν βρῶσιν J 6: 27 can, when it is alone, mean *work for, earn the food* (Hes., Op. βίον ἐ.; Hdt. 1, 24 χρήματα; cf. Pla., Laches 183A; X., Mem. 2, 8, 2; Theod. Pr 21: 6. Also βρῶμα: Palaeph. p. 28, 10). However, in this context βρῶσις seems to be not so much a thing to be earned, as a free gift of the Son of Man. As in the similar case of the Samaritan woman (cf. J 4: 35 w. 4: 14) the hearer is simply prepared for the statement that he is to accept what is freely given. But ἐργάζεσθαι can also mean, when used w. food, *prepare for use, digest, assimilate* sc. τὴν τροφήν (Aristot., De Vita et Morte 4;

Maximus Tyr. 15, 5a [ἐργ. τὴν τροφήν of the activity of the jaws]; more often ἐργασία τ. τροφῆς). The compound κατεργάζεσθαι is more common in this sense, but it is avoided in this passage for the sake of a play on words w. ἐργάζεσθαι in vs. 28. M-M.**

ἐργασία, ας, ἡ (Pind.+; inscr., pap., LXX, Joseph.).

1. *practice, pursuit* τινός *of someth.* (Pla., Gorg. p. 450C τ. τεχνῶν; Ps.-Pla., Eryx. p. 404B; Sir 6: 19; 38: 34) εἰς ἐ. ἀκαθαρσίας πάσης *for the practice of all kinds of sinful things* Eph 4: 19. πολλαπλασιάζειν τὴν ἐ. *do many kinds of work* GH 15 (s. also 4).

2. *working, function* (Pla., Prot. p. 353D τῆς ἡδονῆς) τῶν ἀγγέλων Hm 6, 2, 6.

3. *trade, business* (X., Oec. 6, 8; Diod. S. 1, 80, 1; PLond. 906, 6; PFay. 93, 7; Sir 7: 15) Ac 19: 25.

4. *profit, gain* (X., Mem. 3, 10, 1; Polyb. 4, 50, 3; Artem. 4, 57 ἔχειν . . . ἐργασίαν=have profits or wages; PGM 4, 2438; Wsd 13: 19; Jos., Bell. 2, 109) 16: 19. παρέχειν ἐργασίαν τινί *bring profit to someone* vs. 16; 19: 24. πολλαπλ. τ. ἐ. *multiply the gains* GH 15 (s. 1 above).

5. For δὸς ἐργασίαν Lk 12: 58 s. δίδωμι 7 (ἐργ.= *pains*: Jos., Ant. 3, 35 μὴ σὺν πόνῳ μηδ' ἐργασίᾳ). M-M.*

ἐργαστήριον, ίου, τό (Hdt., Aristoph.+; inscr.; PLond. 897, 18 [84 AD]; POxy. 1455, 9; Philo) *workshop* MPol 13: 1.*

ἐργάτης, ου, ὁ (trag., Hdt.+; inscr.; pap., LXX, Ep. Arist., Philo; Jos., Bell. 4, 557, Ant. 12, 194; Test. Benj. 11: 1; loanw. in rabb.).

1. *workman, laborer*—a. lit. Mt 10: 10; Lk 10: 7; 1 Ti 5: 18; D 13: 2; ὁ ἀγαθὸς ἐ. 1 Cl 34: 1. Esp. of agricultural laborers (Soph., Oed. R. 859 al.; Wsd 17: 16; Philo, Agr. 5 al. γῆς ἐ.) Mt 9: 37f; Lk 10: 2; Js 5: 4. Of workers in a vineyard Mt 20: 1f, 8; ὁ περί τι ἐ. (Ps.-Demosth. 35, 32 οἱ περὶ τὴν γεωργίαν ἐργάται) *workmen engaged in someth.* Ac 19: 25.

b. fig. of apostles and teachers: ἐργάται δόλιοι *deceitful workmen* 2 Cor 11: 13; κακοὶ ἐ. Phil 3: 2; ἐ. ἀνεπαίσχυντος 2 Ti 2: 15.

2. *a doer, one who does* someth. w. gen. (X., Mem. 2, 1, 27 τ. καλῶν κ. σεμνῶν; Aristoxenus, fgm. 43 ἐ. φιλίας; Dio Chrys. 53[70], 1 τ. ἀργῶν; Sextus 384 ἀληθείας; Ep. Arist. 231 ἀγαθῶν; Philo, Leg. All. 1, 54 τ. ἀρετῶν). ἀδικίας *one who does what is wrong, an evildoer* Lk 13: 27 (PHoffmann, ZNW 58 '67, 188–214). ἐ. ἀνομίας (1 Macc 3: 6) 2 Cl 4: 5. M-M.*

ἔργον, ου, τό (Hom.+; inscr., pap., LXX, En., Ep. Arist., Philo, Joseph., Test. 12 Patr.) *work*.

1. *deed, action*—a. in contrast to rest Hb 4: 3, 4 (Gen 2: 2), 10. In contrast to word (X., Hier. 7, 2, Cyr. 6, 4, 5; Cebes 2, 2 λόγῳ καὶ ἔργῳ Πυθαγόρειος; Lucian, Tox. 35. Oft. in Epict.; Dialekt-Inschr. 5039, 20 [Crete] οὔτε λόγῳ οὔτε ἔργῳ; Sir 3: 8; 16: 12; 4 Macc 5: 38; Philo; Jos., Ant. 17, 220, C. Ap. 2, 12) δυνατὸς ἐν ἔργῳ καὶ λόγῳ *mighty in word and deed* Lk 24: 19; cf. Ac 7: 22; ἐν λόγῳ ἢ ἐν ἐ. *in word and deed* Col 3: 17; cf. Ro 15: 18; 2 Cor 10: 11; 2 Th 2: 17; 1 J 3: 18; 2 Cl 17: 7; 4: 3; Tit 1: 16a. A similar contrast betw. the ποιητὴς ἔργου *doer who acts* and the forgetful hearer Js 1: 25, and betw. ἔργα and a πίστις that amounts to nothing more than a verbal statement 2: 14–26 (cf. JHRopes, Exp. 7th Ser. V '08, 547–56 and his comm. '16 ad loc.; HPreisker, ThBl 4, '25, 16f; ETobac, Revue d'histoire ecclés. 22, '26, 797–805; AMeyer, D. Rätsel des Jk '30, 86ff; ASchlatter, D. Brief des Jak. '32, 184–207).

b. *manifestation, practical proof* τὸ ἔ. τῆς πίστεως
1 Th 1: 3; 2 Th 1: 11. ἔ. διακονίας Eph 4: 12. τὸ ἔ. τοῦ
νόμου *acting in accordance with the law* Ro 2: 15 (perh.
also *the bringing of the law into effect*, as Polyaenus 1, 19
τοῦ λογίου τὸ ἔργον=the realization or fulfilment of the
oracular response). ἡ ὑπομονὴ ἔ. τέλειον ἐχέτω *let endurance show itself perfectly in practice* Js 1: 4.

c. *deed, accomplishment*—α. of the deeds of God and
Jesus, specif. the miracles (Epict. 3, 5, 10 ἰδεῖν ἔργα τὰ
σά [=τοῦ θεοῦ]; Ael. Aristid. 50, 17 K.=26 p. 506 D.:
ἔργον τοῦ θεοῦ θαυμαστόν; Quint. Smyrn. 9, 481 ἔργον
ἀθανάτων of the healing of Philoctetes; Josh 24: 29; Ps 45:
9; 65: 5 al.; Jos., Bell. 5, 378 τ. ἔργα τοῦ θεοῦ, C. Ap. 2,
192) Mt 11: 2; J 5: 20, 36; 7: 3, 21 (Diod. S. 5, 33, 5 ἓν
ἔργον=just one practice); 9: 3; 10: 25, 37f; 14: 10, 11, 12;
15: 24; Ac 13: 41 (Hab 1: 5); Rv 15: 3.

β. of the deeds of men, exhibiting a consistent moral
character, referred to collectively as τὰ ἔργα (Ps 105: 35;
Job 11: 11; Jon 3: 10) J 3: 20f; 7: 7; Js 3: 13; 1 J 3: 12; Rv 2:
2, 19 al. πάντα τὰ ἔργα (Am 8: 7; Mi 6: 16) Mt 23: 5.
κατὰ τὰ ἔργα *in accordance w. the deeds* (Ps 27: 4; 61: 13;
Pr 24: 12) Ro 2: 6; 2 Ti 4: 14; Rv 2: 23; 20: 12f. Also κατὰ
τὸ ἔργον (Sir 11: 20) Gal 6: 4; Hb 6: 10; Rv 22: 12. The ἔργον or
ἔργα is (are) characterized by the context as good or bad
Lk 11: 48; 1 Cor 5: 2; 2 Cor 11: 15; 2 Ti 4: 14; 3 J 10; Rv
14: 13; 16: 11; 18: 6 (since in all these passages except Rv
14: 18 ἔ. refers to something bad, it is well to point out that
ἔργον when used alone also means *an evil* or *disgraceful
deed*, e.g., Appian, Bell. Civ. 2, 22 §83 ἔργον οὐδὲν
αὐτοῖς ἀπῆν=they abstained from no shameful deed;
Apollon. Rhod. 4, 476; 742; Arrian, Anab. 3, 21, 4). Or
they are characterized by an added word: ἔ. ἀγαθόν Ro 2:
7; 13: 3; 2 Cor 9: 8; Phil 1: 6; Col 1: 10 al. Pl. Eph 2: 10;
1 Ti 2: 10. πλήρης ἔργων ἀγαθῶν *rich in good deeds* Ac
9: 36. ἔ. καλόν Mt 26: 10; Mk 14: 6; J 10: 33. Pl. (Dio
Chrys. 3, 52) Mk 5: 16; J 10: 32; 1 Ti 5: 10a, 25; 6: 18; Tit
2: 7, 14; 3: 8; Hb 10: 24; 1 Pt 2: 12 (WCvanUnnik, NTS 1,
'54/'55, 92–110; cf. Diod. S. 16, 1, 1), 2 Cl 12: 4. ἔργα
ὅσια, δίκαια 6: 9. ἔ. δικαιοσύνης B 1: 6. ἐξ ἔργων τῶν ἐν
δικαιοσύνῃ *righteous deeds* Tit 3: 5. τὰ ἔ. τοῦ θεοῦ *the
deeds that God desires* (Jer 31: 10; 1 Esdr 7: 9, 15) J 6: 28;
cf. vs. 29. τὰ ἔ. μου (i.e. Χριστοῦ) Rv 2: 26. ἔργα
πεπληρωμένα ἐνώπιον τ. θεοῦ 3: 2. ἔ. ἄξια τ. μετανοίας
Ac 26: 20. ἔ. τῆς πίστεως *the deeds that go with faith* Hs
8, 9, 1. ἔ. αἰώνιον *an imperishable deed* IPol 8: 1. τὰ ἔ.
τοῦ Ἀβραάμ *deeds like those of Abraham* J 8: 39. τὰ ἔ. τ.
πέμψαντός με 9: 4.—ἔργα πονηρά *evil deeds* (1 Esdr 8:
83) Col 1: 21; 2 J 11; cf. J 3: 19; 7: 7; 1 J 3: 12. Also ἔ. τῆς
πονηρᾶς Β 4: 10. νεκρά *dead works*, i.e., those that
lead to death Hb 6: 1; 9: 14. ἄκαρπα *unfruitful actions*
Eph 5: 11. ἄνομα *lawless deeds* 2 Pt 2: 8. Also ἔ. τῆς
ἀνομίας Β 4: 1; Hs 8, 10, 3. ἔργα ἀσεβείας *impious deeds*
Jd 15. τοῦ σκότους *deeds of darkness* (i.e. unbelief) Ro 13:
12; cf. Eph 5: 11. ἔ. τῆς σαρκός *deeds that originate in the
flesh* (i.e. sin) Gal 5: 19. τὰ ἔ. τοῦ πατρὸς ὑμῶν *deeds
such as your father* (the devil) *commits* J 8: 41.—κρύφια,
φανερὰ ἔ. *secret, open deeds* 2 Cl 16: 3. Freq. in Paul
ἔργα νόμου *deeds that the law commands you to do* Ro 3:
20, 28; Gal 2: 16; 3: 2, 5, 10. Also simply ἔργα, w. the
same meaning Ro 4: 2, 6; 9: 12, 32; 11: 6; Eph 2: 9; cf.
ELohmeyer, ZNW 28, '29, 177–207.—δικαιοσύνη 3, end.

2. *work, occupation, task* (cf. Aristoph., Av. 862; X.,
Mem. 2, 10, 6; Arrian, Anab. 5, 23, 1; Epict. 1, 16, 21; Sir
11: 20) w. gen. of the one who assigns the task τοῦ κυρίου
1 Cor 15: 58; 16: 10; Phil 2: 30. διδόναι τινὶ τὸ ἔ. αὐτοῦ
assign his task to someone Mk 13: 34; πληροῦν ἔ.
accomplish a task Ac 14: 26. τ. ἔ. τελειοῦν *finish the work*

(Dionys. Hal. 3, 69, 2 τ. οἰκοδομῆς τ. πολλὰ εἰργάσατο,
οὖ μὴν ἐτελείωσε τὸ ἔργον; 2 Esdr 16 [Neh 6]: 3, 16) J 17:
4; cf. 4: 34. Of the task and work of the apostles Ac 13: 2;
15: 38. οἱ πιστευθέντες παρὰ θεοῦ ἔργον τοιοῦτο *those
who were entrusted by God with so important a duty* 1 Cl
43: 1. καρπὸς ἔργου *fruit of work* Phil 1: 22. To love
someone διὰ τὸ ἔ. αὐτοῦ *because of what he has done* 1 Th
5: 13. Of an office 1 Ti 3: 1 (4 is also poss.). ἔ. ποιεῖν
εὐαγγελιστοῦ *do the work of an evangelist* 2 Ti 4: 5.—ἔ.
συγγενικὸν ἀπαρτίζειν *accomplish a proper, natural
task* IEph 1: 1.

3. of that which is brought into being by work (Hom+;
Gen 2: 2; 3 Km 7: 15, 19; Jer 10: 3; 1 Esdr 5: 44) *work* in
the passive sense. W. special ref. to buildings (Aristoph.,
Av. 1125; Polyb. 5, 3, 6; Diod. S. 1, 31, 9; Appian,
Mithrid. 30 §119; Arrian, Anab.. 6, 18, 2; Dionys. Byz.
§27; IG IV² 1, 106, 56; 114, 31 al.; 1 Macc 10: 11; PPetr.
III 43[2] col. 1, 2 [III BC] εἰς τὰ ἔργα=for the buildings al.
Sib. Or. 4, 59; EPeterson, Biblica 22, '41, 439–41) 1 Cor 3:
13, 14, 15. Perh. a building is also meant in 1 Cor 9: 1 and
Ro 14: 20 (s. καταλύω 1bβ). γῆ κ. τὰ ἐν αὐτῇ ἔ. 2 Pt 3: 10
(FWDanker, ZNW 53, '62, 82–86, would read καὶ γῆ
κατὰ τὰ ἐν αὐτῇ ἔργα). Idols as ἔργα ἀνθρώπων 2 Cl 1:
6 (Herodas 4, 26 ἔργα καλά of works of sculpture). τὸ ἔ.
τῶν χειρῶν τινος *the work of someone's hands*=what
someone has made Ac 7: 41 (cf. Herodas 7, 2f ἔργον τῶν
χειρῶν τινος; Epict. 3, 7, 24; Jos., Bell. 3, 268). Of the
world as created by God (Celsus 4, 99) Hb 1: 10 (Ps 101:
26); B 5: 10; 15: 3. τὰ ἔ. τοῦ διαβόλου *the devil's
undertakings* or *enterprises* (Arrian, Anab. 1, 11, 7 Τρωι-
κὸν ἔ.=the Trojan undertaking, of the Trojan War) 1 J 3:
8. τὰ ἔργα τῆς θηλείας *the works of the female* (w. ref. to
sensual desire like Horapollo 1, 11 p. 18 θηλείας ἔργον
and Longus 4, 19, 5 ἔργα γυναικῶν) GEg 3.

4. weakened to *thing, matter* (Hom. +) Ac 5: 38. κρεῖττον IRo 2: 1. ἔ. εὐφροσύνης *a joyful thing* B 10: 11; οὐ
πεισμονῆς τὸ ἔ. *not a matter of persuasion* IRo 3: 3. οὐ
νῦν ἐπαγγελίας τὸ ἔ. *it is not a matter of what we now
profess* IEph 14: 2. Perh. also 1 Ti 3: 1 (s. 2 above).—
JAKleist, 'Ergon' in the Gospels: CBQ 6, '44, 61–8—many
alternative mngs.; GBertram, TW II 631–49. M-M. B. 540
for ἔργον, etc.

ἐργοπαρέκτης, ου, ὁ (hapax legomenon) *one who gives
work, an employer* 1 Cl 34: 1.*

ἐρεθίζω 1 aor. ἠρέθισα (Hom.+; Epict., Ench. 20; LXX)
arouse, provoke mostly in bad sense *irritate, embitter*, as
τὰ τέκνα Col 3: 21 (cf. Epict., loc. cit., where ἐ. takes up
the preceding λοιδορεῖν and τύπτειν; 1 Macc 15: 40;
Philo, Ebr. 16; Jos., Bell. 2, 414, Ant. 4, 169; 20, 175). In
a good sense of an encouraging example (Ael. Aristid. 28,
75 K.=49 p. 516 D.; Appian, Iber. 26 §103) 2 Cor 9: 2.
M-M.*

ἐρείδω 1 aor. ἤρεισα (Hom.+; LXX; Jos., Bell. 7, 283,
Ant. 8, 133; Sib. Or. 4, 106) *jam fast, become fixed*
(Aeschyl., Ag. 976; Plut., Numa 2, 2, Crass. 19, 4) of the
bow of a ship Ac 27: 41. M-M.*

ἐρεύγομαι fut. ἐρεύξομαι (Hom.+; LXX; Sib. Or. 4, 81)
orig. 'belch', then *utter, proclaim* (so Callimachus: POxy.
1011 fol. 1 vers., 7) τὶ someth. κεκρυμμένα Mt 13: 35.
ῥῆμα *a word* 1 Cl 27: 7 (Ps 18: 3). M-M.*

ἐρευνάω s. ἐραυνάω.

ἐρευνητής s. ἐραυνητής.

ἐρημία, ας, ἡ *uninhabited region, desert* (so Aeschyl.,
Hdt.+; BGU 888, 15 [II AD]; PGrenf. II 84, 4; LXX;

Philo; Jos., Bell. 3, 515 [near the Jordan]; loanw. in rabb.) Mt 15: 33; Mk 8: 4; (w. ὄρη) Hb 11: 38; (in contrast to πόλις, as Ezk 35: 4; Jos., Ant. 2, 24, Vi. 11) 2 Cor 11: 26. M-M.*

ἔρημος, ον (Hom.+; inscr., pap., LXX; on the accent cf. Bl-D. §13; Mlt.-H. 58).
1. adj.—a. of a place *abandoned, empty, desolate* τόπος (Diod. S. 15, 49, 1 ἐν ἐρ. τόπῳ; Plut., Numa 4, 1; Arrian, Ind. 22, 4; Dit., Or. 580, 7; Philo, Spec. Leg. 4, 141; Jos., C. Ap. 1, 308) Mt 14: 13, 15; Mk 1: 35, 45; 6: 31f, 35; Lk 4: 42; 9: 12. οἶκος (Artem. 2, 33 p. 130, 10; Philo, Spec. Leg. 2, 133; Jos., Vi. 376) Mt 23: 38 v.l. ἔπαυλις Ac 1: 20. ὁδός *lonely* 8: 26 (Arrian, Anab. 3, 3, 3 ἐρήμη ἡ ὁδός; 3, 21, 7; s. on Γάζα). χωρίον Papias 3.
b. of persons *desolate, deserted* (trag., Thu.) a childless woman (Charito 3, 5, 5) Gal 4: 27; 2 Cl 2: 1 (both Is 54: 1; cf. Philo, Exsecr. 158). ἐ. ἀπὸ τ. θεοῦ *deserted by God* 2: 3 (cf. Appian, Bell. Civ. 4, 30 §130 ἐρ. ἐκ παραπομπῆς= deserted by his escort).
2. subst. ἡ ἐ. (Hdt. 3, 102 al.; LXX; En. 10, 4; Jos., C. Ap. 1, 89; sc. χώρα) *desert, grassland, wilderness* (in contrast to cultivated and inhabited country) Mt 24: 26; Rv 12: 6, 14; 17: 3. Pl. *lonely places* (cf. PTebt. 61a, 151 [118 BC]) Lk 1: 80; 5: 16; 8: 29. *Steppe, grassland* as pasture 15: 4. Of the Judaean wilderness, the stony, barren eastern declivity of the Judaean mountains toward the Dead Sea and lower Jordan Valley (1 Macc 2: 29; 5: 24, 28; 2 Macc 5: 27) Mt 3: 1 (ἡ ἔ. τῆς Ἰουδαίας) Mk 1: 3, 4 (cf. IQS 8, 12–14 w. ref. to Is 40: 3 and s. HPRüger, ZNW 60, '69, 142–4; GWNebe, ibid. 63, '72, 283–89); Lk 3: 2; J 11: 54. Gathering-place of a band of revolutionaries Ac 21: 38 (on the language cf. Jos., Bell. 7, 438; on the Egyptian, Bell. 2, 261f ἐκ τῆς ἐρημίας, Ant. 20, 169). Of the Arabian desert (LXX) ἡ ἔ. τοῦ ὄρους Σινᾶ (Ex 19: 1f; cf. vs. 3 al.) Ac 7: 30; cf. vss. 36, 38, 42 (Am 5: 25), 44; 1 Cor 10: 5; Hb 3: 8 (Ps 94: 8), 17. As the place where the prophets Eldad and Modat preached Hv 2, 3, 4.—AJonsen, Die bibl. Wüste, Diss. Würzb. '23; UMauser, Christ in the Wilderness (Mk) '63; RWFunk, JBL 78, '59, 205–14; GerhKittel, TW II 654–7. M-M.

ἐρημόω in our lit. only pass.—pf. ptc. ἠρημωμένος; 1 aor. ἠρημώθην (Pind., Hdt.+; inscr., pap., LXX, Philo, Joseph., Test. 12 Patr.) *lay waste, depopulate* a city (Thu., also PSI 71, 11; Cat. Cod. Astr. VIII 3, p. 169, 14; 1 Esdr 2: 17; 2 Esdr 12 [Neh 2]: 3; Is 6: 11 al.; Jos., Bell. 2, 279, Ant. 11, 24) Rv 18: 19; fig. 17: 16. βασιλεία a *kingdom depopulated* by civil war (Philo, Decal. 152) Mt 12: 25; Lk 11: 17. Of a vineyard ἐρημοῦται ὑπὸ τῶν βοτανῶν *is laid waste by weeds* Hs 9, 26, 4.—*Ruin* (Sir 16: 4) of wealth (Sir 21: 4) Rv 18: 17. M-M.*

ἐρημώδης, ες (found nowhere else) *desert-like* of a mountain Hs 9, 1, 9; 26, 1. Of persons 9, 26, 3.*

ἐρήμωσις, εως, ἡ *devastation, destruction, depopulation* (Arrian, Anab. 1, 9, 7; 5, 1, 5; Cat. Cod. Astr. VIII 3 p. 136, 25 τόπων ἐνδόξων ἐρημώσεις; LXX; Test. Levi 17: 10; Jos., Ant. 12, 322) of Jerusalem Lk 21: 20. On τὸ βδέλυγμα τῆς ἐ. Mt 24: 15; Mk 13: 14 s. βδέλυγμα 3 and cf. HBévenot, RB 45, '36, 53–65.*

ἐρίζω fut. ἐρίσω *quarrel, wrangle* (Hom.+; Lucian; Plut.; BGU 1043, 5; PGM 13, 202; LXX; Jos., Bell. 4, 396; 5, 414) abs. (Epict. Schenkl fgm. 25 fr. Stob.) Mt 12: 19 (w. κραυγάζειν; MBlack, An Aramaic Approach³, '67, 257). M-M.*

ἐριθεία, ας, ἡ (W-H. ἐριθία; s. Mlt.-H. 339) found before

NT times only in Aristot., Polit. 5, 3 p. 1302b, 4; 1303a, 14, where it denotes a self-seeking pursuit of political office by unfair means. Its meaning in our lit. is a matter of conjecture. A derivation fr. ἔρις is not regarded w. favor by recent NT linguistic scholarship; it is also unlikely for the sources fr. which Paul possibly derived the lists of vices in 2 Cor 12: 20; Gal 5: 20, since ἔρις and ἐριθεῖαι are both found in these lists. Nevertheless, this is not absolutely valid for Paul and his followers, so that for them the mng. *strife, contentiousness* (so recently Ltzm., MDibelius, JSickenberger) cannot be excluded (cf. Phil 1: 17 w. 15 and s. Anecd. Gr. p. 256, 17 ἐρ.=φιλονεικία). But *selfishness, selfish ambition* (recently PAlthaus on Ro 2: 8; M-M.) in all cases gives a sense that is just as good, and perh. better. W. ζῆλος Js 3: 14, 16. κατὰ ἐριθείαν Phil 2: 3; IPhld 8: 2; ἐξ ἐ. Phil 1: 17; οἱ ἐξ ἐ. Ro 2: 8 (cf. Rdm.² p. 26; 217, 4). Pl. *disputes* or *outbreaks of selfishness* (Bl-D. §142) 2 Cor 12: 20; Gal 5: 20. KAFFritzsche, Comm. in Ep. ad Rom. 1836 on 2: 8 p. 143-8; ChBruston, RThPh 41, '09, 196–228; FBüchsel, TW II 657f. M-M.*

ἔριον, ου, τό (Hom.+; inscr., pap., LXX, En., Philo; Jos., Ant. 4, 80; 208 al.) *wool* B 7: 11; 8: 5f. λευκόν *white wool* (PGM 2, 70f; Da 7: 9) Rv 1: 14; cf. 1 Cl 8: 4 (Is 1: 18). κόκκινον *red* Hb 9: 19; B 7: 8; 8: 1ab. Pl. (class.; inscr., pap., LXX) a large white chair ἐξ ἐρίων χιονίνων γεγονυῖαν *cushioned with snow-white woolen cloth* Hv 1, 2, 2. M-M. B. 400.*

ἔρις, ιδος, ἡ (Hom.+; Aelian, V.H. 2, 21; Zen.-P. 48 [= Sb 6754], 16; PGrenf. I, 1, 21; LXX; Ep. Arist. 250; Philo; Jos., Ant. 14, 470; Sib. Or. 3, 640) acc. ἔριν (Od. 3, 136 al.) Phil 1: 15; Tit 3: 9. Pl. ἔριδες 1 Cor 1: 11 or ἔρεις 1 Cl 35: 5; 46: 5 (Ps 138: 20 Swete); Bl-D. §47, 3 app.; Mlt.-H. 131. *Strife, discord, contention* Tit 3: 9; IEph 8: 1. In a list of vices Ro 1: 29; (w. ζῆλος) 13: 13; 1 Cor 3: 3; cf. 2 Cor 12: 20; Gal 5; 20; 1 Cl 5: 5; 6: 4; 9: 1; (w. φθόνος as Appian, Bell. Civ. 2, §6) Phil 1: 15; 1 Ti 6: 4; (w. στάσις as Appian, Bell. Civ. 3, 86 §357) 1 Cl 3: 2; 14: 2; 54: 2. ἔστιν ἐπὶ τινος *there is strife about someth.* 44: 1. Pl. *quarrels* (Maximus Tyr. 22, 3f; Philo) Ro 13: 13 v.l. (w. ζήλοις); 1 Cor 1: 11; Tit 3: 9 v.l.; 1 Cl 35: 5; 46: 5. M-M. B. 1360.*

ἐριστικός, ή, όν *contentious, quarrelsome* (Pla., Lys. 211B; Aristot., Rhet. 1, 11; Lucian, Hermot. 16; Herm. Wr. 12, 9; Philo) in a list of vices D 3: 2.*

ἐρίφιον, ου, τό (Athen. 14 p. 661B; PThéad. 8, 11 al.; Tob 2: 13) dim. of ἔριφος, lit. *kid*, but also *goat* (cf. the interchange betw. ἐ. and ἔριφος Tob 2: 12, 13) Lk 15: 29 v.l.; Mt 25: 33 (cf. vs. 32 ἔριφος). M-M.*

ἔριφος, ου, ὁ (Hom.+; Lucian; Inschr. v. Priene 362, 12 [IV BC]; Dialekt-Inschr. 1654, 15 [Achaia]; PHib. 54, 18; PStrassb. 24, 49; LXX; Ep. Arist.; Jos., Ant. 3, 239; 8, 396) *kid, he-goat*. Pl. w. πρόβατα prob. simply *goats* (cf. ἄρνας κ. ἐρίφους POxy. 244, 10 [23 AD]; Molpis in Athen. 4 p. 141E ἄρνες, ἔριφοι; Longus 3, 33, 2; Ep. Arist. 146) Mt 25: 32.—*Kid* Lk 15: 29 (as a roast: Alcaeus 44 Diehl²; Maximus Tyr. 30, 5a). B. 166.*

Ἑρμᾶς, ᾶ, ὁ *Hermas* (Dit., Or. 48, 1; BGU 79, 8; 11; 264, 5; PLond. 1178, 14; PMich. 157, 18 [250 AD]. Cf. Rouffiac p. 91; MDibelius on Hv 1, 1, 4) short form of a name beg. w. Ἑρμ- (Bl-D. §125, 1; Rob. 172).
1. receiver of a greeting Ro 16: 14.—2. author of the Shepherd of Hermas, acc. to the Muratorian Fgm. (ll. 73ff) brother of the Roman bishop Pius Hv 1, 1, 4; 1, 2, 2-4; 1, 4, 3; 2, 2, 2; 2, 3, 1; 3, 1, 6; 9; 3, 8, 11; 4, 1, 4; 7. M-M.*

ἑρμηνεία, ας, ἡ (since Pre-Socr., X., Pla.; Vett. Val. p. 4, 5; Philo) W-H. ἑρμηνία Mlt.-H. 339 *translation, interpretation* (BGU 326 I, 1; II, 15; POxy. 1466, 3; Sir Prol. l. 20; Ep. Arist. 3; 11 al.) γλωσσῶν 1 Cor 12: 10; cf. 14: 26. Of words of Jesus Papias 2: 3.*

ἑρμηνευτής, οῦ, ὁ (Pla., Pol. 290c) *translator* (Gen 42: 23) 1 Cor 14: 28 v.l. Mark is called the ἑ. *interpreter* of Peter, Papias 2: 15. M-M.*

ἑρμηνεύω (trag. +)—1. *explain, interpret* (Pla., Ion p. 535A al.; BGU 140, 20 [201/2 AD]; Philo) τινί τι *someth. to someone* Lk 24: 27 v.l. Ἰουδαϊσμὸν ἑ. ὑμῖν *proclaim Judaism to you, depending upon interpretation* IPhld 6: 1 (ἑρμ. also means simply *proclaim, discourse on,* without the idea of interpreting: Soph., Oed. C. 399; Philostrat., Vi. Soph. 2, 14; 2, 22 al.; Celsus 3, 55; Dit., Syll.³ 1168, 88 [IV BC]; Suppl. Epigr. Gr. VIII 551, 39 [I BC]).

2. *translate* (so the act. and mid., X., An. 5, 4, 4; BGU 326 II, 22; PRyl. 62; 2 Esdr [Ezra] 4: 7; Job 42: 17b; Ep. Arist. 39; Philo; Jos., Ant. 6, 156, C. Ap. 2, 46) J 1: 38 v.l., 42; 9: 7 (Stephan. Byz. s.v. Ἱστός: κέλλα ῥαρσάθ, ὃ ἑρμηνεύεται ἱστὸς νηός). Μελχισέδεκ is ἑρμηνευόμενος βασιλεὺς δικαιοσύνης Hb 7: 2.—Of translation of Matthew's work Papias 2: 16. JBehm, TW II 659–62. M-M.*

Ἑρμῆς, οῦ, ὁ *Hermes*—1. the Greek god (SEitrem, Hermes: Pauly-W. VIII 1, '12, 738–92) Ac 14: 12 (s. the lit. on Λύστρα and cf. Ael. Aristid. 46 p. 135 D.: Ἑρμῆν ῥητορικὴν ἔχοντα; 46 p. 398 D. of Demosth., ὃν ἐγὼ φαίην ἂν Ἑρμοῦ τινος λογίου τύπον εἰς ἀνθρώπους κατελθεῖν; Orph. Hymn. 28, 4 Q.: Hermes as λόγου θνητοῖσι προφήτης).

2. receiver of a greeting Ro 16: 14 (H. as a man's name [cf. Dit., Or. 481, 4; 597, 4; PWien Bosw. 6, 2 (250 AD); 4, 2; Jos., Ant. 14, 245] is either simply the name of the god [HMeyersahm, Deorum nomina hominibus imposita, Diss. Kiel 1891; HUsener, Götternamen 1896, 358] or a short form like Ἑρμᾶς [q.v.]; Bl-D. §125, 1; Rob. 172). M-M.*

Ἑρμογένης, ους, ὁ (Dit., Syll. and Or. ind.; POxy. 1292, 1 [30 AD]; Jos., C. Ap. 1, 216) *Hermogenes,* a Christian fr. Asia Ti 1: 15. M-M.*

ἑρπετόν, οῦ, τό (Hom. +; PGM 1, 116; LXX; En.; Ep. Arist.; Philo; Joseph.; Sib. Or. fgm. 3, 8) *reptile* (w. τετράποδα and πετεινά; cf. Palaeph. p. 50, 8) Ac 10: 12; Ro 1: 23; (w. τετρ., πετ. and θηρία) Ac 11: 6; (w. still others, as Herm. Wr. 1, 11b) PK 2, p. 14, 18; (w. θηρία) Hs 9, 26, 1 (s. below); θηρία, πετεινά, ἑ., ἐνάλια *four-footed animals, birds, reptiles, fish* Js 3: 7 (cf. Gen 1: 25f; 9: 2f; En. 7, 5; Philo, Spec. Leg. 4, 110–16; PGM 1, 118f). Esp. of the *snake* (Eur., Andr. 269; Theocr. 24, 56; Jos., Ant. 17, 109) ἑ. θανατώδη *deadly snakes* Hs 9, 1, 9; cf. also 9, 26, 1 (s. above). M-M.*

ἐρρέθην s. εἶπον.

ἐ(ρ)ριμμένος s. ῥίπτω.

ἔρρωσο s. ῥώννυμι.

ἐρυθρός, ά, όν *red* (Hom. +; inscr., LXX) of roses AP 3: 8. ἡ ἐρυθρὰ θάλασσα *the Red Sea* (Aeschyl., Hdt. +; Diod. S. 19, 100, 5; Dit., Or. 69; 186, 6; 199, 25 al. [s. index II p. 590]; PGM 4, 3054; Ex 10: 19 al.; En. 32, 2; Philo, Mos. 1, 165; 2, 1; Jos., Ant. 2, 315) Ac 7: 36; Hb 11: 29; 1 Cl 51: 5. MCopisarow, Vetus Testamentum 12, '62, 1–14; NHSnaith, ibid. 15, '65, 395–98. M-M. B. 1056.*

ἔρχομαι imper. ἔρχου, ἔρχεσθε; impf. ἠρχόμην; fut. ἐλεύσομαι; pf. ἐλήλυθα; 2 aor. ἦλθον, ἦλθα (Bl-D. §81,

3 app.; Mlt.-H. 208f) (Hom. +; inscr., pap., LXX, Ep. Arist., Joseph., Test. 12 Patr.).

I. *come*—1. lit.—a. of pers.—α. abs. ἔρχου καὶ ἔρχεται Mt 8: 9; Lk 7: 8; cf. Mt 22: 3; Lk 14: 17; J 5: 7; Ac 10: 29; 1 Cor 11: 34; Rv 8: 3 and oft. κραυγὴ γέγονεν· ἰδοὺ ὁ νυμφίος ἔρχεται Mt 25: 6 t.r. (Jos., Bell. 5, 272 βοῶντες· ὁ υἱὸς ἔρχεται). οἱ ἐρχόμενοι καὶ οἱ ὑπάγοντες Mk 6: 31. Also w. the specif. mng. *come back, return* (Hom. +; Bar 4: 37; 1 Esdr 5: 8; Tob 2: 3 BA) J 4: 27; 9: 7; Ro 9: 9. *Come before the judgment-seat of God* 2 Cl 9: 4. *Come in a hostile sense* Lk 11: 22 𝔓⁷⁵ et al. (cf. X., Hellenica 6, 5, 43).

β. used w. prepositions: ἀπό w. gen. of the place (Herodian 1, 17, 8 ἀ. τοῦ λουτροῦ) Mk 7: 1; 15: 21; Ac 18: 2; 2 Cor 11: 9; w. gen. of the pers. Mk 5: 35; J 3: 2b; Gal 2: 12.—ἐκ w. gen. of the place Lk 5: 17; J 3: 31b.—εἰς w. acc. of place *into* Mt 2: 11; 8: 14; 9: 1; Mk 1: 29; 5: 38; J 11: 30; *to, toward* J 11: 38; 20: 3. εἰς τὸ πέραν Mt 8: 28; 16: 5; ἐκ . . . εἰς J 4: 54; διὰ w. gen. of place and εἰς Mk 7: 31; J 10: 2 𝔓⁷⁵; εἰς τ. ἑορτήν *to the festival,* i.e. to celebrate it J 4: 45b; 11: 56.

ἐν w. dat. of the thing w. which one comes Ro 15: 29. ἐν ῥάβδῳ 1 Cor 4: 21, also to denote the state of being in which one comes ἐν πνεύματι Lk 2: 27; ὁ Ro 15: 32; w. dat. of the pers. who accompanies someone Jd 14.—ἐπί w. acc. of place *over* Mt 14: 28, *to* (Jos., Ant. 7, 16) Lk 19: 5; Ac 12: 10; w. acc. of the thing *to* (PTurin I 1, II, 29 [116 BC] ἔρχεσθαι ἐπὶ τὸ κριτήριον; Jos., Ant. 12, 395) Mt 3: 7; Mk 11: 13b; w. acc. of the pers. *to* J 19: 33; Ac 24: 8 v.l., *against* Lk 14: 31 (1 Macc 5: 39 ἔρχ. ἐπί τινα εἰς πόλεμον; Jos., Ant. 7, 233).—κατά w. acc. of place *to* Lk 10: 33; Ac 16: 7.—παρά w. acc. of place *to* Mt 15: 29; w. gen. of the pers. *from* Lk 8: 49.—πρός w. acc. of the pers. *to* (X., Mem. 1, 2, 27; Jos., Ant. 2, 106; 11, 243) Mt 3: 14; 7: 15; Mk 9: 14; Lk 1: 43; J 1: 29, 47; 2 Cor 13: 1 and oft. ἀπό τινος (gen. of pers.) πρός τινα 1 Th 3: 6.

γ. w. an adverb of place ἄνωθεν ἔ. J 3: 31. ἐκεῖ 18: 3. ἐνθάδε 4: 16. ὄπισθεν Mk 5: 27. πόθεν (Jdth 10: 12) J 3: 8; 8: 14; Rv 7: 13. ποῦ Hb 11: 8. ὧδε Mt 8: 29; Ac 9: 21. The adv. w. a case as an improper prep. ἄχρι τινός Ac 11: 5. ἐγγύς τινος Hv 4, 1, 9. ἕως τινός Lk 4: 42.

δ. w. a case, without a prep.: dat. of the pers. *come to someone* (Aeschyl., Prom. 358; Thu. 1, 13, 3; X., An. 7, 7, 30; BGU 1041, 16 [II AD] ὅτι ἔρχομαί σοι) Mt 21: 5 (Zech 9: 9); Rv 2: 5, 16.

ε. The purpose of the coming is expressed by the inf. (Eur., Med. 1270, also Palaeph. p. 62, 12; 1 Macc 16: 22; Bel 40 Theod.; 1 Esdr 1: 23; 5: 63) Mt 2: 2; 12: 42; Mk 15: 36; Lk 1: 59; 3: 12 al.; by the fut. ptc. (Hom. +) Mt 27: 49; Ac 8: 27; by the pres. ptc. Lk 13: 6; by ἵνα J 10: 10; 12: 9b; εἰς τοῦτο ἵνα Ac 9: 21; διά τινα J 12: 9a.

ζ. Single forms of ἑ. are used w. other verbs to denote that a person, in order to do someth., must first come to a certain place: in parataxis ἔρχεται καί, ἦλθεν καί etc. (Ex 19: 7; 2 Km 13: 36; 2 Esdr 5: 16) Mt 13: 19, 25; Mk 2: 18; 4: 15; 5: 33; 6: 29; 12: 9; 14: 37; Lk 8: 12, 47; J 6: 15; 11: 48; 12: 22; 19: 38; 20: 19, 26; 21: 13; 3 J 3; Rv 5: 7; 17: 1; 21: 9. ἔρχου καὶ ἴδε J 1: 46; 11: 34. ἔρχεσθε καὶ ὄψεσθε 1: 39. A ptc. of ἑ. followed by a finite verb ἐλθών (Hdt. 2, 115; LXX) Mt 2: 8; 8: 7; 9: 10, 18; 12: 44; 14: 12; 18: 31; 27: 64; 28: 13; Mk 7: 25; 12: 14, 42; 14: 45; 16: 1; Ac 16: 37, 39. ἐρχόμενος Lk 13: 14; 16: 21; 18: 5. The participial constr. is best transl. *come and.* In some places ἐλθών is to be rendered *when (someone) has come* J 16: 8; 2 Cor 12: 20; Phil 1: 27 (opp. ἀπών).

η. Freq. the coming has rather the sense *appear, make an appearance, come before the public.* So esp. of the Messiah Lk 3: 16; J 4: 25; 7: 27, 31, who for this reason (on the basis of pass. like Ps 117: 26; Hab 2: 3; Da 7: 13

Theod.) is called ὁ ἐρχόμενος Mt 11: 3; Lk 7: 19f; Hb 10: 37 (Hab 2: 3), or ὁ ἐρχόμενος ἐν ὀνόματι κυρίου Mt 21: 9; 23: 39; Mk 11: 9; Lk 13: 35; 19: 38; J 12: 13 (in all cases Ps 117: 26); also in John, in whose writings the idea of Jesus' having come fr. heaven to the earth, sent by the Father, is of considerable importance J 16: 28: (ὁ προφήτης) ὁ ἐρχόμενος εἰς τ. κόσμον J 6: 14; 11: 27. Of the appearance of Jesus among men (cf. Harnack, 'Ich bin gekommen': ZThK 22, '12, 1–30; AFrövig, D. Sendungsbewusstsein Jesu u. d. Geist '24, 129ff) Mt 11: 19; Lk 7: 34; J 5: 43; 7: 28; 8: 42. Foll. by the inf. of purpose Mt 5: 17; 10: 34f; Lk 19: 10. W. ἵνα foll. J 10: 10b (ἦλθον, as here, Herm. Wr. 1, 30). W. εἰς τ. κόσμον and ἵνα foll. 12: 46; 18: 37; εἰς κρίμα, ἵνα 9: 39; w. inf. foll. 1 Ti 1: 15. ἔ. ἐν σαρκί come in the flesh 1 J 4: 2; 2 J 7; B 5: 10f. ἔ. δι' ὕδατος καὶ αἵματος 1 J 5: 6 could be transl. go through water and blood (s. II below), that is, in his (Christ's) baptism and death on the cross, if it were not for the continuation ἐν τῷ ὕδατι with the water where ἔρχεσθαι must be supplied and evidently means come. The context demands that ἔ. be rendered by an ambivalent term, denoting both 'come' and 'go', and the English language can in this instance not furnish an expression of the required kind. ἔ. ὀπίσω w. gen. come after of Christ in relation to his forerunner Mt 3: 11; Mk 1: 7; J 1: 15, 27, 30. The idea of coming is even plainer in connection w. the coming of the Son of Man fr. heaven, the return of Jesus fr. his home in heaven Mt 10: 23; Ac 1: 11 (opp. πορεύεσθαι); 1 Cor 4: 5; 11: 26; 2 Th 1: 10. W. ἐν τῇ δόξῃ Mt 16: 27; 25: 31; Mk 8: 38; Lk 9: 26. ἐπὶ τ. νεφελῶν μετὰ δυνάμεως καὶ δόξης Mt 24: 30. ἐν νεφέλαις, νεφέλη etc. Mk 13: 26; Lk 21: 27. ἐν τ. βασιλείᾳ αὐτοῦ in his kingdom Mt 16: 28; Lk 23: 42 v.l.

θ. appear also of forerunners of the Messiah: Elijah Mt 11: 14; 17: 10, 11, 12; Mk 9: 11, 12, 13. John the Baptist Mt 11: 18; Lk 7: 33; J 1: 31; w. εἰς μαρτυρίαν for testimony 1: 7. Of false teachers, false Messiahs, and the Antichrist in his various forms: Mt 24: 5; Mk 13: 6; Lk 21: 8 (ἐπὶ τ. ὀνόματί μου calling on my name); J 10: 8; 2 Cor 11: 4; 2 Pt 3: 3; 1 J 2: 18.

b. of time—a. ἔρχονται ἡμέραι in future sense (1 Km 2: 31; Am 8: 11) Lk 23: 29; Hb 8: 8 (Jer 38: 31); ἐλεύσονται ἡμ. Mt 9: 15; Mk 2: 20; Lk 5: 35; 17: 22; 21: 6. ἦλθεν ἡ ἡμέρα 22: 7; Rv 6: 17.—ἔρχεται ὥρα ὅτε the time is coming when J 4: 21, 23; 5: 25; 16: 25; also ἔ. ὥρα ἐν ᾗ 5: 28; Mk 14: 16: 2, 32. ἦλθεν ἡ ὥρα the hour has come—the hour is here Mk 14: 41b; J 16: 4; Rv 14: 7, 15; w. ἵνα foll. J 13: 1 (ἥκω 𝔓⁶⁶). ἐλήλυθεν ἡ ὥ. ἵνα 12: 23; 16: 32; without ἵνα 17: 1; cf. 7: 30; 8: 20.—ἔρχεται νύξ 9: 4 (Appian, Bell. Civ. 2, 40 §159 νυκτὸς ἐρχομένης). ἡμέρα κυρίου 1 Th 5: 2. καιροὶ Ac 3: 20. τὸ πλήρωμα τ. χρόνου Gal 4: 4.

β. of events and situations that are connected w. a certain time ὁ θερισμός J 4: 35. ὁ γάμος τ. ἀρνίου Rv 19: 7. ἡ κρίσις 18: 10. So also the ptc. ἐρχόμενος coming, future, imminent: αἰὼν ἐ. (= הַעוֹלָם הַבָּא) the age to come Mk 10: 30; Lk 18: 30; ἑορτὴ ἐ. the coming festival Ac 18: 21 t.r.; σάββατον ἐ. 13: 44; ὀργὴ ἐ. the wrath which will be revealed (at the Judgment) 1 Th 1: 10. τὰ ἐρχόμενα what is to come (Is 44: 7 τὰ ἐπερχόμενα) J 16: 13. Of God in Rv ὁ ὢν κ. ὁ ἦν κ. ὁ ἐρχόμενος 1: 4, 8; 4: 8.

c. of things and events—a. of natural phenomena (Hom. +) ποταμοί Mt 7: 25, 27. κατακλυσμός Lk 17: 27. λιμός Ac 7: 11. Of rain ἔ. ἐπὶ τῆς γῆς come upon the earth Hb 6: 7. Sim. of the coming down of birds fr. the air Mt 13: 4, 32; Mk 4: 4; of a voice resounding fr. heaven ἦλθεν φωνὴ ἐκ τ. οὐρανοῦ J 12: 28 (cf. Il. 10, 139).

β. of objects in the sense be brought (Hom. +; Thu. 6, 71, 2 χρήματα; Arrian, Anab. 2, 13, 5 ἀγγελία) ὁ λύχνος

the lamp is brought Mk 4: 21. Sim. ἐλθούσης τ. ἐντολῆς when the commandment came Ro 7: 9. In the last-mentioned passages the transition to the non-literal use can be detected.

2. non-literal use—a. of spiritual coming of God J 14: 23; of Christ ibid. and vss. 3, 18, 28; of the Paraclete 15: 26; 16: 7, 13.

b. of states of being, etc. come, appear τ. σκάνδαλα Mt 18: 7; Lk 17: 1. τὰ ἀγαθά Ro 3: 8 (cf. Jer. 17: 6). τὸ τέλειον 1 Cor 13: 10. ἡ πίστις Gal 3: 23, 25. ἡ ἀποστασία 2 Th 2: 3. ἡ βασιλεία τ. θεοῦ Mt 6: 10; Lk 11: 2 (MBurrows, JBL 74, '55, 1–8); 17: 20; 22: 18 al.; 1 Cl 42: 3.

c. in var. prepositional combinations ἔ. ἐκ τ. θλίψεως have suffered persecution Rv 7: 14. ἔ. εἰς τὸ χεῖρον Mk 5: 26 (PVat. A, 12 [168 BC= Witkowski² p. 65] τοῦ παιδίου εἰς τὰ ἔσχατα ἐληλυθότος). εἰς τοσαύτην ἀπόνοιαν, ὥστε 1 Cl 46: 7 (Hyperid. 2, 5 εἰς τοῦτο ἀπονοίας ἔ., ὥστε). εἰς πειρασμόν Mk 14: 38 (cf. Himerius, Or. 48 [Or. 14], 19 εἰς ἐπιθυμίαν ἐλθεῖν). εἰς ἀπελεγμόν Ac 19: 27. εἰς τὴν ὥραν ταύτην J 12: 27. ἔ. εἰς κρίσιν submit to judgment (letter of Philip in Demosth. 12, 11; 16) 5: 24. εἰς ἐπίγνωσιν 1 Ti 2: 4; 2 Ti 3: 7 (Polyb. 6, 9, 12; Appian, Mithr. 31 §123 ἔρχεσθαι ἐς γνῶσίν τινος; Cebes 12, 3 εἰς τὴν ἀληθινὴν παιδείαν ἐλθεῖν). come to light Mk 4: 22; Lk 8: 17. εἰς προκοπὴν result in furthering Phil 1: 12 (cf. Wsd 15: 5). ἔ. εἴς τι of the writer of a letter come to, i.e. deal with someth. (a new subject) 2 Cor 12: 1. εἰς ἑαυτόν come to oneself (= to one's senses) (Diod. S. 13, 95, 2; Epict. 3, 1, 15; Test. Jos. 3: 9; Sb 5763, 35) Lk 15: 17. ἐπί τινα of serious misfortunes come over someone (Dt 28: 15; Jos., Ant. 4, 128) J 18: 4 (cf. PIand. 21, 2 ἡμῶν τὰ ἐρχόμενα οὐκ οἶδα); tortures IRo 5: 3; blood upon the murderers Mt 23: 35; the Holy Spirit comes down upon someone (cf. Ezk 2: 2) Mt 3: 16; Lk 11: 2 v.l.; Ac 19: 6; peace Mt 10: 13; the wrath of God Eph 5: 6 (cf. Col 3: 6); ἡ βασιλεία Lk 11: 2 D; ἔ. πρός τ. Ἰησοῦν come to Jesus= become disciples of Jesus J 5: 40; 6: 35, 37, 44f, 65; πρός τ. πατέρα 14: 6. ἔ. ὑπὸ τὸν ζυγόν 1 Cl 16: 17.—Not infreq. the pres. ἔρχομαι has the mng. of the fut.: Lk 12: 54 (corresp. to καύσων ἔσται vs. 55); 19: 13; Mt 17: 11; J 14: 3. Esp. also ἕως ἔρχομαι until I shall come J 21: 22f; 1 Ti 4: 13; Hs 5, 2, 2; 9, 10, 5; 6; 9, 11, 1. Cf. Bl-D. §323; 383, 1; Rob. 869. S. also 1ba above.

II. go (Hom. +; LXX) ὀπίσω τινός go with (lit. 'after') someone fig., of a disciple Mt 16: 24; Mk 8: 34; Lk 9: 23; 14: 27. ἐπί τι go to someth. Mt 21: 19; Mk 11: 13a (w. indir. quest. foll.). πρός τινα Lk 15: 20. σύν τινι J 21: 3. ἔ. ὁδόν travel on a journey (Hom. +) Lk 2: 44. S. also I 1aη above. M-M. B. 696.

ἐρῶ s. εἶπον. M-M.

ἔρως, ωτος, ὁ (Hom. +; Herm. Wr., pap.; Pr 7: 18; 30: 16; Philo; Jos., Ant. 1, 302, C. Ap. 2, 244) passionate love ὁ ἐμὸς ἔ. ἐσταύρωται my passionate love (for the world) has been crucified (cf. Gal 6: 14) IRo 7: 2.—S. ἀγάπη I, end. B. 1110.*

ἐρωτάω fut. ἐρωτήσω; 1 aor. ἠρώτησα—1. ask, ask a question (Hom. +; so also inscr., pap. and nearly always LXX; Ep. Arist., Philo; Jos., Ant. 6, 115) abs. (Da 2: 10; 1 Macc 10: 72) Lk 22: 68. τινά someone (Lucian, Dial. Deor. 7, 1; Gen 24: 47; 40: 7; Ex 13: 14 al.) J 1: 25; 8: 7; 9: 21; 16: 19, 30 al. τινά τι someone about someth. (X., Mem. 3, 7, 2, Cyr. 3, 3, 48; Job 21: 29; Jos., Ant. 6, 48) ὑμᾶς λόγον ἕνα ask you one question Mt 21: 24= Lk 20: 3 (cf. Pla., Leg. 10 p. 895E; Jer 45: 14); αὐτὸν τὰς παραβολάς ask him about the parables Mk 4: 10. Certainly J 16: 23 belongs here too. τινὰ περί τινος *someone about someth.* (2 Esdr 11 [Neh 1]: 2; Is 45: 11) Mt 19: 17; Lk 9: 45; J 18: 19. W. τινά and direct question (X., An. 1, 6, 7) Mk 8: 5; Lk 19: 31; J 1: 19, 21; 5: 12; 16: 5; the direct quest. introduced by λέγων or λέγοντες Mt 16: 13; J 9: 2, 19. W. τινά and indir. quest. foll. (X., Cyr. 8, 5, 19) 9: 15. Cf. Lk 23: 6 𝔓⁷⁵ (ἐρωτ. εἰ also Thu. 1, 5, 2).

2. *ask, request* (Babrius 42, 3; 97, 3; Apollon. Dysc., Synt. 3, 167 Uhlig ἐρωτῶ σε νῦν ἐν ἴσῳ τῷ παρακαλῶ σε, λιτανεύω, ἱκνοῦμαι; Dit., Syll.³ 705, 56 [112 BC]; 741, 5 [after 88 BC]; POxy. 744, 6; 13 [1 BC]; 292, 7 [c. 25 AD]; 110; 111; 113; 269; 745; 746 al.; Jer 44: 17; Jos., Ant. 7, 164; Test. Sim. 4: 1.—Dssm., B 30; 31; 45, NB 23f [BS 195f; 290f]) τὶ *for someth.* Lk 14: 32 (s. εἰρήνη 1a). περί τινος *for someth.* Hv 3, 1, 6b (w. ἵνα foll.). τὶ περί τινος *for someth. concerning a thing* 3, 1, 6a. W. acc. of the pers.: τινά *someone* J 14: 16 (Field, Notes 101f). τ. κύριον Hv 2, 1 (Jos., Ant. 5, 42 ἐ. τ. θεόν; Sib. Or. 2, 309). Foll. by λέγων, which introduces the request in direct discourse Mt 15: 23; J 4: 31; 12: 21. W. imper. foll. (BGU 423, 11 ἐρωτῶ σε οὖν, γράψον μοι ἐπιστόλιον; POxy. 745, 7; 746, 5) Lk 14: 18f; Phil 4: 3. τινὰ περί τινος *beseech someone on someone's behalf* Lk 4: 38; J 16: 26; 17: 9, 20; *concerning someth.* 1 J 5: 16, sim. ὑπέρ τινος 2 Th 2: 1 (on the interchange of περί and ὑπέρ s. Bl-D. §229, 1; 231; Rob. 629; 632). τινὰ κατὰ τοῦ κυρίου *beseech someone by the Lord* Hv 3, 2, 3 (Bl-D. §225). W. ἵνα foll. (POxy. 744, 13 [1 BC]) Mk 7: 26; Lk 7: 36; 16: 27; J 4: 47; 17: 15; 19: 31, 38; 2 J 5. W. ὅπως foll. (Dit., Syll.³ 741, 5 [after 88 BC]) PTebt. 409, 4; 6; En. 13, 4) Lk 7: 3; 11: 37; Ac 23: 20. W. inf. foll. (Charito 8, 7, 3; PTebt. 410, 11; PRyl. 229, 8 [38 AD]; POxy. 292, 7 [c. 25 AD]; Jos., Ant. 6, 328) Lk 5: 3; 8: 37; J 4: 40; Ac 3: 3; 10: 48; 16: 39; 18: 20; 1 Th 5: 12. Foll. by εἰς and subst. inf. 2 Th 2: 1.—ἐ. and παρακαλέω together (POxy. 744, 6; 294, 28 [22 AD]. S. the quot. fr. Apollon. Dysc. in 2 above) 1 Th 4: 1.—*Urge* w. inf., imper. et al. B 4: 6; 21: 2, 4, 7.—HGreeven, TW II 682-4. M-M. B. 1264; 1271.

ἐρώτησις, εως, ἡ (= 'question' Hippocr.+; Dit., Or. 508, 10; Philo, Rer. Div. Her. 18) *request* (so prob. Syntipas 105, 30) of a prayer Hv 3, 10, 6.*

Ἐσθήρ, ἡ (אֶסְתֵּר) (indecl. in the book of Esther; in Jos., Ant. 11, 199; 225; 227 al. Ἐσθήρ, ῆρος) *Esther*, heroine of the book named after her 1 Cl 55: 6.*

ἐσθής, ῆτος, ἡ (Hom.+; inscr., pap., LXX, Philo, Joseph., Test. 12 Patr.) *clothing* Lk 23: 11; 24: 4; Ac 10: 30 (cf. Dit., Syll.³ 1157, 39, Or. 332, 38 ἐν ἐσθῆσιν λαμπραῖς); 12: 21 (=Jos., Ant. 19, 344 στολὴν ἐνδὺς ἐξ ἀργύρου πεποιημένην πᾶσαν) Js 2: 2f; Dg 5: 4. The dat. pl. form ἐσθήσεσι, which is not unanimously attested either in Ac 1: 10 or Lk 24: 4 (but found 2 Macc 3: 33; 3 Macc 1: 16; Philo, Vi. Mos. 2, 152; BGU 16, 12 [159/60 AD]; PLond. 77, 20; 32. Cf. also Crönert 173, 1. The form ἐσθῆσιν Jos., Bell. 2, 176 becomes ἐσθήσεσιν in Euseb., H.E. 2, 6, 7) does not come from a word ἔσθησις (so L-S-J), for which there is no evidence in the sing., nor in the pl. except for the dative, but belongs to ἐσθής; it is the result of an attempt to make the dat. ending more conspicuous by doubling it (WSchulze, Ztschr. f. vergleich. Sprachforschg. 42, '09, 235, 2). Bl-D. §47, 4; Mlt.-H. 133. M-M. B. 395.*

ἐσθίω (Hom.+; inscr., pap., LXX, Philo, Joseph., Test. 12 Patr.) and, mainly in the ptc., ἔσθω (Hom.+, also in other poets, rare in prose [Plut., Mor. p. 101D]; Coan inscr. [III BC]; RHerzog, ARW 10, '07, 400ff; 23; 27; 42];

POsl. 153, 15 [beg. II AD]; PGiess. 80, 5; ostraca [BGU 1507, 14; 1508, 3; 4: III BC]; LXX. ἔσθων Lev 17: 14; 1 Km 14: 30; Sir 20: 17; Mk 1: 6; Lk 7: 33f v.l.; 10: 7. ἔσθητε Num 15: 19; Lk 22: 30. Bl-D. §101 w. app.; Mlt.-H. 238; ESchwyzer, Griech. Gramm. I '39, 704 note 1); impf. ἤσθιον; fut. ἔδομαι (LXX) 1 Cl 39: 9; 57: 6; 2 aor. ἔφαγον, Ps 77: 29 ἐφάγοσαν; fut. φάγομαι (Bl-D. §74, 2; Mlt.-H. 238), 2 sing. φάγεσαι (Lk 17: 8; Ruth 2: 14; Bl-D. §87; Mlt.-H. 198) *eat.*

1. lit.—**a.** w. acc. of the thing (Hom.+; X., Cyr. 6, 2, 28; POxy. 1185, 10; PGiess. 80, 6; 10; LXX) τί φάγωσιν (after neg.) *anything to eat* Mt 15: 32; Mk 6: 36; 8: 1f; cf. Mt 6: 25, 31; Lk 12: 22 (s. Epict. 1, 9, 8; 19). τοὺς ἄρτους τῆς προθέσεως *the consecrated bread* Mt 12: 4; Mk 2: 26; Lk 6: 4. Locusts and wild honey Mk 1: 6. Manna (Ps 77: 24) J 6: 31, 49. Vegetables Ro 14: 2b. Meat 14: 21; 1 Cor 8: 13; GEb 6. τὰ εἰδωλόθυτα 1 Cor 8: 10; cf. vs. 7; Rv 2: 14, 20. τὰς θυσίας (Sir 45: 21; Ps 105: 28) 1 Cor 10: 18. τὰ ἐκ τοῦ ἱεροῦ *food from the temple* 9: 13. τὴν σάρκα τ. υἱοῦ τ. ἀνθρώπου J 6: 53 (which passage many interpret as referring to the Eucharist while others explain it as speaking of receiving Christ spiritually through faith). πάντα *all kinds of food* Ro 14: 2a. τὰ παρατιθέμενα *the food that is set before (one)* Lk 10: 8; 1 Cor 10: 27. τὸ ἐν μακέλλῳ πωλούμενον 10: 25. τὸ βιβλαρίδιον Rv 10: 10 (cf. Ezk 2: 8; 3: 3). τὸ πάσχα *the Passover meal,* esp. *the Passover lamb* (2 Esdr [Ezra] 6: 21; 2 Ch 30: 18; ESchürer, Über φαγεῖν τὸ πάσχα 1883; Dalman, Jesus 81f) Mt 26: 17; Mk 14: 12, 14; Lk 22: 8, 11, 15; J 18: 28. κυριακὸν δεῖπνον φαγεῖν 1 Cor 11: 20. ἄρτον ἐσθίειν *eat a meal,* w. bread as its main part (Ex 2: 20; 1 Km 20: 34; 2 Km 9: 7; 3 Km 13: 15 al.) Mt 15: 2; Mk 3: 20; 7: 2, 5; Lk 14: 1 (s. Billerb. IV 611–39: E. altjüd. Gastmahl); of the Messianic banquet Lk 14: 15. τὸν ἑαυτοῦ ἄρτον ἐ. *eat one's own bread* 2 Th 3: 12. ἄρτον φαγεῖν παρά τινος *eat someone's bread* vs. 8. τὰ παρά τινος *what someone provides* Lk 10: 7. Neg. οὐκ ἔφαγεν οὐδέν *he ate nothing* at all Lk 4: 2 (cf. Job 21: 25 οὐ φαγὼν οὐδὲν ἀγαθόν). Of complete abstinence μὴ ἐσθίων ἄρτον μήτε πίνων οἶνον 7: 33. οὐδέποτε ἔφαγον πᾶν κοινόν *I have never eaten anything common at all* Ac 10: 14 (cf. 1 Macc 1: 62). Allegorical interpretation of Mosaic laws against eating forbidden foods B 10 (cf. Hierocles 26 p. 480 reinterpretation of the Pythagorean laws against forbidden foods as moral laws). —Of animals (Hom.+; Aelian, V.H. 1, 1; 2, 40; 3 Km 13: 28; Is 65: 25; Da 4: 33 Theod.): birds τὰς σάρκας τινός *eat someone's flesh* (Gen 40: 19) Rv 19: 18; cf. 17: 16. Swine Lk 15: 16 (ὧν here is for ἅ by attraction, not a gen. dependent on ἐ., as it prob. is in X., Hell. 3, 3, 6; Ps.-Lucian, Asin. 21; this constr. would be wholly isolated in our lit.).

b. w. prepositions, to denote the thing of which one partakes:—**α.** w. ἀπό τινος (Lev 22: 6; Num 15: 19; Dt 14: 12, 19; Pr 13: 2; Da 4: 30a) dogs: ἐ. ἀπὸ τῶν ψιχίων *eat the crumbs* Mt 15: 27; Mk 7: 28 (on the pl. ἐσθίουσιν after the neut. κυνάρια (cf. Lk 11: 7; 1 Cl 42: 2; Bl-D. §133; cf. Rob. 403f). ἀπὸ τραπέζης *partake of a meal* D 11: 9. ἀπὸ τῆς εὐχαριστίας 9: 5.

β. w. ἔκ τινος (Jdth 12: 2; Sir 11: 19) ἐκ τοῦ ἄρτου *eat (some of) the bread* (2 Km 12: 3; Tob 1: 10) 1 Cor 11: 28; cf. J 6: 26, 50f. ἐκ τῶν καρπῶν αὐτῶν Hs 9, 1, 10. ἐκ τοῦ γάλακτος τοῦ ποιμνίου *get sustenance fr. the milk of the flock* 1 Cor 9: 7. ἐκ τ. θυσιαστηρίου Hb 13: 10. ἐκ τ. ξύλου τ. ζωῆς *from the tree of life* Rv 2: 7 (s. En. 32, 6); cf. μηκέτι ἐκ σοῦ μηδεὶς καρπὸν φάγοι Mk 11: 14.

c. used with other prep. expressions ἐ. μετά τινος *eat w. someone* (1 Km 9: 19; Jdth 12: 11; Job 1: 4; Ezk 47: 22) Mt 9: 11; 24: 49; Mk 2: 16; 14: 18 (cf. Ps 40: 10) Lk 5: 30; 7:

36. ἐνώπιόν τινος *in someone's presence* (cf. ἐναντίον τ. θεοῦ Ex 18: 12; Ezk 44: 3) 13: 26; 24: 43. ἐπὶ τ. τραπέζης τινός *at someone's table* (2 Km 9: 11; cf. vs. 13; Da 11: 27) Lk 22: 30. διὰ προσκόμματος ἐ. *eat with offense* (i.e., so that one takes offense in doing so; perh. also so that one gives offense) Ro 14: 20.

d. abs. Mt 12: 1; 14: 20; 26: 21, 26; Mk 7: 3f; 14: 18a, 22; Ac 27: 35; D 12: 3; B 7: 5 al. Used w. λαμβάνειν (Gen 3: 22) λάβετε φάγετε Mt 26: 26b; οἱ ἐσθίοντες 14: 21; 15: 38. φάγωμεν κ. πίωμεν *let us eat and drink* 1 Cor 15: 32 (Is 22: 13). φάγε, πίε, εὐφραίνου Lk 12: 19 (Aristobulus of Cass. [III BC]: 139 fgm. 9 Jac. [cited in Strabo 14, 5, 9], statue of Sardanapalus w. the inscr. ἔσθιε, πῖνε, παῖζε· ὡς τἆλλα τούτου οὐκ ἄξια. This saying of Sardanapalus is also found in Arrian, Anab. 2, 5, 4. A similar thought in the Phrygian grave-inscr.: Inschr. Gal. no. 78, 11ff). τὸ φαγεῖν *eating* Mt 15: 20; 1 Cor 11: 21. διδόναι τινὶ φαγεῖν *give someone someth.* to eat (Ex 16: 8, 15; Num 11: 18, 21) Mt 14: 16; 25: 35; Mk 5: 43; 6: 37; Lk 8: 55; 9: 13; J 6: 52; Rv 2: 7. φέρειν τινὶ φαγεῖν (cf. 2 Km 17: 29) J 4: 33. εὐκαιρέω φαγεῖν *I find time to eat* Mk 6: 31. ἔχω βρῶσιν φαγεῖν *I have food to eat* J 4: 32.—With the principle given in 2 Th 3: 10 cf. Lucian, Parasite 13: when a pupil progresses well δότε αὐτῷ φαγεῖν; when he does not, μὴ δῶτε.

e. ἐ. and πίνω are freq. found together, as in some pass. already quoted (Hom. + ; very oft. LXX; En. 102, 9; Philo, Det. Pot. Ins. 113; Jos., C. Ap. 2, 234).

α. = receive support 1 Cor 9: 4.—β. = eat a meal Lk 5: 30; 17: 8; 1 Cor 11: 22. Of a solemn sacrificial meal 10: 7 (Ex 32: 6).

γ. in contrast to fasting (which is expressed by ἐ. and πίνω w. a neg. [Iambl., Vi. Pyth. 28, 141 οὔτε πίνων οὔτε ἐσθίων]: Mt 11: 18; Lk 4: 2 v.l.; 7: 33; Ac 9: 9; 23: 12, 21) Mt 11: 19; Lk 5: 33; 7: 34; B 7: 5.

δ. of ordinary daily activities Lk 17: 27f.—ε. of carefree, even luxurious or dissipated living Mt 24: 49; Lk 12: 19, 45; 1 Cor 15: 32 (cf. Is 22: 13).—HRiesenfeld, Coniect. Neot. 9, '44, 10f.

2. fig. (Hom+; LXX) *consume, devour* (of fire Il. 23, 182; Is 10: 17; 26: 11) πυρὸς ἐσθίειν μέλλοντος τ. ὑπεναντίους *fire, which is about to consume the adversaries* Hb 10: 27 (Is 26: 11). ὁ ἰὸς . . . φάγεται τ. σάρκας ὑμῶν ὡς πῦρ *the rust will eat your flesh like fire* Js 5: 3 (cf. Aeschyl., fgm. 253 φαγέδαινα [an ulcer] σάρκας ἐσθίει ποδός; Is 30: 27 ἡ ὀργὴ τοῦ θυμοῦ ὡς πῦρ ἔδεται).—JBehm, TW II 686–93. M-M. B. 327.

ἔσθω s. ἐσθίω.

Ἐσλί, ὁ indecl. *Esli,* in the genealogy of Jesus Lk 3: 25. *

ἐσόμενος s. εἰμί.

ἔσοπτρον, ου, τό (Pind., Nem. 7, 20; Anacreontea 7, 3; 22, 5 Pr.; Plut., Mor. 139E; Epict. 2, 14, 21; 3, 22, 51; Proclus on Plato, Timaeus 33B Diehl II p. 80, 20; PRainer 27, 10 [190 AD]; POxy. 978; 1449, 19 ἔσοπτρον ἀργυροῦν; Wsd 7: 26; Sir 12: 11; Philo, Migr. Abr. 98; Jos., Ant. 12, 81) *mirror* κατανοεῖν τὸ πρόσωπον ἐν ἐ. *look at one's face in a mirror* Js 1: 23. δι' ἐσόπτρου βλέπειν ἐν αἰνίγματι *see dimly* or *indirectly in a mirror* (because one sees not the thing itself, but its mirror-image; cf. Herm. Wr. 17) 1 Cor 13: 12. On this s. RSeeberg: D. Reformation 10, '11, 137–9; Rtzst., Hist. Mon. 238–55; HAchelis, Bonwetsch-Festschr. '18, 56ff; PCorssen, ZNW 19, '20, 2–10; SEBassett, 1 Cor 13: 12: JBL 47, '28, 232ff; JBehm, D. Bildwort v. Spiegel 1 Cor 13: 12: RSeeberg-Festschr. I '29, 315–42; GerhKittel, TW I 177–9; WLKnox, St. Paul

and the Church of the Gentiles '39, 121 n. 4; ASPerry, ET 58, '46/'47, 279; NHugedé, La Métaphore du miroir dans 1 et 2 Cor, '57; FWDanker, CTM 30, '60, 428f. S. the lit. on 1 Cor 13 s.v. ἀγάπη I 1a, esp. HRiesenfeld, Coniect. Neot. 5. M-M.*

ἑσπέρα, ας, ἡ (Pind., Hdt.+; inscr., pap., LXX; Ep. Arist. 202; Joseph.) *evening* Ac 4: 3; τῇ ἑ. *in the evening* 20: 15 v.l. ἕως ἑσπέρας (Jos., Ant. 6, 364): ἀπὸ πρωῒ ἕως ἑσπέρας *from morning till evening* (3 Km 22: 35) 28: 23. Also ἀπὸ προΐθεν ἕως ἑσπέρας (Ex 18: 13; Sir 18: 26) 1 Cl 39: 5 (Job 4: 20). ἀφ' ἑσπέρας ἕως πρωΐ (Lev 24: 3) gospel-fgm. in POxy. 655 (Kl. Texte 8³ p. 23 l. 15). πρὸς ἑ. ἐστίν *it is getting toward evening* Lk 24: 29 (X., Hell. 4, 3, 22 ἐπεὶ πρὸς ἑσπέραν ἦν; Ex 12: 6; Jos., Ant. 5, 195). M-M. B. 997.*

ἑσπερινός, ή, όν (since X., Resp. Lac. 12, 6; POxy. 901, 5; BGU 1024 VI, 6; LXX) *of* or *pertaining to the evening* φυλακή the first watch of the night, six to nine p.m. Lk 12: 38 v.l. M-M.*

Ἑσρώμ, ὁ indecl. *Hezron,* in the genealogy of Jesus (1 Ch 2: 5 v.l., 9; in Ruth 4: 18f v.l.) Mt 1: 3; Lk 3: 33. *

ἑσσόομαι 1 aor. ἡσσώθην (Ionic—Hdt. 1, 82; 2, 169; 8, 130; cf. JWackernagel, Hellenistica 1907, 17–19; Bl-D. §34, 1; Mlt.-H. 107; 240; 396; differently W-S. §15, p. 127) *be defeated, be overpowered, be weaker than* or *inferior to* τί γάρ ἐστιν ὃ ἡσσώθητε ὑπὲρ τὰς λοιπὰς ἐκκλησίας; *in what respect, then, are you worse off than the other churches?* 2 Cor 12: 13 𝔓⁴⁶ א* BD*.—FZorell, BZ 9, '11, 160f.*

ἑστάναι, ἑστώς s. ἵστημι.

ἔστωσαν s. εἰμί.

ἔσχατος, η, ον (Hom.+; inscr., pap., LXX, En., Philo; Jos., Bell. 7, 272, C. Ap. 2, 272; Test. 12 Patr.) *last.*

1. of place ὁ ἔσχατος τόπος, perh. to be understood locally of the place in the farthest corner Lk 14: 9f (but s. 2 below).—Subst. τὸ ἔσχατον *the end* (schol. on Apollon. Rhod. 4, 1515a p. 319, 19 εἰς τὸ ἔσχατον τῆς νήσου; PTebt. 68, 54 [II BC] of a document) ἕως ἐσχάτου τῆς γῆς *to the end of the earth* (Is 48: 20; 62: 11; 1 Macc 3: 9) Ac 1: 8 (CBurchard, D. Dreizehnte Zeuge, '70, 134 n. 309); 13: 47; B 14: 8 (the two last Is 49: 6). Pl. (Hes., Theog. 731 and an oracle in Hdt. 7, 140 ἔσχατα γαίης; X., Vect. 1, 6; Diod. S. 1, 60, 5; Ael. Aristid. 35, 14 K. = 9 p. 103 D.: ἔσχ. γῆς; Crates, Ep. 31 and Demosth., Ep. 4, 7 ἐπ' ἔσχατα γῆς) τὰ ἔ. τῆς γῆς *the ends of the earth* 1 Cl 28: 3 (Theocr. 15, 8; schol. on Apollon. Rhod. 2, 413–18b. With εἰς before it Ps 138: 9).

2. of rank and succession (opp. πρῶτος as Hierocles 23 p. 468: man is ἔσχατος μὲν τῶν ἄνω, πρῶτος δὲ τῶν κάτω) *the last, least, most insignificant*: (οἱ) πρῶτοι ἔσχατοι καὶ (οἱ) ἔσχατοι πρῶτοι Mt 19: 30; 20: 16; Mk 9: 35; 10: 31; Lk 13: 30; LJ 2: 4a, b; τὸν ἔ. τόπον κατέχειν *take the poorest place* (in this sense the ἔσχ. τόπος would be contrasted with the ἐνδοξότερος, as Diog. L. 2, 73) Lk 14: 9; cf. vs. 10 (but s. 1 above). Of the apostles, whom God has exhibited as the *least* among men, by the misfortunes they have suffered (Diod. S. 8, 18, 3 the ἔσχατοι are the people living in the most extreme misery; Dio Chrys. 21[38], 37 the tyrants treat you as ἐσχάτους; Cass. Dio 42, 5, 5, Πομπήιος . . . καθάπερ τις τῶν Αἰγυπτίων ἐσχάτων) 1 Cor 4: 9. ἔ. τῶν πιστῶν IEph 21: 2; cf. ITr 13: 1; IRo 9: 2; ISm 11: 1.

3. of time *least, last,* coming last or the last of someth. that is left

a. w. ref. to its relation with someth. preceding Mt 20: 12, 14; Mk 12: 6; J 8: 9 v.l. (opp. πρῶτος; 2 Ch 9: 29 al.; Sir 24: 28; 41: 3) ἀπὸ τῶν ἐ. ἕως τῶν πρώτων Mt 20: 8; cf. 27: 64; 1 Cor 15: 45 (ἔσ. also the later of two, as Dt 24: 3f ἔσ.—πρότερος; hence 1 Cor 15: 47 replaced by δεύτερος. Cf. Mt 21: 31 v.l. ὁ. ἔσ. the latter); Rv 2: 19; Hv 1, 4, 2. τὰ ἔσχατα (in contrast to τὰ πρῶτα as Job 8: 7) the last state Mt 12: 45; Lk 11: 26; 2 Pt 2: 20. Of the creation in the last days ποιῶ τ. ἔσχατα ὡς τ. πρῶτα (apocryphal quot.; cf. Hippolytus, Comm. on Daniel 4: 37) B 6: 13.
b. w. ref. to a situation in which there is nothing to follow the ἔ. (Diod. S. 19, 59, 6 κρίσιν ἐσχάτην τῆς περὶ Δημήτριον βασιλείας = the last [final] crisis in the reign of Demetrius): ἡ ἐ. ἡμέρα τ. ἑορτῆς (cf. 2 Esdr 18 [Neh 8]: 18) J 7: 37. ὁ ἐ. κοδράντης (cf. 2 Esdr 15 [Neh 5]: 15) Mt 5: 26; Lk 12: 59 v.l.; cf. 1 Cor 15: 26, 52; Rv 15: 1; 21: 9. As a self-designation of the Risen Lord ὁ πρῶτος καὶ ὁ ἐ. the first and the last Rv 1: 17; 2: 8; 22: 13. Esp. of the last days, which are sometimes thought of as beginning w. the birth of Christ, somet. w. his second coming ἡ ἐ. ἡμέρα the last day (PViereck, Sermo Gr., quo senatus pop. Rom. magistratusque . . . usi sunt 1888 inscr. 29, 9 [116 BC] εἰς ἐσχάτην ἡμέραν = forever) J 6: 39f, 44, 54; 11: 24; 12: 48 (BAebert, D. Eschatol. des J, Diss. Bres. '36); Hv 2, 2, 5. Pl. (Is 2: 2) Ac 2: 17; 2 Ti 3: 1; Js 5: 3; D 16: 3; B 4: 9. ἐπ' ἐσχάτου τῶν ἡμερῶν τούτων (Num 24: 14; Jer 23: 20; 25: 19) in these last days Hb 1: 2. ἐπ' ἐσχάτων τ. ἡμερῶν (Hos 3: 5; Jer 37: 24; Ezk 38: 16) 2 Pt 3: 3 (cf. ἐπ' ἐσχάτων χρόνων 1 Pt 1: 20𝔓⁷² et al.); 2 Cl 14: 2; B 12: 9; 16: 5.—ἐπ' ἐσχάτου τοῦ χρόνου Jd 18. ἐπ' ἐσχάτου τ. χρόνων 1 Pt 1: 20.—ἐ. καιρός vs. 5; D 16: 2. Pl. (Test. Is 6: 1 ἐν ἐσχάτοις καιροῖς) IEph 11: 1.—ἐ. ὥρα (Teles p. 17, 5) 1 J 2: 18.—The neut. ἔσχατον as adv. finally (Dit., Syll.³ 1219, 11 [III BC]; POxy. 886, 21; Num 31: 2; Pr 29: 21) ἐ. πάντων last of all Mk 12: 22; 1 Cor 15: 8.—Gerh Kittel, TW II 694f. S. lit. s.v. παρουσία. M-M. B. 940. **

ἐσχάτως adv. (Hippocr. +; X., An. 2, 6, 1) finally ἐ. ἔχειν (cf. Lat. 'in extremis esse') be at the point of death (Artem. 3, 60) Mk 5: 23. M-M. *

ἔσω adv. of place (Hom. + in the form εἴσω, and predom. so in later times. In our lit., as in the LXX [Thackeray 82] only ἔσω, likew. Dit., Syll.³ 989, 2 [II BC]; UPZ 13, 17 [160 BC]; BGU 1127, 9 [18 BC].—Jos., Bell. 6, 265 εἴσω, but Ant. 15, 398 ἔσω).
1. in, into εἰσελθὼν ἔ. he went in (Bel 19 Theod.) Mt 26: 58. ἕως ἔ. εἰς τὴν αὐλήν right into the courtyard Mk 14: 54 (ἔσω εἰς τὴν αὐλήν as Pap-urkunden der Bibl. der Univ. Basel I '17 no. 19 [c. 600 AD]). W. gen. of place (class.) ἔ. τῆς αὐλῆς into the palace 15: 16 (mng. 2 is also poss. here).
2. inside, within Ac 5: 22 D, 23; ἦσαν ἔ. they were inside J 20: 26. αἱ ἔ. φλέβες the inner veins MPol 2: 2. ὁ ἔ. ἄνθρωπος the inner nature Ro 7: 22; Eph 3: 16. Also ὁ. ἔ. ἡμῶν ἄ. 2 Cor 4: 16 (cf. ἄνθρωπος 2cα and ἔξω 1αγ).—οἱ ἔ. those within the church (Aeneas Tact. 1312 of those in the city) = the Christians 1 Cor 5: 12; τὸ ἔ. the inside (Lucian, Navig. 38, Sacrif. 13.—Opp. τὸ ἔξω; cf. ἔξω 1αγ) = the soul 2 Cl 12: 2, 4 (a saying of Jesus, and an explanation of it).—JBehm, TW II 696f. M-M. *

ἔσωθεν adv. of place (Aeschyl., Hdt. +; pap., LXX).—**1.** from inside (Hdt. 7, 36, 2; Aeneas Tact. 1636) Lk 11: 7. ἐ. ἐκπορεύεσθαι come fr. within Mk 7: 23; fuller ἔ. ἐκ τῆς καρδίας vs. 21.
2. inside, within (Hdt. +; Epict.; POxy. 1449, 44; LXX; Ep. Arist. 89; Jos., Ant. 14, 477; 15, 424) Mt 7: 15; 23: 25, 27f; IRo 7: 2. Used w. ἔξωθεν (Epict. 4, 11, 18; Gen 6: 14;

Ex 25: 11) 2 Cor 7: 5. ἐ. καὶ ἔξωθεν inward and outward IRo 3: 2; Rv 5: 1 v.l., the text has ἔσωθεν κ. ὄπισθεν (s. γράφω 3). κυκλόθεν καὶ ἔ. all around and within 4: 8.—τὸ ἐ. ὑμῶν (ὑμῖν 𝔓⁷⁵) your inner nature Lk 11: 39. τὸ ἔξωθεν κ. τὸ ἔ. vs. 40. τὸ ἔσωθεν = οἱ ἔσω (s. ἔσω 2) 1 Cor 5: 12 𝔓⁴⁶. M-M. *

ἐσώτερος, α, ον (PMagd. 29, 10 [218 BC]; Mayser 14; 301; Catal. of the Gk. and Lat. Pap. in the JRyl. Libr. III '38 no. 478, 120 ὁ οἶκος ὁ ἐσώτερος; LXX) comp. of ἔσω; inner ἡ ἐ. φυλακή the inner prison Ac 16: 24 (on the subject-matter s. Mommsen, Röm. Strafrecht 1899, 302).—In τὸ ἐσώτερον τοῦ καταπετάσματος, ἐ. is an improper prep. w. gen. (cf. 1 Km 24: 4) what is inside (= behind) the curtain, the Holy of Holies Hb 6: 19 (Lev 16: 2, 12, 15). M-M. *

ἑταῖρος, ου, ὁ (Hom. +; Vett. Val. 331, 13; Dit., Syll.³ 798, 6 [37 AD], Or. 573, 1 [I AD]; pap.; LXX; Jos., Bell. 3, 362, Vi. 124) comrade, companion, friend of one's neighbor D 14: 2. Of playmates Mt 11: 16 v.l. Of Jesus' disciples (X., Mem. 2, 8, 1 al. Socrates refers to his pupils as ἐ.; Ael. Aristid. 47 p. 421 D. οἱ Πλάτωνος ἑτ.; Porphyr., Vi. Pythag. 55 of Pythag.—Philo, Vi. Cont. 40 of Odysseus' companions) Mt 26: 50 (ἑταῖρε; cf. Jos., Ant. 12, 302 ὦ ἑταῖροι); GP 7: 26. As a general form of address to someone whose name one does not know: ἑταῖρε my friend (Theognis 753 Diehl; Aristoph., Pla., et al.) Mt 20: 13; 22: 12.—Instead of being an itacized variant of ἕτερος, the reading ἑταῖροι Lk 23: 32 𝔓⁷⁵ may well connote political partisans (cf. Lysias 43, 28).—JPAErnstman, Οἰκεῖος, Ἑταῖρος, Ἐπιτήδειος, Φίλος, Diss. Utrecht '32; KH Rengstorf, TW II 697-9. M-M. *

ἔτεκον s. τίκτω.

ἑτερόγλωσσος, ον (Polyb. 23, 13, 2; Strabo 8, 1, 2; Philo, Conf. Lingu. 8; Aq. Ps 113: 1; Is 33: 19) speaking a foreign language ἐν ἑτερογλώσσοις λαλεῖν speak through people of strange tongues 1 Cor 14: 21 (after Is 28: 11, where Aq. seems to have written ἑτερόγλ.). Paul interprets it as having to do w. speaking w. tongues. M-M. *

ἑτερογνώμων, ον, gen ονος (Vett. Val. 79, 18; Agathias 4, 2.—ἑτερογνωμοσύνη: Jos., Ant. 10, 281) of a different opinion γυναικὸς ἑτερογνώμονος ὑπαρχούσης who was of a different opinion 1 Cl 11: 2. M-M. under preceding word. *

ἑτεροδιδασκαλέω (only in Christian wr.) teach a different (i.e. heretical) doctrine 1 Ti 1: 3; 6: 3 (cf. IQH 4, 16); IPol 3: 1. *

ἑτεροδοξέω (Pla., Theaet. 190E; Philo, Rer. Div. Her. 247.—Jos., Bell. 2, 129 ἑτερόδοξος of those who do not belong to the Essenes) hold different, i.e. heretical opinions ISm 6: 2. *

ἑτεροδοξία, ας, ἡ (Pla., Theaet. 193D; Philo, fgm. 72 Harris) strange, erroneous opinion of false doctrine IMg 8: 1. *

ἑτεροζυγέω (κτήνη ἑτερόζυγα = draft animals that need different kinds of yokes, because they are of different species [i.e., an ox and a donkey]: Lev 19: 19; Philo, Spec. Leg. 4, 203; cf. Jos., Ant. 4, 228.—ἑτερόζυγος is found in a different sense in Ps.-Phoc. 15, and generally = 'not belonging together' as early as Zen.-P. 59 038, 11 [257 BC]) be unevenly yoked, be mismated τινι with someone μὴ γίνεσθε ἑτεροζυγοῦντες ἀπίστοις 2 Cor 6: 14 (JAFitzmyer, Qumran and 2 Cor 6: 14-7: 1, CBQ 23, '61, 271-80, yoking associated with doctrine). M-M. *

ἑτεροκλινής, ές gen. **οῦς** (Hippocr. +) *leaning to one side,* transf. to the mental realm (Epict. 3, 12, 7 ἑτεροκλινῶς ἔχω πρὸς ἡδονήν; the adv. also 1 Ch 12: 34) *rebellious, apostate* 1 Cl 11: 1; 47: 7.*

ἕτερος, α, ον (Hom. +; inscr., pap., LXX, Ep. Arist.; Jos., Bell. 2, 163; Test. 12 Patr. In the NT it is entirely lacking in 1 and 2 Pt; 1, 2, and 3 J; Rv; found in Mk only in the bracketed ending 16: 12; in J only 19: 37) *other* adj. and subst.

1. of number—**a.** *other* of two, contrasting a definite person or thing w. another (Appian, Hann. 43 §185 Ἄννων ἕτερος=the other of the two Hannos) ἐν τῷ ἑτέρῳ πλοίῳ *in the other boat* Lk 5: 7; cf. 23: 40. ὁ ἕ. in contrast to ὁ πρῶτος (X., An. 3, 4, 25) Mt 21: 30 v.l.; ὁ εἷς —ὁ ἕ. (s. εἷς 5d) 6: 24; Lk 7: 41; 16: 13; 17: 34f; 18: 10; Ac 23: 6; 1 Cor 4: 6. ἕ. βασιλεύς *another king* (of two mentioned) Lk 14: 31.

b. of more than two—**α.** *another* ἕ. τῶν μαθητῶν Mt 8: 21; cf. Gal 1: 19. ἕ. προσδοκῶμεν; *are we to look for someone else?* Mt 11: 3. ἐν ἑ. σαββάτῳ Lk 6: 6. ἑτέρα γραφή *another Scripture passage* J 19: 37; 2 Cl 2: 4; cf. Lk 9: 56, 59, 61; 16: 18 (cf. Job 31: 10); Ac 1: 20 (Ps 108: 8); 7: 18 (Ex 1: 8); Ro 7: 3. ἕ. τις *someone else, any other* Ac 8: 34; Ro 8: 39; 13: 9 (cf. Cicero, Tusc. 4, 7, 16); 1 Ti 1: 10; Hv 3, 8, 4.

β. likew. in the pl. ἕτεροι *other(s)* Ac 2: 13 (ἕτεροι δέ joins the opinion of other people to an opinion previously expressed, as schol. on Pind., Pyth. 9, 183), Ac 10: 1. ἕτεραι γενεαί *other generations* (cf. Ps 47: 14; 77: 4, 6 al.) Eph 3: 5. ἑτέρους διδάσκειν (Da 11: 4) 2 Ti 2: 2. At the end of lists ἕτεροι πολλοί (cf. Demosth. 18, 208; 219; 19, 297; Appian, Bell. Civ. 2, 62 §260) Mt 15: 30; Ac 15: 35; ἕ. πολλαί Lk 8: 3; ἕ. πολλά (Jos., Vi. 39; 261) 22: 65. πολλὰ κ. ἕτερα 3: 18. τινὲς ἕ. (Jos., Vi. 15) Ac 27: 1; cf. Papias 2: 4. ἑπτὰ ἕ. πνεύματα an evil spirit takes *seven other evil spirits* with it Mt 12: 45; Lk 11: 26. Differently, to indicate a difference in kind, καὶ ἕ. (ἑταῖροι 𝔓⁷⁵) κακοῦργοι δύο *also two others, who were criminals* 23: 32 (cf. Test. Jud. 9: 6; PTebt. 41, 9 [c. 119 BC] τινῶν ἡμῶν [men] καὶ ἑτέρων γυναικῶν; Dio Chrys. 30[47], 24 ἑτέραν γυναῖκα Σεμίρ.=and in addition, a woman, Semiramis). οἱ ἕ. *the others, the rest* Mt 11: 16; Lk 4: 43.

γ. used interchangeably w. ἄλλος, which is felt to be its equivalent (Ps.-Pla., Alcib. I p. 116ε; Apollon. Rhod. 4, 141; Dio Chrys. 57[74], 22; Arrian, Anab. 5, 21, 2; 3; Herm. Wr. 11, 12a; PRainer 103, 21 ἀπό τε ἄλλων πρασέων ἢ ἑτέρων οἰκονομιῶν; 3, 19; 6, 17. Cf. also POxy. 276, 11 σὺν ἄλλοις σιτολόγοις w. PGenève 36, 10 σὺν ἑτέροις ἱερεῦσι, POslo. 111, 246 μηδένα ἄλλον with l. 292 μηδένα ἕτερον and Mt 10: 23 with v.l.; Mlt.-Turner 197f): εἰς ἕ. εὐαγγέλιον ὃ οὐκ ἔστιν ἄλλο *to another gospel, which is no (other) gospel at all* Gal 1: 6f (ἄλλος 1eβ). For another view cf. 2 below. ἄλλον Ἰησοῦν . . . πνεῦμα ἕ. . . . εὐαγγέλιον ἕ. 2 Cor 11: 4. S. also δ.

δ. In lists ὁ μὲν . . . καὶ ἕτερον . . . καὶ ἕ. . . . καὶ ἄλλος *some . . . some* etc. Lk 8: (5), 6, 7, 8. ὃς μὲν . . . ἄλλος δέ . . . ἕτερος . . . ἄλλος δὲ . . . ἄλλος δὲ . . . ἕτερος . . . 1 Cor 12: (8), 9, 10; τίς . . . ἕ. 3: 4; τίς . . . ἕ. . . . . ἄλλος τις Lk 22: (56), 58, (59). πρῶτος . . . ἕ. 16: (5), 7; πρῶτος . . . καὶ ἕ. 14: (18), 19f. ὁ πρῶτος . . . ὁ δεύτερος . . . ὁ ἕ. *the first . . . the second . . . the third* 19: (16, 18), 20; δοῦλος . . . ἕ. δοῦλος . . . τρίτος 20: (10), 11, (12). Pl. τινὲς ἕτεροι Lk 11: (15), 16. ἄλλοι . . . ἕ. (PPar. 26, 31 [163/2 BC]) Hb 11: (35), 36. οἱ μὲν . . . ἄλλοι δὲ . . . ἕ. δὲ . . . Mt 16: 14.

ε. ὁ ἕτερος *one's neighbor* (the contrast here is w. αὐτός: Demosth. 34, 12 ἕ. ἤδη ἦν καὶ οὐχ ὁ αὐτός. Cf. Is 34: 14)

Ro 2: 1; 13: 8 (WMarxsen, ThZ 11, '55, 230-37; but s. FWDanker, FWGingrich-Festschr. '72, 111 n. 2); 1 Cor 6: 1; 10: 24, 29; 14: 17; Gal 6: 4. Without the article διδάσκων ἕτερον σεαυτὸν οὐ διδάσκεις; Ro 2: 21 (cf. Ael. Aristid. 28, 1 K.=49 p. 491 D.: νουθετεῖν ἑτέρους ἀφέντες ἑαυτούς); 1 Cl 38: 2. Pl. Phil 2: 4.

ζ. τῇ ἑτέρᾳ (sc. ἡμέρᾳ) *on the next day* (X., Cyr. 4, 6, 10) Ac 20: 15; 27: 3.—ἐν ἑτέρῳ *in another place* (in Scripture; cf. Jos., Ant. 14, 114) 13: 35; Hb 5: 6. εἰς οὐδὲν ἕτερον . . . ἤ Ac 17: 21 (PRainer 32, 15 οὐδὲν δὲ ἕτερον; Jos., Ant. 8, 104).

2. *another, different* fr. what precedes, externally or internally (cf. Pla., Symp. 186β ἕτερος καὶ ἀνόμοιος al.; Dit., Or. 458, 8 [c. 9 BC] ἑτέραν ὄψιν; POxy. 939, 18; Wsd 7: 5; Jdth 8: 20 al.): ἐν ἑ. μορφῇ *in a different form* Mk 16: 12. εἶδος ἕτερον Lk 9: 29. ἑτέρα . . . δόξα, ἑτέρα . . . *glory of one kind, . . . of a different kind* 1 Cor 15: 40. ἕ. νόμος Ro 7: 23. ἑ. γνῶσις B 18: 1. ἑ. ὁδός Js 2: 25. On ἕ. in this sense in Gal 1: 6 s. M-M. s.v. Also actually *strange* ἐν χείλεσιν ἑτέρων *through the lips of strangers* 1 Cor 14: 21 (cf. Is 28: 11). λαλεῖν ἑτέραις γλώσσαις Ac 2: 4 may mean either *speak with different* (even *other* than their own) *tongues* or *speak in foreign languages* (cf. Is 28: 11; Sir prol. l. 22; IQH 4, 16). γλῶσσα 3.—JKElliott, ZNW 60, '69, 140f; HWBeyer, TW 699-702. M-M.

ἑτέρως adv. (Hom. +, more common Pla. +; Dit., Syll.³ 851, 10; POxy. 34, 15 [II AD]; Philo, Aet. M. 28; Jos., C. Ap. 1, 26) *differently, otherwise* ἑ. φρονεῖν Phil 3: 15. M-M.*

ἔτι adv. (Hom. +; inscr., pap., LXX, Ep. Arist., Philo, Joseph., Test. 12 Patr.) *yet, still.*

1. of time—**a.** in positive statements, to denote that a given situation is continuing *still, yet.*

α. of the present Lk 14: 32; Hb 11: 4. ἔ. σαρκικοί ἐστε 1 Cor 3: 3. ἔ. ἐστὲ ἐν ταῖς ἁμαρτίαις 15: 17. ἔ. ὑπὸ κίνδυνόν εἰμι ITr 13: 3. εἰ ἔτι ἀνθρώποις ἤρεσκον *if I were still trying to please men* Gal 1: 10; 5: 11a.

β. of the past, w. the impf. (Arrian, Anab. 6, 13, 2 ἔτι ἠπίστουν=they still disbelieved) ἔ. ἐν τῇ ὀσφύϊ ἦν *he was still in the loins* (i.e. not yet begotten) Hb 7: 10; cf. J 11: 30. Oft. w. the pres. ptc., which stands for the impf. (Diog. L. 9, 86 ἔτι ὁ ἥλιος ἀνίσχων) ἔ. αὐτοῦ λαλοῦντος *while he was still speaking* (cf. Job 1: 16, 17, 18; Jos., Ant. 8, 282) Mt 12: 46; 17: 5; 26: 47; Mk 5: 35a; 14: 43; Lk 8: 49; Ac 10: 44 al. εἶπεν ἔτι ζῶν *while he was still living* Mt 27: 63 (Jos., Ant. 4, 316; 8, 2 ζῶν ἔ.). ἔ. προσερχομένου αὐτοῦ *while he was still approaching* Lk 9: 42. ἔ. αὐτοῦ μακρὰν ἀπέχοντος *while he was still a long way off* 15: 20. σκοτίας ἔ. οὔσης *while it was still dark* J 20: 1. ἔ. ὢν πρὸς ὑμᾶς *when I was still with you* 2 Th 2: 5; cf. Lk 24: 6, 41, 44; Ac 9: 1; Ro 5: 6, 8; Hb 9: 8.

γ. of the future πλησθήσεται ἔ. ἐκ κοιλίας *he will be filled while he is still in his mother's womb* Lk 1: 15 (ἔ. ἐκ κοι. Is 48: 8; cf. 43: 13 and Anth. Pal. 9, 567, 1 ἔ. ἐκ βρέφεος; Ps.-Plut., Consol. ad Apoll. 6 p. 104D). καὶ ἔ. ῥύσεται *and he will deliver us again* 2 Cor 1: 10.

b. in negat. statements—**α.** οὐδὲ ἔ. νῦν *not even yet* 1 Cor 3: 2 (s. νῦν 1c).

β. to denote that someth. is stopping, has stopped, or should stop *no longer* (Arrian, Anab. 5, 25, 3 and 6; 6, 29, 2a οὐ ἔτι= not any longer; Aesop, Fab. 243 H. μὴ ἔτι= no longer; Jos., C. Ap. 1, 72) οὐ δύνῃ ἔ. *you can no longer* Lk 16: 2; cf. Mt 5: 13; Lk 20: 36; Rv 12: 8 al.; οὐ μὴ ἔ. *never again* Hb 8: 12; 10: 17 (both Jer 38: 34); Rv 18: 21, 22, 23. Sim. in rhetorical questions τί ἔ. σκύλλεις τ. διδάσκαλον; *why should you bother the Teacher any further?* you should not bother him any further Mk 5: 35b. Cf. *what* *further need have we of witnesses?* Mt 26: 65; Mk 14: 63; Lk 22: 71.—Ro 6: 2.

c. of time not yet come ἔ. (χρόνον) μικρόν *a little while longer* J 7: 33; 12: 35; 13: 33; 14: 19; Hb 10: 37. ἔ. τετράμηνός ἐστιν καί *there are still four months before* J 4: 35 (PPar. 18 ἔτι δύο ἡμέρας ἔχομεν καί φθάσομεν εἰς Πηλοῦσι).

2. in a sense other than temporal—**a.** of what is left or remaining ἔ. ἕνα εἶχεν υἱόν Mk 12: 6. τί ἔ. ὑστερῶ; *what do I still lack?* Mt 19: 20; cf. Lk 18: 22; J 16: 12; Rv 9: 12.

b. of that which is added to what is already at hand *in addition, more, also, other* ἔ. ἕνα ἢ δύο *one or two others* Mt 18: 16. ἔ. δέ (X., Mem. 1, 2, 1; Diod. S. 1, 74, 1; 13, 81, 3; Strabo 10, 3, 7; Dio Chrys. 36[53], 1; 2 Macc 6: 4) Hb 11: 36. ἔ. δὲ καί *furthermore* (X., An. 3, 2, 28 al.; UPZ 61, 10 [161 BC]; PMich. 174, 7 [146 AD]; 2 Esdr 19 [Neh 9]: 18; Ep. Arist. 151; Jos., Bell. 2, 546, Ant. 7, 70) Ac 2: 26 (Ps 15: 9); 1 Cl 17: 1, 3; Hs 5, 2, 5; B 4: 6 and oft. ἔ. τε καί (Jos., Ant. 14, 194) Lk 14: 26; Ac 21: 28. ἔ. ἄνω, ἔ. κάτω *farther up, farther down* Mt 20: 28 D=Agr 22. ἔ. ἅπαξ *once again* (2 Macc 3: 37) Hb 12: 26f (Hg 2: 6). W. a comp. ἔ. μᾶλλον (Hom.+; POxy. 939, 3; Jos., Ant. 20, 89) Phil 1: 9; περισσότερον ἔ. Hb 7: 15 ἔ. καί ἔ. *again and again* B 21: 4.

c. in logical inference, in interrog. sentences τίς ἔ. χρεία; *what further need would there be?* 7: 11. τί ἔ. μέμφεται; *why, then, does he still find fault?* Ro 9: 19; cf. 3: 7; Gal 5: 11b. M-M.

ἑτοιμάζω fut. ἑτοιμάσω; 1 aor. ἡτοίμασα; pf. ἡτοίμακα; 1 aor. pass. ἡτοιμάσθην; pf. pass. ἡτοίμασμαι (Hom.+; inscr., pap., LXX, En., Ep. Arist.; Jos., Ant. 12, 304, Vi. 223) *put* or *keep in readiness, prepare.*

1. of things that are being put in readiness τὶ *someth.* a way Mt 3: 3; Mk 1: 3; Lk 3: 4 (all three Is 40: 3); 1: 76; Rv 16: 12; a pyre MPol 13: 2; *prepare* a meal (Gen 43: 16; Ep. Arist. 181) Mt 22: 4; Lk 17: 8; cf. 1 Cl 39: 9; τὸ πάσχα (q.v. 3 and 2) Mt 26: 19; Mk 14: 16; Lk 22: 13; cf. GEb 6.—Mk 15: 1; Lk 23: 56; 24: 1. ἃ ἡτοίμασας *what you have prepared* 12: 20. τινί τι *someth. for someone* Hs 1: 6. Of the preparations for receiving and entertaining someone (PTebt. 592 . . . σοῦ ταχὺ ἐρχομένου . . . ἑτοιμάκειν σοι πάντα; POxy. 1299, 9; 1490, 7) ἑτοίμαζέ μοι ξενίαν Phlm 22. ἑ. τινὶ τόπον J 14: 2, 3 (cf. Appian, Bell. Civ. 2, 53 §219 of those who go before, who ἀσφαλῆ τὰ ἐκεῖ προετοιμάσαι= prepare a safe place for those who follow; 1 Ch 15: 1). So also without an object acc. ἑ. τινί *make preparations for someone* Lk 9: 52. In a different sense *prepare (a meal)* Mk 14: 15. Abs. (1 Esdr 1: 4; Jer 26: 14; Job 28: 27) Lk 12: 47; 22: 9, 12. τινί w. inf. foll. Mt 26: 17. W. ἵνα foll. Mk 14: 12. τινί τι w. ἵνα foll. Lk 22: 8.—ἡτοιμασμένος *ready, prepared* εἴς τι *for someth.* (3 Macc 6: 31) of a vessel 2 Ti 2: 21; of horses εἰς πόλεμον Rv 9: 7 (cf. Pr 21: 31 ἵππος ἑτοιμάζεται εἰς ἡμέραν πολέμου, also 1 Macc 13: 22; 12: 27).

2. of pers. (En. 99, 3; Jos., Vi. 203) ἑ. στρατιώτας Ac 23: 23 (AMeuwese, De rer. gest. Divi Augusti vers. graeca '20, 82). Of a bride Rv 21: 2. ἑ. ἑαυτόν *prepare oneself* (Ezk 38: 7; cf. POsl. 88, 13 ἑτοιμάζεσθαι ἑαυτόν) 19: 7; w. ἵνα foll. 8: 6; w. εἰς foll. (Appian, Mithrid. 26 §103). Of angels ἡτοιμασμένοι εἰς τ. ὥραν *held in readiness for that hour* 9: 15. Of Jesus, ὃς εἰς τοῦτο ἡτοιμάσθη, ἵνα B 14: 5. God comes ἐφ' οὓς τ. πνεῦμα ἡτοίμασεν *to those whom the Spirit has prepared* D 4: 10; B 19: 7. Of a people that is made ready (2 Km 7: 24) B 3: 6; 5: 7; 14: 6; κυρίῳ (Sir 49: 12) Lk 1: 17. Here God is referred to several times as the one who brought the preparation about, and the way is prepared for sense

3. God as the One who prepares, w. pers. or thing as obj. (Ex 23: 20; En. 25, 7) Mt 20: 23; 25: 34, 41; Mk 10: 40; Lk 2: 31; 1 Cor 2: 9=1 Cl 34: 8 (quot. of unknown orig.); cf. 2 Cl 14: 5; Hb 11: 16 (πόλιν ἑ. as Hab 2: 12); Rv 12: 6; 1 Cl 35: 3. M-M.**

ἑτοιμασία, ας, ἡ (Hippocr.; BGU 625, 17; PHermopol. 95, 20; LXX) *readiness, preparation* (so Hippocr., Decent. 12 vol. IX 240 L.; Ps 9: 38; Ep. Arist. 182; Jos., Ant. 10, 9 v.l.) τοῦ εὐαγγελίου τῆς εἰρήνης *for the gospel of peace* Eph 6: 15. The mng. *equipment* (here specif. 'boots'), as in Mod. Gk., is favored by AFBuscarlet, ET 9, 1897f, 38f; EHBlakeney, ET 55, '43f, 138; JAFGregg, ET 56, '44, 54; L-S-J. W. ἄσκησις MPol 18: 2. M-M.*

Ἕτοιμας s. Ἐλύμας.

ἕτοιμος, η, ον (also an adj. of two endings in pl. according to Jdth 9: 6; Mt 25: 10; Bl-D. §59, 2; Mlt.-H. 157) *ready* (loanw. in rabb.).

1. of things (Hom.+; inscr., pap., LXX, Philo; Jos., Ant. 7, 339 πάντα), of an altar IRo 2: 2. Of preparations for a meal (cf. Dt 32: 35) Mt 22: 4 (Appian, Bell. Civ. 1, 56 §246 πάντα ἕτοιμα; BGU 625, 13 [III AD] πάντα ἕ.), 8; Lk 14: 17 (of a meal, 'served': Ps.-Clem., Hom. 5, 30.—A call to a meal just before it is to be served, as Esth 6: 14; Philo, Op. M. 78; Lucian, De Merc. Cond. 14). Of a dining room: *put in readiness* Mk 14: 15. Of the collection for the saints 2 Cor 9: 5. τὰ ἕ. *what has been accomplished* (by someone else) 10: 16. καιρὸς ἕτοιμος *the time is ready= is here* J 7: 6. W. inf. of purpose (Esth 1: 1e) σωτηρία ἑ. ἀποκαλυφθῆναι *ready to be revealed* 1 Pt 1: 5.

2. of pers. (Pind.+; PHib. 44, 7 [253 BC]; LXX; Philo; Joseph.) *ready, prepared* Mt 25: 10. ἕ. εἰμι *I am ready* (Thu. et al.; PTebt. 419, 10; LXX) Ac 23: 21; Hs 9, 2, 4; w. inf. foll. (Diod. S. 13, 98, 1 ἕτοιμός εἰμι τελευτᾶν; 1 Macc 7: 29; 2 Macc 7: 2; 4 Macc 9: 1; Jos., Ant. 10, 9) Lk 22: 33; w. τοῦ and inf. foll. (Mi 6: 8; 1 Macc 13: 37) Ac 23: 15; Hs 8, 4, 2. ἕ. γίνεσθαι *be ready, prepare oneself* (Diod. S. 4, 49, 5 ἑτοίμους γενομένους; Ps.-Callisth. 2, 11, 1; 6; Ex 19: 15; Num 16: 16) Mt 24: 44; Lk 12: 40; D 16: 1; w. ἵνα foll. Hs 1: 6. ἕ. πρός τι (X., Mem. 4, 5, 12; Aelian, V.H. 14, 49; BGU 1209, 17 [23 BC]; Tob 5: 17 BA) Tit 3: 1; 1 Pt 3: 15. ἕ. εἴς τι (Hdt. 8, 96 al.; 1 Macc 4: 44; 12: 50 al.; Jos., Ant. 15, 357) 1 Cl 2: 7; ISm 11: 3; IPol 7: 3.—ἐν ἑτοίμῳ *in readiness* (Epicurus in Diog. L. 10, 127; Theocr. 22, 61, Epigr. 16, 5; Dionys. Hal. 8, 17; 9, 35; PGenève 76, 8; PGM 13, 375; 3 Macc 6: 31) ἐν ἑτοίμῳ ἔχειν *be ready* (Polyb. 2, 34, 2; Philo, Leg. ad Gai. 259) w. inf. foll. 2 Cor 10: 6.—Comp. ἑτοιμότερος (Agatharchides [II BC]; 86 fgm. 6 Jac.; PFlor. 123, 4) *more ready, more willing* 2 Cl 15: 4. M-M.*

ἑτοίμως adv. (Aeschyl.+; inscr., pap., LXX; Philo, Spec. Leg. 1, 49) *readily* ἑ. ἔχειν *be ready, be willing* w. inf. foll. (Aeneas Tact. 582; Diod. S. 16, 28, 2; PAmh. 32, 6 [II BC]; BGU 80, 17; POxy. 1469, 21; Da 3: 15 LXX; Jos., Ant. 12, 163) 2 Cor 12: 14; 13: 1 v.l.; 1 Pt 4: 5. ἀποθανεῖν Ac 21: 13 (cf. Jos., Ant. 13, 6 ἀποθνῄσκειν). M-M.*

ἔτος, ους, τό (Hom.+; inscr., pap., LXX, En., Philo, Joseph., Test. 12 Patr.) *year* Ac 7: 30; 13: 21; Hb 1: 12 (Ps 101: 28); 3: 10, 17 (Ps 94: 10); 2 Pt 3: 8 (Ps 89: 4); Rv 20: 3-7; 1 Cl 25: 5 al.—ἔτη ἔχειν *be—years old* (Jos., Ant. 1, 198) J 8: 57; differently w. the addition ἐν τ. ἀσθενείᾳ αὐτοῦ *be ill for—years* 5: 5. εἶναι, γίνεσθαι ἐτῶν w. a numeral to indicate age (X., Mem. 1, 2, 40 al.; Gen 7: 6; 12: 4 and oft.; Jos., Ant. 10, 50) Mk 5: 42; Lk 2: 42; Ac 4: 22; 1 Ti 5: 9 (Kyr.-Inschr. l. 16 μηδένα νεώτερον πέντε κ. εἴκοσι ἐτῶν); ὡς or ὡσεὶ ἐτῶν w. numeral *about—*

years old (X., An. 2, 6, 20 ἦν ἐτῶν ὡς τριάκοντα; PTebt. 381, 4f [123 вс]; cf. Dssm. on PMMeyer, Griech. Texte aus Ägypt. '16, p. 26, 48) Lk 3: 23; 8: 42.—Acc. to denote duration of time in answer to the quest.: how long? (X., Cyr. 1, 2, 9; Dit., Syll.³ 1168, 3; 8; 14; 95; ² 847, 4; 850, 6 and oft.; 2 Km 21: 1; EpJer 2; Jdth 8: 4; 1 Macc 1: 7, 9 and oft.) δώδεκα ἔτη *for twelve years* Mt 9: 20; cf. Mk 5: 25; Lk 2: 36; 13: 7f, 11, 16; 15: 29; Ac 7: 6 (Gen 15: 13), 36, 42 (Am 5: 25); B 10: 6; MPol 9: 3 al. The dat. is also used in almost the same sense (Appian, Illyr. 25 §71 ἔτεσι δέκα= for ten years; Polyaenus 1, 12; Lucian, Dial. Merc. 8, 2 al.; Dit., Syll.³ 872, 17; 898, 28; 966, 17; inscr. concerning a Lycaon. bishop [Exp. 7th Ser. VI '08, p. 387, 12] εἴκοσι πέντε ὅλοις ἔτεσιν τ. ἐπισκοπὴν διοικήσας; Bl-D. §201 w. app.; Rob. 523) of the temple τεσσεράκοντα καὶ ἓξ ἔτεσιν οἰκοδομήθη *it was under construction for forty-six years* J 2: 20; cf. Ac 13: 20. Likew. ἐπί w. acc. (Dit., Syll.³ 1219, 27 ἐπὶ δέκα ἔτη; Wilcken, Chrest. 327, 16 [107 вс]; Jos., Ant. 5, 211) Lk 4: 25; Ac 19: 10. Other prep. combinations: ἀπό (Dit., Syll.³ 762, 14; 820, 8) ἐτῶν δώδεκα *for twelve years* Lk 8: 43; ἀπὸ ἱκανῶν ἐ. Ro 15: 23. Also ἐκ πολλῶν ἐ. Ac 24: 10; cf. 9: 33. δι' ἐ. πλειόνων *after several years* 24: 17; cf. Gal 2: 1. εἰς ἔ. πολλά *for many years to come* Lk 12: 19 (cf. Dit., Syll.³ 707, 19f; 708, 43). ἐν ἔτει πεντεκαιδεκάτῳ 3: 1 (cf. Dit., Syll.³ 736, 11; 52; 54; 90; 3 Km 6: 1; 15: 1 al.). ἕως ἐτῶν . . . *until—years of age* (cf. Jo 2: 2; Jos., Ant. 5, 181) 2: 37. κατ' ἔτος *every year* (Dialekt-Inschr. 4195, 30f [Rhodes]; PAmh. 86, 11 [78 ad]; POxy. 725, 36; 2 Macc 11: 3; Jos., Ant. 7, 99) 2: 41; μετὰ τρία ἔ. *after three years* Gal 1: 18; 3: 17 (cf. Dit., Syll.³ 708, 26; Tob 14: 2 BA; Is 23: 15; Da 4: 33a; 1 Macc 1: 29). πρὸ ἐτῶν δεκατεσσάρων *fourteen years ago* 2 Cor 12: 2. M-M. B. 1011f.**

εὖ adv. (Hom.+; inscr., pap., LXX, Ep. Arist., Philo, Joseph.) *well* εὖ ποιεῖν *do good, show kindness* (X., Cyr. 1, 6, 30; Demosth. 20, 37; POxy. 1292, 3 [c. 30 ad]; LXX; Jos., Ant. 14, 378) τινί (Ex 1: 20; Sir 12: 2, 5. Usu. the acc. follows) Mk 14: 7. εὖ δουλεύειν 1 Cl 16: 12 (Is 53: 11). εὖ πράσσειν means as a rule *get along well, be prosperous* (Pind.; X., Mem. 1, 6, 8; 2, 4, 6; 4, 2, 26, Oec. 11, 8; Pla., Prot. 333d; Ps.-Pla., Alc. 1 p. 116b; Philo, Virt. 170, Decal. 43; Jos., Ant. 12, 156 al. As epistolary formula in Diog. L. 3, 61, also POxy. 115, 12; 120, 27; 527, 9; 822; PGenève 59, 24; 2 Macc 9: 19). This mng. is poss. in Ac 15: 29. However, the mng. *do well*, i.e. *act correctly* or *rightly* gives a better sense; it is supported by the Vulgate, Armenian and Coptic transl. (so Simonides, fgm. 4, 10 D.³; X., Mem. 3, 9, 14; Ps.-Pla., Eryx. 4 p. 393e; Epict. 4, 6, 20; Artem. 2, 3 p. 86, 13; M. Ant. 3, 13; Philo, Mut. Nom. 197; Jos., Ant. 4, 286; Justin, Apol. 1, 28, 3). Furthermore, it is the only mng. poss. in IEph 4: 2; ISm 11: 3. ἵνα εὖ σοι γένηται *that you may prosper* Eph 6: 3 (cf. Gen 12: 13; Ex 20: 12; Dt 4: 40; 5: 16; the last pass. is quoted in Eph). εὖ ἔχειν πρός τινα *be well-disposed* or *gracious to someone* Hs 9, 10, 7. Abs. *well done! excellent!* (Ps.-X., Cyneg. 6, 20 Rühl v.l.) Mt 25: 21, 23; Lk 19: 17 v.l. (for εὖγε). M-M.*

Εὖα (Εὖα.—Schmiedel prefers Ἕνα, ας, ἡ (חַוָּה) *Eve* (Gen 4: 1; Tob 8: 6; Philo, Leg. All. 2, 81; Jos., Ant. 1, 49; Sib. Or. 1, 29) 1 Ti 2: 13. Deception of Eve by the serpent 2 Cor 11: 3; B 12: 5; Dg 12: 8.—WStaerk, Eva-Maria: ZNW 33, '34, 97–104.*

εὐαγγελίζω 1 aor. εὐηγγέλισα. The act., found in our lit. only Rv 10: 7; 14: 6; Ac 16: 17 D*, belongs to later Gk. (Polyaenus 5, 7; Cass. Dio 61, 13, 4; PGiess. 27, 6 [II ad]; PAmh. 2, 16; 1 Km 31: 9; 2 Km 18: 19f; cf. Phryn. 268

L.), and does not differ in mng. (cf. Bl-D. §309, 1) from the much more common (fr. class. times) mid. εὐαγγελίζομαι (Aristoph., Demosth.+; Philo, Joseph.; predom. in LXX) impf. εὐηγγελιζόμην; 1 aor. εὐηγγελισάμην (on the augment cf. Bl-D. §69, 4; Rob. 367). The foll. tenses are used in a passive sense: pres.; pf. εὐηγγέλισμαι; 1 aor. εὐηγγελίσθην. *Bring* or *announce good news.*

1. gener. τί τινι (Jos., Bell. 3, 503, Ant. 7, 250) Lk 1: 19 (ταῦτα εὐ. of the announcement by an angel of the impending birth of a much-desired child Jos., Ant. 5, 282; cf. 277 εὐ. αὐτῇ παιδὸς γονήν); 2: 10; 1 Th 3: 6. τὶ ἐπί τινα Rv 14: 6. τινά *to someone* (for the usage s. 2 below) 10: 7.

2. mostly specif. of the divine message of salvation, the Messianic proclamation, the gospel (cf. Is 60: 6; Ps 67: 12; PsSol 11, 1 al. S. also PGM 5, 142 εὐάγγελος τ. θεοῦ=a glad messenger of God) *proclaim, preach.*

a. mid.—α. w. mention of the thing proclaimed, as well as of the pers. who receives the message τί τινι Lk 4: 43; Ac 8: 35 (τὸν Ἰησοῦν); Gal 1: 8b; Eph 2: 17; 3: 8; B 8: 3; 14: 9. τὸ εὐαγγέλιον εὐ. τινι 1 Cor 15: 1; 2 Cor 11: 7. τί τινα *someth. to someone* (on the constr. s. below) Ac 13: 32. εὐ. τὸν υἱὸν τ. θεοῦ ἐν τ. ἔθνεσιν *proclaim the Son of God among the heathen* Gal 1: 16.

β. w. mention of the object of the proclamation τί (Lucian, Tyrannic. 9 τὴν ἐλευθερίαν; Synes., Prov. 1, 7 p. 96a [the heavenly σημεῖα] τὴν βασιλείαν Αἰγυπτίοις εὐηγγελίζετο [mid.]=brought the Egyptians news of the fortunate reign; Ps 39: 10; 95: 2) Lk 8: 1; Ac 8: 4; 10: 36; 15: 35; 17: 18; Ro 10: 15 (Is 52: 7); Gal 1: 23. Also w. pers. obj. in acc. to denote the object of the proclamation τινά someone τ. Χριστὸν Ἰ. Ac 5: 42; τ. κύριον Ἰ. 11: 20; cf. 17: 18. εὐ. περὶ τῆς βασιλείας 8: 12 (Jos., Ant. 15, 209 περὶ τούτων εὐηγγελίζετο). W. acc. and inf. foll. (Plut., Mar. 22, 4; Jos., Ant. 6, 56) Ac 14: 15; 1 Cl 42: 3.

γ. w. mention of the one who receives the message τινί (Aristoph., Eq. 643 al.; Jer 20: 15; Philo, De Jos. 250; Jos., Ant. 5, 24) Lk 4: 18 (Is 61: 1); Ro 1: 15; 1 Cor 15: 2; Gal 1: 8a; 4: 13; 1 Pt 1: 12ᴾ⁷². εἰς τ. ὑπερέκεινα ὑμῶν εὐ. *preach the gospel in lands beyond you* 2 Cor 10: 16 (cf. 1 Pt 1: 25). τινά (Alciphr. 2, 9, 2 v.l.; Heliod. 2, 10, 1 ed. IBekker [acc. to mss.]; Jos., Ant. 18, 228; Euseb., H.E. 3, 4) Lk 1: 28 v.l.; 3: 18; Ac 8: 25, 40; 14: 21; 16: 10; Gal 1: 9; 1 Pt 1: 12; Pol 6: 3; PK 3 p. 15, 19.

δ. abs. *preach* Lk 9: 6; 20: 1; Ac 14: 7; Ro 15: 20; 1 Cor 1: 17; 9: 16, 18.

b. pass.—α. w. a thing as subj. *be preached* Lk 16: 16; Gal 1: 11 (τὸ εὐαγγέλιον); 1 Pt 1: 25. Impers. νεκροῖς εὐηγγελίσθη 1 Pt 4: 6.

β. w. pers. subj. *have good news (the gospel) preached to one* (2 Km 18: 31; Jo 3: 5) Mt 11: 5; Lk 7: 22; Hb 4: 2, 6. ἀπό τινος *by someone* 1 Cl 42: 1. M-M. B. 1478.*

εὐαγγέλιον, ου, τό (Hom.+; LXX, Joseph.) orig. *a reward for good news*, then simply *good news* (so Plut., Sertor. 11, 8; 26, 6, Phoc. 16, 8; 23, 6 al.; Appian, Bell. Civ. 3, 93 §384; 4, 20 §78; Ps.-Lucian, Asin. 26; Jos., Bell. 2, 420; 4, 618; 656; IG III 10=² 1081 [OWeinreich, ARW 18, '15, p. 43, 3]; papyrus letter [after 238 ad] in Dssm., LO 313f [LAE 371]=Sb 421.—Also in religious use: Diod. S. 15, 74, 2 Διονύσιος τοῖς θεοῖς εὐαγγέλια θύσας= offered a sacrifice for good news to the gods; Dit., Or. 458 =Inschr. v. Priene 105, 40f ἦρξεν δὲ τῷ κόσμῳ τῶν δι' αὐτὸν εὐαγγελίων ἡ γενέθλιος τοῦ θεοῦ [cf. AHarnack, Red. u. Aufs. I² '06, 310ff; PWendland, ZNW 5, '04, 335ff, D. urchristl. Literaturformen '12, 409f]; Philostrat., Vi. Apollon. 1, 28 of the appearing of Apollon.; Ael. Aristid. 53, 3 K.=55 p. 708 D.: Ζεὺς Εὐαγγέλιος) in our lit. only in the specif. sense God's *good news* to men, the *gospel.*

1. abs.—a. τὸ εὐαγγέλιον Mk 1: 15; 8: 35; 10: 29; Ro 1: 16; 10: 16; 11: 28; 1 Cor 4: 15; 9: 18, 23; 2 Cor 8: 18; Gal 2: 2; Eph 3: 6; Phil 1: 5; 2: 22; 4: 3; 1 Th 2: 4; 2 Ti 1: 8, 10; IPhld 5: 1, 2; 8: 2; 9: 2; ISm 5: 1; 7: 2; MPol 1: 1; 22: 1.

b. in gen., dependent on another noun ὁ λόγος τοῦ εὐ. Ac 15: 7; τὸ μυστήριον τ. εὐ. Eph 6: 19; cf. vs. 15; Phil 1: 7, 12, 16; ἡ ἀλήθεια τοῦ εὐ. Gal 2: 5, 14; Col 1: 5 (but the last passage can also be transl. *the true message of the gospel*). ἡ ἐλπὶς τοῦ εὐ. *the hope that is kindled by the gospel* vs. 23; ἡ πίστις τοῦ εὐ. *faith in the gospel* Phil 1: 27; ἐν τ. δεσμοῖς τοῦ εὐ. Phlm 13; ἡ ἐξουσία τοῦ εὐ. *authority over* (i.e. *to preach*) *the gospel* B 8: 3; ἀρχὴ τοῦ εὐ. *beginning* (of the preaching) *of the gospel* Phil 4: 15; cf. 1 Cl 47: 2 (s. on this WHartke, D. Sammlung u. d. ältesten Ausgaben der Paulusbriefe '17, 55); Mk 1: 1 (s. 3 below).

c. in certain combinations w. verbs τὸ εὐ. κηρύσσειν Mt 26: 13; Mk 13: 10; 14: 9 (JoachJeremias, ZNW 44, '53, 103-7: apocalyptic proclamation); 16: 15 (cf. Mt 4: 23; 9: 35; 24: 14; Mk 1: 14; Ac 1: 2 D; B 5: 9). καταγγέλλειν 1 Cor 9: 14. γνωρίζειν 15: 1. εὐαγγελίζεσθαι Gal 1: 11 (cf. 2 Cor 11: 7).

2. in combination—a. w. adj. εὐ. αἰώνιον Rv 14: 6. ἕτερον 2 Cor 11: 4; Gal 1: 6 (EGrässer, ZThK 66, '69, 306-44).

b. w. gen. (cf. OSchmitz, D. Christusgemeinschaft des Pls im Lichte seines Genetivgebrauchs '24, 45-88).

α. objective genitive εὐ. τῆς βασιλείας Mt 4: 23; 9: 35; 24: 14. τ. θεοῦ Mk 1: 14. τ. χάριτος τ. θεοῦ *of God's grace* Ac 20: 24. τ. εἰρήνης Eph 6: 15. τ. σωτηρίας 1: 13. τ. δόξης τ. Χριστοῦ *of the glory of Christ* 2 Cor 4: 4; cf. 1 Ti 1: 11. εὐ. τ. Χριστοῦ is usu. interpr. as the *gospel* (*good news*) *about Christ* (because of Ro 1: 1-3; 2 Cor 4: 4; 1 Th 3: 2, cf. Ro 15: 16) Ro 15: 19; 1 Cor 9: 12; 2 Cor 2: 12 (here and Ro 1: 1 εἰς εὐαγγέλιον=for the purpose of bringing the good news, as Appian, Bell. Civ. 4, 113 §474); 9: 13; 10: 14; Gal 1: 7; Phil 1: 27; 1 Th 3: 2; cf. Ro 1: 9; 2 Th 1: 8; B 5: 9; MPol 19: 1. εὐ. τῆς ἀκροβυστίας *the gospel for the uncircumcised* Gal 2: 7.

β. subjective genitive (τοῦ) θεοῦ Ro 1: 1; 15: 16; 2 Cor 11: 7; 1 Th 2: 2, 8, 9; 1 Pt 4: 17. The man who is commissioned to do the preaching can be mentioned in the subj. gen. εὐ. μου, ἡμῶν Ro 2: 16; 16: 25; 2 Cor 4: 3; 1 Th 1: 5; 2 Th 2: 14; 2 Ti 2: 8. S. LBaudiment, 'L'Évangile' de St. Paul '25; Molland (below) 83-97.

3. The transition to the later Christian usage, in which εὐ. means a book dealing with the life and teaching of Jesus (Justin, Apol. 1, 66), is felt in D 8: 2; 11: 3; 15: 3f; MPol 4: 1; 2 Cl 8: 5, perh. also Mk 1: 1 (LEKeck, The Introduction to Mark's Gospel, NTS 12, '66, 352-70); IPhld 8: 2; ISm 7: 2.

4. The later mng. (sense 3) is certain for Dg 11: 6 (supplement).—ASeeberg, D. Evangelium Christi '05; Harnack, Entstehg. u. Entwicklg. d. Kirchenverfassung '10, 199-239; PZondervan, Het woord 'Evangelium': ThT 48, '14, 187-213; MBurrows, The Origin of the Word 'Gospel': JBL 44, '25, 21-33; JSchniewind, Euangelion 1; 2; '27, '31, Die Begriffe Wort u. Evglm. b. Pls, Diss. Halle '10; AFridrichsen, Τὸ εὐαγγέλιον hos Pls: Norsk Teol. Tidsskr. 13, '12, 153-70; 209-56, Der Begriff Evgl. b. Irenäus, Hippolyt, Novatian: ibid. '17, 148-70; AOepke, D. Missionspredigt des Ap. Pls. '20, 50ff; EDBurton, ICC Gal '21, 422f; EMolland, D. Paulin. Euangelion; D. Wort u. d. Sache '34; RAsting, D. Verkündigung im Urchristentum '39 (on Word of God, Gospel, Witness); GFriedrich, TW II 705-35; KHRengstorf, ZNW 31, '32, 54-6; MAlbertz, D. Botschaft des NT, vols. I and II, '47-'57; JAEvDodewaard, Biblica 35, '54, 160-73; HKoester, TU 65, '57, 6-12; JWBowman, 'Gospel' and its Cognates in Palestinian Syriac, NTEssays (TWManson memorial) ed. Higgins '59, 54-67. M-M. *

εὐαγγελιστής, οῦ, ὁ (acc. to ADieterich ZNW 1, '00, 336-8, title of pagan priests: IG XII 1, 675.—Dialekt-Inschr. 5702, 22; 37 [Ionic] εὐαγγελίς is the official title of the priestess of Hera) *preacher of the gospel, evangelist* Eph 4: 11 (DYHadidian, CBQ 28, '66, 317-21: gospel writer). Acc. to Ac 21: 8 a designation of Philip, one of the seven. 2 Ti 4: 5 Timothy is so called.—Harnack, Mission u. Ausbreitung⁴ '24, 334, 6 al. (s. 983 index). M-M. *

εὐανθής, ές, gen. οῦς (Hom.+; Plut., Lucian, Aelian et al.; Suppl. Epigr. Gr. VIII 548, 8 [I BC]; Philo, Somn. 1, 205) *beautifully blooming* φυτά *beautifully blooming plants* AP 5: 15. *

εὐαρεστέω 1 aor. εὐηρέστησα; pf. εὐηρέστηκα; on the augment s. Bl-D. §69, 4 app.

1. *please, be pleasing* τινί *to someone* (Diod. S. 14, 4, 2; Epict. 1, 12, 8; 2, 23, 42; Dit., Syll.³ 611, 19; LXX) τῷ θεῷ (Gen 6: 9; Philo, Abr. 35, Exsecr. 167; cf. Test. Gad 7: 6) 1 Cl 41: 1; Hv 3, 1, 9. Of Enoch, who pleased God (Gen 5: 22, 24; Sir 44: 16) Hb 11: 5, and in the same context vs. 6, where the verb stands abs.; τῷ παντοκράτορι θεῷ ὁσίως εὐ. 1 Cl 62: 2. Of Jesus εὐηρέστησεν τῷ πέμψαντι αὐτόν IMg 8: 2; *please the Lord* (Christ) Pol 5: 2.

2. *be pleased, take delight—a.* act. (Lysippus Com. [V BC] 7 ed. Kock I 702) τινί *with* or *in someth.* (Dionys. Hal. 11, 60, 1; Ep. Arist. 286; cf. Ps 25: 3) τῷ νόμῳ *with the law* Hs 8, 3, 5 (but here mng. 1 cannot be finally ruled out).

b. the pass. is mostly used in this sense εὐαρεστοῦμαι τινι *be satisfied w. someth.* (Diod. S. 3, 55, 9; 20, 79, 2; Diog. L. 10, 137). τοιαύταις θυσίαις *with such sacrifices* Hb 13: 16. M-M. *

εὐαρέστησις, εως, ἡ (Diod. S. 26, 1, 1; Dionys. Hal.; Epict. 1, 12 tit.; Aq., Sym., Theod. Ex 29: 18; Sym. Ezk 20: 41; Theod. Lev 1: 9; Philo, Deus Imm. 116; Jos., Ant. 12, 269; Test. Iss. 4: 1) *being pleased* εἰς εὐ. τῷ ὀνόματι αὐτοῦ *that they may be well-pleasing to his name* (i.e., to him) 1 Cl 64. *

εὐάρεστος, ον *pleasing, acceptable* (said of pers. and things: Diod. S. 15, 46, 5; Inschr. v. Priene 114, 15 [after 84 BC]; Inscr. of Nisyros: Mitteil. des Deutsch. Arch. Inst. Ath. Abt. 15, 1890, p. 134, 11f; PFay. 90, 17; PFlor. 30, 30; PStrassb. 1, 9; Wsd; Philo, De Jos. 195) τινί *to someone.*

1. in our lit. almost without exception of God, to whom someth. is acceptable τῷ θεῷ (Wsd 4: 10; Philo, Spec. Leg. 1, 201, Virt. 67; Test. Dan 1: 3) Ro 12: 1; 14: 18; 2 Cor 5: 9; Phil 4: 18; 1 Cl 49: 5; ISm 8: 2; Hs 5, 3, 2. τῷ κυρίῳ Eph 5: 10. τ. κυρίῳ τοῦ θεοῦ Hb 13: 21; cf. 1 Cl 21: 1; 60: 2; 61: 2. ἐν κυρίῳ Col 3: 20. εὐ. δοῦλος τ. θεοῦ Hm 12, 3, 1. Of the content of the divine will τὰ εὐάρεστα (καὶ εὐπρόσδεκτα) αὐτῷ 1 Cl 35: 5. Abs. τὸ εὐάρεστον (w. ἀγαθόν, τέλειον) *what is acceptable* to God Ro 12: 2.

2. of slaves εὐ. εἶναι *give satisfaction* to their masters Tit 2: 9. In a parable *well thought of* Hs 5, 2, 2. M-M. *

Εὐάρεστος, ου, ὁ (in inscr. of Smyrna CIG 3148; 3152; 3162 and also found elsewh., e.g. Ael. Aristid. 50, 23 K.=26 p. 508 D.; Sb 3988; Jos., Ant. 19, 145) *Evarestus,* a Christian of Smyrna, writer of the church's letter about the martyrdom of Polycarp MPol 20: 2. *

εὐαρέστως adv. (X., Mem. 3, 5, 5; Epict. 1, 12, 21; fgm.

34 Sch.; CIG 2885, 20; Dit., Syll.³ 587, 10; 708, 20 [II BC]) *in an acceptable manner* εὐ. λατρεύειν τῷ θεῷ Hb 12: 28. M-M.*

Εὔβουλος, ου, ὁ (Diod. S. 16, 66, 1; freq. in inscr. [cf. Dit., Syll.² index I] and pap. [cf. Preisigke, Namenb.]) *Eubulus*, a Christian 2 Ti 4: 21 (Third Corinthians 1, 1).*

εὖγε adv. (Aristoph., Pla.; Arrian, Cyneg. 18, 1; Lucian, LXX) *well done! excellent!* Lk 19: 17.*

εὐγενής, ές, gen. οὖς (trag.+; inscr., pap., LXX, Philo, Joseph., Test. 12 Patr., loanw. in rabb.) comp. εὐγενέστερος (Wilcken, Chrest. 131, 33f [IV AD]).
   1. *well-born, high-born* (X., Hell. 4, 1, 7; Philo, De Jos. 106; Jos., Ant. 10, 186) 1 Cor 1: 26. ἄνθρωπός τις εὐ. *a certain nobleman* Lk 19: 12.
   2. *noble-minded, high-minded* οὗτοι ἦσαν εὐγενέστεροι τῶν ἐν Θεσσαλονίκῃ *these were more high-minded than those in Th.* Ac 17: 11 (cf. Cicero, Ad Att. 13, 21, 7; Jos., Ant. 12, 255).—EbNestle, ZNW 15, '14, 91f; FW Danker, Menand. and the NT, NTS 10, '64, 366f. M-M.*

εὐγλωττία, ας, ἡ (Eur.+; Maximus Tyr. 25, 2d) *glibness, fluency of speech* Ro 16: 18 v.l.*

εὐδαιμονέω *be happy, fortunate* (trag., Hdt.+; Epict.; POxy. 1593, 2; Philo; Jos., C. Ap. 1, 224) Dg 10: 5.*

εὐδία, ας, ἡ—1. *fair weather* (X., Pla. et al.; Plut., Mor. p. 8c; POxy. 1223, 12; Sir 3: 15; Philo, Gig. 51) Mt 16: 2.
   2. oft. in figurative speech, to represent peace and rest (opp. χειμών: Pind., al.; X., An. 5, 8, 20; Epict. 2, 18, 30), then in the mng. *tranquillity, peace* (Herodas 1, 28; Dit., Or. 90, 11 [196 BC] τ. Αἴγυπτον εἰς εὐδίαν ἀγαγεῖν; Philo, Spec. Leg. 1, 69; Jos., Ant. 14, 157) ISm 11: 3. M-M.*

εὐδοκέω impf. ηὐδόκουν (1 Th 2: 8, where v.l. has εὐδοκοῦμεν; s. Bl-D. §67, 1 w. app.; Rob. 1215); 1 aor. εὐδόκησα and ηὐδόκησα (Polyb., Diod. S., Dionys. Hal.; inscr., pap., LXX; cf. Anz 358) *be well pleased.*
   1. *consider good, consent, determine, resolve* w. inf. foll. (Polyb. 1, 78, 8; PGrenf. I 1, 17 [II BC] εὐδοκῶ ζήλῳ δουλεύειν; PTebt. 591; Esth 4: 17d; 1 Macc 6: 23; 14: 46f. Of God Ps 67: 17) Lk 12: 32; 1 Cor 1: 21; Gal 1: 15; 1 Th 2: 8; 3: 1. ἐν αὐτῷ εὐδόκησεν πᾶν τὸ πλήρωμα κατοικῆσαι *all the fullness willed to dwell in him* Col 1: 19. εὐ. μᾶλλον w. inf. *wish rather, prefer* (cf. Polyb. 18, 35, 4; Sir 25: 16) 2 Cor 5: 8. W. acc. and inf. (Polyb. 1, 8, 4; 2 Macc 14: 35) Ro 15: 26. Abs. (Dit., Syll.³ 683, 59; ²853, 2; PRyl. 120, 24; 155, 17; 1 Macc 11: 29) vs. 27.
   2. *be well pleased, take delight*—a. w. pers. obj. ἔν τινι *with* or *in someone* (of God's delight in someone 2 Km 22: 20; Is 62: 4 v.l.; Mal 2: 17; Ps 43: 4) Mt 3: 17; 17: 5; Mk 1: 11 (on the aor. s. BWBacon, JBL 20, '01, 28–30); Lk 3: 22; 1 Cor 10: 5; Hb 10: 38 (Hab 2: 4); GEb 3. Also ἐπί τινα (Is 54: 17 v.l.) ibid. εἴς τινα 2 Pt 1: 17. τινά (Dit., Syll.³ 672, 27 [162/0 BC]; Gen 33: 10) Mt 12: 18. Abs. Ro 9: 16 v.l.
   b. w. a thing as obj., also *delight in, like, approve* τὶ (Eccl 9: 7; Sir 15: 17) Hb 10: 6, 8; 1 Cl 18: 16 (on all three pass. cf. Ps 50: 18). τινί (Polyb. 2, 38, 7; Diod. S. 14, 110, 4; PLond. 1168, 15 [18 AD]; POxy. 261, 17 [55 AD]; 1 Esdr 4: 39; 1 Macc 1: 43) 2 Th 2: 12. ἔν τινι (Polyb. 2, 12, 3; Sb 4512, 57 [II BC] συγχώρησιν, ἐν ᾗ οὐκ εὐδοκεῖ ὁ πατήρ; Hg 1: 8; Sir 34: 19) 2 Cor 12: 10; 2 Th 2: 12 v.l.—abs. Ro 9: 16 L. M-M.*

εὐδόκησις, εως, ἡ (Polyb. 16, 20, 4; Diod. S. 15, 6, 4; Dionys. Hal. 3, 13; Dit., Syll.³ 685, 108 [139 BC], Or. 335,

122 [II BC]; PLond. 289, 35 [91 AD]; POxy. 1200, 35) *approval, satisfaction, good pleasure* γίνεσθαι ἐν εὐ. 1 Cl 40: 3.*

εὐδοκία, ας, ἡ (Hippocr.: CMG I 1 p. 32, 7 εὐδοκίη; Philod., π. εὐσεβ. 25, 5 [TGomperz, Herculan. Studien II 1866 p. 145]; FJacobs, Anth. Gr. II 1814 p. 815 no. 179; IG XIV 102*. Elsewh. only in Jewish—LXX; PsSol 3: 4; 8: 33; En.; Philo, Somn. 2, 40 v.l.—and Christian wr.; Hesychius; Suidas).
   1. *good will* of men δι' εὐδοκίαν *from good will* Phil 1: 15; ὑπὲρ τῆς εὐ. *above and beyond good will* or *in his* (God's) *good will* 2: 13. εὐ. ἀγαθωσύνης *good will of uprightness* (subj. gen. like the foll. ἔργον πίστεως) or *desire for goodness* (obj. gen.), as 3 below, 2 Th 1: 11. Lk 2: 14 ἐν ἀνθρώποις εὐδοκίας has frequently been interpreted *among men characterized by good will* (on the text cf. AMerx, D. vier kanon. Ev. II 2, '05, 198–202; on the content GAicher, BZ 9, '07, 381–91; 402f; Harnack, SAB '15, 854–75 [= Studien I '31, 153–79], cf. JHRopes, HTR 10, '17, 52–6; JoachJeremias, ZNW 28, '29, 13–20; Gv Rad, ibid. 29, '30, 111–15; EBöklen, Deutsches Pfarrerblatt 36, '32, 309f; JWobbe, BZ 22, '34, 118–52; 224–45; 23, '36, 358–64; ERSmothers, Rech de Sc rel 24, '34, 86–93; FHerklotz, ZkTh 58, '34, 113f; Gdspd., Probs. 75f; C-HHunzinger, ZNW 44, '52f, 85–90; JAFitzmyer, Theological Studies [Baltimore] 19, '58, 225–27 [Qumran parallels]). But evidence from Qumran (see Hunzinger above) and recent literary analysis of Lk points to mng. 2 below, whether εὐδοκία or εὐδοκίας is the rdg. preferred.
   2. *favor, good pleasure*; this would refer to the persons upon whom divine favor rests (so oft. LXX; En. 1, 8), and the mng. (w. the rdg. εὐδοκίας) would be *among men with whom he is pleased* or *whom he favors* (Bl-D. §165 app.). On οὕτως εὐ. ἐγένετο ἔμπροσθέν σου Mt 11: 26; Lk 10: 21 cf. ἔμπροσθεν 2d; κατὰ τὴν εὐ. τ. θελήματος αὐτοῦ Eph 1: 5; cf. vs. 9.—The mng. 'favor' is close to
   3. *wish, desire*, inasmuch as a desire is usually directed toward someth. that causes satisfaction or favor (cf. Ps 144: 16 ἐμπιπλᾷς πᾶν ζῷον εὐδοκίας = thou givest freely to every living thing whatever it desireth; Sir 39: 18; also 1: 27; 35: 3) εὐ. τῆς ἐμῆς καρδίας *the desire of my heart* Ro 10: 1. Cf. 2 Th 1: 11, and s. 1 above.—On the whole word s. GSchrenk, TW II 736–48. M-M.*

εὐειδής, ές, gen. οὖς (Hom.+; LXX; En. 24, 2) comp. εὐειδέστερος, superl. εὐειδέστατος *well-formed, beautiful* of women (Hom.+) εὐειδέστατος τῷ χαρακτῆρι *very beautiful in outward appearance* Hs 9, 9, 5. Of a young man (Cornutus 32 p. 66, 16; Da 1: 4) *handsome* Hv 2, 4, 1. Of fruits *more beautiful* s 9, 28, 3.*

εὐείκτως (Etymol. Magn.) adv. of εὐείκτος (Cass. Dio 69, 20) *tractably* 1 Cl 37: 2.*

εὐεργεσία, ας, ἡ (Hom.+; inscr., pap., LXX, Ep. Arist., Philo, Joseph.).
   1. *the doing of good* (Diod. S. 20, 25, 2) or *service* (Herm. Wr. 1, 30; Wsd 16: 11; Ep. Arist. 205) τῆς εὐ. ἀντιλαμβάνεσθαι *devote oneself to* or *benefit by service* (s. ἀντιλ. 2 and 3) 1 Ti 6: 2.
   2. *good deed, benefit, a kindness* (Jos., Ant. 6, 211; 11, 213) w. the obj. gen. of the one who benefits by it (Pla., Leg. 850B εὐ. πόλεως) εὐ. ἀνθρώπου ἀσθενοῦς *a good deed to a sick man* Ac 4: 9. Pl. *good deeds* (Appian, Bell. Civ. 5, 60 §255; Chio 16, 7; inscr., pap.; 2 Macc 9: 26; Jos., Ant. 16, 146) of God (Diod. S. 2, 25, 8 ἡ τῶν θεῶν εὐ.; 3, 56, 5; Ael. Aristid. 50, 68 K. = 26 p. 522 D.: εὐ. τοῦ

θεοῦ; Ps 77: 11; Philo) 1 Cl 19: 2; 21: 1; 38: 3; Dg 8: 11; 9: 5. M-M.*

εὐεργετέω (trag+; inscr., pap., LXX; Jos., Ant. 6, 211 al.) *do good to, benefit* τινά *someone* (Aeschyl.+; Philo, Mut. Nom. 18) τὰ πάντα *do good to all things* 1 Cl 20: 11 (cf. Ep. Arist. 210). τὸν ἐλαττούμενον Dg 10: 6. Abs. (Soph.+) Ac 10: 38. Pass. *be treated well* (X., Pla.+; inscr., POxy. 899, 45; LXX, Philo; Jos., Ant. 14, 370) εὐεργετούμενοι χείρους γίνονται *when they are well treated, they become even worse* IRo 5: 1.—HBolkestein, Wohltätigkt. u. Armenpflege im vorchr. Altertum '39.*

εὐεργέτης, ου, ὁ (Pind.+; inscr., pap., LXX) *benefactor* as a title of princes and other outstanding men (Hdt. 8, 85; X., Hell. 6, 1, 4 al.; esp. inscr. [Dit., Syll.² Ind. III 5 p. 175, VI p. 321]; POxy. 38, 13 [I AD]; 486, 27. Coins [Dssm., LO 215, 4-LAE 249, 1]. Esth 8: 12 n; 2 Macc 4: 2; 3 Macc 3: 19; Philo, Omn. Prob. Lib. 118, In Flacc. 81; Jos., Bell. 3, 459. Cf. JOehler, Pauly-W. VI 978-81; Magie 67f) Lk 22: 25. Of God (Ael. Aristid. 43, 29 K.=1 p. 11 D. of Zeus; Plut., Mor. 355E Osiris μέγας βασιλεὺς εὐ.; Philo of Byblus in Euseb., Praep. Ev. 1, 9, 29; CIG 5041=Wilcken, Chrest. 116, 6 Isis and Sarapis as εὐεργέται. Philo of Alex., Spec. Leg. 1, 209, Congr. Erud. Grat. 171 and oft.; PGM 4, 992; 1048.—PWendland, D. hellenist.-röm. Kultur²⁻³ '12, 103; 121f; RKnopf on 1 Cl 19: 2) εὐ. πνευμάτων 1 Cl 59: 3.—ESkard, Zwei relig.-politische Begriffe: Euergetes-Concordia '32; ADNock, Soter and Euergetes: The Joy of Study (FCGrant-Festschr.) '51, 127-48; FWDanker, Proclamation Commentaries: Luke, '76, 6-17. M-M.*

εὐεργετικός, ή, όν (Aristot.+; Diod. S. 6, 1, 8; Vett. Val. 9, 18; 11, 8f; Dit., Or. 90, 11; 34; Wilcken, Chrest. 352, 11; Wsd 7: 22; Jos., Ant. 16, 150) *beneficent* of God (Antipat. of Tarsus [c. 150 BC] in Plut., Stoic. Repugn. 38 p. 1051E; Arius Didym. [c. birth of Christ] in Euseb., Praep. Ev. 15, 15, 5; Diod. S. 1, 25, 3: τὸ εὐεργετικόν= the will to do good, of Isis; Musonius 90, 11 H.; Philo, Plant. 90) 1 Cl 23: 1.*

εὐθαλέω (Nicander, fgm. 74, 16; Plut. et al.; Da 4: 4 Theod.) *flourish, thrive* of trees (POxy. 729, 22 [137 AD]; PWien Bosw. 8, 22) Dg 12: 1.*

εὐθαλής, ές *flourishing, thriving*—1. lit. of plants (Moschus 3, 107; Dio Chrys. 13[7], 15; Plut., Mor. p. 409A; Da 4: 21 Theod.; Philo, Rer. Div. Her. 270 [fig.]) Hs 9, 1, 7; 9, 24, 1. Of vines in a well-kept vineyard 5, 2, 4f.—2. fig. (Aeschyl., fgm. 290, 5D al.; POxy. 902, 15) Hs 4: 3.*

εὔθετος, ον (Aeschyl., Hippocr.+; Polyb. 26, 5, 6; Diod. S.; Dit., Syll.³ 736, 74; 148; 154; PTebt. 27, 44 [113 BC]; PFlor. 3, 8; LXX; Ep. Arist. 122) orig. *well-placed,* then *fit, suitable, usable, convenient* τινί *for someth.* (Nicol. Com. [IV BC] in Stob., Flor. 14, 7 vol. III p. 471, 14 H. τῷ πράγματι) τῇ βασιλείᾳ τοῦ θεοῦ Lk 9: 62; *for someone* Hb 6: 7. εἴς τι *for someth.* (Diod. S. 2, 57; Dionys. Hal., Comp. Verb. 1; Diosc. 2, 65) of salt οὔτε εἰς γῆν οὔτε εἰς κοπρίαν *of no use either for the soil or for the dunghill* Lk 14: 35 (on the difficult εἰς γῆν s. FPerles, ZNW 19, '20, 96). καιρὸς εὐ. *a convenient time* or *opportunity* (Diod. S. 14, 80, 1; Ps 31: 6; Artapanus in Euseb., Pr. Ev. 9, 27, 7) καιρὸν εὐ. λαμβάνειν (Diod. S. 5, 57, 4 οἱ Αἰγύπτιοι καιρ. εὐ. λαβόντες) Pol 13: 1. M-M. B. 644.*

εὐθέως adv. of εὐθύς (Soph.+; in H. Gk., including LXX [Helbing 23] and Ep. Arist., more common than the adv. εὐθύς and εὐθύ. In Philo and Jos. [Bell. 1, 527, Ant. 19,

362] less freq. than the adv. εὐθύς. Mayser 245; WSchmid, Der Atticismus III 1893, 126; loanw. in rabb.) *at once, immediately* Mt 4: 20, 22; 8: 3; 13: 5; 14: 31 (quick rescue from danger at sea; cf. BGU 423, 8 [II AD] of Serapis: ἔσωσε εὐθέως) and oft. (10-11 times in Mt; 6 times in Lk; 3 times in J; 9 times in Ac. Also Gal 1: 16; Js 1: 24; 3 J 14; Rv 4: 2; 7 times in Apostolic Fathers, e.g. 1 Cl 12: 4; MPol 6: 1; Hm 6, 2, 3). On the difference betw. εὐθέως and εὐθύς cf. HermvSoden, D. Schriften d. NT I 2, '11, §314 p. 1391; HPernot, Études sur la langue des Évangiles '27, 181ff; DDaube, The Sudden in the Scriptures '64, 46-72; LRydbeck, Fachprosa 167-76. S. also παραχρῆμα. M-M.

εὐθηνέω (epic, Ionic, and later by-form for Att. εὐθενέω) —1. act. (Aeschyl.+; Dit., Syll.³ 526, 42; 46; BGU 1122, 23 al.; LXX; Philo, Det. Pot. Ins. 106; Jos., Ant. 7, 297) *thrive, flourish, be in good condition* ὅλον τὸ ὄρος εὐθηνοῦν ἦν *the whole mountain was flourishing* Hs 9, 1, 8; 9, 24, 1 (cf. Da 4: 4 Theod. ἐγὼ εὐθηνῶν ἤμην).

2. mid., w. aor. pass. (Hdt. 1, 66 al.; POxy. 1381, 238 [II AD]; Ps 72: 12), w. sim. mng., of patience εὐθηνουμένη ἐν πλατυσμῷ μεγάλῳ *prospering in a spacious area* Hm 5, 2, 3 (cf. 1: 2).*

εὐθηνία, ας, ἡ *well-being, prosperity, good condition* (so Aristot.; Dit., Or. 90, 13 [196 BC]; 669, 4; Sb 7027, 3; LXX; Philo, Congr. Erud. Grat. 173, Abr. 1; Jos., Bell. 4, 88; 6, 216) εὐ. ἔχειν (Philo, Mut. Nom. 260); εὐθηνίαν πάντοτε ἕξεις μετὰ πάντων Hm 2: 3. ἔχειν τὴν εὐ. ἐν ἑαυτῷ m 5, 1, 2. The older Lat. transl. of Hermas (the so-called Vulgate) renders the word in both pass. 'pax', *peace,* prob. rightly.*

εὐθής, ές (LXX; Philo, Leg. All. 3, 309 codd.; Test. Ash. 1: 2; Georg. Mon. 58, 21; 213, 8 de Boor [1892]; Chron. Pasch. 186, 18 LDindorf [1832]) by-form in H. Gk. for the adj. εὐθύς *upright* 1 Cl 18: 10 (Ps 50: 12).*

εὐθυδρομέω 1 aor. εὐθυδρόμησα of a ship *run a straight course* (Philo, Agr. 174 πνεῦμα εὐθυδρομοῦν τὸ σκάφος ἀνέωσεν, Leg. All. 3, 223 ναῦς εὐθυδρομεῖ) εἰς Σαμοθρᾴκην Ac 16: 11 (w. εἰς as Agathias Hist. 2, 21 [VI AD]: LDindorf, Historici Gr. Min. II 71). Abs. (Laud. Therap. 28 εὐθυδρομήσας διέφυγεν) εὐθυδρομήσαντες ἤλθομεν *we ran a straight course and came* 21: 1 (εὐθυδρόμος in Polyb. 34, 4, 5; Orph. Hymns 21, 10 Qu.).*

εὐθυμέω (trans.='cheer, delight' Aeschyl.+; mid.='be cheerful' X., Pla. et al.) in our lit. only intr. *be cheerful* (Eur., Cycl. 530; Plut., Mor. 465c; 469F; PAmh. 133, 4 [beg. II AD]; PLeipz. 111, 5 al. in letters; Sym. Pr 15: 15; Jos., Ant. 18, 284) Js 5: 13; *cheer up, keep up one's courage* Ac 27: 22, 25. M-M.*

εὔθυμος, ον (Hom.+) *cheerful, in good spirits* (Pind., Pla. et al.; Sb 6222, 10; 2 Macc 11: 26; Jos., Bell. 1, 272, Ant. 14, 369) εὔθυμοι γενόμενοι πάντες *they were all encouraged* Ac 27: 36. εὔθυμόν τινα ποιεῖν *encourage someone* Hm 8: 10. Comp. εὐθυμότερος (Dit., Or. 669, 7 [I AD]; POxy. 939, 19; Philo, De Jos. 162; 198) εὐθυμότερον γίνεσθαι IPol 7: 1. M-M.*

εὐθύμως adv. (Aeschyl., X. et al.; M. Ant. 3, 16, 4; Dit., Or. 669, 4 [I AD]; Jos., Ant. 10, 174; 258) *cheerfully* ἀπολογεῖσθαι *make one's defence cheerfully* Ac 24: 10 (v.l. εὐθυμότερον, cf. X., Cyr. 2, 2, 27; PGiess. 41 II, 12). M-M.*

εὐθύνω 1 aor. εὔθυνα (W-S. §13, 13) (trag.+; Kyr.-Inschr. 68-71 al.; BGU V [Gnomon], 220 [II AD]; LXX; Philo; Jos., Ant. 15, 76).

1. *straighten, make straight* J 1: 23 (cf. Sir 2: 6; 37: 15; 49: 9, but here εὐ. τ. ὁδούς is fig., as Test. Sim. 5: 2).

2. *guide straight* (cf. Num 22: 23), of a ship *steer* (so Eur., Cycl. 15; Appian, Bell. Civ. 2, 89 §374; Philo, Abr. 70, Leg. All. 3, 224, Conf. Lingu. 115) ὁ εὐθύνων *the pilot* Js 3: 4. M-M.*

εὐθύς, εἶα, ὑ gen. **εως** (Pind.+; inscr., pap., LXX) *straight.*

1. lit., of a way (Thu. 2, 100, 2; Arrian, Anab. 3, 4, 5; Vi. Aesopi W c. 4 εὐθεῖα ὁδός; Philo, Deus Imm. 61 [metaph.]; Jos., Ant. 19, 103) εὐθείας ποιεῖν τὰς τρίβους *make the paths straight* Mt 3: 3; Mk 1: 3; Lk 3: 4 (all 3 times Is 40: 3. Cf. Diod. S. 14, 116, 9 εὐθείας ποιῆσαι τὰς ὁδούς; Carmina Pop. 47 Diehl εὐρυχωρίαν ποιεῖτε τῷ θεῷ). τὴν ὁδὸν τὴν εὐθεῖαν τιθέναι *take the straight road* 2 Cl 7: 3. As the name of a street ἡ ῥύμη ἡ καλουμένη Εὐθεῖα *the street called 'Straight (Street)'* Ac 9: 11. ἡ εὐθεῖα w. ὁδός to be supplied (so as early as class., e.g. Pla., Leg. 4 p. 716A, also Sallust. 7 p. 14, 5; Ps 142: 10 v.l.) Lk 3: 5 (Is 40: 4).

2. fig. (since Pind., trag., Thu.)—**a.** of a way in fig. sense (Tob 4: 19 BA; Ps 106: 7; Pr 20: 11 al.) αἱ ὁδοὶ τ. κυρίου αἱ εὐ. Ac 13: 10 (cf. Hos 14: 10; Sir 39: 24). καταλείποντες εὐ. ὁδὸν *leaving the straight way* (= teaching) 2 Pt 2: 15 (cf. Pr 2: 13).

b. of the καρδία: *right, upright* (Ps 7: 11; 10: 2 al.) ἔναντι τοῦ θεοῦ *before God* Ac 8: 21. Also εὐ. μετ᾽ αὐτοῦ 1 Cl 15: 4 (Ps 77: 37). M-M.*

εὐθύς adv. (arising fr. the nom. masc. sg. of εὐθύς) *immediately, at once* (so Pind.+; Epict.; pap. [Mayser 244; also POxy. 744, 7 [1 BC]; PRyl. 234, 4]; LXX; Philo; Jos., Ant. 11, 236 al.; Test. 12 Patr.; cf. Phryn. 144f L.; WSchmid, D. Atticismus I 1887, 121; 266; II 1889, 113) Mt 3: 16; 13: 20f; 14: 27; 21: 2f; 26: 74; Mk 1: 10, 12 al. (on the originality of the word—not the form—in Mk s. JWeiss, ZNW 11, '10, 124-33) Lk 6: 49; J 13: 30, 32; 19: 34; Ac 10: 16; ISm 3: 2; Hv 3, 13, 2; 5: 2, 4; m 5, 1, 3; 11: 12; s 7: 4.—For the inferential use, weakened to *then, so then* e.g. in Mk 1: 21, 23, 29 s. Mlt.-H. 446f.—PVannutelli, Synoptica 1, '38, CXIV-CXXVI; GRudberg, Con. Neot. 9, '44, 42-6. Mlt.-Turner 229. S. on εὐθέως. M-M.

εὐθύτης, ητος, ἡ *straightness* (Aristot. et al.) in our lit. only fig. (LXX; Test. Iss. 3: 1, Gad 7: 7; Syntipas p. 125, 8; Psellus p. 238, 1 with δικαιοσύνη and φιλανθρωπία) *righteousness, uprightness* ἡ ῥάβδος τῆς εὐθύτητος (gen. of quality) *the righteous scepter* Hb 1: 8 (Ps 44: 7); 1 Cl 14: 5 (Ps 36: 37). πορεύεσθαι ἐν τῇ εὐ. τοῦ κυρίου *walk in the uprightness of the Lord* Hv 3, 5, 3.*

εὐκαιρέω impf. εὐκαίρουν Mk 6: 31 and ηὐκαίρουν Ac 17: 21 (s. W-S. §12, 5b); 1 aor. subj. εὐκαιρήσω (Polyb. et al.; inscr., pap.) *have (a favorable) time, leisure, opportunity* (Phryn. 125 L. οὐ λεκτέον, ἀλλ᾽ εὖ σχολῆς ἔχειν) abs. (Polyb. 20, 9, 4; pap.) ἐλεύσεται ὅταν εὐκαιρήσῃ *as soon as he finds an opportunity* 1 Cor 16: 12 (cf. PEleph. 29, 7 [III BC] ἐὰν δὲ μὴ εὐκαιρῇς τοῦ διαβῆναι; UPZ 71, 18 [152 BC]). W. inf. foll. (Plut., Mor. 223D; Ps.-Lucian, Amor. 33) φαγεῖν *have time to eat* Mk 6: 31 (cf. PSI 425, 29 [III BC] εἰ δὲ μὴ εὐκαιρεῖ τις τῶν παρὰ σοι γραμματέων, ἀπόστειλόν μοι κτλ.). W. εἴς τι and inf. foll. εἰς οὐδὲν ἕτερον ηὐκαίρουν ἢ λέγειν *used to spend their time in nothing else than telling* Ac 17: 21. M-M.*

εὐκαιρία, ας, ἡ *favorable opportunity, the right moment* (so since Pla., Phaedr. p. 272A, also BGU 665 II, 4 [I AD] al.; Ps 144: 15; 1 Macc 11: 42) ζητεῖν εὐκαιρίαν *watch for*

a favorable opportunity (Jos., Ant. 20, 76) w. ἵνα foll. Mt 26: 16. Foll. by gen. of the inf. w. the art. (cf. BGU 46, 18 [193 AD] ἐὰν εὐκαιρίας τύχω τοῦ εὑρεῖν) Lk 22: 6. Cf. Bl-D. §400, 1; Mlt. 216-18; Mlt.-H. 448-50. M-M.*

εὔκαιρος, ον (Soph., Hippocr.+; inscr., pap., LXX, Ep. Arist.; Jos., Ant. 15, 112) in our lit. only of time *well-timed, suitable* ἡμέρα *a suitable day* Mk 6: 21 (Herodian 1, 9, 6 καιρὸς εὔκαιρος; 2 Macc 14: 29; JCGGreig, ET 65, '53f, 158f) *coming at the right time* (Plut., Lib. Educ. 14 p. 10E εὔκαιρος σιγή; Ps 103: 27) βοήθεια *help in time of need* Hb 4: 16 (Dit., Or. 762, 4 βοηθείτω κατὰ τὸ εὔκαιρον). M-M.*

εὐκαίρως adv. (since X., Ages. 8, 3; Dit., Syll.³ 495, 43; PHal. 17, 6 [III BC]; PLond. 33, 28 [161 BC]; Sir 18: 22; Philo, Somn. 2, 252; Jos., Ant. 14, 323) *conveniently* παραδιδόναι Mk 14: 11. εὐ. ἀκαίρως *in season and out of season,* i.e. *when it is convenient and when it is inconvenient* 2 Ti 4: 2 (on the asyndeton s. Kühner-G. II 346d). εὐκαίρως ἔχειν *have leisure* (Polyb. 5, 26, 10; pap.) Mk 6: 31 D. M-M.*

εὐκατάλλακτος, ον (Aristot., Rhet. 2, 4) *easily placated, favorable* of God (3 Macc 5: 13) Hv 1, 1, 8.*

εὐκλεής, ές, gen. **οῦς** (Hom.+; Wsd 3: 15; Jer 31: 17; Philo; Jos., Bell. 4, 250, Ant. 19, 240) *famous, renowned* (w. σεμνός) κανὼν τῆς παραδόσεως *renowned standard given us by tradition* 1 Cl 7: 2.*

εὐκλεῶς adv. (Aeschyl.+) *gloriously* φέρειν 1 Cl 45: 5.*

εὐκόλως adv. (since X., Mem. 4, 8, 2; Herm. Wr. 13, 16; Maspéro 2 III, 23; 4, 19) *easily* Hm 12, 3, 5 as v.l. for εὐκόπως; also s 7: 6 v.l.*

εὔκοπος, ον (Polyb. 18, 18, 2; LXX) *easy* in our lit. only in comp. εὐκοπώτερος (Diosc. I 39 W.) Hm 12, 4, 5. In the NT always in the expr. εὐκοπώτερόν ἐστιν *it is easier* w. inf. foll. (cf. Sir 22: 15) Mt 9: 5; Mk 2: 9; Lk 5: 23. W. acc. foll. and inf. (cf. 1 Macc 3: 18) Mt 19: 24; Mk 10: 25; Lk 16: 17; 18: 25. M-M.*

εὐκόπως adv. (Hippocr., Aristoph., Diod. S.; Plut., Mor. 726E; POxy. 1467, 14; Ep. Arist. 208; 250) *easily* φυλάσσειν Hm 12, 3, 5.*

εὐκταῖος, α, ον *prayed for, wished for* (so Aeschyl., Pla.+; PGiess. 68, 3 [II AD]; Philo; Jos., Ant. 1, 292 al.) εἰρήνη 1 Cl 65: 1 (w. ἐπιπόθητος).*

εὐλάβεια, ας, ἡ (trag., Pla.+; Dit., Or. 315, 69; UPZ 42, 22 [162 BC]; LXX, Philo, Joseph.) in our lit. prob. only of reverent *awe in the presence of God, fear of God* (Diod. S. 13, 12, 7 ἡ πρὸς τὸ θεῖον εὐ.; Plut., Camill. 21, 2, Numa 22, 7, Aemil. Paul. 3, 2, Mor. 549E, 568C ['hesitation']; UPZ [s. above]; Pr 28: 14; Philo, Cherub. 29 εὐ. θεοῦ, Rer. Div. Her. 22; 29) μετὰ εὐ. καὶ δέους *with awe and reverence* Hb 12: 28; μετὰ φόβου καὶ πάσης εὐ. *with fear and all reverence* Pol 6: 3. So prob. also εἰσακουσθεὶς ἀπὸ τῆς εὐ. Hb 5: 7 (ἀπό V 1. Cf. JoachJeremias, ZNW 44, '52/'53, 107-11; AStrobel, ZNW 45, '54, 252-66) *heard because of his piety.* But others (e.g. Harnack, SAB '29, 69-73= Studien I 245-52; HStrathmann⁴ '47 ad loc.) prefer to take the word here in the sense *fear, anxiety* (as Demosth. 23, 15; Plut., Fab. 1, 2; Herodian 5, 2, 2; Wsd 17: 8; Philo, Leg. All. 3, 113, Virt. 24; Jos., Ant. 11, 239; 12, 255) *heard (and rescued) from his anxiety.* εὐ. has the sense *scruple, hesitation* Plut., Mor. 568C. M-M.*

εὐλαβέομαι pass. dep.; 1 aor. ptc. εὐλαβηθείς (trag., Pla.+; inscr., pap., LXX, En., Philo, Joseph.).

1. *be afraid, be concerned* (Soph., Oed. R. 47 al.; Polyb. 18, 23, 5; Diod. S. 4, 73, 2; 16, 22, 2; UPZ 119, 5 [156 BC]; LXX; Jos., Ant. 1, 283) w. μή foll. *lest, that* (Polyb. 3, 111; Diod. S. 2, 13, 4; Epict. 4, 13, 4; 1 Macc 12: 40; En. 106, 6; Jos., Ant. 6, 157; 8, 333) Ac 23: 10 t.r.; 1 Cl 44: 5. So perh. also Νῶε . . . εὐλαβηθεὶς κατεσκεύασεν κιβωτόν *Noah . . . became afraid and built an ark* Hb 11: 7; or better yet *Noah took care* (cf. Pla., Gorg. 519A ἐὰν μὴ εὐλαβῇ; Sb 4650, 13 εὐλαβήθητι μήπως μὴ καταλάβουσίν σε; Sir 18: 27; EpJer 4). But many prefer the next mng.

2. *reverence, respect* (Pla., Leg. 9 p. 879E τ. ξενικὸν θεόν; Pr 2: 8; 30: 5; Na 1: 7 al.; Philo, Rer. Div. Her. 29; Jos., Ant. 6, 259 τὸ θεῖον) εὐλαβηθείς (sc. θεόν) *out of reverent regard* (for God's command).—KKerényi, Εὐλάβεια: Byz.-Neugr. Jahrb. 8, '30, 306-16; WSchmid, Phil. Wochenschr. 51, '31, 708f; JCAvanHerten, Θρησκεία, Εὐλάβεια, Ἱκέτης, Diss. Utrecht '34; RBultmann, TW II 749-51. M-M.*

εὐλαβής, ές, gen. **οὖς** comp. εὐλαβέστερος (Pla.+; inscr., pap., LXX, Philo; Jos., Ant. 2, 217; 6, 179 al.) in our lit. only of relig. attitudes *devout, God-fearing.* (cf. Demosth. 21, 61 εὐλαβῶς w. εὐσεβῶς; Mi 7: 2 the same two words occur in the text and as v.l.) κατὰ τὸν νόμον *by the standard of the law* Ac 22: 12; (w. δίκαιος, as Pla., Pol. 311B) Lk 2: 25; ἄνδρες εὐ. *devout men* Ac 2: 5; 8: 2. εὐλαβέστερος *reverent enough* MPol 2: 1. M-M.*

εὔλαλος, ον (Anth. Pal. 5, 148, 1 [Meleager I BC]; 9, 525, 6; 570, 2; Orph., Argon. 244; Achmes 39, 27; LXX) *sweetly speaking, talkative* (Cat. Cod. Astr. XI 2 p. 125, 5); subst. ὁ εὐ. *the talkative person* 1 Cl 30: 4 (Job 11: 2).*

εὐλογέω impf. ηὐλόγουν and εὐλόγουν (W-S. §12, 5b); fut. εὐλογήσω; 1 aor. εὐλόγησα; pf. εὐλόγηκα; pf. pass. ptc. εὐλογημένος; 1 fut. pass. εὐλογηθήσομαι (trag.+; Ps.-Pla., Min. 320E; Isocr., Archid. 43; Ps.-Aristot., Rhet. ad Alex. 4 p. 1426a, 3ff; Polyb. 1, 14, 4; Cass. Dio 42, 28; Herm. Wr.; inscr.: PSI 405, 5 [III BC]; LXX, En.; Ep. Arist. 249; Philo, Joseph., Test. 12 Patr.; Christian pap.).

1. *speak well of, praise, extol* (so quite predom. in secular Gk.) τὸν θεόν (cf. CIG 4705b, 2 εὐλογῶ τὸν θεόν, i.e. Pan; 4706c, 2 τὴν Εἶσιν. Of a Jew: εὐ. τὸν θεόν Dit., Or. 73, 1 [III BC]; PGM 4, 3050f; LXX; En. 106, 11; Jos., Ant. 7, 380; Sib. Or. 4, 25) Lk 1: 64; 2: 28; 24: 53 (v.l. αἰνοῦντες); Js 3: 9; MPol 14: 2f. Christ 19: 2. Also abs. *give thanks and praise* Mt 14: 19; 26: 26; Mk 6: 41; 14: 22; Lk 24: 30; 1 Cor 14: 16 (beside εὐχαριστέω as Herm. Wr. 1, 27. S. also the confession inscr. in FSteinleitner, D. Beicht '13, 112). ἐπ' αὐτούς *over them* Lk 9: 16 D.

2. *bless,* i.e., call down God's gracious power (LXX).

a. upon pers. τινά *bless someone* Lk 24: 50f; Hb 7: 1, 6f (cf. Gen 14: 19). Opp. καταρᾶσθαι (Gen 12: 3; EpJer 65; Philo, Fuga 73, Mos. 2, 196; Jos., Bell. 6, 307) 1 Cl 15: 3 (Ps 61: 5). εὐ. τοὺς καταρωμένους *those who curse* Lk 6: 28; D 1: 3. τοὺς διώκοντας (ὑμᾶς v.l.) *your persecutors* Ro 12: 14a. Of paternal blessings by Isaac (Gen 27) and Jacob (Gen 48) Hb 11: 20f; B 13: 4f. Abs. (Philo, Migr. Abr. 113 opp. καταρᾶσθαι) λοιδορούμενοι εὐλογοῦμεν *when we are reviled we bless* 1 Cor 4: 12; cf. Ro 12: 14b; 1 Pt 3: 9; Dg 5: 15.—Of the word of blessing w. which one greets a person or wishes him well (4 Km 4: 29; 1 Ch 16: 43) Lk 2: 34. Also the acclamation εὐλογημένος ὁ ἐρχόμενος ἐν ὀνόματι κυρίου (Ps 117: 26) Mt 21: 9; 23: 39; Mk 11: 9; Lk 13: 35; J 12: 13; cf. Lk 19: 38; Mk 11: 10.

b. upon things, which are thereby consecrated τί *bless,*

consecrate (Ex 23: 25; 1 Km 9: 13; cf. Jos., Bell. 5, 401) Mk 8: 7; Lk 9: 16. In the language of the Eucharist 1 Cor 10: 16. Perh. Mt 26: 26; Mk 14: 22 also belong here, in which case the obj. is to be supplied fr. the context; likew. possibly Mt 14: 19; Mk 6: 41 (s. 1 above).

3. w. God or Christ as subj. *provide with benefits* (Eur., Suppl. 927; PGM 4, 3050a; LXX; En. 1, 8) τινά *someone* Ac 3: 26; 1 Cl 10: 3 (Gen 12: 2); 33: 6 (Gen 1: 28); ἐκκλησίαν Hv 1, 3, 4. εὐλογῶν εὐλογήσω σε *surely I will bless you* Hb 6: 14 (Gen 22: 17). τινὰ ἔν τινι *someone with someth.* (Ps 28: 11; Test. Jos. 18: 1 v.l.) ἐν πάσῃ εὐλογίᾳ Eph 1: 3 (cf. Test. Iss. 5: 6 ἐν εὐλογίαις τῆς γῆς.—On the form cf. BGU βεβαιώσει πάσῃ βεβαιώσει). Pass. Gal 3: 9; 1 Cl 31: 2. ἐν τῷ σπέρματί σου εὐλογηθήσονται Ac 3: 25 v.l. (Gen 12: 3). Pf. ptc. εὐλογημένος *blessed* (LXX) 1 Cl 30: 5 (Job 11: 2), 8. Of a child (Dt 28: 4) Lk 1: 42b. εὐλογημένη ἐν γυναιξίν *among women* vs. 28 v.l.; 42a. ἐν πᾶσιν *in every respect* IEph 2: 1. ἐν χάριτι θεοῦ *by the grace of God* IMg inscr.; cf. IEph inscr. εὐλογημένοι τοῦ πατρός *those blessed by the Father* Mt 25: 34 (cf. Is 61: 9 σπέρμα ηὐλογημένον ὑπὸ θεοῦ).—Lit. on εὐλογέω and εὐλογία in ThSchermann, Allg. Kirchenordnung '14/'16 II 640, 4. Also JHempel, D. israel. Ansch. v. Segen u. Fluch im Lichte d. altoriental. Parallelen: ZDMG n.F. 4, '25, 20-110; EMaass, Segnen, Weihen, Taufen: ARW 21, '22, 241-81; LBrun, Segen u. Fluch im Urchristentum '32; JZdevsar, Eulogia u. Eulogein im NT, Diss. Rome '54; AMurtonen, Vetus Test. 9, '59, 158-77; EKleszmann, Monatsschr. für Past.-Theol., 48, '59, 26-39. HWBeyer, TW II 751-63. Cf. BFWestcott, Hebrews, 1889, 203-10. M-M. B. 1479.*

εὐλογητός, ή, όν in our lit. only (as predom. LXX; cf. also En. 22, 14; Herm. Wr. 1, 32 εὐλογητὸς εἶ πάτερ) of God (and Christ) εὐ. κύριος ὁ θεὸς τ. Ἰσραήλ (3 Km 1: 48; 2 Ch 2: 11; 6: 4; Ps 71: 18) *blessed, praised* Lk 1: 68 (PVielhauer, ZThK 49, '52, 255-72; AVanhoye, Structure du 'Benedictus', NTS 12, '66, 382-89. εὐ. εἰς τ. αἰῶνας (Ps 88: 53) Ro 1: 25; 9: 5; 2 Cor 11: 31; cf. 1: 3; Eph 1: 3; 1 Pt 1: 3; B 6: 10; IEph 1: 3 (on this form of praise s. Elbogen 4f and PSchorlemmer, 'Die Hochkirche' '24, 110ff; 151). Of Christ MPol 14: 1. ὁ εὐ. as periphrasis for the name of God, which is not mentioned out of reverence Mk 14: 61 (Dalman, Worte 163f).—EFFBishop, IGoldziher Memorial Vol., vol. I '49, 82-8; SEsh, Der Heilige (Er Sei Gepriesen) '57.*

εὐλογία, ας, ἡ (Pind.+; Herm. Wr.; inscr., pap., LXX, En., Philo, Joseph., Test. 12 Patr.).

1. *praise* (class.; Dit., Or. 74 [III BC] θεοῦ εὐλογία· Θεύδοτος Ἰουδαῖος σωθεὶς ἐκ πελάγους; Sb 317; 1117; Herm. Wr. 1, 30 εὐ. τ. πατρὶ θεῷ; 2 Esdr 19 [Neh 9]: 5; Sir 50: 20; Jos., Ant. 11, 80 εἰς θεόν) Rv 5: 12f; 7: 12.

2. *fine speaking* (Pla., Rep. 3 p. 400D; Lucian, Lexiph. 1), also in a bad sense (Aesop 274 and 274b Halm=160 Hausr. uses the adj. εὔλογος of an argument that sounds good but is false. Cf. Lucian, Abdic. 22) *well chosen* (but untrue) *words, false eloquence,* or *flattery* Ro 16: 18.

3. *blessing*—**a.** act. *the act of blessing*—**α.** by which men call down upon other men the grace of God (opp. κατάρα, as Gen 27: 12; Sir 3: 9; Philo, Mos. 1, 283; Jos., Ant. 4, 302; Test. Benj. 6: 5) Js 3: 10. Often the explanation of Hb 12: 17 is thought to be given in Gen 27: 38. Others place the passage under ba.

β. of God's activity in blessing (Wsd 15: 19; Sir 11: 22 al.) 1 Cl 31: 1. ὁδοὶ τ. εὐλογίας *the ways of blessing* i.e., those which God blesses, ibid.

b. a *blessing* as a benefit—**α.** bestowed by God or Christ

(Gen 49: 25; Ex 32: 29; Lev 25: 21 al.) μεταλαμβάνει εὐλογίας *shares the blessing* Hb 6: 7 (but s. 5 below). εὐ. πνευματική *spiritual blessing* Eph 1: 3. εὐ. Χριστοῦ Ro 15: 29; κληρονομεῖν τὴν εὐ. Hb 12: 17 (s. aa above); 1 Pt 3: 9. εὐ. τοῦ Ἀβραάμ Gal 3: 14 (cf. Gen 28: 4).

β. *brought by men* (Gen 33: 11; 1 Km 25: 27; 4 Km 5: 15.—Cyrillus of Scyth. uses εὐλογία = 'gift, bounty' [from men] without biblical influence: p. 68, 17 and 28; 217, 15; 238, 12; also εὐλογέω = bestow p. 137, 9) 2 Cor 9: 5a; mng. 5 is also poss.

4. *consecration* (εὐλογέω 2b) τὸ ποτήριον τῆς εὐ. *the consecrated cup* 1 Cor 10: 16 (Joseph and Aseneth 8, 11 καὶ πιέτω ποτήριον εὐλογίας σου; HGressmann, Sellin-Festschr. '27, 55ff; ROtto, The Kingdom of God and the Son of Man, transl. FVFilson and BLee-Woolf, '57, 265ff).

5. Since the concept of blessing carries with it the idea of bounty, εὐ. gains the mng. *generous gift, bounty* (opp. πλεονεξία) 2 Cor 9: 5b; perh. also 5a, s. 3bβ above. ἐπ' εὐλογίαις (opp. φειδομένως) *bountifully* 9: 6a, b (Philo, Leg. All. 3, 210: ἐπ' εὐλογίαις = in order that blessed influence might be felt). This may perh. be the place for Hb 6: 7 (s. 3ba above) γῆ…μεταλαμβάνει εὐλογίας ἀπὸ τ. θεοῦ *the earth receives rich bounty from God.* M-M.*

εὔλογος, ον (Aeschyl. +; Dit., Or. 504, 9; 669, 10; UPZ 162 V, 2 [117 BC]; Philo; Jos., C. Ap. 1, 259) *reasonable, right* IMg 7: 1. εὐλογόν ἐστιν *it is reasonable* w. inf. foll. (Pla., Crat. 396B; cf. Philo, Deus Imm. 127) ISm 9: 1.*

εὐμετάδοτος, ον (M. Ant. 1, 14, 4; 6, 48, 1; Vett. Val. 7, 13; 11, 7 al.; Vi. Aesopi I c. 26 p. 289, 1) *generous* 1 Ti 6: 18. M-M.*

εὔμορφος, ον (trag., Hdt. +; POxy. 471, 79; 109) *well-formed, beautiful* of women (Artem. 1, 78 p. 73, 9 al.; Xenophon Eph. 1, 4, 3; Sir 9: 8; Philo, Virt. 110; Test. Jud. 13: 3.—εὐμορφία Jos., Ant. 15, 23) Hs 9, 13, 8.*

Εὐνίκη, ης, ἡ (name of mythological figures in Hes., Theogon. 246 Rz.; Theocr. 13, 45; Ps.-Apollod. 1, 2, 7; CIG IV 8139.—Gentile women bear this name: Dialekt-Inschr. no. 4033 [Rhodes]; Κυπρ. I p. 93 no. 40; PFay. 130, 18) *Eunice,* mother of Timothy 2 Ti 1: 5.*

εὐνοέω (trag., Hdt. +; inscr., pap., LXX) *be well-disposed, make friends* τινί *to* or *with someone* (Soph., Aj. 689 al.; Polyb. 3, 11, 7; Herodian 8, 8, 5; Dit., Syll.³ 524, 17; 985, 23; 1268, 15, Or. 532, 9 [3 BC]; PRyl. 153, 10; POxy. 494, 9; Da 2: 43; Jos., Bell. 4, 214, C. Ap. 1, 309; 2, 121) ἴσθι εὐνοῶν τῷ ἀντιδίκῳ σου ταχύ *make friends quickly with your opponent* Mt 5: 25 (εὔνοια appears in a comparable passage Plut., Mor. 489C; for the constr. cf. PHolm. 5, 16 ἔστω κρεμάμενα = they are . . . to hang. Bl-D. §353, 6; Rob. 375). M-M.*

εὔνοια, ας, ἡ (Aeschyl., Hdt. +; inscr., pap., LXX, Ep. Arist., Philo; Jos., Ant. 2, 161) *good will.*

1. *favor, affection, benevolence* (Diod. S. 1, 51, 5; 1, 54, 1; Jos., Bell. 4, 213, Ant. 11, 132; 18, 376) ἡ κατὰ θεὸν εὐ. (your) *godly benevolence* ITr 1: 2. εὐ. εἴς τινα *affection for someone* (Thu. 2, 8, 4 al.; Dit., Syll.³ 390, 18; 2 Macc 9: 26; 11: 19) MPol 17: 3. Abstr. for concr. παρακαλῶ ὑμᾶς, μὴ εὐ. ἄκαιρος γένησθέ μοι *I beg of you, do not show* (lit. *be to*) *me an unseasonable kindness* IRo 4: 1 (cf. the proverb ἄκαιρος εὐνοι' οὐδὲν ἔχθρας διαφέρει [Zenob., Paroem. 1, 50]). ὀφειλομένη εὐ. (s. ὀφείλω 2aα) 1 Cor 7: 3 t.r.

2. *zeal, enthusiasm* (Dit., Syll.³ 799, 27 σπουδὴ καὶ εὐ.;

BGU 1121, 19 [5 BC]) as a virtue of slaves (POxy. 494, 6 [156 AD]; cf. Lucian, Bis Accus. 16) μετ' εὐνοίας δουλεύοντες Eph 6: 7 (on μετ' εὐν. cf. Pla., Phaedr. 241C; Demosth. 18, 276; Dit., Syll.³ 330, 8; Sir Prol. l. 16). M-M.*

εὐνουχία, ας, ἡ (so far found only in Christian wr., e.g. Athenagoras, Legat. 33) *the state of being unmarried* Agr 18.*

εὐνουχίζω (Clearchus, fgm. 49; Appian, Bell. Civ. 3, 98 §409; Lucian, Sat. 12; Archigenes [II AD] in Oribas. 8, 2, 8; Galen: CMG V 4, 2 p. 334, 8; 335, 4; Cass. Dio 68, 2, 4; Jos., Ant. 10, 33.—Fig., Philostrat., Vi. Apoll. 6, 42 p. 252, 27 τὴν γῆν) *castrate, emasculate, make a eunuch of* ἑαυτόν *oneself* Mt 19: 12b; pass., ibid. a. From ancient times it has been disputed whether the word is to be taken literally in both occurrences, fig. in both, or fig. in the first and lit. in the second (cf. WBauer, Heinrici-Festschr. '14, 235–44). The context requires the fig. interpr. (s. εὐνουχία) for the second occurrence, and the lit. for the first (cf. JAKleist, CBQ 7, '45, 447–9).—ADNock, Eunuchs in Anc. Rel.: ARW 23, '25, 25–33 (= Essays in Religion and the Anc. World I, '72, 7–15); LHGray, Eunuch: Enc. of Rel. and Eth. V 579–85; JBlinzler, BRigaux-Festschr., '70, 45–55 (Justin); JSchneider, TW II 763–7.*

εὐνοῦχος, ου, ὁ (Hdt., Aristoph. +; Vett. Val. 18, 19; 86, 34; BGU 725, 14; 29; LXX; Philo; Jos., Bell. 1, 488, Ant. 17, 44; Test. 12 Patr.) *emasculated man, eunuch.*

1. of physically castrated men Mt 19: 12b. They served, esp. in the orient, as keepers of the harem (Esth 2: 14) and not infreq. rose to high positions in the state (Hdt. 8, 105): the εὐ. δυνάστης of Queen Candace Ac 8: 27, 34, 36, 38f.—S. on Κανδάκη.—Diod. S. 11, 69, 1 Mithridates is physically a εὐνοῦχος and holds the position of κατακοιμιστής (= the chamberlain) τοῦ βασιλέως (Xerxes). In 17, 5, 3 Βαγώας as χιλίαρχος bears the title of a high official at the Persian court (18, 48, 4f). Since he is also described as εὐνοῦχος, the word must be understood literally. So also in Ac 8, 27ff the man baptized by Philip performs the function of δυνάστης Κανδάκης βασιλίσσης. Here also 'eunuch' can only refer to his physical state.

2. of those who, without a physical operation, are by nature incapable of marrying and begetting children (Wsd 3: 14) εὐ. ἐκ κοιλίας μητρός Mt 19: 12a.

3. of those who abstain fr. marriage, without being impotent Mt 19: 12c.—Cf. εὐνουχίζω.—JBlinzler, ZNW 48, '57, 254–70. M-M. B. 141.*

Εὐοδία, ας, ἡ (Dit., Syll.² 868, 19, Or. 77; Κυπρ. I p. 46 no. 72 Greek grave inscr. from Cyprus; BGU 550, 1) *Euodia,* a Christian woman Phil 4: 2.*

εὐοδόω 1 fut. pass. εὐοδωθήσομαι (Soph., Hdt. +; pap., LXX; on the latter Anz 290) in our lit. only the pass. is used, and not in its literal sense, 'be led along a good road'; *get along well, prosper, succeed* of pers., abs. (Josh 1: 8; Pr 28: 13; 2 Ch 18: 11; En. 104, 6; Test. Gad 7: 1) εὔχομαί σε εὐοδοῦσθαι κ. ὑγιαίνειν *I pray that all may go well with you and that you may be in good health* 3 J 2; cf. εὐοδοῦταί σου ἡ ψυχή *it is well with your soul* ibid.; εὐ. ἔν τινι *succeed in someth.* (2 Ch 32: 30; Sir 41: 1; Jer 2: 37; Da 6: 4) Hs 6, 3, 5f. W. inf. foll. (cf. 1 Macc 16: 2) εἴ πως ἤδη ποτὲ εὐοδωθήσομαι ἐλθεῖν πρὸς ὑμᾶς *whether I will finally succeed in coming to you* Ro 1: 10. θησαυρίζων ὅ τι ἐὰν εὐοδῶται *save as much as he gains* 1 Cor 16: 2. However, in this pass. the subj. may be a thing (Hdt. 6, 73 τῷ Κλεομένεϊ εὐοδώθη τὸ πρῆγμα; 2 Esdr [Ezra] 5: 8; Tob 4: 19 BA; 1 Macc 3: 6) understood, such as business or profit. M-M.*

εὐοικονόμητος, ον (since Diphilus [IV/III BC] in Athen. 2 p. 54D) *well arranged* of a beginning: *auspicious* IRo 1: 2 (the adv. εὐοικονομήτως 'suitably' in Eustath.).*

εὐπάρεδρος, ον (Hesychius: εὐπάρεδρον· καλῶς παραμένον) *constant* πρὸς τὸ εὐ. τῷ κυρίῳ *that you might be devoted to the Lord* 1 Cor 7: 35 (t.r. εὐπρόσεδρος).*

εὐπειθής, ές gen. οῦς (Aeschyl., X., Pla.+; Musonius 83, 19; Epict. 3, 12, 13; Plut., Mor. 26D; BGU 1104, 23; 1155, 17; POxy. 268, 6; 4 Macc 12: 6; Philo, Virt. 15) *obedient, compliant* Js 3: 17. M-M.*

εὐπερίσπαστος, ον (Ps.-X., Cyn. 2, 7 'easy to pull away'; the verbal in -τος is indifferent as to voice, Mlt. 221) *easily distracting* (cf. ἀπερίσπαστος 'not distracted' Polyb., Plut.; Sir 41: 1; its adv. 1 Cor 7: 35) Hb 12: 1 𝔓⁴⁶ (FWBeare, JBL 63, '44, 390f).*

εὐπερίστατος, ον (Hesychius=εὔκολον, εὐχερῆ; Suidas=μωρόν, ταχέως περιτρεπόμενον; Mlt.-H. 282) *easily ensnaring* of sin Hb 12: 1. M-M. also 'easily avoided', 'admired', 'dangerous'. S. εὐπερίσπαστος.*

Εὔπλους, ου, ὁ (CIG 1211; 2072; Inscr. v. Hierap. 194; 270; Inscr. Or. Sept. Ponti Eux. I 58; 61; 63 Latyschev; CIL III 2571; Suppl. 9054; IX 4665; X 7667; 7700; BGU 665 II, 7 [I AD]) *Euplus*, a Christian IEph 2: 1.*

εὐποιΐα, ας, ἡ—1. *the doing of good* (Epict. in Stob., fgm. 45 Schenkl; Arrian, Anab. 7, 28, 3; Polyaenus, Exc. 1 τῶν πλησίον; Lucian, Abd. 25; Diog. L. 10, 10; Inschr. v. Perg. 333; IG III 1054) Hb 13: 16.
2. *a good deed* (Chio, Ep. 7, 3; Syntipas p. 24, 7; POxy. 1773, 34; PLond. 1244, 8; Philo, Mut. Nom. 24; Jos., Ant. 2, 261; 19, 356) IPol 7: 3.—S. on εὐεργετέω. M-M.*

εὐπορέω impf. 3 sg. mid. εὐπορεῖτο (on the augm. s. W-S. §12, 5b) *have plenty, be well off* (the mid. is used now and then in this sense, which usu. belongs to the active: e.g. the mid. is found Aristot., Oec. 2, 23; Polyb. 1, 66, 5; 5, 43, 8; Jos., Ant. 17, 214, Vi. 28. Cf. Lev 25: 26, 49) abs. (as Theopomp. in Athen. 6 p. 275c; Lucian, Bis Acc. 27; Dit., Syll.³ 495, 66; PGM 4, 3215) καθὼς εὐπορεῖτό τις *according to his* (financial) *ability* Ac 11: 29. M-M.*

εὐπορία, ας, ἡ (Thu.+ in var. mngs.; LXX 4 Km 25: 10 v.l. Oft. Aq., Philo, Joseph.) *means,* then abundant means, *prosperity* (X., Demosth. et al.; cf. POxy. 71 I, 17 οὐδεμία δέ μοι ἑτέρα εὐπορία ἐστὶν ἢ τὰ χρήματα ταῦτα; Jos., Bell. 7, 445) ἡ εὐ. ἡμῖν ἐστιν *we get our prosperity* Ac 19: 25; another poss. mng. is *easy means of earning a living.* M-M.*

εὐπραγέω 1 aor. εὐπράγησα (Thu.+, mostly='be well off'; so also Jos., Ant. 13, 284; Test. Gad 4: 5) *do what is right* (cf. Sym., Ps 35: 4) 2 Cl 17: 7.*

εὐπρέπεια, ας, ἡ (Thu.+; Epict. 1, 8, 7; Dit., Syll.³ 358; 880, 17; LXX; Philo, Aet. M. 126; Jos., Ant. 4, 131) *fine appearance, beauty* AP 3: 10. ἡ εὐ. τοῦ προσώπου αὐτοῦ *the beauty of its* (i.e., the flower's) *appearance* Js 1: 11. περιτιθέναι τὴν εὐ. τινι *clothe someth. w. beauty* Hv 1, 3, 4. M-M.*

εὐπρεπής, ές gen. οῦς (Aeschyl., Hdt.+; Diod. S. 1, 45, 4 Vogel v.l. [the text has ναοῖς ἐκπρεπέσι]; Epict. 1, 2, 18 al.; inscr.; POxy. 1380, 130 [II AD]; LXX, Philo; Jos., Ant. 6, 160). Comp. εὐπρεπέστερος (Aeschyl. et al.; Wsd 7: 29) Dg 2: 2; Hs 5, 2, 4. Superl. εὐπρεπέστατος (Hdt. et al.; Jos., Ant. 1, 200) Hs 2: 1; 9, 1, 10; 9, 10, 3.

1. *looking well* of a vineyard carefully dug and weeded εὐπρεπέστερος ἔσται *it will look better* Hs 5, 2, 4. Of a white mountain εὐπρεπέστατον ἦν ἑαυτῷ τὸ ὄρος *the mountain by itself* (without any trees) *was most beautiful* 9, 1, 10. Of a place that has been cleaned *very attractive* 9, 10, 3. Of a building *magnificent* 9, 9, 7. οὐδὲν εὐπρεπέστερον w. gen. *no better to look at than* Dg 2: 2.
2. *suited* τινι *to someth.* of the elm and the vine εὐπρεπέσταταί εἰσιν ἀλλήλαις *they are very well suited to each other* Hs 2: 1.*

εὐπρεπῶς adv. (Aeschyl.+; Dit., Syll.³ 1109, 110; 1 Esdr 1: 10; Wsd 13: 11; Jos., Ant. 13, 31).
1. *beautifully* Hs 5, 2, 5. This mng. is also poss. for 9, 2, 4. But here the sense can also be—**2.** *fittingly, properly* of women περιεζωσμέναι εὐ.*

εὐπρόσδεκτος, ον (easily) *acceptable, pleasant, welcome* (Plut., Mor. 801c).
1. of things: of offerings (schol. on Aristoph., Pax 1054 εὐπρόσδεκτος ἡ θυσία) προσφορά Ro 15: 16. Of a time which is favorable for bringing God's grace to fruition καιρὸς εὐ. 2 Cor 6: 2. Of the willingness to give, which is said to be acceptable 8: 12. W. the dat. of the one to whom someth. is acceptable: men Ro 15: 31; to God θυσίαι εὐ. θεῷ 1 Pt 2: 5 (cf. Vi. Aesopi W c. 8 εὐπρόσδεκτον παρὰ τῷ θεῷ τὸ ἀγαθοποιεῖν; Cat. Cod. Astr. VII 178, 6 εὐ. αἱ εὐχαὶ πρὸς θεόν; Dit., Syll.³ 1042, 8 ἀπρόσδεκτος ἡ θυσία παρὰ τ. θεοῦ). ἱλαρότης Hm 10, 3, 1. λειτουργία s 5, 3, 8. εὐ. τῷ θελήματι αὐτοῦ *acceptable to his will* 1 Cl 40: 3; τὰ εὐ. *what is acceptable* to God 35: 5.—**2.** of pers. 40: 4. M-M.*

εὐπρόσεδρος, ον *constant* 1 Cor 7: 35 t.r. (s. εὐπάρεδρος).*

εὐπροσωπέω 1 aor. εὐπροσώπησα (PTebt. 19, 12 [114 BC] ὅπως εὐπροσωπῶμεν) *make a good showing* ἐν σαρκί *before men* Gal 6: 12. M-M.*

εὐρακύλων, ωνος, ὁ (a hybrid formation of Lat.-Gk. sailor's language, made fr. εὖρος and Lat. aquilo, Bl-D. §5, 1d; 115, 1; Rob. 166) *the northeast wind, Euraquilo* Ac 27: 14 (v.l. εὐροκλύδων, q.v.). JSmith, The Voyage and Shipwreck of St. Paul⁴ 1880, 119ff; 287ff. M-M.*

εὕρημα, ατος, τό (trag., Hdt.+; POxy. 472, 33 [II AD]; Philo; Jos., C. Ap. 2, 148; the LXX has the later form εὕρεμα [Phryn. p. 445f L.; Dio Chrys. 59[76], 1]; s. Thackeray p. 80) *discovery, invention* Dg 7: 1.*

εὑρίσκω (Hom.+; inscr., pap., LXX, En., Ep. Arist., Philo, Joseph., Test. 12 Patr.) impf. εὕρισκον; fut. εὑρήσω; pf. εὕρηκα; 2 aor. εὗρον, 1 pl. εὕραμεν (BGU 1095, 10 [57 AD]; Sb 6222, 12 [III AD]) Lk 23: 2, mid. εὑράμην Hb 9: 12 (Bl-D. §81, 3 w. app.; cf. Mlt.-H. 208). Pass. εὑρίσκομαι; impf. 3 sg. ηὑρίσκετο; 1 aor. εὑρέθην; 1 fut. εὑρεθήσομαι (W-S. §15 s.v.).

1. *find*—a. after seeking *find, discover, come upon* abs. (opp. ζητεῖν, Pla., Gorg. 59 p. 503D; Epict. 4, 1, 51 ζήτει καὶ εὑρήσεις; PTebt. 278, 30 [I AD] ζητῶι καὶ οὐχ εὑρίσκωι) Mt 7: 7f; Lk 11: 9f; LJ 2: 2; GH 27. τινὰ ζητεῖν κ. εὐ. (3 Km 1: 3) 2 Ti 1: 17. τινὰ ἢ τὶ ζητεῖν κ. οὐχ εὐ. (PGiess. 21, 5; Sextus 28; 4 Km 2: 17; 2 Esdr 17 [Neh 7]: 64; Ps 9: 36; Pr 1: 28; SSol 5: 6; Ezk 22: 30) Mt 12: 43; 26: 60; Mk 14: 55; Lk 11: 24; 13: 6f; J 7: 34, 36; Rv 9: 6. εὐ. τινά Mk 1: 37; Lk 2: 45; 2 Cor 2: 13. τὶ Mt 7: 14; 13: 46; 18: 13; Lk 24: 3. νομήν *pasture* J 10: 9 (cf. La 1: 6); Ac 7: 11. The obj. acc. can be supplied fr. the context Mt 2: 8; Ac 11: 26. W. the place given ἐν τῇ φυλακῇ 5:22. πέραν τῆς θαλάσσης J 6:25. Pass. w. neg. εἴ τις οὐχ εὑρέθη ἐν τῇ βίβλῳ τῆς ζωῆς γεγραμμένος *if anyone('s name) was not found written in the book of life* Rv 20:15 (cf. PHib. 48, 6 [255 bc] οὐ γὰρ εὑρίσκω ἐν τοῖς βιβλίοις; 2 Esdr 18 [Neh 8]:14). The pass. w. neg. can also mean: *no longer to be found*, despite a thorough search= *disappear* (PReinach 11, 11 [111 bc]) of Enoch οὐχ ηὑρίσκετο Hb 11:5 (Gen 5:24). ὄρη οὐχ εὑρέθησαν Rv 16:20; cf. 18:21. The addition of the neg., which is actually found in the Sahidic version, would clear up the best-attested and difficult rdg. of 2 Pt 3:10 καὶ γῆ καὶ τὰ ἐν αὐτῇ ἔργα εὑρεθήσεται (אBKP min. Arm.); other proposals in Nestle. See also Danker s.v. 2.

b. *find, come upon* accidentally, without seeking τινά *someone* (PGenève 54, 31 εὑρήκαμεν τὸν πραιπόσιτον; Gen 4:14f; 18:28ff; 1 Km 10:2; 3 Km 19:19; Sir 12:17) Mt 18:28; 27:32; J 1:41a, 43, 45; 5:14; 9:35; Ac 13:6; 18:2; 19:1; 28:14 (Diog. L. 1, 109 τὸν ἀδελφὸν εὑρών= he came upon his brother). Foll. by ἐν w. dat. to designate the place (3 Km 11:29; 1 Macc 2:46) J 2:14; τὶ *someth.* (Gen 11:2; 26:19; Judg 15:15; 4 Km 4:39 al.) Mt 13:44 (Biogr. p. 324 εὑρὼν θησαυρόν); 17:27; Lk 4:17; J 12:14 (Phot., Bibl. 94 p. 74b on Iambl. Erot. [Hercher I 222, 38] εὑρόντες ὄνους δύο ἐπέβησαν); Ac 17:23. Also foll. by ἐν and the dat. to indicate the place (Herodian 3, 8, 6; 2 Ch 21:17) Mt 8:10; Lk 7:9. Pass. *be found, find oneself, be* (Dt 20:11; 4 Km 14:14; 1 Esdr 1:19; 8:13; Bar 1:7) Φ. εὑρέθη εἰς Ἄζωτον Philip *found himself or was present at Azotus* Ac 8:40 (cf. Esth 1:5 τοῖς ἔθνεσιν τοῖς εὑρεθεῖσιν εἰς τ. πόλιν), but a Semitic phrase . . . בְּהִמָּצֵא=to arrive in, or at, may underlie the expr. here and in εὑρεθῆναι εἰς τ. βασιλείαν Hs 9, 13, 2 (cf. MBlack, Aramaic Studies and the NT, JTS 49, '48, 164). οὐδὲ τόπος εὑρέθη αὐτῶν ἔτι ἐν τ. οὐρανῷ *there was no longer any place for them in heaven* Rv 12:8 (s. Da 2:35 Theod.); cf. 18:22, 24. οὐδὲ εὑρέθη δόλος ἐν τ. στόματι αὐτοῦ 1 Pt 2:22; 1 Cl 16:10 (both Is 53:9); cf. Rv 14:5 (cf. Zeph 3:13). ἵνα εὑρεθῶ ἐν αὐτῷ (i.e. Χριστῷ) *that I might be found in Christ* Phil 3:9 (JMoffatt, ET 24, '13, 46).

c. w. acc. and ptc. or adj., which denotes the state of being or the action in which someone or someth. is or is involved (Bl-D. §416, 2; cf. Rob. 1120f).

α. w. ptc. (Thu. 2, 6, 3; Demosth. 19, 332; Epict. 4, 1, 27; PTebt. 330, 5 [II ad] παραγενομένου εἰς τ. κώμην εὖρον τ. οἰκίαν μου σεσυλημένην; Num 15:32; Tob 7:1 S; 8:13; D 6:14; 6:12 Theod.; Jos., Bell. 6, 136 τ. φύλακας εὖρον κοιμωμένους) εὑρίσκει αὐτὸν σχολάζοντα *he finds it unoccupied* (that gives the condition for his return: HSNyberg, Con. Neot. 2, '36, 22-35) Mt 12:44. εὑρεν ἄλλους ἑστῶτας *he found others standing there* 20:6 (cf. Jdth 10:6); cf. 21:2; 24:46; 26:40, 43; Mk 11:2; 13:36; 14:37, 40; Lk 2:12; 7:10; 8:35; 11:25; 12:37, 43; 19:30; Ac 5:23; 9:2; 10:27; 27:6; 2 Cl 6:9; ITr 2:2 and oft. W. ellipsis of the ptc. εὑρέθη μόνος (sc. ὤν) Lk 9:36. οὐδὲ εὑρίσκω αἴτιον (ὄν) 23:4; cf. vs. 22.

β. w. adj. εὖρον αὐτὴν νεκράν Ac 5:10. εὕρωσιν ὑμᾶς ἀπαρασκευάστους 2 Cor 9:4.

γ. elliptically w. a whole clause οὐχ οἵους θέλω εὕρω ὑμᾶς *I may find you not as I want* (to find you) 2 Cor 12:20. Several times w. καθώς foll.: εὖρον καθὼς εἶπεν αὐτοῖς *they found it just as he had told them* Mk 14:16; Lk 19:32; cf. 22:13. ἵνα. . .εὑρεθῶσιν καθὼς καὶ ἡμεῖς *that they may be found* (leading the same kind of life) *as we* 2 Cor 11:12.

2. fig., of intellectual discovery based upon reflection, observation, examination, or investigation *find, discover*

(X., Hell. 7, 4, 2; M. Ant. 7, 1; Wsd 3:5; Da 1:20 Theod.; Jos., Ant. 10, 196) τὶ *someth.*: *I find it to be the rule* Ro 7:21. ὧδε εὑ. ἐντολήν *here I find a commandment* B 9:5. τινά w. ptc. foll. *find someone* doing someth. (Anonymi Vi. Platonis p. 7, 18 Westerm.) Lk 23:2; Ac 23:29. Likew. τὶ w. ptc. foll. Rv 3:2. τινά w. adj. foll. 2:2. W. ὅτι foll. B 16:7. Of the result of a judicial investigation εὑ. αἰτίαν θανάτου *find a cause for putting to death* Ac 13:28. εὑ. αἰτίαν, κακόν, ἀδίκημα ἔν τινι J 18:38; 19:4, 6; Ac 23:9. εἰπάτωσαν τί εὗρον ἀδίκημα *let them say what wrongdoing they have discovered* 24:20. ποιεῖτε ἵνα εὑρεθῆτε ἐν ἡμέρᾳ κρίσεως *act in order that you may pass muster in the day of judgment* B 21:6. This may be the sense of εὑρ. in 2 Pt 3:10 w. an emendation of καὶ γῆ κατὰ τὰ (for καὶ γῆ καὶ τὰ) ἐν αὐτῇ ἔργα εὑρεθήσεται (cf. PsSol 17:8) *and the earth will be judged according to the deeds done on it* (FWDanker, 2 Pt 3:10 and PsSol 17:10, ZNW 53, '62, 82-86).—W. acc. of a price or measure calculated εὗρον *they found* 19:19; 27:28. W. indir. quest. foll. Lk 5:19 which, by the use of the article, can become an object acc.: εὑ. τὸ τί ποιήσωσιν 19:48. τὸ πῶς κολάσωνται αὐτούς Ac 4:21. W. inf. foll. ἵνα εὕρωσιν κατηγορεῖν αὐτοῦ *in order to find a charge against him* Lk 6:7; 11:54 D (however, there is no accusative with εὕρωσιν; cf. PPar. 45, 7 [153 bc] προσέχων μὴ εὕρῃ τι κατὰ σοῦ ἰπῖν= εἰπεῖν. For this reason it is perhaps better to conclude that εὑρίσκω with inf.= *be able*: Astrampsychus p. 5 1. 14 εἰ εὑρήσω δανείσασθαι ἄρτι=whether I will be able to borrow money now; p. 6 1. 72; p. 42 Dek. 87, 1. Then the transl. would be: *in order that they might be able to bring an accusation against him*). Of seeking and finding God (Is 55:6; Wsd 13:6, 9. Cf. Philo, Spec. Leg. 1, 36, Leg. All. 3, 47) Ac 17:27. Pass. εὑρέθην τοῖς ἐμὲ μὴ ζητοῦσιν *I have let myself be found by those who did not seek me* Ro 10:20 (Is 65:1).—As נִמְצָא *be found, appear, prove, be shown* (to be) (Cass. Dio 36, 27, 6; Dit., Syll.³ 736, 51; 1109, 73; 972, 65; POxy. 743, 25 [2 bc]; Jos., Bell. 3, 114) εὑρέθη ἐν γαστρὶ ἔχουσα *it was found that she was to become a mother* Mt 1:18. εὑρέθη μοι ἡ ἐντολὴ εἰς θάνατον (sc. οὖσα) *the commandment proved to be a cause for death to me* Ro 7:10. οὐχ εὑρέθησαν ὑποστρέψαντες; *were there not found to return?* Lk 17:18; cf. Ac 5:39; 1 Cor 4:2 (cf. Sir 44:20); 15:15; 2 Cor 5:3; Gal 2:17; 1 Pt 1:7; Rv 5:4; 1 Cl 9:3; 10:1; B 4:14; Hm 3:5 and oft. ἄσπιλοι αὐτῷ εὑρεθῆναι *be found unstained in his judgment* 2 Pt 3:14. σχήματι εὑρεθεὶς ὡς ἄνθρωπος *when he appeared in human form* Phil 2:7.

3. *find (for oneself), obtain*. The mid. is used in this sense in Attic wr. (Bl-D. §310, 1; cf. Rob. 814; Phryn. p. 140 L.); in our lit. it occurs in this sense only Hb 9:12. As a rule our lit. uses the act. in such cases (poets; Lucian, Lexiph. 18; LXX; Jos., Ant. 5, 41) τὴν ψυχήν Mt 10:39; 16:25. ἀνάπαυσιν (Sir 11:19; 22:13; 28:16; 33:26) ταῖς ψυχαῖς ὑμῶν *rest for your souls* 11:29. μετανοίας τόπον *have an opportunity to repent* or *for changing the (father's) mind* Hb 12:17. σκήνωμα τῷ θεῷ Ἰακώβ *maintain a dwelling for the God of Jacob* Ac 7:46b v.l. (Ps 131:5). χάριν *obtain grace* (SSol 8:10 v.l.) Hb 4:16. χάριν παρὰ τῷ θεῷ *obtain favor with God* Lk 1:30; also ἐνώπιον τοῦ θεοῦ Ac 7:46a (LXX as a rule ἐναντίον w. gen.). ἔλεος παρὰ κυρίου *obtain mercy from the Lord* 2 Ti 1:18 (cf. Gen 19:19; Da 3:38). M-M. B. 765.

εὐροκλύδων, ωνος, ὁ *Euroclydon*, explained as the southeast wind, that stirs up waves; another form is εὐρυκλύδων= the wind that stirs up broad waves; only Ac 27:14 v.l., where εὐρακύλων (q.v.) is the correct rdg., and the two other forms are prob. to be regarded as scribal errors (but s. Etym. Magn. p. 772, 30 s.v. τυφών: τυφών γάρ ἐστιν ἡ τοῦ ἀνέμου σφόδρα πνοή, ὃς καὶ εὐρυκλύδων καλεῖται).*

εὐρυκλύδων s. εὐροκλύδων.

εὐρύχωρος, ον broad, spacious, roomy (Aristot., H. Anim. 10, 5 p. 637a, 32; Diod. S. 19, 84, 6; LXX; Philo, Sacr. Abel. 61; Jos., Ant. 1, 262; Sib. Or. 3, 598) of a road spacious Mt 7: 13; τὸ εὐ. a large room (Appian, Bell. Civ. 4, 41 §171; 2 Ch 18: 9; 1 Esdr 5: 46), in which one can live comfortably and unmolested (cf. Ps 30: 9 ἐν εὐρυχώρῳ; Hos 4: 16) Hm 5, 1, 2. M-M.*

εὐσέβεια, ας, ἡ (Pre-Socr., Aeschyl.+; inscr., pap. as 'piety, reverence, loyalty, fear of God') in our lit and in the LXX only of the duty which man owes to God piety, godliness, religion (Pla., Rep. 10 p. 615c εἰς θεούς; X., Cyr. 8, 1, 25; Posidon.: 87 fgm. 59, 107 Jac. περὶ τὸ δαιμόνιον; Diod. S. 4, 39, 1 εἰς τὸν θεόν; 7, 14, 6; 19, 7, 3; Epict., Ench. 31, 1 περὶ τ. θεούς; Herm. Wr. 4, 7 πρὸς τ. θεόν; inscr. [Dit., Syll.³, Or. indices]; UPZ 41, 10 [161/0 bc] πρὸς τὸ θεῖον; PHermop. 52: 19; PTebt. 298, 45; PGiess. 66, 10; LXX, esp. 4 Macc.; Ep. Arist. 2; 42 πρὸς τ. θεὸν ἡμῶν al.; Philo, Deus Imm. 17 πρὸς θεόν; 69, Poster. Cai. 181; Jos., Ant. 18, 117, C. Ap. 1, 162 περὶ τὸ θεῖον) ἰδίᾳ εὐσεβείᾳ by our own piety Ac 3: 12; cf. διὰ τ. ἡμετέρας εὐ. 1 Cl 32: 4. ἐν πάσῃ εὐ. in all piety 1 Ti 2: 2; cf. 4: 7f; 6: 5f, 11. μετ' εὐσεβείας in godliness (cf. 2 Macc 12: 45) 1 Cl 15: 1. τὰ πρὸς εὐσέβειαν what belongs to piety 2 Pt 1: 3 (cf. Jos., Ant. 11, 120 τὸ πρὸς τ. θρησκείαν). ἔχειν μόρφωσιν εὐσεβίας have the outward form of religion= be religious only in appearance 2 Ti 3: 5 (cf. Philo, Plant. 70 εἰσί τινες τῶν ἐπιμορφαζόντων εὐσέβειαν). W. φιλοξενία 1 Cl 11: 1. Godliness as a result of steadfastness and cause of brotherly love 2 Pt 1: 6f (on the list of virtues cf. Lucian, Somn. 10; Dit., Or. 438, Dssm. LO 270 [LAE 322]). ἡ ἐν Χριστῷ εὐ. Christian piety 1 Cl 1: 2. περὶ τὴν εὐ. φιλοπονεῖν show a concern for piety 2 Cl 19: 1.—Godly faith, religion (Diod. S. 16, 60, 3; Jos., C. Ap. 1, 60) ἡ κατ' εὐσέβειαν διδασκαλία teaching which is in accordance with godly faith 1 Ti 6: 3; ἡ ἀλήθεια ἡ κατ' εὐ. Tit 1: 1. τὸ τῆς εὐ. μυστήριον the mystery of our religion 1 Ti 3: 16 (MOMassinger, Biblioth. Sacra 96, '40, 479–89).—Pl. godly acts 2 Pt 3: 11 (cf. PGM 13, 717).—OKern, D. Rel. der Griechen I '26, 273–90; FBräuninger, Unters. zu d. Schriften des Hermes Trismeg., Diss. Berlin '26, esp. on εὐσέβεια and γνῶσις; FTillmann, Past. Bonus 53, '42, 129–36; 161–5 ('Frömmigkt' in den Pastoralbr.; WFoerster, NTS 5, '59, 213–18 (Pastorals). S. ὅσιος, end. M-M. B. 1462.*

εὐσεβέω (trag.+; inscr., pap., LXX) be reverent, respectful, devout (w. εἰς, πρός, περί τινα) in our lit. only w. acc. show piety toward someone (trag.+; inscr., LXX).
1. of divine beings worship (Aeschyl., Ag. 338 τοὺς θεούς; Dit., Syll.³ 814, 36 εὐσεβῶν τ. θεούς; Sb 6828, 7; 4 Macc 11: 5; Philo, Spec. Leg. 1, 312, Praem. 40; Jos., Ant. 10, 45, C. Ap. 2, 125 τὸν θεόν) ὃν οὖν ἀγνοοῦντες εὐσεβεῖτε Ac 17: 23.
2. of men τὸν ἴδιον οἶκον εὐ. show piety toward the members of one's own household 1 Ti 5: 4. M-M.*

εὐσεβής, ές (Theognis, Pind.+; inscr., pap., LXX) devout, godly, pious, reverent in our lit. only of one's relation to God (Pla., Euthyphr. 5c, Phil. 39e; X., Apol. 19, Mem. 4, 6, 4; 4, 8, 11; Epict. 2, 17, 31; Lucian, De Calumn. 14; Dit., Syll.³ 821c, 3; 1052, 5 μύσται καὶ ἐπόπται εὐ.;

LXX; Ep. Arist. 233; Philo, Leg. All. 3, 209 al.; Jos., Ant. 9, 236) στρατιώτης εὐ. Ac 10: 7. W. φοβούμενος τ. θεόν vs. 2. πεποίθησις devout confidence 1 Cl 2: 3.—Subst. ὁ εὐ. the godly or devout man (X., Mem. 4, 6, 2, Cyr. 8, 1, 25; Diod. S. 1, 92, 5 οἱ εὐσεβεῖς; Suppl. Epigr. Gr. VIII 550, 4 [I bc] pl. = believers in Isis; Sir 13: 4; 39: 27; Pr 13: 19; Eccl 3: 16 v.l.; En. 102, 4; 103, 3) 2 Pt 2: 9; 2 Cl 19: 4. χῶρος εὐσεβῶν a place among the godly (s. χῶρος I) 1 Cl 50: 3; τὸ εὐ. (opp. τὸ κερδαλέον) piety, religion (Soph., Oed. Col. 1127 al.; Epict. 1, 29, 52; Philo, Agr. 128; Jos., Ant. 12, 43) 2 Cl 20: 4.—BSEaston, Pastoral Epistles, '47, 218. S. also ὅσιος, end. M-M.*

εὐσεβῶς adv. (Pind., X., Pla.+; inscr., pap., LXX) in our lit. of man's relation to God in a godly manner (oft. inscr. [Dit., Syll.³ index]; 4 Macc 7: 21 v.l.; Ep. Arist. 37; 261; Philo, Aet. M. 10) 1 Cl 61: 3. ζῆν 2 Ti 3: 12; Tit 2: 12 (s. βιοῦν εὐ.: Ps.-Pla., Axioch. 372a). W. δικαίως (Dit., Syll.³ 772; Jos., Ant. 8, 300) 1 Cl 62: 1. W. δικ. and σωφρόνως (Socrat., Ep. 15, 1 ἐβίωσε σωφρόνως κ. ὁσίως κ. εὐ.) Tit 2: 12. M-M.*

εὔσημος, ον (trag., Hippocr.+; inscr., pap.; Ps 80: 4) easily recognizable, clear, distinct (Aeschyl., Suppl. 714; Theophr., Caus. Pl. 6, 19, 5; Artem. 2, 44 εὐσήμου ὄντος τ. λόγου; Porphyr., Abst. 3, 4 of speech; Dit., Or. 90, 43; 665, 13) εὐ. λόγον διδόναι utter intelligible speech 1 Cor 14: 9. M-M.*

εὐσπλαγχνία, ας, ἡ (Ps.-Eur., Rhes. 192; Theod. Prodr. 8, 317 H.; Nicetas Eugen. 8, 238; Maspéro 97d, 69; Test. Zeb. 5: 1 al.) mercy w. γλυκύτης (as Theophilus, Ad Autol. 2, 14) 1 Cl 14: 3.*

εὔσπλαγχνος, ον (in the mng. 'with healthy intestines': Hippocr., Prorrh. 2, 6; Hesychius) tenderhearted, compassionate (so Prayer of Manasseh [=Ode 12]: 7; Test. Zeb. 9: 7; PGM 12, 283) of God (as in the pass. already given) w. ἐπιεικής 1 Cl 29: 1.—Of men (Test. Sim. 4: 4; Syntipas p. 106, 23; Leontios 46 p. 99, 15; Nicetas Eugen. 6, 193 H.) 54: 1. (W. φιλάδελφος, ταπεινόφρων) 1 Pt 3: 8. W. numerous other qualifications of deacons Pol 5: 2 and elders 6: 1 (for the mng. courageous in 1 Pt 3: 8 and Pol 6: 1 s. EGSelwyn, First Peter, '46, 188f). εὐ. εἴς τινα toward someone Eph 4: 32.*

εὐστάθεια, ας, ἡ (Epicurus in Plut., Mor. p. 135c; Epict. 2, 5, 9; Vett. Val. 183, 3; Dit., Syll.³ 1109, 15, Or. 669, 4; 45; PGiess. 87, 18; LXX; Ep. Arist. 216; 261; Philo; Jos., Ant. 18, 207) good disposition, tranquility, stability, firmness 1 Cl 61: 1 (w. εἰρήνη as Philo, De Jos. 57, In Flacc. 135); 65: 1.*

εὐσταθέω imper. εὐστάθει; impf. 3 pl. εὐσταθοῦσαν Mlt.-H. 194f) be stable, be tranquil, at rest (outwardly and inwardly: Dionys. Hal., Plut., Lucian, Epict.; Vett. Val. 42, 21; Herm. Wr. 466, 22 Sc.; Dit., Or. 54, 19, Syll.³ 708, 35; BGU 1764, 14 [I bc]; 2 Macc 14: 25; Jos., Ant. 15, 137 περὶ τ. βίον) lead a quiet life Hm 5, 2, 2; be at rest (in contrast to affliction) s 7: 3; be calm (Epict. 1, 29, 61), or stand firm εὐστάθει IPol 4: 1. Of sheep οὐκ εὐσταθοῦσαν they had no peace Hs 6, 2, 7.*

εὐσταθής, ές (Hom.+; LXX) stable, firm, calm τὸ εὐσταθές calmness, composure (Epict., Ench. 33, 11; Philo, Conf. Lingu. 43) MPol 7: 2.*

εὐσυνείδητος, ον with a good conscience (M. Ant. 6, 30, 15) εὐσυνείδητον εἶναι have a good conscience IMg 4. ἔν τινι about someone IPhld 6: 3.*

εὐσχημονέω (Pla., Leg. 732c; Menand.; Philod.; PSI V 541, 5; not LXX) *behave with dignity* or *decorum*; in our lit. only as rdg. of 𝔓⁴⁶ in 1 Cor 13: 5 for ἀσχημονεῖ. If it is not a scribal error here, it must have the sense *behave in an affected manner, play the gentleman* or *lady* (cf. εὐσχήμων 2), which is not found elsewh. S. ADebrunner, Con. Neot. XI, '47, 37–41.*

εὐσχημόνως adv. (Aristoph., Vesp. 1210; X., Mem. 3, 12, 4, Cyr. 1, 3, 8 al.; Epict. 2, 5, 23; Dit., Syll.³ 598E, 5 al.; 717, 14; Jos., Ant. 15, 102) *decently, becomingly* εὐ. περιπατεῖν *behave decently* Ro 13: 13 (as of one properly attired; s. εὐσχημοσύνη); 1 Th 4: 12 (Dit., Syll.³ 1019, 7ff ἀναστρέφεσθαι εὐ.). πάντα εὐ. καὶ κατὰ τάξιν γινέσθω *everything is to be done properly and in good order* 1 Cor 14: 40 (Dit., Syll.³ 736, 42 εὐ. πάντα γίνηται; Ael. Aristid. 46 p. 364 D.: εὐ. καὶ τεταγμένος [i.e. ταῦτα ἐπράττετο]). M-M.*

εὐσχημοσύνη, ης, ἡ (Hippocr., Pla., X.+; Diod. S. 5, 32, 7; Epict. 4, 9, 11; Dit., Or. 339, 32; Inscr. Gr. 545, 8f [II bc]; 4 Macc 6: 2; Ep. Arist. 284) *propriety, decorum, presentability* of clothing (cf. Maximus Tyr. 15, 3b; Dit., Syll.³ 547, 37; 4 Macc 6: 2) of modest concealment τὰ ἀσχήμονα ἡμῶν εὐ. περισσοτέραν ἔχει *our unpresentable* (parts) *receive greater presentability* (= are treated with greater modesty) 1 Cor 12: 23. M-M.*

εὐσχήμων, ον, gen. ονος (Eur., Hippocr.+; inscr., pap.; Pr 11: 25)—1. *proper, presentable* τὰ εὐ. (sc. μέλη) *the presentable parts* 1 Cor 12: 24 (cf. Socrat., Ep. 31 tongue and head τὸ θειότατον . . . τῶν μερῶν ἁπάντων; Diod. S. 20, 63, 3 head and face τὰ κυριώτατα μέρη τοῦ σώματος; Maximus Tyr. 40, 2f κεφαλή and ὄμματα are nobler than μηροί and σφυρά. τὸ εὐ. *good order* (cf. Epict. 4, 1, 163; 4, 12, 6) 7: 35.
2. *prominent, of high standing* or *repute, noble* (Plut., Mor. 309c; Vett. Val. index; PFlor. 61, 61 [85 ad]; 16, 20; PHamb. 37, 7; Dit., Or. 485, 3 ἄνδρα ἀπὸ προγόνων εὐσχήμονα; Jos., Vi. 32; Phryn. p. 333 L.) Ac 13: 50; 17: 12 (*well-to-do*; VeraFVanderlip, Amer. Stud. in Papyrology 12, '72, 25), 34 D. εὐ. βουλευτής *a prominent counsellor* (Joseph of Arimathaea) Mk 15: 43.—HGreeven, TW II 768–70. M-M.*

εὐτάκτως adv. (since Aeschyl., Pers. 399; Hippocr.; X., Cyr. 2, 2, 3; Epict. 3, 24, 95; Dit., Syll.³ 717, 25; 736, 42; PTebt. 5, 55; BGU 1147, 12) *in good order* ἐγένοντο ἀμφότερα εὐ. *both originated in good order* 1 Cl 42: 2 (on the pl. of the verb w. the neut. pl. s. ἐσθίω 1ba). As a military t.t.: of soldiers εὐ. ἐπιτελεῖν τὰ διατασσόμενα *carry out orders with good discipline* 37: 2.*

εὐταξία, ας, ἡ (Thu.+; inscr., pap.; 2 Macc 4: 37; 3 Macc 1: 10; Ep. Arist. 246; Philo, De Jos. 204; Jos., Bell. 2, 151) *good order*, esp. also (military t.t.) *good discipline* (Thu. 6, 72, 4; Ps.-Pla., Alc. 1 p. 122c al.; Jos., Bell. 2, 529) IEph 6: 2.*

εὔτεκνος, ον *with many children, w. good children, fortunate because of children* (Eur.+; Philo). In ISm 13: 2 the word is understood by Zahn and Hilgenfeld as an adj., but by Lghtf., Funk, Krüger, Bihlmeyer as a proper name, because εὐ. as an adj. seems not to fit well into the context. Εὐ. as a name is, however, unattested to date; but s. Dit., Or. 53 and the grammarian Εὐτέκνιος in Pauly-W. VI 1492.*

εὐτόνως adv. (Aristoph., Plut. 1095; X., Hier. 9, 6 al.; Josh 6: 8; Philo, Agr. 70; Jos., Bell. 4, 423) *powerfully,*

vigorously, vehemently εὐ. κατηγορεῖν τινος *accuse someone vehemently* Lk 23: 10. εὐ. διακατελέγχεσθαί τινι *refute someone vigorously* Ac 18: 28. M-M.*

εὐτραπελία, ας, ἡ (Hippocr.+, mostly in a good sense: 'wittiness', 'facetiousness'; so also Posidipp. Com. [III bc], fgm. 28, 5 K.; Diod. S. 15, 6, 5; Philo, Leg. ad Gai. 361; Jos., Ant. 12, 173; 214. Acc. to Aristot., Eth. Nic. 2, 7, 13 it is the middle term betw. the extremes of buffoonery [βωμολοχία] and boorishness [ἀγροικία]; acc. to Aristot., Rhet. 2, 12 it is πεπαιδευμένη ὕβρις) in our lit. only in a bad sense *coarse jesting, buffoonery* Eph 5: 4. M-M.*

Εὔτυχος, ου, ὁ (IG III 1095; 1113; 1122 al.; CIL III 2784; 3028 al.; PPetr. I 12, 8; Preisigke, Namenbuch; Joseph.) *Eutychus*, a young man in Troas Ac 20: 9. M-M.*

εὐφημία, ας, ἡ (Pind.+ in var. mngs.; Sym.; Ep. Arist. 191; Philo; Jos., Ant. 16, 14; 17, 200) *good report, good repute* (so Diod. S. 1, 2, 4; Aelian, V.H. 3, 47; Dit., Or. 339, 30; Inscr. Gr. 394, 39; PLond. 891, 9 ἡ εὐφημία σου περιεκύκλωσεν τ. κόσμον ὅλον) opp. δυσφημία 2 Cor 6: 8. M-M.*

εὔφημος, ον (Aeschyl.+ in var. mngs.; inscr.; Sym. Ps 62: 6; Philo; Jos., C. Ap. 2, 248) ὅσα εὔφημα Phil 4: 8 can be interpreted in various ways: *auspicious, well-sounding, praiseworthy, attractive, appealing.* M-M.*

εὐφορέω 1 aor. εὐφόρησα *bear good crops, yield well, be fruitful* (Hippocr.+; Philo, De Jos. 159; Jos., Bell. 2, 592) of farm land (Philostrat., Vi. Apoll. 6, 39 p. 251, 8 of γῆ) Lk 12: 16. M-M.*

εὐφραίνω 1 aor. inf. εὐφρᾶναι Hm 12, 3, 4; B 21: 9; 1 aor. pass. ηὐφράνθην; 1 fut. εὐφρανθήσομαι (Hom.+; inscr., pap., LXX).
1. act. *gladden, cheer* (*up*) τινά *someone* (Hom.+; Dit., Or. 504, 10 εὐφρᾶναι ὑμᾶς; PFlor. 154 II, 12; LXX; En. 107, 3; Philo, Spec. Leg. 3, 186; Jos., Ant. 4, 117) τίς ὁ εὐφραίνων με; *who makes me glad?* 2 Cor 2: 2. εἰς τὸ εὐφρᾶναι ὑμᾶς *so to cheer you* B 21: 9. Of the commandments of the angel of repentance δυνάμεναι εὐφρᾶναι καρδίαν ἀνθρώπου *be able to gladden the heart of a man* Hm 12, 3, 4 (cf. Ps 18: 9; 103: 15 εὐφραίνει καρδίαν ἀνθρώπου; Pr 23: 15; Sir 40: 20; Aelian, V.H. 1, 32; Ramsay, Phrygia II 386 no. 232, 19 τὴν ψυχὴν εὐφραίνετε πάντοτε).
2. pass. (Hom.+; inscr., pap., LXX, Philo; Jos., Bell. 1, 91) *be glad, enjoy oneself, rejoice* ἐπί τινι (Aristoph., Acharn. 5; X., Symp. 7, 5; Epict. 4, 4, 46; BGU 1080, 7; Sir 16: 1, 2; 18: 32; 1 Macc 11: 44; 12: 12; Philo, Mos. 1. 247; Test. Levi 18: 13) Rv 18: 20; B 10: 11. ἐπί τινα (Is 61: 10; Ps 31: 11) Rv 18: 20 t.r. ἔν τινι *in, about,* or *over someone* or *someth.* (X., Hier. 1, 16; BGU 248, 28; Sir 14: 5; 39: 31; 51: 15, 29; Philo, Spec. Leg. 2, 194) Hs 9, 18, 4; Rv 18: 20 A. ἐν τοῖς ἔργοις τῶν χειρῶν Ac 7: 41; ἐν τοῖς δικαιώμασιν αὐτοῦ εὐ. *take delight in his ordinances* B 4: 11 (cf. Ps 18: 9). διά τινος *be gladdened by someth.* = *rejoice in someth.* (X., Hier. 1, 8; Philo, Spec. Leg. 2, 194) 1: 8. Abs. (PGM 3, 24; 4, 2389; En. 25, 6; Philo, Cher. 86; Sib. Or. 3, 785) Lk 15: 32; Ac 2: 26 (Ps 15: 9); Ro 15: 10 (Dt 32: 43); Gal 4: 27 (Is 54: 1); Rv 11: 10; 12: 12; 1 Cl 52: 2 (Ps 68: 32); 2 Cl 2: 1 (Is 54: 1); 19: 4; Dg 12: 9; Hv 3, 4, 2; m 5, 1, 2; s 5, 7, 1; 9, 11, 8. Esp. of the joys of eating (Od. 2, 311; X., Cyr. 8, 7, 12; Dt 14: 26; 27: 7) φάγε, πίε, εὐφραίνου *eat, drink, be merry* Lk 12: 19 (cf. Eccl 8: 15; Eur., Alcest. 788); cf. 15: 23f, 29; 16: 19.—RBultmann, TW II 770–3. M-M.*

Εὐφράτης, ου, ὁ (פְּרָת) (Hdt.+; Dit., Or. 54, 13f; 17; Gen 2: 14 al.; LXX; Philo; Joseph.; Sib. Or.) *the Euphrates,* the westernmost of the two rivers that include Mesopotamia betw. them. ὁ ποταμὸς ὁ μέγας Εὐ. *the great river Euphrates* (Gen 15: 18; Ex 23: 31.—Cf. Diod. S. 17, 75, 2 μέγας ποταμὸς . . . Στιβοίτης) Rv 9: 14; 16: 12.*

εὐφροσύνη, ης, ἡ (Hom.+; Lucian; M. Ant. 8, 26, 1; PLeipz. 119 II, 1; LXX, Ep. Arist., Philo; Jos., Ant. 15, 50; 17, 112; Test. 12 Patr.; Sib. Or. 3, 786) *joy, gladness, cheerfulness* Ac 2: 28 (Ps 15: 11); 14: 17 (cf. Sir 30: 22 εὐφροσύνη καρδίας. Cf. καί I 1d). W. ἀγαλλίασις 1 Cl 18: 8 (Ps 50: 10); B 1: 6. ἀγάπη εὐφροσύνης *love that goes with joy* ibid. τέκνα εὐφροσύνης *children of gladness=* children for whom gladness is in store 7: 1. ἔργον εὐφροσύνης *a work of gladness* 10: 11; ἡμέραν ἄγειν εἰς εὐ. *celebrate a day with gladness* 15: 9 (s. Jdth 12: 13 and Esth 9: 18). M-M.*

εὐχαριστέω 1 aor. εὐχαρίστησα (ηὐχ- Ro 1: 21 s. Mlt.-H. 191f); 1 aor. pass. subj. 3 sg. εὐχαριστηθῇ.
1. *be thankful, feel obligated to thank* (decrees of the Byzantines in Demosth. 18, 91f). This mng. is poss. in some passages, but is not absolutely necessary in any; e.g. Lk 18: 11; Ro 16: 4. The latter verse is the only passage in our lit. that deals w. thankfulness toward men (as 2 Macc 12: 31). As a rule εὐ. is used of thanks to God, in the sense
2. *give thanks, render* or *return thanks* (as 'return thanks' since Polyb. 16, 25, 1; Posidon. in Athen. 5 p. 213E; Diod. S. 20, 34, 5; Plut., Mor. 505D; Epict., inscr., pap., LXX, Philo; Jos., Ant. 20, 12. Cf. Phryn. p. 18 L.—In a relig. sense: Diod. S. 14, 29, 4; 16, 11, 1 τοῖς θεοῖς περὶ τῶν ἀγαθῶν; Epict. 1, 4, 32; 1, 10, 3; 2, 23, 5 τῷ θεῷ; Artem. 4, 2 p. 206, 4 θῦε καὶ εὐχαρίστει; Herm. Wr. 1, 29 τ. θεῷ; Dit., Syll.³ 995, 11 τ. θεοῖς; 1173, 9f; UPZ 59, 10 [168 BC] τ. θεοῖς; PTebt. 56, 9; BGU 423, 6 τ. κυρίῳ Σεράπιδι; PGM 13, 706 [w. δέομαι]; Jdth 8: 25; 2 Macc 1: 11; 10: 7; 3 Macc 7: 16; Ep. Arist. 177 ὑμῖν, . . . τῷ θεῷ; Philo, Spec. Leg. 2, 204; 3, 6 θεῷ; Jos., Ant. 3, 193 τ. θεῷ; Test. Jos. 8: 5 τῷ κυρίῳ) αὐτῷ (of Jesus, who reveals himself as God in the miracle) Lk 17: 16. τῷ θεῷ (μου) Ac 28: 15; 1 Cor 14: 18; Phil 1: 3; Col 1: 3, 12; 3: 17; Phlm 4; 1 Cl 38: 4; 41: 1 v.l.; B 7: 1; IEph 21: 1; Hv 4, 1, 4. Elliptically Ro 1: 21, where τῷ θεῷ is to be understood fr. the preceding ὡς θεόν (though εὐ. occasionally is used w. the acc. *praise someone w. thanks:* Dit., Syll.³ 1172, 3 εὐχαριστεῖ Ἀσκληπιόν. Cat. Cod. Astr. VII 177, 17); 1 Th 5: 18; 2 Cl 18: 1. Esp. of grace before meals, w. dat. added τῷ θεῷ Ac 27: 35; Ro 14: 6. Abs. Mt 15: 36; 26: 27; Mk 8: 6, 7 v.l.; 14: 23; Lk 22: 17, 19; J 6: 11, 23; 1 Cor 11: 24; D 9: 1; Hs 2: 6; 5, 1, 1. W. mention of the obj., for which one gives thanks τινί τι (*to*) *someone for someth.* Hs 7: 5 (εὐ. τι='thank for someth.' is found so far only in Hippocr., Ep. 17, 46; s. 2 Cor 1: 11 below). περί τινος *for someone, because of someone* (Philo, Spec. Leg. 1, 211) 1 Th 1: 2; also foll by ὅτι *because* (Ps.-Callisth. 2, 22, 11; Berl. Pap.: APF 12, '37, 247) Ro 1: 8; 1 Cor 1: 4f; 2 Th 1: 3; 2: 13. ὑπέρ τινος w. gen. of the pers. *on whose behalf* one thanks 2 Cor 1: 11; Eph 1: 16; also foll. by ὅτι *because* IPhld 11: 1; ISm 10: 1. ὑπέρ τινος w. gen. of the thing *for someth.* (Philo, Congr. Erud. Gr. 96) 1 Cor 10: 30; Eph 5: 20; D 9: 2f; 10: 2. W. ἐπί τινι *because of, for* (Inschr. v. Perg. 224A, 14; Sb 7172, 25 [217 BC] εὐχαριστῶν τοῖς θεοῖς ἐπὶ τῷ συντελέσαι αὐτοὺς ἃ ἐπηγγείλαντο αὐτῷ; UPZ 59, 10f [168 BC]; Philo, Spec. Leg. 1, 67; Jos., Ant. 1, 193) 1 Cor 1: 4; Hs 9, 14, 3. (W. τινί and) ὅτι foll. Lk 18: 11 (cf. IQH 7, 34); J 11: 41; 1 Cor 1: 14; 1 Th 2: 13; Rv 11: 17; 1 Cl 38: 2; IPhld 6: 3; D 10: 4. Abs. σὺ εὐχαριστεῖς

you offer a prayer of thanksgiving 1 Cor 14: 17; cf. D 10: 1, 3, 7. As a parenthetical clause εὐχαριστῶ τῷ θεῷ *thanks be to God* vs. 18. Pass. (cf. Dssm., B 119 [BS 122]; Philo, Rer. Div. Her. 174 ἵνα ὑπὲρ τ. ἀγαθῶν ὁ θεὸς εὐχαριστῆται) ἵνα ἐκ πολλῶν προσώπων τὸ εἰς ἡμᾶς χάρισμα διὰ πολλῶν εὐχαριστηθῇ ὑπὲρ ἡμῶν *in order that thanks may be given by many persons on our behalf for the blessing granted to us* 2 Cor 1: 11 (on εὐ. τι s. above).—PSchubert, Form and Function of the Pauline Thanksgivings '39. In a few passages the word could also mean
3. *pray gener.* (PTebt. 56, 9 [II BC] εὐχαριστῆσαι τοῖς θεοῖς; PLond. 413, 3; 418, 3; BGU 954, 4).—FJAHort, Εὐχαριστία, εὐχαριστεῖν (in Philo): JTS 3, '02, 594-8; ThSchermann, Εὐχαριστία and εὐχαριστεῖν: Philol. 69, '10, 375-410; GHBoobyer, 'Thanksgiving' and the 'Glory of God' in Paul, Diss. Heidelb. '29. M-M. B. 1166.*

εὐχαριστία, ας, ἡ (since Hippocr. and Menand., fgm. 693 K.; inscr.; PLond. 1178, 25 [194 AD]; LXX; Philo; Joseph.).
1. *thankfulness, gratitude* (decrees of the Byzantines in Demosth. 18, 91; Polyb. 8, 12, 8; Diod. S. 17, 59, 7; Dit., Or. 227, 6; 199, 31 [I AD] ἔχω πρὸς τ. μέγιστον θεόν μου Ἄρην εὐχαριστίαν; BGU 1764, 21 [I BC]; 2 Macc 2: 27; Esth 8: 12d; Philo, Leg. All. 1, 84) μετὰ πάσης εὐ. *with all gratitude* Ac 24: 3.
2. *the rendering of thanks, thanksgiving* (Dit., Syll.³ 798, 5 [c. 37 AD] εἰς εὐχαριστίαν τηλικούτου θεοῦ εὑρεῖν ἴσας ἀμοιβάς; Wsd 16: 28; Sir 37: 11; Philo, Spec. Leg. 1, 224; Jos., Ant. 1, 156; 2, 346; 3, 65; 4, 212) abs. Eph 5: 4 (cf. OCasel, BZ 18, '29, 84f, who, after Origen, equates εὐχαριστία w. εὐχαριστία='the mark of fine training'). τῷ θεῷ *toward God* 2 Cor 9: 11. μετὰ εὐχαριστίας *with thanksgiving* (Philo, Spec. Leg. 1, 144) Phil 4: 6; 1 Ti 4: 3f; ἐν εὐ. Col 4: 2. περισσεύειν ἐν εὐ. *overflow w. thanksg.* 2: 7; περισσεύειν τὴν εὐ. *increase the thanksg.* 2 Cor 4: 15. εὐχαριστίαν τῷ θεῷ ἀνταποδοῦναι περὶ ὑμῶν *render thanks to God for you* 1 Th 3: 9. Also εὐ. διδόναι (Theodor. Prodr. 8, 414 H. θεοῖς) Rv 4: 9. Esp. *prayer of thanksgiving* (Herm. Wr. 1, 29) 1 Cor 14: 16; Rv 7: 12. Pl. 2 Cor 9: 12; 1 Ti 2: 1.
3. *the observance and elements of the Lord's Supper: Lord's Supper, Eucharist* ποτήριον τῆς εὐχ. 1 Cor 10: 16 v.l.—D 9: 1, 5; IEph 13: 1; IPhld 4; ISm 8: 1. W. προσευχή 7: 1. Cf. Justin, Apol. 1, 65; 66; RKnopf, Hdb. on D 9: 1.—JRéville, Les origines de l'Eucharistie '08; MGoguel, L'Euch. des origines à Justin mart. '09; FWieland, D. vorirenäische Opferbegriff '09; GLoeschcke, Zur Frage nach der Einsetzung u. Herkunft der Eucharistie: ZWTh 54, '12, 193-205; ALoisy, Les origines de la Cène euch.: Congr. d'Hist. du Christ. I '28, 77-95. GHCMacGregor, Eucharistic Origins '29; KGGoetz, D. Ursprung d. kirchl. Abendmahls '29; HHuber, D. Herrenmahl im NT, Diss. Bern '29; WGoossens, Les origines de l'Euch. '31; RHupfeld, D. Abendmahlsfeier, ihr ursprüngl. Sinn usw. '35; JoachJeremias, D. Abendmahlsworte Jesu '35, ²'49, ³'60 (Eng. transl. The Eucharistic Words of Jesus, AEhrhardt '55; cf. also KGKuhn, ThLZ 75, '50, 399-408), D. paul. Abdm.—e. Opferdarbtg?: StKr 108, '37, 124-41; AArnold, D. Ursprung d. Chr. Abdmahls '37, ²'39; LDTPoot, Het oudchristelijk Avondmaal '36; ELohmeyer, D. Abdm. in d. Urgem.: JBL 56, '37, 217-52; EKäsemann, D. Abdm. im NT: Abdm. gemeinschaft? '37, 60-93; HSasse, D. Abdm. im NT: V. Sakr. d. Altars '41, 26-78; EGaugler, D. Abdm. im NT '43; NJohansson, Det urkristna nattvardsfirandet '44; ESchweizer, D. Abdm. e. Vergegenwärtigg des Todes Jesu od. e. eschat. Freudenmahl?: ThZ 2, '46, 81-101; ThPreiss, ThZ 4, '48, 81-101 (Eng. transl., Was the Last Supper a Paschal Meal? in Life in Christ,

chap. 5, '54, 81-99); F-JLeenhardt, Le Sacrement de la Sainte Cène, '48; GWalther, Jesus, das Passalamm des Neuen Bundes usw., '50; RBultmann, Theol. of the NT (transl. KGrobel), '51, I, 144-52; AJBHiggins, The Lord's Supper in the NT, '52; OCullmann, Early Christian Worship (transl. ATodd and JTorrance), '53; HLessig, D. Abendmahlsprobleme im Lichte der NTlichen Forschung seit 1900, Diss. Bonn, '53; ESchweizer, ThLZ 79, '54, 577-92 (lit.); GBornkamm, Herrenmahl u. Kirche bei Paulus, NTS 2, '55/'56, 202-6; CFDMoule, The Judgment Theme in the Sacraments, in Background of the NT and its Eschatology (CHDodd-Festschr.) '56, 464-81; MBlack, The Arrest and Trial of Jesus and the Date of the Last Supper, in NT Essays (TWManson memorial vol.) '59, 19-33; PNeuenzeit, Das Herrenmahl, '60; The Eucharist in the NT, five essays transl. fr. French by EMStewart, '64; EJKilmartin, The Eucharist in the Primitive Church, '65; BIersel, Nov Test 7, '64/'65, 167-94; HBraun, Qumran II, '66, 29-54; JFAudet, TU 73, '59, 643-62; HSchürmann, D. Paschamahlbericht, '53, D. Einsetzungsbericht, '55, Jesu Abschiedsrede, '57 (all Lk 22); HPatsch, Abendmahl u. Historischer Jesus, '72. S. also the lit. on ἀγάπη II. M-M.*

εὐχάριστος, ον (Hdt.+; inscr., pap., Pr 11: 16; Philo) *thankful* (so X., Cyr. 8, 3, 49; Dit., Or. 267, 36; 339, 60 and oft. in inscr. of cities and their people who are grateful to their benefactors; Jos., Ant. 16, 162) εὐχάριστοι γίνεσθε Col 3: 15 (Inschr. v. Priene 103, 8 [c. 100 BC] γενόμενος ὁ δῆμος εὐ.; Philo, Spec. Leg. 2, 209). M-M.*

εὐχερής, ές, gen. **ους** (Soph., Hippocr.+; inscr.; UPZ 162 VIII, 13 [117 BC] εὐχερῶς; LXX).
1. *easy* εὐχερές ἐστιν w. inf. foll. *it is easy* (Batr. 62; Dit., Syll.³ 674, 65; Jdth 7: 10) ὑμῖν εὐχερές ἐστιν ποιῆσαι *it is easy for you to do* IRo 1: 2.
2. *easily inclined, prone, reckless* (Demosth. 21, 103; Aristot., Metaph. 1025a, 2; PGM 4, 2504 εὐχερῶς; Philo, Somn. 1, 13; Jos., Vi. 167) ἐν καταλαλιᾳ *prone to slander* B 20: 2.*

εὐχή, ῆς, ἡ (Hom.+; inscr., pap., LXX)—1. *prayer* (X., Symp. 8, 15; Diod. S. 20, 50, 6 εὐχὰς τοῖς θεοῖς ἐποιοῦντο; Dio Chrys. 19[36], 36; Dit., Or. 383, 233 [I BC]; BGU 531 I, 5 [I AD]; PGiess. 23, 5 [II AD]; LXX; Philo, Sacr. Abel. 53 and oft. [on Philo: CWLarson, JBL 65, '46, 185-203]; Jos., Bell. 7, 155, Ant. 15, 52; Test. 12 Patr.) ἡ εὐ. τῆς πίστεως *the prayer offered in faith* Js 5: 15; πληρῶσαι τὴν εὐ. *finish a prayer* MPol 15: 1. Pl. D 15: 4; νήφειν πρὸς τὰς εὐ. *be watchful in prayer(s)* Pol 7: 2.
2. *oath, vow* (X., Mem. 2, 2, 10; Diod. S. 1, 83, 2; Jos., Bell. 2, 313) Ac 18: 18; 21: 23 (JThUbbink, NThSt 5, '22, 137-9). θυσίαι εὐχῶν *votive offerings* (cf. Lev 22: 29.—Diod. S. 3, 55, 8 θυσίαι as the result of εὐχαί) 1 Cl 41: 2. ἀποδιδόναι τῷ ὑψίστῳ τὰς εὐ. (ἀποδίδωμι 1) 52: 3 (Ps 49: 14).—AWendel, D. israel.-jüd. Gelübde '31. HSalmanowitsch, D. Nasiräat nach Bibel u. Talmud, Diss. Giessen '31; HHGowen, The Hair-Offering: Journ. of the Soc. of Oriental Research 11, '27, 1-20; HGreeven, TW II 775f. M-M.*

εὔχομαι impf. εὐχόμην (Ac 27: 29 Tdf., s. Proleg. p. 121) and ηὐχόμην Ro 9: 3; Ac 27: 29; 1 aor. εὐξάμην (Hom.+; inscr., pap., LXX, Ep. Arist., Philo, Joseph., Test. 12 Patr.).
1. *pray* τῷ θεῷ (Hom.; Thu. 3, 58, 5; X., Cyr. 7, 1, 1; Plut., Pericl. 8, 6; Epict. 1, 29, 37; Dit., Or. 219, 21; POxy. 1298, 4; PRyl. 244, 3; Sir 38: 9; Philo, Ebr. 125; Jos., Ant. 14, 22; 18, 211.—On εὐχ. τ. θεοῖς cf. GGhedini, Aegyptus 2, '21, 191ff) Ac 26: 29; IRo 1: 1. πρὸς τ.

θεόν *to God* (X., Mem. Ī, 3, 2, Symp. 4, 55; 2 Macc 9: 13; 15: 27; Ep. Arist. 305) 2 Cor 13: 7. That which is requested of God is expressed either by the simple acc. *pray for someth.* (Pind.+; Jos., Ant. 12, 98) 2 Cor 13: 9; or by the acc. w. inf. (Hom.+) Ac 26: 29; 2 Cor 13: 7. W. inf. alone ITr 10: 1. ὑπέρ τινος πρὸς τὸν κύριον Hs 5, 3, 7 (cf. Aeschin. 3, 18 ὑπέρ τινος πρὸς τοὺς θεούς). εὐ. ὑπέρ τινος *for someone* (X., Mem. 2, 2, 10; Longus 2, 24, 2; Diog. L. 8, 9 εὐ. ὑπὲρ ἑαυτῶν; PMMeyer, Griech. Texte aus Aegypt. '16, no. 24, 4; Jos., Ant. 11, 119) w. ὅπως foll. (cf. Epict. 2, 16, 13; Polyaenus 1, 26 εὐ. Διὶ ὅπως; PRyl. 244, 3 εὔχομαι θεοῖς πᾶσιν ὅπως ὑγιαίνοντας ὑμᾶς ἀπολάβω; Jos., Ant. 11, 17) Js 5: 16 v.l.; also ἵνα (cf. Dionys. Hal. 9, 53; Epict. 2, 6, 12; Ep. Arist. 45) Hs 5, 2, 10.—For lit. s. προσεύχομαι, end.
2. *wish* (Pind.+; inscr., pap., Philo; perh. Jos., Ant. 12, 98) τί *for someth.* (X., Hell. 5, 1, 3) IMg 1: 2. W. inf. foll. (Περὶ ὕψους p. 16, 11 V.; Alexandr. graffito in UvWilamowitz, SAB '02, 1098 εὔχομαι κἀγὼ ἐν τάχυ σὺν σοὶ εἶναι; Sib. Or. 4, 111) ITr 10. Foll. by acc. and inf. (X., An. 1, 4, 7; Ep. 46 of Apoll. of Ty.: Philostrat. I 355, 24 K.) Ac 27: 29; 3 J 2 (cf. POxy. 292, 11 [perh. 25 AD] πρὸ δὲ πάντων ὑγιαίνειν σε εὔχομαι; PFay. 117, 27; PMich. 203, 2); IEph 1: 3; 2: 1; ITr 12: 3; IRo 5: 2; ISm 11: 1; 13: 2; IPol 8: 3; MPol 22: 1. Foll. by nom. and inf. Ro 9: 3, on the analogy of θέλω w. inf. (cf. Aeschyl., Eum. 429; TReub. 1, 7)=opt. w. ἄν. Foll. by ἵνα μή IPhld 6: 3. As a greeting-formula εὐ. πλεῖστα χαίρειν IMg inscr.; ITr inscr. M-M.*

εὔχρηστος, ον (Hippocr.+; inscr., pap., LXX; Ep. Arist. 136; Joseph.) *useful, serviceable* abs. (opp. ἄχρηστος) Hv 3, 6, 7. Of gold Hv 4, 3, 4. τινί *to or for someone or someth.*: w. dat. of the pers. (PPetr. III 53[n], 5) σκεῦος εὐ. τ. δεσπότῃ *a vessel that is useful to the master* 2 Ti 2: 21. W. a play on the name Onesimus (opp. ἄχρηστος) σοί κ. ἐμοὶ εὐ. Phlm 11.—Hv 3, 6, 6b; m 5, 1, 6; s 9, 26, 4. Of members εὐ. ὅλῳ τ. σώματι 1 Cl 37: 5. εὐ. γίνεσθαι w. dat. of the pers. (Inschr. v. Priene 102, 5 [c. 100 BC] προγόνων γεγενημένων εὐχρήστων τῷ δήμῳ) Hv 3, 6, 6c; 7b; m 5, 1, 5; s 9, 15, 6. εὐ. εἴς τι *for someth.* (Diod. S. 5, 40, 1; Inscr. Rom. IV 818, 23 εἰς χρίας κυριακὰς εὔχρηστον γενόμενον; Wsd 13: 13; Jos., Ant. 4, 281) 2 Ti 4: 11; Hv 3, 5, 5; 3, 6, 1; 6a. M-M.*

εὐψυχέω (BGU 1097, 15 [I AD] ἐγὼ εὐψυχοῦσα παραμένω; POxy. 115, 1; Poll. 3, 28, 135; Jos., Ant. 11, 241) *be glad, have courage* Phil 2: 19. Imper. εὐψύχει (on grave inscr.='farewell': CIG 4467 and very oft. in Sb [II Allgem. Wörterliste p. 404]) *have courage* Hv 1, 3, 2. M-M.*

εὐωδία, ας, ἡ (X., Pla.+; LXX; En. 25, 4; Philo) *aroma, fragrance* ὀσμὴ εὐωδίας (=רֵיחַ הַנִּיחֹחַ Gen 8: 21; Ex 29: 18 al. of the fragrance fr. a sacrifice, pleasing to God) *a fragrant odor* w. θυσία (Test. Levi 3: 6) Phil 4: 18; Eph 5: 2; B 2: 10. Of the apostles Χριστοῦ εὐ. ἐσμὲν τῷ θεῷ *we are the aroma of Christ for God* 2 Cor 2: 15 (ἐν εὐωδίᾳ χρηστότητος κυρίου Ode of Solomon 11, 15). When Polycarp was burned at the stake, a similar *fragrance* was noted MPol 15: 2.—ELohmeyer, Vom göttl. Wohlgeruch: Sitzgs.-Ber. d. Heidelb. Ak. '19, Abhdlg. 9; Rtzst., Erlösungsmyst. 34; 143ff, Mysterienrel.³ 82f; 393ff; HKees, Totenglauben u. Jenseitsvorstellungen d. alt. Ägypter '26, 148; HVorwahl, ARW 31, '34, 400f; PDeBoer, Studies in the Religion of Anc. Israel, '72, 37-47 (fragrance); A Stumpff, TW II 808-10. M-M.*

εὐώνυμος, ον (Hes., Pind.+) *left*, as opposed to 'right' (Aeschyl., Hdt.+; Dit., Syll.³ 827 III, 9; 16; 1167; PRyl. 63, 4; LXX; Philo; Jos., Ant. 12, 429) Rv 10: 2. καταλιπόντες αὐτὴν (i.e. τὴν Κύπρον) εὐώνυμον leaving it on the left Ac 21: 3. ἐξ εὐωνύμων at the left (Diod. S. 4, 56, 3; Ex 14: 22, 29; 2 Ch 4: 8 al.) Mt 20: 23; 25: 33, 41; 27: 38 (cf. 2 Ch 3: 17); Mk 10: 40; Hv 3, 2, 4. ἐξ εὐωνύμων τινός at someone's left (2 Km 16: 6; 3 Km 22: 19 al.) Mt 20: 21; Mk 15: 27. A quite isolated use: εὐώνυμα on the left (w. δεξιά='on the right') Hs 9, 12, 8. M-M. B. 866.*

εὐωχία, ας, ἡ (Aristoph., Hippocr.+; inscr., pap., LXX, Philo; Diod. S. 2, 26, 4; Jos., Ant. 6, 163, C. Ap. 2, 138) banquet, feasting Jd 12 v.l.*

ἔφαγον s. ἐσθίω.

ἐφάλλομαι 2 aor. ἐφαλόμην (Hom.+; inscr., pap., LXX) leap upon ἐπί τινα someone (1 Km 10: 6; 16: 13 of the coming of the Spirit of God upon a person) of a 'possessed' man Ac 19: 16. M-M.*

ἐφάπαξ adv.—1. at once, at one time (PLond. 483, 88; 1708, 242; PFlor. 158, 10) ἐπάνω πεντακοσίοις ἀδελφοῖς ἐ. to more than 500 brethren at once 1 Cor 15: 6.
2. once for all (Eupolis Com. [V BC] 175 Kock) Ro 6: 10; Hb 7: 27; 9: 12; 10: 10. M-M.*

Ἐφέσιος, ία, ιον Ephesian οἱ Ἐ. the Ephesians (oft. inscr.; Philo, Leg. ad Gai. 315; Jos., Ant. 14, 224f) Ac 18: 27 D; 19: 28, 34, 35a (ἄνδρες Ἐ. as Achilles Tat. 7, 9, 2); 20: 4 D; 21: 29; Eph inscr. (lit. on the Letter to the Eph s. SHanson, The Unity of the Church in the NT, '46, 173-90); IEph 8: 1; 11: 2; IMg 15; ITr 13: 1; IRo 10: 1; IPhld 11: 2; ISm 12: 1. ἡ Ἐφεσίων πόλις (cf. ἡ τῶν Ἱεροσολυμιτῶν π. Jos., Ant. 5, 82; 10, 109 al.) Ac 19: 35b; ἡ Ἐφεσίων ἐκκλησία 2 Ti subscr. (s. the foll. entry).*

Ἔφεσος, ου, ἡ Ephesus (Hdt.+; oft. in inscr.; Joseph.; Sib. Or.), a seaport of Asia Minor in the plain of the Caÿster River. Famous for its temple of Artemis (s. Ἄρτεμις). The Christian church at Ephesus was either founded by Paul, or its numbers greatly increased by his ministry (GSDuncan, St. Paul's Ephesian Ministry '29). Ac 18: 19, 21, 24, 27 D; 19: 1, 17, 26; 20: 16f; 1 Cor 15: 32; 16: 8; subscr. v.l. (Eph 1: 1; here it is lacking in 𝔓⁴⁶ אB Marcion [who has instead: to the Laodiceans]; cf. Harnack, SAB '10, 696ff; JSchmid, D. Eph des Ap. Pls '28; Gdspd., Probs. 171-3); 1 Ti 1: 3; 2 Ti 1: 18; 4: 12; Rv 1: 11 (the order Eph., Smyrna, Perg., Sardis also in an official inscr. fr. Miletus [56-50 BC]: ThWiegand, Milet Heft 2 [city hall] p. 101f); 2: 1; IEph inscr.—OBenndorf, Z. Ortskunde u. Stadtgesch. von Eph. '05; LBürchner, Ephesos: Pauly-W. V '05, 2773-822; Österr. Archäol. Institut: Forschungen in Ephesos Iff, '06ff, preliminary reports in the 'Jahreshefte' '22ff; JKeil, Ephesos² '30; WMRamsay, The Church in the Roman Empire before A.D. 170 '12, 135-9; JNBakhuizen v. d. Brink, De oudchristelijke monumenten van Ephesus '23; VSchultze, Altchr. Städte u. Landsch. II 2, '26, 86-120; Dssm., D. Ausgrabungen in Eph. 1926: ThBl 6, '27, 17-19, The Excav. in Eph.: Biblical Review 15, '30, 332-46; RPRTonneau, E. au temps de S. Paul: RB 38, '29, 5-34; 321-63; PAntoine, Dict. de la Bible, Suppl. II '34, 1076-1104; FRienecker, Der Eph. (w. illustrated supplement) '34; Biblical Archaeologist 8, '45, 61-80. S. Δημήτριος 2.*

ἐφευρετής, οῦ, ὁ (Anacreontea 38, 3 Preisend.; Porphyr., Against the Chr. [ABA '16] 15, 1; Etym. Mag. p. 435, 28) inventor, contriver ἐφευρεταὶ κακῶν contrivers of evil Ro 1: 30 (cf. Theophyl. Sim., Ep. 29 p. 772 H. κακῶν ἐφευρετικόν; Philo, In Flacc. 20 κακῶν εὑρεταί; 73;

2 Macc 7: 31; Vergil, Aen. 2, 164 scelerum inventor; Tacit., Annal. 4, 11 Seianus facinorum omnium repertor). M-M.*

Ἔφηβος, ου, ὁ (cf. e.g. Inscr. Hisp. Lat. ed. Huebner 1869 no. 4970, 172; Inscr. Pariet. Pomp. ed. Zangemeister 1871 no. 1478) Ephebus, whose first name is Claudius, a Roman Christian 1 Cl 65: 1.*

ἐφήδομαι (X.+) (take) delight in, mostly in a bad sense 'delight in someone's misfortune' or 'enjoy bad things' (Dio Chrys. 3, 103; 10[11], 64; Ael. Aristid. 36 p. 690D; Jos., C. Ap. 2, 5); τινί (in) someth. (X., Hell. 4, 5, 18; Jos., Ant. 16, 127) τοῖς ἁμαρτήμασιν Dg 9: 1.*

ἐφημερία, ας, ἡ (Suppl. Epigr. Gr. VII 29 [I BC]) a class or division of priests who performed the daily (hence the name) duties in the temple at Jerusalem (LXX; cf. Jos., Ant. 12, 265). There were 24 such divisions, each one of which took care of the temple duties for one week (1 Ch 23: 6; 28: 13 al.). Schürer II⁴ 286ff; Billerb. II 55ff. The ἐ. Ἀβιά Lk 1: 5 was the eighth division. ἐν τῇ τάξει τ. ἐφημερίας αὐτοῦ in the order of his division vs. 8. M-M.*

ἐφήμερος, ον (Pind., Thu.+; Philo) for the day ἡ ἐ. τροφή food for the day, daily food (Diod. S. 3, 32, 3; Dionys. Hal. 8, 41, 5; Ael. Aristid. 28, 139 K.=49 p. 537 D.; Stob. 1, 1, 13 [I p. 27 W.]; Vett. Val. p. 62, 17 ἐνδεεῖς τῆς ἐ. τροφῆς; PSI 685, 9) Js 2: 15.—HFränkel, Transactions of the Amer. Philol. Assoc. 77, '46, 131-45. M-M.*

ἐφικνέομαι 2 aor. ἐφικόμην (Hom.+; Inschr. v. Priene 105, 47; Sir 43: 27 cod. C; Sib. Or. 11, 215) come to, reach εἴς τινα someone 2 Cor 10: 14. ἄχρι τινός as far as someone vs. 13.*

ἐφίστημι (Hom.+; inscr., pap., LXX, Ep. Arist., Joseph.) 2 aor. ἐπέστην, imper. ἐπίστηθι, ptc. ἐπιστάς; pf. ptc. ἐφεστώς, mid. 3 sg. indic. ἐπίσταται 1 Th 5: 3 v.l. (on the form s. W-S. §5, 10c). 1 aor. pass. ἐπεστάθην 1 Cl 12: 4; Hv 3, 1, 6. This aor. pass. can have mid. mng. (Eur., Iph. T. 1375 al.) and as a rule the mid. has, like the 2 aor., pf. and plpf. act., intransitive sense; it is only this intr. sense that is found for ἐφίστημι in our lit.
1. pres. and aor. stand by or near, approach, appear oft. w. the connotation of suddenness.
a. of pers. w. dat. of the pers. Lk 2: 9; 24: 4 (of angels, as Diod. S. 1, 25, 5 of Isis in a dream; Lucian, Dial. Deor. 17, 1 of Hephaestus; Dit., Syll.³ 1168, 37 ὁ θεὸς ἐπιστάς; Jos., Ant. 3, 188. Of a figure in a dream Hdt. 5, 56); Ac 4: 1; 12: 7 D; 23: 11. ἐπεστάθη μοι she approached me Hv 3, 1, 6. W. dat. of the thing attack τῇ οἰκίᾳ Ἰ. Ac 17: 5. ἐπί τι approach or stand by someth. (Sir 41: 24) Ac 10: 17; 11: 11. ἐπάνω τινός stand at someone's head Lk 4: 39 (cf. 2 Km 1: 9). Abs. (Ep. Arist. 177) Lk 2: 38; 10: 40; 20: 1; Ac 6: 12; 12: 7; 22: 13; 23: 27; 1 Cl 12: 4; MPol 6: 1. ἐπίστηθι stand by=be ready, be on hand (Eur., Andr. 547; Demosth. 18, 60) 2 Ti 4: 2.
b. of things, esp. of misfortunes, which (suddenly) come upon someone (Soph., Oed. R. 777; Thu. 3, 82, 2; LXX) w. dat. of the pers. (cf. Cornutus 10 p. 11, 17; Wsd 6: 8; 19: 1) αἰφνίδιος αὐτοῖς ἐφίσταται ὄλεθρος 1 Th 5: 3. ἐπί τινα Lk 21: 34.
2. perf.—a. stand by, be present αὐτὸς ἤμην ἐφεστώς I (myself) was standing by Ac 22: 20 (cf. Jos., Vi. 294). διὰ τ. ὑετὸν τὸν ἐφεστῶτα because it had begun to rain 28: 2 (Polyb. 18, 20, 7 διὰ τὸν ἐφεστῶτα ζόφον). But the mng. here could also be because it threatened to rain, in accordance w. the next mng.

b. *stand before, be imminent* (Il. 12, 326; Demosth. 18, 176; Jos., Ant. 13, 241, Vi. 137 al.) ὁ καιρὸς τῆς ἀναλύσεώς μου ἐφέστηκεν *the time of my departure is imminent* 2 Ti 4: 6.

c. *be over, be in charge of* as leader or overseer (Eur., Aristoph. et al.: Jdth 8: 10; 12: 11; Synes., Ep. 140 p. 276ʙ ὁ ἐφεστὼς θεός) εἴς τι: οἱ ἄνδρες οἱ εἰς τὴν οἰκοδομὴν ἐφεστῶτες *the men who had been in charge of the construction* Hs 9, 6, 2. M-M.*

ἐφόδιον, ου, τό *travel allowance, provisions for a journey* (used Aristoph., Hdt. + in sg. and pl.; inscr., pap.; Dt 15: 14; Jos., Vi. 224 al.) fig. of the provisions which Christ gives his followers for the journey of life 1 Cl 2: 1 (for the fig. mng. cf. Menand., fgm. 472, 1 ἐ. βίῳ; Epict. 3, 21, 9 ἔχοντάς τι ἐ. τοιοῦτον εἰς τὸν βίον; Plut., Mor. p. 160ʙ; Sextus 551; Philo, Rer. Div. Her. 273; Jos., Bell. 1, 463; 6, 80).*

ἐφοράω (Hom. +; inscr., pap., LXX; Philo, Aet. M. 83; Jos., Bell. 1, 630; Sib. Or. fgm. 3, 42) *gaze upon τὶ someth.* AP 10: 25. S. also ἐπεῖδον.*

Ἐφραίμ, ὁ indecl. (אֶפְרַיִם) (LXX, Philo.—Translit. into Gk. in var. ways: Jos., index) *Ephraim.*
1. son of Joseph, blessed by Jacob in place of his older brother Manasseh (cf. Gen 48: 14, 17ff) B 13: 5.
2. name of a city, 'near the desert', to which, acc. to J 11: 54, Jesus retired for a short time toward the end of his life. On the location of this place acc. to ancient and modern concepts s. Hdb. ad loc. D has εἰς τὴν χώραν Σαμφουρειν (= Sepphoris) ἐγγὺς τῆς ἐρήμου εἰς Ἐφραὶμ λεγομένην πόλιν.—ThZahn, NKZ 19, '08, 31-9; SJCase, Jesus and Sepphoris: JBL 45, '26, 14-22.*

ἐφφαθά Aram. word, translated διανοίχθητι *be opened* Mk 7: 34. It is a contraction of the form of the ethpeel (אֶתְפְּתַח); s. Wlh. ad loc.—Dalman, Gramm.² 278; IRabinowitz, ZNW 53, '62, 229-38; JEmerton, JTS 18, '67, 427-31; MBlack, BRigaux-Festschr., '70, 57-60.

ἐχθές adv. (Soph. +; also found in Attic prose; it is the proper Koine form: PEleph. 29, 6 [III ʙᴄ]; PSI 442, 21 [III ʙᴄ]; PLeipz. 105, 1 [I/II ᴀᴅ]; PFay. 108, 7 [II ᴀᴅ]; LXX [Thackeray 97]; Jos., C. Ap. 2, 14 al.) *yesterday* J 4: 52; Ac 16: 35 D; 7: 28; 1 Cl 4: 10 (the two last pass. Ex 2: 14). More generally it can mean the past as a whole (Soph., Ant. 456 νῦν κἀχθές; Ael. Aristid. 53 p. 623 D.: χθές κ. πρῴην; cf. Jos., C. Ap. 2, 154) w. σήμερον = 'the present' (Sir 38: 22; Himerius, Ecl. 31, 1 W.) Hb 13: 8. M-M.*

ἔχθρα, ας, ἡ (Pind., Thu. +; inscr., pap., LXX) *enmity* Dg 5: 17; Eph 2: 14, 16 (opp. φιλία, as Hyperid., fgm. 209; Ael. Aristid. 38 p. 713 D.; Dit., Syll.³ 826ᴄ, 10; PHib. 170 [247 ʙᴄ]). ἐ. τοῦ θεοῦ *enmity toward God* Js 4: 4. Also ἐ. εἰς θεόν Ro 8: 7. ἐν ἐ. εἶναι (cf. 1 Esdr 5: 49) πρός τινα *live at enmity w. someone* Lk 23: 12 (ἐ. πρός τινα as Lucian, Hermot. 85; Philo, Spec. Leg. 1, 108; Jos., Ant. 4, 106). Pl. of hostile feelings and actions (Pla., 7th Epistle p. 337ʙ; Philo, Sacr. Abel. 96) Gal 5: 20. M-M. B. 1132f.*

ἐχθρός, ά, όν (Hom. +; inscr., LXX) *hostile*—1. pass. *hated* (Hom.; θεοῖς ἐ. since Hes., Theog. 766, also Pla., Rep. 1, 23 p. 352ʙ; Epict. 3, 22, 91; Ael. Aristid. 28, 15 K. = 49 p. 495 D.; Alciphr. 3, 12, 5; Achilles Tat. 7, 6, 3, likew. X., Cyr. 5, 4, 35 καὶ θεοῖς ἐ. καὶ ἀνθρώποις.— Philo, Spec. Leg. 3, 88 πᾶς ἐ. θεῷ) Ro 11: 28, where the pass. sense becomes at least quite probable because of the contrast w. ἀγαπητός.
2. act. *hating, hostile* (Pind., Hdt. +; LXX)—a. adj.

(X., An. 1, 3, 12; 20; PGM 36, 144; Sir 36: 9; Jos., Ant. 11, 27) ἐ. ἄνθρωπος (Horapollo 2, 35) Mt 13: 28. The position of ἐ. before ἄ. (differently Esth 7: 6) suggests that ἐ. is an adj. here; but ἄ. by itself could also serve to emphasize the uncertainty: *an enemy at all* (s. EKlostermann, Hdb. ad loc.). Then this example would also belong to b.

b. subst. (Hes., Pind.; Zen.-P. 14 [= Sb 6720], 18 [257/6 ʙᴄ]; LXX, En., Ep. Arist., Philo, Joseph., Test. 12 Patr.; Sib. Or. 3, 727) ὁ ἐ. *the (personal) enemy.*
α. abs. 2 Cl 6: 3. Enemies of men Lk 1: 74; 2 Th 3: 15; D 1: 3b; B 16: 4. Enemies of God or Christ Ro 5: 10; 1 Cor 15: 25; Col 1: 21; 1 Cl 36: 5. Death as the last enemy 1 Cor 15: 26. The devil as the enemy (cf. Test. Dan 6: 3f) Lk 10: 19; cf. Mt 13: 39.
β. w. gen. of the pers. who is the obj. of the enmity: men Mt 5: 43f; Lk 6: 27, 35 (Delph. commands: Dit., Syll.³ 1286 I, 15; 16 [III ʙᴄ] φίλοις εὐνόει, ἐχθροὺς ἀμύνου; Sextus 213 εὔχου τοὺς ἐχθροὺς εὐεργετεῖν; Pittacus in Diog. L. 1, 78 φίλον μὴ λέγειν κακῶς, ἀλλὰ μηδὲ ἐχθρόν; Epict. 3, 22, 54 as a principle of the Cynic philosopher: δερόμενον φιλεῖν [δεῖ] αὐτοὺς τοὺς δέροντας . . . ὡς ἀδελφόν; Hierocles 7 p. 430 οὐδεὶς ἐχθρὸς τῷ σπουδαίῳ . . . μισεῖ οὐδένα ἄνθρωπον . . . φιλία πρὸς πάντας ἀνθρώπους.—HHaas, Idee u. Ideal d. Feindesliebe in d. ausserchr. Welt '27; MWaldmann, D. Feindesliebe in d. ant. Welt u. im Christent. '02; ThBirt. Chr. Welt 29, '15, 475-83; FKattenbusch, StKr 89, '16, 1-70; PFiebig, ibid. 91, '18, 30-64; 305f; JEYates, Theology 44, '42, 48-51); Mt 10: 36; 13: 25; Lk 1: 71; 19: 27; Ro 12: 20 (Pr 25: 21); Gal 4: 16. God or Christ as the object of enmity Mt 22: 44; Mk 12: 36; Lk 20: 43; Ac 2: 35; Hb 1: 13; 10: 13; 1 Cl 36: 5 (all Ps 109: 1). ἐχθρὸς τ. θεοῦ Js 4: 4 (cf. Aeschyl., Prom. 120 ὁ Διὸς ἐ.).
γ. w. gen. of the thing which is the obj. of the enmity (Demosth. 45, 66; Philo, Conf. Lingu. 48 ἀληθείας ἐ., Somn. 2, 90 λογισμοῦ; Jos., C. Ap. 2, 291 ἀδικίας) ἐ. πάσης δικαιοσύνης *enemy of all righteousness* Ac 13: 10. ἐ. τοῦ σταυροῦ τ. Χριστοῦ Phil 3: 18 (OLinton, Con. Neot. IV '36, 9-21).—WFoerster, TW II 810-15. M-M. B. 1345.

ἔχιδνα, ης, ἡ (Hes.; Hdt. +; Aq. Is 59: 5; loanw. in rabb.) *viper,* usu. a poisonous snake (Diod. S. 4, 38, 2; Conon [I ʙᴄ/I ᴀᴅ]: 26 fgm. 1, 8 Jac.; Lucian, Alex. 10; Artem. 2, 13) Ac 28: 3.—Fig. of persons (Aeschyl., Choeph. 994; Eur., Ion 1262) γεννήματα ἐχιδνῶν *brood of vipers* (cf. Theophyl. Sim., Ep. 73 τὰ τῆς ἐχίδνης κυήματα; Third Corinthians 3: 38) Mt 3: 7; 12: 34; 23: 33; Lk 3: 7. M-M. B. 194.*

ἔχω (Hom. +; inscr., pap., LXX, En., Ep. Arist., Philo, Joseph., Test. 12 Patr.) fut. ἕξω; impf. εἶχον, 1 pl. εἴχαμεν 2 J 5 (Mlt.-H. 194), 3 pl. εἶχαν (Bl-D. §82 app.) Mk 8: 7; Rv 9: 8 or εἴχοσαν (Bl-D. §84, 2; Mlt.-H. 194; Kühner-Bl. II p. 55) J 15: 22, 24; 2 aor. ἔσχον; pf. ἔσχηκα; plpf. ἐσχήκειν.
I. act. trans.—1. *have, hold*—a. lit. *hold in the hands* ἔ. τι ἐν τῇ χειρί *have someth. in one's hand* (since Il. 18, 505) Rv 1: 16; 6: 5; 10: 2; 17: 4. Of holding in the hand without ἐν τῇ χειρί (Josh 6: 8) ἔ. κιθάραν 5: 8. λιβανωτὸν χρυσοῦν 8: 3, cf. vs. 6; 14: 17 and s. ἀλάβαστρον Mt 26: 7; Mk 14: 3.
b. of clothing, weapons, etc. *have on, wear* (Hom. +; LXX) τὸ ἔνδυμα Mt 3: 4; 22: 12. κατὰ κεφαλῆς ἔχων w. τὶ to be supplied *while he wears (a covering) on his head* 1 Cor 11: 4. ἔ. θώρακας Rv 9: 9, 17. ἔ. μάχαιραν *wear a sword* (Jos., Ant. 6, 190) J 18: 10. Sim. of trees ἔ. φύλλα *have leaves* Mk 11: 13.

c. keep, preserve—α. lit., a mina ('pound') in a handkerchief *keep safe* Lk 19: 20.

β. fig. τὴν μαρτυρίαν Rv 6: 9; 12: 17; 19: 10; the mystery of the faith 1 Ti 3: 9; an example of sound teaching 2 Ti 1: 13; *keep* (Diod. S. 17, 93, 1 τὴν βασιλείαν ἔχειν=keep control) Mk 6: 18.

d. of states of being *hold, hold in its grip, seize* (Hom. +; PGiess. 65a, 4 παρακαλῶ σε κύριέ μου, εἰδότα τὴν ἔχουσάν με συμφορὰν ἀπολῦσαί μοι; Job 21: 6; Is 13: 8; Jos., Ant. 3, 95 δέος εἶχε τοὺς Ἑβρ.; 5, 63) εἶχεν αὐτὰς τρόμος καὶ ἔκστασις *trembling and amazement had seized them* Mk 16: 8.

2. have as one's own, possess (Hom. +)**—α.** lit. κτήματα πολλά *have much property* Mt 19: 22; Mk 10: 22. πρόβατα Lk 15: 4; J 10: 16. θησαυρόν Mt 19: 21; Mk 10: 21b. βίον *living* Lk 21: 4; 1 J 3: 17. δραχμὰς δέκα Lk 15: 8. πλοῖα Rv 18: 19. κληρονομίαν Eph 5: 5. θυσιαστήριον Hb 13: 10a; μέρος ἔ. ἔν τινι *have a share in someth.* Rv 20: 6. Gener. μηδὲν ἔ. (Sib. Or. 3, 244) 2 Cor 6: 10. ὅσα ἔχεις Mk 10: 21; cf. 12: 44; Mt 13: 44, 46; 18: 25. τί ἔχεις ὃ οὐκ ἔλαβες; *what do you have that you have not been given?* 1 Cor 4: 7. The obj. acc. is often used w. an adj. or ptc.: ἔ. ἄπαντα κοινά *have everything in common* Ac 2: 44 (cf. Jos., Ant. 15, 18). ἔ. πολλὰ ἀγαθὰ κείμενα *have many good things stored up* Lk 12: 19.—Hb 12: 1. Abs. ἔ. *have (anything)* (Soph.+; Sir 13: 5; 14: 11) Mt 13: 12a; Mk 4: 25a; Lk 8: 18a. ἐκ τοῦ ἔχειν *in accordance w. what you have* 2 Cor 8: 11. ἔ. εἰς ἀπαρτισμόν *have (enough) to complete* Lk 14: 28. W. neg. ἔ. *have nothing* Mt 13: 12b; Mk 4: 25b; Lk 8: 18b.—ὁ ἔχων *the one who has, who is well off* (Soph., Aj. 157; Eur., Alc. 57; X., An. 7, 3, 28). πᾶς ὁ ἔχων *everyone who has (anything)* Mt 25: 29a; Lk 19: 26a. ὁ μὴ ἔχων *the one who has nothing* (X., An. 7, 3, 28; 1 Esdr 9: 51, 54; 2 Esdr 18 [Neh 8]: 10) Mt 25: 29b; Lk 19: 26b; 1 Cor 11: 22.

b. to denote the possession of persons to whom one has close relationships.

α. of relatives πατέρα ἔ. J 8: 41. ἀδελφούς Lk 16: 28. ἄνδρα (Aristot. p. 15b, 28 λεγόμεθα δὲ καὶ γυναῖκα ἔχειν καὶ ἡ γυνὴ ἄνδρα; Tob 3: 8 BA) *be married (of the woman)* J 4: 17f; 1 Cor 7: 2b, 13; Gal 4: 27 (Is 54: 1). γυναῖκα of the man (cf. Lucian, Tox. 45; Dit., Syll.³ 1160 γυναικὸς Ἀΐ., τῆς νῦν ἔχει; PGM 13, 320; 1 Esdr 9: 12, 18. As early as Od. 11, 603 Heracles ἔχει Ἥβην) 1 Cor 7: 2a, 12, 29 (for the play on words cf. Heliod. 1, 18, 4 in connection w. the handing over of a virgin: σὺ ἔχων οὐκ ἕξεις; Crates, Ep. 7 πάντ' ἔχοντες οὐδὲν ἔχετε). τέκνα Mt 21: 28; 22: 24; 1 Ti 3: 4; 5: 4; Tit 1: 6. υἱούς (Artem. 5, 42 τὶς τρεῖς ἔχων υἱούς) Lk 15: 11; Gal 4: 22. σπέρμα *have children* Mt 22: 25. W. acc. as obj. and in predicate ἔ. τινὰ πατέρα *have someone as father* Mt 3: 9. ἔ. τινὰ γυναῖκα (w. γυναῖκα to be understood fr. the context) 14: 4; cf. Mk 6: 18; ὥστε γυναῖκά τινα τοῦ πατρὸς ἔ. *that someone has taken his father's wife* (as his own wife: ἔχειν alone in this sense as Plut., Cato Min. 21, 3; Appian, Bell. Civ. 3, 10 §34; Jos., C. Ap. 1, 147. Perh. an illicit relationship is meant, as Longus 4, 17; Hesychius Miles. [VI AD], Viri Ill. c. 4 JFlach [1880] ἔχω Λαΐδα) 1 Cor 5: 1 (Diod. S. 20, 33, 5 of a man who had illicit relations with his stepmother: ἔχειν λάθρα τοῦ πατρὸς τὴν Ἀλκίαν).

β. more gener. φίλον *have a friend* Lk 11: 5. ἀσθενοῦντας *have sick people* Lk 4: 40 and χήρας *widows* 1 Ti 5: 16 to care for; παιδαγωγοὺς ἔ. 1 Cor 4: 15. δοῦλον Lk 17: 7. οἰκονόμον 16: 1; κύριον ἔ. *have a master,* i.e., be under a master's control Col 4: 1; δεσπότην ἔ. 1 Ti 6: 2; βασιλέα J 19: 15. ἀρχιερέα Hb 4: 14; 8: 1. ποιμένα Mt 9: 36. ἔχων ὑπ' ἐμαυτὸν στρατιώτας *I have soldiers under*

me Lk 7: 8. ἔ. τινὰ ὑπηρέτην *have someone as an assistant* Ac 13: 5. ἔ. τινὰ τύπον *have someone as an example* Phil 3: 17. Of the relation of Christians to God and to Jesus ἔ. θεόν, τὸν πατέρα, τὸν υἱόν *have God, the Father, the Son* i.e., be in communion w. them 1 J 2: 23; 2 J 9.—HHanse, at end of this entry.

c. of the whole in relation to its parts *have, possess—α.* of living beings, of parts of the body in men and animals μέλη Ro 12: 4a; cf. 1 Cor 12: 12. σάρκα καὶ ὀστέα Lk 24: 39. ἀκροβυστίαν Ac 11: 3. οὖς Rv 2: 7, 11. ὦτα Mt 11: 15; Mk 7: 16; Lk 8: 8. χεῖρας, πόδας, ὀφθαλμούς Mt 18: 8f; Mk 9: 43, 45, 47. Of animals and animal-like beings ἔ. πρόσωπον Rv 4: 7. πτέρυγας vs. 8. κέρατα 5: 6. ψυχάς 8: 9. τρίχας 9: 8. κεφαλάς 12: 3 al.

β. of inanimate things: of cities τ. θεμελίους ἔ. Hb 11: 10; cf. Rv 21: 14. Of plants ῥίζαν ἔ. Mt 13: 6; Mk 4: 6.

d. have at hand, have at one's disposal ἄρτους Mt 14: 17; cf. 15: 34. οὐκ ἔχω ὃ παραθήσω αὐτῷ *I have nothing to set before him* Lk 11: 6. μὴ ἐχόντων τί φάγωσι *since they had nothing to eat* Mk 8: 1; cf. Mt 15: 32 (Soph., Oed. Col. 316 οὐκ ἔχω τί φῶ). οὐκ ἔχω ποῦ συνάξω *I have no place to store* Lk 12: 17. ἄντλημα *a bucket* J 4: 11a. οἰκίας ἔ. *have houses (at one's disposal)* 1 Cor 11: 22. Of pers.: *have (at one's disposal)* (PAmh. 92, 18 οὐχ ἕξω κοινωνόν and oft. in pap.) Moses and the prophets Lk 16: 29. παράκλητον *an advocate, a helper* 1 J 2: 1. οὐδένα ἔ. ἰσόψυχον Phil 2: 20. ἄνθρωπον οὐκ ἔ. J 5: 7.

e. of all conditions of body and soul (Hom.+; LXX)—**α.** of illness, etc. (Jos., C. Ap. 1, 305) ἀσθενείας *have diseases* Ac 28: 9. μάστιγας *diseases* Mk 3: 10. πληγὴν τῆς μαχαίρης Rv 13: 14. θλῖψιν J 16: 33b; 1 Cor 7: 28; Rv 2: 10. Esp. of demon possession: δαιμόνιον ἔ. *be possessed by a demon* Mt 11: 18; Lk 7: 33; 8: 27; J 7: 20; 8: 48f, 52; 10: 20. Βεελζεβούλ Mk 3: 22. πνεῦμα ἀκάθαρτον vs. 30; 7: 25; Ac 8: 7. πνεῦμα δαιμονίου ἀκαθάρτου Lk 4: 33. πνεῦμα πονηρόν Ac 19: 13. πνεῦμα ἄλαλον Mk 9: 17. πνεῦμα ἀσθενείας *spirit of sickness* Lk 13: 11. τὸν λεγιῶνα (the demon called) *Legion* Mk 5: 15.

β. gener. of conditions, characteristics, capabilities, emotions, inner possession: ἀγάπην ἔ. *have love* (cf. Diod. S. 3, 58, 3 φιλίαν ἔχειν) J 5: 42; 13: 35; 15: 13; 1 J 4: 16; 1 Cor 13: 1ff; 2 Cor 2: 4; Phil 2: 2; 1 Pt 4: 8. ἀγνωσίαν θεοῦ *fail to know God* 1 Cor 15: 34. ἁμαρτίαν J 9: 41; 15: 22a. ἀσθένειαν Hb 7: 28. γνῶσιν 1 Cor 8: 1, 10. ἐλπίδα Ac 24: 15; Ro 15: 4; 2 Cor 3: 12; 10: 15; Eph 2: 12; 1 J 3: 3. ἐπιθυμίαν Phil 1: 23. ἐπιποθίαν Ro 15: 23b; ζῆλον ἔ. *have zeal* Ro 10: 2. ἔ. ζηλον J 9: 17: 9. *Have jealousy* Js 3: 14. θυμόν Rv 12: 12. λύπην J 16: 21f; 2 Cor 2: 3; Phil 2: 27; μνείαν τινὸς ἔ. *remember someone* 1 Th 3: 6. παρρησίαν Phlm 8; Hb 10: 19; 1 J 2: 28; 3: 21; 4: 17; 5: 14. πεποίθησιν 2 Cor 3: 4; Phil 3: 4. πίστιν Mt 17: 20; 21: 21; Ac 14: 9; Ro 14: 22; 1 Cor 13: 2; 1 Ti 1: 19 al. προφητείαν *have the gift of prophecy* 1 Cor 13: 2. σοφίαν (X., Mem. 2, 3, 10) Rv 17: 9. συνείδησιν ἁμαρτιῶν Hb 10: 2. καλὴν συνείδησιν 13: 18; ἀγαθὴν σ. 1 Ti 1: 19; 1 Pt 3: 16; ἀπρόσκοπον σ. Ac 24: 16; ὑπομονήν Rv 2: 3. φόβον 1 Ti 5: 20. χαρὰν Phlm 7. χάριν ἔ. τινί *be grateful to someone* Lk 17: 9; 1 Ti 1: 12; 2 Ti 1: 3; σιγὴν ἔ. *be silent* Hs 9, 11, 5.

f. w. indications of time and age: πεντήκοντα ἔτη οὔπω ἔχεις *you are not yet fifty years old* J 8: 57 (cf. Jos., Ant. 1, 198). τριάκοντα κ. ὀκτὼ ἔτη ἔχων ἐν τῇ ἀσθενείᾳ αὐτοῦ *who had been sick for 38 years* 5: 5 (Cyranides p. 63, 25 πολὺν χρόνον ἔχων ἐν τῇ ἀρρωστίᾳ. W. cardinal numeral POxy. 1862, 17 τέσσαρες μῆνας ἔχει. Mirac. S. Georgii 44, 7 [JBAufhauser '13] ἔσχεν ... ἔτη ἑπτά); cf. Mt 9: 20 v.l. τέσσαρας ἡμέρας ἔ. ἐν τῷ μνημείῳ *have lain in the grave for four days* J 11: 17 (Jos.,

Ant. 7, 1 αὐτοῦ δύο ἡμέρας ἔχοντος ἐν). πολὺν χρόνον ἔ. *be* (somewhere or in a certain condition) *for a long time* 5: 6. ἡλικίαν ἔχειν *be of age* (Pla., Euthyd. 32 p. 306D; Plut., Mor. 547A; BGU 168 τοῖς ἀτελέσι ἔχουσι τὴν ἡλικίαν) 9: 21, 23. τέλος ἔχειν *have an end, be at an end* (Lucian, Charon 17; UPZ 81 III, 20 [II AD] τέλος ἔχει πάντα) Mk 3: 26; Lk 22: 37 (on the latter pass. s. τέλος 1a, end); cf. Hb 7: 3.

g. of advantages, benefits, or comforts which one enjoys: ἔ. τὰ αἰτήματα *to have been granted the requests* 1 J 5: 15; ἀνάπαυσιν ἔ. *have rest* Rv 4: 8; 14: 11; ἀπόλαυσιν τινος ἔ. *enjoy someth.* Hb 11: 25. βάθος γῆς Mt 13: 5b; Mk 4: 5b; γῆν πολλήν Mt 13: 5a; Mk 4: 5a. εἰρήνην Ro 5: 1. ἐλευθερίαν Gal 2: 4. Cf. ἐξουσία, ἐπαγγελία, ἔπαινος, ζωή, ἰκμάς, καιρός, καρπός, καύχημα, καύχησις, λόγος, μισθός, νοῦς, πνεῦμα, προσαγωγή, πρόφασις, τιμή, χάρις (=grace), χάρισμα (s. those entries).

h. *have=hold in one's charge* or *keeping* ἔ. τὰς κλεῖς *hold the keys* Rv 1: 18; cf. 3: 7. τὸ γλωσσόκομον *the money-box* J 12: 6; 13: 29.

i. *have=have someth. over one, be under someth.*: ἀνάγκην ἔχειν *be under necessity* 1 Cor 7: 37a; w. inf. foll. *be compelled, one must* (ἀνάγκη 1) Lk 14: 18; Hb 7: 27; χρείαν ἔ. *be in need* abs. Eph 4: 28b, τινός *need someth.* (Aeschyl.+; Dit., Syll.³ 333, 20; 421, 35 al.; PPetr. III 42G 9, 7 [III BC] ἐάν τινος χρείαν ἔχῃς) Mt 6: 8; 9: 12a; Mk 11: 3; Lk 19: 31, 34; J 13: 29; 1 Cor 12: 21; Hb 10: 36 al.; w. inf. foll. Mt 3: 14; 14: 16; J 13: 10; 1 Th 1: 8; 4: 9; 5: 1. νόμον J 19: 7. ἐπιταγήν 1 Cor 7: 25. ἐντολήν (Dit., Syll.³ 559, 9 ἔ. τὰς ἰντολάς; 1 Esdr 4: 52; 2 Macc 3: 13; Jos., Bell. 1, 261) Hb 7: 5; 1 J 2: 7; 4: 21; 2 J 5; cf. J 14: 21. διακονίαν 2 Cor 4: 1. ἀγῶνα Phil 1: 30; Col 2: 1. πρᾶξιν Ro 12: 4b. ἔγκλημα Ac 23: 29.

j. *have within oneself* var. constr. w. ἐν: of women ἐν γαστρὶ ἔ. *be pregnant* (γαστήρ 2) Mt 1: 18, 23 (Is 7: 14); 24: 19; Mk 13: 17; Lk 21: 23; 1 Th 5: 3; Rv 12: 2. ἔ. τινὰ ἐν τῇ καρδίᾳ *have someone in one's heart* Phil 1: 7 (Ovid, Metam. 2, 641 aliquem clausum pectore habere). ἔ. τι ἐν ἑαυτῷ (Jos., Ant. 8, 171): ζωήν J 5: 26. τὴν μαρτυρίαν 1 J 5: 10 v.l.; τὸ ἀπόκριμα τοῦ θανάτου *have a sentence of death within oneself* 2 Cor 1: 9.

3. *have with oneself* or *in one's company*, also w. μεθ' ἑαυτοῦ (X., Cyr. 1, 4, 17) τινά *someone* Mt 15: 30; 26: 11; Mk 2: 19; 14: 7; Lk 2: 42 D; J 12: 8.—The ptc. w. acc.=simply *with* (Diod. S. 12, 78, 1 ἔχων δύναμιν with a [military] force; 18, 61, 1 ὁ θρόνος ἔχων τὸ διάδημα the throne with the diadem) ἀνέβησαν ἔχοντες αὐτόν they went up with him Lk 2: 42 D.

4. *have* or *include in itself, bring about, cause* w. acc. (Hom.+; Wsd 8: 16) ὑπομονή: ἔργον τέλειον Js 1: 4. Of πίστις: ἔργα 2: 17. Of φόβος: κόλασιν 1 J 4: 18. Of παρρησία: μεγάλην μισθαποδοσίαν Hb 10: 35.

5. *consider, look upon, view* w. acc. as obj. and predicate acc. (POxy. 292, 6 [c. 25 AD] ἔχειν αὐτὸν συνεσταμένον='look upon him as recommended'; 787 [16 AD] PGiess. 71, 4; Job 30: 9; Ps.-Clem., Hom. 16, 19) ἔχε με παρῃτημένον *consider me excused* Lk 14: 18b, 19 (cf. Martial 2, 79 excusatum habeas me). ἔ. τινὰ ὡς προφήτην *consider someone a prophet* Mt 14: 5; 21: 26, 46 v.l. (cf. Ev. Nicod. 5 ἔχειν Ἰαννῆν καὶ Ἰαμβρῆν ὡς θεούς). τινὰ ἔντιμον ἔ. *hold someone in honor* Phil 2: 29. ἔ. τινὰ εἰς προφήτην *consider someone a prophet* Mt 21: 46 (cf. Duris [III BC]: 76 fgm. 21 Jac. ὂν εἰς θεοὺς ἔχουσιν). εἶχον τ. Ἰωάννην ὄντως ὅτι προφήτης ἦν they thought that John was really a prophet Mk 11: 32.

6. ἔ. w. inf. foll.—a. *have the possibility, can, be able, be in a position* (Hom.+; cf. Eur., Hec. 761; Hdt. 1, 49;

Pla., Phaedo p. 76D; Demosth., Ep. 2, 22; Theocr. 10, 37 τὸν τρόπον οὐκ ἔχω εἰπεῖν I cannot specify the manner; Lucian, Dial. Mort. 21, 2, Herm. 55; Epict. 1, 9, 32; 2, 2, 24 al.; Ael. Aristid. 51, 50 K.=27 p. 546 D.: οὐκ ἔχω λέγειν; PPetr. II 12, 1, 16; PAmh. 131, 15; Pr 3: 27; Jos., Ant. 1, 338; 2, 58) ἔ. ἀποδοῦναι *be able to pay* Mt 18: 25a; Lk 7: 42; 14: 14. μὴ ἔ. περισσότερον τι ποιῆσαι *be in a position to do nothing more* 12: 4. οὐδὲν ἔ. ἀντειπεῖν *be able to make a reply* Ac 4: 14; cf. Tit 2: 8. ἔ. κατηγορεῖν αὐτοῦ J 8: 6 v.l. ἀσφαλές τι γράψαι οὐκ ἔχω I have nothing definite to write Ac 25: 26a; cf. 26b. ἔ. μεταδιδόναι Eph 4: 28a. ἔ. τὴν τούτων μνήμην ποιεῖσθαι *be able to recall these things to mind* 2 Pt 1: 15. κατ' οὐδενὸς εἶχεν μείζονος ὀμόσαι *he could swear by no one greater* Hb 6: 13. In the same sense without the actual addition of the inf., which is automatically supplied fr. context (X., An. 2, 1, 9) ὃ ἔσχεν (i.e. ποιῆσαι) ἐποίησεν *she has done what she could* Mk 14: 8.

b. *one must* (Ps.-Callisth. 2, 1, 3 καθαιρεθῆναι ἔχεις= you must be deposed; Porphyr., Against the Christians 63 Harnack [ABA '16] παθεῖν; Gen 18: 31; Jos., Ant. 19, 348 τοῦ τεθνάναι) βάπτισμα ἔχω βαπτισθῆναι I must undergo a baptism Lk 12: 50. ἔχω σοί τι εἰπεῖν *I have someth. to say to you* (Lucian, Philops. 1 ἔχεις μοι εἰπεῖν. Without dat. Aelian, V.H. 2, 23; Jos., Ant. 16, 312) 7: 40. ἀπαγγεῖλαι Ac 23: 17, 19; cf. vs. 18. πολλὰ γράφειν 2 J 12; 3 J 13.

7. special combinations—a. w. prep. ἐν: τὸν θεὸν ἔ. ἐν ἐπιγνώσει *acknowledge God* Ro 1: 28 (cf. ἐν ὀργῇ ἔ. τινά='be angry at someone', Thu. 2, 18, 5; 2, 21, 3; ἐν ὀρρωδίᾳ ἔ. τ. 2, 89, 1; ἐν ἡδονῇ ἔ. τ.='be glad to see someone' 3, 9, 1; ἐν εὐνοίᾳ ἔ. Demosth. 18, 167). ἐν ἑτοίμῳ ἔ. 2 Cor 10: 6 (ἕτοιμος 2). ἐν ἐμοὶ οὐκ ἔχει οὐδέν *he has no hold on me* J 14: 30 (Appian, Bell. Civ. 3, 32 §125 ἔχειν τι ἔν τινι=have someth. [hope of safety] in someone). κατά τινος: on 1 Cor 11: 4 s. above I 1b. ἔ. τι κατά τινος *have someth. against someone* Mt 5: 23; Mk 11: 25; w. ὅτι foll. Rv 2: 14. ἔ. κατά τινος w. sim. mng. Hm 2: 2; s 9, 23, 2; w. ὅτι foll. Rv 2: 4, 20. ἔ. τινὰ κατὰ πρόσωπον *meet someone face to face* Ac 25: 16. μετά: ἔ. τι μετά τινος *have someth.* w. *someone* κρίματα *lawsuits* 1 Cor 6: 7. περί: ἔ. περί τινος *have* (a word, a reference, an explanation) *about someth.* B 12: 1; with adv. τελείως 10: 10. πρός τινα *have someth. against someone* (Ps.-Callisth. 2, 21, 21 ὅσον τις ὑμῶν ἔχει πρὸς ἕτερον) Ac 24: 19. ζητήματα ἔ. *have questions at issue* w. *someone* 25: 19. λόγον ἔ. πρός τινα 19: 38. πρᾶγμα (=Lat. causa, 'lawsuit': BGU 19 I, 5; 361 II, 4) ἔ. πρός τινα (POxy. 743, 19 [2 BC] εἰ πρὸς ἄλλους εἶχον πρᾶγμα; BGU 22: 8) 1 Cor 6: 1. πρός τινα ἔ. μομφήν *have a complaint against someone* Col 3: 13.

b. τοῦτο ἔχεις ὅτι *you have this* (in your favor), *that* Rv 2: 6. ἔ. ὁδόν *be situated* (a certain distance) *away* (cf. Peripl. Eryth. 37: Ὡραία ἔχουσα ὁδὸν ἡμερῶν ἑπτὰ ἀπὸ θαλάσσης) of the Mt. of Olives ὅ ἐστιν ἐγγὺς Ἱερουσαλὴμ σαββάτου ἔχον ὁδόν Ac 1: 12.—ἴδε ἔχεις τὸ σόν *here you have what is yours* Mt 25: 25. ἔχετε κουστωδίαν *there you have a guard* (=you can have a guard) 27: 65 (cf. POxy. 33 III, 4).

II. act. intr. *be, be situated* w. adv. (Hom.+; inscr., pap., LXX).

1. pers. πῶς ἔχουσιν *how they are* Ac 15: 36 (cf. Gen 43: 27; Jos., Ant. 4, 112). ἑτοίμως ἔ. *be ready, hold oneself in readiness* w. inf. foll. (BGU 80, 17 [II AD] ἡ Σωτηρία ἑτοίμως ἔχουσα καταγράψαι; Da 3: 15 LXX; Jos., Ant. 13, 6) 21: 13; 2 Cor 12: 14; 1 Pt 4: 5. Also ἐν ἑτοίμῳ ἔ. 2 Cor 10: 6 (s. ἕτοιμος 2, end). εὖ ἔ. *be*

well-disposed πρός τινα *toward someone* Hs 9, 10, 7 (cf. Demosth. 9, 63 ἥδιον ἔχειν πρός τινα; Dit., Syll.³ 1094, 4 φιλανθρώπως ἔχει πρὸς πάντας). κακῶς ἔ. *be sick* (Aristoph. +; POxy. 935, 15; Ezk 34: 4) Mt 4: 24; 8: 16; 9: 12b; 17: 15 (see πάσχω 2). καλῶς ἔ. *be well, healthy* (Epict. 1, 11, 4; PGenève 54, 8; PFlor. 230, 24) Mk 16: 18; ἐσχάτως ἔ. (s. ἐσχάτως) 5: 23; κομψότερον ἔ. *feel better* (κομψῶς ἔ.: Epict. 2, 18, 14; 3, 10, 13; PPar. 18; PTebt. 414, 10 ἐὰν κομψῶς σχῶ) J 4: 52.

2. impers. *it is, the situation is* (Himerius, Or. 48 [= Or. 14], 10 πῶς ὑμῖν ἔχειν ταῦτα δοκεῖ; *how does this situation seem to you?*) ἄλλως 1 Ti 5: 25. οὕτως (Antig. Car. 20; Cebes 4, 1; POxy. 294, 11 [22 AD] εἰ ταῦτα οὕτως ἔχει; Jos., Ant. 15, 261) Ac 7: 1; 12: 15; 17: 11; 24: 9. τὸ καλῶς ἔχον *what is right* 1 Cl 14: 2 (Inscr. Gr. 543, 12 [c. 200 BC] καλῶς ἔχον ἐστὶ τιμᾶσθαι τοὺς εὔνους ἄνδρας). τὸ νῦν ἔχον *for the present* Ac 24: 25 (cf. Plut., Amator. 1; Lucian, Anachars. 40, Catapl. 13 τὸ δὲ νῦν ἔχον μὴ διάτριβε; Tob 7: 11).

III. mid. *hold oneself fast, cling to* (Hom. +) in NT only ptc.

1. of inner belonging and close association; the 'to' of belonging and the 'with' of association are expressed by the gen. (Theognis 1, 32 ἀεὶ τῶν ἀγαθῶν ἔχεο=ever hold fast to the good people; X., Oec. 6, 1; Pla., Leg. 7 p. 811D; Lucian, Hermot. 69 ἐλπίδος οὐ μικρᾶς ἐχόμενα λέγεις; Sallust. 14 p. 26, 24 τ. θεῶν; Philo, Agr. 101 τὰ ἀρετῆς ἐχόμενα; Jos., Ant. 10, 204 οὐδὲν ἀνθρωπίνης σοφίας ἐχόμενον, C. Ap. 1, 83 παλαιᾶς ἱστορίας ἐχόμενον) τὰ ἐχόμενα σωτηρίας *things that belong to salvation* Hb 6: 9.

2. of place: ἐχόμενος *neighboring* (Isocr. 4, 96 νῆσος; Hdt. 1, 134 al. οἱ ἐχόμενοι='the neighbors'; Diod. S. 5, 15, 1; Appian, Bell. Civ. 2, 71 §294; Arrian, Peripl. 7, 2; PPar. 51, 5 and oft. in pap.; 1 Esdr 4: 42; Jos., Ant. 6, 6 πρὸς τὰς ἐχομένας πόλεις; 11, 340) κωμοπόλεις Mk 1: 38.

3. of time: *immediately following* (Thu. 6, 3, 2 τ. ἐχομένου ἔτους al.; Dit., Syll.³ 800, 15; BPGrenfell and JPMahaffy, Revenue Laws of Ptol. Philad. [1896] 34, 20; PAmh. 49, 4; PTebt. 124, 43; LXX) τῇ ἐ. (sc. ἡμέρᾳ, as Polyb. 3, 112, 1; 5, 13, 9; 2 Macc 12: 39; Jos., Ant. 6, 235; 7, 18 al.; cf. εἰς τὴν ἐχομένην [i.e. ἡμέραν] PMich. 173, 16 [III BC]) *on the next day* Lk 13: 33; Ac 20: 15; w. ἡμέρᾳ added (PAmh. 50, 17) 21: 26. τῷ ἐχομένῳ σαββάτῳ 13: 44 v.l. (for ἐρχομένῳ; cf. 1 Macc 4: 28, where the witnesses are similarly divided).—On the whole word HHanse, TW II 816-27, 'Gott Haben' in d. Antike u. im frühen Christentum '39. M-M. B. 641; 740.

ἕως (Hom. +; inscr., pap., LXX, En., Ep. Arist., Philo, Joseph., Test. 12 Patr., Sib. Or.).

I. temporal conjunction—1. to denote the end of a period of time *till, until.*

a. w. the aor. ind. (Lysias 25, 26; Ps.-Demosth. 47, 58; Wsd 10: 14; 1 Macc 10: 50; Jdth 10: 18; Sib. Or. 5, 528) ἕως ἐστάθη *until it stood still* Mt 2: 9. ἕως ἦλθεν ὁ κατακλυσμὸς *until the flood came* 24: 39.—Ac 19: 10 D.

b. w. the aor. subj. and, as the rule requires (s. AFuchs, D. Temporalsätze mit d. Konj. 'bis' u. 'so lange als.' '02), ἄν (X., An. 5, 1, 11; Dit., Syll.³ 966, 11; 1207, 10; PPetr. II 40a, 28; POxy. 1124, 7; Gen 24: 14; 49: 10; Ex 33: 22; Lev 22: 4 and oft. LXX; Jos., Ant. 13, 400), to denote that the commencement of an event is dependent on circumstances: ἕως ἂν εἴπω *until I tell you* Mt 2: 13.—S: 18 (AMHoneyman, NTS 1, '54/'55, 141f.), 26 (cf. Dit., Syll.³ 731, 16ff ἕως ἂν ἀποδῷ); 22: 44 (Ps 109: 1); Mk 6: 10; 9: 1; 12: 36 (Ps 109: 1); Lk 20: 43 (Ps 109: 1); 21: 32; Ac 2:

35 (Ps 109: 1); 1 Cor 4: 5; Hb 1: 13; B 12: 10 (the two last Ps 109: 1).—Without ἄν (Soph., Aj. 555, Phil. 764; Dit., Syll.³ 976, 79; UPZ 18, 10 [II BC]; PGrenf. II 38, 16 [I BC]; POxy. 531, 6; 1125, 15; 1159, 21; Sir 35: 17; Tob 14: 5 BA; Sib. Or. 5, 217; Polyb. 35, 2, 4): Mt 10: 23; 18: 30; Mk 14: 32; Lk 15: 4; 22: 34; 2 Th 2: 7; Js 5: 7; Hb 10: 13; Rv 6: 11.

c. w. the pres. ind. (cf. Plut., Lycurg. 29, 3) ἕως ἔρχομαι *until I come* J 21: 22f; 1 Ti 4: 13; Hs 5, 2, 2; 9, 10, 5f; cf. 9, 11, 1.

d. w. the fut. ind. (cf. PHolm. 26, 7; Jdth 10: 15) in a text-critically doubtful pass. (Bl-D. §382, 2; Rob. 971f; 976) ἕως ἥξει ὅτε εἴπητε (ἥξει ὅτε is lacking in אB) *until (the time) comes when you say* Lk 13: 35 (AD).

2. to denote contemporaneousness *as long as, while*—a. w. ind. (Hom. +; Jdth 5: 17) in our lit. only the pres. (Appian, Bell. Civ. 2, 53 §218 ἕως χειμάζουσιν and ibid. ἕως Πομπήιος ἡγεῖται=while Pompey imagines; Jos., Bell. 7, 347) ἔ. ἡμέρα ἐστὶν *while it is day* J 9: 4 (v.l. ὡς. On this interchange cf. LRadermacher, Philol. 60, '01, 495f; Bl-D. §455, 3 app.); 12: 35f t.r.; ἔ. αὐτὸς ἀπολύει τ. ὄχλον *while he himself dismissed the crowd* Mk 6: 45. ἔ. ἔτι ἔχομεν *while we still have* 2 Cl 16: 1 (cf. Pla., Phaedo 89C ἔ. ἔτι φῶς ἐστιν, Parmen. 135D ἔ. ἔτι νέος εἶ; Appian, Bell. Civ. 3, 32 §127 ἕως ἔτι δύνασαι; PEleph. 14, 24 [223 BC]; Sir 33: 21 ἕως ἔτι ζῇς).

b. w. subjunctive (PTebt. 6, 42 [140 BC] ἕως...μένωσι; Dio Chrys. 27[44], 5 ἕως ἂν...φέρῃ='as long as'; Appian, Numid. 4 §2) Mk 14: 32; Lk 17: 8.

II. improper prep. (appears first at the end of the IV cent. BC [ESchwyzer, Gramm. II '50, 550]) *until, up to* (Aristot. +; inscr., pap., LXX; Sib. Or. 5, 57; 118); so almost always (s. 1 bγ).

1. of time—a. w. the gen. of a noun or an equivalent expr. (Dit., Syll.³ 588, 64 [196 BC] ἔ. τοῦ τ. συνθήκης χρόνου, Or. 90, 16 ἔ. τοῦ πρώτου ἔτους; BGU 1128, 8 [14 BC]; oft. LXX) ἕως τῆς ἡμέρας (Jdth 12: 14; 1 Esdr 4: 55; 1 Macc 13: 39) Mt 27: 64; Lk 1: 80. ἔ. τῆς ἡμέρας ἐκείνης (Jdth 1: 15) Mt 26: 29; Mk 14: 25. ἔ. τ. ἡμ. ταύτης (4 Km 17: 23; 1 Macc 8: 10; 13: 30; 1 Esdr 8: 73; Bar 1: 13) 1 Cl 11: 2. ἔ. ὥρας ἐνάτης Mk 15: 33; Lk 23: 44. ἔ. τῆς πεντηκοστῆς 1 Cor 16: 8. ἔ. τῆς σήμερον (sc. ἡμέρας) Mt 27: 8. ἔ. τέλους *until the end* 1 Cor 1: 8. ἔ. αἰῶνος *forever* Hv 2, 3, 3. Of someone's age or a period of life ἔ. ἐτῶν ὀγδοήκοντα τεσσάρων *until the age of 84*, prob.=*until she was now 84 years old* (so Gdspd., Probs. 79-81) Lk 2: 37 (cf. Jos., Ant. 5, 181). Used w. proper names (Polyb. 2, 41, 5; Diod. S. 1, 50, 6) ἔ. Ἰωάννου *up to the time of John* Mt 11: 13. ἔ. Σαμουήλ Ac 13: 20. In such cases, as well as in others, ἔ. often looks back to a preceding ἀπό: *from—to* (Bar 1: 19; 1 Esdr 8: 73; Sir 40: 1; 1 Macc 16: 2; 3 Macc 6: 38 al.): ἀπὸ Ἀβραὰμ ἔ. Δαυὶδ Mt 1: 17a. ἀπὸ τ. βαπτίσματος Ἰωάννου ἔ. τῆς ἡμέρας Ac 1: 22. ἀπὸ τ. ἕκτης ὥρας ἔ. ὥρας ἐνάτης Mt 27: 45 (cf. Dit., Syll.³ 736, 109 [92 BC] ἀπὸ τετάρτας ὥρας ἔ. ἑβδόμας; 1 Esdr 9: 41). ἀπὸ πρωῒ ἔ. ἑσπέρας Ac 28: 23 (cf. Jos., Ant. 6, 364).—ἔ. τοῦ νῦν *until now* (Ps.-Lucian, Halc. 4; Dit., Syll.³ 705, 44f [112 BC]; UPZ 122 [157 BC]; Gen 15: 16; 18: 12; Num 14: 19; 1 Macc 2: 33) after ἀπ' ἀρχῆς Mt 24: 21; Mk 13: 19 (cf. BGU 1197, 8 [4 BC] ἕως τ. νῦν ἀπὸ τοῦ ἐννεακαιδεκάτου ἔτους Καίσαρος; Ezk 4: 14). ἀπὸ Δαυὶδ ἔ. τ. μετοικεσίας Βαβυλῶνος *to the Babylonian exile* Mt 1: 17b.—As here, a historical event forms the boundary (cf. 1 Esdr 5: 71) in ἔ. τ. τελευτῆς Ἡρῴδου 2: 15.—W. the articular inf. (on the acc. with it cf. Bl-D. §406, 3) ἔ. τοῦ ἐλθεῖν αὐτὸν εἰς Καισάρειαν *until he came to Caesarea* Ac 8: 40 (s. Dit., Syll.³ 588, 93f;

Gen 24: 33; 28: 15; 1 Macc 3: 33; 5: 19; Polyb., Joseph. [Bl-D. §403 w. app.]); but s. also 2a below.

b. w. the gen. of the relative pron. in the neut. (οὗ or ὅτου)—**α.** ἕ. οὗ *until* (Hdt. 2, 143; Plut. et al.; LXX; in local mng. Dit., Syll.³ 495, 101) w. aor. ind. (Judg 3: 30; 4: 24 B; 4 Km 17: 20; Tob 1: 21; 2: 4, 10; Jdth 10: 10; 15: 5; Jos., Ant. 10, 134) Mt 1: 25; 13: 33; Lk 13: 21; Ac 21: 26. W. aor. subj. (BGU 1209, 8 [23 bc]; PRyl. 229, 14 [38 ad]; Judg 5: 7 B; Ps 71: 7; Jdth 6: 5, 8) Mt 18: 34; Lk 15: 8; 22: 18; 24: 49; Ac 25: 21; 2 Pt 1: 19. After neg.=*until, before* Mt 17: 9; J 13: 38; Ac 23: 12, 14, 21.

β. ἕ. ὅτου *until* w. aor. ind. (Diod. S. 19, 108, 3; 3 Km 10: 7; 11: 16; Da 2: 34; 7: 4) J 9: 18. W. aor. subj. (POxy. 1061, 16 [22 bc]; 1 Km 22: 3; 2 Esdr 14: 5) Lk 13: 8; 15: 8 v.l.; 22: 16, 18 v.l.

γ. In a few cases ἕως in these combinations has the sense *while* ἕ. οὗ (Jos., Ant. 3, 279 [ἔχουσι]) w. subj. Mt 14: 22; 26: 36 (but s. EDBurton, Moods and Tenses '00, §325).—ἕ. ὅτου (SSol 1: 12) w. ind. Mt 5: 25.

c. w. adv. of time ἕ. ἄρτι *until now* (s. ἄρτι 3), Mt 11: 12; J 2: 10; 5: 17; 16: 24; 1 J 2: 9; 1 Cor 4: 13; 8: 7; 15: 6. ἕ. σήμερον (Sir 47: 7) 2 Cor 3: 15. ἕ. πότε; *how long?* (Ps 12: 2, 3; 2 Km 2: 26; 1 Macc 6: 22) Mt 17: 17a, b; Mk 9: 19a, b; Lk 9: 41; J 10: 24; Rv 6: 10.

2. of place—**a.** w. gen. of the place *as far as, to* (Polyb. 3, 76, 2; Diod. S. 1, 27, 5; Dit., Syll.³ 588, 32 [196 bc] ἕ. θαλάσσης; 1231, 12 ἀπὸ . . . ἕως; PTebt. 33, 5 [112 bc]; LXX; Jos., Bell. 1, 512) ἕ. Φοινίκης Ac 11: 19. ἕ. Βηθλεέμ Lk 2: 15. ἕ. οὐρανοῦ, ᾅδου Mt 11: 23; Lk 10: 15. ἕ. τῆς αὐλῆς Mt 26: 58; cf. Lk 4: 29. ἕ. ἐσχάτου τ. γῆς (Is 48: 20; 62: 11; 1 Macc 3: 9) Ac 1: 8. ἕ. τρίτου οὐρανοῦ 2 Cor 12: 2. ἀπὸ . . . ἕ.: ἀπὸ ἀνατολῶν ἕ. δυσμῶν Mt 24: 27. ἀπ' ἄκρων οὐρανῶν ἕ. ἄκρων αὐτῶν vs. 31 (cf. Dt 30: 4). ἀπ' ἄκρου γῆς ἕ. ἄκρου οὐρανοῦ Mk 13: 27 (cf. Jdth 11: 21).—Also w. gen. of a pers., who is in a certain place (Aelian, V.H. 3, 18 ἕ. Ὑπερβορέων; 4 Km 4: 22; 1 Macc

3: 26) ἦλθον ἕ. αὐτοῦ Lk 4: 42. διελθεῖν ἕ. ἡμῶν Ac 9: 38. Perh. Ac 8: 40 also belongs here (s. above II 1a, end); then pass. like Gen 10: 19 would be comparable.

b. w. adv. of place (LXX) ἕ. ἄνω (2 Ch 26: 8) *to the brim* J 2: 7. ἕ. ἔσω *right into* Mk 14: 54. ἕ. κάτω (Ezk 1: 27; 8: 2 looking back to ἀπό) ἀπ' ἄνωθεν ἕ. κάτω *fr. top to bottom* Mt 27: 51; Mk 15: 38. ἕ. ὧδε (Gen 22: 5; 2 Km 20: 16; 3 Km 18: 45) ἀρξάμενος ἀπὸ τ. Γαλιλαίας ἕ. ὧδε Lk 23: 5.

c. w. proper and improper prep. ἕ. πρός (Polyb. 3, 82, 6; 12, 17, 4; Gen 38: 1; Ezk 48: 1) ἕ. πρὸς Βηθανίαν *as far as B.* Lk 24: 50. For the v.l. ἕ. εἰς B. cf. Polyb. 1, 11, 14; Diod. S. 1, 27, 5; Aelian, V.H. 12, 22; Dt 31: 24; 4 Km 2: 6; Jos., Ant. 16, 90. ἕ. καὶ εἰς *even into* Ac 26: 11. ἕ. ἔξω τῆς πόλεως 21: 5.

3. of order in a series ἀρξάμενος ἀπὸ τῶν ἐσχάτων ἕ. πρώτων Mt 20: 8. ὁ δεύτερος καὶ ὁ τρίτος ἕ. τῶν ἑπτά 22: 26. ἀπὸ μικροῦ ἕ. μεγάλου *great and small* (Bar 1: 4; 1 Macc 5: 45; Jdth 13: 4) Ac 8: 10; Hb 8: 11 (Jer 38: 34).—J 8: 9 v.l.

4. of degree and measure, denoting the upper limit ἕ. ἑπτάκις (4 Km 4: 35) *as many as seven times* Mt 18: 21f; cf. vs. 22. ἕ. ἡμίσους τῆς βασιλείας μου (Esth 5: 3; 7: 2) Mk 6: 23. οὐκ ἔστιν ἕ. ἑνός (cf. PTebt. 56, 7 [II bc] οὐκ ἔχομεν ἕ. τῆς τροφῆς τῶν κτηνῶν ἡμῶν='we do not even have enough to feed our cattle'; Leontios, Vi. Joh. [ed. HGelzer 1893] 66, 21ff οὐ . . . ἕως ἑνὸς νομίσματος= 'not even a single coin') *there is not even one* Ro 3: 12 (Ps 13: 3). ἐᾶτε ἕ. τούτου *stop! No more of this* Lk 22: 51 (ἕ. τούτου='to this point' Aristot., H.A. 9, 46; Polyb. 9, 36, 1; cf. 2 Km 7: 18). ἕ. θανάτου *unto death* (Antig. Car. 16; Sir 34: 12; 51: 6; 4 Macc 14: 19): *contend* (Sir 4: 28. Cf. Dit., Or. 266, 29 [III bc] μαχοῦμαι ἕως ζωῆς καὶ θανάτου) 1 Cl 5: 2. περίλυπός ἐστιν ἡ ψυχή μου ἕ. θανάτου Mt 26: 38; Mk 14: 34 (cf. Jon 4: 9 σφόδρα λελύπημαι ἐγὼ ἕ. θανάτου). M-M.

ς

ς'= the stigma or vau, an obsolete letter used as the numeral *six* or *sixth* in the titles of Hm 6 and s 6. Cf. the

entry χξς' Rv 13: 18 v.l. *

Z

ζ' numeral=7 (ἑπτά) Ac 12: 10 D; =*seventh* (ἑβδόμη) Hm 7; [s 7] in the superscriptions (Apollon. Paradox. 33: Θεόφραστος ἐν τῷ ζ' περὶ φυτῶν). *

Ζαβουλών, ὁ indecl. (זְבוּלֻן) (LXX; Philo, Fuga 73; Test. 12 Patr.—Joseph. acc. to his ordinary usage would prob. decline Ζαβουλῶν [Ant. 1, 308; 2, 179] -ῶνος) *Zebulun* (Gen 30: 20), an Israelite tribe Rv 7: 8; its territory (beside Naphtali) Mt 4: 13, 15; Lk 4: 31 D. *

Ζακχαῖος, ου, ὁ (זַכַּי) (in this form also in WECrum, Coptic Ostraca ['02] 435, 7 acc. to Wilcken's restoration: APF 2, '03, p. 174, 3; 2 Macc 10: 19. In the form Σακχαῖος Jos., Vi. 239. On Ζαχαῖος s. Preisigke, Namenbuch) *Zacchaeus*, a chief tax-collector of Jericho Lk 19: 2, 5, 8. M-M. *

Ζάρα, ὁ (זֶרַח) *Zerah* in the genealogy of Jesus Mt 1: 3 (cf. 1 Ch 2: 4). *

ζαφθάνι is the rdg. of Cod. D Mt 27: 46; Mk 15: 34 for σαβαχθάνι; it is a scholarly correction based on the Hebr. (read ἀζαφθάνι= עֲזַבְתַּנִי and cf. Dalman, Worte 43; Wlh., Mk² '09 on 15: 34; AMerx, D. vier kanon. Ev. II 1, '02, 424). *

Ζαχαρίας, ου, ὁ (זְכַרְיָה) *Zechariah* (freq. name: OT; Ep. Arist.; Joseph., index Niese; Preisigke, Namenbuch).

1. a priest, father of John the Baptist Lk 1: 5, 12f, 18, 21, 40, 59, 67; 3: 2; GEb 1.—**2.** Z. Lk 11: 51, designated as son of Barachiah (q.v.) in Mt 23: 35 (ENestle, ZNW 6, '05, 198–200).

3. In Mt 27: 9 Z. (meaning the prophet) is v.l. for Jeremiah; s. comm. *

[ζάω] contr. ζῶ (Hom.+; inscr., pap., LXX, En., Ep. Arist., Philo, Joseph., Test. 12 Patr.) impf. ἔζων (Ro 7: 9 B ἔζην; on this form cf. Bl-D. §88; Mlt.-H. 194, both w. ref.); fut. ζήσω (uniformly attested Ro 6: 2; Hb 12: 9; accepted by Nestle also J 5: 25; 6: 51b, 57c, 58; 14: 19b; 2 Cor 13: 4b; Js 4: 15); the later (since Hippocr. VII p. 536 L.; Jos., Ant. 1, 193 al.) form ζήσομαι (Bl-D. §77 app.; Rob. 356) is more common; 1 aor. ἔζησα. On the LXX usage s. Thackeray 269.

1. *live*—**a.** of physical life in contrast to death—**α.** gener. Ro 7: 1, 2, 3; 14: 8a, c; 1 Cor 7: 39. ψυχὴ ζῶσα *a living soul* (Gen 1: 20 al.) 1 Cor 15: 45 (Gen 2: 7). ὅσα ἔτη ζῆ *as many years as he lives* B 10: 6 (cf. Dit., Syll.³ 663, 6; Sb 173, 6 Αὐρήλιος ζήσας ἔτη νε'). τὸ ζῆν *life* (Attic wr., inscr., pap., LXX) ὥστε ἐξαπορηθῆναι ἡμᾶς καὶ τοῦ ζῆν *so that we even despaired of life* 2 Cor 1: 8. διὰ παντὸς τοῦ ζῆν *during the whole lifetime* Hb 2: 15 (cf. Diod. S. 1, 74, 3 διατελεῖν πάντα τὸν τοῦ ζῆν χρόνον. ἔτι ζῶν *while he was still living*=before his death Mt 27: 63 (Ramsay, Phrygia II p. 660 no. 618 Ζώσιμος ἔτι ζῶν κατεσκεύασεν; 3 Km 12: 6). ζῶντες ἐβλήθησαν ... εἰς τὴν λίμνην τοῦ πυρός *they were thrown alive into the lake of fire* Rv 19: 20. ζῶσα τέθνηκεν *though alive she is dead* 1 Ti 5: 6 (cf. Sextus 7). ἡμεῖς οἱ ζῶντες *we during our (earthly) life* 2 Cor 4: 11; the same phrase=*we who are still living* 1 Th 4: 15, 17. Here the opp. is νεκροί, as in Mt 22: 32; Mk 12: 27; Lk 20: 38a. ζῶντες καὶ νεκροί *the living and the dead* Ac 10: 42; Ro 14: 9b; 2 Ti 4: 1; 1 Pt 4: 5; 2 Cl 1: 1; B 7: 2.—Occasionally the contrast betw. νεκρός and ζῆν is used fig. with ref. to the realm of religion and ethics Lk 15: 24 v.l., 32.

β. of dead persons who return to life *become alive again* of men (3 Km 17: 23) Mt 9: 18; Ac 9: 41; 20: 12; Rv 20: 4, 5. Of Jesus Mk 16: 11; Lk 24: 5, 23; Ac 1: 3; Ro 14: 9a; 2 Cor 13: 4a; Rv 2: 8.

γ. of sick persons, if their illness terminates not in death but in recovery *be well, recover* (Artem. 4, 4 ἔζησεν ὁ παῖς =became well; 5, 71; 72; PGM 1, 188; 4 Km 1: 2; 8: 8 εἰ ζήσομαι ἐκ τῆς ἀρρωστίας μου ταύτης; Jos., Vi. 421) Mk 5: 23; J 4: 50, 51, 53.—Of removal of anxiety 1 Th 3: 8.

δ. also of healthy persons *live on, remain alive* (X., An. 3, 2, 39 ὅστις δὲ ζῆν ἐπιθυμεῖ πειράσθω νικᾶν; Ep. 56 of Apollonius of Tyana [Philostrat. I 359, 14]) Ac 25: 24; 28: 4. ἐὰν ὁ κύριος θελήσῃ ζήσομεν Js 4: 15.

ε. of beings that in reality, or as they are portrayed, are not subject to death: of Melchizedek Hb 7: 8 (opp. ἀποθνῄσκοντες ἄνθρωποι).—In this sense it is most comprehensively applied to God (ὁ θεὸς ὁ ζῶν (cf. 4 Km 19: 4, 16; Is 37: 4, 17; Hos 2: 1; Da 6: 21 Theod.; 3 Macc 6: 28; Sib. Or. 3, 763; POxy. 924, 11 [IV AD, Gnostic]; PGM 4, 1038 ὁ μέγας ζῶν θεός; 7, 823; 12, 79; Philo, Decal. 67 ὁ ζῶν ἀεὶ θεός.—The phrase 'the living God' is not found in Joseph.) Mt 16: 16; 26: 63; Ac 14: 15; Ro 9: 26 (Hos 2: 1); 2 Cor 3: 3; 6: 16; 1 Ti 3: 15; 4: 10; Hb 3: 12; 9: 14; 10: 31; 12: 22; Rv 7: 2; 2 Cl 20: 2; also ὁ ζῶν πατήρ J 6: 57. W. the addition εἰς τοὺς αἰῶνας τῶν αἰώνων Rv 15: 7; cf. 4: 9 (cf. Tob 13: 2; Sir 18: 1). God takes an oath by himself in the words ζῶ ἐγώ *as surely as I live* (Num 14: 28 al.) Ro 14: 11 (Is 49: 18); classical parallels GStählin, NovT 5, '62, 142 n. 2.

b. w. more precise mention of the sphere (Artem. 3, 62 ἐν ἀγορᾷ ζ.=spend his life in the marketplace) ζ. ἐν σαρκί *live in the flesh* in contrast to the heavenly life Phil 1: 22; Gal 2: 20c; ζ. ἐν κόσμῳ *live in the world* Col 2: 20. ζ. ἐν θεῷ *live in God* (as the Being who penetrates and embraces everything) Ac 17: 28 (s. κινέω 3).

c. w. mention of that upon which life depends ἐπί τινι *on the basis of someth.* (Andoc. 1, 100; Isocr. 10, 18; Ael.

Aristid. 28, 103 K.=49 p. 525 D.) ζ. ἐπ' ἄρτῳ *live on bread* Mt 4: 4; Lk 4: 4 (both Dt 8: 3). ζ. ἔκ τινος *obtain one's living fr. someth.* (Aristoph., Eccl. 591; Demosth. 57, 36; POxy. 1117, 19; 1557, 12) 1 Cor 9: 14.

2. *live* of the supernatural life of the child of God (ζῆν in the sense of a higher type of life than the animal: X., Mem. 3, 3, 11; Cass. Dio 69, 19 βιοὺς μὲν ἔτη τόσα, ζήσας δὲ ἔτη ἑπτά).

a. in the world ἐγὼ ἔζων χωρὶς νόμου ποτέ *I was once (truly) alive without law* (this has been interpr. to mean *when no law existed*; Paul is then regarded as speaking fr. the viewpoint of a man in paradise before the command Gen 2: 16f; 3: 3. Another interpr. thinks of Paul as referring to the period in his life when he was not conscious of the existence and significance of the law) Ro 7: 9. Even now those who listen to the voice of the Son of God enjoy this life J 5: 25; likew. those who receive him into their being 6: 57c; cf. Ro 6: 11, 13 (ἐκ νεκρῶν ζῶντας); Gal 2: 19; Rv 3: 1. This heavenly life on earth is a ζ. πνεύματι Gal 5: 25 or a life not of man, but of Christ who lives in him 2: 20a, **b.** Also of the superhuman power of the apostle ζήσομεν σὺν αὐτῷ ἐκ δυνάμεως θεοῦ εἰς ὑμᾶς *we shall live with him* (Christ) *through God's power in our dealings with you* 2 Cor 13: 4.

b. in the glory of the life to come (Sir 48: 11; cf. Dt 4: 1; 8: 1; 30: 16).

α. abs. Lk 10: 28; J 11: 25; 14: 19; Ro 8: 13b; Hb 12: 9. ἐμοὶ τ. ζῆν Χριστός =*life is possible for me only where Christ is* (hence death is gain) Phil 1: 21 (cf. OSchmitz, GHeinrici-Festschr. '14, 155–69). Another common interpr. is *for me to live is Christ*, i.e. while I am alive I work for Christ; w. death comes a joyful existence in the presence of Jesus.

β. more specifically εἰς τὸν αἰῶνα *have eternal life* (Ps.-Lucian, Philopatr. 17 ζῆν εἰς τὸν αἰῶνα) J 6: 51, 58 (in J the blessed life which the follower of Jesus enjoys here and now in the body is simply continued in the heavenly life of the future. In other respects also the dividing line betw. the present and the future life is somet. non-existent or at least not discernible) B 6: 3; 8: 5; 9: 2; 11: 10f; ἅμα σὺν αὐτῷ (i.e. Χριστῷ) ζ. *live together with Christ* 1 Th 5: 10; ζ. δι' αὐτοῦ (i.e. Chr.) 1 J 4: 9; ζ. κατὰ θεὸν πνεύματι *live, as God (lives), in the Spirit* 1 Pt 4: 6. ὁ δίκαιος ἐκ πίστεως ζήσεται (cf. Hab 2: 4) *he that is just through faith will have life* Ro 1: 17 (AFeuillet, NTS 6, '59, 52–80); Gal 3: 11; Hb 10: 38. This life is τὸ ἀληθινὸν ζῆν ITr 9: 2; IEph 11: 1. Christ is called τὸ ἀδιάκριτον ἡμῶν ζῆν *our unshakable* or *inseparable life* 3: 2.—The law-directed man believes concerning the doing of the law: ὁ ποιήσας αὐτὰ ζήσεται ἐν αὐτοῖς (Lev 18: 5) Gal 3: 12; cf. Ro 10: 5 (cf. Dio Chrys. 58[75], 1 οἱ τοῦτον [=τ. νόμον] φυλάττοντες ἔχονται τῆς σωτηρίας.

3. *live* of the conduct of life (Hom.+)—**a.** used w. adverbs or other modifiers: adv. (Sallust. c. 19 p. 34, 25 κακῶς ζῆν; Dit., Syll.³ 889, 13ff; Wsd 14: 28; Philo; Jos., Ant. 12, 198) ἀσώτως Lk 15: 13. ἐθνικῶς and ἰουδαϊκῶς Gal 2: 14. εὐσεβῶς 2 Ti 3: 12. σωφρόνως κ. δικαίως κ. εὐσεβῶς Tit 2: 12 (Plut., Mor. 2, 1108c=adv.; Colot. 2 [Pohlenz '52] ζῆν σωφρόνως κ. δικαίως. Cf. Diog. L. 10, 132; 140).—Φαρισαῖος *live as a Pharisee* Ac 26: 5. ἐν πίστει Gal 2: 20d. ἐν ἁμαρτίᾳ Ro 6: 2; ζ. ἐν τούτοις *live in these* (sins) Col 3: 7. κατὰ ἀλήθειαν *in keeping w. the truth* IEph 6: 2 (cf. Philo, Post. Cai. 73 κατὰ βούλημα τὸ τοῦ θεοῦ ζ.; Jos., Ant. 4, 302 κατὰ τ. νόμους ζ.). κατὰ θεόν 8: 1 (cf. Dit., Syll.³ 910A; B). κατὰ Ἰησοῦν Χριστόν IPhld 3: 2. κατὰ Χριστιανισμόν *live in accordance w. (our) Christianity* IMg 10: 1. κατὰ σάρκα Ro 8: 12f; Dg 5: 8; κατὰ κυριακὴν ζ. (opp. σαββατίζειν) *include the* observance of the Lord's day in one's life IMg 9: 1. Of a married woman ζ. μετὰ ἀνδρός live w. her husband Lk 2: 36 (for the added acc. of extent of time cf. Ael. Aristid. 46 p. 332 D.; Pr 28: 16; ἥτις ἔξησεν καλῶς μετ' ἐμοῦ ἔτη 18, μῆνας 4, ἡμέρας 5: Suppl. Epigr. Gr. 2, '24/'25, 384, also FWDanker, Jesus and the New Age, '72, 36).

b. τινί live for someone or someth., for his benefit (Hom.+; Demosth. 7, 17 οἳ οὐκ αἰσχύνονται Φιλίππῳ ζῶντες καὶ οὐ τῇ ἑαυτῶν πατρίδι; Dionys. Hal. 3, 17 . . . παῖδες, τῷ πατρὶ ζῶντες) ζ. τῷ θεῷ (4 Macc 7: 19; 16: 25; Philo, Mut. Nom. 13, Rer. Div. Her. 111) Lk 20: 38b (cf. Soph., Ajax 970); Ro 6: 10, 11; Gal 2: 19; Hm 3: 5; τῷ κυρίῳ Ro 14: 8b (cf. Plut., Vit. Cleom. 31, 5). For Christ 2 Cor 5: 15; τῇ δικαιοσύνῃ ζ. 1 Pt 2: 24; ἑαυτῷ ζ. live for oneself (Menand., fgm. 507 Kock οὐχ ἑαυτῷ ζῆν μόνον; Diod. S. 10, 33, 2 ζ. ἑαυτοῖς=live for themselves) Ro 14: 7.

4. The ptc. is used fig. w. respect to things—a. of spring water in contrast w. cistern water ὕδωρ ζῶν (Gen 26: 19; Lev 14: 5; Jer 2: 13 v.l.; Zech 14: 8.—Stagnant water is called ὕ. νεκρόν: Synes., Ep. 114 p. 254D) J 4: 10f (Hdb. exc. on J 4: 14); 7: 38; D 7: 1f.

b. of everything that possesses or brings life from God (Dit., Syll.³ 1173 [138 AD], 5 ζῶσαι ἀρεταὶ ἐγένοντο= miracles occurred that were full of divine life) λόγια ζῶντα words of life Ac 7: 38. λόγος ζῶν θεοῦ 1 Pt 1: 23; cf. Hb 4: 12. ὁδὸς ζῶσα a living way 10: 20. ἐλπὶς ζῶσα a living hope 1 Pt 1: 3.—ζ. is also used of things which serve as descriptions of pers. who communicate divine life: of Christ ὁ ἄρτος ὁ ζῶν J 6: 51a. λίθος ζῶν 1 Pt 2: 4. Of Christians: θυσία ζῶσα a living sacrifice Ro 12: 1. λίθοι ζῶντες 1 Pt 2: 5.—Lit. s. ζωή, end. M-M.

ζβέννυμι (PGM 7, 364 in the ms.; 1 Th 5: 19 B* D* FG) s. σβέννυμι. M-M.

Ζεβεδαῖος, ου, ὁ (וְבַדְיָה) (Jos., Ant. 5, 33; PGrenf. II 113, 42) Zebedee, a father of the apostles John and James, Mt 4: 21; 10: 2; 20: 20; 26: 37; 27: 56; Mk 1: 19f; 3: 17; 10: 35; Lk 5: 10; J 21: 2.*

ζεστός, ή, όν (mng. 'boiled, cooked' in Appian; of 'boiling' water in Nicander, fgm. 70, 11f ζεστὸν ὕδωρ; Strabo; Soranus p. 37, 2 al.; Diosc., Sext. Emp.; Sib. Or. 3, 461) hot; in Rv 3: 15f the underlying idea is that water can be used when it is hot or cold (ψυχρός), but when lukewarm it is unpalatable and will be spat out (on its application to pers. cf. Etym. Mag. 413, 23 ζεστὸν ἄνθρωπον φαμὲν τὸν εὐκίνητον κ. θερμόν). MJSRudwick and EMBGreen, ET 69, '57/'58, 176–8.*

ζεύγνυμι (Hom.+; inscr., LXX) connect, join (with a yoke) Mt 10: 9 v.l. (of marital union also Parthenius 17, 3; Appian, Basil. 1 §1, Bell. Civ. 2, 14 §50; Athen. 12 p. 554B; Sb 6647, 5; Jos., Ant. 16, 11). B. 843.*

ζεῦγος, ους, τό—1. yoke of two animals united by a yoke, ζεῦγος βοῶν (Hom.+; Diod. S. 14, 18, 5; Arrian, Anab. 2, 3, 2; PPetr. III 31, 5 [240 BC]; 3 Km 19: 21; Job 1: 3, 14; 42: 12; cf. Jos., Ant. 8, 353; 12, 192) Lk 14: 19. But here the term can also have the more general mng. 2 (in both senses it is a rabb. loanw.).

2. pair (Aeschyl., Ag. 44; Hdt. 3, 130; X., Oec. 7, 18; Dit., Or. 533, 6; 47; POxy. 267, 6 [36 AD] ἐνωτίων ζ.; BGU 22, 31 [114 AD] ζ. ψελλίων) ζ. τρυγόνων a pair of turtle doves 2: 24 (Lev 5: 11. Of doves also Sb 7814, 21; 24 [256 AD]). M-M.*

ζευκτηρία, ας, ἡ bands, the ropes that tied the rudders (the nautical t.t. is 'pendant' or 'pennant': LCasson, Ships,

etc. in the Ancient World '71, 228) Ac 27: 40 (the adj. ζευκτήριος since Aeschyl., Pers. 736. The subst. neut.= 'yoke' in sg. in Aeschyl., Ag. 515; PHermopol. 95, 18, in pl. τὰ ζευκτήρια PLond. 1177, 167 [113 AD] σχοινίων καὶ ζευκτηρίων; POxy. 934, 5; PFlor. 16, 26 al. in pap.). M-M.*

Ζεύς, Διός, acc. Δία (Hom.+; 2 Macc 6: 2; Ep. Arist. 16; Philo, Joseph., Sib. Or.) Zeus, king of the Greek gods, thought by the people of Lystra to have appeared in the pers. of Barnabas Ac 14: 12. ὁ ἱερεὺς τ. Διὸς τ. ὄντος πρὸ τ. πόλεως the priest of (the temple of) Zeus located before the city vs. 13 (cf. Charito 4, 4, 9 εἰς Ἀφροδίτην βαδίζειν; Philostrat. I 363, 17 ἐν Ἀρτέμιδι=in the temple of Artemis).—Lit. s. Λύστρα.*

ζέω ptc. ζέων boil, seethe (lit. Hom.+; Dialekt-Inschr. p. 1034 no. 3 [Crete, II BC] religious regulation καταχέαι τινὶ ὕδωρ ζέον; pap.; Job 32: 19; Jos., Bell. 3, 271, Ant. 13, 345) fig. of emotions, anger, love, eagerness to do good or evil (trag.; Pla., Rep. 4 p. 440c; Charito 1, 5, 1; Plut., Mor. 1088f; 4 Macc 18: 20; Philo, Mos. 2, 280) ζέων τῷ πνεύματι of Apollos before he became a full-fledged member of the Christian community with burning zeal Ac 18: 25 (cf. Eunap. p. 82 ζέοντος δαίμονος, i.e. of the orator.—S. also HPreisker, ZNW 30, '31, 301–4). But the admonition to Christians to be τῷ πνεύματι ζέοντες Ro 12: 11 directs them to maintain the spiritual glow. M-M. B. 676.*

ζηλεύω (Democrit. 55 v.l. Diels; Simplicius in Epict. p. 56D; Leontios 44a p. 89, 2; Cat. Cod. Astr. X 219, 8) w. same mng. as ζηλόω abs. be eager, earnest Rv 3: 19.*

ζῆλος, ου, ὁ and ζῆλος, ους, τό Ac 5: 17 v.l.; 2 Cor 9: 2; Phil 3: 6; ITr 4: 2 and 1 Cl (the neut. is also poss. in a few other pass.). For LXX usage s. Thackeray 158, 5.

1. in a good sense zeal, ardor (since Soph., Aj. 503; Aristot., Rhet. 2, 11, 1; LXX) 2 Cor 9: 2. W. σπουδή (Dio Chrys. 17[34], 48) 7: 11; κατὰ ζ. as far as zeal is concerned Phil 3: 6. W. obj. gen. (Soph., Oed. Col. 943; Strabo 13, 2, 4; Plut., Cor. 4: 3; Lucian, Adv. Ind. 17; 1 Macc 2: 58. Oft. Philo; Jos., C. Ap. 2, 271) ζ. θεοῦ zeal for God (Jdth 9: 4) Ro 10: 2. ζ. τοῦ οἴκου σου zeal for thy house J 2: 17 (Ps 68: 10). In the same sense ὑπέρ τινος: τὸν ὑμῶν ζ. ὑπὲρ ἐμοῦ your ardor on my behalf 2 Cor 7: 7. W. gen. of quality θεοῦ ζῆλος a zeal like that of God 2 Cor 11: 2 (cf. Is 9: 6; Philo, Post. Cai. 183; on the idea FKüchler, ZAW 28, '08, 42ff; BRenaud, Je suis un Dieu jaloux, '63). Of the fire of judgment which, with its blazing flames, appears like a living being intent on devouring God's adversaries πυρὸς ζῆλος ἐσθίειν μέλλοντος τ. ὑπεναντίους Hb 10: 27 (cf. Is 26: 11; Zeph 1: 18; 3: 8; Ps 78: 5).

2. in a bad sense jealousy, envy (Hes., Op. 195; Plut., Thes. 6, 9, Lycurg. 4, 3; PGrenf. I 1, 13 [II BC]; Eccl 4: 4; 9: 6; Sir 30: 24; 40: 4 [both w. θυμός]; Jos., Ant. 14, 161; Cicero, Tusc. Disp. 4, 8, 17) 1 Cl 6: 1ff; 43: 2; 63: 2. W. ἔρις Ro 13: 13; 1 Cl 6: 4; cf. 1 Cor 3: 3; 2 Cor 12: 20; Gal 5: 20 (in the three last passages ζῆλος seems to be coördinate with ἔρις in the sense 'rivalry' or 'party-attachment'). W. ἐριθεία Js 3: 14, 16. W. φθόνος (Democr. 191; Lysias 2, 48; Pla., Phileb. 47E; 50C; 1 Macc 8: 16) 1 Cl 3: 2; 4: 7 al. πλησθῆναι ζήλου become filled w. jealousy Ac 5: 17; 13: 45. ζ. leads to death 1 Cl 9: 1; 39: 7 (Job 5: 2). μυσερὸν ζ. 14: 1; μιαρὸν κ. ἄδικον ζ. 45: 4. ἔχειν ζῆλόν τινα ἐν ἀλλήλοις περί τινος be jealous of one another because of someth. Hs 8, 7, 4. The pl. ζῆλοι found as v.l. Ro 13: 13; 2 Cor 12: 20; Gal 5: 20 denotes the var. outbreaks of jealousy and the forms it takes (cf. Pla., Leg. 3 p. 679c

ζῆλοί τε καὶ φθόνοι).—BReicke, Diakonie, Festfreude u. Zelos usw., '51, 231-393; AStumpff, TW II 879-84. M-M.**

ζηλοτυπία, ας, ἡ (Aeschines+; Polyb. 4, 87, 4; Plut.; Dio Chrys. 14[31], 99 al.; Lucian; Num 5: 15, 18, 25, 29; Philo; Jos., Ant. 7, 386, C. Ap. 2, 123) jealousy D 5: 1. B. 1139.*

ζηλόω 1 aor. ἐζήλωσα (Hom. Hymns, Hesiod+; inscr., pap., LXX, Ep. Arist., Philo, Joseph., Test. 12 Patr.).
1. in a good sense strive, desire, exert oneself earnestly
a. w. a thing as obj. τὶ (for) someth. (Eur., Hec. 255; Thu. 2: 37; Demosth. 20, 141; Polyb. 6, 25, 11 τὸ βέλτιον; Diod. S. 1, 95; PSI 94, 9 ζηλοῖ τ. μάθησιν; Wsd 1: 12; Sir 51: 18 τὸ ἀγαθόν; Jos., C. Ap. 2, 261) ζ. τὰ χαρίσματα τὰ μείζονα strive for the more valuable spiritual gifts 1 Cor 12: 31. τὸ προφητεύειν 14: 39. τὰ πνευματικά vs. 1 (where beside the acc. a ἵνα-clause depends on ζ.).
b. w. a personal obj. τινά be deeply concerned about someone, court someone's favor (Περὶ ὕψους 13, 2 οἱ ζηλοῦντες ἐκείνους; Pr 23: 17; 24: 1; pass. Jos., C. Ap. 1, 225) Gal 4: 17a, b; 2 Cor 11: 2. μηδέν με ζηλῶσαι let nothing attract me (and turn me away fr. my purpose) IRo 5: 3.
c. abs. manifest zeal (Thu. 2, 64, 4); pass. καλὸν ζηλοῦσθαι ἐν καλῷ πάντοτε it is commendable if zeal is shown at all times in what is good Gal 4: 18.
2. in a bad sense be filled w. jealousy, envy τινά toward someone (Hes., Op. 310; Hom. Hymns, Cer. 168; 223; Gen 26: 14; 30: 1) τὸν Ἰωσήφ Ac 7: 9 (cf. Gen 37: 11). Abs. Ac 17: 5; 1 Cor 13: 4; Js 4: 2; 2 Cl 4: 3.—AStumpff, TW II 884-90. M-M.*

ζηλωτής, οῦ, ὁ (Isocr., Pla.+; inscr., LXX, Philo, Joseph.) zealot, enthusiast, fanatic.
1. w. additions indicating what the ζ. ardently desires to join, promote, actively support, possess or defend.
a. w. gen.—α. of the pers. (Dio Chrys. 38[55], 6 Ὁμήρου ζ.; Dit., Syll.³ 717, 33, Or. 339, 90; Jos., Vi. 11) ζ. τοῦ θεοῦ one who is zealous for God Ac 22: 3 (Musonius 37, 3 ζ. τοῦ Διός; Epict. 2, 14, 13).
β. of the thing (Diod. S. 1, 73 τ. πολεμικῶν ἔργων; Epict. 2, 12, 25; 3, 24, 40; Dit., Syll³ 675, 27f ζ. τῆς αὐτῆς αἱρέσεως; 756, 32; Philo, Praem. 11 ἀρετῆς, Spec. Leg. 1, 30, Virt. 175; Jos., C. Ap. 1, 162) ζ. ἐστε πνευμάτων you are eager to possess spirits (i.e., spiritual gifts) 1 Cor 14: 12. ζ. καλῶν ἔργων eager to perform good deeds Tit 2: 14. τοῦ ἀγαθοῦ 1 Pt 3: 13. τοῦ νόμου an ardent observer of the law Ac 21: 20 (cf. 2 Macc 4: 2; Philo, Spec. Leg. 2, 253; Jos., Ant. 12, 271). ζ. τ. πατρικῶν μου παραδόσεων Gal 1: 14 (Thrasyll. [I AD] in Diog. L. 9, 38: Democritus as ζ. τῶν Πυθαγορικῶν; Philo, Mos. 2, 161 ζ. τῶν Αἰγυπτιακῶν πλασμάτων).—Also rather in the sense of an enthusiastic adherent of a person or a cause (Strabo 10, 5, 6 p. 486 τοῦ Βίωνος ζηλωτής; Appian, Bell. Civ. 2, 2 §4 Σύλλα φίλος καὶ ζ.; Polyaenus 5, 2, 22; Diog. L. 2, 113; Memnon [I BC/I AD]: no. 434 fgm. 1, 35, 1 Jac. ζ. τῆς Λαμάχου προαιρέσεως=of the party of Lamachus).
b. w. περί to introduce a thing—a. w. gen. 1 Cl 45: 1
β. w. acc. Pol 6: 3.
2. abs. (Iambl., Vi. Pyth. 5, 29; Marinus, Vi. Procli 38 Boiss.), in a bad sense (w. ἐριστικός, θυμικός) D 3: 2. ζηλωτής is the cognomen of one of the Twelve, called Simon the Zealot to distinguish him fr. Simon Peter Lk 6: 15; Ac 1: 13; GEb 2. Cf. Jos., Bell. 2, 651; 4, 160 and s. Καναναῖος. WRFarmer, Maccabees, Zealots and Josephus '56; MHengel, Die Zeloten (Herod I to 70 AD), '61; MSmith, HTR 64, '71, 1-19; SGFBrandon, Jesus and the

Zealots, '67; s. Brandon's answer to criticism NTS 17, '70/'71, 453 and cf. JGGriffiths, ibid. 19, '73, 483-89; HPKingdon, ibid. 19, '72, 74-81. M-M.*

ζημία, ας, ἡ (Soph., Hdt.+; inscr., pap., LXX, Philo, Joseph., Test. 12 Patr.; loanw. in rabb. Class. usu. 'punishment') in our lit. only in the mng. damage, disadvantage, loss, forfeit (Philo, Somn. 1, 124 al.; Jos., Ant. 4, 211) Hs 6, 3, 4. μετὰ πολλῆς ζ. τινός with heavy loss of someth. Ac 27: 10; κερδῆσαι τὴν ζ. avoid, save oneself damage vs. 21. ἡγοῦμαί τι ζημίαν I consider someth. (a) loss (X., Mem. 2, 4, 3; cf. 2, 3, 2; Epict. 2, 10, 15; 3, 26, 25 [opp. κέρδος, as Lysias 7, 12; Pla., Leg. 835в al.]) Phil 3: 8; cf. vs. 7. M-M. B. 809.*

ζημιόω 1 aor. pass. ἐζημιώθην, subj. ζημιωθῶ, ptc. ζημιωθείς; 1 fut. pass. ζημιωθήσομαι (Eur., Hdt.+; inscr., pap., LXX, Philo, Joseph., Test. 12 Patr.) inflict injury or punishment, in our lit. only pass.
1. suffer damage or loss, forfeit, sustain injury (PFlor. 142, 8 of a sale ὥστε μήτε τὸν πιπράσκοντα ζημιοῦσθαι; Pr 22: 3) w. acc. τὶ suffer loss w. respect to someth., forfeit someth. (Thu. 3, 40, 3; Pla., Leg. 916в; Philo, Spec. Leg. 3, 143 τ. τιμήν; Jos., Ant. 11, 214; cf. Bl-D §159, 2; Rob. 485) τὴν ψυχήν Mt 16: 26; Mk 8: 36; cf. Lk 9: 25; 2 Cl 6: 2. ἐν μηδενὶ ζ. ἔκ τινος suffer loss through someone in no respect 2 Cor 7: 9; permit oneself to sustain loss w. acc. δι' ὃν τὰ πάντα ἐζημιώθην for whose sake I forfeited everything Phil 3: 8.
2. be punished (Lysias 31, 26 al.; Dit., Or. 669, 40; PTebt. 5, 92; Pr 19: 19; Jos., Ant. 15, 16) 1 Cor 3: 15.—AStumpff, TW II 890-4. M-M.*

Ζηνᾶς, acc. -ᾶν, ὁ (Inschr. v. Magn. 323; Preisigke, Namenbuch) Zenas, a Christian and νομικός (q.v. 2) Tit 3: 13. M-M.*

Ζήνων, ωνος, ὁ (freq. in lit., incl. Joseph., inscr. and pap.) Zeno 2 Ti 4: 19 v.l. as son of Aquila.*

ζητέω impf. ἐζήτουν, 3 sg. pass. ἐζητεῖτο Hb 8: 7; fut. ζητήσω; 1 aor. ἐζήτησα; 1 fut. pass. ζητηθήσομαι (Hom.+; inscr., pap., LXX; En. 103, 13; Philo, Joseph., Test. 12 Patr.; Sib. Or. 5, 297).
1. seek, look for in order to find (s. εὑρίσκω 1a)—a. lit.
α. what one possessed and has lost, w. acc. τινά Mt 28: 5; Mk 1: 37; Lk 2: 48f; J 6: 24, 26; 7: 34, 36. τὶ Mt 18: 12; Lk 19: 10. Abs. 15: 8.
β. what one desires somehow to bring into relation w. oneself or to obtain without knowing where it is to be found τινά 2 Ti 1: 17; J 18: 4, 7f; Ac 10: 19, 21. ζητεῖν τ. θεόν, εἰ ἄρα γε αὐτὸν εὕροιεν search for God, in the hope that they may find him 17: 27 (cf. Wsd 1: 1; 13: 6; Philo, Spec. Leg. 1, 36); Ro 10: 20 (Is 65: 1). τὶ Mt 2: 13; 12: 43; 13: 45 (in the special sense seek to buy as X., Cyr. 2, 2, 26; Theophr., Char. 23, 8 ἱματισμὸν ζητῆσαι εἰς δύο τάλαντα); Lk 11: 24 τ. εἴν τινι someth. on someth. fruit on a tree 13: 6f. Abs. Mt 7: 7f; Lk 11: 9f (Epict. 4, 1, 51).
b. look for, search out τινά someone Mk 3: 32; Ac 9: 11; IPol 4: 2. For the purpose of arrest, pass. GP 7: 26.
c. investigate, examine, consider, deliberate (X., Cyr. 8, 5, 13; Lucian, Hermot. 66; Aelian, V.H. 2, 13; 4 Macc 1: 13; cf. דרשׁ in post-bibl. Hebr. and Aram.: Dalman, Aram.-neuhebr. Handwörterbuch² '22; HLStrack, Einleitg. in Talmud u. Midraš⁵ '21, 4) παραλόγως ζ. engage in irrational investigations Dg 11: 1. ἐν ἑαυτῷ ζ. περί τινος ponder someth. Hs 2: 1. περὶ τούτου ζητεῖτε μετ' ἀλλήλων ὅτι; are you deliberating with each other on the fact that? J 16: 19. W. indir. discourse foll. consider

(Diod. S. 1, 51, 6 πόσαι. . .) πῶς Mk 11: 18; 14: 1, 11. τί Lk 12: 29. τὸ πῶς 22: 2. εἰ B 11: 1.—As legal t.t. *investigate* (Dinarchus 1, 8; POxy. 237 VI, 41; 726, 16; Theban Ostraca '13, 134, 4; EBickermann, Rev. de l'Hist. des Rel. 112, '35, 214f) ἔστιν ὁ ζητῶν κ. κρίνων *there is one who investigates and judges* J 8: 50b (cf. Philo, De Jos. 174). J 11: 56 may also have this technical sense.

2. somewhat removed fr. the basic mng. of seeking—**a.** *try to obtain, desire to possess* τὶ *someth.* (Lucian, Hermot. 66 τ. εὐδαιμονίαν) τ. βασιλείαν Mt 6: 33; Lk 12: 31. εὐκαιρίαν Mt 26: 16; Lk 22: 6. ψευδομαρτυρίαν Mt 26: 59; cf. Mk 14: 55. τὴν δόξαν J 5: 44; 7: 18; 8: 50a. τιμὴν κ. ἀφθαρσίαν Ro 2: 7; cf. 1 Cor 7: 27b; 2 Cor 12: 14; Col 3: 1; 1 Pt 3: 11 (Ps 33: 15).

b. *strive for, aim (at), desire, wish*—**a.** τὶ *someth.* τὸν θάνατον Rv 9: 6. λύσιν 1 Cor 7: 27a. τὸ θέλημά τινος *be intent on someone's will*=aim to satisfy it J 5: 30. τὸ σύμφορόν τινος *someone's benefit* (Hermogenes 283 ed. HRabe '13 p. 301, 11 v.l. ἐμοῦ οὐ τὸ Φιλίππου συμφέρον ζητοῦντος) 1 Cor 10: 33; τὰ (τὸ) ἑαυτοῦ ζητεῖν *strive for one's own advantage* 10: 24; 13: 5; Phil 2: 21.

β. w. interrog. pron. τί ζητεῖτε; (cf. Gen 37: 15) *what do you want?* J 1: 38; cf. 4: 27 (JFoster, ET 52, '40/'41, 37f).

γ. w. inf. foll. (Hdt. 3, 137) mostly aor. (Plut., Thes. 35, 6; Dit., Syll.³ 372, 7; Wsd 8: 2; Sir 7: 6; 27: 1; Tob 5: 14 BA; Jos., Ant. 11, 174; 13, 7) Mt 12: 46; 21: 46; Mk 12: 12; Lk 5: 18; 9: 9; 17: 33; J 5: 18; 7: 1; Ac 13: 7 D, 8; 16: 10 (cf. 3 Km 11: 22); Ro 10: 3; Gal 2: 17. Rarely the pres. inf. (X., An. 5, 4, 33; Esth 8: 12c) Lk 6: 19; Gal 1: 10 (ζ. ἀρέσκειν as Ael. Aristid. 34, 39 K.=50 p. 560 D.)—ἵνα for the inf. 1 Cor 14: 12.

δ. OT lang. apparently is reflected in ζ. τὴν ψυχήν τινος *seek the life of someone* Mt 2: 20 (cf. Ex 4: 19); Ro 11: 3 (3 Km 19: 10); cf. also 3 Km 19: 14; Sir 51: 3; Ps 34: 4; 37: 13; 39: 15; 53: 5; 62: 10; 85: 14.

c. *ask for, request, demand* τὶ *someth.* σημεῖον Mk 8: 12. σοφίαν 1 Cor 1: 22. δοκιμήν 2 Cor 13: 3. τινά J 4: 23. τὶ παρά τινος *demand someth. fr. someone* (Demosth. 4, 33; Sir 7: 4; 28: 3; 1 Esdr 8: 50; Tob 4: 18) Mk 8: 11; Lk 11: 16; 12: 48. Also τὶ ἀπό τινος B 21: 6. ζητεῖται ἐν τ. οἰκονόμοις ἵνα *it is required of managers that* 1 Cor 4: 2 (AFridrichsen, Con. Neot. 7, '42, 5;. M-M. B. 655; 764).

ζήτημα, ατος, τό (Soph., Hippocr.+; inscr., pap.; Ezk 36: 37 v.l.; loanw. in rabb.) in our lit. only in Ac, w. the mng. it still has in Mod. Gk. *(controversial) question, issue* Ac 15: 2; 26: 3. ζ. περί τινος *questions about someth.* (Pla., Leg. 891 c) 18: 15; 25: 19.—In 23: 29, since περί had been already used, the subj. of the discussion is added in the gen., ζ. τοῦ νόμου αὐτῶν. M-M.*

ζήτησις, εως, ἡ (Soph., Hdt.+; inscr., pap., Philo, Joseph.).

1. *investigation* (Pla. et al.; Jos., Vi. 302, esp. as legal t.t.: Dinarchus 1, 10; Dit., Or. 629, 9; POxy. 237 VIII, 39; 513, 45 ζ. περὶ τούτου) ἀπορούμενος ἐγὼ τὴν περὶ τούτων ζ. *because I was at a loss concerning the investigation of these things* Ac 25: 20. In the Past. Epistles it may denote the investigation of relig. and theol. problems (Alex. Aphr., Fat. 2, II 2 p. 166, 14 ζήτησις περὶ τῆς εἱμαρμένης. Cf. Philo, Migr. Abr. 76): 1 Ti 6: 4; 2 Ti 2: 23; Tit 3: 9. But here the context permits other interpr. as well; mng. 2 is poss. for the last two pass.

2. *controversial question, controversy* (Jos., Ant. 15, 135, C. Ap. 1, 11) s. above; for 1 Ti 6: 4 (w. λογομαχία) mng. 3 is poss.

3. *discussion, debate* (Diod. S. 15, 48, 4) Ac 15: 2, 7. ἐγένετο ζ. ἐκ τ. μαθητῶν Ἰωάννου μετὰ Ἰουδαίου περὶ καθαρισμοῦ *there arose a debate betw. the disciples of John and a Jew on purification* J 3: 25 (cf. Hdt. 5, 21 ζ. τῶν ἀνδρῶν τούτων μεγάλη ἐκ τ. Περσέων ἐγίνετο; Dionys. Hal. 8, 89, 4 ζ. πολλὴ ἐκ πάντων ἐγίνετο.—ζ. περί τινος as Athen. 3 p. 83a; Jos., Ant. 14, 195; ζ. betw. Christians and Jews Celsus 3, 1). M-M.*

ζιζάνιον, ου, τό (Apoc. of Mos. ch. 16 [CTischendorf, Apocalypses Apocr. 1866]; Geopon.; Etym. Mag. p. 411, 47) prob. (Suidas: ζιζάνιον· ἡ ἐν τῷ σίτῳ αἶρα) *darnel, cheat* a troublesome weed in the grainfields (Geopon. 2, 43 τὸ ζιζάνιον, τὸ λεγόμενον αἶρα, φθείρει τὸν σῖτον. Concerning αἶρα [without ζιζ.] the same statement in Theophr., Hist. Pl. 8, 8, 3, Caus. Pl. 4, 4, 8); resembling wheat, in our lit. only pl. (Geopon. 10, 87, 1; 14, 1, 5) in Mt in the parable of the 'weeds (tares) among the wheat' (cf. also Psellus p. 268, 17 οἱ τὰ ζιζάνια ἐπισπείροντες Mt 13: 25ff, 29f, 36, 38, 40 (s. RLiechtenhan, Kirchenblatt 99, '43, 146-9; 167-9). The word is supposedly Semitic: ILöw, Aramäische Pflanzennamen 1881, 133; HLewy, D. semit. Fremdwörter im Griech. 1895, 52. On the subj. cf. LFonck, Streifzüge durch die bibl. Flora '00, 129f; Sprenger, Pj 9, '13, 89ff; HGuthe, ZDPV 41, '18, 164f; ILöw, D. Flora d. Juden I '28, 723-9.*

Ζμύρνα (Dit., Or. 458, 41 [c. 9 BC]; PRyl. 153, 18 [II AD]; coins of Smyrna since the time of Trajan) s. Σμύρνα. M-M.

Ζοροβαβέλ, ὁ indecl. (זְרֻבָּבֶל) (in Joseph. Ζοροβάβηλος, ου [Ant. 11, 95]) *Zerubbabel* (Zech 4: 6, 9f; Hg 1: 1; 2: 21, 23; 1 Ch 3: 19; 1 Esdr 4: 13; 5: 5, 8 al.; 2 Esdr [Ezra] 2: 2; 3: 8; 17 [Neh 7]: 7; Sir 49: 11), descendant of David, Persian governor of Jerusalem after the return of the first exiles (ESellin, Serubbabel 1899), in the genealogy of Jesus Mt 1: 12f; Lk 3: 27.*

ζόφος, ου, ὁ (Hom.+; Plut., Lucian; Epict., fgm. p. 487, 2 Sch.; Sym., Philo).

1. *darkness, gloom* Hb 12: 18.—**2.** esp. the Darkness of the nether regions (Od. 20, 356), and these regions themselves (Il. 15, 191; 21, 56; Od. 11, 57) ὁ ζόφος τοῦ σκότους either *black darkness* or *gloomy hell* 2 Pt 2: 17; Jd 13 (the juxtaposition of ζ. and σκότος as Ael. Aristid. 24, 44 K.=44 p. 838 D.; Lucian, Catapl. 2); σειραὶ ζόφου *chains of hell* 2 Pt 2: 4 𝔓⁷² and t.r. ὑπὸ ζόφον *in* (lit. 'under') *darkness* (cf. Aeschyl., Pers. 839.—Quint. Smyrn. 2, 619 ὑπὸ ζ. of the underworld) Jd 6. M-M.*

ζυγός, οῦ, ὁ (Hom. Hymns, Cer. 217 and prose since Pla., Tim. 63B; Polyb., Epict.; PFay. 121, 4 εἰς τὸν ζ.; PStrassburg 32, 12; LXX [Thackeray p. 154]; En. 103, 11) for Attic τὸ ζυγόν (Hom.+; Jos., Ant. 12, 194).

1. *yoke*, in our lit. only fig. of any burden: ζ. δουλείας *yoke of slavery* (Soph., Aj. 944; cf. Hdt. 7, 8, 3; Pla., Leg. 6 p. 770E; Demosth. 18, 289; Gen 27: 40) Gal 5: 1. ὑπὸ ζυγὸν δοῦλοι *slaves under the yoke* (i.e. under the y. of sl.) 1 Ti 6: 1. ζυγὸς ἀνάγκης *yoke of necessity* (Eur., Or. 1330) B 2: 6. Of the teaching of Jesus Mt 11: 29f (cf. Sir 51: 26, also 6: 24-28; ThHaering, Mt 11: 28-30; ASchlatter-Festschr. '22, 3-15; TArvedson, D. Mysterium Christi '37, 174-200; HDBetz, JBL 86, '67, 10-24); D 6: 2. ὑπὸ τὸν ζυγὸν τῆς χάριτος ἔρχεσθαι *come under the yoke of grace* 1 Cl 16: 17. ἐπιθεῖναι ζυγὸν ἐπὶ τ. τράχηλόν τινος *put a yoke on the neck of someone* Ac 15: 10 (sim. expr. have become formal since Hes., Op. 815; Orph. Hymns 59, 5; Zosimus 2, 37, 8; Sib. Or. 3, 448).

2. *lever of a balance,* then *balance, pair of scales* (Pla. et al.) Rv 6: 5, where the gender of the noun cannot be definitely determined; for this mng., however, the lang. seems to prefer the neut. (s. LXX in Thackeray, loc. cit.; Inscr. Gr. 1222, 4 [II BC]).—On the whole word GBertram and KHRengstorf, TW II 898–904. M-M. B. 726.*

ζύμη, ης, ἡ (Aristot., Gen. An. 3, 4; Plut., Mor. 289F; PTebt. 375, 27; LXX; Philo, Spec. Leg. 1, 291; 2, 182; Jos., Ant. 3, 252) *yeast, leaven.*

1. lit. Mt 13: 33; Lk 13: 21. More fully ζ. τῶν ἄρτων Mt 16: 12. μικρὰ ζύμη ὅλον τὸ φύραμα ζυμοῖ *a little yeast ferments the whole lump of dough* 1 Cor 5: 6 (Cyranides p. 64, 22 μετὰ ζύμης μικρᾶς)=Gal 5: 9, shown by its repeated use to be a proverbial saying, serves to picture the influence of apparently insignificant factors in the moral and relig. sphere.

2. fig. ζ. is also used metaphorically of the attitudes of the Pharisees and of Herod Mk 8: 15. Of the hypocrisy of the Pharisees Lk 12: 1. Of the teaching of the Pharisees and Sadducees Mt 16: 6, 11. In IMg 10: 2 the *yeast that has grown old and sour* means a life regulated by the principles of Judaism. It is contrasted w. Jesus Christ, the νέα ζ., ibid. Employing the language of the Passover rules (Ex 12: 15, 19; 13: 7; Dt 16: 3f) Paul admonishes ἐκκαθάρατε τ. παλαιὰν ζ. 1 Cor 5: 7 and explains that *the old leaven* is ζ. κακίας κ. πονηρίας vs. 8.—HWindisch, TW II 904–8. M-M.*

ζυμόω (Hippocr.+; Plut., Mor. 659B; LXX) *to ferment, leaven* 1 Cor 5: 6; Gal 5: 9. Pass. (Philo, Vi. Cont. 81) Mt 13: 33; Lk 13: 21.*

ζωγρέω pf. pass. ptc. ἐζωγρημένος (Hom.+; Epigr. Gr. 841, 7; LXX) *capture alive* (Suidas: ζωγρεῖ ζῶντας λαμβάνει. So as early as Hom.; also Hdt. 1, 86; X., An. 4, 7, 22; Polyb. 3, 84, 10; Num 31: 18; 2 Ch 25: 12; Philo, Virt. 43; Jos., Bell. 2, 448, Ant. 9, 194; 20, 210) fig. ἀνθρώπους ἔσῃ ζωγρῶν *you will catch men* i.e., win them for God's kgdm. Lk 5: 10 (on the metaphor of fishing cf. Aristaen., Ep. 2, 23 ἀντὶ ἰχθύων παρθένους ζ.). ἐζωγρημένοι ὑπ' αὐτοῦ εἰς τὸ ἐκείνου θέλημα *held captive by him* (the devil) *to perform his* (the devil's; cf. Bl-D. §291, 6; Rob. 707.—Vi. Aesopi W c. 106 εἱμαρμένη ἐζώγρησεν someone to destroy him) *will* 2 Ti 2: 26 (differently LHBunn, ET '30, 235–7). M-M.*

ζωή, ῆς, ἡ (Hom.+; inscr., pap., LXX, En., Ep. Arist., Philo; Jos., Bell. 2, 131 al.; Test. 12 Patr., Sib. Or.) *life.*

1. of life in the physical sense—**a.** opp. θάνατος (Pind. et al.; Lucian, Tox. 38; Sir 37: 18; Pr 18: 21; Philo) Ro 8: 38; 1 Cor 3: 22; Phil 1: 20. ἐν τῇ ζωῇ σου *during your life* Lk 16: 25 (s. Sir 30: 5); cf. 12: 15; Ac 8: 33 (Is 53: 8); Js 4: 14; 1 Cl 16: 8 (Is 53: 8). ἐν τῇ ζ. ταύτῃ *in this life* 1 Cor 15: 19; also ζ. ἡ νῦν (opp. ἡ μέλλουσα) 1 Ti 4: 8. τέλος ζωῆς *end of life* Hb 7: 3. ζωὴ κ. πνοή *life and breath* Ac 17: 25 (cf. Gen 2: 7; 7: 22). πνεῦμα ζωῆς *breath of life* Rv 11: 11 (cf. Gen 6: 17; 7: 15). ψυχὴ ζωῆς *living thing* 16: 3 (cf. Gen 1: 30). πρὸς ζωῆς *necessary for life* 1 Cl 20: 10. Of the indestructible life of those clothed in the heavenly body 2 Cor 5: 4. The life of the risen Christ also has this character Ro 5: 10; 2 Cor 4: 10f; ζ. ἀκατάλυτος Hb 7: 16. ὁδοὶ ζωῆς Ac 2: 28 (Ps 15: 11). Christ is ἐν θανάτῳ ζ. ἀληθινή IEph 7: 2.

b. *means of sustenance, livelihood* (Hdt. et al.; Sir 4: 1; 29: 21) Hs 9, 26, 2.

2. of the supernatural life belonging to God and Christ, which the believers will receive in the future, but which they also enjoy here and now.

a. God and Christ—**α.** God as ζωή Dg 9: 6b; as ζωὴ αἰώνιος 1 J 5: 20. It is true of him that ἔχει ζωὴν ἐν ἑαυτῷ J 5: 26a. His commandment is eternal life 12: 50 (cf. Philo, Fug. 198 God is the πρεσβυτάτη πηγὴ ζωῆς; Herm. Wr. 11, 13; 14; 12, 15 God the πλήρωμα τ. ζωῆς; PGM 3, 602 [cf. Rtzst., Mysterienrel.³ 286, l. 11]; the deity called Νοῦς as ζωή and φῶς Herm. Wr. 1, 9; 12; 17; 21; 32; 13, 9; 18; 19. Cf. also Ps 35: 10; 55: 14; Sib. Or. fgm. 3, 34).

β. of Christ, who received life fr. God J 5: 26b. ἐν αὐτῷ ζ. ἦν 1: 4a; cf. 1 J 5: 11b. He is the ἀρχηγὸς τ. ζωῆς Ac 3: 15, the λόγος τ. ζωῆς 1 J 1: 1; cf. vs. 2, the ἄρτος τ. ζωῆς J 6: 35, 48; cf. vs. 33 (EJanot, Le pain de vie: Gregorianum 11, '30, 161–70), also simply ζωή 11: 25; 14: 6 or ἡ ζ. ἡμῶν Col 3: 4. Since the life in him was τὸ φῶς τ. ἀνθρώπων J 1: 4b, men through following him obtain τὸ φῶς τ. ζωῆς 8: 12 (on the combinations of φῶς and ζ. cf. IQS 3, 7 and the Orph. Hymns to Helios no. 8, 18 Qu. ζωῆς φῶς, and the Christian inscr. of Rome [Ramsay, Luke the Physician '08 p. 375: 238 AD], where a father calls his dead son γλυκύτερον φωτὸς καὶ ζοῆς; s. also α above).—SBartina, La vida como historia en J 1: 1–18, Biblica 49, '68, 91–6.

b. The discussion now turns naturally to the life of the believers, which proceeds fr. God and Christ.

a. without (clear) eschatol. implications, of the life of grace and holiness ἐν καινότητι ζωῆς περιπατεῖν *walk in* (i.e. *live) a new life* Ro 6: 4; cf. IEph 19: 3. ἀπηλλοτριωμένοι τ. ζωῆς τ. θεοῦ *estranged fr. the life of God* Eph 4: 18 (cf. Philo, Post. Cai. 69 τῆς θεοῦ ζωῆς ἀπεσχοινίσθαι). ἡ ζωὴ τ. ἀνθρώπων the (true) *life of men* (in God) Hm 2: 1.—Of the life of salvation and of glory. It is ζ. κυρίου B 1: 4 (cf. PGM 12, 255 κύριε τ. ζωῆς; 13, 783) or ζ. ἐν Χρ. Ἰησοῦ 2 Ti 1: 1, effected by his words or by the preaching of the gospel: ῥήματα ζ. αἰωνίου J 6: 68; cf. vs. 63. τὰ ῥήματα τῆς ζ. ταύτης Ac 5: 20. λόγος ζωῆς *word of life* Phil 2: 16; cf. 2 Ti 1: 10; 2 Cor 4: 12. Hence the apostle, proclaiming the gospel, can term himself the bearer of the 'fragrance of Christ', leading those appointed to this bliss, the rescued ἐκ ζωῆς εἰς ζωήν *from life to life* (i.e., as it seems, ever more deeply into the divine life) 2 Cor 2: 16.—The Spirit stands w. Christ as the power of life πνεῦμα τῆς ζωῆς ἐν Χρ. Ἰησοῦ *the spirit of life in Chr. J.* Ro 8: 2; cf. vss. 6, 10 and J 6: 63.—Like the words of Christ, the divine ἐντολή is also to bring life Ro 7: 10. This ζ. is regarded as God's gift ζ. ἐν ἀθανασίᾳ 1 Cl 35: 2. W. ἀφθαρσία 2 Ti 1: 10; 2 Cl 14: 5. W. γνῶσις D 9: 3. W. εὐσέβεια 2 Pt 1: 3. W. εἰρήνη Ro 8: 6. W. σωτηρία 2 Cl 19: 1. The Christians, who truly belong to the ἐκκλησία τῆς ζωῆς 2 Cl 14: 1, are heirs of life, the gift of grace 1 Pt 3: 7. This life, as long as they are in the body, κέκρυπται σὺν τ. Χριστῷ ἐν τῷ θεῷ *is hidden with Christ in God* Col 3: 3. Whoever has forfeited his ζ. is excluded fr. the life of glory Hv 1, 1, 9.—Cf. also Ac 11: 18 (and IQS 3, 1); 13: 46, 48. Esp. in Johannine usage the concept ζ. is copiously employed, as a rule to designate the result of faith in Christ; in most cases it is stated expressly that the follower of Jesus possesses eternal life even in this world: ἔχειν ζωήν (Theophr. in a scholion on Pla. 631c εἰ ζωὴν εἶχεν ὁ πλοῦτος='had life, were alive') J 3: 15f, 36a; 5: 24a, 40; 6: 40, 47, 51, 53f; 10: 10; 20: 31; 1 J 3: 15; 5: 12a, b, 13. διδόναι ζωήν (cf. Sb 8202, 3 [105 BC]) J 10: 28; 17: 2; 1 J 5: 11.—Cf. 5: 16. ὁρᾶν ζωήν J 3: 36b. μεταβεβηκέναι ἐκ τ. θανάτου εἰς τ. ζωήν *to have passed fr. death into life* J 5: 24; 1 J 3: 14. Hence in the eschatol. pass. J 5: 29 ἀνάστασις ζωῆς means not a resurrection to enter life (cf. 2 Macc 7: 14 and MPol 14: 2, where ἀνάστασις ζωῆς αἰ., it seems, is *res. to everlasting life*), but a resurrection which corresponds to the Christian's possession of life here and now, a *resurrection proceeding from life*. J is fond of calling this Life ζ. αἰώνιος, as in many pass. just cited (s. αἰώνιος 3) J 3: 15f, 36; 4: 14, 36; 5: 24, 39; 6: 27, 40, 47, 54, 68; 10: 28; 12: 25, 50; 17: 2f; 1 J 1: 2; 2: 25; 3: 15; 5: 11, 13, 20. But the use of this expr. in our lit. is by no means limited to J and 1 J; it is also found in Mt, Mk, Lk, Ac, Ro, Gal, 1 Ti, Tit, Jd, 2 Cl, Ign, MPol, Herm, D, oft. w. unmistakable eschatol. connotation.

β. ζ. (and ζ. αἰώνιος; cf. IQS 4, 7 and s. J 3: 15 al.) is used of life in the blessed period of final consummation, in the foll. pass.: ἐν τῷ αἰῶνι τῷ ἐρχομένῳ ζ. αἰ. *in the coming age eternal life* Mk 10: 30; Lk 18: 30; cf. Mt 19: 29. τί ποιήσω ἵνα ζ. αἰ. κληρονομήσω; Mk 10: 17; cf. Lk 18: 18; 10: 25; Mt 19: 16f. As a result of the Last Judgment ἀπελεύσονται οἱ δίκαιοι εἰς ζ. αἰ. Mt 25: 46; s. also Ro 2: 7 (cf. IQS 4, 6–8).—Cf. also Mt 7: 14; 18: 8f; Mk 9: 43, 45; Ro 5: 17f, 21; 6: 22f; ζ. ἐκ νεκρῶν *life for those who have come out of the state of death* Ro 11: 15.—Gal 6: 8; 1 Ti 1: 16; 6: 12, 19; 1 Pt 3: 10 (Ps 33: 13); Jd 21; 2 Cl 8: 4, 6. W. ἀνάπαυσις τ. μελλούσης βασιλείας 5: 5. This life is called ἡ ὄντως ζ. *the real, true life* 1 Ti 6: 19; ἡ ἐπουράνιος ζ. 2 Cl 20: 5; ἀΐδιος ζ. IEph 19: 3 (s. ἀΐδιος). Hope is directed toward it, ζωῆς ἐλπίς B 1: 6; cf. Tit 1: 2; 3: 7.—The references to future glory include the foll. concepts: βίβλος or βιβλίον (τῆς) ζωῆς (s. βίβλος 2) Phil 4: 3; Rv 3: 5; 13: 8; 17: 8; 20: 12, 15; 21: 27. τὸ ξύλον (τῆς) ζωῆς *the tree of life* (4 Macc 18: 16; cf. Pr 3: 18; Gen 2: 9; PsSol 14: 3; Philo.—ξύλον 3) Rv 2: 7; 22: 2, 14, 19; Dg 12: 2. στέφανος τ. ζωῆς (cf. Bousset, Rel.³ 277f; MDibelius on Js 1: 12; FCumont, Études syriennes '17, 63ff) Js 1: 12; Rv 2: 10. ὕδωρ (τῆς ζωῆς) 2) 21: 6; 22: 1, 17. πηγὴ ζωῆς B 11: 2 (cf. Jer 2: 13; Ps 35: 10). ζωῆς πηγαὶ ὑδάτων *springs of living water* Rv 7: 17.—FCBurkitt, Life, ζωή, hayyim: ZNW 12, '11, 228–30; RHCharles, A Critical Hist. of the Doctrine of a Fut. Life in Israel, in Judaism and in Christianity² '13; FLindblom, D. ewige Leben '14; Bousset, Rel.³ 269–95; JBFrey, Biblica 13, '32, 129–68.—EvDobschütz, D. Gewissheit des ew. Leb. nach d. NT: 'Dienet einander' 29, '20/'21, 1–8; 43–52; 65–71; 97–101; JThUbbink, Het eeuwige leven bij Pls '17; ESommerlath, D. Ursprung d. neuen Lebens nach Pls² '26; JMüller, D. Lebensbegr. d. Hl. Pls '40; NvArseniew, D. neue Leben nach dem Eph: Internat. Kirchl. Ztschr. 20, '30, 230–6; EvSchrenk, D. joh. Anschauung vom 'Leben' 1898; JBFrey, 'Vie' dans l'Év. de St. Jean: Biblica 1, '20, 37–58; 211–39; RBultmann, D. Eschatol. d. Joh Ev.: Zwischen d. Zeiten 6, '28, 1ff; HPribnow, D. joh. Anschauung v. 'Leben' '34; DBLyons, The Concept of Eternal Life in J '38; JLKoole, Diorama Johanneum. Ζωή: Geref. Th. Tijdschr. 43, '42, 276–84; FMussner, ΖΩΗ (Joh. lit.), Diss. Munich '52; DHill, Gk. Words and Hebrew Mngs. '67, 163–201.—GvRad, GBertram, RBultmann TW II 833–77. M-M. B. 285.**

ζώνη, ης, ἡ (Hom.+; Epigr. Gr. 482, 3; pap., LXX, Ep. Arist., Philo, Joseph., Test. 12 Patr., loanw. in rabb.) *belt, girdle,* in our lit. only of a man's belt or girdle, unless the ref. is to heavenly beings (Rv). Of the Baptist ζ. δερματίνη (4 Km 1: 8=Jos., Ant. 9, 22) Mt 3: 4; Mk 1: 6; GEb 2 (cf. DBuzy, Pagne ou ceinture?: Rech de Sc rel 23, '33, 589–98 and on Ἰωάννης 1). Of Paul Ac 21: 11a, b. Of the Son of Man περιεζωσμένος πρὸς τ. μαστοῖς ζ. χρυσᾶν Rv 1: 13; sim. of angels περιεζωσμένοι περὶ τὰ στήθη ζ. χρυσᾶς 15: 6 (cf. 4 Km 3: 21 Ἰωράμ περιεζωσμένοι ζ.—The golden belt or girdle as Ps.-Callisth. 2, 21, 17). λύειν τὴν ζ. *loose,* i.e. *remove the belt* (Hyperid., fgm. 67) MPol 13: 2. This belt is also used to keep money in

(Plut., Mor. p. 665в ἀνθρώπου . . . ζώνην δὲ χαλκοῦς ἔχουσαν ὑπεζωσμένου; PRyl. 127, 32 [29 AD] ζ. ἐν ᾗ κέρματος (δραχμαί) δ'; 141, 22) Mt 10: 9; Mk 6: 8. M-M. B. 434.*

ζώννυμι by-form **ζωννύω** 2 sg. impf. ἐζώννυες (Bl-D. §92; Mlt.-H. 202f); fut. ζώσω; 1 aor. ἔζωσα; 1 aor. mid. imper. ζῶσαι *gird* (Hom.+; inscr., LXX) τινά *someone* J 21: 18 a, b. Mid. *gird oneself* (Jos., Bell. 2, 129) Ac 12: 8.*

ζωογονέω fut. ζωογονήσω (Aristot., Theophr.+; Herm. Wr. 9, 6; LXX, Philo).
1. *give life to, make alive* (Theophr., Causa Plant. 4, 15, 4; Athen. 7 p. 298c; 1 Km 2: 6) τὶ *someth.* (s. Theophr. and Athen., loc. cit.) τὰ πάντα 1 Ti 6: 13.
2. *keep* or *preserve alive* (Diod. S. 1, 23, 4; Ex 1: 17f; Judg 8: 19; 1 Km 27: 9, 11; 3 Km 21: 31; Philopon. in Aristot., An. p. 332, 9 Hayduck; Theophanes Conf. 337, 31; 379, 21 de Boor; Georg. Mon. 166, 9 de B.) τὴν ψυχήν Lk 17: 33. Pass. Ac 7: 19. M-M.*

ζῷον, ου, τό (Pre-Socr., Hdt.+; Aristoph., Herm. Wr., inscr., pap., LXX, Philo; Jos., Ant. 8, 111).
1. *living thing* or *being,* to denote beings that are not human and yet not really animals of the usual kind (cf. Dit., Or. 90, 31 τῷ τε ῎Απει καὶ τῷ Μνεύει . . . καὶ τοῖς ἄλλοις ἱεροῖς ζῴοις τοῖς ἐν Αἰγύπτῳ; PTebt. 5, 78 [118 BC]; 57, 12; POxy. 1188, 4; Herm. Wr. 11, 7) of the miraculous bird, the phoenix 1 Cl 25: 3. Of the four peculiar beings at God's throne, whose description Rv 4: 6–9 reminds us of the ζῷα in Ezk 1: 5ff, the cherubim. S. also Rv 5: 6, 8, 11, 14; 6: 1, 3, 5–7; 7: 11; 14: 3; 15: 7; 19: 4.
2. (as usu.) *animal* (Diod. S. 3, 31, 2; 5, 45, 1; Epict. 3, 1, 1; Jos., Ant. 3, 228) Hb 13: 11; 1 Cl 20: 4, 10; 33: 3; B 10: 7f; GOxy 4 (s. JoachJeremias, Con. Neot. 11, '48, 98). ἄλογα ζῷα (s. ἄλογος 1) 2 Pt 2: 12; Jd 10.
3. One isolated pass. in our lit. has ζῷα in the sense *living creatures,* including both men and animals (Cornutus 16 p. 20, 20; Ael. Aristid. 45, 32 K.; Jos., Ant. 1, 41) 1 Cl 9: 4. M-M. B. 137.*

ζῳοποιέω fut. ζῳοποιήσω; 1 aor. inf. ζῳοποιῆσαι; 1 aor. pass. ἐζῳοποιήθην Hm 4, 3, 7, Third Corinthians 3: 8, ptc. ζῳοποιηθείς (Aristot. and Theophr.+; Herm. Wr.; LXX; Ep. Arist. 16; inscr.) *make alive, give life to.*
1. lit., of God, who ζ. τὰ πάντα *gives life to all things* 1 Ti 6: 13 v.l. (cf. 2 Esdr 19 [Neh 9]: 6). Esp. of supernatural life: of dead persons who are called to life τοὺς νεκρούς (Test. Gad 4: 6) *bring the dead to life* J 5: 21a (cf. inscr. in MSchwabe, Israel Exploration Journ. 4, '54, 249–61); cf. b; Ro 4: 17. τὰ θνητὰ σώματα ὑμῶν 8: 11. θανατοῦνται καὶ ζῳοποιοῦνται Dg 5: 12 (on the contrast betw. the two verbs cf. 4 Km 5: 7). Christ θανατωθεὶς μὲν σαρκὶ ζῳοποιηθεὶς δὲ πνεύματι 1 Pt 3: 18. Through his suffering (='death'; cf. πάσχω 3aα) Christ gives life to the believers B 7: 2; 12: 5. αὐτὸς ὢν νεκρὸς δύναται ζῳοποιῆσαι *although it* (the serpent typifying Christ) *is dead it can bestow life* 12: 7. ἐν τ. Χριστῷ πάντες ζῳοποιηθήσονται 1 Cor 15: 22. The Spirit is called life-giving J 6: 63; (contrasted w. the letter) 2 Cor 3: 6. So Christ, ὁ ἔσχατος Ἀδάμ, ἐγένετο εἰς πνεῦμα ζῳοποιοῦν 1 Cor 15: 45. Baptism makes alive Hs 9, 16, 2; 7. The law cannot do so Gal 3: 21. ζῳοποιούμενοι *endowed w. life* B 6: 17b; Dg 5: 16.
2. in a less pointed sense and fig.—a. ἐζῳοποιήθην *I feel new life* Hm 4, 3, 7.—b. of a child γάλακτι ζῳοποιεῖται *it is kept alive with milk* B 6: 17a.

c. of the sprouting of seed (Geopon. 9, 11, 7; Herm. Wr. 9, 6) ὃ σπείρεις οὐ ζωοποιεῖται ἐὰν μὴ ἀποθάνῃ 1 Cor 15: 36. M-M.*

Ζώσιμος, ου, ὁ (inscr., pap. [Preisigke, Namenbuch]),

Zosimus, a martyr Pol 9: 1 (with Rufus as here CIG 192; 244; 1969; 3664).*

Ζωτίων, ωνος, ὁ (usu. [inscr., pap.] spelled Σωτίων elsewh.) Zotion, a deacon in Magnesia IMg 2.*

H

η΄numeral=8 (Jos., C. Ap. 1, 126) B 9: 8. As ordinal numeral eighth (ὀγδόη) Hm 8; [s 8] in the superscriptions (Apollon. Paradox. 41 Θεόφραστος ἐν τῷ η΄περὶ φυτῶν).*

ἤ particle (Hom.+; inscr., pap., LXX; Philo, Joseph., Test. 12 Patr.).

1. disjunctive (Bl-D. §446; Rob. 1188f)—a. or, separating—α. opposites, which are mutually exclusive λευκὴν ἢ μέλαιναν Mt 5: 36. ψυχρὸς ἢ ζεστός Rv 3: 15. ἐξ οὐρανοῦ ἢ ἐξ ἀνθρώπων from God or fr. men Mt 21: 25. δοῦναι ἢ οὔ to give or not (to give) 22: 17; cf. Mk 12: 14. ἀγαθὸν ποιῆσαι ἢ κακοποιῆσαι 3: 4. Cf. Lk 2: 24; Ro 14: 4; 1 Cor 7: 11.

β. related and similar terms, where one can take the place of the other or one supplements the other τὸν νόμον ἢ τοὺς προφήτας Mt 5: 17; (schol. on Soph., Oed. Col. 380 Papag. ἢ ἀντὶ τοῦ καὶ ἐστί) πόλιν ἢ κώμην 10: 11. ἔξω τ. οἰκίας ἢ τ. πόλεως ἐκείνης vs. 14. πατέρα ἢ μητέρα vs. 37. τέλη ἢ κῆνσον 17: 25. πρόσκομμα ἢ σκάνδαλον Ro 14: 13. εἰς τίνα ἢ ποῖον καιρόν 1 Pt 1: 11. νοῆσαι ἢ συνιέναι B 10: 12. Cf. Mk 4: 17; 10: 40; Lk 14: 12; J 2: 6; Ac 4: 34; 1 Cor 13: 1. In enumerations as many as six occurrences of ἤ are found: Mk 10: 29; Ro 8: 35; cf. Mt 25: 44; Lk 18: 29; 1 Cor 5: 11; 1 Pt 4: 15.—ἢ καί or (even, also) (PLond. 962, 5; EpJer 58) ἢ καὶ ὡς οὗτος ὁ τελώνης Lk 18: 11; cf. 11: 12; 12: 41; Ro 2: 15; 4: 9; 14: 10; 1 Cor 16: 6; 2 Cor 1: 13b.

b. ἤ—ἤ either—or Mt 6: 24; 12: 33; Lk 16: 13. ἤ—ἤ—ἤ either—or—or (Philod., οἰκ. col. 22, 41 Jensen) 1 Cor 14: 6 (ἤ four times as Libanius, Or. 28 p. 48, 15 F., Or. 31 p. 130, 7). ἤτοι—ἤ (Hdt., Thu. et al. [cf. Kühner-G. II 298]; PTebt. 5, 59; PRyl. 154, 25; Wsd 11: 18; Philo, Op. M. 37; Jos., Ant. 18, 115) either—or Ro 6: 16.

c. In neg. statements ἤ comes to mean nor, or, when it introduces the second, third, etc. item ἰῶτα ἐν ἢ μία κεραία οὐ μὴ παρέλθῃ Mt 5: 18. πῶς ἢ τί how or what 10: 19; cf. Mk 7: 12; J 8: 14; Ac 1: 7. οὐκ ἐδόξασαν ἢ ηὐχαρίστησαν Ro 1: 21. διαθήκην οὐδεὶς ἀθετεῖ ἢ ἐπιδιατάσσεται Gal 3: 15. ἵνα μή τις δύνηται ἀγοράσαι ἢ πωλῆσαι so that no one can either buy or sell Rv 13: 17.—Phil 3: 12.—Likew. in neg. rhetorical questions; here present-day English idiom, making the whole sentence neg., requires the transl. or Mt 7: 16; cf. Mk 4: 21; 1 Cor 1: 13; Js 3: 12.

d. Gener., ἤ oft. occurs in interrog. sentences—α. to introduce and to add rhetorical questions ἢ δοκεῖς ὅτι; or do you suppose that? Mt 26: 53. ἢ Ἰουδαίων ὁ θεὸς μόνον; or is God the God of the Jews alone? Ro 3: 29. ἢ ἀγνοεῖτε; or do you not know? 6: 3; 7: 1; also ἢ οὐκ οἴδατε; 11: 2; 1 Cor 6: 9, 16, 19; cf. 10: 22; 2 Cor 11: 7.

β. to introduce a question which is parallel to a preceding one or supplements it Mt 7: 10; οὐκ ἀνέγνωτε...; ἢ οὐκ ἀνέγνωτε...; have you not read...? Or have you not read...? Mt 12: (3), 5; cf. Lk 13: 4; Ro 2: 4; 1 Cor 9: 6.—Mt 20: 15; 1 Cor 11: 22; 2 Cor 3: 1.

γ. in the second member of direct or indir. double

questions: πότερον—ἤ (Aeschyl., Hdt.+) whether, if—or J 7: 17; B 19: 5; D 4: 4; Hs 9, 28, 4. ἤ—ἤ—ἤ—ἤ whether—or—or—or (Hom.; Theognis 913f; oracle in Hdt. 1, 65, 3; Theocr. 25, 170f et al.; cf. Kühner-G. II 530, 12) Mk 13: 35. Usu. the first member is without the particle Mt 27: 17; J 18: 34; Ac 8: 34; Ro 4: 10; 1 Cor 4: 21; Gal 1: 10; 3: 2, 5.

δ. used w. an interrog. word, mostly after another interrog. sentence ἢ τίς; Mt 7: 9; Mk 11: 28; Lk 14: 31; 20: 2; J 9: 21; Ro 3: 1; 2 Cl 1: 3; 6: 9. τίς...; τίς...; ἢ τίς...; 1 Cor 9: 7. τί...; ἢ τί...; what...? Or what? Mt 16: 26; 1 Cor 7: 16.—ἢ πῶς: ἢ πῶς ἐρεῖς; or how can you say? Mt 7: 4; cf. 12: 29.

2. as a particle denoting comparison—a. after a comparative before the other member of the comparison ἀνεκτότερον—ἤ more tolerable—than Mt 10: 15; cf. 11: 22, 24; Lk 10: 12. εὐκοπώτερον—ἤ Mt 19: 24; Mk 10: 25; cf. Lk 9: 13; J 4: 1. μᾶλλον ἤ more, rather—than Mt 18: 13; J 3: 19; Ac 4: 19; 5: 29; 1 Cor 9: 15; 1 Cl 2: 1a; 14: 1; 21: 5.

b. also without a preceding comp. (Kühner-G. II 303; Bl-D. §245, 3 w. app.).

α. w. verbs without μᾶλλον (Job 42: 12) χαρὰ ἔσται ἐπὶ ἑνὶ ἢ ἐπὶ ἐνενήκοντα ἐννέα there will be more joy over one than over 99 Lk 15: 7. λυσιτελεῖ... ἢ it would be better... than 17: 2 (cf. Andoc. 1, 125 τεθνάναι νομίσασα λυσιτελεῖν ἢ ζῆν; Tob 3: 6 BA). θέλω—ἤ I would rather—than 1 Cor 14: 19 (cf. Epict. 3, 1, 41; BGU 846, 16 [II AD] θέλω πηρὸς γενέσθαι [=γενέσθαι], εἰ [=ἢ] γνοῦναι, ὅπως ἀνθρόπῳ ἔτι ὀφείλω ὀβολόν; Hos 6: 6; 2 Macc 14: 42; Jos., Ant. 18, 59; βούλομαι... ἤ as early as Hom.).

β. after the positive degree (as early as Hdt. 9, 26) καλόν ἐστιν—ἤ it is better—than Mt 18: 8, 9; Mk 9: 43, 45, 47; 1 Cl 51: 3 (Gen 49: 12; Ps 117: 8f; Sir 20: 25; 22: 15; Jon 4: 3, 8; 4 Macc 9: 1. Cf. also Polyaenus 8, 49 καλὸν ἀποθανεῖν ἢ ζῆν; Philemo Com. no. 203 θανεῖν κράτιστόν [=far better] ἐστιν ἢ ζῆν ἀθλίως).

γ. ἤ is used in comparison, w. the idea of exclusion (Ps.-Callisth. 1, 37, 4 μέμφεσθε τὸν ἑαυτῶν βασιλέα ἢ ἐμέ= 'blame your own king, not me'; Gen 38: 26 δεδικαίωται Θαμὰρ ἢ ἐγώ; 2 Km 19: 44; Just., Apol. I 15, 8 on Lk 5: 32 θέλει ὁ πατὴρ τὴν μετάνοιαν ἢ τὴν κόλασιν) δεδικαιωμένος ἢ ἐκεῖνος rather than (=and not) the other man Lk 18: 14 v.l. (cf. Gen 38: 26).

c. οὐδὲν ἕτερον ἤ nothing else than (cf. X., Cyr. 2, 3, 10; 7, 5, 41; Jos., Ant. 8, 104) Ac 17: 21. τί... ἤ what other... than (X., Oec. 3, 3; cf. Kühner-G. II 304, 4) 24: 21.

d. πρὶν ἤ before (Ionism, very rare in Attic wr., but common in the Koine [e.g. Nicol. Dam.: 90 fgm. 130, 14 p. 397, 9 Jac.; Diod. S. 1, 64, 7; 1, 92, 4; Jos., Ant. 8, 345]: ATschuschke, De πρίν particulae apud scriptores aetatis Augusteae prosaicos usu, Bresl. Diss. '13, 31; 33. S. also πρίν 1).

α. w. aor. inf. foll. (Aelian, V.H. 1, 5; Herodian 2, 3, 2; Wsd 2: 8; Sir 11: 8 al.) and accompanying acc. (Nicol.

Dam., Βίος 14 p. 397, 9 Jac.; Aelian, V.H. 1, 21; PSI 171, 25 [II BC]; Sir 48: 25; Tob 2: 4; 3: 8; 8: 20; Test. Reub. 1: 1) Mt 1: 18; Mk 14: 30; Ac 7: 2.

β. foll. by aor. subj. and ἄν Lk 2: 26 (without ἄν Jos., Ant. 4, 10)—γ. foll. by pres. opt. Ac 25: 16.

e. used w. other particles—a. ἀλλ' ἤ s. ἀλλά 1a.—β. ἤπερ than (Hom., Hdt.; Polyb. 2, 51; 61; 2 Macc 14: 42; 4 Macc 15: 16; Jos., Bell. 5, 10, Ant. 18, 62) after μᾶλλον J 12: 43 (cf. Tob 14: 4 S ἐν τ. Μηδίᾳ ἔσται σωτηρία μᾶλλον ἤπερ ἐν Ἀσσυρίοις; Diod. S. 13, 60, 3 πλείονα ἤπερ).—ἤ γάρ Lk 18: 14 v.l. may derive from ἤ + περ'. M-M.

ἤ adv. truly; the word is perh. so to be accented 1 Cor 9: 10, 15. Hb 6: 14 t.r. reads ἤ μήν (Hom. +; Jos., Ant. 15, 368; 17, 72) indeed (for εἰ μήν, which is to be read w. 𝔓⁴⁶ ℵABCD).—Hs 9, 17, 5 Funk has μᾶλλον δὲ ἤ χείρονες. The right rdg. prob. is μ. δ. καὶ χ. M-M.*

ἤγαγον s. ἄγω.

ἡγεμονεύω (Hom. +; Dit., Syll.³ 877, 5, Or. 493, 24; PTebt. 302, 7; PRyl. 113, 20; PStrassb. 41, 17; Philo; Joseph.; Sib. Or. 5, 348) be leader, command, rule, order of the administration of imperial legates (governors; s. ἡγεμών 2; the verb in this mng. POsl. 99, 3 [160/1 AD]; Jos., Ant. 15, 345) ἡγεμονεύοντος τῆς Συρίας Κυρηνίου while Quirinius was governor of Syria Lk 2: 2. On the governorship of Quirinius cf. FBleckmann, Klio 17, '20, 104-12; HDessau, ibid. 252-8. S. also on ἀπογραφή and Κυρήνιος.—Of Pontius Pilate ἡγεμονεύοντος Π. Π. τῆς Ἰουδαίας while P.P. was procurator of Judaea Lk 3: 1. M-M.*

ἡγεμονία, ας, ἡ (Hdt. +; inscr., pap., LXX, Ep. Arist., Philo, Joseph.; Test. Sim. 5: 6; loanw. in rabb.) chief command, direction, management of any high office.
1. of the imperial government (of the royal dignity Hdt. 1, 7; 7, 2; Ep. Arist. 219; Jos., Ant. 2, 348; inscr. fr. the age of Augustus: ZNW 22, '23, 16. Of Nero, Dit., Syll.³ 810, 16; of Caligula, Philo, Leg. ad Gai. 8; 168; of Vespasian, Jos., Vi. 423) Lk 3: 1; 1 Cl 61: 1.
2. of the office of governor (Jos., Ant. 18, 88 of Syrian legates; Dit., Or. 614, 4 of the propraetor of Arabia; POxy. 59, 10; 237 V, 6; PRyl. 77, 36) ἐν καιρῷ τῆς ἡ. Ποντίου Πιλάτου at the time of the procuratorship of P.P. IMg 11. M-M.*

ἡγεμονικός, ή, όν (X., Pla.; UPZ 144, 28 [164 BC]; LXX; Philo; Jos., Bell. 2, 305, C. Ap. 2, 125) guiding, leading πνεῦμα ἡ. the guiding Spirit 1 Cl 18: 12 (Ps 50: 14). On πνεῦμα ἡ. and its philosophical presuppositions cf. Knopf, Hdb. ad loc., exc.; JSchneider, ZNW 34, '35, 62-9.*

ἡγεμών, όνος, ὁ (Hom. +; inscr., pap., LXX, Ep. Arist., Philo, Joseph., loanw. in rabb.).
1. prince (Soph., Oed. R. 103; Dit., Syll.³ 814, 25; Ex 15: 15; Job 42: 17d; Jos., Ant. 19, 217. Perh. 'chieftain' Gen 36: 15ff; 1 Ch 1: 51ff) ἐν τοῖς ἡγεμόσιν Ἰούδα among the princes of Judah Mt 2: 6 (after Mi 5: 1; the rendering ἐν τ. ἡγεμόσιν instead of the LXX ἐν χιλιάσιν, following rabbinic methods of interpretation, is suggested by ἡγούμενον in 2 Km 5: 2, cited in the last part of Mt 2: 6).
2. of imperial governors in the provinces (Dio Chrys. 31[48], 1; Ael. Aristid. 50, 12 K. = 26 p. 505 D.; Dit., Or. index; pap.; Jos., Ant. 15, 405) Mt 10: 18; Mk 13: 9; Lk 21: 12; 1 Pt 2: 14. Esp. of the procurators or prefects in Judaea: Pontius Pilate (Jos., Ant. 18, 55 Πιλᾶτος δὲ ὁ τ.

Ἰουδαίας ἡγεμών; JVardaman, A New Inscr. [Lat.] which Mentions Pilate as 'Prefect', JBL 81, '62, 70f) Mt 27: 2, 11, 14f, 21, 27; 28: 14; Lk 20: 20; Felix Ac 23: 24, 26, 33; 24: 1, 10; Festus 26: 30.—WLiebenam, Beiträge z. Verwaltungsgesch. d. röm. Reiches I 1886, 1ff. M-M.*

ἡγέομαι 1 aor. ἡγησάμην; pf. ἥγημαι (Hom. +; inscr., pap., LXX, En., Ep. Arist., Philo, Joseph.; Sib. Or., fgm. 1, 35).
1. lead, guide; in our lit. only pres. ptc. (ὁ) ἡγούμενος of men in any leading position (Soph., Phil. 386; freq. Polyb.; Diod. S. 1, 4, 72; Lucian, Alex. 44; 57; inscr., pap., LXX, Ep. Arist.; Test. Zeb. 10: 2) ruler, leader (opp. ὁ διακονῶν the servant) Lk 22: 26. Of princely authority (Ezk 43: 7; Sir 17: 17; 41: 17) Mt 2: 6; 1 Cl 32: 2; 61: 1.—Of high officials Ac 7: 10; MPol 9: 3; 1 Cl 5: 7; 51: 5; 55: 1. Of military commanders (Appian, Iber. 78 §333, Bell. Civ. 3, 26 §97; 1 Macc 9: 30; 2 Macc 14: 16) 37: 2f. Also of leaders of religious bodies (PTebt. 525 Παεῦς ἡγούμενος ἱερέων; PLond. 281, 2 [66 AD]; PWien Bosw. 1, 31 [87 AD] τῶν τ. ἱεροῦ ἡγουμένων κ. πρεσβυτέρων. Cf. also Sir 33: 19 οἱ ἡγούμενοι ἐκκλησίας; Sb 7835 [I BC], 10; 14 the [monarchic] ἡγούμενος of the cultic brotherhood of Zeus Hypsistos) of heads of a Christian church Hb 13: 7, 17, 24; 1 Cl 1: 3. ἄνδρας ἡγουμένους ἐν τοῖς ἀδελφοῖς leading men among the brethren Ac 15: 22. FBüchsel, TW II 909f.—Of Paul taken to be Hermes ὁ ἡγούμενος τοῦ λόγου the chief speaker 14: 12 (Cyranides p. 15, 30 Hermes as λόγων ἡγούμενος; Iambl., Myst. [Scott, Hermet. IV p. 28, 4] Hermes ὁ τῶν λόγων ἡγεμών; s. also Ἑρμῆς 1).
2. think, consider, regard (trag., Hdt. +; inscr., pap., LXX) ἀναγκαῖον w. inf. foll. (s. ἀναγκαῖος 1 and cf. BGU 824, 4; PRyl. 235, 4) 2 Cor 9: 5; Phil 2: 25. δίκαιον w. inf. foll. I consider it my duty to 2 Pt 1: 13. περισσὸν ἡγεῖσθαι w. articular inf. foll. consider superfluous (POxy. 1070, 17 τὸ μὲν οὖν γράφειν ... περιττὸν νῦν ἡγησάμην) Dg 2: 10. Foll. by acc. w. inf. (Hdt. 3, 8; Dit., Syll.³ 831, 13; Philo, Agr. 67; Jos., Ant. 19, 107) Phil 3: 8a (cf. also ζημία). W. double acc. look upon, consider someone or someth. (as) someone or someth. (Aeschyl., Hdt. +; Wsd 1: 16; 7: 8; Philo, Cher. 70; Jos., Ant. 7, 51) Ac 26: 2 (the perf. ἥγημαι here has pres. mng., as Hdt. 1, 126; Pla., Tim. 19E; POsl. 49, 3 [c. 100 AD]; Job 42: 6); Phil 2: 3, 6; 3: 7, 8b; 1 Ti 1: 12; 6: 1; Hb 10: 29; 11: 11, 26; 2 Pt 2: 13; 3: 15; in vs. 9 one acc. is supplied by the context; Hv 2, 1, 2; Dg 2: 6. Also τινὰ ὡς τινα 2 Th 3: 15; cf. 2 Cl 5: 6; Hb 1, 1, 7 (ὡς as Philo, Agr. 62; cf. Job 19: 11; 33: 10) πᾶσαν χαρὰν ἡγήσασθε, ὅταν ... deem it pure joy, when ... Js 1: 2 (cf. POxy. 528, 8 πένθος ἡγούμην). Also pass. ἐκείνη βεβαία εὐχαριστία ἡγείσθω let (only) that observance of the Eucharist be considered valid ISm 8: 1. In 1 Th 5: 13 there emerges for ἡ. the mng. esteem, respect (cf. Wilcken, Chrest. 116, 4 [II/III AD] ἡγοῦ μάλιστα τοὺς πατρῴους καὶ σέβου Ἶσιν). M-M. B. 711; 1204.**

ἤδειν s. οἶδα.

ἡδέως adv. (Soph., Hippocr. +; inscr., pap., LXX; Ep. Arist. 198; Philo; Joseph.) gladly (Aristoph., Thu. et al.) λαμβάνειν (Aristoph., Equ. 440) ITr 6: 2. ἡ. ἀκούειν like to hear (Jos., Ant. 3, 191) Mk 6: 20; 12: 37; Hm 2: 2. ἀνέχεσθαι gladly tolerate 2 Cor 11: 19. ἡ. ποιεῖν (Menand., fgm. 704; POxy. 113, 30; PGrenf. II 73, 20) do gladly Hs 6, 5, 5. βαστάζειν s 8, 10, 3; 9, 14, 6. ὑποδέχεσθαι s 8, 10, 3; 9, 27, 2. πάσχειν s 8, 10, 4. Ἰσαὰκ ἡ. προσήγετο θυσία. I. gladly let himself be led as a sacrifice 1 Cl 31: 3.—Comp. ἥδιον (Lysias 7, 40; Inschr. v.

Priene 105, 19 [c. 9 BC] BGU 372 I, 15; Sir 22: 11) *more gladly* ἥ. διδόναι 1 Cl 2: 1. ὑπομιμνῄσκειν 62: 3. Superl. as elative (Bl-D. §60, 2; Rob. 278f; 670) ἥδιστα *very gladly* (Pla., Theaet. 183D; Lucian, Scyth. 8; POxy. 1061, 21 [22 BC]; 933, 5; PLond. 897, 8; Jos., Vi. 365) 2 Cor 12: 15; Ac 13: 8 D. ἥδιστα μᾶλλον καυχήσομαι *I will rather boast all the more gladly* 2 Cor 12: 9 (cf. Bl-D. §246). M-M.*

ἤδη adv. (Hom.+; inscr., pap., LXX) *now, already, by this time.*

1. of time—a. w. pres. tense: Mt 3: 10; 15: 32; Mk 4: 37; 8: 2; 11: 11; Lk 7: 6; 21: 30 (w. ἐγγὺς εἶναι as Jos., Ant. 6, 223); J 4: 36 (if ἤδη belongs to the preceding sentence vs. 35, cf. on its position Tob 3: 6 BA; Jos., Ant. 3, 48); 11: 39 al. *now* (Appian, Bell. Civ. 5, 21 §82 ἤδη λέγουσα), ἤδη καί *even now* (3 Macc 3: 10; 6: 24; Jos., Ant. 16, 100) Lk 3: 9. Sim. νῦν ἤδη 1 J 4: 3.—*at once* (Polyaenus 6, 8) γινώσκεται ἤδη=*we know at once* Lk 21: 30 v.l. a.

b. w. a past tense: Mt 14: 15, 24; 17: 12; Mk 6: 35; 13: 28; 15: 42, 44; Lk 12: 49 al.

c. ἤδη ποτέ *now at length* (Heraclit. Sto. 62 p. 82, 14; Epict. 3, 24, 9; ostracon fr. Thebes in Dssm., LO 167 [LAE 186]) is somet. used w. a past tense Phil 4: 10; 2 Cl 13: 1, somet. w. the fut. (Jos., Ant. 3, 300) εἴ πως ἤδη ποτὲ εὐοδωθήσομαι ἐλθεῖν *whether now at last I may perh. succeed in coming* Ro 1: 10.

2. to denote logical proximity and immediateness Mt 5: 28. ἥ. κέκριται J 3: 18. ἥ. ἥττημα ὑμῖν ἐστιν 1 Cor 6: 7.—In Mt 5: 28 and 1 Cor 6: 7 ἤδη approaches the sense *really.* M-M.

ἥδιον, ἥδιστα s. ἡδέως.

ἥδομαι (Hom.+; inscr., pap., LXX, Philo; Jos., Vi. 226) *be pleased with, delight in* τινί someth. (Hdt. et al.; PGM 13, 657) τροφῇ φθορᾶς *perishable food* IRo 7: 3. B. 1099.*

ἡδονή, ῆς, ἡ (Pre-Socr., trag., Hdt.+; inscr., pap., LXX, Ep. Arist., Philo, Joseph., Test. 12 Patr.).

1. *pleasure, enjoyment, pleasantness* (Diod. S. 3, 10, 2; Pr 17: 1; Jos., Ant. 3, 19; 4, 88) ἡδονὴν ἡγεῖσθαί τι *consider someth. pleasure* 2 Pt 2: 13. ἡδονὴν ἔχει τί τινι someth. *causes pleasure to someone* 2 Cl 15: 5. Of a *desire* to do good (Pla., Aristot.; Jos., C. Ap. 2, 189) Hs 6, 5, 7.— Usu. in a bad sense: (evil) *pleasure, lust* (Demosth. 18, 138 ἐπὶ τ. λοιδορίαις ἡδ.; Musonius 89, 16f; opp. ἀρετή. Oft. Philo, Herm. Wr.) more fully ἡδ. κακή ITr 6: 2; IPhld 2: 2. Usu. pl. (Vett. Val. 76, 1; 4 Macc 5: 23; 6: 35) τοῦ βίου *pleasures of life* Lk 8: 14; IRo 7: 3. Abs. (w. ἐπιθυμίαι, as Dio Chrys. 32[49], 9; Ael. Aristid. 35, 27 K.=9 p. 108 D.; 4 Macc 5: 23; Philo, Agr. 83; 84 al.) Tit 3: 3; Dg 9: 1.—Js 4: 1, 3; Dg 6: 5; Hs 8, 8, 5; 8, 9, 4 (cf. Third Corinthians 3: 11).

2. *agreeable taste* (Sopater in Athen. 14 p. 649A ἡδ. τραγημάτων al.; Wsd 16: 20; Jos., Ant. 3, 28) ἡδονὴν ἔχειν *have a pleasant taste* Hm 10, 3, 3. ἡδονὴ τοῦ οἴνου 12, 5, 3.—GStählin, TW II 911-28. M-M.*

ἡδύοσμον, ου, τό (Theophr., Hist. Pl. 7, 7, 1; Strabo 8, 3, 14; Diosc. 3, 34; Galen XI 882, 16 K.; XII 928, 9) *mint* (garden plant) ἀποδεκατοῦν τὸ ἡ. *pay tithes of mint* Mt 23: 23; Lk 11: 42 (w. πήγανον as Hippiatr. I p. 12, 15). M-M.*

ἡδυπάθεια, ας, ἡ (X., Cyr. 7, 5, 74; Cebes 9, 3; 28, 1; Plut., Mor. 132c; 4 Macc 2: 2, 4) *enjoyment, comfort* in the sense of a luxurious mode of life; pl. (Athen. 4 p. 165E)

ἀποτάσσεσθαι ταῖς ἡ. *renounce the enjoyments* 2 Cl 16: 2. μισεῖν τὰς ἡ. τῆς ψυχῆς *hate the evil pleasures of the soul* 17: 7.*

ἡδύς, εῖα, ύ (Hom.+; inscr., pap., LXX, En., Ep. Arist., Philo; Jos., Ant. 12, 47 ἡδὺ τῷ θεῷ) *pleasant*, lit. 'sweet'; αὕτη ἡ ὁδὸς ἡδυτέρα αὐτοῖς ἐφαίνετο *this way appeared more suitable to them* Hs 9, 9, 1 (Ps.-Dicaearchus p. 140 F. ὁδὸς ἡδεῖα) B. 1032.*

ἦθος, ους, τό (Hom.+) *custom, usage, habit* (so Hes., Hdt.+; inscr., pap., LXX) τῆς ἀγνείας *the habit of purity* 1 Cl 21: 7. τῆς φιλοξενίας 1: 2. Pl. τὰ ἤθη *habits*, ἤθη χρηστά *good habits* (cf. Philo, Spec. Leg. 2, 104.—Ep. Arist. 290 and POxy. 642 [II AD] ἦθος χρηστόν) 1 Cor 15: 33 (φθείρουσιν ἤ. χρ. ὁμιλίαι κακαί is a proverb, occurring in Menander's comedy Thais [fgm. 218 Kock] and perh. as early as Eur. [PHib. 7, 94—III BC; Socrates, Ch. H. 3, 6]. According to Diod. S. 12, 12, [3]4 Charondas the lawgiver [V BC] champions the principle that good men would easily have their characters ruined by association with evil men [τὰ ἤθη πρὸς κακίαν]. In 16, 54, 4 it is said of a tyrant: πονηραῖς ὁμιλίαις διέφθειρε τὰ ἤθη τῶν ἀνθρώπων.—S. also χρηστός 1aβ. Similar ideas as early as Theognis 1, 35f; 305-8). Of Jewish laws as v.l. Ac 16: 21 and 26: 3 (s. ἔθος 2). M-M.*

ἥκω (Hom.+; inscr., pap., LXX, En., Ep. Arist.; Jos., Ant. 16, 329; 341 al.; Test. 12 Patr.); since it has the mng. of a perf., its conjugation somet. has perf. forms (as in pap. [Mayser I 2² '38, 148]; LXX [Helbing 104]; Joseph. [WSchmidt 470]) Mk 8: 3 v.l.; 1 Cl 12: 2. Impf. ἧκον; fut. ἥξω; 1 aor. ἧξα (POxy. 933, 13) Rv 2: 25; *have come, be present.*

1. of pers.—a. w. mention of the starting point ἀπό τινος Mt 8: 11; Lk 13: 29. ἔκ τινος J 4: 47; Ro 11: 26. μακρόθεν Mk 8: 3 v.l. (cf. Josh 9: 6, 9; Is 60: 4, FWDanker, JBL 82, '63, 215f).

b. w. mention of the goal εἴς τι J 4: 47 (s. a above); ἥ. εἰς θάνατον *go to one's death* 1 Cl 16: 9. ἥ. εἰς τὴν πύρωσιν τῆς δοκιμασίας D 16: 5. πρός τινα (PSI 326, 4 [261 BC]) Ac 28: 23 t.r. ἐπί τινα *have come to someone* (UPZ 78, 44 [159 BC]), also w. hostile intent (Pla., Rep. 336B al.; 2 Ch 20: 2) Rv 3: 3b. ἐπί τι (Lucian, Jupp. Tr. 24; Achilles Tat. 5, 10, 1) B 4: 3. W. inf. foll. 1 Cl 12: 2. ἔως ὧδε 20: 7. ἐκεῖ *there* (POsl. 58, 5) Hv 3, 1, 3.

c. abs. Mt 24: 50; Lk 12: 46; 15: 27; J 8: 42; Hb 10: 7, 9 (both Ps 39: 8), 37 (Hab 2: 3); 1 J 5: 20; Rv 2: 25; 3: 3a, 9; 1 Cl 23: 5 (Mal 3: 1); D 16: 7.

d. as a relig. term—α. of the coming of the deity (PGM 1, 26; 29; Zosimus: Hermet. IV p. 111, 5 θεὸς ἥξει πρός σε; 9; Synes., Provid. 2, 2 p. 118B; Sib. Or. 3, 49) who makes a solemn appearance, expressed by ἥκω (PGiess. 3, 2 [ἄγνωστος, beg.]; cf. OWeinreich, ARW 18, '15, 38ff) J 8: 42.

β. of the coming of the worshiper to the deity (Dit., Or. 186, 6 ἥκω πρὸς τὴν κυρίαν Ἶσιν; 196, 2; Sb 1059, 8402 [I BC], 8411 [79 BC], 8412 [66 BC] al.; 3 Km 8: 42; Jer 27: 5) J 6: 37; Rv 15: 4 (Ps 85: 9).

2. used impersonally (Demosth. 23, 12; Diod. S. 18, 58, 2 ἧκε γράμματα='a letter came'; Plut., Philop. 21, 1; Epict. 2, 2, 20; Ael. Aristid. 48, 13 K.=24 p. 468 D.) of time (Ezk 7: 12 ἥκει ὁ καιρός; Ps 101: 14) or of events Mt 24: 14; J 2: 4; 2 Pt 3: 10; Rv 18: 8. Of the kingdom of God 2 Cl 12: 2. ἕως ἥξει ὅτε *until the time comes when* Lk 13: 35. ἐπί τινα *upon someone* (Is 47: 9) of the final tribulations Mt 23: 36; Lk 19: 43.—JSchneider, TW II 929f. M-M.*

ἠλάμην s. ἄλλομαι.

ἦλθα, ἦλθον s. ἔρχομαι.

ἠλί (v.l. ἐλωί; other spellings ἠλι, ἠλει, ἡλει)=אֵלִי my God (Hebr. Ps 22: 2) Mt 27: 46.—GDalman, Jesus-Jeshua, '29 [tr. PLevertoff], 204-7; FWBuckler, Am. Journ. of Sem. Lang. and Lit. 55, '38, 378-91; WJKenneally, CBQ 8, '46, 124-34; FZimmerman, JBL 66, '47, 465f. M-M. s.v. Ἠλεί.*

Ἡλί, ὁ indecl. (עֵלִי) (cf. e.g. 1 Km 1: 3; 2: 12, 20, 22; 3 Km 2: 27.—In Jos., Ant. 5, 340f al. Ἠλ[ε]ίς, gen. Ἠλεῖ 5, 341; 350) Heli, the father (or, acc. to some, the grandfather) of Joseph, in the genealogy of Jesus Lk 3: 23.*

Ἠλίας, ου, ὁ (אֵלִיָּה or אֵלִיָּהוּ) Elijah (Gk. Elias) the Tishbite, a prophet (3 Km 17-20; 4 Km 1f; 2 Ch 21: 12; Mal 3: 22; Sir 48: 1, 4, 12; Joseph.; Sib. Or. 2, 247), whose life and deeds were invested w. great importance by the Jewish contemporaries of Jesus (Schürer II⁴ 407; 610ff; Billerb. IV 764-98). Mt 11: 14; 16: 14; 17: 3f (PDabeck, Biblica 23, '42, 175-89), 10ff; 27: 47, 49; Mk 6: 15; 8: 28; 9: 4f, 11ff; 15: 35f; Lk 1: 17; 4: 25f; 9: 8, 19, 30, 33, 54 v.l.; J 1: 21, 25; Js 5: 17; 1 Cl 17: 1. ἐν Ἠλίᾳ in the story of Elijah Ro 11: 2.—JoachJeremias, TW II 930-43 (lit.); JATRobinson, Elijah, John and Jesus: 12 NT Studies '62, 28-52; GFohrer, Elia '68.²*

ἡλικία, ας, ἡ (Hom.+; inscr., pap., LXX, En., Ep. Arist., Philo, Joseph.).
   1. age, time of life—a. gener. of time that is past. Mt 6: 27=Lk 12: 25 προσθεῖναι ἐπὶ τ. ἡλικίαν αὐτοῦ πῆχυν ἕνα, where acc. to the context the ref. is to someth. insignificant (Lk 12: 26 has expressly ἐλάχιστον.—Paus. Attic. σ. 22 evaluates as τὸ ἐλάχιστον the expression σπιθαμὴ τοῦ βίου='a span [the distance between thumb and little finger of the extended hand] of life'), must refer to length of life (so Gdspd., Probs. 24-6, following Wettstein), not to bodily size, and πῆχυς is a measure of time (cf. Hebr. Ps 39: 6 and s. πῆχυς). Likew. prob. in the parallel in the apocr. gospel fgm. POxy. 655 (=Kl. T. 8³, p. 23, 15). S. 2 below.—Fr. the context the age can be more closely defined as youthfulness (4 Macc 8: 10, 20) IMg 3: 1; MPol 3, or old age 7: 2; 9: 2 (cf. 4 Macc 5: 6, 11, 36).
   b. of age gener., including the years lying ahead προκόπτειν ἐν ἡλικίᾳ increase in years (but s. 2 below) Lk 2: 52 (cf. Dit., Syll.³ 708, 18: inscr. in honor of a young man of Istropolis [II BC] τῇ τε ἡλικίᾳ προκόπτων καὶ προαγόμενος εἰς τὸ θεοσεβεῖν ὡς ἔπρεπεν αὐτῷ πρῶτον μὲν ἐτείμησεν τοὺς θεούς; Biogr. p. 266.—On σοφία, ἡλικία, χάρις: AFridrichsen, Symb. Osl. 6, '28, 33-8).
   c. of the age which is sufficient or requisite for certain things (Jos., Ant. 1, 68; 2, 230a).
   α. the age of strength (2 Macc 5: 24; 7: 27; En. 106, 1), also of women (αἱ ἐν ἡλ. παρθένοι or γυναῖκες in Hippocr., Pla., Plut.) παρὰ καιρὸν ἡλικίας past the normal age (παρά III 3) Hb 11: 11 (cf. καταβολή 1 and 2 and s. Philo, Abr. 195). Thus fig. Eph 4: 13: εἰς ἄνδρα τέλειον, εἰς μέτρον ἡλικίας τοῦ πληρώματος τ. Χριστοῦ, ἵνα μηκέτι ὦμεν νήπιοι to the measure of the full maturity of Christ, who is a mature person (τέλειος), not a (νήπιος) minor (cf. Diod. S. 18, 57, 2 εἰς ἡλικίαν ἔρχεσθαι); but cf. 2 below.
   β. the age of legal maturity, majority (oft. in pap.) ἡλικίαν ἔχειν be of age (Pla., Euthyd. 306D; Plut., Mor.

547A; BGU 168, 5 τοῖς ἀτελέσι ἔχουσι τ. ἡλικίαν) J 9: 21, 23.
   2. bodily stature (Hdt. 3, 16; Pla., Euthyd. 271B; Demosth. 40, 56; Diod. S. 3, 35, 6; Plut., Philop. 11, 2; Lucian, V.H. 1, 40; Jos., Ant. 2, 230b) τῇ ἡλικίᾳ μικρὸς ἦν small of stature Lk 19: 3. Some scholars hold that Mt 6: 27; Lk 12: 25 should be listed here (cf. Field, Notes, 6f); many would prefer stature for Lk 2: 52; Eph 4: 13.— JSchneider TW II 943-5. M-M. B. 956.*

ἡλίκος, η, ον (Soph.+) how great (Aristoph., Pla. et al.; Dit., Syll.³ 850, 11; PTebt. 27, 78 [123 BC]; Jos., Bell. 1, 626, Ant. 8, 208) ἡλίκον ἀγῶνα ἔχω how great a struggle I have Col 2: 1. ἡλίκην ἔχει βάσανον what great torment someth. causes 2 Cl 10: 4. ἡλίκοις γράμμασιν Gal 6: 11 v.l.; ἡ. may also mean how small (Antiphanes Com. 166, 6; Lucian, Herm. 5; Epict. 1, 12, 26); in a play on words ἰδοὺ ἡλίκον πῦρ ἡλίκην ὕλην ἀνάπτει see how large a forest a little fire sets ablaze Js 3: 5. M-M.*

ἥλιος, ου, ὁ (Hom.+; inscr., pap., LXX, En., Philo, Joseph., Test. 12 Patr., loanw. in rabb.) the sun (with and without art.: Bl-D. §253, 1) Mt 13: 43; 17: 2 (cf. Ode of Solomon 11, 13); Lk 21: 25; Ac 2: 20 (Jo 3: 4); 26: 13; 27: 20; 1 Cor 15: 41; Rv 1: 16; 6: 12; 8: 12; 10: 1; 12: 1; 16: 8; 19: 17; 21: 23; 1 Cl 20: 3; B 5: 10; 15: 5; Dg 7: 2; IEph 19: 2; Hs 9, 2, 2; 9, 17, 4; 9, 21, 1; 3. ἥ.=heat of the sun (Polyaenus 8, 10, 3; Is 49: 10; Jon 4: 8b) Rv 7: 16;=light of the sun Ac 13: 11 (cf. Diod. S. 10, 20, 3 ἐφορᾶν τὸν ἥλιον; 18, 27, 2; Maximus Tyr. 27, 3d ἥλιος for ἐξ ἡλίου αὐγή; Ps 57: 9; Jos., Ant. 16, 204 τ. ἥλιον βλέπ.). ἀνατέλλειν (cf. ἀνατέλλω 1 and 2) Mt 5: 45; 13: 6; Mk 4: 6; 16: 2; Js 1: 11. λάμπειν GP 6: 22. ἐκλάμπειν shine forth Hv 4, 1, 6. ἐπικαίειν s 9, 1, 6. δύνειν (q.v.) Mk 1: 32; Lk 4: 40; GP 2: 5; 5: 15. ἐπιδύειν Eph 4: 26. σκοτίζεσθαι be darkened Mt 24: 29; Mk 13: 24; Lk 23: 45 v.l. σκοτοῦσθαι Rv 9: 2. ἐκλείπειν be in eclipse (Ps.-Lucian, Philopatris 24) Lk 23: 45. ἀνατολὴ ἡλίου east (ἀνατολή 2a) Rv 7: 2; 16: 12. φῶς ἡλίου sunlight (Lycurgus the orator, fgm. 77; Ael. Aristid. 45, 29 K.) 22: 5. πρὸ ἡλίου κ. σελήνης before the creation of sun and moon 2 Cl 14: 1. ὁ τοῦ ἡλίου βωμός the altar of the sun or of Helios 1 Cl 25: 4 (ἥλ. as a deity: Dio Chrys. 3, 73; Maximus Tyr. 19, 3d [Pythag.]; Jos., C. Ap. 2, 265).— FBoll, D. Sonne im Glauben u. in d. Weltanschauung d. alten Völker '22; GHHalsberghe, The Cult of Sol Invictus '72. M-M. B. 54.*

Ἡλιούπολις, εως, ἡ (Socrat., Ep. 26, 1 [Ἡλίου πόλις]; Arrian, Anab. 3, 1, 3 [Ἡλιούπολις]; Ex 1: 11 [Ἡλίου πόλις]; Philo, Somn. 1, 77; Jos., C. Ap. 1, 250; 261; 265) Heliopolis, a city of Lower Egypt w. a temple of the sun god; it plays a role in the legend of the bird Phoenix 1 Cl 25: 3.*

ἧλος, ου, ὁ (Hom.+; inscr., pap., LXX; Jos., Ant. 5, 208. —In crucifixion: Asclepiades Junior [physician I/II AD] in Alexander Trallianus 1, 15) nail GP 6: 21; MPol 13: 3. ὁ τύπος τῶν ἥλων the imprint of the nails J 20: 25a. Also ὁ τόπος τ. ἥλων the place of the nails vs. 25b.—JWHewitt, The Use of Nails in the Crucifixion: HTR 25, '32, 29-45. M-M. B. 597.*

ἡμεῖς s. ἐγώ.

ἡμέρα, ας, ἡ (Hom.+; inscr., pap., LXX, En., Ep. Arist., Philo, Joseph., Test. 12 Patr.; loanw. in rabb.) day.
   1. of the natural day, the period betw. the rising and setting of the sun.

a. lit. (opp. νύξ) Mt 4: 2 (fasting for 40 days and 40 nights as Ex 34: 28.—Cf. Lucian, V.H. 1, 10 ἑπτὰ ἡμέρας κ. τὰς ἴσας νύκτας); 12: 40 and oft. ἡμέρα γίνεται day is breaking (X., An. 2, 2, 13; 7, 2, 34; Appian, Iber. 74 §315; Jos., Ant. 10, 202, Vi. 405) Lk 4: 42; 6: 13; 22: 66; Ac 12: 18; 16: 35; 27: 29, 39. ἡμέρα διαυγάζει the day dawns 2 Pt 1: 19. κλίνει declines, evening approaches Lk 9: 12; 24: 29. φαίνει shines Rv 8: 12. In the gen. to denote a point of time ἡμέρας in daylight (Lucian, V.H. 1, 10; Hippocr., Ep. 19, 7; Arrian, Ind. 13, 6) 1 Cl 25: 4. ἡμέρας μέσης at midday, noon (Lucian, Nigr. 34; cf. Jos., Ant. 5, 190) Ac 26: 13. But also, as in class. wr., of time within which someth. occurs, ἡμέρας during the day Rv 21: 25. ἡμέρας καὶ νυκτός (by) day and night (Appian, Liby. 121, §576; Arrian, Anab. 7, 11, 4; Jos., Ant. 11, 171; also in reverse order as Is 34: 10) Mk 5: 5; Lk 18: 7; Ac 9: 24; 1 Th 2: 9; 3: 10; 2 Th 3: 8. The acc. of time νύκτα καὶ ἡμέραν (in this sequence Dio Chrys. 7[8], 15; Ael. Aristid. 51, 1 K.=27 p. 534 D.; Esth 4: 16) (throughout the) day and (the) night Mk 4: 27; Lk 2: 37; Ac 20: 31; 26: 7. τὰς ἡμέρας every day (opp. τὰς νύκτας; cf. Dio Chrys. 4, 36; Jos., C. Ap. 1, 199) Lk 21: 37; cf. πᾶσαν ἡμέραν (throughout) every day Ac 5: 42 (cf. Hdt. 7, 203). τὴν ἡμέραν ἐκείνην (throughout) that day (Ael. Aristid. 49, 45 K.) J 1: 39. ὅλην τ. ἡ. (Jos., Ant. 6, 22) Mt 20: 6. The acc. in a distributive sense συμφωνεῖν ἐκ δηναρίου τὴν ἡμέραν on a denarius a day Mt 20: 2 (cf. Meisterhans³-Schw. 205; pap. in Mlt., CIR 15, '01, 436; 18, '04, 152). ἡμέρας ὁδός a day's journey Lk 2: 44 (cf. X., An. 2, 2, 12; Gen 31: 23; 1 Macc 5: 24; Jos., C. Ap. 2, 21; 23). Daylight lasts for twelve hours, during which a person can walk without stumbling J 11: 9a, **b.** ἡ ἐν ἡμέρᾳ τρυφή dissipation in broad daylight 2 Pt 2: 13.

b. fig. (Sib., Or. 5, 241) the Christians as υἱοὶ φωτὸς καὶ υἱοὶ ἡμέρας sons of light and of the day 1 Th 5: 5; cf. vs. 8 (in contrast, Aristophanes, fgm. 573 K. calls Chaerephon, the friend of Socrates νυκτὸς παῖδα, in a derogatory sense). In J 9: 4 day denotes the period of human life; cf. Ro 13: 12f.

2. of civil or legal day, including the night Mt 6: 34; 15: 32; Mk 6: 21; Lk 13: 14; B 15: 3ff. Opp. the hours Mt 25: 13; hours, months, years Rv 9: 15; cf. Gal 4: 10.—In the gen., answering the question, how long? (Nicostrat. Com., fgm. 5 K. ἡμερῶν τριῶν ἤδη='now for three days'; Porphyr., Vi. Plotini 13 W. τριῶν ἡμ.; BGU 37, 7 [50 AD]; 249, 11 [70–80 AD] ἡμερῶν δύο διαμένομεν) τεσσεράκοντα ἡμερῶν during 40 days Ac 1: 3 D.*—In the dat., answering the quest., when? (X., An. 4, 7, 11; Jdth 7: 6; Esth 7: 2; Bel 40 Theod.) τῇ τρίτῃ ἡμέρᾳ (cf. Arrian, Anab. 6, 4, 1 τρίτῃ ἡμέρᾳ) Mt 16: 21; 17: 23; Lk 9: 22; 24: 7, 46; 1 Cor 15: 4. ᾗ δὲ ἡμέρᾳ on the day on which (PLille 15, 1 [242 BC] ᾗ ἡμέρᾳ; 1 Esdr 1: 49; Jos., Ant. 20, 26) Lk 17: 29; cf. vs. 30. μιᾷ ἡμέρᾳ in (the course of) one day (Appian, Iber. 58 §244) 1 Cor 10: 8.—In the acc., usu. answering the quest., how long? (X., An. 4, 7, 18; Nicol. Dam.: 90 fgm. 130, 26 p. 410, 30 Jac. τὴν ἡμέραν ἐκείνην='throughout that day'; Polyaenus 6, 53 τρεῖς ἡμέρας; Arrian, Anab. 6, 2, 3; Lucian, Alex. 15 ἡμέρας= several days; Philo, Vi. Cont. 30 τὰς ἓξ ἡμέρας) ὅλην τ. ἡμέραν the whole day long Ro 8: 36 (Ps 43: 23), 10: 21 (Is 65: 2). ἡμέραν μίαν for one day Ac 21: 7. ἔμειναν οὐ πολλὰς ἡμέρας J 2: 12; cf. 4: 40; 11: 6; Ac 9: 19; 10: 48; 16: 12; 20: 6c; 21: 4, 10; Gal 1: 18; Rv 11: 3, 9. ἡμέραν ἐξ ἡμέρας day after day (Ps.-Euripides, Rhes. 445f, Henioch. 5, 13 Kock; Gen 39: 10; Num 30: 15; Is 58: 2; Ps 95: 2; Sir 5: 7; En.) 2 Pt 2: 8; 2 Cl 11: 2 (quot. of unknown orig.). Only rarely does the acc. answer the quest., when? (Antiphanes Com. [IV BC] fgm. 280; Ps.-Lucian, Halc. 3

τρίτην ἡ.) τὴν ἡμέραν τῆς πεντηκοστῆς on the Day of Pentecost Ac 20: 16. Peculiar is the expr. τεσσαρεσκαιδεκάτην σήμερον ἡμέραν προσδοκῶντες this is the fourteenth day you have been waiting Ac 27: 33 (cf. X., An. 4, 5, 24 ἐνάτην ἡμέραν γεγαμημένην).—ἑπτάκις τῆς ἡμέρας seven times a day Lk 17: 4.—Used w. prep.: ἀπό w. gen. from—(on) Mt 22: 46; J 11: 53; Ac 20: 18. ἀφ' ἧς ἡμέρας (PRev. 9, 1 [258 BC]; Ep. Arist. 24) Col 1: 6, 9; Hm 4, 4, 3. ἀπὸ... ἄχρι... Phil 1: 5. ἀπὸ... μέχρι ... Ac 10: 30. ἄχρι w. gen. until Mt 24: 38b; Lk 1: 20; 17: 27; Ac 1: 2; 2: 29. ἄχρι ἡμερῶν πέντε five days later Ac 20: 6b. μέχρι τῆς σήμερον (ἡμέρας) up to the present day (1 Esdr 8: 74) Mt 28: 15. ἕως τ. ἡμέρας Mt 27: 64; Ac 1: 22; Ro 11: 8 (Dt 29: 3). δι' ἡμερῶν after (several) days Mk 2: 1 (cf. Hdt. 6, 118 δι' ἐτέων εἴκοσι; Thu. 2, 94, 3; Pla., Hipp. Maj. 281A διὰ χρόνου=after a [long] time). διὰ τριῶν ἡμερῶν within three days (PPetr. II 4 [6], 8 δι' ἡμερῶν ε'='in the course of 5 days') Mt 26: 61; Mk 14: 58. δι' ἡμερῶν τεσσεράκοντα Ac 1: 3 (s. διά A II 1a). διὰ τ. ἡμέρας in the course of the day Lk 9: 37 D. εἰς τ. ἡμέραν for the day J 12: 7; Rv 9: 15; ἐν τῇ ἡμ. in the daytime J 11: 9b. ἐν μιᾷ τῶν ἡμερῶν one day Lk 5: 17; 8: 22; 20: 1. ἐν οn w. dat. sing. Mt 24: 50; Lk 1: 59; J 5: 9; Hb 4: 4 (cf. Gen 2: 2); in, within w. dat. pl. (Alexis Com. 246, 2 K. ἐν πένθ' ἡμέραις; Philo, Somn. 2, 112) ἐν τρισὶν ἡμέραις (PTebt. 14, 5 [114 BC]; Porphyr., Vi. Plot. 17 p. 111, 26 W.; Ep. Arist. 24) Mt 27: 40; Mk 15: 29; J 2: 19f.—ἐπί w. acc. over a period of ἐπὶ ἡμέρας πλείους over a period of many days (PTurin I, 2, 15 [116 BC] ἐφ' ἱκανὰς ἡ.; Jos., Ant. 4, 277) Ac 13: 31; cf. 27: 20; ἐπὶ πολλὰς ἡ. (Jos., Ant. 18, 57) 16: 18; cf. Hb 11: 30. καθ' ἡμέραν every day (Hyperid. 6, 23; 26; Polyb. 1, 57, 7; 4, 18, 2 al.; Diod. S. 1, 36, 7 and 8; 2, 47, 2 al.; Dit., Syll.³ 656, 22; UPZ 42, 13 [162 BC]; PGiess. 17, 1; Tob 10: 7; Sus 8; 12 Theod.; 1 Macc 8: 15; Ep. Arist. 304; Jos., Bell. 2, 265, Ant. 20, 205) Mt 26: 55; Mk 14: 49 ('by day': AWArgyle, ET 63, '51f, 354); Lk 16: 19; 22: 53; Ac 2: 46f; 3: 2; 16: 5; 19: 9; 1 Cor 15: 31; 2 Cor 11: 28; Hb 7: 27; 10: 11. Also (w. the art., which has no mng.: Bl-D. §160; cf. Rob. 766) τὸ καθ' ἡμ. (Aristoph., Equ. 1126; Pla.; Polyb. 4, 18, 2; POxy. 1220, 4) Lk 11: 3; 19: 47; Ac 17: 11; καθ' ἑκάστην ἡμ. every day (X., Mem. 4, 2, 12, Equ. 5, 9; PTebt. 412, 2; Wilcken, Chrest. 327, 18; Ex 5: 8; Esth 2: 11; Job 1: 4; Bel 4: 6) Hb 3: 13. κατὰ πᾶσαν ἡμ. w. same mng. (Jos., Ant. 6, 49) Ac 17: 17. μεθ' ἡμέρας ἓξ six days later (PSI 502, 16 [257 BC] μεθ' ἡμέρας ιβ'; 436, 3) Mt 17: 1; cf. 26: 2; 27: 63; Mk 8: 31; Lk 1: 24; J 4: 43; 20: 26; Ac 1: 5; 15: 36; 24: 1; 28: 13. πρὸ ἓξ ἡμερῶν τοῦ πάσχα six days before the Passover J 12: 1 (not a Latinism, since it is found as early as Hippocr. πρὸ τριῶν ἡμερῶν τῆς τελευτῆς [WSchulze, Graeca Latina '01, 15; LRydbeck, Fachprosa, '67, 64f]. Cf. Plut., Symp. 8 p. 717D; Lucian, De Morte Peregr. 1; Aelian, H.A. 11, 19; mystery inscr. of Andania [Dit., Syll.³ 736, 70 πρὸ ἀμερᾶν δέκα τῶν μυστηρίων]; PFay. 118, 15; PHolm. 4, 23; PGM 13, 26; 671; Am 1: 1; 2 Macc 15: 36; Jos., Ant. 15, 408. Cf. WSchmid, D. Attizismus III 1893, 287f; IV 1897, 629; Mlt. 100f; Bl-D. §213 w. app.). —It is striking to find the nom. denoting time in the expression ἤδη ἡμέραι τρεῖς προσμένουσίν μοι Mt 15: 32; Mk 8: 2; cf. Lk 9: 28 (s. Bl-D. §144; Rob. 460).—Of festive days: ἡ ἡμέρα τῶν σαββάτων (σάββατον 1b) or τοῦ σαββάτου (σάββ. 1a) Lk 4: 16; 13: 14b, 16; J 19: 31; Ac 13: 14. ἡ ἡμέρα or αἱ ἡμέραι τ. ἀζύμων Lk 22: 7; Ac 12: 3; 20: 6. ἡ ἡμέρα τ. πεντηκοστῆς Ac 2: 1; 20: 16. μεγάλη ἡμέρα the great day (of atonement) PK 2 p. 14, 29. ἡ κυριακὴ ἡμέρα the Lord's Day, Sunday Rv 1: 10. Festive days are spoken of in the foll. passages: ὃς μὲν κρίνει ἡμέραν παρ' ἡμέραν, ὃς δὲ κρίνει πᾶσαν ἡμέραν one man considers one day better than another, another man considers every day good Ro 14: 5. φρονεῖν τ. ἡμέραν concern oneself w. (= observe) the day vs. 6. ἡμέρας παρατηρεῖσθαι observe days Gal 4: 10.—Used w. gen. to denote what happens or is to be done on the day in question ἡμ. τοῦ ἁγνισμοῦ Ac 21: 26. τ. ἐνταφιασμοῦ day of burial J 12: 7. ἕως ἡμέρας ἀναδείξεως αὐτοῦ πρὸς τὸν Ἰσραήλ Lk 1: 80 (s. ἀνάδειξις).—OT terminology is reflected in the expr. the fulfilling of the days (Ex 7: 25; 1 Ch 17: 11; Tob 10: 1b; cf. מְלֹאת) ἐπλήσθησαν αἱ ἡμ. τῆς λειτουργίας αὐτοῦ the days of his service came to an end Lk 1: 23. ἐπλήσθησαν ἡμ. ὀκτὼ τοῦ περιτεμεῖν αὐτόν the eighth day had come, on which he was to be circumcised 2: 21; cf. vs. 22. Cf. ἐκπλήρωσις, συμπληρόω, συντελέω, τελειόω. The Hebr. has also furnished the expr. ἡμέρα καὶ ἡμέρᾳ day after day (Esth 3: 4 יוֹם וָיוֹם = LXX καθ᾽ ἑκάστην ἡμέραν; יוֹם יוֹם Ps 68: 20 = LXX 67: 20 ἡμέραν καθ᾽ ἡμέραν) 2 Cor 4: 16.—ἡμέραν ἐξ ἡμέρας (rather oft. in the OT for various Hebr. expressions, but also in Henioch. Com. 5, 13 K.) day after day 2 Pt 2: 8; prophetic quot. of unknown origin 2 Cl 11: 2.

3. of a day appointed for very special purposes (UPZ 66, 5 [153 bc]) ἡ ἡμ.=the wedding day).
   a. τακτῇ ἡμέρᾳ Ac 12: 21. ἡμέραν τάξασθαι (Polyb. 18, 19, 1) 28: 23. στῆσαι (Dionys. Hal. 6, 48) 17: 31. ὁρίζειν (Polyb., Dionys. Hal.; Epict., Ench. 51, 1) Hb 4: 7; Hv 2, 2, 5. Of the day for childbirth J 16: 21 𝔓⁶⁶ et al.
   b. esp. of the day of judgment, fixed by the judge—α. ἀνθρωπίνη ἡμ. a day appointed by a human court 1 Cor 4: 3 (cf. the inscr. on a coin amulet [II/III AD] where these words are transl. 'human judgment' by CBonner, HTR 43, '50, 165-8). This expr. is formed on the basis of ἡμ. as designating
   β. the day of God's final judgment. ᾗ ἡμ. ὁ υἱὸς τοῦ ἀνθρώπου ἀποκαλύπτεται the day on which the Son of Man reveals himself Lk 17: 30; ἡ τοῦ θεοῦ ἡμ. 2 Pt 3: 12. ἡ ἡμέρα ἡ μεγάλη τοῦ θεοῦ τ. παντοκράτορος Rv 16: 14. ἡμ. κυρίου (Jo 1: 15; 2: 1, 11; Is 13: 6, 9 al.) occurring only once in the NT of the day of God, the Lord, in an OT quot. πρὶν ἐλθεῖν ἡμ. κυρίου τ. μεγάλην κ. ἐπιφανῆ Ac 2: 20 (Jo 3: 4). Otherw. Jesus Christ is the Lord of this day: 1 Cor 5: 5; 1 Th 5: 2 (P-ÉLangevin, Jesus Seigneur, '67, 107-67); 2 Th 2: 2; 2 Pt 3: 10. He is oft. mentioned by name or otherw. clearly designated, e.g. as υἱὸς τ. ἀνθρώπου, Lk 17: 24; 1 Cor 1: 8; 2 Cor 1: 14; Phil 1: 6, 10; 2: 16. ἡ ἐσχάτη ἡμ. the last day (of this age) (s. ἔσχατος 3b) J 6: 39f, 44, 54; 11: 24; 12: 48; Hv 2, 2, 5. ἡμ. (τῆς) κρίσεως (Pr 6: 34; Jdth 16: 17; PsSol 15: 12; En.; cf. Test. Lev. 3: 2, 3) Mt 10: 15; 11: 22, 24; 12: 36; 2 Pt 2: 9; 3: 7; 1 J 4: 17; 2 Cl 17: 6; B 19: 10; AP fgm. 4. ᾗ ἡμέρᾳ κρίνει ὁ θεὸς διὰ Χρ. Ἰ. the day on which . . . ; Ro 2: 16 (RBultmann, ThLZ 72, '47, 200f considers this a gloss). ἡμ. ὀργῆς καὶ ἀποκαλύψεως δικαιοκρισίας τοῦ θεοῦ 2: 5 (ἡμ. ὀργῆς as Zeph 1: 15, 18; 2: 3; Ezk 7: 19 v.l.; cf. Rv 6: 17). ἡ ἡμ. ἡ μεγάλη (Jer 37: 7; Mal 3: 22) Rv 6: 17; 16: 14. ἡμ. μεγάλη καὶ θαυμαστή B 6: 4. ἡμ. ἀπολυτρώσεως Eph 4: 30. ἡμ. ἐπισκοπῆς (s. ἐπισκοπή 1; 2) 1 Pt 2: 12. ἡμ. ἀνταποδόσεως B 14: 9 (Is 61: 2); ἐκείνη ἡ ἡμ. (Zeph 1: 15; Am 9: 11; Zech 12: 3f; Is 10: 20; Jer 37: 7f) Mt 7: 22; Lk 6: 23; 10: 12; 21: 34; 2 Th 1: 10; 2 Ti 1: 12, 18; 4: 8. Perh. ἡμ. σφαγῆς (cf. Jer 12: 3; En. 16, 1) Js 5: 5 belongs here (s. σφαγή). Abs. ἡμ. 1 Cor 3: 13; Hb 10: 25; B 7: 9; 21: 3; cf. 1 Th 5: 4.—ἡμέρα αἰῶνος (Sir 18: 10) day of eternity 2 Pt 3: 18 is also eschatological in mng.; it means the day on which eternity commences, or the day which itself constitutes eternity. In the latter case the pass. would belong to the next section.

4. of a longer period (like יוֹם, but not unknown among the Greeks: Soph., Aj. 131; 623; Eur., Ion 720; Aristot., Rhet. 2, 13 p. 1389b, 33f; PAmh. 30, 43 [II bc] ἡμέρας αἰτοῦσα='she asked for time', or 'a respite') time.

   a. in sg. ἐν τ. ἡμέρᾳ τ. πονηρᾷ when the times are evil (unless the ref. is to the final judgment) Eph 6: 13. ἐν ἡμ. σωτηρίας of the blessed time which has come for Christians 2 Cor 6: 2 (Is 49: 8). Of the time of the rescue fr. Egypt ἐν ἡμέρᾳ ἐπιλαβομένου μου τ. χειρὸς αὐτῶν at the time when I took them by the hand Hb 8: 9 (Jer 38: 32; on the constr. cf. Bar 2: 28 and Bl-D. §423, 5; Rob. 514). ἐν ἐκείνῃ τ. ἡμέρᾳ at that time Mk 2: 20b; J 14: 20; 16: 23, 26. τ. ἡμέραν τ. ἐμήν my time (era) 8: 56.

   b. chiefly in the pl. αἱ ἡμέραι of time of life or activity, w. gen. of the pers. (1 Km 17: 12 A; 2 Km 21: 1; 3 Km 10: 21; Esth 1: 1s; Sir 46: 7; 47: 1 and oft.) ἐν ἡμέραις Ἡρῴδου Mt 2: 1; Lk 1: 5; Νῶε 17: 26a; 1 Pt 3: 20; Ἠλίου Lk 4: 25. ἐν ταῖς ἡμ. τοῦ υἱοῦ τ. ἀνθρώπου 17: 26b; cf. Mt 23: 30. ἀπὸ τ. ἡμερῶν Ἰωάννου Mt 11: 12. ἕως τ. ἡμερῶν Δαυίδ Ac 7: 45; cf. 13: 41 (Hab 1: 5). W. gen. of the thing ἡμέραι ἐκδικήσεως time of vengeance Lk 21: 22; τ. ἀπογραφῆς Ac 5: 37; cf. Rv 10: 7; 11: 6. ἐν τ. ἡμέραις τῆς σαρκὸς αὐτοῦ in the time of his appearance in the flesh Hb 5: 7.—ἡμέραι πονηραί corrupt times Eph 5: 16; cf. B 2: 1; 8: 6. ἡμ. ἀγαθαὶ happy times (Artem. 4, 8) 1 Pt 3: 10 (Ps 33: 13). ἀφ᾽ ἡμερῶν ἀρχαίων Ac 15: 7; αἱ πρότερον ἡμ. Hb 10: 32. πάσας τὰς ἡμέρας all the time, always Mt 28: 20 (cf. Dt 4: 40; 5: 29). νῦν τ. ἡμέραις at the present time Hs 9, 20, 4. ἐν (ταῖς) ἐσχάταις ἡμ. Ac 2: 17; 2 Ti 3: 1; Js 5: 3; B 4: 9; D 16: 3. ἐπ᾽ ἐσχάτου τῶν ἡμερῶν τούτων Hb 1: 2; cf. 2 Pt 3: 3. ἐν τ. ἡμέραις ἐκείναις at that time Mt 3: 1; 24: 19, 38; Mk 1: 9; Lk 2: 1; 4: 2b; 5: 35b. ἐν τ. ἡμ. ταύταις at this time Lk 1: 39; 6: 12; Ac 1: 15. εἰς ταύτας τ. ἡμέρας w. respect to our time (opp. πάλαι) Hs 9, 26, 6. πρὸ τούτων τ. ἡμερῶν before this (time) Ac 5: 36; 21: 38; πρὸς ὀλίγας ἡμ. for a short time Hb 12: 10; ἐλεύσονται ἡμ. there will come a time: w. ὅταν foll. Mt 9: 15; Mk 2: 20a; Lk 5: 35a; w. ὅτε foll. Lk 17: 22. ἥξουσιν ἡμέραι ἐπὶ σε καὶ a time is coming upon you when Lk 19: 43. ἡμ. ἔρχονται καὶ Hb 8: 8 (Jer 38: 31). ἐλεύσονται ἡμ. ἐν αἷς Lk 21: 6; 23: 29.—Esp. of time of life πάσαις τ. ἡμέραις ἡμῶν all our lives Lk 1: 75. μήτε ἀρχὴν ἡμερῶν μήτε ζωῆς τέλος ἔχων without either beginning or end of life Hb 7: 3. προβεβηκὼς ἐν ταῖς ἡμ. advanced in years Lk 1: 7, 18; cf. 2: 36 (s. Gen 18: 11; 24: 1; Josh 13: 1; 23: 1; 3 Km 1: 1; προβαίνω 2).—GvRad and GDelling, TW II 945-56. M-M. B. 991.

ἥμερος, ον (Hom. +; LXX; Ep. Arist.; Philo; Jos., C. Ap. 2, 137; 212. Loanw. in rabb.) tame; of pers. (Pind. +; Dit., Syll.³ 932, 7, Or. 116, 7; Philo, Leg. ad Gai. 243, Mos. 2, 279) gentle, merciful opp. ἄγριος (cf. Dio Chrys. 11[12], 28) IEph 10: 2. Of words mild Hv 1, 3, 3. Comp. ἡμερώτερος (since Aeschyl., Ag. 1632) of commandments Hm 12, 4, 5.*

ἡμερόω (Aeschyl., Hdt. +; Wsd 16: 18; Philo) to tame fig. of wicked desires Hm 12, 1, 2.*

ἡμέτερος, α, ον (Hom. +; inscr., pap., LXX, Joseph.) our used w. nouns Ac 2: 11; 19: 35 D; 24: 6 t.r.; 26: 5; Ro 15: 4; 2 Ti 4: 15; 1 J 1: 3; 2: 2; 1 Cl 7: 4; 32: 4; 33: 5; B 5: 5; 7: 3; Dg 9: 2, 6; ISm 5: 1; Hs 9, 11, 3; 9, 24, 4; MPol 12: 2.—τὸ ἡμ. what is ours (=the true riches vs. 11) Lk 16: 12 (opp. τὸ ἀλλότριον, q.v., and cf. SAntoniadis, Neotestamentica: Neophilologus 14, '29, 129-35). οἱ ἡμ. our people (cf. Leo 4, 8; PGiess. 84 II, 7f; Jos., Ant. 14, 228, Vi. 401; 406)=the Christians Tit 3: 14; MPol 9: 1. S. ἐμός, end. M-M.*

ἦ μήν s. ἦ.

ἡμιθανής, ές (Dionys. Hal. 10, 7; Diod. S. 12, 62, 5; Strabo 2, 3, 4; Anth. Pal. 11, 392, 4; PAmh. 141, 13; PLeipz. 37: 21; 4 Macc 4: 11; Proseuche Aseneth 27 Batiffol) *half dead* Lk 10: 30 (for a similar situation in Egyptian law cf. Diod. S. 1, 77, 3). M-M. and suppl.*

ἡμίξηρος, ον (PFlor. 118, 3 [III AD]; Test. Sim. 2, 12; Etym. Mag. p. 535, 23) *half dry, half withered* of branches Hs 8, 1, 8f; 8, 4, 6; 8, 5, 2ff; 8, 7, 1f. Of vegetation 9, 1, 6.*

ἥμισυς, εια, υ gen. ἡμίσους (Dssm., NB 14 [BS 186]) Mk 6: 23; neut. pl. ἡμίση (Theophr., Char. 11, 5; Polyaenus 6, 15; some mss. have the spelling ἡμίσια.—Rdm.² 63) Lk 19: 8 (Hom.+; inscr., pap., LXX, Ep. Arist., Philo, Joseph.) *half.*
1. as adj., used w. a noun, it takes the latter's gender and number (Thu. 5, 31, ἡ ἡμίσεια τῆς γῆς; X., Cyr. 4, 5, 1 τοῦ σίτου ὁ ἥμισυς, 2, 3, 17 οἱ ἡμίσεις τῶν ἀνδρῶν, 4, 5, 4 τῶν ἄρτων οἱ ἡμίσεις; Demosth. 4, 16 οἱ ἡμίσεις τῶν ἱππέων; 1 Macc 3: 34, 37; Jos., Bell. 6, 290) τὰ ἡμίση τῶν ὑπαρχόντων (Tob 10: 10 BA v.l.) Lk 19: 8.
2. as noun τὸ ἥ. *one half* (Hom.+; Jos., Ant. 7, 275) Rv 12: 14 (Da 12: 7); Hs 8, 1, 11; 8, 5, 2; 8, 8, 1; AP 12: 27. ἕως ἡμίσους τῆς βασιλείας μου *up to one half of my kingdom* (Esth 5: 3; 7: 2) Mk 6: 23. οἱ ἡμίσεις Hs 9, 8, 5. ἡμέρας τρεῖς καὶ ἥμισυ *three and one-half days* Rv 11: 9, 11 (cf. Athen. 6 p. 274c τῶν δυοῖν δραχμῶν καὶ ἡμίσους; Ex 25: 17; 26: 16. Without καὶ Plut., Mar. 34, 4).—Gerh Kittel, Rabbinica '20, 39ff. M-M. B. 935.*

ἡμίωρον, ου, τό or v.l. ἡμιώριον (the latter form in Menand.; Strabo 2, 5, 36; Archigenes [II AD] in Aëtius p. 160, 13. On the development of both forms cf. Kühner-Bl. II 323; s. Mlt.-H. 176; 280; 341) *a half hour* Rv 8: 1. M-M.*

ἤνεγκα s. φέρω.

ἠνεῳγμένος, ἠνεῴχθην s. ἀνοίγω.

ἡνίκα particle denoting time (Hom.+; inscr., pap., LXX, Philo; Jos., Ant. 12, 138 al.; Sib. Or. 3, 797) *when, at the time when;* w. pres. subj. and ἄν *whenever* 2 Cor 3: 15; *when, as soon as* 1 Cl 57: 4 (Pr 1: 26). W. aor. subj. and ἐάν (*at the time*) *when, every time that* (POxy. 104, 26 [96 AD] ἡνίκα ἐὰν ἀπαλλαγῇ τ. ἀνδρός; PTebt. 317, 18 ἡνίκα ἐὰν εἰς τὸν νόμον παραγένηται; Gen 27: 40) 2 Cor 3: 16 (Ex 34: 34, but w. ἄν and impf.). M-M.*

ἤπερ s. ἤ 2eβ.

ἤπιος, α, ον (Hom.+; Epict. p. 487, 3; grave inscr. APF 5, '13, 166 no. 17, 4 the deceased is described as ἤπιον ἀνθρώποισι; POxy. 1380, 11; 86; 155; Philo, Mos. 1, 72) *gentle* 1 Th 2: 7 (v.l. νήπιοι, q.v.). ἤ. πρός τινα *kind toward someone* 2 Ti 2: 24 (here also νήπ. is a v.l.). M-M.*

ἠπίως adv. (since Soph., El. 1439; Hdt. 7, 105; also Paus. 10, 11, 4) *kindly* 1 Cl 23: 1.*

Ἤρ, ὁ indecl. (עֵר) *Er* (Gen 38: 3; Philo, Poster. Cai. 180), in the genealogy of Jesus Lk 3: 28.*

ἦρα, ἤρθην s. αἴρω.

ἤρεμος, ον (Lucian, Tragodop. 207; Dit., Or. 519, 10 ἤρεμον καὶ γαληνὸν τὸν βίον διαγόντων; Paroem. Gr.: Zenob. 2, 65 [Hadrian] βίον ἄλυπον καὶ ἠρ. ἔχειν; Esth 3: 13b acc. to cod. A; Hesychius) *quiet, tranquil,* of life: ἵνα ἤρεμον κ. ἡσύχιον βίον διάγωμεν 1 Ti 2: 2. M-M. B. 840f.*

Ἡρῴδης, ου, ὁ (freq.; also in inscr. [Dit., Or. index I] and pap. [Preisigke, Namenbuch], where it is not infrequently found in the correct [Bl-D. §26 w. app.; M-M.; Mlt.-H. 84] spelling with ι; cf. Schürer I⁴ 375, 20) *Herod,* name of Idumaean princes forming a dynasty, whose rule in Palestine was established through the favor of Mark Antony and Octavian toward 1; the dynasty continued to rule, though in varied forms, until after the death of 3.—WOtto, Herodes. Beiträge z. Gesch. d. letzten jüd. Königshauses '13; HWillrich, D. Haus des H. zwischen Jerusalem u. Rom '29.
1. Herod I, the Great (41[37]-4 BC) Mt 2: 1-22; Lk 1: 5. A palace built by him and named after him is mentioned Ac 23: 35.—Schürer I⁴ 348-418; here, 360f, sources and lit.; EMeyer II 322-7; ASchalit, König Herodes '69 (transl. by JAmir from the Hebr. of '60).
2. the son of 1, Herod Antipas (4 BC-39 AD), tetrarch of Galilee and Perea (Jos., Ant. 17, 318), mentioned in the NT because of (among other things) his clash w. John the Baptist, whom he had executed (s. Ἰωάννης 1). The synoptics give as the reason for this clash the fact that John raised objections to the tetrarch's marriage to Herodias (q.v.), who forsook one of his brothers to marry him. Acc. to Lk (and GP) this Herod played a role in the passion story (AWVerrall, JTS 10, '09, 322-53; MDibelius, ZNW 16, '15, 113-26; KBornhäuser, NKZ 40, '29, 714-18; JBlinzler, Her. Ant. u. Jes. Chr. '47; VEHarlow, The Destroyer of Jesus. The Story of Herod Antipas '54). Mt 14: 1, 3, 6; Mk 6: 14-22; 8: 15; Lk 3: 1, 19; 8: 3; 9: 7, 9; 13: 31; 23: 7-15; Ac 4: 27; 13: 1; ISm 1: 2; GEb 1; GP 1: 1f; 2: 4f. Called βασιλεύς Mk 6: 14; cf. Mt 14: 9; GEb 1; GP 1: 2.—Schürer I⁴ 431-49; here, 431, sources and lit.
3. Herod Agrippa I (s. Ἀγρίππας 1) Ac 12: 1, 6, 11, 19, 21.—4. an irenarch in Smyrna (s. εἰρήναρχος) MPol 6: 2; 8: 2; 17: 2, 21.—SPerowne, The Later Herods '58; HWHoehner, Herod Antipas, '72. M-M.*

Ἡρῳδιανοί, ῶν, οἱ *the Herodians,* partisans of Herod the Great and his family (Jos., Ant. 14, 450 οἱ τὰ Ἡρῴδου φρονοῦντες. Cf. Appian, Bell. Civ. 3, 82 §334 οἱ Πομπηιανοί; 3, 91 §376 Καισαριανοί) Mt 22: 16; Mk 3: 6; 8: 15 v.l.; 12: 13.—BWBacon, JBL 39, '20, 102-12; EBickermann, RB 47, '38, 184-97; PJoüon, Rech de Sc rel 28, '38, 585-8; HHRowley, JTS 41, '40, 16-27.*

Ἡρῳδιάς, άδος, ἡ *Herodias,* granddaughter of Herod the Great (Ἡρῴδης 1), daughter of his son Aristobulus, mother-in-law of Philip the tetrarch who married her daughter Salome (q.v.), and wife of Herod who was a half-brother of Herod Antipas (Jos., Ant. 18, 110f). In Mk 6: 17 and Mt 14: 3 (here D omits the name Philip) the first husband of Herodias is called (some hold erroneously) Philip. Mt 14: 3, 6; Mk 6: 17, 19, 22; Lk 3: 19.—Schürer I⁴ 435ff; WLillie, Salome or Herodias?: ET 65, '53f, 251.*

Ἡρῳδίων, ωνος, ὁ (grave-inscr. fr. Kom-el-Gadi: Sb 351 [6/7 AD]. S. also Preisigke, Namenbuch) *Herodion,* a Jewish Christian, greeted Ro 16: 11.*

Ἠσαΐας, ου, ὁ (יְשַׁעְיָהוּ) *Isaiah* (Gk. form Esaias), the prophet (LXX; Joseph.) Mt 3: 3; 4: 14; 8: 17; 12: 17; 13: 14, 35 v.l.; 15: 7; Mk 7: 6; Lk 3: 4; 4: 17; J 1: 23; 12: 38f, 41; Ac 28: 25; Ro 9: 27, 29; 10: 16, 20; 15: 12; B 12: 11. Of the book of Isaiah γέγραπται ἐν τῷ Ἠ. *it is written in I.* Mk 1: 2; ἀνεγίνωσκεν τ. προφήτην Ἠ. Ac 8: 28, cf. vs. 30; λέγει ἐν τῷ Ἠ. *he* (the preëxistent Christ) *says in I.* 2 Cl 3: 5.*

'Ησαῦ, ὁ (עֵשָׂו) indecl. (LXX; Philo; Test. 12 Patr. In Joseph. 'Ησαῦς, αῦ [Ant. 2, 5]) *Esau* Hb 11: 20. 'Hated' by God Ro 9: 13 (Mal 1: 2f). Typical of an immoral and vulgar person (on Esau in this light cf. Book of Jubilees 35, 13f; Philo, Virt. 208; s. Gen 27: 41; 28: 7f) Hb 12: 16. The flight of Jacob fr. Esau (Gen 27: 41ff) 1 Cl 4: 8.—HOdeberg, TW II 957f.*

ἦσθα s. εἰμί.

ἥσσων (Hom.+; inscr. [Dit., Syll.³ 709, 3]; pap. [UPZ 113, 12: 156 BC; PTebt. 105, 36]; LXX [Thackeray 122]), ἥττων (Aristoph., Pla.+; inscr. [Dit., Syll.³ 851, 10]; pap. [PPetr. II 47, 26: 208 BC; PTebt. 329, 29]; LXX; Ep. Arist. 257; Joseph.), ον, gen. ονος. Comp. without a positive *lesser, inferior, weaker* ἥ. ἁμαρτία a lesser sin 1 Cl 47: 4. ἥ. κίνδυνος 55: 6. ἥ. τόπος Mt 20: 28 D=Agr 22.—Subst. ὁ ἥ. Mt 20: 28 D b; οἱ ἥ. 1 Cl 39: 9 (Job 5: 4). τὸ ἧσσον (opp. τὸ κρεῖσσον): εἰς τὸ ἥ. συνέρχεσθε (when) you come together (it is) for the worse (but the comp. sense is no longer strongly felt: AFridrichsen, Horae Soederblom. I 1, '44, 30f) 1 Cor 11: 17.—The neut. as adv. *less* (M. Ant. 3, 2, 6; Jos., Ant. 4, 194; 5, 206) εἰ περισσοτέρως ὑμᾶς ἀγαπῶ ἧσσον ἀγαπῶμαι; *if I love you much more, am I on that account to be loved less?* 2 Cor 12: 15. M-M.*

ἡσυχάζω 1 aor. ἡσύχασα, imper. ἡσύχασον (Aeschyl., Thu.+; pap., LXX, Philo, Joseph., Test. 12 Patr.) in our lit. only intrans.
1. *be quiet, rest* (Appian, Bell. Civ. 4, 72 §306; Jos., Ant. 18, 354) 1 Cl 4: 5 (Gen 4: 7); *abstain fr. work* (Herodian 7, 5, 3) of the conduct prescribed in the law for the sabbath Lk 23: 56 (Neptunianus [II AD] ed. WGemoll, Progr. Striegau 1884, 53 the ants are said τὸ σάββατον ἡσυχάζειν κ. σχολὴν ἄγειν). Of a quiet life (Thu. 1, 120, 3; BGU 372 II, 14; PSI 41, 23 σωφρονεῖν καὶ ἡσυχάζειν; Philo, Abr. 27) 1 Th 4: 11.
2. *be quiet, remain silent* (Aeschyl., Prom. 327; Job 32: 1; 2 Esdr 15 [Neh 5]: 8; Philo, Somn. 2, 263; Jos., Bell. 3, 263, Ant. 1, 339) Lk 14: 4; Ac 11: 18; 21: 14; 22: 2 D.
3. w. gen. *cease from* (cf. Job 32: 6) τῆς ματαίας στάσεως 1 Cl 63: 1.
4. *have rest* (Diog. L. 3, 21) ἀπό τινος *from someth.* 1 Cl 57: 7 (Pr 1: 33), unless the ἀπό-clause goes w. ἀφόβως, in which case this pass. belongs under mng. 1. M-M.*

ἡσυχία, ας, ἡ (Hom.+; inscr., pap., LXX, Ep. Arist., Philo, Joseph.; Test. Benj. 6: 5).
1. *quietness, rest* (Diog. L. 9, 21 of inner peace; Pind., Pyth. 1, 70 of peace and harmony among citizens) w. πραότης Hm 5, 2, 6. Of undisturbed life (Jos., Ant. 18, 245) 2 Th 3: 12 (μετὰ ἡσυχίας as Diod. S. 4, 2, 2; 16, 13, 2; 18, 9, 3; Dit., Syll.³ 1109, 64f; UPZ 8, 17 [161 BC]; BGU 614; Sir 28: 16). ἡσυχίαν ἔχειν ἀπό τινος *have rest from someth.* AP 17: 32.
2. *silence* (Pla., Ep. 2 p. 312C; Pr 11: 12; Philo, Rer. Div. Her. 14; Jos., Ant. 3, 67) IEph 15: 2. ἐν ἥ. *in silence* (Philo, Somn. 2, 263) 1 Ti 2: 11f; IEph 19: 1. παρέχειν ἡσυχίαν *be quiet, silent* (cf. Jos., Ant. 5, 235) Ac 22: 2 (is it possible that here such concepts as 'reverence', 'devotion' may have some influence? Cf. Dio Chrys. 68[18], 10: Herodotus should be read μετὰ πολλῆς ἡσυχίας). ἡσυ-

χίας γενομένης 21: 40 D (cf. Dio Chrys. 13[7], 26; Philo, Vi. Cont. 75). M-M.*

ἡσύχιος, ον (Hom.+; inscr., pap.; Is 66: 2; Joseph.) *quiet* D 3: 8. W. πραΰς 1 Cl 13: 4; B 19: 4 (both Is 66: 2); Hm 5, 2, 3; 6, 2, 3; 11: 8. Again w. πραΰς: πνεῦμα 1 Pt 3: 4 (s. PsSol 12, 5 ψυχὴ ἡσ.). βίος (Pla., Demosth.; Dit., Syll.³ 866, 15; POxy. 129, 8 εἰρηνικὸν καὶ ἡσύχιον βίον διάξαι; Jos., Ant. 13, 407) 1 Ti 2: 2. ἡσύχιον εἶναι Hm 8: 10. M-M. B. (ἥσυχος) 840.*

ἡσύχως adv. (trag.+) *quietly*, λειτουργεῖν 1 Cl 44: 3.*

ἦτα, τό indecl. *eta* seventh letter of the Gk. alphabet, as numeral=*eight* B 9: 8 Funk.*

ἤτοι s. ἤ 1b.

ἡττάομαι in our lit. only in pass.; perf. ἥττημαι; 1 aor. ἡττήθην (so Soph., Hdt.+; pap., LXX [Thackeray 122]; Jos., Bell. 1, 57 al. On the spelling w. ττ s. Bl-D. §34, 1; Mlt.-H. 107; JWackernagel, Hellenistica '07, 12ff) *be defeated, succumb* τινί *to (by) a pers.* or *thing* (Plut., Cato Min. 16, 7; Is 51: 7; Jos., Ant. 1, 288; Test. Reub. 5: 3) 2 Pt 2: 19; cf. vs. 20.—*Be inferior* ὑπέρ τι *to someth.* 2 Cor 12: 13 v.l.; s. ἐσσόομαι. M-M.*

ἥττημα, ατος, τό (Is 31: 8) *defeat* Ro 11: 12. ὅλως ἥ. ὑμῖν ἐστιν *it is an utter defeat for you* 1 Cor 6: 7 (Field, Notes 160f.). M-M.*

ἥφιε s. ἀφίημι.

ἠχέω (Hes.+) in our lit. only intrans. (cf. 3 Km 1: 41; Is 16: 11) *sound, ring out* of brass instruments χαλκὸς ἠχῶν (cf. Hdt. 4, 200; Pla., Prot. 329A) 1 Cor 13: 1. *Roar, thunder* of the sea (cf. Himerius, Or. 40 [=Or. 6], 1 ἠχοῦσα θάλασσα; Ps 45: 4; Jer 5: 22) Lk 21: 25 t.r. (on the Peshitta here, s. MBlack, An Aramaic Approach³, '67, 261f).*

ἦχος, ου, ὁ (Pre-Socr.+; Herm. Wr. 1, 4; Sb 8339, 8 [inscr. 123 AD] τοῦ θεοῦ τὸν ἦχον; PGM 13, 399; 401; 532; LXX; En. 102, 1; Ep. Arist. 96; Philo; Jos., Bell. 4, 299 al.; Sib. Or. 5, 253).
1. *sound, tone, noise* Ac 2: 2. σάλπιγγος (Diod. S. 3, 17, 3; Achilles Tat. 3, 2, 3; 3, 13, 1; Ps 150: 3; Jos., Ant. 11, 83) Hb 12: 19. φωνῆς (Lucian, Nigr. 7) Hv 4, 1, 4.
2. *report, news* ἐξεπορεύετο ἥ. περὶ αὐτοῦ *a report about him went out* Lk 4: 37.—Lk 4: 37; Ac 2: 2 and Hv 4, 1, 4 may belong to the following entry. M-M. B. 1037.*

ἦχος, ους, τό (Ps.-Callisth. p. 61, 2; 9; PGM 13, 201; 204; 394; 545 ἐκ τοῦ ἤχους. In the LXX only the acc. ἦχος Jer 28: 16 can w. certainty be listed here. S. also Reinhold 54) *sound, tone, noise* ἐν ἀπορίᾳ ἤχους θαλάσσης Lk 21: 25 (cf. Nymphis [III BC] no. 432 fgm. 3 Jac., where the masc. pl. [s. preceding entry] refers to the roar of the waves, as well as the masc. sing. Dio Chrys. 13[7], 5 ὁ ἦχος τῆς θαλ.; Ps 64: 8).—If w. W-H. we accentuate ἠχοῦς, this pass. must be assigned to the next entry.*

ἠχώ, οῦς, ἡ (trag.+; Philostrat., Vi. Soph. 2, 3, 1; Herm. Wr. 444, 19 Sc.; Job 4: 13; Wsd 17: 18) *sound*; fig. πάλιν ἔσομαι ἥ. *I shall again be nothing but a sound* IRo 2: 1 (but ἠχώ in this pass. is only a conjecture by Bunsen, Zahn et al.).*

Θ

θ΄ numeral (Jos., C. Ap. 1, 122)=*ninth* (ἐνάτη) Hm 9; [s 9] in superscriptions.*

θάβιτα Mk 5: 41 D; s. ῥαβιθά.*

Θαβώρ, ὁ indecl. (תָּבוֹר) *Tabor*, a mountain on the south border of the Galilean highland (Judg 4: 6ff; Ps 88: 13) GH 5.—JBoehmer, ARW 12, '09, 313-21, D. Name Th.: Ztschr. f. Semitistik 7, '29, 161-9; CKopp, The Holy Places of the Gospels (tr. RWalls) '63, 242-47.*

Θαδδαῖος, ου, ὁ (תַּדַּי, Talmud. תַּדְּאָי. Cf. MLidzbarski, Handbuch d. nordsem. Epigr. 1898, 388; DDiringer, Le Iscrizioni antico-ebraiche palestinesi '34, 183; prob.= Θεόδοτος or a sim. form, MLidzbarski, Ephemeris für semit. Epigr. II '08, 16) *Thaddaeus* Mt 10: 3; Mk 3: 18. In both pass. Λεββαῖος is found as v.l. It has been suggested that originally one of these names was found in one gospel, and the other name in the other, and that the variants in both cases are to be explained as an attempt to bring the lists of apostles into agreement. In Lk (6: 16=Ac 1: 13) Ἰούδας Ἰακώβου occurs in place of these names.*

θάλασσα, ης, ἡ (Hom.+; inscr., pap., LXX, En., Ep. Arist., Philo, Joseph., Test. 12 Patr.).
   1. *sea*—a. gener. Mk 9: 42; 11: 23; Lk 17: 2, 6; Rv 8: 8f; 1 Cl 33: 3. W. γῆ (Epict. 3, 26, 1; Inscr. Gr. 521, 10; Dit., Syll.³ IV 260b: index IV; Philo; Jos., Ant. 1, 282) Rv 7: 1-3; 21: 1 (cf. Artem. 1, 2 p. 6, 8-10 ἥλιου δὲ καὶ σελήνης καὶ τῶν ἄλλων ἄστρων ἀφανισμὸν ἢ τελείαν ἔκλειψιν γῆς τε καὶ θαλάσσης).—W. ἡ ξηρά, the dry land Mt 23: 15. W. γῆ and οὐρανός to denote the whole universe (Ex 20: 11; Hg 2: 6, 21; Ps 145: 6; Jos., Ant. 4, 40, C. Ap. 2, 121) Ac 4: 24; 14: 15; Rv 5: 13; 10: 6; 14: 7. W. γῆ and ἀήρ PK 2 p. 14, 17. κίνδυνοι ἐν θαλάσσῃ 2 Cor 11: 26 (cf. BGU 423, 7; Jos., Vi. 14 πολλὰ κινδυνεύσας κατὰ θάλασσαν). τὴν θ. ἐργάζεσθαι *have work on the sea* Rv 18: 17 (s. ἐργάζ. 2d). The sand of the seashore as symbol of numberlessness Ro 9: 27 (Is 10: 22); Hb 11: 12 (Gen 22: 17). Waves of the sea Js 1: 6; Jd 13. τὸ πέλαγος τῆς θ. *the high seas* Mt 18: 6 (cf. Apollon. Rhod. 2, 608); ἡ ἄπειρος θ. 1 Cl 20: 6.
   b. of specific seas—α. of the Red Sea ἡ ἐρυθρὰ θ. (s. ἐρυθρός) Ac 7: 36; Hb 11: 29. Without adj., but w. ref. to the same sea 1 Cor 10: 1f (s. FJDölger, Antike u. Christent. II '31, 63-79).
   β. of the Mediterranean Sea (Hdt. et al.) Ac 10: 6, 32; 17: 14; 27: 30, 38, 40.
   2. *lake* (a Semitic usage, cf. the expl. in Aristot., Meteor. 1, 13 p. 351a, 8 ἣ ὑπὸ τὸν Καύκασον λίμνη ἣν καλοῦσιν οἱ ἐκεῖ θάλατταν. Cf. Num 34: 11) of Lake Gennesaret ἡ θ. τῆς Γαλιλαίας *the Lake* (or *Sea*; Murray, New [Oxford] Engl. Dict. s.v. 'sea', I 3) *of Galilee* Mt 4: 18; 15: 29; Mk 1: 16; 7: 31. For the same lake ἡ θ. τῆς Τιβεριάδος J 21: 1. Both together 6: 1 ἡ θ. τῆς Γαλιλαίας τῆς Τιβεριάδος *the Galilean Lake of Tiberias*. Simply θάλασσα Mt 8: 24; 13: 1; 14: 24ff (on walking on the θάλ.: Dio Chrys. 3, 30); Mk 2: 13; 3: 7 al. M-M. B. 36.

θάλλω impf. ἔθαλλον (Hom. Hymns and Hes.+; inscr., pap., LXX; Sib. Or. 5, 400) *grow up, flourish* of plants (Diog. L. 7, 86 θάλλει τὰ φυτά='the plants flourish') Hs 9, 1, 8.*

θάλπω (Hom.+; inscr., pap., LXX) lit. *keep warm* (Jos., Ant. 7, 343); fig. *cherish, comfort* (Theocr. 14, 38; M.

Ant. 5, 1, 1; Alciphr. 4, 19, 9; Dit., Or. 194, 5 [42 BC] τὴν πόλιν ἔθαλψε) of children whom the mother cherishes 1 Th 2: 7. Of a wife, whom her husband is to care for as his own flesh (PRainer 30, 20 of the husband to his wife ἀγαπᾶν καὶ θάλπειν καὶ θεραπεύειν; Sb 4658, 12) Eph 5: 29. M-M.

Θαμάρ, ἡ indecl. (תָּמָר) (LXX, Philo, Test. Jud.—Joseph. has the same name, of David's daughter, as Θαμάρα, as [Ant. 7, 162; 178]) *Tamar*, daughter-in-law of Judah and mother of his twin sons Perez and Zerah (Gen 38: 6, 29f). In the genealogy of Jesus Mt 1: 3. GerhKittel, Θαμάρ, Ῥαχάβ, Ῥούθ, ἡ τοῦ Οὐρίου: TW III '35, 1-3.*

θαμβέω (Hom.+; pap., LXX)—1. intr. *be astounded* (this is the orig. sense) τρέμων κ. θαμβῶν *trembling and astounded* Ac 9: 6 t.r.
   2. elsewh. in our lit. only trans. and in the pass.—Impf. ἐθαμβούμην; 1 aor. ἐθαμβήθην, also ἐθαμβώθην AP 3, 8; 1 fut. θαμβηθήσομαι; *astound, amaze*, pass. *be astounded, amazed* (Plut., Caes. 45, 7, Brut. 20, 9; POxy. 645, 7; PGM 13, 527; Wsd 17: 3; 1 Macc 6: 8) Mk 1: 27; 10: 32; Ac 3: 11 D; AP 3, 8. ἐπί τινα at someth. Mk 10: 24.—W. less force, *wonder, be surprised* GH 27 (=LJ 2: 2).—GBertram, TW III '35, 3-7. M-M.*

θάμβος, ους, τό (Hom. +; LXX so certainly Ac 3: 10, text, and **θάμβος, ου, ὁ** (Simonides 237 Bergk, also LXX) so certainly θάμβου Ac 3: 10 C. θ. μέγας Lk 4: 36 D (Jos., Bell. 5, 324; 7, 30 the gender cannot be determined) *astonishment, fear* ἐγένετο ἐπὶ πάντας *came upon them all* Lk 4: 36. περιέσχεν αὐτόν *had seized him* 5: 9. ἐπλήσθησαν θάμβους Ac 3: 10. M-M. B. 1093.*

θαμβόω (Lucian, Syr. Dea 25) s. θαμβέω 2.

θανάσιμος, ον (Aeschyl.+) *deadly* θ. φάρμακον (Eur., Ion 616; Diod. S. 4, 45, 2; Diosc. 2, 24; Dit., Syll.³ 1180, 2; Philo, Plant. 147; Jos., Ant. 4, 279; 17, 69) *deadly poison* ITr 6: 2. Cf. Hs 9, 1, 9 Lghtf. as v.l. for θανατώδης.—Subst. (so the pl. Diosc. 2, 19; 2, 81, 1; Jos., Ant. 14, 368) θανάσιμόν τι Mk 16: 18. M-M.*

θανατηφόρος, ον (Aeschyl., Hippocr.+; Diod. S. 3, 3, 6; 3, 5, 3; Vett. Val. 225, 7; 237, 7; 9 al.; Kyr.-Inschr. 1. 9; 21; pap.; LXX) *death-bringing* ἰός *poison* (Sib. Or., fgm. 3, 33 p. 231 G.) Js 3: 8; καρπὸς θ. ITr 11: 1. M-M.*

θάνατος, ου, ὁ (Hom.+; inscr., pap., LXX; Ep. Arist. 233; Philo, Joseph., Test. 12 Patr.) *death*.
   1. lit.—a. of natural death J 11: 4, 13; Hb 7: 23; 9: 15f; Rv 18: 8; 1 Cl 9: 3. Opp. ζωή Ro 8: 38; 1 Cor 3: 22; 2 Cor 1: 9; Phil 1: 20. γεύεσθαι θανάτου *taste death=die* (γεύομαι 2) Mt 16: 28; Mk 9: 1; Lk 9: 27; J 8: 52; Hb 2: 9b. Also ἰδεῖν θάνατον (Astrampsychus p. 26 Dek. 48, 2. Also θεάομαι θάν. p. 6 l. 53) Lk 2: 26; Hb 11: 5; ζητεῖν τὸν θ. Rv 9: 6. θανάτου καταφρονεῖν *despise death* ISm 3: 2; Dg 10: 7a. περίλυπος ἕως θανάτου *sorrowful even to the point of death* (Jon 4: 9 σφόδρα λελύπημαι ἕως θανάτου; Sir 37: 2) Mt 26: 38; Mk 14: 34; ἄχρι θ. *to the point of death* of a devotion that does not shrink even fr. the sacrifice of one's life Rv 2: 10; 12: 11. διώκειν ἄχρι θανάτου *persecute even to the death* Ac 22: 4. Also διώκειν ἐν θανάτῳ. εἰς θ. πορεύεσθαι *go to one's death* Lk 22: 33. ἀσθενεῖν παραπλήσιον θανάτῳ *be nearly dead with illness* Phil 2: 27; ἐσφαγμένος εἰς θ.

receive *a fatal wound* Rv 13: 3a. ἡ πληγὴ τοῦ θανάτου *a fatal wound* 13: 3b, 12. φόβος θανάτου Hb 2: 15.

b. of death as a penalty (Thu. et al.; Diod. S. 14, 66, 3: the tyrant is μυρίων θανάτων τυχεῖν δίκαιος='worthy of suffering countless deaths')—**a.** as inflicted by secular courts ἔνοχος θανάτου ἐστίν *he deserves death* (ἔνοχος 2bα) Mt 26: 66; Mk 14: 64; παραδιδόναι εἰς θ. *betray, give over to death* Mt 10: 21; Mk 13: 12. θανάτῳ τελευτᾶν *die the death=be punished w. death* Mt 15: 4; Mk 7: 10 (both Ex 21: 17). ἄξιον θανάτου, *deserving death, capital crime* (Jos., Ant. 11, 144) Lk 23: 15; Ac 23: 29; 25: 11, 25. αἴτιον θανάτου Lk 23: 22 (cf. αἴτιος 2). Also αἰτία θανάτου (Lucian, Tyrannic. 11) Ac 13: 28; 28: 18; κρίμα θ. *sentence of death*: παραδιδόναι εἰς κρίμα θ. *sentence to death* Lk 24: 20; fig. ἐν ἑαυτοῖς τὸ ἀπόκριμα τοῦ θ. ἐσχήκαμεν 2 Cor 1: 9. κατακρίνειν τινὰ εἰς θάνατον *condemn someone to death* Mt 20: 18.—Several of the pass. just quoted refer to the death sentence passed against Christ; sim., θάνατος is freq. used

β. of the death of Christ gener.: Ro 5: 10; 6: 3ff; 1 Cor 11: 26; Phil 2: 8a; 3: 10; Col 1: 22; Hb 2: 14a; IEph 7: 2; 19: 1; IMg 9: 1; ITr 2: 1. τὸ πάθημα τ. θανάτου *the suffering of death* Hb 2: 9. ἕως θανάτου καταντῆσαι *even to meet death* Pol 1: 2.—GWiencke, Pls über Jesu Tod '39.—The expr. ὠδῖνες τοῦ θανάτου, used Ac 2: 24 in a passage referring to Christ, comes fr. the LXX, where in Ps 17: 5 and 114: 3 it renders חֶבְלֵי־מָ֫וֶת (cf. IQH 3, 7-12). This would lit. be 'bonds of death'. But an interchange of חֶ֫בֶל 'bond' and חֵ֫בֶל 'pain', specif. 'birth-pangs', has made of it *pangs of death* (cf. a sim. interchange in 2 Km 22: 6 al. LXX, and the expr. in Pol 1: 2 λύσας τ. ὠδῖνας τοῦ ᾅδου). This results in a remarkable mixed metaphor in Ac 2: 24, in which death is regarded as being in labor, and unable to hold back its child, the Messiah (s. Beginn. IV ad loc.; Field, Notes 112).

γ. of natural death as divine punishment Ro 5: 12 a, b; 1 Cor 15: 21; B 12: 2, 5.

c. of the danger of death (2 Ch 32: 11) σῴζειν τινὰ ἐκ θανάτου *save someone fr. death* (Ael. Aristid. 45 p. 120 D.) Hb 5: 7. Also ῥύεσθαι ἐκ θ. 2 Cor 1: 10. θάνατοι (Epict. 4, 6, 2; Ptolem., Apotel. 2, 9, 5; Ael. Aristid. 46 p. 307 D.: ὥσπερ Ὀδυσσεὺς θ.; Maximus Tyr. 15, 8a; Philo, In Flacc. 175 προαποθνῄσκω πολλοὺς θανάτους) *danger(s) of death* 11: 23. μέχρι θανάτου ἐγγίζειν *come close to dying* Phil 2: 30. 2 Cor 4: 11, cf. vs. 12, is reminiscent of the constant danger of death which faced the apostle as he followed his calling.

d. of the manner of death (Artem. 1, 31 p. 33, 10; 4, 83 p. 251, 16 μυρίοι θ.='countless kinds of death'; Ps.-Hecataeus in Jos., C. Ap. 1, 191) ποίῳ θ. *by what kind of death* J 12: 33; 18: 32; 21: 19. θ. σταυροῦ Phil 2: 8b.

e. θάνατος can, through the context, come to mean a particular manner of death; e.g. *fatal illness, pestilence* (Job 27: 15; Jer 15: 2; θάνατος . . . μάχαιρα . . . λιμός) Rv 2: 23. ἀποκτεῖναι ἐν ῥομφαίᾳ κ. ἐν λιμῷ κ. ἐν θανάτῳ 6: 8b; 18: 8.

f. death is thought of as a person Ro 5: 14, 17; 6: 9; 1 Cor 15: 26 (cf. Plut., Is. et Os. 47 p. 370c τέλος ἀπολεῖσθαι [for ἀπολείπεσθαι] τὸν "Αιδην), 54-6 (s. on κέντρον); Rv 1: 18; 6: 8a; 20: 13f; 21: 4; B 5: 6; 16: 9 (this concept among Jews [Hos 13: 14; Sir 14: 12; 4 Esdr 8, 53; Syr. Baruch-Apc. 21, 23; Bousset, Rel.³ 253] and Greeks [ERohde, Psyche³ '03, II 241; 249; CRobert, Thanatos 1879]. Cf. JKroll, Gott u. Hölle '32; Dibelius, Geisterwelt 114ff; JThUbbink, Paulus en de dood: NThSt 1, '18, 3-10 and s. on ἁμαρτία 3).

2. fig. (Philo)—**a.** of spiritual death, to which everyone

is subject unless he has been called to the life of grace. θάνατον οὐ μὴ θεωρήσῃ J 8: 51. Opp. ζωή 5: 24; 1 J 3: 14; Ro 7: 10; 8: 6. This death stands in the closest relation to sin: Ro 7: 13b; Js 1: 15; 5: 20; 2 Cl 1: 6; Hv 2, 3, 1; also to the flesh: Paul thinks of the earthly body as σῶμα τ. θανάτου Ro 7: 24. θάνατος=*cause of death* vs. 13a. The unredeemed are ἐν χώρᾳ καὶ σκιᾷ θανάτου Mt 4: 16; cf. Lk 1: 79 (both Is 9: 2). This mng. of θάνατος cannot always be clearly distinguished fr. the foll., since spiritual death merges into

b. eternal death. θαν. αἰώνιος B 20: 1. This kind of death is meant Ro 1: 32; 6: 16, 21, 23; 7: 5; 2 Cor 7: 10; 2 Ti 1: 10; Hb 2: 14b; B 10: 5; 2 Cl 16: 4; Dg 10: 7b; Hv 1, 1, 8; m 4, 1, 2. ἁμαρτία πρὸς θάνατον 1 J 5: 16f (Polyaenus 8, 32 bravery πρὸς θ.='to the point of death'; s. ἁμαρτάνω 5 and Test. Iss. 7: 1 ἁμαρτία εἰς θάνατον). ὀσμὴ ἐκ θανάτου εἰς θάνατον *a fragrance* that comes *from death* and leads *to death* 2 Cor 2: 16. In Rv this (final) death is called *the second death* (ὁ δεύτερος θ. also Plut., Mor. 942ϝ) 2: 11; 20: 6, 14b; 21: 8 (s. ThZahn, comm. 604-8).—GQuell, Die Auffassung des Todes in Israel '26; RBultmann, TW III '35, 7-25; JLeipoldt, D. Tod bei Griechen u. Juden '42; TBarrosse, Death and Sin in Ro: CBQ 15, '53, 438-59; ELohse, Märtyrer u. Gottesknecht '55 (lit.); SBrandon, The Personification of Death in Some Ancient Religions, Bull. of the JRylands Lib. 43, '61, 317-35. M-M. B. 287.

θανατόω fut. θανατώσω; 1 aor. ἐθανάτωσα, pass. ἐθανατώθην (Aeschyl., Hdt.+; LXX; Philo, Joseph., Test. 12 Patr.) *put to death.*

1. lit. τινά *kill someone, hand someone over to be killed,* esp. of the death sentence and its execution (as X., An. 2, 6, 4; Pla., Leg. 9, p. 872c; Aelian, V.H. 5, 18; Ex 21: 12ff; Sus 28; 1 Macc 1: 57; 4 Macc 8: 25) Mt 10: 21; 26: 59; 27: 1; Mk 13: 12; 14: 55. The obj. acc. is easily supplied in θανατώσουσιν ἐξ ὑμῶν *they will put some of you to death* Lk 21: 16. Pass. 2 Cor 6: 9 (for the play on words ἀποθνῄσκοντες . . . καὶ μὴ θανατούμενοι cf. Ps.-Callisth. 1, 33, 11 p. 36, 21 θανὼν καὶ μὴ θανών); 1 Pt 3: 18; 1 Cl 12: 2; B 12: 2; Dg 5: 12. *Be in danger of death* Ro 8: 36 (Ps 43: 23).—Vi. Aesopi W c. 9 of ill treatment over a period of time: κατὰ πᾶσαν ἀποκτείνεις ἡμέραν).

2. fig.—**a.** of spiritual or eternal death 1 Cl 39: 7 (Job 5: 2); Hs 9, 20, 4. θ. τινὰ ἔν τινι *bring death to someone by someth.* m 12, 1, 3; cf. 12, 2, 2.

b. of the death which the believer dies through mystic unity w. the body of the crucified Christ; τῷ νόμῳ (dat. of disadvantage) Ro 7: 4 (on rabbinic associations s. WDiezinger, NovT 5, '62, 268-98).

c. *put to death, extirpate* τὶ someth. τὰς πράξεις τοῦ σώματος Ro 8: 13.*

θανατώδης, ες (Hippocr.+) *deadly, fatal* (so Aelian, N.A. 7, 5; Polyaenus 4, 3, 28; Suppl. Epigr. Gr. VIII 549, 7 [I BC]; Philo, Abr. 46) of poisonous reptiles Hs 9, 1, 9. Of desires Hm 12, 2, 3.*

θάπτω impf. ἔθαπτον; 1 aor. ἔθαψα; 2 aor. pass. ἐτάφην (Hom.+; inscr., pap., LXX; En. 22, 10; Joseph., Test. 12 Patr.) *bury* τινά *someone* (Jos., Bell. 4, 317, Ant. 4, 78) Mt 8: 21f; 14: 12; Lk 9: 59f (νεκρός 2b); Ac 5: 9; GP 2: 5. τὶ *someth.* τὸ σῶμα 6: 23. W. obj. acc. to be supplied Ac 5: 6, 10 (cf. Polyb. 12, 26, 7 τοὺς πρεσβυτέρους ὑπὸ τῶν νέων θάπτεσθαι). Pass. (Jos., Ant. 4, 202) Lk 16: 22; Ac 2: 29; 1 Cor 15: 4. M-M. B. 291f.*

Θάρα, ὁ indecl. (תֶּ֫רַח) (LXX; Philo [Θάρρα].—In Joseph. Θέρρος [v.l. Θάρρος], ου [Ant. 1, 252]) *Terah,* father of

Abraham (Gen 11: 24ff; Josh 24: 2; 1 Ch 1: 26); in the genealogy of Jesus Lk 3: 34.*

θαρρέω (increasing in frequency beside θαρσέω [q.v.] from the later Attic writers [Pla.], but found even earlier, and occurring also in inscr., pap., LXX [Thackeray 123]. Likew. Philo; Jos., Ant. 6, 181; 20, 175; Vi. 143; on associations of this term in the Eleusinian Mysteries s. RJoly, Revue des Études Grecques 68, '55, 164–70.—Thumb 77) 1 aor. inf. θαρρῆσαι *be confident, be courageous* 2 Cor 5: 6, 8. ὥστε θαρροῦντας ἡμᾶς λέγειν *so that we can say w. confidence* Hb 13: 6. θ. ἔν τινι *be able to depend on someone* 2 Cor 7: 16; *be bold* εἴς τινα *toward someone* 10: 1; cf. vs. 2 (s. δέομαι 2).—WGrundmann, TW III '35, 25–7. M-M.*

θαρσέω (Hom.+; inscr., pap., LXX; Jos., Ant. 1, 187; 8, 293; 11, 334) in the NT (and quite predom. in LXX) only imper. θάρσει, θαρσεῖτε. 1 aor. ἐθάρσησα *be cheerful, be courageous* AP 2: 5; Hv 4, 1, 8. θάρσει *have courage! don't be afraid!* (Il. 4, 184 al.; Gen 35: 17; Zeph 3: 16) Mt 9: 2, 22; Mk 10: 49; Lk 23: 43 D; Ac 23: 11. Pl. (Ex 14: 13) Mt 14: 27; Mk 6: 50; J 16: 33. M-M. B. 1149.*

θάρσος, ους, τό (Hom.+; Epict. 1, 24, 8; 2, 13, 3; Dit., Syll.³ 709, 25; Maspéro 158, 16. LXX, Philo, Joseph.; Sib. Or. 1, 241) *courage* θ. λαμβάνειν *take courage* (Jos., Ant. 9, 55) Ac 28: 15; Hv 3, 1, 5. W. χαρά MPol 12: 1.*

θᾶττον s. ταχέως 2.

θαῦμα, ατος, τό (Hom.+; inscr., LXX; Jos., Ant. 15, 395).

1. *an object of wonder* (Herm. Wr. 1, 16; PMich. 149 III, 19 [II AD]; Philo, Plant. 3).—a. gener. *a wonder, marvel* (Bacchylides 17, 123 of a divine miracle; Appian, Bell. Civ. 1, 16, §67; Philostrat., Imag. 2, 12 p. 358, 1; 2, 18 p. 371, 6; Himerius, Or. 6 [=Or. 2], 25: Xerxes penetrates the strait; Sib. Or. 3, 281) 2 Cor 11: 14.

b. *wonder* in special sense, *portent, miracle* (Philostrat., Vi. Apoll. 1, 39 p. 41, 5; Suppl. Epigr. Gr. VIII 551, 35 [I BC] ἰδεῖν θ. *see a wonder, miracle* MPol 15: 1 (cf. Henioch. Com. 3 ὁρῶ θαῦμ' ἄπιστον; Lucian, Adv. Ind. 8 θ. μέγα τοῖς ὁρῶσιν).

2. *wonder, amazement* (Hom.+; Plut., Timol. 12, 9 μετὰ θαύματος; Job 18: 20) ἐθαύμασα ἰδὼν αὐτὴν θαῦμα μέγα *when I saw her I wondered in great amazement* Rv 17: 6. M-M. B. 1093f.*

θαυμάζω impf. ἐθαύμαζον; fut. θαυμάσομαι; 1 aor. ἐθαύμασα; 1 aor. pass. ἐθαυμάσθην; 1 fut. pass. θαυμασθήσομαι (Hom.+; inscr., pap., LXX, En., Ep. Arist., Philo, Joseph.).

1. act.—a. intr. *wonder, marvel, be astonished* (the context determines whether in a good or bad sense)—a. abs. (X., Cyr. 7, 1, 6; Herm. Wr. 14, 4; Jos., Ant. 6, 56) Mt 8: 10; 15: 31; 22: 22; 27: 14; Mk 5: 20; 15: 5; Lk 1: 63; 8: 25; 11: 14; 24: 41; J 5: 20; 7: 21; Ac 4: 13; 13: 12 D, 41; Rv 17: 7.—Somet. the expr. of amazement is added w. λέγων, λέγοντες Mt 8: 27; 9: 33; 21: 20; J 7: 15; Ac 2: 7.—θαυμ. θαῦμα μέγα Rv 17: 6, s. θαῦμα 2.

β. used w. prep. expr.: διά τι *wonder at someth.* (Isocr. 4, 59; Strabo 17, 1, 5; Aelian, V.H. 12, 6; 14, 36) Mk 6: 6. W. same mng. ἔν τινι: ἐν τῷ χρονίζειν αὐτόν *that he stayed, at his delay* Lk 1: 21 (in case it is so to be understood here [cf. Sir 11: 21 μὴ θαύμαζε ἐν ἔργοις ἁμαρτωλοῦ; Is 61: 6; En. 25, 1], and the words are not to be taken in the sense: *during his stay*; cf. Bl-D. §404, 3; Rob. 1073). On the other hand θ. ἐν ἑαυτῷ *wonder to oneself* Hs 8, 1, 4; 9, 2, 5. ἐπί τινι *at someth.* (X., Mem. 1, 4, 2; 4, 2, 3; Diod. S. 2, 33, 1; Dio Chrys. 7[8], 27; 62 [79], 1; 6; Job 41:

1; 42: 11; Jdth 11: 20) Lk 2: 33; 4: 22; 9: 43; 20: 26; Ac 3: 12; Hs 9, 2, 2. περί τινος Lk 2: 18.

γ. w. ὅτι foll. (freq. w. πῶς in the pap., cf. POxy. 2728, 5f; 2729, 4 et al.). *wonder, be surprised that* (Ps.-X., Cyn. 1, 3; Philo, Somn. 2, 183 μὴ θαυμάσῃς ὅτι; Jos., Vi. 339; POxy. 1348 [III AD]; 2783, 6 [III AD]) Lk 11: 38; J 3: 7; 4: 27; Gal 1: 6. Also w. εἰ foll. (s. εἰ II and cf. Hyperid. 3, 1; Philo Mech. 77, 41; Polyb. 3, 33, 17; PHib. 159 [III BC] θαυμάζω εἰ πιστεύεις. Philo, Migr. Abr. 26; Jos., C. Ap. 1, 68, Ant. 1, 57 al.; Third Corinthians 3: 2) Mk 15: 44; 1 J 3: 13; Dg 10: 4; MPol 16: 1.

b. trans. *admire, wonder at* w. acc.—a. τί *someth.* (Diod. S. 3, 56, 5; Alciphr. 4, 6, 3; Herm. Wr. 4, 5; Da 8: 27 Theod.; Philo, Abr. 103 al.; Jos., Vi. 222) Lk 24: 12 v.l.; J 5: 28; Ac 7: 31 (but here θ. in the impf. is probably rather ='wish to learn to know [about],' as Chio, Ep. 9 θ. τὴν συντυχίαν='wish to know what happened'); 1 Cl 1: 2; 2 Cl 13: 4, cf. vs. 3; MPol 2: 2f; 3; 7: 2.—The expression θαυμάζειν πρόσωπα Jd 16 is found in the LXX (Lev 19: 15; Dt 10: 17; Job 22: 8 al.); but those passages hardly support any sense that is usable for the NT. The addition of the words ὠφελείας χάριν gives an unfavorable turn to the mng. 'admire': *render admiration to someone for one's own advantage.* Hence the transl. *flatter* seems as good as any.

β. τινά *someone* (Diod. S. 1, 93, 2; Diog. L. 9, 4; Himerius, Or. [Ecl.] 3, 20; Jos., C. Ap. 2, 125) Lk 7: 9; Dg 10: 7f.—Pass. *be marvelled at* (Hdt. 3, 82; Dit., Syll.³ 1073, 41; PGiess. 47, 5 ὡς καὶ ὑπὸ πάντων τῶν ἰδόντων θαυμασθῆναι; LXX) 2 Th 1: 10.

2. as dep. w. 1 aor. and 1 fut. pass. (Kühner-Bl. II 439f. Once thus in LXX, Esth 4: 17 p [Thackeray 240, 1]) *wonder, be amazed* Rv 17: 8. In pregnant constr. ἐθαυμάσθη ὅλη ἡ γῆ ὀπίσω τ. θηρίου *the whole world followed the beast, full of wonder* 13: 3 (here wonder becomes worship: cf. Ael. Aristid. 13 p. 290 D.; 39 p. 747 of Dionysus and Heracles, οἳ ὑφ' ἡμῶν ἐθαυμάσθησαν. Sir 7: 29; Jos., Ant. 3, 65.—The act. is also found in this sense: Cebes 2, 3 θ. τινά='admire' or 'venerate' someone; Epict. 1, 17, 19 θ. τὸν θεόν).—GBertram, TW III '35, 27–42. M-M.*

θαυμάσιος, α, ον later also, though rarely, w. two terminations (since Hom. Hymns and Hes.; inscr., pap., LXX) *wonderful, remarkable, admirable.*

1. of things (Ep. Arist. 89; Jos., Vi. 208), subst. τὰ θαυμάσια *wonderful things, wonders* (Hdt. 2, 35; Ex 3: 20 and oft.; Philo; Test. Sim. 6: 7) Mt 21: 15; Hv 4, 1, 3.

2. of pers. (Dit., Syll.³ 798, 11 [37 AD], Or. 504, 12: θαυμασιώτατος. Also superl. POxy. 940 verso; PGiess. 57 verso; Philo, Abr. 38; Jos., C. Ap. 1, 51) ὁ θαυμασιώτατος Π. MPol 5: 1; 16: 2. M-M.*

θαυμαστός, ή, όν (since Hom. Hymns, Pind., Hdt.; inscr., pap., LXX, Ep. Arist., Philo; Jos., Bell. 3, 516, Ant. 7, 209) *wonderful, marvelous, remarkable* (Diod. S. 1, 36, 7 θ. is heightened to παντελῶς ἄπιστον), in our lit. not of human personalities, but

1. of God (Da 9: 4 Theod.; Ps 92: 4b) 1 Cl 60: 1.

2. of things which are often related to God: his name (Ps 8: 2, 10) Hs 9, 18, 5; D 14: 3; his light 1 Pt 2: 9, cf. 1 Cl 36: 2; his glory Hm 12, 4, 2; his course of action (note for the neuter as a result of literal transl. fr. the Hebr.; cf. Bl-D. §138, 2; Rob. 254) Mt 21: 42; Mk 12: 11 (both Ps 117: 23); the judgment day B 6: 4; the deeds of God Rv 15: 3 (cf. Tob 12: 22 BA; Sir 11: 4; Ael. Aristid. 48, 30 K.=24 p. 473 D.).—W. μέγας (as in some of the pass. already mentioned; cf. also Dit., Syll.³ 1073, 26 μέγα τι

καὶ θαυμαστόν; LXX; Philo, Mos. 2, 10) Rv 15: 1; 1 Cl
26: 1; 50: 1; 53: 3; 2 Cl 2: 6; 5: 5. W. μέγας and ἰσχυρός
Hm 12, 4, 2. W. μακάριος 1 Cl 35: 1. W. παράδοξος
(Menand., fgm. 593) Dg 5: 4.—τί θαυμαστὸν εἰ; what
wonder is it, if? (Epict. 1, 25, 33; 2, 9, 9; 4 Macc 2: 1;
Philo, Aet. M. 137) 1 Cl 43: 1. ἐν τούτῳ τὸ θαυμαστόν
ἐστιν the remarkable thing about it is this J 9: 30.—2 Cor
11: 14 v.l. M-M.*

θαυμαστῶς adv. (Pla. et al.; Dit., Syll.³ 796A, 8; Herm.
Wr. 506, 17 Sc.; LXX) wonderfully ἤκουσα μεγάλως καὶ
θ. I have heard great and wonderful things Hv 1, 3, 3 (the
mng. is unmistakable, but the text is prob. damaged; cf.
MDibelius, Hdb. ad loc.). μεγάλως καὶ θαυμαστῶς
πάντα ἐστι s 5, 5, 4. μεγάλως καὶ θ. ἔχει τὸ πρᾶγμα
τοῦτο this is a great and wonderful thing v 3, 4, 1 (θ. ἔχειν
as Ep. Arist. 58).*

θεά, ᾶς, ἡ (Hom.+; inscr., pap.) goddess, of Artemis ἡ
μεγάλη θεά (cf. Greek Inscr. Brit. Mus. III 481, 324 τῇ
μεγίστῃ θεᾷ Ἐφεσίᾳ Ἀρτέμιδι.—θεὰ μεγάλη of Isis:
Dit., Or. 92, 3 [about 200 BC]) Ac 19: 27, 37 v.l.; ὡς θεάν
σε ἡγησάμην I have regarded you as a goddess Hv 1, 1, 7.
M-M.*

θεάομαι 1 aor. ἐθεασάμην; pf. τεθέαμαι; 1 aor. pass. (w.
pass. mng.) ἐθεάθην (Att. [Kühner-Bl. II 441]; also inscr.,
pap., LXX) see, look at, behold.
1. w. physical eyes—a. quite literally (POxy. 963; Sb
1800; Jos., Ant. 3, 132; 6, 340) interchanging w. ὁρᾶν Hv
3, 8, 1. W. acc. as obj. (Hes., Works 482; PSI 41, 19; Tob
2: 2 BA; 2 Macc 2: 4; En. 6, 2; 21, 2) Mt 11: 7; Lk 7: 24;
Ac 21: 27; 22: 9; 1 J 1: 1 (τοῖς ὀφθαλμοῖς ἡμῶν. Cf. Philo,
Mos. 1, 278 θ. αὐτοὺς ὀφθαλμοῖς); 4: 12 (PWvan der
Horst, ZNW 63, '72, 280-82 [word-play]). The obj. acc. is
oft. found w. a ptc. that indicates what has been observed
in the pers. or thing seen (En. 9, 1; 23, 2; Philo, Vi. Cont.
89; Jos., Vi. 28; 281; Bl-D. §416, 1): Mk 16: 14. ἐθεάσατο
τελώνην καθήμενον Lk 5: 27; 6: 5 D (JoachJeremias,
The Unknown Sayings of Jesus [tr. Fuller] '57, 49-54). Cf.
J 1: 38; Ac 1: 11. W. ὅτι foll. J 6: 5. W. acc. and ὅτι:
θεάσασθε τ. χώρας, ὅτι λευκαί εἰσιν see that the fields
are white 4: 35. W. acc. and ὡς: ἐθεάσαντο τὸ μνημεῖον
καὶ ὡς ἐτέθη τὸ σῶμα αὐτοῦ Lk 23: 55. W. acc. and
ὅπως in an interlocking constr. ὅταν θεάσωνται τοὺς
ἀρνησαμένους ὅπως κολάζονται when they see how those
who have denied are punished 2 Cl 17: 7. W. relative
clause foll. J 11: 45 (ὁράω ℙ⁴⁵, ⁶⁶). θεασάμενος ἦν ὅσα
ἀγαθὰ ἐποίησεν he (Joseph) had seen all the good things
that he (Jesus) had done GP 6: 23.
b. see in the sense come to see, visit (Appian, Samn. 7,
§1 θ. τὴν Ἑλλάδα τινά someone (2 Ch 22: 6; Jos., Ant.
16, 6) Ro 15: 24. Here belongs also εἰσελθὼν ὁ βασιλεὺς
θεάσασθαι τ. ἀνακειμένους the king went in to greet the
guests Mt 22: 11.
c. The passive means either—a. be seen ὑπό τινος by
someone Mk 16: 11, or
β. be noticed, attract attention τινί by or of someone
Mt 6: 1; 23: 5 (cf. Bl-D. §191, 1 app.; Rob. 542, cf. 534).
2. see, behold w. physical eyes, but in such a way that a
supernatural impression is gained (cf. PPar. 51, 38 [160
BC] of a vision in the temple of Serapis at Memphis τὸ
ὅραμα τοῦτο τεθέαμαι; Dit., Syll.³ 730, 20; 2 Macc 3: 36;
Tob 13: 7; Jdth 15: 8) τεθέαμαι τὸ πνεῦμα καταβαῖνον
ὡς περιστεράν J 1: 32 (he sees the dove and also becomes
aware that it is the Spirit); ἐθεασάμεθα τ. δόξαν αὐτοῦ 1:
14 (we saw the person and work of Christ and perceived in
them the divine glory; cf. Tob 13: 16 BA θεασάμενοι
πᾶσαν τ. δόξαν σου). Cf. 1 J 4: 14.

3. The perception is wholly supersensual=see, perceive
(X., Hier. 2, 5. W. ὅτι foll. Pla., Prot. p. 352A; Demosth.
4, 3) Dg 10: 7. θεασάμενος ἐν ἡμῖν πολλὴν πλάνην he
perceived much error in us 2 Cl 1: 7. M-M.*

θεατρίζω (inscr. fr. Gerasa: Journ. of Rom. Stud. 18, '28,
p. 144ff no. 14, 18 [c. 102-14 AD], where the word certainly
appears, though its mng. is uncertain; cf. HJCadbury,
ZNW 29, '30, 60-3; Achmes 21, 5 ἀτίμως θεατρισθή-
σεται; 51, 11; Suidas II 688, 26; Byz. Chron. in Psaltes
p. 328; ἐκθεατρίζω in Polyb. 3, 91, 10 and Diod. S.
34+35 fgm. 2, 46) put to shame, expose publicly ὀνειδισμοῖς τε καὶ θλίψεσιν θεατριζόμενοι publicly exposed
to reproach and affliction Hb 10: 33 (Posidon.: 87 fgm.
108 [app.]t Jac. ἐξεθεάτριζον ὀνειδίζοντες).*

θέατρον, ου, τό ([Hdt.], Thu.+; inscr., pap., Philo;
loanw. in rabb.)—1. theater, as a place for public assemblies (Diod. S. 16, 84, 3 δῆμος ἅπας συνέδραμεν εἰς τὸ
θέατρον; Charito 8, 7, 1; Greek Inscr. Brit. Mus. III 481,
395 φερέτωσαν κατὰ πᾶσαν ἐκκλησίαν εἰς τὸ θέατρον
[Ephesus]. Inscr. fr. the theater at Ephesus [103/4 AD] in
Dssm., LO 90f [LAE 114]=Dit., Or. 480, 9. S. also Dit.,
Syll.³ index; Jos., Bell. 7, 47; 107, Ant. 17, 161) Ac 19: 29,
31.
2. what one sees at the theater, a play, spectacle (Ps.-
Pla., Axioch. 371c; Achilles Tat. 1, 16, 3) fig. θ. ἐγενήθημεν τῷ κόσμῳ we have become a spectacle for the world
1 Cor 4: 9 (Synes., Prov. 1, 10 p. 100c θεαταὶ δὲ ἄνωθεν
οἱ θεοὶ τῶν καλῶν τούτων ἀγώνων). M-M.*

Θεγρί, ὁ indecl. Thegri Hv 4, 2, 4, an angel in charge of
the animals. On him and his name s. MDibelius, Hdb.,
exc. ad loc., and s. Σεγρί.*

θεῖον, ου, τό (since Homer [θέειον and θήιον]; pap.,
LXX; Jos., Bell. 7, 189; Sib. Or. 3, 691) sulphur Lk 17: 29
(Gen 19: 24); Rv 9: 17f (w. καπνός and πῦρ as Philo, Mos.
2, 56); 14: 10; 19: 20; 20: 10; 21: 8; 1 Cl 11: 1.*

θεῖος, θεία, θεῖον (Hom.+; inscr., pap., LXX.—RMu-
quier, Le sens du mot θεῖος chez Platon '30; JvanCamp
and PCanart, Le sens du mot theios chez Platon '56).
1. of the godhead and everything that belongs to it—a.
adj. divine δύναμις (Pla., Leg. 3 p. 691E φύσις τις
ἀνθρωπίνη μεμιγμένη θείᾳ τινὶ δυνάμει; Dio Chrys.
14[31], 95; decree of Stratonicea CIG II 2715a, b [Dssm.,
B 277ff-BS 360ff]; Ep. Arist. 157 al.; Philo, Det. Pot. Ins.
83 al.; Sib. Or. 5, 249) 2 Pt 1: 3. φύσις (Diod. S. 5, 31, 4;
Dio Chrys. 11[12], 29; Ael. Aristid. 37, 9 K.=2 p. 16 D.;
Manetho in Jos., C. Ap. 1, 232; Dit., Syll.³ 1125, 8; Philo,
Decal. 104 τῶν θείας φύσεως μετεσχηκότων; Jos., Ant.
107) vs. 4. κρίσις (Simplicius in Epict. p. 20, 30; Philo,
Spec. Leg. 3, 121) 2 Cl 20: 4. γνῶσις (cf. 4 Macc 1: 16) 1
Cl 40: 1. πνεῦμα (Menand., fgm. 482, 3; PGM 4, 966;
Aristobulus in Euseb., Pr. Ev. 8, 10, 4; Philo; Jos., Ant. 6,
222; 8, 408; 10, 239) Hm 11: 2, 5, 7ff, 12, 21. ἔργα of the
deeds of the Virtues v 3, 8, 7.
b. subst. τὸ θεῖον divine being, divinity (Hdt. 3, 108;
Thu. 5, 70; X., Cyr. 4, 2, 15, Hell. 7, 5, 13, Mem. 1, 4, 18;
Pla., Phaedr. p. 242c; Polyb. 31, 15, 7; Diod. S. 1, 6, 1;
13, 3, 2; 16, 60, 2; Epict. 2, 20, 22; Lucian, De Sacrif. 1,
Pro Imag. 13; 17; 28; Herm. Wr. 11, 21b codd.; inscr.
[Dit., Syll.³ index p. 377f]; UPZ 24, 11; 36, 13; 22; 39, 5;
Wilcken, Chrest. 70, 14; 116, 2 σέβου τὸ θεῖον; PGM 3,
192.—Philo, Op. M. 170, Agr. 80, Leg. ad Gai. 3; Jos.,
Ant. 1, 85; 194; 2, 275; 5, 133; 11, 127; 12, 281; 302;
13, 242; 300; 14, 183; 17, 41, Bell. 3, 352; 4, 190.—LXX,
En., Ep. Arist., Sib. Or. and Test. 12 Patr. do not have τὸ
θεῖον) Ac 17: 27 D, 29; Tit 1: 9 v.l.

2. of persons who stand in close relation to the divinity (Diog. L. 7, 119: the Stoa says of the σοφοί: θείους εἶναι· ἔχειν γὰρ ἐν ἑαυτοῖς οἱονεὶ θεόν.—Cf. on ἄνθρωποι θεῖοι Rtzst., Mysterienrel.³ 25f; 237ff; 298; HWindisch, Pls u. Christus '34, 1–114; LBieler, Θεῖος Ἀνήρ I '35; II '36) in the superl. (Oenomaus in Euseb., Pr. Ev. 5, 28, 2 Lycurgus as ὁ θειότατος ἀνθρώπων; Iambl., Vi. Pyth. 29, 161 ὁ θειότατος Πυθαγόρας; used of the emperors in inscr. [Dit., Syll.³ index p. 378a] and pap. [PLond. 1007, 1; 1012, 4]) οἱ θειότατοι προφῆται *the prophets, those men so very near to God* IMg 8: 2 (cf. Philo, Mos. 2, 188; Jos., Ant. 10, 35 ὁ προφήτης θεῖος, C. Ap. 1, 279 [Moses]). Of angels Papias 4.

3. gener., of that which exceeds the bounds of human or earthly possibility, *supernatural* (Lucian, Alex. 12 θεῖόν τι καὶ φοβερόν) of a monster ὑπενόησα εἶναί τι θεῖον *I suspected that it was something supernatural* Hv 4, 1, 6. M-M.*

θειότης, ητος, ἡ (of a divinity: Plut., Mor. 398A; 665A; Lucian, Calumn. 17; Herm. Wr. 9, 1c; Dit., Syll.³ 867, 31 of Artemis, who made Ephesus famous διὰ τῆς ἰδίας θειότητος; POxy. 1381, 165 πληρωθεὶς τ. σῆς [Imouthes-Asclepius] θειότητος; PGM 7, 691; Wsd 18: 9; Ep. Arist. 95; Philo, Op. M. 172 v.l.—Of persons who stand in close relation to a divinity: Heraclit. Sto. 76 p. 102, 4 Homer; Jos., Ant. 10, 268 Daniel; inscr., pap., princes and emperors) *divinity, divine nature* Ro 1: 20.—HSNash, θειότης–θεότης Ro 1: 20, Col 2: 9; JBL 18, 1899, 1–34. M-M.*

θειώδης, ες (Diod. S. 2, 12, 2; Strabo 1, 3, 18; Hero Alex. I p. 12, 8; III 214, 7; Aretaeus 170, 12; Galen: CMG V 4, 2 p. 107, 33; 186, 5 al.) *sulphurous* Rv 9: 17.*

Θέκλα, ης, ἡ *Thecla* (so far found only as a Christian name: CIG 8683; 9138; 9139; PBodl. Uncatal.: Journ. Egypt. Arch. 23, '37, 10f [gen. Θέκλας]; Acts of Paul) 2 Ti 3: 11 v.l.*

θέλημα, ατος, τό (Antipho Soph. 58; Aristot., De Plant. 1, 1 p. 815b, 21; Aeneas Tact. 2, 8; 18, 19; POxy. 924, 8 [IV AD]; LXX) *will*.

1. objective, *what is willed*, what one wishes to happen —**a.** gener. ἐὰν τὸ θ. ᾖ *if it is his* (God's or Christ's) *will* IEph 20: 1; IRo 1: 1 (θέλημα abs.=*God's will* also ISm 11: 1; IPol 8: 1 and in Paul Ro 2: 18; cf. also b below). γενηθήτω τὸ θέλημά σου Mt 6: 10; 26: 42; Lk 11: 2 v.l. τοῦτό ἐστιν τὸ θ. τ. πέμψαντός με J 6: 39f. μὴ τὸ θ. μου ἀλλὰ τὸ σὸν γινέσθω Lk 22: 42. Cf Ac 21: 14; Col 4: 12; Hb 10: 10 (only here in the NT w. ἐν; cf. Third Corinthians 3: 26). οὕτως οὐκ ἔστιν θέλημα ἔμπροσθεν τοῦ πατρὸς ἵνα *so it is not the Father's will that* Mt 18: 14 (οὐκ ἔστιν θ. as Mal 1: 10; Eccl 5: 3; 12: 1).

b. what one wishes to bring about by one's own action, since one has undertaken to do what he has willed οὐ ζητῶ τὸ θ. τὸ ἐμόν *I do not aspire (to do) my own will* J 5: 30a; 6: 38. τὸ μυστήριον τοῦ θελήματος αὐτοῦ *the secret purpose of his will*, i.e. the carrying out of his plan of salvation Eph 1: 9. οὐκ ἦν θ., ἵνα ἔλθῃ *he was not willing to come* 1 Cor 16: 12 (but this passage could also belong under the abs. use of θελ. 1a).

c. what one wishes to bring about by the activity of others, to whom one assigns a task.

a. of persons ὁ δοῦλος ὁ γνοὺς τὸ θ. τοῦ κυρίου αὐτοῦ *what his master wants* Lk 12: 47 (in a parable). τὸ θ. τοῦ πατρός Mt 21: 31.—**β.** of the devil εἰς τὸ ἐκείνου θ. *to do his will* 2 Ti 2: 26.

γ. predom. of God (or Christ) τὸ θέλημα τοῦ θεοῦ (cf.

Herm. Wr. 5, 7; 13, 2; Philo, Leg. All. 3, 197; Test. Iss. 4: 3, Napht. 3: 1) Ro 12: 2; Eph 5: 17; 1 Th 4: 3; 5: 18; 1 Pt 2: 15; 4: 2; cf. J 5: 30b. γινώσκειν τὸ θέλημα *know the will* Ro 2: 18; Ac 22: 14. ἡ ἐπίγνωσις τοῦ θ. αὐτοῦ Col 1: 9; ποιεῖν τὸ θ. (1 Esdr 9: 9; 4 Macc 18: 16) Mt 7: 21; 12: 50; Mk 3: 35; J 4: 34; 6: 38b; 7: 17; 9: 31; Eph 6: 6; Hb 10: 7, 9 (both Ps 39: 9), 36; 13: 21; 1 J 2: 17; Pol 2: 2. Also ποιεῖν τὰ θελήματα (Ps 102: 21; Is 44: 28; 2 Macc 1: 3) GEb 4; Mk 3: 35 v.l.; Ac 13: 22.

δ. ποιεῖν τὰ θελήματα τ. σαρκός *do what the flesh desires* Eph 2: 3.

2. subjective, *will*, the act of willing or desiring—**a.** of the human will (Ps 1: 2) θελήματι ἀνθρώπου *by an act of the human will* 2 Pt 1: 21; ἐξουσίαν ἔχειν περὶ τ. ἰδίου θ. *have control over one's desire* 1 Cor 7: 37; here θ. acc. to many has the connotation of sexual desire, as J 1: 13 (θ. σαρκός, θ. ἀνδρός. Cf. PGM 4, 1430; 1521; 1533). Of the will of the Jews, directed toward the death of Jesus Lk 23: 25.

b. as a rule of the will of God (or Christ) ἡ βουλὴ τοῦ θ. Eph 1: 11; ἡ εὐδοκία τοῦ θ. vs. 5 (cf. CD 3, 15). εἰ θέλοι τὸ θ. τοῦ θεοῦ *if the will of God should so decree* 1 Pt 3: 17. θελήματι θεοῦ *by God's will* ITr 1: 1; Pol 1: 3. Also διὰ θελήματος θεοῦ Ro 15: 32; 1 Cor 1: 1; 2 Cor 1: 1; 8: 5; Eph 1: 1; Col 1: 1; 2 Ti 1: 1, and διὰ τὸ θέλημα Rv 4: 11 or ἐν τ. θελήματι τ. θεοῦ Ro 1: 10; cf. 1 Cl inscr.; IEph inscr., or ἐκ θελήματος θεοῦ (cf. Ps 27: 7) 1 Cl 42: 2; πρὸς τὸ θ. *according to his will* Hs 9, 5, 2. Also κατὰ τὸ θ. (1 Esdr 8: 16) Gal 1: 4; 1 J 5: 14; 1 Pt 4: 19; ISm 1: 1. M-M.**

θέλησις, εως, ἡ (acc. to Pollux 5, 47 an ἰδιωτικόν 'vulgar word'; cf. Phryn. p. 353 L. But also found Stoic. III 41; Philod., Rhet. II 297 Sudh.; PGM 4, 1429 θέλησις τῶν θελημάτων; Ezk 18: 23; 2 Ch 15: 15; Pr 8: 35 al. The Doric pl θελήσιες='wishes': Melissa, Epist. ad Char. p. 62 Orell.) *will*, the act of willing, of God (Herm. Wr. 4, 1a; 10, 2; Iambl., Myst. 2, 11 p. 97, 15 Parthey ἡ θεία θ.) κατὰ τὴν αὐτοῦ θ. *according to his will* Hb 2: 4; τῇ αὐτοῦ θ. *by his will* (Tob 12: 18; 2 Macc 12: 16) 2 Cl 1: 6.*

θέλω (on its relation to the Attic ἐθέλω, which is not found in NT, LXX, or En., s. Kühner-Bl. I 187f; II 408f; Bl-D. §101 p. 45; Mlt.-H. 88; 189; Rob. 205f. θέλω is found since 250 BC in the Attic inscr. [Meisterhans³-Schw. p. 178], likew. quite predom. in the pap. [Mayser I² 2, '38, 119]; Jos., Ant. 18, 144, C. Ap. 2, 192) impf. ἤθελον; fut. θελήσω (Rv 11: 5 v.l.); 1 aor. ἠθέλησα (on the augment s. Bl-D. §66, 3; Mlt.-H. 188); 1 aor. pass. subj. θεληθῶ IRo 8: 1.

1. *wish* of desire (on the difference betw. θ. and βούλομαι s. the latter), *wish to have, desire, want* τὶ someth. (Diogenes the Cynic, fgm. 2: Trag. Gr. p. 809 Nauck²; Sotades [280 BC: not the comic poet] in Stob. 3, 1, 66 t. III p. 27, 5 H.; Theocr. 14, 11 πάντα) Mt 20: 21; Mk 14: 36 (DDaube, A Prayer Pattern in Judaism, TU 73, '59, 539–45); Lk 5: 39; J 15: 7; 1 Cor 4: 21; 2 Cor 11: 12. W. pres. inf. foll. τί πάλιν θέλετε ἀκούειν; *why do you want to hear (it) again?* J 9: 27a. εἰ θέλεις τέλειος εἶναι Mt 19: 21 (Lucian, Dial. Deor. 2, 2 εἰ ἐθέλεις ἐπέραστος εἶναι). ἤθελεν ἀπολογεῖσθαι *wished to make a defense* Ac 19: 33. ἤθελον παρεῖναι πρὸς ὑμᾶς ἄρτι *I wish I were with you now* Gal 4: 20. ἤθελον *I would like* w. aor. inf. (Epict. 1, 29, 38; PLond. 897, 20 [84 AD]) Hv 3, 8, 6; 3, 11, 4 (cf. Bl-D. §359, 2 w. app.; cf. Rob. 923). θέλω w. aor. inf. foll. also occurs Mt 5: 40; 12: 38; 16: 25; 19: 17; Mk 10: 43; Lk 8: 20; 23: 8; J 12: 21 (Diog. L. 6, 31 ξένων δέ ποτε θεάσασθαι θελόντων Δημοσθένην); Ac 25:

9b; Gal 3: 2; Js 2: 20 (cf. Seneca, Ep. 47, 10: vis tu cogitare); 1 Pt 3: 10; B 7: 11. Abs., though the inf. is to be supplied fr. the context: Mt 17: 12 (sc. ποιῆσαι); 27: 15; Mk 9: 13; J 21: 18. Foll. by acc. w. inf. Mk 7: 24; Lk 1: 62; J 21: 22f; Ac 16: 3; Ro 16: 19; 1 Cor 7: 7, 32; 14: 5; Gal 6: 13. Negative οὐ θέλω (other moods take μή as neg.) I do not wish, I am not willing, I will not foll. by (acc. and) aor. inf. Mt 23: 4; Lk 19: 14, 27; 1 Cor 10: 20; IRo 2: 1. οὐ θέλω (θέλομεν) ὑμᾶς ἀγνοεῖν I do not wish you to be ignorant=I want you to know (BGU 27, 5 and PGiess. 11, 4 [118 AD] γινώσκειν σε θέλω ὅτι) Ro 1: 13; 11: 25; 1 Cor 10: 1; 12: 1; 2 Cor 1: 8; 1 Th 4: 13. W. ἵνα foll. (Epict. 1, 18, 14; 2, 7, 8) Mt 7: 12; Mk 6: 25; 9: 30; 10: 35; Lk 6: 31; J 17: 24 (on Mt 7: 12=Lk 6: 31 cf. LPhilippidis, D. 'Goldene Regel' religionsgesch. untersucht '29, Religionswissensch. Forschungsberichte über die 'goldene Regel' '33; GBKing, The 'Negative' Golden Rule, Journ. of Religion 8, '28, 268-79; ADihle, D. Goldene Regel, '62). Foll. by aor. subj. (deliberative subj.; cf. Kühner-G. I 221f; Bl-D. §366, 3; 465, 2; Rob. 935; Epict. 3, 2, 14 θέλεις σοι εἴπω; ='do you wish me to tell you'?; Wilcken, Chrest. 14 III, 6 καὶ σοὶ [=σὺ] λέγε τίνος θέλεις κατηγορήσω) θέλεις συλλέξωμεν αὐτά; do you want us to gather them? Mt 13: 28. τί θέλετε ποιήσω ὑμῖν; what do you want me to do for you? 20: 32 (cf. Plautus, Merc. 1, 2, 49 [l. 159]: quid vis faciam?); cf. 26: 17; 27: 17, 21; Mk 10: 36 (AJBHiggins, ET 52, '41, 317f), 51; 14: 12; 15: 9, 12 v.l.; Lk 9: 54; 18: 41; 22: 9. W. ἤ foll.: I would rather . . . than . . . or instead of (Trypho Alex. [I BC], fgm. 23 [AvVelsen 1853] περιπατεῖν θέλω ἢ περ ἑστάναι; Epict. 3, 22, 53; BGU 846, 15 [II AD] θέλω πηρὸς γενέσθαι, ἢ γνῶναι, ὅπως ἀνθρώπῳ ἔτι ὀφείλω ὀβολόν; 2 Macc 14: 42) 1 Cor 14: 19. W. εἰ foll. (Is 9: 4f; Sir 23: 14) τί θέλω εἰ ἤδη ἀνήφθη how I wish it were already kindled! Lk 12: 49.

2. wish, will, of purpose, resolve wish, want, be ready (cf. Pla., Ap. 41A) to do τὶ someth. Ro 7: 15f, 19f (Epict. 2, 26, 1 and 2 ὃ μὲν θέλει οὐ ποιεῖ . . . θέλει πρᾶξαι οὐκ ὃ μὲν θέλει ποιεῖ; 2, 26, 4 [s. on ποιέω I 1be]); 1 Cor 7: 36; Gal 5: 17. W. aor. inf. foll. (Judg 20: 5) Mt 20: 14; 23: 37; 26: 15. ἤθελεν παρελθεῖν αὐτούς he was ready to pass by them Mk 6: 48. Ἡρῴδης θέλει σε ἀποκτεῖναι Herod wants to kill you Lk 13: 31. Cf. J 1: 43. ὑμεῖς δὲ ἠθελήσετε ἀγαλλιασθῆναι you were minded to rejoice 5: 35; 6: 21; 7: 44; Ac 25: 9a; Gal 4: 9; Col 1: 27; 1 Th 2: 18; Rv 11: 5. Also pres. inf. (2 Esdr 11 [Neh 1]: 11) J 6: 67; 7: 17; 8: 44; Ac 14: 13; 17: 18; Ro 7: 21; 2 Cl 6: 1; B 4: 9. Abs., but w. the inf. supplied fr. the context Mt 8: 2 (cf. what was said to the physician in Epict. 3, 10, 15 ἐὰν σὺ θέλῃς, κύριε, καλῶς ἔξω; εἰ θέλετε δέξασθαι if you are prepared to accept (it) 11: 14; Mk 3: 13; 6: 22; J 5: 21; Ro 9: 18a, b; Rv 11: 6. W. acc. and inf. foll. 1 Cl 36: 2.—Abs. ὁ θέλων the one who wills Ro 9: 16. τοῦ θεοῦ θέλοντος if it is God's will (Jos., Ant. 7, 373; PMich. 211, 4 τοῦ Σεράπιδος θέλοντος; PAmh. 131, 5 ἐλπίζω θεῶν θελόντων διαφεύξεσθαι; PGiess. 18, 10; BGU 423, 18 τῶν θεῶν θελόντων; 615, 4f) Ac 18: 21. Also ἐὰν ὁ κύριος θελήσῃ (Pla., Phaedo 80D; Ps.-Pla., Alcib. 1 p. 135D; Demosth. 4, 7; 25, 2 ἂν θεὸς θέλῃ; Ps.-Demetr., Form. Ep. 11, 12; PPetr. I 2, 3) 1 Cor 4: 19; cf. Js 4: 15; 1 Cl 21: 9. ὅτε θέλει καὶ ὡς θέλει 27: 5 (cf. BGU 27, 11 ὡς ὁ θεὸς ἠθέλησεν). καθὼς ἠθέλησεν (i.e. ὁ θεός) 1 Cor 12: 18; 15: 38 (Hymn to Isis: Suppl. Epigr. Gr. VIII 549, 19f [I BC] πᾶσι μερίζεις οἶσι θέλεις). οὐ θέλω I will not, do not propose, am not willing, do not want w. pres. inf. foll. (Gen 37: 35; Is 28: 12) J 7: 1; 2 Th 3: 10; 2 Cl 13: 1. W. aor. inf. foll. (2 Km 23: 16; Jer 11: 10) Mt 2: 18 (cf. Jer

38: 15); 15: 32; 22: 3; Mk 6: 26; Lk 15: 28; J 5: 40; Ac 7: 39; 1 Cor 16: 7; Dg 10: 7 al. Abs., but w. the inf. to be supplied fr. the context Mt 18: 30; Lk 18: 4. οὐ θέλω I will not Mt 21: 30.—Of purpose, opp. ἐνεργεῖν Phil 2: 13. Opp. κατεργάζεσθαι Ro 7: 18. Opp. ποιεῖν 2 Cor 8: 10. Opp. πράσσειν Ro 7: 15, 19.

3. τί θέλει τοῦτο εἶναι; what can this mean? Ac 2: 12; cf. 17: 20; Lk 15: 26 D.

4. take pleasure in, like—a. w. inf. foll.: to do someth. Mk 12: 38 (later in the same sentence w. acc.; cf. b τί); Lk 20: 46 (w. φιλεῖν).

b. τινά (Gorgias in the Gnomolog. Vatic. 166 [Wiener Stud. 10, p. 36] the suitors and Penelope; Vi. Aesopi W c. 31 θέλω αὐτήν; Ps 40: 12; Tob 13: 8) Mt 27: 43 (Ps 21: 9); IMg 3: 2. τί (Epict. 1, 4, 27; Ezk 18: 32) Mt 9: 13; 12: 7 (both Hos 6: 6); Hb 10: 5, 8 (both Ps 39: 7). ἔν τινι (neut.: Test. Ash. 1: 6 v.l. ἐὰν ἡ ψυχὴ θέλῃ ἐν καλῷ; Ps 111: 1; 146: 10. Masc.: 1 Km 18: 22; 2 Km 15: 26; 3 Km 10: 9) θέλων ἐν ταπεινοφροσύνῃ taking pleasure in humility Col 2: 18 (Augustine, Ep. 149, 27 [Migne, Patrol. Lat. 33, 641f; AFridrichsen, ZNW 21, '22, 135f cites Epict. 2, 19, 16).

c. abs. feel affection perh. w. obj. for me understood (opp. μισεῖν) IRo 8: 3.

5. maintain contrary to the true state of affairs (Paus. 1, 4, 6 Ἀρκάδες ἐθέλουσιν εἶναι; 8, 36, 2; Herodian 5, 3, 5 εἰκόνα ἡλίου ἀνέργαστον εἶναι θέλουσιν) λανθάνει αὐτοὺς τοῦτο θέλοντας in maintaining this it escapes them (=they forget) 2 Pt 3: 5.—GSchrenk, TW III '35, 43-63; HRiesenfeld, Zu θέλω im NT (Ntl. Seminar Uppsala I) '36. M-M. B. 1160.

θέμα, ατος, τό (Cebes; Plut.; inscr., pap., LXX; Sib. Or. 2, 46; 49) deposit, specif. a prize offered contestants, in so far as it consists of money, not a wreath (Dit., Syll.³ 1063, 21 w. note 4, Or. 339, 81f; 566, 28) θ. ἀφθαρσία the prize is immortality IPol 2: 3 (Zahn in his edition has unnecessarily changed ἀφθαρσία, which is the rdg. of the mss., to the gen.).*

θεμέλιον, ου, τό (designated by Moeris p. 185, together w. its pl. θεμέλια, as the real Attic form. This is, however, not in agreement w. what is found in literature. We have the neut. e.g. in Aristot., Phys. Auscult. 2, 9 p. 200a, 4; Heraclit. Sto. 38 p. 55, 20; Paus. 8, 32, 1; Vett. Val. index; Ps.-Lucian, Salt. 34, also in pap. [Mayser 289]; LXX [Thackeray 154]) foundation, basis. In our lit. the sg. is found Hs 9, 4, 2; 9, 14, 6; the pl. Ac 16: 26; B 6: 2 (Is 28: 16); Hs 9, 5, 4; 9, 15, 4; 9, 21, 2, in lit. as well as fig. mng. In the other passages either the gender cannot be determined or the words in question belong to the following entry, where the ambiguous pass. are also given. But the dat. τοῖς θεμελίοις Hs 9, 4, 3 is not to be classed w. the latter, since H always uses the neut. elsewh.*

θεμέλιος, ου, ὁ (Thu. 1, 93, 2; Polyb. 1, 40, 9; Lucian, Calum. 20; Macho in Athen. 8 p. 346A; Epict. 2, 15, 8; Dit., Syll.³ 888, 55; 70; LXX [cf. Thackeray 154]; En. 18, 1; Philo, Cher. 101, Spec. Leg. 2, 110; Jos., Bell. 5, 152, Ant. 5, 31; 11, 19; loanw. in rabb.) foundation.

1. lit.—a. foundation stone (cf. Aristoph., Aves 1137 θεμέλιοι λίθοι) Rv 21: 14, 19a, b.

b. foundation of a building (Diod. S. 11, 63, 1 ἐκ θεμελίων; Philo, Exsecr. 120 ἐκ θεμελίων ἄχρι στέγους οἰκίαν) χωρὶς θεμελίου Lk 6: 49. τιθέναι θεμέλιον (cf. Hyperid. 6, 14) 14: 29; ἐπί τι on someth. 6: 48. The foundations of the heavenly city built by God Hb 11: 10 (cf. RKnopf, Heinrici-Festschr. '14, 215; LMMuntingh,

Hb 11: 8-10 in the Light of the Mari Texts: AvanSelms Festschr. '71, 108-20 [contrasts 'tents of Abraham' w. the city]).

2. fig.—a. of the elementary beginnings of a thing; of the founding of a congregation Ro 15: 20; 1 Cor 3: 10, 12. Of elementary teachings θεμέλιον καταβάλλεσθαι *lay a foundation* (Dionys. Hal. 3, 69; Jos., Ant. 11, 93; 15, 391) Hb 6: 1.

b. of the indispensable prerequisites for someth. to come into being: God's will is the foundation of an orderly creation 1 Cl 33: 3. The foundation of the Christian church or congregation: Christ 1 Cor 3: 11 (AFridrichsen, TZ 2, '46, 316f); the apostles and prophets Eph 2: 20; cf. 2 Ti 2: 19.

c. about equal to *treasure, reserve* (Philo, Sacr. Abel. 81 θεμέλιος τῷ φαύλῳ κακία, Leg. All. 3, 113) 1 Ti 6: 19.— KLSchmidt, TW III '35, 63f. M-M.*

θεμελιόω fut. θεμελιώσω; 1 aor. ἐθεμελίωσα; pf. pass. τεθεμελίωμαι; plpf. 3 sg. τεθεμελίωτο (on the missing augment s. Bl-D. §66, 1; Mlt.-H. 190) (since X., Cyr. 7, 5, 11; Dit., Syll.³ 1104, 15; synagogue inscr. fr. Jerus.: Suppl. Epigr. Gr. VIII 170, 9 [before 70 AD]; LXX; En.; Philo, Op. M. 102) *found, lay the foundation of.*

1. lit. τὶ someth. τὴν γῆν (Job 38: 4; Pr 3: 19) Hb 1: 10 (Ps 101: 26). θεμελιώσας τ. γῆν ἐπὶ ὑδάτων (who) *founded the earth upon the waters* Hv 1, 3, 4 (cf. Ps 23: 2). In the same sense ἐπί w. acc. τεθεμελίωτο ἐπὶ τὴν πέτραν Mt 7: 25; Lk 6: 48 v.l.

2. fig. *establish, strengthen* (Diod. S. 11, 68, 7 βασιλεία καλῶς θεμελιωθεῖσα; 15, 1, 3).

a. of the believers, whom God establishes 1 Pt 5: 10, or to whom he gives a secure place Hv 1, 3, 2. Pass. Eph 3: 17; Col 1: 23; Hv 3, 13, 4; 4, 1, 4.

b. of the revelations which H. receives: πάντα τεθεμελιωμένα ἐστίν *they are all well-founded* Hv 3, 4, 3.—Of the church viewed as a tower: τεθεμελίωται τῷ ῥήματι τοῦ παντοκράτορος καὶ ἐνδόξου ὀνόματος *it has been established by the word of the almighty and glorious name* (of God) Hv 3, 3, 5. M-M.*

θεμιτός, ή, όν (Hom. Hymns, Hdt.+; inscr., pap.; Jos., Bell. 6, 432) *allowed, permitted, right* θεμιτόν ἐστιν *it is right* w. inf. foll. (Sext. Emp., Adv. Gramm. 81; Dit., Syll.³ 965, 16f) 1 Cl 63: 1. Mostly w. neg. (Hdt. 5, 72 al.; Ael. Aristid. 45 p. 25 D.; Tob 2: 13 BA; Philo, Op. M. 17 οὐ θ.; Jos., Ant. 14, 72) οὐ θ. *it is not right* (without copula as Hyperid. 6, 27) Dg 6: 10.*

θεοδίδακτος, ον (Prolegomenon Syll. p. 91, 14 [HRabe '31] θεοδίδακτος ἡ ῥητορική. Elsewh. in eccl. wr.: Athenag., Leg. 11; 32; Theophil. 2, 9. Cf. δίδακτος 1 and Maximus Tyr. 26, 1c Ἀπόλλωνος διδάγματα; Ps.-Callisth. 1, 13, 5 ὑπὸ θεοῦ τινος διδασκόμενος; Damascius, Princ. 111 p. 229 R. παρ' αὐτῶν τ. θεῶν διδαχθέντες) *taught, instructed by God* 1 Th 4: 9; B 21: 6. M-M.*

θεοδρόμος, ου, ὁ *God's runner* (obviously a new word formed by Ignatius; he may have based it on pass. like Gal 5: 7; 1 Cor 9: 24-6; 2 Ti 4: 7) IPhld 2: 2; IPol 7: 2.*

θεολόγος, ου, ὁ (Aristot.+; Diod. S. 5, 80, 4; Philod., Plut., Mor. 417F; Sext. Emp., Math. 2, 31; Diog. L. 1, 119; Porphyr., Abst. 2, 36-43 ἅ τε λέγει ὁ θεολόγος [Orpheus]; inscr., esp. w. ref. to the emperor cult in Asia Minor [Dit., Or. 513 w. note 4]; PGM 13, 933 ὡς ὁ θεολόγος Ὀρφεὺς παρέδωκεν διὰ τῆς παραστιχίδος; Apollon. Paradox. 4 of Abaris; Philo, Praem. 53 [Moses]) *one who speaks of God* or *divine things, God's herald* Rv inscr. v.l.—Dssm., NB 58f (BS 231f), LO 297 (LAE 353,

n. 1); Rtzst., Hist. Mon. 135ff; FKattenbusch, D. Entstehung e. christl. Theologie. Z. Gesch. der Ausdrücke θεολογία, θεολογεῖν, θεολόγος: ZThK n.s. 11, '30, 161-205. M-M.*

θεομακάριστος, ον *blessed by God* of Polycarp θεομακαριστότατος IPol 7: 2. Also of Christ's passion ISm 1: 2 acc. to Funk and Lghtf.*

θεομακαρίτης, ου, ὁ (hapax legomenon) *one blessed by God, deceased,* used as adj. (like μακαρίτης Aristoph., Pl. 555) *divinely blessed* of Christ's passion ISm 1: 2, acc. to Zahn (s. θεομακάριστος).*

θεομαχέω (Eur., Iph. A. 1409; X., Oec. 16, 3; Menand., fgm. no. 187 p. 54 Kock; Manetho in Jos., C. Ap. 1, 246; 263; Diod. S. 14, 69, 2; Epict. 3, 24, 21; 24; 4, 1, 101; Philostrat., Vi. Apoll. 4, 44; 2 Macc 7: 19) *fight against God, oppose God* and his works Ac 23: 9 t.r.—WNestle, Philologus 59, '00, 48-50 (Eur. and Ac); OWeinreich, Gebet u. Wunder '29, 172f. M-M.*

θεομάχος, ον (Scymnus the geographer [II BC] 637 CMüller; Heraclit. Sto. 1 p. 1, 7; Lucian, Jupp. Tr. 45; Vett. Val. 331, 12; Sym. Job 26: 5; Pr 9: 18; 21: 16; cf. Jos., Ant. 14, 310) *fighting against God* Ac 5: 39.—AVögeli, Lk and Eur.: ThZ 9, '53, 415-38. M-M.*

θεόπνευστος, ον (Ps.-Phoc. 129 τῆς θεοπνεύστου σοφίης λόγος ἐστὶν ἄριστος; Plut., Mor. 904F; Vett. Val. 330, 19; Sib. Or. 5, 308; 406; on these texts and others, s. BBWarfield, Revelation and Inspiration '27, 229-59) *inspired by God* 2 Ti 3: 16. M-M.*

θεοπρεπής, ές (Pind., Nem. 10, 2; cf. Diod. S. 11, 89, 5; Plut., Dio 28, 4; Philo, Mos. 2, 15; Dit., Or. 383, 57) *fit for God, revered, venerable, godly,* superl. θεοπρεπέστατος (Plut., Mor. 780F).

1. of pers. (Lucian, Alex. 3) θ. πρεσβύτης MPol 7: 2. Also of a group of pers.: θ. πρεσβυτέριον ISm 12: 2. συμβούλιον ἄγειν θεοπρεπέστατον *call a council invested with all the splendor of God* IPol 7: 2. ἐκκλησία θεοπρεπεστάτη ISm inscr.

2. of things: Ign. is proud to have ὄνομα θεοπρεπέστατον *a name radiant w. divine splendor* IMg 1: 2, though it is not certain what he means by it (cf. Maximus Tyr. 35, 2e θεοπρεπῆ ὀνόματα in contrast to ἀνθρωπικὰ ὀν.). He uses θ. also of his bonds ISm 11: 1.*

θεοπρεσβευτής, οῦ, ὁ *an ambassador of God,* one commissioned or empowered by God (cf. also IPhld 10: 1) ISm 11: 2; v.l. θεοπρεσβύτης Funk; see πρεσβύτης.*

θεός, οῦ, ὁ and **ἡ** (Hom.+; Herm. Wr.; inscr., pap., LXX, En., Ep. Arist., Philo, Joseph., Test. 12 Patr., Sib. Or.); voc. θεέ (Pisid. Inscr. [JHS 22, '02, 355] θέ; PGM 4, 218 θεὲ θεῶν; 7, 529 κύριε θεέ μέγιστε; 12, 120 κύριε θεέ; 13, 997; LXX [Thackeray 145; PKatz, Philo's Bible '50, 152f]; Jos., Ant. 14, 24 ὦ θεὲ βασιλεῦ τ. ὅλων; Sib. Or. 13, 172 βασιλεῦ κόσμου θεέ) Mt 27: 46, more frequently (s. 2 and 3c, h below) ὁ θεός (LXX; Bl-D. §147, 3 w. app.; JWackernagel, Über einige antike Anredeformen '12; Mlt.-H. 120). On the inclusion or omission of the art. gener. s. W-S. §19, 13d; Bl-D. §254, 1; 268, 2; Rob. 758; 761; 780; 786; 795; Mlt.-Turner 174; BWeiss, D. Gebr. des Artikels bei den Gottesnamen, StKr 84, '11, 319-92; 503-38 (also available separately). *God, god.*

1. of divine beings gener.: Ac 28: 6; 2 Th 2: 4 (cf. Sib. Or. 5, 34 ἰσάζων θεῷ αὐτόν). θεὸς Ῥομφά Ac 7: 43 (Am 5: 26). οὐδεὶς θεὸς εἰ μὴ εἷς *there is no God but one* 1 Cor 8: 4. θεοῦ φωνὴ καὶ οὐκ ἀνθρώπου Ac 12: 22.—ἡ θεός *the*

goddess (Att., later more rarely; Peripl. Eryth. c. 58; Lucian, Dial. Deor. 17, 2; Dit., Syll.³ 695, 28; inscr., one of which refers to Artemis, in Hauser p. 81f; Jos., Ant. 9, 19) Ac 19: 37.—Pl. Ac 7: 40 (Ex 32: 1). Cf. 14: 11; 19: 26; PK 2 p. 14, 21. εἴπερ εἰσὶν λεγόμενοι θεοί *even if there are so-called gods* 1 Cor 8: 5a; cf. b (on θεοὶ πολλοί cf. Jos., Ant. 4, 149.—Maximus Tyr. 11, 5a: θ. πολλοί w. εἷς θ. πατήρ). οἱ φύσει μὴ ὄντες θεοί *those who by nature are not really gods* Gal 4: 8b.

2. Some writings in our lit. use the word θ. w. ref. to Christ (without necessarily equating Christ with the Father), though the interpretation of some of the pass. is in debate. In Ro 9: 5 the interpr. depends on the punctuation. If a period is placed before ὁ ὢν κτλ., the doxology refers to God (so EAbbot, JBL 1, 1881, 81–154; 3, 1883, 90–112; RALipsius; HHoltzmann, Ntl. Theol.² II '11, 99f; EGünther, StKr 73, '00, 636–44; FCBurkitt, JTS 5, '04, 451–5; Jülicher; PFeine, Theol. d. NTs⁶ '34, 176; OHoltzmann; Ltzm.; AMBrouwer; RSV text).—If a comma is used in the same place, the reference is to Christ (so BWeiss; EBröse, NKZ 10, 1899, 645–57; ASchlatter; ThZahn; EKühl; PAlthaus; M-JLagrange; JSickenberger; RSV mg. S. also εἰμί I1.—Undecided: ThHaering.—The conjecture of the Socinian scholar JSchlichting [died 1661] ὧν ὁ='to whom belongs' is revived by JWeiss, most recently in D. Urchristentum '17, 363; WWrede, Pls '05, 82; CStrömman, ZNW 8, '07, 319f). In 2 Pt 1: 1; 1 J 5: 20 the interpretation is open to question. On the other hand, θ. certainly refers to Christ in the foll. NT pass.: J 1: 1b (w. ὁ θεός 1: 1a, which refers to God the Father; on θεός w. and without the article, acc. to whether it means God or the Logos, s. Philo, Somn. 1, 229f; JGGriffiths, ET 62, '50f, 314–16; BMMetzger, ET 63, '51f, 125f), 18b. ὁ κύριός μου καὶ ὁ θεός μου *my Lord and my God!* (nom. w. art.=voc.; s. beg. of this entry.—On the resurrection as proof of divinity cf. Diog. L. 8, 41, who quotes Hermippus: Pythagoras returns from a journey to Hades and appears among his followers [εἰσέρχεσθαι εἰς τὴν ἐκκλησίαν], and they consider him θεῖόν τινα] 20: 28 (on the combination of κύριος and θεός s. 3c below). Tit 2: 13 (μέγας θ.). Hb 1: 8, 9 (in a quot. fr. Ps 44: 7, 8). S. TFGlasson, NTS 12, '66, 270–72. Jd 5 𝔓⁷². But above all Ignatius calls Christ θεός in many pass.: θεὸς Ἰησοῦς Χριστός ITr 7: 1; Χριστὸς θεός ISm 10: 1. ὁ θεὸς ἡμῶν IEph inscr.; 15: 3; 18: 2; IRo inscr. (twice); 3: 3; IPol 8: 3; τὸ πάθος τοῦ θεοῦ μου IRo 6: 3. ἐν αἵματι θεοῦ IEph 1: 1. ἐν σαρκὶ γενόμενος θεός 7: 2. θεὸς ἀνθρωπίνως φανερούμενος 19: 3. θεὸς ὁ οὕτως ὑμᾶς σοφίσας ISm 1: 1.—Hdb. exc. 193f; MRackl, Die Christologie d. hl. Ign. v. Ant. '14.—StLösch, Deitas Jesu u. antike Apotheose '33.

3. quite predom. of the true God, somet. with, somet. without the art.

a. ὁ θεός Mt 1: 23; 3: 9; 5: 8, 34; Mk 2: 12; 13: 19; Lk 2: 13; J 3: 2b; Ac 2: 22b; Gal 2: 6 al. With prep. εἰς τὸν θ. Ac 24: 15. ἐκ τοῦ θεοῦ J 8: 42b, 47; 1 J 3: 9f; 4: 1ff, 6f; 5: 1, 4; 2 Cor 3: 5; 5: 18 al.; ἐν τῷ θ. Ro 5: 11; Col 3: 3. ἔναντι τοῦ θεοῦ Lk 1: 8; ἐπὶ τὸν θ. Ac 15: 19; 26: 18, 20; ἐπὶ τῷ θ. Lk 1: 47; παρὰ τοῦ θ. J 8: 40; παρὰ τῷ θ. Ro 2: 13; 9: 14; πρὸς τὸν θ. J 1: 2; Ac 24: 16. τὰ πρὸς τὸν θεόν Hb 2: 17; 5: 1; Ro 15: 17 is acc. of respect: *with respect to one's relation to God* or *the things pertaining to God, in God's cause* (cf. Bl-D. §160; Rob. 486. For τὰ πρὸς τ. θ. s. Soph., Phil. 1441; X., De Rep. Lac. 13, 11; Aristot., De Rep. 5, 11; Lucian, Pro Imag. 8; Wilcken, Chrest. 109, 3 [III BC] εὐσεβὴς τὰ πρὸς θεούς; Ex 4: 16; 18: 19; Jos., Ant. 9, 236 εὐσεβὴς τὰ πρὸς τ. θεόν).

b. without the art. Mt 6: 24; Lk 2: 14; 20: 38; J 1: 18a;

Ro 8: 8, 33b; 2 Cor 1: 21; 5: 19; Gal 2: 19; 4: 8f; 2 Th 1: 8; Tit 1: 16; 3: 8; Hb 3: 4. W. prep. ἀπὸ θεοῦ J 3: 2a; 16: 30. εἰς θεόν IPhld 1: 2. ἐκ θεοῦ (Pind., Ol. 11, 10, Pyth. 1, 41; Jos., Ant. 2, 164) Ac 5: 39; 2 Cor 5: 1; Phil 3: 9. κατὰ θεόν acc. to God's will (Appian, Iber. 19 §73; 23 §88; 26 §101, Liby. 6 §25, Bell. Civ. 4, 86 §364) Ro 8: 27; 2 Cor 7: 9ff; IEph 2: 1. ἡ κατὰ θ. ἀγάπη *godly love* IMg 1: 1; cf. 13: 1; ITr 1: 2. παρὰ θεῷ (Jos., Bell. 1, 635) Mt 19: 26; Lk 2: 52.

c. w. gen. foll. to denote a special relationship: ὁ θ. Ἀβραάμ Mt 22: 32; Mk 12: 26; Lk 20: 37; Ac 3: 13; 7: 32 (all Ex 3: 6). ὁ θ. (τοῦ) Ἰσραήλ (Ezk 44: 2) Mt 15: 31; Lk 1: 68; cf. Ac 13: 17; 2 Cor 6: 16; Hb 11: 16. ὁ θ. μου Ro 1: 8; 1 Cor 1: 4 v.l.; 2 Cor 12: 21; Phil 1: 3; 4: 19; Phlm 4. OT κύριος ὁ θ. σου (ἡμῶν, ὑμῶν, αὐτῶν) Mt 4: 7 (Dt 6: 16); 22: 37 (Dt 6: 5); Mk 12: 29 (Dt 6: 4); Lk 1: 16; 4: 8 (Dt 6: 13); 10: 27 (Dt 6: 5); Ac 2: 39. ὁ κύριος καὶ ὁ θ. ἡμῶν Rv 4: 11 (the combination of κύριος and θεός is freq. in the OT: 2 Km 7: 28; 3 Km 18: 39; Jer 38: 18; Zech 13: 9; Ps 29: 3; 34: 23; 85: 15. But s. also Epict. 2, 16, 13 κύριε ὁ θεός [GBreithaupt, Her. 62, '27, 253–5], Herm. Wr.: Cat. Cod. Astr. VIII 2, p. 172, ὁ κύριε ὁ θεὸς ἡμῶν, the ref. at the beg. of this entry, and the sacral uses τ. θεῷ κ. κυρίῳ Σοκνοπαίῳ [Dit., Or. 655, 3f—24 BC]; PTebt. 284, 6; τῷ κυρίῳ θεῷ Ἀσκληπίῳ [Sb 159, 2]; deo domino Saturno [inscr. fr. imperial times fr. Thala in the prov. of Africa: BPhW 21, '01, 475], also Suetonius, Domit. 13 dominus et deus noster). ὁ θ. τοῦ κυρίου ἡμῶν Ἰ. Χ. Eph 1: 17.

d. used w. πατήρ (s. πατήρ 3a) ὁ θ. καὶ πατὴρ τοῦ κυρίου ἡμῶν Ἰησοῦ Χριστοῦ Ro 15: 6; 2 Cor 1: 3; Eph 1: 3; Col 1: 3; 1 Pt 1: 3. ὁ θ. καὶ πατὴρ ἡμῶν Gal 1: 4; Phil 4: 20; 1 Th 1: 3; 3: 11, 13. ὁ θ. καὶ πατήρ 1 Cor 15: 24; Eph 5: 20; Js 1: 27. ὁ πατήρ Phil 2: 11; 1 Pt 1: 2; cf. 1 Cor 8: 6. ἀπὸ θεοῦ πατρὸς ἡμῶν Ro 1: 7b; 1 Cor 1: 3; 2 Cor 1: 2; Gal 1: 3; Eph 1: 2; Phil 1: 2; Col 1: 2; Phlm 3; ἀπὸ θ. π. Gal 1: 3 v.l.; Eph 6: 23; 2 Th 1: 2; 2 Ti 1: 2; Tit 1: 4; παρὰ θεοῦ π. 2 Pt 1: 17; 2 J 3.

e. w. gen. of what God brings about, in accordance w. his nature: ὁ θ. τῆς εἰρήνης Ro 15: 33; 1 Th 5: 23. τῆς ἐλπίδος *the God fr. whom hope comes* Ro 15: 13. πάσης παρακλήσεως 2 Cor 1: 3b. ὁ θ. τῆς ἀγάπης 13: 11. ὁ θ. πάσης χάριτος 1 Pt 5: 10. In οὐ γάρ ἐστιν ἀκαταστασίας ὁ θεός 1 Cor 14: 33, θεός is to be supplied before ἀκατ.: *for God is not a God of disorder.*

f. The genit. (τοῦ) θεοῦ is—α. subj. gen., extremely freq. depending on words like βασιλεία, δόξα, θέλημα, ἐντολή, εὐαγγέλιον, λόγος, ναός, οἶκος, πνεῦμα, υἱός, υἱοί, τέκνα and many others. Here prob. belongs τὸ μωρὸν τ. θ. the (*seeming*) *foolishness of G.* 1 Cor 1: 25.

β. obj. gen. ἡ ἀγάπη τοῦ θ. *love for God* Lk 11: 42; J 5: 42; ἡ προσευχὴ τοῦ θ. *prayer to God* Lk 6: 12. πίστις θεοῦ *faith in God* Mk 11: 22. φόβος θεοῦ *fear of, reverence for God* Ro 3: 18 al. (s. φόβος 2ba).

γ. τὰ τοῦ θεοῦ *the things, ways, thoughts,* or *secret purposes of God* 1 Cor 2: 11. φρονεῖν τὰ τ. θ. Mt 16: 23; Mk 8: 33 s. φρονέω 2. ἀποδιδόναι τὰ τ. θ. τῷ θεῷ *give God what belongs to God* Mt 22: 21; Mk 12: 17; Lk 20: 25.

δ. Almost as a substitute for the adj. *divine* IMg 6: 1f; 15.

g. The dat. τῷ θεῷ is (s. Bl-D. §188, 2; 192; Rob. 538f; WHavers, Untersuchungen z. Kasussyntax d. indogerm. Sprachen '11, 162ff)

α. dat. of advantage *for God* 2 Cor 5: 13. Perh. (s. β) ὅπλα δυνατὰ τῷ θ. 10: 4. The dat. of Ro 6: 10f rather expresses the possessor.

β. ethical dat. *in the sight of God,* hence w. superl. force (s. Beginn. IV, 75, on Ac 7: 20) *very:* μεγάλοι τῷ θ.

B 8: 4 (cf. Jon 3: 3). ἀστεῖος τῷ θ. Ac 7: 20. Perh. (s. a) ὅπλα δυνατὰ τ. θ. *weapons powerful in the sight of God* 2 Cor 10: 4. This idea is usu. expressed by ἐνώπιον τοῦ θ.

h. ὁ θ. is used as a vocative Mk 15: 34 (Ps 21: 2. θεός twice at the beginning of the invocation of a prayer: Ael. Dion. θ, 8; Paus. Attic. θ, 7 'θεὸς θεός' ταῖς ἀρχαῖς ἐπέλεγον ἐπιφημιζόμενοι); Lk 18: 11; Hb 1: 8 (Ps 44: 7); 10: 7 (Ps 39: 9). S. also 2 and 3c and the beginn. of this entry.

i. θ. τῶν αἰώνων s. αἰών 3 and 4; θ. αἰώνιος s. αἰώνιος 2; θ. ἀληθινός s. ἀληθινός 3; εἷς ὁ θεός s. εἷς 2b; (ὁ) θ. (ὁ) ζῶν s. [ζάω] 1aε.—ὁ μόνος θεός *the only God* (4 Km 19: 15, 19; Ps 85: 10; Is 37: 20; Da 3: 45; Philo, Leg. All. 2, 1f. Cf. Norden, Agn. Th. 145) J 5: 44 (some mss. lack τοῦ μόνου); 1 Ti 1: 17.—ὁ μόνος ἀληθινὸς θ. (Demochares in Athen. 6, 62 p. 253c μόνος θ. ἀληθινός) J 17: 3. Cf. the sim. combinations w. μόνος θ. Ro 16: 27; Jd 25.—θ. σωτήρ s. σωτήρ 1.—OHoltzmann, D. chr. Gottesglaube, s. Vorgesch. u. Urgesch. '05; EvDobschütz, Rationales u. irrat. Denken über Gott im Urchristent.: StKr 95, '24, 235-55; RAHoffmann, D. Gottesbild Jesu '34; PAlthaus, D. Bild Gottes b. Pls: ThBl 20, '41, 81-92; Dodd 3-8; KRahner, Theos im NT: Bijdragen (Maastricht) 11, '50, 212-36; 12, '51, 24-52.

4. fig., of that which is worthy of reverence or respect (Artem. 2, 69 p. 161, 17: γονεῖς and διδάσκαλοι are like gods; Simplicius in Epict. p. 85, 27 acc. to ancient Roman custom children had to call their parents θεοί).

a. of persons θεοί (as אֱלֹהִים) J 10: 34f (Ps 81: 6; men are called θ. in the OT also Ex 7: 1; 22: 27. Cf. Philo, Det. Pot. Insid. 161f, Somn. 1, 229, Mut. Nom. 128, Omn. Prob. Lib. 43, Mos. 1, 158, Decal. 120, Leg. All. 1, 40, Migr. Abr. 84.—Arcesilaus [III BC] describes Crates and Polemo as θεοί τινες='a kind of gods' [Diog. L. 4, 22]; Antiphanes says of the iambic poet Philoxenus: θεὸς ἐν ἀνθρώποισιν ἦν [Athen. 14, 50 p. 643D]; Diod. S. 1, 4, 7 and 5, 21, 2 of Caesar; Dio Chrys. 30[47], 5 Πυθαγόρας ἐτιμᾶτο ὡς θεός; Heliod. 4, 7, 8 σωτὴρ κ. θεός, addressed to a physician; BGU 1197, 1 [4 BC] a high official, and 1201, 1 [2 BC] a priest θεός and κύριος; PMich. 209, 11f [II/III AD] οἶδας ἄδελφε, ὅτει οὐ μόνον ὡς ἀδελφόν σε ἔχω, ἀλλὰ καὶ ὡς πατέρα κ. κύριον κ. θεόν).—JAEmerton, JTS 11, '60, 329-32.

b. of the belly (=appetite) as the god of certain people Phil 3: 19 (cf. Athen. 3 p. 97c γάστρων καὶ κοιλιοδαίμων. Also Eupolem. in Athen. 3 p. 100B).

5. of the devil ὁ θ. τοῦ αἰῶνος τούτου 2 Cor 4: 4 (s. αἰών 2a and WMüllensiefen, StKr 95, '24, 295-9).—TW III '36, 65-123. M-M. B. 1464.

θεοσέβεια, ας, ἡ (X., An. 2, 6, 26; Pla., Epin. p. 985D; 989E; Gen 20: 11; Job 28: 28; Sir 1: 25; Bar 5: 4; Philo.— The word is found as a title in Christian inscr.) *reverence for God, piety, religion* 1 Ti 2: 10; 2 Cl 20: 4; Dg 1; 3: 3; 4: 5 (Third Corinthians 3: 10); ἀόρατος θ. *invisible religion* (i.e., without images, sacrifices, or elaborate ceremonies) 6: 4. τὸ τῆς θ. μυστήριον 4: 6. M-M.*

θεοσεβέω (Pollux 1, 22; Cass. Dio 54, 30, 1; Dit., Syll.³ 708, 18 [II BC]; Test. Jos. 6: 7) *worship God* κατὰ τὰ αὐτὰ Ἰουδαίοις *in the same way as the Jews* Dg 3: 1.*

θεοσεβής, ές (Soph., Hdt.+; Vett. Val. 17, 1; 19; 18, 16; Herm. Wr. 9, 4b; Inscr. Graec. et It. 1325; Epigr. Gr. 729, 2; PGiess. 55, 1; UPZ 14, 20 [158 BC], on which s. the editor's note p. 159; LXX; Ep. Arist. 179; Philo, Mut. Nom. 197; Jos., C. Ap. 2, 140. Cf. also Jos., Ant. 12, 284; 20, 195, and the Jewish inscr. in the theater at Miletus in Dssm., LO 391f [LAE 446f] and Schürer III⁴ 174, 70, SAB 1897, 221ff) *god-fearing, devout* J 9: 31. W. θεοφιλής: γένος τῶν Χριστιανῶν MPol 3. Of Job 1 Cl 17: 3 (Job 1: 1).—GBertram, TW III '36, 124-8. M-M.*

θεοστυγής, ές quotable fr. earlier times only in the pass. sense *hated by a god* (Eur., Tro. 1213, Cycl. 396; 602), then *godforsaken*. In the list of vices Ro 1: 30 the act. mng. *hating God* seems preferable (ADebrunner, Griech. Wortbildungslehre, 1917, 52 §105). It is obviously act. in Ps.-Clem., Hom. 1, 12 ἄδικοι κ. θεοστυγεῖς. The noun θεοστυγία 1 Cl 35: 5 is also to be taken as act.—CFA Fritzsche (1836) on Ro 1: 30.*

θεοστυγία, ας, ἡ *hatred* or *enmity toward God* 1 Cl 35: 5 (s. θεοστυγής).*

θεότης, ητος, ἡ (Plut., De Def. Orac. 10 p. 415BC οὕτως ἐκ μὲν ἀνθρώπων εἰς ἥρωας, ἐκ δὲ ἡρώων εἰς δαίμονας αἱ βελτίονες ψυχαὶ τὴν μεταβολὴν λαμβάνουσιν. ἐκ δὲ δαιμόνων ὀλίγαι μὲν ἔτι χρόνῳ πολλῷ δι' ἀρετῆς καθαρθεῖσαι παντάπασι θεότητος μετέσχον; Lucian, Icarom. 9; Herm. Wr. 12, 1; 13, 7a; Proclus, Theol. 137 p. 122, 5 al.; Kleopatra l. 62; 117; 137) *deity, divinity*, used as abstract noun for θεός: τὸ πλήρωμα τῆς θ. *the fullness of deity* Col 2: 9 (s. Nash on θειότης). ἐπιζητεῖν περὶ τῆς θ. *inquire concerning the deity* Hm 10, 1, 4; cf. 5f. δύναμις τῆς θ. *power of the deity* Hm 11: 5; πνεῦμα (τῆς) θ. m 11: 10, 14.*

θεοφιλής, ές *(be)loved by God* (so Pind., Hdt.+; Diod. S. 5, 34, 1; Dio Chrys. 16[33], 21; Dit., Or. 383, 42 [I BC]; PGM 13, 225; Ep. Arist. 287; Jos., Ant. 1, 106; 14, 22; 455), also act. *loving God* (Isocr. 4, 29; Philo, Praem. 43) w. θεοσεβής MPol 3.*

Θεόφιλος, ου, ὁ (in lit. as well as [since III BC] in inscr. and pap. for Jews [Ep. Arist. 49; Joseph.] and Gentiles) *Theophilus*, a Christian of prominence, to whom Lk (1: 3) and Ac (1: 1) are dedicated (cf. Third Corinthians 1: 1). M-M.*

θεοφόρος, ον *god-bearing, inspired* (Aeschyl., fgm. 225; Philod., π. θεῶν 1 col. 4, 12 Diels: 'bearing the divine spirit within oneself'; Leontios 12 p. 22, 14; 15 p. 30, 15; American Journ. of Arch. 37, 244 [inscr. II AD; Bacchic mysteries].—Heraclitus, Ep. 8, 2 the Σίβυλλα as θεοφορουμένη γυνή); subst. ὁ θ. *the God-bearer* IEph 9: 2 (s. the foll. entry and cf. the v.l. for 1 Cor 6: 20 in the Vulgate 'portate [=ἄρατε] deum in corpore vestro').*

Θεοφόρος, ου, ὁ (not found as proper name before Ign., and perh. coined by him or for him; on the word and name cf. Hdb., Ergänzungsband '23, 189-91.—Ael. Aristid., because of his close relationship to Asclepius, receives the surname Θεόδωρος: 50, 53f K.=26 p. 518 D.) *Theophorus*, surname of Ignatius, IEph inscr.; IMg inscr.; ITr inscr.; IRo inscr.; IPhld inscr.; ISm inscr.; IPol inscr.*

θεραπεία, ας, ἡ (Eur., Hdt.+; inscr., pap., LXX, Ep. Arist., Philo, Joseph.) *serving, service, care.*

1. of *treatment* of the sick, esp. *healing* (Hippocr.+; PTebt. 44, 6 [114 BC] ὄντος μου ἐπὶ θεραπείᾳ ἐν τῷ Ἰσιείῳ χάριν τ. ἀρρωστίας; Sb 159, 4f; 1537b).

a. lit. (Diod. S. 1, 25, 7 [Pl.]; 17, 89, 2; Lucian, Abdic. 7; Philo, Deus Imm. 63; Jos., Vi. 85) Lk 9: 11. θεραπείας ποιεῖν *perform healings* LJ 1: 6.

b. fig., w. obj. gen. (cf. Pla., Prot. 345A τ. καμνόντων; Sb 1537b; θ. ὅλου σώματος; Dit., Syll.³ 888, 125; Philo, Spec. Leg. 1, 191 θ. ἁμαρτημάτων) θ. τῶν ἐθνῶν Rv 22: 2.

2. =οἱ θεράποντες *servants* (Hdt. +; Gen 45: 16; Esth 5: 2b; Philo, In Flacc. 149; Jos., Bell. 1, 82, Ant. 4, 112) καταστῆσαί τινα ἐπὶ τῆς θ. *put someone in charge of the servants* (cf. Polyb. 4, 87, 5 ὁ ἐπὶ τῆς θ. τεταγμένος) Lk 12: 42; Mt 24: 45 t.r. M-M.*

θεραπεύω impf. ἐθεράπευον, pass. ἐθεραπευόμην; fut. θεραπεύσω; 1 aor. ἐθεράπευσα; perf. pass. ptc. τεθεραπευμένος; 1 aor. pass. ἐθεραπεύθην (Hom. +; inscr., pap., LXX) *serve, be a servant.*
1. *serve a divinity* (Hes., Hdt. +; Diod. S. 5, 44, 2 οἱ θεραπεύοντες τοὺς θεοὺς ἱερεῖς; Arrian, Anab. 7, 2, 4; Dit., Or. 90, 40, Syll.³ 663, 6; 996, 30; 1042, 10; Inscr. Gr. 982, 14; PGiess. 20, 20; LXX [Thackeray p. 8]; Ep. Arist. 256; Philo, Spec. Leg. 2, 167; Jos., Bell. 7, 424, Ant. 4, 67) pass. ὑπό τινος: οὐδὲ ὑπὸ χειρῶν ἀνθρωπίνων θεραπεύεται *nor is he served by human hands* Ac 17: 25 (Field, Notes 127).
2. *care for, wait upon, treat* (medically), then also *heal, restore* (in the latter mng. Athen. 12 p. 522ʙ; Dit., Syll.³ 1004, 21; 1168, 126; 1170, 20; 1171, 7; 1172, 5; Tob 12: 3; Sir 38: 7) τινά *someone* (Jos., Bell. 1, 272) Mt 4: 24; 8: 7, 16; Mk 1: 34; 3: 2, 10; Lk 4: 23 (Horapollo 2, 76 ὑφ᾽ ἑαυτοῦ θεραπευθείς), 40; 10: 9 and oft. τινὰ ἀπὸ τινος *heal* or *cure someone from an illness* (BGU 956, 2 ἐξορκίζω ὑμᾶς κατὰ τοῦ ἁγίου ὀνόματος θεραπεῦσαι τὸν Διονύσιον ἀπὸ παντὸς ῥίγου [=ῥίγους] καὶ πυρετοῦ) 7: 21. Pass. 5: 15; 6: 18; 8: 2. ἀπό τινος has a different mng. in vs. 43 οὐκ ἴσχυσεν ἀπ᾽ οὐδενὸς θεραπευθῆναι *she could not be healed by anybody.*—θ. νόσον καὶ μαλακίαν (cf. Philo, Det. Pot. Ins. 43; Jos., Ant. 17, 150) Mt 4: 23; 9: 35; 10: 1; Lk 9: 1. Of wounds, pass. Rv 13: 3, 12; wounds healed by a plaster IPol 2: 1. Abs. Mt 12: 10; Mk 6: 5; Lk 6: 7; 9: 6; 13: 14; 14: 3.—Fig. in isolated instances (e.g., Vi. Aesopi I c. 98 τὴν ὀργὴν ὁ λόγος θεραπεύσει): of God (Wsd 16: 12) ὁ θεραπεύων θεός *God, who can heal* 2 Cl 9: 7 (cf. Shmone Esre 8 רוֹפֵא ... אֵל).—JHempel, Heilung als Symbol u. Wirklichkeit '58; HWBeyer, TW III '36, 128–32. M-M. B. 306.

θεράπων, οντος, ὁ (Hom. +; Alciphr. 4, 19, 9 Διονύσου θ. καὶ προφήτης; Dit., Syll.³ 219, 12; 1168, 114f οἱ θεράποντες of the temple of Asclepius; BGU 361 III, 18; LXX [Thackeray p. 7f]; Philo) *servant* in our lit. only of Moses (as Ex 14: 31; Num 12: 7; Wsd 10: 16) Hb 3: 5; 1 Cl 4: 12; 43: 1; 51: 3; cf. vs. 5; 53: 5; B 14: 4. M-M. B. 1334.*

θερεία, ας, ἡ subst. of θέρειος (Hdt. +; Diod. S.; pap.) *summertime* Hs 4: 2 v.l. for θέρος.*

θερίζω fut. θερίσω; 1 aor. ἐθέρισα, pass. ἐθερίσθην (Pre-Socr., trag. +; inscr., pap., LXX, Philo; Jos., Ant. 3, 251 al.) *reap, harvest.*
1. lit. Mt 6: 26; Lk 12: 24; 1 Cl 56: 15 (Job 5: 26) ὁ θερίσας *the harvester* Js 5: 4 (cf. BGU 349, 10 ἐμοῦ τοῦ μισθωσαμένου θερίζοντος τῷ μισθῷ); cf. J 4: 36.—Dalman, Arbeit III.
2. fig.—**a.** esp. in proverbial expr. (Paroem. Gr.: Diogenian. 2, 62) ἄλλος ἐστὶν ὁ σπείρων καὶ ἄλλος ὁ θερίζων *one sows, and another reaps* J 4: 37, cf. 38. ὃ γὰρ ἐὰν σπείρῃ ἄνθρωπος, τοῦτο καὶ θερίσει *whatever a man sows he will also reap* Gal 6: 7 (cf. Aristot., Rhet. 3, 3, 4 σὺ δὲ ταῦτα αἰσχρῶς μὲν ἔσπειρας κακῶς δὲ ἐθέρισας; Pla., Phaedr. 260ʙ; Philo, Leg. ad Gai. 293). θερίζειν ὅπου οὐκ ἔσπειρας *reaping where you did not sow* Mt 25: 24, 26; Lk 19: 21f. Of a reward gener. (Test. Levi 13: 6 ἐὰν σπείρητε πονηρά, πᾶσαν ταραχὴν καὶ θλῖψιν θερίσετε; Philo, Conf. Lingu. 152; Jer 12: 13; Pr 22: 8) φθοράν, ζωὴν αἰώνιον Gal 6: 8. τὰ σαρκικὰ ὑμῶν *reap*

(=lay claim to) *your material benefits* 1 Cor 9: 11. Abs. Gal 6: 9; 2 Cor 9: 6.
b. of the harvest of the Last Judgment, which brings devastation Rv 14: 15. ἐθερίσθη ἡ γῆ vs. 16 (cf. Plut., Mor. 182ᴀ θερίζειν τὴν Ἀσίαν). M-M. B. 506.*

θερινός, ἡ, όν (Pind. +; Sb 358, 7; 14 [inscr. III ʙᴄ]; BGU 1188, 9 [I ʙᴄ]; POxy. 810; LXX; Philo; Jos., Ant. 15, 54) *of summer* καιροὶ *seasons of summer* 1 Cl 20: 9.*

θερισμός, οῦ, ὁ (X., Oec. 18, 3; Polyb. 5, 95, 5; PLille 1 verso, 9 [III ʙᴄ]; PHib. 90, 5; BGU 594, 5; LXX; Ep. Arist. 116; Philo, Somn. 2, 23) *harvest.*
1. the process (and time) of harvesting ἕως τ. θερισμοῦ Mt 13: 30a. ἐν καιρῷ τ. θερισμοῦ ibid. b (cf. Jer 27: 16 ἐν καιρῷ θ.); Mk 4: 29. In these parables, θερισμός serves to explain the situation in the kingdom of God, as Mt 13: 39 plainly shows; J 4: 35a.
2. in fig. sense *the crop to be harvested*—**a.** of persons to be won Mt 9: 37f; Lk 10: 2; J 4: 35b.
b. of the judgment ἐξηράνθη ὁ θ. τῆς γῆς *the earth's harvest is dry* (=fully ripe) Rv 14: 15. M-M.*

θεριστής, οῦ, ὁ (X., Hier. 6, 10 al.; Plut.; Philostrat., Her. 158, 31; PHib. 44, 4; PFlor. 80, 6; Bel 33; Philo, Virt. 90) *reaper, harvester* Mt 13: 30, 39. M-M.*

θερμαίνω (Hom. +; LXX) in our lit. only θερμαίνομαι (PSI 406, 37 [III ʙᴄ]; Jos., Bell. 3, 274) impf. ἐθερμαινόμην *warm oneself* at a fire (Is 44: 16) Mk 14: 67; J 18: 18a, b, 25. πρὸς τὸ φῶς *at the fire* Mk 14: 54. Of clothing (Hg 1: 6; Job 31: 20) θερμαίνεσθε *dress warmly! keep warm!* Js 2: 16.*

θέρμη (and θέρμα; s. Phryn. 331 L.; WGRutherford, New Phryn. 1881, 198; 414. Thu. +; inscr., pap.; Job 6: 17; Ps 18: 7; Sir 38: 28; Jos., Bell. 3, 272), ης, ἡ *heat* ἀπὸ τῆς θ. *because of the heat* Ac 28: 3. M-M.*

θερμός, ή, όν (Hom. +; LXX; En. 14, 13; Jos., Vi. 85) *warm* of water for baptism ὕδωρ (cf. Soranus p. 41, 8; Philumen. p. 23, 17; 26, 12; Dit., Syll.³ 1170, 12; Philo, Mos. 1, 212) D 7: 2. B. 1077.*

θέρος, ους, τό (Hom. +; Dit., Or. 56, 41; PHib. 27, 33; LXX, Philo; Jos., Ant. 5, 190; 212) *summer* Mt 24: 32; Mk 13: 28; Lk 21: 30 (ZNW 10, '09, 333f; 11, '10, 167f; 12, '11, 88). Fig. for heavenly bliss Hs 4: 2f, 5. M-M. B. 511; 1014f.*

θέσις, εως, ἡ (Pind. +; inscr., pap., LXX, Ep. Arist., Philo) *position* ἰσχυρὰ ἡ θέσις *the position is secure* Hv 3, 13, 3.*

Θεσσαλία, ας, ἡ (Hdt. +; inscr.; Philo, Leg. ad Gai. 281; Sib. Or.) *Thessaly,* a region in northeast Greece Ac 17: 15 D.*

Θεσσαλονικεύς, έως, ὁ *Thessalonian,* an inhabitant of Thessalonica Ac 20: 4; 27: 2; 1 Th 1: 1, inscr.; 2 Th 1: 1, inscr.*

Θεσσαλονίκη, ης, ἡ (Polyb. 23, 11, 2; Strabo 7 fgm. 24; Ps.-Lucian, Asin. 46; anon. history of the Diadochi [time unknown]: 155 fgm. 2, 3 Jac.; inscr. [Dit., Syll.³ index vol. IV 94]) *Thessalonica,* a city in Macedonia on the Thermaic Gulf. Paul founded a church here Ac 17: 1, 11, 13; Phil 4: 16; 2 Ti 4: 10.*

Θευδᾶς, ᾶ, ὁ (CIG 2684; 3563; 5689; Bull. de corr. hell. 11, 1887, p. 213–15) *Theudas,* the short form of a name compounded w. θεός, but perh. not Θεόδωρος, since in

CIG 3920=Dit., Syll.³ 1229 two brothers Theodore and Theudas are mentioned (cf. Bl-D. §125, 2; Mlt.-H. 88; 91). Ac 5: 36 mentions a Jewish insurrectionist named Theudas; the only such pers. known to history revolted and was killed in the time of the procurator Cuspius Fadus, 44 AD and later (Jos., Ant. 20, 97-9). For the grave chronological difficulties here s. the comm., e.g. EHaenchen and Beginn. IV ad loc.—Schürer I⁴ 566 (lit. here, note 6); JWSwain, HTR 37, '44, 341-9. M-M.*

θέω (Hom.+) *run* w. acc. of place (Ps.-X., Cyneg. 4, 6 τὰ ὄρη) θ. τὴν ὁδὸν τὴν εὐθεῖαν *run the straight course* 2 Cl 7: 3.*

θεωρέω impf. ἐθεώρουν; 1 aor. ἐθεώρησα (Aeschyl., Hdt.+; inscr., pap., LXX, En., Ep. Arist., Philo, Joseph.).
   1. *be a spectator, look at, observe, perceive, see* (w. physical eyes) abs. (2 Macc 3: 17) Mt 27: 55; Mk 15: 40; Lk 14: 29; 23: 35 (cf. Ps 21: 8). W. indir. quest. foll. Mk 12: 41; 15: 47. W. acc. foll. τινά J 6: 40; 12: 45; 14: 19a; 16: 10, 16f, 19; Ac 3: 16; 25: 24; Rv 11: 11f; 1 Cl 16: 16 (Ps 21: 8); 35: 8 (Ps 49: 18). W. acc. of the pers. and a ptc. Mk 5: 15; Lk 10: 18; 24: 39; J 6: 19, 62; 10: 12; 20: 12, 14; 1 J 3: 17. W. acc. of the pers. and ὅτι J 9: 8. τὶ *someth.* (X., Cyr. 4, 3, 3; Jos., Ant. 12, 422) Lk 21: 6; 23: 48. πνεῦμα *a ghost* 24: 37.—J 2: 23; 6: 2 v.l.; 7: 3. ἔν τινί τι *see someth. in someone*: the whole church in the envoys IMg 6: 1; cf. ITr 1: 1. W. acc. of the thing and ptc. foll. J 20: 6; Ac 7: 56; 8: 13; 10: 11; 17: 16. W. ἀκούειν Ac 9: 7 (Apollon. Rhod. 4, 854f: when a deity [in this case Thetis] appears, only those who are destined to do so can see and hear anything; none of the others can do so). θεωρεῖν καὶ ἀκούειν ὅτι 19: 26.—Pass. *become visible* MPol 2: 2.—Rather in the sense *view* (Cebes 1, 1 ἀναθήματα) τὸν τάφον Mt 28: 1.—*Catch sight of, notice* Mk 3: 11. τὶ *someth.* θόρυβον 5: 38. W. ὅτι foll. Mk 16: 4.—The expr. *see someone's face* for *see someone in person* is due to OT infl. (cf. Jdth 6: 5; 1 Macc 7: 28, 30) Ac 20: 38.
   2. *of perception by the mind or spirit*—a. *notice, perceive, observe, find,* esp. on the basis of what one has seen and heard τὶ *someth.* (Apollodor. Com., fgm. 14 K. θ. τὴν τοῦ φίλου εὔνοιαν=ʼbecome aware of the friendʼs goodwill by the actions of the doorkeeper and the dogʼ; Sallust. c. 4 p. 4, 24 τὰς οὐσίας τ. θεῶν θ.=ʼperceive the true nature of the godsʼ) Ac 4: 13. W. acc. of the thing and ptc. (Ep. Arist. 268) 28: 6. W. acc. of the pers. and predicate adj. (cf. Diod. S. 2, 16, 8) δεισιδαιμονεστέρους ὑμᾶς θ. *I perceive that you are very religious people* Ac 17: 22. W. ὅτι foll. (2 Macc 9: 23) J 4: 19; 12: 19. Foll. by ὅτι and inf. w. acc. (Bl-D. §397, 6 w. app.; Mlt. 213) Ac 27: 10. W. indir. quest. foll. 21: 20; Hb 7: 4.
   b. *of the spiritual perception of the one sent by God,* which is poss. only to the believer (s. Herm. Wr. 12, 20b; Philo, e.g. Praem. 26) J 14: 17, 19b; cf. also 17: 24.
   c. *experience* θάνατον (OT expr.; cf. Ps 88: 49; also Lk 2: 26; Hb 11: 5. S. ὁράω 1b) J 8: 51 (εἶδον 𝔓⁶⁶ et al.) M-M.*

θεωρία, ας, ἡ (Aeschyl., Hdt.+; Herm. Wr., inscr., pap., LXX, Philo; Jos., Ant. 8, 138) obj., *that which one looks at, spectacle, sight* (so mostly of public spectacles, religious festivals, processions, etc., cf. DHagedorn and LKoenen, ZPE 2, '68, 74) συνπαραγενόμενοι ἐπὶ τὴν θ. ταύτην *who had gathered for this spectacle* Lk 23: 48 (w. sim. mng. IG IV² 1, 123, 26 θ. for the ὄχλος; 3 Macc 5: 24.—Wilcken, Chrest. 3, 6 [112 BC] ἐπὶ θεωρίαν). M-M.*

θήκη, ης, ἡ *receptacle* (Aeschyl., Hdt.+; inscr., pap., LXX; En. 17, 3; Joseph., Test. 12 Patr.; loanw. in rabb.).

1. *grave* (trag., Hdt.+; Dit., Syll.³ 1233, 1; POxy. 1188, 4; 21 [13 AD]; PGM 4, 2215; Jos., Ant. 8, 264; 16, 181) 1 Cl 50: 4.
2. *sheath* for a sword (Posidon.: 87 fgm. 15, 1 Jac.; Pollux 10, 144; PPetr. III 140a, 4; Jos., Ant. 7, 284) J 18: 11. M-M.*

θηλάζω 1 aor. ἐθήλασα—1. *give suck* (Lysias, Aristot. +; pap., LXX; En. 99, 5) abs. Mt 24: 19; Mk 13: 17; Lk 21: 23.
   2. *suck* (Hippocr., Aristot.+; PRyl. 153, 18; LXX; Philo, Det. Pot. Ins. 118) μαστοὶ οὓς ἐθήλασας *the breasts you have sucked* Lk 11: 27 (cf. SSol 8: 1; Job 3: 12; Hippocr. VIII 594 L. θ. τὸν μαστόν; Theocr. 3, 16 μασδὸν ἐθήλαξεν). οἱ θηλάζοντες *sucklings* Mt 21: 16 (Ps 8: 3). M-M. B. 334.*

θηλυκός, ή, όν (Aristot.+; PLille 10, 5 [III BC]; POxy. 1458, 11; PGM 4, 2518; Num 5: 3; Dt 4: 16; Philo, Deus Imm. 141) *female* ἵνα ἀδελφὸς ἰδὼν ἀδελφὴν οὐδὲν φρονῇ περὶ αὐτῆς θηλυκόν *that a brother when he sees a sister should not think of her as a female* 2 Cl 12: 5.*

θῆλυς, εια, υ (Hom.+; inscr., pap., LXX, En.; Ep. Arist. 250; Philo; Jos., Ant. 4, 79, C. Ap. 2, 244; Test. 12 Patr.) *female* ἡ θ. *the woman* (Hdt. 3, 109; X., Mem. 2, 1, 4 al.; Lev 27: 4-7; En. 15, 5; 7) Ro 1: 26f; 1 Cl 55: 5; 2 Cl 12: 2, 5 (both the latter pass. are quot. fr. an apocryphal gospel, presumably GEg); GEg 3. Also τὸ θ. (PTebt. 422, 18) ἄρσεν καὶ θ. *male and female* (LXX; Philo; Jos., Ant. 1, 32; cf. Pla., Rep. 454D; Aristot., Metaph. 988a, 5) Mt 19: 4; Mk 10: 6; 1 Cl 33: 5; 2 Cl 14: 2 (all Gen 1: 27); Gal 3: 28.—GNaass 1; GEg 2a, b; 2 Cl 12: 2 (s. above); cf. B 10: 7. M-M. B. 84f.*

θημωνιά, ᾶς, ἡ (LXX; Etym. Mag. p. 451, 8; Anecd. Gr. p. 264, 18=σωρὸς καρπῶν) *heap* (*of sheaves*) θ. ἅλωνος *a heap on the threshing-floor* 1 Cl 56: 15 (Job 5: 26).*

θήρ, ός, ὁ (Hom.+; Sb 4011, 4; LXX) (*wild*) *animal* 1 Cl 20: 4. θῆρες ἄγριοι *wild animals* 56: 12 (Job 5: 23).*

θήρα, ας, ἡ (Hom.+; inscr., pap., LXX; Philo, Mos. 1, 298; Jos., Ant. 1, 274; 18, 45, usu. in the mng. ʼhuntʼ or ʼpreyʼ) *net, trap* (so Horapollo 2, 26 w. παγίς; Ps 34: 8; Pr 11: 8) Ro 11: 9. M-M.*

θηρεύω 1 aor. ἐθήρευσα (Hom.+; inscr., pap., LXX) *to hunt, catch* fig. (so in many ways Pind.+; Diod. S. 2, 5, 1; Ps 139: 12; Philo; Jos., Ant. 19, 308) θ. τι ἐκ τοῦ στόματος αὐτοῦ *catch him in someth. he might say* Lk 11: 54 (Pla., Gorg. 489B ὀνόματα θηρεύειν=ʼto hunt for the words [of other people] to see whether they might perhaps commit errors [ἐάν τις ῥήματι ἁμάρτῃ].—θ.=catch by treachery: Ps.-Clem., Hom. 8, 22). M-M.*

θηριομαχέω 1 aor. ἐθηριομάχησα *be forced to fight with wild animals* as a punishment (cf. Diod. S. 3, 43, 7; Artem. 2, 54; 5, 49; Ptolem., Apotel. 4, 9, 10; Vett. Val. 129, 33; 130, 21; Jos., Bell. 7, 38) lit. IEph 1: 2; ITr 10; ἐπισήμως θ. MPol 3. It is uncertain whether θ. is used lit. or fig. in 1 Cor 15: 32. It is quite unlikely that Paul could have engaged in a real struggle w. wild animals (but. s. Bowen below). He says nothing about such an experience in 2 Cor 11: 23-9, and Ac does not mention it. Also the apostle could not have been sentenced ʼad bestiasʼ without losing his Roman citizenship, which he still held at a later date, and which formed the basis for his appeal to the emperor. If, nevertheless, the verb is to be taken as lit., the expr. is to be considered (w. JWeiss on 1 Cor 15: 32 and WMichaelis, Die Gefangenschaft d. Paulus in Ephesus

'25, 118ff) a contrary to fact (unreal) conditional sentence: 'if I had fought w. wild animals' (against this JSchmid, Zeit u. Ort d. paul. Gefangenschaftsbr. '31, 39-60; WG Kümmel, Hdb. '49). But the expr. can also be fig., as it certainly is in IRo 5: 1 ἀπὸ Συρίας μέχρι 'Ρώμης θηριομαχῶ . . . δεδεμένος δέκα λεοπάρδοις, ὅ ἐστι στρατιωτικὸν τάγμα *from Syria to Rome I am fighting with wild animals, bound to ten leopards, that is, a detachment of soldiers* (cf. Dit., Or. 201, 15 ἐπολέμησα ἀπὸ Π. ἕως Τ.); here Ign. describes the sufferings of his journey as a prisoner with a word that suggests the struggle w. wild animals, for which he longed, and which filled all his thoughts (cf. Appian, Bell. Civ. 2, 61 §252, where Pompey says in sim. fig. language: οἵοις θηρίοις μαχόμεθα; Philo, Mos. 1, 43f).—CRBowen, JBL 42, '23, 59-68; CPCoffin, ibid. 43, '24, 172-6; JWHunkin, ET 39, '28, 281f; RE Osborne, JBL 85, '66, 225-30; AJMalherbe, JBL 87, '68, 71-80. M-M.*

θηρίον, ου, τό (Hom.+; inscr., pap., LXX, En., Ep. Arist., Philo, Joseph.), in form, but not in mng., dim. of θήρ: *(wild) animal, beast*.

1. lit.—**a.** gener. Hb 12: 20. τὰ θ. τῆς γῆς (Gen 1: 24, 25, 30) B 6: 12; cf. vs. 18. W. adj. θ. ἄγρια (X., An. 1, 2, 7) 1 Cl 56: 11 (Job 5: 22).

β. of animals of a particular kind: quadrupeds (Ps.-Clem., Hom. 3, 36) Js 3: 7;—wild animals (Diod. S. 1, 87, 3; Jos., Bell. 3, 385, Ant. 9, 197) Mk 1: 13 (FSpitta, ZNW 5, '04, 323ff; 8, '07, 66ff.—Himerius, Or. 39 [=Or. 5], 5: Orpheus in the Thracian mountains, where he has no one to listen to him θηρίων τὴν ἐκκλησίαν ἐργάζεται= 'forms a community for himself from the wild animals'); so perh. Ac 11: 6 (s. Hs 9, 26, 1 below);—dangerous animals (Antig. Car. 29 [wolf]; Diod. S. 17, 92, 2 and 3 [lion]; Maximus Tyr. 20, 2b; Jos., Ant. 2, 35) Rv 6: 8 (cf. Hdt. 6, 44); IEph 7: 1;—specif. *snake* (Diod. S. 20, 42, 2, alternating with ὄφις; Polyaenus 2, 3, 15 with ἔχις; Aretaeus 159, 8 τὸ διὰ τ. θηρίων φάρμακον; 163, 2; Galen IV 779 K.; θήρ=snake: Simias [III BC], Ov. fgm. 21, 17 ed. HFränkel '15) Ac 28: 4f; Hs 9, 26, 7b; so also ibid. a and prob. 9, 26, 1 w. ἑρπετά (cf. Ac 11: 6; Jos., Ant. 17, 117). Cf. PK 2 p. 14, 18.

γ. oft. of the *wild animals* in fighting w. animals in the arena (Diod. S. 36, 10, 3; Artem. 2, 54; Jos., Bell. 7, 38) IRo 4: 1f; 5: 3; ISm 4: 2a, b; MPol 3f; 11: 1f; Dg 7: 7; Hv 3, 2, 1. εἰς τὰ θηρία κρίνεσθαι *be condemned to fight w. wild animals* MPol 2: 4.

b. of animal-like beings of a supernatural kind (Paus. 1, 24, 6: griffins, 2, 37, 4 the hydra; cf. Da 7: 3ff) B 4: 5 (Da 7: 7). Of a monstrous dragon (schol. on Apollon. Rhod. 4, 156-66a the guardian of the golden fleece; Damascius, Vi. Isid. 140) Hv 4, 1, 6; 8; 10; 4, 2, 1; 3ff; 4, 3, 1; 7. The 'beasts' or 'animals' of Rv: 11: 7; 13: 1ff, 11f, 14f, 17f; 14: 9, 11; 15: 2; 16: 2, 10, 13; 17: 3, 7f, 11ff, 16f; 19: 19f; 20: 4, 10.—Lit. s.v. δράκων. BMurmelstein, StKr 101, '29, 447-57; RSchütz, D. Offb. d. Joh. u. Kaiser Domitian '33; PSMinear, JBL 72, '53, 93-101.

2. fig., persons w. a 'bestial' nature, *beast, monster* (Aristoph., Equ. 273, Plutus 439, Nub. 184; Appian [s. θηριομαχέω, end]; Alciphr. 2, 17, 4 al.; Achilles Tat. 6, 12, 3; Jos., Bell. 1, 624; 627, Ant. 17, 117; 120. Cf. Vett. Val. 78, 9; BGU 1024 IV, 5ff) Tit 1: 12 (Damascius, Vi. Isid. 301 the wife of Isid. is called a κακὸν θ.). θ. ἀνθρωπόμορφα *beasts in human form* (Philo, Ab. 33) ISm 4: 1. M-M. B. 137.**

θησαυρίζω 1 aor. ἐθησαύρισα; pf. pass. ptc. τεθησαυρισμένος (Hdt.+; Dit., Syll.³ 954, 80; LXX; En. 97, 9; Philo) *store up, gather, save*.

1. lit. τὶ *someth.* (Diod. S. 5, 21, 5; 20, 8, 4) ὅ τι ἐὰν εὐοδῶται *in keeping with his gains* 1 Cor 16: 2. τί τινι someth. *for someone* θησαυροὺς ἑαυτῷ *store up treasures for oneself* Mt 6: 19. Abs. (Philod., Oec. p. 71 Jensen; Ps 38: 7) *store up treasure* Js 5: 3. τινί *for someone* Lk 12: 21; 2 Cor 12: 14.

2. fig. (Diod. S. 9, 10, 3 words ἐν ταῖς ψυχαῖς τεθησαυρισμέναι; Philostrat., Vi. Soph. 2, 1, 2 θ. ἐν ταῖς γνώμαις=in the hearts)—**a.** of treasures in heaven (cf. Tob 4: 9; PsSol 9: 5 θ. ζωὴν αὐτῷ παρὰ κυρίῳ) Mt 6: 20.

b. *store up* (plentifully) ὀργὴν ἑαυτῷ *anger for oneself* Ro 2: 5 (cf. Diod. S. 20, 36, 4 φθόνος; Appian, Samn. 4, 3; Vi. Aesopi I c. 107 κακά; Inschr. v. Priene 112, 15 ἐθησαύρισεν ἑαυτῷ παρὰ μὲν τ. ζώντων ἔπαινον, παρὰ δὲ τ. ἐπεσομένων μνήμην; Pr 1: 18 κακά. S. also ὀργή 2b; on θ. ἐν ἡμ. cf. Tob 4: 9).

c. *save up, reserve* (4 Macc 4: 3; Philo, Sacr. Abel. 62, Deus Imm. 156) heaven and earth τεθησαυρισμένοι εἰσίν *are reserved* 2 Pt 3: 7. M-M.*

θησαυρός, οῦ, ὁ (Hes., Hdt.+; inscr., pap., LXX, En., Philo, Joseph.; Test. Ash. 1: 9; Sib. Or. 5, 184; loanw. in rabb.).

1. *the place where someth. is kept*—**a.** lit.—**α.** *treasure box* or *chest* (cf. X., An. 5, 4, 27; Diod. S. 17, 71, 1; PTebt. 6, 27; PAmh. 41, 8; En. 97, 9; Jos., Ant. 9, 163) Mt 2: 11.

β. *storehouse, storeroom* (Appian, fgm. 6; PRyl. 231, 8; PFay. 122, 4; POxy. 101, 29; Am 8: 5; Pr 8: 21) Mt 13: 52 (with ἐκβάλλειν ἐκ τοῦ θησ. cf. Arrian, Cyneg. 34, 1 ἐμβάλλειν ἐς τὸν θησ.).

b. fig. (Test. Ash. 1: 9) of the heart as the treasury for heavenly possessions θ. τῆς καρδίας Lk 6: 45; cf. Mt 12: 35 (on ἀγαθὸς θ. s. Dt 28: 12).

2 *that which is stored up, treasure* Mt 6: 21; Lk 12: 34.—**a.** lit. (Diod. S. 17, 71, 1) Mt 6: 19; 13: 44 (for θ. buried in the ground: Maximus Tyr. 15, 5h; Artem. 2, 58; Philostrat., Vi. Apoll. 6, 39 p. 250, 4ff; JDMDerrett, Law in the NT, '70, 1-16). The treasures of Egypt Hb 11: 26.

b. fig. (on θησ. that is dug up in fig. sense cf. Philemo Com. 169 K. ἐὰν γυνὴ γυναικὶ κατ' ἰδίαν ὁμιλεῖ, μεγάλων κακῶν θησαυρὸς ἐξορύσσεται. Fig. use also bγ, end)—**a.** of the treasures in heaven Mt 6: 20. θ. ἀνέκλειπτος ἐν τ. οὐρανοῖς Lk 12: 33. θησαυρὸν ἔχειν ἐν οὐρανῷ *have treasure in heaven* which is, as it were, deposited there and becomes available to men after death Mt 19: 21; Mk 10: 21; Lk 18: 22.—WPesch, Biblica 41, '60, 356-78 (Mt 6: 19-21; Lk 12: 33f).

β. θησαυροὶ σκοτεινοί *treasures lying in darkness* B 11: 4 (Is 45: 3).

γ. of the gospel and its glory 2 Cor 4: 7. Of Christ: ἐν ᾧ εἰσιν πάντες οἱ θησαυροὶ τῆς σοφίας καὶ γνώσεως ἀπόκρυφοι *in whom all the treasures of wisdom and knowledge lie hidden* Col 2: 3 (ἐν θησαυροῖς σοφίας Sir 1: 25; cf. X., Mem. 1, 6, 14; 4, 2, 9 θησαυροὶ σοφίας; Pla., Phileb. 15E; Diod. S. 9, 10, 3 κάλλιστος θησ.; Himerius, Or. [Ecl.] 3, 20 θησ. ἀθάνατος of the possession of virtue; Pr 2: 3ff; Philo, Congr. Erud. Gr. 127). M-M. B. 777.*

θιγγάνω 2 aor. ἔθιγον (trag.+—though not in Attic prose [WGRutherford, New Phryn. 1881, 169f; 391]; Hippocr. [Anz 293]; inscr., pap.; Ex 19: 12) *touch* τινός someth. (Aeschyl.+; Ep. Arist. 106) Hb 12: 20 (cf. Dio Chrys. 31, 10). In a hostile sense τινός *someone* (Eur., Iph. A. 1351; Act. Thom. 12 p. 118, 5 B. παῖδες, ὧν αἱ βλάβαι αὐται θιγγάνουσι) Hb 11: 28. Abs. Col 2: 21 (IG XII 3, 451 μὴ θίγγανε; but cf. ἅπτω 2a. M-M.*

θλάω pf. τέθλακα (Hom.+; PFay. 112, 20 [99 AD]; Jos., Ant. 10, 7=4 Km 18: 21) *break* a seal (which in this case is not a natural, purposeful act, but one greatly to be regretted, since the seal appears as a means of protection, whose destruction is followed by dire consequences) Hs 8, 6, 3.*

θλίβω pf. pass. ptc. τεθλιμμένος; 2 aor. pass. ἐθλίβην (Hom.+; inscr., pap., LXX, Philo; Jos., Bell. 3, 330, Ant. 20, 111; Test. 12 Patr., Sib. Or.).
1. *press upon, crowd* τινά someone (Sir 16: 28 v.l.) Mk 3: 9 (cf. Appian, Bell. Civ. 4, 45, §194 ἐπιθλίβω τινά= 'crowd around someone').
2. *press together, compress, make narrow.* Pass.—**a.** *be jammed full* (Theocr. 21, 18 θλιβομένα καλύβη; Lucian, Alex. 49 τ. πόλεως θλιβομένης ὑπὸ τ. πλήθους) τόπος τεθλιμμένος *a place jammed full* AP 10: 25.
b. *become restricted, narrow* (Dionys. Hal. 8, 73 βίοι τεθλιμμένοι, provisions that have become scarce) of a road (w. a corresp. στενὴ πύλη) ὁδὸς τεθλιμμένη *a narrow, confined road* Mt 7: 14 (cf. KBornhäuser, Die Bergpredigt '23, 177ff).
3. *oppress, afflict* τινά someone (Dt 28: 53; Lev 19: 33; Sib. Or. 3, 630) 2 Th 1: 6. τὸ πνεῦμα τὸ ἅγιον *oppress the Holy Spirit* Hm 10, 2, 5; χρεώστας θ. *oppress debtors* m 8: 10.—Pass. *be afflicted, distressed* (UPZ 42, 22 [162 BC]) 2 Cor 1: 6; 4: 8; 7: 5; Hb 11: 37; Hm 2: 5. θλιβεὶς *by suffering* B 7: 11. θλιβεὶς τῇ γνώμῃ τινός *distressed by someone's scheming* IPhld 6: 2. ψυχὴ θλιβομένη *distressed soul* Hs 1: 8 (PGM 1, 213 θλίβεταί [?]μου ἡ ψυχή; Proclus on Pla., Crat. p. 72, 3 Pasqu. δαίμονες θλίβουσι τ. ψυχάς; Nicetas Eugen. 2, 27 H. ψυχὴ τεθλιμμένη; cf. Philo, De Jos. 179). Cf. Hs 8, 10, 4.—Subst. ὁ θλιβόμενος *the oppressed (one)* (Diod. S. 13, 109, 5 οἱ θλιβόμενοι ='those who were hard pressed') 1 Ti 5: 10; ISm 6: 2; B 20: 2; D 5: 2. Esp., as in some of the aforementioned pass., of the persecution of Christians 1 Th 3: 4; 2 Th 1: 7. θλιβῆναι πάσῃ θλίψει *suffer every kind of affliction* Hs 6, 3, 6; cf. 7: 1ff; 8, 10, 4. ὑπὲρ τοῦ νόμου θλιβέντες *persecuted for the law* (i.e., for the Christian faith) 8, 3, 7. M-M.*

θλίψις, εως, ἡ (on the accent s. Bl-D. §13; Mlt.-H. 57.—KHALipsius, Grammat. Untersuchungen über d. bibl. Gräz. 1863, 34f prefers to write θλῖψις; so also W-H.) rare in extra-Biblical Gk., and there lit., *pressing, pressure* (Strabo, Galen). Freq. in the LXX and our lit., in the fig. sense *oppression, affliction, tribulation* (so Vett. Val. 71, 16; Cat. Cod. Astr. VIII 3 p. 175, 5; 178, 8; pl. 169, 2 [cf. Boll 134f]; Dit., Or. 444, 15 [II or I BC] διὰ τὰς τ. πόλεων θλίψεις; BGU 1139, 4 [I BC]; POxy. 939, 13; PAmh. 144, 18).
1. of distress that is brought about by outward circumstances (Jos., Ant. 4, 108), in sg. and pl. Ac 11: 19; Ro 5: 3b; 12: 12; 2 Cor 1: 8; 6: 4; 8: 2; Rv 1: 9; 2, 9, 22; 1 Cl 22: 7 (Ps 33: 18); 59: 4; 2 Cl 11: 4 (quot. of unknown orig.); Hs 7: 4ff. ἐπὶ πάσῃ τῇ θ. ἡμῶν 2 Cor 1: 4a; 7: 4; 1 Th 3: 7; ἐν πάσῃ θ. (Test. Gad 4: 4) 2 Cor 1: 4b; ἐν (τ.) θ. Ro 5: 3a; Eph 3: 13; 1 Th 1: 6; 3: 3. θ. μεγάλη *great tribulation* (Sib. Or. 3, 186) Mt 24: 21 (1 Macc 9: 27); Ac 7: 11; Hv 4, 2, 4. Pl. Hv 3, 2, 1. ἡ θ. ἡ μεγάλη *the great tribulation* Rv 7: 14; τὸ ἐλαφρὸν τῆς θ. *slight affliction* 2 Cor 4: 17. ἀνταποδοῦναί τινι θλῖψιν *repay someone w. affliction* 2 Th 1: 6. W. ἀνάγκη (q.v. 2) 1 Th 3: 7. W. διωγμός Mt 13: 21; Mk 4: 17; Ac 8: 1 D; 13: 50 D; pl. 2 Th 1: 4. W. δεσμά (Test. Jos. 2: 4) Ac 20: 23. W. ὀνειδισμός Hb 10: 33. W. στενοχωρία (q.v.) Ro 2: 9. W. στενοχωρία and διωγμός 8: 35. ἡμέρα θλίψεως *day of affliction* (Gen 35: 3; 2 Km 22: 19; cf. En. 103, 9; Test. Levi 5: 5) 1 Cl 52: 3 (Ps 49: 15).—Of the tribulations of the last days (as Da 12:

1) Mt 24: 21, 29; Mk 13: 19, 24. ἡ θ. ἡ ἐρχομένη ἡ μεγάλη *the great tribulation to come* Hv 2, 2, 7; cf. 2, 3, 4; 4, 1, 1; 4, 2, 5; 4, 3, 6.—Distress caused by war 1 Cl 57: 4 (Pr 1: 27). θ. θανάτου *affliction of death* B 12: 5. *Difficult circumstances* 2 Cor 8: 13; Js 1: 27; συνκοινωνεῖν τῇ θ. *show an interest in (someone's) distress* Phil 4: 14. Of a woman's birth-pangs J 16: 21.—ὅταν γένηται θ. *when persecution comes* Hv 3, 6, 5. θλῖψιν ἀκούειν *hear of persecution* Hs 9, 21, 3. θλῖψιν ἔχειν J 16: 33; 1 Cor 7: 28; Rv 2: 10; Hv 2, 3, 1. ἐὰν ὑπενέγκῃ τὰς θλίψεις τὰς ἐπερχομένας αὐτῷ Hs 7: 4. ἐξείλατο αὐτὸν ἐκ πασῶν τῶν θλίψεων αὐτοῦ Ac 7: 10. διὰ πολλῶν θ. εἰσελθεῖν εἰς τ. βασιλείαν 14: 22. τότε παραδώσουσιν ὑμᾶς εἰς θλῖψιν Mt 24: 9; cf. B 12: 5.—Of the sufferings of Christ θλίψεις τοῦ Χριστοῦ Col 1: 24 (s. on ἀνταναπληρόω and πάθημα 1).
2. fig., of mental and spiritual states of mind, *affliction* in the spiritual sense, *trouble* θ. καὶ συνοχὴ καρδίας *trouble and anguish of heart* 2 Cor 2: 4. θλῖψιν ἐγείρειν τοῖς δεσμοῖς μου *cause trouble for me in my imprisonment* Phil 1: 17.—HSchlier, TW III '36, 139-48. M-M.**

θνῄσκω (Hom.+; M. Ant. 10, 18; inscr., pap., Philo, Joseph. [Schmidt 482]. On the spelling cf. Kühner-Bl. I 133; II 442; Bl-D. §26 app.; 27 app.; Mlt.-H. 84) pf. τέθνηκα, inf. τεθνηκέναι (Ac 14: 19 τεθνάναι t.r. as Jos., Vi. 59); plpf. (3 sg. ἐτεθνήκει J 11: 21 t.r.) 2 pl. τεθνήκειτε Hs 9, 28, 6: *die, be dead.*
1. lit. Mt 2: 20; Mk 15: 44; Lk 8: 49; J 19: 33; Ac 14: 19; 25: 19. Subst. perf. ptc. (ὁ) τεθνηκώς *the man who had died* (class.; LXX) Lk 7: 12; J 11: 44.
2. fig. (w. ζῆν: Charito 7, 5, 4) of spiritual death (Ael. Aristid. 52, 2 K.=28 p. 551 D.: τὸ τεθνηκὸς τῆς ψυχῆς; Bar 3: 4; Philo, Fug. 55 ζῶντες ἔνιοι τεθνήκασι καὶ τεθνηκότες ζῶσι) ζῶσα τεθνήκειν *have died, but she is dead though she is still alive* 1 Ti 5: 6. (Timocles Com. [IV BC] 35 οὗτος μετὰ ζώντων τεθνηκώς) οὔτε ζῶσιν οὔτε τεθνήκασιν Hs 8, 7, 1; 9, 21, 2; 4. διὰ τὰς ἁμαρτίας ὑμῶν τεθνήκειτε [ἂν] τῷ θεῷ *because of your sins you would have died to God* s 9, 28, 6.*

θνητός, ή, όν (Hom.+; Dit., Syll.³ 798, 10; LXX; Sib. Or. 3, 236) *mortal* opp. ἀθάνατος (Dio Chrys. 20[37], 30; Plut., Mor. 960B; Herm. Wr. 1, 15; Philo, Rer. Div. Her. 265; Jos., Ant. 11, 56) D 4: 8; Dg 6: 8. σάρξ (Heraclit. Sto. 74, 1) 2 Cor 4: 11. σῶμα (Hyperid. 6, 24; Philo, Mut. Nom. 36; Jos., Bell. 7, 344) Ro 6: 12; 8: 11. θ. ἐπίνοια Dg 7: 1. ὁ θ. *the mortal=man* (Empedocles: Vorsokrat. 31 B 112 ὁ θν.='man' in contrast to θεός; Job 30: 23; Pr 3: 13; 20: 24; Philo, Praem. 87) 1 Cl 39: 2; οἱ θ. *mortals* (Hom.+; Sb 4456, 4; 5829, 14; Wsd 9: 14) Dg 9: 2 (opp. ὁ ἀθάνατος). τὸ θ. (oft. Philo) 1 Cor 15: 53f (opp. ἀθανασία as Philo, Aet. M. 46); 2 Cor 5: 4 (opp. ἡ ζωή). M-M.*

θορυβάζω pres. pass. 2 sg. θορυβάζῃ (Dositheus 71, 16; En. 14, 8; Etym. Mag. p. 633, 34; also Euseb. of Alex. [Migne, Patrol., Ser. Gr. LXXXVI 1 p. 444c]) *cause trouble.* Pass. *be troubled* or *distracted* περί τι *by* or *about* someth. of a busy housewife Lk 10: 41 (v.l. τυρβάζῃ, q.v.).*

θορυβέω impf. ἐθορύβουν, pass. ἐθορυβούμην (Soph., Hdt.+; inscr., pap., LXX, Joseph.).
1. act. *throw into disorder* w. acc. (cf. Wsd 18: 19; Jos., Vi. 401, Ant. 18, 65) πόλιν *set the city in an uproar* Ac 17: 5. καρδίαν 21: 13 D (but here θορ. may also be used abs.).
2. pass. *be troubled, distressed, aroused* (Charito 5, 8, 3; Appian, Bell. Civ. 1, 25 §110; Polyaenus 8, 23, 19; Jos., Ant. 17, 251) GP 5: 15. μὴ θορυβεῖσθε Mk 13: 7 D; Ac 20:

10 (PTebt. 411, 12 μηδὲν μέντοι θορυβηθῇς). τί θορυ-βεῖσθε; Mk 5: 39. Of an ὄχλος: θορυβούμενος aroused, in disorder Mt 9: 23 (Appian, Bell. Civ. 5, 10 §42 ἡ χώρα θορυβουμένη). M-M.*

θόρυβος, ου, ὁ (Pind., Hdt.+; Dit., Or. 48, 9; Inschr. v. Magn. 114, 3; pap., LXX, Philo, Joseph.; loanw. in rabb.).
1. noise, clamor Ac 21: 34; MPol 8: 3. θ. μέγας (Jos., Ant. 17, 184) Hs 9, 3, 1; MPol 9: 1.—2. confusion, unrest 1 Cl 57: 4 (Pr 1: 27).
3. turmoil, excitement, uproar (X., An. 3, 4, 35; Appian, Bell. Civ. 2, 118, §494)—a. of the milling about of a throng in a house of mourning Mk 5: 38 (though mngs. 1 and 2 are also poss.).
b. of the noise and confusion of excited crowds (Philo, In Flacc. 120; Jos., Bell. 1, 201; 2, 611) Mk 14: 2; Ac 20: 1; γίνεται θ. (cf. PTebt. 15, 3 [114 BC] θορύβου γενομένου ἐν τῇ κώμῃ) Mt 26: 5; 27: 24. μετὰ θορύβου (cf. Polyaenus 6, 41, 1; Ezk 7: 11; Jos., Ant. 5, 216) with a disturbance Ac 24: 18. M-M.*

θράσος, ους, τό (Hom.+; LXX, Ep. Arist., Philo; Jos., Ant. 16, 66, Vi. 120) boldness, arrogance, shamelessness 1 Cl 30: 8. οὐ δώσεις τῇ ψυχῇ σου θράσος you must not give (=admit) arrogance to your soul, you must not become arrogant B 19: 3; D 3: 9 (cf. Diod. S. 5, 29, 3 τὸ θράσος τῆς ψυχῆς).—JWackernagel, Hellenistica, '07, 15f.*

θρασύτης, ητος, ἡ (Thu.+) boldness, arrogance (Dio Chrys. 48[65], 5; Sb 6026, 1 [III AD]; Philo, Spec. Leg. 3, 175 al.) B 20: 1; D 5: 1.*

θραυματίζω break Lk 4: 18 D; s. θραύω 2b.*

θραύω pf. pass. ptc. τεθραυσμένος; 1 aor. pass. ἐθραύσ-θην (Pind., Hdt.+; Vett. Val., inscr., pap., LXX) break in pieces.
1. lit. (Diod. S. 20, 93, 2; Dit., Syll.² 588, 27 [II BC]; Epigr. Gr. 1003; Jos., Ant. 8, 390) Mk 14: 3 v.l. Of pottery Hm 11: 13.
2. fig. (Maximus Tyr. 14, 6e; Cat. Cod. Astr. VIII p. 147, 12; Jos., Bell. 1, 323).
a. of an oath break Dg 11: 5.—b. break, weaken, oppress (Orph. Hymns 87, 3 ψυχήν; Plut., Anton. 17, 4 θραυόμενος τὸν λογισμόν; M. Ant. 4, 49, 2) Hv 3, 11, 3. τεθραυσμένοι the downtrodden Lk 4: 18; B 3: 3 (both Is 58: 6). M-M.*

θρέμμα, ατος, τό (trag.+) (domesticated) animal, esp. a sheep or goat (X., Oec. 20, 23 al.; Dit., Syll.³ 636, 26; 826G, 20; Dit., Or. 200, 11; 629, 175; POxy. 246, 16; BGU 759, 11; PAmh. 134, 5; Test. Gad 1: 6; Philo; Jos., Ant. 7, 148) J 4: 12 (Timaeus Hist. [IV/III BC]: no. 566 fgm. 56a Jac. αὐτοὶ καὶ τὰ θρέμματα αὐτῶν). M-M.*

θρηνέω impf. ἐθρήνουν; fut. θρηνήσω; 1 aor. ἐθρήνησα (Hom.+; LXX).
1. intr.—a. mourn, lament (w. κλαίειν; cf. Jo 1: 5) J 16: 20.—b. esp. sing a dirge (LXX) Mt 11: 17; Lk 7: 32.
2. trans. mourn for, lament τινά someone (Herodian 3, 4, 6; Nicetas Eugen. 7, 182 H.; LXX; Philo, Leg. All. 3, 231; Jos., Bell. 3, 436) Lk 23: 27 (w. κόπτεσθαι as Xenophanes, fgm. 13 Diels; Mi 1: 8; Jos., Ant. 6, 377). M-M.*

θρῆνος, ου, ὁ (Hom.+; pap., LXX; Philo, Ebr. 95; Jos., Ant. 7, 42) dirge Mt 2: 18 CD (Jer 38: 15).*

θρησκεία, as, ἡ (Hdt.+; inscr., pap., LXX, Philo, Jo-seph.) the worship of God, religion, esp. as it expresses itself in religious service or cult; the Being who is wor-shipped is given in the obj. gen. (Aelian, N.A. 10, 28 τοῦ Σαράπιδος; Herodian 4, 8, 7 τοῦ θεοῦ; Delph. inscr. in Dit., Syll.³ 801D, 4 τοῦ Ἀπόλλωνος; Wsd 14: 27 τ. εἰδώλων; Philo, Spec. Leg. 1, 315 τῶν θεῶν; Jos., Ant. 1, 222; 12, 271 τοῦ θεοῦ) θρησκεύειν τὴν θρησκείαν τοῦ ὑψίστου 1 Cl 45: 7. θ. τῶν ἀγγέλων Col 2: 18 (MDi-belius, Hdb. exc. 2: 23 [lit.; also ALWilliams, JTS 10, '09, 413–38].—Ramsay, Phryg. I 2 p. 541 no. 404 and p. 741 no. 678 testify to the worship of angels in Phrygia. The Council of Laodicea, Can. 35 rejects it. Theodoret on Col 2: 16 ed. Hal. III 490 deplores its tenacious survival in Phrygia and Pisidia). Of Judaism ἡμετέρα θ. our religion Ac 26: 5 (cf. 4 Macc 5: 7 and Jos., Ant. 12, 253 Ἰουδαίων [subj. gen] θ.; Ps.-Clem., Hom. 5, 27). Of Christianity τὰ ἀνήκοντα τῇ θ. ἡμῶν the things that befit our religion 1 Cl 62: 1. τὴν θ. προσάγειν θεῷ offer service to God Dg 3: 2. Js contrasts the μάταιος θ. 1: 26 w. vs. 27, the θ. καθαρὰ καὶ ἀμίαντος παρὰ τ. θεῷ, which consists in good deeds (Herm. Wr. 12, 23 θρησκεία τ. θεοῦ μία ἐστί, μὴ εἶναι κακόν).—S. on εὐλαβέομαι and KLSchmidt, TW III '36, 155–9. M-M. B. 1463.*

θρησκεύω (Hdt.+; Dit., Syll.³ 783, 42f [27 BC] τοὺς θεοὺς ἐθρήσκευσεν εὐσεβῶς; Sb 991, 7 [III AD]; Herm. Wr. 12, 23 τοῦτον τὸν λόγον, ὦ τέκνον, προσκύνει καὶ θρή-σκευε; Wsd 11: 15; 14: 17) practice religious observances, worship w. the acc. of that which is worshipped or served (Dionys. Hal. 2, 23, 1 τοὺς θεούς; Celsus 8, 66; Dit., Syll. [s. above]; Herm. Wr. [s. above]; Wsd 11: 15; Jos., Ant. 8, 248; 9, 289; Sib. Or. 5, 77) πῶς θρησκεύουσι αὐτόν (i.e. τ. θεόν) how you worship him Dg 1. τινά τινι serve or worship someone by means of someth. 2: 8; θ. θρησκείαν practice religion 1 Cl 45: 7.*

θρησκός, όν (Hesychius; Etym. Mag. p. 455, 9) religious Js 1: 26.*

θριαμβεύω 1 aor. ἐθριάμβευσα (Ctesias; Polyb.; Dio-nys. Hal.; Epict. 3, 24, 85 al.; not a Lat. loanw.—s. Bl-D. §5, 1 app. and L-S-J s.v. θρίαμβος II).
1. lead in a triumphal procession τινά someone as a captive (Plut., Rom. 33, 4, Pomp. 83, 3, Arat. 54, 8; Appian, Mithrid. 77 §338; 103 §482; cf. Theophyl. Sim., Ep. 68), hence gener. triumph over θριαμβεύσας αὐτοὺς ἐν αὐτῷ through him (Christ) he (God) has triumphed over them (the hostile supernatural powers) Col 2: 15. Many scholars (Heinrici, Bousset, Bachmann, Schlatter, Kümmel, RSV ad loc.) find the same mng. in 2 Cor 2: 14 τῷ θεῷ χάρις τῷ πάντοτε θριαμβεύοντι ἡμᾶς ἐν τ. Χριστῷ, which they render about as follows: thanks be to God, who always leads us in triumph with him in Christ. Others prefer the sense
2. cause to triumph (Ctesias, Pers. 13 θριαμβεύσας τὸν μάγον=after he had procured a triumph for the μάγος [but LWilliamson, Jr., Interpretation 22, '68, 317–32, renders θρ. 'hold up to ridicule'].—So Klöpper, Schmie-del, Belser, GGodet, Sickenberger ad loc.; sim. Weiz-säcker), or
3. simply lead or exhibit in a public procession (Ctesias, Pers. 58, of the head and right hand of a slain enemy.—Cf. Ltzm., Hdb. ad loc.). Windisch leaves the choice open betw. 2 and 3.—Field, Notes 181f; RMPope, ET 21, '10, 19–21; 112–14; ABKinsey, ibid. 282f; FPrat, Rech de Sc rel 3, '12, 201–29. M-M.*

θρίξ, τριχός, ἡ (Hom.+; inscr., pap., LXX, Philo, Jo-seph., Test. 12 Patr.) hair.

1. of the hair of animals τρίχες καμήλου *camel's hair*: ἔνδυμα ἀπὸ τρ. κ. *a garment of camel's hair* Mt 3: 4. So Mk 1: 6 says of John the Baptist that he was ἐνδεδυμένος τρίχας κ. *dressed in camel's hair*, somewhat as we say: 'in wool'.—Of apocalyptic animals w. long hair Rv 9: 8 (JEMichl, BZ 23, '35, 266-88; Biblica 23, '42, 192f).

2. of human hair (Jos., Ant. 15, 86, C. Ap. 1, 282) white, black hair Mt 5: 36; cf. Rv 1: 14. τρίχες πρεσβύτεραι *belonging to an older person*, i.e. gray Hv 3, 10, 4f; 3, 12, 1. τρ. λευκαί ν 4, 2, 1. Coming out easily (ἐκ or ἀπὸ τ. κεφαλῆς) Lk 21: 18; Ac 27: 34 (cf. 1 Km 14: 45). αἱ τρίχες τῆς κεφαλῆς πᾶσαι *all the hairs of the head* Mt 10: 30; Lk 12: 7 (Alcaeus 80, 10 D.² παρὰ μοῖραν Διὸς οὐδὲ τρίχες [here the text breaks off]='against the will of Zeus not even the hairs are' . . .—The hair as someth. quite worthless: Paroem. Gr. Zenob. [time of Hadrian] 2, 4 ἡ θρὶξ οὐδενὸς ἀξία); cf. 7: 38 (αἱ τρ. τῆς κεφαλῆς as Jdth 10: 3; Ps 39: 13; Philo, Leg. ad Gai. 223), 44; J 11: 2; 12: 3. ἐμπλοκὴ τριχῶν *braiding the hair* 1 Pt 3: 3. τρίχας λελυμένη *with the hair loose* Hs 9, 9, 5; cf. 9, 13, 8. λαμβάνειν τινὰ ἐν μιᾷ τῶν τρ. αὐτοῦ *take someone by one of his hairs* GH 5. τρίχες ὀρθαί *hair standing on end* (Il. 24, 359; Lucian, Philops. 22) Hv 3, 1, 5. M-M.*

θροέω 1 aor. pass. ptc. θροηθείς (trag.+, in act. and mid. w. the mng.: 'cry out, tell out, speak, announce', etc.—The act.: Jos., Ant. 18, 234; 19, 137) in the NT only pass. in the sense *be inwardly aroused* (cf. Tetrast. Iamb. 2, 1, 4 p. 286; Malalas 41, 12 LDind. [1831]; SSol 5: 4), *be disturbed* or *frightened* 2 Th 2: 2. μὴ θροεῖσθε Mt 24: 6; Mk 13: 7. θροηθέντες καὶ ἔμφοβοι γενόμενοι Lk 24: 37 𝔓⁷⁵ B 1241.*

θρόμβος, ου, ὁ (trag., Hdt.+) *drop* θ. αἵματος (Aeschyl., Choëph. 533; 546; Pla., Critias p. 120A; medical wr. [Hobart 82f]) *small amount of* (flowing) *blood, clot of blood* Lk 22: 44.—WSurbled-Sleumer, D. Moral in ihren Beziehungen z. Medizin u. Hygiene II² '19, 183ff. M-M.*

θρόνος, ου, ὁ (Hom.+; inscr., pap., LXX, En.; Jos., Ant. 7, 353; 8, 399; Test. Levi; loanw. in rabb.).

1. throne—**a.** of human kings and rulers (Hdt. 1, 14; X., Cyr. 6, 1, 6; Herodian 1, 8, 4) καθελεῖν ἀπὸ θρόνων *dethrone* Lk 1: 52. The throne of David (2 Km 3: 10), the ancestor of the Messiah 1: 32; Ac 2: 30.

2. of God (Soph., Ant. 1041; inscr. of Antiochus of Commagene [Dit., Or. 383] 42 πρὸς οὐρανίους Διὸς θρόνους; Ps 46: 9; Ezek. Trag. in Euseb., Pr. Ev. 9, 29, 5) Hb 12: 2; Rv 7: 15; 12: 5; 22: 1, 3; cf. 1: 4; 3: 21b; 4: 2ff, 9; 5: 1, 6f, 11, 13 al.—ὁ θρόνος τ. χάριτος Hb 4: 16; τ. μεγαλωσύνης 8: 1.—Of heaven as the throne of God (after Is 66: 1) Mt 5: 34; 23: 22; Ac 7: 49; B 16: 2 (the two last pass. are direct quot. of Is 66: 1.—Cf. Theosophien 56, 33f. For heaven as the throne of Zeus s. Orpheus: Hymn. 62, 2f Q. and Demosth. 25, 11).

c. of Christ, who occupies the throne of his ancestor David (s. a above). It is a θ. δόξης αὐτοῦ Mt 19: 28a; 25: 31; an eternal throne Hb 1: 8 (Ps 44: 7), which stands at the right hand of the Father's throne Pol 2: 1 or is even identical w. it Rv 22: 1, 3; cf. 3: 21b. His own are to share this throne w. him vs. 21a.

d. of the thrones of the 12 apostles as judges (Philochorus [IV/III bc]: no. 328 fgm. 64bβ the νομοφύλακες...ἐπὶ θρόνων ἐκάθηντο; Plut., Mor. 807b; Paus. 2, 31, 3; Ps 121: 5; Jos., Ant. 18, 107) or rulers in the time of the final consummation Mt 19: 28b (Galen X 406 K. Θέσσαλος ἅμα τοῖς ἑαυτοῦ σοφισταῖς ἐφ' ὑψηλοῦ θρόνου καθήμενος); Lk 22: 30; cf. Rv 20: 4.

e. of the thrones of the 24 elders of Rv 4: 4; 11: 16.—Rv

also mentions thrones of infernal powers; the throne of the dragon, which the beast receives 13: 2; cf. 16: 10.—ὁ θ. τοῦ Σατανᾶ 2: 13 in the letter to Pergamum is freq. (e.g. Dssm., LO 240, 8 [LAE 280, 2]; Lohmeyer ad loc.; Boll 112, 4) taken to be the famous Altar of Zeus there (cf. En. 25, 3 the mountain whose peak is like a throne); others (Zahn; JWeiss, RE X 551; cf. Hadorn) prefer to think of the temple of Asclepius, and Bousset of Perg. as the center of the emperor-cult.—ThBirt, D. Thron d. Satans: Philol. Wochenschr. 52, '32, 259-66.

2. fig.—**a.** *dominion, sovereignty* (a mng. perh. poss. in some aforementioned pass.) θ. αἰώνιος of Jesus Christ 1 Cl 65: 2; MPol 21.

b. name of a class of supernatural beings (Test. Levi 3: 8. Cf. the astrol. PMich. 149 XVI, 23; 24 [II AD].—Kephal. I 117, 24-26, personification of the one who sits on the throne, the judge) Col 1: 16.—OSchmitz, TW III '36, 160-7. M-M. B. 481.*

θρύπτω (Pla. et al.; POxy. 471, 80 [II AD]; Ps 57: 8 Sym.; Philo; Jos., Bell. 4, 563) *break in* (*small*) *pieces* θρυπτόμενον as a supplement to τὸ σῶμα τὸ ὑπὲρ ὑμῶν 1 Cor 11: 24 in D (cf. Dio Chrys. 60+61[77+78], 41; Soranus p. 34, 10 θρυπτόμενον τὸ σῶμα; Nicander, Ther. 108 ἂν σάρκες θρύπτωνται; Galen: CMG V 4, 2 p. 148, 23 θρύμμα ἄρτου; Diod. S. 1, 83, 3 καταθρύπτοντες τοὺς ἄρτους).*

Θυάτιρα (-ειρα W-H.), ων, τά (Polyb. 16, 1, 7; 32, 27, 10; Strabo 13, 4, 4; Ptolem. 5, 2, 14; Appian, Syr. 30 §150; inscr. On the acc. in -αν Rv 1: 11 v.l., s. Bl-D. §57 w. app.; Mlt.-H. 128) *Thyatira* a city in Lydia in Asia Minor, on the Lycus R. betw. Pergamum and Sardis, founded by Macedonian Greeks (s. Strabo loc. cit.; Dit., Or. 211 w. note 2). Its busy industrial life included notably the dyeing of purple cloth. There was in Th. a guild of dyers (βαφεῖς), the existence of which is attested by numerous inscr. (CIG 3496-8; other inscr. in WHBuckler, Monuments de Thyatire: Rev. de philol. 37, '13, 289-331. Also the inscr. which the guild of purple-dyers in Thessalonica dedicated to a certain Menippus of Thyatira: LDuchesne et ChBayet, Mission au Mont Athos 1876, p. 52 no. 83). Ac 16: 14; Rv 1: 11; 2: 18, 24.—EZiebarth, RhM 51, 1896, 632ff; AWikenhauser, Die Ap-Gesch. '21, 410f (lit.). M-M.*

θυγάτηρ, τρός, ἡ (Hom.+; inscr., pap., LXX, Ep. Arist., Philo; Jos., C. Ap. 1, 96 al.; Test. 12 Patr.) voc. θύγατερ, for which the nom. without the art. is also used (Lk 8: 48; J 12: 15; W-S. §29, 4; Mlt.-H. 136); pl. θυγατέρες etc.; *daughter*.

1. lit. Mt 10: 35, 37; Lk 8: 42; 12: 53. Foll. by gen. of the father or mother Mt 9: 18; 14: 6; 15: 22, 28; Mk 5: 35; 6: 22; 7: 26, 29; Lk 2: 36; 8: 49; Ac 2: 17 (Jo 3: 1); 7: 21; Hb 11: 24; B 19: 5; D 4: 9; cf. Ac 21: 9.

2. fig. (Epict. 4, 11, 35; Paus. 8, 20, 3; Paradoxogr. Vat. 60 Keller; Phalaris, Ep. 142, 3 θ.=girl)—**a.** voc. in a friendly greeting to girls or women Mt 9: 22; Mk 5: 34; Lk 8: 48.

b. to denote a more general relationship—**α.** among persons θυγατέρες Ἀαρών *the female descendants of Aaron*, i.e., the women of priestly families Lk 1: 5. θ. Ἀβραάμ 13: 16 (cf. 4 Macc 15: 28). Of the women who are readers of B, and are therefore his pupils B 1: 1.

β. fig. (Procop. Soph., Ep. 93 the letters are θυγατέρες of their writers) of doubt θ. ἐστὶ τοῦ διαβόλου *the devil's daughter* Hm 9: 9; cf. 12, 2, 2 (Pind., Olymp. 10, 5 ἀλάθεια as θυγάτηρ Διός). Of virtues, one of which is the daughter of the other in turn Hv 3, 8, 4f.

c. of the daughters of God as his children in the spiritual sense 2 Cor 6: 18 (cf. Is 43: 6; Wsd 9: 7).

d. θυγατέρες Ἰερουσαλήμ Lk 23: 28 is an OT expr. to designate the individual female inhabitants of the city (cf. SSol 2: 7; 3: 5; Is 3: 16; 4: 4). But the situation is different

e. w. the sing. θυγάτηρ Σιών which—also in OT fashion (cf. Zech 2: 14; 9: 9; Jer 4: 31 al.—Sib. Or. 3, 324 θυγατέρες δυσμῶν=peoples of the west)—denotes the city of Zion and its inhabitants Mt 21: 5; J 12: 15 (both Is 62: 11). M-M. B. 106.*

θυγάτριον, ου, τό (Strattis Com. [c. 400 bc], fgm. 63 Kock; Menand., fgm. 428 K.; Machon in Athen. 13 p. 581 c; Plut., Mor. 179e; Epict. 1, 11, 4; Dio Chrys. 10[11], 54; Dit., Syll.³ 364, 55; PPetr. III 53 r, 3; PLond. 24, 6; Jos., Ant. 19, 200.—WSchmid, D. Attizismus IV 1897, 305) dim. of θυγάτηρ little daughter (though the word can denote one who is marriageable: Lucian, Tox. 22), also a term of endearment Mk 5: 23; 7: 25. M-M.*

θύελλα, ης, ἡ (Hom.+; Ps.-Aristot., De Mundo 4 p. 395a, 6: θύελλα πνεῦμα βίαιον κ. ἄφνω προσαλλόμενον; Jos., Bell. 2, 396; 3, 368; Sib. Or. 4, 115) storm, whirlwind Hb 12: 18 (cf. Dt 4: 11; 5: 22).*

θύϊνος, η, ον (Strabo 4, 6, 2 al., perh. also PLond. 928, 20) from the citron tree ξύλον citron wood (Diosc. 1, 21; 3 Km 10: 11 Sym.) Rv 18: 12. M-M.*

θῦμα, ατος, τό (trag., Thu.+; Dit., Or. 332, 40 [II bc] al. inscr.; Wilcken, Chrest. I 111, 3 [III bc]; oft. LXX) sacrifice, offering PK 2 p. 14, 20.*

θυμίαμα, ατος, τό (Soph., Hdt.+; inscr., pap., LXX, Philo, Joseph.; Test. Levi 8: 10).
1. incense—a. sing. (Hdt. 1, 198; PTebt. 112, 22 [112 bc]; Jos., Ant. 3, 197) B 2: 5 (Is 1: 13). More often—b. in the pl. (Soph., Oed. R. 4; Hdt. 2, 86; Pla., Rep. 2 p. 373a; Dit., Syll.³ 999, 15f; LXX, Philo; Jos., Ant. 4, 32) Rv 5: 8; 8: 3f; 18: 13.
2. incense burning, incense offering (LXX) τὸ θυσιαστήριον τοῦ θ. the altar of incense (Ex 30: 1, 27; 2 Macc 2: 5) Lk 1: 11; ἡ ὥρα τοῦ θ. the hour of the incense offering vs. 10. M-M.*

θυμιατήριον, ου, τό (Hdt., Thu.+; inscr., pap., LXX) properly a place or vessel for the burning of incense (Kühner-Bl. II p. 281, 5), usu. a censer. However Hb 9: 4 altar of incense (as Hdt. 4, 162; Aelian, V.H. 12, 51; esp. of the altar of incense in the Jewish temple: Philo, Rer. Div. Her. 226, Mos. 2, 94; Jos., Bell. 5, 218, Ant. 3, 147; 198). M-M.*

θυμιάω 1 aor. inf. θυμιᾶσαι (Pind., Hdt.+; Diod. S. 16, 11, 1; Dit., Or. 352, 37 [II bc]; pap. [Kl. T. 135 no. 5, 46]; LXX, Philo; Jos., Ant. 3, 199 al.) make an incense offering ἔλαχε τοῦ θυμιᾶσαι it fell to his lot to make the incense offering Lk 1: 9. M-M.*

θυμικός, ή, όν (Aristot. et al.; Philo) hot-tempered, irascible (so Aristot., Rhet. 2, 14 p. 1389a, 9; Cornutus 20 p. 39, 16; Athen. 2, 45 p. 55f) D 3: 2.*

θυμομαχέω be very angry τινί at someone (Polyb. 27, 8, 4 ἐπί τινι) Ac 12: 20.*

θυμός, οῦ, ὁ (Hom.+; inscr., pap., LXX, En., Ep. Arist., Philo; Jos., Vi. 393 al.; Test. 12 Patr.; Sib. Or., fgm. 3, 19).
1. passion, passionate longing (Hom.+; Pla., Cratyl. 419e θυμὸς ἀπὸ τῆς θύσεως κ. ζέσεως τ. ψυχῆς; Philo) ἐκ τ. οἴνου τοῦ θυμοῦ τῆς πορνείας αὐτῆς πεπότικεν τ.

ἔθνη she has caused the nations to drink the wine of her passionate immorality Rv 14: 8; cf. 18: 3. τὸ ποτήριον τ. οἴνου τ. θυμοῦ τ. ὀργῆς αὐτοῦ the wine-cup of his passionate wrath 16: 19; cf. 19: 15. But in all these cases mng. 2 may be the correct one; for the other pass. in Rv where θ. occurs, mng. 2 is prob. the only one possible.
2. anger, wrath, rage Rv 12: 12 (θυμὸν ἔχειν as Theognis 747 Bergk). ὁ οἶνος τ. θυμοῦ τ. θεοῦ the wine of God's wrath (s. ἄκρατος) 14: 10; cf. vs. 19; 15: 1, 7; 16: 1 (the figure of the outpouring of wrath freq. in OT). If this mng. holds true for all the Rv pass., the combination of genitives of θυμός and ὀργή in 16: 19; 19: 15 is to be taken as a strengthening of the thought (cf. Ex 32: 12; Jer 32: 37; La 2: 3; CD 10, 9), and in 14: 8; 18: 3 we have a mixed metaphor: the wine of harlotry, w. which Babylon intoxicates the nations, becomes the wine of God's wrath for them. —In the other occurrences of θ. in our lit., the same mng. is indicated: of God (w. ὀργή; both words are oft. used together thus in the LXX) Ro 2: 8; 1 Cl 50: 4. Of men Hb 11: 27; (w. ὀργή, as Aelian, V.H. 15, 54; Ael. Aristid. 35, 10 K. =9 p. 101 D.; Herodian 8, 4, 1; Sir 45: 18; Jos., Bell. 2, 135, Ant. 20, 108) Col 3: 8; (w. πικρία and ὀργή) Eph 4: 31; cf. Hm 5, 2, 4 and Js 3: 11 𝔓⁴⁶. ἐξερίσαι εἰς τοσοῦτο θυμοῦ reach such a pitch of fury 1 Cl 45: 7; ἀκατάσχετος θ. MPol 12: 2. πλησθῆναι θυμοῦ be filled w. anger Lk 4: 28; cf. Ac 19: 28.—Pl. θυμοί (Herm. Wr. 12, 4; Philo, Rer. Div. Her. 64; Jos., Bell. 4, 314) outbursts of anger 2 Cor 12: 20; Gal 5: 20; 1 Cl 46: 5.—FBüchsel, TW III '36, 167–73. M-M. B. 1087; 1134.*

θυμόω make angry pass. become angry (Aeschyl., Hdt.+; Dio Chrys. 10[11], 20; LXX; Ep. Arist. 254; Jos., Bell. 1, 221, Ant. 12, 270) 1 aor. ἐθυμώθην. Abs. (Polyb. 5, 16, 4; Test. Dan 4: 4) Mt 2: 16.*

θύρα, ας, ἡ (Hom.+; inscr., pap., LXX; Ep. Arist. 158; Philo, Joseph.) door. As is oft. the case in class. wr., the pl. can be used of one door (Phlegon: 257 fgm. 36, 1, 3 Jac.; Philo, Ebr. 49; cf. Jos., C. Ap. 2, 119.—Bl-D. §141, 4; Rob. 408).
1. lit.—a. ἀνοίγειν open the door (Jos., Vi. 246) Ac 5: 19; B 16: 9. Pass. Ac 16: 26f (Achilles Tat. 7, 13, 1 Λευκίππη τὰς θύρας ἀνεῳγμένας ὁρῶσα. (ἀπο)κλείειν shut Mt 6: 6; Lk 13: 25a. Pass (Jos., Ant. 18, 74) Mt 25: 10; Lk 11: 7; J 20: 19, 26; Ac 21: 30; κρούειν τὴν θ. knock at the door 12: 13; Lk 13: 25b; διὰ τῆς θ. J 10: 1f. ἐπὶ τ. θυρῶν before the door(s) Ac 5: 23. Also ἐπὶ θύραις (Aesop, Fab. 466 P.; Jos., Ant. 17, 90. Also with art.: Clearchus, fgm. 24 p. 17, 21; Appian, Bell. Civ. 3, 93 §385) 1 Cl 39: 9 (Job 5: 4); ἐπὶ τῇ θ. Ac 5: 9. πρὸ τῆς θύρας 12: 6 (schol. on Nicander, Ther. 860 πρὸ τ. θυρῶν). πρὸς (τὴν) θ. at the door (Hegesippus Com. [III bc] 1, 24) Mk 1: 33; 11: 4; τὰ πρὸς τὴν θ. the place near the door 2: 2. πρὸς τῇ θ. ἔξω outside the door J 18: 16 (cf. Lucian, Herm. 7, 7 ὁ παρὰ τὴν θύραν ἔξω ἑστώς).—θ. τοῦ πύργου Hv 3, 9, 6.—On the θύρα ὡραία Ac 3: 2 s. under ὡραῖος.—1 Cl 43: 3 v.l. Funk.
b. of the door-like opening of a cave-tomb entrance (cf. Od. 9, 243; Suppl. Epigr. Gr. VIII 200 [I ad, Jerus.]) ἡ θ. τοῦ μνημείου Mt 27: 60; Mk 15: 46; 16: 3. θ. τοῦ μνήματος GP 8: 32; cf. 9: 37; 12: 53f.—The firm vault of heaven has a 'door' (cf. Ps 77: 23), which opens to admit favored ones Rv 4: 1 (differently, GRinaldi, CBQ 25, '63, 336–47).
2. fig. (Maximus Tyr. 19, 5d ὁ ἔρως ἐστὶ ἐπὶ θύραις τ. ψυχῆς; Iambl., Myst. [Scott, Hermet. IV p. 39, 5ff] ἡ ἱερατικὴ δόσις καλεῖται 'θύρα πρὸς θεόν').
a. ἐγγύς ἐστιν ἐπὶ θύραις he is near, at your very door (cf. X., An. 6, 5, 23) Mt 24: 33; Mk 13: 29. Also πρὸ τῶν

θυρῶν ἕστηκεν Js 5: 9; cf. also Ac 5: 9. ἕστηκα ἐπὶ τ. θύραν καὶ κρούω Rv 3: 20a; s. also b.

b. of the door to the kgdm. of heaven: εἰσελθεῖν διὰ τῆς στενῆς θύρας *come in through the narrow door* Lk 13: 24. Perh. the same door is meant in δέδωκα ἐνώπιόν σου θύραν ἠνεῳγμένην Rv 3: 8. But here sense

c. is also conceivable, acc. to which the opening of the door represents something made possible or feasible: θύρα μοι ἀνέῳγεν μεγάλη 1 Cor 16: 9 (HNie, Vox Theologica 10, '40, 185–92); cf. 2 Cor 2: 12; Col 4: 3. Sim. ὁ θεὸς . . . ἤνοιξεν τοῖς ἔθνεσιν θύραν πίστεως Ac 14: 27 (πίστις 2da).

d. In John Jesus calls himself ἡ θύρα J 10: 9, certainly *the door for* the sheep; ἡ θύρα (ὁ ποιμήν 𝔓[75] et al.) τῶν προβάτων vs. 7, however, has the sense which is prominent in the context, *the door to the sheep* (s. Hdb. ad loc.; EFascher, Ich bin d. Thür! Deutsche Theologie '42, 34–57; 118–33).—Jesus as the θύρα τοῦ πατρός *the door to the Father* IPhld 9: 1.—JoachJeremias, TW III '36, 173–80. M-M. B. 466.*

θυρεός, οῦ, ὁ (Polyb. 6, 23, 2; Diod. S. 5, 33, 4 al.; PSI 428, 36 [III BC]; LXX; Jos., Ant. 8, 179; Sib. Or. 3, 729; loanw. in rabb.) a long, oblong *shield*; fig. θ. τῆς πίστεως *shield of faith* Eph 6: 16. M-M. B. 1402.*

θυρίς, ίδος, ἡ *window* (so Aristot.+; inscr., pap., LXX En. 101, 2; Philo, Plant. 169; Joseph.; Test. Jos. 14: 1; loanw. in rabb.) καθέζεσθαι ἐπὶ τῆς θ. *sit at (in) the window* Ac 20: 9. διὰ θυρίδος *through the window* 2 Cor 11: 33 (Palaeph. p. 20, 5; Josh 2: 15; 1 Km 19: 12; Jos., Bell. 6, 252, Ant. 6, 217). M-M.*

θυρωρός, οῦ *doorkeeper*—1. ὁ of a man (Sappho+; pap., LXX; Jos., Ant. 11, 108) Mk 13: 34; J 10: 3.

2. ἡ of a woman (BGU 1061, 10 [14 BC]; PRyl. 36, 6 [34 AD]; PStrassb. 24: 17; 2 Km 4: 6; Jos., Ant. 7, 48) J 18: 16f (MBlack, An Aramaic Approach³, '67, 258f [Sin. Syriac]). M-M.*

θυσία, ας, ἡ (Pind., Hdt.+; inscr., pap., LXX, Ep. Arist., Philo, Joseph., Test. 12 Patr.).

1. *the act of offering* fig. ἐπὶ τῇ θυσίᾳ τ. πίστεως ὑμῶν *as you offer your faith* Phil 2: 17 (though mng. 2b is not impossible for this difficult pass.; s. below).

2. *sacrifice, offering*—a. lit. (stated gener. Dg 3: 5) Mt 9: 13; 12: 7 (both Hos 6: 6); Mk 9: 49 v.l., s. ἁλίζω; Hb 10: 5 (Ps 39: 7), 26. Pl. Mk 12: 33; Lk 13: 1 (cf. Jos., Bell. 2, 30 παρὰ ταῖς ἰδίαις θυσίαις ἀπεσφάχθαι); Hb 10: 1, 8; 1 Cl 4: 2 (Gen 4: 3. Cf. Diod. S. 12, 20, 2 τῶν θεῶν οὐ χαιρόντων ταῖς τῶν πονηρῶν θυσίαις); B 2: 4, 5 (Is 1: 11), 7 (Jer 7: 22). The various kinds are specified 1 Cl 41: 2. ἀνάγειν θυσίαν *bring an offering* Ac 7: 41 (ἀνάγω 2). Also ἀναφέρειν θ. Hb 7: 27 (ἀναφέρω 2); δοῦναι θ. Lk 2: 24. προσφέρειν (Ex 32: 6; Lev 2: 1, 8 and oft.) Ac 7: 42 (Am 5: 25); Hb 5: 1; 8: 3; 10: 11; 11: 4; 1 Cl 10: 7. Pass. Hb 9: 9; φέρειν θ. (2 Ch 29: 31, Jer 17: 26) 1 Cl 4: 1 (Gen 4: 3). προσάγεσθαι θ. (cf. 1 Esdr 1: 16) *be led as a sacrifice* 1 Cl 31: 3. Of a sacrificial meal (Polycrates: no. 588 fgm. 1 Jac. equated w. θοίνη ['feast']; Ps.-Callisth. 3, 29, 9 τὴν θυσίαν ἐποιησάμεθα τῶν Σωτηρίων='the meal to celebrate deliverance') ἐσθίειν τὰς θ. *eat the sacrifices* (Ps 105: 28; Num 25: 2) 1 Cor 10: 18. The Eucharist is spoken of as a *sacrifice* or *offering* and sacrificial meal D 14: 1ff (s. Knopf, Hdb. exc. on D 9 and 10, p. 24f).—Of the sacrificial death of Christ which, in contrast to the earthly sacrifices, is to be classed among the κρείττονες θυσίαι Hb 9: 23; 10: 12. διὰ τῆς θυσίας αὐτοῦ 9: 26. παρέδωκεν ἑαυτὸν ὑπὲρ ἡμῶν θυσίαν τ. θεῷ Eph

5: 2 (Diod. S. 4, 82, 2 τὴν θυσίαν ὑπὲρ ἁπάντων τ. Ἑλλήνων).—B 7: 3.

b. fig. (Sextus 47: the doing of good as the only θυσία pleasing to God) a broken spirit designated as θ. 1 Cl 18: 16f; 52: 4; B 2: 10 (all three Ps 50: 19; 51: 17). θ. αἰνέσεως *praise-offering* (s. on αἴνεσις) is used fig. in our lit. of spiritual sacrifice 1 Cl 35: 12 (Ps 49: 23); 52: 3 (Ps 49: 14). It is explained Hb 13: 15 as καρπὸς χειλέων ὁμολογούντων τῷ ὀνόματι αὐτοῦ (=τ. θεοῦ).—εἰ σπένδομαι ἐπὶ τῇ θυσίᾳ τῆς πίστεως ὑμῶν *even if I must pour out my blood over the sacrifice of your faith* (i.e., consisting in your faith) Phil 2: 17 (cf. Arrian, Exp. Alex. 6, 19, 5 σπείσας ἐπὶ τῇ θυσίᾳ τὴν φιάλην. But s. 1 above). θ. δεκτή *an acceptable sacr.* (cf. δεκτός) Phil 4: 18; Hs 5, 3, 8; cf. Hb 13: 16; πνευματικαὶ θ. *spiritual sacrifices* 1 Pt 2: 5 (cf. Herm. Wr. 13, 18; 19; 21 λογικαὶ θυσίαι; s. on this Rtzst., Mysterienrel.³ 38; 328f.—Sib. Or. 8, 408 ζῶσα θυσία). Of the sacrifice of martyrdom IRo 4: 2; MPol 14: 2. παρακαλῶ ὑμᾶς παραστῆσαι τὰ σώματα ὑμῶν θυσίαν ζῶσαν *I appeal to you to present your bodies as a living sacrifice* Ro 12: 1 (παριστάναι θυσίαν is a t.t. of sacrificial procedure: Dit., Or. 332, 17; 42; 456, 20f; 764, 23; 33 al., Syll.² 554, 6; ³694, 50.—PSeidensticker, Lebendiges Opfer Röm 12: 1, diss. Münster, '54).—OSchmitz, Die Opferanschauung d. spät. Judentums u. die Opferaussagen d. NTs '10; HWenschkewitz, D. Spiritualisierung der Kultusbegriffe Tempel, Priester u. Opfer im NT '32; WvLoewenich, Z. Verständnis d. Opfergedankens im Hb: ThBl 12, '32, 167–72; JBrinktrine, D. Messopferbegr. in den ersten 2 Jahrh. '18; RKYerkes, ATR 29, '47, 28–33; RdeVaux, Les Sacrifices de l'Ancien Testament '64. S. also εὐχαριστία 3. M-M. B. 1467.*

θυσιαστήριον, ου, τό (LXX; Ep. Arist. 87; Philo, Mos. 2, 105; Jos., Ant. 8, 88; 105; Test. Levi 16: 1) *altar*.

1. lit.—a. of the altar of burnt offering in the inner forecourt of the temple at Jerusalem (s. Schürer II⁴ 344f) Mt 5: 23f; 23: 18–20, 35; Lk 11: 51; Hb 7: 13; Rv 11: 1; 1 Cl 41: 2; B 7: 9 (cf. Lev 16: 7–9, 18). λειτουργεῖν τῷ θ. *serve at the altar* 1 Cl 32: 2; παρεδρεύειν τῷ θ. (s. παρεδρεύω) 1 Cor 9: 13a; συμμερίζεσθαι τῷ θ. (s. συμμερίζω) vs. 13b; κοινωνοὶ τοῦ θ. *partners, sharers in the altar*=closely united w. the altar (=w. God; s. 10: 20) 10: 18, cf. κοινωνός 1 ba (but s. GVJourdan, JBL 67, '48, 122f).

b. of the altar of incense—α. in the temple at Jerusalem τὸ θ. τοῦ θυμιάματος (Ex 30: 1, 27) Lk 1: 11.

β. the heavenly altar of Rv also seems to be thought of as an altar of incense: 6: 9; 8: 3, 5; 9: 13; 14: 18; 16: 7. Hermas also speaks of a θ. τοῦ θεοῦ in heaven Hm 10, 3, 2f; s 8, 2, 5.

c. of an *altar* gener.: the one erected by Abraham (Gen 22: 9) Js 2: 21; B 7: 3. Pl. Ro 11: 3 (3 Km 19: 10).

2. fig. in var. ways—a. ἐντὸς (τοῦ) θ. εἶναι *be inside the sanctuary* (lit., *the place of sacrifice* or *of the altar*) in this mng. perh. also Rv 14: 18 and Procop., Aed. 1, 65; inscr. Ἀρχαιολογικὸν Δελτίον 12, '27, 69), i.e. in the church, under the care and control of its constituted authorities IEph 5: 2; ITr 7: 2. This is in accord w. Ignatius' emphatic assertion that there is only one θ. IMg 7: 2; IPhld 4.

b. IRo 2: 2 Ign. speaks of the altar that is ready to receive his death as a martyr.

c. Pol 4: 3 the Christian widows are called a θυσιαστήριον θεοῦ, since they are to bring to God none but perfect gifts (cf. Sextus 46b, the pure heart as a θ. for God).

d. The pass. ἔχομεν θ. ἐξ οὗ φαγεῖν οὐκ ἔχουσιν ἐξουσίαν οἱ τῇ σκηνῇ λατρεύοντες *we have an altar from* *which those who serve the tabernacle have no right to eat* Hb 13: 10 is difficult. Scholars more recently fr. FBleek to ASeeberg and BHaensler, BZ 11, '13, 403-9, interpret the θ. as the cross of Christ, others [e.g. ThHaering, Der Brief an die Hebr. '25, 103] as the communion table. HWindisch rejects both these interpr. BWeiss and ERiggenbach²,³ '22 give up the attempt to understand it. Cf. also JMCreed, ET 50, '38, 13-15; JPWilson, ibid. 380f; JEL Oulton, ibid. 55, '44, 303-5.—προσέρχεσθαι ἐν τῷ θ. λειτουργεῖν τὸ θεῖον Tit 1: 9 v.l. is also to be interpr. fr. the viewpoint of Christian institutions. B. 1467.*

θύω impf. ἔθυον; 1 aor. ἔθυσα; pf. pass. ptc. τεθυμένος; 1 aor. pass. ἐτύθην (Hom.+; inscr., pap., LXX, Philo, Joseph., Test. 12 Patr.).

1. *sacrifice* (this is the proper mng. and the one most commonly found. Used also of human sacrifice: Apollodorus [II BC]: 244 fgm. 125 Jac.=Porphyr., Abst. 2, 55) τινί τι *someth. in honor of someone* (Diod. S. 16, 18, 5; 17, 100, 1; Lucian, Dial. Deor. 2, 4; Dit., Syll.³ 589, 48; 993, 11f; Gen 46: 1; Jos., Bell. 2, 214 τῷ θεῷ χαριστήρια; Sib. Or. 3, 626) 1 Cor 10: 20 (Dt 32: 17). τ. θεῷ θυσίαν *offer a sacr. to God* 1 Cl 52: 3 (Ps 49: 14). τινί *in honor of someone* (X., Cyr. 8, 7, 3; Wilcken, Chrest. 116, 2 θύε πᾶσι τοῖς θεοῖς; BGU 287, 7; LXX; Ep. Arist. 138; Jos., Bell. 1, 56 τῷ θεῷ) Ac 14: 18; 2 Cl 3: 1. Abs. (Lucian, Jupp. Trag. 22, beg.; PHib. 28, 7; LXX) Ac 14: 13; MPol 12: 2.

2. *slaughter, kill* (Aesop, Fab. 122 P.=195 H.; 143 P.=262 H.; 290 P.—Babr. 21.—On the close relation betw. sacrifice and slaughter cf. Ltzm., Hdb. on 1 Cor 10: 25) τι *someth.* (Tob 7: 8; Jos., Ant. 1, 197 μόσχον) a calf Lk 15: 23, 27, 30. Pass. Mt 22: 4. τὸ πάσχα *the Passover lamb* (Ex 12: 21; Dt 16: 2, 5f; 1 Esdr 1: 6; 7: 12) Mk 14: 12. Pass. Lk 22: 7; hence τὸ πάσχα ἡμῶν ἐτύθη Χριστός

1 Cor 5: 7 (θύω of the sacrifice of a person, s. 1 above). Abs. Ac 10: 13; 11: 7.

3. gener. *kill* (Eur., Iph. T. 621; Sir 34: 20; 1 Macc 7: 19) abs. J 10: 10.

4. *celebrate,* but perh. only when an animal is slaughtered in the same connection (Polyaenus 1, 44. θ. εὐαγγέλια='a joyous festival'; Appian, Syr. 4 §17; 16 §69 γάμους both times; Athen. 12, 43 p. 532Ε θ. τὰ ἐπινίκια; Achilles Tat. 8, 19, 3 θ. τοὺς γάμους.—Philochorus no. 328 fgm. 65 Jac. uses θυσία of domestic family festivals) Mk 14: 12; Lk 22: 7 (s. 2 above).—GDKilpatrick, Biblical Translator 12, '61, 130-32 (kill for food J 10: 10). JBehm, TW III '36, 180-91. M-M.*

θῶ s. τίθημι.

Θωμᾶς, ᾶ, ὁ (the Aram. תְּאוֹמָא='twin', which was never used simply as a surname [MLidzbarski, Handb. der nordsem. Epigraphik 1898, 383], came to coincide in Gk.-speaking regions w. the Gk. name Θωμᾶς [RHerzog, Philol. 56, 1897, 51]. Cf. Dalman, Gramm.² 145, 6; Wuthnow 55; Bl-D. §53, 2d; 125, 2) *Thomas,* one of the 12 apostles (s. Δίδυμος) Mt 10: 3; Mk 3: 18; Lk 6: 15; J 11: 16; 14: 5; 20: 24, 26-8; 21: 2; Ac 1: 13; LJ 2: 1; Papias 2: 4. M-M.*

θώραξ, ακος, ὁ—1. *breastplate* (so Hom.+; Lind. Tempelchron. C, 36; 41; 47; PPetr. III 6a, 26 [237 BC]; PGiess. 47, 6; LXX; Philo, Leg. All. 3, 115; Jos., Ant. 8, 414, Vi. 293; Test. Jud. 3: 5; loanw. in rabb.) Rv 9: 9b, 17.—Fig. ἐνδύεσθαι τὸν θώρακα τῆς δικαιοσύνης *put on the breastplate of righteousness* Eph 6: 14 (cf. Is 59: 17; Wsd 5: 18). θ. πίστεως 1 Th 5: 8.

2. *the part of the body covered by the breastplate, the chest* (Eur.; Pla., Tim. 69Ε; Aristot., Hist. An. 1, 7; Diod. S. 15, 87, 1; 5; Polyaenus 3, 9, 22) Rv 9: 9a (though mng. 1 is not to be excluded). M-M. B. 1399.*

I

ι´ numeral=10 (δέκα: Jos., C. Ap. 1, 157; cf. Sib. Or. 5, 14) B 9: 8; Hs 9, 3, 3; 9, 4, 2; 3; 9, 5, 4; 9, 15, 4. As an ordinal numeral *tenth* (δεκάτη) Hm 10 superscr.*

ια´ numeral= *eleventh* (ἐνδεκάτη) Hm 11 superscr.*

Ἰάϊρος, ου, ὁ Ἰάειρος W-H. (=יָאִיר 'he—God—will enlighten' or rarely [1 Ch 20: 5]=יָעִיר 'he will arouse') *Jairus* (Ἰαΐρ Num 32: 41; Dt 3: 14; 1 Ch 2: 22f al. Ἰάϊρος 1 Esdr 5: 31; Esth 1: 1a; Jos., Bell. 2, 447. Cf. PThomsen, Inschr. d. Stadt Jerusalem [=ZDPV 43, '20, 138ff] no. 190; Ostraka II 1231) a synagogue official Mk 5: 22; Lk 8: 41. M-M.*

Ἰακώβ, ὁ indecl. (יַעֲקֹב) *Jacob.* This, the un-Grecized form of the OT, is reserved for formal writing, and esp. for the patriarch (so also Philo, e.g. Leg. Alleg. 3, 18, Sacrif. Abel. 5, Ebr. 82, Migr. Abr. 200; Test. 12 Patr.; Sib. Or. 2, 247; also in magic: PGM 4, 1736; 1803; also in the spelling Ἰακούβ [Fluchtaf. 3, 2]. Differently Josephus, s. Ἰάκωβος. Cf. Dssm. B 184, 3 [BS 282]).

1. son of Isaac Mt 1: 2; Lk 3: 34; J 4: 5f, 12; Ac 7: 8, 12, 14f, 46 (but s. below); Ro 9: 13 (Mal 1: 2f); Hb 11: 9, 20f; 1 Cl 4: 8; 31: 4; B 11: 9 (quot. of unknown orig.); 13: 4f. Of the nation of Israel, *the descendants of Jacob* (Num 23: 7; Sir 23: 12; Is 9: 7; 40: 27 al.) Ro 11: 26 (Is 59: 20); so

perh. also in οἶκος Ἰ. Ac 7: 46. Also (Ex 19: 3; Is 2: 5) Lk 1: 33; cf. 1 Cl 29: 2 (Dt 32: 9). The triad Abraham, Isaac, and Jacob (also in magic [s. Ἀβραάμ] and grave inscr. Sb 2034, 11; 3901, 12) Mt 8: 11; Lk 13: 28; B 8: 4; IPhld 9: 1. Esp. the God of Abraham, Isaac, and Jacob (Ex 3: 6; also in magic: PGM 4, 1231f; Fluchtaf. 5, 2; 37) Mt 22: 32; Mk 12: 26; Lk 20: 37; Ac 3: 13; 7: 32.—Cf. B 6: 8 (Ex 33: 1).

2. the father of Joseph, in the genealogy of Jesus Mt 1: 15f; Lk 3: 23 D. M-M.*

Ἰάκωβος, ου, ὁ (Grecized form of the preceding, W-S. §10, 3; Ep. Arist. 48; 49. Oft. in Joseph., even for the patriarch [s. Ἰακώβ]. In the spelling Ἰάκουβος: POxy. 276, 5 [77 AD]; BGU 715 II, 11; 1 Esdr 9: 48) *James* (for the history of this name s. Murray, New [Oxford] Engl. Dict. s.v. James).

1. son of the Galilean fisherman Zebedee, brother of John, member of the Twelve, executed by Herod Agrippa I not later than 44 AD: Mt 4: 21; 10: 2; 17: 1; Mk 1: 19, 29; 3: 17; 5: 37; 9: 2; 10: 35, 41; 13: 3; 14: 33; Lk 5: 10; 6: 14; 8: 51; 9: 28, 54; Ac 1: 13a; 12: 2; GEb 2.—ESchwartz, Über d. Tod der Söhne Zeb. '04; JBlinzler and ABöhling, Novum Testamentum 5, '62, 191-213.

2. James, the son of Alphaeus (q.v.) also belonged to the Twelve Mt 10: 3; Mk 2: 14 v.l. (s. 6 below); 3: 18; Lk 6: 15; Ac 1: 13b. This James is perh. identical with

3. James, the son of Mary Mt 27: 56; Mk 16: 1; Lk 24: 10 (s. Bl-D. §162, 3), who is called Mk 15: 40 'Ι. ὁ μικρός, *James the small* or *the younger* (μικρός 1a, b.—ThZahn, Forschungen VI '00, 345f; 348ff).

4. James, the Lord's brother (Jos., Ant. 20, 200), later head of the church at Jerusalem, confused w. 2 at an early date; Mt 13: 55; Mk 6: 3; 1 Cor 15: 7; Gal 1: 19; 2: 9, 12; Ac 12: 17; 15: 13; 21: 18; GH 21 (Lat.); most probably Papias 2: 4. This J. is certainly meant Js 1: 1 (MMeinertz, D. Jk u. sein Verf. '05; AMeyer, D. Rätsel des Jk '30) and Jd 1.—GerhKittel, D. Stellg. des Jak. zu Judentum u. Heidenchristentum: ZNW 30, '31, 145–57, D. geschichtl. Ort des Jk: ibid. 41, '42, 71–105; KAland, D. Herrenbr. Jak. u. Jk: ThLZ 69, '44, 97–104; GerhKittel, D. Jak. u. die Apost. Väter: ZNW 43, '50/'51, 54–112; WKPrentice, in Studies in Roman Economic and Social Hist. in honor of ACJohnson '51, 144–51; PGaechter, Petrus u. seine Zeit '58, 258–310.

5. James, father of an apostle named Judas, mentioned only by Luke: Lk 6: 16a; Ac 1: 13c.

6. Mk 2: 14 D the tax-collector is called James (instead of Levi. S. FCBurkitt, JTS 28, '27, 273f).—HHoltzmann, Jak. der Gerechte u. seine Namensbrüder: ZWTh 23, 1880, 198–221; FMaier, Z. Apostolizität des Jak. u. Jud.: BZ 4, '06, 164–91; 255–66; HKoch, Z. Jakobusfrage Gal 1: 19: ZNW 33, '34, 204–9. M-M.*

ἴαμα, ατος, τό (Hdt.+ w. the mng. 'remedy') *healing* (Pla., Leg. 7 p. 790D; Lucian, Calumn. 17; Dit., Syll.³ 1168, 2 ἰάματα τ. 'Απόλλωνος καὶ τ. 'Ασκλαπιοῦ; 24; 35. Cf. Jer 40: 6) χαρίσματα ἰαμάτων (*spiritual*) *gifts of healing* 1 Cor 12: 9, 28, 30. Cf. ἰάματα B 3: 4 v.l. (for ἰμάτια) Funk. M-M.*

'Ιαμβρῆς, ὁ *Jambres*, s. 'Ιάννης.

'Ιανναί, ὁ indecl. *Jannai*, in the genealogy of Jesus Lk 3: 24.*

'Ιάννης, ὁ *Jannes*, named w. Jambres as one of the Egyptian sorcerers who (Ex 7: 11ff) opposed Moses before Pharaoh 2 Ti 3: 8. The names go back to Jewish tradition (Schürer III⁴ 402ff; MDibelius, Hdb. ad loc.), whence Numenius of Apamea [II AD] in Euseb., Pr. Ev. 9, 8, 1 got them. Μαμβρῆς appears as v.l. for 'Ιαμβρῆς, reflecting variation in the mss. A Jewish apocryphal work bearing both names has disappeared except for the title (Schürer, loc. cit.).—RJames, JTS 2, '01, 572ff.; The Damascus Document (Kl. T. 167) 5, 19f (cf. CD 5, 18f and SSchechter, Fragments of a Zadokite Work '10 p. xxxvii and lixf); Billerb. III 660–4; HOdeberg, TW III 192f.*

ἰάομαι mid. dep., impf. ἰώμην; 1 aor. ἰασάμην; pass. forms w. pass. mng. 1 aor. ἰάθην, imper. ἰαθήτω; 1 fut. ἰαθήσομαι; pf. ἴαμαι (Bl-D. §311, 1). (Hom.+; Dit., Syll.³ 1168, 108; 113; 117; 1169, 7; PSI 665, 5 [III BC]; BGU 1026 XXII, 15; LXX, Philo; Jos., Ant. 9, 105) *heal, cure.*

1. lit. τινά *someone* Lk 5: 17; 6: 19; 9 (in vs. 2 τοὺς ἀσθενεῖς is v.l.), 11, 42; 14: 4; 22: 51; J 4: 47; Ac 9: 34; 10: 38; 28: 8; 1 Cl 59: 4.—Pass. Mt 8: 8, 13; 15: 28; Lk 7: 7; 8: 47; 17: 15; J 5: 13; Ac 5: 16 D. ἰαθῆναι ἀπό τινος *be cured of an illness*: ἀπὸ τῆς μάστιγος *of the terrible suffering* Mk 5: 29. ἀπὸ τῶν νόσων αὐτῶν Lk 6: 18. ἰᾶθαι διά τινος *be cured by someth.* B 8: 6.

2. fig. of deliverance from other ills of many kinds (Ael. Aristid. 13 p. 273 D.; Julian, Epistle 61 p. 424A, fr. the evils of ignorance; Sallust. 14 p. 28, 3 κακίαν; Jos., Ant. 2, 119 λύπην) *restore* (En. 10, 7) τινά *someone* fr. sin and its consequences Mt 13: 15; J 12: 40; Ac 28: 27 (all three Is 6: 10); the brokenhearted Lk 4: 18 t.r.; B 14: 9 (both Is 61: 1). τὶ *someth.* (Philostrat., Vi. Soph. 1, 22 p. 38, 9) *heal* (cf. the proverb in Hdt. 3, 53; Thu. 5, 65, 2; Apollon. Rhod. 4, 1081; Appian, Ital. 5 §10, Bell. Civ. 1, 3 §9, and in Prov. Aesopi 91 P.: κακὸν κακῷ ἰᾶσθαι) τὰ ἁμαρτήματα Hv 1, 1, 9 (Appian, Hann. 31 §131 ἁμάρτημα ἰ.). τὰ προγεγονότα πονηρά *all the past evils* 1, 3, 1; cf. s 9, 23, 5. Abs. of the results of God's punishment, which he brings to an end 1 Cl 56: 7 (Job 5: 18).—Pass. of sin Js 5: 16; 2 Cl 9: 7; Hs 9, 28, 5. The figure of sin as a wound or disease is also plain in ἵνα τὸ χωλὸν ἰαθῇ Hb 12: 13, and τῷ μώλωπι αὐτοῦ ἡμεῖς ἰάθημεν 1 Cl 16: 5; B 5: 2; cf. 1 Pt 2: 24 (all three Is 53: 5).—AOepke, TW III 194–215. M-M.*

'Ιάρετ, ὁ indecl. (יֶרֶד, in pause יָרֶד) *Jared,* father of Enoch (Gen 5: 15, 18; 1 Ch 1: 2; En. 106, 13; 'Ιάρεδ in all these, but 'Ιάρετ as v.l. in Gen 5: 18 [ARahlfs, Genesis '26].— Jos., Ant. 1, 79; 84 'Ιάρεδος, ου), in the genealogy of Jesus Lk 3: 37.*

ἴασις, εως, ἡ (Archilochus [VII BC]+; Dit., Syll.³ 244 I, 53; LXX; En. 10, 7; Philo, Joseph.) *healing.*

1. lit. (Hippocr., Pla. et al.; LXX; Jos., Ant. 7, 294) J 5: 7 v.l. εἰς ἴασιν *for healing=to heal* Ac 4: 30; τὸ σημεῖον τῆς ἰ. *the miracle of healing* vs. 22. ἰάσεις ἀποτελεῖν (s. Vett. Val. on 2) *perform cures* Lk 13: 32; δέησις περὶ τῆς ἰ. *prayer for healing* B 12: 7.

2. fig. (Pla., Leg. 9 p. 862C ἴασις τῆς ἀδικίας; Lucian, Jupp. Trag. 28; Alciphr. 3, 13, 2; Vett. Val. 190, 30 τῶν φαύλων ἴασιν ἀποτελεῖ; Sir 43: 22; Philo, Leg. All. 2, 79 ἰ. τοῦ πάθους; Jos., Ant. 5, 41) of *forgiveness of sins* (Arrian, Anab. 7, 29, 2 μόνη ἴασις ἁμαρτίας ὁμολογεῖν τε ἁμαρτόντα καὶ δῆλον εἶναι ἐπ' αὐτῷ μεταγινώσκοντα='the only cure for a sin is for the sinner to confess it and to show repentance for it'; Sir 28: 3; cf. also ἰάομαι 2) ἴασιν δοῦναι *grant forgiveness* Hm 4, 1, 11; s 5, 7, 3f. ἴασιν δοῦναί τινι s 7: 4. ποιεῖν ἴασιν τοῖς ἁμαρτήσίν τινος *forgive someone's sins* m 12, 6, 2. λαμβάνειν ἴασιν παρὰ τοῦ κυρίου τῶν ἁμαρτιῶν *receive forgiveness of sins fr. the Lord* s 8, 11, 3 (λαμβ. ἰ. as Philo, Post. Cai. 10). M-M.*

ἴασπις, ιδος, ἡ (Pla.+; Dit., Syll.² 587, 87f [IV BC]; PGM 12, 203 ἴασπιν; LXX; Jos., Bell. 5, 234, Ant. 3, 168. Occasionally also masc., e.g., Petosiris, fgm. 29) *jasper*, a precious stone found in various colors, mostly reddish, somet. green (Cyranides p. 23, 22 λίθος χλωρός), brown, blue, yellow, and white. In antiquity the name was not limited to the variety of quartz now called jasper, but could designate any opaque precious stone. Rv 21: 18f. W. λίθος 4: 3. λίθος ἴασπις κρυσταλλίζων *a stone of crystal-clear jasper* 21: 11 (cf. Is 54: 12); perh. the opal is meant here; acc. to some, the diamond. S. on ἀμέθυστος. M-M.*

'Ιάσων, ονος, ὁ (freq. found, also in LXX; Ep. Arist. 49; Joseph. It was a favorite practice among Jews to substitute the purely Gk. name 'Ιάσων for the Jewish-Gk. 'Ιησοῦς: Dssm., B 184, 1 [BS 315, 2]; Bl-D. §53, 2d) *Jason.*

1. host of Paul and Silas in Thessalonica Ac 17: 5–7, 9.

2. one who sends a greeting Ro 16: 21, hardly the same as 1.

3. 'Ιάσονι is found for Μνάσωνι Ac 21: 16 in ℵ, the Bohairic version et al. M-M.*

ἰατρός, οῦ, ὁ (Hom.+; inscr., pap., LXX, Philo; Jos., Bell. 1, 272, Vi. 404) *physician.*

1. lit. Mt 9: 12; Mk 2: 17; Lk 5: 31 (cf. on these pass. Plut., Mor. 230F, Phocion 10, 5; Stob., Floril. III p. 462,

14 H. οὐδὲ γὰρ ιατρὸς ὑγιείας ὢν ποιητικὸς ἐν τοῖς ὑγιαίνουσι τὴν διατριβὴν ποιεῖται); LJ 1: 6 (cf. Dio Chrys. 8[9], 4 νοσοῦντες ἐπιδημοῦντος ιατροῦ μὴ προσῄεσαν); Mk 5: 26 (Sb 8266, 13ff [161/60 BC] when the physicians refuse to help, the god Amenothis intervenes with a miracle). ιατροῖς προσαναλίσκειν ὅλον τὸν βίον spend all of one's money on physicians Lk 8: 43 v.l. (PStrassb. 73, 18f, a physician's fee of 20 drachmas; Diod. S. 32, 11, 3 a physician διπλοῦν ἀπῄτει τὸν μισθόν). Given as Luke's profession Col 4: 14 (Heraclid. Pont., fgm. 118 W. Ἀσκληπιάδης ὁ ι.; Strabo 10, 5, 6 p. 486 Ἐ. ὁ ι.; Sb 8327 [inscr. II AD] Ἀπολλώνιος ιατρός). In a proverb (s. Jülicher, Gleichn. 172f; EKlostermann and FHauck ad loc.) ιατρὲ θεράπευσον σεαυτόν physician, heal yourself Lk 4: 23 (Eur., fgm. 1086 Nauck² ἄλλων ιατρὸς αὐτὸς ἕλκεσιν βρύων. Aesop, Fab. 289 P.=H. 78 and 78b=Babr. 120 πῶς ἄλλον ιήσῃ, ὃς σαυτὸν μὴ σώζεις;).—Papias 3. 2. fig. (Diog. L. 3, 45 an epigram calls Plato the ιητήρ ψυχῆς; schol. on Pla. 227A ὁ Σωκράτης ιατρὸς περὶ ψυχήν; Diod. S. 34+35 fgm. 17, 1 τῆς λύπης ὁ κάλλιστος ιατρὸς χρόνος; Philo, Spec. Leg. 2, 31 ι. ἁμαρτημάτων) of God (Aristoph., Av. 584 and Lycophron 1207; 1377 of Apollo; Simplicius in Epict. p. 41, 51 God as ιατρός; Ael. Aristid. 47, 57 K.=23 p. 459 D.: Asclepius as ἀληθινὸς ιατρός) Dg 9: 6. Of Jesus Christ ι. σαρκικὸς καὶ πνευματικός physician of body and soul (or ph. who is flesh and spirit) IEph 7: 2. Cf. JOtt, D. Bezeichnung Christi als ιατρός in d. urchristl. Literatur: Der Katholik 90, '10, 457f; AvHarnack, Mission I⁴ '23, 129ff. M-M. B. 308.*

Ἰαχίν, ὁ indecl. Jachin, in the genealogy of Jesus, Lk 3: 23ff D.*

ιβ′ numeral=12 (δώδεκα as Jos., C. Ap. 1, 122) Mk 6: 7 D. Postscript to Mk in the Ferrar group (s. Ῥωμαϊστί): ἐγράφη ιβ′ ἔτη τῆς ἀναλήψεως τ. κυρίου; Ac 1: 26 D; =twelfth (δωδεκάτη) Hm 12 superscr.*

Ἰγνάτιος, ου, ὁ (on the name s. Hdb., Ergänzungsband '23, 189. In addition to the examples given there of the name in this spelling see also Sb 8802b, 6 [82/83 AD]; 7662, 23 [II AD]) Ignatius, bishop of Antioch IEph IMg ITr IRo IPhld ISm IPol inscr.; Pol 9: 1; 13: 1f.*

ἴδε (on the accentuation s. εἶδον) properly imper. of εἶδον, but stereotyped as a particle, and hence used when more than one pers. is addressed, and when that which is to be observed is in the nom. (Bl-D. §144 app. This use of the imper. begins in Hom.; cf. Kühner-G. I 84, 4) (you) see, mostly at the beginning of a sentence, but somet. in the middle (J 3: 26). 1. pointing out someth. to which the speaker wishes to draw attention (Gen 27: 6; Sir 28: 24) Mk 2: 24; 13: 1; J 5: 14; 18: 21; B 8: 1; 12: 10. ι. οὖν B 6: 14; 15: 7. W. indir. quest. foll. J 11: 36; cf. 16: 29; 19: 4; Gal 5: 2; B 12: 11. W. εἰ foll. see whether Hm 11: 18a, b. 2. introducing someth. unexpected J 3: 26; 7: 26; 11: 3; 12: 19. 3. here is (are) (like French voici) ι. ὁ τόπος here is the place Mk 16: 6. ι. ἡ μήτηρ μου καὶ οἱ ἀδελφοί μου here are my mother and my brothers (or brothers and sisters? s. ἀδελφός 1) 3: 34; cf. 26, 20, 22; Mk 11: 21; J 1: 29, 36, 47; 19: 14, 26f. Cf. GDalman, Jesus-Jeshua (tr. PLevertoff) '29, 201-3. W. adv. of place ἴδε ὧδε . . . ι. ἐκεῖ here is . . . there is Mk 13: 21. 4. w. obvious loss of its fundamental mng. (schol. on Pla. 130c: Ἀλκιβιάδης, ἴδε, τί λέγει='hear') ι. νῦν

ἠκούσατε there, now you have heard Mt 26: 65. ἴδε πόσα σου κατηγοροῦσιν you hear how many charges they bring against you Mk 15: 4. ι. Ἠλίαν φωνεῖ listen! he is calling Elijah vs. 35. 5. simply here ι. ἔχεις τὸ σόν here you have what is yours Mt 25: 25. S. bibliog. s.v. ἰδού, esp. Fiedler. M-M.*

ἰδέα, ας, ἡ (Pind., Hdt.+; pap., LXX, Philo, Joseph.— CRitter on εἶδος). 1. appearance, aspect (Theognis, Pind. et al.; POxy. 1277, 10; Gen 5: 3; EpJer 62; 2 Macc 3: 16; Jos., Bell. 3, 508, Ant. 8, 177) Hs 9, 17, 1f; ἡ ι. αὐτοῦ ἱλαρὰ ἦν his appearance was pleasant 6, 1, 6. κατηφὴς τῇ ι. downcast in appearance Hv 1, 2, 3; cf. s 6, 2, 5; 9, 3, 1. ἠλλοιώθη ἡ ι. αὐτοῦ his appearance changed v 5: 4; cf. Lk 9: 29 D. ἄλλην ι. ἔχειν Hs 9, 1, 4. (For the mng. face, which is poss. in Hv 1, 2, 3; s 6, 1, 6, s. on εἰδέα Mt 28: 3). 2. form, kind (Aristoph., Ran. 384 ἑτέρα ὕμνων ἰδέα; Thu. 1, 109, 1; 3, 102, 7; 4 Macc 1: 14, 18; Philo, Op. M. 22, Praem. 90; Jos., Ant. 15, 416) ἄλλαις βασάνων ἰδέαις with other kinds of torture(s) MPol 2: 4 (cf. Thu. 3, 81, 5 πᾶσα ι. θανάτου). M-M. B. 1212.*

ἴδιος, ια, ον (Hom.+; inscr., pap., LXX, Ep. Arist., En., Philo, Joseph., Test. 12 Patr. Cf. Bl-D. §286; Rob. 691f; Mlt.-Turner 191f.—For the spelling ἴδιος s. on ὀλίγος) one's own. 1. belonging to an individual—a. in contrast to what is public property or belongs to another: private, one's own, peculiar to oneself. α. (opp. κοινός, as Pla., Pol. 7 p. 535B; Appian, Bell. Civ. 5, 41 §171) οὐδὲ εἷς τι τῶν ὑπαρχόντων αὐτῷ ἔλεγεν ἴδιον εἶναι nor did anyone claim that anything he had belonged to him alone Ac 4: 32; cf. D 4: 8. β. (opp. ἀλλότριος) κατὰ τὴν ἰδίαν δύναμιν according to his own capability (in contrast to that of others) Mt 25: 15. τὴν δόξαν τὴν ι. ζητεῖ J 7: 18; cf. 5: 18, 43. ἕκαστος τῇ ι. διαλέκτῳ ἡμῶν Ac 2: 8; cf. vs. 6. ἰδίᾳ δυνάμει 3: 12; cf. 28: 30; τὴν ι. (δικαιοσύνην) Ro 10: 3; cf. 11: 24; 14: 4f. ἕκαστος τ. ι. μισθὸν λήμψεται κατὰ τ. ι. κόπον each one will receive his own wages according to his own labor 1 Cor 3: 8. ἑκάστη τὸν ἴδιον ἄνδρα her own husband 7: 2 (Diog. L. 8, 43 πρὸς τὸν ἴδιον ἄνδρα πορεύεσθαι). ἕκαστος ἴδιον ἔχει χάρισμα 7: 7. ἕκαστος τὸ ἴδιον δεῖπνον προλαμβάνει (s. προλαμβάνω 2a) 11: 21 (Eratosth.: 241 fgm. 16 Jac. of the festival known as Lagynophoria τὰ κομισθέντα αὑτοῖς δειπνοῦσι κατακλιθέντες . . . κ. ἐξ ἰδίας ἕκαστος λαγύνου παρ' αὑτῶν φέροντες πίνουσιν. Judgment: συνοίκια [unification-festival] ταῦτα ρυπαρὰ· ἀνάγκη γὰρ τὴν σύνοδον γίνεσθαι παμμιγοῦς ὄχλου). Cf. 1 Cor 9: 7; 15: 38. ἕκαστος τὸ ι. φορτίον βαστάσει Gal 6: 5.—Tit 1: 12; Hb 4: 10; 7: 27; 9: 12; 13: 12. In ἰδία ἐπίλυσις 2 Pt 1: 20 one's own private interpretation is contrasted with the meaning intended by the author himself or with the interpretation of another person who is authorized or competent (s. WHWeeda, NThSt 2, '19, 129-35). b. without any clearly felt contrast belonging to or peculiar to an individual ἕκαστον δένδρον ἐκ τ. ἰδίου καρποῦ γινώσκεται every tree is known by its own fruit Lk 6: 44. τὰ ἴδια πρόβατα his (own) sheep J 10: 3f. εἰς τὸν τόπον τ. ἴδιον to his own peculiar place Ac 1: 25; cf. 20: 28; Ro 8: 32 (ὁ ἴδιος υἱός without emphasis: Diod. S. 17, 80, 1 of Parmenio; 17, 118, 1 of Antipater. In relating an instance in which a son was not spared Polyaenus 8, 13 has υἱὸς αὐτοῦ, for which Exc. 3, 7 inserts ἴδιος υἱός. Hence the latter can be without special emphasis on feeling in Ro 8: 32); 1 Cor 7: 4a, b. ἕκαστος ἐν τ. ἰδίῳ τάγματι *each one in his (own) turn* 15: 23 (cf. En. 2, 1 τ. ἰδ. τάξιν). καιροὶ ἴδιοι *the proper time* (cf. Diod. S. 1, 50, 7 ἐν τοῖς ἰδίοις χρόνοις; likew. 5, 80, 3; Jos., Ant. 11, 171; Ps.-Clem., Hom. 3, 16) 1 Ti 2: 6; 6: 15; Tit 1: 3; 1 Cl 20: 4; cf. 1 Ti 3: 4f, 12; 4: 2; 5: 4. ἴδιαι λειτουργίαι...ἴδιος ὁ τόπος...ἴδιαι διακονίαι in each case *proper: ministrations,...place,...services* 1 Cl 40: 5. These pass. are close to mng. 2; it is esp. difficult to fix the boundaries here.

2. ἴ. is used for the gen. of αὐτός or the possess. pron., or for the possess. gen. ἑαυτοῦ, ἑαυτῶν (this use found in Hellenistic wr. [Schmidt 369], in Attic [Meisterhans³-Schw. 235] and Magnesian [Thieme 28f] inscr.; pap. [Kuhring—s. ἀνά beg.—14]. S. also Dssm., B 120f [BS 123f], and against him Mlt. 87–91. LXX oft. uses ἴ. without emphasis to render the simple Hebr. personal suffix [Gen 47: 18; Dt 15: 2; Job 2: 11; 7: 10, 13; Pr 6: 2 al.], but somet. also employs it without any basis for it in the original text [Job 24: 12; Pr 9: 12; 22: 7; 27: 15]. Da 1: 10, where LXX has ἴδ., Theod. uses μου. 1 Esdr 5: 8 εἰς τὴν ἰδίαν πόλιν=2 Esdr 2: 1 εἰς πόλιν αὐτοῦ).

a. with the first pers. (UPZ 13, 14 [158 BC] εἰμὶ μετὰ τ. ἀδελφοῦ ἰδίου=w. my brother) κοπιῶμεν ταῖς ἰ. χερσὶν *with our own hands* 1 Cor 4: 12.

b. with the second pers. (Jos., Bell. 6, 346 ἰδίαις χερσίν =w. your own hands) ἐν τῷ ἰ. ὀφθαλμῷ *in your own eye* Lk 6: 41; cf. Eph 5: 22 (s. also vs. 28 τὰς ἑαυτῶν γυναῖκας); 1 Th 2: 14; 1 Pt 3: 1; 2 Pt 3: 17.

c. with the third pers. ἐν τῇ ἰδίᾳ πατρίδι J 4: 44 (=ἐν τῇ πατρίδι αὐτοῦ: Mt 13: 57; Mk 6: 4; Lk 4: 24); cf. Mt 9: 1. ἐπὶ τὸ ἴδιον ἐξέραμα 2 Pt 2: 22 (=ἐπὶ τὸν ἑαυτοῦ ἔμετον Pr 26: 11). εἰς τὸν ἴδιον ἀγρόν Mt 22: 5; cf. 25: 14; Mk 4: 34b; Lk 10: 34; J 1: 41 (UPZ 13 ob. 2a: ἀδ. ἴδ.); Ac 1: 7, 19; 24: 24; 25: 19; 1 Cor 6: 18; 7: 37a, b; 1 Ti 6: 1; Tit 2: 5, 9; 1 Pt 3: 5; Js 1: 14; Jd 6; MPol 17: 3; Papias 3.

3. subst.—**a.** οἱ ἴδιοι (comrades in battle: Polyaenus, Exc. 14, 20; Dit., Syll.³ 709, 19; 22; 2 Macc 12: 22; Jos., Bell. 1, 42, Ant. 12, 405; compatriots: Philo, Mos. 1, 177) fellow-Christians Ac 4: 23; 24: 23. The disciples (e.g., of a philosopher: Epict. 3, 8, 7) J 13: 1. Relatives (BGU 37; POxy. 932; PFay. 110; 111; 112; 116; 122 al.; Vett. Val. 70, 5 ὑπὸ ἰδίων κ. φίλων; Sir 11: 34) 1 Ti 5: 8; J 1: 11b (the worshipers of a god are also so called: Herm. Wr. 1, 31).

b. τὰ ἴδια *home* (Polyb. 2, 57, 5; 3, 99, 4; Appian, Iber. 23; Peripl. Eryth. 65 εἰς τὰ ἴδια; POxy. 4 ἡ ἀνωτέρα ψυχὴ τ. ἴδια γεινώσκει; 487, 18; Esth 5: 10; 6: 12; 1 Esdr 6: 31 [τὰ ἴδια αὐτοῦ=2 Esdr 6: 11 ἡ οἰκία αὐτοῦ]; 3 Macc 6: 27, 37; 7: 8; Jos., Ant. 8, 405; 416, Bell. 1, 666; 4, 528) J 16: 32 (EFascher, ZNW 39, '41, 171–230); 19: 27; Ac 5: 18 D; 14: 18 v.l.; 21: 6. Many (e.g. Gdspd., Probs. 87f; 94–6; Field, Notes 84; RSV; but not Bultmann 34f) prefer this sense for J 1: 11a and Lk 18: 28; another possibility in both these pass. is the mng. *property, possessions* (POxy. 489, 4; 490, 3; 491, 3; 492, 4 al.). ἐκ τῶν ἰδίων *from his own well-stocked supply* (oft. in inscr. e.g. fr. Magn. and Priene, also Dit., Syll.³ 547, 37; 1068, 16; Jos., Ant. 12, 158) J 8: 44. The sg. can also be used in this way τὸ ἴδιον (Dit., Syll.³ 1257, 3; BGU 1118, 31 [22 BC]) J 15: 19.—τὰ ἴδια *one's own affairs* (X., Mem. 3, 4, 12; 2 Macc 9: 20; 11: 23, 26, 29) 1 Th 4: 11.

4. adv. ἰδίᾳ (Aristoph., Thu.+; inscr., pap., 2 Macc 4: 34; Philo; Jos., Bell. 4, 224, C. Ap. 1, 225) *by oneself, privately* 1 Cor 12: 11; IMg 7: 1.—κατ' ἰδίαν (Machon in Athen. 8 p. 349B; Polyb. 4, 84, 8; Diod. S. 1, 21, 6, also inscr. [Dit., Syll.³ 1157, 10 καὶ κατὰ κοινὸν καὶ κατ' ἰδίαν ἑκάστῳ and oft.]; 2 Macc 4: 5; 14: 21; Philo, Sacr. Abel. 136) *privately, by oneself* (opp. κοινῇ: Jos., Ant. 4, 310)

Mt 14: 13, 23; 17: 1, 19; 20: 17; 24: 3; Mk 4: 34a; 6: 31f; 7: 33 (Diod. S. 18, 49, 2 ἕκαστον ἐκλαμβάνων κατ' ἰδίαν= 'he took each one aside'); 9: 2 (w. μόνος added), 28; 13: 3; Lk 9: 10; 10: 23; Ac 23: 19; Gal 2: 2 (on the separate meeting cf. Jos., Bell. 2, 199 τ. δυνατοὺς κατ' ἰδίαν κ. τὸ πλῆθος ἐν κοινῷ συλλέγων; Appian, Bell. Civ. 5, 40 §170); ISm 7: 2. M-M.

ἰδίως adv. (Pla. et al.; Hero Alex. I p. 432, 4; Dit., Syll.³ 1002, 13; Wsd 17: 10 v.l.; Philo, Plant. 13, Migr. Abr. 50) *in a special way, especially* ἀγαπᾶν B 4: 6; perh. ἰ. is intended to form a contrast to πάντας, in which case it could mean *individually.* *

ἰδιώτης, ου, ὁ (Hdt.+; inscr., pap.; Pr 6: 8b; Ep. Arist.; Philo; Joseph.; loanw. in rabb.).

1. *layman, amateur* in contrast to an expert or specialist of any kind (the uncrowned person as over against the king [Hdt. 2, 81; 7, 199; Ep. Arist. 288f; Philo, Decal. 40; Jos., Bell. 1, 665]; the private soldier as over against the officer [Polyb. 1, 69, 11]; as over against the physician [Thu. 2, 48, 3; Philo, Conf. Lingu. 22], the philosopher [Plut., Mor. 776E; Epict., index Sch.; Philo, Omn. Prob. Lib. 3], the orator [Isocr. 4, 11; Lucian, Jupp. Trag. 27], the μάντις [Paus. 2, 13, 7], the poet [Alexis Com. 269], the priest [Dit., Or. 90, 52; Philo, Spec. Leg. 3, 134], the educated man [Lucian, Lexiph. 25]: any person who does not belong to any one of these groups. The civilian as over against the soldier [Jos., Bell. 2, 178], the private citizen in contrast to the official [Sb 3924, 9; 25; POxy. 1409, 14]) ἰ. τῷ λόγῳ *unskilled in speaking* (cf. Jos., Ant. 2, 271 of Moses: ἰδ....λόγοις) 2 Cor 11: 6 (WGemoll, Phil. Wochenschr. 52, '32, 28). (W. ἄνθρωπος ἀγράμματος) *an untrained man* Ac 4: 13.

2. In 1 Cor 14: 23f ἰδιῶται and ἄπιστοι together form a contrast to the Christian congregation. The ἰδ. are neither similar to the ἄπιστοι (against Ltzm., Hdb. ad loc.), nor are they full-fledged Christians; obviously they stand betw. the two groups as a kind of proselytes or catechumens; perh. *inquirer* (ἰδιώτης as a t.t. of religious life e.g. Dit., Or. 90, 52 [196 BC], Syll.³ 1013, 6; mystery inscr. fr. Andania [92 BC=Syll.³ 736] 16ff αἱ μὲν ἰδιώτιες...αἱ δὲ ἱεραί. In relig. associations the term is used for non-members who may participate in the sacrifices: FPoland, Gesch. des griech. Vereinswesens '09, 247*; 422.—Cf. also Cratin. Jun. Com. [IV BC] 7 vol. II 291 K. of the Pythagoreans: ἔθος ἐστὶν αὐτοῖς, ἄν τιν' ἰδιώτην ποθὲν λάβωσιν εἰσελθόντα κτλ.). The closer relation which they, in contrast to the ἄπιστοι, held w. the Christian group (so as early as Severian of Gabala [died after 409 AD]: KStaab, Pauluskommentare aus. d. griech. Kirche '33, p. xxxv; 268) is clearly shown by the fact that they had a special place in the room where the Christians assembled 1 Cor 14: 16 (ἀναπληρόω 4).—HSchlier, TW III 215–17. M-M. *

ἰδιωτικός, ή, όν (Hdt.+; inscr., pap.; 4 Macc 4: 3, 6; Philo, In Flacc. 133 πράγματα [opp. δημόσια]; Jos., Bell. 5, 228) *private* θλίψεις ἰ. *troubles of one's own* Hv 2, 3, 1. M-M. s.v. ἰδιώτης. *

ἰδού demonstrative particle (Soph.+; inscr., pap., LXX, Test. 12 Patr.; Sib. Or. fgm. 1, 28; 30. It is actually the aor. mid. imper. of εἶδον, ἰδοῦ, except that it is accented w. the acute when used as a particle) *(you) see, look, behold*, variously translated, somet. w. no exact Engl. equiv. (for var. renderings s. EFSiegman, CBQ 9, '47, 77f, fr. RLKnox's transl.).

1. Like הִנֵּה it somet. serves to enliven a narrative—**a.** by arousing the attention of hearers or readers (in 1 Cl,

2 Cl and B only in quots. fr. the OT) Lk 22: 10; J 4: 35; 1 Cor 15: 51; 2 Cor 5: 17; Js 5: 9; Jd 14; Rv 1: 7; 9: 12; 11: 14; Hv 1, 3, 4 al.

b. by introducing someth. new—**α.** after a gen. abs., in order to introduce someth. new, which calls for special attention in the situation generally described by the gen. abs.: Mt 1: 20; 2: 1, 13; 9: 18; 12: 46; 17: 5; 26: 47; 28: 11.

β. With other constructions καὶ ἰδού introduces someth. new: Mt 2: 9; 3: 16; 4: 11; 8: 2, 24, 29, 32, 34; 9: 2, 3, 20 al.; Lk 1: 20, 31, 36; 2: 25; 9: 30, 38; 10: 25 al.; Ac 12: 7; 16: 1. Also someth. quite extraordinary *and yet ὡς ἀποθνῄσκοντες κ. ἰδοὺ ζῶμεν* 2 Cor 6: 9; cf. Mt 7: 4; Ac 27: 24 (contrary to all appearances).

γ. Whole stories may be introduced by ἰδού to attract attention Mt 13: 3.

δ. ἰδού in the middle of a statement to enliven it Mt 23: 34; Ac 2: 7; 13: 11; 20: 22, 25.

ε. used to emphasize the size or importance of someth. *ἰ. ἡμεῖς ἀφήκαμεν πάντα* Mt 19: 27; Mk 10: 28. *ἰ. δέκα κ. ὀκτὼ ἔτη eighteen long years* Lk 13: 16 (cf. BGU 948, 6 ἡ μήτηρ σου ἀσθενεῖ, ἰδοὺ δέκα τρεῖς μῆνες; Dt 8: 4); vs. 7; 15; 29; 19: 8; 2 Cor 12: 14.—*καὶ ἰ. ἐγὼ μεθ' ὑμῶν εἰμι πάσας τὰς ἡμέρας* Mt 28: 20; cf. 20: 18; 23: 38; Lk 2: 34; 6: 23; 13: 30 al.

c. as a call to closer consideration and contemplation *remember, consider,* etc. Mt 10: 16; 11: 8; 22: 4; Mk 14: 41; Lk 2: 48; 7: 25; Hv 2, 3, 4. Likew. ἰδοὺ γάρ Lk 1: 44, 48; 2: 10; Ac 9: 11; 2 Cor 7: 11. The citing of examples Js 3: 4f; 5: 4, 7, 11 belongs here.

2. used w. a noun without a finite verb *here* or *there is (are), here* or *there was (were), here* or *there comes (came)* (old Attic inscr. in Meisterhans³-Schw. p. 203 ἰδοὺ χελιδών; Epict. 4, 11, 35; LXX) *καὶ ἰ. φωνὴ ἐκ τ. οὐρανῶν and a voice came from heaven* Mt 3: 17. *καὶ ἰ. ἄνθρωπος and there was a man* Mt 12: 10. *ἰ. ἄνθρωπος φάγος here is a man who is a glutton* 11: 19; Lk 7: 34; cf. 5: 12, 18; 7: 37; 11: 31; 13: 11; 17: 21a; 19: 2, 20; 22: 38, 47; 23: 50; Ac 8: 27 (WCvanUnnik, ZNW 47, '56, 181-91), 36; 2 Cor 5: 2; Rv 12: 3; 21: 3. *ἰ. ὁ νυμφίος here is the bridegroom* Mt 25: 6. *ἰ. ὁ ἄνθρωπος here is the man* J 19: 5. In Rv as a formula εἶδον κ. ἰδού 4: 1; 6: 2, 5, 8; 7: 9; 14: 14; cf. 19: 11. The godly man answers *ἰ. ἐγώ here I am* to the divine call, in order to signify his willingness to obey God's command (1 Km 3: 4) Ac 9: 10. (In Mt *ἰ.* is found 62 times, in Mk 8 times [including once as a v.l. and once in a quot.], in Lk 56 times, in J 4 times [including once in a quot.], in Ac 23 times, in Paul 9 times [including once in a quot.], Hb 4 times in quotations, Js 6 times, Jd once, 1 Pt once in a quot., Rv 26 times; it is not found at all in 1-3 J, 2 Pt, Eph, Phil, Col, 1 and 2 Th, Pastorals, Phlm, Dg, Ign, Pol). Cf. Mlt. 11, w. note 1; MJohannessohn, Ztschr. f. vergl. Sprachforschung 64, '37, 145-260; 66, '39, 145-95; 67, '40, 30-84 (esp. on καὶ ἰδού); PVannutelli, Synoptica 2, '38, XLVI-LII; ἰδού in the Syn. Gosp.; PFiedler, D. Formel 'Und Siehe' im NT: Studien z. A. u. NT 20, '69; AVargas-Machucha, (καὶ) ἰδού en el estilo narrativo de Mt, Biblica 50, '69, 233-44. See ἴδε. M-M.

Ἰδουμαία, ας, ἡ *Idumaea,* Grecized form (Diod. S. 19, 98; Appian, Mithrid. 106 §499; LXX; Joseph.) of אֱדוֹם (Edom); a mountainous district south of Judaea Mk 3: 8; Ac 2: 9 v.l. *

ἰδρόω 1 aor. imper. ἰδρωσάτω (Hom.+; POxy. 1242, 52; 4 Macc 3: 8; 6: 11) *sweat, perspire* fig. *ἰδρωσάτω ἡ ἐλεημοσύνη σου εἰς τὰς χεῖράς σου let your alms sweat in your hands,* i.e., do not give alms without due consideration D 1: 6 (quot. of unknown orig.; cf. Sib. Or. 2, 79.—S. ἐλεημοσύνη). *

ἰδρύω pf. pass. ptc. ἰδρυμένος (Hom.+; inscr.; PGiess. 99, 16; 4 Macc 17: 3; Philo; Jos., Ant. 1, 60, C. Ap. 2, 36) act. *cause to sit down,* in our lit. only pass. *be seated, sit, be established.* Perf. pass. *be established* of faith ἵδρυται *it is established* Dg 11: 6. ὁ ἰδρυμένος αὐτοῖς τόπος *the place established for them* 1 Cl 44: 5. *

ἰδρώς, ῶτος, ὁ (Hom.+; PGM 5, 152 ἰδ. . . . ἐπὶ τ. γῆν; LXX; Philo; Jos., Bell. 3, 5, Ant. 7, 282) *sweat, perspiration* Lk 22: 44 (on this LBrun, ZNW 32, '33, 265-76.—Bloody sweat as an extraordinary phenomenon: Apollon. Rhod. 4, 1282f; Appian, Bell. Civ. 4, 4 §14).—διὰ κόπου καὶ ἰδρῶτος (cf. Philo, Leg. All. 3, 251) B 10: 4. M-M. B. 264. *

Ἰεζάβελ, ἡ indecl. (אִיזֶבֶל; 3 Km 16: 31 al.—In Joseph. Ἰεζαβέλη, ης [Ant. 8, 356]) *Jezebel,* Ahab's queen, who favored the cult of the Phoenician Baal in Israel and persecuted the prophets of Yahweh (3 Km 16-4 Km 9), and who was also addicted to harlotry and magic (4 Km 9: 22). Hence the name was applied to a woman who endangered orthodox teaching within the Christian church at Thyatira Rv 2: 20. ESchürer (Weizsäcker-Festschr. 1892, 39-58) considers that the name refers to a prophetess of the temple of the Chaldaean Sibyl in that city. Zahn, in Einl.³ II 620ff and in his comm., prefers the rdg. γυναῖκά σου and takes it to mean the bishop's wife. M-M. *

Ἰεζεκιήλ, ὁ indecl. (יְחֶזְקֵאל; in Joseph. Ἰεζεκίηλος) *Ezekiel,* OT prophet (Ezk 1: 3) 1 Cl 17: 1. λέγει ἡ γραφὴ ἐν τῷ Ἰεζεκιήλ 2 Cl 6: 8 (on the quot. fr. Ezk 14: 14, 16, 18 cf. Knopf, Hdb. ad loc.). *

Ἰεράπολις, εως, ἡ *Hierapolis,* a city in Phrygia in Asia Minor, on the Lycus R. (Altertümer v. Hierap.: Jahrb. d. Deutsch. Arch. Inst., Ergänzungsheft 4, 1898; SEJohnson, Biblical Archaeologist 13, '50, 12-18; Sib. Or. 5, 318; 12, 280) Col 4: 13 (Bl-D. §115, 2 claim it should be written Ἱερᾷ πόλει; cf. Mlt.-H. 278, νέος 3 and Ἡλιούπολις). M-M. *

ἱερατεία, ας, ἡ (Aristot., Pol. 7, 8 p. 1328b, 12f; Dionys. Hal. 2, 73; inscr. fr. before 335 BC [Inschr. v. Priene 139, 7], cf. Dit., Or. 90, 52, Syll.³ Index IV p. 390a; PTebt. 298, 14; LXX, Test. 12 Patr.) *the priestly office* or *service κατὰ τὸ ἔθος τῆς ἱ. according to the custom of the priestly office* Lk 1: 9. τὴν ἱ. λαμβάνειν *receive the priestly office* (cf. Dionys. Hal. loc. cit. παραλαμβάνει τὴν ἱερατείαν ὁ δοκιμασθείς) Hb 7: 5.—*Priesthood* Rv 5: 10 v.l. M-M. *

ἱεράτευμα, ατος, τό (only in the Gk. of Bibl. wr. and others dependent on them) *priesthood οἰκοδομεῖσθαι εἰς ἱ. ἅγιον be built up into a holy priesthood* 1 Pt 2: 5; *βασίλειον ἱ. a priesthood of royal rank* or *in royal service* vs. 9 (Ex 19: 6; 23: 22). PDabin, Le sacerdoce royal des fidèles dans l. livres saints '41, 179-97; WArndt, CTM 19, '48, 241-9; JBlinzler, Episcopus [Faulhaber-Festschr.] '49, 49-65; JHElliott, The Elect and the Holy (1 Pt 2: 4-10) '66. M-M. *

ἱερατεύω (late Gk. word: Herodian 5, 6, 3; Heliod. 10, 40 al.; inscr. fr. II BC: Dit., Or. 90, 51 [196 BC]; Inschr. v. Magn. 178, 6 [II BC]; other exx. fr. inscr. in Dssm., NB 43 [BS 215f]; PGiess. 11, 10 [118 AD]; LXX; Jos., Ant. 3, 189; 15, 253) *hold the office* or *perform the service of a priest* Lk 1: 8. W. λειτουργεῖν 1 Cl 43: 4. M-M. *

Ἰερεμίας, ου, ὁ (יִרְמְיָה, יִרְמְיָהוּ; LXX; Ep. Arist. 50; Philo, Cher. 49; Joseph.) *Jeremiah,* prophet at the time of the fall of the Jewish state ῥηθὲν διὰ Ἰερεμίου τοῦ προφήτου (cf. Jos., Ant. 11, 1) Mt 2: 17; 27: 9. Some Jews

considered that Jesus was Jeremiah come again (s. Billerb.
I 730) Mt 16: 14.—HFDSparks, JTS n.s. 1, '50, 155f;
JCarmignac, KGKuhn-Festschr., '71, 283-98; JoachJere-
mias, TW III 218-21.*

ἱερεύς, έως, ὁ (Hom.+; inscr., pap., LXX, Ep. Arist.,
Philo, Joseph., Test. 12 Patr.) *priest.*
  1. lit.—**a.** of pagan priests Ac 14: 13; 1 Cl 25: 5. οἱ
ἱερεῖς τ. εἰδώλων B 9: 6.
  b. of Jewish priests (Diod. S. 40, 3, 4 and 5)—**a.** of
ordinary priests: ὁ ἱερεύς *the priest* who officiates in a
given situation (Lev 13: 2ff) Mt 8: 4; Mk 1: 44; Lk 5: 14.
Otherwise of an individual priest 1: 5; 10: 31; Hb 8: 4; 10:
11. Pl. Mt 12: 4f; Mk 2: 26; Lk 6: 4; 17: 14; 20: 1 v.l.; J 1:
19; Ac 4: 1; 6: 7; Hb 7: 14f, 20, 23; 9: 6; GP 7: 25; IPhld 9:
1; B 7: 6. W. Λευῖται 1 Cl 32: 2 (cf. Lk 10: 31 and 32.
Named before the Levites as Jos., Ant. 11, 80f and oft. in
Joseph. [Schmidt 358]). W. the Lev. and the ἀρχιερεύς 40:
5. οἱ ἱ. τοῦ ναοῦ B 7: 3.
  β. of the high priest (Diod. S. 34+35 fgm. 1, 3; 3 Km 1:
8; Bar 1: 7; 1 Macc 15: 1) Ac 5: 27 D. Ἀαρὼν ὁ ἱερεύς (cf.
Ex 35: 19; Lev 13: 2.—ἱ. also of pagan high priests in
Mayser II 2 p. 465; Appian, Bell. Civ. 4, 134 §562 Caesar,
the Pontifex Maximus, is called a ἱ.; Synes., Prov. 2, 3 p.
122A) GEb 1 (s. GH 21 servus sacerdotis).
  2. fig.—**a.** of Christ, who is called in Hb ἱερεὺς (in
sense 1β; s. 5: 5f) εἰς τὸν αἰῶνα κατὰ τὴν τάξιν
Μελχισέδεκ (Ps 109: 4) 5: 6; 7: 17, 21; also ἱερεὺς μέγας
(1 Macc 12: 20; cf. Sir 50: 1; Jdth 4: 6, 8, 14; Philo, Spec.
Leg. 1, 161 al.=ἀρχιερεύς) 10: 21. Cf. also 7: 1, 3, 11 and
s. ἀρχιερεύς 2a, and s. CSpicq, MGoguel-Festschr. '50,
258-69.
  b. of the Christians ἱερεῖς τοῦ θεοῦ *priests of God* Rv
20: 6; cf. 1: 6; 5: 10 (Diog. L. 7, 119: acc. to the Stoa the
σοφοί are the only real priests).—GSchrenk, TW III
257-65; AHGunneweg, Leviten u. Priester '65. M-M. B.
1472.*

Ἰεριχώ, ἡ indecl. (יְרִיחוֹ; LXX. On the word s. W-S. §10,
1a. Joseph. varies betw. Ἰεριχώ, gen. -οῦς and Ἰεριχοῦς,
gen. -οῦντος; s. Niese index. Ἰεριχοῦς, -οῦντος also
Galen XI 693 K., but in Strabo 16, 2, 41 Ἰερικοῦς. On the
spelling cf. Bl-D. §38 app.; 39, 1) *Jericho,* a city in Judaea,
not far from the ford across the Jordan just north of the
Dead Sea Mt 20: 29; Mk 10: 46; Lk 18: 35; Hb 11: 30; 1 Cl
12: 2. Since a much-travelled road led to Jerusalem, 150
stades (Jos., Bell. 4, 474) or about 18 mi. away, a customs
house was located here Lk 19: 1. The road fr. Jerusalem to
Jericho, which leads through desolate mountainous country (Jos., loc. cit. ἔρημον κ. πετρῶδες), was notoriously
unsafe Lk 10: 30 (AvVeldhuizen, ThSt 25, '07, 41-3).—
ESellin and CWatzinger, Jericho '13; Dalman, Orte'
257ff; PThomsen, Jericho: Reallex. d. Vorgesch. VI '26,
153ff; JBPritchard, The 1951 Campaign at Herodian Jer.:
Bull. of the Amer. Schools of Or. Research no. 123, '51,
8-17; JLKelso, NT Jericho: Bibl. Archeologist 14, '51,
34-43; Lucetta Mowry, ibid. 15, '52, 26-42.*

ἱερόθυτος, ον (Pind., fgm. 78 refers to death for one's
fatherland as ἱερόθυτος θάνατος; this is one of the earliest
occurrences of the word; Dit., Syll.³ 624, 43; 736, 23;
PGM 4, 2899) *devoted* or *sacrificed to a divinity,* subst.
τὸ ἱ. *meat sacrificed to idols* (Ps.-Aristot., Mirabilia 123 p.
824b, 1f; Plut., Mor. 729c ἐγεύοντο τῶν ἱεροθύτων)
1 Cor 10: 28. M-M.*

ἱερόν, οῦ, τό (subst. neut. of the adj. ἱερός) *sanctuary,
temple* (so Hdt.+; inscr., pap., LXX).
  1. of pagan temples (Diod. S. 13, 7, 6 τ. Διὸς ἱερόν;

Appian, Liby. 81 §383 al.; Bel 22 Theod.; 1 Macc 10: 84;
Philo, Leg. ad Gai. 139 al.; Jos., Ant. 18, 65) the temple of
Artemis at Ephesus (s. 2, end, below) Ac 19: 27.
  2. of the temple at Jerusalem, including the whole
temple precinct w. its buildings, courts, etc. (LXX; Ezk
45: 19; 1 Ch 29: 4 and oft. in the Apocrypha; Ep. Arist.;
Philo, Joseph.; Polyb. 16, 39, 4; Diod. S. 40, 3, 3; Strabo
16, 2, 34; Dit., Or. 598, 3; PGM 13, 233) Mt 12: 6; 24: 1b;
Mk 13: 3; Lk 21: 5; Ac 24: 6; 25: 8; GOxy 9 and oft.
στρατηγὸς τ. ἱεροῦ *captain of the temple* (Jos., Bell. 6,
294) Ac 4: 1; 5: 24; pl. Lk 22: 52. (εἰσ)ελθεῖν εἰς τὸ ἱ. Mt
21: 12a, 23; Mk 11: 11, 15a; Lk 2: 27 al.; ἐξελθεῖν ἀπὸ
τοῦ ἱ. Mt 24: 1a; ἐκπορεύεσθαι ἐκ τοῦ ἱ. Mk 13: 1. Cf. Mt
26: 55; Mk 14: 49; Lk 19: 47; 21: 37; 22: 53; 24: 53; J 5: 14;
7: 14, 28; Ac 3: 2a al. As the place where the priests
worked Mt 12: 5. Provided w. porticoes J 10: 23. Even
when the action takes place in the Court of the Gentiles,
where merchants and money-changers had their places Mt
21: 12; Mk 11: 15f; Lk 19: 45; J 2: 14f, or in the Court of
Women Lk 2: 37, the choice of the word ἱ. emphasizes the
fact that the holy precinct is the scene of the action (τὸ ἱ.
w. ὁ ναός the temple bldg: Jos., Bell. 2, 400. On the
cleansing of the temple cf. ACaldecott, JTS 24, '23, 382ff;
FCBurkitt, ibid. 25, '24, 386ff; FMBraun, RB 38, '29,
178-200; ELohmeyer, ThBl 20, '41, 257-64.—Appian,
Bell. Civ. 2, 120 §507 ἐν τοῖς ἱεροῖς the robbers encamp in
the temples; Ep. 65 of Apollonius of Tyana [Philostrat. I
363, 23] the ἱερόν of Artemis at Ephesus as τῶν ἀπο-
στερούντων μυχός=hideaway for robbers). On τὸ πτερύγιον τοῦ ἱεροῦ (Mt 4: 5; Lk 4: 9) s. πτερύγιον.—
PJoüon, Les mots employés pour désigner 'le temple' dans
AT, NT et Josèphe: Rech de Sc rel 25, '35, 329-43; OWolf,
D. Tempel v. Jerus. '31; ELohmeyer, Kultus u. Evglm.
'42; GLMay, ET 62, '50f, 346f; CKopp, The Holy Places
in the Gospels (tr. RWalls) '63, 283-304; REClements,
God and Temple, '65; GSchrenk, TW III 230-47. M-M.
B. 1465.

ἱεροπρεπής, ές *befitting a holy pers. or thing, holy,
worthy of reverence* (X., Symp. 8, 40; Pla., Theag. 122D;
Cass. Dio 56, 46; Lucian, Sacrif. 13; Plut., Lib. Educ. 14
p. 11c; 4 Macc 9: 25; 11: 20; Philo, Abr. 101, Decal. 60,
Leg. All. 3, 204; Jos., Ant. 11, 329) of the conduct of the
older women of the congregation Tit 2: 3. The more
specialized mng. *like a priest(ess),* resulting fr. the use of
the word in describing the conduct of a priest (Inscr. Gr.
163, 21; Inschr. v. Priene 109, 216; Dit., Syll.³ 708, 24;
Philo, Omn. Prob. Lib. 75) may perh. be poss. here.—
GSchrenk, TW III 253f. M-M.*

ἱερός, ά, όν (Hom.+; inscr., pap., LXX, Philo, Joseph.)
holy.
  1. adj. (Jos., Ant. 16, 27; 28) ἱερὰ γράμματα (γράμμα
2c) 2 Ti 3: 15. Also ἱεραὶ βίβλοι (βίβλος 1) 1 Cl 43: 1. ἱ.
γραφαί (γραφή 2ba) 45: 2; 53: 1. ἱ. κήρυγμα short
ending of Mk; ἱ. χεῖρες *holy hands,* that touch nothing
profane 1 Cl 33: 4. αὕτη ἡ πολυτέλεια καλὴ καὶ ἱερά
such extravagance is good and holy Hs 1: 10.
  2. subst. τὰ ἱερά *the holy things,* everything belonging
to the temple and its service (Demosth. 57, 3 τῶν ἱερῶν
καὶ κοινῶν μετέχειν; Philo, Spec. Leg. 3, 40; Jos., Ant.
14, 214) τὰ ἱερὰ ἐργάζεσθαι *perform the holy services in
the temple* (cf. Ael. Aristid. 51, 66 K.=27 p. 550 D.: ἱερὰ
ποιεῖν) 1 Cor 9: 13a.—GSchrenk, TW III 221-30.—Ἰερᾷ
πόλει s. Ἱεράπολις. M-M. B. 1475.*

Ἰεροσόλυμα, τά and **ἡ,** and **Ἰερουσαλήμ, ἡ** indecl.
(יְרוּשָׁלַיִם‎, יְרוּשָׁלֵם‎) *Jerusalem.* On the breathing cf. Bl-D.
§39, 1; Mlt.-H. 101; on the form of the name cf. Bl-D.

§56, 1; 4 app.; Mlt.-H. 147f; Ramsay, Exp. 7th ser. III '07, 110ff, 414f; Harnack, D. Apostelgesch. '08, 72ff; RSchütz, ZNW 11, '10, 169-87.—τὰ Ἱεροσόλυμα (Polyb. 16, 39, 4; Diod. S. 34+35, fgm. 1; 1, 2, 3, 5; Strabo 16, 2, 34; 36; 40; Appian, Syr. 50 §252; Cass. Dio 37, 15; 17; Timochares in Euseb., Pr. Ev. 9, 35; Ps.-Hecataeus in Jos., C. Ap. 1, 197; Agatharchides ibid. 1, 209; Manetho ibid. 1, 241; Lysimachus ibid. 1, 311; PGM 13, 997; LXX in Apocr. [Thackeray 168]; Ep. Arist. 32; 35; 52; Philo, Leg. ad Gai. 278; Joseph. [Niese index]) is the form found in Mt (the sole exception 23: 37 is obviously fr. a quot.), Mk and J; it is also found in Lk and Ac, as well as Gal 1: 17f; 2: 1; PK 4 p. 15, 35.—πᾶσα Ἱεροσόλυμα Mt 2: 3; GEb 2 p. 13, 30 seems to go back to a form ἡ Ἱεροσόλυμα, ης (cf. Pel.-Leg. 14, 14 πᾶσα [ἡ] Ἱεροσόλυμα; Tob 14: 4; Bl-D. §56, 4 app.—S. also PGM 4, 3069 ἐν τῇ καθαρᾷ Ἱεροσολύμῳ and 13, 233 ἐν Ἱερωσολύμῳ).—ἡ Ἱερουσαλήμ (quite predom. in LXX; Test. 12 Patr.; Philo, Somn. 2, 250.—Jos., C. Ap. 1, 179 Clearchus is quoted as reporting remarks of his teacher Aristotle in which the latter uses the form Ἱερουσαλήμη [doubted by Niese; Euseb., Pr. Ev. 9, 5, 6 has the same quot. fr. Clearchus w. the form Ἱερουσαλήμ]) besides Mt 23: 37 (s. above) in Lk, Ac (cf. P-LCouchoud et RStahl, Rev. d'Histoire des Rel. 97, '28, 9-17), predom. in Paul, Hb 12: 22; Rv; 1 Cl 41: 2; GH 6; GP.—Mostly without the art. Bl-D. §261, 3 w. app.; 275, 2; W-S. §18, 5e; w. the art. only J 2: 23; 5: 2; 10: 22; 11: 18; cf. Ac 5: 28; Gal 4: 25f; Rv 3: 12. No certain conclusions can be drawn concerning the use of the two forms of the name (they are used in the same immediate context by Hecataeus in Euseb., Pr. Ev. 9, 4, 2); the mss. vary considerably in their practice.

1. The name refers—**a.** to the city itself Mt 2: 1 and oft.; Mk 3: 8 and oft.; Lk 2: 25, 41; J 1: 19; Ro 15: 19, 25f; Gal 1: 17f; 2: 1 al. ἀναβαίνειν εἰς 'I. Mt 20: 17f; Mk 10: 32f; Lk 19: 28; J 2: 13; 5: 1; 11: 55; Ac 25: 1; Lk 18: 31; Ac 11: 2; 21: 12, 15. καταβαίνειν ἀπὸ 'I. Mk 3: 22; Ac 11: 27; 25: 7; Lk 10: 30; Ac 8: 26. θυγατέρες 'I. cf. θυγάτηρ 2d.

b. to its inhabitants πᾶσα 'I. *the whole city of Jerusalem* (Caecilius Calactinus, fgm. 75 p. 57, 11 says πᾶσα ἡ Ἑλλάς [Thu. 1, 6, 1] stands ἀντὶ τῶν Ἑλλήνων; Pla., Ep. 7 p. 348Α πᾶσα Σικελία; Demosth. 18, 18; Psellus p. 43, 12 πᾶσα ἡ Πόλις='all Byzantines') Mt 2: 3; cf. 3: 5; 23: 37 (Aeschines, Ctesiph. 133 Θῆβαι, Θῆβαι; Ps.-Demetr. in Eloc. c. 267 adds to this Aeschines passage the comment, 'The repetition of the name produces a powerful effect'.—HvanderKwaak, NovT 8, '66, 56-70); Lk 2: 38; 13: 34; Ac 21: 31.—For a geographical and historical treatment HGuthe, RE VIII 666ff; XXIII 671f; HVincent and F-MAbel, Jérusalem I '12; II '26; GDalman, J. u. s. Gelände '30; MJoin-Lambert, Jerusalem (tr. CHaldane) '58; PWinter, 'Nazareth' and 'Jer.' in Lk 1 and 2, NTS 3, '56/'57, 136-42 (lit.); CKopp, The Holy Places of the Gospels '63 (tr. RWalls), 283-417. On its cultural history JoachJeremias, Jerus. in the Time of Jesus (tr. FH and CHCave) '69. For its theol. significance, JBlinzler in Wikenhauser-Festschr. '52, 20-52; JSchneider, ibid., 207-29.

2. In fig. and eschatol. usage ἡ νῦν 'I. *the present J.* is contrasted w. the ἄνω 'I. *the heavenly J.* Gal 4: 25f. For the latter also 'I. ἐπουράνιος Hb 12: 22 and ἡ καινὴ 'I. *the new J.* Rv 3: 12; 21: 2, also ἡ ἁγία 'I. 21: 10; cf. vs. 2. On the theol. usage s. JdeYoung, Jerus. in the NT '60.—For lit. s. on πόλις 2. M-M.

Ἱεροσολυμίτης, ου, ὁ (Sir 50: 27; 4 Macc 4: 22; 18: 5; Joseph. [Niese index]) *an inhabitant of Jerusalem* Mk 1: 5; J 7: 25.*

ἱεροσυλέω (Aristoph.+; Polyb. 30, 26, 9; Artem. 3, 3; Heraclitus, Ep. 7, 4H.; Dit., Syll.³ 417, 8; 10; 2 Macc 9: 2; Philo; Jos., C. Ap. 1, 249, Ant. 17, 163) *rob temples* (prob. to be taken literally) Ro 2: 22 (w. κλέπτω and μοιχεύω as Philo, Conf. Lingu. 163; cf. also Herm. Wr. 12, 5).— GSchrenk, TW III 254-6. M-M.*

ἱερόσυλος, ον (Aristoph.+; Aristot., Pol. 5, 4 p. 1304a, 3f; Diod. S. 16, 25, 2; Plut., Sol. 17, 1; inscr.; 2 Macc 4: 42; Jos., Bell. 1, 654, Ant. 16, 164) *pertaining to a temple robber*; subst. ὁ ἱ. *temple robber* (Draco in Plut., Solon 17, 2; Dio Chrys. 31[14], 82; Alciphr. 3, 7, 5; Philo, De Jos. 84; Jos., Ant. 16, 168) Ac 19: 37. But a more general mng. is also poss. (KLatte, Hlg. Recht '20, 83ff) *one who commits irreverent acts against a holy place, a sacrilegious person* (Dit., Syll.³ 578, 47ff [II BC] ὁ δὲ εἴπας ἢ πρήξας τι παρὰ τόνδε τὸν νόμον...ἔστω ἱερόσυλος; 1016, 8; ²680, 10. S. also Menand., Dyscolus 640 ἱερόσυλε συ= *you rogue!*, Epitr. 551; 666 J.). M-M.*

ἱερουργέω (Plut., Num. 14, 1, Alex. 31, 4; Herodian 5, 6, 1; 5, 5, 9; Philostrat., Vi. Soph. 2, 10, 2 p. 91, 25; CIG add. to 4528 [III p. 1175]; IG ed. min. I 4, 4; 8 [V BC]; 4 Macc 7: 8 v.l.; Philo, Mos. 1, 87 al.; Jos., Ant. 6, 102; 7, 333) *perform holy service, act as a priest* τὶ w. *regard to* someth. τὸ εὐαγγέλιον *serve the gospel as a priest* (perh. w. emphasis on sacrifice; Field, Notes 165) Ro 15: 16. M-M.*

Ἱερουσαλήμ s. Ἱεροσόλυμα.

ἱερωσύνη, ης, ἡ *priestly office, priesthood* (Hdt.+; Pla., Demosth.; Diod. S. 5, 58, 2; Plut. et al.; inscr.; PBrem. 70, 6; LXX; Philo; Jos., Ant. 2, 216, C. Ap. 1, 31; Test. 12 Patr. On the word-formation s. Mayser 15; 154, 11 [lit.]; Mlt.-H. 358) 1 Cl 43: 2; ἡ Λευιτικὴ ἱ. *the Levitic priesthood* Hb 7: 11; μετατιθεμένης τῆς ἱ. *when the priesthood changes* vs. 12; ἀπαράβατον ἔχειν τὴν ἱ. vs. 24 (Ps.-Aristot., Mirabilia 137 τ. ἱερωσύνην ἔχειν= 'possess the priestly office'). M-M.*

Ἰεσσαί, ὁ indecl. (יִשַׁי; in Joseph. Ἰεσσαῖος, ου [Ant. 6, 162]) *Jesse*, David's father (1 Km 16: 1, 10; 17: 12; 20: 27) Ac 13: 22; 1 Cl 18: 1. In the genealogy of Jesus (cf. Ruth 4: 22) Mt 1: 5f; Lk 3: 32; ἡ ῥίζα τοῦ 'I. *the Scion of Jesse* of the Messianic king Ro 15: 12 (Is 11: 10).*

Ἰεφθάε, ὁ indecl. (יִפְתָּח; in Joseph. Ἰάφθας [v.l. Ἰεφθας], α [Ant. 5, 271]) *Jephthah*, son of Gilead, one of the judges of Israel (Judg 11f) Hb 11: 32.*

Ἰεχονίας, ου, ὁ (יְכָנְיָהוּ=יְהוֹיָכִין) *Jechoniah*, a king of Judah (Jos., Bell. 6, 103, Ant. 10, 229f). Acc. to the genealogy Mt 1: 11f he was a son of Josiah and had brothers. In 1 Ch 3: 15f Ἰεχονία is the son of Ἰωακίμ and the grandson of Josiah, and only one brother is mentioned. 1 Ch 3: 17; Mt 1: 12 and Lk 3: 23ff D agree that he was the father of Salathiel.*

Ἰησοῦς (יֵשׁוּעַ Jeshua, later form for יְהוֹשׁוּעַ Joshua; s. MLidzbarski, Handb. d. nordsem. Epigr. 1898, 291; FPraetorius, ZDMG 59, '05, 341f; FXSteinmetzer, BZ 14, '17, 193ff; FJWaele, Wetenschappelijke Tijdingen 5, '42, 177-81), gen. οῦ, dat. οῦ, acc. οῦν, voc. οῦ, ὁ *Jesus*. This name, which was common among Jews (several persons w. it in LXX and Joseph. [Niese, index]; Ep. Arist. 48; 49; inscr. fr. the time of Augustus [Rev. Épigraphique n.s. 1, '13 no. 12]; POxy. 816 [I BC]; PLond. 1119a, 2. Ostraca: Sb 5812; 5817; 5820; 5822), usu. takes the article in the gospels, except when it is accompanied by a word in apposition w. the art.; in the epistles and Rv it does not regularly take the art. (Bl-D. §260, 1; W-S. §18, 6;

HermvSoden, D. Schriften des NTs I 2, '11, 1406-9; RCNevius, NTS 12, '65, 81-85 (4th Gosp.).

1. *Joshua,* successor of Moses and military leader of the people when they entered Canaan (Josh; 1 Macc 2: 55; 2 Macc 12: 15; Philo; Joseph.; Sib. Or. 2, 247) Ac 7: 45; Hb 4: 8. Fully 'Ι. υἱὸς Ναυή (Josh 1: 1; cf. Sir 46: 1) B 12: 8f or 'Ι. ὁ τοῦ Ναυή 1 Cl 12: 2.

2. *Jesus,* son of Eliezer, in the genealogy of Jesus Lk 3: 29.

3. *Jesus Christ,* more definitely designated as 'Ι. Χριστός, Χριστὸς 'Ι., ὁ κύριος 'Ι. (Χριστός), ὁ σωτήρ 'Ι. Χριστός etc. Mt 1: 1, 21, 25 and oft. S. Χριστός, κύριος, σωτήρ. On the use of the names in Paul s. EvDobschütz, D. Th. Briefe in Meyer[7] '09, 60f. On the abbreviation of the names in mss. cf. LTraube, Nomina sacra '07, 113ff; EbNestle, ZNW 9, '08, 248ff.—The older lit. on Jesus in ASchweitzer, Gesch. der Leben-Jesu-Forschung[2] '13. Further RGG III[3], '59, 619-53 (bibliog. 651-53); Marie Veit, D. Auffassung v. d. Pers. Jesu im Urchristent. nach d. neuesten Forschungen, Diss. Mbg. '46. Lives fr. more recent times: REisler, 'Ιησοῦς Βασιλεύς '28-'30; RBultmann, Jesus[2] '29 (reprinted '51), D. Urchristentum '49; PFeine, Jesus '30; FPrat, Jésus-Christ '33; JKlausner, J. von Nazareth[2] '34 (Engl. version '26); MGoguel, La Vie de J. '32 (Engl. '44); KAdam, Jes. Christus[4] '35; FMWillam, D. Leben J. im Lande u. Volke Israel[4] '34; JPickl, Messiaskönig J. in d. Auffassung seiner Zeitgenossen[3] '39; RGuardini, D. Herr '37; MDibelius, Jesus '39 ([3]'60) (Engl. '49); ALoisy, Hist. et mythe à propos de J-Ch. '38; HFelder, Jes. v. Naz.[2] '39; CNoel, The Life of J. '39; VGrønbech, J. d. Menschensohn '41; RMeyer, D. Proph. aus Galil. '40; CJCadoux, The Hist. Mission of J. '41; ATOlmstead, J. in the Light of History '42; WManson, J. the Messiah '43, 6th impr. '52; AEJRawlinson, Christ in the Gospels '44; GRicciotti, Life of Christ '47; FBüchsel, Jesus '47; HJCadbury, J.: What Manner of Man '47; GSDuncan, J., Son of Man '47; JGHHoffmann, Les Vies de Jésus et le Jésus de l'Histoire '47; WGKümmel, Verheissung u. Erfüllung[2] '53; GBornkamm, J. von Nazareth '56 (Engl. transl. McLuskey and Robinson '60); JKnox, Jesus, Lord and Christ '58; HRistow u. KMatthiae, ed., D. historische Jesus u. d. kerygmatische Christus '60; E Schweizer, Jesus (transl. DEGreen) '71; HBraun, Qumran u. d. NT II '66, 54-118 (lit.).—On the name: WLowrie, Theol. Today 8, '51, 11-19; VTaylor, Names of Jesus '53.

4. *Jesus Barabbas* s. Βαραββᾶς.—5. 'Ι. ὁ λεγόμενος 'Ιοῦστος *Jesus who is called Justus* (on the double name cf. Dssm., B. 183f [BS 315]), συνεργὸς ἐκ περιτομῆς Col 4: 11. It has been conjectured (Zahn, Einl. I 321, 4; EAmling, ZNW 10, '09, 261f) that this Jesus is referred to again in Phlm 23. On this ADeissmann, D. Name J.: Mysterium Christi '31, 13-41.—WFoerster, TW III 284-94. M-M.

ἱκανός, ή, όν (trag., Hdt.+; inscr., pap., LXX, Ep. Arist., Philo, Joseph., Test. Napht. 2: 4; loanw. in rabb.).

1. *sufficient, adequate, large enough,* also gener. *large, much* of number and quantity.

a. κεράμια ἱκανώτατα *a large number of jars* Hm 12, 5, 3 (Dit., Syll.[3] 736, 108 ξύλα ἱ.). ὄχλος *a large crowd* Mk 10: 46; Lk 7: 12; Ac 11: 24, 26; 19: 26 (Dit., Syll.[3] 569, 14 πλῆθος ἱ.; PPetr. II 20 II, 7; PLille 3, 76 [III BC]; Jos., Ant. 5, 250). κλαυθμός *weeping aloud* 20: 37. ἀργύρια *a large sum of* (lit. 'enough') *money* Mt 28: 12 (cf. Inscr. Rom. IV 514, 5 ἱ. ἀργύριον; Dit., Syll.[3] 1106, 74; 77). λαμπάδες *a good many lamps* Ac 20: 8. ἀγέλη χοίρων ἱκανῶν Lk 8: 32. φῶς *a very bright light* Ac 22: 6. ἐν λόγοις ἱ. w. *many words*=*at length* Lk 23: 9.—ἱκανὸν ἡ

ἐπιτιμία *the punishment is severe enough* 2 Cor 2: 6 (on the lack of agreement in gender cf. Bl-D. §131; Rob. 411).

b. also esp. of time ἱ. χρόνος *a considerable time* (Aristoph.; Pla., Leg. 5 p. 736c; Dit., Syll.[3] 665, 12; UPZ 161, 29 [119 BC] ἐφ' ἱ. χρόνον; Jos., Ant. 7, 22, C. Ap. 1, 237) ἱ. χρόνον διέτριψαν Ac 14: 3. ἱ. χρόνου διαγενομένου 27: 9. ἱκανῷ χρόνῳ *for a long time* Lk 8: 27; Ac 8: 11 (on the dat. s. Bl-D. §201; Rob. 527). Pl. Lk 20: 9 (Bl-D. §201; Rob. 470). ἐξ ἱ. χρόνων *for a long time* 23: 8; also ἀπὸ χρόνων ἱ. 8: 27 D. ἀπὸ ἱ. ἐτῶν *for many years* Ro 15: 23 (cf. 2 Macc 1: 20). ἡμέραι ἱ. (UPZ 162 II, 15 [117 BC] ἐφ' ἱκανὰς ἡμέρας) Ac 9: 23; ἡμέρας ἱ. *for many days* 9: 43; 18: 18. Also ἐν ἱ. ἡμέραις 27: 7.

c. abs. ἱκανοί *in large numbers, many* (Wilcken, Chrest. 11 B Fr. (a), 10 [123 BC]; PTebt. 41, 13 ἱκανῶν ἡμῶν; 1 Macc 13: 49; Jos., Ant. 14, 231) Ac 12: 12; 14: 21; 19: 19; 1 Cor 11: 30; cf. Lk 7: 11 t.r.—ἱκανόν ἐστιν *it is enough* (Epict. 1, 2, 36; 3 Km 16: 31; the copula is oft. omitted: Gen 30: 15; Ezk 34: 18) Lk 22: 38 (WWestern, ET 52, '40/'41, 357 'large' or 'long enough'). εἴ τινι μὴ δοκοίη κἂν ταῦτα ἱκανά *if this should seem insufficient to anyone* Dg 2: 10. Latinism (Bl-D. §5, 3b; Mlt. 20f) τὸ ἱκανὸν ποιεῖν τινι satisfacere alicui=*satisfy* (Polyb. 32, 7, 13; Appian, Lib. 74; Diog. L. 4, 50; BGU 1141, 13 [14 BC] ἐάν σοι Ἔρως τὸ ἱκανὸν ποιήσῃ γράψον μοι; POxy. 293, 10; PGiess. 40 I, 5); also possible is *do someone a favor* (so plainly Diog. L. 4, 50) Mk 15: 15; Hs 6, 5, 5; τὸ ἱ. *pledge, security, bond* (POxy. 294, 23 [22 AD]; BGU 530, 38; PStrassb. 41, 51) λαμβάνειν τὸ ἱ. satis accipere=*take security* (Dit., Or. 484, 50; 629, 101 [both II AD]) Ac 17: 9.—ἐξ ἱκανοῦ *for a long time* Lk 23: 8 v.l. ἐφ' ἱκανόν *enough, as long as one wishes,* esp. of time *for a long time* (Polyb. 11, 25, 1; Diod. S. 11, 40, 3; 13, 100, 1; Dit., Syll.[3] 685, 34; 2 Macc 7: 5; 8: 25; Ep. Arist. 109) Ac 20: 11.

2. *fit, appropriate, competent, qualified, able,* w. the connotation *worthy* (Thu.; Diod. S. 13, 106, 10; POxy. 1672, 15; Ex 4: 10) πρός τι *for someth.* (Pla., Prot. 322B; 2 Macc 10: 19; Ep. Arist. 211) 2 Cor 2: 16. W. inf. foll. (Hdt. 8, 36; Jos., Ant. 1, 29; 5, 51; Bl-D. §393, 4; Rob. 658) Mt 3: 11; Mk 1: 7; Lk 3: 16; J 1: 27 𝔓[66 75]; 1 Cor 15: 9; 2 Cor 3: 5 (Dodd 15f); 2 Ti 2: 2 (Jos., Ant. 3, 49 εἰπεῖν ἱ.); 1 Cl 50: 2. Also w. ἵνα foll. (Bl-D. §393, 4; Rob. 658; cf. PHolm. 4, 23) Mt 8: 8; Lk 7: 6.—Cf. ITr 3: 3 v.l.— KHRengstorf, TW III 294-7. M-M. B. 927.*

ἱκανότης, ητος, ἡ *fitness, capability, qualification* (Lysias the orator in Pollux 4, 23; Pla., Lysis 11 p. 215A; Stoic. III 68, 3) 2 Cor 3: 5.*

ἱκανόω 1 aor. ἱκάνωσα (outside the NT the pass. is used: Teles p. 39, 6; 42, 4; Dionys. Hal. 2, 74; PTebt. 20, 8; LXX; Test. Iss. 1: 7; cf. Anz 353) *make sufficient, qualify* (perh. shading into the sense *empower, authorize* [PTebt. 20, 8]) w. double acc. *someone for someth.* 2 Cor 3: 6. τινὰ εἴς τι *someone for someth.* Col 1: 12. M-M.*

ἱκανῶς adv. (Soph., Hdt.+; PPetr. III 53n, 3; POxy. 1088, 56; PTebt. 411, 6; Job 9: 31; 3 Macc 1: 4; Philo, Op. M. 90; Jos., C. Ap. 1, 58; 287, Ant. 2, 31) *sufficiently* ἱ. ἐπεστείλαμεν 1 Cl 62: 1. ἱ. ἐλέγχειν *ably refute* Epil Mosq 1.*

ἱκεσία, ας, ἡ (Eur.+; inscr., pap.; 2 Macc 10: 25; 12: 42; Philo; Jos., Ant. 11, 326; 12, 300) *prayer, supplication* ἱ. ποιεῖσθαι *pray* (Aeschines 3, 121; Dionys. Hal. 8, 43, 5) ἐκτενῆ τὴν δέησιν καὶ ἱ. ποιεῖσθαι *pray w. eager supplication* 1 Cl 59: 2 (ἱ. w. δέησις as Dit., Or. 569, 11; Wilcken, Chrest. 6, 3).*

ἱκετεύω (Hom.+; inscr., pap., LXX; Jos., C. Ap. 2, 213) *supplicate, beseech θεόν* (curse of Artemisia [pap. in Sb 5103—III BC] 9f ἱκετεύουσα τοὺς θεούς; Appian, Bell. Civ. 2, 104 §431 θεοὺς πάντας ὁ Καῖσαρ ἱκέτευεν; Ps 36: 7; 2 Macc 11: 6; Ep. Arist. 197; Philo, Cherub. 47; Jos., Ant. 3, 6) 1 Cl 7: 7; 48: 1. W. inf. foll. 2: 3.*

ἱκετηρία, ας, ἡ (actually the fem. of the adj. ἱκετήριος, w. ἐλαία or ῥάβδος to be supplied: the olive branch was the sign of the suppliant. As subst. = 'sign of a suppliant' Aeschyl., Hdt.+) *supplication* (so Isocr.+; POsl. 148, 12 [II/I BC]; 2 Macc 9: 18; Philo, Leg. ad Gai. 228) w. δέησις (Isocr. 8, 138 Blass v.l.; Job 40: 27; Philo, Leg. ad Gai. 276). As a supplication made to God, *prayer* (Ael. Aristid. 49, 38 K.=25 p. 498 D.; Aelian, fgm. 304; Sb 5103, 9; 11 [s. ἱκετεύω above]) w. δέησις (Polyb. 3, 112, 8 θεῶν ἱκετηρίαι καὶ δεήσεις; Philo, Cher. 47 v.l.) δεήσεις κ. ἱκετηρίας πρὸς τὸν δυνάμενον σῴζειν αὐτὸν προσενέγκας Hb 5: 7. CSpicq, RB 56, '49, 549f. M-M.*

ἱκέτης, ου, ὁ (Hom.+; inscr., LXX, Philo; Jos., C. Ap. 2, 207) *suppliant* ἱκέται γενόμενοι τοῦ ἐλέους αὐτοῦ as *suppliants of his mercy* 1 Cl 9: 1 (cf. Jos., Ant. 7, 361 ἱκέτης γίνεται τ. θεοῦ and the Delphic commands in Dit., Syll.³ 1268, 24 ἱκέτας ἐλέει).—S. on εὐλαβέομαι.*

ἰκμάς, άδος, ἡ (Hom.+; LXX; Philo, Op. M. 38. Exx. fr. Joseph., Plut., Lucian in HJCadbury, The Style and Literary Method of Luke VI '19, 43) *moisture* of the moisture in the soil, without which plants cannot live (Theophr., Hist. Pl. 6, 4, 8 ἰκμάδα ἔχειν in contrast to ξηραίνεσθαι; Jos., Ant. 3, 10; Jer 17: 8) Lk 8: 6; Hs 8, 2, 7; 9. Of the juices secreted by decaying flesh 1 Cl 25: 3 (on the medical use of the word s. Hobart 57f). M-M.*

Ἰκόνιον, ου, τό (on the spelling s. Bl-D. §42, 3; Rob. 197) *Iconium* (acc. to X., An. 1, 2, 19 belonging to Phrygia, likew. Pliny, Nat. Hist. 5, 41; Acta Justini 4. On the other hand, Strabo 12, 6, 1 puts it in Lycaonia), visited by Paul several times Ac 13: 51; 14: 1, 19, 21; 16: 2; 2 Ti 3: 11.—Ramsay, most recently Bearing 53ff [Phrygia]; Bludau (s. on Λύστρα); AWikenhauser, Die Apostelgesch. '21, 336f; VSchultze, Altchr. Städte u. Landschaften II 2, '26. M-M.*

ἰκτῖνος, ου, ὁ (metaplastic acc. ἰκτῖνα [Cyranides p. 24, 8]) *hawk, kite* (Hdt., X., Pla. et al.), whose flesh the Jews were forbidden to eat (Lev 11: 14; Dt 14: 13) B 10: 4.*

ἱλαρός, ά, όν (Aristoph., X.+; inscr., pap., LXX, En., Ep. Arist., Philo; Jos., Bell. 6, 364, Ant. 18, 291; Test. Jos. 8: 5) *cheerful, glad, merry* of things (Appian, fgm. 7 βοὴ ἱλαρά; Aesop, Fab. 314 P.=Babr. 24 Cr. ἱ. κῶμοι; Synes., Kingship 1 p. 1c λόγοι ἱ.; Philo, Spec. Leg. 2, 48 ἱ. βίος) πάντα ὁμαλὰ κ. ἱλαρά *everything is smooth and cheerful* Hm 2: 4.—Of animals (Philostrat., Imag. 1, 15): sheep s 6, 1, 6.—Of persons (Diod. S. 3, 17, 1; Hv 1, 2, 3; 1, 4, 3; 3, 3, 1 al. λειτουργία καλὴ καὶ ἱλαρά *a good and joyful service* s 5, 3, 8. δότης *one who gives cheerfully, gladly* 2 Cor 9: 7 (cf. Pr 22: 8a). But here the mng. might easily pass over into *kind, gracious* (s. Nägeli 65f and Artem. 1, 5 θεοί; POxy. 1380, 127 the ἱλαρὰ ὄψις of Isis; Philo, Spec. Leg. 4, 74 ἱ. μεταδόσεις=gracious gifts).—RBultmann, TW III 298-300. M-M.**

ἱλαρότης, ητος, ἡ (Diod. S. 3, 17, 1; Cornutus 24 p. 45, 11; Plut., Ages. 2, 4; Alciphr. 3, 43; Vita Philonidis 21, 4 Crönert [SAB 1900, II 942ff]; Pr 18: 22; Philo, Plant. 166; Test. Napht. 9: 2) *cheerfulness, gladness, graciousness* Ro 12: 8; Hm 5, 1, 2; 10, 3, 1; 4; s 9, 15, 2 (personified in the last pass.). M-M.*

ἱλάσκομαι mid. dep.; 1 aor. pass. imper. ἱλάσθητι (Hom.+; inscr.; LXX [Thackeray 270f; CHDodd, Ἱλάσκεσθαι . . . in the LXX: JTS 32, '31, 352-60]).

1. *propitiate, conciliate* (Strabo 4, 4, 6 τὸν θεόν; Cornutus 34 p. 73, 5; Heraclit. Sto. 16 p. 24, 9 τὸν Ἥλιον; Appian, Samn. 12 §6, Hann. 27 §115 θυσίαις κ. εὐχαῖς ἱλ. τ. θεούς; Herm. Wr. 1, 22; Philo, Spec. Leg. 1, 116; Jos., Ant. 6, 124 τὸν θεὸν ἱ.; 8, 112, C. Ap. 1, 308 ἱ. τοὺς θεούς; Sib. Or. 3, 625; 628). Pass. *be propitiated, be merciful* or *gracious* (4 Km 24: 4; La 3: 42; Da 9: 19 Theod.) w. dat. (of advantage, Esth 4: 17h ἱλάσθητί τ. κλήρῳ σου. Cf. also Ps 78: 9) ἱλάσθητί μοι τῷ ἁμαρτωλῷ (dat. of advantage) *have mercy on me, sinner that I am* Lk 18: 13 (Sb 8511, 7 [inscr., imperial times] ἵλαθι μοι, Μανδοῦλι [a divinity]).

2. *expiate*: of Christ as high priest εἰς τὸ ἱλάσκεσθαι τὰς ἁμαρτίας τοῦ λαοῦ *to expiate the sins of the people* Hb 2: 17 (cf. Dit., Syll.³ 1042, 15f [II/III AD] ἁμαρτίαν ὀφιλέτω Μηνὶ Τυράννῳ ἣν οὐ μὴ δύνηται ἐξειλάσασθαι; Ps 64: 4 τὰς ἀσεβείας ἱ.; Dssm., NB 52[BS 225]).—Dodd 82-95 on ἱ. and related words; (against Dodd: LMorris, ET 62, '51, 227-33; RRNicole, Westminster Theol. Journ. 17, '55, 117-57); SLyonnet, Verbum Domini 37, '59, 336-52, Sin, Redemption and Sacrifice, '70, 120-66, 256-61; DHill, Gk. Words and Hebrew Mngs. '67, 23-48; JHerrmann and FBüchsel, TW III 300-24. M-M.*

ἱλασμός, οῦ, ὁ—1. *expiation, propitiation* (τῶν θεῶν Orph., Arg. 39; Plut., Fab. 18, 3; cf. Plut., Sol. 12, 5. In these cases we have the pl., prob. referring to the individual actions to be expiated. But also sg.: Plut., Mor. 560D, Camill. 7, 5; Lev 25: 9; Ps 129: 4; Philo, Leg. All. 3, 174) so perh. abstr. for concr. of Jesus as the ἱ. περὶ τ. ἁμαρτιῶν ἡμῶν 1 J 2: 2; 4: 10. But mng. 2 is just as possible.

2. *sin-offering* (Ezk 44: 27 προσοίσουσιν ἱ. Cf. Num 5: 8; 2 Macc 3: 33) s. above.—CHDodd, The Johannine Epistles '46. M-M.*

ἱλαστήριον, ου, τό (subst. neut. of ἱλαστήριος, ον [PFay. 337 I, 3ff—II AD; 4 Macc 17: 22; Jos., Ant. 16, 182]) *that which expiates* or *propitiates*, concr. a *means of expiation, gift to procure expiation* (WRPaton and ELHicks, Inscr. of Cos 1891, no. 81 ὁ δᾶμος ὑπὲρ τᾶς Αὐτοκράτορος Καίσαρος θεοῦ υἱοῦ Σεβαστοῦ σωτηρίας θεοῖς ἱλαστήριον; 347; Lind. Tempelchr. B 49 Ἀθάναι ἱλατήριον; Dio Chrys. 10[11], 121. The mng. is uncertain in POxy. 1985, 11) of Christ, ὃν προέθετο ὁ θεὸς ἱλαστήριον Ro 3: 25 (GFitzer, ThZ 22, '66, 161-83). For the view that ἱ. means *place of propitiation* (as Ezk 43: 14, 17, 20; cf. also Luther's 'Gnadenstuhl', and on Hb 9: 5 below) in this pass., s. TWManson, JTS 46, '45, 1-10.—Cf. also Dssm., ZNW 4, '03, 193-212 (cf. EB III, 3027-35); PFiebig and GKlein ibid. 341-4; SFraenkel, ibid. 5, '04, 257f; CBruston, ibid. 7, '06, 77-81; GottfrKittel, StKr 80, '07, 217-33; E da SMarco, Il piano divino della salute in Ro 3: 21-6: Diss. Rome '37; VTaylor, ET 50, '39, 295-300; GABarton, ATR 21, '39, 91f; WDDavies, Paul and Rabbinic Judaism² '55, 227-42; ELohse, Märtyrer u. Gottesknecht '55; LMorris, NTS 2, '55/'56, 33-43; DEHWhitely, JTS n.s. 8, '57, 240-55; SLyonnet, Sin, Redemption and Sacrifice, '70, 155-66.—The LXX uses ἱ. of the lid on the ark of the covenant, which was sprinkled w. the blood of the sin-offering on the Day of Atonement (Ex 25: 16ff al. Likew. Philo, Cher. 25, Fuga 100, Mos. 2, 95.—JHStelma, Christus' offer bij Pls [w. Philo] '38). So Hb 9: 5, transl. *mercy-seat*; for the history of this word s. Murray, New (Oxford) Engl. Dict. s.v. M-M.*

ἱλατεύομαι 1 aor. ἱλατευσάμην (the act. Jdth 16: 15 v.l.; Da 9: 19) *be gracious* τινί *to someone* Hv 1, 2, 1.*

ἵλεως, ων (Bl-D. §44, 1; Mlt. 240; Mlt.-H. 121.—Hom.+ as ἵλαος; ἵλεως is the Attic form. Also inscr., pap., LXX, Philo, Joseph.) *gracious, merciful*, mostly—in our lit. and the LXX always—of God (also Diod. S. 4, 24, 4; Lucian, Pro Imag. 12; Oenomaus [time of Hadrian] in Euseb., Pr. Ev. 5, 19, 1 θεὸς ἵ. ἔσται; M. Ant. 12, 36; Philo; Jos., Ant. 4, 222; 7, 290; Sib. Or. 1, 161) ἵ. ἔσομαι τ. ἀδικίαις αὐτῶν *I will be merciful toward their iniquities* Hb 8: 12 (Jer 38: 34). ἱλέῳ τινος τυγχάνειν *find someone merciful=find mercy in someone's sight* (Herm. Wr. 5, 2; Philo, De Jos. 104) 1 Cl 61: 2. ἵ. γενέσθαι τινί *be gracious or forgiving to someone* (Archilochus, fgm. 75 Ἥφαιστε, μοί ἵλαος γενεῦ; Sallust. 4 p. 10, 4; Num 14: 19; Dt 21: 8; 2 Macc 2: 22) Hv 2, 2, 8. Abs. ἵ. γενέσθαι (Alciphr. 4, 18, 17; UPZ 78, 24 [159 BC]; Ezek. the trag. in Euseb., Pr. Ev. 9, 29, 11) 1 Cl 2: 3; 48: 1; Hs 9, 23, 4.—ἵλεώς σοι, κύριε (sc. εἴη ὁ θεός, as, in a way, Herodas 4, 25; Plut., Mor. 983E ἵλεως ὁ θεὸς εἴη) *may God be gracious to you, Lord*, i.e. may God in his mercy spare you this, *God forbid!* Mt 16: 22 (cf. Inscr. Rom. 107, 10 ἵλεώς σοι, Ἀλύπι=may [Serapis] help you, Alypis; Dit., Or. 721, 10; Gen 43: 23; 2 Km 20: 20; 1 Ch 11: 19.—Bl-D. §128, 5, differently PKatz, ThLZ 82, '57, 113f and the Eng. transl. of Bl-D. by RWFunk '61; Rob. 395f; HMaehler, ZPE 4, '69, 99f). M-M.*

Ἰλλυρικόν, οῦ, τό (the adj. Ἰλλυρικός, ή, όν in Apollon. Rhod. 4, 516; Strabo) *Illyricum*, a district across the Adriatic Sea fr. Italy, in official usage Dalmatia (Illyris Superior) and Pannonia (I. Inferior). Ro 15: 19 ἀπὸ Ἰερουσαλὴμ καὶ κύκλῳ μέχρι τοῦ Ἰ. is the only reference extant to missionary activity of Paul in this part of the world. Yet in view of the close connection of Illyricum with Macedonia (Appian, Bell. Civ. 3, 63 §258; 4, 75 §317 τῆς Ἰλλυρίδος ἐπὶ τῇ Μακεδονίᾳ; 5, 145 §602) there is no difficulty in assuming that Paul visited Ill. from Mac.—WWeber, Untersuchungen z. Gesch. des Kaisers Hadrianus '07, 55. S. on Δαλματία. M-M.*

ἱμάς, άντος, ὁ (Hom.+; inscr., pap., LXX; Jos., Ant. 12, 192-4) leather *strap* or *thong*, on sandals (X., An. 4, 5, 14; Menand., fgm. no. 109, 2 Kock; Plut., Mor. 665B; Is 5: 27) Mk 1: 7; Lk 3: 16; J 1: 27. The interpr. of ὡς προέτειναν αὐτὸν τ. ἱμᾶσιν Ac 22: 25 is in doubt. It can be instrumental dat., *with the thongs*, used for tying him to the post. It is better taken as a dat. of purpose *for the thongs*, in which case οἱ ἱμάντες=*whips* (Posidonius: 87 fgm. 5 Jac.; POxy. 1186, 2 τὴν διὰ τῶν ἱμάντων αἰκείαν. —Antiphanes 74, 8, Demosth. 19, 197 and Artem. 1, 70 use the sing. in this way). M-M.*

ἱματίζω pf. pass. ptc. ἱματισμένος (PLond. 24, 14 [163 BC]; BGU 1125, 8; PTebt. 385, 15, al. in pap.) *dress, clothe* Mk 5: 15; Lk 8: 35. M-M.*

ἱμάτιον, ου, τό (Hdt., Aristoph.+; inscr., pap., LXX, Philo; Jos., Ant. 9, 111, C. Ap. 1, 281; Test. 12 Patr.) *garment*.
1. gener. of any garment (PRyl. 154, 8; PPetr. II 32, 18; PSI 94, 16; LXX) sing. Mt 9: 16; Mk 2: 21; 5: 27; Lk 5: 36; 8: 27; Hb 1: 11f (Ps 101: 27); B 6: 2 (Is 50: 9) al. Pl. *clothing* (Philo, Leg. All. 3, 239) Mt 27: 35; Mk 5: 28, 30; 9: 3; 15: 24 al. The pl. in the foll. pass. is explained by the fact that each one of a number of persons contributed one piece of clothing: Mt 21: 7f; Mk 11: 7f; Lk 19: 35, 36 (on these pass. s. Plut., Cato Min. 12, 1); Ac 9: 39 (Paradoxogr. Vat. 20 Keller ἱμάτια ἐπιδεικνύναι).—ἀποθέσθαι

ἑαυτῷ πάντα τὰ ἱ. *take off all one's (own) clothes* MPol 13: 2. ἱ. μαλακά *soft clothing* Lk 7: 25. λευκά *white clothing* Rv 3: 5, 18; 4: 4; cf. Mt 17: 2; μέλανα ἱ. Hs 9, 15, 1; 3 (in such cases ἱ. can be omitted, as we say 'dressed in white' or 'in black': J 20: 12; Hv 4, 2, 1. Cf. Bl-D. §241, 7 and λευκός 2, end). Ruined by moths Js 5: 2. σύνθεσις ἱματίων Hs 6, 1, 5. ἔνδυσις ἱματίων *putting on clothing* 1 Pt 3: 3.
2. of outer clothing *cloak, robe* (Lucian, Alex. 11) Mt 9: 20f; 24: 18; Lk 8: 44; 22: 36; J 19: 2; Rv 19: 16. W. χιτών, the under garment (Diod. S. 4, 38, 1; Dio Chrys. 13[7], 61; Diogenes, Ep. 30, 3; Diog. L. 6, 6; Dit., Syll.³ 736, 17 [92 BC]; Zen.-P. 11=Sb 6717, 9 [257 BC]) Ac 9: 39; D 1: 4; Mt 5: 40 (here the order is χιτ.–ἱ.; the situation is that of a lawsuit, in which the defendant is advised to give up not only the indispensable χιτών demanded by his opponent, but the ἱ. as well); Lk 6: 29 (here the order is ἱ.–χ., a sequence that suggests highway robbery, in which the robber first deprives his victim of his outer garment. Cf. UPZ 122, 14 [157 BC], the report of a robbery: βουλόμενός μου περιελέσθαι τὸ ἱμάτιον. Also PLille 6, 9 ἐξέδυσαν χιτῶνα ... ἱμάτιον.—But Lk may have had Dt 24: 10–13 in mind [ἱμ. as a pledge]. Through nonretaliation the debtor shows the shamelessness of the creditor: FW Danker, Jesus and the New Age, '72, 85.). ἱ. περιβάλλειν, περιβάλλεσθαι (PFay. 12, 19 [c. 103 BC]; Gen 28: 20; 1 Km 28: 8 al.) J 19: 2; Ac 12: 8; Rv 19: 13. The outer garment was laid off in order to leave the arms free Ac 7: 58; 22: 20; so perh. also vs. 23. It was torn as a sign of grief (oft. LXX) 14: 14, and removed from a person who was to be flogged 16: 22.
3. Certain pass. fall betw. 1 and 2; they speak of τὰ ἱμάτια, but involve only one person, who obviously is doing someth. to one outer garment: ὁ ἀρχιερεὺς διέρρηξεν τὰ ἱ. αὐτοῦ Mt 26: 65 (cf. Gen 37: 29, 34; Josh 7: 6; Jdth 14: 16 al.). Cf. J 13: 4, 12; Ac 18: 6.—B 3: 4 ἱμάτια is an uncertain rdg.; ℵ reads ἱάματα; CLat. have ἱμάτια; it is a quot. fr. Is 58: 8 (s. the variants there, ed. JZiegler).—Dalman, Arbeit V '37. M-M. B. 395; 416.

ἱματισμός, οῦ, ὁ (Theophr., Char. 23, 8; Polyb. 6, 15, 4; Diod. S. 17, 94, 2; Plut., Alex. 39, 10; Dit., Syll.³ 999, 5; 1015, 36; PHib. 54, 16 [c. 245 BC]; PTebt. 381, 13; 384, 19; LXX; Philo, Migr. Abr. 105) *clothing, apparel* J 19: 24 (Ps 21: 19); Ac 20: 33; D 13: 7; B 6: 6 (Ps 21: 19); Hs 8, 2, 4; 9, 13, 3; 5. ἱ. ἔνδοξος *fine clothing* Lk 7: 25. ἱ. πολυτελής *expensive apparel* (Pel.-Leg. p. 4, 8; cf. Plut., Mor. 229A ἱμάτια πολυτελῆ) 1 Ti 2: 9. ἱ. λαμπρότατος *shining apparel* Hv 1, 2, 2. White clothing (Aeneas Tact. 1488 ἱμ. λευκός) Lk 9: 29; Hs 8, 2, 3. M-M.*

ἱμείρομαι s. ὁμείρομαι. M-M.

ἵνα (Hom.+; inscr., pap., LXX, En., Ep. Arist., Philo, Joseph., Test. 12 Patr.) conjunction, the use of which increased considerably in H.Gk. as compared w. class. times because it came to be used periphrastically for the inf. and imper. Bl-D. §369; 379; 388–94 al.; Mlt. index; Rob. index.
I. in final sense to denote purpose, aim, or goal *in order that, that*.
1. w. subjunctive, not only after a primary tense, but also (in accordance w. Hellenistic usage) after a secondary tense (Bl-D. §369, 1; Rob. 983; Mlt.-Turner 100–102; JKnuenz, De enuntiatis Graecorum finalibus '13, 15ff).
a. after a present tense Mk 4: 21; 7: 9; Lk 6: 34; 8: 16; J 3: 15; 5: 34; 6: 30; Ac 2: 25 (Ps 15: 8); 16: 30; Ro 1: 11; 3: 19; 1 Cor 9: 12; Gal 6: 13; Phil 3: 8; Hb 5: 1; 6: 12; 1 J 1: 3 and oft.

b. after a perfect Mt 1: 22; 21: 4; J 5: 23, 36; 6: 38; 12: 40, 46; 14: 29; 16: 1, 4; 17: 4; 1 Cor 9: 22b al.

c. after a pres. or aor. imper. Mt 7: 1; 14: 15; 17: 27; 23: 26; Mk 11: 25; J 4: 15; 5: 14; 10: 38; 1 Cor 7: 5; 11: 34; 1 Ti 4: 15; Tit 3: 13. Likew. after the hortatory subj. in the first pers. pl. Mk 1: 38; Lk 20: 14; J 11: 16; Hb 4: 16.

d. after a fut. Lk 16: 4; 18: 5; J 5: 20; 14: 3, 13, 16; 1 Cor 15: 28; Phil 1: 26.

e. after a secondary tense: impf. Mk 3: 2; 6: 41; 8: 6; Lk 6: 7; 18: 15 al.—Plpf. J 4: 8.—Aor. Mt 19: 13; Mk 3: 14; 11: 28; 14: 10; Lk 19: 4, 15; J 7: 32; 12: 9; Ro 7: 4; 2 Cor 8: 9; Hb 2: 14; 11: 35; 1 J 3: 5.

2. w. fut. ind. (Dit., Syll³ 888, 87ff, Or. 665, 35; POxy. 299; 1071, 5 ἵνα ποιήσουσιν καὶ πέμψουσιν; Gen 16: 2 [Swete; ARahlfs, Genesis '26 v.l.] al.), beside which the aor. subj. is usu. found in the mss. (Bl-D. §369, 2; Rob. 984; Mlt.-Turner 100) ἵνα σταυρώσουσιν Mk 15: 20 v.l. ἵνα ἐρεῖ σοι Lk 14: 10. ἵνα δώσουσιν 20: 10. ἵνα θεωρήσουσιν J 7: 3. ἵνα δώσει 17: 2 v.l.; Rv 8: 3. ἐπισκιάσει Ac 5: 15 v.l.; ξυρήσονται 21: 24. κερδανῶ 1 Cor 9: 21 v.l.; καυθήσομαι 13: 3. καταδουλώσουσιν Gal 2: 4. κερδηθήσονται 1 Pt 3: 1. The fut. ind. is also used oft. when ἵνα has no final mng., esp. in Rv: 1 Cor 9: 18 (ἵνα as answer, as Epict. 4, 1, 99); Rv 6: 4, 11 v.l.; 9: 4, 5, 20; 13: 12; 14: 13; 22: 14. Occasionally the fut. ind. and aor. subj. are found in the same sentence Rv 3: 9; cf. also Phil 2: 10 v.l. (on this interchange cf. Reinhold 106; JVogeser, Zur Sprache d. griech. Heiligenlegenden, Diss. München '07, 34f; Knuenz, op. cit. 23ff; 39; Dio Chrys. 26[43], 7 ἵνα μὴ παρῶ...μηδὲ ἔξουσιν; POxy. 1068, 5 ἵνα διαπέμψεται, ἵνα δυνηθῶ...).—On the interchange of pres. subj. and fut. ind. in J 15: 8 s. GMLee, Biblica 51, '70, 239f.

3. ἵνα is found w. the pres. ind. only in passages where the subj. is also attested in the mss.; its presence is prob. due to corruption of the text (Bl-D. §369, 6; Rob. 984f; Mlt.-Turner 100f. But see the clear instance in Antinoöpolis Pap. III '67, 188, 15: ἵνα μή ἐσμεν, and cf. BGU 1081, 3 ἐχάρην, ἵνα σε ἀσπάζομαι; Test. Napht. 8: 2; Martyr. Petr. et Pauli 60 p. 170, 8 Lips. ἵνα κατευθύνει; Acta Petr. et Paul. 58 p. 203, 17 Lips.; Act. Pauli et Thecl. 11 p. 243, 11 L. v.l.). φυσιοῦσθε 1 Cor 4: 6 and ζηλοῦτε Gal 4: 17 could be subj. (Bl-D. §91; Rob. 984). But Gal 6: 12 διώκονται 𝔓⁴⁶ ACFG; Tit 2: 4 σωφρονίζουσιν ℵAF; J 5: 20 θαυμάζετε ℵL; 17: 3 γινώσκουσιν ADGL; 1 J 5: 20 γινώσκομεν ℵABL; Rv 12: 6 τρέφουσιν ℵC; 13: 17 δύναται B; ἵνα συνίετε B 6: 5 ℵ (συνιῆτε G, συνῆτε C); ἵνα...ᾄδητε IEph 4: 2 G¹ (Lghtf. ᾄδητε); μετέχετε ibid. G¹ (al. μετέχητε). διατάσσομαι ITr 3: 3 G¹ (al. διατάσσωμαι). βλασφημεῖται 8: 2 G¹ G² (al. βλασφημῆται).

4. The opt. after ἵνα is never found in our lit. (Bl-D. §369, 1; 386, 3; Rob. 983). In Mk 12: 2 only ℵ has ἵνα λάβοι (for λάβῃ). Eph 1: 17 ἵνα δῴη (v.l. δῷ) is certainly subj., and δώῃ is the correct rdg. (Bl-D. §95, 2; Mlt. 196f). Likew. ἵνα παραδοῖ J 13: 2.

5. after a demonstrative (Epict. 2, 5, 16 ἐν τούτῳ...ἵνα) εἰς τοῦτο for this (purpose, namely) that J 18: 37; 1 J 3: 8; Ro 14: 9; 2 Cor 2: 9; 1 Pt 3: 9; 4: 6; B 5: 1, 11; 14: 5. εἰς αὐτὸ τοῦτο for this very purpose, that Eph 6: 22; Col 4: 8. διὰ τοῦτο for this reason...that (Himerius, Or. 14, 3) 2 Cor 13: 10; Phlm 15; 1 Ti 1: 16; the ἵνα clause can also precede διὰ τοῦτο J 1: 31. τούτου χάριν...ἵνα for this reason...that Tit 1: 5.

6. ἵνα with 'I should like to say this' supplied is found in class. usage Mk 2: 10 (Bl-D. §470, 3. Differently [a virtual imper.] DSSharp, ET 38, '27, 427f). The necessary supplement precedes in ἵνα δείξῃ (he said this), in order to show B 7: 5.

II. Very oft. the final mng. is greatly weakened or disappears altogether. In this case the ἵνα-constr. serves

1. as a substitute for an inf. that supplements a verb, or an acc. w. inf. (cf. Od. 3, 327. A spurious document in Demosth. 18, 155 p. 279, 8. Later very common, also in inscr., pap. [Rdm.² 191ff]; LXX).

a. after verbs w. the sense—α. 'wish, desire, strive' (PGiess. 17, 5 [II AD] ἠγωνίασα...ἵνα ἀκούσω; BGU 1081, 3 ἐχάρην ἵνα σὲ ἀσπάζομαι) θέλειν ἵνα Mt 7: 12; Mk 9: 30; 10: 35; Lk 6: 31; J 17: 24; 1 Cor 14: 5. βουλεύεσθαι J 11: 53; 12: 10. συμβουλεύεσθαι Mt 26: 4. συντίθεσθαι J 9: 22. ἀγαλλιᾶσθαι joyfully strive after 8: 56 (s. ἀγαλλιάομαι). ζητεῖν 1 Cor 4: 2; 14: 12. ζηλοῦν 14: 1. εὔχεσθαι 'wish' IPhld 6: 3.

β. 'take care, be ashamed, be afraid' φυλάσσεσθαι 2 Pt 3: 17. προσέχειν take care that B 16: 8. βλέπειν see to it, that 1 Cor 16: 10.

γ. 'request, demand': δεῖσθαι request (Dionys. Hal. 4, 12, 1; Lucian, Dom. 9; Jos., Ant. 6, 321; 12, 125 al.) Lk 9: 40; 21: 36; 22: 32; B 12: 7; Pol 6: 2; Hv 3, 1, 2; s 5, 4, 1. ἐρωτᾶν request (s. ἐρωτάω 2) Mk 7: 26; Lk 7: 36; 16: 27; J 4: 47; 17: 15 al. (JCEarwaker, ET 75, '64, 316f so interprets the third ἵνα in 17: 21). παρακαλεῖν request, exhort (Ep. Arist. 318; 321; Jos., Ant. 14, 168) Mt 14: 36; Mk 5: 18; 6: 56; 7: 32; 8: 22; Lk 8: 32; 1 Cor 1: 10 al. αἰτεῖσθαι Col 1: 9. προσεύχεσθαι Mt 24: 20; 26: 41; Mk 14: 35; Lk 22: 46; 1 Cor 14: 13 al. εὔχεσθαι pray (s. εὔχομαι 1, end) Hs 5, 2, 10. εὐχαριστεῖν Eph 1: 16f. ἀξιοῦν demand, request (CIG 4892, 13 [III AD]; Jos., Ant. 14, 22) Hv 4, 1, 3. καταξιοῦν ISm 11: 1; IPol 7: 2.

δ. 'summon, encourage, order' (Epict. 4, 11, 29; 1 Esdr 8: 19; Ep. Arist. 46) ἀπαγγέλλειν Mt 28: 10. παραγγέλλειν (CIG 4957, 48 [68 AD]) Mk 6: 8. διαμαρτύρεσθαι 1 Ti 5: 21. ἐντέλλεσθαι (Jos., Ant. 7, 356) Mk 13: 34; J 15: 17. κηρύσσειν Mk 6: 12. διαστέλλεσθαι Mt 16: 20 v.l.; Mk 5: 43; 7: 36; 9: 9. ἐπιτιμᾶν warn Mt 16: 20; 20: 31; Mk 8: 30; 10: 48; Lk 18: 39. ἐξορκίζειν Mt 26: 63. ὁρκίζειν Hs 9, 10, 5. λέγειν order Mt 4: 3; 20: 21; Mk 3: 9; 9: 18; Lk 4: 3; 10: 40; Hv 2, 2, 6. γράφειν write (Jos., Ant. 11, 7; 127) Mk 9: 12; 12: 19; Lk 20: 28. ἀποστέλλειν Ac 16: 36.

ε. 'cause, bring about' πείθειν Mt 27: 20. ποιεῖν J 11: 37; Col 4: 16; cf. Rv 3: 9; 13: 16. τιθέναι appoint J 15: 16. ἀγγαρεύειν Mt 27: 32; Mk 15: 21.

ζ. 'permit, grant' ἀφιέναι Mk 11: 16. διδόναι 10: 37; Rv 9: 5.—η. συνευδοκεῖν Hs 5, 2, 8.

b. after impers. expr.: ἀρκετόν (ἐστι) it is sufficient Mt 10: 25. λυσιτελεῖ (εἰ...ἢ ἵνα) Lk 17: 2. συμφέρει Mt 5: 29f; 18: 6; J 11: 50. ἐμοὶ εἰς ἐλάχιστόν ἐστιν it is a matter of little consequence to me 1 Cor 4: 3. ἔδει B 5: 13. πολλὰ λείπει Hv 3, 1, 9.

c. after nouns and adjs., esp. when they are parts of fixed expressions:

α. χρείαν ἔχειν J 2: 25; 16: 30; 1 J 2: 27. ἔστιν συνήθεια J 18: 39. θέλημά ἐστιν Mt 18: 14; J 6: 40; 1 Cor 16: 12b. βουλὴ ἐγένετο Ac 27: 42. ἐντολή (cf. Polyb. 36, 17, 10 νόμος) J 15: 12; 11: 57; 13: 34; Ac 17: 15. δέησις Eph 6: 19. ἐξουσία Ac 8: 19. ἐμὸν βρῶμά ἐστιν J 4: 34. τίς ἐστιν ὁ μισθός; ἵνα... 1 Cor 9: 18.

β. οὐκ εἰμὶ ἱκανός Mt 8: 8; Lk 7: 6. οὐκ εἰμὶ ἄξιος J 1: 27; cf. Hs 9, 28, 5. Cf. Bl-D. §379 w. app.; Rob. 996.

d. after nouns mng. time: χρόνον διδόναι, ἵνα give time Rv 2: 21. ἔρχεται ἡ ὥρα the time comes (Aesop, Fab. 242 H. ἡ ἡμέρα, ἵνα=the day on which) J 12: 23; 13: 1; 16: 2, 32. Cf. Bl-D. §382, 1; 393.

e. ἵνα can also take the place of the explanatory inf. after a demonstrative (Bl-D. §394; Rdm.² 192.—Wsd 13: 9) Mk 11: 28. πόθεν μοι τοῦτο ἵνα ἔλθη (for τὸ ἐλθεῖν τὴν κτλ.) Lk 1: 43. τοῦτο προσεύχομαι ἵνα Phil 1: 9. Cf. 1 Cor 9: 18. This is a favorite usage in J: τοῦτό ἐστιν τὸ ἔργον τοῦ θεοῦ ἵνα πιστεύητε (for τὸ πιστεύειν ὑμᾶς) 6: 29; cf. vs. 50. μείζονα ταύτης ἀγάπην οὐδεὶς ἔχει ἵνα . . . θῇ (for τοῦ θεῖναι) 15: 13; cf. 3 J 4.—J 6: 39; 17: 3; 1 J 3: 11, 23; 4: 21; 5: 3; 2 J 6a. ἐν τούτῳ· ἐν τούτῳ ἐδοξάσθη ὁ πατήρ μου ἵνα . . . φέρητε (for ἐν τῷ φέρειν ὑμᾶς ἐδοξάσθη) J 15: 8; cf. 1 J 4: 17.—S. also Hs 9, 28, 4, and ποταπὴν ἀγάπην ἵνα 1 J 3: 1.

2. as a substitute for the inf. of result ('ecbatic' or consecutive use of ἵνα: Bl-D. §391, 5 w. app.; Mlt. 206-9; Rob. 997-9 and in SJCase, Studies in Early Christianity [FCPorter-BWBacon Festschr.] '28, 51-7; EHBlakeney, ET 53, '41/'42, 377f), when the result is considered probable, but not actual. But this distinction is not always strictly observed. Cf. Epict. 1, 24, 3; 25, 15; 27, 8 al.; 2, 2, 16 οὕτω μωρὸς ἦν, ἵνα μὴ ἴδῃ; Vett. Val. 185, 31; 186, 17; 292, 20; Jos., Bell. 6, 107; PLond. 964, 13. Very many exx. in ANJannaris, An Historical Greek Grammar 1897 §1758 and 1951. So that ἦν παρακεκαλυμμένον ἀπ' αὐτῶν ἵνα μὴ αἴσθωνται αὐτό Lk 9: 45. τίς ἥμαρτεν, ἵνα τυφλὸς γεννηθῇ; J 9: 2. Cf. 2 Cor 1: 17; Gal 5: 17; 1 Th 5: 4; 1 J 1: 9; Rv 9: 20; 13: 13; Hs 7: 2; 9, 1, 10.—In many cases purpose and result cannot be clearly differentiated, and hence ἵνα is used for the result which follows according to the purpose of the subj. or of God. As in Jewish and pagan thought, purpose and result are identical in declarations of the divine will (Ps.-Callisth. 2, 16, 10 the rule of the Persian king is being overthrown by the deity ἵνα Δαρεῖος . . . φυγὰς γενόμενος κτλ. Here ἵνα means both 'in order that' and 'so that'): Lk 11: 50; J 4: 36; 12: 40; 19: 28; Ro 3: 19; 5: 20; 7: 13; 8: 17; 11: 31f al. (EFSutcliffe, Effect or Purpose, Biblica 35, '54, 320-27). The formula ἵνα πληρωθῇ is so to be understood, since the fulfillment is acc. to God's plan of salvation: Mt 1: 22; 2: 15; 4: 14; 12: 17; 21: 4; 26: 56; J 12: 38; 17: 12; 19: 24, 36.—The ἵνα of Mk 4: 12=Lk 8: 10, so much in dispute, is surely to be taken as final (w. AvVeldhuizen, NThSt 8, '25, 129-33; 10, '27, 42-4; HWindisch, ZNW 26, '27, 203-9; JGnilka, Die Verstockung Israels '61, 45-8; Bl-D. §369, 2 app. [here the lit. on 'causal' ἵνα, which is allowed at least for Rv 22: 14 and perh. 14: 13; see Bl-D.-Funk §369, 2 and III 2, below]. S. also FLaCava, Scuola Cattol. 65, '37, 301-4; MBlack, An Aramaic Approach³, '67, 211-16).

III. ἵνα is used elliptically—1. ἀλλ' ἵνα but this has happened that, where the verb to be supplied must be inferred fr. the context (Epict. 1, 12, 17): ἀλλ' ἵνα μαρτυρήσῃ (sc. ἦλθεν) J 1: 8. ἀλλ' (ἐγένετο ἀπόκρυφον) ἵνα ἔλθῃ εἰς φανερόν but it was hidden that it might be revealed Mk 4: 22 (but cf. CJCadoux, JTS 42, '41, 169 n. 3). ἀλλ' (κρατεῖτέ με) ἵνα πληρωθῶσιν but you are holding me (prisoner), that 14: 49. ἀλλ' (ἐγένετο τυφλὸς) ἵνα φανερωθῇ J 9: 3. ἀλλ' (ἀποθνῄσκει) ἵνα . . . συναγάγῃ 11: 52.—13: 18.

2. ἵνα w. subjunctive as a periphrasis for the imper. (Bl-D. §387, 3; Mlt. 178; 210f; 248; Rob. 994; Mlt.-Turner 94f; FSlotty, D. Gebr. des Konj. u. Opt. in d. griech. Dialekten I '15, 35; CJCadoux, The Imper. Use of ἵνα in the NT: JTS 42, '41, 165-73; in reply HGMeecham, ibid. 43, '42, 179f, cf. ET 52, '40/'41, 437; ARGeorge, JTS 45, '44, 56-60. Gdspd., Probs. 57f.—Soph., Oed. Col. 155; Epict. 4, 1, 41, Enchir. 17; PTebt. 408, 17 [3 AD]; BGU 1079, 20; PFay. 112, 12; POxy. 299, 5 ἵν' εἰδῇς 'know'; PGM 4, 2135; Tob 8: 12 BA; 2 Macc 1: 9) ἵνα ἐπιθῇς τὰς χεῖρας αὐτῇ (please) lay your hands on her Mk 5: 23. ἡ δὲ γυνὴ ἵνα φοβῆται τ. ἄνδρα the wife is to respect her husband Eph 5: 33. Cf. Mt 20: 33; Mk 10: 51; 1 Cor 7: 29; 16: 16; 2 Cor 8: 7; Gal 2: 10. ἵνα ἀναπαή-

σονται let them rest Rv 14: 13. W. θέλω: θέλω ἵνα δῷς Mk 6: 25 (=δός Mt 14: 8.).—On Mk 2: 10 s. I 6 above.

3. ἵνα without a finite verb, which can be supplied fr. the context (Epict. 3, 23, 4 ἵνα ὡς ἄνθρωπος, i.e. ἐργάζῃ) ἵνα ἡμεῖς εἰς τὰ ἔθνη, αὐτοὶ δὲ εἰς τὴν περιτομήν (i.e. εὐαγγελιζώμεθα and εὐαγγελίζωνται) Gal 2: 9. ἵνα κατὰ χάριν (γένηται) Ro 4: 16. ἵνα ἄλλοις ἄνεσις (γένηται) 2 Cor 8: 13. ἵνα (γένηται) καθὼς γέγραπται 1 Cor 1: 31 (Bl-D. §481; Rob. 1202f).

IV. At times, contrary to regular usage, ἵνα is placed elsewhere than at the beginning of its clause, in order to emphasize the words that come before it (Bl-D. §475, 1 app.): τὴν ἀγάπην ἵνα γνῶτε 2 Cor 2: 4. εἰς τὸν ἐρχόμενον μετ' αὐτὸν ἵνα πιστεύσωσιν Ac 19: 4. τῷ ὑμετέρῳ ἐλέει ἵνα Ro 11: 31. Cf. J 13: 29; 1 Cor 7: 29; Gal 2: 10; Col 4: 16b.—EStauffer, Ἵνα u. d. Problem d. teleol. Denkens b. Pls: StKr 102, '30, 232-57, TW III 324-34; JHGreenlee, ἵνα Substantive Clauses in the NT: Asbury Seminarian 2, '47, 154-63; HRiesenfeld, Zu d. johanneischen ἵνα-Sätzen, Studia Theologica 19, '65, 213-20; MBlack, An Aramaic Approach³, '67, 76-81. M-M.

ἱνατί (oft. written separately; for ἵνα τί γένηται; 'in order that what might happen?' Bl-D. §12, 3; W-S. §5, 7e; Rob. 739) why, for what reason? (Aristoph., Nub. 1192; Pla., Apol. 14 p. 26D, Symp. 205A; Epict. 1, 29, 31; LXX; Jos., Bell. 6, 347; Test. Jos. 7: 5) Mt 9: 4; 27: 46 (Ps 21: 2); Lk 13: 7; Ac 4: 25 (Ps 2: 1); 7: 26; 1 Cor 10: 29; 1 Cl 4: 4 (Gen 4: 6); 35: 7 (Ps 49: 16); 46: 5, 7; B 3: 1 (Is 58: 4). W. εἰς τί why and for what? D 1: 5. Bl-D. §299, 4. M-M. s.v. ἵνα.*

ἰνδάλλομαι (Hom.+; Sib. Or. 13, 71) form false ideas, entertain strange notions (Dio Chrys. 11[12], 53; Sext. Emp., Math. 11, 122 ὁ τὸν πλοῦτον μέγιστον ἀγαθὸν ἰνδαλλόμενος; Clem. Alex., Protr. 10, 103, 2) ἐπί τινι about someth. 1 Cl 23: 2 (s. Harnack, Lghtf., Knopf ad loc.).*

Ἰόππη, ης, ἡ (Antig. Car. 151; Diod. S. 19, 59, 2; 19, 93, 7; Strabo 16, 2, 28; 34; Dionys. Perieg. in Müller, Geogr. Gr. Min. II 160; Dit., Or. 602, 2; 1 Esdr 5: 53; 1 Macc 10: 75 al.; 2 Macc 4: 21; Ep. Arist. 115; Joseph.; Sib. Or. 5, 251. On the spelling w. one π or two [so Bibl. mss. throughout] s. Bl-D. §40; Mlt.-H. 102; Rob. 214; Schürer II⁴ 128, 140) Joppa, modern Jaffa, seaport and city on the Philistine coast Ac 9: 36, 38, 42f; 10: 5, 8, 23, 32; 11: 5, 13.—Schürer II⁴ 128-32 (lit.); FScholten, Palästina I: Jaffa '31. M-M.*

Ἰορδάνης, ου, ὁ (יַרְדֵּן) (Strabo 16, 2, 16; Galen XI 693 K.; Tacitus, Hist. 5, 6; LXX, Ep. Arist., Philo, Joseph.; Sib. Or. 7, 67 ['Ιόρδανος, also found in Joseph. and Paus. 5, 7, 4]. On the use of the art. w. it cf. Bl-D. §261, 8) the Jordan, chief river of Palestine (Ep. Arist. 116). It arises at the foot of Mt. Hermon, flows through the Sea of Galilee, and empties into the Dead Sea Mt 3: 5f, 13; 4: 15 (Is 8: 23), 25; 19: 1; Mk 1: 5, 9; 3: 8; 10: 1; Lk 3: 3; 4: 1; J 1: 28; 3: 26; 10: 40; GEb 1; UGosp 66; HGuthe, RE XIV 573ff, Palästina², '27; Dalman, Orte³, index; OWaser, V. Flussgott J.: AKaegi-Festschr. '19, 191-217; NGlueck, The River Jordan '46; WvSoden, ZAW n.s. 16, '39, 153f.*

ἰός, οῦ, ὁ—1. poison (Pind.+; pap., LXX)—a. lit. ἰὸς ἀσπίδων (cf. Appian, Mithr. 88 §490 ἰὸς ὄφεων; Philo, Leg. ad Gai. 166; Jos., Bell. 1, 601; Constant. Manasse 4, 39 H.) Ro 3: 13 (Ps 13: 3; 139: 4). Of animal (i.e. snake; cf. θηρίον 1aβ) poison also Hs 9, 26, 7. These passages, as well as Hv 3, 9, 7 and ITr 6: 2 v.l. Funk, show that the transition to the fig. use was easy.

b. fig. (Aeschyl., Eum. 730 al.; Herm. Wr. p. 480, 15
Sc.; Test. Reub. 5: 6) Js 3: 8.

2. *rust* (Theognis 451; Pla., Tim. 59c, Rep. 10 p. 609A;
Theocr. 16, 17 al.; Dit., Syll.² 587, 310 [329 BC] σίδηρος
καταβεβρωμένος ὑπὸ τοῦ ἰοῦ;³ 284, 15; Herm. Wr. 14, 7;
Ezk 24: 6, 11f; EpJer 10; 23; Philo, Rer. Div. Her. 217
[χρυσὸς] ἰὸν οὐ παραδέχεται) Js 5: 3; Dg 2: 2.—
OMichel, TW III 334-6. M-M.*

Ἰουδαία, ας, ἡ (יְהוּדָה; but the word is to be derived fr.
Aram. יְהוּד) (fr. the adj. Ἰουδαῖος with γῆ or χώρα
supplied, as Philo, Leg. ad Gai. 281) *Judaea* (since Clearchus, the pupil of Aristotle in Jos., C. Ap. 1, 179; inscr.
[Schürer I⁴ 643, 1]; PRyl. 189, 5; LXX; Philo).

1. properly, of the southern part of Palestine in contrast
to Samaria, Galilee, Peraea and Idumaea (cf. Mk 3: 7f; Ac
9: 31; so LXX and oft. Joseph. Also Strabo 16, 2, 34 w.
Galil. and Samar.) Mt 2: 1, 5, 22; 3: 1; 4: 25; 24: 16; Mk 1:
5 (see also Ἰουδαῖος 1); 3: 7; 13: 14; Lk 1: 65; 2: 4; 3: 1; 5:
17; 6: 17; 21: 21; J 4: 3, 47, 54; 7: 1, 3; 11: 7; Ac 1: 8; 8: 1;
9: 31; 12: 19; 15: 1; 21: 10; 28: 21; Ro 15: 31; 2 Cor 1: 16;
Gal 1: 22. Metaph. of the inhabitants Mt 3: 5.—Buhl
64-75; HGuthe, RE IX 556-85; XXIII 713f (lit.).

2. in a wider sense, the region occupied by the Jewish
nation (Nicol. Dam. in Jos., Ant. 14, 9; Diod. S. 40, 3, 2;
Strabo 16, 2, 34; Memnon [I BC/I AD]: no. 434 fgm. 1, 18,
9; Ptolem. 5, 16, 1; cf. 15, 6-8; Cass. Dio 37, 16; 47, 28;
Tacitus, Hist. 5, 9; LXX; Ep. Arist. 4; 12; Philo, Leg. ad
Gai. 200; Joseph.—On the NT: ELevesque, Vivre et
Penser 3, '43/'44, 104-11 denies the wider use) Lk 1: 5; 4:
44 (v.l. Γαλιλαίας); 7: 17; 23: 5; Ac 10: 37; 11: 1, 29; 1 Th
2: 14. πᾶσα ἡ χώρα τῆς Ἰ. *the whole Jewish country* Ac
26: 20. εἰς τὰ ὅρια τῆς Ἰ. πέραν τοῦ Ἰορδάνου *into the
Jewish territory beyond the Jordan* Mt 19: 1; cf. Mk 10: 1.
On the mention of Judaea Ac 2: 9 cf. the variants and
conjectures in Nestle; EvDobschütz, ZWTh 45, '02, 407-
10; Harnack, AG '08, 65f; SKrauss, ZDPV 33, '10, 225;
OLagercrantz, Eranos 10, '10, 58-60; LKöhler, ET 22,
'11, 230f. Also BZ 1, '03, 219; 7, '09, 219; 9, '11, 218;
ZNW 9, '08, 253f; 255f. M-M.**

ιουδαΐζω live as a Jew, acc. to Jewish customs (so Plut.,
Cic. 7, 6; Esth 8: 17; Jos., Bell. 2, 454 μέχρι περιτομῆς ἰ.;
s. also 463; Acta Pilati A 2, 1) Gal 2: 14; IMg 10: 3.*

Ἰουδαϊκός, ή, όν (Dit., Or. 543, 16; 586, 7; Cleomedes [II
AD] in DBDurham, The Vocabulary of Menander '13, 27;
2 Macc 8: 11 v.l.; 13: 21; Ep. Arist. 28; 121; Philo, In
Flacc. 55; Jos., Ant. 12, 34; 14, 228; 20, 258 al.) *Jewish* Ἰ.
μῦθοι Tit 1: 14. M-M.*

Ἰουδαϊκῶς adv. (Jos., Bell. 6, 17) *in a Jewish manner, acc.
to Jewish custom* Ἰ. ζῆν Gal 2: 14. M-M.*

Ἰουδαῖος, αία, αῖον (Clearchus, the pupil of Aristotle, in
Jos., C. Ap. 1, 179; Theophr., fgm. 151 W. [WJaeger,
Diokles v. Karystos '38, 134-53: Theophrastus and the
earliest Gk. report concerning the Jews]; Hecataeus of
Abdera [300 BC] in Diod. S. 1, 28, 2 al.; Polyb.; Diod. S.;
Strabo; Plut.; Epict. 1, 11, 12f, al.; Appian, Syr. 50 §252f,
Mithrid. 106 §498, Bell. Civ. 2, 90 §380; Artem. 4, 24 p.
217, 13; Diog. L. 1, 9; Dit., Or. 73, 4; 74, 3; 726, 8; CIG
3418; Ramsay, Phrygia I 2 p. 538 no. 399b τ. νόμον τῶν
Εἰουδέων; Wilcken, Chrest. 55; 56 [both III BC]; 57 [II
BC]; BGU 1079, 25 [41 AD]; PFay. 123, 16 [100 AD]; POxy.
1189, 9; LXX; Ep. Arist.; Philo; Joseph.; Sib. Or.) *Jewish.*

1. as a real adj. (Philo, In Flacc. 29; Jos., Ant. 10, 265)
ἀνὴρ Ἰ. (1 Macc 2: 23; 14: 33) *a Jew* Ac 10: 28; 22: 3.
ἄνθρωπος 21: 39. ἀρχιερεύς 19: 14. ψευδοπροφήτης 13:
6. ἐξορκισταί 19: 13. γυνή (Jos., Ant. 11, 185) 16: 1.

χώρα Mk 1: 5.—γῆ J 3: 22; here, however, it is to be taken
of Judaea in the narrower sense (s. Ἰουδαία 1), and means
the Judaean countryside in contrast to the capital city.

2. as a noun (so predom.).—**a.** ὁ Ἰ. *the Jew* (w. respect to
birth, race, or religion. The term is used by non-Jews also;
s. Ἰσραήλ 2, end) J 3: 25; (Wilcken, Chrest. 57, 5 [II BC]
παρ' Ἰουδαίου=from a Jew) 4: 9; 18: 35; Ac 18: 2, 24; 19:
34; Ro 1: 16; 2: 9f, 17, 28f (on the 'genuine' Jew cf. Epict.
2, 9, 20f τῷ ὄντι Ἰουδαῖος . . . λόγῳ μὲν Ἰουδαῖοι, ἔργῳ
δ' ἄλλο τι); 10: 12; Gal 2: 14; 3: 28; Col 3: 11.—Collect.
sing. (Thu. 6, 78, 1 ὁ Ἀθηναῖος, ὁ Συρακόσιος; Ep. Arist.
13 ὁ Πέρσης; Bl-D. §139; Rob. 408) Ro 3: 1.

b. ἡ Ἰουδαία, as *the Jewess* Ac 24: 24.

c. οἱ Ἰ. (on the use of the art. Bl-D. §262, 1; 3) *the Jews*
οἱ Φαρισαῖοι κ. πάντες οἱ Ἰ. Mk 7: 3; τὸ πάσχα τῶν Ἰ.
J 2: 13; cf. 5: 1; 6: 4; 7: 2; ὁ βασιλεὺς τῶν Ἰ. (Appian,
Mithrid. 117 §573 Ἰουδαίων βασιλεὺς Ἀριστόβουλος)
Mt 2: 2; 27: 11, 29; Mk 15: 2 and oft. πόλις τῶν Ἰ. Lk 23:
51; ἔθνος τῶν Ἰ. Ac 10: 22; λαὸς τῶν Ἰ. 12: 11. χώρα
τῶν Ἰ. 10: 39; ἄρχων τῶν Ἰ. J 3: 1; συναγωγὴ τῶν Ἰ.
Ac 14: 1a. Cf. J 2: 6; 4: 22. Ἰ. καὶ Ἕλληνες (on the
combination of the two words s. Bl-D. §444, 2: w. τε . . .
καί) Jews and Gentiles Ac 14: 1b; 18: 4; 19: 10; 20: 21;
1 Cor 1: 24; 10: 32; 12: 13; PK 2 p. 15, 7; ἔθνη τε καὶ Ἰ.
Gentiles and Jews Ac 14: 5; cf. ISm 1: 2. Ἰ. τε καὶ προσήλυτοι *Jews and proselytes* Ac 2: 11; cf. 13: 43; οἱ κατὰ τὰ
ἔθνη Ἰ. *the Jews who live among the Gentiles* (in the
Diaspora) 21: 21. Jews and Gentiles as persecutors of
Christians MPol 12: 2; cf. also 13: 1; 17: 2; 18: 1; 1 Th 2:
14.—Dg 1.

d. of Jewish Christians Gal 2: 13; cf. Ac 21: 20.

e. in J the Ἰουδαῖοι are the enemies of Jesus 1: 19; 2: 18,
20; 5: 10, 15f; 6: 41, 52; 7: 1, 11, 13; 9: 18, 22; 10: 24, 31,
33; 11: 8; 13: 33; 18: 14. Cf. Hdb. exc. on J 1: 19 and, fr.
another viewpoint, JEBelser, ThQ 84, '02, 265ff; WLütgert, Heinrici-Festschr. '14, 147ff, Schlatter-Festschr. '22,
137-48. Further on anti-Jewish feeling in J, s. EGraesser,
NTS 11, '64, 74-90; DRAHare, Religious Studies Review,
July, '76, 15-22 (lit.).—On the whole word s. Ἰσραήλ,
end. M-M.

Ἰουδαϊσμός, οῦ, ὁ *Judaism*= the Jewish way of belief and
life (2 Macc 2: 21; 8: 1; 14: 38; 4 Macc 4: 26; synagogue
inscr. at Stobi l. 8: ZNW 32, '33, 93f) Gal 1: 13f.
Contrasted w. Χριστιανισμός IMg 10: 3; IPhld 6: 1. κατὰ
(νόμον is prob. a gloss) Ἰουδαϊσμὸν ζῆν live in accordance w. Judaism IMg 8: 1.*

Ἰούδας, α, ὁ (יְהוּדָה; Judah; LXX, Ep. Arist., Philo,
Joseph., Test. 12 Patr.—The indecl. form Ἰουδά, which
occasionally occurs in the LXX [e.g. Gen 29: 35; 2 Macc
14: 13 Swete; Thackeray 163] is not to be postulated for
our lit., not even Mt 2: 6; Lk 1: 39) *Judah* (Hebr.), *Judas*
(Gk.), *Jude* (s. 8); cf. Bl-D. §53, 1; 55, 1a; Mlt.-H. 143f.

1. *Judah,* son of the patriarch Jacob—**a.** in pers.: in the
genealogy of Jesus Mt 1: 2f; Lk 3: 33. κατὰ τὸν Ἰούδαν
through Judah 1 Cl 32: 2.

b. the tribe of Judah (Judg 1: 2) ἐξ Ἰούδα ἀνατέταλκεν
ὁ κύριος Hb 7: 14. Also φυλὴ Ἰούδα Rv 5: 5; 7: 5.

c. the country belonging to the tribe of Judah (Josh 11:
21; 2 Ch 28: 18) Βηθλεὲμ γῆ Ἰούδα Mt 2: 6a; cf. Lk 2: 4
D; ἡγεμόνες Ἰ. Mt 2: 6b; πόλις Ἰ. (2 Ch 23: 2) Lk 1: 39
(cf. CCTorrey, HTR 17, '24, 83-91). ὁ οἶκος Ἰ. (w. ὁ οἶκος
Ἰσραήλ) the inhabitants of the land Hb 8: 8 (Jer 38: 31).

2. *Judas,* a name in the genealogy of Jesus Lk 3: 30.

3. *Judas,* called ὁ Γαλιλαῖος, a revolutionary in the time
of Quirinius 'in the days of the census' (cf. Jos., Ant. 18,
4-10, 23-5; 20, 102, Bell. 2, 118; 433; 7, 253.—Schürer I⁴
420f; 486f; 526f; 532; 542) Ac 5: 37.—WLodder, J. de

Galileër: NThSt 9, '26, 3-15.—4. *Judas* of Damascus,
Paul's host Ac 9: 11.

5. *Judas,* an apostle, called 'Ι. 'Ιακώβου *son of Jacob* or
James (linguistically speaking, ἀδελφός might also be
supplied: Alciphr. 4, 17, 10 Τιμοκράτης ὁ Μητροδώρου,
i.e., his brother), to differentiate him fr. the betrayer. He
is mentioned in lists of apostles only in the Lucan writings,
where two men named Judas are specifically referred to Lk
6: 16 and presupposed Ac 1: 13; cf. J 14: 22.

6. *Judas,* several times called 'Ισκαριώθ or (ὁ) 'Ισκαριώτης (s. this entry), the betrayer of Jesus Mt 10: 4; 26: 14,
25, 47; 27: 3; Mk 3: 19; 14: 10, 43; Lk 6: 16; 22: 3, 47f;
J 12: 4; 13: 29; 18: 2f, 5; Ac 1: 16, 25; GEb 2; Agr 23b;
MPol 6: 2. Manner of his death Papias 3. His father was
Simon J 13: 2, and this Simon is also called 'Ισκαριώτης
6: 71; 13: 26. On Judas himself and the tradition concerning him s. Papias (in EPreuschen, Antileg.² '05, 98.
Lit. on it in EHennecke, Ntl. Apokryphen² '24, 124) as well
as GMarquardt, D. Verrat des J. Isch.—eine Sage '00;
WWrede, Vorträge u. Studien '07, 127-46; FKFeigel, D.
Einfluss d. Weissagungsbeweises '10, 48ff; 95; 114; WB
Smith, Ecce Deus '11, 295-309; KWeidel, StKr 85, '12,
167-286; GSchläger, Die Ungeschichtlichkeit des Ver-
räters J.: ZNW 15, '14, 50-9; MargPlath, ibid. 17, '16,
178-88; WHCadman, The Last Journey of Jesus to Jerus.
'23, 129-36; JMRobertson, Jesus and J. '27; DHaugg, J.
Isk. in den ntl. Berichten '30 (lit.); JFinegan, D. Überl. d.
Leidens- u. Auferstehungsgesch. Jesu '34; FWDanker,
The Literary Unity of Mk 14: 1-25, JBL 85, '66, 467-72.
Esp. on the death of J.: RHarris, AJTh 4, '00, 490-513;
JHBernard, Exp. 6th Ser. IX '04, 422-30; KLake, Beginn.
V '33, note 4, 22-30; PBenoit, La mort de Judas, AWiken-
hauser-Festschr. '53, 1-19; KLüthi, Judas Iskarioth in d.
Geschichte d. Auslegung von d. Reformation bis zur
Gegenwart '55; MSEnslin, How the Story Grew: Judas in
Fact and Fiction: FWGingrich-Festschr., ed. Barth and
Cocroft, '72, 123-41; and s. on πρηνής.

7. *Judas,* called Βαρσαββᾶς (s. this entry), a Christian
prophet in a leading position in the Jerusalem church Ac
15: 22, 27, 32 (34).

8. *Judas,* the brother of Jesus Mt 13: 55; Mk 6: 3. Prob.
the same man is meant by the *Jude* of Jd 1. M-M.*

'Ιουδίθ, ἡ indecl. (יְהוּדִית) *Judith,* an Israelite heroine
(Jdth 8-16) 1 Cl 55: 4.*

'Ιουλία, ας, ἡ *Julia,* a common name, found even among
slave women in the imperial household. She receives a
greeting Ro 16: 15 ('Ιουλίαν 𝔓⁴⁶). GMilligan, The NT
Documents '13, 183.—This woman's name is read by 𝔓⁴⁶
(w. Vulg. mss., Boh., Ethiopic) also vs. 7 for Ιουνιαν (s.
'Ιουνιᾶς, end). M-M.*

'Ιούλιος, ου, ὁ *Julius,* a common name (also in Joseph.),
borne by a centurion of the imperial cohort Ac 27: 1, 3 (A:
'Ιουλιανός, which is the name of a ἑκατοντάρχης Jos.,
Bell. 6, 81).*

'Ιουνιᾶς, ᾶ, ὁ *Junias* (not found elsewh., prob. short form
of the common Junianus; cf. Bl-D. §125, 2; Rob. 172) a
Jewish convert to Christianity, who was imprisoned w. Paul
Ro 16: 7; s. on 'Ανδρόνικος.—The possibility, fr. a purely
lexical point of view, that this is a woman's name 'Ιουνία,
ας, *Junia* (Mlt.-H. 155; ancient commentators took Andr.
and Junia as a married couple. S. 'Ιουλία), is prob. ruled
out by the context (s. Ltzm., Hdb. ad loc.). M-M.*

'Ιοῦστος, ου, ὁ (Κυπρ. I p. 42 no. 27 name of the
ἀρχιερεὺς τῆς νήσου [Cyprus]; PWarr. 16, 4 [III AD]); a
name commonly borne by Jews and proselytes (s. Lghtf. on
Col 4: 11) *Justus,* surname

1. of Joseph Barsabbas, one of the two candidates in
the election for apostle Ac 1: 23.

2. of Titius, a Corinthian proselyte Ac 18: 7. Cf. Gdspd.
s.v. Τίτιος.

3. of a Jewish Christian named Jesus, who supported the
prisoner Paul in his work Col 4: 11. Deissmann on 'Ιησοῦς
5.—On the double name s. Dssm., B 183f (BS 315f).*

ἱππεύς, έως, ὁ (Hom.+; inscr., pap., LXX, Philo; Jos.;
Vi. 157 al.; Sib. Or. 3, 612; 805) acc. pl. τοὺς ἱππεῖς
(Polyaenus 1, 29, 1; 8, 23, 12; Dit., Syll.³ 502, 9 [228/5
BC]; 627, 15 [183 BC]) *horseman, cavalryman* Ac 23: 23,
32; MPol 7: 1. M-M.*

ἱππικός, ή, όν (Aeschyl.+; inscr., pap.; 1 Macc 15: 38;
3 Macc 1: 1; Philo; Jos., Bell. 2, 117; 308) *pertaining to a
horseman* τὸ ἱ. *the cavalry* (Hdt. 7, 87 al.; Dit., Syll.³
697E, 5 Diocles, of the στρατηγῶν ἐπὶ τὸ ἱππικόν) τὰ
στρατεύματα τοῦ ἱ. *the troops of cavalry* Rv 9: 16. M-M.*

ἵππος, ου, ὁ (Hom.+; inscr., pap., LXX; En. 100, 3;
Philo, Joseph.) *horse, steed* Js 3: 3; Rv 9: 9; 14: 20; 18: 13;
19: 18. Horses of var. colors play a large role in Rv (s. on
πυρρός) a white *horse* (Aeneas Tact. 1488) 6: 2; 19: 11,
14; cf. vss. 19, 21; fiery red 6: 4; black vs. 5; pale, dun vs.
8. Grasshoppers like horses 9: 7; horses w. lions' heads vs.
17; cf. 19. Cf. MWMüller, D. Apocal. Reiter: ZNW 8, '07,
290ff; GHoennicke, D. apokal. Reiter: Studierstube 19,
'21, 3ff; AvHarnack, D. apokal. Reiter: Erforschtes u.
Erlebtes '23, 53ff; LKöhler, D. Offenb. d. Joh. '24, 59-68;
Boll 78ff, agreeing w. him GBaldensperger, RHPhr 4, '24,
1ff, against him JFreundorfer, Die Apk. des Ap. Joh. '29,
67-123; FDornseiff, ZNW 38, '39, 196f; OMichel, TW III
336-9. M-M. B. 167f.*

ἶρις, ιδος, ἡ—**1.** *rainbow* (Hom. +) Rv 10: 1; AP 3: 10.—
2. (colored) *halo, radiance* (Aristot., Meteor. 3, 4; 5;
Theophr., Ostent. 1, 13; Lucian, Dom. 11) ἶρις ὅμοιος
ὁράσει σμαραγδίνῳ *a halo that was like an emerald* (*in
appearance*) Rv 4: 3.—KHRengstorf, TW III 340-3.
M-M.*

'Ισαάκ (יִצְחָק), in 𝔓⁴⁶ and D always 'Ισάκ (Bl-D. §39, 3
app.), ὁ indecl. (LXX, Philo, Test. 12 Patr.; Sib. Or. 2,
247.—Joseph. and Ep. Arist. 'Ίσακος, ου [Ant. 1, 227];
Ep. Arist. 49 'Ίσαχος) *Isaac,* son of Abraham (Gen 21:
3ff) Ac 7: 8a. Father of Jacob, ibid. b. Named w. him and
Abraham (s. 'Αβραάμ and 'Ιακώβ) Mt 8: 11; Lk 13: 28; B
8: 4; IPhld 9: 1. God as the God of Abr., Is., and Jac. (Ex
3: 6) Mt 22: 32; Mk 12: 26; Lk 20: 37; Ac 3: 13; 7: 32; B 6:
8. Bearer of the promises Ro 9: 7 (Gen 21: 12), 10; Gal 4:
28; cf. Hb 11: 9, 18 (Gen 21: 12), 20. Husband of Rebecca
Ro 9: 10; B 13: 2 (Gen 25: 21), 3. Sacrifice of Isaac (Gen
22: 1ff) Hb 11: 17; Js 2: 21; 1 Cl 31: 3; B 7: 3. In the
genealogy of Jesus Mt 1: 2; Lk 3: 34.—HJSchoeps, The
Sacrifice of Isaac in Paul's Theology: JBL 65, '46, 385-92.
M-M.*

ἰσάγγελος, ον (Iambl. in Stob., Ecl. I 457, 9 W.; Hierocles, in Aur. Carm. c. 4 ἀνθρώπους σέβειν...τοὺς
ἰσοδαίμονας καὶ ἰσαγγέλους. Christian grave-inscr.:
Epigr. Gr. 542, 6f. Cf. Philo, Sacr. Abel. 5 ἴσος ἀγγέλοις
γεγονώς) *like an angel* of the glorified ones Lk 20: 36.
M-M.*

ἴσθι s. εἰμί.

'Ισκαριώθ (Mk 3: 19; 14: 10; Lk 6: 16; 22: 47 D) indecl.,
and **'Ισκαριώτης, ου, ὁ** *Iscariot,* surname of Judas the
betrayer, as well as of his father (s. 'Ιούδας 6). The mng.
of the word is obscure; s. Wlh. on Mk 3: 19; Dalman,
Jesus 26 (Eng. tr. 51f). It is usu. taken to refer to the place

of his origin, *from Kerioth* (in southern Judaea; Buhl 182) אִישׁ קְרִיּוֹת (agreeing w. this we have the v.l. ἀπὸ Καρυώτου J 6: 71 א al.; 12: 4 D; 13: 2 D, 26 D; 14: 22 D). Another interpr. connects it w. σικάριος (q.v.), 'assassin, bandit' (among others FSchulthess, D. Problem der Sprache Jesu '17, 41; 55, ZNW 21, '22, 250ff). Cf. also CCTorrey, HTR 36, '43, 51-62 ('false one'). Mt 10: 4; 26: 14; Mk 14: 43 v.l.; Lk 22: 3; J 6: 71; 12: 4; 13: 2, 26; 14: 22; GEb 2.—HIngholt, Iscariot: JPedersen Festschr. '53; BGärtner, D. rätselhafte Termini Nazaräer u. Iskariot '57, 37-68; OCullmann, RevHistPhilRel 42, '62, 133-40; KLüthi, J. Isk. in d. Geschichte der Auslegung (Reformation to present) '55. M-M.*

'Ισοκράτης, ους, ὁ (lit., inscr., pap.) *Isocrates*, a Christian scribe Epil Mosq 4a, b.*

ἴσος, η, ον (Hom.+; inscr., pap., LXX, Ep. Arist., Philo; Jos., Ant. 10, 131, C. Ap. 2, 35; Sib. Or. 5, 3) *equal in number, size, quality* τράγοι B 7: 10. τὸ μῆκος καὶ τὸ πλάτος καὶ τὸ ὕψος αὐτῆς ἴσα ἐστίν Rv 21: 16. ἡ ἴ. δωρεά *the same gift* Ac 11: 17. τὴν ἀγάπην τινὶ ἴ. παρέχειν *show the same* (degree of) *love* 1 Cl 21: 7. Of testimony given by witnesses *consistent* Mk 14: 56, 59. ἴσον ποιεῖν τινά τινι *treat someone equally w. someone else* (Polyb. 2, 38, 8; 2 Macc 9: 15 αὐτοὺς ἴσους Ἀθηναίοις ποιήσειν) Mt 20: 12. ἑαυτὸν τῷ θεῷ *make oneself equal to God* J 5: 18 (cf. Philo, Leg. All. 1, 49 ἴσος θεῷ).— Subst. τὰ ἴσα *an equal amount* (PRyl. 65, 7 [I BC] εἰς τὸ βασιλικὸν τὰ ἴσα) ἀπολαβεῖν τὰ ἴ. *receive an equal amount in return* Lk 6: 34.—The neut. pl. ἴσα (like the neut. sing. ἴσον) is used as an adv. (Hom.+; Diod. S. 1, 89, 1; Wsd 7: 3) w. dat. (Demosth. 19, 314; oft. Philostrat. [Schmid IV 48]; Himerius, Or. 20, 4 W. ἴσα ποιηταῖς; PTebt. 278, 33 [I AD]; Job 11: 12; 30: 19) ἴσα εἶναί τινι *be equal with someone* Phil 2: 6 (ἴσα εἶναι as Thu. 3, 14, 1; ἴσα θεῷ as Dionys. Byz. §24 p. 12, 14; §41 p. 17, 12; Himerius, Or. [Ecl.] 3, 20. Cf. Bl-D. §434, 1; W-S. §28, 3. Aeschyl., Pers. 856 ἰσόθεος of a king, Philod., Rhet. II p. 57, 11 Sudh. of a philosopher; Nicol. Dam.: 90 fgm. 130, 97 Caesar τὸν ἴσα κ. θεὸν τιμώμενον; 117; Ael. Aristid. 46 p. 319 D.: ἐξ ἴσου τοῖς θεοῖς ἐθαυμάζετο). ἐξ ἴσου (Soph., Hdt. et al.; Dit., Syll.³ 969, 84; pap.) *equally, alike* Pol 4: 2.—GStählin, TW III 343-56. M-M. B. 910.*

ἰσότης, ητος, ἡ (Eur.+; oft. Philo; only twice LXX; Ep. Arist. 263).
1. *equality* (Ps.-Phoc. 137) ἐξ ἰσότητος *as a matter of equality* 2 Cor 8: 13; also ὅπως γένηται ἰ. *that there may be equality* vs. 14.
2. *fairness* (Menand., Monost., 259; Polyb. 2, 38, 8 ἰ. κ. φιλανθρωπία; Diod. S. 5, 71, 2; Vett. Val. 332, 34) w. τὸ δίκαιον (cf. Diog. L. 7, 126; Philo, Spec. Leg. 4, 231 ἰσότης μήτηρ δικαιοσύνης) *justice and fairness* Col 4: 1. M-M.*

ἰσότιμος, ον (Strabo 15, 3, 20; Dio Chrys. 24[41], 2; Plut. et al.; Dit., Or. 234, 25 [c. 200 BC]; 544, 33 [adv.]; PRyl. 253; Wilcken, Chrest. 13, 10; Philo; Jos., Ant. 12, 119) *equal in value*, also simply *of the same kind* (Aelian, N.A. 10, 1; Herodian 2, 3, 6; Herm. Wr. 12, 12) ἰσότιμον ἡμῖν πίστιν *a faith of the same kind as ours* 2 Pt 1: 1. M-M.*

ἰσόψυχος, ον (Aeschyl., Agam. 1470; schol. on Eur., Andr. 419; Ps 54: 14) *of like soul* or *mind* Phil 2: 20 (AFridrichsen, Symb. Osl. 18, '38, 42-9 would supply ὑμῖν: *having much in common with you.* The same scholar Con. Neot. 7, '42, 3, w. ref. to ἰσοψύχως in the Acta Pauli '36, p. 44; PChristou, JBL 70, '51, 293-6: *confidant*). M-M.*

'Ισραήλ, ὁ indecl. (יִשְׂרָאֵל) *Israel* (LXX, Philo, Test. 12 Patr.; Sib. Or. 1, 360; 366; PGM 4, 3034; 3055 al.—Jos., Ant. 1, 333 'Ισράηλος).
1. the patriarch Jacob; οἱ ἐξ 'Ι. *the descendants of Israel* Ro 9: 6a. Also ἐκ γένους 'Ι. Phil 3: 5 (cf. 1 Esdr 1: 30; Jdth 6: 2); οἶκος 'Ι. *the house of Israel*=all the descendants of the patr. (cf. Jdth 14: 5; 3 Macc 2: 10) Mt 10: 6; 15: 24; Ac 2: 36; 7: 42 (Am 5: 25); Hb 8: 10 (Jer 38: 33); 1 Cl 8: 3 (quot. of unknown orig.). Also υἱοὶ 'Ι. (Mi 5: 2; Sir 46: 10; 47: 2 and oft.) Mt 27: 9; Lk 1: 16; Ac 5: 21; 7: 23, 37; Ro 9: 27b. On the other hand, ὁ οἶκος 'Ι. Hb 8: 8 in contrast to οἶκος 'Ιούδα (after Jer 38: 31) means the people of the Northern Kingdom. Some of the pass. mentioned here may belong under
2. the nation of *Israel* τὸν λαόν μου τὸν 'Ι. Mt 2: 6; ἄκουε 'Ι. Mk 12: 29 (Dt 6: 4).—Lk 1: 54; Ro 9: 27a; 11: 25f; 1 Cl 29: 2 (Dt 32: 9); 43: 5; ἐν τῷ 'Ι. Mt 8: 10; 9: 33; Lk 2: 34; 4: 25, 27; 1 Cl 43: 6; B 4: 14; κατὰ τοῦ 'Ι. Ro 11: 2; πρὸς τὸν 'Ι. Lk 1: 80; Ro 10: 21; B 5: 2; τὶς τοῦ 'Ι. PK 3; βασιλεὺς τοῦ 'Ι. Mt 27: 42; Mk 15: 32; J 1: 49; 12: 13; GP 3: 7; 4: 11; 1 Cl 4: 13; διδάσκαλος τοῦ 'Ι. J 3: 10; πολιτεία τοῦ 'Ι. Eph 2: 12; πόλεις τοῦ 'Ι. Mt 10: 23. ὁ θεὸς (τοῦ) 'Ι. 15: 31; Lk 1: 68; γῆ 'Ι. Mt 2: 20f; ὁ λαὸς 'Ι. Lk 2: 32; Ac 4: 10. The pl. λαοὶ 'Ι. vs. 27 because of the quot. Ps 2: 1 in vs. 25. αἱ φυλαὶ τοῦ 'Ι. *the tribes of Israel* (CIG IV 9270 [Iconium; prob. Jewish] ὁ θεὸς τ. φυλῶν τοῦ 'Ισραήλ) Mt 19: 28; Lk 22: 30; cf. Rv 7: 4. τὸ δωδεκάφυλον τοῦ 'Ι. *the twelve tribes of Israel* 1 Cl 55: 6. τὸ δωδεκάσκηπτρον τοῦ 'Ι. 31: 4; ἡ ἐλπὶς τοῦ 'Ι. Ac 28: 20.—'Ι. is the main self-designation of the Jews; fr. this as a starting-point it is also used
3. in a fig. sense of the Christians as the true nation of Israel, in contrast to ὁ 'Ι. κατὰ σάρκα *Israel in the physical sense* 1 Cor 10: 18. ὁ 'Ι. τοῦ θεοῦ *the* (true) *divine Israel* Gal 6: 16. οὐ γὰρ πάντες οἱ ἐξ 'Ι. οὗτοι 'Ι. *not all who are descended fr. Israel* (=Jacob), or *who belong to the Israelite nation, are really Israelites* Ro 9: 6.—FW Maier, I. in d. Heilsgesch. nach Rö 9-11, '29.—JJocz, A Theology of Election: Israel and the Church '58; JMunck, Paul and the Salvation of Mankind (tr. GClarke) '59; WTrilling, Das Wahre Israel (Mt)³ '64; JvanGoudoever, NovT 8, '66, 111-23 (Lk); GStrecker, D. Weg d. Gerechtigkeit, '66, esp. 99-118.—On the whole word, GvRad, KGKuhn and WGutbrod, 'Ισραήλ, 'Ιουδαῖος, 'Εβραῖος and related words: TW III 356-94.

'Ισραηλίτης, ου, ὁ יִשְׂרְאֵלִי; LXX; Joseph. index; Test. 12 Patr.—As a fem.: Inscr. 44 of the Villa Torlonia in Rome, ed. HWBeyer and HLietzmann '30) *the Israelite* J 1: 47 (cf. Plut., Is. et Os. 3 p. 352c 'Ισιακός ἐστιν ὡς ἀληθῶς of a genuine worshiper of Isis); Ro 9: 4; 11: 1; 2 Cor 11: 22. As a form of address ἄνδρες 'Ισραηλῖται *men of Israel* (Jos., Ant. 3, 189) Ac 2: 22; 3: 12; 5: 35; 13: 16; 21: 28. M-M.*

'Ισσαχάρ, ὁ indecl. (יִשָּׂשׁכָר; LXX; Philo; Test. 12 Patr. ['Ισαχάρ].—Jos., Ant. 1, 308 'Ισσαχάρης; 2, 178 'Ισακχάρου) *Issachar*, a son of the patriarch Jacob (Gen 30: 18), and hence an Israelite tribe Gen 49: 14; Num 1: 26 al.) Rv 7: 7 (v.l. 'Ισαχάρ; so Test. 12 Patr. and variants in Philo).*

ἴστε s. οἶδα.

ἵστημι (Hom.+; inscr., pap. [Mayser 353]; LXX [Thackeray 247f]; Ep. Arist., Philo, Joseph., Test. 12 Patr., Sib. Or.) and also ἱστάνω (since I BC Dit., Syll.³ 1104, 26 ἱστανόμενος; pap. [Mayser, loc. cit.; ἀνθιστάνω can be quoted here as early as III BC]; Epict. 3, 12, 2; LXX [Ezk 17: 14; Thackeray, loc. cit.]. Later wr. in StBPsaltes, Gramm. d. byz. Chroniken '13, 236) Ro 3: 31. Cf. Bl-D.

§93; Mlt.-H. 202. Fut. στήσω; 1 aor. ἔστησα; 2 aor. ἔστην, imper. στῆθι, inf. στῆναι, ptc. στάς; pf. ἔστηκα (*I stand*), ptc. ἑστηκώς, ός and ἑστώς (J 12: 29), ὧσα (J 8: 9 v.l.), neut. ἑστός (Rv 14: 1 v.l.). Cf. Bl-D. §96; Mlt.-H. 222) and ἑστός, inf. always ἑστάναι; plpf. εἰστήκειν (*I stood*) or ἱστήκειν GP 2: 3, third pl. εἰστήκεισαν (Mt 12: 46; J 18: 18; Ac 9: 7; Rv 7: 11. W-H. spell it ἱστ. everywhere); fut. mid. στήσομαι (Rv 18: 15); 1 aor. pass. ἐστάθην; 1 fut. pass. σταθήσομαι.

I. trans. (pres., impf., fut., 1 aor. act.; cf. Bl-D. §97, 1; Mlt.-H. 241) *put, place, set.*

1. gener.—a. lit.—α. *set, place, bring, allow to come* τινά *someone* ἐν τῷ συνεδρίῳ Ac 5: 27. εἰς αὐτούς *before them* 22: 30. ἐκ δεξιῶν τινος *at someone's right (hand)* Mt 25: 33. ἐν μέσῳ *in the midst, among* 18: 2; Mk 9: 36; J 8: 3. ἐνώπιόν τινος *before someone* Ac 6: 6. Also κατενώπιόν τινος Jd 24. ἐπί τι *upon someth.* Mt 4: 5; Lk 4: 9. παρά τινι *beside someone* 9: 47.

β. *put forward, propose* for a certain purpose: the candidates for election to the apostleship Ac 1: 23. μάρτυρας ψευδεῖς 6: 13.

2. fig.—a. *establish, confirm, make* or *consider valid* τὶ someth. (cf. Gen 26: 3 τὸν ὅρκον; Ex 6: 4; 1 Macc 2: 27 τὴν διαθήκην) τὸν νόμον Ro 3: 31. τὸ δεύτερον (opp. ἀναιρεῖν τὸ πρῶτον) Hb 10: 9. τὴν ἰδίαν δικαιοσύνην Ro 10: 3.

b. *make someone* (τινά) *stand* δυνατεῖ ὁ κύριος στῆσαι αὐτόν Ro 14: 4.

c. *set, fix* ἡμέραν (s. ἡμέρα 3a) Ac 17: 31. This mng. is perh. correct for Mt 26: 15 (Zech 11: 12) οἱ δὲ ἔστησαν αὐτῷ τριάκοντα ἀργύρια *they set out (=offered, allowed) (for) him 30 silver coins* (Wlh., OHoltzmann, Schniewind). Others (BWeiss, HHoltzmann, JWeiss; FSchulthess, ZNW 21, '22, 227f; Field, Notes 19f), prob. rightly, prefer the mng. *weigh out* on the scales (Hom.; X., Cyr. 8, 2, 21, Mem. 1, 1, 9 al.; Dialekt-Inschr. p. 870, ⁿ49 A [Ephesus VI BC] 40 minas ἐστάθησαν; Is 46: 6; Jer 39: 9; 2 Esdr [Ezra] 8: 25). The same sense is found by Weizsäcker, BWeiss, Hoennicke, Zahn, OHoltzmann et al. in κύριε, μὴ στήσῃς αὐτοῖς ταύτην τ. ἁμαρτίαν Ac 7: 60. On the other hand, Overbeck, Blass, HHoltzmann, Wendt seek the correct transl. w. 1ba above: *confirm, hold against.*

II. intrans. (2 aor., pf., plpf. act.; fut. mid. and pass.; 1 aor. pass.).

1. the aorist and future forms—a. *stand still, stop* (Hom., Aristot.; Philostrat., Ep. 36, 2 ὁ ποταμὸς στήσεται) Lk 24: 17. στὰς ὁ Ἰησοῦς ἐφώνησεν αὐτούς Mt 20: 32.—Mk 10: 49; Lk 7: 14; 17: 12; 18: 40. στῆναι τὸ ἅρμα Ac 8: 38. ἀπὸ μακρόθεν ἔστησαν Rv 18: 17; cf. vs. 15. ἔστη ἐπὶ τόπου πεδινοῦ *he took his stand on a level place* Lk 6: 17. Of a star ἐστάθη ἐπάνω οὗ ἦν τὸ παιδίον Mt 2: 9. Of a flow of blood *come to an end* ἔστη ἡ ῥύσις τ. αἵματος Lk 8: 44 (cf. Ex 4: 25 [though HKosmala, Vetus Test. 12, '62, 28 renders it as an emphatic εἶναι] Heraclid. Pont., fgm. 49 W.; POxy. 1088, 21 [I AD]; Cyranides p. 117 note γυναικί . . . αἷμα ἵστημι παραχρῆμα). στῆθι *stand* Js 2: 3.

b. *come up, stand, appear* ἔμπροσθέν τινος *before someone* Mt 27: 11; Lk 21: 36. Also ἐνώπιόν τινος Ac 10: 30 or ἐπί τινος: σταθήσεσθε *you will have to appear* Mt 10: 18 D; Mk 13: 9. στῆθι εἰς τὸ μέσον Lk 6: 8; cf. vs. 8b; J 20: 19, 26 (Vi. Aesopi I c. 6 p. 243, 15 Αἴσωπος στὰς εἰς τὸ μέσον ἀνέκραξεν) Lk 24: 36; Ac 17: 22. Also ἐν μέσῳ Lk 24: 36; Ac 17: 22. Cf. J 21: 4; Rv 12: 18; Lk 7: 38; POxy. 1, 3 (JoachJeremias, Unknown Sayings of Jesus, tr. Fuller, '57, 69f). *Step up* or *stand* to say someth. or make a speech Lk 18: 11. Cf. 19: 8; Ac 2: 14; 5: 20; 11: 13 al.

c. *offer resistance* πρός w. acc. *to* (Thu. 5, 104) Eph 6: 11. Abs. *resist* (Ex 14: 13) vs. 13.

d. *stand firm, hold one's ground* (Ps 35: 13) in battle (X., An. 1, 10, 1) Eph 6: 14. σταθήσεται *he will stand firm* Ro 14: 4a. τίς δύναται σταθῆναι; Rv 6: 17. εἰς ἣν στῆτε *stand fast in it* (Gdspd., Probs. 198) 1 Pt 5: 12. Of house, city, or kingdom Mt 12: 25f; Mk 3: 24f; Lk 11: 18. Cf. Mk 3: 26. The OT expr. (Dt 19: 15) ἵνα ἐπὶ στόματος δύο μαρτύρων ἢ τριῶν σταθῇ πᾶν ῥῆμα Mt 18: 16; 2 Cor 13: 1 may be classed here.

e. *stand up* firmly ἐπὶ τοὺς πόδας *upon one's feet* (Ezk 2: 1) Ac 26: 16; Rv 11: 11. Abs. Ac 3: 8.

2. perf. and plpf. *I stand, I stood*—a. of bodily position, e.g. of a speaker J 7: 37; Ac 5: 25, of hearers J 12: 29 or spectators Mt 27: 47; Lk 23: 35; Ac 1: 11, of accusers Lk 23: 10. Cf. J 18: 5, 16, 18a, b, 25; 19: 25; Ac 16: 9 al.

b. Very oft. the emphasis is less on 'standing' than on *being, existing.*

α. w. adv. of place ἔξω Mt 12: 46f; Lk 8: 20; 13: 25. μακρόθεν Lk 18: 13. ἀπὸ μακρόθεν *at a distance* 23: 49; Rv 18: 10. ἐκεῖ Mk 11: 5. ὅπου 13: 14. ὧδε Mt 16: 28; 20: 6b. αὐτοῦ Lk 9: 27.

β. w. place indicated by a prep.—א. ἐκ δεξιῶν τινος *at the right (hand) of someone* or *someth.* Lk 1: 11; Ac 7: 55f (HPOwen, NTS 1, '54/'55, 224-26). ἐν αὐτοῖς *among them* Ac 24: 21; w. ἐν and dat. of place Mt 20: 3; 24: 15; J 11: 56; Rv 19: 17. ἐνώπιόν τινος 7: 9; 11: 4; 12: 4; 20: 12. ἐπί w. gen. (X., Cyr. 3, 3, 66; Apollodorus [II BC]: 244 fgm. 209 Jac. ἐπί τ. θύρας) Ac 5: 23; 21: 40; 24: 20; 25: 10; Rv 10: 5, 8; w. dat. Ac 7: 33; w. acc. Mt 13: 2; Rv 3: 20; 7: 1; 14: 1; 15: 2. παρά w. acc. of place Lk 5: 1f. πέραν τῆς θαλάσσης J 6: 22. πρό w. gen. of place Ac 12: 14. πρός w. dat. of place J 20: 11. σύν τινι Ac 4: 14. κύκλῳ τινός *around someth.* Rv 7: 11.

ℶ. *attend upon, be the servant of* Rv 8: 2 (RHCharles, Rv ICC vol. 1, p. 225).

γ. abs. (Epict. 4, 1, 88 ἑστῶσα of the citadel, simply standing there) Mt 26: 73; J 1: 35; 3: 29; 20: 14; Ac 22: 25. The verb standing alone in the sense *stand around idle* (Eur., Iph. Aul. 860; Aristoph., Av. 206, Eccl. 852; Herodas 4, 44) Mt 20: 6a. ἀργός can be added (Aristoph., Eccl. 879f, Pax 256 ἔστηκας ἀργός) vs. 6a v.l., b (w. the question cf. Eubulus Com., fgm. 15, 1 K. τί ἔστηκας ἐν πύλαις; Herodas 5, 40). W. modifying words Plato, Phaedr. 275D ἔστηκε ὡς ζῶντα τὰ ἔκγονα) εἰστήκεισαν ἐνεοί *they stood there speechless* Ac 9: 7. ὡς ἐσφαγμένον Rv 5: 6. Cf. Ac 26: 6.

c. fig.—a. *stand firm* (opp. πεσεῖν) 1 Cor 10: 12; 2 Cl 2: 6. τ. πίστει ἔστηκας *you stand firm because of your faith* Ro 11: 20. ὃς ἕστηκεν ἐν τ. καρδίᾳ αὐτοῦ *whoever stands firm in his heart* 1 Cor 7: 37. ὁ θεμέλιος ἔστηκεν *the foundation stands (unshaken)* 2 Ti 2: 19 (Stob. 4, 41, 60 [vol. V, p. 945]: Apelles, when he was asked why he represented Tyche [Fortune] in a sitting position, answered οὐχ ἔστηκεν=because she can't stand, i.e., has no stability; Hierocles 11 p. 441 ἑστῶτος τοῦ νόμου=since the law stands firm [unchanged]; Procop. Soph., Ep. 47 μηδὲν ἑστηκὸς κ. ἀκίνητον; 75).

β. *stand* or *be in* grace (Hierocles 12 p. 446 ἐν ἀρετῇ) Ro 5: 2; within the scope of the gospel 1 Cor 15: 1; in faith 2 Cor 1: 24; in truth J 8: 44.—The pres. middle also has intr. mng. in the expr. (as old as Hom.) μὴν ἱστάμενος *the month just beginning* (oft. inscr.) MPol 21. M-M. B. 835.

ἱστίον, ου, τό *a sail* (so, mostly in pl., Hom. +; inscr.; pap.; Is 33: 23) συστέλλειν τὰ ἱ. *shorten the sails* or *furl them* altogether Ac 27: 16 v.l. B. 736.*

ἱστορέω 1 aor. ἱστόρησα (Aeschyl., Hdt. + in the sense 'inquire', etc.; inscr., pap., 1 Esdr) *visit for the purpose of coming to know someone or someth.* (Plut., Thes. 30, 3, Pomp. 40, 2, Lucull. 2, 9, Mor. 516c; Epict. 2, 14, 28; 3, 7, 1; Dit., Or. 694; Sb 1004; PLond. 854, 5; Jos., Bell. 6, 81, Ant. 1, 203) Gal 1: 18 (GDKilpatrick, TWManson memorial vol., ed. AJBHiggins '59, 144–9 'to get information from'). Cf. Ac 17: 23 v.l. M-M.*

ἰσχνόφωνος, ον (Hdt. +; Ex; Ezek. Trag. in Euseb., Pr. Ev. 9, 29, 9) *weak-voiced,* but also *having an impediment in one's speech* 1 Cl 17: 5 (Ex 4: 10).*

ἰσχυροποιέω fut. ἰσχυροποιήσω; 1 aor. ἰσχυροποίησα; pres. pass. imper. ἰσχυροποιοῦ (Polyb. et al.; Ezk 27: 27 Aq.) *strengthen* (Diod. S. 17, 65; Herm. Wr. 16, 12) τινά *someone* Hv 1, 3, 2; 4, 1, 3. τινὰ ἐν τῇ πίστει Hm 12, 6, 1. Pass. (Antig. Car. 175; Epict. 2, 18, 7; 4, 9, 15; Vett. Val. 333, 7; 347, 5 al.) s 6, 3, 6. εἰς τὸ ἀγαθόν *to do good* v 3, 13, 2. ἐν ταῖς ἐντολαῖς *in keeping the commandments* v 5: 5.*

ἰσχυροποίησις, εως, ἡ (Clem. Alex., Strom. 4, 12, 85; Aëtius 12, 21) *strengthening* Hv 3, 12, 3.*

ἰσχυρός, ά, όν (Aeschyl. +; inscr., pap., LXX, Philo, Jos., Ant. 5, 285, C. Ap. 2, 218) comp. ἰσχυρότερος (Hdt. +; inscr., pap., LXX) *strong, mighty, powerful.*
1. of living beings: in physical strength, or mental or spiritual power.
a. of superhuman beings: of God (Dit., Syll.³ 216, 1 [IV BC] ἰσχυρῷ θειῷ [= θεῷ s. note 4] Σανέργει; Dt 10: 17; 2 Macc 1: 24 and oft.; Philo, Spec. Leg. 1, 307; PGM 10, 11; 12, 374; 36, 105) Rv 18: 8. Of angels (PGM 3, 71f ἄγγελος κραταιὸς κ. ἰσχυρός) 5: 2; 10: 1; 18: 21. Of Christ 1 Cor 10: 22; cf. also Lk 11: 22 (s. below on Lk 11: 21). Of the one to come after John the Baptist ἰσχυρότερός μου (cf. Judg 5: 13 A; PGM 13, 202) Mt 3: 11; Mk 1: 7; Lk 3: 16. τὸ ἀσθενὲς τ. θεοῦ ἰσχυρότερον τ. ἀνθρώπων 1 Cor 1: 25 (cf. Philo, Ebr. 186 τὸ ἀσθενές—τὸ ἰ.). Of Satan, who may be the ἰσχυρός of the parable Mt 12: 29; Mk 3: 27; Lk 11: 21 (cf. PGM 5, 147 the δαίμων, who calls himself ἰσχυρός, and the ἰσχυρός of 13, 203 who, acc. to 197 is ἔνοπλος, as well as the Φόβος καθωπλισμένος 528 fighting the ἰσχυρότερος 543). In case Satan is not meant, these passages, together w. Lk 11: 22 (s. above) belong under b below.
b. of human beings (opp. ἀσθενής as Philo, Somn. 1, 155) 1 Cor 4: 10; Agr 4.—1 J 2: 14. ἰ. ἐν πολέμῳ *mighty in war* Hb 11: 34. οἱ ἰσχυροί (Ps.-Xenophon, Respublica Athen. ['The Old Oligarch'] 1, 14; 4 Km 24: 15; Da 8: 24 Theod.) Rv 6: 15; 19: 18. Even the neut. τὰ ἰσχυρά refers to persons 1 Cor 1: 27.
2. of things ἄνεμος *violent* (Dio Chrys. 60 and 61 [77 and 78], 7 χειμὼν ἰ.) Mt 14: 30 v.l.; βροντή *loud* Rv 19: 6. κραυγή Hb 5: 7. λίθος *solid, mighty* (Sir 6: 21) B 6: 2. λιμός *a severe famine* Lk 15: 14 (cf. Petosiris, fgm. 6 l. 49 λιμὸς ἰ.; Hdt. 1, 94; Dit., Syll.³ 495, 59 [c. 230 BC] σιτοδείας γενομένης ἰσχυρᾶς; Gen 41: 31). πόλις *mighty* (Is 26: 1 v.l.; Test. Judah 5: 1) Rv 18: 10 (cf. also τεῖχος X., Cyr. 7, 5, 7; 1 Macc 1: 33 v.l. Kappler; πύργος Judg 9: 51 B). φωνή *loud* (Aesop, Fab. 420 P. ἰσχυρᾷ τῇ φωνῇ; Ex 19: 19; Da 6: 21 Theod.) Rv 18: 2; παράκλησις ἰ. *strong encouragement* Hb 6: 18. ῥῆμα *mighty* Hv 1, 3, 4. (W. βέβαια and τεθεμελιωμένα) πάντα ἰσχυρά *everything is secure* s 4, 3. θέσις Hv 3, 13, 3. (W. βαρεῖαι, as Test. Judah 9: 2) ἐπιστολαί *weighty and effective* (cf. X., Cyr. 3, 3, 48; Wsd 6: 8) *letters* 2 Cor 10: 10. M-M. B. 295.**

ἰσχυρότης, ητος, ἡ (Dionys. Hal. 3, 65, 2 Jac. v.l.; Philo, Leg. All. 3, 204) *power, strength* προσῆλθεν ὑμῖν ἰ. *you received power* Hv 3, 12, 3. Of stones: *solidity, strength* (cf. Job 6: 12 ἰσχὺς λίθων) s 9, 8, 7.*

ἰσχυρόω (Is 41: 7) *strengthen* Hm 5, 2, 8 v.l. for ἰσχύω.*

ἰσχυρῶς adv. (Hdt. +; LXX; Philo, Aet. M. 21; Jos., Ant. 12, 368, C. Ap. 1, 127) *strongly, dependably* (w. ἀνδρείως) ἀναστρέφεσθαι *conduct oneself dependably and manfully* Hs 5, 6, 6. ὑποφέρειν *bear bravely* 7: 5. ἀνθεστηκέναι m 12, 5, 4. ἑστάναι *stand firmly* v 3, 13, 3. ταπεινοφρονῆσαι *be extremely humble* s 7: 4 (simply='very much': Antig. Car. 35; Appian, Liby. 96, §454; Diog. L. 1, 75 ἰ. ἐτίμησαν).*

ἰσχύς, ύος, ἡ (Hes. +; rare in later times and in inscr. and pap. [e.g. PMich. 156—II AD], but oft. LXX; Ep. Arist.; Philo; Jos., C. Ap. 1, 19 al.; Test. 12 Patr.) *strength, power, might* 1 Cl 13: 1 (Jer 9: 22); 39: 2; B 6: 3; 12: 11 (Is 45: 1); Hv 3, 12, 2; ἐξ ἰ. *by the strength* 1 Pt 4: 11. ἐξ ὅλης τῆς ἰ. *with all one's strength* Mk 12: 30, 33; 1 Cl 33: 8; cf. Lk 10: 27 (s. Herm. Wr. 1, 30 ἐκ ψυχῆς κ. ἰσχύος ὅλης); ἰσχύειν τῇ ἰ. Hs 9, 1, 2. (W. δύναμις, as Dio Chrys. 14[31], 11; 30[47], 3; Appian, Bell. Civ. 4, 71 §302; PLond. 1319, 5; cf. Thu. 7, 66, 3; 2 Ch 26: 13; Jos., Ant. 11, 44) ἄγγελοι ἰσχύϊ κ. δυνάμει μείζονες 2 Pt 2: 11. Used w. δύναμις and sim. words as attributes of God (ἰ. as divine attribute in trag. and oft. LXX) Rv 5: 12; 7: 12. Cf. also 1 Cl 60: 1; Dg 9: 6. Of God κράτος τῆς ἰ. (cf. Job 12: 16 παρ' αὐτῷ κράτος καὶ ἰσχύς. Philo, De Prov. in Euseb., Pr. Ev. 8, 14, 38) Eph 1: 19; 6: 10 (for the Eph passages cf. the Qumran parallels noted by KGKuhn, NTS 7, '61, 335, e.g. 1QH iv 32, xviii 8; 1QS xi 19f) 1 Cl 27: 5. Of the Lord ἀπὸ τῆς δόξης τῆς ἰ. αὐτοῦ (10, 19, 21) 2 Th 1: 9. Of the *power* of prayer IEph 5: 2 (cf. Lucian, Hist. 43 τῆς ἑρμηνείας ἰσχύς; Alex. Aphr., Fat. 16, II 2 p. 186, 23 of the power of truth; Phalaris, Ep. 70, 1).—Grundmann, s. δύναμις, end, also TW III 400–5. M-M.*

ἰσχύω fut. ἰσχύσω; 1 aor. ἴσχυσα (Pind. +; inscr., pap., LXX, Philo, Joseph., Test. 12 Patr.) *be strong, powerful.*
1. *be in possession of one's powers, be in good health* οἱ ἰσχύοντες *those who are healthy* (Soph., Tr. 234; X., Cyr. 6, 1, 24, Mem. 2, 7, 7) Mt 9: 12; Mk 2: 17.
2. *have power, be competent, be able*—**a.** πολύ *be able to do much* (cf. Diod. S. 1, 60, 2 πλέον ἰ.; 4, 23, 3; Appian, Bell. Civ. 2, 88 §371 τοσοῦτον ἰ.; Jos., C. Ap. 1, 77 μεῖζον ἰ., Ant. 15, 88 πλεῖστον ἰ.) Js 5: 16. πάντα Phil 4: 13. εἰς οὐδέν *be good for nothing* Mt 5: 13.
b. w. inf. foll. (Diod. S. 1, 83, 8; Plut., Pomp. 58, 6; PEleph. 17, 23; POxy. 396; 533, 16; 1345 οὐκ ἴσχυσα ἐλθεῖν σήμερον. LXX; Philo, Leg. All. 3, 27; Jos., Bell. 6, 367, Ant. 2, 86) Mt 8: 28; 26: 40; Mk 5: 4; 14: 37; Lk 6: 48; 8: 43; 14: 6, 29f; 20: 26; J 21: 6; Ac 6: 10; 15: 10; 25: 7; 27: 16; Hv 1, 3, 3. *Be strong enough* σκάπτειν *to dig* Lk 16: 3; cf. Hv 3, 8, 8. Abs., though the inf. can easily be supplied fr. the context (as Sir 43: 28) οὐκ ἴσχυσαν (ἐκβαλεῖν) Mk 9: 18. οὐκ ἰσχύσουσιν (εἰσελθεῖν) Lk 13: 24.
3. *have power, be mighty* (Diod. S. 11, 23, 3; PPetr. II 18, 12) ὁ λόγος ηὔξανεν κ. ἴσχυεν Ac 19: 20. μέχρι πότε θάνατος ἰσχύσει; *how long will death hold its power?* GEg: Kl. T. 8³ p. 15 app. to l. 20ff; ἰ. ἐν ταῖς ἐντολαῖς *be strong in keeping the commandments* Hm 5, 2, 8. *Win out, prevail* (Thu. 3, 46, 3; Dio Chrys. 17[34], 19) ὁ δράκων οὐκ ἴσχυσεν Rv 12: 8. κατά τινος *over, against someone* Ac 19: 16.
4. *have meaning, be valid,* esp. as legal t.t. (Diod. S. 2, 33, 1; Aelian, V.H. 2, 38 νόμον ἰσχύειν; Dit., Syll.³ 888,

59; 151 ἴσχυσεν τὰ προστάγματα; PTebt. 286, 7 νομὴ
ἄδικος οὐδὲν εἰσχύει) of a will μήποτε ἰσχύει ὅτε ζῇ ὁ
διαθέμενος Hb 9: 17. οὔτε περιτομή τι ἰσχύει, οὔτε
ἀκροβυστία neither circumcision nor uncircumcision
means anything Gal 5: 6.—Have the value of (Inscr. Rom.
IV 915a, 12 ἡ δραχμὴ ἰσχύει ἀσσάρια δέκα; Jos., Ant.
14, 106) ὅλον ἐνιαυτὸν ἰσχύει ἡ ἡμέρα the day is equal to
a whole year Hs 6, 4, 4. M-M.**

ἴσως adv. (Theognis+='equally'; inscr., pap., LXX)
perhaps, probably (Attic wr., also PAmh. 135, 16; PTebt.
424, 3; POxy. 1681, 4 ἴσως με νομίζετε, ἀδελφοί,
βάρβαρόν τινα εἶναι. 4 Macc 7: 17; Philo, Aet. M. 60;
134; Jos., Bell. 4, 119, Ant. 4, 11) Lk 20: 13. M-M.*

Ἰταλία, ας, ἡ (Hdt. 1, 24 al.; Dit., Syll.³ 1229, 2 πλεύσας
εἰς Ἰταλίαν; Philo; Sib. Or.; oft. Joseph.) nearly always
w. the art.—Bl-D. §261, 6. Italy Ac 18: 2 (Jos., Ant. 16, 7
ἧκον ἀπὸ τῆς Ἰτ.); 27: 1, 6; Hb subscr. (no art.). οἱ ἀπὸ
τ. Ἰταλίας Hb 13: 24 s. ἀπό IV 1b.*

Ἰταλικός, ή, όν (Pla.+; Dit., Syll.³ 726, 4 [97/6 bc]; 746,
19; 1171, 10; Philo, Vi. Cont. 48; Jos., Ant. 9, 85; 18, 44;
loanw. in rabb.) Italian σπεῖρα Ἰ. the Italian cohort
(Arrian, Alan. 13 ed. AGRoos II '28 p. 181, 6 ἡ σπεῖρα ἡ
Ἰταλική) Ac 10: 1—Lit. on ἑκατοντάρχης. M-M.*

ἰταμός, ή, όν (Aristoph., Demosth.+; Lucian; Aelian;
Ael. Aristid. 31, 5 K.=11 p. 128 D.; Jer 6: 23; 27: 42)
bold, impetuous Hm 11: 12.*

ἰτέα, ας, ἡ (Hom.+; Diod. S. 5, 41, 5; LXX; Jos., Ant. 3,
245) willow tree Hs 8, 1, 1f; 8, 2, 7.*

Ἰτουραῖος, αία, αῖον (since Eupolemus [II bc] in Euseb.,
Pr. Ev. 9, 30, 3, mostly in the pl. of the subst. masc.
Ἰτουραῖοι [Appian, Mithrid. 106 §499, Bell. Civ. 5, 7,
§31; Arrian, Alans 1 and 18; Jos., Ant. 13, 318]. Schürer I⁴
707ff) ἡ Ἰ. χώρα Ituraea, a region along the Lebanon and
Anti-Lebanon ranges belonging to the Tetrarchy of Philip,
w. Chalcis as its capital city Lk 3: 1. Cf. Schürer loc. cit.
for sources and lit. M-M.*

ἰχθύδιον, ου, τό (Aristoph.+; pap.) dim. of ἰχθύς little
fish (Aelian, N.A. 6, 24 p. 150, 11) Mt 15: 34; Mk 8: 7.
Obviously without diminutive sense fish (PFay. 117, 7 [108
ad]; PFlor. 119, 7 [254 ad]; Synes., Ep. 4 p. 166a) B 10: 5
(=ἰχθύς 10: 10).*

ἰχθύς (poss. to be accented ἰχθῦς; cf. Bl-D. §13; Mlt.-H.
141f), ύος, ὁ (Hom.+; inscr., pap., LXX; En. 101, 7;
Philo, Joseph.) acc. pl. ἰχθύας (Epict. 4, 1, 30; Arrian,
Anab. 5, 4, 3; PFay. 113, 13 [100 ad].—The acc. form
ἰχθῦς [Athen. 7 p. 327b] is not found in our lit.) fish, as
food Mt 7: 10; 14: 17, 19; 15: 36; 17: 27 (s. RMeyer, OLZ
40, '37, 665-70; JDMDerrett, Law in the NT, '70, 258-60);
Mk 6: 38, 41, 43; Lk 5: 6, 9; 9: 13, 16; 11: 11; 24: 42; J 21:
6, 8, 11 (Jos., Bell. 3, 508 the γένη ἰχθύων in the Lake of
Gennesaret.—Test. Zeb. 6: 6 extraordinary catches of fish
caused by divine intervention). The flesh of fishes 1 Cor
15: 39. ἰχθύες τ. θαλάσσης B 6: 12 (Gen 1: 26, 28); cf. vs.
18; 10: 10. Fish that by nature have no scales may not be
eaten by the Jews B 10: 1 (cf. Lev 11: 9-12; Dt 14: 9f).
M-M. B. 184.*

ἴχνος, ους, τό (Hom.+; inscr., pap., LXX, Philo; Jos., Vi.
283)—1. footprint, in our lit. only in fig. sense (as Sir 21:
6; Philo, Op. M. 144) περιπατεῖν τοῖς ἴ. walk in the
footsteps 2 Cor 12: 18. στοιχεῖν τοῖς ἴ. τινος Ro 4: 12
(Dit., Syll.³ 708, 6 αὐτὸς στοιχεῖν βουλόμενος καὶ τοῖς ἴ.
ἐκείνων ἐπιβαίνειν; Philo, Gig. 58). ἐπακολουθεῖν τοῖς
ἴ. τινος follow in someone's footsteps 1 Pt 2: 21. πρὸς τὰ ἴ.

τινὸς εὑρεθῆναι be found in the footsteps of someone
MPol 22: 1.

2. sole, of the foot itself or of the footwear, both of
which as a whole can be referred to as ἴχνος (Eur., Bacch.
1134; Hippocr., Art. 62 vol. IV p. 266 L.; Herodas 7, 12;
113; 119; Arrian, Ind. 16, 5; Galen X p. 876 K.; Anth.
Pal. 9, 371, 2; POxy. 1449, 51 [III ad]; 2130, 18 [267 ad];
Dt 11: 24). Then the expression ὑπὸ τὰ ἴ. τινὸς εὑρεθῆναι
IEph 12: 2 would belong to the excessively humble sayings
of Ign., to which later pap. (Preisigke, W.-B. I col. 706)
offer comparable examples: under or below, at the soles or
the feet. M-M.*

ἰχώρ, ῶρος, ὁ (Hom.+) serum of blood (so in Pythagoras,
acc. to Diog. L. 8, 28; Pla.+; PGM 4, 2577; 2645; 4 Macc
9: 20; Philo, Spec. Leg. 4, 119), also serous discharge, pus
(Memnon [I bc/I ad]: no. 434 fgm. 1, 2, 4 Jac.; Job 2: 8; 7:
5; Jos., Ant. 2, 296) AP 11: 26; Papias 3.*

Ἰωαθάμ, ὁ indecl. (יוֹתָם; 1 Ch 3: 12 Ιωαθαν) Jotham, in
the genealogy of Jesus Mt 1: 9; Lk 3: 23ff D (Ἰωαθάν).*

Ἰωακίμ, ὁ indecl. (יְהוֹיָקִים; s. Ἰεχονίας) Jehoiakim Mt 1:
11 v.l.; Lk 3: 23ff D.*

Ἰωανάν, ὁ indecl. (יוֹחָנָן; Bl-D. §53, 2 app.—2 Esdr
[Ezra] 10: 6; 22: 22f; 2 Ch 17: 15; 23: 1) Joanan, in the
genealogy of Jesus Lk 3: 27.*

Ἰωάν(ν)α, ας, ἡ (on the spelling cf. Bl-D. §40; 53, 3)
Joanna Lk 8: 3; 24: 10.*

Ἰωάν(ν)ης, ου, ὁ (on the spelling cf. FBlass, Philology of
the Gospels 1898, 75f; 81; Bl-D. §40; 55, 1c; Mlt.-H. 102;
Rob. 194; 214; GRudberg, Ntl. Text u. Nomina sacra '15,
13f.—The name is also found 1 Macc 2: 1f; 9: 36, 38; 13:
53; 1 Esdr 8: 38; 9: 29; Ep. Arist. 47; 49; 50 and in
Joseph.) John.

1. John the Baptist (Jos., Ant. 18, 116-19) Mt 3: 1, 4,
13; 4: 12 al.; Mk (cf. JStarr, JBL 51, '32, 227-37) 1: 4,
6, 9, 14; 2: 18; 6: 14, 16ff; 8: 28; 11: 30, 32; Lk 1:
13, 60, 63; 3: 2, 15f, 20 al.; J 1: 6, 15, 19, 26, 28, 32,
35 al.; Ac 1: 5, 22; 10: 37; 11: 16; 13: 24f; 18: 25;
19: 3f; GEb 1; 2b; 3; ISm 1: 1.—Schürer I⁴ 436ff;
JThomas, Le mouvement baptiste en Palest. et Syrie '35;
MDibelius, Die urchr. Überlieferung von Joh. d. Täufer
'11; CABernoulli, J. der Täufer und die Urgemeinde '18;
CRBowen: Studies in Early Christianity, ed. SJCase
(Festschr. for FCPorter and BWBacon) '28, 127-47; EW
Parsons: ibid. 149-70; WMichaelis, Täufer, Jesus, Urge-
meinde '28; MGoguel, Jean-Baptiste '28; ELohmeyer, Joh.
d. T. '32; WFHoward, J. the Bapt. and Jesus: Amicitiae
Corolla '33, 118-32; PGuénin, Y a-t-il conflit entre Jean B.
et Jésus? '33; GHCMacgregor, John the Bapt. and the
Origins of Christianity: ET 46, '35, 355-62; CHKraeling,
John the Bapt. '51.—HWindisch, D. Notiz üb. Tracht u.
Speise d. Täuf. Joh.: ZNW 32, '33, 65-87; PJoüon, Le
costume d'Élie et celui de J. Bapt.: Biblica 16, '35, 74-81.
Esp. on his baptism: JoachJeremias, ZNW 28, '29, 312-20;
his death: HWindisch, ZNW 18, '18, 73-81; PZondervan,
NThT 7, '18, 131-53; 8, '19, 205-40; 10, '21, 206-17;
DVölter, ibid. 10, '21, 11-27; his disciples: HOort, ThT
42, '08, 299-333; WMichaelis, NKZ 38, '27, 717-36.—
JWDoeve, Nederl. Th. Tijdschrift 9, '55, 137-57; DFlus-
ser, Johannes d. Täufer '64; ASGeyser, The Youth of J.
the Bapt., NovT 1, '56, 70-75; CHScobie, John the Bapt.
'64; HBraun, Qumran u. d. NT '66, II, 1-29; WWink,
John the Bapt. in the Gosp. Trad. '68; JMRife, The
Standing of the Baptist: FWGingrich-Festschr., ed.
EHBarth and RECocroft, '72, 205-08. On the Mandaeans
s. RGG³ IV '60. 709-12 (lit.).

2. *John,* son of Zebedee, one of the 12 disciples, brother of James (s. Ἰάκωβος 1) Mt 4: 21; 10: 2; 17: 1; Mk 1: 19, 29; 3: 17; 5: 37 al.; Lk 5: 10; 6: 14; 8: 51 al.; Ac 1: 13; 3: 1, 3f, 11; 4: 13, 19; 8: 14; 12: 2; Gal 2: 9; GEb 2a; Papias 2: 4. Title of the Fourth Gospel κατὰ Ἰωάννην.—WHGThomas, The Apostle John '46. **3.** The tradition of the church equates J., son of Zebedee (2), w. the *John* of Rv: 1: 1, 4, 9; 22: 8.—On 2 and 3 cf. the comm. on the Johannine wr., also Zahn, RE IX 272ff, Forsch. VI '00, 175–217; Harnack, Die Chronologie der altchristl. Lit. 1897, 320–81; ESchwartz, Über d. Tod der Söhne Zebedäi '04; WHeitmüller, ZNW 15, '14, 189–209; BWBacon, ibid. 26, '27, 187–202. **4.** *John,* father of Peter J 1: 42; 21: 15–17; GH 9 (s. Ἰωνᾶς 2 and cf. 1 Esdr 9: 23 with its v.l.).—Schürer II⁴ 275f. **5.** *John,* an otherw. unknown member of the high council Ac 4: 6 (v.l. Ἰωνάθας). **6.** *John* surnamed Mark, son of Mary. His mother was a prominent member of the church at Jerusalem. He was a cousin of Barnabas and accompanied Paul and Barn. on the first missionary journey Ac 12: 12, 25; 13: 5, 13; 15: 37; s. Μᾶρκος and BTHolmes, Luke's Description of John Mark: JBL 54, '35, 63–72.

Ἰωάς, ὁ indecl. (יוֹאָשׁ) 2 Kings [=4 Km] 14: 1) *Joash,* king of Judah (Joseph.: Ἰώασος, ου [Ant. 9, 158]) Mt 1: 8 v.l.; Lk 3: 23ff D.*

Ἰώβ, ὁ indecl. (אִיּוֹב) LXX; Philo, Mut. Nom. 48.—Cf. Jos., Ant. 2, 178 Ἰῶβος, the son of Issachar) *Job,* hero of the book of the same name, example of patient suffering Js 5: 11; 1 Cl 17: 3 (Job 1: 1); 26: 3; 2 Cl 6: 8 (Ezk 14: 14).*

Ἰωβήδ, ὁ indecl. (עוֹבֵד) *Obed,* David's grandfather (1 Ch 2: 12 v.l. Likew. as v.l. in the book of Ruth 4: 21f [D. Buch Ruth griech. herausgeg. v. ARahlfs '22, 28]), in the genealogy of Jesus Mt 1: 5; Lk 3: 32 (t.r. Ὠβήδ.—Jos., Ant. 5, 336; 6, 157 Ὠβήδης, ου).*

Ἰωδά, ὁ indecl. *Joda* (1 Esdr 5: 56), in the genealogy of Jesus Lk 3: 26 (t.r. Ἰούδας).*

Ἰωήλ, ὁ indecl. (יוֹאֵל) *Joel,* the OT prophet. τὸ εἰρημένον διὰ τοῦ προφήτου Ἰωήλ (i.e. Jo 3: 1–5a) Ac 2: 16.*

Ἰωνάθας, ου, ὁ (cf. PPetr III 7, 15 [236 bc]; 1 Esdr 8: 32; Ep. Arist. 48 and 49; 50 has Ἰωνάθης, like Joseph. [gen. -ου: Ant. 6, 234]) *Jonathas* Ac 4: 6 D instead of Ἰωάννης (s. Ἰωάν(ν)ης 5; Jos., Ant. 18, 95a Ἰωνάθης is mentioned, a son of Annas, who followed Caiaphas as high priest). M-M.*

Ἰωνάμ, ὁ indecl. *Jonam,* in the genealogy of Jesus Lk 3: 30 (t.r. Ἰωνάν as 1 Esdr 9: 1 v.l.).*

Ἰωνᾶς, ᾶ, ὁ (יוֹנָה) *Jonah*—1. the OT prophet (4 Km 14: 25; Book of Jonah; Tob 14: 4, 8 BA; 3 Macc 6: 8; Jos., Ant. 9, 206–14; Sib. Or. 2, 248). He is meant by the enigmatic saying about the 'sign of Jonah' Mt 12: 39–41; 16: 4; Lk 11: 29f, 32 (Mt 12: 40 the sign consists in Jonah's stay inside the monster for three days and nights. Lk thinks perh. of the preaching of the prophet to the Ninevites; s. on σημεῖον 1 and AVögtle, Synoptische Studien [Wikenhauser-Festschr.] '53, 230–77); 1 Cl 7: 7. **2.** a Galilean fisherman, father of Simon Peter and Andrew Mt 16: 17 v.l.; GH 11 (Lat.). Acc. to J 1: 42; 21: 15–17 his name was Ἰωάν(ν)ης (s. Ἰωάν(ν)ης 4); the J pass. all have Ἰωνᾶ as v.l. Cf. Βαριωνᾶς and s. Bl-D. §53, 2 app.; W-S. §5, 26c.—On 1 and 2 JoachJeremias,

TW III 410–13; HMGale, JBL 60, '41, 255–60; OGlombitza, NTS 8, '61/'62, 359–66.—RAEdwards, The Sign of Jonah in the Theology of the Evangelists and Q, '71.*

Ἰωράμ, ὁ indecl. (יְהוֹרָם); in Joseph. Ἰώραμος, ου [Ant. 9, 58]) *Joram* (in OT *Jehoram*), king of Judah (4 Km 8: 16ff; 2 Ch 21: 3ff.—The name also 1 Esdr 1: 9); in the genealogy of Jesus Mt 1: 8; Lk 3: 23ff D.*

Ἰωρίμ, ὁ indecl. *Jorim,* in the genealogy of Jesus Lk 3: 29.*

Ἰωσαφάτ, ὁ indecl. (יְהוֹשָׁפָט); in Joseph. Ἰωσάφατος, ου [Ant. 8, 399]) *Jehoshaphat,* king of Judah (3 Km 22: 41ff; 2 Ch 17–20); in the genealogy of Jesus Mt 1: 8; Lk 3: 23ff D w. final δ.*

Ἰωσῆς, ῆ or ῆτος (s. Mayser 274), ὁ (the name is found IG Sic. It. 949 Κλαύδιος Ἰωσῆς; inscr. fr. Cyrene: Sb 1742. S. ibid. 3757 [I ad]; BGU 715 I, 4 [= Schürer III⁴ 47] Ἰ. ὁ καὶ Τεύφιλος; Jos., Bell. 4, 66 v.l. Cf. Bl-D. §53, 2; 55, 2; Rob. 263; Wuthnow 60) *Joses.* **1.** name of a brother of Jesus Mk 6: 3; Mt 13: 55 t.r.; s. Ἰωσήφ 5. **2.** son of a Mary and brother of James the younger Mk 15: 40, 47; Mt 27: 56 v.l. (for Ἰωσήφ, q.v. 9; on the text s. AMerx, D. Vier kanon. Ev. II 1, '02, 430ff). **3.** name of a member of the early church better known as Barnabas Ac 4: 36 v.l. (s. Ἰωσήφ 7). M-M.*

Ἰωσήφ, ὁ indecl. (יוֹסֵף); Apollonius Molon [I bc] in Euseb., Pr. Ev. 9, 19, 3; Sb II 250, word-list; LXX; Philo; Test. 12 Patr.—Ep. Arist.: Ἰωσήφος; Josephus: Ἰώσηπος, ου [Ant. 2, 17], also C. Ap. 1, 92) *Joseph.* **1.** the patriarch (Gen 30: 24 and oft.; Philo, Mut. Nom. 90f and oft.; Test. 12 Patr.) J 4: 5; Ac 7: 9, 13f, 18; Hb 11: 21f; 1 Cl 4: 9; B 13: 4f; φυλὴ Ἰ. in Rv 7: 8 stands for the half-tribe Ephraim which, w. its other half Manasseh vs. 6 brings the number of the tribes to twelve once more, after the loss of the tribe of Dan, to which acc. to tradition the Antichrist belongs (WBousset, Der Antichrist 1895, 112f). **2.** son of Jonam, in the genealogy of Jesus Lk 3: 30. **3.** son of Mattathias Lk 3: 24. **4.** husband of Mary the mother of Jesus Mt 1: 16 (PWSchmiedel, PM 6, '02, 88–93, SchThZ 31, '14, 69–82; ibid. 32, '15, 16–30; ERiggenbach, ibid. 31, '14, 241–9; GKuhn, NKZ 34, '23, 362–85; UHolzmeister, De S. Jos. Quaestiones Biblicae '45), 18–20, 24; 2: 13, 19; Lk 1: 27; 2: 4, 16, 33 v.l.; 3: 23 (a genealogy in which the first name is given without the article, and all subsequent names have the article, as Theopomp. [IV bc]: 115 fgm. 393 Jac.—in ascending order to Heracles. Diod. S. 5, 81, 6 Λέσβος ὁ Λαπίθου τοῦ Αἰόλου τοῦ Ἱππότου; Nicol. Dam.: 90 fgm. 30 p. 343, 30 Jac. Δηιφόντῃ τῷ Ἀντιμάχου τοῦ Θρασυάνορος τοῦ Κτησίππου τοῦ Ἡρακλέους. Other exx. in Klostermann ad loc.; Bl-D. §162, 2 app.); 4: 22; J 1: 45; 6: 42 (PHMenoud, RThPh 63, '30, 275–84). **5.** a brother of Jesus Mt 13: 55. Cf. Ἰωσῆς 1.—**6.** *Joseph* of Arimathaea, member of the Sanhedrin, in whose tomb Jesus was buried Mt 27: 57, 59; Mk 15: 43, 45; Lk 23: 50; J 19: 38; GP 6: 23. Acc. to GP 2: 3 he was a friend of Pilate.—EvDobschütz, ZKG 23, '02, 1–17. **7.** *Joseph,* surnamed Barnabas Ac 4: 36. Cf. Ἰωσῆς 3.—**8.** *Joseph,* surnamed Barsabbas (s. Βαρσαβ[β]ᾶς 1), also called Justus (s. Ἰοῦστος 1) 1: 23. **9.** son of a certain Mary Mt 27: 56 (s. Ἰωσῆς 2). M-M.*

Ἰωσήχ, ὁ indecl. (Mlt.-H. 108f) *Josech,* son of Joda, in the genealogy of Jesus Lk 3: 26.*

'Ιωσίας, ου, ὁ (יֹאשִׁיָּהוּ) *Josiah,* king of Judah (4 Km 22f; 2 Ch 34f; Sir 49: 1, 4; Bar 1: 8; 1 Esdr 1: 1–32; Jos., Ant. 10: 48, 67–78); in the genealogy of Jesus Mt 1: 10f; Lk 3: 23ff D.*

ἰῶτα, τό indecl. (written out as a word Aeneas Tact. 1506; Sb 358, 12; 20 [III BC]) *iota.* In Mt 5: 18 it is evidently the Gk. equivalent of the Aram. yod which, in the orig. form of the saying, represented the smallest letter of the alphabet (s. MLidzbarski, Handb. d. nordsemit. Epigraphik 1898, 190ff; EFSutcliffe, Biblica 9, '28, 458–62). As numeral=*ten* B 9: 8. S. ι' as numeral. M-M.*

K

κάβος, ου, ὁ (Geopon. 7, 20, 1; 4 Km 6: 25) *the cab,* a measure (usu. for grain, etc.) equal to approx. two quarts Lk 16: 6 v.l.; s. κάδος.*

κἀγώ (since Il. 21, 108, also inscr. [Meisterhans³-Schw. 72]; pap. [Mayser 159 w. exx. for all cases; cf. also UPZ 78, 15 [159 BC]; PSI 540, 17; PTebt. 412, 4 καιγώ]; LXX [Thackeray 137f]; Jos., Ant. 7, 212. Formed by crasis fr. καὶ ἐγώ) dat. κἀμοί, acc. κἀμέ. Cf. Bl-D. §18; Mlt.-H. 84.

1. *and I* ὁ πατήρ σου κἀγώ Lk 2: 48. Cf. Mt 11: 28; J 6: 57; 7: 28; 8: 26; 10: 28; 17: 22; IPhld 11: 1 al.—In a narrative told in the first pers. sg. it connects one member w. another J 1: 31, 33, 34. It oft. expresses a reciprocal relation *and I, as I* ἐν ἐμοὶ μένει κἀγὼ ἐν αὐτῷ J 6: 56. μείνατε ἐν ἐμοὶ κἀγὼ ἐν ὑμῖν 15: 4. Cf. 10: 15, 38; 14: 20; also 2 Cor 12: 20; Gal 6: 14.

2. *but I:* Jesus in contrast to the prince of this world J 12: 32. Cf. Ac 22: 19. ὑμεῖς . . . κἀμοί *you . . . but to me* 10: 28. σὺ πίστιν ἔχεις, κἀγὼ ἔργα ἔχω *you have faith, but I have deeds* Js 2: 18a.

3. *I also, I too*—a.=I, as well as others δοκῶ κἀγὼ πνεῦμα θεοῦ ἔχειν *I believe that I, too, have the Spirit of God* 1 Cor 7: 40. κἀγὼ προσκυνήσω αὐτῷ Mt 2: 8. Cf. Lk 1: 3; Ac 8: 19. Cf. J 5: 17; 2 Cor 11: 21, 22a, b, c.—καθὼς . . . κἀγώ *just as . . . I also* J 15: 9; 17: 18; 20: 21.

b. *I for my part, I in turn* Mt 10: 32f; 18: 33; 21: 24; Lk 22: 29; B 1: 4; ISm 4: 2. ὅτι ἐτήρησας . . . κἀγώ σε τηρήσω *because you have kept . . . I, in turn, will keep you* Rv 3: 10.—Introducing the moral of a parable κἀγὼ ὑμῖν λέγω *I, for my part, say to you* Lk 11: 9 (cf. 16: 9).—κἀγὼ δέ *but I, for my part* Mt 16: 18.

c. The καί in κἀγώ is redundant in comparisons τοιούτους ὁποῖος κἀγὼ εἰμι *such as I am* Ac 26: 29 v.l. ἐὰν μείνωσιν ὡς κἀγώ *if they remain as I am* 1 Cor 7: 8. Cf. 10: 33; 11: 1. Sim. διὰ τοῦτο κἀγὼ οὐ παύομαι *for that reason I do not cease* Eph 1: 15; cf. 1 Th 3: 5.

4. *I in particular* or *I for instance* τί ἔτι κἀγὼ ὡς ἁμαρτωλὸς κρίνομαι; Ro 3: 7. M-M.

κάδος, ου, ὁ (Anacr., Hdt.+; Dialekt-Inschr. 5220 [Sicily—18 times]; pap.; Is 40: 15; 2 Ch 2: 9 v.l., ἐλαίου κάδ.) *jar, container* Lk 16: 6 D; s. κάβος.*

καθά conj. or adv. (since Polyb. 3, 107, 10 [FKälker, Quaest. de elocut. Polyb. 1880, 300]; Diod. S. 4, 81, 3; 19, 48, 2; 19, 71, 7; inscr. [Meisterhans³-Schw. 257; Dit., Syll.³ index]; PRyl. 160 II, 18; POxy. 1473, 10; LXX; Jos., Ant. 19, 96; 298; 20, 6) *just as* Mt 6: 12 v.l.; 27: 10; Lk 1: 2 D (cf. Bl-D. §453); IMg 10: 1; Hs 1: 8. M-M.*

καθαίρεσις, εως, ἡ (Thu.+; inscr., pap., LXX; Jos., Ant. 14, 437) *tearing down, destruction.*

1. lit. (τ. τειχῶν X., Hell. 2, 2, 15; 5, 1, 35; Polyb. 23, 7, 6; Dit., Syll.² 587, 76; PMagd. 9; Ex 23: 24 καθαιρέσει καθελεῖς τ. στήλας αὐτῶν. Jos., Ant. 17, 163) as a type of someth. spiritual (cf. Philo, Conf. Lingu. 130 πρὸς τὴν τοῦ ὀχυρώματος τούτου καθαίρεσιν) *for the tearing down of bulwarks* 2 Cor 10: 4.

2. fig. (Diod. S. 34+35, fgm. 7, 1 of removal from office; Philo; opp. οἰκοδομή='edification'; s. this entry) εἰς οἰκοδομὴν καὶ οὐκ εἰς καθαίρεσιν 2 Cor 13: 10. W. obj. gen. of the pers. εἰς καθαίρεσιν ὑμῶν 10: 8 (cf. 1 Macc 3: 43 καθ. τοῦ λαοῦ). M-M.*

καθαιρέτης, ου, ὁ (since Thu. 4, 83, 5; BGU 14 V, 12 [255 AD]) *destroyer* ὁ τῶν ἡμετέρων θεῶν κ. MPol 12: 2.*

καθαιρέω 2 fut. καθελῶ Lk 12: 18; 2 aor. καθεῖλον, ptc. καθελών (Hom.+; inscr., pap., LXX, Ep. Arist., Philo, Joseph.).

1. *take down, bring down, lower* τινά or τὶ *someone* or *someth.:* someone fr. a carriage MPol 8: 3. Of raised hands *let (them) drop* B 12: 2 (w. τὰς χεῖρας to be supplied); the body fr. the cross (Polyb. 1, 86, 6; Philo, In Flacc. 83; Jos., Bell. 4, 317) Mk 15: 36, 46; Lk 23: 53. ἀπὸ τοῦ ξύλου (Josh 8: 29; 10: 27) Ac 13: 29. δυνάστας ἀπὸ θρόνων *bring down the rulers fr. their thrones* Lk 1: 52 (κ. abs. in this mng.: Hdt. 7, 8, 1; Aelian, V.H. 2, 25; Jos., Ant. 8, 270).

2. *tear down, destroy, overpower*—a. lit.—α. of buildings *tear down* (X., Hell. 4, 4, 13 τῶν τειχῶν=a part of the walls; Dit., Syll.³ 826E, 31 τ. οἰκίαν; PAmh. 54, 3; Is 5: 5; 22: 10; Jos., Vi. 65) in contrast to οἰκοδομέω (Jer 49: 10; 51: 34; Ezk 36: 36): the temple B 16: 3 (cf. Diod. S. 20, 93, 1 ἱερά; Is 49: 17). Barns Lk 12: 18. Pass. B 16: 4.

β. *conquer, destroy* (Thu. 1, 4; 1, 77, 6 al.; Aelian, V.H. 2, 25; POxy. 1408, 23 τοὺς λῃστάς; Ep. Arist. 263; Philo, Agr. 86; Jos., Ant. 10, 209) ἔθνη Ac 13: 19. Pass. καθαιροῦνται αἱ δυνάμεις τοῦ σατανᾶ IEph 13: 1.

b. fig. (Epict. 1, 28, 25 τὰ δόγματα τὰ ὀρθὰ κ.; Zech 9: 6 καθελῶ ὕβριν ἀλλοφύλων; Jos., Ant. 6, 179 τ. ἀλαζονείαν) λογισμοὺς *destroy sophistries* 2 Cor 10: 4. Pass. ἄγνοια IEph 19: 3. καθαιρεῖσθαι τῆς μεγαλειότητος αὐτῆς *suffer the loss of her magnificence* Ac 19: 27 (cf. Achmes 13, 22 ὁ κριτὴς . . . καθαιρεῖται τῆς ἀξίας αὐτοῦ =the judge suffers the loss of his dignity; Bl-D. §180, 1 app.; Rob. 518. Field, Notes 129f would supply τὶ and transl. *diminish*). M-M.*

καθαίρω 1 aor. ptc. καθάρας; pf. pass. ptc. κεκαθαρμένος (Hom.+; inscr., pap., LXX, Philo, Joseph.) *make clean.*

1. lit., of a place that has been swept (cf. Diod. S. 19, 13, 4 τόπον ἀνακαθαίρειν=clear [out] a place): πάντα κεκάθαρται *everything is clean* Hs 9, 10, 4. Of a vine *clear, prune* by removing the superfluous wood (cf. Philo, Agr. 10, Somn. 2, 64) J 15: 2.

2. fig. (Diod. S. 4, 31, 4; 4, 69, 4; Dio Chrys. 60+61 [77+78], 40 τὴν αὐτοῦ διάνοιαν καθαίρει τῷ λόγῳ; Himerius, Or. 41 [= Or. 7], 1 'Ηλίῳ Μίθρᾳ ψυχὴν καθάραντες=after we have cleansed our souls by the agency of Helios Mithra; Philo, Somn. 1, 198 καθαίρει ψυχὴν ἁμαρτημάτων; Jos., Ant. 5, 42) οἱ κεκαθαρμένοι *those*

who are purified Hs 9, 18, 3. καθᾶραι ἑαυτὸν ἀπὸ τῶν λογισμῶν *clear oneself from the thoughts* Dg 2: 1 (κ. ἀπό as Appian, Bell. Civ. 2, 1 §2; Jos., Ant. 13, 34). M-M.*

καθάπερ conj. or adv. (Attic wr.; inscr., pap.; LXX; Ep. Arist. 11; Philo; Jos., Bell. 4, 406, C. Ap. 1, 74; 130 and oft. [BBrüne, Josephus '12, 34]) *just as,* in our lit. only Paul, Hb, Dg. κ. γέγραπται Ro 3: 4; 9: 13; 10: 15; 11: 8 (these pass. have καθώς as v.l.; cf. Philod., π. εὐσεβ. 60 Gomp. καθάπερ ἐν Ἠοίαις=as it says in the Eoiai [a work of Hesiod lost except for fragments].—1 Cor 10: 10; 2 Cor 3: 13, 18 (v.l. καθώσπερ); 1 Th 2: 11. *As it were* (Diod. S. 14, 1, 4a) Dg 3: 3. καθάπερ καί *as also* Ro 4: 6; 2 Cor 1: 14; 1 Th 3: 6, 12; 4: 5; Dg 2: 1. It is oft. used elliptically, as Hb 4: 2, but the verb can easily be supplied fr. the context: οὐ κ. . . . οὕτως ἀλλά *not as . . . but* Dg 7: 2; κ. . . . οὕτως *just as . . . so* (Diod. S. 23, 14, 3; 23, 15, 11; 27, 18, 2; Ps.-Demetr. c. 186; 2 Macc 2: 29; 6: 14; 15: 39; 4 Macc 15: 31f) Ro 12: 4; 1 Cor 12: 12; without a verb 2 Cor 8: 11.—FWDanker, FWGingrich-Festschr., '72, 99f. M-M.*

καθάπτω 1 aor. καθῆψα (in mid. Hom.+; in act. trag.+) *take hold of, seize* (it is usu. the mid., found here as a v.l., that has this mng. [cf. Jos., Bell. 3, 319; 385], but the act. also has it [Ps.-Xenophon, Cyneg. 6, 9; Polyb. 8, 8, 3]) τινός *someth.* (quot. in Pollux 1, 164; Epict. 3, 20, 10 ὁ τοῦ τραχήλου καθάπτων) of a snake καθῆψεν τ. χειρὸς αὐτοῦ *it fastened on his hand* Ac 28: 3. M-M.*

καθαρεύω (Aristoph., Pla.+; pap., Philo; Test. Reub. 6: 1, 2) *be pure, clean* GOxy 23; 24. κ. τινός *be free fr. someth.* (Pla., Ep. 8 p. 356ε; Plut., Phoc. 37, 2 φόνου, Cato Min. 24, 6 ἁμαρτημάτων; Ael. Aristid. 44 p. 828 D.: τῶν αἰσχρῶν; Herm. Wr. 6, 3 τ. κακίας; PRainer 232, 34 πάσης αἰτίας; Philo, Rer. Div. Her. 7 ἁμαρτημάτων; Jos., Ant. 1, 102 φόνου, Vi. 79) τοῦ αἵματός τινος *free fr. someone's blood* GP 11: 46.*

καθαρίζω (καθερίζω s. Bl-D. §29, 1; Mlt.-H. 67) Attic fut. καθαριῶ (Hb 9: 14; J 15: 2 D; Bl-D. §101 s.v. καθαίρειν; cf. Mlt.-H. 218); 1 aor. ἐκαθάρισα, imper. καθάρισον; 1 aor. pass. ἐκαθαρίσθην (also ἐκαθερίσθην: Mt 8: 3b v.l.; Mk 1: 42 v.l.), καθαρίσθητι; pf. ptc. κεκαθαρισμένος. Cf. Reinhold 38f; Thackeray 74. (H.Gk. substitute for the class. καθαίρω: as agricultural t.t. PLond. 131 recto, 192 [78/9 AD]; PStrassb. 2, 11; PLeipz. 111, 12. In the ritual sense, mystery inscr. fr. Andania= Dit., Syll.³ 736, 37; likew. 1042, 3; Jos., Ant. 10, 70; 11, 153; 12, 286. The word is also found BGU 1024 IV, 16; Ep. Arist. 90 and in var. mngs. in LXX—Dssm., NB 43f [BS 216f]) *make clean, cleanse, purify.*

1. lit.—a. of physical uncleanness τί *someth.* Mt 23: 25f; Lk 11: 39. The much-discussed passage καθαρίζων πάντα τὰ βρώματα Mk 7: 19 may belong here (so BWeiss; HHoltzmann; Schniewind), but s. 2a below.

b. of the healing of diseases which make a person ceremonially unclean, esp. leprosy.

α. τινά *make someone clean* Mt 8: 2; 10: 8; Mk 1: 40; Lk 5: 12. Pass. (Lev 14: 7 al.) Mt 11: 5; Mk 1: 42; Lk 4: 27; 7: 22; 17: 14, 17. καθαρίσθητι (cf. 4 Km 5: 13) *be clean!* Mt 8: 3a; Mk 1: 41; Lk 5: 13.

β. τί *remove someth. by* or *for the purpose of purification* (cf. Od. 6, 93 καθαίρειν ῥυπά; Epict. 2, 16, 44; 3, 24, 13) pass. ἐκαθαρίσθη αὐτοῦ ἡ λέπρα *his leprosy disappeared* Mt 8: 3b.

2. fig.—a. a Levitical cleansing of foods *make clean, declare clean* (cf. Lev 13: 6, 23) ἃ ὁ θεὸς ἐκαθάρισεν Ac 10: 15; 11: 9. Many (Origen; Field, Notes 31f; Jülicher;

Gleichn. 59; ASchlatter, JWeiss, Wohlenberg, EKlostermann, OHoltzmann, FHauck, Lohmeyer) prefer to take καθαρίζων πάντα τ. βρώματα Mk 7: 19 (s. 1a above) in this sense, regarding the words as an observation of the evangelist or a marginal note by a reader: *he* (Jesus) (hereby) *declares all foods clean.*—WBrandt, Jüd. Reinheitslehre u. ihre Beschreibung in den Evang. '10.

b. of moral and religious cleansing—α. *cleanse, purify* fr. sin (LXX) τινά or τί: τὴν καρδίαν Hs 6, 5, 2. τὰς καρδίας v 3, 9, 8. χεῖρας Js 4: 8. τὸ ἐντὸς τ. ποτηρίου *the contents of the cup,* which must not be acquired in a sinful manner, nor used for a sinful purpose Mt 23: 26. ἐλθέτω τὸ ἅγ. πνεῦμά σου ἐφ᾽ ἡμᾶς κ. καθαρισάτω ἡμᾶς *let thy Holy Spirit come upon us and make us pure* Lk 11: 2 v.l. Marcion.—Pass. Hv 4, 3, 4. ἅπαξ κεκαθαρισμένους Hb 10: 2. καθαρισθήσεται ἡ ἐκκλησία Hs 9, 18, 2; cf. 3. τινὰ (τί) ἀπό τινος (on the constr. w. ἀπό s. the two pass. fr. Dit., Syll.³ at the beg. of this entry; Lev 16: 30 καθαρίσαι ὑμᾶς ἀπὸ τ. ἁμαρτιῶν; Ps 18: 14; 50: 4; Sir 23: 10; 38: 10 and oft.; Jos., Ant. 12, 286; Test. Reub. 4: 8) κ. τινὰ ἀπὸ πάσης ἁμαρτίας 1 J 1: 7; cf. vs. 9. κ. ἑαυτὸν ἀπὸ μολυσμοῦ σαρκός *cleanse oneself from defilement of the body* 2 Cor 7: 1. ἀπὸ τῆς λύπης Hm 10, 3, 4. ἀπὸ πάσης ἐπιθυμίας Hs 7: 2. κ. τὴν καρδίαν ἀπὸ τῆς διψυχίας *cleanse the heart of doubt* m 9: 7. ἀπὸ τῶν ματαιωμάτων *from vanities* m 9: 4. κ. ἑαυτῶν τὰς καρδίας ἀπὸ τῶν ἐπιθυμιῶν m 12, 6, 5. κ. τὴν συνείδησιν ἡμῶν ἀπὸ νεκρῶν ἔργων Hb 9: 14. Pass. καθαρίζεσθαι ἀπὸ τ. ἁμαρτιῶν Hv 2, 3, 1; ἀπὸ τ. ὑστερημάτων v 3, 2, 2a; cf. b and 3, 8, 11.—κ. τινά (τί) τινι (dat. of instr.): τῇ πίστει καθαρίσας (i.e. God) τὰς καρδίας αὐτῶν Ac 15: 9. Of Christ and the church καθαρίσας τῷ λουτρῷ τοῦ ὕδατος ἐν ῥήματι Eph 5: 26 (OCasel, Jahrb. für Liturgiewiss. 5, '25, 144ff).—καθάρισον ἡμᾶς τὸν καθαρισμὸν τῆς σῆς ἀληθείας *purify us w. the cleansing of thy truth* 1 Cl 60: 2.—Of Christ and the Christians κ. ἑαυτῷ λαὸν περιούσιον Tit 2: 14.

β. *remove by* or *for the purpose of purification* τί *someth.* (s. above 1bβ and cf. Dt 19: 13) τὰς ἁμαρτίας τινός Hs 5, 6, 2f.

c. Hb 9: 22f occupies an intermediate position, since ceremon. purification and moral purification merge, and the former becomes the shadow-image of the latter.

d. *set free* τινά τινος *someone from someth.* 1 Cl 16: 10 (Is 53: 10). M-M.**

καθαρισμός, οῦ, ὁ (occurs as an agricultural t.t. [s. καθαρίζω, beg.] PMich. 185, 16 [122 AD]; PLond. 168, 11 [162 AD]; in the sense 'propitiation' in Ps.-Lucian, Asin. 22; found also in LXX and in Achmes 92, 19 v.l. It replaces the much more common καθαρμός) *purification.*

1. in the cultic sense (2 Macc 2: 16 of the dedication of a temple) J 3: 25. W. subj. gen. κ. τῶν Ἰουδαίων 2: 6. W. obj. gen. of the pers.: Mk 1: 44; Lk 5: 14 (Manetho in Jos., C. Ap. 1, 282 deals with the ceremonies that a person who has been healed of leprosy undergoes). αἱ ἡμέραι τ. καθαρισμοῦ αὐτῶν (cf. Ex 29: 36) Lk 2: 22 includes Joseph in the purification, whereas only the woman was required to undergo purification (Aristot., Hist. An. 7, 10 p. 587b, 1ff this is called καθαρμός).

2. fig. (Test. Levi 14: 6 v.l.) 1 Cl 60: 2 (s. καθαρίζω 2bα). κ. τῶν ἁμαρτιῶν ποιεῖσθαι *bring about purification from sin* (cf. Job 7: 21) Hb 1: 3. Cf. 2 Pt 1: 9. M-M.*

κάθαρμα, ατος, τό (trag.+; of persons: Aristoph., Plutus 454; Demosth. 21, 185; Dio Chrys. 13[7], 30; Diog. L. 6, 32 ἀνθρώπους ἐκάλεσα, οὐ καθάρματα; Philostrat., Vi. Apoll. 1, 12; Synes., Ep. 148 p. 288A [of the Cyclopes];

Philo, Virt. 174; Jos., Bell. 4, 241) for περικάθαρμα (q.v.) 1 Cor 4: 13 v.l.*

καθαρός, ά, όν (Hom.+; inscr., pap., LXX; Ep. Arist. 2; Philo, Joseph., Test. 12 Patr.) *clean, pure.*

1. lit., in the physical sense, of a cup Mt 23: 26. σινδών *clean linen* (PGM 4, 1861; 2189; 3095; 5, 217) Mt 27: 59. λίνον καθαρὸν λαμπρόν (v.l. λίθον; on this Philo, Mos. 2, 72) Rv 15: 6. βύσσινον λαμπρὸν καθ. 19: 8; cf. vs. 14; ὠμόλινον καθ. Hs 8, 4, 1. ὕδωρ *pure, clean water* (Eur., Hipp. 209; Dit., Syll.³ 972, 169; PGM 4, 3252; Ezk 36: 25; Philo, Spec. Leg. 3, 58) Hb 10: 22. Of metals (Hdt. 4, 166; Aristot., Meteor 383b, 1; Theocr. 15, 36 ἀργύριον; Plut., Alex. 32, 9 ἄργυρος; Sb 4481, 13 σίδηρος) χρυσίον κ. *pure gold* (Diod. S. 3, 14, 4; Ex 25: 31; 2 Ch 3: 5) Rv 21: 18a, 21; ὕαλος κ. *clear crystal* vs. 18b. In the fig. lang. of Ignatius, referring to martyrdom, we have the concept καθ. ἄρτος (Hdt. 2, 40; Teles p. 40, 11; Dio Chrys. 13[7], 76 al.; POxy. 736, 26) *pure* (wheat) *bread,* without admixture IRo 4: 1.–ὁ λελουμένος ἐστὶν καθαρὸς ὅλος *a person who has bathed is clean all over* J 13: 10a.

2. *ceremonially pure* (inscr.; PGM 4, 3084; 3085; LXX) of the temple τὸ ἱερὸν . . . καθαρόν GOxy 17f. πάντα καθαρά *everything is ritually pure,* hence fit for use Ro 14: 20; Tit 1: 15a, c.

3. in the moral and relig. sense: *pure, free* fr. sin (Pind., Pyth. 5, 2; Pla., Rep. 6 p. 496ᴅ καθαρὸς ἀδικίας τε καὶ ἀνοσίων ἔργων, Crat. 403ᴇ; 405ᴮ al.; LXX, Ep. Arist., Philo, Joseph.; Test. Benj. 8: 2f). **a.** of pers. οἱ καθαροί Tit 1: 15b. C J 13: 10b, 11; 15: 3. Christendom is Christ's λαὸς κ. Hs 9, 18, 4. οἱ καθαροὶ τῇ καρδίᾳ (Ps 23: 4) Mt 5: 8. καθαρὸς τῇ συνειδήσει ITr 7: 2b; *guiltless* Ac 18: 6. ἀπό τινος *free from* (Ps.-Demosth. 59, 78; Cass. Dio 37, 24, 2. Exx. fr. pap. and inscr. in Dssm., NB 24 [BS 196]; PGM 13, 648; 1004; Gen 24: 8; Pr 20: 9; Tob 3: 14; Jos., Ant. 4, 222) ἀπό τ. αἵματος (Sus 46 Theod.) Ac 20: 26.—Also of the Holy Spirit Hm 5, 1, 2. **b.** of things κ. καρδία (Lucian, Nigr. 14 κ. ἦθος; Simplicius in Epict. p. 93, 49 ζωή κ.; Gen 20: 5; Ps 50: 12; cf. κ. ψυχή: Pythagoras in Diog. L. 8, 31; Diod. S. 12, 20, 2; 13, 29, 6) 1 Ti 1: 5; 2 Ti 2: 22; 1 Pt 1: 22 v.l.; B 15: 1. κ. συνείδησις (POsl. 17, 10 [136 ᴀᴅ]) 1 Ti 3: 9; 2 Ti 1: 3 (cf. κ. συνειδός: Philo, Spec. Leg. 1, 203, Praem. 84); θρησκεία κ. Js 1: 27. χεῖρες καθαραί (Aeschyl., Eum. 313, also Plut., Pericl. 8, 8; Dit., Syll.³ 983, 5; Job 9: 30; 22: 30; Philo, Virt. 57; Jos., Bell. 5, 380, Ant. 4, 222) B 15: 1.

4. Ritual and moral purity merge (Simplicius in Epict. p. 111, 18) Lk 11: 41. After a confession of sins καθαρὰ ἡ θυσία ὑμῶν D 14: 1. ὁ ἐντὸς θυσιαστηρίου ὢν καθαρός ἐστιν ITr 7: 2a.—ThWächter, Reinheitsvorschriften im griech. Kult '10; FPfister, Katharsis: Pauly-W. Suppl. IV '35, 146ff; RMeyer and FHauck, TW III 416-34: καθαρός and related words. M-M.**

καθαρότης, ητος, ἡ (X., Mem. 2, 1, 22 al.; Caecilius the orator [I ʙᴄ] p. 98, 7; 107, 1 EOfenloch ['07] of purity of speech; Epict. 4, 11, 5; POxy. 67, 6; 904, 2; Ex 24: 10 v.l.; Wsd 7: 24; Ep. Arist. 234; Test. Napht. 3: 1) *purity* in the ritual sense: τῆς σαρκός Hb 9: 13. M-M.*

καθαρῶς adv. (Hes. and Hom. Hymns+; UPZ 144, 29 [164 ʙᴄ]; 2 Macc 7: 40 v.l.; Philo; Jos., Ant. 18, 100) *in purity* fig. Dg 12: 3.*

καθέδρα, ας, ἡ (Thu.+; inscr., pap., LXX, En.; Jos., Ant. 5, 130; 19, 100; loanw. in rabb.) *chair, seat* (so Polyb. 1, 21, 2; Herodian 2, 3, 7; Lucian, Jupp. Tr. 11; BGU 717, 14; LXX) Hv 1, 2, 2; 1, 4, 1; 3; 3, 10, 3; 3, 11, 2; 4.

καθέδρα λοιμῶν B 10: 10 (after Ps 1: 1). *Seat* of those selling someth. (but s. Dalman, Arbeit VII 192) Mt 21: 12; Mk 11: 15; the *teacher's chair* (Dit., Syll.³ 845, 2f ὁ ἐπὶ τῆς καθέδρας σοφιστής) Hm 11: 1; ἡ Μωϋσέως κ. Mt 23: 2 (cf. Pj 23, '27, 44). κ. κρίσεως *judge's seat* GP 3: 7 (cf. Ps 106: 32 ἐν καθέδρᾳ πρεσβυτέρων). M-M. B. 482.*

καθέζομαι impf. ἐκαθεζόμην (Hom.+; inscr., pap., LXX). In our lit., at least quite predom., it means

1. *sit* (as Lysias 13, 37; Epict. 1, 29, 55; 3, 24, 18; Paus. 10, 5, 2; Vett. Val. 78, 24; Dit., Or. 201, 13; LXX; Jos., Bell. 5, 73, Ant. 12, 171) ἐν τῷ ἱερῷ of teachers Mt 26: 55. Of pupils Lk 2: 46. ἐν τῷ συνεδρίῳ *in the council* Ac 6: 15. ἐπὶ τῆς θυρίδος 20: 9 (Ael. Aristid. 47, 23 K.=23 p. 451 D.: καθ. ἐπὶ βήματος). ἐπὶ τῇ πύλῃ 3: 10 D. ἐν τῷ οἴκῳ *sit, remain at home* I 11: 20. Abs. *sit there* 20: 12. The more general *be, be situated* is also poss. in some pass. (Paus. Attic. σ, 8 ἐν νησίῳ καθεζόμεναι=stay; Stephan. Byz. s.v. Σκίρος· ἐν τῷ τόπῳ τούτῳ; Biogr. p. 265; Lev 12: 5; Jos., Ant. 6, 32, Vi. 286).

2. *sit down* (class.; Jos., Vi. 222; Sib. Or. 5, 460.—The impf. w. aor. mng.: 'I sat down'; Bl-D. §101; cf. Rob. 837ff; 882f) ἐκαθέζετο αὐτὴ ἐκ δεξιῶν she herself sat down at the right Hv 3, 2, 4. εἰς καθέδραν *on a chair* 3, 11, 4. Ἰησοῦς ἐκαθέζετο οὕτως ἐπὶ τῇ πηγῇ *Jesus sat down, just as he was, by the well* J 4: 6 (on the word and the idea s. Jos., Ant. 2, 257 and Marinus, Vi. Procli 10 Boiss. As early as Demosth. 21, 219 οὑτωσὶ καθεζόμενος). Cf. also 6: 3 v.l. M-M.**

καθεῖλον and **καθελεῖν** s. καθαιρέω.

καθεῖς (καθ' εἷς) s. εἷς 5e.

καθεξῆς adv. (Plut., Mor. 615ʙ; Aelian, V.H. 8, 7; Test. Judah 25: 1) *in order, one after the other* of sequence in time, space, or logic: διερχόμενος κ. τὴν Γαλατικὴν χώραν καὶ Φρυγίαν one place after the other in Galatia and Phrygia Ac 18: 23. κ. τινί (τι) γράφειν write someth. *for someone in orderly sequence* Lk 1: 3 (cf. PScheller, De hellenist. historiae conscr. arte, Diss. Leipz. '11, 45. HConzelmann, Die Mitte der Zeit' '60, Eng. tr. GBuswell '60 [theology dominates the structure of Lk]). ἐκτίθεσθαι τινι κ. *explain to someone point by point* Ac 11: 4.—W. the art. οἱ κ. the successors Ac 3: 24; τὸ κ. *what follows:* ἐν τῷ κ. *in what follows* MPol 22: 3; *afterward* Lk 8: 1. τὸ κ. *and so forth* 1 Cl 37: 3. M-M.*

καθερίζω s. καθαρίζω.

καθεύδω impf. ἐκάθευδον (Hom.+; Dit., Syll.³ 1004, 44; BGU 1141, 32; PSI 94, 17; LXX; Philo; Jos., Vi. 248; Test. 12 Patr.) *sleep.*

1. lit. Mt 8: 24; 13: 25; 25: 5; 26: 40, 43, 45; Mk 4: 27, 38; 13: 36; 14: 37, 40f; Lk 22: 46; 1 Th 5: 7. The mng. is in doubt in Mt 9: 24; Mk 5: 39 (REKer, ET 65, '53f, 315f); Lk 8: 52; in these pass. the following mng. is commonly accepted.

2. fig.—**a.** of the sleep of death (Ps 87: 6; Da 12: 2). So certainly 1 Th 5: 10. **b.** of spiritual laziness and indifference (cf. X., An. 1, 3, 11; Oenomaus in Euseb., Pr. Ev. 5, 19, 2 of dull indifference) 1 Th 5: 6.—The word is also used fig. in the quot. fr. an unknown hymn: ἔγειρε ὁ καθεύδων *awake, O sleeper!* Eph 5: 14.—AOepke, TW III 434-40. M-M. B. 269.*

καθηγητής, οῦ, ὁ *teacher* (so Dionys. Hal., Jud. de Thu. 3, 4; Plut., Mor. 327ꜰ of Aristotle; Vett. Val. 115, 18;

PGiess. 80, 7; 11; POxy. 930, 6; 20) Mt 23: 10. This verse is deleted by Blass, Wlh., Dalman, Worte 279; 276 as a variant of vs. 8. In the latter καθ. is v.l. M-M.*

καθῆκα s. καθίημι.

καθηκόντως adv. of the pres. ptc. of καθήκω (q.v.) *as is fitting*, in accordance w. obligation or duty (Polyb. 5, 9, 6; Plut., Mor. p. 448ε; Dit., Or. 90, 28 [II вс]; Ep. Arist. 181; Philo, Cher. 14) 1 Cl 1: 3.*

καθῆκω (Aeschyl., Hdt. +) *come* or *reach to, be proper* or *fitting* καθήκουσα ἡ τιμή *the proper respect* 1 Cl 1: 3. Usu. impers. **καθῆκει** *it comes* (to someone), *it is proper, it is fitting* (X. +, oft. inscr., pap., LXX) foll. by acc. and inf. (Diod. S. 16, 1, 1; Jos., Ant. 7, 131) οὐ καθῆκεν αὐτὸν ζῆν *he should not be allowed to live* Ac 22: 22 (on the impf. cf. Bl-D. §358, 2; Rob. 886f).—τὸ καθῆκον *what is proper, duty* (Menand., fgm. 575, 2 Kock; Stoic wr. since Zeno [s. Ltzm., Hdb. on Ro 1: 28; GNebel, Her. 70, '35, 439-60; MPohlenz, D. Stoa I '48, 487: index]; Polyb. 6, 6, 7; Ep. Arist. 227; Philo, Leg. All. 2, 32a) πολιτεύεσθαι κατὰ τὸ κ. τῷ Χριστῷ *conduct oneself in accordance with one's duty toward Christ* (dat. of advantage) 1 Cl 3: 4. παρὰ τὸ κ. (Diog. L. 7, 108; Dit., Syll.³ 643, 6 [171 вс]; POxy. 1203, 3; Philo, Leg. All. 2, 32b; Jos., Ant. 13, 66): παρὰ τὸ κ. τῆς βουλήσεως αὐτοῦ ποιεῖν τι *do anything contrary to the duty imposed by his will* 1 Cl 41: 3. Pl. τὰ κ. (X., Cyr. 1, 2, 5 al.; Ep. Arist. 245; Philo, Leg. All. 1, 56) τὰ μὴ καθήκοντα (UPZ 191, 8 [III вс]; 2 Macc 6: 4; 3 Macc 4: 16) ποιεῖν τὰ μὴ καθήκοντα *do what is improper* Ro 1: 28 (M-JLagrange, Le catalogue des vices dans Ro 1: 28-31, RB 8, '11, 534-49).—On probability of a contractual metaphor in Ro 1: 28 s. FWDanker, FW Gingrich-Festschr., '72, 95f.—HSchlier, TW III 440-3. M-M. B. 643.*

καθηλόω 1 aor. καθήλωσα; pf. pass. ptc. καθηλωμένος (Polyb. 1, 22, 5; Diod. S. 20, 85; Hero I 442, 10; Plut., Alex; 24, 7; Dit., Syll.³ 969, 57; 84; PLond. 1384, 41; LXX) *nail on, fasten w. nails* of one condemned to be burned at the stake MPol 14: 1 (cf. Ps.-Callisth. 2, 18, 2 ἐδέδεντο ἐν πέδαις καθηλωταῖς). Of Christ on the cross: τὰς σάρκας B 5: 13 (Ps 118: 120); ISm 1: 2. Hence of the Christians ὥσπερ καθηλωμένοι ἐν τῷ σταυρῷ τοῦ κυρίου Ἰ. Χρ. σαρκί τε καὶ πνεύματι *as if nailed to the cross of the Lord Jesus Christ in body and in spirit* 1: 1.*

κάθημαι (Hom. +; inscr., pap., LXX; En. 13, 9; Jos., Ant. 5, 192) 2 sg. κάθη (since Hyperid., fgm. 115 [OLautensach, Glotta 8, '17, 186]; POxy. 33 verso III, 13 [II ad]) Ac 23: 3, imper. κάθου (Moeris 215: κάθησο Ἀττικῶς, κάθου κοινῶς; later Attic [Lautensach, Glotta 9, '18, 88; cf. also AMaidhof, Z. Begriffsbestimmung der Koine '12, 300]) twice in Js 2: 3 and seven times in a quot. fr. Ps 109: 1 (Bl-D. §100; Mlt.-H. 206f; s. 2 below); impf. ἐκαθήμην (on the augment cf. Bl-D. §69, 1; Mlt.-H. 192); fut. καθήσομαι (oft. LXX) Mt 19: 28; Lk 22: 30.

1. *sit*—a. lit.—α. w. the place indicated by a prep. ἀπέναντί τινος *opposite someth.* Mt 27: 61.—εἴς τι *on someth.* (Pel.-Leg. p. 4, 4 καθημένη εἰς βαδιστήν='sitting on a donkey'; cf. also Musonius 43, 18 H. καθῆσθαι εἰς τὸ ὄρος=ἐλαιῶν Mk 13: 3; cf. Hs 5, 1, 1. ἐκ δεξιῶν τινος *at someone's right* (hand) Mt 26: 64; Mk 14: 62; Lk 22: 69.—ἐν: Mt 11: 16; 26: 69; Lk 7: 32. ἐν σάκκῳ κ. σποδῷ 10: 13. ἐν δεξιᾷ τινος *at someone's right* Col 3: 1. ἐν τοῖς δεξιοῖς *on the right* (side) Mk 16: 5.— ἐπάνω τινός *on* or *upon someth.* Mt 23: 22; Rv 6: 8; ἐπί τινος *on someth.* (Babrius 57, 14; UPZ 79, 10 [160 вс]) Mt

24: 3. ἐπὶ τοῦ θρόνου (Aeschines in Ps.-Demetr. c. 205; Cebes 21, 3 ἐπὶ θρόνου ὑψηλοῦ; Ex 11: 5; Jos., Ant. 5, 192) Rv 4: 9f; 5: 1, 7, 13; 6: 16 al. ἐπὶ τῆς νεφέλης 14: 15. ἐπὶ τοῦ ἄρματος Ac 8: 28. ἐπὶ τ. ἵππων Rv 9: 17 (cf. Test. Jud. 3: 2). Of judges (κ.='sit in judgment': Pla., Ap. 35c; Hyperid. 3, 6) ἐπὶ τοῦ βήματος Mt 27: 19.—ἐπὶ τῇ ὡραίᾳ πύλῃ *at the 'Beautiful Gate'* Ac 3: 10. ἐπί τι w. acc. of place (Lev 8: 35) Mt 9: 9; 19: 28; Mk 2: 14; Lk 5: 27; J 12: 15; Rv 4: 2, 4; 6: 2, 4f; 11: 16; 17: 3; 19: 11.—παρά τι *beside someth.* παρὰ τὴν ὁδόν *at the side of the road* Mt 20: 30; Mk 10: 46; Lk 18: 35.—περί τινα *around someone* Mk 3: 32, 34.—πρὸς τὸ φῶς *by the fire* Lk 22: 56 (Aristoph., Vesp. 773 πρὸς τὸ πῦρ κ. Likewise Menand., fgm. 832 πρὸς τὸ πῦρ κ.).

β. w. the place indicated by an adv. of place: ἐκεῖ Mk 2: 6; οὗ Ac 2: 2; Rv 17: 15; ὅπου vs. 9.

γ. abs. *sit, sit there* (Epict. 2, 16, 13 εὔχου καθήμενος; 33) Mt 27: 36; Lk 5: 17; J 2: 14; 9: 8; 1 Cor 14: 30; B 10: 4.

δ. w. some indication of the state or characteristics of the pers. sitting (Ex 18: 14 σὺ κάθησαι μόνος; κ. of a judge Ael. Aristid. 46 p. 318 D.; 327) σὺ κάθῃ κρίνων με; *do you sit there to judge me?* Ac 23: 3.

ε. in the special sense *sit quietly* Mk 5: 15; Lk 8: 35. *Be enthroned* in majesty (Od. 16, 264) κάθημαι βασίλισσα Rv 18: 7.

b. fig. *stay, be, live, reside, settle* (Hom. +; Hdt. 5, 63 ἐν Δελφοῖς; Musonius p. 59, 7 ἐν πόλει; Ael. Aristid. 50, 14 K. =26 p. 505 D.; Is 9: 8 v.l.; 2 Esdr 21 [Neh 11]: 6; Jdth 4: 8; 5: 3) Lk 21: 35; Rv 14: 6. πρός τινα w. *someone* D 12: 3; 13: 1. ἐν σκοτίᾳ, ἐν σκιᾷ θανάτου (Ps 106: 10) Lk 1: 79 (cf. Pind., Ol. 1, 133 ἐν σκότῳ καθήμενος [=useless]; Ael. Aristid. 46 p. 272 D.: ἐν τ. στενοῖς τ. ἐλπίδων ἐκάθηντο).

2. *sit down*; the occurrence of this sense in our lit. can scarcely be disputed; the same is true of the LXX (W-S. §14, 3). It is to be assumed for the imperative in all its occurrences; seven of them are connected w. Ps 109: 1: κάθου ἐκ δεξιῶν μου Mt 22: 44; Mk 12: 36; Lk 20: 42; Ac 2: 34; Hb 1: 13; 1 Cl 36: 5; B 12: 10. The imper. has the same mng. twice in Js 2: 3. But this sense is also quite probable for the foll. pass.: ἐν τῇ θαλάσσῃ Mk 4: 1. ἐπάνω τινός Mt 28: 2. μετά τινος 26: 58; J 6: 3 (καθίζω v.l.). παρὰ τὴν θάλασσαν Mt 13: 1.—ἐκεῖ Mt 15: 29.— μέσος αὐτῶν Lk 22: 55.—Abs. Mt 13: 2.—CSchneider, TW III 443-7. M-M. B. 455.

καθημέραν for καθ' ἡμέραν s. ἡμέρα 2.

καθημερινός, ή, όν (Theophr. +; Plut., Lyc. 10, 1, Pyrrh. 14, 12; Polyaenus 4, 2, 10; Alciphr. 1, 5, 2; Athen. 6 p. 259ϝ; PTebt. 275, 21; PGM 7, 218; Jdth 12: 15; Jos., Ant. 3, 238; 11, 297) fr. καθ' ἡμέραν *daily* διακονία Ac 6: 1. λόγος *the word repeated daily* Hv 1, 3, 2. M-M.*

καθίζω (Hom. +; inscr., pap., LXX; En.; Ep. Arist.; Joseph.; Test. 12 Patr.) fut. καθίσω Mt 25: 31 and καθιῶ Is 47: 8, mid. καθίσομαι and καθιοῦμαι Hv 3, 1, 9; 1 aor. ἐκάθισα, imper. κάθισον Mk 12: 36 v.l.; pf. κεκάθικα Hb 12: 2 (Bl-D. §101; W-S. §14, 2; 15; Rob. 1216).

1. trans. *cause to sit down, seat, set*—a. lit. καθίσας ἐν δεξιᾷ αὐτοῦ *he had* (him) *sit at his right hand* Eph 1: 20. τινὰ ἐπί τι Hs 9, 1, 4. God took an oath to David ἐκ καρποῦ τῆς ὀσφύος αὐτοῦ καθίσαι ἐπὶ τὸν θρόνον αὐτοῦ *to 'set one of his descendants upon his throne* Ac 2: 30. ἐν ὄνῳ MPol 8: 1. ἐκάθισαν αὐτὸν ἐπὶ καθέδραν κρίσεως *they seated him on the judge's chair* GP 3: 7. J 19: 13 is probably to be understood in this sense, since the trial is evidently in progress (cf. Dio Chrys. 4, 67; Loisy; PCors-

sen, ZNW 15, '14, 339f; IdelaPotterie, Biblica 41, '60, 217-47; s. CBQ 25, '63, 124-26); but s. 2aα below.

b. fig. *appoint, install* (Pla., Leg. 9 p. 873ε δικαστήν; Polyb. 40, 5, 3; Jos., Ant. 20, 200 καθίζει συνέδριον κριτῶν, Vi. 368; POxy. 1469, 7) τοὺς ἐξουθενημένους ἐν τῇ ἐκκλησίᾳ καθίζετε; *do you appoint as judges men who have no standing in the church?* 1 Cor 6: 4 (on καθ.= 'appoint as judge' cf. Jos., Ant. 13, 75).

2. intrans.—a. act.—**α.** lit. *sit down* (LXX; En.; Ep. Arist. 94) abs. (Diod. S. 8, 10, 4; Polyaenus 2, 21) Mt 5: 1; 13: 48; Mk 9: 35; Lk 4: 20; 5: 3; 7: 15 v.l.; 14: 28, 31; 16: 6; J 8: 2; Ac 13: 14; 16: 13; Hv 1, 2, 2. W. inf. foll. ἐκάθισεν φαγεῖν καὶ πεῖν 1 Cor 10: 7 (Ex 32: 6). W. an adv. of place ὧδε (Sb 4117, 5; Ruth 4: 1, 2; 4 Km 7: 4) Mk 14: 32 (perh. *stay here*). αὐτοῦ *here* (Gen 22: 5) Mt 26: 36. W. prep. εἰς τὸν ναὸν τοῦ θεοῦ *in the temple of God* (PSI 502, 21 [III BC]) καθίσαντες εἰς τὸ ἱερόν 2 Th 2: 4. εἰς τὴν κλίνην *on the bed* (cf. Dicaearchus, fgm. 20 W. εἰς θρόνον) Hv 5: 1 (on sitting down after prayer cf. the Pythagorean precept: Philosophenspr. p. 508, 60 καθῆσθαι προσκυνήσαντες= after prayer we should sit down. Similarly Numa: Plut., Numa 14, 7.—HLewy, Philol. 84, '29, 378-80). ἐκ δεξιῶν τινος *at someone's right* Mt 20: 21, 23; Mk 10: 37, 40; 16: 19. Also ἐν δεξιᾷ τινος Hb 1: 3; 8: 1; 10: 12; 12: 2. ἐν τῷ θρόνῳ μου *on my throne* Rv 3: 21a, b (Hdt. 5, 25 ἐν τῷ κατίζων θρόνῳ). ἐπί τινος (Diod. S. 1, 92, 2; 17, 116, 3 ἐκάθισεν ἐπὶ τοῦ θρόνου= sat down on; Jos., Ant. 8, 344) Mt 19: 28a; 23: 2 (Bl-D. §342, 1 app.; cf. Rob. 837); 25: 31; ἐπί τι (Thu. 1, 126, 10; Aesop, Fab. 393 H.) θρόνους Rv 20: 4; on an animal (Achilles Tat.: 1, 12, 2 ἐπὶ τ. ἵππον) Mk 11: 2, 7; Lk 19: 30; J 12: 14. Of the Holy Spirit as a flame of fire ἐκάθισεν ἐφ' ἕνα ἕκαστον αὐτῶν *it rested upon each one of them* Ac 2: 3; κατέναντί τινος *opposite someth.* Mk 12: 41. σύν τινι *sit down w. someone* Ac 8: 31. Esp. of a judge (Pla., Leg. 2 p. 659B; Ps 9: 5) κ. ἐπὶ (τοῦ) βήματος *sit down in the judge's seat* to open the trial (Jos., Bell. 2, 172 ὁ Πιλᾶτος καθίσας ἐπὶ βήματος, Ant. 20, 130) J 19: 13 (JBlinzler, Der Prozess Jesu³, '60, 257-62; s. 1a above); Ac 12: 21; 25: 6, 17.

β. *settle, stay, live* (Thu. 3, 107, 1; 4, 93, 1) ἐν τῇ πόλει Lk 24: 49 (cf. 1 Ch 19: 5; 2 Esdr 21 [Neh 11]: 1f; Jos., Bell. 1, 46, Ant. 18, 86; Dit., Syll.³ 685, 28 ἐν τῷ ἱερῷ). W. acc. of time Ac 18: 11.

b. mid. *sit down* (Pla.+) Mt 19: 28b v.l.; J 6: 3 v.l. M-M.**

καθίημι 1 aor. καθῆκα (Hom.+; LXX) *let down* τινά *someone* διὰ κεράμων εἰς (cf. Jos., Ant. 2, 31; 35 K. εἰς τὸν λάκκον) Lk 5: 19. διὰ τοῦ τείχους Ac 9: 25 (Polyaenus 6, 49 αὐτοὺς ἀπὸ τῶν τειχῶν καθῆκαν; 8, 21). Pass. ἐπὶ τ. γῆς 10: 11; ἐκ τοῦ οὐρανοῦ 11: 5. M-M.*

καθιστάνω s. καθίστημι.

καθίστημι and **καθιστάνω** (Ac 17: 15; 1 Cl 42: 4; Ep. Arist. 280; 281; Jos., Ant. 16, 129; POxford [ed. EPWegener '42] 16, 12). Fut. καταστήσω; 1 aor. κατέστησα; pf. pass. ptc. καθεσταμένος (1 Cl 54: 2; Jos., Ant. 12, 268); 1 aor. pass. κατεστάθην; 1 fut. pass. κατασταθήσομαι. (Hom.+; inscr., pap., LXX, Ep. Arist., Philo, Joseph.).

1. *bring, conduct, take* someone somewhere (Od. 13, 274; Thu. 4, 78, 6; X., An. 4, 8, 8; UPZ 78, 14 [159 BC]; BGU 93, 22 κατάστησον αὐτοὺς εἰς Μέμφιν; Josh 6: 23; 1 Km 5: 3; 2 Ch 28: 15; Jos., Ant. 7, 279) Ac 17: 15.

2. *appoint, put in charge* (Hdt. et al.).—**a.** someone over (of) someth. or someone τινὰ ἐπί τινος (Arrian, Exp. Al. 3, 6, 6 ἐπὶ τ. χρημάτων; Gen 41: 41; Num 3: 10; Da 2: 48; Jos., Ant. 2, 73) Mt 24: 45; cf. 25: 21, 23; Lk 12: 42;

Ac 6: 3. τινὰ ἐπί τινι *over someth.* (Jos., Ant. 12, 278) Mt 24: 47; Lk 12: 44. τινὰ ἐπί τι (Isocr. 12, 132; X., Cyr. 8, 1, 9; Da 3: 12 Theod.) Hb 2: 7 v.l. (Ps 8: 7). W. acc. of the pers. and inf. of purpose ὁ υἱὸς κατέστησε τ. ἀγγέλους ἐπ' αὐτοὺς τοῦ συντηρεῖν αὐτούς Hs 5, 6, 2.

b. w. acc. *ordain, appoint* (Pla., Rep. 10 p. 606D ἄρχοντα; 1 Macc 3: 55; Jos., Ant. 9, 4 κρίτας) πρεσβυτέρους Tit 1: 5. Cf. 1 Cl 42: 5 (Is 60: 17); 43: 1; 44: 2. Pass. 44: 3; 54: 2; foll. by εἰς w. inf. of the high priest: εἰς τὸ προσφέρειν δῶρα καθίσταται *is appointed to offer gifts* Hb 8: 3. Sim. ὑπὲρ ἀνθρώπων καθίσταται τὰ πρὸς τὸν θεόν, ἵνα προσφέρῃ *is appointed (to act) on behalf of men in relation to God, to bring* Hb 5: 1.—A second acc. (predicate) can be added to τινά: *make* or *appoint someone someth.* (Hdt. 7, 105 al.; PHib. 82 I, 14 [239/8 BC]; Sir 32: 1; 1 Macc 9: 25; 10: 20; Jos., Ant. 12, 360) Lk 12: 14; Ac 7: 10; Hb 7: 28 (Diog. L. 9, 64 ἀρχιερέα κ. αὐτόν). τίς σε κατέστησεν ἄρχοντα; Ac 7: 27, 35; 1 Cl 4: 10 (all three Ex 2: 14).

3. *make, cause* (someone to become someth.) τινά τι (Eur., Androm. 635 κλαίοντά σε καταστήσει; Pla., Phileb. p. 16Β ἐμὲ ἔρημον κατέστησεν; POxy. 939 σε εὐθυμότερον; Jos., Ant. 6, 92; 20, 18) ταῦτα οὐκ ἀργοὺς οὐδὲ ἀκάρπους καθίστησιν *this does not make (you) useless and unfruitful* 2 Pt 1: 8.—Pass. *be made, become* (Menand., fgm. 769 K. ἄπαντα δοῦλα τοῦ φρονεῖν καθίσταται. Herodas 1, 40 ἱλαρὴ κατάστηθι=be(come) cheerful; Diod. S. 17, 70, 3; Περὶ ὕψους 5; PReinach 18, 40 [108 BC] ἀπερίσπαστος κατασταθήσεται='be left undisturbed'; Ep. Arist. 289 σκληροὶ καθίστανται; Philo, Aet. M. 133) ἁμαρτωλοὶ κατεστάθησαν... δίκαιοι κατασταθήσονται Ro 5: 19 (FWDanker in FW Gingrich-Festschr. '72, 106f, quoting POxy. 281, 14-24 [20-50 AD] in possible legal sense). The two pass. in Js where the word occurs prob. belong here also (φίλος τ. κόσμου) ἐχθρὸς τ. θεοῦ καθίσταται 4: 4; cf. 3: 6 where, however, the text may not be in order.—JdeZwaan, Rö 5: 19; Jk 3: 6; 4: 4 en de Κοινή: ThSt 31, '13, 85-94. M-M.*

καθό adv. (Pla. et al.; inscr., pap., LXX; Jos., Ant. 16, 26)=καθ' ὅ.

1. of kind and manner (Inscr. Gr. 731, 22 [II BC] καθὸ πάτριόν ἐστιν; Ep. Arist. 11) *as* κ. δεῖ *as is fitting, as one should* Ro 8: 26 (Diod. S. 8, 15, 1 κατὰ τὴν ἀξίαν οὐδὲ θελήσαντες δυνάμεθα τιμῆσαι τὸ δαιμόνιον=we cannot honor the divinity in a worthy manner, even though we may wish [to do so]).

2. of degree *in so far as, to the degree that* καθὸ κοινωνεῖτε τοῖς τοῦ Χριστοῦ παθήμασιν *in so far as you share the sufferings of Christ* 1 Pt 4: 13. καθὸ ἐὰν ἔχῃ 2 Cor 8: 12a; cf. vs. 12b. M-M.*

καθολικός, ή, όν (Hippocr.+; Polyb.; Dionys. Hal., Comp. Verb. 12; Iambl., Vi. Pyth. 15, 65; Porphyr., Vi. Pyth. 30; Ps.-Plut., Hom. 201 κ. λόγοι; Dit., Syll.³ 785, 4 [6 BC], Or. 668, 47; BGU 19 I, 5 [135 AD]; Philo. Later a much-used title) *general, universal, catholic* ἡ κ. ἐκκλησία *the universal church* (in contrast to a single congregation [cf. the contrast μερικὰ κ. καθολικά in Zosimus 7: Hermetica IV p. 105, 24]; s. Hdb. on ISm 8: 2) ISm 8: 2; MPol inscr.; 8: 1; 19: 2. Not in contrast to a single congregation MPol 16: 2; but the text is not certain. ὁ ἐκκλησιαστικὸς κανὼν καὶ κ. (Artem. 1, 2 p. 4, 23 ὅρος κ.=a generally valid definition; 4, 2 p. 205, 1 λόγος; Aëtius p. 30, 20 of a law of general validity; Herm. Wr. 2 inscr. v.l. Ἑρμοῦ...λόγος καθολικός; Epict. 4, 4, 29; 4, 12, 7 τὰ καθολικά=the laws or truths of general validity) Epil Mosq 1. Ἐπιστολαὶ καθολικαί (καθολικὴ ἐπιστολή first in the Antimontanist Apollonius [c. 197 AD] in Euseb., H.E. 5, 18, 5. Eusebius himself speaks, as we do, of 'the' seven catholic epistles: 2, 23, 25) Js inscr. v.l. M-M.*

καθόλου adv. (class. [Bl-D. §225; 12, 3]; inscr., pap., LXX, Ep. Arist.; Jos., Bell. 4, 460; 5, 390, Ant. 4, 286) *entirely, completely,* μὴ κ. *not at all* (Sb 4369a, 36; Ex 22: 10 v.l.) κ. μὴ φθέγγεσθαι *not to speak at all* Ac 4: 18 (on the v.l. τὸ καθόλου s. Bl-D. §399, 3 app.; Ezk 13: 3; Test. Gad 5: 5. μηδὲν τὸ καθόλου λαβεῖν: BGU 1058, 25; 1106, 24; 1165, 24 [all I BC]).—Papias 3. M-M.*

καθοπλίζω (Soph.+) act. *arm fully, equip* (X.+; LXX; Ep. Arist. 14; Jos., Ant. 2, 341). Mid. καθοπλίζομαι *arm* or *equip oneself* (Polyb. 3, 62, 7 al.; 4 Macc 3: 12). 1 aor. ptc. καθοπλισάμενος; pf. pass. ptc. καθωπλισμένος (PGM 13, 528; 4 Macc 4: 10; 7: 11; Jos., Ant. 5, 244).
1. lit. ὁ ἰσχυρὸς καθωπλισμένος *the strong man in his armor* Lk 11: 21.
2. fig. (Diod. S. 9, 1, 4 of souls equipped w. [the] armor [of Solon's legislation]; 4 Macc 11: 22) καθωπλίσασθαι τὸν φόβον κυρίου *arm oneself w. the fear of God* Hm 12, 2, 4. καθωπλισμένος τῷ φόβῳ τ. θεοῦ ibid. M-M.*

καθοράω (Hom.+; Abercius Inscr. 5; PLond. 342, 13; LXX) *perceive, notice,* also of spiritual seeing (Pind., Pyth. 9, 87; Aristot., Rhet. 3, 9 τὸ τέλος πάντες βούλονται καθορᾶν; Philostrat., Vi. Soph. 1, 22 p. 38, 10 al.; 3 Macc 3: 11; Philo; Jos., Ant. 8, 168) τὰ ἀόρατα αὐτοῦ 7. ποιήμασι νοούμενα καθορᾶται *his* (God's) *invisible attributes are perceived with the eye of reason in the things that have been made* Ro 1: 20 (on the play on words cf. Ps.-Aristot., De Mundo 399b, 14ff ἀόρατος τοῖς ἔργοις ὁρᾶται; Sib. Or. 4, 12 ὃς καθορῶν ἅμα πάντας ὑπ' οὐδενὸς αὐτὸς ὁρᾶται.—Philostrat., Ep. 41 νοῦς ὁρῇ). M-M.*

καθότι (Hdt., Thu.+; inscr., pap., LXX, Joseph.)—1. *as, to the degree that* καθότι ἄν (Inscr. Gr. 534, 28 [III BC] καθότι ἂν δοκεῖ αὐτοῖς; Lev 25: 16; 27: 12) Ac 2: 45; 4: 35.
2. *because, in view of the fact that* (Polyb. 18, 21, 6; Jos., Ant. 18, 90) Lk 1: 7; 19: 9; Ac 2: 24; 17: 31; ITr 5: 2. M-M.*

καθώς adv. (its use strongly opposed by Phryn. p. 425 L.; Aristot.+; inscr., pap., LXX, En., Ep. Arist., Philo; Jos., Ant. 12, 158 al.; Test. 12 Patr.).
1. indicating comparison: *just as* w. οὕτως foll. (*just) as . . . so* Lk 11: 30; 17: 26; J 3: 14; 2 Cor 1: 5; 10: 7; Col 3: 13; 1 J 2: 6; 1 Cl 20: 6; Hs 9, 4, 1. κ. . . . ὁμοίως *as . . . so, likewise* Lk 6: 31. κ. . . . ταῦτα J 8: 28; τὰ αὐτὰ . . . κ. 1 Th 2: 14. κ. . . . καί *as . . . so* or *so also* J 15: 9; 17: 18; 20: 21; 1 J 2: 18; 4: 17; 1 Cor 15: 49. οὕτως καθώς *just as* Lk 24: 24. Freq. the demonstrative is omitted: ποιήσαντες κ. συνέταξεν αὐτοῖς ὁ Ἰησοῦς *they did as Jesus had directed them* Mt 21: 6; cf. 28: 6; Mk 16: 7; Lk 1: 2, 55, 70; 11: 1; J 1: 23; 5: 23; Ac 15: 8; Ro 1: 13; 15: 7; 1 Cor 8: 2; 10: 6; 2 Cor 1: 14; 9: 3; 11: 12; Eph 4: 17; Hm 12, 2, 5; 1 Cl 16: 2. As a formula κ. γέγραπται *as it is written* (cf. Sb 7532, 16 [74 BC] καθὰ γέγραπται and see s.v. καθάπερ) Mt 26: 24; Mk 1: 2; 9: 13; 14: 21; Lk 2: 23; Ac 15: 15; Ro 1: 17; 2: 24; 3: 10; 4: 17; 8: 36 and very oft. in Paul; cf. κ. προείρηκα Ro 9: 29. κ. διδάσκω *as I teach* 1 Cor 4: 17. The accompanying clause is somet. to be supplied fr. the context: κ. παρεκάλεσά σε (POxy. 1299, 9 καθὼς ἐνετειλάμην σοι= [act, do] as I have commanded you) 1 Ti 1: 3; cf. Gal 3: 6. ἤρξατο αἰτεῖσθαι (ἵνα

ποιήσῃ αὐτοῖς) κ. ἐποίει αὐτοῖς *as he was accustomed to do for them* Mk 15: 8. In combination w. εἶναι: ὀψόμεθα αὐτὸν κ. ἐστιν *we will see him (just) as he is* 1 J 3: 2. κ. ἀληθῶς ἐστιν *as it actually is* 1 Th 2: 13. Somet. an expression may be condensed to such an extent that opposites are compared ἀγαπῶμεν ἀλλήλους οὐ κ. Κάϊν 1 J 3: 11f. οὗτός ἐστιν ὁ ἄρτος. . .οὐ κ. ἔφαγον οἱ πατέρες *quite different from that which the fathers ate* J 6: 58.
2. *as, to the degree that* (Num 26: 54) κ. ἠδύναντο ἀκούειν *so far as they were able to understand* Mk 4: 33. κ. εὐπορεῖτό τις *each according to his ability* Ac 11: 29. κ. βούλεται (*just) as he wills* 1 Cor 12: 11; cf. vs. 18. κ. ἔλαβεν χάρισμα *to the degree that he has received a gift* 1 Pt 4: 10. Cf. Ac 2: 4; 1 Cor 15: 38.
3. in a causal sense, esp. as a conjunction beginning a sentence (Bl-D. §453, 2; Rob. 968; 1382) *since, in so far as* J 17: 2; Ro 1: 28; 1 Cor 1: 6; 5: 7; Eph 1: 4; 4: 32; Phil 1: 7.
4. The temporal mng. of κ. is disputed, but seems well established (2 Macc 1: 31; 2 Esdr 15 [Neh 5]: 6; Ep. Arist. 310; cf. ὡς): κ. (A ὡς) ἤγγιζεν ὁ χρόνος *when the time came near* Ac 7: 17 (Ep. Arist. 236 καθὼς εὔκαιρον ἐγένετο).
5. After verbs of saying it introduces indirect discourse (=ὡς, πῶς) Συμεὼν ἐξηγήσατο, κ. ὁ θεὸς ἐπεσκέψατο *Symeon has related how God visited* Ac 15: 14. μαρτυρούντων σου τῇ ἀληθείᾳ, κ. σὺ ἐν τῇ ἀληθείᾳ περιπατεῖς *who testify to your truth, namely how you walk in the truth* 3 J 3. M-M.

καθώσπερ adv. (Himerius, Or. 1, 20; Paroem. Gr. II p. 73, 11; 473, 13; Nicetas Eugen. 8, 106 H.) (*just) as* κ. καὶ Ἀαρών *just as Aaron also* (was) Hb 5: 4 (2 Cor 3: 18 many mss. read κ. for καθάπερ).*

καί conjunction (Hom.+; inscr., pap., LXX), found most frequently by far of all Gk. particles in the NT; since it is not only used much more commonly here than in literary Gk., but oft. in a different sense, or rather in different circumstances, it contributes greatly to the distinctive coloring of the NT style.—HKMcArthur, ΚΑΙ Frequency in Greek Letters, NTS 15, '68/'69, 339–49.
I. connective *and.* As such it serves—1. to connect single words.
a. gener. Ἰάκωβος καὶ Ἰωσὴφ καὶ Σίμων καὶ Ἰούδας Mt 13: 55. χρυσὸν καὶ λίβανον καὶ σμύρναν 2: 11. ἡ ἐντολὴ ἀγία καὶ δικαία καὶ ἀγαθή Ro 7: 12. πολυμερῶς κ. πολυτρόπως Hb 1: 1. ὁ θεὸς κ. πατήρ *God, who is also the Father* 1 Cor 15: 24; cf. 2 Cor 1: 3; 11: 31; Eph 1: 3; Js 1: 27; 3: 9 al.—Connects two occurrences of the same word, so used for emphasis (Dit., Or. 90, 19 [196 BC] Ἑρμῆς ὁ μέγας κ. μέγας; pap. in Mayser II 1, 54) μείζων κ. μείζων *greater and greater* Hv 4, 1, 6. ἔτι κ. ἔτι *again and again* B 21: 4 (Bl-D. §493, 1; 2 app.; cf. Rob. 1200).
b. w. numerals, w. the larger number first δέκα καὶ ὀκτώ Lk 13: 16. τεσσεράκοντα κ. ἕξ J 2: 20. τετρακόσιοι κ. πεντήκοντα Ac 13: 20.—The καί in ἐπὶ στόματος δύο μαρτύρων καὶ τριῶν σταθήσεται πᾶν ῥῆμα *by the statement of two and* (= 'or' [א has ἢ τριῶν, as it reads Mt 18: 16]; cf. Js 4: 13 t.r. σήμερον καὶ αὔριον='today or tomorrow', but s. above all Thu. 1, 82, 2; Pla., Phaedo 63E; X., De Re Equ. 4, 4 ἁμάξας τέτταρας καὶ πέντε; Heraclides, Pol. 28 τρεῖς καὶ τέσσαρας; Polyb. 3, 51, 12 ἐπὶ δυεῖν καὶ τρισὶν ἡμέραις; 5, 90, 6; Diod. S. 34+35 fgm. 2, 28, εἶς καὶ δύο=one or two; schol. on Apollon. Rhod. 4, 1091 p. 305, 22 W. τριέτης καὶ τετραέτης) *three witnesses every charge must be sustained* 2 Cor 13: 1 is explained by Dt 19: 15.

c. adding the whole to the part *and in general* (Aristoph., Nub. 1239 τὸν Δία καὶ τοὺς θεούς; Thu. 1, 116, 3; 7, 65, 1) Πέτρος καὶ οἱ ἀπόστολοι *Peter and the rest of the apostles* Ac 5: 29. οἱ ἀρχιερεῖς κ. τὸ συνέδριον ὅλον *the high priest and all the rest of the council* Mt 26: 59. Vice versa, adding a (specially important) part to the whole *and especially* (πᾶς Ἰουδα καὶ Ἰερουσαλήμ 2 Ch 35: 24; cf. 32, 33; 1 Macc 2: 6) τοῖς μαθηταῖς κ. τῷ Πέτρῳ Mk 16: 7. σὺν γυναιξὶ κ. Μαριάμ Ac 1: 14.

d. The expr. connected by καί can be united in the form of a hendiadys (Alcaeus 117, 9f D.[2] χρόνος καὶ κάρπος=time of fruit; Soph., Aj. 144; 749; Polyb. 6, 9, 4; 6, 57, 5 ὑπεροχὴ καὶ δυναστεία=1, 2, 7; 5, 45, 1 ὑπεροχὴ τῆς δυναστείας; Diod. S. 5, 67, 3 πρὸς ἀνανέωσιν καὶ μνήμην=renewal of remembrance; 15, 63, 2 ἀνάγκη καὶ τύχη=compulsion of fate; 16, 93, 2 ἐπιβουλὴ κ. θάνατος=a fatal plot; Jos., Ant. 12, 98 μετὰ χαρᾶς κ. βοῆς=w. a joyful cry; 17, 82 ἀκρίβεια κ. φυλακή) ἐξίσταντο ἐπὶ τῇ συνέσει καὶ ταῖς ἀποκρίσεσιν αὐτοῦ *they were amazed at his intelligent answers* Lk 2: 47. δώσω ὑμῖν στόμα κ. σοφίαν *I will give you wise utterance* 21: 15. τροφὴ κ. εὐφροσύνη *joy concerning (your) food* Ac 14: 17. ἐλπὶς κ. ἀνάστασις *hope of a resurrection* 23: 6 (2 Macc 3: 29 ἐλπὶς καὶ σωτηρία; cf. OLagercrantz, ZNW 31, '32, 86f; GBjörck, Con. Neot. 4, '40, 1-4).

e. A colloquial feature is the coordination of two verbs, one of which should be a ptc. (cf. Bl-D. §471 w. app.; Rob. 1135f) ἀποτολμᾷ κ. λέγει=ἀποτολμῶν λέγει *he is so bold as to say* Ro 10: 20. ἔσκαψεν κ. ἐβάθυνεν (=βαθύνας) Lk 6: 48. ἐκρύβη κ. ἐξῆλθεν (=ἐξελθών) J 8: 59. Sim. χαίρων κ. βλέπων *I am glad to see* Col 2: 5.

2. to connect clauses and sentences—a. gener.: ἐν γαστρὶ ἕξει κ. τέξεται υἱόν Mt 1: 23 (Is 7: 14). εἰσῆλθον . . . κ. ἐδίδασκον Ac 5: 21. διακαθαριεῖ τὴν ἅλωνα αὐτοῦ κ. συνάξει τὸν σῖτον Mt 3: 12 and very oft. Connecting two questions Mt 21: 23, or quotations (e.g., Ac 1: 20), and dialogue (Lk 21: 8), or alternate possibilities (13: 18).

b. Another common feature is the practice, drawn fr. Hebrew or fr. the speech of everyday life, of using κ. as a connective where more discriminating usage would call for other particles: καὶ εἶδον καὶ (for ὅτι) σεισμὸς ἐγένετο Rv 6: 12. καὶ ἤκουσεν ὁ βασιλεύς. . .καὶ (for ὅτι) ἔλεγον *and the king learned that they were saying* Mk 6: 14 (cf. HLjungvik, ZNW 33, '34, 90-2; on this JBlinzler, Philol. 96, '43/'44, 119-31). τέξεται υἱὸν καὶ καλέσεις τὸ ὄνομα αὐτοῦ (for οὖ τὸ ὄνομα καλ.) Mt 1: 21; cf. Lk 6: 6; 11: 44. καλόν ἐστιν ἡμᾶς ὧδε εἶναι καὶ ποιήσωμεν σκηνάς Mk 9: 5. Esp. freq. is the formula in historical narrative καὶ ἐγένετο (ἐγένετο δέ). . .καὶ (like ׳ . . . ׳וַיְהִי) *and it happened* or *came about. . .that* Mt 9: 10; Mk 2: 15; Lk 5: 1, 12, 17; 6: 12; 14: 1; 17: 11 al. Cf. KBeyer, Semitische Syntax im NT I, 1 '62, 29-62; Mlt.-Turner 334f.—As in popular speech, κ. is used in rapid succession Mt 14: 9ff; Mk 1: 12ff; Lk 18: 32ff; 1 Cor 12: 5f; Rv 6: 12ff; 9: 1ff. On this kind of colloquial speech, which joins independent clauses rather than subordinating one to the other (parataxis rather than hypotaxis) cf. Bl-D. §458; Rdm.[2] p. 222; Rob. 426; Dssm., LO 105ff (LAE 129ff), w. many references and parallels fr. secular sources. This is a favorite, e.g., in Polyaenus 2, 3, 2-4; 2, 4, 3; 3, 9, 10; 3, 10, 2; 4, 6, 1; 7, 36 al.

c. It is also coordination rather than subordination when κ. connects an expr. of time with that which occurs in the time (Od. 5, 362; Hdt. 7, 217; Thu. 1, 50, 5; Pla., Symp. 220c; Aeschin. 3, 71 νὺξ ἐν μέσῳ καὶ παρῆμεν. Cf. Bl-D. §442, 4; KBrugmann[4]-AThumb, Griechische

Gramm. '13, 640*): ἤγγικεν ἡ ὥρα κ. παραδίδοται *the time has come when he is to be given up* Mt 26: 45. κ. ἐσταύρωσαν αὐτόν *when they crucified him* Mk 15: 25. κ. ἀνέβη εἰς Ἱεροσόλυμα *when he went up to Jerusalem* J 2: 13. κ. συντελέσω *when I will make* Hb 8: 8 (Jer 38: 31); cf. J 4: 35; 7: 33; Lk 19: 43; 23: 44; Ac 5: 7.

d. καί introducing an apodosis is really due to Hebr. infl. (Bl-D. §442, 7; Abel §78a, 6 p. 341; Mlt.-H. 422; KBeyer, Semitische Syntax im NT I, 1 '62, 66-72; but s. Il. 1, 478; Thu. 2, 93, 4 ὡς ἔδοξεν αὐτοῖς, καὶ ἐχώρουν εὐθύς; Herm. Wr. 13, 1 . . ., καὶ ἔφης) καὶ ὅτε ἐπλήσθησαν ἡμέραι ὀκτὼ . . ., κ. ἐκλήθη τὸ ὄνομα αὐτοῦ Lk 2: 21. Cf. Rv 3: 20 v.l. For this κ. ἰδού in an apodosis Lk 7: 12; Ac 1: 10.

e. connecting negative and affirmative clauses Lk 3: 14. οὔτε ἄντλημα ἔχεις κ. τὸ φρέαρ ἐστὶ βαθύ *you have no bucket, and the well is deep* J 4: 11; cf. 3 J 10 (οὔτε. . .καὶ Eur., Iph. Taur. 591f; Longus, Past. 1, 17; 4, 28; Aelian, N. An. 1, 57; 11, 9; Lucian, Dial. Meretr. 2, 4 οὔτε πάντα ἡ Λεσβία, Δωρί, πρὸς σὲ ἐψεύσατο καὶ σὺ τἀληθῆ ἀπήγγελκας Μυρτίῳ). After a negative clause, which influences the clause beginning w. καί: μήποτε καταπατήσουσιν. . .κ. στραφέντες ῥήξωσιν ὑμᾶς Mt 7: 6; cf. 5: 25; 10: 38; 13: 15 (Is 6: 10); 27: 64; Lk 12: 58; 21: 34; J 6: 53; 12: 40 (Is 6: 10); Ac 28: 27 (Is 6: 10); 1 Th 3: 5; Hb 12: 15; Rv 16: 15.

f. to introduce a result, which comes fr. what precedes: *and then, and so* Mt 5: 15; 23: 32; 2 Cor 11: 9; Hb 3: 19; 1 J 3: 19. καὶ ἔχομεν *and so we have* 2 Pt 1: 19. Esp. after the imper., or expr. of an imperative nature (Soph., Oed. Col. 1410ff θέσθε . . . καὶ . . . οἴσει; El. 1207; Sir 2: 6; 3: 17) δεῦτε ὀπίσω μου καὶ ποιήσω and *then I will make* Mt 4: 19. εἰπὲ λόγῳ, κ. ἰαθήσεται ὁ παῖς μου *speak the word, and then my servant will be cured* Mt 8: 8; Lk 7: 7; cf. Mt 7: 7; Mk 6: 22; Lk 10: 28; J 14: 16; Js 4: 7, 10; Rv 4: 1.—καί introduces a short clause that confirms the existence of someth. that ought to be: ἵνα τέκνα θεοῦ κληθῶμεν, κ. ἐσμέν *that we should be called children of God; and so we really are* (καλέω 1aδ) 1 J 3: 1 (Appian, Bell. Civ. 2, 40 §161 they were to conquer Sardinia, καὶ κατέλαβον =and they really took it; 4, 127 §531 one day would decide [κρίνειν] the fate of Rome, καὶ ἐκρίθη).

g. emphasizing a fact as surprising or unexpected or noteworthy: *and yet, and in spite of that, nevertheless* (Eur., Herc. Fur. 509; Philostrat., Her. 11 [II 184, 29 Kayser] ῥητορικώτατον καὶ δεινόν; Longus, Past. 4, 17 βουκόλος ἦν Ἀγχίσης καὶ ἔσχεν αὐτὸν Ἀφροδίτη) κ. σὺ ἔρχῃ πρὸς μέ; *and yet you come to me?* Mt 3: 14; cf. 6: 26; 10: 29; Mk 12: 12; J 1: 5, 10; 3: 11, 32; 5: 40; 6: 70; 7: 28; 1 Cor 5: 2; 2 Cor 6: 9; Hb 3: 9 (Ps 94: 9); Rv 3: 1. So also, connecting what is unexpected or otherw. noteworthy with an attempt of some kind: *but* ζητεῖ κ. οὐχ εὑρίσκει *but he does not find* Mt 12: 43. ἐπεθύμησαν ἰδεῖν κ. οὐχ εἶδαν *but did not see (it)* 13: 17; cf. 26: 60; Lk 13: 7; 1 Th 2: 18. Perhaps Mk 5: 20. Introducing a contrasting response καὶ ἀποδώσεις μοι Hv 2, 1, 3.

h. to introduce an abrupt question, which may often express wonder, ill-will, incredulity, etc. (Bl-D. §442, 8. For class. exx. of this usage s. Kühner-G. II p. 247f; for later times ECColwell, The Gk. of the Fourth Gospel '31, 87f): κ. πόθεν μοι τοῦτο; *how have I deserved this?* Lk 1: 43. κ. τίς; *who then?* Mk 10: 26; Lk 10: 29; J 9: 36. καὶ τί γέγονεν ὅτι . . .; *how does it happen that . . .?* 14: 22. W. a protasis εἰ γὰρ ἐγὼ λυπῶ ὑμᾶς, κ. τίς ὁ εὐφραίνων με; *for if I make you sad, who then will cheer me up?* 2 Cor 2: 2 (cf. Ps.-Clem., Hom. 2, 43; 44 εἰ [ὁ θεὸς] ψεύδεται, καὶ τίς ἀληθεύει;). Thus Phil 1: 22 is prob. to be punctuated as follows (cf. ADebrunner, GGA '26, 151): εἰ δὲ τὸ ζῆν ἐν σαρκί, τοῦτό μοι καρπὸς ἔργου, καὶ τί αἱρήσομαι; οὐ γνωρίζω then which shall I choose? καὶ πῶς αὐτοῦ υἱός ἐστιν; how, then, is he his son? Lk 20: 44 (cf. Gen 39: 9).

i. to introduce a parenthesis (Eur., Orest. 4, Hel. 393; X., Equ. 11, 2.—Bl-D. §465, 1; Rob. 1182) κ. ἐκωλύθην ἄχρι τοῦ δεῦρο but so far I have been prevented Ro 1: 13.

3. oft. explicative; i.e., a word or clause is connected by means of καί w. another word or clause, for the purpose of explaining what goes before it and so, that is, namely (PPetr. II 18 [1], 9 πληγὰς . . . καὶ πλείους=blows . . . indeed many of them.—Kühner-G. II p. 247; Bl-D. §442, 9; Rob. 1181; Mlt.-Turner 335) χάριν κ. ἀποστολήν grace, that is, the office of an apostle Ro 1: 5. ἀπήγγειλαν πάντα καὶ τὰ τ. δαιμονιζομένων they told everything, namely what had happened to the demoniacs Mt 8: 33. καὶ χάριν ἀντὶ χάριτος that is, grace upon grace J 1: 16. Cf. 1 Cor 3: 5; 15: 38.—Mt 21: 5.—Other explicative uses are καὶ οὗτος, καὶ τοῦτο, καὶ ταῦτα (the first and last are class.; cf. Kühner-G. I p. 647; II p. 247) and, also ascensive and indeed, and at that Ἰ. Χρ., καὶ τοῦτον ἐσταυρωμένον, J. Chr., and him on the cross 1 Cor 2: 2. καὶ τοῦτο Ro 13: 11; 1 Cor 6: 6, 8; Eph 2: 8. καὶ ταῦτα w. ptc. and to be sure Hb 11: 12. Cf. Bl-D. §290, 5; 425, 1; 442, 9.—The ascensive force of καί is also plain in Ῥωμαῖον καὶ ἀκατάκριτον a Roman citizen, and uncondemned at that Ac 22: 25. ἔρχεται ὥρα καὶ νῦν ἐστιν an hour is coming, indeed it is already here J 5: 25.

4. After πολύς and before a second adj. καί is pleonastic fr. the viewpoint of modern lang. (class. [Kühner-G. II p. 252, 1]. Cf. Cebes 1, 1 πολλὰ καὶ ἄλλα ἀναθήματα; 2, 3; Bl-D. §442, 11) πολλὰ . . . κ. ἄλλα σημεῖα many other signs J 20: 30 (cf. Jos., Ant. 3, 318). πολλὰ κ. βαρέα αἰτιώματα many severe charges Ac 25: 7. πολλὰ . . . καὶ ἕτερα Lk 3: 18 (cf. Himerius, Or. 40 [=Or. 6], 6 πολλὰ καὶ ἄλλα). πολλοὶ καὶ ἀνυπότακτοι Tit 1: 10 v.l.

5. introducing someth. new, w. loose connection: Mt 4: 23; 8: 14, 23, 28; 9: 1, 9, 27, 35; 10: 1; 12: 27; Mk 5: 1, 21; Lk 8: 26; J 1: 19 and oft.

6. καί . . . καί both . . . and, not only . . . , but also (Synes., Dreams 10 p. 141в καὶ ἀπιστεῖν ἔξεστι καὶ πιστεύειν.—Bl-D. §444, 3; Rob. 1182; Mlt.-Turner 335) connecting single expressions Mt 10: 28; Ro 11: 33; Phil 2: 13; 4: 12. κ. ἐν ὀλίγῳ κ. ἐν μεγάλῳ Ac 26: 29. κ. ἅπαξ κ. δίς (s. ἅπαξ 1) Phil 4: 16; 1 Th 2: 18. Connecting whole clauses or sentences Mk 9: 13; J 7: 28; 9: 37; 12: 28; 1 Cor 1: 22. Introducing contrasts: although . . . yet (Anthol. VII no. 676 Δοῦλος Ἐπίκτητος γενόμην καὶ σῶμ' ἀνάπηρος καὶ πενίην Ἴρος καὶ φίλος ἀθανάτοις) J 15: 24; Ac 23: 3. καὶ . . . οὐ Lk 5: 36; J 6: 36. καὶ οὐ . . . καί 17: 25; κ. . . . κ. now . . . now Mk 9: 22. On τὲ . . . καί s. τέ.—HJCadbury, Superfluous καί in the Lord's Prayer [i.e. Mt 6: 12] and Elsewhere: Munera Studiosa (=WHPHatch-Festschr.) '46.

II. Rather as an adv. also, likewise—1. simply κ. τὴν ἄλλην the other one also Mt 5: 39; cf. vs. 40; 6: 21; 12: 45; Mk 1: 38; 2: 26; 8: 7 and oft. Freq. used w. pronouns κἀγώ (q.v.). καὶ σύ Mt 26: 73. κ. ὑμεῖς 20: 4, 7; Lk 21: 31; J 7: 47 and oft. κ. αὐτός (s. αὐτός 1g).

2. ascensive: even Mt 5: 46f; 10: 30; Mk 1: 27; 4: 41; Lk 10: 17; Ac 5: 39; 22: 28; 1 Cor 2: 10; 2 Cor 1: 8; Gal 2: 17; Eph 5: 12; Phlm 21; Hb 7: 25; 1 Pt 4: 19; Jd 23. CBlackman, JBL 87, '68, 203f would transl. Ro 3: 26b: . . . even in the act of declaring righteous. In formulas expressing a wish: ὄφελον καί if only, would that Gal 5:

12. In connection w. a comparative: κ. περισσότερον προφήτου one who is even more than a prophet Mt 11: 9. κ. μείζονα ποιήσει J 14: 12.

3. In sentences denoting a contrast καί appears in var. ways, somet. in both members of the comparison, and oft. pleonastically, to our way of thinking καθάπερ . . . , οὕτως καὶ as . . . , thus also 2 Cor 8: 11. ὥσπερ . . . , οὕτως καί (Hyperid. 1, 2, 5–8) Ro 5: 19; 11: 30f; 1 Cor 11: 12; 15: 22; Gal 4: 29. ὡς . . . , οὕτως καί Ro 5: 15, 18. ὃν τρόπον . . . , οὕτως καί 2 Ti 3: 8.—οὕτως καί thus also Ro 6: 11. ὡσαύτως καί in the same way also 1 Cor 11: 25. ὁμοίως καί (Jos., Bell. 2, 575) J 6: 11; Jd 8. ὡς καί Ro 15: 7; Ac 11: 17; 1 Cor 7: 7; 9: 5. καθὼς καί Ro 15: 7; 1 Cor 13: 12; 2 Cor 1: 14; Eph 4: 17. καθάπερ καί Ro 4: 6; 2 Cor 1: 14.—καί can also stand alone in the second member w. the mng. so also, so. ὡς . . . καί Mt 6: 10; Ac 7: 51; Gal 1: 9; Phil 1: 20. καθὼς . . . καί Lk 6: 31 v.l.; J 6: 57; 13: 15; 1 Cor 15: 49.—οἷος . . . , τοιοῦτος καί 1 Cor 15: 48. After a comp. ὅσῳ καί by so much also Hb 8: 6. καί is found in both members of the comparison (cf. Kühner-G. II 256; 2 Macc 2: 10; 6: 14) Ro 1: 13; 1 Th 2: 14. καθὼς καί . . . οὕτως καί Col 3: 13 (cf. Hyperid. 1, 40, 20–5 ὥσπερ καί . . . οὕτως καί; 3, 38).

4. w. expressions that introduce cause or result, here also pleonastic to a considerable degree διὰ τοῦτο καί for this reason (also) Lk 11: 49; J 12: 18. διὸ καί Lk 1: 35; Ac 10: 29; Ro 4: 22; Hb 13: 12. εἰς τοῦτο καί 2 Cor 2: 9. ὥστε καί 1 Pt 4: 19. ὅθεν καί Hb 7: 25; 11: 19.

5. after an interrogative (class.; cf. Kühner-G. II 255. S. also Bl-D. §442, 14) at all, still ἱνατί καί τ. γῆν καταργεῖ; Lk 13: 7. τί καί; (Hyperid. 3, 14 τί καὶ ἀδικεῖ; what kind of wrong, then, is he committing?) τί καὶ ἐλπίζει; why does he still (need to) hope? Ro 8: 24. τί καὶ βαπτίζονται; why are they baptized (at all)? 1 Cor 15: 29; cf. vs. 30.

6. used w. a relative, it oft. gives greater independence to the foll. relative clause: Lk 10: 30; Ac 1: 3, 11; 7: 45; 10: 39; 11: 30; 12: 4; 13: 22; 28: 10; Ro 9: 24; 1 Cor 11: 23; Gal 2: 10; Col 1: 29 al.

7. used pleonastically w. prep.—a. μετά (BGU 412, 6 μετὰ καὶ τ. υἱοῦ) Phil 4: 3.

b. σύν (inscr. in Papers of the American School of Class. Stud. at Athens III 612; PFay. 108; BGU 179, 19; 515, 17) 1 Cl 65: 1.—Dssm., NB 93 [BS 265f].

8. w. double names ὁ καί who is also called . . . (the earliest ex. in a fragment of Ctesias, c. 400 BC [cf. Hatch 141]; Dit., Or. 565; 574; 583; 589; 603; 604; 620; 623; 636; POxy. 45; 46; 54; 101; 485; 1279; PFay. 30; BGU 22, 25; 36, 4; Jos., Ant. 1, 240; 5, 85; 12, 285; 13, 320; 18, 35. Further material in WSchmid, Der Atticismus III 1893, 338; Dssm., B 181ff [BS 313–17]. Lit. in Bl-D. §268, 1 w. app.) Σαῦλος, ὁ καὶ Παῦλος Ac 13: 9. Ἰγνάτιος, ὁ καὶ Θεοφόρος inscr. of all the letters of Ign.—On κ. . . . γάρ, καὶ γε, κ. . . . δέ, δὲ καί, s. γάρ, γέ, δέ. On ἀλλὰ κ., ἐὰν κ., εἰ κ., ἦ κ. see ἀλλά, ἐάν, εἰ, ἦ. M-M.

Καϊάφας, α, ὁ (N.: Καϊαφᾶς) Caiaphas (Jos., Ant. 18, 35; 95), high priest 18–36 AD, who played an important role in the condemnation of Jesus. Cf. Mt 26: 3, 57; Lk 3: 2; J 11: 49; 18: 13f, 24, 28; Ac 4: 6; GEb 1. Acc. to J 18: 13 he was son-in-law to Annas (s. Ἄννας).—Schürer II⁴ 256; 271.— KHRengstorf, Rabb. Texte, Erste Reihe, vol. 3, '33ff, p. 16f on Tos. Jeb. 1, 10. On the name cf. Bl-D. §37; Dalman, Gramm. 161, 2; EbNestle, Theol. Studien f. ThZahn, '08, 251ff, FCBurkitt, The Syriac Forms of NT Proper Names (Proceed. of the Brit. Acad. '11/'12) 385. M-M.*

καίγε s. γέ 3c.

Κάιν, ὁ indecl. (נֵר ; W-H. Κάιν; LXX; En. 22, 7; Philo; Test. Benj. 7: 5.—In Jos., Ant. 1, 52; 65f; 57 Κάις, Κάιος, Κάιν) Cain, son of Adam (Gen 4: 1ff) Hb 11: 4; 1 J 3: 12; Jd 11; 1 Cl 4: 1ff.—NDahl, D. Erstgeborene Satans usw., Apophoreta (Haenchen-Festschr.) '64, 70–84; PBretscher, Cain, Come Home! '76. S. on Ἄβελ.*

Καϊνάμ, ὁ indecl. (Καϊνάν, Hebr. קֵינָן Gen 5: 9) Cainan, in the genealogy of Jesus.
1. son of Arphaxad (LXX Gen 10: 24; 11: 12; 1 Ch 1: 18) Lk 3: 36. The name is lacking in 𝔓⁷⁵ D.—2. son of Enos (Gen 5: 9ff.—Jos., Ant. 1, 79; 84 Καινᾶς, ᾶ) vs. 37.*

καινίζω (trag.+) make new B 6: 11 v.l. Funk (for ἀνακ.).*

καινός, ή, όν (Aeschyl., Hdt.+; inscr., pap., LXX, Philo, Joseph., Test. 12 Patr.) comp. καινότερος; new.
1. in the sense unused (X., Hell. 3, 4, 28; PGM 36, 265; Judg 15: 13; 2 Km 6: 3; 4 Km 2: 20) ἀσκοί wineskins (Josh 9: 13) Mt 9: 17; Mk 2: 22; Lk 5: 38. ἱμάτιον (Artem. 2, 3 p. 86, 3; 3 Km 11: 29f) vs. 36. μνημεῖον Mt 27: 60; J 19: 41 (w. ἐν ᾧ οὐδέπω οὐδεὶς ἦν τεθειμένος added). τὸ κ. the new piece=πλήρωμα Mk 2: 21; Lk 5: 36. καινὰ καὶ παλαιά Mt 13: 52 (perh. with ref. to coins; cf. PGrenf. II 74, 9; 77, 7f).
2. in the sense of someth. not previously present, unknown, strange, remarkable, also w. the connotation of the marvelous or unheard-of (Pla., Apol. 24c; X., Mem. 1, 1, 1 ἕτερα καὶ καινὰ δαιμόνια) διδαχή Mk 1: 27; Ac 17: 19. ἐντολή (κ. νόμος: Menand., fgm. 272, 3) J 13: 34; 1 J 2: 7f (Polyaenus 2, 1, 13 οὐ καινοὺς νόμους . . . ἀλλὰ τ. παλαιούς); 2 J 5. ὄνομα (Is 62: 2; 65: 15) Rv 2: 17 (here w. ὁ οὐδεὶς οἶδεν εἰ μὴ ὁ λαμβάνων); 3: 12. ᾠδή 5: 9 (Ps 143: 9; cf. Is 42: 10; Ps 32: 3.—Philo, Vi. Cont. 80 ὕμνος κ. [opp. ἀρχαῖος]); 14: 3. γλῶσσαι Mk 16: 17. κ. γένος of the Christians Dg 1. Christ as ὁ κ. ἄνθρωπος the new kind of man IEph 20: 1. ἢ λέγειν τι ἢ ἀκούειν τι καινότερον either to hear or to say someth. quite new Ac 17: 21 (cf. Kühner-G. II 306f; Norden, Agn. Th. 333ff [but s. HAlmqvist, Plutarch u. d. NT '46, 79f, w. ref. to Plut.]; Bl-D. §244, 2; Rdm.² p. 70 and s. Demosth. 4, 10 ὦ ἄνδρες Ἀθηναῖοι . . . λέγεταί τι καινόν; γένοιτ' ἄν τι καινότερον . . . ; Theophr., Char. 8, 2; BGU 821, 6 [II AD] ὅταν ἦ τι καινότερον, εὐθέως σοι δηλώσω; Simplicius, Coroll. De Tempore, in Aristot., Phys. p. 788, 36ff καινοτέραν ἐβάδισεν ὁδόν=he traveled a rather new road [of interpretation]; Jos., Ant. 14, 104).
3. in contrast to someth. old—a. w. no criticism of the old implied Herodas 4, 57 καινὴ Ἀθηναίη; Lucian, M. Peregr. 12 κ. Σωκράτης. Of the Son of God or Logos, who is old and new at the same time Hs 9, 12, 1ff; Dg 11: 4.
b. in the sense that what is old has become obsolete, and should be replaced by what is new. In such a case the new is, as a rule, superior in kind to the old ἡ κ. διαθήκη the new covenant or declaration (Jer 38[31]: 31) Mt 26: 28 v.l.; Mk 14: 24 v.l.; Lk 22: 20; 1 Cor 11: 25; 2 Cor 3: 6; Hb 8: 8 (Jer 38[31]: 31), 13; 9: 15. κ. νόμος (Timocles Com. [IV BC] 32, 4 κατὰ τὸν νόμον τ. καινόν) B 2: 6. λαὸς κ. 5: 7; 7: 5; cf. B 15: 7.—Esp. in eschatol. usage κ. οὐρανοί, κ. γῆ (Is 65: 17; 66: 22) 2 Pt 3: 13; Rv 21: 1. Ἰερουσαλὴμ καινή vs. 2; 3: 12. καινὰ πάντα ποιεῖν 21: 5. καινὸν πίνειν τὸ γένημα τῆς ἀμπέλου Mt 26: 29; Mk 14: 25.—Of the renewing of a person who has been converted κ. ἄνθρωπος Eph 4: 24; Dg 2: 1. κ. κτίσις a new creature 2 Cor 5: 17a; cf. b (Ps.-Pla., Axioch. 11 p. 370E ἐκ τῆς ἀσθενείας ἐμαυτὸν συνείλεγμαι καὶ γέγονα καινός=out of weak-

ness I have brought myself together and become new); Gal 6: 15; cf. B 16: 8. All the Christians together appear as κ. ἄνθρωπος Eph 2: 15.—RAHarrisville, The Concept of Newness in the NT, '60; GSchneider, Καινὴ Κτίσις (Paul and background), diss. Trier, '59, Neuschöpfung oder Wiederkehr? '61; JBehm, TW III 450–6 καινός and related words. M-M. B. 957.*

καινότης, ητος, ἡ (since Thu. 3, 38, 5; Plut., Pericl. 13, 5; Lucian, Tyrann. 22; 3 Km 8: 53a; Ezk 47: 12; Philo, Vi. Cont. 63) newness w. the connotation of someth. extraordinary (καινός 2) of a star IEph 19: 2. Hebraistically, the noun for an adj. κ. πνεύματος=πνεῦμα καινόν a new spirit Ro 7: 6. κ. ζωῆς a new life 6: 4; cf. IEph 19: 3 (for lit. s. παλιγγενεσία 2). κ. ἐλπίδος a new hope IMg 9: 1.*

καινοφωνία s. κενοφωνία.

καινῶς adv. (Dit., Or. 669, 46; 49) newly καὶ τοῦτο οὐ κ. (sc. ἐγένετο) and this was nothing new 1 Cl 42: 5. καινῶς (τ. θεὸν) σεβόμενοι worshiping God in a new way PK 2 p. 15, 3; cf. 8.*

καίπερ conj. (since Od. 7, 224; Dit., Syll.³ 709, 18; 1108, 8; PGiess. 47, 22; PSI 298, 17; LXX) although w. ptc. (so usu., also Diod. S. 8, 9, 2; 10, 19, 2; 17, 114, 1; Wsd 11: 9; Jos., Ant. 3, 280; Test. Jos. 10: 5) Phil 3: 4; Hb 5: 8; 7: 5; 12: 17; 2 Pt 1: 12; 1 Cl 7: 7; 16: 2; ISm 3: 3; MPol 17: 1; Hv 3, 2, 9; s 8, 6, 4; 8, 11, 1 (Bl-D. §425, 1; Rob. 1129; FScheidweiler, καίπερ nebst e. Exkurs zum Hb: Her. 83, '55, 220–30). M-M.*

καιρός, οῦ, ὁ (Hes.+; inscr., pap., LXX; En. 99, 5; Ep. Arist.; Philo; Joseph.; Test. 12 Patr.; Sib. Or.; loanw. in rabb.) time, i.e. point of time as well as period of time.
1. gener. κ. δεκτός a welcome time 2 Cor 6: 2a (Is 49: 8); cf. b. καιροὶ χαλεποί difficult times 2 Ti 3: 1. καιροὶ καρποφόροι fruitful times or seasons (so Achmes 156, 15f: καρποφόρος is the καιρός in which the tree bears fruit, in contrast to late autumn, when there is no more.—TW III 416, 45f; 459, 19) Ac 14: 17 (OLagercrantz, ZNW 31, '32, 86f proposes, on the basis of Mod. Gk., the mng. 'weather', but the pl. is against this mng.). καιροὶ ἐαρινοί 1 Cl 20: 9.—ἔσται καιρὸς ὅτε there will come a time when 2 Ti 4: 3; εἰς τίνα ἢ ποῖον κ. to what time or what sort of time (unless τίνα here=what person [RSV], but cf. PTebt. 25, 18 [117 BC] καὶ διὰ τίνος καὶ ἀπὸ ποίου ἐπιδείγματος) 1 Pt 1: 11. ἄχρι καιροῦ until (another) time, for a while Lk 4: 13; Ac 13: 11; ἐν παντὶ κ. at all times, always (Aristot. 117a, 35; Sir 26: 4) Lk 21: 36; Eph 6: 18; Hm 5, 2, 3. κατὰ καιρὸν from time to time, regularly (Lucian, Hermot. 10; Plut., Mor. 984D) J 5: 4 (s. 3 also); 1 Cl 24: 2; πρὸς κ. for a limited time (perh. also for the present moment; cf. Strabo 6, 2, 3; Ps.-Plut., Fluv. 23 Arax. 1; BGU 265, 20 [II AD] 618, 19; 780, 14; Wsd 4: 4; Philo, Post. Cai. 121; Jos., Bell. 6, 190) Lk 8: 13; 1 Cor 7: 5. πρὸς καιρὸν ὥρας (a combination of πρὸς κ. and πρὸς ὥραν [2 Cor 7: 8; Gal 2: 5; Phlm 15; J 5: 35]) 1 Th 2: 17.—The present (time) Ro 13: 11 (for the view that κ. here is used in an eschatological sense, see 3 below); 12: 11 v.l. ὁ καιρὸς (personified=your Christian contemporaries) ἀπαιτεῖ σε the times call upon you IPol 2: 3 (Diod. S. 17, 27, 2 ὑπὸ τῶν καιρῶν προεκλήθησαν=they were called out by the [circumstances of the] times). Also ὁ νῦν κ. (PSI 402, 7 [III BC] ἐν τῷ νῦν καιρῷ) Ro 3: 26; 8: 18; 11: 5; 2 Cor 8: 14. ὁ νῦν τῆς ἀνομίας the present godless time 18: 2 (s. also 4 below). ὁ κ. ὁ ἐνεστηκώς (Polyb. 1, 60, 9; Jos., Ant. 16, 162) Hb 9: 9; ἐν ἐκείνῳ τῷ κ. at that time, then (Gen 21: 22; Is 38: 1) Mt 11: 25; 12: 1; 14: 1; cf. Eph 2: 12. Also

καιρός—Καῖσαρ

κατ᾽ ἐκεῖνον τὸν κ. (Jos., Ant. 1, 171, Vi. 49.—Diod. S. 2, 27, 1 and Vi. Aesopi I c. 81 κατ᾽ ἐκείνους τοὺς καιρούς =at that time) Ac 12: 1; 19: 23. ἔτι κατὰ καιρὸν ὑπὲρ ἀσεβῶν for those who at that time were still godless Ro 5: 6, though κατὰ κ. here may=at the right time, as in mng. 2a below (cf. Bl-D. §255, 3 app.). Of the future κατὰ τ. καιρὸν τοῦτον at this time 9: 9 (Gen 18: 10, 14). ἐν αὐτῷ τῷ κ. just at that time (2 Esdr [Ezra] 5: 3) Lk 13: 1. W. attraction of the relative ἐν ᾧ κ. at that time, then Ac 7: 20.

2. the right, proper, favorable time—**a.** gener. ἐν καιρῷ at the right time (X., An. 3, 1, 39; Diod. S. 36, 7, 2; Appian, Bell. Civ. 3, 8 §29; Dit., Syll.³ 1268 [Praecepta Delphica II, 6; III BC]) Mt 24: 45; Lk 12: 42 (cf. on both Ps 103: 27, w. v.l.). καιρῷ (Thu. 4, 59, 3; Diog. L. 1, 41) Lk 20: 10. τῷ καιρῷ Mk 12: 2. ὁ καιρὸς ὁ ἐμός, ὁ καιρὸς ὁ ὑμέτερος the proper time for me (you) J 7: 6, 8 (Eunap., Vi. Iambl. p. 459 Didot: the worker of miracles acts ὅταν καιρὸς ᾖ).—καιρὸν λαβεῖν find a favorable time, seize the opportunity (Lysias, C. Agor. 6; Cleanthes [III BC]: Stoic. I no. 573; Diod. S. 2, 6, 5; Ep. Arist. 248; Jos., Bell. 1, 527, Ant. 4, 10. Cf. PTebt. 332, 9). καιρὸν μεταλαβεῖν (s. μεταλαμβάνω 2) Ac 24: 25. λαβεῖν κ. εὔθετον find a convenient opportunity Pol 13: 1. κ. ἔχειν have opportunity (Thu. 1, 42, 3; Pla., Ep. 7 p. 324B; Plut., Lucull. 16, 3; PFlor. 259, 3; 1 Macc 15: 34; Jos., Ant. 16, 73; 335) Gal 6: 10; Hb 11: 15; 2 Cl 16: 1; ISm 9: 1; IRo 2: 1. ὀλίγον καιρὸν ἔχειν Rv 12: 12. ἐξαγοράζεσθαι τὸν κ. make the most of the opportunity Col 4: 5; Eph 5: 16 (s. ἐξαγοράζω 2). κατὰ κ. Ro 5: 6 is more naturally construed with ἀπέθανεν than with ἀσεβῶν (cf. κατὰ καιρὸν θεριζόμενος reaped in its proper time Job 5: 26).

b. καιρός is often used w. qualifying phrases to define the specific character of the κ. in question: definite, fixed time. Abs. καιροί festal seasons (Ex 23: 14, 17; Lev 23: 4.—So perh. also beside θυσίαι in the Inscr. de Sinuri ed. LRobert ᾽45 no. 42) Gal 4: 10.—Not infreq. w. a gen., which indicates the reason why the time is set apart (Pla., Leg. 4 p. 709c χειμῶνος καιρός; Aesop, Fab. 258 P.=255 H. ἀπολογίας κ., also oft. LXX; Philo, Spec. Leg. 1, 191 κ. εὐφροσύνης; Jos., Ant. 18, 74) κ. θερισμοῦ time of harvest Mt 13: 30. κ. τῶν καρπῶν time when the fruit is ripe 21: 34; cf. vs. 41. κ. σύκων time when the figs are ripe Mk 11: 13 (cf. Horapollo 2, 92 ὁ κ. τῶν ἀμπέλων). κ. μετανοίας time for repentance 2 Cl 8: 2. κ. πειρασμοῦ Lk 8: 13b. ὁ κ. τῆς ἀναλύσεως the time of death 2 Ti 4: 6. κ. ἐπισκοπῆς σου Lk 19: 44. κ. διορθώσεως Hb 9: 10. κ. ἡλικίας 11: 11. κ. τῆς ἡγεμονίας Ποντίου Πιλάτου the time of the procuratorship of P.P. IMg 11. ὁ αὐτοῦ καιρός (Num 9: 7) 2 Th 2: 6. ὁ κ. αὐτῶν the time set for the fulfilment of Gabriel's words Lk 1: 20. ὁ κ. μου my time= the time of my death Mt 26: 18. κ. τοῦ ἰαθῆναι time to be healed 2 Cl 9: 7. κ. τοῦ ἄρξασθαι τὸ κρίμα 1 Pt 4: 17. Cf. the extraordinary ἦλθεν ὁ κ. τῶν νεκρῶν κριθῆναι καὶ δοῦναι=ἵνα κριθῶσιν οἱ νεκροὶ καὶ δῷς Rv 11: 18.—Pl. (Heraclit. Sto. 11 p. 18, 18 οἱ μεταξὺ καιροί=the periods of time between; Maximus Tyr. 1, 2f πολλοὶ κ.; Test. Napht. 7: 1 δεῖ ταῦτα πληρωθῆναι κατὰ τοὺς καιροὺς αὐτῶν) καιροὶ ἐθνῶν times of the Gentiles (in which they may punish God's people or themselves be converted) Lk 21: 24.—κατὰ καιρόν at the appropriate time (Arrian, Anab. 4, 5, 1; PSI 433, 4 [261 BC]) J 5: 4; 1 Cl 56: 15 (Job 5: 26). Also ἐν καιρῷ (Himerius, Or 13 [Ecl. 14], 3): ἐν καιρῷ αὐτοῦ B 11: 6, 8 (Ps 1: 3). καιρῷ ἰδίῳ in due time Gal 6: 9. καιροῖς ἰδίοις at the right time 1 Ti 2: 6; 6: 15; Tit 1: 3; cf. 1 Cl 20: 4.—κατὰ τὸν ἴδιον καιρόν vs. 10. πεπλήρωται ὁ κ. the time (determined by God) is fulfilled Mk 1: 15. Pl. (cf. Ps 103: 19) ὁρίσας προστεταγμένους

καιρούς he (God) has determined allotted times (MDibelius, S. Hdlbg. Ak. d. W. ᾽38/᾽39, 2. Abh. p. 6f, ᾽seasons'; cf. IQM 10, 12–15; FMussner, Einige Parallelen [Qumran and Areopagus speech], BZ 1, ᾽57, 125–30) Ac 17: 26; cf. 1 Cl 40: 1f. Definite, fixed time can also refer to the last things, hence κ. becomes

3. one of the chief eschatological terms. ὁ καιρός the time of crisis, the last times (FBusch, Z. Verständnis d. synopt. Eschatol. Mk 13 neu untersucht ᾽38; GDelling, D. Zeitverständn. des NTs ᾽40; WMichaelis, D. Herr verzieht nicht d. Verheissung ᾽42; WGKümmel, Verheissung. u. Erfüllung ᾽45, ³᾽56; OCullmann, Christus u. d. Zeit ᾽46 [tr. FVFilson, Christ and Time ᾽50, 39–45; 79; 121]) ὁ κ. ἤγγικεν Lk 21: 8. ὁ κ. ἐγγύς Rv 1: 3; 22: 10. οὐκ οἴδατε πότε ὁ καιρός ἐστιν Mk 13: 33. Cf. Ro 13: 11 (s. 1 above) if it is to be interpreted as eschatological (cf. Plut., Mor. 549F). πρὸ καιροῦ before the end-time and the judgment Mt 8: 29; 1 Cor 4: 5. ἐν καιρῷ 1 Pt 5: 6. Also ἐν καιρῷ ἐσχάτῳ 1: 5; D 16: 2. Pl. πλήρωμα τῶν καιρῶν Eph 1: 10. τὰ σημεῖα τ. καιρῶν the signs of the Messianic times Mt 16: 3. The Messianic times described as καιροὶ ἀναψύξεως Ac 3: 20.—ἔσχατοι καιροί (or ὕστεροι καιροί 1 Ti 4: 1) come before the ἔσχατος κ. IEph 11: 1; χρόνοι ἢ καιροί times and seasons (Artem. 4, 2 p. 203, 25f the χρόνος is divided into καιροὶ καὶ ὧραι), which must be completed before the final consummation Ac 1: 7 (Strato of Lamps. in FWehrli, Die Schule des Aristoteles, V fgm. 10, 32f κατὰ τοὺς καιροὺς καὶ τοὺς χρόνους; quoted in JBarr, Biblical Words for Time, ᾽62, 33; see also Diog. L. 5, 64 [Loeb]); cf. 1 Th 5: 1. συντέμνειν τοὺς καιρούς shorten the (last) times B 4: 3. Sim. in sg. ὁ καιρὸς συνεσταλμένος ἐστίν 1 Cor 7: 29.—The expr. καιρὸν καὶ καιροὺς κ. ἥμισυ καιροῦ also belongs to the eschatol. vocab.; it means the apocalyptic time of 1+2+½=3½ years, during which acc. to Da 12: 7 (cf. 7: 25) the Antichrist is to reign on earth Rv 12: 14.—ὁ κ. οὗτος the present age (cf. αἰών 2a) Mk 10: 30; Lk 12: 56; 18: 30. Also ὁ νῦν κ. B 4: 1. As ruled by the devil: ὁ ἄνομος κ. 4: 9. καταργεῖν τὸν κ. τοῦ ἀνόμου destroy the age of the lawless one 15: 5.—Dg 12: 9 καιροί is considered to be a textual error; s. the editions of vGebh.-Harnack and Bihlmeyer.—JMánek, NTS 6, ᾽59, 45–51; JBarr, Biblical Words for Time, ᾽62. M-M. B. 954.**

Καῖσαρ, αρος, ὁ (=Lat. Caesar; on the distribution of this word, freq. found in lit., inscr., pap. s. Hahn [sources and lit. here 123, 3] and Magie.—Philo, Joseph., Sib. Or., loanw. in rabb.—In our lit. w. the art. only J 19: 12 [cf. Bl-D. §254, 1]) emperor, Caesar (orig. a proper name, then used as a title) Mt 22: 17, 21a; Mk 12: 14, 16; Lk 20: 22, 24; 23: 2 (s. φόρος); J 19: 12b (cf. Philo, In Flacc. 40 [523 M]), Ac 17: 7; 25: 8, 10–12, 21; 26: 32; 27: 24; 28: 19; κύριος Κ. MPol 8: 2. ὀμνύναι τὴν Καίσαρος τύχην (s. τύχη) 9: 2; 10: 1. τὰ Καίσαρος what belongs to the emperor Mt 22: 21b; Mk 12: 17; Lk 20: 25 (HWindisch, Imperium u. Evangelium im NT ᾽31; KPieper, ThGl 25, ᾽33, 661–9; EStauffer, Gott u. Kaiser im NT ᾽35; GKittel, Christus u. Imperator ᾽39; JBenum, Gud och Kejsaren ᾽40; HLoewe, ᾽Render Unto Caesar' ᾽40; NJHommes, God en Kejzer in het NT ᾽41; OEck, Urgem. u. Imperium ᾽41; MDibelius, Rom u. die Christen im 1. Jahrh. ᾽42; JDM Derrett, Law in the NT, ᾽70). φίλος τ. Καίσαρος friend of the emperor (as official title CIG 3499, 4; 3500, 4; Epict. 3, 4, 2; 4, 1, 8; 45–8; 95; 4, 4, 5; Jos., Ant. 14, 131) J 19: 12a. οἱ ἐκ τῆς Καίσαρος οἰκίας those (slaves) who belong to the emperor's household Phil 4: 22 (cf. Lghtf., Phil 171ff; Dssm., LO 127, 1; 202, 3; 380 [LAE 382]; and s. οἰκία 3).—W. proper names Τιβέριος Κ. Emperor

395

Tiberius Lk 3: 1. K. Νέρων 2 Ti subscr. But Καῖσαρ Αὐγοῦστος *Caesar Augustus* Lk 2: 1, since here K. is not a title, but a part of the name (Bl-D. §5, 3a). M-M. B. 1324.*

Καισάρεια, ας, ἡ (Καισαρία a wrong accent; s. W-S. §5, 13c, end) *Caesarea.*

1. Καισάρεια ἡ Φιλίππου *C. Philippi,* a city at the foot of Mt. Hermon, once known as Paneas, rebuilt by Philip the Tetrarch and made an important city; he named it Caesarea in honor of Tiberius Caesar (Jos., Ant. 18, 28, Bell. 2, 168) Mt 16: 13. αἱ κῶμαι K. τῆς Φ. are villages near the city Mk 8: 27.—Schürer II⁴ 204-8 (sources and lit.); Dalman, Orte³ (index).

2. Καισάρεια without further designation is *Caesarea* 'by the sea' (Philo, Leg. ad Gai. 305; Jos., Bell. 7, 23 [here both Caesareas together]), located south of Mt. Carmel, founded by Herod the Great on the site of the ancient Strato's Tower, named C. in honor of Augustus Caesar; later became the seat of the Roman procurators (Jos., Ant. 13, 313; 15, 293; 331ff; 19, 343, Bell. 1, 408-14 s. index). Ac 8: 40; 9: 30; 10: 1, 24; 11: 11; 12: 19; 18: 22; 21: 8, 16; 23: 23, 33; 25: 1, 4, 6, 13.—Schürer II⁴ 134-8 (sources and lit.); LHaefeli, Caesarea am Meere '23; CKopp, The Holy Places of the Gospels, tr. RWalls, '63, 231-35.*

καίτοι (since Il. 13, 267; inscr., pap.; 4 Macc 2: 6; 5: 18; 7: 13) particle (Bl-D. §425, 1; 450, 3; Rob. 1129; 1154) w. a finite verb (Chio, Ep. 3, 1; Jos., Ant. 5, 78) *and yet* Ac 14: 17. W. gen. absol. foll. (BGU 850, 4 [76 AD] καίτοι ἐμοῦ σε πολλὰ ἐρωτήσαντος; 898, 26; Jos., Ant. 2, 321. Also καίτοι γε Dit., Syll.³ 685, 76 [139 BC]) Hb 4: 3. M-M.*

καίτοιγε or καίτοι γε (since Aristoph., Ach. 611; not really class. [MMeister, De Axiocho Dial., Bresl. Diss. '15, p. 31, 5]; Ps.-Pla., Axioch. 364B; Jos., Bell. 1, 7, Ant. 5, 36; Dit., Syll.³ 685, 76; 82 [139 BC]), particle w. the same mng. as καίτοι *and yet* J 4: 2; Ac 14: 17 t.r.; Dg 8: 3. M-M.*

καίω (Hom. +; inscr., pap., LXX, En., Philo, Joseph.) 1 aor. ἔκαυσα; pf. pass. ptc. κεκαυμένος; 1 aor. pass. inf. καυθῆναι (MPol 5: 2) and 2 aor. (Bl-D. §76, 1; Rob. 349f) καῆναι (MPol 12: 3); 1 fut. pass. καυθήσομαι (καυθήσωμαι 1 Cor 13: 3 v.l., s. Bl-D. §28; Mlt.-H. 219).

1. *light* someth., *have* or *keep* someth. *burning*—a. lit. λύχνον *a lamp* (Posidon.: 87 fgm. 94 Jac.; cf. Lev 24: 2, 4; Jos., C. Ap. 1, 308; PGM 4, 2372) Mt 5: 15 (so act. καίω τι X., An. 4, 4, 12; 4, 1, 11; EpJer 18. But, in contrast to ἅπτω, κ. lays the emphasis less upon the act of lighting than on keeping a thing burning; cf. Jülicher, Gleichn. 80. —Diod. S. 13, 111, 2 πυρὰ κάειν=keep fires burning). Pass. *be lit, burn* Mk 4: 21 v.l. λύχνοι καιόμενοι (Artem. 2, 9; cf. Phlegon: 257 fgm. 36, 1, 1 Jac. καιομένου τοῦ λύχνου; Ex 27: 20; Jos., Ant. 8, 90) Lk 12: 35; J 5: 35; Rv 4: 5; 8: 10. πῦρ καιόμενον (Hdt. 1, 86; Is 4: 5; Sib. Or. 7, 6) MPol 11: 2. κλίβανος καιόμενος *a burning* or *heated oven* (Hos 7: 4) 2 Cl 16: 3. W. πυρί added (Pla., Phaedo 113A εἰς τόπον μέγαν πυρὶ πολλῷ καιόμενον) Hb 12: 18 (cf. Dt 4: 11; 5: 23; 9: 15); Rv 8: 8. πυρὶ καὶ θείῳ w. *fire and brimstone* (cf. Is 30: 33) 21: 8; cf. 19: 20.

b. fig. (schol. on Apollon. Rhod. 3, 762 ἡ ὀδύνη καίουσα; Philo, Decal. 49 καιόμενοι κ. κατακαιόμενοι ὑπὸ τ. ἐπιθυμιῶν) of the heart οὐχὶ ἡ καρδία ἡμῶν καιομένη ἦν; *were not our hearts burning?* Lk 24: 32 (cf. PGM 7, 472 καιομένην τὴν ψυχὴν κ. τὴν καρδίαν; Test. Napht. 7: 4 ἐκαιόμην τοῖς σπλάγχνοις. PGrenf. I 1, 9 [II BC] συνοδηγὸν ἔχω το πολὺ πῦρ τὸ ἐν τῇ ψυχῇ μου καιό-

μενον. Cf. Ps 38: 4. On the variants s. in addition to the comm. WCAllen, JTS 2, '01, 299).

2. *burn* (*up*) act. trans. (Hom. +; Job 15: 34) MPol 18: 1. Pass. intr. *be burned* (Is 5: 24; Jos., Ant. 4, 248 [ἡ παιδίσκη] καιέσθω ζῶσα) J 15: 6; Hs 4: 4. The stones being burned Hv 3, 2, 9; 3, 7, 2 are to be understood as representing apostates.—MPol 12: 3a. σὰρξ καιομένη 15: 2. δεῖ με ζῶντα καυθῆναι *I must be burned alive* 5: 2; cf. 12: 3b (Ael. Aristid. 36, 67 K.=48 p. 465 D.: καυθήσεσθε ζῶντες; 45 p. 74 D.; Appian, Hann. 31, §132 ζῶντας ἔκαυσε). The mng. is disputed in ἐὰν παραδῶ τὸ σῶμά μου ἵνα καυθήσομαι (v.l. καυχήσωμαι; s. καυχάομαι 1) 1 Cor 13: 3. Most scholars in this connection think of martyrdom (most recently Ltzm., JSickenberger, H-D Wendland.—Cf. e.g. Da 3: 19f; 2 Macc 7: 5; 4 Macc 6: 26; 7: 12; Jos., Ant. 17, 167. Also Dio Chrys. 7[8], 16 μαστιγούμενον κ. τεμνόμενον κ. καόμενον).—JWeiss (in Meyer⁹) and FJDölger (Antike u. Christentum I '29, 254-70) prefer to interpret it as voluntary self-burning (Diod. S. 17, 107, 1-6 Κάλανος; Lucian, M. Peregr., cf. ch. 20 καύσων ἑαυτόν; RFick, D. ind. Weise Kalanos u. s. Flammentod: NGG, Phil.-hist. Kl. '38; NMacnicol, ET 55, '43/'44, 50-2). KLSchmidt (TW III 466-9) leaves the choice open betw. the two possibilities mentioned.— Preuschen (ZNW 16, '15, 127-38) interprets it to mean *brand, mark as a slave by branding,* i.e., to sell oneself as a slave, and present the purchase price to charity (for the idea s. 1 Cl 55: 2). M-M. B. 75.*

κἀκεῖ adv. (formed by crasis [on crasis in the NT cf. HermvSoden, D. Schriften d. NT I 2, '11, 1380f] fr. καὶ ἐκεῖ. Found Eratosth. p. 22, 11; 31, 10; Diod. S. 4, 34, 1; 4, 85, 5; Att. inscr. fr. I BC [Meisterhans³-Schw.]; 3 Macc 7: 19; in other LXX pass. in individ. mss. [Thackeray 138]; Jos., Ant. 16, 299).

1. *and there* Mt 5: 23; 10: 11; 28: 10 (v.l. καὶ ἐκεῖ); Mk 1: 35; 14: 15 v.l. (for καὶ ἐκεῖ); J 11: 54; Ac 14: 7; 22: 10; 25: 20; 27: 6; AP 18: 33.

2. *there also* Mk 1: 38 v.l. (for καὶ ἐκεῖ); Ac 17: 13. κἀκεῖ δέ *but there also* 1 Cl 41: 2.*

κἀκεῖθεν adv. (formed by crasis fr. καὶ ἐκεῖθεν. Inscr. fr. Athens in Dit., Syll.³ 640, 8 [175/4 BC]; not LXX [Thackeray 138]).

1. of place *and from there* (Lucian, Dial. Deor. 7, 4; Jos., Ant. 14, 379) Mk 9: 30; Lk 11: 53; Ac 7: 4; 14: 26; 16: 12; 20: 15; 21: 1; 27: 4; 28: 15; MPol 7: 1.

2. of time (ἐκεῖθεν in this mng. in Diod. S. and Cass. Dio) *and then* Ac 13: 21.*

κἀκεῖνος, η, ο (formed by crasis fr. καὶ ἐκεῖνος; X., Cyr. 5, 5, 29 codd.; Diod. S. 3, 17, 5; 4, 84, 4; 11, 56, 8; PPar. 2 col. 15 [before 165 BC]; Wsd 18: 1; Is 57: 6; 2 Macc 1: 15 [cf. Thackeray 138]).

1. denoting what is relatively more distant—a. *and that one, and he* Lk 11: 7; 22: 12; J 10: 16; Ac 18: 19; Hb 4: 2. After ταῦτα *this . . . and that, the one . . . and the other* Mt 23: 23; Lk 11: 42.

b. *that one also, also he* (Lucian, Dial. Deor. 2, 2; 7, 3) Ac 15: 11; 1 Cor 10: 6. κἀκεῖνοι δέ Ro 11: 23.

2. denoting what is relatively closer—a. *and he, and it* (*that*) Mt 15: 18; Mk 16: 11; J 7: 29; 19: 35 v.l. (for καὶ ἐ.).

b. *he also, he too* (Jos., Ant. 14, 474) Mk 12: 4f; 16: 13; Lk 20: 11; J 6: 57; 14: 12; 17: 24; Ac 5: 37; 2 Ti 2: 12.*

κἀκεῖσε adv. (formed by crasis fr. καὶ ἐκεῖσε; Appian, Iber. 26 §103; Herodian 4, 8, 6; Jos., Ant. 7, 327) *and there, and thither,* always w. ὧδε (Aesop 62 Halm) Hm 5, 2, 7; s 6, 1, 6; 6, 2, 7; 9, 3, 1.*

κακία, ας, ἡ (Theognis, Pre-Socr.+; Dit., Syll.³ 1268, 18 κακίας ἀπέχου; pap., LXX, En., Ep. Arist., Philo, Joseph., Test. 12 Patr.) *badness, faultiness.*

1. in the moral sense—**a.** *depravity, wickedness, vice* gener. opposed to virtue (X., Mem. 1, 2, 28; Aristot., Rhet. 2, 6; Cicero, Tusc. 4, 15; Appian, Bell. Civ. 4, 129 §544 κακία-ἀρετή; Herm. Wr. 9, 4b; Dit., Syll. s. above; Sb 4127, 6; Wsd 7: 30; 12: 2, 10; Sir 14: 6, 7 al.; LXX; oft. Philo; Jos., Ant. 8, 252) περισσεία κακίας *excess of wickedness* Js 1: 21. δεσμὸς κακίας *fetter of wickedness* IEph 19: 3. W. πονηρία in the same general mng. (cf. Ael. Aristid. 33 p. 625 D.; Sir 25: 17, 19) 1 Cor 5: 8. πάσης κ. πλήρης 1 Cl 45: 7. τῇ κακίᾳ νηπιάζειν *be a child as far as wickedness is concerned* i.e., have as little wickedness as a child 1 Cor 14: 20; cf. Hs 9, 29, 1; 3. μετανόησον ἀπὸ τ. κακίας σου ταύτης Ac 8: 22; cf. 2 Cl 10: 1. ὡς ἐπικάλυμμα ἔχοντες τ. κακίας τὴν ἐλευθερίαν *use freedom as a cloak for wickedness* 1 Pt 2: 16.

b. a special kind of moral inferiority, w. other deficiencies, someth. like *malice, ill-will, malignity* (Diod. S. 1, 1; PReinach 7, 15 [II BC]; POxy. 1101, 7; Philo) w. other vices Ro 1: 29; Eph 4: 31; Col 3: 8; Tit 3: 3; 1 Pt 2: 1; B 20: 1; D 5: 1. τὸ στόμα σου ἐπλεόνασεν κακίαν 1 Cl 35: 8 (Ps 49: 19). Cf. B 2: 8 (Zech 8: 17).

2. *trouble, misfortune* (Thu. 3, 58, 1 opp. ἡδονή; 1 Km 6: 9; Eccl 7: 14 ἐν ἡμέρᾳ κακίας; 12: 1; Sir 19: 6; Am 3: 6; 1 Macc 7: 23; Jos., Ant. 1, 97) ἀρκετὸν τῇ ἡμέρᾳ ἡ κ. αὐτῆς *each day has enough trouble of its own* Mt 6: 34—GBaumbach, Das Verständnis des Bösen in den synopt. Evv., '63. M-M.*

κακοδιδασκαλέω (Sext. Emp., Math. 2, 42; s. κακοδιδασκαλία and καλοδιδάσκαλος) *teach evil* τινά to someone τὰς ἀναιτίους ψυχάς *to innocent souls* 2 Cl 10: 5.*

κακοδιδασκαλία, ας, ἡ *evil* or *false teaching* IPhld 2: 1 (=κακὴ διδασκαλία IEph 16: 2).*

κακοήθεια, ας, ἡ (X., Pla. et al.) *malice, malignity, craftiness* (so Polyb. 5, 50, 5; Vett. Val. 44, 20; PGrenf. I 60, 13 [cf. Sb 5112, 15]; Esth 8: 12f; 3 Macc 3: 22; Jos., Ant. 1, 50; 16, 68, C. Ap. 1, 222 [w. φθόνος]) in a catalogue of vices (Epistle 43 of Apollonius of Tyana [Philostrat. I 354, 6]: φθόνου, κακοηθείας, μίσους, διαβολῆς, ἔχθρας) Ro 1: 29; 1 Cl 35: 5 (Aristot., Rhet. 2, 13 p. 1389b, 20f defines it thus: ἔστι κακοήθεια τὸ ἐπὶ τὸ χεῖρον ὑπολαμβάνειν ἅπαντα; Ammonius [100 AD] p. 80 Valck. defines it as κακία κεκρυμμένη. Cf. 4 Macc 1: 4; 3: 4). M-M.*

κακοήθης, ες (Pla., Menand. et al.; Vett. Val. 47, 2; 4; PGiess. 40 II, 11; 4 Macc 1: 25; 2: 16; Philo, Somn. 2, 192; Jos., Ant. 1, 42) *malicious, spiteful* D 2: 6.*

κακολογέω (Lysias 8, 5; Plut., Vett. Val. et al.; PFay. 12, 15 [II BC]; PRyl. 150, 9; LXX) *speak evil of, revile, insult* τινά someone (Jos., Ant. 20, 180) Mk 9: 39. πατέρα ἢ μητέρα Mt 15: 4; Mk 7: 10 (both Ex 21: 16; cf. Pr 20: 9a; Ezk 22: 7). τὶ someth. τὴν ὁδὸν *the Way* (i.e. Christianity) Ac 19: 9. Abs. D 2: 3. M-M.*

κακοπάθεια, ας, ἡ (Tdf., BWeiss, vSoden after AL) and **κακοπαθία, ας, ἡ** (W-H., Nestle after BP. This spelling in the inscr. since III BC; also BGU 1209, 7 [23 BC]), which may differ fr. the first form in formation as well as spelling (cf. W-S. §5, 13c, p. 44f); both occur in the pass. sense as *suffering, misfortune, misery* that come to a person (Thu. 7, 77, 1 al.; Mal 1: 13; 2 Macc 2: 26f; Ep. Arist. 208; Philo, De Jos. 223), as well as in the active mng. *suffering* that a person endures, *a strenuous effort* that one makes, or *perseverance* that he practices (Polyb. 3, 42,

9; 4, 8, 3; Plut., Numa 3, 5; Vett. Val. 277, 16; 4 Macc 9: 8; Ep. Arist. 92; 259. The inscr. since Dit., Or. 244, 12 [III BC]; s. the editor's note. Also the papyrus mentioned above. Cf. Dssm., NB 91f [BS 263f]; Thieme 29). The latter mng. is apparently the preferred one in later times, and is hence to be accepted in Js 5: 10, where it has the further advantage of fitting better into the context. Differently GBjörck, Con. Neot. 4, '40, 3, who takes κ. w. μακροθ. as hendiadys. M-M.*

κακοπαθέω 1 aor. ἐκακοπάθησα, imper. κακοπάθησον.

1. *suffer misfortune* (X., Mem. 1, 4, 11; Polyb. 3, 72, 5; Teles 61, 6; Musonius 28, 9; Vett. Val. 106, 10; Zen.-P. 14, 17 [=Sb 6720—257/6 BC]; PLond. 98 recto, 73; PRyl. 28, 84; Jon 4: 10; Ep. Arist. 241; Philo, Somn. 2, 181; Jos., Ant. 12, 336, C. Ap. 2, 203) 2 Ti 2: 9; Js 5: 13; 2 Cl 19: 3.

2. *bear hardship patiently* (Aristot., Eth. Nic. 10, 6 p. 1176b, 29; Appian, Bell. Civ. 5, 87 §364; Philo, Virt. 88; Jos., Ant. 10, 220) 2 Ti 4: 5. M-M.*

κακοπαθία s. κακοπάθεια.

κακοποιέω 1 aor. ἐκακοποίησα (Aeschyl.+; inscr., pap., LXX).

1. intr. *do wrong, be an evil-doer* or *a criminal* (X., Oec. 3, 11; PHib. 59, 10 [III BC]; Pr 4: 16; Test. Ash. 2: 8) 1 Pt 3: 17; 3 J 11. Even Mk 3: 4=Lk 6: 9 could belong here. But in these pass. the word may possibly mean

2. *harm, injure* (X., Mem. 3, 5, 26 al.; Musonius 32, 17; Dit., Syll.³ 736, 103; 1243, 15; Ep. Arist. 164; 168; Gen 31: 7; Num 35: 23). In all four NT pass. it is contrasted w. ἀγαθοποιέω. M-M.*

κακοποιός, όν (Pind.+) *doing evil* (Aristot., Eth. Nic. 4, 9 p. 1125a, 18f; Polyb. 15, 25, 1; Sallust. 9 p. 18, 19; Pr 12: 4) subst. *evil-doer, criminal, sorcerer* (NEB) (schol. on Nicander, Alex. 569; PMich. 149 [II AD], 10; 16 al.; Pr 24: 19; J 18: 30 v.l.; 1 Pt 2: 12; 4: 15. Opp. ἀγαθοποιός 2: 14 (Artem. 4, 59 p. 238, 9; 11). M-M.*

κακός, ή, όν (Hom.+; inscr., pap., LXX, En., Ep. Arist., Philo, Joseph., Test. 12 Patr.) *bad, worthless, inferior.*

1. in the moral sense *bad, evil* (Hom.+; LXX)—**a.** of pers. ὁ κ. δοῦλος *the bad slave* Mt 24: 48. κ. ἐργάτης *evil-doer* Phil 3: 2. Subst. without art. (Sir 20: 18) Rv 2: 2. κακοὺς κακῶς ἀπολέσει Mt 21: 41 (cf. Hipponax [VI BC] 27 D.²; Soph., Phil. 1369; Aristippus in Diog. L. 2, 76 κακοὶ κακῶς ἀπόλοιντο; Nicol. Dam.: 90 fgm. 66, 33 Jac.; Cebes 21; Alciphron 2, 2, 1 κακὸς κακῶς ἀπόλοιτο; Jos., Ant. 2, 300; 7, 291; 12, 256; Dit., Syll.³ 526, 46f [III BC] ἐξόλλυσθαι κακῶς κακούς; POxy. 1238, 5 κακὸς κακῶς ἀπόλ.).

b. of the characteristics, actions, emotions, plans, etc., of men (POxy. 532, 22 [II AD] ὑπὸ κακοῦ συνειδότος κατεχόμενος; 2 Macc 5: 8; 4 Macc 17: 2) διαλογισμοὶ *evil thoughts* Mk 7: 21. ἐπιθυμία *base desire* (Menand., fgm. 535, 7; Pr 12: 12) Col 3: 5; ἔργον κ. *bad deed* Ro 13: 3. ὁμιλίαι *bad company, evil associations* 1 Cor 15: 33 (s. ἦθος). διδασκαλία IEph 16: 2; cf. 9: 1.

c. neut. as subst. (Hom.+; inscr., pap., LXX, Philo) τὸ κακόν *evil, what is contrary to law; crime, sin* J 18: 23; Ro 7: 21 (Maximus Tyr. 34, 2a: the soul falls victim to [the] κακόν, contrary to its own efforts and in spite of its struggles); 16: 19; 1 Cor 13: 5; Hb 5: 14; 1 Pt 3: 10f (Ps 33: 15); 3 J 11. Perh. also Ro 14: 20 (s. 2 below). οὐδὲν κ. *nothing wrong* Ac 23: 9. Pl. *evil deeds* (Ael. Aristid. 45 p. 74 D.) Ro 1: 30; 1 Cor 10: 6; Js 1: 13 (s. ἀπείραστος); πάντα τὰ κ. *all evils* 1 Ti 6: 10.—κακὸν ποιεῖν *do* (what is) *evil* (Menand., Sam. 307 J.; Plut., Mor. 523A) Mt 27: 23; Mk 15: 14; Lk 23: 22; J 18: 30; 2 Cor 13: 7; 1 Pt 3: 12

(Ps 33: 17). Also τὸ κ. ποιεῖν Ro 13: 4a. τὰ κ. ποιεῖν (Pt 16: 12) 3: 8; cf. GP 4: 13. (τὸ) κ. πράσσειν Ro 7: 19; 13: 4b. κατεργάζεσθαι τὸ κ. 2: 9.

2. *evil, injurious, dangerous, pernicious* (Pr 16: 9 ἡμέρα κ.) ἕλκος κ. καὶ πονηρόν Rv 16: 2. κ. θηρία Tit 1: 12 (cf. POxy. 1060, 7 ἀπὸ παντὸς κακοῦ ἑρπετοῦ. On transfer to human beings s. θηρίον 2). Subst. of harmful things, conditions, etc. τὸ κακόν (*the*) *evil* (Susario Com. [VI BC] κακὸν γυναῖκες; Fgm. Iamb. Adesp. 29 Diehl δῆμος ἄστατον κακόν; Ps.-Pla., Eryxias 8 p. 395E: opp. τὸ ἀγαθόν; Apollon. Rhod. 3, 129; Theocr. 14, 36; Plut., Lysander 18, 9 of ἄγνοια; Maximus Tyr. 24, 4a μέγιστον κακὸν ἀνθρώπῳ ἐπιθυμία; Philo, Rer. Div. Her. 287 [λιμὸς] . . . κακὸν χεῖρον) of the tongue ἀκατάστατον κακόν Js 3: 8 (s. ἀκατάστατος). (τὰ) κακά *misfortunes* (Appian, Iber. 79, §338; Maximus Tyr. 41, 3a ff; schol. on Soph., Trach. 112 p. 286 Papag.; Is 46: 7; Ep. Arist. 197; 207; Jos., Bell. 6, 213, Ant. 3, 86) Lk 16: 25; Ac 8: 24 D; 2 Cl 10: 1. κακόν τι πάσχειν *suffer harm* Ac 28: 5 (cf. Jos., Ant. 12, 376). πράσσειν ἑαυτῷ κ. *do harm to oneself* 16: 28. τί κ. ἐστιν; w. inf. foll. *what harm is there?* MPol 8: 2. It may be that Ro 14: 20 (s. 1c above) κ. τῷ ἀνθρώπῳ *harmful for the man* belongs here.

3. Certain passages fall betw. 1 and 2; in them the harm is caused by evil intent, so that 1 and 2 are combined: *evil, harm, wrong* Ro 12: 21a, b (cf. the proverb s.v. ἰάομαι 2. Also Polyaenus 5, 11 οὐ κακῷ κακὸν ἠμυνάμην, ἀλλ᾽ ἀγαθῷ κακόν; but cf. SRobertson, ET 60, '48/'49, 322). κακά τινι ποιεῖν Ac 9: 13 (the dat. as Vi. Aesopi I c. 11; Witkowski 64, 12 [95 BC] ἡμῖν κακὸν ἐποίησεν. Cf. Bl-D. §157). κακόν τινι ἐργάζεσθαι Ro 13: 10. κακά τινι ἐνδείκνυσθαι 2 Ti 4: 14. (τινί) κακὸν ἀντὶ κακοῦ ἀποδιδόναι (cf. Paroem. Gr.: Apostol. 18, 33 χρὴ μὴ τὸ κακὸν διὰ κακοῦ ἀμύνασθαι) Ro 12: 17; 1 Th 5: 15; 1 Pt 3: 9.—WGrundmann, TW III 470-83; WFLofthouse, Poneron and Kakon in O and NT: ET 60, '48/'49, 264-8; GBaumbach s.v. κακία. M-M. B. 1177.**

κακοτεχνία, ας, ἡ (Pla.+; inscr., pap.) *craftiness, deceit* pl. *intrigues* (Lucian, Calumn. 12, Alex. 4) of the devil, w. ἐνέδραι IPhld 6: 2.—IPol 5: 1, where there is no ref. to the devil, and where Polycarp is advised to make κακοτεχνίαι the subject of preaching, the word seems to mean *evil arts*, i.e. the arts and trades which are forbidden for a Christian, esp. magic. Cf. Zahn, Ign. von Ant. 1873, 321; Lghtf. and Hdb. ad loc.*

κακουργέω (Eur., Thu.+; inscr., pap.; Ep. Arist. 271) *treat badly* (Jos., Bell. 2, 277, Ant. 2, 101 al.) pass. *be badly treated* of the soul κακουργουμένη σιτίοις καὶ ποτοῖς ἡ ψυχή *the soul when badly treated w. respect to food and drink, when stinted in food and drink* Dg 6: 9.*

κακοῦργος, ον (Soph., Hdt.+; Sib. Or. 5, 386; 419) usu. as subst. ὁ κ. *criminal, evil-doer* (Thu. 1, 134, 4 al.; Menand., Dyscolus 258; Dit., Or. 669 17 [I AD]; PLille 7, 20 [III BC]; PFay. 108, 11; LXX; Philo, In Flacc. 75; Jos., Ant. 2, 59), one who commits gross misdeeds and serious crimes (Diod. S. 20, 81, 3 of pirates; Ep. Socr. 30, 6 w. παράνομος; Syntipas p. 61, 7; 114, 1 w. λῃστής) Lk 23: 32f, 39 (Plut., Mor. 554B); 2 Ti 2: 9; GP 4: 10, 13; 7: 26; GOxy 5. M-M.*

κακουχέω (since Teles p. 34, 8; pap. [in marriage contracts]) *maltreat, torment* pass. (Diod. S. 3, 23, 3; 19, 1, 4; Cass. Dio 35, 9; Plut., Mor. 114E; 3 Km 2: 26) Hb 11: 37; 13: 3. M-M.*

κακόω fut. κακώσω; 1 aor. ἐκάκωσα; pf. pass. inf. κεκακῶσθαι.

1. *harm, mistreat* w. acc. (Hom.+; PTebt. 407, 9 [II AD]; LXX; Philo, Spec. Leg. 2, 135; Jos., Vi. 121) Ac 7: 6 (Gen 15: 13), 19; 12: 1; 18: 10; 1 Pt 3: 13. Pass. 1 Cl 16: 7 (Is 53: 7).

2. *make angry, embitter* τὰς ψυχάς τινων κατά τινος *poison the minds of some persons against another* Ac 14: 2 (cf. Jos., Ant. 16, 10; pass., 16, 205; 262; Ps 105: 32). M-M.*

κακῶς adv. (Hom.+; inscr., pap., LXX; Ep. Arist. 37; Philo; Jos., Ant. 11, 161, Vi. 192) *badly*.

1. in the physical sense κ. ἔχειν *be ill, sick* (ἔχω II 1) Mt 4: 24; 8: 16; 9: 12; 14: 35; 17: 15; Mk 1: 32, 34; 2: 17; 6: 55; Lk 5: 31; 7: 2. κ. πάσχειν (Aeschyl., Prom. 759; Polyb. 3, 90, 13) *suffer severely* Mt 17: 15 v.l. δαιμονίζεσθαι *be severely tormented by a demon* 15: 22.—κακοὺς κ. ἀπολέσει (κακός 1a) 21: 41.

2. in the moral sense: κ. διακονεῖν Hs 9, 26, 2. κ. λαλεῖν *speak wrongly, wickedly* (1 Macc 7: 42) J 18: 23. Also κ. εἰπεῖν (Libanius, Or. 51 p. 9, 11 F. [opp. ἐπαινεῖν]; Jos., Ant. 6, 299) w. acc. *against* or *about someone* (Pittacus in Diog. L. 1, 78 φίλον μὴ λέγειν κακῶς; Diod. S. 27, 4, 4; Artem. 3, 48; Lucian, Pisc. 6; Procop. Soph., Ep. 161 p. 596) Ac 23: 5 (Ex 22: 27; Is 8: 21). κ. αἰτεῖσθαι *ask with wrong motives* Js 4: 3. M-M.*

κάκωσις, εως, ἡ (Thu.+; Vett. Val. index; PSI 158, 16; LXX; Philo; Jos., Bell. 1, 444, Ant. 13, 151; Test. Napht. 4: 2) *mistreatment, oppression* (Appian, Samn. 2 §2; Sextus 96) Ac 7: 34 (Ex 3: 7). W. πληγή 1 Cl 16: 4 (Is 53: 4). M-M.*

καλάμη, ης, ἡ (Hom.+; pap., LXX) *stalk, straw* as a building material (cf. Diod. S. 5, 21, 5 οἰκήσεις ἐκ τῶν καλάμων ἢ ξύλων) 1 Cor 3: 12 (collective singular, as Arrian, Ind. 27, 9); the mng. *stubble* (Hom.+, pap.) is poss., but less likely. M-M.*

κάλαμος, ου, ὁ (Pind., Hdt.+; pap., LXX, Joseph., loanw. in rabb.).

1. *reed* (Theophrastus [RStrömberg, Theophrastea '37, 100f]; 3 Km 14: 15; Job 40: 21), swaying in the wind (Lucian, Hermot. 68 ἐοικὼς . . . καλάμῳ . . . πρὸς πᾶν τὸ πνέον καμπτομένῳ) Mt 11: 7; Lk 7: 24; easily broken κ. συντετριμμένος *a bent reed* Mt 12: 20 (cf. Is 42: 3 and s. PvanDijk, Het gekrookte riet en de rookende vlaswiek [Mt 12: 18 vv.]: Geref. Theol. Tijdschr. 23, '23, 155-72).

2. *stalk, staff* (cf. Artem. 2, 48 p. 150; 4 Km 18: 21 ἡ ῥάβδος ἡ καλαμίνη=Jos., Ant. 10, 7 κάλαμος) Mt 27: 29f, 48; Mk 15: 19, 36; GP 3: 9.

3. *measuring rod* (PRyl. 64, 2; Ezk 40: 3ff; 42: 16ff) Rv 11: 1; 21: 15f.

4. *reed pen* (Pla., Phaedr. 61 p. 276C; Plut., Demosth. 29, 4; Lucian, Hist. Conscr. 38; Themist., In Constant. p. 31C ἐν καλάμῳ καὶ μέλανι; PGrenf. II 38, 7 [81 BC]; POxy. 326; 521, 21; Ps 44: 2; 3 Macc 4: 20) 3 J 13. M-M. B. 1290.*

καλάνδαι, ῶν, αἱ (Lat. loanw.: calendae.—Dionys. Hal. 6, 48; 8, 55; 9, 67; 16, 3; Plut., Numa 3, 6, Mar. 12, 3; inscr. [indices in Dit., Syll.³, Or.]; pap. [Preisigke, Wörterb. III p. 90]; Jos., Ant. 14, 228; loanw. in rabb.) *the calends*, the first day of the month in the Roman calendar πρὸ ἐννέα καλανδῶν Σεπτεμβρίων=on *August 24* IRo 10: 3. πρὸ ἑπτὰ καλ. Μαρτίων *on February 23* MPol 21.*

καλέω impf. ἐκάλουν; fut. καλέσω (Jos., Ant. 11, 266.—Bl-D. §74, 1; Mlt.-H. 242); 1 aor. ἐκάλεσα; pf. κέκληκα, pass. κέκλημαι; 1 aor. pass. ἐκλήθην; 1 fut. pass. κληθήσομαι (W-S. §15). (Hom.+; inscr., pap., LXX, En., Ep. Arist., Philo, Joseph., Test. 12 Patr.).

1. *call*—**a**. *call by name, name*—**α**. *call* (to someone) abs. (opp. ὑπακούειν; cf. PHamb. 29, 3 [89 AD] κληθέντων τινῶν καὶ μὴ ὑπακουσάντων) 1 Cl 57: 4 (Pr 1: 24).

β. *call, address as, designate as* w. double acc. αὐτὸν καλῶμεν κύριον 2 Cl 4: 1; cf. Mt 22: 43, 45; 23: 9 (here the sense supplies the second acc.: *you are to call no one your father*); Lk 20: 44; Ac 14: 12; Ro 9: 25; Hb 2: 11; 1 Pt 1: 17 P⁷²; 3: 6. A voc. can take the place of the second acc. τί με καλεῖτε κύριε, κύριε; Lk 6: 46. Pass. καλεῖσθαι ὑπὸ τῶν ἀνθρώπων ῥαββί Mt 23: 7. ὑμεῖς μὴ κληθῆτε ῥαββί *you are not to have people call you 'rabbi'* vs. 8; vs. 10. Cf. Lk 22: 25; Js 2: 23. ὁ οἶκός μου οἶκος προσευχῆς κληθήσεται Mt 21: 13; Mk 11: 17 (both Is 56: 7). κληθήσονται υἱοὶ θεοῦ Ro 9: 26 (Hos 2: 1).

γ. *name, provide with a name* w. double acc. ἐκάλουν αὐτὸ Ζαχαρίαν *they were going to name him Z.* Lk 1: 59 (on ἐπὶ τῷ ὀνόματι τ. πατρός *after his father*['s name] cf. 1 Esdr 5: 38; Sir 36: 11 and s. Hs 9, 17, 4).—Pass. *be given a name, be named* (Jos., Ant. 1, 34) κληθήσεται Ἰωάννης *his name is to be John* Lk 1: 60; cf. vs. 62. σὺ κληθήσῃ Κηφᾶς J 1: 42. Also of localities Mt 27: 8; Ac 1: 19.—*Have as a name, be called* (Lucian, Jud. Voc. 7 Λυσίμαχος ἐκαλεῖτο ὃς καλεῖται τ. ὀνόματι τούτῳ *who bears this name* Lk 1: 61. Also of localities (Appian, Bell. Civ. 3, 70 §289; 3, 91 §374; Dit., Syll.³ 599, 5 τὸ φρούριον ὃ καλεῖται Κάριον) πόλις Δαυὶδ ἥτις καλεῖται Βηθλέεμ Lk 2: 4. Cf. Ac 28: 1; Rv 11: 8.—Lk, Ac, Rv, GP add to a pers. or thing the name or surname which (he, she) it bears, by means of the pres. pass. ptc. (cf. Dit., Syll.³ 685, 39 νῆσον τὴν καλουμένην Λεύκαν; 826ε, 22; 1063, 5; PPetr. II 45 II, 20; BGU 1000, 6; PGoodspeed 9, 4; Ostraka II 1210, 4). The name: ἀδελφὴ καλουμένη Μαριάμ *a sister named Mary* Lk 10: 39 (Maspéro 23, 16 τ. ἀδελφὴν καλουμένην Πρόκλαν). Cf. 19: 2; Ac 7: 58; Rv 19: 11, also 12: 9. πόλις καλουμένη Ν. Lk 7: 11; cf. 9: 10; 19: 29; 21: 37; 23: 33; Ac 1: 12; 3: 11; 8: 10; 9: 11; 10: 1; 27: 8, 14, 16; Rv 1: 9; 16: 16; GP 6: 24. The surname (2 Macc 10: 12 Πτολεμαῖος ὁ καλούμενος Μάκρων; 1 Macc 3: 1; Jos., Ant. 13, 367): Σίμων ὁ κ. ζηλωτής *Simon the Zealot* Lk 6: 15. Cf. 8: 2; 22: 3; Ac 1: 23; 13: 1; 15: 22, 37.—The example of the OT (Gen 17: 19; 1 Km 1: 20; Hos 1: 9; 1 Macc 6: 17) has influenced the expr. καλεῖν τὸ ὄνομά τινος, the name added in the acc. καλέσεις τὸ ὄνομα αὐτοῦ Ἰησοῦν Mt 1: 21. Cf. vs. 23 (Is 7: 14); 25; Lk 1: 13, 31. Pass. Lk 2: 21; Rv 19: 13.

δ. Very oft. the emphasis is to be placed less on the fact that the name is such and such, than on the fact that the bearer of the name actually is what the name says about him. The pass. *be named* thus approaches closely the mng. *to be*, and it must be left to the feeling of the interpreter whether this transl. is to be attempted in any individual case (Quint. Smyrn. 14, 434 οὔτ' ἔτι σεῖο κεκλήσομαι= I do not wish any longer to be yours, i.e., your daughter). Among such pass. are these: Ναζωραῖος κληθήσεται *he is to be a Nazarene* Mt 2: 23. υἱοὶ θεοῦ κληθήσονται 5: 9. Cf. vs. 19a, b. υἱὸς ὑψίστου κληθήσεται (in parallelism w. ἔσται μέγας) Lk 1: 32; cf. vss. 35, 36, 76; 2: 23. οὐκέτι εἰμὶ ἄξιος κληθῆναι υἱός σου 15: 19, 21. οὐκ εἰμὶ ἱκανὸς καλεῖσθαι ἀπόστολος 1 Cor 15: 9. ἵνα τέκνα θεοῦ κληθῶμεν, καὶ ἐσμέν *that we should be called children of God; and so we really are* 1 J 3: 1 (καλεῖσθαι beside εἶναι as Plut., Demetr. 25, 6). ἄχρις οὗ τὸ σήμερον καλεῖται *as long as it is called 'today', as long as 'today' lasts* Hb 3: 13 (WLLorimer, NTS 12, '66, 390f, quoting Pla., Phaedo 107c).—Here we may also class ἐν Ἰσαὰκ κληθήσεταί σοι σπέρμα *in (through) Isaac you are to have your descendants* Ro 9: 7 (Gen 21: 12).

b. *invite* (Hom.+; pap.; 2 Km 13: 23; Esth 5: 12;

LRobert, Nouvelles Inscriptions de Sardes, 1, '64, p. 9, lines 1-4) τινά *someone* εἰς (τοὺς) γάμους *to the wedding* (Diod. S. 4, 70, 3; POxy. 1487, 1 καλεῖ σε Θέων εἰς τοὺς γάμους) Mt 22: 3b, 9; Lk 14: 8; cf. J 2: 2; Rv 19: 9. Abs. *invite* τινά *someone* 1 Cor 10: 27 (Diog. L. 7, 184 of Chrysippus: ἐπὶ θυσίαν [sacrificial meal] ὑπὸ τῶν μαθητῶν κληθῆναι). Cf. Lk 7: 39; 14: 9, 12f. οἱ κεκλημένοι *the invited guests* (Demox. in Athen. 3, 59 p. 102c; Jos., Ant. 6, 48; 52) Mt 22: 3 (οἱ κεκλημένοι εἰς τ. γάμους as Diphilus Com. [IV/III BC] 17: 1), 4, 8; Lk 14: 7, 17; cf. vs. 24.

c. *call together* τινάς *people* workmen to be paid Mt 20: 8. Slaves to receive orders 25: 14; Lk 19: 13. Guests, when the banquet is ready, Mt 22: 3a.

d. *summon* τινά *someone* (Appian, Bell. Civ. 4, 82 §347; 4, 86 §362; 1 Macc 1: 6) ἀπέστειλαν πρὸς αὐτὸν καλοῦντες αὐτόν *they sent to him to summon him* Mk 3: 31. Cf. Mt 2: 7. Of God: the Israelites fr. Egypt (as a type of Christ) Mt 2: 15.—*Call upon* (Himerius, Or. 48 [= Or. 14], 10; 4 Macc 3: 19) Hb 11: 8.

e. a legal t.t. *call in, summon before a court* (oft. pap.) τινά *someone* (Jos., Ant. 14, 169) Ac 4: 18; 24: 2.—The transition to mng. 2 is well illustrated by Mt 4: 21; Mk 1: 20, where the summons is also a call to discipleship.

2. From the mngs. 'summon' and 'invite' there develops the fig. *call* (Paus. 10, 32, 13 οὓς ἂν ἡ Ἶσις καλέσῃ δι' ἐνυπνίων; Ael. Aristid. 30, 9 K.=10 p. 116 D.: ὑπὸ τοῦ θεοῦ κληθείς) τινα εἴς τι *someone to someth.*, in the usage of the NT, as well as that of the LXX, of the choice of pers. for salvation: God (much more rarely Christ) calls εἰς τὴν αὐτοῦ δόξαν 1 Pt 5: 10. εἰς ζωὴν αἰώνιον 1 Ti 6: 12. εἰς κοινωνίαν τοῦ υἱοῦ αὐτοῦ *to fellowship with his son* 1 Cor 1: 9. ἐκ σκότους εἰς τὸ αὐτοῦ φῶς *from darkness to his light* 1 Pt 2: 9. ἀπὸ σκότους εἰς φῶς 1 Cl 59: 2. διὰ τ. χάριτος αὐτοῦ Gal 1: 15. εἰς ὃ ἐκάλεσεν ὑμᾶς διὰ τοῦ εὐαγγελίου ἡμῶν εἰς περιποίησιν δόξης *for this he called you through our preaching (of the gospel), namely to obtain the glory* 2 Th 2: 14. Without further modification Ro 8: 30; 9: 24; 1 Cor 7: 17f, 20-2, 24; 2 Cl 9: 5; 10: 1.—κ. κλήσει ἁγίᾳ *call with a holy calling* 2 Ti 1: 9. ἀξίως τῆς κλήσεως ἧς (attraction, instead of ἣν) ἐκλήθητε *worthily of the calling by which you were called* Eph 4: 1 (on the constr. cf. W-S. §24, 4b; Rob. 478). Of God: ὁ καλῶν τινα Gal 5: 8; 1 Th 5: 24. Abs. ὁ καλῶν Ro 9: 12. ὁ καλέσας τινά Gal 1: 6; 1 Pt 1: 15; 2 Pt 1: 3. Likew. of Christ ὁ καλέσας τινά 2 Cl 5: 1. Pass. οἱ κεκλημένοι *those who are called* Hb 9: 15. κεκλημένοι ὑπὸ τοῦ θεοῦ δι' αὐτοῦ (=Ἰ. Χρ.) 1 Cl 65: 2. οἱ κεκλημένοι ὑπ' αὐτοῦ (=υἱοὶ τ. θεοῦ) Hs 9, 14, 5. οἱ κληθέντες Hm 4, 3, 4.—More closely defined: ἐν δικαιοσύνῃ B 14: 7 (Is 42: 6). ἐπ' ἐλευθερίᾳ (s. ἐλευθερία) Gal 5: 13. οὐκ ἐπὶ ἀκαθαρσίᾳ ἀλλ' ἐν ἁγιασμῷ *not for impurity, but in consecration* 1 Th 4: 7. ἐν εἰρήνῃ *in peace* 1 Cor 7: 15. ἐκλήθητε ἐν μιᾷ ἐλπίδι τῆς κλήσεως ὑμῶν *you were called in one hope, that belongs to your call* Eph 4: 4. ἡμεῖς διὰ θελήματος αὐτοῦ (=θεοῦ) ἐν Χριστῷ Ἰησοῦ κληθέντες 1 Cl 32: 4. εἰς εἰρήνην τοῦ Χριστοῦ ἐν ἑνὶ σώματι Col 3: 15. ἐν τῇ σαρκί 2 Cl 9: 4. πόθεν ἐκλήθημεν καὶ ὑπὸ τίνος καὶ εἰς ὃν τόπον 1: 2. εἰς τοῦτο ἵνα *for this reason, that* 1 Pt 3: 9; cf. 2: 21. Of Christ: οὐκ ἦλθον καλέσαι δικαίους ἀλλὰ ἁμαρτωλούς (+εἰς μετάνοιαν t.r.) Mt 9: 13; Mk 2: 17; 2 Cl 2: 4; cf. 7. Lk 5: 32. Of God: ἐκάλεσεν ἡμᾶς οὐκ ὄντας *he called us when we did not exist* 2 Cl 1: 8. ὁ καλῶν τὰ μὴ ὄντα ὡς ὄντα *the one who calls into being what does not exist* Ro 4: 17 (Philo, Spec. Leg. 4, 187 τὰ μὴ ὄντα ἐκάλεσεν εἰς τὸ εἶναι. Cf. Is 41: 4; 48: 13). κ. εἰς μετάνοιαν *call to repentance* Lk 5: 32.—Of the call to an office by God Hb 5: 4.—JHempel,

Berufung u. Bekehrung (also GBeer-Festschr.) '35; HWildberger, Jahwes Eigentumsvolk usw. '60; KL Schmidt, TW III 488-92. M-M. B. 1276.

καλλιέλαιος, ου, ἡ the cultivated olive tree (opp. ἀγριέλαιος wild olive tree; this contrast as early as Aristot., De Plant. 1, 6 p. 820b, 40) Ro 11: 24.—OPlasberg, APF 2, '03, 219ff; here, fr. a Strassburg pap. the words εἰς καλλιελαίαν. The word as adj. also Zen.-P. 21=Sb 6727, 3 [257/6 BC]. Cf. Nicetas, De Manuele Comn. 4, 4 (Migne, S. Gr. 139, 480) of a Hungarian son-in-law at the Byzantine court: μὴ τὸν ἐκ φυταλιᾶς ἑτεροφύλου ῥάδαμνον εἰς καλλιέλαιον μετεγκεντρίζειν πιότατον. An expression very much like this Psellus p. 99, 17.—Lit. on ἀγριέλαιος and ἐλαία 2. M-M.*

κάλλιον s. καλῶς 7.

καλλονή, ῆς, ἡ (Eur., Hdt.+; Dit., Syll.³ 783, 46; 51; PFlor. 65, 12; PLond. 1764, 4; LXX; En. 24, 2; Ep. Arist.) beauty of the future glory 1 Cl 35: 3. τὸ μεγαλεῖον τῆς κ. τοῦ θεοῦ great beauty 49: 3.*

κάλλος, ους, τό (Hom.+; LXX; Philo; Jos., C. Ap. 1, 195; 2, 167; Test. 12 Patr.) beauty 1 Cl 16: 3 (Is 53: 2); Hv 1, 1, 2; 3, 10, 5; s 9, 13, 9. κ. τῆς ὄψεως of the face AP 3: 7.*

καλλωπίζω (X., Pla.; LXX; Jos., Ant. 1, 121) beautify the face (Galen, Protr. 10 p. 34, 2 J.), also gener. adorn, beautify (Philostrat., Ep. 27 p. 239, 28 ἵππους) GOxy 38.*

καλοδιδάσκαλος, ον (not found elsewh.) teaching what is good of the old women Tit 2: 3.*

Καλοὶ λιμένες, Καλῶν λιμένων, οἱ Fair Havens, the name, not found elsewh. in ancient sources, of a bay on the south coast of Crete, near the city of Lasaea Ac 27: 8. Diod. S. 3, 44, 7 describes a harbor named Charmuthas as λιμὴν κάλλιστος. In general καλός is not infrequently found as an adj. applied to a serviceable harbor: Diod. S. 5, 10, 1 λιμέσι καλοῖς; 5, 13, 3. καλὸς λιμήν is a coastal place on the Black Sea in Arrian, Peripl. 19, 5.—Breusing 158f. Maps in JSmith, Voyage and Shipwreck of St. Paul⁴ 1880, 82f; HBalmer, D. Romfahrt d. Ap. Pls. '05, 313f (lit.).*

καλοκἀγαθία, ας, ἡ (Aristoph., X.+; Diod. S. 1, 79; Epict. 1, 7, 8; 4, 1, 164; inscr., pap., 4 Macc, Ep. Arist. Oft. in Philo) nobility of character, excellence Js 5: 10 v.l.; IEph 14. 1.—JJüthner, Alois Rzach-Festschr. '30, 99ff.*

καλοποιέω (Etym. Mag. 189, 24; PLond. 1338, 28; Lev 5: 4 v.l. Swete; cf. Philo, Somn. 2, 296 v.l.) do what is right, good 2 Th 3: 13. M-M.*

καλός, ή, όν (Hom.+; inscr., pap., LXX, Ep. Arist., Philo, Joseph., Test. 12 Patr.).
1. beautiful in outward appearance λίθοι κ. beautiful stones Lk 21: 5. Of pers. (Lucian, Tim. 16, Dial. Mort. 1, 3) Hs 9, 3, 1.
2. of quality, in accordance w. the purpose of someth. or someone: good, useful.
a. in the phys. sense free from defects, fine, precious opp. σαπρός (PLond. 356, 4ff [I AD]) of fish Mt 13: 48; of a tree and its fruit 12: 33; Lk 6: 43. Opp. πονηρός of fruits Mt 7: 17ff. Otherw. of fruits (Menand., Mon. 303 καρπός) 3: 10; Lk 3: 9. τράγοι B 7: 6, 10. γῆ good soil Mt 13: 8, 23; Mk 4: 8, 20; Lk 8: 15. σπέρμα Mt 13: 24, 27, 37f. οἶνος J 2: 10a, b. μαργαρῖται fine pearls Mt 13: 45. Subst. (Epict. 1, 12, 12 καλόν τι ἐλευθερία ἐστί) καλὸν τὸ ἅλας salt is a good thing Mk 9: 50; Lk 14: 34.

b. morally good, noble, praiseworthy, contributing to salvation etc. ἔργον καλόν, ἔργα καλά (Hippocr., Ep. 27, 30; Athen. 1, 15 p. 8F ἐν τοῖς καλοῖς ἔργοις; Sib. Or. 3, 220) Mt 5: 16; 26: 10; Mk 14: 6; J 10: 32f; 1 Ti 5: 10, 25; 6: 18; Tit 2: 7, 14; 3: 8a, b, 14; Hb 10: 24; 1 Pt 2: 12. καλόν· ἐν καλῷ Gal 4: 18b; cf. Pol 6: 3. (Opp. κακόν) διάκρισις καλοῦ τε καὶ κακοῦ Hb 5: 14 (Sext. Emp., Pyrrh. Hyp. 3, 19 διάκρισις τῶν τε καλῶν κ. κακῶν). τὸ κ. (opp. κακ.) ποιεῖν (2 Ch 14: 1; 31: 20) Ro 7: 21; 2 Cor 13: 7. Without the contrast w. κακ. Gal 6: 9; Js 4: 17. κατεργάζεσθαι Ro 7: 18. ἐργάζεσθαι B 21: 2. καλὰ προνοεῖσθαι ἐνώπιόν τινος (Pr 3: 4) Ro 12: 17; 2 Cor 8: 21.—ἀναστροφή (cf. 2 Macc 6: 23) Js 3: 13; 1 Pt 2: 12. συνείδησις Hb 13: 18 (cf. PReinach 52, 5 οὐ καλῷ συνειδότι χρώμενοι). μαρτυρία κ. a good reputation 1 Ti 3: 7. ἐν καρδίᾳ καλῇ κ. ἀγαθῇ in a noble and good heart Lk 8: 15 (w. ἀγ., as freq. in secular wr., also Jos., Ant. 4, 67; 10, 188 al.). Of the law morally unobjectionable (Maximus Tyr. 20, 9a) Ro 7: 16; cf. 1 Ti 1: 8. οὐ καλὸν τὸ καύχημα ὑμῶν 1 Cor 5: 6. τοῦτο καλὸν καὶ ἀπόδεκτον ἐνώπιον τ. θεοῦ 1 Ti 2: 3.

c. in every respect unobjectionable, blameless, excellent —α. of pers. κύριος B 7: 1; cf. 19: 11 (κ. of God: Celsus 4, 14). μαθητής IPol 2: 1. ἱερεῖς IPhld 9: 1; διάκονος Χριστοῦ Ἰ. 1 Ti 4: 6a. οἰκονόμος 1 Pt 4: 10; στρατιώτης Χρ. Ἰ. 2 Ti 2: 3. ποιμήν J 10: 11a, b, 14.
β. of things μέτρον good, full measure Lk 6: 38. θεμέλιος 1 Ti 6: 19. βαθμός 3: 13. ἔργον office 3: 1. παραθήκη 2 Ti 1: 14. ὁμολογία 1 Ti 6: 12b, 13. ἀγών 6: 12a; 2 Ti 4: 7. στρατεία 1 Ti 1: 18. κτίσμα (3 Macc 5: 11) 4: 4. πλάσμα B 6: 12. καλὸν θεοῦ ῥῆμα (cf. Josh 21: 45; 23: 15; Zech 1: 13) Hb 6: 5. τὸ καλὸν ὄνομα τὸ ἐπικληθὲν ἐφ' ὑμᾶς Js 2: 7 (in a Pompeian graffito [Dssm., LO 237; LAE 277] a lover speaks of the καλὸν ὄνομα of his beloved). τὸ καλόν what passes the test 1 Th 5: 21.

3. καλόν (ἐστιν) it is good (Pr 17: 26.— בָּרַח =καλόν loanw. in rabb.).
a. it is pleasant, desirable, advantageous (Jos., Bell. 4, 163) Mt 17: 4; 18: 8f; Mk 9: 5; Lk 9: 33.—1 Cor 7: 26a.
b. it is morally good, pleasing to God, contributing to salvation 1 Cor 7: 1 (cf. Gen 2: 18), 8, 26b; Hb 13: 9.—οὐ καλόν Mt 15: 26; Mk 7: 27.
c. καλόν ἐστιν αὐτῷ μᾶλλον it is better for him Mk 9: 42; cf. 1 Cor 9: 15. καλόν (σοί) ἐστιν...ἤ it is a(n) (greater) advantage (for you) . . . , than (cf. Jon 4: 3) Mt 18: 8f; Mk 9: 43, 45, 47 (cf. Bl-D. §190, 2). καλὸν ἦν αὐτῷ it would have been better for him Mt 26: 24; Mk 14: 21 v.l. (Bl-D. §358, 1; 360, 1). Without the copula 1 Cl 51: 3; IRo 6: 1.—That which is good or better is added in the inf., which forms the subject of καλόν ἐστιν (Appian, Bell. Civ. 3, 13 §46 καλὸν εἴη τινὶ θνῄσκειν; Polyaenus 8, 9, 2; Jos., Bell. 1, 650; 4, 163) Mt 15: 26; 18: 8f; Mk 7: 27; Gal 4: 18a; also the articular inf. (Menand., Monost. 283; 291 καλὸν τὸ θνῄσκειν al.). κ. τὸ μὴ φαγεῖν κρέα Ro 14: 21; 1 Cor 7: 26b; w. acc. and inf. ἡμᾶς ὧδε εἶναι Mt 17: 4; Mk 9: 5; Lk 9: 33; cf. Mk 9: 43, 45, 47; B 21: 1; with εἰ Mt 26: 24; Mk 9: 42; 14: 21; with ἐάν 1 Cor 7: 8. Cf. Bl-D. §409, 3; KBeyer, Semitische Syntax im NT '62, 76-8.— Superlat. κάλλιστος, η, ον very beautiful (Diod. S. 5, 13, 1; Jos., Ant. 16, 142) τὰ κάλλιστα the specially good ones Mt 13: 48 D. ὑπόδειγμα an illustrious example 1 Cl 6: 1.—WGrundmann, TW III 539-53. M-M. B. 1176; 1191.**

κάλυμμα, ατος, τό (Hom.+; Delian inscr. [III BC]: Bull. de corr. hell. 32, 13 no. 3a, 42; LXX; Philo, Leg. All. 2, 53; Test. Judah 14: 5) covering, veil.
1. lit., of the veil w. which Moses covered his face (Ex 34: 33-5) 2 Cor 3: 13.—καλ. is v.l. for ἐξουσία 1 Cor 11: 10.

2. fig. *veil, covering* that prevents right understanding τὸ αὐτὸ κ. ἐπὶ τῇ ἀναγνώσει...μένει *the same veil remains when...is read* 3: 14. κ. ἐπὶ τὴν καρδίαν κεῖται *a veil lies on the mind* vs. 15; περιαιρεῖται τὸ κ. *the cover is taken away* vs. 16 (cf. Ex 34: 34).—JGöttsberger, D. Hülle des Mos. nach Ex 34 u. 2 Cor 3: BZ 16, '24, 1-17; SSchulz, Die Decke des Moses (2 Cor 3: 7-18), ZNW 49, '58, 1-30; AOepke, TW III 560-2. M-M. B. 436.*

καλύπτω fut. καλύψω; 1 aor. ἐκάλυψα; pf. pass. ptc. κεκαλυμμένος (in Hom., Pind., trag.; rare in Attic prose [X., Cyr. 5, 1, 4 κεκαλυμμένη, Equ. 12, 5]; on the other hand, in Aristot., Plut., Paus., Ael. Aristid. [Anz 271], also inscr., PRainer 239, 5; LXX; En. 14, 13; Ep. Arist. 87; Test. Levi 10: 3; Philo, Leg. All. 3, 158; Jos., Ant. 13, 208; Sib. Or. 4, 53. Prob. passed into the Koine fr. Ionic [Nägeli 27]) *cover, hide, conceal*.

1. lit. τινά *cover someone (up)* Lk 23: 30, perh. in the special sense *bury* (exx. in HGüntert, Kalypso '19, 31ff. Also inscr. in Ramsay, Phryg. I 2 p. 476 no. 342). τί τινι *cover someth. w. someth.* (Num 4: 12) λύχνον σκεύει κ. *a lamp with a vessel* 8: 16 (cf. Num 4: 9). Of a boat καλύπτεσθαι ὑπὸ τῶν κυμάτων *be covered by the waves* Mt 8: 24 (Achilles Tat. 3, 2, 6; Ps 77: 53; Ex 15: 10).

2. fig.—**a.** *cover (up), remove from sight* πλῆθος ἁμαρτιῶν (cf. Ps 84: 3; s. also Philosophenspr. p. 490, 56 ἡ εὔνοια τὴν ἁμαρτίαν περιστέλλει) 1 Pt 4: 8; Js 5: 20; 1 Cl 49: 5; 2 Cl 16: 4 (for the last 4 cf. also Prov 10: 12). ἁμαρτίας Dg 9: 3.

b. *hide* (Hos 10: 8) pf. pass. *be hidden* (=unknown) of the gospel: κεκαλυμμένον τὸ εὐαγγέλιον ἡμῶν 2 Cor 4: 3; cf. Mt 10: 26 (Vi. Aesopi W. c. 110 πάντα τὰ καλυπτόμενα ὁ χρόνος εἰς φῶς ἄγει).

c. *veil* of the καρδία (q.v. 1bβ) of uncomprehending disciples: *was our heart not veiled?* Lk 24: 32 D. M-M. B. 849.*

καλῶς adv. (Hom.+; inscr., pap., LXX; En. 102, 9; Ep. Arist., Philo, Joseph., Test. 12 Patr.; loanw. in rabb.) *well, beautifully*.

1. *fitly, appropriately, in the right way, splendidly* (Is 23: 16) κ. πάντα πεποίηκεν *he has done everything very well, indeed* Mk 7: 37. διὰ τὸ κ. οἰκοδομῆσθαι αὐτήν *because it was well built* Lk 6: 48; σὺ κάθου ὧδε κ. *be seated here in a good place* Js 2: 3 (Lucian, Paras. 50 καλῶς κατακείμενος; cf. Field, Notes 236), unless κ. here =*please* (so JHRopes, ICC '16 ad loc.; RSV). σὺ κ. εὐχαριστεῖς *you may give thanks well enough* 1 Cor 14: 17; ἐτρέχετε κ. *you were running so well* Gal 5: 7. Cf. 1 Ti 3: 4, 12, (Diog. L. 1, 70 Chilon advises that one must μανθάνειν τῆς αὑτοῦ οἰκίας καλῶς προστατεῖν) 13; 5: 17. In these pass. the mng. approaches 2.

2. in a moral sense *commendably, in a manner free from objection* ζηλοῦσιν οὐ καλῶς Gal 4: 17. κ. ἀναστρέφεσθαι (s. ἀναστρέφω 2 ba) Hb 13: 18.

3. *beneficially, acceptably* κ. ποιεῖν *do good* (Lucian, Ep. Sat. 3, 31) Mt 12: 12. W. dat. (Zeph 3: 20) τοῖς μισοῦσιν ὑμᾶς Mt 5: 44 v.l.; Lk 6: 27. κ. λέγειν w. acc. *speak well of* 6: 26. Cf. Bl-D. §151, 1 κ. ἔχειν *be well, in good health* Mk 16: 18 (ἔχω II 1).

4. *rightly, correctly*—**a.** κ. ποιεῖν *do what is right, act rightly, do well* (Dio Chrys. 30[47], 25; Ael. Aristid. 36 p. 685 D.) 1 Cor 7: 37f; Js 2: 8, 19. W. ptc. (Appian, Bell. Civ. 3, 75 §305; Sb 5216, 7 [I BC]; 6265, 8 [I AD]; POsl. 55, 7; Jos., Ant. 11, 279; Bl-D. §414, 5; Rob. 1121) *be kind enough to do someth.* Ac 10: 33; Phil 4: 14; 3 J 6; *do well in doing someth.* 2 Pt 1: 19; GEg 1 c.

b. w. verbs of speaking, hearing, understanding κ. ἀποκρίνεσθαι *answer rightly, well* Mk 12: 28. εἰπεῖν (Simpli-

cius in Epict. p. 44, 50; 47, 51; Jos., Ant, 8, 380) Ll: 20: 39; J 4: 17. λαλεῖν Ac 28: 25. λέγειν J 8: 48; 13: 13; cf. 18: 23. προφητεύειν *prophesy rightly* Mt 15: 7; Mk 7: 6; cf. κ. ἀκούειν *hear correctly* (Menand., fgm. 623) Hm 4, 3, 2. κ. ἐπίστασθαί τι *know someth. well* 1 Cl 53: 1 (Appian, Bell. Civ. 2, 98 §406 εἰδέναι κ.; Procop. Soph., Ep. 18 ἴσθι κ.=you may be quite sure). Papias 2: 3.

c. as exclamation καλῶς *quite right, that is true, well said* (Arrian, Cyneg. 18, 1; Ael. Aristid. 33 p. 617 D.; 45 p. 44; Lucian, Dial. Deor. 20, 10; 3 Km 2: 18) Mk 12: 32; Ro 11: 20.

5. *fortunately* καλῶς ἐξέφυγες *fortunately you escaped* Hv 4, 2, 4.

6. ironically (Soph., Ant. 739; Aelian, V.H. 1, 16 al.) κ. ἀνέχεσθε *you put up with it well enough* 2 Cor 11: 4 (cf. PKirberg, Die Toleranz der Korinther '10; JGMachen, The Origin of Paul's Religion '21, 131ff). κ. ἀθετεῖν Mt 7: 9. But here perh. the καλῶς of vs. 6, which is not ironic, may require a similar interpr., and the sentence should be a question: *are you doing the right thing in rejecting God's commandment?*

7. comp. κάλλιον (for the superl., as Galen, Protr. 8 p. 24, 19 J.; cf. Bl-D. §244, 2) ὡς καὶ σὺ κ. ἐπιγινώσκεις *as also you know very well* Ac 25: 10. M-M.**

καμάρα, ας, ἡ (Hdt.+; Dit., Syll.³ 1243, 4; pap.) *arch, vault, vaulted room* (Is 40: 22) MPol 15: 2 (on the mngs. of the Carian word fr. which it may be derived s. FSolmsen, BPhW 26, '06, 853).*

καμέ s. κἀγώ.

κάμηλος, ου, ὁ and ἡ (Aeschyl., Hdt.; inscr., pap., LXX, Philo; Jos., Ant. 1, 252; 8, 167 al.) *camel* τρίχες καμήλου *camel's hair* Mt 3: 4; Mk 1: 6; GEb 2b (here there is naturally no thought of the soft τρίχες καμήλου from which the garments of distinguished people are made acc. to Ctesias in Apollon. Paradox. 20). Proverbially εὐκοπώτερόν ἐστιν κάμηλον διὰ τρήματος ῥαφίδος εἰσελθεῖν *it is easier for a camel to go through a needle's eye* of someth. impossible, w. the contrast emphasized greatly (for a proverb comparing someth. very small w. someth. very large, cf. Lucian, Ep. Sat. 1, 19 μύρμηξ ἢ κάμηλος): the largest animal and the smallest opening Mt 19: 24; Mk 10: 25; Lk 18: 25 (s. GAicher, Kamel u. Nadelöhr '08; ERostan, Les Paradoxes de Jésus '08, 11ff; WBleibtreu [s. μισέω] 17f; RLehmann u. KLSchmidt, ThBl 11, '32, 336-40; EBöklen, Deutsches Pfarrerblatt 37, '33, 162-5; CLattey, Verb. Dom. 31, '53, 291f; EBest, ET 82, '70, 83-9. S. κάμιλος). To strain out a gnat τὴν δὲ κ. καταπίνειν *but swallow a camel*=be over-zealous in small matters and careless in important ones Mt 23: 24 (s. κώνωψ.—The camel is contrasted w. the elephant in Phalaris, Ep. 86; Ps.-Libanius, Ep. 1597, 1 ed. F. XI p. 593, 1.—Artem. 4 p. 199, 9 explains that camel and elephant would have the same mng. in figurative interpretation).—OMichel, TW III 597-9. M-M. B. 189f.*

κάμιλος, ου, ὁ *rope, ship's cable* is the rdg. of several mss., and of several versions (e.g. Armenian; FHerklotz, BZ 2, '04, 176f) Mt 19: 24; Mk 10: 25; Lk 18: 25 instead of κάμηλος (q.v.). κάμιλος, found only in Suidas 1967c and the scholia on Aristoph. (Vesp. 1035), may be ancient (Bl-D. §24; Mlt.-H. 72—'Byzantine invention'), but has no place in the NT.—EBoisacq, Dict. Étym. '16 p. 403, 1; Bröndal, BPhW 38, '18, 1081f; PHaupt, Camel and Cable: AJPh 45, '24, 238ff.*

κάμινος, ου, ἡ (Aeschyl., Hdt.+; pap., LXX, Joseph., loanw. in rabb. Cf. Bl-D. §49, 1) *oven, furnace* καπνὸς κάμινου (Ex 19: 18; Job 41: 12) Rv 9: 2. κ. τοῦ πυρός *fiery oven, kiln* (Da 3: 6, 11 al.) of potters' kilns (Sir 27: 5) 2 Cl 8: 2. Of smelters' furnaces (X., Vectig. 4, 49; Diod. S. 5, 13, 1; 5, 27, 2; Ezk 22: 20, 22) Rv 1: 15; MPol 15: 2. κ. πυρός as the place of the fiery trial of the three young men (Da 3: 20ff; 4 Macc 16: 21; Jos., Ant. 10, 213) 1 Cl 45: 7. Fig. of hell: Mt 13: 42, 50. M-M.*

κάμμύω 1 aor. ἐκάμμυσα (contracted fr. καταμύω; despite the protests of Phryn. 339f L., it spread fr. the poets [Batr. 191; Alexis Com. 319; Apollon. Dysc., Synt. 323, 22; 326, 9] into popular speech: X., Cyr. 8, 3, 27 codd.; Hero Alex. I p. 412, 5; PGM 4, 586; 958; 1057; 1069; 7, 855; 13, 945; LXX [Thackeray 99]; Philo [s. below].—W-S. §5, 22c; 12, 6; Bl-D. §69, 1; Mlt.-H. 92; 243; 398; Thumb 63f; Crönert 64, 4) *close (the eyes)* τοὺς ὀφθαλμούς (so Ps.-Callisth. 3, 33, 27 w. ref. to the dying Alexander) fig. (Philo, Somn. 1, 164 καμμύσαντες τὸ τ. ψυχῆς ὄμμα; La 3: 45) of an attitude of hostility toward the gospel Mt 13: 15; Ac 28: 27 (both Is 6: 10). M-M.*

κάμνω 2 aor. ἔκαμον; pf. κέκμηκα Rv 2: 3 t.r., ptc. κεκμηκώς.
1. *be weary, fatigued* (so Hom. +; PGiess. 47, 8; PLond. 1708, 50; 4 Macc 3: 8) τῇ ψυχῇ *in spirit* Hm 8: 10. Here we may think of a weariness of the soul (for weariness of this kind cf. Diod. S. 20, 96, 3 κάμνοντες ταῖς ψυχαῖς; Philo, Post. Cai. 31 [the wandering soul]; Jos., Ant. 2, 290). But another interpretation may perh. be derived from Diod. S. 15, 38, 2: κάμνειν τῇ συνεχείᾳ τῶν πολέμων=be tired or weary of the continued succession of the wars. Then the κάμνοντες τῇ ψυχῇ would be not the weary in spirit but those who are tired of living (as Job 10: 1).—Hb 12: 3 it may be abs. (as Jos., Vi. 209), i.e., if τ. ψυχαῖς ὑμῶν belongs w. ἐκλυόμενοι. Of documents σχεδὸν ἐκ τοῦ χρόνου κεκμηκότα *almost worn out by time* MPol 22: 3; Epil Mosq 4 (Diog. L. 9, 113: in Timon's house the works of the poets lie about unprotected, many of them half eaten up [ἡμίβρωτα]).
2. *be ill* (so Soph., Hdt. +) ὁ κάμνων *the sick man* (Strabo 8, 6, 15; Musonius 20, 8 θεραπείαν τῶν καμνόντων; Epict., fgm. 19; M. Ant. 6, 55; Dit., Syll.³ 943, 9f ἐπιμέλεια τῶν καμνόντων; Philo, Omn. Prob. Lib. 12, Migr. Abr. 124 τὴν τῶν καμνόντων σωτηρίαν) Js 5: 15. Another possibility here is the mng. *be hopelessly sick, waste away* (schol. on Apollon. Rhod. 4, 1091 p. 306, 23 W.; Jos., Ant. 8, 266), or even—3. *die* (Crinagoras [I BC/I AD] no. 25, 1; Diod. S. 14, 71, 1 and 4; Dionys. Byz. §109; 110; Epigr. Gr. 321, 8 καμών=dead; grave inscr. [AD Nock, Sallust. p. XXXIII 94 ὅταν κάμῃς, τοῦτο τὸ τέλος=when you die, this is the end]; Wsd 4: 16; 15: 9; Sib. Or. 3, 588). M-M. B. 540.*

κάμοί s. κἀγώ.

Καμπανός, ή, όν *Campanian,* belonging to the district of Campania in south central Italy (incl. Naples, Cumae) ἡ ὁδὸς ἡ Κ.=*Via Campana* (CIL VI 2107, 3; 14; 10250; 29772) Hv 4, 1, 2. Cf. MDibelius, Hdb. ad loc.*

κάμπτω fut. κάμψω; 1 aor. ἔκαμψα (Hom. +; pap., LXX, Philo).
1. trans. *bend, bow* τὸν τράχηλον *the neck* B 3: 2 (Is 58: 5). γόνυ (also pl.) *bend the knee* as a sign of (religious) devotion (LXX) τινί *before someone* (Sib. Or. 3, 616f) τῇ Βάαλ Ro 11: 4. Also πρός τινα Eph 3: 14. Fig. κ. τὰ γόνατα τῆς καρδίας (s. γόνυ) 1 Cl 57: 1.
2. intr. (Polyaenus 3, 4, 3 ἔκαμψεν=he bent inward) *bend (itself)* ἐμοὶ κάμψει πᾶν γόνυ *every knee shall bend before me* Ro 14: 11 (Is 45: 23). ἐν τῷ ὀνόματι Ἰησοῦ *when the name of Jesus is proclaimed* Phil 2: 10 (also infl. by Is 45: 23). M-M. B. 542.*

κἄν (formed by crasis fr. καὶ ἐάν, quotable Hes. +; pap., LXX [Thackeray 138]; Philo, Aet. M. 134 al.; Joseph.; Sib. Or. 3, 18; Bl-D. §18; 371; Rob. 208) particle w. subjunctive.
1. *and if* Mt 10: 23 v.l.; Mk 16: 18; Lk 6: 34 D; 13: 9 (here the suppression of the first apodosis [καλῶς ἔχει] is quite class.; Bl-D. §454, 4; cf. Rob. 1023); J 8: 55; Js 5: 15; Hs 5, 5, 4. κἄν . . . δέ *but if* IRo 5: 2. κἄν . . . κἄν . . . *and if . . . and if . . . and if* 1 Cor 13: 2f in text and v.l. κἄν . . . κἄν *and if . . . and if, whether . . . whether* (Demosth. 25, 15; Test. Jud. 15: 5, Reub. 4: 7) Lk 12: 38.
2. *even if, even though* οὐ μόνον . . . ἀλλὰ κἄν εἴπητε *not only . . . but even if you say* Mt 21: 21.—26: 35 (κἄν δέῃ ἀποθανεῖν as Jos., Ant. 6, 108; 11, 228); J 8: 14; 10: 38; 11: 25; 2 Cl 19: 3; *even if . . . just* Hb 12: 20.
3. *(even) if only, at least* (Soph., El. 1483; Lucian, Tim. Tim. 20 κἄν ὄνος 'at least a donkey'; PReinach 52, 6; POxy. 1593, 5ff κἄν νῦν 'now at least') κἄν τῶν ἱματίων *even his clothes* Mk 5: 28. Cf. 6: 56 (cf. Athen. 5, 212ғ ἑκάστου σπεύδοντος κἄν προσάψασθαι τῆς ἐσθῆτος). κἄν ἡ σκιά *at least his shadow* Ac 5: 15. κἄν ὡς ἄφρονα δέξασθέ με *accept me at least as a fool* 2 Cor 11: 16.—2 Cl 18: 2; IEph 10: 1. In the apodosis of a conditional sentence 2 Cl 7: 3; GP 12: 52, 54.—κἄν ταῦτα *even if this=this, little though it be* Dg 2: 10 (cf. Lucian, Dial. Mar. 1, 3). M-M.*

Κανά, ἡ indecl. *Cana,* name of a city in Galilee (cf. Jos., Vi. 86), the location of which can no longer be determined. Among the possibilities are the sites now known as Khirbet Kānā=Kānat el Jelīl (Dalman, Orte³ 108ff) and Kefr Kennā (ThaddSoiron, D. Evangelium u. d. hl. Stätten in Palästina '29), or even 'Ain Kānā south of er-Rêne. Place of Jesus' first miracle in J 2: 1, 11 (lit. in Hdb. exc. after J 2: 12; CKopp, The Holy Places of the Gospels, tr. RWalls, '63, 143–54).—4: 46. Home of Nathanael 21: 2; according to many, also Simon Mt 10: 4 (s. Καναναῖος).—Heinz Noetzel, Christus und Dionysus '60. M-M.*

Καναναῖος, ου, ὁ *Cananaean,* surname of the second Simon among the 12 disciples Mt 10: 4; Mk 3: 18 (the t.r. has Κανανίτης in both pass.). Not *from Cana* (Jerome) nor *Canaanite,* but fr. Aram. קַנְאָן *enthusiast, zealot* (cf. Lk 6: 15; Ac 1: 13, where he is called ζηλωτής), prob. because he had formerly belonged to the party of the Zealots (Schürer I⁴ 486f; 573f; 617ff; JKlausner, Jesus v. Naz.² '34, 272ff [Eng. transl. '26, 205f; 284f]; against this view Børge Salomonsen, NTS 12, '66, 164–76); s. FCBurkitt, Syriac Forms of NT Proper Names '12, 5, and Σίμων 2. M-M.*

Κανανίτης, ου, ὁ *Cananite, man from Cana.* Acc. to Strabo 14, 5, 14 one of the two Stoics named Athenodorus received this name to distinguish him fr. the other Ath.; ἀπὸ κώμης τινος (Cana near Tarsus) was added. The t.r. has Κ. in Mt 10: 4; Mk 3: 18 for Καναναῖος, and so interprets it.*

Κανδάκη, ης, ἡ *Candace* (Bion of Soli [II BC], Aethiopica 668 F. 1 Jac. βασιλέως μητέρα καλοῦσι Κ.; Strabo 17, 1, 54 p. 820; Ps.-Callisth. 3, 18; Cass. Dio 54, 5; Pliny, H.N. 6, 35, 7; Sb 8366 [inscr. 109 AD]) title of the queen of Ethiopia (on Egypt. monuments she is called k[e]nt[e]ky) Ac 8: 27.—RPietschmann, Pauly-W. I 1894, 1095ff; Grohmann, ibid. X 2, '19, 1858f; WMaxMüller, Aethiopien '04; GRöder, Klio 12, '12, 72ff; AWikenhauser, Die ApGesch. '21, 361f; StLösch, ThQ 111, '30, 477–519. M-M.*

κανών, όνος, ὁ (Hom. +; inscr., pap., LXX. For the mngs. of the word [basically 'straight rod'] s. ThZahn, Grundriss d. Gesch. d. ntl. Kanons² '04, 1ff; HOppel, ΚΑΝΩΝ: Philol. Suppl. 30, 4, '37; LWenger, Canon: Ak. d. W. Wien, Phil.-hist. Kl. Sitzgsber. 220, 2, '42) the mngs. found in our lit. are:

1. *rule, standard* (Eur., Hec. 602; Demosth. 18, 296; Aeschin., In Ctesiph. 66; Sext. Emp., Log. 2, 3; Ps.-Plut., Consol. ad Ap. 103Α; Epict., index Sch.; Lucian, Pisc. 30; UPZ 110, 58 [164 BC]; PLond. 130, 12; 4 Macc 7: 21; Ep. Arist. 2; Philo; Jos., Ant. 10, 49, C. Ap. 2, 174; Test. Napht. 2: 3) τῷ κανόνι τούτῳ στοιχεῖν Gal 6: 16; Phil 3: 16 t.r.; ἔλθωμεν ἐπὶ τὸν τῆς παραδόσεως ἡμῶν κανόνα 1 Cl 7: 2 (cf. Epict. 1, 28, 28 ἔλθωμεν ἐπὶ τοὺς κανόνας).

2. *sphere* of action or influence, *province, limits* ἐν τῷ κανόνι τῆς ὑποταγῆς ὑπάρχειν 1 Cl 1: 3. παρεκβαίνειν τὸν ὡρισμένον τῆς λειτουργίας κανόνα 41: 1. Cf. 2 Cor 10: 13, 15f.

3. In the second century in the Christian church κ. came to stand for revealed truth, *rule of faith* (Zahn, RE VI 683ff.—Cf. Philo, Leg. All. 3, 233 ὁ διαφθείρων τὸν ὑγιῆ κανόνα τῆς ἀληθείας; Synes., Ad. Paeon. 4 p. 310D τῆς ἀληθείας κανών of mathematics). ἐκκλησιαστικὸς καὶ καθολικὸς κ. Epil Mosq 1.—HWBeyer, TW III 600-6. M-M.*

Καπερναούμ s. Καφαρναούμ.

καπηλεύω (Aeschyl., Hdt. +; inscr., pap.; Philo, Virt. 112, Leg. ad Gai. 203; cf. Dio Chrys. 8, 9) *trade in, peddle, huckster* (of retail trade; cf. the contrast καπηλεία–ἐμπορία Jos., C. Ap. 1, 61) τὶ *someth.*, also fig. (Pla., Prot. 5 p. 313D οἱ τὰ μαθήματα καπηλεύοντες. Sim., Nicol. Dam.: 90 fgm. 132, 2 Jac.; Iambl., Vi. Pyth. 34, 245; Philostrat., Vi. Apoll. 1, 13 τὴν σοφίαν καπηλεύειν) τὸν λόγον τ. θεοῦ 2 Cor 2: 17 (Anon. Vi. Pla. p. 8, 48 Westerm. κάπηλος λόγων). Because of the tricks of small tradesmen (Dio Chrys. 14[31], 37f; Lucian, Hermot. 59 φιλόσοφοι ἀποδίδονται τὰ μαθήματα ὥσπερ οἱ κάπηλοι, . . . δολώσαντες καὶ κακομετροῦντες; Is 1: 22 οἱ κάπηλοί σου τ. οἶνον ὕδατι) the word comes to mean almost *adulterate* (so Vulg., Syr., Goth.).—Hug, Pauly-W. X 2 '19, col. 1888f; HWindisch, TW III 606-9. M-M. B. cf. 821.*

καπνός, οῦ, ὁ (Hom. +; BGU 1026 XXII, 17; LXX; Jos., Ant. 5, 284; 12, 310) *smoke* Rv 9: 2f; 18: 9, 18. ἀναβαίνει (Horapollo 2, 16 εἰς οὐρανόν; Ex 19: 18; Josh 8: 20; Is 34: 10) 8: 4; 9: 2a; 14: 11; 19: 3. καπνὸς καμίνου (Ex 19: 18; Job 41: 12) 9: 2b. Of the cloud of smoke in which God appears (Is 6: 4) 15: 8. W. fire and brimstone (cf. θεῖον) 9: 17f. W. fire and blood ἀτμὶς καπνοῦ *steaming smoke* Ac 2: 19 (Jo 3: 3). M-M. B. 73.*

Καππαδοκία, ας, ἡ (Menand., Kolax fgm. 2, 2; Strabo 11, 13, 15; 12, 2, 11 al.; Joseph., ind.; inscr.) *Cappadocia,* a province in the interior of Asia Minor. Mentioned w. other parts of Asia Minor (Posidon.: 87 fgm. 36, 50 Jac.) Ac 2: 9; 1 Pt 1: 1 (Ps.-Callisth. 2, 11, 1 Alexander sends a circular letter—ἐγκύκλιος ἐπιστολή—to five adjoining satrapies, among them Cappadocia).—JMarquardt, Röm. Staatsverwaltung I² 1881, 365ff; Ramsay, Hist. Geogr. 281ff, Church 443ff.*

καραδοκία, ας, ἡ (Aq.—καραδοκέω Eur., Hdt. +; Jos., Bell. 4, 305; 5, 28, Ant. 17, 86) *eager expectation* Phil 1: 20 v.l. (for ἀποκαραδοκία).*

καρδία, ας, ἡ (since Hom. [καρδίη, κραδίη]. Rather rare in secular wr. in the period of the Gk. Bible [cf. Diod. S. 32, 20; Plut., Mor. p. 30A; 63A; Epict. 1, 27, 21; M. Ant. 2, 3,

3; 7, 13, 3; Ps.-Apollod. 1, 4, 1, 5; Lucian; pap., incl. PGM 5, 157; 13, 263; 833; 1066; s. below 1bη], but common LXX, Test. 12 Patr.; Ep. Arist. 17. On Philo and Joseph. s. ASchlatter, D. Theol. d. Judentums nach d. Bericht d. Jos. '32, 21).

1. *heart* as the seat of physical, spiritual and mental life —a. as the center and source of physical life (Ps 101: 5; 103: 15) ἐμπιπλῶν τροφῆς τὰς κ. *satisfying the hearts w. food* Ac 14: 17. τρέφειν τὰς κ. *fatten the hearts* Js 5: 5.

b. as center and source of the whole inner life, w. its thinking, feeling, and volition (νοῦν κ. φρένας κ. διάνοιαν κ. λογισμὸν εἰπέ τις ποιητής [Hes., fgm. 247 Rz.] ἐν καρδίᾳ περιέχεσθαι), in the case of the natural man as well as the redeemed man.

a. in the all-inclusive sense: said of God or Christ γινώσκειν τὰς καρδίας (cf. 1 Km 16: 7; 1 Ch 28: 9) Lk 16: 15; δοκιμάζειν 1 Th 2: 4; ἐρευνᾶν Ro 8: 27; Rv 2: 23 (νεφροὺς κ. καρδίας as Ps 7: 10; Jer 17: 10; 20: 12). τὰ κρυπτὰ τῆς κ. 1 Cor 14: 25 (cf. Test. Reub. 1: 4). ὁ κρυπτὸς τῆς κ. ἄνθρωπος 1 Pt 3: 4. ἐκ καρδίας *from* the *bottom of the heart*=sincerely (Aristoph., Nub. 86) Ro 6: 17; 1 Pt 1: 22. Also ἀπὸ τῶν καρδιῶν (M. Ant. 2, 3, 3 ἀπὸ καρδίας εὐχάριστος τ. θεοῖς; Lucian, Jupp. Trag. 19; Is 59: 13; La 3: 33) Mt 18: 35. ἐκ καθαρᾶς καρδίας 1 Ti 1: 5; 2 Ti 2: 22. ἐξ ὅλης τ. καρδίας (Test. Levi 13: 1) Ac 8: 37 v.l. Opp. πρόσωπον and καρδία externals and inner attitude of heart (cf. 1 Km 16: 7 ἄνθρωπος ὄψεται εἰς πρόσωπον, ὁ δὲ θεὸς ὄψεται εἰς καρδίαν) 2 Cor 5: 12. The same contrast προσώπῳ οὐ καρδίᾳ *outwardly, not inwardly* 1 Th 2: 17. As the seat of the inner life in contrast to the mouth or lips, which either give expression to the inner life or deny it Mt 15: 8; Mk 7: 6 (both Is 29: 13); Mt 15: 18; Ro 10: 8 (Dt 30: 14); vs. 9f; 2 Cor 6: 11.

β. of the faculty of thought, of the thoughts themselves, of understanding, as the organ of natural and spiritual enlightenment (see the 'poet' under 1b above; Aesop, Fab. 254 P.=232 H.; 3 Km 10: 2; Job 12: 3; 17: 4). In this area κ. may oft. be transl. *mind:* 2 Cor 4: 6; Eph 1: 18; 2 Pt 1: 19. τῇ κ. συνιέναι *understand* Mt 13: 15b; Ac 28: 27b (both Is 6: 10). νοεῖν τῇ κ. *think* J 12: 40b. ἐν τῇ κ. λέγειν (Dt 8: 17; 9: 4; Ps 13: 1. Also Aesop 62 Halm=179 Chambry βοῶν ἐν τῇ καρδίᾳ alternating w. ταῦτα καθ' ἑαυτὸν λέγοντος) *say to oneself,* i.e. think, reflect, without saying anything aloud Mt 24: 48; Lk 12: 45; Ro 10: 6; Rv 18: 7; διαλογίζεσθαι Mk 2: 6, 8; Lk 3: 15; 5: 22; Hv 1, 1, 2; 3, 4, 3. The κ. as the source of διαλογισμοί Mt 15: 19; Mk 7: 21; Lk 2: 35; 9: 47. διαλογισμοὶ ἀναβαίνουσιν ἐν τῇ καρδίᾳ Lk 24: 38. ἀναβαίνει τι ἐπὶ τὴν καρδίαν τινός *someth.* enters *someone's mind*=someone thinks of someth. (s. ἀναβαίνω 2) Ac 7: 23; 1 Cor 2: 9; Hv 3, 7, 2; m 12, 3, 5; s 5, 7, 2. Also of memory Hv 3, 7, 6; m 4, 2, 2; 6, 2, 8. διατηρεῖν ἐν τ. καρδίᾳ Lk 2: 51 (cf. Test. Levi 6: 2). συμβάλλειν vs. 19. ἐνθυμεῖσθαι Mt 9: 4. διακρίνειν Hv 1, 2, 2. —Likew. of a lack of understanding: ἡ ἀσύνετος κ. *the senseless mind* Ro 1: 21; βραδὺς τῇ κ. *slow of comprehension* Lk 24: 25 (cf. Tetr. Iamb. 2, 31a, 6 the mocking words of the fox ὦ ἀνόητε κ. βραδὺ τῇ καρδίᾳ). ἐπαχύνθη ἡ κ. τοῦ λαοῦ Mt 13: 15a; Ac 28: 27a (both Is 6: 10). πωροῦν τὴν κ. J 12: 40a; κ. πεπωρωμένη Mk 6: 52; 8: 17; ἡ πώρωσις τῆς κ. 3: 5; Eph 4: 18. ἀπατᾶν καρδίαν ἑαυτοῦ Js 1: 26; cf. Ro 16: 18. κάλυμμα ἐπὶ τὴν κ. κεῖται 2 Cor 3: 15.—As the seat of thought, κ. is also the seat of doubt διακρίνεσθαι ἐν τῇ κ. Mk 11: 23. διστάζειν Hm 9: 5.—God opens the heart Ac 16: 14 or the eyes of the heart 1 Cl 59: 3 to Christian knowledge.

γ. of the will and its decisions (Diod. S. 32, 20) ἕκαστος καθὼς προῄρηται τῇ κ. *each one as he has made up his mind* 2 Cor 9: 7 (cf. Test. Jos. 17: 3 ἐπὶ προαιρέσει καρδίας). θέτε ἐν ταῖς καρδίαις ὑμῶν (s. 1 Km 21: 13) *make up your minds* Lk 21: 14; cf. Ac 5: 4. πρόθεσις τ. καρδίας 11: 23. βάλλειν εἰς τὴν κ. ἵνα *put it into someone's heart to* J 13: 2. Also διδόναι εἰς τ. κ. (2 Esdr 17 [Neh 7]: 5) w. inf. foll. Rv 17: 17, or πληροῦν τὴν κ. w. inf. foll. Ac 5: 3. Cf. 1 Cor 4: 5; 7: 37; Hb 3: 8 (Ps 94: 8) al. God's law written in the hearts of men Ro 2: 15; 2 Cor 3: 2f; Hb 8: 10 (Jer 38[31]: 33).

δ. of moral decisions, the moral life, of vices and virtues: ἀγνίζειν τὰς κ. Js 4: 8; καθαρίζειν τὰς κ. Ac 15: 9; Hv 3, 9, 8; w. ἀπό τινος Hm 12, 6, 5; καθαρὸς τῇ κ. *pure in heart* (Ps 23: 4) Mt 5: 8; καθαρὰ κ. (Sextus 46b) Hv 4, 2, 5; 5: 7; m 2: 7. ῥεραντισμένοι τὰς κ. ἀπὸ συνειδήσεως πονηρᾶς *with hearts sprinkled clean from a consciousness of guilt* Hb 10: 22. κ. ἄμεμπτος 1 Th 3: 13. ἀμετανόητος Ro 2: 5. κ. πονηρὰ ἀπιστίας Hb 3: 12; λίθιναι κ. B 6: 14 (Ezk 36: 26). γεγυμνασμένη πλεονεξίας *trained in greediness* 2 Pt 2: 14. Cf. Lk 21: 34; Ac 8: 21f. περιτομὴ καρδίας (cf. Jer 9: 25; Ezk 44: 7, 9) Ro 2: 29.—B 9: 1; 10: 12; Ac 7: 51.

ε. of the emotions, wishes, desires (Theognis 1, 366; Bacchylides 17, 18): ἐπιθυμίαι τῶν κ. *desires of the heart* Ro 1: 24. ἐπὶ τὴν κ. σου ἀνέβη ἡ ἐπιθυμία τ. πονηρίας Hv 1, 1, 8; cf. s 5, 1, 5. ἐνθύμησις m 4, 1, 2; 6, 2, 7. μὴ ἀναβαινέτω σου ἐπὶ τὴν κ. περὶ γυναικός m 4, 1, 1; cf. Hv 1, 2, 4; Mt 5: 28.—6: 21; 12: 34; Lk 12: 34; 24: 32 (s. καίω 1b); Js 3: 14; 5: 8. Of joy: ηὐφράνθη ἡ κ. Ac 2: 26 (Ps 15: 9). χαρήσεται ἡ κ. J 16: 22. Of sorrow: ἡ λύπη πεπλήρωκε τὴν κ. 16: 6; λύπη ἐγκάθηται εἰς τὴν κ. *grief sits in the heart* Hm 10, 3, 3. ἡ κ. ταράσσεται (Job 37: 1; Ps 142: 4) J 14: 1, 27; ὀδύνη τῇ κ. Ro 9: 2. συνοχὴ καρδίας *anguish of heart* 2 Cor 2: 4; διαπρίεσθαι ταῖς κ. Ac 7: 54; κατανυγῆναι τὴν κ. 2: 37; συνθρύπτειν τὴν κ. 21: 13. κ. συντετριμμένη *a broken heart* B 2: 10 (Ps 50: 19). παρακαλεῖν τὰς κ. Eph 6: 22; Col 4: 8. Of hope (Ps 111: 7) Hm 12, 5, 2. Of repentance Hv 3, 13, 4; m 5, 1, 7; 12, 6, 1. Of the feeling for good and evil, someth. like *conscience* (1 Km 24: 6; 2 Km 24: 10) 1 J 3: 20, 21 (cf. ASkrinjar, Verb. Dom. 20, '40, 340-50). Of a wish εὐδοκία τῆς κ. (s. εὐδοκία 3) Ro 10: 1. Of a longing for God τὴν κ. ἔχειν πρὸς κύριον Hm 10, 1, 6. ἐπιστρέφεσθαι πρὸς τὸν κύριον ἐξ ὅλης τῆς κ. 12, 6, 2 (cf. 3 Km 8: 48). προσέρχεσθαι μετὰ ἀληθινῆς κ. *with sincere desire* (cf. Is 38: 3; Test. Dan 5: 3 ἀλ. κ.) Hb 10: 22. Cf. the opposite Ac 7: 39.—Also of the wish or desire of God ἀνὴρ κατὰ τὴν κ. (τοῦ θεοῦ) *after God's heart* i.e. *as God wishes him to be* Ac 13: 22 (cf. 1 Km 13: 14).

ζ. esp. also of love (Aristoph., Nub. 86 ἐκ τῆς κ. φιλεῖν; M. Ant. 7, 13, 3 ἀπὸ κ. φιλεῖν τ. ἀνθρώπους) ἀγαπᾶν τινα ἐξ ὅλης τ. καρδίας Mk 12: 30, 33; Lk 10: 27 (cf. Dt 6: 5 and APF 5, '13, 393 no. 312, 9 ἐκ ψυχῆς κ. καρδίας). ἐν ὅλῃ τ. καρδίᾳ Mt 22: 37; εἶναι ἐν τῇ κ. *have a place in the heart* 2 Cor 7: 3; ἔχειν τινὰ ἐν τῇ κ. Phil 1: 7; Hm 12, 4, 3; s 5, 4, 3; cf. m 12, 4, 5.—The opp. κατά τινος ἐν τῇ κ. ἔχειν *have someth. against someone* v 3, 6, 3.

η. of disposition ἁπλότης (τ.) καρδίας (Test. Reub. 4: 1, Sim. 4: 5 al.) Eph 6: 5; Col 3: 22. κ. καὶ ψυχὴ μία Ac 4: 32 (combination of ψυχή and καρδία as PGM 7, 472; Fluchtaf. 3, 15; Dt 11: 18; 1 Km 2: 35; 4 Km 23: 3 and oft. LXX). πραῢς καὶ ταπεινὸς τῇ κ. Mt 11: 29 (cf. Test. Reub. 6: 10).

θ. The human heart as the dwelling-place of heavenly powers and beings (PGM 1, 21 ἔσται τι ἔνθεον ἐν τῇ σῇ κ.): of the Spirit Ro 5: 5; 2 Cor 1: 22; Gal 4: 6; of the Lord Eph 3: 17; of the angel of righteousness Hm 6, 2, 3; 5.

2. fig. *heart* in the sense *interior, center* (Ezk 27: 4, 25; Jon 2: 4; Ps 45: 3; EpJer 19) τῆς γῆς Mt 12: 40.—S., in addition to the works on Bibl. anthropology and psychology (πνεῦμα, end): HKornfeld, Herz u. Gehirn in altjüd. Auffassung: Jahrb. für jüd. Gesch. u. Lit. 12, '09, 81 to 89; ASchlatter, Herz. u. Gehirn im l. Jahrh.: ThHaering-Festschr. '18, 86-94; FBaumgärtel u. JBehm, TW III 609-16; RBultmann, Theologie des NT '48, 216-22 (Paul), Engl. transl., Theol. of the NT, KGrobel, '51, I, 220-227; RJewett, Paul's Anthropological Terms, '71, 305-33. M-M. B. 251.

καρδιογνώστης, ου, ὁ (only in Christian wr., e.g. Ps.-Clem., Hom. 10, 13; other reff. in Haenchen ad loc.) *knower of hearts, one who knows the hearts* of God Ac 1: 24; 15: 8; Hm 4, 3, 4. M-M.*

καροῦχα, ας, ἡ (Sym. Is 66: 20; Chron. Pasch. 571, 7 LDind. [1832] and in Byz. wr.) *carriage* (actually a Celtic word, Lat. carruca) MPol 8: 2f.—AMau, Pauly-W. III 1614f.*

καρπάσινος, η, ον (Dionys. Hal. 2, 68, 5; Strabo 7, 2, 3; Esth 1: 6) *made of fine flax* (Lat. carbasus; פַּרְכָּס) λέντιον κ. (v.l. καρπάσιον) *a fine linen cloth* Hv 3, 1, 4 (Tibullus 3, 2, 21 carbasea lina).—Olck, Pauly-W. III 1572ff.*

Κάρπος, ου, ὁ (Artem. 3, 38; Dit., Syll.² 438, 20; Inschr. aus Hierap. 120; coin fr. Magnesia [Thieme 40]; pap. [Preisigke, Namenbuch]) *Carpus*, a Christian 2 Ti 4: 13. M-M.*

καρπός, οῦ, ὁ (Hom.+; inscr., pap., LXX, Ep. Arist., Philo, Joseph., Test. 12 Patr., Sib. Or.) *fruit* (the sing. used collectively: Diod. S. 3, 24, 1).

1. lit.—a. of the fruits of trees Mt 12: 33; 21: 19; Mk 11: 14; Lk 6: 44; 13: 6f. Of the fruit of the vine (Jos., Ant. 2, 67) Mt 21: 34; Mk 12: 2; Lk 20: 10; 1 Cor 9: 7. Of field crops (Diod. S. 4, 4, 2; Ps.-Phoc. 38; Sib. Or. 4, 16) 2 Ti 2: 6; Js 5:7; συνάγειν τοὺς κ. (Lev 25: 3) Lk 12: 17; cf. J 4: 36; ὅταν παραδοῖ ὁ κ. *when the* (condition of the) *crop permits* Mk 4: 29 ('fruit'=grain as Ps.-Scylax, Peripl. §93 p. 36 Fabr. [πυροὺς κ. κριθάς]). βλαστάνειν τὸν κ. *produce crops* Js 5: 18 (βλαστάνω 1). ποιεῖν κ. (=עָשָׂה פְּרִי) *bear* or *yield fruit* (Gen 1: 11f; 4 Km 19: 30; Ezk 17: 23.—Diosc., Mat. Med. 2, 195) Mt 3: 10 (s. δένδρον); 7: 17ff; 13: 26; Lk 3: 9; 6: 43; 8: 8; 13: 9; Rv 22: 2a. Also διδόναι (=נָתַן פְּרִי; Lev 26: 20; Dt 11: 17; Ps 1: 3; Zech 8: 12) Mt 13: 8; Mk 4: 7f; B 11: 6 (Ps 1: 3); Hs 2: 4. φέρειν (Apollon. Rhod. 4, 1396-99b; Jo 2: 22; Hos 9: 16; Jos., Ant. 3, 11; Sib. Or. 2, 320) Mt 7: 18; J 12: 24; 15: 2, 4. ἀποδιδόναι *bear fruit* (Lev 26: 4) Rv 22: 2b, cf. Hb 12: 11, but *pay* someone *his portion of the fruit* Mt 21: 41. γεννᾶν καρπὸν θανατηφόρον *bear deadly fruit* ITr 11: 1.

b. Hebraistically of offspring ὁ κ. τῆς κοιλίας *the fruit of the womb* (Gen 30: 2; Ps 131: 11; Mi 6: 7; La 2: 20; in the Ps and Mi pass. κοιλία is used of the male and= 'body') Lk 1: 42. Fr. the standpoint of the father: ὁ κ. τῆς ὀσφύος *the fruit of his loins* Ac 2: 30.

2. fig., in the mental and spiritual realm; sometimes the orig. figure is quite prominent; somet. it is more or less weakened.

a. *result, outcome, product* (cf. Epict. 2, 1, 21 τῶν δογμάτων καρπός; Inschr. v. Priene 112, 14 [I BC] μόνη μεγίστους ἀποδίδωσιν καρπούς; Dio Chrys. 23[40], 34 τῆς ἔχθρας καρπός) κ. τοῦ πνεύματος Gal 5: 22 (a list of virtues following a list of vices as Cebes 19, 5; 20, 3; Ael. Aristid. 37, 27 K.=2 p. 287 D.) τοῦ φωτός Eph 5: 9; κ. πολὺν φέρειν *be very fruitful* J 15: 5, 8, 16. κ. δικαιοσύνης *fruit of righteousness* (cf. Epicurus, fgm. 519 δικαιοσύνης καρπὸς μέγιστος ἀταραξία; Am 6: 12; Pr 11: 30; 13: 2; Ep. Arist. 232) Phil 1: 11; Js 3: 18; Hs 9, 19, 2a; κ.

εἰρηνικὸς δικαιοσύνης *peaceful fruit of righteousness* Hb 12:11. κ. ἀληθείας Hs 9, 19, 2b. The outcome of acting is a deed: ἀπὸ τῶν καρπῶν τινος ἐπιγινώσκειν τινά *know someone by his deeds,* as one knows a tree by its fruits Mt 7:16, 20 (Proverbia Aesopi 51 P.: Δῆλος ἔλεγχος ὁ καρπὸς γενήσεται Παντὸς δένδρου ἣν ἔχει φύσιν=its fruit will be a clear proof for every tree of the nature that it has). ποιεῖν τοὺς καρποὺς αὐτῆς (=τῆς βασιλείας τ. θεοῦ) *prove fruitful for the kingdom* 21:43. ποιεῖν καρπὸν ἄξιον τῆς μετανοίας *bear fruit consistent with repentance* 3:8; the pl. in the parallel Lk 3:8 is farther removed fr. the orig. picture: καρποί=ἔργα (cf. Pr 10:16). καρποὶ ἀγαθοί Js 3:17. Cf. Dg 12:1. Of the outcome of life in sin and in righteousness Ro 6:21f (of the results of evil e.g., Oenomaus in Euseb., Pr. Ev. 5, 20, 10); ταχὺς κ. (s. ταχ. 1) 2 Cl 20:3.—Of the proceeds of the collection Ro 15:28.

b. *advantage, gain, profit* (Polyaenus 3, 9, 1 κ. τῆς ἀνδραγαθίας; Ep. Arist. 260 σοφίας κ.; Philo, Fug. 176 ἐπιστήμης; Jos., Ant. 20, 48 εὐσεβείας) κ. ἔργου *gain from the labor* Phil 1:22. οὐ δόμα, ἀλλὰ τὸν καρπόν *not the gift, but the advantage* (accruing to the Philippians fr. their generous giving) 4:17; κ. ἔχειν *have fruit* Ro 1:13.

c. Hebraistically, a praise-offering as καρπὸς χειλέων (Hos 14:3; Pr 18:20; 31:31 v.l.) Hb 13:15. M-M. B. 511.**

καρποφορέω fut. καρποφορήσω; 1 aor. ἐκαρποφόρησα *bear fruit* or *crops.*
1. lit. (X.+; Theophr., Hist. Pl. 3, 3, 7; Diod. S. 2, 49, 4; Zen.-P. Mich. 106, 6 [III BC]; Wsd 10:7; Hab 3:17) of land Mk 4:28 (γῆ κ. as Jos., C. Ap. 1, 306). Of a vine Hs 2:3.
2. fig., of practical conduct as the fruit of the inner life (Philo, Cher. 84 κ. ἀρετάς; cf. Ode of Solomon 11, 23) Mt 13:23; Mk 4:20; Lk 8:15; Hs 4:5, 8. κ. ἐν τῇ καρδίᾳ *bear fruit in the heart,* i.e. in a resolve to do what is right B 11:11. Of faith τῆς πίστεως ῥίζα καρποφορεῖ εἰς τὸν κύριον ἡμῶν Ἰησοῦν Χριστόν *the root of faith yields fruit in* (or *to*) *our Lord Jesus Christ* Pol 1:2. W. dat. of advantage κ. τῷ θεῷ Ro 7:4. Also θανάτῳ vs. 5. κ. ἐν παντὶ ἔργῳ ἀγαθῷ *bear fruit in all kinds of good deeds* Col 1:10.—Mid. (Gk. Inscr. Brit. Mus. 918) *bear fruit of itself* 1:6. M-M.*

καρποφόρος, ον (Pind., Hdt.+; inscr.; PSI 171, 40 [II BC]; Gk. Parchments fr. Avroman: JHS 35, '15, 22ff, no. 1A, 13 [88 BC]; Sb 991, 5; 6598, 7; LXX; Philo; Jos., Bell. 3, 44, Ant. 4, 85; Sib. Or., fgm. 3, 5) *fruitbearing, fruitful* καιροὶ κ. (s. καιρός 1) Ac 14:17. Cf. J 15:2 D. (Ode of Solomon 11, 23). M-M.*

καρτερέω 1 aor. ἐκαρτέρησα (Soph., Thu.+; pap., LXX; Jos., Ant. 11, 52) *be strong, be steadfast, hold out, endure* (Thu. 2, 44, 3; Pla., Theaet. 157D, Lach. 193A; Diod. S. 3, 5, 3 καρτερῆσαι μέχρι τῆς τελευτῆς; PGrenf. I 1, 19 [II BC]; PAmh. 130, 6; Job 2:9; Sir 2:2; 12:15; 2 Macc 7:17 al.) τὸν ἀόρατον ὡς ὁρῶν ἐκαρτέρησεν *he persevered as if he saw him who is invisible* Hb 11:27. Cf. Windisch; Strathmann.—GAWhitaker, in ET 27, '16, 186 prefers the mng. *fix one's eyes upon,* on the basis of certain pass. in Plut.—But the proper understanding of this word must surely proceed from the fact that the ptc. with καρτερεῖν does not denote an accompanying circumstance, but rather the quality in which someone endures or is steadfast (Diod. S. 8, 18, 3 τοιοῦτον βίον ζῶντα καρτερεῖν=keep on living a life like this; 14, 65, 4 μέχρι τίνος καρτερήσομεν ταῦτα πάσχοντες; =how long will we continue to suffer this?; 18, 60, 1 καρτερεῖν δεσποζόμενος=allow

oneself to be continually dominated; Arrian, Anab. 7, 8, 3 οὐκοῦν σιγῇ ἔχοντες ἐκαρτέρησαν=they did not continue, then, in silence; Ps.-Dicaearchus p. 141 l. 11F. ἀκούων καρτ.=listen continually). Accordingly Hb 11:27, giving the reason for Moses' fearlessness: *he kept the one who is invisible continually before his eyes* (i.e., in faith), *as it were.* M-M.*

[ἀπὸ] **Καρυώτου** s. Ἰσκαριώθ.

κάρφος, ους, τό (Aeschyl., Hdt.+; Gen 8:11) *speck, chip,* a small piece of straw, chaff, wood, etc., to denote someth. quite insignificant (cf. the proverb κινεῖν μηδὴ κ. Aristoph., Lysias 474 and Herodas 1, 54; 3, 67.—Ion of Chios [V BC]: no. 392 fgm. 6 p. 280, 7 Jac. of a tiny foreign object in a wine cup. Grave inscr., Epigr. Gr. 980, 9 [ὁ εὐσεβὴς] οὐδὲ κάρφος ἐβλάβη) Mt 7:3ff; Lk 6:41f; LJ 1:1.—For lit. s. on δοκός. M-M.*

κατά (Hom.+; inscr., pap., LXX, En., Ep. Arist., Philo, Joseph., Test. 12 Patr., Sib. Or.) prep. (s. the lit. s.v. ἀνά beg.).
I. with the gen. (so 73 times in NT)—1. of place—a. *down from someth.* (Hom.+; LXX) ὁρμᾶν κ. τοῦ κρημνοῦ *rush down* (*from*) *the bank* (cf. Polyb. 39, 9, 7 κατὰ τῶν κρημνῶν ῥίπτειν; Jos., Bell. 1, 313) Mt 8:32; Mk 5:13; Lk 8:33. κ. κεφαλῆς ἔχειν *have someth. on one's head* (lit. hanging down fr. the head, as a veil. Cf. Plut., Mor. 200F ἐβάδιζε κατὰ τῆς κεφαλῆς ἔχων τὸ ἱμάτιον. Wilcken, Chrest. 499, 5 of a mummy ἔχων τάβλαν κατὰ τοῦ τραχήλου) 1 Cor 11:4.
b. *into someth.* (Od. 9, 330 κατὰ σπείους 'into the depths of the cave'; Hdt. 7, 235; X., An. 7, 1, 30) ἡ κ. βάθους πτωχεία *extreme* (lit. 'reaching down into the depths'; cf. Strabo 9, 3, 5 p. 419 ἄντρον κοῖλον κατὰ βάθους) or *abysmal poverty* 2 Cor 8:2. This may perh. be the mng. of πλήσσειν τινὰ κατὰ τῶν ὀφθαλμῶν *strike someone deep into the eyes* AP 11:26 (cf. Demosth. 19, 197 ξαίνει κατὰ τοῦ νώτου; PPetr. II 18[2b], 15 [246 BC] ἔτυπτεν αὐτὸν κατὰ τοῦ τραχήλου).
c. *throughout* (so in the Lucan writings; Polyb. 3, 19, 7 κατὰ τῆς νήσου διεσπάρησαν; PGiess. 48, 8 κατὰ κυριακῆς γῆς; Jos., Ant. 8, 297; Sib. Or. 3, 222; 4, 24; 5, 305) γνωστὸν γενέσθαι κ. ὅλης Ἰόππης *become known throughout all Joppa* Ac 9:42. κ. ὅλης τῆς Ἰουδαίας 9:31; 10:37; Lk 23:5. φήμη ἐξῆλθεν κ. ὅλης τῆς περιχώρου 4:14.
2. fig. *down upon, toward, against someone* or *someth.*
—a. w. verbs of swearing, to denote what one swears by (Thu. 5, 47, 8; Lysias 32, 13; Isaeus 7, 28; Demosth. 21, 119; 29, 26; Dit., Syll.³ 526, 4ff; 685, 25; UPZ 110, 39 [164 BC]; BGU 248, 13; Jdth 1:12; Is 45:23; 2 Ch 36:13) *by* ἐξορκίζειν (q.v.) Mt 26:63. ὀμνύναι (q.v.) Hb 6:13, 16. ὁρκίζειν (q.v.) Hs 9, 10, 5. Sim. ἐρωτᾶν κ. τινος *request, entreat by someone* Hv 3, 2, 3.
b. in a hostile sense: *against*—α. after verbs that express hostile action, etc. διχάζειν Mt 10:35. ἐπαίρεσθαι 2 Cor 10:5. ἰσχύειν Ac 19:16. κακοῦν 14:2. στρατεύεσθαι 1 Pt 2:11. φυσιοῦσθαι 1 Cor 4:6.
β. after words and expressions that designate hostile speech, esp. an accusation ἔχειν (τι) κατά τινος *have or hold someth. against someone* Rv 2:4, 14, 20. ἐγκαλεῖν Ro 8:33. ἐντυγχάνειν τινὶ κατά τινος 11:2. κατηγορεῖν Lk 23:14. ποιεῖν κρίσιν Jd 15a. τὸ κ. ἡμῶν χειρόγραφον *the bond that stands against us* Col 2:14. ἐμφανίζειν Ac 24:1; 25:2. αἰτεῖσθαί τι 25:3, 15. αἰ. κ. τινος αἰτίαι vs. 27. εἰπεῖν πονηρόν Mt 5:11 (cf. Soph., Phil. 65 κακὰ λέγειν κατά τινος. X., Hell. 1, 5, 2; Isocr., C. Nic. 13; Plut., Mor. p. 2A λέγειν κ.; Dit., Syll.³ 1180, 1

λέγειν κατά τινος). λαλεῖν ῥήματα Ac 6: 13; cf. Jd 15b. μαρτυρεῖν κατὰ τ. θεοῦ give testimony in contradiction to God 1 Cor 15: 15. ζητεῖν μαρτυρίαν κατά τινος testimony against someone Mk 14: 55. ψευδομαρτυρεῖν 14: 56f. ψευδομαρτυρία Mt 26: 59. γογγύζειν 20: 11. στενάζειν Js 5: 9. διδάσκειν Ac 21: 28. συμβούλιον διδόναι (ποιεῖν v.l.) Mk 3: 6; σ. λαβεῖν Mt 27: 1. ψεύδεσθαι Js 3: 14 (Lysias 22, 7; X., Ap. 13).

γ. after expressions which designate such a position or state of mind in a different way εἶναι κ. τινος be against someone (opp. ὑπέρ) Mk 9: 40 (WNestle, ZNW 13, '12, 84–87; AFridrichsen, ibid., 273–80); Ro 8: 31; (opp. μετά) Mt 12: 30; Lk 11: 23. δύνασθαί τι be able to do someth. against someone 2 Cor 13: 8. ἔχειν τι κατά τινος have someth. against someone (on one's heart) Mt 5: 23; Mk 11: 25; Hs 9, 24, 2; cf. ibid. 23, 2, where the acc. is to be supplied. ἐξουσίαν ἔχειν J 19: 11. ἐπιθυμεῖν Gal 5: 17. μερίζεσθαι καθ' ἑαυτῆς Mt 12: 25. Cf. 1 Cl 39: 4 (Job 4: 18). κατά prob. means against also in ἔβαλεν κατ' αὐτῆς ἄνεμος Ac 27: 14. ἐτελείωσαν κατὰ τ. κεφαλῆς αὐτῶν τὰ ἁμαρτήματα they completed the full measure of sins against their own head GP 5: 17.

II. With the acc. (so 391 times in NT)—1. of place—a. of extension in space along, over, through, in, upon (Hom. +; Dit., Or. 90, 7 ἐκ τῶν κατὰ τ. χώραν ἱερῶν; PHib. 82, 19; PTebt. 5, 188; LXX) Ac 24: 12. καθ' ὅλην τ. πόλιν through the whole city Lk 8: 39. ἐγένετο λιμὸς κατὰ τὴν χώραν ἐκείνην 15: 14. κατὰ τὰς κώμας 9: 6. κατὰ πόλεις καὶ κώμας 13: 22.—κατὰ τόπους in place after place Mt 24: 7; Mk 13: 8; Lk 21: 11 (Theophr., περὶ σημ. 1, 4 p. 389W.; Cat. Cod. Astr. III 28, 11 ἐν μέρει τ. ἀνατολῆς κατὰ τόπους, VIII 3, 186, 1 λιμὸς καὶ λοιμὸς καὶ σφαγαὶ κατὰ τόπους). οἱ ὄντες κ. τὴν Ἰουδαίαν those throughout Judaea or living in Judaea Ac 11: 1. διασπαρῆναι κ. τὰς χώρας τῆς Ἰουδαίας be scattered over the regions of Judaea 8: 1. κ. τὴν οὖσαν ἐκκλησίαν in the church there 13: 1. τοῖς κ. τὴν Ἀντιόχειαν καὶ Συρίαν καὶ Κιλικίαν ἀδελφοῖς 15: 23. τοὺς κ. τὰ ἔθνη Ἰουδαίους the Jews (dispersed) among the heathen 21: 21. τοῖς κ. τὸν νόμον γεγραμμένοις throughout the law=in the law 24: 14b. κ. τὴν ὁδόν along or on the way (Lucian, Catapl. 4; Jos., Ant. 8, 404) Lk 10: 4; Ac 25: 3; 26: 13. τὸ κ. Κιλικίαν καὶ Παμφυλίαν πέλαγος the sea along the coast of Cilicia and Pamphylia 27: 5. On the other hand, the geographical designation τὰ μέρη τ. Λιβύης τῆς κατὰ Κυρήνην 2: 10 prob. belongs to b: the parts of Libya toward Cyrene.

b. of direction toward, to, up to ἐλθεῖν κ. τὸν τόπον come up to the place (Jos., Vi. 283) Lk 10: 32. ἐλθόντες κ. τὴν Μυσίαν to Mysia Ac 16: 7; cf. 27: 7. πορεύεσθαι κ. μεσημβρίαν (s. μεσημβρία 2) toward the south 8: 26 (cf. Jos., Bell. 5, 505). κ. σκοπὸν διώκειν run (over the course) toward the goal Phil 3: 14. λιμὴν βλέπων κ. λίβα καὶ κ. χῶρον a harbor open to the southwest and northwest Ac 27: 12 (s. βλέπω 8).—κ. πρόσωπον to the face (cf. Jos., Ant. 5, 205) Gal 2: 11. ἔχειν τινὰ κ. πρόσωπον meet someone face to face (Thieme 19 has reff. for the use of κατὰ πρόσωπον as a legal formula) Ac 25: 16. κ. πρόσωπον ταπεινός humble when personally present 2 Cor 10: 1. κ. πρόσωπόν τινος in the presence of someone Lk 2: 31; Ac 3: 13. τὰ κ. πρόσωπον what lies before one's eyes, i.e., is obvious 2 Cor 10: 7. κ. ὀφθαλμοὺς προγράφειν portray before one's eyes Gal 3: 1.

c. κατά serves to isolate or separate by (Thu. 1, 138, 6 οἱ καθ' ἑαυτοὺς Ἕλληνες 'the Greeks by themselves'; Polyb. 1, 24, 4; 5, 78, 3; 11, 17, 6; Diod. S. 13, 72, 8; Gen 30: 40; 43: 32; 2 Macc 13: 13; Philo, Migr. Abr. 87; 90) ἔχειν τι καθ' ἑαυτόν keep someth. to oneself Ro 14: 22 (cf. Jos.,

Ant. 2, 255; Heliod. 7, 16, 1). κ. ἑαυτὸν μένειν live by oneself of the private dwelling of Paul in Rome Ac 28: 16. πίστις νεκρὰ κ. ἑαυτήν faith by itself is dead Js 2: 17 (Simplicius in Epict. p. 3, 43 τὸ σῶμα καθ' αὐτὸ νεκρόν ἐστιν). ἡ κατ' οἶκον ἐκκλησία the church in the house Ro 16: 5; 1 Cor 16: 19. κατ' ἰδίαν s. ἴδιος 4. κατὰ μόνας (Thu. 1, 32, 5; Menand., Epitr. 594 J, fgm. 158 Kock; Polyb. 4, 15, 11; Diod. S. 4, 51, 16; BGU 813, 15 [s. APF 2, '03, 97]; LXX) alone, by oneself Mk 4: 10; Lk 9: 18; Hm 11: 8 (here, as well as BGU loc. cit. and LXX, written as one word καταμόνας).

d. as a distributive (Arrian, Anab. 4, 21, 10 κατὰ σκηνήν=tent by tent) κατ' οἰκίαν (οἶκον) in the various houses (PLond. 904, 20 ἡ κατ' οἰκίαν ἀπογραφή) Ac 2: 46b; 5: 42. Likew. the pl. κατὰ τοὺς οἴκους εἰσπορευόμενος 8: 3. κατὰ τὰς συναγωγάς 22: 19. κατὰ πόλιν (Jos., Ant. 6, 73) from city to city IRo 9: 3, but in every (single) city Ac 15: 21; 20: 23; Tit 1: 5. Also κατὰ πόλιν πᾶσαν (cf. Herodian 1, 14, 9) Ac 15: 36; κατὰ πᾶσαν πόλιν 20: 23 D. κατὰ πόλιν καὶ κώμην Lk 8: 1; cf. vs. 4.

2. of time (Hdt. et al.; inscr., pap., LXX)—a. in definite indications of time: at, on, during κ. ἀρχάς in the beginning (cf. ἀρχή 1c) Hb 1: 10 (Ps 101: 26). κ. τὴν ἡμέραν τοῦ πειρασμοῦ in the day of trial 3: 8 (Ps 94: 8.—Cf. Antig. Car. 173 κατὰ τὸν σπόρου καιρόν). Of the future: κ. τὸν καιρὸν τοῦτον at that time, then Ro 9: 9 (Gen 18: 10). Of the past: κ. ἐκεῖνον τὸν καιρόν at that time, then (2 Macc 3: 5; Jos., Ant. 8, 266) Ac 12: 1; 19: 23. κατὰ καιρόν at that time, then Ro 5: 6 (cf. Dit., Or. 90, 28 καθ' ὃν καιρόν), unless καιρός here means the right time (s. καιρός 2, end). κατ' ὄναρ (as καθ' ὕπνον Gen 20: 6) during a dream, in a dream Mt 1: 20; 2: 12.

b. with indefinite indications of time: toward, about κ. τὸ μεσονύκτιον about midnight Ac 16: 25; cf. 27: 27.—8: 26 (s. μεσημβρία 1).

c. distributively: κ. ἔτος every year (s. ἔτος) Lk 2: 41. Also κ. ἐνιαυτόν (s. ἐνιαυτός 1) Hb 9: 25; 10: 1, 3. κ. ἡμέραν daily, every day (s. ἡμέρα 2) Mt 26: 55; Mk 14: 49; Lk 16: 19; 22: 53; Ac 2: 46f; 3: 2; 16: 5; 19: 9; 1 Cor 15: 31; Hb 7: 27; 10: 11. Also τὸ κ. ἡμέραν (s. ἡμέρα 2) Lk 11: 3; 19: 47; Ac 17: 11. ἡ ἐπίστασις ἡ κ. ἡμέραν (s. ἐπίστασις) 2 Cor 11: 28. κ. πᾶσαν ἡμέραν every day (Jos., Ant. 6, 49) Ac 17: 7. Also καθ' ἑκάστην ἡμέραν (s. ἡμέρα 2) Hb 3: 13. κ. μίαν σαββάτου on the first day of every week 1 Cor 16: 2. κ. πᾶν σάββατον every Sabbath Ac 13: 27; 15: 21b; 18: 4. κ. μῆνα ἕκαστον each month Rv 22: 2 (κατὰ μῆνα as Dit., Syll.³ 153, 65; POxy. 275, 18; 2 Macc 6: 7). κ. ἑορτήν at each festival Mt 27: 15; Mk 15: 6.

3. distributively (apart from indications of place [s. above II 1d] and time [s. above II 2c]), indicating the division of a greater whole into individual parts:

a. used w. numerals: κ. δύο ἢ τὸ πλεῖστον τρεῖς two or, at the most, three at a time (i.e., in any one meeting, cf. ἀνὰ μέρος) 1 Cor 14: 27 (Dio Chrys. 80[30], 42 κατὰ δύο κ. τρεῖς; Jos., Ant. 3, 142 κατὰ ἕξ; 5, 172 κατὰ δύο κ. τρεῖς). κ. ἕνα (on this and the foll. s. εἷς 5e) singly, one after the other vs. 31. κ. ἕνα each individual stone Hs 9, 3, 5; 9, 6, 3. κ. ἕν ἕκαστον one by one, in detail Ac 21: 19; 1 Cl 32: 1. εἷς καθ' εἷς Mk 14: 19; J 8: 9; cf. Ro 12: 5 (Bl-D. §305; Rob. 460). κ. ἑκατὸν καὶ κ. πεντήκοντα in hundreds and in fifties Mk 6: 40.

b. περί τινος λέγειν κ. μέρος speak of someth. in detail Hb 9: 5 (s. μέρος 1c). κ. ὄνομα (each one) by name (BGU 27, 18 ἀσπάζομαι πάντας τοὺς φιλοῦντάς σε κατ' ὄνομα; PTebt. 422, 16; Jos., Vi. 86) J 10: 3; 3 J 15; ISm 13: 2.

4. of goal, purpose for the purpose of, for, to (Thu. 6,

31, 1 κατὰ θέαν ἥκειν=to look at something; cf. Sb 7263, 6 [254 BC]; X., An. 3, 5, 2 καθ' ἁρπαγὴν ἐσκεδασμένοι; Arrian, Anab. 1, 17, 12; 4, 5, 1; 21, 9; 6, 17, 6; 26, 2; Lucian, Ver. Hist. 2, 29; Anton. Lib., Fab. 24, 1 Δημήτηρ ἐπῄει γῆν ἅπασαν κατὰ ζήτησιν τῆς θυγατρός; 38; Jdth 11: 19) κατὰ τὸν καθαρισμὸν τῶν Ἰουδαίων *for the Jewish ceremonial purification* J 2: 6. κατ' ἀτιμίαν λέγω *to my shame* 2 Cor 11: 21 (cf. Jos., Ant. 3, 268 κατὰ τιμὴν τ. θεοῦ τοῦτο ποιῶν). ἀπόστολος...κατὰ πίστιν... καὶ ἐπίγνωσιν *an apostle...for the faith...and the knowledge* Tit 1: 1 (but the mng. 'in accordance with' is also poss.).

5. of the norm, of similarity, homogeneity *according to, in accordance with, in conformity with, corresponding to.*

a. to introduce the norm which governs someth.—**α.** the norm of the law, etc. (Dit., Or. 56, 33; Wilcken, Chrest. 352, 11 κατὰ τὰ κελευσθέντα; POxy. 37 II, 8) κατὰ τὸν νόμον (Jos., Ant. 14, 173; 15, 51; κατὰ τοὺς νόμους Ἀρεοπαγείτης, letter of MAurelius: ZPE 8, '71, 169, l. 27) Lk 2: 22; J 18: 31; 19: 7; Hb 7: 5. τὰ κατὰ τ. νόμον *what is to be done according to the law* Lk 2: 39 (cf. Ep. Arist. 32). κατὰ τὸ ὡρισμένον *in accordance w. what has been determined* 22: 22. Cf. 1: 9; 2: 24, 27, 42; Ac 17: 2; 22: 3. κατὰ τὸ εὐαγγέλιόν μου Ro 2: 16; 16: 25a; 2 Ti 2: 8. κατὰ τὸ εἰρημένον Ro 4: 18. κατὰ τὰς γραφάς (cf. Paus. 6, 21, 10 κατὰ τὰ ἔπη=according to the epic poems) 1 Cor 15: 3; cf. Js 2: 8. κατὰ τὴν παράδοσιν Mk 7: 5.—κατὰ λόγον *as one wishes* (exx. in Dssm., B 209 [not in BS]; also PEleph. 13, 1; 3 Macc 3: 14) Ac 18: 14 (though II 5bβ is also poss.).—It can also stand simply w. the acc. of the pers. according to whose will, pleasure, or manner someth. occurs κατὰ θεόν (cf. Socrat., Ep. 14, 5 κ. θεόν; 26, 2; Nicol. Dam.: 90 fgm. 4 p. 332, 1 Jac. and Appian, Bell. Civ. 2, 84 §352 κατὰ δαίμονα; Jos., Ant. 4, 143 ὁ κατὰ τοῦτον [=θεόν] βίος) Ro 8: 27; 2 Cor 7: 9–11; κατὰ Χριστὸν Ἰ. Ro 15: 5. κατὰ κύριον 2 Cor 11: 17. Cf. 1 Pt 1: 15. κατὰ τ. Ἕλληνας *in the manner of the Greeks,* i.e. *heathen* PK 2, p. 14, 1; 7. κατὰ Ἰουδαίους l. 25.

β. the norm according to which a judgment is rendered, or rewards or punishments are given ἀποδοῦναί τινι κατὰ τ. πρᾶξιν or ἔργα αὐτοῦ (Ps 61: 13; Pr 24: 12) Mt 16: 27; Ro 2: 6; 2 Ti 4: 14; Rv 2: 23. μισθὸν λήμψεται κατὰ τ. ἴδιον κόπον 1 Cor 3: 8. κρίνειν κατὰ J 7: 24; 8: 15; 1 Pt 1: 17; cf. Ro 2: 2.

γ. of a standard of any other kind κατὰ τ. χρόνον ὃν ἠκρίβωσεν *in accordance w. the time which he had ascertained* Mt 2: 16. κατὰ τ. πίστιν ὑμῶν *acc. to your faith* 9: 29. κατὰ τ. δύναμιν *acc. to his capability* 25: 15. Cf. Lk 1: 38; 2: 29; Ro 8: 4; 10: 2; Eph 4: 7. ἀνὴρ κατὰ τ. καρδίαν μου Ac 13: 22 (καρδία 1bε).

δ. Oft. the norm is at the same time the reason, so that *in accordance with* and *because of* are merged οἱ κατὰ πρόθεσιν κλητοί Ro 8: 28. κατ' ἐπιταγὴν θεοῦ 16: 26; 1 Ti 1: 1; Tit 1: 3. κατὰ ἀποκάλυψιν Eph 3: 3. οἱ καθ' ὑπομονὴν ἔργου ἀγαθοῦ Ro 2: 7. κατ' ἐκλογήν 11: 5. Cf. Eph 1: 11; 2 Th 2: 9; Hb 7: 16. κατὰ τί γνώσομαι τοῦτο *by what shall I know this?* (cf. Gen 15: 8) Lk 1: 18.—The mng. 'in accordance w.' can also disappear entirely, so that κ. means simply *because of, as a result of, on the basis of* (Ael. Aristid. 46 p. 219 D.: κ. τοὺς νόμους; Jos., Ant. 1, 259; 278). κατὰ πᾶσαν αἰτίαν *for any and every reason* (αἰτία 1) Mt 19: 3. κατὰ ἀποκάλυψιν Gal 2: 2. Cf. Ro 2: 5; 1 Cor 12: 8 (κατὰ τ. πνεῦμα=διὰ τοῦ πν.); Eph 1: 5; 4: 22b; Phil 4: 11; 1 Ti 5: 21; 2 Ti 1: 9; Tit 3: 5; Phlm 14; IPol 1: 3. ὁ κατὰ τὸ πολὺ αὐτοῦ ἔλεος ἀναγεννήσας ἡμᾶς 1 Pt 1: 3.—καθ' ὅσον (Thu. 4, 18, 4) *in so far as, inasmuch as* Hb 3: 3. καθ' ὅσον ..., κατὰ τοσοῦτο *in so far*

as ..., *just so far* (Lysias 31, 8; Galen, De Dignosc. Puls. 3, 2 vol. VIII p. 892 K.) 7: 20, 22.

b. of equality, similarity, example *in accordance with, just as, similar(ly) to* (schol. on Nicander, Ther. 50: sheep are not burden-bearers κατὰ τοὺς ὄνους=as donkeys are).

α. κατὰ τὰ ἔργα αὐτῶν μὴ ποιεῖτε *do not do as they do* Mt 23: 3. κατὰ Ἰσαάκ *just as Isaac* Gal 4: 28. κατὰ θεὸν κτισθείς Eph 4: 24 (Synes., Prov. 2, 2 p. 118c κατὰ θεόν=just as a god). Cf. Col 3: 10. κατὰ τὸν τύπον Hb 8: 5 (Ex 25: 40). Cf. 5: 6 (Ps 109: 4); 8: 9 (Jer 38[31]: 32); Js 3: 9.—κατὰ τὰ αὐτά *in (just) the same way* (Dit., Or. 56, 66; PEleph. 2, 6; 1 Macc 8: 27; 12: 2) Lk 6: 23, 26; 17: 30; Dg 3: 1. On the other hand, the sing. κατὰ τὸ αὐτό Ac 14: 1 means *together* (marriage contract PEleph. 1, 5 [IV BC] εἶναι ἡμᾶς κατὰ ταὐτό; 1 Km 11: 11). καθ' ὃν τρόπον *just as* (2 Macc 6: 20; 4 Macc 14: 17) Ac 15: 11; 27: 25. καθ' ὅσον ..., οὕτως (*just*) as ..., so Hb 9: 27. κατὰ πάντα τρόπον *in every way* (PSI 520, 16 [250 BC]; Zen.-P. 59631, 2; 3 Macc 3: 24) Ro 3: 2. κατὰ μηδένα τρόπον (PMagd. 14, 9 [221 BC]; PReinach 7, 31; 3 Macc 4: 13; 4 Macc 4: 24 v.l.) 2 Th 2: 3. Cf. MJohannessohn, Der Gebrauch der Kasus, Diss. Berlin '10, 82. κατὰ w. acc. serves in general

β. to indicate the nature, kind, peculiarity or characteristics of a thing (freq. as a periphrasis for the adv.; e.g., Antioch. of Syracuse [V BC]: no. 555 fgm. 12 Jac. κατὰ μῖσος=out of hate, filled with hate) κ. ἐξουσίαν *with authority* or *power* Mk 1: 27. κ. συγκυρίαν *by chance* Lk 10: 31. κ. ἄγνοιαν *without knowing* Ac 3: 17 (ἄγνοια 1). κ. ἄνθρωπον 1 Cor 3: 3 al. (ἄνθρωπος 1c). κ. κράτος *powerfully,* Ac 19: 20 (κράτος 1). κατὰ λόγον *reasonably, rightly* (Pla.; Polyb. 1, 62, 4; 5, 110, 10; Jos., Ant. 13, 195; PYale 42, 24 [12 Jan., 229 BC]) 18: 14 (but s. above II 5aα). λέγειν τι κ. συγγνώμην, οὐ κ. ἐπιταγήν *say someth. as a concession, not as a command* 1 Cor 7: 6; cf. 2 Cor 8: 8. κ. τάξιν *in (an) order(ly manner)* 1 Cor 14: 40 (τάξις 2). κατὰ ὀφθαλμοδουλίαν *with eye-service* Eph 6: 6. μηδὲν κ. ἐριθείαν μηδὲ κ. κενοδοξίαν Phil 2: 3. κ. ζῆλος *zealously* 3: 6a, unless this pass. belongs under 6 below, in its entirety. κ. σάρκα *on the physical plane* Ro 8: 12f; 2 Cor 1: 17; also 5: 16a, b, if here κ. σ. belongs w. οἴδαμεν or ἐγνώκαμεν (as Bachmann, JWeiss, H-D Wendland, Sickenberger take it. S. 7a below). καθ' ὑπερβολήν (PTebt. 42, 5 [c. 114 BC] ἠδικημένος καθ' ὑπερβολὴν ὑπὸ Ἀρμιύσιος; 4 Macc 3: 18) *beyond measure, beyond comparison* Ro 7: 13; 1 Cor 12: 31; 2 Cor 4: 17. καθ' ὁμοιότητα (Aristot.; Gen 1: 12; Philo, Fug. 51) *in a similar manner* Hb 4: 15b. κατὰ μικρόν *in brief* B 1: 5 (μικρός 3a).

6. denoting relationship to someth., *with respect to, in relation to* κ. σάρκα *w. respect to the flesh, physically* of human descent Ro 1: 3; 4: 1; 9: 3, 5. κ. τὸν ἔσω ἄνθρωπον 7: 22 (cf. POxy. 904, 6 πληγαῖς κατακοπτόμενον κατὰ τὸ σῶμα). Cf. Ro 1: 4; 11: 28; Phil 3: 5, 6b; Hb 9: 9b. τὰ κ. τινα (Hdt. 7, 148; Diod. S. 1, 10, 73; Aelian, V.H. 2, 20; PEleph. 13, 3; POxy. 120, 14; Tob 10: 9; 1 Esdr 9: 17; 2 Macc 3: 40; 9: 3 al.) *someone's case, circumstances* Ac 24: 22 (cf. PEleph. 13, 3 τὰ κατὰ σέ); 25: 14; Eph 6: 21; Phil 1: 12; Col 4: 7. κ. πάντα *in all respects* (since Thu. 4, 81, 3; Sb 4324, 3; 5761, 22; Dit., Syll.³ 834, 7; Gen 24: 1; Wsd 19: 22; 2 Macc 1: 17; 3 Macc 5: 42) Ac 17: 22; Col 3: 20, 22a; Hb 2: 17 (Artem. 1, 13 αὐτῷ ὅμοιον κ. π.); 4: 15a.

7. Somet. the κατά-phrase can best be understood as an adj., or acts as the periphrasis of a possessive pron. or of a gen. It stands for

a. an adj. (Synes., Kingdom 4 p. 4D τὰ κατ' ἀρετὴν ἔργα=the virtuous deeds; PHib. 27, 42 ταῖς κατὰ σελήνην ἡμέραις; 4 Macc 5: 18 κατ' ἀλήθειαν=ἀληθής) οἱ κατὰ φύσιν κλάδοι *the natural branches* Ro 11: 21. ἡ κατ' εὐσέβειαν διδασκαλία 1 Ti 6: 3; cf. Tit 1: 1b. οἱ κατὰ σάρκα κύριοι *the earthly masters* Eph 6: 5. Cf. 2 Cor 5: 16b, in case (s. 5bβ above) κ. σ. belongs w. Χριστόν (as the majority, most recently Ltzm., take it): *a physical Christ, a Christ in the flesh,* in his earthly relationships (σάρξ 6). Correspondingly in vs. 16a κ. σ. would be taken w. οὐδένα: *no one simply as a physical being.*—JLMartyn, JKnox-Festschr., '67, 269–87.

b. a possessive pron. (Demosth. 2, 27 τὰ καθ' ὑμᾶς ἐλλείμματα; Aelian, V.H. 2, 42 ἡ κατ' αὐτὸν ἀρετή; 3, 36; Dit., Or. 168, 17 παραγεγονότες εἰς τοὺς καθ' ὑμᾶς τόπους, Syll.³ 646, 6; 807, 15 al.; UPZ 20, 9 [II bc] ἐπὶ τῆς καθ' ἡμᾶς λειτουργίας; PTebt. 24, 64; 2 Macc 4: 21) τῶν καθ' ὑμᾶς ποιητῶν τινες *some of your (own) poets* Ac 17: 28. ἡ καθ' ὑμᾶς πίστις Eph 1: 15. ὁ καθ' ὑμᾶς νόμος Ac 18: 15. τὸ κατ' ἐμὲ πρόθυμον *my wish* Ro 1: 15.

c. the gen. of a noun (Polyb. 3, 113, 1 ἡ κατὰ τὸν ἥλιον ἀνατολή; 2, 48, 2; 3, 8, 1 al.; Diod. S. 14, 12 ἡ κατὰ τὸν τύραννον ὠμότης; Dionys. Hal. 2, 1; Dit., Syll.³ 873, 5 τῆς κατὰ τ. μυστήρια τελετῆς; 569, 22; 783, 20; PTebt. 5, 25; PLond. 1164k, 20 ὑπὸ τοῦ κατὰ πατέρα μου ἀνεψιοῦ) τὰ κ. Ἰουδαίους ἔθη *the customs of the Jews* Ac 26: 3. Cf. 27: 2. ἡ κατὰ πίστιν δικαιοσύνη *the righteousness of faith* Hb 11: 7. ἡ κατ' ἐκλογὴν πρόθεσις *purpose of election* Ro 9: 11.—Here also belong the titles of the gospels εὐαγγέλιον κατὰ Ματθαῖον etc., where κατά is likew. periphrasis for a gen. (cf. Jo. Lydus, De Mag. 3, 46 p. 136, 10 Wünsch τῆς κατὰ Λουκανὸν συγγραφῆς; Herodian 2, 9, 4 of an autobiography ἐν τῷ καθ' αὑτὸν βίῳ; Jos., C. Ap. 1, 18 τ. καθ' αὑτὸν ἱστορίαν; 2 Macc 2: 13. Cf. Bl-D. §163; 224, 2; Zahn, Einleitung §49; BW Bacon, Why 'According to Mt'? Expositor, 8th Series, 20, '20, 289–310).—On the periphrasis of the gen. by κατά cf. Rudberg (ἀνά, beg.) w. many exx. fr. Pla. on. But it occurs as early as Thu. 6, 16, 5 ἐν τῷ κατ' αὐτοὺς βίῳ. M-M.

καταβαίνω impf. κατέβαινον; fut. καταβήσομαι; 2 aor. κατέβην, imper. κατάβηθι and κατάβα (Diog. L. 2, 41) Mk 15: 30 t.r.; pf. καταβέβηκα (Hom.+; inscr., pap., LXX, En., Philo, Joseph.) *come down, go down, climb down.*

1. lit.—a. of pers.:—α. w. indication of the place fr. which one comes or goes down: ἀπό τινος (Pind., Nem. 6, 87; X., Cyr. 5, 5, 6; Ael. Aristid. 51, 22 K.=27 p. 538 D.: ἀπὸ τ. ὄρους; Gen 38: 1; Ex 32: 15 ἀπὸ τ. ὄρους; 4 Km 1: 16; Na 3: 7 v.l.; Ezk 47: 1; Jos., Ant. 6, 108) Mt 8: 1; Mk 9: 9 v.l. *Come down* fr. a cross (Charito 4, 3, 6 κατέβαινε τοῦ σταυροῦ, after the command κατάβηθι) Mt 27: 40, 42; Mk 15: 30, 32. *Get out* of a boat (cf. Ezk 27: 29) Mt 14: 29. W. ἔκ τινος: ἐκ τ. ὄρους (Il. 13, 17; X., An. 7, 4, 12; Ex 19: 14; 32: 1; Dt 9: 15; 10: 5; Josh 2: 23) 17: 9; Mk 9: 9. ἐντεῦθεν 1 Cl 53: 2 (Dt 9: 12). Abs., though it is clear fr. the context where the descent is from Mk 13: 15; Lk 19: 5f; J 5: 7; Ac 20: 10; 23: 10; B 4: 8; 14: 3 (the two last Ex 32: 7, where ἐντεῦθεν is added); MPol 7: 2. W. inf. foll. (Gen. 11: 5; 43: 20; Ex 3: 8) Mt 24: 17; Lk 17: 31. καταβὰς ἔστη 6: 17.

β. as in LXX (for יָרַד 3 Km 22: 2; 4 Km 8: 29; 10: 13 al.) of going away fr. Jerusalem or Palestine: ἀπὸ Ἰεροσολύμων Mk 3: 22; Lk 10: 30 (cf. 1 Macc 16: 14); Ac 25: 7; cf. Lk 10: 31; Ac 24: 1, 22. W. geograph. reff. in general (oft. LXX; Jos., Vi. 68 εἰς Τιβεριάδα) εἰς Αἴγυπτον 7: 15. εἰς Ἀντιόχειαν 18: 22.—14: 25; 16: 8; 25: 6; Lk 2: 51; J 2: 12. Abs. J 4: 47, 49, 51; Ac 8: 15; 10: 20.

γ. of coming down fr. heaven (Maximus Tyr. 11, 12e κ. ἐκ τ. θεοῦ μέχρι γῆς) ἀπὸ τοῦ οὐρανοῦ (Diogenes, Ep. 38, 1; Da 4: 13, 23 Theod.; Philo, Migr. Abr. 185) J 6: 38; 1 Th 4: 16. ἐξ οὐρανοῦ (Charito 6, 3, 4 τὶς ἐξ οὐρ. καταβέβηκε. Of things (Dt 28: 24; 4 Km 1: 10) Mt 28: 2; J 3: 13 (for the contrast ἀναβαίνω εἰς τ. οὐρ.—καταβαίνω cf. Pr 30: 4; PGM 4, 546f); 6: 33, 41f, 50f, 58; Rv 10: 1; 18: 1; 20: 1. Abs. (Aristob. in Euseb., Pr. Ev. 8, 10, 13; PGM 4, 3024; 36, 299) Ac 7: 34 (Ex 3: 8); J 1: 51; Eph 4: 10.

δ. w. indication of the place to which one goes or comes down Mk 13: 15 v.l. εἰς τὴν ἄβυσσον Ro 10: 7. εἰς ᾅδου (Diod. S. 4, 25, 4 and Artem. 2, 55 with ἀναβαίνειν ἐξ ᾅδου) 1 Cl 51: 4 (Num 16: 30; Ps 54: 16). εἰς τὰ κατώτερα μέρη τῆς γῆς (s. κατώτερος) Eph 4: 9. Esp. of baptism κ. εἰς (τὸ) ὕδωρ *go down into the water* Ac 8: 38; B 11: 8, 11; Hm 4, 3, 1; s 9, 16, 4 and 6. εἰς τὸν οἶκον αὐτοῦ (from the temple) *home(ward)* Lk 18: 14. εἰς τὴν θάλασσαν (X., Ages. 1, 18; cf. Gen 24: 16, 45) J 6: 16. πρὸς τοὺς ἄνδρας (cf. 1 Km 10: 8; 4 Km 1: 15; 1 Macc 10: 71) Ac 10: 21; cf. 14: 11. ἄγγελος κατέβαινεν ἐν τ. κολυμβήθρᾳ *into the pool* J 5: 4 (cf. Judg 7: 9f B κ. ἐν τ. παρεμβολῇ). Of the descent of the devil: πρός τινα Rv 12: 12 (cf. Philo, Gig. 12 [ψυχαί] πρὸς σώματα κατέβησαν).

b. of things etc.: a sheet fr. heaven (cf. Sib. Or. 2, 20) *come down* Ac 10: 11; 11: 5. Every good gift comes down ἀπὸ τοῦ πατρὸς τῶν φώτων Js 1: 17. Of the New Jerusalem κ. ἐκ τ. οὐρανοῦ ἀπὸ τοῦ θεοῦ Rv 3: 12; 21: 2, 10. Of the Holy Spirit at the baptism of Jesus: καταβ. εἰς αὐτόν *come down* and enter *into him* Mk 1: 10. ἐπ' αὐτόν *upon him* Mt 3: 16; Lk 3: 22; J 1: 32f. Of rain (cf. Ps 71: 6; Is 55: 10; Jos., Ant. 2, 343) *fall* Mt 7: 25, 27. Of a storm *come down* Lk 8: 23. Of fire *fall down* ἀπὸ τοῦ οὐρανοῦ (cf. Jos., Ant. 2, 343) 9: 54. ἐκ τοῦ οὐρανοῦ εἰς τὴν γῆν Rv 13: 13. ἐκ τ. οὐρανοῦ (4 Km 1: 10, 14; 2 Macc 2: 10) 20: 9. Of hail ἐκ τοῦ οὐρανοῦ ἐπί τινα *fall down fr. heaven upon someone* 16: 21. Of drops of blood ἐπὶ τὴν γῆν Lk 22: 44 (cf. Sir 35: 15 δάκρυα ἐπὶ σιαγόνα). Of a road *lead away* ἀπὸ Ἰερουσαλήμ Ac 8: 26. M-M.

2. fig. *be brought down* ἕως ᾅδου (cf. Is 14: 11, 15. ἕως as Ps 106: 26) Mt 11: 23; Lk 10: 15 (both w. καταβιβασθήσῃ as v.l.). M-M.*

καταβάλλω (Hom.+; inscr., pap., LXX, En., Ep. Arist., Philo, Joseph.).

1. act. and pass. *throw down, strike down* (X., Cyr. 1, 3, 14 al.) τινά *someone* (Diod. S. 14, 17, 10; Appian, Liby. 111, §527; Lucian, Dial. Deor. 14, 2; Philo, Agr. 120) pass. καταβαλλόμενοι ἀλλ' οὐκ ἀπολλύμενοι *struck down, but not destroyed* 2 Cor 4: 9. Cf. Rv 12: 10 t.r.

2. mid. *found, lay (a foundation)* θεμέλιον (Dionys. Hal. 3, 69 τοὺς θεμελίους; Porphyr., Abst. 8, 10; Jos., Ant. 11, 93; 15, 391; cf. 2 Macc 2: 13 βιβλιοθήκην; Ep. Arist. 104) fig. (so e.g. of the founding of a philos. school Plut., Mor. 329A) Hb 6: 1. M-M.*

καταβαρέω 1 aor. κατεβάρησα (Polyb.; Diod. S. 19, 24, 5 et al.; Kyr.-Inschr. l. 11; POxy. 487, 10) *burden, be a burden to* τινά *someone* (Appian, Bell. Civ. 5, 67 §283) 2 Cor 12: 16. Abs. αἱ ἁμαρτίαι ὑμῶν κατεβάρησαν *your sins weighed heavily* (the context supplies ὑμᾶς) *upon you* Hs 9, 28, 6. M-M.*

καταβαρύνω (Theophr. et al.; LXX) *weigh down, burden, oppress* τὴν ζωήν *make someone's life hard* (cf. τὸν βίον Antip. in Stob. 4, 22, 25 vol. IV 511, 7 H.) Hm 12, 6, 2. Pass. (Herm. Wr. 2, 9) of the eyes ἦσαν καταβαρυνόμενοι *were heavy*=fell shut Mk 14: 40.*

κατάβασις, εως, ἡ (Hdt.+; inscr., pap., LXX, Philo, Joseph.) *descent, road leading down* (Polyb. 3, 54, 5; Diod. S. 4, 21, 2; 14, 28, 5; Jos., Bell. 2, 547), also *slope, declivity* (Ps.-Demetr., Eloc. §248; Josh 10: 11) ἐγγίζειν πρὸς τῇ κ. τοῦ ὄρους τῶν ἐλαιῶν *come close to the slope of the Mount of Olives* Lk 19: 37. M-M.*

καταβῇ s. καταβαίνω.

καταβιβάζω 1 fut. pass. καταβιβασθήσομαι (Hdt.+; PLond. 130, 105; LXX) *bring down, drive down* τινά *make someone come down* Ac 19: 33 v.l. (in text in Blass). Pass. (cf. Philo, Deus Imm. 120) ἕως ᾅδου Mt 11: 23 v.l.; Lk 10: 15 v.l. (s. καταβαίνω 2). M-M.*

καταβοάω (Hdt.+; Dit., Or. 669, 5; 51; PSI 440, 19; 551, 2; 4; 6; LXX; Jos., Bell. 3, 410, Ant. 3, 307) *cry out, bring charges, complain* Ac 18: 13 D.*

καταβολή, ῆς, ἡ (Hippocr., Demosth. et al.; inscr., pap., 2 Macc 2: 29; Ep. Arist.; Philo, Joseph.).
1. *foundation, beginning* (Jos., Bell. 2, 260 ἀποστάσεως καταβολή) τ. καταβολὴν τ. στάσεως ποιεῖν *be responsible for beginning the dissension* (cf. Polyb. 13, 6, 2 καταβολὴν ἐποιεῖτο τυραννίδος) 1 Cl 57: 1. Esp. καταβολὴ κόσμου (Plut., Mor. 956A ἅμα τῇ πρώτῃ καταβολῇ τ. ἀνθρώπων): ἀπὸ καταβολῆς κόσμου *from the foundation of the world* (Polyb. 1, 36, 8; 24, 8, 9; Diod. S. 12, 32, 2—all three ἐκ καταβολῆς) Mt 25: 34; Lk 11: 50; Hb 4: 3; 9: 26; Rv 13: 8; 17: 8; B 5: 5. πρὸ καταβολῆς κόσμου J 17: 24; Eph 1: 4; 1 Pt 1: 20.—OHofius, ZNW 62, '71, 123-8. Also abs. (without κόσμου; cf. Ep. Arist. 129) Mt 13: 35. This may be the mng. of Hb 11: 11, where it is said of Sarah δύναμιν εἰς καταβολὴν σπέρματος ἔλαβεν *she received power to establish a posterity* (most recently Strathmann). But
2. κ. is a t.t. for the *sowing* of the seed, for begetting (τοῦ σπέρματος [εἰς γῆν ἢ μήτραν M. Ant. 4, 36]: Plut., Mor. 320B σπορὰ κ. καταβολή *of the procreation of Romulus by Ares and Silvia*; 905E; Ps.-Lucian, Amor. 19; Galen, Aphorism. 4, 1 vol. XVII 2 p. 653 K.; cf. Philo, Op. M. 132; Epict. 1, 13, 3; Herm. Wr. 9, 6; cf. Field, Notes 232). If this mng. is correct for Hb 11: 11, there is prob. some error in the text, since this expression could not be used of Sarah, but only of Abraham (e.g. αὐτῇ Σάρρᾳ ='together w. Sarah' is read by W-H. margin; Riggenbach; Michel; Bl-D. §194, 1. This use of the dat. is class., also Diod. S. 20, 76, 1; Appian, Samn. 7 §2; Polyaenus 6, 18, 2 and 7, 15, 3; 8, 28; Theod. Prodr. 6, 148 H. αὐτῇ Ῥοδάνῃ). Windisch, Hdb. ad loc. and s. on αἷμα 1a.—MBlack, An Aramaic Approach³, '67, 83-9. M-M.*

καταβραβεύω (Demosth., 21, 93; Vett. Val. 344, 30; Sb 4512 B, 57 [II BC]) *decide against* (as umpire), *rob of a prize, condemn* τινά (Didymus [I BC/I AD] p. 179 M Schmidt; cf. Field, Notes 196f) Col 2: 18. M-M.*

καταγγελεύς, έως, ὁ (Dit., Or. 456, 10 [I BC]; IG XII 8, 190, 39f [I AD]; Pel.-Leg. 18, 21) *proclaimer, preacher* ξένων δαιμονίων *of strange divinities* Ac 17: 18. M-M.*

καταγγέλλω impf. κατήγγελλον; 1 aor. κατήγγειλα; pf. κατήγγελκα; 2 aor. pass. κατηγγέλην (Ac 17: 13). (Since X., An. 2, 5, 11; inscr., pap., 2 Macc; Philo, Op. M. 106; Joseph.) *proclaim* (*solemnly* [Dit., Syll.³ 797, 5]).
1. w. a thing as obj. τι *someth.*: the gospel 1 Cor 9: 14; customs Ac 16: 21. τ. ἡμέρας ταύτας 3: 24 (Jos., Ant. 3, 206 ἑορτήν). τὸν θάνατον τοῦ κυρίου καταγγέλλετε *you proclaim* (by celebrating the sacrament rather than w. words) *the Lord's death* 1 Cor 11: 26. τὸν λόγον τοῦ θεοῦ

ἐν ταῖς συναγωγαῖς Ac 13: 5; cf. 15: 36. Pass. 17: 13. ἐν τῷ Ἰησοῦ τὴν ἀνάστασιν τὴν ἐκ νεκρῶν *proclaim in the person of Jesus the resurrection from the dead* 4: 2. Pass. ἡ πίστις ὑμῶν καταγγέλλεται ἐν ὅλῳ τῷ κόσμῳ *your faith is well known throughout the world* Ro 1: 8; cf. Pol 1: 2.—τινί τι *someth. to someone* (Philo, Aet. M. 68; Jos., Ant. 2, 15) ἄφεσιν ἁμαρτιῶν Ac 13: 38; ὁδὸν σωτηρίας 16: 17. τὸ μαρτύριον (μυστήριον v.l.) τοῦ θεοῦ *the secret purpose of God* 1 Cor 2: 1. φῶς τῷ τε λαῷ καὶ τοῖς ἔθνεσιν *proclaim light to the people and to the Gentiles* Ac 26: 23; cf. 17: 23. εἴς τι: εἰς τὸ εὐαγγέλιον *direct one's proclamation toward the gospel, i.e. foreshadow the gosp.* IPhld 5: 2.
2. w. personal obj.: τινά *someone* τὸν Χριστόν Phil 1: 17; cf. vs. 18; Col 1: 28. τινά τινι *someone to someone* Ac 17: 3. οἱ προφῆται κ. εἰς αὐτόν *the prophets directed their proclamation toward him* (Jesus) IPhld 9: 2.—JSchniewind, TW I 68-71. M-M.*

καταγέλαστος, ον (Aristoph., Hdt.+; Dio Chrys. 57[74], 12; Ael. Aristid. 43, 1 K. =1 p. 1 D.; Celsus 6, 78; Wsd 17: 8; Philo; Jos., C. Ap. 1, 254) *ridiculous* Dg 4: 1.*

καταγελάω impf. κατεγέλων; 1 aor. κατεγέλασα (Aeschyl., Hdt.+; Dit., Syll.³ 1168, 122 [III BC]; BGU 814, 21; LXX) *laugh at, ridicule* τινός (Hdt. 5, 68 al.; Achilles Tat. 1, 1, 13 [ed. SGaselee '47]; Philo, Omn. Prob. Lib. 156; Jos., Ant. 5, 144) Mt 9: 24; Mk 5: 40; Lk 8: 53; 1 Cl 56: 11 (Job 5: 22); 2 Cl 13: 4.—KHRengstorf, TW I 656-60. M-M.*

καταγίνομαι (Demosth., Teles et al.; inscr., pap., LXX; Manetho in Jos., C. Ap. 1, 77) ἔν τινι *busy oneself, be taken up with someth.* (Polyb. 31, 29, 6; Diog. L. 6, 70) ἡ διάνοια ἐν ταῖς πράξεσιν (their) *mind is taken up w. their own affairs* Hm 10, 1, 5.*

καταγινώσκω pf. pass. ptc. κατεγνωσμένος (Aeschyl., Hdt.+; inscr., pap., LXX) *condemn, convict* (Thu. 6, 60, 4; Lysias 1, 32 al.; PYale 42, 24. Of God's unfavorable judgment Jos., Bell. 7, 327) τινός *someone* or *someth.* (Ps.-Pla., Demod. 382E; Dit., Or. 691, 2; POxy. 1062, 14; Dt 25: 1; Philo, Omn. Prob. Lib. 79; Jos., Ant. 4, 5) κ. ἡμῶν ἡ καρδία 1 J 3: 20 (Test. Gad 5: 3 οὐχ ὑπ' ἄλλου καταγινωσκόμενος ἀλλ' ὑπὸ τ. ἰδίας καρδίας. Sir 14: 2). Vs. 21 the obj. is to be supplied fr. what precedes; likew. Mk 7: 2 D; τ. ἀπάτης τοῦ κόσμου *condemn the deceit of the world* Dg 10: 7.—κατεγνωσμένος ἦν *he stood condemned* (by his own actions or by his opinions publicly expressed, cf. Diod. S. 34+35 fgm. 29 κατεγνώσθη=he was condemned [by his outrageous deed or by his opinion publicly expressed], i.e., the faithless friend of Gracchus; Diog. L. 6, 33 καταγινωσκομένους [by their public opinions]; Jos., Bell. 2, 135) Gal 2: 11.—FWMozley, Exp. 8th Ser. IV '12, 143-6. M-M.*

κατάγνυμι fut. κατεάξω Mt 12: 20; 1 aor. κατέαξα; 2 aor. pass. κατεάγην (Bl-D. §66, 2; 101 under ἄγνυμι; Mlt.-H. 189; 226 under ἄγνυμι). (Hom.+; inscr., pap., LXX, Philo; Jos., Bell. 6, 402, Ant. 5, 225) *break* a reed Mt 12: 20; limbs of the body (Menand., Epitr. 628; Prov. Aesopi 10 P. λόγος καλὸς ὀστοῦν κατεάξει) τὰ σκέλη *the legs* J 19: 31, 32, 33 (Euseb., H.E. 5, 21, 3 κατεάγνυται τὰ σκέλη; Philostorg. 3, 27 Ἀέτιον ἀμφοῖν τοῖν σκέλοιν κατεαγῆναι.—Hitzig, Pauly-W. IV 1731. S. on σκέλος). M-M.*

κατάγνωσις, εως, ἡ (Thu.+; PStrassb. 40, 29; Sb 4670, 5; 4681, 5; 4835, 5; Sir 5: 14; Philo, Ebr. 205; Jos., Bell. 6, 34, Vi. 93) *condemnation* μᾶλλον ἑαυτῶν κ. φέρουσιν ἢ τῆς ὁμοφωνίας they would rather bear condemnation of themselves than of the harmony 1 Cl 51: 2.*

καταγράφω impf. κατέγραφον (Eur., Pla.+; inscr., pap., LXX) *write,* also *draw figures* (so Paus. 1, 28, 2; Serenus Antinoensis [IV AD] p. 280, 13; 282, 22 al. [ILHeiberg 1896].—But καταγρ. also means 'write down an accusation': Zen.-P. 59 140, 17 [256 BC] κατὰ τούτων καταγέγραφεν σοι) εἰς τὴν γῆν on the ground J 8: 6 (v.l. ἔγραφεν), vs. 8 D.—On the subject matter s. Diog. L. 2, 127: Menedemus the philosopher (300 BC), in whose presence someone behaved improperly διέγραφεν εἰς τοὔδαφος and thereby shamed him. M-M.*

κατάγω 2 aor. κατήγαγον; 1 aor. pass. κατήχθην, ptc. καταχθείς (Hom.+; inscr., pap., LXX, Joseph., Test. 12 Patr.) *lead* or *bring down* τινά someone, w. the destination given (fr. Jerusalem) εἰς Καισάρειαν Ac 9: 30 (Zen.-P. 59 150, 2 [256 BC] εἰς τὴν Ἀλεξάνδρειαν). (Fr. the barracks, located on higher ground) εἰς τὸ συνέδριον into the council building 23: 20, 28; cf. vs. 15; 22: 30. εἰς ᾅδου (1 Km 2: 6; ᾅδης 1, end) into the underworld 1 Cl 4: 12. Χριστὸν κ. bring Christ down (fr. heaven) (Iambl., Vi. Pyth. 13, 62 an eagle fr. the air) Ro 10: 6.—Of things: τὰ πλοῖα ἐπὶ τὴν γῆν bring the boats to land (fr. the 'high' seas) (cf. Hdt. 8, 4; Cass. Dio 50, 13, 2) Lk 5: 11. Hence the pass. of ships and seafarers *put in* εἴς τι at a harbor (Jos., Ant. 13, 332; 14, 378) εἰς Σιδῶνα Ac 27: 3. εἰς Συρακούσας 28: 12.—21: 3 t.r. M-M.*

καταγωνίζομαι mid. dep.; 1 aor. κατηγωνισάμην (Polyb.+; inscr.) *conquer, defeat, overcome* (Polyb. 2, 42, 3; 2, 45, 4; 3, 4, 10 al.; Plut., Num. 19, 6; Aelian, V.H. 4, 8; Lucian, Dial. Deor. 13, 1; Alciphr. 1, 20, 3; Philo, Abr. 105; Jos., Ant. 4, 153; 7, 53; w. acc. in many of these pass.; Dit., Or. 553, 7 κ. τοὺς ὑπεναντίους) w. acc. of the pers. MPol 19: 2. βασιλείας Hb 11: 33. M-M.*

καταδέχομαι mid. dep.; 1 aor. κατεδεξάμην (Hippocr., Pla.+; inscr., pap., LXX; Jos., C. Ap. 1, 292) *receive, accept* τὶ someth. (Pla., Rep. 3, 401E τὶ εἰς τὴν ψυχήν) τὰ λόγια θεοῦ 1 Cl 19: 1.*

καταδέω 1 aor. κατέδησα (Hom.+; inscr., pap., LXX; Jos., Ant. 5, 309 al.) *bind up* τὶ someth. (Hdt. 2, 122 τ. ὀφθαλμούς; Jos., Ant. 8, 390) τὰ τραύματα *bandage the wounds* (cf. Sir 27: 21 and s. Hobart 27) Lk 10: 34. M-M.*

κατάδηλος, ον (Soph., Hdt.+; PLeipz. 64=Wilcken, Chrest. 281, 28; 33; 37 τοῦτο κατάδηλον; 47; Jos., Ant. 10, 191, Vi. 167) *very clear, quite plain* περισσότερον ἔτι κ. ἐστιν it is clearer still Hb 7: 15. M-M.*

καταδιαιρέω (Polyb. 2, 45, 1; Hero Alex. III p. 66, 2; Dionys. Hal. 4, 19; Sext. Emp., Math. 5, 23; Herm. Wr. 3, 1b; PRainer 22, 25; 27, 21; Ps 54: 10; 135: 13) *divide, make a distinction between* τὰς τῶν καιρῶν ἀλλαγάς Dg 4: 5.*

καταδικάζω 1 aor. κατεδίκασα, pass. κατεδικάσθην *condemn, find* or *pronounce guilty* (Hdt.+, though mostly w. gen. of the pers.; inscr., pap., LXX, Philo; Jos., Bell. 4, 274) τινά someone (so Diod. S. 14, 4, 2 τ. πονηροτάτους; 15, 40, 1; La 3: 36; Jos., Ant. 7, 271) τοὺς ἀναιτίους the innocent Mt 12: 7. τὸν δίκαιον Js 5: 6. Abs. Lk 6: 37a. Pass. (Artem. 2, 9 p. 95, 2; Herm. Wr. 2, 17a; En. 10, 14; Philo; Jos., Bell. 3, 391; Polyb. 6, 37, 1) vs. 37b (αἰσχύνω 𝔓72). ἐκ τῶν λόγων σου by, on the basis of, your words Mt 12: 37. M-M.*

καταδίκη, ης, ἡ (Thu.+; Herm. Wr. 10, 8a; inscr., pap.; Wsd 12: 27; Philo; Jos., Ant. 17, 338; loanw. in rabb.)

condemnation, sentence of condemnation (so Epicharmus [V BC] in Athen. 2, 3 p. 36D; Polyb.; Plut.; Philo, Spec. Leg. 3, 116; Jos., Bell. 4, 317) αἰτεῖσθαι κατά τινος κ. *ask for a sentence of condemnation against someone* Ac 25: 15. M-M.*

καταδιώκω 1 aor. κατεδίωξα (Thu.+; pap., LXX, nearly always 'pursue' in a hostile sense) *search for eagerly, hunt for* τινά someone Mk 1: 36 (in a good sense in Polyb. 6, 42, 1; Ps 37: 21. W. acc. of the pers. Ps 22: 6. κ. μετά τινος=go w. someone 1 Km 30: 22. ὀπίσω τινός Sir 27: 17). M-M.*

καταδουλόω fut. καταδουλώσω (Hdt.+; inscr.; PGM 9, 4 καταδούλωσον πᾶν γένος ἀνθρώπων; 9; LXX, Philo, Test. 12 Patr., Sib. Or. 2, 175) *enslave, reduce to slavery,* in our lit. only in fig. sense (the act. is so used in PGM 9, 9; Menand., fgm. 338, 1 Kock; Plut., Mor. 828c) τινά someone 2 Cor 11: 20; Gal 2: 4. M-M.*

καταδυναστεύω (X.+; PPetr. III 36(a) verso, 2 [pass.]; POxy. 67, 15 [act.]; LXX, Ep. Arist.; Jos., Ant. 12, 30) *oppress, exploit, dominate* τινός someone (Diod. S. 13, 73; Ep. Arist. 148 v.l.) of exploitation by the rich (oft. in LXX of outrages against the poor, widows, and orphans) Js 2: 6; Dg 10: 5.—Of the tyrannical rule of the devil (Plut., Is. et Os. 41 p. 367D of the evil spirit Typhon) Hm 12, 5, 1f; pass. *be oppressed* Ac 10: 38 (ὑπό τινος as Strabo 6, 2, 4 p. 270; Horapollo 1, 6). M-M.*

κατάθεμα, ατος, τό (Audollent, Defix. Tab. 22, 23; Act. Phil. 28 p. 15, 12 B.) *that which is devoted* or *given over to a deity,* i.e. under a curse (חֵרֶם), hence *accursed thing* (s. ἀνάθεμα 2) Rv 22: 3. The passage D 16: 5 is (perh. purposely) obscure: σωθήσονται ὑπ' αὐτοῦ τοῦ κ. *they will be saved by the accursed one himself* (i.e. by Christ who, in the minds of those offended by him, is accursed; cf. also Gal 3: 13, κατάρα). M-M.*

καταθεματίζω (Act. Phil. 17, p. 9, 23B; Irenaeus 1, 13, 4; 16, 3; PGlaue, ZNW 45, '54, 94) *curse* Mt 26: 74. M-M.*

καταιγίς, ίδος, ἡ (Democr. 14; Ps.-Aristot., De Mundo 4; Aelian, N.A. 15, 2 p. 367, 20; Herm. Wr. 16, 10b; LXX, Philo, Deus Imm. 60; Test. Judah 21: 9) *a sudden blast of wind* 1 Cl 57: 4 (Pr 1: 27).*

καταισχύνω (Hom.+; LXX) pass.: impf. κατῃσχυνόμην; 1 aor. κατῃσχύνθην; 1 fut. καταισχυνθήσομαι; pf. ptc. κατῃσχυμμένος (Hm 12, 5, 2; Bl-D. §72).

1. *dishonor, disgrace, disfigure* (Diod. S. 11, 46, 2; 13, 106, 10; Epict. 2, 8, 21; Philo, Spec. Leg. 3, 14; Jos., Ant. 20, 89 σποδῷ τ. κεφαλήν) τὴν κεφαλήν 1 Cor 11: 4f.

2. *put to shame* (Appian, Bell. Civ. 4, 126 §526) τινά someone of God τοὺς σοφούς, τὰ ἰσχυρά 1 Cor 1: 27. Pass. *be put to shame, be humiliated* (Diod. S. 19, 72, 7; LXX), also *be ashamed* (Diod. S. 2, 4, 3 καταισχυνθεῖσα=because she was ashamed) Mt 20: 28 D; Lk 13: 17; 2 Cor 7: 14; 9: 4; 1 Pt 3: 16 (𝔓75 has δικάζετε and δικασθῆτε in Lk 6: 37 a, b); Hm 12, 5, 2.—*Humiliate* (Test. Judah 12: 5) τοὺς μὴ ἔχοντας those who have nothing (cf. Ruth 2: 15) 1 Cor 11: 22.

3. of the shame and disappointment that come to one whose faith or hope is shown to be vain—a. act. causative (anonymous iambic poet [III/II BC] ed. Diehl III, XIII l. 68: a god τὸ θεῖον οὐ καταισχύνει=cause to be ruined or lost; Ps 118: 31 ἡ ἐλπὶς οὐ καταισχύνει hope does not disappoint Ro 5: 5.

b. pass. *be disappointed* (anonymous iambic poet in Ps.-Callisth. 1, 46a, 9 τὸ θράσος κατῃσχύνθη=boldness has been put to shame; Is 50: 7 v.l.; Ps 30: 2; Sir 2: 10) Ro 9: 33; 10: 11; 1 Pt 2: 6 (on all three cf. Is 28: 16). M-M.*

κατακαίω (Hom.+; inscr., pap., LXX) impf. κατέκαιον; fut. κατακαύσω; 1 aor. κατέκαυσα. Pass.: 2 aor. κατεκάην (Jos., Bell. 6, 191) and 1 aor. κατεκαύθην (MPol 12: 3; Jos., Bell. 7, 450); 2 fut. κατακαήσομαι (1 Cor 3: 15; 2 Pt 3: 10 v.l. This form also Nicol. Dam.: 90 fgm. 68 p. 371, 32 Jac.; Sib. Or. 3, 507) and 1 fut. κατακαυθήσομαι (Rv 18: 8; Hs 4: 4). Cf. Bl-D. §76, 1; Mlt.-H. 242 (s.v. καίω) *burn down, burn up, consume* by fire τὶ someth.: weeds Mt 13: 30; books Ac 19: 19 (cf. PAmh. 30, 36 [II bc] ἠναγκάσθην ἐνέγκαι τὰς συνγραφὰς καὶ ταύτας κατακαῦσαι. Acc. to Diog. L. 9, 52, books of Protagoras were burned by the Athenians in the marketplace); a heifer B 8: 1 (cf. Num 19: 5, 8).—Pass. ἔργον 1 Cor 3: 15; cf. γῆ καὶ τὰ ἐν αὐτῇ ἔργα κατακαήσεται 2 Pt 3: 10 v.l. Bodies of animals Hb 13: 11. A third of the earth w. its trees and grass Rv 8: 7a, b, c. ὡς ξύλα Hs 4: 4. Of being burned at the stake as a martyr MPol 12: 3 (Diod. S. 1, 59, 3; 12, 25, 3 [in Roman admin. of justice]; Dio Chrys. 9[10], 26 κατεκαύθη ζῶν; 29[46], 7; Artem. 2, 52 [as the result of a court sentence]; 2, 49 p. 151, 16; Jos., Bell. 7, 450 [in Roman admin. of justice]).—W. the addition of πυρί *burn, consume* someth. w. *fire* (Ex 29: 14, 34; Lev 9: 11) chaff Mt 3: 12; Lk 3: 17. Pass., weeds Mt 13: 40. W. ἐν πυρί added (oft. LXX): κ. τινὰ ἐν π. Rv 17: 16. Pass. 18: 8.—Of a pillow ὑπὸ πυρὸς κατακαίεσθαι *be consumed by fire* MPol 5: 2. M-M.*

κατακαλύπτω pf. pass. ptc. κατακεκαλυμμένος (Hom. +; inscr., LXX) *cover, veil.*
1. act. (Is 6: 2) and pass. (Sus 32 Theod.) of a young woman κατακεκαλυμμένη ἕως τοῦ μετώπου *covered* or *veiled to the forehead* Hv 4, 2, 1. But here the form could also be
2. mid. *cover oneself* w. a veil, abs. (s. Jos., Ant. 7, 254) 1 Cor 11: 6a, b. W. acc. (either of the obj. or of specification, as Gen 38: 15) τὴν κεφαλήν vs. 7 (Ps.-Dicaearchus p. 144 l. 16ff F. of the Theban women: τὸ τῶν ἱματίων ἐπὶ τῆς κεφαλῆς κάλυμμα τοιοῦτόν ἐστιν, ὥσπερ προσωπιδίῳ δοκεῖν πᾶν τὸ πρόσωπον κατειλῆφθαι. In case the text is in order, it may be transl. about as follows: the covering of the clothes on the head is of such a kind that the whole face seems to be covered as with a mask).—AJeremias, D. Schleier v. Sumer bis heute '31; RdeVaux, RB 44, '35, 395–412; AOepke, TW III 563–5. M-M.*

κατακάλυψις, εως, ἡ (Περὶ ὕψους 17, 3; Galen XIII 99 K.; XIX 445; Proclus on Pla., Tim. III p. 149, 17 Diehl) *covering* ἐν μίτρᾳ ἦν ἡ κ. αὐτῆς *her head was covered with a snood* Hv 4, 2, 1.*

κατάκαρπος, ον (Aristodem. in Athen. 11 p. 495 F.; Leontios, Prooem. p. 2, 16 and 21 of vine and olive tree; LXX) *very fruitful* δένδρα Hs 9, 1, 10.*

κατακαυχάομαι 2 pers. sing. κατακαυχᾶσαι (Zech 10: 12; Jer 27: 11, 38; grave-inscr. of Asia Minor: SAB '32, p. 855 κατακαυχᾶσθαι κατά τινος of a gladiator over his defeated foe).
1. *boast against, exult over* τινός *someone* or *someth.* τῶν κλάδων the branches Ro 11: 18a.—Abs. *boast, brag* Ro 11: 18b; Js 3: 14; 4: 16 v.l.
2. *triumph over* τινός (Rhet. Gr. I 551, 13; 589, 23; Constantinus Manasse. 1, 59 Hercher; Psellus p. 183, 3 τῆς φύσεως κατεκαυχήσατο) κ. ἔλεος κρίσεως *mercy triumphs over judgment* Js 2: 13.*

κατάκειμαι impf. κατεκείμην (Hom.+; grave-inscr.: Sb 6089, 1; pap., LXX, Joseph.) *lie down.*
1. of sick people (Hdt. 7, 229; Aristoph., Eccl. 313; Lucian, Icarom. 31; Plut., Cic. 43, 3; Jos., Ant. 6, 214; PRyl. 68, 16 [89 bc]; PTebt. 422, 19) J 5: 3, 6. W. the sickness given: Ac 28: 8. κατέκειτο πυρέσσουσα *she lay sick w. a fever* Mk 1: 30. Also of one who has already died 5: 40 v.l. W. indication of the place where: ἐπί τινος *lie on someth.* Ac 9: 33. ἐπί τι *on someth.* Lk 5: 25. Cf. Mk 2: 4.
2. of those who are resting (M. Ant. 5, 1, 1) MPol 7: 1. Also of animals lying in the meadow Hs 9, 1, 9.
3. *recline* on a couch at table, *dine* (X., An. 6, 1, 4, Symp. 1, 14; Pla., Symp. 177D, Rep. 2, 372D) abs. (Dio Chrys. 31[48], 3 οἱ κατακείμενοι; Jos., Vi. 222) Mk 14: 3; Lk 5: 29. W. ἐν foll. (Diog. L. 7, 1, 19 ἐν συμποσίῳ) Mk 2: 15; Lk 7: 37; ἐν εἰδωλείῳ κ. *dine in a temple* 1 Cor 8: 10. M-M.*

κατακεντέω 1 aor. κατεκέντησα *pierce, stab* (Pla., Tim. 76B; Diod. S. et al.; Jdth 16: 12; Ezk 23: 47; Philo, Poster. Cai. 182; Jos., Ant. 14, 292 τ. ἄνδρα) w. acc. B 7: 8, 9.*

κατακλάω 1 aor. κατέκλασα (Hom.+; Ezk 19: 12; Philo, Somn. 2, 236; Jos., Bell. 7, 204, Ant. 2, 305) *break in pieces* τοὺς ἄρτους Mk 6: 41; Lk 9: 16. M-M.*

κατακλείω 1 aor. κατέκλεισα (Hdt., Thu.+; inscr., pap., LXX; Philo, Aet. M. 135 κ. ἐν; Jos., Bell. 4, 327, Ant. 13, 380 κ. ἐν) *shut up, lock up* κ. ἐν φυλακῇ *in prison* Lk 3: 20. Also ἐν φυλακαῖς Ac 26: 10 (cf. Jer 39: 2f ἐν αὐλῇ τ. φυλακῆς..., ἐν ᾗ κατέκλεισεν αὐτόν...; Dit., Or. 669, 17 [I ad]). M-M.*

κατακληροδοτέω (Theophyl. Sim., Hist. 6, 7, 12; Dt 1: 38 v.l.; 21: 16; 1 Macc 3: 36) *parcel out by lot* Ac 13: 19 t.r. (s. κατακληρονομέω). M-M.*

κατακληρονομέω 1 aor. κατεκληρονόμησα (LXX; Test. Benj. 10: 5 v.l.).
1. *give (over) as an inheritance* (Dt 3: 28; 12: 10; 31: 7 al.) τὶ someth. a country Ac 13: 19 (where the t.r. has κατεκληροδότησεν).—2. *receive as an inheritance* (Num 13: 30; Dt 2: 21; Ps 36: 34) B 6: 8.*

κατακλίνω 1 aor. κατέκλινα, pass. κατεκλίθην (Hom. +; inscr., pap., LXX, Ep. Arist.; Philo, Op. M. 85; Joseph.). Act. *cause to lie down* or *sit down* to eat; τινά *someone* (Hdt. 1, 126; X., Cyr. 2, 3, 21 ἐπὶ τὸ δεῖπνον; PGM 1, 168; Jos., Ant. 6, 52 κ. ἐπάνω τῶν κεκλημένων) κατακλίνατε αὐτοὺς κλισίας Lk 9: 14; cf. vs. 15.—Pass. *recline at table* (Aristoph., Vesp. 1208; 1210; X., Cyr. 5, 2, 15; Dit., Syll.³ 1042, 25; Jdth 12: 15; Jos., Ant. 6, 163) Lk 7: 36; 24: 30. εἰς τὴν πρωτοκλισίαν *in the place of honor* 14: 8. M-M.*

κατακλύζω 1 aor. pass. κατεκλύσθην (Pind., Aeschyl., Hdt.+; inscr., pap., LXX, Philo; Jos., Bell. 5, 566; Sib. Or. 3, 690) *flood, inundate* pass. κόσμος ὕδατι κατακλυσθεὶς ἀπώλετο *the world was destroyed by being flooded w. water* 2 Pt 3: 6. M-M.*

κατακλυσμός, οῦ, ὁ (Pla.+; Marmor Par. [III bc]: 239A 4 Jac. [Deucalion]; Celsus 1, 19; 4, 11; PMagd. 28, 18 [III bc]; BGU 1121, 27; LXX; En., Philo, Joseph., Test. 12 Patr.) *flood, deluge*, in our lit. only of the flood in Noah's time (Gen 6–9; Jos., Ant. 1, 92f; 10, 147, C. Ap. 1, 130; Nicol. Dam. in Jos., Ant. 1, 95; Berosus in Jos., Ant. 1, 158; Sib. Or. 4, 53) Mt 24: 38f; Lk 17: 27. κατακλυσμὸν ἐπάγειν *bring a flood* (Gen 6: 17) τινί *upon someth.* 2 Pt 2: 5. M-M.*

κατακολουθέω 1 aor. κατηκολούθησα (Teles p. 57, 10; Polyb.; Dio Chrys. 59[76], 4; inscr., pap., LXX) *follow* (Longus 3, 15) τινί *someone* Ac 16: 17. Abs. Lk 23: 55. Fig. (so mostly, incl. Ep. Arist.; Jos., Ant. 6, 147, C. Ap. 2, 281 al.) τῇ σοφίᾳ τινός *approach* or *attain the wisdom of someone* Pol 3: 2. M-M.*

κατακόπτω impf. κατέκοπτον (Hdt.+; inscr., pap., LXX; Jos., Ant. 17, 213). 1. *beat, bruise* τινά τινι *someone w. someth.* ἑαυτὸν λίθοις *beat oneself w. stones* Mk 5: 5 (Epigr. Gr. 316f; PLeipz. 37, 20 κατέκοψαν πληγαῖς αὐτόν; PSI 313, 10. S. other exx. in Field, Notes 27). The basic mng. of κ., *cut,* is also poss. here.—2. *break in pieces* (Pla., Euthyd. 301c; 2 Ch 15: 16; 34: 7) of stones (Is 27: 9) Hv 3, 2, 7; cf. 3, 6, 1. M-M.*

κατακρημνίζω 1 aor. κατεκρήμνισα (X., Cyr. 1, 4, 7; 8, 3, 41; Diod. S. 4, 31, 3; 2 Ch 25: 12; 4 Macc 4: 25; Philo, Agr. 68; Jos., Bell. 4, 312, Ant. 6, 114) *throw down (from) a cliff* τινά *someone* (Phylarchus [III BC]: 81 fgm. 24 Jac.; Philod., Ira p. 56 W.; Jos., Ant. 9, 191) Lk 4: 29.*

κατάκριμα, ατος, τό prob. not 'condemnation', but the punishment following sentence, *punishment, doom* (Dionys. Hal. 6, 61 κατακριμάτων ἀφέσεις; POxy. 298, 4 [I AD]; PRainer 1, 15ff; 188, 14f; Wilcken, Chrest. 28, 12; Dssm., NB 92f [BS 264f]) οὐδὲν κ. τοῖς ἐν Χριστῷ Ἰησοῦ *there is no doom for those who are in Christ Jesus* Ro 8: 1. εἰς πάντας ἀνθρώπους εἰς κ. (sc. ἐγένετο) (led) *to punishment* or *doom for all men* 5: 18. In a play on words w. κρίμα vs. 16.—FWDanker, FWGingrich-Festschr., '72, 105 (Ro). M-M.*

κατακρίνω fut. κατακρινῶ; 1 aor. κατέκρινα; 1 aor. pass. κατεκρίθην; 1 fut. pass. κατακριθήσομαι; pf. κατακέκριμαι (Pind., Hdt.+; inscr., pap., LXX; En. 13, 5; Jos., Ant. 3, 308; 10, 238) *condemn* τινά *someone* (Wsd 4: 16; Esth 2: 1; Sus 53) J 8: 10f. In a play on words w. κρίνω Ro 2: 1. Pass. Mt 27: 3; Dg 5: 12; w. διακρίνομαι Ro 14: 23. τινὰ θανάτῳ *condemn someone to death* (Da 4: 37a; Jos., Ant. 10, 124) Mk 10: 33; Hs 8, 11, 3. Also κ. εἰς θάνατον Mt 20: 18 (v.l. θανάτῳ). εἰς πῦρ αἰώνιον Dg 10: 7. Of cities καταστροφῇ κ. *condemn to destruction* 2 Pt 2: 6 (on the dat. cf. Bl-D. §195, 2; Rob. 533 and s. Dit., Syll.³ 736, 160ff τὸν μὴ ποιοῦντα κατακρινάτω εἴκοσι δραχμαῖς). W. acc. and inf. foll. (Sus 41 Theod. κατέκριναν αὐτὴν ἀποθανεῖν) κατέκριναν αὐτὸν ἔνοχον εἶναι θανάτου *they condemned him as being worthy of death* Mk 14: 64. Abs. Ro 8: 34. Of God's condemnation Mk 16: 16; 1 Cor 11: 32 (play on words w. κρίνειν). The conduct of one person, since it sets a standard, can result in the condemnation before God of another person whose conduct is inferior (Wsd 4: 16; cf. Ro 2: 27) Mt 12: 41f [JoachJeremias, Jesus' Promise to the Nations, '58, 50 n. 3); Lk 11: 31f; Hb 11: 7. ὁ θεὸς ... κατέκρινεν τὴν ἁμαρτίαν ἐν τῇ σαρκί *God has pronounced his sentence on sin in the flesh* Ro 8: 3. M-M.*

κατάκρισις, εως, ἡ (Vett. Val. 108, 4; 117, 35; Syntipas p. 43, 11 θεόθεν κ. Act. Thom. 84 p. 200, 9 B.; 128 p. 236, 20; 135 p. 242, 10) *condemnation* κατάκρισιν ἔχειν τινί *bring condemnation for someone* 2 Cl 15: 5. πρὸς κ. οὐ λέγω *I do not say this to condemn* 2 Cor 7: 3. Of OT religion: διακονία κατακρίσεως *the ministry of condemnation* (s. διακονία 3) 3: 9. M-M.*

κατάκριτος, ον (Diod. S. 33, 2; Plut., Mor. 188A; Ps.-Lucian, Am. 36; 52; Suppl. Epigr. Gr. VIII 13, 21; Philo, Virt. 139; Jos., Bell. 1, 639; 6, 108; Act. Jo. 10 p. 157, 12 B.) *condemned* abs. IEph 12: 1; ITr 3: 3; IRo 4: 3.*

κατακροάομαι mid. dep.; impf. 3 sing. κατηκροᾶτο (Eupolis Com. [V BC] fgm. 245 K.) *listen attentively* τινός *to someone* (Jos., Bell. 4, 38) προσευχομένου μου Hv 3, 1, 6.*

κατακύπτω 1 aor. κατέκυψα (Hom.+; Epict. 2, 16, 22; Lucian, Icarom. 15 al.; 4 Km 9: 32; Ep. Arist. 91) *bend down* (Appian, Bell. Civ. 2, 62 §258 [ὑπ᾽ αἰδοῦς=out of shame]; Jos., Bell. 2, 224) J 8: 8. M-M.*

κατακυριεύω fut. κατακυριεύσω; 1 aor. κατεκυρίευσα, imper. κατακυρίευσον; 1 aor. pass. κατεκυριεύθην. 1. *become master, gain dominion over, subdue* (Diod. S. 14, 64, 1; Num 21: 24; 32: 22; Ps 9: 26 al.) τινός (LXX) Ac 19: 16. Fig. *become master, gain power* τινός *over someone* (Test. Jud. 15: 5) or *someth.* τοῦ διαβόλου Hm 7: 2; 12, 4, 7; 12, 6, 4. τῶν ἔργων τοῦ διαβόλου m 12, 6, 2. τῶν πονηρῶν ἐπιθυμιῶν m 5, 1, 1. τῆς διψυχίας *master doubt* m 9: 10. τῆς ἐπιθυμίας 12, 2, 5. ἃ βλέπεις, ἐκείνων κατακυρίευε *what you see, strive to master that* s 9, 2, 7.—Pass. ὑπό τινος *let oneself be overcome by someth.* Hm 12, 2, 3. 2. *be master, lord it (over), rule* τινός *of, over someone* or *someth.* (Ps 118: 133; Gen 1: 28; Sir 17: 4) Mt 20: 25; Mk 10: 42. τῆς γῆς B 6: 13, 17. τῶν ὑπὸ τὸν οὐρανὸν πάντων *be master of everything under heaven* Hm 12, 4, 2; cf. 3. τῶν κλήρων 1 Pt 5: 3.*

καταλαλέω (Aristoph.+; Polyb.; Stoic. III 237, 6 al.; Dit., Syll.³ 593, 6 [II BC]; PHib. 151 [c. 250 BC]; LXX; Philo [only in connection w. the OT: Leg. All. 2, 66f= Num 12: 8 and Leg. All. 2, 78=Num 21: 7]) *speak against, speak evil of, defame, slander* τινός *someone* (Ps 77: 19 τοῦ θεοῦ; 100: 5 τοῦ πλησίον αὐτοῦ; Test. Iss. 3: 4, Gad 5: 4. Cf. Diod. S. 11, 44, 6) Js 4: 11a, b; 2 Cl 4: 3; Hm 2: 2a. ἵνα ἐν ᾧ καταλαλοῦσιν ὑμῶν 1 Pt 2: 12 (cf. Dit., Syll.³ loc. cit. ἵνα μηδ᾽ ἐν τούτοις ἔχωσιν ἡμᾶς καταλαλεῖν οἱ ...). Also κατά τινος (so mostly LXX, En.) 1 Cl 35: 8 (Ps 49: 20). Pass. 1 Pt 3: 16.—Fig. (Ps.-Lucian, As. 12 τοῦ λύχνου) νόμου *speak against the law* Js 4: 11c.—Abs. ὁ καταλαλῶν *one who speaks evil* Hm 2: 2 (three times). M-M.*

καταλαλιά, ᾶς, ἡ (Leontios 18 p. 36, 9; Wsd 1: 11; Test. Gad 3: 3; Act. Phil. 142 p. 81, 8 B.—Thom. Mag.: καταλαλιὰ οὐδεὶς εἶπε τῶν ἀρχαίων, ἀλλ᾽ ἀντὶ τούτου κατηγορία) *evil speech, slander, defamation, detraction* in lists of vices (s. on πλεονεξία) in sing. and pl. (to denote individual instances) 2 Cor 12: 20; 1 Cl 35: 5; B 20: 2; Pol 2: 2; 4: 3; Hm 8: 3; s 9, 15, 3. ἀποτίθεσθαι πάσας καταλαλιάς *put away all slanders* 1 Pt 2: 1. φεύγειν καταλαλιάς *avoid evil speaking* 1 Cl 30: 1; cf. vs. 3; πιστεύειν τῇ κ. *believe the slander* Hm 2: 2; πονηρὰ ἡ κ. 2: 3; κ. is injurious to faith s 9, 23, 2; cf. 3.*

κατάλαλος, ον *speaking evil of others, slanderous* w. δίψυχοι Hs 8, 7, 2. W. δόλιοι s 9, 26, 7. Subst. ὁ κ. (POxy. 1828 r, 3) *slanderer* (in a list of vices) Ro 1: 30; Hs 6, 5, 5.*

καταλαμβάνω (Hom.+; inscr., pap., LXX, Ep. Arist., Philo, Joseph., Test. 12 Patr.) 2 aor. κατέλαβον; pf. κατείληφα; 2 aor. mid. κατελαβόμην; pf. pass. 3 sing. κατείληπται, ptc. κατειλημμένος; 1 aor. pass. κατελήμφθην (Phil 3: 12; Bl-D. §101 p. 46 s.v. λαμβ.; Mlt.-H. 246f, s.v. λαμβ.; on the form κατειλήφθη J 8: 4 in the older NT editions cf. W-S. §12, 1). 1.—a. act. and pass. *seize, win, attain, make one's own* (Plut., Cleom. 4, 2; POxy. 1101, 26.—Diog. L. 5, 12 καταλαμβάνω means 'come into possession of an inheritance') abs. (though τὸ βραβεῖον is to be supplied fr. the context) of the winning of a prize 1 Cor 9: 24. As a result of διώκειν (cf. Diod. S. 17, 73, 3 ἐπιδιώκων ... τὸν Δαρεῖον ... καταλαβών; Sir 11: 10 ἐὰν διώκῃς, οὐ μὴ καταλάβῃς; 27: 8) Phil 3: 12a, 13: Χριστόν, corresp. to κατελήμφθην ὑπὸ Χριστοῦ Ἰ. vs. 12b. δικαιοσύνην Ro 9: 30. ἐπίγνωσιν πατρός Dg 10: 1. The pass. is found in the mng. *make one's own* in the ending of Mark in the Freer ms. 3 (KHaacker, ZNW 63, '72, 125–29).—This may also be the mng. of κ. in J 1: 5 ἡ σκοτία αὐτὸ (=τὸ φῶς) οὐ κατέλαβεν *the darkness did not grasp it* (Hdb. ad loc.; so also Bultmann, and similarly JADyer, JBL 79, '60, 70f: *appreciate*), in which case *grasp* easily passes over to the sense *comprehend* (the act. [for the mid. in the same sense s. 2 below] has the latter sense in Pla., Phaedr. 250D; Polyb. 8, 4, 6; Dionys. Hal. 5, 46, 3; PTebt. 15, 5; 38, 18; Ep. Arist. 1; Philo, Mut. Nom. 4; Jos., Vi. 56). Most Greek commentators since Origen take κ. here as *overcome, suppress* (Hdt. 1, 46 κ. τινῶν αὐξανομένην τὴν δύναμιν; 1, 87 τὸ πῦρ; WNagel, ZNW 50, '59, 132–37). So Gdspd. *put out* (Probs. 93f). But perh. J intended to include both mngs. here (so FWGingrich, Classical Weekly 37, '43, 77), and some such transl. as *master* would suggest this (so MSmith, JBL 64, '45, 510f).

b. *seize w. hostile intent, overtake, come upon* (Hom. +; oft. LXX; numerous exx. in JJWettstein on J 1: 5 and in Zahn[5,6] '21, p. 63, 40. Cf. also Dit., Syll.[3] 434/5, 14) μὴ ἡμᾶς καταλάβῃ κακά *lest evil overtake us* (cf. Gen 19: 19; Num 32: 23) 2 Cl 10: 1; cf. B 4: 1. Of a demon ὅπου ἐὰν αὐτὸν καταλάβῃ *wherever it seizes him* (the sick man) Mk 9: 18. Of the coming of 'the day', unexpected by the 'sons of darkness' and fraught w. danger for them 1 Th 5: 4. Esp. used of night, evening, darkness coming upon a pers. (Dionys. Hal. 2, 51, 3 ἑσπέρα γὰρ αὐτοὺς κατέλαβεν; Lucian, Tox. 31; 52; Philo, De Jos. 145; Jos., Ant. 5, 61 καταλαβοῦσα νύξ, Vi. 329. But the thought in these instances is not necessarily always that of night as of something fearsome, the friend of no man. κ. can also mean simply 'arrive', 'come on', as Dionys. Hal. 10, 56, 1 ἐπεὶ κατέλαβεν ὁ ἀρχαιρεσιῶν καιρός; Strabo 3, 1, 5; Jos., Ant. 4, 78) J 12: 35; 6: 17 v.l.

c. *catch, detect* (PLille 3, 58 [III BC]; PRyl. 138, 15. Esp. of the detection of adultery Epict. 2, 4, 1; BGU 1024 III, 11; Sus 58) τινὰ ἐπί τινι *someone in someth.* ἐπὶ μοιχείᾳ *in adultery* (Diod. S. 10, 20, 2 ἐπὶ μοιχείᾳ κατειλημμένῃ) J 8: 3. Pass. w. ptc. indicating the punishable act ἐπ' αὐτοφώρῳ *in the act* vs. 4.

2. mid. *grasp, find, understand* (Dionys. Hal. 2, 66, 6; Sext. Emp., Math. 7, 288; Vett. Val. 225, 8; Philo, Mos. 1, 278; Jos., Ant. 8, 167) w. acc. and inf. Ac 25: 25. W. ὅτι foll. 4: 13; 10: 34. W. indirect discourse foll. Eph 3: 18. M-M. B. 701; 1207.*

καταλάμπω (Eur., Pla. +; PGM 7, 704; Philo; Test. Gad 7: 3[?]) *shine upon*, pass. *be illuminated, be bright* (Eur., Tro. 1069, Ion 87; X., Mem. 4, 7, 7) τινί *by* or *with someth.* (Cebes 17, 1 φωτὶ καταλαμπόμενος; Wsd 17: 19; Philo, Somn. 1, 218) ἀκτῖσιν ἡλίου AP 5: 15 (Dio Chrys. 19[36], 45 τὸ καταλαμπόμενον Ἡλίῳ).*

καταλέγω (Hom. +; LXX; Philo, Aet. M. 114; Jos., Ant. 19, 301, C. Ap. 1, 131 al.) *select* as a member of a group, *enlist, enroll* (of soldiers Aristoph. +. Of reception into the circle of the gods Diod. S. 4, 39, 4; into the Senate, Plut., Pomp. 13, 11. Cf. Inscr. Gr. 165, 2; BGU 1073, 10) pass. χήρα καταλεγέσθω μὴ ἔλαττον ἐτῶν ἑξήκοντα γεγονυῖα either gener. *be selected* or specif. *be enrolled* 1 Ti 5: 9 (of reception into a religious body κ. is also used POxy. 416, 4. On the constr. cf. the double acc. Pla., Leg. 742E κ. τινὰ πλούσιον). M-M.*

κατάλειμμα, ατος, τό (Galen; LXX; En. 106, 18[?]) *remnant* (so Galen XIV p. 456, 13 K.) Ro 9: 27 t.r. (Is 10: 22); s. ὑπόλειμμα.*

καταλείπω (Hom. +; inscr., pap., LXX; En. 106, 16; Philo, Joseph., Test. 12 Patr.) impf. κατέλειπον; fut. καταλείψω; 1 aor. κατέλειψα (Ac 6: 2; Hs 8, 3, 5; PRainer 102; Jos., Bell. 1, 504, Ant. 10, 277); 2 aor. κατέλιπον (on the aor. forms s. Bl-D. §75 app.; W-S. §13, 10; Rob. 348; Helbing 90f; Thackeray 234; Dssm., NB 18 [BS 190]; Crönert 234, 6; KDieterich, Untersuchungen 1898, 238; Mayser 364); pf. pass. inf. καταλελεῖφθαι, ptc. καταλελειμμένος (W-S. §5, 13e); 1 aor. pass. κατελείφθην; *leave behind.*

1. of pers. τινά *leave someone—a. leave* someone (*behind*) when one leaves a place (Diod. S. 1, 55, 4; 5, 51, 4; Da 10: 13) καταλείψει ἄνθρωπος τὸν πατέρα κτλ. Mt 19: 5; Mk 10: 7; Eph 5: 31 (all three Gen 2: 24); Mt 16: 4; 21: 17. κἀκείνους κατέλιπεν αὐτοῦ Ac 18: 19. κατέλιπόν σε ἐν Κρήτῃ, ἵνα Tit 1: 5 v.l. ὁ Φῆλιξ κατέλιπεν τ. Παῦλον δεδεμένον Ac 24: 27 (the ptc. as Test. Reub. 3: 14); cf. the pass. *be left behind* 25: 14.—Elsewh. the pass. has the mng. *remain behind* (X., An. 5, 6, 12) J 8: 9. ἐν Ἀθήναις 1 Th 3: 1. W. inf. foll. to denote purpose: τοῦ φυλάσσειν τὸν πύργον *to guard the tower* Hs 9, 5, 1.

b. *die and leave (behind)* (Hom. +; oft. pap. and LXX) γυναῖκα Mk 12: 19. σπέρμα *descendants* vs. 21. τέκνα (Dt 28: 54; cf. Pr 20: 7; Jos., Ant. 12, 235) Lk 20: 31.

c. *leave over*, see to it that someth. *is left* (cf. Sir 24: 33) κατέλιπον ἐμαυτῷ ἑπτακισχιλίους ἄνδρας *I have kept 7,000 men for myself* Ro 11: 4 (3 Km 19: 18; the Lucianic text and the Hebr. have the first pers.).

d. *leave without help* τινά w. the inf. of result (not of purpose; s. Bl-D. §392, 1f; Rob. 1090, and cf. Il. 17, 151) ἡ ἀδελφή μου μόνην με κατέλειπεν διακονεῖν *my sister has left me without help, so that now I must serve alone* Lk 10: 40 (cf. Jos., Vi. 301 κ. ἐμὲ μόνον).—*Desert* MPol 17: 2.

2. w. impers. obj.—a. *leave (behind)* (s. 1a) πρόβατα ἐν τῇ ἐρήμῳ Lk 15: 4. πάντα ἐπὶ τ. γῆς *everything on land* 5: 11 D.—IRo 4: 2.

b. *leave* a place when going away (Dio Chrys. 30[47], 2 τ. πατρίδα) τὴν Ναζαρά Mt 4: 13. Αἴγυπτον Hb 11: 27. Fig. καταλείποντες εὐθεῖαν ὁδὸν ἐπλανήθησαν 2 Pt 2: 15.

c. *leave to one side, give up* 2 Cl 10: 1. Also in the sense *set to one side, neglect* (Ps.-X., Cyneg. 3, 10 τὰ αὑτῶν ἔργα; Dt 29: 24 τ. διαθήκην; Jos., Ant. 8, 190 τ. τῶν πατρίων ἐθισμῶν φυλακήν; Test. Iss. 6: 1 τὴν ἁπλότητα) τὸν λόγον τ. θεοῦ Ac 6: 2. τ. ἀλήθειαν Hs 8, 9, 1. ἄμπελος Hs 9, 26, 4.

d. *leave, abandon, give up* (e.g. schol. on Apollon. Rhod. 272–74 τὴν τέχνην give up one's trade); *lose* (Petosiris, fgm. 12 l. 22; 120 τὸν θρόνον) πάντα Lk 5: 28; cf. 1 Cl 10: 2; τὴν παροικίαν τ. κόσμου τούτου 2 Cl 5: 1; of a youth fleeing fr. the police Mk 14: 52 (Aesop, Fab. 419 P.=196 H.: κατέλιπε τὸν ἑαυτοῦ χιτῶνα; Gen 39: 12; Test. Jos. 8: 3).

e. *leave someth.* as it is, located in its own place, of an island καταλιπόντες αὐτὴν εὐώνυμον Ac 21: 3.

f. *leave over* (Alex. Aphr., Fat. 28, II 2 p. 199, 8) pass. *remain* (Jos., Bell. 4, 338 σωτηρίας ἐλπίς), specif. in the sense *be incomplete, unfinished, open* (X., Cyr. 2, 3, 11 μάχη; PLond. 1171, 43 [8 BC]) καταλειπομένη ἐπαγγελία *a promise that is still open* Hb 4: 1.

g. *leave behind* of an inheritance Hv 3, 12, 2. M-M.*

καταλιθάζω fut. καταλιθάσω (only in Christian wr. But καταλιθοβολέω Ex 17: 4; Num 14: 10 and καταλιθόω in

Paus.; Jos., Ant. 4, 282 al.) *stone to death* τινά *someone* Lk 20: 6. *

καταλλαγή, ῆς, ἡ *reconciliation* (so Aeschyl., Sept. 767; Demosth. 1, 4) with God (2 Macc 5: 20; Philo, Exs. 166 αἱ πρὸς τὸν πατέρα [=God] καταλλαγαί [in Philo always pl.]), which, acc. to Paul, is brought about by God alone; he 'reconciles men to himself' (s. καταλλάσσω). κ. κόσμου (opp. ἀποβολὴ) Ro 11: 15; λόγος τῆς κ. *the word of reconciliation* 2 Cor 5: 19. διακονία τῆς κ. *ministry of rec.* vs. 18. Since men are not active in this dispensation fr. God, they are said τ. καταλλαγὴν λαμβάνειν *to receive reconciliation* Ro 5: 11.—EGvanLeeuwen, De καταλλαγή: ThSt 28, '10, 159–71; ANygren, D. Versöhnung als Gottestat '32. M-M.*

καταλλάσσω 1 aor. κατήλλαξα; 2 aor. pass. κατηλλάγην, ptc. καταλλαγείς; *reconcile* (so Hdt. +; 2 Macc.).
1. act. τινά (Hdt. 5, 29; 6, 108; Aristot., Oec. 2, 15) *someone* τινι *to someone*. Of God ἡμᾶς ἑαυτῷ διὰ Χριστοῦ *us to himself through Christ* 2 Cor 5: 18=ἐν Χριστῷ κόσμον ἑαυτῷ vs. 19.
2. pass. *be reconciled, become reconciled* (BGU 1463, 3 [247 BC]; Philo, Leg. All. 3, 134) w. dat. of the pers. (cf. X., An. 1, 6, 2; Pla., Rep. 8 p. 566E; 2 Macc 1: 5; 7: 33; 8: 29; Jos., Ant. 7, 184).
a. of man's relation to God (Soph., Aj. 744; Jos., Ant. 6, 143 θεὸν καταλλάττεσθαι τῷ Σαούλῳ) καταλλαγῆναι τῷ θεῷ be(come) *reconciled to God* Ro 5: 10a; 2 Cor 5: 20 (cf. Vi. Aesopi I c. 100 καταλλάγηθι Σαμίοις). Abs. Ro 5: 10b.
b. of reconciliation betw. human beings Ac 12: 22 D. (γυνὴ) τῷ ἀνδρὶ καταλλαγήτω *let her become reconciled to her husband* 1 Cor 7: 11 (cf. POxy. 104, 27 [I AD]; the hypothesis [summary] by Aristophanes the Grammarian, of Menander's Dyscolus, l. 9: κατηλλάγη τῇ γυναικί).—FBüchsel, TW I 254–8. M-M.*

κατάλοιπος, ον (Pla. +; inscr., pap., LXX) *left, remaining* οἱ κ. τῶν ἀνθρώπων *the rest of mankind* Ac 15: 17 (Am 9: 12). M-M.*

κατάλυμα, ατος, τό (Polyb. 2, 36, 1; 32, 19, 2; Diod. S. 14, 93, 5; IG V 1, 869; Dit., Syll.³ 609, 1; UPZ 120, 5 [II BC] al. in pap.; LXX; s. Bl-D. §109, 2; Rob. 151) *inn*. This sense is possible in Lk 2: 7, but in 10: 34 Lk uses πανδοχεῖον, the more specific term for *inn*. κ. is perh. best understood here as *lodging* (PSI 341, 8 [256 BC]; Ep. Arist. 181) or *guest-room*, as in 22: 11; Mk 14: 14, where the contexts also permit the sense *dining-room* (cf. 1 Km 1: 18; 9: 22; Sir 14: 25).—PBenoit, BRigaux-Festschr., '70, 173–86 (Lk 2: 7). M-M.*

κατάλυσις, εως, ἡ (Thu. +; inscr., PMagd. 8, 10 [218 BC] κ. τοῦ βίου; LXX, Philo; Jos., Bell. 2, 594, Ant. 18, 55; 19, 301 al.) *dissolution, abolition*, also *downfall* (of a tyrant: Diod. S. 14, 64, 4; 14, 67, 1) θανάτου IEph 19: 3.*

καταλύω fut. καταλύσω; 1 aor. κατέλυσα; 1 aor. pass. κατελύθην; 1 fut. pass. καταλυθήσομαι (Hom. +; inscr., pap., LXX, Philo, Joseph.).
1. trans.—a. *throw down, detach* of a stone fr. a building Mt 24: 2; Mk 13: 2; Lk 21: 6.
b. *destroy, demolish, dismantle* of buildings (Hom. +; 2 Esdr [Ezra] 5: 12; Jos., Ant. 9, 161 τ. ναοῦ [τ. θεοῦ] καταλυθέντος; Sib. Or. 3, 459).
α. lit. τ. ναὸν τοῦ θεοῦ Mt 26: 61; cf. 27: 40; Mk 14: 58; 15: 29. τὸν τόπον τοῦτον *this place* Ac 6: 14.
β. fig. (opp. οἰκοδομεῖν) *tear down, demolish* Gal 2: 18. Of the body as an earthly tent ἐὰν ἡ ἐπίγειος ἡμῶν οἰκία

τοῦ σκήνους καταλυθῇ *if the earthly tent we live in is destroyed* or *taken down* 2 Cor 5: 1. τὸ ἔργον τοῦ θεοῦ *tear down the work* (i.e. the Christian church which, because of vs. 19, is prob. thought of as a building) *of God* Ro 14: 20. On the contrary, the figure of the building is not present, and the gener. mng. *destroy, annihilate* (Strabo 13, 2, 3 p. 617; Ael. Aristid. 29 p. 570 D.: ἐλπίδας; Test. Benj. 3: 8) is found in τὰ ἔργα τῆς θηλείας (s. ἔργον 3, end) GEg 3.
c. *do away with, abolish, annul, make invalid* (Hdt. +) κ. τὸν νόμον *do away with, annul* or *repeal the law* Mt 5: 17a (cf. X., Mem. 4, 4, 14; Isocr. 4, 55; Diod. S. 34+35 fgm. 3 and 40, 2 [of the intention of the Seleucids against the Jews: καταλύειν τοὺς πατρίους νόμους]; Philostrat., Vi. Apoll. 4, 40; 2 Macc 2: 22; Philo, Somn. 2, 123; Jos., Ant. 16, 35; 20, 81). τ. νόμον κ. τ. προφήτας (as also Mt 5: 17a) Lk 23: 2 Marcion and It. τὰς θυσίας *abolish sacrifices* GEb 5. Abs. Mt 5: 17b (opp. πληροῦν); D 11: 2. *Ruin, bring to an end* (Appian, Prooem. C. 10 §42 ἀρχάς=empires; Arrian, Anab. 4, 10, 3 τυραννίδα; 4 Macc 4: 24 τὰς ἀπειλάς; Jos., Ant. 12, 1 τὴν Περσῶν ἡγεμονίαν) ἡ βουλὴ καταλυθήσεται *the plan will fail* Ac 5: 38. Also of pers. (Diod. S. 16, 47, 2 τοὺς μάγους; Appian, Bell. Civ. 1, 48 §210) *put down, stop* vs. 39. Of rulers who are *deposed* (Diod. S. 1, 66, 6; 9, 4, 2 [a tyrant]; 14, 14, 7 al.; Polyaenus 7, 3 and 10; 8, 29) καταλύεται ὁ ἄρχων τοῦ αἰῶνος τούτου *the ruler of this age is deposed* ITr 4: 2.
2. intr. *halt* (lit. 'unharness the pack animals'), *rest, find lodging* (Thu. +; Dit., Syll.³ 978, 8; UPZ 12, 37 [158 BC]; 62, 34; BGU 1097, 5; Gen 19: 2; 24: 23, 25; Sir 14: 25, 27; 36: 27; Jos., Vi. 248; cf. En. 5, 6) Lk 9: 12. W. εἰσέρχεσθαι 19: 7. M-M. B. 758.*

καταμανθάνω 2 aor. κατέμαθον (Hdt. +; inscr., pap., LXX; En. 3, 1; Philo; Jos., Ant. 6, 230f, Vi. 10) *observe* (*well*), *notice, learn* τὶ *someth*. τοὺς καιρούς IPol 3: 2. W. ὅτι foll. (Hippocr., Art. 8 p. 122, 2 Kühlewein) 1 Cl 7: 5. W. acc. and ὅτι foll. (Aristot., Pol. 3, 14 p. 1285a, 1; Philo, Leg. All. 3, 183) 2 Cl 13: 3. W. acc. and πῶς foll.: τὰ κρίνα τοῦ ἀγροῦ πῶς αὐξάνουσιν Mt 6: 28. τοὺς ἑτεροδοξοῦντας ... πῶς ἐναντίοι εἰσὶν ISm 6: 2. M-M.*

καταμαρτυρέω (Lysias, Demosth.; PPetr. III 17 I, 9; UPZ 162 V, 33 [117 BC]; LXX; Philo, Leg. All. 3, 199; Jos., Ant. 8, 358; 359) *bear witness against, testify against* τὶ τινος *testify someth. against someone* (Plut., Ages. 3, 9; Pr 25: 18; Sus 43; 49 Theod.) Mt 26: 62; 27: 13; Mk 14: 60. M-M.*

καταμένω fut. καταμενῶ (Hdt., Aristoph. +; inscr., pap., LXX, Ep. Arist., Philo; Jos., Ant. 6, 249; 7, 180) *stay, live* οὗ ἦσαν καταμένοντες *where they were staying* Ac 1: 13. κ. πρός τινα *stay w. someone* 1 Cor 16: 6 (v.l. παραμενῶ). M-M.*

καταμόνας s. μόνος 3.

κατανάθεμα Rv 22: 3 t.r. (s. κατάθεμα).*

καταναθεματίζω (Justin, Dial. 47) *curse* Mt 26: 74 t.r. (s. καταθεματίζω).*

καταναλίσκω (X., Pla. +; Dit., Syll.³ 672, 39 [II BC]; PSI 41, 20; LXX; Jos., Bell. 4, 242) *consume* of fire (Aristot., De Juv. 469b, 29): God is πῦρ καταναλίσκον *a consuming fire* Hb 12: 29 (Dt 4: 24). M-M.*

καταναρκάω fut. καταναρκήσω; 1 aor. κατενάρκησα (in Hippocr., Art. 48 p. 182, 18 Kühlewein, Epidem. 6, 7, 3 ed. Littré V 340='stupefy, disable'; Philod., παρρ. col.

XIIb, 10 Oliv.—Jerome, Ep. 121, 10, 4 maintains that the Cilicians used it for Lat. gravare, 'weigh down, burden'. At any rate the Latin and Syriac versions understand it in that sense; Chrysostom and Theodoret take for granted that this is the mng.) *burden, be a burden to* τινός *someone* 2 Cor 11: 9; 12: 13. Abs. 12: 14. M-M.*

κατανεύω 1 aor. κατένευσα (Hom.+; BGU 1119, 24; 1120, 30 [I BC]; Philo, Post. Cai. 169; Jos., Vi. 156 al.) *signal* by means of a nod τινί *to someone.* The message to be given by the signal is added in the inf. (w. art.; cf. Bl-D. §400, 7; Rob. 1068) Lk 5: 7 (cf. Polyb. 39, 1, 3 κ. τινὶ προϊέναι). M-M.*

κατανοέω impf. κατενόουν; 1 aor. κατενόησα (Hdt., Thu.+; inscr., pap., LXX, En., Ep. Arist., Philo, Joseph.).
1. *notice, observe* carefully τὶ someth. δοκόν Mt 7: 3; Lk 6: 41. πτελέαν καὶ ἄμπελον Hs 2: 1. κόλπον Ac 27: 39.
2. *look at* (*with reflection*), *consider, contemplate* τὶ someth. (Herm. Wr. 1, 13a; En. 2, 1; Philo, Leg. ad Gai. 358; Jos., Ant. 3, 302; 5, 5) κεράμια *pay attention to the jars* Hm 12, 5, 3a, b. τὰ κρίνα Lk 12: 27. τ. κόρακας 12: 24. τὸ ἑαυτοῦ σῶμα νενεκρωμένον Ro 4: 19. τ. ῥάβδους Hs 8, 1, 5; 8, 2, 5; 8, 3, 8; 8, 6, 1. τ. πύργον s 9, 5, 6f al. Abs., though the obj. is easily supplied fr. the context Ac 7: 31f; 11: 6.—Also simply *look at* (Gen 3: 6) τὸ πρόσωπον Js 1: 23. ἑαυτὸν vs. 24.
3. *consider, notice* in a spiritual sense, *fix the eyes of the spirit upon* τινά *someone* Hb 3: 1; 10: 24; someth. τὴν πανουργίαν *notice the trickery* Lk 20: 23 (cf. BGU 1011 II, 17 [II BC]; Jos., Ant. 14, 291, Vi. 72).—*Consider, contemplate* (Antig. Car. 31; Is 57: 1; Ep. Arist. 3; Philo, Ebr. 137; Jos., Ant. 7, 204) τὶ someth. 1 Cl 32: 1. W. indir. question foll. (Antiphanes Com. 33, 1) 24: 1; 47: 5. W. acc. and indir. question foll. 34: 5; 37: 2. M-M.**

κατανtάω 1 aor. κατήντησα; pf. κατήντηκα 1 Cor 10: 11 (Polyb., Diod. S.; inscr., pap., LXX; En. 17, 6; Jos., Ant. 3, 246) *come* (to), *arrive* (at).
1. lit. w. εἰς and acc. of place (Aristot., Dialog. fgm. 11 Rose εἰς τοὺς λιμένας; Diod. S. 3, 34, 7; 12, 55, 5; PTebt. 59, 3 [99 BC] εἰς τ. πόλιν Σοκονώφεως; Inschr. v. Priene 112, 97 [I BC]; 2 Macc 4: 21, 44) εἰς Ἰκόνιον Ac 13: 51 D. εἰς Δέρβην 16: 1. Cf. 18: 19, 24; 21: 7; 25: 13 (w. ἀσπάζω; cf. ἀπήντησεν αὐτῷ κ. ἠσπάσατο, Plut., Mor. 488E) 27: 12; 28: 13. ἀντικρυς Χίου *off Chios* 20: 15.
2. fig.—a. *arrive at* someth., so that one comes to possess it, *attain* (to) someth. μέχρι καταντήσωμεν εἰς τ. ἑνότητα τ. πίστεως Eph 4: 13 (εἰς as Polyb. 6, 9, 10; BGU 1101, 5 εἰς τ. αὐτὸν βίον). W. εἴς τι also Ac 26: 7; Phil 3: 11; εἰς πέπειρον κ. *come to ripeness* 1 Cl 23: 4. ἕως θανάτου καταντῆσαι *meet death* Pol 1: 2. W. ἐπί τι (Epicurus p. 63, 8 Us.; Diod. S. 1, 79, 2; Ammon. Herm. In Lib. Aristot. De Interpret. p. 264, 22 Busse κ. ἐπὶ τὸ ἔσχατον) ἐπὶ τὸν σκοπὸν κ. *arrive at the goal, reach the goal* 1 Cl 63: 1. Likew. ἐπὶ τὸν βέβαιον δρόμον κ. 6: 2.
b. The person does not come to someth., but someth. comes to him (κ. εἰς as t.t. for the inheritance that comes to an heir: BGU 1169, 21 [10 BC]; POxy. 75, 5; 248, 11; 274, 19. Cf. 2 Km 3: 29). Of the word of God: ἡ εἰς ὑμᾶς μόνους κατήντησεν; *or has it come to you alone?* 1 Cor 14: 36. On εἰς οὓς τὰ τέλη τ. αἰώνων κατήντηκεν 10: 11 cf. αἰών 2b, end.—OMichel, TW III 625-8. M-M.*

καταντικρύ (Hom.+) and **καταντικρύς** (later form, cf. Phryn. p. 444 L.; PGM 36, 3) *directly opposite* τινός someth. or *someone* (cf. Pla., Phaedo 112E; X., Hell. 4, 8,

5; Arrian, Anab. 3, 16, 8; Eubul. in Athen. 11 p. 473D; PGM 4, 89) AP 6: 21; 14: 29.*

κατάνυξις, εως, ἡ (Cyrillus of Scyth. p. 19, 25; 34, 21; 97, 1; 206, 27 [=deep emotion]; Leontios 1 p. 6, 20; Pel.-Leg. p. 3, 7; LXX; Hesychius) *stupefaction* πνεῦμα κατανύξεως (Is 29: 10) *a spirit of stupor* Ro 11: 8. M-M.*

κατανύσσομαι 2 aor. pass. κατενύγην (Pel.-Leg. 7, 16; LXX; Hesychius.—The act. in Phlegon [II AD]: 257 fgm. 36 IV Jac.) *be pierced, stabbed* fig., of the feeling of sharp pain connected w. anxiety, remorse, etc. (Photius: κατανυγείς· λυπηθείς; Ps.-Callisth. 2, 36 Müller κατανυγεὶς ἐπὶ τοῖς λόγοις=taken aback; Cyrillus of Scyth. p. 53, 14; 96, 19; 108, 2 be deeply moved; Leontios 14 p. 30, 13 al.) κατενύγησαν τὴν καρδίαν *they were cut to the heart* Ac 2: 37 (κ. τῇ καρδίᾳ Ps 108: 16). M-M.*

καταξαίνω 1 aor. pass. ptc. καταξανθείς (Aeschyl.+; Judg 8: 7 A, 16 A) *tear to shreds* (lit. 'comb, card', as wool) μάστιγι καταξανθέντες *torn to shreds with whips* MPol 2: 2.*

καταξιοπιστεύομαι *pretend to be trustworthy, simulate honesty* (Polyb. 12, 17, 1: καταξιοπιστέομαι) ITr 6: 2.*

καταξιόω 1 aor. κατηξίωσα, pass. κατηξιώθην (Aeschyl.+; Polyb. 1, 23, 3; Diod. S. 2, 60, 3; inscr., pap., LXX, Ep. Arist. 175; Jos., Ant. 15, 76) *consider worthy.*
1. w. God or Jesus Christ as subj., act. τινά *someone* 1 Cl 50: 2; IEph 20: 1. W. inf. foll. IRo 2: 2.—Pass. *be considered worthy* τινός *of a thing* (CIA III 690, 9f; 4 Macc 18: 3) τῆς βασιλείας τοῦ θεοῦ 2 Th 1: 5. πλείονος γνώσεως 1 Cl 41: 4. ὀνόματος θεοπρεπεστάτου (on the idea s. Hdb. ad loc.) IMg 1: 2. τοῦ κλήρου ITr 12: 3. τῆς τοιαύτης διακονίας *of such a service* IPhld 10: 2: cf. IPol 1: 1; MPol 14: 2 v.l. Funk. W. inf. foll. (PAmh. 145, 4; PGM 13, 707; Jos., Ant. 4, 281) Lk 20: 35; 21: 36 t.r.; Ac 5: 41. Also ἵνα ISm 11: 1.
2. w. a human subj., pass., w. ἵνα foll. IPol 7: 2. W. subst. inf. foll. τοῦ εἰς Συρίαν πορεύεσθαι 8: 2. M-M.*

καταπαλαίω 1 aor. κατεπάλαισα (Eur., Aristoph., Pla.+; 4 Macc 3: 18; Philo, Vi. Cont. 43) *win a victory over, defeat* (*in wrestling*) (w. ἀντιπαλαίειν) τινά *someone* Hs 8, 3, 6. Abs. m 12, 5, 2.*

καταπατέω fut. καταπατήσω; 1 aor. κατεπάτησα, pass. κατεπατήθην (Hom., Hdt., Thu.+; Dit., Syll.³ 1169, 115; pap., LXX, Joseph.) *trample under foot.*
1. lit.—a. *trample* τὶ ἔν τινι someth. *with* (*under*) someth. Mt 7: 6 (of swine πατέω: Ananius Lyricus [VI BC] in Athen. 7, 282B).—Pass. (Diod. S. 25, 3, 1) *be trampled under foot* Mt 5: 13; Lk 8: 5.
b. *tread upon* of a milling crowd (Arrian, Anab. 2, 11, 3 ἀπ᾽ ἀλλήλων καταπατούμενοι=hard-pressed by each other, getting in each other's way; Polyaenus 4, 3, 21 ὑπ᾽ ἀλλήλων καταπατούμενοι) ὥστε καταπατεῖν ἀλλήλους *so that they trod on one another*('s feet) Lk 12: 1.
2. fig. *trample under foot, treat with disdain* (Il. 4, 157 [in tmesis]; Pla., Leg. 4 p. 714A τοὺς νόμους, Gorg. 484A; Epict. 1, 8, 10; Lucian, Lexiph. 23; 2 Macc 8: 2; Hos 5: 11; Jos., Bell. 4, 386.—Cf. the underlying reality in Diod. S. 33, 5, 3 τὰ τῶν θεῶν ἀγάλματα ὑβριστικῶς κατεπάτησαν) τὸν υἱὸν τοῦ θεοῦ Hb 10: 29. M-M.*

κατάπαυσις, εως, ἡ (Hdt.+, but act., 'stopping, causing to rest'; also Jos., Ant. 17, 43) intr.
1. *rest* (2 Macc 15: 1 ἡ τῆς καταπαύσεως ἡμέρα of the Sabbath) τόπος τ. καταπαύσεως *place of rest,* i.e. the

place where one rests and lives Ac 7: 49; B 16: 2 (both Is 66: 1).

2. abstract for concrete *place of rest* (Dt 12: 9; Ps 131: 14 al.) εἰσελεύσονται εἰς τὴν κ. μου (Ps 94: 11); this OT pass. is typologically interpreted fr. a Christian viewpoint Hb 3: 11, 18; 4: 1, 3, 5, 10f.—GvRad, Zwischen den Zeiten 11, '33, 104-11; WRHutton, ET 52, '41, 316f.*

καταπαύω fut. καταπαύσομαι (B 15: 5); 1 aor. κατέπαυσα (Hom.+; LXX; En. 106, 18; Philo, Joseph.; Anz 294f).

1. trans.—**a.** *(cause to) stop, bring to an end* τὶ someth. (Hom.+; LXX; Philo, Leg. All. 1, 5; Jos., Vi. 422) τὸν διωγμόν MPol 1: 1. τ. προσευχήν 8: 1.

b. *bring to rest—α.* τινά someone, in such a way that he gives up someth. he has begun to do and is quiet τινά τινος *restrain, dissuade someone fr. someth.* (cf. Jos., Ant. 3, 14 κ. τῆς ὀργῆς) κατέπαυσαν τ. ὄχλους τοῦ μὴ θύειν αὐτοῖς Ac 14: 18 (on the constr. s. Bl-D. §400, 4; Rob. 1094; 1102).

β. τινά someone, so that he has rest. Concr., *bring to a place of rest* (Ex 33: 14; Dt 3: 20; Josh 1: 13; Sir 24: 11) Hb 4: 8.—**γ.** τὶ someth. τὰ πάντα B 15: 8.

2. intr. *stop, rest* (Eur., Hec. 918; comic poet in Diod. S. 12, 14 vol. II 371, 19 Vogel εὐημερῶν κατάπαυσον; Gen 2: 2; Ex 31: 18) of God κατέπαυσεν ἐν τῇ ἡμέρᾳ τῇ ἑβδόμῃ *he rested on the seventh day* B 15: 3, 5 (both Gen 2: 2). κ. ἀπὸ τῶν ἔργων αὐτοῦ *from his work* Hb 4: 4, 10 (also Gen 2: 2).

3. mid. and pass. have the same mng. as the intr. act. (Aristoph.+; Appian, Bell. Civ. 5, 132 §548; Ex 16: 13; Philo, Leg. All. 1, 18) B 15: 5, 7. M-M.*

καταπέτασμα, ατος, τό (Heliod. 10, 28) *curtain* (inscr. of Samos of 346/5 BC, listing the furnishings of the Temple of Hera [in OHoffmann, D. griech. Dialekte III 1898, 72; Dssm., LO 80-LAE 101]; LXX; Ep. Arist. 86; Philo; Joseph.). In the temple at Jerusalem one curtain separated the holy of holies fr. the holy place, and another covered the entrance fr. the forecourt to the temple proper. κ. means the latter in Ex 26: 37; 38: 18; Num 3: 26; Ep. Arist. 86; Jos., Ant. 8, 75, Bell. 5, 212; the former in Ex 26: 31ff; Lev 21: 23; 24: 3; Philo, Mos. 2, 86; 101; Jos., Ant. 8, 75. Our lit. knows only the inner curtain, τὸ δεύτερον κ. Hb 9: 3 (cf. Philo, Gig. 53 τὸ ἐσωτάτω καταπέτασμα). It is called simply τὸ κ. τοῦ ναοῦ, and Mt 27: 51; Mk 15: 38; Lk 23: 45; GP 5: 20 tell how it was torn at the death of Jesus. (EbNestle, NovT Suppl. 1896, 79¹, concludes, on the basis of GH 20, that פָּרֹכֶת 'curtain' was confused w. כַּפְתֹּר 'lintel', and thinks the lintel burst [but כַּפְתֹּר never means 'lintel'; rather 'capital of a column']; cf. Zahn, NKZ 13, '02, 729-56; HLaible, NKZ 35, '24, 287-314; PFiebig, Neues Sächs. Kirchenbl. 40, '32, 227-36; ASchmidtke, Neue Fgmte u. Untersuchungen zu d. judenchristl. Evangelien: TU 37, 1, '11 p. 257-64.—GLindeskog, The Veil of the Temple: Coniect. Neot. 11, '47, 132-7.)—τὸ ἐσώτερον τοῦ κ. (cf. Lev 16: 2, 12) *the inner sanctuary behind the curtain, the holy of holies* as a figure for heaven Hb 6: 19. κ. is used similarly in the fig. language of this epistle 10: 20: we have an εἴσοδος τ. ἁγίων, since Jesus has opened a ὁδὸς διὰ τοῦ καταπετάσματος *a way through the curtain.*—CSchneider, TW III 630-2. M-M.*

καταπίμπρημι (Plut., Polyaenus+) *burn to ashes* κατέπ[ρ]ησεν as v.l. from 𝔓⁷² mg in 2 Pt 2: 6.*

καταπίνω 2 aor. κατέπιον; 1 aor. pass. κατεπόθην (Hes., Hdt.+; inscr., pap., LXX, En., Philo; Jos., Bell. 5, 472; 566 al.) *drink down, swallow.*

1. lit., though more or less transferred—**a.** *swallow, swallow up* τὶ someth. (of the earth, that drinks up water Pla., Critias p. 111D; Diod. S. 1, 32, 4) ἤνοιξεν ἡ γῆ τὸ στόμα αὐτῆς καὶ κατέπιεν τὸν ποταμόν Rv 12: 16 (Philostephanus Hist. [III BC], fgm. 23 [ed. CMüller III 1849] p. 32 ποταμὸς ὑπὸ γῆς καταπίνεται; Simplicius in Epict. p. 95, 35; cf. Num 16: 30, 32). On the camel Mt 23: 24 cf. κώνωψ.

b. *devour* (Hes., Theog. 459 υἱούς. Of animals that devour Tob 6: 2; Jon 2: 1; Jos., Ant. 2, 246) the devil like a lion ζητῶν τίνα καταπιεῖν 1 Pt 5: 8 (Damasc., Vi. Isid. 69 ὁ λέων καταπίνει τὸν ἄνθρωπον.

c. of water, waves *swallow up* (Polyb. 2, 41, 7 πόλις καταποθεῖσα ὑπὸ τ. θαλάσσης; Diod. S. 18, 35, 6; 26, 8; En. 101, 5; Philo, Virt. 201) pass. *be drowned* (Ex 15: 4 v.l. κατεπόθησαν ἐν ἐρυθρᾷ θαλάσσῃ) Hb 11: 29.—Transferred to mental and spiritual states (cf. Philo, Gig. 13, Deus Imm. 181) μή πως τ. περισσοτέρᾳ λύπῃ καταποθῇ *so that he may not be overwhelmed by extreme sorrow* 2 Cor 2: 7.

2. fig. *swallow up* w. total extinction as a result (cf. PGM 12, 44 κατέπιεν ὁ οὐρανός; Ps 106: 27; Philo, Leg. All. 3, 230; Test. Jud. 21: 7) pass. τὸ θνητὸν ὑπὸ τῆς ζωῆς *what is mortal may be swallowed up in life* 2 Cor 5: 4. ὁ θάνατος εἰς νῖκος *death has been swallowed up in victory* (after Is 25: 8; s. on this κέντρον 1 and ARahlfs, ZNW 20, '21, 183f) 1 Cor 15: 54. M-M. and suppl.*

καταπίπτω 2 aor. κατέπεσον (Hom.+; inscr., pap., LXX; Ep. Arist. 144; Philo, Joseph.) *fall (down)* εἰς τὴν γῆν *fall on the ground* Ac 26: 14. ἐπὶ τὴν πέτραν (cf. Jos., Bell. 6, 64) Lk 8: 6. Abs. (Jos., Ant. 5, 27) καταπίπτειν νεκρόν *fall down dead* Ac 28: 6 (cf. 4 Macc 4: 11). M-M.*

καταπιστεύω *trust* (Polyb.; Plut., Lys. 8, 3; pap.; Mi 7: 5) w. dat. (Polyb. 2, 3, 3 al.) ἑαυτῷ *trust oneself* Hm 9: 10.*

καταπλέω 1 aor. κατέπλευσα (Hom.+; inscr., pap.) *sail down* fr. the 'high seas' toward the coast, *sail toward* w. εἰς (X., Hell. 1, 7, 29 εἰς τ. γῆν; Appian, Basil. 1 §1 ἐς τινα αἰγιαλόν; Dit., Or. 344, 2 εἰς Βιθυνίαν; Jos., Bell. 1, 610, Ant. 13, 86) εἰς τὴν χώραν τῶν Γερασηνῶν Lk 8: 26. On the expr. κ. εἰς τοὺς ἀγῶνας *go to the contests* (κ. gener. ='go through' Sib. Or. 11, 203 κόσμον κ.) 2 Cl 7: 1, 3 cf. Harnack, Lghtf., Knopf ad loc. M-M.*

κατάπληξις, εως, ἡ (Thu.+; Diod. S. 17, 84, 3; Celsus 6, 75; BGU 1209, 16 [23 BC]; 2 Esdr [Ezra] 3: 3; Philo; Jos., Bell. 6, 89) *terror* Dg 7: 3.*

καταπλήσσω (Hom.+; inscr., pap., LXX) *amaze, astound, terrify* (lit. *strike down*) τινά someone (Philo, Omn. Prob. Lib. 100; Jos., Ant. 14, 370) IPol 3: 1. Perf. pass. καταπέπληγμαι *be amazed, astounded* τὶ at someth. (class.; PSI 502, 8 [III BC]; cf. 2 Macc 3: 24; Philo, Post. Cai. 147; Jos., Vi. 120) οὗ καταπέπληγμαι τὴν ἐπιείκειαν *at whose gentleness I am amazed* IPhld 1: 1.*

καταπονέω (Hippocr.+; Polyb., Diod. S. 11, 6, 3, pap., LXX, Joseph.) *subdue, torment, wear out, oppress* τινά someone B 20: 2b; D 5: 2b. In our lit. predom. in pres. pass. ptc. καταπονούμενος (Aelian, V.H. 3, 27 ὑπὸ πενίας καταπονούμενος; Jos., Bell. 2, 313, Ant. 7, 124) Ac 4: 2 D. Of Lot 2 Pt 2: 7.—Subst. ὁ καταπονούμενος *the one who is oppressed, mistreated, weary* (UPZ 110, 88 [164 BC]) ποιεῖν ἐκδίκησιν τῷ κ. *see to it that justice is done for the oppressed* Ac 7: 24; πονεῖν ἐπὶ κ. *toil for him who is downtrodden* B 20: 2a; D 5: 2a. M-M.*

καταποντίζω 1 aor. pass. κατεποντίσθην (Epicharmus [ca. 480 BC]: Vorsokrat.⁵ 23 B, 44a; Lysias, Demosth.+; Polyb., Diod. S.; PPetr. II 40 (a), 27 [III BC]; LXX; Jos., Ant. 10, 122, C. Ap. 2, 245) *throw into the sea*, then gener. *drown*, pass. *be sunk, be drowned* ἐν τῷ πελάγει θαλάσσης *be sunk or be drowned in the high seas* Mt 18: 6. εἰς τὴν θάλασσαν 1 Cl 46: 8 (Plut., Tim. 13, 10 εἰς τὸ πέλαγος; Ps.-Callisth. 1, 39, 5 εἰς βυθὸν θαλάσσης). Abs. ἀρξάμενος καταποντίζεσθαι *as he began to sink* Mt 14: 30. M-M.*

κατάρα, ας, ἡ (Aeschyl. +; Ps.-Pla., Alc. 2 p. 143B; Polyb. 24, 8, 7; Diod. S. 1, 45, 2; Ael. Aristid. 33, 32 K. =51 p. 582 D.; Dit., Syll.³ 1241, 1; LXX; En.; Philo; Jos., Ant. 4, 118; 307; Test. 12 Patr.) *curse, imprecation* w. εὐλογία (as Dt 11: 26; 30: 1, 19; Sir 3: 9; Philo, Det. Pot. Ins. 71) Js 3: 10. ἀποδιδόναι κατάραν ἀντὶ κατάρας *repay a curse with a curse* Pol 2: 2. Of infertile land, full of thorns and thistles κατάρας ἐγγύς *almost cursed* Hb 6: 8 (cf. Gen 3: 17.—κ. ἐγγύς as Ael. Aristid. 26, 53 K.=14 p. 343 D.). Of the way of death κατάρας μεστή *full of cursing* B 20: 1; D 5: 1. Of persons κατάρας τέκνα (cf. Sir 41: 9 ἐὰν γεννηθῆτε εἰς κατάραν γεννηθήσεσθε) *accursed* 2 Pt 2: 14.—In Paul of the adherents of the law ὑπὸ κατάραν εἰσίν *they are under a curse* (this expr. corresponds to ἐξαποστελῶ [i.e., the κύριος] ἐφ᾿ ὑμᾶς τ. κατάραν Mal 2: 2. Cf. Judg 9: 57) Gal 3: 10. Of Christ: ἡμᾶς ἐφηγόρασεν ἐκ τῆς κ. τοῦ νόμου *he ransomed us from the curse of the law* vs. 13a. Abstract for concrete γενόμενος ὑπὲρ ἡμῶν κ. *by becoming a curse-offering* (or *an object of a curse*) *in our behalf* vs. 13b. M-M.*

καταράομαι mid. dep.; 1 aor. κατηρασάμην (Hom. +; LXX, En., Philo, Joseph.) *to curse* τινά *someone* (Plut., Cato Min. 32, 1; Ps.-Lucian, Asinus 27; Gen 12: 3; 27: 29 al.; Philo, Det. Pot. Ins. 103; Test. 12 Patr.) Lk 6: 28; Js 3: 9; 1 Cl 10: 3 (Gen 12: 3); a tree Mk 11: 21. W. dat. τινί (so Hdt. 4, 184; X., An. 7, 7, 48; Diod. S. 1, 45, 2; 14, 70, 2; EpJer 65; Philo, Fuga 73, Leg. All. 3, 65 τῷ ὄφει [but 75 τὸν ὄφιν]; Jos., Bell. 3, 297, C. Ap. 1, 204) *curse someone* Lk 6: 28 t.r.; D 1: 3. Abs. (Aristoph., Vesp. 614; Demosth. 18, 283) *curse* (w. εὐλογεῖν as Philo, Rer. Div. Her. 177) Ro 12: 14; 1 Cl 15: 5 (Ps 61: 5). W. ἀρνεῖσθαι and ὀμνύναι GH 16.—Perf. ptc. κατηραμένος w. pass. mng. (Plut., Lucull. 18, 6; 4 Km 9: 34; Wsd 12: 11) κατηραμένοι *accursed ones* Mt 25: 41. οἱ κ. ὑπὸ τοῦ θεοῦ (cf. Dt 21: 23; Herm. Wr. 2, 17a) 1 Cl 30: 8.—Lit. s. on εὐλογέω, end; also KLatte, Heil. Recht ’20, 61–96; F Büchsel, TW I 449–51. M-M. B. 1481.*

καταργέω fut. καταργήσω; 1 aor. κατήργησα; pf. κατήργηκα; 1 aor. pass. κατηργήθην; 1 fut. καταργηθήσομαι; pf. κατήργημαι (since Eur., Phoen. 753; Polyb.; POxy. 38, 7 [49/50 AD]; PFlor. 176, 7; 218, 13; PStrassb. 32, 7; 2 Esdr)

1. *make ineffective, powerless, idle*—a. lit., of a tree κ. τὴν γῆν *use up, exhaust, waste* Lk 13: 7 (ἀργεῖ οὐδὲν ἀλλὰ καρποφορεῖ Ode of Solomon 11, 23).

b. fig. (so, above all, in Paul and the writings dependent on him; cf. Herm. Wr. 13, 7 καταργηθέν τ. σώματος τὰς αἰσθήσεις) *make ineffective, nullify* τὴν πίστιν τοῦ θεοῦ *God's faithfulness* Ro 3: 3. ἐπαγγελίαν Gal 3: 17; cf. Ro 4: 14; τὰ ὄντα κ. *nullify the things that* (actually) *exist* 1 Cor 1: 28. τὸν νόμον *make the law invalid* Eph 2: 15; cf. Ro 3: 31. Also in B of the OT laws, which have lost their validity for the Christians 2: 6; 9: 4; 16: 2.

2. *abolish, wipe out, set aside* τὶ someth. τὰ τοῦ νηπίου *set aside childish ways* 1 Cor 13: 11. Of God or Christ: God will *do away with* both stomach and food 6: 13; *bring to an* end πᾶσαν ἀρχήν, ἐξουσίαν, δύναμιν 15: 24. τὸν ἄνομον 2 Th 2: 8. τὸν καιρὸν τοῦ ἀνόμου *put an end to the time of the lawless one* (i.e., the devil) B 15: 5. τὸν θάνατον *break the power of death* 2 Ti 1: 10; B 5: 6; pass. 1 Cor 15: 26 (MEDahl, The Resurrection of the Body [1 Cor 15], ’62, 117–19). τὸν τὸ κράτος ἔχοντα τοῦ θανάτου *destroy the one who has power over death* Hb 2: 14. ἵνα καταργηθῇ τὸ σῶμα τ. ἁμαρτίας *in order that the sinful body may be done away with* Ro 6: 6. In 2 Cor 3: 14 the subject may be ἡ παλαιὰ διαθήκη or, more probably, κάλυμμα; in the latter case the mng. is *remove*.—Pass. *cease, pass away* προφητεία, γνῶσις 1 Cor 13: 8. τὸ ἐκ μέρους *what is imperfect* vs. 10. ἄρα κατήργηται τὸ σκάνδαλον τοῦ σταυροῦ *the cross has ceased to be an obstacle* Gal 5: 11. πᾶς πόλεμος καταργεῖται *every war is brought to an end* IEph 13: 2. καταργούμενος *doomed to perish* of the ἄρχοντες τοῦ αἰῶνος τούτου 1 Cor 2: 6. Of the radiance on Moses' face 2 Cor 3: 7. Subst. τὸ καταργούμενον *what is transitory* vss. 11, 13.

3. καταργοῦμαι ἀπό τινος *be released from an association with someone* or *someth., have nothing more to do with*, of a woman upon the death of her husband κατήργηται ἀπὸ τοῦ νόμου τοῦ ἀνδρός Ro 7: 2. Of the Christians κ. ἀπὸ τοῦ νόμου *be released fr. the law* vs. 6. Of those who aspire to righteousness through the law κ. ἀπὸ Χριστοῦ *be estranged from Christ* Gal 5: 4.—GDelling, TW I 453–5. M-M.*

καταριθμέω pf. pass. ptc. κατηριθμημένος (Eur., Pla.+; inscr., pap., LXX, Philo, Joseph.).

1. *count* (Jos., Ant. 11, 73) ὁ ἀριθμὸς ὁ κατηριθμημένος τῶν ἐκλεκτῶν *the number of the chosen, that has been counted* 1 Cl 59: 2.

2. *count among* pass. *belong to* w. ἐν (Pla., Polit. 266A al.; Diod. S. 4, 85, 5; 16, 83, 3; Dit., Syll.³ 810, 24 ἀνδρὸς παρ᾿ ὑμεῖν ἐν τοῖς ἐπιφανεστάτοις καταριθμουμένου; UPZ 110, 99 [164 BC]; 2 Ch 31: 19; Philo, Spec. Leg. 2, 118) of the traitor: κατηριθμημένος ἦν ἐν ἡμῖν *he belonged to our number* Ac 1: 17. M-M.*

καταρρέω impf. κατέρρεον (Hom.+; PMagd. 24, 5 [III BC]; LXX; Joseph.) *flow down* of pus (Horapollo 2, 57) and foulness AP 11: 26.*

καταρτίζω fut. καταρτίσω; 1 aor. κατήρτισα, mid. κατηρτισάμην, 2 pers. sing. κατηρτίσω; pf. pass. κατήρτισμαι (Hdt.+; inscr., pap., LXX).

1. *put in order, restore*—a. *restore to its former condition, put to rights* (since Hdt. 5, 28; 106; Dionys. Hal. 3, 10) τὶ someth. nets (by cleaning, mending, folding together) Mt 4: 21; Mk 1: 19 (cf. GRWynne, Exp. 7th Ser. VIII ’09, 282–5). Fig. κ. τινά *restore someone* ἐν πνεύματι πραΰτητος *in a spirit of gentleness*, i.e. in a gentle manner Gal 6: 1. Pass. καταρτίζεσθε *mend your ways* 2 Cor 13: 11.

b. *put into proper condition, complete, make complete* τὶ someth. καταρτίσαι τὰ ὑστερήματα τ. πίστεως ὑμῶν *to complete what is lacking in your faith* 1 Th 3: 10. τινά *someone:* ὑμᾶς ἐν παντὶ ἀγαθῷ *make you complete in every good thing* Hb 13: 21. κατηρτισμένοι ἐν τῷ αὐτῷ νοΐ καὶ ἐν τῇ αὐτῇ γνώμῃ *made complete in the same mind and the same conviction* 1 Cor 1: 10. ἐν μιᾷ ὑποταγῇ IEph 2: 2. ἐν ἀκινήτῳ πίστει ISm 1: 1. Abs. 1 Pt 5: 10. κατηρτισμένος *(fully) trained, practiced* (Polyb. 5, 2, 11 τ. εἰρεσίαις κατηρτισμένοι) κ. πᾶς (μαθητὴς) ἔσται ὡς ὁ διδάσκαλος αὐτοῦ *when he* (the pupil) *is fully trained, he will be like his teacher* Lk 6: 40.

2. *prepare, make, create*—a. act. and pass., of God (w. ποιεῖν) B 16: 6. (W. κτίζειν) τὰ πάντα Hm 1: 1. Pass. ὁ

κόσμος κατηρτίσθη Hv 2, 4, 1; also οἱ αἰῶνες (s. αἰών 3) ῥήματι θεοῦ Hb 11: 3. κατηρτισμένος εἴς τι made, created for someth.: σκεύη ὀργῆς κατηρτισμένα εἰς ἀπώλειαν vessels of wrath, designed for destruction Ro 9: 22. ἄνθρωπος εἰς ἕνωσιν κατηρτισμένος a man set on (lit. made for) unity IPhld 8: 1.

b. mid. (PGM 4, 1147) καταρτίζεσθαί τί τινι prepare someth. for someone σῶμα Hb 10: 5 (Ps 39: 7 BSA). W. reflexive mng.: for oneself κατηρτίσω αἶνον thou hast prepared praise for thyself Mt 21: 16 (Ps 8: 3). M-M.*

κατάρτισις, εως, ἡ (Plut., Alex. 7, 1 'training', Them. 2, 7) being made complete, completion εὐχόμεθα τὴν ὑμῶν κ. we pray that you may be made complete 2 Cor 13: 9.*

καταρτισμός, οῦ, ὁ (medical t.t. [Soranus p. 150, 8]: 'setting of a bone', etc. But more gener. PTebt. 33, 12 [112 BC] 'preparation' αὐλῆς; PRyl. 127, 28; Sym. Is 38: 12 'restoration') equipment, equipping εἴς τι for someth. πρὸς τὸν κ. τῶν ἁγίων εἰς ἔργον διακονίας to equip the saints for service Eph 4: 12, though training, discipline (L-S-J) is also poss. M-M.*

κατασβέννυμι 1 aor. inf. κατασβέσαι (Hom.+; PGM 12, 57 Dieterich; LXX; Philo, Aet. M. 91) put out, quench τὶ someth. τὸ πῦρ (Il. 21, 381) MPol 16: 1.*

κατασείω 1 aor. κατέσεισα (Thu.+; 1 Macc 6: 38; Philo, Joseph.) in our lit. (Ac) always used w. χείρ and in the mng. 'give a signal'.

1. shake, wave (rapidly) w. acc. τὴν χεῖρα (Vi. Aesopi W c. 87 τὴν χεῖρα τῷ ὄχλῳ κατασείσας; Philo, De Jos. 211, Leg. ad Gai. 181 τὴν δεξιὰν χεῖρα) Ac 19: 33.

2. motion, make a sign w. dat. τῇ χειρί (Polyb. 1, 78, 3; Jos., Ant. 4, 323; 8, 275) 13: 16. Still another dat. can indicate the person(s) for whom the signal is intended (cf. X., Cyr. 5, 4, 4 κατασείω τινί; Jos., Ant. 17, 257. Sim. PGM 5, 453 κ. τῷ λύχνῳ='motion toward the lamp') κατέσεισεν τ. χειρὶ τ. λαῷ 21: 40. The purpose of the signal is given in the inf. (s. Appian, Bell. Civ. 4, 2 §5 ἥκειν and Jos. in the pass. quoted, but not Ant. 8, 275) κατασείσας αὐτοῖς τ. χειρὶ σιγᾶν he motioned to them (with his hand) to be silent 12: 17. M-M.*

κατασκάπτω 1 aor. κατέσκαψα tear down, raze to the ground (so trag., Hdt.+; inscr., LXX; Philo, Leg. ad Gai. 132) τὶ someth. cities (Hdt. 7, 156; Ael. Aristid. 32 p. 604 D.; Dit., Syll.³ 344, 7; Jos., Ant. 4, 313; 8, 128) 1 Cl 6: 4. Altars Ro 11: 3 (3 Km 19: 10). τὰ κατεσκαμμένα αὐτῆς the parts of it that had been torn down Ac 15: 16 v.l. (s. καταστρέφω 2). M-M.*

κατασκευάζω fut. κατασκευάσω; 1 aor. κατεσκεύασα, pass. κατεσκευάσθην; pf. ptc. κατεσκευασμένος (Anaxagoras, Hdt.+; inscr., pap., LXX. Oft. Ep. Arist., Philo, Joseph.).

1. make ready, prepare τὶ someth. τὴν ὁδόν (Dit., Syll.³ 313, 22 [320 BC] of the ὁδοί along which the procession in honor of Zeus and Dionysus was to pass: ὅπως κατασκευασθῶσιν ὡς βέλτιστα) Mt 11: 10; Mk 1: 2; Lk 7: 27.—Fig., in a mental or spiritual sense (Aristot., Rhet. 3, 19 κ. τὸν ἀκροατήν; Wsd 7: 27; Jos., C. Ap. 2, 188 πλῆθος κατεσκευασμένον πρὸς τ. εὐσέβειαν) λαὸς κατεσκευασμένος a people made ready Lk 1: 17.

2. build, construct, erect, create (Phylarch. [III BC]: 81 fgm. 29 Jac. ναούς; Plut., Mor. 189c, Num. 10, 9 οἶκος; Herodian 5, 6, 6; 9; Dit., Syll.³ 495, 140; 145; 1100, 20; 1229; PAmh. 64, 2 βαλανεῖον; POxy. 892, 8; Philo, Rer. Div. Her. 112 σκηνήν; Jos., Bell. 6, 191, Vi. 65 οἶκος) κιβωτόν construct an ark (κ. is a favorite word for

construction of ships: Diod. S. 1, 92, 2; 11, 62, 2; Palaeph. 29, 4; 31, 9; 1 Macc 15: 3) Hb 11: 7. Pass. 1 Pt 3: 20. οἶκον Hb 3: 3f. Of God (Is 40: 28; 45: 7; Philo, Aet. M. 39; 41; Aristob. in Euseb., Pr. Ev. 13, 12, 9) ὁ πάντα κατασκευάσας the builder of all things Hb 3: 4b (cf. Epict. 1, 6, 7). Pf. pass. ptc. as subst. τὸ κατεσκευασμένον what is produced or supplied Dg 2: 2.

3. In addition to the erection of a building it is also used in the sense furnish, equip (X., An. 4, 1, 8, Hiero 2, 2, Cyr. 5, 5, 2: σκηνή; Num 21: 27) σκηνὴ κατεσκευάσθη ἡ πρώτη the foremost tent or tabernacle was furnished (an enumeration of its furnishings follows) Hb 9: 2. τούτων δὲ οὕτως κατεσκευασμένων such are the furnishings, and so vs. 6. M-M.*

κατασκηνόω (X.+; oft. in Polyb. and Plut.; LXX) inf. κατασκηνοῦν as v.l. in Mt 13: 32 and Mk 4: 32 (Bl-D. §91; Rdm.² 95; Mlt. 53; Mlt.-H. 197); fut. κατασκηνώσω; 1 aor. κατεσκήνωσα.

1. trans. (Ps 22: 2) cause to dwell of the name in the hearts D 10: 2.

2. intr. (so mostly; Philo, Leg. All. 3, 46; Jos., Ant. 3, 202) live, settle of birds (Ps 103: 12): ἐν τοῖς κλάδοις nest in the branches (Da 4: 21 Theod.) Mt 13: 32; Lk 13: 19 (cf. Joseph and Aseneth 15). ὑπὸ τὴν σκιάν Mk 4: 32.—Of persons live, dwell (Diod. S. 13, 96, 2; 14, 62, 3 ἐν τῷ νεῷ; 19, 94, 10 ἐν οἰκίαις; Ps 14: 1; Jos., Ant. 9, 34) 1 Cl 58: 1. ἡ σάρξ μου κατασκηνώσει ἐπ' ἐλπίδι (Ps 15: 9) my flesh will dwell ἐπ' ἐλπίδι (ἐλπίς 2a) Ac 2: 26; cf. 1 Cl 57: 7 (Pr 1: 33). On a Christian gravestone (Sb 1540, 9[408 AD]) κ. means 'rest'. M-M.*

κατασκήνωσις, εως, ἡ—1. taking up lodging (so Polyb. 11, 26, 5; LXX) ἔχειν τόπον κατασκηνώσεως have a place to dwell Hs 5, 6, 7.

2. a place to live (so Diod. S. 17, 95, 2; Dit., Or. 229, 57 [III BC]) of birds: nest Mt 8: 20; Lk 9: 58. M-M.*

κατασκιάζω (Hes.+; Epigr. Gr. 495) overshadow of the winged cherubim in the sanctuary κατασκιάζοντα τὸ ἱλαστήριον Hb 9: 5 (for the idea s. Ex 25: 20: συσκιάζοντες ἐν ταῖς πτέρυξιν αὐτῶν ἐπὶ τ. ἱλαστηρίου). M-M.*

κατάσκιος, ον (Hes., Hdt.+; Aelian, V.H. 12, 38; LXX; Philo, Aet. M. 63) shaded of a mountain covered w. trees (cf. Zech 1: 8) Hs 9, 1, 9.*

κατασκοπεύω 1 aor. inf. κατασκοπεῦσαι (PTebt. 230 [II BC]; LXX. Cf. Anz 379) spy out τὴν χώραν (cf. τὴν γῆν Gen 42: 30; Josh 2: 2f; 14: 7) 1 Cl 12: 2.*

κατασκοπέω 1 aor. κατεσκόπησα (Eur., Hel. 1607; 2 Km 10: 3; 1 Ch 19: 3. Elsewh. usu. in mid.) spy out, lie in wait for τὴν ἐλευθερίαν ἡμῶν our freedom Gal 2: 4. M-M.*

κατάσκοπος, ου, ὁ (trag., Hdt.+; LXX, Philo; Jos., Ant. 3, 302; 312; 16, 236) a spy Hb 11: 31; Js 2: 25 v.l.; 1 Cl 12: 2, 4. κ. τῆς γῆς B 12: 9. M-M.*

κατασοφίζομαι mid. dep.; 1 aor. κατεσοφισάμην (Diod. S. 17, 116, 4; Lucian, LXX, Philo; Jos., Ant. 6, 219; 8, 412. Anz 366) get the better of or take advantage of by trickery τινά someone (after Ex 1: 10) τὸ γένος ἡμῶν Ac 7: 19.*

κατασπείρω (Eur., Pla.+; LXX) sow (upon) UGosp 69 (the Gk. proverbial expr. σπείρειν πόντον: Theognis, Eleg. 1, 106; Ps.-Phoc. 152 [cf. also Plut. ed. Bern. VII 463, 11 εἰς ὕδωρ σπείρεις], denoting an action that can hope for no results, may lie in the background here).*

κατάστασις, εως, ἡ (trag., Hdt.+; inscr., pap.; Wsd 12: 12; Philo; Jos., C. Ap. 1, 58, Ant. 12, 267) *state* (*of being*), *character* τῆς πολιτείας *of the way of life* Dg 5: 4.*

καταστέλλω 1 aor. κατέστειλα; pf. pass. ptc. κατεσταλμένος (Eur.+; pap., LXX) *restrain, quiet* w. acc. (Plut., Mor. 207ε; 3 Macc 6: 1; Jos., Bell. 2, 611; 4, 271, Ant. 20, 174) τὸν ὄχλον Ac 19: 35 (cf. Wilcken, Chrest. 10, 10f). κατεσταλμένος *calm, quiet* (Diod. S. 1, 76, 3; Epict. 4, 4, 10) δέον ἐστὶν ὑμᾶς κατεσταλμένους ὑπάρχειν *you must be calm* vs. 36. M-M.*

κατάστημα, ατος, τό (Epicurus+) *behavior, demeanor* (Plut., Marcell. 23, 6, Tib. Gracch. 2, 2; Dit., Or. 669, 3; 3 Macc 5: 45 [κατάστεμα]; Ep. Arist. 122; 210; 278; Jos., Bell. 1, 40, Ant. 15, 236) ἐν κ. *in their behavior* Tit 2: 3.—ITr 3: 2. M-M.*

καταστολή, ῆς, ἡ (Hippocr.; Wilcken, Chrest. 12, 15; Is 61: 3; Ep. Arist., Joseph.) *deportment*, outward, as it expresses itself in *clothing* (Jos., Bell. 2, 126; cf. Is 61: 3), as well as inward (Inschr. v. Priene 109, 186f [120 bc]; Plut., Pericl. 5, 1; Epict. 2, 10, 15; Ep. Arist. 284f), and prob. both at the same time (Epict. 2, 21, 11) ἐν κ. κοσμίῳ 1 Ti 2: 9. M-M.*

καταστρέφω 1 aor. κατέστρεψα; pf. pass. ptc. κατεστραμμένος (Hom. Hymns+; inscr., LXX; Jos., Bell. 1, 199, Ant. 8, 200 al.).
1. *upset, overturn* τὶ *someth.* (Diog. L. 5, 82 τὰς εἰκόνας) money-changers' tables Mt 21: 12; Mk 11: 15; J 2: 15 v.l.
2. *destroy, ruin* (Herodian 8, 4, 22; LXX; PGM 36, 299) of God δύναται αὐτὰ (=τὰ πάντα) καταστρέψαι (cf. Job 11: 10) 1 Cl 27: 4. πόλεις 1 Cl 6: 4 Funk. τὰ κατεστραμμένα *ruins* Ac 15: 16 (v.l. κατεσκαμμένα, cf. Am 9: 11 with v.l.).
3. *turn away, mislead* τινά *someone* Hm 6, 2, 4. τινὰ ἀπό τινος s 6, 2, 1. τινά τινι *someone by means of someth.* m 5, 2, 1. M-M.*

καταστρηνιάω 1 aor. κατεστρηνίασα *become wanton against* (Bl-D. §181; Mlt.-H. 316) ὅταν καταστρηνιάσωσιν τοῦ Χριστοῦ *when they feel sensuous impulses that alienate them from Christ* 1 Ti 5: 11 (cf. Ps.-Ignatius, Ad Antioch. 11).*

καταστροφή, ῆς, ἡ (Aeschyl., Hdt.+; LXX; En. 102, 10; Jos., Ant. 15, 287; 376) *ruin, destruction* gener. 1 Cl 57: 4 (Pr 1: 27). Of a city 7: 7. καταστροφῇ κατακρίνειν *condemn to destruction* 2 Pt 2: 6 (v.l. omits καταστρ. Cf. Gen 19: 29).—Fig. ἐπὶ καταστροφῇ τινος *to the ruin of the hearers* (the opp. would be edification) 2 Ti 2: 14. M-M.*

καταστρώννυμι 1 aor. κατέστρωσα, pass. κατεστρώθην (Eur., Hdt.+; UPZ 77 II, 28 [II bc] al. pap.; LXX).
1. *lay low, kill* (Hdt. 8, 53; 9, 76; X., Cyr. 3, 3, 64; Jdth 7: 14; 14: 4; 2 Macc 5: 26 al.) of the Israelites killed in the desert (cf. Num 14: 16) 1 Cor 10: 5.
2. ἐὰν καταστρώσω εἰς τὰς ἀβύσσους, a quot. of Ps 138: 8f which differs considerably fr. the LXX, seems to presuppose for κ. the mng. *spread out* (a bed, cf. Hierocles in Stob., Flor. 85, 21 κλίνην; PTurin I 8, 17 [116 bc] κονίαν ἐπὶ τοῦ δρόμου=sand on the racecourse) 1 Cl 28: 3. M-M.*

κατασύρω (Hdt.+; LXX; Jos., Bell. 2, 190; Test. 12 Patr.) *drag* (*away by force*) (Parthenius 19; Dio Chrys. 1, 196; Philo, In Flacc. 174, Leg. ad Gai. 131) τινά *someone* πρὸς τὸν κριτήν *before the judge* Lk 12: 58. See σύρω.*

κατασφάζω (Jos., Ant. 6, 120) or -σφάττω (cf. Bl-D. §71) *slaughter, strike down* (trag., Hdt.+; Aelian, V.H. 13, 2; Herodian 5, 5, 8; PGiess. 82, 11; LXX; En. 10, 12; Jos., Bell. 7, 362 al.) τινά *someone* ἔμπροσθέν τινος *before someone's eyes* Lk 19: 27. M-M.*

κατασφραγίζω pf. pass. ptc. κατεσφραγισμένος (Aeschyl.+; inscr., pap., LXX) *seal* (*up*) of a book closed by a seal Rv 5: 1 (Dit., Or. 266, 42 [III bc] τά τε γράμματ' ἀνοίσω κατεσφραγισμένα, Syll.³ 1157, 43; PSI 358). M-M.*

κατάσχεσις, εως, ἡ (LXX; Philo, Rer. Div. Her. 194 [after Num 35: 8]; Jos., Ant. 9, 9 v.l.).
1. *possession, taking into possession* (Memnon Hist. [I ad], fgm. 52, 3 CMüller) τὴν γῆν δοῦναι εἰς κ. *give the land as a possession* (as Gen 17: 8; Ezk 33: 24; 36: 5; Test. Benj. 10: 4) Ac 7: 5; cf. 13: 33 D and 1 Cl 36: 4 (both Ps 2: 8). W. gen. ἐν τῇ κ. τῶν ἐθνῶν prob. *when they took possession of* (the land of) *the Gentiles* Ac 7: 45. S. Field, Notes 114; 116.
2. *holding back, restraining* (Hippocr., π. διαίτης 2, 64) μήποτε γενηθῇ αὐτῷ κατάσχεσις *in order that he might experience no delay* Ac 20: 16 D.*

κατάσχωμεν s. κατέχω.

κατατίθημι 1 aor. κατέθηκα; 2 aor. mid. κατεθέμην (Hom.+; inscr., pap., LXX).
1. *lay* (*down*), *place* τινὰ ἐν μνήματι place a body in a *tomb* (schol. on Apollon. Rhod. 4, 1091 p. 306, 24 W.) Mk 15: 46.
2. mid. (Ep. Arist. 321; Jos., Ant. 6, 232; 11, 213) χάριτα κ. τινί *grant* or *do someone a favor* (X., Cyr. 8, 3, 26; BGU 596, 13 [84 ad] τοῦτο οὖν ποιήσας ἔσῃ μοι μεγάλην χάριτα κατατεθειμένος) Ac 24: 27. Also χάριν κ. 25: 9 (Philo, De Jos. 231.—τὴν χάριν καταθέσθαι Thu. 1, 33, 1; Hdt. 6, 41 means 'lay up a store of gratitude'). M-M.*

κατατομή, ῆς, ἡ (Theophr., H. Pl. 4, 8, 12; Synes., Ep. 15 p. 272ᴅ; Eutecnius p. 23, 28; CIG I 160, 27f; Sym. Jer 48[31]: 37, always 'incision, notch', etc.) *mutilation, cutting in pieces* w. περιτομή in a play on words, perh. to denote those for whom circumcision results in (spiritual) destruction Phil 3: 2 (for a similar play on words cf. Diog. L. 6, 24 τ. μὲν Εὐκλείδου σχολὴν ἔλεγε χολήν, τ. δὲ Πλάτωνος διατριβὴν κατατριβήν). M-M.*

κατατοξεύω 1 fut. pass. κατατοξευθήσομαι (Hdt.+; LXX) *shoot down* βολίδι *with a missile* Hb 12: 20 t.r. (Ex 19: 13).*

κατατρέχω 2 aor. κατέδραμον *run down* (Hdt., Aristoph. +; inscr., pap., LXX; En. 17, 5; Jos., Ant. 8, 204 al.) w. ἐπί and acc. *run down to* (X., An. 7, 1, 20; Da 4: 24; Job 16: 10 v.l.) Ac 21: 32. M-M.*

καταυγάζω (Heraclid. Pont. [300 bc], fgm. 116 W. [pass.]; Apollon. Rhod. 4, 1248 [mid.]; Cornutus 32 p. 69, 10; Sext. Emp.; Heliod. et al.; Herm. Wr. 10, 4b; PGM 13, 749 [pass.]; LXX; Philo, Cher. 62 [pass.]; Jos., Ant. 19, 344 [pass.]) *shine upon, illuminate* 2 Cor 4: 4 CD (for αὐγάσαι; but s. αὐγάζω and διαυγάζω 1).*

καταφαγεῖν s. κατεσθίω.

καταφέρω 1 aor. κατήνεγκα, pass. κατηνέχθην (Hom. +; inscr., pap., LXX, En.; Philo, Aet. M. 33; Joseph.).
1. *bring down* abs. (sc. the tables of the law fr. the mountain) B 14: 2.
2. κατά='against' makes its influence felt in ψῆφον κ. τινός *cast one's vote against someone*, i.e., *vote for*

someone's condemnation Ac 26: 10 (Aristot. 1437a, 19 τὴν διαβολὴν κ. τινός. Cf. Jos., Ant. 10, 91 πάντες ἤνεγκαν τὰς ψήφους κατ᾽ αὐτοῦ. αἰτιώματα κ. bring charges 25: 7.

3. pass. καταφέρεσθαι τινι get into a state of being ὕπνῳ βαθεῖ sink into a deep sleep (cf. Lucian, D. Mer. 2, 4; Herodian 2, 1, 2; 2, 9, 5; Jos., Ant. 2, 82 εἰς ὕπνον. καταφέρεσθαι abs. also has this mng.: Aristot. p. 456b, 31; 462a, 10) Ac 20: 9a. κατενεχθεὶς ἀπὸ τοῦ ὕπνου overwhelmed by sleep vs. 9b. M-M.*

καταφεύγω 2 aor. κατέφυγον (Eur., Hdt.+; inscr., pap., LXX; Ep. Arist. 141; Philo, Joseph., Test. 12 Patr.).
1. lit. flee εἰς τὰς πόλεις τῆς Λυκαονίας Ac 14: 6 (cf. κ. εἴς τ. πόλ. Aeneas Tact. 1794; Lev 26: 25; Dt 4: 42.—Jos., Bell. 6, 201, Ant. 18, 373).
2. fig. take refuge (PSI 383, 15 [248 BC]; PMagd. 25, 8; Alex. Aphr., Fat. 32, II 2 p. 204, 26 to Asclepius; Stephan. Byz. s.v. Σύβαρις: κ. ἐπὶ τὴν θεόν =to the goddess; Philo) w. inf. foll. οἱ καταφυγόντες κρατῆσαι τῆς προκειμένης ἐλπίδος we who have taken refuge, to seize the hope that is placed before us Hb 6: 18. M-M.*

καταφθείρω pf. pass. ptc. κατεφθαρμένος; 2 aor. pass. κατεφθάρην; 2 fut. καταφθαρήσομαι (Aeschyl., Pla.,+; inscr., pap., LXX, Ep. Arist.; Philo, Deus Imm. 141; 142).
1. destroy (Aeschyl., LXX) pass. be destroyed (Polyb. 2, 64, 3; Lev 26: 39; 2 Km 14: 14 v.l.; 2 Macc 5: 14) 2 Pt 2: 12 t.r.
2. ruin, corrupt τινά someone; of grief παρὰ πάντα τὰ πνεύματα κ. τὸν ἄνθρωπον it ruins a man more than all the (other) spirits Hm 10, 1, 2. Pass. be ruined, become useless (Dit., Syll.³ 1157, 74 [I BC] δένδρα; pap.) ἀπό τινος for someth. ἀπὸ τῶν βιωτικῶν πράξεων for the duties of everyday life Hv 1, 3, 1b; cf. s 6, 2, 4. κ. ὑπό τινος εἴς τι: εἰς θάνατον be injured by someone so that one dies s 9, 26, 6. κατεφθαρμένος τὸν νοῦν depraved in mind 2 Ti 3: 8 (Menand., Epitr. 461 J. καταφθαρεὶς τὸν βίον). Abs. Hv 1, 3, 1a; m 10, 1, 4; s 9, 14, 3; 9, 26, 4. M-M.*

καταφθορά, ᾶς, ἡ (trag.; Dit., Or. 339, 5 [c. 120 BC]; UPZ 110, 126 [164 BC]; 162 III, 8; LXX) destruction, downfall, death παραδιδόναι τι εἰς κ. give someth. up to destruction B 5: 1; 16: 5 (quot. of uncertain origin); ἀπόλλυσθαι εἰς κ. be destroyed (by someone) unto corruption Hs 6, 2, 2ff (w. θάνατος, as Sir 28: 6).*

καταφιλέω impf. κατεφίλουν; 1 aor. κατεφίλησα (X., Cyr. 6, 4, 10; 7, 5, 32; Polyb. 15, 1, 7; Aelian, V.H. 13, 4; Plut., Brut. 16, 5; Lucian, Dial. Deor. 4, 5; 5, 3; M. Ant. 11, 34; PGrenf. I 1, 3 [II BC]; LXX; Jos., Ant. 7, 284; 8, 387; Test. 12 Patr.) kiss τινά someone in greeting or in farewell (Philo, Rer. Div. Her. 41) Mt 26: 49; Mk 14: 45; Lk 15: 20; Ac 20: 37; Hs 9, 6, 2; 9, 11, 4. τὶ someth. (Menand., Epitr. 56 J.; Epict. 4, 10, 20 τὰς χεῖρας; PGM 4, 707) the feet (Epict. 4, 1, 17; Sb 4323, 5 τοὺς πόδας) Lk 7: 38, 45. M-M.*

καταφρονέω fut. καταφρονήσω; 1 aor. κατεφρόνησα (Eur., Hdt.+; inscr., pap., LXX, Philo, Joseph.).
1. look down on, despise, scorn, treat with contempt τινός (X., Mem. 3, 4, 12; Menand., fgm. 301, 10 K. τῶν πτωχῶν; Diod. S. 1, 67, 7; PMagd. 8, 11; 23, 4 [221 BC]; Jos., Bell. 1, 633) someone or someth. (opp. ἀντέχεσθαι) Mt 6: 24; Lk 16: 13.—Dg 2: 7. ἑνὸς τῶν μικρῶν τούτων Mt 18: 10 (differently κατ. τῶν μικρῶν [neut.]: Socrat., Ep. 29, 3); the church 1 Cor 11: 22; doubt Hm 9: 10; grief 10, 3, 1. κυριότητος 2 Pt 2: 10. μηδείς σου τῆς νεότητος

καταφρονείτω let no one look down on you because you are young 1 Ti 4: 12 (καταφρονήσας τῆς Ἀλεξάνδρου νεότητος Diod. S. 17, 7, 1 [Field, Notes 209]; Herodian 1, 3, 5; cf. PGenève 6, 13 [146 AD]). Cf. Tit 2: 15 v.l. Pass. Hm 7: 2.—Think lightly, have wrong ideas τινός of or about someth. τοῦ πλούτου τῆς χρηστότητος entertain wrong ideas about God's goodness Ro 2: 4 (s. Ltzm. ad loc.—Phylarch. [III BC]: 81 fgm. 24 Jac. οἱ πολλοὶ κ. τοῦ θείου). Abs. (sc. αὐτῶν) 1 Ti 6: 2.
2. care nothing for, disregard, be unafraid of (Diod. S. 3, 50, 5; Epict. 4, 1, 70 τοῦ ἀποθανεῖν; 71; Arrian, Anab. 7, 4, 3; Dit., Syll.³ 705, 36 [112 BC] καταφρονήσαντες τοῦ τῆς συγκλήτου δόγματος; Ep. Arist. 225; Joseph.) αἰσχύνης Hb 12: 2 (cf. Jos., Ant. 7, 313 τ. ὀλιγότητος = their small number); death (Diod. S. 5, 29, 2 τοῦ θανάτου κ.) Dg 1: 1; 10: 7 (opp. φοβεῖσθαι); ISm 3: 2; torture MPol 2: 3; cf. 11: 2. M-M.*

καταφρονητής, οῦ, ὁ (on Duris: 76 fgm. 30 Jac.; Epict. 4, 7, 33; Plut., Brut. 12, 1; Vett. Val. 47, 33; LXX; Philo, Leg. ad Gai. 322; Jos., Bell. 2, 122, Ant. 6, 347) despiser, scoffer Ac 13: 41 (Hab 1: 5). M-M.*

καταφωνέω (Hesychius) for ἐπιφωνέω (q.v.) Ac 22: 24 v.l.*

καταχαίρω fut. mid. καταχαροῦμαι (Hdt.+; IG XIV 2410, 11; Suppl. Epigr. Gr. II 844) rejoice at the misfortune of others 1 Cl 57: 4 (Pr 1: 26).*

καταχέω 1 aor. 3 sing. κατέχεεν (Hom.+; inscr., pap., LXX) pour out or down over w. gen. of what the liquid is poured over (Hdt. 4, 62; Pla., Leg. 7, 814B; PMagd. 24, 4; 9 [III BC]; Philo, Cher. 59; Jos., C. Ap. 2, 256 μύρον αὐτοῦ καταχέας) αὐτοῦ τῆς κεφαλῆς (Epict. 4, 5, 33; Jos., Ant. 9, 108; as early as Alcaeus 86, 1 D.²: Κὰτ τᾶς κεφαλᾶς κακχέατω μύρον =pour ointment on my head) Mk 14: 3. Also ἐπὶ τῆς κεφαλῆς αὐτοῦ Mt 26: 7. M-M.*

καταχθόνιος, ον (Hom.+; Dionys. Hal. 2, 10; Strabo 6, 2, 11; Cornutus 34 p. 72, 18; IG III 2, 1423; 1424; XIV 1660; Dit., Or. 382, 1; Sb 5762; PGM 4, 1918 mostly θεοὶ κ.; PGM 4, 2088 κ. δαίμων; Audollent, Defix. Tab. 74, 1 ἄγγελοι κ.) under the earth, subterranean οἱ κ. beings or powers under the earth (w. ἐπουράνιοι, ἐπίγειοι) Phil 2: 10 (cf. ἐπίγειος 2b). M-M.*

καταχράομαι 1 aor. κατεχρησάμην (Pla. et al.; inscr., pap., LXX, Philo; Jos., Bell. 2, 109). As a rule the prep. gives the simple verb a special coloring ('make full use of', 'misuse', 'use up'); in the only two pass. where it occurs in our lit. (both 1 Cor), this word differs little, if at all, fr. the simple verb: use (Charito 7, 1, 8; Dit., Or. 669, 19, Syll.³ 736, 61 [92 BC] κ. ἄλλο τι καταχρήσασθαι; PPetr. III 39 II, 15; 46 [3], 3; POxy. 494, 20 καταχρᾶσθαι εἰς τὸ ἴδιον 'use for one's own needs' [fr. a will]; Jos., Ant. 3, 303) τινί someth. (Eunap. p. 61 παρρησίᾳ; Philo, Op. M. 171, Det. Pot. Ins. 101; Jos., Ant. 12, 184) τῇ ἐξουσίᾳ μου to make full use of my authority 1 Cor 9: 18. Abs. οἱ χρώμενοι τὸν κόσμον ὡς μὴ καταχρώμενοι using the world as if they did not use (it) 7: 31 (in quite similar language, Plotin., Enn. 5, 3, 3 p. 498D interchanges προσχράομαι and χράομαι). M-M.*

κατάχυμα, ατος, τό (Themist. 23 p. 354, 18; Suidas. The form κατάχυσμα Aristoph.+.—Ammonius [100 AD] p. 78 Valck. and Thomas Mag. make a difference in the mng. of the two words) sauce, broth, soup ἐκ καταχύματος μεταλαμβάνειν to fish out of the soup, i.e., get everything for oneself Hv 3, 9, 2. The expr. seems to be proverbial. Dibelius, Hdb. ad loc., would prefer to take it as figurative, mng. *surplus, abundance*, though this sense has not been found elsewh. *

καταψεύδομαι (Eur.+; Dit., Or. 8, 14f; PFlor. 382, 57; Wsd 1: 11; Philo) *tell lies (against)* τινός *in contradiction* or *in opposition to someone* (Hyperid. 3, 18 τ. θεοῦ; Dio Chrys. 6, 17 τῆς θεοῦ; Charito 5, 6, 10; Philostrat., Vi. Apoll. 5, 37 p. 198, 10; Sextus 367; En. 104, 9; Jos., Bell. 6, 288) ITr 10. τινός w. ptc. foll. *say falsely about someone that* Dg 4: 3. τινός τι *charge someone falsely w. someth.* (Pla., Phaedo 85A, Euthyd. 283F, Rep. 2, 381D; 3, 391D al.; Philo, Op. M. 7 τοῦ θεοῦ ἀπραξίαν κ.) Hv 1, 1, 7. *

καταψηφίζομαι (mid. dep., Thu.+; pap.; Philo, Leg. All. 3, 74; Jos., Bell. 6, 250, Ant. 17, 153; the act. is rare and late) pass. *be enrolled* (as the result of a vote) Ac 1: 26 v.l. (for συγκαταψηφίζομαι). *

καταψύχω 1 aor. κατέψυξα (Hippocr.+; Zen.-P. 27 [=Sb 6733], 5 [256/5 BC]; Gen 18: 4, but intr. here) *cool off, refresh* τὶ *someth.* (Theophr., C. Pl. 4, 12, 9; Philo, Migr. Abr. 210; Jos., Bell. 1, 66 τ. ὁρμήν) *the tongue* Lk 16: 24. M-M. *

κατεάγην, κατέαξα s. καταγνυμι.

κατείδωλος, ον (only in Christian wr.: Prochorus, Acta Jo. 117, 4 Zahn; Georg. Syncell. [c. 800 AD] p. 177, 5 Bonn) *full of idols* of Athens Ac 17: 16. M-M. *

κατειλημμένος s. καταλαμβάνω.

κάτειμι (fr. εἶμι. Hom.+; inscr., pap.; Philo, Aet. M. 58; Jos., Bell. 3, 343, Ant. 14, 50) *come down, get down* ἀπὸ τῆς καρούχας MPol 8: 3. *

κατείργω 1 aor. pass. κατείρχθην (Eur., Hdt.+; Jos., Ant. 18, 322, C. Ap. 2, 241) *shut up, enclose* εἰς κάμινον πυρός 1 Cl 45: 7. *

κατέναντι adv. *opposite.* JWackernagel, Hellenistica '07, 3–6; JWaldis, Präpositionsadverbien mit d. Bedeutung 'vor' in d. LXX '22; Bl-D. §214, 4; Rob. 643f.
1. used as an adv. εἰς τ. κατέναντι κώμην *into the village opposite* (us) Lk 19: 30 (cf. 2 Ch 4: 10; Ezk 11: 1; 40: 10; Act. Phil. 98 p. 38, 23 B.).
2. as improper prep. w. gen. (Lucian, Fug. 1; Inschr. v. Priene 37, 170 [II BC] κ. τοῦ ὄρευς; UPZ 79, 11 [159 BC]; LXX).
a. of place (En. 14, 15) κ. τοῦ ἱεροῦ *opposite the temple* Mk 13: 3. κ. τοῦ γαζοφυλακείου 12: 41. κ. μου *opposite* or *before me* Hv 1, 2, 2; cf. 3, 2, 4; 3, 9, 10. κ. αὐτῶν *before them* Mk 6: 41 D (MBlack, An Aramaic Approach³, '67, 116). εἰς τὴν κώμην τὴν κ. ὑμῶν *into the village lying before you* Mt 21: 2; Mk 11: 2. κ. τοῦ ὄχλου *in the presence of the crowd* Mt 27: 24.
b. fig. *in the sight of* someone, *before* someone (Sir 28: 26; Jdth 12: 15, 19) κ. θεοῦ ἐν Χριστῷ λαλοῦμεν *before God* (Sir 50: 19; Sib. Or. 3, 499) 2 Cor 2: 17; 12: 19. κ. οὗ ἐπίστευσεν θεοῦ (=κ. τοῦ θεοῦ ᾧ ἐπίστευσεν, Bl-D. §294, 2; Rob. 717) *before the God in whom he believed* Ro 4: 17. M-M. *

κατενεχθείς s. καταφέρω.

κατενύγην s. κατανύσσομαι.

κατενώπιον (Leo Gramm. 273, 18 IBekker [1842]; Theodos. Melitenus 191 Tafel [1859]; Georg. Mon. 365, 21 de B. [1892]. Cf. StBPsaltes, Gramm. der Byz. Chroniken '13, 337. For other lit. s. on κατέναντι, beg.; AWikenhauser, BZ 8, '10, 263–70) adv. as improper prep. w. gen.

(LXX [Johannessohn 197]; Christian amulet BGU 954, 6 [VI AD] κλίνω τ. κεφαλήν μου κ. σου) in our lit. only in relation to God *before, in the presence of,* and used w. a word that means 'blameless'.
a. actually *in the presence of God* (cf. Lev 4: 17) on the day of judgment κ. τῆς δόξης αὐτοῦ Jd 24 (cf. En. 104, 1).
b. *in the sight of God* on his heavenly throne κ. αὐτοῦ *before him* Eph 1: 4; Col 1: 22. κ. αὐτοῦ τῆς δικαιοσύνης Pol 5: 2. M-M. *

κατεξουσιάζω (scarcely to be found in secular Gk.— though κατεξουσία occurs IG XIV 1047, 5 and CIG 4710. The verb Act. Thom. 45 p. 162 B. v.l.; 98 p. 211, 2 and Julian, C. Galil. 100c of the God of the Jews κ. τῶν ὅλων) *exercise authority,* perh. *tyrannize* τινός *over someone* of the mighty ones of the earth Mt 20: 25; Mk 10: 42. M-M. *

κατεπίθυμος, ον *very eager, desirous* (Jdth 12: 16 κ. τοῦ συγγενέσθαι μετ' αὐτῆς) w. inf. foll καθίσαι Hv 3, 2, 2. τοῦ θεάσασθαι 3, 8, 1. *

κατεπόθην s. καταπίνω.

κατεργάζομαι mid. dep., 1 aor. κατειργασάμην, pass. κατειργάσθην (on κατηργασάμην and κατηργάσθην s. Bl-D. §67, 3 w. app.; Mlt.-H. 189), perf. mid. κατείργασμαι. (Soph., Hdt.+; inscr., pap., LXX, Ep. Arist., Philo, Joseph.).
1. *achieve, accomplish, do* τὶ *someth.* (Hdt. 5, 24 πρήγματα μεγάλα; X., Mem. 3, 5, 11; Jos., Vi. 289) Ro 7: 15, 17f, 20; 1 Cor 5: 3; 1 Cl 32: 3f. τὴν ἀσχημοσύνην κατεργαζόμενοι *committing shameless acts* Ro 1: 27. τὸ κακόν *do what is wrong* 2: 9. τὸ βούλημα τῶν ἐθνῶν *do what the heathen like to do* 1 Pt 4: 3. ἅπαντα κατεργασάμενοι *after you have done* or *accomplished everything* (in this case the reference would be to the individual pieces of armor mentioned in what follows, which the reader is to employ as is prescribed. But s. 4 below) Eph 6: 13. ὧν οὐ κατειργάσατο Χριστὸς δι' ἐμοῦ *of anything except what Christ has accomplished through me* Ro 15: 18. Pass. τὰ σημεῖα τοῦ ἀποστόλου κατειργάσθη ἐν ὑμῖν *the signs by which an apostle demonstrates his authority have been done among you* 2 Cor 12: 12.
2. *bring about, produce, create* (Hdt. 7, 102 ἀρετὴ ἀπὸ σοφίης κατεργασμένη; Philo, Plant. 50; Test. Jos. 10: 1) τὶ *someth.* νόμος ὀργὴν Ro 4: 15. θλῖψις ὑπομονήν 5: 3 (Test. Jos. 10: 1 πόσα κατεργάζεται ἡ ὑπομονή); cf. Js 1: 3. λύπη θάνατον 2 Cor 7: 10; cf. vs. 11 (where a dat. of advantage is added). φθόνος ἀδελφοκτονίαν 1 Cl 4: 7. μνησικακία θάνατον Hv 2, 3, 1. ἡ ἁμαρτία κ. ἐν ἐμοὶ πᾶσαν ἐπιθυμίαν *sin called forth every desire within me* Ro 7: 8. τινί τι *bring about someth. for someone* (Eur., Her. 1046 πόλει σωτηρίαν) μοι θάνατον 7: 13. αἰώνιον βάρος δόξης ἡμῖν 2 Cor 4: 17. εὐχαριστίαν τῷ θεῷ *bring about thankfulness to God* 9: 11; θάνατον ἑαυτῷ κ. *bring death upon oneself* Hm 4, 1, 2; cf. s 8, 8, 5.—*Work out* τὶ *someth.* (Pla., Gorg. 473D ὁ κατειργασμένος τὴν τυραννίδα ἀδίκως) τὴν ἑαυτῶν σωτηρίαν κατεργάζεσθα Phil 2: 12 (JHMichael, Phil 2: 12: Exp. 9th Ser. II '24, 439–50).
3. κ. τινα εἴς τι *prepare someone for someth.* (cf. Hdt. 7, 6, 1; X., Mem. 2, 3, 11) ἡμᾶς εἰς αὐτὸ τοῦτο *for this very purpose* 2 Cor 5: 5.
4. *overpower, subdue, conquer* (Hdt. 6, 2 νῆσον; Thu. 6, 11, 1 al. τινά; 1 Esdr 4: 4; Philo, Sacr. Abel. 62; Jos., Ant. 2, 44) ἅπαντα κατεργασάμενοι στῆναι *after proving victorious over everything, to stand your ground* Eph 6: 13 (but s. 1 above).—GBertram, TW III 635–7. M-M. *

κατέρχομαι 2 aor. κατῆλθον (κατῆλθα Ac 27: 5 s. Bl-D. §81, 3; cf. Mlt.-H. 208f) (Hom.+; Herm. Wr. 10, 25 οὐδεὶς τῶν οὐρανίων θεῶν ἐπὶ γῆν κατελεύσεται; inscr., pap., LXX, Philo, Joseph., Test. 12 Patr.) *come down.*

1. lit., w. indication of the place fr. which ἀπό τινος: ἀπὸ τοῦ ὄρους (cf. Jos., Ant. 1, 109) Lk 9: 37. ἀπὸ τῆς Ἰουδαίας Ac 15: 1; 21: 10.—18: 5. ἐκεῖθεν GP 9: 36. The place from which is supplied fr. the context 11: 44. W. indication of the place fr. which and the goal ἀπό τινος εἰς τι *from—to* Ac 11: 27; 12: 19. W. indication of the goal εἴς τι (Jos., Ant. 8, 106 θεὸς κ. εἰς τὸ ἱερόν) Lk 4: 31; Ac 8: 5; 13: 4; 15: 30; 19: 1 v.l. πρός τινα *to someone* 9: 32. Of ships and those who sail in them, who 'come down' fr. the 'high seas': *arrive, put in* (Eustath. ad Hom. 1408, 29 [Od. 1, 182] κατελθεῖν, οὐ μόνον τὸ ἁπλῶς κάτω που ἐλθεῖν, ἀλλὰ καὶ τὸ ἐς λιμένα ἐλθεῖν, ὥσπερ καὶ καταβῆναι καὶ καταπλεῦσαι κ. καταχθῆναι κ. κατᾶραι, τὸ ἐλλιμενίσαι λέγεται. 1956, 35 [Od. 24, 115]) εἴς τι *at someth.* a harbor 18: 22; 21: 3; 27: 5.

2. fig. (cf. Philo, Det. Pot. Ins. 117 ὅταν κατέρχηται [ἡ τῆς θείας σοφίας πηγή]) ἡ σοφία ἄνωθεν κατερχομένη *that comes from above* i.e. fr. God Js 3: 15. M-M.*

κατεσθίω and **κατέσθω** (Mk 12: 40; PGM 5, 279 κατέσθεται; En. 103, 15; 104, 3. S. on ἐσθίω, also Bl-D. §101 under ἐσθίω; Mlt.-H. 238 under ἐσθίω) 2 aor. κατέφαγον; fut. καταφάγομαι (Bl-D. §74, 2; Mlt.-H. 198. S. also PIand. 26, 23 [98 AD]; LXX) and κατέδομαι (1 Cl 8: 4; LXX) *eat up, consume, devour, swallow* (Hom.+; pap., LXX, En., Philo; Jos., C. Ap. 1, 261).

1. lit. τὶ *someth.* (PFlor. 150, 6 ἀπὸ τῶν μυῶν κατεσθιόμενα) of birds (Sib. Or. 5, 471) Mt 13: 4; Mk 4: 4; Lk 8: 5 (τὰ πετεινὰ τ. οὐρανοῦ κ. as 3 Km 12: 24m; 16: 4). σάρκας (cf. Da 7: 5) B 10: 4. Of the animals that are to devour Ignatius IRo 5: 2 (cf. Babrius 103, 10 [lion]; Gen 37: 20, 33; Sib. Or. 5, 470). Of the apocalyptic dragon τὸ τέκνον αὐτῆς *devour her child* Rv 12: 4. A book 10: 9f (cf. Ezk 3: 1 and BOlsson, ZNW 32, '33, 90f.—Artem. [of Ephesus] 2, 45 p. 149, 6 speaks of ἐσθίειν βιβλία, experienced in a dream, which is interpreted to mean a quick death). The moth that eats clothing, as a type σὴς καταφάγεται ὑμᾶς B 6: 2 (Is 50: 9).

2. fig. *destroy* (Heraclitus, Ep. 7, 10 τὰ ζῶντα κατεσθίετε. Pass. Diog. L. 6, 5 'the jealous ones by their own vileness') of fire *consume* τινά *someone* (cf. Num 26: 10; Job 20: 26; Ps 77: 63) Rv 11: 5; 20: 9. Of the sword (Jer 2: 30; 2 Km 18: 8) ὑμᾶς κατέδεται 1 Cl 8: 4 (Is 1: 20). Of zeal *consume* (Test. Sim. 4: 9; cf. Jos., Ant. 7, 163) J 2: 17 (Ps 68: 10).—τὸν βίον *devour property* (cf. Od. 3, 315; Hipponax 39 Diehl; Diog. L. 10, 8, τὴν πατρῴαν οὐσίαν, that was divided among the sons; Aesop., Fab. 169 P.=304 H.; POxy. 58, 6; 10 [288 AD]; Gen 31: 15) Lk 15: 30. τὰς οἰκίας τῶν χηρῶν *eat up widows' houses* i.e. appropriate them illegally (cf. Od. 2, 237f κατέδουσι βιαίως οἶκον Ὀδυσσῆος; Alcaeus, fgm. 43, 7 D.²; Mnesimachus Com. [IV BC] 8 πόλιν; Jos., Bell. 4, 242) Mk 12: 40; Lk 20: 47 (Mt 23: 13 t.r.). Of spiteful party strife: betw. δάκνω and ἀναλίσκω (q.v.), *someth.* like *tear to pieces* Gal 5: 15 (cf. Philo, Leg. All. 3, 230 the fig. triad κατεσθίει, βιβρώσκει, καταπίνει). Abs. εἴ τις κ. *if anyone devours* (you) (i.e. exploits, robs; cf. Ps 13: 4; Is 9: 12) 2 Cor 11: 20. M-M.*

κατευθύνω 1 aor. κατεύθυνα, opt. 3 sing. κατευθύναι, imper. κατεύθυνον, inf. κατευθῦναι (Pla.+; Plut., LXX, Ep. Arist.; Philo, Decal. 60; Jos., Bell. 3, 118) *make straight, lead, direct* τὶ εἴς τι *someth.* to *someth.* τοὺς πόδας εἰς ὁδὸν εἰρήνης *the feet in the way of peace* Lk 1: 79. κ. τὰ διαβήματα *direct the steps* (Ps 39: 3) 1 Cl 60: 2. τ. καρδίας (1 Ch 29: 18 πρὸς σέ; 2 Ch 12: 14; 19: 3) *the hearts* to the love of God 2 Th 3: 5. τ. ὁδόν *direct the way* (cf. Jdth 12: 8) τὴν ὁδὸν ἡμῶν πρὸς ὑμᾶς *direct our way to you* 1 Th 3: 11. κ. τὴν πορείαν ἐν ὁσιότητι *direct their course in holiness* 1 Cl 48: 4. M-M.*

κατευλογέω impf. κατευλόγουν (Plut., Mor. 66A; 1069C; Ps.-Plut., Amator. 4 p. 750C; Tob 10: 14; 11: 17 BA) *bless* Mk 10: 16.*

κατευοδόω 1 aor. pass. κατευοδώθην (LXX; Test. Jud. 1: 6) pass. *prosper* (Achmes 13, 14; 39, 16; Cat. Cod. Astr. XII 128, 14; 162, 15) πάντα . . . κατευοδωθήσεται *everything . . . will prosper* B 11: 6 (Ps 1: 3). The same Ps-pass. influences IMg 13: 1, where the Gk. tradition κατευοδωθῆτε is to be preferred w. Lghtf., Funk, Bihlmeyer (Zahn changes it to κατευοδωθῇ): *you prosper in everything you do, both in the flesh and in the spirit.**

κατέφαγον s. κατεσθίω.

κατεφίσταμαι 2 aor. κατεπέστην (hapax legomenon) *rise up* τινί *against someone* Ac 18: 12.*

κατέχω impf. κατεῖχον; 2 aor. κατέσχον (Hom.+; inscr., pap., LXX, Philo, Joseph.).

1. trans.—a. *hold back, hold up*—α. *hold back, hinder, prevent from going away* (Hom.+; BGU 1205, 27 [28 BC]; 37, 6 [50 AD]; PFay. 109, 11; Gen 24: 56; cf. Jos., Ant. 7, 76) Hs 9, 11, 6. ὃν ἐβουλόμην πρὸς ἐμαυτὸν κ. *whom I wished to keep with me* Phlm 13. Foll. by gen. of the inf. w. article (Bl-D. §400, 4) οἱ ὄχλοι κατεῖχον αὐτὸν τοῦ μὴ πορεύεσθαι ἀπ' αὐτῶν Lk 4: 42.

β. *hold down, suppress* τὶ *someth.* (γέλωτα X., Cyr. 2, 2, 1; Charito 3, 7, 4 τ. λύπην; WECrum, Coptic Ostraca p. 4, 522=Dssm., LO 260=PGM II p. 209 Κρόνος, ὁ κατέχων τὸν θυμὸν ὅλων τ. ἀνθρώπων, κάτεχε τ. θυμὸν Ὠρι; Jos., Vi. 233 τ. ὀργήν) τ. ἀλήθειαν ἐν ἀδικίᾳ Ro 1: 18 (differently, FWDanker, FWGingrich-Festschr. '72, 93).

γ. *restrain, check* (Thu. 6, 29, 3; Appian, Bell. Civ. 2, 149 §622 τοῦ δαίμονος κατέχοντος τὸ πέλαγος=the god held the sea back until Alexander reached the other shore; PGiess. 70, 3 [II AD] ἡ ἀναγραφὴ κατέσχεν ἡμᾶς μέχρι ὥρας ἕκτης) τὸ κατέχον (Themistocl., Ep. 13, 4) 2 Th 2: 6 and ὁ κατέχων vs. 7 mean *that which restrains* and *he who restrains,* i.e., what prevents the adversary of God fr. coming out in open opposition to him, for the time being. Present-day interpr., as did the exegesis of the ancient church, generally takes τὸ κατ. to be the Roman Empire and ὁ κ. the Emperor (OBetz, NTS 9, '63, 276-91). An alternative view, as old as Theodore of Mops., would make τὸ κατ. the preaching of Christian missionaries and ὁ κ. the apostle Paul (so OCullmann, CHDodd-Festschr. '56, 409-21). In any case, the concept of the temporary restraining of the forces of hell (cf. Rtzst., Poim. 27 late Egyptian prayer 6, 4 Horus as κατέχων δράκοντα=PGM 4, 994f; cf. 2770 Μιχαὴλ . . . κατέχων, ὃν καλέουσι δράκοντα μέγαν) was given a new interpr. by the NT writer.—WBousset, D. Antichrist 1895; NFFreese, StKr 93, '21, 73-7; VHartl, ZkTh 45, '21, 455-75; WSchröder, D. 2. Thess. '29, 8-15; DBuzy, Rech de Sc rel 24, '34, 402-31; OCullmann, Recherches théol. 1, '38, 26-61; JSchmid, ThQ 129, '49, 323-43; OBetz, NTS 9, '63, 276-91.

δ. *hold back* τὶ *someth.* κ. ἐν μυστηρίῳ τὴν σοφὴν αὐτοῦ βουλήν *hold back his wise plan as a secret* Dg 8: 10.

b. *hold fast*—α. *keep in one's memory* (Theophr., Char. 26, 2, a word of Homer) εἰ κατέχετε *if you hold it fast* 1 Cor 15: 2.

β. *hold fast, retain* faithfully (X., Symp. 8, 26 τ. φιλίαν; Test. Judah 26: 1) τὸν λόγον Lk 8: 15. τὰς παραδόσεις *guard the traditions* 1 Cor 11: 2. τὸ καλόν *hold fast what is good* 1 Th 5: 21; Agr 11. W. double acc. τὴν παρρησίαν βεβαίαν κ. *keep the confidence firm* Hb 3: 6; cf. vs. 14. κ. τὴν ὁμολογίαν ἀκλινῆ 10: 23.

γ. *keep* in one's possession, *possess* (Ps.-Aristot., Mirabilia 159; 160; Polyb. 1, 2, 3; Inschr. v. Magn., 105, 51 [II BC] ἵνα ἔχωσιν κατέχωσίν τε καρπίζωνται τε; Ezk 33: 24; Da 7: 18, 22) τὶ *someth.* Mt 21: 38 v.l.; ὡς μηδὲν ἔχοντες καὶ πάντα κατέχοντες 2 Cor 6: 10. Abs. 1 Cor 7: 30.

δ. *keep, confine* in prison (Diod. S. 12, 65, 9 ἐν φυλακῇ κατέχειν τινά; PFlor. 61, 60; BGU 372 I, 16; Gen 39: 20; Philo, Leg. All. 3, 21) pass. Χριστιανοὶ κατέχονται ὡς ἐν φρουρᾷ τῷ κόσμῳ *they are confined in the world as in a prison* Dg 6: 7.

c. *take into one's possession, occupy* (Hdt. 5, 72 al.; PAmh. 30, 26 [II BC] τὴν οἰκίαν) τὸν ἔσχατον τόπον Lk 14: 9 (cf. Jos., Ant. 8, 104). Cf. GP 5: 15.

d. pass. *be bound*—α. by the law: ἀποθανόντες ἐν ᾧ κατειχόμεθα *having died to that by which we were bound* Ro 7: 6 (cf. PAmh. 97, 17 οὐ κατασχεθήσομαι τῇ ὑποσχέσει; PRyl. 117, 13).

β. by disease (Diod. S. 4, 14, 5; Philo, Op. M. 71, Congr. Erud. Grat. 138; PSI 299, 3 κατεσχέθην νόσῳ; act., Jer 13: 21; Jos., Vi. 48) Lk 4: 38 D; J 5: 4 t.r.

2. intr., nautical t.t. *make for, head for, steer toward* (Hdt. 7, 188 κατέσχε ἐς τὸν αἰγιαλόν; Dicaearchus, fgm. 85 εἰς Δῆλον κατέσχε; Polyb. 1, 25, 7; Philostrat., Vi. Apoll. 4, 13 p. 133, 5; 5, 18 p. 178, 13; cf. Jos., Ant. 1, 204) Ac 27: 40. M-M.*

κατηγορέω impf. κατηγόρουν; fut. κατηγορήσω; 1 aor. κατηγόρησα (trag., Hdt.+; inscr., pap., LXX, Philo, Joseph.; loanw. in rabb.) *accuse,* and nearly always as

1. legal t.t.: *bring charges* in court—a. before a human judge: τινός *against someone* (class., also Dit., Syll.³ 172, 37; 780, 8; PPetr. III 21g, 14; Zen.-P. 33 [=Sb 6739], 4) Mt 12: 10; Mk 3: 2; Lk 6: 7; 11: 54 v.l.; 23: 2, 10; J 8: 6; Ac 25: 5. τί τινος *accuse someone of a thing* (class., also 1 Macc 7: 25) κατηγόρουν αὐτοῦ πολλά Mk 15: 3 (for πολλά cf. PLond. 893, 12 [40 AD] πολλά κ.); cf. vs. 4. οὐχ ὡς τοῦ ἔθνους μου ἔχων τι κατηγορεῖν *not that I had any charge to bring against my own people* Ac 28: 19. This may also be the place for περὶ πάντων τούτων, ὧν ἡμεῖς κατηγοροῦμεν αὐτοῦ *of which we accuse him* 24: 8; sim. 25: 11, if this is a case of attraction of the relative ὧν = τούτων ἅ. But it is also poss. to take it as a double gen. (cf. Demosth. 21, 5 παρανόμων ἔμελλον αὐτοῦ κατηγορεῖν; Dositheus 68, 2 βίας σου κατηγορῶ).—Also τινὸς περί τινος (Thu. 8, 85, 2; X., Hell. 1, 7, 2; Jos., Ant. 13, 104) Ac 24: 13. κατά τινος (X., Hell. 1, 7, 9) w. gen. or (in the case of attraction, s. above) acc. of the thing Lk 23: 14. Abs. (Dit., Or. 218, 95 [III BC]; POxy. 237 VIII, 21) Ac 24: 2, 19. Pass. *be accused* ὑπό τινος *by someone* (Thu. 1, 95, 3 ἀδικία κατηγορεῖτο αὐτοῦ ὑπό τ. Ἑλλήνων; 2 Macc 10: 13; Philo, Mut. Nom. 206) Mt 27: 12. τί κατηγορεῖται ὑπὸ τ. Ἰουδαίων Ac 22: 30. ὁ κατηγορούμενος *the accused* (Maspéro 63, 2) 25: 16.

b. before God's tribunal κατηγορήσω ὑμῶν πρὸς τ. πατέρα J 5: 45a (for the constr. w. πρός cf. 1 Macc 7: 6; 2 Macc 10: 13). ὁ κατήγωρ . . . ὁ κατηγορῶν αὐτοὺς ἐνώπιον τ. θεοῦ ἡμῶν Rv 12: 10 (for the acc. s. PLond. 41, 10 [161 BC] ὁ βουκόλος κατηγόρησεν αὐτάς). Subst. ὁ κατηγορῶν *the accuser* (cf. Jos., C. Ap. 2, 137) J 5: 45b.

2. without legal connotation *accuse, reproach* (X., Mem. 1, 3, 4; Aelian, V.H. 9, 17; Herodian 6, 9, 1; Philo,

Plant. 80) Job αὐτὸς ἑαυτοῦ κατηγορεῖ *he accuses himself* 1 Cl 17: 4. Abs., of thoughts Ro 2: 15. M-M. B. 1439.*

κατηγορία, ας, ἡ (Hdt.+; inscr.; POxy. 237 VIII, 7; Mitteis, Chrest. 68, 19; Philo; Jos., Ant. 2, 49, C. Ap. 2, 137; loanw. in rabb.) *accusation* τίνα κ. φέρετε τοῦ ἀνθρώπου τούτου; *what accusation do you bring against this man?* J 18: 29. κ. παραδέχεσθαι κατά τινος *entertain an accusation against someone* 1 Ti 5: 19 (κατά τινος, as Isocr. 5, 147; Dit., Syll.³ 704F, 7; 705, 32). εὑρεῖν κ. Lk 6: 7 v.l. W. gen. of the content of the accusation (Demosth. 18, 279; Philo, Fuga 36) κ. ἀσωτίας *charge of profligacy* Tit 1: 6. M-M.*

κατήγορος, ου, ὁ (Soph., Hdt.; inscr., pap.; Pr 18: 17; 2 Macc 4: 5; Philo; Jos., Bell. 4, 339, C. Ap. 2, 132) *accuser* Ac 23: 30, 35; 24: 8 t.r.; 25: 16, 18; Rv 12: 10 v.l.; IMg 12 (Pr 18: 17). M-M.*

κατήγωρ, ορος, ὁ (loanw. in rabb., by no means either a Hebr. [Bousset, Offb. Joh.⁶ '06, 342] or an Aram. [W-S. §8, 13 p. 85f] modification of the Gk. κατήγορος, but rather a colloquial formation starting fr. the fact that the gen. pl. is κατηγόρων whether the word belongs to the second or third declension. This form is found also PGM 10, 25. Cf. Dssm., LO 72f [LAE 90f]; Rdm.² 19; Mlt.-H. 127f; Bl-D. §52; StBPsaltes, Gramm. der Byz. Chroniken '13, 175; ADebrunner, GGA '26, 137ff) *accuser,* designation of the devil (Billerb. I 141f) κ. τῶν ἀδελφῶν ἡμῶν Rv 12: 10. M-M.*

κατήφεια, ας, ἡ (Hom.+; Dionys. Hal.; Plut.; Philo, Spec. Leg. 3, 193; Jos., Ant. 13, 406; 19, 260) *gloominess, dejection* (Charito 6, 8, 3; 7, 3, 3; cf. Plut., Mor. 528E τ. κατήφειαν ὁρίζονται λύπην κάτω βλέπειν ποιοῦσαν. Sim., Etym. Mag. 496, 53) μετατραπήτω . . . ἡ χαρὰ εἰς κ. *let your joy be turned into gloominess* Js 4: 9. M-M.*

κατηφής, ές (Hom.+; POxy. 471, 92; Wsd 17: 4; Jos., Ant. 2, 55) *downcast* τί οὕτω κ. τῇ ἰδέᾳ; *why do you look so downcast?* Hv 1, 2, 3.*

κατηχέω 1 aor. κατήχησα, pass. κατηχήθην; pf. pass. κατήχημαι (late word; PStrassb. 41, 37 [III AD]; not LXX, but Philo, Joseph.) *make oneself understood.*

1. gener., of information that comes to someone's attention, of a communication that one receives *report, inform* (Jos., Vi. 366 αὐτός σε πολλὰ κατηχήσω='I myself will give you much information') pass. *be informed, learn* (Philo, Leg. ad Gai. 198; Ps.-Plut., Fluv. 7, 2; 8, 1; 17, 1 κατηχηθείς περὶ συμβεβηκότων; PPrinceton Univ. II '36 no. 20, 1 [II AD]) κατηχήθησαν περὶ σοῦ ὅτι *they have been informed concerning you that* Ac 21: 21; cf. vs. 24.

2. *teach, instruct* (Lucian, Jupp. Trag. 39; Ps.-Lucian, Asin. 48) in our lit. only of instruction in religious matters.

a. gener. τινά *someone* 1 Cor 14: 19. ὁ κατηχῶν *the teacher* Gal 6: 6b. Pass. (Ps.-Lucian, Philopatr. 17 of teaching about God: κατηχούμενος πείθου παρ' ἐμοῦ) κατηχούμενος ἐκ τοῦ νόμου *instructed in the law* Ro 2: 18. W. acc. of what is taught κατηχημένος τὴν ὁδὸν τοῦ κυρίου *in the way of the Lord* Ac 18: 25. ὁ κατηχούμενος τὸν λόγον *in (Christian) teaching* Gal 6: 6a. ἵνα ἐπιγνῷς περὶ ὧν κατηχήθης λόγων τὴν ἀσφάλειαν (=τὴν ἀ. τῶν λόγων περὶ ὧν κ.) *in order that you may know the truth about the things you have been taught* Lk 1: 4 (so BWeiss, HHoltzmann, FHauck, Rengstorf, Gdspd., though Zahn, JWeiss, EKlostermann; FVogel, NKZ 44, '33, 203–5; Beyer, RSV prefer mng. 1: *the things of which you have been informed.* S. on παρακολουθέω 3).

b. in the specif. sense of catechetical instruction by the church *give instruction to catechumens* 2 Cl 17: 1.—PCarrington, The Primitive Christian Catechism '40; CHDodd in NT Essays (TWManson memorial vol.) '59, 106-18; HWBeyer, TW III 638-40. M-M.*

κατήχθημεν s. κατάγω.

κατ' ἰδίαν s. ἴδιος 4.

κατιόω (Sir 12: 11) pf. pass. 3 sing. κατίωται; pass. *become rusty, tarnished, corroded* (Strabo 16, 2, 42; Epict. 4, 6, 14) of gold and silver (cf. EpJer 10) Js 5: 3.*

κατισχύω impf. κατίσχυον; fut. κατισχύσω; 1 aor. κατίσχυσα (Soph.+; oft. in later wr. and in LXX; Ep. Arist.; Jos., Ant. 14, 357; Test. 12 Patr., but scarcely at all in inscr., pap. [PGM 13, 797]) intrans. *be strong, powerful, gain the ascendancy* (s. ἰσχύω).
1. abs. *be dominant, prevail* (Polyb. 11, 13, 3; Ex 17: 11; En. 104, 6) κατίσχυον αἱ φωναὶ αὐτῶν *their voices prevailed* Lk 23: 23 (Antig. Car. 152 κατίσχυκεν ἡ φήμη). W. inf. foll. *be able, be in a position* 21: 36.
2. used w. gen. *win a victory over* (Dio Chrys. 12[13], 4 al.; Aelian, H.A. 5, 19; Wsd 7: 30; Jer 15: 18; Jos., Bell. 2, 464 κατισχύσας πλειόνων='conqueror of a superior force'; Test. Reub. 4: 11) πύλαι ᾅδου οὐ κατισχύσουσιν αὐτῆς (i.e. τῆς ἐκκλησίας) Mt 16: 18 (s. on πύλη 1). πάσης πονηρίας Hv 2, 3, 2. κ. τῶν ἔργων τοῦ διαβόλου *win the victory over the works of the devil* Hm 12, 6, 4. M-M.*

κατοικέω fut. κατοικήσω; 1 aor. κατῴκησα (Soph., Hdt.+; inscr., pap., LXX, Philo, Joseph., Test. 12 Patr.).
1. intrans. *live, dwell, reside, settle (down)*—**a.** w. the place indicated by ἔν τινι (X., An. 5, 3, 7; Inschr. v. Hier. 212 τῶν ἐν Ἱεραπόλει κατοικούντων Ἰουδαίων; P Magd. 25, 2 [221 BC]; PTebt. 5, 180; Lev 23: 42; Gen 14: 12; Philo, Sobr. 68; Jos., Vi. 31; PMerton 63, 9) Ac 1: 20 (cf. Ps 68: 26); 2: 5 v.l. (for εἰς, s. below); 7: 2, 4a, 48; 9: 22; 11: 29; 13: 27; 17: 24; Hb 11: 9; Rv 13: 12; B 11: 4; IEph 6: 2; Hs 3: 1. Also used w. εἰς and acc. (Ps.-Callisth. 1, 38, 3 εἰς φθαρτὰ σώματα ἀθανάτων ὀνόματα κατοικεῖ; schol. on Soph., Trach. 39 p. 281 Papag.; Bl-D. §205; Rob. 592f) Mt 2: 23; 4: 13; Ac 2: 5; 7: 4b. εἰς τὰ τείχη Hs 8, 7, 3. εἰς τὸν αἰῶνα τὸν ἐρχόμενον s 4: 2. ἐπὶ τῆς γῆς *live on the earth* Rv 3: 10; 6: 10; 8: 13; 11: 10; 13: 8, 14a, b; 17: 8. ἐπὶ παντὸς προσώπου τῆς γῆς *live on the whole earth* Ac 17: 26. ἐπὶ ξένης (i.e. χώρας) Hs 1: 6. τοῦ, ὅπου Rv 2: 13a, b. Abs. (Ramsay, Phryg. I 2 p. 461 nos. 294 and 295 οἱ κατοικοῦντες Ῥωμαῖοι) ὑπὸ πάντων τῶν (sc. ἐκεῖ) κατοικούντων Ἰουδαίων *by all the Jews who live there* Ac 22: 12.
b. in relation to the possession of human beings by God, Christ, the Holy Spirit, and other supernatural beings, virtues, etc. (cf. Wsd 1: 4; Test. Dan 5: 1, Joseph 10: 2f) ὁ θεὸς κ. ἐν ἡμῖν B 16: 8. Of Christ Eph 3: 17. Of the Holy Spirit Hm 5, 2, 5; 10, 2, 5; s 5, 6, 5; ὁ κύριος ἐν τῇ μακροθυμίᾳ κ. m 5, 1, 3. ἐν αὐτῷ κ. πᾶν τὸ πλήρωμα τῆς θεότητος Col 2: 9; cf. 1: 19; ἐν οἷς δικαιοσύνη κ. 2 Pt 3: 13 (cf. Is 32: 16). ἡ μακροθυμία κατοικεῖ μετὰ τῶν τ. πίστιν ἐχόντων *patience dwells with those who have faith* Hm 5, 2, 3. Of demonic possession Mt 12: 45; Lk 11: 26 (κ. ἐκεῖ as Palaeph. 39 p. 44, 4).
2. trans. *inhabit* τὶ *someth.* (Demosth., Ep. 4, 7 τ. Ἰνδικὴν χώραν; Ps.-Aristot., Mirabilia 136; Dit., Syll.³ 557, 17 τ. Ἀσίαν; PMagd. 9, 1 [III BC]; PTurin 4, 8 [117 BC] τὴν αὐτὴν πόλιν; Gen 13: 7; Ezk 25: 16; Philo, Leg. All. 3, 2; Jos., Vi. 27 Δαμασκόν) Ἱερουσαλήμ Lk 13: 4; Ac 1: 19; 2: 14; 4: 16. Cf. 2: 9 (cf. Diod. S. 18, 11, 2 Μεσσήνιοι καὶ οἱ τὴν Ἀκτὴν κατοικοῦντες); 9: 32, 35; 19: 10, 17. οἱ κατοικοῦντες τὴν γῆν *the inhabitants of*

the earth Rv 17: 2. κ. πόλεις (Hdt. 7, 164) Dg 5: 2. Of God ὁ κ. τὸν ναόν *the One who dwells in the temple* (cf. Jos., Bell. 5, 458f) Mt 23: 21; cf. Js 4: 5 t.r. M-M.**

κατοίκησις, εως, ἡ (Thu.+; PLond. 1708, 111; LXX; En.; Jos., Ant. 6, 321, C. Ap. 2, 34; 35) *living (quarters), dwelling* κ. ἔχειν ἐν τοῖς μνήμασιν *live among the tombs* Mk 5: 3. ἐν τῷ πύργῳ κ. ἔχειν Hv 3, 8, 8. ἐγένετο ἡ κ. αὐτῶν (cf. Gen 10: 30) εἰς τὸν πύργον *they found a home in the tower* Hs 8, 7, 5; 8, 8, 5 (ἐν τῷ πύργῳ 8, 9, 2).*

κατοικητήριον, ου, τό (LXX; Cat. Cod. Astr. VIII 1 p. 189, 10; Christian inscr. CIA III 3508.—The adj. κατοικητήριος Soranus p. 37, 16) *dwelling-(place)* ἐγένετο κ. δαιμονίων *it has become a dwelling-place of demons* i.e. they have taken possession of it Rv 18: 2 (cf. Jer 9: 10 κ. δρακόντων). Of the Christians συνοικοδομεῖσθε εἰς κ. τοῦ θεοῦ *you are built up together for a dwelling-place of God* Eph 2: 22. τὸ κ. τῆς καρδίας *the habitation of the heart* a temple of God B 6: 15; cf. 16: 7f.*

κατοικία, ας, ἡ *dwelling-(place), habitation* (Polyb. 2, 32, 4; Diod. S. 18, 7, 7; Strabo 5, 4, 8; Mitteis, Chrest. 31 I, 23 [116 BC]; Sb 5620, 3; 1 Esdr 9: 12, 37; 1 Macc 1: 38; 2 Macc 3: 39; Jos., Ant. 10, 223; 18, 37) Ac 17: 26. εἰς τὸν πύργον *in the tower* Hs 8, 7, 3; 8, 8, 2f; 8, 9, 4; 8, 10, 1; 4; 9, 13, 5; cf. s 8, 3, 4; 8, 6, 3; 6. M-M.*

κατοικίζω 1 aor. κατῴκισα *cause to dwell, establish, settle* (so Hdt.+; POxy. 705, 24; LXX; Ep. Arist.; Jos., Ant. 1, 110 εἰς; 11, 19 ἐν) of the Spirit τὸ πνεῦμα ὃ κατῴκισεν ἐν ἡμῖν *the Spirit which he (God) has caused to live in us* Js 4: 5. τὸ πνεῦμα ὃ ὁ θεὸς κ. ἐν τῇ σαρκὶ ταύτῃ Hm 3: 1. τὸ πνεῦμα κατῴκισεν ὁ θεὸς εἰς σάρκα *God caused the Spirit to dwell in flesh* s 5, 6, 5. M-M.*

κατοικτίρω 1 aor. inf. κατοικτεῖραι (Soph., Hdt.+; 4 Macc) *have pity* τὶ *on someth.* (Alciphr. 3, 39, 3) τὴν ἡλικίαν (cf. 4 Macc 8: 20 τὸ τ. μητρὸς γῆρας) MPol 3.*

κατοπτρίζω (act. ='produce a reflection' in Plut., Mor. 894F; mid. ='look at oneself in a mirror' in Diog. L. 2, 33; 3, 39; 7, 17; Artem. 2, 7; Athen. 15 p. 687c. In the same mng. ἐγκατοπτρίξασθαι εἰς τὸ ὕδωρ Dit., Syll.³ 1168, 64 [III BC]. Pass. τὰ κατοπτριζόμενα='what is seen in a mirror' POxy. 1609, 19) occurs once in our lit., in the middle, prob. in the mng.: *look at someth. as in a mirror, contemplate someth.* (cf. Philo, Leg. All. 3, 101. The Itala and Vulg. transl. 'speculantes'; Tert., Adv. Marc. 5, 11 'contemplantes'. Likew. the Peshitto and Bohairic and Sahidic versions) τὴν δόξαν κυρίου *the glory of the Lord* 2 Cor 3: 18.—Rtzst., NGG '16, 411, Hist. Mon. 242ff, Mysterienrel.³ 357; PCorssen, ZNW 19, '19/'20, 2-10; AEBrooke, JTS 24, '23, 98; NHugedé, La Métaphore du Miroir dans 1 et 2 Cor, '57 ('contemplate').—Schlatter, Allo, WLKnox, St. Paul and the Church of the Gentiles '39, 132; JDupont, RB 56, '49, 392-411 (a good review) prefer the mng. *reflect*. See s.v. ἔσοπτρον. M-M.*

κατορθόω fut. κατορθώσω; 1 aor. mid. κατωρθωσάμην (trag., Thu.+; inscr., pap., LXX, Ep. Arist.; oft. Philo; Jos., Bell. 7, 13, C. Ap. 2, 231) *set straight, complete, bring to a successful conclusion* of God (Menand., Epitr. 339; Alex. Aphr., Fat. 34, II 2 p. 206, 31; cf. Jos., Ant. 12, 312) τὰς μερίμνας *he will set your cares straight* Hv 4, 2, 5 (Polyaenus 8, 23, 30 of τοὺς πολέμους—to bring them to a fortunate end). Mid. κ. τὰς ἐντολὰς *carry out the commands* v 3, 5, 3. τὰς ὁδούς (cf. Ps 118: 9) v 2, 2, 6.—Pass. v 1, 1, 8.—Hs 8, 11, 4 v.l.*

κατόρθωμα, ατος, τό (Aristot., Polyb. et al.; Philo; Jos., Bell. 1, 55; 7, 5) *success, prosperity, good order*, pl. (as

Charito 7, 6, 5; Xenophon Eph. 1, 1, 4; Dit., Syll.³ 783, 15; PHermopol. 125 II, 4 τ. μέγιστα κατορθώματα τῇ πατρίδι Ac 24: 2 t.r. (s. διόρθωμα). M-M.*

κάτω adv. of place (Hom.+; inscr., pap., LXX, En., Philo, Joseph.).—1. *below* κ. ἐν τῇ αὐλῇ *below in the courtyard* Mk 14: 66. ἐπὶ τῆς γῆς κ. (Dt 4: 39; Josh 2: 11; 3 Km 8: 23) Ac 2: 19. κ. τοῦ βυθοῦ *at the bottom of the sea* B 10: 5. Subst. τὰ κάτω (opp. τὰ ἄνω) *this world* (in contrast to 'that' world as Maximus Tyr. 11, 10c) J 8: 23 (for the opp. τὰ ἄνω—τὰ κάτω cf. Ael. Aristid. 36, 32 K.=48 p. 449 D.; Herm. Wr. 11, 5; 14, 5; Dit., Syll.³ 610, 52f [190 BC]). *Under* w. a number Mt 2: 16 D.
2. *downwards, down* (Herodian 3, 11, 3; En. 14, 25; Jos., Ant. 19, 349) βάλλειν κάτω J 12: 31 v.l.; βάλλειν σεαυτὸν κ. *throw yourself down* Mt 4: 6; Lk 4: 9. κ. κύπτειν J 8: 6, 8 v.l.; πίπτειν κ. Ac 20: 9; ἀπενεχθῆναι κ. *be brought down* Hs 9, 4, 7. ἔτι κ. χώρει *go down farther* Mt 20: 28 D=Agr 22. ἀπ᾽ ἄνωθεν ἕως κ. *from top to bottom* (cf. Aëtius p. 86, 5 ἄνωθεν κάτω) Mt 27: 51; Mk 15: 38 (ἕως κ. as Ezk 1: 27; 8: 2). M-M.*

κατώτερος, α, ον comp. of κάτω (Hippocr.+; Vett. Val. 34, 21; IG XIV 2476; Gen 35: 8; Test. Levi 3: 1) *lower* κατέβη εἰς τὰ κατώτερα μέρη τῆς γῆς *he went down into the lower regions of the earth* Eph 4: 9 (on the expr. cf. Galen VIII p. 894 K. μέρη τῆς καρδίας κατωτέρω; Ps 138: 15 ἐν τοῖς κατωτάτοις τῆς γῆς; Tob 13: 2 S; ἐκ τοῦ κατωτάτου ᾅδου Third Corinthians 3: 30). Some think the pass. refers to Jesus' burial. Many (Tert., Chrysost., FCBaur, Wohlenberg, Clemen² 90, OHoltzmann) take τὰ κατ. μέρη τ. γῆς to be Hades (cf. Ael. Aristid. 26, 103 K.=14 p. 367 D. of the Titans: εἰς τ. κατωτάτους μυχοὺς τῆς γῆς ἀπελθεῖν). Others hold that Jesus' coming on earth, the incarnation, is meant.—AHJLindroth, Descendit ad inferna: Svensk Teol. Kvartalskrift 8, '32, 121-40; FBüchsel, TW III 641-3; Bl-D. §167 app. S. on πνεῦμα 2 and 4c. M-M.*

κατωτέρω adv. (Aristoph.+; Jos., Bell. 4, 505, Ant. 8, 154) *lower, below* w. numbers ἀπὸ διετοῦς καὶ κατωτέρω *two years old and under* Mt 2: 16 (cf. 1 Ch 27: 23 ἀπὸ εἰκοσαετοῦς καὶ κάτω.—Bl-D. §62; Rob. 297f).*

Καῦδα s. Κλαῦδα. M-M.

καῦμα, ατος, τό (Hom.+; Epigr. Gr. 649, 5; PLond. 1166, 6 [42 AD]; PSI 184, 6; LXX; Jos., Bell. 3, 312, Ant. 18, 192) *burning, heat* Rv 7: 16 (Crinagoras no. 14, 4 ἠελίου καῦμα τὸ θερμότατον). καυματίζεσθαι κ. μέγα *be burned with a scorching heat* 16: 9. M-M.*

καυματίζω 1 aor. ἐκαυμάτισα, pass. ἐκαυματίσθην (Epict. 1, 6, 26; 3, 22, 52; M. Ant. 7, 64, 3. Of fever Plut., Mor. 100D; 691E) *burn (up)* τινὰ ἐν πυρί *someone with fire* Rv 16: 8. Pass. *be burned, be scorched* of plants withering in the heat Mt 13: 6; Mk 4: 6. κ. καῦμα μέγα Rv 16: 9 (s. καῦμα).*

καυματόω (only in Eustathius Macrembolita 8, 4 p. 18 ἀνδρὶ διψῶντι καὶ καυματουμένῳ) *be scorched by the heat* Mt 13: 6 B.*

καῦσις, εως, ἡ (Hdt.+; Inschr. v. Magn. 179, 11; Wilcken, Chrest. 70, 10 [57/6 BC]; PLond. 1166, 14 [42 AD]; 1177, 74; LXX; En. 102, 1; Philo, Decal. 150) *burning* ἧς τὸ τέλος εἰς καῦσιν *its* (the land's) *end is to be burned over* Hb 6: 8. M-M.*

καυσόω (Ptolem., Apotelesm. 1, 4, 4 Boll-B.; PHolm. 25, 27) pass. *be consumed by heat, burn up* (Diosc. 2, 134 W.; Antyllus in Oribas. 9, 13, 1; Galen, CMG V 9, 1 p. 264,

13; Philumen. p. 26, 21 of fever) στοιχεῖα καυσούμενα λυθήσεται *the elements will be destroyed by burning* 2 Pt 3: 10; cf. vs. 12.—On the destruction of the world by fire cf. Rtzst., Weltuntergangsvorstellungen '24; s. also FOlivier, 2 Pt 3: 10: Religio 11, '35, 481-9.*

καυστηριάζω pf. pass. ptc. κεκαυστηριασμένος (Strabo 5, 1, 9 ed. GKramer [1844] v.l.; Leontios 40 p. 79, 9; perh. BGU 952, 4.—καυτηριάζω in Hippiatr. 1, 28 vol. I p. 12, 4) *brand with a red-hot iron* (Strabo), *sear* fig., pass. κεκαυστηριασμένοι τὴν ἰδίαν συνείδησιν *seared in their own consciences* 1 Ti 4: 2 (schol. on Lucian 137, 11 Rabe is dependent on this). M-M.*

καύσων, ωνος, ὁ *heat, burning* (sun) (so Diphilus [c. 300 BC] in Athen. 3, 2 p. 73A; Leo 9, 5; Syntipas collection of Aesop's fables 54 p. 547 P.; Cyrill. Scyth. p. 94, 23 and 25; 109, 21; Gen 31: 40 A; Sir 18: 16; Test. Gad 1: 4) Mt 20: 12. κ. ἔσται *it will be a hot day* Lk 12: 55. ἀνέτειλεν ὁ ἥλιος σὺν τῷ κ. *the sun came up with its scorching heat* Js 1: 11 (since the sun brings w. it burning heat, but not the scorching east wind, which is usu. meant by καύσων in the LXX, it is not likely that a hot wind is meant in the Js passage. On the combination of κ. with ἥλιος cf. Is 49: 10). M-M.*

καυτηριάζω 1 Ti 4: 2 t.r., s. καυστηριάζω.*

καυχάομαι (Pind., Hdt.+; Dit., Syll.³ 1268, 23; POxy. 1160, 7ff; PSI 26, 16; LXX) mid. dep.; 2 sing. καυχᾶσαι Ro 2: 17, 23; 1 Cor 4: 7 (cf. Mayser 328; JWackernagel, ThLZ 33, '08, 639; Thackeray 218; Mlt.-H. 198); fut. καυχήσομαι; 1 aor. ἐκαυχησάμην; pf. κεκαύχημαι. In our lit. restricted to Paul (who has it c. 35 times), except for two pass. each in Js and Ign., and one in 1 Cl (a quot. fr. the OT).
1. intr. *boast, glory, pride oneself* (Sappho, fgm. 26, 10 D.²) ἔν τινι *in* or *about a person* or *thing* (schol. on Apollon. Rhod. 3, 976 οἱ καυχώμενοι ἐν ἑτέρων διαβολαῖς; LXX; Test. Judah 13: 2.—Bl-D. §196 w. app.; cf. Rob. 532) ἐν θεῷ Ro 2: 17. ἐν τῷ θεῷ 5: 11. ἐν κυρίῳ 1 Cor 1: 31b; 2 Cor 10: 17b (cf. on both Jer 9: 23). ἐν Χριστῷ Ἰησοῦ Phil 3: 3. ἐν ἀνθρώποις 1 Cor 3: 21.—ἐν νόμῳ (cf. Sir 39: 8) Ro 2: 23; in afflictions 5: 3; in the work of others 2 Cor 10: 15; in weaknesses 12: 9; in high position Js 1: 9; wisdom, etc. 1 Cl 13: 1 (Jer 9: 22f). ἐν τῇ ὑμετέρᾳ σαρκί Gal 6: 13. ἐν τῷ σταυρῷ vs. 14. ἐν τῷ προσώπῳ κ., opp. ἐν τῇ καρδίᾳ *pride oneself on externals—on the heart* 2 Cor 5: 12. ἐν ᾧ καυχῶνται 11: 12.—The ἐν is to be taken somewhat differently Js 4: 16 (s. ἀλαζονεία).—εἴς τι *boast with regard to someth.* 2 Cor 10: 16. Differently εἰς τὰ ἄμετρα κ. *boast beyond limit* (s. ἄμετρος) vss. 13, 15.—ἐπί τινι *based on someth., in someth.* (Cratinus Com. [V BC] 95; Diod. S. 15, 6, 2 ἐπὶ τοῖς ποιήμασιν; 16, 70, 2; iambic poet in Ps.-Callisth. 2, 20, 11 ἐπὶ τέκνοισι; Dit., Syll.³ loc. cit. ἐπὶ ῥώμη; Ps 5: 12 v.l. [11]) Ro 5: 2 (JMBover, Biblica 22, '41, 41-5). ὑπέρ τινος *on behalf of someone* 2 Cor 12: 5a, b. κατά τι *in accordance with someth.* 2 Cor 11: 18a.—ἐνώπιον τ. θεοῦ *before God* 1 Cor 1: 29.—W. ὅτι foll. (Strabo 13, 1, 27) IPhld 6: 3.—Abs. (Test. Reub. 3: 5) 1 Cor 1: 31a; 4: 7; 2 Cor 10: 17a; 11: 18b, 30a; 12: 1; Eph 2: 9; IPol 5: 2.—1 Cor 13: 3, 𝔓⁴⁶ ℵ AB Orig. and the Egypt. versions have καυχήσωμαι (defended e.g. by Harnack, SAB '11, 139ff; Gdspd., Probs. 162-5; KWClark, Studia Paulina [deZwaan-Festschr.] '53, 61f) instead of καυθήσομαι, which is preferred by most (Heinrici, B and JWeiss, Bachmann, Ltzm., Sickenberger, H-DWendland, E Preuschen [ZNW 16, '15, 127ff]; JKElliott, ZNW 62, '71, 297f).—S. καίω 2.

2. trans. *boast about, mention in order to boast of, be proud of* τὶ *someth.* (Philemo Com. 141 p. 521; Diod. S. 20, 63, 4) τὰ τῆς ἀσθενείας μου *boast about my weaknesses* 2 Cor 11: 30b (cf. Pr 27: 1 κ. τὰ εἰς αὔριον). τὶ περί τινος 10: 8. τί τινι ὑπέρ τινος *say someth. boastingly* (or *in pride*) *to someone concerning someone* 7: 14; 9: 2 (here a ὅτι-clause defines τὶ more closely). μικρόν τι 11: 16.—JBosch, 'Gloriarse' según San Pablo, Sentido y teologia de καυχάομαι, '70. M-M. B. 1281.*

καύχημα, ατος, τό (Pind., Isth. 5, 65; LXX).—1. *boast, object of boasting* (Ael. Aristid. 32, 5 K.=12 p. 135 D.), then also used when the boast is not made in words, to denote *the thing of which one is proud*, in this sense *pride* (Dt 33: 29; Pr 17: 6) κ. ἔχει *he has someth. to boast about* Ro 4: 2. οὐκ ἔστιν μοι κ. *I have nothing to boast about* 1 Cor 9: 16. εἰς ἑαυτὸν τὸ κ. ἔχειν *have a reason for boasting on one's own account* Gal 6: 4 (PhHaeuser, BZ 12, '14, 45-56). With gen. (Ps.-Callisth. 2, 22, 7 and 11 Περσῶν κ.) τὸ κ. μου οὐδεὶς κενώσει 1 Cor 9: 15. κ. τινος εἶναι *be someone's pride* 2 Cor 1: 14. εἰς κ. ἐμοὶ εἰς ἡμέραν Χριστοῦ *as my pride (and joy) in the day of Christ* Phil 2: 16. τὸ κ. ἡμῶν *what we are proud of* 1 Cl 34: 5. τὸ κ. ὑμῶν *what you can be proud of* Phil 1: 26. οὐ καλὸν τὸ κ. ὑμῶν *what your are so proud of* 1 Cor 5: 6. τὸ κ. τῆς ἐλπίδος *that for which we are proud to hope* (cf. Ro 5: 2) Hb 3: 6.

2. *boast, what is said in boasting* ἵνα μὴ τὸ κ. ἡμῶν τὸ ὑπὲρ ὑμῶν κενωθῇ *so that what we say in praise of you may not prove to be empty words* 2 Cor 9: 3.—Almost= *boasting* (cf. Pind., Isth. 5, 51 καύχημα=act. 'boasting') ἀφορμὴν διδόναι τινὶ καυχήματος ὑπέρ τινος *give someone an occasion to be proud of someone* 5: 12.—Genths, D. Begriff des καύχημα b. Pls: NKZ 38, '27, 501-21.*

καύχησις, εως, ἡ (Epicurus fgm. 93; Philod., περὶ κακιῶν p. 27 J.; Philo, Congr. Erud. Gr. 107; LXX).

1. *boasting* (Jer 12: 13) Ro 3: 27; 2 Cor 11: 10, 17; Js 4: 16; IEph 18: 1. In a list of vices Hm 8: 3. στέφανος καυχήσεως *crown of pride*, i.e. to be proud of (Ezk 16: 12; Pr 16: 31) 1 Th 2: 19. κ. ὑπέρ τινος *pride that one has in someone* 2 Cor 7: 4; 8: 24. ἡ καύχησις ἡμῶν ἐπὶ Τίτου *our boasting in the presence of Titus* 7: 14. ἐν κ. ἀπολέσθαι *be lost because of boasting* ITr 4: 1. ἔχω τὴν κ. ἐν Χριστῷ Ἰησοῦ τὰ πρὸς τὸν θεόν *I may boast in Christ of my relation to God* Ro 15: 17; νὴ τὴν ὑμετέραν κ. *as surely as I may boast of you* 1 Cor 15: 31.

2. *object of boasting, reason for boasting* 2 Cor 1: 12.—RAsting, Kauchesis '25; AFridrichsen, Symb. Osl. 7, '28, 25-9; 8, '29, 78-82; RBultmann, TW III 646-54.*

Καφαρναούμ, ἡ indecl. (כְּפַר נַחוּם; Καφαρν. also 𝔓⁴⁵ Lk 10: 15 and in the two gosp.-fgm. [V AD] POxy. 847 [J 2: 12]; 1596 [J 6: 17]. In the later tradition the form Καπερναούμ predominates; on the spelling cf. Bl-D. §39, 2; Rob. 184; 219; FCBurkitt, The Syriac Forms of NT Proper Names '12, 27f, JTS 34, '33, 388-90; F-MAbel, Le nom de C.: Journ. of the Palest. Orient. Soc. 8, '28, 24-34) *Capernaum* (Ptolem. 5, 16, 4 Καπαρναούμ; cf. Jos., Bell. 3, 519 Καφαρναούμ, Vi. 403 εἰς κώμην Κεφαρνωκόν. Not in OT), a city on Lake Gennesaret, whose location is still uncertain. Acc. to some (so the Onomastica), its ruins are to be found at Tell Ḥûm (or Telḥûm); this view has the best support at present. Acc. to others the site was at Khan Minyeh (so perh. Jos., Bell. 3, 519) Mt 4: 13; 8: 5; 11: 23; 17: 24; Mk 1: 21; 2: 1; 9: 33; Lk 4: 23, 31; 7: 1; 10: 15; J 2: 12; 4: 46; 6: 17, 24, 59; GEb 2.—HGuthe, RE X 27ff (lit.); BMeistermann, C. et Bethsaïde '21; Dalman, Orte³ 149ff; HHBörge, Kapernaum '40; BHjerl-Hansen, Kapernaum

'41; JSKennard, Jr., Was C. the Home of Jesus?: JBL 65, '46, 131-41; EFFBishop, Jesus and C.: CBQ 15, '53, 427-37; CKopp, The Holy Places of the Gospels, tr. RWalls, '63, 171-79. Further lit. s.v. συναγωγή 2. M-M.*

κε' as numeral *twenty-five* Hs 9, 4, 3; 9, 5, 4; 9, 15, 4.*

Κεγχρεαί, ῶν, αἱ (Thu. [Κεγχρειαί], X.+) *Cenchreae*, the seaport of Corinth (Philo, In Flacc. 155: K., τὸ Κορίνθιον ἐπίνειον) on the eastern side of the isthmus (Strabo 8, 6, 22) Ac 18: 18; Ro 16: 1; subscr. The port on the western side was Lechaeum (Diod. S. 11, 16, 3 ἀπὸ Λεχαίου μέχρι Κεγχρεῶν).—WMichaelis, ZNW 25, '26, 144-54.*

κέδρος, ου, ἡ (Hom.+; LXX; Philo, Aet. M. 64; Jos., Ant. 8, 44) *cedar tree* J 18: 1 v.l.; 1 Cl 14: 5 (Ps 36: 35). S. the foll. entry. M-M.*

Κεδρών, ὁ indecl. (קִדְרוֹן; Jos., Bell. 5, 70; 252 Κεδρών, ῶνος, Ant. 8, 17 τὸν χειμάρρουν Κεδρῶνα) *Kidron* ὁ χειμάρρους τοῦ Κ. (the Rahlfs LXX does not have the article before Κ. anywhere; this is in accord w. the good text tradition: 2 Km 15: 23; 3 Km 2: 37; 15: 13; 4 Km 23: 6, 12) *the Kidron valley*, a wadi or watercourse (dry except in the rainy season), adjoining Jerusalem on the east and emptying into the Dead Sea J 18: 1.—GDalman, Jerusalem u. s. Gelände '30, 182ff. M-M. s.v. κέδρος.*

κεῖμαι impf. 3 sing. ἔκειτο (Hom.+; inscr., pap., LXX, Ep. Arist., Philo, Test. 12 Patr.; Sib. Or. 4, 66; 5, 225 al.) *lie, recline*; can serve as passive of τίθημι.

1. lit.—a. of pers.: w. indication of place ἔν τινι *in someth.* of a child ἐν φάτνῃ Lk 2: 12, 16. Of a dead person (Hom.+; also in Palest. [Philol. Wochenschr. 49, '29, 247] and Alexandrian [Sb 1397] grave inscr.; PRyl. 114, 17 τοῦ σώματος κειμένου) w. οὗ or ὅπου (PGM 4, 2038) Mt 28: 6; Lk 23: 53; J 20: 12.

b. of things *lie* ἐπί τι *on someth.* 2 Cor 3: 15. Also ἐπάνω τινός Mt 5: 14 (κ. of location of a place since Hdt., Thu.; Dit., Syll.³ 685, 46 [139 BC]; Tob 5: 6 S ἐν τῷ ὄρει; Jos., Ant. 9, 7).—Abs. (as Hom.+; Josh 4: 6) of a throne, a bench *stand* (Hdt. 1, 181, 5 κλίνη κ.; Arrian, Anab. 6, 29, 6 τράπεζα κ.; Charito 5, 4, 5; Polyaenus 4, 3, 24 and Paus. 2, 31, 3 θρόνος κ.) Rv 4: 2; Hv 3, 1, 4. Of cloths *lie (there)* J 20: 5, 6, 7.—21: 9. Of vessels *stand (there)* (X., Oec. 8, 19; Paus. 9, 31, 3 τρίποδες. Cf. 1 Esdr 6: 25; Jer 24: 1) 2: 6; 19: 29. Of goods *be stored up* Lk 12: 19 (Hom.+; cf. PSI 365, 20 [251/0 BC] ὁ σῖτος ἐπὶ τῆς ἅλω κείμενος).—Of a foundation *be laid* 1 Cor 3: 11. ἡ πόλις τετράγωνος κεῖται *is laid out as a square* Rv 21: 16. κ. πρός τι *be laid at someth.* the ax at the roots Mt 3: 10; Lk 3: 9. κ. πρός w. acc. also means *be very close to someone* in ὁ ἄγγελος τ. προφητικοῦ πνεύματος ὁ κείμενος πρὸς αὐτόν (i.e. τ. ἄνθρωπον) Hm 11: 9 (the text in POxy. 5 says: ἐπ' αὐτόν).

2. fig.—a. *be appointed, set, destined* εἴς τι *for someth.* εἰς πτῶσιν καὶ ἀνάστασιν *for the fall and rising* Lk 2: 34. εἰς ἀπολογίαν τοῦ εὐαγγελίου Phil 1: 16. εἰς τοῦτο 1 Th 3: 3.—κ. ἐπί τινος *be put in charge of someth.* of the angel of punishment ἐπὶ τῆς τιμωρίας *in charge of the punishment* Hs 6, 3, 2.

b. *be given, exist, be valid* of legal matters (legal t.t. Eur.; Thu.+; s. also BGU 1002, 14 [55 BC] πᾶσαι αἱ κατ' αὐτῶν κείμεναι συγγραφαί; PTebt. 334, 7 of a marriage contract κατὰ τ. κειμένην ἡμῖν συγγραφήν; 2 Macc 4: 11) τινί *for someone* of law (Menand., Pap. Did. 14 J. ἐστ' ἀνδρὶ κ. γυναικὶ κείμενος νόμος; Dio Chrys. 64[14], 13; Dit., Or. 111, 30 [II BC] ὁ κείμενος νόμος; pap.; Ep.

Arist. 15; Philo, Det. Pot. Ins. 18 νόμος κεῖται) 1 Ti 1: 9.
Of powers κ. ἐπί τινι *exist for someth.*, *relate* or *apply to*
someth. Hm 6, 1, 1.

c. *occur, appear, be found* (Hellanicus [V BC] 4 fgm. 93
Jac. αὕτη [i.e., Πιτάνη] παρ᾽ Ἀλκαίῳ κεῖται=is found
in Alcaeus) ἐν παραβολαῖς B 17: 2. διὰ τί ὁ υἱὸς τοῦ θεοῦ
εἰς δούλου τρόπον κεῖται ἐν τῇ παραβολῇ; *why does the
Son of God appear in the parable as a slave?* Hs 5, 5, 5; cf.
5, 6, 1.

d. *find oneself, be,* in a certain state or condition (Hdt.
8, 102 al.; Menand., fgm. 576, 2 K. τὴν ἐν ἑτέρῳ
κειμένην ἁμαρτίαν; PTebt. 27 I, 7 [113 BC] ἐν περι-
στάσει κειμένων; 2 Macc 3: 11; 4: 31, 34; 3 Macc
5: 26) ὁ κόσμος ἐν τῷ πονηρῷ κ. *the world lies in* (*the
power of*) *the evil one* 1 J 5: 19 (another possibility is the
mng. κ. ἔν τινι *be dependent on someone* [Soph., Oed. R.
247f; Polyb. 6, 15, 6]). M-M. B. 834.**

κειρία, ας, ἡ (Aristoph.; Plut., Alcib. 16, 1; Pr 7: 16; cf.
κιρία Zen.-P. 69 [=Sb 6775], 9; PSI 341, 7; 387, 4. On the
spelling Bl-D. §24; cf. Mlt.-H. 71f) *bandage, grave-clothes*
(schol. on Aristoph., Av. 816 κειρία· εἶδος ζώνης ἐκ
σχοινίων, παρεοικὸς ἱμάντι, ᾗ δεσμοῦσι τὰς κλίνας) J
11: 44. M-M.*

κείρω 1 aor. ἔκειρα, mid. ἐκειράμην (Hom.+; inscr.,
pap., LXX; Jos., Bell. 6, 5; Sib. Or. 3, 359) *shear a sheep*
(Artem. 4, 51 πρόβατον; Babrius 51, 3; Jos., Ant. 6, 297
after 1 Km 25: 2; Test. Jud. 12: 1) ὁ κείρων (Aesop, Fab.
212 P.=382 H.) Ac 8: 32 or ὁ κείρας 1 Cl 16: 7; B 5: 2 (all
three after Is 53: 7, where both readings are found) *the
shearer.* Mid. *cut one's hair* or *have one's hair cut* (Bl-D.
§317; Rob. 809.—X., Hell. 1, 7, 8) τὴν κεφαλήν *have
one's hair cut* (as the result of a vow; s. εὐχή 2) Ac 18: 18.
Abs. (Quint. Smyrn. 3, 686 and 688) 1 Cor 11: 6a, b.
M-M.*

κέκμηκα s. κάμνω.

κέλευσμα, ατος, τό (Aeschyl., Hdt.+; Sb 4279, 3 [I AD];
Pr 30: 27; Philo, Abr. 116; Jos., Ant. 17, 140; 199; on the
spelling s. Bl-D. §70, 3) *signal,* (*cry of*) *command* (Hdt. 4,
141 al.) ὁ κύριος ἐν κ. καταβήσεται *the Lord will come
down with a cry of command* 1 Th 4: 16 (cf. on the
κέλευσμα of God, Galen XIX p. 179 K. τοῦ δημιουργοῦ;
Philo, Praem. 117 and Descensus Mariae in Rtzst., Poim.
5, 3).—LSchmid, TW III 656-9. M-M.*

κελεύω impf. ἐκέλευον; 1 aor. ἐκέλευσα (Hom.+; inscr.,
pap., LXX, Ep. Arist.; Philo, Leg. All. 2, 28; Joseph.;
Test. 12 Patr.) *command, order, urge* foll. by the aor. inf.
(Bl-D. §338, 2; Rob. 857), which indicates the action to be
carried out; the pers. who receives the order is in the acc.
(Sib. Or. 3, 298) κέλευσόν με ἐλθεῖν πρός σε *command
me to come to you* Mt 14: 28, cf. vs. 19; Ac 4: 15; 22: 30;
23: 10; 24: 8 v.l.; 1 Cl 43: 2. This constr. can also be
understood simply as the acc. w. inf. as such, as plainly Ac
8: 38.—The constr. in which κ. is followed by the acc. and
the pass. inf., indicating that something is to happen to
someone or something without giving the person who is to
carry out the command, is more in accord w. Lat. usage
than w. class. Gk. (Bl-D. §5, 3b; 392, 4; Rob. 111)
ἐκέλευσεν αὐτὸν ὁ κύριος πραθῆναι Mt 18: 25. Cf. 27:
64; Lk 18: 40; Ac 12: 19; 25: 6, 17.—W. inf. alone,
so that everything else must be supplied fr. the context
Mt 8: 18; 14: 9; 27: 58; Ac 5: 34; 21: 33.—More rarely and
actually as an exception (Bl-D. §338, 2) we have the pres.
inf.: w. acc. (X., An. 2, 1, 8; Charito 7, 6, 2) Ac 21: 34; 22:
24; 23: 3, 35; 25: 21; 27: 43; 1 Cl 33: 3; 40: 1f. Without
acc. (X., Cyr. 2, 2, 2; Appian, Liby. 55 §241; Herodian

2, 3, 3) Ac 16: 22.—Abs. κελεύσαντος τοῦ Φήστου *at
Festus' command* Ac 25: 23 (cf. Inscr. Gr. 594, 53 [279 BC]
ἐπιμελητῶν κελεόντων; Jos., Ant. 11, 78 Δαρείου
κελεύσαντος).—W. dat. of the pers. and inf. (Longus 3,
8, 2; Polyaenus 3, 10, 11; Tob 8: 18 BA [aor.].—Thu.
1, 44, 1; Diod. S. 19, 17, 3; Herm. Wr. 1, 29; 2 Macc
5: 12; Ep. Arist. 184; Jos., Ant. 20, 132 [pres.]) Mt 15: 35
v.l. (κ. is also toned down to *urgently request, invite*: Nicol.
Dam.: 90 fgm. 4 p. 332, 9ff Jac.; Epict., fgm. 17 in an
invitation; Arrian, Anab. 2, 6, 1 his friends do this to Alex.
the Great; 3, 9, 3; 7, 2, 1; 7, 8, 3). M-M. B. 1337.

κενεμβατεύω a form supplied purely by conjecture as v.l.
for ἐμβατεύω Col 2: 18 (q.v.). The closely related κενεμ-
βατέω *step on emptiness, make a misstep* in rope-walking
is found Plut., Lucian et al. Mlt.-H. 273f; Bl-D. §154.*

κενοδοξέω *hold a false opinion, vainly imagine* (Polyb. 12,
26c, 4; Dio Chrys. 21[38], 29; 4 Macc 5: 10; 8: 24; Philo,
Mut. Nom. 226) MPol 10: 1.*

κενοδοξία, ας, ἡ—1. *vanity, conceit, excessive ambition*
(Polyb. 3, 81, 9; Plut., De Adulat. 14 p. 57D; Lucian, Dial.
Mort. 20, 4; Vett. Val. 358, 31; 4 Macc 2: 15; 8: 19; Philo,
De Jos. 36) κατὰ κενοδοξίαν *from empty conceit* Phil 2: 3;
IPhld 1: 1. In a catalogue of vices (as Cebes 24, 2) 1 Cl 35:
5; Hm 8: 5.

2. *illusion, delusion, error* (since Epicurus p. 78, 7 Us.;
Wsd 14: 14; Philo, Mut. Nom. 96, Leg. ad Gai. 114)
ἐμπίπτειν εἰς τὰ ἄγκιστρα τῆς κ. *be caught on the
fishhooks of false doctrine* IMg 11. πείθεσθαι ταῖς κ.
τινός *let oneself be misled by someone's delusions* Hs 8, 9,
3.—FrWilhelm, RhM 70, '15, 188; 72, '17/'18, 383f w.
many exx. M-M.*

κενόδοξος, ον *conceited, boastful* (so Polyb. 27, 7, 12; 38,
7, 1; Epict. 3, 24, 43; M. Ant. 5, 1, 6; Vett. Val. 271, 2;
Ep. Arist. 8; Philo, Somn. 2, 105) D 3: 5. μὴ γινώμεθα
κενόδοξοι *let us not become boasters* Gal 5: 26. M-M.*

κενός, ή, όν (Hom.+; inscr., pap., LXX, Ep. Arist., Philo,
Joseph.) *empty*—1. lit. (Jos., Vi. 167) κεράμιον *empty jar*
Hm 11: 15. σκεῦος (4 Km 4: 3) m 11: 13. κ. ἀποστέλλειν
τινά *send someone away empty-handed* (cf. PReinach 55,
9 [III AD] μὴ ἀναπέμψῃς αὐτὸν κενόν; Gen 31: 42; Dt 15:
13; Job 22: 9) Mk 12: 3; cf. Lk 1: 53; 20: 10f.

2. fig.—**a.** of things—**α.** *without content, without any
basis, without truth, without power* κ. λόγοι *empty words*
(Pla., Laches 196B; Menand., Mon. 512; Herm. Wr. 16, 2;
Ex 5: 9; Dt 32: 47; Jos., C. Ap. 2, 225; Test. Napht. 3: 1.
—PPar. 15, 68 [120 BC] φάσει κενῇ) 1 Cor 3: 18 D; Eph 5:
6; Dg 8: 2; cf. D 2: 5. πνεῦμα Hm 11: 11, 17. κ. ἀπάτη
empty deceit Col 2: 8 (cf. Arrian, Anab. 5, 10, 4 κενὸς
φόβος=false alarm). Of the things of everyday life *vain*
Hm 5, 2. τρυφή m 12, 2, 1. πεποίθησις s 9, 22, 3. Of
preaching and faith 1 Cor 15: 14a, b; Js 2: 20 𝔓74 (cf.
Demosth. 18, 150 κ. πρόφασις; Aeschyl., Pers. 804 κ.
ἐλπίς; cf. Wsd 3: 11; Sir 34: 1). As κ. here=μάταιος (vs.
17), the two words are found together in the same sense
(cf. Demosth. 2, 12; Plut., Artax. 15, 6, Mor. p. 1117A;
Oenomaus in Euseb., Pr. Ev. 5, 21, 5 κενὰ καὶ μάταια of
oracles; Hos 12: 2; Job 20: 18; Ep. Arist. 205) 1 Cl 7: 2; cf.
κενὴ ματαιολογία Pol 2: 1.

β. *without result, without profit, without effect, without
reaching its goal* κενὰ μελετᾶν *imagine vain things* Ac 4:
25 (Ps 2: 1). κενὸν γενέσθαι *be in vain*: ἡ χάρις αὐτοῦ οὐ
κενὴ ἐγενήθη 1 Cor 15: 10. ἡ εἴσοδος ἡμῶν ἡ πρὸς ὑμᾶς
οὐ κ. γέγονεν 1 Th 2: 1. κόπος 1 Cor 15: 58.—εἰς κενόν *in
vain, to no purpose* (Diod. S. 19, 9, 5; Heliod. 10, 30;
PPetr. II 37, 1b recto, 12 [III BC]; Epigr. Gr. 646, 10; Lev

26: 20; Is 29: 8; 65: 23; Jer 6: 29; Jos., Ant. 19, 27; 96) 2 Cor 6: 1. εἰς κ. τρέχειν *run in vain* (cf. Menand., Mon. 51 ἀνὴρ ἄβουλος εἰς κ. μοχθεῖ τρέχων) Gal 2: 2; Phil 2: 16a; cf. vs. 16b; 1 Th 3: 5; Pol 9: 2 (Phil 2: 16a).

b. of pers. (Pind.+; Soph., Ant. 709; Plut., Mor. 541A ἀνόητοι καὶ κενοί; Epict. 2, 19, 8; 4, 4, 35; Judg 9: 4; 11: 3 B; Philo, Spec. Leg. 1, 311): *foolish, senseless, empty* Hm 12, 4, 5. ἄνθρωπος κ. Js 2: 20; Pol 6: 3. ἄνθρωπος κενὸς ἀπὸ τοῦ πνεύματος τοῦ δικαίου *empty of the righteous spirit* Hm 5, 2, 7. κ. ἀπὸ τῆς ἀληθείας m 11: 4; ἀπὸ τῆς πίστεως κ. s 9, 19, 2. In paronomasia (cf. Job 27: 12) αὐτὸς κ. ὢν κενῶς καὶ ἀποκρίνεται κενοῖς *he himself, empty (of God's Spirit) as he is, gives empty answers to empty people* m 11: 3.—vs. 13. M-M. B. 932.*

κενόσπουδος, ον *concerning oneself about worthless things* (Plut., Mor., p. 560B; 1061C; 1069B; Diog. L. 9, 68) ἐὰν κ. μὴ εὑρεθῇς *if it is not found that you concern yourself about worthless things* Hs 9, 5, 5.*

κενοφωνία, ας, ἡ (Diosc., Mat. Med. Praef. 2 W.; Porphyr., Adv. Christ. 58, 15 Harnack; Hesychius and Suidas=ματαιολογία) *chatter, empty talk* βέβηλοι κενοφωνίαι *godless chatter* 1 Ti 6: 20; 2 Ti 2: 16 (as v.l. in both pass. καινοφωνίαι *contemporary jargon*, unless this is simply a phonetic variant, since in this period αι was pronounced as ε). M-M.*

κενόω fut. κενώσω; 1 aor. ἐκένωσα, pass. ἐκενώθην; pf. pass. κεκένωμαι (trag., Hdt.+; pap.; Jer 14: 2; 15: 9; Philo; Jos., Ant. 8, 258 v.l.) *make empty*.

1. *to empty* pass. κενοῦται ὁ ἄνθρωπος *the man is emptied* Hm 11: 14. Of Christ, who gave up the appearance of his divinity and took on the form of a slave, ἑαυτὸν ἐκένωσεν *he emptied himself, divested himself of his privileges* Phil 2: 7 (s. on ἁρπαγμός and JRoss, JTS 10, 1909, 573f, supported by WWarren, On ἑαυτὸν ἐκένωσεν: JTS 12, '11, 461-3; KPetersen, ἑαυτ. ἐκέν.: Symb. Osl. 12, '33, 96-101; WEWilson, ET 56, '45, 280; ELewis, Interpretation 1, '47, 20-32; ESchweizer, Erniedrigung u. Erhöhung bei Jesus u. seinen Nachfolgern '62; HWRobinson, The Cross in the OT '55, 103-5; RPMartin, An Early Christian Confession '60; JoachJeremias, TW V, 708 holds that the kenosis is not the incarnation but the cross [Is 53: 12], and defends his position NovT 6, '63, 182-88; D Georgi, Der Vorpaulinische Hymnus Phil 2: 6-11 in Bultmann-Festschr., '64, 263-93; JHarvey, ET 76, '65, 337-39 [Adam typology]).

2. *destroy; render void, of no effect* (Vett. Val. 90, 7) τὸ καύχημά μου οὐδεὶς κενώσει *no one will deprive me of my reason for boasting* 1 Cor 9: 15. Pass. κεκένωται ἡ πίστις *faith is made invalid* Ro 4: 14. ἵνα μὴ κενωθῇ ὁ σταυρὸς τοῦ Χριστοῦ 1 Cor 1: 17.—Also of pers. πολλοὶ ἐκενώθησαν *many have been ruined* Hs 9, 22, 3.

3. *deprive of (its) justification* pass. *lose its justification* 2 Cor 9: 3 (c. καύχημα 2). M-M.*

κέντρον, ου, τό (Hom.+; BGU 544, 12; LXX, Philo; Jos., Bell. 2, 385, Ant. 7, 169).

1. *the sting* of an animal (Aristot. et al.; Aelian, N.A. 16, 27 σκορπίου) Rv 9: 10 (s. Ctesias, Ind. 7, a strange beast of India τὸ πρόσωπον ἐοικὸς ἀνθρώπῳ ... ὥσπερ λέων ... horrible teeth ... σκορπίος ... τὸ κέντρον in its tail, whose sting is deadly). Fig. (Aesop, Fab. 276 P.=Babr. no. 185 Cr. κ. τῆς λύπης) of death 1 Cor 15: 55f after Hos 13: 14 (s. ESellin, RSeeberg-Festschr. I '29, 307-14).

2. *a goad*, a pointed stick that served the same purpose as a whip (Hom.+; Pr 26: 3), in a proverbial expr. (cf.

Pind., Pyth. 2, 173 [s. Ael. Aristid. 45 p. 70 D.]; Aeschyl., Ag. 1624, Prom. 323; Eur., Bacch. 795 [WNestle, Anklänge an Eur. in AG: Philol. 59, '00, 46-57]: Fgm. Iamb. Adesp. 13 Diehl: ἵππος ὄνῳ· 'πρὸς κέντρα μὴ λακτιζέτω'; inscr. fr. Asia Minor [JHS 8, 1887, 261]: λακτίζεις πρὸς κέντρα; AOtto, D. Sprichwörter d. Römer 1890, 331f) πρὸς κέντρα λακτίζειν *kick against the goads* of a balking animal, fig. of a man who resists the divine call Ac 9: 5 t.r.; 26: 14 (on the pl. cf. Eur., loc. cit., the iambic fragment, the inscr., and PGM 4, 2911 κέντροισι βιαίοις of the stings of passion; Herm. Wr. p. 482, 26 Sc.; Philo, Det. Pot. Ins. 46 πάθους κέντροις).—FSmend, Ἄγγελος I '25, 34-45, esp. 41ff, but s. WG Kümmel, Rö 7 u. die Bekehrung des Paulus '29, 155-7; HWindisch, ZNW 31, '32, 10-14; further lit. in EHaenchen, Acts '56, p. 616, 2 (Eng. tr. '71, p. 685, 3); LSchmid, TW III 662-8. M-M. B. 864.*

κεντυρίων, ωνος, ὁ (Lat. loanw.; since Polyb. 6, 24, 5; inscr., pap. [exx. in Hahn 122, 7; 227, 8; 233, 3]; loanw. in rabb.) *centurion* (=ἑκατοντάρχης) Mk 15: 39, 44f; GP 8: 31; 10: 38; 11: 45, 47, 49; MPol 18: 1.—S. on ἑκατοντάρχης and CSchneider, D. Hauptmann am Kreuz: ZNW 33, '34, 1-17. M-M.*

Κενχρεαί s. Κεγχρεαί.

κένωμα, ατος, τό (Philo Mech. 57, 17; 21; Polyb. 6, 31, 9; 11; Hero Alex. I p. 432, 5; Plut., Aemil. 20, 8, Mor. 655B al.; PAmh. 48, 8 [106 BC]; POxy. 1292, 4 [c. 30 AD]; Aq.) *empty space, emptiness* τοῦ ἀνθρώπου of a man who does not possess the divine Spirit Hm 11: 3.*

κενῶς adv. (Aristot.+) *in an empty manner, idly, in vain, to no purpose* (Epict. 2, 17, 8; Plut., Mor. 35E; 40C; PLond. 908, 28 κενῶς κ. ἀνωφελῶς; Is 49: 4) ἀποκρίνεσθαι Hm 11: 3. λαλεῖν 11: 13. λέγειν Js 4: 5.*

κεραία, ας, ἡ (Aeschyl., Thu.+; Dit., Syll.³ 374, 14; PMagd. 11, 4 of a sailyard; Jos., Bell. 3, 419) lit. 'horn'; *projection, hook* as part of a letter, a *serif* (of letters, Sib. Or. 5, 21; 24; 25 al.; of accents and breathings in IG II 4321, 10; Apollon. Dysc.; Plut., Numa 13, 9, Mor. 1100A. In the last-named pass. in the sense of someth. quite insignificant: ζυγομαχεῖν περὶ συλλαβῶν καὶ κεραιῶν. Likew. Dio Chrys. 14[31], 86 κεραίαν νόμου τινός ἢ ψηφίσματος μίαν μόνην συλλαβὴν ἐξαλείφειν; Philo, In Flacc. 131 τὰ γράμματα κατὰ συλλαβήν, μᾶλλον δὲ καὶ κεραίαν ἑκάστην) Mt 5: 18; Lk 16: 17 (s. on ἰῶτα). M-M.*

κεραμεύς, έως, ὁ (Hom.+; inscr., pap., LXX) *potter* Dg 2: 3, and his clay (cf. Is 45: 9; 29: 16; Jer 18: 6; Sir 33: 13; Wsd 15: 7; IQS 11, 21f) Ro 9: 21; 2 Cl 8: 2. ὁ ἀγρὸς τοῦ κ. *the potter's field* Mt 27: 7, 10. M-M.*

κεραμικός, ή, όν (Aristoph., Hippocr.+; inscr.; PGM 7, 867; Da 2: 41) *belonging to the potter* or *made of clay* (depending on the derivation: Bl-D. §113, 2 app.; Mlt.-H. 379) τὰ σκεύη τὰ κ. Rv 2: 27. M-M.*

κεράμιον, ου, τό (Hdt.+; inscr., pap., LXX) *an earthenware vessel, jar* ὕδατος (*water*) *jar* (Theophr., Caus. Plant. 3, 4, 3) Mk 14: 13; Lk 22: 10. οἴνου (X., An. 6, 1, 17; Polyb. 4, 56, 3; Dit., Syll.³ 1109, 162; POxy. 1211, 5; Ostraka II 757, 3; Jer 42: 5), ἐλαίου (Jos., Ant. 8, 322; cf. 9, 48) (*wine, oil*) *jar* D 13: 6. κ. κενόν *an empty jar* Hm 11: 15. κεράμια ἱκανώτατα *very many jars* 12, 5, 3. κ. μέλιτος (*honey*) *jar* m 5, 1, 5.—Hv 4, 1, 6 v.l. for κέραμος, q.v. M-M.*

κέραμος, ου, ὁ (Hom.+; inscr., pap.; 2 Km 17: 28; Jos., Bell. 4, 462).

1. *clay*, also *earthenware vessel* (Hom.+; PHib. 54, 26; 2 Km loc. cit.) κεφαλὴν εἶχεν ὡς κεράμου *it had a head as if made of clay* Hv 4, 1, 6 (the text is uncertain; cod. אᶜ and the Lat. versions read καιραμίου [=κεραμίου], which would be identical w. the second mng. of κέραμος given above: *like a* [large] *jar* [?]).

2. *a roof tile* (Herodas 3, 44; Paus. 1, 13, 8; schol. on Apollon. Rhod. 2, 1075a) Lk 5: 19 (LFonck, Biblica 2, '21, 30–44; KJäger, D. Bauernhaus in Palästina '12, 11ff; 22ff; HThiersch, ZDPV 37, '14, 81f; CCMcCown, JBL 58, '39, 213–16). Then collectively *tile roof* (so Aristoph.+; Appian, Bell. Civ. 1, 32 §145; Dit., Syll.³ 1200, 6f; Inscr. Gr. 594, 52; 1387, 123) ἀπὸ τοῦ κεράμου a drop *from the roof* hollows out the stone Hm 11: 20. M-M. B. 618f.*

κεράννυμι 1 aor. ἐκέρασα, pass. ἐκράθην; pf. pass. ptc. κεκερασμένος (Hom.+; inscr., pap., LXX, Philo; Sib. Or. 11, 126) *mix*.

1. lit. χολὴν μετὰ ὄξους, supplied fr. the context w. the abs. κεράσαντες, GP 5: 16.—Fig. ἐν τῷ ποτηρίῳ ᾧ ἐκέρασεν κεράσατε αὐτῇ διπλοῦν *in the cup in which she has mixed, mix her a double portion* Rv 18: 6. But perh. κ. means *pour* (*in*), as 14: 10 ἐκ τ. οἴνου τ. θυμοῦ τ. θεοῦ τ. κεκερασμένου ἀκράτου ἐν τῷ ποτηρίῳ τ. ὀργῆς αὐτοῦ (some) *of the wine of God's wrath, poured out unmixed into the cup of his anger* (cf. Anth. Pal. 11, 137, 12; Is 19: 14; PsSol 8: 14).

2. fig. (Oenomaus in Euseb., Pr. Ev. 5, 24, 7 ἐκέρασε τὸ λόγιον =he made the oracle a mixture [of favorable and unfavorable things]) κραθέντες τῇ σαρκὶ αὐτοῦ καὶ τῷ πνεύματι *closely united w. his flesh and spirit* ISm 3: 2. M-M. B. 335.*

κέρας, ατος, τό (Hom.+; inscr., pap., LXX, Philo; Jos., Ant. 4, 281; 5, 223) *horn*.

1. lit., in the description of the apocal. beasts (Achmes 189, 16ff, interpretation of three, four, and more horns of an ox seen in a dream, as referring to the corresponding number of the χρόνοι of a ruler) Rv 5: 6; 12: 3; 13: 1, 11; 17: 3, 7, 12, 16; B 4: 5 (Da 7: 7f). Of a calf κέρατα ἐκφέρειν *grow horns* 1 Cl 52: 2 (Ps 68: 32).

2. the horn-shaped *corners* or simply the *ends, extensions* (Apollon. Rhod. 4, 282 κ. Ὠκεανοῖο of a river at the end of the Ocean) of the altar (cf. Ex 27: 2; 29: 12; Lev 4: 7 al.; Philo) Rv 9: 13.

3. fig., as an expr. for the might, power (cf. Ps 88: 18; 131: 17; 1 Km 2: 1, 10; Sir 47: 7, 11; 1 Macc 2: 48. But also Cephalio [c. 120 AD]: 93 fgm. 7 p. 445, 29 Jac. as a poetic expr. κέρας . . . , ὅπερ ἐστὶ . . . δύναμις), hence κ. σωτηρίας *horn of salvation* (of God Ps 17: 3; 2 Km 22: 3) of the Messiah ἤγειρεν κ. σωτ. ἡμῖν Lk 1: 69 (Gdspd., Probs. 70f a *mighty Savior*). IScheftelowitz, D. Hörnermotiv in den Religionen: ARW 15, '12, 451–87; WFoerster, TW III 668–71. M-M. B. 209.*

κεράτιον, ου, τό (Aristot.; Polyb. 26, 1, 4) dim. of κέρας, 'little horn'; in pl. of the fruits of the carob tree, *carob pods* (Diosc. 1, 114; Aëtius 160, 3; PLond. 131, 7) Lk 15: 16 (as fodder for swine Lycophron from 675 to 678). —ESchmitz, D. Johannisbrotbaum im Hl. Land: Das Hl. Land 50, '17, 171–3. M-M.*

κερβικάριον, ου, τό (Lat. loanw., cervical. Exx. in CWessely, Wiener Studien 24, '02, 99ff. Cf. e.g. PFay. 347; BGU 814, 11; Sb 7994, 15; Herodian Gramm. [II AD] in the Lex. Vind. p. 312, 2 declares that the use of the foreign word κερβ. for ὑπαυχένιον ='a pillow under the neck' is a

barbarism; loanw. in rabb.) *pillow* κ. λινοῦν *a linen p.* Hv 3, 1, 4.*

κερδαίνω (Hes., Hdt.+; pap.; not LXX and Test. 12 Patr., but occasionally Ep. Arist., Philo, Joseph.) fut. κερδήσω (Jos., Bell. 2, 324; 5, 74); 1 aor. ἐκέρδησα (Jos., Ant. 8, 210) and ἐκέρδανα (Jos., Ant. 4, 129 κερδᾶναι.—Subj. κερδάνω 1 Cor 9: 21, where W-H. accent κερδανῶ and read it as a future); 1 fut. pass. κερδηθήσομαι (Bl-D. §101; Mlt.-H. 243).

1. *to gain*—a. lit. τὶ someth. πέντε τάλαντα Mt 25: 16f; cf. vss. 20, 22. τὸν κόσμον ὅλον *the whole world*, i.e. the sum total of earthly riches Mt 16: 26; Mk 8: 36; Lk 9: 25; 2 Cl 6: 2. Abs. (POxy. 1477, 10; Ep. Arist. 270) *make a profit* Js 4: 13.

b. fig. τινά *someone* for the Kgdm. of God Mt 18: 15; 1 Cor 9: 19–22. Pass. 1 Pt 3: 1.—Χριστὸν κ. *gain Christ, make him one's own* Phil 3: 8 (Third Corinthians 3: 35).— ASchlier, TW III '38 p. 672; DDaube, κερδαίνω as a Missionary Term: HTR 40, '47, 109–20.

2. Since the avoidance of loss is a gain, κ. can also mean *spare oneself someth., avoid someth.* (cf. Eur., Cycl. 312 ζημίαν; Philemo Com. 92, 10; Diog. L. 7, 14; Himerius, Ecl. 3, 8 W. τ. δίκην; Jos., Ant. 2, 31; 10, 39) ὕβριν καὶ ζημίαν *injury and loss* Ac 27: 21 (Field, Notes 145). M-M.*

κερδαλέος, α, ον (Hom.+; Artem. 4, 62) *profitable, gainful* τὸ κ. διώκειν *pursue gain* 2 Cl 20: 4.*

κέρδος, ους, τό (Hom.+; rare in inscr., pap.; not at all in LXX, Ep. Arist., Test. 12 Patr., but in Aq., Symm., Theod.; Philo; Jos., Bell. 4, 102, Ant. 15, 158, Vi. 325) *a gain* (Fgm. Mel. Chor. Adesp. no. 11 Diehl² ['42] ἄδικον κ.) Tit 1: 11; IPol 1: 3.—Of someth. advantageous (Chio, Ep. 8; Philo, Spec. Leg. 3, 154) ἐμοὶ τὸ ἀποθανεῖν κέρδος Phil 1: 21 (Aeschyl., Prom. 747; Soph., Ant. 461–64; Aelian, V.H. 4, 7 τ. κακοῖς οὐδὲ τὸ ἀποθανεῖν κέρδος; Pla., Apol. 32 p. 40D θαυμάσιον κέρδος ἂν εἴη ὁ θάνατος). Pl. Phil 3: 7. M-M. B. 807.*

κερέα s. κεραία.

κέρμα, ατος, τό (Aristoph., Demosth.+) *piece of money, coin* (usu. copper), small *change*. In J 2: 15 B, Orig. have the pl. τὰ κέρματα (Attic [Pollux 9, 87], also UPZ 81 IV, 20 [II BC]; Jos., Bell. 2, 295); א, A have the collective sing. τὸ κέρμα (Eubul. Com. [IV BC] 84; PSI 512, 13 [253/2 BC]; POxy. 114, 14; PGenève 77, 5; PTebt. 418, 12 ἐὰν χρείαν ἔχῃ κέρματος) ἐκχέειν τ. κ. *pour out the coins* (Diog. L. 6, 82 τὸ κέρμα διερρίπτει =throw the coins of a money-changer into confusion). M-M.*

κερματιστής, οῦ, ὁ (not found in secular usage; the rdg. κερμ. [for χρηματιστής] in Maximus Tyr. 31, 2b and d has no support in the ms. tradition) *money-changer*. In the outer fore-court of the temple (Schürer II⁴ 76; 314f) J 2: 14. M-M.*

κεφάλαιον, ου, τό (Pind.+; inscr., pap., LXX)—1. *main thing, main point* (Thu. 4, 50, 2; Isocr. 4, 149 κεφ. δὲ τῶν εἰρημένων; Pla., Phaedo 44 p. 95B; Demosth. 13, 36; Epict. 1, 24, 20; POxy. 67, 18; Philo, Leg. All. 2, 102; Jos., C. Ap. 1, 219, Ant. 17, 93) Hv 5: 5. κ. ἐπὶ τοῖς λεγομένοις *the main point in what has been said* (is this) Hb 8: 1 (Menand., in Plut., Mor. 103D τὸ δὲ κεφ. τῶν λόγων).—*Summary, synopsis* (limited to the main points) ἐν κ. *in summary, in brief* (X., Cyr. 6, 3, 18; Appian, Bell. Civ. 4, 93 §388 ἐν κ. εἰπεῖν; PLeipz. 105, 35; POxy. 515, 6 al. pap.) MPol 20: 1.

2. financial *capital* (Pla., Demosth., inscr., pap.), then a *sum of money* gener. (Artem. 1, 17 p. 21, 19; 1, 35 p. 36, 17 and 37, 16; Dialekt-Inschr. 2503, 14 [Delphi]; Kyr.-Inschr. 132; BGU 1200, 17 [I вс] οὐ μικρῷ κεφαλαίῳ; POxy. 268, 7; Lev 5: 24; Num 5: 7; 31: 26; Ep. Arist. 24; Jos., Ant. 12, 30; 155) πολλοῦ κ. τὴν πολιτείαν ταύτην ἐκτησάμην *I acquired this citizenship for a large sum of money* Ac 22: 28. M-M.*

κεφαλιόω (Thu. +; Philod., Οἰκ. col. 7, 40 Jensen; Diog. L. 7, 125; 'sum up', etc.) Mk 12: 4, better (Bl-D. §108, 1 app.; Mlt.-H. 395) κεφαλιόω, q.v. M-M.*

κεφαλή, ῆς, ἡ (Hom. +; inscr., pap., LXX, En., Ep. Arist., Philo, Joseph.) *head*—**1.** lit.—**a.** actually of the head of man or beast; man: Mt 5: 36 (on swearing by the head s. Athen. 2, 72 p. 66c; cf. Juvenal, Satires 6, 16f; PGM 4, 1917); 6: 17; 14: 8, 11; 26: 7; 27: 29f; Mk 6: 24f, 27f; 14: 3; 15: 19; Lk 7: 46; J 13: 9; 19: 2; 20: 7; 1 Cor 11: 4b, 5ab, 7, 10; 12: 21; Rv 18: 19 (cf. Josh 7: 6; La 2: 10); 1 Cl 37: 5; 56: 5 (Ps 140: 5); B 13: 5 (Gen 48: 14); Hm 11: 20; Papias 3.—Animals: B 7: 8 (of the scapegoat Lev 16; cf. vs. 21).—In apocal. presentations in connection w. human figures: Rv 1: 14; 4: 4; 12: 1; 14: 14; 19: 12; w. animals: 9: 7, 17, 19; 12: 3 (s. δράκων); 13: 1, 3; 17: 3, 7, 9 (cf. Ael. Aristid. 50, 50 K.=26 p. 517 D.: ὤφθη τὸ ἔδος [of Asclepius] τρεῖς κεφαλὰς ἔχον. A person sees himself in a dream provided with a plurality of heads Artem. 1, 35 p. 37, 14: δύο ἔχειν κεφαλὰς ἢ τρεῖς. Also the many-headed dog Cerberus of the underworld in Hesiod, Theog. 311 al. as well as Heraclit. Sto. 33 p. 49, 14); of angels Rv 10: 1.—The hair(s) of the *head* (Philo, Leg. ad Gai. 223) Mt 10: 30; Lk 7: 38; 12: 7; 21: 18; Ac 27: 34. τὴν κ. κλίνειν *lay down the head* to sleep Mt 8: 20; Lk 9: 58. Sim. J 19: 30 (s. Hdb. ad loc.). κινεῖν τὴν κ. (s. κινέω 2a) Mt 27: 39; Mk 15: 29; 1 Cl 16: 16 (Ps 21: 8); ἐπαίρειν τὴν κ. (s. ἐπαίρω 1) Lk 21: 28; *shear the head*, i.e. *cut the hair* as a form of a vow Ac 21: 24; cf. 18: 18. Of the anointing of Jesus' head IEph 17: 1. κατὰ κεφαλῆς ἔχειν *have* (someth.) *on the head* (s. κατά I 1a) 1 Cor 11: 4a. ἐπάνω τῆς κ. *above his head* Mt 27: 37. Also πρὸς τῇ κ. J 20: 12.—Well-known expr. fr. the OT: ἄνθρακας πυρὸς σωρεύειν ἐπὶ τὴν κ. τινος Ro 12: 20 (s. ἄνθραξ). A curse-formula: τὸ αἷμα ὑμῶν ἐπὶ τὴν κ. ὑμῶν *your blood be on your own heads* (s. αἷμα 2a and cf. Demosth., Ep. 4, 10 τ. ἄδικον βλασφημίαν εἰς κεφαλὴν τῷ λέγοντι τρέπουσι; 6, 1; Maximus Tyr. 5, 1d; Aesop, Fab. 206 P.=372 H. ὃ θέλεις σὺ τούτοις ἐπὶ τῇ σῇ κεφαλῇ γένοιτο; Phalaris, Ep. 102 εἰς κεφαλὴν σοί τε καὶ τῷ σῷ γένει)=you are responsible for your own destruction Ac 18: 6; cf. GP 5: 17.

b. metaph. (Plut., Galba 4, 5 G. as κεφ. ἰσχυρῷ σώματι) Christ the κ. of the ἐκκλησία thought of as a σῶμα Col 1: 18; cf. 2: 19 (Artem. 2, 9 p. 92, 25 ἡ κεφαλὴ ὑπερέχει τοῦ παντὸς σώματος; schol. on Nicander, Alexiph. 215 ἡ κεφαλὴ συνέχει πᾶν τὸ σῶμα. SBedale, JTS 5, '54, 211-15).

2. fig.—**a.** in the case of living beings, to denote superior rank (cf. Artem. 4, 24 p. 218, 8 ἡ κεφ. is the symbol of the father; Judg 11: 11; 2 Km 22: 44) *head* (Zosimus of Ashkelon [500 AD] hails Demosth. as his master: ὦ θεία κεφαλή [Biogr. p. 297]) of the husband in relation to his wife 1 Cor 11: 3b; Eph 5: 23a. Of Christ in relation to the church Eph 4: 15; 5: 23b. But Christ is the head not only of the church, but of the universe as a whole: κ. ὑπὲρ πάντα Eph 1: 22, and of every cosmic power κ. πάσης ἀρχῆς καὶ ἐξουσίας *the head of all might and power* Col 2: 10. The divine influence on the world results in the series (for the growing distance from God with corre-

sponding results cf. Ps.-Aristot. De Mundo 6, 4): God the κ. of Christ, Christ the κ. of man, the man the κ. of the woman 1 Cor 11: 3c, a, b (s. on γυνή 1).

b. of things *the uppermost part, extremity, end, point* (Mathem. Pappus of Alex. [IV AD] in the 8th book [ed. CJGerhardt 1871 p. 379 τῇ κεφαλῇ τοῦ κοχλίου=at the point of the screw; Judg 9: 25; En. 17, 2; Jos., Bell. 2, 48, Ant. 3, 146; oft. pap. of plots of ground) κ. γωνίας the *cornerstone* (forming the farthest extension [cf. PFlor. 50, 83] of the corner, though JoachJeremias, Ἄγγελος I '25, 65-70, ZNW 29, '30, 264-80 thinks of it as the *keystone* or *capstone* above the door; RJMcKelvey, NTS 8, '62, 352-59. Cf. HGressmann, Pj 6, '10, 38-45; GHWhitaker, Exp. 8th Ser. XXII '21, 470ff) Mt 21: 42; Mk 12: 10; Lk 20: 17 (on the last three pass. s. JDMDerrett, TU 102, '68, 180-86; Ac 4: 11; 1 Pt 2: 7; B 6: 4 (all Ps 117: 22).—κ.=*capital* (city) (Appian, Illyr. 19 §54) Ac 16: 12 D (but 'frontier city' ACClark, Acts of the Apostles '33, 362-5 and JAOLarsen, CTM 17, '46, 123-5).—HSchlier, TW III 672-81. M-M. B. 212.**

κεφαλιόω 1 aor. ἐκεφαλίωσα (Phryn. p. 95 Lob.; Bl-D. §108, 1 app.; Mlt.-H. 395) *strike on the head* Mk 12: 4 v.l. (in אBL; in the text κεφαλαιόω [q.v.]).—GBjörck, Con. Neot. 1, '36, 1-4: 'ruin, kill outright'.—Field, Notes 36f.*

κεφαλίς, ίδος, ἡ (in var. mngs. Aristot. +; PLond. 755 B, 6; LXX; Ep. Arist. 68; Philo, Mos. 2, 77; Jos., Ant. 12, 73 [after Ep. Arist.]) in our lit. only once, modelled after the OT (Ezk 2: 9) and in a quot. fr. Ps 39: 8 κ. βιβλίου *the roll of a book* (cf. ThBirt, RhM n.F. 62, '07, 488; VGardthausen, Griech. Paläographie² I '11, 141) Hb 10: 7. M-M.*

κέχρημαι s. χράομαι.

κηδεύω 1 aor. inf. κηδεῦσαι (trag. +; inscr., pap.) *take care of, bury* a corpse (Soph., El. 1141; Polyb. 5, 10, 4; IG XIV 1860; PPar. 18b, 4; PLond. 932, 10; Philo, Migr. Abr. 159; Jos., Ant. 3, 262; 9, 227) Mk 6: 29 v.l.*

κημόω fut. κημώσω *to muzzle* (X., R. Equ. 5, 3) βοῦν ἀλοῶντα an ox that is treading out the grain 1 Cor 9: 9.*

κῆνσος, ου, ὁ (Lat. loanw., census, also in rabb., quotable in Gk. since I BC [inscr.: Annual of the British School at Athens 12, '05/'06, p. 178]. Cf. BGU 917, 6; PAmh. 83, 2) *tax, poll-tax* κῆνσον διδόναι *pay a tax* Mt 22: 17; Mk 12: 14. λαμβάνειν *collect taxes* Mt 17: 25. τὸ νόμισμα τοῦ κ. *the coin with which the tax is paid* 22: 19 (cf. Hesychius κῆνσος· εἶδος νομίσματος, ἐπικεφάλαιον).—Kubitschek, Pauly-W. III 1899, 1914ff. M-M.*

κῆπος, ου, ὁ (Hom. +; inscr., pap., LXX; Jos., Bell. 5, 410, Ant. 9, 227) *garden* Lk 13: 19; J 18: 1, 26; 19: 41; GP 6: 24. M-M. B. 490.*

κηπουρός, οῦ, ὁ (Pla. +; Polyb. 18, 6, 4; Epict. 3, 5, 17; 24, 44f; Plut., Mor. 927в, Aratus 5, 5; 6, 3; 7, 3; Dit., Syll.³ 120в, 6 [c. 400 BC κηπορός]; Monum. As. Min. Ant. III '31, no. 13; PSI 336, 6; 13 [257/6 BC]; BGU 111 I, 21; PLeipz. 97 XIV, 3) *gardener* J 20: 15. M-M.*

κηρίον, ου, τό (Hes. +; inscr., pap., LXX; Jos., Ant. 6, 118; 126) *wax, honey-comb* B 6: 6 (Ps 117: 12); Lk 24: 42 t.r. (s. μελίσσιος). M-M.*

κήρυγμα, ατος, τό—**1.** *proclamation, announcement* by a herald (so Soph., Hdt. +; inscr., PPetr. III 125, 9; PHamburg 29, 10; LXX; Philo, Agr. 117 al.; Jos., Ant. 10, 236) κηρύγματι καλεῖν *call together by a proclamation* B 12: 6.

2. elsewh. in our lit. *proclamation, preaching* by a herald sent by God (cf. Herm. Wr. 4, 4; Himerius, Or. 69 [=Or. 22], 7 and 8 the religious speaker makes the κήρυγμα known to the μύσται and ἐπόπται; Jon 3: 2; Philo, Mos. 2, 167; 170; Jos., Bell. 6, 288 τὰ τοῦ θεοῦ κ.): of prophetic preaching τὸ κ. Ἰωνᾶ Mt 12: 41; Lk 11: 32. τὸ κ. Ἰησοῦ Χριστοῦ *preaching about Jesus Christ* Ro 16: 25. Abs. of apostolic preaching 1 Cor 1: 21; 2 Ti 4: 17; Hs 8, 3, 2. τὸ κ. μου *my preaching* 1 Cor 2: 4; cf. 15: 14. διδάσκαλοι τοῦ κ. τοῦ υἱοῦ τοῦ θεοῦ *teachers of the preaching about the Son of God* Hs 9, 15, 4. κ. τῆς σωτηρίας *short ending of Mk* (Polyaenus 4, 7, 6 τὸ κήρ. τῆς ἐλευθερίας); σφραγὶς τοῦ κ. *the seal on the preaching* i.e., baptism Hs 9, 16, 5. κήρυγμα ὃ ἐπιστεύθην ἐγώ *the preaching w. which I have been entrusted* Tit 1: 3.— CHDodd, The Apostolic Preaching and its Developments '36. KGoldammer, ZNW 48, '57, 77-101; WBaird, JBL 76, '57, 181-91. M-M.*

κῆρυξ, υκος, ὁ (on the accent according to Herodian Gr. cf. Bl-D. §13; Mlt.-H. 57).

1. *herald,* whose duty it is to make public proclamations (Hom. +; inscr., pap., LXX; Philo, Agr. 112; Jos., Bell. 2, 624, Ant. 10, 75) MPol 12: 1f.

2. in a relig. sense (in the usage of the mystery cults: X., Hell. 2, 4, 20 ὁ τῶν μυστῶν κῆρυξ; Philostrat., Vi. Soph. 2, 33, 4 τοῦ Ἐλευσινίου ἱεροῦ κῆρυξ; Dit., Syll.³ 728ʙ, 7 κῆρυξ τοῦ θεοῦ, 773, 5 κ. τοῦ Ἀπόλλωνος, 845, 2 ὁ τῶν ἱερῶν κ. Cf. FPoland, Gesch. d. griech. Vereinswesens '09, 395.—The Cynic preacher, as a messenger fr. God, calls himself a κ.: Epict. 3, 22, 69; 3, 21, 13.—Herm. Wr. 4, 4) *preacher, one who proclaims:* of Noah δικαιοσύνης κ. 2 Pt 2: 5. Of the ap. Paul (w. ἀπόστολος) 1 Ti 2: 7; (w. ἀπόστολος and διδάσκαλος) 2 Ti 1: 11. Likew. of Paul 1 Cl 5: 6.

3. the *trumpet-shell* (Aristot., Hist. An. 5 p. 544, 546, 547 al.; Macho in Athen. 8 p. 349c), a large, sharp seashell, used in torturing MPol 2: 4.—GFriedrich, TW III 682-95. M-M.*

κηρύσσω impf. ἐκήρυσσον; fut. κηρύξω; 1 aor. ἐκήρυξα, inf. κηρύξαι (κηρῦξαι Tdf.); 1 aor. pass. ἐκηρύχθην; 1 fut. κηρυχθήσομαι (Hom. +; inscr., pap., LXX, Philo, Joseph.; loanw. in rabb.).

1. *announce, make known* by a herald (Maximus Tyr. 1, 6c κηρύττομαι=I am being announced by the herald) MPol 12: 1.—Rv 5: 2.—2. *proclaim aloud*—a. gener. *speak of, mention publicly* w. acc. κ. πολλὰ τὸν λόγον *spread the story widely* Mk 1: 45. The hospitality of the Cor. church 1 Cl 1: 2. W. indir. discourse foll. Mk 5: 20; Lk 8: 39. Abs. Mk 7: 36.—S. below 2bβ.

b. of proclamation that is relig. in nature (Epict. 3, 13, 12 of the peace of the wise men, which does not originate w. the emperor, but is ὑπὸ τοῦ θεοῦ κεκηρυγμένη διὰ τ. λόγου).

α. of the proclamation or preaching of the older prophets (Jo 2: 1; 4: 9; Jon 1: 2; 3: 2; Jos., Ant. 10, 117) Ἰωνᾶς Νινευίταις καταστροφὴν ἐκήρυξεν 1 Cl 7: 7 (Jonah as Jos., Ant. 9, 214); cf. vs. 6; 9: 4 (Noah as Sib. Or. 1, 128); 17: 1 (Elijah and Elisha, also Ezekiel); B 6: 13 (ὁ προφήτης).

β. of the proclamation of contemporary preachers (POxy. 1381, 35; 144 [II AD]: of the great deeds of the gods; Herm. Wr. 1, 27; 4, 4.—Philo, Agr. 112 κήρυξον κήρυγμα τοιοῦτον. S. κῆρυξ 2.—Also of false prophets: Jos., Bell. 6, 285), of Jewish propaganda, the preaching of John the Baptist, and proclamation of the Christian message in the widest sense: Μωϋσῆν *preach Moses* i.e. the keeping of the law Ac 15: 21. περιτομὴν *preach*

circumcision i.e. the necessity of it Gal 5: 11 (here and 2a the mng. *praise publicly* is also poss.: X., Cyr. 8, 4, 4; Polyb. 30, 29, 6). κ. μὴ κλέπτειν *preach against stealing* Ro 2: 21.—κ. τι *preach, proclaim* someth. Mt 10: 27; pass. Lk 12: 3. ἐνιαυτὸν κυρίου δεκτόν 4: 19 (cf. Is 61: 1f). τὸν λόγον 2 Ti 4: 2. τὸ ῥῆμα τῆς πίστεως *the word of faith* Ro 10: 8. τὴν βασιλείαν τοῦ θεοῦ Lk 8: 1; 9: 2; cf. Ac 20: 25; 28: 31. τὸ εὐαγγέλιον Mk 16: 15; Ac 1: 2 D; Gal 2: 2; B 5: 9. τὸ εὐ. τ. βασιλείας Mt 4: 23; 9: 35. τὸ ὄνομα τοῦ υἱοῦ τοῦ θεοῦ Hs 9, 16, 5. Pass. Hs 9, 16, 4. W. dat. of the pers. 1 Cor 9: 27; 1 Pt 3: 19 (CEBCranfield, ET 69, '57/'58, 369-72; see lit. s.v. πνεῦμα; GP 10: 41. εἰς τὰς συναγωγάς *in the synagogues* Mk 1: 39; Lk 4: 44. τινί τι someth. to someone 4: 18; B 14: 9 (both Is 61: 1). τὶ εἴς τινα someth. to someone τὸ εὐαγγέλιον εἰς ὑμᾶς 1 Th 2: 9. εἰς ὅλον τὸν κόσμον Hs 9, 25, 2. Pass. εἰς τὰ ἔθνη Mk 13: 10 (DBosch, Die Heidenmission in der Zukunftsschau Jesu '59, 159-71); κ. τὸ εὐ. Mt 24: 14; 26: 13; Mk 14: 9; Col 1: 23.—βάπτισμα *preach baptism* i.e., the necessity of it Mk 1: 4; Lk 3: 3; Ac 10: 37. μετάνοιαν εἰς ἄφεσιν ἁμαρτιῶν *repentance for the forgiveness of sins* Lk 24: 47. ἵνα μετανοῶσιν Mk 6: 12.—τινά (τινι) *someone (to someone)* Χριστόν Ac 8: 5; cf. 1 Cor 1: 23; Phil 1: 15. Ἰησοῦν Ac 19: 13; 2 Cor 11: 4. οὐχ ἑαυτοὺς κηρύσσομεν ἀλλὰ Χριστὸν Ἰησοῦν κύριον *we preach not ourselves, but Christ Jesus as Lord* 4: 5. Pass. ὃς (Χριστός). . .ἐκηρύχθη 1 Ti 3: 16; cf. Hs 8, 3, 2; 9, 17, 1; Dg 11: 3. διά τινος *through someone* (cf. Epict. 3, 13, 12) Χρ. Ἰ. ὁ ἐν ὑμῖν δι᾽ ἡμῶν κηρυχθείς 2 Cor 1: 19. W. an addition that indicates the content of the preaching, introduced by ὅτι (cf. Epict. 4, 5, 24): κ. w. acc. and ὅτι foll. Mk 1: 14 v.l.; Ac 9: 20; pass. Χρ. κηρύσσεται ὅτι ἐκ νεκρῶν ἐγήγερται *Christ is preached as having risen fr. the dead* 1 Cor 15: 12. κ. τινί, ὅτι Ac 10: 42; οὕτως κ. 1 Cor 15: 11. The content of the preaching is introduced by λέγων Mt 3: 1f; 10: 7; Mk 1: 7; cf. vs. 14; IPhld 7: 2. Beside λέγειν w. direct discourse (Epict. 4, 6, 23) Mt 4: 17. Abs. Mt 11: 1; Mk 1: 38; 3: 14; 16: 20; Ro 10: 15; 1 Cl 42: 4; B 5: 8; 8: 3. κηρύσσων *a preacher* Ro 10: 14. M-M. B. 1478.*

κῆτος, ους, τό (Hom. +; Diod. S. 17, 41, 5 κῆτος ἄπιστον τὸ μέγεθος; LXX; Test. Judah 21: 7) *sea-monster* (such as tried to swallow Andromeda: Eur., Andr. fgm. 121; 145 ANauck² 1889) of Jonah's fish (דָּג גָּדוֹל) ἐν τῇ κοιλίᾳ τ. κήτους (Jon 2: 1; cf. 3 Macc 6: 8; Jos., Ant. 9, 213; Third Corinthians 3: 29) Mt 12: 40 (all the details are from Jon 2: 1. But Tzetzes on Lycophron 34 has Heracles staying in the belly of the κῆτος for three days when he rescues Hesione). Of an apocalyptic animal Hv 4, 1, 6; 9.*

Κηφᾶς, ᾶ, ὁ (כֵּיפָא 'rock') *Cephas,* Aram. surname of Simon; the Gk. form of the surname is Peter (s. the lit. on πέτρα 1 b and Πέτρος) 1 Cor 1: 12; 3: 22; 9: 5; 15: 5; Gal 1: 18; 2: 9, 11, 14; 1 Cl 47: 3. Κ., ὁ ἑρμηνεύεται Πέτρος J 1: 42.*

κιβώριον, ου, τό *ciborium, the seed-vessel of the Egyptian bean* (WWeber, Ägypt.-griech. Terrakotten '14, 63f), also a *vessel* of similar shape (Diod. S. 1, 34, 6; Nicander, fgm. 81; Strabo; Didym. in Athen. 11 p. 477ᴇ; POxy. 105, 18 [II AD]; Am 9: 1 Sym., Theod.) Ac 19: 24 v.l. after ναοὺς ἀργυροῦς; ἴσως ὡς κιβώρια μικρά.*

κιβωτός, οῦ, ἡ (Aristoph., Lysias et al.; inscr., pap., LXX) *box, chest,* in our lit.—1. *the ark* of Noah (Gen 6: 14ff; 4 Macc 15: 31; Sib. Or. 1, 266) Mt 24: 38; Lk 17: 27 (both Gen 7: 7); Hb 11: 7; 1 Pt 3: 20; 1 Cl 9: 4.

2. *the ark* in the Holy of Holies ἡ κ. τῆς διαθήκης *the ark of the covenant* (Ex 39: 14 al.; Philo; Jos., Ant. 3, 134

al.) Hb 9: 4; also found in the temple in heaven Rv 11: 19. M-M.*

κιθάρα, ας, ἡ (Hom. Hymns, Hdt.+; LXX; Philo; Jos., Ant. 1, 64; Sib. Or. 8, 119) *lyre, harp* Rv 5: 8; 14: 2. κ. τοῦ θεοῦ lit. *harps of God* Rv 15: 2, i.e., *belonging to* or *given by God* (cf. ἐν σάλπιγγι θεοῦ 1 Th 4: 16), or *harps used in the praise of God.* It is also possible that the expression may be a Semitic superlative formation, *great harps,* analogous to ὄρη θεοῦ=mighty mountains Ps 35: 7; cf. 79: 11; cf. also ἀστεῖος τῷ θεῷ Ac 7: 20 and s. θεός 3gβ. W. the flute (s. αὐλός; Philo, Leg. All. 2, 75; 3, 221) 1 Cor 14: 7. The strings of the harp IEph 4: 1; IPhld 1: 2.—Lit. on κύμβαλον.*

κιθαρίζω (Hom.+; Dit., Syll.³ 578, 18 [II BC] κιθαρίζειν ἢ ψάλλειν; Is 23: 16; Jos., C. Ap. 2, 242) *play the lyre* or *harp* w. blowing the flute (Dio Chrys. 2, 55; 52[69], 3; Polyaenus 5, 3, 3; Achmes 207, 16) 1 Cor 14: 7. κ. ἐν κιθάρᾳ Rv 14: 2. M-M.*

κιθαρῳδός, οῦ, ὁ (Hdt., Pla.; Diphil. in Athen. 6 p. 247D; Plut., Mor. 166A; Aelian, V.H. 4, 2; Dit., Syll.³ [index], Or. 51, 41 [III BC]; 352, 67; Inschr. v. Priene 113, 80; Zen.-P. 77 [=Sb 6783], 17 [257 BC]; Philo) *lyre-player, harpist* who plays an accompaniment to his own singing (the κιθαριστής plays the instrument without singing; both words together Philo, Agr. 35; differentiated Diog. L. 3, 88; Aristoxenus, fgm. 102 carries the contrast back to two different instruments: κίθαρις [=λύρα] and κιθάρα) Rv 14: 2; 18: 22. M-M.*

Κιλικία, ας, ἡ (Hdt.+; inscr., LXX; Philo, Leg. ad Gai. 281; Joseph.) *Cilicia,* a province in the southeast corner of Asia Minor, whose capital is Tarsus; home of Paul Ac 6: 9; 15: 23, 41; 21: 39; 22: 3; 23: 34; 27: 5; Gal 1: 21 (on the connection with Συρία s. that entry); IPhld 11: 1.—Ramsay, Hist. Geogr. 361ff; RHeberdey-AWilhelm, Reisen in Kilikien 1896; FXSchaffer, Cilicia '03; VSchultze, Altchristl. Städte u. Landschaften II 2, '26. M-M.*

Κίλιξ, ικος, ὁ (Hom.+; inscr., Joseph., Sib. Or.) *a Cilician* Ac 23: 34 v.l.*

κινδυνεύω impf. ἐκινδύνευον (Pind., Hdt.+; inscr., pap., LXX, Joseph.) *be in danger, run a risk* abs. (Dit., Syll.³ 708, 8; BGU 423, 7; Is 28: 13) Lk 8: 23 (cf. Jos., Vi. 14). οἱ κινδυνεύοντες *those who are in danger* (Dit., Syll.³ 570, 4) 1 Cl 59: 3. κ. πᾶσαν ὥραν *be in peril every hour* (in danger of one's life, at that; cf. κινδυνεύω used abs. Diog. L. 9, 57) 1 Cor 15: 30. κινδυνεύειν τινὸς χάριν *face danger for the sake of someone* 1 Cl 55: 6.—W. inf. foll. (X., Mem. 2, 3, 16; Diod. S. 12, 51, 1; Dit., Syll.³ 852, 32f; 888, 68f; UPZ 161, 10 [119 BC]; BGU 530, 12; 30; POxy. 44, 9; 3 Macc 5: 41; Jos., Ant. 4, 188; cf. Bl-D. §392, 2) κινδυνεύομεν ἐγκαλεῖσθαι στάσεως *we run the risk of being charged w. rioting* Ac 19: 40. τοῦτο κινδυνεύει ἡμῖν τὸ μέρος εἰς ἀπελεγμὸν ἐλθεῖν *there is danger that this trade of ours may come into disrepute* vs. 27. M-M.*

κίνδυνος, ου, ὁ (Pind., Hdt.+; inscr., pap., LXX; Ep. Arist. 199; Jos., Vi. 272) *danger, risk* Ro 8: 35. That which brings the danger is expressed with the gen. alone (Pla., Euthyd. p. 279E τῆς θαλάσσης, Rep. 1 p. 332E; Heliod. 2, 4, 1; Hippiatr. II 234, 13 ποταμῶν; Ps 114: 3; Sir 43: 24) 2 Cor 11: 26a, or by ἐκ ibid. b. The words ἐν πόλει, ἐν ἐρημίᾳ, ἐν θαλάσσῃ (Plut., Mor. 603E κινδύνους ἐν θαλ.), ἐν ψευδαδέλφοις ibid. c have a somewhat different sense, and indicate the place where the danger lurks (cf. Ps.-Ael. Aristid. 25, 20 K.=43 p. 804 D.: θάνατοι κατ'

οἰκίας, ἐν ἱεροῖς, ἐν θύραις, ἐν πύλαις; Ps.-Pla. 11th Letter p. 358E κινδυνεύειν κατά τε γῆν καὶ κατὰ θάλατταν, καὶ νῦν πάντα κινδύνων ἐν ταῖς πορείαις ἐστὶ μεστά). ὑπὸ κίνδυνον *in danger* IEph 12: 1; ITr 13: 3. κ. ὑποφέρειν *incur danger* 1 Cl 14: 2. κινδύνῳ ὑποκεῖσθαι *incur a risk* 41: 4. κ. ἑαυτῷ ἐπεξεργάζεσθαι *bring danger upon oneself* 47: 7. παραδοῦναι ἑαυτὸν τῷ κ. *expose oneself to danger* 55: 5; also παραβαλεῖν vs. 6. κινδύνῳ ἑαυτὸν ἐνδῆσαι *involve oneself in danger* 59: 1. M-M. B. 1155.*

κινέω fut. κινήσω; 1 aor. ἐκίνησα, pass. ἐκινήθην (Hom.+; inscr., pap., LXX, En., Philo, Joseph.; Sib. Or. 3, 534) *move.*

1. *move away, remove* τὶ *someth.* (Lysimachus [200 BC]: no. 382 fgm. 2 Jac.; Diod. S. 20, 110, 1 κινῆσαι τὸ ἔθος= put an end to the custom; Jos., C. Ap. 2, 272 τὰ νόμιμα κ. ='remove the law fr. its proper place') τῷ δακτύλῳ φορτία *move burdens w. so much as a finger* Mt 23: 4 (Artem. 1, 31 p. 32, 18f φορτία κινούμενα). κ. τι ἔκ τινος *remove someth. from someth.* κ. τὴν λυχνίαν ἐκ τοῦ τόπου αὐτῆς Rv 2: 5. Pass. 6: 14 (cf. Astrampsychus p. 5 l. 12 εἰ κινηθήσομαι τοῦ τόπου μοῦ=whether I lose my place).

2. *move, set in motion*—a. *shake* the head (Hom.+; Job 16: 4; Da 4: 19; Sir 12: 18; 13: 7) as a sign of scorn and derision (Nicol. Dam.: 90 fgm. 4 p. 335, 18 Jac.) Mt 27: 39; Mk 15: 29; 1 Cl 16: 16 (Ps 21: 8).

b. *arouse* pass. (Jos., Ant. 3, 13) ἐκινήθη ἡ πόλις ὅλη *the whole city was aroused* Ac 21: 30. ἐπὶ τῇ διδαχῇ 14: 7 D.

3. pass. *be moved, move* (Hom.+; Gen 7: 14, 21 al.; En. 101, 8; Philo) Hv 4, 1, 9. ἐν αὐτῷ (God) ζῶμεν καὶ κινούμεθα καὶ ἐσμέν *in him we live and move and have our being* Ac 17: 28 (on the mng. and origin of this saying, specif. of ἐν αὐτῷ κινεῖσθαι s. Norden, Agn. Th. 19ff; MDibelius, Pls auf. d. Areop. '39, 26; MPohlenz, Pls u. d. Stoa: ZNW 42, '49, 69–104, esp. 88ff.—Perh. κ. in this passage, coming as it does betw. 'living' and 'being', emphasizes 'moving' less than 'existence'; cf. Achilles Tat. 2, 37, 1 τὸ κινούμενον ἐν φθορᾷ='that which exists amid corruptibility').

4. fig.—a. *cause, bring about* (Pla., Rep. 8 p. 566E πολέμους; Jos., Bell. 2, 175 ταραχήν; PPar. 68A, 6 θόρυβος ἐκινήθη) στάσεις Ac 24: 5.

b. in the mental and spiritual realm *move, cause* (Plut., Cim. 16, 10; Ael. Aristid. 19, 6 K.=41 p. 764 D.: ἐκίνησέν με ὁ θεός; POxy. 1121, 16 τίνι λόγῳ ἢ πόθεν κεινηθέντες;) pass. w. inf. foll. (PFlor. 58, 15) Dg 11: 8. M-M. B. 662.*

κίνησις, εως, ἡ (Pla.+; Dit., Or. 543, 15 [II AD]; pap., LXX, Ep. Arist., oft. Philo; Jos., Ant. 1, 31; 17, 251) *motion* τοῦ ὕδατος J 5: 3 t.r. (Diod. S. 11, 89, 4 κίνησις of a movement in water caused by a god; Epict. 3, 3, 21 ὅταν τὸ ὕδωρ κινηθῇ). M-M.*

κιννάμωμον, ου, τό (Semitic loanw., s. Hdt. 3, 111; Aristot.; Diod. S. 2, 49, 3; Dit., Or. 214, 59 [III BC]; PTebt. 190; 250; PSI 628, 8; PGM 13, 100; 358; LXX, En.; Jos., Bell. 6, 390) *cinnamon* Rv 18: 13 (t.r. κινάμ.). M-M.*

Κίς, ὁ indecl. (קִישׁ) *Kish,* father of Saul (1 Km 9: 1 al.; Jos., Ant. 6, 45f; 130 [Κείς]; 56; 62 [Κείσαιος]; 268 [Κείσος]) Ac 13: 21.*

κισσάω 1 aor. ἐκίσσησα *crave* (Aristoph.+; of the cravings of pregnant women for strange food Aristot.+); *become pregnant with* τινά *someone* 1 Cl 18: 5 (Ps 50: 7).*

κίχρημι 1 aor. ἔχρησα (Hdt.+; inscr., pap., LXX) *lend* τινί τι (Hdt. 3, 58; Plut., Pomp. 29, 4; Dit., Syll.³ 241в, 87; 1 Km 1: 28; Jos., Bell. 3, 359) Lk 11: 5. M-M.*

κλάδος, ου, ὁ (trag.+; Hdt. 7, 19 [τῆς ἐλαίης τ. κλάδους]; inscr., pap., LXX; Philo, Aet. M. 63; Jos., Ant. 8, 136; Test. 12 Patr.) *branch* Mt 13: 32; 24: 32; Mk 13: 28; Lk 13: 19; Hs 8, 1, 4; 8, 2, 9; 8, 3, 1. ποιεῖν κλάδους *produce branches* Mk 4: 32 (birds on the branches as Da 4: 12, 14 Theod.). κόπτειν κλάδους ἀπό τινος *cut branches from someth.* Mt 21: 8; Hs 8, 1, 2.—Paul speaks fig. (cf. Menand., fgm. 716 Kock; Sir 23: 25; 40: 15; Sib. Or. 5, 50) of root and branches of the olive tree (Epigr. Gr. 368, 7 a girl who has died is called κλάδος ἐλέας) Ro 11: 16ff, 21. Also fig., orthodox Christians are called κλάδοι τοῦ σταυροῦ *branches of the cross* ITr 11: 2. M-M. B. 523.*

κλαίω (Hom.+; inscr., pap., LXX, Joseph., Test. 12 Patr.) impf. ἔκλαιον; fut. (Bl-D. §77 w. app.; Mlt.-H. 244) κλαύσω and κλαύσομαι (Rv 18: 9 v.l.; Hv 3, 3, 2; Jos., Bell. 1, 628; Sib. Or. 5, 170); 1 aor. ἔκλαυσα.

1. *weep, cry* Mk 14: 72; Lk 7: 38; J 11: 31, 33; 20: 11, 13, 15; Ac 9: 39; 21: 13; 1 Cl 48: 1; Hv 4, 1, 7. πικρῶς (q.v.) Mt 26: 75; Lk 22: 62. πολύ *vehemently* Rv 5: 4. πολλά Ac 8: 24 D; λίαν κ. *weep bitterly* Hm 3: 3. μὴ κλαῖε, μὴ κλαίετε *do not weep* Lk 7: 13; 8: 52b; 23: 28a, b; Rv 5: 5. Of mourning for the dead (s. on ἀλαλάζω) Mk 5: 38f; Lk 7: 32; 8: 52. ἐπί w. acc. *over* (Judg 14: 17 A; cf. Bl-D. §233, 2) Lk 19: 41; 23: 28a, b. Also ἐπί τινι (Plut., Mor. 216D; Synes., Ep. 140 p. 277A; Sir 22: 11) Lk 19: 41 t.r. (on weeping and lamenting over the imminent destruction of Jerusalem cf. τὸν ἐπὶ τῇ πόλει θρῆνον by Jesus, son of Ananias: Jos., Bell. 6, 304-9). W. κόπτεσθαι (Jos., Ant. 13, 399) Lk 8: 52; Rv 18: 9; GP 12: 52, 54. W. λυπεῖσθαι (Test. Zeb. 4: 8) GP 14: 59. W. πενθεῖν (POxy. 528, 8 νυκτὸς κλαίων ἡμέρας δὲ πενθῶν) Mk 16: 10; Lk 6: 25; Js 4: 9; Rv 18: 11, 15, 19; GP 7: 27.—As an expression of any feeling of sadness, care, or anxiety J 16: 20 (w. θρηνεῖν); 1 Cor 7: 30; Js 5: 1. (Opp. γελᾶν) Lk 6: 21, 25. (Opp. χαίρειν as Hippocr., Ep. 17, 49) J 16: 20; Ro 12: 15; Hv 3, 3, 2. κλαίων λέγω *I say with tears* Phil 3: 18; Hv 1, 2, 2.

2. trans. *weep for, bewail* τινά *someone* (as early as Hom.; Sb 4313, 15; Jer 8: 23; 22: 10; 1 Macc 9: 20; Test. Sim. 9) Mt 2: 18; Rv 18: 9 t.r. (Bl-D. §148, 2; Rob. 475).—KHRengstorf, TW III 721-5. M-M. B. 1129.*

κλάσις, εως, ἡ (Pla.+; Philo) *breaking*—1. ἡ κ. τοῦ ἄρτου *the breaking of bread* Lk 24: 35; Ac 2: 42.—Th Schermann, D. 'Brotbrechen' im Urchristentum: BZ 8, '10, 33-52; 162-83; JWeiss, D. Urchristentum '17, 41ff; JGewiess, D. urapostol. Heilsverkünd. nach d. AG '39, 146-57. JBehm, TW III 726-43. S. on ἀγάπη II and εὐχαριστία 3, end.

2. ἡ τῶν σκελῶν κ. *breaking of the legs* (s. σκέλος) Phlm subscr.*

κλάσμα, ατος, τό (Ps.-X., Cyn. 10, 5; Diod. S. 17, 13, 4; Plut., Tib. Gr. 19, 1; Vett. Val. 110, 31; 34; Dit., Syll.³ 588, 192; 196; Inscr. Gr. 833; PLond. 1431, 26; 36; 1435, 158; LXX; Jos., Ant. 10, 244) *fragment, piece, crumb* (cf. Artem. 4, 33 p. 224, 7 and Ezk 13: 19 v.l. κλάσματα ἄρτων) of the remains of a meal Mt 14: 20; 15: 37; Mk 6: 43; 8: 8, 19f; Lk 9: 17; J 6: 12f. Of the pieces of bread at the Lord's Supper D 9: 3f (CFDMoule, JTS 6, '55, 240-43). M-M.*

Κλαῦδα *Clauda,* a small island south of Crete Ac 27: 16. The mss. vary: Κλαυδα אA and Καυδα B. The reason for this is prob. not a confusion betw. two different islands

(W-S. §5, 31, p. 68 note 72); it is rather that the name of the same island is variously written (RHarris, ET 21, '10, 17ff). M-M.*

Κλαυδία, ας, ἡ (s. e.g., Sb index) *Claudia,* a Christian woman 2 Ti 4: 21. M-M.*

Κλαύδιος, ου, ὁ (freq. found) *Claudius*—1. Tiberius Claudius Drusus Nero Germanicus, Roman emperor (41–54 AD); his measures taken against the Jews in Rome (Sueton., Claudius 25; Cass. Dio 60, 6. Cf. Schürer III⁴ 61ff; Zahn on Ac 18: 2; ABludau, Der Katholik 83, '03, 113ff; 193ff; Harnack, SAB '12, 674ff; JJuster, Les Juifs dans l'empire romain '14, II 171; 199; AWikenhauser, Die AG '21, 323f; ROHoerber, CTM 31, '60, 690-94) Ac 18: 2. A famine during his reign (Schürer I⁴ 567, 8; VWeber, D. antiochen. Kollekte '17, 38f; Wikenhauser, op. cit. 407ff; KSGapp, The Universal Famine under Claudius: HTR 28, '35, 258-65; EHaenchen, Acts ad loc.) Ac 11: 28.—HDessau, Gesch. d. röm. Kaiserzeit II 1, '26.

2. Claudius Lysias, Rom. official in Jerusalem (χιλίαρχος τ. σπείρης Ac 21: 31; cf. Schürer I⁴ 464) at the time Paul was arrested 23: 26.

3. Claudius Ephebus, Rom. Christian, sent to Corinth as representative of the Rom. church 1 Cl 65: 1.*

κλαυθμός, οῦ, ὁ (Hom.+; inscr. [Sb 7541, 15: II AD]; LXX) *weeping, crying* (w. ὀδυρμός) Mt 2: 18 (Jer 38: 15; θρῆνος, which is found w. both of them here as well as Mt 2: 18 v.l., occurs also Philo, Vi. Cont. 73 and Jos., Ant. 20, 112 w. κλαυθμός). ἱκανὸς κ. ἐγένετο πάντων *they all began to weep loudly* Ac 20: 37. ὁ κ. with ὁ (the art. indicates the unique and extreme character of the action) βρυγμὸς τ. ὀδόντων Mt 8: 12; 13: 42, 50; 22: 13; 24: 51; 25: 30; Lk 13: 28 (on these passages s. BSchwanke, BZ 16, '72, 121f). M-M.*

κλάω 1 aor. ἔκλασα (Hom.+; inscr. of Gaza: Suppl. Epigr. Gr. VIII 269, 6 [III/II BC]; PLeipz. 39, 12; LXX; Philo; Jos., Bell. 5, 407, Vi. 212 al.) *break* in our lit. only of the breaking of bread (cf. Jer 16: 7; PGM 4, 1392f. But as early as Anacr., fgm. 69 Diehl² ἰτρίου λεπτοῦ μικρὸν ἀποκλάς. Also Diod. S. 17, 41, 7 οἱ διακλώμενοι τῶν ἄρτων =those of the loaves that were broken through).—LXX also has διαθρύπτειν τ. ἄρτον: Is 58: 7), by which the father of the household gave the signal to begin the meal (פרס, פתת לחם). This was the practice of Jesus Mt 14: 19; 15: 36; 26: 26; Mk 8: 6, 19; 14: 22; Lk 22: 19; 24: 30; 1 Cor 11: 24. Likew. of the religious meals of the early Christians Ac 2: 46; 20: 7, 11; 27: 35; 1 Cor 10: 16; D 14: 1; IEph 20: 2.—Lit. on κλάσις. M-M. B. 563.*

κλεῖθρον, ου, τό (X., Pla. et al.; Sb 6253, 9 [137 BC]; PGM 4, 2261; 2294; LXX; Sib. Or. 2, 228) lit. a *bar* or *bolt* for closing a door; fig., a *barrier,* of the coast as a barrier for the sea 1 Cl 20: 6 (Appian, Mithr. 24 §96 of the 'bars' with which an endangered seaport was closed). B. 467.*

κλείς, κλειδός, ἡ (Hom.+; inscr., pap., LXX; loanw. in rabb.) acc. κλεῖδα Lk 11: 52 (POxy. 113, 3; LXX [Thackeray 150]) and κλεῖν Rv 3: 7; 20: 1 (Dit., Syll.³ 996, 24; POxy. 1127, 25), pl. κλεῖδας Mt 16: 19; 1 Cl 43: 3 (Dit., Or. 229, 96; 98; PHermopol. 8 II, 5; BGU 253, 18) and κλεῖς Rv 1: 18 (Ctesias, Pers. 14 ὃς τὰς κλεῖς πάσας τῶν βασιλείων εἶχε; POxy. 729, 23 [137 AD]; BGU 75, 13.— Bl-D. §47, 3; Mlt.-H. 131f; Mayser 272 [lit.]; Reinhold 51) anything used for locking, esp. a *key.*

1. lit. σφραγίζειν τὰς κ. 1 Cl 43: 3 (inscr. [218 BC]: ΕΛΛΗΝΙΚΑ 7, '34 p. 179, 9f κλείδας ἐχέτωσαν . . . σφραγιζέσθωσαν).—The foll. exprs. come close to the

fig. mng.: κ. τοῦ θανάτου καὶ τοῦ ᾅδου (ᾅδης 1) Rv 1: 18. κ. τῆς ἀβύσσου 20: 1 or κ. τοῦ φρέατος τῆς ἀβύσσου 9: 1 (ἄβυσσος 2). Likew. the portrayal of Peter as the keeper of heaven's gate δώσω σοι τὰς κλεῖδας τῆς βασιλείας τῶν οὐρανῶν Mt 16: 19 (s. JGrill, D. Primat des Petrus '04; WKöhler, ARW 8, '05, 214ff [lit.]; ADell, ZNW 15, '14, 27ff, esp. 33ff; VBurch, JBL 52, '33, 147–52; HvCampenhausen, D. Schlüsselgewalt der Kirche: Evang. Theol. 4, '37, 143–69. S. also on πέτρα 1b and Πέτρος, end). ἔχειν τὴν κ. Δαυίδ (cf. Is 22: 22 v.l. τὴν κ. οἴκου Δ.) hold the key of David Rv 3: 7 (on authority over the keys cf. Parmenides 1, 14 Δίκη ἔχει κληῖδας, i.e., of the gate that leads to the realm of light and knowledge; Dit., Or. 229, 56 [III BC] κυριεύσοντα τῶν κλειδῶν likewise Polyb. 4, 18, 2. The phrase ἔχειν τὰς κλεῖς=hold the keys Rv 1: 18; 3: 7; 20: 1 is as early as Pind., Pyth. 8, 4).

2. fig. (Diod. S. 2, 8, 3 καθαπερεὶ τὰς κλεῖς ἔχειν= hold the keys as it were; Artem. 3, 54 κλείς is a symbol of πίστις=trust) αἴρειν τὴν κλεῖδα τῆς γνώσεως take away the key (to the door) of knowledge Lk 11: 52. Cf. here the badly damaged apocryphal gospel fragment POxy. 655, 41ff (=Kl. T. 8³, '29, 23) with the restoration τὴν κλεῖδα τῆς [γνώσεως].—JoachJeremias, TW III 743–53. M-M. B. 468f.*

κλείω fut. κλείσω Rv 3: 7; 1 aor. ἔκλεισα, pass. ἐκλείσθην; pf. pass. κέκλεισμαι, ptc. κεκλεισμένος (Hom.+; inscr., pap., LXX, Joseph.) shut, lock, bar.

1. lit. τὴν θύραν (Aristopho Com. [IV BC] 7 ed. Kock II p. 278; Herodas 6, 98; Epict. 3, 22, 14; 2 Ch 28: 24) Mt 6: 6; Rv 3: 8. Pass. (Menand., Epitr. 642; Jos., Ant. 18, 74; cf. X., Cyr. 7, 5, 27) Mt 25: 10; Lk 11: 7; J 20: 19, 26; Ac 21: 30. οἱ πυλῶνες the gates (of the heavenly Jerusalem; cf. Is 60: 11) Rv 21: 25.—Of structures close, lock (BGU 1116, 15 [13 BC]; Is 24: 10) κ. τὴν σκηνήν close the tabernacle 1 Cl 43: 3. Pass. Ac 5: 23.—Abs. shut (Jos., Vi. 153) Rv 3: 7a, b (cf. Is 22: 22 v.l.); 20: 3.

2. fig. κ. τὸν οὐρανόν shut the heavens, so that it does not rain Rv 11: 6; pass. Lk 4: 25. In a vision ἐκλείσθησαν οἱ οὐρανοί the heavens were closed Hv 1, 2, 1. κ. τὴν βασιλείαν τῶν οὐρανῶν shut the kingdom of heaven i.e., prevent people fr. entering it Mt 23: 13 (MBlack, An Aramaic Approach³, '67, 259–61 [Sin. Syriac]). κ. τὰ σπλάγχνα ἀπό τινος close one's heart against someone 1 J 3: 17 (cf. a sim. figure στόμα κεκλεισμένον Sir 30: 18). M-M. B. 847f.*

κλέμμα, ατος, τό stealing, theft (so, denoting an action, Eur.+.—LXX only='stolen goods') μετανοεῖν ἐκ τῶν κλεμμάτων repent of the thefts Rv 9: 21. In a list of vices Hm 8: 5; cf. Mk 7: 22 D. M-M.*

Κλεοπᾶς, ᾶ, ὁ Cleopas (Ostraka II 1438; 1442; 1448 [all II AD]; short form of Κλεόπατρος). This genuinely Gk. name, which evidently takes the place of the Semitic Κλωπᾶς (q.v.), without necessarily denoting the identity of the two persons w. these names in the gospels, is borne by an otherwise unknown disciple in Jerusalem Lk 24: 18. Cf. Bl-D. §53, 2d; 125, 2; Dssm., B 184, 6 [BS 315, 2]; Dalman, Gramm.² 179, 4; Mlt.-H. p. 88. M-M.*

κλέος, ους, τό (Hom.+; pap.; Job 28: 22; 30: 8; Philo; Jos., Ant. 4, 105; 115; 19, 223; Sib. Or. 3, 431; 5, 428) fame, glory τὸ γενναῖον τῆς πίστεως κ. 1 Cl 5: 6. κ. περιποιεῖσθαι ἑαυτῷ win fame for oneself 54: 3. ποῖον κ. w. εἰ foll. what credit is it, if 1 Pt 2: 20. M-M.*

κλέπτης, ου, ὁ (Hom.+; pap., LXX, Philo; Jos., Ant. 16, 3) thief Mt 6: 19f; 24: 43; Lk 12: 33, 39; J 10: 1 (w. λῃστής as vs. 8 and EpJer 57. Opp. ποιμήν as Il. 3, 11; Maximus

Tyr. 19, 4e), 10; 1 Pt 4: 15; 1 Cl 35: 8 (Ps 49: 18). Excluded fr. the kgdm. of God 1 Cor 6: 10. Of Judas the traitor J 12: 6. The breaking in of a thief as a figure for someth. sudden, surprising, unexpected; used of the Parousia (as in Mt 24: 43; Lk 12: 39 above) ὡς κ. ἐν νυκτὶ ἔρχεσθαι come as a thief in the night 1 Th 5: 2 (the thief in the night: Dio Chrys. 52[69], 8; Job 24: 14; Philo, Spec. Leg. 4, 10); cf. vs. 4; 2 Pt 3: 10; Rv 3: 3; 16: 15.—GFörster, ZNW 17, '16, 169–77; WHarnisch, Eschatologische Existenz, '73: Exkurs II, 84–116.—In the saying concerning the shepherds, the relig. leaders who came before Jesus are fig. called thieves J 10: 8.—HPreisker, TW III 753–6. M-M.*

κλέπτω fut. κλέψω; 1 aor. ἔκλεψα; 2 aor. pass. ἐκλάπην Dg 2: 2 (Hom.+; inscr., pap., LXX, Philo; Jos., Ant. 4, 272; 18, 169; Test. 12 Patr.) steal τὶ someth. Pass. Dg 2: 2, 7. τινά someone of a dead pers. (Charito 3, 2, 7; 2 Km 21: 12; Tob 1: 18 BA) of Jesus Mt 27: 64; 28: 13; GP 8: 30. Abs. Mt 6: 19f; 19: 18; Mk 10: 19; Lk 18: 20; Ro 13: 9; D 2: 2 (the last five Ex 20: 14.—In Epict. 3, 7, 12 the command takes the form: μὴ κλέπτετε); J 10: 10; Ro 2: 21; Eph 4: 28. M-M. B. 789.*

κλῆμα, ατος, τό branch, esp., of a vine (Aristoph. +; Pla., Rep. 1 p. 353A ἀμπέλου κλῆμα; Theophr., H. Pl. 4, 13, 5; Pollux 1, 237 ὁ τῆς ἀμπέλου [sc. κλάδος] κλῆμα; PFlor. 148, 9; LXX; Jos., Ant. 2, 64; 12, 75 κλ. ἀμπέλων; Sib. Or. 7, 148) in the saying about the vine and branches J 15: 2, 4–6 (ESchweitzer, in TWManson mem. vol. '59, 230–45). M-M.*

Κλήμης, εντος, ὁ Clement (the Gk. form of this Lat. name [Clemens] is found e.g. Philostrat., Vi. Soph. 2, 27, 2; Jos., Ant. 19, 37–47; Dit., Or. 207, 1; 574, 9; POxy. 241, 1; 340; Sb 4613; 8089, 1 [beg. II AD]).

1. a member of the church at Philippi, honored by Paul w. the title 'co-worker' (a Clement of Philippi is mentioned CIL III 633) Phil 4: 3.

2. a member of the church at Rome, in charge of relations w. other churches Hv 2, 4, 3. Identified by older scholars w. 1, though without sufficient reason. The pers. meant is certainly the author of 1 Cl; he is named in the subscr. of that letter; also subscr. of 2 Cl Funk. M-M.*

κληρονομέω fut. κληρονομήσω; 1 aor. ἐκληρονόμησα; pf. κεκληρονόμηκα (Demosth. et al.; inscr., pap., LXX, En., Philo, Joseph.).

1. inherit, τινά someone (Posidon.: 87 fgm. 36 p. 243, 32 Jac.; POxy. 1067, 8; PRyl. 28, 226 δοῦλος αὐτὸν κληρονομήσει; Gen 15: 3; Pr 13: 22; Tob 3: 15; Jos., Ant. 20, 241) 1 Cl 16: 13 (Is 53: 12).—Abs. inherit, be an heir (Epict. 3, 2, 8; Dit., Syll.³ 833, 8; Sb 4638, 12 [II BC] Gal 4: 30 (Gen 21: 10); B 13: 1. Jesus as ὁ κληρονομῶν the heir 14: 5.

2. acquire, obtain, come into possession of τὶ someth. (H. Gk. [Phryn. 129 L.; Moeris 149]; cf. Polyb. 18, 38, 8 φήμην; 15, 22, 3; Lucian, Dial. Mort. 11, 3; BGU 19 II, 1; 1024 VIII 16; PRyl. 117, 13; LXX; Philo, Rer. Div. Her. 98 σοφίαν) esp. of participation in Messianic salvation: τὴν γῆν (Ps 24: 13; 36: 9, 11, 22; En. 5, 6; 7) Mt 5: 5; D 3: 7. βασιλείαν θεοῦ the kgdm. of God (cf. 1 Macc 2: 57) 1 Cor 6: 9f(= Pol 5: 3); 15: 50a; Gal 5: 21; IEph 16: 1; IPhld 3: 3; cf. Mt 25: 34. ζωὴν αἰώνιον receive, share in eternal life (cf. Sib. Or. fgm. 3, 47) 19: 29; Mk 10: 17; Lk 10: 25; 18: 18; Hv 3, 8, 4. δόξαν καὶ τιμήν 1 Cl 45: 8. τὴν ἐν τ. οὐρανῷ πνευματικὴν καὶ ἄφθαρτον τῆς δικαιοσύνης δόξαν κ. ending of Mk in the Freer ms. 10ff. σωτηρίαν Hb 1: 14. τὰς ἐπαγγελίας what is promised 6: 12; 1 Cl 10: 2. τὴν ἀφθαρσίαν 1 Cor 15: 50b. (τὴν

εὐλογίαν Hb 12: 17; 1 Pt 3: 9. διαφορώτερον ὄνομα Hb 1: 4 (= 1 Cl 36: 2.—κλ. ὄνομα as Dionys. Byz. §7; Themist., Paraphrases Aristot. II p. 172, 13 Spengel [1866]). ταῦτα all this Rv 21: 7. JHerrmann and WFoerster, TW III 757-86: κλ. and related words. M-M.*

κληρονομία, ας, ἡ (Isocr., Demosth. et al.; inscr., pap., LXX; En. 99, 14; Philo; Jos., Bell. 2, 249).
1. inheritance (so almost always in secular wr., also Num 26: 54, 56) Mt 21: 38; Mk 12: 7; Lk 20: 14; Hv 3, 12, 2; s 5, 6, 4. μερίσασθαι μετά τινος τὴν κ. divide the inheritance w. someone Lk 12: 13. λαὸς κληρονομίας people of the inheritance B 14: 4. At his coming again the Beloved shall come to his inheritance 4: 3. Inheritance, of Israel 1 Cl 29: 2 (Dt 32: 9).
2. possession, property (Sir 22: 23; 24: 20; Jdth 16: 21; 1 Macc 2: 56; 6: 24) διδόναι τινὶ κληρονομίαν give someone property Ac 7: 5; 13: 33 D; 1 Cl 36: 4 (the two last Ps 2: 8). λαμβάνειν τι εἰς κ. receive someth. as a possession (cf. Aristot., Eth. Nic. 7, 14 p. 1153b, 33; Test. Benj. 10: 5) Hb 11: 8.
3. in specif. Christian usage (corresp. to the LXX) (the possession of) salvation (as the inheritance of God's children) Gal 3: 18. ἀπολαμβάνειν τὴν ἀνταπόδοσιν τῆς κ. receive salvation as a reward Col 3: 24. ἡ ἐπαγγελία τῆς αἰωνίου κ. the promise of the eternal inheritance Hb 9: 15. κ. ἄφθαρτος an imperishable possession 1 Pt 1: 4. ἡ κ. ἡμῶν our salvation Eph 1: 14; granted by God vs. 18. δοῦναι τὴν ἐν τοῖς ἡγιασμένοις grant salvation among those who are consecrated Ac 20: 32. κ. ἔχειν ἐν τῇ βασιλείᾳ τοῦ Χριστοῦ have a share in the kgdm. of Christ Eph 5: 5 (PLHammer, JBL 79, '60, 267-72).
4. abstr. for concr. =the heirs (s. ἀκροβυστία 3) Ro 11: 1 𝔓⁴⁶ G. M-M.*

κληρονόμος, ου, ὁ (Pla. et al.; inscr., pap., LXX, Philo; Jos., Ant. 13, 322) heir—1. lit. (Appian, Bell. Civ. 3, 11 §36 υἱὸς καὶ κλ.) Mt 21: 38; Mk 12: 7; Lk 20: 14; Gal 4: 1; Hs 5, 2, 6.
2. fig., of the pers. who, as God's son, receives someth. as a possession fr. him (cf. also Hs 5, 2, 6).
a. of Christ ὃν ἔθηκεν κ. πάντων whom he (God) has appointed heir of all things Hb 1: 2.
b. of the believers; as τέκνα they are: κληρονόμοι, κληρονόμοι θεοῦ Ro 8: 17; cf. Gal 4: 7. More definitely κ. τῆς διαθήκης τοῦ κυρίου, where διαθήκη (q.v. 2) fluctuates betw. 'last will and testament' and 'decree' B 6: 19; 13: 6. κατ' ἐπαγγελίαν κληρονόμοι heirs according to the promise Gal 3: 29; cf. Hb 6: 17. κ. τῆς βασιλείας heirs of the kingdom Js 2: 5. ἵνα κληρονόμοι γενηθῶμεν κατ' ἐλπίδα ζωῆς αἰωνίου that we might become heirs in accordance w. the hope of eternal life Tit 3: 7. τῆς κατὰ πίστιν δικαιοσύνης ἐγένετο κ. he (Noah) became an heir of the righteousness that comes by faith Hb 11: 7 (on the gen. of the abstract noun cf. Demosth. 22, 34 κ. τῆς ἀτιμίας). Abraham and all those who are expecting the 'righteousness of faith' as he did, are κ. κόσμου, in contrast to those who depend on the law Ro 4: 13f (cf. Philo, Somn. 1, 175 τῶν τοῦ κόσμου κληρονόμον μερῶν). —On inheritance in Paul, esp. in Gal, cf. MConrat, ZNW 5, '04, 204-27; OEger, ibid. 18, '18, 84-108; WMCalder, JTS 31, '30, 372-4. M-M. B. 779.*

κλῆρος, ου, ὁ (Hom. +; inscr., pap., LXX, Philo, Joseph., Test. 12 Patr.; Sib. Or. 7, 139; loanw. in rabb.).
1. lot (i.e. pebble, small stick, etc.; Diod. S. 13, 34, 6 κλήρῳ=by lot) βάλλειν κ. (ἐπί τι) cast lots (for someth.) Mt 27: 35; Mk 15: 24; Lk 23: 34; J 19: 24; B 6: 6 (Ps 21: 19. The expr. as such is oft. found in LXX, also Jos., Ant. 6,

61; schol. on Soph., Antig. 275 p. 232 Papag.; IQS 6, 16-22). ἔπεσεν ὁ κ. ἐπί τινα the lot fell upon someone (Jon 1: 7) Ac 1: 26b. ἔδωκαν κλήρους αὐτοῖς they gave them (the candidates) lots vs. 26a. On this LSThornton, JTS 46, '45, 51-9. JLindblom, Vetus Test. 12, '62, 164-78 (OT background); WABeardslee, NovT 4, '60, 245-52 (Qumran).
2. that which is assigned by lot, portion, share (Pla.; Diod. S. 40, 3, 7 in connection with the distribution of the country conquered by the Jews; Wilcken, Chrest. I pp. 280-83; Jos., Bell. 2, 83) esp. what comes to someone by divine grace (Ael. Aristid. 30, 23 K.=10 p. 123 D.; Hierocles 4 p. 426 ἀθάνατος κλ.=the eternal portion bestowed by the gods; LXX) λαγχάνειν τὸν κ. τῆς διακονίας ταύτης Ac 1: 17; cf. vs. 25 v.l. λαβεῖν κ. ἐν τοῖς ἡγιασμένοις receive a place among those who are consecrated 26: 18 (cf. Wsd 5: 5 ἐν ἁγίοις ὁ κ. αὐτοῦ). μερίς and κλῆρος together (schol. on Apollon. Rhod. 1, 1082a; Dt 10: 9; 12: 12 al.; Is 57: 6) οὐκ ἔστιν σοι μερὶς οὐδὲ κ. ἐν τῷ λόγῳ τούτῳ you have neither part nor share in this matter 8: 21. μερὶς τοῦ κ. τῶν ἁγίων ἐν τῷ φωτί a share in the inheritance of the saints in light Col 1: 12 (cf. IQH 11, 11f). κ. Ἐφεσίων the class of the Ephesians IEph 11: 2.—1 Pt 5: 3 the κλῆροι seem to denote the 'flock' as a whole, i.e., the various parts of the congregation which have been assigned as 'portions' to the individual presbyters or shepherds (of the various portions that combine to form a whole, Simplicius in Epict. p. 71, 10. Here the κλῆροι of good and evil [acc. to the teaching of those who assume two original principles] are differentiated ἐξ ἀϊδίου [eternally]).
3. lot in the sense of fate, destiny esp. of martyrs τὸν ἴδιον κ. ἀπαρτίζειν fulfill one's own destiny MPol 6: 2; cf. ITr 12: 3; IRo 1: 2; IPhld 5: 1.—Pauly-W., art. Losung, XIII 2, '27, 1451-1504; WFoerster, TW III 757-63. M-M.*

κληρόω pf. pass. ptc. κεκληρωμένος; 1 aor. pass. ἐκληρώθην (Pind., Hdt.+; inscr., pap., LXX, Philo; Sib. Or. 5, 322).
1. act. appoint by lot (Diod. S. 15, 18, 3 κληρώσαντες) pass. be appointed by lot (Appian, Mithrid. 102 §471 τοὺς κληρονομένους=those chosen by lot) gener. ὡς ἕκαστος ἐκληρώθη as each one's lot is cast Dg 5: 4. W. relig. connotation ἐν ᾧ ἐκληρώθημεν in whom our lot is cast Eph 1: 11. Linguistically it is also poss. that εἰς τὸ εἶναι . . . vs. 12 is dependent on ἐκληρώθημεν, in which case the mng. would be be destined, chosen (cf. PIand. 27, 4 ἐκληρώθημεν εἰς γεωργίαν; BGU 625, 5 ἐκληρώθην εἰς τὰ βουκόλια).
2. mid. obtain by lot, also simply receive, have τὶ someth. (since Eur., Tro. 29; Herm. Wr. 16, 14; Philo, Mos. 2, 101 al.; Sb 7031, 23 [72 AD]; 7032, 22) ὁ κεκληρωμένος τὸ αὐτὸ ὄνομα who bore the same name MPol 6: 2. M-M.*

κλῆσις, εως, ἡ (Aristoph., X., Pla.; pap., LXX, Philo).
1. call, calling, invitation. In our lit. almost exclusively in a relig. sense (cf. a κλῆσις, ἣν κέκληκεν [ὁ θεός] in Epict. 1, 29, 49. Cf. Maximus Tyr. 11, 11a) of the divine call, of the invitation to enter the kgdm. of God κ. ἐπουράνιος a heavenly (=divine) call Hb 3: 1. ἡ κ. τοῦ θεοῦ the call that comes fr. God Ro 11: 29; Lk 11: 42 v.l. ἡ ἐλπὶς τῆς κ. αὐτοῦ (=τοῦ θεοῦ) the hope to which God calls Eph 1: 18. ἐλπὶς τ. κλήσεως ὑμῶν the hope that your calling brings you 4: 4. ἡ ἄνω κ. τοῦ θεοῦ ἐν Χριστῷ the upward call of God in Christ Phil 3: 14; cf. 1 Cl 46: 6. καλεῖν κλήσει ἁγίᾳ call with a holy calling 2 Ti 1: 9; cf. Eph 4: 1, 4; ἀξιοῦν τινα τῆς κ. 2 Th 1: 11 (s. 1b). ἡ κ.

τινος the call that has come to someone 2 Pt 1: 10. βλέπετε τὴν κ. ὑμῶν consider your call i.e., what happened when it occurred 1 Cor 1: 26. κ. τῆς ἐπαγγελίας the calling of (i.e. that consists in) his promise B 16: 9. Of baptism (cf. HKoch, Die Bussfrist des Pastor Hermae: Festgabe für AvHarnack '21, 175f) μετὰ τὴν κ. ἐκείνην τὴν μεγάλην καὶ σεμνήν after that great and sacred call Hm 4, 3, 6; cf. s 8, 11, 1.

2. station in life, position, vocation (Libanius, Argum. Orat. Demosth. 2 vol. VIII p. 601, 6F. τὴν τοῦ μαχαιροποιοῦ κλῆσιν ἔλαβεν='took up the occupation'; Progymn. 9, 2, 1 vol. VIII p. 290, 14 ἐν τῇ κλήσει ταύτῃ=in this characteristic, i.e., as Phrygians; Philo, Leg. ad Gai. 163 θεοῦ κλῆσις=the position of a god [is a thing so sacred to the Alexandrians that they even give animals a share in it]) ἕκαστος ἐν τῇ κ. ᾗ ἐκλήθη, ἐν ταύτῃ μενέτω everyone is to remain in the station in which he found himself when he was called 1 Cor 7: 20.—KHoll, D. Gesch. des Wortes Beruf: SAB '24, p. xxixff; ENorden, Antike Menschen im Ringen um ihre Berufsbestimmung: SAB '32, p. xxxviiiff).—WBieder, D. Berufung im NT '61; KLSchmidt, TW III 492–5. M-M.*

κλητός, ή, όν (Hom.; Aeschin. 2, 162; Aelian, Nat. An. 11, 12; PAmh. 79, 5; LXX) called, invited to a meal (3 Km 1: 41, 49; 3 Macc 5: 14) as a fig. for invitation to the kgdm. of God Mt 22: 14 (=B 4: 14); cf. 20: 16 t.r.—Also without the figure consciously in the background called to God's kgdm. κ. ἅγιοι saints who are called (by God) Ro 1: 7; 1 Cor 1: 2.Cf. B 4: 13.—Subst. (Sib. Or. 8, 92) κλητοὶ Ἰησοῦ Χριστοῦ called by Jesus Christ Ro 1: 6 (for the gen. cf. 3 Km 1: 49 οἱ κλητοὶ τοῦ Α.). κατὰ πρόθεσιν κ. ὄντες called in accordance w. (God's) purpose 8: 28. οἱ κλητοί those who are called 1 Cor 1: 24; Jd 1. οἱ μετ' αὐτοῦ κλητοὶ κ. ἐκλεκτοὶ κ. πιστοί Rv 17: 14. κ. ἡγιασμένοι ἐν θελήματι θεοῦ διὰ τοῦ κυρίου ἡμῶν Ἰ. Χρ. those who are called and consecrated acc. to the will of God through our Lord Jesus Christ 1 Cl inscr.—Of calling to an office: κ. ἀπόστολος called (by God) as an apostle Ro 1: 1; 1 Cor 1: 1.—KLSchmidt, TW III 495–7. M-M.*

κλίβανος, ου, ὁ (Ion. form [Hdt. 2, 92, also PPetr. III 140a, 3; BGU 1117, 10; 28; LXX; Philo, Rer. Div. Her. 311] for the Att. κρίβανος; cf. Phryn. 179 L.; Crönert 77, 4) an oven (made of pottery) εἰς κ. βάλλειν put into the furnace Mt 6: 30; Lk 12: 28. The Day of Judgment ὡς κ. καιόμενος like a burning oven (cf. Hos 7: 4) 2 Cl 16: 3. As v.l. for κλίνη Rv 2: 22. M-M. B. 340.*

κλίμα, ατος, τό (Aristot.+; BGU 1549, 7; 1550, 5 [III BC]; Judg 20: 2 A; Ep. Arist. On the accent cf. Bl-D. §13; 109, 3; Mlt.-H. 57; 354) district (Polyb. 5, 44, 6; 7, 6, 1; Dit., Or. 519, 18; Philo; Jos., Bell. 5, 506, Ant. 14, 401; Sib. Or. 5, 339) τὰ κ. τῆς Ἀχαΐας the region of Achaia, the province in its entirety 2 Cor 11: 10. τὰ κ. τῆς Συρίας καὶ τῆς Κιλικίας Gal 1: 21. ἐν τοῖς κ. τούτοις in these regions Ro 15: 23.—On νερτέρων ἀνεκδιήγητα κλίματα 1 Cl 20: 5 s. ἀνεκδιήγητος. M-M.*

κλῖμαξ, ακος, ἡ (Hom.+; inscr., pap., LXX, Philo; Jos., Vi. 396) ladder, flight of stairs GOxy 26.*

κλινάριον, ου, τό (Aristoph., fgm. 239; Epict. 3, 5, 13; M. Ant. 11, 18, 3; Artem. 2, 57 v.l.; PSI 616, 14; POxy. 1645, 9.—Bl-D. §111, 3) dim. of κλίνη bed (w. κράβαττος) Ac 5: 15. M-M.*

κλίνη, ης, ἡ (Eur., Hdt.+; inscr., pap., LXX, Ep. Arist. 320) bed, couch, a place for those who are resting (2 Km 4: 7; Ps 6: 7), suffering (Gen 48: 2; 49: 33), or dining

(Xenophanes 18, 2 Diehl²; Ezk 23: 41) Mk 4: 21; 7: 30; Lk 8: 16; 17: 34; dining couch Mk 7: 4 t.r. καθίσαι εἰς τὴν κ. sit on the bed Hv 5: 1.—Pallet, stretcher on which a sick man was carried (Appian, Bell. Civ. 1, 45 §199 ἔφυγεν ἐπὶ κλίνης διὰ νόσον; as a bier for the dead Pla., Leg. 12 p. 947B; Jos., Ant. 7, 40=2 Km 3: 31.—2 Ch 16: 14), prob. not differentiated fr. 'bed' Mt 9: 2, 6; Lk 5: 18 (φέρειν ἐπὶ κλίνης as Dit., Syll.³ 1169, 31; Jos., Ant. 17, 197). βάλλειν τινὰ εἰς κ. lay someone on a sickbed i.e. strike her w. an illness Rv 2: 22 (a lingering illness as a divine punishment: Diod. S. 16, 61, 3. Cf. also PUps. 8, 4 s.v. ξηραίνω 2b). M-M. B. 480.*

κλινίδιον, ου, τό (Dionys. Hal. 7, 68; Artem. 1, 2 p. 7, 22; M. Ant. 10, 28, 2; Plut., Mor. p. 466c, Coriol. 24, 5 p. 225B; Pollux 10, 7; Jos., Ant. 17, 161.—Bl-D. §111, 3; Mlt.-H. 346) dim. of κλίνη (q.v.) bed=pallet, stretcher Lk 5: 19, 24. M-M.*

κλίνω 1 aor. ἔκλινα; pf. κέκλικα; 1 aor. pass. ἐκλίθην (Bl-D. §76, 1; W-S. §13, 9f) (Hom.+; inscr., pap., LXX, Philo, Joseph., Test. 12 Patr.).

1. trans.—a. incline, bend, bow τὴν κεφαλήν the head of Jesus as he was dying J 19: 30 (but since the bowing of the head came before the giving up of his spirit, and since esp. in the Fourth Gosp. the Passion is a voluntary act of Jesus to the very last, the bowing must not be regarded as a sign of weakness; the Crucified One acted of his own accord. Cf. BGU 954, 5 κλίνω τ. κεφαλήν μου κατενώπιόν σου). τὸ πρόσωπον εἰς τὴν γῆν bow one's face to the ground Lk 24: 5.—b. lay (down) τὴν κεφαλήν (to sleep) Mt 8: 20; Lk 9: 58.

c. pass. lean, fall (over) λέγει κύριος (where?) ὅταν ξύλον κλιθῇ καὶ ἀναστῇ B 12: 1.—d. fig. cause to fall, turn to flight (as early as Hom.; Jos., Ant. 14, 416) παρεμβολὰς κ. ἀλλοτρίων Hb 11: 34.

2. intr. (Bl-D. §308; Rob. 800) decline, be far spent (X.+; PHib. 38, 8 [252/1 BC]) of the day Lk 9: 12; 24: 29 (cf. Apollon. Rhod. 1, 452 κλίνοντος ἠελίοιο; Polyb. 3, 93, 7; Arrian, Anab. 3, 4, 2; Jer 6: 4 κέκλικεν ἡ ἡμέρα). M-M.*

κλισία, ας, ἡ (Hom.+; Lucian, Dial. Deor. 24, 1; Plut., Sert. 26, 9 Ziegler v.l.; Dit., Syll.³ 1109, 74; 3 Macc 6: 31; Ep. Arist. 183; Jos., Ant. 12, 96) a group of people eating together κατακλίνατε αὐτοὺς κλισίας have them sit down in groups (to eat) Lk 9: 14. M-M.*

κλοπή, ῆς, ἡ (Aeschyl.+; inscr., pap., LXX, Philo; Jos., Ant. 18, 169) theft, stealing in list of vices (Jos., Bell. 2, 581) D 3: 5a. Pl. (Jos., Bell. 5, 402; Test. Reub. 3: 6) Mt 15: 19; Mk 7: 21; D 3: 5b; 5: 1. M-M.*

κλύδων, ωνος, ὁ (Hom.+; Sb 8026, 19; LXX; Jos., Bell. 3, 423, rarely in pl. [as Polyb. 10, 3, 3; Vett. Val. 344, 15; 4 Macc 15: 31]) rough water, (a succession of) waves κ. τοῦ ὕδατος Lk 8: 24; surf κ. θαλάσσης (Philo, Op. M. 58, Gig. 51; cf. Jon 1: 4, 11; Jos., Ant. 9, 210) Js 1: 6. M-M.*

κλυδωνίζομαι (Vett. Val. 354, 26; Aristaen., Ep. 1, 27 H.; Is 57: 20; Jos., Ant. 9, 239 ὁ δῆμος ἅπας ταρασσόμενος κ. κλυδωνιζόμενος; Sib. Or. 1, 289) be tossed here and there by waves fig. κλυδωνιζόμενοι καὶ περιφερόμενοι παντὶ ἀνέμῳ τ. διδασκαλίας Eph 4: 14. M-M.*

Κλωπᾶς, ᾶ, ὁ Clopas. Among the women who were standing at the cross of Jesus acc. to J 19: 25 there was a Μαρία ἡ Κλωπᾶ Mary, the wife of Clopas. This woman can scarcely be identical w. the sister of Jesus' mother who has just been mentioned (without being named), since then we should have to postulate two sisters w. the same name,

Mary (but s. Artem. 4, 30 p. 222, 3f, where we find a woman with her ἀδελφὴ ὁμώνυμος). Hegesippus mentions a Clopas as a brother of Joseph (in Euseb., H.E. 3, 11; 32, 1-4; 6; 4, 22, 4).—The name cannot be explained w. certainty, but is prob. Semit. (Palmyr. קלופא; Journ. Asiat. 10, 1897, 327). Cf. Κλεοπᾶς. M-M.*

κνήθω (Aristot.+='scratch'; acc. to Moeris p. 234 H. Gk., not Att. There is an older form κνάω which, as ἐπικνάω, is found as early as Il. 11, 639. The aor. mid. is found in Lucian, Bis Accusatus 1 οὐδ᾽ ὅσον κνήσασθαι τὸ οὖς σχολὴν διάγων=he does not even have enough time to scratch his ear) *itch* pass. *feel an itching* κνηθόμενοι τὴν ἀκοήν (s. ἀκοή 1c). Fig. of curiosity, that looks for interesting and spicy bits of information. This itching is relieved by the messages of the new teachers. W. the same concepts as a background, one might transl.: *to have one's ear tickled* (a κνῆσις ὤτων takes place τρυφῆς ἕνεκα: Plut., Mor. 167в) 2 Ti 4: 3 (s. Clement of Alex., Strom. I 3, 22, 5 p. 15 Stähl.). M-M.*

Κνίδος, ου, ἡ (Hom. Hymns, Hdt.+; Jos., Ant. 13, 370; 1 Macc 15: 23) *Cnidus*, a peninsula w. a city of the same name on the coast of Caria in Asia Minor, touched by Paul on his journey to Crete Ac 27: 7.*

κνῖσα, ης, ἡ (Hom.[κνίση]+; Philo, Somn. 1, 49 v.l. [for κνίσσα]) *the odor of burning fat* on a sacrifice Dg 2: 8; 3: 5 (used both times w. αἷμα).*

κοδράντης, ου, ὁ (Lat. loanw., 'quadrans'; also in rabb.; actually one quarter of an 'as'. Cf. Plut., Cic. 29, 5 τὸ λεπτότατον τοῦ χαλκοῦ νομίσματος κουαδράντην ἐκάλουν [the Romans]. For the spelling s. Bl-D. §41, 2) *quadrans, penny*=two λεπτά Mk 12: 42 (DSperber, Mk 12: 42 and its Metrological Background, NovT 9, '67, 178-90). Its value was approximately one quarter of a cent in normal times. ἕως ἂν ἀποδῷς τὸν ἔσχατον κ. *until you have paid the last cent* Mt 5: 26; Lk 12: 59 D; D 1: 5 (Sextus 39 μέχρις οὗ καὶ τ. ἔσχατον κοδράντην ἀπολάβῃ [the punishing demon]).—Lit. under ἀργύριον 2c. M-M.*

Κοδρᾶτος, ου, ὁ *Quadratus* (Epict. 3, 23, 23; Ael. Aristid. 47, 22 K.=23 p. 451 D.; Herodian; Dit., Or. 683, 5; Jos., Bell. 2, 241) MPol 21; s. Στάτιος.*

κοιλία, ας, ἡ (Hdt., Aristoph.+; inscr., pap., LXX, Philo; Jos., Ant. 3, 273; 19, 346; Test. 12 Patr.; loanw. in rabb.) *body-cavity, belly* (Gen 3: 14 w. στῆθος).
1. as an organ of nourishment: the digestive apparatus in its fullest extent (Jer 28: 34; Ezk 3: 3; Sir 36: 18 al.) εἰς τὴν κ. χωρεῖν (cf. Plut., Mor. 699ϝ εἴπερ εἰς κοιλίαν ἐχώρει διὰ στομάχου πᾶν τὸ πινόμενον. Even the last part of the alimentary canal is κ.: Herodian 1, 17, 10) Mt 15: 17; cf. Mk 7: 19. *Belly, stomach* (so Diod. S. 2, 58, 3 between φάρυγξ [gullet] and σπλάγχνα [intestines]; Aelian, V.H. 1, 1 al.) of Jonah's fish (Jon 2: 1f) Mt 12: 40. Of the human *stomach* 1 Cor 6: 13. γεμίσαι τὴν κ. ἐκ τινος *fill the stomach w. someth.* i.e., eat one's fill of someth. Lk 15: 16. Of the working of a scroll eaten by the writer of the Apoc. (cf. Ezk 3: 3) πικρανεῖ σου τὴν κ. Rv 10: 9; cf. vs. 10; δουλεύειν τῇ κ. *be a slave to one's stomach* Ro 16: 18; ὧν ὁ θεὸς ἡ κ. *whose god is their stomach* Phil 3: 19.
2. as an organ of reproduction, esp. *womb, uterus* (Epict. 2, 16, 43; 3, 22, 74; Dt 28: 4, 11; Job 1: 21; Ruth 1: 11) Lk 1: 41, 44; 2: 21; 11: 27; 23: 29; J 3: 4; B 13: 2 (Gen 25: 23). ἐκ κοιλίας *from birth* (Judg 16: 17 ms. A; Is 49: 1) Mt 19: 12; Lk 1: 15; Ac 3: 2; 14: 8; Gal 1: 15; καρπὸς τῆς κ. *fruit of the womb* (cf. Mi 6: 7; La 2: 20) Lk 1: 42.

3. κ. denotes the hidden, innermost recesses of the human body (Job 15: 35; Pr 18: 20; 20: 27, 30; Sir 19: 12; 51: 21), so that a variation betw. κοιλία and καρδία becomes poss. (Ac 2: 30 v.l.; Rv 10: 9; Hab 3: 16; Ps 39: 9. Cf. schol. on Nicander, Alexiph. 21 τοῦ στόματος τῆς κοιλίας, ἣν οἱ μὲν καρδίαν καλοῦσιν, οἱ δὲ δοχεῖον τῶν ἐντέρων τῆς βρώσεως [καρδία of the upper opening of the stomach: Theocr. 2, 49]; PGM 4, 3141: the κοιλία is the place where the καρδία is found). ποταμοὶ ἐκ τῆς κ. αὐτοῦ ῥεύσουσιν ὕδατος ζῶντος *rivers of living water shall flow from his heart* J 7: 38 (thought of as a scripture quot., though its source can no longer be determined w. certainty. The expr. may be proverbial; cf. the Cicero ref. below. The κ. has often been taken to be that of the believer, but there is an increasing tendency to punctuate w. a period after ἐμέ in vs. 38 rather than after πινέτω at the end of vs. 37 [s. RSV mg.] and understand κ. of Jesus; cf. Hdb. ad loc.; JoachJeremias, Golgotha '26, 80-4; HBornhäuser, Sukka '35, 34-9; Bultmann, Ev. d. Joh. '41, 228-30. For the patristic interpr., HRahner, Biblica 22, '41, 269-302; 367-403. Differently, A-MDubarle, Vivre et Penser 3, '43/'44, 238-41. Cf. Cicero, De Orat. 2, 39[162]; JBlenkinsopp, NTS 6, '59, 95-99; JBehm, TW III 788f. M-M. B. 253.*

κοιμάω 1 aor. pass. ἐκοιμήθην; 1 fut. κοιμηθήσομαι; pf. κεκοίμημαι (Hom.+; inscr., pap., LXX, En., Philo, Joseph.) in our lit. only in pass. *sleep, fall asleep.*
1. lit. (Hom.+ usu.; Diod. S. 15, 25, 2; PGM 36, 151; 305; Jos., Bell. 4, 306, Ant. 8, 28, Vi. 132; Test. 12 Patr., Sib. Or. 3, 794) Mt 28: 13; Lk 22: 45; J 11: 12; Ac 12: 6; Hv 2, 4, 1; s 9, 11, 3; 6. Fig. of the night (as of the sun: Pythag. in Gemin., Elem. Astr. p. 22ε) κοιμᾶται ἡ νὺξ *the night falls asleep* 1 Cl 24: 3.
2. fig. of the sleep of death, in which case additional words often emphasize the figurative nature of the expression (as early as Il. 11, 241; Dit., Or. 383, 43 [I вс]; IG Sic. It. 549, 1; 929, 13 κοιμᾶται τ. αἰώνιον ὕπνον). Yet the verb without these additions can have this mng. (Soph., Electra 509 Μυρτίλος ἐκοιμάθη; Aeschrio Lyr. [IV bc] 6, 2 Diehl², grave-epigram, ἐνταῦθα κεκοίμημαι; PFay. 22, 28 [I вc]; Gen 47: 30; Dt 31: 16; 3 Km 11: 43; Is 14: 8; 43: 17; 2 Macc 12: 45.—OMerlier, Bull. de corr. hell. 54, '30, 228-40; MBOgle, The Sleep of Death: Memoirs of the Amer. Acad. in Rome 11, '33, 81-117; JCBowmer, ET 53, '42, 355f [on 1 Cor 15: 20, 22]).
a. *fall asleep, die, pass away* J 11: 11; Ac 7: 60; 13: 36; 1 Cor 7: 39; 11: 30; 15: 6, 51; 2 Pt 3: 4; 1 Cl 44: 2; Hm 4, 4, 1. ἐκοιμήθην καὶ ὕπνωσα (Ps 3: 6) is interpr. to mean 'die' in 1 Cl 26: 2. ἐν δικαιοσύνῃ ἐκοιμήθησαν *they fell asleep as righteous men* Hs 9, 16, 7. κοιμηθείς *after my death* IRo 4: 2. οἱ διδάσκαλοι . . . κοιμηθέντες ἐν δυνάμει καὶ πίστει τ. υἱοῦ τ. θεοῦ *teachers who died in the power of the Son of God, and in faith in him* Hs 9, 16, 5. οἱ κοιμηθέντες *those who have already died* 1 Th 4: 14f. οἱ κ. ἐν Χριστῷ *those who died in communion w. Christ* 1 Cor 15: 18.
b. the pres. ptc. and perf. ptc. denoting a state of being, w. art., subst. *the one who has fallen asleep* οἱ κοιμώμενοι 1 Th 4: 13; GP 10: 41.—οἱ κεκοιμημένοι 1 Cor 15: 20; Hs 9, 16, 3. Not subst. οἱ κεκοιμημένοι ἅγιοι Mt 27: 52. οἱ μὲν κεκοιμημένοι, οἱ δὲ ἔτι ὄντες *some are dead, the others are still living* Hv 3, 5, 1. M-M. B. 269.*

κοίμησις, εως, ἡ *sleep*—1. lit. (Pla., Symp. 10 p. 183ᴀ) ἡ κ. τοῦ ὕπνου (epexeg. gen.) *the sleep of slumber* J 11: 13.
2. fig. *death* (Sir 46: 19; 48: 13; inscrs. on Jewish graves in Rome [ABerliner, Gesch. d. Juden in Rom I 1893, 72f;

Schürer II⁴ 441 ἐν εἰρήνῃ ἡ κοίμησις αὐτοῦ]; Sb 1540, 5; Fluchtaf. 4, 30; Pel.-Leg. p. 15, 16) Hv 3, 11, 3; s 9, 15, 6. M-M.*

κοινῇ s. κοινός 1c.

κοινός, ή, όν (Hes.+; inscr., pap., LXX) *common—* 1. *communal, common* (so secular wr., also LXX; Ep. Arist., Philo, Joseph., Sib. Or.).
a. adj. τράπεζα (Diod. S. 4, 74, 2) Dg 5: 7a. πίστις Tit 1: 4. σωτηρία (cf. Dit., Syll.³ 409, 33f [ca. 275 Bc]; X., An. 3, 2, 32; Diod. S. 37, 2, 5; Polyaenus 5, 31) Jd 3. κ. ἐλπίς IEph 21: 2; IPhld 5: 2; 11: 2. κ. ὄνομα (Philo, Abr. 7, Leg. ad Gai. 194) IEph 1: 2; εἶχον ἅπαντα κ. *they had everything in common* (κοινὰ πάντα ἔχειν: Strabo 7, 3, 9.—Diod. S. 5, 9, 4: the inhabitants of Lipara τὰς οὐσίας κοινὰς ποιησάμενοι καὶ ζῶντες κατὰ συσσίτια=they made their possessions common property and lived acc. to the custom of common meals; Iambl., Vi. Pyth. 30, 168 of the Pythagoreans: κοινὰ πᾶσι πάντα... ἦν, ἴδιον δὲ οὐδεὶς οὐδὲν ἐκέκτητο. Porphyr., Vi. Pyth. 20. The word occurs in a sim. context w. ref. to the Essenes: Philo, Prob. Lib. 85; 86; Jos., Ant. 18, 20, and the Therapeutae: Philo, Vi. Cont. 32; 40; HBraun, Qumran u. d. NT, I, '66, 43–50. Even Pla., Phaedr. 279c κοινὰ τὰ τῶν φίλων) Ac 2: 44; cf. 4: 32 (cf. IQS 6, 2).—PWSchmiedel, Die Gütergemeinschaft der ältesten Christenheit: PM 2, 1898, 367–78; EvDobschütz, Probleme des apost. Zeitalters '04, 39ff; JBehm, Kommunismus im Urchristentum: NKZ 31, '20, 275–97; KLake: Beginn. I 5, '33, 140–51; EHaenchen, Acts '56, 191–6 (lit.).—Of body and spirit ἀμφότερα κ. ἐστι *both are in communion=belong together, cannot be separated* Hs 5, 7, 4.
b. subst. τὸ κοινόν *what is (in) common* τὸ κ. τῆς ἐλπίδος *the common ground of hope* 1 Cl 51: 1.—τὸ κ. *the society, church* (t.t. to designate all those who belong to a given group: POxy. 53, 2 τὸ κ. τῶν τεκτόνων; 84, 3; Jos., Vi. 65) διακονία εἰς τὸ κ. *service for the church* IPhld 1: 1. Also the *common treasury* (Appian, Iber. 8, §31 τὸ κ.=the state treasury) of slaves ἐλευθεροῦσθαι ἀπὸ τοῦ κ. *to be freed at the expense of the church treasury* IPol 4: 3 (cf. X., An. 4, 7, 27; 5, 1, 12 ἀπὸ κοινοῦ='at state expense'; Jos., Vi. 297 ἐκ τοῦ κ. 298).
c. adv. κοινῇ *together, collectively* (Soph., Thu.+; inscr., PMagd. 29, 2; LXX; Jos., C. Ap. 1, 70; 2, 166) IEph 20: 2; ISm 12: 2 (both in contrast to κατ' ἄνδρα ['man for man', 'individually'], as Dit., Syll.³ 1073, 18); 7: 2 (opp. κατ' ἰδίαν, as Diod. S. 11, 24, 4; Dio Chrys. 34[51], 9; Dit., Syll.³ 630, 15; 2 Macc 9: 26). τὸ κοινῇ συμφέρον *the common good* B 4: 10.
2. *of that which comes into contact w. anything and everything, and is therefore common, ordinary, profane* (cf. Alcman [VII Bc], fgm. 49 D.² τὰ κοινά of that which ordinary people eat, in contrast to those of more refined tastes; Plut., Eroticus 4 p. 751B καλὸν γὰρ ἡ φιλία καὶ ἀστεῖον, ἡ δὲ ἡδονὴ κοινὸν καὶ ἀνελεύθερον [Ltzm., Hdb. on Ro 14: 14]. Then 1 Macc 1: 47, 62; Ep. Arist. 315=Jos., Ant. 12, 112 κοινοὶ ἄνθρωποι; 13, 4). εἰκαιότης *silliness* Dg 4: 6. Of that which is ceremonially impure Rv 21: 27. χεῖρες (ceremon.) *impure* Mk 7: 2, 5 (MSmith, Tannaitic Parall. to the Gosp. '51, 31f); οὐδὲν κ. δι' ἑαυτοῦ *nothing is unclean of itself* Ro 14: 14a; cf. b, c. κ. ἡγεῖσθαί τι *consider someth. unclean* Hb 10: 29. οὐδέποτε ἔφαγον πᾶν κ. καὶ ἀκάθαρτον *I have never eaten anything common or unclean* (1 Macc 1: 62) Ac 10: 14; cf. vs. 28; 11: 8.—Dg 5: 7b (see κοίτη 1b).—FHauck, TW III 789–810: κοινός and related words. M-M. B. 1365.*

κοινόω 1 aor. ἐκοίνωσα; pf. κεκοίνωκα, pass. ptc. κεκοι-

νωμένος (Pind., Thu.+ in the sense of κοινός 1; Jos., Ant. 5, 267; 18, 231). In our lit. only in the sense of κοινός 2.
1. *make common* or *impure, defile* in the ceremonial sense (4 Macc 7: 6. Cf. Malalas 277, 2 LDind. [1831] κοινώσας τὰ ὕδατα).
a. τινά *someone* Mt 15: 11, 18, 20; Mk 7: 15, 18, 20, 23. Pf. pass. ptc. w. the art., subst. οἱ κεκοινωμένοι *those who are ceremonially unclean* Hb 9: 13.
b. τι *someth.* the temple *profane, desecrate* Ac 21: 28. Pass., of a sacrifice *become defiled* D 14: 2.—c. abs. Rv 21: 27 t.r.
2. *consider* or *declare* (ceremonially) *unclean* Ac 10: 15; 11: 9. M-M.*

Κόϊντος, ου, ὁ (Diod. S. 11, 27, 1 of a contemporary of the battle of Salamis [480 Bc]; Plut. et al.; Dit., Syll.² 588, 34; ³1127, 3, Or. 684, 1; pap. [Preisigke, Namenbuch]; 2 Macc 11: 34; Jos., Ant. 14, 219) *Quintus*, a Christian in Smyrna MPol 4.*

κοινωνέω fut. κοινωνήσω; 1 aor. ἐκοινώνησα; pf. κεκοινώνηκα (Aeschyl.+; inscr., pap., LXX; En. 11, 2).
1. *share, have a share—*a. τινός *in someth.* (X., Rep. Lac. 1, 9, Mem. 2, 6, 23; Pla., Leg. 12 p. 947A; Diod. S. 5, 49, 6 τοὺς τῶν μυστηρίων κοινωνήσαντας=those who participated in, i.e., were initiated into, the mysteries; 5, 68, 3 τῆς τροφῆς ταύτης; 15, 68, 1; 19, 4, 3; Herodian 3, 10, 8; inscr. [Kl. T. 121 no. 32, 41]; pap.; Pr 1: 11; 3 Macc 2: 31; Philo, Post. Cai. 160 al.; Jos., Ant. 4, 75, C. Ap. 2, 174.—Bl-D. §169, 1; Rob. 509f) of human beings αἵματος καὶ σαρκός *share in flesh and blood* Hb 2: 14 (inscr. fr. Commagene in KHumann u. OPuchstein, Reisen in Kleinasien u. Nordsyrien, Textband 1890 p. 371 [I Bc] πᾶσιν ὅσοι φύσεως κοινωνοῦντες ἀνθρωπίνης).
b. τινί *in someth.* (Demosth., Prooem. 25, 2 [bracketed by Blass]; Plut., Arat. 8, 3; but Wsd 6: 23 'associate with'; s. JYCampbell, JBL 51, '32, 359).
α. τοῖς πνευματικοῖς *in spiritual blessings* Ro 15: 27. τοῖς τοῦ Χριστοῦ παθήμασιν 1 Pt 4: 13 (cf. Achilles Tat. 7, 2, 3 εἰς τὸ παθεῖν κοινωνία='fellowship in suffering'). Of a martyr's body: *receive a part of* i.e. a part of the body as a 'relic' κ. τῷ ἁγίῳ σαρκίῳ MPol 17: 1.
β. To *share, participate* in the deeds of others means to be equally responsible for them ἁμαρτίαις ἀλλοτρίαις 1 Ti 5: 22 (Artem. 3, 51 κ. τῶν ἁμαρτημάτων ἐκείνῳ). τοῖς ἔργοις αὐτοῦ τ. πονηροῖς 2 J 11.
γ. Participation in someth. can reach such a degree that one claims a part in it for oneself *take an interest in, share* (Philostrat., Vi. Apoll. 5, 25; Pr 1: 11) ταῖς χρείαις τῶν ἁγίων Ro 12: 13. The transition to the next mng. is easy.
2. *give* or *contribute a share* (Philo, Spec. Leg. 2, 107) w. dat. of the pers. (cf. Demosth. 25, 61; Appian, Bell. Civ. 1, 31 §139; Artem. 5 p. 252, 14; Sextus 350; Jos., C. Ap. 2, 258) foll. by ἔν τινι *give someone a share of someth.* Gal 6: 6. κοινωνήσεις ἐν πᾶσιν τῷ πλησίον σου B 19: 8. Also τινί εἴς τι (cf. Pla., Rep. 5 p. 453A; PLond. 1794, 7; Test. Zeb. 3: 1) οὐδεμία μοι ἐκκλησία ἐκοινώνησεν εἰς no church made me its partner in Phil 4: 15.
3. Ms. D uses κ. Mt 15: 11 (twice), 18, 20 in the sense of κοινόω 1a (so Diod. S. 5, 33, 5 κ.=partake [in uncleanness]). M-M.*

κοινωνία, ας, ἡ (Pind.+; inscr., pap., LXX, Philo [Mos. 1, 158 of communion w. God]; Joseph.; loanw. in rabb.).
1. *association, communion, fellowship, close relationship* (hence a favorite expr. for the marital relationship as the most intimate betw. human beings Isocr. 3, 40; BGU 1051, 9 [I AD]; 1052, 7; POxy. 1473, 33; 3 Macc 4: 6; Jos., Ant. 1, 304. But s. also Diod. S. 10, 8, 2 ἡ τοῦ βίου κ.=the

common type or bond of life that unites the Pythagoreans) τινός *with* or *to someone* (Amphis Com. [IV BC] 20, 3; Herodian 1, 10, 1); so it is linguistically poss. to transl.: κ. τοῦ υἱοῦ αὐτοῦ *fellowship with his Son* 1 Cor 1: 9 (s. 4 below) and κ. τοῦ ἁγίου πνεύματος *fellowship w. the Holy Spirit* 2 Cor 13: 13 (so Sickenberger in the Trinitarian sense). Others take the latter gen. as a subjective gen. or gen. of quality *fellowship brought about by the* Holy Spirit (Heinrici, Bachmann, Bousset; TSchmidt, D. Leib Christi '19, 135; s. 4 below). Corresp. κ. πνεύματος *fellowship w. the Spirit* Phil 2: 1 (Synes., Prov. 1, 15 p. 108c κ. γνώμης=community of will and s. 2 below).—κοινωνία(ν ἔχειν) μετά τινος (*have) fellowship w. someone* (cf. Job 34: 8) w. God 1 J 1: 3b, 6 (cf. Epict. 2, 19, 27 περὶ τῆς πρὸς τὸν Δία κοινωνίας βουλευόμενον; Jos., Bell. 7, 264, C. Ap. 1, 35 [both πρὸς w. acc.]); w. the Christian brethren vss. 3a, 7. εἴς τι (POxford [ed EPWegener '42] 5f) ἡ κ. εἰς τὸ εὐαγγέλιον *close relationship w. the gospel* Phil 1: 5. ηὐδόκησαν κ. τινὰ ποιήσασθαι εἰς τοὺς πτωχούς *they have undertaken to establish a rather close relation w. the poor* Ro 15: 26 (but s. 3 below).—κ. πρός w. acc. *connection with, relation to* (Pla., Symp. 188c; Galen, Protr. 9 p. 28, 7 J.; Dit., Syll.³ 646, 54 [170 BC]; Philo, Leg. ad Gai. 110 τίς οἰκείων πρὸς Ἀπόλλωνα τῷ μηδὲν οἰκεῖον ἐπιτετηδευκότι; cf. Jos., C. Ap. 2, 208) τίς κ. φωτὶ πρὸς σκότος; *what does darkness have in common with light?* 2 Cor 6: 14 (Aristoph., Thes. 140 τίς κατόπτρου καὶ ξίφους κοινωνία;).—Abs. *fellowship*, (brotherly) *unity* Ac 2: 42 (cf. JAFitzmyer, PSchubert-Festschr. '66, 242-44 [Acts-Qumran] suggests that 'community of goods' [יחד] may be meant here, as IQS 1, 11-13; 6, 17. On the problem of this term s. HBraun, Qumran u. d. NT, I, '66; 143-50; s. also ACarr, The Fellowship of Ac 2: 42 and Cognate Words: Exp. 8th Ser. V '13, 458ff). δεξιὰς κοινωνίας διδόναι τινί *give someone the right hand of fellowship* Gal 2: 9.—κ. also has the concrete mng. *society, brotherhood* as a closely knit majority, naturally belonging together; Maximus Tyr. 15, 4b τί ἐστιν τὸ τῆς κοινωνίας συμβόλαιον; what is the contribution (i.e., of the philosopher) to the community or (human) society? 16, 2m δημώδεις κοινωνίαι= meetings of the common people.

2. *generosity, fellow-feeling, altruism* (Epict. in Stob. 43 Sch. χρηστότητι κοινωνίας; Arrian, Anab. 7, 11, 9 κ. beside ὁμόνοια; Herm. Wr. 13, 9 [opp. πλεονεξία]) ἁπλότης τῆς κ. εἴς τινα 2 Cor 9: 13. W. εὐποιΐα Hb 13: 16. The context permits this mng. also Phil 2: 1 (s. 1 above). The transition to the next sense is easy.

3. abstr. for concr. *sign of fellowship, proof of brotherly unity*, even *gift, contribution* (Lev 5: 21; inscr., of Asia Minor: κ.='subsidy' [Rdm.² 10]) Ro 15: 26 (s. 1 above). Under this head we may perh. classify κοινωνία τ. αἵματος (σώματος) τοῦ Χριστοῦ *a means for attaining a close relationship with the blood (body) of Christ* 1 Cor 10: 16a, b (s. 4 below).

4. *participation, sharing* τινός in someth. (Appian, Bell. Civ. 1, 67 §306 κ. τῶν παρόντων=in the present undertakings; 5, 71 §299 κ. τῆς ἀρχῆς in the rule; Polyaenus 6, 7, 2 κ. τοῦ μιάσματος in the foul deed; Maximus Tyr. 19, 3b τῆς ἀρετῆς; Synes., Kgdm. 13 p. 12c. κ. τῶν ἔργων=in the deeds of others; Wsd 8: 18; Jos., Ant. 2, 62) ὅπως ἡ κ. τῆς πίστεώς σου ἐνεργὴς γένηται *that your participation in the faith may be made known through your deeds* Phlm 6. γνῶναι κοινωνίαν παθημάτων αὐτοῦ *become aware of sharing his sufferings* Phil 3: 10. ἡ κ. τῆς διακονίας τῆς εἰς τοὺς ἁγίους *taking part in the relief of the saints* 2 Cor 8: 4. Perh. this is the place for 1 Cor 1: 9 (s. 1 above); 2 Cor 13: 13 (*participation*

in the Holy Spirit: Ltzm., Kümmel, Windisch, Seesemann [s. below] 70; Gdspd., Probs. 169f;—s. 1 above); 1 Cor 10: 16 (*participation in the blood [body] of Christ*. So recently ASchlatter, Pls der Bote Jesu '34, 295f; s. 3 above. But perh. here κοινωνία w. gen. means *the common possession* or *enjoyment of someth*. [Diod. S. 8, 5, 1 ἀγελῶν κ. = of the flocks; Maximus Tyr. 19, 3b ἐπὶ κοινωνίᾳ τῆς ἀρετῆς= for the common possession of excellence; Diog. L. 7, 124; Synes., Kgdm. 20 p. 24B; Hierocles 6 p. 428: we are to choose the best man as friend and unite ourselves with him πρὸς τὴν τῶν ἀρετῶν κοινωνίαν=for the common possession or enjoyment of the virtues; 7 p. 429 τῶν καλῶν τὴν κ.]. Then 1 Cor 10: 16 would be: Do not the cup and the bread mean the common partaking of the body and blood of Christ? After all, we all partake of one and the same bread).—JYCampbell, Κοινωνία and its Cognates in the NT: JBL 51, '32, 352-80; EPGroenewald, Κοινωνία (gemeenskap) bij Pls, Diss. Amst. '32; HSeesemann, D. Begriff Κοινωνία im NT '33; PJTEndenburg, Koinoonia . . . bij de Grieken in den klass. tijd '37; HWFord, The NT Conception of Fellowship: Shane Quarterly 6, '45, 188-215; GVJourdan, Κοινωνία in 1 Cor 10: 16: JBL 67, '48, 111-24; KFNickle, The Collection, A Study in Paul's Strategy, '66. M-M.*

κοινωνικός, ή, όν (since Ps.-Pla., Def., and Aristot.; Vett. Val., pap., Philo; Jos., Bell. 2, 122) *giving* or *sharing* what is one's own, *liberal, generous* (Aristot., Rhet. 2, 24, 2 p. 1401a, 20; Polyb. 2, 44, 1; Lucian, Tim. 56 ἀνὴρ τῶν ὄντων κοινωνικός; Iambl., Protr. 21, 19 and 30 p. 117, 8; 123, 6 Pistelli) w. εὐμετάδοτος 1 Ti 6: 18. M-M.*

κοινωνός, οῦ, ὁ and ἡ (trag.+; inscr., pap., LXX, Philo, Joseph.) *companion, partner, sharer*.

1. *one who takes part in someth. with someone*—a. *with someone*, expressed
α. by the dat. (Philo, Spec. Leg. 1, 131 θεῷ τινος ['in someth.']; Jos., Ant. 8, 239 σοί τινος; Himerius, Or. 48 [=Or. 14], 15 κ. ἐκείνοις τῆς γνώμης=with those men [the seven wise men] in knowledge) ἦσαν κοινωνοὶ τῷ Σίμωνι (who) *were partners* (in business) *with Simon* Lk 5: 10 (cf. PAmh. 100, 4: Hermes the fisherman takes Cornelius as his κ.='partner'; ὁ κ.=partner Diod. S. 8, 5, 3; BGU 1123, 4).
β. by the gen. (Pr 28: 24; Is 1: 23; Mal 2: 14) κ. τῶν οὕτως ἀναστρεφομένων γενηθέντες Hb 10: 33. Of a martyr (who shares a bloody death w. Christ) Χριστοῦ MPol 6: 2; cf. 17: 3. κ. τῶν δαιμονίων *be a partner w. the demons* (in the sacrifices offered to them) 1 Cor 10: 20 (HGressmann, Ἡ κοινωνία τῶν δαιμονίων: ZNW 20, '21, 224-30; Clemen² 182-8).
γ. by μετά and gen. μετὰ τοῦ πνεύματος κ. Hs 5, 6, 6.
b. *in someth.*, expressed—a. by the gen. of the thing (Diod. S. 14, 61, 5; Epict. 3, 22, 63 κ. τῆς βασιλείας [of the Cynic]; Plut., Mor. 45E; 819c, Brut. 13, 5; Aelian, V.H. 2, 24; Appian, Samn. 10 §12 τ. ἀγαθῶν; Maximus Tyr. 31, 5c; Sir 6: 10; Esth 8: 12n; Jos., Vi. 142, Ant. 4, 177 κ. τῆς ταλαιπωρίας). κ. τοῦ θυσιαστηρίου 1 Cor 10: 18 (Pla., Ep. 7 p. 350c κοινωνὸς ἱερῶν; Philo, Spec. Leg. 1, 221 κοινωνὸν τοῦ βωμοῦ). τῶν παθημάτων (Diod. S. 4, 20, 2 τῶν κακοπαθειῶν κ.), τῆς παρακλήσεως 2 Cor 1: 7. ὁ τῆς μελλούσης ἀποκαλύπτεσθαι δόξης κ. 1 Pt 5: 1. θείας φύσεως 2 Pt 1: 4 (cf. the inscr. fr. Commagene under κοινωνέω 1a). τῆς μοιχείας a partner in adultery Hm 4, 1, 5 (Socrat., Ep. 7, 1 κοι. τ. ἀδικήματος; Polyaenus 2, 14, 1 κ. τῆς ἐπαναστάσεως in the uprising). ἀμφότεροι κοινωνοὶ τοῦ ἔργου τ. δικαίου Hs 2: 9 (Pla., Ep. 7 p. 325A ἀνοσίων αὐτοῖς ἔργων κοι.).

β. by ἐν: D 4: 8. ἐν τῷ ἀφθάρτῳ κ. *in what is imperishable* B 19: 8.—c. *with someone in someth.* αὐτῶν κ. ἐν τῷ αἵματι τῶν προφητῶν Mt 23: 30.

d. abs. (4 Km 17: 11) κ. ἐμὸς καὶ συνεργός 2 Cor 8: 23 (for the combination of κ. and συνεργός cf. the first two Plut.-pass. given under ba). ἔχειν τινὰ κοινωνόν *consider someone a partner* Phlm 17 (cf. Diod. S. 18, 53, 6 ἔσχε κοινωνοὺς τ. αὐτῶν ἐλπίδων).

2. *one who permits someone else to share in someth.* τινί τινος: τῶν ἀποκαλυφθέντων ἡμῖν γινόμεθα ὑμῖν κοινωνοί *we let you share in what has been revealed to us* Dg 11: 8.—The concrete mng. 'member' (Idomeneus Hist. [III BC] no. 338 fgm. 8 Jac. κ. τῆς προαιρέσεως='member of the party') does not seem to be found in our lit. M-M.*

κοινῶς adv. (Eur.+) *in the common language* or *dialect* (Apollon. Dysc., Pron. 82, 27 al.) Mk 3: 17 W et al.*

κοινωφελής, ές (Epict. 4, 10, 12; M. Ant. 1, 16, 4; 3, 4, 1; 4, 12, 2; POxy. 1409, 19 [III AD]; Philo, De Jos. 34; 73, Mos. 2, 9; 28, Spec. Leg. 4, 157; 170 al.) *generally useful* ζητεῖν τὸ κ. πᾶσιν *seek the common good of all* 1 Cl 48: 6.*

κοίτη, ης, ἡ (Hom.+; inscr., pap., LXX, Joseph., Sib. Or., Test. 12 Patr.; loanw. in rabb.).

1. *bed*—a. gener. (Cass. Dio 61, 13, 5; Herm. Wr. 1, 29; 2 Km 4: 5; Jos., Ant. 6, 52 κοίτης ὥρα) εἰς τὴν κ. εἶναι *be in bed* Lk 11: 7 (Jos., Ant. 1, 177 τ. ἐν ταῖς κοίταις ὄντας).

b. esp. (trag.+; Sib. Or. 4, 33) *marriage-bed* (w. γάμος) Hb 13: 4 (on the 'defiling' of the marriage-bed by adultery cf. Ps.-Plut., Fluv. 8, 3 and Jos., Ant. 2, 55 τ. κοίτην μιαίνειν; Artem. 2, 26; Synes., Dreams 11 p. 143в κοίτην ἀμόλυντον; Gen 49: 4; Test. Reub. 1: 6). Dg 5: 7 emend.

2. euphem. for—a. *sexual intercourse* (Eur., Med. 152, Alc. 249; Lev 15: 21-6; Wsd 3: 13, 16) pl. (w. ἀσέλγειαι) *sexual excesses* Ro 13: 13.

b. *seminal emission* (Num 5: 20 ἔδωκέν τις τὴν κοίτην αὐτοῦ ἐν σοί. In full κοίτη σπέρματος: Lev 15: 16f, 32; 18: 20; 22: 4) κοίτην ἔχειν ἐξ ἑνός *conceive children by one man* Ro 9: 10. M-M. B. 480.*

κοιτών, ῶνος, ὁ (this word, rejected by the Atticists [Phryn. p. 252 L.], in Diod. S. 11, 69, 2; Epict. et al.; inscr., pap., LXX; Jos., Vi. 382; Test. Reub. 3, 13; loanw. in rabb.) *bedroom*; as a title: ὁ ἐπὶ τοῦ κοιτῶνος *the one in charge of the bed-chamber, the chamberlain* (Epict. 4, 7, 1; Dit., Or. 256, 5 [c. 130 BC] ἐπὶ τ. κοιτῶνος τῆς βασιλίσσης. Other exx. in Magie 73) Ac 12: 20. M-M.*

κοκκάριον, ου, τό (Rufus [II AD] in Oribasius 8, 47, 11) dim. of κόκκος, *little grain* of a hailstone Hm 11: 20.*

κόκκινος, η, ον (Herodas 6, 19; Martial 2, 39; Plut., Fab. 15, 1; Epict.; PHamb. 10, 24; PLond. 191, 5; 193, 22; LXX, Philo; Jos., Ant. 8, 72 v.l.) *red, scarlet* χλαμὺς κ. *a red cloak* of the 'sagum purpureum (paludamentum)' of Roman soldiers Mt 27: 28; ἔριον κ. Hb 9: 19; B 7: 8ff; 8: 1. As the color of an apocalyptic beast or its covering Rv 17: 3.—τὸ κ. *scarlet cloth, a scarlet garment* (Epict. 3, 22, 10 ἐν κοκκίνοις περιπατεῖν; 4, 11, 34; 2 Km 1: 24.—Gen 38: 28; Ex 25: 4; Josh 2: 18; 2 Ch 2: 13) ἡ γυνὴ ἦν περιβεβλημένη πορφυροῦν κ. κόκκινον Rv 17: 4; cf. 18: 16 (on the comb. πορφ. κ. κόκκ. cf. PTebt. 405, 5; Ex 39: 12; 2 Ch 2: 6), vs. 12; (opp. ἔριον 'white wool') 1 Cl 8: 4 (Is 1: 18); *scarlet cord* 12: 7.—Eva Wunderlich, Die Bed. der roten Farbe im Kultus der Griechen u. Römer '25; RGradwohl, D. Farben im AT, Beih. ZAW 83, '63, 73-8; OMichel, TW III 812-15. M-M. B. 1056.*

κόκκος, ου, ὁ (Hom. Hymns, Hdt.+; Dit., Syll.³ 1173, 12; PGM 7, 638) *seed, grain*

1. of various plants: mustard Mt 13: 31; 17: 20; Mk 4: 31; Lk 13: 19; 17: 6; of wheat, etc. (Favorinus [beg. II AD] in Diog. L. 6, 88) J 12: 24 (Ocellus [II BC] c. 16 H.: the ἀνάλυσις of the fruit makes the seed free. Cf. Philo, Aet. M. 94ff); 1 Cor 15: 37 (HRiesenfeld, TU 77, '61, 43-55).

2. of the *scarlet 'berry'*, the female of a scale insect (similar to the cochineal) which clings to the leaves of an oak tree; the dried bodies of these insects, known as kermes, were used by the ancients to prepare a purplishred dye (s. Theophr., H. Plant. 3, 7, 3; 3, 16, 1), hence also *scarlet, scarlet dye* (Dromo in Athen. 6 p. 240D; PHolm. 22, 1; Sir 45: 10; Jos., Bell. 6, 390) 1 Cl 8: 3 (quot. of unknown orig.).—OMichel, TW III 810-12. M-M.*

κοκκύζω (Hes.+) *crow* of a cock (Cratinus+; Plato Com. [V/IV BC] 209 p. 659 K.; Hyperid., fgm. 239) gospel fragment fr. Fayum (Kl. T. 8³, p. 23, 10; cf. Mk 14: 30.).*

κολαβρίζω 1 aor. pass. ἐκολαβρίσθην (Hesychius) *mock, ridicule* (Suidas) 1 Cl 39: 9 (Job 5: 4).*

κολάζω fut. κολάσω; 1 aor. mid. ἐκολασάμην; 1 fut. pass. κολασθήσομαι *punish* (so trag., Pla.+; Dit., Or. 90, 28; PSI 446, 14; BGU 341, 14; PRyl. 62, 9; LXX; Ep. Arist. 208; Philo; Jos., Ant. 3, 317, Vi. 133; Test. 12 Patr.) act. τινά *someone* lit., of the punishment of slaves Hs 9, 28, 8. Fig.=*do someone an injury* Dg 2: 8. In hell there are οἱ κολάζοντες ἄγγελοι AP 6: 21b (Charito 4, 2, 7 οἱ κολάζοντες='constables, police'; Sallust. 19 p. 34, 25 δαίμονες κολάζοντες).—Mid. (Aristoph., Vesp. 405; Pla., Protag. 324c; 3 Macc 7: 3) Ac 4: 21.—Mostly pass. of the punishment of Christians 1 Pt 2: 20 𝔓⁷² et al.; Dg 5: 16; 6: 7; 8; 10: 7; MPol 2: 4. Of the Last Judgment 2 Pt 2: 9. βασάνοις 2 Cl 17: 7 (on the dat., cf. Appian, Bell. Civ. 2, 90 §377 κ. θανάτῳ; Polyaenus 3, 9, 56; Lucian, Dial. Mort. 17, 2; Jos., Ant. 18, 314 κ. πληγαῖς). δισσῶς *be punished doubly* Hs 9, 18, 2. Of hell οἱ κολαζόμενοι ἐκεῖ AP 6: 21a. (Of punishment by God: Diod. S. 16, 32, 1; Epict. 3, 11, 3; Dio Chrys. 59[76], 5; Aesop, Fab. 77 P.=127 H. ὑπὸ θεῶν κολάζονται; oft. in inscr. in FSteinleitner, D. Beicht '13, p. 10ff; LRobert, Nouvelles Inscriptions de Sardes, '64, 24ff; LXX; Jos., Bell. 2, 163). M-M.*

κολακεία, ας, ἡ (Pla.+; Philod. [Περὶ κολακείας: RhM n. F. 56, '01, 623]; Dit., Syll.³ 889, 30 κολακεία; PLond. 1727, 24; Philo; Jos., Bell. 4, 231, Ant. 16, 301. On the spelling cf. Bl-D. §23; Mlt.-H. 339) *flattery* λόγος κολακείας *flattering words* 1 Th 2: 5. M-M.*

κολακεύω fut. κολακεύσω; 1 aor. ἐκολάκευσα (Aristoph., Pla.+; PSI 586, 4; LXX; Philo; Jos., Bell. 2, 213, Vi. 367) *flatter*. In our lit. only in Ign., and here in a good sense, someth. like *entice, deal graciously with*, w. acc. (Philo, Spec. Leg. 1, 60) τὰ θηρία (Vi. Aesopi W c. 49 κολακεύω τὴν κύνα=stroke the dog) IRo 4: 2; 5: 2. τὰ φαινόμενά σου εἰς πρόσωπον *the things that appear before your face* IPol 2: 2.—IRo 6: 2 v.l. Funk.*

κόλασις, εως, ἡ *punishment* (so Hippocr.+; Diod. S. 1, 77, 9; 4, 44, 3; Aelian, V.H. 7, 15; Dit., Syll.² 680, 13; LXX; Philo, Leg. ad Gai. 7, Mos. 1, 96; Jos., Ant. 17, 164; Sib. Or. 5, 388).

1. lit. κ. ὑπομένειν *undergo punishment* GOxy 6; δειναί κ. (4 Macc 8: 9) MPol 2: 4; ἡ ἐπίμονος κ. *long-continued torture* ibid. κακαὶ κ. τοῦ διαβόλου IRo 5: 3. Of the martyrdom of Jesus PK 4 p. 15, 34. The smelling of the

odor arising fr. sacrifices ironically described as *punishment, injury* (s. κολάζω) Dg 2: 9.

2. of divine retribution (Diod. S. 3, 61, 5; 16, 61, 1; Epict. 3, 11, 1; Dio Chrys. 80[30], 12; 2 Macc 4: 38 al. in LXX; Philo, Spec. Leg. 1, 55; 2, 196; Jos., Ant. 1, 60 al.): w. αἰκισμός 1 Cl 11: 1. Of eternal damnation (w. θάνατος) Dg 9: 2 (Diod. S. 8, 15, 1 κ. ἀθάνατος). Of hell: τόπος κολάσεως AP 6: 21 (Simplicius in Epict. p. 13, 1 εἰς ἐκεῖνον τὸν τόπον αἱ κολάσεως δεόμεναι ψυχαὶ καταπέμπονται. ἀπέρχεσθαι εἰς κ. αἰώνιον go away into eternal punishment Mt 25: 46; MPol 11: 2 (κ. αἰ. as Test. Reub. 5: 5, Ash. 7: 5; Celsus 8, 48). ῥύεσθαι ἐκ τῆς αἰωνίου κ. rescue fr. eternal punishment 2 Cl 6: 7. τὴν αἰώνιον κ. ἐξαγοράζεσθαι buy one's freedom fr. eternal pun. MPol 2: 3. κακαὶ κ. τοῦ διαβόλου IRo 5: 3. κ. τινος punishment for someth. (Ezk 14: 3, 4, 7; 18: 30; Philo, Fuga 65 ἁμαρτημάτων κ.) ἔχειν κόλασίν τινα τῆς πονηρίας αὐτοῦ Hs 9, 18, 1. ὁ φόβος κόλασιν ἔχει fear has to do with punishment 1 J 4: 18 (cf. Philo, In Flacc. 96 φόβος κολάσεως). M-M.*

Κολασσαεύς (Κολοσσαεύς, Κολοσαεύς, Κολασαεύς), έως, ὁ *a Colossian* (s. Κολοσσαί). Only as v.l. (but as early as 𝔓⁴⁶) in the title of Col.—Bl-D. §42, 3 app.; Mlt.-H. 73; 350.*

Κολασσαί s. Κολοσσαί.

κολαφίζω 1 aor. ἐκολάφισα (non-Attic, vernacular word; s. Lobeck, Phryn. 175; Mlt.-H. 364; 407. Found almost exclusively in Christian lit.; also in Paus. Attic. κ, 38; a pagan letter: Sb 6263, 23 [Rom. times]; Test. Jos. 7: 5 v.l.—Hesychius: κολαφιζόμενος· ῥαπιζόμενος; Etym. Mag. p. 525, 4) *strike with the fist, beat, cuff* τινά *someone.*

1. lit. Mt 26: 67; Mk 14: 65 (KLSchmidt, MGoguel-Festschr. '50, 218-27); MPol 2: 4 (Funk v.l.). Of mistreatment in general: κολαφιζόμεθα *we are roughly treated* 1 Cor 4: 11. εἰ κολαφιζόμενοι ὑπομενεῖτε *if you endure being beaten* 1 Pt 2: 20 (κολαζόμενοι v.l.).

2. fig., of painful attacks of an illness, described as a physical beating by a messenger of Satan 2 Cor 12: 7, variously held to be

a. epilepsy: MKrenkel, Beiträge 1890, 47ff; Schmiedel and Bousset ad loc.; WWrede, Paulus² '07, 17; HFischer, M.D., D. Krankheit d. Ap. Pls. '11; cf. WWeber [psychiatrist], ThLZ 37, '12, 623; FCConybeare in WBundy, The Psychic Health of Jesus '22, 226f; ASchweitzer, D. Mystik des Ap. Pls. '30, 152; JKlausner, From Jesus to Paul '43, 325-30.

b. hysteria: ELombard, Les extases et les souffrances de l'apôtre Paul: RThPh 36, '03, 450-500; Windisch ad loc.; FFenner, D. Krankheit im NT '30, 30-40.

c. periodic depressions: KBonhoeffer, M.D., in Ltzm., Hdb. ad loc.

d. headaches, severe eye-trouble: Seeligmüller, M.D., War Paulus Epileptiker? '10; cf. WWeber, ThLZ 36, '11, 235; Uhle-Wettler, Evang. Kirchenztg. 87, '13, 130ff; 145ff.

e. malaria: Ramsay, Church² 63ff; Sickenberger ad loc.

f. leprosy: EPreuschen, ZNW 2, '01, 193f; REisler, Ιησους βασιλευς II '30, 426ff; 794.

g. an impediment in his speech [stammering]: WKL Clarke, ET 39, '28, 458-60. S. also on σκόλοψ). On interpretations (formerly favored by many) in the direction of spiritual temptations, brought about by opponents, or pangs of conscience, or distressed states of mind s. GHeinrici in Meyer⁸ '00 ad loc. PHMenoud: JdeZwaan-

Festschr. '53 thinks of the anxieties of a missionary's life.—KLSchmidt, TW III 818-21. B. 553 s.v. κόλαφος.*

κολλάω 1 aor. pass. ἐκολλήθην; 1 fut. pass. κολληθήσομαι (Aeschyl. +; Pla., Diod. S., Plut., inscr., pap., LXX; Ep. Arist. 97; Philo, Test. 12 Patr.) *join closely together, unite.*

1. act., fig. *bind closely, unite* τινά τινι *someone with* or *to someone* ἡ ἀγάπη κολλᾷ ἡμᾶς τῷ θεῷ *love unites us w. God* 1 Cl 49: 5. ἡ νουθέτησις...κολλᾷ ἡμᾶς τῷ θελήματι τοῦ θεοῦ *admonition unites us w. God's will* 56: 2.

2. pass.—a. *cling (closely) to someth.* —α. lit. τινί (Job 29: 10) of stones ἐκολλῶντο ἀλλήλοις *they were close to each other* Hv 3, 2, 6. Of dust: τὸν κονιορτὸν τὸν κολληθέντα ἡμῖν ἐκ τῆς πόλεως ὑμῶν *the dust of your city that clings to us* Lk 10: 11.

β. fig. *cling to=come in close contact with* (cf. Ps 21: 16; 43: 26 ἐκολλήθη εἰς γῆν ἡ γαστὴρ ἡμῶν. The act. = 'bring into contact' PGM 5, 457 κολλήσας τ. λίθον τῷ ὠτίῳ) ἐκολλήθησαν αἱ ἁμαρτίαι ἄχρι τ. οὐρανοῦ *the sins have touched the heaven=reached the sky* (two exprs. are telescoped) Rv 18: 5.

γ. fig. of the Spirit, which is (*closely*) *joined* to the flesh 2 Cl 14: 5.

b. *join oneself to, join, cling to, associate with*—a. of a pers., w. dat. of the thing κολλήθητι τῷ ἅρματι τούτῳ Ac 8: 29.—W. dat. of the pers. (which may very rarely be replaced w. a prepositional constr., as Tob 6: 19 S) 1 Cl 30: 3; cf. 46: 1. τοῖς εἰρηνεύουσι 15: 1. τοῖς ἁγίοις 46: 2 (quot. of unknown orig.); Hv 3, 6, 2; s 8, 8, 1. τοῖς δούλοις τοῦ θεοῦ Hs 9, 20, 2; 9, 26, 3. τοῖς δικαίοις s 8, 9, 1. τοῖς ἀθῴοις κ. δικαίοις 1 Cl 46: 4. τοῖς διψύχοις καὶ κενοῖς *the doubters and the senseless* Hm 11: 13. τοῖς ἀκαθάρτοις B 10: 8; 10: 3ff. Also μετά τινος (cf. Ruth 2: 8) 10: 11; 19: 2, 6; D 3: 9. τῷ κυρίῳ *join oneself to the Lord* (cf. 4 Km 18: 6; Sir 2: 3) 1 Cor 6: 17; Hm 10, 1, 6. τῇ γυναικὶ αὐτοῦ *be joined to his wife* Mt 19: 5 (cf. Vi. Aesopi Ic. 30, where a woman says to Aesop: μή μοι κολλῶ=don't come too near me; 1 Esdr 4: 20; Philo, Leg. All. 2, 50). τῇ πόρνῃ *join oneself to a harlot* 1 Cor 6: 16 (cf. Sir 19: 2). *Associate with* on intimate terms, *join* Ac 5: 13; 9: 26; 10: 28 (CBurchard, ZNW 61, '70, 159f). *Become a follower* or *disciple of someone* (cf. 2 Km 20: 2; 1 Macc 3: 2; 6: 21) 17: 34. *Hire oneself out to someone* Lk 15: 15. *Have someth. to do with* lying spirits Hm 11: 4.

β. of impers. things: of anger ὅταν κολληθῇ τῷ ἀνθρώπῳ *when it attaches itself to a pers.* Hm 10, 2, 3. Also of punishment s 6, 5, 3.

c. w. the dat. of the thing *cling to, enter into a close relation w.* (Ps 118: 31; Test. Iss. 6: 1, Dan 6: 10 τ. δικαιοσύνῃ, Gad 5: 2) ταῖς δωρεαῖς *cling to the gifts* 1 Cl 19: 2. τῷ ἀγαθῷ *be attached* or *devoted to what is good* Ro 12: 9; B 20: 2; D 5: 2 (cf. Test. Ash. 3: 1 τῇ ἀγαθότητι; Plut., Mor. 481 c). τῇ εὐλογίᾳ *cling to the blessing* 1 Cl 31: 1. κρίσει δικαίᾳ B 20: 2. M-M.*

κολλούριον, ου, τό (this is the later spelling, attested by AP; also Philumen. p. 9, 16; PHolm. 1, 16; PFlor. 177, 20 [257 AD]; PGM 4, 1316; 2691; 2893. On the other hand אBC have κολλύριον, as do Epict. 2, 21, 20; 3, 21, 21; Galen: CMG V 4, 2 p. 192, 30; Philumen. p. 33, 18; 22; Aëtius very oft.; Dit., Syll.³ 1173, 16 [138 AD]; POxy. 1088, 1; 42 [I AD]; PGM 4, 2682; LXX [Thackeray 92].—Cf. Bl-D. §42, 4 w. app.; Mlt.-H. 78f; Crönert 130; KDieterich, Untersuchungen z. griech. Sprache 1898, 23) *eyesalve* (so Epict., Dit., PFlor., loc. cit.) Rv 3: 18.—FW Bayer: Reallex. f. Ant. u. Christent. 7, '44, 973ff. M-M.*

κολλυβιστής, οῦ, ὁ (Lysias in Pollux 7, 33; 170; Menand. in Phryn. 440 L. [but the Atticists reject the word, ibid.]; PPetr. III 59a I, 7 [III bc]) money-changer Mt 21: 12; Mk 11: 15; Lk 19: 45 D; J 2: 15. M-M.*

κολλύριον s. κολλούριον.

κολοβός, όν (X.+; PGenève 23, 5 [70 ad]; PPetr. III 19g, 2; POxy. 43 verso V, 9; Aq. and Sym. Is 37: 27).
1. mutilated, of hewn stones: damaged (opp. ὁλοτελής) Hv 3, 6, 4; s 9, 6, 4; 9, 8, 4; 9, 26, 7. κ. ἀπὸ τῆς πίστεως damaged in the faith 9, 26, 8.
2. short, stocky (Peripl. Eryth. c. 65; Galen, De Usu Part. I p. 58, 19 Helmr.; Procopius of Caesarea, Anecdota 8, 12 [opp. μακρός]; 10, 11) ἄνθρωπος (opp. μακρός) Gospel of Eve: Kl. T. 8³, p. 18.*

κολοβόω 1 aor. ἐκολόβωσα; 1 aor. pass. ἐκολοβώθην; 1 fut. pass. κολοβωθήσομαι; pf. ptc. κεκολοβωμένος (Aristot., H.A. 1, 1 p. 487b, 24; Diod. S. 1, 78, 5; 2 Km 4: 12 'cut off, cut short') mutilate, curtail (so Polyb. 1, 80, 13; Epict. 2, 10, 20).
1. lit., of stones κεκολοβωμένοι damaged Hv 3, 2, 8; 3, 6, 4. ὅλως ἐξ αὐτῶν οὐδὲν ἐκολοβώθη nothing at all was damaged about them s 9, 8, 5.
2. fig. shorten the last days Mt 24: 22a, b; Mk 13: 20a, b. M-M.*

Κολοσσαεύς, έως (Suidas on 'Ρόδος: IV p. 297, 15) Colossian; subst. ὁ Κ. the Colossian Col inscr.—𝔓⁴⁶ AB* K write Κολασσ. (q.v.), which is also found in Suidas, loc. cit., as v.l. (Strabo 12, 8, 16 uses the form Κολοσσηνός).*

Κολοσσαί, ῶν, αἱ Colossae, once a flourishing city (Hdt. 7, 30; X., An. 1, 2, 6), later less important (Strabo 12, 8, 13 πόλισμα), in Phrygia in Asia Minor. The church there was prob. founded by Epaphras (Col 1: 7), who was from Colossae (4: 12). Col 1: 2; Phlm subscr. v.l.—Lghtf., Col and Phlm p. 1ff; Ramsay, Church 465ff, Phrygia I 208ff; VSchultze, Altchr. Städte u. Landschaften II 1, '22, 445ff; Zahn, Einl. I³ 318, who, like Lghtf. 16, 4, deals w. the var. forms of the name (Κολασσαί, Κολασαί).*

κόλπος, ου, ὁ (Hom.+; inscr., pap., LXX, Philo, Joseph.).
1. bosom, breast, chest ἀνακεῖσθαι ἐν τῷ κόλπῳ τινός lie (at a meal) w. one's head on someone's breast (s. ἀνάκειμαι 2) J 13: 23. ἐν τοῖς κόλποις αὐτοῦ (=τοῦ Ἀβραάμ. In this case ἀνακείμενον is to be supplied) lying in Abraham's bosom (in the place of honor at the banquet in the next world. On the pl. s. Bl-D. §141, 5; cf. Rob. 408; Theocr. 2, 120 and below; Plut., Cato Min. 33. Cf. also Sb 2034, 11 ἐν κόλποις Ἀβρὰμ κ. Ἰσὰκ κ. Ἰακώβ) Lk 16: 23. ἀπενεχθῆναι εἰς τὸν κ. Ἀβραάμ be carried to Abraham's bosom vs. 22. The mng. lap is also poss. for κόλπος: Ael. Aristid. 13 p. 163 D.: ἐκ τῶν κόλπων τ. γῆς; Diog. L. 3, 44; Meleager, Anth. Pal. 5, 165 ἐν κόλποισιν ἐκείνης=lying on her lap; Anonymous Vita Pla. ed. Westerm. 1850 p. 5, 31 ἐντὸς κόλπων for 2, 44 ἐν τοῖς γόνασιν. The sing. in this sense: Epict. 2, 5, 16; 4, 7, 24; Vi. Aesopi I c. 82; 137 P.; Ps.-Clem., Hom. 8, 12. (Piers Plowman, version C 9, 283 'in Abrahammes lap'; PHaupt, AJPh 42, '21, 162-67; ESchwyzer, Der Götter Knie—Abrahams Schoss: JWackernagel-Festschr. '23, 283-93; MMieses, Im Schosse Abr. s: OLZ 34, '31, 1018-21. Opposing him BHeller, ibid. 36, '33, 146-9. —Rabb. in RMeyer [s. below] 825). ἐὰν ἦτε συνηγμένοι ἐν τῷ κ. μου if you are gathered in my bosom 2 Cl 4: 5 (a saying of Jesus; cf. GH 7b twice). Furthermore, apart fr. the idea of eating together on the same couch, 'being in

someone's bosom' denotes the closest communion (cf. Plut., Pericl. 1, 1, Demosth. 31, 6, Cato Min. 33, 7 Ziegler v.l.: Gabinius, an ἄνθρωπος ἐκ τῶν Πομπηίου κόλπων; Longus, Past. 4, 36, 3; Num 11: 12; Dt 13: 7; 28: 54, 56; 2 Km 12: 3; 3 Km 17: 19; Ruth 4: 16): ὁ ὢν εἰς τὸν κ. τοῦ πατρός who rests in the bosom of the Father J 1: 18 (M-EBoismard, RB 59, '52, 23-39).
2. the fold of a garment, formed as it falls from the chest over the girdle (Hom.+; Jos., Ant. 2, 273). Fr. early times (e.g. Od. 15, 468; Herodas 6, 102; Diod. S. 25, 16; Appian, Iber. 13 §49; Polyaenus 7, 48; 8, 64; Dio Chrys. 67[17], 22; Ex 4: 6f; Jos., Bell. 6, 195) this fold was used as a pocket. διδόναι τι put someth. into the fold of someone's garment (cf. Ps 78: 12; Is 65: 6; Jer 39: 18) Lk 6: 38.
3. bay, gulf of the sea (Hom.+; Dit., Or. 441, 218; Philo, Op. M. 113; Jos., Ant. 3, 25) Ac 27: 39.—RMeyer, TW 824-6. M-M. B. 39.*

κολυμβάω (Pla. et al.)—1. swim up and down, lit. 'dive' B 10: 5.
2. swim (Paradoxogr. Flor. 10; Palaeph. p. 36, 5; Babrius 165, 1; 3; Aq. Is 25: 11; Jos., Ant. 20, 248) τοὺς δυναμένους κ. those who could swim Ac 27: 43. M-M.*

κολυμβήθρα, ας, ἡ (Pla.+; Diod. S. 4, 78, 1; 11, 25, 4; Jos., Ant. 9, 239; 15, 54; POxy. 147, 2; LXX) pool, swimming-pool (used for bathing: Ael. Aristid. 48, 21 K.=24 p. 470 D.). Of Bethzatha (s. Βηθζαθά and cf. JoachJeremias, D. Wiederentdeckung von Bethesda '49) J 5: 2, 4, 7; Siloam 9: 7 (2 Esdr 13 [Neh 3]: 15 S κολυμβήθρα τοῦ Σιλωάμ). M-M.*

κολωνία, ας, ἡ (Lat. loanw., colonia; found also in rabb. Exx. in Hahn 271 Lat. word-index; edict of Claudius in Jos., Ant. 19, 291) colony, of Philippi in Macedonia, which was changed into a military colony by Augustus (s. Φίλιπποι) Ac 16: 12. M-M.*

κομάω (Hom.+; BGU 16, 11; Philo, Deus Imm. 88; Jos., Ant. 4, 72) wear long hair, let one's hair grow long (Diod. S. 20, 63, 3) 1 Cor 11: 14, 15 (Greek men do not do this: Hdt. 1, 82, 7; Plut., Mor. 267b; Ps.-Phoc. 212 ἄρσεσιν οὐκ ἐπέοικε κομᾶν). M-M.*

κόμη, ης, ἡ (Hom.+; WSchubart, Der Gnomon des Idios Logos '19 [=BGU V], 71; 76 [II ad]: ἱερεῦσι οὐκ ἐξὸν κόμην φορεῖν; LXX; Philo, Sacr. Abel. 25; Jos., Bell. 4, 561, Ant. 14, 45; loanw. in rabb.) (long) hair of women (Xenophon Eph. 1, 2, 6; Achilles Tat. 8, 6, 8) 1 Cor 11: 15. κ. οὔλη curly hair AP 3: 10. M-M.*

κομίζω 1 aor. ἐκόμισα, mid. ἐκομισάμην; fut. mid. κομίσομαι and κομιοῦμαι (Hom.+; inscr., pap., LXX, En., Ep. Arist., Philo, Joseph.; Sib. Or. 3, 253).
1. act. bring (Dit., Syll.³ 409, 29; 434, 42; 559, 28; PPetr. III 53k, 5; PTebt. 55, 4; 1 Esdr 4: 5; 3 Macc 1: 8) τὶ someth. (Jos., Vi. 50 ἐπιστολάς; Test. Jos. 6: 2) a jar of ointment Lk 7: 37.
2. mid.—a. carry off, get (for oneself), receive (Diod. S. 17, 69, 1; 20, 28, 3; Appian, Bell. Civ. 5, 60, §252 γράμματα) τὰ ὀψώνια pay, wages IPol 6: 2. μισθόν (Polystrat. p. 22; Lucian, Paras. 2, 5; Dit., Syll.³ 193, 9; 11; 1077, 4; 2 Macc 8: 33) 2 Cl 11: 5; cf. B 4: 12, where μισθόν is to be supplied (as En. 100, 7). μισθὸν ἀδικίας reward for wrongdoing 2 Pt 2: 13 v.l. (ἀδικέω 2b, end). τῆς δόξης στέφανον 1 Pt 5: 4 (cf. Eur., Hipp. 432 codd. κ. δόξαν; 1 Macc 13: 37). τὴν ἐπαγγελίαν the promise (i.e. what is promised) Hb 10: 36; 11: 13, 39. τὸ τέλος τῆς πίστεως σωτηρίαν ψυχῶν obtain as an outcome of faith the salvation of souls 1 Pt 1: 9. κ. τὰ διὰ τοῦ σώματος πρὸς ἃ

ἔπραξεν *receive a recompense for what he has done during his life in the body* 2 Cor 5: 10; cf. Col 3: 25. τοῦτο κομίσεται παρὰ κυρίου Eph 6: 8 (PSI 438, 11 [III BC] κεκόμισμαι παρὰ Φανίου ἐπιστολήν).—
b. *get back, recover* (Eur., Thu. +; Isaeus 8, 8; Polyb. 1, 83, 8; 3, 40, 10; 10, 34, 3; Sir 29: 6; Philo, De Jos. 210; 231; Jos., Ant. 13, 80) τὸ ἐμὸν σὺν τόκῳ *what is mine with interest* Mt 25: 27. Of Abraham: *receive his son back* (cf. Jos., Ant. 1, 236) Hb 11: 19 (Himerius, Or. 6[2], Demeter τὴν ζητουμένην κομίζεται=*receives the girl whom she sought [her daughter]*). M-M.*

κόμπος, ου, ὁ (Hom. +) *boasting, pomp* (so trag., Hdt.; Esth 8: 12d; 3 Macc 6: 5; Philo, Congr. Erud. Gr. 61; Jos., Bell. 6, 260) 1 Cl 16: 2.*

κομφέκτωρ, ορος, ὁ (Lat. loanw., confector, Suetonius, Octav. 43, Nero 12. The Gk. form: Acta S. Meletii 39) an *executioner*, who gave the coup de grâce to wounded gladiators MPol 16: 1 (s. Lghtf. ad loc.).*

κομψότερον adv. of the comp. of κομψός (the word Eur. +; the comp. in Pla., Crat. 429D; POxy. 935, 5 [III AD]) *better* of sick persons: κ. ἔχειν *begin to improve* J 4: 52 (κομψῶς ἔχειν in this sense in Epict. 3, 10, 13; PPar. 18, 3; PTebt. 414, 10. On the comp. cf. POxy. 935, 5 θεῶν συνλαμβανόντων ἡ ἀδελφὴ ἐπὶ τὸ κομψότερον ἐτράπη; FBilabel, Badische Papyri '23 no. 34, 4 [I AD] κομψότερον ἔσχεν). M-M. s.v. -ως.*

κονιάω pf. pass. ptc. κεκονιαμένος (Demosth. +; Inscr. Gr. 594, 96; Dit., Syll.³ 695, 88. Pass. CIG I 1625, 16; Dt 27: 2, 4; Pr 21: 9) *whitewash* τοῖχος κ. *a whitewashed wall* Ac 23: 3 (s. τοῖχος). τάφοι κ. *whitewashed tombs* Mt 23: 27; GNaass 6 (Aesop, Fab. 121 P.=193 H. ἐν κεκονιαμένῳ οἴκῳ).—KHRengstorf, Rabb. Texte, 1. Reihe III '33ff, p. 34f. M-M.*

κονιορτός, οῦ, ὁ (Hdt. +; Wilcken, Chrest. 198, 16 [III BC]; LXX; Philo, Exs. 133; Jos., Ant. 3, 193) *dust* ἐκτινάσσειν τὸν κ. τῶν ποδῶν (cf. Heraclit. Sto. 10 p. 17, 8 after Il. 2, 150 ποδῶν . . . κονίη; Na 1: 3 κ. ποδῶν αὐτοῦ) *shake the dust from the feet* Mt 10: 14; cf. Lk 9: 5; 10: 11; Ac 13: 51 (s. on ἐκτινάσσω 1). Of an unruly mob κονιορτὸν βάλλειν εἰς τὸν ἀέρα *throw dust into the air* Ac 22: 23. κ. ἐγείρειν *raise dust* (cf. Appian, Mithrid. 87 §396 κονιορτὸς ἠγείρετο; Jos., Bell. 5, 471) Hv 4, 1, 5b.—*A cloud of dust* (Aristodem. [IV AD]: 104 fgm. 1, 8 Jac.) κ. ὡς εἰς τ. οὐρανόν *a cloud of dust reaching, as it were, to heaven* 4, 1, 5a (Quint. Smyrn. 2, 469f κόνις ἄχρις ἐς οὐρανόν). γινομένου μείζονος καὶ μείζονος κονιορτοῦ *when the dust-cloud became greater and greater* 4, 1, 6. M-M. B. 19.*

κοπάζω 1 aor. ἐκόπασα (Hdt. +; LXX and fr. Num 17: 13 in Philo, Somn. 2, 235, fr. Gen 8: 8 in Sib. Or. 1, 246; AWilhelm, Symb. Osl., Suppl. 13, '50, 32, a Gk. epigram: ἡ μακρὴ κατ' ἐμοῦ δυσπλοΐη κοπάσει) *abate, stop, rest, cease*, ὁ ἄνεμος ἐκόπασεν *the wind fell* (so Hdt. 7, 191; cf. Aelian in Suid. [Anz 316]) Mt 14: 32; Mk 4: 39; 6: 51. M-M.*

κοπετός, οῦ, ὁ (Eupolis Com. [V BC], fgm. 347; Dionys. Hal. 11, 31; Plut., Fab. 17, 7; Epigr. Gr. 345, 4; LXX, Joseph.; Sib. Or. 5, 193) *mourning, lamentation*; acc. to oriental custom this was accompanied by breast-beating ἐποίησαν κ. μέγαν ἐπ' αὐτῷ *they made loud lamentation over him* Ac 8: 2 (Mi 1: 8 κ. ποιεῖσθαι [MWilcox, The Semitisms of Ac, '65, 136f]; Zech 12: 10 κ. ἐπί τινα; cf. Jer 9: 9; Jos., Bell. 2, 6). M-M.*

κοπή, ῆς, ἡ (Strabo et al.; pap.) *cutting down, slaughter* (Josh 10: 20; Jdth 15: 7) ὑποστρέφειν ἀπὸ τῆς κ. τῶν βασιλέων *return fr. the defeat of* (i.e., fr. defeating) *the kings* Hb 7: 1 (Gen 14: 17). M-M.*

κοπιάω (Aristoph. +; Hippocr.; Epicurus 59, 3 Us.; inscr., pap., LXX, En., Philo, Joseph.) 1 aor. ἐκοπίασα; pf. κεκοπίακα, 2 sing. κεκοπίακες (Bl-D. §83, 2; Mlt.-H. 221; the ms. tradition varies).
1. *become weary, tired* (Aristoph. et al.; Sir 16: 27; 1 Macc 10: 81; 4 Macc 9: 12; Jos., Bell. 6, 142) Rv 2: 3. ἔκ τινος *from someth.* ἐκ τῆς ὁδοιπορίας *from the journey* J 4: 6 (cf. Jos., Ant. 2, 321 ὑπὸ τῆς ὁδοιπορίας κεκοπωμένοι; Is 40: 31). οἱ κοπιῶντες *those who are weary* (Diocles 142 p. 186, 28; cf. IQH 8, 36) Mt 11: 28 (s. on φορτίζω).
2. *work hard, toil, strive, struggle* (Vett. Val. 266, 6; Syntipas p. 107, 15; POsl. 160, 1; Philo, Mut. Nom. 254, Cher. 41) of physical, but also mental and spiritual exertion, abs. (Aesop, Fab. 391 P.) Mt 6: 28; Lk 5: 5; 12: 27 t.r.; J 4: 38b; Ac 20: 35; 1 Cor 4: 12; 16: 16; Eph 4: 28; 2 Ti 2: 6. τὶ *labor for someth.* (En. 103, 9 κόπους κ.) J 4: 38a. πολλά *work hard* Ro 16: 6, 12b; Hs 5, 6, 2; 2 Cl 7: 1. περισσότερον 1 Cor 15: 10. κ. ἔν τινι *work hard in preaching and teaching* 1 Ti 5: 17. διὰ λόγου *labor by word of mouth* B 19: 10. The sphere in which the work is done: ἐν ὑμῖν *among you* 1 Th 5: 12. The manner: ἐν κυρίῳ Ro 16: 12a, b; εἴς τινα *work hard for someone* vs. 6; Gal 4: 11. εἰς τοῦτο *for this* 1 Ti 4: 10. εἰς ὃ κοπιῶ *this is what I am toiling for* Col 1: 29. εἰς κενόν *toil in vain* (cf. Is 49: 4 κενῶς ἐκοπίασα; 65: 23 κοπιάσουσιν εἰς κενόν) Phil 2: 16. Also εἰς μάτην (Ps 126: 1) Hs 9, 4, 8. M-M. B. 312.*

κόπος, ου, ὁ—1. *trouble, difficulty* (trag.; pap.; Ps 106: 12; Sir 22: 13; 1 Macc 10: 15; Jos., Ant. 2, 257) κόπους (κόπον) παρέχειν τινί (*cause*) *trouble (for) someone, bother someone* (κόπος παρέχειν τινί PTebt. 21, 10 [115 BC]; BGU 844, 12; PGM 14b; κόπον παρέχειν τινί Sir 29: 4) Mt 26: 10; Mk 14: 6; Lk 11: 7; 18: 5; Gal 6: 17; Hv 3, 3, 2. πολλοὺς κόπους ἠντληκώς *after he had endured many hardships* s 5, 6, 2a.
2. *work, labor, toil* (Eur., Aristoph.; Dit., Syll.³ 761, 6 [I BC]; PAmh. 133, 11; POxy. 1482, 6; LXX; En.; Jos., Ant. 3, 25; 8, 244) sing. κ. τῆς ἀγάπης *labor of love*, i.e., *loving service* 1 Th 1: 3. W. ἔργα Rv 2: 2. W. ἱδρώς B 10: 4. W. μόχθος (q.v.) 2 Cor 11: 27; 1 Th 2: 9; 2 Th 3: 8; Hs 5, 6, 2b. ὁ κ. ὑμῶν οὐκ ἔστιν κενός *your labor is not in vain* 1 Cor 15: 58. μήπως εἰς κενὸν γένηται ὁ κ. ἡμῶν *that our work may not be fruitless* 1 Th 3: 5. Fig. of work at harvest time εἰς τὸν κ. τινὸς εἰσέρχεσθαι *enter into someone's labor* i.e., reap the rewards of another person's work J 4: 38; τὸν μισθὸν λαμβάνειν κατὰ τὸν κ. *receive pay in accordance w. the work done* 1 Cor 3: 8. ὅπου πλείων κ., πολὺ κέρδος *the greater the toil, the richer the gain* IPol 1: 3.—Pl., of individual acts (En. 7, 3) 2 Cor 6: 5; 10: 15; 11: 23; Rv 14: 13. Also abstr. for concr. *reward for labor* (Sir 14: 15) Hm 2: 4; s 9, 24, 2f.—AvHarnack, Κόπος (κοπιᾶν, οἱ κοπιῶντες) im frühchristl. Sprachgebr.: ZNW 27, '28, 1–10; HTKuist, Bibl. Review 16, '31, 245–9. M-M. B. 540.*

κοπρία, ας, ἡ (Strattis Com. [V BC], fgm. 43; Strabo 7, 5, 7; 16, 4, 26; Epict. 2, 4, 5; M. Ant. 8, 51, 2; POxy. 37 I, 6 [49 AD]; PRyl. 162, 17; LXX.—UWilcken, APF 2, '03, 311f) *dung-heap, rubbish-heap* Lk 14: 35. M-M.*

κόπριον, ου, τό (Heraclitus 96; Epict. 2, 4, 5; Plut., Pomp. 48, 2; Dit., Or. 483, 81 [II BC]; PFay. 110, 5; 10; POxy.

502, 32 καθαρὰ ἀπὸ κοπρίων; Jer 32: 33; Sir 22: 2) *dung, manure* κόπρια βάλλειν *put manure on* Lk 13: 8 (Theophr., Caus. Pl. 3, 9, 5 παραβάλλειν κόπρον). *Filth, dirt* τὰ κ. αἴρειν (PGM 4, 1441) *take away the dirt* Hs 9, 10, 3. M-M.*

κόπρον, ου, τό (Galen XII 290 K.—For the LXX ἡ κόπρος [s. the foll. entry] is surely correct wherever the gender can be established. But there is also the acc. κόπρον which, without the article, may be fem. or neut. [Is 30: 22; 36: 12, which latter form has τήν w. it as a v.l.] and likew. the gen. κόπρου [4 Km 6: 25; Ezk 4: 12; Jos., Ant. 9, 62; PGM 7, 485]) Hs 9, 10, 3 if the restoration τὰ κό[πρα] in FXFunk² '01 is correct, and perh. κόπρον Lk 13: 8 v.l.*
But the latter form more likely belongs under

κόπρος, ου, ἡ (Hom.+; Diod. S. 4, 13, 3; Dio Chrys. 13[7], 16; 15[32], 87; inscr., pap., LXX [s. κόπρον]) *dung, manure.* Since this form is so incomparably better attested than the neut. in the entry above, it is almost certain that the doubtful cases mentioned there belong under this word.*

κόπτω (Hom.+; inscr., pap., LXX) impf. ἔκοπτον; 1 aor. ἔκοψα, mid. ἐκοψάμην; fut. mid. κόψομαι; pf. pass. ptc. κεκομμένος (Hs 8, 1, 4); 2 aor. pass. ἐκόπην (Hs 8, 1, 4). 1. act. (Jos., Vi. 171) *cut (off)* τὶ ἀπό (or ἔκ) τινος *someth. fr. someth.* (Quint. Smyrn. 11, 71 κ. τι ἀπό τινος) κλάδους ἀπὸ τ. δένδρων Mt 21: 8. κλάδους ἀπὸ τῆς ἱτέας Hs 8, 1, 2; cf. 4; 8, 3, 1; 8, 4, 4f. στιβάδας ἐκ τῶν ἀγρῶν *leafy branches from the fields* Mk 11: 8 (cf. X., Hell. 5, 2, 43; POsl. 17, 7 [136 AD]; Is 44: 14 ξύλον ἐκ τοῦ δρυμοῦ; 2 Ch 2: 15; Sib. Or. 3, 651). 2. mid. *beat one's breast as an act of mourning* (Aeschyl., Pers. 683; Pla., Phaedo 60B; LXX; Jos., Ant. 7, 41) κ. τὰ στήθη *beat their breasts* (PGM 36, 139) GP 8: 28. Then abs. *mourn (greatly)* (Lucian, De Sacrific. 15; 3 Km 13: 29 v.l.; Zech 7: 5) Mt 24: 30; GP 7: 25; (w. θρηνεῖν, q.v. 2 and Jos., Ant. 8, 273) Mt 11: 17; Lk 23: 27; (w. κλαίειν, q.v. 1) GP 12: 52, 54. κ. ἐπὶ σάκκου καὶ σποδοῦ *mourn in sackcloth and ashes* B 7: 5 (the unusual use of ἐπί is prob. to be explained by the fact that the mourner sat on ashes; cf. 3: 2). W. acc. foll. *mourn someone* (Aristoph., Lys. 396; Pla., Rep. 10 p. 619c; Anth. Pal. 11, 135, 1; Gen 23: 2; 1 Km 25: 1 al.; Jos., Ant. 13, 399) Lk 8: 52; cf. 23: 27. Also ἐπί τινα *mourn for someone* (2 Km 1: 12; 11: 26 v.l.) Rv 1: 7; 18: 9.—GStählin, TW III 829-51. M-M. B. 553; 557.*

κόραξ, ακος, ὁ (Hom.+; PMagd. 21, 5; LXX; Jos., Ant. 1, 91 al.) *crow, raven* Lk 12: 24. The Jews were forbidden to eat it B 10: 1, 4 (Lev 11: 15; Dt 14: 14). M-M.*

κοράσιον, ου, τό (Pla. in Diog. L. 3, 33; Philippides Com. [IV/III BC] 36; Epict. 2, 1, 28; 3, 2, 8; 4, 10, 33; Anth. Pal. 9, 39, 1; IG VII 3325; PStrassb. 79, 2 [16/15 BC]; BGU 887, 9; 913, 7; LXX. Cf. Lobeck on Phryn. p. 73f; PKretschmer, D. Entstehung der Κοινή '00, 17; FSolmsen, RhM 59, '04, 503f) dim. of κόρη *girl*; (acc. to Wellhausen transl. of the Aramaic רְבִיתָא for which the more elegant טְלִיתָא was inserted as a correction: s. Wlh., EKlostermann ad loc.) Mk 5: 41 (on τὸ κ. as a voc., cf. Bl-D. §147, 3; Rob. 461).—Mt 9: 24f; 14: 11; Mk 5: 42; 6: 22, 28. M-M.*

κορβᾶν indecl. (קָרְבָּן) Hebr. word, explained by the notation ὅ ἐστι δῶρον (transl. corresp. by the LXX Lev 2: 1, 4, 12, 13) *corban*, a *gift consecrated to God*, to be used for relig. purposes (cf. Jos., Ant. 4, 73 of the Nazirites οἱ κορβᾶν αὑτοὺς ὀνομάσαντες τῷ θεῷ, δῶρον δὲ τοῦτο

σημαίνει κατὰ Ἑλλήνων γλῶτταν, C. Ap. 1, 167) Mk 7: 11. On this subject cf. Philo, Spec. Leg. 2, 16f; Billerb. I 711ff; Dalman, Gramm.² 174, 3; HOrt, De verbintenissen met 'Korban': ThT 37, '03, 284-314; JHAHart, Corban: JQR 19, '07, 615-50; HLaible, Korban: Allg. Ev.-Luth. Kirchenzeitung 54, '21, 597ff; 613ff; MBlack, Aramaic Approach³, '67, 139; HHommel, D. Wort Korban u. seine Verwandten: Philologus 98, '54, 132-49; JAFitzmyer, JBL 78, '59, 60-65; SZeitlin, JQR 53, '62, 160-63; KHRengstorf, TW III 860-6.*

κορβανᾶς, ᾶ, ὁ (קָרְבָּן; Aram. קָרְבָּנָא) *temple treasury* (Jos., Bell. 2, 175 ἱερὸς θησαυρός, καλεῖται δὲ κορβωνᾶς.—Dalman, Gramm.² 174, 3) εἰς τὸν κ. βάλλειν *put into the temple treasury* Mt 27: 6.*

Κόρε, ὁ indecl. (קֹרַח) *Korah*, head of a rebellion against Moses (Num 16; Sir 45: 18; Philo, Fuga 145.—Jos., Ant. 4, 14ff; Κορῆς, έου) Jd 11.*

κορέννυμι pf. pass. ptc. κεκορεσμένος; 1 aor. ἐκορέσθην (Hom.+; Jos., Ant. 2, 86; 10, 261) *satiate, fill* pass. *be satiated, have enough* w. gen. *of that with which one is satiated* (Hom.+; Sib. Or. 3, 697). 1. lit. κορεσθέντες τροφῆς *when they had eaten enough* Ac 27: 38. 2. fig. (Appian, Hann. 27 §115, Bell. Civ. 1, 3, §10; Philo; Jos., Bell. 4, 314) ironically ἤδη κεκορεσμένοι ἐστέ *you already have all you could wish*, i.e., you think you already have all the spiritual food you need 1 Cor 4: 8. M-M.*

κόρη, ης, ἡ *pupil* or *'apple'* of the eye (lit. 'girl', then 'image'; *pupil* trag., Hippocr.+; Dit., Syll.³ 1169, 67; LXX; Philo) in full κ. τοῦ ὀφθαλμοῦ fig. ἀγαπᾶν ὡς κ. τ. ὀ. *love as the apple of one's eye* B 19: 9 (cf. Dt 32: 10; Ps 16: 8; Pr 7: 2).*

Κορίνθιος, ου, ὁ *the Corinthian* (trag., Hdt.+; inscr.) Ac 18: 8, 27 D; 2 Cor 6: 11; 1 Cl 47: 6. Also in the title of 1 and 2 Cor and 1 and 2 Cl and the subscr. of Ro, 1 Cl; 2 Cl 20: 5 (subscr.) Funk.*

Κόρινθος, ου, ἡ (Hom.+; inscr., Philo, Sib. Or. 3, 487 al.) *Corinth*, a city in Greece on the isthmus of the same name. From 27 BC capital of the senatorial province of Achaia, and seat of the proconsul. The Christian church there was founded by Paul on his so-called second missionary journey, Ac 18: 1, 27 D; 19: 1; 1 Cor 1: 1, 23; 2 Cor 1: 1, 23; 2 Ti 4: 20; 1 Cl inscr.; MPol 22: 2; Epil Mosq 4. Also subscr. of Ro and 1 Th.—ECurtius, Peloponnesos II 1852, 514ff; JCladder, Korinth '23; Byvanck u. Lenschau: Pauly-W. Suppl. IV '29, 991-1036; OBroneer, Biblical Archeologist 14, '51, 78-96.—Cf. the Corinthian inscr. (Dssm., LO 12, 8 [LAE 13, 7]):⟨συνα⟩γωγὴ Ἑβρ⟨αίων⟩. The low state of morals in Cor. is indicated by the proverb: οὐ παντὸς ἀνδρὸς ἐς Κόρινθον ἔσθ' ὁ πλοῦς (Strabo 8, 6, 20. Cf. Ael. Aristid. 29, 17 K.=40 p. 755 D.). But on the proverb cf. L-S-J s.v. Κόρινθος I.*

Κορνήλιος, ου, ὁ (found frequently: s. Diod. S. 11, 27, 1 [of a man contemporary with the battle of Salamis, 480 BC]; 11, 86, 1; 14, 110, 1; Dit., Syll. and Or. indices; Preisigke, Namenbuch; Joseph.) *Cornelius*, a Roman centurion (ἑκατοντάρχης) in Caesarea by the sea Ac 10: 1, 3, 17, 22, 24f, 30f.—CBurchard, D. dreizehnte Zeuge, '70, 54 n. 11.*

κόρος, ου, ὁ (PSI 554, 14 [259 BC]; LXX; Eupolem. the Jew in Euseb., Pr. Ev. 9, 33; Joseph.; Test. Jud. 9: 8) *cor, kor* (כֹּר; HLewy, D. Semit. Fremdwörter im Griech. 1895, 116) a measure of capacity for grain, flour, etc., acc. to Jos., Ant. 15, 314=ten Attic medimni, hence about 393 liters or betw. ten and twelve bushels; *measure* Lk 16: 7.—Lit. under βάτος. M-M.*

κοσμέω impf. ἐκόσμουν; 1 aor. ἐκόσμησα; pf. pass. 3 sing. κεκόσμηται, ptc. κεκοσμημένος; plpf. 3 sing. ἐκεκόσμητο (Hom.+; inscr., pap., LXX, Philo, Joseph., Test. 12 Patr.).

1. *put in order* (Od. 7, 13; X., Cyr. 8, 2, 6; 6, 11; Dit., Syll.³ 1038, 11 τράπεζαν; PThéad. 14, 18; Sir 29: 26; 50: 14) *trim*, of lamps Mt 25: 7. For Mt 12: 44; Lk 11: 25 s. mng. 2aβ.

2. *adorn, decorate* (Hes.+; LXX; Sib. Or. 3, 426)—**a.** lit.—**α.** of pers. τινά ἔν τινι *someone w. someth.* (Diod. S. 17, 53, 3 ἐν ὅπλοις=with [splendid] weapons; Test. Jud 13: 5 ἐν χρυσίῳ καὶ μαργαρίταις) 1 Ti 2: 9. Pass. (Xenophon Eph. 1, 2, 2 παρθένοι κεκοσμημέναι; Jos., Bell. 2, 444) νύμφη κεκοσμημένη *a bride adorned* for her husband (Achilles Tat. 3, 7, 5; s. Test. Jud. 12: 1) Rv 21: 2; cf. Hv 4, 2, 1. Of women (POxy. 1467, 5 γυναῖκες κεκοσμημέναι) κοσμηθεῖσαι πρὸς μοιχείαν *adorned for adultery* AP 9: 24 (cf. Test. Reub. 5: 5 κ. πρὸς ἀπάτην διανοίας, Test. Jos. 9: 5).

β. of things τὶ *someth.* Pass. οἶκος κεκοσμημένος *a decorated house* Mt 12: 44; Lk 11: 25 (Philo, Deus Imm. 150; Dit., Syll.³ 326, 15 κεκοσμημένην τὴν πόλιν), though *put in order* (s. mng. 1 above) is also poss. The temple λίθοις καλοῖς καὶ ἀναθήμασιν κεκόσμηται *is adorned w. beautiful stones and votive offerings* (Dit., Syll.³ 725, 2f τὸ ἱερὸν ἀναθέμασι κεκόσμηται; 1100, 21f; 1050, 6; 2 Macc 9: 16; Philo, Det. Pot. Ins. 20) 21: 5; cf. Rv 21: 19. κ. τὰ μνημεῖα (cf. X., Mem. 2, 2, 13; Jos., Ant. 14, 284 κ. τάφον) Mt 23: 29. δένδρα καρποῖς κεκοσμημένα *trees adorned w. fruit* Hs 9, 1, 10; 9, 28, 1.

b. fig.—**α.** *make beautiful* or *attractive* spiritually, religiously, morally (Pind., Nem. 6, 78; Thu. 2, 42, 2 αἱ ἀρεταὶ ἐκόσμησαν; X., Cyr. 8, 1, 21; Inscr. Rom. IV 288, 9 κεκόσμηκε τὸν αὐτοῦ βίον τῇ καλλίστῃ παρρησίᾳ. Inschr. v. Priene 105, 36) κ. ἑαυτόν *adorn oneself* 1 Pt 3: 5 (cf. Epict. 3, 1, 26).—Pass., w. dat. of the thing that adorns (Diod. S. 16, 65, 2 ἀρεταῖς κεκοσμημένος; 3 Macc 6: 1; Philo, Op. M. 139) παντὶ καλῷ ἐκεκόσμητο *he was adorned w. every good thing* MPol 13: 2. καρποῖς Dg 12: 1. τ. παναρέτῳ πολιτείᾳ 1 Cl 2: 8. τῷ ἐνδόξῳ ὀνόματι 43: 2. Also ἔν τινι (Sir 48: 11 BSA οἱ ἐν ἀγαπήσει κεκοσμημένοι) ἐν ἔργοις ἀγαθοῖς 1 Cl 33: 7. ἐν τ. ἐντολαῖς Ἰησοῦ Χριστοῦ *with the commandments of Jesus Christ* IEph 9: 2.

β. *adorn, do credit to* (Theognis 947 Diehl πατρίδα κοσμήσω) ἵνα τὴν διδασκαλίαν κοσμῶσιν ἐν πᾶσιν *that they may do credit to the teaching in all respects* Tit 2: 10. M-M.*

κοσμικός, ή, όν (Aristot., Phys. 2, 4 p. 196a, 25 τοὐρανοῦ τοῦδε καὶ τῶν κοσμικῶν πάντων; Vett. Val. Index II; Lucian, Paras. 11 [opp. ἀνθρώπινος]; Ps.-Plutarch, Consol. ad Apoll. 34 p. 119ε κοσμικὴ διάταξις; inscr.; PGM 4, 2533 τὰ κοσμικὰ πάντα; 2553; Philo, Aet. M. 53; Jos., Bell. 4, 324; Test. Jos. 17: 8; loanw. in rabb.).

1. *earthly* (Test. Jos. 17: 8) τὸ ἅγιον κ. *the earthly sanctuary* (opp. heavenly) Hb 9: 1. τὸ κ. μυστήριον ἐκκλησίας *the earthly mystery of the church* D 11: 11. κοσμικαὶ βάσανοι *earthly tortures* MPol 2: 3.—Subst. τὰ κ. ταῦτα *these earthly things* 2 Cl 5: 6.

2. *worldly*, w. the connotation of that which is at enmity w. God or morally reprehensible αἱ κοσμικαὶ ἐπιθυμίαι *worldly desires* Tit 2: 12; 2 Cl 17: 3.*

κόσμιος, (ία), ον (Aristoph., Pla.+; inscr., pap.; Eccl 12: 9) *respectable, honorable.*

1. of pers. (Nicopho Com. [V/IV bc 16]; Dit., Or. 485, 3 ἄνδρα κόσμιον; Philo, Spec. Leg. 3, 89) w. σώφρων (IG IV² 1, 82, 27 [40/42 AD]) honorary inscr. for a man) 1 Ti 3: 2.

2. used w. an impers. noun, yet w. ref. to a pers. (cf. Inschr. v. Magn. 165, 6 κ. ἀναστροφή; 179, 4) ἐν καταστολῇ κ. *in modest apparel* (of women, as Epict., Ench. 40; Dio Chrys. 5, 14; PSI 97, 1) 1 Ti 2: 9. M-M.*

κοσμίως adv. (Aristoph., Pla.+; inscr.; Philo, Spec. Leg. 1, 153) *modestly* 1 Ti 2: 9 v.l. M-M.*

κοσμοκράτωρ, ορος, ὁ *world-ruler* (used of world-ruling gods [Orph. Hymns 8, 11 Helios; 11, 11 Pan; Vett. Val. 170, 36 κ. Ζεύς; 171, 6; 314, 16 κ. Ἥλιος; PGM 4, 1599; 2198; 5, 400 and 17b, 1 Ἑρμῆς; 13, 619 Σάραπις] and of the emperor Caracalla [Egypt. inscr. APF 2, '03, 449 no. 83]. Then gener. of spirit beings, who have parts of the cosmos under their control: Vett. Val. 278, 2; 360, 7; Iambl., Myst. 2, 9; 3, 10.—FCumont, Compt. rend. Acad. des inscr. '19, 313f; EPeterson, Εἷς θεός '26, p. 238, 3. Also loanw. in rabb., e.g. of the angel of death) of evil spirits (w. ἀρχαί and ἐξουσίαι) οἱ κ. τοῦ σκότους τούτου *the world-rulers of this darkness* i.e. the rulers of this sinful world Eph 6: 12 (s. Test. of Solomon in Dibelius, Geisterwelt 230: spirits come to Sol. and call themselves οἱ κοσμοκράτορες τ. σκότους τούτου. On the subject cf. Hdb. on J 12: 31 and FJDölger, D. Sonne d. Gerechtigkeit '18, 49ff; GHCMacgregor, Principalities and Powers: ACPurdy-Festschr. '60, 88–104).*

κοσμοπλανής, ῆτος, ὁ *deceiver of the world*, of the anti-Christ D 16: 4 (Harnack and Knopf read κοσμοπλάνος).*

κοσμοπλάνος s. κοσμοπλανής.

κόσμος, ου, ὁ (Hom.+; inscr., pap., LXX)—1. *adornment, adorning* (Hom.+; Diod. S. 20, 4, 5 τῶν γυναικῶν τὸν κόσμον; Dit., Or. 531, 13; PEleph. 1, 4; PSI 240, 12 γυναικεῖον κόσμον; LXX; Philo, Migr. Abr. 97 γυναικῶν κ.; Jos., Ant. 1, 250; 15, 5; Test. Jud. 12: 1) of women's attire, etc. ὁ ἔξωθεν . . . κόσμος *external adorning* 1 Pt 3: 3 (Vi. Hom. 4 of the inward adornment of a woman, beside σωφροσύνη; Crates, Ep. 9; Pythag., Ep. 11, 1; Plut., Mor. 141ε).

2. in philosoph. usage *the world* as the sum total of everything here and now, *the (orderly) universe* (so, acc. to Plut., Mor. 886β, as early as Pythagoras; certainly Heraclitus, fgm. 66; Pla., Gorg. 508A, Phaedr. 246c; Chrysipp., fgm. 527 v. Arnim κόσμος σύστημα ἐξ οὐρανοῦ καὶ γῆς καὶ τῶν ἐν τούτοις περιεχομένων φύσεων. Likew. Posidonius in Diog. L. 7, 138; Ps.-Aristot., De Mundo 2 p. 391b, 9ff; 2 and 4 Macc; Wsd; Ep. Arist. 254; Philo, Aet. M. 4; Jos., Ant. 1, 21; Test. 12 Patr.; Sib. Or. 7, 123.— The other philosoph. usage, in which κ. denotes the heaven in contrast to the earth, is prob. without mng. for our lit. [unless perh. Phil 2: 15 κ.='sky'?]). ἡ ἀέναος τοῦ κ. σύστασις *the everlasting constitution of the universe* 1 Cl 60: 1 (cf. Dit., Or. 56, 48 εἰς τὸν ἀέναον κ.). Sustained by four elements Hv 3, 13, 3. πρὸ τοῦ τὸν κ. εἶναι *before the world existed* J 17: 5. ἀπὸ καταβολῆς κόσμου *from the beginning of the world* Mt 13: 35 v.l. (the text omits κόσμου); 25: 34; Lk 11: 50; Hb 4: 3; 9: 26; Rv 13: 8; 17: 8. Also ἀπ' ἀρχῆς κ. Mt 24: 21 or κτίσεως κ. Ro 1: 20.—B 5: 5 ἀπὸ καταβ. κ. evidently means *at the foundation of the world* (cf. Windisch, Hdb. ad loc.). πρὸ καταβολῆς κ. *before the foundation of the world* J 17: 24; Eph 1: 4; 1 Pt

1: 20 (on the uses w. καταβολή s. that word, 1). οὐδὲν εἴδωλον ἐν κ. *there is (really) no such thing as an idol in the world* 1 Cor 8: 4. Of the creation in its entirety 3: 22. ὁ κόσμος ὅλος=πᾶσα ἡ κτίσις (Sallust. 21 p. 36, 13) Hs 9, 14, 5. φωστῆρες ἐν κόσμῳ *stars in the universe* Phil 2: 15 (s. above). Esp. of the universe as created by God (Epict. 4, 7, 6 ὁ θεὸς πάντα πεποίηκεν, τὰ ἐν τῷ κόσμῳ καὶ αὐτὸν τὸν κόσμον ὅλον; Wsd 9: 9; 2 Macc 7: 23 ὁ τοῦ κ. κτίστης; 4 Macc 5: 25) ὁ ποιήσας τὸν κ. *who has made the world* Ac 17: 24. ὁ κτίστης τοῦ σύμπαντος κ. 1 Cl 19: 2; ὁ κτίσας τὸν κ. Hv 1, 3, 4; cf. m 12, 4, 2. ὁ τοῦ παντὸς κ. κυριεύων B 21: 5. Christ is called παντὸς τοῦ κ. κύριος 5: 5. The world was created for the sake of the church Hv 2, 4, 1.—The universe, as the greatest space conceivable, is not able to contain someth. (Philo, Ebr. 32) J 21: 25.

3. *the world* as the sum total of all beings above the level of the animals θέατρον ἐγενήθημεν (i.e. οἱ ἀπόστολοι) τῷ κόσμῳ καὶ ἀγγέλοις καὶ ἀνθρώποις 1 Cor 4: 9. Here *the world* is divided into *angels and men* (cf. the Stoic definition of the κόσμος in Stob., Ecl. I p. 184, 8 τὸ ἐκ θεῶν καὶ ἀνθρώπων σύστημα; likew. Epict. 1, 9, 4.— Acc. to Ocellus Luc. c. 37, end, the κ. consists of the sphere of the divine beyond the moon and the sphere of the earthly on this side of the moon).

4. *the world* as the earth, the planet upon which we live (Dit., Syll.³ 814, 31 [67 AD] Nero, ὁ τοῦ παντὸς κόσμου κύριος, Or. 458, 40 [=Inschr. v. Priene 105]; 2 Macc 3: 12; Jos., Ant. 9, 241; 10, 205).

a. gener. Mk 16: 15. τὰς βασιλείας τοῦ κ. Mt 4: 8; ἐν ὅλῳ τῷ κ. 26: 13. Cf. 13: 38; Mk 14: 9; Hs 9, 25, 2. τὸ φῶς τοῦ κ. τούτου *the light of this world* (the sun) J 11: 9. In rhetorical exaggeration ἡ πίστις ὑμῶν καταγγέλλεται ἐν ὅλῳ τ. κόσμῳ Ro 1: 8 (cf. the Egypt. grave inscr. APF 5, '13, 169 no. 24, 8 ὧν ἡ σωφροσύνη κατὰ τὸν κ. λελάληται). Abraham as κληρονόμος κόσμου *heir of the world* 4: 13.—Cf. 1 Cor 14: 10; Col 1: 6. ἡ ἐν τῷ κ. ἀδελφότης *the brotherhood in the (whole) world* 1 Pt 5: 9. ἐγένετο ἡ βασιλεία τοῦ κ. τοῦ κυρίου ἡμῶν *our Lord has assumed the sovereignty of the world* Rv 11: 15. τὰ ἔθνη τοῦ κ. (not LXX, but prob. rabbinic אֻמּוֹת הָעוֹלָם =humankind apart fr. Israel; Billerb. II 191; Dalman, Worte 144f) *the heathen in the world* Lk 12: 30. In this line of development, κόσμος alone serves to designate the *pagan world* Ro 11: 12, 15.—Other worlds (lands) beyond the ocean 1 Cl 20: 8.—In several of these pass. the mng. was

b. *the world* as the habitation of mankind (as Sib. Or. 1, 160). So also Hs 9, 17, 1f. εἰσέρχεσθαι εἰς τὸν κ. of entrance into the world by being born 1 Cl 38: 3. ἐκ τοῦ κ. ἐξελθεῖν *leave this present world* (Philo, Leg. All. 3, 5 ἔξω τ. κόσμου φεύγειν) 1 Cor 5: 10b; 2 Cl 8: 3. γεννηθῆναι εἰς τὸν κ. *be born into the world* Hs 12: 2; ἐσμὲν ἐν τούτῳ τῷ κ. 2 Cl 8: 2. οὐδὲν εἰσφέρειν εἰς τὸν κ. (Philo, Spec. Leg. 1, 294 τὸν μηδὲν εἰς τὸν κόσμον εἰσενηνοχότα) 1 Ti 6: 7. πολλοὶ πλάνοι ἐξῆλθαν εἰς τὸν κ. 2 J 7.—J 12: 25.

c. *earth, world* in contrast to heaven (Dio Chrys. 19 [36], 59) ἐν τῷ κόσμῳ τούτῳ 2 Cl 19: 3.—Esp. when mention is made of the preëxistent Christ, who came fr. the other world into the κόσμος. So, above all, in John (Bultmann, Reg. I κόσμος) ἔρχεσθαι εἰς τὸν κ. (τοῦτον) J 6: 14; 9: 39; 11: 27; 16: 28a; 18: 37; specif. also *come into the world as light* 12: 46; 1: 9; 3: 19. Sending of Jesus into the world 3: 17a; 10: 36; 1 J 4: 9. His εἶναι ἐν τῷ κόσμῳ J 9: 5a. Leaving the world and returning to the Father 13: 1; 16: 28b. His kingship is not ἐκ τοῦ κ. τούτου *of this world* 18: 36a, b.—Also Χρ. Ἰησοῦς ἦλθεν εἰς τ. κόσμον 1 Ti 1: 15; cf. ἐπιστεύθη ἐν κόσμῳ (opp. ἀνελήμφθη ἐν δόξῃ) 3: 16.—εἰσερχόμενος εἰς τὸν κ. Hb 10: 5.

d. *the world* outside in contrast to one's home PK 3 p. 15, 13; 19.

5. *the world* as mankind (Sib. Or. 1, 189)—**a.** gener. οὐαὶ τῷ κ. ἀπὸ τῶν σκανδάλων *woe to mankind because of vexations* Mt 18: 7; τὸ φῶς τοῦ κ. *the light for mankind* 5: 14; cf. J 8: 12; 9: 5. ὁ σωτὴρ τοῦ κ. 4: 42; 1 J 4: 14 (this designation is found in the inscrs., esp. oft. of Hadrian [WWeber, Untersuchungen z. Geschichte des Kaisers Hadrianus '07, 225; 226; 229]).—J 1: 29; 3: 17b; 17: 6.—κρίνειν τὸν κ. (Sib. Or. 4, 184) Ro 3: 6; B 4: 12; cf. Ro 3: 19. ἡ ἁμαρτία εἰς τὸν κ. εἰσῆλθεν 5: 12; likew. θάνατος εἰσῆλθεν εἰς τὸν κ. 1 Cl 3: 4 (Wsd 2: 24; 14: 14). Cf. Ro 5: 13; 1 Cor 1: 27f. περικαθάρματα τοῦ κ. *the refuse of mankind* 4: 13.—6: 2a, b (Sallust. 21 p. 36, 13 the souls of the virtuous, together w. the gods, will rule the whole κόσμος); 2 Cor 1: 12; 5: 19; Js 2: 5; 1 J 2: 2; 4: 1, 3. ἀρχαῖος κόσμος *the men of the ancient world* 2 Pt 2: 5a; cf. b; 3: 6.—ὅλος ὁ κ. *all the world, everybody* Ac 2: 47 D. Likew. ὁ κόσμος (cf. Philo, De Prov. in Euseb., Pr. Ev. 8, 14, 58) ὁ κ. ὀπίσω αὐτοῦ ἀπῆλθεν J 12: 19. ἐγὼ παρρησίᾳ λελάληκα τῷ κ. 18: 20; cf. 7: 4; 14: 22.

b. of all mankind, but especially of believers, as the object of God's love J 3: 16, 17c; 6: 33, 51; 12: 47.

6. *the world* as the scene of earthly joys, possessions, cares, sufferings (cf. 4 Macc 8: 23) τὸν κ. ὅλον κερδῆσαι *gain the whole world* Mt 16: 26; Mk 8: 36; Lk 9: 25; 2 Cl 6: 2 (cf. Procop. Soph., Ep. 137 the whole οἰκουμένη is an unimportant possession compared to ἀρετή). τὰ τερπνὰ τοῦ κ. *the delightful things in the world* IRo 6: 1. οἱ χρώμενοι τὸν κ. ὡς μὴ καταχρώμενοι *those who use the world as though they were not using it to the full* 1 Cor 7: 31a. ἔχειν τὸν βίον τοῦ κ. *possess worldly goods* 1 J 3: 17. τὰ τοῦ κόσμου *the affairs of the world* 1 Cor 7: 33f; cf. 1 J 2: 15f. The latter pass. forms an easy transition to the large number of exprs. (esp. in Paul and John) in which

7. *the world,* and everything that belongs to it, appears as that which is hostile to God, i.e. lost in sin, wholly at odds w. anything divine, ruined and depraved (Herm. Wr. 6, 4 [the κόσμος is τὸ πλήρωμα τῆς κακίας]; 13, 1 [ἡ τοῦ κ. ἀπάτη], in Stob. p. 428, 24 Sc.; En. 48, 7; Test. Iss. 4: 6; Hdb., exc. on J 1: 10; Bultmann 33-5.—Cf. Sotades Maronita [III BC] 11 Diehl: the κόσμος is unjust and hostile to great men) IMg 5: 2; IRo 2: 2. ὁ κόσμος οὗτος *this world* (in contrast to the other world) J 8: 23; 12: 25, 31a; 13: 1; 16: 11; 18: 36; 1 J 4: 17; 1 Cor 3: 19; 5: 10a; 7: 31b; Hv 4, 3, 2ff; D 10: 6; 2 Cl 5: 1, 5; (opp. ὁ ἅγιος αἰών) B 10: 11. 'This world' is ruled by the ἄρχων τοῦ κ. τούτου *the prince of this world,* the devil J 12: 31b; 16: 11; without τούτου 14: 30. Cf. also ὁ κ. ὅλος ἐν τῷ πονηρῷ κεῖται *the whole world lies in the power of the evil one* 1 J 5: 19. Cf. 4: 4; also ὁ αἰὼν τοῦ κ. τούτου Eph 2: 2 (s. αἰών 4).—The Christian must have nothing to do with this world of sin and separation fr. God: instead of desiring it IRo 7: 1, one is to ἄσπιλον ἑαυτὸν τηρεῖν ἀπὸ τοῦ κ. *keep oneself unstained by the world* Js 1: 27. ἀποφεύγειν τὰ μιάσματα τοῦ κ. 2 Pt 2: 20; cf. 1: 4 (s. ἀποφεύγω).—Pol 5: 3. ἡ φιλία τοῦ κ. ἔχθρα τ. θεοῦ ἐστιν Js 4: 4a; cf. b. When he takes this attitude the Christian is naturally hated by the world IRo 3: 3; J 15: 18, 19a, d; 17: 14a; 1 J 3: 13, as his Lord was hated J 7: 7; 15: 18. Cf. 1: 10c; 14: 17; 16: 20.— Also in Paul: God and world in opposition τὸ πνεῦμα τοῦ κ. and τὸ πνεῦμα τὸ ἐκ θεοῦ *the spirit of the world* and *the Spirit that comes fr. God* 1 Cor 2: 12. ἡ κατὰ θεὸν λύπη and ἡ τοῦ κ. λύπη *godly grief* and *worldly grief* 2 Cor 7: 10. The world is condemned by God 1 Cor 11: 32; but also the object of the divine plan of salvation 2 Cor 5: 19; cf. 1 Cl 9: 4. The Christian is dead as far as this world is concerned: δι' οὗ (i.e. Ἰ. Χρ.) ἐμοὶ κ. ἐσταύρωται κἀγὼ κόσμῳ *through Christ the world has been crucified for*

me, and I have been (crucified) *to the world* Gal 6: 14. For στοιχεῖα τοῦ κ. Col 2: 8, 20 s. στοιχεῖον.—The use of κ. in this sense is even further developed in John. The κ. stands in opposition to God 1 J 2: 15f and hence is incapable of knowing God J 17: 25; cf. 1 J 4: 5, and excluded fr. Christ's intercession J 17: 9. Neither Christ himself 17: 14c, 16b; 14: 27, nor his own 15: 19b; 17: 14b, 16a; 1 J 3: 1 belong in any way to the 'world'. Rather Christ has chosen them 'out of the world' J 15: 19c, even though for the present they must still live 'in the world' 17: 11b; cf. vss. 15, 18b. All the trouble that they must undergo because of this, 16: 33a, means nothing compared w. the victorious conviction that Christ (and the believers w. him) has overcome 'the world' vs. 33b; 1 J 5: 4f, and that it is doomed to pass away 2: 17 (Kephal. I 154, 21: the κόσμος τῆς σαρκός will pass away).

8. *totality, sum total* (Dit., Syll.³ 850, 10 τὸν κόσμον τῶν ἔργων; Pr 17: 6a) ὁ κ. τῆς ἀδικίας ἡ γλῶσσα καθίσταται *the tongue becomes* (or *proves to be*) *the sum total of iniquity* Js 3: 6 (so, approx., in recent times Meinertz; FHauck.—MDibelius, Windisch and ASchlatter find mng. 7 here, while ACarr, Exp. 7th Ser. VIII '09, 318ff thinks of mng. 1). Χρ. τὸν ὑπὲρ τῆς τοῦ παντὸς κόσμου τῶν σῳζομένων σωτηρίας παθόντα *Christ, who suffered* or *died* (s. πάσχω 3aα) *for the salvation of the sum total of those who are saved* MPol 17: 2.—FBytomski, D. genet. Entwicklung des Begriffes κόσμος in d. Hl. Schrift: Jahrb. für Philos. und spekul. Theol. 25, '11, 180–201; 389–413 (only the OT); CSchneider, Pls u. d. Welt: Ἄγγελος IV '32, 11–47; EvSchrenck, Der Kosmos-Begriff bei Joh.: Mitteilungen u. Nachrichten f. d. evang. Kirche in Russland 51, 1895, 1–29; RLöwe, Kosmos u. Aion '35; RBultmann, D. Verständnis v. Welt u. Mensch im NT u. im Griechentum: ThBl 19, '40, 1–14; GBornkamm, Christus u. die Welt in der urchr. Botschaft: ZThK 47, '50, 212–26; RVölkl, Christ u. Welt nach dem NT '61; GJohnston, οἰκουμένη and κ. in the NT, NTS 10, '64, 352–60; NHCassem, ibid. 19, '72/'73, 81–91; HSasse, TW III 867–96. M-M. B. 13; 440.

Κούαρτος, ου, ὁ (on the accent s. Bl-D. §41, 2; 3; Rob. 235f) *Quartus,* an otherw. unknown Christian Ro 16: 23; 1 Cor subscr.*

κούμ (אBC as over against κουμι AD) Mesopotamian form of the imper. קוּם, for which Palestinian Aramaic has קוּמִי, *stand up* Mk 5: 41 (Wlh. ad loc.).*

Κούμαι, ῶν, αἱ (the Gk. form: Paradoxogr. Flor. 28; Ptolem. 3, 1, 6) *Cumae* a city in Campania, Italy, not far fr. Naples; an old Gk. colony, famed for its Sibyl (on Cumae as the residence of the Sibyl s. MDibelius, Hdb. exc. on Hv 2, 4, 1). Hv 1, 1, 3; 2, 1, 1.*

κουμι s. **κούμ.**

κουστωδία, ας, ἡ (POxy. 294, 20 [22 AD]; PRyl. 189, 2; BGU 341, 3; cf. Hahn 233, 6; 234, 7 w. lit. Lat. loanw., custodia, also in rabb.) *a guard* composed of soldiers Mt 27: 66; 28: 11. ἔχειν κουστωδίαν *take a guard* 27: 65. M-M.*

κουφίζω impf. ἐκούφιζον (Hes. +) *make light, lighten* (so trag.; Dio Chrys. 80[30], 40; inscr., pap., LXX; Jos., Bell. 2, 96, Ant. 18, 149) τὶ someth. (1 Km 6: 5) τὸ πλοῖον *lighten the ship* by throwing out the cargo Ac 27: 38 (Polyb. 20, 5, 11; Jon 1: 5). M-M.*

κούφισμα, ατος, τό (Eur., Phoen. 860; Plut., Mor. 114c) *lightening, alleviation* of almsgiving κ. ἁμαρτίας γίνεται *lightens the load of sin* 2 Cl 16: 4 (after 1 Esdr 8: 84 σύ,

κύριε, ἐκούφισας τὰς ἁμαρτίας ἡμῶν. Cf. 2 Esdr [Ezra] 9: 13).*

κόφινος, ου, ὁ (Aristoph., X.+; inscr., pap.; Judg 6: 19 B; Ps 80: 7) *basket,* in the NT prob. a large, heavy basket for carrying things (FJAHort, JTS 10, '09, 567ff; Artem. 2, 24; Jos., Bell. 3, 95) Mt 14: 20; Mk 6: 43; Lk 9: 17; J 6: 13; but of var. sizes, and considered typical of the Jews (Juvenal 3, 14; 6, 542; RCHorn, Lutheran Quarterly 1, '49, 301). W. σφυρίς (Mt 16: 10; Mk 8: 20; cf. on this APF 6, '20, 220 no. 8, 4f [III BC] Φίλωνι κόφινοι β′, Πτολεμαίῳ σφυρίδιον) Mt 16: 9; Mk 8: 19. κ. κοπρίων *a basket of manure* Lk 13: 8 D (Nicol. Dam.: 90 fgm. 66, 13 Jac. κόπρον ἐν κοφίνῳ). M-M. B. 623.*

κράβαττος, ου, ὁ (a loanw., found also in rabb., but of uncertain origin and late in appearing [Phryn. 62 L. Acc. to Pollux 10, 35 in the form κράββατος in the comic poets Rhinto—III BC—and Crito—II BC—, also Epict. 1, 24, 14; Aesop, Fab. 413 H.; PLond. 191, 16—II AD—κράββατος. Ostracon in Mélanges Nicole '05 p. 184=Sb 4292, 9 and Moeris p. 58; 354 κράβατος. The form κράβακτος also occurs: PTebt. 406, 19.—Aq. Am 3: 12]. On the form of the word s. Bl-D. §42, 4 w. app.; Mlt. 244, Einleitung 60, 1; Mlt.-H. 102; Rob. 119; 213) *mattress, pallet,* the poor man's *bed* Mk 2: 4; 6: 55. W. κλινάριον Ac 5: 15. αἴρειν τὸν κ. Mk 2: 9, 11f; J 5: 8–11 (cf. Lucian, Philopseud. 11 ὁ Μίδας αὐτὸς ἀράμενος τὸν σκίμποδα, ἐφ' οὗ ἐκεκόμιστο, ᾤχετο ἐς τὸν ἀγρὸν ἀπιών). κατακεῖσθαι ἐπὶ κραβάττου *lie in bed* Ac 9: 33. M-M.*

κράζω (Aeschyl. +; pap., LXX, En., Philo, Joseph.) neut. ptc. κράζον (Bl-D. §13; Rob. 231); impf. ἔκραζον; fut. κράξω and κεκράξομαι (Bl-D. §77; Rob. 361); 1 aor. ἔκραξα and ἐκέκραξα (Ac 24: 21, s. Bl-D. §75; W-S. §13, 2; 10 note 10); pf. κέκραγα.

1. *cry out, scream, shriek,* when one utters loud cries, but no words capable of being understood: of insane persons, epileptics, or the evil spirits living in them Mk 5: 5; 9: 26; Lk 4: 41 v.l.; 9: 39. Of the death-cry of Jesus on the cross Mk 15: 39 v.l. Of the cry of a woman in childbirth Rv 12: 2. ἀπὸ τοῦ φόβου *cry out in fear* Mt 14: 26. φωνῇ μεγάλῃ *cry out in a loud voice* Mt 27: 50; Ac 7: 57; Rv 10: 3.

2. *call, call out, cry*—a. lit. κράζει ὄπισθεν ἡμῶν *she is calling out after us* Mt 15: 23. τὶ someth. of a crowd Ac 19: 32. φωνὴν κ. *call out a thing loudly* 24: 21. W. direct discourse foll. (Bl-D. §397, 5 app.) Mk 10: 48; 11: 9; 15: 14; Lk 18: 39; Ac 19: 34; 21: 28, 36; 23: 6. W. φωνῇ μεγάλῃ and direct discourse foll. Mk 5: 7; Ac 7: 60. Also ἐν φωνῇ μεγάλῃ Rv 14: 15. Used w. λέγειν (Bl-D. §420, 2 app.) of loud speaking κράζω λέγων *I say loudly* (Ex 5: 8) Mt 8: 29; 14: 30; 15: 22; 20: 30f; 21: 9; 27: 23; Mk 3: 11; J 7: 37; Ac 16: 17; Rv 18: 18f. Also pleonast. κ. φωνῇ μεγάλῃ λέγων *I call out w. a loud voice and say* Rv 6: 10; 7: 10. κ. ἐν φωνῇ μεγάλῃ λέγων 19: 17; cf. 18: 2. κράξας ἔλεγε Mk 9: 24. κ. καὶ λέγειν Mt 9: 27; 21: 15; Mk 10: 47; Lk 4: 41 v.l.; Ac 14: 14f. ἔκραξεν καὶ εἶπεν J 12: 44. ἔκραξεν διδάσκων καὶ λέγων *he cried out as he was teaching, and said* 7: 28. The pf. κέκραγα has present mng. (Hippocr., Περὶ ἱερ. νούσ. 15 vol. VI 388 Littré βοᾷ καὶ κέκραγεν; Menand., Sam. 11; 24 J.; Plut., Cato Min. 58, 1 μαρτυρόμενος καὶ κεκραγώς; Lucian, Demon. 48 κεκραγότα κ. λέγοντα; Ex 5: 8; 2 Km 19: 29; Is 15: 4; Job 30: 20, 28; 34: 20; Ps 4: 4; 140: 1) Ἰωάννης μαρτυρεῖ περὶ αὐτοῦ καὶ κέκραγεν λέγων J 1: 15. κ. τινι (ἐν) φωνῇ μεγάλῃ (λέγων) *call out to someone in a loud voice* Rv 7: 2; 14: 15.—Of angel choirs 1 Cl 34: 6 (Is 6: 3).

b. fig.—α. of the urgent speech of the prophet (Jos., Ant. 10, 117: Jerem.) or what his book says (Ammonius

Herm. in Aristot. Lib. De Interpret. p. 183, 30 Busse: ἀκουέτω τοῦ Ἀριστοτέλους κεκραγότος ὅτι ...) Ἠσαΐας κράζει ὑπὲρ τοῦ Ἰσραήλ Ro 9: 27. Of prayer, rather fervent than loud 8: 15. ἐκέκραξεν ὁ δίκαιος 1 Cl 22: 7 (Ps 33: 18). Of the divine Spirit in the heart Gal 4: 6.

β. of things (Epict. 1, 16, 11 κέκραγεν ἡ φύσις; Achilles Tat. 5, 17, 4 κέκραγέ σου ἡ μορφή τ. εὐγένειαν): stones, that cry out if the disciples were to hold back with their confession of Jesus' messiahship Lk 19: 40. The laborers' wages, held back, κράζει Js 5: 4 (cf. Gen 4: 10; 18: 20; Philo, Ebr. 98 κ. ἐν ἡμῖν αἱ ἄλογοι ὁρμαί; Jos., Bell. 1, 197).—WGrundmann, TW III 898–904 κράζω and related words. M-M. B. 1250.*

κραιπάλη, ης, ἡ both carousing, intoxication, and its result drunken headache, hangover, since it means dizziness, staggering, when the head refuses to function (Aristoph.; Plut., Mor. 127F; Lucian, Bis Accus. 16; Soranus p. 16, 26; Aretaeus p. 110, 2) ἐν κ. καὶ μέθη w. dissipation and drunkenness Lk 21: 34 (cf. Herodian 2, 6, 6 παρὰ μέθην κ. κρ.; Is 24: 20). πολυτέλεια μεθυσμάτων καὶ κραιπαλῶν extravagance in drunkenness and carousing Hm 6, 2, 5.—HJCadbury, The Style and Literary Method of Luke '19, 54. M-M.*

κρανίον, ου, τό (Hom.+; pap., LXX; Jos., Bell. 3, 245, Ant. 8, 390) skull κρανίου (epexegetic gen.) τόπος the place that is called (a) Skull as a transl. of Γολγοθᾶ (q.v.) Mt 27: 33; Mk 15: 22; J 19: 17. Cf. Lk 23: 33, where 'Calvary' of the KJ is not a NT place name, but the Lat. transl. of κ. (s. Gdspd., Probs. 89f). Schol. on Lucian 251, 20f Κρανίον· ἐστὶ τόπος ἐν Κορίνθω.—For other lit. s. on Γολγοθᾶ. M-M. B. 213f.*

κράσπεδον, ου, τό (trag., X.+; LXX; loanw. in rabb.) —1. edge, border, hem of a garment (Theocr. 2, 53; Appian, Bell. Civ. 1, 16 §68 τὸ κρ. τοῦ ἱματίου of the Pontifex Maximus; Ael. Aristid. 47 p. 416 D.; Athen. 4, 49 p. 159D; 9, 16 p. 374A; PGM 7, 371 ἐξάψας κράσπεδον τοῦ ἱματίου σου; Zech 8: 23) ἥψατο τοῦ κ. τοῦ ἱματίου αὐτοῦ Mt 9: 20; Lk 8: 44; cf. Mt 14: 36; Mk 6: 56.—But mng. 2 is also poss. for these passages, depending on how strictly Jesus followed the Mosaic law, and also upon the way in which κρ. was understood by the authors and first readers of the gospels.

2. tassel (ציצת), which the Israelite was obligated to wear on the four corners of his outer garment, acc. to Num 15: 38f; Dt 22: 12 (Schürer II⁴ 566 [sources and lit.]; Billerb. IV 276–92). Of the Pharisees μεγαλύνειν τὰ κ. make the tassels on their garments long Mt 23: 5. M-M. B. 859f.*

κραταιός, ά, όν (in Hom. and other poets; in prose it appears late: Philo Mech. 80, 22; Polyb. 2, 69, 8; Cornutus 31 p. 63, 1; Plut., Crass. 24, 4, Mor. p. 967c; Lucian, Anach. 28; Vett. Val. index; Wilcken, Chrest. 122, 1 [6 AD] τῷ μεγίστῳ κραταιῷ θεῷ Σοκνοπαίῳ; PGM 7, 422 θεοὶ κραταιοί; 563; 789; LXX; Philo, Spec. Leg. 1, 307 θεὸς μέγας κ. ἰσχυρὸς κ. κραταιός) powerful, mighty of God's hand (oft. LXX; Test. Jos. 1, 5; PGM 4, 1279; 1307) 1 Pt 5: 6; 1 Cl 28: 2; 60: 3. δύναμις mighty power (cf. Philo, Conf. Lingu. 51) Hv 1, 3, 4. M-M.*

κραταιόω (later form for class. κρατύνω. Hippocr.: CMG I 1 p. 88, 12; LXX.—Philo has the mid. in act. sense: Conf. Lingu. 101; 103] impf. pass. ἐκραταιούμην; 1 aor. pass. inf. κραταιωθῆναι strengthen. Pass. become strong (Philo, Agr. 160, Omn. Prob. Lib. 27; Test. Napht. 1: 4) 1 Cor 16: 13 (w. ἀνδρίζεσθαι, as Ps 30: 25; 2 Km 10: 12);

w. αὐξάνειν Lk 2: 40. κ. πνεύματι grow strong 1: 80. δυνάμει κ. διὰ τοῦ πνεύματος be mightily strengthened through the Spirit Eph 3: 16.*

κρατέω impf. ἐκράτουν; fut. κρατήσω; 1 aor. ἐκράτησα; pf. inf. κεκρατηκέναι; impf. pass. ἐκρατούμην; pf. pass. κεκράτημαι, 3 pl. κεκράτηνται (Hom.+; inscr., pap., LXX, Ep. Arist., Philo, Joseph., Test. 12 Patr.).

1. take into one's possession or custody—a. arrest, take into custody, apprehend τινά someone (cf. Ps 136: 9) Mt 14: 3; 21: 46; 26: 4, 48, 50, 55, 57 (on the arrest of Jesus cf. Feigel, Weidel, Finegan s.v. Ἰούδας 6); Mk 6: 17; 12: 12; 14: 1, 44, 46, 49, 51; Ac 24: 6; Rv 20: 2.

b. take hold of, grasp, seize forcibly and also without the use of force (cf. 2 Km 6: 6; SSol 3: 4); w. acc. of the pers. or thing Mt 12: 11; 18: 28; 22: 6; 28: 9; Mk 3: 21. κ. ῥάβδον τῇ χειρί take hold of a staff w. the hand Hs 9, 6, 3 (cf. PGM 5, 451 κράτει τῇ ἀριστερᾷ σου τὸν δάκτυλον; Synes., Ep. 58 p. 202 πόδα). τῆς χειρός (τινος) take hold of (someone's) hand (Bl-D. §170, 2; Rob. 475; 1391; Ps 72: 23; Gen 19: 16; Jos., Bell. 1, 352) Mt 9: 25; Mk 1: 31; 5: 41; 9: 27; Lk 8: 54; B 14: 7 (Is 42: 6). τινὰ τῆς χειρός take someone by the hand Mk 9: 27 t.r.; cf. B 12: 11 (Is 45: 1).

c. attain (Diod. S. 3, 54, 7 κ. τῆς ἐπιβολῆς attain the purpose; likew. 17, 77, 4 and 20, 25, 3; Appian, Bell. Civ. 3, 61 §249 οὐ ... ἐκράτησε) τῆς προθέσεως the purpose Ac 27: 13 (s. Field, Notes 144).

2. hold—a. hold τινά someone (fast) w. the hand, so that he cannot go away Ac 3: 11.

b. hold in the hand (Sib. Or. 3, 49) τὶ ἐν τῇ δεξιᾷ Rv 2: 1 (Polemo Perieg. [c. 200 BC] in Athen. 11, 67 p. 484C ἐν τῇ δεξιᾷ κώθωνα κρ.; cf. Plut., Mor. 99D).

c. hold upright, support τὶ someth. Hs 9, 8, 5. τὰς χεῖρας v 3, 8, 3 (cf. MDibelius, Hdb. ad loc.). Pass. be supported ὑπό τινος by someth. Hv 3, 3, 5; 3, 8, 7. W. διά instead of ὑπό: ὁ κόσμος διὰ τεσσάρων στοιχείων κρατεῖται the world is supported by four elements 3, 13, 3.

d. hold back or restrain from, hinder in an action w. acc., foll. by ἵνα μή Rv 7: 1. Pass. be prevented foll. by τοῦ μή and inf. (Bl-D. §400, 4; Rob. 1061; 1425) their eyes ἐκρατοῦντο τοῦ μὴ ἐπιγνῶναι Lk 24: 16. But it is not certain whether physical eyes or the eyes of the spirit are meant (cf. διανοίγω 1b).

e. hold fast and so prevent fr. escaping—a. hold in one's power (PTebt. 61b, 229; POxy. 237 VIII, 34; Jos., C. Ap. 1, 84) pass. οὐκ ἦν δυνατὸν κρατεῖσθαι αὐτὸν ὑπ' αὐτοῦ it was impossible for him (Christ) to be held in its (death's) power Ac 2: 24.

β. hold fast (to) someone or someth., and hence remain closely united to it or him. W. acc. τὴν κεφαλήν hold fast to the Head (i.e. to Christ) Col 2: 19 (cf. SSol 3: 4 ἐκράτησα αὐτὸν καὶ οὐκ ἀφήσω αὐτόν). τὴν παράδοσιν Mk 7: 3 (cf. Test. Napht. 3: 1 τὸ θέλημα τ. θεοῦ); cf. vss. 4, 8; 2 Th 2: 15. τὴν διδαχήν Rv 2: 14f. τὸ ὄνομά μου vs. 13.—W. gen. of the thing (Stephan. Byz. s.v. Γυναικόπολις: in the absence of the men τὰς γυναῖκας κρατῆσαι τοῦ πολέμου=they kept the war going; Pr 14: 18; Jos., Ant. 6, 116 τοῦ λογισμοῦ) τῆς ὁμολογίας hold fast to our confession Hb 4: 14. τῆς ἐλπίδος 6: 18. τῶν ἔργων τινός Hv 3, 8, 8.

γ. hold fast, keep hold of someth. that belongs to oneself, so that it cannot be taken away fr. him Rv 2: 25; 3: 11.

δ. keep to oneself a saying, in order to occupy oneself w. it later Mk 9: 10.

ε. retain τὰς ἁμαρτίας the sins (opp. ἀφιέναι) J 20: 23. M-M. B. 746.*

κράτιστος, η, ον (Hom. +; inscr., pap., LXX, Ep. Arist., Philo, Joseph. Isolated superl. of κρατύς) *most noble, most excellent,* honorary form of address used to persons who hold a higher official or social position than the speaker.

1. official rendering of the Latin title *vir egregius* (Magie 31; 112; Hahn 259; OSeeck in Pauly-W. V 2006f; O Hirschfeld, Kleine Schriften '13, 651, 5; 654; Wilcken, Her. 20, 1885, 469ff; WSchubart, Einf. in d. Papyruskunde '18, 259.—Jos., Ant. 20, 12), in addressing the Procurator of Judaea Ac 23: 26; 24: 3; 26: 25.

2. as a form of polite address with no official connotation (Theophr., Char. 5; Dionys. Hal., De Orat. Ant. 1 ὦ κράτιστε Ἀμμαῖε; Jos., Vi. 430 κράτιστε ἀνδρῶν Ἐπαφρόδιτε [a freedman of Domitian, to whom Joseph. dedicated his Antiquities and his books against Apion]; likew. C. Ap. 1, 1 [but 2, 1 τιμιώτατέ μοι Ἐ.; 2, 296 simply his name]. κ. is also found in dedications Galen X 78; XIV 295; XIX 8 Kühn.—Bl-D. §60, 2) Lk 1: 3; Dg 1: 1. Cf. Zahn, Einl. II³ 340; 365; 390, Ev. des Lk.³·⁴ '20, 56f. M-M.*

κράτος, ους, τό (Hom. +; inscr., pap., LXX, Philo, Joseph.)—**1.** *power, might* of God's power (Theognis 376 al.; Ael. Aristid. 37, 8 K.=2 p. 15 D.; 2 Macc 3: 34; 7: 17; 11: 4. S. also 4 below) 1 Cl 33: 3; 61: 1; 64. Of the power of Jesus 2 Cl 17: 5.—τὸ κ. τῆς δόξης αὐτοῦ *his glorious* (divine) *might* Col 1: 11. κατὰ κράτος αὐξάνειν *grow mightily, wonderfully* Ac 19: 20 (κατὰ κράτος like Menand., Per. 407; Dio Chrys. 26[43], 11; IG XII 5, 444, 103 [264/3 bc]; PTebt. 27, 83 [113 bc]; AWArgyle, ET 75, '64, 151 connects κατὰ κρ. with τ. κυρίου, *by the might of the Lord*).

2. *mighty deed* ποιεῖν κ. (cf. עָשָׂה חַיִל Ps 118: 15) *do mighty deeds* Lk 1: 51.

3. *strength, intensity* (cf. Appian, Bell. Civ. 2, 35 §141 κατὰ κράτος=with all his might; Ps.-Callisth. 1, 8, 2 ἡλίου κρ.; Ps 89: 11) τὸ κρ. τῆς ἰσχύος αὐτοῦ Eph 1: 19; 6: 10; 1 Cl 27: 5 (cf. Is 40: 26; Da 4: 30 Theod.; IQS 11, 19f; IQH 4, 32).

4. *power, rule, sovereignty* (Arrian, Anab. 4, 20, 3 the ruling might of the great king; POxy. 41 I, 2 εἰς αἰῶνα τὸ κράτος τῶν Ῥωμαίων. Of divinities: Apollon. Rhod. 4, 804 Zeus; UPZ 81 II, 17 [II bc] of Isis: ἐλθέ μοι θεὰ θεῶν, κράτος ἔχουσα μέγιστον; PSI 29, 21 τὸ κρ. τοῦ Ἀδωναΐ; POxy. 1380, 238 ἀστραπῶν τὸ κρ. ἔχεις; Philo, Spec. Leg. 1, 307 τ. ὅλων τὸ κρ.; Jos., Ant. 10, 263 τὸ πάντων κρ. ἔχων) τὸν τὸ κ. ἔχοντα τοῦ θανάτου *the one who has power over death* Hb 2: 14 (τὸ κρ. ἔχειν τινός since Hdt. 3, 69).—In a doxology 1 Ti 6: 16; 1 Pt 4: 11; 5: 11; Jd 25; Rv 1: 6; 5: 13; 1 Cl 65: 2; MPol 20: 2.— WMichaelis, TW III 905–14 κράτος and related words. M-M.*

κραυγάζω impf. ἐκραύγαζον; fut. κραυγάσω; 1 aor. ἐκραύγασα (poet. fgm. in Pla., Rep. 10 p. 607ʙ [of a dog]; Demosth. 54, 7; Epict. 3, 1, 37 [of a raven]; 3, 4, 4; 2 Esdr [Ezra] 3: 13 λαὸς ἐκραύγασεν φωνῇ μεγάλῃ) *cry (out), utter a (loud) sound.*

1. of animal sounds, as the grunting of hungry swine B 10: 3.

2. of the human voice—**a.** *cry out, cry for help, scream* excitedly (Epict. 1, 18, 19; Polemo, Decl. 1, 40 p. 14, 16) Mt 12: 19; Ac 22: 23. Also w. λέγοντες foll., which introduces direct discourse J 18: 40; 19: 6, 12. Without λέγ. w. direct discourse foll. vs. 15.—Of demons coming out of persons, and speaking in human languages δαιμόνια κραυγάζοντα καὶ λέγοντα ὅτι w. direct discourse foll. Lk 4: 41 𝔓⁷⁵ DE.

b. *cry* loudly, in a moment of exaltation κ. ὡσαννά J 12: 13. κ. φωνῇ μεγάλῃ w. direct discourse foll. J 11: 43; IPhld 7: 1. B 1250.*

κραυγή, ῆς, ἡ (Eur., X. +; Vett. Val. 2, 35; PPetr. II 45 III, 25 [246 bc]; POxy. 1242 III, 54; PTebt. 15, 3; LXX; En. 104, 3; Ep. Arist.; Joseph.).

1. lit.—**a.** *shout(ing), clamor* of excited persons Eph 4: 31. Of people shouting back and forth in a quarrel: ἐγένετο κ. μεγάλη *there arose a loud outcry* Ac 23: 9 (cf. Ex 12: 30; without μεγ. X., Cyr. 7, 5, 28). Also *crying* in grief or anxiety (cf. Ex 3: 7; 11: 6; Esth 4: 3; Is 65: 19) Rv 21: 4.

b. *a loud* (articulate) *cry* κ. γέγονεν w. direct discourse foll. *there arose a shout* Mt 25: 6 (EGrässer, D. Problem der Parousieverzögerung, ZNW Beih. 22, '57, 124f). ἀνεφώνησεν κραυγῇ μεγάλῃ καὶ εἶπεν w. direct discourse foll. Lk 1: 42; cf. Rv 14: 18 v.l. Of fervent prayer (Ps 17: 7; Jon 2: 3) μετὰ κ. ἰσχυρᾶς *with loud crying* Hb 5: 7 (cf. Diod. S. 19, 83, 3 μετὰ πολλῆς κραυγῆς.—μετὰ κ. as Diod. S. 11, 36, 1; Nicol. Dam. 90, fgm. 130, 25 p. 409, 20 Jac.; UPZ 8, 17 [161 bc]; Ep. Arist. 186; Jos., Bell. 2, 517). ἀκουσθῆναι ἐν κ. τὴν φωνὴν ὑμῶν *so that your voice is heard in loud cries* B 3: 1 (Is 58: 4).

2. fig.: the virginity of Mary, her childbearing, and the death of Jesus are called τρία μυστήρια κραυγῆς, ἅτινα ἐν ἡσυχίᾳ θεοῦ ἐπράχθη *three mysteries (to be) loudly proclaimed, which were accomplished in the stillness of God* IEph 19: 1. M-M.*

κρέας, κρέως and later **κρέατος** (s. Thumb 96; Meisterhans³-Schw. p. 143 [an Attic inscr. of 338 bc w. κρέατος]; Thackeray 149, 3), *τό meat* (Hom. +; inscr., pap., LXX, Philo) pl. τὰ κρέα (Bl-D. §47, 1; Jos., Ant. 10, 261) φαγεῖν κρέα (Test. Judah 15: 4) Ro 14: 21; 1 Cor 8: 13; κρέας GEb 6. M-M. B. 202.*

κρείσσων s. **κρείττων.**

κρείττων, ον, gen. **ονος,** and **κρείσσων** (Bl-D. §34, 1 w. app.; Mlt.-H. 107; JWackernagel, Hellenistica '07, 12–25; Reinhold 43f; Thackeray 121, 2. The ms. tradition fluctuates in most places betw. ττ and σσ. The word occurs Hom. +; inscr., pap., LXX, Philo; Jos., Bell. 1, 57) in our lit. always a real comp. (of κρατύς, but functions as comp. of ἀγαθός).

1. *more prominent, higher in rank, preferable, better* (Pind., Hdt. et al.) of pers. IPhld 9: 1; Hb 7: 7 (opp. ἐλάττων). τοσούτῳ κ. γενόμενος τῶν ἀγγέλων *as much superior to the angels* 1: 4 (Jos., Ant. 8, 111 τ. ἄλλων ... κρείττονες γεγόναμεν).—Of things 7: 19, 22; 8: 6; 9: 23; 10: 34; 11: 16, 35; IRo 2: 1. κρεῖττον 1 Cor 12: 31 t.r. (for the continuation of vs. 31b here cf. Appian, Mithrid. 60 §247 ἑτέραν ὁδὸν ἔχειν κρείττονα= know another way, a better one). W. gen. foll. *better than* (Jos., C. Ap. 1, 273) Dg 2: 2. κρεῖττόν τι someth. *better* Hb 11: 40. ἐν ᾧ κρείσσων ἐστίν *in the respect in which he is better off* (than the other man) Dg 10: 6. ἡ ἀπὸ τῶν κρειττόνων ἐπὶ τὰ χείρω μετάνοια *a change of mind from better to worse* MPol 11: 1.

2. *more useful, more advantageous, better* πεπείσμεθα περὶ ὑμῶν τὰ κ. *we are sure of better things concerning you* Hb 6: 9. εἰς τὸ κ. συνέρχεσθαι (opp. εἰς τὸ ἧσσον; s. ἥσσων) 1 Cor 11: 17. W. gen. *better, more advantageous than* (Artem. 2, 11 p. 98, 24 κρεῖττον τὸ κακοῦν τοῦ ὑπό τινος κακοῦσθαι) 2 Cl 16: 4. κρεῖττον (v.l. -σσ-) ἐστιν w. inf. foll. *it is better* (Diod. S. 12, 16, 2 κρεῖττον γάρ ἐστιν ἀποθανεῖν ἢ ... πειρασθῆναι; Demosth., Ep. 2, 21 εἰ ..., τεθνάναι με κρεῖττον ἦν) 1 Cor 7: 9; cf. 1 Pt

3: 17. κρεῖττον ἦν αὐτοῖς w. inf. foll. *it would be better for them* 2 Pt 2: 21 (s. Bl-D. §410; Rob. 1084); cf. 1 Cl 46: 8. Pleonast. πολλῷ μᾶλλον κ. *much better indeed* Phil 1: 23.—κ. ἐλευθερία IPol 4: 3.

3. adv. *better* κρεῖσσον ποιεῖν 1 Cor 7: 38. κρεῖττον λαλεῖν Hb 12: 24 (παρά w. acc. *than*). M-M.*

κρέμαμαι s. κρεμάννυμι 2.

κρεμάννυμι (this form of the present not in the Gk. Bible, but Job 26: 7 has κρεμάζω. The word, in mngs. 1 and 2, Hom.+; inscr., pap., LXX, Philo; Jos., Vi. 147 al.) 1 aor. ἐκρέμασα, pass. ἐκρεμάσθην.

1. trans. *hang (up)* ἐπὶ ξύλου *on the tree* i.e., *cross* (cf. Gen 40: 19; Dt 21: 22; Esth 8: 7) Ac 5: 30; 10: 39. The verb κρ. by itself can also mean *crucify* (Diod. S. 17, 46, 4; Appian, Mithrid. 8 §25; 29 §114 δούλους ἐκρέμασε, Bell. Civ. 2, 90 §377; Arrian, Anab. 6, 17, 2; 6, 30, 2; 7, 14, 4). Pass. Lk 23: 39 (cf. Appian, Bell. Civ. 3, 3 §9; Sb 6739 [255BC], 9).—ἵνα κρεμασθῇ μύλος ὀνικὸς περὶ τὸν τράχηλον αὐτοῦ *that a millstone would be hung around his neck* Mt 18: 6.—1 Cl 12: 7 v.l. Funk.

2. intrans., dep. κρέμαμαι (cf. Bl-D. §93; Rob. 316f) *hang*—a. lit. (Jos., Ant. 7, 241) ἐπί τινος *on a thing* (X., An. 3, 2, 19) ἐπὶ ξύλου (s. 1 above) Gal 3: 13 (Dt 21: 23). Of the branch of a vine μὴ κρεμαμένη ἐπὶ τῆς πτελέας *if it does not hang on the elm tree* Hs 2: 3; cf. vs. 4. ἔκ τινος *on someth.* (Pla., Leg. 8 p. 831c; Dit., Syll.² 588, 201. Cf. Jdth 8: 24) of a snake κ. ἐκ τῆς χειρός *hung on the hand* Ac 28: 4. Of those being punished in hell ἐκ τῆς γλώσσης κρεμάμενοι AP 7: 22.

b. fig. (Philo, Post. Cai. 24; 25; Sib. Or. 7, 55) ἐν ταύταις τ. δυσὶν ἐντολαῖς ὅλος ὁ νόμος κρέμαται καὶ οἱ προφῆται *all the law and the prophets hang (depend) on these two commandments* Mt 22: 40 (as a door hangs on its hinges, so the whole OT hangs on these two comm. For the thought cf. Plut., Mor. 116D.—On κρ. ἐν cf. 2 Km 18: 9).—GBertram, TW III 915-20 κρεμάννυμι and related words. M-M.*

κρεπάλη (cf. Mlt.-H. 81) is preferred by W-H. in place of κραιπάλη (q.v.). But Aristoph., Ach. 277, Wasps 1255 prove the length of the first syllable.

κρημνός, οῦ, ὁ (Hom.+; Epigr. Gr. 225, 2; PPetr. III 39 II, 8; 2 Ch 25: 12; Ep. Arist. 118; Test. 12 Patr.; Jos., Ant. 3, 76) *steep slope* or *bank, cliff* κατὰ τοῦ κ. *down the steep bank* (Dio Chrys. 7, 3; Philo, Agr. 76; Jos., Bell. 1, 313) Mt 8: 32; Mk 5: 13; Lk 8: 33. ἀπὸ κ. μεγάλου *down from a high cliff* AP 17: 32 (ἀπὸ κ. as Celsus 6, 34). M-M.*

κρημνώδης, ες (since Thu. 7, 84, 4; Jos., Bell. 7, 280) *steep, precipitous* ἦν ὁ τόπος κ. *the place was precipitous* (Stephan. Byz. s.v. Ὄαξος: τὸν τόπον κρημνώδη ὑπάρχειν) Hv 1, 1, 3. Cf. s 6, 2, 6.*

Κρής, ητός, ὁ pl. Κρῆτες (Hom.+; inscr.; UPZ 20, 32 [163 BC]; 29, 2; Jos., Ant. 13, 86, C. Ap. 2, 172; Sib. Or. 3, 140) *a Cretan,* inhabitant of the island of Crete Ac 2: 11 (OEissfeldt, Kreter u. Araber: ThLZ 72, '47, 207-12); subscr. of Tit. An unfavorable estimate of Cretan character (s. on this ἀργός 2) Tit 1: 12.—RHarris, Exp. '06 II 305-17; '07 III 332-7; '12 IV 348-53; '15 I 29-35; MGöbel, Ethnica, Diss. Breslau '15, 77ff.*

Κρήσκης, εντος, ὁ (Lat. Crescens; the Gk. form is quite rare, the Lat. form common, incl. Pol 14, which is preserved only in Lat.) *Crescens,* a companion of Paul 2 Ti 4: 10. S. Κρίσπος.*

Κρήτη, ης, ἡ (Hom.+; inscr.; 1 Macc 10: 67; Philo, Spec. Leg. 3, 43; Joseph.; Sib. Or.) *Crete* Ac 27: 7, 12f, 21; Tit 1: 5 (as early as Il. 2, 649 Crete was famous for its many cities; Ps.-Scylax [ed. BFabricius 1878] has the names of many cities).*

κριθή, ῆς, ἡ (Hom.+, but in class. wr. only in pl. On the other hand, in later wr. [Dionys. Hal. 2, 25; Cornutus 28 p. 54, 4; Libanius, De Vita Sua 8 Förster v.l.; Herm. Wr. 14, 10; Philo, Spec. Leg. 2, 175; 3, 57; Jos., Bell. 5, 427], in inscr., pap., LXX also in sing.) *barley,* used in the preparation of cheaper kinds of bread (s. Hdb. on J 6: 9; Appian, Illyr. 26 §76 κριθὴ ἀντὶ σίτου for inferior soldiers). τρεῖς χοίνικες κριθῶν *three quarts of barley* (t.r. κριθῆς) Rv 6: 6; GDalman, Arbeit II '32, 252f; III '33, 300ff. M-M. B. 516.*

κρίθινος, η, ον (since Hipponax [VI BC] 39, 6 Diehl; PEleph. 5, 25 [284/3 BC]; BGU 1092, 28; LXX; Philo, Spec. Leg. 2, 175; Jos., Ant. 5, 219) *made of barley flour* ἄρτος κ. *barley bread* (Plut., Anton. 45, 8; Artem. 1, 69; above all 4 Km 4: 42) J 6: 9, 13. M-M.*

κρίκος, ου, ὁ (Hom.+; inscr., pap., LXX; Jos., Ant. 3, 109f; 136) *ring* κάμπτειν ὡς κρίκον τὸν τράχηλον *bend the neck as a ring,* i.e. so it is as round as a ring B 3: 2 (Is 58: 5).*

κρίμα, ατος, τό (Aeschyl.+; inscr.; PPetr. III 26, 2; 36 verso, 20 [III BC]; LXX; Philo, Conf. Lingu. 128; Joseph. —On the accent s. Bl-D. §13; 109, 3; Mlt.-H. 57).

1. *dispute, lawsuit* (Ex 18: 22) κρίματα ἔχετε μεθ' ἑαυτῶν *you have lawsuits with one another* 1 Cor 6: 7.

2. *decision, decree* (Inschr. Gal. no. 25, 2 [II AD] κατὰ τὸ κρ. τῆς βουλῆς; Ps 18: 10; 118: 75; Jos., Ant. 14, 318; 321), also of the fixed purposes of divine grace Ro 11: 33.

3. *judging, judgment,* the action or function of a judge κρίμα ἐδόθη αὐτοῖς *authority to judge was given to them* Rv 20: 4.—Of God's judgment: τὸ κρίμα τὸ μέλλον Ac 24: 25. κρ. αἰώνιον *judgment whose decision is valid eternally* Hb 6: 2. God's judgment begins with the church 1 Pt 4: 17. Pl.: God is δίκαιος ἐν τοῖς κρίμασιν *righteous in his judgments* 1 Cl 27: 1; 60: 1.—1 Cl 20: 5 Funk.

4. *judicial verdict*—a. gener. (Polyb. 24, 1, 12) τὸ κρ. ἐξ ἑνὸς εἰς κατάκριμα *the verdict came as the result of one transgression, and led to punishment* Ro 5: 16.

b. mostly in an unfavorable sense, of the *sentence of condemnation,* also of the *condemnation* and the subsequent *punishment* itself 2 Pt 2: 3; Jd 4. τὸ κ. τοῦ θεοῦ *the condemnation of God* (i.e., pronounced by him) Ro 2: 2f. ὧν τὸ κ. ἔνδικόν ἐστιν *their condemnation is just* 3: 8 (but WOFitch, ET 59, '47/'48, 26 'verdict'). πρόδηλον ἐγενήθη *their condemnation has been made plain* 1 Cl 51: 3. τὸ κρ. τῆς πόρνης *the condemnation and punishment of the harlot* Rv 17: 1. εἰς κρ. συνέρχεσθαι 1 Cor 11: 34. κρ. ἑαυτῷ ἐσθίειν *eat condemnation upon oneself* vs. 29; λαμβάνεσθαι κρ. *be condemned* Mt 23: 13 t.r.; Mk 12: 40; Lk 20: 47; Ro 13: 2; Js 3: 1. ἔχουσαι κρ., ὅτι *they are subject to condemnation because* 1 Ti 5: 12; βαστάζειν τὸ κρ. Gal 5: 10. εἰς κρ. γίνεσθαι *incur condemnation* 1 Cl 11: 2. εἰς κρ. γίνεσθαί τινι *turn out to be condemnation for someone* 21: 1; IEph 11: 1. ἐν τῷ αὐτῷ κρ. εἶναι *be under the same condemnation* Lk 23: 40. εἰς κρ. ἐμπίπτειν τοῦ διαβόλου 1 Ti 3: 6. κρ. θανάτου (cf. Sir 41: 3) *death sentence* Lk 24: 20.—Pl. (cf. BGU 471, 9 [II AD]) τὰ μέλλοντα κρίματα *the punishments to come* 1 Cl 28: 1.—GPWetter, Der Vergeltungsgedanke bei Pls '12, 1ff.

5. The OT is the source of—a. the expr. κρίνειν τὸ κρ. (cf. Zech 7: 9; 8: 16; Ezk 44: 24) ἔκρινεν ὁ θεὸς τὸ κρίμα

ὑμῶν ἐξ αὐτῆς *God has pronounced judgment for you against her* or *God has pronounced on her the judgment she wished to impose on you* (HJHoltzmann, Hdb. 1893 ad loc.) Rv 18: 20.

b. the close relation betw. κρ. and δικαιοσύνη, and the expr. ποιεῖν κρ. καὶ δικαιοσύνην (Jer 23: 5; Ezk 33: 14) *do justice and righteousness* 1 Cl 13: 1.

6. of the judgment of a man upon his fellowman Mt 7: 2; Ro 2: 1 v.l.

7. In J κρ. shows the same two-sidedness as the other members of the κρίνω family ('judgment' and 'separation'; s. Hdb. on J 3: 17), and means the judicial decision which consists in the separation of those who are willing to believe fr. those who are unwilling to do so 9: 39. M-M. B. 1422.*

κρίνον, ου, τό (Aristoph., Hdt.+; Longus 2, 3, 4 [ῥόδα, κρίνα, ὑάκινθος as spring flowers]; Epigr. Gr. [I AD]; PSI 297, 8; LXX; Ep. Arist. 68; 75. Cf. Jos., Ant. 8, 77; Test. Sim. 6, 2; loanw. in rabb.) *lily*. In this connection many think of the autumn crocus, Turk's cap lily, anemone, or gladiolus. Perh. Jesus had no definite flower in mind, but was thinking of all the wonderful blooms that adorn the fields of Galilee. As an extremely beautiful flower (as Theodor. Prodr. 6, 296 H.) it is mentioned Mt 6: 28; Lk 12: 27.—LFonck, Streifzüge durch die biblische Flora '00, 53ff; JBoehmer, Die Lilien auf dem Felde: Studierstube 6, '08, 223ff; FLundgreen, Die Pflanzen im NT: NKZ 28, '17, 828ff; GDalman, Die Lilie der Bibel: Pj 21, '25, 98ff, Arbeit I, '28, 357ff al.; ILöw, D. Flora d. Juden II '24, 160ff, also IV '34, 669 (indices); GVKing, Consider the Lilies: Crozer Quarterly 10, '33, 28-36; TCSkeat, The Lilies of the Field: ZNW 37, '39, 211-14; M. et Mme. EHa-Reubeni, RB 54, '47, 362-4 (anthemis or Easter daisy, Fr. pâquerette). M-M.*

κρίνω (Hom.+; inscr., pap., LXX, En., Ep. Arist., Philo, Joseph., Test. 12 Patr., Sib. Or.) fut. κρινῶ; 1 aor. ἔκρινα; pf. κέκρικα; plpf. 3 sing. κεκρίκει (on the lack of augment cf. Bl-D. §66, 1; Mlt.-H. 190). Pass.: impf. ἐκρινόμην; pf. κέκριμαι; 1 aor. ἐκρίθην; 1 fut. κριθήσομαι.

1. *separate, distinguish*, then *select, prefer* (Aeschyl., Suppl. 39 τί; Pla., Rep. 3 p. 399ᴇ κρίνειν τινὰ πρό τινος 'prefer someone to someone', Phil. p. 57ᴇ; Himerius, Or. 40 [= Or. 6], 3 κρ. τί τινι = select someth. because of someth. [a place because of its size]) ὃς μὲν γὰρ κρίνει ἡμέραν παρ' ἡμέραν *the one prefers one day to another* Ro 14: 5a. In the other half of the sentence ὃς δὲ κρίνει πᾶσαν ἡμέραν, κρ. prob. has the sense *recognize, approve* (X., Hell. 1, 7, 34 ἔκριναν τὴν τῆς βουλῆς γνώμην) *the other holds every day in esteem* vs. 5b.

2. *judge, think, consider, look upon* w. double acc. of the obj. and the predicate (Soph., Oed. R. 34; Pla., Rep. 9 p. 578ʙ and s. Cebes 39, 4; 3 Macc 2: 33) οὐκ ἀξίους κρίνετε ἑαυτούς *you do not consider yourselves worthy* Ac 13: 46 (Jos., Ant. 6, 159 ὃν αὐτὸς τ. βασιλείας ἄξιον ἔκρινεν. Ep. Arist. 98); cf. PK 3 p. 15, 17. τὰ ὑστερήματα αὐτῶν ἴδια ἐκρίνετε *you considered their shortcomings as your own* 1 Cl 2: 6. Pass. (Thu. 2, 40, 3; Jos., Ant. 4, 193) τί ἄπιστον κρίνεται παρ' ὑμῖν; *why do you think it is incredible?* Ac 26: 8 (Jos., Ant. 18, 76 ἄπιστα αὐτὰ κρίνειν).—Foll. by acc. w. inf. (Pla., Gorg. p. 452c, Rep. 9 p. 578ʙ; X., An. 1, 9, 5; 28) κεκρίκατέ με πιστὴν . . . εἶναι Ac 16: 15.—W. inf. foll. κρίνω μὴ παρενοχλεῖν τοῖς κτλ. 15: 19.—Foll. by τοῦτο ὅτι 2 Cor 5: 14.—W. direct quest. foll. ἐν ὑμῖν αὐτοῖς κρίνατε *judge, decide for yourselves* 1 Cor 11: 13.—W. indirect quest.

foll. (Thu. 4, 130, 7 κρίναντες ἐν σφίσιν αὐτοῖς, εἰ . . . ; X., Cyr. 4, 1, 5) εἰ δίκαιόν ἐστιν, ὑμῶν ἀκούειν μᾶλλον ἢ τοῦ θεοῦ, κρίνατε *decide whether it is right to obey you rather than God* Ac 4: 19.—κρίνατε ὑμεῖς ὅ φημι *pass your own judgment on what I say* 1 Cor 10: 15.—ὀρθῶς ἔκρινας *you have judged rightly* Lk 7: 43.

3. *reach a decision, decide, propose, intend* (Isocr. 4, 46; Polyb. 3, 6, 7; 5, 52, 6; 9, 13, 7; Epict. 2, 15, 7; Appian, Bell. Civ. 14, 118 §497 ὅταν οἱ θεοὶ κρίνωσιν; LXX w. inf. (Diod. S. 4, 33, 10; 17, 95, 1; UPZ 42, 37 [162 ʙᴄ]; PTebt. 55, 4 [II ʙᴄ] ἔκρινα γράψαι; PLond. 897, 11; 1 Macc 11: 33; 3 Macc 1: 6; Jdth 11: 13; Wsd 8: 9; Jos., Ant. 7, 33; 12, 403; 13, 188) Ac 3: 13; 20: 16; 25: 25; 1 Cor 2: 2; 5: 3; Tit 3: 12. W. τοῦ and inf. (Bl-D. §397, 2) ἐκρίθη τοῦ ἀποπλεῖν ἡμᾶς Ac 27: 1. ἐπεὶ ἤδη σεαυτῷ κέκρικας τοῦ μὴ δύνασθαι τὰς ἐντολὰς ταύτας ὑπὸ ἀνθρώπου φυλαχθῆναι *since you have already decided in your own mind that these commandments cannot be kept by a man* Hm 12, 3, 6.—W. acc. and inf. (2 Macc 11: 25, 36; 3 Macc 6: 30; Sib. Or. 3, 127) Ac 21: 25 (even in the substantially different rdgs. of D and t.r.). τοῦτο κέκρικεν . . . , τηρεῖν τὴν ἑαυτοῦ παρθένον *he has determined this, namely to keep his own virgin* (pure and undefiled) 1 Cor 7: 37 (Diod. S. 4, 73, 2 of a father: κρῖναι ταύτην [i.e., his daughter] παρθένον διαφυλάττειν). τοῦτο κρῖναι μᾶλλον, τὸ μὴ τιθέναι πρόσκομμα *but rather decide this, (namely) to give no offense* Ro 14: 13b. ἔκρινα ἐμαυτῷ τοῦτο, τὸ . . . ἐλθεῖν 2 Cor 2: 1. τὰ δόγματα τὰ κεκριμένα ὑπὸ τ. ἀποστόλων Ac 16: 4 (cf. Polyb. 5, 52, 6 πράξας τὸ κριθέν; Epict. 2, 15, 7 τοῖς κριθεῖσιν ἐμμένειν δεῖ).

4. as a legal t.t. *judge, decide, hale before a court, condemn*, also *hand over for judicial punishment* (in a forensic sense Hom.+; inscr., pap., LXX).

a. of a human court—α. act. and pass. abs. Ac 13: 27. W. adv. GP 3: 7. κρ. τινά: κατὰ τὸν νόμον J 18: 31; Ac 23: 3; 24: 6 t.r. Of the right of the apostle and the church to judge believers 1 Cor 5: 12a, b. μὴ ὁ νόμος ἡμῶν κρίνει τὸν ἄνθρωπον *does our law* (personified) *punish a man?* J 7: 51 (Appian, Bell. Civ. 3, 50 §205 certain senators desire that before Mark Antony is declared a public enemy he should be brought to trial, ὡς οὐ πάτριον σφίσιν ἀκρίτου καταδικάζειν). ἐκ τ. στόματός σου κρινῶ σε *I will punish you on the basis of your own statement* Lk 19: 22. Pass. Ac 25: 10. κρίνεσθαι ἐπί τινι *be on trial because of a thing* 26: 6 (Appian, Basil. 12 κρινόμενος ἐπὶ τῷδε = be brought to trial because of this thing; likew. Iber. 55 §233). Also περί τινος (Diod. S. 12, 30, 5) 23: 6; 25: 20; w. addition of ἐπί w. gen. of the court of judicature *before someone* (schol. on Hes., Op. 9) 24: 21; 25: 9.—τί δὲ καὶ ἀφ' ἑαυτῶν οὐ κρίνετε τὸ δίκαιον; Lk 12: 57, which leads over into the sphere of jurisprudence (vs. 58), means: *why cannot you yourselves decide what is right?* (cf. the prayer for vengeance fr. Amorgos [Bull. de corr. hell. 25, '01 p. 416; Dssm., LO 94—LAE 118] ἐπάκουσον, θεά, καὶ κρῖναι τὸ δίκαιον). Cf. Appian, Mithrid. 89 §403 κρίνειν τὴν μάχην = decide the battle.

β. mid. and pass. (*dispute, quarrel, debate*, also) *go to law* (so Thu. 4, 122, 4 δίκῃ κρίνεσθαι; Hos 2: 4 al. in LXX) τινί *with someone* (Job 9: 3; 13: 19) Mt 5: 40. Also μετά τινος (Vi. Aesopi W c. 76 κριθῆναί με μετὰ τῆς κυρίας μου ἐπὶ σοί = I am pleading my case with my mistress before you; Eccl 6: 10) 1 Cor 6: 6. ἐπὶ τινος *before someone* (as judge) vs. 1 (on the beginning of 1 Cor 6 cf. the decree of Alexander to the Greeks in Ps.-Callisth. 2, 21, 21: βούλομαι δὲ μὴ ἐν ἑαυτοῖς κρίνειν ὅσον τις ὑμῶν ἔχει πρὸς ἕτερον, οὐδὲ ἐφ' οὗ βούλεσθε = it is my will that you are not to go to law among yourselves, no matter what any of you may have against another, nor before anyone you wish).

b. of the divine tribunal—**α.** occupied by God or Christ: abs. *administer justice, judge* J 5: 30; 8: 16, 50; cf. vs. 26; Rv 6: 10; B 5: 7. Pass. *be judged* Mt 7: 1b, 2b; Lk 6: 37b; Rv 11: 18.—W. acc. foll. (PGM 4, 1013 of Horus ὁ κρίνων τὰ πάντα) J 5: 22; 8: 15b. τοὺς ἔξω 1 Cor 5: 13. ζῶντας καὶ νεκρούς *judge the living and the dead* 2 Ti 4: 1; 1 Pt 4: 5; B 7: 2. τὰ κρυπτὰ τῶν ἀνθρώπων Ro 2: 16. τὸν κόσμον B 4: 12. τὴν οἰκουμένην Ac 17: 31. κρ. κατὰ τὸ ἑκάστου ἔργον *judge each one by what he does* 1 Pt 1: 17; cf. Rv 20: 13. ἐκρίθησαν οἱ νεκροὶ ἐκ τῶν γεγραμμένων ἐν τοῖς βιβλίοις κατὰ τὰ ἔργα αὐτῶν *the dead were judged by what was written in the books* (of life and of death), *in accordance w. their deeds* vs. 12; δικαίως κρ. *judge righteously* (Sotades [280 BC] in Stob. 4, 34, 8 vol. V p. 826, 5 ὁ παντογενής ... οὐ κρίνει δικαίως) 1 Pt 2: 23; B 19: 11. Also ἐν δικαιοσύνῃ Rv 19: 11. διὰ νόμου κρίνεσθαι *be judged on the basis of the law* Js 2: 12.—Oft. the emphasis is unmistakably laid upon that which follows the Divine Judge's verdict, upon the condemnation or punishment: *condemn, punish* (opp. σῴζειν) J 3: 17; cf. 18a, b; 12: 47a, b, 48a; cf. b; Ac 7: 7 (Gen 15: 14). διὰ νόμου κρ. *punish on the basis of the law* Ro 2: 12.—3: 6f; 1 Cor 11: 31f (here of the temporal punishment which God brings upon sinners; 2 Th 2: 12; Hb 10: 30 (κρινεῖ κύριος τὸν λαὸν αὐτοῦ *the Lord will judge=punish his people* is derived fr. Dt 32: 36=Ps 134: 14, where the judgment of God is spoken of, resulting in the vindication of the innocent [the thought prominent in the two OT pass.] and the punishment of the guilty [the thought prominent in the Hb pass.]); 13: 4; Js 5: 9; 1 Pt 4: 6 (s. also 6a); Rv 18: 8; 19: 2; B 15: 5.—W. the punishment given κρ. διὰ πυρός 1 Cl 11: 1. κεκριμένοι ἤδη τῷ θανάτῳ *already condemned to death* B 10: 5. Also εἰς θάνατον *condemned to death* Hs 9, 18, 2. οἱ κρινόμενοι ἀσεβεῖς *the godless, who are condemned* 2 Cl 18: 1. Of the devil ὁ ἄρχων τοῦ κόσμου τούτου κέκριται J 16: 11.—ταῦτα ἔκρινας *thou hast imposed these punishments* Rv 16: 5.—On κρίνειν τὸ κρίμα 18: 20 cf. κρίμα 5a.

β. occupied by men, who have been divinely commissioned to judge: the 12 apostles judge the 12 tribes Mt 19: 28; Lk 22: 30 (PBatiffol, RB n.s. 9, '12, 541–3. But here κρ. could have the broader sense *rule*; cf. 4 Km 15: 5; Ps 2: 10; 1 Macc 9: 73; PsSol 17: 29). κρινεῖ ἡ ἐκ φύσεως ἀκροβυστία ... σέ *the one who is physically uncircumcised will sit in judgment upon you* Ro 2: 27. οἱ ἅγιοι as judges of the cosmos 1 Cor 6: 2a, b (κρίνεσθαι ἐν: Diod. S. 19, 51, 4.—On the saints as co-rulers with God cf. Epict., Ench. 15; Sallust. 21 p. 36, 14) as well as of the angels vs. 3 (cf. Da 7: 22).

5. *see to it that justice is done* (LXX) τινί *to someone* 1 Cl 8: 4 (Is 1: 17).

6. of the judgment which people customarily pass upon (and thereby seek to influence) the lives and actions of their fellowmen.

a. *judge, pass judgment upon, express an opinion about* Mt 7: 1a, 2a; Lk 6: 37a; 1 Cl 13: 2 (Sextus 183 ὁ κρίνων ἄνθρωπον κρίνεται ὑπὸ τ. θεοῦ). κρ. δικαίως B 19: 11. κρ. κατ' ὄψιν *by the outward appearance* J 7: 24a. κατὰ τὴν σάρκα 8: 15. τὴν δικαίαν κρίσιν κρ. *pass a right judgment* 7: 24b (on the expr. cf. Dt 16: 18). This is perh. the place for 1 Pt 4: 6 ἵνα κριθῶσιν κατὰ ἀνθρ. (cf. Wsd 3: 4).

b. esp. in an unfavorable sense *pass an unfavorable judgment upon, criticise, find fault with, condemn* (Epict. 2, 21, 11) Ro 2: 1a, b, c, 3; 14: 3f, 10, 13a (a play on

words, w. κρίνειν used in two different mngs. in the same vs.; s. 3 above on vs. 13b); Col 2: 16; Js 4: 11, 12. μή τι κρίνετε *do not pronounce judgment on anything* 1 Cor 4: 5. ἱνατί γὰρ ἡ ἐλευθερία μου κρίνεται ὑπὸ ἄλλης συνειδήσεως; *why is my freedom* (of action) *to be unfavorably judged by another man's scruples?* 1 Cor 10: 29. μακάριος ὁ μὴ κρίνων ἑαυτόν *happy is the man who finds no fault w. himself* Ro 14: 22.—Also of a human judgment directed against God ὅπως ἂν νικήσεις ἐν τῷ κρίνεσθαί σε *that thou mayest prevail when thou art judged* Ro 3: 4 (OMichl in KEK [Meyer series] prefers active sense); 1 Cl 18: 4 (both Ps 50: 6).—JBüchsel and VHerntrich, TW III 920–55 κρίνω and related words. M-M. B. 1428.**

κριός, οῦ, ὁ (Hom.+; inscr., pap., LXX; Jos., Ant. 3, 221; 5, 223; 8, 228) a *ram* MPol 14: 1 (ἐπίσημος 1); B 2: 5 v.l. (Is 1: 11).*

κρίσις, εως, ἡ (Aeschyl., Hdt.+; inscr., pap., LXX, En.; Ep. Arist. 252; Philo, Joseph., Test. 12 Patr.).

1. *judging, judgment*——**a.** of the activity of God or the Messiah as judge, esp. on the Last Day.

α. ἡ δικαία κρ. τοῦ θεοῦ *God's righteous judgment* 2 Th 1: 5. ἡ κρίσις ἡ ἐμὴ δικαία ἐστιν J 5: 30. κρίσιν ποιεῖν *execute judgment, act as judge* (Aristoph., Ran. 778; 785; X., Hell. 4, 2, 6; 8; Dt 10: 18.—Likew. κρ. ποιεῖσθαι: 1 Macc 6: 22; Jos., Ant. 6, 34) vs. 27. τ. κρίσιν διδόναι τινί *commit judgment* or *judging to someone* vs. 22. ἡ ἡμέρα (τῆς) κρίσεως *the Day of Judgment* (Jdth 16: 17; Is 34: 8; Pr 6: 34) Mt 10: 15; 11: 22, 24; 12: 36; 2 Pt 2: 9; 3: 7; 1 J 4: 17; 2 Cl 16: 3; 17: 6; B 19: 10; 21: 6.— ἡ κρ. ἡ μέλλουσα *the judgment to come* 2 Cl 18: 2; MPol 11: 2. ἡ κρ. ἡ ἐπερχομένη *the approaching judgment* Hv 3, 9, 5. Denial of the Last Judgment Pol 7: 1. κρ. μεγάλης ἡμέρας *the judgment of the Great Day* Jd 6. ἡ ὥρα τῆς κρ. αὐτοῦ *the hour when he is to judge* Rv 14: 7. οὐκ ἀναστήσονται οἱ ἀσεβεῖς ἐν κρ. *the wicked will not rise in the judgment* (or *on the J. Day*) B 11: 7 (Ps 1: 5); cf. Mt 12: 41f; Lk 10: 14; 11: 31f. δικαιοσύνη κρίσεως ἀρχὴ καὶ τέλος *righteousness* (on the part of the judge) *is the beginning and end of judging* B 1: 6. Divine judgment (cf. Iambl., Vi. Pyth. 8, 40 τῶν ἀθανάτων κ.; Hierocles 11 p. 441 and 442 al. θεία κρίσις) is also mentioned 1 Ti 5: 24; Hb 9: 27 (cf. Diog. L. 3, 79 after Plato: one must fulfill the δικαιοσύνη θεοῦ, ἵνα μὴ καὶ μετὰ τὸν θάνατον δίκας ὑπόσχοιεν οἱ κακοῦργοι); 2 Pt 2: 4, 9; 2 Cl 20: 4; D 11: 11.

β. The word oft. means *judgment that goes against a person, condemnation,* and the *punishment* that follows (Sib. Or. 3, 670) GP 7: 25. δισσὴν ἕξουσιν τὴν κρ. *they will receive double punishment* 2 Cl 10: 5. ἡ κρ. σου *your judgment* Rv 18: 10. κἀκείνοις κρ. ἐστίν *judgment comes upon them, too* ISm 6: 1. φοβερά τις ἐκδοχὴ κρίσεως *a fearful prospect of judgment* Hb 10: 27 (Iambl., Vi. Pyth. 30, 179 a reference to the κρ. τῶν ψυχῶν serves to arouse φόβος τ. ἀδικίας). ἡ κρ. αὐτοῦ ἤρθη *his punishment was taken away* Ac 8: 33; 1 Cl 16: 7 (both Is 53: 8). ὑπὸ κρίσιν πίπτειν *come under judgment* Js 5: 12; cf. 2: 13a, b. ἡ κρ. τῆς γεέννης *being punished in hell* Mt 23: 33 (gen. as Diod. S. 1, 82, 3 θανάτου κρ.=punishment by death). κρ. κατά τινος *upon, against someone* (Aelian, V.H. 2, 6) ποιῆσαι κρίσιν κατὰ πάντων *execute judgment upon all* Jd 15 (En. 1, 9).—(Opp. ζωή) ἔχει ζωὴν αἰώνιον καὶ εἰς κρ. οὐκ ἔρχεται J 5: 24 (cf. Philip [=Demosth. 12, 16] εἰς κρ. ἐλθεῖν). ἀνάστασις ζωῆς— ἀνάστασις κρίσεως vs. 29. κρίσις τοῦ κόσμου τούτου *judgment of* (or *upon*) *this world* 12: 31; cf. 16: 8, interpreted as a judgment on the prince of this world 16: 11 (cf. 12: 31b; 1QM 1, 5; but s. also LJLutkemeyer, CBQ 8, '46, 225f 'good judgment', and BNoack, Satanas u. Soteria '48, 79; also s. on δικαιοσύνη 2, end).—In 3: 19 κρ. has in addition to the senses 'judgment' and 'condemnation' the clear connotation of 'separation, division' (Hecataeus [320 BC] in Diod. S. 40, 3, 2 Dind. κρίσις τῶν κακῶν='separation fr. the evils'.—A double sense as in J is found in Artem. 5, 5 κριτής='judge' and 'divider'). The 'judgment', which is operative here and now, consists in the fact that men divide themselves into those who accept Christ and those who reject him (Hdb.; Bultmann).—Pl. judgments, punishments (Diod. S. 1, 75, 2; Appian, Bell. Civ. 1, 96 §446 κρίσεις πικραί=severe punishments) ἀληθιναὶ καὶ δίκαιαι αἱ κρίσεις σου Rv 16: 7; 19: 2.—Bousset, Rel.³ 257ff; LRuhl, De Mortuorum Judicio '03; JBlank, Krisis (J), diss. Freiburg, '64.

b. of the judgment of one person upon or against another—α. of men toward men κρ. δικαία B 20: 2; D 5: 2. κρ. ἄδικος unjust judgment Pol 6: 1; ἀπότομος ἐν κρ. relentless in judgment ibid. τὴν δικαίαν κρίσιν κρίνατε J 7: 24 (κρίνω 6a). Cf. ἡ κρ. ἡ ἐμὴ ἀληθινή ἐστιν 8: 16.
β. of the archangel against the devil οὐκ ἐτόλμησεν κρίσιν ἐπενεγκεῖν βλασφημίας he did not presume to pronounce a reviling judgment Jd 9. Cf. the corresp. pass. in 2 Pt 2: 11 ἄγγελοι οὐ φέρουσιν κατ' αὐτῶν παρὰ κυρίῳ βλάσφημον κρίσιν angels do not pronounce a reviling judgment against them before the Lord.

2. board of judges, court, specif. a local court (cf. Schürer II⁴ 226f; Diod. S. 17, 80, 2; Aesop, Fab. 190 H.; Theod. Prodr. 1, 402 H.) ἔνοχος ἔσται τῇ κρ. he will have to answer to a (local) court Mt 5: 21f.—RGuelich, ZNW 64, '73, 44ff.

3. right in the sense of justice, righteousness (Inscr. Gr. 542, 6 [II BC] πίστιν ἔχοντα καὶ κρίσιν ὑγιῆ; Dit., Or. 383, 207 [I BC]; LXX; cf. מִשְׁפָּט) ἀφήκατε τὴν κρίσιν κ. τὸ ἔλεος κ. τὴν πίστιν Mt 23: 23; cf. Lk 11: 42. κρίσιν τ. ἔθνεσιν ἀπαγγελεῖ he will proclaim justice for the Gentiles Mt 12: 18 (Is 42: 1). ἐκζητεῖν κρ. seek out justice 1 Cl 8: 4 (Is 1: 17). ἕως ἂν ἐκβάλῃ εἰς νῖκος τ. κρίσιν until he leads justice to victory vs. 20 (cf. Is 42: 3.—Other poss. mngs. are legal action, trial, case [X., An. 1, 6, 5; Diod. S. 2, 42, 4 αἱ κρίσεις=legal suits, transactions; En. 9, 3 εἰσαγάγετε τὴν κρίσιν ἡμῶν πρὸς τὸν ὕψιστον] and, influenced by νῖκος, a [military] decision [Dionys. Hal. 9, 35; 2 Macc 14: 18]). The mng. right, justice may also play a role in such passages as J 7: 24; 12: 31; 16: 8, 11; Ac 8: 33 [so RSV] and perh. others.—GPWetter on κρίμα 4, end; HBraun, Gerichtsgedanke u. Rechtfertigungslehre b. Pls '30; FVFilson, St. Paul's Conception of Recompense '31. M-M.*

Κρίσπος, ου, ὁ (Diod. S. 15, 38, 1; Crinagoras no. 48, 2; inscr., pap.; Jos., Vi. 33; on the accent s. Bl-D. §41, 3 app.; Rob. 235) Crispus, leader of the synagogue in Corinth Ac 18: 8; baptized by Paul 1 Cor 1: 14. As v.l. (Syr., Goth.) 2 Ti 4: 10. M-M.*

κριτήριον, ου, τό—1. lawcourt, tribunal (so since Pla., Leg. 6 p. 767ᴮ, also Polyb.; Diod. S.; Dit., Syll.³ 683, 48; 807, 9; UPZ 118, 15; PHib. 29=Wilcken, Chrest. 259, 5; BGU 1054, 1; LXX; cf. Philo, Virt. 66) ἕλκειν τινὰ εἰς κριτήρια drag someone into court Js 2: 6 (cf. PTurin I 1 VI, 11 [117 BC] ἐλκυσθέντων ἀπάντων εἰς τὸ κριτήριον). It is not easy to fit this mng. into the two other pass. in our lit. where κρ. is found. ἀνάξιοί ἐστε κριτηρίων ἐλαχίστων; could perh. mean: are you unfit to form even the most insignificant courts (i.e., those that have juris-

diction over the petty details of everyday life)? 1 Cor 6: 2. Likew. βιωτικὰ κριτήρια ἐὰν ἔχητε, τοὺς ἐξουθενημένους καθίζετε; if you have (need for) courts for the matters of everyday life, do you appoint insignificant men (as judges)? vs. 4 (καθίζειν κριτήριον as Polyb. 9, 33, 12). However, in both cases the tendency is now to prefer for κρ. the sense

2. lawsuit, legal action (most recently JWeiss, Ltzm., Sickenberger, H-DWendland). Cf. Kyr.-Inschr. l. 21 θανατηφόρα κριτήρια=lawsuits involving capital punishment (corresp. to Lat. judicia capitis); Suppl. Epigr. Gr. VIII 13 (=Διάταγμα Καίσαρος [I AD] l. 14 κριτήριον γενέσθαι=the lawsuit to be tried. Sim. Diod. S. 1, 72, 4; 36, 3, 3. M-M.*

κριτής, οῦ, ὁ (trag., Hdt.+; inscr., pap., LXX; Philo, Joseph., loanw. in rabb.) one who reaches a decision, passes judgment.

1. a judge—a. lit., in jurisprudence (not class. in this sense, but Diod. S. 1, 92, 4; Epict. 3, 7, 30; inscr.; POxy. 97, 5; 726, 20; 1195, 1; PTebt. 317, 20; LXX).
α. of men Mt 5: 25; Lk 12: 14, 58; 18: 2. ὁ κρ. τῆς ἀδικίας the unjust judge 18: 6 (W-S. §30, 8; Mlt.-H. 440; JDMDerrett, NTS 18, '71/'72, 178-91). πενήτων ἄνομοι κρ. lawless judges of the poor B 20: 2; D 5: 2. Of Herod Antipas' judges GP 1: 1. Of the procurator Ac 24: 10 (v.l. κρ. δίκαιος; so of a human judge Epict., fgm. Stob. 48). Of the proconsul κρ. τούτων οὐ βούλομαι εἶναι I do not wish to render a decision on these matters Ac 18: 15.
β. of God (LXX; Philo; Jos., Bell. 5, 390; Test. Jud. 20: 5. Cf. Ael. Aristid. 13 p. 230 D.; τὶς τῶν ἐξ οὐρανοῦ κριτής) and Christ Hb 12: 23; Js 4: 12; δίκαιος κρ. 2 Ti 4: 8; Hs 6, 3, 6. Of God or Christ κρ. ζώντων καὶ νεκρῶν judge of the living and the dead 2 Cl 1: 1.—Ac 10: 42; Pol 2: 1. ὁ κρ. πρὸ τῶν θυρῶν ἔστηκεν the judge stands at the door Js 5: 9.

b. in a more general mng. (Appian, Liby. 52 §227 κριτής τινος judge, critic of someth.) κριταὶ διαλογισμῶν πονηρῶν Js 2: 4. κριτής (νόμου) a judge of the law 4: 11. Of the 'sons' of the Pharisees κριταὶ ἔσονται ὑμῶν they will be your judges i.e. they will convict you of wrongdoing Mt 12: 27; Lk 11: 19. Of Moses 1 Cl 4: 10 (cf. Ex 2: 14).

2. in a special sense in the historical accounts of the theocratic period, judge, a leader of the people in the period before the rise of the Hebrew kgdm. (cf. Judg 2: 16, 18f; Ruth 1: 1; Jos., Ant. 6, 85; 11, 112) Ac 13: 20. M-M.*

κριτικός, ή, όν (Pla.+; Strabo, Plut., Lucian et al.; Philo, Mut. Nom. 110) able to discern or judge foll. by obj. gen. κρ. ἐνθυμήσεων καὶ ἐννοιῶν καρδίας able to judge the thoughts and deliberations of the heart Hb 4: 12.*

Κρόκος, ου, ὁ (not a very common name; in the Gk. form e.g. Dit., Or. Inscr. 140; CIG add. 4716d, 44; Κυπρ. I p. 100 no. 74; PLond. 257, 221; 223; BGU 90, 1; 537, 1) Crocus, an Ephesian Christian: θεοῦ ἄξιος καὶ ὑμῶν IEph 2: 1. τὸ ποθητόν μοι ὄνομα a person dear to me IRo 10: 1.*

κροκώδης, ες (Diod. S. 2, 52, 5; Diosc. 1, 27; Heraclides [KDeichgräber, D. griech. Empirikerschule '30, 195, 22]; Aretaeus p. 58, 24) saffron-yellow Hs 6, 1, 5.*

κρούω 1 aor. ἔκρουσα (since Soph. and X., De Re Equ. 11, 4; PGM 5, 75; 92 al.; LXX; Philo, Mut. Nom. 139; Jos., Ant. 7, 306) strike, knock, in our lit. only of knocking at a door; abs. (on the contrast κρ.—ἀνοίγω cf. SSol 5: 2 κρούει ἐπὶ τὴν θύραν Ἄνοιξόν μοι and UPZ 79, 7 [159

BC] κρούει θύραν κ. ἀνοίγεται; Eunap., Vi. Soph. p. 94, where it is said fig. of a sophist: ἔκρουε μὲν τὴν θύραν ἱκανῶς, ἠνοίγετο δὲ οὐ πολλάκις) Mt 7: 7f; Lk 11: 9f; 12: 36; Ac 12: 16; Rv 3: 20. W. acc. τὴν θύραν knock at the door (Aristoph., Eccles. 317; 990; X., Symp. 1, 11; Pla., Prot. 310A; 314D, Symp. 212C; PGM 4, 1854. Further exx. fr. later Gk. in Field, Notes 120. The Atticists reject this expr. in favor of κόπτειν τ. θύραν [Phryn. p. 177 Lob.].—Judg 19: 22) Lk 13: 25; Ac 12: 13. M-M. B. 553.*

κρύβω s. κρύπτω.

κρύπτη, ης, ἡ (Strabo 17, 1, 37; Athen. 5 p. 205A; Jos., Bell. 5, 330 [Niese accents κρυπτή]; PSI 547, 18 [III BC]) a dark and hidden place, a cellar λύχνον εἰς κρ. τιθέναι put a lamp in a cellar Lk 11: 33. M-M.*

κρυπτός, ή, όν (Hom.+; pap., LXX) hidden, secret—1. adj. (Herodian 5, 6, 3 κρ. καὶ ἀόρατος; Dit., Syll.³ 973, 5f; BGU 316, 28; 3 Km 6: 4; Ezk 40: 16; 2 Macc 1: 16; Jos., Ant. 15, 424) ὁ κρυπτὸς τῆς καρδίας ἄνθρωπος the hidden man of the heart 1 Pt 3: 4 (s. ἄνθρωπος 2ca). οὐδὲν... κρ. ὃ οὐ γνωσθήσεται there is nothing secret that shall not be made known Mt 10: 26; Lk 12: 2; cf. Mk 4: 22 (Philemo Com. 192 χρόνος τὰ κρυπτὰ πάντα εἰς φάος ἄγει).

2. subst. τὸ κρυπτόν—a. a hidden thing (Menand., Mon. 225) Lk 8: 17. Esp. in pl. τὰ κρυπτά (Dt 29: 28; Is 29: 10; Sus 42 Theod.; Jos., Bell. 5, 402; 413 ὁ θεὸς τὰ κρ. πάντα ἐφορᾷ) τὰ κρ. ἐλέγχει it exposes the secret things (so, word for word, Artem. 1, 14 p. 19, 4 and 1, 44 p. 42, 8) IPhld 7: 1. τὰ κρ. τινος someone's secret thoughts, plans, purposes (Philemo Com. 233 φίλου; Iambl., Myst. 6, 5 Partey; PGM 57, 13 τὰ κρ. τ. θεᾶς Ἴσιδος; Sir 1: 30; Jer 30: 4) Ro 2: 16; IEph 15: 3; IPhld 7: 1. τὰ κρ. τῆς καρδίας αὐτοῦ (cf. Is 22: 9 τὰ κρ. τῶν οἴκων τῆς ἄκρας) the secret thoughts of his heart 1 Cor 14: 25; cf. Pol 4: 3. τὰ κρ. τοῦ σκότους what is hidden in darkness 1 Cor 4: 5. τὰ κρ. τῆς αἰσχύνης the things that are hidden out of a sense of shame 2 Cor 4: 2.

b. a hidden place ἐν τῷ κρ. in secret (Vi. Aesopi W c. 104) Mt 6: 4a, b, 6a, b, 18 t.r.; ἐν κρ. in a secret place J 7: 4; 18: 20; in secret, secretly (Test. Jud. 12: 5) ὁ ἐν τῷ κρ. Ἰουδαῖος the Jew who is one inwardly, not only by the outward sign of circumcision Ro 2: 29; ἀνέβη ὡς ἐν κρ. he went up privately, as it were J 7: 10.—On Lk 11: 33 s. κρύπτη. M-M.*

κρύπτω (Hom.+; inscr., pap., LXX; Philo, Leg. All. 3, 23; Jos., Ant. 18, 105, C. Ap. 2, 207; Test. 12 Patr.; Sib. Or. 5, 45.—**κρύβω** [PGM 12, 322; Jos., Ant. 8, 410, C. Ap. 1, 292], whence the impf. mid. ἐκρυβόμην GP 7: 26, is a new formation in H. Gk. fr. the aor. ἐκρύβην [Bl-D. §73; Mlt.-H. 214; 245; Reinhold 72. On the LXX s. Helbing 83f]) 1 aor. ἔκρυψα; pf. pass. 3 sing. κέκρυπται, ptc. κεκρυμμένος; 2 aor. pass. ἐκρύβην (Hellenistic: Lobeck, Phryn. p. 317; LXX; Jos., Ant. 8, 384); 2 fut. pass. κρυβήσομαι (Plut., Mor. 576D) hide, conceal, cover.

1. lit.—a. hide in the sense prevent someth. fr. being seen τὶ someth. money Mt 25: 18; a treasure that has been found 13: 44b. κρ. τινα ἀπὸ προσώπου τινός Rv 6: 16. Fig. of the key of knowledge Lk 11: 52 v.l. Pass. (Philo, Det. Pot. Ins. 128 τὰ ἀποκείμενα ἐν σκότῳ κέκρυπται) of a city on an eminence οὐ δύναται κρυβῆναι Mt 5: 14; LJ 1: 7. Of Moses, who escaped detection Hb 11: 23. τὸ μάννα τὸ κεκρυμμένον the hidden manna, concealed fr. human eyes because it is laid up in heaven Rv 2: 17.—If mention is made of the place to which persons or things are

brought to hide them fr. view, the word plainly comes to mean

b. conceal, etc. (acc. to the context) κ. τι ἐν τῇ γῇ hide someth. in the earth (Apollon. Rhod. 4, 480 κρ. τι ἐν γαίῃ) Mt 25: 25; likew. in pass. θησαυρὸς κεκρυμμένος ἐν τῷ ἀγρῷ a treasure hidden in a field 13: 44a. Cf. Ac 7: 24 D. Of living persons (Paus. 9, 19, 1) Ῥαὰβ αὐτοὺς ἔκρυψεν εἰς τὸ ὑπερῷον ὑπὸ τὴν λινοκαλάμην Rahab concealed them in the upper room under the flax 1 Cl 12: 3 (Diod. S. 4, 33, 9 κ. εἰς; Ps.-Apollod. 1, 4, 1, 4 ὑπὸ γῆν ἔκρυψε).—κρύπτειν ἑαυτόν hide oneself (Nicander in Anton. Lib. 28, 3) εἴς τι in someth. ἔκρυψαν ἑαυτοὺς εἰς τὰ σπήλαια they hid themselves in the caves (Diod. S. 4, 12, 2 ἔκρυψεν ἑαυτὸν εἰς πίθον) Rv 6: 15.

c. κρυβῆναι hide or conceal oneself (Gen 3: 8, 10; Judg 9: 5; 1 Km 13: 6; 14: 11; Job 24: 4; 29: 8) Ἰησοῦς ἐκρύβη J 8: 59. ἐκρύβη ἀπ' αὐτῶν 12: 36.—ποῦ κρυβήσομαι ἀπὸ τοῦ προσώπου σου; 1 Cl 28: 3.—ἐκρυβόμεθα we remained in hiding GP 7: 26.

d. without the purpose, yet w. the result, of hiding someth. fr. view, (Hipponax [VI BC] 25 D. ἀσκέρῃσι τοὺς πόδας δασείῃσιν ἔκρυψας=you have put my feet in furlined shoes) put (in), mix (in) τὶ εἴς τι someth. in someth. (ζύμην) γυνὴ ἔκρυψεν εἰς ἀλεύρου σάτα τρία Lk 13: 21 (v.l. ἐνέκρυψεν 𝔓⁷⁵ et al.).

2. fig.—a. withdraw from sight or knowledge, hide, conceal, keep secret (Delphic commandments: Dit., Syll.³ 1268 II, 16 [III BC] ἀπόρρητα κρύπτε) τὶ ἀπό τινος someth. fr. someone (Synes., Ep. 57 p. 195D; Gen 18: 17) Mt 11: 25. Pass. Lk 18: 34. ἐκρύβη ἀπὸ ὀφθαλμῶν σου it is hidden from your (spiritual) eyes 19: 42. Of the moral conduct of a person κρυβῆναι οὐ δύναται 1 Ti 5: 25 (Diod. S. 14, 1, 3 ἀδυνατεῖ κρύπτειν τὴν ἄγνοιαν).—κεκρυμμένα hidden, unknown things (Philo, Spec. Leg. 3, 61) Mt 13: 35. μαθητὴς κεκρυμμένος a secret disciple J 19: 38.

b. cause to disappear pass. ἵνα ἀνομία πολλῶν ἐν δικαίῳ ἑνὶ κρυβῇ that the lawlessness of so many should be made to disappear in one who is righteous Dg 9: 5.

c. hide in a safe place ἀπὸ μάστιγος γλώσσης σε κρύψει he will hide you from the scourge of the tongue 1 Cl 56: 10 (Job 5: 21). Pass. ἡ ζωὴ ὑμῶν κέκρυπται σὺν τῷ Χριστῷ ἐν τῷ θεῷ Col 3: 3.—AOepke, TW III 959-79 κρύπτω and related words. M-M. B. 850.*

κρυσταλλίζω (hapax legomenon) shine like crystal, be as transparent as crystal of jasper Rv 21: 11 (s. κρύσταλλος).*

κρύσταλλος, ου, ὁ rock-crystal (so Diod. S. 2, 52, 2; Strabo 15, 1, 67; Dio Chrys. 12[13], 34; Aelian, N.A. 15, 8; Arrian, Anab. 3, 4, 4 of a kind of salt: καθαρὸς ὥσπερ κρύσταλλος; Is 54: 12; Ep. Arist. 67; Philo, Somn. 1, 21) Rv 4: 6 (cf. PLond. 130, 150 ὁμοία κρυστάλλῳ; Aëtius p. 4, 2 προσέοικε κρυστάλλῳ); 22: 1. Or is it poss. that, since κρ. is compared w. θάλασσα and ποταμὸς ὕδατος in the two pass., the older mng. ice (Hom.; Hdt.; Antig. Car. 144; Diod. S. 3, 34, 2; 17, 82, 5; Longus 3, 3, 2; Job 6: 16; Wsd 16: 22; Jos., Ant. 1, 30; Test. Levi 3: 2; Sib. Or. 14, 151, fgm. 1, 34) is to be preferred? M-M. B. 69.*

κρυφαῖος, αία, αῖον (Pind., Pla.+; LXX) hidden ἐν τῷ κρ. in secret Mt 6: 18a, b (cf. ἐν κρυφαίοις Jer 23: 24; La 3: 10).*

κρυφῇ adv. (κρυφῆ Tdf.; s. W-S. §5, 11c; Bl-D. §26 app.; cf. 73; Mlt.-H. 84.—Soph., X.+; ostracon: APF 6, '20, 220 no. 8, 3 κρυφῆι [III BC]; POxy. 83, 14; LXX; Test. Sim. 8: 2) in secret τὰ κρ. γινόμενα ὑπ' αὐτῶν the things they do in secret Eph 5: 12. M-M.*

κρύφιος, ία, ιον (Hes.+; LXX) *hidden, secret* τὰ κρύφια ἔργα 2 Cl 16: 3. Subst. τὰ κ. *hidden* or *secret things* (LXX) 1 Cl 18: 6 (Ps 50: 8); B 6: 10; IMg 3: 2.—ἐν κρυφίᾳ *in secret* Mt 6: 18 D.*

κτάομαι fut. κτήσομαι; 1 aor. ἐκτησάμην; pf. κέκτημαι (Hom.+; inscr., pap., LXX, En., Ep. Arist., Philo; Jos., Bell. 2, 285, Ant. 1, 284; Test. 12 Patr.) *procure for oneself, acquire, get.*

1. τὶ *someth.* 2 Cl 5: 7. πάντα ὅσα κτῶμαι *my whole income* Lk 18: 12. W. acc. and εἴς τι foll.: χρυσὸν . . . εἰς τὰς ζώνας *acquire gold* (in order to put it) *into your (money-) belts* Mt 10: 9. *Procure* τὶ *someth.* (Plut., Mor. 189D βιβλία κτᾶσθαι) τὴν δωρεὰν τ. θεοῦ διὰ χρημάτων κτᾶσθαι *secure the gift of God with money* Ac 8: 20 (Herodian 2, 6, 5 χρήμασι κτ. τι). Also ἐκ: χωρίον ἐκ μισθοῦ τ. ἀδικίας *acquire a field w. the reward of his wickedness* 1: 18 (JSickenberger, BZ 18, '29, 69–71). Also w. gen. of price πολλοῦ κεφαλαίου *for a large sum* Ac 22: 28. τὸ ἑαυτοῦ σκεῦος κτᾶσθαι ἐν ἁγιασμῷ καὶ τιμῇ *take a wife for himself* (or: *gain control over his own body*; s. σκεῦος 2) *in consecration and honor* 1 Th 4: 4 (cf. κτᾶσθαι γυναῖκα X., Symp. 2, 10; Sir 36: 24). ἐν τῇ ὑπομονῇ ὑμῶν κτήσεσθε τὰς ψυχὰς ὑμῶν *you will win your lives by your endurance* Lk 21: 19.

2. of misfortunes, etc. *bring upon oneself* (Soph.; Eur.; Thu. 1, 42, 2 ἔχθραν; Pr 3: 31) εὔχομαι, ἵνα μὴ εἰς μαρτύριον αὐτὸ κτήσωνται *I pray that they may not bring it* (my message) *upon themselves as a witness* (against them) IPhld 6: 3.

3. The pf. (only in Ign. in our lit.) has present mng. *possess* (Appian, Bell. Civ. 5, 67 §282 οἱ κεκτημένοι= those who possessed [slaves]; En. 97, 10; Ep. Arist. 229; Philo, Cher. 119, Mos. 1, 157 al.; Jos., C. Ap. 1, 66) τινά *someone* ἐπίσκοπον IEph 1: 3. τὶ *someth.* ὄνομα 1: 1. ἀγάπην 14: 2. λόγον Ἰησοῦ 15: 2. πνεῦμα IMg 15; IPol 1: 3. διακονίαν IPhld 1: 1. γνώμην IPol 8: 1. M-M.*

κτῆμα, ατος, τό (Hom.+; inscr., pap., LXX, Philo, Joseph.)—1. gener. *property, possession* of any kind. πᾶν κτ. D 13: 7. Pl. *possessions* (PRyl. 28, 182; 76, 11; Jos., Ant. 14, 157) τὰ κτήματα καὶ αἱ ὑπάρξεις Ac 2: 45. Beside fields and houses of movable property, furniture Hs 1: 9. ἔχειν κτ. πολλά Mt 19: 22; Mk 10: 22 (cf. Diog., Ep. 38, 5, a rich youth follows Diogenes διανείμας τὴν οὐσίαν. Porphyr., Vi. Plotini 7: Rogatianus the senator gives away πᾶσα κτῆσις and becomes a Cynic).

2. In later usage κτ. came to be restricted to the mng. *landed property, field, piece of ground* (since Demosth. 18, 41; Plut., Crass. 1, 5; Herodian 2, 6, 3; PTebt. 5, 52; 120, 9; BGU 530, 20; Pr 23: 10; 31: 16; Philo, Spec. Leg. 2, 116; Jos., Bell. 4, 574) Ac 5: 1 (=χωρίον vs. 3). M-M. B. 769.*

κτῆνος, ους, τό *animal,* i.e. *domesticated animal, pet, pack-animal, animal used for riding* (mostly in pl. as collective: since Hom. Hymns and Hdt.; inscr., pap., LXX, Ep. Arist., Philo; Sib. Or., fgm. 3, 12; infreq. in sing.: X., An. 5, 2, 3; Dit., Syll.[3] 986, 8; Ex 22: 4; Test. Reub. 2: 9) of livestock (PTebt. 56, 8; LXX) Hv 4, 1, 5; s 9, 1, 8 (in contrast to wild and dangerous animals 9, 1, 9; cf. M. Ant. 5, 11 and Philo, Op. M. 64: κτ.—θηρίον); 9, 24, 1. Also 1 Cor 15: 39; PK 2 p. 14, 18 refer to domesticated animals. *Cattle* alone seem to be meant in the combination κτήνη καὶ πρόβατα Rv 18: 13 (cf. PRyl. 126, 15 τὰ ἑατοῦ πρόβατα κ. βοικὰ κτήνη).—Of animals used for riding (POxy. 2153, 20 [III AD]; Jos., Ant. 8, 241) Lk 10: 34; Ac 23: 24. M-M.*

κτήτωρ, ορος, ὁ (Diod. S. 34+35, 2, 31; POxy. 237 VIII, 31; 718, 13; PTebt. 378, 24; Sym. Jo 1: 11) *owner* of houses and lands χωρίων ἢ οἰκιῶν Ac 4: 34 (cf. 1QS 1, 11f). M-M.*

κτίζω 1 aor. ἔκτισα; pf. pass. ἔκτισμαι; 1 aor. pass. ἐκτίσθην (Hom.+; inscr., pap., LXX) *create,* in our lit. of God's creative activity (LXX; En., Ep. Arist. 185; Eupolis in Euseb., Pr. Ev. 9, 31; Philo, Decal. 97; Jos., Bell. 3, 369; 379, Ant. 1, 27; Sib. Or. 3, 20; Fluchtaf. 4, 1; PGM 5, 98ff) τὶ *someth.* 1 Ti 4: 3. κτίσιν Mk 13: 19. τὸν οὐρανὸν καὶ τὰ ἐν αὐτῷ *the heaven and what is in it* Rv 10: 6. τὰ πάντα (Herm. Wr. 13, 17) 4: 11a; cf. b. ὁ θεὸς ὁ τὰ πάντα κτίσας Eph 3: 9; Hm 1: 1; cf. s 5, 5, 2 and D 10: 3; pass. Col 1: 16a, b (cf. ἐν I 5a). ὁ θεὸς κτίσας ἐκ τοῦ μὴ ὄντος τὰ ὄντα *what is from what is not* Hv 1, 1, 6. τὸν κόσμον v 1, 3, 4. τὸν κόσμον ἕνεκα τοῦ ἀνθρώπου m 12, 4, 2. τὰ ἔθνη s 4: 4. τὸν λαόν s 5, 6, 2. Pass. ἐκτίσθη ἀνήρ 1 Cor 11: 9. Of the church πάντων πρώτη ἐκτίσθη Hv 2, 4, 1. Of the angels οἱ πρῶτοι κτισθέντες v 3, 4, 1; s 5, 5, 3. Abs. ὁ κτίσας *the Creator* (Jos., Bell. 3, 354) Ro 1: 25; Mt 19: 4 (v.l. ποιήσας). ὁ τὰ πάντα κτίσας *the Creator of the universe* Hs 7: 4 (PGM 13, 62 τὸν πάντα κτίσαντα; 983).—Also of the Spirit τὸ πνεῦμα τὸ κτίσαν πᾶσαν τὴν κτίσιν Hs 5, 6, 5.—Of the divine creative activity w. regard to the inner life of man: of men who were κτισθέντες ἐν Χριστῷ Ἰησοῦ ἐπὶ ἔργοις ἀγαθοῖς *created* (by God) *in Christ Jesus for good deeds* Eph 2: 10. ἵνα τοὺς δύο κτίσῃ ἐν αὐτῷ εἰς ἕνα καινὸν ἄνθρωπον *in order that he* (Christ) *might make them both* (Jews and Gentiles) *one new man in him* vs. 15. τὸν καινὸν ἄνθρωπον τὸν κατὰ θεὸν κτισθέντα ἐν δικαιοσύνῃ *the new man, created in the likeness of God in righteousness* 4: 24. Corresp. τὸν νέον (ἄνθρωπον) τὸν ἀνακαινούμενον εἰς ἐπίγνωσιν κατ' εἰκόνα τοῦ κτίσαντος αὐτόν *the new man, who is renewed in knowledge according to the image of his Creator* Col 3: 10. ἐγενόμεθα καινοί, πάλιν ἐξ ἀρχῆς κτιζόμενοι *we became new, created again from the beginning* B 16: 8. καρδίαν καθαρὰν κτίσον ἐν ἐμοί 1 Cl 18: 10 (Ps 50: 12). S. on ἐκλογή, end, and Teschendorf under γίνομαι I 2a.—PKatz, The Mng. of the root קנה: Journal of Jewish Studies 5, 126–31; WFoerster, TW III 999–1034 κτίζω and related words. M-M.**

κτίσις, εως, ἡ (Pind.+; inscr., pap., LXX, En., Ep. Arist., Joseph., Test. 12 Patr., Sib. Or.).

1. *creation*—**a.** of the act of creation: ἀπὸ κτίσεως κόσμου *since the creation of the world* Ro 1: 20 (cf. PsSol 8, 7; Jos., Bell. 4, 533). The Son of God was σύμβουλος τῷ πατρὶ τῆς κτίσεως αὐτοῦ *counselor to the Father in his creative work* Hs 9, 12, 2.

b. *that which is created* as the result of that creative act (Ep. Arist. 136; 139; Test. Reub. 2: 9).

α. of individual things or beings created, *creature* (Tob 8: 5, 15) *created thing* τὶς κτ. ἑτέρα *any other creature* Ro 8: 39. οὐκ ἔστιν κτ. ἀφανὴς ἐνώπιον αὐτοῦ *no creature is hidden from his sight* Hb 4: 13. πᾶν γένος τῆς κ. τοῦ κυρίου *every kind of creature that the Lord made* Hs 9, 1, 8; πᾶσα κτ. *every created thing* (cf. Jdth 9: 12) MPol 14: 1. Of Christ πρωτότοκος πάσης κτ. Col 1: 15. Of the name of God ἀρχέγονον πάσης κτ. 1 Cl 59: 3. τὸ εὐαγγέλιον . . . τὸ κηρυχθὲν ἐν πάσῃ κτίσει *the gospel . . . which has been preached to every creature* (here limited to human beings) Col 1: 23.—Pl. (En. 18, 1) δοξάζειν τὰς κτίσεις τοῦ θεοῦ *praise the created works of God* Hv 1, 1, 3.—The Christian is described by Paul as καινὴ κτ. *a new creature* 2 Cor 5: 17, and the state of being in the new faith by the same words as *a new creation*

Gal 6: 15 (cf. Jos., Ant. 18, 373 καιναί κτίσεις). S. on ἐκλογή, end.

β. the sum total of everything created, *creation, world* (Sib. Or. 5, 152) ἡ κτ. αὐτοῦ Hv 1, 3, 4. ἐν ἀρχῇ τῆς κτ. *at the beginning of the world* B 15: 3; ἀπ᾽ ἀρχῆς κτ. *from the beginning of the world* Mk 13: 19; 2 Pt 3: 4. Likew. Mk 10: 6; πᾶσα ἡ κτ. *the whole creation* (Jdth 16: 14; Ps 104: 21 v.l.; Test. Levi 4: 1, Napht. 2: 3; PGM 12, 85) Hv 3, 4, 1; m 12, 4, 2; s 5, 6, 5; 9, 14, 5; 9, 23, 4; 9, 25, 1. The whole world is full of God's glory 1 Cl 34: 6. ἀόργητος ὑπάρχει πρὸς πᾶσαν τὴν κτίσιν αὐτοῦ 19: 3. ὁ υἱὸς τ. θεοῦ πάσης τ. κτίσεως αὐτοῦ προγενέστερός ἐστιν *the Son of God is older than all his creation* Hs 9, 12, 2. πᾶσα ἡ κτ. limited to mankind Mk 16: 15; Hm 7: 5. Also ἡ κτίσις τῶν ἀνθρώπων D 16: 5.—αὕτη ἡ κτ. *this world* (earthly in contrast to heavenly) Hb 9: 11.—κτ. *the creation, what was created* in contrast to the Creator (Wsd 16: 24) Ro 1: 25 (Ep. Arist. 139 θεὸν σεβόμενοι παρ᾽ ὅλην τὴν κτίσιν).—Of Christ ἡ ἀρχὴ τῆς κτίσεως τοῦ θεοῦ Rv 3: 14 (s. ἀρχή 2).—The mng. of κτ. is in dispute in Ro 8: 19-22, though the pass. is usu. taken to mean the waiting of the whole creation below the human level (animate and inanimate—so, e.g. OCullmann, Christ and Time [tr. FVFilson] '50, 103).—HBiedermann, D. Erlösg. der Schöpfung beim Ap. Pls. '40.

2. Corresponding to 1a κτίσις is also the act by which an authoritative or governmental body is created (inscr. in Ramsay, Phrygia I 2 p. 468 no. 305 [I AD]: founding of the Gerousia [Senate]. Somewhat comparable, of the founding of a city: Scymnus Chius v. 89 κτίσεις πόλεων). But then, in accordance with 1b, it is prob. also the result of the act, *the institution* or *authority* itself 1 Pt 2: 13 (Diod. S. 11, 60, 2 has κτίστης as the title of a high official. Cf. νομοθεσία in both meanings: 1. lawgiving, legislation; 2. the result of the action, i.e., law.)—BRBrinkman, 'Creation' and 'Creature' I, Bijdragen (Nijmegen) 18, '57, 129-39, also 359-74; GWHLampe, The NT Doctrine of κτίσις, Scottish Journ. of Theol. 17, '64, 449-62. M-M.*

κτίσμα, ατος, τό (Polyb. 4, 70, 3; Dionys. Hal. 1, 59; Strabo 7, 5, 5; Vett. Val. 213, 6; Dit., Syll.³ 799, 7 [38 AD]; PGM 7, 483; BGU 3, 19; LXX; loanw. in rabb.) in our lit. always (as Wsd 9: 2; 13: 5; 14: 11; Sir 36: 14; 38: 34; 3 Macc 5: 11; Ep. Arist. 17) *that which is created* (by God), *creature* (created by God) πᾶν κτ. θεοῦ καλόν *everything created by God is good* 1 Ti 4: 4. πᾶν κτ. ὃ ἐν τῷ οὐρανῷ *every creature in heaven* Rv 5: 13.—Pl., of the component parts of creation (Herm. Wr. 1, 18 πάντα τὰ κτ.; Sextus 439) Dg 8: 3.—τὰ κτ. τὰ ἐν τῇ θαλάσσῃ Rv 8: 9.—τὰ κτ. τοῦ θεοῦ *what God has created* Hv 3, 9, 2; m 8: 1; man is lord of it 12, 4, 3. The Christians are ἀπαρχή τις τῶν αὐτοῦ κτ. *a kind of first-fruits of his creatures* (here κτ. is to be thought of as referring chiefly to men; for a similar restriction in the use of κτίσις s. that entry 1bα, β) Js 1: 18. M-M.*

κτίστης (on the accent cf. Kühner-Bl. I §107, 4eβ p. 392; Rob. 231) ου, ὁ (the word Aristot.+; inscr., pap., LXX, Ep. Arist., Philo; Jos., Ant. 1, 214; Sib. Or.—As designation of rulers and others of high rank: Dit., Syll.³ 751, 2; 839, 8 [both κτ., sc. τῆς πόλεως, w. σωτήρ]; Inschr. v. Priene 229, 4; CIG II 2572 the Rom. emperor as τῆς οἰκουμένης κτ.; Jos., C. Ap. 2, 39.—Also w. ref. to a deity: PGM 4, 591 φωτὸς κτίστα; 5, 248; 7, 963) in our lit. only of God as *the Creator* (hymn to Isis: Suppl. Epigr. Gr. VIII 549, 11 [I BC] the god Σοκονῶπις as κτ. καὶ γαίης τε καὶ οὐρανοῦ; Herm. Wr. 13, 17; Sir 24: 8 ὁ κτ. ἀπάντων; 2 Macc 1: 24; 4 Macc 11: 5; Ep. Arist. 16;

Philo, Spec. Leg. 1, 30 al.; Sib. Or., fgm. 3, 17 al.) 1 Pt 4: 19; 1 Cl 62: 2. κτ. τοῦ σύμπαντος κόσμου *Creator of the whole universe* 19: 2 (cf. ὁ τοῦ κόσμου κτ. 2 Macc 7: 23; 4 Macc 5: 25; PGM 4, 1200). κτ. παντὸς πνεύματος *Creator of every spirit* 59: 3.—HFWeiss, TU 97, '66, 55-8 (cosmology). M-M.*

κυβεία, ας, ἡ *dice-playing* (Pla., Phaedr. 274D; X., Mem. 1, 3, 2, Oec. 1, 20; Dio Chrys. 53[70], 4. As a loanw. קוביא in the Bab. Talmud, Sabb. 149b) ἡ κυβεία τῶν ἀνθρώπων is shown by the succeeding phrase, ἐν πανουργίᾳ κτλ., to be *craftiness, trickery* Eph 4: 14 (κυβεύω= 'deceive' Epict. 2, 19, 28; 3, 21, 22). M-M.*

κυβέρνησις, εως, ἡ (Pind.+; Plut., Mor. 162A [θεοῦ κ.]; PLond. 1349, 20; Pr 1: 5; 11: 14; 24: 6) *administration*; the pl. indicates proofs of ability to hold a leading position in the church 1 Cor 12: 28.—HWBeyer, TW III 1034-6. M-M.*

κυβερνήτης, ου, ὁ (Hom.+; inscr., pap., LXX, Philo; Jos., Vi. 163; Test. Napht. 6: 2; loanw. in rabb.) *captain, steersman, pilot.*

1. lit. Rv 18: 17; IPol 2: 3. W. ναύκληρος, the 'shipowner' (Plut., Mor. 807B ναύτας μὲν ἐκλέγεται κυβερνήτης καὶ κυβερνήτην ναύκληρος; Jos., Ant. 9, 209) Ac 27: 11 (LCasson, Ships and Seamanship in the Ancient World, '71, 316-18).

2. fig. (Pla., Polit. 272E of God; Vett. Val. 340 κυβερνήτης βίου. Oft. Philo, somet. of God, and Migr. Abr. 67 of the λόγος θεῖος; Herm. Wr. 12, 4 of the νοῦς) of Christ κυβ. τῶν σωμάτων ἡμῶν *the Pilot of our bodies* MPol 19: 2 (the figure of the κυβερνήτης is also used in the martyr-narrative in 4 Macc 7: 1). M-M.*

κυβία s. κυβεία.

κύθρα, ας, ἡ (Herodas 7, 76; Etymol. Mag. p. 454, 43; PTebt. 112, 42; 47, 75 [112 BC]; PAmh. 125, 5; cf. Mayser p. 184. For the LXX cf. Thackeray p. 103) *a pot* 1 Cl 17: 6 (quot. of unknown origin; s. RHarris, JBL 29, '10, 190f).*

κυκλεύω 1 aor. ἐκύκλευσα (Strabo 6, 3, 7; PLond. 131 recto, 508; PGrenf. I 58, 7; 4 Km 3: 25) *surround* τὴν παρεμβολὴν τῶν ἁγίων Rv 20: 9. τινά *someone* J 10: 24 v.l.—Cf. Hs 9, 9, 6 v.l. Cf. κυκλόω. M-M.*

κυκλόθεν adv. of place (Lysias 7, 28; Epigr. Gr. 546, 7f; BGU 1117, 25 [13 BC]; LXX) *all around, from all sides.*

1. as adv. (Sib. Or. 3, 706) κυκλόθεν κ. ἔσωθεν Rv 4: 8.—2. as (improper) prep. w. gen. (Sb 6152, 20 [93 BC]; Sir 50: 12; 4 Macc 14: 17; Aristob. in Euseb., Pr. Ev. 8, 10, 14) κ. τοῦ θρόνου *around the throne* 4: 3f. M-M.*

κυκλόω 1 aor. ἐκύκλωσα, pass. ἐκυκλώθην (Pind.+; LXX; Philo, Leg. All. 1, 85; 86; Jos., Bell. 4, 557, Ant. 10, 137; Sib. Or. 5, 233).

1. *surround, encircle*, mostly w. hostile intent (Eur., Thu. et al.; LXX) τινά *someone* J 10: 24; Ac 14: 20; B 6: 6 (cf. Ps 21: 17). A place (cf. Jos., Vi. 114) pass. κυκλουμένην ὑπὸ στρατοπέδων Ἱερουσαλήμ Lk 21: 20.—For protection, fig., of mercy 1 Cl 22: 8 (Ps 31: 10).

2. *go around, circle round* τὸν πύργον Hs 9, 9, 6 (cf. Gen 2: 11; Dt 2: 1, 3). Pass., of Jericho's walls ἔπεσαν κυκλωθέντα ἐπὶ ἑπτὰ ἡμέρας *they fell after the Israelites had marched around them seven days* Hb 11: 30 (cf. Josh 6: 20).*

κύκλῳ dat. (of κύκλος) of place, fixed as an adv. (Bl-D. §199; Rob. 295f; 644) *around, all around*, lit. *in a circle*

(Hom.+; inscr., pap., LXX, En., Ep. Arist., Philo, Joseph.).

1. used as adv. (Jos., Ant. 14, 418; 15, 337)—**a.** κ. περιτειχίζειν MPol 15: 2. οἱ περὶ αὐτὸν κύκλῳ καθήμενοι Mk 3: 34 (cf. 1 Esdr 4: 11 and κύκλῳ περί τι Hdt. 1, 185; Pla., Phaedo 111c; Ep. Arist. 63). περιῆγεν τ. κώμας κ. *he went around among the villages* 6: 6. ἀπὸ Ἰερουσαλὴμ καὶ κύκλῳ Ro 15: 19 (ASGeyser, Un Essai d'Explication de Ro 15: 19, NTS 6, '60, 156–59) is either (*beginning*) *from Jerusalem and its environs* (BWeiss) or prob. better *beginning from Jerus. and traveling around* (*describing a circle*) (Zahn, Ltzm., Sickenberger, Althaus). This avoids giving the impression that Paul travelled in a straight line, and agrees better w. the comprehensive nature of his activity (cf. PLond. 891, 9 ἡ εὐφημία σου περιεκύκλωσεν τ. κόσμον ὅλον='travel about in'. Maximus Tyr. 25, 1c Ἀνάχαρσις περιῄει τὴν Ἑλλάδα ἐν κύκλῳ). Perhaps it would be better to render κύκλῳ with *in an arc* or *curve* (Appian, Mithrid. 101 §467: Mithridates, on his march from Dioscurias on the east shore of the Black Sea wishes to go around τὸν Πόντον ὅλον ἐν κύκλῳ=the whole Black Sea in a curved path, as far as Lake Maeotis=the Sea of Azov).

b. preceded by the art., and used as an adj. *around, nearby* (X., Cyr. 4, 5, 5; 7, 2, 23; Arrian, Anab. 6, 15, 7 τὰ κύκλῳ ἔθνη; Bar 2: 4b; 2 Macc 4: 32 αἱ κ. πόλεις) εἰς τοὺς κ. ἀγρούς *into the farms nearby* Mk 6: 36. εἰς τὰς κ. κώμας *into the villages around here* Lk 9: 12.

2. as (improper) prep. w. gen. (X., Cyr. 4, 5, 5; Polyb. 4, 21, 9; Dit., Or. 455, 12; PRainer 42, 10; PFay. 110, 7; PTebt. 342, 26; Gen 35: 5; Ex 7: 24; 16: 13 al.; En. 14, 11) κ. τοῦ θρόνου *around the throne* Rv 4: 6; 5: 11; 7: 11. κ. τοῦ πύργου *around the tower* Hv 3, 2, 8; 3, 4, 2; s 9, 9, 6. κ. τοῦ πεδίου *around the plain* s 9, 1, 4. M-M. Cf. B. 905.**

κύλισμα, ματος, τό s. κυλισμός.

κυλισμός, οῦ, ὁ *rolling, wallowing* (Hippiatr. 75, 12 [=I p. 291, 23]; Pr 2: 18 Theod.) of a swine λουσαμένη εἰς κ. βορβόρου (s. on βόρβορος) 2 Pt 2: 22 (κύλισμα t.r. is prob. on the analogy of ἐξέραμα. κύλισμα is found Ezk 10: 13 Sym.; JZiegler, Ezk p. 126). M-M.*

κυλίω impf. pass. ἐκυλιόμην; 1 aor. ἐκύλισα, pass. ἐκυλίσθην (perh. as early as class. Gk. [Kühner-Bl. II 453]; Polyb. 26, 10, 16; Hero Alex. I p. 342, 19; LXX; Joseph.).

1. act. *roll* (*up*) τὶ someth. λίθον (BGU 1290, 10; 19 [II bc]; 1 Km 14: 33; Pr 26: 27; Jos., Ant. 6, 121 [pass.]; Test. Judah 6: 4) GP 8: 32; Lk 23: 53 v.l.

2. pass. *roll* (*oneself*) (Aristot., H.A. 5, 19, 18; Polyb. 26, 1, 14; Dionys. Hal. 8, 39; Aelian, N.A. 7, 33; Epict. 4, 11, 29; LXX; En. 18, 15) of one possessed by a demon Mk 9: 20. Of sinners in the place of punishment AP 15: 30. Of stones: in the intr. sense: *roll* (Alex. Aphr., Fat. 36 II 2 p. 208, 24 κυλίεσθαι=roll [of a ball on an inclined plane]; Quint. Smyrn. 2, 384 κυλίνδεσθαι roll, of a stone; cf. Zech 9: 16; Jos., Ant. 5, 219) ἐκ τῆς ὁδοῦ εἰς τὴν ἀνοδίαν or εἰς τὸ ὕδωρ *from the road into the pathless ground* or *into the water* Hv 3, 2, 9; 3, 7, 1; cf. 3; GP 9: 37. M-M.*

κυλλός, ή, όν (Aristoph., Hippocr.+) of a limb of the human body that is in any way abnormal or incapable of being used; also of persons who have such limbs *crippled, deformed*: w. ref. to the hand (Anth. Pal. 11, 84; Galen II 394, 1 K. =ἄχρηστον ἔχων τ. χεῖρα) Mt 18: 8; Mk 9: 43. The subst. (ὁ) κυλλός also has the special sense (*the*)

cripple, injured person Mt 15: 30f (acc. to Ael. Dion. χ 23 the Attic writers used the word of hands and feet; κ, 43). M-M.*

κῦμα, ατος, τό (Hom.+; PChicag. col. 6, 15 p. 85 Coll. [II ad] κῦμα θαλάττης; PGM 5, 276 τὰ τ. θαλάσσης κύματα; LXX, Ep. Arist., Philo; Jos., C. Ap. 2, 33) *wave* pl. Mt 8: 24; 14: 24; Mk 4: 37; Ac 27: 41 t.r.; 1 Cl 20: 7 (Job 38: 11). As a figure of the inconstancy and stormy confusion (Appian, Bell. Civ. 3, 20 §76 ὁ δῆμος ἐστιν ἀστάθμητος ὥσπερ ἐν θαλάσσῃ κῦμα κινούμενον) of the false teachers κύματα ἄγρια θαλάσσης *wild waves of the sea* Jd 13 (ἄγρια κύματα as Wsd 14: 1). M-M. B. 40.*

κύμβαλον, ου, τό (Pind.+; PHib. 54, 13 [c. 245 bc]; PGM 4, 2296; 36, 158; LXX; Jos., Bell. 5, 385, Ant. 7, 80; 306; 11, 67; Sib. Or. 8, 114) *cymbal,* a metal basin, also used in ritual observances; when two of them were struck against each other, a shrill sound resulted. κ. ἀλαλάζον *a clashing cymbal* 1 Cor 13: 1 (s. ἀλαλάζω).—JQuasten, Musik u. Gesang in den Kulten d. hdn. Antike u. christl. Frühzeit '30. FJDölger, Antike u. Christent. I '29, 184f: 'D. gellende Klingel' b. Pls 1 Cor 13: 1; KLSchmidt, TW III 1037f; HRiesenfeld, Con. Neot. 12, '48, 50–3. M-M.*

κύμινον, ου, τό (a word of Phoenician origin; Hippocr., Theophr. et al.; PTebt. 112, 13; 314, 19; PFay. 101 I, 9; Is 28: 25, 27) *cum*(*m*)*in.* The tiny fruits ('seeds') of the cumin were tithed despite their slight value Mt 23: 23 (to show how relative this slightness of value was cf. Sb. 7667 [320 ad], a contract for the delivery of cumin to be paid for in advance).—Schürer II⁴ 305; Billerb. I 933. M-M.*

κυνάριον, ου, τό (Theopomp. Com. [V bc] 90; Pla., Euthyd. 298d; X., Cyr. 8, 4, 20; Epict. 4, 1, 111; PGM 4, 2945; 2947; 2951. Rejected by Phryn. p. 180 L. in favor of κυνίδιον) dim. of κύων; a house-dog or lap-dog in contrast to a dog of the street or farm (cf. Bl-D. §111, 3; Mlt.-H. 346f), but also used with no diminutive force at all (Plut., Arat. 7, 3) *little dog, dog* Mt 15: 26f; Mk 7: 27f (Eutecnius 1 p. 17, 11f, house-dogs that eat the scraps fr. the τράπεζα. Cf. Ael. Dion., α, 159: ψωμὸς εἰς ὃν ἐκματτόμενοι τὰς χεῖρας μετὰ τὸ δεῖπνον ἐρρίπτουν τοῖς κυσίν. Similarly Paus. Attic., α, 134). M-M.*

κυνηγέσιον, ου, τό (Eur., Hdt.+) *animal hunt* (usu. in pl., as e.g. Dit., Or. 529, 14; CIG 2511), instituted on some festival days by certain officials, e.g. in Smyrna by the Asiarchs. MPol 12: 2. B. 190.*

κυοφορέω (Hippocr.+; M. Ant. 9, 3, 2; Eccl 11: 5; Philo, Sacr. Abel. 102 and oft.) *be pregnant* fig. *be fruitful* γῆ κυοφοροῦσα *the fruitful earth* 1 Cl 20: 4 (cf. Philo, Opif. Mundi 43). Pass. (Artem. 4, 84; Galen XIX p. 174 K.) of Jesus ἐκυοφορήθη ὑπὸ Μαρίας *he was conceived by Mary* IEph 18: 2.*

Κύπριος, ου, ὁ (Pind., Hdt.+; inscr.; 2 Macc 4: 29; Joseph.) *a Cyprian, an inhabitant of Cyprus* Μνάσων τις Κ. Ac 21: 16; ἄνδρες Κ. 11: 20; Κ. τῷ γένει 4: 36.*

Κύπρος, ου, ἡ (Hom.+; inscr.; 1 Macc 15: 23; 2 Macc 10: 13; Philo, Leg. ad Gai. 282; Joseph.; Sib. Or.) *Cyprus,* an island in the bay formed by the south coast of Asia Minor and the Syrian coast. From 22 bc it was a senatorial province governed by a proconsul. Visited by Paul on his so-called first missionary journey Ac 13: 4. But Christianity had already been brought there by fugitives fr. Jerusalem 11: 19. Cf. also 15: 39; 21: 3; 27: 4.—WHEngel,

Kypros 1841; ASMurray-AHSmith-HBWalters, Excavations in Cyprus '00, EOberhummer, D. Insel Cypren '03, Pauly-W. XII '24, 59-117; Baedeker 363ff; Ramsay, Bearing 150ff; EPower, Dict. de la Bible, Suppl. II '34, 1-23.*

κύπτω 1 aor. ἔκυψα bend (oneself) down (so Hom.+; LXX) Mk 1: 7. κάτω κ. bend down to the ground (Aristoph., Vesp. 279; Theophr., Char. 24, 8; Charito 2, 3, 6; 2, 5, 5; Pel.-Leg. 23, 18) J 8: 6, 8 v.l. M-M.*

Κυρεῖνος Lk 2: 2 v.l. see Κυρήνιος.

Κυρηναῖος, ου, ὁ (Hdt.+; Dit., Or. 767, 31; Inscr. Gr. 897, 26; PPetr. I 16[1], 3; 22[1], 3; 2 Macc 2: 23; Joseph.) a Cyrenian (s. Κυρήνη) with the article Ac 13: 1 (Socrates, Ep. 28, 1 Θεόδωρος ὁ Κ.; Athen. 7, 14 p. 281c). Without the article Mk 15: 21; Lk 23: 26 (Diod. S. 11, 84, 1 Πολύμναστος Κυρηναῖος).—Adj. ἄνθρωπος Κ. Mt 27: 32. ἄνδρες Κ. Ac 11: 20. In Jerusalem the Cyrenian Jews had a synagogue, either for themselves alone, or together w. other Jews of the Diaspora 6: 9 (Schürer¹ II 502; III 53).—BZimolong, BZ 21, '33, 184-8; EFFBishop, ET 51, '39/'40, 148-53; WBarclay, ET 72, '60, 28-31. M-M.*

Κυρήνη, ης, ἡ (Pind., Hdt.+; inscr.; 1 Macc 15: 23; Joseph.; Sib. Or. 5, 198) Cyrene, capital city of the N. African district of Cyrenaica (Pentapolis); from 27 BC Cyrenaica was combined w. Crete as a senatorial province, and ruled by a proconsul. Cyrene was an old Greek colony, and many Jews settled there (Schürer III¹ 52f). τὰ μέρη τῆς Λιβύης τῆς κατὰ Κυρήνην the parts of Libya near Cyrene, i.e. Libya Cyrenaica Ac 2: 10.—LMalten, Kyrene '11; Italian researches: Rivista di filologia e di istruzione classica, N.S. VI, fasc. 2; 3, '28; UvWilamowitz, Kyrene '28. M-M.*

Κυρήνιος (IG III 1 no. 599 Μᾶρκον Κυρήνιον; AGRoos, Mnemos. 9, '41, 306-18), more correctly **Κυρίνιος** (Bl-D. §41; Mlt.-H. 72), ου, ὁ which is also found in some mss. Quirinius (P. Sulpicius. Cf. Jos., Bell. 2, 433; 7, 253, Ant. 17, 355; 18, 1; 26; 29; 20, 102), imperial governor of Syria, mentioned in the NT in connection w. the census Lk 2: 2.—Concerning him s. the lit. on ἀπογραφή and ἡγεμονεύω, also FSpitta, ZNW 7, '06, 290-303; WmWeber, ibid. 10, '09, 307-19; Ramsay, Bearing 275-300, Journ. of Rom. Studies 7, '17, 273ff; WLodder, D. Schätzung des Qu. bei Fl. Josephus '30; GOgg, ET 79, '68, 231-6; Schürer I (rev. ed. '73), 399-427. M-M.*

κυρία, ας, ἡ (fem. form of the subst. adj. κύριος [q.v. I]. Rare and late as a proper name: Preisigke, Namenbuch 188; HWBeyer-HLietzmann, D. jüd. Katakombe der Villa Torlonia '31, inscr. 41) lady, mistress.
1. used in addressing a definite person (Plut., Mor. 271D; Epict., Ench. 40; Cass. Dio 48, 44; POxy. 112, 1; 3; 7; 744, 2=Ltzm., Griech. Papyri² '10, 7; letter in Dssm., LO 160 [LAE² 193, n. 6].—LXX uses κ. to designate the mistress as opposed to the slave; so also Philo, Congr. Erud. Gr. 154; Jos., Ant. 17, 137; 139; PTebt. 413, 1; 6; 20; Hv 1, 1, 5; 1, 2, 2; 1, 3, 3; 1, 4, 2; 2, 1, 3; 3, 1, 3; 8; 3, 2, 4; 3, 3, 1; 4f; 3, 4, 1; 3; 3, 5, 3; 3, 6, 5f; 3, 8, 2; 5f; 4, 2, 2f; 4, 3, 1. Many take 2 J 1; 5 in this sense (e.g. LHug; BFWestcott, The Epistles of St. John 1886, 214; HPoggel, D. 2. u. 3. Brief d. Apostels Joh. 1896, 127ff; RHarris, Exp. 6th Ser. III '01, 194ff; M-M. 'dear').—But it is far more probable that
2. κ. is fig. here, and refers to a congregation (Demetr. of Phal. [c. 300 BC] says in his work περὶ τῆς Ἀθηναίων νομοθεσίας [228 fgm. 4 Jac.]: κυρία ἡ ἐκκλησία; Leges

Graecorum Sacrae II [ed. LZiehen '06] 37, 5 [III BC] ἐκκλησία κυρία. Aristoph., Acharn. 19 κυρία ἐκκλησία. This is the regular Athenian ecclesia [=assembly], and it can also be called simply ἡ κυρία [Lex. Cantabr. ed. Nauck-Dobree p. 347]) or church (s. ἀδελφή 4), which is usually translated the chosen (or elect) lady (so BWeiss, HHoltzmann, Zahn, Jülicher, Belser, Baumgarten, Meinertz, Windisch, Vrede, OHoltzmann, FHauck. Cf. BennonaBresky, Das Verhältnis des zweiten Johannesbriefs zum dritten '06, 2ff; FJDölger, Antike u. Chr.-tum V 3, '36, 211-17, Domina mater ecclesia u. d. 'Herrin' im 2 J; AEBrooke, ICC). The proposal (HJGibbins, Exp. 6th Ser. VI '02, 228f) to make ἐκλεκτή a proper noun and κυρία an adj. has little to recommend it. M-M.*

κυριακός, ή, όν belonging to the Lord, the Lord's (oft. in inscr. [since 68 AD: Dit., Or. 669, 13; 18] and pap.= 'imperial' in certain exprs.: imperial treasury, service, etc. S. Dssm., NB 44ff [BS 217ff], LO 304ff [LAE² 362ff]; Hatch 138f) κ. δεῖπνον the Lord's Supper 1 Cor 11: 20. κ. ἡμέρα the Lord's day (Kephal. I 192, 1; 193, 31) i.e. certainly Sunday (so in Mod. Gk.) Rv 1: 10 (WStott, NTS 12, '65, 70-75). For this κυριακὴ κυρίου D 14: 1. Without κυρίου (Kephal. I 194, 9; 195, 6) GP 9: 35; 12: 50. κατὰ κυριακὴν ζῆν observe the Lord's day (opp. σαββατίζειν) IMg 9: 1 (on the omission of ἡμέρα cf. Jer 52: 12 δεκάτῃ τοῦ μηνός and s. ἀγοραῖος 2).—SVMcCasland, The Origin of the Lord's Day: JBL 49, '30, 65-82; JBoehmer, D. christl. Sonntag nach Urspr. u. Gesch. '31; PCotton, From Sabbath to Sunday '33; WRordorf, Der Sonntag... im ältesten Christentum '62 (Eng. tr. AGraham '68); HRiesenfeld, Sabbat et Jour du Seigneur: TWManson memorial vol. '59, 210-17.—κ. λογίων Papias 2: 15. M-M. B. 1008.*

κυριεύω fut. κυριεύσω; 1 aor. ἐκυρίευσα (X.+; inscr., pap., LXX, En., Ep. Arist., Philo, Joseph., Test. 12 Patr.) be lord or master, rule, lord it (over), control.
1. of persons, w. gen. of that over which rule is exercised (X., Mem. 2, 6, 22; Polyb. 4, 18, 2; Dit., Or. 229, 56 [III BC]; Gen 3: 16; 37: 8; Jos., Bell. 1, 39) οἱ βασιλεῖς τ. ἐθνῶν κυριεύουσιν αὐτῶν Lk 22: 25.—Ac 19: 16 v.l. θλιβέντα κυριεῦσαι αὐτοῦ gain it through suffering B 7: 11. ἐντολῆς κ. master a commandment, i.e. make it one's own Hm 5, 2, 8. κ. τῆς πίστεως τινος lord it over someone's faith 2 Cor 1: 24.—Of God (Theod. Da 4: 25, 32; 5: 21; En. 22, 14; Ep. Arist. 45; 269 δόξης πάσης; PGM 1, 214 ὁ κυριεύων πάντων ἀγγέλων; 12, 115 ὁ κυριεύων τοῦ παντὸς κόσμου) ὁ πάντων κυριεύων Hs 9, 23, 4. ὁ τοῦ παντὸς κόσμου κυριεύων B 21: 5. Of Christ νεκρῶν καὶ ζώντων κ. Ro 14: 9.—Abs. B 6: 18. οἱ κυριεύοντες lords 1 Ti 6: 15.
2. of things, likew. w. the gen. (Sextus 41; 363a; Philo, Leg. All. 3, 187 πάθος; Test. Sim. 3: 2, Iss. 7: 7): of the law κυριεύει τοῦ ἀνθρώπου Ro 7: 1 (JDMDerrett, Law in the NT, '70, 461-71). Of sin 6: 14. Of death vs. 9. M-M. B. 1319.*

I. κύριος, ία, ιον (Pind.+; inscr., pap.) strong, authoritative, valid, ruling; then principal, essential (Aeschyl.+; 4 Macc 1: 19; Jos., Ant. 20, 41, C. Ap. 1, 19; 2, 177) τὸ δὲ κυριώτερον but what is more important IMg 1: 2 (cf. Diog. L. 4, 26 ἐν τῷ κυρίῳ=quite definitely).*

II. κύριος, ου, ὁ (the masc. form of the subst. adj. κύριος [s. I], Aeschyl.+; Appian, Bell. Civ. 4, 92 §385 [=ὁ τὸ κῦρος ἔχων]; inscr., pap., LXX, En., Ep. Arist., Philo, Joseph., Test. 12 Patr.; loanw. in rabb.) lord, Lord, master.

1. gener.—a. *owner* of possessions (X., Symp. 6, 1; Diod. S. 4, 15, 3; 14, 7, 6; inscr., pap., LXX) κ. πάντων Gal 4: 1 (Diod. S. 33, 7, 1; Philostrat., Vi. Apoll. 1, 13 p. 12, 10 of one who has come of age and controls his own property).

a. w. impers. obj. κ. τοῦ ἀμπελῶνος *owner of the vineyard* (cf. Dit., Syll.³ 742, 6 κύρ. τῆς χώρας) Mt 20: 8; 21: 40; Mk 12: 9; Lk 20: 13, 15; ὁ κ. τῆς οἰκίας the *master of the house* (Ex 22: 7; Dit., Syll.³ 1215, 28; PTebt. 5, 147 [118 bc] τοὺς κ. τῶν οἰκιῶν) Mk 13: 35. Of a πῶλος: οἱ κύρ. αὐτοῦ *its owners* (PHib. 34, 3 a span of oxen; Ex 21: 29 [αὐτοῦ=τοῦ ταύρου]) Lk 19: 33 (ASouter, Exp. 8th Ser. VIII '14, 94f, in connection w. the pl. here and Ac 16: 16, 19 thinks of the owners as man and wife; the pl. οἱ κύριοι has this mng. Diod. S. 34+35, fgm. 2, 10 and 2, 37: a married couple who are slave-owners. On the other hand in the Syntipas collection of Aesop's Fables 16 p. 534 P. οἱ κύριοι of a dog are a number of metalworkers). The mng. *owner* easily passes into that of *lord, master,* one who has full control of someth. (Diod. S. 5, 42, 5 θανάτου κύριοι= lords over [life and] death; 10, 17, 1 and 2 κύρ. τοῦ σώματος=master of one's own body; Ptolem., Apotel. 3, 11, 10 ὁ κύρ. τῆς ζωῆς; Philo, Spec. Leg. 3, 67; Jos., C. Ap. 2, 200) ὁ κ. τοῦ θερισμοῦ *the Lord of the harvest* (Jos., Ant. 4, 227 κύριος ἔστω τὰ φυτὰ καρποῦσθαι) Mt 9: 38; Lk 10: 2. κ. τοῦ σαββάτου *Lord of the Sabbath* Mt 12: 8; Mk 2: 28; Lk 6: 5.

β. w. a personal obj.: opp. δοῦλος J 13: 16; foll. by gen. of the pers. (cf. Judg 19: 11; Gen 24: 36) Mt 10: 24f; 18: 31f; 24: 48; Lk 12: 36. ὁ κ. τοῦ δούλου Lk 12: 46. Abs., though the sense is unmistakable (Diod. S. 8, 5, 3) 12: 37, 42b; 14: 23; J 15: 15; cf. Ro 14: 4a; Eph 6: 9a; Col 4: 1. Several masters of the same slave (Billerb. I 430.—Test. Jos. 14: 2): δυσὶν κυρίοις δουλεύειν Mt 6: 24; Ac 16: 16, 19 (s. Souter under a above). κατὰ σάρκα designates more precisely the sphere in which the service-relation holds true οἱ κατὰ σάρκα κ. Eph 6: 5; Col 3: 22. As a form of address used by slaves κύριε Mt 13: 27; 25: 20, 22, 24; Lk 13: 8; 14: 22; 19: 16, 18, 20, 25.

b. as a designation of any pers. of high position: the husband in contrast to the wife 1 Pt 3: 6 (Gen 18: 12. Cf. Plut., De Virt. Mul. 15 p. 252в; Dit., Syll.³ 1189, 7; 1190, 5; 1234, 1); of a father by his son Mt 21: 29 (cf. BGU 423, 2 Ἀπίων Ἐπιμάχῳ τῷ πατρὶ καὶ κυρίῳ; 818, 1; 28; Gen 31: 35); of an official in high position, by those who have dealings with him (cf. PFay. 106, 15; 129, 1; 134, 2; BGU 648, 16) Mt 27: 63. As a form of address to respected pers. gener.; here, as elsewhere, = our *sir* (as Mod. Gk.) Mt 25: 11; J 12: 21; 20: 15; Ac 16: 30; Rv 7: 14 (cf. Epict. 3, 23, 11; 19; Gen 23: 6; 44: 18).

2. in religious usage—a. as a designation of God (for this custom, which has its roots in the Orient, s. the references in Ltzm., Hdb. exc. on Ro 10: 9; Bousset, Kyrios Christos² '21, 95-8; Dssm., LO 298f [LAE 353ff]; LXX; En.; Philo; FDoppler, D. Wort 'Herr' als Götter-name im Griech.: Opusc. philol. v. kath. akad. Philologenverein in Wien I '26, 42-7) ὁ κ. Mt 5: 33; Mk 5: 19; Lk 1: 6, 9, 28, 46; 2: 15, 22; Ac 4: 26 (Ps 2: 2); 7: 33; 8: 24; Eph 6: 7 (perh. w. ref. to Christ); 2 Th 3: 3; 2 Ti 1: 16, 18; Hb 8: 2; Js 1: 7; 4: 15. Without the art. (on the inclusion or omission of the art. s. BWeiss [θεός, beg.]; Mlt.-Turner 174), almost like a personal name Mt 27: 10; Mk 13: 20; Lk 1: 17, 58; Ac 7: 49; Hb 7: 21 (Ps 109: 4); 12: 6 (Pr 3: 12); 2 Pt 2: 9; Jd 5 (θεὸς Χριστός 𝔓⁷²); 9. ἄγγελος κυρίου Mt 1: 20, 24; 2: 13, 19; 28: 2; Lk 1: 11; 2: 9a; Ac 5: 19; 8: 26; 12: 7, 23. δόξα κυρίου (Is 40: 5) Lk 2: 9; δούλη κ. 1: 38; ἡμέρα κ. Ac 2: 20 (Jo 3: 4); νόμος κ. Lk 2: 23f, 39; τὸ ὄνομα κ. Mt 21: 9 (Ps 117: 26); Ac 2: 21 (Jo 3: 5); πνεῦμα

κ. Lk 4: 18 (Is 61: 1); Ac 8: 39; τὸ ῥῆμα κ. 1 Pt 1: 25; φωνή κ. Ac 7: 31; χεὶρ κ. Lk 1: 66. ὁ Χριστὸς κυρίου 2: 26.—W. the sphere of his lordship more definitely given (Diod. S. 3, 61, 5 Zeus is κ. τοῦ σύμπαντος κόσμου; 6 θεὸς καὶ κύρ. εἰς τὸν αἰῶνα τοῦ σύμπαντος κόσμου; Jos., Ant. 20, 90 τῶν πάντων κ.) κ. τοῦ οὐρανοῦ καὶ τῆς γῆς (PGM 4, 640f) Mt 11: 25; Lk 10: 21; cf. Ac 17: 24. κ. τῶν κυριευόντων *Lord of lords* 1 Ti 6: 15. ὁ κ. ἡμῶν 1: 14; 2 Pt 3: 15; Rv 11: 15. κ. ὁ θεός Lk 1: 32; Rv 1: 8; with μου (σου, etc.) Mt 4: 7 (Dt 6: 16), 10 (Dt 6: 13); 22: 37 (Dt 6: 5); Mk 12: 29f (Dt 6: 4f); Lk 1: 16 al. κ. ὁ θεὸς τοῦ Ἰσραήλ 1: 68. κ. θεὸς (ἡμῶν) ὁ παντοκράτωρ *God, the (our) Lord, the Almighty* Rv 4: 8; 15: 3; 16: 7; 19: 6; 21: 22. κ. Σαβαώθ Ro 9: 29 (Is 1: 9); Js 5: 4.—W. prep. ἐνώπιον κυρίου Lk 1: 15. παρὰ κυρίου Mt 21: 42; Mk 12: 11 (both Ps 117: 23). παρὰ κυρίῳ 2 Pt 3: 8. πρὸς τὸν κύριον Hs 9, 12, 6.

b. Closely connected w. the custom of applying the term κ. to divinities is that of honoring (deified) rulers with the same title (exx. [2a, beg.] in Ltzm., op. cit.; Bousset 93; Dssm., 299ff [LAE 356]; FKattenbusch, Das apostol. Symbol II '00, 605ff; KPrümm, Herrscherkult u. NT: Biblica 9, '28, 3-25; 119-40; 289-301). Fr. the time of Claudius (POxy. 37, 6; Ostraka II 1038, 6) we find the Rom. emperors so designated in increasing measure; in isolated cases, even earlier (Dit., Or. 606, 1). Ac 25: 26.

c. κύριος is also used in ref. to Jesus:—a. in OT quotations, where it is understood of the Lord of the new community ἡ ὁδὸς κ. (Is 40: 3) Mt 3: 3; Mk 1: 3; Lk 3: 4; J 1: 23. εἶπεν κύριος τ. κυρίῳ μου (Ps 109: 1: the first κ. is God, the second Christ; s. Billerb. IV 452-65: Der 110. Ps. in d. altrabb. Lit.) Mt 22: 44 (cf. vss. 43, 45); Mk 12: 36 (cf. vs. 37); Lk 20: 42 (cf. vs. 44); Ac 2: 34. ὁ καυχώμενος ἐν κυρίῳ καυχάσθω 1 Cor 1: 31 (cf. Jer 9: 22f). τὸ ὄνομα κυρίου Ro 10: 13 (cf. Jo 3: 5). σὺ κατ' ἀρχάς, κύριε, τὴν γῆν ἐθεμελίωσας Hb 1: 10 (cf. Ps 101: 26). εἰ ἐγεύσασθε ὅτι χρηστὸς ὁ κύριος 1 Pt 2: 3 (cf. Ps 33: 9). 1 Pt 3: 15 adds Χριστόν to κύριον ἁγιάσατε Is 8: 13.

β. Apart from OT quots., Mt and Mk speak of Jesus as κύριος only in one pass. (words of Jesus himself) Mk 11: 3=Mt 21: 3 (but cf. RGBratcher, ET 64, '52f, 93). However, they record that he was addressed as 'Lord' (κύριε), once in Mk (7: 28) and more oft. in Mt, 8: 2, 6, 8, 21, 25; 9: 28; 14: 28, 30; 15: 22, 25, 27; 16: 22 al.—Lk refers to Jesus much more frequently as ὁ κ.: 7: 13; 10: 1, 39 (Ἰησοῦ 𝔓⁷⁵; τοῦ Ἰησοῦ 𝔓⁴⁵ et al.), 41; 11: 39; 12: 42a; 13: 15; 17: 5f; 18: 6; 19: 8 al. The voc. κύριε is also found oft.: 5: 8, 12; 9: 54; 61; 10: 17, 40; 11: 1; 12: 41 al.—In J the designation ὁ κ. occurs rarely, in the first 19 chapters only in passages that are text-critically uncertain (4: 1 v.l.; 6: 23) or that have been suspected on other grounds (11: 2); then 20: 2, 18, 20, 25; cf. vss. 13, 28; 21: 7a, b, 12. On the other hand, κύριε in address is extraordinarily common throughout the whole book: 4: 11, 15, 19, 49; 5: 7; 6: 34, 68 al. (about 30 times).—In the long ending of Mk we have the designation ὁ κ. twice, 16: 19, 20. In GP ὁ κ. occurs 1: 2; 2: 3a, b; 3: 6, 8; 4: 10; 5: 19; 6: 21, 24; 12: 50a, b; 14: 59, 60 (in the last pass. without the art.); the fragment that has been preserved hardly affords any opportunity for the use of the voc. 2 Cl introduces apocryphal sayings of Jesus with λέγει ὁ κ. 5: 2; λ. ὁ κ. ἐν τ. εὐαγγελίῳ 8: 5.—Repeated κύριε, κύριε Mt 7: 21f; Lk 6: 46; 2 Cl 4: 2 (cf. KKöhler, StKr 88, '15, 471-90).

γ. Even in the passages already mentioned the use of the word κ. raises Jesus above the human level (Mani is also κ. for his people: Kephal. I 183, 11; 13; 16); this tendency becomes even more clear in the following places: ὁ κύριος

Ac 5: 14; 9: 10f, 42; 11: 23f; 22: 10b; Ro 12: 11; 14: 8; 1 Cor 6: 13f, 17; 7: 10, 12; 2 Cor 5: 6, 8; Gal 1: 19; Col 1: 10; 1 Th 4: 15b; 2 Th 3: 1; Hb 2: 3; Js 5: 7f; B 5: 5; IEph 10: 3.—Without the art. 1 Cor 4: 4; 7: 22b; 10: 21a, b; 2 Cor 12: 1; 1 Th 4: 15a; 2 Ti 2: 24. So esp. in combinations w. preps.: ἀπὸ κυρίου Col 3: 24. κατὰ κύριον 2 Cor 11: 17. παρὰ κυρίου Eph 6: 8. πρὸς κύριον 2 Cor 3: 16. σὺν κυρίῳ 1 Th 4: 17b. ὑπὸ κυρίου 1 Cor 7: 25b; 2 Th 2: 13. Esp. freq. is the Pauline formula ἐν κυρίῳ (lit. on ἐν I 5d), which appears outside Paul's letters only Rv 14: 13; IPol 8: 3 (cf. Pol 1: 1 ἐν κυρίῳ ἡμῶν Ἰ. Χριστῷ): 1 Cor 11: 11; Phlm 16; πιστὸς ἐν κ. 1 Cor 4: 17; cf. Eph 6: 21; Hm 4, 1, 4; φῶς ἐν κ. Eph 5: 8. ἡ σφραγίς μου τ. ἀποστολῆς ὑμεῖς ἐστε ἐν κ. 1 Cor 9: 2. W. verbs: ἀσπάζεσθαι Ro 16: 22 (GBahr, CBQ 28, '66, 465f renders: in the service of my master, i.e., Paul); 1 Cor 16: 19. ἐνδυναμοῦσθαι Eph 6: 10. καλεῖσθαι 1 Cor 7: 22a. καυχᾶσθαι 1: 31. κοπιᾶν Ro 16: 12a, b; μαρτύρεσθαι Eph 4: 17. παραλαμβάνειν διακονίαν Col 4: 17. πεποιθέναι εἴς τινα Gal 5: 10. ἐπί τινα Phil 1: 14; 2: 24. προΐστασθαι 1 Th 5: 12. προσδέχεσθαι Ro 16: 2; Phil 2: 29. στήκειν 4: 1; 1 Th 3: 8. ὑπακούειν Eph 6: 1. τὸ αὐτὸ φρονεῖν Phil 4: 2. θύρας μοι ἀνεῳγμένης ἐν κ. 2 Cor 2: 12.—W. διδάσκαλος J 13: 13f. W. σωτήρ 2 Pt 3: 2; cf. 1: 11; 2: 20. W. Χριστός Ac 2: 36; cf. Χριστὸς κύριος (La 4: 20; PsSol 17, 32; 18 inscr.) Lk 2: 11. Esp. freq. are the formulas ὁ κ. Ἰησοῦς Ac 1: 21; 4: 33; 8: 16; 11: 20; 15: 11; 16: 31; 19: 5, 13, 17; 20: 24, 35; 21: 13; 1 Cor 11: 23; 16: 23; 2 Cor 4: 14; 11: 31; Eph 1: 15; 1 Th 2: 15; 4: 2; 2 Th 1: 7; 2: 8; Phlm 5.—ὁ κ. Ἰησοῦς Χριστός Ac 11: 17; 28: 31; Ro 13: 14; 2 Cor 13: 13; Phil 4: 23; 2 Th 3: 6; Phlm 25. Without the art. mostly in introductions to letters Ro 1: 7; 1 Cor 1: 3; 2 Cor 1: 2; Gal 1: 3; Eph 1: 2; 6: 23; Phil 1: 2; 3: 20; 1 Th 1: 1; 2 Th 1: 2, 12b; Js 1: 1; Χριστὸς Ἰησοῦς κ. 2 Cor 4: 5; Χριστὸς Ἰησοῦς ὁ κ. Col 2: 6. Χριστὸς ὁ κ. 2 Cl 9: 5. In an appeal κύριε Ἰησοῦ (cf. PGM 7, 331 κύριε Ἄνουβι) Rv 22: 20.—W. gen. of the pers. (in many places the mss. vary considerably in adding or omitting this gen.) ὁ κ. μου ISm 2; 1 κ. ἡμῶν 2 Ti 1: 8; Hb 7: 14; IPhld inscr.; ὁ κ. ἡμῶν Ἰησοῦς Ac 20: 21; 1 Cor 5: 4; 2 Cor 1: 14; 1 Th 2: 19; 3: 11, 13; 2 Th 1: 8; Hb 13: 20. Ἰησοῦς ὁ κ. ἡμῶν 1 Cor 9: 1. ὁ κ. ἡμῶν Χριστός Ro 16: 18. ὁ κ. ἡμῶν Ἰησοῦς Χριστός Ac 15: 26; Ro 5: 1, 11; 15: 6, 30; 1 Cor 1: 2, 7f, 10; 6: 11 v.l.; 15: 57; 2 Cor 1: 3; 8: 9; Gal 6: 14, 18; Eph 1: 3; 5: 20; 6: 24; Col 1: 3; 1 Th 1: 3; 5: 9, 23, 28; 2 Th 2: 1, 14, 16; 3: 18; 1 Ti 6: 3, 14; Js 2: 1; 1 Pt 1: 3; 2 Pt 1: 8, 14, 16; Jd 4, 17, 21. Ἰησοῦς Χριστὸς ὁ κ. ἡμῶν Ro 1: 4; 5: 21; 7: 25; 1 Cor 1: 9; Jd 25. (ὁ) Χριστὸς Ἰησοῦς ὁ κ. ἡμῶν Ro 6: 23; 8: 39; 1 Cor 15: 31; Eph 3: 11; 1 Ti 1: 2, 12; 2 Ti 1: 2. Χριστὸς Ἰησοῦς ὁ κ. μου Phil 3: 8. ὁ κ. αὐτῶν Rv 11: 8.—W. other genitives: πάντων κ. Lord over all (cf. Pind., Isth. 5, 33 Ζεὺς ὁ πάντων κ.; Plut., Mor. 355ε Osiris; PGM 13, 202) Ac 10: 36; Ro 10: 12. κ. κυρίων (cf. En. 9, 4) Rv 17: 14; 19: 16.—That 'Jesus is κύριος' (perh. 'our κύριος is Jesus') is the confession of the (Pauline) Christian church: Ro 10: 9; 1 Cor 12: 3; cf. 8: 6; Phil 2: 11 (on the latter pass. s. under ἁρπαγμός and κενόω 1. Cf. also Diod. S. 5, 72, 1: after Zeus was raised ἐκ γῆς εἰς τὸν οὐρανόν, there arose in the ψυχαῖς of all those who had experienced his benefactions, the belief ὡς ἁπάντων τῶν γινομένων κατὰ οὐρανὸν οὗτος εἴη κύριος).—In J the confession takes the form ὁ κύριός μου καὶ ὁ θεός μου J 20: 28 (on the combination of κύριος and θεός cf. θεός, beg., and 3c).

d. In many places it is not clear whether God or Christ is meant, cf. Ac 9: 31; 1 Cor 4: 19; 7: 17; 2 Cor 8: 21; Col 3: 22b; 1 Th 4: 6; 2 Th 3: 16 al.

e. of other supernatural beings—α. an angel Ac 10: 4. —β. in contrast to the one κύριος of the Christians there are θεοὶ πολλοὶ καὶ κύριοι πολλοί many gods and many lords 1 Cor 8: 5 (we cannot say just what difference Paul makes betw. these θεοί and κύριοι, but evidently the κ. are of lower rank than the θ. On the many κύριοι as 'gods of lower rank' cf. Maximus Tyr. 11, 5a, b θεὸς εἷς πάντων βασιλεὺς κ. πατήρ, κ. θεοὶ πολλοί, θεοῦ παῖδες [=δαίμονες 11, 12a], συνάρχοντες θεοῦ. Ταῦτα κ. ὁ Ἕλλην λέγει, κ. ὁ βάρβαρος; 8, 8e; f. Also Diog. L. 8, 23 the saying of Pythagoras, that mankind must τοὺς θεοὺς δαιμόνων προτιμᾶν = honor the gods more than the δαίμονες; Heraclitus, fgm. 5 divides the celestial realm into θεοὶ καὶ ἥρωες. S. also κυριότης 3 and, in a way, PGM 36, 246 κύριοι ἄγγελοι).—On the whole word s. WGraf Baudissin, Kyrios als Gottesname im Judentum u. s. Stelle in d. Religionsgesch., 4 vols. '26–'29; SvenHerner, Die Anwendung d. Wortes κ. im NT '03; Dssm., LO 298ff [LAE 353ff]; BWBacon, Jesus as Lord: HTR 4, '11, 204–28; WHeitmüller, ZNW 13, '12, 333ff; HBöhlig, D. Geisteskultur v. Tarsos '13, 53ff, Zum Begriff κύριος bei Pls: ZNW 14, '13, 23ff, Ἐν κυρίῳ: Heinrici-Festschr. '14, 170ff; WBousset, Kyrios Christos '13; ²'21; PWernle, ZThK 25, '15, 1-92; PAlthaus, NKZ 26, '15, 439ff; 513ff; Heitmüller, ZThK 25, '15, 156ff; Bousset, Jesus der Herr '16; GVos, The Continuity of the Kyrios Title in the NT: PTR 13, '15, 161-89, The Kyrios Christos Controversy: ibid. 15, '17, 21-89; EWeber, Zum Gebrauch der κύριος-Bez.: NKZ 31, '20, 254ff; ERohde, Gottesglaube u. Kyriosglaube bei Paulus: ZNW 22, '23, 43ff; RSeeberg, D. Ursprung des Christenglaubens '14; JWeiss, D. Urchristentum '17, 351ff; Ltzm., Hdb. exc. on Ro 10: 9; ED Burton, ICC Gal '21, 399-404; WFoerster, Herr ist Jesus '24; AFrövig, D. Kyriosglaube des NTs '28; ELohmeyer, Kyr. Jesus '28; EvDobschütz, Κύριος Ἰησοῦς: ZNW 30, '31, 97-123 (lit.); OMichel, D. Christus des Pls: ZNW 32, '33, 6-31; also 28, '29, 324-33; Dodd 9-11; LCerfaux, 'Kyrios' dans les citations paul. de l'AT: Ephem. Theol. Lovanienses 20, '43, 5-17; FCGrant, An Introd. to NT Thought '50, 130-7; PÉLangevin, Jésus Seigneur '67; IdelaPotterie, BRigaux-Festschr. '70, 117-46 (Luke); JD Kingsbury, JBL 94, '75, 246-55 (Mt); FDanker, Luke '76, 18-43; GQuell and WFoerster, TW III 1038-98 κύριος and related words. M-M. B. 1330.

κυριότης, ητος, ἡ (Memnon Hist. [I BC/I AD] no. 434 fgm. 1, 4, 6 Jac. κ. πολλῶν = 'rule over many'; Achmes 229, 17 κ. λαοῦ; Soranus p. 10, 23 κ. πρὸς τὸ ζῆν = 'mng. for life'; Dositheus 1, 1, of the special mng. of a thing [w. δύναμις]; schol. on Pla. 111A κ. τῶν ὀνομάτων = meaning of the words. Elsewh. in eccl. writers and Byz. authors, as well as late pap.: Maspéro 151, 199 [VI AD] παρακαλῶ πάντα κριτὴν κ. δικαστὴν κ. ἐξουσίαν κ. κυριότητα; 132 ἐπὶ πάσης ἀρχῆς κ. ἐξουσίας κ. θρόνου κ. κυριότητος ὑφ' ἡλίῳ).

1. the essential nature of the κύριος, the Lord's nature, w. ref. to God D 4: 1.

2. esp. the majestic power that the κύριος wields, ruling power, lordship, dominion ὁ υἱὸς τοῦ θεοῦ εἰς ἐξουσίαν μεγάλην κεῖται καὶ κυριότητα the Son of God appears in great authority and ruling power Hs 5, 6, 1 (κεῖμαι 2c). κυριότητα ἀθετεῖν Jd 8 and κυριότητος καταφρονεῖν 2 Pt 2: 10, which is usu. considered dependent on it, is oft. (Ritschl, Spitta, HermvSoden, BWeiss, Kühl, Mayor, Windisch, Knopf, Vrede. —FHauck leaves the choice open betw. 2 and 3) taken to mean the glory of the Lord which is rejected or despised by the false teachers. Perh. it is abstr. for concr. κυριότης for κύριος; s. the foll.

3. of a special class of angelic powers (cf. En. 61, 10; Slav. En. 20 and s. κύριος II 2eβ) *bearers of the ruling power, dominions* Col 1: 16; Eph 1: 21.—GHMacGregor, Principalities and Powers; the Cosmic Background of Paul's Thought: NTS 1, '54, 17-28. ADupont-Sommer, Jahrb. f. kleinasiat. Forschung 1, '50, 210-18.*

κυρόω 1 aor. ἐκύρωσα; pf. pass. ptc. κεκυρωμένος (Aeschyl., Hdt.+; inscr., pap., LXX, Ep. Arist., Joseph.).
1. *confirm, ratify, validate* (Dio Chrys. 59[76], 1; Dit., Syll.³ 368, 25; 695, 68f τὸ κεκυρωμένον ψήφισμα, Or. 383, 122; Inscr. gr. 478, 6; PAmh. 97, 14; 17; PTebt. 294, 16; Ep. Arist. 26; cf. OEger, ZNW 18, '18, 88ff) κεκυρω-μένην διαθήκην ἀθετεῖν *set aside a will that has been ratified* Gal 3: 15.
2. *conclude, decide in favor of* (Hdt. 6, 86, 8; 6, 126; Thu. 8, 69, 1; Jos., Bell. 4, 362, Ant. 2, 18) κ. εἴς τινα ἀγάπην *decide in favor of love for someone* 2 Cor 2: 8 (though perh. the act. may have the same mng. as the middle in Pla., Gorg. 451B=*make valid, affirm*; in the 2 Cor passage *reaffirm* is also very good). M-M.*

κυσί see κύων.

κύτος, ους, τό (since Alcman [VII bc] 49 Diehl; Galen XIX p. 168 K.; Herm. Wr. 16, 8; LXX; Jos., Ant. 8, 79) *hollow (place)* τὸ κύτος τῆς ἀπείρου θαλάσσης *the hollow of the boundless sea* 1 Cl 20: 6 (κύτος τ. θαλάσσης as Ps 64: 8).*

κύω (Hom. Hymns+; PSI 167, 19 [II bc]; Is 59: 4, 13; Philo; Joseph.) *conceive, become pregnant* (Jos., Ant. 1, 257) τῷ στόματι *through the mouth* of the weasel B 10: 8 (for the idea s. Windisch, Hdb. ad loc., and the passages given under γαλῆ; also TSDuncan, The Weasel in Myths, Superstition and Religion: Washington Univ. Studies, Humanist. Ser. XII '25, 33ff).*

κύων, κυνός, ὁ (Hom.+ in lit. and fig. mngs.; inscr., pap., LXX, Philo; Jos., Bell. 4, 324, Ant. 15, 289) *dog.*
1. lit. Lk 16: 21 (licking sores: Dit., Syll.³ 1169, 37) 2 Pt 2: 22 (Pr 26: 11. Cf. Paroem. Gr.: Gregor. Cypr. 2, 83 κ. ἐπὶ τὸν ἴδιον ἔμετον); PK 2 p. 14, 20. As an unclean animal w. χοῖρος GOxy 33 (Ps.-Aristot., Mirabilia 116 κύνες and ὕες as unclean animals that eat human filth; cf. KHRengstorf, Rabb. Texte, Series I, vol. III '33ff, p. 35f); this pass. is taken fig. of unclean persons (s. 2 below) by JoachJeremias, Con. Neot. XI, '47, 104f. μὴ δῶτε τὸ ἅγιον τ. κυσίν Mt 7: 6 (s. χοῖρος) must be a proverbial saying, which at an early date was taken in a
2. non-literal sense, mng. those who are unbaptized and therefore impure D 9: 5. The mng. must be that holy words, things, and truths have to be treated w. reverence and are not to be permitted to become the butt of jests and ridicule of wicked people. The fig. use (s. Dio Chrys. 8[9], 3; BGU 814, 19; Ps 21: 17) also Phil 3: 2; Rv 22: 15. Heretics are compared to mad dogs IEph 7: 1 (s. Philo, Omn. Prob. Lib. 90).—OMichel, TW III 1100-3. M-M. B. 179.*

κῶλον, ου, τό (Aeschyl.+ = 'limb') in LXX and NT only pl., and in the sense *dead body, corpse* (1 Km 17: 46; Lev 26: 30; Is 66: 24), esp. still unburied ὧν τὰ κῶλα ἔπεσεν ἐν τῇ ἐρήμῳ *whose bodies fell in the desert* Hb 3: 17 (cf. Num 14: 29, 32).*

κωλύω impf. ἐκώλυον; 1 aor. ἐκώλυσα, pass. ἐκωλύθην (Pind.+; inscr., pap., LXX, En., Ep. Arist., Philo, Joseph., Test. 12 Patr.).
1. in relation to persons *hinder, prevent, forbid* abs. (X., An. 4, 2, 25b) Lk 9: 50; Ac 19: 30 D. ἐάνπερ ὑμεῖς μὴ

κωλύσητε *if you do not stand in the way* IRo 4: 1. τινά *someone* Mk 9: 38f; 10: 14; Lk 9: 49; 11: 52; 18: 16; Ac 11: 17; 3 J 10. W. λέγων and direct discourse foll. GEb 3. Pass. ἐκωλύθην Ro 1: 13.—τινά τινος *prevent someone fr. (doing) someth.* (X., Cyr. 2, 4, 23, An. 1, 6, 2, Hell. 3, 2, 21; PPetr. II 11[1], 3 [III bc] μηθέν σε τῶν ἔργων κωλύει; Dit., Syll.³ 1109, 100. Cf. 1 Esdr 6: 6) ἐκώλυσεν αὐτοὺς τοῦ βουλήματος *he kept them fr. carrying out their plan* Ac 27: 43.—τινά *forbid* or *prevent someone w.* inf. foll. *to do* or *from doing someth.* (X., Cyr. 6, 2, 18; Herodian 1, 2, 4; Jos., Ant. 11, 61.—Bl-D. §392, 1f; Rob. 1089. On the omission of μή w. the inf., contrary to the usage of Attic Gk., cf. PMagd. 2, 5 [222 bc] κεκώλυκεν οἰκοδομεῖν; PEleph. 11, 6.—Bl-D. §400, 4; 429; s. Küh-ner-G. II 214f; Rob. 1171) Mt 19: 14; Ac 24: 23; 1 Th 2: 16. τινὰ τοῦ μή w. inf. *someone fr. doing someth.* Ac 11: 17 D. τί κωλύει με βαπτισθῆναι; *what is there to prevent me from being baptized?* Ac 8: 36 (cf. Ael. Aristid. 46 p. 240 D.: τί κωλύει ἡμᾶς ἐξετάσαι; Jos., Bell. 2, 395, Ant. 16, 51; Plut., Mor. 489B; s. OCullmann, D. Tauf-lehre des NTs '48, 65-73 [Eng. tr. JReid, '50, 71-80]). Pass. (X., Mem. 4, 5, 4) 16: 6; 17: 15 D; Hb 7: 23. Of the flesh τ. ἡδοναῖς κωλύεται χρῆσθαι Dg 6: 5.
2. in relation to things *hinder, prevent, forbid* τὶ some-th. (X., An. 4, 2, 24; Diod. S. 17, 26, 5 τὸ πῦρ κωλύειν; Herodian 3, 1, 6; 1 Macc 1: 45) τὴν τοῦ προφήτου παραφρονίαν *restrain the prophet's madness* 2 Pt 2: 16. τὸ λαλεῖν γλώσσαις *speaking in tongues* 1 Cor 14: 39. W. inf. without the art. (Herodian 2, 4, 7; Is 28: 6; Jos., C. Ap. 1, 167) κ. γαμεῖν *forbid marriage* 1 Ti 4: 3. Cf. Lk 23: 2; Dg 4: 3 (the specific mng. *forbid* in Philochorus [IV/III bc] no. 328 fgm. 169a Jac.).
3. *refuse, deny, withhold, keep back* τὶ someth. τὸ ὕδωρ Ac 10: 47. τὶ ἀπό τινος someth. fr. someone (Gen 23: 6; Test. Sim. 2: 12; cf. Bl-D. §180, 1) Lk 6: 29. M-M. B. 1275; 1355.*

κώμη, ης, ἡ (Hes., Hdt.+; inscr., pap., LXX) *village, small town.*
1. lit., with (and in contrast to [cf. Dio Chrys. 3, 38; 23(40), 22; Herodian 3, 6, 9; Ep. Arist. 113; Jos., Bell. 4, 241, Vi. 235; 237]) πόλις Mt 9: 35; 10: 11; Lk 8: 1; 13: 22. W. ἀγρός Mk 6: 36; Lk 9: 12. W. πόλις and ἀγρός Mk 6: 56. In the pl., used w. the gen. of a larger district, to denote the villages located within it (s. Num 21: 32; 32: 42 and oft. in LXX) Mk 8: 27. Mentioned by name: Bethany (near the Mt. of Olives) J 11: 1, 30. Bethsaida Mk 8: 23, 26; Bethlehem J 7: 42. Emmaus Lk 24: 13, 28.—Also Mt 14: 15; 21: 2; Mk 6: 6; 11: 2; Lk 5: 17; 9: 6, 52, 56; 10: 38; 17: 12; 19: 30; Ac 21: 16 D.
2. fig. *the inhabitants of a village* Ac 8: 25. M-M. B. 1310.*

κωμόπολις, εως, ἡ (Strabo 12, 2, 6 al. Freq. in Byz. authors) lit. *a city that 'has only the position of a κώμη as far as its constitution is concerned'* (Schürer II⁴ 227), in Mk 1: 38 someth. *like market-town.*

κῶμος, ου, ὁ (Hom. Hymns, Hdt.+; Dit., Syll.³ 1078 κῶμοι τῷ Διονύσῳ; APF 5, '13, 180 no. 38, 5; LXX) orig. *a festal procession* in honor of Dionysus, then *a joyous meal* or *banquet*, in the NT (as Polyb. 10, 26, 3; in the only two LXX pass. [Wsd 14: 23; 2 Macc 6: 4] and in Philo; Jos., Ant. 17, 65; Sib. Or. 8, 118) only in a bad sense *excessive feasting*, w. μέθαι (cf. Philo, Cher. 92; Polyaenus 2, 2, 7 μεθύειν καὶ κωμάζειν) *carousing, revelry* Ro 13: 13; Gal 5: 21. Likew. w. πότοι (Epicurus in Diog. L. 10, 132; Plut., Mor. 12B; Appian, Bell. Civ. 1, 113 §526) 1 Pt 4: 3. M-M.*

κώνωψ, ωπος, ὁ (Aeschyl., Hdt.) *gnat, mosquito* in a proverb διυλίζειν τὸν κ. *strain out a gnat* (s. διυλίζω) Mt 23: 24 (or is it possible that the reference is to a certain worm found in wine, which Aristot., H. An. 5, 19 p. 552b describes as a κώνωψ?).—CCTorrey, HTR 14, '21, 195f.*

Κώς, Κῶ, ἡ acc. Κῶ (Meisterhans³-Schw. 128f.—The t.r. has Κῶν) *Cos* (Hom.+; inscr.; 1 Macc 15: 23 εἰς Κῶ; Joseph.), an island in the Aegean Sea Ac 21: 1.—WR Paton and ELHicks, The Inscriptions of Cos 1891; RHerzog, Koische Forschungen u. Funde 1899. M-M.*

Κωσάμ (קֵיסָם), ὁ indecl. *Cosam*, in the genealogy of Jesus Lk 3: 28.*

κωφός, ή, όν (Hom.+; inscr., pap., LXX) *blunt, dull*—1. *dumb, mute* (Hdt.; Wsd 10: 21; Philo, In Flacc. 20; Jos., Ant. 18, 135) ἐλάλησεν ὁ κωφός Mt 9: 33; cf. vs. 32; Mt 12: 22a, b; 15: 30f; Lk 1: 22; 11: 14a, b.
2. *deaf* (Hom. Hymns; X., Cyr. 3, 1, 19 al.; fgm. of

Ostanes [JBidez-FCumont, Les mages hellénisés '38 II p. 334]: it praises a θεῖον ὕδωρ, which heals all infirmities: ὀφθαλμοὶ βλέπουσι τυφλῶν, ὦτα ἀκούουσι κωφῶν, μογιλάλοι τρανῶς λαλοῦσιν; Ex 4: 11; Is 43: 8; Ps 37: 14; Philo, Mut. Nom. 143 οὐδὲ κωφὸς ἀκούειν) κωφοὶ ἀκούουσιν Mt 11: 5; Mk 7: 32, 37; 9: 25; Lk 7: 22 (Mt 11: 5; Lk 7: 22 have also been taken fig. [so Parmenides 6, 7 κωφοὶ κ. τυφλοί of those without knowledge; Heraclitus B, 34; Epict. 2, 23, 22; 2, 24, 19; Dio Chrys. 80(30), 42 τυφλοὶ κ. κωφοί]: HHoltzmann; Wlh.; JMoffatt, ET 18, '07, 286f; OHoltzmann; EKlostermann].
3. *deaf and dumb* (Philo, Spec. Leg. 4, 197; Sib. Or. 4, 28) fig. of the idols, that neither hear nor answer (Hab 2: 18; 3 Macc 4: 16) Dg 2: 4; 3: 3, 5. M-M. B. 320f.*

κωφόω *make blunt* or *dull* in our lit. only pass.—1. *become deaf* (Hippocr., Aphor. 4, 90 ed. Littré IV 524; Philo, Det. Pot. Ins. 175) ITr 9: 1.
2. *be rendered speechless* (Ps 38: 3, 10; Philo, Conf. Lingu. 9) Hm 11: 14.*

Λ

λʹ numeral=30, Lk 3: 23 D; Hv 4, 2, 1; s 6, 4, 4.*

λαβ- s. λαμβάνω.

Λαβάν, ὁ indecl. (לָבָן; LXX, Philo, Test. 12 Patr.—In Joseph. Λάβανος, ου [Ant. 1, 278]) *Laban*, Jacob's uncle and father-in-law. Jacob's flight to him (Gen 28ff) as an example of his humility 1 Cl 31: 4.*

λαγχάνω 2 aor. ἔλαχον, subj. λάχω, ptc. λαχών (Hom. +; inscr., pap., LXX, Philo, Joseph., Sib. Or. 3, 580; 5, 101) for its constr. s. Bl-D. §171, 2; Rob. 509.
1. *receive, obtain* (by lot, or by divine will; Hom. +) τὶ someth. ἔλαχεν τὸν κλῆρον τῆς διακονίας ταύτης Ac 1: 17. πίστιν 2 Pt 1: 1.
2. *be appointed* or *chosen by lot* (Hom.+; Pla., Pol. 290E ὁ λαχὼν βασιλεύς; Dit., Syll.³ 486, 9; 762, 12 λαχὼν ἱερεύς. Oft. used sim. in inscrs.; Jos., Bell. 3, 390) ἔλαχεν τοῦ θυμιᾶσαι *he was chosen by lot to burn incense* Lk 1: 9 (on the constr. s. Bl-D. §400, 3; Rob. 1060; 1 Km 14: 47 v.l. Σαοὺλ ἔλαχεν τοῦ βασιλεύειν).
3. *cast lots* (Isocr. 7, 23; Diod. S. 4, 63, 3b) περί τινος *for someth.* (Ps.-Demosth. 21 Hyp. 2 §3.—Bl-D. §229, 2; cf. Rob. 509) J 19: 24. M-M.*

λαγώς, οῦ, ὁ (epic and late for Attic λαγώς [λαγῶς]; Ps.-X., Cyn. 10, 2 and not infreq. in later writers [Phryn. p. 179 L.]; Ps 103: 18 v.l.; Herm. Wr. p. 510, 2 Sc.) *hare* B 10: 6 (s. ἀφόδευσις).*

Λάζαρος, ου, ὁ *Lazarus* (לְעָזָר, rabbinic abbreviation of אֶלְעָזָר; s. Schürer II⁴ 439, 104.—Jos., Bell. 5, 567 Μαναῖος ὁ Λαζάρου; Thomsen, Inschr. [s. Ἰάϊρος] no. 199).
1. In J, brother of Mary and Martha, resident in Bethany in Judaea J 11: 1f, 5, 11, 14, 43; 12: 1f, 9f, 17. Following others, FVFilson, JBL 68, '49, 83–8, identifies L. as the disciple whom Jesus loved. Likew. JNSanders, NTS 1, '54, 29–41.
2. name of a beggar in the parable Lk 16: 20, 23ff.—Jülicher, Gleichn. 621; HOort, Lazarus: ThT 53, '19, 1–5; HGressmann, Vom reichen Mann u. armen L.: ABA '18; MvRhijn, Een blik in het onderwijs van Jesus (attempt at a new interpr. of Lk 16: 19–31) '24; HWindisch, NThT 14, '25, 343–60; HÅkerhielm, Svensk exegetisk Årsbok 1, '37,

63–83; LThLefort, Le nom du mauvais riche: ZNW 37, '39, 65–72; on the relation betw. the reff. in J and Lk s. RDunkerley, NTS 5, '59, 321–27.—JDMDerrett, Law in the NT, '70, 78–99. M-M.*

λαθ- s. λανθάνω.

λάθρᾳ adv. (on the spelling with or without ι s. Bl-D. §26 app.; W-S. §5, 11c; Mlt.-H. 84; EBoisacq, Dictionnaire étymologique '16 p. 549) (Hom. [λάθρη]+; Dit., Syll.³ 609, 6[?]; UPZ 19, 28 [163 BC]; BGU 1141, 48).
1. used as adv. *secretly* (Diod. S. 11, 88, 4; 11, 91, 2; Dt 13: 7 λ. λέγειν; 1 Macc 9: 60; Jos., Bell. 2, 408) opp. φανερῶς (Diod. S. 16, 24, 2; Appian, Bell. Civ. 3, 91 §376; Cass. Dio 69, 13, 1) IPhld 6: 3. ἀπολύειν Mt 1: 19. ἐκβάλλειν Ac 16: 37. καλεῖν (Jos., Vi. 388) Mt 2: 7. ποιεῖν Mk 5: 33 v.l. φωνεῖν J 11: 28.
2. as (improper) prep. w. gen. *without the knowledge of* (Hom.+; Diod. S. 5, 65, 4 λ. τοῦ πατρός; Sb 6222, 17; perh. Ps 100: 5 λ. τοῦ πλησίον αὐτοῦ) λ. ἐπισκόπου ISm 9: 1. M-M.*

λαθροδήκτης, ου, ὁ (Phryn. in Bekker, Anecdot. p. 50; Chrysostom, Hom. 15 on Eph opp. XI p. 115A οἱ λαθροδῆκται τῶν κυνῶν.—Aesop, Fab. 332 P. =224 H.=Babr. 104 Cr. λάθρη κύων ἔδακνε; Paroem. Gr.: Zenob. 4, 90 κύων λάθρα δάκνων) *one who bites in secret, stealthily* of dogs IEph 7: 1.*

λαϊκός, ή, όν (lit. 'belonging to the people, common'; PLille 10, 4; 7 [III BC]; PStrassburg 93, 4 [II BC]; BGU 1053 II, 10 [I BC]; not LXX, but 1 Km 21: 4 Aq., Sym., Theod.; Ezk 48: 15 Sym., Theod., 22: 26 Sym.; Ps.-Clem., Hom. p. 7, 38 Lagarde; Clem. Alex., Strom. 3, 90, 1; 5, 33, 3 and in later Christian wrs.) *belonging to the laity, lay* as opposed to clergy, ὁ λ. ἄνθρωπος *the layman* 1 Cl 40: 5. τὰ λ. προστάγματα *ordinances for the layman* ibid. Here λ. is contrasted w. the OT priesthood, but clearly w. ref. to the situation within the Christian church.*

λαῖλαψ, απος, ἡ (Hom.+; Plut., Tim. 28, 3; Sb 4324, 15; LXX; Philo, Mut. Nom. 214; Sib. Or. 8, 204) *whirlwind, hurricane* (Ps.-Aristot., De Mundo 4 p. 395a, 7 defines it as πνεῦμα εἱλούμενον κάτωθεν ἄνω) 2 Pt 2: 17. λ.

ἀνέμου (Test. Napht. 6: 4) *a fierce gust of wind* Mk 4: 37; Lk 8: 23 (Semonides 1, 15ff Diehl² ἐν θαλάσσῃ λαίλαπι . . . κ. κύμασιν πολλοῖσι. . .θνήσκουσιν). M-M.*

λακάω (PGM 4, 3074 σίδηρος λακᾷ='iron breaks apart, bursts'; Hippiatr. I 423, 16f φλύκταιναι . . . διαλακῶσιν [as pres. ind.]='blisters burst'. Hence the ambiguous forms [Aristoph., Nub. διαλακήσασα; Act. Thom. 33 p. 150, 18ʙ ἐλάκησεν; PGM 12, 197 λακηθῇ] are also to be referred tc a pres. λακάω rather than λακέω [as Bl-D. §101 p. 46; Mlt.-H. 246]) *burst apart, burst open* ἐλάκησεν μέσος *he burst open in the middle* Ac 1: 18. M-M. s.v. λακέω.*

λάκκος, ου, ὁ (Hdt., Aristoph.+; Dialekt-Inschr. 5056, 4; 5060, 6; 64 [Crete]; Sb 7167, 7; LXX; Philo; Jos., Bell. 5, 164; 7, 291 al.; Test. 12 Patr.) *pit, den* λ. λεόντων 1 Cl 45: 6 (cf. Da 6: 6ff; Jos., Ant. 10, 253).*

λακτίζω (Hom.+; Herodas 7, 118; BGU 1007, 7 [III ʙc]; PTebt. 798, 15 [II ʙc]; Jos., Ant. 4, 278) *kick* of draught animals, as a figure for unreasoning resistance: πρὸς κέντρα *against the goad* of the driver Ac 9: 5 t.r.; 26: 14 (s. κέντρον 2). M-M.*

λαλέω impf. ἐλάλουν; fut. λαλήσω; 1 aor. ἐλάλησα; pf. λελάληκα, pass. λελάλημαι; 1 aor. pass. ἐλαλήθην; 1 fut. pass. λαληθήσομαι (Soph.+, in class. Gk. usu. 'chatter, babble'; inscr., pap., but not nearly as freq. in secular authors as in LXX—also En., Ep. Arist., Philo, Joseph., Test. 12 Patr.—and our lit.).
1. of inanimate things *sound, give forth sounds* or *tones* which form a kind of speech (e.g. of the echo, Cass. Dio 74, 21, 14; of streams of water Achilles Tat. 2, 14, 8), of the thunder ἐλάλησαν αἱ βρονταί Rv 10: 4a, b. ἐλάλησαν αἱ βρονταί τὰς ἑαυτῶν φωνάς vs. 3. Of the trumpet 4: 1 (cf. Aristot., De Aud. p. 801a, 29 διὰ τούτων =flutes, etc.; Achilles Tat. 2, 14, 8 of the κιθάρα). Of the blood of Christ, that *speaks more effectively than that of Abel* (Gen 4: 10) Hb 12: 24; s. 11: 4 (Gdspd., Probs. 188). Cf. J 12: 29.
2. of pers.—a. *speak*—α. (*be able to*) *speak*; to have and use the faculty of speech, in contrast to one who is incapable of speaking (cf. Ps 113: 13; 3 Macc 4: 16) Mt 9: 33; 12: 22; 15: 31; Mk 7: 37; Lk 1: 20, 64; 11: 14. ἐλάλει ὀρθῶς *he could speak plainly* (in contrast to the unintelligible utterances of a deaf-mute) Mk 7: 35.
β. *speak* in contrast to keeping silent (Lucian, Vit. Auct. 3) οὐκ ἤφιεν λαλεῖν τ. δαιμόνια Mk 1: 34; Lk 4: 41 (λέγειν 𝔓⁷⁵, 485). λάλει καὶ μὴ σιωπήσῃς Ac 18: 9.—In contrast to listening (Plut., Mor. 502c λαλοῦντι μὲν πρὸς τ. ἀκούοντας μὴ ἀκούοντι δὲ τ. λαλούντων) Js 1: 19.—In contrast to acting 2: 12.
γ. *speak, express oneself* οὐ γὰρ ὑμεῖς ἐστε οἱ λαλοῦντες *it is not you who* (*will*) *speak* Mt 10: 20. προφῆται δύο ἢ τρεῖς λαλείτωσαν *two or three prophets are to express themselves* 1 Cor 14: 29. ἔτι αὐτοῦ λαλοῦντος *while he was still speaking* Mt 17: 5; 26: 47; Mk 5: 35; 14: 43; Lk 8: 49; 22: 47, 60.—Lk 5: 4; 1 Cor 14: 11a, b, al.
δ. The pers. to whom or with whom one is speaking is mentioned in various ways: in the dat. λ. τινί *speak to* or *with someone* (Aristoph., Equ. 348; Philemo Com. 11 p. 481; Menander, Per. 220 σοί; Aelian, Ep. 14 p. 181, 1; Diog. L. 9, 64, λ. ἑαυτῷ=with oneself; Lev 1: 1f; Ezk 33: 30b) Mt 12: 46a, b, 47; 13: 10; Mk 16: 19; Lk 1: 22; 24: 6, 32; J 4: 26 (cf. Ramsay, Phryg. I 2 p. 566f no. 467-69 'Ἀθάνατος 'Ἐπιτύγχανος says of himself: ἐγὼ εἰμι ὁ λαλῶν πάντα); 9: 29; 12: 29; 15: 22; Ac 9: 27; Ro 7: 1; 1 Cor 3: 1; 1 Th 2: 16; Hb 1: 1f; by πρός

and the acc. (Plut. [2αβ]; Ps.-Lucian, Asin. 44; Gen 27: 6; Ex 30: 11, 17, 22; Sib. Or. 3, 669) Lk 1: 19, 55; Ac 4: 1; 8: 26; 11: 20; 26: 31; by μετά and the gen. (Gen 35: 13) Mk 6: 50; J 4: 27; 9: 37; 14: 30; Rv 1: 12; 10: 8; 17: 1; 21: 9, 15.—The pers. or thing spoken about is expressed by περί w. the gen. (PSI 361, 5 [251 ʙc] λαλήσας περί μου; PFay. 126, 4 [c. 200 ᴀᴅ]; Gen 19: 21; Ezk 33: 30a; Philo, Fuga 33, 30a) J 8: 26; 12: 41; Ac 2: 31; Hb 2: 5; 4: 8.—τινὶ περί τινος (PPetr. II 13, 6, 9 [III ʙc]) Lk 2: 38; 9: 11; pass. Ac 22: 10.
ε. The speaking can be more closely defined: κακῶς, καλῶς J 18: 23. ὡς νήπιος 1 Cor 13: 11. ὡς δράκων (*hissed?*) Rv 13: 11. στόμα πρὸς στόμα *face to face* (cf. Num 12: 8) 2 J 12; 3 J 14. εἰς ἀέρα 1 Cor 14: 9. κατὰ κύριον 2 Cor 11: 17. ἐκ τοῦ περισσεύματος τ. καρδίας τὸ στόμα λαλεῖ Mt 12: 34; Lk 6: 45. ἐκ τῆς γῆς J 3: 31 (cf. Lev 1: 1 λ. ἐκ τῆς σκηνῆς). ἐκ τῶν ἰδίων J 8: 44. παρρησίᾳ 7: 13, 26. ἐν παρρησίᾳ 16: 29. ἐν παραβολαῖς Mt 13: 10, 13. χωρὶς παραβολῆς Mk 4: 34. λ. ψαλμοῖς *speak in psalms* Eph 5: 19. Of prophets λ. ἐν πνεύματι D 11: 7. Of God λ. διὰ στόματος τ. προφητῶν Lk 1: 70; Ac 28: 25.
ζ. as subst. ptc. τὰ λαλούμενα (Paradox. Vat. 2 Keller; Jos., Ant. 16, 321) ὑπό τινος Ac 13: 45; 16: 14. τὰ λελαλημένα (Ep. Arist. 299) αὐτῇ παρὰ κυρίου Lk 1: 45.—For λαλεῖν γλώσσῃ and λ. γλώσσαις s. γλῶσσα 3.
b. trans. *speak and thereby assert, proclaim, say* τὶ *someth.* (X., Cyr. 1, 4, 1 πολλά; Demosth. 45, 77 μέγα; Paradox. Vat. 2 τὰ ὀνόματα) τὰ ῥήματα τ. θεοῦ J 3: 34. ῥῆμα Mt 12: 36; cf. J 8: 20. τὸν λόγον Mk 8: 32; J 12: 48; Ac 4: 29, 31 (λαλ. τι μετὰ παρρησίας as Jos., Ant. 16, 113); 8: 25; 14: 25; 16: 6, 32. τὰ μεγαλεῖα τ. θεοῦ Ac 2: 11. βλασφημίας Lk 5: 21; cf. Ac 6: 11. σοφίαν 1 Cor 2: 6f. μυστήρια 14: 2; cf. Col 4: 3. τὰ μὴ δέοντα 1 Ti 5: 13. τὸ στόμα λαλεῖ ὑπέρογκα Jd 16; μεγάλα Rv 13: 5. τί Mt 10: 19; Mk 13: 11; J 12: 49. ὁ λαλεῖ Mk 11: 23; cf. J 10: 6; 12: 50. ταῦτα Lk 24: 36; J 8: 28, 30; 12: 36; 17: 1. ἐλάλησέν τι περὶ σοῦ πονηρόν Ac 28: 21 (cf. 3 Km 22: 8, 13b).—Pass. λαλεῖταί τι *someth. is said, proclaimed, reported* (cf. the inscr. for mother and brother [APF 5, '13, 169 no. 24, 8] ὧν καὶ ἡ σωφροσύνη κατὰ τ. κόσμον λελάληται, also Ps 86: 3) Mt 26: 13; Mk 14: 9; cf. Hb 2: 3; 9: 19 ἡ λαλουμένη διδαχή Ac 17: 19. ὁ λαληθεὶς λόγος Hb 2: 2.—Oft., in addition, the pers. spoken to is mentioned, in the dat. ἄλλην παραβολὴν ἐλάλησεν αὐτοῖς Mt 13: 33. ἐλάλει αὐτοῖς τὸν λόγον *he proclaimed the word to them* Mk 2: 2; 4: 33; J 15: 3; Ac 11: 19. ἐλάλησεν αὐτοῖς πολλὰ ἐν παραβολαῖς Mt 13: 3; cf. vs. 34. τὸ ῥῆμα . . . αὐτοῖς Lk 2: 50; cf. J 6: 63.—8: 40 (ἀλήθειαν λ. as Eph 4: 25 below); 14: 25; 15: 11; 16: 1, 4, 6. ἀνθρώποις λαλεῖ οἰκοδομήν 1 Cor 14: 3; w. πρός and acc. (Gen 18: 19; Zech 8: 16) λόγους . . . ἐλάλησα πρὸς ὑμᾶς Lk 24: 44 (cf. Dt 10: 4).—Ac 3: 22; 11: 14; 1 Th 2: 2; w. ἐν and the dat. σοφίαν λαλοῦμεν ἐν τ. τελείοις *we discourse of wisdom among those who are mature* 1 Cor 2: 6; w. μετά and the gen. λαλεῖτε ἀλήθειαν ἕκαστος μετὰ τοῦ πλησίον αὐτοῦ Eph 4: 25 (cf. Zech 8: 16). ὅσα ἂν λαλήσω μετὰ σοῦ Hs 5, 3, 2, Cf. Hs inscr.—W. the speaking definitely characterized ταῦτα ἐν παροιμίαις λελάληκα ὑμῖν J 16: 25a. κατὰ ἄνθρωπον ταῦτα λαλῶ 1 Cor 9: 8. ἐν ἐκκλησίᾳ θέλω πέντε λόγους τῷ νοΐ μου λαλῆσαι 14: 19. πάντα ἐν ἀληθείᾳ ἐλαλήσαμεν ὑμῖν 2 Cor 7: 14. ἀφόβως τὸν λόγον τ. θεοῦ λαλεῖν Phil 1: 14. λ. τι εἰς τὰ ὦτα *someth. communicate someth. to someone personally* (cf. Dt 5: 1) Hv 3, 8, 11 (cf. 4, 3, 6). λ. τι πρὸς τὸ οὖς *whisper someth. in someone's ear* (so that no one else hears it; cf. Jos., Ant. 6, 165) Lk 12: 3.

3. In a number of passages the content of the speaking is introduced by λέγων (s. λέγω I 8a), just as in the OT (Gen 34: 8; 41: 9; 42: 22; Ex 31: 12; Lev 20: 1) Mt 13: 3; 14: 27; 23: 1; 28: 18; J 8: 12; Ac 8: 26; Rv 4: 1; 17: 1 al. M-M. B. 1254.

λαλιά, ᾶς, ἡ (Aristoph. +, mostly in an unfavorable sense ='gossip, common talk'; so also Sb 2266, 13) in our lit. always in a good sense.

1. *speech, speaking* (Epict. 3, 16, 1; Himerius, Or. 64 [=Or. 18] superscription [of a speech by Himerius]; Ps.-Callisth. 1, 17, 3; Is 11: 3; SSol 4: 3; Job 33: 1; 2 Macc 8: 7; Jos., Bell. 2, 132; Test. Reub. 2: 6) οὐκ εἰσὶν λόγοι οὐδὲ λαλιαί *there is neither word nor speech* 1 Cl 27: 7 (Ps 18: 4). διὰ τ. σὴν λ. *because of what you said* J 4: 42.

2. also of the manner of expressing oneself, *form of speech, way of speaking.*
a. lit., of dialectical peculiarities Mt 26: 73 (cf. Zahn, Einl. I³ 19.—Similarly Ps.-Callisth. 2, 15, 7 of Alexander at the Persian court: ἡ φωνὴ αὐτὸν ἤλεγξε).—**b.** of the characteristic way in which Jesus spoke J 8: 43. M-M.*

λαμά (לָמָה, Aram. לְמָא) *why?* Mt 27: 46 v.l.; Mk 15: 34. M-M.*

λαμβάνω (Hom. +; inscr., pap., LXX, En., Ep. Arist., Philo, Joseph., Test. 12 Patr., Sib. Or.) impf. ἐλάμβανον; fut. λήμψομαι (PTurin II 3, 48; POxy. 1664, 12; on the μ cf. Mayser 194f; Thackeray 108ff; Bl-D. §101 p. 64, Eng. p. 53; Mlt.-H. 106; 246f; Reinhold 46f; WSchulze, Orthographica 1894.—On the middle s. Bl-D. §77); 2 aor. ἔλαβον, imper. λάβε (Bl-D. §101 p. 64; Eng. p. 53; §13; Mlt.-H. 209 n. 1); pf. εἴληφα, 2 sing. εἴληφας and εἴληφες (Rv 11: 17; W-S. §13, 16 note; Mlt.-H. 221), ptc. εἰληφώς; pf. pass. 3 sing. εἴ λ η π τ α ι.

1. (more actively) *take*—**a.** *take in the hand, take hold of, grasp* ἄρτον (Diod. S. 14, 105, 3 ῥάβδον) Mt 26: 26a; Mk 14: 22a; Ac 27: 35. τ. βιβλίον (Tob 7: 14) Rv 5: 8f. τ. κάλαμον Mt 27: 30. λαμπάδας *take (in hand)* (Strattis Com. [V BC], fgm. 37 λαβόντες λαμπάδας) 25: 1, 3. μάχαιραν *draw the sword* (Gen 34: 25; Jos., Vi. 173) 26: 52. Abs. λάβετε *take* (this) Mt 26: 26b; Mk 14: 22b.— *Take hold of* (me) GH 22=ISm 3: 2.—ἔλαβε με ἡ μήτηρ μου τὸ ἅγιον πνεῦμα ἐν μιᾷ τῶν τριχῶν μου *my mother, the Holy Spirit, took me by one of my hairs* GH 5. λαβών is somet. used pleonastically to enliven the narrative, as in class. Gk., but also in accord w. Hebr. usage (JViteau, Étude sur le Grec du NT 1893, 191; Dalman, Worte 16ff; Wlh., Einleitung² '11, 14; Bl-D. §419, 1; 2; cf. Rob. 1127) s., e.g., Josh 2: 4; Horapollo 2, 88 τούτους λαβὼν κατορύττει) Mt 13: 31, 33; Mk 9: 36; Lk 13: 19, 21; J 12: 3; Ac 9: 25; 16: 3; Hs 5, 2, 4. At times the ptc. can actually be rendered by the prep. *with* (Bl-D. §418, 5; Rob. 1127) λαβὼν τὴν σπεῖραν ἔρχεται *he came with a detachment* J 18: 3 (cf. Soph., Trach. 259 στρατὸν λαβὼν ἔρχεται). λαβὼν τὸ αἷμα...τὸν λαὸν ἐρράντισε *with the blood he sprinkled the people* Hb 9: 19. Freq. parataxis takes the place of the ptc. constr. (Bl-D. §419, 5) ἔλαβε τὸν Ἰησοῦν καὶ ἐμαστίγωσεν (instead of λαβὼν τ. Ἰ. ἐ.) *he had Jesus scourged* J 19: 1. λαβεῖν τὸν ἄρτον...βαλεῖν *throw the bread* Mt 15: 26; Mk 7: 27. ἔλαβον τὰ ἱμάτια αὐτοῦ καὶ ἐποίησαν τέσσερα μέρη *they divided his garments into four parts* J 19: 23.—Also fig. ἀφορμὴν λ. *find opportunity* Ro 7: 8, 11 (s. ἀφορμή); ὑπόδειγμα λ. *take as an example* Js 5: 10; so also λ. alone, λάβωμεν Ἐνώχ 1 Cl 9: 3.—Of the cross as the symbol of the martyr's death *take upon oneself* Mt 10: 38 (cf. Pind., Pyth. 2, 172 λ. ζυγόν). We may class here ἔλαβεν τὰ ἱμάτια αὐτοῦ *he put his clothes on* J 13: 12 (cf. Hdt. 2, 37;

4, 78). Prob. sim. μορφὴν δούλου λ. *put on the form of a slave* Phil 2: 7.—Of food and drink *take* (cf. Bel 37 Theod.) Mk 15: 23. ὅτε ἔλαβεν τὸ ὄξος J 19: 30. λαβὼν τροφὴν ἐνίσχυσεν Ac 9: 19.—1 Ti 4: 4 (s. 2 below) could also belong here.

b. *take away, remove* with or without the use of force τὰ ἀργύρια *take away the silver coins* (fr. the temple) Mt 27: 6. τὰς ἀσθενείας *diseases* 8: 17. τὸν στέφανον Rv 3: 11. τὴν εἰρήνην ἐκ τῆς γῆς *remove peace from the earth* 6: 4 (λ. τι ἐκ as UPZ 125, 13 ὃ εἴληφεν ἐξ οἴκου; 2 Ch 16: 2).

c. *take (into one's possession)* τὶ *someth.* τὸν χιτῶνα Mt 5: 40. οὐδέν J 3: 27. ἑαυτῷ βασιλείαν *obtain kingly power for himself* Lk 19: 12 (cf. Jos., Ant. 13, 220). λ. γυναῖκα *take a wife* (Eur., Alc. 324; X., Cyr. 8, 4, 16; Gen 4: 19; 6: 2; Tob 1: 9; Jos., Ant. 1, 253) Mk 12: 19–21; Lk 20: 28–31 (s. also the reading of ms D in 14: 20; 1 Cor 7: 28). Of his life, that Jesus voluntarily gives up, in order to *take possession* of it again on his own authority J 10: 18a. ἑαυτῷ τ. τιμὴν λ. *take the honor upon oneself* Hb 5: 4.—*Lay hands on, seize* w. acc. of the pers. who is seized by force (Hom. +; LXX) Mt 21: 35, 39; Mk 12: 3, 8. Of an evil spirit that seizes the sick man Lk 9: 39 (cf. PGM 7, 613 εἴλημπται ὑπὸ τοῦ δαίμονος; Jos., Ant. 4, 119 ὅταν ἡμᾶς τὸ τοῦ θεοῦ λάβῃ πνεῦμα).—Esp. of feelings, emotions *seize, come upon* τινά *someone* (Hom. +; Ex 15: 15; Wsd 11: 12; Jos., Ant. 2, 139; 14, 57) ἔκστασις ἔλαβεν ἅπαντας *amazement seized (them) all* Lk 5: 26. φόβος 7: 16. Sim. πειρασμὸς ὑμᾶς οὐκ εἴληφεν εἰ μὴ ἀνθρώπινος 1 Cor 10: 13.—Of hunting and fishing: *catch* (X., Cyr. 1, 4, 9; Aelian, V.H. 4, 14) οὐδέν Lk 5: 5. Fig. εἴ τις λαμβάνει (ὑμᾶς) *if someone 'takes you in', takes advantage of you* (Field, Notes, 184f; CLattey, JTS 44, '43, 148) 2 Cor 11: 20; δόλῳ τινὰ λ. *catch someone by a trick* 12: 16.

d. *receive, accept* of taxes, etc. *collect* the two-drachma tax Mt 17: 24; *tithes* Hb 7: 8f; his portion of the fruit as rent Mt 21: 34. τὶ ἀπό τινος *someth. fr. someone* (Plut., Mor. 209D, Aem. Paul. 5, 9) 17: 25. παρὰ τῶν γεωργῶν λ. ἀπὸ τῶν καρπῶν *collect a share of the fruit fr. the vinedressers* Mk 12: 2.—τὶ παρά τινος *someth. fr. someone* (Jos., Ant. 5, 275) οὐ παρὰ ἀνθρώπου τὴν μαρτυρίαν λ. *the testimony which I receive is not from man* or *I will not let a man bear witness to me* (PSI 395, 6 [241 BC] σύμβολον λαβὲ παρ' αὐτῶν=have them give you a receipt) J 5: 34; cf. vs. 44; 3: 11, 32f.

e. *take up, receive*—**α.** τινα *someone* εἰς *into* (Wsd 8: 18) lit. εἰς τὸ πλοῖον *take someone (up) into the boat* J 6: 21. εἰς οἰκίαν *receive someone into one's house* 2 J 10. εἰς τὰ ἴδια *into his own home* J 19: 27. *Receive someone* in the sense of recognizing his authority J 1: 12; 5: 43a, b; 13: 20a, b, c, d.—οἱ ὑπηρέται ῥαπίσμασιν αὐτὸν ἔλαβον Mk 14: 65 does not mean 'the servants took him into custody with blows' (BWeiss, al.), but is a colloquialism (Bl-D. §198, 3 app. αὐτὸν κονδύλοις ἔλαβεν; Act. Jo. 90) *the servants treated him to blows* (cf. Moffatt), or even *'got' him w. blows* (perh. a Latinism; Cicero, Tusc. 2, 14, 34 verberibus accipere. Bl-D. §5, 3b; cf. Rob. 530f); the v.l. ἔβαλον is the result of failure to recognize this rare usage.

β. τὶ *someth.* fig. τὰ ῥήματά τινος *receive someone's words* (and use them as a guide) J 12: 48; 17: 8. τὸν λόγον *receive the teaching* Mt 13: 20; Mk 4: 16 (for μετὰ χαρᾶς λ. cf. PIand. 13, 18 ἵνα μετὰ χαρᾶς σε ἀπολάβωμεν).— The OT is the source of λαμβάνειν πρόσωπον (s. πρόσωπον 1b, end) Lk 20: 21; Gal 2: 6; B 19: 4; D 4: 3.

f. *choose, select* πᾶς ἀρχιερεὺς ἐξ ἀνθρώπων λαμβανόμενος *who is chosen fr. among men* Hb 5: 1 (cf. Num 8: 6; Am 2: 11).

g. *make one's own, apprehend* or *comprehend* mentally or spiritually (class.) of the mystical apprehension of Christ (opp. κατελήμφθην ὑπὸ Χριστοῦ) ἔλαβον (i.e. Χριστόν) *I have made (him) my own* Phil 3: 12.

h. special constructions θάρσος λ. *take courage* s. θάρσος; πεῖράν τινος λ. *try someth.* (Pla., Prot. 342A; 348A, Gorg. 448A; X., Cyr. 6, 1, 28; Polyb. 1, 75, 7; 2, 32, 5; 5, 100, 10; Aelian, V.H. 12, 22; Dio Chrys. 50, 6; Dt 28: 56; Jos., Ant. 8, 166) Hb 11: 29 (this expr. has a different mng. in vs. 36; s. 2 below).—συμβούλιον λαμβάνειν *consult (with someone)*, lit. 'take counsel', is a Latinism (consilium capere; cf. Bl-D. §5, 3b; Rob. 109) Mt 27: 7; 28: 12; w. ὅπως foll. 22: 15; foll. by κατά τινος *against someone* and ὅπως 12: 14; foll. by κατά τινος and ὥστε 27: 1. οὐ λήψῃ βουλὴν πονηρὰν κατὰ τοῦ πλησίον σου D 2: 6.

2. (more passively) *receive, get, obtain* abs. λαβών (of a hungry swine) *when it has received someth.* B 10: 3. (Opp. αἰτεῖν, as Appian, fgm. [I p. 532–36 Viereck-R.] 23 αἰτεῖτε καὶ λαμβάνετε; PGM 4, 2172) Mt 7: 8; Lk 11: 10; J 16: 24. (Opp. διδόναι as Thu. 2, 97, 4 λαμβάνειν μᾶλλον ἢ διδόναι. Ael. Aristid. 34 p. 645 D.; Herm. Wr. 5, 10b; Philo, Deus Imm. 57; Sib. Or. 3, 511) Mt 10: 8; Ac 20: 35; B 14: 1; on the other hand in D 1: 5 λ. rather has the 'active' sense *accept a donation*.—W. acc. of the thing τὶ *someth.* (Da 2: 6) τὸ ψωμίον *receive the piece of bread* J 13: 30. ὕδωρ ζωῆς δωρεάν *water of life without cost* Rv 22: 17. μισθόν (q.v. 1) Mt 10: 41a, b; J 4: 36; 1 Cor 3: 8, 14. Money: ἀργύρια Mt 28: 15. ἀνὰ δηνάριον *a denarius each* Mt 20: 9f; ἐλεημοσύνην Ac 3: 3. βραχύ τι *a little* J 6: 7; *eternal life* Mk 10: 30 (Jos., C. Ap. 2, 218 βίον ἀμείνω λαβεῖν); the Spirit J 7: 39; Ac 2: 38; cf. Gal 3: 14; 1 Cor 2: 12; 2 Cor 11: 4; forgiveness of sin Ac 10: 43; grace Ro 1: 5; cf. 5: 17; the victor's prize 1 Cor 9: 24f; the crown of life Js 1: 12 (cf. Wsd 5: 16 λ. τὸ διάδημα); the early and late rain 5: 7. ἔλεος *receive mercy* Hb 4: 16. λ. τὸ ὄνομα τοῦ υἱοῦ (θεοῦ) *receive the name of the Son of God* (in baptism) Hs 9, 12, 4. διάδοχον *receive a successor* Ac 24: 27 (cf. Pliny the Younger, Epist. 9, 13 successorem accipio). τὴν ἐπισκοπὴν αὐτοῦ λαβέτω ἕτερος *let another man receive his position* 1: 20 (Ps 108: 8). τόπον ἀπολογίας λ. (τόπος 2c) 25: 16. λ. τι μετὰ εὐχαριστίας *receive someth. w. thankfulness* 1 Ti 4: 4 (but s. above 1a, end.—On the construction with μετά cf. Libanius, Or. 63 p. 392, 3 F. μετὰ ψόγου λ.). τί ἔχεις ὃ οὐκ ἔλαβες; *what have you that you did not receive?* 1 Cor 4: 7 (Alciphr. 2, 6, 1 τί οὐ τῶν ἐμῶν λαβοῦσα ἔχεις;). Of punishments (cf. δίκην λ. Hdt. 1, 115; Eur., Bacch. 1312. ποινάς Eur., Tro. 360. πληγάς Philyllius Com. [V BC] 11 K.; τιμωρίαν Jos., Ant. 14, 336) λ. περισσότερον κρίμα *receive a punishment that is just so much more severe* Mt 23: 14 t.r.; Mk 12: 40; Lk 20: 47; cf. Js 3: 1. οἱ ἀνθεστηκότες ἑαυτοῖς κρίμα λήμψονται *those who oppose will bring punishment upon themselves* Ro 13: 2. πεῖράν τινος λ. *become acquainted with, experience, suffer someth.* (X., An. 5, 8, 15; Polyb. 6, 3, 1; 28, 9, 7; 29, 3, 10; Diod. S. 12, 24, 4 τὴν θυγατέρα ἀπέκτεινεν, ἵνα μὴ τῆς ὕβρεως λάβῃ πεῖραν; 15, 88; Jos., Ant. 2, 60; Preisigke, Griech. Urkunden des ägypt. Museums zu Kairo ['11] 2, 11; 3, 11 πεῖραν λ. δαίμονος) μαστίγων πεῖραν λ. Hb 11: 36 (the phrase in a different mng. vs. 29; s. 1h above).—Also used as a periphrasis for the passive: οἰκοδομὴν λ. *be edified* 1 Cor 14: 5. περιτομὴν *be circumcised* J 7: 23. τὸ χάραγμα *receive a mark=be marked* Rv 14: 9, 11; 19: 20; 20: 4. καταλλαγὴν *be reconciled* Ro 5: 11. ὑπόμνησιν τινος *be reminded of=remember someth.* 2 Ti 1: 5; λήθην τινὸς λ. *forget someth.* (Timocles Com. [IV BC], fgm. 6, 5 K.; Aelian, V.H. 3, 18 end, H. An. 4, 35; Jos.,

Ant. 2, 163; 202; 4, 304) 2 Pt 1: 9; ἀρχὴν λ. *be begin, have its beginning* (Pla. et al.; Polyb. 1, 12, 9; Sext. Emp., Phys. 1, 366; Aelian, V.H. 2, 28; 12, 53; Dio Chrys. 40, 7; Philo, Mos. 1, 81 τρίτον [σημεῖον] . . . τὴν ἀρχὴν τοῦ γίνεσθαι λαβὸν ἐν Αἰγύπτῳ) Hb 2: 3.—λ. τι ἀπό τινος *receive someth. from someone* (Epict. 4, 11, 3 λ. τι ἀπὸ τῶν θεῶν; Herm. Wr. 1, 30) 1 J 2: 27; 3: 22. Also τί παρά τινος (Pisander Epicus [VI BC] in Athen. 11 p. 469c; Diod. S. 5, 3, 4 λαβεῖν τι παρὰ τῶν θεῶν.—παρά I 3b) J 10: 18b; Ac 2: 33; 3: 5; 20: 24; Js 1: 7; 2 J 4; Rv 2: 28. λ. τὸ ἱκανὸν παρὰ τοῦ Ἰάσονος *receive security from Jason* Ac 17: 9 (s. ἱκανός 1c). λ. τι ὑπό τινος *be given someth. by someone* 2 Cor 11: 24. λ. τι ἔκ τινος *receive someth. fr. a large supply* ἐκ τοῦ πληρώματος αὐτοῦ ἐλάβομεν χάριν *from his fulness we have received grace* J 1: 16. ἐκ τοῦ πνεύματος αὐτοῦ ἐλάβετε Hs 9, 24, 4.—λ. ἐξ ἀναστάσεως τοὺς νεκροὺς αὐτῶν (s. ἀνάστασις 2a) Hb 11: 35. M-M. B. 743.

Λάμεχ, ὁ indecl. (לֶמֶךְ, in pause לָמֶךְ) *Lamech* (Gen 4: 18ff; 5: 25ff; Philo; Test. Benj. 7: 4.—En. 10, 1 Raderm. has Λέμεχ, but 106, 1; 4 al. Bonner Λάμεχ; Joseph. Λάμεχος, ου [Ant. 1, 79]), father of Noah; in the genealogy of Jesus Lk 3: 36 (cf. 1 Ch 1: 3).*

λαμπάς, άδος, ἡ (Aeschyl., Hdt.+; inscr., pap., LXX, Philo, Joseph., Sib. Or., loanw. in rabb.).

1. *torch* (in this mng. in trag.; Thu. 3, 24, 1; Polyb. 3, 93, 4; Herodian 4, 2, 10; Dit., Or. 764, 43; 50; 54; Sir 48: 1; Jos., Bell. 6, 16, Ant. 5, 223; Sib. Or. fgm. 3, 44), so prob. J 18: 3 w. φανοί (=lanterns; both articles together Dionys. Hal. 11, 40, 2; PLond. 1159, 59=Wilcken, Chrest. p. 493).—Celestial phenomena that resemble burning torches (Diod. S. 16, 66; Ps.-Aristot., De Mundo 4; Erot. Gr. fgm. pap. ed. BLavagnini '22, Herp. 47; PGM 4, 2939ff ἀστέρα ὡς λαμπάδα) ἀστὴρ μέγας καιόμενος ὡς λαμπάς Rv 8: 10 (Diod. S. 15, 50, 2 ὤφθη κατὰ τὸν οὐρανὸν ἐπὶ πολλὰς νύκτας λαμπὰς μέγας καιομένη; Artem. 2, 9 p. 92, 22 λαμπάδες ἐν οὐρανῷ καιόμεναι). Cf. ἑπτὰ λαμπάδες πυρὸς καιόμεναι ἐνώπιον τ. θρόνου 4: 5 (λαμπάδες πυρός as Eutecnius 4 p. 39, 6; Gen 15: 17; Na 2: 5; Da 10: 6; Philo, Rer. Div. Her. 311.—λαμπάδες καιόμεναι as Artem. [see above]; Job 41: 11).

2. *lamp* (so POxy. 1449 [III AD]; Jdth 10: 22; Da 5: 5 Theod.) w. a wick and space for oil Mt 25: 1, 3f, 7f (acc. to FZorell, Verbum Domini 10, '30, 176–82; HAlmqvist, Plut. u. d. NT '46, 46 [Mor. 263F] the wedding torch [s. 1] is meant here); Ac 20: 8. M-M. B. 484.*

λαμπηδών, όνος, ἡ (Hippocr. V 632 L.; Epicurus 45, 8 Us.; Diod. S. 3, 37, 9; Plut.; Aelian, N.A. 2, 8 p. 36, 16; Artem. 5, 90; Herm. Wr. 10, 4b; PGM 4, 531; Is 58: 11 Aq.; Jos., Ant. 3, 207) *brightness, brilliance* Hs 9, 2, 2.*

λαμπρός, ά, όν (Hom.+; inscr., pap., LXX, Philo, Joseph., Test. 12 Patr.) *bright, shining, radiant*.

1. of heavenly bodies (Hom.+; X., Mem. 4, 7, 7; EpJer 59; Test. Napht. 5: 4) the sun (Philo, Somn. 2, 282) Hs 9, 17, 4. the morning star Rv 22: 16.

2. of water, *clear, transparent* (Aeschyl., Eum. 695; X., Hell. 5, 3, 19) ποταμὸν ὕδατος ζωῆς λαμπρὸν ὡς κρύσταλλον Rv 22: 1.

3. of garments, esp. white ones *bright, shining* (Od. 19, 234; Polyb. 10, 4, 8; 10, 5, 1; Dit., Syll.³ 1157, 39f ἐν ἐσθῆσιν λαμπραῖς; Philo, De Jos. 105 λ. ἐσθής) ἱματισμὸς λαμπρότατος *a brightly shining garment* Hv 1, 2, 2. ἐσθὴς λ. Lk 23: 11 (PJoüon, Rech de Sc rel 26, '36, 80–5); Ac 10: 30; Js 2: 2f. στολή (Jos., Vi. 334) GP 13: 55. βύσσινον λ. καθαρόν Rv 19: 8 (cf. Jos., Ant. 8, 72). λίνον καθαρὸν λ. 15: 6.

4. of other objects *gleaming, bright* stones Hv 3, 2, 4b; s 9, 3, 3; 9, 4, 6; 9, 6, 7f; 9, 8, 7; 9, 9, 3f; 9, 17, 3; 9, 30, 2 and 4. ἐπάρασα ῥάβδον τινὰ λαμπράν *as she lifted up a sort of glittering staff* Hv 3, 2, 4a.

5. subst. τὰ λαμπρά *splendor* (Philo, In Flacc. 165, Leg. ad Gai. 327), in which a rich man takes delight (cf. Jos., Ant. 12, 220 δωρεὰς δοὺς λαμπράς) Rv 18: 14. M-M.*

λαμπρότης, ητος, ἡ (Hdt.+; inscr., pap., LXX, Ep. Arist., Philo, Joseph.) *brilliance, splendor.*
1. lit. (X., An. 1, 2, 18 of the splendor of weapons; Jos., Bell. 5, 271, Ant. 12, 81) *brightness* of the sun (Vi. Aesopi W c. 115. Of a constellation Diod. S. 15, 50, 3) Ac 26: 13.
2. fig., of a mental or spiritual state, someth. like *joyousness, greatness of soul* (Polyb. 32, 8, 1; Diod. S. 2, 22, 3; 4, 10, 2; 4, 40, 1 ψυχῆς λαμπρότητι; Ep. Arist. 16; Jos., Ant. 11, 342) λ. ἐν δικαιοσύνῃ 1 Cl 35: 2. M-M.*

λαμπρῶς adv. (Aeschyl.+; Dit., Syll.³ 545, 12; 1045, 15; PSI 406, 30; Jos., Ant. 6, 15 al.) *splendidly* εὐφραίνεσθαι καθ᾽ ἡμέραν λαμπρῶς *fare sumptuously every day* Lk 16: 19 (PGM 1, 111 ἐξαρτίσαι τὸ δεῖπνον λαμπρῶς; cf. δαπανάω 1). M-M.*

λάμπω fut. λάμψω; 1 aor. ἔλαμψα (Hom.+; LXX, En., Joseph., Test. 12 Patr., Sib. Or.; Christian inscr. in Dit., Or. 610, 1f [VI AD] φῶς σωτήριον ἔλαμψεν ὅπου σκότος ἐκάλυπτεν).
1. lit.—a. *shine, flash* (Jos., Ant. 3, 218) of a lamp Mt 5: 15; lightning Lk 17: 24.
b. *shine out, shine forth, gleam* (Charito 1, 9, 5 of a gleaming sword; Jos., Ant. 5, 284) light Ac 12: 7; a star (cf. Isishymn. v. Andros [I BC] 23; Bar 3: 34; Sib. Or. 3, 334 ἀστὴρ λάμψει) IEph 19: 2; sun (Archilochus [VII BC] 74, 4 Diehl²) GP 6: 22. Of the face of the transfigured Jesus ὡς ὁ ἥλιος (cf. EpJer 66; En. 14, 18; 106, 2; Test. Levi 18: 4) Mt 17: 2. Of the light that shone forth at creation by God's command 2 Cor 4: 6a.
2. used fig. w. φῶς (cf. Pr 4: 18; Tob 13: 13 S; Is 9: 1) *shine* λαμψάτω τ. φῶς ὑμῶν ἔμπροσθεν τ. ἀνθρώπων Mt 5: 16.—Of God, prob. *shine forth* θεὸς . . . ὃς ἔλαμψεν ἐν ταῖς καρδίαις ἡμῶν *God, who has shone in our hearts* 2 Cor 4: 6b (perh. *reflect*, as PGM 13, 770 of the heavenly eyes of the divinity λάμποντες ἐν ταῖς κόραις τ. ἀνθρώπων. GWMacRae, Anti-Dualist Polemic in 2 Cor 4: 6? TU 102, '68, 420-31.—AOepke, TW IV 17-28 λάμπω and related words. M-M.*

λανθάνω 2 aor. ἔλαθον (Hom.+; inscr., pap., LXX, Ep. Arist., Philo, Joseph.) *escape notice, be hidden* abs. (Jos., Bell. 3, 343) Mk 7: 24; Lk 8: 47; MPol 6: 1.—λανθάνει τί τινα *someth. is hidden from someone, escapes someone's notice* (Hom.+; BGU 531 II, 13; POxy. 34 vers. III, 3; 1253, 22; Job 34: 21 λέληθεν αὐτὸν οὐδέν. Ep. Arist. 132; Jos., Ant. 17, 38, Vi. 83) IEph 19: 1; 2 Pt 3: 8. οὐδὲν λέληθεν αὐτόν 1 Cl 21: 3; cf. 27: 6; IEph 14: 1; 15: 3; Pol 4: 3. λανθάνειν αὐτὸν τούτων οὐ πείθομαι οὐθέν *I cannot bring myself to believe that any of these things has escaped his notice* Ac 26: 26.—That which escapes notice can also be expressed by a ὅτι-clause (X., Mem. 3, 5, 24; Isocr., Ep. 6, 12; Dio Chrys. 16[33], 37) λανθάνει αὐτοὺς τοῦτο θέλοντας ὅτι *when they maintain this, it escapes their notice* (i.e. they forget) *that* 2 Pt 3: 5 (s. θέλω 5). Likew. by the ptc. (Maximus Tyr. 4, 6b; Jos., Vi. 425; Bl-D. §414, 3; Rob. 1120) ἔλαθόν τινες (sc. ἑαυτούς) ξενίσαντες ἀγγέλους *some, without knowing it, have entertained angels* Hb 13: 2 (cf. Hdt. 1, 44 φονέα τοῦ παιδὸς ἐλάνθανε βόσκων=he fed the murderer of his son

without knowing it; X., Mem. 4, 3, 9 al.; Lucian, De Merc. Cond. 7 ἔλαθον γηράσαντες=they had grown old without noticing it). M-M.*

λαξευτός, ή, όν (Dt 4: 49; Aq. Num 21: 20; 23: 14; Dt 34: 1; Josh 13: 20. Cf. Bl-D. §2) *hewn in the rock* μνῆμα a *tomb* Lk 23: 53. M-M.*

Λαοδίκεια, ας, ἡ (Strabo 12, 8, 16; inscr.; Sib. Or.) *Laodicea* a city in Phrygia (in Asia Minor) on the Lycus R. There was a large colony of Jews there (Jos., Ant. 14, 241ff; Schürer III⁴ 16f; 110, 37), and Christianity also took root at an early date. Col 2: 1; 4: 13, 15f. Subscr. of 1 and 2 Ti; Rv 1: 11; 3: 14.—Ramsay, Phrygia I 1, 32ff; 341f; I 2, 512; 542ff; Lghtf., Col 1ff.—Paul wrote a letter to the church at Laodicea, Col 4: 16. Cf. Harnack, D. Adresse des Eph des Pls: SAB '10, 696-709; Gdspd., Introd. to the NT, '37, 114-24; CPAnderson, JBL 85, '66, 436-40.*

Λαοδικεύς, έως, ὁ (inscr.; Jos., Ant. 14, 241; Appian, Mithrid. 20 §78; 117 §573; Artem. 4, 1 p. 202, 8) *a Laodicean,* inhabitant of Laodicea in Phrygia Col 4: 16. Cf. also the superscr. of Eph in Marcion. M-M.*

λαός, οῦ, ὁ (Hom.+; inscr.; pap. [here the pl. λαοί, Mayser 27; 29]; LXX, En., Philo, Joseph., Test. 12 Patr.; Sib. Or. 7, 119) *people.*
1. the people gener.—a. in the mass, *crowd* Lk 1: 21; 3: 15, 18; 7: 1; 20: 1; Ac 3: 12; 4: 1f; 13: 15; 21: 30. πᾶς ὁ λ. *the whole crowd, all the people* (Jos., Ant. 13, 201) Mt 27: 25; Lk 8: 47; 9: 13; 18: 43; 21: 38; J 8: 2; Ac 3: 9, 11. Also ἅπας ὁ λ. (Jos., Ant. 7, 63; 211) Lk 3: 21. ὁ λ. ἅπας (Jos., Ant. 6, 199; 8, 101) 19: 48; GP 8: 28. λ. ἱκανός Ac 5: 37 t.r. πᾶν τὸ πλῆθος τ. λαοῦ Lk 1: 10; cf. Ac 21: 36. πλῆθος πολὺ τοῦ λαοῦ *a large crowd of people* Lk 6: 17; 23: 27.
b. *the people* distributively, *populace* Mt 27: 64. ἐν τῷ λαῷ *among the people* Mt 4: 23; Ac 6: 8.
c. *the people*—a. in contrast to their leaders Mt 26: 5; Mk 11: 32 v.l.; 12: 12; Lk 19: 48; 20: 6, 19, 26; 23: 13; Ac 2: 47; 4: 17, 21; 5: 26; 6: 12; 12: 4.
β. the people in contrast to the Pharisees and legal experts Lk 7: 29.—γ. the people in contrast to the priests Hb 2: 17; 5: 3; 7: 5, 27.—RMeyer, Der 'Am hā-'Āreṣ, Judaica 3, '47, 169-99.
2. *people* as nation (w. φυλή, ἔθνος, γλῶσσα; cf. Da 3: 4) Rv 5: 9; 13: 7; 14: 6. Pl. (a Sibylline oracle in Appian, Maced. 2; En. 10, 21) 7: 9; 10: 11; 11: 9; 17: 15.—Lk 2: 31. Of a monstrous animal θηρίον δυνάμενον λαοὺς διαφθεῖραι *a beast capable of destroying (whole) peoples* Hv 4, 2, 3.
3. the people of God—a. of the people of Israel ὁ λαός (s. also the Jewish inscriptions in Dit., Syll.³ 1247; GKittel, ThLZ 69, '44, 13; En. 20, 5.—λαός of the native Egyptian population since III BC at least: UWilcken on UPZ 110, 100f) Ac 3: 23; 7: 17; 28: 17; 2 Pt 2: 1. Without the art. (Sir 46: 7; Wsd 18: 13) Jd 5; οὗτος ὁ λ. Mt 15: 8; Mk 7: 6 (both Is 29: 13); Lk 21: 23; B 9: 3; 10: 2; πᾶς ὁ λ. Lk 2: 10 (here, however, the evangelist may have intended the word to have its universal sense: *all the people*=everyone); B 12: 8. πᾶς ὁ λ. Ἰσραήλ Ac 4: 10. οἱ ἀρχιερεῖς τοῦ λ. Mt 2: 4; 26: 47; 27: 1; τὸ πρεσβυτέριον τοῦ λ. Lk 22: 66; οἱ ἄρχοντες τοῦ λ. Ac 4: 8; B 9: 3; UGosp l. 6; οἱ πρῶτοι τοῦ λ. Lk 19: 47. Opp. τὰ ἔθνη *Gentiles, heathen* (s. ἔθνος 2 and cf. Appian, Bell. Civ. 5, 67 §283 the contrast τὰ ἔθνη—τὴν Ἰταλίαν) Ac 26: 17, 23; Ro 15: 10 (Dt 32: 43).—W. a gen. that denotes the possessor ([τοῦ] θεοῦ, αὐτοῦ, μοῦ etc. Cf. Jos., Ant. 10, 12): λ. τοῦ θεοῦ Lk 1: 68;

Hb 11: 25. ὁ λαός μου Ac 7: 34 (Ex 3: 7). Rv 18: 4 (pl. verb with λαός in sing. as Περὶ ὕψους 23, 2 after a poet λαός. . . κελάδησαν).—Lk 7: 16. λ. σου Ἰσραήλ Lk 2: 32. ὁ λ. μου ὁ Ἰσραήλ Mt 2: 6. ὁ λ. Ἰσραήλ B 16: 5. Pl. of the tribes of Israel (Jos., C. Ap. 2, 159, unless the pl. here means 'the people', as Hes., Op. 763f πολλοὶ λαοί; Aristoph., Equ. 163, Ran. 216; 677 πολὺν λαῶν ὄχλον; Callim., Epigr. 47; Isyllus [III вс]: Coll. Alex. p. 133, 37 θεὸν ἀείσατε, λαοί=ἐνναέται Ἐπιδαύρου [inhabitants of Epidaurus]; Diod. S. 1, 45, 1; 3, 45, 6 διὰ τὴν τῶν λαῶν ἀπειρίαν=because of the inexperience of the people; 4, 67, 6; 5, 7, 6; 5, 48, 1 συναγαγεῖν τ. λαοὺς σποράδην οἰκοῦντας=gather the people who live in scattered places; 5, 59, 5 al.; Orph. Hymn. 34, 10 Q; Herm. Wr. 1, 27; PRev. 42, 17 [258 вс] γραφέτωσαν οἱ λαοί=the people are to submit a written statement; Jos., Ant. 18, 352; Basilius, Ep.: Migne, S. Gr. XXXII p. 481A; Theophanes, Chron. 172, 7 de Boor ἀπέθανον λαοὶ πολλοί) Ac 4: 25 (Ps 2: 1), 27; Ro 15: 11 (Ps 116: 1). b. of the Christians Ac 15: 14; 18: 10; Ro 9: 25 (Hos 2: 25); Hb 4: 9; 1 Pt 2: 10; 1 Cl 59: 4; 2 Cl 2: 3; B 13: 1ff. Prepared by Christ B 3: 6; cf. Hs 5, 5, 2. Protected by angels 5, 5, 3; specif. entrusted to Michael 8, 3, 3; cf. 8, 1, 2.—Also in pl. (s. 3a, end) λαοὶ αὐτοῦ Rv 21: 3; cf. Hs 8, 3, 2.—λ. εἰς περιποίησιν a people (made) his own possession 1 Pt 2: 9. Also λ. περιούσιος (Ex 19: 5) Tit 2: 14; 1 Cl 64. λ. κατεσκευασμένος a people made ready Lk 1: 17. λ. καινός B 5: 7; 7: 5.—OKern, ARW 30, '33, 205-7; EKäsemann, D. wandernde Gottesvolk '39; NA Dahl, D. Volk Gottes: E. Untersuchg. z. Kirchenbewusstsein des Urchristent. '41; HSahlin, D. Messias u. d. Gottesvolk '45; AOepke, D. neue Gottesvolk '50; HStrathmann u. RMeyer, TW IV 29-57. M-M. B. 1313; 1315.

λέρυγξ, γγος, ὁ (Eur.+; LXX; cf. Bl-D. §46, 4; Mlt.-H. 108) throat, gullet (orig. 'larynx'), fig. τάφος ἀνεῳγμένος ὁ λάρυγξ αὐτῶν (ἀνοίγω 1b) Ro 3: 13 (Ps 5: 10; 13: 3).*

Λασαία, ας or Λασέα, ας (W-H.), ἡ Lasaea, a city on the south coast of the island of Crete. Ac 27: 8. M-M.*

λάσκω 1 aor. ἐλάκησα, crash, etc., erroneously thought to be the source of ἐλάκησεν Ac 1: 18; s. λακάω.

λατομέω 1 aor. ἐλατόμησα; pf. pass. ptc. λελατομημένος (Antig. Car. 161; Posidonius: 87 fgm. 57 Jac.; Diod. S. et al.; Dit., Syll.³ 1169, 25 [III вс] λατομήσας τ. πέτραν; PPetr. II 4(9), 3 [255 вс]; PCair. Zen. 296, 34 [III вс]; LXX; Artapanus in Euseb., Pr. Ev. 9, 27, 11; Jos., Ant. 8, 59). 1. hew out of the rock (2 Ch 26: 10; 2 Esdr 19 [Neh 9]: 25) a grave (Is 22: 16 μνημεῖον) Lk 23: 53 v.l. λελατομημένον ἐκ πέτρας Mk 15: 46. λ. ἐν τῇ πέτρᾳ cut in the rock Mt 27: 60. 2. hew, shape stones (1 Ch 22: 2; Is 51: 1) Hv 3, 5, 3; s 9, 3, 3; 9, 4, 5; 9, 5, 3; 9, 6, 8; 9, 7, 4; 9, 8, 2ff; 6; 9, 9, 3. M-M.*

λατόμος, ου, ὁ (Ptolem., Apotel. 4, 4, 5; Pollux 7, 118; Dit., Or. 660, 3 [I AD]; PSI 423, 1; 37 [III вс]; PPetr. III 47 [a], 2 al.; LXX; Jos., Ant. 11, 78) stone-mason Hs 9, 9, 2.*

λατρεία, ας, ἡ (Pind.+; LXX. On the cultic t.t. עֲבוֹדָה cf. Elbogen 4) in relig. usage service or worship (of God) (Pla., Apol. 23в τοῦ θεοῦ, Phaedr. 244E; Sb 1934, 3 [?]; LXX; Philo, Ebr. 144 al.; Jos., Bell. 2, 409) Ro 9: 4; λογικὴ λ. 12: 1 (s. λογικός). δικαιώματα λατρείας regulations for worship Hb 9: 1. τὰς λ. ἐπιτελεῖν perform the rites vs. 6. λ. προσφέρειν τῷ θεῷ offer a service to

God J 16: 2. Of idolatry λ. θεῶν νεκρῶν D 6: 3; cf. Dg 3: 2. M-M.*

λατρεύω fut. λατρεύσω; 1 aor. ἐλάτρευσα (trag. et al.; inscr., LXX, En., Philo, Sib. Or. 4, 104) serve, in our lit. only of the carrying out of relig. duties, esp. of a cultic nature, by human beings: λ. θεῷ (Eur., Ion 152; Plut., Mor. 405c; 407E; Philo, Spec. Leg. 1, 300 ὅλῃ τ. ψυχῇ. Cf. En. 10, 21) Mt 4: 10; Lk 4: 8 (both Dt 6: 13); 1: 74; Ac 7: 7 (cf. Ex 3: 12); 24: 14; 27: 23; Hb 9: 14; Rv 7: 15; 22: 3; Pol 2: 1. τῷ ὀνόματι (θεοῦ) 1 Cl 45: 7; τῷ διαβόλῳ λ. serve the devil (in reality) ISm 9: 1. Of the Jews λ. ἀγγέλοις PK 2 p. 14, 26. Of idolatry (Ex 20: 5; 23: 24; Ezk 20: 32; En. 99, 7) Ac 7: 42; Ro 1: 25.—W. indication of the manner in which the service (τῷ θεῷ) is performed ἐν καθαρᾷ συνειδήσει serve God w. a clear conscience 2 Ti 1: 3. (διὰ χάριτος) λ. εὐαρέστως τῷ θεῷ μετὰ εὐλαβείας καὶ δέους (in thankfulness) serve God acceptably with reverence and awe Hb 12: 28. (τῷ θεῷ) λ. ἐν τῷ πνεύματί μου ἐν τῷ εὐαγγελίῳ I serve God with my spirit in the gospel Ro 1: 9 (cf. Phil 3: 3 v.l.).—Without the dat. of the one to whom the service is given: ἐν ἐκτενείᾳ νύκτα κ. ἡμέραν λ. serve (God) earnestly night and day Ac 26: 7. νηστείαις κ. δεήσεσιν λ. νύκτα κ. ἡμέραν serve (God) night and day w. fasting and prayer Lk 2: 37. οἱ πνεύματι θεοῦ λατρεύοντες those who worship by the Spirit of God Phil 3: 3 (HKoester, NTS 8, '62, 320f: work as a missionary in the Spirit of God). ὁ λατρεύων the worshiper (who is concerned w. the rituals prescribed by the law) Hb 9: 9; 10: 2.—Hb also adds to λ. in the dat. the holy objects by means of which the priest renders service 8: 5; 13: 10.—WBrandt, Dienst u. Dienen im NT '31; CEB Cranfield, Interpretation 12, '58, 387-98; BReicke, NT Studies: TWManson memorial vol., '59, 194-209; HStrathmann, TW IV 58-66. M-M.*

λαχ- s. λαγχάνω.

λάχανον, ου, τό (Cratinus+; pap., LXX; Jos., Bell. 5, 437) edible garden herb, vegetable Mt 13: 32; Mk 4: 32. πᾶν λάχανον every kind of garden herb Lk 11: 42.—Of one who is a vegetarian for religious reasons ὁ ἀσθενῶν λάχανα ἐσθίει the one who is weak (in his convictions) eats (only) vegetables Ro 14: 2 (cf. the Neopythagoreans in Diog. L. 8, 38 ἐσθίουσι λάχανα; Philostrat., Vi. Apoll. 1, 8 λάχανα ἐσιτεῖτο.—JHaussleiter, D. Vegetarismus in der Antike '35). M-M. B. 369.*

λαχμός, οῦ, ὁ lot (schol. on Soph., Aj. 1281; schol. on Eur., Hippol. 1057; schol. on Theocr. 8, 30; Etym. Mag. p. 519, 10; Eustath.) λαχμὸν βάλλειν ἐπί τινι cast lots for someth. GP 4: 12.*

λε΄ numeral=35, Hs 9, 4, 3; 9, 5, 4; 9, 15, 4.*

Λεββαῖος, ου, ὁ (לֶבַּי) Lebbaeus, in the list of apostles Mt 10: 3 and Mk 3: 18 as v.l. for Θαδδαῖος (q.v.).—Dalman, Worte 40; MLidzbarski, Handbuch der nordsem. Epigr. 1898, 301.*

λεγιών, ῶνος, ἡ (Lat. loanw.: legio, also in rabb. In Gk. since Diod. S. 26, 5; Nicol. Dam.: 90 fgm. 130 §132 Jac.; inscr. fr. the time of the triumvirs [fr. Ephesus, Jahreshefte des Österreich. Archäol. Inst. 2, 1899, Beiblatt, col. 83/4]; pap., fr. about the beginning of our era [BGU 1108, 5-3 вс; PLond. 256 recto (a), 3-15 AD]; Sib. Or. 8, 78. The spellings λεγεών [t.r.] and λεγιών [crit. editions] are about equally attested [s. the reff. in Hahn, Wortregister; Dit., Or. index]; cf. on this ThEckinger, D. Orthographie latein. Wörter in griech. Inschriften, Zürich Diss. 1892,

30; APMMeuwese, De rerum gestarum D. Augusti versione graeca, Diss. Amsterdam '20, 15; Bl-D. §41, 1; Mlt.-H. 76) a *legion*, numbering in the time of Augustus about 6,000 soldiers, usu. w. approx. an equal number of auxiliary troops. The angels divided into legions Mt 26: 53 (for this concept cf. Maximus Tyr. 4, 4c after Pla., Phaedr. 26 p. 246E: Zeus with the heavenly στρατιά made up of eleven hosts [Maximus Tyr. 10, 9c the souls of good men are counted as members of the στρατιὰ θεῶν]; Aristodem. [IV AD]: 104 fgm. 1, 8 Jac.: at Salamis οἱ θεοὶ συνεμάχησαν τ. Ἕλλησιν . . . κονιορτὸν ὡς δισμυρίων ἀνδρῶν). As the name of a demon Mk 5: 9, 15 (ὁ λ. here is explained by the fact that the demon was masculine: cf. correspondingly Dio Chrys. 46 [63], 1 ἡ δαίμων); Lk 8: 30.—HPreisker, TW IV 68f. M-M.*

λέγω (Hom.+; on the mng. of the word ADebrunner, TW IV 71-3) impf. ἔλεγον (3 pl. ἔλεγαν s. Bl-D. §82 app.; Mlt.-H. 194; KBuresch, RhM 46, 1891, 224). Only pres. and impf. are in use; the other tenses are supplied by εἶπον (q.v., also Bl-D. §101 p. 46; Mlt.-H. 247); *say* (so very rarely in Hom. and Hes., more freq. in Pind.; the usual word since the Attic writers; inscr., pap., LXX, En., Ep. Arist., Philo, Joseph., Test. 12 Patr., Sib. Or.).

I. gener. *utter in words, say, tell, give expression to* orally, but also in writing.

1. w. an indication of what is said—a. in the acc. ταύτην τ. παραβολήν Lk 13: 6. (τὴν) ἀλήθειαν (Teles p. 4, 14) J 8: 45f; Ro 9: 1; 1 Ti 2: 7. ἀληθῆ (cf. Herodian 4, 14, 4) J 19: 35. παροιμίαν οὐδεμίαν 16: 29. τὶ καινότερον Ac 17: 21 (w. ἀκούω as Pla., Prot. 310A; Dio Chrys. 3, 28; 4, 37). τὶ λέγουσιν *what they say* Mt 21: 16; cf. Lk 18: 6; 1 Cor 14: 16. τὶ λέγω; *what shall I say?* Hb 11: 32. ὃ λέγει Lk 9: 33; cf. 2 Ti 2: 7; Phlm 21. ἃ λέγουσιν 1 Ti 1: 7. ταῦτα (τοῦτο) λ. (Jos., Vi. 291) Lk 9: 34; 11: 45b; 13: 17; J 2: 22; τοιαῦτα λ. Hb 11: 14. τὸ αὐτὸ λέγειν *be in agreement* (not only in words: Thu. 4, 20, 4; 5, 31, 6; Polyb. 2, 62, 4; 5, 104, 1; Jos., Ant. 18, 375; 378) 1 Cor 1: 10.—Also τινί τι *tell someone someth.* παραβολὴν αὐτοῖς Lk 18: 1. μυστήριον ὑμῖν 1 Cor 15: 51. τ. ἀλήθειαν ὑμῖν J 16: 7. ὃ λέγω ὑμῖν Mt 10: 27. μηδενὶ λ. τοῦτο Lk 9: 21. οὐδὲν αὐτῷ λέγουσιν *they say nothing to him* J 7: 26. ταῦτα ἔλεγον ὑμῖν 2 Th 2: 5.—τὶ πρός τινα: παραβολὴν πρὸς αὐτούς Lk 5: 36; cf. 14: 7; 20: 9.—24: 10; 11: 53 v.l.

b. expressed in some other way—α. by direct discourse or direct question foll., mostly abs. (extremely freq.) Mt 9: 34; 12: 44; Mk 3: 30; Lk 5: 39; J 1: 29, 36; 1 Cor 12: 3; Js 4: 13. Also oft. introduced by recitative ὅτι Mt 9: 18; Mk 1: 15; 2: 12; 3: 21f; 5: 28; 6: 14f, 35; 7: 20; Lk 1: 24; 4: 41; 17: 10; 21: 8 v.l.; J 6: 14; 7: 12; 8: 33; Ac 2: 13; 11: 3 and oft.—καὶ ἔλεγεν Mk 4: 21, 24, 26, 30 may = *he used to say* (so that they might memorize): WGEssame, ET 77, '66, 121.

β. by indirect discourse or indirect question foll.; abs. Mt 21: 27; Mk 11: 33c; Lk 20: 8.—Introduced by ὅτι (Diod. S. 11, 4, 3; 11, 6, 2; 14, 4, 3; Petosiris, fgm. 14c; Jos., Bell. 4, 543) Lk 22: 70; Ac 20: 23.—In acc. w. inf. τινα λέγουσιν οἱ ἄνθρωποι εἶναι τ. υἱὸν τ. ἀνθρώπου; Mt 16: 13; cf. vs. 15; Lk 9: 20; 11: 18; 23: 2b; 24: 23b; J 12: 29a; Ac 4: 32; 8: 9; 17: 7.—W. the inf. only Lk 24: 23a; Js 2: 14; 1 J 2: 6, 9.

2. w. indication of the pers. or thing about which someth. is said, or that is meant by someth.—a. by a prep. περί τινος (Soph., Thu.+) οἱ Φαρισαῖοι ἔγνωσαν ὅτι περὶ αὐτῶν λέγει *the Pharisees perceived that he was talking about them* Mt 21: 45. λέγει περὶ αὐτοῦ *he said*

concerning him J 1: 47; cf. 2: 21; 11: 13; 13: 18, 22. εἴς τινα (Eur., Med. 453; X., Mem. 1, 5, 1) Ac 2: 25; Eph 5: 32. ἐπί τινα Hb 7: 13. πρός τινα Lk 12: 41; Hb 1: 7.

b. by the acc. alone *mean someone* or *someth.* (Demosth. 18, 88; Diod. S. 15, 23, 5; Phalaris, Ep. 142, 1 ἢν λέγω; Ael. Aristid. 48, 35 K. = 24 p. 474 D.: τὸν Φιλάδελφον λέγων; Aelian, N. An. 8, 3 ὃ δὲ λέγω, τοιοῦτόν ἐστιν, V.H. 3, 36; Lucian, Dial. Deor. 3; 10, 2; 2 Macc 14: 7; Jos., Ant. 6, 86) τ. ἄνθρωπον τοῦτον ὃν λέγετε *this man whom you mean* Mk 14: 71. ἔλεγεν τὸν Ἰούδαν J 6: 71. συνείδησιν λέγω οὐχὶ τὴν ἑαυτοῦ *I mean not your own conscience* 1 Cor 10: 29. τοῦτο δὲ λέγω *but this is what I mean* Gal 3: 17; cf. 1 Cor 1: 12a (Ptolem., Apotel. 2, 3, 12; 2, 11, 1 λέγω δέ . . . but I mean).—Mt 26: 70; Mk 14: 68; Lk 22: 60.

3. w. an indication of the one to whom someth. is said (on the synoptics and Ac s. WLarfeld, Die ntl. Ev. '25, 237f); mostly in dat. (Aeschyl., Ag. 103; Herodas 4, 42 σοι; POxy. 413, 99; s. also 1a above) Mt 8: 7; Mk 2: 8, 17f; Lk 3: 7; 5: 24; J 1: 39, 41, 43 and oft.—πρός τινα (Epict. 2, 17, 34 πρὸς ἄλλους ἐρεῖς; s. also 1a above) Mk 4: 41; 16: 3; Lk 4: 21; 8: 25 (λ. πρὸς ἀλλήλους as Jos., Ant. 2, 108; 9, 239); 9: 23; 12: 1; 16: 1; J 2: 3; 3: 4; Ac 2: 12; 28: 4. μετά τινος: ἔλεγον μετ' ἀλλήλων *they said to each other* J 11: 56.

4. in other (cf. 1a, 2a, 3) prep. uses ἀφ' ἑαυτοῦ (= ἀπὸ σεαυτοῦ v.l.) σὺ τοῦτο λέγεις; *do you say this of your own accord?* J 18: 34. εἴς τινα *against someone* Lk 22: 65. τὶ περί τινος *say someth. about* or *concerning someone* J 1: 22; Ac 8: 34; Tit 2: 8. λ. περὶ τοῦ ἱεροῦ, ὅτι *say, with reference to the temple, that* Lk 21: 5. τὶ σὺ λέγεις περὶ αὐτοῦ, ὅτι; *what have you to say about him, since?* J 9: 17b (λ. τι περί τινος ὅτι as Jos., Bell. 7, 215). τινὶ περί τινος *say to someone about someone* w. direct discourse foll. Mt 11: 7. Also πρός τινα περί τινος (Jos., C. Ap. 1, 279 πρὸς αὐτὸν περὶ Μωϋσέως) Lk 7: 24. πρός τινα ἐπί τινος *bring charges against someone before someone* Ac 23: 30 (λ. ἐπί τινος as Jos., Vi. 258). λ. ὑπέρ τινος *say* (someth.), *speak in someone's defense* 26: 1.

5. in connection w. adverbs and adv. exprs.: Λυκαονιστὶ λ. *say in* (the) *Lycaonian* (language) Ac 14: 11. καλῶς *correctly* (X., Mem. 2, 7, 11; 3, 3, 4; Ep. Arist. 125; 196) J 8: 48; 13: 13. ὡσαύτως *in the same way* Mk 14: 31. ἀληθῶς λέγω ὑμῖν *truly, I tell you* Lk 12: 44; 21: 3. κατὰ ἄνθρωπον (s. ἄνθρωπος 1c) Ro 3: 5; Gal 3: 15. κατὰ συγγνώμην, οὐ κατ' ἐπιταγήν (s. ἐπιταγή) 1 Cor 7: 6; cf. 2 Cor 8: 8. καθ' ὑστέρησιν Phil 4: 11.

6. w. emphasis on a certain kind of saying: φωνῇ μεγάλῃ *in a loud voice* Rv 5: 12; 8: 13. Also ἐν φωνῇ μεγάλῃ 14: 7; 9. Opp. ἐν τῇ καρδίᾳ (cf. Ps 13: 1) 18: 7. Also ἐν ἑαυτῷ Mt 3: 9; 9: 21; Lk 3: 8; 7: 39, 49.

7. in quotations fr. scripture (but s. also Epict. 1, 28, 4 ὡς λέγει Πλάτων with a quotation) Ἠσαΐας λέγει *Isaiah says* Ro 10: 16, 20; 15: 12. Μωϋσῆς λέγει 10: 19. Δαυὶδ λέγει 11: 9. ἡ γραφὴ λέγει (Paus. 2, 16, 4 τὰ ἔπη λέγει = the epic poets say) 4: 3; 10: 11; Gal 4: 30; 1 Ti 5: 18; Js 4: 5; cf. 2: 23; 2 Cl 14: 2. In the case of the quot. formula λέγει without the subj. expressed, ἡ γραφή or ὁ θεός is easily understood (Bl-D. §130, 3; Rob. 392.—On the omission of the subj. cf. Epict. 1, 24, 12 λέγει σοι 'θὲς κτλ.' = someone says to you). It could prob. be translated indefinitely *it says*: Ro 15: 10; 2 Cor 6: 2; Gal 3: 16; Eph 4: 8; 5: 14. ὁ θεός is obviously the subj. (Clearch., fgm. 69c; Epict. 1, 1, 10 λέγει ὁ Ζεύς, followed by a divine revelation to Epictetus) Hb 5: 6. λέγει ὁ κύριος 2 Cl 13: 4; cf. Hb 8: 8-10. W. the passage more definitely indicated (schol. on Pind., Ol. 7, 66 ἐν τοῖς Μουσαίου λέγεται; schol. on

Apollon. Rhod. 3, 1179 Wendel v.l. ἐν τῇ γ΄ τῆς Μουσαίου Τιτανογραφίας λέγεται ὡς) ἐν Ἡλίᾳ . . . λέγει ἡ γραφή Ro 11: 2 (Epict. 2, 17, 34 τί λέγει Χρύσιππος ἐν τοῖς περὶ τοῦ ψευδομένου). Δαυὶδ λέγει ἐν βίβλῳ ψαλμῶν Lk 20: 42 (Epict. 2, 19, 14 Ἑλλάνικος λέγει ἐν τοῖς Αἰγυπτιακοῖς with quot.). ἐν τ. Ὡσηὲ λέγει Ro 9: 25. λέγει ἐν τῷ Ἡσαΐᾳ 2 Cl 3: 5; cf. ἐν Δαυὶδ Hb 4: 7. ὁ νόμος λέγει (cf. Pla., Crito 12 p. 50c; Epict. 3, 24, 43 τί γὰρ λέγει; [i.e. ὁ νόμος θεῖος]) 1 Cor 14: 34. λέγει τὸ πνεῦμα τὸ ἅγιον Hb 3: 7. Of words of Jesus: λέγει ὁ κύριος ἐν τῷ εὐαγγελίῳ 2 Cl 8: 5. λέγει ὁ κύριος 5: 2; 6: 1. λέγει αὐτός (i.e. ὁ Χριστός 2: 7) 3: 2. λέγει 4: 2.

8. Hebraistic, though by no means limited to the OT (cf. EKieckers, IndogF 35, '15, 34ff; Bl-D. §420; Mlt.-H. 454), is the freq. use of λ. to introduce

a. direct discourse (like לֵאמֹר), even though it is preceded by a verb of saying, or one that includes the idea of saying. Esp. λέγων is so used, as in the LXX, e.g. after ἀναβοᾶν, ἀνακράζειν (Mk 1: 23; cf. Phlegon: 257, fgm. 36, 3, 9 Jac. ἀνεκεκράγει λέγων), ἀπαγγέλλειν, ἀποκρίνεσθαι, ἀρνεῖσθαι, βοᾶν, γογγύζειν, διαγογγύζειν, διαμαρτύρεσθαι, διαστέλλεσθαι, διαλογίζεσθαι, διδάσκειν, δοξάζειν, εἰπεῖν Mt 22: 1; Lk 12: 16; 20: 2 (cf. Bl-D. §101, p. 46; cf. Rob. 882f; Kieckers, loc. cit. 36f), ἐμβριμᾶσθαι, ἐντέλλεσθαι, ἐπερωτᾶν, ἐπιτιμᾶν, ἐπιφωνεῖν, ἐρωτᾶν, κατηγορεῖν, κηρύσσειν, κράζειν, κραυγάζειν, λαλεῖν, μαρτυρεῖν, μεριμνᾶν, παραινεῖν, παρακαλεῖν, παρατιθέναι παραβολήν, προσεύχεσθαι, προσφωνεῖν, προφητεύειν, συζητεῖν, συλλαλεῖν, φωνεῖν, ψευδομαρτυρεῖν; s. these entries. Also after such verbs as denote an action accompanied by a statement of some kind: ἄγγελος κυρίου . . . ἐφάνη αὐτῷ λέγων *appeared to him and said* Mt 1: 20; cf. 2: 13; προσεκύνει αὐτῷ λ. *fell before him and said* 8: 2; 9: 18; cf. 14: 33. ἅπτεσθαι 8: 3; 9: 29. ἔρχεσθαι Mk 5: 35; Lk 18: 3; 19: 18 al.; cf. Lk 1: 66; 5: 8; 8: 38; 15: 9; Ac 8: 10, 19; 12: 7; 27: 23f; 1 Cor 11: 25 al.

b. the content of a written document (2 Km 11: 15; 4 Km 10: 6.—1 Macc 8: 31; 11: 57; Jos., Ant. 11, 26) ἔγραψεν λέγων (=לֵאמֹר יִכְתֹּב) *he wrote as follows* Lk 1: 63.

c. orders or instructions to be carried out by other persons: ἔπεμψεν λέγων *he sent and had them say* Lk 7: 19. ἀπέστειλεν λ. (Judg 11: 14f; Jdth 3: 1) Mt 22: 16 v.l.; 27: 19; Lk 7: 20; 19: 14; J 11: 3. If the persons carrying out the orders are named, the ptc. can refer to them Mt 22: 16, text.

d. When it is used w. the ptc. λ. appears in its finite forms ἐμπαίζοντες ἔλεγον *they mocked and said* Mt 27: 41. προσελθὼν αὐτῷ λέγει *he approached him and said* Mk 14: 45. διαρήξας . . . λέγει *he tore his clothes as he said* vs. 63; cf. vs. 67; 15: 35; Lk 6: 20; J 1: 36; Hb 8: 8a al.—Also pleonastically ἀποκριθεὶς λέγει *he answered* Mk 8: 29b; 9: 5, 19; 10: 24; 11: 22; Lk 3: 11; 11: 45; 13: 8. κράξας λέγει *he cried out* Mk 5: 7; 9: 24.

9. Now and then short exprs. w. λ. are inserted as parentheses (Bl-D. §465, 2; Rob. 434): πολλοί, λέγω ὑμῖν, ζητήσουσιν *many, I tell you, will seek* Lk 13: 24. ἐν ἀφροσύνῃ λέγω 2 Cor 11: 21b. ὡς τέκνοις λέγω 6: 13.

10. ptc. w. the article τὰ λεγόμενα *what was said* (Ep. Arist. 215; 298; Jos., Ant. 3, 85; 207) Lk 18: 34. προσεῖχον τ. λεγομένοις ὑπὸ τ. Φιλίππου (προσέχω 1αβ) Ac 8: 6 (προσέχ. τοῖς λεγ. as Jos., Ant. 13, 303; τὰ λ. ὑπό τινος as Bell. 7, 56; 423; Esth 3: 3, also Nicol. Dam.: fgm. 24, p. 408, 19 ὑπὸ τῶν μάντεων; fgm. 30 p. 417, 23 Jac.; Epict. 1, 18, 1; Dit., Syll.³ 679, 85). τὰ ἢ λεχθέντα ἢ πραχθέντα (Ps.-Libanius, Charact. Ep. p. 48, 18; 64, 18;

Jos., C. Ap. 1, 55) Papias in Euseb., H.E. 3, 39, 15 (= Geb., Harn., Zahn 15, p. 72, 17).

II. in the specific sense—**1.** of special forms of saying—
a. *ask* w. direct question foll: Mk 9: 14; 15: 1; 18: 1; Mk 5: 30f. ὁ διδάσκαλος λέγει *the Master asks* 14: 14. W. dat. of the pers. and a direct question foll.: Mt 9: 28a; 15: 34; 16: 15; 20: 6.

b. *answer* (Lucian, Syr. Dea 18) Mt 17: 25; Mk 8: 24; J 1: 21; 18: 17b. W. dat. of the pers. and direct discourse: Mt 4: 10; 8: 26; 9: 28b; 14: 17; 15: 33; 18: 22; 19: 7, 20 al. W. dat of the pers. and direct discourse introduced by ὅτι Mt 19: 8.

c. *order, command, direct, enjoin, recommend* more or less emphatically (Syntipas p. 9, 4; Num 32: 27) τί someth. 2 Cl 6: 4. ἃ λέγω Lk 6: 46. τί τινι *command someone* (to do) *someth.* ὅ τι ἂν λέγῃ ὑμῖν J 2: 5b; cf. Ac 21: 23 (s. Num 32: 31). ὃ ὑμῖν λέγω, πᾶσιν λέγω, γρηγορεῖτε *the order I give to you I give to everyone: be on your guard!* Mk 13: 37. Gener. w. dat. of the pers. and direct discourse foll.: Mt 5: 44; 6: 25; 8: 4, 9; 26: 52; Mk 3: 3, 5; 5: 8; 6: 10; Lk 6: 27; 7: 8; J 2: 7f. W. dat. of the pers. and inf. foll. Rv 10: 9; 13: 14; w. an inf. and a negative *forbid* (X., An. 7, 1, 40) Mt 5: 34, 39.—Here belongs χαίρειν τινὶ λέγειν (Epict. 3, 22, 64) *extend a greeting to someone*, since the greeting consists in saying χαῖρε='may you prosper' 2 J 10f. W. ἵνα foll. *recommend that, tell to* τῷ λαῷ λέγων . . . ἵνα πιστεύσωσιν Ac 19: 4. οὐ περὶ ἐκείνης λέγω ἵνα ἐρωτήσῃ *I do not recommend that anyone should pray about that* (sin) 1 J 5: 16. W. inf. foll. Ro 2: 22.—τάδε λέγει is the formal style of one who is giving an order (introductory formula for the edicts of the Persian kings [Inschr. v. Magnes. 115]; in the OT a favorite method of introducing a prophetic statement [Thackeray p. 11]) Ac 21: 11; Rv 2: 1, 8, 12, 18; 3: 1, 7, 14 (cf. GAGerhard, Philol. 64, '05, 27ff; Thieme 23; GRudberg, Eranos 11, '11, 177f; LLafoscade, De epistulis imperatorum '02, 63; 77).

d. *assure, assert*; w. direct discourse foll. Esp. in the formulas λέγω σοι, λ. ὑμῖν, ἀμὴν (ἀμήν) λ. ὑμῖν Mt 11: 22; 12: 31; 19: 24; 23: 39; Mk 11: 24; Lk 4: 25; 7: 9, 28; 9: 27.—Mt 5: 26; 6: 2, 5; 8: 10; Mk 3: 28; 9: 41; 10: 15; Lk 4: 24; 18: 17, 29; 23: 43; J 1: 51; 3: 3, 5, 11; 5: 19, 24f; 6: 26, 32 al.

e. *maintain, declare, proclaim* as teaching, w. direct discourse foll.: Gal 4: 1; 1 J 2: 4. Foll. by acc. and inf. (X., Symp. 5, 5) Mt 22: 23; Mk 12: 18; Lk 20: 41; 23: 2b; Ro 15: 8; 2 Ti 2: 18. Foll. by ὅτι and direct discourse Mk 12: 35b; 1 Cor 15: 12. W. dat. of the pers. and direct discourse after ὅτι Mt 5: 20, 22, 28, 32; 8: 11 al. Someth. like *interpret* εἰς w. ref. to Eph 5: 32.—σὺ λέγεις (that is what) *you maintain* Mt 27: 11; Mk 15: 2; Lk 23: 3 (cf. σὺ εἶπας Mt 26: 25 and s. εἶπον 1). Cf. also Lk 22: 70; J 18: 37 (s. OMerlier, Rev. des Étud. Grecques 46, '33, 204-9; Gdspd., Probs. 64-8 [strong affirmative, *yes*]; MSmith, JBL 64, '45, 506-10 [intentionally ambiguous, *so you say*, Tannaitic Parallels to the Gospels, '51, 27-30]; DRCatchpole, NTS 17, '70/'71, 213-26). τί λέγει ἡ γνῶσις; *what does Gnosis teach* about this? with the answer in direct discourse B 6: 9 (cf. Epict. 3, 13, 11 καὶ τί λέγει [i.e., ὁ λόγος ὁ τῶν φιλοσόφων = philosophy]; direct discourse follows).

f. of written communications (Hdt. 3, 40; 122; 8, 140; UPZ 68, 5 [152 BC]; Jos., Ant. 13, 80) 1 Cor 6: 5; 7: 6; 15: 51; 2 Cor 6: 13; 8: 8; Gal 5: 2; Phil 4: 11; Col 2: 4; Phlm 21, al. in Paul.

2. *speak, report, tell of* someth. (Diog. L. 1, 31) τινί *to someone* Mk 7: 36. τί *about* someth. (X., Cyr. 1, 2, 16 νῦν λέξομεν τὰς Κύρου πράξεις) τὴν ἔξοδον αὐτοῦ of his death (lit., departure) Lk 9: 31. τὰ περὶ τ. βασιλείας Ac 1: 3. τὰ γινόμενα ὑπ' αὐτῶν αἰσχρόν ἐστιν καὶ λέγειν it is a disgrace even to speak of the things they do Eph 5: 12 (Demosth. 10, 27 ὅ...οὔτε λέγειν ἄξιον). τινὶ περὶ τινος bring a report about someone to someone Mk 1: 30; 8: 30. Likew. τινί τινα Phil 3: 18.

3. call, name (Aeschyl.+) w. double acc. (Epict. 2, 19, 19 τί Στωικὸν ἔλεγες σεαυτόν; Diog. L. 8, 88 τὴν ἡδονὴν λέγειν τὸ ἀγαθόν = call pleasure the [real] good; 2 Macc 4: 2) τινά τι describe someone as someth. τί με λέγεις ἀγαθόν; why do you call me good? Mk 10: 18; Lk 18: 19. Δαυὶδ λέγει αὐτὸν κύριον David calls him Lord Mk 12: 37. πατέρα ἴδιον ἔλεγεν τὸν θεόν he called God his Father J 5: 18. οὐκέτι λέγω ὑμᾶς δούλους I no longer call you slaves 15: 15; cf. Ac 10: 28; Rv 2: 20. Pass. be called, named Mt 13: 55; Hb 11: 24. ὁ λεγόμενος the so-called (Epict. 4, 1, 51 οἱ βασιλεῖς λεγόμενοι; Socrat., Ep. 14, 7 ὁ λ. θάνατος) λεγόμενοι θεοί so-called gods 1 Cor 8: 5 (Herm. Wr. 2, 14 the λεγόμενοι θεοί in contrast to μόνος ὁ θεός. Somewhat differently Jos., Ant. 12, 125 Ἀντίοχος ὁ παρὰ τοῖς Ἕλλησιν θεὸς λεγόμενος). οἱ λεγόμενοι ἀκροβυστία ὑπὸ τῆς λ. περιτομῆς those who are called 'the uncircumcised' (i.e. Gentiles) by the so-called circumcision (i.e. Jews) Eph 2: 11. ὁ λεγόμενος (Bl-D. §412, 2; Rob. 1107. Cf. BGU 1117, 9 [13 BC]; PRyl. 133, 11; 137, 19; 2 Macc 12: 17; 14: 6; 3 Macc 1: 3) who is called ... Mt 1: 16; 27: 17; whose surname is (Appian, Liby. 49 §213 Ἄννων ὁ μέγας λεγόμενος; Jos., Ant. 13, 370, Vi. 4) 10: 2; Col 4: 11; by name Mt 9: 9; 26: 3, 14; 27: 16; Mk 15: 7; Lk 22: 47; J 9: 11.—Of things: of the name of a star Rv 8: 11. Of place-names (BGU 326, 19 [II AD]; 2 Macc 9: 2; 12: 21) Mt 2: 23; 26: 36; J 4: 5; 11: 54; 19: 13; Ac 3: 2; 6: 9; Hb 9: 3. Of the local, vernacular name λ. Ἑβραϊστί J 19: 17b.—In the transl. of foreign words (which) means: ὅ ἐστιν κρανίου τόπος λεγόμενος which means 'Place of a Skull' Mt 27: 33b. Cf. also J 4: 25; 11: 16; 20: 24; 21: 2. Also ὁ λέγεται 20: 16. ὁ λ. μεθερμηνευόμενον which, when translated, means 1: 38. ἣ διερμηνευομένη λέγεται Ac 9: 36.—Other exx. of the significance mean (Aeschyl.+) are 1 Cor 10: 29; Gal 4: 1; 2 Cl 6: 4; 8: 6.—ADebrunner, HKleinknecht, OProcksch, Gerh Kittel, TW IV 69-147: λέγω, λόγος, ῥῆμα, λαλέω. M-M. B. 1253f; 1257; 1277.

λεῖμμα, ατος, τό (Hdt. 1, 119; Plut., Mor. 78A; W-H. read λίμμα.—PTebt. 115, 2 [115/13 BC] τὸ γεγονὸς [=ὃς] λίμμα [Mayser p. 843]; 4 Km 19: 4 A λίμματος [Thackeray p. 84]; W-S. §5; 13e) remnant λ. κατ' ἐκλογὴν χάριτος γέγονεν there is a remnant chosen by grace Ro 11: 5 (cf. CD 1, 4).—JoachJeremias, D. Gedanke des 'Heiligen Restes' usw., ZNW 42, '49, 154-94.—VHerntrich and GSchrenck, TW IV 198-221; λεῖμμα and related words. M-M.*

λεῖος, α, ον (Hom.+; Dit., Syll.³ 972, 119; BGU 162, 5; 781 II, 15; LXX; En. 22, 2; Ep. Arist. 76; Philo; Jos., Ant. 15, 400) smooth, level of a road (opp. τραχὺς rough, as X., Mem. 3, 10, 1; Philo, Abr. 239) Lk 3: 5 (Is 40: 4 v.l.). M-M. B. 1068.*

λειποτακτέω or **λιποτακτέω** milit. t.t. leave the ranks, desert (Plut., Mor. 241A; Polemo, Decl. 2, 44 p. 31, 17; PLeipz. 45, 18; 46, 15; PLond. 1247, 14; 4 Macc 9: 23) fig. turn away (Philo, Gig. 43) ἀπό τινος from someth. ἀπὸ τοῦ θελήματος (θεοῦ) 1 Cl 21: 4.*

λείπω 2 aor. ἔλιπον, subj. 3 sing. λίπῃ Tit 3: 13 v.l. (Hom.+; inscr., pap., LXX, Joseph., Sib. Or. 3, 416).

1. trans. leave (behind); mid. and pass.—a. be left (behind), fall short, be inferior (Hdt. 7, 8, 1; Diod. S. 17, 46, 1; Jos., Bell. 3, 482, Ant. 14, 474) ἔν τινι in someth. (Sb 620, 6 [97/6 BC] of a temple λείπεσθαι ἐν τῷ μὴ εἶναι ἄσυλον; Dit., Syll.³ 618, 15; 800, 29; PGM 4, 2347) ἐν μηδενί fall short in no respect Js 1: 4.

b. be or do without, lack, be in need or want (of) w. gen. (Bl-D. §180, 4; cf. Soph., El. 474; Ps.-Pla., Axioch. 366D; later, e.g. Libanius, Progym.: Confirm. 1, 1 vol. VIII p. 138F. τῆς ἐνθέου μανίας) σοφίας be deficient in wisdom Js 1: 5. τῆς ἐφημέρου τροφῆς be in need of daily food 2: 15. θεοῦ lack God ITr 5: 2b. μηδενός lack nothing IPol 2: 2.

2. intr., act. lack, fall short (λείπει τί τινι: Polyb. 10, 18, 8; Epict. 2, 14, 19; Jos., Ant. 12, 36) σοὶ πολλὰ λείπει you fall far short Hv 3, 1, 9. πολλὰ ἡμῖν λείπει we lack much ITr 5: 2a. ἔτι ἕν σοι λείπει there is one thing that you still lack Lk 18: 22 (cf. Jos., Bell. 4, 257 τοῖς τολμήμασιν ἓν μόνον λείπει). ἵνα μηδὲν αὐτοῖς λείπῃ that they may lack nothing Tit 3: 13. τὰ λείποντα (Lucian, Syr. Dea 26) what is lacking, the defects 1: 5. W. inf. foll. λείπει τῷ πύργῳ ἔτι μικρὸν οἰκοδομηθῆναι the tower still lacks a little of being finished, is still not quite finished Hs 9, 9, 4. M-M. B. 839.*

λειτουργέω impf. ἐλειτούργουν; 1 aor. ἐλειτούργησα (X.+; inscr., pap., LXX, Ep. Arist., Philo, Joseph. On the spelling cf. Mayser 127; Mlt.-H. 76f) perform a public service, serve in a (public) office, in our lit. exclusively of religious and ritual services both in a wider and a more restricted sense (Dit., Syll.³ 717, 23f [100 BC] ἐλειτούργησαν ἐν τῷ ἱερῷ εὐτάκτως; 736, 73; 74f λειτουργούντω τοῖς θεοῖς; 97f [92 BC]; PLond. 33, 3 [II BC]; 41 B, 1; UPZ 42, 2 [162 BC]; 47, 3; BGU 1006, 10; LXX; Ep. Arist. 87; Dssm., B 137 [BS 140f]; Anz 346f).

1. lit., of the service performed by priests and Levites in the temple (cf. Ex 28: 35, 43; 29: 30; Num 18: 2; Sir 4: 14; 45: 15; Jdth 4: 14; 1 Macc 10: 42; Philo, Mos. 2, 152; Jos., Bell. 2, 409, Ant. 20, 218) abs. Hb 10: 11. λ. τῷ θυσιαστηρίῳ τοῦ θεοῦ perform services at the altar of God 1 Cl 32: 2 (cf. Jo 1, 9, 13); (w. ἱερατεύειν as Sir 45: 15) λ. τῷ θεῷ 43: 4.—Of Christian services ἐν τ. θυσιαστηρίῳ λ. τὸ θεῖον perform service to God at the altar Tit 1: 9 v.l.

2. fig., of the various ways in which the religious man serves God (Dionys. Hal. 2, 22 ἐπὶ τῶν ἱερῶν), including prayer (w. νηστεύειν, and of the prophets and teachers) τ. κυρίῳ Ac 13: 2. λ. τῷ θεῷ (cf. Jo 1: 13b) Hm 5, 1, 2; cf. 3; s 7: 6. Of OT worthies οἱ τελείως λειτουργήσαντες those who have rendered perfect service to God 1 Cl 9: 2.

3. serve gener. (X., Mem. 2, 7, 6; Chares in Athen. 12, 54 p. 538E) ἐν τοῖς σαρκικοῖς λ. do a service in material things Ro 15: 27.—Of the officials of Christian churches: λ. ἀμέμπτως τῷ ποιμνίῳ τοῦ Χριστοῦ serve Christ's flock blamelessly 1 Cl 9: 2; 44: 3. Of the bishops Hs 9, 27, 3. Of the bishops and deacons λ. τὴν λειτουργίαν τῶν προφητῶν καὶ διδασκάλων perform the service of prophets and teachers D 15: 1 (s. 2 above on Ac 13: 2.—λειτ. λ. oft. in LXX; also Philo, Spec. Leg. 1, 82; Dit., Syll.³ 409, 61).—Of angels (Test. Levi 3: 5) τῷ θελήματι αὐτοῦ (sc. θεοῦ) λειτουργοῦσιν παρεστῶτες they stand at his side and serve his will 1 Cl 34: 5; cf. vs. 6 (Da 7: 10 Theod.).—On this entry and the foll. one s. Elbogen 5; 511; FOertel, D. Liturgie, '17; WBrandt, D. Wortgruppe λειτουργεῖν im Hb u. 1 Kl: Jahrb. d. Theol. Schule Bethel 1, '30, 145-76; OCasel, λειτουργία—munus: Oriens Christ. III 7, '32, 289-302; EPeterson, Nuntius 2, '49, 10f; HStrathmann u. RMeyer, TW IV 221-38 λειτ.

and related words; ARomeo, Miscellanea Liturgica (L Mohlberg-Festschr.), vol. 2, '49, 467-519; FWDanker, FWGingrich-Festschr. '72, 108ff. M-M.*

λειτουργία, ας, ἡ (Pla.+; inscr., pap., LXX, Ep. Arist., Philo, Joseph., loanw. in rabb.) *service,* the usual designation for a service performed by an individual for the state (oft. free of charge), in our lit. always used w. some sort of relig. connotation.

1. of ritual and cultic services (Diod. S. 1, 21, 7; Dit., Syll.³ 1109, 111; UPZ 17, 17 [163 BC] λ. τῷ θεῷ; 40, 19 [161 BC]; PTebt. 302, 30 [cf. Dssm. B 138—BS 141]; Ex 37: 19; Num 8: 22; 16: 9; 18: 4; 2 Ch 31: 2; Ep. Arist.; Philo, Virt. 54 al.; Jos., Bell. 1, 26, Ant. 3, 107 al.) *service as priest* Lk 1: 23. τὰς προσφορὰς καὶ λειτουργίας ἐπιτελεῖσθαι *bring offerings and perform (other) ceremonial services* 1 Cl 40: 2. τὰ σκεύη τῆς λ. *the vessels used in priestly service* Hb 9: 21. Of the high priest's service 1 Cl 40: 5. Fig., of the high-priestly office of Christ Hb 8: 6.

2. of other kinds of service to God 1 Cl 20: 10. Of Noah 1 Cl 9: 4. Of Paul (w. θυσία, q.v.; cf. BGU 1201, 7 [2 AD] πρὸς τὰς λιτουργείας καὶ θυσείας τῶν θεῶν) *sacrificial service* Phil 2: 17. Of Epaphroditus' services to Paul ἵνα ἀναπληρώσῃ τὸ ὑμῶν ὑστέρημα τῆς πρός με λειτουργίας *in order that he might supply what was lacking in your service to me* vs. 30.—Of officials in Christian churches διαδέχεσθαι τὴν λ. αὐτῶν *succeed to their office* 1 Cl 44: 2; ἡ αὐτοῖς τετιμημένη λ. *the office held in honor by them* 44: 6; ἀποβάλλεσθαι τῆς λ. *be removed from office* 44: 3. On D 15: 1 cf. λειτουργέω 3.—Also of the activities of the layman in the church service μὴ παρεκβαίνειν τὸν ὡρισμένον τῆς λ. αὐτοῦ κανόνα *not overstepping the fixed boundaries of his ministry* 1 Cl 41: 1. W. ref. to the collection ἡ διακονία τῆς λ. ταύτης 2 Cor 9: 12. Of acts that show forth Christian charity and other virtues, and thus call forth God's approval: αἱ λ. αὗται *these services* Hs 5, 3, 3; cf. 8.—ESchweizer, D. Leben d. Herrn in d. Gemeinde u. ihren Diensten, '46, 19-23. M-M.*

λειτουργικός, ή, όν (PPetr. II 39[e] [6 times; s. Dssm., B 138 (BS 141)]; PTebt. 5, 49 [118 BC]; 102, 3. But also in a ritual sense PTebt. 88, 3 [115/14 BC] ἡμέραι λιτουργικαί = the days when the prophets of the temple are permitted to perform certain holy acts [Wilcken, Chrest. p. 94; WOtto, Priester u. Tempel im hellenist. Ägypt. II '08 p. 33, 2; 39, 2]; likew. Wilcken, Chrest. no. 115, 15; 146; Ex 31: 10; 39: 12; Num 4: 12, 26; 2 Ch 24: 14) *engaged in holy service of angels* Hb 1: 14 (cf. Philo, Virt. 74 ἄγγελοι λειτουργοί). M-M.*

λειτουργός, οῦ, ὁ (Polyb.+; inscr., pap., LXX) *servant,* in our lit. always w. relig. connotations (λ. τῶν θεῶν Dionys. Hal. 2, 2, 3; 2, 73, 2; Plut., Mor. 417A; inscr. [I BC: Rev. des Études anciennes 32, '30, p. 5] θεοῖς λιτουργοί; inscr. fr. Miletus: GKawerau and ARehm, D. Delphinion in M. '14, 396; LXX; Ep. Arist. 95; Philo).

1. lit., of pagan government officials λ. θεοῦ *servants of God* Ro 13: 6 (cf. AvanVeldhuizen, Wie zijn λειτουργοί θεοῦ in Ro 13: 6: ThSt 32, '14, 302-11). Of heavenly beings as *servants* of God Hb 1: 7; 1 Cl 36: 3 (both Ps 103: 4; cf. 102: 21; Philo, Virt. 74 ἄγγελοι λειτουργοί).

2. of priests 1 Cl 41: 2. Of Christ, the true High Priest τῶν ἁγίων λ. καὶ τῆς σκηνῆς τῆς ἀληθινῆς *a minister in the sanctuary and in the true tabernacle* Hb 8: 2 (Philo, Leg. All. 3, 135 λειτουργὸς τῶν ἁγίων).—Also of the prophets οἱ λειτουργοὶ τῆς χάριτος τοῦ θεοῦ 1 Cl 8: 1. Of

Paul, apostle to the Gentiles, λ. Χριστοῦ Ἰησοῦ εἰς τὰ ἔθνη *a servant of Christ Jesus for the Gentiles* Ro 15: 16.

3. fig. of Epaphroditus λειτουργὸς τῆς χρείας μου *the one who has served my needs* Phil 2: 25. M-M.*

λείχω (Aeschyl., Hdt.+; LXX) *lick* τὶ *someth.,* of dogs (3 Km 20: 19) Lk 16: 21 D. B. 267.*

Λέκτρα, ας, ἡ *Lectra* 2 Ti 4: 19 v.l. as wife of Aquila.*

λεμά Mt 27: 46; s. λαμά.

λέντιον, ου, τό (Lat. loanw.: linteum, also in rabb.; Peripl. Eryth. c. 6; Arrian, Peripl. 4; Inschr. v. Magn. 116, 34; POxy. 929, 10 λίνον καὶ λέντιον; Ostraka II 1611, 1; Hahn 235; 262; 266) *linen cloth* Hv 3, 1, 4; *towel* J 13: 4f (Vi. Aesopi I c. 61 of a woman who is preparing to wash another person's feet: περιζωσαμένη λέντιον). M-M.*

λεόπαρδος, ου, ὁ (Galen: CMG V 4, 1, 1 p. 86, 15; Anecdota Astrol. [ALudwich, Maximi et Ammonis carmina 1877] p. 122, 2; Theognost.: Anecd. Gr. p. 1394; Acta Phil. 36; 50 Bonnet; Athanasius, Vi. Anton. 9 vol. I 640) *leopard,* fig. for rough soldiers δεδεμένος (ἐνδεδεμένος Lghtf.) δέκα λεοπάρδοις *bound to ten 'leopards'* IRo 5: 1 (the addition of ὅ ἐστι στρατιωτικὸν τάγμα establishes the fact that the language is fig. here; it is all the more appropriate because Ignatius is being taken as a prisoner to Rome to fight w. wild beasts).*

λεπίς, ίδος, ἡ (Hdt.+; Inscr. Gr. 833, 11 [279 BC]; BGU 544, 8; PGM 4, 258 al.; LXX; Philo; Jos., Ant. 3, 149) *scale.*

1. lit., of the scales of fish B 10: 1 (cf. Lev 11: 9ff; Dt 14: 9f).

2. fig. ἀπέπεσαν αὐτοῦ ἀπὸ τῶν ὀφθαλμῶν ὡς λεπίδες *someth. like scales fell fr. his eyes,* i.e. he suddenly regained his sight Ac 9: 18. For the expr. cf. Galen: CMG V 4, 1, 1 p. 77, 3 οἷον λεπὶς ἀπέπιπτε='someth. like a scale fell off' (other exx. in Hobart 39). On the figure cf. Tob 11: 12. M-M.*

λέπρα, ας, ἡ (Hdt.+; Galen: CMG V 4, 2 p. 333, 5; 429, 11; LXX, Philo; Jos., Ant. 3, 265, C. Ap. 1, 235) *leprosy.* In pre-Bibl. Gk. λ. = 'psoriasis'. There is abundant evidence that not all the צָרַעַת (cf. Lev 13 and 14) and λέπρα of the Bible is true *leprosy* caused by Hansen's bacillus as known in modern times; indeed, there are many (see Gramberg and Cochrane below) who hold that Hansen's disease was unknown in biblical times, or known by a different name than leprosy. λέπρα in LXX and NT prob. refers to such skin diseases as psoriasis, lupus, ringworm, and favus: Mt 8: 3; Mk 1: 42; Lk 5: 12f; UGosp 39 (= AHuck⁹-HLietzmann, Synopse '36, p. 37 note [in Engl., Gosp. Parallels, '49, p. 32 note]).—GNMünch, Die Zaraath (Lepra) der hebr. Bibel 1893; ELMcEwen, Biblical World 38, '11, 194-202; 255-61; LSHuizinga, Leprosy: Bibliotheca Sacra 83, '26, 29-46; 202-12; Billerb. IV '28, 745-63; Handb. d. Haut- u. Geschlechtskrankheiten, ed. JJadassohn, vol. X: Die Lepra '30; FCLendrum, The Name 'Leprosy': Amer. Journ. of Tropical Medicine and Hygiene 1, '52, 999-1008. Series of articles in the Bible Translator: KPCAGramberg, 11, '60, 10-20; JLSwellengrebel, 11, '60, 69-80, with note by EANida; RGCochrane, Biblical Leprosy, 12 '61, 202f, w. mention of a separate publ. of the same title; '61; DHWallington, 12, '61, 75-79; SGBrowne, ET 73, '62, 242-45.*

λεπράω 1 aor. ἐλέπρησα (Hdt., Hippocr.+; Num 12: 10) *be* or *become leprous, scaly* restored ἐλ[έπρησα] UGosp

1, 35; reproduced KAland, Synopsis 4 Evangeliorum '64, p. 315.*

λεπρός, ά, όν (Aristoph., fgm. 723 K.; Theophr.; Herodas 6, 36 et al.; LXX; orig. 'scaly') *leprous* (so Theophr., Caus. Pl. 2, 6, 4; LXX) λεπροὶ ἄνδρες Lk 17: 12.—Subst. ὁ λ. *the leper* (Philo, Leg. All. 3, 7; Jos., Ant. 3, 264, C. Ap. 1, 278) Mt 8: 2; 10: 8; 11: 5; Mk 1: 40 (ChMasson, La péricope du lépreux [Mk 1: 40-5]: RThPh n.s. 23, '39, 287-95); Lk 4: 27; 7: 22 (on Mt 11: 5 and Lk 7: 22 s. κωφός 2); UGosp 32. As surname of Simon of Bethany (cf. Sb 7638, 4f [257 BC] τὴν Νικάνορος τοῦ ποδαγρικοῦ οἰκίαν) Mt 26: 6; Mk 14: 3.*

λεπτός, ή, όν (Hom.+; Dit., Syll.³ 567, 6; pap., LXX, Philo; Jos., Bell. 2, 154; Sib. Or. 1, 361).
1. *small, thin, light* ὄστρακον λ. Hs 9, 10, 1; θηρία λ. *tiny animals* AP fgm. 2 p. 12, 27.
2. τὸ λ. (sc. νόμισμα with Artem. 2, 58; Pollux 9, 92 or κέρμα w. Alciphr. 1, 9, 1) *small copper coin*, worth normally about one-eighth of a cent. Mk 12: 42; Lk 12: 59; 21: 2. (Cf. Dit., Or. 484, 35, Syll.³ 1109, 80; 98f.)—S. on ἀργύριον 2c. M-M. B. 889.*

Λευί (לֵוִי), ὁ indecl. (Bl-D. §53, 1) and **Λευίς** gen. Λευί, acc. Λευίν (Bl-D. §55, 1e; W-S. §10, 5; Wuthnow 67. Mlt.-H. 146 Λευείς) *Levi* (LXX; Ep. Arist. 48; Philo, Joseph., Test. 12 Patr.).
1. son of Jacob Hb 7: 9. οἱ υἱοὶ Λευί vs. 5; φυλὴ Λ. Rv 7: 7.
2. son of Melchi; in the genealogy of Jesus Lk 3: 24.—
3. son of Symeon; in the genealogy of Jesus vs. 29.
4. a disciple of Jesus, called by him fr. the tax-collector's office Lk 5: 27, 29. Acc. to Mk 2: 14 this disciple was a son of Alphaeus (s. Ἀλφαῖος 1). GP 14: 60 also speaks of a Λευ(ε)ὶς ὁ τοῦ Ἀλφαίου as a disciple of Jesus. On Mt 9: 9 s. Ματθαῖος.
5. name of a high priest, partly restored by conjecture GOxy 10.—HStrathmann, TW IV 241-5.*

Λευίτης, ου, ὁ (LXX, Philo, Joseph.; Plut., Mor. 671ε) *a Levite*, member of the tribe of Levi, esp. one who did not belong to the family of Aaron, and whose duty it was to perform the lowlier services connected w. the temple ritual. W. ἱερεύς Lk 10: 32; J 1: 19; 1 Cl 32: 2; 40: 5. Of Joseph Barnabas Ac 4: 36.—JAEmerton, Vetus T 12, '62, 129-38 (Deut.); AHJGunneweg, Leviten u. Priester, '65; RMeyer, TW IV 245-7.*

Λευιτικός, ή, όν (Lev, title; Philo) *Levitical* Λ. ἱερωσύνη the Levitical (i.e. OT) *priesthood* Hb 7: 11.*

λευκαίνω 1 aor. ἐλεύκανα (Bl-D. §72; Mlt.-H. 214f), inf. λευκᾶναι (Hom.+; Apollod. [II BC]: 244 fgm. 107c Jac.; Sb 6754, 18; LXX; Philo, Leg. All. 2, 43) *make white*.
1. lit. of clothes whitened by the fuller (Aesop, Fab. 29 P.=59 H.) Mk 9: 3.
2. fig., *make* blood-red sins *white* 1 Cl 8: 4 (Is 1: 18); cf. 18: 7 (Ps 50: 9). In the apocal. figure, of the martyrs: ἐλεύκαναν τὰς στολὰς αὐτῶν ἐν τῷ αἵματι τοῦ ἀρνίου *they have made their robes white in the blood of the Lamb* Rv 7: 14. M-M.*

λευκοβύσσινος s. λευκός 2, end.

λευκός, ή, όν (Hom.+; inscr., pap., LXX, En., Philo, Joseph., Test. 12 Patr.; Sib. Or. 3, 617; 622; loanw. in rabb.).
1. *bright, shining, gleaming* (Hom.+) λ. ὡς τὸ φῶς (Il. 14, 185 λ. ἠέλιος ὡς) *brilliant as light* Mt 17: 2. λ.

ἐξαστράπτων Lk 9: 29. This mng. is also poss. for some of the foll. pass.
2. *white* (including, for the Greeks, many shades of that color; cf. our 'white' wine) of hair (Tyrtaeus [VII BC] 7, 23 of an old man's hair; Soph., Ant. 1092; Lev 13: 3ff) Mt 5: 36 (opp. μέλας as Menand., Sam. 262 of A., who dyes his white hair); Rv 1: 14a. Of a goatskin Hv 5: 1; s 6, 2, 5. Of a pebble, used for voting etc. (Lucian, Harmonides 3 p. 855f ψῆφον...τὴν λευκὴν καὶ σῴζουσαν) Rv 2: 17. Of wool (PRyl. 146, 15 [39 AD]; Da 7: 9 ὡσεὶ ἔριον λ.; En. 106, 2) 1: 14b. Of apocal. horses (Zech 1: 8. S. πυρρός) 6: 2; 19: 11, 14a. Of an apocal. monster w. the colors black, red, gold and white Hv 4, 1, 10; cf. 4, 3, 5. Of a cloud Rv 14: 14. Of stones (Inscr. Gr. 509, 17 [241 BC]; Dit., Or. 219, 36; 268, 17; 339, 34; 105 al. in inscr.) Hv 3, 2, 8; 3, 5, 1; 3, 6, 5; s 9, 4, 5; 9, 6, 4; 9, 8, 5; 9, 9, 1. Of a chair v 1, 2, 2. Of fields of ripe grain λ. πρὸς θερισμόν *white for the harvest* J 4: 35. Of a mountain Hs 9, 1, 10; 9, 29, 1; 9, 30, 1f; 4. Of a rock 9, 2, 1. Of a throne Rv 20: 11. Of garments (Plut., Aristid. 21, 4 festive garment; Inschr. v. Priene 205 εἰσίναι εἰς τὸ ἱερὸν ἁγνὸν ἐν ἐσθῆτι λευκῇ; POxy. 471, 95ff; 531, 13; PGM 4, 636; Eccl 9: 8; 2 Macc 11: 8; Jos., Bell. 2, 1, Ant. 11, 327; Test. Levi 8: 2) Mk 9: 3; 16: 5 (Lucian, Philops. 25 of a heavenly messenger: νεανίας πάγκαλος λευκὸν ἱμάτιον περιβεβλημένος); Ac 1: 10; Rv 3: 5, 18; 4: 4; 6: 11; 7: 9, 13. A garment is λ. ὡς χιών (Da 7: 9 Theod.) Mt 28: 3; Mk 9: 3 t.r.; Hs 8, 2, 3. ἐν λευκοῖς (sc. ἱματίοις) *in white* (Artem. 2, 3 p. 86, 17; 4, 2 p. 205, 9) J 20: 12; Rv 3: 4; Hv 4, 2, 1; s 8, 2, 4 v.l.; βύσσινον λ. *a white linen garment* Rv 19: 14b (v.l. λευκοβύσσινον). Of a priest's clothing made of white linen (cf. Schürer II⁴ 338f) GOxy 27. Of shoes Hv 4, 2, 1.—GRadke, D. Bedeutg. d. weissen u. schwarzen Farbe in Kult u. Brauch d. Griech. u. Römer, Diss. Berlin '36; RGradwohl, D. Farben im AT, '63, 34-50; WMichaelis, TW IV 247-56. M-M. B. 1052; 1054.*

λέων, οντος, ὁ (Hom.+; inscr.; BGU 957, 4 [10 BC]; PGrenf. II 84, 7; LXX; Philo; Jos., Ant. 8, 389 [lit.]; Test. 12 Patr.) *lion*.
1. lit. Hb 11: 33; MPol 12: 2. Symbol of rapacity 1 Cl 35: 11 (Ps 49: 22 v.l. [ARahlfs, Psalmi cum Odis '31]). λάκκος λεόντων (s. λάκκος) 45: 6. Of the devil ὡς λ. ὠρυόμενος περιπατεῖ *he goes about like a roaring lion* 1 Pt 5: 8 (Ps 21: 14; cf. Joseph and Asenath 12, 9 ὁ λέων ὁ ἄγριος ὁ παλαιὸς καταδιώκει με). Apocalyptic usage also makes comparisons w. the lion, or parts of his body, or his actions (Il. 6, 181; Strabo 16, 4, 16 fabulous beings: σφίγγες κ. κυνοκέφαλοι κ. κῆβοι [monkeys] λέοντος μὲν πρόσωπον ἔχοντες τὸ δὲ λοιπὸν σῶμα πάνθηρος κτλ.; quite similarly Diod. S. 3, 35, 6) Rv 4: 7; 9: 8 (cf. Jo 1: 6), 17; 10: 3; 13: 2.
2. fig. ῥυσθῆναι ἐκ στόματος λ. *be rescued from the jaws of the lion*, i.e. fr. great danger 2 Ti 4: 17 (cf. Ps 21: 22).—Of a lion-hearted hero (cf. Lycophron 33 [Heracles]; Ael. Aristid. 46 p. 191f D. [Pericles]; Esth 4: 17s; Jos., Ant. 18, 228), the Messiah ὁ λ. ὁ ἐκ τῆς φυλῆς Ἰούδα *the lion fr. the tribe of Judah* Rv 5: 5 (cf. Gen 49: 9).—ERGoodenough, Jewish Symbols VII, '58, 29-86; W Michaelis, TW IV 256-9. M-M. B. 185.*

λήθη, ης, ἡ (Hom.+; Vett. Val. 242, 4; Maspéro 4, 4; LXX; En. 5, 8; Philo; Jos., Ant. 15, 376) *forgetfulness* λήθην λαμβάνειν τινός *forget someth.* (s. λαμβάνω 2) 2 Pt 1: 9. M-M.*

λῆμμα, ατος, τό (Soph., Pla.+; pap., LXX, Philo; Jos., Bell. 1, 289, Ant. 14, 393) *gain* διὰ τ. ἐπιθυμίαν τοῦ λ. *because of the desire for gain* Hs 9, 19, 3.*

λῆμψις, εως, ἡ (Soph., Thu.+; PTebt. 238 [II BC]; POxy. 71 I, 18. On the spelling cf. the lit. given s.v. λαμβάνω on λήμψομαι) receiving, credit κοινωνεῖν εἰς λόγον δόσεως καὶ λ. Phil 4: 15 (s. on δόσις 2). ἐν πικρίᾳ γίνεσθαι . . . περὶ δόσεως καὶ λ. become bitter . . . about giving and receiving, 'debit and credit' Hm 5, 2, 2. M-M.*

ληνός, οῦ, ἡ wine-press (so Theocr.; Diod. S. 3, 63, 4; inscr.: Sb 7541, 11 [II AD]; PAmh. 48, 7 [106 BC]; POxy. 729, 19; LXX; Jos., Ant. 5, 213 al.) γεννήματα λ. produce of the wine-press (cf. Num 18: 30) D 13: 3 (s. on γέννημα). Hewn in the rock (cf. POxy. 502, 36 [164 AD] τὰς ληνοὺς λιθίνας) Mt 21: 33.—In Rv fig. πατεῖν τὴν λ. tread the wine-press (i.e. the grapes in it; Diod. S. 4, 5, 1 πατῆσαι τ. σταφυλὰς ἐν ληνῷ; s. also 2 Esdr 23 [Neh 13]: 15; La 1: 15; cf. Jer 31: 33) Rv 19: 15; pass. 14: 20a. βάλλειν εἰς τὴν ληνόν pour into the wine-press (cf. Anacreontea 59, 4 Pr. κατὰ ληνὸν βάλλειν . . . πατεῖν) 14: 19. Blood (cf. the 'blood of the grape') flows fr. the wine-press vs. 20b.—GBornkamm, TW IV 259-62. M-M.*

λῆρος, ου, ὁ (Aristoph.+; X., An. 7, 7, 41; PSI 534, 16; 4 Macc 5: 11; Philo, Post. Cai. 165; Jos., Bell. 3, 405) idle talk, nonsense, humbug ἐφάνησαν ἐνώπιον αὐτῶν ὡσεὶ λῆρος τὰ ῥήματα ταῦτα these words seemed to them to be nonsense Lk 24: 11. M-M.*

ληρώδης, ες (Pla.+; BGU 1011 II, 15 [II BC]; 2 Macc 12: 44; Philo, Leg. ad Gai. 168) foolish, silly, frivolous Dg 8: 2.*

λῃστής, οῦ, ὁ (Soph., Hdt.+; inscr., pap., LXX, Joseph.; loanw. in rabb.).
1. robber, highwayman, bandit (in Palestine: Jos., Bell. 2, 125; 228 al.) Lk 10: 30, 36; 2 Cor 11: 26 (Charito 6, 4, 6 λῃσταῖς θαλάττῃ). Crucified Mt 27: 38, 44; Mk 15: 27. W. κλέπτης (Pla., Rep. 351c; Ep. 63 of Apollonius of Tyana [Philostrat. I 363, 21]) J 10: 1, 8. σπήλαιον λῃστῶν a den of robbers (Jer 7: 11) Mt 21: 13; Mk 11: 17; Lk 19: 46; 2 Cl 14: 1 (GWBuchanan, Hebrew Union Coll. Annual 30, '59, 169-77: 'cave of brigands'; s. ἱερόν 2, end).—This mng. was extended to signify
2. revolutionary, insurrectionist (Jos., Bell. 2, 254= σικάριος; 253; 4, 504, Ant. 14, 159f; 20, 160f; 167) of Barabbas (cf. μετὰ τῶν στασιαστῶν Mk 15: 7) J 18: 40 (HARigg, Jr., JBL 64, '45, 444 n. 95; HGWood, NTS 2, '55/'56, 262-66 and JJTwomey, Scripture (Edinburgh) 8, '56, 115-19 support this, but see MHengel, Die Zeloten, '61, 25-47; 344-48); prob. also in the words of Jesus Mt 26: 55; Mk 14: 48; Lk 22: 52; MPol 7: 1 (cf. Mt 26: 55).—KHRengstorf, TW IV 262-7. M-M. B. 791.*

λῆψις s. λῆμψις.

λίαν adv. (Hom.+ as λίην; as λίαν Pind.+; inscr., pap., LXX, En., Ep. Arist., Joseph.) very (much), exceedingly.
1. used w. verbs: preceding them (Ep. Arist. 312; Jos., Vi. 404) λ. ἀντέστη he vehemently opposed 2 Ti 4: 15. λ. πρόσεχε be scrupulously on your guard D 6: 3. Following them (Gen 4: 5) ἐθυμώθη λ. he became very angry Mt 2: 16. θαυμάζειν . . . λ. 27: 14; ἔκλαυσα λ. I wept bitterly Hm 3: 3; J. he was very glad Lk 23: 8. In a letter ἐχάρην λίαν I was very glad (BGU 632, 10; PGiess. 21, 3) 2 J 4; 3 J 3. Strengthened λίαν ἐκ περισσοῦ altogether Mk 6: 51.
2. used w. adjs., which—a. serve as attribute (Dit., Syll.³ 1102, 12 αἱ λίαν ἄκαιροι δαπάναι) ὄρος ὑψηλὸν λ. very high Mt 4: 8; χαλεποὶ λ. very dangerous 8: 28.

b. serve as predicate: preceding (Diod. S. 14, 58, 2 λίαν ὀχυρός; PTebt. 315, 18 ὁ ἄνθρωπος λείαν ἐστὶν αὐστηρός) αἰσχρὰ καὶ λ. αἰσχρά shameful, very shameful 1 Cl 47: 6. λ. ἄφρων εἰμί Hm 4, 2, 1; cf. 8: 6; s 2: 5 al. Following (Gen 1: 31; Tob 6: 12 S) ἐγένετο λευκὰ λ. Mk 9: 3; περίλυπος ἤμην λ. I was extremely unhappy Hv 3, 10, 6.
3. used w. an adv., following it (Da 11: 25) πρωΐ ἔννυχα λ. early in the morning, when it was still quite dark Mk 1: 35. Preceding it (2 Macc 11: 1; Ep. Arist. 230; Jos., C. Ap. 1, 286; 2, 3; PMich. 154, 17 λ. νυκτός) λ. πρωΐ very early in the morning 16: 2. Cf. ὑπερλίαν. M-M.**

λίβα s. λίψ.

Λίβανος, ου, ὁ (Theophr., On Plants 9, 7, 1; Diod. S. 19, 58, 2f) (the) Lebanon a mountain range in Syria following the coast of the Mediterranean, famous for its cedars 1 Cl 14: 5 (Ps 36: 35).—Pauly-W. XIII, 1, 1-11; IDB III 105-7.*

λίβανος, ου, ὁ (= the tree Hdt.+; = the resinous gum Pind.+; inscr., pap.; LXX; Jos., Ant. 3, 143; cf. Phryn. 187 L.) frankincense, a white resinous gum, obtained fr. several kinds of a certain tree in Arabia, used both medicinally and for cult purposes (EHMaehler, ZPE 4, '69, 99). 1 Cl 25: 2; Rv 18: 13. W. gold and myrrh as a precious gift Mt 2: 11 (cf. Diod. S. 19, 94, 5; Is 60: 6; for frankincense and myrrh together s. Diod. S. 3, 46, 3; Strabo 16, 4, 14 p. 774; Polyaenus 8, 26; En. 29, 2; PGM 13, 354.—As early as Empedocles 128, ὁ σμύρνη and λίβανος are valuable as sacrificial gifts to the gods. Sib. Or. III, 772: a messianic gift).—ILöw, D. Flora d. Juden I '28, 312-14. M-M.*

λιβανωτός, οῦ, ὁ—1. (frank)incense (so Hdt.+; Diod. S. 2, 49, 2 [offered to the gods throughout the world]; Dit., Or. 383, 142 [I BC] λιβανωτοῦ κ. ἀρωμάτων al. in inscr.; PHib. 121, 54 [III BC]; POxy. 118, 20; 234 II, 38; Mayser 40; 1 Ch 9: 29 λ. κ. τῶν ἀρωμάτων; 3 Macc 5: 2; Philo, Spec. Leg. 1, 275; Jos., Ant. 3, 256) ὡς λιβανωτοῦ πνέοντος ἢ ἄλλου τινὸς τῶν ἀρωμάτων MPol 15: 2.
2. censer, in which incense is burned Rv 8: 3, 5. M-M.*

Λιβερτῖνος, ου, ὁ (Lat. loanw.: libertinus; IG XIV 1781) Freedman Ac 6: 9, a designation for certain Jews in Jerusalem who had their own synagogue (Schürer II⁴ 87; 502, 7; III⁴ 128, 23; Ltzm., ZNW 20, '21, 172) like the Libertini in Pompeii (GBdeRossi, Bull. di arch. christ. 1864, 70; 92f). The name describes these people as former slaves or their descendants. The change to Λιβυστίνων (this word in Stephan. Byz. s.v. Λίβυς)='Libyans' (so the Armen. version) was first proposed in the 16th cent. (RHarris, ET 6, 1895, 378-90), and more recently favored by FrBlass, Philol. of the Gospels 1898, 69f; Moffatt; Gdspd., Probs. 127-30.—HStrathmann, TW IV 269f. M-M.*

Λιβύη, ης, ἡ (Hom.+; Dit., Or. 54, 5 [III BC]; Sb 4456 gravestone [II BC] al. in inscr., pap. [Mayser 101]; Philo, Joseph., Sib. Or.) Libya, a district in N. Africa betw. Egypt and Cyrene; the western part, Libya Cyrenaica, is meant by τὰ μέρη τῆς Λ. τῆς κατὰ Κυρήνην the parts of Libya near Cyrene Ac 2: 10 (Jos., Ant. 16, 160 ἡ πρὸς Κυρήνην Λιβύη).*

Λιβυστῖνος s. Λιβερτῖνος.

λιθάζω 1 aor. ἐλίθασα, pass. ἐλιθάσθην (since Anaxandrides Com. [IV BC], fgm. 16; Aristot., mostly abs. 'throw stones'; 2 Km 16: 6, 13; Jos., C. Ap. 2, 206 cod.) *stone* τινά *someone*. In the OT and the Mishna (Sanhedrin 6; 7, 4–8, 5, ed. SKrauss '33, 181ff; 215ff) a means of capital punishment for certain crimes: adultery J 8: 5; esp. blasphemy; somet. the populace became aroused and took upon itself the task of pronouncing and carrying out such a sentence: 10: 31ff (on λιθάζετε vs. 32 *you are trying to stone* cf. Rob. 880); 11: 8; Ac 5: 26; 14: 19; 2 Cor 11: 25; 1 Cl 5: 6; GP 11: 48. W. other forms of death Hb 11: 37; cf. 1 Cl 45: 4.—RHirzel, Die Strafe der Steinigung: Abh. d. Sächs. Ges. d. Wiss. 27, '09, 223–66; JBlinzler, CFD Moule-Festschr. '70, 147–61. M-M.*

λίθινος, ίνη, ον (Pind., Hdt.+; inscr., pap., LXX; Jos., Ant. 14, 57; 15, 401) (*made of*) *stone*.
1. lit. εἴδωλα Rv 9: 20; cf. Dg 2: 7 (s. Da 5: 4, 23 Theod.; Hermocles [IV/III BC] p. 174, 19 Coll. [= Athen. 6, 63 p. 253E] in contrast to a ξύλινος or λίθινος θεός, Demetrius Poliorcetes is an ἀληθινός.—Diod. S. 22, 9, 4 ἀγάλματα [= θεοί] λίθινα κ. ξύλινα). ὑδρίαι *water-jars* J 2: 6 (cf. POxy. 937, 13 τῆς φιάλης τῆς λιθίνης). Of the tables of the law πλάκες λ. (LXX) 2 Cor 3: 3; B 4: 7 (Ex 31: 18).
2. fig. (Herodas 7, 109; Dio Chrys. 71[21], 13; Ps.-Aeschin., Ep. 10, 10; Alciphr. 4, 16, 7; Libanius, Or. 25, 47 vol. II p. 559, 12 F.; Philo, Mos. 2, 202 λ. ψυχή) of the heart καρδία λ. *a stony heart*, i.e. one without feeling B 6: 14 (Ezk 11: 19; 36: 26). M-M.*

λιθοβολέω impf. ἐλιθοβόλουν; 1 aor. ἐλιθοβόλησα; 1 fut. pass. λιθοβοληθήσομαι.
1. *throw stones at* someone (Diod. S. 13, 10, 6; 17, 41, 8; Plut., Mor. 1011E) Mt 21: 35; Mk 12: 4 t.r.; Ac 14: 5 (for the acc. to denote the goal, *at somebody* or *someth.* cf. Ps.-Demetr. c. 115).
2. *stone* (*to death*) (LXX) τινά *someone* God's messengers Mt 23: 37; Lk 13: 34. Stephen Ac 7: 58f. (Arrian, Anab. 4, 14, 3: the conspirators against Alexander are stoned after the trial by those present [πρὸς τῶν παρόντων]. Pass. (Aristodemus [II BC]: no. 383 fgm. 6 Jac.) J 8: 5 v.l. An animal Hb 12: 20 (cf. Ex 19: 13). M-M.*

λιθοξόος, ου, ὁ (Timon in Diog. L. 2, 19) *sculptor* (so Plut., Mor. 74D; Ptolem., Apotel. 4, 4, 5; IG III 1372) Dg 2: 3.*

λίθος, ου, ὁ (Hom.+; inscr., pap., LXX, En., Ep. Arist., Philo, Joseph., Test. 12 Patr. In our lit. always masc.) *stone*.
1. lit.—a. gener., of stones of any kind: Mt 3: 9 (ZNW 9, '08, 77f; 341f); 4: 3, 6 (Ps 90: 12); 7: 9; Mk 5: 5; Lk 3: 8; 4: 3, 11 (Ps 90: 12); 11: 11 v.l.; 19: 40 (cf. 4 Esdr 5: 5 and the 'hearing' πέτραι PGM 36, 263); 22: 41; J 8: 7, 59; 10: 31; LJ 1: 5 (cf. Lucian, Hermotim. 81 p. 826 ὁ θεὸς οὐκ ἐν οὐρανῷ ἐστιν, ἀλλὰ διὰ πάντων πεφοίτηκεν, οἷον ξύλων κ. λίθων κ. ζῴων).
b. of stones used in building (Dio Chrys. 57[74], 26; Oenomaus in Euseb., Pr. Ev. 5, 24, 4 λίθοι καὶ ξύλοι; Palaeph. p. 62, 7; PPetr. II 13[18a], 7 [258 BC]; Dt 27: 5f; 3 Km 6: 7) Mt 24: 2; Mk 13: 1f (LGaston, No Stone on Another, '70 [fall of Jerus.]); Lk 19: 44; 21: 6 (λίθος ἐπὶ λίθῳ as Aristippus in Diog. L. 2, 72); Hv 3, 2, 4ff; 3, 4, 3; 3, 5, 1ff; 3, 6, 3; 6f; 3, 7, 1; 5; s 9, 3, 3ff al.; λ. καλοί *costly stone(s)* (prob. kinds of marble; cf. Diod. S. 1, 66, 3 κάλλιστοι λίθοι; Jos., Ant. 15, 392) Lk 21: 5.—1 Cor 3: 12 is also classed here by Blass and Dssm., Pls² '25, 245f (Paul, '26, 212ff); s. c below.
c. of precious stones, jewels (Jos., Ant. 17, 197; Synes., Ep. 3 p. 158B) λίθος καθαρός Rv 15: 6 v.l. Mostly in the combination λίθος τίμιος (τιμιώτατος) and mentioned

beside gold, silver, or even pearls (Appian, Liby. 66 §297; Herodian 5, 2, 4; Da 11: 38 Theod.; 2 Km 12: 30) Rv 17: 4; 18: 12, 16; 21: 11, 19 (s. the lit. s.v. ἀμέθυστος. Also FCumont³ 246, 87). Also in 1 Cor 3: 12 the way in which the word is used scarcely permits another mng., and hence we must assume (unless it is enough to think of the edifice as adorned w. precious stones [Diod. S. 3, 47, 6f: the use of gold, silver, and precious stones in the building of palaces in Sabae; Lucian, Imag. 11 ὁ νεὼς λίθοις τ. πολυτελέσιν ἠσκημένος κ. χρυσῷ]) that Paul either had in mind imaginary buildings (Ps.-Callisth. 3, 28, 4: in the city of Helios on the Red Sea there are 12 πύργοι χρυσῷ καὶ σμαράγδῳ ᾠκοδομημένοι· τὸ δὲ τεῖχος ἐκ λίθου Ἰνδικοῦ κτλ.) as Rv 21: 18ff; Is 54: 11f; Tob 13: 17, or simply mentioned the costliest materials, without considering whether they could actually be used in erecting a building (in Phoenix of Colophon [III BC] 1, 9: Anth. Lyr. Gr. I 3² '36 EDiehl the rich snob thinks of houses ἐγ [= ἐκ] λίθου σμαραγδίτου. S. χρυσίον.—Cf. b above).—λ. ἴασπις (q.v.) Rv 4: 3.
d. of millstones λ. μυλικός Lk 17: 2. λ. ὡς μύλινος Rv 18: 21.
e. of large stones used to seal graves (Charito 3, 3, 1 παραγενόμενος εὗρε τ. λίθους κεκινημένους κ. φανερὰν τὴν εἴσοδον) Mt 27: 60, 66; 28: 2; Mk 15: 46; 16: 3f; Lk 24: 2; J 11: 38f, 41; 20: 1; GP 8: 32 al. Also of the tables of the Mosaic law 2 Cor 3: 7.
f. of stone images of the gods (Dt 4: 28; Ezk 20: 32) Ac 17: 29; cf. PK 2 p. 14, 14; Dg 2: 2.
2. fig. (in the pass. fr. Hv 3 and s 9 mentioned in 1b above, the tower and its stones are symbolic) of Christ λ. ζῶν 1 Pt 2: 4. Likew. of the Christians λίθοι ζῶντες *living stones* (in the spiritual temple) vs. 5 (JCPlumpe, Vivum saxum vivi lapides: Traditio 1, '43, 1–14). 1 Pt and B 6: 2 (cf. LWBarnard, Studia Evangelica. ed. FLCross, '64, III, 306–13: NT and B) also refer to Christ as the λ. ἐκλεκτος ἀκρογωνιαῖος vs. 6 (cf. Is 28: 16; EFSiegman, CBQ 18, '56, 364–79; JElliott, The Elect and the Holy '66, esp. 16–38), the λ., ὃν ἀπεδοκίμασαν οἱ οἰκοδομοῦντες vs. 7 (Ps 117: 22)—likew. Mt 21: 42; Mk 12: 10; Lk 20: 17; cf. Ac 4: 11 (for lit. s. on κεφαλή 2b)—, and finally the λ. προσκόμματος 1 Pt 2: 8 (Is 8: 14)—likew. Ro 9: 32f. The same OT (Is 8: 14f) infl. is felt in Mt 21: 44; Lk 20: 18 (Daimachus [IV BC]: 65 fgm. 8 Jac. speaks in his work περὶ εὐσεβείας of the fall of a holy stone fr. heaven πεσεῖν τὸν λίθον).—JoachJeremias, TW IV 272–83. M-M. B. 51; 442.**

λιθόστρωτος, ον (Soph.+; Epict. 4, 7, 37 v.l.; POxy. 2138, 15; PFlor. 50, 97 [268 AD] ἐπὶ τοῦ λιθοστρώτου δρόμου Ἕρμου; 2 Ch 7: 3; Esth 1: 6; SSol 3: 10; Ep. Arist. 88; Jos., Bell. 6, 85; 189) *paved w. blocks of stone*, also subst. τὸ λιθόστρωτον (IG IV² 1, 110, 19 [IV/III BC] Κυπρ. I p. 58 no. 1 ἀπὸ τοῦ Ἡραίου ἕως τοῦ λιθοστρώτου; 2 Ch 7: 3) *stone pavement* or *mosaic* (in J 19: 13 either *pavement* or *mosaic* is poss.; the place meant is the one called 'in Hebrew Gabbatha' (q.v.), where Pilate pronounced judgment on Jesus.—REngelmann, BPhW 27, '07, 341; 1652ff; Vincent-Abel, Jérusalem II '26, 570; LHVincent, RB 42, '33, 83–113; 46, '37, 563–70; 59, '50, 513–30; EACerny, CBQ 4, '42, 159f; PBenoit, RB 59, '50, 531–50. M-M.*

λικμάω fut. λικμήσω (in the sense 'winnow' Hom.+; PSI 522, 2 [248/7 BC]; BGU 1040, 11; LXX; Philo, De Jos. 112; Jos., Ant. 5, 328); in our lit. only Mt 21: 44 = Lk 20: 18 ἐφ' ὃν δ' ἂν πέσῃ (i.e. ὁ λίθος, q.v., end), λικμήσει αὐτόν, where the Sin. and Cur. Syriac and Vulgate take it to mean *crush* (for this mng. cf. schol. on

Nicander, Ther. 114 [beside τοὺς στάχυας τρίβω]; Da 2: 44 Theod. and BGU 146, 8, the latter a complaint against those who ἐλίκμησάν μου τὸ λάχανον 'stamped on, destroyed my vegetables' [Dssm., NB 52f; BS 225f], and s. Boll 130, 1). M-M.*

λιμήν, ένος, ὁ (Hom.+; inscr., pap., LXX; Ep. Arist. 115; Philo; Jos., Ant. 17, 87 al.; loanw. in rabb.) *harbor* Ac 27: 12a, b. Fig. (trag.+; Περὶ ὕψους p. 15, 6 V.; Herm. Wr. 7, 1b; Philo, Decal. 67 and oft.) λιμένος τυγχάνειν *reach the harbor* ISm 11: 3. The storm-tossed sailor longs for it IPol 2: 3.—As a place name: Καλοὶ λιμένες (q.v. as a separate entry. On the pl. cf. Jos., Ant. 13, 261; 14, 76) Ac 27: 8. M-M. B. 738.*

λίμμα s. λεῖμμα.

λίμνη, ης, ἡ (Hom.+; inscr., pap., LXX; Philo, Aet. M. 147; 148; Jos., Ant. 5, 81).
1. *lake*, of the Lake of Gennesaret (usu. called θάλασσα elsewh.; s. this and cf. ◌ृ) ἡ λ. Γεννησαρέτ Lk 5: 1. The abs. ἡ λ. also has this sense (Jos., Vi. 96; 165; 304; Ant. 14, 450) vs. 2; 8: 22f, 33. Of the *lake of fire* Rv 20: 14a, b, 15 (cf. Joseph and Aseneth 12, 10 ἄβυσσος τ. πυρός) or *of fire and brimstone* vs. 10; cf. 19: 20; 21: 8, in which the enemies of God are punished. AP 8: 23 sinners are punished in a λίμνη μεγάλη πεπληρωμένη βορβόρου φλεγομένου.
2. *pool* ἡ λ. τοῦ Δαυὶδ *the pool of David*, acc. to GOxy 25 a basin in the temple inclosure used by the priests for bathing (ZNW 9, '08, 6f; 15, '14, 338; JoachJeremias, Unbek. Jesusworte '48, 37-45 [tr. Fuller, '57, 36-49]). M-M. B. 38.*

λιμός, οῦ, ὁ and ἡ (for the fem. s. Lk 4: 25 v.l.; 15: 14; Ac 11: 28; Bl-D. §2 end, app.; 49, 1; Mlt.-H. 123f; Phryn. 188 L.; Ael. Dion. λ, 16; Thumb 67.—The word Hom.+; UPZ 11, 27 and 19, 21 τῷ λ.; 42, 9 τῆς λ.; PSI 399, 10 [III BC] τῇ λ.; LXX [Thackeray 146]).
1. *hunger* Ro 8: 35. λιμῷ ἀπόλλυμαι *I am dying of hunger* (Ael. Aristid. 46 p. 271 D.) Lk 15: 17; (w. δίψος. Cf. Aeschyl., Pers. 483; X., Mem. 1, 4, 13; Is 5: 13; Jos., Bell. 3, 189) 2 Cor 11: 27.
2. *famine* (schol. on Aristoph., Plut. 31 λιμοῦ γενομένου ἐν τῇ Ἀττικῇ; Gen 12: 10; Philo, Rer. Div. Her. 287) Lk 4: 25 (4 Km 6: 25 ἐγέν. λ. μέγας); 15: 14; Ac 7: 11 (cf. Gen 41: 54); 11: 28 (Jos., Ant. 3, 320; 20, 101 μέγας λ.—KSGapp, The Universal Famine under Claudius: HTR 28, '35, 258-65; RWFunk, JBL 75, '56, 130-36; EHaenchen, Acts '56, 323-30; Rv 6: 8; 18: 8. ἐν λιμῷ *in famine* 1 Cl 56: 9 (Job 5: 20). λιμοὶ *famines* among the tribulations of the last days Mt 24: 7; Mk 13: 8; Lk 21: 11; in the last pass. and Mt 24: 7 v.l. λοιμοί are connected w. them (for this combination cf. Hes., Op. 243; Hdt. 7, 171; Plut., Mor. 370B; Cat. Cod. Astr. VII 166, 13; VIII 3, 186, 1; Herm. Wr. 414, 9 Sc.; Philo, Mos. 1, 110; 2, 16; Jos., Bell. 1, 377; 4, 361; Test. Judah 23: 3; Sib. Or. 2, 23; 8, 175.—For an enumeration of περιστάσεις [crises, troubles] see Ptolem., Apotel. 2, 1, 4 πολέμων ἢ λιμῶν ἢ λοιμῶν ἢ σεισμῶν ἢ κατακλυσμῶν καὶ τῶν τοιούτων). M-M. B. 332.*

λινοκαλάμη, ης, ἡ (schol. on Pla., Ep. 13 p. 363A; oft. in pap. fr. III BC) *a stalk of flax* 1 Cl 12: 3 (Josh 2: 6; the sing. is collective).*

λίνον, ου, τό (Hom.+; pap., LXX; Jos., Bell. 5, 275, Ant. 5, 9) *flax, linen*, then someth. made of them. In the latter sense in our lit.
1. *lamp-wick* λ. τυφόμενον *a smoldering wick* Mt 12: 20 (cf. Is 42: 3).—S. on κάλαμος 1.

2. *linen garment* (since Aeschyl., Suppl. 120; 132; IG IV² 1, 118, 71 [III BC]; POxy. 1281, 6 [21 AD]; PTebt. 314, 16; 406, 18 λίνα λευκά; PGM 13, 313 στόλισον αὐτὸν λίνῳ καθαρῷ. Cf. 650) Rv 15: 6.
3. *a fish-net* (Il. 5, 487; Antig. Car. 27; Philo, Agr. 24, Poster. Cai. 116) GP 14: 60. M-M. B. 401.*

Λίνος, ου, ὁ (Diog. L. 1, 3f; Biogr. p. 78; Sb 1283; 3169; 3625 a potter's stamp Λίνου) *Linus*, otherw. unknown Christian, acc. to tradition (Iren. 3, 3, 3) the first bishop of Rome 2 Ti 4: 21.*

λινοῦς, ῆ, οῦν (Hdt., Aristoph.+; inscr., pap., LXX; Jos., Ant. 20, 216) (*made of*) *linen* κερβικάριον λ. *a linen pillow* Hv 3, 1, 4a. λ. χιτών (Philostrat., Ep. 60; Dit., Syll.³ 736, 17 [92 BC]; POxy. 285, 11 [c. 50 AD]; BGU 816, 19; Lev 6: 3; 16: 4) *linen garment, linen shirt* s 9, 2, 4; 9, 11, 7. λέντιον λινοῦν καρπάσινον *a fine linen cloth* v 3, 1, 4b.*

λιπαίνω 1 aor. ἐλίπανα, imper. λιπανάτω *anoint* τὶ someth. (Philo Mech. 61, 37; Philostrat., Imag. 1, 18 p. 320, 18; PGM 36, 212) 1 Cl 56: 5 (Ps 140: 5).*

λιπαρός, ά, όν (Hom.+; pap., LXX) *oily, fat*—1. fig. (Jos., Ant. 4, 107 δέησις λ.; 8, 2 γῆρας λ.) εἰρήνη *rich, fruitful peace* 1 Cl 2: 2.—2. *bright, costly, rich* (Jos., C. Ap. 2, 229; Sib. Or. 7, 18) subst. τὰ λιπαρά (w. τὰ λαμπρά; cf. Suppl. Epigr. Gr. VIII 550, 10 [I BC]) *luxury* Rv 18: 14.*

λιποτακτέω s. λειποτακτέω.

λιτανεύω 1 aor. ἐλιτάνευσα (Hom.+; Ps 44: 13) *pray to, petition* τινὰ ὑπέρ τινος *someone on someone's behalf* τὸν Χριστὸν ὑπὲρ ἐμοῦ IRo 4: 2 (of praying to a divinity: Strabo 15, 1, 60; Dionys. Hal. 4, 76; Theosophien 39; Ep. Arist. 227). M-M. s.v. -εία.*

λίτρα, ας, ἡ (Lat. loanw.: libra, also in rabb.; Polyb. 22, 26, 19; Diod. S. 14, 116, 7; Plut., Tib. et G. Gracch. 2, 3; Jos., Ant. 14, 106; Test. Judah 3: 3; Dit., Syll.³ 890, 13; 23; 24 [251 AD]; 954, 7; 11; 13f al., Or. 521, 4; POxy. 1454, 5; 1513, 7; 1543, 6) *a (Roman) pound* (twelve ounces; 327.45 grams) J 12: 3; 39. M-M.*

λίψ, λιβός, acc. λίβα, ὁ (Hdt.+; inscr., pap., LXX; Jos., Bell. 1, 409, Ant. 3, 294; cf. Dssm., B 139 [BS 141f]) *the southwest*, of a harbor: βλέπειν κατὰ *be open toward the southwest* Ac 27: 12 (cf. EJGoodspeed, Exp. 6 ser. VIII, '03, 130f, APF, 3, '06, 406f). In the OT it almost always means *south* (s. Dssm., loc. cit.) 1 Cl 10: 4 (Gen 13: 14). M-M.*

λογεία, ας, ἡ (inscr., pap.: many exx. in the works named below) *collection* of money (λογεία is etymologically correct; λογία predominates in the mss.; cf. Bl-D. §23; Mlt.-H. 339), esp. a collection for religious purposes (PSI 262, 3 [I AD] λ. τοῦ θεοῦ; Ostraka no. 412; 414; 415; s. Wilcken) 1 Cor 16: 1. λογεῖαι γίνονται *collections are made* vs. 2.—Dssm., B 139ff, NB 46f [BS 142ff; 219f]; LO 83f [LAE 104]; Mayser 417; Wilcken, Ostraka I 253ff; WOtto, Priester u. Tempel I '05, 359ff; KHoll, SAB '21, 939f; WMFranklin, D. Koll. des Pls, Diss. Hdlbg. '38. M-M.*

λογίζομαι impf. ἐλογιζόμην; 1 aor. ἐλογισάμην, pass. ἐλογίσθην; 1 fut. pass. λογισθήσομαι. Mid. dep. (Bl-D. §311; Rob. 816; 819) (Soph., Hdt.+; inscr., pap., LXX; En. 99, 2; Ep. Arist., Philo, Joseph., Test. 12 Patr.). A word esp. used by Paul; cf. GThomas, ET 17, '06, 211ff.
1. *reckon, calculate*—**a.** *count, take into account* τὶ someth. ἡ ἀγάπη οὐ λογίζεται τὸ κακόν *love does not*

take evil into account 1 Cor 13: 5 (cf. Zech 8: 17). λ. τί
τινι *count someth. against someone,* to punish him for it
(Simplicius in Epict. p. 79, 15 τὴν ἁμαρτίαν οὐ τῷ
πράττοντι λογίζονται; Test. Zeb. 9: 7) μὴ λογιζόμενος
αὐτοῖς τὰ παραπτώματα 2 Cor 5: 19.—οὐ οὐ μὴ λογίσηται κύριος ἁμαρτίαν Ro 4: 8 (Ps 31: 2). Pass. (Lev 17:
4) μὴ αὐτοῖς λογισθείη (on the form s. Mlt.-H. 217) 2 Ti
4: 16.—But 'place to one's account' can also mean *credit*
τῷ ἐργαζομένῳ ὁ μισθὸς οὐ λογίζεται κατὰ χάριν *a
workman's wages are not credited to him as a favor* (but as
a claim) Ro 4: 4. ᾧ ὁ θεὸς λογίζεται δικαιοσύνην vs. 6.
Pass. εἰς τὸ λογισθῆναι αὐτοῖς τ. δικαιοσύνην vs. 11.—
λ. τινί τι εἴς τι *credit someth. to someone as someth.*
pass. ἐλογίσθη αὐτῷ εἰς δικαιοσύνην (after Gen 15: 6;
cf. Ps 105: 31; 1 Macc 2: 52) Ro 4: 3, 5, 9, 22 (WDiezinger,
NovT 5, '62, 288-98 [rabbinic use of λογ.]); Gal 3: 6; Js 2:
23.—Cf. also Ro 4: 10, 23f.—H-WHeidland, D. Anrech-
nung des Glaubens zur Gerechtigkeit '36; FWDanker,
FWGingrich-Festschr., '72, 104.—λ. εἴς τινα *put on
someone's account, charge to someone* (commercial t.t.:
Dit., Or. 595, 15 τὰ ἕτερα ἀναλώματα ἑαυτοῖς ἐλογισά-
μεθα, ἵνα μὴ τὴν πόλιν βαρῶμεν; PFay. 21, 9) μή τις εἰς
ἐμὲ λογίσηται *in order that no one may credit me* 2 Cor
12: 6.
   b. *as a result of a calculation evaluate, estimate, look
upon as, consider* (Hyperid. 2, 20) εἰς οὐθὲν λογισθῆναι
be looked upon as nothing (Is 40: 17; Wsd 3: 17; 9: 6) Ac
19: 27. τὰ τέκνα τ. ἐπαγγελίας λογίζεται εἰς σπέρμα
the children of the promise are looked upon as seed Ro 9: 8
(cf. La 4: 2). οὐχ ἡ ἀκροβυστία αὐτοῦ εἰς περιτομὴν
λογισθήσεται; *will not his uncircumcision be regarded as
circumcision?* 2: 26.—*Count, class* (PLond. 328, 8 of a
camel's colt: λογιζομένου νυνὶ ἐν τελείοις= 'which is
now classed among the full-grown') μετὰ ἀνόμων ἐλογίσθη *he was classed among the criminals* (Is 53: 12) Mk
15: 28 t.r.; Lk 22: 37. Also (exactly like the LXX) ἐν τοῖς
ἀνόμοις ἐλογίσθη 1 Cl 16: 13. μετὰ τῶν ἐθνῶν ἐλο-
γίσθησαν *they were counted with the heathen* Hs 8, 9,
3.—οὐκ ἐλογίσθη *he was held in disrespect* 1 Cl 16: 3 (Is
53: 3).—λ. τινα ὡς w. acc. *consider, look upon someone
as:* ἡμᾶς λογιζέσθω ἄνθρωπος ὡς ὑπηρέτας Χριστοῦ
1 Cor 4: 1. λ. ἡμᾶς ὡς κατὰ σάρκα περιπατοῦντας 2 Cor
10: 2b. Pass. ἐλογίσθημεν ὡς πρόβατα σφαγῆς Ro 8: 36
(Ps 43: 23). λ. τινα foll. by acc. and inf. (Is 53: 4)
λογίζεσθε ἑαυτοὺς εἶναι νεκροὺς *consider yourselves
dead* Ro 6: 11.
   2. *think (about), consider, ponder, let one's mind dwell
on* (PsSol 2, 28b; Philo, Leg. All. 3, 227 ταῦτα; Jos., Ant.
6, 211) Phil 4: 8. Foll. by ὅτι (PsSol 2, 28a; Philo, Somn. 2,
169; Jos., Ant. 11, 142) J 11: 50; Hb 11: 19; B 1: 5.
τοῦτο λ. ὅτι 2 Cor 10: 11, 7 (here ἐφ' [v.l. ἀφ'] ἑαυτοῦ *in
his own mind* is added). W. ἐν ἑαυταῖς and a direct
question foll. Lk 24: 1 D.—*Have in mind, propose,
purpose* w. inf. foll. (X., An. 2, 2, 13; 1 Macc 6: 19)
2 Cor 10: 2a. *Think out* τὶ *someth.* (Ps 51: 4) ὡς ἐξ
ἑαυτῶν as *(if) of ourselves* 3: 5. *Reason or make plans*
(Wsd 2: 1) ὡς νήπιος *like a child* 1 Cor 13: 11.
   3. *think, believe, be of the opinion* w. ὅτι foll. Ro 8: 18.
W. acc. and ὅτι foll.: λογίζῃ τοῦτο..., ὅτι; *do you
imagine that?* 2: 3. Foll. by acc. and inf. (Wsd 15: 12)
λογιζόμεθα δικαιοῦσθαι ἄνθρωπον *we hold that a man is
justified* 3: 28. λ. τι κοινὸν εἶναι 14: 14. ἐμαυτὸν οὔπω λ.
κατειληφέναι *I consider that I have not yet attained* Phil
3: 13. ὃν λογίζομαι καὶ τοὺς ἀθέους ἐντρέπεσθαι *whom,
I believe, even the godless respect* ITr 3: 2. Foll. by the inf.
alone 2 Cor 11: 5.—ὡς λογίζομαι *as I think* 1 Pt 5: 12; Dg
7: 3.—H-WHeidland, TW IV 287-95. M-M.**

λογικός, ή, όν (a favorite expr. of philosphers since
Aristot.; Dit., Syll.³ 803, 5. Not LXX, but oft. Philo)
rational, spiritual λογικὴ λατρεία *a spiritual service* Ro
12: 1 (cf. Herm. Wr. 1, 31 λογικὴ θυσία; 13, 18; 21;
Epict. 1, 16, 20f the singing of hymns is the religious
service of man, as a λογικός= a being endowed with
reason; 3, 1, 26 τὸ λογικὸν ἔχεις ἐξαίρετον· τοῦτο
κόσμει καὶ καλλώπιζε. Philo, Spec. Leg. 1, 277 God
places no value on sacrificial animals, but on τοῦ θύοντος
πνεῦμα λογικόν. Test. Levi 3: 6 λ. καὶ ἀναίμακτος
προσφορά [v.l. θυσία]; Euseb., H.E. 4, 23, 13 Schwartz;
cf. the paraenetic pattern of Plut., Mor. 478D-E.—Rtzst.,
Mysterienrel.³ 328f; Ltzm., Hdb. exc. on Ro 12: 1; B
Schmidt, D. geistige Gebet, Diss. Bresl. '16; OCasel,
Jahrb. f. Liturgiewissensch. 4, '24, 38ff; CFDMoule, JTS
n.s. I, '50, 34f). Most likely τὸ λογικὸν ἄδολον γάλα
1 Pt 2: 2 is to be taken in the same way *pure spiritual milk*;
it is to be borne in mind that λ. means *spiritual* not only in
the sense of πνευματικός, but also in contrast to 'literal',
w. the mng. 'metaphorical' (cf. Pel-Leg. p. 20: the bishop
is the shepherd τῶν λογικῶν προβάτων τοῦ Χριστοῦ;
Euseb., H.E. 1, 1, 4 ἐκ λογικῶν λειμώνων).—Gerh
Kittel, TW IV 145-7. M-M.*

λόγιον, ου, τό (Eur., Hdt.+, mostly of short sayings
originating fr. a divinity: Hdt. 8, 60, 3; Thu. 2, 8, 2; Polyb.
3, 112, 8; 8, 30, 6; Diod. S. 2, 14, 3; 2, 26, 9; 4, 65, 3 al.;
Aelian, V.H. 2, 41. Likew. LXX [TWManson, Goguel-
Festschr. '50, 142f]; Ep. Arist. 177; Philo, Congr. Erud.
Grat. 134, Fuga 60, Mos. 2, 262, Praem. 1, Vi. Cont. 25;
Jos., Bell. 6, 311) *a saying,* in our lit. only pl. (as also
predom. in secular wr.); of the revelations received by
Moses λόγια ζῶντα Ac 7: 38. Of God's promises to the
Jews Ro 3: 2 (JWDoeve, Studia Paulina [JdeZwaan-Fest-
schr.] '53, 111-23). Of words fr. Scripture gener. (as Plut.,
Fab. 4, 5 of words fr. the Sibylline books): τὰ λόγια τοῦ
θεοῦ (LXX) Hb 5: 12.—1 Cl 13: 4; 19: 1; 53: 1. τὰ λ. τῆς
παιδείας τοῦ θεοῦ *the oracles of God's teaching* 62: 3.
Also of NT sayings 2 Cl 13: 3 (cf. vs. 4). Likew. τὰ λόγια
τοῦ κυρίου *the sayings of the Lord* (Jesus; Marinus, Vi.
Procli 26 p. 163, 50 Boiss. τὰ Ὀρφέως λόγια) Pol 7: 1 (cf.
Clem. Alex., Quis Div. Salv. 3, 1; Irenaeus I Praef. 1;
Papias in Euseb., H.E. 3, 39, 1=Geb., Harn., Zahn,
Papias 2: 15, 16; PNepper-Christensen, Mt ein Juden-
christliches Evangelium? '58, 37-56). Of the utterances of
those Christians gifted w. the charisma of the word 1 Pt 4:
11.—GerhKittel, TW IV 140-5. M-M.*

λόγιος, ία, ιον (Pind.+; inscr., pap.)—1. *eloquent* (Plut.,
Pomp. 51, 8; Lucian, Pseudolog. 24, Pro Merc. Cond. 5
Hermes as ὁ λόγιος; Philo, Mut. Nom. 220, Cher. 116.
This mng. rejected by Phryn. [p. 198 L.]; defended by
Field [Notes, 129]).
   2. *learned, cultured* (Hdt. 1, 1; 2, 3; Aristot., Pol. 2, 8;
Heliod. 4, 7, 4 of an ἰατρός; Ep. Arist. 6; Philo, Mos. 1, 23
al.; Jos., Bell. 1, 13, Ant. 17, 149). In Ac 18: 24, where
Apollos is called ἀνὴρ λ. (as Ps.-Libanius, Charact. Ep. p.
20, 12; PLond. 2710 r., 6—s. HTR 29, '36, 40f; 45; Philo,
Poster. Cai. 53), either mng. is poss., even though the
ancient versions (Lat., Syr., Armen.) prefer the first.—
EOrth, Logios '26. M-M.*

λογισμός, οῦ, ὁ (Thu.+; inscr., pap., LXX; oft. Philo;
Jos., Ant. 17, 228; Sib. Or. 2, 314).
   1. *calculation, reasoning, reflection, thought* in our lit.
in pl. W. ἔννοιαι *thoughts and sentiments* Pol 4: 3.
μεταξὺ ἀλλήλων τῶν λ. κατηγορούντων *as their
thoughts accuse one another* Ro 2: 15. Not infreq. in an

unfavorable sense (as e.g. Vett. Val. 49, 8; 173, 11; λ. κακοί Pr 6: 18. Cf. Wsd 1: 3, 5; 11: 15) οἱ προκατέχοντές σου τὴν διάνοιαν λογισμοί the (prejudiced) *thoughts that occupy your mind* Dg 2: 1. λογισμοὶ ἐθνῶν *the designs of the heathen* 1 Cl 59: 3. λογισμοὺς καθαιροῦντες *we demolish sophistries* 2 Cor 10: 4.

2. *reasoning power, wisdom* (Epicurus in Diog. L. 10, 132 νήφων λογισμός= *sober reasoning*; Test. Gad 6: 2 τὸ πνεῦμα τοῦ μίσους ἐτάρασσέ μου τὸν λογισμὸν πρὸς τὸ ἀνελεῖν αὐτόν; Jos., Bell. 2, 31) ἄνθρωπος αἴσθησιν ἔχει κ. λογισμόν *a man has the power to feel and think* Dg 2: 9 (λ. w. αἴσθησις as Philo, Praem. 28). M-M.*

λογομαχέω (Eustath., Opusc. p. 47, 96) *dispute about words, split hairs* 2 Ti 2: 14.*

λογομαχία, ας, ἡ (Conon [I BC/I AD], Narrat. 38 in Photius, Bibl. Cod. 186; Porphyr. in Euseb., Praep. Ev. 14, 10, 2; Cat. Cod. Astr. VIII 1 p. 167, 21) *word-battle, dispute about words* 1 Ti 6: 4; Tit 3: 9 G.*

λόγος, ου, ὁ (Hom.+; inscr., pap., LXX, En., Ep. Arist., Philo, Joseph., Test. 12 Patr., Sib. Or.).

1. *speaking*—**a.** gener.—**α.** *word* (opp. ἔργον, 'deed'; Polystrat. p. 33 μὴ λόγῳ μόνον ἀλλ᾽ ἔργῳ δυνατὸς ἐν ἔργῳ κ. λόγῳ Lk 24: 19 (Diod. S. 13, 101, 3 ἄνδρας λόγῳ δυνατούς). Cf. Ro 15: 18; 2 Cor 10: 11; Col 3: 17; 2 Th 2: 17; 1 J 3: 18 (cf. Theognis, Eleg. 1, 87f Diehl² μή μ᾽ ἔπεσιν μὲν στέργε κτλ.—For the contrast λόγῳ—ἀληθείᾳ cf. Diod. S. 13, 4, 1). In contrast to a sinful deed we also have the λόγος ἁμαρτίας *sinful word* GH 10. (W. γνῶσις) ἐν παντὶ λόγῳ κ. πάσῃ γνώσει 1 Cor 1: 5. ἰδιώτης τῷ λόγῳ, ἀλλ᾽ οὐ τῇ γνώσει 2 Cor 11: 6. (Opp. δύναμις 'revelation of power') 1 Cor 4: 19, 20. τὸ εὐαγγέλιον οὐκ ἐγενήθη ἐν λόγῳ μόνον, ἀλλὰ καὶ ἐν δυνάμει 1 Th 1: 5. (W. ἐπιστολή) 2 Th 2: 2, 15. (W. ἀναστροφή) 1 Ti 4: 12; 1 Pt 3: 1b. (Opp. 'be silent') IRo 2: 1.—μόνον εἰπὲ λόγῳ *just say the word* Mt 8: 8; cf. Lk 7: 7 (Phalaris, Ep. 121, 1 λόγῳ λέγειν. Cf. schol. on Pla. 341A ἐν λόγῳ μόνον εἰπεῖν). οὐδεὶς ἐδύνατο ἀποκριθῆναι αὐτῷ λόγον *no one was able to answer him a (single) word* Mt 22: 46; cf. 15: 23.—*The (mighty) word* (of one who performs miracles) ἐξέβαλεν τὰ πνεύματα λόγῳ Mt 8: 16.—διὰ λόγου *by word of mouth* (opp. 'by letter') Ac 15: 27.—In the textually uncertain pass. Ac 20: 24 the text as it stands in N., οὐδενὸς λόγου ποιοῦμαι τὴν ψυχὴν τιμίαν, may well mean: *I do not consider my life worth a single word* (cf. λόγου ἄξιον [ἄξιος 1a] and our 'worth mention').

β. The expression may take any one of many different forms, so that the exact transl. of λ. depends on the context: *what you say* Mt 5: 37; *statement* (PGM 4, 334) Lk 20: 20; *question* (Sext. Emp., Math. 8, 295; 9, 133; Diog. L. 2, 116) ἐρωτήσω ὑμᾶς λόγον *I will ask you a question* (cf. Jos., Ant. 12, 99) Mt 21: 24; cf. Mk 11: 29; Lk 20: 3; *prayer* (PGM 1, 25; 4, 90; 179; 230 al.; 5, 180; 196 al.) Mt 26: 44; Mk 14: 39. ἡγούμενος τοῦ λ. *principal speaker* Ac 14: 12. W. ἐξεγεῖτ. gen. λ. παρακλήσεως 13: 15. (W. κήρυγμα perh.) *pastoral counselling* w. an individual 1 Cor 2: 4a. (W. διδασκαλία) *preaching* 1 Ti 5: 17; *prophecy* (Biogr. p. 364 [Pythia]) J 2: 22; 18: 32; *command* (Aeschyl., Pers. 363) Lk 4: 36; 2 Pt 3: 5, 7. *Report, story* (X., An. 1, 4, 7; Diod. S. 3, 40, 9; 19, 110, 1 λ. διαδιδόναι= *spread a report*; Appian, Iber. 80 §346, Maced. 4 §1 [both= *rumor*]; Diod. S. 32, 15, 3 ἦλθεν ὁ λ. ἐπί τινα= *the report came to someone*; Arrian., Anab. 7, 22, 1 λόγος λέγεται τοιόσδε= *a story is told like this*, Ind. 9, 2; Diod. S. 3, 18, 3 λ.= *story, account*; Jos., Ant. 19, 132) Mt 28: 15; Mk 1: 45; Lk 5: 15 (λ. περί τινος as

X., An. 6, 6, 13; Jos., Ant. 19, 127); J 21: 23. ἠκούσθη ὁ λόγος εἰς τὰ ὦτα τ. ἐκκλησίας *the report came to the ears of the church* Ac 11: 22. λόγον ἔχειν σοφίας *have the appearance of wisdom, pass for wisdom* Col 2: 23 (cf. Pla., Epinomis 987B ἔχει λόγον; Demosth., C. Lept. 462 [20, 18] λόγον τιν᾽ ἔχον; but mng. 2f is possible). *Proverb* (Pla., Phaedr. 17 p. 240c, Symp. 18 p. 195B, Gorg. 54 p. 499c, Leg. 6, 5 p. 757A; Socrat., Ep. 22, 1) J 4: 37. *Proclamation, instruction, teaching, message* Lk 4: 32; 10: 39; J 4: 41; 17: 20; Ac 2: 41; 4: 4; 10: 44; 1 Cor 1: 17; 2: 1. λόγος σοφίας *proclamation of wisdom, speaking wisely* 12: 8a (Ps.-Phoc. 129 τῆς θεοπνεύστου σοφίης λ.); corresp. λ. γνώσεως ibid. b. Cf. 14: 9; 15: 2; 2 Cor 1: 18; 6: 7; 10: 10. ὁ κατὰ τ. διδαχὴν πιστὸς λ. *the message of faith, corresponding to the teaching* Tit 1: 9. *A speech* (Aristot. p. 14b, 2; Diod. S. 40, 5a) διὰ λόγου πολλοῦ *in a long speech* Ac 15: 32; cf. 20: 2; *speaking gener.* 2 Cor 8: 7; Eph 6: 19; Col 4: 6; D 2: 5. ἐν λόγῳ πταίειν *make a mistake in what one says* Js 3: 2.

γ. of a statement of definite content: *assertion, declaration, speech* ἀκούσαντες τὸν λ. *when they heard the statement* Mt 15: 12. Cf. 19: 11, 22; 22: 15; Mk 5: 36. διὰ τοῦτον τὸν λ. *because of this statement of yours* 7: 29. Cf. 10: 22; 12: 13; Lk 1: 29; J 4: 39, 50; 6: 60; 7: 36; 15: 20a; 18: 9; 19: 8; Ac 6: 5; 7: 29; 1 Th 4: 15. ὃς ἐὰν εἴπῃ λόγον κατὰ τοῦ υἱοῦ τοῦ ἀνθρώπου *whoever makes a (blasphemous) statement against the Son of Man* Mt 12: 32; cf. Lk 12: 10 (λ. εἰπεῖν κατά τινος as Jos., Ant. 15, 81). λόγον ποιεῖσθαι *make a speech* Ac 11: 2 D (cf. Hyperid. 3, 20; Jos., Ant. 11, 86).

δ. the pl. (οἱ) λόγοι is used (1) either of words uttered on various occasions, of speeches made here and there (Jos., Ant. 4, 264) ἐκ τῶν λόγων σου δικαιωθήσῃ (καταδικασθήσῃ) Mt 12: 37a, b; 24: 35; Mk 13: 31; Lk 21: 33; Ac 2: 40; 7: 22 (ἐν λόγοις καὶ ἔργοις αὐτοῦ. Cf. Dio Chrys. 4, 6 the λόγοι and ἔργα of Diogenes. On the contrast betw. λ. and ἔργ. s. a above); 15: 24; 20: 35; 1 Cor 2: 4b, 13; 14: 19a, b; κενοὶ λ. Eph 5: 6; Dg 8: 2; πλαστοὶ λ. 2 Pt 2: 3. λ. πονηροί 3 J 10; (2) or of words and exprs. that form a unity, whether it be connected discourse (Jos., Ant. 15, 126), a conversation, or parts of one and the same teaching, or expositions on the same subject (Diod. S. 16, 2, 3 μετέσχε τῶν Πυθαγορίων λόγων; Dio Chrys. 37[54], 1; Ael. Aristid. 50, 55 K.= 26 p. 519 D.: οἱ Πλάτωνος λόγοι) πᾶς ὅστις ἀκούει μου τοὺς λόγους τούτους Mt 7: 24; cf. vss. 26, 28; 10: 14; Mk 10: 24; Lk 1: 20; 6: 47. ἐπηρώτα αὐτὸν ἐν λόγοις ἱκανοῖς *he questioned him at some length* 23: 9. τίνες οἱ λ. οὗτοι οὓς ἀντιβάλλετε; *what is this conversation that you are holding?* 24: 17.—J 14: 24a; Ac 2: 22; 2 Ti 4: 15; 1 Cl 13: 1; 46: 7.

ε. the *subject* under discussion, *matter, thing* gener. (Theognis 1055 Diehl; Hdt. 8, 65 μηδενὶ ἄλλῳ τὸν λόγον τοῦτον εἴπῃς. Cf. Hebr. רָבָד) τὸν λ. ἐκράτησαν *they took up the subject* Mk 9: 10. οὐκ ἔστιν σοι μερὶς ἐν τῷ λόγῳ τούτῳ *you have no share in this matter* Ac 8: 21. ἰδεῖν περὶ τ. λόγου τούτου *look into this matter* 15: 6. ἔχειν πρός τινα λόγον *have a complaint against someone* (cf. Demosth. 35, 55 ἐμοὶ πρὸς τούτους ὁ λόγος; Pland. 16, 3 δίκαιον λόγον ἔχει πρὸς σέ) 19: 38. παρεκτὸς λόγου πορνείας Mt 5: 32 (2d is also poss.).—Perh. also Mk 8: 32 *he discussed the subject quite freely* (but s. 1bβ below).

ζ. of written words and speeches: of the separate books of a work (Hdt. 5, 36 ἐν τῷ πρώτῳ τ. λόγων; Pla., Parmen. 2, 127D ὁ πρῶτος λόγος; Philo, Omn. Prob. Lib. 1 ὁ μὲν πρότερος λόγος ἦν ἡμῖν, ὦ Θεόδοτε, περὶ τοῦ...) *treatise* Ac 1: 1 (cf. on the prologue to Ac: AHilgenfeld,

ZWTh 41, 1898, 619ff; AGercke, Her. 29, 1894, 373ff; RLaqueur, Her. 46, '11, 161ff; Norden, Agn. Th. 311ff; JMCreed, JTS 35, '34, 176-82; Gdspd., Probs. 119-21).—περὶ οὗ πολὺς ἡμῖν ὁ λόγος *about this we have much to say* Hb 5: 11. Hb is described as ὁ λ. τῆς παρακλήσεως a *word of exhortation* (in literary form) 13: 22. Of writings that are part of Holy Scripture ὁ λ. Ἡσαΐου J 12: 38. ὁ λ. ὁ ἐν τῷ νόμῳ γεγραμμένος 15: 25; ὁ προφητικὸς λ. 2 Pt 1: 19; 2 Cl 11: 2 (quot. of unknown orig.). ὁ ἅγιος λ. *the holy word* 1 Cl 56: 3. ὁ λ. ὁ γεγραμμένος 1 Cor 15: 54 (Is 25: 8 and Hos 13: 14 follow). Pl. οἱ λόγοι τ. προφητῶν Ac 15: 15. ὡς γέγραπται ἐν βίβλῳ λόγων Ἡσαΐου Lk 3: 4 (Pla., 7th Epistle p. 335A πείθεσθαι ἀεὶ χρὴ τοῖς παλαιοῖς καὶ ἱεροῖς λόγοις).—Of the content of Rv: ὁ ἀναγινώσκων τ. λόγους τῆς προφητείας 1: 3. οἱ λόγοι (τ. προφητείας) τ. βιβλίου τούτου 22: 7, 9f, 18f.

b. of revelation by God—**α.** of God's word, command, commission (Ael. Aristid. hears a ἱερὸς λ. at night fr. a god: 28, 116 K.=49, p. 529 D.; Sextus 24) ἠκυρώσατε τ. λόγον τοῦ θεοῦ Mt 15:6; cf. Mk 7: 13.—J 5: 38; 8: 55; 10: 35; Ro 3: 4 (Ps 50: 6). Of God's promise Ro 9: 6, 9, 28 (Is 10: 22f). Cf. Hb 2: 2; 4: 2 (s. ἀκοή 2b); 7: 28; 12: 19. οἱ δέκα λόγοι *the ten commandments* (Ex 34: 28; Dt 10: 4; Philo, Rer. Div. Her. 168, Decal. 32; Jos., Ant. 3, 138; cf. 91f) B 15: 1. The whole law, acc. to Ro 13: 9; Gal 5: 14 is summed up in the λόγος Lev 19: 18.—That which God has created ἁγιάζεται διὰ λόγου θεοῦ 1 Ti 4: 5; in line w. the context, this hardly refers to God's creative word (so Sib. Or. 3, 20; PK 2), but to table prayers which use biblical expressions.

β. of the divine revelation through Christ and his messengers θεὸς ἐφανέρωσεν τὸν λ. αὐτοῦ ἐν κηρύγματι Tit 1: 3. δέδωκα αὐτοῖς τὸν λ. σου J 17: 14; cf. vss. 6, 17; 1 J 1: 10; 2: 14. ἵνα μὴ ὁ λ. τοῦ θεοῦ βλασφημῆται Tit 2: 5. The apostles and other preachers, w. ref. to the λόγος of God, are said to: λαλεῖν Ac 4: 29, 31; 13: 46; Phil 1: 14; Hb 13: 7; καταγγέλλειν Ac 13: 5; 17: 13; διδάσκειν 18: 11; μαρτυρεῖν Rv 1: 2. Of their hearers it is said: τὸν λ. τοῦ θεοῦ ἀκούειν Ac 13: 7; δέχεσθαι 8: 14; 11: 1. Of the λ. τοῦ θεοῦ itself we read: ηὔξανεν Ac 6: 7; 12: 24 v.l.; οὐ δέδεται 2 Ti 2: 9. In these places and many others ὁ λόγος τοῦ θεοῦ is simply *the Christian message, the gospel:* Lk 5: 1; 8: 11, 21; 11: 28 (Simplicius in Epict. p. 1, 20 μὴ μόνον ἀκουόντων ἀλλὰ πασχόντων ὑπὸ τῶν λόγων=let the message have its effect on oneself); Ac 6: 2 (s. καταλείπω 2c); 13: 44; 16: 32; 1 Cor 14: 36; 2 Cor 2: 17; 4: 2; Col 1: 25; 1 Pt 1: 23; Rv 1: 9; 6: 9; IPhld 11: 1. Cf. 1 Th 2: 13a, b; 1 J 2: 5.—Since this 'divine word' is brought to men through Christ, his word can be used in the same sense: ὁ λόγος μου J 5: 24; cf. 8: 31, 37, 43, 51f; 12: 48; 14: 23f; 15: 3; Rv 3: 8. ὁ λόγος τοῦ Χριστοῦ Col 3: 16; cf. Hb 6: 1. ὁ λ. τοῦ κυρίου Ac 8: 25; 12: 24; 13: 44 v.l., 48f; 15: 35, 36; 19: 10; 1 Th 1: 8; 2 Th 3: 1. Pl. Mk 8: 38; 1 Ti 6: 3.—Or it is called simply ὁ λόγος=*the 'Word'*, since no misunderstanding would be possible among Christians: Mt 13: 20-3; Mk 2: 2; 4: 14-20, 33; 8: 32 (s. above 1ae); 16: 20; Lk 1: 2; 8: 12f, 15; Ac 6: 4; 8: 4; 10: 36; 11: 19; 14: 25; 16: 6; 17: 11; 18: 5; Gal 6: 6; Col 4: 3; 1 Th 1: 6; 2 Ti 4: 2; Js 1: 21; 1 Pt 2: 8; 3: 1; 1 J 2: 7.—Somet. the 'Word' is more closely defined by a gen.: ὁ λ. τῆς βασιλείας *the word of the kingdom* or *kingship* (of God) Mt 13: 19. τῆς σωτηρίας Ac 13: 26. τῆς καταλλαγῆς 2 Cor 5: 19. τοῦ σταυροῦ 1 Cor 1: 18. δικαιοσύνης (q.v. 4) Hb 5: 13. ζωῆς Phil 2: 16. (τῆς) ἀληθείας Eph 1: 13; Col 1: 5; 2 Ti 2: 15; Js 1: 18. τῆς χάριτος αὐτοῦ (=τοῦ κυρίου) Ac 14: 3; 20: 32. (Differently the pl. οἱ λόγοι τ. χάριτος *gracious words* Lk 4: 22; cf. Marcellinus, Vi. Thucyd. 57 Hude λόγοι εἰρω-

νείας.) ὁ λ. τοῦ εὐαγγελίου Ac 15: 7; ὁ τοῦ Χριστιανισμοῦ λ. MPol 10: 1. In Rv (3: 10) the gospel is described as ὁ λ. τῆς ὑπομονῆς μου *my* (the Son of Man's) *word of endurance* (W-S. §30, 12c).—The pastoral letters favor the expr. πιστὸς ὁ λόγος (sc. ἐστίν and s. πιστός 1b) 1 Ti 1: 15; 3: 1; 4: 9; 2 Ti 2: 11; Tit 3: 8; cf. Rv 21: 5; 22: 6. λ. ὑγιής *sound preaching* Tit 2: 8; cf. the pl. ὑγιαίνοντες λόγοι 2 Ti 1: 13.—The pl. is also used gener. of Christian teachings, the words of the gospel Lk 1: 4 (s. κατηχέω 2a); 1 Th 4: 18. οἱ λ. τῆς πίστεως 1 Ti 4: 6.—JSchniewind, Die Begriffe Wort und Evangelium bei Pls, Diss. Bonn '10; RAsting (εὐαγγέλιον, end).

2. *computation, reckoning*—**a.** *account, accounts, reckoning* λόγον δοῦναι (Hdt. 8, 100; X., Cyr. 1, 4, 3; Diod. S. 3, 46, 4; Dit., Syll.³ 1099, 16; BGU 164, 21; Jos., Ant. 16, 120) *give account, make an accounting* ἕκαστος περὶ ἑαυτοῦ λόγον δώσει τ. θεῷ Ro 14: 12. Also λ. ἀποδοῦναι abs. (Diod. S. 16, 56, 4; 19, 9, 4) Hb 13: 17. τινί *to someone* (Diod. S. 16, 27, 4; Plut., Alcib. 7, 3; Charito 7, 6, 2; Dit., Syll.³ 631, 13 τᾷ πόλει; 2 Ch 34: 28; Da 6: 3 Theod.; Jos., Bell. 1, 209) τῷ ἑτοίμως ἔχοντι κρῖναι 1 Pt 4: 5. τινὸς of someth. (Dit., Syll.³ 1044, 46; 1105, 10 τοῦ ἀναλώματος; Jos., Ant. 19, 307) Lk 16: 2 (here λ. w. the art.). Likew. περὶ τινος (Diod. S. 18, 60, 2 δοὺς αὑτῷ περὶ τούτων λόγον=taking account [considering] with himself; BGU 98, 25 περὶ τούτου) Mt 12: 36; Ac 19: 40. ὑπέρ τινος *concerning someone* Hv 3, 9, 10.—αἰτεῖν τινα λόγον περὶ τινος *call someone to account for someth.* 1 Pt 3: 15 (cf. Pla., Pol. 285E; Dio Chrys. 20[37], 30).

b. *settlement (of an account)* (εἰς λόγον commercial t.t. 'in settlement of an account' POxy. 275, 19; 21) εἰς λόγον δόσεως κ. λήμψεως *in settlement of a mutual account* (lit., 'of giving and receiving', 'of debit and credit') Phil 4: 15 (cf. Plut., Mor. 11B λόγον δοῦναι καὶ λαβεῖν). The same ideas are in the background of εἰς λόγον ὑμῶν *credited to your account* vs 17.—συναίρειν λόγον *settle accounts* (BGU 775, 18f. The mid. in the same mng. PFay. 109, 6 [I AD]; POxy. 113, 27f.—Dssm., LO 94 [LAE 118f]) μετά τινος Mt 18: 23; 25: 19.

c. *respect, regard* εἰς λόγον τινός *with regard to, for the sake of* (Thu. 3, 46, 4; Demosth. 19, 142 εἰς ἀρετῆς λόγον; Polyb. 11, 28, 8; Ael. Aristid. 39 p. 743 D.: εἰς δεινότητος.) εἰς λ. τιμῆς IPhld 11: 2. εἰς λ. θεοῦ ISm 10: 1.

d. *reason, motive* (Dio Chrys. 64[14], 18 ἐκ τούτου τ. λόγου; Appian, Hann. 29 §126 τῷ αὐτῷ λόγῳ; Iambl., Vi. Pyth. 28, 155) τίνι λόγῳ; *for what reason?* Ac 10: 29 (cf. Pla., Gorg. 512C τίνι δικαίῳ λ.; Appian, Mithrid. 57 §232 τίνι λόγῳ;). κατὰ λόγον 18: 14 (s. κατά II 5bβ). παρεκτὸς λόγου Mt 5: 32 (though 1ae is also poss.).

e. πρὸς ὃν ἡμῖν ὁ λόγος (ἐστίν) *with whom we have to do* (i.e. *to reckon*) (exx. in FBleek, Hb II 1, 1836, 590ff, in his capacity as judge (Libanius, Legat. Ulixis [=Declamatio IV] 2 F. τοῖς δὲ ἀδίκως ἀποκτενοῦσι καὶ πρὸς θεοὺς καὶ πρὸς ἀνθρώπους ὁ λόγος γίγνεται) Hb 4: 13. οὐ πρὸς σάρκα ὁ λόγος, ἀλλὰ πρὸς θεόν *he has to do not with flesh, but with God* IMg 3: 2.

f. In Col 2: 23 (s. 1aβ) λόγον μὲν ἔχοντα σοφίας may= *have a concern for wisdom* (cf. λόγος ἡμῖν οὐδείς, Plut., Mor. 870).

3. *the Logos.* Our lit. shows traces of a way of thinking that was widespread in contemporary syncretism, as well as in Jewish wisdom lit. and Philo, the most prominent feature of which is the concept of the Logos, the independent, personified 'Word' (of God): J 1: 1a, b, c, 14. It is the distinctive teaching of the Fourth Gospel that this divine 'Word' took on human form in a historical person, that is, in Jesus. (Cf. RSeeberg, Festgabe für AvHarnack '21, 263-81.—Aelian, V.H. 4, 20 ἐκάλουν τὸν Πρωταγόραν Λόγον. Similarly Favorinus [II AD] in Diog. L. 9, 50 of Democritus: ἐκαλεῖτο Σοφία. Equating a divinity with an abstraction that she personifies: Artem. 5, 18 φρόνησις εἶναι νομίζεται ἡ θεός [Athena]). Cf. 1 J 1: 1; Rv 19: 13. εἷς θεός ἐστιν, ὁ φανερώσας ἑαυτὸν διὰ Ἰ. Χριστοῦ τοῦ υἱοῦ αὐτοῦ, ὅς ἐστιν αὐτοῦ λόγος, ἀπὸ σιγῆς προελθών *there is one God, who has revealed himself through Jesus Christ his Son, who is his 'Word' proceeding from silence* IMg 8: 2 (s. σιγή). The Lord as νόμος κ. λόγος PK 1. Cf. Dg 11: 2, 3, 7, 8; 12: 9.—HClavier, TWManson memorial vol., '59, 81-93: the Alexandrian eternal λόγος is also implied in Hb 4: 12; 13: 7.—S. also the 'Comma Johanneum' (to the bibliography in RGG³ I, 1854 [HGreeven] add AJülicher, GGA '05, 930-5; AvHarnack, SAB '15, 572f [= Studien I '31, 151f]; MMeinertz, Einl. in d. NT⁴ '33, 309-11; AGreiff, ThQ 114, '33, 465-80; CHDodd, The Joh. Epistles '46) ὁ πατήρ, ὁ λόγος καὶ τὸ ἅγιον πνεῦμα 1 J 5: 7 t.r. (such interpolations were not unheard of. According to Diog. L. 1, 48 some people maintain that Solon inserted the verse mentioning the Athenians after Iliad 2, 557).—On the Logos: EZeller, D. Philosophie der Griechen III 2⁴ '03, 417-34; MHeinze, D. Lehre v. Logos in d. griech. Philosophie 1872; PWendland, Philo u. d. kynisch-stoische Diatribe [Beiträge z. Gesch. der griech. Philosophie u. Religion by Wendl. and OKern 1895, 1-75]; AAall, Gesch. d. Logosidee 1896, 1899; MPohlenz, D. Stoa '48f, I 482; 490 (index); LDürr, D. Wertung des göttl. Wortes im AT u. im ant. Orient '38 (§9 of the Joh. Logos); EBréhier, Les idées philosophiques et religieuses de Philon d'Alexandrie '07, 83-111; (² '25); JLebreton, Les théories du Logos au début de l'ère chrétienne '07; E Schwartz, NGG '08, 537-56; GVos, The Range of the Logos-Title in the Prologue of the Fourth Gospel: PTR 11, '13, 365-419; 557-602; RHarris, The Origin of the Prologue to St. John's Gospel '17, Athena, Sophia and the Logos: Bull. of the JRylands Libr. 7, 1, '22 p. 56-72; M-JLagrange, Vers le Logos de S. Jean: RB 32, '23, 161-84, Le Logos de Philon: ibid. 321-71; HLeisegang, Logos: Pauly-W. XIII '26, 1035-81; TFGlasson, Heraclitus' Alleged Logos Doctr., JTS 3, '52, 231-8.—NJWeinstein, Z. Genesis d. Agada '01, 29-90; Billerb. II 302-33. —Rtzst., Zwei religionsgeschichtl. Fragen '01, 47-132, Mysterienrel.³ '27, 428 index; WBousset, Kyrios Christos² '21, 304ff; 316f; JKroll, D. Lehren d. Hermes Trismegistos '14, 418 index.—RBultmann, D. religionsgesch. Hintergrund des Prol. z. Joh.: HGunkel-Festschr. '23, II 1-26, Comm. '41, 5ff; ABDAlexander, The Johannine Doctrine of the Logos: ET 36, '25, 394-9; 467-72; (Rtzst. and) HHSchaeder, Studien z. antiken Synkretismus '26, 306-37; 350; GAvdBerghvanEysinga, In den beginne was de Logos: NThT 23, '34, 105-23; JDillersberger, Das Wort von Logos '35; RGBury, The 4th Gosp. and the Logos-Doctrine '40; EMay, CBQ 8, '46, 438-47; GAFKnight, From Moses to Paul '49, 120-9. TW IV 76-89; 126-40 (on this s. SLyonnet, Biblica 26, '45, 126-31); CStange, Zsyst Th 21, '50, 120-41; MEBoismard, Le Prologue de St. Jean '53; HLangkammer, BZ 9, '65, 91-4; HRinggren, Word and Wisdom [hypostatization in Near East] '47; WEltester, Haenchen-Festschr., '64, 109-34; HFWeiss, Untersuchungen zur Kosmologie etc., TU 97, '66, 216-82; MRissi, Die Logoslieder im Prolog des vierten Evangeliums, ThZ 31, '75, 321-36. M-M. B. 1262.

λόγχη, ης, ἡ (Pind., Hdt.+; inscr., pap., LXX; Jos., Bell. 3, 95, Ant. 16, 315; Sib. Or. 3, 688; loanw. in rabb.) *spear,*

lance Mt 27: 49 t.r. (HJVogels, BZ 10, '12, 396-405); J 19: 34. In the latter pass. the mng. *spear-point* (Hdt. 1, 52; X., An. 4, 7, 16; Dit., Syll.³ 1168, 95; 1169, 65) is also poss. M-M. B. 1390.*

λοιδορέω 1 aor. ἐλοιδόρησα (since Pind., Ol. 9, 56 λ. θεούς; Dio Chrys. 15[32], 89 θεούς; Epict. 3, 4, 7 τὸν Δία; Dit., Syll.³ 1109, 75ff; PPetr. III 21 [g], 19 [III BC]; BGU 1007, 6; LXX) *revile, abuse* τινά *someone* (X., An. 7, 5, 11; Theophr., Char. 28, 5; Dt 33: 8; Jos., Bell. 2, 302, C. Ap. 2, 148) J 9: 28; Ac 23: 4. τὸν Χριστόν MPol 9: 3. Pass. λοιδορούμενοι εὐλογοῦμεν *when we are reviled, we bless* 1 Cor 4: 12; cf. Dg 5: 15. Of Christ λοιδορούμενος οὐκ ἀντελοιδόρει *when he was reviled he did not revile in return* 1 Pt 2: 23. M-M.*

λοιδορία, ας, ἡ (Aristoph., Thu.+; PPetr. II 18 [1], 8; PSI 222, 14 μεθ' ὕβρεως κ. λοιδοριῶν; LXX; Philo; Jos., Ant. 17, 37, C. Ap. 2, 4) *verbal abuse, reproach, reviling* ἀποδιδόναι λοιδορίαν ἀντὶ λοιδορίας *return abuse for abuse* 1 Pt 3: 9 (= Pol 2: 2; cf. Philo, Agr. 110). μηδεμίαν ἀφορμὴν διδόναι τῷ ἀντικειμένῳ λοιδορίας χάριν *give the opponent no occasion* (for criticism) *because of the abuse* (which it might produce); perh. also simply: *for abuse, abusing us* (if the opponent is human; s. ἀντίκειμαι) 1 Ti 5: 14. M-M.*

λοίδορος, ου, ὁ (Eur.+; Plut.; Inscr. Rom. I 307, 3) *reviler, abusive person* (so Plut., Mor. 177D; Sir 23: 8; Test. Benj. 5: 4) 1 Cor 5: 11; 6: 10. M-M.*

λοιμικός, ή, όν (Hippocr.+; Lycophron, vs. 1205; IG XII 1, 1032, 7; Dit., Syll.³ 731, 7 [I BC]; PMich. 149, 5, 8; 10 [II AD]; Philo, Gig. 10) *pestilential* λ. καιρός *a time of pestilence* 1 Cl 55: 1.*

I. λοιμός, οῦ, ὁ *pestilence* (Hom.+; Dit., Syll.³ 620, 15; 921, 58 λ. ἢ πόλεμος; POxy. 1666, 20; 4 Macc 15: 32 v.l.; Philo; Jos., Ant. 9, 289f al.) λοιμοί *plagues, diseases* (pl. as Pla., Leg. 4 p. 709A; Hymn to Isis [I BC] 24 P.) among the signs of the last time (w. λιμός, q.v. 2) Mt 24: 7 t.r.; Lk 21: 11. M-M.*

II. λοιμός, ή, όν (LXX) comp. λοιμότερος *pestilential, diseased, pernicious* of birds of prey, looked upon as typical of certain persons ὄρνεα ... ὄντα λοιμὰ τῇ πονηρίᾳ αὐτῶν B 10: 4. Subst. (1 Macc 15: 21) vs. 10 (Ps 1: 1). οἱ λοιμότεροι *the more troublesome ones* IPol 2: 1. εὑρόντες τὸν ἄνδρα τοῦτον λοιμόν *we have found this man to be a plague-spot* Ac 24: 5 (the noun λοιμός as designation of a person dangerous to the public weal in Demosth. 25, 80; Aelian, V.H. 14, 11. The adj. in Libanius, Or. 1, 186 F. τὸν λοιμὸν Γερόντιον. Cf. Ἐλύμας and OHoltzmann, ZKG 14, 1894, 495-502).*

λοιπός, ή, όν (Pind., Hdt.+; inscr., pap., LXX, Ep. Arist.; Philo, Aet. M. 130; Joseph.; Test. 12 Patr.) *remaining.*

1. *left*—a. adj. αἱ λοιπαὶ φωναί *the remaining blasts* Rv 8: 13.

b. subst. οἱ λοιποί *those who were left* Rv 11: 13. W. gen. (Iambl., Vi. Pyth. 35, 251) οἱ λ. τῶν ἀνθρώπων 9: 20.

2. *other*—a. adj. (Jos., Ant. 5, 129 αἱ λ. φυλαί) οἱ λ. ἀπόστολοι *the other apostles* Ac 2: 37; 1 Cor 9: 5. αἱ λ. παρθένοι Mt 25: 11. τὰ λ. ἔθνη *the rest of the Gentiles* Ro 1: 13. οἱ λ. Ἰουδαῖοι Gal 2: 13. αἱ λ. ἐκκλησίαι 2 Cor 12: 13. οἱ λ. συνεργοί *the other coworkers* Phil 4: 3. αἱ λ. γραφαί *the rest of the scriptures* 2 Pt 3: 16.

b. subst.—**α.** οἱ λοιποί, αἱ λοιπαί *the others* (Plut., Mor. 285ᴅ; Herodian 4, 2, 10; Jos., Bell. 3, 497) Mt 22: 6; 27: 49; Mk 16: 13; Lk 8: 10; 18: 9; 24: 10; Ac 5: 13 (differently CCTorrey, ET 46, '35, 428f); 16: 30 D; 17: 9; 27: 44; Ro 11: 7; 1 Cor 7: 12; 2 Cor 2: 17 v.l.; Eph 2: 3; 1 Th 5: 6; 1 Ti 5: 20; Rv 19: 21. οἱ λ. πάντες *all the others* 2 Cor 13: 2; Phil 1: 13 (Dit., Syll.³ 593 καὶ ἐν τοῖς λοιποῖς πᾶσιν φανερὰν πεποιήκαμεν τὴν προαίρεσιν). πάντες οἱ λ. *all the rest* Lk 24: 9. οἱ λ. ἔχοντες ἀσθενείας *the others who were sick* Ac 28: 9. οἱ λ. οἱ μὴ ἔχοντες ἐλπίδα *the rest who have no hope* 1 Th 4: 13. οἱ λ. οἱ ἐν Θυατίροις Rv 2: 24. W. gen. foll. (Lucian, Tox. 28 οἱ λ. τῶν οἰκετῶν) οἱ λ. τῶν ἀνθρώπων *other people* Lk 18: 11. οἱ λ. τῶν νεκρῶν *the rest of the dead* Rv 20: 5. οἱ λ. τοῦ σπέρματος αὐτῆς *the others of her descendants* 12: 17.

β. τὰ λοιπά *the other things, the rest* (Appian, Bell. Civ. 5, 67 §284; Jos., Ant. 2, 312) Lk 12: 26; 1 Cor 11: 34; 15: 37; Rv 3: 2. αἱ περὶ τὰ λοιπὰ ἐπιθυμίαι *desires for other things* Mk 4: 19.

3. adverbial uses—**a.** of time—**α.** (τὸ) λοιπόν *from now on, in the future, henceforth* (Pind. +) 1 Cor 7: 29 (but see 'b' below); Dg 9: 2. λοιπὸν ἀπόκειταί μοι *for the future there is reserved for me* 2 Ti 4: 8 (but see 'b' below). τὸ λοιπὸν ἐκδεχόμενος *then waiting* Hb 10: 13. καθεύδετε (τὸ) λοιπόν, which is variously interpreted, may mean: *you are still sleeping!* or: *do you intend to sleep on and on?* Also poss.: *meanwhile, you are sleeping! you are sleeping in the meantime?* (so τὸ λ. Jos., Ant. 18, 272) Mt 26: 45; Mk 14: 41.—λοιπόν *finally* (Jos., Ant. 6, 46) Ac 27: 20; MPol 9: 1.

β. τοῦ λοιποῦ *from now on, in the future* (Hdt. 2, 109; Aristoph., Pax 1084; X., Cyr. 4, 4, 10, Oec. 10, 9; Dit., Syll.³ 611, 17; 849, 12; PHal. 1, 171 [III ʙᴄ]; POxy. 1293, 14; Jos., Ant. 4, 187.—Bl-D. §186, 2; Rob. 295) Gal 6: 17.—In Eph 6: 10 the mng. is prob. rather *finally*, bringing the matter to a conclusion (s. b below; a v.l. has τὸ λοιπόν).

b. (τὸ) λοιπόν (Herodas 2, 92; Longus 2, 22, 2) *as far as the rest is concerned, beyond that, in addition, finally* λοιπὸν οὐκ οἶδα *beyond that I do not know* 1 Cor 1: 16 (POxy. 120, 1 [IV ᴀᴅ] λοιπὸν . . . οὐκ οἶδα. σκάψω λοιπὸν τ. ἀμπελῶνα *in addition I will dig the vineyard* Hs 5, 2, 4. As a transition to someth. new (Phil 3: 1), esp. when it comes near the end of a work *finally* (UPZ 78, 43 [159 ʙᴄ]; POxy. 119, 13) 2 Cor 13: 11; Phil 4: 8; 1 Th 4: 1 (λ. οὖν as BGU 1079, 6 [41 ᴀᴅ]); 2 Th 3: 1; Hm 10, 3, 2.—ὧδε λοιπόν (Epict. 2, 12, 24) *in this connection, then; furthermore* 1 Cor 4: 2.—Inferentially *therefore* (Epict. 1, 24, 1; 1, 27, 2 al.; POxy. 1480, 13 [32 ᴀᴅ]) IEph 11: 1; perh. also 1 Cor 7: 29; 2 Ti 4: 8.—ACavallin, Eranos 39, '41, 121-44; AFridrichsen, K. Human. Vetenskaps-Samfundet i Upp. Årsbok '43, 24-8. M-M.**

Λουκᾶς, ᾶ, ὁ (as a pagan name CIG III 4759; III add. 4700k; 4790; inscr. in Pisidian Antioch: Ramsay, Bearing 370-84; CIL VI 17 685; Ephem. Epigr. VIII 3 no. 477; Sb 224) *Luke* (an affectionate or pet name for Lucius [another inscr. fr. Pisidian Antioch closely connected w. the one mentioned above—Ramsay, loc. cit.—calls the man Λούκιος who is named Λουκᾶς in the former one]: WSchulze, Graeca Latina '01, 12; Bl-D. §125, 2; Mlt.-H. 88 [favors Lucanus]; Dssm., Festgabe für AvHarnack '21, 117-20 = LO 372-7 [LAE² 435ff]; EKlostermann, Hdb. on Lk 1: 1 [considers still other possibilities], companion and co-worker of Paul Phlm 24; 2 Ti 4: 11; 2 Cor subscr.; acc. to Col 4: 14 a physician (cf. Lucian, M. Peregr. 44 Ἀλέξ. ὁ ἰατρός), and in line w. tradition (Iren. 3, 3, 1f; Murat. Canon 2-8; 34-9) author of the third gospel (title κατὰ Λουκᾶν) and of Ac. The proposition that the language of these books shows that their author was a physician (so Hobart; Harnack [s. below] 122ff; Zahn, Einl.³ II 433ff et al.) is disputed by GAvdBerghvanEysinga, De geneesher L.: NThT 5, '16, 228-50; HJCadbury, The Style and Literary Method of Luke I '19, 39ff, JBL 45, '26, 190-209 et al. The idea, known since Origen, In Rom. Comm. 10, 39, that Luke is to be identified w. the Lucius of Ro 16: 21 (Λούκιος 2) has been revived by Dssm., loc. cit. Ephraem Syrus identified L. with Lucius of Cyrene (Λούκιος 1) Ac 13: 1 (AMerk, D. neuentdeckte Komm. d. hl. E. zur AG: ZkTh 48, '24, 54).—Harnack, Lukas d. Arzt '06; Ramsay, Luke the Physician '08; AvanVeldhuizen, Lukas de medicijnmeester '26; HJCadbury, The Making of Luke-Acts '27, reprinted '58; EMeyer I 1ff; 46ff; 100ff; 304ff. WS Reilly, CBQ 1, '39, 314-24. M-M.*

Λούκιος, ου, ὁ (Diod. S. 11, 81, 1; 12, 43, 1; 14, 38, 1; Dit., Syll.³ 1173, 7; Sb II p. 258f; PFay. 110, 1 [94 ᴀᴅ]; PWarr. 1, 1; PWien Bosw. 2, 11; Jos., Bell. 6, 188; Bl-D. §41, 1; Mlt.-H. 88) *Lucius*.

1. of Cyrene, a teacher or prophet at Antioch Ac 13: 1.—HJCadbury, Beginn. I 5, '33, 489-95.—**2.** an otherw. unknown Christian, sender of a greeting Ro 16: 21.—On both s. Λουκᾶς. M-M.*

λουτρόν, οῦ, τό (since Hom. [λοετρόν], contracted since Hes.; inscr., pap.; SSol 4: 2; 6: 6; Sir 34: 25; Jos., Ant. 8, 356) *bath, washing* of baptism (for the ceremonial usage cf. Ael. Aristid. 48, 71 K.=24 p. 483 D.: λουτρὰ θεῖα; Arrian, Tact. 33, 4; Philostrat. Junior [III ᴀᴅ] at the end of his Εἰκόνες [APF 14, '41] l. 77, p. 8; 19 λουτρὰ σεμνά; mystery inscr. fr. Andania: Dit., Syll.³ 736, 106 [92 ʙᴄ]; Philo, Cher. 95 al. S. also λούω 2aβ) τὸ λ. τοῦ ὕδατος *the washing in water* Eph 5: 26 (Jos., C. Ap. 1, 282 ὑδάτων λουτροῖς). λ. παλιγγενεσίας *the bath that brings about regeneration* Tit 3: 5 (cf. Philo, Mut. Nom. 124 τοῖς φρονήσεως λουτροῖς χρησαμένη [ἡ ψυχή]). M-M.*

λούω 1 aor. ἔλουσα; pf. pass. ptc. λελουμένος (J 13: 10) and λελουσμένος (Hb 10: 22; Bl-D. §70, 3; Mlt.-H. 248; Helbing 100f) *wash*, as a rule of the whole body, *bathe*.

1. act., lit., abs. of the washing of a corpse (Hom. +) Ac 9: 37; GP 6: 24. Of persons who have been scourged ἔλουσεν ἀπὸ τῶν πληγῶν *he washed their wounds* (lit., 'by washing he freed them from the effects of the blows') Ac 16: 33 (on the constr. w. ἀπό s. 2aβ below. Also Antig. Car. 163 of Europa: λούσασθαι ἀπὸ τῆς τοῦ Διὸς μίξεως = wash off the traces of intercourse with Zeus).—Sim., fig. τῷ λούσαντι ἡμᾶς ἀπὸ τῶν ἁμαρτιῶν ἡμῶν ἐν τῷ αἵματι αὐτοῦ Rv 1: 5 t.r. On this rdg. s. PvonderOstenSacken, ZNW 58, '67, 258 n. 17.

2. mid.—**a.** *I wash myself, I bathe myself* (Hom. +)—**α.** lit., of man or beast: of a woman λουμένη εἰς τὸν ποταμόν *bathing in the river* Hv 1, 1, 2 (λ. εἰς also Ptolem. Euerg. II [II ʙᴄ]: 234 fgm. 3 Jac.; Alciphr. 3, 7, 1 λουσάμενοι εἰς τὸ βαλανεῖον; Cyranides p. 57, 6). ὗς λουσαμένη 2 Pt 2: 22 (s. βόρβορος 2).

β. of relig. washings (Soph., Ant. 1201 τὸν μὲν λούσαντες ἁγνὸν λουτρόν; Apollon. Rhod. 3, 1203 λοέσσατο ποταμοῖο . . . θεῖοιο . . . before the sacrifice Jason washed himself clean of pollution, in the divine river; Plut., Mor. 264ᴅ λούσασθαι πρὸ τῆς θυσίας; Ael. Aristid. 33, 32 K.=51 p. 582 D.: πρὸς θεῶν λούσασθαι κέρδος ἐστὶ ζῶντα, ἢ καὶ τελευτήσαντι μένει; Dssm., NB 54 [BS 226f] cites for this usage three inscrs., all of which have the mid., two in combination w. ἀπό τινος; Sb 4127, 14 ἐν ᾧ καὶ ἁγίῳ τῷ τῆς ἀθανασίας ὕδατι λουσάμενος; Ramsay, Exp. 7th Ser. VIII '09, p. 280, 1; LXX;

Jos., Vi. 11 λ. πρὸς ἀγνείαν) of the act of purification necessary before entering the temple GOxy 14; 19; 24f (ἐν τῇ λίμνῃ τοῦ Δαυίδ); 32 (ὕδασιν). ὁ λελουμένος the one who has bathed (in contrast to the one who has his feet washed, and with allusion to the cleansing of the whole body in baptism [λελουμένος 'newly bathed, after the bath' Hdt. 1, 126; Aristoph., Lysist. 1064; Plut., Mor. 958в λουσαμένοις ἢ νιψαμένοις; Lev 15: 11 τ. χεῖρας νίπτεσθαι, λούεσθαι τὸ σῶμα]; differently HWindisch, Johannes u. d. Synoptiker '26, 77. On foot-washing s. also GAFKnight, Feetwashing: Enc. of Rel. and Ethics V 814–23; PFiebig, Αγγελος III '30, 121–8; BWBacon, ET 43, '32, 218–21; HvCampenhausen, ZNW 33, '34, 259–71; FMBraun, RB 44, '35, 22–33; ELohmeyer, ZNW 38, '39, 74–94; AFridrichsen, ibid. 94–6; Bultmann, J '41, 355–65; JDDunn, ZNW 61, '70, 247–52) J 13: 10 (λού. beside νίπτ. in eating Tob 7: 95; λού. before eating Act. Thom. 89). λούσασθε wash yourselves 1 Cl 8: 4 (Is 1: 16).—The sense is in doubt in εἴ τις μεταλάβῃ τὸ σῶμα τοῦ κυρίου καὶ λούσεται if anyone receives the body of the Lord (in the Eucharist) and then rinses out his mouth or bathes himself Agr 19.

b. I wash for myself w. obj. in acc. (Hes.+) τὸ σῶμα ὕδατι καθαρῷ (cf. Dt 23: 12) Hb 10: 22 (of baptism).—AOepke, TW IV 297–309 λούω and related words. M-M. B. 579.*

Λύδδα (לֹד.—1 Macc 11: 34; Joseph. index), gen. Λύδδας Ac 9: 38 (cf. Thackeray 161), where Λύδδης is also attested. The acc. Λύδδα (Jos., Bell. 2, 242; 515 beside Λύδδαν Ant. 20, 130) vss. 32, 35 functions as an indecl. form or a neut. pl. (Jos., Bell. 1, 302 ἐν Λύδδοις; 2, 244; 4, 444; cf. Bl-D. §56, 2 app.), **ἡ**, Lydda, a city about 10½ miles southeast of Joppa on the road to Jerusalem. Ac 9: 32, 35, 38. Schürer index, esp. II⁴ 232, 35. M-M.*

Λυδία, ας, ἡ (as a woman's name Horace, Odes 1, 8, 1; 1, 13, 1; 1, 25, 8; 3, 9, 6f; Martial, Epigr. 11, 21. In Gk. preserved in the form Λύδη: CIG 653; 6975; CIA III 3261f) Lydia, a merchant fr. Thyatira in Lydia (the province of L. in Asia Minor as v.l. Ac 2: 9) who dealt in purple cloth; she was converted by Paul in Philippi, after having been σεβομένη τ. θεόν (s. σέβω 2a) Ac 16: 14, 40. M-M.*

Λυκαονία, ας, ἡ (X.+; inscr.) Lycaonia, a province in the interior of Asia Minor, bounded by Cappadocia, Galatia (s. Γαλατία), Phrygia, Pisidia and Cilicia. Its main cities were those visited by Paul: Lystra, Iconium, and Derbe. Ac 14: 6.—Ramsay, Histor. Comm. on Gal 1899, 19ff.*

Λυκαονιστί adv. in (the) Lycaonian (language), a dialect spoken in Lycaonia, no longer known to us Ac 14: 11.— PKretschmer, Einleitung in die Geschichte der griech. Sprache 1896, 396; KHoll, Her. 43, '08, 240ff. M-M.*

Λυκία, ας, ἡ (Hdt.+; inscr.; 1 Macc 15: 23; Sib. Or.) Lycia, a projection on the south coast of Asia Minor between Caria and Pamphylia Ac 27: 5.—OBenndorf et al., Reisen im südwestl. Kleinasien I; II, 1884; 1889; EKalinka, Zur histor. Topographie Lykiens: HKiepert-Festschr. 1898, 161f.*

λύκος, ου, ὁ (Hom.+; inscr., pap., LXX, Philo, Test. 12 Patr.; Sib. Or. 8, 41; 13, 28; loanw. in rabb., but s. KH Rengstorf, ELittmann-Festschr. '35, 55–62) wolf.

1. lit., as a symbol Mt 10: 16; Lk 10: 3; J 10: 12a, b; D 16: 3 (in all these pass. in contrast to sheep; cf. Dio Chrys. 64[14], 2; Philostrat., Vi. Apoll. 8, 22; Philo, Praem. 86).

2. fig. (as early as Il. 4, 471; 16, 156; Epict. 1, 3, 7 al.

Cf. Zeph 3: 3; Jer 5: 6; Ez 22: 27; Rhodon [in Euseb., H.E. 5, 13, 4] refers to Marcion as ὁ Ποντικὸς λύκος), of evil men IPhld 2: 2; 2 Cl 5: 2–4 (fr. a non-canonical gospel). λ. ἅρπαγες ravenous wolves Mt 7: 15. λ. βαρεῖς fierce wolves Ac 20: 29.—GBornkamm, TW IV 309–13. M-M. B. 185.*

λυμαίνω 1 aor. inf. λυμᾶναι; impf. mid. ἐλυμαινόμην, quite predom., in earlier times exclusively, used as a mid. dep. (Aeschyl., Hdt.+; inscr., pap., LXX; En. 19, 1; Ep. Arist. 164; Philo; Jos., Bell. 2, 271; 4, 534 al.) harm, injure, damage, spoil, ruin, destroy (so Thu.+) τὶ someth. Σαῦλος ἐλυμαίνετο τὴν ἐκκλησίαν Saul was trying to destroy the church Ac 8: 3. Of gluttons who, by their intemperance, damage τὴν σάρκα αὐτῶν their bodies Hv 3, 9, 3a (Epict. 3, 22, 87 τὸ σῶμα λυμαίνεται= he injures his body).—Also used as a passive (UPZ 187, 20 [127/6 bc]) λυμαίνεται ἡ σὰρξ αὐτῶν their bodies become injured Hv 3, 9, 3b (cf. Jos., Ant. 12, 256 λ. τὰ σώματα). —The act. λυμαίνω appears quite late (Libanius, Decl. 13, 6 vol. VI p. 10, 13 F.; PGM 13, 302 πῦρ, οὐ μή μου λυμάνῃς σάρκα; Herm. Wr. 10, 20). It has the same mng. πόλιν λυμᾶναι destroy a city Hv 4, 1, 8. τινά hurt someone 4, 2, 4. M-M. B. 760.*

λυπέω 1 aor. ἐλύπησα; pf. λελύπηκα; 1 aor. pass. ἐλυπήθην; 1 fut. pass. λυπηθήσομαι (Hes.+; inscr., pap., LXX, En., Ep. Arist., Philo, Joseph., Test. 12 Patr.) grieve, pain.

1. act. τινά someone (Dio Chrys. 28[45], 3; BGU 531 II, 18 [I ad].—Also rather in the sense vex, irritate, offend, insult: Herodas 5, 7, 3) 2 Cor 2: 2a; 7: 8a, b. The object of λυπεῖν can also be a divinity (Diod. S. 1, 65, 7 and 8 τὸν θεόν; schol. on Apollon. Rhod. 2, 313 λ. τὸν Δία) μὴ λυπεῖτε τὸ πνεῦμα τὸ ἅγιον τοῦ θεοῦ Eph 4: 30; Hm 10, 2, 2; 10, 3, 2; cf. 10, 2, 4. χάριν Dg 11: 7. In εἴ τις λελύπηκεν 2 Cor 2: 5 λ. used abs. is certainly more than cause pain or vexation. In Polyaenus 8, 47 it is used of the severe humiliation or outrage experienced by a king who has been deposed by his subjects.

2. pass.—**a.** aor. λυπηθῆναι become sad, sorrowful, distressed (BGU 1079, 9 [41 ad]; Esth 2: 21; Ps 54: 3; 2 Esdr 15 [Neh 5]: 6; Jos., Ant. 8, 356) Mt 14: 9; 17: 23; 18: 31; J 16: 20; 2 Cor 2: 4; 7: 9a; 1 Pt 1: 6; 1 Cl 4: 3 (Gen 4: 5 Cain took offense); Dg 1. W. ὅτι foll. become distressed because (cf. En. 102, 5) J 21: 17. λυπηθῆναι εἰς μετάνοιαν become sorry enough to repent 2 Cor 7: 9b. λ. κατὰ θεόν as God would have it vss. 9c, 11.

b. pres. λυπεῖσθαι be sad, be distressed, grieve (La 1: 22) 1 Th 4: 13. λυπῇ; are you grieved or hurt? Hv 3, 1, 9b. λυπούμενος (being) sad, sorrowful Mt 19: 22; 26: 22; Mk 10: 22; Hv 1, 2; 2; 3, 13, 2 (Jos., Vi. 208). (Opp. χαίρων as Dio Chrys. 50[67], 5; Philo, Virt. 103) 2 Cor 6: 10. λυπουμένου (μου) ὅτι because Hv 3, 1, 9a. ἤμην λυπούμενος 1, 2, 1. ὁ λυπούμενος the mournful man (Ael. Aristid. 46 p. 404 D.) m 10, 3, 3. ὁ λ. ἐξ ἐμοῦ 2 Cor 2: 2b gives the source of the pain or sadness. ἤρξατο λυπεῖσθαι he began to be sorrowful Mt 26: 37; cf. Mk 14: 19. λ. διά τι because of someth. (schol. on Apollon. Rhod. 4, 1090): εἰ διὰ βρῶμα ὁ ἀδελφός σου λυπεῖται if your brother's feelings are hurt because of food Ro 14: 15 (but λ. can also mean injure, damage: X., Mem. 1, 6, 6, Cyr. 6, 3, 13). μὴ λυπείσθω ὁ εὐσεβὴς ἐάν the godly man is not to grieve if 2 Cl 19: 4. λ. ἐπί τινι at someth. (X., Mem. 3, 9, 8; Lucian, Dial. Mort. 13, 5, Tox. 24; Artem. 2, 60; PGrenf. II 36, 9 [95 bc]; Jon 4: 9; Philo, Abr. 22) Hm 10, 2, 3; cf. s 6, 3, 1.—Impf. ἐλυπούμην I was sad GP 7: 26; cf. 14: 59. —RBultmann, TW IV 314–25: λυπέω and related words. M-M.*

λύπη, ης, ἡ (Aeschyl., Hdt.+; inscr., pap., LXX; En. 102, 5; 7; Ep. Arist., Philo; Jos., Vi. 205 al.; Test. 12 Patr.) *grief, sorrow, pain* of mind or spirit, *affliction* J 16: 6; Hm 10, 1, 2; 10, 2, 1-6; 10, 3, 1; 3f. περισσοτέρα λ. *excessive sorrow* 2 Cor 2: 7. Opp. χαρά (X., Hell. 7, 1, 32; Eth. Epic. col. 3, 16; Philo, Abr. 151, Leg. ad Gai. 15) J 16: 20; Hb 12: 11. λύπην ἔχειν *have pain, be sorrowful* (Dio Chrys. 46[63], 1) in child-birth J 16: 21; cf. vs. 22. λ. ἔχειν ἀπό τινος *be pained by someone* 2 Cor 2: 3. λύπην ἐπὶ λύπην ἔχειν *sorrow upon sorrow* Phil 2: 27. Cf. Hs 1: 10. λ. μοί ἐστιν μεγάλη *I am greatly pained* Ro 9: 2 (cf. Test. Judah 23: 1 πολλὴ λύπη μοί ἐστι.—λ. μεγάλη as Jon 4: 1). βαλεῖν τινα εἰς λύπην *plunge someone into grief* 1 Cl 46: 9. τὸ μὴ πάλιν ἐν λ. πρὸς ὑμᾶς ἐλθεῖν *not to come to you again in sorrow* 2 Cor 2: 1. σεαυτῷ λύπην ἐπισπᾶσθαι *bring sorrow on yourself* Hs 9, 2, 6. ἀποβαλεῖν πᾶσαν λ. *lay aside all sorrow* Hv 4, 3, 4. Also αἴρειν ἀφ' ἑαυτοῦ τὴν λ. m 10, 1, 1. συγκόπτεσθαι ἀπὸ τῆς λύπης *be crushed with sorrow* v 5: 4. ἀπὸ τῆς λ. *from sorrow* Lk 22: 45 (UPZ 18, 13 [163 bc] ἀποθνῄσκει ὑπὸ τῆς λ. Jos., Ant. 6, 337). ἐκ λύπης *reluctantly* 2 Cor 9: 7 (Aesop, Fab. 275 P. ἐκ τῆς λύπης); ἡ κατὰ θεὸν λ. *sorrow that God approves* 7: 10a (leading to μετάνοια as Plut., Mor. 961d). In contrast to this ἡ τοῦ κόσμου λύπη *the sorrow of the world* vs. 10b. λύπην ἐπάγειν τῷ πνεύματι *bring grief to the spirit* Hm 3: 4.—Pl. (Demosth., Ep. 2, 25; Dio Chrys. 80[30], 14; Gen 3: 16f; 5: 29; Pr 15: 13; 31: 6) αἱ πρότεραι λῦπαι *the former sorrows* Hv 3, 13, 2. ὑποφέρειν λύπας 1 Pt 2: 19. παλαιοῦσθαι ταῖς λύπαις *be made old by sorrows* Hv 3, 11, 3. λύπη personified Hs 9, 15, 3. M-M. B. 1118.*

λυπηρός, ά, όν (trag., Hdt.+; pap., LXX, Philo; Jos., Ant. 15, 61)—1. act. *painful, distressing* τινί *to someone* (PPetr. II 13 [19], 13 [III bc] οὐθέν σοι μὴ γενηθῇ λυπηρόν; Gen 34: 7; Jos., Ant. 17, 175) ἀμφότερα λυπηρά ἐστι τῷ πνεύματι Hm 10, 2, 4.

2. pass. *sad, mournful, downcast* ἀνήρ (Pr 17: 22) 10, 3, 2.*

Λυσανίας, ου, ὁ (on the gen. s. Mlt.-H. 119) *Lysanias,* tetrarch of Abilene Lk 3: 1. There was a Lysanias, son of the dynast Ptolemaeus of Chalcis, who ruled 40-36 bc and was executed by Mark Antony. If Luke had meant this Lysanias (so HHoltzmann and Wlh. ad loc. and E Schwartz, NGG '06, 370f), he would have committed a grave chronological error. There was, however, a younger Lysanias in the period 25-30 ad, to whom Josephus' expressions Ἄβιλαν τὴν Λυσανίου (Ant. 19, 275) and Ἀβέλλα (= Ἄβιλα) as Λυσανία τετραρχία (20, 138) are best referred, and to whom the inscrs. CIG 4521 = Dit., Or. 606; CIG 4523 refer.—Schürer I⁴ 717ff (719, 44 the older lit.); EKlostermann and Zahn ad loc.; RSavignac, Texte complet de l'inscription d'Abila relative à Lysanias: RB n.s. 9, '12, 533-40; Ramsay, Bearing 297-300; EMeyer I 47ff; HLeclercq, Dict. d'Arch. X '31, 405-11. M-M.*

Λυσίας, ου, ὁ (lit., inscr., pap., LXX, Joseph.) *(Claudius) Lysias* (s. Κλαύδιος 2) Ac 23: 26; 24: 7, 22.*

λύσις, εως, ἡ (Hom.+; inscr., pap., LXX; En. 5, 6; Philo; Jos., Ant. 9, 70; Test. 12 Patr.; Diod. S. 18, 25, 2 [λύσις τῶν κακῶν = resolution, removal of difficulties]) *release, separation,* (in marriage) *a divorce* 1 Cor 7: 27. M-M.*

λυσιτελέω (Hdt., Aristoph.+; LXX; Jos., Ant. 15, 110 al.) *be advantageous, be better* impers. λυσιτελεῖ *it is better, it profits* (Pla.+) w. dat. (Dio Chrys. 48[65], 3;

Dit., Syll.³ 344, 96 [c. 303 bc]; PHamb. 27, 17 [250 bc]; Tob 3: 6; Philo, Det. Pot. Ins. 68) λυσιτελεῖ αὐτῷ εἰ περίκειται . . . ἢ ἵνα *it would be better for him if . . . , than that* Lk 17: 2 (Andoc. 1, 125 τεθνάναι λυσιτελεῖ ἢ ζῆν). M-M.*

λυσσάω (Soph.+; Sib. Or. 5, 96) *be raving, be mad* of dogs (Aristoph.+) κύνες λυσσῶντες *mad dogs* (fig. as Jos., Bell. 6, 196) IEph 7: 1.*

Λύστρα (Ptolem. 5, 4, 12; Dit., Or. 536. Cf. Pliny, Nat. Hist. 5, 147; CIL Suppl. 6786; 6974) acc. Λύστραν; dat. Λύστροις (on its declension cf. Bl-D. §57; Mlt. 48; Mlt.-H. 147; Thackeray 167f) ἡ or τά *Lystra,* a city in Lycaonia in Asia Minor, where a church was founded by Paul. Ac 14: 6, 8, 21; 16: 1f; 27: 5 v.l.; 2 Ti 3: 11.—ABludau, Pls in L., Ac 14: 7-21: Der Katholik 87, '07, 91-113; 161-83; WMCalder, Zeus and Hermes at Lystra: Exp. 7th ser. X '10, 1-6, The 'Priest' of Zeus at Lystra: ibid. 148-55; AWikenhauser, D. AG '21, 362f; LCurtius, Zeus u. Hermes '31; MMeunier, Apoll. de Ty. ou le séjour d'un dieu parmi les hommes '36; SEitrem, Con. Neot. 3, '39, 9-12. M-M.*

λύτρον, ου, τό (Pind., Hdt.+; inscr., pap., LXX, Philo, Joseph.) *price of release, ransom* (esp. also the ransom money for the manumission of slaves, mostly in pl.: Diod. S. 19, 85, 3; Polyaenus 4, 10, 1; POxy. 48, 6 [86 ad]; 49, 8; 722, 30; 40; Mitteis, Chrest. 362, 19; Jos., Ant. 12, 46, but also in sing.: Diod. S. 20, 84, 6 δοῦναι λύτρον; inscr. in KBuresch, Aus Lydien 1898 p. 197; Jos., Ant. 14, 371.—LMitteis, Reichsrecht und Volksrecht 1891, 388; FSteinleitner, Die Beicht '13, 36ff; 59; 111) give up one's life λ. ἀντὶ πολλῶν *as a ransom for many* (s. πολύς I 2aα) Mt 20: 28; Mk 10: 45 (BBlake, ET 45, '34, 142; WFHoward, ET 50, '38, 107-10; JoachJeremias, Judaica 3, '48, 249-64; ELohse, Märtyrer u. Gottesknecht, '55, 116-22; CKBarrett, NT Essays: TWManson mem. vol. '59, 1-18 [refers to 2 Macc 7: 37].—Cf. Diod. S. 12, 57, 2; Dio Chrys. 64[14], 11 λύτρα διδόναι; Jos., Ant. 14, 107 λ. ἀντὶ πάντων; Philo Bybl. in Euseb., Pr. Ev. I, 16, 44 ἀντὶ τῆς πάντων φθορᾶς . . . λ.). God gave his Son λ. ὑπὲρ ἡμῶν *as a ransom for us* Dg 9: 2 (Lucian, Dial. Deor. 4, 2 κριὸν λύτρον ὑπὲρ ἐμοῦ; schol. on Nicander, Alexiph. 560 λύτρα ὑπὲρ τῶν βοῶν; Philo, Spec. Leg. 2, 122; Jos., Ant. 14, 371 λ. ὑπὲρ αὐτοῦ). λ. τῶν ἁμαρτιῶν *a ransom for sins* B 19: 10.—S. on ἀπολύτρωσις, end; also NLevinson, Scottish Journal of Theol. 12, '59, 277-78; DHill, Gk. Words and Heb. Mngs. '67, 49-81. M-M.*

λυτρόω (Pla.+) in our lit. only mid. (and pass.) **λυτρόομαι** (Demosth.+; inscr., pap., LXX, Philo; Joseph.) 1 aor. mid. ἐλυτρωσάμην, imper. λύτρωσαι; 1 aor. pass. ἐλυτρώθην.

1. *free by paying a ransom, redeem*—a. lit. (Demosth. 19, 170) of prisoners (Diod. S. 5, 17, 3; Jos., Ant. 14, 371) 1 Cl 55: 2.

b. fig. λύτρωσαι τ. δεσμίους ἡμῶν (in a prayer) 59: 4.—Pass. ἀργυρίῳ ἢ χρυσίῳ λυτρωθῆναι ἐκ τῆς ματαίας ἀναστροφῆς *be ransomed with silver or gold from the futile way of life* 1 Pt 1: 18 (on λ. ἔκ τινος s. 2 below.— WCvanUnnik, De verlossing 1 Pt 1: 18, 19 en het problem van den 1 Pt '42).

2. gener. *set free, redeem, rescue* (Ps.-Callisth. 2, 7, 4 τὴν Ἑλλάδα λυτρώσασθαι; 3, 19, 10; LXX; Philo) τινά *someone* B 14: 8. Of Christ in his coming again λυτρώσεται ἡμᾶς *he will redeem us* 2 Cl 17: 4. Of the Messiah ὁ μέλλων λυτροῦσθαι τὸν Ἰσραήλ Lk 24: 21 (cf. Is 44: 22-4; 1 Macc 4: 11; PsSol 8: 30; 9: 1). τινὰ ἀπό τινος

λυτρόω – λύω

someone fr. someth. (Ps 118:134; cf. the ancient Christian prayer: CSchmidt, Heinrici-Festschr. '14, p. 69, 32f) λ. ἡμᾶς ἀπὸ πάσης ἀνομίας Tit 2:14 (Test. Jos. 18:2 ἀπὸ παντὸς κακοῦ). Also τινὰ ἔκ τινος (pagan inscr. in Ramsay, Phrygia II 566f ἐλυτρώσατο πολλοὺς ἐκ κακῶν βασάνων; Dt 13:6; Ps 106:2; Sir 51:2) someone fr. a monster Hv 4, 1, 7. ἐξ ἀναγκῶν m 8:10. ἐκ τοῦ σκότους B 14:5f; cf. 7. ἐκ θανάτου (Hos 13:14) 19:2. τ. ψυχὴν ἐκ θανάτου Ac 28:19 v.l.—Pass. (Aristot., Eth. Nicom. 10, 2 p. 1164b, 34; LXX) be redeemed ἐν τῇ χάριτι by grace IPhld 11:1 (on λ. ἐν cf. 2 Esdr 11 [Neh 1]:10 ἐν τ. δυνάμει; Ps 76:16; Sir 48:20). M-M.*

λύτρωσις, εως, ἡ (as legal and commercial t.t. in pap.) —1. ransoming, releasing, redemption (Plut., Arat. 11, 2 λ. αἰχμαλώτων; Palaeph. exc. Vat. p. 99, 10; LXX; Test. Jos. 8:1) ποιεῖν λύτρωσιν τῷ λαῷ bring about a deliverance for the people Lk 1:68. προσδέχεσθαι λύτρωσιν Ἰερουσαλήμ wait for the redemption of Jerusalem 2:38; αἰωνία λ. Hb 9:12. διὰ τοῦ αἵματος τοῦ κυρίου λ. ἔσται πᾶσιν τοῖς πιστεύουσιν redemption will come 1 Cl 12:7.
2. abstr. for concr. ransom (-money) δώσεις λ. ἁμαρτιῶν σου you must give a ransom for your sins D 4:6; B 19:10 Funk. M-M.*

λυτρωτής, οῦ, ὁ redeemer (not in secular wr.; LXX of God: Ps 18:15; 77:35) of Moses Ac 7:35. M-M.*

λυχνία, ας, ἡ (Hero Alex. I p. 264, 20; Plut., Dio 9, 2; Ps.-Lucian, Asin. 40; Artem. 1, 74; inscr.; pap. since PEleph. 5, 7 [284/3 BC]; LXX, Philo; Joseph. [s. λύχνος, beg.]; cf. Phryn. p. 313f L.) lampstand upon which lamps were placed or hung (s. λύχνος, beg.); not a candlestick. τιθέναι ἐπὶ τὴν λ. (ἐπὶ λυχνίας) put on the (lamp)stand Mt 5:15; Mk 4:21; Lk 8:16; 11:33. Of the seven-branched lampstand (Ex 25:31ff; Jos., Ant. 14, 72) Hb 9:2. In Rv the seven churches of Asia appear as seven lampstands Rv 1:12f, 20a, b; 2:1. Cf. also κινήσω τὴν λ. σου ἐκ τοῦ τόπου αὐτῆς I will remove your lampstand from its place, i.e. remove you fr. the circle of the churches 2:5. Rv also likens the two witnesses of Christ to two lampstands 11:4 (cf. Zech 4:11). M-M.*

λύχνος, ου, ὁ (Hom.+; inscr., pap., LXX) the (oil-burning: Posidonius: 87 fgm. 94 Jac.; Diod. S. 1, 34, 11; Charito 1, 1, 15; PGM 7, 359-64.—Made of metal or clay [Artem. 2, 9 p. 96, 20f λύχνος χαλκοῦς, ὀστράκινος]) lamp (s. λυχνία.—λυχνία beside λύχνος: Artem. 1, 74 p. 67, 12; Inscr. of Cos [Paton and Hicks 1891] 36d, 7; 8; Philo, Spec. Leg. 1, 296 καίεσθαι λύχνους ἐπὶ τῆς λυχνίας; Jos., Bell. 7, 429, Ant. 3, 182; 199).
1. lit. Lk 11:36; GP 5:18. φῶς λύχνου (Charito 1, 1, 15) light of a lamp Rv 22:5; cf. 18:23; ἔρχεται ὁ λ. a lamp is brought in Mk 4:21; καίειν λ. Mt 5:15 (Paus. 3, 17, 8 τὸν καιόμενον λύχνον). λ. ἅπτειν light a lamp (ἅπτω 1.—As a symbol of someth. out of place Paroem. Gr.: Diogenian 6, 27 λ. ἐν μεσημβρίᾳ ἅπτειν. Likew. an unknown comic poet: fgm. 721 K.) Lk 8:16; 11:33; 15:8.—Use of the lamp as a symbol: ἔστωσαν ὑμῶν...οἱ λύχνοι καιόμενοι Lk 12:35 (Artem. 2, 9 λ. καιόμενος); cf. D 16:1. The Baptist as ὁ λύχνος ὁ καιόμενος κ. φαίνων J 5:35. The believers are to pay attention to the prophetic word ὡς λύχνῳ φαίνοντι 2 Pt 1:19 (cf. Ps 118:105 λ....ὁ λόγος σου).
2. fig. (Lycophron vs. 422 λύχνοι are the eyes as vs. 846 λαμπτήρ an eye) ὁ λ. τοῦ σώματός ἐστιν ὁ ὀφθαλμός the lamp of the body is the eye Mt 6:22; Lk 11:34 (F Schwencke, ZWTh 55, '13, 251-60; WBrandt, ZNW 14, '13, 97-116; 177-201; BWBacon, Exp. 8th ser. VII '13,

275-88; JDMDerrett, Law in the NT, '70, 189-207; GSchneider, Das Bildwort von der Lampe usw., ZNW 61, '70, 183-209.—Further lit. s.v. ἁπλοῦς). Of the Spirit of God λ. ἐρευνῶν τὰ ταμιεῖα τῆς γαστρός 1 Cl 21:2 (Pr 20:27 A). Of the heavenly Jerusalem ὁ λ. αὐτῆς τὸ ἀρνίον Rv 21:23.—KGalling, D. Beleuchtungsgeräte im isr.-jüd. Kulturgebiet: ZDPV 46, '23, 1-50; RHSmith, Biblical Archaeologist 27, '64, 1-31, 101-24; 29, '66, 2-27; W Michaelis, TW IV 325-9: λύχνος, λυχνία. M-M. B. 484.*

λύω impf. ἔλυον; 1 aor. ἔλυσα. Pass.: impf. ἐλυόμην; pf. λέλυμαι, 2 sing. λέλυσαι, ptc. λελυμένος; 1 aor. ἐλύθην; 1 fut. λυθήσομαι (Hom.+; inscr., pap., LXX, Ep. Arist., Philo, Joseph., Test. 12 Patr., Sib. Or.).
1. loose, untie bonds (Da 5:12 Theod.), fetters (Lucian, Dial. Mar. 14, 3; Job 39:5 δεσμούς; Philo, Somn. 1, 181) or someth. similar used to hold someth. together or to secure it.
a. lit. τὸν ἱμάντα Mk 1:7; Lk 3:16; J 1:27. σφραγῖδας break (Polyaenus 5, 2, 12) Rv 5:2 (of the broken seals of a will: BGU 326 II, 21 ἡ διαθήκη ἐλύθη; POxy. 715, 19.—λύω of the opening of a document: Plut., Dio 31, 4 [a letter]; Vi. Aesopi W c. 92).
b. fig. ἐλύθη ὁ δεσμὸς τ. γλώσσης αὐτοῦ Mk 7:35; cf. Lk 1:63 D.
2. set free, loose, untie—a. lit. a pers., animal, or thing that is bound or tied: a prisoner (Jos., Bell. 2, 28, Ant. 13, 409; Ps 145:7) Ac 22:30; cf. vs. 29 v.l. Angels that are bound Rv 9:14f. Also more gener. (Isisaretal. v. Kyme 48 P. ἐγὼ τοὺς ἐν δεσμοῖς λύω) release, set free prisoners Ac 24:26 t.r. Of Satan, bound and imprisoned in the abyss Rv 20:3. λυθήσεται ὁ σατανᾶς ἐκ τῆς φυλακῆς αὐτοῦ vs. 7.—Of Lazarus, bound in grave-clothes λύσατε αὐτόν unbind him J 11:44 (Vi. Aesopi I 83 λύσατε αὐτόν=take off his fetters).—Of animals (X., An. 3, 4, 35) a colt that is tied up Mt 21:2; Mk 11:2, 4f; Lk 19:30f, 33a. b. τὸν βοῦν ἀπὸ τῆς φάτνης untie the ox from the manger Lk 13:15 (λ. ἀπό as Quint. Smyrn. 4, 373; Is 5:27; Jer 47:4). —λ. τὸ ὑπόδημα untie the sandal Ac 7:33 (Ex 3:5; Josh 5:15); 13:25.—Pass. τὰς τρίχας λελυμέναι with unbound hair Hs 9, 9, 5.
b. fig. free, set free, release ἀπό τινος (Cyranides p. 97, 12) λυθῆναι ἀπὸ τ. δεσμοῦ τούτου be set free from this bond Lk 13:16. λέλυσαι ἀπὸ γυναικός; are you free from a wife, i.e. not bound to a wife? 1 Cor 7:27 (a previous state of being 'bound' need not be assumed; cf. Chio, Ep. 7, 3 λελυμένως=[speak] in an unrestrained manner. See also Simplicius in Epict. p. 129, 3: 'he who does not found a family is εὔλυτος', i.e.,=free). ἐκ instead of ἀπό: λ. τινὰ ἐκ τῶν ἁμαρτιῶν αὐτοῦ free someone from his sins Rv 1:5. τινὰ ἐκ χειρὸς σιδήρου 1 Cl 56:9 (Job 5:20).
3. break up into its component parts, destroy, of a building tear down (Il. 16, 10; X., An. 2, 4, 17f; Herodian 7, 1, 7; 1 Esdr 1:52; Jos., Bell. 6, 32; Sib. Or. 3, 409) τ. ναὸν τοῦτον J 2:19. τὸ μεσότοιχον Eph 2:14 (as a symbol).—ἡ πρύμνα ἐλύετο the stern began to break up Ac 27:41 (PLond. 1164h, 19 [III AD] uses λ. of the dismantling of a ship). Of the parts of the universe, as it is broken up and destroyed in the final conflagration 2 Pt 3:10-12.—Of a meeting (Il. 1, 305; Od. 2, 257; Apollon. Rhod. 1, 708; X., Cyr. 6, 1, 2; Diod. S. 19, 25, 7; Ep. Arist. 202; Jos., Ant. 14, 388 λυθείσης τ. βουλῆς) λυθείσης τ. συναγωγῆς when the meeting of the synagogue had broken up Ac 13:43.
4. destroy, bring to an end, abolish, do away with (Socrat., Ep. 28, 2 and 4 'dispel' slanders) λ. τὰ ἔργα τ. διαβόλου destroy the works of the devil 1 J 3:8. Pass. ἐλύετο πᾶσα μαγεία all magic began to be dissolved IEph

483

19: 3. λύεται ὁ ὄλεθρος ἐν τ. ὁμονοίᾳ *his destructiveness comes to an end through the unity* 13: 1.—λ. τ. ὠδῖνας τ. θανάτου must mean in this context: *he brought the pangs to an end* (IG IV² 128, 49 [280 BC] ἔλυσεν ὠδῖνα; Lycophron vs. 1198 ὠδῖνας ἐξέλυσε γονῆς; Himerius, Or. 64 [= Or. 18], 1 λυθῆναι τὰς ὠδῖνας of the cessation of labor pains; Job 39: 2; Aelian, H.A. 12, 5 τοὺς τῶν ὠδίνων λῦσαι δεσμούς; Eutecnius 3 p. 30, 26), so that the 'birth' which is to bring Christ to light may attain its goal Ac 2: 24 (but s. on θάνατος 1bβ; originally it is probable that 'the bonds of death' went with 'loose').—Of commandments, laws, statements *repeal, annul, abolish* (Hdt. 1, 29, 1 νόμον. Text fr. Nysa in Diod. S. 1, 27, 4 ὅσα ἐγὼ ἐνομοθέτησα, οὐδεὶς αὐτὰ δύναται λῦσαι; Ael. Aristid. 30 p. 573 D.: νόμους; Achilles Tat. 3, 3, 5; Dit., Syll.³ 355, 21; 1219, 12; Jos., Ant. 11, 140) ἐντολήν Mt 5: 19. τὸ σάββατον *abolish the Sabbath* J 5: 18 (in John, Jesus is accused not of breaking the Sabbath, but of doing away w. it). Pass. (Dio Chrys. 58[75], 10 τ. νόμου λυθέντος) 7: 23; 10: 35 (RJungkuntz, CTM 35, '64, 556-65 [J 10: 34-6]).— λύειν τὸν Ἰησοῦν *annul* (the true teaching about) *Jesus* (by spurning it); (opp. ὁμολογεῖν; cf. Alex. Aphr., Fat. 26, II 2 p. 196, 18 λ. τινὰ τῶν Ζήνωνος λόγων = certain teachings of Zeno) 1 J 4: 3 v.l. (for the rdg. λύει cf. Harnack, SAB '15, 556-61 = Studien I '31, 132-7; A Rahlfs, ThLZ 40, '15, 525; OAPiper, JBL 66, '47, 440-4 [exorcistic, *break a spell*]).

5. On the combination and contrast of δέειν and λύειν Mt 16: 19; 18: 18 s. δέω 4; also GLambert, Vivre et Penser, IIIe s., '43/'44, 91-103.—OProcksch and FBüchsel, TW IV 329-59: λύω and related words. M-M. B. 1239f. **

Λωΐς, ΐδος, ἡ (PPetr. II 39b, 15 [III BC] has the genitive Λωΐτος from a nominative Λωΐς. Or does the name—which is found nowhere else—belong to a positive degree of comparison λῶϊς [claimed by Buttmann for the not uncommon λωΐων, a nom. sing. = more pleasant, more desirable]? Cf. Semonides 7, 30 D.² οὐκ ἔστιν ἄλλη τῆσδε λωΐων γυνή = no other woman is more worthy of being desired than this one) *Lois*, grandmother of Timothy 2 Ti 1: 5.*

Λώτ, ὁ indecl. (לוֹט.—LXX, Philo.—In Joseph. Λῶτος, ου [Ant. 1, 201]) *Lot*, son of Haran, nephew of Abraham (Gen 11: 27); he lived in Sodom Lk 17: 28f; was rescued fr. that doomed city, having led a virtuous life 2 Pt 2: 7; 1 Cl 11: 1 (SRappaport, D. gerechte Lot: ZNW 29, '30, 299-304). As they left the city his wife perished because she looked back, contrary to God's command Lk 17: 32 (on the whole s. Gen 19). His separation fr. Abraham 1 Cl 10: 4 (cf. Gen 13, esp. vss. 14-16).—(On the spelling s. JWordsworth-HJWhite on Mt 1: 17.)*

M

μ´ numeral = *forty* (Diod. S. 22, 13, 2) Ac 10: 41 D; Hs 9, 4, 3; 9, 5, 4; 9, 15, 4; 9, 16, 5.*

Μάαθ, ὁ indecl. (cf. the name מַחַת 1 Ch 6: 20 [Μεθ]; 2 Ch 29: 12 [Μααθ]; 31: 13) *Maath*, in the genealogy of Jesus Lk 3: 26.*

Μαγαδάν, ἡ indecl. *Magadan*, place of uncertain location on Lake Gennesaret Mt 15: 39; Mk 8: 10, the parallel pass., has Δαλμανουθά (q.v.), whose location is similarly uncertain; t.r. substitutes Μαγδαλά in Mt, which is also a v.l. in Mk, where furthermore D offers Μελεγαδά.— JBoehmer, ZNW 9, '08, 227-9; CKopp, Dominican Studies 4, '50, 344-50.*

Μαγδαληνή, ῆς, ἡ (subst. fem. of Μαγδαληνός, ή, όν) *Magdalene, woman from Magdala*, surname of a certain Mary (s. Μαρία 2), prob. fr. the town of Magdala which, acc. to the Talmud, lay about a twenty minutes' walk fr. Tiberias on the west side of the Lake of Gennesaret (Buhl 225f; CKopp, The Holy Places of the Gospels, tr. RWalls, '63, 190-7) Mt 27: 56, 61; 28: 1; Mk 15: 40, 47; 16: 1, 9; Lk 8: 2; 24: 10; J 19: 25; 20: 1, 18; GP 12: 50.*

Μαγεδών s. Ἀρμαγεδ(δ)ών.

μαγεία, ας, ἡ (Pla.+; on the spelling cf. Bl-D. §23; cf. Mlt.-H. 339) *magic* (Theophr., H. Pl. 9, 15, 7; Vett. Val. 210, 4; Fluchtaf. 4, 15; PGM 1, 127; Zosimus 7: Hermet. IV p. 105 Sc.; the Herm. document Κόρη κόσμου in Stob. I 407, 4 W. = p. 494, 7 Sc.; Jos., Ant. 2, 286) in a list of vices B 20: 1. ἐλύετο πᾶσα μαγεία IEph 19: 3 (λύω 4). Pl. *magic arts* (Jos., Ant. 2, 284) in a list of vices D 5: 1. Of Simon Ac 8: 11 (cf. PGM 4, 2447ff; Παχράτης, ὁ προφήτης Ἡλιουπόλεως, Ἀδριανῷ βασιλεῖ ἐπιδεικνύμενος τ. δύναμιν τῆς θείας αὐτοῦ μαγείας).—Lit. s.v. Σίμων 9. M-M (-ία). B. 1494.*

μαγεύω fut. μαγεύσω *practice magic* (Eur., Iph. 1338; Plut., Artax. 3, 6, Numa 15, 8; Gk.-Aram. inscr. in CClemen, D. Einfluss d. Mysterienreligionen auf d. älteste Christentum '13 p. 10, 3 στρατηγὸς . . . ἐμάγευσε Μίθρῃ) Ac 8: 9. In a list of vices D 2: 2. M-M.*

μαγία s. μαγεία.

Μαγνησία, ας, ἡ (Hdt.+; inscr.) *Magnesia*, a city in Asia Minor a short distance southeast of Ephesus, IMg inscr. In order to differentiate this city from Magnesia in Thessaly, which was considered its mother (Dit., Or. 503 Μάγνητες οἱ πρὸς τῷ Μαιάνδρῳ ποταμῷ, ἄποικοι ὄντες Μαγνήτων τῶν ἐν Θεσσαλίᾳ, also the note, Syll.³ 636; 1157), and fr. another Magnesia in Asia Minor near Mt. Sipylus (Dit., Or. 501, 13; 229 s. note 12), it is called Magnesia on the Maeander, despite the fact that it lies on the Lethaeus, about four miles distant fr. the Maeander. The name of the river is usu. added w. a prep., in our passage πρός w. dat., as also in Dit., Or. 229, 84; 503 (s. above). OKern, Die Inschriften von M. am Mäander '00, no. 40, 11; 16; 44, 4; 101, 8. An inhabitant of the city is called Μάγνης, ητος (Hdt. + in lit.; on inscr. and coins [cf. the material in Lghtf. on IMg inscr., also Dit., Or. 12; 231; 232; 234; 319; 501. Kern, op. cit. p. 206]).*

μάγος, ου, ὁ—1. *a Magus*, a (Persian [SNyberg, D. Rel. d. alten Iran '38], then also Babylonian) wise man and priest, who was expert in astrology, interpretation of dreams and various other secret arts (so Hdt.+; Jos., Ant. 20, 142, and Da 2: 2, 10; in still other pass. in Da, Theod.). After Jesus' birth μάγοι *Magi* Mt 2: 7 (s. Jos., Ant. 10, 216), 16a, b or more definitely μάγοι ἀπὸ ἀνατολῶν *Magi from the east* vs. 1 came to Palestine and declared that they had read in the stars of the birth of the Messianic King. Diog. L. 2, 45 φησὶ δ' Ἀριστοτέλης μάγον τινὰ ἐλθόντα ἐκ Συρίας εἰς

Άθήνας in order to announce to Socrates that he would come to a violent end.—ADieterich, ZNW 3, '02, 1-14; FXSteinmetzer, D. Gesch. der Geburt u. Kindheit Christi '10; GFrenken, Wunder u. Taten der Heiligen '29, 186-93; KBornhäuser, D. Geburts- u. Kindheitsgesch. Jesu '30. FCumont, L'Adoration des Mages: Memorie della Pontif. Acc. Rom. di Archeol. 3, '32, 81-105. EJHodous, CBQ 6, '44, 71-4; 77-83.—On the Magi HUMeyboom, Magiërs: ThT '39, '05, 40-70; GMessina, D. Ursprung der Magier u. d. zarath. Rel., Diss. Berl. '30, I Magi a Betlemme e una predizione di Zoroastro '33 (against him GHartmann, Scholastik 7, '32, 403-14); RPettazzoni, Revue d'Hist. des Rel. 103, '31, 144-50; Gdspd., Probs. 14f.—On the star of the Magi HHKritzinger, Der Stern der Weisen '11; HGVoigt, Die Geschichte Jesu u. d. Astrologie '11; OGerhardt, Der Stern des Messias '22; DAFrövig, D. Stern Bethlehems in der theol. Forschung: Tidsskrift for Teologi og Kirke 2, '31, 127-62; CSSmith, ChQR 114, '32, 212-27; WVischer, D. Ev. von den Weisen aus dem Morgenlande: EVischer-Festschr. '35, 7-20; ELohmeyer, D. Stern d. Weisen: ThBl 17, '38, 288-99; GHartmann, Stimmen d. Zeit 138, '41, 234-8; JSchaumberger, Ein neues Keilschriftfragment über d. angebl. Stern der Weisen: Biblica 24, '43, 162-9. Cf. ποιμήν 1.

2. *magician* (trag.+; Aeschin. 3, 137 [μάγος=πονηρός]; Diod. S. 5, 55, 3; 34+35 fgm. 2, 5 τὶς ... ἄνθρωπος μάγος, a false prophet, who πολλοὺς ἐξηπάτα; Vett. Val. 74, 17; Philo, Spec. Leg. 3, 93; Test. Reub. 4: 9) of Barjesus=Elymas on Cyprus Ac 13: 6, 8. Cf. Hm 11: 2 v.l. —On the history of the word ADNock, Beginn. I 5, '33, 164-88=Essays on Religion and the Ancient World I, '72, 308-30.—GDelling, TW IV 360-3: μάγος and related words. M-M. B. 1494f.*

Μαγώγ, ὁ indecl. (מָגוֹג) *Magog*, mentioned w. Gog (s. Γώγ) among the enemies of God in the last days Rv 20: 8. The idea and the names are fr. Ezk 38: 2-39: 16; but there Gog is prince of Magog, and in Rv G. and M. are two peoples (cf. Sib. Or. 3, 319 χώρα Γὼγ ἠδὲ Μαγώγ; 512).—Lit. s.v. Γώγ; also RdeVaux, Magog-Hierapolis: RB 43, '34, 568-71.*

Μαδιάμ, ὁ indecl. (מִדְיָן; also Philo, Mut. Nom. 110.—Jos., Ant. 2, 257 Μαδιανή, ῆς) *Midian*, a people in Arabia. γῆ M. is (after Ex 2: 15) the place where Moses stayed for a while Ac 7: 29.*

μαζός, οῦ, ὁ (Hom.+; Epigr. Gr. 644, 4; 690, 2; PSI 253, 134) *breast*—1. of a man (oft. Hom.; Apollon. Rhod. 3, 119; Achilles Tat. 3, 8, 6; Etym. Mag. *574, 220) Rv 1: 13 A.

2. of a woman's breast (Hom.+; Artem. 1, 16; Test. Napht. 1: 7), also of an animal's udder (Callim. 1, 48 Schn.; Aratus, Phaen. 163; Crinagoras no. 26, 6). Fig. (Philo, Aet. M. 66) of springs (Pampretius of Panopolis [V AD] 1, 90 [ed. HGerstinger: SB d. Wien. Ak. d. W. 208, 3, 1928]) which offer to men τοὺς πρὸς ζωῆς μαζούς *their life-giving breasts* 1 Cl 20: 10. M-M.*

μαθεῖν s. μανθάνω.

μάθημα, ατος, τό (Soph., Hdt.+; inscr., pap.; Jer 13: 21; Philo) *someth. that is learned, knowledge, teaching* Dg 5: 3.*

μαθηματικός, ή, όν (Pla.+; Sib. Or. 13, 67), subst. μαθηματικός, οῦ, ὁ (Aristot.+), in the sense *astrologer* (M. Ant. 4, 48; Sext. Emp., Adv. Math.; Philo, Mut. Nom. 71) D 3: 4.*

μαθητεία, ας, ἡ *lesson, instruction* (Timo [III BC] 54 in HDiels, Poetarum philos. fgm. '01; Dio Chrys. 4, 41; Suidas) οὗ τὸ κατάστημα μεγάλη μ. *whose demeanor is a great lesson* ITr 3: 2.*

μαθητεύω 1 aor. ἐμαθήτευσα, pass. ἐμαθητεύθην.

1. intr. *be* or *become a pupil* or *disciple* (Plut., Mor. 832B; 837C; Iambl., Vi. Pyth. 23, 104 μ. τῷ Πυθαγόρᾳ; schol. on Apollon. Rhod. Proleg. Aa) τινί *of someone* (Ἰωσήφ) ἐμαθήτευσεν τῷ Ἰησοῦ *Joseph had become a disciple of Jesus* Mt 27: 57 v.l. Likew. as

2. pass. dep. μαθητεύομαι *become a disciple* τινί: (Ἰ.) ἐμαθητεύθη τῷ Ἰησοῦ Mt 27: 57. ὑμῖν μαθητευθῆναι *become your disciples, be instructed by you* IEph 10: 1. γραμματεὺς μαθητευθεὶς τῇ βασιλείᾳ τ. οὐρανῶν *a scribe who has become a disciple of the kgdm. of heaven or who has been trained for the kgdm.* Mt 13: 52 (γραμματεύς 3). Abs. IEph 3: 1. μᾶλλον μαθητεύομαι *I am becoming a disciple more and more* IRo 5: 1. This gave rise to a new active form (Bl-D. §148, 3; Rob. 800)

3. trans. *make a disciple of, teach* τινά Mt 28: 19. ἱκανούς *make a number of disciples* Ac 14: 21. Abs. ἃ μαθητεύοντες ἐντέλλεσθε *what you command when you are instructing* or *winning disciples* IRo 3: 1. M-M.*

μαθητής, οῦ, ὁ (Hdt.+; inscr.; BGU 1125, 9 [I BC]; POxy. 1029, 25. In LXX only in two places in Jer [13: 21; 20: 11], and then as v.l. of codex A; Philo; Joseph.) *learner, pupil, disciple.*

1. gener. *pupil, apprentice* (in contrast to the teacher) Mt 10: 24f; Lk 6: 40 (TWManson, The Teaching of Jesus, '55, 237-40).

2. *disciple, adherent* (Pla., Apol. 33A; X., Mem. 1, 6, 3; Dio Chrys. 11[12], 5; Lucian, M. Peregr. 28 al.; Diog. L. 7, 7, 179; 8, 1, 3; 10, 11, 22; Iambl., Vi. Pyth. 35, 254 οἱ μ.; Dit., Syll.³ 1094, 5f αὐτὸς καὶ οἱ μαθηταὶ αὐτοῦ; Jos., Ant. 9, 68; 13, 289), oft. w. an indication of the pers. whose disciple one is, mostly in the gen. (Jos., C. Ap. 1, 176 Ἀριστοτέλους μ., Ant. 9, 33; 15, 3; Theosophien 66 Φορφυρίου μ.).

a. μ. Ἰωάννου Mt 9: 14a; 11: 2; 14: 12; Mk 2: 18a, b; 6: 29; Lk 5: 33; 7: 18; 11: 1; J 1: 35, 37; 3: 25. τ. Μωϋσέως 9: 28b; τῶν Φαρισαίων Mt 22: 16; Mk 2: 18c. τοῦ Πολυκάρπου MPol 22: 2; Epil Mosq 1.

b. esp. of the disciples of Jesus—α. of the Twelve οἱ δώδεκα μ. αὐτοῦ *his twelve disciples* Mt 10: 1; 11: 1; οἱ ἕνδεκα μ. 28: 16. οἱ μαθηταὶ αὐτοῦ (or w. another gen. of similar mng.—Yet it is somet. doubtful whether a particular pass. really means the Twelve and not a larger [s. β below] or smaller circle; ERMartinez, CBQ 23, '61, 281-92 [restricted to the 12, even in Mt 18]) 12: 1; 15: 2; Mk 5: 31; 6: 1, 35, 45; 8: 27; Lk 8: 9; J 2: 2; 3: 22 and oft. Also without a gen. οἱ μ. Mt 8: 21; 13: 10; 14: 19; 16: 5; Mk 8: 1; 9: 14; 10: 24; Lk 9: 16; J 4: 31; 11: 7f and oft.—LBrun, D. Berufung der ersten Jünger Jesu: Symb. Osl. 11, '32, 35-54; SvanTilborg, The Jewish Leaders in Mt, '72, 99-141; ULuz, Die Jünger im Mt, ZNW 62, '71, 141-7; on the 'beloved disciple' of J 13: 23 al. cf. FVFilson, JBL 68, '49, 83-8; ELTitus, ibid. '50, 323-8.

β. of Jesus' disciples gener. ὄχλος πολὺς μ. αὐτοῦ *a large crowd of his adherents* Lk 6: 17; ἅπαν τὸ πλῆθος τῶν μ. *the whole crowd of the disciples* 19: 37. οἱ μ. αὐτοῦ ἱκανοί *a large number of his disciples* 7: 11 v.l. πολλοὶ ἐκ τῶν μ. αὐτοῦ J 6: 66.—Papias 2: 4.

γ. Even after Jesus' departure fr. this life those who followed him were called μ. (generations later, as Socrates is called the μ. of Homer: Dio Chrys. 38[55], 3ff) οἱ μ. τοῦ κυρίου Ac 9: 1; μ. Ἰησοῦ Χριστοῦ IMg 9: 2 (opp. ὁ μόνος διδάσκαλος, who also had the prophets as his μαθηταί vs. 3; 10: 1. Ac uses μ. almost exclusively to denote the members of the new religious community (cf. Rtzst., Erlösungsmyst. 127f), so that it almost= *Christian* (cf. 11: 26) 6: 1f, 7; 9: 19; 11: 26, 29; 13: 52; 15: 10 al. τῶν μαθητῶν (without τινές) *some Christians* 21: 16 (cf. X., Cyr. 1, 4, 20, An. 3, 5, 16; Herodas 2, 36 τῶν πορνέων; Polyaenus 5, 17, 2 καὶ ἦσαν τῶν Μακεδόνων).—καλοὶ μαθηταί IPol 2: 1. Individuals (Aberciusinschr. 3: 'A., ὁ μ. ποιμένος ἀγνοῦ): Ananias Ac 9: 10; Mnason 21: 16b; Timothy 16: 1.

δ. The martyrs (s. on μάρτυς 3) are specif. called μ. κυρίου MPol 17: 3. Also absol. μ. IEph 1: 2; ITr 5: 2; IRo 5: 3; IPol 7: 1. As long as a Christian's blood has not been shed, he is only a beginner in discipleship (IRo 5: 3), not a μαθητὴς ἀληθὴς τοῦ Χριστοῦ IRo 4: 2.—For lit. s. on ἀπόστολος and cf. also JWach, Meister and Jünger '25; ESchweizer, Lordship and Discipleship, '60, 464–66; GBornkamm, Bultmann-Festschr., '64, 171–91 (Mt 28: 16–20); KHRengstorf, TW IV 392–465; μαθητής, μανθάνω and related words. M-M. B. 1225.

μαθήτρια, ας, ἡ (Diod. S. 2, 52, 7; Diog. L. 4, 2; 8, 42) *a (woman) disciple* of Mary Magdalene μ. τοῦ κυρίου GP 12: 50. —Also abs. *Christian woman* (s. μαθητής 2bγ) of Tabitha in Joppa Ac 9: 36. M-M.*

Μαθθάθ s. Ματθάτ.

Μαθθαῖος s. Ματθαῖος. M-M.

Μαθθάν s. Ματθάν.

Μαθθάτ s. Ματθάτ.

Μαθθίας s. Ματθίας. M-M.

Μαθουσάλα, ὁ indecl. (מְתוּשֶׁלַח.—So also Philo and En. 106, 1; 107, 3, the latter in the form Μεθουσάλεκ.—Joseph. has Μαθουσάλας, but only in nom.) *Methuselah*, son of Enoch and grandfather of Noah (Gen 5: 21ff); in the genealogy of Jesus Lk 3: 37.*

Μαίανδρος, ου, ὁ (Hom.+; inscr.; Sib. Or. 4, 149; 151) *Maeander*, a river in Caria in Asia Minor IMg inscr.; s. Μαγνησία.*

Μαϊνάν s. Μεννά.

μαίνομαι (Hom.+; POxy. 33 IV, 9ff; PHermopol. 7 I, 18; LXX; Philo; Jos., Bell. 1, 352, C. Ap. 1, 204; Test. Jos. 8: 3; Sib. Or. 4, 83) *be mad, be out of one's mind* beside δαιμόνιον ἔχειν and as a result of it *have no control over oneself* J 10: 20 (cf. Eur., Bacch. 291ff; Hdt. 4, 79 ὁ δαίμων τὸν βασιλέα λελάβηκε καὶ ὑπὸ τ. θεοῦ μαίνεται; Dio Chrys. 11 [12], 8: the owl warns the mad birds about men. The birds, however, ἀνόητον αὐτὴν ἡγοῦντο καὶ μαίνεσθαι ἔφασκον; the same Aesop, Fab. 437 P. = 105 H.; Diog. L. 1, 49 the members of the Athenian council concerning Solon: μαίνεσθαι ἔλεγον αὐτόν). Opp. ἀληθείας καὶ σωφροσύνης ῥήματα ἀποφθέγγεσθαι Ac 26: 25. μαίνῃ *you are mad*, said to one who has brought incredible news 12: 15; *you are out of your mind*, said to one whose enthusiasm seems to have overcome his better judgment 26: 24 (Sallust. c. 4 p. 6, 8 μ. as a judgment on a man proclaiming certain teachings; Porphyr., Vi. Plotini c. 15 μαίνεσθαι τὸν Πορφύριον as a judgment on a poem that has been recited). Of the impression made by speakers in 'tongues' on strangers 1 Cor 14: 23 (Herm. Wr. 9, 4 those who were filled w. divine Gnosis made the same impression on the outsiders: μεμηνέναι δοκοῦσι).—HPreisker, TW IV 363–5. M-M.*

μακαρίζω Att. fut. μακαριῶ; 1 aor. ἐμακάρισα (Hom.+; Vett. Val. 88, 25; LXX; Philo, Exs. 152; Joseph.) *call or consider blessed, happy, fortunate* τινά someone (Hippocr., Ep. 17; Diod. S. 13, 58, 2; Charito 5, 8, 3; Gen 30: 13; Sir 11: 28; Jos., Bell. 7, 356) or τὶ someth. (Herodian 5, 1, 5; Jos., C. Ap. 2, 135) Lk 1: 48; IEph 5: 1. τοὺς ὑπομείναντας *those who showed endurance* Js 5: 11. ἑαυτόν *oneself* Hs 9, 28, 6. τὴν τελείαν γνῶσιν 1 Cl 1: 2. τὴν εἰς θεὸν αὐτοῦ γνώμην *his* (the bishop's) *attitude toward God* IPhld 1: 2. Perh. abs. (X., Mem. 1, 6, 9) Dg 10: 8. M-M.*

μακάριος, ία, ιον (Pind., Pla., X.+; inscr., pap., LXX, En., Philo, Joseph.) *blessed, fortunate, happy*, usu. in the sense *privileged recipient of divine favor.*

1. of human beings—a. with less obvious relig. coloring (Chrysippus in Diog. L. 7, 179 calls himself a μακάριος ἀνήρ; Epict. 2, 18, 15; Jos., Ant. 16, 108; 20, 27) ἥγημαι ἐμαυτὸν μακάριον Ac 26: 2. Of the widow who remains unmarried μακαριωτέρα ἐστίν *she is happier* 1 Cor 7: 40. μ. ἤμην εἰ τοιαύτην γυναῖκα εἶχον Hv 1, 1, 2 (Charito 6, 2, 9 μ. ἦν εἰ). Cf. Lk 23: 29.

b. with a more obvious relig. connotation (Jos., Ant. 9, 264), of Biblical persons: Moses 1 Cl 43: 1. Judith 55: 4. Paul 47: 1; Pol 3: 2; (11: 3). Of other prominent Christians, esp. martyrs: Ignatius, Zosimus, Rufus Pol 9: 1. Polycarp MPol 1: 1; 19: 1, 21; 22: 1, 3. Of presbyters who have died 1 Cl 44: 5. μ. εἶναι ἐν τῇ ποιήσει αὐτοῦ *be blessed in what he does* Js 1: 25.—In various sentence combinations, in which the copula belonging with μ. is often omitted (Bl-D. §127, 4; Rob. 395; Maximus Tyr. 14, 6f; μ. [opp. δυστυχής] εὐσεβὴς φίλος θεοῦ): as the apodosis of a conditional sentence Lk 6: 5 D (JoachJeremias, Unknown Sayings of Jesus, tr. Fuller, '57, 49–54); 1 Pt 3: 14; 4: 14; Hm 8: 9. The conditional sentence follows J 13: 17; 1 Cl 50: 5; Hs 6, 1, 1a. W. relative clause foll. Mt 11: 6; Lk 7: 23; 14: 15 (μ. ὅστις Menand., fgm. 114, Mon. 340 al.); Ro 4: 7f (Ps 31: 1f); Js 1: 12 (Sext. 40 μακ. ἀνήρ w. rel.); 1 Cl 56: 6 (Job 5: 17); B 10: 10 (Ps 1: 1.—Maximus Tyr. 33, 5e ὁ μ. ἀνήρ, ὅν); 11: 8; Hv 2, 2, 7; s 9, 29, 3. μ. ἐν Ἰησοῦ Χριστῷ, ὅς IPhld 10: 2. The relative clause precedes Hv 3, 8, 4; s 5, 3, 9b; 6, 1, 1b. As a predicate w. a subst. or subst. adj. or ptc. μ. ὁ *blessed is he who* . . . (2 Ch 9: 7; Da 12: 12) Mt 5: 3ff (the transl. *O, the happiness of* or *hail to those*, favored by some [Zahn, Wlh., EKlostermann, JWeiss; KBornhäuser, Die Bergpredigt '23, 24 al.] may be exactly right for the Aramaic original [=Hebr. אַשְׁרֵי], but it scarcely exhausts the content which μακάριος had in the mouths of Gk.-speaking Christians [cf. e.g. Maximus Tyr. 14, 6f μακάριος εὐσεβὴς φίλος θεοῦ, δυστυχὴς δὲ ὁ δεισιδαίμων; Artem. 4, 72 the state of μακ. εἶναι is brought about by ascension into heaven and the ὑπερβάλλουσα εὐδαιμονία enjoyed there].—CCMcCown, The Beatitudes in the Light of Ancient Ideals: JBL 46, '27, 50–61; JRezevskis [Resewski], D. Makarismen bei Mt u. Lk, ihr Verhältnis zu einander u. ihr histor. Hintergrund: Studia Theologica I [=IBenzinger-Festschr.] '35, 157–70; JDupont, Les Béatitudes '54; GStrecker, Die Makarismen der Bergpredigt, NTS 17, '70/'71, 255–75; see lit. s.v. ὄρος); 24: 46; Lk 1: 45; 6: 20ff; 11: 28; 12: 37; cf. vs. 38, 43; J 20: 29; Ro 14: 22; Rv 1: 3; 14: 13; 16: 15; 19: 9; 20: 6; 22: 7, 14; 2 Cl 16: 4; 19: 3; D 1: 5; Pol 2: 3 (=Lk 6: 20). W. ὅτι foll. Mt 16: 17; Lk 14: 14. W. ὅταν Mt 5: 11. Acc. to the reading of the Michigan Pap. (ed. CBonner '34, p. 46) and of a parchment leaf at Hamburg (SAB '09, 1081) Hs 5, 1, 3 contains the words μακάριόν με ποιήσεις, ἐάν *you will make me happy, if.*

2. of God (Aristot., Eth. Nicom. 10, 8 p. 1178b, 25f τοῖς θεοῖς ἅπας ὁ βίος μακάριος; Epicurus in Diog. L. 10, 123 τ. θεὸν ζῷον ἄφθαρτον κ. μακάριον νομίζων; Herm. Wr. 12, 13b; Sextus 560; Philo, Cher. 86, Deus Imm. 26 ὁ ἄφθαρτος κ. μακάριος, Leg. ad Gai. 5 [other pass. in MDibelius, Hdb. on 1 Ti 1: 11]; Jos., C. Ap. 2, 190, cf. Ant. 10, 278) 1 Ti 1: 11; 6: 15 (BSEaston, Pastoral Epistles '47, 179).

3. of impersonal things (Eur.+; Eccl 10: 17)—**a.** of parts of the body of persons who are the objects of special grace, which are themselves termed blessed: μ. οἱ ὀφθαλ-μοί Mt 13: 16; Lk 10: 23. μ. ἡ κοιλία 11: 27 (Kleopatra 1. 168f. Prob. Christian despite the ref. to Cleop. Of the secular parallels, the next closest is Musaeus, Hero 137 . . . γαστήρ τ' ἢ σ' ἐλόχευσε μακαρτάτη).

b. of things that stand in a very close relationship to the divinity: τὰ δῶρα τ. θεοῦ 1 Cl 35: 1. Of the πνεύματα implanted in the Christians B 1: 2 (cf. Maximus Tyr. 41, 51 ἡ εὐδαίμων κ. μακαρία ψυχή). Of the age to come 2 Cl 19: 4 (cf. Dit., Or. 519, 9 ἐν τοῖς μακαριοτάτοις ὑμῶν καιροῖς; 17).

c. of martyrdoms MPol 2: 1. Of the object of the Christian hope προσδεχόμενοι τὴν μ. ἐλπίδα Tit 2: 13 (cf. Dit., Or. 383, 108 μακαριστὰς ἐλπίδας). μακάριόν ἐστιν μᾶλλον διδόναι ἢ λαμβάνειν Ac 20: 35 (cf. Pla., Rep. 496c ὡς μακάριον τὸ κτῆμα; Thu. 2, 97, 4 λαμβά-νειν μᾶλλον ἢ διδόναι; Beginn. IV 264; JoachJeremias, Unknown Sayings of Jesus, tr. Fuller, '58, 78-81; EHaen-chen, Ac ad loc.).—FHauck u. GBertram, TW IV 365-73: μακάριος, -ίζω, -ισμός. S. the lit. s.v. ὄρος. M-M. B. 1105.**

μακαρισμός, οῦ, ὁ (Pla., Rep. 9 p. 591D; Aristot., Rhet. 1, 9, 34; Plut., Sol. 27, 7, Mor. 471c; Stob., Ecl. III 57, 14 H.; Philo, Somn. 2, 35; Jos., Bell. 6, 213; Sib. Or. 13, 117) *blessing*, of a quot. fr. the Psalms beginning w. אַשְׁרֵי= μακάριον Ro 4: 6, 9; 1 Cl 50: 7 (both Ps 31: 1f). ποῦ οὖν ὁ μ. ὑμῶν; *where, then, is your blessing?* i.e. the frame of mind in which you *blessed* yourselves Gal 4: 15.—GL Dirichlet, De veterum macarismis '14. Also εὐλογέω, end. M-M.*

Μακεδονία, ας, ἡ (Hdt.+; inscr., Philo, Joseph., Sib. Or. [ίη]) *Macedonia*, a Roman province since 146 B.C., in Paul's day a senatorial province. Visited by Paul several times Ac 16: 9f, 12; 18: 5; 19: 21f; 20: 1, 3; 2 Cor 2: 13; 7: 5; Phil 4: 15; 1 Th 1: 7f; 4: 10. Travel plans w. ref. to Mac. 1 Cor 16: 5a, b; 2 Cor 1: 16a, b; 1 Ti 1: 3. Support for Paul fr. the Macedonian brethren 2 Cor 11: 9. They were also active in the collection for Jerusalem Ro 15: 26; 2 Cor 8: 1.*

Μακεδών, όνος, ὁ (Hdt.+; Περὶ ὕψους 18, 1; Arrian: 156 fgm. 9, 17 Jac.; Polyaenus 1, Prooem., 1 [all three M. ἀνήρ]; inscr., pap.; Esth 8: 12k; Philo, Omn. Prob. Lib. 94; Joseph.; Sib. Or.) *a Macedonian* Ac 16: 9 (AWiken-hauser, Religionsgesch. Parallelen zu Ac 16: 9; BZ 23, '35, 180-6). Of Gaius and Aristarchus 19: 29. Of Aristarchus 27: 2. Pl. of the Maced. Christians or their representatives 2 Cor 9: 2, 4.*

μάκελλον, ου, τό (not originally a Lat. word taken into Gk. [as Rob. 109], since it is quotable in Gk. fr. c. 400 BC in an inscr. fr. Epidaurus [Sammlg. griech. Dialekt-inschr., ed. HCollitz and FBechtel III 1, 1899, 3325= IG 4² (I) 102, 107; 296; 298; 301 in the form μάκελλον w. the mng. 'enclosure, grating']. The sense 'meat market' is found for the Lat. macellum Plautus and Terence+ [III/II BC]; the earliest Gk. ex. of μ. in this sense is Dit., Syll.³ 783

[IG 5(2), 268], 45 [I BC]; here it is masc., μάκελλος, as also schol. on Aristoph., Eq. 137; Vi. Aesopi I c. 51 ὁ μάκελ-λος in which pork can be bought; cf. macellus in Martial, and Sahidic and Bohairic versions of 1 Cor 10: 25. S. Cad-bury below 134 n. 2. Elsewh. the word is neut. [so also Peshîttâ and Harclean Syriac] or the gender cannot be determined. μ. may have reëntered H.Gk. in this new sense; so Hahn 249 n. 6. Ultimately μ. may be of Semitic origin [AWalde, IndogF 39, '21, 82; Bl-D. §5, 1 app.], though Doric-Ionic acc. to Varro, De Lingua Lat. 5, 146 Goetz-Scholl. Cf. JSchneider, TW IV 373f.—Plut., Mor. 277D; Cass. Dio 61, 18, 3 τ. ἀγορὰν τῶν ὀψῶν, τὸ μάκελλον; IG 5[1], 149; 150; Bull. de corr. hell. 17, 1893, 261; 20, 1896, 126; PHermopol. 127[3] verso, 5) *meat market, food market* (s. the plan of one at Pompeii in AMau, Pompeii² '08, 90-7, fr. here in Ltzm., Hdb. on 1 Cor 10: 25. Also HJCadbury, The Macellum of Corinth: JBL 53, '34, 134-41 w. a Lat. inscr. found at Corinth containing the word 'macellum': Corinth, Results of Ex-cavations VIII 2, '31, no. 124; 125) τὸ ἐν μ. πωλούμενον ἐσθίειν *eat what is sold in the meat market* 1 Cor 10: 25. M-M. B. 365.*

μακράν (a fixed form, orig. an acc. of extent of space, w. ὁδόν to be supplied.—Aeschyl.+; pap., LXX, En., Philo, Joseph.) *far (away)*—**1.** as adv.—**a.** of place—**α.** lit. μ. ἀπέχειν *be far away* Lk 15: 20 (Zen.-P. 59 605, 3 οὐ μακράν σου ἀπέχομεν). εἰς ἔθνη μακρὰν ἐξαποστελῶ σε *I will send you far away to the heathen* Ac 22: 21. μ. ἀπό τινος (Polyb. 3, 45, 2; LXX; Jos., C. Ap. 1, 60; Sib. Or. 8, 33f): ῥίπτειν μ. ἀπὸ τοῦ πύργου *throw far away from the tower* Hv 3, 2, 7. μ. εἶναι ἀπό τινος *be far away fr. someone or someth.* Mt 8: 30; J 21: 8; Hs 1: 1. μ. ἀπέχειν ἀπό τινος (Pr 15: 29; 1 Macc 8: 4) Lk 7: 6; MPol 5: 1. Of God οὐ μ. ἀπὸ ἑνὸς ἑκάστου ἡμῶν ὑπάρχοντα *he is not far from each one of us* Ac 17: 27 (cf. Dio Chrys. 11[12], 28 οὐ μακρὰν οὐδ' ἔχω τοῦ θείου . . . , ἀλλὰ ἐν αὐτῷ μέσῳ [s. σύμφυτος], Ant. 8, 108).

β. fig. (Epict. 3, 22, 11 μ. ἀπ' αὐτοῦ=far from a true Cynic) μ. ὄντες ἀπὸ τοῦ κυρίου Hm 12, 4, 4. οὐ μ. εἶ ἀπὸ τῆς βασιλείας τοῦ θεοῦ *you are not far from the kgdm. of God* i.e., you are almost ready to enter it Mk 12: 34 (cf. Ps 21: 2 μ. ἀπὸ τ. σωτηρίας μου). οἱ μ. (opp. οἱ ἐγγύς; cf. Is 57: 19; Da 9: 7 Theod.; Esth 9: 20) *those who are far away* of Gentiles (in contrast to the Jews) Eph 2: 17. οἳ ποτε ὄντες μ. *who once were far away* vs. 13.

b. of time: τοῖς τέκνοις ὑμῶν κ. πᾶσιν τοῖς εἰς μ. Ac 2: 39 prob. refers to future generations (cf. 2 Km 7: 19 εἰς μ.=vs. 16 εἰς τὸν αἰῶνα; Sir 24: 32 ἐκφανῶ αὐτὰ ἕως εἰς μ.—εἰς μ. also Demosth. 18, 36; Polyaenus 6, 7, 1; Jos., Ant. 6, 278; 20, 153; Test. Sim. 6: 2. Ostraca of the Deissmann collection ed. PMMeyer [Griech. Texte aus Aegypt. '16 p. 107ff] 66, 2). But the spatial interpr. is also poss.

2. as a(n improper) prep. μ. τινος *far away fr. someone or someth.* (Herodas 7, 111 θεῶν ἐκεῖνος οὐ μακρὴν ἀπῴκισται; Polyb. 3, 50, 8; Polyaenus 5, 2, 10; Zen.-P. 59 605, 3 [s. 1aa above, beginning]; POxy. 113, 18; Sir 15: 8) Lk 7: 6 v.l. μ. πάσης ἁμαρτίας Ro 3: 3; cf. 4: 3; 6: 1. ὢν μ. πραΰτης D 5: 2. ὢν μ. καὶ πόρρω πραΰτης B 20: 2. M-M.**

μακρόβιος, ον (Hippocr.+; LXX; Philo; Jos., Bell. 2, 151) *long-lived* σπέρμα μ. *a long-lived posterity* 1 Cl 16: 11 (after Is 53: 10).*

μακρόθεν adv. (H.Gk.: Chrysippus in Athen. 4, 137f; Polyb. 29, 8, 4; Strabo 3, 3, 4; Epict. 1, 16, 11; Dio Chrys.

1, 68 al.; Aelian, Nat. An. 2, 15; 15, 12; PTebt. 230 [II вс]; LXX; En. 32, 3; Philo; cf. Phryn. 93 L.) *from far away, from a distance* (Ezk 23: 40 ἔρχεσθαι μ.; Tob 13: 13) μ. ἀκολουθεῖν *follow at a distance* Lk 22: 54. ἑστὼς μ. *stood some distance away* 18: 13 (Syntipas collection of Aesop's Fables 37 p. 541 P. μ. ἑστῶσα).—Mostly ἀπὸ μ. (Ps.-Polemo Physiogn. 15 p. 319, 9 F.; Ps 137: 6; 2 Esdr [Ezra] 3: 13), since the suffix -θεν has lost its orig. separative force (Bl-D. §104, 3 app.; Rob. 300; KDieterich, Untersuchungen z. Geschichte d. griech. Sprache 1898, 183f.—Cf. ἀπ᾽ οὐρανόθεν: Eratosthenes [III вс] 16, 11 Coll.; PGM 2, 83; Sib. Or. 3, 691.—ἀπὸ μικρόθεν: POxy. 1216, 6 [II/III AD]). ἀκολουθεῖν ἀπὸ μ. *follow at a distance* Mt 26: 58 (the rdg. varies; Tdf. deletes ἀπό); Mk 14: 54. ἀπὸ μ. θεωρεῖν *look on from a distance* Mt 27: 55; Mk 15: 40. ὁρᾶν ἀπὸ μ. 5: 6; 11: 13; Lk 16: 23. ἀπὸ μ. ἑστηκέναι *stand at a distance* (Ps 37: 12) Lk 23: 49 (for the whole situation as well as details in expression cf. Appian, Bell. Civ. 2, 85 §360 τὸ γύναιον τοῦ Πομπηίου καὶ οἱ φίλοι ταῦτα [i.e., the murder of Pompey] μακρόθεν ὁρῶντες); Rv 18: 10, 15, 17. ἀπὸ μ. εἶναι *live far away* Mk 8: 3.*

μακροθυμέω 1 aor. ἐμακροθύμησα—**1.** *have patience, wait* (Plut., Mor. 593f; Job 7: 16; Sir 2: 4; Bar 4: 25; Test. Jos. 2: 7) abs. Hb 6: 15; Js 5: 8. μ. ἐπί τινι *wait patiently for someth.* Js 5: 7b. μ. ἕως τ. παρουσίας τ. κυρίου *have patience until the coming of the Lord* vs. 7a.

2. *be patient, forbearing* (LXX) abs. (Pr 19: 11) of God Dg 9: 2. Of love 1 Cor 13: 4. ἀγάπη πάντα μακροθυμεῖ *love is patient about everything* 1 Cl 49: 5. πρός τινα *toward someone* 1 Th 5: 14. μετά τινος w. *someone* IPol 6: 2. εἴς τινα *toward someone* 2 Pt 3: 9. ἐπί τινι w. *someone* (Sir 18: 11; 29: 8) Mt 18: 26, 29.

3. Lk 18: 7 μακροθυμεῖ ἐπ᾽ αὐτοῖς; which is textually uncertain and difficult to interpret (but cf. Mt 18: 12 for the mixture of tenses in a question), may best be transl.: *will he delay long over them?* (RSV; cf. Weizsäcker³⁻⁸; Sir 35: 19 Rahlfs; μ.=delay: Artem. 4, 11).—Jülicher, Gleichn. 286ff; HSahlin, Zwei Lk-Stellen: Lk 6: 43–5; 18: 7: Symb. Bibl. Ups. 4, '45, 9–20; HRiesenfeld, NT Aufsätze (JSchmid-Festschr.), '63, 214–17 (Lk 18: 7); but see KBeyer, Semit. Syntax im NT, '62, 268 n. 1. M-M.*

μακροθυμία, ας, ἡ (Menand.+; Strabo 5, 4, 10; LXX)—**1.** *patience, steadfastness, endurance* (Menand., fgm. 19; Plut., Lucull. 32, 3; 33, 1; Is 57: 15; 1 Macc 8: 4; Test. Dan 2: 1; Jos., Bell. 6, 37) w. ὑπομονή (Test. Jos. 2: 7) Col 1: 11; 1 Cl 64; IEph 3: 1; cf. 2 Ti 3: 10. διὰ πίστεως καὶ μακροθυμίας *through faith and steadfastness* Hb 6: 12. ὑπόδειγμα τ. κακοπαθίας κ. τ. μακροθυμίας Js 5: 10. W. ταπεινοφροσύνη Hs 8, 7, 6; cf. 9, 15, 2.

2. *forbearance, patience* toward others (Artem. 2, 25 p. 119, 10)—**a.** of men (Pr 25: 15; Sir 5: 11; Test. Jos. 17: 2) w. other virtues 2 Cor 6: 6; Gal 5: 22; 1 Cl 62: 2. W. ἐπιείκεια cf. Ep. Arist. 188) 1 Cl 13: 1. W. πραΰτης Col 3: 12. W. ἐγκράτεια B 2: 2. ἐν πάσῃ μακροθυμίᾳ 2 Ti 4: 2. In contrast to ὀξυχολία: Hm 5, 1, 3; 6; 5, 2, 3; 8. μετὰ μακροθυμίας ἀνεχόμενοι ἀλλήλων Eph 4: 2.

b. of divine beings—**α.** of God himself Ro 2: 4; 9: 22; 1 Pt 3: 20; IEph 11: 1.

β. of Christ 1 Ti 1: 16; 2 Pt 3: 15.—S. ὑπομονή 1, end.—JHorst, TW IV 377–90 μακροθυμία and related words. M-M.*

μακρόθυμος, ον (M. Ant. 6, 30, 10; Anth. Pal. 11, 317, 1; LXX) *patient, forbearing, even-tempered.*

1. of men (Pr 14: 29; 15: 18; 16: 32 al.) Hv 1, 2, 3; m 5, 1, 1; cf. 2; D 3: 8. μακρόθυμον εἶναι Hm 8: 10.

2. of God (Ex 34: 6; Num 14: 18; 2 Esdr 19 [Neh 9]: 17 al.) Hs 8, 11, 1. W. φιλάνθρωπος Dg 8: 7; ὁ μ. *he who is patient* i.e. God B 3: 6. τὸ μ. αὐτοῦ βούλημα 1 Cl 19: 3.*

μακροθύμως adv. *patiently* ἀκούειν τινός *listen to someone with patience* Ac 26: 3.*

μακρός, ά, όν (Hom.+; inscr., pap., LXX, Philo, Joseph.; Sib. Or. 3, 274; loanw. in rabb.).

1. of extension in time or space *long*; the neut. as adv. (since Hom., e.g. Il. 2, 224 μακρὰ βοᾶν; Jos., Ant. 6, 241) μακρὰ προσεύχεσθαι *make long prayers* Mt 23: 14 t.r.; Mk 12: 40; Lk 20: 47.

2. of distance *far away, distant* (Aeschyl., Prom. 814 μ. ἀποικία; Mi 4: 3 εἰς γῆν μακράν) εἰς χώραν μ. Lk 15: 13; 19: 12. M-M. B. 882.*

μακροχρόνιος, ον (Hippocr.+; Philo, Rer. Div. Her. 34) *long-lived* (Porphyr., Vi. Pyth. 24 N.) ἵνα ... ἔσῃ μ. ἐπὶ τῆς γῆς *that you may have a long life on the earth* Eph 6: 3 (Ex 20: 12; Dt 5: 16). M-M.*

μαλακία, ας, ἡ (Hdt.+; pap., LXX, Philo; Jos., Ant. 4, 169; 17, 109; Test. Jos. 17: 7; loanw. in rabb.) *softness, weakness, weakliness, ailment.*

1. of bodily weakness, *sickness* (Menand., fgm. 201, 5 Kock; Vit. Hom. 36; Dt 7: 15; 28: 61; Is 38: 9) w. νόσος (as in the Christian amulets, which are obviously dependent upon NT language: POxy. 1151, 27; BGU 954, 12) Mt 4: 23; 9: 35; 10: 1. εἰδὼς φέρειν μαλακίαν *who knows how to endure weakness* 1 Cl 16: 3 (Is 53: 3).

2. of weakness of spirit (Thu. 1, 122, 4; Demosth. 11, 22) *faint-heartedness, despondency, lack of energy* pl. (w. διψυχία) Hv 3, 11, 2; 3, 12, 3. M-M.*

μαλακίζομαι perf. mid.-pass. 3 sing. μεμαλάκισται; 1 aor. pass. ἐμαλακίσθην (Thu.+; Dit., Syll.² 850, 24; PSI 420, 16 [III вс]; PPetr. II 19, 2, 6 [III вс]; Sb 158; LXX; Philo; Jos., Bell. 4, 43, Ant. 6, 365; 18, 205; Test. 12 Patr.) *be* or *become soft, weak, weakly, discouraged, sick* μαλακισθέντες ἀπὸ τῶν βιωτικῶν πραγμάτων *weakened by the duties of everyday life* Hv 3, 11, 3 (μαλακίζεσθαι ἀπό as Test. Gad 1: 4 v.l.).—μεμαλάκισται διὰ τὰς ἀνομίας ἡμῶν *he was made to suffer for our misdeeds* 1 Cl 16: 5; cf. B 5: 2 (both Is 53: 5).*

μαλακός, ή, όν (Hom.+; inscr., pap., LXX, Philo; Jos., Ant. 8, 72 βύσσος μ.) *soft.*

1. of things: clothes (Hom.+; Artem. 1, 78 p. 73, 10 ἱματίων πολυτελῶν κ. μαλακῶν; PSI 364, 5 ἱμάτιον μαλ.) μ. ἱμάτια *soft garments*, such as fastidious people wear Lk 7: 25. (τὰ) μ. *soft clothes* (Sb 6779, 57; cf. λευκός 2, end) Mt 11: 8a, b.

2. of pers. *soft, effeminate*, esp. of *catamites*, men and boys who allow themselves to be misused homosexually (Dionys. Hal. 7, 2, 4; Dio Chrys. 49[66], 25; Ptolem., Apotel. 3, 15, 10; Vett. Val. 113, 22; Diog. L. 7, 173; PHib. 54, 11 [c. 245 вс] a musician called Zenobius ὁ μαλακός [cf. Dssm., LO 131, 4-LAE 150, 4]. Sim. a Macedon. inscr. in LDuchesne and CBayet, Mémoire sur une Mission au Mont Athos 1876 no. 66 p. 46; Plautus, Miles 668 cinaedus malacus) 1 Cor 6: 9=Pol 5: 3.—S. lit. s.v. ἀρσενοκοίτης. M-M. B. 1065.*

Μαλελεήλ, ὁ indecl. (מַהֲלַלְאֵל; in Jos., Ant. 1, 79; 84 Μαλάηλος, ου) *Maleleel* (Gen 5: 12), in the genealogy of Jesus Lk 3: 37.*

μάλιστα (superl. of the adv. μάλα; Hom.+; inscr., pap., LXX; En. 25, 2; Ep. Arist., Joseph.).

1. *most of all, above all, especially, particularly, (very) greatly* Ac 20: 38; 1 Ti 4: 10; 5: 17; 2 Ti 4: 13; Tit 1: 10; Phlm 16; 1 Cl 13: 1; Dg 1; 3: 1; IEph 20: 1; IPhld inscr.; MPol 13: 1; Hv 1, 1, 8. καί *μ. and above all, particularly* (Plut., Mor. 835E; Jos., C. Ap. 1, 27) Ac 25: 26; 1 Ti 5: 8; Hv 1, 2, 4. μ. δέ *but especially* (Il. 1, 16; Lesbonax Gramm. [II AD] p. 8 [ed. RMüller 1900]; Jos., Vi. 14) Gal 6: 10; Phil 4: 22; 2 Pt 2: 10; IPol 3: 1; Hm 12, 1, 2; s 8, 6, 5; 9, 10, 7. μ. γνώστην ὄντα σε *since you are outstandingly familiar* Ac 26: 3 (cf. Appian, Bell. Civ. 2, 26 §100 ὁ μάλιστα ἐχθρός= the bitterest enemy).

2. in answer to a question: *most assuredly, certainly* 1 Cl 43: 6. M-M.*

μᾶλλον (comp. of the adv. μάλα; Hom.+; inscr., pap., LXX, Ep. Arist.; Jos., Ant. 5, 350; 13, 407 al.; Sib. Or. 3, 242) *more, rather.*

1. *to a greater degree* Phil 1: 12. πολλῷ μᾶλλον ἔκραζεν *he cried out even more loudly* Mk 10: 48; Lk 18: 39. ἔτι μᾶλλον καὶ μᾶλλον *more and more* (Diog. L. 9; 10, 2 μ. ἔτι καὶ μ.) Phil 1: 9; Hs 9, 1, 8. ἐγὼ μᾶλλον *I can do so even more* Phil 3: 4. The thing compared is introduced by ἤ (Apollon. Paradox. 9; Appian, Iber. 90 §392; Lucian, Adv. Ind. 2) Mt 18: 13 or stands in the gen. of comparison (X., Mem. 4, 3, 8, Cyr. 3, 3, 45) πάντων ὑμῶν μ. γλώσσαις λαλῶ *I (can) speak in tongues more than you all* 1 Cor 14: 18.—Abs. μ. can mean *to a greater degree* than before, *even more, now more than ever* Lk 5: 15; J 5: 18; 19: 8; Ac 5: 14; 22: 2; 2 Cor 7: 7. Somet. it is also added to verbs: Σαῦλος μ. ἐνεδυναμοῦτο Ac 9: 22.— In combination w. an adj. it takes the place of the comparative (class.; Synes., Ep. 123 p. 259D μ. ἄξιος) μακάριόν ἐστιν μᾶλλον Ac 20: 35 (s. 3c below). καλόν ἐστιν αὐτῷ μᾶλλον Mk 9: 42; cf. 1 Cor 9: 15. πολλῷ μ. ἀναγκαῖά ἐστιν *they are even more necessary* 1 Cor 12: 22. πολλὰ τ. τέκνα τῆς ἐρήμου μᾶλλον ἢ τῆς ἐχούσης τ. ἄνδρα *the children of the desolate woman are numerous to a higher degree than* (the children) *of the woman who has a husband*= *the children are more numerous* Gal 4: 27 (Is 54: 1).—Pleonastically w. words and expressions that already contain the idea 'more' (Kühner-G. I 26; O Schwab, Histor. Syntax der griech. Komparation III 1895, 59ff; Bl-D. §246; Rob. 278) μ. διαφέρειν τινός Mt 6: 26; Lk 12: 24. περισσεύειν μᾶλλον 1 Th 4: 1, 10; w. a comp. (trag.; Hdt. 1, 32; X., Cyr. 2, 2, 12; Lucian, Gall. 13; Ps.-Lucian, Charid. 6; Synes., Ep. 79 p. 227c; 103 p. 241D) πολλῷ μᾶλλον κρεῖσσον Phil 1: 23. μᾶλλον περισσότερον ἐκήρυσσον Mk 7: 36. περισσοτέρως μᾶλλον ἐχάρημεν *we rejoiced still more* 2 Cor 7: 13. μ. ἐνδοξότεροι Hs 9, 28, 4. ὅσῳ δοκεῖ μ. μείζων εἶναι *the more he seems to be great* 1 Cl 48: 6b.

2. *for a better reason*—a. *rather, sooner* μ. χρῆσαι *rather take advantage of it* (i.e., either freedom or slavery) 1 Cor 7: 21 (lit. on χράομαι 1a.). The slaves who have Christian masters μᾶλλον δουλευέτωσαν *rather they are to continue as slaves* 1 Ti 6: 2. νῦν πολλῷ μ. ἐν τ. ἀπουσίᾳ μου *much more in my absence* Phil 2: 12. οὐ πολὺ μ. ὑποταγησόμεθα τ. πατρί; *should we not much rather submit to the Father?* Hb 12: 9. τοσούτῳ μ. ὅσῳ *all the more, since* 10: 25.

b. *more (surely), more (certainly)* πόσῳ μ. σοί *how much more surely to you* Phlm 16 (Diod. S. 1, 2, 2). πολλῷ μ. Ro 5: 9 (cf. HMüller, Qal-Wachomer Schluss. in paul. Theol., ZNW 58, '67, 73-92). Very oft. a conditional clause (εἰ) precedes it (Epicurus in Diog. L. 10, 91 εἰ..., πολλῷ μᾶλλον= if..., how much more surely) εἰ τὸν χόρτον ὁ θεὸς οὕτως ἀμφιέννυσιν, οὐ πολλῷ μ. ὑμᾶς; *if God so clothes the grass,* (will he) *not*

much more surely (clothe) *you?* Mt 6: 30. Likew. εἰ... πολλῷ μ. Ro 5: 10, 15, 17; 2 Cor 3: 9, 11; εἰ... πόσῳ μ. *if... how much more surely* Mt 7: 11; 10: 25; Lk 11: 13; 12: 28; Ro 11: 12, 24; Hb 9: 14. εἰ—πῶς οὐχὶ μ.; *if—why should not more surely?* 2 Cor 3: 8. εἰ... πολὺ μ. ἡμεῖς *if... then much more surely we* Hb 12: 25. εἰ ἄλλοι... οὐ μᾶλλον ἡμεῖς; *if others* (have a claim, then) *do we not more surely* (have one)? 1 Cor 9: 12 (μ. can also mean *above all, especially,* e.g., Himerius, Or. 40 [Or. 6], 2).—CMaurer, Der Schluss 'a minore ad majus' als Element paul. Theol., ThLZ 85, '60, 149-52.

3. *rather* in the sense *instead* (of someth.)—a. following a negative which

α. is expressed: μὴ εἰσέλθητε. πορεύεσθε δὲ μ. *do not enter* (into); *go instead* Mt 10: 6. μὴ φοβεῖσθε—φοβεῖσθε δὲ μ. vs. 28; ἵνα μὴ τὸ χωλὸν ἐκτραπῇ, ἰαθῇ δὲ μ. Hb 12: 13. μὴ..., μᾶλλον δέ Eph 4: 28; 5: 11. μὴ or οὐ..., ἀλλὰ μ. (Syntipas p. 17, 3; 43, 17) Mt 27: 24; Mk 5: 26; Ro 14: 13; Eph 5: 4.

β. the negative can be unexpressed, though easily supplied fr. the context: πορεύεσθε μ. (do not turn to us,) *rather go* Mt 25: 9. ἵνα μ. τὸν Βαραββᾶν *that he should* (release) *Barabbas instead* (of Jesus) Mk 15: 11. ἥδιστα μᾶλλον καυχήσομαι (I will not pray for release,) *rather I will gladly boast* 2 Cor 12: 9. μᾶλλον παρακαλῶ (I do not order,) *rather I request* Phlm 9; τοὐναντίον μ. *on the other hand rather* 2 Cor 2: 7.

b. οὐχὶ μᾶλλον *not rather* follows a positive statement: ὑμεῖς πεφυσιωμένοι ἐστέ, καὶ οὐχὶ μᾶλλον ἐπενθήσατε; *you are puffed up; should you not rather be sad?* 1 Cor 5: 2. διὰ τί οὐχὶ μ. ἀδικεῖσθε; *why do you not rather suffer wrong* (instead of doing wrong to others)? 6: 7a; cf. b.

c. μᾶλλον ἤ(περ) usually (exceptions: Ac 20: 35 [JoachJeremias, Unknown Sayings of Jesus, tr. Fuller, '57, 77-81: this is not an exception, and renders 'giving is blessed, not receiving']; 1 Cor 9: 15; Gal 4: 27) excludes fr. consideration the content of the phrase introduced by ἤ (Appian, Iber. 26 §101 θαρρεῖν θεῷ μᾶλλον ἢ πλήθει στρατοῦ= put his trust in God, not in...) ἠγάπησαν οἱ ἄνθρωποι μ. τὸ σκότος ἢ τὸ φῶς *men did not love light, but rather darkness* J 3: 19; cf. 12: 43. ὑμῶν ἀκούειν μ. ἢ τοῦ θεοῦ, *not obey God, but you instead* Ac 4: 19; cf. 5: 29.—1 Ti 1: 4; 2 Ti 3: 4. τῷ ναυκλήρῳ μ. ἐπείθετο ἢ τοῖς ὑπὸ Παύλου λεγομένοις *he did not pay attention to what Paul said, but to the owner of the ship* Ac 27: 11. Likew. μᾶλλον ἑλόμενος ἤ *he chose the one rather than the other* Hb 11: 25.

d. μᾶλλον δέ *but rather, or rather,* or simply *rather,* introduces an expr. or thought that supplements and thereby corrects what has preceded (Aristoph., Plut. 634; X., Cyr. 5, 4, 49; Demosth. 18, 65; Philo, Aet. M. 23 μ. δέ) Χρ. Ἰ. ὁ ἀποθανών, μᾶλλον δὲ ἐγερθείς *Chr. J. who died, yes rather was raised* Ro 8: 34. γνόντες θεόν, μᾶλλον δὲ γνωσθέντες ὑπὸ θεοῦ *since you have known God, or rather have been known by God* Gal 4: 9; cf. 1 Cor 14: 1, 5. M-M.**

Μάλχος, ου, ὁ (Porphyr., Pyth. Vi. inscr. Πορφύριος ὁ καὶ Μ. [fr. Tyre] and Porphyr., Vi. Plot. 17 p. 111, 3ff Westerm.; Joseph. index, almost entirely of Gentiles, in fact of Nabataean Arabs; Dit., Or. 640, 3 [Palmyra]; inscr. in RDussaud, Mission dans les régions désertiques de la Syrie moyenne '02, p. 644 no. 9; inscr. from the Hauran: RB 41, '32, p. 403 no. 12; p. 578 no. 130; 131; PBrem. 5, 3 [117/19 AD] 6, 3; HWuthnow, E. palmyren. Büste: ELittmann-Festschr. '35, 63-9.—Zahn ad loc. [w. lit.]) *Mal-*

chus, slave of the high priest, whom Peter wounded when Jesus was arrested J 18: 10. M-M.*

μάμμη, ης, ἡ (orig. 'mother', later) *grandmother* (so Menand., Sam. 28; Herodas 3, 34; 38; Plut., Mor. 704B al.; Dit., Syll.³ 844B, 5; POxy. 1644, 12 [63/2 BC]; PReinach 49, 14; BGU 19 II, 7 al.; 4 Macc 16: 9; Philo, Spec. Leg. 3, 14; Jos., Ant. 10, 237.—Lob. on Phryn. 133-5) 2 Ti 1: 5 (μάμμη and μήτηρ mentioned together by name as Plut., Agis 4, 1.—Cf. also the influence of his grandmother Macrina and his mother Emmelia on the religious life of the fourth-century church father Basilius as he was growing up [Basilius, Ep. 223, 3 ἐκ παιδὸς ἔλαβον ἔννοιαν περὶ θεοῦ παρὰ τῆς μακαρίας μητρός μου καὶ τῆς μάμμης Μακρίνης]). M-M. B. 109.*

μαμωνᾶς, ᾶ, ὁ (Aram. מָמוֹנָא, emphat. state מָמוֹנָא) *wealth, property* Lk 16: 9, 11. Personified, 'Mammon' Mt 6: 24; Lk 16: 13; 2 Cl 6: 1.—EbNestle, Encyclopaedia Biblica 2912ff (here [2914f] the etymology of the word is also treated in detail); EKautzsch, Gramm. des Bibl.-Aram. 1884, 10; Dalman, Gramm.² 170f, RE³ XII '03, 153f; HZimmern, Akkadische Fremdwörter² '17, 20; ERiggenbach, ASchlatter-Festschr. '22, 21ff; MBlack, An Aramaic Approach, 102; FHauck, TW IV 390-2.—The word is also found Mishna Aboth 2, 17 and in the Damascus document p. 14, 20 Schechter '10=LRost (Kl. T. 167) '33, p. 26, which cannot be dated w. certainty (s. Bousset, Rel. 15f); EMeyer, ABA '19, 9, Abhdlg. p. 50. M-M.*

Μαναήν, ὁ indecl. (מְנַחֵם; 4 Km 15: 14 Μαναήμ; Jos., Ant. 9, 229; 232 Μαναῆμος, ου [15, 374]. Other Jews w. this name in Schürer⁴ index) *Manaen*, one of the prophets and teachers in the Antioch church, described as Ἡρῴδου τοῦ τετραάρχου σύντροφος Ac 13: 1.—On the name ThNöldeke, Beiträge z. semit. Sprachwissensch. '04, 99. M-M.*

Μανασσῆς, ῆ, acc. **ῆ, ὁ** (מְנַשֶּׁה) *Manasseh* (predominantly a Jewish name. But a Cyprian inscr. [OHoffmann, D. griech. Dialekte I 1891 p. 75 no. 140] gives it as the name of a pagan as well. See ἀββᾶ, end)—1. first-born son of Joseph (Gen 41: 51; Philo, Joseph.), father of a tribe B 13: 5 (cf. Gen 48: 14). Of the tribe Rv 7: 6.
2. son of Hezekiah, Hebrew king (4 Km 21: 1ff; 2 Ch 33: 1ff; Joseph.); in the genealogy of Jesus Mt 1: 10; Lk 3: 23ff D.*

μάνδρα, ας, ἡ (Soph.+; pap., LXX) *sheep-fold* B 16: 5 (for quotation cf. En. 89, 56; 66f).*

μανθάνω 2 aor. ἔμαθον, imper. pl. μάθετε, ptc. μαθών, perf. act. ptc. μεμαθηκώς (Hom.+; inscr., pap., LXX, En., Ep. Arist., Philo, Joseph., Test. 12 Patr.) *learn.*
1. lit., through instruction, abs. 1 Cor 14: 31; 1 Ti 2: 11; 2 Ti 3: 7. παρά τινος *learn from someone* as teacher (X., Cyr. 2, 2, 6; Appian, Iber. 23 §89 παρὰ τοῦ θεοῦ μ.; Sextus 353 μ. παρὰ θεοῦ; Philo, Deus Imm. 4) vs. 14b; *be someone's disciple* (μαθητής) Epil Mosq 1. ἀπό τινος *from someone* (Theognis 1, 28f: Theognis teaches what 'I myself as a παῖς ἔμαθον ἀπὸ τῶν ἀγαθῶν'; 1, 35; Jos., Ant. 8, 317) Mt 11: 29; Col 1: 7. W. acc. of the thing learned τί *someth.* 1 Cor 14: 35. πάντα Hs 9, 1, 3. Teaching Ro 16: 17. τὴν θεοσέβειαν τ. Χριστιανῶν Dg 1; cf. 11: 2. τὰ δικαιώματα τ. κυρίου *the ordinances of the Lord* B 21: 1. τὸν Χριστόν=Christian teaching Eph 4: 20 (Chio, Ep. 16, 8 θεὸν ἔμαθες=you have learned to know God). W. attraction of a relative μένε ἐν οἷς (=ἐν τούτοις ἃ) ἔμαθες *stand by what you have learned* 2 Ti 3: 14a. W. obj. to be supplied fr. the context (γράμματα) J 7: 15

(Gdspd., Probs. 102-4). μ. τι ἀπό τινος *learn someth. from someone* B 9: 9. μ. περὶ πάντων *receive instruction concerning all things* vs. 7 (περί τινος as Philo, Spec. Leg. 1, 42). μ. τι ἔν τινι *learn fr. someone's example* 1 Cor 4: 6 (Bl-D. §220, 2; Rob. 587).—μ. τι ἀπό τινος *learn someth. fr. someth.*: ἀπὸ τ. συκῆς μάθετε τ. παραβολήν Mt 24: 32; Mk 13: 28.—W. ὅτι foll. (Philo, Leg. All. 3, 51) B 9: 8. W. inf. foll. (Aristoxenus, fgm. 96 αὐλεῖν) 1 Cl 8: 4 (Is 1: 17); 57: 2. W. indirect question foll. 1 Cl 21: 8. τί ἐστιν *what this means* Mt 9: 13. W. the question preceding B 5: 5; 6: 9; 14: 4; 16: 2, 7; Dg 4: 6. Used w. other verbs: ἀκούειν κ. μ. (Pla., Ap. 33B, Ep. p. 344D; Theocr. 5, 39; Ael. Aristid. 45 p. 33 D. p. 40; cf. Polyb. 3, 32, 9 ὅσῳ διαφέρει τὸ μαθεῖν τοῦ μόνον ἀκούειν, τοσούτῳ...) J 6: 45. μ. καὶ παραλαμβάνειν Phil 4: 9.
2. *learn* or *come to know* τὸν τοῦ Χριστιανισμοῦ λόγον *Christian teaching* MPol 10: 1. τί παρά τινος *someth. fr. someone* (Sir 8: 8f; Ep. Arist. 198; Philo, Fuga 8, Leg. All. 3, 194; Jos., Vi. 62) Dg 4: 1. *Take note* τί *of someth.* MPol 20: 1.
3. *find out* (trag., X.; PRyl. 77, 42; POxy. 1067, 6; 1671, 20; LXX) τί ἀπό τινος *find someth. out fr. someone* Gal 3: 2. W. ὅτι foll. (Arrian, Anab. 2, 5, 7; Esth 1: 1n; Jos., Ant. 12, 208) Ac 23: 27.
4. *learn, appropriate to oneself* less through instruction than through experience or practice: ἔμαθεν ἀφ᾽ ὧν ἔπαθεν τὴν ὑπακοήν *he learned obedience through what he suffered* Hb 5: 8 (for the consonance cf. Aeschyl., Agam. 177 τῷ πάθει μάθος; Hdt. 1, 207, 1 τὰ δέ μοι παθήματα...μαθήματα; schol. on Pla. 222B ἐὰν μὴ πάθῃς, οὐ μὴ μάθῃς; Philo, Fuga 138 ἔμαθον μὲν ὃ ἔπαθον. Further exx. in HWindisch ad loc. and CSpicq, RB 56, '49, 551.—A similar play on words in Theognis 1, 369f μωμεῖσθαι—μιμεῖσθαι=[they can] find fault [with me, but not] do as I do).—W. inf. foll. (X., Cyr. 1, 6, 6; Lucian, Dial. Deor. 14, 2; Dt 14: 23; Is 2: 4) τ. ἴδιον οἶκον εὐσεβεῖν 1 Ti 5: 4; cf. Tit 3: 14. μ. κατὰ Χριστιανισμὸν ζῆν IMg 10: 1, cf. IRo 4: 3. ἔμαθον ἐν οἷς εἰμι αὐτάρκης εἶναι *I have learned, in whatever state I am, to be content* (s. αὐτάρκης) Phil 4: 11. ἀργαὶ μανθάνουσιν περιερχόμεναι τὰς οἰκίας 1 Ti 5: 13 presents many difficulties fr. a linguistic point of view. Perh. εἶναι or ζῆν is to be inserted after ἀργαί (X., An. 3, 2, 25 ἂν ἅπαξ μάθωμεν ἀργοὶ ζῆν; so Bl-D. §416, 2; Mlt. 229; Dibelius, Hdb. ad loc.). Others substitute λανθάνουσιν by conjecture (most recently PWSchmiedel, ThBl 1, '22, 222, Zürcher Bibelübers. '31, appendix to NT, note 12).
5. οὐδεὶς ἐδύνατο μαθεῖν τ. ᾠδήν Rv 14: 3 seems to mean *no one was able to hear the song* (Boll 18ff; Lohmeyer; Behm). But linguistically the mngs. *learn* (e.g. Bousset; Allo; RSV) or *understand* (Lysias 10, 15; Pla., Meno 84D, Tht. 174B, Euthyd. 277E.—So e.g. JWeiss) are also poss. M-M. B. 1222.*

μανία, ας, ἡ (Pind.+; pap., LXX, Philo; Jos., Bell. 1, 506, Ant. 2, 330) *madness, frenzy, delirium,* also in weakened sense *eccentricity, queerness, excitement* (so perh. the passage [II BC] fr. an unedited Tebtunis papyrus in M-M s.v. φαίνη εἰς μανίαν ἐμπεπτωκέναι, διὸ λόγον σαυτοῦ οὐ ποιεῖς καὶ ὑπομεμένηκας. So Solon is reproached with μανία by his opponents: Solon 9, 1 D.² Cf. μαίνομαι) τὰ πολλά σε γράμματα εἰς μανίαν περιτρέπει *all your study is driving you mad* Ac 26: 24. M-M.*

μάννα, τό indecl. (מָן. The Gk. form μάννα [LXX—only Ex 16 μάν; Philo, Leg. Alleg. 2, 84, Det. Pot. Insid. 118; Jos., Ant. 3, 32] is prob. explained by the influence of the Gk. word ἡ μάννα='little grain, granule' [Hippocr.+;

POxy. 1088, 21; PGM 4, 1874]. The fem. inflection also Jos., Ant. 3, 296; 5, 21; Sib. Or. 7, 149) *manna*, called a miraculous food, often identified with the sweetish exudate of the manna tamarisk and related trees, produced by the sting of an insect; it dries and falls down in the form of small grains. S. on it, fr. more recent times: AKaiser, Der heutige Stand der Mannafrage: Mitteilungen d. Thurgauischen Naturforsch. Gesellschaft, Heft 25, '24, Wanderungen u. Wandlungen in d. Sinaiwüste 1886-1927: ibid. '28, 21ff; HSDarlington, Open Court 42, '28, 372-81; FSBodenheimer and OTheodor, Ergebnisse d. Sinai-Exped. 1927 der hebr. Univers. Jerus. '30; BJMalina, The Palestinian Manna Tradition, '68.

1. lit. J 6: 31, 49. Of the *manna* which, acc. to Ex 16: 32ff, was kept in the tabernacle Hb 9: 4. Of the honey eaten by the Baptist: οὗ ἡ γεῦσις ἡ τοῦ μ. *that tasted like manna* GEb 2.

2. τὸ μ. τὸ κεκρυμμένον *the hidden manna*, a heavenly food Rv 2: 17.—W-S. 10A. 2 p. 92; RMeyer, TW IV 466-70. M-M.*

μαντεύομαι (Hom.+; inscr., LXX, Philo, Joseph.) mid. dep., also w. pass. mng. for pass. forms; in our lit., as well as LXX, always in an unfavorable sense.

1. *prophesy, divine, give an oracle* (Hom.+; 1 Km 28: 8=Jos., Ant. 6, 330; Sib. Or. 4, 3) of a demoniac pagan slave-girl Ac 16: 16.

2. *consult an oracle* (Pind.+; Artem. 3, 20; Jos., C. Ap. 1, 306) of doubting Christians Hm 11: 4. M-M.*

μάντις, εως, ὁ (Hom.+; inscr., LXX, Philo; Jos., Bell. 1, 80, C. Ap. 1, 257 al.) *soothsayer, diviner, prophet* of false Christian prophets, to whom the poorly grounded believers go, as to soothsayers Hm 11: 2.*

Μάξιμος, ου, ὁ a name freq. (Polyb. 3, 87, 6 al.; inscr., pap., Joseph.) found, *Maximus*, a Christian Hv 2, 3, 4.*

μαραίνω pass.: pf. ptc. μεμαραμμένος (Bl-D. §72); 1 aor. ἐμαράνθην; 1 fut. μαρανθήσομαι (Hom.+; inscr., pap., LXX) *quench, destroy*, in our lit. only pass. gradually *die out, fade, disappear, wither* of plants (schol. on Nicander, Ther. 677; Job 15: 30; Wsd 2: 8) ὡς μεμαραμμέναι *as if withered* Hs 9, 1, 7; cf. 9, 23, 1f. Of one's spirit v 3, 11, 2 (cf. Appian, Bell. Civ. 5, 90 §379 μαραίνεσθαι of the πνεῦμα, wind=abate fully, die down; Jos., Ant. 11, 56 of beauty). Of pers. (Aristaen., Ep. 1, 10 μαραινόμενος τ. νοῦν) ὁ πλούσιος ἐν ταῖς πορείαις αὐτοῦ μαρανθήσεται *the rich man will fade away, together with his undertakings* Js 1: 11 (s. the grave-inscription Sb 5199, 2 ἐμαράνθη; Jos., Bell. 6, 274 λιμῷ μαραινόμενοι; Test. Sim. 3: 3). M-M.*

μαρὰν ἀθᾶ=מָרַן אֲתָא (our) *Lord has come*, better separated μαράνα θᾶ=מָרַנָא תָא (our) *Lord, come!* an Aramaic formula which D 10: 6 associates with what appears to be the early Christian liturgy of the Lord's Supper (on D 10: 6 s. JAEmerton, Maranatha and Ephphatha, JTS 18, '67, 427-31 and Moule below. On both passages P-ÉLangevin, Jésus Seigneur, '67, 168-208; 236-98). Used without explanation by Paul 1 Cor 16: 22.—EKautzsch, Gramm. d. Bibl.-Aram. 1884, 12; 174, StKr. 74, '01, 296; EbNestle, Theol. Studien aus Württemb. 5, 1884, 186ff; ThNöldeke, GGA 1884, 1023; Dalman, Gramm.² 152, 3; 357, 1, Worte 269; FSchulthess, D. Problem d. Sprache Jesu '17, p. 28, 50; Dssm., D. Urgeschichte d. Christentums im Lichte der Sprachforschung '10, 26ff; Zahn, Einl. I³ 216f; WBousset, Jesus der Herr '16, 22ff; EHommel, ZNW 15, '14, 317-22ff [מָרַן אֲתָא='our Lord is the sign'='the א and the

ת'. So earlier ChBruston, Rev. de Théol. et des Quest. Rel. 22, '13, 402-8]; FJDölger, Sol Salutis '20, 153ff; CFabricius, Urbekenntnisse d. Christenheit: RSeeberg-Festschr. '29 I 21-41; Field, Notes, 180; HJCadbury, JBL 58, '39, p. X; Gdspd., Probs. 166-8; CFDMoule, NTS 6, '60, 307-10; SSchulz, ZNW 53, '62, 125-44.—KGKuhn, TW IV 470-5. M-M.*

μαργαρίτης, ου, ὁ (Theophr.; Strabo; Aelian, N.A. 10, 13; pap.; En. 18, 7; Test. Jud. 13: 5; loanw. in rabb.) *pearl*.

1. lit., w. gold 1 Ti 2: 9. W. gold and precious stones Rv 17: 4; 18: 12, 16. Of the pearls that serve as gates for the heavenly city 21: 21 (each gate a single pearl): EBurrows, JTS 43, '42, 177-9). καλοὶ μ. Mt 13: 45; πολύτιμος μ. *a very valuable pearl* vs. 46 (μ. more in demand than gold, Chares of Mitylene [IV BC]: 125 fgm. 3 Jac. Among the Indians worth 3 times as much as pure gold: Arrian, Ind. 8, 13 and always in great demand: ibid. 8, 9).

2. fig., in a proverb (s. χοῖρος) βάλλειν τοὺς μ. ἔμπροσθεν τ. χοίρων *throw pearls to swine* i.e. entrust someth. precious (on the value placed on pearls in antiquity s. also HUsener, Die Perle: Weizsäcker-Festschr. 1892, 203-13) to people who cannot or will not appreciate it Mt 7: 6 (differently GSchwartz, NovT 14, '72, 18-25). πνευματικοὶ μ. *spiritual pearls* of a martyr's bonds IEph 11: 2.—FHauck, TW IV 475-7.*

Μάρθα, ας, ἡ (מַרְתָּא) 'mistress'. Plut., Mar. 17, 2 Σύραν γυναῖκα, Μάρθαν ὄνομα; BGU 1153 I, 3 [14 BC]; 1155, 4 [10 BC]) *Martha*, acc. to Lk 10: 38, 40f sister of Mary, acc. to J 11: 1, 5, 19ff, 24, 30, 39 also sister of Lazarus of Bethany.—12: 2. M-M.*

Μαρία, ας, ἡ (vase-inscr. fr. Samaria-Sebaste: Suppl. epigr. Gr. VIII 110 [I BC/I AD]; two ostraca in PMMeyer, Griech. Texte aus Ägypt. '16, 107ff nos. 33 and 56 [both II AD]; cf. Dssm., LO 97f; 302; a third ostracon in Dssm., LO 260 [cf. LAE² 121, n. 11; 122; 306, n. 6]; Jos., Bell. 6, 201) and **Μαριάμ** indecl. (מִרְיָם Μαριαμ, Miriam, sister of Moses Ex 15: 20f al.; Ezech. Trag. in Clem. of Alex., Strom. 1, 23, 155, 4; Philo.—Joseph. writes the name Μαριά[μ]μη, ης [Ant. 3, 54].—On the name and its various forms s. Bl-D. §53, 3; Mlt.-H. 144f; OBardenhewer, Der Name Maria 1895; HermvSoden, Die Schriften des NTs I '06, 1373f; FZorell, ZkTh 30, '06, 356ff; EKönig, ZNW 17, '16, 257-63; MNoth, D. isr. Personennamen '29) *Mary*.

1. the mother of Jesus. The foll. forms of the name are attested in the var. cases: Μαρία as nom. Lk 2: 19, otherw. only occasionally as v.l. (DLk 1: 30, 39, 56; C and D vss. 34, 38, 46). Μαρίας Mt 1: 16, 18; 2: 11; Mk 6: 3; Lk 1: 41; IEph 7: 2; 18: 2; 19: 1; ITr 9: 1. Μαρίαν Mt 1: 20. Μαριάμ as nom. Mt 13: 55; Lk 1: 27, 34, 38f, 46, 56; 2: 19 v.l.; as acc. Mt 1: 20 v.l.; Lk 2: 16; as voc. Lk 1: 30; σὺν Μαριάμ Lk 2: 5; Ac 1: 14; πρὸς Μαριάμ Lk 2: 34. Little is known about the life of this Mary; in the infancy narratives Mt 1f; Lk 1f and esp. in the apocryphal gospels she plays a great role; s. HUsener, ZNW 4, '03, 1ff. In Mk 3: 31f and parallels, where she and the brothers and sisters of Jesus are prominently mentioned, no indication of any interest in his movement is given. But Ac 1: 14 mentions Mary and his brothers (brothers and sisters? s. ἀδελφός 1) among the members of the early church. The mother of Jesus is also mentioned in the Fourth Gospel, though not by name.—RSeeberg, Die Herkunft der Mutter Jesu: Bonwetsch-Festschr. '18, 13ff; JBlinzler, Jes. u. s. Mutter nach dem Zeugn. der Evv.: Klerusblatt 23, '42; 24, '43; UHolzmeister, De anno mortis Deip. Virg.: Marianum 4, '42,

167–82; FMWillam, D. Leb. Marias³ '42; HRäisänen, D. Mutter Jesu im NT, '69.

2. *Mary Magdalene* (s. Μαγδαληνή). Forms of her name: Μαρία Mt 27: 56; 28: 1 v.l.; Mk 15: 40, 47; 16: 1, 9 (Μαρίᾳ); Lk 8: 2; 24: 10; J 19: 25; 20: 1, 11, 18 v.l. Μαριάμ Mt 27: 56 v.l., 61; 28: 1; Mk 15: 40 v.l.; J 19: 25 v.l.; 20: 1 v.l., 11 v.l., 16 (voc.), 18; GP 12: 50. Acc. to the gospels this woman, one of Jesus' most faithful followers, was cured by Jesus of a seven-fold demonic possession (Mk 16: 9; Lk 8: 2). She appears in the Passion Narrative w. women companions; also in the synoptic account of Easter morning. In the Fourth Gosp. she is the only one mentioned at the grave, and sees the resurrected Lord (likew. in the long ending of Mk). Later tradition identified her w. the sinful woman who anointed Jesus in the house of the Pharisee (Lk 7: 37, 39). UHolzmeister, Die Magdalenenfrage in der kirchl. Überl.: ZkTh 46, '22, 402ff; JSickenberger, Ist die Magdalenenfrage wirklich unlösbar? BZ 17, '26, 63ff; PKetter, D. Magdalenenfrage '29. S. Simpson and Burkitt under 5 below.

3. the 'other' *Mary,* mother of James (s. Ἰάκωβος 3) and Joses (s. Ἰωσῆς 2). Form of the name Μαρία Mt 27: 56, 61 (ἡ ἄλλη Μαρία); 28: 1 (ἡ ἄλλ. Μ.—JRMackay, The Other M.: ET 40, '29, 319–21); Mk 15: 40, 47; 16: 1; Lk 24: 10. She was one of the followers of Jesus present as a spectator at the tragedy on Golgotha. Hence she could be identical with

4. Μαρία (v.l. Μαριάμ) ἡ τοῦ Κλωπᾶ Μ., *the wife of Clopas* J 19: 25.

5. *Mary,* acc. to Lk 10: 39, 42 sister of Martha, acc. to J 11: 1f, 19f, 28, 31f, 45; 12: 3 also sister of Lazarus, resident in Bethany. Forms of the name: Μαρία Lk 10: 42 v.l.; J 11: 2 v.l., 20 v.l., 32 v.l.; 12: 3 v.l.; Μαρίας J 11: 1; Μαρίαν J 11: 19 v.l., 28 v.l., 31 v.l., 45 v.l. Μαριάμ Lk 10: 39, 42; J 11: 2, 20, 32; 12: 3; as acc. J 11: 19, 28, 31, 45.— ARSimpson, M. of Bethany, M. of Magdala, and Anonyma: ET 20, '09, 307–18; FCBurkitt, M. Magd. and M., Sister of Martha: ET 42, '31, 157–9.

6. *Mary,* mother of John Mark, owner of a house in Jerusalem (οἰκία τῆς Μαρίας), who placed it at the disposal of the Christian church for its meetings Ac 12: 12.

7. *Mary,* an otherw. unknown Christian, probably of Jewish descent (yet Μαρία appears in Ramsay, Phrygia I 2 p. 557f no. 439 and 440 as the fem. form of the Roman name Marius), who is greeted Ro 16: 6 (ἀσπάσασθε Μαρίαν; v.l. Μαριάμ [as early as 𝔓⁴⁶]), w. the additional note that she had rendered outstanding service to the receivers of the letter. M-M.*

Μαριάμ, ἡ indecl. (on the form of the name see the beginning of the preceding entry) *Miriam,* prophetess, and sister of Aaron and Moses (Ex 15: 20f; Num 12) 1 Cl 4: 11.*

Μαρκίων, ωνος, ὁ *Marcion,* a rather rare name (Sb 4604, 3).

1. a Christian of Smyrna MPol 20: 1 (Μάρκου is also attested, as well as the form Μαρκιανοῦ, which is in the Lat. version and is preferred by Lghtf.; s. on this OvGebhardt, ZWTh 18, 1875, 370ff).

2. the famous heretic Epil Mosq 2.—AvHarnack, Marcion² '24; MSEnslin, The Pontic Mouse: ATR 27, '45, 1–16.*

Μαρκιωνιστής, οῦ, ὁ *Marcionite, follower of Marcion* Epil Mosq 2 (s. Μαρκίων 2).*

Μᾶρκος, ου, ὁ (on the accent s. Bl-D. §41, 3; Rob. 235) *Mark,* a name found rather freq. (Diod. S. 11, 63, 1; Plut.,

inscr., pap.; Philo, Leg. ad Gai. 62; 294; Joseph.); surname of John (s. Ἰωάν[ν]ης 6), son of Mary of Jerusalem (s. Μαρία 6). Perh. introduced to Paul by Barnabas, his cousin (Col 4: 10); he accompanied Paul and Barnabas on the so-called first missionary journey, but left them before it was completed, and later became the cause of an open break betw. them. Ac 12: 12, 25; 15: 37, 39. The same pers. is certainly referred to Phlm 24; 2 Ti 4: 11; 1 Pt 5: 13; Papias 2: 15. Title of the second gosp. κατὰ Μᾶρκον (on the two names of a man who was active and well known, among Semites and Greeks, we may compare the circumstance that the Carthaginian Ἀσδρούβας [Hasdrubal, II BC] was known as Κλειτόμαχος among the Greeks [Diog. L. 4, 67]).—Zahn, Einl. II³ 204ff; Jülicher, RE XII 288ff; EBarnikol, Personenprobleme d. AG, Joh. Markus u. Titus '31; WSReilly, CBQ 1, '39, 223–31; ROPTaylor, ET 54, '43, 136–8; KNiederwimmer, ZNW 58, '67, 172–87. M-M.*

μάρμαρος, ου, ὁ (Hom.+ in the sense 'stone, block of rock') *marble* (so since Theophr., Lap. 9; Strabo 9, 1, 23; IG IV² 1, 109 III, 103 [III BC]; PLeid. X 10, 12; BGU 952, 10; EpJer 71; Jos., Bell. 4, 532; both masc. and fem.) as precious material Rv 18: 12. M-M.*

Μάρτιος, ίου, ὁ (Lat. loanw.: Martius) *March* πρὸ ἑπτὰ καλανδῶν Μαρτίων = February 23, MPol 21.*

μαρτυρέω impf. ἐμαρτύρουν; fut. μαρτυρήσω; 1 aor. ἐμαρτύρησα; pf. μεμαρτύρηκα. Pass.: impf. ἐμαρτυρούμην; pf. μεμαρτύρημαι; 1 aor. ἐμαρτυρήθην (Hb 11: 2, 4, 39). (Semonides, Hdt.+; inscr., pap., LXX, Philo, Joseph.).

1. act.—a. *bear witness, be a witness* ὑμεῖς μαρτυρεῖτε *you are witnesses* J 15: 27. ἐὰν θέλωσιν μαρτυρεῖν *if they are willing to appear as witnesses* Ac 26: 5.—J 12: 17; 1 J 5: 6f. Parenthetically, emphasizing the correctness of a statement, μαρτυρῶ *I can testify* (POxy. 105, 13 Σαραπίων μαρτυρῶ= 'I, S., am witness'; PLond. 1164[f], 35 al.— Bl-D. §465, 2; Rob. 434) 2 Cor 8: 3. περί τινος *bear witness, testify concerning someone* or *someth.* (PGrenf. II 73, 16 ὅταν ἔλθῃ σὺν θεῷ, μαρτυρήσει σοι περὶ ὧν αὐτὴν πεποιήκασιν; Jos., C. Ap. 1, 217, Vi. 259) J 1: 7f, 15 (in the very likely case that μαρτυρεῖ refers to the past, cf. Caecil. Calact., fgm. 75 p. 58, 2ff, where examples are given of the interchange of tenses: Demosth. 59, 34 τοὺς ὁρῶντας for τ. ἑωρακότας; Eur., Androm. fgm. 145 Nauck² ὁρῶ ἀντὶ τοῦ εἶδον; Thu. 2, 35, 1 ἐπαινοῦσι ἀντὶ τοῦ ἐπῄνεσαν); 2: 25; 5: 31, 32a, 36f, 39; 7: 7; 8: 13f, 18a, b; 10: 25; 15: 26; 21: 24; 1 J 5: 9. μαρτύρησον περὶ τοῦ κακοῦ *testify concerning the wrong* J 18: 23 (μ. = furnish proof X., Symp. 8, 12). Also ἐπί τινι Hb 11: 4b (on ἐπί w. dat. in this pass. s. Gen 4: 4). W. dat. of the thing (Jos., Ant. 12, 135) μ. τῇ ἀληθείᾳ *bear witness to the truth* J 5: 33; 18: 37. μ. σου τῇ ἀληθείᾳ *testify to the truth of you(r way of life)* 3 J 3; σου τῇ ἀγάπῃ vs. 6. W. dat. of the pers. about whom testimony is given (Appian, Bell. Civ. 3, 73 §298.—It is dat. of advantage or disadv.) Ac 10: 43; 22: 5; w. ptc. foll. θεὸς ἐμαρτύρησεν αὐτοῖς δοὺς κτλ. *God testified for them by giving* Ac 15: 8 (though αὐτοῖς can also be taken w. δούς); w. ὅτι foll. *bear someone witness that* J 3: 28; Ro 10: 2; Gal 4: 15; Col 4: 13. μ. ἑαυτῷ, ὅτι *bear witness to oneself that* Mt 23: 31. The dat. can also designate the pers. who is informed or instructed by the testimony: *bear witness to someone* Hb 10: 15; Rv 22: 18.—μ. ὅτι *testify that* (Aelian, V.H. 9, 11) J 1: 34; 4: 44; 12: 17 v.l.; 1 J 4: 14. ὅτι introducing direct discourse J 4: 39. μ. κατὰ τ. θεοῦ ὅτι *bear witness against God by*

declaring that 1 Cor 15: 15 (PPetr. II 21 [d], 12 [III вc] καθ᾽ οὖ μαρτυρῶ). ἐμαρτύρησεν καὶ εἶπεν w. direct discourse foll. J 13: 21. μ. λέγων w. direct disc. foll. J 1: 32. Of God μοι μαρτυρεῖ λέγων (Ps 89: 4 follows) *he testifies (of it) to me by saying* B 15: 4.

b. *bear witness to, declare, confirm* (Eunap., Vi. Soph. p. 76 ὁ θεὸς ἐμαρτύρησε) τὶ *someth.* (Demosth. 57, 4 ἀκοήν; Aeschines 1, 46 τἀληθῆ) ὃ ἑωράκαμεν μαρτυροῦμεν J 3: 11; cf. vs. 32. τὸν λόγον τ. θεοῦ Rv 1: 2. ταῦτα 22: 20. τινί τι *someth. to* or *for someone* (Dionys. Hal. 3, 67, 1; Jos., Ant. 6, 355) vs. 16. ὑμῖν τ. ζωήν 1 J 1: 2. The acc. is to be supplied fr. the context J 19: 35; Ac 23: 11. W. ptc. ἀκούσαντες μαρτυρήσωσιν *they must admit that they have heard* PK 3 p. 15, 23.—μαρτυρίαν μ. *bear witness* (Ps.-Pla., Eryx. 399в; Epict. 4, 8, 32) περί τινος *concerning someone* J 5: 32b; 1 J 5: 10.

c. *testify favorably, speak well (of), approve (of)* (Dio Chrys. 23[40], 19; Dit., Syll.³ 374, 37 [III вc]; POxy. 930, 16) w. dat. of the pers. (Appian, Samn. 11, §2 τοῖς ὑπάτοις, Liby. 105 §495, Bell. Civ. 4, 92 §387; Aelian, V.H. 1, 30; Jos., Ant. 12, 134) or of the thing approved Lk 4: 22; J 3: 26. Of God toward David Ac 13: 22. μὴ ἑαυτῷ μαρτυρείτω *he must not testify (favorably) concerning himself* 1 Cl 38: 2. W. dat. to be supplied 3 J 12b. μαρτυρίᾳ, ᾗ ἐμαρτύρησεν αὐτῷ ὁ δεσπότης Hs 5, 2, 6. Of the flesh ἵνα τὸ πνεῦμα . . . μαρτυρήσῃ αὐτῇ Hs 5, 7, 1.—ὁ κύριος ὁ μαρτυρῶν ἐπί (which a v.l. omits; μ. ἐπί τινι as Jos., Ant. 3, 189) τῷ λόγῳ τ. χάριτος αὐτοῦ *the Lord, who attested the word of his grace* Ac 14: 3. With συνευδοκέω Lk 11: 48 𝔓⁷⁵ et al.

d. in eccl. usage w. regard to martyrdom *bear witness, testify, be a witness (unto death), be martyred*: of Paul μαρτυρήσας ἐπὶ τῶν ἡγουμένων . . . εἰς τὸν ἅγιον τόπον ἐπορεύθη 1 Cl 5: 7; cf. vs. 4; MPol 1: 1; 19: 1; 21f; Epil Mosq 3. Prob. 1 Ti 6: 13 also belongs here: Χριστοῦ Ἰησοῦ τοῦ μαρτυρήσαντος ἐπὶ Ποντίου Πιλάτου τ. καλὴν ὁμολογίαν *Christ Jesus, who made the good confession before Pontius Pilate* (cf. GBaldensperger, RHPhr 2, ᾽22, 1-25; 95-117); otherwise the passage may be classed under 1a above.

2. pass.—a. *be witnessed, have witness borne* ὑπό τινος *by someone* (Philo, Leg. All. 3, 46 σοφία μαρτυρουμένη ὑπὸ θεοῦ) Ro 3: 21 (the witness of the law and prophets points to God's righteousness). Foll. by ὅτι and a quot. in direct discourse Hb 7: 17. μαρτυρούμενος ὅτι ζῇ *one of whom it is testified that he lives* vs. 8.

b. *be well spoken of, be approved* (Ep. 12 of Apollonius of Tyana: Philostrat. I 348, 26. Exx. fr. inscr. in Dssm., NB 93 [BS 265], LO 69, 2 [LAE 84, 5]) ἀνὴρ μαρτυρούμενος or μεμαρτυρημένος *a man of good reputation* Ac 6: 3; IPhld 11: 1. Of OT worthies to whom God made himself known *men of attested merit* 1 Cl 17: 1; 19: 1. Of David 18: 1. Of Abraham μεγάλως ἐμαρτυρήθη *his merit was gloriously attested* 17: 2. Of the apostles 47: 4. Of Paul IEph 12: 2. Of church leaders 1 Cl 44: 3.—Foll. by nom. and inf. Hb 11: 4a; cf. vs. 5. διά τινος *be praised for someth.* 11: 4a, 39. ἐν ἔργοις καλοῖς μαρτυρούμενος *well attested in good deeds* 1 Ti 5: 10; cf. Hb 11: 2. ὑπό τινος *be well spoken of by someone* (M. Ant. 7, 62; Dit., Syll.³ 799, 28; Jos., Ant. 3, 59) Ac 10: 22; 16: 2; 22: 12; IPhld 5: 2.—Impersonally μαρτυρεῖταί τινι ὑπό τινος *a good testimony is given by someone to someone* (Dionys. Hal., Thu. 8 μαρτυρεῖται τῷ ἀνδρὶ τάχα μὲν ὑπὸ πάντων φιλοσόφων; BGU 1141, 15 [14 вc] ὡς καὶ μαρτυρηθήσεταί σοι ὑπὸ τῶν φίλων) Δημητρίῳ μεμαρτύρηται ὑπὸ πάντων καὶ ὑπὸ αὐτῆς τῆς ἀληθείας *Demetrius has received a good testimony from everyone*

and from the truth itself 3 J 12a.—Dg 12: 6.—OMichel, Bibl. Bekennen u. Bezeugen, Ὁμολογεῖν und μαρτυρεῖν im bibl. Sprachgebr.: Evang. Theologie 2, ᾽35, 231-45; EBurnier, La notion de témoignage dans le NT ᾽39; HStrathmann, TW IV 477-520: μαρτυρέω, μάρτυς and related words. M-M.*

μαρτυρία, ας, ἡ (Hom.+; inscr., pap., LXX, Philo, Joseph.—KLatte, Martyria: Pauly-W. XIV 2, ᾽30, 2032-9).

1. act. *testimony, testifying* (Pla., Leg. 11 p. 937A εἰς μαρτυρίαν κληθείς; Epict. 3, 22, 86 the μ. of the Cynic; PHal. 1, 222 εἰς μαρτυρίαν κλῆσις) οὗτος ἦλθεν εἰς μαρτυρίαν J 1: 7. Of the two witnesses: ὅταν τελέσωσιν τ. μαρτυρίαν αὐτῶν Rv 11: 7.

2. pass. *testimony*—a. of testimony in court (Demosth. 29, 7 al.; Jos., Ant. 4, 219) Mk 14: 56, 59; Lk 22: 71. κατά τινος *against someone* Mk 14: 55; δύο ἀνθρώπων ἡ μ. *the testimony of two persons* J 8: 17.

b. of historical *attestation* or *testimony* (Diod. S. 11, 38, 6 τῆς ἱστορίας δικαία μαρτυρία) J 19: 35; 21: 24 (JChapman, JTS 31, ᾽30, 379-87).

c. in the religious and moral senses, of a judgment on relig. or moral matters, passed by one person upon another (Jos., Ant. 6, 346) 1 J 5: 9a; 3 J 12; Tit 1: 13. ἡ μ. τῆς ἀγαθῆς πράξεως *testimony concerning good deeds* 1 Cl 30: 7. μαρτυρίαν καλὴν ἔχειν ἀπὸ τῶν ἔξωθεν *have a good standing with outsiders* 1 Ti 3: 7 (μ.=recommendation: Dio Chrys. 28[45], 9; Chio, Ep. 2; Dit., Syll.³ 1073, 17 [II AD]).—In the obscure concatenation of clauses B 1: 6, love seems to be ἔργων δικαιοσύνης μαρτυρία *a testimony of righteous deeds.*—Of a good testimony fr. God (Dio Chrys. 16[33], 12 τῆς μεγίστης ἔτυχε μαρτυρίας παρὰ τοῦ δαιμονίου) Hs 5, 2, 6.

d. esp. w. ref. to Jesus—a. of human testimony concerning Jesus: by the Baptist J 1: 19. By Paul Ac 22: 18. By the believers Rv 12: 11. Human testimony rejected J 5: 34.

β. of superhuman testimony concerning Jesus: he bears witness to himself as the central point of the Christian message: J 3: 11, 32f; 8: 14. His self-attestation is rejected vs. 13; cf. 5: 31. Jesus also testifies concerning himself in Rv 1: 2, 9.—God attests him (cf. Ael. Aristid. 45 p. 12 D.: μ. παρὰ Ἀπόλλωνος, p. 13 ἐκ Διός; Dexippus Athen. [III AD]: 100 fgm. 1, 7 Jac. ἡ τοῦ θεοῦ μ. for the 'god' Lycurgus) J 5: 32, 36 (μαρτυρία μείζων as Dionys. Soph., Ep. 77); 1 J 5: 9b, c, 10a, b, 11.—RAsting (εὐαγγέλιον, end).—On John s. ECHoskyns, The Fourth Gosp. ᾽40 I p. 93-104.

γ. Rv speaks of the μαρτυρία or the μ. Ἰησοῦ which the Christians, or certain Christians (martyrs, prophets), possess: 6: 9; 12: 17; 19: 10a, b; 20: 4.

3. *a martyr's death, martyrdom* MPol 1: 1; 13: 2; 17: 1. M-M.*

μαρτύριον, ου, τό (Pind., Hdt.+; inscr., pap., LXX; Ep. Arist. 306; Philo, Joseph.).

1. *that which serves as testimony* or *proof, testimony, proof*—a. consisting of an action, a circumstance, or a thing that serves as a testimony (Pla., Leg. 12 p. 943C τ. στέφανον ἀναθεῖναι μαρτύριον εἰς κρίσιν; Jos., Ant. 6, 66) προσένεγκον τὸ δῶρον εἰς μαρτύριον αὐτοῖς Mt 8: 4 (JZoller, 'Z. Zeugnis für sie': Ricerche Relig. 5, ᾽29, 385-91 against SZeitlin: Rev. des Études juives 87, ᾽29, 79-82); cf. Mk 1: 44; Lk 5: 14. ἐκτινάξατε τὸν χοῦν εἰς μ. αὐτοῖς Mk 6: 11; cf. Lk 9: 5 (ἐπ᾽ αὐτούς). ἐπὶ ἡγεμόνας ἀχθήσεσθε ἕνεκεν ἐμοῦ εἰς μαρτύριον αὐτοῖς Mt 10: 18; cf. Mk 13: 9; ἀποβήσεται ὑμῖν εἰς μ. Lk 21: 13 (s. ἀποβαίνω 2). κηρυχθήσεται ἐν ὅλῃ τ. οἰκουμένῃ εἰς

μ. Mt 24: 14.—A spoken statement serves εἰς μ. *as a testimony* B 9: 3; IPhld 6: 3; a written statement εἰς μ. ἐν ὑμῖν (cf. Dt 31: 26) ITr 12: 3. The circumstance that certain numbers occur in the OT serves as an indication, amounting to a testimony, of certain details in the plan of salvation B 8: 3f; cf. GEb 2. The redeeming death of Jesus was a testimony (of God) 1 Ti 2: 6. The rust on the money of the wealthy will turn out εἰς μ. for them Js 5: 3. Moses as a servant (whose service is directed) εἰς μ. τῶν λαληθησομένων, toward testifying about revelations still to come Hb 3: 5. The μείωσις τῆς σαρκός as μ. ἐκλογῆς *testimony* or *proof of (s)election* Dg 4: 4.

b. consisting of a statement that is brought out as testimony: w. subj. gen. τὸ μ. τῆς συνειδήσεως *the testimony that our conscience gives* 2 Cor 1: 12. W. obj. gen. ἀπεδίδουν τὸ μ.... τῆς ἀναστάσεως *they gave testimony to the resurrection* Ac 4: 33. τὸ μ. τοῦ σταυροῦ *the testimony of the cross* Pol 7: 1. Of Christian preaching and the gospel gener. τὸ μ. τοῦ Χριστοῦ *the testimony to Christ* 1 Cor 1: 6; cf. 2 Ti 1: 8. τὸ μ. τοῦ θεοῦ *the testimony of God* 1 Cor 2: 1. ἐπιστεύθη τὸ μ. ἡμῶν ἐφ' ὑμᾶς *our testimony to you was believed* 2 Th 1: 10.

2. used in the LXX as the transl. of מוֹעֵד in the expr. ἡ σκηνὴ τοῦ μ.= אֹהֶל מוֹעֵד *tent of meeting, tent* or *tabernacle of testimony* (Ex 28: 43 al.) Ac 7: 44; Rv 15: 5; 1 Cl 43: 2, 5.

3. *martyrdom* MPol 1: 1; 2: 1; 18: 2; 19: 1; Epil Mosq 1; Phlm subscr. M-M.*

μαρτύρομαι (trag., Thu.+; pap., LXX)—1. *testify, bear witness* (Pla., Phileb. 47D; Jos., Bell. 3, 354; POxy. 1120, 11; PAmh. 141, 17; PStrassb. 5, 14; 1 Macc 2: 56 τῇ ἐκκλησίᾳ) τινί *to someone* μικρῷ τε καὶ μεγάλῳ *to great and small* Ac 26: 22; τινί w. ὅτι foll. 20: 26; Gal 5: 3.

2. *affirm, insist, implore* (someone Polyb. 13, 8, 6; Jdth 7: 28; Jos., Ant. 10, 104) w. λέγειν and acc. w. inf. foll. Eph 4: 17. τινά foll. by εἰς and subst. inf. w. acc. παρακαλοῦντες ὑμᾶς καὶ παραμυθούμενοι καὶ μαρτυρόμενοι εἰς τὸ περιπατεῖν ὑμᾶς ἀξίως 1 Th 2: 12. M-M.*

μάρτυς, μάρτυρος, ὁ dat. pl. μάρτυσιν (Pind., Hdt.+; inscr., pap., LXX, Philo, Joseph.) *witness*.

1. lit., in the legal sense Ac 7: 58; Mt 18: 16; 2 Cor 13: 1; 1 Ti 5: 19 (the last 3 after Dt 19: 15; cf. Jos., Vi. 256 and Hipponax [VI BC] 47 D.² ἐλθὼν σὺν τριοῖσι μάρτυσιν); Hb 10: 28 (Dt 17: 6.—ἐπὶ μάρτυσι also Appian, Bell. Civ. 3, 14 §49). τί ἔτι χρείαν ἔχομεν μαρτύρων; *what further need have we of witnesses?* (Pla., Rep. 1 p. 340A τί δεῖται μάρτυρος; αὐτὸς γὰρ ὁ Θρασύμαχος ὁμολογεῖ) Mt 26: 65; Mk 14: 63. μάρτυρες ψευδεῖς *false witnesses* (Demosth. 29, 28) Ac 6: 13. There is also someth. 'legal' about the prudent and blameless men whom the Roman church sent to Corinth and who μάρτυρες ἔσονται μεταξὺ ὑμῶν κ. ἡμῶν 1 Cl 63: 3.

2. fig. of anyone who can or should testify to anything
—a. of God (or the exalted Christ) as witness (gods as witnesses oft. Pind.+; Philo; Jos., Bell. 1, 595, Ant. 1, 209; Test. Levi 19: 3; Sib. Or., fgm. 1, 4); as a formula μ. μού (ἐστιν) ὁ θεός *God is my witness* (that I am telling the truth) Ro 1: 9; Phil 1: 8; shortened θεὸς μ. 1 Th 2: 5; cf. vs. 10 (here also Jos., Ant. 15, 130 μ. ὑμᾶς ποιούμενος). μ. μοι ἐν ᾧ δέδεμαι IPhld 7: 2. μάρτυρα τὸν θεὸν ἐπικαλεῖσθαι *call upon God as witness* 2 Cor 1: 23 (cf. 1 Km 12: 5f; 20: 23; Polyb. 11, 6, 4 τ. θεοὺς ἐπικαλέσεσθε μάρτυρας; Heliod. 1, 25, 1; Galen VI 775 Kühn).

b. of any kind of human witnessing by eye and ear (X., Ages. 4, 5; Pla., Ep. 1 p. 309A; Aelian, V.H. 10, 6; Jos., Ant. 18, 299) 1 Th 2: 10; 1 Ti 6: 12; 2 Ti 2: 2.—Also of

those witnesses whose faith is tried and true τοσοῦτον νέφος μαρτύρων Hb 12: 1.—Of witnesses of events which they know about, without having experienced them personally (acc. to Strabo 7, 3, 7 p. 300 Hesiod is μάρτυς with regard to the Scythians): the teachers of the law bear witness to the murder of the prophets by their ancestors, by erecting tombs for the prophets Lk 11: 48 (μαρτυρεῖτε 𝔓⁷⁵ et al.).

c. of witnesses who bear a divine message (Epict. 3, 26, 28 God uses the wise men as his μάρτυρες) Rv 11: 3 (though the mng. approaches *martyr* [s. 3 below] here; cf. vs. 7. S. DHaugg, D. zwei Zeugen-Apk 11: 1–13, '36; JSConsidine, CBQ 8, '46. 377–92). In this sense, above all, of Jesus' disciples as the witnesses of his life, death, and resurrection: μού μάρτυρες *my witnesses* Ac 1: 8; cf. 13: 31 (Ps.-Demetr. c. 222 μάρτυς σου γίνεται). W. obj. gen. of the thing witnessed: *witness for, of* (Jos., C. Ap. 1, 4 τῶν ὑπ' ἐμοῦ λεγομένων μ., Ant. 4, 40) Lk 24: 48; Ac 1: 22; 3: 15; 5: 32; 10: 39; 26: 16. μ. τῶν τοῦ Χριστοῦ παθημάτων *a witness of the sufferings of Christ* 1 Pt 5: 1. ἔσῃ μ. αὐτῷ πρὸς πάντας ἀνθρώπους *you will be a witness for him to all men* Ac 22: 15 (Epict. 3, 24, 113 μ. πρὸς τοὺς ἄλλους). —10: 41.

3. In the usage of the persecuted church μάρτυς became one who witnessed unto death, a martyr τὸ αἷμα Στεφάνου τοῦ μάρτυρός σου Ac 22: 20. Of Antipas ὁ μ. μου ὁ πιστός μου Rv 2: 13 (cf. Pind., Pyth. 1, 88 μάρτυρες πιστοί= dependable witnesses). Onesimus μ. Χριστοῦ γεγένηται Phlm subscr. Gener. μάρτυρες Ἰησοῦ Rv 17: 6; cf. MPol 2: 2; 14: 2; 15: 2; 16: 2; 17: 3; 19: 1. Since Rv also calls Jesus (as well as Antipas) ὁ μάρτυς ὁ πιστός 1: 5; 3: 14, these pass. are prob. to be classed here (cf. Ps 88: 38). The death of Jesus was early regarded as the first martyrdom.—For an analysis of the question how μάρτυς= 'witness' came to mean 'martyr', cf. FKattenbusch, ZNW 4, '03, 111ff; KHoll, variously, now Gesamm. Aufsätze II '28, 103ff; ASchlatter, BFChTh 19, 3, '15; PCorssen, NJklA 35, '15, 481ff, 37, '16, 424ff, ZNW 15, '14, 221ff w. several continuations until 18, '17, 249ff, Sokrates 6, '18, 106ff; Rtzst., Hist. Mon. '16, 85; 257, NGG '16, 417ff, Her. 52, '17, 442ff; FDornseiff, ARW 22, '23/'24, 133ff; HDelehaye, Analecta Bollandiana 39, '21, 20ff, Sanctus '27 (²'33), 74ff (75, 1 lit.). ELohmeyer, D. Idee des Martyriums im Judent. u. Urchristent.: ZsystTh 5, '27/'28, 232–49; GFitzer, D. Begriff des μ. im Judent. u. Urchristent., Diss. Bresl. '29; HLietzmann, Martys: Pauly-W. XIV 2, '30, 2044–52; OMichel, Prophet u. Märt. '32; RPCasey, Μάρτυς: Beginn. I 5, '33, 30–7; EStauffer, Märtyrertheologie u. Täuferbewegg.: ZKG 52, '33, 545–98; DWRiddle, The Martyr Motif in Mk: Journal of Religion 4, '24, 174–91, Hb, 1 Cl and the Persecution of Domitian: JBL 43, '24, 329–48, From Apocalypse to Martyrology: ATR 9, '27, 260–80, The Martyrs: A Study in Social Control '31, Die Verfolgungslogien im formgesch. u. soziol. Bed.: ZNW 33, '34, 271–89; HvCampenhausen, D. Idee des Martyriums in d. alten Kirche ²'64; EPeterson, Zeuge d. Wahrh. '37; HWSurkau, Martyrien in jüd. u. frühchristl. Zt. '38; HAFischel, Martyr and Prophet (in Jewish lit.), JQR 37, '46/'47, 265–80; 363–86; EGünther, Μάρτυς, D. Gesch. eines Wortes '41, Zeuge u. Märtyrer, ZNW 47, '56, 145–61. ELohse, Märtyrer u. Gottesknecht '55; HvanVliet, No Single Testimony (Dt 19: 15) '58; NBrox, Zeuge u. Märtyrer '61. M-M. B. 1436.*

μαρυκάομαι (a Doric form of μηρυκ., taken over into colloq. Gk. [Aelian, N.A. 2, 54; Lev 11: 26= Dt 14: 8; cf. Thackeray 76]) *chew the cud* Hs 9, 1, 9. πᾶν μαρυκώμενον *all ruminants* B 10: 11.—PKatz, Philo's Bible '50, 157–9.*

μασάομαι impf. ἐμασώμην (Aristoph., Hippocr.+; Artem. 4, 33; Philostrat., Vi. Apoll. 7, 21 p. 276, 2; PGM 5, 280; Job 30: 4; Jos., Bell. 6, 197) *bite* w. acc. τὰς γλώσσας *bite their tongues* Rv 16: 10; AP 14: 29. τὰ χείλη *bite their lips* 13: 28. M-M.*

μασθός s. μαστός.

μαστιγόω fut. μαστιγώσω; 1 aor. ἐμαστίγωσα, pass. ἐμαστιγώθην (Hdt.+; inscr., pap., LXX; Philo, In Flacc. 85; Joseph.; Test. Jos. 8: 4) *whip, flog, scourge.*
  1. lit., of flogging as a punishment decreed by the synagogue (Dt 25: 2f; cf. the Mishna Tractate Sanhedrin-Makkoth, edited w. notes by SKrauss '33) w. acc. of the pers. Mt 10: 17; 23: 34. Of the beating (Lat. verberatio) given those condemned to death (ThMommsen, Röm. Strafrecht 1899, 938f; Jos., Bell. 2, 308; 5, 449) J 19: 1; cf. Mt 20: 19; Mk 10: 34; Lk 18: 33. As a punishment for cheating in athletic contests (Ps.-Dionys. Hal., Ars Rhet. 7, 6 μάστιγες...κ. τὸ ἐκβάλλεσθαι ἐκ τ. σταδίων κ. ἀγώνων) 2 Cl 7: 4.
  2. fig.—a. *punish, chastise* of God (Jer 5: 3; Jdth 8: 27) for discipline (Maximus Tyr. 19, 5e of the soul) Hb 12: 6; 1 Cl 56: 4 (both Pr 3: 12).
  b. gener. *afflict, torment, mistreat* (Artem. 1, 24 p. 25, 16 μ. τὰ ὦτα= pulling the ears; UPZ 119, 29; 44 [156 BC]; Sir 30: 14) ITr 4: 1; Hs 6, 3, 1.—CSchneider, TW IV 521-5. M-M.*

μαστίζω (Hom.+; Diod. S. 14, 112; 2; Plut., Mor. 165E; Lucian, Pro Imag. 24; Palestin. inscr.: Suppl. Epigr. Gr. VIII 246, 17 [II AD]; LXX) *strike with a whip* GP 3: 9. Specif. *scourge* of the punishment known in Lat. as verberatio Ac 22: 25 (it was prohibited to impose the punishment of verberatio on a Roman citizen: Appian, Bell. Civ. 2, 26 §98. Further, s. HJCadbury, Beginn. V '33, 297-338; EHaenchen, Ac 568, 1). M-M.*

μάστιξ, ιγος, ἡ (Hom.+; inscr., pap., LXX) *whip, lash.*
  1. lit. Hs 6, 2, 5. Mostly pl. *lashing* or *lashes* (Jos., Bell. 2, 306, Vi. 147) B 5: 14 (Is 50: 6); MPol 2: 2; Hv 3, 2, 1. μάστιξιν ἀνετάζειν τινά *examine someone by scourging* Ac 22: 24. W. ἐμπαιγμός Hb 11: 36.
  2. fig. *torment, suffering* (sent by God to men: Il. 12, 37 Διὸς μ.; Proverbia Aesopi 105 P.; Ps 38: 11; 2 Macc 7: 37; 9: 11; En. 25, 6; 100, 13; inscr. in Ramsay, Phrygia II 520 no. 361 λήψεται παρὰ τοῦ θεοῦ μάστειγα αἰώνιον) of bodily illness Mk 3: 10; 5: 29, 34; Lk 7: 21. Of the afflictions of the sinner 1 Cl 22: 8 (Ps 31: 10); Hv 4, 2, 6. W. αἰκίσματα of the Egyptian plagues 1 Cl 17: 5. μ. γλώσσης *the scourge of the tongue* 1 Cl 56: 10 (Job 5: 21).—Eitrem (s. πειράζω 2d, end) 12f. M-M.*

μαστός, οῦ, ὁ (collateral forms μασθός [Heracld. Miles. (I AD), fgm. 25 LCohn 1884; IG III 238b; POsl. 95, 19 (96 AD); PGM 7, 208; Thackeray 104] and μαζός [q.v.], both of which are found in mss. in all passages; cf. Kühner-Bl. I 157; Bl-D. §34, 5 w. app.; Mlt.-H. 110) *breast* pl. (Jos., Bell. 7, 189).
  1. of a man (X., An. 4, 3, 6; Eratosth. p. 33, 2; Dit., Syll.³ 1170, 24) περιεζωσμένος πρὸς τοῖς μ. ζώνην χρυσᾶν *with a golden belt around his breast* Rv 1: 13 (Diod. S. 1, 72, 2 περιεζωσμένοι ὑποκάτω τῶν μαστῶν).
  2. of a woman (Hdt.+; Sb 6706, 9; LXX; Philo, Op. M. 38) Lk 11: 27; 23: 29. M-M. B. 248.*

μαστώδης, ες *rounded*, lit. *breast-shaped*, of a mountain Hs 9, 1, 4 (Strabo 14, 6, 3 ὄρος μαστοειδὲς Ὄλυμπος; Diod. S. 17, 75, 2 πέτρα μαστοειδής; Jos., Bell. 1, 419, Ant. 15, 324).*

ματαιολογία, ας, ἡ (Plut., Lib. Educ. 9 p. 6F; Vett. Val. 150, 24; 257, 23; 360, 4; Diogenianus Epicureus [II AD] in Euseb., Praep. Ev. 6, 8, 11; Porphyr., Abst. 4, 16; Herm. Wr. 14, 5) *empty, fruitless talk* ἐκτρέπεσθαι εἰς μ. *turn to fruitless discussion* 1 Ti 1: 6. Tautologically(?) κενὴ μ. Pol 2: 1. M-M.*

ματαιολόγος, ον (Telestes Lyr. [IV BC] 1, 9 Diehl; Vett. Val. 301, 11; Physiogn. I 379, 10; II 231, 5) *talking idly*, subst. ὁ μ. *an idle talker* Tit 1: 10. M-M.*

ματαιοπονία, ας, ἡ (Strabo 17, 1, 28; Plut., Mor. 119E; Lucian, Dial. Mort. 10, 8) *fruitless toil* 1 Cl 9: 1.*

μάταιος, αία, αιον (Pind., Hdt.+; Zen.-P. 11 [=Sb 6717], 3 [257 BC]; POxy. 58, 20; LXX, En., Ep. Arist., Philo; Jos., C. Ap. 1, 6; Test. 12 Patr.) also, as somet. in Attic wr., varying betw. two and three endings (Bl-D. §59, 2; Mlt.-H. 157) *idle, empty, fruitless, useless, powerless, lacking truth* τούτου μ. ἡ θρησκεία *his religion is worthless* Js 1: 26; νηστεία μ. *useless fasting* Hs 5, 1, 4; ἀνωφελὴς καὶ μ. *useless and fruitless* Tit 3: 9. ἐλπίς *vain, empty* (Artem. 1, 67 p. 62, 5; Lucian, Alex. 47; Is 31: 2) B 16: 2. διαλογισμοὶ *foolish thoughts* 1 Cor 3: 20 (Ps 93: 11). φροντίδες 1 Cl 7: 2. ἐπιθυμία *futile desire*, directed toward worthless things Hm 11: 8; pl. 2 Cl 19: 2; Hm 12, 6, 5. πίστις μ. *empty* 1 Cor 15: 17. τρυφαὶ *idle luxury* Hs 6, 2, 2. ἐπιθυμία ἐδεσμάτων πολλῶν ματαίων *a desire for many needless things to eat* m 12, 2, 1. οἰκήματα *dwellings that will pass away* s 1: 1. ἡ μ. στάσις *futile dissension* 1 Cl 63: 1. ἡ μ. ἀναστροφὴ *futile way of living* 1 Pt 1: 18.—μάταιον (sc. ἐστίν) *it is useless* B 2: 5 (Is 1: 13). οὐ μὴ λάβης ἐπὶ ματαίῳ τὸ ὄνομα κυρίου *you must never use the Lord's name for an unworthy purpose* 19: 5 (Ex 20: 7; Dt 5: 11).—Subst. μάταια *what is worthless, empty* (Vett. Val. 356, 16; Zech 10: 2; Pr 12: 11; Jos., Bell. 7, 330) ἀγαπᾶν B 20: 2; D 5: 2; λαλεῖν IPhld 1: 1. τὰ μάταια (or οἱ μάταιοι, i.e. θεοί) *idols* (Esth 4: 17 p; Jer 2: 5; 8: 19; 3 Macc 6: 11) Ac 14: 15.—OBauernfeind, TW IV 525-30. M-M.*

ματαιότης, ητος, ἡ (Philod., Rhet. II p. 26, 6 Sudh. μ. ἀνθρώπων; Sext. Emp., Math. 1, 278; Pollux 6, 134; LXX; Philo, Conf. Lingu. 141. Perh. also CIG IV 8743, 6) *emptiness, futility, purposelessness, transitoriness* τῇ μ. ἡ κτίσις ὑπετάγη *the creation was subjected to frustration* Ro 8: 20. Of the heathen περιπατεῖν ἐν μ. τοῦ νοός *walk with their minds fixed on futile things* Eph 4: 17. φεύγειν ἀπὸ πάσης μ. *flee from all idle speculations* B 4: 10; cf. Pol 7: 2. ὑπέρογκα ματαιότητος φθέγγεσθαι *utter high-sounding but empty words* 2 Pt 2: 18 (cf. Ps 37: 13). ἐπὶ ματαιότητι *out of folly* (Arrian, Ind. 36, 1 ἐπὶ τῆς ἀγγελίης τῇ ματαιότητι) ITr 8: 2. M-M.*

ματαιόω 1 aor. pass. ἐματαιώθην (Herodian, Gramm. I 453, 13; schol. on Soph., Trach. 258 Papag.; Dositheus 71, 17; otherw. in bibl. and eccl. usage; LXX) *render futile, worthless*; pass. *be given over to worthlessness, think about idle, worthless things, be foolish* (1 Ch 21: 8) ἐματαιώθησαν ἐν τοῖς διαλογισμοῖς αὐτῶν *their thoughts became directed to worthless things* Ro 1: 21 (w. ref. to idolatry; s. μάταιος and cf. Jer 2: 5 ἐπορεύθησαν ὀπίσω τῶν ματαίων καὶ ἐματαιώθησαν).*

ματαίωμα, ατος, τό *emptiness, worthlessness* τὰ μ. τοῦ αἰῶνος τούτου *the worthless things of this age* Hm 9: 4; s 5, 3, 6.*

μάτην adv. (Hom. Hymns, Hdt.+; inscr., pap., LXX; Jos., Bell. 7, 135, C. Ap. 1, 142) *in vain, to no end* Mt 15: 9; Mk 7: 7 (both Is 29: 13); Hs 5, 4, 2a. Also εἰς μ. (Ael.

Aristid. 33, 3 K.=51 p. 572 D.; Ps.-Lucian, Tragodop. 28; Tetrast. Iamb. 1, 14, 4 p. 269; Ps 62: 10; 126: 1a, b, 2) s 5, 4, 2b; 6, 1, 3; 9, 4, 8; 9, 13, 2. M-M.*

Ματθαῖος, ου, ὁ (אBD spell it Μαθθαῖος; cf. FCBurkitt, JTS 34, '33, 387-90. Also Μαθαῖος; Preisigke, Namenb.; HJMMilne, Catal. of the Lit. in the Brit. Mus. '27, no. 99, 2) *Matthew*. His name is included in all the lists of the 12 apostles: Mk 3: 18; Lk 6: 15; Ac 1: 13. The first gospel (title κατὰ M -ον) describes him in its list as ὁ τελώνης Mt 10: 3, thereby identifying him w. the tax-collector of 9: 9; sim. GEb 2; Papias 2: 4, 16.—AJülicher, RE XII '03, 428ff; Zahn, Einl. II³ 258ff; EvDobschütz, Matth. als Rabbi u. Katechet: ZNW 27, '28, 338-48.*

Ματθάν, ὁ indecl. (מַתָּן; the name is found 2 Ch 23: 17; Jer 45: 1) *Matthan*, in the genealogy of Jesus Mt 1: 15; Lk 3: 23ff D (Μαθθαν).*

Ματθάτ, ὁ indecl. (מַתְּתָה; א writes Μαθθαθ, B in Lk 3: 29 Μαθθατ, A in vs. 29 Ματταθ) *Matthat*, in the genealogy of Jesus
1. son of Levi, father of Eli and grandfather of Joseph Lk 3: 24.—2. son of Levi, father of Jorim vs. 29, usu. Μαθθάτ.*

Ματθίας, ου, ὁ (Joseph.—Prob. a short form of Ματταθίας; BD write Μαθθίας) *Matthias*, the successful candidate in the election to replace the traitor Judas Ac 1: 23, 26 (PGaechter, Petrus u. seine Zeit, '58, 31-66; KHRengstorf, OPiper-Festschr. '62, 178-92).*

Ματταθά, ὁ indecl. (מַתִּתָה 2 Esdr [Ezra] 10: 33 Μαθαθα and v.l. Μαθθαθα) *Mattatha*, son of Nathan, grandson of David; in the genealogy of Jesus Lk 3: 31.*

Ματταθίας, ου, ὁ (מַתִּתְיָה 2 Esdr [Ezra] 10: 43 Μαθαθια, v.l. Μαθθαθιας; 18: 4 [Neh 8: 4] v.l. Ματθαθιας, in the text Ματταθίας, as 1 Ch 9: 31; 16: 5; 1 Macc 2: 1, 14 al.; Ep. Arist. 47; Joseph.) *Mattathias*, in the genealogy of Jesus
1. son of Amos Lk 3: 25.—2. son of Semein vs. 26.*

μάχαιρα, ης, ἡ (Hom.+; inscr., pap., LXX; Jos., Ant. 6, 190; Test. 12 Patr. The Ptolemaic pap. decline it as a rule [Mayser p. 12] μαχαίρας, -χαίρᾳ; likew. LXX [Thackeray p. 141f; Helbing p. 31ff]; ISm 4: 2b. The pap. fr. Roman times prefer -ρης, -ρῃ [isolated exx. fr. earlier times: PTebt. 16, 14—114 BC; 112, 45—112 BC]; likew. the NT) *sword, saber.*
1. lit. Mt 26: 47, 55; Mk 14: 43, 48; Lk 22: 36, 38 (ASchlatter, Die beiden Schwerter: BFChTh 20, 6, '16; TMNapier, ET 49, '38, 467-70; IZolli, Studi e Mat. di Storia delle Rel. 13, '38, 227-43. Field, Notes 76f suggests 'knives' here), 52; Rv 6: 4; 13: 10. ἐν φόνῳ μαχαίρης ἀποθανεῖν *be killed with the sword* Hb 11: 37 (Ex 17: 13; Dt 13: 16). ἀποσπᾶν τὴν μ. *draw the sword* Mt 26: 51. Also σπάσασθαι τὴν μ. (1 Ch 21: 5; 1 Esdr 3: 22; Jos., Vi. 303) Mk 14: 47; Ac 16: 27. λαμβάνειν μάχαιραν *take, grasp the sword* (Jos., Vi. 173) Mt 26: 52b (HKosmala, NovT 4, '60, 3-5: Targum Is 50: 11 as parallel); ἑλκύειν μ. J 18: 10; πατάσσειν ἐν μ. *strike w. the sword* Lk 22: 49. βάλλειν τὴν μ. εἰς τὴν θήκην *put the sword into its sheath* J 18: 11; cf. Mt 26: 52a. Of execution by the sword ISm 4: 2a, b. ἀναιρεῖν μαχαίρῃ *have someone put to death w. the sword* Ac 12: 2; ἔχειν πληγὴν τῆς μ. *have a sword-wound* Rv 13: 14. στόμα μαχαίρης *the edge of the sword* (cf. Gen 34: 26; 2 Km 15: 14; Theod. Prodr. 1, 19 Hercher; 2, 264; 6, 101) Lk 21: 24; Hb 11: 34 (OHofius, ZNW 62, '71, 129f); the corresponding figure μ. κατέδεται (cf. 2 Km 11: 25; Theod. Prodr. 6, 122 H. ἔτρωγεν

. . . τὸ ξίφος κρέα, ἔπινεν ἡ μάχ. πηγὰς αἱμάτων) 1 Cl 8: 4 (Is 1: 20). μ. δίστομος *a double-edged sword* (Judg 3: 16; Pr 5: 4) Hb 4: 12.
2. fig., μ. stands for violent death Ro 8: 35; for war (Gen 31: 26; Sib. Or. 8, 120.—Opp. εἰρήνη) Mt 10: 34 (Harnack, ZThK 22, '12, 4-6). Symbol of the power of the authorities to punish evildoers τὴν μάχαιραν φορεῖν *carry the sword* Ro 13: 4 (cf. Philostrat., Vi. Soph. 1, 25, 3 δικαστοῦ ξίφος ἔχοντος). ἡ μ. τοῦ πνεύματος *the sword of the Spirit*, explained as the Word of God Eph 6: 17 (cf. Hb 4: 12 in 1 above). M-M. B. 559; 1392.*

μάχη, ης, ἡ (Hom.+; inscr., pap., LXX; Jos., Bell. 3, 365, Ant. 1, 172 al.; Test. 12 Patr.; Sib. Or. 5, 516) *battle* (one fighter on each side is enough: Maximus Tyr. 22, 4b), in our lit. only in pl. and only of battles fought without actual weapons *fighting, quarrels, strife, disputes* (Pythag., Ep. 5, 7; Dit., Syll.³ 1109, 72; Epigr. Gr. 522, 5; PRyl. 28, 203 μάχας ἕξει διὰ θῆλυ; Cat. Cod. Astr. XII 160, 1 of marital discord; LXX, Philo) w. πόλεμοι (Il. 5, 891 πόλεμοί τε μάχαι τε; Dio Chrys. 21[38], 11; Plut., Mor. 108A) Js 4: 1. ἔξωθεν μάχαι ἔσωθεν φόβοι 2 Cor 7: 5. γεννᾶν μάχας *breed quarrels* 2 Ti 2: 23. μάχαι νομικαί *strife about the law* Tit 3: 9 (cf. Pla., Tim. p. 88A μάχας ἐν λόγοις ποιεῖσθαι). M-M.*

μάχομαι impf. ἐμαχόμην mid. dep. (Hom.+; inscr., pap., LXX, Philo; Jos., Bell. 3, 365, Ant. 19, 243 al.) *fight.*
1. of an actual fight (betw. two persons Ex 21: 22) Ac 7: 26.
2. fig., of fighting without weapons *fight, quarrel, dispute* (Hom.+; Dit., Syll.³ 1109, 95 ἐκβάλλειν τοὺς μαχομένους; POxy. 120, 6; Gen 26: 20; 31: 36; Jos., C. Ap. 1, 38) abs. *be quarrelsome* 2 Ti 2: 24. W. πολεμεῖν Js 4: 2. μαχομένους συναγαγεῖν *bring together those who are at enmity* B 19: 12; cf. D 4: 3. πρός τινα (Ep. Arist. 13; Philo, Leg. All. 2, 106) *dispute with someone* πρὸς ἀλλήλους *among themselves* J 6: 52 (πρ. ἀλλ. fig. as Lucian, Tim. 9; Aesop, Fab. 62 P.=116 H.). M-M. B. 1370.*

μεγαλαυχέω (Aeschyl.+; Polyb. 12, 13, 10; 8, 23, 11; Diod. S. 15, 16, 3; Vett. Val. 257, 19; 262, 4; 358, 29; LXX, Philo) *become proud, boast* Js 3: 5 t.r. (for μεγάλα αὐχεῖ, s. αὐχέω). M-M.*

μεγαλεῖος, α, ον (X.+; inscr., pap., LXX) *magnificent, splendid, grand*; in our lit. only subst. τὸ μ. *greatness, sublimity* (Polyb. 3, 87, 5; 8, 1, 1; Artem. 3 p. 169, 1 τὸ μ. τῆς σοφίας; Dit., Syll.³ 798, 4 [37 AD]; Sir 17: 8; Philo; Jos., Ant. 8, 49; 15, 187) τῆς ἐπαγγελίας 1 Cl 26: 1. τὸ μ. τῆς καλλονῆς αὐτοῦ *his* (or *its*) *sublime beauty* 49: 3.—Pl. τὰ μ. *the mighty deeds* (Dt 11: 2; Ps 70: 19; Sir 36: 7; 42: 21) τὰ μ. τοῦ θεοῦ Ac 2: 11; cf. Hv 4, 2, 5; s 9, 18, 2. Abs. v 4, 1, 8. Of the great and good deeds of God Lk 1: 49 v.l. (cf. Ps 70: 19). μ. τῶν δωρεῶν *the greatness of (God's) gifts* 1 Cl 32: 1. M-M.*

μεγαλειότης, ητος, ἡ (Athen. 4, 6 p. 130F; Vett. Val. 70, 4; Dit., Or. 666, 26 [I AD]; 669, 9 [I AD]; PGiess. 40 I, 19; LXX) *grandeur, sublimity, majesty*; in our lit. only of a divinity or of divine attributes. Of God (Aristob. in Euseb., Pr. Ev. 8, 10, 17; Jos., Ant. 1, 24; 8, 111, C. Ap. 2, 168) Lk 9: 43; Dg 10: 5; IRo inscr. Of Christ 2 Pt 1: 16. Of Artemis Ac 19: 27. ἡ μ. τῆς προνοίας τοῦ δεσπότου *the Master's wondrous providence* 1 Cl 24: 5. M-M.*

μεγαλοπρέπεια, ας, ἡ (Hom.+; Dit., Syll.³ 695, 14; pap. [as honorary title]; LXX [only Ps, but not rare there]) *majesty, sublimity* of God, w. ἰσχύς 1 Cl 60: 1.*

μεγαλοπρεπής– μέγας

μεγαλοπρεπής, ές (Hdt., Aristoph. +; inscr., pap., LXX; En. 32, 3; Philo; Jos., Ant. 9, 182; 13, 242) *magnificent, sublime, majestic* δόξα 2 Pt 1: 17; 1 Cl 9: 2. κράτος θεοῦ 61: 1. βούλησις θεοῦ 9: 1. δωρεαί θεοῦ 19: 2 (Diod. S. 3, 54, 6 δῶρα μεγαλοπρεπῆ). ἡ μ. θρησκεία τοῦ ὑψίστου *the exalted worship of the Most High* 45: 7 (Appian, Bell. Civ. 5, 4 §15 τῇ θεῷ μεγαλοπρεπῶς ἔθυε). τὸ μ. καὶ ἅγιον ὄνομα Χριστοῦ 1 Cl 64 (cf. 2 Macc 8: 15).—τὸ μ. τῆς φιλοξενίας ὑμῶν ἦθος *the remarkable character of your hospitality* 1: 2. M-M.*

μεγαλο(ρ)ρημονέω 1 aor. ἐμεγαλορημόνησα (Strabo 13, 1, 40; LXX) *use great words, boast* 1 Cl 17: 5.*

μεγαλο(ρ)ρημοσύνη, ης, ἡ *proud* or *boastful talking* (Anonymus in Suidas s.v. σεμνομυθοῦσιν=Polyb. 38, 19 Bü-W. v.l.; Philostrat., Her. 2, 19 p. 161, 19; 1 Km 2: 3) pl. IEph 10: 2.*

μεγαλο(ρ)ρήμων, ονος (Philostrat., Vi. Apoll. 6, 11 p. 222, 21) *boastful* γλῶσσα (Ps 11: 4; 3 Macc 6: 4; Jos., Ant. 20, 90 v.l.) 1 Cl 15: 5.*

μεγαλύνω impf. ἐμεγάλυνον, mid. ἐμεγαλυνόμην; fut. μεγαλυνῶ; 1 aor. pass. ἐμεγαλύνθην (Aeschyl. +; Thu. 5, 98; POxy. 1592, 3; LXX) *make large* or *long, magnify.*
1. lit. τὶ someth. τὰ κράσπεδα (τῶν ἱματίων: addition of the t.r., correct as to subject matter) *the tassels (on their garments)* Mt 23: 5. μ. τὸ ἔλεος μετά τινος *show someone great mercy* Lk 1: 58 (cf. Gen 19: 19 ἐμεγάλυνας τ. δικαιοσύνην σου). μ. τὸ ὄνομά τινος *magnify someone's name* 1 Cl 10: 3 (Gen 12: 2).—Pass. *increase, grow* (1 Km 2: 21; 3 Km 10: 26) 2 Cor 10: 15.
2. fig. *exalt, glorify, praise, extol* (Eur., Thu. et al.; LXX) w. the acc. of the one praised τὸν κύριον (Sir 43: 31) Lk 1: 46. τὸν θεόν (Ps 68: 31.—Cf. Diod. S. 1, 20, 6 μ. τοῦ θεοῦ τὴν δύναμιν) Ac 10: 46. Of the apostles ἐμεγάλυνεν αὐτοὺς ὁ λαός *the people held them in high esteem* 5: 13. The boasters say: τ. γλῶσσαν ἡμῶν μεγαλυνοῦμεν *we will praise (or magnify?) our tongue* 1 Cl 15: 5 (Ps 11: 5).—Pass. *be glorified, praised* (2 Km 7: 26) τὸ ὄνομα τοῦ κυρίου Ac 19: 17 (μ. τὸ ὄνομά τινος as Gen 12: 2; Eur., Bacch. 320). μεγαλυνθήσεται Χριστὸς ἐν τῷ σώματί μου *Christ will be glorified in my person* (i.e. in me) Phil 1: 20. W. δοξασθῆναι 1 Cl 32: 3. M-M.*

μεγάλως adv. (Hom. +; inscr., pap., LXX) *greatly* μ. εἶναι (w. θαυμαστῶς) *be great* Hs 5, 5, 4. Used to strengthen a verb *very (much), greatly* (Polyb. 1, 52, 2; Herodian 4, 15, 2; Jos., Vi. 154; Sib. Or. 5, 61) ἐμαρτυρήθη μ. Ἀβραάμ *Abraham had received a glorious witness* 1 Cl 17: 2; χαρῆναι μ. *be very glad* (PAmh. 39, 8 [II BC] μεγάλως ἐχάρημεν; Ep. Arist. 42; 312) Phil 4: 10; παραδέχεσθαι μ. *be welcomed heartily* Ac 15: 4 D.—GP 11: 45 (s. ἀγωνιάω). It is textually uncertain whether the verb w. μ. in 1 Cl 1: 1 is βλασφημηθῆναι or βλαφθῆναι. M-M.**

μεγαλωσύνη, ης, ἡ (Herodian, Gramm. I 335, 18; LXX; En. 98, 2; 101, 3; the other ms. has [5, 4] μεγαλοσύνη; Ep. Arist. 192; Test. Levi 3: 9; 18: 8; Suidas; Etym. Mag. p. 275, 44; Byz. Chron. in Psaltes p. 267) *majesty,* lit. *greatness* used only of God; in a doxology w. δόξα (and other sim. ideas; En. 14, 16) Jd 25; 1 Cl 20: 12; 61: 3; 64; 65: 2; MPol 20: 2; 21: 1 (here referred to Christ). τὸ σκῆπτρον τῆς μ. τοῦ θεοῦ *the scepter of the majesty of God* 1 Cl 16: 2; ἐν λόγῳ τῆς μ. *by his majestic word* 27: 4. ἀπαύγασμα τῆς μ. *a reflection of his majesty* 36: 2 (cf. Hb 1: 3). τὸ τῆς μ. ὄνομα αὐτοῦ *his glorious name* 58: 1.—As a periphrasis for God himself ἐν δεξιᾷ τῆς μ. *at the right hand of the Majesty* Hb 1: 3. ὁ θρόνος τῆς μ. 8: 1. M-M.*

μέγας, μεγάλη, μέγα (Hom. +; inscr., pap., LXX, En., Ep. Arist., Philo, Joseph., Test. 12 Patr.) comp. μείζων and beside it, because of the gradual disappearance of feeling for its comp. sense, μειζότερος 3 J 4 (APF 3, '06, 173; POxy. 131, 25; BGU 368, 9; Bl-D. §61, 2; Mlt.-H. 166). Superl. μέγιστος (2 Pt 1: 4); *large, great.*
1. lit.—a. of any extension in space in all directions λίθος Mt 27: 60; Mk 16: 4. δένδρον Lk 13: 19 t.r. κλάδοι Mk 4: 32. Buildings 13: 2. Fish J 21: 11. A mountain (Tyrtaeus [VII BC], fgm. 4, 8 D.²; Ps.-Aristot., Mirabilia 138; Theopomp. [IV BC]: 115 fgm. 78 Jac.) Rv 8: 8. A star vs. 10. A furnace 9: 2. A dragon (Esth 1: 1e; Bel 23 Theod.) 12: 3, 9. ἀετός (Ezk 17: 3) vs. 14. μάχαιρα *a long sword* 6: 4. ἅλυσις *a long chain* 20: 1.
b. with the concept of spaciousness ἀνάγαιον *a spacious room upstairs* Mk 14: 15; Lk 22: 12. θύρα *a wide door* 1 Cor 16: 9. A winepress Rv 14: 19. χάσμα *a broad chasm* (2 Km 18: 17) Lk 16: 26. οἰκία (Jer 52: 13) 2 Ti 2: 20.
c. with words that include the idea of number ἀγέλη μ. *a large herd* Mk 5: 11. δεῖπνον *a great banquet,* w. many invited guests (Da 5: 1 Theod.) Lk 14: 16. Also δοχὴ μ. (Gen 21: 8) Lk 5: 29.
2. fig.—a. of measure—α. of age (Jos., Ant. 12, 207 μικρὸς ἢ μέγας='young or old'); to include all concerned μικροὶ καὶ μεγάλοι *small and great* (PGM 15, 18) Rv 11: 18; 13: 16; 19: 5, 18; 20: 12. μικρῷ τε καὶ μεγάλῳ Ac 26: 22. ἀπὸ μικροῦ ἕως μεγάλου (Gen 19: 11; 4 Km 23: 2; 2 Ch 34: 30; POxy. 1350) 8: 10; Hb 8: 11 (Jer 38: 34). μέγας γενόμενος *when he was grown up* 11: 24 (Ex 2: 11). ὁ μείζων *the older* (Ostraka II 144, 3 [128 AD]; 213, 3; 1199, 2; cf. Polyb. 18, 18, 9 Σκιπίων ὁ μέγας; 32, 12, 1) Ro 9: 12; B 13: 2 (both Gen 25: 23).
β. of quantity: *rich* μισθαποδοσία Hb 10: 35. πορισμός *a great means of gain* 1 Ti 6: 6.
γ. of intensity: δύναμις Ac 4: 33; 19: 8 D. Esp. of sound: *loud* φωνή Mk 15: 37; Lk 17: 15; Rv 1: 10; φωνῇ μεγάλῃ (LXX) Mt 27: 46, 50; Mk 1: 26; 5: 7; 15: 34; Lk 4: 33; 8: 28; 19: 37; 23: 23 (φωναῖς μεγάλαις), 46; J 11: 43; Ac 7: 57, 60; 8: 7; Rv 5: 12; 6: 10 al.; μεγ. φωνῇ Ac 14: 10; 16: 28; μεγ. τῇ φωνῇ (Jos., Bell. 6, 188) 14: 10 v.l.; 26: 24; ἐν φωνῇ μ. Rv 5: 2. μετὰ σάλπιγγος μεγάλης *with a loud trumpet call* Mt 24: 31. κραυγή (Ex 11: 6; 12: 30) Lk 1: 42; Ac 23: 9; cf. μεῖζον κράζειν *cry out all the more* Mt 20: 31. κοπετός (Gen 50: 10) Ac 8: 2.—Of natural phenomena: ἄνεμος *a strong wind* J 6: 18; Rv 6: 13; λαῖλαψ μ. (Jer 32: 32) Mk 4: 37. βροντή (Sir 40: 13) Rv 14: 2. χάλαζα Rv 11: 19; 16: 21a. σεισμὸς μ. (Jer 10: 22; Ezk 3: 12; 38: 19; Jos., Ant. 9, 225) Mt 8: 24; 28: 2; Lk 21: 11a; Ac 16: 26. γαλήνη μ. *a deep calm* Mt 8: 26; Mk 4: 39; φῶς μ. *a bright light* (Plut., Mor. 567F: a divine voice sounds forth from this light; Petosiris, fgm. 7 l. 39 τὸ ἱερὸν ἄστρον μέγα ποιοῦν φῶς) Mt 4: 16 (Is 9: 1). καῦμα μ. *intense heat* Rv 16: 9.—Of surprising or unpleasant events or phenomena of the most diverse kinds (ἀπώλεια Dt 7: 23; θάνατος Ex 9: 3; Jer 21: 6; κακόν Philo, Agr. 47) σημεῖα (Dt 6: 22; 29: 2) Mt 24: 24; Lk 21: 11b; Ac 6: 8. δυνάμεις 8: 13. ἔργα μ. *mighty deeds* (cf. Judg 2: 7) Rv 15: 3. μείζω τούτων *greater things than these* J 1: 50 (μείζονα 𝔓⁶⁶ et al.); cf. 5: 20; 14: 12. διωγμὸς μ. *a severe persecution* Ac 8: 1; θλῖψις μ. *(a time of) great suffering* (1 Macc 9: 27) Mt 24: 21; Ac 7: 11; Rv 2: 22; 7: 14. πληγή (Judg 15: 8; 1 Km 4: 10, 17 al.; Philo, Sacr. Abel. 134) 16: 21b. λιμὸς μ. (4 Km 6: 25; 1 Macc 9: 24) Lk 4: 25; Ac 11: 28; ἀνάγκη μ. Lk 21: 23; πυρετὸς μ. *a high fever* (s. πυρετός) 4: 38.—Of emotions: χαρά *great joy* (Jon 4: 6; Jos., Ant. 12, 91) Mt 2: 10; 28: 8; Lk 2: 10; 24: 52. φόβος (X., Cyr. 4, 2, 10; Menand., fgm. 454; Jon 1: 10, 16; 1 Macc 10: 8) Mk 4: 41; Lk 2: 9; 8: 37; Ac 5: 5, 11; θυμὸς μ. *fierce anger* (1 Macc 7: 35) Rv 12: 12. ἀγάπη J 15: 13.

z
497

λύπη *profound* (Jon 4: 1; 1 Macc 6: 4, 9, 13) Ro 9: 2. πίστις *firm* Mt 15: 28. ἔκστασις (Gen 27: 33) Mk 5: 42.

b. of rank and dignity—**α.** of pers.; of God and other divinities (Dit., Syll.³ 985, 34 θεοὶ μεγάλοι; 1237, 5 ὀργὴ μεγάλη τ. μεγάλου Διός, Or. 50, 7; 168, 6; 716, 1; PStrassb. 81, 14 [115 BC] Ἴσιδος μεγάλης μητρὸς θεῶν; POxy. 886, 1; PTebt. 409, 11; 22 ὁ θεὸς μ. Σάραπις, al.; PGM 4, 155; 482; 778 and oft.; 3052 μέγ. θεὸς Σαβαώθ; 5, 474; Dt 10: 17 al. in LXX; En. 103, 4; 104, 1; Philo, Cher. 29 al.; Jos., Ant. 8, 319; Sib. Or. 3, 19; 71 al.—Thieme 36f) Tit 2: 13 (Christ is meant). Ἄρτεμις (q.v.) Ac 19: 27f, 34f (cf. Ael. Aristid. 48, 21 K.=24 p. 471 D. the outcry: μέγας ὁ Ἀσκληπιός). Simon the magician is called ἡ δύναμις τ. θεοῦ ἡ καλουμένη μεγάλη Ac 8: 10b (s. δύναμις 6).—Of men who stand in relation to the Divinity or are otherw. in high position: ἀρχιερεύς (s. ἀρχιερεύς 2a and cf. ἱερεύς 2a.—ἀρχ. μέγ. is also the appellation of the priest-prince of Olba in Cilicia: Monum. As. Min. Antiqua III '31 p. 67, inscr. 63; 64 [I BC]) Hb 4: 14. προφήτης (Sir 48: 22) Lk 7: 16. ποιμήν Hb 13: 20. Gener. of rulers: οἱ μεγάλοι *the great men, those in high position* Mt 20: 25; Mk 10: 42. Of men prominent for any reason Mt 5: 19; 20: 26; Mk 10: 43; Lk 1: 15, 32; Ac 5: 36 D; 8: 9 (MSmith, HAWolfson-Festschr., '65, 741: μ. here and Lk 1: 32 may imply a messianic claim).—μέγας in the superl. sense (2 Km 7: 9.—The positive also stands for the superl. e.g., Sallust. c. 4 p. 6, 14, where Paris calls Aphrodite καλή=the most beautiful. Diod. S. 17, 70, 1 πολεμία τῶν πόλεων=the most hostile [or especially hostile] among the cities) Lk 9: 48 (opp. ὁ μικρότερος).—Comp. μείζων *greater* of God (Ael. Aristid. 27, 3 K.=16 p. 382 D.; PGM 13, 689 ἐπικαλοῦμαί σε, τὸν πάντων μείζονα) J 14: 28; Hb 6: 13; 1 J 3: 20; 4: 4. *More prominent* or *outstanding* because of certain advantages Mt 11: 11; Lk 7: 28; 22: 26f; J 4: 12; 8: 53; 13: 16a, b; 1 Cor 14: 5. More closely defined: ἰσχύϊ καὶ δυνάμει μείζων *greater in power and might* 2 Pt 2: 11. μεῖζον τοῦ ἱεροῦ *someth. greater than the temple* Mt 12: 6. μείζων with superl. mng. (Ps.-Apollod., Epit. 7, 8 Wagner: Ὀδυσσεὺς τρεῖς κριοὺς ὁμοῦ συνδέων . . . καὶ αὐτὸς τῷ μείζονι ὑποδύς; Appian, Bell. Civ. 2, 87 §366 ἐν παρασκευῇ μείζονι=in the greatest preparation; Vett. Val. 62, 24) Mt 18: 1, 4; 23: 11; Mk 9: 34; Lk 9: 46; 22: 24, 26.

β. of things: *great, sublime, important* μυστήριον (Philo, Leg. All. 3, 100 al.) Eph 5: 32; 1 Ti 3: 16. Of the sabbath day that begins a festival period J 19: 31; MPol 8: 1b. Esp. of the day of the divine judgment (LXX) Ac 2: 20 (Jo 3: 4); Jd 6; Rv 6: 17; 16: 14.—μέγας in the superl. sense (Plut., Mor. 35A w. πρῶτος; Himerius, Or. 14 [Ecl. 15], 3 μέγας=greatest, really great; Bl-D. §245, 2; cf. Rob. 669) ἐντολή Mt 22: 36, 38. ἡμέρα ἡ μ. τῆς ἑορτῆς *the great day of the festival* J 7: 37 (cf. Lucian, Pseudolog. 8 ἡ μεγάλη νουμηνία [at the beginning of the year]).—μείζων as comp. (Chio, Ep. 16, 8 philosophy as νόμος μείζων=higher law; Sir 10: 24) J 5: 36; 1 J 5: 9. μ. ἁμαρτία J 19: 11 (cf. schol. on Pla. 189D ἁμαρτήματα μεγάλα; Ex 32: 30f). τὰ χαρίσματα τὰ μείζονα *the more important spiritual gifts* (in the sense Paul gave the word) 1 Cor 12: 31. As a superl. (Epict. 3, 24, 93; Stephan. Byz. s.v. Ὕβλαι: the largest of three cities is ἡ μείζων [followed by ἡ ἐλάττων, and finally ἡ μικρά=the smallest]. The comparative also performs the function of the superlative, e.g., Diod. S. 20, 22, 2, where πρεσβύτερος is the oldest of 3 men) Mt 13: 32; 1 Cor 13: 13 (by means of the superl. μ. Paul singles out from the triad the one quality that interests him most in this connection, just as Ael. Aristid. 45, 16 K. by means of αὐτός at the end of the θεοί singles out Sarapis, the only one that affects him).—The

superl. μέγιστος, found not infrequently in contemporary authors, occurs only once in the NT, where it is used in the elative sense *very great* (Diod. S. 2, 32, 1) ἐπαγγέλματα 2 Pt 1: 4.—Neut. μέγα εἰ . . . θερίσομεν; *is it an extraordinary thing* (i.e. are we expecting too much) *if we wish to reap?* 1 Cor 9: 11. οὐ μέγα οὖν, εἰ *it is not surprising, then, if* 2 Cor 11: 15 (on this constr. cf. Pla., Menex. 235D; Plut., Mor. 215F; Gen 45: 28; AFridrichsen, Coniect. Neot. 2, '36, 46). On the adv. usage Ac 26: 29 s. ὀλίγος 3b.—Neut. pl. μεγάλα ποιεῖν τινι *do great things for someone* Lk 1: 49 (cf. Dt 10: 21). λαλεῖν μεγάλα καὶ βλασφημίας *utter proud words and blasphemies* Rv 13: 5 (Da 7: 8. Cf. En. 101, 3). WGrundmann, TW IV 535–50: μέγας and related words. M-M. B. 878f; 1309.

μέγεθος, ους, τό (Hom.+; inscr., pap., LXX, Ep. Arist., Philo; Jos., Ant. 14, 370) *greatness, size*.

1. lit. (Appian, Bell. Civ. 1, 50 §219 ἀνὴρ μεγέθει μέγας; Ps.-Dicaearch. p. 145 l. 5 F. μεγάλη τῷ μεγέθει) ὑψηλὸς τῷ μεγέθει *very tall indeed* Hs 9, 6, 1.

2. fig. of God (inscr. in Ramsay, Phrygia II 700 no. 635, 4 τὸ μέγεθος τ. θεοῦ; Philo, Spec. Leg. 1, 293 τὸ τ. θεοῦ μ.) τί τὸ ὑπερβάλλον μέγεθος τ. δυνάμεως αὐτοῦ *how surpassingly great his* (God's) *power* Eph 1: 19 (cf. Philo, Op. M. 23, end τὸ μ. [τῶν δυνάμεων θεοῦ]). ἐν μεγέθει IEph inscr., to be sure, does not belong grammatically w. θεοῦ, which rather goes w. πληρώματι foll.; nevertheless it describes the nature of God. τὸ μ. τῆς μαρτυρίας *the greatness of his martyrdom* MPol 17: 1. ἀπολαμβάνειν τὸ ἴδιον μ. *recover their proper greatness* of a congregation ISm 11: 2. μεγέθους ἐστὶν ὁ Χριστιανισμός *Christianity is* (truly) *great* IRo 3: 3. M-M.*

μεγιστάν, ᾶνος, ὁ almost exclusively in our lit. always, in pl. μεγιστᾶνες, ων (Manetho 4, 41; Artem. 1, 2 p. 8, 16; 3, 9; Jos., Ant. 11, 37; 20, 26, Vi. 112; 149; LXX; PGM 13, 251 [sing.]; Phryn. 196f L.—Bl-D. §2: Dorism) *great man, courtier, magnate* at Herod's court Mk 6: 21. Gener. οἱ μ. τῆς γῆς Rv 18: 23; (w. βασιλεῖς) 6: 15. C-HHunzinger, ZNW Beih. 26, '60, 209–20: Gospel of Thomas. M-M.*

μέγιστος s. μέγας 2bβ. M-M.

μεθερμηνεύω (Polyb. 6, 26, 6; Diod. S. 1, 11, 2; Plut., Cato Maj. 2, 6; Herm. Wr. 12, 13a; PTebt. 164 I, 1 [II BC]; BGU 1002 II, 1 al.; Sir Prol., l. 30; Ep. Arist. 38; Jos., Ant. 8, 142, C. Ap. 1, 54) *translate* οὕτως μεθερμηνεύεται τὸ ὄνομα αὐτοῦ *that is the meaning of his name when it is translated* Ac 13: 8. Mostly in the formula ὅ ἐστιν μεθερμηνευόμενον *which means* (when translated) (Theophilus: 296 fgm. 3 Jac.) Mt 1: 23; Mk 5: 41; 15: 22, 34; J 1: 41; Ac 4: 36. Also ὃ λέγεται μ. J 1: 38. M-M.*

μέθη, ης, ἡ (Antipho+; Epict. 3, 26, 5; Herm. Wr. 1, 27; pap., LXX, Philo; Jos., Ant. 1, 301; 11, 42; Test. 12 Patr.) *drunkenness* ἐν κραιπάλῃ καὶ μ. *with dissipation and drunkenness* Lk 21: 34. Also pl. w. the same mng. (class.; Vett. Val. 90, 13; PGiess. 3, 8; Jdth 13: 15) 1 Cl 30: 1. (W. κῶμοι) Ro 13: 13. In a list of vices Gal 5: 21 (yet it seems that in the last two passages the proximity of κῶμοι= 'unrestrained revelry' may influence μέθαι in the direction of *drinking-bout*. On this cf. Diod. S. 16, 19, 2, where all mss. agree in the reading οἱ στρατηγοὶ ἐκ τῆς μέθης μεθύοντες=the generals who were drunken from the revelry).—HPreisker, TW IV 550–4: μέθη and related words. M-M.*

μεθίστημι by-form μεθιστάνω (Hv 1, 3, 4; 1 Cor 13: 2 t.r.) 1 aor. μετέστησα, pass. μετεστάθην, subj. μετασταθῶ (Hom. + ; inscr., pap., LXX, Joseph.) *remove from one place to another.*

1. *remove* τὶ *someth.* ὄρη 1 Cor 13: 2 (Is 54: 10). Heavens, mountains, hills, seas Hv 1, 3, 4. (ἡμᾶς) μετέστησεν εἰς τὴν βασιλείαν *he transferred us to the kingdom* Col 1: 13 (cf. Jos., Ant. 9, 235 μ. εἰς τ. αὐτοῦ βασιλείαν.—μ. εἰς='transplant into' also Alex. Aphr., Mixt. II 2 p. 219, 28; 230, 29).—Also of persons *remove, depose* (3 Km 15: 13; 1 Macc 11: 63; Jos., Ant. 19, 297; 20, 16) τινὰ ἀπὸ τοῦ τόπου *remove someone from his place* 1 Cl 44: 5. Pass. *be removed* ὅταν μετασταθῶ ἐκ τ. οἰκονομίας *when I am discharged fr. my position as manager* Lk 16: 4 (Vi. Aesopi I c. 9 μεταστήσω σε τῆς οἰκονομίας=I will remove you from your position as steward.—μ. ἐκ as Jos., Vi. 195).—This is prob. also the place for Ac 13: 22 μεταστήσας αὐτόν *after he had removed him* (fr. the throne; cf. Da 2: 21). The expr., in its fullest form μ. τινὰ ἐκ τοῦ ζῆν 'put someone to death' (Diod. S. 2, 57, 5; 4, 55, 1; cf. 3 Macc 6: 12), scarcely seems applicable here.

2. mentally and spiritually *to bring to a different point of view, cause someone to change his position,* also in an unfavorable sense *turn away, mislead* (X., Hell. 2, 2, 5; Plut., Galba 14, 3 τοὺς πλείους μετέστησαν; Josh 14: 8) ἱκανὸν ὄχλον Ac 19: 26. M-M.*

μεθοδεία, ας, ἡ (POxy. 136, 18; 24; 1134, 9 al., though only in later pap. [421 AD and later], and in the sense 'method', etc.; Hesychius; Suidas) in our lit. (only Eph) only in an unfavorable sense (s. μεθοδεύω) *scheming, craftiness* πρὸς τὴν μ. τῆς πλάνης *in deceitful scheming* Eph 4: 14. Pl. *wiles, stratagems* (Suidas: μεθοδείας· τέχνας ἢ δόλους) αἱ μ. τοῦ διαβόλου (Cyrill. of Scyth. p. 30, 21 μ. τῶν δαιμόνων) 6: 11, 12 𝔓⁴⁶. M-M.*

μεθοδεύω (found not infreq. in later wr., incl. PGM 13, 713; LXX, Philo) in an unfavorable sense *defraud, deceive, pervert* (Charito 7, 6, 10 μεθοδεύεται γυνὴ ἐπαγγελίαις =is deceived by promises; Philo, Mos. 2, 212 ὅπερ μεθοδεύουσιν οἱ λογοθῆραι καὶ σοφισταί; 2 Km 19: 28) τὰ λόγια τοῦ κυρίου πρὸς τὰς ἰδίας ἐπιθυμίας *pervert the words of the Lord to suit one's own desires* Pol 7: 1.*

μεθόριον, ου, τό (subst. neut. of μεθόριος [w. two or three endings]; the subst. in Thu. et al.; Josh 19: 27 A; Philo; Jos., Ant. 18, 111; loanw. in rabb.) *boundary*; pl. (Thu. 4, 99; X., Cyr. 1, 4, 16; 17) also the *region* included by the boundaries (Ael. Aristid. 38 p. 721 D.: ἐν μεθορίοις τῆς Ἀττικῆς) Mk 7: 24 t.r. (for ὅρια, q.v.). M-M.*

μεθύσκω (Pla. et al.; LXX) *cause to become intoxicated;* in our lit. only pass. μεθύσκομαι, 1 aor. ἐμεθύσθην (Eur., Hdt. + ; Pr 4: 17; 23: 31; Jos., Bell. 2, 29; Test. Judah 14: 1) *get drunk, become intoxicated* οἴνῳ *with wine* Eph 5: 18 (as Pr 4: 17; cf. Bl-D. §195, 2; Rob. 533). οἱ μεθυσκόμενοι (Cornutus 30 p. 59, 21; Dio Chrys. 80[30], 36) 1 Th 5: 7 (s. μεθύω 1). W. πίνειν (X., Cyr. 1, 3, 11) Lk 12: 45. μεθυσθῆναι *drink freely, be drunk* (Diod. S. 23, 21 μεθυσθέντες=those who had become drunk. Likewise 5, 26, 3; 17, 25, 5; Jos., Vi. 225) J 2: 10. ἐκ τοῦ οἴνου (like שָׁכַר מְיַיִן) Rv 17: 2. M-M.*

μέθυσμα, ατος, τό (LXX; Philo, Agr. 157, Deus Imm. 158 al.) *intoxicating drink* μ. ἀνομίας *intox. drink that leads to lawlessness* Hm 8: 3. Pl. (w. ἐδέσματα) m 6, 2, 5; 12, 2, 1.*

μέθυσος, ου, ὁ (masc. subst. of the adj., which is found Aristoph. + ; POxy. 1828, 3; LXX; Test. Jud. 14: 8. From Menand. [fgm. 67] on it is used of both sexes [Lucian,

Tim. 55; Plut., Brut. 5, 4; Sext. Emp., Hyp. 3, 24; Pr 23: 21; 26: 9], though the older writers used it only of women: Phryn. 151f L.) *drunkard*; w. those addicted to other vices (as Cebes 34, 3 and in the pap. above) Hs 6, 5, 5. Likew., but closely connected w. λοίδορος, 1 Cor 5: 11; 6: 10. M-M.*

μεθύω (Hom. + ; PHal. 1, 193f; PGM 7, 180 πολλὰ πίνειν καὶ μὴ μεθύειν, al. in pap.; LXX, Philo; Jos., Bell. 6, 196, Vi. 225; 388) *be drunk.*

1. lit. Ac 2: 15; LJ 1: 3=POxy. 1, 11–21 (JoachJeremias, Unknown Sayings of Jesus, tr. Fuller, '57, 69–74). Opp. πεινᾶν 1 Cor 11: 21. οἱ μεθυσκόμενοι νυκτὸς μεθύουσιν *those who get drunk are drunk at night* 1 Th 5: 7. οἱ μεθύοντες *those who are drunken* (Diod. S. 4, 5, 3; Cornutus 30 p. 61, 6; Job 12: 25) Mt 24: 49.

2. fig. (X., Symp. 8, 21; Pla., Lysias 222c; Philostrat., Vi. Soph. 2, 1, 2 πλούτῳ μ.; Achilles Tat. 1, 6, 1 ἔρωτι; Philo) of the apocal. woman who has sated her thirst for blood εἶδον τὴν γυναῖκα μεθύουσαν ἐκ τ. αἵματος τ. ἁγίων Rv 17: 6. M-M.*

μείγνυμι or **μειγνύω** (the pres. is lacking in our lit. [Bl-D. §92; Mlt.-H. 249], as well as in the Ptolemaic pap. [Mayser I 2², '38, 187].—On the spelling cf. Bl-D. §23; Kühner-Bl. II 482; Mayser 91; Mlt.-H. 249.—The word is found Hom. [μίσγω]+ ; inscr., pap., LXX, Joseph.) 1 aor. ἔμειξα; pf. pass. ptc. μεμειγμένος; 2 aor. pass. ἐμίγην *mix, mingle.*

1. lit. τί τινι *mingle someth. with someth.* Rv 15: 2 (Charito 3, 10, 2 αἵματι μεμειγμένον ὕδωρ; Quint. Smyrn. 6, 281 οἴνῳ δ' αἷμα μέμικτο; schol. on Nicander, Alexiph. 353). Also τί ἔν τινι (cf. Ps 105: 35) 8: 7. τὶ μετά τινος (Pla., Tim. 35β) οἶνον μετὰ χολῆς μεμειγμένον Mt 27: 34. ὧν τὸ αἷμα Πιλᾶτος ἔμειξεν μετὰ τ. θυσιῶν αὐτῶν *whose blood Pilate mingled with (the blood of) their sacrifices,* i.e. whom P. ordered slain while they were sacrificing Lk 13: 1. ὄξος καὶ οἶνος μεμειγμένα ἐπὶ τὸ αὐτό *vinegar and wine mixed together* Hm 10, 3, 3b.

2. fig. *mix, blend* τί τινι *someth. with someth.* (Jos., Bell. 5, 332, Ant. 15, 52) ἡ ὀξυχολία τῇ μακροθυμίᾳ Hm 5, 1, 6. τὶ μετά τινος: ἡ λύπη μετὰ τῆς ἐντεύξεως, . . . μετὰ τοῦ ἁγίου πνεύματος m 10, 3, 3a, c. M-M. s.v. μίγν-. B. 335.*

μειζότερος s. μέγας.

μείζων s. μέγας. M-M.

μειόω 1 aor. ἐμείωσα (X., Pla. + ; Strabo in Jos., Ant. 15, 10; PFay. 26, 15 [II AD] al. in pap.; Sir 43: 7; Philo, Rer. Div. Her. 140; Sib. Or. 12, 134) *lessen* τὶ *someth.* τὸ σεμνὸν τῆς φιλαδελφίας ὑμῶν *the respect that is due your brotherly love* 1 Cl 47: 5 (cf. Dit., Syll.³ 783, 8f οὐκ ἐμίωσέν τι τῆς πατρῴας ἀρετῆς).*

μείωσις, εως, ἡ (Hippocr. + ; Polyb. 9, 43, 5; Sext. Emp., Math. 9, 400; Vett. Val. index; Philo) *lessening, diminution* τῆς σαρκός *mutilation of the flesh* Dg 4: 4.*

μέλαν, τό s. μέλας, end.

μελανέω fut. μελανήσω; 1 aor. ἐμελάνησα (Theophr. et al.; PLond. 897, 23 [84 AD]) *turn black* of stones Hs 9, 30, 2.—In 9, 8, 7 the ἐμελάνωσαν of the mss. has been corrected by Gebhardt to ἐμελάνησαν.—Reinhold §14, 3.*

μέλας, μέλαινα, μέλαν gen. ανος, αίνης, ανος (Hom. + ; inscr., pap., LXX, Philo, Joseph., Sib. Or. 4, 75) comp. μελανώτερος (Strabo 16, 4, 12) 1 Cl 8: 3; *black* hair (Lev 13: 37) Mt 5: 36 (opp. λευκός as Artem. 1, 32 p. 34, 5; 9f).

Of clothing used in mourning (Polyaenus 6, 7, 1 ἐν μελαίνῃ ἐσθῆτι; Jos., Vi. 138) μ. ὡς σάκκος τρίχινος Rv 6: 12; cf. 1 Cl 8: 3. Apocal. color: w. others Rv 6: 5 (cf. Zech 6: 2, 6 and s. πυρρός); Hv 4, 1, 10; 4, 3, 2; named alone, and as the color of evil, forming a contrast to the world of light (*evil, malignant* in the moral realm Solon, Pind. +; Diphilus Com. [IV/III BC] 91 of a woman; Plut., Mor. p. 12D μ. ἄνθρωποι; M. Ant. 4, 28 μ. ἦθος; Philostrat., Vi. Apoll. 5, 36 p. 196, 19 gold) Hs 9, 1, 5; 9, 6, 4; 9, 8, 1f; 4f; 9, 9, 5; 9, 13, 8; 9, 15, 1; 3; 9, 19, 1. Hence ὁ μ. *the Black One* of the devil B 4: 9; 20: 1 (Lucian, Philops. 31 ὁ δαίμων μελάντερος τοῦ ζόφου).—FJDölger, D. Sonne der Gerechtigkeit u. der Schwarze '18; LZiehen, ARW 24, '26, 48ff; RGradwohl, Die Farben im AT Beih. ZAW 83, '63, 50–3. S. also Act. Thom. 55; 64.—Neut. τὸ μέλαν, ανος ink (Pla., Phaedr. 276c; Demosth. 18, 258; Plut., Mor. 841E, Solon 17, 3; Synes., Ep. 157 p. 294B κάλαμον κ. χάρτην κ. μέλαν; PGrenf. II 38, 8[81 BC]; POxy. 326; PLeid. X 10, 1ff; loanw. in rabb.) ἐπιστολὴ ἐγγεγραμμένη μέλανι 2 Cor 3: 3. διὰ μέλανος καὶ καλάμου γράφειν write with pen and ink 3 J 13. διὰ χάρτου καὶ μέλανος 2 J 12.—GRadke (on λευκός); WMichaelis, TW IV 554–6. M-M. B. 1052; 1055; 1291. *

Μελεά, ὁ indecl. (מְלֵאָה??; in a list of indecl. names scarcely Μελεᾶ as gen. of Μελεᾶς) *Melea*, in the genealogy of Jesus Lk 3: 31. *

μέλει third pers. sing. of μέλω, used impersonally and personally; impf. ἔμελεν; 1 aor. ἐμέλησεν, subj. μελήσῃ (B 1: 5) (Hom. +; pap., LXX) w. dat. of the pers.: *it is a care* or *concern to someone*.
   1. w. gen. of the thing about which concern is felt (class.; Ael. Aristid. 51, 34 K.=27 p. 542 D.: τούτων ἐμέλησε τῷ θεῷ; Oenomaus in Euseb., Pr. Ev. 5, 34, 14 satirical statement by a Cynic: τί μέλει τοῖς φιλανθρώποις θεοῖς ἀνθρώπων; Jos., Ant. 7, 45 θεός, ᾧ μέλει πάντων) μὴ τῶν βοῶν μ. τῷ θεῷ; *is it about oxen that God is concerned?* 1 Cor 9: 9 (Ael. Dion. τ, 35; Paroem. Gr.: Apostol. 17, 43 τῶν δ' ὄνων οὔ μοι μέλει. For the idea cf. Ep. Arist. 144; Philo, Spec. Leg. 1, 260 οὐ γὰρ ὑπὲρ ἀλόγων ὁ νόμος).
   2. foll. by περί τινος *about someone* or *someth.* (Aeschyl., Hdt. +; Diod. S. 4, 38, 3 περὶ τῶν λοιπῶν Διῒ μελήσειν=Zeus will care for the rest; Alciphr. 4, 6, 5; PLond. 897, 27; POxy. 1155, 5; 1 Macc 14: 42, 43; Wsd 12: 13; Jos., Ant. 6, 253) οὐ μ. σοι περὶ οὐδενός *you care for no man* i.e., *you court no man's favor* Mt 22: 16; Mk 12: 14. περὶ τῶν προβάτων *care for the sheep* J 10: 13. περὶ τῶν πτωχῶν 12: 6; cf. 1 Pt 5: 7; Hv 2, 3, 1. περὶ ἀγάπης οὐ μ. αὐτοῖς *they are not concerned about love* ISm 6: 2.
   3. foll. by ὅτι (Hdt. 9, 72; PSI 445; Tob 10: 5 BA) *someone is concerned that* Mk 4: 38; Lk 10: 40. W. inf. foll. (POxy. 930, 11) *someone takes care* or *is pleased to do someth.* B 11: 1. W. περί τινος and a subst. inf. foll. τοῦ μεταδοῦναι 1: 5.
   4. abs. (X., Cyr. 4, 3, 7; IG IX 1, 654 τῇ θεῷ μελήσει) μή σοι μελέτω *never mind* 1 Cor 7: 21.
   5. a rather clear case of the personal constr. (class.; Ep. Arist. 92) οὐδὲν (subj.) τούτων (partitive gen.) τῷ Γαλλίωνι ἔμελεν *none of these things concerned Gallio= he paid no attention to this* Ac 18: 17 (cf. Bl-D. §176, 3 app.; Rob. 508f. But s. οὐδείς 2bγ). Sim. πάντα σοι μ. *you are concerned about everything*, lit. 'everything is a care to you' Hs 9, 13, 6. M-M. *

μελετάω 1 aor. ἐμελέτησα (Hom. Hymns, Thu. +; Vett. Val. 330, 22; pap., LXX, Philo).

1. *take care, endeavor* (Hes. et al.; PSI 94, 18) εἰς τὸ σῶσαι ψυχήν *to save a soul* B 19: 10.
   2. *practice, cultivate, take pains with* w. acc. (Aristoph., Plut. 511; Hdt. 6, 105; Philo; Jos., Bell. 6, 306 al.) ταῦτα (Epict. 2, 1, 29 ταῦτα μελετᾶτε; 1, 1, 25 ταῦτα μελ. . . . ἐν τούτοις . . .) 1 Ti 4: 15; B 21: 7. μ. τὸν φόβον τοῦ θεοῦ *cultivate the fear of God* B 4: 11; cf. 11: 5 (=Is 33: 18). Pass. διὰ τὸ μελετᾶσθαι θανάτου κατάλυσιν *because the destruction of death was being carried out* IEph 19: 3.
   3. *think about, meditate upon* (Ps.-Demosth. 61, 43) τὶ someth. (Job 27: 4; Pr 15: 28; Ep. Arist. 160; Jos., Ant. 4, 183) κενά *think vain thoughts, conspire in vain* (הָגָה רִיק) Ac 4: 25 (Ps 2: 1). διάσταλμα ῥήματος B 10: 11.—Abs. μηδὲ μελετᾶτε *and do not rack your brains* Mk 13: 11 t.r. M-M. *

μελέτη, ης, ἡ (Hes. et al.; IG II² 1028, 19 al.; BGU 1125, 7 [13 BC]; LXX, Philo; Jos., C. Ap. 2, 276, Ant. 16, 43) *meditation, study* B 10: 11. B. 1092. *

μέλι, ιτος, τό (Hom. +; inscr., pap., LXX; Ep. Arist. 112; Philo; Jos., Ant. 5, 288; 6, 118) *honey; sweet* Rv 10: 9f (Ezk 3: 3); Hm 5, 1, 5f. W. milk as food for children (Diod. S. 5, 70, 3; Philostrat., Her. 19, 19; Is 7: 15, 22) B 6: 17; sign of fertility (schol. on Pind., Ol. 1, 157c γῆ μέλι ῥέουσα) 6: 8, 10, 13 (Ex 33: 3; on the formula cf. HUsener [on γάλα 2]; NADahl, MGoguel-Festschr. '50, 62–70). μ. ἄγριον (s. ἄγριος 1) Mt 3: 4; Mk 1: 6; GEb 2.—SKrauss, Honig in Palästina: ZDPV 32, '09, 151–64; Dalman, Arbeit VII (s. οἰκία 1a). M-M. B. 384. *

μέλισσα, ης, ἡ (Hom. +; PSI 426, 13; Ps.-Phoc. 127; Philo in Euseb., Pr. Ev. 8, 11, 8; Jos., Ant. 5, 288; 6, 118) *bee* B 6: 6 (Ps 117: 12). B. 192. *

μελίσσιος, ιον *pertaining to the bee* (Syntipas p. 28, 9; 29, 3) μελίσσιον κηρίον (bee-)*honeycomb* (Biogr. p. 93; Syntipas 28, 7) ἀπὸ μελισσίου κηρίου *some honeycomb* Lk 24: 42 t.r. The v.l. ἀπὸ μελισσίου κηρίον rather belongs to μελισσ(ε)ῖον, ου, τό *bee-hive* (PCair. Zen. 467 [III BC]; Hesychius) *a honeycomb from a bee-hive.*— EbNestle, ZDPV 30, '07, 209f; EGrafvMülinen, ibid. 35, '12, 105ff; LKöhler, ibid. 54, '31, 289ff; GDalman, ibid. 55, '32, 80f. *

Μελίτη, ης, ἡ *Malta*, an island located south of Sicily (M. is attested as the name of this island in Diod. S. 15, 12, 2; Strabo 6, 2, 11; 17, 3, 16; Ps.-Scylax 94 [p. 37 BFabricius 1878]; inscr.) Ac 28: 1.—AMayr, D. Insel Malta im Altertum '09; Zahn, AG 841–4. M-M. *

Μελιτήνη v.l. for Μελίτη.

μέλλω (Hom. +; inscr., pap., LXX, En., Ep. Arist., Philo, Joseph., Test. 12 Patr.) fut. μελλήσω; impf. ἔμελλον and ἤμελλον (Bl-D. §66, 3; W.-S. §12, 3; Mlt.-H. 188. In Att. inscr. the ἠ- appears after 300 BC [Meisterhans³-Schw. 169]. In the inscr. from Priene ἐ- occurs only once: 11, 5 [c. 297 BC]).

1. used w. an inf. foll.—a. only rarely w. the fut. inf., w. which it is regularly used in class. Gk., since in colloquial language the fut. inf. and ptc. were gradually disappearing and being replaced by combinations with μέλλω (Bl-D. §338, 3; 350; cf. Rob. 882; 889). W. the fut. inf. μ. denotes certainty that an event will occur in the future μ. ἔσεσθαι (Dit., Syll.³ 914, 10 μέλλει ἔσεσθαι; 247 I, 74 [?]; Jos., Ant. 13, 322) *will certainly take place* or *be* Ac 11: 28; 24: 15; 27: 10; 1 Cl 43: 6; cf. Dg 8: 2.
   b. w. the aor. inf. (rarely in class. Gk. [but as early as Hom., and e.g. X., Cyr. 1, 4, 16]; Herodas 3, 78 and 91;

UPZ 70, 12 [152/1 BC]; PGiess. 12, 5; POxy. 1067, 17; 1488, 20; Ex 4: 12; Job 3: 8; 2 Macc 14: 41; cf. Phryn. p. 336; 745ff L.; WGRutherford, New Phryn. 1881, 420ff).

a. *be on the point of, be about to* μ. ἀποκαλυφθῆναι *be about to be revealed* Ro 8: 18. τὸ δωδεκάφυλον τοῦ Ἰσραὴλ μέλλον ἀπολέσθαι *the twelve tribes of Israel that were about to be destroyed* 1 Cl 55: 6. ἤμελλεν προαγαγεῖν Ac 12: 6. ἀποθανεῖν Rv 3: 2. ἐμέσαι vs. 16. τεκεῖν 12: 4.

β. *be destined, inevitable* (acc. to God's will) ἀποκαλυφθῆναι *that is destined to be revealed* Gal 3: 23.

c. w. the pres. inf. So mostly (84 times in the NT.; oft. in lit., inscr., pap., LXX, Ep. Arist.; cf. HGMeecham, Letter of Aristeas '25, 118 and 124).

a. *be about to, be on the point of* ἤμελλεν τελευτᾶν *he was at the point of death* (Aristot. in Apollon. Paradox. 27 and Diod. S. 6, 4, 3 μέλλων τελευτᾶν; cf. Jos., Ant. 4, 83; 12, 357) Lk 7: 2. Also ἤμελλεν ἀποθνῄσκειν (Artem. 4, 24 p. 217, 5 γραῦς μέλλουσα ἀποθνῄσκειν; Aesop, Fab. 131 P. = 202 H.; 233 P. = 216 H.; 2 Macc 7: 18; 4 Macc 10: 9) J 4: 47. ἤμελλεν ἑαυτὸν ἀναιρεῖν *he was about to kill himself* Ac 16: 27. Of God's Kgdm. μέλλειν ἔρχεσθαι 1 Cl 42: 3. Of heavenly glory ἡ μέλλουσα ἀποκαλύπτεσθαι 1 Pt 5: 1. Cf. Lk 19: 4; J 6: 6; Ac 3: 3; 5: 35; 18: 14; 21: 27; 22: 26; 23: 27.—Occasionally almost= *begin* ἤμελλον γράφειν Rv 10: 4. ὅταν μέλλῃ ταῦτα συντελεῖσθαι πάντα *when all these things are* (or *begin*) *to be accomplished* Mk 13: 4; cf. Lk 21: 7; Rv 10: 7.

β. in a weakened sense it serves simply as a periphrasis for the fut. (PMich. III 202, 8ff; 13ff [105 AD].—Mayser II 1, 226) ὅσα λαλῶ ἢ καὶ μ. λαλεῖν (=ἢ καὶ λαλήσω) *what I tell or shall tell* Hm 4, 4, 3. So esp. oft. in Hermas: μ. λέγειν v 1, 1, 6; 3, 8, 11; m 11: 7, 18; s 5, 2, 1. μ. ἐντέλλεσθαι v 5: 5; m 5, 2, 8. μ. κατοικεῖν s 1: 1; 4: 2. μ. χωρεῖν (=χωρήσω) IMg 5: 1.—Substitute for the disappearing fut. forms (inf. and ptc. Bl-D. §356 w. app.); for the fut. inf.: προσεδόκων αὐτὸν μέλλειν πίμπρασθαι Ac 28: 6; for the fut. ptc.: ὁ μέλλων ἔρχεσθαι Mt 11: 14. ὁ τοῦτο μέλλων πράσσειν *the one who was going to do this* Lk 22: 23; cf. 24: 21; Ac 13: 34. οἱ μέλλοντες πιστεύειν *those who were to believe* (in him) *in the future* 1 Ti 1: 16; 1 Cl 42: 4; Hm 4, 3, 3. μέλλοντες ἀσεβεῖν *those who were to be ungodly in the future* 2 Pt 2: 6. Of Christ ὁ μέλλων κρίνειν 2 Ti 4: 1; B 7: 2. οἱ μέλλοντες ἀρνεῖσθαι=οἱ ἀρνησόμενοι Hv 2, 2, 8. πυρὸς ζῆλος ἐσθίειν μέλλοντος τοὺς ὑπεναντίους *that will devour the opponents* Hb 10: 27.

γ. denoting an intended action: *intend, propose, have in mind* μέλλει Ἡρῴδης ζητεῖν τὸ παιδίον *Herod intends to search for the child* Mt 2: 13. οὗ ἤμελλεν αὐτὸς ἔρχεσθαι *where he himself intended to come* Lk 10: 1. μέλλουσιν ἔρχεσθαι *they intended to come* J 6: 15. Cf. vs. 71; 7: 35; 12: 4; 14: 22; Ac 17: 31; 20: 3, 7, 13a, b; 23: 15; 26: 2; 27: 30; Hb 8: 5; 2 Pt 1: 12. τί μέλλεις ποιεῖν; *what do you intend to do?* Hs 1: 5. οὐ μ. ποιεῖν *I have no intention of doing* MPol 8: 2. μ. προσηλοῦν *they wanted to nail him fast* 13: 3. μ. λαμβάνειν *we wanted to take him out* 17: 2.

δ. denoting an action that necessarily follows a divine decree *is destined, must, will certainly* . . . μ. πάσχειν *he is destined to suffer* Mt 17: 12; B 7: 10; 12: 2; cf. 6: 7. μ. σταυροῦσθαι *must be crucified* 12: 1. μ. παραδίδοσθαι Mt 17: 22; Lk 9: 44; B 16: 5. ἤμελλεν ἀποθνῄσκειν J 11: 51; 12: 33; 18: 32. ἐν σαρκὶ μ. φανεροῦσθαι B 6: 7, 9, 14. Cf. Mt 16: 27; 20: 22; Ro 4: 24; 8: 13; Rv 12: 5. οὐκέτι μέλλουσιν . . . θεωρεῖν *they should no more see* . . . Ac 20: 38. τὰ μ. γίνεσθαι *what must come to pass* 26: 22; cf. Rv 1: 19. διὰ τοὺς μέλλοντας κληρονομεῖν σωτηρίαν

those who are to inherit salvation Hb 1: 14. μέλλομεν θλίβεσθαι *that we were to be afflicted* 1 Th 3: 4.—Mk 10: 32; Lk 9: 31; J 7: 39; Hb 11: 8.

2. The ptc. is used abs. in the mng. *future, to come* (Pind., Ol. 10, 7 ὁ μέλλων χρόνος) ὁ αἰὼν ὁ μέλλων *the age to come* (s. αἰών 2b), which brings the reign of God (opp. ὁ αἰὼν οὗτος or ὁ νῦν αἰών) Mt 12: 32; Eph 1: 21; 2 Cl 6: 3; Pol 5: 2; cf. Hb 6: 5. Also ὁ μ. καιρός (opp. ὁ νῦν κ.) B 4: 1. ἡ μ. ζωή (opp. ἡ νῦν ζ.) 1 Ti 4: 8. ὁ μ. βίος (opp. ὁ νῦν β.) 2 Cl 20: 2. ἡ μ. βασιλεία 5: 5; ἡ οἰκουμένη ἡ μ. *the world to come* Hb 2: 5. ἡ μέλλουσα πόλις (as a play on words, opp. [οὐ . . .] μένουσα π.) 13: 14. ἡ μ. ἐπαγγελία *the promise for the future* 2 Cl 10: 3f. τὰ μ. ἀγαθά Hb 9: 11 v.l.; Hv 1, 1, 8. ἡ μ. ἀνάστασις 1 Cl 24: 1; τὸ κρίμα τὸ μ. *the judgment to come* Ac 24: 25; cf. 1 Cl 28: 1; 2 Cl 18: 2; MPol 11: 2. ἡ μ. ὀργή Mt 3: 7; IEph 11: 1. ἡ μ. θλῖψις Hv 4, 2, 5. τὰ μ. σκάνδαλα B 4: 9.—ἡ μέλλουσά σου ἀδελφή *your future sister*= the one who in the future will be your sister, no longer your wife Hv 2, 2, 3. Several times the noun can be supplied fr. the context: τύπος τοῦ μέλλοντος, i.e. Christ Ro 5: 14.—Subst. τὸ μέλλον *the future* (Aeneas Tact. 422; 431 al.; Antiphanes Com. [IV BC] 227 K.; Menand., Monostich. 412; Anacreont. 36; Plut., Caes. 14, 4; Herodian 1, 14, 2; Dit., Syll.³ 609, 5; Philo) 1 Cl 31: 3. εἰς τὸ μ. *for the future* 1 Ti 6: 19; specif. (*in the*) *next year* (PLond. 1231, 4 [144 AD] τὴν εἰς τὸ μέλλον γεωργείαν; s. Field, Notes 65) Lk 13: 9. τὰ μ. *the things to come* (X., Conv. 4, 47; Aeneas Tact. 1050; Artem. 1, 36; Wsd 19: 1; Philo) Col 2: 17; PK 3 p. 15, 21. (Opp. τὰ ἐνεστῶτα *the present* as PGM 5, 295) Ro 8: 38; 1 Cor 3: 22; B 1: 7; 5: 3; 17: 2.

3. *delay* τί μέλλεις; *why are you delaying?* cf. Aeschyl., Prom. 36; Eur., Hec. 1094; Thu. 8, 78; Lucian, Dial. Mort. 10, 13; Jos., Bell. 3, 494 τί μέλλομεν; 4 Macc 6: 23; 9: 1) Ac 22: 16. M-M. B. 974.

μέλος, ους, τό (Hom.+; inscr., pap., ostr., LXX, Ep. Arist., Philo; Jos., Bell. 1, 656, Ant. 9, 240; Test. 12 Patr.) *member, part, limb.*

1. lit., of parts of the human body καθάπερ ἐν ἑνὶ σώματι πολλὰ μ. ἔχομεν *as we have many members in one body* Ro 12: 4a, b; cf. 1 Cor 12: 12a, 14, 18-20, 25f; Js 3: 5 (Apollod. [II BC]: 244 fgm. 307 Jac. κράτιστον τῶν μελῶν ἡ γλῶσσα). τὰ μ. τοῦ σώματος *the parts of the body* (Diod. S. 5, 18, 12; Philo, In Flacc. 176) 1 Cor 12: 12b, 22; 1 Cl 37: 5; Dg 6: 2. W. σάρξ 6: 6. μ. σκοτεινόν Lk 11: 36 𝔓⁴⁵. W. gen. of the pers. Mt 5: 29f (cf. Sextus 13); Ro 6: 13a, b, 19a, b; 7: 5, 23a, b; Js 3: 6; 4: 1 (the pl. τὰ μέλη can also mean the body, sing.: Pind., Nem. 11, 15 θνατὰ μέλη= mortal body). συγκοπὴ μελῶν *mangling of limbs* (leading to martyrdom. Diod. S. 17, 83, 9 describes a procedure of this kind) IRo 5: 3.

2. There is no fixed boundary betw. parts of the body as taken lit. and fig.; Col 3: 5 νεκρώσατε τὰ μέλη τὰ ἐπὶ τῆς γῆς, which may be paraphrased: *put to death whatever in your nature belongs to the earth.*

3. fig., of the many-sided organism of the Christian community (on the figure of the body and its members, a favorite one in ancient lit., s. Ltzm., Hdb. on 1 Cor 12: 12; WNestle, D. Fabel des Menenius Agrippa: Clio 21, '27, 350-60): the individual Christians are members of Christ, and together they form his body (for this idea cf. Simplicius in Epict. p. 70, 51: souls are μέρη τοῦ θεοῦ; 71, 5.—In p. 80, 54 the soul is called μέρος ἢ μέλος τοῦ θεοῦ) 1 Cor 12: 27; Eph 5: 30; 1 Cl 46: 7; IEph 4: 2; ITr 11: 2; cf. Eph 4: 16 v.l. ἀλλήλων μέλη *members of each other* Ro 12: 5; Eph 4: 25; 1 Cl 46: 7b. In 1 Cor 6: 15a for a special reason the σώματα of the Christians are called μέλη Χριστοῦ. Since acc. to Paul's understanding of Gen

2: 24 sexual intercourse means fusion of bodies (vs. 16), relations w. a prostitute fr. this point of view become particularly abhorrent vs. 15b.—FHorst, TW IV 559–72. M-M.*

Μελχί, ὁ indecl. (מַלְכִּי) *Melchi,* in the genealogy of Jesus —1. son of Jannai, father of Levi Lk 3: 24.—2. son of Addi, father of Neri vs. 28.*

Μελχισέδεκ, ὁ indecl. (מַלְכִּי־צֶדֶק; Gen 14: 18; Philo, Leg. All. 3, 79; Jos., Ant. 1, 180f.—FCBurkitt, The Syriac Forms of NT Proper Names '12, 82) *Melchizedek* king of Salem and priest of God Most High in the time of Abraham (both after Gen 14: 18). In the typology of Hb, a type of Christ as High Priest (Mel. is not called ἀρχιερεύς in LXX, Philo, or Joseph., but ὁ μέγας ἱερεύς Philo, Abr. 235) 5: 6, 10; 6: 20; 7: 1, 10f, 15, 17 (nearly always Ps 109: 4b has influenced these passages, if it is not quoted in full: σὺ εἶ ἱερεὺς εἰς τὸν αἰῶνα κατὰ τὴν τάξιν Μελχισέδεκ). —On Mel. in the NT: FrJJérome, D. gesch. M-Bild u. s. Bed. im Hb., Diss. Freib. '20; GWuttke, M., der Priesterkönig von Salem: E. Studie zur Gesch. der Exegese '27; RGyllenberg, Kristusbilden i Hebréer brevet '28; GBardy, M. dans la trad. patrist.: RB 35, '26, 496–509; 36, '27, 25–45; HStork, D. sog. Melchisedekianer '28; HWindisch, Hdb., exc. on Hb 7: 4 (²'31); EKäsemann, D. wandernde Gsvolk '39; HEdelMedico, ZAW 69, '57, 160–70; JJPetuchowski, Hebrew Union Coll. Annual 28, '57, 127–36; JAFitzmyer, CBQ 25, '63, 305–21; MdeJonge and ASvd Woude, 11 Q Melch. and the NT, NTS 12, '66, 301–26; SLyonnet, Sin, Redemption and Sacrifice, '70, 310–12 (lit.); OMichel, TW IV 573–5. M-M.*

μεμβράνα, ης, ἡ (Lat. loanw.: membrana; cf. Bl-D. §5, 1 [μεμβράνη]; Rob. 109; GMeyer, D. lat. Lehnworte im Neugriech.: SAWien 132, 1895, 44 [μεμβράνα];—Charax of Pergamum [II/III AD]: 103 fgm. 37 Jac.; Acta Barn. 6 p. 66 Tisch. τὰς μεμβράνας; POxy. 2156, 9 [c. 400 AD]) *parchment,* used for making books. τὰ βιβλία, μάλιστα τὰς μ. *the books, especially the parchments* 2 Ti 4: 13 (perh. 'scrolls'; cf. Theodoret III 695 Sch. μεμβράνας τὰ εἰλητὰ κέκληκεν· οὕτω γὰρ Ῥωμαῖοι καλοῦσι τὰ δέρματα. ἐν εἰλητοῖς δὲ εἶχον πάλαι τὰς θείας γραφάς. οὕτω δὲ καὶ μέχρι τοῦ παρόντος ἔχουσιν οἱ Ἰουδαῖοι. But WHPHatch [letter of Sept. 12, '53] now believes the μεμβράνα of 2 Ti to be parchment *codices,* pointing to Martial, Ep. 14, 7; 184 pugillares membranei='parchments of a size to be held in one's fist'; cf. Ep. 14, 186; 188; 190; 192; MRJames, Companion to Latin Studies³ '43, 238. So also CCMcCown, HTR 34, '41, 234f). M-M. B. 1289.*

μέμνημαι s. μιμνήσκομαι.

μέμφομαι 1 aor. ἐμεμψάμην (Hes.+; inscr., pap., LXX) *find fault with, blame* w. acc. τινά *someone* (Hes.+; PFay. 111, 3 [95/96 AD]; POxy. 1481, 5; PRyl. 239, 13; Philo; Jos., Ant. 13, 109; Sib. Or. 5, 237) and τί *someth.* (Pind.+), or w. dat. τινί *someone* (Aeschyl.+; Alex. Polyhistor [I BC]: 273 fgm. 46 Jac.; Jos., C. Ap. 1, 142; Sir 41: 7; 2 Macc 2: 7.—Bl-D. §152, 1; Rob. 473; RSchekira, De imperatoris Marci Aurelii Ant. librorum τὰ εἰς ἑαυτόν sermone, Diss. Greifswald '19, 147) μεμφόμενος αὐτοὺς λέγει *he finds fault with them when he says* Hb 8: 8 (acc. to אAD; but αὐτοῖς t.r., B P⁴⁶). οὐκ ἔχει ἡμῶν οὐδὲν μέμψασθαι *he will have nothing to blame us for* Hs 9, 10, 4. γνῶσιν Dg 12: 5. Abs. (Sir 11: 7) Mk 7: 2 v.l.—τί ἔτι μέμφεται; (Aristippus in Diog. L. 2, 77: τί οὖν ἐμέμφου; Ael. Aristid. 32 p. 604 D.: τί μέμφονται;) *why does he*

still find fault? or *what fault can he still find?* Ro 9: 19 (Appian, Maced. 11 §5 εἴ τι μέμφονται= if they have any fault to find. —*Complain* is also poss., as Jos., Ant. 2, 63; Ps.-Pla., Axioch. 7, p. 368A). For the subject matter cf. Oenomaus in Euseb., Pr. Ev. 6, 7, 36: ὁ Ζεὺς οὗτος, under whose control everything is found, τί ἡμᾶς τίνυται [punish]; ... τί δὲ καὶ ἀπειλεῖ ἡμῖν;). M-M.*

μεμψίμοιρος, ον (Isocr. 12, 8; Aristot., H.A. 608b, 10; cf. Theophr., Char. 17[22], 1; Lucian, Cynic. 17, Tim. 55; Plut., De Ira Cohib. 13 p. 461B; Ptolem., Apotel. 3, 14, 23; Vett. Val. 17, 12) *fault-finding, complaining* (w. γογγυστής) Jd 16. M-M.*

μέμψις, εως, ἡ (Aeschyl.+; BGU 926, 6; POxy. 140, 16; 1255, 19; LXX; Philo; Jos., C. Ap. 2, 242, Vi. 266) *reason for complaint* Col 3: 13 D.*

μέν affirmative particle, a weakened form of μήν (Hom. +; inscr., pap., LXX). One of the commonest particles in class. Gk., but its usage declines sharply in post-class. times. Found only 182 times in the NT. In seven of these places the editions vary (in Tdf. it is omitted Mk 9: 12; Ro 7: 25; 16: 19; 1 Cor 2: 15; in W-H. Ac 23: 8; 1 Cor 12: 20—in Ro 16: 19; Gal 4: 23 they bracket the word). The mss. show an even greater variation. In Rv, 2 Th, 1 Ti, Tit, Phlm, 2 Pt, 1, 2, 3 J it does not occur at all; Eph, Col, 1 Th, Js have only one occurrence each. It is also quite rare in 1, 2 Cl, Ign, GP, but is common in Ac, Hb, B and esp. in Dg. It never begins a clause. Cf. Kühner-G. II p. 264ff; Bl-D. §447 w. app.; Rob. 1150–3; Mlt.-Turner 331f.

1. used correlatively w. other particles—a. introducing a concessive clause, followed by another clause w. an adversative particle: *to be sure. . . but, on the one hand . . . on the other hand,* though in many cases the translation will not fit this scheme; rather, the contrast is to be emphasized in the second clause, often with *but.*

α. μέν. . .δέ: ἐγὼ μὲν ὑμᾶς βαπτίζω. . .ὁ δὲ ὀπίσω μου ἐρχόμενος Mt 3: 11. ὁ μὲν θερισμός. . .οἱ δὲ ἐργάται 9: 37. τὸ μὲν ποτήριόν μου πίεσθε. . .τὸ δὲ καθίσαι 20: 23. ὁ μὲν υἱὸς τοῦ ἀνθρώπου. . .οὐαὶ δὲ τῷ ἀνθρώπῳ ἐκείνῳ Mk 14: 21. τοῦ μὲν πρώτου κατέαξαν τὰ σκέλη . . .ἐπὶ δὲ τὸν Ἰησοῦν ἐλθόντες J 19: 32 and oft. Cf. Mt 22: 8; Ro 6: 11; 1 Cor 9: 24; 11: 14; 12: 20; 2 Cor 10: 10; Hb 3: 5; 1 Pt 1: 20.—In combination w. conjunctions: εἰ μὲν . . . εἰ δέ *if . . . but if* Dg 3: 2. εἰ μὲν οὖν . . . εἰ δέ *if then . . . but if* Ac 19: 38f; cf. 25: 11. εἰ μὲν . . . νῦν δέ *if. . . but now* Hb 11: 15. μὲν οὖν. . .δέ *(now) indeed. . . but* J 19: 24; 20: 30; Ac 8: 4; 12: 5; 1 Cor 9: 25. μὲν γάρ. . .δέ *for indeed. . .but* (Wsd 7: 30; Job 28: 2) 1 Cor 11: 7; Ro 2: 25. κἂν μὲν . . . , εἰ δὲ μήγε *if . . . but if not* Lk 13: 9. ἐὰν μὲν . . . , ἐὰν δὲ μή Mt 10: 13. W. prep. εἰς μὲν . . . εἰς δέ Hb 9: 6.

β. μέν. . .ἀλλά *to be sure. . .but* (Thu. 3, 2, 1; X., Oec. 3, 6; Tetr. Iamb. 1, 2, 3) Mk 9: 12 (Tdf. omits μέν). πάντα μὲν καθαρὰ ἀλλὰ κακὸν τῷ ἀνθρώπῳ *to be sure everything is clean, but. . .* Ro 14: 20. σὺ μὲν γὰρ καλῶς . . . ἀλλ᾽ ὁ ἕτερος 1 Cor 14: 17. Cf. Ac 4: 16.

γ. μέν. . .πλήν *indeed. . . but* (Galen, Inst. Log. c. 8, 2 Kalbfl. [1896]) Lk 22: 22.

b. without any real concessive sense on the part of μέν, but adversative force in δέ, so that μέν need not be translated at all: αὐτοὶ μὲν. . .ὑμεῖς δέ Lk 11: 48; cf. Ac 13: 36. ἐγὼ μὲν. . .ἐγὼ δέ 1 Cor 1: 12. τοῖς μὲν ἀπολλυμένοις. . .τοῖς δὲ σῳζομένοις vs. 18. Ἰουδαίοις μέν. . .ἔθνεσι δέ vs. 23. ἐμοὶ μὲν. . .ὑμῖν δέ Phil 3: 1. εἰ μέν. . .εἰ δέ Ac 18: 14; Dg 2: 8.

c. Somet. the combination μέν...δέ does not emphasize a contrast, but separates one thought from another in a series, so that they may be easily distinguished: πρῶτον μέν...ἔπειτα δέ *in the first place...then* Hb 7: 2. ὁ μέν...ὁ δέ *the one...the other* Mt 13: 8, 23 (cf. Lucian, Hermot. 66 ὁ μὲν ἑπτά, ὁ δὲ πέντε, ὁ δὲ τριάκοντα); Ro 9: 21. ὃς μέν...ὃς δέ *the one...the other* Mt 21: 35; 25: 15; Lk 23: 33; Ac 27: 44; Ro 14: 5; 1 Cor 11: 21; Jd 22. ἃ μέν...ἃ δέ *some...others* 2 Ti 2: 20. ὁ μὲν...ὁ δὲ *the one...the other, but pl. some...others* Ac 14: 4; 17: 32; Gal 4: 23; Eph 4: 11; Phil 1: 16; Dg 2: 2f. ἕκαστος...,ὁ μὲν οὕτως ὁ δὲ οὕτως *each one...,one in one way, one in another* 1 Cor 7: 7. ὃς μὲν πιστεύει φαγεῖν πάντα, ὁ δὲ ἀσθενῶν *the one believes he may eat anything, but the weak man* Ro 14: 2. τινὲς μέν...τινὲς δέ *some...but still others* Phil 1: 15. ἄλλη μέν..., ἄλλη δέ...1 Cor 15: 39. ἑτέρα μέν..., ἑτέρα δέ vs. 40. οἱ μέν..., ἄλλοι δέ..., ἕτεροι δέ Mt 16: 14. ᾧ μὲν γάρ..., ἄλλῳ δέ..., ἑτέρῳ 1 Cor 12: 8ff. ἃ μέν..., ἄλλα δέ..., ἄλλα δέ Mt 13: 4ff. τοῦτο μέν..., τοῦτο δέ *in part...in part* (Hdt. 3, 106; Isocr. 4, 21; 22) Hb 10: 33 (μέν followed by more than one δέ: two, Libanius, Or. 18, p. 251, 3f; Or. 59 p. 240, 13. Four, Or. 64 p. 469, 14).

2. Frequently μέν is found in anacolutha—a. when the contrast can be supplied fr. the context, and therefore can be omitted as obvious: λόγον μὲν ἔχοντα σοφίας (sc. ὄντα δὲ ἄλογα or someth. sim.) *they have the reputation of being wise* (but are foolish) Col 2: 23. τὰ μὲν σημεῖα τοῦ ἀποστόλου κατειργάσθη ἐν ὑμῖν *the signs that mark a true apostle were performed among you* (but you paid no attention) 2 Cor 12: 12. ἤδη μὲν οὖν ἥττημα *indeed it is already a defeat for you* (but you make it still worse) 1 Cor 6: 7.—μέν serves to emphasize the subject in clauses which contain a report made by the speaker concerning his own state of being, esp. intellectual or emotional; so ἐγὼ μ. Παῦλος 1 Th 2: 18. ἡ μ. εὐδοκία τῆς ἐμῆς καρδίας Ro 10: 1.

b. Somet. the contrast is actually expressed, but not in adversative form (Diod. S. 12, 70, 6 Ἀθηναῖοι μὲν οὖν ἐπιβουλεύσαντες τοῖς Βοιωτοῖς τοιαύτῃ συμφορᾷ περιέπεσον=the Ath., after plotting against the B., became involved [however] in such a disaster; Polyaenus 4, 3, 20 οἱ μέν..., Ἀλέξανδρος...; 2, 3, 2) τότε μέν...ἔπειτα (here we expect δέ) J 11: 6f. ἐφ' ὅσον μὲν οὖν εἰμι ἐγὼ ἐθνῶν ἀπόστολος *in so far, then, as I am an apostle to the Gentiles* Ro 11: 13 (the contrast follows in vs. 14); cf. 7: 12 and 13ff.

c. We notice anacoluthon in enumerations, either if they are broken off or if they are continued in some manner that is irregular in form πρῶτον μέν *in the first place* Ro 1: 8; 3: 2; 1 Cor 11: 18. πρῶτον μέν—ἔπειτα (X., Cyr. 7, 5, 1) Js 3: 17. In the prologue to Ac (s. λόγος 1aζ) the clause w. δέ corresponding to τὸν μὲν πρῶτον λόγον 1: 1 (Diod. S. 11, 1, 1 Ἡ μὲν οὖν πρὸ ταύτης βίβλος...τὸ τέλος ἔσχε τῶν πράξεων...ἐν ταύτῃ δέ...The preceding book...contained...; in this one, however...) may have been omitted through editorial activity acc. to Norden, Agn. Th. 311ff; 397.

d. μέν followed by καί is an inexact usage (Ael. Aristid. 31, 19 K.=11 p. 133 D.; Tituli Lyciae 325, 10ff Kalinka μέν...καί; POxy. 1153, 14 [I AD] two armbands ἐν μὲν σανδύκινον καὶ ἐν πορφυροῦν) Mk 4: 4ff; Lk 8: 5ff.

e. μέν οὖν denotes continuation (Bl-D. §451, 1 app.; Kühner-G. II 157f; Mayser II 3, 152f; Rob. 1151; 1191) *so, then* Lk 3: 18. Esp. in Ac: 1: 6, 18; 2: 41; 5: 41; 8: 25; 9: 31; 11: 19; 13: 4; 14: 3 (DSSharp, ET 44, '33, 528); 15: 3, 30; 16: 5; 17: 12, 17, 30; 19: 32; 23: 18, 22, 31; 25: 4; 26:

4, 9; 28: 5. Also 1 Cor 6: 4 (Bl-D. §450, 4); Hb 9: 1. εἰ μὲν οὖν *now if* Hb 7: 11; 8: 4.

f. μενοῦν and μενοῦνγε s. under these entries. M-M.

Μεννά, ὁ indecl. (in a series of indecl. names, hardly Μεννᾶ as gen. of Μεννᾶς) *Menna* in the genealogy of Jesus Lk 3: 31 (Μαινάν t.r.).*

μενοῦν Lk 11: 28; Ro 9: 20 v.l.; Phil 3: 8 v.l. and

μενοῦνγε (μενοῦν γε), particles used esp. in answers, to emphasize or correct (Bl-D. §450, 4; Rob. 1151f), even—contrary to class. usage—at the beginning of a clause (Phryn. 342 L.) *rather, on the contrary* (Soph., Aj. 1363; Pla., Crito 44Β; X., Cyr. 8, 3, 37) Lk 11: 28. *Indeed* Ro 10: 18. ἀλλὰ μενοῦνγε *more than that* Phil 3: 8. μενοῦνγε σὺ τίς εἶ; *on the contrary, who are you?* Ro 9: 20. M-M.*

μέντοι particle (trag., Hdt.+; inscr., pap., LXX; Jos., Ant. 14, 162, C. Ap. 1, 8; 13 al.).

1. *really, actually* Js 2: 8.—2. mostly adversative *though, to be sure, indeed* οὐδεὶς μ. εἶπεν *though no one said* J 4: 27; cf. 7: 13. οὐ μ. *though not, indeed not* 20: 5; 21: 4; Hs 6, 1, 6; Papias 2: 15. ὁ μ. θεμέλιος ἕστηκεν *nevertheless the firm foundation stands* 2 Ti 2: 19. ὅμως μ. *yet, despite that* (Kühner-G. II 280) J 12: 42.—Weakened to *but* Jd 8 (Bl-D. §450, 1; Rob. 1154; 1188). M-M.*

μένω (Hom.+; inscr., pap., LXX, Philo, Joseph.) impf. ἔμενον; fut. μενῶ; 1 aor. ἔμεινα, imper. μεῖνον (Hv 3, 1, 9); plpf. μεμενήκειν (1 J 2: 19; on the lack of augment s. Bl-D. §66, 1; Mlt.-H. 190).

1. intr. *remain, stay*—a. a pers. or thing remains where he or it is.

α. lit. *stay,* oft. in the special sense *live, dwell, lodge* (Horapollo 2, 49 μ. alternating w. οἰκέω) w. ἐν and the dat. (Ps.-Demosth. 43, 75 μ. ἐν τοῖς οἴκοις; Vi. Aesopi I c. 12 p. 259, 6) ἐν οἰκίᾳ Lk 8: 27; J 8: 35a; ἐν τ. οἴκῳ σου Lk 19: 5; cf. 10: 7. ἐν τῷ πλοίῳ *remain in the ship* Ac 27: 31. μ. ἐν τῇ Γαλιλαίᾳ J 7: 9.—Ac 9: 43; 16: 15; 18: 20; 20: 15 v.l.; 2 Ti 4: 20. κατὰ πόλιν *remain in the city* MPol 5: 1. W. an adv. of place ἐκεῖ Mt 10: 11; Mk 6: 10; Lk 9: 4; J 2: 12; 10: 40; 11: 54; Hs 9, 11, 7. ὧδε Mt 26: 38; Mk 14: 34; Hs 9, 11, 1. ποῦ μένεις; *where do you live?* J 1: 38; cf. vs. 39 (Sb 2639 ποῦ μένι θερμοῦθις; Pel.-Leg. 7, 27; Nicetas Eugen. 1, 230 H. ποῦ μένεις;). W. acc. of time (Jos., Ant. 1, 299) J 1: 39b; 4: 40b; 11: 6; Ac 21: 7; D 11: 5; 12: 2. W. time-indications of a different kind ἕως ἂν ἐξέλθητε Mt 10: 11. ὡς μῆνας τρεῖς Lk 1: 56. εἰς τὸν αἰῶνα J 8: 35b. W. prep. παρά τινι μ. *stay with someone* (Cebes 2; Jos., Ant. 20, 54) J 1: 39b; 4: 40a; Ac 18: 3 (*live with* is also poss.: Lucian, Timon 10); 21: 7, 8. παρ' ὑμῖν μένων *when I was (staying) with you* J 14: 25. πρός τινα *with someone* Ac 18: 3 D; D 12: 2. ἐπί τινα *remain on someone* J 1: 32f. σύν τινι *with someone* (4 Macc 18: 9) Lk 1: 56; 24: 29b. Also μ. μετά τινος (Gen 24: 55) Lk 24: 29a; Hs 9, 11, 1; 3; 6; 7. καθ' ἑαυτόν *live by oneself,* in one's own quarters Ac 28: 16 (of what is called in Lat. custodia libera). Of a corpse μ. ἐπὶ τοῦ σταυροῦ *stay (hanging) on the cross* J 19: 31. Of the branch: ἐν τῇ ἀμπέλῳ *remain on the vine,* i.e. not be cut off 15: 4b. Of stones μ. ἐν τῇ ὁδῷ *stay on the road* Hv 3, 2, 9. Of stones that *remain* in the divine structure, and are not removed Hs 9, 13, 4; 9. Also symbolically τὸ κάλυμμα ἐπὶ τῇ ἀναγνώσει τῆς παλαιᾶς διαθήκης μένει *the veil remains unlifted at the reading of the OT* (and hinders the right understanding of it) 2 Cor 3: 14.

β. fig., of someone who does not leave the realm or sphere in which he finds himself: *remain, continue, abide*

(Pla., Ep. 10 p. 358c μένε ἐν τοῖς ἤθεσιν, οἷσπερ καὶ νῦν μένεις; Alex. Aphr., An. II 1 p. 2, 15 μ. ἐν ταῖς ἀπορίαις = remain overcome by doubts; Jos., Ant. 4, 185; Test. Jos. 1: 3 ἐν τ. ἀληθείᾳ; Third Corinthians 3: 36) ἐν ἀγνείᾳ IPol 5: 2; cf. IEph 10: 3. ἐν τῇ διδαχῇ τοῦ Χριστοῦ *remain in the teaching of Christ* 2 J 9a; cf. b (2 Macc 8: 1 μ. ἐν τῷ Ἰουδαϊσμῷ). ἐν πίστει καὶ ἀγάπῃ 1 Ti 2: 15. μένε ἐν οἷς ἔμαθες *continue in what you have learned* 2 Ti 3: 14. ἐν τῷ λόγῳ τῷ ἐμῷ J 8: 31. μείνατε ἐν τῇ ἀγάπῃ τῇ ἐμῇ *continue in my love* 15: 9f; cf. 1 J 4: 16. ἐν τῷ φωτί 2: 10. ἐν τῷ θανάτῳ 3: 14. ἐν τῇ σκοτίᾳ J 12: 46. The phrase μ. ἔν τινι is a favorite of J to denote an inward, enduring personal communion. So of God in his relation to Christ ὁ πατὴρ ἐν ἐμοὶ μένων *the Father, who abides in me* J 14: 10. Of the Christians in their relation to Christ J 6: 56; 15: 4a, c, 5–7; 1 J 2: 6, 24c. Of Christ in his relation to the Christians J 15: 4a, 5 (Gdspd., Probs. 112–15). Of the Christians in their relationship to God 1 J 2: 24c, 27f; 3: 6, 24a; 4: 13. Of God in his relation to the Christians 1 J 3: 24; 4: 12f, 15.—Vice versa, of someth. that remains in someone; likew. in Johannine usage: of the word of God 1 J 2: 14. Of the words of Christ J 15: 7b; cf. 1 J 2: 24a, b. Of the anointing fr. heaven vs. 27. Of the love of God 1 J 3: 17. Of the seed of God 3: 9. Of truth 2 J 2. The possession is shown to be permanent by the expr. ἔχειν τι μένον ἐν ἑαυτῷ *have someth. continually, permanently* 1 J 3: 15; the word of God J 5: 38. Instead of μ. ἔν τινι also μ. παρά τινι *remain with someone*: of the Spirit of truth J 14: 17. On the other hand, of the wrath of God, μένει ἐπ' αὐτὸν *it remains upon him* 3: 36.— GPercorara, De verbo 'manere' ap. Jo.: Div. Thomas Piac. 40, '37, 159–71.

b. a pers. or thing remains in the state in which he or it is found (Lucian, Laps. 16 ἐν τῇ τάξει μ.) 1 Cor 7: 20, 24. μένει ἱερεὺς εἰς τὸ διηνεκές *he remains a priest forever* Hb 7: 3. αὐτὸς μόνος μένει *it remains alone* J 12: 24. μενέτω ἄγαμος 1 Cor 7: 11. ἀσάλευτος Ac 27: 41. πιστός 2 Ti 2: 13. ἀόρατος Dg 6: 4. μ. μετά τινος *remain in fellowship w. someone* 1 J 2: 19. Of one who has divorced his wife *remain by himself, remain unmarried* Hm 4, 1, 6; 10; 4, 4, 2. οὐχὶ μένον σοὶ ἔμενεν; *was it (the piece of ground) not yours, as long as it remained (unsold)?* Ac 5: 4 (cf. 1 Macc 15: 7 and OHoltzmann, ZKG 14, 1893, 327–36).—W. adv. οὕτως μ. *remain as one is* (i.e., unmarried) 1 Cor 7: 40. ἁγνῶς B 2: 3. μ. ὡς ἐγώ *remain as I am* 1 Cor 7: 8.

c. remain, last, persist, continue to live—**a.** of pers. (Ps 9: 8 ὁ κύριος εἰς τ. αἰῶνα μ.; 101: 13; Da 6: 27) ὁ Χριστὸς μ. εἰς τὸν αἰῶνα *Christ remains (here) forever* J 12: 34; cf. Hb 7: 24; 1 J 2: 17. Pregnant *remain (alive), be alive* (Epict. 3, 24, 97; Diog. L. 7, 174; Achilles Tat. 8, 10. μένειν ἐν τῷ ζῆν Plut., Mor. 1042D; Eccl 7: 15) J 21: 22f; 1 Cor 15: 6; Phil 1: 25; Rv 17: 10.

β. of things (Maximus Tyr. 4, 8b and Polyaenus 7, 34: γῆ μένει; Socrat., Ep. 31[=33]; Hierocles 15 p. 454 ὁ πόνος παρῆλθεν, τὸ καλὸν μένει) τι ἔμενεν ἂν μέχρι τῆς σήμερον *it would have lasted until today* Mt 11: 23. μένουσα πόλις *a permanent city* Hb 13: 14.—ἡ φιλαδελφία μενέτω *continue* 13: 1 (JCambier, Salesianum 11, '49, 62–96).—J 9: 41; 15: 16. εἰ τὸ ἔργον μενεῖ *if the work survives* 1 Cor 3: 14. ὕπαρξις Hb 10: 34. δικαιοσύνη 2 Cor 9: 9 (Ps 111: 9). ἡ κατ' ἐκλογὴν πρόθεσις τοῦ θεοῦ Ro 9: 11 (of God's counsel Ps 32: 11). λόγος θεοῦ *endure* 1 Pt 1: 23 (cf. 1 Esdr 4: 38 ἡ ἀλήθεια μένει). τ. ῥῆμα κυρίου μένει εἰς τ. αἰῶνα vs. 25 (Is 40: 8). ἡ βρῶσις ἡ μένουσα εἰς ζωὴν αἰώνιον J 6: 27. τὸ μένον *what is permanent* (Philo, Leg. All. 3, 100.—Opp. τὸ καταργούμενον) 2 Cor 3: 11. μένει πίστις ἐλπὶς ἀγάπη

1 Cor 13: 13 (WMarxsen, D. 'Bleiben' im 1 Cor 13: 13, OCullmann-Festschr., '72, 223–9; on the eschatology cf. Enoch 97, 6–10 and s. the lit. on ἀγάπη I 1a.—For the contrast πίπτει [vs. 8]—μένει cf. Pla., Crat. 44 p. 440A εἰ μεταπίπτει πάντα χρήματα καὶ μηδὲν μένει).

2. trans. *wait for, await*—**a.** of pers.: *wait for* someone who is arriving (Hom.; Thu. 4, 124, 4; X., An. 4, 4, 20; Pla., Leg. 8 p. 833c; Polyb. 4, 8, 4; Tob 2: 2 BA; 2 Macc 7: 30; Jos., Ant. 13, 19) τινά w. the place indicated ἔμενον ἡμᾶς ἐν Τρωάδι *they were waiting for us in Troas* Ac 20: 5.

b. of dangers, misfortunes, etc. that *await* or *threaten* someone (trag.; Epigr. Gr. 654, 9 κἀμὲ μένει τὸ θανεῖν; Sib. Or. 4, 114 v.l. σὲ) θλίψεις με μένουσιν Ac 20: 23.— Of the 112 passages in which μένω occurs in the NT, 66 are found in the Johannine writings (gosp. 40, 1 J 23, 2 J three).—JHeise, Bleiben: Menein in d. Johan. Schr., '67; FHauck, TW IV 578–93: μένω and related words. M-M. B. 836. **

μερίζω Att. fut. μεριῶ 1 Cl 16: 13 (LXX); 1 aor. ἐμέρισα, pf. μεμέρικα, pass. μεμέρισμαι; 1 aor. mid. inf. μερίσασθαι; 1 aor. ἐμερίσθην (X. +; inscr., pap., LXX, En., Ep. Arist.; Philo, Poster. Cai. 92 [pass.]; Joseph.; Sib. Or. 3, 107) *divide, separate.*

1. *divide* into its component parts—**a.** act. and pass., fig. (Procop. Soph., Ep. 17 ψυχὴ μεριζομένη) μεμέρισται ὁ Χριστός; *has Christ been divided?* 1 Cor 1: 13 (Third Corinthians 3: 10; GHWhitaker, Chrysostom on 1 Cor 1: 13: JTS 15, '14, 254–7). *Divide* ὑμᾶς IMg 6: 2. βασιλεία, πόλις, οἰκία μερισθεῖσα καθ' ἑαυτῆς *a kingdom, city, family divided against itself, disunited* Mt 12: 25. ἐφ' ἑαυτὸν ἐμερίσθη *he is disunited* vs. 26; cf. Mk 3: 24–6. Abs. ὁ γαμήσας μεμέρισται *the married man* (i.e., his attention) *is divided*, since he tries to please the Lord and his wife at the same time 1 Cor 7: 34.

b. mid. μερίζεσθαί τι μετά τινος *share someth. with someone* (Demosth. 34, 18; cf. Jos., Ant. 1, 169 τὶ πρός τινα) Lk 12: 13.

2.—**a.** *distribute* τί τισιν *someth. to some people* (PTebt. 302, 12; POxy. 713, 29; Pr 19: 14) τοὺς δύο ἰχθύας πᾶσιν Mk 6: 41. Without dat. τῶν ἰσχυρῶν μεριεῖ σκῦλα *he will distribute the spoils of the strong* 1 Cl 16: 13 (Is 53: 12).

b. *deal out, assign, apportion* τί τινι *someth. to someone* (Polyb. 11, 28, 9; Diod. S. 13, 22, 8 μ. τινὶ τὸν ἔλεον; UPZ 19, 20 [163 Bc]; 146, 38; Sb 8139, 19f [inscr. I Bc, of Isis] πᾶσι μερίζεις, οἷσι θέλεις, ζωὴν παντοδαπῶν ἀγαθῶν; PGM 13, 635 μερίσόν μοι ἀγαθά; Sir 45: 20; Ep. Arist. 224 [θεός]) ἑκάστῳ μέτρον πίστεως Ro 12: 3. κατὰ τὸ μέτρον τοῦ κανόνος οὗ ἐμέρισεν ἡμῖν ὁ θεὸς μέτρου *according to the measure of the limit* (or *area*) *which God has assigned us* 2 Cor 10: 13. ᾧ δεκάτην ἀπὸ πάντων ἐμέρισεν Ἀβραάμ *to whom Abraham apportioned a tenth of everything* Hb 7: 2. W. dat. of the pers. alone (En. 27, 4) ἑκάστῳ ὡς μεμέρικεν ὁ κύριος 1 Cor 7: 17. M-M. *

μέριμνα, ης, ἡ (Hes.; Vett. Val. 131, 3; 6; 271, 3; PGiess. 19, 8; 22, 11; Ep. Arist. 271; LXX.—In LXX the pl. only Da 11: 26, as Hes., Op. 178 al.; PRyl. 28, 219) *anxiety, worry, care* πᾶσα ἡ μ. ὑμῶν *all your anxiety* 1 Pt 5: 7 (Ps 54: 23); cf. Hv 3, 11, 3; 4, 2, 4f. W. obj. gen. μ. πασῶν τῶν ἐκκλησιῶν *anxiety about all the churches* 2 Cor 11: 28. μ. τοῦ βίου *the worries of life* (in case our β. belongs w. μ.—UPZ 20, 29 [163 Bc] τὴν τ. βίου μέριμναν) Lk 8: 14. Also μ. βιωτικαί 21: 34. ἡ μ. τοῦ αἰῶνος *the worry of the world* i.e. of the present age Mt 13: 22; pl. Mk 4: 19. M-M. B. 1092. *

μεριμνάω fut. μεριμνήσω; 1 aor. ἐμερίμνησα (since Soph., Oed. Rex 1124; X., Pla.; Ep. Arist. 296; Sib. Or. 3, 222; 234).

1. *have anxiety, be anxious, be (unduly) concerned* (PTebt. 315, 9 [II AD] γράφω ὅπως μὴ μεριμνῆς; Ps 37: 19) μηδέν *have no anxiety* Phil 4: 6 (WHWeeda, Filipp. 4: 6 en 7: ThSt 34, '16, 326–35). περί τινος Mt 6: 28; Lk 12: 26; Dg 9: 6. W. indir. question foll.: πῶς ἢ τί λαλήσητε *about how you are to speak or what you are to say* Mt 10: 19; cf. Lk 12: 11. W. dat. and a question foll. μὴ μεριμνᾶτε τῇ ψυχῇ (dat. of advantage: *for your life*, Bl-D. §188, 1; Rob. 539) ὑμῶν τί φάγητε Mt 6: 25; Lk 12: 22. Abs. Mt 6: 31; in ptc. (s. Mlt. 230) Mt 6: 27; Lk 12: 25. Beside θορυβάζεσθαι περὶ πολλά of the distracting cares of housekeeping 10: 41 (the text is uncertain; s. Zahn and EKlostermann, also Strähl, Krit. u. exeget. Beleuchtung von Lk 10: 41f; SchThZ 4, 1887, 116–23). εἰς τὴν αὔριον *do not worry about tomorrow* Mt 6: 34a.

2. *care for, be concerned about* τι someth. (Soph., loc. cit.; cf. Bar 3: 18) τὰ τοῦ κυρίου *the Lord's work* 1 Cor 7: 32; 34a. τὰ τοῦ κόσμου vss. 33, 34b. τὰ περί τινος *someone's welfare* Phil 2: 20. τὰ ἑαυτῆς *its own affairs* Mt 6: 34b (t.r.). This pass. is textually uncertain; the newer editions read, after אB, ἡ αὔριον μεριμνήσει ἑαυτῆς *will worry about itself* (It. 'sibi'.—Bl-D. §176, 2 app.; Rob. 509). τί ὑπέρ τινος· ἵνα τὸ αὐτὸ ὑπὲρ ἀλλήλων μεριμνῶσιν τὰ μέλη *that the parts may have the same concern for one another* 1 Cor 12: 25.—RBultmann, TW IV 593–8: μεριμνάω and related words. M-M.*

μερίς, ίδος, ἡ (Antipho, Thu.+; inscr., pap., LXX, Philo; Jos., Ant. 11, 292, Vi. 36; Test. 12 Patr.).

1. *part of a whole that has been divided* (Pla., Soph. p. 266A; Diod. S. 15, 31, 2; 15, 64, 1 [where comparison with 15, 63, 4 τέτταρα μέρη—ἡ πρώτη μερίς shows that it is not necessary to assume that there is a difference in the meanings of these word-forms]. In inscr. and pap. oft.= *district*: Dit., Or. 177, 9; 179, 8; PPetr. III 32[r], 3 τῆς Θεμίστου μερίδος; BGU 975, 6 [45 AD]; PTebt. 302, 4; 315, 13; Diod. S. 1, 54, 3; Josh 18: 6). The wording of Ac 16: 12 in describing Philippi ἥτις ἐστὶν πρώτη τῆς μερίδος Μακεδονίας πόλις (אAC.—B has the article before Μακ. instead of before μερ. HLP have it in both positions) is difficult because of τῆς μερίδος. The transl. *leading city of the district of Macedonia* (in question) (most recently Beyer, Steinmann, Bauernfeind, RSV) is tolerable only through lack of a better one. As far as the form is concerned, the article is lacking w. πρώτη, and as far as subject matter goes, Philippi was not the capital city (which πρώτη means in such a context: Ps.-Scylax, Peripl. 35 [BFabricius 1878]; schol. on Pind., Ol. 8, 1h; cf. 6, 144g; Eunap. 7; 96; Procop., Aedif. 5, 4, 18 μητρόπολις . . . οὕτω πόλιν τ. πρώτην τοῦ ἔθνους καλοῦσι 'Ρωμαῖοι) either of the province of Macedonia or of any of its districts. Blass favors the earlier conjecture of Johannes Clericus πρώτης μερίδος τῆς Μακεδονίας *of the first district of Macedonia*, w. ref. to the fact that the Romans (Livy 45, 29) divided Macedonia into four μερίδες= districts in 167 BC (so also Hoennicke, Preuschen, Wlh., Zahn; Field, Notes 124; EHaupt, Gefangenschaftsbriefe⁷ '02, 83f; Belser; Zürcher Bibel '31; Haenchen. Cf. AC Clark and JAOLarsen s.v. κεφαλή 2b, end.—If the restoration of the apparently damaged text should result in a wording that would make it possible for πρώτη to refer to the progress of a journey, we might compare Arrian, Anab. 4, 13 ἡ πρώτη καθ' ὁδὸν πόλις; Appian, Bell. Civ. 2, 35 §137 Ariminum ἐστὶν 'Ιταλίας πρώτη [i.e., πόλις] μετὰ τὴν Γαλατίαν= the first city in Italy after

[leaving] Gaul; Ps.-Scylax §67: from Thessaly the πρώτη πόλις Μακεδονίας is 'Ηράκλειον.—Linguistically πρ. πόλ. can, of course, be understood of time as well, and can mean the first city in connection with which someth. happens [Diod. S. 12, 67, 2 Acanthus was the first city—πρ. πόλ.—to revolt from Athens]).

2. *share, portion* (Demosth. 43, 82; Plut., Ages. 17, 5; Lucian, De Merc. Cond. 26; Vett. Val. 345, 16; Dit., Syll.³ 1013, 4; BGU 996 III, 1; PLond. 880, 18ff; POxy. 1482, 21; LXX) τὴν ἀγαθὴν μ. ἐκλέγεσθαι *choose the better portion* Lk 10: 42 (fig., of food? Cf. Mft., transl., and s. Gen 43: 34; 1 Km 9: 23, but against him TGillieson, ET 59, '47/'48, 111f. For other reff. Field, Notes 63f; HAlmqvist, Plutarch u. d. NT '46, 65). μ. κυρίου *the Lord's portion* 1 Cl 29: 2 (Dt 32: 9); cf. 30: 1. τίς μερὶς πιστῷ μετὰ ἀπίστου; *what has a believer in common with an unbeliever?* 2 Cor 6: 15. Sim. μετὰ μοιχῶν τὴν μερίδα σου ἐτίθεις *you cast your lot w. adulterers* 1 Cl 35: 8 (Ps 49: 18). οὐκ ἔστιν σοι μ. οὐδὲ κλῆρος ἐν τῷ λόγῳ τούτῳ *you have neither share nor lot in this matter* Ac 8: 21 (cf. Dt 12: 12 οὐκ ἔστιν αὐτῷ μ. οὐδὲ κλῆρος μεθ' ὑμῶν.—μ. καὶ κλῆρος also in Philo, Plant. 60.—μ. ἐν as 2 Km 20: 1). ἡ μερὶς τοῦ κλήρου τῶν ἁγίων *a share in the inheritance of the saints, the holy ones* (cf. IQS 11, 7f) Col 1: 12. M-M.*

μερισμός, οῦ, ὁ (Pla.+; inscr., pap., LXX, Philo; Jos., C. Ap. 2, 203).

1. *division, separation*—a. ἄχρι μερισμοῦ ψυχῆς καὶ πνεύματος *to the separation of soul and spirit*, i.e. *so as to separate soul and spirit* Hb 4: 12.

b. in Ign. w. ref. to the heretics, who have separated themselves: *(the) division* partly as action, partly as result IPhld 2: 1; 3: 1; 8: 1. Pl. ISm 7: 2. ὥσπερ εἰδότα τὸν μ. τινων *as one who knew of the division caused by certain people* IPhld 7: 2.

2. *distribution, apportionment* (Aeneas Tact. 1, 27; Polyb. 31, 10, 1; Dit., Syll.³ 1017, 17 [III BC]; Josh 11: 23; Philo, Poster. Cai. 90) ἁγίου πνεύματος μερισμοί *distributions of the Holy Spirit*, i.e. of the various gifts proceeding from the Holy Spirit Hb 2: 4. M-M.*

μεριστής, οῦ, ὁ (Suppl. Epigr. Gr. VIII 551, 25 [I BC]; Pollux 4, 176; Vett. Val. 62, 4; PGM 13, 638 epithet of Sarapis) *divider, arbitrator* Lk 12: 14 (omitted in v.l.). M-M.*

μέρος, ους, τό (Pind., Hdt.+; inscr., pap., LXX, Ep. Arist., Philo, Joseph.).

1. *part, in contrast to the whole*—a. gener. (Ocellus Luc. c. 12 τὸ πᾶν ἢ μέρος τι τοῦ παντός; Alex. Aphr., An. II 1 p. 13, 16 μ. ἐν ὅλῳ; Gen 47: 24; Philo, Spec. Leg. 3, 189 τ. ὅλου κ. τῶν μερῶν al.) w. the gen. of the whole τὸ ἐπιβάλλον μ. τῆς οὐσίας *the part of the property that falls to me* Lk 15: 12 (Dit., Syll.³ 346, 36 τὸ μέρος τὸ ἐπιβάλλον; 1106, 80). μ. τι τοῦ ἀγροῦ *a part of the field* Hs 5, 2, 2. δύο μέρη τῆς ῥάβδου *two thirds of the stick* (Thu. 1, 104 τῆς Μέμφιδος τῶν δύο μερῶν πρὸς τὸ τρίτον μέρος; Dit., Syll.³ 975, 24f) Hs 8, 1, 12f; cf. 8, 5, 3ff; 8, 8, 4; 8, 9, 1. τὸ πλεῖστον μ. αὐτῶν Hs 8, 2, 9; cf. 9, 7, 4 and 8, 1, 16. Also without gen., when it is plain fr. the context how much of a contrast betw. part and whole is involved μὴ ἔχον μέρος τι σκοτεινόν *with no dark part* Lk 11: 36; cf. J 19: 23 (Jos., Ant. 1, 172 μέρη τέσσαρα ποιήσαντες); Ac 5: 2; Rv 16: 19; Hv 4, 3, 4f. Of the Christians ἐκλογῆς μ. *a chosen portion* fr. among all mankind 1 Cl 29: 1.

b. specialized uses—a. *component part, element* τινὰ μέρη ἔχουσιν τ. ἀνομίας *they still have certain elements of lawlessness* Hv 3, 6, 4b.

β. of parts of the body (Diod. S. 32, 12, 1 τὰ τοῦ σώματος μέρη; Dio Chrys. 16[33], 62; Plut., Mor. 38A μ. τ. σώματος; Artem. 3, 51 al.; Herodian 8, 4, 10; PRyl. 145, 14 [38 AD]; PGM 4, 2390; 2392) fig., of the body whose head is Christ Eph 4: 16 (on the text cf. μέλος 3; for the idea σῶμα, end).

γ. τὰ μέρη *the parts* of a country, *region, district* (Herodian 6, 5, 7; Jos., Ant. 12, 234; Bl-D. §141, 2; cf. Rob. 408) τῆς Γαλιλαίας Mt 2: 22. τὰ μ. τῆς Λιβύης τῆς κατὰ Κυρήνην Ac 2: 10; cf. 20: 2. Also of a district in or around a city (cf. UPZ 180b, 8 [113 BC] οἰκίας τῆς οὔσης ἐν τῷ ἀπὸ νότου μέρει Διὸς πόλεως) τὰ μ. Τύρου καὶ Σιδῶνος *the district of Tyre and Sidon* Mt 15: 21; cf. 16: 13; Mk 8: 10; J 6: 1 D; Ac 7: 43 D. τὰ ἀνωτερικὰ μέρη *the upper= inland regions, interior* (cf. PHamb. 54 I, 14 τὰ ἄνω μέρη of the upper Nile valley) Ac 19: 1.—Eph 4: 9 (cf. κατώτερος).

δ. *side* (Diod. S. 2, 9, 3 ἐφ᾿ ἑκάτερον μέρος= on both sides; Ex 32: 15; 1 Macc 9: 12) Hs 9, 2, 3. τὰ δεξιὰ μ. *on the right side,* τὰ ἀριστερὰ μ. *on the left side* v 3, 1, 9; 3, 2. 1. Of a vessel τὰ δεξιὰ μ. τοῦ πλοίου *the right side of the boat* as the lucky side J 21: 6. τὰ ἐξώτερα μ. τῆς οἰκοδομῆς *the outside of the building* Hs 9, 9, 3.

ε. *piece* ἰχθύος ὀπτοῦ μέρος *a piece of broiled fish* Lk 24: 42.—μ. τι λαμβάνειν *take a portion* Hv 3, 1, 6.

ζ. *party* (Jos., Bell. 1, 143; POxy. 1278, 24; PFlor. 47, 17; PLond. 1028, 18 τοῦ πρασίνου μέρους= 'of the green party') Ac 23: 6. τινὲς τ. γραμματέων τ. μέρους τ. Φαρισαίων vs. 9.

η. *branch* or *line of business* (cf. PFlor. 89, 2 after Preisigke, Berichtigungsliste '22, 147 τὰ μέρη τῆς διοικήσεως= 'the branches of the administration') Ac 19: 27.

θ. *matter, affair* (Menand., Epitr. 17, Per. 107 J.; Diod. S. 2, 27, 1; Περὶ ὕψους 12, 5 [μέρη=objects]; Jos., Ant. 15, 61 τούτῳ τῷ μέρει; PRyl. 127, 12 [29 AD] ἀναζητῆσαι ὑπὲρ τοῦ μέρους= 'begin an investigation concerning the matter') ἐν τούτῳ τῷ μέρει *in this case, in this matter* (cf. Polyb. 18, 18, 2 τ. πίστιν ἐν τούτῳ τῷ μέρει διαφυλάττειν) 2 Cor 3: 10; 9: 3 (s. also ἐν μέρει in c below). Cf. 1 Pt 4: 16 v.l.

c. used w. prepositions: ἀνὰ μέρος *one after the other, in succession* (s. ἀνά 2) 1 Cor 14: 27.—ἀπὸ μέρους *in part* (Dio Chrys. 28[45], 3; Ael. Aristid. 32, 4 K.=12 p. 135 D.; Ptolem., Apotel. 2, 10, 2; Epict. 1, 27, 17 δι᾿ ὅλων ἢ ἀ. μ.; PRyl. 133, 17; BGU 1201, 15 [2 AD]; PTebt. 402, 2; POxy. 1681, 9) πώρωσις ἀ. μ. *a partial hardening* Ro 11: 25. τολμηροτέρως . . . ἀ. μ. *very boldly on some points* 15: 15. καθὼς ἐπέγνωτε ἡμᾶς ἀ. μ. *as you have understood us in part* 2 Cor 1: 14. Also *for a while*: ἀ. μ. ἐμπλησθῆναί τινος *enjoy someone's company for a while* Ro 15: 24; cf. 2 Cor 2: 5 *in some degree.*—ἐκ μέρους *in part, individually* (Ael. Aristid. 54 p. 695 D.; 698; Dit., Syll.³ 852, 30 . . . ὅλη, ἐκ μέρους δέ . . . ; PLond. 1166, 14 [42 AD]; BGU 538, 33; PRyl. 233, 6; Philo, Mos. 2, 1 al.) *individually* 1 Cor 12: 27. ἐκ μ. γινώσκειν *know in part* 13: 9a, 12; cf. vs. 9b. τὸ ἐκ μ. *what is 'in part'= imperfect* vs. 10.—ἐν μέρει *in the matter of, with regard to* (Antig. Car. 124; Diod. S. 20, 58, 5; Plut., Mor. 102E; Horapollo 1, 57 ἐν τροφῆς μέρει= 'as food'; Dialekt-Inschr. 5185, 30 [Crete]; ἐν χάριτος μέρει; Philo, Det. Pot. Ins. 5 ἐν μέρει λόγου al.) ἐν μέρει ἑορτῆς *with regard to a festival* Col 2: 16 (s. bθ above).—κατὰ μέρος *part by part, in detail* (inscr. [s. Dit., Syll.³ ind. IV p. 444a]; PTebt. 6, 24) περὶ ὧν οὐκ ἔστιν νῦν λέγειν κατὰ μέρος (κ. μ. of the detailed treatment of a subj. as Pla., Theaet. 157B, Soph. 246C;

Polyb. 1, 4, 6; 3, 19, 11; 3, 28, 4; 10, 27, 7 λέγειν κ. μ.; Ptolem., Apotel. 2, 11, 7; 2 Macc 2: 30; Jos., Ant. 12, 245) *point by point* Hb 9: 5.—παρὰ μέρος *to one side* (Appian, Liby. 14 §55 γιγνόμενος παρὰ μ.= going to one side, Bell. Civ. 5, 81 §345; PGM 13, 438 βάλε παρὰ μέρος= 'put to one side') ὁ λίθος ὑπεχώρησε παρὰ μ. *the stone went back to one side* GP 9: 37.

d. as adv. acc. μέρος τι *in part, partly* (Thu. 2, 64; 4, 30, 1; X., Eq. 1, 12; Dit., Syll.³ 976, 65; 1240, 8 ἤ τι μέρος ἢ σύμπας; 3 Km 12: 31) 1 Cor 11: 18; τὸ πλεῖστον μ. *for the most part* (Menand., fgm. 739; Diod. S. 22, 10, 5) Hs 8, 5, 6; 8, 10, 1. τὸ πλεῖον μ. *for the greater part* v 3, 6, 4a.

2. *share* (trag.+) μ. τι μεταδοῦναι ἀπό τινος *give a share of someth.* B 1: 5 (on μέρος ἀπό τινος cf. PStrassb. 19, 5 [105 AD] τοῦ ὑπάρχοντος αὐτῷ μέρους ἑνὸς ἀπὸ μερῶν ἐννέα). ἔχειν μ. ἔν τινι *have a share in someth.* (cf. Synes., Ep. 58 p. 203A οὐκ ἔστι τῷ διαβόλῳ μέρος ἐν παραδείσῳ) Rv 20: 6 (Dalman, Worte 103f). ἀφελεῖ ὁ θεὸς τὸ μέρος αὐτοῦ ἀπὸ τοῦ ξύλου τῆς ζωῆς 22: 19.— *Place* (Appian, Bell. Civ. 1, 34 §154 ἐν ὑπηκόων ἀντὶ κοινωνῶν εἶναι μέρει= to be in the place of subjects instead of partners) τὸ μ. αὐτῶν ἐν τ. λίμνῃ *their place is in the lake* Rv 21: 8. ἔχειν μ. μετά τινος *have a place with someone* J 13: 8. τὸ μ. τινος μετὰ τῶν ὑποκριτῶν τιθέναι *assign someone a place among the hypocrites* Mt 24: 51; cf. Lk 12: 46. μετ᾿ αὐτῶν μοι τὸ μ. γένοιτο σχεῖν ἐν (v.l. παρὰ) θεῷ *may I have my place with them in* (or *with*) *God* IPol 6: 1. τοῦ λαβεῖν μ. ἐν ἀριθμῷ τῶν μαρτύρων MPol 14: 2. M-M. B. 934.*

μεσάζω (Hippocr.+; Diod. S. 1, 32, 9; PSI 151, 6; Wsd 18: 14) *be in* or *at the middle* J 7: 14 𝔓⁶⁶ et al. (Ps.-Callisth. 3, 26, 7 p. 127, 2 θέρους μεσάζοντος); s. μεσόω.*

μεσημβρία, ας, ἡ (Aeschyl., Hdt.+; inscr., pap., LXX, Philo, Joseph.) *midday, noon.*

1. of time (Aeschyl., Hdt. et al.; PRyl. 27, 66; PGM 7, 157. So as a rule in LXX; Jos., Ant. 11, 155) Ac 22: 6; GP 5: 15. κατὰ μεσημβρίαν Ac 8: 26 *about noon* (Philo, Somn. 1, 202; so EbNestle, StKr 65, 1892, 335–7; Wendt, HHoltzmann, BWeiss, Schlatter, Hoennicke, Knopf, Steinmann, Beyer).

2. of place *the south* (Hdt. 1, 6; 142; 2, 8 al.; Dit., Syll.³ 972, 96; 1112, 26; Da 8: 4, 9; Philo; Jos., Bell. 5, 505; Sib. Or. 3, 26) as the position of the sun at midday κατὰ μεσημβρίαν Ac 8: 26 *toward the south* (so Bl-D. §253, 5 app.; Preuschen, Zahn, Felten, Bauernfeind, Haenchen, Engl. transl. gener.—OHoltzmann is undecided betw. 1 and 2). M-M. B. 873; 996.*

μεσιτεύω 1 aor. ἐμεσίτευσα *mediate, act as surety* (Aristot.+; Dit., Or. 437, 76 [I BC]; 79; BGU 906, 7; PRainer 1, 19; 206, 13; Philo) intr. (Jos., Ant. 7, 193; 16, 118 'act as mediator, peacemaker') *guarantee* ὅρκῳ *by means of an oath* Hb 6: 17. M-M.*

μεσίτης, ου, ὁ (since Polyb. 28, 17, 8; Ps.-Lucian, Amor. 47 θεὸν μεσίτην λαβόντες; pap.; Job 9: 33; Philo; Jos., Ant. 4, 133; 16, 24. On this many-sided t.t. of Hellenistic legal language cf. LMitteis, Her. 30, 1895, 616ff; JBehm, D. Begriff Διαθήκη im NT '12, 77ff w. numerous exx.; s. lit. in JModrzejewski, Private Arbitration in Greco-Roman Egypt, Journ. of Juristic Papyrology 6, '52, 247 n. 79) *mediator, arbitrator,* one who mediates betw. two parties to remove a disagreement or reach a common goal. Of Christ (Mithras as μεσίτης: Plut., Is. et Osir. 46) w. gen. of the pers. betw. whom he mediates μ. θεοῦ καὶ ἀνθρώπων *mediator between God and man* (cf. Test. Dan 6: 2)

1 Ti 2: 5; w. gen. of the thing that he mediates: κρείττονος Hb 8: 6, καινῆς 9: 15, νέας διαθήκης 12: 24 (s. διαθήκη. Ascension of Moses p. 15, end, Clemen [= Kl. T. 10], Moses calls himself τῆς διαθήκης μεσίτης). Of the law διαταγεὶς δι' ἀγγέλων ἐν χειρὶ μεσίτου ordered through the angels, by the hand of a mediator Gal 3: 19 (Moses, as mediator betw. God and the people, called μεσίτης e.g. Philo, Mos. 2, 166, Somn. 1, 143). The sense of vs. 20, ὁ δὲ μ. ἑνὸς οὐκ ἔστιν an intermediary does not exist for one party alone, is disputed. It prob. means that the activity of an intermediary implies the existence of more than one party, and hence may be unsatisfactory because it must result in a compromise. The presence of an intermediary would prevent the εἶς θεός from attaining his purpose in the law without let or hindrance.—NKZ 39, '28, 21-4; 549-52; 552f; HStegmann, BZ 22, '34, 30-42; AOepke, TW IV, 602-29. M-M.*

μεσονύκτιον, ου, τό (subst. neut. of μεσονύκτιος [Pind. +]; as a noun Hippocr.+; Diod. S. 20, 48, 6; Charito 1, 9, 1; POxy. 1768, 6; LXX. The spelling μεσανύκτιον is not well attested [POxy. 1768, 6—III AD. Cf. Bl-D. §35, 2; Mlt.-H. 73]. On its formation s. Bl-D. §123, 1; Mlt.-H. 341; Phryn. p. 53 L.) midnight μεσονύκτιον acc. of time at midnight Mk 13: 35 (Hippocr. VII p. 72 Littré; Ps 118: 62.—PGM 13, 680 τὸ μεσονύκτιον). Also the gen. (which is read in the Hippocr.-pass. just quoted, by the edition of Kühn II p. 260; cf. Bl-D. §186, 2) μεσονυκτίου Lk 11: 5. κατὰ τὸ μ. about midnight (Strabo 2, 5, 42) Ac 16: 25. μέχρι μεσονυκτίου until midnight 20: 7 (on the omission of the article s. Bl-D. §255, 3; Rob. 792). M-M.*

Μεσοποταμία, ας, ἡ (subst. fem. of μεσοποτάμιος, α, ον = 'located betw. rivers'. ἡ μεσοποταμία, sc. χώρα = 'the land betw. rivers'. [Polyb. 5, 44, 6; Strabo 11, 12, 2], esp. that betw. the Euphrates and Tigris) Mesopotamia (Diod. S. 2, 11, 2; 18, 6, 3; Appian, Syr. 48 §246; 53 §269; Arrian, Anab. 3, 7, 3; 7, 7, 3; Polyaenus, Exc. 9, 2; Ptolem., Apotel. 2, 3, 22; 28; Dit., Or. 54, 18; LXX, Philo, Joseph.; Test. Judah 9: 1; 10: 1) Ac 2: 9. In the narrative about Abraham (cf. Gen 24: 10) 7: 2.*

μέσος, η, ον (Hom.+; inscr., pap., LXX, En., Ep. Arist., Philo, Joseph., Test. 12 Patr.) middle, in the middle.

1. as adj. ὁ μέσος αὐτῶν ἀνήρ the man in their midst Hs 9, 12, 7. μέσης νυκτός at midnight (3 Km 3: 20.—Bl-D. §270, 2; Rob. 495; Lobeck, Phryn. p. 53; 54; 465) Mt 25: 6. ἡμέρας μέσης at midday (Jos., Bell. 1, 651, Ant. 17, 155) Ac 26: 13. ἐν μέσοις τοῖς ὀργάνοις τοῦ διαβόλου in the midst of the tools of the devil 2 Cl 18: 2 (cf. Gen 2: 9 ἐν μέσῳ τῷ παραδείσῳ). εἰς μέσην τὴν οἰκοδομήν into the middle of the building Hs 9, 7, 5; cf. 9, 8, 2; 4; 6 (cf. Philo, Fuga 49 εἰς μέσον τὸν ποταμόν; Jos., Ant. 4, 80 εἰς μέσον τὸ πῦρ. ἐσταύρωσαν . . . μέσον τὸν Ἰησοῦν they crucified Jesus between (them) J 19: 18. ἐσχίσθη τὸ καταπέτασμα μέσον the curtain was torn in two Lk 23: 45 (cf. Artem. 4, 30 τὸ ἱμάτιον μέσον ἐρρωγέναι). ἐλάκησεν μέσος Ac 1: 18 (cf. Aristoph., Ran. 955). ἐκάθητο ὁ Πέτρος μέσος αὐτῶν Peter was sitting among them Lk 22: 55 (cf. Jos., Ant. 9, 107). μέσος ὑμῶν στήκει J 1: 26 (Pla., Rep. 330β, Pol. 303α; Jos., Ant. 14, 23).

2. the subst. neut. τὸ μ. the middle (on the absence of the art. s. Bl-D. §264, 4; W-S. §19, 1a; cf. Rob. 792) ἀνὰ μέσον τινός (s. ἀνά 1) among someth. Mt 13: 25. ἀνὰ μέσον τῶν ὁρίων within or through the region Mk 7: 31. ἀνὰ μ. αὐτῶν between them GP 4: 10; Hs 9, 2, 9, 15, 2. διακρῖναι ἀνὰ μ. τοῦ ἀδελφοῦ 1 Cor 6: 5 (s. ἀνά 1b. Perh. μέσος prompted a shortening of the sentence tending to obscurity; cf. the Stoic expr. μέσα καθήκοντα=καθή-

κοντα ἃ ἐν μέσῳ ἐστὶ κατορθωμάτων κ. ἁμαρτημάτων: MPohlenz, D. Stoa II '49, 73f). τὸ ἀρνίον τὸ ἀ. μ. τοῦ θρόνου the lamb who is (seated) on the center of the throne Rv 7: 17.—διὰ μέσου αὐτῶν through the midst of them (X., An. 1, 4, 4; Aesop. Fab. 147 P.; Am 5: 17; Jer 44: 4; Jdth 11: 19; 1 Macc 5: 46) Lk 4: 30; J 8: 59 t.r. διὰ μέσον Σαμαρείας καὶ Γαλιλαίας Lk 17: 11 prob. can only mean through Samaria and Galilee; this raises a practical difficulty, since we should expect to find the provinces mentioned in the opposite order. Perh. the text is damaged (s. Bl-D. §222; cf. Rob. 648; JBlinzler, AWikenhauser-Festschr. '54, 46ff. If the v.l. διὰ μέσου Σ. καὶ Γ. should be correct, we could compare Maximus Tyr. 28, 4a διὰ μέσου πίστεως κ. ἀπιστίας=throughout between). For the view that μέσον signifies the area betw. S. and G. s. the comm.—εἰς τὸ μέσον into the middle or center (X., Cyr. 3, 1, 6; Dio Chrys. 19[36], 24; 3 Km 6: 8; Jos., Ant. 9, 149) Mk 3: 3; Lk 4: 35; 5: 19; 6: 8; J 20: 19, 26 (ἔστη εἰς τὸ μέσον as Vi. Aesopi I c. 82); Hs 9, 8, 5; also in the middle 9, 6, 1. W. gen. (X., An. 1, 5; 14a; Jer 21: 4; 48: 7; Sb 6270, 13) εἰς τὸ μ. αὐτῶν in the midst of them 9, 11, 7. Without the art. (LXX; Jos., Vi. 334; Sib. Or. 3, 674) εἰς μ. τοῦ πεδίου in the middle of the plain s 9, 2, 1 (εἰς μ.= 'in the middle', as Ps.-Clem., Hom. 3, 30 p. 44, 21 Lag.). εἰς μ. τῶν ἀκανθῶν τιθέασιν Β 7: 11. ἀναστὰς εἰς μ. he arose (and came) forward Mk 14: 60 (cf. Theocr. 22, 82 ἐς μέσον=into the middle; Himerius, Or. 63 [= Or. 17], 2 εἰς μέσον ἔρχεσθαι=come into the open; X., Cyr. 4, 1, 1 στὰς εἰς τὸ μ.).—ἐν τῷ μ. among, before (more closely defined by the context, or= in public [so Clearch., fgm. 45 οἴκοι καὶ μὴ ἐν τῷ μέσῳ; Appian, Liby. 15 §63]) Mt 14: 6 (Dio Chrys. 30[79], 39 ὀρχεῖσθαι ἐν τῷ μέσῳ; Lucian, M. Peregr. 8) and into the middle, before (them) (Vi. Aesopi W c. 86 στὰς ἐν τῷ μέσῳ ἔφη) Ac 4: 7. Without the art. (LXX) ἐν μέσῳ (on the spelling ἐμ μέσῳ, which occurs several times as v.l., cf. Bl-D. §19, 1 app.; Mlt.-H. 105) abs. into the middle, before (someone) (Appian, Hann. 16 §67, Liby. 14 §59; Jos., Ant. 7, 278) J 8: 3; MPol 18: 1 and in the middle (Pla., Rep. 558α; Herm. Wr. 4, 3; PLille recto, 5 [259 BC]) J 8: 9. W. gen. of place (Aeneas Tact. 1529; 1532) τῆς θαλάσσης (En. 97, 7) in the middle of the lake Mk 6: 47. τῆς πλατείας through the middle of the street Rv 22: 2. ἐν μ. τῆς αὐλῆς in the middle of the courtyard Lk 22: 55a; τοῦ τάφου GP 13: 55. ἐν μ. αὐτῆς within it (the city of Jerusalem) Lk 21: 21; cf. Dg 12: 3; MPol 12: 1; Β 12: 2(?). ἐν μ. τοῦ θρόνου καὶ τῶν τεσσάρων ζῴων on the center of the throne and among the four living creatures Rv 5: 6a (w. double gen. also between: Appian, Hann. 14 §60, Bell. Civ. 5, 23 §92; Arrian, Anab. 1, 20, 2; 3, 28, 8 al.; Lucian, Fugit. 10 ἐν μ. ἀλαζονείας κ. φιλοσοφίας). ἐν μέσῳ τοῦ θρόνου around (on every side of) the throne 4: 6 (but between the throne and a more remote point: RRBrewer, JBL 71, '52, 227-31).—ἐν μέσῳ ἐκκλησίας Hb 2: 12 (Ps 21: 23). Cf. Ac 17: 22. W. gen. pl. in the midst of, among in answer to the questions where and whither (Bl-D. §215, 3 app.) w. gen. of the pers. Mt 18: 2, 20; Mk 9: 36; Lk 2: 46; 24: 36; Ac 1: 15; 2: 22; 6: 15 D; 27: 21; Rv 5: 6b; cf. 6: 6. Of close personal relationship ἐν μέσῳ ὑμῶν among you= in communion with you Lk 22: 27; 1 Th 2: 7.—ἐν μ. λύκων among wolves Mt 10: 16; Lk 10: 3; 2 Cl 5: 2.—W. gen. pl. of things (Alciphr. 3, 24, 3) Lk 8: 7; Rv 1: 13; 2: 1. ἐκ (τοῦ) μ. from among (X., An. 1, 5, 14b; oracular response in Diod. S. 9, 3, 2; LXX=מִתּוֹךְ): αἴρειν τι (or τινά) ἐκ (τοῦ) μέσου (τινῶν) Col 2: 14; 1 Cor 5: 2 (s. αἴρω 4). ἁρπάσαι αὐτὸν ἐκ μ. αὐτῶν Ac 23: 10 (s. ἁρπάζω 2a). ἀφορίζειν τοὺς πονηροὺς ἐκ μ. τῶν δικαίων Mt 13: 49 (s. ἀφορίζω 1). γίνεσθαι ἐκ μ. 2 Th 2: 7 (s.

γίνομαι I 4cβ). ἐξέρχεσθαι ἐκ μ. αὐτῶν *from among them* Ac 17: 33; cf. 2 Cor 6: 17 (cf. Is 52: 11). κύριος λαμβάνει ἑαυτῷ ἔθνος ἐκ μ. ἔθνῶν 1 Cl 29: 3 (cf. Dt 4: 34). κατὰ μέσον (Jos., Bell. 5, 207; Sib. Or. 3, 802 κατὰ μέσον = 'in the middle' [of the day]) κατὰ μ. τῆς νυκτός *about midnight* Ac 16: 25 D; 27: 27.

3. The neut. μέσον serves as an adv. (e.g., Appian, Bell. Civ. 3, 43 §175 μ.=meanwhile)—a. ἦν μέσον ὡς he *was in the center of it* as MPol 15: 2.

b. used w. gen. as (improper) prep. (Bl-D. §215, 3 app.; Rob. 644. Cf. Hdt. 7, 170; Polyb. 8, 25, 1; Epict. 2, 22, 10; LXX; Jos., Ant. 6, 65; Sib. Or. 3, 319) μ. τῆς θαλάσσης *in the middle of the lake* Mt 14: 24 v.l.; μ. γενεᾶς σκολιᾶς *in the midst of a crooked generation* Phil 2: 15 (cf. Maximus Tyr. 36, 5a ἐν μέσῳ τῷ σιδηρῷ τούτῳ γένει). M-M. B. 864.*

μεσότοιχον, ου, τό (the noun ὁ μεσότοιχος = *dividing wall* in Eratosthenes: Athen. 7, 14 p. 281D; inscr. fr. Argos: Bull. de corr. hell. 33, '09, 452 no. 22, 16.—But an inscr. fr. Didyma: ABA '11, 56 l. 13 ἐπὶ τοῦ μεσοτοίχου and PAmh. 98, 9 μέρος μεσοτοίχων can just as well come fr. τὸ μεσότοιχον; this occurs in Vi. Aesopi W c. 75. Cf. Jos., Ant. 8, 71 ὁ μέσος τοῖχος) *dividing wall* τὸ μ. τοῦ φραγμοῦ *the barrier formed by the dividing wall* between us Eph 2: 14. M-M.*

μεσουράνημα, ατος, τό (Posidon.: 87 fgm. 85 p. 273, 15 Jac.; Manetho; Plut.; Sext. Emp.; POxy. 235, 13 [I AD]) lit., in astronomy the 'meridian' ('culmination'; μεσουρανεῖν means 'be at the zenith', of the sun [Aristot.; Plut.; schol. on Apollon. Rhod. 1, 450; PGM 4, 2992]) *zenith* ἐν μεσουρανήματι *in midheaven* Rv 8: 13; 14: 6; 19: 17. M-M.*

μεσόω (Aeschyl., Hdt.+; LXX) *be in* or *at the middle* in gen. abs. (Thu. 6, 30, 1 θέρους μεσοῦντος; Ael. Aristid. 13 p. 274 D.: πολέμου μεσοῦντος; Ex 12: 29; 34: 22; 3 Macc 5: 14; Philo, Spec. Leg. 1, 183 μεσοῦντος ἔαρος; Jos., Ant. 5, 190) τῆς ἑορτῆς μεσούσης *when the festival was half over* J 7: 14 (v.l. μεσαζούσης; s. μεσάζω).*

Μεσσίας, ου, ὁ Hellenized transliteration of מָשִׁיחַ, Aram. מְשִׁיחָא (s. Schürer II⁴ 613 w. lit.; Dalman, Gramm.² 157, 3) *the Messiah = the Anointed One* (ThNöldeke, ZDMG 32, 1878, 403; W-S. §5, 26c p. 57 note 54) in our lit. only twice, and in J: in the mouth of a disciple J 1: 41 and of the Samaritan woman 4: 25, in both cases translated by Χριστός, q.v.*

μεστός, ή, όν (trag., X., Pla.+; inscr., pap., LXX, Joseph.) *full.*

1. lit., w. gen. of the thing (X., An. 1, 4, 19; Alciphr. 2, 11; Jos., Ant. 4, 93; PGrenf. I, 14, 9; POxy. 1070, 31f [III AD]) σκεῦος ὄξους μ. *full of vinegar* J 19: 29a. Likew. of a sponge μ. τοῦ ὄξους vs. 29b. τὸ δίκτυον μ. ἰχθύων μεγάλων *the net full of large fish* 21: 11. As a symbol, of the tongue μ. ἰοῦ *full of poison* Js 3: 8.

2. fig. w. gen.—a. of pers. *filled w. someth.* (Dio Chrys. 51[68], 4; Ael. Aristid. 46 p. 267 D.: ὕβρεων κ. κακῶν μ.; 47 p. 435 εὐλαβείας; PRainer 19, 15 μ. ψευδολογίας; POxy. 130, 6 μ. ἐλεημοσύνης; Pr 6: 34; Jos., Ant. 16, 351) μ. ὑποκρίσεως καὶ ἀνομίας *full of hypocrisy and lawlessness* Mt 23: 28. μ. φθόνου (Maximus Tyr. 35, 4e; Tetrast. Iamb. 1, 31, 2 p. 276) Ro 1: 29. μ. πολλῆς ἀνοίας καὶ πονηρίας 2 Cl 13: 1 (Isocr. 5, 45 πολλῆς ἀνοίας μ.; Dio Chrys. 15[32], 15 μ. πονηρίας). μ. ἀγαθωσύνης Ro 15: 14. μ. μ. ἐλέους Js 3: 17 (plus μεστὴ καρπῶν ἀγαθῶν 𝔓⁷⁴). μ. ὁσίας βουλῆς 1 Cl 2: 3.

b. of things (Epicurus in Diog. L. 10, 146 πάντα ταραχῆς μεστά; Menand., fgm. 452 μεστόν ἐστι τὸ ζῆν φροντίδων; Philo, Op. M. 2; 22 al.) ὀφθαλμοὶ μ. μοιχαλίδος (s. μοιχαλίς 1) 2 Pt 2: 14. The way of death is κατάρας μ. B 20: 1; D 5: 1. M-M. B 931.*

μεστόω pf. pass. ptc. μεμεστωμένος *fill* w. gen. of the thing (so mostly, e.g. 3 Macc 5: 10) γλεύκους μεμεστωμένοι *full of new wine* Ac 2: 13. W. dat. of the thing (3 Macc 5: 1) λόγος μεμεστωμένος πράξει *speech filled with* (= *fulfilled in*) *action* D 2: 5. M-M.*

μετά (Hom. +; inscr., pap., LXX, En., Ep. Arist., Philo, Joseph., Sib. Or.) prep. w. gen. and acc., in the NT not (Bl-D. §203; Rob. 610) w. dat.—For lit. s. ἀνά, beg.; also for μετά (and σύν) Tycho Mommsen, Beiträge zu d. Lehre v. den griech. Präp. 1895.

A. with genitive: *with*—I. of place *with, among, in company with* someone (Gen 42: 5; Ep. Arist. 180) or someth. ἦν μετὰ τῶν θηρίων *he was among the wild animals* Mk 1: 13 (Diog. L. 6, 92 μόσχοι μετὰ λύκων). ἦν συγκαθήμενος μ. τῶν ὑπηρετῶν *he sat down among the servants* 14: 54. μετὰ ἀνόμων ἐλογίσθη *he was classed among the criminals* Mk 15: 28; Lk 22: 37. τὸ μέρος αὐτοῦ μ. τῶν ἀπίστων θήσει *he will assign him his lot among the faithless* (unbelievers?) Lk 12: 46; cf. Mt 24: 51. ζητεῖν τὸν ζῶντα μ. τῶν νεκρῶν *seek the living among the dead* Lk 24: 5. μὴ γογγύζετε μετ' ἀλλήλων *do not grumble among yourselves* J 6: 43. εἱστήκει Ἰούδας μετ' αὐτῶν 18: 5. ἡ σκηνὴ τ. θεοῦ μετὰ τ. ἀνθρώπων Rv 21: 3a. μετὰ τῶν νεφελῶν *in the midst of the clouds* 1: 7.

II. denoting the company within which someth. takes place.

1. w. gen. of the pers. in company with whom someth. happens.

a. w. verbs of going, remaining, etc. προσέρχεσθαι μ. τινος *come* (*in company*) *with* someone Mt 20: 20; cf. 5: 41; Mk 1: 29; 3: 7; 5: 24, 37; 11: 11; 14: 17; Lk 2: 51; 6: 17; 9: 49; 14: 31; J 3: 22; 11: 54; Ac 24: 1; Gal 2: 1. Angels accompanying the Messiah Mt 25: 31; cf. 16: 27; Mk 8: 38; 1 Th 3: 13; 2 Th 1: 7. περιπατεῖν μ. τινος (Menand., fgm. 202, 2, Sam. 242) J 6: 66. γίνεσθαι μ. τινος *be, remain with* someone Ac 7: 38; 9: 19; 20: 18. οἱ μ. αὐτοῦ γενόμενοι *his companions* Mk 16: 10. μένειν μ. τινος *stay with* someone 1 J 2: 19. ζήσασα μ. ἀνδρός Lk 2: 36. ἀκολουθεῖν μ. τινος *follow* (*after*) *someone* Rv 6: 8; 14: 13 (s. ἀκολουθέω 2).

b. used w. trans. verbs ἄγειν τινὰ μ. ἑαυτοῦ *bring someone along* (cf. ἄγω 1b) 2 Ti 4: 11. παραλαμβάνειν τινὰ μεθ' ἑαυτοῦ *take* or *bring someone along* (*as a companion*) (Gen 22: 3) Mt 12: 45; 18: 16; Mk 14: 33. ἔχειν τι μ. ἑαυτοῦ *have someth. with oneself*: bread 8: 14; τινά *someone* (PGM 4, 1952): the lame Mt 15: 30; the poor Mk 14: 7; Mt 26: 11; J 12: 8; the bridegroom Mk 2: 19b. Pass. συγκατεψηφίσθη μετὰ τ. ἕνδεκα ἀποστόλων *he was chosen* (*to serve*) *with the eleven apostles* Ac 1: 26 (cf. Himerius, Or. 44 [= Or. 8], 3 μετὰ τῶν θεῶν ἀριθμούμενος = *numbered with the gods*).

c. esp. εἶναι μ. τινος *be with someone, in someone's company*—a. lit., of close association: the disciples w. Jesus Mt 26: 69, 71; Mk 3: 14; 14: 67; Lk 22: 59; J 15: 27; 17: 24. Also of accompaniment for a short time Mt 5: 25; J 3: 26; 9: 40; 12: 17; 20: 24, 26. Of Jesus' association w. his disciples 13: 33; 14: 9; 16: 4; 17: 12. Of the bishop and the church μετὰ τ. ἐπισκόπου εἶναι *be with, on the side of, the bishop* IPhld 3: 2. οἱ μ. τινος (sc. ὄντες) *someone's friends, companions,* etc. (Diod. S. 17, 96, 2 οἱ μεθ' Ἡρακλέους; Dit., Syll.³ 175, 5; 659, 5; 826E II, 30;

Am 4: 2; 8: 10; Gen 24: 59; 1 Macc 7: 23; Jos., Vi. 397, Ant. 7, 20) Mt 12: 3f; 26: 51; Mk 1: 36; 2: 25; Lk 6: 3f. Of things ἄλλα πλοῖα ἦν μ. αὐτοῦ *other boats were with him, accompanied him* Mk 4: 36. ὁ μισθός μου μετ᾽ ἐμοῦ (sc. ἐστιν) Rv 22: 12.

β. fig., of aid or help *be with someone, stand by, help someone* of God's help (Gen 21: 20; 26: 3; 28: 20 al.; Jos., Ant. 15, 138) J 3: 2; 8: 29; 16: 32; Ac 7: 9 (cf. Gen 39: 2, 21); 10: 38; cf. Mt 1: 23 (Is 8: 8); Lk 1: 28; Ro 15: 33. Of God's hand (1 Ch 4: 10) Lk 1: 66; Ac 11: 21. Of Christ: Mt 28: 20; Ac 18: 10.

γ. a favorite expr. in conclusions of letters ὁ θεὸς τῆς ἀγάπης καὶ εἰρήνης ἔσται μ. ὑμῶν *will be with you* 2 Cor 13: 11; cf. Phil 4: 9; ὁ κύριος κτλ. 2 Th 3: 16 (cf. Ruth 2: 4); 2 Ti 4: 22. ἡ χάρις τοῦ κυρίου Ἰησοῦ μ. ὑμῶν (sc. ἔσται) 1 Cor 16: 23; cf. 1 Th 5: 28; 1 Cl 65: 2. μ. τοῦ πνεύματος ὑμῶν Gal 6: 18; Phil 4: 23; Phlm 25; B 21: 9. μ. πάντων ὑμῶν 2 Th 3: 18; cf. Eph 6: 24. Short and to the point: ἡ χάρις μ. ὑμῶν Col 4: 18; 1 Th 6: 21; cf. Tit 3: 15; Hb 13: 25. ἔσται μεθ᾽ ἡμῶν χάρις ἔλεος εἰρήνη 2 J 3.—ἡ ἀγάπη μου μ. πάντων ὑμῶν ἐν Χριστῷ Ἰησοῦ *my love is with you all in Christ Jesus* 1 Cor 16: 24. ἡ χάρις τοῦ κυρίου Ἰ. Χρ. καὶ ἡ ἀγάπη τ. θεοῦ καὶ ἡ κοινωνία τοῦ ἁγίου πνεύματος μετὰ πάντων ὑμῶν 2 Cor 13: 13 (WCvanUnnik, Dominus Vobiscum: liturg. formula, TWManson memorial vol., '59, 270–305; on the Trinitarian formula s. the lit. on πνεῦμα 8).—In the expr. ὅσα ἐποίησεν ὁ θεὸς μ. αὐτῶν Ac 14: 27; 15: 4 (cf. Hs 5, 1, 1) ὧν could be supplied *what God has done in helping them;* but ποιεῖν can just as well go w. μ. αὐτῶν *has done for them,* after the analogy of עָשָׂה עִם (Tob 12: 6; 13: 7 ἃ ποιήσει μεθ᾽ ὑμῶν; Jdth 8: 26 ὅσα ἐποίησεν μετὰ Ἀβραάμ; 15: 10; 1 Macc 10: 27. But cf. also BGU 798, 8 εὐχαριστοῦμεν τῇ ἡμῶν δεσποίνῃ εἰς πάντα τὰ καλὰ ἃ ἐποίησεν μετὰ τ. δούλων αὐτῆς). Here also belongs ποιεῖν ἔλεος μ. τινος *have mercy on someone, show mercy to someone* (Gen 24: 12; 2 Km 3: 8) Lk 1: 72; 10: 37 (MWilcox, The Semitisms in Ac, '65, 84f). ἐμεγάλυνεν κύριος τὸ ἔλεος αὐτοῦ μετ᾽ αὐτῆς *the Lord has shown great mercy to her* 1: 58 (cf. 1 Km 12: 24; Ps 125: 2f).—In πληρώσεις με εὐφροσύνης μ. τοῦ προσώπου σου Ac 2: 28= Ps 15: 11 the LXX has literally translated אֶת־פָּנֶיךָ; it means *in thy presence.*

δ. in contrast to εἶναι κατά τινος *be against someone* is εἶναι μ. τινος *be with someone, on someone's side* Mt 12: 30a; Lk 11: 23a (AFridrichsen, ZNW 13, '12, 273–80).

2. to denote the company in which an activity or experience takes place: ἀνακεῖσθαι μ. τινος *recline at table with someone* (for a meal) Mt 26: 20. ἀνακλιθῆναι 8: 11; cf. Lk 24: 30. βασιλεύειν Rv 20: 4, 6. γρηγορεῖν Mt 26: 38, 40. δειπνεῖν Rv 3: 20. δουλεύειν Gal 4: 25. ἐμπαίζειν Mt 27: 41. ἐσθίειν 9: 11; 24: 49; Mk 2: 16a, b; 14: 14, 18; Lk 5: 30. ἠρώτα . . . ἵνα φάγῃ μ. αὐτοῦ *he asked (him) to eat with him* 7: 36. εὐφραίνεσθαι 15: 29; Ro 15: 10 (Dt 32: 43). κλαίειν 12: 15b. κληρονομεῖν Gal 4: 30 (Gen 21: 10). πίνειν Mt 26: 29. ποιεῖν τὸ πάσχα *celebrate the Passover (with someone)* 26: 18. συνάγειν 12: 30b; Lk 11: 23b. συνεσθίειν Gal 2: 12. ταράττεσθαι Mt 2: 3. τρώγειν J 13: 18 v.l. χαίρειν Ro 12: 15a.

3. The fact that the activity or experience took place in the company of others can also be made clear by the influence which two opposite parties exert upon each other or together, or, on the other hand, by which one party brings the other to adopt a corresponding, and therefore common attitude.

a. in hostile fashion; after verbs of fighting, quarreling, etc. to denote the pers. w. whom the strife is being carried on πολεμεῖν μ. τινος *carry on war with= against someone* (נִלְחַם עִם פ׳ 1 Km 17: 33; 3 Km 12: 24. But s. also Dit., Or. 201, 3 ἐπολέμησα μετὰ τῶν Βλεμύων; BGU 1035, 9; 11. Also in Mod. Gk. [AThumb, Hdb. der neugriech. Volkssprache² '10 §162, 1 note]) Rv 2: 16; 12: 7; 13: 4; 17: 14 (Bl-D. §193, 4 w. app.; Rob. 610). Also πόλεμον ποιεῖν (Gen 14: 2; 1 Ch 5: 19) 11: 7; 12: 17; 13: 7 (Da 7: 21 Theod.); 19: 19. ζητεῖν μ. τινος *deliberate* or *dispute w. someone* J 16: 19; cf. 3: 25. κρίνεσθαι *go to law w. someone* 1 Cor 6: 6. κρίματα ἔχειν μ. τινος *have lawsuits w. someone* vs. 7.

b. in friendly, or at least not in hostile, fashion: εἰρηνεύειν (3 Km 22: 45) Ro 12: 18; cf. 2 Ti 2: 22; Hb 12: 14. εὐθηνίαν ἔχειν Hm 2: 3. κοινωνίαν ἔχειν 1 J 1: 3a, 7. λαλεῖν μετά τινος (cf. Gen 31: 24, 29; 1 Macc 7: 15) Mk 6: 50; J 4: 27a, b. συλλαλεῖν μ. τινος Mt 17: 3; Ac 25: 12. συμβούλιον διδόναι Mk 3: 6. συνάγεσθαι Mt 28: 12; J 18: 2. συνᾶραι λόγον Mt 18: 23; 25: 19. ἐγένοντο φίλοι ὅ τε Ἡρῴδης καὶ ὁ Πιλᾶτος μετ᾽ ἀλλήλων· Lk 23: 12. οἱ μοιχεύοντες μετ᾽ αὐτῆς *those who commit adultery with her* Rv 2: 22. πορνεύειν (cf. Ezk 16: 34) 17: 2; 18: 3, 9. μολύνεσθαι 14: 4.

4. of any other relation betw. persons, whether already existing or brought about in some manner εἶδον τὸ παιδίον μ. Μαρίας Mt 2: 11. ἀνταποδοῦναι ὑμῖν ἄνεσιν μ. ἡμῶν 2 Th 1: 7. ἐκδέχομαι αὐτὸν μ. τῶν ἀδελφῶν 1 Cor 16: 11. Of delegations, composed of several units Mt 22: 16; 2 Cor 8: 18. συμφωνεῖν Mt 20: 2.

5. of things ὧν τὸ αἷμα ἔμιξεν μ. τῶν θυσιῶν αὐτῶν Lk 13: 1. Pass. πιεῖν οἶνον μ. χολῆς μεμιγμένον Mt 27: 34.

6. to show a close connection betw. two nouns, upon the first of which the main emphasis lies (Thu. 7, 75, 3 λύπη μ. φόβου; Pla., Rep. 9 p. 591B ἰσχύν τε καὶ κάλλος μετὰ ὑγιείας λαμβάνειν) ἀγάπη μ. πίστεως Eph 6: 23. πίστις μ. σωφροσύνης 1 Ti 2: 15. εὐσέβεια μ. αὐταρκείας 6: 6. Cf. Eph 4: 2b; Col 1: 11; 1 Ti 1: 14. φάρμακον μ. οἰνομέλιτος ITr 6: 2.

III. to denote the attendant circumstances of someth. that takes place.

1. of moods, emotions, wishes, feelings, excitement, states of mind or body (Xenophon Eph. p. 345, 2; 355, 7 H.; PAmh. 133, 11 μετὰ πολλῶν κόπων; PLond. 358, 8; Dit., Syll.³ index IV p. 445f; LXX [Johannessohn 209ff]) μ. αἰδοῦς *with modesty* 1 Ti 2: 9. μ. αἰσχύνης *with shame* (s. αἰσχύνη 2) Lk 14: 9. μ. εὐνοίας Eph 6: 7. μ. εὐχαριστίας Phil 4: 6; 1 Ti 4: 3f; cf. Ac 24: 3. μετὰ χαρᾶς (2 Macc 15: 28; 3 Macc 5: 21; 6: 34 al.; s. χαρά 1) 1 Th 1: 6; Hb 10: 34; 13: 17; cf. Phil 2: 29. μ. φόβου καὶ τρόμου 2 Cor 7: 15; Eph 6: 5; Phil 2: 12. μ. φόβου καὶ χαρᾶς Mt 28: 8. μ. πραΰτητος καὶ φόβου 1 Pt 3: 16. μ. παρρησίας (Lev 26: 13; 1 Macc 4: 18; s. παρρησία 3a) Ac 2: 29; 4: 29, 31; 28: 31; Hb 4: 16. μ. πεποιθήσεως 1 Cl 31: 3. μ. σπουδῆς (3 Macc 5: 24, 27) Mk 6: 25; Lk 1: 39. μ. ταπεινοφροσύνης Eph 4: 2a; cf. Ac 20: 19. μ. ὀργῆς (3 Macc 6: 23) Mk 3: 5. μ. δακρύων *in tears* (3 Macc 1: 16; 4: 2; 5: 7; s. δάκρυον) Mk 9: 24 v.l.; Hb 5: 7; 12: 17. μ. εἰρήνης (s. εἰρήνη 1b) Ac 15: 33; Hb 11: 31.

2. of other accompanying phenomena (Antig. Car. 148 μετὰ φλογὸς καίεσθαι) μ. διωγμῶν *though with persecutions* Mk 10: 30. μ. ἐπιθέσεως τῶν χειρῶν 1 Ti 4: 14. μ. νηστειῶν Ac 14: 23. μ. θορύβου (Jos., Ant. 5, 216) 24: 18. μ. παρακλήσεως 2 Cor 8: 4. μ. παρατηρήσεως Lk 17: 20. μ. ὕβρεως καὶ πολλῆς ζημίας Ac 27: 10 (s. ὕβρις 3). μ. φαντασίας 25: 23. μ. δυνάμεως καὶ δόξης Mt 24: 30; Mk 13: 26; Lk 21: 27. μ. ἐξουσίας καὶ ἐπιτροπῆς Ac 26: 12 (Jos., Ant. 20, 180 μετ᾽ ἐξουσίας). μ. βραχίονος

ὑψηλοῦ ἐξάγειν τινά (cf. βραχίων) Ac 13: 17. μ. φωνῆς μεγάλης w. a loud voice Lk 17: 15 (cf. Ep. Arist. 235; 281). μ. σάλπιγγος with a trumpet call Mt 24: 31 (Plut., De Mus. 14=Mor. 1135ϝ μετ' αὐλῶν=with the sound of flutes). σφραγίσαντες τ. λίθον μετὰ τ. κουστωδίας makes the stationing of the guard an accompaniment to the sealing of the stone Mt 27: 66 (another possibility here is the instrumental use of μετά [Lycurgus the orator 124 μ. παραδειγμάτων διδάσκειν; Suppl. Epigr. Gr. VIII 246, 8 μετὰ κυνῶν—an instrument of torture—βασανίσαι; CWessely, Neue griech. Zauberpap. 1893, 234 γράφε μ. μέλανος; 2 Macc 6: 16]: secure the stone by means of a guard; s. σφραγίζω 2a).

3. of concrete objects, which serve as equipment (Appian, Maced. 9 §4 μετὰ χρυσῶν στεφάνων; POxy. 123, 15; 19 μετὰ τῶν χλαμύδων εἰσβῆναι; 1 Esdr 5: 57; Jdth 15: 13) μ. μαχαιρῶν καὶ ξύλων Mt 26: 47; 55; Mk 14: 43, 48; Lk 22: 52. μ. φανῶν καὶ λαμπάδων καὶ ὅπλων (Xenophon Eph. p. 336, 20 μ. λαμπάδων) J 18: 3.

B. with the accusative. In our lit. only in the mng. after, behind.

I. of place (Hom.+; Polyb., not LXX) μ. τὸ δεύτερον καταπέτασμα behind the second curtain Hb 9: 3.

II. of time (Hom.+; inscr., pap., LXX)—1. with the time expressly given μ. πολὺν χρόνον (2 Macc 6: 1.—μετ' οὐ πολὺν χρ.: Hero Alex. I p. 340, 6; Dit., Syll.³ 1169, 54; Jos., Vi. 407) Mt 25: 19. μ. τοσοῦτον χρόνον (4 Macc 5: 7) Hb 4: 7. μ. χρόνον τινά (Diod. S. 9, 10, 2; Witkowski 26, 9 [III вс]; Jos., Ant. 8, 398) Hv 1, 1, 2f; s 5, 2, 5; 9, 13, 8. μ. ἡμέρας ἕξ after six days Mt 17: 1; Mk 9: 2. μ. τρεῖς ἡμέρας (Artem. 4, 33 p. 224, 5; Polyaenus 6, 53; 8, 62; Ep. Arist. 301; Jos., Ant 7, 280) Mt 27: 63; Mk 8: 31; 10: 34; Lk 2: 46; cf. Mt 26: 2; Mk 14: 1 (cf. Caesar, Bell. Gall. 4, 9, 1 post tertiam diem= on the third day). μ. τινας ἡμέρας Ac 15: 36; 24: 24. μετ' οὐ πολλὰς ἡμέρας (Artem. 1, 78 p. 72, 30; Jos., Ant. 5, 328, Vi. 309) Lk 15: 13. οὐ μ. πολλὰς ταύτας ἡμέρας not long after these days=within a few days Ac 1: 5 (Bl-D. §226; 433, 3; Rob. 612; 1158; Dssm., Ztschr. für vergleich. Sprachforschg. 45, '13, 60). W. gen. foll. μ. ἡμέρας εἴκοσι τῆς προτέρας ὁράσεως twenty days after the former vision Hv 4, 1, 1 (cf. Biogr. p. 31 μετὰ ξ' ἔτη τοῦ Ἰλιακοῦ πολέμου; Gen 16: 3; Test. Reub. 1, 2). μ. τρεῖς μῆνας Ac 28: 11. μ. τρία ἔτη Gal 1: 18. ὁ μ. τετρακόσια καὶ τριάκοντα ἔτη γεγονὼς νόμος 3: 17.

2. w. designations that are general, but include the idea of time: μ. τὴν ἄφιξίν μου Ac 20: 29. μ. τὸ πάσχα after the Passover 12: 4. μ. τὴν μετοικεσίαν Βαβυλῶνος Mt 1: 12.

3. gener. μ. τὴν θλῖψιν after the (time of) tribulation Mk 13: 24; cf. μ. τὴν θλῖψιν τῶν ἡμερῶν ἐκείνων Mt 24: 29. μ. τὴν ἔγερσιν 27: 53. μ. τὴν ἀνάγνωσιν Ac 13: 15. μ. τὸ βάπτισμα 10: 37. μ. μίαν καὶ δευτέραν νουθεσίαν Tit 3: 10. μ. τὸ ψωμίον after he had eaten the piece of bread J 13: 27.—Quite gener. μ. τοῦτο after this, afterward (Lucian, Hermot. 31; Gen 18: 5; Lev 14: 19; Ep. Arist. 258) J 2: 12; 11: 7, 11; 19: 28; Hb 9: 27; Rv 7: 1. μ. ταῦτα after this (Aeneas Tact. 240; 350; Diod. S. 1, 7, 1; Ex 3: 20; 11: 8 and oft.) Mk 16: 12; Lk 5: 27; 10: 1 and oft. μ. οὐ πολύ (Dio Chrys. 56[73], 8; Lucian, Scyth. 1; Herodian 1, 9, 7; BGU 614, 14; Mitteis, Chrest. 96 II, 9; 1 Esdr 3: 22; Jos., Ant. 12, 132) not long afterward Ac 27: 14. μ. μικρόν a short while afterward Mt 26: 73; Mk 14: 70. Also μ. βραχύ Lk 22: 58 (cf. μετ' ὀλίγον: Lucian, Dial. Mort. 15, 3; PRyl. 77, 41; Wsd 15: 8; Jdth 13: 9; Jos., Ant. 12, 136).

4. w. subst. aor. inf. foll.—a. w. acc. (Dit., Syll.³ 633, 105; 640, 13; 695, 78; 1233, 1; Sir 46: 20; Jdth 16: 25; Bar 1: 9; 1 Macc 1: 1, 9.—Bl-D. §406, 3; Rob. 979) μ. τὸ

ἐγερθῆναί με after I am raised up Mt 26: 32; Mk 14: 28. μ. τὸ παραδοθῆναι τὸν Ἰωάννην after John was arrested Mk 1: 14.—Ac 1: 3; 7: 4; 10: 41; 15: 13; 19: 21; 20: 1; Hv 2, 1, 3; m 4, 1, 7; s 8, 2, 5.

b. without acc. (Aelian, V.H. 12, 1 p. 118, 27; Herodian 2, 9, 5; Dit., Syll.³ 976, 39; UPZ 110, 193 [164 вс]; Sir 23: 20; 32: 18 v.l.; 1 Macc 1: 20) μ. τὸ λαλῆσαι αὐτοῖς after he had spoken to them Mk 16: 19.—Lk 12: 5; 1 Cor 11: 25; Hb 10: 26.—W. perf. inf. 10: 15. M-M.

μεταβαίνω (Hom.+; inscr., pap., LXX; Philo, Migr. Abr. 194; Jos., Ant. 3, 100 al.) fut. μεταβήσομαι; 2 aor. μετέβην, imper. μετάβηθι (J 7: 3) and μετάβα (Mt 17: 20; cf. Bl-D. §95, 3; Mlt.-H. 209f); pf. μεταβέβηκα.

1. lit.—a. go or pass over (fr. one place to another).

α. of pers., w. indications of the place from which ἀπὸ τῶν ὁρίων αὐτῶν from their district Mt 8: 34. ἐντεῦθεν J 7: 3. ἐκεῖθεν Mt 11: 1; 12: 9; 15: 29; Ac 18: 7. ἐκ τοῦ κόσμου τούτου πρὸς τ. πατέρα J 13: 1.

β. of things (Epict. 3, 19, 4 a stone; Jos., Bell. 2, 163) ἐρεῖτε τῷ ὄρει· μετάβα ἔνθεν ἐκεῖ, καὶ μεταβήσεται Mt 17: 20.

b. specif. change one's place of residence, move (Diog. L. 5, 89 εἰς θεούς=go over or be removed to the gods; PTebt. 316, 20; 92; Jos., Bell. 6, 299) w. the goal given εἰς ἕτερον ἀγρίδιον MPol 6: 1. W. the place fr. which and place to which given: ἐξ οἰκίας εἰς οἰκίαν go from one house to another Lk 10: 7 (μ. ἐξ—εἰς as Jos., Ant. 11, 204).

2. fig. (Pla. et al.; Anth. Pal. 9, 378 κοιμῶ μεταβὰς ἀλλαχόθι; Dit., Or. 458, 7 [c. 9 вс]; Jos., Vi. 149).

a. ἐκ τοῦ θανάτου εἰς τὴν ζωὴν pass (perh. 'move') from death into life (s. 1b) J 5: 24; 1 J 3: 14 (Sb 6648, 3 vice versa of one deceased: τὸν μεταβάντα εἰς μυχὸν αἰώνων ἐν σκοτίᾳ διάγειν).

b. rhetor. t.t. pass on to another subject (Pla., Phaedr. 265c, Crat. 438a) ἐπὶ ἑτέραν γνῶσιν καὶ διδαχὴν pass on to a different kind of knowledge and teaching B 18: 1 (cf. 2 Macc 6: 9). M-M.*

μεταβάλλω 2 aor. mid. μετεβαλόμην (Hom.+; inscr., pap., LXX, Philo, Joseph.) in our lit. only mid.

1. turn εἴς τι to someth. (Jos., Ant. 5, 256; Test. Dan 4: 3) εἰς νέαν ζύμην to the new leaven (=Christ) IMg 10: 2 (cf. Ode of Solomon 11, 19).

2. change one's mind (Thu. et al.) abs. (Pla., Gorg. 481ε μεταβαλόμενος λέγεις; X., Hell. 2, 3, 31; Inschr. v. Magn. 115, 20; 4 Macc 6: 18; Philo, Mos. 1, 147; Jos., Bell. 1, 296) Ac 28: 6. M-M.*

μεταγράφω 1 aor. mid. μετεγραψάμην (Eur., Thu.+; inscr., pap., Ep. Arist.) in our lit. only mid.: copy, transcribe τὶ ἔκ τινος someth. from someth. (cf. the act. Philo, Spec. Leg. 4, 61) MPol 22: 2; Epil Mosq 1; 4. βιβλίδιον copy a little book Hv 2, 1, 3; cf. 4.*

μετάγω 2 aor. μετήγαγον (X.+; inscr., pap., LXX, Ep. Arist.) guide (in another direction) (= 'lead to another place': Polyb., Diod. S. et al.; POxy. 244, 3 [πρόβατα]; 259, 19; 1 Esdr 1: 43; 3 Km 8: 48; 2 Ch 36: 3).

1. lit., the bodies of horses Js 3: 3 (Philosophenspr. p. 486, 18 οἱ ἵπποι τοῖς χαλινοῖς μετάγονται). Pass. of a ship μετάγεται is steered, guided vs. 4. Of corpses be brought (back) Ac 7: 16 D.

2. fig. (Plut., Mor. 225ϝ; Ep. Arist. 227) τινὰ ἔκ τινος force someone out of someth. i.e. remove someone from an office 1 Cl 44: 6. M-M. and suppl.*

μεταδίδωμι 2 aor. subj. μεταδῶ, imper. μεταδότω, inf. μεταδοῦναι (Theognis, Hdt.+; inscr., pap., LXX, Ep.

Arist., Philo; Jos., Ant. 4, 237; 6, 255; Test. 12 Patr.) *give (a part of), impart, share* τινί τι (Hdt. 9, 34; X., An. 4, 5, 5; Tob 7: 10 BA; Ep. Arist. 43) *someth. to* or *with* someone (Bl-D. §169, 1; Rob. 510) ἵνα τι μεταδῶ χάρισμα ὑμῖν πνευματικόν *in order that I might impart some spiritual gift to you* Ro 1: 11. ὑμῖν τὸ εὐαγγέλιον τοῦ θεοῦ *share the gospel of God with you* 1 Th 2: 8 (cf. Wsd 7: 13 of the wise man's teaching). W. omission of the acc., which is supplied fr. the context Lk 3: 11; of alms-giving *to the needy* Eph 4: 28; cf. Hv 3, 9, 2; 4. Without the dat., which is to be supplied fr. the context B 1: 5. Abs. ὁ μεταδιδοὺς ἐν ἁπλότητι *he who gives, (let him do it) with liberality,* or *in all sincerity,* i.e., without grudging Ro 12: 8.—S. on εὐεργετέω. M-M.*

μετάθεσις, θέσεως, ἡ (Thu. +; pap.; 2 Macc 11: 24; Ep. Arist., Philo, Joseph.).
1. *removal* (Diod. S. 1, 23, 3) τῶν σαλευομένων Hb 12: 27. Of the *taking up* or *translation* of Enoch (Philo, Praem. 17) 11: 5.
2. *change, transformation* (Thu. 5, 29, 3 al.; PSI 546, 3; Ep. Arist. 160; Philo, Gig. 66; Jos., C. Ap. 1, 286) νόμου 7: 12. M-M.*

μεταίρω 1 aor. μετῆρα (Demosth. 19, 174; Dit., Or. 573, 15; LXX; Jos., Ant. 1, 161) in our lit. (exclusively Mt) only intr. (Bl-D. §308; cf. Rob. 799) *go away* w. indication of the place from which ἀπὸ τῆς Γαλιλαίας Mt 19: 1. ἐκεῖθεν 13: 53 (Aq. Gen 12: 9). M-M.*

μετακαλέω 1 aor. mid. μετεκαλεσάμην; fut. μετακαλέσομαι (Thu. et al.; pap., LXX, Philo, Joseph.) in our lit. (exclusively Ac) only mid. *call to oneself, summon* (POxy. 33 verso II, 2 μετεκαλέσατο αὐτόν; 1252 recto, 26; Jos., Vi. 78) τινά *someone* (Jos., Ant. 2, 226) Ac 24: 25. Ἰακώβ 7: 14.—10: 32. τ. πρεσβυτέρους τῆς ἐκκλησίας 20: 17. M-M.*

μετακινέω (Hdt. +; inscr., LXX; Jos., Ant. 5, 179, C. Ap. 2, 184; Sib. Or. 3, 209) *shift, remove* mid. (cf. Hdt. 9, 51) fig. μὴ μετακινούμενοι ἀπὸ τῆς ἐλπίδος *without shifting from the hope* Col 1: 23. M-M.*

μετακόσμιος, ον (Diog. L. 10, 89; Plut.; Philo, Somn. 1, 184, Conf. Lingu. 134) *between* or *after the world(s);* elsewh. an Epicurean expr., denoting the space betw. heaven and earth (intermundia: Cicero, Nat. Deor. 1, 8, 18); here prob. *what is to come after this world* (in time) Dg 12: 9 (text uncertain).*

μεταλαμβάνω impf. μετελάμβανον; 2 aor. μετέλαβον, inf. μεταλαβεῖν, ptc. μεταλαβών; pf. μετείληφα (Pind., Hdt. +; inscr., pap., LXX, Ep. Arist., Philo, Joseph.) *receive one's share, share in* or *receive* gener.
1. w. gen. of the thing (so as a rule; cf. Bl-D. §169, 1; Rob. 510; 519) καρπῶν *receive his share of the crops* 2 Ti 2: 6 (Paroem. Gr.: Zenob. [II AD] 5, 71 ἔφη μὴ μεταλήψεσθαι τὸν δεσπότην τοῦ καρποῦ). τῶν ἐπηγγελμένων δωρεῶν 1 Cl 35: 4. τῆς τιμῆς Dg 3: 5. εὐλογίας Hb 6: 7. τῆς ἁγιότητος 12: 10. μετειληφότες πράξεων *have a share in the* (blessings *of the) deeds* 1 Cl 19: 2. τῆς ἐν Χριστῷ παιδείας 21: 8. τοῦ ῥήματος τοῦ δικαίου Hv 3, 7, 6. τοῦ πνεύματος 2 Cl 14: 3b, 4. τοσαύτης χρηστότητος *since we have shared in such great kindness* 15: 5. τοῦ ἐλέους Ἰησοῦ *experience the mercy of Jesus* 16: 2.— Esp. μ. τροφῆς (Jos., Bell. 2, 143; PRyl. 77, 19 τροφῶν μεταλαβεῖν) *take, eat food* Ac 2: 46; 27: 33f.
2. w. acc. of the thing (Eur., Pla. +; Diod. S. 5, 75, 1 τὴν εἰρήνην; PTebt. 79, 49; PAmh. 39, 6; Jos., Bell. 2, 1) τὸ αὐθεντικόν *receive the original* 2 Cl 14: 3a. ζωήν

receive life 14: 5. τὰ κτίσματα τοῦ θεοῦ *take possession of what God has created* Hv 3, 9, 2; καιρὸν μ. *have an opportunity=find time* (Polyb. 2, 16, 15; Diod. S. 19, 69, 2; Jos., Ant. 4, 10) Ac 24: 25. M-M.*

μετάλημψις (t.r. μετάληψις; on the μ cf. λαμβάνω, beg.) εως, ἡ (Pla. +; Dit., Or. 764, 15; POxy. 1200, 36; 1273, 39; Philo, Plant. 74) *sharing, taking, receiving* ἃ ὁ θεὸς ἔκτισεν εἰς μ. τοῖς πιστοῖς *which God created for the faithful to receive* 1 Ti 4: 3. M-M.*

μεταλλάσσω 1 aor. μετήλλαξα (Hdt. +; inscr., pap., LXX; Berosus in Jos., C. Ap. 1, 136; Sib. Or. 7, 96) *exchange* τι ἔν τινι *someth. for someth.* τὴν ἀλήθειαν τοῦ θεοῦ ἐν τῷ ψεύδει *the truth of God* (= *the true God) for a lie* (= *the false god;* s. ψεῦδος) Ro 1: 25. Also τι εἴς τι (Diod. S. 4, 51, 5) τὴν φυσικὴν χρῆσιν εἰς τὴν παρὰ φύσιν *exchange natural sex relations for those that are contrary to nature* vs. 26 (the same connection between perversion in religion and in sex Test. Napht. 3: 4 ἐνήλλαξε τάξιν φύσεως). M-M.*

μεταμέλομαι pass. dep.; impf. μετεμελόμην; 1 aor. pass. μετεμελήθην; 1 fut. pass. μεταμεληθήσομαι (Thu. +; Dit., Or. 458, 11; BGU 1040, 20; LXX) *(feel) regret, repent* (Simplicius in Epict. p. 107, 21 μεταμελομένων τῶν ἁμαρτανόντων) Mt 21: 30, 32 (in these places it can also mean simply *change one's mind* as Polyb. 4, 50, 6); 27: 3; 2 Cor 7: 8a, b; Hb 7: 21 (Ps 109: 4.—Of God changing his mind also Jos., Ant. 6, 145). EFThompson, Μετανοέω and Μεταμέλει in Gk. Lit. until 100 AD, '08; Windisch, Exc. on 2 Cor 7: 8; OMichel, TW IV 630-3. M-M.*

μεταμορφόω pf. pass. ptc. μεταμεμορφωμένος; 1 aor. pass. μετεμορφώθην (Diod. S. 4, 81, 5; Castor of Rhodes [50 BC]: 250 fgm. 17 Jac. εἰς ἕτερα μεταμορφοῦσθαι σώματα; Plut., Mor. 52D al.; Athen. 8 p. 334C; Aelian, V.H. 1, 1; Ps.-Lucian, Asin. 11; Herm. Wr. 16, 9; PGM 1, 117; 13, 70; Sym. Ps 33: 1; Philo, Mos. 1, 57, Leg. ad Gai. 95) *transform, change in form* in our lit. only in pass.
1. of a transformation that is outwardly visible: of Jesus, who took on the form of his heavenly glory and *was transfigured* Mt 17: 2; Mk 9: 2 (cf. IQH 7, 24.—RHartstock, Visionsberichte in den syn. Evangelien: JKaftan-Festschr. '20, 130-44; AvHarnack, SAB '22, 62-80; E Lohmeyer, ZNW 21, '22, 185-215; UvWilamowitz, Red. u. Vorträge⁴ II '26, 280-93: D. Verklärung Christi; JB Bernardin, The Transfiguration: JBL 52, '33, 181-9; JBlinzler, D. ntl. Berichte üb. d. Verklärg. Jesu '37; JHöller, D. Verkl. Jesu '37; EDabrowski, La transfiguration de Jésus '39; GHBoobyer, St. Mark and the Transfiguration Story '42; HRiesenfeld, Jésus transfiguré '47; HBaltensweiler, Die Verklärung Jesu '59; SHirsch on βαπτίζω 2a). Of the transformation of raw material into a statue Dg 2: 3.
2. of a transformation invisible to the physical eye τὴν αὐτὴν εἰκόνα μεταμορφοῦσθαι *be changed into the same form* 2 Cor 3: 18 (on the acc. cf. Bl-D. §159, 4 app.; Rob. 486; for the idea Rtzst., Mysterienrel.³ 262-5; cf. Seneca, Ep. 6, 1, esp. 94, 48). μεταμορφοῦσθε τῇ ἀνακαινώσει τοῦ νοός *let yourselves be transformed by the renewing of your minds* Ro 12: 2. M-M.*

μετανοέω fut. μετανοήσω; 1 aor. μετενόησα (Antipho +; inscr., pap., LXX, Philo, Joseph., Test. 12 Patr.) *change one's mind* Hv 3, 7, 3; m 11: 4 (cf. Diod. S. 15, 47, 3 μετενόησεν ὁ δῆμος; 17, 5, 1; Epict. 2, 22, 35; Appian, Hann. 35 §151, Mithrid. 58 §238; Stob., Ecl. II 113, 5ff

W.; PSI 495, 9 [258 BC]; Jos., Vi. 110; 262), then *feel remorse, repent, be converted* (in religio-ethical sense: X., Hell. 1, 7, 19 οὐ μετανοήσαντες ὕστερον εὑρήσετε σφᾶς αὐτοὺς ἡμαρτηκότας τὰ μέγιστα ἐς θεούς τε καὶ ὑμᾶς αὐτούς; Plut., Camill. 29, 3, Ag. 19, 5, Galba 6, 4, Adulat. 36 p. 74c; M. Ant. 8, 2; 53; Ps.-Lucian, De Salt. 84 μετανοῆσαι ἐφ᾽ οἷς ἐποίησεν; Herm. Wr. 1, 28; Dit., Or. 751, 9 [II BC] θεωρῶν οὖν ὑμᾶς μετανενοηκότας τε ἐπὶ τοῖς προημαρτημένοις, Syll.³ 1268 II, 8 [III BC] ἁμαρτὼν μετανόει; PSI 495, 9 [258/7 BC]; BGU 747 I, 11; 1024 IV, 25; PTebt. 424, 5; Is 46: 8; Jer 8: 6; Sir 17: 24; 48: 15; oft. Test. 12 Patr. [s. index]; Philo [s. μετάνοια]; Jos., Bell. 5, 415, Ant. 7, 153; 320) ἐν σάκκῳ καὶ σποδῷ μ. *repent in sackcloth and ashes* Mt 11: 21; Lk 10: 13. As a prerequisite for attaining the Kgdm. of God in the preaching of John the Baptist and Jesus Mt 3: 2; 4: 17; Mk 1: 15. As the subject of the disciples' preaching 6: 12; Ac 17: 30; 26: 20. Failure to repent leads to destruction Lk 13: 3, 5; Mt 11: 20. Repentance saves (cf. Philo, Spec. Leg. 1, 239 ὁ μετανοῶν σῴζεται; 253) 12: 41; Lk 11: 32; cf. 15: 7, 10; 16: 30. μ. εἰς τὸ κήρυγμά τινος *repent at* or *because of someone's preaching* Mt 12: 41; Lk 11: 32 (Bl-D. §207, 1; Rob. 593; s. εἰς 6a). W. ἐπί τινι to denote the reason *repent of, because of someth.* (Charito 3, 3, 11; Ps.-Lucian, Salt. 84; M. Ant. 8, 2; 10; 53; Jo 2: 13; Jon 3: 10; 4: 2; Am 7: 3, 6; Prayer of Manasseh [=Ode 12] 7; Philo, Virt. 180; Jos., Ant. 7, 264; Test. Judah 15: 4.—Bl-D. §235, 2) ἐπὶ τῇ ἀκαθαρσίᾳ *of their immorality* 2 Cor 12: 21. ἐπὶ τοῖς ἁμαρτήμασιν *of their sins* 1 Cl 7: 7. ἐπί w. subst. inf. foll. MPol 7: 2. Also διά τι Hv 3, 7, 2. Since in μ. the negative impulse of turning away is dominant, it is also used w. ἀπό τινος: *repent and turn away from someth.* ἀπὸ τῆς κακίας (Jer 8: 6) Ac 8: 22 (MWilcox, The Semitisms of Ac, '65, 102–5). ἀπὸ τῆς ἀνομίας 1 Cl 8: 3 (quot. of unknown orig.). Also ἔκ τινος Rv 2: 21b, 22; 9: 20f; 16: 11. W. ἐπιστρέφειν ἐπὶ τὸν θεόν Ac 26: 20. μ. εἰς ἑνότητα θεοῦ *turn in repentance to the unity of God* (which precludes all disunity) IPhld 8: 1b; cf. ISm 9: 1. But μ. εἰς τὸ πάθος *repent concerning the suffering* (of Christ, which the Docetists deny) 5: 3. W. inf. foll. Rv 16: 9. W. ὅτι foll. *repent because* or *that* (Jos., Ant. 2, 315) Hm 10, 2, 3. W. adv. ἀδιστάκτως s 8, 10, 3. βραδύτερον s 8, 7, 3; 8, 8, 3b. πυκνῶς m 11: 4. ταχύ Hs 8, 7, 5; 8, 8, 3a; 5b; 8, 10, 1; 9, 19, 2; 9, 21, 4; 9, 23, 2c. μ. ἐξ ὅλης (τῆς) καρδίας *repent w. the whole heart* 2 Cl 17: 1; 19: 1; Hv 1, 3, 2; 2, 2, 4; 3, 13, 4b; 4, 2, 5; m 5, 1, 7; 12, 6, 1; s 7: 4; 8, 11, 3. μ. ἐξ εἰλικρινοῦς καρδίας *repent w. a sincere heart* 2 Cl 9: 8.—The word is found further, and used abs. (Diod. S. 13, 53, 3; Epict., Ench. 34; Oenomaus [time of Hadrian] in Euseb., Pr. Ev. 5, 19, 1; Philo, Mos. 2, 167 al.; Jos., Ant. 2, 322) Lk 17: 3f; Ac 2: 38; 3: 19; Rv 2: 5a (Vi. Aesopi I c. 85 μετανόησον) take counsel with yourself), b, 16, 21; 3: 3, 19; 2 Cl 8: 1, 2, 3; 13: 1; 15: 1; 16: 1; IPhld 3: 2; 8: 1a; ISm 4: 1; Hv 1, 1, 9; 3, 3, 2; 3, 5, 5; 3, 13, 4a; 5: 7; m 4, 1, 5; 7ff; 4, 2, 2; 4, 3, 6; 9: 6; 10, 2, 4; 12, 3, 3; s 4: 4; 6, 1, 3f; 6, 3, 6; 6, 5, 7; s 7: 2; 4f; 8, 6, 1ff; 8, 7, 2f; 8, 8, 2; 5a; 8, 9, 2; 4; 8, 11, 1f; 9, 14, 1f; 9, 20, 4; 9, 22, 3f; 9, 23, 2; 5; 9, 26, 6; 8; D 10: 6; 15: 3; PK 3 p. 15, 11; 27.—S. also MPol 9: 2; 11: 1f, in the sense *repent* from Christianity.—Windisch, Exc. on 2 Cor 7: 10 p. 233f; Norden, Agn. Th. 134ff; AHDirksen, The NT Concept of Metanoia, Diss. Cath. Univ. of America, Washington, '32; FPShipham, ET 46, '35, 277–80; EKDietrich, D. Umkehr (Bekehrg. u. Busse) im AT u. im Judent. b. bes. Berücksichtigg. der ntl. Zeit '36; HPohlmann, D. Metanoia '38; OMichel, Ev. Theol. 5, '38, 403–14; BPoschmann, Paenitentia secunda '40, 1–205 (NT and Apost. Fathers); JBehm and EWürthwein, TW IV 972–1004. S. μεταμέλομαι, end. M-M. B. 1123. *

μετάνοια, ας, ἡ *a change of mind* (Thu. 3, 36, 4; Polyb. 4, 66, 7; Appian, Mithrid. 16 §57; Jos., C. Ap. 1, 274, Ant. 16, 125), *remorse* (as regret for shortcomings and errors: Batr. 69; Lycon the Peripatetic [III BC] in Diog. L. 5, 66; Polyb. 18, 33, 7; Stoic. III p. 147, l. 21f; Cebes 10, 4; 11, 1; Plut., Mor. 56A; 68F; 961D, Alex. 11, 4, Mar. 10, 4; 39, 3; Charito 1, 3, 7; Appian, Liby. 52 §225; 102 §482; 116 §553; M. Ant. 8, 10; Ps.-Lucian, Calumn. 5; Jos., Ant. 13, 314) in our lit. w. an expressly religious coloring (cf. Hierocles 14 p. 451; Sir 44: 16; Wsd 12: 10, 19; Prayer of Manasseh [=Ode 12] 8; Philo, Det. Pot. Ins. 96, Spec. Leg. 1, 58, Virt. 175ff [περὶ μετανοίας] al.; Ep. Arist. 188; Jos., Ant. 9, 176; Test. Reub. 2: 1, Judah 19: 2, Gad 5: 7f; Sib. Or. 1, 129; 168) *repentance, turning about, conversion*; as a turning away μετάνοια ἀπὸ νεκρῶν ἔργων *turning away from dead works* Hb 6: 1. Mostly of the positive side of repentance, as the beginning of a new religious and moral life: ἡ εἰς θεὸν μ. *repentance that leads to God* Ac 20: 21. ἄξια τῆς μετανοίας ἔργα *deeds that are consistent with repentance* 26: 20. Also καρπὸν ἄξιον τῆς μ. Mt 3: 8; cf. Lk 3: 8. βαπτίζειν εἰς μ. *baptize for repentance* Mt 3: 11 (s. βαπτίζω 2a; also εἰς 6a). βάπτισμα μετανοίας Mk 1: 4; Lk 3: 3; cf. Ac 13: 24; 19: 4. χρείαν ἔχειν μετανοίας *need repentance or conversion* Lk 15: 7. κηρύσσειν μ. εἰς ἄφεσιν ἁμαρτιῶν *preach repentance that leads to the forgiveness of sins* 24: 47; cf. 1 Cl 7: 6. ἔχειν καιρὸν μετανοίας *still have time for repentance* 2 Cl 8: 2. τόπον μετανοίας διδόναι *give an opportunity for repentance* (Wsd 12: 10) 1 Cl 7: 5. μετανοίας τόπον εὑρίσκειν Hb 12: 17. διδόναι τινὶ (τὴν) μ. (cf. Wsd 12: 19; M. J. Brutus, Ep. 7) Ac 5: 31; 11: 18; 2 Ti 2: 25; B 16: 9; cf. Hv 4, 1, 3; s 8, 6, 2; 8, 11, 1. τιθέναι τινὶ μετάνοιαν *prescribe repentance for someone* Hm 4, 3, 4; cf. 5; καλεῖν τινα εἰς μ. Lk 5: 32; Mt 9: 13 t.r.; Mk 2: 17 t.r. περὶ μετανοίας λαλεῖν 1 Cl 8: 1. ἀκούσαντες ταύτην τὴν μετάνοιαν *when they heard of this repentance* Hs 8, 10, 3; παιδεύεσθαι εἰς μ. *be disciplined so as to repent* 1 Cl 57: 1. εἰς μ. ἄγειν τινά (Ep. Arist. 188; Jos., Ant. 4, 144) Ro 2: 4; ἀνακαινίζειν εἰς μ. Hb 6: 6; χωρῆσαι εἰς μ. *come to repentance* 2 Pt 3: 9. μετάνοιαν λαμβάνειν *receive repentance* (after denying Christ) Hs 9, 26, 6a. μετανοίας μετασχεῖν 1 Cl 8: 5. μετάνοιαν ἔχειν *have the possibility of repentance* Hm 4, 3, 3; s 8, 8, 2. ἐστί τινι μετάνοιαν *have a possibility of repentance* Hv 2, 2, 5c; 3, 7, 5; s 8, 8, 5; 8, 9, 4a; 9, 19, 1; 9, 20, 4. τινι μετάνοιά ἐστι μία *have (only) one possibility of repentance* m 4, 1, 8; cf. 4, 3, 1. μ. κεῖται τινι *repentance is ready, available for someone* s 9, 19, 2f; 9, 22, 4; 9, 26, 6b. ἐπίκειταί τινι 8, 7, 2a. γίνεταί τινι 9, 26, 5; εἰς μάτην ἐστὶν ἡ μ. *is in vain* s 6, 1, 3. ταχινὴ ὀφείλει εἶναι *must follow quickly* 8, 9, 4b. ἡ μ. σύνεσίς ἐστιν μεγάλη *is great understanding* m 4, 2, 2. μ. καθαρά m 12, 3, 2; cf. s 7: 6. μ. ἁμαρτίας *rep. for sin* 2 Cl 16: 4; cf. Hm 4, 3, 3. μ. ζωῆς *rep. that leads to life* s 6, 2, 3; cf. 8, 6, 6. ἐλπὶς μετανοίας *hope of repentance* or *conversion* IEph 10: 1; Hs 6, 2, 4; 8, 7, 2b; 8, 10, 2. W. πίστις and other Christian virtues 1 Cl 62: 2. The ἄγγελος τῆς μ. appears in Hermas as a preacher of repentance: v 5: 8; m 12, 4, 7; 12, 6, 1; s 9, 1, 1; 9, 14, 3; 9, 23, 5; 9, 24, 4; λυπεῖσθαι εἰς μ. *feel pain that leads to repentance* 2 Cor 7: 9. λύπη μετάνοιαν ἐργάζεται (cf. Plut., Mor. 476F) vs. 10.—W. the Christian use of the word in mind Polycarp says ἀμετάθετος ἡμῖν ἡ ἀπὸ τῶν κρειττόνων ἐπὶ τὰ χείρω μετάνοια *for us 'repentance' from the better to the worse is impossible* MPol 11: 1.—WHolladay, The Root Šûbh in the OT, '58. M-M. **

μεταξύ adv. (Hom.+; inscr., pap., LXX [Johannessohn 173f]; En., Philo, Joseph.).

1. used as adv.—a. of space (Hom. +) *between, in the middle* τὸ μεταξύ *what lies between* (Aeneas Tact. 1420; Dio Chrys. 18[35], 1) Dg 7: 2 (cf. Philo, Det. Pot. Ins. 80 τὰ μ.).

b. of time—a. *between* (Pla., Rep. 5 p. 450c; Jos., Ant. 2, 169) ἐν τῷ μεταξύ *in the meanwhile* (X., Symp. 1, 14; BGU 1139, 8 [5 вс]; PTebt. 24, 42; 72, 190; PFlor. 36, 5; Jos., Ant. 14, 434; Test. Zeb. 2: 7) J 4: 31.

β. *afterward, thereupon* (Plut., Mor. 58в; 240а; Achilles Tat. 1, 13, 1; Mitteis, Chrest. 57, 11 [40/41 AD]; 64, 5; Jos., Bell. 2, 211, Ant. 10, 45) εἰς τὸ μεταξὺ σάββατον *on the next sabbath* Ac 13: 42. Cf. 23: 24 v.l.; 1 Cl 44: 2f. ὁ λαὸς ὁ μεταξύ *the people yet to come* B 13: 5.

2. as improper prep. w. gen. (Hdt. et al.) *between, in the middle of*—a. of space (Polyb. 14, 1, 9; Aelian, V.H. 3, 1; En. 14, 11; 18, 3; Jos., Ant. 3, 147 μ. αὐτῆς [τ. λυχνίας] καὶ τ. τραπέζης) μ. τοῦ ναοῦ καὶ τοῦ θυσιαστηρίου *between the sanctuary and the altar* Mt 23: 35; cf. Lk 11: 51. μ. ἡμῶν καὶ ὑμῶν 16: 26. μ. δύο στρατιωτῶν *between two soldiers* Ac 12: 6. μ. θηρίων μ. θεοῦ (to be) *among the wild beasts (is to be) with God* ISm 4: 2. W. a relative foll. μ. ὧν ἐλάλουν *between the words of my discourse* IPhld 7: 1 (the text is uncertain; s. Hdb. ad loc.; Lake reads ὧν and transl. μ. *with* [you]).

b. of a reciprocal relation, a difference (PReinach 44, 16 [104 AD] τῆς συμφωνίας τῆς γενομένης μεταξὺ αὐτοῦ κ. Ἰσιδώρας; POxy. 1117, 3 μ. ἡμῶν κ. ἀρχόντων) μ. σοῦ καὶ αὐτοῦ μόνου *between you and him alone* Mt 18: 15. Witnesses μ. ὑμῶν καὶ ἡμῶν *betw. us and you* 1 Cl 63: 3. —διακρίνειν μ. τινος καὶ τινος *make a distinction between* Ac 15: 9. τοσαύτη τις διαφορὰ μ. τῶν τε ἀπίστων κ. τῶν ἐκλεκτῶν MPol 16: 1. διαφορὰ πολλὴ μ. τῶν δύο ὁδῶν *a great difference between* D 1: 1.—μεταξὺ ἀλλήλων (PGenève 48, 11 μ. ἡμῶν ἀλλήλων) *among themselves, with one another* Ro 2: 15. M-M.*

μεταπαραδίδωμι (Vett. Val. 163, 25; Iambl., Vi. Pyth. 32, 226; inscr., pap.; PGM 4, 501) in our lit. only intr. and only once *give place to, succeed, follow* ἀλλήλοις *one another* of the seasons 1 Cl 20: 9.*

μεταπέμπω (Hdt. +; inscr., pap., LXX, Joseph.) in our lit. only mid. and pass.; 1 aor. mid. μετεπεμψάμην, imper. μετάπεμψαι; 1 aor. pass. ptc. μεταπεμφθείς; *send for, summon* τινά *someone* (Hippocr., Ep. 6; Appian, Iber. 10 §38; Gen 27: 45; Num 23: 7; Ep. Arist. 179; Jos., Vi. 69) Ac 10: 5, 29b; 11: 13; 20: 1; 24: 24, 26. W. acc. of the pers. and indication of the place to which: μεταπέμψασθαί σε εἰς τὸν οἶκον αὐτοῦ *to summon you to his house* 10: 22. αὐτὸν εἰς Ἱερουσαλήμ 25: 3 (Jos., C. Ap. 1, 92 τ. ἀδελφοὺς εἰς τὴν Αἴγυπτον). Without the acc. (easily supplied fr. the context) w. indication of the place from which ἀπὸ ἀνατολῆς μεταπεμψάμενος *since* (God) *has summoned* (the bishop) *from the east* IRo 2: 2.—Pass. μεταπεμφθείς *when I was sent for* Ac 10: 29a (Jos., Ant. 6, 164 ἧκεν μεταπεμφθείς). M-M.*

μεταστρέφω 1 aor. μετέστρεψα; 2 aor. pass. μετεστράφην, imper. μεταστραφήτω; 2 fut. μεταστραφήσομαι (Hom. +; PGM 4, 2625; LXX) *change, alter, pervert* τὶ εἰς τι *someth. into someth.*, oft. its opposite (Ps 77: 44; Sir 11: 31 τὰ ἀγαθὰ εἰς κακά. Cf. Test. Ash. 1: 8) *sun into darkness* Ac 2: 20 (Jo 3: 4). *Laughter to grief* Js 4: 9 v.l. (cf. Am 8: 10; 1 Macc 9: 41). W. acc. of the thing μ. τὸ εὐαγγέλιον τοῦ Χριστοῦ *pervert the gospel of Christ* Gal 1: 7. M-M.*

μετασχηματίζω fut. μετασχηματίσω; 1 aor. μετεσχημάτισα *change the form of, transform, change* (Pla., Leg. 10 p. 903е; 906c; Aristot., De Caelo 3, 1 p. 298b, 31;

Plut., Ages. 14, 2, Mor. 426е; 680а; Sext. Emp., Math. 10, 335; LXX; Philo, Aet. M. 79; Jos., Ant. 7, 257) μ. τὸ σῶμα τ. ταπεινώσεως ἡμῶν *change our lowly body* to be like the glorious body Phil 3: 21 (cf. Philo, Leg. ad Gai. 80). Mid. *change or disguise oneself* (Jos., Ant. 8, 267) abs. 2 Cor 11: 15. W. εἰς τι *into* or *as someth.* (Diod. S. 3, 57, 5 εἰς ἀθανάτους φύσεις; 4 Macc 9: 22) ὁ σατανᾶς εἰς ἄγγελον φωτός *Satan disguises himself as an angel* (fr. the kgdm.) *of light* vs. 14 (cf. Test. Reub. 5: 6 the guardian angels μετεσχηματίζοντο εἰς ἄνδρα). Of the false apostles μετασχηματιζόμενοι εἰς ἀποστόλους Χριστοῦ *who disguise themselves as apostles* vs. 13 (JHColson, JTS 17, '16, 379ff).—1 Cor 4: 6 is more or less unique (on it s. σχηματίζειν and σχῆμα in Philostrat., Vi. Soph. 2, 17, 1; 2, 25, 1. In Ps.-Demetr., Eloc. 287; 292-4 σχηματίζειν means 'say someth. with the aid of a figure of speech'): ταῦτα μετεσχημάτισα εἰς ἐμαυτὸν κ. Ἀπόλλων *I have applied this to Apollos and myself*= I have given this teaching of mine the form of an exposition concerning Apollos and myself. M-M.*

μετατίθημι 1 aor. μετέθηκα; 2 aor. ptc. μεταθείς; 1 aor. pass. μετετέθην (Hom. +; inscr., pap., LXX, Ep. Arist. 188; Philo, Joseph., Sib. Or. 4, 162) *change (the position of)*.

1. lit. *convey to another place, put in another place, transfer* τὴν χεῖρα ἐπί τι *transfer your hand to someth.* B 13: 5. W. acc. of the pers. and indication of the goal μεταθέντες αὐτὸν ἐπὶ τὴν καροῦχαν *they had him transferred to the carriage* MPol 8: 2. Pass.: of corpses μετετέθησαν εἰς Συχέμ *they were brought back to Shechem* Ac 7: 16. W. indication of the place fr. which ἐκ τῶν βασάνων *be removed from* (the place of) *torment* Hv 3, 7, 6 (μετατίθημι ἐκ as a grave-inscr. fr. Amastris: Jahreshefte d. Oesterr. Arch. Inst. 28 Beibl. '33, col. 81f no. 39). Of Enoch *be taken up, translated* Hb 11: 5a; 1 Cl 9: 3 (cf. Sir 44: 16; Wsd 4: 10); the act. in the same sense and of the same person Hb 11: 5b (Gen 5: 24).

2. non-literally—a. *change, alter* (Hdt. 5, 68 al.; Jos., Ant. 15, 9) τὶ εἴς τι *someth. into someth.* (Esth 4: 17s μετάθες τὴν καρδίαν αὐτοῦ εἰς μῖσος) τὴν τοῦ θεοῦ ἡμῶν χάριτα εἰς ἀσέλγειαν *pervert the grace of our God to dissoluteness* Jd 4. Pass. μετατιθεμένης τῆς ἱερωσύνης *when the priesthood is changed*, i.e. passed on to another Hb 7: 12 (Jos., Ant. 12, 387 of the transfer of the office of high priest to another person).

b. mid. *change one's mind, turn away, desert, turn apostate* (Polyb. 5, 111, 8; 24, 9, 6; Diod. S. 11, 4, 6; 2 Macc 7: 24 ἀπὸ τ. πατρίων.—ὁ μεταθέμενος means a turncoat who leaves one philosoph. school for another one: Diog. L. 7, 166; Athen. 7 p. 281d) ἀπό τινος εἴς τι *from someth. to someth.* μ. ἀπὸ τοῦ καλέσαντος ὑμᾶς...εἰς ἕτερον εὐαγγέλιον *desert him who called you* (and turn) *to another gospel* Gal 1: 6 (cf. Hierocles 7 p. 429: there is to be no yielding to μεταβαλλομένοις ἐκ τῆς περὶ φιλοσοφίαν σπουδῆς εἰς ἑτέραν τινὰ τοῦ βίου πρόθεσιν; Field, Notes 188). ἀπὸ τῶν χαλεπῶν ἐπὶ τὰ δίκαια *turn away from evil to good* MPol 11: 1. M-M.*

μετατρέπω 2 aor. pass. μετετράπην, imper. μετατραπήτω (Hom. +; 4 Macc; Ep. Arist. 99; Philo) *turn around* pass. *be turned* (Quint. Smyrn. 11, 270) laughter into grief Js 4: 9. M-M.*

μεταφέρω 1 aor. pass. μετηνέχθην (trag., X., Pla. +; inscr., pap., LXX, Ep. Arist.) *carry away* pass. (Jos., Ant. 3, 103) of stones ἐκ τοῦ πύργου Hs 9, 6, 5; 9, 8, 1.*

μεταφυτεύω 1 aor. pass. imper. μεταφυτεύθητι (Theophr., H.Pl. 2, 6, 3; 4; Aq., Sym., Theod. Ps 91: 14; Aq. also Ps 1: 3) *transplant* pass. *be transplanted* Lk 17: 6 D.*

μετέβη s. μεταβαίνω.

μετέπειτα adv. (Hom.+; Dit., Or. 177, 14; LXX, Ep. Arist.; Jos., Ant. 6, 66) *afterwards* Hb 12: 17; Hv 2, 4, 2. M-M.*

μετέχω 2 aor. μετέσχον, inf. μετασχεῖν; pf. μετέσχηκα (Pind., Hdt.+; inscr., pap., LXX, En., Ep. Arist., Philo; Jos., C. Ap. 1, 31; 51 al.; Sib. Or. 8, 56) *share, have a share, participate* w. gen. of the thing *in* or *of someth.* (Bl-D. §169, 1; Rob. 509) πάντων Dg 5: 5. μετανοίας 1 Cl 8: 5. φυλῆς ἑτέρας *belong to another tribe* Hb 7: 13 (cf. Thu. 8, 86, 3). τῶν εὐεργεσιῶν *share in the benefits* Dg 8: 11; θεοῦ μ. *share in God* IEph 4: 2 (cf. Jos., C. Ap. 1, 232 θείας μ. φύσεως). τραπέζης κυρίου, δαιμονίων *share in, partake of the table of the Lord, of demons* i.e. in the Lord's Supper and in idolatrous banquets 1 Cor 10: 21 (Philostrat., Vi. Soph. 2, 15, 1 μ. τοῦ ἱεροῦ.—μ. τραπέζης as Lucian, Cyn. 7; Philo, De Jos., 196). μετέσχεν τῶν αὐτῶν *he shared the same things* (i.e. flesh and blood) Hb 2: 14.—Participation can also mean *eat, drink, enjoy*, esp. w. foods: ὁ μετέχων γάλακτος *whoever lives on milk* Hb 5: 13. Abs. ἐπ' ἐλπίδι τοῦ μετέχειν (sc. τῶν καρπῶν) *in the hope of enjoying the crops* 1 Cor 9: 10. εἰ ἐγὼ χάριτι μετέχω (sc. τῆς τροφῆς) *if I eat with thanks* 10: 30. Also of rights: τῆς ὑμῶν ἐξουσίας μ. *enjoy authority over you* 1 Cor 9: 12. Instead of the gen. μ. ἔκ τινος: ἐκ τοῦ ἑνὸς ἄρτου *share, eat one and the same loaf* 10: 17 (s. Thieme 29f).—The poorly attested rdg. ἄνδρα μ. Lk 1: 34 means *have a husband.*—HHanse, TW II 830f. M-M.*

μετεωρίζομαι (Aristoph.+ in sense 'raise up'; pap., LXX, Philo, Joseph.) in our lit. only in one place, pass. and fig. μὴ μετεωρίζεσθε Lk 12: 29. In the context this can hardly mean anything other than *do not be anxious, worried* (the verb has this meaning Polyb. 5, 70, 10; POxy. 1679, 16 μὴ μετεωρίζου, καλῶς διάγομεν='do not worry, we are getting along well'; Jos., Ant. 16, 135.—Likew. the adj. μετέωρος='hovering between hope and fear, restless, anxious': Thu. 2, 8, 1; Polyb. 3, 107, 6; BGU 417, 4; 6 [opp. ἀμέριμνος]). The alternate transl. *be overbearing, presumptuous*, though possible on purely linguistic grounds (Diod. S. 13, 80, 1; 13, 92, 2.—Simplicius in Epict. p. 32, 13 μετεωρισμός=pride), supported by the LXX, and favored by Vulg., Luther, Tyndale et al., can no longer be seriously considered.—AHarnack, Sprüche u. Reden Jesu '07, 10; KKöhler, StKr 86, '13, 456ff. M-M.*

μετῆρα s. μεταίρω.

μετοικεσία, ας, ἡ (Leonidas of Tarentum [III bc]: Anth. Pal. 7, 731, 6; Psellus p. 222, 5; LXX) *removal to another place of habitation, deportation* ἐπὶ τῆς μ. Βαβυλῶνος *at the time of the Babylonian captivity* Mt 1: 11. μετὰ τὴν μ. Βαβυλῶνος vs. 12; ἕως τῆς μ. Β. vs. 17; ἀπὸ τῆς μ. Β. ibid. (of the Bab. exile 4 Km 24: 16; 1 Ch 5: 22; Ezk 12: 11). M-M.*

μετοικίζω Attic. fut. μετοικιῶ (Bl-D. §74, 1; cf. Mlt.-H. 218); 1 aor. μετῴκισα (Aristoph.+; inscr., LXX, Ep. Arist., Philo, Joseph.) *remove to another place of habitation, resettle* τινά εἴς τι *someone to a certain place* (Dit., Or. 264, 7 μετῴκισεν αὐτοὺς εἰς τὴν παλαιὰν πόλιν; 1 Ch 8: 6; Ep. Arist. 4; Jos., C. Ap. 1, 132) αὐτὸν εἰς τὴν γῆν ταύτην *he removed him to this country* Ac 7: 4. Of forcible deportation μετοικιῶ ὑμᾶς ἐπέκεινα Βαβυλῶνος *I will deport you beyond Babylon* vs. 43 (Am 5: 27). M-M.*

μετοπωρινός, όν (Hes., Thu.+; Philostrat., Vi. Apoll. 5, 6 p. 168, 24; Philo) *autumnal* καιροὶ μ. *the autumn* 1 Cl 20: 9.*

μετοχή, ῆς, ἡ (Hdt.+; pap.; Ps 121: 3; PsSol 14: 6; Philo, Leg. All. 1, 22) *sharing, participation* (BGU 1123, 11 [I bc]; PLond. 941, 8 al.) τίς μ. δικαιοσύνῃ καὶ ἀνομίᾳ; *what have righteousness and lawlessness in common?* 2 Cor 6: 14 (there is a purely formal parallel to 2 Cor 6: 14-16 in Himerius, Or. [Ecl.] 3, 6 ποῦ δὲ συμβαίνει κ. μίγνυται ἡδονὴ πόνοις, καρτερία τρυφῇ, ἀκαδημία καὶ πόρναι, φιλοσοφία καὶ πότος, σωφρονούντων βίος καὶ ἀκόλαστα μειράκια;). M-M.*

μέτοχος, ον (Eur., Hdt.+; pap., LXX)—1. *sharing or participating in* w. gen. of the pers. or thing (Hdt. 3, 52; Pr 29: 10; Ep. Arist. 207; Sib. Or. 12, 174) κλήσεως ἐπουρανίου *sharing in a heavenly calling* Hb 3: 1. In the Lord's discipline 12: 8. In the Holy Spirit 6: 4. In the promises 1 Cl 34: 7. *Share in prayer* IEph 11: 2. μ. εἰ τῆς ἁμαρτίας αὐτοῦ *you share in his sin* Hm 4, 1, 9.—μ. τοῦ Χριστοῦ *sharing in Christ* (cf. Epigr. Gr. 654, 5 πρόσθεν μὲν θνητή, νῦν δὲ θεῶν μέτοχος) Hb 3: 14. But perh. this pass. belongs under 2.

2. subst. ὁ μ. *partner, companion* (Ps.-Demosth. 61, 31; PPetr. III 37a II, 7 [259 bc]; BGU 1123, 4 al.; pap.; En. 104, 6; Test. Benj. 2: 5) Lk 5: 7; Hb 1: 9 (Ps 44: 8). M-M.*

μετρέω 1 aor. ἐμέτρησα; 1 fut. pass. μετρηθήσομαι (Hom.+; inscr., pap., LXX, Philo; Jos., Bell. 6, 167, Ant. 2, 124) *measure.*

1. *take the dimensions of, measure*—a. lit., w. acc. of the thing: τὸν ναόν *measure the temple* Rv 11: 1 (PKetter, Past. Bonus 52, '41, 93-9). τὴν πόλιν *measure the city* 21: 15. αὐλήν 11: 2. τὸν οὐρανόν B 16: 2 (Is 40: 12). W. the measuring-instrument given in the dat. (Ex 16: 18) τῷ καλάμῳ *measure with the rod* Rv 21: 16; cf. 11: 1. The measure arrived at is expressed by the gen. of quality ἐμέτρησεν τὸ τεῖχος ἑκατὸν τεσσεράκοντα τεσσάρων πηχῶν *he measured the wall (and it was) 144 cubits* Rv 21: 17; also by ἐπί and the gen. vs. 16, where a v.l. has ἐπί and acc. (on the latter cf. Da 3: 47).

b. fig. αὐτοὶ ἐν ἑαυτοῖς ἑαυτοὺς μετροῦντες *they measure themselves by one another* 2 Cor 10: 12. ἐμαυτὸν μετρῶ *I keep myself within bounds* ITr 4: 1 (Sotades Mar. [III bc] 10, 8 Diehl ἡ σωφροσύνη πάρεστιν, ἂν μετρῇς σεαυτόν).

2. *give out, deal out, apportion* τινί τι *someth. to someone* (Eur.; Ps.-Demosth. 46, 20; PPetr. III 89, 2; PTebt. 459, 4 [5 bc] ὃ ἐὰν περισσὸν γένηται μέτρησον αὐτοῖς) in the proverbial expr. ἐν ᾧ μέτρῳ μετρεῖτε, μετρηθήσεται ὑμῖν *the measure you give will be the measure you get* Mk 4: 24; Mt 7: 2. Likew., except without ἐν, Lk 6: 38 v.l. (Maximus Tyr. 27, 7b has a play on words μετρεῖ—μετρεῖται.—Philo, Rer. Div. Her. 229 μέτροις μεμέτρηται.—The pass.='receive as one's portion': Jos., Bell. 3, 185).—1 Cl 13: 2 the saying reads ᾧ μέτρῳ μετρεῖτε, ἐν αὐτῷ μετρηθήσεται ὑμῖν. The text of Lk 6: 38 has ᾧ μέτρῳ μετρεῖτε, ἀντιμετρηθήσεται ὑμῖν, which is repeated word for word in Pol 2: 3.—KDeissner, TW IV 635-8: μετρέω and related words. M-M. B. 877f.*

μετρητής, οῦ, ὁ *measure*, a liquid measure orig. fr. Attica (Demosth. 42, 20; Aristot. H.A. 8, 9; Polyb. 2, 15, 1; inscr. [fr. IV bc]; pap., LXX; Ep. Arist. 76; loanw. in rabb.), similar in content to the Hebr. בַּת, containing 72 sextarii (Jos., Ant. 8, 57) or pints=39.39 liters, or about nine gallons (cf. FHultsch, Griech. u. röm. Metrologie² 1882, 101f; 108f; 703). As a measure for wine (Dit., Syll.³ 672, 54 [162-0 bc], Or. 266, 4; Gk. Pap. fr. Gurob ['21] 8, 14; 1 Esdr 8: 20; Bel 3 Theod.) J 2: 6. M-M.*

μετριοπαθέω (Sext. Emp., Pyrrh. Hyp. 3, 235; 236; Dositheus 71, 11; Philo, Abr. 257; Jos., Ant. 12, 128.

μετριοπαθής and μετριοπάθεια are more common) *moderate one's feelings, deal gently* w. dat. of the pers.: τοῖς ἀγνοοῦσιν *deal gently with the sinners* (ἀγνοέω 4) Hb 5: 2. M-M.*

μέτριος, ία, ιον (Hes., Thu.+; Dit., Syll.³ 783, 53; POxy. 120, 7; 1117, 19; Sir 31: 20; Philo; Jos., Bell. 1, 552, Vi. 22; 122) *moderate* μέτρια νοεῖν *be moderate, practice self-restraint* 1 Cl 1: 3 (μέτρια φρονεῖν in the same sense: Diod. S. 23, 15, 4; 8).*

μετρίως adv. (Eur., Hdt.+; Plut., Tit. Flam. 9, 5 οὐ μ.; UPZ 71, 5 [152 BC]; PRyl 150, 9 ὕβρισεν οὐ μετρίως; PGiess. 17, 5 οὐ μ.; Sb 4323, 2 οὐ μ.; 2 Macc 15: 38; Ep. Arist. 197) *moderately, somewhat* οὐ μ. *greatly* (Diod. S. 18, 45, 4; 20, 83, 2; Plut., Mor. 838F; Procop. Soph., Ep. 5; Philo; Jos., Ant. 15, 194; 276; s. above) Ac 20: 12. M-M.*

μέτρον, ου, τό (Hom.+; inscr., pap., LXX, En., Ep. Arist., Philo; Jos., Ant. 13, 294, C. Ap. 2, 216; Test. 12 Patr.; Sib. Or. 3, 237) *measure.*
1. as an instrument for measuring—a. of measures of capacity ἐν μέτρῳ μετρεῖν Mt 7: 2; Mk 4: 24; 1 Cl 13: 2b. μέτρῳ μετρεῖν (Maximus Tyr. 32, 9c; 35, 2i) Lk 6: 38b; 1 Cl 13: 2a; Pol 2: 3. W. heaping up of attributes μ. καλὸν πεπιεσμένον σεσαλευμένον ὑπερεκχυννόμενον *good measure, pressed down, shaken together, running over* Lk 6: 38a. Symbolically πληροῦν τὸ μ. τινός *fill up a measure that someone else has partly filled* Mt 23: 32.
b. of linear measure Rv 21: 15. μέτρον ἀνθρώπου, ὅ ἐστιν ἀγγέλου *a human measure, used also by angels* vs. 17.
2. *measure as the result of measuring, quantity, number*
a. lit. τὰ μ. τῶν τῆς ἡμέρας δρόμων φυλάσσειν *keep the measure of its daily courses* Dg 7: 2.
b. fig. (Maximus Tyr. 40, 3c ὑγιείας μ.; Alex. Aphr., Quaest. 3, 12 II 2 p. 102, 2 μ. τῆς ἀληθείας) ὡς ὁ θεὸς ἐμέρισεν μέτρον πίστεως as God has apportioned the *measure of faith* Ro 12: 3 (CEBCranfield, NTS 8, '62, 345–51: Christ is the measure of faith). ἑνὶ ἑκάστῳ ἐδόθη ἡ χάρις κατὰ τὸ μ. τῆς δωρεᾶς τοῦ Χριστοῦ *grace was given to each one according to the measure (of it) that Christ gave* Eph 4: 7. κατὰ τὸ μ. τοῦ κανόνος οὗ ἐμέρισεν ἡμῖν ὁ θεὸς μέτρου *according to the measure of the limit (=within the limits) which God has apportioned us (as a measure)* (cf. Bl-D. §294, 5 app.; Rob. 719) 2 Cor 10: 13. κατ' ἐνέργειαν ἐν μέτρῳ ἑνὸς ἑκάστου μέρους *according to the power that corresponds to the measure of each individual part* Eph 4: 16 (ἐν μ. as Synes., Ep. 12 p. 171c). καταντᾶν εἰς μ. ἡλικίας τοῦ πληρώματος τοῦ Χριστοῦ *attain to the measure of mature age (or stature of the fulness) of Christ* vs. 13 (s. ἡλικία 1ca and cf. μ. ἡλικίας Plut., Mor. 113D; μ. ἥβης Il. 11, 225; Od. 11, 317).—οὐκ ἐκ μέτρου J 3: 34, an expr. not found elsewh. in the Gk. language, must mean in its context *not from a measure, without measure* (the opp. is ἐν μέτρῳ Ezk 4: 11, 16; Jdth 7: 21). M-M.*

μέτωπον, ου, τό (Hom.+; inscr., pap., LXX; Jos., Ant. 6, 189; 15, 399) *forehead* Lk 23: 48 D. Of a maiden: veiled ἕως τοῦ μ. Hv 4, 2, 1. As the place marked w. a sign of some kind (cf. BStade, D. Kainszeichen: ZAW 14, 1894, 250ff; PsSol 15: 9; Diphilus Com. [IV BC], fgm. 66, 8 K.; Herodas 5, 79; Lucian, Pisc. 46; Porphyr., Vi. Pyth. 15; of a branded slave, Martial 3, 21) Rv 7: 3; 9: 4; 13: 16; 14: 1, 9; 17: 5; 20: 4; 22: 4 (Dit., Syll.³ 1168, 48; 54 [letters]; PLille 29 II, 36; Ezk 9: 4 al.).—CSchneider, TW IV 638–40. M-M. B. 218.*

μέχρι even before vowels as in Attic Lk 16: 16; Job 32: 12.

In three places in the NT (Mk 13: 30 and Gal 4: 19 μέχρις οὗ, Hb 12: 4 μέχρις αἵματος) as well as Hv 4, 1, 9 (μέχρις ὅτε), s 9, 11, 1 (μέχρις ὀψέ) the form used before vowels is μέχρις (Vett. Val. 357, 19; IG XII 5, 647; Dit., Syll.³ 888, 150 [before a conson.]; 958, 16; 1109, 41; pap. [Mayser p. 244]. On the LXX cf. Thackeray p. 136.—Bl-D. §21; Mlt.-H. 113; 331) *until.*
1. prep. w. gen. foll. (Hom.+; inscr., pap., LXX, En., Ep. Arist., Philo, Joseph., Test. 12 Patr.; Sib. Or. 3, 568).
a. of space *as far as* μ. τοῦ οὐρανοῦ GP 10: 40. μ. τῆς Ἀσίας Ac 20: 4 D. ἀπὸ Ἰερουσαλήμ . . . μ. τοῦ Ἰλλυρικοῦ Ro 15: 19 (ἀπὸ—μ. as Dit., Syll.³ 973, 6f). μ. τῶν ἔσω φλεβῶν MPol 2: 2 (Jos., Bell. 6, 304 μ. ὀστέων).
b. of time μ. (τῆς) νῦν IMg 8: 1; Papias 3 (Chio, Ep. 16, 4; Longus 4, 16, 2; Xenophon Eph. 1, 4, 1; Jos., Ant. 7, 386; 17, 114; cf. μ. τοῦ νῦν X., Cyr. 7, 3, 15; PTebt. 50, 26 [112/11 BC]; BGU 256, 9). μ. ὀψέ Hs 9, 11, 1. μέχρι τίνος; *how long?* (Alciphr. 4, 17, 2; Achilles Tat. 2, 5, 1) v 3, 10, 9. μ. τῆς σήμερον *until today* (Jos., Ant. 9, 28) Mt 11: 23; cf. 28: 15; Hv 2, 2, 4. μ. μεσονυκτίου *until midnight* Ac 20: 7. μ. Ἰωάννου *until (the time of) John* Lk 16: 16. μ. τῆς ἐπιφανείας τοῦ κυρίου ἡμῶν Ἰησοῦ Χριστοῦ 1 Ti 6: 14. μ. καιροῦ διορθώσεως Hb 9: 10. μ. τοῦ θερισμοῦ (v.l. ἕως, ἄχρι) *until harvest time* Mt 13: 30. μ. τέλους Hb 3: 6, 14.—ἀπὸ . . . μ. (POxy. 1647, 20 ἀπὸ ἀνατολῆς ἡλίου μέχρι δύσεως; Ep. Arist. 298): ἀπὸ τετάρτης ἡμέρας μ. ταύτης τῆς ὥρας *from the fourth day to this hour* Ac 10: 30. ἀπὸ Ἀδὰμ μ. Μωϋσέως Ro 5: 14.
c. of degree, measure (Appian, Bell. Civ. 3, 69 §284 μ. τοῦ τέλους=to the end; Jos., Ant. 11, 81 μ. θρήνων) κακοπαθεῖν μ. δεσμῶν *suffer even to the point of being imprisoned* 2 Ti 2: 9. μ. αἵματος ἀντικαταστῆναι *resist to the point of shedding one's blood* in being wounded or killed Hb 12: 4 (μ. αἵμ. as Herodian 2, 6, 14). μ. θανάτου διωχθῆναι καὶ μ. δουλείας ἐλθεῖν 1 Cl 4: 9 (cf. 2 Macc 13: 14; Jos., Bell. 2, 141). Of Christ ὑπήκοος μ. θανάτου *obedient unto death* Phil 2: 8. Of Epaphroditus διὰ τὸ ἔργον Χριστοῦ μ. θανάτου ἤγγισεν vs. 30 (μέχρι θανάτου to denote degree: Diod. S. 15, 27, 2; Cebes 26, 3; Appian, Bell. Civ. 2, 113 §471; 3, 77 §314; 3, 90 §372; 4, 135 §570 al.; Polyaenus 7, 30; 8, 49; schol. on Apollon. Rhod. 3, 427–31a; 2 Macc 13: 14).
2. as a conjunction *until* (Bl-D. §383, 2 w. app.; Rob. 975) μ. καταντήσωμεν Eph 4: 13 (cf. Hdt. 4, 119, 4; Dit., Syll.³ 976, 71 μέχρι ποιήσωσιν; PKairo ed. Preisigke ['11] 48, 7 μέχρι τὸ πλοιάριον εὑρῶμεν; Sib. Or. 3, 570. On the omission of ἄν cf. Mlt. 168f; LRydbeck, Fachprosa, '67, 144–53). μ. οὗ w. subjunctive (Herodas 2, 43; POxy. 293, 7 [27 AD] μέχρι οὗ ἀποστείλῃς; Da 11: 36 Theod.; Ep. Arist. 298) Mk 13: 30 (μ. ὅτου B); Gal 4: 19. μ. ὅτε (ὅτου ℵ°) Hv 4, 1, 9 (cf. Bl-D. §455, 3). M-M.**

μή (Hom.+; inscr., pap., LXX, En., Ep. Arist., Philo, Joseph., Test. 12 Patr., Sib. Or.) negative particle, *not.* 'μή is the negative of will, wish, doubt. If οὐ denies the fact, μή denies the idea' (Rob. 1167). For the Koine of the NT the usage is simplified to such a degree that οὐ is generally the neg. used w. the indicative, and μή is used w. the other moods (Bl-D. §426; Rob. 1167).
A. as a negative particle—I. negativing clauses—1. in conditional clauses after ἐάν Mt 5: 20; 6: 15; 10: 13; 12: 29; 18: 3, 16, 35; 26: 42; Mk 3: 27; 7: 3f; 10: 30; 12: 19; Lk 13: 3, 5; J 3: 2f, 5, 27 al. After ὃς ἄν (=ἐάν) Mt 10: 14; 11: 6; 19: 9; Mk 6: 11; 10: 15; Lk 8: 18; 18: 17. After ὅσοι ἄν Lk 9: 5; Rv 13: 15. After ὅστις ἄν Ac 3: 23. After εἰ in a contrary to fact condition (Bl-D. §428, 2; Rob. 1169) Mt 24: 22; Mk 13: 20; J 9: 33; 15: 22, 24; 18: 30; 19: 11; Ac 26: 32; Ro 7: 7. εἰ μή *if not, except (that)*, εἰ δὲ μήγε *otherwise* with verb and elliptically (Bl-D. §428, 3;

439, 1; Rob. 1024f) Mt 5: 13; 6: 1; 9: 17; 11: 27; 12: 4, 24 and very oft. (GHarder, 1 Cor 7: 17: ThLZ 79, '54, 367-72).

2. in purpose clauses ἵνα μή *in order that not* Mt 5: 29f; 7: 1; 17: 27; Mk 3: 9; 4: 12; Lk 8: 10, 12; 16: 28; J 3: 20; 7: 23; Ac 2: 25 (Ps 15: 8); 4: 17; 24: 4; Ro 11: 25; 15: 20 al. ὅπως μή *in order that not* Mt 6: 18; Lk 16: 26; Ac 20: 16; 1 Cor 1: 29. On the inf. w. neg. as periphrasis for purpose clauses s. below.

3. in result clauses ὥστε μή w. inf. foll. (cf. PHib. 66, 5) *so that not* Mt 8: 28; Mk 3: 20; 1 Cor 1: 7; 2 Cor 3: 7; 1 Th 1: 8; w. imper. foll. 1 Cor 4: 5.

4. in interrog. clauses w. an element of doubt: δῶμεν ἢ μὴ δῶμεν; *should we pay (them) or should we not?* Mk 12: 14.

5. in a few relative clauses (Bl-D. §428, 4; Mlt. 171; 239f) διδάσκοντες ἃ μὴ δεῖ Tit 1: 11 (cf. Lucian, Dial. Deor. 13, 1; PGM 4, 2653 ὃ μὴ θέμις γενέσθαι; PRain. 19, 17; 2 Macc 12: 14; Sir 13: 24). The literary language is the source of ᾧ μὴ πάρεστιν ταῦτα τυφλός ἐστιν 2 Pt 1: 9, where the relat. clause has a hypothetical sense. ὅσα μὴ θέλετε Ac 15: 29 D. Cf. Col 2: 18 v.l. On ὃ μὴ ὁμολογεῖ (v.l. ὃ λύει) 1 J 4: 3 s. ARahlfs, ThLZ 40, '15, 525.

6. in a causal clause contrary to the rule, which calls for οὐ: ὅτι μὴ πεπίστευκεν εἰς τὸ ὄνομα J 3: 18 (cf. Epict. 4, 4, 8; Jos., C. Ap. 1, 217 διήμαρτον, ὅτι μὴ ταῖς ἱεραῖς ἡμῶν βίβλοις ἐνέτυχον; Ps.-Clem., Hom. 8, 4; 11, 8; 32; Dio Chrys. 31, 94; 110.—Bl-D. §428, 5; Mlt. 171; 239; Mlt.-Turner 284; Rahlfs, loc. cit.).

II. used with various moods—1. w. the inf. (Bl-D. §399, 3; 400, 4; 5; Mlt.-Turner 285f)—a. after verbs expressing a negative concept, usu. omitted in translation ἀντιλέγοντες ἀνάστασιν μὴ εἶναι Lk 20: 27 (v.l. λέγοντες). ἀπαρνεῖσθαι 22: 34. παραιτεῖσθαι Hb 12: 19. ἐγκόπτειν τινά Gal 5: 7. προσέχειν Mt 6: 1. οὐ δύναμαι μὴ *I can do nothing else than* Ac 4: 20.

b. gener., after verbs of saying, reporting, ordering, judging, etc.

α. in declarative clauses: after ἀποκρίνεσθαι Lk 20: 7. λέγειν Mt 22: 23; Mk 12: 18; Lk 20: 27 v.l.; Ac 23: 8. ὀμνύναι Hb 3: 18. θέλειν Ro 13: 3. χρηματίζεσθαι Lk 2: 26.

β. in clauses denoting a summons or challenge: after λέγειν Mt 5: 34, 39; Ac 21: 4; Ro 2: 22; 12: 3. γράφειν 1 Cor 5: 9, 11. κηρύσσειν Ro 2: 21. παραγγέλλειν Ac 1: 4; 4: 18; 5: 28, 40; 1 Cor 7: 10f (w. acc.); 1 Ti 1: 3; 6: 17. αἰτεῖσθαι Eph 3: 13. εὔχεσθαι 2 Cor 13: 7 (w. acc.). χρηματίζεσθαι Mt 2: 12. ἀξιοῦν Ac 15: 38. βοᾶν 25: 24.

c. after predicates that contain a judgment upon the thing expressed by the inf. (with or without the art.): καλόν (sc. ἐστιν) 1 Cor 7: 1; Gal 4: 18; cf. Ro 14: 21. ἄλογον Ac 25: 27 (w. acc.). κρεῖττον ἦν 2 Pt 2: 21. αἱρετώτερον ἦν αὐτοῖς τὸ μὴ γεννηθῆναι Hv 4, 2, 6. Cf. δεῖ Ac 27: 21.

d. The gen. of the subst. inf. τοῦ μή *that not* (Lat. *ne*) comes—α. after verbs of hindering κατέχειν Lk 4: 42. παύειν J 3: 10 (Ps 33: 14). καταπαύειν Ac 14: 18. κωλύειν 10: 47. κρατεῖσθαι Lk 24: 16; cf. ἀνένδεκτόν ἐστιν τοῦ . . . μὴ ἐλθεῖν 17: 1.

β. also after other expressions: ὀφθαλμοὶ τοῦ μὴ βλέπειν, ὦτα τοῦ μὴ ἀκούειν *eyes that should not see, ears that should not hear* Ro 11: 8, 10 (Ps 68: 24). In place of a result clause: τοῦ μὴ εἶναι αὐτὴν μοιχαλίδα *so that she commits no adultery, if . . .* 7: 3.

e. the subst. inf. comes after prepositions: εἰς τὸ μή *so that . . . not; to the end that . . . not* Ac 7: 19; 1 Cor 10: 6; 2 Cor 4: 4. W. acc. and inf. foll. 2 Th 2: 2; 1 Pt 3: 7.—διὰ τὸ μή *because . . . not* (PPetr. II 11, 1, 7 [III BC]

τοῦτο δὲ γίνεται διὰ τὸ μὴ ἀθροῦν ἡμᾶς; 2 Macc 2: 11) Mt 13: 5f; Mk 4: 5f; Lk 8: 6; Js 4: 2 (w. acc.).—πρὸς τὸ μή *in order that . . . not* (Ptolem. Pap. aus Alexandria 4, 3 in Witkowski p. 51 πρὸς τὸ μὴ γίνεσθαι τῷ βασιλεῖ τὸ χρήσιμον; Esth 3: 13d, e; Bar 1: 19; 2: 5) 2 Cor 3: 13; 1 Th 2: 9; 2 Th 3: 8.

f. w. the dat. of the subst. inf. τῷ μή *because . . . not* 2 Cor 2: 13.

g. w. the nom. or acc. of the subst. inf. (2 Esdr [Ezra] 6: 8; cf. Bl-D. §399, 3; cf. Rob. 1038) Ro 14: 13; 2 Cor 2: 1; 10: 2; 1 Th 4: 6.

2. very oft. w. the ptc., in keeping w. the tendency of later Gk. to prefer μή to οὐ; exceptions in Bl-D. §430 w. app.; cf. Rob. 1172.

a. μή is regularly used to negative the ptc. used w. the article, when the ptc. has a hypothet. sense or refers to no particular person, and has a general mng. (Artem. 4, 22 p. 215, 14 οἱ μὴ νοσοῦντες): ὁ μὴ ὢν μετ' ἐμοῦ *every one who is not with me* Mt 12: 30a, b; Lk 11: 23a, b; ὁ μὴ πιστεύων J 3: 18. πᾶς ὁ μή . . . Mt 7: 26; 1 J 3: 10a, b; 2 J 9. πάντες οἱ μή 2 Th 2: 12. μακάριοι οἱ μή J 20: 29; cf. Ro 14: 22. τῶν τὴν ψυχὴν μὴ δυναμένων ἀποκτεῖναι Mt 10: 28b and oft.

b. w. the ptc. when it has conditional, causal, or concessive sense: πᾶν δένδρον μὴ ποιοῦν Mt 3: 10; 7: 19. Cf. 9: 36; 13: 19; Lk 11: 24. θερίσομεν μὴ ἐκλυόμενοι *we will reap, if we do not become weary* (before the harvest) Gal 6: 9. μὴ ὄντος νόμου *when there is no law* Ro 5: 13. νόμον μὴ ἔχοντες *although they have no law* 2: 14. μὴ ὢν αὐτὸς ὑπὸ νόμον *though I am not under the law* 1 Cor 9: 20. μὴ μεμαθηκώς *without having learned (them)* J 7: 15. μὴ ἔχοντος δὲ αὐτοῦ ἀποδοῦναι *but since he could not pay it back* Mt 18: 25.

c. when it is to be indicated that the statement has subjective validity: ὡς μὴ λαβών *as though you had not received* 1 Cor 4: 7. ὡς μὴ ἐρχομένου μου vs. 18. Gk. would require οὐ: τὰ μὴ ὄντα *what does not exist* (in reality, not only in Paul's opinion) Ro 4: 17; 1 Cor 1: 28 (Philo, Op. M. 81 τὸ τὰ μὴ ὄντα εἰς τὸ εἶναι παραγαγεῖν); Hv 1, 1, 6. τὰ μὴ βλεπόμενα *what is unseen* 2 Cor 4: 18a, b. τὰ μὴ δέοντα 1 Ti 5: 13. τὰ μὴ καθήκοντα (3 Macc 4: 16) Ro 1: 28. τὰ μὴ σαλευόμενα Hb 12: 27. τὸν μὴ γνόντα ἁμαρτίαν 2 Cor 5: 21. τυφλὸς μὴ βλέπων Ac 13: 11. S. also μὴ ἀσθενήσας τῇ πίστει κατενόησεν Ro 4: 19 where, as oft., the main idea is expressed by the ptc.

III. In a prohibitive sense in independent clauses, to express a negative wish or a warning.

1. with subjunctive *let us not, we should not*: pres. subj. μὴ γινώμεθα κενόδοξοι Gal 5: 26. μὴ ἐγκακῶμεν 6: 9. μὴ καθεύδωμεν 1 Th 5: 6; cf. 1 Cor 5: 8. W. aor. subj. μὴ σχίσωμεν αὐτόν J 19: 24.

2. w. optative (Bl-D. §427, 4; Rob. 1170) μὴ αὐτοῖς λογισθείη 2 Ti 4: 16 (cf. Job 27: 5). ἐμοὶ δὲ μὴ γένοιτο καυχᾶσθαι Gal 6: 14 (cf. 1 Macc 9: 10; 13: 5). Esp. in the formula μὴ γένοιτο (s. γίνομαι I 3a) Lk 20: 16; Ro 3: 4, 31; 6: 2, 15; 7: 7, 13; 9: 14; 11: 1, 11; 1 Cor 6: 15; Gal 2: 17; 3: 21.

3. w. the pres. imperative—a. to express a command that is generally valid (Test. Reub. 2: 10) μὴ γίνεσθε ὡς οἱ ὑποκριταί Mt 6: 16; cf. vs. 19. μὴ μεριμνᾶτε τῇ ψυχῇ ὑμῶν vs. 25; Lk 12: 22.—Mt 7: 1; 10: 31; 19: 6; Lk 6: 30; 10: 4, 7; 1 Cor 6: 9; 7: 5, 12f, 18; Eph 4: 26 (Ps 4: 5), 29 and oft.

b. to bring to an end a condition now existing (Aeschyl., Sept. 1036; Charito 2, 7, 5 μὴ ὀργίζου='be angry no longer'; PHib. 56, 7 [249 BC]; PAmh. 37, 7; POxy. 295, 5; Wsd 1: 12 and elsewh. LXX; Mlt. 122ff) μὴ φοβεῖσθε *do not be afraid (any longer)* Mt 14: 27; 17: 7; Lk 2: 10; cf. 1: 13, 30. μὴ κλαῖε *do not weep (any more)* 7: 13; cf. 23: 28. μὴ σκύλλου *do not trouble yourself (any further)* 7: 6; cf. 8: 49 t. r.—9: 50; Mk 9: 39; J 2: 16; 6: 43. μὴ γράφε *do not write (any longer)=* it must no longer stand written 19: 21. μή μου ἅπτου *do not cling to me any longer= let go of me* 20: 17. μὴ γίνου ἄπιστος vs. 27.—Ac 10: 15; 20: 10; Ro 11: 18, 20; 1 Th 5: 19; Js 2: 1 and oft.

4. w. aor. imper. (Od. 16, 301; Lucian, Paras. μὴ δότε; 1 Km 17: 32) μὴ ἐπιστρεψάτω Mt 24: 18; Lk 17: 31b. μὴ καταβάτω Mt 24: 17; Mk 13: 15; Lk 17: 31a. μὴ γνώτω Mt 6: 3.

5. W. the aor. subj. μή serves—a. almost always to prevent a forbidden action fr. beginning (Plut., Alex. 54, 6 μὴ φιλήσῃς='don't kiss'; PPetr. II 40a, 12 [III BC]; POxy. 744, 11; BGU 380, 19; LXX.—This is the sense of μὴ θαυμάσῃς Herm. Wr. 11, 17; s. b below) μὴ φοβηθῇς Mt 1: 20; 10: 26. μὴ δόξητε 3: 9; cf. 5: 17. μὴ ἅψῃ Col 2: 21. μὴ ἀποστραφῇς Mt 5: 42. μὴ κτήσησθε 10: 9 and oft. Also w. the third pers. of the aor. subj. μή τις αὐτὸν ἐξουθενήσῃ *no one is to slight him* 1 Cor 16: 11. μή τίς με δόξῃ εἶναι 2 Cor 11: 16. μή τις ὑμᾶς ἐξαπατήσῃ 2 Th 2: 3. μὴ σκληρύνητε Hb 3: 8, 15 (quot. fr. Ps 94: 8) is hardly a pres. subj.; it is rather to be regarded as an aor.

b. only rarely is the aor. subj. used, as the pres. imper. regularly is (s. above III 3b), to put an end to a condition already existing μὴ θαυμάσῃς *you need no longer wonder* J 3: 7 ('with an effect of impatience': Mlt. 124; 126. S. a above).

6. in abrupt expressions without a verb: μὴ ἐν τῇ ἑορτῇ (we must) *not* (proceed against him) *during the festival* Mt 26: 5; Mk 14: 2. Cf. J 18: 40. καὶ μὴ (ποιήσωμεν) Ro 3: 8. μὴ ὀκνηροί (γίνεσθε) 12: 11. Cf. 14: 1; Gal 5: 13; Eph 6: 6 al.

B. as a conjunction—1. after verbs of fearing, etc. *that . . .* (*not*), *lest*—a. w. pres. subj. (3 Macc 2: 23) ἐπισκοποῦντες . . . μή τις ῥίζα . . . ἐνοχλῇ Hb 12: 15.

b. w. aor. subj. (Pla., Apol. 1 p. 17A) φοβηθεὶς μὴ διασπασθῇ Ac 23: 10. Also after a pres. 27: 17 (cf. Tob 6: 15). After βλέπειν in the mng. *take care* (PLond. 964, 9 βλέπε μὴ ἐπιλάθῃ οὐδέν) Mt 24: 4; Mk 13: 5; Lk 21: 8; Ac 13: 40; 1 Cor 10: 12; Gal 5: 15; Hb 12: 25. σκοπῶν σεαυτόν, μὴ καὶ σὺ πειρασθῇς Gal 6: 1. στελλόμενοι τοῦτο, μή τις ἡμᾶς μωμήσηται 2 Cor 8: 20. ὁρᾶν Mt 18: 10; 1 Th 5: 15. Elliptically, like an aposiopesis ὅρα μή *take care! you must not do that!* Rv 19: 10; 22: 9 (Bl-D. §480, 5; Rob. 932; 1203).

c. the fut. ind. follows instead of the subj. (X., Cyr. 4, 1, 18 ὅρα μὴ πολλῶν ἑκάστῳ ἡμῶν χειρῶν δεήσει) βλέπετε μή τις ἔσται Col 2: 8; cf. Hb 3: 12.

2. taking the place of a purpose clause: w. aor. subj. Mk 13: 36; Ac 27: 42; 2 Cor 12: 6.

C. μή is used as an interrogative particle when a negative answer is expected to the question (Bl-D. §427, 2; 4; 440; Rob. 1168; 1175; Mlt.-Turner 283).

1. in direct questions (Xenophon Eph. 398, 26 H.; Job 1: 9; 8: 11) *perhaps,* usu. left untranslated, but cf. μή τινος ὑστερήσατε; *you did not lack anything, did you?* Lk 22: 35. Cf. Mt 7: 9f; 9: 15; Mk 2: 19; Lk 5: 34; 11: 11; 17: 9; J 3: 4; 4: 12, 33; 6: 67; 7: 35, 51f; 21: 5 (cf. μήτι); Ac 7: 28 (Ex 2: 14), 42 (Am 5: 25); Ro 3: 3, 5 (cf. Job 8: 3); 9: 14, 20 (Is 29: 16); 1 Cor 1: 13; 9: 8f; 10: 22 al. μὴ γάρ J 7: 41; 1 Cor 11: 22.—In cases like Ro 10: 18f; 1 Cor 9: 4f μή is an interrog. word and οὐ negatives the verb. The double negative causes one to expect an affirmative answer (Bl-D. §427, 2; cf. Rob. 1173f; Tetrast. Iamb. 17, 2 p. 266 μὴ οὐκ ἔστι χλόη; = 'there is grass, is there not?').

2. in indirect questions *whether. . . not* Lk 11: 35 (cf. Epict. 4, 5, 18a; Arrian, Anab. 4, 20, 2 μή τι βίαιον ξυνέβη = whether anything violent has happened [hopefully not]; Jos., Ant. 6, 115).

D. in combination w. οὐ, μή has the effect of strengthening the negation (Kühner-G. II 221-3; Mlt. 187-92 [a thorough treatment of NT usage]; RLudwig: D. prophet. Wort 31 '37, 272-9; Bl-D. §365.—Class. [Kühner-G. loc. cit.]; Dit., Syll.³ 1042, 16; POxy. 119, 5, 14f; 903, 16; PGM 5, 279; 13, 321; LXX). οὐ μή is the most decisive way of negativing someth. in the future.

1. w. the subj.—a. aor. subj. (Ael. Aristid. 50, 107 K. = 26 p. 533 D.: οὐ μὴ ἡμῶν καταφρονήσωσι; Diogenes, Ep. 38, 5; UPZ 62, 34; 79, 19) *never, certainly not,* etc. Mt 5: 18, 20, 26; 24: 2; Mk 13: 2; Lk 1: 15; 6: 37a, b; J 8: 52; 10: 28; 11: 26; 13: 8; 1 Cor 8: 13; Hb 8: 12 (Jer 38: 34); 13: 5; 1 Pt 2: 6 (Is 28: 16); Rv 2: 11; 3: 12; 18: 21-3 al.—Also in a rhetorical question, when an affirmative answer is expected οὐ μὴ ποιήσῃ τὴν ἐκδίκησιν; *will he not vindicate?* Lk 18: 7. οὐ μὴ πίω αὐτό; *shall I not drink it?* J 18: 11. τίς οὐ μὴ φοβηθῇ; *who shall not fear?* Rv 15: 4.—In relative clauses Mt 16: 28; Mk 9: 1; Ac 13: 41 (Hab 1: 5); Ro 4: 8 (Ps 31: 2); cf. Lk 18: 30.—In declarative and interrogative sentences after ὅτι Mt 24: 34; Lk 22: 16 (οὐκέτι οὐ μή); J 11: 56; without ὅτι Mt 26: 29; Lk 13: 35.—Combined w. οὐδέ: οὐδ᾽ οὐ μὴ γένηται (Wilcken, Chrest. 122, 4 [6 AD]) Mt 24: 21.

b. w. pres. subj. Hb 13: 5 where, however, only Tdf. has accepted ἐγκαταλείπω, which is well attested (so 𝔓⁴⁶), while L., W-H., N., vSoden read ἐγκαταλίπω.

2. w. fut. ind. (En. 98, 12; 99, 10) οὐ μὴ ἔσται σοι τοῦτο Mt 16: 22.—Hm 9: 5; s 1: 5. Cf. Mt 15: 6; 26: 35; Lk 21: 33; J 4: 14; 6: 35b; 10: 5; Hb 10: 17. οὐκέτι οὐ μὴ εὑρήσουσιν Rv 18: 14. οὐ γὰρ μὴ κληρονομήσει Gal 4: 30 (Gen 21: 10 v.l.); but the tradition wavers mostly betw. the fut. and aor. subj. (s. Mlt. and Bl-D. loc. cit.). M-M.

μήγε in the formula εἰ δὲ μήγε *otherwise* s. γέ 3b.

μηδαμῶς adv. (Aeschyl., Hdt. +; pap. [Mayser 182; also POxy. 901, 11; PStrassb. 40, 34]; LXX; Jos., Ant. 18, 20; 70) and **μηθαμῶς** (UPZ 79, 8 [159 BC]) 1 Cl 33: 1; 45: 7; 53: 4 (s. Bl-D. §33; W-S. §5, 27f; Reinhold §6, 3) *by no means, certainly not, no* stating a negative reaction (Chio, Ep. 16, 7; Lucian, Dial. Deor. 4, 2; Ael. Aristid. 23, 79 K. = 42 p. 794 D.) Ac 10: 14; 11: 8; Hv 1, 2, 4. Also the passages fr. 1 Cl above. M-M. *

μηδέ negative disjunctive particle (Hom. +; inscr., pap., LXX, En., Ep. Arist., Joseph., Test. 12 Patr., Sib. Or. 3, 550).

1. *and not, but not, nor* continuing a preceding negation (almost always w. μή).

a. in such a way that both negatives have one verb in common: in the ptc. Mt 22: 29; Mk 12: 24; in the pres. subj. 1 Cor 5: 8; 1 J 3: 18; in the imper. Mt 6: 25; Lk 12: 22; 1 J 2: 15. More than one μηδέ can also follow μή: (Diod. S. 18, 56, 5 μὴ κατιέναι is followed by μηδέ used five times with the same verb) Mt 10: 9f; Lk 14: 12.

b. in such a way that μή and μηδέ each have a verb for themselves: introduced by ὃς ἄν (ἐάν) Mt 10: 14; Mk 6: 11; by ἵνα J 4: 15; ὅπως Lk 16: 26. Both verbs in ptc. 2 Cor 4: 2; in imper. Mk 13: 15; J 14: 27; Ro 6: 12f; Hb 12: 5 (Pr 3: 11). The imperatives can also be wholly or partly replaced by equivalent subjunctive forms: Mt 7: 6; 23: 9f; Lk 17: 23; 1 Pt 3: 14. Both verbs in inf. (depending on παραγγέλλω) Ac 4: 18; 1 Ti 1: 4; 6: 17; cf. Ac 21: 21. More than one μηδέ after μή (Appian, Bell. Civ. 4, 11 §42 μηδεὶς μηδένα followed by μηδέ three times) Col 2: 21; 2 Cl 4: 3; cf. Ro

14: 21; 1 Cor 10: 7-10. The first verb can also be connected w. any compound of μή: μηδείς (Jos., Ant. 8, 395) Lk 3: 14; 1 Ti 5: 22. μήπω Ro 9: 11.

c. in the apodosis of a conditional sentence εἴ τις οὐ θέλει ἐργάζεσθαι, μηδὲ ἐσθιέτω *if anyone is not willing to work, he is not to be given anything to eat* 2 Th 3: 10.

2. *not even* (X., Mem. 1, 2, 36; PMagd. 28, 4 [218 BC]; PTebt. 24, 76) preceded by ὥστε μή (or μηκέτι) Mk 3: 20. μηδὲ τὰ πρὸς τὴν θύραν *not even about the door* Mk 2: 2. μηδὲ εἰς τὴν κώμην εἰσέλθῃς *do not even go into the village* (before returning home) Mk 8: 26. τῷ τοιούτῳ μηδὲ συνεσθίειν *not even to eat with such a person* 1 Cor 5: 11. μηδὲ ὀνομαζέσθω ἐν ὑμῖν *should not even be mentioned among you* Eph 5: 3. M-M.

μηδείς, μηδεμία, μηδέν (Hom.+; inscr., pap., LXX, Ep. Arist.; Jos., Bell. 1, 43, Ant. 8, 395 al.; Test. 12 Patr.— For μηθέν Ac 27: 33; Hm 2: 6, which is found freq. since Aristot. in lit., inscr. [Meisterhans³-Schw. 258f] and pap. [Mayser 180-2], cf. Bl-D. §33; Mlt.-H. 111; Thumb 14. The LXX usage in Thackeray 58-62; Ep. Arist. 182).

1. adj. *no* μηδεμία αἰτία Ac 13: 28; 28: 18. Cf. 25: 17; 1 Cor 1: 7; 1 Ti 5: 14; Hb 10: 2.—Used w. another neg. *no. . . at all* 2 Cor 6: 3; 13: 7; 1 Pt 3: 6. κατὰ μηδένα τρόπον (τρόπος 1) 2 Th 2: 3.

2. subst.—**a.** μηδείς *nobody* ἀκούοντες μὲν τ. φωνῆς μηδένα δὲ θεωροῦντες Ac 9: 7. μηδενὶ εἴπῃς Mt 8: 4; cf. 9: 30; 16: 20; 17: 9; Mk 5: 43; 7: 36; Lk 3: 14; 5: 14; 10: 4; J 15: 24 𝔓⁶⁶; Ac 11: 19; Ro 12: 17; 1 Cor 3: 18; 10: 24; Gal 6: 17; Eph 5: 6; 1 Ti 4: 12; Tit 2: 15; Js 1: 13; 1 J 3: 7; Rv 3: 11 and oft.—Used w. another neg. *nobody at all:* Mk 11: 14; Ac 4: 17.

b. μηδέν *nothing*—**α.** μηδὲν αἴρειν εἰς (τὴν) ὁδόν Mk 6: 8; Lk 9: 3. Cf. 6: 35; Ac 8: 24; 1 Cor 10: 25, 27. ἐκ τοῦ μηδενός *out of nothing*, i.e. *for no good reason at all* Hm 5, 2, 2.—Used w. another neg. (Lucian, Dial. Deor. 24, 1 μὴ λέγε τοιοῦτον μηδέν= 'anything'; Xenophon Eph. 356, 11 H.) ὅρα μηδενὶ μηδὲν εἴπῃς *see to it that you say nothing to anyone* Mk 1: 44. μηδενὶ μηδὲν ὀφείλετε Ro 13: 8. Cf. Phil 1: 28.

β. as acc. of the inner obj. μηδέν almost comes to mean *not . . . at all, in no way* (class.; Lucian, Dial. Deor. 2, 4, Tim. 43; PHib. 43, 6 [III BC]; PAmh. 111, 20; 2 Macc 14: 28; 3 Macc 3: 9; Jos., Ant. 14, 402) μηδὲν ὠφεληθεῖσα *she received no benefit at all* Mk 5: 26. μηδὲν βλάψαν αὐτόν *without harming him in any way* Lk 4: 35.—Ac 4: 21; 10: 20; 11: 12; Js 1: 6; Rv 2: 10 v.l. μεριμνᾶν Phil 4: 6. ὑστερεῖν 2 Cor 11: 5. μ. ἐμποδίζειν 1 Cl 20: 2. μ. ἐναντιοῦσθαι 61: 1. μ. ἀδικεῖσθαι *suffer no harm at all* Dg 6: 5.

γ. μηδὲν εἶναι *be nothing* (Soph., Aj. 767; 1094; Pla., Apol. 33 p. 41E) Gal 6: 3.

δ. ἐν μηδενί *in no way* or *respect* (Hero Alex. III p. 214, 2) 2 Cor 7: 9; Js 1: 4. Cf. also the pass. mentioned above, 2 Cor 6: 3; Phil 1: 28. M-M.

μηδέποτε adv. (X., Pla.+; inscr., pap., LXX; Jos., Ant. 14, 142, Vi. 259) *never* w. ptc. (Diod. S. 20, 78, 1; Galen, Inst. Log. 14, 7 Kalbfl. [1896]; PTebt. 57, 6 [114 BC]) 2 Ti 3: 7; MPol 2: 3; Hm 2: 3; 10, 1, 4; s 8, 7, 2. W. inf. B 16: 10. M-M.*

μηδέπω adv. (Aeschyl.+; POxy. 471, 6; BGU 1210, 63) *not yet* w. ptc. (BGU 1124, 10; Jos., Ant. 17, 202; 312) μ. βλεπόμενα Hb 11: 7. M-M.*

Μῆδος, ου, ὁ (Aeschyl.+; inscr., LXX, Joseph., Sib. Or.) *a Mede,* inhabitant of Media, where there was a Jewish Diaspora (Schürer III⁴ 8f) Ac 2: 9.*

μηθαμῶς s. μηδαμῶς.

μηθέν s. μηδείς, beg.

μηκέτι adv. (Hom.+; inscr., pap., LXX, Joseph.) *no longer, not from now on* in the same usages as μή.

1. in purpose clauses: after ἵνα (POxy. 528, 23) 2 Cor 5: 15; Eph 4: 14.—**2.** in result clauses: after ὥστε (2 Macc 4: 14) Mk 1: 45; 2: 2. W. the inf. of result 1 Pt 4: 2.

3. w. the ptc. (Tob 5: 10 S; Jos., Ant. 13, 399; Test. Reub. 3: 15) Ac 13: 34; Ro 15: 23; 1 Th 3: 1, 5; B 15: 7; IMg 9: 1.

4. w. the inf. (Josh 22: 33; 2 Ch 16: 5; 2 Macc 10: 4; En. 103, 10; Jos., Ant. 8, 45; 47) Ac 4: 17; 25: 24; Ro 6: 6; Eph 4: 17.

5. in a relative clause MPol 2: 3.—**6.** in independent clauses—**a.** w. the imper. (Ex 36: 6; 1 Macc 13: 39) Lk 8: 49; J 5: 14; 8: 11; Eph 4: 28; 1 Ti 5: 23; Hv 3, 3, 2.—Instead of this the aor. subj. (Tob 14: 9 BA) Mk 9: 25; Hv 2, 3, 1. W. piling up of negatives (s. b and c below) οὐ μ. ἐκ σοῦ καρπὸς γένηται εἰς τὸν αἰῶνα *no fruit shall ever come from you again* Mt 21: 19.

b. w. the opt., in double negation μ. . . . μηδεὶς καρπὸν φάγοι *may no one ever eat fruit from you again* Mk 11: 14 (cf. μηδείς 2a).

c. w. the hortatory subjunctive (Sir 21: 1 μὴ προσθῇς μηκέτι) Ro 14: 13. M-M.**

μῆκος, ους, τό (Hom.+; inscr., pap., LXX, Ep. Arist., Philo; Jos., Bell. 4, 467; 482, Ant. 12, 231; Sib. Or. 3, 649) *length* in our lit. only of space: w. breadth, height, depth Eph 3: 18 (cf. βάθος 1). W. breadth Rv 21: 16a, and w. breadth and height (Diod. S. 13, 82, 2 μῆκος, πλάτος ὕψος of the temple of Zeus at Acragas with exact measurements; 16, 83, 2) vs. 16b. τῷ μήκει *in length= long* w. the measurement given Hv 4, 1, 6 (Da 4: 12 οἱ κλάδοι τῷ μήκει ὡς σταδίων τριάκοντα). M-M.*

μηκύνω (Pind., Hdt.+; PLond. 1708, 131; LXX; Ep. Arist. 8) *make long* (cause to grow large Is 44: 15) mid. *become long, grow* (*long*) (Philo, Agr. 17 fig. of trees; Jos., Ant. 12, 357) of sprouting grain Mk 4: 27. M-M.*

μηλωτή, ῆς, ἡ (Philemo Com. [IV/III BC] 25; Pamphilus [I BC/I AD] in Ael. Dion. ω, 1; cf. ο, 5; Apollon. Dysc., Synt. 191, 9; Dit., Or. 629, 32; PTebt. 38, 22 [II BC]; LXX) *sheepskin* of the cloak worn by prophets (3 Km 19: 13, 19; 4 Km 2: 8, 13f) Hb 11: 37; 1 Cl 17: 1. M-M.*

μήν particle (Hom.+; UPZ 59, 27 [168 BC]; LXX) used w. other particles.

1. εἰ μήν q.v.—**2.** καὶ μήν (class.; BGU 1024, 7; 24; Jos., C. Ap. 2, 257, Vi. 256).

a. in contrast to what precedes *and yet* (Kühner-G. II 137; Bl-D. §450, 4 app.) B 9: 6.—**b.** *indeed* (Diod. S. 2, 18, 8 οὐ μήν= of course not; Ep. Arist. 158) Hm 4, 1, 8; 5, 1, 7.

3. μήτε μήν *not even* GOxy 15. M-M.**

μήν, μηνός, ὁ (Hom.+; inscr., pap., LXX, Philo, Joseph., Test. 12 Patr.).

1. *month* Lk 1: 36; PK 2 p. 14, 27. Acc. of time answering the question: how long? (Bl-D. §161, 2; Rob. 469f) *for five months* Lk 1: 24; cf. vs. 56; 4: 25 v.l.; Ac 7: 20; 18: 11; 20: 3; Js 5: 17; Rv 9: 5, 10; 11: 2; 13: 5. W. prep.: εἰς μ. (w. hour, day, year) Rv 9: 15. ἐν μ. Lk 1: 26; ἐπὶ μῆνας τρεῖς *for a period of three months* (s. Jos., Bell. 2, 180) Ac 19: 8; cf. Lk 4: 25. κατὰ μῆνα ἕκαστον *every month* Rv 22: 2 (PRev. 16, 2 [258 BC] καθ᾽ ἕκαστον μῆνα; X., Oec. 9, 8 κατὰ μῆνα). μετὰ τρεῖς μῆνας *after three*

months Ac 28: 11. In an exact date: μηνὸς Ξανθικοῦ δευτέρᾳ ἱσταμένου=February 22, MPol 21; on this s. ἵστημι, end and ESchwartz, Christl. u. jüd. Ostertafeln: AGG new series VIII '05, 127ff.
2. new moon (festival) Gal 4: 10; Dg 4: 5.—GDelling, TW IV 641-5. M-M. B. 1010.*

μηνιάω H.Gk. for class. μηνίω (Apollon. Rhod. 2, 247; Dionys. Hal., Rhet. 9, 16; Aelian, N.A. 6, 17; Charito 1, 2; Sir 10: 6; Philo, Abr. 213; Jos., Ant. 8, 112 v.l.—Phryn. p. 82 L.) cherish anger, rage τινί against someone ἀλλήλοις Hs 9, 23, 3.*

μῆνις, ιος and later ιδος, ἡ (Hom.+; PRyl. 67, 3 [II BC]; BGU 1026, 22, 14; LXX; Jos., Ant. 9, 104; Test. Dan 5: 2; Sib. Or. 4, 135) vengefulness, implacable anger, w. ὀργή described as the source of μ. Hm 5, 2, 4 (on the relationship betw. ὀργή and μῆνις in the Stoa s. Diog. L. 7, 113. Andronicus, περὶ παθῶν 4 [Stoic. III no. 397]; Ps.-Phoc. 64; Sir 27: 30). Described as an incurable sin, ibid.*

μηνύω 1 aor. ἐμήνυσα; pf. μεμήνυκα; 1 aor. pass. ptc. μηνυθείς (Pind., Hdt.+; inscr., pap., LXX, Philo, Joseph.) make known, reveal w. an affirmative clause preceding (ὅτι; cf. Jos., Ant. 1, 198) Lk 20: 37 (of scripture as Philo, Op. M. 15; 77). Obj. easily supplied fr. the context ὁ μηνύσας the man who informed you 1 Cor 10: 28. Report in a written communication MPol 20: 1. Esp. also in a forensic sense report, give information to the authorities (Appian, Bell. Civ. 4, 7 §30; UPZ 121, 15; 25 [156 BC]; PLond. 1171 verso c, 7; PGiess. 61, 7 al.; Jos., Ant. 4, 220) J 11: 57. Pass. μηνυθείσης μοι ἐπιβουλῆς after it became known to me that there was a plot Ac 23: 30 (the dat. as Diod. S. 2, 28, 4 μηνυθείσης αὐτῷ τῆς πράξεως=after the deed had been reported to him; APF VIII p. 214, 9 [79 BC] τοῖς στρατηγοῖς). M-M.*

μὴ οὐ s. μή C 1.

μήποτε (Hom.+; inscr., pap., LXX, En., Ep. Arist., Philo; Jos., Ant. 16, 107 al.; Test. Gad 6: 4. On separating it μή ποτε s. KHALipsius, Gramm. Unters. über die bibl. Gräzität 1863, 129f).
1. negative particle w. the indicative (freq. in H.Gk.) ἐπεὶ μήποτε ἰσχύει since it is never in force Hb 9: 17 (v.l. μὴ τότε).
2. a conjunction, freq. used as an emphatic form of μή —a. after verbs of fearing, being concerned, etc. that . . . not, lest (Diod. S. 11, 20, 2 φοβεῖσθαι μήποτε)—a. w. aor. subj. προσέχετε ἑαυτοῖς μ. βαρηθῶσιν αἱ καρδίαι ὑμῶν take care that . . . not . . . Lk 21: 34 (cf. Sir 11: 33). βλέπε μ. ἀναβῇ Hs 5, 7, 2.—β. w. pres. subj. Hb 4: 1.—γ. w. fut. ind. (En. 106, 6) Hb 3: 12.
b. denoting purpose, (in order) that . . . not, oft. expressing apprehension:
α. w. the aor. subj. (Diod. S. 15, 20, 1; Gen 38: 23; 2 Esdr [Ezra] 4: 22; SSol 1: 7) Mt 4: 6 (Ps 90: 12); 5: 25; 13: 15 (Is 6: 10), 29; 15: 32; 27: 64; Mk 4: 12 (Is 6: 10); Lk 4: 11 (Ps 90: 12); 14: 12; Ac 5: 39; 16: 39 D; 20: 16 D; 28: 27 (Is 6: 10); Hb 2: 1; Hm 10, 2, 5; s 9, 28, 7. After ἵνα Lk 14: 29.—β. w. pres. subj. 12: 58; 14: 8.—γ. w. fut. ind. Mt 7: 6; Mk 14: 2; but the rdg. varies in the Mt pass.
δ. in a double negation μήποτε οὐ μὴ φοβηθήσονται lest they cease to fear D 4: 10.
3. interrog. particle: whether perhaps—a. in a direct quest. (Judg 3: 24; Tob 10: 2; Ep. Arist. 15) μήποτε ἀληθῶς ἔγνωσαν οἱ ἄρχοντες; can it be that the authorities have really come to know? J 7: 26.
b. in indirect quest.—a. w. opt. (Jos., Bell. 1, 609) μ.

αὐτὸς εἴη ὁ Χριστός whether perhaps he himself was the Messiah Lk 3: 15.
β. w. subj. μ. δῴη (s. δίδωμι, beg.) αὐτοῖς ὁ θεὸς μετάνοιαν (seeing) whether God may perhaps grant them repentance 2 Ti 2: 25.
γ. w. the aor. ind., when the content of the question refers to the past (Arrian, Anab. 7, 24, 3 'whether perhaps', with an indirect question referring to the past) GP 5: 15 (s. also ἀγωνιάω).
4. Somet. the negation is weakened to such a degree that μήποτε introduces someth. conjectured probably, perhaps (Aristot., Eth. Nic. 10, 1; 10; M. Ant. 4, 24; Job 1: 5; Sir 19: 13f; Philo, Sacr. Abel. 72, Det. Pot. Ins. 168) μήποτε οὐκ ἀρκέσῃ Mt 25: 9 t.r. perhaps there might not be enough (cf. PJoüon, Rech de Sc rel 15, '25, 438; Mayser II 2, p. 548). The tone is sharper in the wording μήποτε οὐ μὴ ἀρκέσῃ (BCD) certainly there would never be enough. M-M.**

μήπου or μή που conj. (Hom.+; BGU 446, 15; Jos., Bell. 7, 397, Ant. 18, 183) lest or that . . . somewhere after φοβεῖσθαι Ac 27: 29.*

μήπω adv. (Hom.+; POxy. 1062, 15) not yet w. acc. and inf. μ. πεφανερῶσθαι τὴν τῶν ἁγίων ὁδόν Hb 9: 8. W. ptc. (Pla., Symp. 187D; Sb 5343, 37 [182 AD]; Jos., Ant. 1, 217) μ. γεννηθέντων Ro 9: 11. μ. φυγών 2 Cl 18: 2. M-M.*

μήπως or μή πως conj. (Hom.+; pap.; Sir 28: 26).
1. denoting purpose—a. actually in purpose clauses so that . . . (perhaps) not, lest somehow w. aor. subj. 1 Cor 9: 27; 2 Cor 2: 7; 9: 4.
b. after verbs of apprehension that perhaps, lest somehow w. aor. subj. after φοβεῖσθαι (Test. Zeb. 4: 2) Ac 27: 29 t.r.; 2 Cor 11: 3; 12: 20a; cf. b, where the verb (γένωνται) is to be supplied. After βλέπετε take care that . . . not somehow 1 Cor 8: 9 (cf. Sir 28: 26). Referring to someth. that has already taken place, w. perf. ind. Gal 4: 11 (Bl-D. §370, 1; Rob. 995; 1169). Elliptically μ. οὐδὲ σοῦ φείσεται (it is to be feared) that perhaps he will not spare you, either Ro 11: 21 t.r. μ. ἐπείρασεν ὑμᾶς ὁ πειράζων καὶ εἰς κενὸν γένηται ὁ κόπος ἡμῶν (in the fear) that the tempter might really have tempted you (ind., as Gal 4: 11 above), and then our work might have been in vain 1 Th 3: 5.
2. introducing an indirect question μ. εἰς κενὸν τρέχω ἢ ἔδραμον (fearing) that perhaps I may be running or might have run in vain Gal 2: 2. M-M.*

μηρός, οῦ, ὁ (Hom.+; pap. [of a camel marked on the thigh: PLond. 1132b, 5. Likew. Ps.-Callisth. 1, 15, 2 of Bucephalus: ἐν τῷ μηρῷ αὐτοῦ]; LXX; Jos., Ant. 1, 243) thigh Rv 19: 16. M-M.*

μήτε (Hom.+; pap., LXX, En., Ep. Arist., Joseph.) negative copula (Bl-D. §445; Rob. 1189) and not, in the ms. tradition not always carefully distinguished fr. μηδέ (Bl-D. §445, 1; Rob. 1189); continues μή not . . . and not, neither . . . nor Lk 7: 33 (where Tdf. has μή—μηδέ, and μήτε—μήτε is also attested) Mk 3: 20 t.r.; Eph 4: 27 t.r. More than one after μή neither . . . nor . . . nor Ac 23: 8; Rv 7: 1, 3. μήτε . . . μήτε neither . . . nor (Jos., Bell. 5, 533, Ant. 15, 168) Mt 11: 18; Ac 23: 12, 21; 27: 20 (continued w. τέ as X., An. 4, 4, 6); Hb 7: 3; B 16: 10; 19: 11. καὶ μ. . . . μ. and neither . . . nor ISm 7: 2.—A preceding negatived item is divided into its component parts by more than one μήτε foll.: μὴ ὀμόσαι ὅλως, μήτε ἐν τ. οὐρανῷ . . . , μήτε ἐν τῇ γῇ . . . , μήτε . . . not

..., *either* ..., *or* ..., *or* Mt 5: 34ff. Cf. 1 Ti 1: 7; Js 5: 12. μηδὲν ... μήτε ... μήτε *nothing* ..., *neither* ... *nor* Lk 9: 3. μὴ ... μηδὲ ..., μήτε ..., μήτε ... μήτε 2 Th 2: 2 (the first two members are equivalent; the second is then divided into three parts. On the piling up of negatives cf. Phalaris, Ep. 91 μήτε—μήτε ... μηδεὶς ... μηδὲν ... μηδ'; Aelian, V.H. 14, 22 μηδένα μηδενὶ διαλέγεσθαι μήτε κοινῇ μήτε ἰδίᾳ; Synes., Dreams 19 p. 153c τὰ μηδαμῇ μηδαμῶς μήτε ὄντα μήτε φύσιν ἔχοντα; IG IV² 1, 68, 60-5 [302 вс] μή—μήτε—μηδέ).**

μήτηρ, τρός, ἡ (Hom.+; inscr., pap., LXX, Ep. Arist., Philo, Joseph., Test. 12 Patr.) *mother.*

1. lit. Mt 1: 18; 13: 55; 14: 8, 11; 20: 20; Mk 6: 24, 28 and oft. W. the child (cf. Ep. Arist. 27) Mt 2: 11, 13f, 20f. W. the father 10: 37; 15: 4a (Ex 20: 12). Cf. b (Hes., Works 331-34 also knows that whoever abuses or speaks harshly to his aged father is punished by Zeus); 19: 5 (Gen 2: 24), 19 (Ex 20: 12), 29; Mk 5: 40 al. W. brothers Mt 12: 46; Mk 3: 31-3. W. the grandmother 2 Ti 1: 5 (s. μάμμη).

2. GH 5 has the extraordinary notion that the Holy Spirit (רוּחָא דְקוּדְשָׁא—fem. gender) was the mother of Christ; cf. πνεῦμα 5ca, end.

3. transferred also to those who are respected or loved as mothers (Diod. S. 17, 37, 6 ὦ μῆτερ addressed to an aged lady who is well thought of; POxy. 1296, 8; 15; 1678; PGiess. 78, 1) Mt 12: 49f; Mk 3: 34f; J 19: 27 (Duris [III вс]: 76 fgm. 63 Jac.: Polycrates introduces the mothers of those slain in battle to rich citizens w. the words μητέρα σοι ταύτην δίδωμι; Lucian, Tox. 22); Ro 16: 13.

4. of cities (like אֵם) in relation to their citizens; so allegor. of the heavenly Jerusalem, i.e. the Messianic community in relation to its members Gal 4: 26; cf. vs. 22.—JCPlumbe, Mater Ecclesia: An Inquiry into the Concept of Church as Mother in Early Christianity, '43.

5. symbolically (Theognis 1, 385 D.²; Hippocr. in Synes., Ep. 115 p. 255в τ. ἐνδείαν ὑγιείας μητέρα; X., Oec. 5, 17 τ. γεωργίαν τ. ἄλλων τεχνῶν μητέρα εἶναι; Tob 4: 13; Ps.-Phoc. 42 μ. κακότητος; Philo; Test. Sim. 5: 3) of faith, as the source of Christian virtues (Hierocles 11 p. 442 ἡ εὐσέβεια μήτηρ τῶν ἀρετῶν) Hv 3, 8, 5; cf. 7. Babylon ἡ μήτηρ τ. πορνῶν κτλ. Rv 17: 5. M-M. B. 103.

μήτι interrog. particle in questions that expect a negative answer (Aeschyl., Prom. 959; Epict. 2, 11, 20; 4, 1, 133; Mal 3: 8 v.l.—Bl-D. §427, 2; 440; Rob. 1172; 1176): usu. left untranslated, but cf. μήτι συλλέγουσιν κτλ. *surely they do not gather* ..., *do they?* Mt 7: 16; cf. 26: 22, 25; Mk 4: 21; 14: 19; Lk 6: 39; J 8: 22; 18: 35 (in J 21: 5 the best rdg. is not μήτι but μή τι προσφάγιον ἔχετε; *you probably have no fish, have you?*); Ac 10: 47; 2 Cor 12: 18; Js 3: 11; Hv 3, 10, 8; s 9, 12, 5.—Also in questions in which the questioner is in doubt concerning the answer *perhaps* (Ps.-Callisth. 2, 14, 9 μήτι σὺ ὁ 'Αλέξανδρος;) Mt 12: 23; J 4: 29; Hm 4, 4, 1.—Used w. other particles μ. ἄρα (*then*) *perhaps* 2 Cor 1: 17 (Bl-D. §440, 2; Rob. 1190). μήτιγε, s. this entry. After εἰ s. εἰ VI 9. M-M.*

μήτιγε really μήτι γε, in an elliptical expression (Bl-D. §427, 3) *not to speak of, let alone* (Demosth. 2, 23 μὴ τί γε δὲ θεοῖς; Nicol. Dam.: 90 fgm. 130, 29 p. 415, 9 Jac.; Plut., Mor. 14A) 1 Cor 6: 3. M-M.*

μήτρα, ας, ἡ (Hdt., Pla. et al.; pap. [BGU 1026, 22, 20; APF 5, '13, 393 no. 312, 10ff]; LXX; Philo; Sib. Or., fgm. 3, 2; loanw. in rabb.) *womb* ἡ νέκρωσις τῆς μ. Σάρρας *the barrenness of Sarah's womb* Ro 4: 19. Of first-born πᾶν ἄρσεν διανοῖγον μήτραν *every male that opens the womb* Lk 2: 23 (s. διανοίγω 1a). M-M.*

μητραλῴας for which in the NT the mss. more strongly attest the later **μητρολῴας, ου, ὁ** (Bl-D. §26 app.; 35, 2; 119, 2; Mlt.-H. 68.—Attic μητραλοίας Aeschyl.+; Pla., Phaedo 113E; 114A πατραλοῖαι καὶ μητραλοῖαι, Leg. 9 p. 881A μητραλοῖαι ... ὃς ἂν τολμήσῃ μητέρα τύπτειν.— Lysias 10, 8; Lucian, Deor. Conc. 12) *one who murders his mother, a matricide* (w. πατρολῴας. On these very strong words in a catalogue of vices cf. Physiogn. I 327, 15 πατροφόνοι τε καὶ μητροφόνοι παιδοφθόροι τε καὶ φαρμακοὶ κ. τὰ ὅμοια τούτων) 1 Ti 1: 9.*

μητρόπολις, εως, ἡ (Pind., Hdt.+) *capital city* (so X., An. 5, 2, 3; 5, 4, 15; Diod. S. 17, 70, 1; Strabo 16, 2, 44; Dio Chrys. 16[33], 17; inscr., pap., LXX, Philo; Jos., Ant. 4, 82; 12, 119) 1 Ti subscr. (s. Πακατιανός). M-M.*

μηχανάομαι impf. 3 sing. ἐμηχανᾶτο *devise, contrive* τὶ *someth.* in a bad sense (Hom.+; PRainer 19, 19 ταῦτα πάντα ἐμηχανήσατο='all this he has thought up himself'; 3 Macc 6: 24; Philo, Virt. 42; Jos., Ant. 17, 17, Vi. 53; Sib. Or. 126; 172) κατά τινος *devise stratagems against someone* (Test. Reub. 5: 3; cf. Vi. Aesopi I c. 3 κατὰ ἄλλου μηχανεύεσθαι κακόν) MPol 3.*

μηχανή, ῆς, ἡ (Hes.+) *machine* (Aeschyl., Hdt.+; inscr., pap., LXX, Philo; Jos., Ant. 14, 423; 17, 4; loanw. in rabb.), specif. a *crane* for hoisting things (Pla., Crat. 425D) fig. μ. 'Ιησοῦ Χριστοῦ IEph 9: 1. The figure is carried out thus: the parts of the 'crane of Christ' are the cross (Hdt. 2, 125 μηχ. ξύλων='made of wood') and the Holy Spirit, the latter being the rope. The crane brings the stones, symbolizing Christians, to the proper height for the divine structure (cf. Chrysostom, Hom. 3 in Eph ὥσπερ διά τινος ἕλκων μηχανῆς εἰς ὕψος αὐτὴν [sc. ἐκκλησίαν] ἀνήγαγε μέγα; Martyr. Andreae 1, 14 p. 55, 4в. ὦ σταῦρε μηχάνημα σωτηρίας).*

μιαίνω (Hom.+; inscr., pap., LXX, Philo, Joseph., Test. 12 Patr.) fut. μιανῶ (Hs 5, 7, 2); 1 aor. ἐμίανα, ptc. μιάνας; 1 aor. pass. ἐμιάνθην; pf. pass. μεμίαμμαι, ptc. μεμιαμμένος (Bl-D. §72; Mlt.-H. 223; 249) *stain, defile* only fig.

1. of ceremonial impurity (Jos., Bell. 4, 201; 215, Ant. 11, 300 al.) pass. ἵνα μὴ μιανθῶσιν J 18: 28 (cf. 1 Macc 1: 63 ἵνα μὴ μιανθῶσιν τοῖς βρώμασι). On this subject s. Schürer II⁴ 92; Bousset, Rel.³ 93f.

2. of moral defilement by sins and vices (Pind., Aeschyl. et al.; Epigr. Gr. 713, 9 οὐ χεῖρα φόνοισι μιάνας. Less freq. in prose, e.g. Dit., Syll.³ 1240, 7 ὑβρίσει μιάνας; PFlor. 338, 18; LXX; Ep. Arist. 166; Philo; Jos., Bell. 4, 323) τὶ *someth.* τὰς χεῖρας Ac 5: 38 D. σάρκα Jd 8; Hm 4, 1, 9; s 5, 7, 2-4. τὸ πνεῦμα s 5, 6, 5; 5, 7, 2. ἑαυτόν s 9, 17, 5. τὴν ἐντολὴν τοῦ κυρίου *defile the commandment of the Lord* m 3: 2; cf. s 9, 29, 2.—Pass. (UPZ 78, 27 [159 вс]; En. 12, 4; oft. Philo; Test. Benj. 8: 3) ἡ πορεία τῆς σαρκὸς ταύτης ... οὐκ ἐμιάνθη s 5, 6, 6. The Holy Spirit, dwelling in a person, is contaminated when the pers. becomes angry m 5, 1, 3; likew. patience 5, 1, 6. The mind of the faithless Tit 1: 15b. Withdrawing fr. the grace of God leads to defilement by sin Hb 12: 15. Subst. ὁ μεμιαμμένος *he who is defiled* Tit 1: 15a (JCPlumpe, Theol. Studies 6, '45, 509-23). M-M.*

μιαρός, ά, όν (Hom.+; Dit., Or. 218, 86; Maspéro 97 II, 45; 2 and 4 Macc; Jos., Ant. 18, 38, C. Ap. 1, 236) lit. *defiled, polluted,* then fig., gener. *abominable, wretched, foul, depraved, wanton* (Soph.+; Hyperid. 5, 32; 2 and 4 Macc; Philo; Sib. Or. 3, 667) ἐπιθυμίαι 1 Cl 28: 1. (W. ἀνόσιος, as Heraclit. Sto. 76 p. 100, 12; PGM 4, 2475) στάσις 1: 1; (w. ἄναγνος) συμπλοκαί 30: 1; (w. ἄδικος) ζῆλος 45: 4.*

μίασμα, ατος, τό (Aeschyl.+; LXX) *defilement, corruption* only fig. of moral corruption through crimes and vices (Antipho 5, 82; Ps.-Demosth. 59, 86 [w. ἀσεβήματα]; Polyb. 36, 16, 6; Jdth 13: 16; Ezk 33: 31; En. 10, 22; Philo; Jos., Bell. 2, 455), also *shameful deed, misdeed, crime* (so plainly Conon [I bc/I ad]: 26 fgm. 1, 48, 3 Jac.: τὸ μίασμα πρᾶξαι; Polyaenus 6, 7, 2 κοινωνία τοῦ μιάσματος = participation in the crime) ἀποφυγεῖν τὰ μ. τοῦ κόσμου 2 Pt 2: 20. τὸ μ. τῆς μοιχείας AP 9: 24. M-M.*

μιασμός, οῦ, ὁ *pollution, corruption* (Plut., Mor. 393c, Sol. 12, 3; Iambl., Protr. 21, 16 p. 116, 5 Pistelli; LXX) only fig. in the moral realm (Proclus on Pla., Rep. II 354, 20 Kr. μ. ψυχῶν; Wsd 14: 26 ψυχῶν μ.; Test. Levi 17: 8, Benj. 8: 2f) of dissipations παραχρῆσθαι τῇ σαρκὶ ἐν μ. τινι *misuse the flesh in some defilement* Hs 5, 7, 2. ὀπίσω σαρκὸς ἐν ἐπιθυμίᾳ μιασμοῦ πορεύεσθαι *follow after the flesh in corrupting desire* 2 Pt 2: 10.*

μίγμα, ατος, τό (μίγ. [perh. μεῖγ.] Bl-D. §13; Mlt.-H. 57.—Aristot.+; Plut., Mor. 997a; Athen. 15, 17 p. 675b and c; PGM 7, 867; Sir 38: 7; Philo, Ebr. 191) *mixture, compound* of an ointment μ. σμύρνης καὶ ἀλόης *a mixture of myrrh and aloes* J 19: 39 (v.l. ἔλιγμα, σμῆγμα, σμίγμα; s. these). M-M.*

μίγνυμι s. μείγνυμι.

μικρολογία, ας, ἡ (Pla.+) *a small matter,* in a disdainful sense *trifle* (Pla., Hipp. Maj. 304b; Lucian, Vit. Auct. 17; Philo, Somn. 1, 94) Hs 5, 2, 2.*

μικρός, ά, όν (Hom.+; inscr., pap., LXX, Ep. Arist., Philo, Joseph., Test. 12 Patr.) comp. μικρότερος, έρα, ον: *small.*
1. of pers.—a. in stature Lk 19: 3. Perh. also Ἰάκωβος ὁ μικρός (ὁ μ. after a person's name: Aristoph., Ran. 708; X., Mem. 1, 4, 2; Aristot., Pol. 5, 10 p. 1311b, 3; Diog. L. 1, 79 of a 'younger' Pittacus; Sb 7576, 6 [I ad]; 7572, 10 [II ad]) Mk 15: 40 (s. Ἰάκωβος 3). This pass. may possibly belong to
b. in age. Subst. *the little one, the child* (ὁ μικρός Menand., Sam. 39f; PLond. 893, 7 [40 ad]; PFay. 113, 14. ἡ μικρά PLond. 899, 6) Mt 18: 6, 10, 14.—For the designation of all the members of a group as μικροὶ κ. μεγάλοι, etc. cf. μέγας 2aa: Ac 8: 10; 26: 22; Hb 8: 11 (Jer 38: 34); Rv 11: 18; 19: 5, 18; 20: 12.
c. in esteem, importance, influence, power, etc. εἷς τῶν μικρῶν τούτων *one of these humble folk* (disciples? so Gdspd.) Mt 10: 42; Mk 9: 42 (Kephal. I 189, 6-19; 201, 30 interprets 'the little ones who believe as the catechumens. But the Gk. word μικρός is not found in the Coptic text); Lk 17: 2. OMichel, 'Diese Kleinen'—e. Jüngerbezeichnung Jesu: StKr 108, '37/'38, 401-15. ὁ μικρότερος ἐν τῇ βασιλείᾳ τ. οὐρανῶν *the one of least importance in the Kingdom of Heaven* (but FDibelius, ZNW 11, '10, 190-2 and OCullmann, Coniect. Neot. 11, '47, 30 prefer 'youngest', and refer it to Christ) Mt 11: 11; cf. Lk 7: 28. ὁ μικρότερος ἐν πᾶσιν ὑμῖν ὑπάρχων *the one who is least among you all* 9: 48.
2. of things—a. *small* in mass and compass (X., Mem. 3, 14, 1 μ. ὄψον) μικρότερον πάντων τ. σπερμάτων *the smallest of all seeds* Mt 13: 32; Mk 4: 31 (s. σίναπι.— Alex. Aphr., An. II 1 p. 20, 14 οὐδὲν κωλυθήσεται τὸ μέγιστον ἐν τῷ μικροτάτῳ γενέσθαι σώματι). μικρὰ ζύμη *a little (bit of) yeast* 1 Cor 5: 6; Gal 5: 9. Of the tongue μικρὸν μέλος *a small member* Js 3: 5 (cf. Eur., fgm. 411).

b. *small* in number (Gen 30: 30; 47: 9) τὸ μικρὸν ποίμνιον Lk 12: 32.
c. *small, insignificant* δύναμις Rv 3: 8. μισθός 2 Cl 15: 1b (cf. a: μ. συμβουλία). ἐπιθυμίαι Hs 8, 10, 1a.
d. *short* of time χρόνον μικρόν (Pla., Rep. 6 p. 498d; Ael. Aristid. 34 p. 661 D.; Is 54: 7) J 7: 33; cf. 12: 35; Rv 6: 11; 20: 3.
3. the neut. (τὸ) μικρόν is used subst. to mean—a. *a little* μικρόν τι (Diod. S. 1, 74, 1; Ael. Aristid. 48, 37 K. = 24 p. 474 D.; UPZ 70, 3 [152/1 bc]) *a little* 2 Cor 11: 16. μ. τι ἀφροσύνης vs. 1 (Procop. Soph., Ep. 80 μοί μικρὸν δίδου νεανιεύεσθαι). παρὰ μικρόν (Isocr. 19, 22; Dionys. Byz. §§3 and 50; Ps 72: 2; Ezk 16: 47; Jos., C. Ap. 2, 270) *except for a little, nearly* Hs 8, 1, 14. κατὰ μικρόν *in brief* (Galen XIX p. 176 K.; Lucian, Catapl. 17, De Merc. Cond. 35) B 1: 5.
b. *what is insignificant, small* τὸ μ. τηρεῖν 2 Cl 8: 5 (apocr. saying of Jesus). μικρὰ φρονεῖν περί τινος *think little of someth.* 2 Cl 1: 1f (μικρὸν φρονεῖν Soph., Aj. 1120; Plut., Mor. p. 28c).—Pl. *insignificant things, trifles* (Aelian, V.H. 2, 27) μικρὰ κατ' ἀλλήλων *have trifling complaints against each other* Hs 8, 10, 1b.
c. *the state of being small* ἐκ μικροῦ αὐξῆσαι Mt 20: 28 D = Agr 22.—d. *a short distance, a little way* (X., Cyr. 1, 2, 15; Dionys. Byz. §§8 and 13) προελθὼν μικρόν (Ps.-Demetr. c. 226) Mt 26: 39; Mk 14: 35.
e. *a short time, a little while* (Jos., Ant. 4, 159; 8, 405) J 13: 33 (cf. Job 36: 2); Hs 9, 4, 4; 9, 5, 1. μικρόν *for a moment* (Menand., Epitr. 474 J.) v 4, 1, 6. μετὰ μικρόν *after a short while* (Phlegon: 257 fgm. 36, 1, 2 Jac.; Lucian, Dial. Mort. 15, 3; Synes., Dio 1 p. 234, 5 NTerzaghi ['44]) Mt 26: 73; Mk 14: 70. (ἔτι) μικρὸν καί . . . in *a little while,* lit. 'yet a little while, and' = *soon* (Ex 17: 4; Jer 28: 33; Hos 1: 4) J 14: 19; 16: 16-19. ἔτι μ. ὅσον ὅσον *in a very little while = soon* Hb 10: 37; 1 Cl 50: 4 (both Is 26: 20; cf. Bl-D. §304; Rob. 733). M-M. B. 880.**

Μίλητος, ου, ἡ (Hom.+; inscr.; Sib. Or. 5, 325) *Miletus,* a seaport city on the west coast of Asia Minor, south of the mouths of the Meander, and 35 mi. south of Ephesus. There was a Jewish community in M. (Schürer III⁴ 16; 110, 37; AvGerkan, E. Synagoge in Milet: ZNW 20, '21, 177-81; Dssm., LO 391f [LAE 451f]). Paul touched at the city on his last journey to Jerusalem Ac 20: 15, 17. Acc. to 2 Ti 4: 20 Trophimus lay ill in Miletus.—Milet. Ergebnisse der Ausgrabungen u. Untersuchungen seit d. Jahre 1899; seit '06 in drei Bdn. im Erscheinen, herausg. v. ThWiegand.*

μίλιον, ου, τό (Eratosthenes [in Julian of Ashkelon, Metr. Script. I 201]; Polyb. 34, 12, 3; Strabo 3, 1, 9; 5, 1, 11 al.; Plut., Cic. 32, 1, C. Gracch. 7, 3; Inscr. Rom. III 1385; Dit., Syll.³ 888, 26; Bull. de corr. hell. 29, '05, 99f; APF 2, '03, 566 no. 122; PStrassb. 57, 6. Latin loanw.: mille. Loanw. in rabb.) a Roman *mile,* lit. a thousand paces, then a fixed measure = eight stades = about 4,854 feet or 1,478.5 meters Mt 5: 41; D 1: 4. M-M.*

μιμέομαι mid. dep.; imper. μιμοῦ; impf. ἐμιμούμην; fut. μιμήσομαι; 1 aor. ἐμιμησάμην (Pind.+; inscr., pap., LXX, Ep. Arist., Philo, Joseph.) *imitate, emulate, follow, use as a model* w. acc. of the pers. (Ael. Aristid. 34 p. 669 D.; Wsd 15: 9; Philo; Jos., Ant. 6, 347, C. Ap. 2, 257) ISm 12: 1. ἡμᾶς 2 Th 3: 7, 9 (PFlor. 367, 3 ἐγὼ οὐ μειμήσομαί σε). θεόν Dg 10: 5 (Heraclitus, Ep. 5, 1 θεόν; Eunap. 104 of Oribasius the physician: ἐμιμεῖτο θεόν [Asclepius]; Ep. Arist. 281; Philo, Spec. Leg. 4, 73, Virt. 168; Test. Ash. 4: 3 κύριον).—Of Christ ἂν ἡμᾶς μιμήσεται, καθὰ πράσσομεν *if he were to imitate our way of acting* IMg 10: 1.

W. acc. of the thing *imitate someth.* (Appian, Samn. 10 §1 τὴν ἀρετήν; Philo, Congr. Erud. Gr. 69 τὸν ἐκείνων βίον al.; Jos., Ant. 12, 241, C. Ap. 1, 165) τὴν πίστιν Hb 13: 7. τὸ κακόν, ἀγαθόν (Epigr. Gr. 85, 3 ἐμιμούμην τὸ καλόν; Ep. Arist. 188) 3 J 11. τὸ μαρτύριον MPol 19: 1.—WMichaelis, TW IV 661-78: μιμέομαι and related words. M-M.*

μίμημα, ατος, τό (Aeschyl.+; Musonius 90, 40 man is μ. θεοῦ; Polemo, Decl. 2, 32 p. 27, 7; Dit., Or. 383, 63; 404, 26; Wsd 9: 8. Oft. Philo; Jos., Bell. 7, 142, Ant. 12, 75; Sib. Or. 8, 116) *copy, image* δέχεσθαι τὰ μ. τῆς ἀληθοῦς ἀγάπης *receive the copies of True Love* (i.e. of Christ), perh. w. ref. to Ign. and fellow prisoners (s. JAKleist, transl., ad loc.) Pol 1: 1 (Herm. Wr. 382, 18 Sc. μ. τ. ἀληθείας).*

μιμητής, οῦ, ὁ (X., Pla. et al.; Philo, Joseph.) *imitator,* in our lit. mostly used w. εἶναι or γίνεσθαι and w. the gen.

1. of the pers. imitated (X., Mem. 1, 6, 3 οἱ διδάσκαλοι τοὺς μαθητὰς μιμητὰς ἀποδεικνύουσιν; Jos., Ant. 1, 109; 12, 203 μιμ. γίν. τοῦ γεγεννηκότος) μιμηταί μου γίνεσθε *use me as your model* 1 Cor 4: 16; 11: 1 (EEidem, Imitatio Pauli: Festskrift for EStave '22, 67-85; WPdeBoer, The Imitation of Paul '62; ELarsson, Christus als Vorbild [Diss. Upsala] '62; ASchulz, Nachfolgen u. Nachahmen '62; further lit. EGüttgemanns, D. leidende Apostel, '66, 185-94; CSpicq, BRigaux-Festschr., '70, 313-22). Cf. 1 Cl 17: 1. μιμηταὶ τῶν κληρονομούντων τὰς ἐπαγγελίας Hb 6: 12. μ. ἡμῶν κ. τοῦ κυρίου 1 Th 1: 6. τ. κυρίου IEph 10: 3; MPol 17: 3; cf. 1: 2. Χριστοῦ IPhld 7: 2; cf. 1 Cor 11: 1. (τοῦ) θεοῦ Eph 5: 1; Dg 10: 4b, 6; IEph 1: 1; ITr 1: 2.—EGGulin, Die Nachfolge Gottes: Studia Orientalia I ed. Societas Orientalis Fennica '25, 34-50; FTillmann, D. Idee der Nachfolge Christi '34; JMNielen in Hlg. Überliefg. (ed. OCasel) '38, 59-85.

2. w. an impersonal gen. (Herodian 6, 8, 2 τ. ἀνδρείας; Philo, Virt. 66; Jos., Ant. 1, 68; 8, 251) τῶν ἐκκλησιῶν τοῦ θεοῦ 1 Th 2: 14. τοῦ ἀγαθοῦ 1 Pt 3: 13 t.r. τῆς χρηστότητος Dg 10: 4a. τῆς ὑπομονῆς Pol 8: 2. τοῦ πάθους τοῦ θεοῦ IRo 6: 3. M-M.*

μιμνήσκομαι 1 aor. ἐμνήσθην; 1 fut. μνησθήσομαι; pf. μέμνημαι (used as a pres. [Ep. Arist. 168]; cf. Bl-D. §341; Rob. 894f) (Hom.+; inscr., pap., LXX, Philo, Joseph., Test. 12 Patr., Sib. Or.)

1. reflexive *remind oneself, recall to mind, remember*
   a. in contrast to 'forget', *remember, keep in mind.*
   α. w. gen. of the thing (1 Macc 6: 12) Mt 26: 75; Lk 24: 8; 2 Ti 1: 4; 2 Pt 3: 2; Jd 17; 1 Cl 13: 1; 46: 7; 50: 4; Hv 3, 1, 5.—β. w. gen. of the pers. (PBad. 48, 17 [126 bc] μνήσθητι ἡμῶν) πάντα μου μέμνησθε *you think of me in every way* 1 Cor 11: 2.
   γ. w. acc. of the thing (Hom.; Hdt. 7, 18; Dt 8: 2; Is 63: 7.—Bl-D. §175; cf. Rob. 482f) μνησθήσῃ ἡμέραν κρίσεως *remember the Day of Judgment* B 19: 10.
   δ. w. ὅτι foll. (X., Cyr. 3, 1, 27; Is 12: 4; Dt 5: 15; Job 7: 7; Jos., Vi. 209) Mt 5: 23; 27: 63; Lk 16: 25; J 2: 17, 22; 12: 16.—W. ὡς foll. (Ps.-Clem., Hom. 2, 47) Lk 24: 6. W. gen. and ὡς foll. Ac 11: 16.—ε. w. rel. clause foll. μνησθεὶς ὡς ἐδίδαξέν με μεγαλείων *I remembered the great things which he had taught me* Hv 4, 1, 8.
   b. *make mention* τινός *of someone* (Pardalas Iamb. in Herodes, Cercidas etc. ed. ADKnox '29 p. 276 μεμνήσομαί σου ἐν ἐμῆσι βύβλοισι=I will mention you in my books) Epil Mosq 1.
   c. *remember, think of, care for, be concerned about* w. gen. (Od. 18, 267 al.; Arrian, Ind. 41, 5 δείπνου; Gen 30: 22; Jos., Bell. 4, 340; Sib. Or. 3, 595) μνήσθητί μου

remember me Lk 23: 42 (Epict. 3, 24, 100 Ο God μοῦ μέμνησο; cf. GDalman, Jesus-Jeshua [tr. PLevertoff] '29, 197-201).—Hb 2: 6 (Ps 8: 5); 13: 3; D 4: 1. μ. διαθήκης (cf. διαθήκη 2) Lk 1: 72 (Lev 26: 42, 45). μ. ἐλέους vs. 54 (Ps 97: 3).—W. gen. and inf. of the purposeful result (Bl-D. §391, 4) μνήσθητι, κύριε, τῆς ἐκκλησίας σου τοῦ ῥύσασθαι αὐτὴν *remember, O Lord, thy church to save her* D 10: 5 (GSchmidt, ΜΝΗΣΘΗΤΙ: Eine liturgiegeschichtliche Skizze, HMeiser-Festschr., '51, 259-64). —μὴ μνησθῆναι τῶν ἁμαρτιῶν τινος *not remember someone's sins, let someone's sins go unpunished* (cf. Ps 24: 7; 78: 8; Sir 23: 18; Is 43: 25) Hb 8: 12; 10: 17 (both Jer 38: 34).

2. pass.—a. *be mentioned* εἰ διὰ τοῦ Ἀβραὰμ ἐμνήσθη (sc. ὁ λαὸς οὗτος) B 13: 7. This may also be the place for μνησθῆναι ἐνώπιον τοῦ θεοῦ *be mentioned before God* Ac 10: 31; Rv 16: 19. But these pass. can also be understood on the basis of the next mng.
   b. *be called to remembrance,* and ἐνώπιον τ. θ. can then take on the mng. of ὑπὸ τ. θ. (ἐνώπιον 5a) αἱ ἐλεημοσύναι σου ἐμνήσθησαν ἐνώπιον τ. θεοῦ *your charities have been called to remembrance by God* Ac 10: 31; cf. Rv 16: 19.—CLKessler, The Memory Motif in the God-man Relationship of the OT, Diss. Northwestern Univ. '56. OMichel, TW IV 678-87: μιμνήσκομαι and related words. M-M. B. 1228f.*

Μισαήλ, ὁ indecl. (מִישָׁאֵל; 1 Esdr 9: 44. In Jos. [Ant. 10, 188f] Μισάηλος) *Mishael* one of the three youths in the fiery furnace (Da 3: 88; also 1: 6f, 11, 19; 2: 17; 1 Macc 2: 59; 4 Macc 16: 3, 21; 18: 12) 1 Cl 45: 7.*

μισέω impf. ἐμίσουν; fut. μισήσω; 1 aor. ἐμίσησα; pf. μεμίσηκα, pass. ptc. μεμισημένος (Hom.+; inscr., pap., though quite rare in both; LXX, Philo, Joseph., Test. 12 Patr.) *hate, persecute in hatred, detest, abhor.*

1. w. acc. of the pers. (opp. ἀγαπάω as Dt 21: 15, 16=Philo, Leg. All. 2, 48. Cf. AFridrichsen, Svensk exegetisk Årsbok 5, '40, 152-62) Mt 5: 43 (PJouon, Rech de Sc rel 20, '30, 545f; MSmith, HTR 45, '52, 71-3. Cf. the prayer of Solon [fgm. 1, 5 Diehl] γλυκὺν φίλοισ', ἐχθροῖσι πικρόν; also IQS 1, 9f and s. EFSutcliffe, Hatred at Qumran, Revue de Qumran 2, '59/'60, 345-55; KStendahl, HTR 55, '62, 343-55; OLinton, Studia Theologica 18, '64, 66-79); 24: 10; Lk 16: 13; 2 Cl 13: 4; D 1: 3; 2: 7.—Lk 1: 71; 6: 22, 27; 14: 26 (JDenney, The Word 'Hate' in Lk 14: 26: ET 21, '10, 41f; WBleibtreu, Paradoxe Aussprüche Jesu: Theol. Arbeiten aus d. wissensch. Prediger-Verein d. Rheinprovinz, new ser. 20, 24, 15-35; RWSockman, The Paradoxes of J. '36); 19: 14; J 7: 7a, b; 15: 18f, 23f; 17: 14; J 2: 9, 11; 3: 13, 15; 4: 20; Rv 17: 16; B 19: 11; Dg 2: 6. ἀλλήλους Mt 24: 10; Tit 3: 3; D 16: 4. μ. τινα δωρεάν (חִנָּם אֲשֶׁר) *hate someone without cause, undeservedly* (s. δωρεάν 2) J 15: 25 (Ps 68: 5.—34: 19). μ. τινα ἀδίκως *hate someone wrongfully* 1 Cl 60: 3. Of God 1 Cl 30: 6; Dg 9: 2; Ro 9: 13 (Mal 1: 2f).

2. w. acc. of the thing (Jos., Ant. 3, 274 τ. ἀδικίαν) τὸ φῶς J 3: 20. ἀλήθειαν B 20: 2; D 5: 2. ἀνομίαν Hb 1: 9 (Ps 44: 8). τὴν γαλῆν B 10: 8. τὰ ἐνθάδε *earthly things* 2 Cl 6: 6. τὴν πονηρὰν ἐπιθυμίαν Hm 12, 1, 1. τὰ ἔργα τῶν Νικολαϊτῶν Rv 2: 6. τὰ ἔργα τῆς πονηρᾶς ὁδοῦ *the deeds of the evil way* B 4: 10. τὰς ἡδυπαθείας 2 Cl 17: 7. παιδείαν 1 Cl 35: 8 (Ps 49: 17). τὴν πλάνην B 4: 1. σοφίαν 1 Cl 57: 5 (Pr 1: 29). τὴν ἑαυτοῦ σάρκα Eph 5: 29 (cf. Herm. Wr. 4, 6 ἐὰν μὴ τὸ σῶμα μισήσῃς, σεαυτὸν φιλῆσαι οὐ δύνασαι). τὴν ψυχὴν αὐτοῦ J 12: 25 or ἑαυτοῦ Lk 14: 26 (Plut., Mor. 556D οὐδ' ἐμίσουν ἑαυτούς). τὴν ψυχὴν Dg 6: 5f. πᾶσαν ὑπόκρισιν B 19: 2b; D

4: 12a. χιτῶνα Jd 23. πᾶν ὃ οὐκ ἔστιν ἀρεστὸν τῷ θεῷ B
19: 2a; D 4: 12b. ὃ μισῶ τοῦτο ποιῶ *I do what I detest* Ro
7: 15.

3. abs. IEph 14: 2; IRo 8: 3; Dg 5: 17.—Pass.: the pres.
ptc. w. εἶναι in periphrastic conjugation, to express the
long duration of the hate (Charito 2, 6, 1 εἰμὶ μισούμενος
ὑπὸ τ. Ἔρωτος) ἔσεσθε μισούμενοι Mt 10: 22; 24: 9; Mk
13: 13; Lk 21: 17 (cf. Herm. Wr. 9, 4b). Of Christianity
ὅταν μισῆται ἀπὸ κόσμου *whenever it is hated by the
world* IRo 3: 3. μεμισημένος beside ἀκάθαρτος *unclean
and loathsome* (for relig. reasons) of birds Rv 18: 2.—
ACarr, The Mng. of 'Hatred' in the NT: Exp. 6th Ser. XII
'05, 153-60.—OMichel, TW IV 687-98. M-M.*

μισθαποδοσία, ας, ἡ (only Hb and eccl. lit. But ἀποδίδωμι [q.v. 1] τὸν μισθόν is quite common) *reward*, lit.
'payment of wages' ἀποβλέπειν εἰς τὴν μ. *look forward to
a reward* Hb 11: 26; of confidence ἥτις ἔχει μεγάλην μ.
10: 35. Also in an unfavorable sense: *punishment, retribution* λαμβάνειν ἔνδικον μ. *receive a just penalty* Hb 2: 2.*

μισθαποδότης, ου, ὁ (only Hb and eccl. lit.) *rewarder*, lit.
'one who pays wages' of God (Act. Thom. 142 p. 249, 10;
159 p. 271, 1B; PGenève [Christian] 14: 27 τῷ μισθαπο-
δότῃ θεῷ) τοῖς ἐκζητοῦσιν αὐτὸν μ. γίνεται *he proves
himself a rewarder of those who seek him* Hb 11: 6. M-M.*

μίσθιος (actually adj. of two or three terminations. In our
lit. only subst.: Jos., Bell. 5, 49; Plut., Lyc. 16, 7 al.;
Anth. Pal. 6, 283, 3; PAmh. 92, 19; Lev 25: 50; Job 7: 1;
Tob 5: 12 BA; Sir 7: 20), ου, ὁ *day laborer, hired man* Lk
15: 17, 19, 21 v.l. (Alciphr. 2, 32, 3 δέχου με μισθωτὸν
κατ' ἀγρόν, πάντα ὑπομένειν ἀνεχόμενον ὑπὲρ τοῦ τὴν
ἀπλήρωτον ἐμπλῆσαι γαστέρα). M-M.*

μισθός, οῦ, ὁ (Hom.+; inscr., pap., LXX, Philo; Jos., Vi.
200 al.) *pay, wages*.
1. lit., as payment for work done Lk 10: 7; 1 Ti 5: 18.
Personified ὁ μ. ὁ ἀφυστερημένος κράζει *the wages which
you have kept back cry out* (to heaven) Js 5: 4. τὸν μ.
ἀποδιδόναι *pay (out) wages* (s. ἀποδίδωμι 1) Mt 20: 8.
μισθὸν λαμβάνειν *receive one's wages* (Diod. S. 12, 53, 2;
Jos., Bell. 2, 296, Ant. 4, 206) J 4: 36. μισθοὺς λαμβάνειν
τινός *accept payment(s) for someth.* Hm 11: 12 (μ. λαμβ.
τινός as Philo, Spec. Leg. 4, 98; for the pl. cf. Aesop 87d,
12 Chambry; Jos., Ant. 1, 183; BGU 1067, 15 [II AD]). μ.
τῆς ἀδικίας *money paid for treachery* Ac 1: 18. μ. ἀδικίας
dishonest gain 2 Pt 2: 15; on ἀδικούμενοι μισθὸν ἀδικίας
vs. 13 cf. ἀδικέω 2b.—In τῇ πλάνῃ τοῦ Βαλαὰμ μισθοῦ
ἐξεχύθησαν, μισθοῦ is gen. of price (as in the anonymous
comic fgm. 218 Kock; Diod. S. 4, 20, 2; 3 μισθοῦ
ἐργάζεσθαι) *for pay or gain* Jd 11 (s. ἐκχέω 3).
2. fig., the recompense given (mostly by God) for the
moral quality of an action (Pla., Rep. 10, 614A τῷ δικαίῳ
παρὰ θεῶν τε καὶ ἀνθρώπων μισθοὶ καὶ δῶρα γίγνεται;
cf. 2, 363D ἡγησάμενοι κάλλιστον ἀρετῆς μισθὸν
μέθην αἰώνιον; Plut., Mor. 183D; Lucian, Vit. Auct. 24;
Jos., Ant. 1, 183; 18, 309; LXX).
a. *reward* 2 Cl 3: 3. μισθὸν ἔχειν *have a reward* 1 Cor 9:
17; Mt 5: 46; 6: 1 (cf. habeo pretium: Horace, Ep. 1, 16,
47). τὸν μ. ἀπέχειν *have received one's reward (in full)*
Mt 6: 2, 5, 16 (s. ἀπέχω 1). μισθὸν λαμβάνειν *receive
one's reward* 1 Cor 3: 8, 14; cf. Mt 10: 41a (Jos., Ant. 6, 48
μὴ λαμβάνειν τὸν προφήτην μισθόν), b. Also μ. ἀπολαμβάνειν 2 Cl 9: 5; Hs 5, 6, 7b. τὸν μ. κομίσασθαι 2 Cl
11: 5. μισθὸν πλήρη ἀπολαμβάνειν *receive a full reward*
2 J 8. τὸν μ. ἀποδιδόναι *pay (out) the reward* (Wsd 10: 17)
2 Cl 20: 4; cf. B 11: 8. ὁ τοῦ μ. ἀνταποδότης B 19: 11; D 4:
7. τὸν μισθὸν εὑρεῖν παρὰ τῷ θεῷ *find one's reward with

God Hs 2: 5 (μ. εὑρ. as Ezk 27: 33). μισθὸν αἰτεῖν *ask as a
reward* 2 Cl 19: 1. ὁ μ. πολὺς ἐν τ. οὐρανοῖς *the reward in
heaven is great* Mt 5: 12; cf. Lk 6: 23, 35. οὐκ ἔστι μικρός
2 Cl 15: 1. Coming w. the parousia Rv 11: 18; B 21: 3. W.
the obj. gen. μ. δικαιοσύνης *reward for righteousness* B
20: 2; D 5: 2. διδόναι μισθὸν ἀντιμισθίας ὧν ἐλάβομεν
give a recompense for what we have received 2 Cl 1: 5 (διδ.
μ. as Ael. Aristid. 28, 10 K.=49 p. 494 D.; Sir 51: 30).
ἀπολέσαι τὸν μ. *lose one's reward* (Jos., Ant. 1, 183a) Mt
10: 42; Mk 9: 41; Hs 5, 6, 7a; ἔσται μοι εἰς μ. *it will bring
me the reward* B 1: 5.—τῷ ἐργαζομένῳ ὁ μ. οὐ λογίζεται
κατὰ χάριν ἀλλὰ κατὰ ὀφείλημα *to the man who works,
his wages are considered not a favor, but what is due him*
Ro 4: 4.
b. in an unfavorable sense, the *reward* that consists in
punishment (trag.; Hdt. 8, 116f; Callim., Hymn. in Dian.
264; Dionys. Hal. 10, 51; 2 Macc 8: 33) ὁ μισθὸς αὐτῆς
(sc. τῆς ἀδικίας) κόλασις κ. θάνατος Dg 9: 2. ὁ μ. τῆς
πονηρίας ἔμπροσθεν αὐτοῦ *the reward of wickedness is in
store for him* B 4: 12.
c. *reward or punishment* as the case may be Rv 22: 12;
1 Cl 34: 3 (both Is 40: 10); B 21: 3.—Billerb. IV 1245f
(index); esp. IV 487-500: Altsynagog. Lohnlehre; KWeiss,
D. Frohbotsch. Jesu über Lohn u. Vollkommenheit (Mt
20: 1-16) '27; MWagner, D. Lohnged. im Ev.: NKZ 43,
'32, 106-12; 129-39; OMichel, D. Lohnged. in d. Verkünd. Jesu: ZsystTh 9, '32, 47-54.—GPWetter, D. Vergeltungsged. b. Pls '12; FVFilson, St. Paul's Conception of
Recompense '32; HWHeidland, D. Anrechng. des Glaubens z. Gerechtigkeit '36; GBornkamm, D. Lohnged. im
NT: Evang. Theol. '44, 143-66; BReicke, The NT Conception of Reward: MGoguel-Festschr. '50, 195-206;
MSmith, Tannaitic Par. to the Gosp. '51, 49-73; WPesch,
Der Lohngedanke in d. Lehre Jesu usw., Diss. Munich '55
(lit.); GdeRu, NovT 8, '66, 202-22; HPreisker u. EWürthwein, TW IV 699-736: μισθός and related words. M-M.
B. 814.*

μισθόω 1 aor. ἐμισθωσάμην (in our lit. [Mt] and LXX
only mid.) the mid. has the mng. *hire, engage* for oneself
(Hdt.+; inscr., pap., LXX) w. acc. ἐργάτας (PLeipz. 111,
11; Jos., Bell. 3, 437, Ant. 11, 174) Mt 20: 1 (on μ. εἰς cf.
Appian, Mithrid. 23 §90 ἐς τὸ ἔργον ἐμισθώσαντο), 7.—
Diod. S. 4, 20, 3 ὁ μισθωσάμενος ἐλεήσας καὶ τὸν
μισθὸν ἀποδοὺς ἀπέλυσε τῶν ἔργων the employer
took pity on a woman who had just given birth, gave her
her wages in full, and released her from work early. It is
his goodness alone that prompts him to grant this favor.
M-M.*

μίσθωμα, ατος, τό act. *contract price, rent* (Hdt.+;
inscr., pap., LXX; Philo, Spec. Leg. 1, 280) and pass.
what is rented, a rented house (this mng. is not found
elsewh. Even Ammonius Gramm. [100 AD] p. 93 Valck.
knows nothing of it. Hence the transl. *at his own expense*
[RSV] is poss.) ἐν ἰδίῳ μισθώματι *in his own rented
lodgings* Ac 28: 30 (for the idea cf. Jos., Ant. 18, 235).—
HJCadbury, JBL 45, '26, 321f. M-M.*

μισθωτός (actually adj. of three terminations. In our lit.
only subst.: Aristoph.+; inscr., pap., LXX; Philo, Spec.
Leg. 2, 82; 83; Jos., Bell. 1, 517), οῦ, ὁ *hired man* of hired
fishermen Mk 1: 20. Of hired shepherds J 10: 12f (μ. as
inferior: Ael. Aristid. 46 p. 206 D.; Hippocr., Ep. 16, 3;
Themist. I p. 10f μ. ἀντὶ βουκόλου; Plut., Mor. 37E μ.
forms a contrast to the θεῖος ἡγεμών, the λόγος). M-M.*

μῖσος, ους, τό (Aeschyl.+; Vett. Val. 242, 25; LXX; Test.
12 Patr.) *hate* ἀγάπη στραφήσεται εἰς μ. *love shall be
turned into hate* D 16: 3. Personif. Hs 9, 15, 3. B. 1132.*

μίτρα, ας, ἡ (Hom.+) *snood* or *turban* as head-covering (Pind., Hdt.+; Ex 29: 6; Lev 8: 9; Jdth 16: 8; Bar 5: 2; Ep. Arist. 98; Philo, Mos. 2, 116; Test. Levi 8: 2) ἐν μ. ἦν ἡ κατακάλυψις αὐτῆς *her head-covering was a snood* Hv 4, 2, 1.—The μίτρα may also have been a piece of clothing worn from the throat or back of the neck (Parthenius 11, 3 τὴν μίτραν ἐνθεῖναι τὸν τράχηλον). In any case, a woman was not considered to be properly covered without it (Quint. Smyrn. 13, 110).*

Μιτυλήνη, ης, ἡ (later [Dit., Syll.³ 344, 30 (303 BC)], Or. 266, 19 (III BC); Strabo, Plut.; Jos., Ant. 15, 350; 16, 20] spelling for the older [Hdt., X., inscr.—Meisterhans³-Schw. p. 29] Μυτιλήνη. Cf. Bl-D. §42, 3 app.; Mlt.-H. 72; 79) *Mitylene*, chief city of the island of Lesbos, in the Aegean Sea off the north-west coast of Asia Minor Ac 20: 14. M-M.*

Μιχαήλ, ὁ indecl. (מִיכָאֵל) *Michael*, archangel (Da 12: 1; 10: 13, 21; En. 9, 1; 10, 11; 20, 5; 24, 6; Wadd. 2263; 2637b; inscr. fr. Asia Minor [Ramsay, Phrygia II 541 no. 404, p. 741 no. 678]; PGM 1, 301; 2, 158; 3, 148; 4, 1815; 2356; 7, 257; 22b, 29 τῷ μεγάλῳ πατρὶ Ὀσίριδι Μιχαήλ) Jd 9; Rv 12: 7 (M. as ἀρχιστράτηγος PGM 13, 928. On his fighting w. the dragon s. PGM 4, 2769ff); Hs 8, 3, 3. In Jewish theology M. was the special patron and protector of the Jewish nation (Da 12: 1).—Bousset, Rel.³ 325ff; Dssm., LO 396ff [LAE 456f]; WLueken, Der Erzengel M. 1898. M-M.*

μνᾶ, μνᾶς, ἡ (Semitic loanw., as early as Attic wr.; inscr., pap., LXX; Jos., Ant. 7, 189; 14, 106; Test. Jos. 16: 4) *mina*, a Gk. monetary unit=100 drachmas; the Attic mina was worth about eighteen to twenty dollars in normal times. Lk 19: 13, 16, 18, 20, 24f (on the parable s. PJoüon, Rech de Sc rel 29, '40, 489–94).—Lit. s.v. ἀργύριον 2c. M-M.*

μνάομαι (Hom.+; Philo) *woo* or *court for one's bride* pf. ptc. μεμνησμένη of the woman *engaged, betrothed* Lk 1: 27 D.*

Μνάσων, ωνος, ὁ (Anth. Pal.; Lucian; Dialektinschr. 2580, 25 [Delphi]; Dit., Syll.³ 585, 43; 47; 77; 81; 85; 90; 94; 234; 238 [197 BC]; PHib. 41, 3 [ca. 261 BC]; Sb 3199) *Mnason*, a Christian fr. Cyprus Ac 21: 16 (Μνασέας, father of Zeno the Stoic, was also fr. Cyprus; Κυπρ. I p. 190 no. 4 a Gk. inscr. from Cyprus contains the name Μνασίας).—HJCadbury, Amicitiae Corolla (for RHarris) '33, 51–3. M-M.*

μνεία, ας, ἡ (Soph.+; inscr., pap., LXX, Ep. Arist., Test. Napht. 8: 5; Ode of Solomon 11, 22).
  1. *remembrance, memory* w. obj. gen. τινός *of someone* (Sib. Or. 5, 486; Bar 4: 27) Ro 12: 13 v.l.; *of someth.* (Dit., Syll.³ 577, 3; Wsd 5: 14) εἴ τίς ἐστιν ἀγαθοῦ μ. *if there is any remembrance of what is good* B 21: 7. μνείαν ἔχειν τινός *think of someone* (Soph., El. 384 al.) ἔχετε μνείαν ἡμῶν ἀγαθὴν πάντοτε *you always think kindly of us* 1 Th 3: 6. ἀδιάλειπτον ἔχω τὴν περὶ σοῦ μ. *I remember you constantly* 2 Ti 1: 3. εἰς μ. ἔρχεταί τινι as in Lat. in mentem venit alicui *comes to someone's recollection* Hv 3, 7, 3.
  2. *mention* μνείαν ποιεῖσθαί τινος *mention someone* (Pla., Phaedr. 254; Diog. L. 8, 2, 66; Inschr. v. Priene 50, 10; Zen.-P. 14 [= Sb 6720], 3 [256 BC]; UPZ 59, 6; cf. Ps 110: 4) in our lit. only of mentioning in prayer (BGU 632, 5 μνείαν σου ποιούμενος παρὰ τοῖς ἐνθάδε θεοῖς; Epigr. Gr. 983, 2ff [79 BC] Δημήτριος ἥκω πρὸς μεγάλην Ἰσιν θεάν, μνείαν ἐπ' ἀγαθῷ τ. γονέων ποιούμενος) Ro 1: 9;

1 Th 1: 2 t.r.; Phlm 4. The gen. is supplied fr. the context Eph 1: 16; 1 Th 1: 2. ἐπὶ πάσῃ τῇ μ. ὑμῶν *as often as I make mention of you* (in prayer) Phil 1: 3. ἡ πρὸς θεὸν μ. *mention* (in prayer) *before God* (though *remembrance* is also poss. here) 1 Cl 56: 1. M-M.*

μνῆμα, ατος, τό lit. a 'sign of remembrance', esp. for the dead (Hom.+), then gener. *grave, tomb* (Hdt., Pla. et al.; Dit., Syll.³ 1221; 1237, 3; BGU 1024 IV, 23; LXX, Philo; Jos., Ant. 7, 19; 8, 240) Mk 16: 2; Lk 24: 1 (μνημεῖον 𝔓⁷⁵ et al.); Ac 2: 29 (David's μ. Jos., Ant. 7, 393); GP 8: 30–2; 11: 44; 12: 50, 52. κατατιθέναι ἐν μ. *lay in a tomb* Mk 15: 46; cf. Ac 7: 16. τιθέναι ἐν μ. λαξευτῷ *lay in a rock-hewn tomb* Lk 23: 53. τιθέναι εἰς μνῆμα Rv 11: 9 (for the idea s. Jos., Bell. 4, 317). Dwelling-place of demoniacs Mk 5: 3, 5; Lk 8: 27. M-M.*

μνημεῖον, ου, τό lit. 'token of remembrance' (Pind.+; Philo, Joseph.), esp. for the dead (Eur., Iph. T. 702; 821; Thu. 1, 138, 5; X., Hell. 2, 4, 17; 3, 2, 15; Pla., Rep. 3 p. 414A).
  1. *monument, memorial* (cf. Jos., Ant. 5, 119 μν. καὶ τάφος): οἰκοδομεῖτε τ. μνημεῖα τῶν προφητῶν Lk 11: 47 (JoachJeremias, Heiligengräber in Jesu Umwelt '58) is prob. to be understood in this sense (for μ. οἰκοδομεῖν cf. Jos., Ant. 13, 211). But μ. in our lit. usu. has the sense
  2. *grave, tomb* (Dit., Syll.³ 1229, 4; 1232; 1234; 1242; 1244; PFlor. 9, 10; Gen 23: 6, 9; Is 22: 16 al.; Jos., Ant. 1, 237; 18, 108); of tombs in caves, etc. (s. PThomsen, Grab: Reallex. d. Vorgesch. IV 2, 473ff), into which a person can enter (Mk 16: 5; J 20: 6) Mt 23: 29; 27: 52f (JBlinzler, ThGl 35, '43, 91–3.—Diod. S. 13, 86, 3: when the Carthaginians besieging Acragas destroyed some tombs lying outside the walls, διὰ νυκτὸς εἴδωλα [ghosts] φαίνεσθαι τῶν τετελευτηκότων.—On the earthquake that opens the graves and frees those inside s. Ps.-Ael. Aristid. 25, 20f K.=43 p. 804 D.: μνήματα ἀνερρήγνυτο ... τὰ μνήματα ἀνερρίπτει τοὺς κειμένους. EFascher, Die Auferweckung der Heiligen Mt 7: 51–53, '51), 60b; 28: 8; Mk 15: 46; 16: 2 v.l., 3, 5, 8; Lk 23: 55; 24: 1 v.l. 𝔓⁷⁵ et al., 2, 9, 12, 22, 24; J 11: 17, 31 (Aesop, Fab. 109 H. γυνὴ ἀπιοῦσα πρὸς τὸ μνημεῖον ἐθρήνει), 38; 12: 17; 19: 42; 20: 1–4, 6, 8, 11a, b; GP 9: 34; 12: 51, 53 (lit. on the Holy Sepulcher: RGG² III 92; also FMBraun, La Sépulture de Jésu '37; RHSmith, The Tomb of Jesus, Biblical Archaeologist 30, '67, 74–90). τιθέναι εἰς μ. *place in the tomb* Ac 13: 29. Also τιθέναι ἐν τῷ μ. Mt 27: 60a; Mk 6: 29. μ. καινόν Mt 27: 60a; J 19: 41; οἱ ἐν τοῖς μ. *those who are in their tombs* 5: 28. The haunt of demoniacs Mt 8: 28; Mk 5: 2 (acc. to Diog. L. 9, 38 Democritus sought solitude among the graves). Graves were somet. not recognizable as such fr. their outward appearance Lk 11: 44; s. ἄδηλος 1. M-M.*

μνήμη, ης, ἡ (trag.+; inscr., pap., LXX, Ep. Arist., Philo, Joseph.) *remembrance, memory.*
  1. memory that one has himself, w. gen. *of someth.* (Ep. Arist. 159) τ. μνήμην τινὸς ποιεῖσθαι *recall someth. to mind* 2 Pt 1: 15 (PFay. 19, 10 [11 AD] τῶν πραγμάτων μνήμην ποιεῖσθαι='hold the things in remembrance'. Likew. schol. on Apollon. Rhod. 4, 839–41a.—The mng. of μ. ποιεῖσθαι, quotable Hdt.+; Jos., Ant. 18, 65= 'make mention' is scarcely applicable here). εἰς τὴν τῶν προηθληκότων μ. *in memory of those who have already contested* MPol 18: 2.
  2. the memory that another pers. has of someth. (Diod. S. 5, 73, 1 and 23, 15, 2 αἰώνιον μνήμην παρὰ πᾶσιν ἀνθρώποις; testament of Epicurus in Diog. L. 10, 18: a memorial meal εἰς τὴν ἡμῶν μνήμην; ΕΛΛΗΝΙΚΑ I,

'28, p. 18, 18 festivals are arranged εἰς μνήμην Εὐρυκλέους εὐεργέτου; Jos., Ant. 13, 63) pl. ἡ τρυφὴ καὶ ἀπάτη μνήμας οὐκ ἔχει= have no remembrance= are not long remembered (like Lat. memoriam non habet) Hs 6, 5, 3. μνήμας μεγάλας ἔχειν have a lasting remembrance= live long in remembrance ibid. (cf. Proverbia Aesopi 111 P. μνήμην ἔχειν; Ep. Arist. 279). M-M.*

μνημονεύω impf. ἐμνημόνευον; 1 aor. ἐμνημόνευσα (Hdt.+; inscr., pap., LXX, Philo, Joseph., Test. 12 Patr.).
1. *remember, keep in mind, think of,* also—w. no fixed boundaries—*mention.*
   a. w. gen. (Pla., Theaet. 191D; Philod., De Piet. 94; Diod. S. 1, 21, 8; Lucian, Dial. Deor. 4, 7; Dit., Syll.³ 284, 8; 620, 25; PSI 502, 2; 651, 2 [III BC]; Wsd 2: 4; Tob 4: 5, 19 BA; Sus 9 Theod.; Ep. Arist. 157), and, to be sure, w. gen. of the pers.: Lk 17: 32; Hb 13: 7; B 21: 7; MPol 8: 1; IEph 12: 2; ISm 5: 3; Hm 4, 1, 1. Of mention in prayer (Heidelb. Pap.-Sammlung I ed. Deissmann '05, no. 6, 15 παρακαλῶ οὖν, δέσποτα, ἵνα μνημονεύῃς μοι [μου?] εἰς τ. ἁγίας σου εὐχάς) IEph 21: 1; IMg 14: 1.—W. the connotation of solicitude (cf. 1 Macc 12: 11) μ. τῶν πτωχῶν *remember the poor* Gal 2: 10.—W. gen. of the thing (Arrian, Peripl. 16, 3 πόλεως ἐμνημόνευσεν; Jos., Ant. 2, 162; 6, 93 al.) τοῦ λόγου J 15: 20; pl. Ac 20: 35. ὧν εἶπεν ὁ κύριος Pol 2: 3. τῶν τοῦ κυρίου ἐνταλμάτων 2 Cl 17: 3. τῶν ἐντολῶν αὐτοῦ Hs 1: 7. τῆς τρυφῆς 6, 5, 4.—J 16: 4, 21.—μου τῶν δεσμῶν *remember my bonds* Col 4: 18. Perh. mention or remembering in prayer is meant here, as in ὑμῶν τοῦ ἔργου τῆς πίστεως *your work of faith* 1 Th 1: 3 (MDibelius, Hdb., exc. ad loc.). τῆς ἐν Συρίᾳ ἐκκλησίας ITr 13: 1; IRo 9: 1.—εἰ ἐκείνης (i.e. πατρίδος) ἐμνημόνευον *if they had thought of,* i.e. meant, that homeland (the earthly one) Hb 11: 15.
   b. w. acc. (Hdt. 1, 36; X., An. 4, 3, 2, also Herodian 6, 1, 7; BGU 1024 V, 20; Jdth 13: 19; 2 Macc 9: 21) of the pers.: Ἰησοῦν Χριστὸν ἐγηγερμένον 2 Ti 2: 8. W. acc. of the thing (Philo, Leg. All. 1, 55) τοὺς πέντε ἄρτους Mt 16: 9. τὸν κόπον ἡμῶν 1 Th 2: 9. τὰ προγεγραμμένα Hv 4, 3, 6.—Papias 2: 3, 15. Of God: ἐμνημόνευσεν τὰ ἀδικήματα αὐτῆς *God has remembered her wicked deeds* to punish them Rv 18: 5.
   c. foll. by περί τινος Hb 11: 22.—W. ὅτι foll. (Pla., Rep. 480A) Ac 20: 31; Eph 2: 11; 2 Th 2: 5. Foll. by indirect quest. (PStrassb. 41, 40 οὐ μνημονεύω δέ, τί ἐν τῇ μεσειτίᾳ ἐγένετο) Rv 2: 5; 3: 3. W. temporal clause foll.: Mk 8: 18.
   d. pass., of Polycarp ὑπὸ πάντων μνημονεύεται *he is remembered by everyone* MPol 19: 1.
2. *retain in one's memory* (like Lat. memoria tenere aliquid) w. acc. of the thing Hv 1, 3, 3a; 2, 1, 3. τὰ ἔσχατα ῥήματα v 1, 3, 3b. M-M.*

μνημοσύνη, ης, ἡ (Hom.+) *memory* εἰς μνημοσύνην αὐτοῦ *in memory of him* GP 12: 54.*

μνημόσυνον, ου, τό (Hdt.+; pap., LXX, En.)—1. *memory* as a mental faculty: ἔγγραφοι ἐγένοντο ἐν τῷ μ. αὐτοῦ *they were inscribed in his memory* 1 Cl 45: 8.
2. *memory* w. obj. gen. (oft. LXX) εἰς μ. τινος *in memory of someone* Mt 26: 13; Mk 14: 9 (JoachJeremias, ZNW 44, '52/'53, 103-7: God's 'eschatological remembrance'). ἐξολεθρεῦσαι ἐκ γῆς τὸ μ. αὐτῶν *root out the memory of them from the earth* 1 Cl 22: 6 (Ps 33: 17; cf. Sir 10: 17; Test. Jos. 7: 5).
3. *a memorial offering* (= אַזְכָּרָה Lev 2: 2, 9, 16; 5: 12; cf. Sir 35: 6; 38: 11; 45: 16) fig. αἱ προσευχαί σου

ἀνέβησαν εἰς μνημόσυνον ἔμπροσθεν τ. θεοῦ Ac 10: 4. M-M.*

μνησικακέω fut. μνησικακήσω, 1 aor. ἐμνησικάκησα (Hdt.+; inscr., LXX; Jos., Bell. 4, 94 al.) *remember evil, bear malice, bear a grudge* τινί *against someone* (Thu. 8, 73; Lysias 30, 9; Philo, Virt. 106, De Jos. 17; Jos., Ant. 1, 323) B 19: 4; Hv 2, 3, 1; s 9, 23, 4b. τινί τι: τοῖς ἐξομολογουμένοις τὰς ἁμαρτίας αὐτῶν *bear a grudge against those who have confessed their sins,* or perh. *cast up their sins to those who confess them* s 9, 23, 4a. ἔκαστος ὑμῶν κατὰ τοῦ πλησίον κακίαν μὴ μνησικακείτω *let no one of you hold a grudge against his neighbor* B 2: 8 (Zech 7: 10). Abs., w. pers. obj. to be supplied *bear a grudge, be resentful* (Diod. S. 31, 8, 2; Lucian, Prom. 8) D 2: 3; Dg 9: 2. οἱ ἄνθρωποι οἱ μνησικακοῦντες *people who hold a grudge* Hm 9: 3.*

μνησικακία, ας, ἡ (Plut., Mor. 860A; Appian, Ital. fgm. 7; Philo, De Jos. 261; Jos., Ant. 16, 292) *bearing a grudge, vengefulness* Hm 8: 3; also vs. 10 in Lake's text; *causing death* Hv 2, 3, 1.*

μνησίκακος, ον (Aristot. et al.; Pr 12: 28) *vengeful* μ. γίνεσθαι Hs 9, 23, 3.*

μνηστεύω (Hom.+; Diod. S. 4, 37, 4; 5; LXX; Jos., C. Ap. 2, 200; the mid. PFlor. 36, 4) pf. pass. ptc. ἐμνηστευμένη, v.l. μεμνηστευμένη (Bl-D. §68; Mlt.-H. 193); 1 aor. pass. ptc. μνηστευθεῖσα *woo and win,* betroth pass. *be betrothed, become engaged* (Dt 22: 25, 27f) τινί *to someone* (Artem. 2, 12 p. 101, 4 H. v.l.; Dt 22: 23; Jos., Bell. 1, 508) Mary Mt 1: 16 v.l., 18; Lk 1: 27; 2: 5. M-M.*

μογγιλάλος, ον (Ptolem., Apotel. 3, 13, 3 p. 151, 2 Boll-B.; Georg. Mon. 492, 14 de Boor [1892]; Is 35: 6 v.l.; s. Thackeray p. 120f.—Bl-D. §34, 6; Mlt.-H. 106) *speaking in a hoarse* or *hollow voice* Mk 7: 32 v.l.*

μογιλάλος, ον (on the form cf. Bl-D. §34, 6; Rob. 169; 210)—1. *speaking with difficulty, having an impediment in one's speech* (Aëtius 8, 38; schol. on Lucian, p. 68, 5 Rabe; Anecd. Gr. I p. 100, 22; cf. JBidez et FCumont, Les mages hellénisés II '38 p. 334, 8 with v.l. μογγιλάλοι); this mng. for Mk 7: 32 is supported by vs. 35 ἐλάλει ὀρθῶς (cf. ASWeatherhead, ET 23, '12, 381).
2. *mute, incapable of speech* (Vett. Val. 73, 12; POxy. 465, 228; Is 35: 6.—Aq. Is 56: 10; Aq., Sym., Theod. Ex 4: 11); the ancient versions take Mk 7: 32, 33 v.l. in this sense. M-M.*

μόγις adv. (Hom.+; Diod. S.; Epict.; Polemo, Decl. 2, 3; 15; Lucian; PMagd. 11, 6 [221 BC]; POxy. 298, 19 [I AD]; PLeipz. 105, 10; PSI 49, 2; Wsd 9: 16 v.l.; 3 Macc 7: 6; Philo, In Flacc. 113 v.l.; Jos., Ant. 8, 130; 16, 345.—Bl-D. §33; cf. Rob. 296) *scarcely, with difficulty* Lk 9: 39 v.l.; Ac 14: 18 D; Ro 5: 7 v.l. (in each case the text has μόλις, q.v.).—Lk 23: 53 D. M-M.*

μόδιος, ίου, ὁ (Lat. loanw. [modius]: Dinarchus 1, 43[?]; Dionys. Hal. 12, 1; Epict. 1, 17, 7; 9; Plut., Demetr. 33, 6; inscr. [Dit., Or. index]; PThéad. 32, 25; PGenève 62, 17; Jos., Ant. 9, 85; 14, 28; 206. Loanw. in rabb.) *a peck-measure,* a grain-measure containing 16 sextarii = about 8.75 liters, almost exactly one peck: Mt 5: 15; Mk 4: 21; Lk 11: 33 (a vessel used to hide a light, as Jos., Ant. 5, 223.—On the figure, ADupont-Sommer, Note archéol. sur le prov. évang.: mettre la lampe sous le boisseau= Mél. Syr. à MRDussaud II '39, 789-94; JoachJeremias, ZNW 39, '41, 237-40). M-M.*

μοῖρα, ας, ἡ (Hom.+; pap., Philo; Jos., Bell. 4, 86, Ant. 17, 303; Sib. Or. 3, 121 al.) *fate* (PLeipz. 40 II, 26) AP fgm. 2.*

μοιχαλίς, ίδος, ἡ (Aëtius [100 AD]: Dox. Gr. 301a, 14; Heliod. 8, 9; Procop., Anecd. 1, 36; Syntipas p. 23, 6 al. [Phryn. 452 L.]; Cat. Cod. Astr. VII p. 109, 6; 20; VIII 1 p. 264, 29; VIII 4 p. 146, 26; Maspéro 97 II, 42; Suidas III p. 421, 10; LXX; Test. Levi 14: 6) *adulteress.*

1. lit. Ro 7: 3a, b (the same case sim. described in Achilles Tat. 8, 10, 11f). ὀφθαλμοὶ μεστοὶ μοιχαλίδος *eyes that are full of (desire for) an adulteress* i.e., always looking for a woman with whom to commit adultery 2 Pt 2: 14 (on the expr. cf. Timaeus Hist. [IV BC] in Περὶ ὕψους 4, 5 of a moral man ἐν ὀφθαλμοῖς κόρας, μὴ πόρνας ἔχων; Plut., Mor. 528E).

2. fig., in a usage found in Hosea (3: 1), in which God's relation to his people is depicted as a marriage, and any beclouding of it becomes adultery (cf. Jer 3: 9; 9: 1; Ezk 16: 32ff, esp. vs. 38).

   a. adj. *adulterous* γενεὰ μοιχαλίς Mt 12: 39; 16: 4; Mk 8: 38.—**b.** subst. μοιχαλίδες of both sexes (W-S. §28, 2b) Js 4: 4 (μοιχοὶ καὶ μοιχαλίδες t.r.). M-M.*

μοιχάω (X.+—JWackernagel, Hellenistica '07, 7ff; Bl-D. §101 p. 46f) *cause to commit adultery* in our lit. (as well as LXX) only pass. *be caused to commit adultery, be an adulterer or adulteress, commit adultery,* lit.

1. of a woman (Ezk 16: 32) ποιεῖ αὐτὴν μοιχᾶσθαι (the man who divorces his wife) *causes her to commit adultery* (if she contracts a new marriage) Mt 5: 32a t.r. αὐτὴ μοιχᾶται *she commits adultery* Mk 10: 12. But also

2. of a man (PsSol 8, 10), who marries a divorced woman Mt 5: 32b; 19: 9 v.l. or who marries again after divorcing his wife 19: 9; Hm 4, 1, 6. μοιχᾶται ἐπ' αὐτὴν *commits adultery against her* (his first wife) Mk 10: 11 (NTurner, Bible Translator 7, '56, 151f: associates w. Jer 5: 9).

3. of a man or woman 2 Cl 4: 3. ὃς ἂν τὰ ὁμοιώματα ποιῇ τοῖς ἔθνεσιν, μοιχᾶται *whoever acts as the heathen do* (i.e., takes part in idol-worship), *commits adultery* (and it cannot be expected of the other marriage-partner to maintain marital relations) Hm 4, 1, 9. M-M.*

μοιχεία, ας, ἡ (Andocides+; Heraclit. Sto. 69 p. 89, 15; PMich. 148 I, 8; LXX; Philo; Jos., Ant. 16, 340 al.) *adultery* lit. Hm 4, 1, 5; 9; AP 9: 24. W. other sins (Hos 4: 2) Gal 5: 19 t.r.; 1 Cl 30: 1; 2 Cl 6: 4; B 20: 1; D 5: 1; Hm 8: 3. Pl. (as in D 5: 1 above) denoting separate acts (Pla., Rep. 4 p. 443A, Leg. 8 p. 839A; PTebt. 276, 16 πορνεῖαι καὶ μοιχεῖαι; Philo, Spec. Leg. 2, 13; Jos., Bell. 5, 402.—Bl-D. §142; cf. Rob. 408) *adulterous acts* Mt 15: 19=Mk 7: 22 (in a list of vices also Plut., Mor. 1050D). Cf. D 3: 3. καταλαμβάνειν ἐπὶ μοιχείᾳ *catch in the act of adultery* J 8: 3 (Plut., Mor. 291F; on the 'adulterous woman' cf. REisler, ZNW 22, '23, 305-7; KBornhäuser, NKZ 37, '26, 353-63; EFFBishop, JTS 35, '34, 40-5; JoachJeremias, ZNW 43, '51, 148f: a temptation story, cf. Mk 12: 13-17; TWManson, ZNW 44, '52/'53, 255f; FASchilling, ATR 37, '55, 91-106; JDMDerrett, Law in the NT, '70, 156-87). Also εὑρίσκειν ἐν μ. Hm 4, 1, 4. M-M. B. 1456.*

μοιχεύω fut. μοιχεύσω; 1 aor. ἐμοίχευσα, pass. inf. μοιχευθῆναι (Aristoph., X.+; LXX; Philo; Jos., Ant. 16, 296 al.; Test. 12 Patr.—HBogner, Was heisst μ.?: Her. 76, '41, 318-20) *commit adultery.*

1. of both sexes, w. ref. to the Ten Commandments (Ex 20: 13; Dt 5: 17) Mt 5: 27; 19: 18; Mk 10: 19; Lk

18: 20; Ro 13: 9; Js 2: 11a, b. One or more of these pass. may refer to the man alone; this is obviously the case under

2. in some instances where μ.—a. is used abs.: Lk 16: 18a, b; Ro 2: 22 (μὴ μοιχεύειν as Jos., Ant. 3, 92); B 19: 4; D 2: 2.

   b. has as obj. τινά (γυναῖκα) *commit adultery w. someone* (Aristoph., Av. 558; Pla., Rep. 2 p. 360B; Lucian, Dial. Deor. 6, 3; Aristaenet., Ep. 1, 20; PSI 158, 45. Cf. Lev 20: 10) Mt 5: 28 (cf. Epict. 2, 18, 15; Sextus 233). This explains the use of the passive in the case of the woman (Charito 1, 4, 6 μοιχευομένην τὴν γυναῖκα; Achilles Tat. 6, 9, 7; Sir 23: 23; Philo, Decal. 124; Jos., Ant. 7, 131) ποιεῖ αὐτὴν μοιχευθῆναι *he causes her to commit adultery* (by contracting a subsequent marriage) Mt 5: 32; 19: 9 v.l. ἡ γυνὴ κατείληπται μοιχευομένη J 8: 4.

   c. οἱ μοιχεύοντες μετ' αὐτῆς Rv 2: 22 is at least on the way to a fig. mng. (cf. Jer 3: 9).—RHCharles, The Teaching of the NT on Divorce '21, 91ff; FJDölger, Christl. u. hdn. Ächtung des Ehebr. in d. Kultsatzung: Antike u. Christent. III '32, 132-48; GDelling, RAC IV, '59, 666-80; JAFitzmyer, Theological Studies 37, '76, 197-226 (Mt).—FHauck, TW IV 737-43: μοιχεύω and related words. M-M.*

μοιχός, οῦ, ὁ (since Hipponax [VI BC] 67 D.²; Soph.; POxy. 1160, 24ff; BGU 1024 III, 12; LXX; Philo) *adulterer.*

1. lit., w. πόρνος Hb 13: 4. W. φθορεύς (cf. Philo, Spec. Leg. 4, 89) B 10: 7. W. other sinners (Test. Levi 17: 11) Lk 18: 11; 1 Cor 6: 9; Hs 6, 5, 5. Parallel w. κλέπτης 1 Cl 35: 8 (Ps 49: 18).—2. fig., w. μοιχαλίς (q.v. 2) Js 4: 4 t.r. M-M.*

μόλιβος, ου, ὁ (Hom.+; PTebt. 121, 52; 84; LXX; Jos., Bell. 6, 278, Ant. 15, 398. On the var. forms and spellings s. Thackeray 96; 116) *lead;* because of its low melting point a symbol of the earth, destroyed in the fire of the last judgment 2 Cl 16: 3.*

μόλις adv. (trag., Thu.+; PTebt. 19, 10 [114 BC]; PRyl. 113, 27; POxy. 1117, 19; PGiess. 4, 15; LXX, Ep. Arist., Philo, Joseph.—Bl-D. §33; Rob. 296; s. μόγις) *scarcely.*

1. *with difficulty* (Lycophron vs. 757; Appian, Liby. 3 §14, Bell. Civ. 1, 8 §33; 1, 77 §351; Ael. Aristid. 48, 43 K.=24 p. 476 D.; Wsd 9: 16=μετὰ πόνου; Sir 29: 6; Philo, Op. M. 80; Jos., Bell. 1, 149) Lk 9: 39; Ac 14: 18; 23: 29 v.l.; 27: 7f, 16; 1 Pt 4: 18 (Pr 11: 31; cf. Artem. 1, 2 p. 4, 13 μόλις ἐσώθη).

2. *not readily, only rarely* (Nicander, Ther. 281; Synes., Prov. 1, 11 p. 101D: μόλις [seldom, scarcely ever] do virtue and good fortune meet; Sir 21: 20; 26: 29; 32: 7; Jos., C. Ap. 1, 66, Vi. 173) Ro 5: 7; another possibility here is—3. *hardly* (Phlegon: 257 fgm. 36, 1; 3 Jac.; Achilles Tat. 2, 26, 1) or *scarcely* (Appian, Bell. Civ. 3, 53 §218 ὀλίγοι μόλις=scarcely a few). M-M.*

Μολόχ, ὁ indecl. (LXX.—מֶלֶךְ, w. the vowels of בֹּשֶׁת) *Moloch,* the Canaanite-Phoenician god of sky and sun (Baudissin, RE XIII 269ff) Ac 7: 43 in a quot. fr. Am 5: 26, where the LXX renders the words סִכּוּת מַלְכְּכֶם by τὴν σκηνὴν τοῦ Μολόχ (סֻכַּת מֶלֶךְ).—OEissfeldt, Molk als Opferbegriff im Punischen u. Hebr. u. d. Ende des Gottes Moloch '35 (on this WvSoden, ThLZ 61, '36, 45f).*

μολύνω 1 aor. ἐμόλυνα, pass. ἐμολύνθην (Aristoph., Pla.+; PSI 1160, 6 [30 BC]; LXX) *stain, defile, make impure, soil.*

1. lit. (Lucian, Anach. 1; Gen 37: 31; SSol 5: 3) μεμολυμμένος *unclean, unwashed* GOxy 16. Unsoiled

garments as symbol of a spotless life ἃ οὐκ ἐμόλυναν τὰ ἱμάτια αὐτῶν Rv 3: 4.
2. fig. (Epict. 2, 8, 13; 2, 9, 17; Porphyr., Abst. 1, 42; Synes., Dreams 10 p. 142ᴅ ἀθέων τῶν μολυνάντων τὸ ἐν αὐτοῖς θεῖον; Sir 21: 28; Jer 23: 11; Test. Ash. 4: 4 τὴν ψυχήν) τ. χεῖρας (Jos., Vi. 244) Ac 5: 38 v.l. ἡ συνείδη-σις . . . μολύνεται the conscience is defiled by eating meat sacrificed to idols 1 Cor 8: 7 (Amm. Marc. 15, 2 conscientiam polluebat). Esp. of immorality (Ep. Arist. 152) οἳ μετὰ γυναικῶν οὐκ ἐμολύνθησαν who have not defiled themselves with women Rv 14: 4. M-M.*

μολυσμός, οῦ, ὁ (Strabo 17, 2, 4; Plut., Mor. 779ᴄ; Heliod. 10, 4, 2; 1 Esdr 8: 80; 2 Macc 5: 27; Jos., C. Ap. 1, 289) defilement fig., of religious and moral things (Vett. Val. 242, 16; Jer 23: 15; Ep. Arist. 166; Test. Sim. 2: 13) ἀπὸ παντὸς μ. σαρκὸς καὶ πνεύματος from all defilement of body and spirit, i.e. outwardly and inwardly 2 Cor 7: 1. M-M.*

μομφή, ῆς, ἡ (Pind.+) blame, (cause for) complaint πρός τινα ἔχειν μ. have a complaint against anyone (ἔχειν μομφήν τινι; Pind. et al.) Col 3: 13.*

μονάζω (Cornutus 14 p. 17, 17; Anth. Pal. 5, 66, 1; Iambl., Vi. Pyth. 3, 14; 35, 253; Apollon. Dysc., Synt. 191, 2, Gramm. Gr. II 2 p. 262, 10; 376, 7; schol. on Soph., Aj. 654, Oed. R. 479; Etym. Mag. p. 627, 13; Ps 101: 8) live alone, separate oneself B 4: 10; Hs 9, 26, 3.*

μονή, ῆς, ἡ (Eur., Hdt.+; inscr., pap.; 1 Macc 7: 38)
—1. staying, tarrying (Eur.+; Dit., Or. 527, 5; Philo, Mos. 1, 316) μονὴν ποιεῖσθαι live, stay (Thu. 1, 131, 1; BGU 742; Jos., Ant. 8, 350; 13, 41) J 14: 23.
2. dwelling(-place), room, abode (Charito 1, 12, 1 μονὴν ποιεῖν; Paus. 10, 31, 7; Dit., Or. 527, 5) of heavenly dwellings J 14: 2 (OSchaefer, ZNW 32, '33, 210–17; understood in an existential sense: RGundry, ZNW 58, '67, 68–72). τῆς ἀμείνονος τυγχάνειν μονῆς attain a better abode AP fgm. 2. M-M.*

μονογενής, ές (Hes.+; LXX; Joseph.; loanw. in rabb.) only (so mostly, incl. Judg 11: 34; Tob 3: 15; 8: 17) of children: of Isaac, Abraham's only son (Jos., Ant. 1, 222) Hb 11: 17. Of an only son (Plut., Lycurgus 31, 8; Jos., Ant. 20, 20) Lk 7: 12; 9: 38. Of the daughter (Diod. S. 4, 73, 2) of Jairus 8: 42.—Also unique (in kind) of someth. that is the only example of its category (Cornutus 27 p. 49, 13 εἷς κ. μονογενὴς ὁ κόσμος ἐστί. μονογενῆ κ. μόνα ἐστίν='unique and alone'; Pla., Timaeus 92c). Of the mysterious bird, the Phoenix 1 Cl 25: 2.—In the Johannine lit. μ. is used only of Jesus. The mngs. only, unique may be quite adequate for all its occurrences here (so M-M., RSV et al.; DMoody, JBL 72, '53, 213–19; FCGrant, ATR 36, '54, 284–87). But some (e.g. WBauer, Hdb.) prefer to regard μ. as somewhat heightened in mng. in J and 1 J to only-begotten or begotten of the Only One, in view of the emphasis on γεννᾶσθαι ἐκ θεοῦ (J 1: 13 al.); in this case it would be analogous to πρωτότοκος (Ro 8: 29; Col 1: 15 al.). τὸν υἱὸν τὸν μ. ἔδωκεν J 3: 16 (Philo Bybl. [100 ᴀᴅ] in Euseb., Pr. Ev. 1, 10, 33: Cronus offers up his μονογενὴς υἱός). ὁ μ. υἱὸς τοῦ θεοῦ vs. 18; cf. J 1: 34 v.l. τὸν υἱὸν τὸν μ. ἀπέσταλκεν ὁ θεός 1 J 4: 9; cf. Dg 10: 2. On the expr. δόξαν ὡς μονογενοῦς παρὰ πατρός J 1: 14 s. Hdb. ad loc. and PWinter, Zeitschrift für Rel. u. Geistesgeschichte 5, '53, 335–65 (Engl.). Cf. also Hdb. on vs. 18 where, beside the rdg. μονογενὴς θεός (considered by many the orig.) an only-begotten one, God (acc. to his real being), or a God begotten of the Only One, another rdg. ὁ μονογενὴς υἱός is found. MPol 20: 2 in the doxology διὰ

παιδὸς αὐτοῦ τοῦ μονογενοῦς Ἰησοῦ Χριστοῦ.—On the mng. of μονογενής in history of religion cf. the material in Hdb.[3] 25f on J 1: 14 (also Plut., Mor. 423ᴀ Πλάτων . . . αὐτῷ δή φησι δοκεῖν ἕνα τοῦτον [sc. τὸν κόσμον] εἶναι μονογενῆ τῷ θεῷ καὶ ἀγαπητόν; Wsd 7: 22 of σοφία: ἔστι ἐν αὐτῇ πνεῦμα νοερὸν ἅγιον μονογενές.—Vett. Val. 11, 32) as well as the lit. given there, also HLeisegang, Der Bruder des Erlösers: Αγγελος I '25, 24–33; RBultmann J, 47, 2; 55f; FBüchsel, TW IV 745–50. M-M.*

μονόλιθος, ον (since Hdt. 2, 175; Diod. S. 1, 46, 1; Strabo 9, 5, 16; pap.; Jos., Bell. 7, 290, Ant. 13, 211) (made of) a single stone of a tower Hs 9, 9, 7; 9, 13, 5.*

μόνον s. μόνος 2.

μόνος, η, ον (Pind.+[as μοῦνος as early as Hom.]; inscr., pap., LXX, En., Ep. Arist., Philo, Joseph., Test. 12 Patr.) only, alone.
1. adj.—a. only, alone—α. used w. verbs like εἶναι, εὑρίσκεσθαι, καταλείπειν: μόνος ἦν ἐκεῖ Mt 14: 23; cf. J 8: 16. Λουκᾶς ἐστιν μόνος μετ' ἐμοῦ 2 Ti 4: 11. εὑρέθη Ἰησοῦς μόνος Lk 9: 36. μόνην με κατέλειπεν 10: 40 (w. inf. foll.); pass. κατελείφθη μόνος J 8: 9; cf. 1 Th 3: 1. κἀγὼ ὑπελείφθην μόνος I am the only one left (Theseus Hist. [Roman times] no. 453 fgm. 2 Jac. μόνος περιλειφθείς of the only survivor of a battle) Ro 11: 3 (cf. 3 Km 19: 10, 14).—Ac 15: 34 D.
β. used w. a noun τὰ ὀθόνια μόνα Lk 24: 12. μόνοι οἱ μαθηταὶ ἀπῆλθον J 6: 22. μόνος ὁ ἀρχιερεύς Hb 9: 7.—Cf. Mt 12: 4 (Jos., Ant. 15, 419 τ. ἱερεῦσιν ἐξὸν ἦν μόνοις).—Used w. pronouns (μόνος αὐτός: Nicol. Dam. 90 fgm. 130, 23 p. 407, 21 Jac.; Ps.-Demetr., El. 97; 2 Macc 7: 37; Philo, Agr. 39; Jos., Ant. 8, 405, C. Ap. 1, 49); αὐτῷ μόνῳ λατρεύσεις (Dt 6: 13 v.l.; cf. Jos., Ant. 3, 91 τοῦτον μ.) Mt 4: 10; Lk 4: 8.—Mt 18: 15; Mk 6: 47; 9: 2; J 6: 15. σὺ μόνος; (1 Km 21: 2) are you the only one? (Field, Notes 82) Lk 24: 18; ἐγὼ μ. Ac 26: 14 v.l.; 1 Cor 9: 6. ὑμεῖς μόνοι 14: 36.
γ. w. a negative and w. ἀλλά foll.: οὐκ ἐπ' ἄρτῳ μόνῳ . . ., ἀλλ' . . . (Dt 8: 3) Mt 4: 4. οὐκ ἐγὼ μ. . . ., ἀλλὰ καὶ . . . Ro 16: 4; 2 J 1. Pleonast. w. εἰ μή after a neg. not . . . except . . . alone Mt 12: 4; 17: 8; 24: 36; Mk 9: 8; Lk 5: 21; 6: 4; Phil 4: 15; Rv 9: 4 t.r.
δ. μόνος θεός (cf. Simonides, fgm. 4, 7 θεὸς μόνος; Da 3: 45; Sib. Or. 3, 629; PGM 13, 983) the only God 1 Ti 1: 17; Jd 25 (GDelling, ThLZ 77, '52, 469–76). W. article preceding ὁ μόνος θ. (Ep. Arist. 139; Philo, Fuga 71; ὁ θεὸς μόνος 4 Km 19: 15, 19; Ps 85: 10; Is 37: 20. Cf. ENorden, Agn. Theos '13, 245, 1) J 5: 44 (without θεοῦ 𝔓[66] [75] et al.). ὁ μ. ἀληθινὸς θεός the only true God 17: 3 (Demochares [c. 300 ʙᴄ]: 75 fgm. 2 Jac. τὸν Δημήτριον οἱ Ἀθηναῖοι ἐδέχοντο . . . ἐπάδοντες ὡς εἴη μόνος θεὸς ἀληθινός. οἱ δ' ἄλλοι καθεύδουσιν ἢ ἀποδημοῦσιν ἢ οὐκ εἰσίν. γεγονὼς δ' εἴη ἐκ Ποσειδῶνος καὶ Ἀφροδίτης). τὸ ὄνομα τ. ἀληθινοῦ καὶ μόνου κυρίου 1 Cl 43: 6. μ. σοφὸς θεός the only wise God Ro 16: 27 (Philo, Fuga 47 ὁ μ. σοφός; Heraclitus, fgm. 32 ἓν τὸ σοφὸν μοῦνον). ὁ μ. δεσπότης the only one who is master Jd 4 (cf. Jos., Bell. 7, 323; 410). ὁ μακάριος καὶ μόνος δυνάστης 1 Ti 6: 15.—vs. 16; Rv 15: 4.
b. alone, deserted, helpless (Hom.+; BGU 180, 23 [172 ᴀᴅ] ἄνθρωπος πρεσβύτης καὶ μόνος τυγχάνων; 385, 4; Wsd 10: 1; La 1: 1) οὐκ ἀφῆκέν με μόνον J 8: 29; 16: 32a, b (ἀφ. μόν. as Dio Chrys. 46[63], 2).
c. isolated, by itself (cf. Bar 4: 16) ἐὰν μὴ ὁ κόκκος τ. σίτου . . . ἀποθάνῃ, αὐτὸς μόνος μένει J 12: 24. In Hv 3, 9, 2 μ. refers to selfish Christians who isolate themselves fr. the needs of the hungry.

2. The neut. μόνον is used as an adv. *only, alone* (Aeschyl., Hdt.+)—**a.** limiting the action or state to the one designated by the verb Mt 9: 21; 14: 36; Mk 5: 36; Lk 8: 50; 1 Cor 15: 19; Gal 1: 23; Hv 3, 2, 1.

b. w. a noun or pron., to separate one pers. or thing fr. others: Mt 5: 47; 10: 42; Ac 18: 25; Ro 3: 29; Gal 2: 10; Hb 9: 10; Hm 12, 4, 7; τοῦτο μ. Gal 3: 2.

c. used w. negatives:—**α.** μ. μή *only not, not only* (POxy. 2153, 22) Gal 5: 13. οὐ (μή) μ. 4: 18; Js 1: 22. οὐ μ. . . . ἀλλά (without καί when the second member includes the first. X., Cyr. 1, 6, 16; Diod. S. 4, 15, 1; Dio Chrys. 1, 22; 62; 64[14], 7; Bl-D. §448, 1) Ac 19: 26 (but ADL 13 add καί) 1 J 5: 6. οὐ (or μή) μ. . . . , ἀλλὰ καί *not only* . . . , *but also* (PMich. 209, 12 [c. 200 AD]; Jos., Bell. 3, 102) Mt 21: 21; J 5: 18; Ac 19: 27; 26: 29; 27: 10; Ro 1: 32; 2 Cor 7: 7; Eph 1: 21 and oft. οὐ (μή). . .μ., ἀλλὰ καί J 11: 52; 12: 9; 13: 9; 17: 20; Ro 4: 12, 16; Phil 2: 27 al. οὐδέπω . . . , μ. δέ *not yet* . . . , *but* . . . *only* Ac 8: 16. οὐ μ. δέ, ἀλλὰ καί *not only this, but also* (ellipsis w. supplementation of what immediately precedes. Mitteis, Chrest. 26, 9=27, 9 [108 BC]. Cf. Sb 7616 [II AD]; Wsd 19: 15; Bl-D. §479, 1 app.; cf. Rob. 1201ff) Ro 5: 3, 11; 8: 23; 9: 10; 2 Cor 8: 19. μὴ μ., ἀλλὰ πολλῷ μᾶλλον *not only,* . . . *but much more* Phil 2: 12. On 1–2c cf. KBeyer, Semitische Syntax im NT '62, 126–9.

β. *in isolation* οὐκ ἐκ πίστεως μόνον *not by faith viewed in isolation* Js 2: 24; cf. Clem., Strom. 3, 15 οὐ γὰρ μόνον ἡ εὐνουχία δικαιοῖ=being a eunuch does not of itself justify. S. also πίστις 2dδ.

d. ἵνα μόνον *solely in order that* B 12: 8.

3. κατὰ μόνας (Thu. 1, 32, 5; X., Mem. 3, 7, 4; Menand., Epitr. 594 J., fgm. 158 K.; Polyb. 4, 15, 11; Diod. S. 4, 51, 16; Gen 32: 16; Ps 4: 9; Jer 15: 17; 1 Macc 12: 36; Jos., Vi. 326, Ant. 17, 336 al.—Also written καταμόνας; cf. BGU 813, 15 in APF 2, '03, 97) *alone* γίνεσθαι κ. μ. *be alone* (Syntipas p. 9, 16) Mk 4: 10.—Lk 9: 18; Hm 11: 8. Bl-D. §241, 6. M-M. B. 937.

μονόφθαλμος, ον (Hdt.+; rejected by the Atticists for 'deprived of one eye' in favor of ἑτερόφθαλμος [Phryn. 136 L.], but used in later colloq. speech in this sense: Polyb. 5, 67, 6; Strabo 2, 1, 9; Lucian, V.H. 1, 3; Ps.-Apollod. 2, 8, 3, 4 al. Perh. BGU 1196, 97 [I BC]) *one-eyed* Mt 18: 9; Mk 9: 47. M-M.*

μονόω pf. pass. ptc. μεμονωμένος (Hom.+; Musonius 73, 1 H.) *make solitary* pass. *be left alone* (Thu. 2, 81, 5; 5, 58, 2; Nicol. Dam.: 90 fgm. 130, 30 p. 416, 15 Jac.; Philo; Jos., Ant. 5, 280, Vi. 95) of a widow *is left alone* (cf. Anacreontea 37, 13 Preis.) 1 Ti 5: 5. M-M.*

μορφή, ῆς, ἡ (Hom.+; inscr., pap., LXX, Philo, Joseph.; Sib. Or. 3, 8; 27) *form, outward appearance, shape* gener. of bodily form 1 Cl 39: 3 (Job 4: 16). Of the shape or form of statues (Jos., Vi. 65) Dg 2: 3. Of appearances in visions, etc., similar to persons (Callisthenes [IV BC] in Athen. 10, 75 p. 452B Λιμὸς ἔχων γυναικὸς μορφήν; Diod. S. 3, 31, 4 ἐν μορφαῖς ἀνθρώπων; Jos., Ant. 5, 213 a messenger fr. heaven νεανίσκου μορφῇ): of the church Hv 3, 10, 2; 9; 3, 11, 1; 3, 13, 1; s 9, 1, 1; of the angel of repentance ἡ μ. αὐτοῦ ἠλλοιώθη *his appearance had changed* m 12, 4, 1. Of Christ (gods ἐν ἀνθρωπίνη μορφῇ: Iambl., Vi. Pyth. 6, 30; cf. Philo, Abr. 118) μορφὴν δούλου λαβών *he took on the form of a slave* Phil 2: 7. The risen Christ ἐφανερώθη ἐν ἑτέρᾳ μορφῇ *appeared in a different form* Mk 16: 12. Of the preëxistent Christ: ἐν μ. θεοῦ ὑπάρχων *although he was in the form of God* (on μορφὴ θεοῦ cf. Pla., Rep. 2 p. 380D; 381B and C; X., Mem. 4, 3, 13; Diog. L. 1, 10 the Egyptians say μὴ εἰδέναι τοῦ θεοῦ μορφήν;

Philo, Leg. ad Gai. 80; 110; Jos., C. Ap. 2, 190; PGM 7, 563; 13, 272; 584.—Rtzst., Mysterienrel.³ 357f) Phil 2: 6. For lit. s. on ἁρπαγμός and κενόω 1; RPMartin, ET 70, '59, 183f).—JBehm, TW IV 750–67: μορφή and related words. M-M.*

μορφόω 1 aor. pass. ἐμορφώθην (Aratus, Phaen. 375; Nilus: Anth. Pal. 1, 33, 1; Is 44: 13 Q in margin and Aq.; Philo, Plant. 3; Ps.-Philo, De Mundo 13; Sib. Or. 4, 182; Justin, Apol. 1, 5, 4 τοῦ λόγου μορφωθέντος καὶ ἀνθρώπου γενομένου) *to form, shape* act. PK 2 p. 14, 13. Pass. *take on form, be formed* (Theophr., Caus. Pl. 5, 6, 7; Diod. S. 3, 51, 3) symbolically as in the formation of an embryo (Galen XIX p. 181 K. ἔμβρυα μεμορφωμένα; Philo, Spec. Leg. 3, 117) μέχρις οὗ μορφωθῇ Χριστὸς ἐν ὑμῖν *until Christ is formed in you* Gal 4: 19 (RHermann, ThLZ 80, '55, 713–26). M-M.*

μόρφωσις, εως, ἡ (Theophr., Caus. Pl. 3, 7, 4 al.; Test. Benj. 10: 1)—**1.** *embodiment, formulation* of the Jew ἔχοντα τὴν μ. τῆς γνώσεως καὶ τῆς ἀληθείας ἐν τῷ νόμῳ *you who have the embodiment of knowledge and truth in the book of the law* Ro 2: 20 (νόμος = 'book of the law' as Jos., Bell. 2, 292, Ant, 12, 256).

2. *outward form, appearance* of teachers of error ἔχοντες μ. εὐσεβείας *who hold to the outward form of religion* 2 Ti 3: 5 (cf. Philo, Plant. 70 ἐπεὶ καὶ νῦν εἰσί τινες τῶν ἐπιμορφαζόντων εὐσέβειαν κτλ.). M-M.*

μοσχοποιέω 1 aor. ἐμοσχοποίησα (only in Christian wr.; εἰδωλοποιέω Pla.+) *make a calf* of the golden calf Ac 7: 41 (for ἐποίησε μόσχον Ex 32: 4). M-M.*

μόσχος, ου, ὁ *calf, young bull* or *ox* (so trag., Hdt.; inscr., pap., LXX, Ep. Arist., Philo; Jos., Ant. 1, 197) ὁ μ. ὁ σιτευτός (Judg 6: 25 A, 28 A; Jer 26: 21) *the fattened calf* Lk 15: 23, 27, 30. As an apocalyptic animal (cf. Ezk 1: 10) Rv 4: 7. As a sacrificial animal (Wilcken, Chrest. 87–9) 1 Cl 52: 2 (Ps 68: 32). Esp. of the sin-offering on the Day of Atonement αἷμα τράγων καὶ μόσχων *the blood of goats and calves* Hb 9: 12; cf. vs. 19. Denotes the 'red heifer' (Num 19), interpreted to mean Christ B 8: 2. M-M. B. 155.*

μουσικός, ή, όν *pertaining to music* (so Aristoph.+; inscr., pap., LXX; Jos., Ant. 16, 137); subst. ὁ μ. *the musician* (X., Cyr. 1, 6, 38; Cornutus 32 p. 67, 17 μ. καὶ κιθαριστής; Dit., Or. 383, 162; PFlor. 74, 6; POxy. 1275, 9 συμφωνίας αὐλητῶν κ. μουσικῶν; Ezk 26: 13; Philo), w. harpists, flute-players and trumpeters Rv 18: 22.—EWerner, The Sacred Bridge (Liturgy and Music) '59. M-M.*

μόχθος, ου, ὁ (Hes. and X.+; PRyl. 28, 117; Epigr. Gr. 851, 1; LXX; Philo, Mos. 1, 284; Sib. Or. 2, 272) *labor, exertion, hardship* w. κόπος (Proverb. Aesopi 11 P.; Anth. Pal. 1, 47, 3; 1, 90, 4; Jer 20: 18 v.l.; cf. Job 2: 9) 2 Cor 11: 27; 1 Th 2: 9; 2 Th 3: 8; Hs 5, 6, 2.—πόνος 2, end. M-M.*

μοχλός, οῦ, ὁ (Hom.+) *bar, bolt* (so Aeschyl., Thu.+; inscr., LXX; Jos., Bell. 6, 293 μ. σιδηρόδετος; loanw. in rabb.) μ. σιδηροῦς συγκλᾶν *break iron bars* B 11: 4 (Is 45: 2).*

μυελός, οῦ, ὁ (Hom.+; Gen 45: 18; Job 21: 24; 33: 24; on the spelling cf. Bl-D. §29, 2) serves to denote the inmost part (Eur., Hipp. 255 πρὸς ἄκρον μυελὸν ψυχῆς) pl. *marrow* (Jos., Bell. 6, 205) Hb 4: 12 (Alciphr. 3, 40, 2; Heliod. 3, 7, 3 ἄχρις ἐπ' ὀστέα κ. μυελούς).*

μυέω pf. pass. μεμύημαι t.t. of the mystery religions *initiate* (*into the mysteries*) (trag., Hdt.+; Dit., Or. 530, 15; 764, 12; 3 Macc 2: 30; Philo, Cher. 49, Sacr. Abel. 62; Jos., C. Ap. 2, 267). Also gener., without the specific sense: pass., w. inf. foll. (Alciphr. 4, 19, 21 v.l., but in all mss., κυβερνᾶν μυηθήσομαι) ἐν παντὶ καὶ ἐν πᾶσιν μεμύημαι καὶ χορτάζεσθαι καὶ πεινᾶν *in any and all circumstances I have learned the secret of being well fed and going hungry* Phil 4: 12. M-M.*

μύθευμα, ατος, τό (Aristot., Poet. 24; Plut., Mar. 11, 10, Mor. p. 28D; Philostrat., Vi. Apoll. 8, 11 p. 327, 29) *story, fable* w. ἑτεροδοξίαι: μυθεύματα τὰ παλαιά *the old fables* IMg 8: 1.*

μῦθος, ου, ὁ (Hom.+; inscr.; Sir 20: 19) *tale, story, legend, myth, fable* (so Pind., Hdt.+; Pla., Tim. 26E μὴ πλασθέντα μῦθον, ἀλλ᾽ ἀληθινὸν λόγον, Phaedo 61B; Epict. 3, 24, 18; Dit., Syll.³ 382, 7; Philo, Congr. Erud. Grat. 61 al.; Joseph.) w. πλάνη 2 Cl 13: 3. Pl. (cf. Diod. S. 1, 93, 3; 2, 46, 6; 23, 13 [all three μῦθοι πεπλασμένοι]; Philo, Exsecr. 162 τοὺς ἄπλαστον ἀλήθειαν ἀντὶ πεπλασμένων μύθων μεταδιώκοντας; Jos., C. Ap. 2, 256) σεσοφισμένοις μ. ἐξακολουθεῖν *follow cleverly devised fables* 2 Pt 1: 16 (Jos., Ant. 1, 22 τ. μύθοις ἐξακολουθεῖν). Of false teachings Ἰουδαϊκοὶ μ. Tit 1: 14. βέβηλοι καὶ γραώδεις μ. *worldly old wives' tales* 1 Ti 4: 7 (cf. Lucian, Philops. 9 γραῶν μῦθοι; Ael. Aristid. 45 p. 133 D. As early as Pla., Gorg. 527A μ. ὥσπερ γραός; Xenophon, Ep. 7). W. γενεαλογίαι (q.v.) 1: 4. ἐπὶ τοὺς μ. ἐκτρέπεσθαι *turn to myths* 2 Ti 4: 4.—EHoffmann, Qua ratione ἔπος, μῦθος, αἶνος λόγος... adhibita sint, Diss. Gött. '22; LMueller, Wort u. Begriff Mythos im kl. Griech., Diss. Hamburg, '54; KGoldammer, ZNW 48, '57, 93-100; CKBarrett, ET 68, '57, 345-48; 359-62; GStählin, TW IV 769-803. M-M.*

μυκάομαι (Hom.+; PGM 13, 942; 945) *roar* of lions (Theocr. 26, 20f) Rv 10: 3. M-M.*

μυκτηρίζω (Hippocr., Epid. 7, 123='have a nose-bleed') *turn up the nose at, treat with contempt* (Lysias in Pollux 2, 78; Sext. Emp., Math. 1, 217; LXX; Sib. Or. 1, 171) τινά *someone* (Pr 15: 20; Ps 79: 7) w. χλευάζειν 1 Cl 39: 1. ἐμοὺς ἐλέγχους 57: 5 (Pr 1: 30). Abs. Lk 23: 35 D. Pass. (PTebt. 758, 11 [II BC]; Jer 20: 7) of God οὐ μ. *he is not to be mocked, treated w. contempt*, perh. *outwitted* Gal 6: 7; Pol 5: 1. M-M.*

μυλικός, ή, όν (schol. on Eur., Hecuba 362; Syntipas p. 108, 11) *belonging to a mill* λίθος μ. *millstone* Mk 9: 42 t.r.; Lk 17: 2; Rv 18: 21 v.l.*

μύλινος, η, ον (CIG 3371, 4; Dit., Syll.³ 996, 16 *belonging to a mill* λίθος ὡς μ. μέγας *a stone like a great millstone* Rv 18: 21. M-M.*

μύλος, ου, ὁ (H.Gk. for ἡ μύλη [so also Joseph.]; Bl-D. §50).
1. *mill* (Diod. S. 3, 13, 2; Plut., Mor. 549E; 830D; PSI 530, 2 [III BC]; POxy. 278, 17; Ex 11: 5; Dt 24: 6; Is 47: 2; Sib. Or. 8, 14), made of two round, flat stones (illustration: Kurzes Bibelwörterbuch 451). ἀλήθειν ἐν τῷ μ. *grind with the* (*hand-*)*mill* (cf. Num 11: 8) Mt 24: 41. φωνὴ μ. *the sound of the mill* (as it turns) Rv 18: 22.
2. *millstone* (Lycophron 233; Strabo 4, 1, 13; Anth. Pal. 11, 246, 2; PRyl. 167, 10; BGU 1067, 5; Judg 9: 53 A; 2 Km 11: 21) Rv 18: 21 t.r.; μ. ὀνικός *a great* (lit. 'donkey') *millstone*, i.e., not a stone fr. the small handmill, but one fr. the large mill, worked by donkey-power (s. ὀνικός). As a heavy weight: ἵνα κρεμασθῇ μ. ὀνικὸς περὶ τὸν τράχη-

λον αὐτοῦ *that a great millstone would be hung around his neck* Mt 18: 6. Also εἰ περίκειται μ. ὀν. περὶ τὸν τράχηλον αὐτοῦ *if a great millstone were hung around his neck* Mt 9: 42. More briefly περιτεθῆναι μύλον *have a millstone hung* (on him) 1 Cl 46: 8.—Rv 18: 21 v.l. M-M. B. 363.*

μυλών, ῶνος, ὁ (Eur.+; Thu. 6, 22; inscr.: Bull. de corr. hell. 27, '03, 64, 146 [250 BC]; Maspéro 139 p. 53, 13; Jer 52: 11) *mill-house* (Ps.-Lucian, Asin. 42) Mt 24: 41 t.r.*

μυλωνικός, ή, όν *belonging to the mill-house* μ. λίθος *millstone* Mk 9: 42 v.l. (μ. as subst. is found Wilcken, Chrest. 323, 7 [II AD]).*

Μύρα (Strabo et al. The spelling w. one ρ is correct, made certain by CIG III 4288, 3-6; Dit., Or. 441, 214. Also, it is to be taken as a neut. pl. Μύρα, ων: CIG III 4288; Pliny 32, 17; Athen. 2, 53 p. 59A; Sib. Or. 4, 109; Acta Pauli et Theclae 40 p. 266, 2; 4 L.; Basilius, Ep. 218. The rdg. Μύραν Ac 27: 5 is found in very few mss.; also Acta Pauli et Theclae 40 p. 266, 4 v.l.—W.-S. p. 58; Mlt.-H. 101) *Myra*, a city on the south coast of Lycia in Asia Minor. Visited by Paul on his journey to Rome Ac 27: 5 (v.l. wrongly Lystra); acc. to 21: 1 D also on his last journey to Jerusalem. M-M.*

μυριάς, άδος, ἡ (Hdt.+; inscr., pap., LXX, En., Ep. Arist., Philo, Joseph.) *myriad* (ten thousand).
1. lit., as a number (Archimedes II 220, 8 Heiberg and oft.) ἀργυρίου μ. πέντε *fifty thousand pieces of silver* (i.e. denarii= about $10,000) Ac 19: 19 (Jos., Ant. 17, 189 ἀργυρίου μυρ. πεντήκοντα).
2. of a very large number, not exactly defined, pl. *myriads* (Eur., Phoen. 837 al.; Ps 3: 7; Philo, Agr. 35; 113; Sib. Or. 4, 139) Lk 12: 1; Ac 21: 20 (cf. Appian, Bell. Civ. 4, 10 §39 τοσάσδε πολιτῶν μυριάδας; Jos., Ant. 7, 318 πόσαι μυριάδες εἰσὶ τ. λαοῦ;). μ. ἀνδρῶν Hv 3, 2, 5. Of angel hosts (cf. the Christian amulet PIand. 6, 10 and the exx. on p. 26 given by the editor ESchaefer; Dt 33: 2; En.; PGM 1, 208; 4, 1203) Hb 12: 22; Jd 14 (En. 1, 9). As an apocalyptic number μυριάδες μυριάδων *countless thousands* Rv 5: 11 (cf. Gen 24: 60 χιλιάδες μυριάδων). μύριαι μυριάδες (En. 14, 22) 1 Cl 34: 6 (Da 7: 10). On δισμυριάδες μυριάδων Rv 9: 16 cf. δισμυριάς. M-M.*

μυρίζω 1 aor. ἐμύρισα (Hdt., Aristoph.+; PGM 4, 180) *anoint* of harlots and flute-girls GOxy 36. Of corpses (Philosophenspr. p. 495, 127 νεκρὸν μυρίζειν) μ. τὸ σῶμα εἰς τὸν ἐνταφιασμόν *anoint a body for burial* Mk 14: 8. M-M.*

μύριοι, αι, *a ten thousand* (Hes., Hdt.+; inscr., pap., LXX) talents (Esth 3: 9; Jos., Ant. 14, 78) Mt 18: 24. μ. μυριάδες 10,000 *myriads* 1 Cl 34: 6 (Da 7: 10). M-M.*

μυρίος, α, ον (Hom.+; APF 5, '13, 383 no. 69A, 12; PFlor. 33, 14; LXX; Philo; Jos., Ant. 5, 180; Sib. Or. 1, 147.—Kühner-Bl. I 629) *innumerable, countless* μ. παιδαγωγοί 1 Cor 4: 15 (cf. Philo, Leg. ad Gai. 54 μυρ. διδάσκαλοι). μ. λόγοι 14: 19.*

μύρον, ου, τό (since Archilochus [VII BC] in Athen. 15 p. 688C; Hdt.; Dit., Or. 629, 35; 45; 149; POxy. 234 II, 9; 736, 13; LXX; Jos., Bell. 4, 561, Ant. 14, 54.—Semit. loanw.= HLewy, Die semit. Fremdwörter im Griech. 1895, 42; 44) *ointment, perfume* (Pla., Polit. 398A μύρον κατὰ τῆς κεφαλῆς [a proverb, according to the schol.]; Ps 132: 2 μ. ἐπὶ κεφαλῆς; Jos., Ant. 19, 239 τὴν κεφ.) Mt 26: 12; Lk 7: 38, 46; J 11: 2; IEph 17: 1; precious Mk 14: 4f; J 12: 3a, 5; strongly aromatic (Philo, Sacr. Abel. 21, end) vs. 3b; kept in alabaster flasks (cf. Dit., Or. 736, 35[?]) Mt 26: 7; Mk 14: 3; Lk 7: 37 (JDMDerrett, Law in the NT, '70, 266–85). W. other articles of trade Rv 18: 13. Dssm., ThBl 1, '22, 13; D 10: 3 v.l., Funk-B. p. XIX l. 5. Pl. (w. ἀρώματα as Plut., Alex. 20, 13; SSol 1: 3) Lk 23: 56 (for embalming a body; cf. POxy. 736, 13; Artem. 1, 5). M-M.*

Μύρρα s. Μύρα.

μῦς, μυός, ὁ (Aeschyl.+; pap.; Lev 11: 29) acc. pl. μῦς (Hdt. 2, 141; Plut., Mor. 537A) *mouse* PK 2 p. 14, 19.*

μυσερός, ά, όν (as μυσαρός Eur., Hdt.+; inscr. from the Asclepieion of Cos A, 22 [III BC]: RHerzog, ARW 10, '07, 402; Sib. Or. 3, 500. On the spelling cf. Bl-D. §29, 1 app. In LXX only Lev 18: 23, where μυσερός is better attested; cf. Thackeray 75.—PGM 2, 148 ἁγνὸς ἀπὸ παντὸς μυσεροῦ; Manetho, Apotel. 4, 269 [ed. AKoechly 1858] μυσερός is v.l.; Etym. Mag. p. 535, 32; 566, 43 μυσε. beside μυσα.; Malalas [VI AD] μυσε. [Psaltes p. 2]) *loathsome, abominable, detestable,* ζῆλος 1 Cl 14: 1. μοιχεία 30: 1.*

Μυσία, ας, ἡ (Eur., Hdt.+; inscr.; Jos., Bell. 1, 425) *Mysia* a province in the northwest of Asia Minor. Paul touched here on his so-called second miss. journey Ac 16: 7f.*

μυστήριον, ου, τό *secret, secret rite, secret teaching, mystery,* a relig. t.t., applied in secular Gk. (predom. pl.) mostly to the mysteries w. their secret teachings, relig. and political in nature, concealed within many strange customs and ceremonies (trag.+; Hdt. 2, 51, 2; Diod. S. 1, 29, 3; 3, 63, 2; Socrat., Ep. 27, 3; Cornutus 28 p. 56, 22; 57, 4; Alciphr. 3, 26, 1; Dit., Or. 331, 54; 528, 13; 721, 2, Syll.³ index; Sb 7567, 9 [III AD]; PGM 1, 131; 4, 719ff; 2477 τὰ ἱερὰ μ. ἀνθρώποις εἰς γνῶσιν; 5, 110; 12, 331; 13, 128 τὸ μυστήριον τοῦ θεοῦ.—OKern, D. griech. Mysterien d. klass. Zeit '27; WFOtto, D. Sinn der eleusin. Myst. '40; MPNilsson, The Dionysiac Mysteries of the Hell. and Rom. Age, '57). Also LXX and other versions of the OT use the word, as well as En. (of the heavenly secret). Philo, Joseph. (C. Ap. 2, 189, 266), Test. Levi 2: 10, Sib. Or. 12, 63 al.; it is a loanw. in rabb. Our lit. uses it to mean the secret thoughts, plans, and dispensations of God which are hidden fr. the human reason, as well as fr. all other comprehension below the divine level, and hence must be revealed to those for whom they are intended.

1. In the gospels μ. is found only in one context, where Jesus says to the disciples who have asked for an explanation of the parable(s) ὑμῖν τὸ μυστήριον δέδοται τῆς βασιλείας τ. θεοῦ Mk 4: 11; the synopt. parallels have the pl. Mt 13: 11 (LCerfaux, NTS 2, '55/'56, 238–49); Lk 8: 10.—WWrede, D. Messiasgeh. in den Evv. '01; HJEbeling, D. Mess. geh. u. d. Botschaft des Mc-Evangelisten '39; NJohansson, Sv. Teol. Kv. 16, '40, 3–38; OAPiper, Interpretation 1, '47, 183–200.

2. The Pauline lit. has μ. in 21 places. A *secret* or *mystery,* too profound for human ingenuity, is God's reason for the partial hardening of Israel's heart Ro 11: 25 or the transformation of the surviving Christians at the Parousia 1 Cor 15: 51. Even Christ, who was understood by so few, is *God's secret* or *mystery* Col 2: 2, hidden ages ago 1: 26 (cf. Herm. Wr. 1, 16 τοῦτό ἐστι τὸ κεκρυμμένον μυστήριον μέχρι τῆσδε τῆς ἡμέρας), but now gloriously revealed among the Gentiles vs. 27, to whom the *secret of Christ* 4:·3 is proclaimed (CLMitton, ET 60, '48/'49, 320f). Cf. Ro 16: 25; 1 Cor 2: 1 v.l. The pl. is used to denote Christian preaching by the apostles and teachers

in the expr. οἰκονόμοι μυστηρίων θεοῦ 1 Cor 4: 1 (Iambl., Vi. Pyth. 23, 104 calls the teachings of Pyth. θεῖα μυστήρια). Not all Christians are capable of understanding all the mysteries. The one who speaks in tongues πνεύματι λαλεῖ μυστήρια *utters secret truths in the Spirit* which he alone shares w. God, and which his fellow-man, even a Christian, does not understand 1 Cor 14: 2. Therefore the possession of *all mysteries* is a great joy 13: 2. And the spirit-filled apostle can say of the highest stage of Christian knowledge, revealed only to the τέλειοι: λαλοῦμεν θεοῦ σοφίαν ἐν μυστηρίῳ *we impart the wisdom of God in the form of a mystery* (ἐν μυστηρίῳ= in a mysterious manner [Laud. Therap. 11] or= secretly, so that no unauthorized person would learn of it [cf. Cyrill. of Scyth. p. 90, 14 ἐν μυστηρίῳ λέγει]) 2: 7 (AKlöpper, ZWTh 47, '05, 525–45).—Eph, for which (as well as for Col) μ. is a predominant concept, sees the μ. τοῦ θελήματος αὐτοῦ (sc. θεοῦ) 1: 9 or μ. τ. Χριστοῦ 3: 4 or μ. τ. εὐαγγελίου 6: 19 in the acceptance of the Gentiles as Christians 3: 3ff, 9ff. A unique *great mystery* is revealed 5: 32, where the relation betw. Christ and the Church is spoken of (cf. WLKnox, St. Paul and the Church of the Gentiles, '39, 183f; 227f; WBieder, ThZ 11, '55, 329–43).—1 Ti uses μ. as a formula: τὸ μ. τῆς πίστεως is simply *faith* 3: 9. τὸ τ. εὐσεβείας μ. *Christian religion* vs. 16.—τὸ μ. τῆς ἀνομίας 2 Th 2: 7 s. ἀνομία 1 (Jos., Bell. 1, 470 calls the life of Antipater κακίας μυστήριον because of his baseness practiced in secret. Cf. also Sib. Or. 8, 58 τὰ πλάνης μυστήρια; 56).—PHFurfey, CBQ 8, '46, 179–91.

3. Elsewh. in the NT μ. occurs only in Rv, w. ref. to the mysterious things portrayed there. The whole content of the book appears as τὸ μ. τοῦ θεοῦ 10: 7. Also τὸ μ. τῶν ἑπτὰ ἀστέρων 1: 20; τὸ μ. τῆς γυναικός 17: 7, cf. vs. 5, where in each case μ. may mean *allegorical significance* (so BSEaston, Pastoral Epistles '47, 215).

4. Outside the NT we have μ.—**a.** in Ign.: the death and resurrection of Jesus as μ. IMg 9: 2. The virginity of Mary, her child-bearing, and the Lord's death are called τρία μ. κραυγῆς *three mysteries (to be) loudly proclaimed* IEph 19: 1. The deacons are οἱ διάκονοι μυστηρίων Ἰ. Χρ. ITr 2: 3.

b. Quite difficult is the saying about the tried and true prophet ποιῶν εἰς μυστήριον κοσμικὸν ἐκκλησίας *who acts in accord with the earthly mystery of the church* D 11: 11. This may refer to celibacy; the prophet lives in such a way as to correspond to the relation betw. Christ and the church; cf. Eph 5: 32 (so Harnack, TU II 1; 2, 1884, 44ff; HWeinel, Die Wirkungen d. Geistes u. der Geister 1899, 131–8; PDrews, Hdb. z. d. ntl. Apokryphen '04, 274ff; RKnopf, Hdb. ad loc.—Differently CTaylor, The Teaching of the Twelve Apost. 1886, 82–92; RHarris, The Teaching of the Ap. 1887; FXFunk, Patr. Apostol.² '01 ad loc.; Zahn, Forschungen III 1884, 301).

c. μ. occurs oft. in Dg: τὸ τῆς θεοσεβείας μ. *the secret of the (Christian) religion* 4: 6. Likew. of Christian teaching πατρὸς μυστήρια 11: 2; cf. vs. 5. Hence the Christian can μυστήρια θεοῦ λαλεῖν 10: 7. In contrast to ἀνθρώπινα μ. 7: 1. οὗ (sc. τ. θεοῦ) τὰ μυστήρια *whose secret counsels* 7: 2. κατέχειν ἐν μυστηρίῳ τ. βουλήν *keep his counsel a secret* 8: 10.—Lghtf., St. Paul's Ep. to the Col. and Phlm. p. 167ff; JARobinson, St. Paul's Ep. to the Eph. '04, 234ff; GWobbermin, Religionsgesch. Studien 1896, 144ff; EHatch, Essays on Bibl. Gk. 1889, 57ff; HansvSoden, ZNW 12, '11, 188ff; TBFoster, AJTh 19, '15, 402–15; OCasel, D. Liturgie als Mysterienfeier⁵ '23; JSchneider, 'Mysterion' im NT: StKr 104, '32, 255–78; TArvedson, D. Mysterium Christi '37; KPrümm, 'Mysterion' v. Pls bis Orig.: ZkTh 61, '37, 391–425, Biblica 37,

'56, 135-61; REBrown, The Semitic Background of 'Mystery' in the NT, '68); cf. KGKuhn, NTS 7, 61, 366 for Qumran parallels to various passages in Eph and Ro; ABöhlig, Mysterion u. Wahrheit, '68, 3-40; ADNock, Hellenistic Mysteries and Christian Sacraments, Essays on Religion and the Ancient World II, '72, 790-820. GBornkamm, TW IV 809-34. M-M. and suppl.*

μυωπάζω (only Christian wr.: Basilius II 825ʙ Migne [S. Gr. XXX]; Epiphan. 59, 11, 1 Holl.; Ps.-Dionys., Eccl. Hierarch. 2, 3, 3) *be short-sighted* fig. τυφλός ἐστιν μυωπάζων *he is so short-sighted that he is blind* 2 Pt 1: 9 (opp. Χριστοῦ ἐπίγνωσις). M-M.*

Μωδάτ, ὁ indecl. *Modad* Hv 2, 3, 4; s. on Ἐλδάδ.*

μώλωψ, ωπος, ὁ (Hyperid., fgm. 200; Plut., Mor. 565ʙ; Herodian Gr. I 247, 20; Artem. 2, 4; LXX) *welt, bruise, wound* caused by blows (Dionys. Hal. 16, 5, 2; Sir 28: 17) οὗ τῷ μώλωπι ἰάθητε *by his wound(s) you have been healed* 1 Pt 2: 24; cf. 1 Cl 16: 5; B 5: 2 (all Is 53: 5). M-M.*

μωμάομαι mid. dep.; 1 aor. ἐμωμησάμην, pass. ἐμωμήθην (Hom.+; Plut., Mor. 346ᴀ; LXX; Philo, Leg. All. 3, 180) *find fault with, censure, blame* τινά *someone* 2 Cor 8: 20. Pass. *have fault found with it* 6: 3.*

μῶμος, ου, ὁ—1. *blame* (Hom.+; Sir 18: 15; Sib. Or. 3, 377) δίχα παντὸς μ. *without any blame* 1 Cl 63: 1.

2. *defect, blemish* bodily (Lev 21: 17f, 21; 24: 19f; Test. Levi 9: 10) and also moral (Sir 11: 31, 33; 20: 24; Philo, Sobr. 11 μ. ἐν ψυχῇ) of teachers of error σπίλοι καὶ μῶμοι *blots and blemishes* 2 Pt 2: 13. M-M.*

μωμοσκοπέομαι mid. dep.; 1 aor. pass. ptc. μωμοσκοπηθείς (Const. Apost. 2, 3. The noun μωμοσκόπος in Philo, Agr. 130; Clem. Alex., Strom. 4, 18, 117) t.t. in sacrificial usage *examine for blemishes*.

1. lit., of a sacrificial animal, etc. 1 Cl 41: 2.—2. fig. of God πάντα μωμοσκοπεῖται *he examines everything (for blemishes)* Pol 4: 3.*

μωραίνω 1 aor. ἐμώρανα, pass. ἐμωράνθην (Eur.+, but intr., also Philo, Cher. 116) in our lit. only trans. (Polemo, Decl. 2, 36 p. 28, 11; LXX).

1. *make foolish, show to be foolish* οὐχὶ ἐμώρανεν ὁ θεὸς τὴν σοφίαν τοῦ κόσμου; *has not God shown that the wisdom of the world is foolish?* 1 Cor 1: 20. Pass. *become foolish* (Sir 23: 14) φάσκοντες εἶναι σοφοὶ ἐμωράνθησαν *although they claimed to be wise, they became fools* Ro 1: 22 (cf. Jer 10: 14).

2. *make tasteless* pass. *become tasteless, insipid* of salt (s. ἄναλος and FPerles, Rev. des Ét. juives 82, '26, 122f; MBlack, Aramaic Approach³, '67, 166f) Mt 5: 13; Lk 14: 34.—S. on ἅλας.*

μωρία, ας, ἡ (Soph., Hdt.+; Maspéro 4, 6; Sir 20: 31; 41: 15; Philo; Jos., Ant. 17, 209) *foolishness* gener. of worldly wisdom μ. παρὰ τῷ θεῷ ἐστιν 1 Cor 3: 19. Conversely, to all those who are lost 1: 18 and esp. to the Gentiles vs. 23, the Christian preaching of a Savior who died a slave's death on the cross was μ. It has pleased God to save the believers διὰ τ. μωρίας τοῦ κηρύγματος vs. 21. The ψυχικὸς ἄνθρ. rejects the things of the spirit as μ., 2: 14. The Jewish temple cult is evaluated as μ. (opp. θεοσέβεια) Dg 3: 3.—WCaspari, Über d. bibl. Begriff der Torheit: NKZ 39, '28, 668-95.*

μωρολογία, ας, ἡ (Aristot., H.A. 1, 11; Plut., Mor. 504ʙ; Jos., C. Ap. 2, 115) *foolish, silly talk* w. αἰσχρότης and εὐτραπελία Eph 5: 4 (cf. 1QS 10, 21-24: KGKuhn, NTS 7, '61, 339). M-M.*

μωρός, ά, όν (trag., X., Pla.+; pap., LXX, Philo; Test. Levi 7: 2; loanw. in rabb.; on the accent s. Bl-D. §13; Mlt.-H. 58) *foolish, stupid*.

1. *of pers.* (Simonides of Ceos 48, 6f, who uses the word with reference to his opponent, Cleobulus; Diod. S. 10, 22; Epict. 2, 2, 16; 3, 24, 86) Mt 5: 22 (s. below); (w. τυφλός) 23: 17, 19 t.r.; (opp. φρόνιμος) 7: 26; 25: 2f, 8. The same contrast 1 Cor 4: 10, where the apostle ironically compares himself w. the Corinthians. (Opp. σοφός as Lucian, Epigr. 1; Dt 32: 6; Sir 21: 26) 3: 18. W. ἀσύνετος (Sir 21: 18) Hv 3, 6, 5; s 9, 22, 4. W. ἀσύνετος and other similar predicates 1 Cl 39: 1. Of the overly ambitious Hs 8, 7, 4. τὰ μ. τοῦ κόσμου *what is considered foolish in the world* 1 Cor 1: 27 also refers to persons, and can do so since it pertains not to individuals but to a general attribute (Bl-D. §138, 1 app.; 263, 4; Rob. 411).

2. *of things* (Sib. Or. 3, 226) ὀξυχολία Hm 5, 2, 4. παράδοσις Mk 7: 13 v.l. ζητήσεις 2 Ti 2: 23; Tit 3: 9. πράγματα Hm 5, 2, 2. τρυφαί m 12, 2, 1. διδαχαί s 8, 6, 5. ἀφροσύνη 9, 22, 2. Of the πνεῦμα ἐπίγειον m 11: 11.—τὸ μ. τοῦ θεοῦ *the foolishness of God* (in the judgment of unbelievers) 1 Cor 1: 25 (cf. Eur., Hipp. 966 τὸ μ.=ʼfoolishnessʼ).

3. The mng. of μωρέ Mt 5: 22 is disputed. Most scholars take it, as the ancient Syrian versions did, to mean *you fool* (Pla., Leg. 9 p. 857ᴅ and Socrat., Ep. 14, 6 ὦ μῶρε [as it is accented in Att.]= you fool! Likew. Biogr. p. 179.—Epict. 2, 16, 13; 3, 13, 17 μωρέ; Philo, Cher. 75 ὦ μωρέ), somet. also w. the connotation of an obstinate, godless person (like נָבָל; cf. Dt 32: 6; Is 32: 6; Sir 50: 26). Fr. the time of HEGPaulus, Comm.² 1804ff I 671 to FSchulthess, ZNW 21, '22, 241, and SIFeigin, Jour. of Near Eastern Stud. 2, '43, 195 it has been held to be a transliteration of מוֹרֶה *rebel* (Dt 21: 18, 20); acc. to KKöhler, ZNW 19, '20, 91-5 it is simply the Gk. translation of ῥακά; acc. to HPernot, Pages choisies des Évang. '25, 61, who refers to Mod. Gk., a simple exclamation w. humorous coloring.— RAGuelich, ZNW 64, '73, 39-52 (Engl.); Field, Notes 3-5; Mlt.-H. 152f; GBertram, TW IV 837-52: μωρός and related words. M-M. B. 1215.*

μωρῶς adv. (X., An. 7, 6, 21 al.) *foolishly* ἀπόλλυσθαι *perish in one's folly* IEph 17: 2.*

Μωσῆς s. Μωϋσῆς.

Μωϋσῆς (the Hebr. מֹשֶׁה seems to have been written so in Gk. orig. [Manetho—III ʙᴄ—in Jos., C. Ap. 1, 250; Diod. S. 1, 94, 2; 34+35 fgm. 1, 3; Nicol. Dam. in Jos., Ant. 1, 95; Numenius of Apamea—II ᴀᴅ—in Clem. Alex., Strom. 1, 150, 4; LXX, Thackeray 163, 3; Ep. Arist. 144; Ezech. Trag. in Clem. 1, 155, 5; Philo, Joseph.; Test. Sim. 9, Levi 12: 2.—PGM 13=8th Book of Moses 3; 21; 343; 383; 730 al. has Μοϋσῆς]; the Μωσῆς of the t.r., also of ISm 5: 1 [but s. ed. Bihlmeyer XXXVI and ad loc.], occurs Diod. S. 40, 3, 3; 6; Strabo 16, 2, 35; 39 and LXX; Sib. Or. On the spelling Bl-D. §38 w. app.; 53, 1; Mlt.-H. 86f; EbNestle, ZAW 27, '07, 111-13; Preisigke, Namenbuch; Wuthnow 79f), ἕως, ὁ dat. εἶ and ῇ (w. ms. variations), acc. mostly ῆν, rarely έα (Lk 16: 29), voc. ῆ B 4: 8; 1 Cl 53: 2. Cf. on the declension Bl-D. §55, 1d; Mlt.-H. 146; W-S. §10, 5 and note 4. *Moses*. Lawgiver of the Hebrews (as such Manetho in Jos., C. Ap. 1, 250; without being named, but as author of Gen 1: 3, 9f, Περὶ ὕψους 9, 9) Mt 8: 4; 19: 7f; 22: 24 (the quite common introductory formula M. εἶπεν, followed by Dt 25: 5, as Epict. 1, 28, 4 ὡς λέγει Πλάτων, i.e., Sophista 228c); Mk 1: 44; 7: 10; 10: 3f; 12: 19; Lk 5: 14; 20: 28; J 1: 17; 7: 19, 22f; 8: 5. Details of his life story: summary of his life Ac 7: 20ff. His flight 1 Cl 4: 10. The theophany at the burning bush Lk 20: 37. The serpent raised up J 3: 14. The giving of the manna 6: 32. Moses' conversation w. God 9: 29, sojourn on Sinai 1 Cl 53: 2; B 4: 7; 14: 2ff; 15: 1, shining face 2 Cor 3: 7 (cf. Ex 34: 29ff), a cover on it vs. 13 (cf. Ex 34: 33). Jannes and Jambres 2 Ti 3: 8. Dathan and Abiram 1 Cl 4: 12. The struggle betw. Michael and the devil for M's. corpse Jd 9. πιστὸς θεράπων 1 Cl 43: 1 (cf. Num 12: 7); cf. 17: 5; 51: 3, 5; Hb 3: 5. ὁ δοῦλος τοῦ θεοῦ Rv 15: 3. Designated a προφήτης (Philo; Jos., Ant. 4, 329; PGM 5, 109 ἐγώ εἰμι Μωϋσῆς ὁ

προφήτης σου, ᾧ παρέδωκας τὰ μυστήριά σου) B 6: 8. ἐν πνεύματι ἐλάλησεν 10: 2, 9; cf. 12: 2. ποιεῖ τύπον τοῦ Ἰησοῦ 12: 5ff. W. Elijah (PDabeck, Biblica 23, '42, 175-89) Mt 17: 3f; Mk 9: 4f; Lk 9: 30, 33. Moses=the Books of Moses (as Plut., Is. et Os. 70, Plato=the writings of Pla.) 2 Cor 3: 15. Correspondingly M. and the prophets Lk 16: 29, 31; 24: 27; Ac 26: 22. Cf. ISm 5: 1.—Lit. on Moses in the Haggadah: Monatsschr. f. Gesch. u. Wiss. d. Judent. 77, '33, 390-2; JoachJeremias, TW IV 852-78. M-M.

N

Ναασσών, ὁ indecl. (נַחְשׁוֹן Ex 6: 23 [quoted by Philo, Poster. Cai. 76]; Num 1: 7; Ruth 4: 20) *Nahshon,* in the genealogy of Jesus Mt 1: 4a, b; Lk 3: 32.*

Ναγγαί, ὁ indecl. *Naggai* in the genealogy of Jesus Lk 3: 25.*

Ναζαρά, Ναζαρέτ, Ναζαρέθ (Ναζαράτ, Ναζαράθ), ἡ indecl. *Nazareth.* On the var. forms of the name s. JKZenner, ZkTh 18, 1894, 744-7; Dalman, Gramm.² 152; FCBurkitt, The Syriac Forms of NT Proper Names '12, 16; 28f, JTS 14, '13, 475f; Zahn on Mt 2: 23; Bl-D. §39, 2 app.; W-S. §5, 27e and p. XVI on §5 note 58; Mlt.-H. 107f. Ναζαρέτ and Ναζαρέθ seem to have the best attestation.—Home of Jesus' parents; the place is not mentioned in the OT, Talmud, Midrash, or Joseph., but plays a significant role in Christian tradition: Mt 2: 23; 4: 13: 21: 11; Mk 1: 9; Lk 1: 26; 2: 4, 39, 51; 4: 16 (BViolet, Z. recht. Verst. der Naz.-Perikope Lk 4: 16-30: ZNW 37, '39, 251-71); J 1: 45f; Ac 10: 38.—On N. see HGuthe, RE XIII '03, 676ff, Palästina² '27, 149ff; Dalman, Orte³ 61-88; GSchumacher, D. jetzige Naz.: ZDPV 13, 1890, 235ff; PViaud, Naz. et ses deux églises '10; MBrückner, Naz. die Heimat Jesu: Pj 7, '11, 74-84; ThSoiron, D. Ev. u. die. hl. Stätten '29, 17-37; PWinter, 'Naz.' and 'Jerus.' in Lk 1 and 2, NTS 3, '56/'57, 136-42; CKopp, The Holy Places of the Gospels, tr. RWalls, '63, 49-86. M-M.*

Ναζαρηνός, ή, όν *coming from Nazareth;* only subst. ὁ N. *the Nazarene, inhabitant of Nazareth* applied only to Jesus Mk 1: 24; 10: 47; 14: 67; 16: 6; Lk 4: 34; 24: 19; J 18: 5 D.*

Ναζωραῖος, ου, ὁ *Nazoraean, Nazarene,* quite predominantly a designation of Jesus, in Mt, J, Ac and Lk 18: 37, while Mk has Ναζαρηνός (q.v.). Of the two places where the latter form occurs in Lk, the one, Lk 4: 34, apparently comes fr. Mk (1: 24), the other, 24: 19, perh. fr. a special source. Where the author of Lk-Ac writes without influence fr. another source he uses Ναζωραῖος. Mt says expressly 2: 23 that Jesus was so called because he grew up in Nazareth. In addition, the other NT writers who call Jesus Ναζωραῖος know Nazareth as his home. But linguistically the transition fr. Ναζαρέτ to Ναζωραῖος is difficult (Dalman, Gramm.² 178; Wlh. on Mt 26: 69; MLidzbarski, Mandäische Liturgien '20, XVIff, Zeitschrift für Semitistik I '22, 230ff, Ginza '25, IXf; FCBurkitt, The Syriac Forms of NT Proper Names '12; AvGall, Βασιλεία τοῦ θεοῦ '26 p. 432, 4; cf. 411f; RBultmann, ZNW 24, '25, 143f, Jesus '26, 26; HHSchaeder in Rtzst. u. Schaeder, Studien zum antiken Synkretismus '26 p. 308, 2) and it is to be borne in mind that Ναζωραῖος meant

someth. different before it was connected w. Nazareth (cf. Celsus 7, 18, who calls Jesus ὁ Ναζωραῖος ἄνθρωπος. JASanders, JBL 84, '65, 169-72 interprets N. in Mt 2: 23 as meaning both 'coming from Nazareth' and 'miraculously born'). The pass. where Jesus is so called are Mt 2: 23; 26: 69 v.l., 71; Lk 18: 37; J 18: 5, 7; 19: 19; Ac 2: 22; 3: 6; 4: 10; 6: 14; 22: 8; 26: 9. Acc. to Ac 24: 5 the Christians were so called; cf. Kl. Texte 3² p. 3, l. 32 and 8³ p. 6, ll. 8, 17, 27; p. 7, note on l. 1ff; p. 8, 5; p. 9, 17; 23; p. 10, 5; 15; p. 11, 28; note on l. 9ff, all passages in which Jewish Christians are called Nazaraei, Nazareni, Ναζωραῖοι.—Laud. Therap. 27 the monks are called ναζιραῖοι (with the v.l. Ναζαραῖοι).—EbNestle, ET 19, '08, 523f, PM 14, '10, 349f; HZimmern, ZDMG 74, '20, 429ff; GFMoore, Nazarene and Nazareth: Beginn. I 1, '20, 426-32 (cf. I 5, '33, 356f); EMeyer II 408f; 423, 2; HGressmann, ZKG 41 = new ser. 4, '22, 166f; WCaspari, ZNW 21, '22, 122-7; HSmith, Ναζωραῖος κληθήσεται: JTS 28, '27, 60; ELohmeyer, Joh. d. Täufer '32, p. 115, 2; HSchlier, Theol. Rundschau new ser. 5, '33, 7f; WOE Oesterley, ET 52, '41, 410-12; SLyonnet, Biblica 25, '44, 196-206; MBlack, An Aramaic Approach³, '67, 197-200; WFAlbright, JBL 65, '46, 397-401, also JSKennard, Jr., ibid. 66, '47, 79-81; HMShires, ATR 29, '47, 19-27; TNicklin, Gospel Gleanings, '50, 257-60; BGärtner, Die rätselhafte Termini Nazoräer u. Iskariot '57, 5-36; E Schweizer, Judentum, Urchrist., Kirche '60, 90-93.— Bl-D. §39, 4 app.; HHSchaeder, TW IV 879-84. M-M.*

Ναθάμ, ὁ indecl. (נָתָן) *Nathan,* son of David (2 Km 5: 14; perh. Zech 12: 12 Ναθάν, as Lk 3: 31 v.l.—In Jos., Ant. 7, 70 Νάθας [acc. -αν]); in the genealogy of Jesus Lk 3: 31.*

Ναθαναήλ, ὁ indecl. (נְתַנְאֵל. Cf. Num 1: 8; 2 Esdr [Ezra] 10: 22; 1 Ch 2: 14; 15: 24.—In Jos., Ant. 6, 161; 20, 14 Ναθαναῆλος, ου) *Nathanael,* a disciple of Jesus, mentioned only in J (1: 45-9; 21: 2). He does not appear in the synoptic lists of the twelve apostles; hence, since antiquity attempts have been made to identify him w. various apostles, esp. Bartholomew, as well as w. other personalities; some have given up the attempt to place him among the twelve. Cf. Hdb.³ exc. on J 1, end. Acc. to J 21: 2 he came fr. Cana in Galilee. S. also the apocryphal gospel fragment fr. the Berlin pap. 11710: ZNW 22, '23, 153f.— REisler, Das Rätsel des Joh-Ev. '36, 475-85; JoachJeremias, D. Berufung des N.: Ἄγγελος III, '28, 2-5); UHolzmeister, Biblica 21, '40, 28-39; GQuispel, ZNW 47, '56, 281-3.*

ναί particle denoting affirmation, agreement, or emphasis (Hom.+; POxy. 1413, 7 al. in pap.; LXX; Ep. Arist. 201 ναί, βασιλεῦ; Jos., Ant. 17, 169).

1. in answer to a question—**a.** asked by another pers., *yes* (Ael. Aristid. 34 p. 663 D.; Lucian, Dial. Deor. 4, 1 al.; Alexander Numenianus [time of Hadrian]: Rhet. Gr. ed. LSpengel III 1856 p. 24f: the answer to a question should be ναὶ ἢ οὔ; Ammonius Herm. In Lib. Aristot. De Interpret. p. 199, 21 Busse ἀποκρίν. τὸ ναὶ ἢ τὸ οὔ; Sb 7696, 57 [250 AD]) Mt 9: 28; 13: 51; 17: 25; 21: 16; J 11: 27; 21: 15f; Ac 5: 8; 22: 27; GP 10: 42; Hs 9, 11, 8.

b. asked by the one who answers: *yes, indeed* ναὶ λέγω ὑμῖν Mt 11: 9; Lk 7: 26 gives an affirmative answer to the question directed to the crowd, thereby confirming the correctness of the crowd's opinion; the people are 'on the right track', but need further instruction.—If the question is put in negative form, the answer may be *of course* Ro 3: 29.

2. in declarations of agreement to the statements of others *certainly, indeed, quite so* (Gen 42: 21; Epict. 2, 7, 9 ναί, κύριε; Diod. S. 13, 26, 1 ναί, ἀλλά=indeed, but; Lucian, Jupp. Trag. 6 and 9 ναί. ἀλλὰ . . .) ναί, κύριε· καὶ γάρ *certainly, Lord* (or *sir*); *and yet* Mt 15: 27; Mk 7: 28 (on the other hand, it may mean an urgent repetition of the request: Zahn; Bl-D. §441, 1; AFridrichsen, Con. Neot. 1, '36, 10–13; Athen. Tafel Elderkin 2 [III AD]: Hesperia 6, '37, 383ff l. 7 a fervent invocation in prayer: ναὶ κύριε Τυφώς, ἐκδίκησον . . . καὶ βοήθησον αὐτῷ; PGM 1, 216 ναί, κύριε; cf. 36, 227); Hv 3, 3, 1; 4, 3, 1; m 6, 1, 1. Prob. Rv 14: 13; 16: 7; 22: 20b t.r. belong here.

3. in emphatic repetition of one's own statement *yes* (*indeed*) Mt 11: 26; Lk 10: 21; 11: 51. ναὶ λέγω ὑμῖν, τοῦτον φοβήθητε *yes, indeed, fear him, I tell you* 12: 5.— Phlm 20; B 14: 1. The repetition can consist in the fact that one request preceded and a similar one follows ναὶ ἐρωτῶ καὶ σέ *yes* (*indeed*), *I ask you, too* Phil 4: 3.—1 Cl 60: 3.

4. in solemn assurance (Herodas 1, 86 ναὶ Δήμητρα= by Demeter) ναὶ ἔρχομαι ταχύ *surely I am coming soon* Rv 22: 20. ναί, ἀμήν *so it is to be, amen* 1: 7.

5. In a play on words, ναί is used w. οὔ: ἤτω ὑμῶν τὸ ναὶ ναί, καὶ τὸ οὒ οὔ *let your 'yes' be yes, and your 'no' no* i.e., the absolute dependability of your statements should make an oath unnecessary Js 5: 12. But Mt 5: 37 reads ἔστω ὁ λόγος ὑμῶν ναὶ ναί, οὒ οὔ i.e., *a clear 'yes', a clear 'no'* and nothing more (ναί doubled also Archilochus [VII BC] 99 Diehl²; Alciphr. 4, 13, 8; Theod. Prodr. 8, 321 Hercher; PGM 1, 90). Yet many (Bl-D. §432, 1; Wlh. and EKlostermann on Mt 5: 37; CCTorrey, The Four Gospels '33, 291; ELittmann, ZNW 34, '35, 23f) assume that Mt 5: 37 has the same sense as Js 5: 12; the Koridethi gosp. (ms. Θ) assimilates the text of the Mt pass. to the one in Js.— Paul denies that, in forming his plans, he has proceeded in such a way ἵνα ᾖ γαρ' ἐμοὶ τὸ ναὶ ναὶ καὶ τὸ οὒ οὔ *that my 'yes' should at the same time be 'no'* 2 Cor 1: 17; cf. vs. 18. This is just as impossible as that in the gospel ναὶ καὶ οὔ *'yes' and 'no'* are preached at the same time vs. 19a. Rather, in Jesus Christ there is only 'yes' vs. 19b to all the promises of God vs. 20. M-M.*

Ναιμάν, ὁ indecl. (נַעֲמָן. On the var. ways of writing the name in the tradition s. Bl-D. §37; 53, 2 app.; Mlt.-H. p. 84) *Naaman*, a Syrian army commander, healed of leprosy by Elisha (4 Km 5: 1ff) Lk 4: 27. M-M.*

Ναΐν, ἡ indecl. (in the Bible only Lk 7: 11. The name is applied to an Idumaean locality in Jos., Bell. 4, 511 v.l.; 517) *Nain*, a city in Galilee Lk 7: 11.—Dalman, Pj 9, '13, 45; CKopp, The Holy Places of the Gospels, tr. RWalls, '63, 236–41.*

ναός, οῦ, ὁ (Hom.+; inscr., pap., LXX; Bl-D. §44, 1; Mlt.-H. 71; 121) *temple.*

1. lit.—a. of the temple at Jerusalem (3 Km 6: 5, 17 al.; Jos., Ant. 8, 62ff; Sib. Or. 3, 575; 657; 702; Stephan. Byz. s.v. Σόλυμα: ὁ ναὸς ὁ ἐν Ἱεροσολύμοις.—ναός [νεώς] of Herod's temple: Philo, In Flacc. 46, Leg. ad Gai. 278 al.; Jos., Bell. 5, 185; 207; 215, Ant. 15, 380; also of the whole temple precinct: Bell. 6, 293, C. Ap. 2, 119) Mt 23: 17, 35; 27: 5, 40; Mk 14: 58 (on this saying cf. RAHoffmann, Heinrici-Festschr. '14, 130–9 and MGoguel, Congr. d'Hist. du Christ. I '28, 117–36. More generally DPlooij, Jes. and the Temple: ET 42, '31, 36–9); 15: 29; Lk 1: 21f; J 2: 20; Ac 7: 48 t.r.; Rv 11: 2; 1 Cl 41: 2; B 16: 1ff; GP 7: 26. οἱ ἱερεῖς τ. ναοῦ B 7: 3. τὸ καταπέτασμα τοῦ ναοῦ *the curtain of the temple* that separated the Holy of Holies fr. the holy place Mt 27: 51; Mk 15: 38; Lk 23: 45; GP 5: 20 (τ. κ. τ. ναοῦ τῆς Ἱερουσαλήμ). An oath by the temple Mt 23: 16, 21. More fully ὁ ναὸς τοῦ θεοῦ (as Jos., Ant. 15, 380; cf. Artem. 2, 26 νεὼς θεοῦ) Mt 26: 61; 2 Th 2: 4 (on this s. WWrede, Die Echtheit des 2 Th '03, 96ff); Rv 11: 1 (on the prophecy of the rescue of the temple fr. the general destruction cf. Jos., Bell. 6, 285). ὁ ναὸς τοῦ κυρίου Lk 1: 9; cf. 1 Cl 23: 5 (Mal 3: 1).

b. of the heavenly sanctuary (cf. Ps 10: 4; 17: 7; Wsd 3: 14 ν. κυρίου; Philo, Spec. Leg. 1, 66; Test. Levi 5: 1 v.l.) of Rv: ὁ ναὸς 14: 15; 15: 6, 8a, b; 16: 1, 17. ὁ ναὸς αὐτοῦ (=τοῦ θεοῦ) 7: 15; 11: 19b. ὁ ναὸς ὁ ἐν τ. οὐρανῷ 14: 17. ὁ ναὸς τοῦ θεοῦ ὁ ἐν τ. οὐρανῷ 11: 19a. ὁ ναὸς τῆς σκηνῆς τ. μαρτυρίου ἐν τ. οὐρανῷ 15: 5. Cf. also 3: 12. Yet there will be no temple in the New Jerusalem 21: 22a; God himself is the sanctuary of the eternal city vs. 22b.

c. of temples gener. (Diod. S. 5, 15, 2 θεῶν ναούς) Ac 17: 24. Specif. of pagan temples: of Artemis at Ephesus 19: 24; but here, beside ἱερόν vs. 27 (cf. Dit., Or. 90, 34 [196 BC]; Sb 8745, 6 [pap. 171/72 AD] ἐν τῷ ἱερῷ Σοκνοβραίσεως ναὸς ξύλινος περικεχρυσωμένος. Likew. 8747, 5; 3 Macc 1: 10; Philo, Leg. ad Gai. 139 ἱερὰ κ. ναοί, Decal. 7; Jos., Ant. 16, 106), ναός can be understood in the more restricted sense *shrine*, where the image of the goddess stood (so Hdt.+; Diod. S. 1, 97, 9; 20, 14, 3; UPZ 5, 27=6, 22 [163 BC], cf. the editor's note; BGU 1210, 191 ἐν παντὶ ἱερῷ, ὅπου ναός ἐστιν; 211; PErlang. 21 [II AD]: APF 14, '41, 100f, a shrine w. a ξόανον of Isis).

2. fig. (Philo, Op. M. 136f of the σῶμα as the νεὼς ἱερὸς ψυχῆς). A border-line instance is J 2: 19, 21 where Jesus, standing in the temple made of stone, speaks of the ναὸς τοῦ σώματος αὐτοῦ (AMDubarle, Le signe du Temple [J 2: 19]: RB 48, '39, 21–44; OCullmann, Theol. Ztschr. 4, '48, 367).—Of the spirit-filled body of the Christians, which is said to be a habitation of God, therefore a temple (cf. Sextus 35); on occasion it may become the habitation of demons, an idol's temple: τὸ σῶμα ὑμῶν ν. τοῦ ἐν ὑμῖν ἁγίου πνεύματός ἐστιν *your body is a temple of the Holy Spirit* (dwelling) *within you* 1 Cor 6: 19. The habitation of the heart is a ν. ἅγιος τῷ κυρίῳ B 6: 15; cf. the development of this thought 16: 6ff (Pythagorean saying in HSchenkl, Wiener Stud. 8, 1886, 273 no. 66 νεὼς θεοῦ σοφὸς νοῦς, ὃν ἀεὶ χρὴ παρασκευάζειν κ. κατακοσμεῖν εἰς παραδοχὴν θεοῦ. Cf. Sextus 46a; Synes., Dio 9 p. 49c νεὼς οὗτος [i.e., the νοῦς οἰκεῖος θεῷ= the Νοῦς is the real temple of God]). Of spirit-filled Christians γίνεσθαι ν. τέλειον τῷ θεῷ 4: 11. φυλάσσειν τὴν σάρκα ὡς ν. θεοῦ 2 Cl 9: 3; τηρεῖν τὴν σάρκα ὡς ν. θεοῦ IPhld 7: 2. Hence individual Christians are called αὐτοῦ (=θεοῦ) ναοί IEph 15: 3. Of the church 1 Cor 3: 16, 17a, b; 2 Cor 6: 16a, b. αὔξει εἰς ναὸν ἅγιον ἐν κυρίῳ Eph 2: 21. The Christians are λίθοι ναοῦ πατρός *stones for the Father's temple* IEph 9: 1. In order to place great emphasis on the oneness of the church community (which permits no division) Christians are challenged thus: πάντες ὡς εἰς ἕνα ναὸν συντρέχετε θεοῦ *come together, all of you, as to one temple of God* IMg 7: 2.—ἱερόν 2.— KBaltzer, HTR 58, '65, 263–77 (Luke); BGärtner, The Temple and the Community in Qumran and in the NT '65; REClements, God and Temple '65 (OT); OMichel, TW IV 884–95. M-M. B. 1465.*

Ναούμ, ὁ indecl. (נַחוּם; cf. Na 1: 1.—In Jos., Ant. 9, 239 Ναοῦμος) *Nahum* in the genealogy of Jesus Lk 3: 25.*

ναοφόρος, ον (hapax legomenon) *bearing the image of a temple* or *shrine* (s. ναός 1c) subst. *the temple-bearer* or *shrine-bearer* w. other compounds of -φόρος IEph 9: 2. Evidently the writer has a pagan relig. procession in mind.*

νάρδος, ου, ἡ (prob. a Semit. loanw. [HLewy, Die sem. Fremdwörter im Griech. 1895, 40], but ultimately of Indo-European orig. [Pers. nārdīn; Sanskr. naladâ]) *(spike)-nard.*
1. as a plant (En. 32, 1) native to India (Onesicritus: 134 fgm. 22 Jac.; Arrian, Anab. 6, 22, 5) στέφανος ἐκ νάρδου στάχυος πεπλεγμένος *a wreath woven of nard blossoms* AP 3: 10 (cf. Theophr., Hist. Plant. 9, 7, 2ff).
2. as *oil of nard* (cf. Peripl. Eryth. c. 39; 48; Diosc., Mat. Med. 1, 6, 75; Pliny, Nat. Hist. 12, 26; 13, 2; 4; PSI 628, 7 [III BC]; Zen.-P. 69 [=Sb 6775], 5 [257 BC]; POxy. 1088, 49; PGM 13, 19; 353; SSol 1: 12; 4: 13f), extracted fr. the root of the nard plant (Nicander, Ther. 937, Alexiph. 402 νάρδου ῥίζαι). μύρον νάρδου *ointment* or *perfume of nard* Mk 14: 3; J 12: 3. In the latter pass. a pound of it is valued at 300 denarii= normally about $55 to $60 (vss. 3 and 5). ILöw, D. Flora d. Juden III '24, 482–8; SANaber, Νάρδος πιστική: Mnemosyne 30, '02, 1–15; WHSchoff, Nard: Journ. of the Amer. Oriental Soc. 43, '25, 216–28; JPBrown, The Mediterranean Vocab. of the Vine, Vetus T 19, '69, 160–64.—S. πιστικός. M-M.*

Νάρκισσος, ου, ὁ *Narcissus*, a name found not infreq. among slaves and freedmen (Tacitus, Ann. 13, 1; Sueton., Claudius 28; Cass. Dio 64, 3, 4; Inschr. v. Magn. [122d, 14] u. Hierap. [80]; IG XII 8, 548, 2; CIL VI 4123; 4346; 5206 al.). Paul greets οἱ ἐκ τῶν Ναρκίσσου οἱ ὄντες ἐν κυρίῳ *those belonging to the household of Narcissus who are Christians* Ro 16: 11 (slaves of N. are meant. Cf. Narcissiani CIL III 3973, VI 15640). M-M.*

ναυαγέω 1 aor. ἐναυάγησα (Aeschyl., Hdt.+; POxy. 839, 6ff; Philo) *suffer shipwreck.*
1. lit. τρὶς ἐναυάγησα *I have been shipwrecked three times* 2 Cor 11: 25.—2. fig. (Cebes 24, 2 ὡς κακῶς διατρίβουσι καὶ ἀθλίως ζῶσι καὶ ναυαγοῦσιν ἐν τῷ βίῳ; Philo, Mut. Nom. 215, Somn. 2, 147) περὶ τὴν πίστιν ἐναυάγησαν *they have suffered shipwreck in their faith* 1 Ti 1: 19. M-M.*

Ναυή, ὁ indecl. (נוּן. Cf. Ex 33: 11; Num 11: 28; Josh 1: 1 al. In all these pass. LXX renders נון with Ναυή; cf. Jos., Bell. 4, 459; 1 Ch 7: 27: Νούμ; PKatz ThZ 9, '53, 230) *Nun*, Joshua's father 1 Cl 12: 2; B 12: 8f.*

ναύκληρος, ου, ὁ (Soph., Hdt.+; Plut.; Jos. [both w. κυβερνήτης, q.v. 1]; Dit., Or. 344, 4 [I BC]; pap. [Preisigke, Fachwörter '15]; En. 101, 4; 9; Philo, Op. M. 147) *ship-owner.* But it can also mean *captain*, since the sailing-master of a ship engaged in state service was called a ναύκληρος (MRostovtzeff, APF 5, '13, 298; LCasson, Ships and Seamanship in the Ancient World, '71, 314–16) Ac 27: 11. M-M.*

ναῦς, ἡ (Hom.+; inscr., pap., LXX; Philo, Aet. M. 138 al.; Jos., Vi. 165 al.; Sib. Or. 8, 348) acc. ναῦν *ship*, only of larger vessels Ac 27: 41. M-M. B. 727.*

ναύτης, ου, ὁ (Hom.+; inscr., pap.; Aq. Ezk 27: 9; Sym. Ezk 27: 29; Jos., Vi. 66, Ant. 9, 209; Test. Napht. 6: 2; loanw. in rabb.) *sailor* Ac 27: 27, 30; Rv 18: 17. M-M.*

Ναχώρ, ὁ indecl. (נָחוֹר) *Nahor* (Gen 11: 22–6; 1 Ch 1: 26f; Philo, Congr. Erud. Gr. 43.—In Joseph. Ναχώρης, ου [Ant. 1, 153]), in the genealogy of Jesus Lk 3: 34.*

νεανίας, ου, ὁ (trag., Hdt.+; inscr.; POxy. 471, 114 [II AD]; LXX; Jos., Bell. 2, 409, Vi. 129; 170; Test. Jos. 12, 3) *youth, young man* (fr. about the 24th to the 40th year; Diog. L. 8, 10; Philo, Cher. 114; Lob. on Phryn. p. 213.—FBoll, D. Lebensalter: NJklA 31, '13, 89ff) Ac 7: 58; 20: 9; 23: 17, 18 t.r., 22 t.r.; Hv 1, 4, 1 (here the mng. *servant* is also poss., cf. Judg 16: 26 B). M-M.*

νεανίσκος, ου, ὁ (Hdt.+; inscr., pap., LXX; Jos., Ant. 6, 179, Vi. 126; Test. 12 Patr.) dim. of νεάν.
1. *youth, young man* (on the chron. limits of this period of life cf. what is said on νεανίας and s. Philo, Op. M. 105) Mt 19: 20, 22; Mk 14: 51; 16: 5; Lk 7: 14; Ac 2: 17 (Jo 3: 1); 20: 12 D; 23: 18, 22; 1 J 2: 13f; Hv 2, 4, 1; 3, 1, 6ff; 3, 2, 5; 3, 4, 1; 3, 10, 1 and 7; s 6, 1, 5; 6, 2, 6; GP 9: 37; 13: 55.
2. *servant* (Lucian, Aiex. 53; Gen 14: 24, perh. as early as Zen.-P. 4 [=Sb 6710], 6 [259 BC]) Mk 14: 51b t.r. οἱ νεανίσκοι; Ac 5: 10 (though here the ref. may simply be to young men of the congregation, who would naturally perform this service). M-M.*

Νεάπολις s. νέος 3.

Νεεμάν s. Ναιμάν.

νεῖκος, εος, τό as v.l. in 1 Cor 15: 54f is not the word for 'strife' w. the same spelling (Hom.+), but an itacistic form of νῖκος, q.v.*

νεκρός, ά, όν—1. adj. (perh. as early as Hom., certainly Pind.+; inscr., pap., LXX) *dead.*
a. lit.—α. of living beings καταπίπτειν νεκρόν *fall dead* Ac 28: 6. ἤρθη νεκρός *he was taken up dead* 20: 9 (another possibility is *as dead, for dead*: Lucian, Ver. Hist. 1, 22; Eunapius, Vi. Soph. 76 συγχωρήσατε τῷ νεκρῷ [the one who is deathly sick] με δοῦναι φάρμακον.—ἤρθη ν. as Test. Jud. 9: 3).—5: 10; Js 2: 26a. ἔπεσα πρὸς τοὺς πόδας αὐτοῦ ὡς ν. *I fell at his feet as if I were dead* Rv 1: 17 (ὡς ν. as Diod. S. 36, 8, 4). ἐγενήθησαν ὡς νεκροί Mt 28: 4. ἐγένετο ὡσεὶ νεκρός Mk 9: 26. Of Christ ἐγενόμην ν. *I was dead* Rv 1: 18; cf. 2: 8.
β. *lifeless* (Wsd 15: 5) of the brass serpent B 12: 7. Of idols PK 2 p. 14, 21. νεκροὶ θεοί 2 Cl 3: 1; D 6: 3.
b. fig.—α. of pers. (Soph., Philoct. 1018 ἄφιλον ἔρημον ἄπολιν ἐν ζῶσιν νεκρόν; Menand., Colax 50; Epict. 3, 23, 28; scholia on Aristoph., Ran. 423 διὰ τὴν κακοπραγίαν νεκροὺς τοὺς Ἀθηναίους καλεῖ; Sextus 175 ν. παρὰ θεῷ; Philo, Leg. All. 3, 35, Conf. Lingu. 55, Fuga 56) of the prodigal son either *thought to be dead, missing*, or morally *dead, depraved* Lk 15: 24, 32. Of a church that is inactive, remiss Rv 3: 1. Of persons before baptism Hs 9, 16, 3f; 6. W. dat. of disadvantage ν. τῇ ἁμαρτίᾳ *dead to sin* Ro 6: 11.—ν. τοῖς παραπτώμασιν *dead in sins* Eph 2: 1, 5; Col 2: 13. Of worldly-minded Christians: τὸ ἥμισυ ν. ἐστι Hs 8, 8, 1.
β. of things ν. ἔργα *dead works* that cannot bring eternal life Hb 6: 1; 9: 14; Hs 9, 21, 2. ἡ πίστις χωρὶς ἔργων ν. ἐστιν *faith apart from deeds* (i.e. without

practical application) *is dead, useless* Js 2: 26b (κενή 𝔓⁷⁴), cf. vss. 17, 20 ℵ et al. Of sin χωρὶς νόμου ἁμαρτία ν. *where there is no law, sin is dead,* is not perceptible Ro 7: 8. Of the believer, in whom Christ lives: τὸ σῶμα νεκρόν *the body* (of σάρξ and sin) *is dead* 8: 10 (Herm. Wr. 7, 2 visible corporeality is called ὁ αἰσθητικὸς νεκρός. Sim. Philo, Leg. All. 3, 69ff, Gig. 15).

2. subst. ὁ ν. (so mostly Hom.+; inscr., pap., LXX, En. 103, 5; Philo; Jos., Bell. 4, 331 al.) *the dead* person.

a. lit. Lk 7: 15; (w. ζῶν as Appian, Liby. 129 §617 τ. νεκροὺς κ. τ. ζῶντας; Aesop, Fab. 69 H.; Ep. Arist. 146) of God οὐκ ἔστιν (ὁ) θεὸς νεκρῶν ἀλλὰ ζώντων Mt 22: 32; Mk 12: 27; Lk 20: 38. καὶ ν. καὶ ζώντων κυριεύειν *rule over the living and the dead* i.e. over all mankind past and present Ro 14: 9. κρίνειν ζῶντας καὶ νεκρούς 2 Ti 4: 1; 1 Pt 4: 5 (cf. vs. 6); B 7: 2; κριτὴς ζώντων καὶ ν. Ac 10: 42; 2 Cl 1: 1; Pol 2: 1. In this combination ν. without the article means all the dead, all those who are in the underworld (νεκροί=the dead: Thu. 4, 14, 5; 5, 10, 12; Lucian, V.H. 1, 39; Polyaenus 4, 2, 5). Likew. in the expr. ἐκ. ν. and ἀπὸ ν. (Bl-D. §254, 2; Rob. 791f). ἐγείρειν ἐκ ν., ἐγείρεσθαι ἐκ ν. Mt 17: 9; Mk 6: 14; Lk 9: 7; J 2: 22; 12: 1, 9, 17; 21: 14; Ac 3: 15; 4: 10; 13: 30; Ro 6: 4; 7: 4; 8: 11a, b, 34 v.l.; 10: 9; 1 Cor 15: 12a, 20; Gal 1: 1; Eph 1: 20; Col 2: 12; 1 Pt 1: 21; IMg 9: 3; ITr 9: 2; Pol 2: 1f (1 Pt 1: 21); 5: 2. ἀναστῆναι ἐκ ν. and ἀναστῆσαί τινα ἐκ ν. Mk 9: 9f; 12: 25; Lk 16: 31; J 20: 9; Ac 10: 41; 13: 34; 17: 3, 31; 1 Cl 24: 1; B 15: 9; GP 8: 30 (KGKuhn, NTS 7, '61, 343f). ἡ ἐκ ν. ἀνάστασις B 5: 6; Lk 20: 35; Ac 4: 2. Also ἡ ἐξανάστασις ἡ ἐκ ν. Phil 3: 11; ἀνάγειν ἐκ ν. *bring up from the realm of the dead* Ro 10: 7; Hb 13: 20. ἀπὸ ν. πορεύεσθαι πρός τινα *come up to someone fr. the realm of the dead* Lk 16: 30. Somet. the art. is included in these prep. combinations without appreciable difference in mng.: ἐγείρεσθαι ἀπὸ τῶν ν. Mt 14: 2; 27: 64; 28: 7 (w. ἐγείρεσθαι ἐκ ν. 17: 9). ἐγείρειν ἐκ τῶν ν. 1 Th 1: 10; πρωτότοκος ἐκ τῶν ν. Col 1: 18 beside ὁ πρωτότοκος τῶν ν. Rv 1: 5. The art. is often omitted w. the gen.; so as a rule in ἀνάστασις ν. *resurrection of the dead,* an expr. that is explained by the locution ἀναστῆναι ἐκ ν. Ac 17: 32; 23: 6; 24: 21; 26: 23; Ro 1: 4; 1 Cor 15: 12b, 13, 21; D 16: 6. Also ἀνάστασις τῶν ν. Mt 22: 31; 1 Cor 15: 42. νεκροὺς ἐγείρειν *raise the dead* Mt 10: 8; Ac 26: 8. Pass. Mt 11: 5; Lk 7: 22 (on the fig. understanding s. κωφός 2); 1 Cor 15: 15f, 29b, 32. Also τοὺς ν. ἐγείρειν J 5: 21; 2 Cor 1: 9. Pass. Lk 20: 37; 1 Cor 15: 35, 52. Of God ζωοποιεῖν τοὺς ν. Ro 4: 17. μετὰ τῶν ν. *among the dead* Lk 24: 5. βαπτίζεσθαι ὑπὲρ τῶν ν. *be baptized for the dead* 1 Cor 15: 29a (s. βαπτίζω 2bγ). τάφοι νεκρῶν IPhld 6: 1. ὀστέα νεκρῶν *the bones of the dead* Mt 23: 27. ἄτονος ὥσπερ νεκροῦ νεῦρα *powerless as the sinews of a corpse* Hm 12, 6, 2. αἷμα ὡς νεκροῦ *blood like that of a dead man* Rv 16: 3.

b. fig. (cf. Philo, Fuga 56) ἄφες τοὺς ν. θάψαι τοὺς ἑαυτῶν ν. *let the dead bury their dead* of those who are lost to the Kgdm. of God Mt 8: 22; Lk 9: 60 (cf. Theophyl. Sim., Ep. 25 τ. θνητοῖς τὰ θνητὰ καταλείψομεν.— FPerles, ZNW 19, '20, 96; 25, '26, 286f; Bleibtreu [s. μισέω 1]. ATEhrhardt, Studia Theologica VI, 2, '53, 128–64.—θάπτειν τοὺς ν. lit. Jos., Bell. 5, 518). The words ἀνάστα ἐκ τ. νεκρῶν Eph 5: 14 belong to a hymn (s. Rtzst., Erlösungsmyst. '21, 136) that may have become part of the baptism ritual (MDibelius, Hdb. ad loc.; FJDölger, Sol Salutis², '25, 364ff).—RBultmann, TW IV 896–9: νεκρός and related words. M-M. B. 290.*

νεκροφόρος, ον *bearing a corpse;* subst. ὁ ν. *the corpsebearer.* It lit. means a man who carries a corpse to its burial-place (Polyb., 35, 6, 2; Plut., Cato Maj. 9, 2). Ign. uses it in a play on words to reject the views of the Docetists, who deny that Christ was a σαρκοφόρος. Whoever does this, he says, is himself a νεκροφόρος, evidently mng. that he is *clothed in a corpse* rather than in flesh ISm 5: 2 (cf. Philo, Agr. 25 [ψυχὴ] νεκροφοροῦσα). *

νεκρόω 1 aor. ἐνέκρωσα; pf. pass. ptc. νενεκρωμένος (Hellenist. word: Hipponax[?]; Epict. 1, 5, 7; Plut., Mor. 954D; Themist., Paraphr. Aristot. II p. 51, 15 Spengel; inscr.; Philo, Aet. M. 125) *put to death* τὰ μέλη τὰ ἐπὶ τῆς γῆς *what is earthly in you* Col 3: 5. Pass. *be worn out, impotent, as good as dead* (Longus 2, 7, 5) νενεκρωμένος *worn out, impotent* of persons whose physical capabilities have failed in a certain respect (comm. on Hipponax: POxy. 2176 fgm. 1, col. 2, 7 [KLatte, Philol. 97, '48, 39f] τ. τράχηλον; Maximus Tyr. 41, 3h; cf. Epict. 4, 5, 21); e.g. of Abraham in his old age ἀφ᾽ ἑνὸς ἐγενήθησαν καὶ ταῦτα νενεκρωμένου *from one man, and him as good as dead, were born* Hb 11: 12. τὸ σῶμα νενεκρωμένον *his worn-out body* Ro 4: 19 (cf. IG III 2, 1355 ἄνθρωπε μή μου παρέλθης σῶμα τὸ νενεκρωμένον.—Dssm., LO 75 [LAE 94]; BHaensler, BZ 12, '14, 168ff; 14, '16, 164ff). M-M.*

νέκρωσις, εως, ἡ (Aretaeus p. 32, 16; Soranus p. 140, 3; Galen: CMG V 9, 2 p. 87, 10; 313, 16 ν. τοῦ σώματος; Porphyr., Abst. 4, 20 p. 262, 20 Nauck; Proclus on Pla., Rep. II 117, 16 Kr. of the trees in spring: ἐκτινάσσειν τὴν ν.; Photius, Bibl. p. 513, 36 οἱ γὰρ κόκκοι μετὰ τ. νέκρωσιν ἀναζῶσι).

1. *death, putting to death* lit. πάντοτε τ. νέκρωσιν τοῦ Ἰησοῦ ἐν τῷ σώματι περιφέροντες *we always carry about in our body the putting to death of Jesus* (of the constant danger of death in which the apostle lives) 2 Cor 4: 10.

2. *deadness, mortification*—a. lit. ἡ ν. τῆς μήτρας Σάρρας *the deadness of Sarah's womb* Ro 4: 19.

b. fig. ἀποτίθεσθαι τὴν ν. τῆς ζωῆς τῆς προτέρας *lay aside the deadness of their former life* i.e. *the dead life they formerly led* (before baptism) Hs 9, 16, 2f. νέκρωσις τῆς καρδίας *deadening* Mk 3: 5 D (cf. Epict. 1, 5, 4 ἀπονέκρωσις τῆς ψυχῆς). M-M.*

νέμομαι impf. ἐνεμόμην (Jos., Ant. 17, 193, C. Ap. 1, 60; 195) *graze, feed* (so Hom.+; pap., LXX) of cattle and birds εἰς τὸ ὄρος *feed on the mountain* Hs 9, 1, 8. Trans. ν. τι *feed on someth.* 9, 24, 1.*

νεομηνία, ας, ἡ (in the contracted form νουμηνία since Aristoph.; X., An. 5, 6, 23; Antig. Car. 126; Appian, Bell. Civ. 5, 97 §404; 98 §406; inscr. [Dit., Syll.³ and Or. index]; PPetr. II 4 [2], 6 [III BC]; BGU 1053, 20 [13 BC]; LXX [Thackeray 98]; Philo; Jos., Bell. 5, 230, Ant. 4, 78. The uncontracted [Ionic] form is found in inscr. [ENachmanson, Laute u. Formen d. magn. Inschr. '03, 69] and pap. [PTebt. 318, 12 (166 AD); BGU 859, 6 (II AD). Cf. Mayser p. 153] not before the second half of the second century AD, also Alciphr. 3, 25, 2.—Proclus on Pla., Cratyl. p. 40, 3 νουμηνίαν μὲν Ἀττικοί φασιν, νεομηνίαν δὲ Κρῆτες; Lob., Phryn. 148) *new moon, first of the month,* oft. celebrated as a festival by Jews and Gentiles: Col 2: 16; B 2: 5; 15: 8 (the two last Is 1: 13 νουμηνία); PK 2 p. 14, 28. τὴν τῆς νουμηνίας εἰρωνείαν *the hypocritical observance of the new moon* Dg 4: 1 (Antig. Car. 126 μύρμηκες ταῖς νουμηνίαις ἀναπαύονται=the ants rest at the time of the new moon). M-M.*

νέος, α, ον (Hom.+; inscr., pap., LXX, Philo, Joseph., Test. 12 Patr.) comp. νεώτερος.

1. adj.—a. *new, fresh*—α. lit., of things ν. φύραμα *fresh dough* w. no yeast in it; symbolically of Christians 1 Cor 5: 7 (s. φύραμα, ζύμη). Also ν. ζύμη of Christ IMg 10: 2. οἶνος ν. *new wine* (Simonides 49 D.; Diocles 141 p. 184, 14; POxy. 729, 19; 92, 2; 3; Sir 9: 10), which is still fermenting Mt 9: 17; Mk 2: 22; Lk 5: 37f; (opp. παλαιὸς οἶ. *old, aged wine*: schol. on Pind., Ol 9, 74f) vs. 39; διαθήκη ν. *the new covenant* (διαθήκη 2) Hb 12: 24.

β. fig., of pers. ἐνδύσασθαι τὸν ν. (ἄνθρωπον) *put on the new man* Col 3: 10. Of Christ πάντοτε νέος ἐν ἁγίων καρδίαις γεννώμενος *he is ever born anew in the hearts of the saints* Dg 11: 4 (Diod. S. 3, 62, 6 of Dionysus, who was torn to pieces but later joined together again by Demeter: ἐξ ἀρχῆς νέον γεννηθῆναι).

b. *young*—α. positive (Appian, Bell. Civ. 5, 136 §566 νέος ἀνήρ; Philo, Post. Cai. 109; Jos., Ant. 8, 23; Jerus. inscr.: Suppl. Epigr. Gr. VIII 209 [I AD]) ὁλοτελῶς νέον εἶναι *be completely young* Hv 3, 13, 4. Also of animals μόσχος νέος *a young ox or calf* 1 Cl 52: 2 (Ps 68: 32).

β. mostly comp.: ὁ νεώτερος υἱός *the younger son* (Gen 27: 15; cf. Philo, Sacr. Abel. 42; Jos., Ant. 12, 235, in all these pass. in contrast to πρεσβύτερος as Lk 15: 25) Lk 15: 13; cf. vs. 12; B 13: 5 (Gen 48: 14). τὴν ὄψιν νεωτέραν ἔχειν *have a more youthful face* Hv 3, 10, 4; 3, 12, 1; cf. s 9, 11, 5. On the other hand, the comp. sense is scarcely felt any longer 3, 10, 5; 3, 13, 1. Likew. in νεώτεραι χῆραι 1 Ti 5: 11; cf. vs. 14, where the noun is to be supplied fr. context. Sim. J 21: 18 (cf. Ps 36: 25).

2. subst.—a. *novice* νέοι ἐν τῇ πίστει Hv 3, 5. 4.

b. on the basis of the mng. 'young'—α. positive (οἱ) νέοι *the young people* (X., Cyr. 5, 1, 25; Diod. S. 14, 115, 3; 2 Macc 5: 13; 6: 28; 15: 17; Jos., C. Ap. 2, 206) w. οἱ πρεσβύτεροι (s. πρεσβύτερος 1a) 1 Cl 1: 3; 3: 3; 21: 6. σκοπὸν πᾶσι τοῖς νέοις τιθέναι *set a goal for all the young people* 2 Cl 19: 1 (οἱ νέοι for young people of both sexes: Nicetas Eugen. 8, 187 H.).—αἱ νέαι *the young women* Tit 2: 4.

β. comp., mostly with little comp. force (POxy. 298, 29; Jos., Ant. 15, 407): οἱ νεώτεροι *young men* (Diod. S. 14, 113, 3 [alternating with οἱ νέοι, and with no difference in mng. 14, 115, 3, as 18, 46, 3 οἱ πρεσβύτεροι . . . οἱ νεώτεροι beside 4 οἱ πρεσβύτεροι . . . οἱ νέοι]; 2 Macc 5: 24) Ac 5: 6; 1 Ti 5: 1 (s. on πρεσβύτερος 1a); Tit 2: 6; Pol 5: 3. Opp. πρεσβύτεροι 1 Pt 5: 5 (X., An. 7, 4, 5; Timaeus Hist.: no. 566 fgm. 11a Jac. διακονεῖν τοὺς νεωτέρους τοῖς πρεσβυτέροις; Dio Chrys. 78[29], 21; Demosth., Ep. 2, 10; Ep. Arist. 14; Philo, Spec. Leg. 2, 226; Jos., Ant. 3, 47; PPar. 66, 24 πρεσβύτεροι καὶ ἀδύνατοι καὶ νεώτεροι; Plut., Mor. 486F. On the other hand, also the inscr. of Ptolemais APF 1, '01, 202 no. 4, 15 οἱ νεώτεροι καὶ οἱ ἄλλοι πολῖται. On νεώτεροι as t.t. s. Schürer III⁴ 91). (αἱ) νεώτεραι *young(er) women* 1 Ti 5: 2.—ὁ νεώτερος beside ὁ μείζων Lk 22: 26 has the force of a superlative (cf. Gen 42: 20); this is influenced by the consideration that the youngest was obliged to perform the lowliest service (cf. Ac 5: 6).

3. The well-known city name (quotable Hdt.+) is prob. to be written Νέα πόλις (cf. Dit., Syll.³ 107, 35 [410/09 BC] ἐν Νέαι πόληι; Meisterhans³-Schw. p. 137; PWarr. 5, 8 [154 AD]; Diod. S. 20, 17, 1 Νέαν πόλιν; 20, 44, 1 ἐν Νέᾳ πόλει; Jos., Bell. 4, 449. Even in 247 AD τῆς Νέας πόλεως is found in pap. [PViereck, Her. 27, 1892, 516 II, 29f]; Mlt.-H. 278) acc. Νέαν πόλιν Ac 16: 11; IPol 8: 1 (where, however, Νεάπολιν is attested and customarily printed). In both places our lit. means by *Neapolis* (New City) the harbor of Philippi in Macedonia (Ptolem. 3, 13; Strabo 7, fgm. 36 p. 331; Appian, Bell. Civ. 4, 106 §446; Pliny, N.H. 4, 42 p. 58 Detl.).—RAHarrisville s.v. καινός. JBehm, TW IV 899-903. M-M. B. 957f.*

νεοσσός s. νοσσός.

νεότης, τητος, ἡ (Hom.+; inscr., pap., LXX, Philo; Jos., Vi. 325; Test. 12 Patr.) *youth* τῆς ν. τινος καταφρονεῖν *look down on someone's youth*, i.e. *on someone because he is young* 1 Ti 4: 12 (Appian, Bell. Civ. 1, 94 §435 ἐπιγελάω τῇ νεότητι. ἀπὸ νεότητος *from youth (up)* (M. Ant. 8, 1, 1; PTebt. 276, 38; Jos., Bell. 4, 33; 1 Macc 1: 6; 16: 2, and used w. a gen. Num 22: 30; Jer 3: 25) 1 Cl 63: 3; B 19: 5; D 4: 9. Also ἐκ ν. (Il. 14, 86; Gen 48: 15; Is 47: 15; 54: 6 and very oft. in LXX w. a gen.) Mt 19: 20 D; Lk 18: 21; Ac 26: 4. ἐκ νεότητός μου Mt 19: 20 v.l.; Mk 10: 20; Lk 18: 21 v.l. M-M.*

νεόφυτος, ον (Aristoph., fgm. 828 I p. 581 Kock; PRyl. 138, 9 [34 AD]; BGU 563 I, 9 al. [Dssm., NB 47f—BS 220f]; Ps 127: 3; 143: 12; Is 5: 7; Job 14: 9) lit. *newly planted*, fig. (only in Christian lit.) newly planted in the Christian church, *newly converted* (cf. 'neophyte') 1 Ti 3: 6. M-M.*

νέρτερος, α, ον (trag.+) comp. without a positive *the lower*, usu. in positive mng. *belonging to the lower world* (τὰ) νέρτερα *the underworld* (Orph. Hymns 3, 10; 57, 2; 78, 5 Qu.) νερτέρων ἀνεκδιήγητα κρίματα *the indescribable verdicts of the underworld* 1 Cl 20: 5 (on the text s. ἀνεκδιήγητος).*

Νέρων, ωνος, ὁ *Nero*, Roman emperor (54-68 AD) 2 Ti subscr.*

Νευης form of the proper name of the rich man Lk 16: 19, only in 𝔓⁷⁵. Another form, found in scholia, is Νινευης. Full discussion by HJCadbury, JBL 81, '62, 399-402. S. also LLefort, Le nom du mauvais riche et la trad. copte, ZNW 37, '38, 65-72; KGrobel, NTS 10, '64, 373-82.*

νεῦρον, ου, τό (Hom.+; Herm. Wr. 5, 6; PGM 36, 156; LXX) *sinew* ὥσπερ νεκροῦ νεῦρα *like the sinews of a corpse* Hm 12, 6, 2 (cf. Philo, In Flacc. 190).*

νεύω 1 aor. ἔνευσα (Hom.+; pap.; Pr 4: 25; 21: 1; Ezech. Trag. in Euseb., Pr. Ev. 9, 29, 5; Jos., Bell. 1, 629, Ant. 7, 175) *nod* ν. τινι *nod to someone* as a signal (Lucian, Catapl. 15; BGU 1078, 9 [39 AD]; Field, Notes 100) J 13: 24. W. inf. foll. (Eur., Hec. 545; Bl-D. §392, 1d) J 13: 24 t.r.; Ac 24: 10. M-M.*

νεφέλη, ης, ἡ (Hom.+; Epigr. Gr. 375; pap., LXX, En., Philo, Joseph.) *cloud* ν. λευκή Rv 14: 14a. Clouds fr. the west bringing rain Lk 12: 54. νεφέλαι σκότους *dark clouds* as a comparison for a swarm of worms AP 10: 25. ν. ἄνυδροι *waterless clouds*, that yield no rain Jd 12; cf. 2 Pt 2: 17 t.r. Jesus at the Transfiguration was overshadowed by a νεφέλη φωτεινή *bright cloud* (ν. as a sign of God's presence: Jos., Ant. 3, 290; 310) Mt 17: 5; cf. Mk 9: 7; Lk 9: 34f (HRiesenfeld, Jésus Transfiguré '47, 130-45). περιβεβλημένος νεφέλην *clothed in a cloud* (Lucian, Jupp. Trag. 16) *clothed in a cloud* Rv 10: 1. Christ ascending in a cloud Ac 1: 9 (cf. Dosiadis [III BC]: no. 458 fgm. 5 Jac. of Ganymede: νέφος ἥρπασεν αὐτὸν εἰς οὐρανόν; Ps.-Apollod. 2, 7, 7, 12 of Heracles). Likew. the believers 1 Th 4: 17 (cf. PGM 5, 277 τὸν περιεχόμενον . . . ὑπὸ τῆς τοῦ ἀέρος νεφέλης); cf. Rv 11: 12. Clouds as the vehicle of Christ at his second coming ἐρχόμενον ἐπὶ τῶν ν. τοῦ οὐρανοῦ (cf. Da 7: 13) Mt 24: 30; 26: 64. ἐν νεφέλαις Mk 13: 26. ἐν νεφέλῃ Lk 21: 27. μετὰ τῶν ν. τοῦ οὐρανοῦ (Da 7: 13 Theod.) Mk 14: 62; cf. Rv 1: 7. ἐπάνω τῶν ν. τοῦ οὐρανοῦ D 16: 8; καθήμενος ἐπὶ τῆς ν. Rv 14: 15f; ἐπὶ τὴν ν. vs. 14b. ὑπὸ τὴν ν. εἶναι *be under the cloud* 1 Cor 10: 1 (for the idea cf. Ex 14: 19ff; Num 14: 14; Ps 104: 39; Wsd 10: 17; 19: 7). πάντες ἐβαπτίσαντο (the v.l. ἐβαπτίσθησαν is better.

Bl-D. §317; Rob. 808) ἐν τῇ νεφέλῃ *they were all baptized in* (*by*) *the cloud* vs. 2 is meant to establish a baptism for those who were in the desert.—AOepke, TW IV 904–12. M-M.*

Νεφθαλίμ, ὁ indecl. (נַפְתָּלִי; Gen 30: 8; 49: 21; Judg 4: 6, 10 al. With μ at the end Is 8: 23 and occas. [Gen 49: 21; Dt 33: 23; Judg 4: 6 B] as v.l.; Philo, Somn. 2, 36. On this s. PKatz, ThLZ 61, '36, 281.—In Jos., Ant. 1, 305 Νεφθάλεις and 2, 181 Νεφθάλις) *Naphtali,* Hebrew tribe and its ancestor. φυλὴ N. Rv 7: 6. Its land γῆ N. Mt 4: 15 (Is 8: 23). (τὰ) ὅρια N. vs. 13; Lk 4: 31 D.*

νέφος, ους, τό (Hom.+; inscr., LXX; Jos., Bell. 6, 298) *cloud* as a symbol of darkness (Charito 3, 9, 11 νέφος ἀνεκάλυψε τῆς ψυχῆς; Isishymnus v. Andros 158 Peek; Philo, Mos. 1, 176; Jos., Ant. 16, 376 ν. ἐπάγειν τοῖς πράγμασιν='spread darkness over the events'; Sib. Or. 3, 173) ἀποθέμενοι ἐκεῖνο ὃ περικείμεθα ν. *we laid aside the cloud that surrounded us* 2 Cl 1: 6. Fig. of a compact, numberless throng (Il. 4, 274 al.; Hdt. 8, 109 νέφος τοσοῦτον ἀνθρώπων; Timon [III BC] in Diog. L. 8, 16; Diod. S. 3, 29, 2; Ps.-Callisth. 1, 2, 2 νέφος ἐχθρῶν. Further exx. in Bleek on Hb 12: 1) *host* τοσοῦτον ἔχοντες περικείμενον ἡμῖν ν. μαρτύρων *since we have so great a host of witnesses about us* Hb 12: 1. M-M.*

νεφρός, οῦ, ὁ (Aristoph., Pla. et al.; LXX; Philo; Jos., Ant. 3, 228) usu. pl. *kidneys;* fig., of the inner life, *mind* (LXX). Of the Son of Man ἐρευνῶν νεφροὺς καὶ καρδίας *who searches minds and hearts* (Diod. S. 1, 91, 5 νεφροὶ καὶ καρδία are the only things left in the body cavity by the Eg. embalmers) Rv 2: 23 (in the OT a similar expr., w. different verbs, is used of God: Ps 7: 10; Jer 11: 20; 17: 10; 20: 12). M-M.*

νεωκόρος, ου, ὁ lit. *temple keeper* (so X., Pla.+; Ael. Aristid. 47, 11 K.=1 p. 23 D.; Inschr. v. Priene 231 [IV BC] Μεγάβυξος νεωκόρος τῆς Ἀρτέμιδος τῆς ἐν Ἐφέσῳ; PMagd. 35 [217 BC]; Philo, Spec. Leg. 1, 156; Jos., Bell. 1, 153; 5, 383; Sib. Or. 12, 274. Loanw. in rabb.), then, w. the rise of the emperor cult in Asia Minor, a title assumed by cities that built and maintained temples in honor of the emperor. In rare cases this custom was extended to other deities; so Ephesus is called ν. τῆς μεγάλης Ἀρτέμιδος *the guardian of the temple of the great Artemis* (νεωκόρος τῆς Ἀρτέμιδος CIG 2966; 2972; OBenndorf, Forschungen in Ephesos I '06, 211 νεωκόρος τῆς ἁγιωτάτης Ἀρτέμιδος; Dit., Or. 481, 1ff; Rouffiac 64f. Also on coins [JWeiss, RE X 543; AWikenhauser, Die AG '21, 366]) Ac 19: 35.—WBüchner, De Neocoria 1888. M-M.*

νεωτερικός, ή, όν *youthful* (so Polyb. 10, 21, 7; Plut., Dion 8, 1; 3 Macc 4: 8; Jos., Ant. 16, 399) ἐπιθυμίαι 2 Ti 2: 22 (cf. Vett. Val. 118, 3 νεωτερικὰ ἁμαρτήματα). προσλαμβάνειν τὴν φαινομένην νεωτερικὴν τάξιν *take advantage of his seemingly youthful appearance* IMg 3: 1. M-M.*

νεωτερισμός, οῦ, ὁ (IG IV² 1, 68, 43 [302 BC]) *innovation,* mostly in a bad sense *uprising, revolution, rebellion* (Pla., Demosth., Plut.; Ep. Arist. 101; Philo, In Flacc. 93; Jos., Ant. 5, 101; 20, 106; Test. Reub. 2: 2). Pl. (Pla., Leg. 6 p. 758c) *revolutionary outbreaks* (w. μέθαι and other vices) 1 Cl 30: 1.*

νεώτερος s. νέος. M-M.

νή particle of strong affirmation (Aristoph.+; pap.; Gen 42: 15f; Jos., C. Ap. 1, 255) *by* w. acc. of the pers. or thing by which one swears or affirms (Bl-D. §149; Rob. 487;

1150) νὴ τὴν ὑμετέραν καύχησιν (yes, truly) *by my pride in you* 1 Cor 15: 31 (cf. Epict. 2, 20, 29 νὴ τ. σὴν τύχην; PGiess. 19, 11 νὴ τὴν σὴν σωτηρίαν; POxy. 939, 20; Gen 42: 15f νὴ τὴν ὑγίειαν Φαραώ). JWerres, D. Beteuerungsformeln in d. att. Komödie, Diss. Bonn '36. M-M.*

νήθω (Cratinus 96; Pla., Pol 289c; Anth. Pal. 11, 110, 6; 14, 134, 3; Ex 26: 31 al. in Ex) *spin* w. κοπιάω Mt 6: 28.—Lk 12: 27.—Dalman, Arbeit V '37. M-M. B. 408.*

νηκτός, ή, όν (Plut., Mor. 636E; 776c; Vett. Val. 344, 15; Philo, Op. M. 63; Jos., Ant. 8, 44) *swimming,* subst. τὸ νηκτόν *that which swims* (Ps.-Aristot., De Mundo 398b, 31; Galen XVIII 1 p. 207 K.) τῆς θαλάσσης τὰ νηκτά *what swims in the sea* PK 2 p. 14, 18.*

νηπιάζω (Hippocr. IX 360 L.; Erinna Lyrica [IV BC]: PSI IX 1090, 55+15 [p. XII]; Memnon Hist. [I AD], fgm. 22, 1 CMüller; Porphyr., πρὸς Γαῦρον [ABA 1895] 12, 3 p. 50, 27; 12, 4 p. 51, 6; schol. on Eur., Phoen. 713) *be* (*as*) *a child* fig., w. dat. (Hippocr., Ep. 17, 25 ἐπιβουλῇσι νηπιάζειν) τῇ κακίᾳ *in evil* 1 Cor 14: 20. M-M.*

νήπιος, ία, ιον (Hom.+; inscr., pap., LXX, Philo, Joseph., Test. 12 Patr., Sib. Or.) *infant, minor.*

1. of very young children—a. lit. (Jos., Ant. 6, 262) ὡς ν. βρέφη *like veritable babes* Hs 9, 29, 1. Usu. subst. οἱ ν. *children* (w. θηλάζοντες) Mt 21: 16 (Ps 8: 3). Sing. 1 Cor 13: 11a, b, c, d; τὰ τοῦ ν. *childish ways* vs. 11e. τὰ ν. (sc. βρέφη) Hm 2: 1.

b. fig.; the transition to the fig. sense is found Hb 5: 13 where the νήπιος, who is fed w. the milk of elementary teaching, is contrasted w. the τέλειος='mature person', who can take the solid food of the main teachings (s. also 1 Cor 3: 1f). In this connection the ν. is one who views spiritual things fr. the standpoint of a child. W. this can be contrasted

α. the state of the more advanced Christian, to which the ν. may aspire (Ps 118: 130; Philo, Migr. Abr. 46) ITr 5: 1. ἵνα μηκέτι ὦμεν νήπιοι Eph 4: 14. The Jew as διδάσκαλος νηπίων Ro 2: 20. νήπιος ἐν Χριστῷ *immature Christian* 1 Cor 3: 1 (cf. JWeiss, Paulin. Probleme: Die Formel ἐν Χριστῷ Ἰησοῦ, StKr 69, 1896, 1–33). Harnack, Die Terminologie d. Wiedergeburt: TU XLII 3, '18, 97ff.

β. The contrast can also be w. the concepts σοφός, συνετός, and then the νήπιοι are the *child-like, innocent* ones, unspoiled by learning, with whom God is pleased Mt 11: 25; Lk 10: 21 (GDKilpatrick, JTS 48, '47, 63f; WGrundmann, NTS 5, '58/'59, 188–205; SLégasse, Jésus et l'enfant [synopt.], '69). Cf. also 1 Cl 57: 7 (Pr 1: 32).

2. in the legal sense *minor, not yet of age* (UPZ 20, 22 [II BC] ἔτι νηπίας οὔσας ὁ πατὴρ ἀπέδωκεν εἰς σύστασιν Πτολεμαίῳ) ἐφ' ὅσον χρόνον ὁ κληρονόμος ν. ἐστιν as *long as the heir is a minor* Gal 4: 1. Fig. vs. 3.—In 1 Th 2: 7 νήπιοι is the rdg. of א* BCD* et al., and is accepted by Lachmann and W-H., as well as by interpreters fr. Origen to Wohlenberg, Frame, and Gdspd., Probs. 177f. Others, incl. N. (also Tischend., HermvSoden, BWeiss, Bornemann, vDobschütz, Dibelius, Steinmann) prefer ἤπιοι (A, t.r. et al.), and regard the ν of νήπιοι as the result of dittography fr. the preceding word. MLacroix, Ηπιος—Νηπιος: Mélanges Desrousseaux '37, 260–72.—GBertram, TW IV 913–25. M-M. B. 92.*

νηπιότης, ητος, ἡ (Pla., Leg. 7 p. 808E; Maximus Tyr. 10, 5c; Lucian, Halc. 3; LXX; Philo, Conf. Lingu. 21; Jos., Ant. 1, 287; 2, 233) *child-likeness* (w. ἁπλότης) (*child-like*) *innocence* Hs 9, 24, 3. ἐν ν. διαμένειν *remain in one's innocence* 9, 29, 1. Also μετὰ νηπιότητος διαμένειν 9, 29, 2.*

Νηρεύς, έως, ὁ *Nereus* (the old mythological name as a personal name e.g. IG III 1053, 11; 1162, 62; 1177, 48 also CIL); not infreq. borne by freedmen and slaves, some of them in the imperial service (Zahn, Einleitung I³ 299). W. his sister, recipient of a greeting: ἀσπάσασθε Νηρέα καὶ τ. ἀδελφὴν αὐτοῦ Ro 16: 15. M-M.*

Νηρί, ὁ indecl. (נֵרִי) *Neri*, in the genealogy of Jesus Lk 3: 27.*

νησίον, ου, τό (Strabo 2, 5, 23; 3, 3, 1; Paradoxogr. Flor. 38; Heliod. 1, 7, 2; loanw. in rabb.) dim. of νῆσος: *little island* (oft. no longer felt to be a dim.: Peripl. Eryth. c. 38 νησίον μικρόν) of the island of Clauda (s. Κλαῦδα) Ac 27: 16.*

νῆσος, ου, ἡ (Hom.+; inscr., pap., LXX, Ep. Arist.; Philo, Aet. M. 120; 138; Jos., Ant. 4, 116 al.; loanw. in rabb.) *island* Ac 27: 26. Cyprus (Jos., Ant. 17, 335) 13: 6. Malta 28: 1, 7, 9, 11. Patmos Rv 1: 9. Removed fr. their places in the last days 6: 14; 16: 20. M-M. B. 29.*

νηστεία, ας, ἡ (since Hdt. 4, 186; pap., LXX, Philo, Joseph., Test. 12 Patr.) *fasting, abstention from food.*
   1. gener., of hunger brought about by necessity: pl. (Bl-D. §142; cf. Rob. 408) of oft-recurring situations (cf. Da 9: 3; 2 Macc 13: 12) ἐν νηστείαις *through hunger* 2 Cor 6: 5. ἐν νηστείαις πολλάκις *often without food* 11: 27.
   2. esp. of fasting as a relig. rite—a. of public fasts: of the Day of Atonement (יוֹם כִּפֻּר; Strabo 16, 2, 40 τὴν νηστείας ἡμέραν [for the Jews]; Philo, Spec. Leg. 2, 193ff; Jos., Ant. 14, 66; 18, 94) Ac 27: 9; B 7: 4.—For D 8: 1 s. on νηστεύω, end.
   b. of private fasting Hs 5, 2, 1; 5, 3, 5. Of Moses on the mountain (w. ταπείνωσις, cf. Jdth 4: 9 v.l.; Ps 34: 13; PsSol 3: 8) 1 Cl 53: 2; likew. of Esther 55: 6. (W. προσευχή; cf. Tob 12: 8; Da 9: 3) Mt 17: 21; Mk 9: 29 v.l. (νηστεία strengthening prayer as 2 Macc 13: 12; Test. Jos. 10: 1f) 1 Cor 7: 5 t.r. (W. δεήσεις; cf. Da 9: 3 Theod.) Lk 2: 37. προσεύχεσθαι μετὰ νηστειῶν *pray and fast* Ac 14: 23. νηστείαν νηστεύειν (= צוֹם צוּם 2 Km 12: 16; 3 Km 20: 9) *keep, observe a fast* Hs 5, 1, 2f; νηστεύειν τὴν ν. *keep the fast* (day) B 7: 3 (ἡ νηστεία =fast day, as Jos., Ant. 18, 94). νηστεύειν τῷ θεῷ νηστείαν *keep a fast to God* Hs 5, 1, 4b. μεγάλην ν. ποιεῖν s 5, 1, 5. φυλάσσειν τὴν νηστείαν s 5, 3, 5; τελεῖν τὴν ν. s 5, 3, 8. ἡ ν. τελεία s 5, 3, 6, acc. to Hermas, includes abstaining fr. all evil as well as fr. food. —προσκαρτερεῖν νηστείαις *persevere in fasting* Pol 7: 2. Fasting better than prayer 2 Cl 16: 4 (cf. Tob 12: 8f). Rejected by God B 3: 1ff (Is 58: 5f). τῆς νηστείας εἰρωνεία *hypocritical observance of fast days* Dg 4: 1.— RArbesmann, D. Fasten b. d. Griech. u. Römern '29; MSFreiberger, D. Fasten im alten Israel '29; JAMontgomery, Ascetic Strains in Early Judaism: JBL 51, '32, 183-213; IAbrahams, Studies in Pharisaism and the Gospels I '17, 121-8; GFMoore, Judaism II '27, 55ff; 257ff; Billerb. IV '28, 77-114: V. altjüd. Fasten; MHShepherd, ATR 40, '58, 81-94; JBehm, TW IV 925-35.*

νηστεύω fut. νηστεύσω; 1 aor. ἐνήστευσα, inf. νηστεῦσαι, imper. νηστεύσατε, ptc. νηστεύσας (Aristoph.; Aristot.; Plut., Mor. 626f; Aelian, V.H. 5, 20; LXX; Philo, Spec. Leg. 2, 197; Jos., C. Ap. 1, 308; Test. 12 Patr.) *to fast* as a relig. rite, among Jews and Christians: as a sign of grief (2 Km 1: 12; 12: 22; Zech 7: 5; Bar 1: 5) Mt 9: 15 v.l.; Mk 2: 19f; Lk 5: 34f (cf. ν. ἐν τῇ ἡμέρᾳ ἐκείνῃ Judg 20: 26; 1 Km 7: 6); GP 7: 27. Moses B 4: 7; 14: 2 (cf. for the idea Ex 34: 28) and Jesus Mt 4: 2 *fast*

for forty days and forty nights (cf. 1 Km 31: 13; 1 Ch 10: 12 ν. ἑπτὰ ἡμέρας; Marinus, Vi. Procli 19 Boiss. τινὰς ν. ἡμέρας). With lamentation B 7: 5. As preparation for prayer (Jos., Ant. 20, 89) Hv 3, 10, 6; for baptism D 7: 4 (on fasting before being received into the pagan mystery cults s. Knopf, Hdb. ad loc.). W. προσεύχεσθαι (cf. Bar 1: 5) Ac 13: 3. W. δέομαι Hv 3, 1, 2. To increase the power of his prayer, Hermas fasts μίαν ἡμέραν *for one whole day* v 3, 10, 7; a fifteen-day fast v 2, 2, 1. His fast consists in taking only bread and water Hs 5, 3, 7. W. λειτουργεῖν τῷ κυρίῳ Ac 13: 2 (EPeterson, Nuntius 2, '49, 9f). Jesus and his disciples did not fast Mt 9: 14; Mk 2: 18; Lk 5: 33 (HJEbeling, D. Fastenfrage [Mk 2: 18-22]: StKr 108, '37/'38, 387-96, but cf. KTSchäfer, Synopt. Studien [Wikenhauser-Festschr.], '53, 124-47; FGCremer, D. Fastenansage Jesu, '65). Right and wrong attitudes in fasting Mt 6: 16-18. ν. νηστείαν *observe a fast* Hs 5, 1, 2f (s. νηστεία 2b). ν. τῷ θεῷ νηστείαν 5, 1, 4b. But ν. τὴν νηστείαν *keep the fast day* B 7: 3 (s. νηστεία 2b). ν. τῷ θεῷ Hs 5, 1, 4a; cf. B 3: 1 (Is 58: 4). Cf. Hs 5, 1, 1. As an act pleasing to God, w. the pers. given, who is to profit from it νηστεύετε ὑπὲρ τῶν διωκόντων ὑμᾶς *fast for those who persecute you* D 1: 3 (where Mt 5: 44 has προσεύχεσθε.—Knopf, Hdb. ad loc.). Pious Jews used to fast twice a week Lk 18: 12, on Monday and Thursday (s. Schürer II⁴ 572f; Elbogen 126f; 225f; 533; 551; Billerb. on Lk 18: 12), the Christians on Wednesday and Friday D 8: 1.—ν. τὸν κόσμον LJ 1: 2 has not yet been satisfactorily explained. Could it be taken fig. *abstain from the world* (see s.v. νηστεία on Hs 5, 3, 6 and cf. Empedocles in Plut., Mor. 464B [Vorsokrat. I⁵ 369, 17] νηστεῦσαι κακότητος; LEWright, JBL 65, '46, 180)? M-M. B. 1483.*

νῆστις, ὁ, ἡ gen. in Ion. and Ep. ιος, Attic ιδος, acc. pl. νήστεις (cf. Bl-D. §47, 3; Mlt.-H. 132 [strictly should be called an adj.]; 287; 374; on the formation of the word IWackernagel, Kl. Schr. 1150) *not eating, hungry* (so Hom.+; Da 6: 19; PKatz, ThLZ 81, '56, 605) Mt 15: 32; Mk 8: 3. M-M.*

νηφαλέος, α, ον (Herodian Gr. I 114, 17 al.; Philo, Leg. All. 3, 82; Etym. Mag. p. 261, 52; 262, 2; Act. Jo. 69. On the accent s. Kühner-Bl. II p. 297, 11) later form for νηφάλιος (q.v.) 1 Ti 3: 2 t.r.; 3: 11 t.r.—Bl-D. §35, 3 app.; Mlt.-H. 76; 362.*

νηφάλιος, ία, ον (Aeschyl.+; Plut.; Dit., Syll.³ 1040, 26) of pers. (cf. Philo, Sobr. 2, Mos. 1, 187; Jos., Ant. 3, 279) lit. *temperate in the use of alcoholic beverages, sober, clear-headed, self-controlled* 1 Ti 3: 2, 11; Tit 2: 2. M-M.*

νήφω 1 aor. ἔνηψα (Soph., Pla., X.+; inscr., pap.) *be sober*, in the NT only fig.=*be free fr. every form of mental and spiritual 'drunkenness'*, fr. excess, passion, rashness, confusion, etc. *be well-balanced, self-controlled* (Aristot.+; Epicurus in Diog. L. 10, 132 νήφων λογισμός=sober reasonableness; Περὶ ὕψους 16, 4; Lucian, Hermot. 47 νῆφε; Herodian 2, 15, 1; Achilles Tat. 1, 13 ν. ἐκ τοῦ κακοῦ; Herm. Wr. 7, 1; BGU 1011 III, 9 [II BC]; POxy. 1062, 13 ἵνα αὐτὴν [sc. τ. ἐπιστολὴν] ἀναγνοῖς νήφων κ. σαυτοῦ καταγνοῖς; Ep. Arist. 209; Philo; Jos., Bell. 2, 225; 4, 42; Sib. Or. 1, 154) 1 Th 5: 8; 1 Pt 1: 13. ν. ἐν πᾶσιν *be self-possessed under all circumstances* (M. Ant. 1, 16, 15) 2 Ti 4: 5. W. γρηγορεῖν (cf. Plut., Mor. 800B ἀγρυπνῶν κ. νήφων κ. πεφροντικώς) 1 Th 5: 6; 1 Pt 5: 8. W. σωφρονεῖν (Lucian, Nigrin. 5f) ν. εἰς προσευχάς *exercise self-restraint, to help you pray* 1 Pt 4: 7; Pol 7: 2 has ν. πρὸς τὰς εὐχάς. ν. ἐπὶ τὸ ἀγαθόν *exercise self-control for (your own) good* 2 Cl 13: 1. W. allusion to the self-control practiced by athletes: νῆφε ὡς θεοῦ ἀθλη-τής IPol 2: 3.—HLevy, Sobria ebrietas '29; OBauernfeind, TW IV 935-40: νήφω and related words. M-M.*

νήχομαι mid. dep. (Hom.+; Hero Alex. I 414, 18; 446, 16; Plut.; Lucian; Job 11: 12[?]; Philo Epicus Jud. [II BC] in Euseb., Pr. Ev. 9, 37, 1; Philo Alex., De Prov. in Euseb., Pr. Ev. 8, 14, 65; Jos., Ant. 15, 55, Vi. 15) *swim* ἐν τῷ βυθῷ B 10: 5. B. 681.*

Νίγερ, ὁ (Lat. loanw.; Dialekt-Inschr. 1555c, 20; e, 24 [Phocis]; ostracon APF 6, '20, 213, 1 [174/5 AD] Αἰβύτιος Νίγερ; Sb 46; Ostraka II 266; 296; wood tablet w. the name of the veteran L. Petronius Niger [94 AD] in Dssm., LO 383 [LAE 443]; Jos., Bell. 2, 520) *Niger* (dark-complexioned), surname of Simeon the prophet Ac 13: 1. M-M.*

Νικάνωρ, ορος, ὁ (Thu. 2, 80, 5 al.; Dit., Or. 21, 4; 196, 11f; 599, 1 al. in inscr.; Sb 1079; 3763; PFrankfurt [ed. HEwald: SA Heidelb. 14, '20] 5 recto, 20 [242/1 BC]; 1, 2 and 4 Macc; Ep. Arist. 182; Joseph.—Bl-D. §29, 3. In rabb. נִיקָנוֹר) name freq. found, *Nicanor*, one of the seven 'deacons' of the Jerusalem church Ac 6: 5. M-M.*

νικάω (Hom.+; inscr., pap., LXX, Philo, Joseph., Test. 12 Patr.) ptc. νικῶν, dat. νικοῦντι (Rv 2: 17 Tregelles, Tdf.; Lachm. also reads νικοῦντι vs. 7; W-H., N. have νικῶντι everywhere; on this exchange of -αω and -εω forms cf. Bl-D. §90 w. app.; Rob. 203; cf. Mlt.-H. 195); fut. νικήσω; 1 aor. ἐνίκησα; pf. νενίκηκα; 1 aor. pass. ptc. νικηθείς.
1. intr. *be victor, prevail, conquer*—a. in a battle or contest (Ep. Arist. 281), of Christ Rv 3: 21b; 5: 5 (the foll. inf. ἀνοῖξαι indicates what the victory enables the victor to do). Of Israel as victorious in battle B 12: 2. ἐξῆλθεν νικῶν κ. ἵνα νικήσῃ 6: 2. Of the good athlete (Lucian, Tim. 50; POxy. 1759, 4 letter to an athlete) IPol 3: 1. The Christian as ὁ νικῶν *he who is victorious* (cf. Bl-D. §322; Rob. 865) Rv 2: 7, 11, 17, 26; 3: 5, 12, 21; 21: 7 (s. Boll 49, 1). οἱ νικῶντες ἐκ τοῦ θηρίου (=τηρήσαντες ἑαυτοὺς ἐκ τ. θ.—Bl-D. §212; GBonaccorsi, Primi saggi di filologia neotest. I '33 p. clxii) 15: 2.—Hs 8, 3, 6 v.l.
b. in a legal action (Aristoph., Equ. 95, Av. 445; 447; Protagoras in Diog. L. 9, 56 [νικάω and νίκη]; Artem. 1, 35 p. 36, 20; 4, 31 p. 222, 17 al.; PSI 551, 7 [III BC]; PHal. 1, 51; 58 [III BC]; Jos., Bell. 2, 284, Ant. 12, 126) ὅπως νικήσεις (or νικήσῃς) ἐν τῷ κρίνεσθαί σε *that you may win when you are accused* Ro 3: 4; 1 Cl 18: 4 (both Ps 50: 6.—IG XI 4, 1299 l. 26f [c. 200 BC] Sarapis and his worshipers win in a lawsuit over the new temple).
2. trans. *conquer, overcome, vanquish*—a. act. w. the obj. in the acc. τινά *overcome someone* (Polyb. 6, 58, 13; Diod. S. 4, 57, 6; Jos., Vi. 81) Lk 11: 22; Rv 11: 7; 13: 7; 17: 14. Of Christ νενίκηκα τὸν κόσμον *I have overcome the world* (i.e. the sum total of everything opposed to God; s. κόσμος 7) J 16: 33 (ν. τι='be stronger than': Isisaretal. v. Kyme 55 Peek). Also said of the Christians 1 J 5: 4f; cf. αὕτη ἐστιν ἡ νίκη ἡ νικήσασα τὸν κόσμον vs. 4b (s. νίκη). Also ν. τὸν πονηρόν *overcome the evil one, the devil* 2: 13f (on this passage and J 16: 33 s. JBruns, JBL 86, '67, 451-53); cf. Rv 12: 11. αὐτούς (=τοὺς ἐκ τοῦ κόσμου) 1 J 4: 4. ν. τὴν ψυχήν *win a victory over the soul* (i.e. the earthly-minded part of man; cf. Sextus 71a νίκα τὸ σῶμα) 2 Cl 16: 2. The conquering power added in the dat. (Eur., Herc. Fur. 342 ἀρετῇ; Ael. Aristid. 13 p. 272 D.: ἐπιει-κείᾳ) τοῖς ἰδίοις βίοις νικῶσι τ. νόμους *in their way of life they surpass* (or *outdo*) *the laws* (i.e., they live better lives than the laws require) Dg 5: 10; by (means of) ἔν τινι

(Pla., Symp. 213E; Himerius, Or. [Ecl.] 3, 11 ἐν δόγμασι νικῶν ἐκείνους): ἐν τῷ μὴ ποιεῖν τὰς ἐπιθυμίας αὐτῆς τὰς πονηράς 2 Cl 16: 2. ν. ἐν τῷ ἀγαθῷ τὸ κακόν *overcome evil with good* Ro 12: 21b (Test. Benj. 4: 3 οὗτος τὸ ἀγαθὸν ποιῶν νικᾷ τὸ κακόν).
b. pass. *be conquered, beaten* (Thu. 1, 76, 2 al.; Posidippus [III BC]: no. 447 fgm. 2 Jac. νικᾶται ὁ Κύ-πριος τῷ σχήματι=the Cyprian is 'conquered' by the picture [of Aphrodite] et al.; Philo, De Jos. 200 νικώμενος ὑπὸ πάθους; Jos., Ant. 1, 302 by the force of necessity) Hm 12, 5, 2. *Let oneself be overcome* μὴ νικῶ ὑπὸ τ. κακοῦ Ro 12: 21a; Dg 7: 7.—OBauernfeind, TW IV 941-5: νικάω and related words. M-M.*

νίκη, ης, ἡ (Hom.+; inscr., pap., LXX; Ep. Arist. 180; Philo, Leg. All. 3, 186 ὅταν νικήσῃ νίκην; Jos., Ant. 6, 145 al.; Sib. Or. 13, 38) *victory,* then as abstr. for concr. *the means for winning a victory* (but cf. also the custom of speaking of the emperor's νίκη as the power that grants him the victory) 1 J 5: 4. M-M. B. 1406.*

Νικήτης, ου, ὁ a not uncommon name (Dit., Syll.³ 287, 2; 491, 73; 540, 44; 1029, 62) *Nicetes* MPol 8: 2; 17: 2.*

Νικόδημος, ου, ὁ a name common among Jews and Gentiles (exx. in Wettstein; Diod. S. 16, 82; 4; Jos., Ant. 14, 37; Dit., Syll.² and Preisigke, Sb in the indices; PHib. 110, 60; 75; 105; PFlor. 6, 20 Νικόδημος βουλευτής) *Nicodemus* (in rabb. נַקְדִּימוֹן), a member of the Sanhedrin who was favorable to Jesus and his cause, mentioned only in the Fourth Gospel. Little is known about him, and the connection w. the Talmudic Nicodemus, whose real name is said to have been Buni ben Gorion, and who was held to be a disciple of Jesus (Billerb. II 413f), is questionable. J 3: 1, 4, 9; 7: 50; 19: 39.—BZimolong, D. Nikod. perikope (J 2: 23-3: 22) nach d. syrosinait. Text, Diss. Bresl. '19; SMendner, JBL 77, '58, 293-323. M-M.*

Νικολαΐτης, ου, ὁ *Nicolaitan,* a follower of Nicolaus, an otherw. unknown founder of a sect, ἔργα τῶν Νικολαϊ-τῶν Rv 2: 6. διδαχὴ τῶν Νικολαϊτῶν vs. 15. On the sect of the Nicolaitans cf. ESchürer, Die Prophetin Isabel: Weizsäcker-Festschr. 1892, 39-58; LSeesemann, StKr 66, 1893, 47-82; GWohlenberg, NKZ 6, 1895, 923ff; Zahn, Einl. II³ 623f; AvHarnack, The Sect of the Nicolaitans and Nicolaus, the Deacon in Jerus.: Journ. of Religion 3, '23, 413-22; MGoguel, Les Nicolaïtes: Rev. de l'Hist. des Rel. 115, '37, 5-36. M-M.*

Νικόλαος, ου, ὁ (Hdt.+; Diod. S. 13, 19, 6; 32, 15, 5; IG XIV 682; 1252; Dit., Syll.² and Preisigke, Sb indices; Joseph.) *Nicolaus,* a proselyte of Antioch and one of the seven 'deacons' of the Jerusalem church Ac 6: 5. It hardly seems poss. that he had anything to do w. the sect of the Nicolaitans, despite the assertions of the ancients (approved by Zahn) that he did. M-M.*

Νικόπολις, εως, ἡ *Nicopolis*; of the many cities bearing this name (Stephan. Byz. names three of them, in Epirus, Bithynia, and Armenia Minor), the one mentioned Tit 3: 12 and in the subscr. of 1 Ti and Tit is usu. taken to be the N. in Epirus (Cass. Dio 50, 13; 51, 1; Strabo 7, 7, 5; 10, 2, 2). MDibelius, Hdb. exc. on Tit 3: 14.*

νῖκος, ους, τό (Manetho, Apot. 1, 358; Orph., Argon. 587; Polemo 1, 12 p. 6, 16; Vett. Val. 358, 5; IG XII 5, 764, 2; BGU 1002, 14 [55 BC]; LXX; Sib. Or. 14, 334; 339; Lob. on Phryn. p. 647) late form for ἡ νίκη (JWackernagel, Hellenistica '07, 26f; EFraenkel, Glotta 4, '13, 39ff; Bl-D. §51, 1; Mlt.-H. 126; 381).

1. *victory* ποῦ σου θάνατε τὸ ν.; *where, O Death, is your victory?* 1 Cor 15: 55 (after Hos 13: 14, where our LXX mss. read ποῦ ἡ δίκη σου, θ.; [cf. WDittmar, V.T. in Novo '03, 217 and s. on κέντρον 1], but Paul, influenced by vs. 54, substitutes νῖκος for δίκη; EEEllis, Paul's Use of the OT, '57, 140). In κατεπόθη ὁ θάνατος εἰς νῖκος *death is swallowed up in* (or *by*) *victory* vs. 54, νῖκος agrees w. the improvement which Theod. made in the LXX wording of Is 25: 8 (s. ARahlfs, ZNW 20, '21, 183f; JZiegler, Is. '39 ad loc.). Vss. 54 and 55 have the v.l. νεῖκος., q.v. διδόναι τινὶ τὸ ν. *give someone the victory* vs. 57 (cf. 2 Macc 10: 38; Jos., Ant. 6, 145). ἕως ἂν ἐκβάλῃ εἰς ν. τὴν κρίσιν *until he brings justice to victory* Mt 12: 20 (cf. 2 Km 2: 26 and variants in Field, Hexapla and the Cambridge LXX; s. κρίσις, end).

2. abstr. for concr. *the prize of victory* (4 Macc 17, 12 τὸ νῖκος ἀφθαρσία) παραδοὺς αὐτῇ τὸ ν. ὃ ἔλαβες *give over to it the prize of victory you have won* Hm 12, 2, 5. M-M.*

Νινευή (less well Νινευί [Bl-D. §39, 1; cf. Rob. 191f]), ἡ, indecl. (Gen 10: 11f; Is 37: 37; Jon 1: 2 al.; Zeph 2: 13 al. LXX; Hebr. נִינְוֵה) *Nineveh,* capital of the later Assyrian Empire Lk 11: 32 t.r.*

Νινευίτης, ου, ὁ *Ninevite*; ἄνδρες Νινευῖται *men of Nineveh* as examples of penitence, contrasted w. the contemporaries of Jesus Mt 12: 41; Lk 11: 32. οἱ Νινευῖται vs. 30. Jonah's preaching of repentance among them 1 Cl 7: 7.*

νιπτήρ, ῆρος, ὁ (Hdt. 2, 172 ποδανιπτήρ; a Cyprian inscr. fr. Roman times has the acc. νιπτῆρα: ASakellarios, Τα Κυπριακα I 1890, p. 191 no. 2; Lex. Vindob. p. 128, 16; Test. Abr. recension A 3: NTS 1, '54, 220) (*wash*)*basin* J 13: 5 (ποδονιπτήρ 𝔓⁶⁶).*

νίπτω 1 aor. ἔνιψα, mid. ἐνιψάμην, imper. νίψαι (Bl-D. §73; Mlt.-H. 250) (Hippocr.; Epict. [s. 1 below]; LXX; Jos., Ant. 8, 87).

1. act. *wash* w. acc. τὶ someth. τοὺς πόδας (Epict. 1, 19, 5 νίπτω τ. πόδας; Vi. Aesopi I c. 10 p. 252, 2; Gen 43: 24; 1 Km 25: 41) J 13: 5f, 8a, 12, 14a, b (on 'foot-washing' s. on λούω 2aβ); 1 Ti 5: 10. τινά *someone* J 13: 8b.

2. mid. *wash oneself* or *for oneself*—a. *I wash myself* J 9: 7b, 11a, b, 15; 13: 10 (if εἰ μὴ τ. πόδας is omitted); GOxy 34f. νίπτεσθαι εἰς τὴν κολυμβήθραν *wash, bathe in the pool* (cf. Epict. 3, 22, 71 ἵν' αὐτὸ [sc. τὸ παιδίον] λούσῃ εἰς σκάφην) J 9: 7a.

b. *I wash* (*for myself*) w. acc., ν. τὸ πρόσωπον *wash one's face* (Artem. 4, 41; Achmes 143, 11) Mt 6: 17. τὰς χεῖρας *wash one's hands* (Diod. S. 23, 2, 1; Ex 30: 19; Lev 15: 11) 15: 2; Mk 7: 3 (cf. FSchulthess, ZNW 21, '22, 233); GP 1: 1. τοὺς πόδας (Artem. 5, 55; Gen 19: 2; Judg 19: 21) J 13: 10 (if εἰ μὴ τ. πόδας is accepted). JHorst, D. Worte Jesu über d. kult. Reinheit: StKr 87, '14, 429-54. Branscomb (s. νόμος, end) 156-60. WKGrossouw, NovT 8, '66, 124-31; JATRobinson, The Significance of Footwashing, OCullmann-Festschr., '62, 144-47. M-M. B. 578f.*

νοέω 1 aor. ἐνόησα; pf. νενόηκα (Hom.+; pap., LXX, En., Ep. Arist., Philo, Joseph., Test. 12 Patr.).

1. of rational reflection or inner comtemplation *perceive, apprehend, understand, gain an insight into.*

a. w. the obj. in the acc. (X., An. 3, 4, 44; Jos., Vi. 298; Sib. Or. 5, 65) τὴν σύνεσίν μου *my insight* Eph 3: 4. δικαίως ν. τὰς ἐντολὰς *understand the commandments rightly* B 10: 12b. τὰς παραβολὰς *understand the parables* Hm 10, 1, 4 (cf. Pr 1: 6); (w. συνιέναι, as B 10: 12a) πάντα τὰ λεγόμενα m 10, 1, 6a; cf. b; τῆς βασάνου τὴν δύναμιν *the power of the torment* s 6, 4, 3a. τὴν πρᾶξιν

ἣν ποιεῖ *what he is doing* 6, 5, 3. οὐδέν 9, 14, 4. τὰ ἐπουράνια *understand heavenly things* ITr 5: 2. τὴν δόξαν τοῦ θεοῦ Hm 12, 4, 2. Relative clause as obj. 1 Ti 1: 7; Dg 8: 11; IRo 6: 3. ταῦτα B 10: 12a; Hs 5, 5, 4. αὐτά 6, 5, 2; 9, 2, 6b; οὐδὲν ν. *comprehend nothing* Hv 3, 6, 5; ὅλως οὐθὲν ν. *understand nothing at all* m 4, 2, 1. Also οὐδὲν ὅλως ν. m 10, 1, 5. ὅσα οὐ δύνασαι νοῆσαι *whatever you cannot comprehend* s 9, 2, 6a. οὐδὲ δύναμαι νοῆσαί τι *nor do I understand anything (about it)* 9, 9, 2.—W. acc. of the pers.: of the angel of wickedness *I do not understand how I am to recognize him* Hm 6, 2, 5.—W. περί τινος instead of the obj. ἔτι οὐ νενόηκα ὅλως περὶ τοῦ χρόνου τῆς ἀπάτης *I have not yet fully understood concerning the time of pleasure* s 6, 5, 1.—Pass. τὰ ἀόρατα . . . νοούμενα καθορᾶται *what is invisible . . . is clearly perceived* (w. the eye of the understanding) Ro 1: 20 (νοῆσαι τὸν θεόν: Herm. Wr. 11, 20b; 12, 20b and PGM 3, 597; Orpheus in Aristobulus: Euseb., Pr. Ev. 13, 12, 5 οὐδέ τις αὐτὸν εἰσορᾷ ψυχῶν θνητῶν, νῷ δ' εἰσοράαται. S. on γνωστός 2). Of the λόγος: ὑπὸ ἀπίστων μὴ νοούμενος Dg 11: 2.

b. w. ὅτι foll. (BGU 114 I, 9; 2 Km 12: 19; Ep. Arist. 224; Philo, Virt. 17, Mos. 1, 287; Bl-D. §397, 2) Mt 15: 17; 16: 11; Mk 7: 18; Ac 16: 10 D; 1 Cl 27: 3; B 7: 1; Hm 10, 1, 2; s 1: 3; (w. οἶδα) s 2: 8.

c. foll. by acc. and inf. (2 Macc 14: 30; Bl-D. §397, 2; Rob. 1036) Hb 11: 3; foll. by acc. and ptc. ἐνόησα ὑμᾶς κατηρτισμένους *I have observed that you are trained* ISm 1: 1 (Epigr. Gr. 278, 3 τὸν φίλον ὄντα νόει).

d. foll. by indirect question (Fluchtaf. 4, 56f ἵνα μὴ νοῶσιν τί ποιῶσιν; Wsd 4: 17; Sib. Or. 3, 796) Hm 6, 1, 1; s 5, 4, 2; οὐ ν. w. indir. quest. preceding *I do not understand* m 10, 1, 3. Elliptically πῶς, οὐ νοῶ *how (this can be) I do not understand* s 5, 6, 1.

e. abs. (Sir 11: 7) B 6: 10; 17: 2; Hs 6, 4, 3b; 9, 28, 6; (beside γινώσκειν w. the acc. [as Pla., Rep. 6, 508D]) οὐ δύναμαι νοῆσαι *I cannot understand* (*them*) s 5, 3, 1. νοῆσαί σε δεῖ πρῶτον *you must understand it first* v 3, 8, 11. *Comprehend, perceive* (Ep. Arist. 153) Mt 16: 9; Mk 8: 17. More fully ν. τῇ καρδίᾳ (Is 44: 18) J 12: 40.

2. *consider, take note of, think over* ὁ ἀναγινώσκων νοείτω *let the reader note* (*these words*) Mt 24: 15; Mk 13: 14. νόει ὃ λέγω *consider what I say* 2 Ti 2: 7 (Pla., Ep. 8 p. 352C νοήσατε ἃ λέγω) ἔτι κἀκεῖνο νοεῖτε *consider this, too* B 4: 14. W. indir. quest. foll. 1 Cl 19: 3; B 8: 2.

3. *think, imagine* (En. 100, 8 ν. τὸ κακόν) ὑπερεκπερισσοῦ ὧν νοοῦμεν *far beyond what we imagine* Eph 3: 20.

4. *be minded* σεμνὰ ν. *be honorably minded* 1 Cl 1: 3. —JBehm, TW IV 947-1016: νοέω, νοῦς and related words. M-M.*

νόημα, ατος, τό (Hom.+; LXX)—1. *thought, mind* (Hom.+; Pla., Symp. 197E; Sib. Or. 3, 585) mostly in pl. (Cornutus 16 p. 21, 2; oft. Philo; Herm. Wr. 9, 3) ἐπωρώθη τὰ νοήματα αὐτῶν 2 Cor 3: 14. ὁ θεὸς τ. αἰῶνος τούτου ἐτύφλωσεν τὰ νοήματα τ. ἀπίστων 4: 4. μή πως φθαρῇ τὰ νοήματα ὑμῶν ἀπὸ τ. ἁπλότητος τῆς εἰς Χριστόν *that perhaps your minds will be led astray from sincere devotion to Christ* 11: 3. τ. καρδίας ὑμῶν καὶ τὰ ν. ὑμῶν *your hearts and minds* Phil 4: 7.

2. *purpose,* in a bad sense *design, plot* (Hom.; Pla., Pol. 260D; Bar 2: 8; 3 Macc 5: 30) of Satan's designs 2 Cor 2: 11. αἰχμαλωτίζοντες πᾶν ν. εἰς τὴν ὑπακοὴν τοῦ Χριστοῦ *we take captive every design to make it obedient to Christ* 10: 5. M-M.*

νόθος, η, ον (Hom.+; pap.; Wsd 4: 3; Philo) *born out of wedlock, illegitimate, baseborn* (opp. γνήσιος [q.v.]

Menand., fgm. 290; Jos., Ant. 5, 233). As a symbol of men who reject God's discipline and hence (after Pr 3: 11f) cannot be his sons: ἄρα νόθοι καὶ οὐχ υἱοί ἐστε *then you are illegitimate children and not real sons* Hb 12: 8. M-M.*

νομή, ῆς, ἡ (Hom.+; inscr., pap., LXX; Ep. Arist. 112; Philo; Jos., Ant. 2, 18; 17, 249).
1. *pasture* in the sense *pasturing-place* (Soph., Hdt., X., Plut., pap.) or mng. *fodder* (Pla., Aristot.) ν. εὑρίσκειν *find pasture* (1 Ch 4: 40; La 1: 6) J 10: 9. Fig. of God as Shepherd of his people (i.e. the Christians); the latter are called πρόβατα τῆς νομῆς σου *sheep of thy pasture* (Ps 73: 1; 78: 13; cf. 99: 3) 1 Cl 59: 4; likew. B 16: 5 in a quot. fr. an unknown document (perh. En. 89, 56; 66f), called γραφή.
2. fig. (after the spreading out of a flock at pasture) in medical language, *spreading,* of an ulcer (Hippocr.+. Cf. Polyb. 1, 81, 6 νομὴν ποιεῖται ἕλκος.—Also 11, 4[5], 4 τὸ πῦρ λαμβάνει νομήν; 1, 48, 5; Memnon Hist. [I BC/I AD]: no. 434 fgm. 1, 2, 4 Jac. [ulcer]; Philo, Aet. M. 127 [conjecture of Usener]; Jos., Bell. 6, 164) ὁ λόγος αὐτῶν ὡς γάγγραινα νομὴν ἕξει *their teaching will spread like a cancer* 2 Ti 2: 17. M-M.*

νομίζω impf. ἐνόμιζον, pass. ἐνομιζόμην; 1 aor. ἐνόμισα (Aeschyl., Hdt.+; inscr., pap., LXX, Ep. Arist., Philo, Joseph., Test. 12 Patr.).
1. *have in common use* pass. *be the custom* (Aeschyl., Hdt.; Diod. S. 10, 3, 4 [τὰ νομιζόμενα]; Joseph., inscr., pap.) οὖ ἐνομίζετο προσευχὴ εἶναι *where, according to the custom, there was a place of prayer* Ac 16: 13 t.r.
2. *think, believe, hold, consider* (Aeschyl., Hdt.; inscr., pap., LXX, Ep. Arist., Philo; Jos., Ant. 1, 196) foll. by acc. and inf. (X., An. 6, 1, 29, Cyr. 1, 4, 5; inscr. [Dit. Syll.³ ind.]; 4 Macc 4: 13; 5: 16, 18, 19; 9: 4; Philo, Congr. Erud. Gr. 139] Lk 2: 44; Ac 7: 25; 14: 19; 16: 27; 17: 29; 1 Cor 7: 26; 1 Ti 6: 5; 1 Cl 1: 1; 26: 1; 44: 3 (pass.); Dg 4: 1, 6. With double acc. 2: 1. οὖ ἐνομίζομεν προσευχὴν εἶναι *where we supposed there was a place of prayer* Ac 16: 13. W. inf. foll. (inscr. [Dit., loc. cit.]; PTebt. 50, 11 [112/11 BC]; PLeipz. 105, 2; 2 Macc 4: 32) Ac 8: 20; 1 Cor 7: 36; Dg 2: 7; 12: 6. W. ὅτι foll. (X., Hell. 5, 4, 62; Lucian, Syr. Dea 28 p. 474; PFay. 109, 4 [I AD]; BGU 248, 29 [c. 75 AD]) Mt 5: 17 (μὴ νομίσητε as 4 Macc 2: 14; Jos., Ant. 5, 109); 10: 34; 20: 10; GP 5: 18. W. acc. and ὅτι foll. Ac 21: 29.—Pass. (Appian, Iber. 18 §68; 2 Macc 8: 35; Ep. Arist. 128; Philo, Spec. Leg. 2, 122) Dg 1. ὤν υἱὸς ὡς ἐνομίζετο Ἰωσήφ *he was, as was supposed, the son of Joseph* Lk 3: 23 (ὡς ἐνομίζετο as Appian, Mithrid. 63 §263; cf. also Appian, Liby. 111 §525 of the Macedonian king τὸν νομιζόμενον υἱὸν εἶναι Περσέως, Bell. Civ. 1, 33 §146; 2, 39 §153 νομιζόμενος εἶναι Ποσειδῶνος; Paus. 2, 10, 3 Ἄρατον Ἀσκληπιοῦ παῖδα εἶναι νομίζουσιν; Olympiodorus, Life of Plato, ed. AWestermann 1850 p. 1, 4: λέγεται ὁ Πλάτων υἱὸς γενέσθαι Ἀρίστωνος, though the writer claims he was of supernatural origin). M-M. B. 1204.*

νομικός, ή, όν (Pla., Aristot. et al.; inscr. [Hatch 134ff]; pap.; 4 Macc 5: 4; Sib. Or. 8, 112).
1. *pertaining to the law* μάχαι ν. *quarrels about the law* (i.e. the validity of the [Mosaic?] law) Tit 3: 9 (cf. Philostrat., Vitae Sophist. 1, 22, 1 ἀγῶνες ν.).
2. *learned in the law;* hence subst. ὁ νομικός *legal expert, jurist, lawyer* (Strabo 12, 2, 9; Epict. 2, 13, 6-8; Inschr. v. Magn. 191, 4 [also Thieme 37]; other exx. from inscriptions in LRobert, Hellenica I 62, 9; BGU 326 II, 22; 361 III, 2; POxy. 237 VIII, 2; PRainer 18, 24 al. in pap.;

4 Macc 5: 4); Tit 3: 13 mentions a certain Zenas the ν., but it is not clear whether he was expert in Jewish or non-Jewish (in that case most prob. Roman) law.—Elsewh. in the NT only once in Mt and several times in Lk, always of those expert in the Jewish law: Mt 22: 35; Lk 10: 25. Pl. 11: 45f, 52; 14: 3. Cf. UGosp line 2. Mentioned w. Pharisees 7: 30; 11: 53 D; 14: 3.—Schürer II⁴ 372ff; GRudberg, Coniect. Neot. II '36, 41f; Kilpatrick s.v. γραμματεύς. M-M. B. 1424.*

νόμιμος, η, ον (Pind., trag., Hdt.+; inscr., pap., LXX) *conformable to law, lawful.* Subst. τὸ νόμιμον, esp. in pl. τὰ νόμιμα (Pind.+; Diog. L. 7, 119 [the θεοσεβεῖς are experts in τῶν περὶ θεοὺς νομίμων]; inscr., pap.; Lev 18: 26; Pr 3: 1 al.; LXX; Ep. Arist. 10; 127; Philo, Mos. 2, 12ff al.; Jos., Ant. 8, 129; 18, 344, Vi. 191) *statutes, laws, commandments* πορεύεσθαι ἐν τοῖς ν. τῶν προσταγμάτων αὐτοῦ *walk according to the laws of his commandments* 1 Cl 3: 4 (cf. Jer 33: 4; Ezk 5: 6f). τοῖς ν. τοῦ δεσπότου ἀκολουθεῖν *follow the ordinances of the Lord* 40: 4. ἐν τοῖς ν. τοῦ θεοῦ πορεύεσθαι *walk according to the statutes of God* 1: 3 (the mss. have ἐν τοῖς νόμοις; the rdg. νομίμοις, which is found Clem. of Alex., Strom. 4, 17, 105, has been taken into the more recent editions). τηρεῖν τὰ ν. τοῦ θεοῦ *keep the commandments of God* Hv 1, 3, 4 (Eur., Suppl. 19 ν. θεῶν).*

νομίμως adv. (since Thu. 2, 74, 3; Dit., Or. 669, 19; 24; 4 Macc 6: 18; Jos., C. Ap. 2. 152; 217; Sib. Or. 11, 82) *in accordance with rule(s)* or *law* of athletes ν. ἀθλεῖν *compete according to the rules* 2 Ti 2: 5 (cf. Epict. 3, 10, 8 ὁ θεός σοι λέγει 'δός μοι ἀπόδειξιν, εἰ νομίμως ἤθλησας'). Paronomasia καλὸς ὁ νόμος, ἐάν τις αὐτῷ ν. χρῆται *the law is good, if anyone uses it lawfully* 1 Ti 1: 8 (Rob. 1201). M-M.*

νόμισμα, ατος, τό (Aeschyl.+) of money introduced into common use by νόμος; *coin* (so Hdt., Aristoph.+; inscr.; PTebt. 485 [II BC]; PGrenf. II 77, 8; 2 Esdr 17 [Neh 7]: 72 v.l.; 1 Macc 15: 6; Ep. Arist. 33; Philo, Spec. Leg. 2, 33; Jos., Bell. 2, 592, Ant. 14, 371) τὸ ν. τοῦ κήνσου *the coin for paying the tax* Mt 22: 19. Pl. (Herodian 1, 9, 7), as a symbol (Philo is also fond of the symbolic usage) νομίσματα δύο, ὁ μὲν θεοῦ, ὁ δὲ κόσμου *two coinages, one of God and the other of the world* of the believers and the unbelievers IMg 5: 2. M-M. B. 775.*

νομοδιδάσκαλος, ου, ὁ (only in Christian wr.; but νομοδιδάκτης in Plut., Cato Maj. 20, 4; Artem. 2, 29.—Synesius has νομοδιδάσκαλος Ep. 105 p. 248A in the general sense, and Ep. 4 p. 162A in specif. Jewish mng.) *teacher of the law* of teachers of false doctrine θέλοντες εἶναι νομοδιδάσκαλοι *they desire to be teachers of the law* 1 Ti 1: 7. The two other pass. in our lit. clearly refer to teachers of the Mosaic law: Gamaliel Ac 5: 34. W. Pharisees Lk 5: 17.—Schürer II⁴ 375. M-M.*

νομοθεσία, ας, ἡ lit. *lawgiving* (Pla., Aristot. et al.), then also its result, *legislation,* collect. *law* (Diod. S. 1, 95, 6; 12, 11, 4; Dionys. Hal. 10, 57f; 11, 6; Ps.-Lucian, Am. 22; Dit., Or. 326; 26 [II BC]; PLeipz. 35, 7; Wilcken, Chrest. 6, 11. Specif. of the Mosaic law 2 Macc 6: 23; 4 Macc 5: 35; 17: 16; Ep. Arist.; Aristob. in Euseb., Pr. Ev. 8, 10, 13; Philo, Mos. 2, 25; 31 al.; Jos., Ant. 6, 93 al.) w. other great gifts of God to Israel Ro 9: 4. M-M.*

νομοθετέω 1 aor. ἐνομοθέτησα; perf. pass. νενομοθέτημαι, ptc. νενομοθετημένος (Lysias, X., Pla. et al.; inscr., pap., LXX, Ep. Arist.; Aristob. in Euseb., Pr. Ev. 8, 10, 12; Philo, Joseph.)—1. *function as lawgiver, legis-*

late of Moses (Philo, Mos. 2, 9; Jos., C. Ap. 1, 284f, Ant. 1, 19) καλῶς ν. B 10: 11. Pass. *receive law(s)* ὁ λαὸς ἐπ᾽ αὐτῆς (i.e. τῆς Λευιτικῆς ἱερωσύνης) νενομοθέτηται *on the basis of it* (i.e. the Levit. priesthood) *the people received the law* Hb 7: 11 (νομοθετεῖν τινα is found only Ps.-Galen [HWagner, Galeni qui fertur libellus Εἰ ζῷον τὸ κατὰ γαστρός, Diss. Marburg '14] p. 17, 8 v.l. ἐνομοθέτησε Ἀθηναίοις ἡ Παλλάς and in LXX Ps 24: 8; 26: 11; 118: 33. Elsewh. in Gk. νομοθετεῖν τινι; but this constr. can also yield a personal passive: Kühner-G. I p. 124). 2. *ordain, enact,* or *found by law* pass. (Appian, Bell. Civ. 4, 2 §6 καινὴν ἀρχὴν νομοθετηθῆναι=a new magistracy is to be established by law; 4, 7 §27) (διαθήκη) ἥτις ἐπὶ κρείττοσιν ἐπαγγελίαις νενομοθέτηται (a *covenant*) *which has been (legally) enacted on the basis of better promises* Hb 8: 6 (cf. Philo, Migr. Abr. 91 τὰ ἐπ᾽ αὐτῇ νομοθετηθέντα). τὰ ὑπ᾽ αὐτοῦ νενομοθετημένα *what was legally ordained by him* (Dit., Or. 329, 13 [II BC] τὰ νενομοθετημένα ὑπὸ τ. βασιλέων.—τὰ νομοθετηθέντα: Philo, Spec. Leg. 1, 198 al.; Jos., Ant. 3, 317 [ὑπ᾽ αὐτοῦ]) 1 Cl 43: 1. M-M.*

νομοθέτης, ου, ὁ (since Antipho 5, 15; Thu. 8, 97, 2; Diod. S. 40, 3, 6 [of Μωσῆς]; inscr.; Nicol. Dam. in Jos., Ant. 1, 95; Ep. Arist., Philo; Jos., Ant. 1, 18; 20; 22 al.; LXX only Ps 9: 21) *lawgiver* of God (Dio Chrys. 19[36], 32; Maximus Tyr. 35, 8d νομοθέτης ὁ θεός; Philo, Sacr. Abel. 131, Op. M. 61.—In the Isisaret. v. Kyme 122, 4 Peek, Isis says: ἐγὼ νόμους ἀνθρώποις ἐθέμην κ. ἐνομοθέτησα) Js 4: 12. ἑαυτῶν γίνεσθε νομοθέται ἀγαθοί *be your own good lawgivers* B 21: 4 (cf. Diod. S. 20, 70, 4 ὁ θεὸς ὥσπερ ἀγαθὸς νομοθέτης).*

νόμος, ου, ὁ (Hes.+; inscr., pap., LXX, Ep. Arist., Aristob. in Euseb., Pr. Ev. 8, 10, 12; Philo, Joseph., Test. 12 Patr., Sib. Or., loanw. in rabb.—On the history of the word MPohlenz, Nomos: Philol. 97, '48, 135–42) *law.*
1. gener., of any law διὰ ποίου ν.; *by what kind of law?* Ro 3: 27. ν. τῆς πόλεως *the law of the city* enforced by the ruler of the city; the penalty for breaking it is banishment Hs 1: 5f. τοῖς ν. χρῆσθαι *observe the laws* s 1: 3; πείθεσθαι τοῖς ὡρισμένοις ν. *obey the established laws* Dg 5: 10; νικᾶν τοὺς ν. ibid. (νικάω 2a). Ro 7: 1f might refer to Roman law (BWeiss, Jülicher); more likely the Mosaic law is meant (s. 3 below).
2. *a rule* governing one's actions, *principle, norm* (Alcman [VII BC], fgm. 93 D.[2] of the tune that the bird sings; Ocellus [II BC] c. 49 Harder ['26] τῆς φύσεως νόμος; Appian, Basil. 1 §2 πολέμου ν., Bell. Civ. 5, 44 §186 ἐκ τοῦδε τοῦ σοῦ νόμου=under this rule of yours governing action; Polyaenus 5, 5, 3 ν. πόμπης; 7, 11, 6 ν. φιλίας; Sextus 123 τοῦ βίου νόμος) κατὰ νόμον ἐντολῆς σαρκίνης *in accordance w. the rule of an external commandment* Hb 7: 16. εὑρίσκω τὸν νόμον *I observe a principle* Ro 7: 21 (ν. as 'principle' Soph., Ant. 908). In general, Paul uses the expression νόμος (which dominates this context) in cases in which he prob. would have preferred another word: he speaks of the *principle* of action that obligates him to keep the moral law as ὁ νόμος τ. νοός μου vs. 23b (s. νοῦς 2). Engaged in a bitter struggle w. this νόμος there is a ἕτερος νόμος which, in contrast to the νοῦς, dwells ἐν τοῖς μέλεσίν μου *in my* (physical) *members* vs. 23a, and hence is a νόμος τῆς ἁμαρτίας vs. 23c or a νόμος τ. ἁμαρτίας καὶ τ. θανάτου 8: 2b.
3. esp. of the law, which Moses received from God (Diod. S. 1, 94, 1; 2: the pagan lawgiver Mneves receives the law from Hermes, Minos from Zeus, Lycurgus from Apollo, Zarathustra from the ἀγαθὸς δαίμων, Zalmoxis from Hestia; παρὰ δὲ τοῖς Ἰουδαίοις, Μωϋσῆς receives

the law from the Ἰαὼ ἐπικαλούμενος θεός). ὁ ν. Μωϋσέως Lk 2: 22; J 7: 23; Ac 15: 5. ν. Μωϋσέως Ac 13: 38; Hb 10: 28. Also ὁ ν. κυρίου Lk 2: 39. ὁ ν. τοῦ θεοῦ Mt 15: 6 v.l. ὁ ν. ἡμῶν, ὑμῶν, αὐτῶν etc. J 18: 31; 19: 7b v.l. (cf. Jos., Ant. 7, 131); Ac 24: 6 t.r.; 25: 8; ὁ πατρῷος ν. 22: 3. Since the law and its observance are the central point of Jewish piety, ὁ νόμος can almost come to mean *(Jewish) religion* Ac 23: 29; ν. ὁ καθ᾽ ὑμᾶς 18: 15.—Abs., without further qualification ὁ ν. Mt 22: 36; 23: 23; Lk 2: 27; J 1: 17; Ac 6: 13; 7: 53; 21: 20, 28; Ro 2: 15 (Diod. S. 1, 94, 1 ν. ἔγγραπτος), 18, 23b, 26; 4: 15a; 7: 1b, 4–7, 12, 14, 16; 8: 3f; 1 Cor 15: 56; Gal 3: 12f, 17, 19, 21a, 24; 5: 3, 14; 1 Ti 1: 8 (GRudberg, Coniect. Neot. 7, '42, 15); Hb 7: 19 (s. Windisch, Hdb. exc. ad loc.), 28; 10: 1; κατὰ τὸν ν. *according to the* (Mosaic) *law* (Jos., Ant. 14, 173; 15, 51 al.) Ac 22: 12; 23: 3; Hb 7: 5; 9: 22. παρὰ τ. νόμον *contrary to the law* (Jos., Ant. 17, 151, C. Ap. 2, 219) Ac 18: 13.—νόμος without the art. in the same sense (on the attempt, beginning w. Origen, In Ep. ad Rom. 3: 7 ed. Lomm. VI 201, to establish a difference in mng. betw. Paul's use of ὁ νόμος and νόμος cf. W-S. §19, 13h; Bl-D. §258, 2; Rob. 796; Mlt.-Turner 177; Grafe [s. below] 7–11) Ro 2: 13a, b, 17, 25a; 3: 31a, b; 5: 13, 20; 7: 1a (s. 1 above); Gal 2: 19b; 5: 23 (JDRobb, ET 56, '45, 279f: κατὰ —νόμος fr. Aristot., Politics 1284a). δικαίῳ νόμος οὐ κεῖται, ἀνόμοις δὲ . . . 1 Ti 1: 9 (in Pla., Polit. and in Stoic thought the wise man needed no commandment [Stoic. III 519], the bad man did; MPohlenz, Stoa '48; '49 I 133; II 75). Used w. prepositions: ἐκ ν. Ro 4: 14; 10: 5; Gal 3: 18, 21c (v.l. ἐν ν.); Phil 3: 9 (ἐκ νόμου can also mean *corresponding to* or *in conformity with the law*: PRev. 15, 11 ἐκ τῶν νόμων). διὰ νόμου Ro 2: 12b; 3: 20b; 4: 13; 7: 7b; Gal 2: 19a, 21; ἐν ν. Ro 2: 12a, 23; Gal 3: 11, 21c v.l.; Phil 3: 6. κατὰ νόμον 3: 5; Hb 8: 4; 10: 8 (make an offering κατὰ νόμον as Arrian, Anab. 2, 26, 4; 5, 8, 2); χωρὶς ν. Ro 3: 21a; 7: 8f; ἄχρι ν. 5: 13a. ὑπὸ νόμον 6: 14f; 1 Cor 9: 20; Gal 3: 23; 4: 4f, 21a; 5: 18.—Dependent on an anarthrous noun παραβάτης νόμου *a law-breaker* Ro 2: 25b; Js 2: 11. ποιητὴς ν. *one who keeps the law* 4: 11d; τέλος ν. *the end of the law* Ro 10: 4 (RBultmann and HSchlier, Christus des Ges. Ende '40). πλήρωμα ν. *fulfilment of the law* 13: 10. ν. μετάθεσις *a change in the law* Hb 7: 12. ἔργα ν. Ro 3: 20a, 28; 9: 32 t.r.; Gal 2: 16; 3: 2, 5, 10a.—(ὁ) ν. (τοῦ) θεοῦ Ro 7: 22, 25a; 8: 7 because it was given by God and accords w. his will. Imperishable Mt 5: 18; Lk 16: 17 (cf. Bar 4: 1; Philo, Mos. 2, 14; Jos., C. Ap. 2, 277).—Used w. verbs, w. or without the art.: πληροῦν ν. *fulfill the law* Ro 13: 8; pass. Gal 5: 14. πληροῦν τὸ δικαίωμα τοῦ ν. *fulfill the requirement of the law* Ro 8: 4. φυλάσσειν (τὸν) ν. *observe the law* Ac 21: 24; Gal 6: 13. τὰ δικαιώματα τοῦ ν. φυλάσσειν *observe the precepts of the law* Ro 2: 26; πράσσειν ν. 2: 25a. ποιεῖν τὸν ν. J 7: 19b; Gal 5: 3, τὸν ν. τηρεῖν Js 2: 10. τὸν ν. τελεῖν Ro 2: 27. κατὰ ν. Ἰουδαϊσμὸν ζῆν IMg 8: 1 is prob. a textual error (Pearson, Lghtf., Funk, Bihlmeyer, Hilgenfeld; Zahn, Ign. v. Ant. 1873 p. 354, 1 [differently in the edition] all omit νόμον as a gloss; this is supported by the Latin versions; s. Hdb. ad loc.). τὰ τοῦ ν. ποιεῖν *carry out the requirements of the law* Ro 2: 14b (FFlückiger, ThZ 8, '52, 17–42).—Pl. διδοὺς νόμους μου εἰς τὴν διάνοιαν αὐτῶν Hb 8: 10; cf. 10: 16 (both Jer 38: 33).—Of an individual stipulation of the law ὁ νόμος τοῦ ἀνδρός *the law insofar as it concerns the husband* (Aristot., fgm. 184 R. νόμοι ἀνδρὸς καὶ γαμετῆς.—Dit., Syll.[3] 1198, 14 κατὰ τὸν νόμον τῶν ἐρανιστῶν; Num 9: 12 ὁ ν. τοῦ πάσχα; Philo, Sobr. 49 ὁ ν. τῆς λέπρας) Ro 7: 2b; cf. δέδεται νόμῳ vs. 2a; 1 Cor 7: 39 t.r.—The law is personified, as it were (Demosth. 43, 59; Aeschin. 1, 18; Herm. Wr. 12, 4 [the law of punishment]; Inschr. v. Magn. 92a, 11 ὁ ν. συντάσσει; b, 16 ὁ ν. ἀγορεύει; Jos., Ant. 3, 274) J 7: 51; Ro 3: 19.

4. of a collection of holy writings precious to the Jews— **a.** in the strict sense the law= the Pentateuch, the work of Moses the lawgiver (Diod. S. 40, 3, 6 προσγέγραπται τοῖς νόμοις ἐπὶ τελευτῆς ὅτι Μωσῆς ἀκούσας τοῦ θεοῦ τάδε λέγει τ. Ἰουδαίοις= at the end of the laws this is appended: this is what Moses heard from God and is telling to the Jews) τὸ βιβλίον τοῦ νόμου Gal 3: 10b (cf. Dt 27: 26). Also simply ὁ νόμος (Jos., Bell. 7, 162 ὁ ν. or 2, 229 ὁ ἱερὸς ν. of the holy book in a concrete sense) Mt 12: 5 (Num 28: 9f is meant); J 8: 5; 1 Cor 9: 8 (cf. Dt 25: 4); 14: 34 (cf. Gen 3: 16); Gal 4: 21b (the story of Abraham); Hb 9: 19. ὁ ν. ὁ ὑμέτερος J 8: 17 (cf. Jos., Bell. 5, 402). ἐν Μωϋσέως νόμῳ γέγραπται 1 Cor 9: 9. καθὼς γέγραπται ἐν νόμῳ κυρίου Lk 2: 23 (γέγραπται ἐν νόμῳ as Athen. 6, 27 p. 235c; Inschr. v. Magn. 52, 35 [III bc]). ἔγραψεν Μωϋσῆς ἐν τῷ νόμῳ J 1: 45 (cf. Cercidas [III bc], fgm. 1 l. 18f Diehl² καὶ τοῦθ᾽ Ὅμηρος εἶπεν ἐν Ἰλιάδι).—The Holy Scriptures of the Jews are referred to as a whole by the phrase ὁ ν. καὶ οἱ προφῆται the law (= הַתּוֹרָה) and the prophets (הַנְּבִיאִים) Mt 5: 17; 7: 12; 11: 13; 22: 40; Lk 16: 16; Ac 13: 15; 24: 14; 28: 23; Ro 3: 21b; cf. Dg 11: 6; J 1: 45. τὰ γεγραμμένα ἐν τῷ ν. Μωϋσέως καὶ τοῖς προφήταις καὶ ψαλμοῖς Lk 24: 44.

b. in the wider sense= Holy Scripture gener., on the principle that the most authoritative part gives its name to the whole: J 10: 34 (Ps 81: 6); 12: 34 (Ps 109: 4; Is 9: 6; Da 7: 14); 15: 25 (Ps 34: 19; 68: 5); 1 Cor 14: 21 (Is 28: 11f); Ro 3: 19 (preceded by a cluster of quotations fr. Psalms and prophets).—Mt 5: 18; Lk 10: 26; 16: 17; J 7: 49. JHänel, Der Schriftbegriff Jesu '19; OMichel, Pls u. s. Bibel '29.

5. fig. of Christianity as a 'new law': ὁ καινὸς ν. τοῦ κυρίου ἡμῶν Ἰησοῦ Χριστοῦ B 2: 6; in brief ν. Ἰησοῦ Χριστοῦ IMg 2. Beginnings of this terminology as early as Paul: ὁ ν. τοῦ Χριστοῦ Gal 6: 2. The gospel is a νόμος πίστεως a law requiring faith Ro 3: 27b (FGerhard, ThZ 10, '54, 401-17) or ὁ ν. τοῦ πνεύματος τῆς ζωῆς ἐν Χρ. Ἰ. the law of the spirit of life in Chr. J. 8: 2a. In the same sense Js speaks of the ν. βασιλικός (s. βασιλικός) 2: 8 or ν. ἐλευθερίας vs. 12 (λόγος ἐλ. 𝔓⁷⁴), ν. τέλειος ὁ τῆς ἐλευθερίας 1: 25 (the association w. IQS 10, 6; 8; 11 made by EStauffer, ThLZ 77, '52, 527-32, is rejected by SNötscher, Biblica 34, '53, 193f); also, where the context makes the mng. unmistakable, simply ὁ νόμος 2: 9 (cf. LAllevi, Scuola Cattol. 67, '39, 529-42).—Hermas too, who in part interprets Jewish tradition as referring to the Christians, sees the gospel as a law. He says of Christ δοὺς αὐτοῖς (i.e. the believers) τὸν ν., ὃν ἔλαβε παρὰ τοῦ πατρὸς αὐτοῦ s 5, 6, 3, cf. s 8, 3, 3. Or he sees in the υἱὸς θεοῦ κηρυχθεὶς εἰς τὰ πέρατα τῆς γῆς, i.e. the preaching about the Son of God to the ends of the earth, the νόμος θεοῦ ὁ δοθεὶς εἰς ὅλον. τ. κόσμον s 8, 3, 2. Similarly to be understood are τηρεῖν τὸν ν. 8, 3, 4. ὑπὲρ τοῦ ν. παθεῖν 8, 3, 6. ὑπὲρ τοῦ ν. θλίβεσθαι 8, 3, 7. ἀρνησάμενοι τὸν νόμον ibid. JMeinhold, Jesus u. das AT 1896; MKähler, Jesus u. das AT² 1896; AKlöpper, Z. Stellung Jesu gegenüber d. Mos. Gesetz, Mt 5: 17-48: ZWTh 39, 1896, 1-23; EKlostermann, Jesu Stellung z. AT '04; AvHarnack, Hat Jesus das atl. Gesetz abgeschafft?: Aus Wissenschaft u. Leben II '11, 225-36, SAB '12, 184-207; KBenz, D. Stellung Jesu zum atl. Gesetz '14; MGoguel, RHPhr 7, '27, 160ff; BWBacon, Jesus and the Law: JBL 47, '28, 203-31; BHBranscomb, Jes. and the Law of Moses '30; WGKümmel, Jes. u. d. jüd. Traditionsged.: ZNW 33, '34, 105-30; JHempel, D. synopt. Jesus u. d. AT: ZAW 56, '38, 1-34;

JJervell, HTR 64, '71, 21-36 (Lk-Ac).—EGrafe, D. paulin. Lehre vom Gesetz² 1893; HCremer, D. paulin. Rechtfertigungslehre 1896, 84ff; 363ff; FSieffert, D. Entwicklungslinie d. paul. Gesetzeslehre: BWeiss-Festschr. 1897, 332-57; WSlaten, The Qualitative Use of νόμος in the Pauline Ep.: AJTh 23, '19, 213ff; HMosbech, Pls' Laere om Loven: Teolog. Tidsskrift IV 3, '22, 108-37; 177-221; EDBurton, ICC, Gal '21, 443-60; PFeine, Theol. des NT⁶ '34, 208-15 (lit.); PBenoit, La Loi et la Croix d'après S. Paul (Ro 7: 7-8: 4): RB 47, '38, 481-509; ChMaurer, D. Gesetzeslehre des Pls '41; PBläser, D. Gesetz b. Pls '41; BReicke, JBL 70, '51, 259-76; GBornkamm, Das Ende d. Gesetzes '63.—Dodd 25-41; HKleinknecht u. WGutbrod, TW IV 1016-84: νόμος and related words. M-M. B. 1358; 1419; 1421.

νοσέω (Aeschyl., Hdt.+; Dit., Syll.³ 943, 5; pap.) be sick, ailing; in our lit. only fig. (X., Mem. 3, 5, 18 al.; Diod. S. 11, 86, 3; Heraclit. Sto. 69 p. 89, 20; Wsd 17: 8; Philo, Leg. All. 3, 211; Jos., Ant. 16, 244; 18, 25) νοσεῖν περί τι be ailing with, have a morbid craving for someth. (Plut., Mor. 546f. ν. περὶ δόξαν) περὶ ζητήσεις καὶ λογομαχίας (s. ζήτησις) 1 Ti 6: 4. M-M.*

νόσημα, ατος, τό (trag., Thu.+; Chio, Ep. 14, 2; Artem. 3, 51; Maspéro 159, 18; Philo; Jos., Ant. 8, 45, C. Ap. 1, 282) disease ᾧ δήποτε κατείχετο νοσήματι no matter what disease he had J 5: 4 t.r.*

νόσος, ου, ἡ (Hom.+; inscr., pap., LXX; Ep. Arist. 233; Philo; Jos., Ant. 12, 279; Test. 12 Patr.) disease, illness.

1. lit. Ac 19: 12; (w. μαλακία θεραπεύειν πᾶσαν ν. Mt 4: 23; 9: 35; 10: 1 (cf. Jos., Bell. 5, 383 πάσῃ ν.). νόσους θεραπεύειν Lk 9: 1. W. βάσανοι Mt 4: 24. ἐθεράπευσεν πολλοὺς κακῶς ἔχοντας ποικίλαις ν. he healed many who were sick w. various diseases Mk 1: 34. ἀσθενοῦντες νόσοις ποικίλαις Lk 4: 40. ἐθεράπευσεν πολλοὺς ἀπὸ νόσων he healed many people of their illnesses 7: 21. Pass. ἰαθῆναι ἀπὸ τῶν ν. 6: 18. As a symbol βαστάζειν τὰς ν. τινός bear someone's diseases (after Is 53: 4 where, however, LXX does not have νόσος) Mt 8: 17; IPol 1: 3.

2. fig. of vices (Bias in Diog. L. 1, 86 νόσος ψυχῆς of a defect of character; Herm. Wr. 12, 3 ἀθεότης; oft. Philo) ὁ μοιχὸς . . . τῇ ἰδίᾳ ν. τὸ ἱκανὸν ποιεῖ the adulterer gives satisfaction to his own diseased inclination Hs 6, 5, 5.—AOepke, TW IV 1084-91: νόσος and related words. M-M.*

νοσσιά, ᾶς, ἡ (H.Gk. for class. νεοσσιά, s. Bl-D. §31, 3 w. app.; Mlt.-H. 92; Thackeray p. 98; Lob. on Phryn. p. 207).

1. nest (this mng. Hdt., Aristoph.+; LXX) νοσσιᾶς ἀφῃρημένης after their nest is robbed B 11: 3.—**2.** brood (Lycurgus the orator [IV bc] 132; Dt 32: 11) Lk 13: 34. M-M.*

νοσσίον, ου, τό (H.Gk. for νεοσσίον; cf. νοσσιά) the young of a bird Mt 23: 37 (the word, in the form νεοττίον Aristoph.+, as νοσσίον also Ps 83: 4). B 175.*

νοσσός, οῦ, ὁ (H.Gk. for νεοσσός [cf. νοσσιά and Jos., C. Ap. 2, 213 νεοττός], as AD et al. read in Lk) the young of a bird (as νεοσσός Hom.+; LXX) B 11: 3 (cf. Is 16: 2). δύο νοσσοὺς περιστερῶν two young doves Lk 2: 24 (Lev 12: 8; 14: 22.—Soranus p. 72, 15 νεοσσοὺς περιστερῶν. —νοσσοὶ of the young of doves: Sb 7814, 15 [256 AD]). M-M.*

νοσφίζω (Hom.+) in our lit. only mid.; 1 aor. ἐνοσφισάμην put aside for oneself, misappropriate (X., Cyr. 4, 2,

42; Polyb. 10, 16, 6; Plut., Lucull. 37, 2, Aristid. 4, 3; Jos., Ant. 4, 274; Dit., Syll.³ 993, 21; PRyl. 116, 10; 2 Macc 4: 32) ἀπό τινος *some of someth.* (PSI 442, 4 [III BC]; Josh 7: 1.—ἔκ τινος Athen. 6 p. 234A) Philo, Mos. 1, 253) ἐνοσφίσατο ἀπὸ τῆς τιμῆς *he misappropriated some of the purchase price* Ac 5: 2f (cf. with this account Josh 7: 1, 19-26. Diod. S. 5, 34, 3: a lot-holder who embezzles [νοσφίζεσθαι] and holds back some of the crops which have been declared common property [κοινοποιεῖσθαι] is subject to the death penalty among the Vaccaei, a Celtic tribe). μηδὲν ὅλως ν. εἰς ἐπιθυμίαν πονηράν keep back or *misappropriate nothing at all for the satisfaction of one's base desire* Hs 9, 25, 2. Abs. (inscr. [I AD]: ΕΛΛΗ-ΝΙΚΑ 1, '28, p. 18 l. 13; PPetr. III 56[b], 10; 12) Tit 2: 10. M-M.*

νότος, ου, ὁ—1. *south wind, southwest wind* (Hom.+; LXX; Philo, Mos. 1, 120.—Appian, Bell. Civ. 5, 98 §410 it is the southwest wind beyond doubt) ὑποπνεύσαντος νότου Ac 27: 13 (s. ὑποπνέω). ἐπιγενομένου νότου *when the southwest wind came up* 28: 13. Bringing heat Lk 12: 55 (cf. Jos., Bell. 7, 318 νότος πνεύσας).

2. *south* (Soph.; Hdt. 6, 139 al.; Dit., Syll.³ 691, 18; POxy. 255, 7; PTebt. 342, 8; LXX; En. 26, 2; Jos., Bell. 5, 145, Ant. 8, 319) ἀπὸ βορρᾶ καὶ ν. *from north and south* (s. βορρᾶς) Lk 13: 29. ἀπὸ νότου *on the south* (ἀπό II 1) Rv 21: 13.

3. *a country in the south* (Ps 125: 4 ἐν τῷ νότῳ) βασίλισσα νότου *the queen of the south* (Sheba) Mt 12: 42; Lk 11: 31. M-M. B. 873.*

νουθεσία, ας, ἡ (Aristoph., Ran. 1009; Diod. S. 15, 7, 1; BGU 613, 21; PAmh. 84, 21; Wsd 16: 6; Philo, Mos. 1, 119 al.; Jos., Ant. 3, 311; Lob. on Phryn. 512) *admonition, instruction, warning* Tit 3: 10. W. παιδεία (as Philo, Deus Imm. 54) Eph 6: 4 (νουθ. κυρίου=Christian instruction). γράφειν πρὸς ν. τινός *write for the instruction of someone* 1 Cor 10: 11 (πρὸς ν. τινός as Philo, Exs. 133). Beside πίστις, ὑπομονή, μακροθυμία IEph 3: 1. M-M.*

νουθετέω fut. νουθετήσω; 1 aor. ἐνουθέτησα (trag.+; PGrenf. II 93, 3; LXX; Philo; Jos., Ant. 4, 260; 20, 162; Test. Jos. 6: 8) *admonish, warn, instruct* w. acc. of the pers. (Dio Chrys. 56[73], 10; Sb 6263, 26) Ac 20: 31; 1 Cor 4: 14 (Wsd 11: 10 τούτους ὡς πατὴρ νουθετῶν; Jos., Bell. 1, 481, Ant, 3, 311); Col 1: 28; 3: 16 (in the last two pass. w. διδάσκειν, as Pla., Leg. 8 p. 845B; Philo, Decal.); 1 Th 5: 12; 2 Th 3: 15; Tit 1: 11 v.l.; 1 Cl 7: 1; 2 Cl 19: 2. ἀλλήλους Ro 15: 14; 2 Cl 17: 2. τοὺς ἀτάκτους *warn the idle* 1 Th 5: 14 (*punish* is also possible: Plut., Sertor. 19, 11 πληγαῖς ν.). τὸν οἶκον Hv 1, 3, 1; also τὰ τέκνα v 1, 3, 2. τὰς χήρας καὶ τοὺς ὀρφανούς v 2, 4, 3. ἁμαρτάνοντας m 8: 10. Pass. νουθετεῖσθαι ὑπό τινος (Philo, Deus Imm. 134; Jos., Ant. 20, 162a) 2 Cl 17: 3; Hv 3, 5, 4.—JBehm, TW IV 1013-16. M-M.*

νουθέτημα, ατος, τό (Aeschyl.+) *admonition, discipline* 1 Cl 56: 6 (Job 5: 17).*

νουθέτησις, εως, ἡ (since Eupolis Com. [V BC] 66; Pla.; Diod. S. 1, 70, 8; 1, 77, 7; 3, 33, 5; Iambl., Vi. Pyth. 33, 231; Jdth 8: 27; Pr 2: 2) *admonition, warning, reproof* ἡ ν., ἣν ποιούμεθα εἰς ἀλλήλους *the reproof which we address to each other* 1 Cl 56: 2.*

νουμηνία s. νεομηνία.

νουνεχῶς adv. (Aristot. 1436b, 33 νουνεχῶς κ. δικαίως; Polyb. 1, 83, 3; 2, 13, 1; 5, 88, 2; Sib. Or. 1, 7) *wisely, thoughtfully* ἀποκρίνεσθαι Mk 12: 34. M-M.*

νοῦς, νοός, νοΐ, νοῦν, ὁ (contracted fr. νόος.—Hom.+; pap., LXX; Ep. Arist. 276; Philo [oft.]; Jos., Ant. 3, 65, Vi. 122 al.; Test. 12 Patr.; Sib. Or. 3, 574.—On its declension cf. Bl-D. §52; W-S. §8, 11; Mlt.-H. 127; 142) in the NT only in Pauline lit. except for Lk 24: 45; Rv 13: 18; 17: 9. Denotes the faculty of physical and intellectual perception, then also the power to arrive at moral judgments.

1. *the understanding, the mind* as the faculty of thinking διανοίγειν τὸν ν. τινος *open someone's mind* Lk 24: 45. ὁ ἔχων νοῦν *whoever has understanding* Rv 13: 18 (ν. ἔχειν as Aristoph., Equ. 482; Hyperid. 3, 23; Dio Chrys. 17[34], 39; 23[40], 26; Ael. Aristid. 23, 12 K.=42 p. 771 D.; Ep. Arist. 276; Philo, Mos. 1, 141; Test. Reub. 3: 8). ὧδε ὁ ν. ὁ ἔχων σοφίαν *here is* (i.e. *this calls for*) *a mind with wisdom* 17: 9. νοῦν διδόναι *grant understanding* Dg 10: 2. Also παρέχειν νοῦν 11: 5. ὁ σοφίαν καὶ νοῦν θέμενος ἐν ἡμῖν τῶν κρυφίων αὐτοῦ *who has placed in us wisdom and understanding of his secrets* B 6: 10. ποικίλος τῇ φρονήσει καὶ τῷ ν. *diverse in thought and understanding* Hs 9, 17, 2a; cf. b. Of the peace of God ἡ ὑπερέχουσα πάντα ν. *which surpasses all power of thought* Phil 4: 7. In contrast to the divine Pneuma which inspires the 'speaker in tongues': ὁ ν. μου ἄκαρπός ἐστιν *my mind is unfruitful*, because it remains inactive during the glossolalia 1 Cor 14: 14. προσεύχεσθαι τῷ ν. (opp. τῷ πνεύματι.—νόῳ as instrumental dat. as Pind., Pyth. 1, 40) *pray w. the understanding* vs. 15a; ψάλλειν τῷ ν. vs. 15b. θέλω πέντε λόγους τῷ ν. μου λαλῆσαι *I would rather speak five words w. my understanding* vs. 19 (cf. 1QS 10, 9).—As a designation of Christ (cf. Sib. Or. 8, 284) in a long series of expressions (w. φῶς) Dg 9: 6 (cf. Epict. 2, 8, 2 τίς οὖν οὐσία θεοῦ; νοῦς, ἐπιστήμη, λόγος ὀρθός. The god Νοῦς in the Herm. Wr.: Rtzst., Mysterienrel.³ 47 al.; JKroll, D. Lehren des Hermes Trismegistos '14, 10ff; 60ff al.; PGM 5, 465 ὁ μέγας Νοῦς).—Also the state of *sensibleness, composure* in contrast to the disturbances of soul brought about by the expectation of the Parousia, σαλευθῆναι ἀπὸ τοῦ νοός *be shaken, and thereby lose your calmness of mind* 2 Th 2: 2.

2. *the mind, intellect* as the side of life contrasted w. physical existence, the higher, mental part of the natural man which initiates his thoughts and plans (Apollonius of Tyana [I AD] in Euseb., Pr. Ev. 4, 13): ὁ νόμος τοῦ νοός μου *the law of my intellect* (νοῦς=ὁ ἔσω ἄνθρωπος vs. 22 v.l.) Ro 7: 23. (Opp. σάρξ) τῷ ν. δουλεύειν νόμῳ θεοῦ *serve the law of God w. one's intellect* vs. 25.

3. *mind, attitude, way of thinking* as the sum total of the whole mental and moral state of being

a. as possessed by every person μεταμορφοῦσθαι τῇ ἀνακαινώσει τοῦ ν. *be transformed by the renewing of the mind*, which comes about when the Christian has his natural νοῦς penetrated and transformed by the Spirit which he received at baptism Ro 12: 2 (s. Ltzm., Hdb. ad loc.). W. the same sense ἀνανεοῦσθαι τῷ πνεύματι τοῦ ν. ὑμῶν *you must adopt a new attitude of mind* Eph 4: 23 (the piling up of synonyms is a distinctive feature of Eph; s. MDibelius, Hdb. exc. on Eph 1: 14). Of the Gentiles παρέδωκεν αὐτοὺς ὁ θεὸς εἰς ἀδόκιμον ν. *God abandoned them to depraved thoughts* Ro 1: 28. τὰ ἔθνη περιπατεῖ ἐν ματαιότητι τοῦ ν. αὐτῶν *the heathen live w. their minds fixed on futile things* Eph 4: 17. Of one who is in error: εἰκῆ φυσιούμενος ὑπὸ τοῦ ν. τῆς σαρκὸς αὐτοῦ *groundlessly conceited* (lit. 'puffed up') *by his mind, fixed on purely physical things* Col 2: 18. κατεφθαρμένος τὸν ν. *with depraved mind* 2 Ti 3: 8; also διεφθαρμένος τὸν ν. 1 Ti 6: 5 (Bl-D. §159, 3; Rob. 486). μεμίανται αὐτῶν καὶ ὁ ν. καὶ ἡ συνείδησις *their minds and consciences are unclean* Tit 1: 15.

b. specif. of the Christian *attitude* or *way of thinking* κατηρτισμένοι ἐν τῷ αὐτῷ νοΐ 1 Cor 1: 10. Through baptism men receive μίαν φρόνησιν καὶ ἕνα νοῦν Hs 9, 17, 4; cf. 9, 18, 4. εἰς νοῦς, μία ἐλπίς is to rule in the church IMg 7: 1.

4. also the result of thinking *mind, thought, opinion, decree* (Hom. + of gods and men) ἕκαστος ἐν τῷ ἰδίῳ ν. πληροφορείσθω *everyone is to be fully convinced in his own mind* Ro 14: 5. τίς γὰρ ἔγνω νοῦν κυρίου; *who has known the Lord's thoughts?* (Is 40: 13) 11: 34; 1 Cor 2: 16a. When Paul continues in the latter passage vs. 16b w. ἡμεῖς νοῦν Χριστοῦ ἔχομεν, he is using the scriptural word νοῦς to denote what he usu. calls πνεῦμα (vs. 14f). He can do this because his νοῦς (since he is a 'pneumatic' person) is filled w. the Spirit (s. above 3a), so that in his case the two are interchangeable. Such a νοῦς is impossible for a 'psychic' person. —OMoe, Vernunft u. Geist im NT: ZsystTh 11, '34, 351–91; RJewett, Paul's Anthropological Terms, '71, 358–90. S. καρδία, end; νοέω, end. M-M. B. 1198.*

Νυμφᾶν Col 4: 15 is in any case an accusative form; it is not clear whether it is from the feminine name Νύμφα, as =Att. Νύμφη, ης (so PHib. 94, 8 [III BC]; CWessely, Studien z. Paläogr. u. Papyruskunde 10, '10, no. 113, 2 [II AD]) *Nympha*, or from the masculine name Νυμφᾶς, ᾶ (CIG I 269, 15; 1240, 18f; prob. a short form for Νυμφόδωρος) *Nymphas*. The choice betw. the two depends on whether one prefers to read αὐτῆς with B, αὐτῶν with אACP 33, or αὐτοῦ with DGKL in connection w. τὴν κατ' οἶκον ἐκκλησίαν.—Bl-D. §125, 1; Mlt. 48. M-M.*

νύμφη, ης, ἡ (Hom. +; inscr., pap., LXX, Philo, Joseph.; Test. Jud. 13: 3; loanw. in rabb.).

1. *bride* (Diod. S. 5, 2, 3) Rv 21: 2. W. νυμφίος (q.v.) Mt 25: 1 t.r. (cf. FCBurkitt, JTS 30, '29, 267–70); J 3: 29; Rv 18: 23 (Jer 7: 34; 16: 9 al.). Of the bride of the Lamb Rv 21: 9; cf. 22: 17 (CChavasse, The Bride of Christ '40).—It can also be *the newly married woman* (Istros [III BC]: no. 334 fgm. 55 Jac.).

2. *daughter-in-law* (Gen 11: 31; 38: 11; Ruth 1: 6, 22 al.; Philo, Leg. All. 3, 74; Jos., Ant. 5, 321; Sib. Or. 1, 206; 3, 827.—='daughter' in inscr. fr. Asia Minor: ENachmanson, Eranos 9, '09, 78) Mt 10: 35; Lk 12: 53 (for both cf. Mi 7: 6).—RABatey, NT Nuptial Imagery '71; JoachJeremias, TW IV 1092–9: νύμφη and related words. M-M. B. 125.*

νυμφίος, ου, ὁ (Hom. +; Dit., Syll.³ 1024, 33f [c. 200 BC]; PRainer 30, 37; Sb 10; LXX) *bridegroom* Mt 9: 15b, c; 25: 1, 5f, 10 (on the coming of the bridegroom, who outshines all other mortals, cf. Sappho 123 Diehl²); Mk 2: 19f; Lk 5: 34f; J 2: 9; 3: 29a, c; Rv 18: 23 (w. νύμφη [q.v. 1] as Diod. S. 5, 18, 1; Philo, Spec. Leg. 1, 110; Jos., Bell. 6, 301). ὁ φίλος τοῦ ν. (1 Macc 9: 39; cf. Jos., Ant. 13, 20) the friend of the bridegroom (שׁוֹשְׁבִין) was a go-between in arranging the marriage, and then had a prominent place in the wedding festivities J 3: 29b. οἱ υἱοὶ τοῦ νυμφίου Mt 9: 15a v.l. is surely not the original rdg. (Jülicher, Gleichn. 180f). M-M.*

νυμφών, ῶνος, ὁ—1. *wedding hall* Mt 22: 10.—2. *bridal chamber* (Paus. 2, 11, 3; Heliod. 7, 8, 3; PLond. 964, 19; Tob 6: 14, 17; Clem. of Alex., Exc. ex Theod. §64f) Hv 4, 2, 1. οἱ υἱοὶ τοῦ νυμφῶνος (gen. as Ps 149: 2; 1 Macc 4: 2 οἱ υἱοὶ τῆς Ἄκρας) *the bridegroom's attendants*, that

group of the wedding guests who stood closest to the groom and played an essential part in the wedding ceremony Mt 9: 15; Mk 2: 19; Lk 5: 34 (cf. FWLewis, ET 24, '13, 285).—Billerb. I 500–18. M-M.*

νῦν adv. of time (Hom. +; inscr., pap., LXX, En., Ep. Arist., Philo, Joseph.) *now*.

1. lit., of time—**a.** *now, at the present time* of the immediate present, designating both a point of time as well as its extent. The verbs w. which it is used are found

α. in the pres. Lk 16: 25; J 4: 18; 9: 21; 16: 29; Ac 7: 4; 2 Cor 13: 2; Gal 1: 23; 1 Pt 3: 21; 1 J 3: 2 and oft.

β. in the perf., when it has pres. mng. ἔρχεται ὥρα καὶ ν. ἐλήλυθεν *it is now here* J 16: 32 t.r.; ν. ἐγνώκαμεν *now we know* 8: 52; cf. 17: 7. ν. οἶδα Ac 12: 11. ν. ἡ ψυχή μου τετάρακται J 12: 27. Cf. 1 J 2: 18.

γ. in the aor., mostly in contrast to the past, denoting that an action or condition is beginning in the present: νῦν ἐδοξάσθη ὁ υἱὸς τοῦ ἀνθρώπου *now the glorification of the Son of Man has begun* J 13: 31. ν. τὴν καταλλαγὴν ἐλάβομεν *we have now entered into the reconciliation* Ro 5: 11. οὗτοι ν. ἠπείθησαν *they have now become disobedient* 11: 31. ν. ἀπεκαλύφθη τοῖς ἁγίοις ἀποστόλοις *now it has been revealed to the holy apostles* Eph 3: 5; cf. vs. 10; 2 Ti 1: 10. ἃ ν. ἀνηγγέλη ὑμῖν *that which is now proclaimed to you* 1 Pt 1: 12. Cf. Ro 5: 9; 16: 26; 1 Pt 2: 10b, 25.—More rarely in contrast to the future: οὐ δύνασαί μοι νῦν ἀκολουθῆσαι, ἀκολουθήσεις δὲ ὕστερον J 13: 36 (νῦν–ὕστερον as Jos., Ant. 4, 295). ἵνα ν. ἔλθῃ· ἐλεύσεται δέ ι 1 Cor 16: 12. ἐὰν μὴ λάβῃ . . . ν., explained by ἐν τῷ καιρῷ τούτῳ Mk 10: 30.

δ. in the imperative, to denote that the order or request is to be complied w. at once; ν. comes after the imper. (Bl-D. §474, 3): καταβάτω ν. ἀπὸ τοῦ σταυροῦ *now let him come down from the cross* Mt 27: 42; Mk 15: 32. ῥυσάσθω ν. *let him deliver (him)* Mt 27: 43. ἀντλήσατε ν. *now draw (some out)* J 2: 8.

b. of time shortly before or shortly after the immediate pres.: ν. ἠκούσατε Mt 26: 65. ν. ἐζήτουν σε λιθάσαι *they were just now trying to stone you* J 11: 8. Cf. 21: 10; Ac 7: 52.—(Soon) *now* (Epict. 3, 24, 94) ν. ἀπολύεις τὸν δοῦλόν σου Lk 2: 29. Cf. J 12: 31a, b; 16: 5; Phil 1: 20.

c. νῦν used w. other particles: ἀλλὰ νῦν *but now* Lk 22: 36; 2 Cor 5: 16b. ἀλλὰ καὶ ν. J 11: 22 v.l.; ἄρα ν. *so or thus now* Ro 8: 1. ν. γάρ *for now* 13: 11. ν. δέ *but now* 1 Cor 5: 17: 13; Col 1: 26; Hb 2: 8. οὐδὲ ἔτι ν. *not even now* 1 Cor 3: 2 (ἔτι ν.='even now'; Plut., Mor. 162D; Ael. Aristid. 13 p. 302 D.; Jos., Ant. 1, 92; 2, 313). καὶ ν. *even now* (cf. Dio Chrys. 13[7], 121) J 11: 22 (perh. *assuredly*, but see HRiesenfeld, Nuntius 6, '52, 41–4); Phil 1: 20; *and now* J 17: 5; Ac 16: 37; 23: 21; 26: 6; Phil 1: 30. ν. οὖν *so now* (Gen 27: 8; 1 Macc 10: 71) Ac 16: 36; 23: 15. καὶ ν. . . . ἤδη *and now* . . . *already* 1 J 4: 3. ν. μέν *now, to be sure* J 16: 22. ποτὲ . . . ν. δέ *once . . . but now* Ro 11: 30; Eph 5: 8; 1 Pt 2: 10. πολλάκις . . . ν. δέ *often . . . but now* Phil 3: 18. τότε (μέν . . .) ν. δέ *then (to be sure . . .) but now* Gal 4: 9; Hb 12: 26. ὥσπερ τότε . . . οὕτως καὶ ν. *just as then . . . so also now* Gal 4: 29.—ALaurentin, עַתָּה.—καὶ νῦν Formule, etc. (J 17: 5), Biblica 45, '64, 168–95; 413–32; HABronyers, . . . adverbiales עַתָּה im AT: Vetus T 15, '65, 289–99.

2. Oft. it is not so much the present time that is meant as much as the situation pertaining at a given moment *as things now stand* (Gen 29: 32; Ps.-Clem., Hom. 10, 22) νῦν ζῶμεν ἐὰν *as the situation now is, we live if* 1 Th 3: 8. So also νῦν δέ, καὶ νῦν, νῦν οὖν: νῦν οὖν τί πειράζετε τ. θεόν; *since this is so, why are you tempting God?* Ac 15:

10; cf. 10: 33 (νῦν οὖν: Lucian, Dial. Deor. 25, 3; Babrius 6, 9). καὶ ν. τί μέλλεις; 22: 16. Cf. 2 J 5.—Somet. in imperative statements (oft. LXX; cf. JoachJeremias, ZNW 38, '39, 119f) καὶ ν. πέμψον *now send* Ac 10: 5. Cf. 16: 36; 23: 15; 1 J 2: 28.—On ἄγε νῦν cf. ἄγε.—Not infreq. νῦν δέ serves to contrast the real state of affairs with an unreal conditional clause: εἰ ἔγνως . . . · νῦν δέ *if you had known; but, as a matter of fact* Lk 19: 42. Cf. J 8: 40; 9: 41; 15: 22, 24; 18: 36; 1 Cor 12: 18, 20; Hb 11: 16.— 1 Cor 5: 11; 7: 14; Js 4: 16.

3. used w. the article—**a.** as an adj. ὁ, ἡ, τὸ νῦν *the present* (X., An. 6, 6, 13 ὁ νῦν χρόνος; Dio Chrys. 19[36], 55 ὁ νῦν κόσμος; PAmh. 68, 66 ὁ νῦν στρατηγός; BGU 19, 5) ὁ ν. αἰών *the present age* 1 Ti 6: 17; 2 Ti 4: 10; Tit 2: 12. ὁ ν. καιρός (Ael. Aristid. 13 p. 239 D.) Ro 3: 26; 8: 18; 11: 5; 2 Cor 8: 14; B 4: 1. ἡ ν. Ἰερουσαλήμ *the present Jerus.* Gal 4: 25. οἱ ν. οὐρανοί 2 Pt 3: 7. ζωὴ ἡ ν. (opp. ἡ μέλλουσα) 1 Ti 4: 8.

b. subst. τὸ νῦν *the present (time)* (Aristot.) w. prep. (X.+; inscr., pap. LXX) ἀπὸ τοῦ ν. *from now on, in the future* (Dit., Syll.³ 982, 22; BGU 153, 14; 193 II, 11; POxy. 479, 6 [other exx. in Dssm., NB 81–BS 253]; Sir 11: 23f; Tob 7: 12; 1 Macc 10: 41; 11: 35; 15: 8; Jos., Ant. 13, 50) Lk 1: 48; 5: 10; 12: 52; 22: 69; Ac 18: 6; 2 Cor 5: 16a; ἄχρι τοῦ ν. *until now* (s. ἄχρι 1a.—μέχρι τοῦ ν.: Diod. S. 1, 22, 2; Dit., Syll.³ 742, 35; BGU 256, 9; 667, 8; 3 Macc 6: 28; Jos., Ant. 3, 322) Ro 8: 22; Phil 1: 5. ἕως τοῦ ν. *until now* (Dit., Syll.³ 705, 44f [112 BC]. PMich. 173, 14 [III BC]. Gen 32: 5; 46: 34; 1 Macc 2: 33) Mt 24: 21; Mk 13: 19.

c. as adv.: neut. pl. τὰ ν. (also written τανῦν; cf. Tdf., Prol. p. 111) *as far as the present situation is concerned=now* (trag., Pla. et al.; POxy. 743, 30 [2 BC]; 811; PTebt. 315, 25; Jos., C. Ap. 1, 217) Ac 4: 29; 17: 30; 20: 32; 27: 22. καὶ τὰ νῦν λέγω ὑμῖν *for now I tell you (this)* 5: 38.— τὸ νῦν ἔχον *for the present* (Dio Chrys. 21[38], 42; Tob 7: 11 BA v.l.) Ac 24: 25.—The ms. tradition oft. varies betw. ν. and νυνί.—PTachau, 'Einst' u. 'Jetzt' im NT, '72; GStählin, TW IV 1099–1117. M-M. B. 962f.

νυνί adv. of time (Hdt. 7, 229 al.; Dit., Syll.³ 259, 11 [338/7 BC]; PPetr. III 42 H [8] f, 4 [III BC]; POxy. 490, 5 [124 AD]; 506, 25; 908, 5; LXX [Thackeray 191]), an emphatic form of νῦν made by adding to it the demonstrative suffix ι (Kühner-Bl. I p. 620; Bl-D. §64, 2; Rob. 296; 523) which does not, however, differ fr. it in mng. (Mayser 456). Except for Ac 22: 1; 24: 13; Hb 8: 6 v.l.; 9: 26; 1 Cl 47: 5; 2 Cl 2: 3, only in the Pauline writings and there always ν. δέ (the ms. tradition oft. varies betw. νῦν and νυνί) *now*.

1. lit., of time—**a.** w. the pres. (Job 30: 9; Jos., Ant. 14, 404) Ac 24: 13; Ro 15: 23, 25; 2 Cor 8: 22; Phlm 9; cf. 11.

b. w. the perf. in pres. sense ν. δὲ . . . πεφανέρωται *but now . . . has been revealed* Ro 3: 21.

c. w. aor. (Job 30: 1) 6: 22; 7: 6; 11: 30 v.l.; Eph 2: 13; Col 1: 22; 2 Cl 2: 3. Imper.: 2 Cor 8: 11; Col 3: 8; 1 Cl 47: 5.

d. w. a subst. (PRyl. 111, 4 [161 AD] τὴν νυνεὶ γυναῖκά μου) ἡ πρὸς ὑμᾶς ν. ἀπολογία *the defense which I now make before you* Ac 22: 1.

2. w. the idea of time weakened or entirely absent— **a.** ν. δέ *but now,* as the situation is Ro 7: 17; 1 Cor 13: 13; 14: 6 t.r.

b. introducing the real situation after an unreal conditional clause or sentence *but, as a matter of fact* 1 Cor 5: 11 t.r.; Tdf.; 12: 18 t.r.; Tdf.; 15: 20; Hb 8: 6 v.l.; 9: 26; 11: 16 t.r. M-M.*

νύξ, νυκτός, ἡ (Hom.+; inscr., pap., LXX, Philo, Joseph., Test. 12 Patr.; Sib. Or. 5, 378) *night.*

1. lit.—**a.** Mt 14: 25 (φυλακῇ τ. νυκτός as Jos., Bell. 5, 510); Mk 6: 48; J 13: 30 (for the short clause cf. εἰμί I 5.— For the scene cf. 1 Km 28: 25; Musaeus, Hero and Leander [V AD] v. 309 [ALudwich '29] νὺξ ἦν); Ac 16: 33; 23: 23; 27: 27a; Rv 21: 25; 22: 5; 1 Cl 27: 7 (Ps 18: 3); GP 5: 18. ἐν ὁράματι τῆς ν. *in a vision at night* Hv 3, 10, 6. κατὰ μέσον τῆς ν. *at midnight* Ac 16: 25 D; 27: 27b. καὶ ἡ ν. ὁμοίως *and likewise the night,* as well as the day (i.e. μὴ φάνῃ τὸ τρίτον αὐτῆς=it is to lose a third of the light fr. moon and stars) Rv 8: 12 (cf. Job 3: 9). W. ἡμέρα (as En. 104, 8; Philo, Aet. M. 19) also 1 Cl 20: 2; 24: 3. κοιμᾶται ἡ ν., ν. ἐπέρχεται *the night sleeps, comes on* vs. 3b.

b. gen. νυκτός *at night, in the night-time* (Hom.+; Diod. S. 18, 34, 6; Dit., Syll.³ 521, 5 [III BC]; PHib. 36, 5 [229 BC]; PAmh. 134, 6; 1 Macc 4: 1, 5; 5: 29; 2 Macc 12: 9; 3 Macc 5: 19; Jos., Ant. 6, 215.—Bl-D. §186, 2; Rob. 495) Mt 2: 14; 28: 13; J 3: 2; 19: 39; Ac 9: 25; 1 Th 5: 7a, b; τῆς ν. *on this night* (X., An. 5, 7, 14; Alexis Com. 148 Kock.—Bl-D. §186, 2) Lk 2: 8. νυκτὸς καὶ ἡμέρας *night and day* (X., Symp. 4, 48, Apol. 31; BGU 246, 12; PGiess. 19, 7; Jdth 11: 17) 1 Th 2: 9; 3: 10; 2 Th 3: 8; 1 Ti 5: 5; 2 Ti 1: 3; B 19: 10; IRo 5: 1; D 4: 1; GP 7: 27; GOxy 34. ἡμέρας καὶ ν. (Dt 28: 66; Josh 1: 8; 2 Ch 6: 20; 2 Esdr 14: 3; Ps 1: 2; Is 60: 11 al.) Lk 18: 7; Rv 4: 8; 7: 15; 12: 10; 14: 11; 20: 10. ἡμέρας τε καὶ ν. (Inschr. v. Magn. 163, 8) Ac 9: 24; 1 Cl 2: 4. διὰ παντὸς νυκτὸς καὶ ἡμέρας *continually, night and day* (cf. UPZ 110, 87 [164 BC]; PTebt. 48, 10 [113 BC]) Mk 5: 5.—W. prep. διὰ νυκτός *through the night* (X., An. 4, 6, 22; Athen. 7 p. 276c; PGM 4, 2052) Ac 23: 31; δι᾽ ὅλης ν. *all through the night, during the night* (s. διά A II 1a). διὰ νυκτός *at night, during the night* (s. διά A II 1b and cf. also Inscr. Rom. IV 860, 10 στρατηγήσαντα διὰ νυκτός; BGU 597, 20; PTebt. 332, 9; Sb 4317, 4; PGM 6, 47; 7, 407) Ac 5: 19; 16: 9; 17: 10 (on the v.l. διὰ τῆς ν. [so Achilles Tat. 8, 19, 1] s. Bl-D. §255, 3; Rob. 791). μέσης ν. *at midnight* Mt 25: 6 (s. μέσος 1).

c. dat., answering the question 'when?' (Bl-D. §200, 1; Rob. 522): νυκτί *at night* (Hom.+; Philo, Aet. M. 88) φαίνειν Dg 7: 2. Pl. ταῖς νυξὶ *at night* 2: 7; ταύτῃ τῇ ν. *this very night, tonight* Mk 14: 30; Lk 12: 20; 17: 34; Ac 27: 23; αὐτῇ τῇ ν. *on the night of that same day* Hv 3, 1, 2; 3, 10, 7. τῇ ν. ἐκείνῃ Ac 12: 6; τῇ ἐπιούσῃ ν. *the following night* 23: 11. Cf. GP 9: 35.—W. prep. ἐν ν. *at night, in the night* (X. et al.; Dit., Syll.³ 527, 40 [c. 220 BC]; Veröffentlichungen aus der Pap.-Sammlung München 6, 43; 3 Macc 5: 11) Ac 18: 9; 1 Th 5: 2; 2 Pt 3: 10 t.r.; ἐν τῇ ν. J 11: 10. ἐν τῇ ν. ταύτῃ Jdth 11: 3, 5; 13: 14) Mt 26: 31. ἐν ταύτῃ τῇ ν. vs. 34; ἐν ἐκείνῃ τῇ ν. (cf. 1 Macc 13: 22) J 21: 3. ἐν τῇ ν. ᾗ παρεδίδοτο 1 Cor 11: 23.

d. acc., answering the question 'how long?' (Hom.+.— Bl-D. §161, 2; Rob. 469–71) ἡμέρας τεσσεράκοντα καὶ τεσσεράκοντα νύκτας Mt 4: 2; 1 Cl 53: 2; B 4: 7; 14: 2 (Ex 24: 18; 34: 28). τρεῖς ἡμέρας καὶ τρεῖς νύκτας Mt 12: 40a, b (Jon 2: 1). τριετίαν νύκτα καὶ ἡμέραν οὐκ ἐπαυσάμην *for three years, night and day, I did not stop* Ac 20: 31. νύκτα καὶ ἡμέραν *night and day* (Hyperid. 5, 13; Aeneas Tact. 380; Palaeph. p. 57, 5; Jos., Ant. 16, 260) Mk 4: 27; Lk 2: 37; Ac 26: 7; MPol 5: 1. τὰς νύκτας *during the nights, at night* (Biogr. p. 428; PHal. 8, 4; Tob 10: 7 BA) Lk 21: 37. ὅλην τὴν ν. *the whole night through* (Amphis Com. [IV BC] 20, 4 Kock; Ex 14: 20f; Lev 6: 2 al.) Hs 9, 11, 8, cf. τὴν νύκτα vs. 6.

2. fig., as the time for rest from work J 9: 4 (as a symbol of death: Epigr. Gr. 1095, 4 νὺξ αὐτοὺς καταλύει). As a time of darkness ἡ ν. προέκοψεν *the night is far gone* Ro 13: 12; cf. 1 Th 5: 5.—GDelling, TW IV 1117–20. M-M. B. 992.*

νύσσω 1 aor. ἔνυξα (Hom.+; Sir 22: 19; Philo, Leg. ad Gai. 42; Jos., Bell. 3, 335 δόρατι; 5, 64 κατὰ πλευρὰν ν.) *prick, stab, pierce* τινά τινι *someone w. someth.* καλάμῳ αὐτόν GP 3: 9 (cf. Diog. L. 2, 109 νυχθῆναι καλάμῳ [Eubulides dies of a stab-wound like this]; Hesychius Miles., Viri Ill. c. 5 JFlach [1880]; Sib. Or. 8, 296). τί τινι *someth. w. someth.* λόγχῃ τὴν πλευράν J 19: 34 (Field, Notes 108); cf. Mt 27: 49 t.r. (Plut., Cleom. 37, 16 νύσσειν w. a dagger serves to determine whether a person is dead).—*Nudge,* to waken someone fr. sleep (Od. 14, 485; Plut., Mor. p. 79E; Diog. L. 6, 53; 3 Macc 5: 14) νύξας τ. πλευρὰν τ. Πέτρου ἤγειρεν αὐτόν Ac 12: 7 D. M-M.*

νυστάζω 1 aor. ἐνύσταξα (s. Bl-D. §71)—1. *nod, become drowsy, doze* (Aristoph., Hippocr.+; LXX) ἐνύσταξαν πᾶσαι *they all became drowsy* Mt 25: 5.
2. fig. *be sleepy, idle* (Pla.; Ps. 118: 28 v.l.; Philo, Congr. Erud. Gr. 81) of Destruction personified ἡ ἀπώλεια αὐτῶν οὐ ν. *their destruction is not asleep,* i.e. it is on its way 2 Pt 2: 3.*

νυχθήμερον, ου, τό (Petosiris, fgm. 7 l. 58; Herm. Wr. in Stob. 1, 21, 9 W.=414, 2 Sc.; Galen VII 508 K.; Cleomedes Astron. [II AD] 1, 6, 30f; 2, 1, 73 HZiegler; Anecdota Astrologica [ALudwich, Maximi et Ammonis Carmina 1877] p. 125, 7; Cyranides p. 58, 14; Themist., Paraphr. Aristot. I p. 372, 3 Spengel; Proclus, in Tim. Platon. index EDiehl. Cf. Mitteis, Chrest. 78, 6 [376/8 AD] ἐπὶ τέσσαρας ὅλας νυχθημέρους [Bl-D. §121 w. app.; cf. Mlt.-H. 269; 283]; Kühner-Bl. II 318.—As adj. as early as Peripl. Eryth. c. 15) *a day and a night*=24 hours 2 Cor 11:

25. EKönig, Kalenderfragen: ZDMG 60, '06, 605ff, esp. 608-12. M-M.*

Νῶε, ὁ indecl. (נֹחַ) *Noah* (Gen 5: 29 al.; En. 107, 3; Philo; in Joseph. Νῶχος, ου [Ant. 1, 99]); in the genealogy of Jesus Lk 3: 36. As a preacher of repentance 1 Cl 7: 6 (cf. Jos., Ant. 1, 74 [SRappaport, Agada u. Exegese bei Fl. Josephus '30, 93f]; Sib. Or. 1, 127ff; Book of Jubilees 7: 20-39). Sim. as δικαιοσύνης κῆρυξ 2 Pt 2: 5 (N. as δίκαιος Gen 6: 9; Wsd 10: 4; Sir 44: 17; Philo, Congr. Erud. Gr. 90, Migr. Abr. 125; cf. Sib. Or. 1, 126 δικαιότατος). πιστὸς εὑρεθείς (cf. Sib. Or. 1, 120 πιστότατος) 1 Cl 9: 4; cf. Hb 11: 7. ἐν (ταῖς) ἡμέραις N. Lk 17: 26; 1 Pt 3: 20 (EGSelwyn, 1 Pt '46, 328-33); cf. Mt 24: 37. N. in the ark Mt 24: 38; Lk 17: 27. W. Job and Daniel 2 Cl 6: 8 (Ezk 14: 14ff).—JPLewis, A Study of the Interpr. of Noah and the Flood in Jewish and Christian Lit., '68.*

νωθρός, ά, όν (Hippocr.+; Herm. Wr. 10, 24a ν. ψυχή; PBrem. 61, 15; LXX) *lazy, sluggish* ν. καὶ παρειμένος ἐργάτης *a lazy and careless workman* 1 Cl 34: 1 (cf. Sir 4: 29). ἵνα μὴ νωθροὶ γένησθε Hb 6: 12. ν. ταῖς ἀκοαῖς *sluggish in hearing=hard of hearing* (cf. ἀκοή 1c and Heliod. 5, 1, 5 νωθρότερος ὢν τὴν ἀκοήν) 5: 11. M-M.*

νῶτος, ου, ὁ (Hom.+ [but in Att. almost always τὸ νῶτον], also X., Equ. 3, 3; Aristot., H.A. 3, 3; 12, 5; LXX [Thackeray p. 155]; Philo, Aet. M. 128 [νῶτα]; Jos., Ant. 12, 338; 424 [τὰ νῶτα]; Test. Iss. 5: 3 [τὸν νῶτον]; Bl-D. §49, 2; Mlt.-H. 124.—PTebt. 21, 8 [II BC] the acc. νῶτον) *back* Ro 11: 10 (Ps 68: 24); B 5: 14 (Is 50: 6). M-M. B. 211.*

Ξ

ξαίνω (Hom.+; Aristoph., Theophr., Anth. Pal.; not LXX; fig. in Jos., Ant. 1, 46, Bell. 6, 304) *comb, card wool,* found in the original rdg. of Cod. א in Mt 6: 28, where it was erased and later revealed by ultra-violet light (TCSkeat, ZNW 37, '38, 211-14 [cf. POxy. 2221 col. 2, 8 and note]): πῶς οὐ ξένουσιν (=ξαίν.), instead of πῶς αὐξάνουσιν of the texts. This may make it possible to restore the logion in POxy. 655, 1a l. 22 (Kl. T. 8³ p. 23 and KAland, Synopsis 4 Evangeliorum, '64, p. 91) ο]ὐ ξα[ί]νει instead of α]ὐξάνει. This could mean that ξαίνω may have stood in the common source of Mt 6: 28=Lk 12: 27; in that case there would be three negations for the lilies of Mt 6: 28 as well as for the birds of vs. 26.—PKatz, JTS 5, 2, '54, 207-9; TFGlasson, Carding and Spinning: POxy. 655, JTS 13, '62, 331f.*

Ξανθικός, ου, ὁ (so Diod. S. 18, 56, 5 in an edict of remission from the Macedonians in the time of the Diadochi τοῦ Ξανθικοῦ μηνός; 2 Macc 11: 30; Joseph., index. The correct form is Ξανδικός; s. Dit., Or. index V; Mayser 180) *Xanthicus,* a month in the Macedonian calendar. The date for the martyrdom of Polycarp μηνὸς Ξανθικοῦ δευτέρα ἱσταμένου MPol 21 is equivalent to Feb. 22 or 23.—Lghtf., Apost. Fathers II² 1, 1889, 677ff; ESchwartz, Jüd. u. christl. Ostertafeln: AGG VIII 6, '05, 125ff.*

ξενία, ας, ἡ (Hom.+; inscr., pap., Sir 29: 27 v.l.; Philo, Joseph., loanw. in rabb.) *hospitality, entertainment* shown a guest (so mostly), less frequently the place where the guest is lodged, *the guest room* (Suidas and sim. Hesychius

equate ξενία with καταγώγιον, κατάλυμα. Cf. also Sb 3924, 7; 17 [19 AD]; PSI 50, 16; Philo, Mos. 2, 33; Jos., Ant. 1, 200; 5, 147; Ps.-Clem., Hom. 1, 15; 8, 2; 12, 24; 14, 1; 8). In the two places in our lit. where ξ. occurs, both mngs. are possible, though the second is perh. more probable. ἑτοιμάζειν τινὶ ξενίαν *prepare a guest room for someone* Phlm 22 (Ps.-Clem., Hom. 12, 2 τὰς ξενίας ἑτοιμάζοντες.—ξενία=guest room also schol. on Nicander, Ther. 486. Cf. Lat. hospitium parare). Of Paul's lodgings in Rome Ac 28: 23 (on the question whether ξ. here=μίσθωμα vs. 30, s. Lghtf. on Phlm 22 and in the comm. on Phil p. 9, also HJCadbury, JBL 45, '26, 320ff). M-M.*

ξενίζω 1 aor. ἐξένισα, pass. ἐξενίσθην; 1 fut. pass. ξενισθήσομαι (Hom.+; inscr., pap., LXX, Philo, Joseph.).
1. *receive as a guest, entertain* (Hom.+) τινά *someone* (X., Cyr. 8, 3, 35; Diod. S. 14, 31, 3; Aelian, V.H. 13, 26) Ac 10: 23. ἀγγέλους Hb 13: 2 (after Gen 18: 3; 19: 2f). The obj. is to be supplied fr. the context (Sir 29: 25) Ac 28: 7.—Pass. *be entertained* as a guest, *stay* ἐν οἰκίᾳ τινός 10: 32. παρά τινι *with someone* (Diod. S. 14, 30, 3; Philo, Abr. 131; Jos., Ant. 12, 171) vs. 6; 21: 16 (on the constr. cf. Bl-D. §294, 5 app.; Rob. 721); 1 Cor 16: 19 DG*. ἐνθάδε Ac 10: 18.
2. *surprise, astonish* w. someth. new or strange (Polyb. 3, 114, 4; Diod. S. 12, 53, 3; Jos., Ant. 1, 45) ξενίζοντά τινα *surprising things* Ac 17: 20.—Pass. *be surprised, wonder* (Polyb.; M.Ant. 8, 15; PStrassb. 35, 6; PIand. 20, 1) w. dat. of the thing causing the surprise (Polyb. 1, 23, 5;

3, 68, 9) μὴ ξενίζεσθε τῇ ἐν ὑμῖν πυρώσει *do not be surprised* (upset, EGSelwyn, 1 Pt '46, 212) *at the fiery ordeal among you* 1 Pt 4: 12; v.l. ἐπὶ τῇ κτλ. (corresponding to Polyb. 2, 27, 4; UPZ 146, 4; 6 [II BC]; Jos., Ant. 1, 35). Also ἔν τινι vs. 4 (Bl-D. §196; cf. Rob. 532). Abs. 2 Cl 17: 5. M-M.*

ξενισμός, οῦ, ὁ (Pla.+; Polyb. 15, 17, 1; Diod. S. 3, 33, 7; inscr.; Pr 15: 17) *surprise, astonishment* ξενισμὸν παρεῖχεν ἡ καινότης αὐτοῦ *the newness of it caused astonishment* IEph 19: 2.*

ξενοδοχέω 1 aor. ἐξενοδόχησα (Maximus Tyr. 26, 9a; Cass. Dio 78, 3; Ps.-Lucian, Amor. 47 p. 450; Graec. Ven. Gen 26: 17. It stands for the older [Eur., Hdt.+] ξενοδοκέω, and is rejected by the Atticists; Phryn. p. 307 L.) *show hospitality* abs. 1 Ti 5: 10. M-M.*

ξένος, η, ον (Hom.+; inscr., pap., LXX, Philo, Joseph., Test. 12 Patr., loanw. in rabb.).
1. adj. *strange*—a. lit. *strange, foreign* ξ. δαιμόνια *foreign divinities* (δαιμόνιον 1 and Achilles Tat. 2, 30, 1; Jos., C. Ap. 2, 251; 267 ξένους θεούς Ac 17: 18. διδαχαὶ strange teachings (coming fr. other religions; cf. Jos., Bell. 2, 414 θρησκεία ξένη) Hb 13: 9; Hs 8, 6, 5.
b. fig.—a. τινός *strange to someth.*, estranged fr. it, unacquainted w. it, without interest in it (Soph., Oed. R. 219; Pla., Apol. 17D; Heliod. 10, 14; POxy. 1154, 8 [I AD] εἰμὶ ξένος τῶν ἐνθάδε.—Bl-D. §182, 3; Rob. 516) ξ. τῶν διαθηκῶν τῆς ἐπαγγελίας Eph 2: 12.
β. *strange in kind, surprising, unheard of, foreign* (Aeschyl., Prom. 688; Diod. S. 3, 15, 6; 3, 52, 2; M. Ant. 8, 14; POxy. 1772, 3 οὐδὲν ξένον; Wsd 16: 2, 16; 19: 5; Philo, Mos. 1, 213) UGosp 64. ὡς ξένου ὑμῖν συμβαίνοντος *as though something unheard of were happening to you* 1 Pt 4: 12. οὐ ξένα ὁμιλῶ *I have nothing strange to say* Dg 11: 1. W. dat. of the pers. ἡ ξένη τοῖς ἐκλεκτοῖς τοῦ θεοῦ στάσις *the uprising* (which is) *foreign to God's chosen people* 1 Cl 1: 1.
2. subst.—a. ὁ ξένος *the stranger, alien* Mt 25: 35, 38, 43f; 27: 7; 3 J 5. Opp. πολίτης (cf. Ael. Aristid. 13 p. 163 D.; Dit., Syll.³ 495, 115; 708, 16f; 729, 4 al., Or. 764, 18; Philo, Poster. Cai. 109; Jos., Ant. 11, 159, Vi. 372) Dg 5: 5. W. πάροικοι (opp. συμπολίτης) Eph 2: 19 (cf. Diod. S. 4, 27, 3 and Dit., Syll.³ 799, 24f ξ. ἢ μέτοικος). W. παρεπίδημοι (Dit., Or. 268, 9 τ. παρεπιδημοῦντας ξένους; 339, 29) Hb 11: 13; οἱ ἐπιδημοῦντες ξ. *the strangers who lived* (or *visited*) *there* Ac 17: 21 (Dit., Syll.³ 1157, 80f τῶν ἐνδημούντων ξένων).
b. ἡ ξένη *a foreign country* (Soph., Phil. 135; POxy. 251, 11; 253, 7) Dg 5: 5. ἐπὶ ξένης (X., Resp. Lac. 14, 4; Epict. 1, 27, 5; Plut., Mor. 576c; BGU 22, 34 [114 AD]; 159, 7; PFay. 136, 10; 2 Macc 5: 9: 28; Philo, Leg. ad Gai. 15; Jos., Ant. 18, 344) ἐπὶ ξένης κατοικεῖν *live in a foreign country* Hs 1: 1, 6.
c. ὁ ξένος *the host*, one who extends hospitality (since Il. 15, 532) w. gen. (X., An. 2, 4, 15) ὁ ξ. μου καὶ ὅλης τῆς ἐκκλησίας *host to me and to the whole church*, prob. because he furnished space for its meetings Ro 16: 23.—GStählin, TW V 1-36: ξένος and related words. M-M. B. 1350-2.*

ξέστης, ου, ὁ (Diosc.; Epict. 1, 9, 33f; 2, 16, 22; Dit., Or. 521, 24; Ostraka II 1186, 2; Sb II word-list p. 360; Jos., Ant. 8, 57, Vi. 75. Loanw. in rabb.—Taken by most to be a corruption of Lat. sextarius; Mlt.-H. 155, w. note 3, expresses some doubts on this point) a liquid measure, about equal to one pint or ½ liter (FHultsch, Griech. u. röm. Metrologie² 1882, 103ff; APF 3, '06, 438; Wilcken,

Ostraka I 762f). But then it comes to mean simply *pitcher, jug*, without reference to the amount contained (POxy. 109, 21 ξέσται χαλκοῦ; 921, 23; Cat. Cod. Astr. VIII 3, 139) w. ποτήριον, χαλκίον Mk 7: 4; cf. vs. 8 v.l. M-M.*

ξηραίνω 1 aor. ἐξήρανα, pass. ἐξηράνθην; pf. pass. ἐξήραμμαι, ptc. ἐξηραμμένος (Hom.+; pap., LXX, En., Joseph.).
1. act. *dry, dry out* τὶ someth. (Thu. 1, 109, 4; schol. on Nicander, Ther. 831 ξηραίνει τὸ δένδρον; PGM 13, 27 ξήρανον i.e. τὰ ἄνθη; Is 42: 15; Jer 28: 36) of the sun τὸν χόρτον Js 1: 11.
2. elsewh. pass. *become dry, dry up, wither*—a. lit. of trees (POxy. 53, 10; Jo 1: 12) Mt 21: 19f; Mk 11: 20f. Of plants without good roots Mt 13: 6; Mk 4: 6; Lk 8: 6.— 1 Pt 1: 24 (Is 40: 7); Rv 14: 15. A vine-branch when cut off J 15: 6. Gener. of plants Hs 9, 21, 1; 3. Of water (Gen 8: 7; 3 Km 17: 7; Is 19: 5f ποταμός; En. 101, 7; Jos., Bell. 5, 409 πηγή; Test. Levi 4: 1) of a river: *dry up* Rv 16: 12. Of a flow of blood εὐθὺς ἐξηράνθη ἡ πηγὴ τοῦ αἵματος αὐτῆς *her hemorrhage stopped at once* Mk 5: 29.
b. As plants are killed by drought, so the human body is damaged by certain harmful things (Hippocr., π. τῶν ἐντὸς παθῶν 22 vol. VII 222 L.—PUps. 8, 4 καταξηρανθήτω τὸ σῶμα ἐν κλίνοις = may her body dry up on the sickbed) ἄνθρωπος ἐξηραμμένην ἔχων τ. χεῖρα *a man with a withered hand* (i.e., one incapable of motion; cf. 3 Km 13: 4) Mk 3: 1, 3 t.r. Likew. the whole body of the boy who was possessed stiffens ξηραίνεται *he becomes stiff* 9: 18 (Theocr. 24, 61 ξηρὸν ὑπαὶ δείους = stiff with fright. Similarly Psellus p. 212, 6). M-M.*

ξηρός, ά, όν (Hdt.+; inscr., pap., LXX, En., Philo; Jos., Bell. 3, 228, Ant. 5, 249; Test. Zeb. 2: 7) *dry, dried* (up).
1. lit., of ξύλον (q.v. 3 and Dialekt-Inschr. 4689, 108 [Messenia] ξηρὰ ξύλα; Zen.-P. 93 [= Sb 6808], 1 [256 BC]; Is 56: 3; Ezk 17: 24) Lk 23: 31. Of trees (Lucian, Sat. 9) Hs 3: 1ff; s 4: 1, 4. Of branches (POxy. 1188, 4 [13 AD]; Epigr. Gr. 1039, 14) s 8, 1, 6f; 11ff; 8, 2, 6; 8, 4, 4ff; 8, 5, 2ff; 8, 6, 4f; 8, 8, 1; 4; 8, 9, 1; 8, 10, 1; 3. Of plants s 9, 1, 6; 9, 21, 1; hence also symbol. θεμέλια (corresp. to ῥίζαι) 9, 21, 2 and even of pers.: δίψυχοι ibid.; cf. s 4: 4. Of seeds 1 Cl 24: 5. ἡ ξ. γῆ *dry land* Hb 11: 29. Also simply ἡ ξηρά *the dry* (land, ground) (X., Oec. 17, 2; 19, 7; Aristot., H.A. 5, 10; Gen 1: 9 al. in LXX) Hb 11: 29 t.r.; Hv 3, 2, 7; 3, 5, 3. W. θάλασσα (Jon 1: 9; Hg 2: 21; 1 Macc 8: 23, 32; En. 97, 7) Mt 23: 15.
2. fig. of diseased states (ξηραίνω 2b; ξηρότης Galen VII 666, 1 K. = a wasting disease.—ξηρός in this sense on the third stele of Epidaurus l. 108 as read by RHerzog, D. Wunderheilungen v. Ep. '31, 32; 138. ἡμίξηρος = half-stiffened Hippiatr. I 185, 9; χεὶρ ἡμίξηρος Test. Sim. 2, 12. Cf. also Hipponax 11 D.² λιμῷ γένηται ξηρός; Hos 9: 14 μαστοὶ ξηροί; Psellus p. 27, 17 νηδὺς ξηρά of the womb of an aged woman) χεὶρ ξηρά *a withered hand* Mt 12: 10; Mk 3: 3; Lk 6: 6, 8. ξηροί *withered, paralyzed* (Lucian, Tox. 24 of a woman ξηρὰ τὸ ἥμισυ) J 5: 3.—On the mng. of the word DCHesseling, Sertum Nabericum '08, 145-54. M-M. B. 1076.*

ξιφίδιον, ου, τό (Aristoph., Thu.+; POxy. 936, 9 [III AD]; Jos., Ant. 20, 164, Vi. 293) *short sword, dagger* MPol 16: 1.*

ξίφος, εος or **ους, τό** (Hom.+; pap., LXX, Philo; Jos., Bell. 3, 364, Vi. 138; Test. Dan 1: 7) *sword* AP 15: 30. B. 1392.*

ξόανον, ου, τό (trag.+; inscr., pap.) a (crude) *wooden image* of idols (so Eur.; X., An. 5, 3, 12; inscr., pap.; Aq.

Ezk 6: 4; Manetho in Jos., C. Ap. 1, 244; 249; Philo, Mos. 1, 298 al.; Sib. Or. 3, 723) AP 18: 33.*

ξύλινος, η, ον (Pind., Hdt.+; inscr., pap., LXX, Philo; Jos., Ant. 11, 13; Test. 12 Patr.) *wooden* τὰ εἴδωλα ... τὰ ξ. *the wooden idols* (cf. Aesop, Fab. 66 H. ἄνθρωπός τις ξύλινον ἔχων θεόν; EpJer 3 θεοὶ ξ., 10, 29, 54, 69, 70; Da 5: 4, 23 Theod.; En. 99, 7) Rv 9: 20. σκεύη *wooden vessels* or *equipment* (cf. Dit., Syll.³ 962, 41ff; 316; Lev 15: 12; Num 31: 20; 35: 18) 2 Ti 2: 20. M-M.*

ξύλον, ου, τό (Hom.+; inscr., pap., LXX, Philo, Joseph., Test. 12 Patr.).

1. *wood* Dg 2: 2; LJ 1: 5 (cf. λίθος 1a). πᾶν ξ. θύϊνον *every kind of citron wood* Rv 18: 12a. ξ. τιμιώτατον *very precious wood* vs. 12b. Pl. *wood* as building material (Diod. S. 5, 21, 5 κάλαμοι and ξύλα; PFlor. 16, 23) 1 Cor 3: 12; for making idols ξύλα κ. λίθους (Sextus 568) together w. other materials 2 Cl 1: 6; PK 2 p. 14, 13. As fuel (POxy. 1144, 15 ξύλα εἰς θυσίαν; Gen 22: 3, 6; Lev 1: 7) MPol 13: 1; Hs 4: 4.

2. *of objects made of wood*—a. of the wooden stocks for the feet of a prisoner (Hdt. 6, 75; 9, 37; Lysias 10, 16; Aristoph., Eq. 367; 394; 705; also Charito 4, 2, 6; Dit., Or. 483, 181 [s. the note]; Job 33: 11) τοὺς πόδας ἠσφαλίσατο αὐτῶν εἰς τὸ ξύλον *he fastened their feet in the stocks* Ac 16: 24.

b. *the pole* (Diod. S. 5, 18, 4; Maximus Tyr. 2, 8b) on which Moses raised the brass serpent (Num 21: 8f) B 12: 7.—*Club, cudgel* (Hdt. 2, 63; 4, 180; Polyb. 6, 37, 3; Herodian 7, 7, 4; PHal. 1, 187; PTebt. 304, 10; Jos., Bell. 2, 176, Vi. 233) pl. (w. μάχαιραι) Mt 26: 47, 55; Mk 14: 43, 48; Lk 22: 52.

c. *gallows*, in NT *cross* (Alexis Com. [IV BC] 220, 10 ἀναπήγνυμι ἐπὶ τοῦ ξύλου; Gen 40: 19; Dt 21: 23; Josh 10: 26; Esth 5: 14; 6: 4; Philo, Somn. 2, 213; Jos., Ant. 11, 246) B 8: 5, cf. vs. 1; 12: 1 (fr. an apocr. prophetic writing, perh. 4 Esdr 5: 5. Cf. UHolzmeister, Verb. Dom. 21, '41, 69–73). κρεμάσαι ἐπὶ ξύλου *hang on the cross* Ac 5: 30; 10: 39. ὁ κρεμάμενος ἐπὶ ξύλου Gal 3: 13 (Dt 21: 23). καθελεῖν ἀπὸ τοῦ ξ. *take down fr. the cross* (cf. Josh 10: 27) Ac 13: 29. πάσχειν ἐπὶ ξύλου B 5: 13. τὰς ἁμαρτίας ἀναφέρειν ἐπὶ τὸ ξ. *bear the sins on* (or *to*) *the cross*, to destroy them on the cross 1 Pt 2: 24=Pol 8: 1.—WSv Leeuwen, NThSt 24, '41, 68–81.

3. *tree* (this usage is perceptible in Eur., Hdt.; Ctesias in Apollon. Paradox. 17 παρ' Ἰνδοῖς ξύλον γίνεσθαι; Theophr., H.Pl. 5, 4, 7; Fgm. Iamb. Adesp. 17 Diehl; Plut., Lycurgus 13, 7; Harpocration s.v. ὀξυθυμία; PTebt. 5, 205 [118 BC]; PFlor. 152, 4; Gen 1: 29; 2: 9; 3: 1ff; Is 14: 8; Eccl 2: 5) Dg 12: 8. ὑγρόν, ξηρὸν ξ. *a green, a dry tree* Lk 23: 31 (s. ξηρός 1 and cf. Polyaenus 3, 9, 7 ξύλα ξηρά [opp. χλωρά].—AJBHiggins, ET 57, '45/'46, 292–4). πάγκαρπον ξ. *a tree bearing all kinds of fruit* Dg 12: 1. ξ. ἄκαρπον *a tree without* (edible) *fruit* (of the elm) Hs 2: 3. ξύλῳ ἑαυτὸν συμβάλλειν *compare oneself to a tree* 1 Cl 23: 4a; 2 Cl 11: 3 (both script. quots. of unknown orig.). τὰ φύλλα τοῦ ξ. Rv 22: 2b; καρπὸς τοῦ ξ. 1 Cl 23: 4b. Of trees by watercourses B 11: 6 (Ps 1: 3). ξ. γνώσεως Dg 12: 2a (cf. Gen 2: 9, 17). ξ. (τῆς) ζωῆς Rv 2: 7; 22: 2a (RSchran, BZ 24, '38/'39, 191–8), 14, 19; Dg 12: 2b (cf. vs. 3 and ζωή end; LvSybel, Ξύλον ζωῆς: ZNW 19, '20, 85–91; UHolmberg, D. Baum d. Lebens '23; HBergema, De Boom des Levens in Schrift en Historie, Diss. Hilversum '38; JSchneider, TW V 36–40. M-M. B. 50. 1385.*

ξυν- s. συν-.

ξυράω (Diod. S. 1, 83, 2; 1, 84, 2; 5, 28, 3; Plut., Mor. 180B; Dio Chrys. 16[33], 63; Longus 4, 10, 1), **ξυρέω** (trag., Hdt., Pla. et al.; Lob. on Phryn. p. 205), **ξύρω** (Hippocr.; Plut., Mor. 336E τὴν κεφαλὴν ξυράμενος; Lucian, De Morte Peregr. 17). In our lit. the foll. verbal forms of the stem ξυρ- are found: mid.: ξύρωνται Ac 21: 24 D; fut. ξυρήσονται 21: 24; aor. subj. ξυρήσωνται ibid. v.l. Pass.: perf. ptc. ἐξυρημένος 1 Cor 11: 5. In 11: 6 ξυρᾶσθαι seems to be marked as a verbal form of ξυράω by ἐξυρημένη vs. 5, and in that case it is to be accented as a pres. mid. inf. ξυρᾶσθαι (cf. Diog. L. 7, 166 ξυρᾶσθαι = to have himself shaved; Jos., Ant. 19, 294 ξυρᾶσθαι and Bell. 2, 313 ξυρήσεσθαι; Philo, Spec. Leg. 1, 5 ξυρῶνται). On the other hand, the immediate proximity of κείρασθαι makes it much more likely that it is an aorist, an aor. mid. inf. of ξύρω, to be accented ξύρασθαι (cf. Bl-D. §101 p. 47; Mlt.-H. 200; 250; Anz 310f) mid. *have oneself shaved* (cf. Bl-D. §317; Rob. 809) τὴν κεφαλήν *have one's head shaved* (Ps.-Callisth. 1, 3, 2; Num 6: 9; Ezk 44: 20) Ac 21: 24 (s. on εὐχή 2 and Jos., Ant. 19, 294). Abs. 1 Cor 11: 6. Pass. ἐξυρημένη *a woman whose head is shaved* vs. 5. M-M.*

O

ὁ, ἡ, τό pl. **οἱ, αἱ, τά** *article*, derived fr. a demonstrative pronoun, *the*. Since the treatment of the inclusion and omission of the art. belongs to the field of grammar, the lexicon can limit itself to exhibiting the main features of its usage. It is difficult to set hard and fast rules for the employment of the art., since the writer's feeling for style had special freedom of play in this area.—Kühner-G. I p. 589ff; Bl-D. §249–76; Mlt. 80–4; Rob. 754–96; W-S. §17ff; Rdm.² p. 112–18; Abel §28–32; HKallenberg, RhM 69, '14, 642ff; FVölker, Syntax d. griech. Papyri I, Der Artikel, Progr. d. Realgymn. Münster '03; FEakin, AJPh 37, '16, 333ff; CWEMiller, ibid. 341ff; ECColwell, JBL 52, '33, 12–21 (for a critique s. Mlt.-H.-Turner III 183f); ASvensson, D. Gebr. des bestimmten Art. in d. nachklass. Epik '37.

I. the art. as demonstrative pronoun, *this one, that one*

1. in accordance w. epic usage (Hes., Works 450: ἡ = this [voice]) in the quot. fr. Arat., Phaenom. 5 τοῦ γὰρ καὶ γένος ἐσμέν *for we are also his* (lit. this One's) *offspring* Ac 17: 28.

2. ὁ μέν ... ὁ δέ *the one ... the other* (PSI 512, 21 [253 BC]), pl. οἱ μέν ... οἱ δέ (Polyaenus 6, 2, 1 ὁ μέν ... ὁ δέ ... ὁ δέ; PSI 341, 9 [256 BC]) *some ... others* w. ref. to a noun preceding: ἐσχίσθη τὸ πλῆθος ... οἱ μὲν ἦσαν σὺν τοῖς Ἰουδαίοις, οἱ δὲ σὺν τοῖς ἀποστόλοις Ac 14: 4; 17: 32; 28: 24; 1 Cor 7: 7; Gal 4: 23; Phil 1: 16f. Also without such a relationship expressed τοὺς μὲν ἀποστόλους, τοὺς δὲ προφήτας, τοὺς δὲ εὐαγγελιστάς Eph 4: 11. οἱ μέν ... ὁ δέ Hb 7: 5f, 20f. οἱ μέν ... ἄλλοι (δέ) J 7: 12. οἱ μὲν ἄλλοι δέ ... ἕτεροι δέ Mt 16: 14. τινὲς ... οἱ δέ Ac 17: 18 (cf. Pla., Leg. 1, 627A; 2, 658 B.; Aelian, V.H. 2, 34; Palaephat. 6, 5).—Mt 26: 67; 28: 17 οἱ δέ introduces a second class; just before this, instead of the first class, the whole group is men-

tioned (cf. X., Hell. 1, 2, 14)= *but some* (as Arrian, Anab. 5, 2, 7; 5, 14, 4; Lucian, Tim. 4 p. 107; Diog. L. 1, 25; 26 and oft.; Hesychius Miles. [VI AD] c. 35 end [JFlach 1880]).

3. To indicate the progress of the narrative, ὁ δέ, οἱ δέ *but he, but they* (lit. this one, they) is also used without ὁ μέν preceding (likew. class.; Clearchus, fgm. 76b τὸν δὲ εἰπεῖν= but this man said; pap. examples in Mayser II 1, '26, 57f) Mt 2: 9, 14; 4: 4; 9: 31 al. ὁ μὲν οὖν Ac 23: 18; 28: 5. οἱ μὲν οὖν 1: 6; 5: 41; 15: 3, 30.—JJO'Rourke, Paul's Use of the Art. as a Pronoun, CBQ 34, '72, 59-65.

II. as the definite article, *the*—**1.** w. nouns—**a.** w. appellatives, or common nouns, where, as in class. Gk., the art. has double significance, specific or individualizing, and generic.

α. In its individualizing use it focuses attention on a single thing or single concept, as already known or otherwise more definitely limited: things and pers. that are unique in kind: ὁ ἥλιος, ἡ σελήνη, ὁ οὐρανός, ἡ γῆ, ἡ θάλασσα, ὁ κόσμος, ἡ κτίσις, ὁ θεός (BWeiss [s. on θεός, beg.]), ὁ διάβολος, ὁ λόγος (J 1: 1, 14), τὸ φῶς, ἡ σκοτία, ἡ ζωή, ὁ θάνατος etc. (but somet. the art. is omitted w. them, esp. when they are used w. preps.; Bl-D. §253, 1-4; Rob. 791f; Mlt.-Turner 171). ἐν συναγωγῇ καὶ ἐν τῷ ἱερῷ J 18: 20.—Virtues, vices, etc. (contrary to Engl. usage): ἡ ἀγάπη, ἡ ἀλήθεια, ἡ ἁμαρτία, ἡ δικαιοσύνη, ἡ σοφία et al.—The individualizing art. stands before a common noun that was previously mentioned (without the art.): τοὺς πέντε ἄρτους Lk 9: 16 (after πέντε ἄρτοι vs. 13). τὸ βιβλίον 4: 17b (after βιβλίον, 17a), τοὺς μάγους Mt 2: 7 (after μάγοι, vs. 1). J 4: 43 (40); 12: 6 (5); 20: 1 (19: 41); Ac 9: 17 (11); Js 2: 3 (2); Rv 15: 6 (1).—The individ. art. also stands before a common noun which, in a given situation, is given special attention as the only or obvious one of its kind (Hipponax [VI BC] 16 D.[2] ὁ παῖς the [attending] slave; Diod. S. 18, 29, 2 ὁ ἀδελφός= his brother; Artem. 4, 71 p. 245, 19 ἡ γυνή= your wife) τῷ ὑπηρέτῃ to the attendant (who took care of the synagogue) Lk 4: 20. εἰς τὸν νιπτῆρα into the basin (that was there for the purpose) J 13: 5. ἰδοὺ ὁ ἄνθρ. here is this (wretched) man 19: 5. ἐκ τῆς παιδίσκης or ἐλευθέρας by the (well-known) slave woman or the free woman (Hagar and Sarah) Gal 4: 22f. τὸν σῖτον Ac 27: 38. ἐν τῇ ἐπιστολῇ 1 Cor 5: 9 (s. ἐπιστολή). τὸ ὄρος the mountain (nearby) Mt 5: 1; 8: 1; 14: 23; Mk 3: 13; 6: 46; Lk 6: 12; 9: 28 al.; ἡ πεισμονή this (kind of) persuasion Gal 5: 8. ἡ μαρτυρία the (required) witness or testimony J 5: 36.—The art. takes on the idea of κατ' ἐξοχήν 'par excellence' (Porphyr., Abst. 24, 7 ὁ Αἰγύπτιος) ὁ ἐρχόμενος the one who is (was) to come simply= the Messiah Mt 11: 3; Lk 7: 19. ὁ προφήτης J 1: 21, 25; 7: 40. ὁ διδάσκαλος τ. Ἰσραήλ 3: 10 (Ps.-Clem., Hom. 5, 18 of Socrates: ὁ τῆς Ἑλλάδος διδάσκαλος); cf. MPol 12: 2. With things (Stephan. Byz. s.v. Μάρπησσα: οἱ λίθοι= the famous stones [of the Parian Marble]) ἡ κρίσις the (last) judgment Mt 12: 41. ἡ ἡμέρα the day of decision 1 Cor 3: 13; Hb 10: 25. ἡ σωτηρία Christian salvation at the consummation of the age Ro 13: 11.

β. In its generic use it singles out an individual who is typical of his class, rather than the class itself: ὁ ἀγαθὸς ἄνθρωπος Mt 12: 35. κοινοῖ τὸν ἄνθρωπον 15: 11. ὥσπερ ὁ ἐθνικός 18: 17. ὁ ἐργάτης Lk 10: 7. ἐγίνωσκεν τί ἦν ἐν τῷ ἀνθρώπῳ J 2: 25. τὰ σημεῖα τοῦ ἀποστόλου 2 Cor 12: 12. ὁ κληρονόμος Gal 4: 1. So also in parables and allegories: ὁ οἰκοδεσπότης Mt 24: 43. Cf. J 10: 11b, 12. The generic art. in Gk. is often rendered in Engl. by the indef. art. or omitted entirely.

b. The use of the art. w. personal names is varied; as a general rule the presence of the art. w. a personal name indicates that the pers. is known; the absence of the art. simply names him (cf. Dssm., BPhW 22, '02, 1467f; BWeiss, D. Gebr. des Art. b. d. Eigennamen [im NT]: StKr 86, '13, 349-89). This rule, however, is subject to considerable modification; there is an unmistakable drift in the direction of Mod. Gk. usage, in which every proper name has the art. (Bl-D. §260; cf. Rob. 759-61; Mlt.-Turner 165f). The ms. tradition varies considerably. In the gospels the art. is usu. found w. Ἰησοῦς; yet it is commonly absent when Ἰ. is accompanied by an appositive that has the art. Ἰ. ὁ Γαλιλαῖος Mt 26: 69; Ἰ. ὁ Ναζωραῖος vs. 71; Ἰ. ὁ λεγόμενος Χριστός 27: 17, 22. Sim. Μαριὰμ ἡ μήτηρ τοῦ Ἰ. Ac 1: 14. The art. somet. stands before oblique cases of indecl. proper names, seemingly to indicate their case (Bl-D. §260, 2; Rob. 760). But here, too, it is impossible to set up a hard and fast rule.—HMTeeple, NTS 19, '73, 302-17 (synopt.).

c. The art. is customarily found w. the names of countries (Bl-D. §261, 4; Rob. 759f); less freq. w. names of cities (Bl-D. §261, 1; 2; Rob. 760; Mlt.-Turner 170-2). W. Ἰερουσαλήμ, Ἱεροσόλυμα it is usu. absent (s. these words); it is only when this name has modifiers that it must have the art. ἡ νῦν Ἰ. Gal 4: 25; ἡ ἄνω Ἰ. vs. 26; ἡ καινὴ Ἰ. Rv 3: 12. But even in this case it lacks the art. when the modifier follows: Hb 12: 22.—Names of rivers have the art. ὁ Ἰορδάνης, ὁ Εὐφράτης, ὁ Τίβερις Hv 1, 1, 2 (Bl-D. §261, 8; Rob. 760; Mlt.-Turner 172). Likew. names of seas ὁ Ἀδρίας Ac 27: 27.

d. The art. comes before nouns that are accompanied by the gen. of a pronoun (μου, σου, ἡμῶν, ὑμῶν, αὐτοῦ, ἑαυτοῦ, αὐτῶν) Mt 1: 21, 25; 5: 45; 6: 10-12; 12: 49; Mk 9: 17; Lk 6: 27; 10: 7; 16: 6; Ro 4: 19; 6: 6 and very oft. (only rarely is it absent: Mt 19: 28; Lk 1: 72; 2: 32; 2 Cor 8: 23; Js 5: 20 al.).

e. When accompanied by the possessive pronouns ἐμός, σός, ἡμέτερος, ὑμέτερος the noun always has the art., and the pron. stands mostly betw. art. and noun: Mt 18: 20; Mk 8: 38; Lk 9: 26; Ac 26: 5; Ro 3: 7 and oft. But only rarely so in John (J 4: 42; 5: 47; 7: 16), who prefers to repeat the article w. the possessive following the noun ἡ κρίσις ἡ ἐμή J 5: 30; cf. 7: 6; 17: 17; 1 J 1: 3 al.

f. Adjectives (or participles), when they modify nouns that have the art., also come either betw. the art. and noun: ἡ ἀγαθὴ μερίς Lk 10: 42. τὸ ἅγιον πνεῦμα 12: 10; Ac 1: 8. ἡ δικαία κρίσις J 7: 24 and oft., or after the noun w. the art. repeated τὸ πνεῦμα τὸ ἅγιον Mk 3: 29; J 14: 26; Ac 1: 16; Hb 3: 7; 9: 8; 10: 15. ἡ ζωὴ ἡ αἰώνιος 1 J 1: 2; 2: 25. τὴν πύλην τὴν σιδηρᾶν Ac 12: 10. Only rarely does an adj. without the art. stand before a noun that has an art. (s. Bl-D. §270, 1; Rob. 777; Mlt.-Turner 185f) ἀκατακαλύπτῳ τῇ κεφαλῇ 1 Cor 11: 5. εἶπεν μεγάλῃ τῇ φωνῇ Ac 14: 10 v.l.; cf. 26: 24. κοιναῖς ταῖς χερσίν Mk 7: 5 D.—Double modifier τὸ πῦρ τὸ αἰώνιον τὸ ἡτοιμασμένον τῷ διαβόλῳ Mt 25: 41. τὸ θυσιαστήριον τὸ χρυσοῦν τὸ ἐνώπιον τοῦ θρόνου Rv 8: 3; 9: 13. ἡ πόρνη ἡ μεγάλη ἡ καθημένη 17: 1.—Mk 5: 36 τὸν λόγον λαλούμενον is prob. a wrong rdg. (B has τὸν λαλ., D τοῦτον τὸν λ. without λαλούμενον).—On the art. w. ὅλος, πᾶς, πολύς s. the words in question.

g. As in the case of the poss. pron. (e) and adj. (f), so it is w. other expressions that can modify a noun: ἡ κατ' ἐκλογὴν πρόθεσις Ro 9: 11. ἡ παρ' ἐμοῦ διαθήκη 11: 27. ὁ λόγος ὁ τοῦ σταυροῦ 1 Cor 1: 18. ἡ ἐντολὴ ἡ εἰς ζωὴν Ro 7: 10. ἡ πίστις ὑμῶν ἡ πρὸς τὸν θεόν 1 Th 1: 8. ἡ διακονία ἡ εἰς τοὺς ἁγίους 2 Cor 8: 4.

ὁ

h. The noun has the art. preceding it when a demonstrative pron. (οὗτος, ἐκεῖνος) belonging with it comes before it or after it; e.g.: οὗτος ὁ ἄνθρωπος Lk 14: 30; J 9: 24. οὗτος ὁ λαός Mk 7: 6. οὗτος ὁ υἱός μου Lk 15: 24. οὗτος ὁ τελώνης 18: 11 and oft. ὁ ἄνθρωπος οὗτος Mk 14: 71; Lk 2: 25; 23: 4, 14, 47. ὁ λαὸς οὗτος Mt 15: 8. ὁ υἱός σου οὗτος Lk 15: 30 and oft.—ἐκείνη ἡ ἡμέρα Mt 7: 22; 22: 46. ἐκ. ἡ ὥρα 10: 19; 18: 1; 26: 55. ἐκ. ὁ καιρός 11: 25; 12: 1; 14: 1. ἐκ. ὁ πλάνος 27: 63 and oft. ἡ οἰκία ἐκείνη Mt 7: 25, 27. ἡ ὥρα ἐκ. 8: 13; 9: 22; ἡ γῆ ἐκ. 9: 26, 31; ἡ ἡμέρα ἐκ. 13: 1. ὁ ἀγρὸς ἐκ. vs. 44 and oft.—ὁ αὐτός s. αὐτός 4.

i. When placed before the nom. of a noun, the art. makes it a vocative (as early as Hom.; cf. KBrugmann⁴-AThumb, Griech. Gramm. '13, 431; Bl-D. §147; Rob. 769. On the LXX MJohannessohn, D. Gebrauch d. Kasus in LXX, Diss. Berlin '10, 14f) ναί, ὁ πατήρ Mt 11: 26. τὸ κοράσιον, ἔγειρε Mk 5: 41. Cf. Mt 7: 23; 27: 29 v.l.; Lk 8: 54; 11: 39; 18: 11, 13 (Gdspd., Probs. 85–7); J 19: 3 and oft.

2. Adjectives become substantives by the addition of the art.—**a.** ὁ πονηρός Eph 6: 16. οἱ σοφοί 1 Cor 1: 27. οἱ ἅγιοι, οἱ πολλοί al. Likew. the neut. τὸ κρυπτόν Mt 6: 4. τὸ ἅγιον 7: 6. τὸ μέσον Mk 3: 3. τὸ θνητόν 2 Cor 5: 4. τὰ ἀδύνατα Lk 18: 27. τὸ ἔλαττον Hb 7: 7. Also w. gen. foll. τὰ ἀγαθά σου Lk 16: 25. τὸ ἀσθενὲς τοῦ θεοῦ 1 Cor 1: 25; cf. vs. 27f. τὸ γνωστὸν τοῦ θεοῦ Ro 1: 19. τὰ ἀόρατα τοῦ θεοῦ vs. 20. τὸ ἀδύνατον τοῦ νόμου 8: 3. τὰ κρυπτὰ τῆς αἰσχύνης 2 Cor 4: 2.

b. adj. attributes whose noun is customarily omitted come to have substantive force and therefore receive the art. (Bl-D. §241; Rob. 652–4) ἡ περίχωρος Mt 3: 5; ἡ ξηρά 23: 15 (i.e. γῆ). ἡ ἀριστερά, ἡ δεξιά (sc. χείρ) 6: 3. ἡ ἐπιοῦσα (sc. ἡμέρα) Ac 16: 11. ἡ ἔρημος (sc. χώρα) Mt 11: 7.

c. The neut. of the adj. w. the art. can take on the mng. of an abstract noun (Thu. 1, 36, 1 τὸ δεδιός=fear; Herodian 1, 6, 9; 1, 11, 5 τὸ σεμνὸν τῆς παρθένου; M. Ant. 1, 1) τὸ χρηστὸν τοῦ θεοῦ God's kindness Ro 2: 4. τὸ δυνατόν power 9: 22. τὸ σύμφορον benefit 1 Cor 7: 35. τὸ γνήσιον genuineness 2 Cor 8: 8. τὸ ἐπιεικές Phil 4: 5 al.

d. The art. w. numerals indicates, as in class. Gk. (HKallenberg, RhM 69, '14, 662ff), that a part of a number already known is being mentioned (Diod. S. 18, 10, 2 τρεῖς μὲν φυλὰς . . . τὰς δὲ ἑπτά='but the seven others'; Plut., Cleom. 8, 4 οἱ τέσσαρες='the other four'; Polyaenus 6, 5 οἱ τρεῖς='the remaining three'; Diog. L. 1, 82 Βίας προκεκριμένος τῶν ἑπτά=Bias was preferred before the others of the seven [wise men]. Bl-D. §265): οἱ ἐννέα the other nine Lk 17: 17. Cf. 15: 4; Mt 18: 12f. οἱ δέκα the other ten (disciples) 20: 24; Mk 10: 41. οἱ πέντε . . . ὁ εἷς . . . ὁ ἄλλος five of them . . . one . . . the last one Rv 17: 10.

3. The ptc. w. the art. receives—**a.** the mng. of a subst. ὁ πειράζων the tempter Mt 4: 3; 1 Th 3: 5. ὁ βαπτίζων Mk 6: 14. ὁ σπείρων Mt 13: 3; Lk 8: 5. ὁ ὀλεθρεύων Hb 11: 28. τὸ ὀφειλόμενον Mt 18: 30, 34. τὸ αὐλούμενον 1 Cor 14: 7. τὸ λαλούμενον vs. 9. τὰ γινόμενα Lk 9: 7. τὰ ἐρχόμενα J 16: 13. τὰ ἐξουθενημένα 1 Cor 1: 28. τὰ ὑπάρχοντα (s. ὑπάρχω 1). In Engl. usage many of these neuters are transl. by a relative clause, as in b below. Bl-D. §413; Rob. 1108f.

b. the mng. of a relative clause ὁ δεχόμενος ὑμᾶς whoever receives you Mt 10: 40. τῷ τύπτοντί σε Lk 6: 29. ὁ ἐμὲ μισῶν J 15: 23. οὐδὲ γὰρ ὄνομά ἐστιν ἕτερον τὸ δεδομένον (ὃ δέδοται) Ac 4: 12. τινές εἰσιν οἱ ταράσσοντες ὑμᾶς Gal 1: 7. Cf. Lk 7: 32; 18: 9; J 12: 12; Col 2:

8; 1 Pt 1: 7; 2 J 7; Jd 4 al. So esp. after πᾶς: πᾶς ὁ ὀργιζόμενος everyone who becomes angry Mt 5: 22. πᾶς ὁ κρίνων Ro 2: 1 al. After μακάριος Mt 5: 4, 6, 10. After οὐαὶ ὑμῖν Lk 6: 25.

4. The inf. w. neut. art. (Bl-D. §398ff; Rob. 1062-8) stands—**a.** for a noun (Bl-D. §399; Rob. 1062-6) τὸ (ἀνίπτοις χερσὶν) φαγεῖν Mt 15: 20. τὸ (ἐκ νεκρῶν) ἀναστῆναι Mk 9: 10. τὸ ἀγαπᾶν 12: 33; cf. Ro 13: 8. τὸ ποιῆσαι, τὸ ἐπιτελέσαι 2 Cor 8: 11. τὸ καθίσαι Mt 20: 23. τὸ θέλειν Ro 7: 18; 2 Cor 8: 10.—Freq. used w. preps. ἀντὶ τοῦ, διὰ τό, διὰ τοῦ, ἐκ τοῦ, ἐν τῷ, ἕνεκεν τοῦ, ἕως τοῦ, μετὰ τό, πρὸ τοῦ, πρὸς τό etc.; s. the preps. in question (Bl-D. §402-4; Rob. 1068-75).

b. The gen. of the inf. w. the art., without a prep., is esp. frequent (Bl-D. §400; Mlt. 216–8; Rob. 1066–8; DEEvans, Classical Quarterly 15, '21, 26ff). The use of this inf. is esp. common in Lk and Paul, less freq. in Mt and Mk, quite rare in other writers. The gen. stands

α. dependent on words that govern the gen.: ἄξιον 1 Cor 16: 4 (cf. ἄξιος 1c). ἐξαπορηθῆναι τοῦ ζῆν 2 Cor 1: 8. ἔλαχε τοῦ θυμιᾶσαι Lk 1: 9 (cf. 1 Km 14: 47 v.l. Σαοὺλ ἔλαχεν τοῦ βασιλεύειν).

β. dependent on a noun (Bl-D. §400, 1; Rob. 1066f) ὁ χρόνος τοῦ τεκεῖν Lk 1: 57. ἐπλήσθησαν αἱ ἡμέραι τοῦ τεκεῖν αὐτήν 2: 6. ἐξουσία τοῦ πατεῖν 10: 19. εὐκαιρία τοῦ παραδοῦναι 22: 6. ἐλπὶς τοῦ σῴζεσθαι Ac 27: 20; τοῦ μετέχειν 1 Cor 9: 10. ἐπιποθία τοῦ ἐλθεῖν Ro 15: 23. χρείαν ἔχειν τοῦ διδάσκειν Hb 5: 12. καιρὸς τοῦ ἄρξασθαι 1 Pt 4: 17. τ. ἐνέργειαν τοῦ δύνασθαι the power that enables him Phil 3: 21. ἡ προθυμία τοῦ θέλειν zeal in desiring 2 Cor 8: 11.

γ. Somet. the connection w. the noun is very loose, and the transition to the consecutive sense (=result) is unmistakable (Bl-D. §400, 2; Rob. 1066f): ἐπλήσθησαν ἡμέραι ὀκτὼ τοῦ περιτεμεῖν αὐτόν Lk 2: 21. ὀφειλέται . . . τοῦ κατὰ σάρκα ζῆν Ro 8: 12. εἰς ἀκαθαρσίαν τοῦ ἀτιμάζεσθαι 1: 24. ὀφθαλμοὺς τοῦ μὴ βλέπειν 11: 8. τὴν ἔκβασιν τοῦ δύνασθαι ὑπενεγκεῖν 1 Cor 10: 13.

δ. Verbs of hindering, ceasing take the inf. w. τοῦ μή (class.; PGenève 16, 23 [207 AD] κωλύοντες τοῦ μὴ σπείρειν; LXX): καταπαύειν Ac 14: 18. κατέχειν Lk 4: 42. κρατεῖσθαι 24: 16. κωλύειν Ac 10: 47. παύειν 1 Pt 3: 10 (Ps 33: 14). ὑποστέλλεσθαι Ac 20: 20, 27. Without μή: ἐγκόπτεσθαι τοῦ ἐλθεῖν Ro 15: 22.

ε. The gen. of the inf. comes after verbs of deciding exhorting, commanding, etc. (1 Ch 19: 19) ἐγένετο γνώμης Ac 20: 3. ἐντέλλεσθαι Lk 4: 10 (Ps 90: 11). ἐπιστέλλειν Ac 15: 20. κατανεύειν Lk 5: 7. κρίνειν Ac 27: 1. παρακαλεῖν 21: 12. προσεύχεσθαι Js 5: 17. τὸ πρόσωπον στηρίζειν Lk 9: 51. συντίθεσθαι Ac 23: 20.

ζ. The inf. w. τοῦ and τοῦ μή plainly has final (=purpose) mng. (Bl-D. §400, 5 app. w. exx. fr. secular lit. and pap.; Rob. 1067): ἐξῆλθεν ὁ σπείρων τοῦ σπείρειν a sower went out to sow Mt 13: 3. ζητεῖν τοῦ ἀπολέσαι=ἵνα ἀπολέσῃ 2: 13. τοῦ δοῦναι γνῶσιν Lk 1: 77. τοῦ κατευθῦναι τοὺς πόδας vs. 79. τοῦ σινιάσαι 22: 31. τοῦ μηκέτι δουλεύειν Ro 6: 6. τοῦ ποιῆσαι αὐτά Gal 3: 10. τοῦ γνῶναι αὐτόν Phil 3: 10. Cf. Mt 3: 13; 11: 1; 24: 45; Lk 2: 24, 27; 8: 5; 24: 29; Ac 3: 2; 20: 30; 26: 18; Hb 10: 7 (Ps 39: 9); 11: 5,

η. as well as consecutive mng. (result): μετεμελήθητε τοῦ πιστεῦσαι αὐτῷ you changed your minds and believed him Mt 21: 32. τοῦ μὴ εἶναι αὐτὴν μοιχαλίδα Ro 7: 3. τοῦ ποιεῖν τὰ βρέφη ἔκθετα Ac 7: 19. Cf. 3: 12; 10: 25.

5. The art. is used w. prepositional expressions (Artem. 4, 33 p. 224, 7 ὁ ἐν Περγάμῳ; 4, 36 ὁ ἐν Μαγνησίᾳ) τῆς ἐκκλησίας τῆς ἐν Κεγχρεαῖς Ro 16: 1. τοῖς ἐν τῇ οἰκίᾳ to those in the house Mt 5: 15. πάτερ ἡμῶν ὁ ἐν τ. οὐρανοῖς 6: 9. οἱ ἀπὸ τῆς Ἰταλίας Hb 13: 24. οἱ ἐν Χριστῷ Ἰησοῦ Ro 8: 1. οἱ ἐξ ἐριθείας 2: 8. οἱ ἐκ νόμου 4: 14; cf. vs. 16. οἱ ἐκ τῆς Καίσαρος οἰκίας Phil 4: 22. οἱ ἐξ εὐωνύμων Mt 25: 41. οἱ παρ' αὐτοῦ Mk 3: 21. οἱ μετ' αὐτοῦ Mt 12: 3. οἱ περὶ αὐτόν Mk 4: 10; Lk 22: 49 al.—Neut. τὰ ἀπὸ τοῦ πλοίου pieces of wreckage fr. the ship Ac 27: 44 (differently FZorell, BZ 9, '11, 159f). τὰ περί τινος Lk 24: 19, 27; Ac 24: 10; Phil 1: 27. τὰ περὶ τινα 2: 23. τὰ κατ' ἐμέ my circumstances Eph 6: 21; Col 4: 7; what has happened to me Phil 1: 12. τὰ κατὰ τὸν νόμου what (was to be done) according to the law Lk 2: 39. τὸ ἐξ ὑμῶν Ro 12: 18. τὰ πρὸς τὸν θεόν 15: 17; Hb 2: 17; 5: 1 (X., Resp. Lac. 13, 11 ἱερεῖ τὰ πρὸς τοὺς θεούς, στρατηγῷ δὲ τὰ πρὸς τοὺς ἀνθρώπους). τὰ παρ' αὐτῶν Lk 10: 7.

6. w. an adv. or adverbial expr. (1 Macc 8: 3) τὸ ἔμπροσθεν Lk 19: 4. τὸ ἔξωθεν Mt 23: 25. τὸ πέραν Mt 8: 18, 28. τὰ ἄνω J 8: 23; Col 3: 1f. τὰ κάτω J 8: 23. τὰ ὀπίσω Mk 13: 16. τὰ ὧδε matters here Col 4: 9. ὁ πλησίον the neighbor Mt 5: 43. οἱ καθεξῆς Ac 3: 24. τὸ κατὰ σάρκα Ro 9: 5. τὸ ἐκ μέρους 1 Cor 13: 10.—Esp. w. indications of time τό, τὰ νῦν s. νῦν 3. τὸ πάλιν 2 Cor 13: 2. τὸ λοιπόν 1 Cor 7: 29; Phil 3: 1. τὸ πρῶτον J 10: 40; 12: 16; 19: 39. τὸ πρότερον 6: 62; Gal 4: 13. τὸ καθ' ἡμέραν daily Lk 11: 3.—τὸ πλεῖστον at the most 1 Cor 14: 27.

7. The art. w. the gen. foll. denotes a relation of kinship, ownership, or dependence: Ἰάκωβος ὁ τοῦ Ζεβεδαίου Mt 10: 2 (Thu. 4, 104 Θουκυδίδης ὁ Ὁλόρου [sc. υἱός]; Plut., Timol. 3, 2; Appian, Syr. 26 §123 Σέλευκος ὁ Ἀντιόχου; Jos., Bell. 5, 5; 11). Μαρία ἡ Ἰακώβου Lk 24: 10. ἡ τοῦ Οὐρίου the wife of Uriah Mt 1: 6. οἱ Χλόης Chloë's people 1 Cor 1: 11. οἱ Ἀριστοβούλου, οἱ Ναρκίσσου Ro 16: 10f. οἱ αὐτοῦ Ac 16: 33. οἱ τοῦ Χριστοῦ 1 Cor 15: 23; Gal 5: 24. Καισάρεια ἡ Φιλίππου Caesarea Philippi i.e. the city of Philip Mk 8: 27.—τό, τά τινος someone's things, affairs, situation (Thu. 4, 83 τὰ τοῦ Ἀρριβαίου; Parthenius 1, 6; Appian, Syr. 16 §67 τὰ Ῥωμαίων) τὰ τοῦ θεοῦ, τῶν ἀνθρώπων Mt 16: 23; 22: 21; Mk 8: 33; cf. 1 Cor 2: 11. τὰ τῆς σαρκός, τοῦ πνεύματος Ro 8: 5; cf. 14: 19; 1 Cor 7: 33f; 13: 11. τὰ ὑμῶν 2 Cor 12: 14. τὰ τῆς ἀσθενείας μου 11: 30. τὰ τοῦ νόμου what the law requires Ro 2: 14. τὸ τῆς συκῆς what has been done to the fig tree Mt 21: 21; cf. 8: 33. τὰ ἑαυτῆς its own advantage 1 Cor 13: 5; cf. Phil 2: 4, 21. τὸ τῆς παροιμίας what the proverb says 2 Pt 2: 22 (Pla., Theaet. 183E τὸ τοῦ Ὁμήρου; Menand., Dyscolus 633 τὸ τοῦ λόγου). ἐν τοῖς τοῦ πατρός μου in my Father's house (so Field, Notes 50-6; Gdspd., Probs. 81-3; differently, 'interests', PJTemple, CBQ 1, '39, 342-52) Lk 2: 49 (Lysias 12, 12 εἰς τὰ τοῦ ἀδελφοῦ; Theocr. 2, 76 τὰ Λύκωνος; pap. in Mayser II ['26] p. 8; POxy. 523, 3 [II AD] an invitation to a dinner ἐν τοῖς Κλαυδίου Σαραπίωνος; PTebt. 316 II, 23 [99 AD] ἐν τοῖς Ποτάμωνος; Esth 7: 9; Job 18: 19; Jos., Ant. 16, 302. Of the temple of a god Jos., C. Ap. 1, 118 ἐν τοῖς τοῦ Διός). Mt 20: 15 is classified here by WHPHatch, ATR 26, '44, 250-53; s. also ἐμός 2.

8. The neut. of the art. stands—a. before whole sentences or clauses (Epict. 4, 1, 45 τὸ Καίσαρα μὴ εἶναι φίλον; Prov. Aesopi 100 P. τὸ Οὐκ οἶδα; Jos., Ant. 10, 205) τὸ Οὐ φονεύσεις, οὐ μοιχεύσεις κτλ. (quot. fr. the Decalogue) Mt 19: 18; Ro 13: 9. τὸ Καὶ μετὰ ἀνόμων ἐλογίσθη (quot. fr. Is 53: 12) Lk 22: 37. Cf. Gal 5: 14. τὸ Εἰ δύνῃ as far as your words 'If you can' are concerned Mk 9: 23. Likew. before indirect questions (Vett. Val. 291, 14 τὸ πῶς τέτακται; Ael. Aristid. 45, 15 K. τὸ ὅστις ἐστίν; Jos., Ant. 20, 28 ἐπὶ πείρᾳ τοῦ τί φρονοῖεν; Pel.-Leg. p. 20, 32 τὸ τί γένηται) τὸ τί ἂν θέλοι καλεῖσθαι αὐτό Lk

1: 62. τὸ τίς ἂν εἴη μείζων αὐτῶν 9: 46. τὸ πῶς δεῖ ὑμᾶς περιπατεῖν 1 Th 4: 1. Cf. Lk 19: 48; 22: 2, 4, 23f; Ac 4: 21; 22: 30; Ro 8: 26; Hs 8, 1, 4.

b. before single words which are taken fr. what precedes and hence are quoted, as it were (Epict. 1, 29, 16 τὸ Σωκράτης; Hierocles, Carm. Aur. 13 p. 448 ἐν τῷ μηδείς) τὸ 'ἀνέβη' Eph 4: 9. τὸ 'ἔτι ἅπαξ' Hb 12: 27. τὸ '' Ἀγάρ' Gal 4: 25.

9. Other notable uses of the art. are—a. the elliptic use, which leaves a part of a sentence accompanied by the art. to be completed fr. the context: ὁ τὰ δύο the man with the two (talents), i.e. ὁ τὰ δύο τάλαντα λαβών Mt 25: 17; cf. vs. 22. τῷ τὸν φόρον Ro 13: 7. ὁ τὸ πολύ, ὀλίγον the man who had much, little 2 Cor 8: 15 after Ex 16: 18 (cf. Lucian, Bis Accus. 9 ὁ τὴν σύριγγα [sc. ἔχων]).

b. Σαῦλος, ὁ καὶ Παῦλος Ac 13: 9; s. καί II 8.

c. the fem. art. is found in a quite singular usage ἡ οὐαί (= ἡ θλῖψις or ἡ πληγή) Rv 9: 12; 11: 14. Sim. ὁ Ἀμήν 3: 14.

10. One art. can refer to several nouns connected by καί—a. when various words, sing. or pl., are brought close together by a common art.: τοὺς ἀρχιερεῖς καὶ γραμματεῖς Mt 2: 4; cf. 16: 21; Mk 15: 1. ἐν τοῖς προφήταις κ. ψαλμοῖς Lk 24: 44. τῇ Ἰουδαίᾳ καὶ Σαμαρείᾳ Ac 1: 8; cf. 8: 1; Lk 5: 17 al.—Even nouns of different gender can be united in this way (Aristoph., Eccl. 750; Ps.-Pla., Axioch. 12 p. 371A οἱ δύο θεοί of Apollo and Artemis; Ps.-Demetr., Eloc. c. 292; PTebt. 14, 10 [114 BC]; En. 18, 14; Ep. Arist. 109) κατὰ τὰ ἐντάλματα καὶ διδασκαλίας Col 2: 22. Cf. Lk 1: 6. εἰς τὰς ὁδοὺς καὶ φραγμούς 14: 23.

b. when one and the same person has more than one attribute applied to him: πρὸς τὸν πατέρα μου καὶ πατέρα ὑμῶν J 20: 17. ὁ θεὸς καὶ πατὴρ τοῦ κυρίου Ἰ. Ro 15: 6; 2 Cor 1: 3; 11: 31; Eph 1: 3; 1 Pt 1: 3. ὁ θεὸς καὶ πατὴρ (ἡμῶν) Eph 5: 20; Phil 4: 20; 1 Th 1: 3; 3: 11, 13. Of Christ: τοῦ κυρίου ἡμῶν καὶ σωτῆρος 2 Pt 1: 11; cf. 2: 20; 3: 18. τοῦ μεγάλου θεοῦ καὶ σωτῆρος Tit 2: 13 (PGrenf. II 15 I, 6 [139 BC] of the deified King Ptolemy τοῦ μεγάλου θεοῦ εὐεργέτου καὶ σωτῆρος ἐπιφανοῦς εὐχαρίστου).

c. On the other hand, the art. is repeated when two different persons are named: ὁ φυτεύων καὶ ὁ ποτίζων 1 Cor 3: 8. ὁ βασιλεὺς καὶ ὁ ἡγεμών Ac 26: 30.

11. In a fixed expression, when a noun in the gen. is dependent on another noun, it is customary to have the article either twice or not at all: τὸ πνεῦμα τοῦ θεοῦ 1 Cor 3: 16; πνεῦμα θεοῦ Ro 8: 9. ὁ λόγος τοῦ θεοῦ 2 Cor 2: 17; λόγος θεοῦ 1 Th 2: 13. ἡ ἡμέρα τοῦ κυρίου 2 Th 2: 2; ἡμ. κ. 1 Th 5: 2. ὁ υἱὸς τοῦ ἀνθρώπου Mt 8: 20; υἱ. ἀ. Hb 2: 6. ἡ ἀνάστασις τῶν νεκρῶν Mt 22: 31; ἀ. ν. Ac 23: 6. ἡ κοιλία τῆς μητρός J 3: 4; κ. μ. Mt 19: 12.—AMPerry, JBL 68, '49, 329-34; MBlack, An Aramaic Approach³, '67, 93-5. M-M.

ὀβελίσκος, ου, ὁ (Aristoph., X.+; inscr.; PEleph. 5, 2; Job 41: 22; 4 Macc 11: 19) dim. of ὀβελός; a (little) skewer or spit w. ξίφος AP 15: 30.*

ὀγδοήκοντα indecl. (Thu. et al.; inscr., pap., LXX; Jos., Bell. 4, 482, Vi. 15; 75; Test. Jos. 16: 5) eighty Lk 2: 37; 16: 7; MPol 9: 3. M-M.*

ὄγδοος, η, ον (Hom.+; inscr., pap., LXX, Ep. Arist., Philo, Joseph., Test. 12 Patr.) the eighth Rv 17: 11; 21: 20; MPol 21; Hs 9, 1, 8; 9, 25, 1; ἡ ἡμέρα ἡ ὀ. Lk 1: 59; Ac 7: 8 (Gen 21: 4; cf. Jos., Ant. 1, 192); B 15: 9; cf. vs. 8. ὄγδοον Νῶε δικαιοσύνης κήρυκα ἐφύλαξεν he preserved Noah as a preacher of righteousness, with seven others (lit. 'as the eighth') 2 Pt 2: 5 (on this expr. cf. Thu. 1, 46, 2; 1, 61, 1; 2, 13, 1; Pla., Leg. 3 p. 695c λαβὼν τὴν ἀρχὴν ἔβδομος; Plut., Pelop. 13, 7 εἰς οἰκίαν δωδέκατος κατελθών; Ps.-Apollod., Epit. 3, 15 ἡ μήτηρ ἐνάτη= the mother with eight [children]; 2 Macc 5: 27 δέκατος γενηθείς= 'with nine others'). M-M.*

ὄγκος, ου, ὁ (Hom.+; Suppl. Epigr. Gr. VIII 802; Philo; Jos., Bell. 4, 319; 7, 443. Loanw. in rabb.) *weight, burden, impediment* ὄγκον ἀποτίθεσθαι πάντα *lay aside every impediment* Hb 12: 1. τῆς κεφαλῆς ὄ. *the bulk of the head* Papias 3.—HSeesemann, TW V 41. M-M.*

ὅδε, ἥδε, τόδε (Hom.+; inscr., pap. [rare in both: Mayser I 308]; LXX [Thackeray p. 191]; En. 106, 16; Ep. Arist. 28; Philo; Jos., Ant. 10, 113) demonstrative pron. (Bl-D. §289 w. app.; Rob. 696f) *this* (*one*) (*here*).

1. w. ref. to what follows (so predom.), esp. in the formula τάδε λέγει *this is what . . . says* (introductory formula in the decrees of the Persian kings: Inschr. v. Magn. 115, 4; Ps.-Pla., Alcib. II 12 p. 149c τ. λ. Ἄμμων; Jos., Ant. 11, 26. In the OT freq. as an introduction to prophetic utterance [Thackeray p. 11]. Also in wills: PGiess. 36, 10 [161 BC] τάδε λέγει γυνὴ Ἑλληνὶς Ἀμμωνία; GRudberg, Eranos 11, '11, 170-9. As introd. to a letter Nicol. Dam.: 90 fgm. 5 p. 336, 22 Jac. Cf. GAGerhard, Unters. z. Gesch. d. gr. Briefes: I d. Anfangsformel, Diss. Hdlbg. '03) Ac 21: 11; Rv 2: 1, 8, 12, 18; 3: 1, 7, 14; B 6: 8; 9: 2 (Jer 7: 3), 5 (Jer 4: 3); cf. IPhld 7: 2.—Simply *this* 1 Cl 50: 3; 63: 2.

2. w. ref. to what precedes (Soph., Hdt.+; Aelian, N.A. 4, 15 p. 85, 28; 9, 63 p. 241, 11; Philostrat., Vi. Apoll. 218, 25; 271, 3 al.; Jos., Ant. 17, 2; 19) γυνή τις . . . καὶ τῇδε ἦν ἀδελφή *she had a sister* Lk 10: 39 (cf. Gen 25: 24; 38: 27; Judg 11: 37 B; MJohannessohn, Ztschr. für vgl. Sprachforschung 66, '39, p. 184, 7). ἥδε ἀπεκρίθη 1 Cl 12: 4.

3. εἰς τήνδε τὴν πόλιν *into this or that city, into such and such a city* Js 4: 13 (τήνδε for Att. τὴν δεῖνα or τὴν καὶ τήν. Cf. Cyrill. Scyth. p. 207, 20 τῆσδε τῆς πόλεως; 185, 13; Plut., Mor. 623ε τήνδε τὴν ἡμέραν [W-S. §23, 1c note 2; Bl-D. §289 w. app.; Rob. 696f.—The same expr. in Appian, Liby. 108 §510 and Ael. Aristid. 46 p. 384 D.], τόνδε τὸν ἄνθρωπον [Hierocles, Carm. Aur. 11 p. 439 M.], τόδε= 'this and that' [Bl-D. loc. cit.; also Plut., Mor. 168ᴅ; Dit., Syll.² 737, 62], τοῦδέ τινος= τοῦ δεῖνος [PMich. 154, 24— c. 300 Aᴅ] and the Mod. Gk. use of ὁ τάδε[ς]= ὁ δεῖνα [KBrugmann, Die Demonstrativpronomina: Abh. d. Sächs. Ges. d. W. 22, '04, 133 note]; JWackernagel, Syntax II² '28, 108). ὅδε is also found as v.l. Ac 15: 23; 2 Cor 12: 19.—LRydbeck, Fachprosa, '67, 88-99. M-M.*

ὁδεύω 1 aor. inf. ὁδεῦσαι (Hom.+; Dit., Or. 199, 28; POxy. 1537, 18; 22; 1771, 10; LXX, Philo, Joseph.; Sib. Or. 3, 367) *go, travel* ὁδὸν ὁδεύειν *make one's way* B 19: 1 (Artem. 2, 12; 37; cf. Philo, Poster. Cai. 155 ἀτραπὸν ὁδ.). δι' ἧς (i.e. ἀνοδίας.—ὁδ. διά as X., An. 7, 8, 8; Jos., Ant. 20, 118) ἄνθρωπος οὐκ ἐδύνατο ὁδεῦσαι *through which a man could not walk* Hv 1, 1, 3. Abs. (Tob 6: 6 BA; Jos., Bell. 1, 264; 3, 115) *travel* Σαμαρίτης ὁδεύων *a Samaritan who was on a journey* Lk 10: 33 (ASouter, Exp. 8th Ser. VIII '14, 94). Pass. (Strabo 5, 1, 7) ῥᾳδίως (Lat. raro) ὁδεύεται ὁ τόπος *the place is easily reached* Hv 4, 1, 2. M-M.*

ὁδηγέω fut. ὁδηγήσω (Aeschyl.+; inscr. fr. Transjordan [NGG Phil.-hist. Kl. Fachgr. V new series I 1, '36 p. 3, 1: divine leading]; PSI 332, 6; LXX) *lead, guide.*

1. lit. (Jos., Vi. 96) τινά *someone* τυφλὸς τυφλόν (cf.

Hesiod, Astron. fgm. 182 Rz. a blind man; Plut., Mor. 139ᴀ τυφλούς; Test. Reub. 2: 9; Ps.-Phoc. 24) Mt 15: 14; Lk 6: 39. τινὰ ἐπί τι *someone to someth.* (cf. M.Ant. 7, 55, 1 ἐπί τί σε ἡ φύσις ὁδηγεῖ; PSI loc. cit.; Ps 106: 30; 22: 3; 24: 5) ἐπὶ ζωῆς πηγὰς ὑδάτων *to springs of living water* Rv 7: 17.

2. fig. *lead, guide, conduct* (Plut., Mor. 954ʙ; Sextus 167 σοφία ψυχὴν ὁδηγεῖ πρὸς θεόν; LXX) of the Spirit ὁδηγήσει ὑμᾶς εἰς τὴν ἀλήθειαν πᾶσαν J 16: 13 (in the Herm. Lit. Hermes-Nous leads the souls to knowledge: Herm. Wr. 10, 21 εἰς τὴν εὐσεβῆ ψυχὴν ὁ νοῦς ὁδηγεῖ αὐτὴν ἐπὶ τὸ τῆς γνώσεως φῶς. Cf. 4, 11; 7, 2; 9, 10; 12, 12. Rtzst., Poim. 23, 5, Mysterienrel.³ 297; PGM 13, 523ff πάντα κινήσεις . . . Ἑρμοῦ σε ὁδηγοῦντος.—Wsd 9: 11; 10: 10, 17; Test. Jud 14: 1 εἰς πλάνην). Of lying ὁδηγεῖ εἰς τὴν κλοπήν *it leads to theft* D 3: 5. Of complaining: εἰς τ. βλασφημίαν 3: 6. Of divination: εἰς τὴν εἰδωλολατρείαν 3: 4 (cf. Test. Jud. 19: 1 ἡ φιλαργυρία πρὸς εἰδωλολατρείαν ὁδηγεῖ). Also ὁδ. πρός τι (Test. Gad 5: 7) 3: 2f. Without further qualification: ἐὰν μή τις ὁδηγήσει με *if no one instructs me* Ac 8: 31. M-M.*

ὁδηγός, οῦ, ὁ *leader, guide*—1. lit. (Polyb. 5, 5, 15; Plut., Alex. 27, 3; Zen.-P. 59 770, 14 [III ʙᴄ]; Jos., Ant. 12, 305; 1 Macc 4: 2; 2 Macc 5: 15; cf. Philo, Mos. 1, 178) of Judas as guide for the men who arrested Jesus Ac 1: 16.

2. as a symbol (Wsd 7: 15; 18: 3; Jos., Ant. 1, 217) ὁδηγὸς τυφλῶν *a guide for the blind* Ro 2: 19. τυφλοί εἰσιν ὁδηγοὶ τυφλῶν *they are blind leaders of the blind* Mt 15: 14. ὁδηγοὶ τυφλοί (Paroem. Gr.: Apostol. 11, 50) 23: 16, 24.*

ὀδμή s. ὀσμή.

ὁδοιπορέω (Soph., Hdt.+; Jos., Vi. 157, Ant. 14, 226; Dit., Syll.³ 885, 28; PGM 7, 181) *travel, be on the way* ὁδοιπορούντων ἐκείνων *as they were on their way* Ac 10: 9. M-M.*

ὁδοιπορία, ας, ἡ (Hom. Hymns, Hdt.+; Diod. S. 5, 29, 1; Epict. 3, 10, 11; POxy. 118 verso, 6; Wsd 13: 18; 18: 3; 1 Macc 6: 41; Philo, Mut. Nom. 165, Leg. ad Gai. 254; Jos., Ant. 5, 53) *walking, journey* κεκοπιακὼς ἐκ τῆς ὁδ. *tired from the journey* J 4: 6 (Jos., Ant. 2, 321 ὑπὸ τῆς ὁδοιπορίας κεκοπωμένος; 3; 2, 257; Dio Chrys. 77[27], 1 οἱ διψῶντες τ. ὁδοιπόρων). Pl. (Hdt. 8, 118; X., Oec. 20, 18) *journeys* 2 Cor 11: 26. M-M.*

ὁδοποιέω *make a way* or *path* (X., An. 3, 2, 24; 4, 8, 8; 5, 1, 13; Appian, Liby. 91 §430, Bell. Civ. 1, 78 §356 al.; Arrian, Anab. 1, 26, 1; Herodian 3, 3, 7; Dit., Or. 175, 10 [II ʙᴄ]; Is 62: 10; Ps 79: 10) of the disciples ἤρξαντο ὁδοποιεῖν τίλλοντες τοὺς στάχυας *they began to make a path as they picked the ears* Mk 2: 23 v.l. M-M.*

ὁδός, οῦ, ἡ (Hom.+; inscr., pap., LXX, En., Ep. Arist., Philo, Joseph., Test. 12 Patr.) *way.*

1. lit.—a. as a place: *way, road, highway* Mt 2: 12; 21: 8a, b; Mk 11: 8; Lk 3: 5 (Is 40: 4 v.l.); 19: 36; ἑτέρα ὁδ. Js 2: 25. ἡ ὁδ. ἡ Καμπανή= Lat. Via Campana *the Campanian Way* Hv 4, 1, 2 (s. MDibelius, Hdb. ad loc.; Hülsen, Pauly-W. III 1434); described as ἡ ὁδ. ἡ δημοσία *the public highway* ibid. (s. δημόσιος 1). ἡ ὁδ. ἡ καταβαίνουσα ἀπὸ Ἰερουσαλὴμ εἰς Γάζαν Ac 8: 26. παρέρχεσθαι διὰ τῆς ὁδ. *pass by* (a certain place) *on the road* Mt 8: 28 (on διὰ τ. ὁδ. cf. Philo, Abr. 269). πίπτειν εἰς τὴν ὁδ. *fall on the road* Hv 3, 7, 1a. ἔρχεσθαι εἰς τὴν ὁδ., μένειν ἐν τῇ ὁδ. v 3, 2, 9. κυλίεσθαι ἐκ τῆς ὁδ. *roll off the road* ibid.; 3, 7, 1b. Of a fig tree ἐπὶ τῆς ὁδοῦ *by the roadside* Mt 21: 19. Of beggars καθῆσθαι παρὰ τὴν ὁδ. *sit*

by the roadside Mt 20: 30; Mk 10: 46; Lk 18: 35 (Stephan. Byz. s.v. Εὕτρησις: κώμη... κεῖται παρὰ τὴν ὁδόν). Of seed that is sown πίπτειν παρὰ τὴν ὁδ. *fall along the road* (Dalman, Pj 22, '26, 121ff) Mt 13: 4; Mk 4: 4; Lk 8: 5; cf. Mt 13: 19; Mk 4: 15; Lk 8: 12. ἐξέρχεσθαι εἰς τὰς ὁδ. *go out into the streets* Mt 22: 10; Lk 14: 23; for διεξόδους τῶν ὁδ. Mt 22: 9 s. διέξοδος; καταβαίνειν ἐν τῇ ὁδ. *go down the road* Lk 10: 31. πορεύεσθαι κατὰ τὴν ὁδ. *go on along the highway* Ac 8: 36. ἐν τῇ ὁδῷ ᾗ ἤρχου (by attraction for ἣν ἤρ.; X., An. 2, 2, 10) 9: 17. ἑτοιμάζειν τὴν ὁδ. τινος *prepare someone's way* Mt 3: 3; Mk 1: 3; Lk 3: 4 (all after Is 40: 3); cf. Lk 1: 76 and for the pass. Rv 16: 12. Also κατασκευάζειν τὴν ὁδ. τινος Mt 11: 10; Mk 1: 2; Lk 7: 27. εὐθύνειν τὴν ὁδ. τινος J 1: 23. κατευθύνειν τὴν ὁδ. τινος 1 Th 3: 11.—W. obj. gen. to indicate direction (Gen 3: 24) Mt 10: 5; Hb 9: 8.—The acc. ὁδόν, following the Hebr. דֶּרֶךְ, and contrary to Gk. usage (but single cases of ὁδός take on the functions of adverbs or prepositions in the Gk. language as well: cf. Diog. L. 7, 156; Synes., Providence 1, 8 ὁδῷ βαδίζειν= 'go straight forward'; Appian, Hann. 47 § ὁδὸν ἐλάσσονα by a shorter [or the shortest] way; Plut., Mor. p. 371c.—The nearest parallel to our situation would be the report of Diog. L. 9, 8 concerning Heraclitus: τὴν μεταβολὴν ἄνω κάτω γίνεσθαι, if it might be translated: 'Change [in the universe] is accomplished in an upward and downward direction') is used as a prep. *toward* (Dt 11: 30; 3 Km 8: 48; 18: 43 ὁδὸν τῆς θαλάσσης. Cf. Bl-D. §161, 1) ὁδ. θαλάσσης *toward the sea* Mt 4: 15 (Is 8: 23 LXX, Aq., Sym.).

b. as an action: *way, journey* (Hes., Theogon. 754; X., Mem. 3, 13, 5; Herodian 2, 11, 1) εἰς (τὴν) ὁδ. *for the journey* (Jos., Ant. 12, 198) Mt 10: 10; Mk 6: 8; Lk 9: 3; *on the journey* Mk 10: 17. ἐν τῇ ὁδῷ *on the way* (Gen 45: 24; Jos., Ant. 6, 55; Ps.-Clem., Hom. 10, 2, end) Mt 15: 32; 20: 17; Mk 8: 3, 27; 9: 33f; 10: 52; Lk 9: 57; 12: 58; 24: 32; Ac 9: 27. τὰ ἐν τῇ ὁδῷ *what had happened to them on the way* Lk 24: 35. εἶναι ἐν τῇ ὁδῷ Mt 5: 25; Mk 10: 32. ἐξ ὁδοῦ *from a journey* (Appian, Bell. Civ. 1, 91 §418; Damasc., Vi. Isid. 203 p. 138, 8 W.; Jos., Vi. 246; 248 ἐκ τ. ὁδοῦ) Lk 11: 6. κατὰ τὴν ὁδ. *along the way* (Arrian, Anab. 1, 26, 5; 3, 19, 3; Jos., Ant. 8, 404; Ps.-Clem., Hom. 10, 2) 10: 4; Ac 25: 3; 26: 13. τ. ὁδὸν αὐτοῦ πορεύεσθαι *go on his way* 8: 39 (cf. X., Cyr. 5, 2, 22). πορεύεσθαι τῇ ὁδῷ 1 Cl 12: 4. ὁδὸν ποιεῖν *take a journey, make one's way* (Judg 17: 8) Mk 2: 23 (so the Lat., Syr., Copt., Armen. versions); s. ὁδοποιέω.—σαββάτου ὁδ. a *Sabbath day's journey* could belong under a or b; it signified the distance a Jew might travel on the Sabbath, two thousand paces or cubits (= about 800 meters), and a nearly equal number of yards.—'Erubin 4, 3; 7; 5, 7 [Die Mischna II 2: 'Erubin, by WNowack '26]; Origen, Princ. 4, 17; Schürer II⁴ 557; 575f; Billerb. II 590ff) Ac 1: 12. ἡμέρας ὁδός a *day's journey* Lk 2: 44 (Diod. S. 19, 17, 3; Appian, Samn. 1 §5; Polyaenus 7, 21, 1; Lucian, Syr. Dea 9; Procop., Aed. 6, 1, 12; cf. Hdt. 4, 101; X., Cyr. 1, 1, 3 παμπόλλων ἡμερῶν ὁδός; Ael Aristid. 36, 87 K.=48 p. 473 D.: τριῶν ἡμ. ὁδ.; Gen 30: 36; 31: 23; Ex 3: 18; Jdth 2: 21; 1 Macc 5: 24; 7: 45; Jos., Ant. 15, 293).

2. fig., but oft. w. the picture prominently in mind (Sib. Or. 3, 233).

a. *way* εἰς ὁδ. ἐθνῶν μὴ ἀπέλθητε *do not go in the way of the Gentiles* i.e. do not turn to the Gentiles Mt 10: 5 (but s. 1a.—JoachJeremias, Jesu Verheissung für d. Völker, '56). εὐρύχωρος ἡ ὁδ. ἡ ἀπάγουσα εἰς τὴν ἀπώλειαν 7: 13 (Pla., Gorg. 524A ἡ ὁδώ, ἡ μὲν εἰς μακάρων νήσους, ἡ δ' εἰς Τάρταρον). Also ἡ ὁδ. τῆς ἀπωλείας AP 1: 1; ἡ τοῦ μέλανος ὁδ. B 20: 1. ἡ τοῦ θανάτου ὁδ. (Herm. Wr. 1,

29) D 5: 1. Cf. 1: 1 (on this Jer 21: 8; Test. Ash. 1: 3, 5 ὁδοὶ δύο, καλοῦ κ. κακοῦ; Sib. Or. 8, 399 ὁδοὶ δύο, ζωῆς θανάτου τε; Ael. Aristid. 30 p. 577 D.: δυοῖν ὁδοῖν τὴν μὲν... τὴν δέ.—The two ὁδοί of Heracles: X., Mem. 2, 1, 21ff; Maximus Tyr. 14, 1a; e; k). ὁδ. σκότους B 5: 4b. Description of the way B 20; D 5: 1ff. τεθλιμμένη ἡ ὁδ. ἡ ἀπάγουσα εἰς τὴν ζωήν Mt 7: 14. Also ἡ ὁδ. τῆς ζωῆς D 1: 2. ἡ ὁδ. τοῦ φωτός B 19: 1. Description of the way B 19; D 1–4. ὁδ. εἰρήνης Lk 1: 79; Ro 3: 17 (Is 59: 8; Ps 13: 3). ὁδ. ζωῆς Ac 2: 28 (Ps 15: 11); cf. D 1: 2 above. ὁδ. σωτηρίας Ac 16: 17. ὁδ. πρόσφατος κ. ζῶσα Hb 10: 20. ὁδ. δικαιοσύνης B 1: 4; 5: 4a. Of love ὁδ. ἡ ἀναφέρουσα εἰς θεόν IEph 9: 1. αὕτη ἡ ὁδ. ἐν ᾗ εὕρομεν τὸ σωτήριον ἡμῶν 1 Cl 36: 1.—Christ calls himself ἡ ὁδ. (i.e., to God) J 14: 6, cf. 4f (s. Hdb. and Bultmann [p. 466ff—Engl. 603ff w. other lit.]; JPascher, Η ΒΑΣΙΛΙΚΗ ΟΔΟΣ; D. Königsweg. z. Wiedergeb. u. Vergottung b. Philon v. Alex. '31).

b. *way of life, way of acting, conduct* (ἡ) ὁδ. (τῆς) δικαιοσύνης (Pr 21: 16, 21; Job 24: 13) Mt 21: 32 (ἐν ὁδῷ δικ. [cf. Pr 8: 20] denotes either the way of life practiced by the Baptist [Zahn; OHoltzmann] or the type of conduct he demanded [HHoltzmann; BWeiss; JWeiss; EKlostermann; Schniewind]. Cf. JAKleist, CBQ 8, '46, 192-6); 2 Pt 2: 21. τῇ ὁδ. αὐτοῦ ἐπλανήθη *he went astray in his path* (= 'in his conduct') 1 Cl 16: 6 (Is 53: 6). ἐκ πλάνης ὁδοῦ αὐτοῦ *from his misguided way of life* Js 5: 20. ἡ ὁδ. τῆς ἀληθείας (Ps 118: 30) vs. 19 v.l. (cf. 2 Pt 2: 2 in c below); 1 Cl 35: 5. ἀφιέναι τὴν ὁδ. τὴν ἀληθινήν Hv 3, 7, 1. τῇ ὁδ. τοῦ Κάϊν πορεύεσθαι *follow the way of Cain* Jd 11. ὁδ. δικαίων, ἀσεβῶν B 11: 7 (Ps 1: 6). (ἡ) ὁδ. (ἡ) δικαία (Jos., Ant. 13, 290) 12: 4; 2 Cl 5: 7. τὸ δίκαιον ὀρθὴν ὁδ. ἔχει *the way of righteousness is a straight one* Hm 6, 1, 2. τῇ ὀρθῇ ὁδ. πορεύεσθαι ibid.; cf. 4. Opp. ἡ στρεβλὴ ὁδ. *the crooked way* m 6, 1, 3. θέωμεν τὴν ὁδ. τὴν εὐθεῖαν *let us run the straight course* 2 Cl 7: 3; cf. 2 Pt 2: 15. Of life among the heathen αὕτη ἡ ὁδ. ἡδυτέρα αὐτοῖς ἐφαίνετο Hs 8, 9, 1. The basic mng. has disappeared to such a degree that one can speak of καρποὶ τῆς ὁδ. 1 Cl 57: 6 (Pr 1: 31) and ἔργα τῆς πονηρᾶς ὁδ. B 4: 10.—Pl. *ways*, of one's conduct as a whole Ac 14: 16; Ro 3: 16 (Is 59: 7; Ps 13: 3a); Js 1: 8; Hv 2, 2, 6. Esp. of the *ways of God*, in part of the ways that God initiates ὡς... ἀνεξιχνίαστοι αἱ ὁδ. αὐτοῦ *how inscrutable are his ways* Ro 11: 33. δίκαιαι καὶ ἀληθιναὶ αἱ ὁδ. σου Rv 15: 3. αἱ ὁδ. τῆς εὐλογίας *the ways of blessing* 1 Cl 31: 1; in part of the ways that are to be adopted by men: οὐκ ἔγνωσαν τὰς ὁδ. μου Hb 3: 10 (Ps 94: 10). διαστρέφειν τὰς ὁδοὺς τοῦ κυρίου Ac 13: 10. διδάσκειν τὰς ὁδ. σου 1 Cl 18: 13 (Ps 50: 15). Likew. the sing. τὴν ὁδ. τοῦ θεοῦ ἐν ἀληθείᾳ διδάσκειν Mt 22: 16; cf. Mk 12: 14; Lk 20: 21. ἀφιέναι τὴν ὁδ. τοῦ θεοῦ AP 20: 34. παρέβησαν ἐκ τῆς ὁδ. 1 Cl 53: 2 (Ex 32: 8).

c. of the whole way of life fr. a moral and relig. viewpoint, *the Way, teaching* in the most comprehensive sense (Lucian, Hermot. 46 ὁδ. of the doctrine of a philosophical school), and specif. of Christianity (SVMcCasland, JBL 77, '58, 222-30: Qumran parallels) κατὰ τὴν ὁδ. ἣν λέγουσιν αἵρεσιν *according to the Way, which they call a sect* Ac 24: 14. ἐάν τινας εὕρῃ τῆς ὁδ. ὄντας *if he should find people who belonged to the Way* 9: 2. ὁδ. κυρίου, θεοῦ of Christian teaching 18: 25f. κακολογεῖν τὴν ὁδ. ἐνώπιον τοῦ πλήθους 19: 9. ταύτην τὴν ὁδ. διώκειν *persecute this religion* 22: 4. ἐγένετο τάραχος περὶ τῆς ὁδ. *there arose a disturbance concerning the Way* 19: 23. τὰ περὶ τῆς ὁδ. *(the things) concerning the teaching* 24: 22. ἡ ὁδὸς τ. ἀληθείας of the true Christian religion 2 Pt 2: 2. Of the way of love καθ' ὑπερβολὴν ὁδ. *a* *far better way* 1 Cor 12: 31. ἡ ὁδ. τῆς δικαιοσύνης AP 7: 22; 13: 28. Likew. the pl. (En. 104, 13 μαθεῖν ἐξ αὐτῶν [= τ. βίβλων] πάσας τ. ὁδοὺς τῆς ἀληθείας) τὰς ὁδούς μου ἐν Χριστῷ Ἰησοῦ *my Christian teachings* 1 Cor 4: 17.—OBecker, D. Bild des Weges u. verwandte Vorstellungen im frühgriech. Denken '37; FNötscher, Gotteswege u. Menschenwege in d. Bibel u. in Qumran, '58; ERepo, D. Weg als Selbstbezeichnung des Urchr., '64 (but s. CBurchard, Der 13te Zeuge, '70, 43, n. 10). WMichaelis, TW V 42-118: ὁδός and related words. M-M. B. 717; 720.**

ὀδούς, ὀδόντος, ὁ (Hom.+; pap., LXX, Philo; Jos., Bell. 6, 197) *tooth* Rv 9: 8 (cf. Jo 1: 6). δι' ὀδόντων θηρίων ἀλήθεσθαι *be ground by the teeth of wild beasts* IRo 4: 1. W. ὀφθαλμός Mt 5: 38 (Ex 21: 24). τρίζειν τοὺς ὀδ. *grind one's teeth* Mk 9: 18. Also βρύχειν τοὺς ὀδ. ἐπί τινα (s. βρύχω) Ac 7: 54. From this, βρυγμὸς τῶν ὀδ. *gnashing* or *grinding of teeth* (w. κλαυθμὸς), only in connection w. the tortures of hell Mt 8: 12; 13: 42, 50; 22: 13; 24: 51; 25: 30; Lk 13: 28 (s. βρυγμός). M-M. B. 231.*

ὀδυνάω *cause pain* in our lit. only pass. ὀδυνάομαι 2 pers. ὀδυνᾶσαι (Bl-D. §87; Mlt.-H. 198; Helbing p. 61) *feel pain* (trag.+; Democr. 159; Pla.; Vett. Val. index; LXX). 1. of physical torment (Aelian, N.A. 11, 32 p. 286, 28) περί τινος *suffer pain for* (the sake of) someone 1 Cl 16: 4 (Is 53: 4). Esp. of the tortures of hell ὀδ. ἐν τῇ φλογί *suffer torment in the flames* Lk 16: 24; cf. vs. 25. 2. of mental and spiritual pain (Dio Chrys. 66[16], 1; Alciphr. 3, 14, 2; Philo, De Jos. 94 ὀδυνώμενος; Jos., Bell. 6, 183 ὀδυνώμενον) ὀδυνώμενοι ζητοῦμέν σε *we have been anxiously looking for you* Lk 2: 48 (two persons of different sex are referred to with a masc. modifier, as Epici p. 20 Achilles and Helen with αὐτούς). ὀδυνώμενοι μάλιστα ἐπὶ τῷ λόγῳ *they were especially pained at his saying* Ac 20: 38 (ὀδυνᾶσθαι ἐπί τινι as Philo, Conf. Lingu. 92). M-M.*

ὀδύνη, ης, ἡ (Hom.+; PGrenf. I 1, 2 [II BC]; Sb 4949, 12; 5716, 12; LXX; En. 102, 11; Ep. Arist. 208; Philo; Jos., Ant. 15, 62 f. Ap. 2, 143; Test. 12 Patr.) *pain, woe* of the tribulations of the last days Mt 24: 8 v.l. Of mental pain: ἀδιάλειπτος ὀδ. τῇ καρδίᾳ μου (sc. ἐστί) *my heart is continually grieved* Ro 9: 2 (Philo, Aet. M. 63 ὀδ. ψυχῆς). Of the remorse of conscience ἑαυτοὺς περιέπειραν ὀδύναις πολλαῖς *they have pierced themselves to the heart with many pangs* 1 Ti 6: 10.—FHauck, TW V 118f. M-M.*

ὀδυρμός, οῦ, ὁ (Aeschyl., Pla.+; Aelian, V.H. 14, 22; Jos., Bell. 5, 31, Ant. 2, 328; 2 Macc 11: 6) *lamentation, mourning* 2 Cor 7: 7. W. κλαυθμός Mt 2: 18 (Jer 38: 15). M-M.*

ὀδύρομαι mid. dep. (Hom.+; inscr. fr. Gaza: Suppl. Epigr. Gr. VIII 269, 8 [III/II BC]; PThéad. 21, 15; Ramsay, Studies in the History and Art of the Eastern Provinces '06 p. 144, 5; Jer 38: 18; Philo, Migr. Abr. 156; Jos., Ant. 11, 222, C. Ap. 2, 243; Test. Zeb. 2: 4) *mourn, lament* w. ἐλεεῖν MPol 2: 2.*

Ὀζίας, ου, ὁ (עֻזִּיָּה, עֻזִּיָּהוּ; Ὀζίας in LXX and Joseph.; cf. EKautzsch, Mitteilungen u. Nachrichten des Deutschen Palästina-Vereins '04, 6f) *Uzziah*, Hebrew king, in the genealogy of Jesus Mt 1: 8f; Lk 3: 23ff D (here, as Jos., Ant. 9, 236, the gen. is Ὀζία).*

ὄζος, ου, ὁ (Hom.+ mng. 'branch') *the knot* on a tree-branch (so Theophr. et al.; Wsd 13: 13) ῥάβδος σκληρὰ

λίαν ὄζους ἔχουσα *a very hard and knotty staff* Hs 6, 2, 5 (cf. Alciphr. 3, 19, 5). B. 523.*

ὄζω (Hom.+; Antig. Car. 117 [given off by a corpse]; Epict. 4, 11, 15; 18 [of an unkempt man]; Ex 8: 10) *smell, give off an odor,* pleasant or unpleasant; ἤδη ὄζει *by this time the smell must be offensive* J 11: 39. M-M. B.*

ὅθεν adv. (Hom.+; inscr., pap., LXX; Philo, Aet. M. 147; Joseph.) *from where, whence, from which.* 1. of place (Jos., Ant. 1, 168; 19, 291) GP 13: 56; Hs 9, 4, 7. ὅθ. ἐξῆλθον Mt 12: 44; Lk 11: 24. εἰς Ἀντιόχειαν ὅθ. ἦσαν παραδεδομένοι Ac 14: 26. εἰς Συρακούσας . . . ὅθ. περιελθόντες κατηντήσαμεν 28: 13. W. attraction (Thu. 1, 89, 3.—Bl-D. §437; Rob. 548) συνάγων ὅθ. (=ἐκεῖθεν ὅπου) οὐ διεσκόρπισας *gathering where you did not winnow* Mt 25: 24, 26. 2. *from which fact* (Jos., Ant. 2, 36) 1 J 2: 18.—3. *for which reason* (Pla., Aristot.; inscr. [Meisterhans³-Schw. p. 253]; UPZ 162 II, 4 [117 BC]; BGU 731 II, 12; LXX); at the beginning of a clause *therefore, hence* (Diod. S. 14, 51, 5; Appian, Liby. 47 §202; Ps.-Callisth. 2, 1, 4; Wsd 12: 23; Jdth 8: 20; Ep. Arist. 110; Jos., Ant. 19, 203, Vi. 338; Test. Napht. 1: 8.—Bl-D. §451, 6; Rob. 962) Mt 14: 7; Ac 26: 19; Hb 2: 17; 3: 1; 7: 25; 8: 3; 9: 18; 11: 19 (or *from among whom,* cf. Gdspd.); 2 Cl 5: 1; IEph 4: 1. M-M.**

ὀθόνη, ης, ἡ (Hom.+; pap.; Jos., Ant. 5, 290; 12, 117) *linen cloth, sheet* (Appian, Bell. Civ. 4, 47 §200) Ac 10: 11; 11: 5. Esp. of a sail (Isishymnus v. Andr. [I BC] 153 Peek; Lucian, Jupp. Trag. 46, Ver. Hist. 2, 38; Test. Zeb. 6: 2) ὀθ. πλοίου *sail of a ship* MPol 15: 2. M-M.*

ὀθόνιον, ου, τό (Aristoph., Hippocr. et al.; inscr. [e.g. the Rosetta Stone: Dit., Or. 90, 18—196 BC]; pap. [e.g. UPZ 85, 8; 42—163/60 BC]; Judg 14: 13 B; Hos 2: 7, 11; Ep. Arist. 320. Cf. Wilcken, Ostraka I p. 266ff. On the origin of the word s. HLewy, Die semit. Fremdwörter im Griech. 1895, 124f; Thumb 111) dim. of ὀθόνη; *linen cloth, bandage* used in preparing a corpse for burial (so UPZ 85, 8; PGiess. 68, 11) J 19: 40; 20: 5ff; Lk 24: 12 t.r.—JBlinzler, ΟΘΟΝΙΑ etc.: Philol. 99, '55, 158-66. M-M.*

οἶδα (Hom.+; inscr., pap., LXX, Philo, Joseph., Test. 12 Patr.) really the perf. of the stem εἰδ- (Lat. video), but used as a pres.; 2 sing. οἶδας (1 Cor 7: 16; J 21: 15f), 2 pl. οἴδατε, 3 pl. οἴδασιν (ἴσασιν only Ac 26: 4. The form οἴδασιν is found as early as Hdt. 2, 43; X., Oec. 20, 14; Dit., Syll.³ 182, 8 [362/1 BC]; PGoodspeed, 3, 7 [III BC]; ἴστε Eph 5: 5; Hb 12: 17; Js 1: 19 can be indic. (so 3 Macc 3: 14) or imper.; subj. εἰδῶ; inf. εἰδέναι; ptc. εἰδώς, εἰδυῖα (Mk 5: 33; Ac 5: 7). Plpf. ᾔδειν, 2 sing. ᾔδεις (Mt 25: 26; Lk 19: 22), 3 pl. ᾔδεισαν (W-S. §13, 20). Fut. εἰδήσω (Hb 8: 11 [Jer 38: 34]) and εἴσομαι (Dg 12: 1). Bl-D. §99, 2; 101 p. 45 (εἰδέναι); W-S. §14, 7; Mlt.-H. 220-2; Helbing p. 108; Mayser 321, 2; 327, 17; 372f.

1. *know*—**a.** w. acc. of the pers. *know someone, know about someone* Mk 1: 34; J 1: 26, 31, 33; 6: 42; 7: 28a; Ac 3: 16; 7: 18 (Ex 1: 8); Hb 10: 30; B 10: 11. (τὸν) θεόν (Herm. Wr. 14, 8) of the heathen, who *know nothing about God* Gal 4: 8; 1 Th 4: 5 (cf. Jer 10: 25). **b.** w. acc. of the thing: οὐ τὴν ἡμέραν οὐδὲ τὴν ὥραν Mt 25: 13; cf. 2 Cl 12: 1. τὰς ἐντολάς Mk 10: 19; Lk 18: 20. βρῶσιν J 4: 32. τ. ἐνθυμήσεις Mt 9: 4 (cf. Jos., Vi. 283). τὴν ἐπιθυμίαν Ro 7: 7. τὰ μυστήρια πάντα 1 Cor 13: 2. τὰ ἐγκάρδια 2 Cl 9: 9. τὰ κρύφια IMg 3: 2. τὴν πόλιν Hs 1: 1. **c.** w. acc. of the pers. and the ptc. in place of the predicate (X., An. 1, 10, 16; Bl-D. §416, 2; cf. Rob. 1103) οἶδα ἄνθρωπον ἐν Χριστῷ . . . ἁρπαγέντα τὸν τοιοῦτον

ἕως τρίτου οὐρανοῦ *I know of a Christian . . . that he was transported into the third heaven* 2 Cor 12: 2. Also without the ptc. εἰδὼς αὐτὸν ἄνδρα δίκαιον (sc. ὄντα) *because he knew that he was a just man* Mk 6: 20 (Chio, Ep. 3, 5 ἴσθι με προθυμότερον [ὄντα]). The obj. more closely defined by a declarative or interrog. clause: οἴδατε τὴν οἰκίαν Στεφανᾶ, ὅτι ἐστὶν ἀπαρχὴ τῆς Ἀχαίας=οἴδατε ὅτι ἡ οἰκία Στεφανᾶ ἐστιν ἀπαρχὴ τῆς Ἀ. 1 Cor 16: 15.—Ac 16: 3 t.r. An indirect quest. may take the place of ὅτι: οἶδά σε τίς εἶ Mk 1: 24; Lk 4: 34. οὐκ οἶδα ὑμᾶς πόθεν ἐστέ *I do not know where you come from* 13: 25; cf. vs. 27 (ὑμᾶς is not found in all the mss. here); 2 Cl 4: 5. τοῦτον οἴδαμεν πόθεν ἐστίν J 7: 27; 9: 29b.

d. foll. by acc. and inf. (Bl-D. §397, 1; cf. Rob. 1036ff) Lk 4: 41; 1 Pt 5: 9; 1 Cl 62: 3.

e. foll. by ὅτι (Aeneas Tact. 579; Dio Chrys. 31[48], 1; Maximus Tyr. 16, 2b.—Bl-D. §397, 1; Rob. 1035) Mt 6: 32; 9: 6; 15: 12; 20: 25; Mk 10: 42; Lk 2: 49; 8: 53; J 4: 25; Ac 3: 17 and very oft. εἰδὼς (εἰδότες) ὅτι Ac 2: 30; 1 Cl 45: 7; 2 Cl 7: 1; 10: 5; B 10: 11; 19: 6; IMg 14; ISm 4: 1; Pol 1: 3; 4: 1; 5: 1; 6: 1; D 3: 10.—τοῦτο, ὅτι 1 Ti 1: 9; 2 Ti 1: 15. ἓν οἶδα, ὅτι *I know just this one thing, that* J 9: 25b (Vi. Aesopi I c. 17 p. 269, 16f οὐκ οἶδα, τί γέγονεν. ἐν δ' οἶδα μόνον, ὅτι . . .).—The formula οἴδαμεν ὅτι is freq. used to introduce a well-known fact that is generally accepted Mt 22: 16; Lk 20: 21; J 3: 2; 9: 31; Ro 2: 2; 3: 19; 7: 14; 8: 22, 28; 2 Cor 5: 1; 1 Ti 1: 8; 1 J 3: 2; 5: 18ff. Paul also uses for this purpose the rhetorical question (ἢ) οὐκ οἴδατε ὅτι; Ro 6: 16; 1 Cor 3: 16; 5: 6; 6: 2f, 9, 15f, 19; 9: 13, 24.

f. w. indirect quest. foll.: τίς, τί Mt 20: 22; Mk 9: 6 (HBaltensweiler, D. Verklärung Jesu '59, 114f); 10: 38; 14: 40; J 5: 13; 6: 6; 9: 21b; 13: 18; 15: 15; Ro 8: 27; 11: 2; 1 Th 4: 2; 2 Ti 3: 14; IEph 12: 1. ποῖος Mt 24: 42f; Lk 12: 39. ἡλίκος Col 2: 1. οἷος 1 Th 1: 5. ποῦ J 3: 8; 8: 14; 12: 35; 14: 5; 20: 2, 13. πῶς (BGU 37, 7) J 9: 21a; Col 4: 6; 2 Th 3: 7; 1 Ti 3: 15. πότε Mk 13: 33, 35. πόθεν J 2: 9a; 3: 8; 7: 28b; 8: 14; 9: 30. Foll. by εἰ *whether* (Lucian, Tox. 22) J 9: 25; 1 Cor 7: 16a, b (JoachJeremias, Bultmann-Festschr. '54, 255–66 understands τί οἶδας εἰ as 'perhaps'; CBurchard, ZNW 61, '70, 170f); Hm 12, 3, 4.—εἴτε 2 Cor 12: 2f.

g. followed by a relat. (PPetr. II 11[1], 7 [III ʙᴄ]) οἶδεν ὁ πατὴρ ὑμῶν ὧν χρείαν ἔχετε Mt 6: 8; cf. Mk 5: 33; 2 Ti 1: 12.

h. foll. by περί τινος *know about someth.* Mt 24: 36; Mk 13: 32 (RBrown, Jesus, God and Man, '67, 59–79).

i. abs. Mt 21: 27; Mk 4: 27; Lk 11: 44; J 2: 9b; 1 Cl 43: 6. καθὼς (αὐτοὶ) οἴδατε *as you (yourselves) know* Ac 2: 22; 1 Th 2: 2, 5; cf. 3: 4. καίπερ εἰδότες *though you know (them)* 2 Pt 1: 12. ὁ θεὸς οἶδεν *God knows (that I do)* 2 Cor 11: 11; cf. B 9: 9. ἴστε Js 1: 19 (indic.: HermvSoden; BWeiss; Weymouth; W-S. §14, 7; imperative: Hollmann; MDibelius; Windisch; OHoltzmann; Hauck; Meinertz; RSV; Bl-D. §99, 2; Mlt. 245).

2. *be* (intimately) *acquainted with, stand in a (close) relation to* οὐκ οἶδα τὸν ἄνθρωπον *I have no knowledge of the man* Mt 26: 72, 74; cf. Mk 14: 71; Lk 22: 57. ὥστε ἡμεῖς ἀπὸ τοῦ νῦν οὐδένα οἴδαμεν κατὰ σάρκα 2 Cor 5: 16.—*To know God*, i.e. not only to know theoretically of his existence, but to have a positive relationship with him, or *not to know God*, i.e. to want to know nothing about him: 2 Th 1: 8; Tit 1: 16.—J 7: 28b; 8: 19 al.—οὐκ οἶδα ὑμᾶς *I have nothing to do with you* Mt 25: 12. Cf. the formula of similar mng. by which a teacher excluded a scholar for seven days: Billerb. I, 469; IV, 293.

3. *know* or *understand how, can, be able* w. inf. foll. (X., Cyr. 1, 6, 46; Philosophenspr. p. 497, 7 εἰδὼς εὔχεσθαι; Herodian 3, 4, 8; Jos., Bell. 2, 91; 5, 407)

οἴδατε δόματα ἀγαθὰ διδόναι *you know how to give good gifts* Mt 7: 11; Lk 11: 13. οἴδατε δοκιμάζειν *you understand how to interpret* 12: 56a; cf. b v.l. οἶδα καὶ ταπεινοῦσθαι, οἶδα καὶ περισσεύειν Phil 4: 12. εἰδέναι ἕκαστον ὑμῶν τὸ ἑαυτοῦ σκεῦος κτᾶσθαι ἐν ἁγιασμῷ *each one of you is to know how to possess his own vessel* (s. σκεῦος 2) *in consecration* 1 Th 4: 4. τοῦ ἰδίου οἴκου προστῆναι οὐκ οἶδεν *does not know how to manage his own household* 1 Ti 3: 5. εἰδὼς καλὸν ποιεῖν Js 4: 17. οἶδεν κύριος εὐσεβεῖς ἐκ πειρασμοῦ ῥύεσθαι 2 Pt 2: 9. οἴδασιν διὰ κόπου . . . πορίζειν ἑαυτοῖς τὴν τροφήν B 10: 4. εἰδὼς φέρειν μαλακίαν *one who knew how to endure pain* 1 Cl 16: 3 (Is 53: 3).—Abs. ἀσφαλίσασθε ὡς οἴδατε *make it* (= the tomb) *as secure as you can* Mt 27: 65.

4. *understand, recognize, come to know, experience* (Sallust. c. 3 p. 4, 8 τοῖς δυναμένοις εἰδέναι=to those who can understand it) w. acc. of the thing τὴν παραβολήν Mk 4: 13. τὰ τοῦ ἀνθρώπου *understand a man's thoughts* 1 Cor 2: 11. τὰ ὑπὸ τοῦ θεοῦ χαρισθέντα ἡμῖν vs. 12. τὰ συνέχοντά με IRo 6: 3. W. indir. quest. foll. εἰδέναι τίς ἐστιν ἡ ἐλπίς *come to know what the hope is* Eph 1: 18. οὐκ οἶδα τί λέγεις *I do not understand what you mean* (Philostrat., Vi. Soph. 1, 7, 4) Mt 26: 70; cf. J 16: 18; 1 Cor 14: 16. οὐκ οἶδα ὃ λέγεις Lk 22: 60 (Oenomaus in Euseb., Pr. Ev. 6, 7, 9 οὐκ οἶσθα ἃ λέγεις). εἴσεσθε ὅσα παρέχει ὁ θεὸς *you will experience what God bestows* Dg 12: 1.—Esp. of Jesus' ability to fathom the thoughts of men: τὰς ἐνθυμήσεις αὐτῶν Mt 12: 25. τὴν ὑπόκρισιν Mk 12: 15. τοὺς διαλογισμοὺς αὐτῶν Lk 6: 8; cf. 11: 17. W. ἐν ἑαυτῷ added and ὅτι foll. J 6: 61.

5. In λοιπὸν οὐκ οἶδα εἴ τινα ἄλλον ἐβάπτισα 1 Cor 1: 16 οὐκ οἶδα takes on the mng. *I do not remember* (cf. Lucian, Dial. Meretr. 1, 1 οἶσθα αὐτόν, ἢ ἐπιλέλησαι τὸν ἄνθρωπον; οὐκ, ἀλλ' οἶδα, ὦ Γλυκέριον. Cf. Field, Notes 187).—εἰδέναι τοὺς κοπιῶντας ἐν ὑμῖν *respect the people who work among you* 1 Th 5: 12 (εἰδέναι τινά can mean *recognize* or *honor someone* [Ael. Aristid. 35, 35 K.=9 p. 111 D. τοὺς κρείττους εἰδέναι], but can also mean *take an interest in someone, care for someone*; Witkowski 30, 7 οἱ θεοί σε εἰδῶσιν; τὸν θεὸν καὶ ἐπίσκοπον εἰδέναι *honor God and the bishop* ISm 9: 1.—τοῦτο ἴστε γινώσκοντες Eph 5: 5 is perh. a Hebraism (so ARobinson '04 ad loc., calling attention to LXX 1 Km 20: 3 γινώσκων οἶδεν and Sym. Jer 49[42]: 22 ἴστε γινώσκοντες).—HSeesemann, TW V 120–2. M-M. B. 1209.

οἰκεῖος, (α), ον (Hes., Hdt.+; inscr., pap., LXX, Philo; Jos., Ant. 4, 86 al.) lit. 'belonging to the house'; in our lit. only subst. οἱ οἰκ. *members of the household* in any sense.

1. lit. (Jos., Vi. 183) of all the members of a household MPol 6: 1. οἱ οἰκ. τοῦ σπέρματός σου *your blood relatives* B 3: 3 (Is 58: 7). W. ἴδιοι of *members of one's family* (schol. on Pla. 20ᴇ λέγονται οἰκεῖοι καὶ οἱ συγγενεῖς) 1 Ti 5: 8 (Diod. S. 5, 18, 1; Appian, Hann. 28 §118; Dit., Syll.³ 317, 38; 560, 21; 591, 59 φίλοι καὶ οἰκεῖοι; Test. Reub. 3: 5 γένος κ. οἰκεῖοι).

2. fig. (w. συμπολῖται τῶν ἁγίων) οἰκ. τοῦ θεοῦ *members of God's household* (cf. Marinus, Vi. Procli 32 τοῦ θεοφιλοῦς ἀνδρὸς ἡ πρὸς τ. θεὸν οἰκειότης) of the Christians Eph 2: 19. οἱ οἰκ. τῆς πίστεως *those who belong to the household of the faith* Gal 6: 10 (cf. Polyb. 5, 87, 3 οἰκ. τῆς ἡσυχίας; 4, 57, 4; 14, 9, 5; Diod. S. 13, 91, 4; 19, 70, 3 οἰκ. τυραννίδος; Strabo 17, 1, 5 οἰκ. σοφίας.—GHWhitaker, Exp. 8th Ser. XXIII '21, 76ff).—S. on ἑταῖρος. M-M.*

οἰκετεία, ας, ἡ (since Dit., Syll.³ 495, 112f [c. 230 ʙᴄ]; Strabo 14, 5, 2; Lucian, De Merc. Cond. 15; Epict., Ench. 33, 7 [s. Schenkl, app.]; Dit., Syll.³ 694, 54f; 695, 61;

PTebt. 285, 6; Sym. Job 1: 3; Ep. Arist. 14; 15; Jos., Ant. 12, 30) *the slaves in a household* καταστῆσαί τινα ἐπὶ τῆς οἰκετείας αὐτοῦ *put someone in charge of* (*the slaves in*) *his household* Mt 24: 45. M-M.*

οἰκέτης, ου, ὁ lit. *member of the household*, then specif. *house slave, domestic*, and *slave* gener. (in the specif. sense Aeschyl., Hdt.+; inscr., pap., LXX; Jos., C. Ap. 2, 181, Vi. 341) Ac 10: 7. Opp. δεσπότης (Dio Chrys. 64[14], 10; Ael. Aristid. 45 p. 40 D.; Pr 22: 7; Philo, Deus Imm. 64) 1 Pt 2: 18; κύριος (Philo, Poster. Cai. 138) Lk 16: 13; 2 Cl 6: 1. ἀλλότριος οἰκ. *another man's servant* Ro 14: 4. M-M. B. 1332.*

οἰκέω fut. οἰκήσω—1. intr. *live, dwell, have one's habitation* (Hom.+; inscr., pap., LXX; Philo, Aet. M. 148 ἐν οἰκ. μετά τινος *live with someone* (M. Ant. 1, 17, 15; Gen 24: 3; 27: 44) Hv 5: 2; in marriage (Soph., Oed. R. 990) 1 Cor 7: 12f. ἔν τινι *in someone* or *someth.* of the Christians ἐν κόσμῳ οἰκ. Dg 6: 3b. Also of the soul ἐν τῷ σώματι ibid. a. Of the Spirit of God, which dwells in a pers. (cf. Test. Gad 5: 4 ὁ φόβος τ. θεοῦ οἰκεῖ ἐν αὐτῷ) Ro 8: 9, 11; 1 Cor 3: 16. Of the good Ro 7: 18. Of sin vs. 20.
2. trans. *inhabit, dwell in* τὶ *someth.* lit. (Mitteis, Chrest. 284, 5 οἰκίαν; PGiess. 2, 23; PTebt. 104, 21; Gen 24: 13; Philo, Conf. Lingu. 106 κόσμον ὡς πατρίδα οἰ.; Jos., Ant. 14, 88, C. Ap. 1, 9) πατρίδας ἰδίας Dg 5: 5. Of God φῶς οἰκῶν ἀπρόσιτον *who dwells in unapproachable light* 1 Ti 6: 16.—On οἰκουμένη see it as a separate entry. M-M.*

οἴκημα, ατος, τό (Pind., Hdt.+; inscr., pap., LXX; Philo, Vi. Cont. 25; Joseph.).
1. gener. *room, apartment* (Hdt. 1, 9; 10; Menand., Sam. 19; Diod. S. 1, 92, 6; Appian, Bell. Civ. 4, 24 §98; Jos., Ant. 8, 134; 137; 14, 455) οἰκήματα μάταια *rooms that will pass away* Hs 1: 1.
2. euphemism for *prison* (Thu. 4, 47, 3; 48, 1; Demosth. 32, 29; Lucian, Tox. 29; Plut., Agis 19, 5; 8; 9; Aelian, V.H. 6, 1) φῶς ἔλαμψεν ἐν τῷ οἰκ. Ac 12: 7. M-M.*

οἴκησις, εως, ἡ *house, dwelling* (so Aeschyl., Hdt.+; Diod. S. 1, 50, 6; 17, 105, 5; Dit., Syll.³ 1216, 11; PMagd. 29, 3 [III BC]; BGU 1113, 19; PTebt. 489; Jdth 7: 14; 1 Macc 13: 48; Philo; Jos., Vi. 159, Ant. 14, 261) Hs 1: 4.*

οἰκητήριον, ου, τό (Eur., Democr.+; Cebes 17, 3 εὐδαιμόνων οἰ.; Plut., Mor. 603B; UPZ 170A, 23 [127 BC]; BGU 1167, 33 [12 BC]; POxy. 281, 11; inscr. in GPlaumann, Ptolemais '10 p. 35 [76/5 BC]; 2 Macc 11: 2; En. 27, 2; Jos., C. Ap. 1, 153) *dwelling, habitation*.
1. lit., of the angels (Ps.-Aristot., De Mundo 2, 2 heaven as the οἰκητήριον θεοῦ or 3, 4 τῶν ἄνω θεῶν) ἀπολιπεῖν τὸ ἴδιον οἰκ. *abandon one's own dwelling* Jd 6 (ἴδιον οἰ. as Cornutus 24 p. 45, 21; on the subject matter cf. En. 15, 3ff; Jos., Ant. 1, 73).
2. fig., of the glorified body of the transfigured Christian (alternating w. οἰκία, οἰκοδομή vs. 1) 2 Cor 5: 2 (s. on σκῆνος and the lit. on γυμνός 4). M-M.*

οἰκήτωρ, ορος, ὁ (Aeschyl., Hdt.+; Diod. S. 5, 41, 2; Aelian, V.H. 9, 16; PLond. 1677, 27; PGM 7, 351; LXX; Philo; Jos., Ant. 14, 75, Vi. 230) *inhabitant* ἔσονται οἰκήτορες γῆς *they will inhabit the earth* 1 Cl 14: 4 (Pr 2: 21).*

οἰκία, ας, ἡ (Hdt.+; inscr., pap., LXX, En., Philo, Joseph.)—1. *house*—a. lit., as a building Mt 2: 11; 7: 24-7; 24: 43; Mk 10: 29f; 13: 34; Lk 6: 48f; 15: 8; 18: 29; J 12: 3; Ac 10: 6; 1 Cor 11: 22; 1 Cl 12: 6 al. W. ἀγρός Hs

1: 4, 8; cf. Mt 19: 29. W. χωρίον Ac 4: 34. εἰς τ. οἰκίαν τινός Mt 8: 14; 9: 23; Mk 1: 29; Lk 4: 38; 7: 44; 22: 54. εἰς οἰκίαν τινός Ac 18: 7. εἰς τὴν οἰκίαν *into the house* Lk 8: 51; 10: 38; 22: 10; *home* (Appian, Bell. Civ. 5, 68 §288; Jos., Vi. 144) Mt 9: 28; 13: 36; 17: 25; *at home* Mk 10: 10. εἰς οἰκίαν *into a house* 6: 10; 7: 24; *into your house* 2 J 10. ἐν τῇ οἰκίᾳ τινός Mk 2: 15; 14: 3; Lk 5: 29; 7: 37. ἐν οἰκίᾳ τινός (POxy. 51, 13 ἐν οἰκίᾳ Ἐπαγαθοῦ) Mt 26: 6; Ac 9: 11; 10: 32; ἐν τῇ οἰκίᾳ *in the house* J 8: 35; 11: 31; *at home* Mt 8: 6; 9: 10; Mk 9: 33. ἐν οἰκίᾳ *in a house* or *at home* Lk 8: 27. οἱ ἐν τῇ οἰκίᾳ *those who are in the house* Mt 5: 15 (πάντες οἱ ἐν τ. οἰ. as Dio Chrys. 64[14], 7); cf. Ac 16: 32. ὁ κύριος τῆς οἰκίας *the master of the house* Mk 13: 35. ὁ οἰκοδεσπότης τῆς οἰκίας Lk 22: 11. κατεσθίειν τὰς οἰκ. τῶν χηρῶν *devour widows' houses* i.e., rob widows of their houses (and household goods; cf. οἶκος 4) Mt 23: 14 t.r.; Mk 12: 40; Lk 20: 47 (Maximus Tyr. 14, 4e κείρειν [=devour] οἶκον βασιλέως). κατοικεῖν οἰκίας πηλίνας *live in houses of clay* 1 Cl 39: 5 (Job 4: 19).— KJäger, D. Bauernhaus in Palästina, m. Rücksicht auf d. bibl. Wohnhaus untersucht '12; Dalman, Arbeit VII: D. Haus, Hühnerzucht, Taubenzucht, Bienenzucht '42.
b. fig., of the body as the habitation of the soul ἡ ἐπίγειος ἡμῶν οἰκ. τοῦ σκήνους *the earthly tent we live in* 2 Cor 5: 1a. In contrast to this the glorified body is called οἰκία ἀχειροποίητος *a dwelling not made with hands* 2 Cor 5: 1b.—S. on οἰκητήριον 2.—Of heaven as God's dwelling-place (cf. Artem. 2, 68 p. 159, 13 ὁ οὐρανὸς θεῶν ἐστιν οἶκος; schol. on Aeschin. 2, 10: acc. to Timaeus, a woman dreamed that she had been snatched up into heaven and had seen there τὰς τῶν θεῶν οἰκήσεις; Sappho 1, 7 D.²: Aphrodite inhabits πατρὸς [Zeus'] δόμον.—Purely formal UPZ 18, 8 [163 BC] ἡ οἰκία τοῦ πατρὸς ἡμῶν) J 14: 2 (differently OSchaefer, ZNW 32, '33, 210-17, against him Bultmann 464, 5).
2. *household, family* (X., Mem. 2, 7, 6; Diod. S. 12, 14, 3; 13, 96, 3; PPetr. II 23[4], 2 καταγράψας τὴν οἰκίαν τοῦ Ὥρου; Philo, Abr. 92; Jos., Ant. 17, 134) Mt 12: 25 (w. πόλις, as Synes., Providence 1, 4 p. 92D); Mk 3: 25 (w. βασιλεία). ἐπίστευσεν αὐτὸς καὶ ἡ οἰκ. αὐτοῦ ὅλη *he and his whole household came to believe* J 4: 53 (Appian, Bell. Civ. 1, 13 §55 Γράκχος αὐτοῦ σὺν ὅλῃ τῇ οἰκίᾳ κατάρχοιτο). ἡ οἰκ. Στεφανᾶ *the family of Stephanas* 1 Cor 16: 15. ἄτιμος εἰ μὴ . . . ἐν τῇ οἰκ. αὐτοῦ *without honor except . . . in his family* Mt 13: 57; Mk 6: 4.
3. a kind of middle position betw. mngs. 1 and 2 is held by Mt 10: 12f; εἰσερχόμενοι εἰς τὴν οἰκίαν ἀσπάσασθε αὐτήν. καὶ ἐὰν ᾖ ἡ οἰκία ἀξία . . . —οἱ ἐκ τῆς Καίσαρος οἰκίας Phil 4: 22 means, whether it be translated *those in the house* or *those in the household of the Emperor*, according to prevailing usage, not members of the emperor's family or relationship, but servants at his court; in early imperial times they were ordinarily slaves or freedmen (cf. Philo, In Flacc. 35; Jos., Ant. 17, 142; Passio Pauli 1 p. 104, 9; 106, 15 L. Cf. also Diog. L. 5, 75 the explanation for the 'ignoble' origin of Demetrius of Phalerum: ἦν γὰρ ἐκ τῆς Κόνωνος οἰκίας. On the other hand Diod. S. 17, 35, 3 αἱ τῆς βασιλικῆς οἰκίας γυναῖκες= the ladies of the royal family.—AdeWaal, Οἱ ἐκ τῆς Καίσαρος οἰκίας [Phil 4: 22]: Röm. Quartalschr. 26, '12, 160-3; Zahn, Einl. I³ 391; GSDuncan, St. Paul's Ephesian Ministry '29 [where the theory of Paul's Ephesian imprisonment is set forth]. S. also Καῖσαρ ad loc.). M-M. B. 133; 458.

οἰκιακός, οῦ, ὁ (Plut., Cic. 20, 3; POxy. 294, 17 [22 AD]; PGiess. 88, 4) *member of a household* Mt 10: 25 (opp. οἰκοδεσπότης), 36 (here rather relatives than members of the household in the stricter sense). M-M.*

οἰκοδεσποτέω (late word [Lob., Phryn. p. 373]; esp. astrolog. t.t. 'rule' of the planet that influences human life: Plut., Mor. 908B; Ps.-Lucian, Astrol. 20; POxy. 235, 16 [20/50 AD] οἰκοδεσποτεῖ Ἀφροδίτῃ; PLond. 130, 163) *manage one's household, keep house* 1 Ti 5: 14. M-M.*

οἰκοδεσπότης, ου, ὁ (later word [Lob., Phryn. p. 373]; Alexis Com. [IV BC] 225; Plut., Mor. 271E; Dit., Syll.³ 888, 57f; Isaurian inscr. in Papers of the Amer. School of Class. Stud. at Athens III p. 150 υἱοὺς τοὺς οἰκοδεσπότας; PLond. 98 recto, 60; PSI 158, 80; Philo; Jos., C. Ap. 2, 128) *the master of the house* Mt 24: 43; Mk 14: 14; Lk 12: 39. Pleonast. οἰκ. τῆς οἰκίας Lk 22: 11 (cf. Dit., Syll.³ 985, 53; Bl-D. §484). Used w. ἄνθρωπος in a figure Mt 13: 52; 20: 1; 21: 33. In parables and figures, of God (cf. Epict. 3, 22, 4; Philo, Somn. 1, 149) Mt 13: 27 (interpreted as Son of Man in vs. 37); 20: 1, 11; 21: 33; Lk 14: 21; Hs 5, 2, 9; cf. IEph 6: 1. Christ of himself Mt 10: 25; Lk 13: 25 (δεσπότης 𝔓⁷⁵). M-M.*

οἰκοδομέω (Hdt.; inscr., pap., LXX, En., Ep. Arist., Philo, Joseph., Test. 12 Patr.) impf. ᾠκοδόμουν; fut. οἰκοδομήσω; 1 aor. ᾠκοδόμησα (on the augment s. W-S. §12, 5a; Mlt.-H. 191). Pass.: impf. 3 sing. ᾠκοδομεῖτο; perf. inf. ᾠκοδομῆσθαι, ptc. οἰκοδομημένος LJ 1: 7, ᾠκοδομημένος Hv 3, 2, 6; plpf. 3 sing. ᾠκοδόμητο; 1 aor. ᾠκοδομήθην or οἰκοδομήθην J 2: 20; 1 fut. οἰκοδομηθήσομαι; *build.*

1. lit., of real buildings—a. w. obj. acc. *build, erect* (Jos., Ant. 15, 403 al.) οἰκίαν (Diod. S. 14, 116, 8; Lucian, Charon 17) Lk 6: 48a. Pass. (Sb 5104, 2 [163 BC] οἰκία ᾠκοδομημένη; PAmh. 51, 11; 23) ibid. b. πύργον (Is 5: 2) Mt 21: 33; Mk 12: 1; Lk 14: 28; Hs 9, 3, 1; 4; 9, 12, 6. Pass. Hv 3, 2, 4ff; 3, 3, 3; 3, 5, 5; 3, 8, 9; Hs 9, 3, 2; 9, 5, 2; 9, 9, 7; cf. s 9, 9, 4. ναόν Mk 14: 58; B 16: 3 (Is 49: 17). Pass. J 2: 20 (Heliodorus Periegeta of Athens [II BC]: 373 fgm. 1 Jac. says of the Acropolis: ἐν ἔτεσι ε΄ παντελῶς ἐξεποιήθη); B 16: 6 (s. below; the 'scripture' pass. is interpreted spiritually). ἀποθήκας Lk 12: 18 (opp. καθαιρεῖν; s. this 2aα). τοὺς τάφους τῶν προφητῶν *the tombs of the prophets* Mt 23: 29 (cf. EKlostermann² ad loc.). τὰ μνημεῖα τῶν προφητῶν *monuments for the prophets* Lk 11: 47 (μνημεῖον 1).—οἰκ. τινί *build someth. for someone* (Gen 8: 20; Ex 1: 11; Ezk 16: 24) συναγωγὴν οἰκ. τινί Lk 7: 5. οἰκ. τινὶ οἶκον Ac 7: 47, 49; B 16: 2 (the last two Is 66: 1).—W. the obj. acc. and foll. by ἐπί w. acc. or w. gen.: τὴν οἰκίαν ἐπὶ τὴν πέτραν *build the house on the rock* Mt 7: 24. ἐπὶ τὴν ἄμμον *on the sand* vs. 26 (proverbial: Plut. VII p. 463, 10 Bern. εἰς ψάμμον οἰκοδομεῖς). πόλις ἐπὶ τ. ὄρους Lk 4: 29 (cf. Jos., Ant. 8, 97). ἐπὶ τὴν γῆν 6: 49. πόλις οἰκοδομημένη ἐπ᾽ ἄκρον ὄρους ὑψηλοῦ *a city that is built on the top of a high mountain* LJ 1: 7. πύργος ἐπὶ ὑδάτων Hv 3, 3, 5; ἐπὶ τὴν πέτραν s 9, 14, 4 (opp. χαμαὶ οὐκ ᾠκοδόμηται).

b. abs.—α. when the obj. can be supplied fr. the context Lk 11: 48; 14: 30.—Cf. Hv 3, 1, 7; 3, 4, 1a; 3, 10, 1; s 9, 4, 1.

β. but also entirely without an obj. ᾠκοδόμουν *they erected buildings* Lk 17: 28. οἱ οἰκοδομοῦντες *the builders, the masons* (after Ps 117: 22) Mt 21: 42; Mk 12: 10; Lk 20: 17; Ac 4: 11 t.r.; 1 Pt 2: 7; B 6: 4. Also with no ref. to the Ps passage: Hs 9, 4, 4; 9, 6, 6.

γ. οἱ λίθοι οἱ ἤδη ᾠκοδομημένοι *the stones already used in the building* Hv 3, 5, 2; cf. s 9, 6, 3.

c. *build up again, restore,* a mng. that οἰκ. can receive fr. the context (Josh 6: 26; Ps 50: 20; 68: 36) Mt 26: 61; 27: 40; Mk 15: 29; B 16: 3 (Is 49: 17).—S. also 2 below.

2. fig. (as in Hermas passages given under 1, where the tower is a symbol of the church): of the building up of the Christian church (cf. Ruth 4: 11 ᾠκοδόμησαν τὸν οἶκον Ἰσραήλ) ἐπὶ ταύτῃ τῇ πέτρᾳ οἰκοδομήσω μου τὴν ἐκκλησίαν *on this rock I will build my church* Mt 16: 18. ὡς λίθοι ζῶντες οἰκοδομεῖσθε οἶκος πνευματικός *like living stones let yourselves be built up* (pass.) or *build yourselves up* (mid., so Gdspd., Probs. 194f) *into a spiritual house* 1 Pt 2: 5. Paul refers to missionary work where another Christian has begun activities as ἐπ᾽ ἀλλότριον θεμέλιον οἰκ. *building on another man's foundation* Ro 15: 20. He also refers to a religious point of view as a building, and speaks of its refutation as a tearing down (καταλύειν), and of returning to it as a *rebuilding* (s. 1c above) Gal 2: 18. This is prob. where B 11: 1 belongs, where it is said of the Israelites that (in accordance with scriptural declarations) they do not accept the baptism that removes sin, but ἑαυτοῖς οἰκοδομήσουσιν *will build up* (someth.) *for themselves.* In another pass. B calls the believer a πνευματικὸς ναὸς οἰκοδομούμενος τῷ κυρίῳ *a spiritual temple built for the Lord* 16: 10; cf. vs. 6f.—In his discourse on the buliding of the temple Hermas speaks of the angels to whom God has entrusted the οἰκοδομεῖν *building up* or *completion* of his whole creation Hv 3, 4, 1b.

3. οἰκ. is also used quite in a non-literal sense, oft. without any consciousness of its basic mng., like *edify* in our relig. usage, but perhaps without the emotional connotations that have been associated with it (the non-literal use is found to a certain degree as early as X., Cyr. 8, 7, 15 and in LXX: Ps 27: 5; Jer 40: 7. Also Test. Benj. 8: 3.—JWeiss on 1 Cor 8: 1). It=someth. like *benefit, strengthen, establish,* as well as *edify,* of the Lord, who is able to strengthen the believers Ac 20: 32. Of the church, which *was being built up* 9: 31.—Esp. in Paul: ἡ ἀγάπη οἰκοδομεῖ *love builds up* (in contrast to γνῶσις, which 'puffs up') 1 Cor 8: 1 (=Dg 12: 5). πάντα ἔξεστιν, ἀλλ᾽ οὐ πάντα οἰκοδομεῖ *everything is permitted, but not everything is beneficial* 10: 23. ὁ λαλῶν γλώσσῃ ἑαυτὸν οἰκοδομεῖ· ὁ δὲ προφητεύων ἐκκλησίαν οἰκοδομεῖ 14: 4; cf. vs. 17. οἰκοδομεῖτε εἰς τὸν ἕνα *strengthen one another* 1 Th 5: 11. In 1 Cor 8: 10 the apostle is prob. speaking ironically, w. ref. to the 'strong' party at Corinth, who declare that by their example they are *benefiting* the 'weak': οὐχὶ ἡ συνείδησις αὐτοῦ οἰκοδομηθήσεται εἰς τὸ τὰ εἰδωλόθυτα ἐσθίειν; *will not his conscience be 'strengthened' so that he will eat meat offered to idols?* (differently MargaretThrall, TU 102, '68, 468-72).—Of Paul's letters, by which δυνηθήσεσθε οἰκοδομεῖσθαι εἰς τὴν δοθεῖσαν ὑμῖν πίστιν *you will be able to build yourselves up in the faith that has been given you* Pol 3: 2.—HCremer, Über den bibl. Begriff der Erbauung 1863; HMScott, The Place of οἰκοδομή in the NT: PTR 2, '04, 402-24; HBassermann, Über den Begriff 'Erbauung': Zeitschr. für prakt. Theol. 4, 1882, 1-22; CTrossen, Erbauen: ThGl 6, '14, 804ff; PhVielhauer, Oikodome (d. Bild vom Bau vom NT bis Clem. Alex.) Diss. Hdlbg. '39; PBonnard, Jésus-Christ édifiant son Église '48. M-M. B. 590.**

οἰκοδομή, ῆς, ἡ (rejected by the Atticists [Lob., Phryn. 421; 487ff; WSchmid, Der Attizismus III 1893, 248], but found since Aristot., Eth. Nic. 5, 14, 7; Diod. S. 1, 46, 4; Plut., Lucull. 39, 2; IG XIV 645, 146 [Dorian]; Dit., Or. 655, 2 [25 BC]; PGrenf. I 21, 17 [126 BC]; BGU 699, 3; 894, 2; LXX; En.; Philo, Mos. 1, 224 v.l., Spec. Leg. 1, 73 v.l.; Joseph. [Schmidt 528f]).

1. *building* as a process, *construction*—a. lit. (2 Ch 3: 2 v.l.; Sir 40: 19; Jos., Ant. 11, 59) ἐτελέσθη ἡ οἰκοδομή *the construction was at an end* Hs 9, 5, 1a. ἀνοχὴ τῆς οἰκ. *a delay in the building* ibid. b; 9, 14, 2.

b. fig., of spiritual strengthening (s. οἰκοδομέω 3) *edifying, edification, building up.*

α. act., w. obj. gen. πρὸς τὴν οἰκ. τῆς ἐκκλησίας *for the building up of the church* 1 Cor 14: 12. ὑπὲρ τῆς ὑμῶν οἰκ. 2 Cor 12: 19. Abs. πρὸς οἰκοδομήν *for edification* Ro 15: 2; 1 Cor 14: 26; cf. Eph 4: 29. Paul has received his authority fr. the Lord εἰς οἰκοδομὴν καὶ οὐκ εἰς καθαίρεσιν 2 Cor 13: 10; cf. 10: 8. τὰ τῆς οἰκ. τῆς εἰς ἀλλήλους *what makes for the edification of each other* Ro 14: 19. Abstr. for concr. ὁ προφητεύων λαλεῖ οἰκοδομήν *the one who prophesies speaks words that edify* 1 Cor 14: 3.

β. pass. οἰκοδομὴν λαβεῖν *receive edification, be edified* 1 Cor 14: 5. εἰς οἰκ. τ. σώματος τ. Χριστοῦ *that the body of Christ might be built up* Eph 4: 12. εἰς οἰκ. ἑαυτοῦ *for its own edification* vs. 16.

2. *building, edifice,* the result of construction—**a.** lit.; pl., of secular buildings (Diod. S. 16, 76, 2; 20, 8, 3) Hs 1: 1 (w. ἀγροί, παρατάξεις, οἰκήματα). Esp. of temple buildings (1 Esdr 5: 70) εἰς τὴν οἰκ. ἐλπίζειν *put one's hope in the building* (alone) B 16: 1. Pl. of the various buildings in the temple area Mk 13: 1f. αἱ οἰκοδομαὶ τοῦ ἱεροῦ Mt 24: 1. Esp. freq. in the symbolism of the tower in Hermas (v 3; s 9). Yet in many pass. mng. 1 is also poss.: ἡ οἰκ. τοῦ πύργου *the tower building* (or *the building of the tower*) Hv 3, 2, 6b; 3, 4, 1f; 3, 5, 1b; 3, 12, 3; s 9, 1, 2; 9, 3, 3; 9, 4, 2ff; 9, 5, 2; 9, 17, 4 al. τὰ ἐξώτερα μέρη τῆς οἰκ. *the outside of the building* s 9, 9, 3b. Of the stones: εὔχρηστοι εἰς (τὴν) οἰκ. v 3, 5, 5; 3, 6, 1; 6. Also εὔχρηστοι τῇ οἰκ. s 9, 15. 6. χρήσιμοι εἰς τὴν οἰκ. τοῦ πύργου v 4, 3, 4; ἀπενεχθῆναι εἰς τὴν οἰκ. s 9, 8, 3a. ἀπέρχεσθαι εἰς τὴν οἰκ. s 9, 5, 3f; 9, 7, 4a; 6f; 9, 10, 2; ἀποβάλλεσθαι ἐκ (ἀπὸ) τῆς οἰκ. s 9, 7, 1; 9, 8, 3b; 9, 9, 5; ἀποδοκιμάζειν ἐκ τῆς οἰκ. s 9, 12, 7. Pass. (without ἐκ) 9, 23, 3; ἁρμόζειν εἰς τὴν οἰκ. s 9, 6, 5; 3, 7, 5. Pass. s 9, 4, 3; 9, 8, 5ff; 9, 4, 9; 15, 4; βάλλειν εἰς τὴν οἰκ. s 9, 7, 4; 6; 9, 8, 2a. Pass. 9, 7, 5; 9, 10, 1; 9, 30, 2; δοκιμάζειν τὴν οἰκ. s 9, 5, 2b; εἰσέρχεσθαι εἰς τὴν οἰκ. s 9, 12, 4; 9, 13, 4; ἐκλέγεσθαι εἰς τὴν οἰκ. s 9, 9, 3a; ἐπιδιδόναι εἰς τὴν οἰκ. s 9, 4, 5; 8; 9, 15, 5. Pass. 9, 4, 6; ἐπιθυμεῖν τὴν οἰκ. s 9, 9, 7. ἐπιτίθεσθαι εἰς τὴν οἰκ. v 3, 5, 2. ἐργάζεσθαι εἰς τὴν οἰκ. *work at the building* s 9, 6, 2b; εὑρεθῆναι εἰς τὴν οἰκ. s 9, 6, 4; ὁ ἐφεστὼς εἰς τὴν οἰκ. s 9, 6, 2a; κατανοεῖν τὴν οἰκ. *examine the building* s 9, 5, 7; 9, 6, 3. συναρμόζεσθαι εἰς τὴν οἰκ. τοῦ πύργου s 9, 16, 7; τιθέναι εἰς τὴν οἰκ. v 3, 2, 6a; 7; s 9, 7, 2; 9, 8, 2b. Pass. v 3, 5, 4; s 9, 6, 8; 9, 8, 4; 9, 9, 2; 9, 13, 6; 9, 16, 1; 9, 17, 3; 9, 29, 4; 9, 30, 1; τίθεσθαι ἐκ τῆς οἰκ. s 9, 8, 1; ὑπάγειν εἰς τὴν οἰκ. v 3, 5, 1a; 3; 6, 2; s 9, 3, 3f.

b. Hermas moves about on the border-line betw. the literal and non-literal uses of οἰκ., but the foll. passages are quite non-literal: θεοῦ οἰκοδομή ἐστε *you are God's building* 1 Cor 3: 9 (AFridrichsen [s. on γεώργιον]). In Eph 2: 21 the Christian community is called an οἰκοδομή, more definitely a ναὸς ἅγιος ἐν κυρίῳ, which is erected on the foundation of the apostles and prophets w. Christ Jesus as the cornerstone (HSchlier, Christus u. d. Kirche im Eph '30).—Of the Christians ὄντες λίθοι ναοῦ πατρὸς ἡτοιμασμένοι εἰς οἰκοδομὴν θεοῦ πατρός *since you are stones for the Father's temple, made ready for the building of God the Father* IEph 9: 1.—Fig., in another way, of the glorified body of the departed Christian οἰκοδομὴν ἐκ θεοῦ ἔχομεν, οἰκίαν ἀχειροποίητον *we have a building fr. God, a house not made w. hands* 2 Cor 5: 1. S. on οἰκητήριον 2.—Lit. on οἰκοδομέω, end. M-M.**

οἰκοδομητός, ή, όν (Strabo 3, 3, 7; 8, 6, 2; Etym. Mag. p. 282, 46; 453, 33) *built* οἰκ. ναὸς διὰ χειρός *a temple built with hands* B 16: 7.*

οἰκοδομία, ας, ἡ (since Thu. 1, 93, 1; 2, 65, 2; Pla.; Polyb. 10, 22, 7; Plut., Pomp. 66, 1; Lucian, Conscr. Hist. 4; Jos., Ant. 11, 7; 118; Dit., Syll.³ 144, 32 [IV bc]; 204, 26f al., Or. 483, 104; 107; PHal. 1, 181 [III bc]; PSI 500, 3; 4.—Lob., Phryn. p. 487) *building*, both as process and result, in our lit. only once as v.l., and in a fig. sense *edification* ἐκζητήσεις παρέχουσιν μᾶλλον ἢ οἰκοδομίαν θεοῦ 1 Ti 1: 4 t.r. (for οἰκονομίαν; D*, Irenaeus et al. have οἰκοδομήν). M-M.*

οἰκοδόμος, ου, ὁ (Hdt.+; Galen, Protr. 13 p. 42, 17, John [w. τέκτων]; Lucian, Icarom. 19; Dit., Or. 770, 7; pap., LXX; Jos., Ant. 7, 66 [w. τέκτων]) *builder* Ac 4: 11. M-M.*

οἰκονομέω pf. ptc. οἰκονομηκώς (on the mng. of οἰκ. and derivatives s. ARobinson on Eph 1: 10).

1. abs., hold the office of an οἰκονόμος (q.v.), *be manager* (Astrampsychus p. 8 Dek. 1, 9) Lk 16: 2.

2. *manage, regulate, administer, plan* (Soph., Pla.+; inscr., pap.; 3 Macc 3: 2; Ep. Arist.) τὶ *someth.* (Jos., Ant. 1, 19) of God πάντα σὺν τῷ παιδὶ οἰκονομηκώς *after he had planned everything with his Son* Dg 9: 1 (Maximus Tyr. 27, 8a ὁ θεὸς οἰ. τὸ πᾶν τοῦτο; M. Ant. 5, 32; Philo, Decal. 53 [θεὸς] οἰκονομεῖ σωτηρίως ἀεὶ τὰ σύμπαντα). M-M.*

οἰκονομία, ας, ἡ (X., Pla.+; inscr., pap.; Is 22: 19, 21; Philo, Joseph.)—**1.** *management* of a household, *direction, office* (X., Oec. 1, 1; Herodian 6, 1, 1; Jos., Ant. 2, 89; PTebt. 27, 21 [114 bc]; PLond. 904, 25).

a. lit., of the work of an οἰκονόμος Lk 16: 2-4 (this passage shows that it is not always poss. to draw a sharp distinction betw. the office itself and the activities associated w. it).

b. Paul applies the idea of administration to the office of an apostle οἰκονομίαν πεπίστευμαι *I have been entrusted with a commission* 1 Cor 9: 17. ἀνθρωπίνων οἰκονομίαν μυστηρίων πεπίστευνται *they have been entrusted with the administration of* (merely) *human mysteries* Dg 7: 1. Of the bishop: ὃν πέμπει ὁ οἰκοδεσπότης εἰς ἰδίαν οἰκ. (=οἰκ. ἰδίου οἴκου) *the one whom the master of the house sent to administer his own household* IEph 6: 1. This is prob. also the place for κατὰ τὴν οἰκ. τοῦ θεοῦ τὴν δοθεῖσάν μοι εἰς ὑμᾶς *according to the divine office which has been granted to me for you* Col 1: 25, but ἠκούσατε τὴν οἰκονομίαν τ. χάριτος τ. θεοῦ τῆς δοθείσης μοι εἰς ὑμᾶς *you have heard of the stewardship of God's grace that was granted to me for you* Eph 3: 2 may be parallel to the usage in vs. 9; s. 2b below.

2. *arrangement, order, plan* (X., Cyr. 5, 3, 25; Polyb. 4, 67, 9; 10, 16, 2; Diod. S. 1, 81, 3)—**a.** ἡ τῆς σαρκὸς οἰκονομία of the *arrangement* or *structure* of the parts of the body beneath the skin; they are laid bare by scourging MPol 2: 2.

b. of God's *plan of salvation*, his *arrangements for* man's *redemption* (in the pap. of the arrangements and directions of the authorities: UPZ 162 IX, 2 [117 bc]; PRainer 11, 26, and in PGM [e.g. 4, 293] of the measures by which one wishes to attain some goal by supernatural help) ἡ οἰκ. τοῦ μυστηρίου *the plan of the mystery* Eph 3: 9 (cf. vs. 2 and JReumann, NovT 3, '59, 282-92). Also in the linguistically difficult passage 1: 10 οἰκ. certainly refers to the *plan of salvation* which God is bringing to reality through Christ, in the fulness of the times. κατ' οἰκονομίαν θεοῦ *according to God's plan of redemption* IEph 18: 2. προσδηλώσω ὑμῖν ἧς ἠρξάμην οἰκονομίας εἰς τὸν καινὸν ἄνθρωπον Ἰησοῦν Χριστόν *I will explain to you further the divine plan which I began* (to discuss), *with reference to the new man Jesus Christ* IEph 20: 1.

c. also of God's *arrangements* in nature pl. αἱ οἰκ. θεοῦ Dg 4: 5.

3. *training* (in the way of salvation); this mng. (found also Clem. Alex., Paed. 1, 8, 69, 3; 70, 1 p. 130 St.) seems to fit best in 1 Ti 1: 4, where it is said of the erroneous teachings of certain persons ἐκζητήσεις παρέχουσιν μᾶλλον ἢ οἰκονομίαν θεοῦ τὴν ἐν πίστει *they promote useless speculations rather than divine training that is in faith* (οἰκοδομήν and οἰκοδομίαν [q.v.] as v.l. are simply 'corrections' to alleviate the difficulty). M-M.*

οἰκονόμος, ου, ὁ (Aeschyl.+; inscr., pap., LXX; Philo, Praem. 113; Joseph.; loanw. in rabb.) *(house)-steward, manager.*

1. lit.—a. of the manager in a private position (Diod. S. 36, 5, 1) ὁ πιστὸς οἰκ. ὁ φρόνιμος Lk 12: 42. Sim. ζητεῖται ἐν τοῖς οἰκ. ἵνα πιστός τις εὑρεθῇ 1 Cor 4: 2. He manages his master's property (cf. Jos., Ant. 12, 200; Artem. 4, 28. The οἰκ. of various persons are mentioned in the pap.: PTebt. 402, 1; POxy. 929, 25) Lk 16: 1, 3. ὁ οἰκ. τῆς ἀδικίας *the dishonest manager* (cf. Lucian, Ep. Sat. 2, 26 ὁ οἰκ. ὑφελόμενος) vs. 8 (cf. on the 'unjust steward' Jülicher, Gleichn. 495–514; LFonck, D. Parabeln³ '19 [lit. here 675f]; ARücker, Bibl. Studien XVII 5, '12; JKögel, BFChTh XVIII 6, '14; ERiggenbach, Schlatter-Festschr. '22, 17ff; FTillmann, BZ 9, '11, 171–84; Gerda Krüger, ibid. 21, '33, 170–81; FHüttermann, ThGl 27, '35, 739–42; HPreisker, ThLZ 74, '49, 85–92; JoachJeremias, Gleichnisse Jesu² '52, 30–3; JDMDerrett, Law in the NT, '70, 48–77; DRFletcher, JBL 82, '63, 15–30); JAFitzmyer, Theological Studies 25, '64, 23–42). With ἐπίτροπος Gal 4: 2 (SBelkin, JBL 54, '35, 52–5).

b. ὁ οἰκ. τῆς πόλεως *the city treasurer* (Dit., Syll.³ 1252 πόλεως Κῴων οἰκονόμος; other exx. in PLandvogt, Epigr. Untersuchungen üb. den οἰκονόμος, Diss. Strassb. '08; HJCadbury, JBL 50, '31, 47ff) Ro 16: 23.

2. fig. (Aristot., Rhet. 3 p. 1406a, 27 οἰκ. τῆς τῶν ἀκουόντων ἡδονῆς) of the administrators of divine things (of an office in the Serapeum UPZ 56, 7 [160 BC]; cult associations also had οἰκ.: Dit., Or. 50, 12; 51, 26); the apostles are οἰκονόμοι μυστηρίων θεοῦ *administrators of the mysteries of God* 1 Cor 4: 1. So the bishop must conduct himself as a θεοῦ οἰκ. Tit 1: 7. But the Christians gener. are also θεοῦ οἰκ. (καὶ πάρεδροι καὶ ὑπηρέται) IPol 6: 1 or καλοὶ οἰκ. ποικίλης χάριτος θεοῦ *good administrators of God's varied grace* 1 Pt 4: 10 (cf. X., Mem. 3, 4, 7 οἱ ἀγαθοὶ οἰκ.).—JReumann, JBL 77, '58, 339–49 (pre-Christian), 'Jesus the Steward', TU 103, '68, 21–9. M-M.*

οἶκος, ου, ὁ (Hom.+; inscr., pap., LXX, Ep. Arist., Philo, Joseph., Test. 12 Patr.).

1. *house*—a. lit.—α. a *dwelling* Lk 11: 17 (cf. πίπτω 1bβ); 12: 39; 14: 23 (unless οἰκ. means *dining room* here as Phryn. Com. [V BC] 66 Kock; X., Symp. 2, 18; Athen. 12 p. 548A); Ac 2: 2; (w. ἀγροί, κτήματα) Hs 1: 9. εἰς τὸν οἶκόν τινος *into* or *to someone's house* (Judg 18: 26) ἀπέρχεσθαι Mt 9: 7; Mk 7: 30; Lk 1: 23; 5: 25; εἰσέρχεσθαι Lk 1: 40; 7: 36; 8: 41; Ac 11: 12; 16: 15b; ἔρχεσθαι Mk 5: 38; καταβαίνειν Lk 18: 14; πορεύεσθαι 5: 24; ὑπάγειν Mt 9: 6; Mk 2: 11; 5: 19; ὑποστρέφειν Lk 1: 56; 8: 39.—κατοικεῖν εἰς τὸν οἶκόν τινος *live in someone's house* Hm 4, 4, 3; s 9, 1, 3. οἱ εἰς τὸν οἶκόν μου *the members of my household* Lk 9: 61.—εἰς τὸν οἶκον *into the house; home*: ἀνάγειν Ac 16: 34. ἀπέρχεσθαι Hs 9, 11, 2. ἔρχεσθαι Lk 15: 6. ὑπάγειν Hs 9, 11, 6. ὑποστρέφειν Lk 7: 10.—εἰς οἶκόν τινος *to someone's house; home* Mk 8: 3, 26. εἰς οἶκόν τινος τῶν ἀρχόντων Lk 14: 1 (on the absence of the art. cf. Bl-D. §259, 1; Rob.

792).—εἰς οἶκον *home* (Aeschyl., Soph.; Diod. S. 4, 2, 1): εἰσέρχεσθαι Mk 7: 17; 9: 28. ἔρχεσθαι 3: 20.—ἐκ τοῦ οἴκου ἐκείνου Ac 19: 16.—ἐν τῷ οἴκῳ τινός *in someone's house* Ac 7: 20; 10: 30; 11: 13; Hs 6, 1, 1.—ἐν τῷ οἴκῳ *in the house, at home* J 11: 20; Hv 5: 1.—ἐν οἴκῳ *at home* (Strabo 13, 1, 38; UPZ 59, 5 [168 BC]; 74, 6; POxy. 531, 3 [II AD]; 1 Km 19: 9) Mk 2: 1 (Gdspd., Probs. 52); 1 Cor 11: 34; 14: 35.—κατὰ τοὺς οἴκους εἰσπορεύεσθαι *enter house after house* Ac 8: 3. κατ᾽ οἴκους (opp. δημοσίᾳ) *from house to house* i.e., in private 20: 20. In the sing. κατ᾽ οἶκον (opp. ἐν τῷ ἱερῷ) *in the various private homes* (Jos., Ant. 4, 74; 163.—Diod. S. 17, 28, 4 κατ᾽ οἰκίαν ἀπολαύσαντες τῶν βρωτῶν=having enjoyed the food in their individual homes) 2: 46; 5: 42. ἡ κατ᾽ οἶκόν τινος ἐκκλησία *the church in someone's house* Ro 16: 5; 1 Cor 16: 19; Col 4: 15; Phlm 2 (cf. ἐκκλησία 4c). τὰ κατὰ τὸν οἶκον *household affairs* (Lucian, Abdic. 22) 1 Cl 1: 3.

β. *house* of any large building οἶκος τοῦ βασιλέως *the king's palace* (Ael. Aristid. 32, 12 K.=12 p. 138 D.; 2 Km 11: 8; 15: 35; 3 Km 7: 31; Jos., Ant. 9, 102) Mt 11: 8. οἶκος ἐμπορίου (s. ἐμπόριον) J 2: 16b. οἶκος προσευχῆς *house of prayer* Mt 21: 13; Mk 11: 17; Lk 19: 46 (all three Is 56: 7). οἶκ. φυλακῆς *prison-(house)* B 14: 7 (Is 42: 7).—Esp. of *God's house* (Herodas 1, 26 οἶκος τῆς θεοῦ [of Aphrodite]; WRPaton and ELHicks, Inscr. of Cos 1891 no. 8, 4 οἶκος τῶν θεῶν.—οἶκ. in ref. to temples as early as Eur., Phoen. 1372; Hdt. 8, 143; Pla., Phaedr. 246E; inscr. [cf. Dit., Syll.³ index IV οἶκος d; Thieme 31]; UPZ 79, 4 [II BC] ἐν τῷ οἴκῳ τῷ Ἄμμωνος; POxy. 1380, 3 [II AD]; LXX) οἶκος τοῦ θεοῦ (Jos., Bell. 4, 281) Mt 12: 4; Mk 2: 26; Lk 6: 4. Of the temple in Jerusalem (3 Km 7: 31 ὁ οἶκος κυρίου) ὁ οἶκός μου Mt 21: 13; Mk 11: 17; Lk 19: 46 (all three Is 56: 7). ὁ οἶκ. τοῦ πατρός μου J 2: 16a; cf. Ac 7: 47, 49 (Is 66: 1). Specif. of the temple building (Eupolem. in Euseb., Pr. Ev. 9, 34, 14; Ep. Arist. 88; 101) μεταξὺ τοῦ θυσιαστηρίου καὶ τοῦ οἴκου *between the altar and the temple building* Lk 11: 51. Of the heavenly sanctuary, in which Christ functions as high priest Hb 10: 21 (the mng. bα is preferred by some here).

γ. in a wider sense οἰκ. occasionally amounts to *city* (cf. the note on POxy. 126, 4.—Jer 22: 5; 12: 7; Test. Levi 10, 4 οἶκος . . . Ἱερουσ. κληθήσεται) Mt 23: 38; Lk 13: 35.

b. fig. (Philo, Cher. 52 ὦ ψυχή, δέον ἐν οἴκῳ θεοῦ παρθενεύεσθαι al.)—a. of Christendom as the spiritual temple of God ὡς λίθοι ζῶντες οἰκοδομεῖσθε οἶκος πνευματικός *as living stones let yourselves be built up into a spiritual house* 1 Pt 2: 5 (EGSelwyn, 1 Pt '46, 286–91). The tower, which Hermas uses as a symbol of the church, is also called ὁ οἶκ. τοῦ θεοῦ: ἀποβάλλεσθαι ἀπὸ τοῦ οἶκ. τοῦ θ. Hs 9, 13, 9. Opp. εἰσέρχεσθαι εἰς τὸν οἶκ. τοῦ θεοῦ 9, 14, 1.—The foll. pass. are more difficult to classify; mng. 2 (the Christians as God's family) may also be poss.: ὁ οἶκ. τοῦ θεοῦ 1 Pt 4: 17; ἐν οἴκῳ θεοῦ ἀναστρέφεσθαι ἥτις ἐστὶν ἐκκλησία θεοῦ ζῶντος 1 Ti 3: 15.

β. *dwelling, habitation* of the human body (Lucian, Gall. 17) as a habitation of demons Mt 12: 44; Lk 11: 24. Corresp. the heathen is called an οἰκ. δαιμονίων B 16: 7.

2. *household, family* (Hom.+; Artem. 2, 68 p. 161, 11 μετὰ ὅλου τοῦ οἴκου) Lk 10: 5; 19: 9; Ac 10: 2; 11: 14; 16: 31; 18: 8. ὅλους οἴκους ἀνατρέπειν *ruin whole families* Tit 1: 11 (cf. Gen 47: 12 πᾶς ὁ οἶκος='the whole household'). ὁ Στεφανᾶ οἶκ. *Stephanas and his family* 1 Cor 1: 16; ὁ Ὀνησιφόρου οἶκ. 2 Ti 1: 16; 4: 19. ὁ οἶκ. Ταουΐας ISm 13: 2. Esp. freq. in Hermas: τὰ ἁμαρτήματα ὅλου τοῦ οἴκου σου *the sins of your whole family* Hv 1, 1, 9; cf. 1, 3, 1; 2, 3, 1; s 7: 2. . . . σε καὶ τὸν οἶκ. σου v 1, 3, 2; cf. m 2: 7; 5, 1, 7; s 7: 5ff. W. τέκνα m 12, 3, 6; s 5, 3, 9. Cf. 1 Ti 3: 4, 12 (on the subj. matter, Ocellus Luc. c. 47 τοὺς ἰδίους

οἴκους κατὰ τρόπον οἰκονομήσουσι; Letter 58 of Apollonius of Tyana [Philostrat. I 362, 3]). ἡ τοῦ Ἐπιτρόπου σὺν ὅλῳ τῷ οἴκῳ αὐτῆς καὶ τῶν τέκνων the (widow) of Epitropus together with all her household and that of her children IPol 8: 2 (Sb 7912 [inscr. 136 AD] σὺν τῷ παντὶ οἴκῳ). ἀσπάζομαι τοὺς οἴκους τῶν ἀδελφῶν μου σὺν γυναιξὶ καὶ τέκνοις I greet the households of my brethren, including their wives and. children ISm 13: 1. In a passage showing the influence of Num 12: 7, Hb 3: 2-6 draws a contrast betw. the οἶκος of which Moses was a member and the οἶκος over which Christ presides. Hence the words of vs. 6 οὗ (i.e. Χριστοῦ) οἶκός ἐσμεν ἡμεῖς whose household we are.—On the Christians as God's family s. also 1ba above. τοῦ ἰδίου οἴκ. προστῆναι manage one's own household 1 Ti 3: 4f; cf. vs. 12 and 5: 4.

3. transferred fr. a single family to a whole clan or tribe of people descended fr. a common ancestor house= descendants, nation (Appian, Bell. Civ. 2, 127 §531 οἶκοι μεγάλοι=famous families [of Caesar's assassins]; Dionys. Byz. 53 p. 23, 1 Güngerich; LXX; Jos., Ant. 2, 202; 8, 111; Sib. Or. 3, 167) ὁ οἶκ. Δαυίδ (3 Km 12: 19; 13: 2) Lk 1: 27, 69. ἐξ οἴκου καὶ πατριᾶς Δ. 2: 4.—οἶκ. Ἰσραήλ Mt 10: 6; 15: 24; Ac 2: 36; 7: 42 (Am 5: 25); Hb 8: 10 (Jer 38: 33); 1 Cl 8: 3 (quot. of unknown orig.). ὁ οἶκ. Ἰσ. combined w. ὁ οἶκ. Ἰούδα Hb 8: 8 (Jer 38: 31). οἶκ. Ἰακώβ (Ex 19: 3; Is 2: 5) Lk 1: 33; Ac 7: 46. οἶκ. τοῦ Ἀμαλήκ B 12: 9.

4. the house and what is in it=property, possessions (Hom.+; s. also Hdt. 3, 53; Isaeus 7, 42; Pla., Lach. 185A; X., Oec. 1, 5; Jos., Bell. 6, 282) ἐπ' Αἴγυπτον καὶ ὅλον τὸν οἶκον αὐτοῦ over Egypt and over all his property Ac 7: 10 (cf. Gen 41: 40; Artem. 4, 61 προέστη τοῦ παντὸς οἴκου).—GDelling, Zur Taufe von 'Häusern' im Urchrist., NovT 7, '65, 285-311=Studien zum NT '70, 288-310; OMichel, TW V 122-61; οἶκος and related words. M-M. B. 133; 458.

οἰκουμένη, ης, ἡ (sc. γῆ. Hdt.+; inscr., pap., LXX; Artapanus in Euseb., Pr. Ev. 9, 27, 22 God as ὁ τῆς οἰκ. δεσπότης; Ep. Arist., Philo, Joseph.; Test. Levi 18: 3; loanw. in rabb.).

1. the inhabited earth, the world—a. as such (Ps 23: 1 and often): πάσας τ. βασιλείας τ. οἰκουμένης Lk 4: 5. Cf. 21: 26; Ro 10: 18 (Ps 18: 5); Hb 1: 6. ὅλη ἡ οἰκ. the whole inhabited earth (Diod. S. 12, 2, 1 καθ' ὅλην τὴν οἰκουμένην) Ep. Arist. 37.—Diod. S. 3, 64, 6 and Dius, Bell. 7, 43 πᾶσα ἡ οἰκ.) Mt 24: 14; Ac 11: 28; Rv 3: 10; 16: 14. οἱ κατὰ τὴν οἰκ. ἄνθρωποι PK p. 15, l. 20. αἱ κατὰ τὴν οἰκ. ἐκκλησίαι the churches throughout the world MPol 5: 1; cf. 8: 1; 19: 2.

b. world in the sense of its inhabitants, humankind Ac 17: 31 (cf. Ps 9: 9); 19: 27. Of Satan: ὁ πλανῶν τὴν οἰκ. ὅλην who deceives all humankind Rv 12: 9. The passage ἐξῆλθεν δόγμα παρὰ Καίσαρος Αὐγούστου ἀπογράφεσθαι πᾶσαν τὴν οἰκουμένην Lk 2: 1 belongs here also. For the evangelist considers it of great importance that the birth of the world's savior coincided w. another event that also affected every person in the world. But it can also be said of Augustus that he ruled the οἰκ., because the word is used in still another specific sense, namely

2.=the Roman Empire (which, in the exaggerated language commonly used in ref. to the emperors, was equal to the whole world [as, e.g., the empire of Xerxes: Ael. Aristid. 54 p. 675 D., and of Cyrus: Jos., Ant. 11, 3]: Dit., Or. 666, 3; 668, 5 τῷ σωτῆρι κ. εὐεργέτῃ τῆς οἰκουμένης [Nero]; 669, 10, Syll.³ 906 A, 3f τὸν πάσης οἰκουμένης δεσπότην [Julian]; POxy. 1021, 5ff; Sb 176, 2.—Cf. 1 Esdr 2: 2; Philo, Leg. ad Gai. 16; Jos., Bell. 4, 656, Ant. 19, 193).

a. as such Ac 24: 5 (as Jos., Ant. 12, 48 πᾶσι τοῖς κατὰ τὴν οἰκουμένην Ἰουδαίοις, where however, οἰκ. has mng. 1. Cf. PLond. 1912 [letter of Emperor Claudius], 100).

b. its inhabitants 17: 6.—GJDAalders, Het Romeinsch Imperium en het NT '38.

3. an extraordinary use: τὴν οἰκ. ἔκτισας 1 Cl 60: 1, where οἰκ. seems to mean the whole world (so far as living beings inhabit it, therefore the realm of spirits as well). S. Johnston s.v. κόσμος.—Also ἡ οἰκ. ἡ μέλλουσα Hb 2: 5= ὁ μέλλων αἰών (6: 5); s. αἰών 2b.—JKaerst, Die antike Idee der Oekumene '03; JVogt, Orbis terrarum '29; MPaeslack, Theologia Viatorum II, '50, 33-47. M-M. B. 13.*

οἰκουργέω keep house τὰ κατὰ τὸν οἶκον οἰκ. fulfill one's household duties 1 Cl 1: 3 (class. οἰκουρεῖν, which the Jerus. ms. restores by erasure). M-M. s.v. -ός.*

οἰκουργός, όν (for class. οἰκουρός. The form w. γ is found elsewh. only in Soranus p. 18, 2 v.l. [for οἰκουρός]: οἰκουργὸν καὶ καθέδριον διάγειν βίον) working at home, domestic of women Tit 2: 5 (cf. Philo, Exsecr. 139 σώφρονας κ. οἰκουροὺς κ. φιλάνδρους; Cass. Dio 56, 3). M-M.*

οἰκουρός, όν (Aeschyl.+; PGM 11a, 11; Philo, Rer. Div. Her. 186) staying at home, domestic Tit 2: 5 t.r. (οἰκουρός, end; Field, Notes 220-2).*

οἰκοφθόρος, ον (Eur., Pla.; Philo, Agr. 73; Sib. Or. 2, 257) destroying houses or families subst. and specif. (after IEph 15: 3; s. οἶκος 1aβ) temple-destroyer IEph 16: 1. Since Ign. is plainly dependent on 1 Cor 6 (vs. 19; cf. also 1 Cor 3: 16f) here, he is prob. thinking of the introduction of immorality as the particular means of destruction (cf. Plut., Mor. p. 12B γυναικῶν οἰκοφθορίαι γαμετῶν; PGrenf. I 53, 19.—Hesychius completes the equation οἰκοφθόρος=μοιχός).*

οἰκτείρω s. οἰκτίρω (Bl-D. §23; 101; Mlt.-H. 78; 250; 402; Kühner-Bl. II 498; Meisterhans³-Schw. 179). M-M.

οἰκτιρμός, οῦ, ὁ (Pind., Pyth. 1, 164; Maspéro 7, 19 [VI AD]; LXX) rarely in sing. (which is not common in the LXX) pity, mercy, compassion ἐνδύσασθαι σπλάγχνα οἰκτιρμοῦ (gen. of quality) put on heartfelt compassion Col 3: 12. Almost always pl., partly to express the concrete forms of expression taken by the abstract concept (Bl-D. §142; cf. Rob. 408), but more oft. without any difference fr. the sing., due to the influence of the Hebr. pl. רַחֲמִים (2 Km 24: 14; Ps 24: 6; Is 63: 15; Test. Jos. 2: 3). Quite gener. χωρὶς οἰκτιρμῶν without pity Hb 10: 28.—Of men: w. σπλάγχνα (hendiadys) Phil 2: 1. ἡ ... μετ' οἰκτιρμῶν μνεία remembrance with compassion 1 Cl 56: 1.—Of God (Ps 24: 6; 39: 12; Ps.-Clem., Hom. 3, 29) οἰκ. τοῦ θεοῦ Ro 12: 1. τὸ πλῆθος τῶν οἰκ. σου thy abundant mercy 1 Cl 18: 2 (Ps 50: 3). ἐπιστρέφειν ἐπὶ τοὺς οἰκ. αὐτοῦ turn to his compassion 9: 1. προσφεύγειν τοῖς οἰκ. αὐτοῦ take refuge in his mercies 20: 11. God as πατὴρ τῶν οἰκ. merciful Father 2 Cor 1: 3 (cf. Bl-D. §165 w. app.; Mlt.-H. 440f). M-M.*

οἰκτίρμων, ον (Gorgias, Palam. 32 Blass; Theocr. 15, 75; Anth. Pal. 7, 359, 1; Sb 3923 οἰκτείρμων; LXX) merciful, compassionate of God (so almost always LXX and, in addition, always combined w. ἐλεήμων) w. πολύσπλαγχνος Js 5: 11. W. εὐεργετικός 1 Cl 23: 1. W. ἐλεήμων 60: 1.—Of men also (Memnon Hist. [I BC/I AD]: 434 fgm. 1, 3, 2 Jac.; Ps 108: 12; La 4: 10) Lk 6: 36.*

οἰκτίρω fut. οἰκτιρήσω (Hom.+; inscr.; Ps.-Phoc. 25; Philo, Migr. Abr. 122; Jos., Bell. 4, 384; 5, 418, Ant. 7,

153; 14, 354; Test. 12 Patr.; for the spelling s. on οἰκτείρω) only in one pass. in our lit., a quot. *have compassion* τινά *on someone* (Pla., Laws 2, 1 p. 653c θεοὶ οἰκτείραντες τὸ τῶν ἀνθρώπων γένος; Epict. 4, 6, 21; Appian, Bell. Civ. 4, 22 §89; Lucian, Tim. 42, Dial. Mort. 28, 2; Ezek. Trag. in Euseb., Pr. Ev. 9, 29, 11; Test. Ash. 2: 2) Ro 9: 15 (Ex 33: 19.—οἰκτίρω of the divinity: Apollon. Rhod. 4, 917; beside ἐλεέω Pla., Euthyd. 288D). —RBultmann, TW V 161-3: οἰκτίρω and related words.*

οἶμαι s. οἴομαι.

οἰνόμελι, ιτος, τό (Carneades [II BC] in Diog. L. 4, 64; Polyb. 12, 2, 7; Diod. S. 5, 34, 2; Plut., Mor. 196E; 733E; Diosc., Mat. Med. 5, 8 W; Sext. Emp., Adv. Math. 6, 44, 9. Loanw. in rabb.) *wine mixed with honey,* a drink someth. like mead. In our lit. only fig., of heretics: θανάσιμον φάρμακον διδόναι μετὰ οἰνομέλιτος *give a deadly poison mixed with honeyed wine* (Anonym. Mimus [II AD] in OCrusius, Herondas⁵ '14 [p. 110-16] l. 161f φάρμακον θανάσιμον μετ' οἰνομέλιτος; 171f) ITr 6: 2.*

οἰνοπότης, ου, ὁ (Anacr. 99 Diehl; Callim., Epigr. 36 Schn.; Polyb. 20, 8, 2; Anth. Pal. 7, 28, 2; UPZ 81 IV, 21 [II BC]; Pr 23: 20) *wine-drinker, drunkard* (w. φάγος) Mt 11: 19; Lk 7: 34. M-M.*

οἶνος, ου, ὁ (Hom.+; inscr., pap., LXX, Philo; Jos., Ant. 3, 279 al.; Test. 12 Patr.) *wine,* normally the fermented juice of the grape (cf. Hastings, Dict. of the Bible 1899, 2, 33f); the word for 'must', or unfermented grape juice, is τρύξ (Anacr.+; pap.).

1. lit. J 2: 3, 9f (HWindisch, Die joh. Weinregel: ZNW 14, '13, 248-57. Further material on the 'marriage at Cana' Hdb.³ '33, exc. after 2: 12. Cf. also HNoetzel, Christus u. Dionysos '60); 4: 46. οἶνος μετὰ χολῆς μεμιγμένος *wine mixed with gall* Mt 27: 34 (s. χολή). ὄξος καὶ οἶν. μεμιγμένα ἐπὶ τὸ αὐτό *vinegar and wine mixed together* Hm 10, 3, 3. ἐσμυρνισμένος οἶν. *wine mixed with myrrh* Mk 15: 23. W. ἔλαιον D 13: 6; used medicinally (Theophr., Hist. Pl. 9, 12; Diosc., Mat. Med. 5, 9) Lk 10: 34; stored in a cellar Hm 11: 15. W. other natural products Rv 18: 13. John the Baptist abstains fr. wine and other intoxicating drink (cf. Num 6: 3; Judg 13: 14; 1 Km 1: 11) Lk 1: 15; to denote the extraordinary degree of his abstinence it is said of him μὴ ἐσθίων ἄρτον μήτε πίνων οἶνον 7: 33 (Diod. S. 1, 72, 2 the Egyptians in mourning for their kings abstain from wheat bread [πυρός] and from wine). Abstinence fr. wine and meat on the part of 'weak' Christians Ro 14: 21 (Ltzm., Hdb. exc. before Ro 14. Lit. on ἀσθενής 2b and λάχανον). ἡ ἡδονὴ τοῦ οἴνου *the flavor of the wine* Hm 12, 5, 3. οἶν. νέος *new wine* (s. νέος 1aa) Mt 9: 17 (WNagel, Vigiliae Christianae 14, '60, 1-8: [Gosp. of Thomas]); Mk 2: 22; Lk 5: 37f.—μεθύσκεσθαι οἴνῳ *get drunk with wine* Eph 5: 18. οἶνος πολύς (Ps.-Anacharsis, Ep. 3 p. 103 H.): οἴνῳ πολλῷ προσέχειν *be addicted to much wine* 1 Ti 3: 8. οἴνῳ πολλῷ δεδουλωμένος *enslaved to drink* Tit 2: 3. οἴνῳ ὀλίγῳ χρῆσθαι *take a little wine* 1 Ti 5: 23 (the moderate use of wine is recommended fr. the time of Theognis [509f]; Plut., Is. et Os. 6 p. 353B of οἶνος: χρῶνται μέν, ὀλίγῳ δέ; Ps.-Plut., Hom. 206; Crates, Ep. 10).—KKircher, D. sakrale Bed. des Weines im Altertum '10; VZapletal, D. Wein in d. Bibel '20; JDöller, Der Wein in Bibel u. Talmud: Biblica 4, '23, 143-67, 267-99; JBoehmer, D. NT u. d. Alkohol: Studierstube 22, '26, 322-64; Else Zurhellen-Pfleiderer, D. Alkoholfrage im NT '27; IWRaymond, The Teaching of the Early Church on the Use of Wine, etc. '27. S. also ἄμπελος 1 and ἄρτος 1a.

2. fig., in apocalyptic symbolism, of the punishments

which God gives to the wicked to 'drink' like wine: ὁ οἶνος τοῦ θυμοῦ τοῦ θεοῦ *the wine of God's wrath* Rv 14: 10. Also ὁ οἶν. τοῦ θυμοῦ τῆς ὀργῆς τοῦ θεοῦ 19: 15; cf. 16: 19. Of Babylon the harlot ὁ οἶνος τοῦ θυμοῦ τῆς πορνείας αὐτῆς 14: 8; 18: 3. Cf. θυμός on all these passages. οἶν. τῆς πορνείας 17: 2.

3. effect for cause: *vineyard* Rv 6: 6; s. ἔλαιον 3.— HSeesemann, TW V 163-7. M-M. B. 390.*

οἰνοφλυγία, ας, ἡ (X., Oec. 1, 22; Aristot., Eth. Nic. 3, 5, 15; Stoic. III 397 οἰνοφλυγία δὲ ἐπιθυμία οἴνου ἄπληστος) *drunkenness* pl. (Polyb. 2, 19, 4; Musonius p. 14, 15 H.; Philo, Mos. 2, 185, Spec. Leg. 4, 91) w. ἀσέλγειαι, κῶμοι, πότοι et al., of the individual occurrences of drunkenness 1 Pt 4: 3. M-M.*

οἴομαι contracted οἶμαι, 1 aor. ᾠήθην ITr 3: 3 (Hom.+; inscr., pap., LXX, Ep. Arist.; Jos., Ant. 8, 241, Vi. 83) *think, suppose, expect* foll. by acc. and inf. (PEleph. 13, 6; POxy. 1666, 2; Gen 37: 7; Job 34: 12; Jos., Ant. 1, 323) J 21: 25; 2 Cl 14: 2; Dg 3: 1. W. inf. foll. (PEleph. 12, 1; PFlor. 332, 8; POxy. 898, 24; 1 Macc 5: 61; 2 Macc 7: 24; Jos., C. Ap. 2, 117) Phil 1: 17; 1 Cl 30: 4 (Job 11: 2); PK 2 p. 14, 25; Dg 2: 7; 3: 4f; 10: 3. W. ὅτι foll. (Lucian, Adv. Indoct. 7 p. 106, Alex. 61 p. 265 al.; Ps.-Aeschines, Ep. 4, 2; Is 57: 8; Ep. Arist. 227) Js 1: 7; 2 Cl 6: 6; 15: 1. The passage . . . εἰς τοῦτο ᾠήθην, ἵνα κτλ. ITr 3: 3 is difficult, no doubt because of damage to the text; in their efforts to make tolerable sense of it, Zahn, Funk and Bihlmeyer remain closer to the text tradition than does Lghtf. They read οὐκ εἰς τ. ᾠ., ἵνα κτλ. *I do not consider myself entitled to,* etc. M-M. s.v. οἶμαι.*

οἷος, α, ον relative pron. (Hom.+; inscr., pap., LXX, Philo, Joseph.) *of what sort, (such) as* οἷος . . . τοιοῦτος *as . . . so* (Oenomaus in Euseb., Pr. Ev. 5, 27, 5; Sir 49: 14) 1 Cor 15: 48a, b; 2 Cor 10: 11; Hs 9, 4, 6. τὸν αὐτὸν ἀγῶνα . . . οἷον *the same struggle . . . as you saw* (οἷον refers to significance, as Dialekt-Inschr. 4999 II, 10 [Crete] θάνατος οἷος διακωλυσεῖ=an instance of death whose significance hinders) in its inexorable nature . . . Phil 1: 30. The correlative can oft. be supplied fr. the context (POxy. 278, 18; PRyl. 154, 28; Gen 44: 15; Jos., Ant. 10, 13): θλῖψις, οἵα οὐ γέγονεν Mt 24: 21 (Da 12: 1 Theod.); Mk 9: 3; 2 Cor 12: 20a, b; 2 Ti 3: 11a; Rv 16: 18 (cf. Da 12: 1 LXX and Theod.); B 10: 8. The pleonastic θλῖψις, οἵα οὐ γέγονεν τοιαύτη Mk 13: 19 is to be explained on the basis of Hebr. In an indir. quest. (Epict. 4, 6, 4; Maximus Tyr. 18, 4e) Lk 9: 55 t.r.; 1 Th 1: 5; *how great* GP 7: 25. In exclamations (Bl-D. §304) οἵους διωγμοὺς ὑπήνεγκα *what persecutions I endured!* 2 Ti 3: 11b.—οὐχ οἷον ὅτι Ro 9: 6 is a mixture of οὐχ οἷον (Hellenistic=οὐ δή που 'by no means' [Alexis Com., fgm. 201 Kock πέτεται, οὐχ οἷον βαδίζει; Diod. S. 1, 83, 4 οὐχ οἷον . . . , τοὐναντίον 'by no means . . . , on the contrary'; Field, Notes 158]; Jos., C. Ap. 2, 238; cf. Phryn. p. 372 L.; Bl-D. §304; cf. Rob. 732) and οὐχ ὅτι 'not as if' (Bl-D. 480, 5; Rob. 1034).—οἱοσδηποτοῦν, also written οἷος δή ποτ' οὖν (Vett. Val. p. 339, 26; 354, 23; BGU 895, 28 [II AD] οἴῳ δήποτε οὖν τρόπῳ), is found only in the textually doubtful vs. J 5: 4: οἵῳ δηποτοῦν κατείχετο νοσήματι *no matter what disease he had.* M-M.**

οἱοσδηποτοῦν s. οἷος, end. M-M.

οἴσω s. φέρω.

οἰωνοσκόπος, ου, ὁ (Eur., Suppl. 500; Strabo 16, 2, 39; Herm. Wr. 480, 7 Sc.; inscr., Philo.—οἰωνοσκοπέω Jos., Ant. 18, 125) *soothsayer, augur* who obtains omens fr. the behavior of birds D 3: 4.*

ὀκνέω 1 aor. ὤκνησα (Hom.+; pap., LXX) *hesitate, delay* w. inf. foll. (Oenomaus in Euseb., Pr. Ev. 5, 21, 2) μὴ ὀκνήσῃς διελθεῖν ἕως ἡμῶν *come over to us without delay* Ac 9: 38 (cf. Lucian, Necyom. 11 μὴ ὀκνήσῃς εἰπεῖν; POxy. 1769, 7; Num 22: 16; Philo, Aet. M. 84; Jos., Vi. 251, C. Ap. 1, 15. Field, Notes 118). ὁ. συγκατατάξαι Papias 2: 3. M-M.*

ὀκνηρός, ά, όν (Pind., Hippocr.+; LXX; Philo; Jos., Ant. 2, 236)—1. possessing ὄκνος *idle, lazy, indolent* of a slave (w. πονηρός) Mt 25: 26 (voc. as Pr 6: 6, 9). W. dat. τῇ σπουδῇ μὴ ὀκ. *when earnestness is needed, never be indolent* (20th Cent.) Ro 12: 11.

2. causing ὄκνος, *causing fear* or *reluctance* ἐμοὶ οὐκ ὀκνηρόν *it is not troublesome to me* w. inf. Phil 3: 1 (the verb with γράφειν PLeid. XVII, 14, 20f; Sb 7353, 14 [c. 200 AD]; PSI 621, 5).—AFridrichsen, StKr 102, '30, 300f; FHauck, TW V 167f. M-M. B. 315.*

ὀκταήμερος, ον (cf. Mlt.-H. p. 176; Gregor. Naz., Or. 25 p. 465D Χριστὸς ἀνίσταται τριήμερος, Λάζαρος τετραήμερος) *on the eighth day* περιτομῇ ὀκ.=*circumcised on the eighth day* Phil 3: 5 (on the dat. of reference cf. Bl-D. §197; Rob. 523). M-M.*

ὀκτώ indecl. (Hom.+; inscr., pap., LXX, Ep. Arist., Philo; Jos., Ant. 5, 181 al.; Test. 12 Patr.; loanw. in rabb.) *eight* B 9: 8. ὀκ. ψυχαί 1 Pt 3: 20; ἡμέραι ὀκ. Lk 2: 21; cf. 9: 28; Ac 25: 6. μεθ' ἡμέρας ὀκ. *after eight days* J 20: 26. ἐξ ἐτῶν ὀκ. *for eight years* Ac 9: 33.—δεκαοκτώ *eighteen* Lk 13: 4, 11. Also δέκα καὶ ὀκ. vs. 16 (Bl-D. §63, 2 w. app.; Rob. 282f). τριάκοντα καὶ ὀκ. *thirty-eight* J 5: 5. M-M.*

ὀλεθρευτής, ὀλεθρεύω s. ὀλοθρευτής, ὀλοθρεύω.

ὀλέθριος, ον (Hom.+; cf. Crönert 186; LXX) act. (so mostly, incl. Polyb. 2, 68, 10; 3 Km 21: 42) *deadly, destructive* δίκη *punishment* 2 Th 1: 9 v.l.*

ὄλεθρος, ου, ὁ (Hom.+; Dit., Syll.³ 527, 82 [c. 220 BC]; BGU 1027 XXVI, 11; LXX; Philo; Jos., Ant. 17, 38, Vi. 264; Sib. Or. 3, 327; 348) *destruction, ruin, death* in our lit. always w. some kind of relig. coloring: ἔρχεταί τινι ὄλ. *ruin comes upon someone* 1 Cl 57: 4 (Pr 1: 26). αἰφνίδιος αὐτοῖς ἐφίσταται ὄλ. *sudden destruction will come upon them* 1 Th 5: 3. βυθίζειν τινα εἰς ὄλ. *plunge someone headlong into ruin* 1 Ti 6: 9. ὄλ. αἰώνιος *eternal death* (Test. Reub. 6: 3) 2 Th 1: 9 (s. ὀλέθριος). παραδοῦναί τινα τῷ σατανᾷ εἰς ὄλ. τῆς σαρκός *hand someone over to Satan for the destruction of his flesh* 1 Cor 5: 5 (handing over to Satan will result in the sinner's death.— EvDobschütz, Die urchristl. Gemeinden '02, 269–72 and s. παραδίδωμι 1b.—Hierocles 14 p. 451b has the thought that the soul of the sinner in Hades is purified by the tortures of hell, and is saved thereby). Destruction brought about by Satan is mentioned also IEph 13: 1 ὅταν πυκνῶς ἐπὶ τὸ αὐτὸ γίνεσθε, καθαιροῦνται αἱ δυνάμεις τοῦ σατανᾶ καὶ λύεται ὁ ὄλ. αὐτοῦ *when you come together frequently, the (spirit-)powers of Satan are destroyed, and his destructiveness is nullified.* M-M.*

ὀλιγόβιος, ον (Aristot., H.A. 8, 28; Sext. Emp., Math. 1, 73; Job) *short-lived* γεννητὸς γυναικὸς ὀλ. *he that is born of woman and is short-lived* 1 Cl 30: 5 (Job 11: 2).*

ὀλιγοπιστία, ας, ἡ (only in Christian wr.; Leontios 7 p. 14, 18; 21; 15, 6; Cosmas and Damian 26, 71) *littleness* or *poverty of faith* Mt 17: 20.*

ὀλιγόπιστος, ον (Sextus 6; elsewh. only in Christian wr.; Third Corinthians 3: 31) *of little faith* or *trust*, in our lit.,

in fact only in the synoptics, only in addressing the disciples Mt 6: 30; 8: 26; 16: 8; Lk 12: 28; Peter alone Mt 14: 31. M-M. and suppl.*

ὀλίγος, η, ον (Hom.+; inscr., pap., LXX, En., Ep. Arist., Philo, Joseph., Test. 12 Patr.—For the NT the spelling ὀλίγος is not infrequently attested [exx. in Bl-D. §14 app.; Mlt.-H. 98f]; like ἐλπίς, ἴδιος and a few others of this kind, this form is found in inscr. and pap. as early as pre-Christian times, and is more freq. later [Crönert 148–53; Helbing 25f; Thackeray 126f; KHauser, Gramm. der griech. Inschr. Lykiens, Zürcher Diss. '16, 60]).

1. pl., quantitative *few* in number—a. used w. a noun ἐργάται Mt 9: 37; Lk 10: 2. ἰχθύδια *a few (small) fish* Mt 15: 34; Mk 8: 7. ἄρρωστοι 6: 5. ἄφρονες *a few foolish persons* ITr 8: 2. ὀνόματα Rv 3: 4. πρόσωπα *persons* 1 Cl 1: 1. W. κεράμια to be understood fr. the immediate context Hm 12, 5, 3. ἡμέραι ὀλίγαι (PFay. 123, 10 [c. 100 AD]; Gen 29: 20; cf. Ps 108: 8; Philo, Somn. 1, 46; Jos., Ant. 1, 91): ἐν ἡμ. ὀλίγαις (Diod. S. 36, 4, 4) Ac 15: 30 D. πρὸς ὀλ. ἡμέρας *for a few days* Hb 12: 10; μετὰ ὀλίγας ὀλ. *after a few days* Hs 5, 2, 9; 7: 1; 8, 4, 1. μετ' ὀλ. ἡμέρας (Teles p. 19, 5; Diod. S. 13, 8, 1) Hs 8, 2, 9; 8, 11, 5; 9, 5, 5f. ὀλ. ῥήματα *a few words* m 4, 2, 1; 12, 5, 1. δι' ὀλ. γραμμάτων *in a few lines* (s. γράμμα 1) IRo 8: 2; IPol 7: 3.

b. abs. ὀλίγοι (a) *few* (opp. πολλοί as Menand., Mon. 443; Polyb. 18, 53, 1; Diod. S. 15, 37, 1; Plut., Mor. 188E; Porphyr., Vi. Pyth. 22) Mt 7: 14 (Cebes 15, 2f there are ὀλίγοι who travel the στενὴ ὁδός . . . , ἡ ἄγουσα to the goal); 20: 16 v.l.; 22: 14=B 4: 14; Lk 13: 23; 1 Pt 3: 20; Hs 8, 5, 4; MPol 5: 1. Used w. the partitive gen. (Arrian, Anab. 5, 15, 4 ὀλίγοι τῶν ἐλεφάντων), and a neg. *not a few, a number (of)* (Jos., Bell. 7, 438) γυναικῶν Ac 17: 4. γυναικῶν . . . καὶ ἀνδρῶν vs. 12.—ὀλ. ἐξ αὐτῶν Hs 9, 8, 6.—ὀλίγα (a) *few things* Lk 10: 42 (opp. πολλά as Menand., Mon. 226; ABaker, CBQ 27, '65, 127–37; Rv 2: 14; ὑποδείξω ὀλ. *I shall point out a few things* B 1: 8. ὀλ. ἐπερωτᾶν τινα *ask someone a few questions* Hm 4, 1, 4. ἐπὶ ὀλίγα ἧς πιστός *you were trustworthy in managing a few things* Mt 25: 21, 23. δαρήσεται ὀλίγας *as he will receive few lashes* Lk 12: 48 (s. δέρω). δι' ὀλίγων γράφειν 1 Pt 5: 12 (βραχέων 𝔓⁷², cf. Hb 13: 22; s. διά III 1b).

2. sing. *little, small, short*—a. of quantity (3 Km 17: 10 ὀλ. ὕδωρ) οἶνος ὀλ. *a little wine* (Artem. 1, 66 p. 59, 25) 1 Ti 5: 23; πῦρ ὀλ. *a little fire* Js 3: 5 t.r. οὐκ ὀλ. ἐργασία *no small profit* Ac 19: 24; of fruit *little* Hs 2: 4; of a country *small* 1 Cl 10: 2.—Subst. τὸ ὀλίγον *a small amount* ὁ τὸ ὀλ. *he who gathered a small amount* (opp. ὁ τὸ πολύ) 2 Cor 8: 15 (cf. Num 11: 32; Ex 16: 18). ᾧ ὀλίγον ἀφίεται *the one to whom little is forgiven* Lk 7: 47a.

b. of degree οὐκ ὀλ. *great, severe*: τάραχον Ac 12: 18; 19: 23. στάσις κ. ζήτησις 15: 2. χειμών 27: 20.

c. of duration (Musaeus vs. 291 ὀλίγον ἐπὶ χρόνον= *for a short time*) ὀλ. καιρός *a short time* Rv 12: 12 χρόνος οὐκ ὀλ. *a long time* (Jos., Bell. 2, 62) Ac 14: 28. ὀλίγον χρόνον *for a short while* (Menand., fgm. 797) 2 Cl 19: 3; Hs 7: 6; ἐν καιρῷ ὀλ. *in a short time* 1 Cl 23: 4.

3. The neut. ὀλίγον in adverbial expressions (Hom.+; Pr 6: 10; Sir 51: 16, 27)—a. ὀλίγον *a little* of distance, etc. (Pla., Prot. 26 p. 339D ὀλίγον προελθών) Mk 1: 19; Lk 5: 3.—Of time (Ps 36: 10) Mk 6: 31; 1 Pt 1: 6; 5: 10; Rv 17: 10.—Of degree or extent *only a little* (Ael. Aristid. 33, 6 K.=51 p. 573 D.) ὀλίγον ἀγαπᾷ *he loves only (to) a little* (extent) Lk 7: 47b.

b. used w. preps. ἐν ὀλίγῳ (cf. Test. Gad 4, 6= 'slightly') *in brief* (Aristot., Rhet. 3, 11 p. 1412b, 23; Dionys. Byz. §3) Eph 3: 3; *in a short time, quickly* (Pind.; Pla., Apol. 22B; Jos., Ant. 18, 145; Lucian, Toxaris 24) Ac

26: 28 (s. πείθω 1b; 3a and reff. there). καὶ ἐν ὀλ. καὶ ἐν μεγάλῳ *whether in a short or a long time* vs. 29 (cf. Bl-D. §195; GHWhitaker, The Words of Agrippa to St. Paul: JTS 15, '14, 82f; AFridrichsen, Symb. Osl. 14, '35, 50; Field, Notes 141–3; cf. Rob. 653).—μετ' ὀλίγον *after a short while* (Diod. S. 14, 9, 6; 15, 6, 5; Appian, Liby. 98 §465; Dit., Syll.³ 1170, 25f; PRyl. 77, 41; Jdth 13: 9; Wsd 15: 8; Jos., Vi. 344) MPol 11: 2.—πρὸς ὀλίγον *for a short time* (Lucian, Dial. Deor. 18, 1; Aelian, V.H. 12, 63; POxy. 67, 14; Jos., Bell. 4, 642, Ant. 4, 128) Js 4: 14. On the other hand, this is not indicated for 1 Ti 4: 8 because of the contrast w. πρὸς πάντα; here πρὸς ὀλίγον ὠφέλιμος means *profitable for (a) little.*—HSeesemann, TW V 137f: ὀλίγος and related words. M-M. B. 925f.*

ὀλιγοχρόνιος, ον (Hdt. et al.; Polyb. 2, 35, 6; Epict. in Stob. p. 463, 1 Sch. Oft. Vett. Val., s. index; Wsd 9: 5; Philo) *of short duration, short-lived* ἡ ἐπιδημία ἡ ἐν τῷ κόσμῳ τούτῳ τῆς σαρκὸς ταύτης μικρά ἐστιν καὶ ὀλ. 2 Cl 5: 5. τὰ ἐνθάδε (w. μικρά and φθαρτά) 6: 6.*

ὀλιγοψυχέω (Isocr. 19, 39; inscr. fr. Pamphylia: JHS 32, '12 p. 273; PPetr. II 40[a], 12; UPZ 63, 1 [158 bc]; POxy. 1294, 13; LXX) *be faint-hearted, discouraged* οἱ ὀλιγοψυχοῦντες *those who are discouraged* 1 Cl 59: 4.*

ὀλιγόψυχος, ον (Artem. 3, 5; PMilan [I '37] 24, 50 [117 ad] ὀλιόψυχος [sic] of a woman; LXX; cf. Cat. Cod. Astr. X 222, 16; 226, 8) *faint-hearted, discouraged* subst. 1 Th 5: 14. M-M.*

ὀλιγωρέω (Thu.+; inscr., pap.; PsSol 3: 4) *think lightly, make light* τινός *of someth.* (Diod. S. 1, 39, 13 τῆς ἀληθείας; PFlor. 384, 86; Philo; Jos., Ant. 5, 132, C. Ap. 2, 172.—Bl-D. §176, 2; Rob. 508) παιδείας κυρίου Hb 12: 5 (Pr 3: 11). M-M.*

ὀλίγως adv. (Hippocr., Aphorisms 2, 7; Ps.-Pla., Second Alcibiades 149A Clark v.l. Strato [II ad]: Anth. Pal. 12, 205, 1; Dit., Or. 669, 11[?]; POxy. 1223, 16; Aq. Is 10: 7) *scarcely, barely* ὀλ. ἀποφεύγειν 2 Pt 2: 18 (t.r. ὄντως). M-M.*

ὄλλυμι fut. ὀλῶ (Hom.+; LXX) *destroy* τινά *someone* (Sib. Or. 5, 509 πάντας κακούς) ἀσεβεῖς 1 Cl 57: 7 (Pr 1: 32). M-M.*

ὀλοθρευτής, οῦ, ὁ (only in Christian wr.; cf. Act. Phil. 130 p. 59, 9B. On the spelling s. ὀλοθρεύω) *the destroyer* 1 Cor 10: 10 (the OT speaks of ὁ ὀλεθρεύων Ex 12: 23=הַמַּשְׁחִית; Wsd 18: 25; cf. Hb 11: 28); the one meant is the destroying angel as the one who carries out the divine sentence of punishment, or perh. Satan (MDibelius, Geisterwelt 44f). M-M.*

ὀλοθρεύω (Vett. Val. 123, 11 ὀλεθρεύει; LXX; Philo, Leg. All. 2, 34; Test. Levi 13, 7; Sib. Or. 5, 304. On its spelling, beside ὀλεθρεύω, s. Bl-D. §32, 1; Mlt.-H. p. 71; Reinhold p. 40; KBuresch, RhM 46, 1891, 216f) *destroy, ruin* τινά *someone* ὁ ὀλοθρεύων *the destroying angel* (s. ὀλοθρευτής) Hb 11: 28 (after Ex 12: 23). JSchneider, TW V 168–72: ὀλεθρεύω and related words. M-M.*

ὀλοκαύτωμα, ατος, τό *whole burnt offering* in which the animal was entirely consumed by fire (not in secular Gk. [but ὀλοκαυτόω X.+]. But LXX; Philo, Sacr. Abel. 110; Jos., Bell. 5, 565, Ant. 10, 70; Test. Levi 9: 7. On the formation of the word s. Dssm., B 135 [BS 138]).
1. lit. (w. θυσία and other sim. concepts) Mk 12: 33; 1 Cl 18: 16 (Ps 50: 18) B 2: 4, 5 (Is 1: 11), 7 (Jer 7: 22). W. περὶ ἁμαρτίας *'sin-offering'* Hb 10: 6, 8 (both Ps 39: 7). ὀλ. ὑπὲρ ἁμαρτιῶν B 7: 6 (cf. Lev 16: 5). θυσίας αὐτῷ δι'

αἵματος καὶ κνίσης καὶ ὀλοκαυτωμάτων ἐπιτελεῖν *offer sacrifices to him* (God) *with blood, burning fat, and whole burnt offerings* Dg 3: 5.
2. fig., of a martyr who was burned at the stake ὀλ. δεκτὸν τῷ θεῷ ἡτοιμασμένον MPol 14: 1. M-M.*

ὀλοκληρία, ας, ἡ (Chrysipp. [Stoic. III 33]; Plut., Mor. 1041E; 1047E τοῦ σώματος; 1063F ὑγεία καὶ ὀλ.; Diog. L. 7, 107; Dit., Syll.³ 1142, 2 [I/II ad] ὀλ. τῶν ποδῶν; POxy. 123, 6; 1478, 3; BGU 948, 4 w. ὑγία; Is 1: 6 v.l.) *wholeness, completeness, soundness* in all parts: of the healing of a lame man ἡ πίστις . . . ἔδωκεν αὐτῷ τὴν ὀλ. ταύτην *faith . . . has given him this perfect health* Ac 3: 16. ADebrunner, Philol. 95, '42, 174–6. M-M.*

ὀλόκληρος, ον (Pla.; Polyb. 18, 45, 9; Ps.-Lucian, Macrob. 2; Epict. 3, 26, 7; 25; 4, 1, 66; 151; Dit., Or. 519, 14, Syll.³ 1009, 10; 1012, 9 and oft.; PLond. 935, 7; POxy. 57, 13; LXX; Philo, Abr. 47, Spec. Leg. 1, 283; Jos., Ant. 3, 228; 278; 14, 366) a qualitative term, *with integrity, whole, complete, undamaged, intact, blameless* πίστις *undiminished faith* Hm 5, 2, 3. In an ethical sense: ὀλ. ὑμῶν τὸ πνεῦμα . . . τηρηθείη *may your spirit . . . be preserved complete* or *sound* 1 Th 5: 23 (PGM 7, 590 διαφύλασσέ μου τὸ σῶμα, τὴν ψυχὴν ὁλόκληρον.—PAvanStempvoort, NTS 7, '60/'61, 262–5: connects πνεῦμα and ἁγιάσαι in 1 Th 5: 23.). W. τέλειος Js 1: 4. M-M. B. 919.*

ὀλολύζω (Hom.+; PGM 11a, 30; LXX) *cry out* in joy or pain; in the latter sense (ἐπί τινι as Lucian, Dial. Deor. 12, 1) κλαύσατε ὀλολύζοντες ἐπὶ ταῖς ταλαιπωρίαις ὑμῶν *wail and cry aloud over your tribulations* Js 5: 1.—LDeubner, Ololyge u. Verwandtes: ABA '41 no. 1. M-M.*

ὅλος, η, ον (Pind.+ [Hom. and Hes. have the Ion. οὖλος]; inscr., pap., LXX, En., Ep. Arist., Philo, Joseph., Test. 12 Patr.) *whole, entire, complete,* in the NT never in the attributive position (W-S. §20, 12a; Bl-D. §275, 2; 4; Rob. 774) and never w. the art. as a substantive, as Third Corinthians 3: 9.
1. used w. a noun that has no art., somet. preceding it, somet. coming after it: ὅλ. οἴκους *whole families* Tit 1: 11. ὅλ. ἄνθρωπον ὑγιῆ ἐποίησα *I have healed a man's whole body* J 7: 23.—ἐνιαυτὸν ὅλ. *for a whole year* Ac 11: 26. διετίαν ὅλ. *for two full years* 28: 30.—δι' ὅλης νυκτός *the whole night through* Lk 5: 5 (Appian, Liby. 134 §636; Lucian, Ver. Hist. 1, 29.—Γit., Syll.³ 1171, 6 δι' ὅλης ἡμέρας. Cf. Jos., Ant. 6, 37, Vi. 15 δι' ὅλης τῆς νυκτός; Inschr. v. Priene 112, 98 διὰ τοῦ χειμῶνος ὅλου). Likew. w. names of cities without the art. ὅλη Ἰερουσαλήμ *all Jerusalem* Ac 21: 31.
2. used w. a noun that has the art.—a. coming before the noun: ὅλ. ἡ περίχωρος ἐκείνη Mt 14: 35. ὅλ. ἡ χώρα ἐκείνη Mk 6: 55. ὅλ. ἡ πόλις 1: 33. ὅλ. τὸ σῶμά σου Mt 5: 29f; 6: 22f. ὅλ. ὁ βίος Lk 8: 43 v.l. ὅλ. τὴν ἡμέραν *the whole day (through)* (Jos., Ant. 6, 22) Mt 20: 6; Ro 8: 36 (Ps 43: 23); 10: 21 (Is 65: 2). ἐξ ὅλης τῆς ἰσχύος ἡμῶν *with all our strength* 1 Cl 33: 8. εἰς ὅλον τὸν κόσμον Hs 9, 25, 2 (ὅλ. ὁ κόσμος; Wsd 11: 22; Aristobulus in Euseb., Pr. Ev. 13, 12, 9; Ep. Arist. 210). ἡ πίστις ὑμῶν καταγγέλλεται ἐν ὅλῳ τῷ κόσμῳ Ro 1: 8 (on the hyperbole cf. PLond. 891, 9 ἡ εὐφημία σου περιεκύκλωσεν τὸν κόσμον ὅλον).
b. after the noun ὁ κόσμος ὅλ. Mt 16: 26; Lk 9: 25; 1 J 5: 19; τὸ συνέδριον ὅλ. Mt 26: 59; τὸ σῶμά σου ὅλ. Lk 11: 36a; ἡ οἰκία αὐτοῦ ὅλ. J 4: 53; ἡ πόλις ὅλ. Ac 21: 30; ἡ οἰκουμένη ὅλ. Rv 3: 10.
c. The noun can also be supplied fr. the context ἕως οὗ ἐζυμώθη ὅλον (i.e. τὸ ἄλευρον) *until (the) whole (batch*

of flour) was leavened Mt 13: 33; Lk 13: 21. ἔσται
φωτεινὸν ὅλον (i.e. τὸ σῶμά σου) Lk 11: 36b.—Sim. the
subst. ptc. ἔστιν καθαρὸς ὅλος (ὁ λελουμένος) (the one
who has bathed) is clean all over J 13: 10.

3. used w. a pron. σὺ ὅλος you altogether, wholly J 9:
34. τοῦτο ὅλον all this Mt 1: 22; 21: 4 t.r.; 26: 56.

4. used w. a prep. δι' ὅλου throughout, through and
through (Philo Mech. 60, 25; POxy. 53, 10; 1277, 8; PGM
5, 154) J 19: 23. M-M. B. 919.

ὁλοτελής, ές (since Aristot., Plant. 1, 2, 20; Plut., Mor.
909B; Galen XIX p. 162 K.; Dit., Syll.³ 814, 45 [67 AD]) a
quantitative term, quite complete, quite undamaged of
stones Hv 3, 6, 4. ἀποκάλυψις a revelation that is quite
complete v 3, 10, 9; 3, 13, 4b. ὅλ. ἐν τῇ πίστει m 9: 6. ὁ
θεὸς ἀγιάσαι ὑμᾶς ὁλοτελεῖς may God sanctify you
wholly or through and through 1 Th 5: 23. M-M.*

ὁλοτελῶς adv. (Petosiris, fgm. 21 l. 260); Peripl. Eryth. c.
30; Vett. Val. 155, 3; Aq. Dt 13: 16[17]) wholly, altogether
μετανοεῖν repent fully Hv 3, 13, 4a. ὅλ. χλωρός quite
green s 8, 5, 2.*

'Ολοφέρνης, ου, ὁ Holofernes, Assyrian commander-in-
chief, slain by Judith in his own tent when he laid siege to
her native city of Bethulia (Jdth 2ff) 1 Cl 55: 5.—On the
name and pers. of H. s. JMarquart, Philol. 54, 1895,
507ff; Schürer III⁴ 233, 22.*

'Ολυμπᾶς, ᾶ, ὁ (IG III 1080, 28.—CIL XIV 1286. Short
form, perh. fr. 'Ολυμπιόδωρος or some other rather long
name compounded w. 'Ολυμπ-. W-S. §16, 9; Rouffiac
91) Olympas, recipient of a greeting Ro 16: 15. M-M.*

ὄλυνθος, ου, ὁ (Hes.+; Theophr., Caus. Pl. 5, 9, 12;
Diosc. 1, 185; SSol 2: 13. Loanw. in rabb.) late or summer
fig Rv 6: 13. VHehn, Kulturpflanzen u. Haustiere⁶ 1894,
94ff.*

ὅλως adv. (Pla.+; inscr., pap.; Job 34: 8 v.l.; Philo)
generally speaking, actually, everywhere ὅλως ἀκούεται it
is actually reported 1 Cor 5: 1 (AFridrichsen, Symb. Osl.
13, '34, 43f: 'to say it at once'; Diod. S. 13, 16, 2
'continually', 'again and again'; Ps.-Demetr., El. c. 175;
199 R. ὅλως='regularly', 'generally', 'everywhere' and
can be parallel w. πανταδαποῦ). ἤδη οὖν ὅλως now
actually 6: 7. Rather oft. w. a neg. not at all (X., Mem. 1,
2, 35; Dio Chrys. 53[70], 5; 8; Philostrat., Vi. Apoll. 1, 39
p. 41, 9; Philo, Op. M. 170, Praem. 40; Jos., Vi. 221, Ant.
8, 241; Test. Jud. 16: 3) μὴ ὅλ. Mt 5: 34.—1 Cor 15: 29;
Hv 4, 1, 9; m 4, 2, 1 al. M-M.**

ὁμαλίζω Att. fut. ὁμαλῶ (X.+; Dit., Syll.³ 313, 10; 22;
PTebt. 375, 30; LXX) make level ὄρη B 11: 4 (Is 45: 2).*

ὁμαλός, ή, όν (Hom.+; inscr.; Aq., Sym., Theod., Philo)
level, smooth, even—1. lit. ὁμαλὸν γίνεσθαι become level
Hs 9, 10, 1; τὰ ὁμ. the level ground v 1, 1, 3.

2. as a symbol τῇ ὀρθῇ ὁδῷ πορεύεσθαι καὶ ὁμ. walk in
the straight and level way m 6, 1, 2. πάντα ὁμ. γίνεται
τοῖς ἐκλεκτοῖς all things will become level for (his) chosen
v 1, 3, 4; cf. m 2: 4 (w. ἱλαρός).*

ὁμαλῶς adv. (Thu. et al.) smoothly, evenly ὁμ. περιπατεῖν walk smoothly Hm 6, 1, 4.*

ὄμβρος, ου, ὁ (Hom.+; inscr., pap., LXX, En., Philo;
Jos., Ant. 1, 101; 2, 343 al.) rain-storm, thunderstorm Lk
12: 54. M-M.*

ὀμείρομαι (CIG III 4000, 7 [IV AD] ὀμειρόμενοι περὶ
παιδός [Ramsay, JHS 38, '18, 157; 160]; Job 3: 21 οἳ
ὀμείρονται τοῦ θανάτου [v.l. ἱμείρ.]; Sym. Ps 62: 2.

Hesychius explains it w. ἐπιθυμεῖν.—Thackeray 97;
GMilligan, Exp. 9th Ser. II '24, 227f) have a kindly
feeling, long τινός for someone 1 Th 2: 8 (W-H. write ὁμ.,
cf. app. 152; Mlt.-H. 251; ADebrunner, IndogF 21, '07,
203f; W-S. §16, 6; Bl-D. §101 p. 47, on the constr. cf.
§171, 1; Rob. 508). M-M.*

ὁμιλέω impf. ὡμίλουν; 1 aor. ὡμίλησα (Hom.+; inscr.,
pap., LXX, Ep. Arist., Philo, Joseph.) speak, converse,
address (class.; LXX) τινί (with) someone (Philemo Com.
169 K. ἐὰν γυνὴ γυναικὶ κατ' ἰδίαν ὁμιλεῖ; Ael. Aristid.
28, 116 K.=49 p. 529 D.: θεῷ; POxy. 928, 5 ὡμείλησας
δέ μοί ποτε περὶ τούτου; Da 1: 19; Jos., Ant. 17, 50)
ὡμίλει αὐτῷ he used to talk with him Ac 24: 26 (Himerius, Or. 48 [=Or. 14], 18 ὁμ. τινι=confer with
someone). Of Christ talking to the martyrs (cf. Herm. Wr.
12, 19 [τῷ ἀνθρώπῳ] μόνῳ ὁ θεὸς ὁμιλεῖ) παρεστὼς ὁ
κύριος ὡμίλει αὐτοῖς the Lord was standing by and
conversing with them MPol 2: 2. Also πρός τινα (X.,
Mem. 4, 3, 2; Jos., Ant. 11, 260 τούτων πρὸς ἀλλήλους
ὁμιλούντων): ὡμίλουν πρὸς ἀλλήλους περὶ πάντων
they were conversing w. each other about all the things Lk
24: 14. W. acc. of the thing οὐ ξένα ὁμιλῶ I have nothing
strange to say Dg 11: 1. ἃ λόγος ὁμιλεῖ 11: 7. Abs. Lk 24:
15. ἐφ' ἱκανὸν ὁμιλήσας ἄχρι αὐγῆς after talking a long
time until daylight Ac 20: 11. M-M.*

ὁμιλία, ας, ἡ— 1. association, intercourse, company
(trag., Thu.+; X., Mem. 1, 2, 20 ὁμιλία τῶν χρηστῶν;
Herm. Wr. in Stob. I 277, 21 W.=432, 20 Sc. τὰς πρὸς
τοὺς πολλοὺς ὁμιλίας παραιτοῦ; POxy. 471, 76; Wsd 8:
18; 3 Macc 5: 18; Jos., Ant. 11, 34, Vi. 67) ὁμιλίαι κακαί
bad company 1 Cor 15: 33 (cf. ἦθος and s. Ep. Arist. 130).

2. a speech (in church), sermon (ὁμ.=speech Diod. S.
16, 55, 2; Ael. Aristid. 42, 9 K.=6 p. 68 D.; Lucian,
Demon. 12; Philostrat., Vi. Apoll. 3, 15 p. 93, 20, Imag.
Prooem. p. 295, 11; Dositheus 1, 1; Jos., Ant. 15, 68;
Ps.-Clem., Hom. p. 6, 28; 12, 11; 28 al. Lag. Acc. to
Moeris 276 this usage is Hellenistic). ὁμιλίαν ποιεῖσθαι
deliver a sermon, preach (as Justin, Dial. 28; 85.—On ὁμ.
ποιεῖσθαι cf. Jos., Vi. 222) περί τινος about someth. IPol
5: 1. M-M.*

ὅμιλος, ου, ὁ (Hom.+; Aq. 1 Km 19: 20; Philo, Agr. 23)
crowd, throng πᾶς ἐπὶ τῶν πλοίων ὁ ὅμ. the whole throng
(of those traveling) on the ships Rv 18: 17 t.r. (Jos., Ant. 5,
17 ὁ πᾶς ὅμιλος). M-M.*

ὁμίχλη, ης, ἡ (Hom.+; Plut., Mor. 460A; Ael. Aristid.
51, 19 K.=27 p. 539 D.; PGM 4, 3024; LXX, En.; Sib.
Or. 3, 806) mist, fog pl. ὁμίχλαι ὑπὸ λαίλαπος ἐλαυνό-
μεναι mists driven by the storm 2 Pt 2: 17 (w. ζόφος and
σκότος as Lucian, Catapl. 2). M-M. B. 66.*

ὄμμα, ατος, τό (Hom.+, more common in poetry than in
prose; Dit., Syll.³ 1168, 120; PLond. 678, 6; BGU 713, 9;
PGM 4, 703; LXX; En. 106, 5; 10; Jos., Bell. 6, 288) eye.

1. lit. pl. (Diod. S. 3, 46, 2) Mt 20: 34; Mk 8: 23.—
2. fig. τὸ ὄμμα τῆς ψυχῆς the eye of the soul (Pla., Rep.
7 p. 533D, Soph. 254A; Porphyr., Vi. Pyth. 47; Philo, Sacr.
Abel. 36, Abr. 70.—PGM 4, 517 ἀθανάτοις ὄμμασι; 3,
474.—Rtzst., Mysterienrel.³ 296f; 318f) ἐμβλέπειν τοῖς
ὄμμ. τῆς ψυχῆς εἴς τι gaze at someth. with the eyes of the
soul 1 Cl 19: 3. M-M. B. 225.*

ὀμνύω (a by-form of ὄμνυμι which is predominant in
H.Gk. and therefore in the NT as well; in the form ὄμνυμι
Hom.+; inscr., pap.; the by-form in Hdt., X. et al.;
inscr., pap., LXX, En., Philo; Jos., Ant. 3, 271, C. Ap. 2,
121. In the NT the older form occurs only in the inf.
ὀμνύναι Mk 14: 71 [in the critical editions, foll. B et al.;

the t.r. reads ὀμνύειν w. אAC et al.]; Bl-D. §92; Mlt.-H. 251) 1 aor. ὤμοσα *swear, take an oath* w. acc. of the pers. or the thing by which one swears (Hom. +; X., An. 7, 6, 18; Diod. S. 1, 29, 4 τὴν Ἶσιν; Appian, Syr. 60 §317 πάντας τ. θεούς, Bell. Civ. 4, 68, §289; UPZ 70, 2 [152/1 bc] τὸν Σάραπιν; POxy. 239, 5 [66 ad] Νέρωνα; Bl-D. §149; Rob. 484. On the LXX s. MJohannessohn, Der Gebr. der Kasus in LXX, Diss. Berlin '10, 77; Jos., Ant. 5, 14; 13, 76) τὸν οὐρανόν, τὴν γῆν *swear by heaven, by the earth* (Apollon. Rhod. 3, 699 and schol. on Apollon. Rhod. 3, 714 ὅμοσον Γαῖάν τε καὶ Οὐρανόν; Aesop, Fab. 140 H.) Js 5: 12. τὴν Καίσαρος τύχην MPol 9: 2; 10: 1. Abs., in the same sense (cf. Jos., Ant. 4, 310) 9: 3; (w. ἐπιθῦσαι) MPol 4.—Instead of the acc., ἐν w. dat. of the pers. or thing is used (as בְּ נִשְׁבַּע in the OT; cf. Johannessohn, loc. cit.) ἐν τῷ οὐρανῷ, ἐν τῇ γῇ Mt 5: 34 (cf. the contrary advice IQS 5, 8; MDelcor, VetusT 16, '66, 8-25 [heaven and earth]); cf. 23: 22 (GHeinrici, Beiträge III '05, 42-5; ERietschel, Das Verbot des Eides in d. Bergpredigt: StKr 79, '06, 373-418; ibid. 80, '07, 609-18; OProksch, Das Eidesverbot Jesu Christi: Thüringer kirchl. Jahrbuch '07; HMüller, Zum Eidesverbot d. Bergpred. '13; OOlivieri, Biblica 4, '23, 385-90; GStählin, Zum Gebrauch von Beteuerungsformeln im NT, NovT 5, '62, 115-43; Billerb. I 321-36.—Warning against any and all oaths as early as Choerilus Epicus [V bc]: Stob., Flor. 3, 27, 1 vol. III p. 611, 3 H. ὅρκον δ' οὔτ' ἄδικον χρεὼν ὀμνύναι οὔτε δίκαιον; Nicol. Dam.: 90 fgm. 103i Jac.: the Phrygians do not swear at all; Pythagoreans acc. to Diog. L. 8, 22; Essenes in Jos., Bell. 2, 135). ἐν τῇ κεφαλῇ σου *by your head* 5: 36. ἐν τῷ ναῷ, ἐν τῷ χρυσῷ τοῦ ναοῦ 23: 16; 21. ἐν τῷ θυσιαστηρίῳ, ἐν τῷ δώρῳ τῷ ἐπάνω vss. 18, 20. ἐν τῷ ζῶντι εἰς τ. αἰῶνας τ. αἰώνων Rv 10: 6. ἐν is replaced by εἰς Mt 5: 35. Also κατά τινος *by someone* or *someth.* (Aristoph.; Demosth. [exx. in FBleek, Hb II 2, 1840, 245a]; Longus, Past. 4, 20, 2; Porphyr., Abst. 3, 16; Ps.-Lucian, Calumn. 18; Dit., Syll.³ 526, 5; 685, 25; BGU 248, 12 [I ad]; Gen 22: 16; 31: 53; Ex 32: 13; 1 Km 30: 15; Am 6: 8; Zeph 1: 5) ἐπεὶ κατ' οὐδενὸς εἶχεν μείζονος ὀμόσαι, ὤμοσεν καθ' ἑαυτοῦ *since he could swear by no one greater, he swore by himself* Hb 6: 13; cf. vs. 16 (Philo, Leg. All. 3, 203 οὐ καθ' ἑτέρου ὀμνύει θεός, οὐδὲν γὰρ αὐτοῦ κρεῖττον, ἀλλὰ καθ' ἑαυτοῦ, ὅς ἐστι πάντων ἄριστος, De Abr. 273). ὤμοσεν ὁ δεσπότης κατὰ τῆς δόξης αὐτοῦ *the Master took an oath by his glory* Hv 2, 2, 5. It is even said of God: ὤμ. κατὰ τοῦ υἱοῦ αὐτοῦ v 2, 2, 8.—Foll. by direct discourse Hb 7: 21 (Ps 109: 4). The dir. disc. is preceded by ὅτι Mt 26: 74 (w. καταθεματίζειν); Mk 14: 71 (w. ἀναθεματίζειν); Rv 10: 6f. As a quot. fr. Ps 94: 11 w. εἰ preceding the dir. disc. Hb 3: 11; 4: 3 (cf. εἰ IV).—W. dat. of the pers. *confirm someth.* (τι) *for someone with an oath* B 6: 8 (Ex 33: 1); Ac 7: 17 t.r. (ἧς by attraction, for ἥν). W. inf. foll. τίσιν ὤμοσεν μὴ εἰσελεύσεσθαι εἰς τὴν κατάπαυσιν αὐτοῦ; *whom did he assure by an oath that they should not enter his rest?* Hb 3: 18 (dat. w. fut. inf. as Plut., Galba 22, 12). διαθήκη ἥν ὤμοσεν τοῖς πατράσι δοῦναι τ. λαῷ *the covenant which he swore to the fathers to give to the people* B 14: 1. Foll. by dir. disc. introduced by ὅτι recitative Mk 6: 23 (JDM Derrett, Law in the NT, '70, 339-58). ὅρκῳ ὀμ. τινί w. inf. foll. Ac 2: 30. Though the dat. ὅρκῳ is quite rare in this combination (cf. En. 6, 4), the acc. ὅρκον (cf. Gen 26: 3; Num 30: 3) is quite common: ὅρκον ὀμ. πρός τινα (ὀμ. πρός τινα Od. 14, 331; 19, 288) *swear an oath to someone* foll. by the gen. of the aor. inf. Lk 1: 73.—RHirzel, D. Eid '02; LWenger, D. Eid in d. griech. Pap.: Z. d. Sav.-St., Rom. Abt. 23, '02, 158ff; JPedersen, Der Eid bei

den Semiten '14; ESeidl, Der Eid in röm.-ägypt. Provinzialrecht,, '33; JSchneider, TW V 177-85. M-M. B. 1437. *

ὁμοήθεια, ας, ἡ (Nicol. Dam.: 90 fgm. 139 Jac.; Philostrat., Vi. Apoll. 2, 11 p. 53, 11; Pollux 3, 62) *similarity in character, agreement in convictions* ὁμοήθειαν θεοῦ λαβόντες *you who have received a divine agreement in your convictions* IMg 6: 2. κατὰ ὁμοήθειαν θεοῦ λαλεῖν *speak on the basis of a divine unity in convictions* IPol 1: 3. *

ὁμοθυμαδόν adv. (Aristoph., X. +; Polyb.; Diod. S. 18, 22, 4; Vett. Val. 286, 27; Herm. Wr. 1, 28; Dit., Syll.³ 742, 13 [82 bc]; 1104, 28; PTebt. 40, 8 [117 bc]; LXX; Ep. Arist. 178; Philo, Mos. 1, 72 al.; Jos., Ant. 15, 277; 19, 357; Test. Napht. 6: 10; Sib. Or. 3, 458. On its formation cf. Kühner-Bl. II p. 307γ; Mlt.-H. 164) *with one mind* or *purpose* or *impulse* Ac 1: 14; 2: 1 t.r., 46; 4: 24; 7: 57; 8: 6; 12: 20; 18: 12; 19: 29; 20: 18 v.l.; MPol 12: 3. (W. ἐν ἑνὶ στόματι) δοξάζειν τὸν θεόν Ro 15: 6; γενόμενοι ὁμ. *unanimously* Ac 15: 25. The weakened mng. *together* is at least possible in 5: 12, as well as in other passages (so EHatch, Essays in Biblical Greek, 1889, 63f; HJCadbury, JBL 44, '25, 216-18; RSV et al.). M-M. *

ὁμοιάζω (only as v.l. in Mt and Mk) *be like, resemble* w. dat. (Leontios 43 p. 88, 6 τὸ παιδίον ὁμοιάζον αὐτῷ) τάφοις κεκονιαμένοις Mt 23: 27 v.l. Abs. ἡ λαλιά σου ὁμοιάζει *your speech is like* (sc.: τῇ λαλιᾷ τῶν Γαλιλαίων) Mt 26: 73 v.l.; likew. Mk 14: 70 t.r. *

ὁμοιοπαθής, ές (Pla., Rep. 3 p. 409b, Tim. p. 45c; Theophr., H.Pl. 5, 7, 2; Wsd 7: 3; 4 Macc 12: 13; Philo, Conf. Lingu. 7) *of similar feelings, circumstances, experiences with the same nature* τινί *as someone* Ac 14: 15; Js 5: 17. M-M. *

ὅμοιος, οἵα, οιον (Hom. +; inscr., pap., LXX, En., Ep. Arist., Philo; Jos., Ant. 2, 73; 12, 364 al.; Test. 12 Patr.—On the accent s. Bl-D. §13; Mlt.-H. 58. On ἡ ὅμοιος Rv 4: 3b s. 1 below and cf. Bl-D. §59, 2; Mlt.-H. 157) *of the same nature, like, similar.*

1. w. dat. of the pers. or thing compared (this is the rule Hom. +) ὅμ. αὐτῷ ἐστιν *he looks like him* J 9: 9.—χρυσῷ ἢ ἀργύρῳ . . . τὸ θεῖον εἶναι ὅμ. *the Deity is like gold or silver* Ac 17: 29. τὰ ὅμ. τούτοις *things like these* Gal 5: 21; cf. Hm 8: 5, 10; 12, 3, 1; (w. παραπλήσιος) 6, 2, 5. ὅμ. ὁράσει λίθῳ ἰάσπιδι *similar in appearance to jasper* Rv 4: 3a; cf. 3b (here ὁμ. is an adj. of two endings, as Aesop 59a, 4 Chambry στήλην ὅμοιον). ὅμ. τῇ ἰδέᾳ *similar in appearance* Hs 9, 3, 1.—Rv 1: 15; 2: 18; 4: 6f; 9: 7, 19; 11: 1; 13: 2; 21: 11, 18; 1 Cl 35: 9 (Ps 49: 21); B 7: 10a; Dg 2: 2f; Hs 9, 19, 2; 9, 21, 2. ὑπὸ ἀνθρώπων σκεύη ὅμοια γενέσθαι τοῖς λοιποῖς *to be made by human hands into vessels like the others* Dg 2: 4. ἄλλος ὅμ. ἐμοί *any other like me* Pol 3: 2. ὅμ. τοῖς φαρμάκοις *like the poisoners* or *magicians* Hv 3, 9, 7. ἡ καταστροφὴ ὅμ. καταιγίδι *the downfall is like a wind-storm* 1 Cl 57: 4 (cf. Pr 1: 27). ὅμοιοι αὐτῷ ἐσόμεθα *we shall be like him* 1 J 3: 2 (cf. Herm. Wr. 11, 5 ὅμ. τῷ θεῷ). ὁ τούτοις τὰ ὅμ. ποιῶν *he who does such things as these* Hs 6, 5, 5. τὸν ὅμοιον τρόπον τούτοις *in the same way as they* Jd 7. ἔσομαι ὅμοιος ὑμῖν ψεύστης *I should be like you, a liar* J 8: 55 (ὅ. αὐτῷ 'what is like him' Sir 13: 15; 28: 4). Freq. in parables *like* ὁμ. ἐστίν *it is like* (Aristippus in Diog. L. 2, 79 in a parable: τίς ὅμοιός ἐστί τινι; Philosophenspr. p. 485, 2 M. ἡ παιδεία ὁμοία ἐστὶ χρυσῷ στεφάνῳ) Mt 11: 16; 13: 31, 33, 44f, 47, 52; 20: 1; Lk 6: 47-9; 7: 31f; 12: 36; 13: 18f, 21. In brachylogy οὐρὰς ὁμοίας σκορπίοις *tails like those of scorpions* Rv 9: 10.

κέρατα δύο ὅμοια ἀρνίῳ 13: 11.—In a special sense *equally great* or *important, as powerful as, equal (to)* (Gen 2: 20; Jos., Ant. 8, 364; cf. the Lat. motto 'nec pluribus impar') τίς ὅμ. τῷ θηρίῳ, καὶ τίς δύναται πολεμῆσαι μετ' αὐτοῦ; *who is a match for the beast, and who is able to fight him?* Rv 13: 4. τίς ὅμ. τῇ πόλει τῇ μεγάλῃ; 18: 18. δευτέρα (i.e. ἐντολή) ὁμοία αὐτῇ (i.e. τῇ πρώτῃ) *a second, just as great as this one* Mt 22: 39; Mk 12: 31 v.l.

2. w. the gen. of what is compared (Theophr., H.Pl. 9, 11, 11; Hero Alex. I p. 60, 16; Aelian, H.A. 8, 1 τέτταρας ὁμοίους ἐκείνου κύνας; Pland. VI 97, 9 [III AD]; Cat. Cod. Astr. VIII 3 p. 197, 16 ὅμ. ὄφεως; Sir 13: 16.—Kühner-G. I p. 413, 10; Bl-D. §182, 4 app.; Rob. 530) ἔσομαι ὅμ. ὑμῶν ψεύστης J 8: 55 v.l. (for ὑμῖν; cf. 1 above; LRydbeck, Fachprosa, '67, 46–9). ἄνθρωποι ὅμ. χοίρων *like swine* B 10: 3. φεῦγε ἀπὸ παντὸς πονηροῦ καὶ ἀπὸ παντὸς ὁμοίου αὐτοῦ *avoid evil of any kind, and everything resembling it* D 3: 1.

3. The acc. of what is compared is a solecism and nothing more in ὅμ. υἱὸν ἀνθρώπου *one like a son of man* Rv 1: 13; 14: 14 (both have υἱῷ as v.l.).—Bl-D. §182, 4 app.; Rob. 530.

4. abs. τράγοι ὅμ. *goats that are alike* B 7: 6, 10b. ὅμοιοι ἐγένοντο λευκοί *they all alike became white* Hs 9, 4, 5. (τὰ δένδρα) ξηρά εἰσι καὶ ὅμοια (*the trees) are all alike dry*= *one is as dry as the other* s 3: 2a; cf. 1b. ὅμοια ἦν πάντα *they (the trees) were all alike* s 3: 1a; cf. 2b and 3ab.—JSchneider, TW V 186–98: ὅμοιος and related words. M-M. B. 912.*

ὁμοιότης, ητος, ἡ (Pre-Socr., Pla., Isocr.+; Polyb. 6, 53, 5; 13, 7, 2; Plut., Mor. 25B; 780E; Epict. 4, 11, 28; Lucian, Dial. Deor. 6, 5; pap., LXX, Philo) *likeness, similarity, agreement* πάντας ὑμᾶς αὐτῷ ἐν ὁμ. εἶναι *you are all to be like him* IEph 1: 3. ἐκπλήττεσθαι ἐπὶ τῇ ὁμ. τινος *be amazed at the similarity w. someth.* B 7: 10. καθ' ὁμοιότητα (Philo, Fuga 51; Herm. Wr. 464, 29; 518, 13 Sc.; BGU 1028, 15; PSI 107, 2; PGM 1, 211; Gen. 1: 11, 12) *in quite the same way* Hb 4: 15. W. gen. foll. (Dionys. Byz. §29; BGU 1028, 15 [II AD]; POxy. 1202, 24; PSI 107, 2; Philo, Rer. Div. Her. 232, Spec. Leg. 1, 296) κατὰ τὴν ὁμ. Μελχισέδεκ *in the same way as M.* 7: 15. M-M.*

ὁμοιοτρόπως adv. (Thu. 6, 20, 3; Aristot., Gen. An. 3, 5; Philo, Aet. M. 20 [all three w. dat.]) *in the same way* ὁμ. τοῖς προειρημένοις *in the same way as those already mentioned* Dg 3: 2.*

ὁμοιόω fut. ὁμοιώσω; 1 aor. pass. ὡμοιώθην (on the form ὁμοιώθην Ro 9: 29 v.l., s. W-H., App. 161); aor. act. subj. also ὁμοιώσω Mk 4: 30; 1 fut. pass. ὁμοιωθήσομαι (Hom.+; LXX; Philo; Jos., Bell. 5, 213).

1. *make like* τινά τινι *make someone like a person* or *thing* pass. *become like, be like* τινί *someone* (Ps.-Apollod. 1, 4, 1, 1; Herm. Wr. 1, 26a; PGM 4, 1859; 2500; Sir 13: 1; Ps 48: 13; Philo, Deus Imm. 48; Test. Benj. 7: 5) τοῖς ἀδελφοῖς Hb 2: 17. Of gods (Diod. S. 1, 86, 3 ὁμοιωθῆναί τισιν ζῴοις) ὁμοιωθέντες ἀνθρώποις κατέβησαν *they have come down in the form of men* Ac 14: 11 (Aesop, Fab. 89 P.=140 H. Ἑρμῆς ὁμοιωθεὶς ἀνθρώπῳ). ἀνδρί Mt 7: 24, 26. αὐτοῖς 6: 8; B 4: 2; cf. vs. 6. ἀνθρώποις τοιούτοις 10: 4f. τοῖς τοιούτοις vs. 6f. ὡμοιώθη ἡ βασιλεία τ. οὐρανῶν *the kingdom of heaven is like, may be compared to* Mt 13: 24; 18: 23; 22: 2. Also, w. a glance at the Parousia in the fut., ὁμοιωθήσεται ἡ β. τ. οὐρ. 25: 1. Used w. ὡς instead of the dat. (cf. Ezk 32: 2) ὡς Γόμορρα ἂν ὡμοιώθημεν *we would have resembled Gomorrah* Ro 9: 29 (Is 1: 9).

2. *compare* τινά τινι *someone with* or *to someone* or *someth.* (Sappho, fgm. 127 D.²; inscr.: Annual of the Brit. School at Athens, vol. 29 p. 35 [IV AD]) τί τινι *someth. with someth.* (Plut., Cim. et Lucull. 1, 5; SSol 1: 9; La 2: 13; Wsd 7: 9; Is 40: 18) Mt 7: 24 t.r. τίνι ... ὁμοιώσω τὴν γενεὰν ταύτην; *to what shall I compare this generation?* Mt 11: 16; cf. Lk 7: 31. τίνι ὁμοιώσω τὴν βασιλείαν τοῦ θεοῦ; 13: 20. Cf. vs. 18. W. combination of two thoughts πῶς ὁμοιώσωμεν τὴν βασιλείαν τοῦ θεοῦ; *how shall I portray the kingdom of God symbolically?* and *to what shall I compare the kgdm. of God?* Mk 4: 30 (cf. Is 40: 18; HWBartsch, ThZ, 15, '59, 126–8).*

ὁμοίωμα, ατος, τό (Pla., Parm. 132D; 133D, Phaedr. 250B; Ps.-Aristot., Hermen. 1 p. 16a, 7f; Dit., Syll.³ 669, 52; PFay. 106, 20; LXX).

1. *likeness* οὖ (Χριστοῦ) καὶ κατὰ τὸ ὁμοίωμα ἡμᾶς ... οὕτως ἐγερεῖ ὁ πατὴρ αὐτοῦ *in accordance with whose likeness* (= *just as he raised him*) *his Father will also raise us in this way* ITr 9: 2. This is prob. the place for Ro 6: 5 εἰ σύμφυτοι γεγόναμεν τῷ ὁμοιώματι τ. θανάτου αὐτοῦ *if we have been united* (i.e. αὐτῷ *with him*; cf. vs. 4 συνετάφημεν αὐτῷ) *in the likeness of his death* (= *in the same death that he died*); but s. PGächter, ZkTh 54, '30, 88–92; OKuss, D. Römerbr. I, '63, 301. On the syntax, Bl-D. §194, 2; Rob. 528. ἁμαρτάνειν ἐπὶ τῷ ὁμοιώματι τῆς παραβάσεως Ἀδάμ *sin in the likeness of Adam's transgression* (= *just as Adam did, who transgressed one of God's express commands*) 5: 14.—Abstr. for concr. τὰ ὁμοιώματα=τὰ ὅμοια: ὃς ἂν τὰ ὁμοιώματα ποιῇ τοῖς ἔθνεσιν *whoever does things similar to* (*the deeds of*) *the heathen*= *acts as the heathen do* Hm 4, 1, 9. περὶ τοιούτων τινῶν ὁμοιωμάτων πονηρῶν (thoughts) *about any other wicked things similar to these* 4, 1, 1.—ἐν τίνι ὁμοιώματι παραβάλωμεν αὐτήν; *with what corresponding thing can we compare it?* Mk 4: 30 v.l.

2. *image, copy* (Dt 4: 16ff; 1 Km 6: 5; 4 Km 16: 10; 1 Macc 3: 48) ὁμοίωμα εἰκόνος φθαρτοῦ ἀνθρώπου (s. εἰκών 2; pleonasm as Maximus Tyr. 27, 3c εἰς μορφῆς εἶδος) Ro 1: 23 (cf. Ps 105: 20).

3. *form, appearance* (schol. on Apollon. Rhod. 4, 825–31a ὁμ. κ. πρόσωπον γυναικός=figure and face of a woman; Dt 4: 12; Josh 22: 28; Ezk 1: 16; Jos., Ant. 8, 195) τὰ ὁμοιώματα τῶν ἀκρίδων ὅμοιοι ἵπποις *the locusts resembled horses in appearance* Rv 9: 7.

4. The mng. is not quite clear in the two related passages in which Paul uses our word in speaking of Christ's earthly life. The expressions ἐν ὁμοιώματι ἀνθρώπων (𝔓⁴⁶, Marcion, Orig.: ἀνθρώπου) Phil 2: 7 and ἐν ὁμοιώματι σαρκὸς ἁμαρτίας Ro 8: 3 could mean that the Lord in his earthly ministry possessed a completely human form and that his physical body was capable of sinning as human bodies are, or that he had only the form of a man and was looked upon as a human being (cf. En. 31, 2 ἐν ὁμ. w. gen. = 'similar to', 'looking like'), whereas in reality he remained a Divine Being even in this world. In the light of what Paul says about Jesus in general it is safe to assert that his use of our word is to bring out both that Jesus in his earthly career was similar to sinful men and yet not absolutely like them (cf. JWeiss, Das Urchristentum '17, 376ff).—S. the lit. on ἁρπαγμός. M-M.*

ὁμοίως adv. (Pind., Hdt.+; inscr., pap., LXX, En., Ep. Arist., Philo, Joseph., Test. 12 Patr.) *likewise, so, similarly, in the same way* Mk 4: 16; Lk 3: 11; 10: 37; 13: 3, 5 v.l. (see ὡσαύτως) al. ὁμ. καὶ *and so, so also* Mt 22: 26; 26: 35; Mk 15: 31; Lk 5: 33; IPol 5: 1. ὁμ. μέντοι καὶ *in the same way, too* Jd 8. ὁμ. δὲ καὶ (pap., Ep. Arist.; Jos.,

Bell. 2, 575, Ant. 14, 216) Lk 5: 10; 10: 32; 1 Cor 7: 3f; Js 2: 25. In Ro 1: 27 the rdg. varies betw. όμ. τε καί (in the text) and όμ. δὲ καί (v.l.). Sim. Mt 27: 41 (t.r. with D et al. όμ. δὲ καί; B et al. όμ. καί, and אAL only όμ.).— καθὼς θέλετε..., ποιεῖτε όμοίως as you wish..., do so Lk 6: 31. όμ. καθώς, in the same way as 17: 28. όμ. πάλιν similarly, again B 12: 1. W. the dat. foll. όμ. πλανᾶσθαι ἐκείνοις to go astray as they did 2: 9. Somet. the idea of similarity fades into the background to such a degree that όμ. means also (UPZ 70, 8 [152/1 BC] όμνύω, ὅτι ψευδῆ πάντα καὶ οἱ παρὰ σὲ θεοὶ όμοίως; 65, 8f; όμ. καὶ Κότταβος, όμ. καί. Χεντοσνεύς) ταῦτα καὶ ὁ υἱὸς όμ. ποιεῖ this the Son also does J 5: 19; cf. 6: 11; 21: 13; cf. Lk 7: 31.—As a connective (Hierocles 26 p. 480 [όμοίως δὲ καί]; oft. pap.); more than one όμ. in the same way... also (an edict of Augustus fr. Cyrenaica, ed. LRadermacher, Anzeiger der Ak. d. Wiss. Wien, phil.-hist. Kl. '28 X p. 76, l. 108; 110) 1 Pt 3: 1, 7. Cf. 5: 5. M-M.

όμοίωσις, εως, ἡ likeness, resemblance (so since Pla., Theaet. 176B; Aristot., De Plant. 2, 6 p. 826b, 32f; Plut., Mor. 53C; Sext. Emp., Hyp. Pyrrh. 75 καθ' όμοίωσιν κρίνειν; LXX; Jos., Ant. 13, 67 καθ' όμοίωσιν; Test. Napht. 2: 2) καθ' όμοίωσιν (w. κατ' εἰκόνα, as also in Philo) Gen 1: 26. This pass. in Genesis is quoted 1 Cl 33: 5; B 5: 5; 6: 12, and Js 3: 9 uses it freely. M-M.*

όμολογέω impf. ὡμολόγουν; fut. όμολογήσω; 1 aor. ὡμολόγησα (Soph., Hdt.+; inscr., pap., LXX, Philo, Joseph., Test. 12 Patr.).

1. promise, assure (class.; Inscr. Rom. IV 542 [Phryg.] εὐχήν..., ἢν ὡμολόγησεν ἐν Ῥώμῃ; Jos., Ant. 6, 40) ἐπαγγελίας ἧς (by attr. of the rel. for ἢν) ὡμολόγησεν ὁ θεὸς τῷ Ἀβραάμ promise that God had made to Abraham Ac 7: 17; μεθ' ὅρκου όμ. w. aor. inf. foll. (Bl-D. §350; Rob. 1031f) promise with an oath Mt 14: 7. Solemnly promise, vow ὁ... όμολογήσας μὴ γῆμαι ἄγαμος διαμενέτω Agr 18.

2. agree, admit (Hdt. 2, 81; X., An. 1, 6, 7; Plut., Mor. 202B όμολογεῖταί γε παρὰ πάντων μέγας θεὸς εἶναι; pap.; 4 Macc 13: 5; Jos., Ant. 3, 322; Sext. Emp., Adv. Eth. 218) καθάπερ καὶ αὐτὸς ὡμολόγησας Dg 2: 1. όμολογήσαντες ὅτι ξένοι εἰσίν admitting that they were (only) foreigners Hb 11: 13. όμολογοῦμεν χάριν μὴ εἰληφέναι we admit that we have not received grace IMg 8: 1.

3. confess (Pla., Prot. 317B όμολογῶ σοφιστὴς εἶναι)
a. in judicial language make a confession, confess abs. MPol 6: 1; 9: 2. τί τινι: όμολογῶ δὲ τοῦτό σοι, ὅτι Ac 24: 14. Foll. by acc. and inf. ὡμολόγησεν ἑαυτὸν Χριστιανὸν εἶναι MPol 12: 1.—The transition to sense b may be illustrated by John the Baptist's action in reply to questioning by the authorities καὶ ὡμολόγησεν καὶ οὐκ ἠρνήσατο καὶ ὡμολόγησεν ὅτι (dir. disc. follows) J 1: 20 (cf. Plut., Mor. 509E in interrogation; the contrast όμ. and ἀρνεῖσθαι as Thu. 6, 60, 3; Phalaris, Ep. 147, 3 όμολογοῦμεν κ. οὐκ ἀρνησόμεθα; Aelian, Nat. An. 2, 43; Jos., Ant. 6, 151; cf. MPol 9: 2 and many of the passages given below).
b. as a term in religious and moral usage (Ps.-Aristot., Mirabilia 152 όμολογοῦντες ἃ ἐπιώρκησαν; Arrian, Anab. 7, 29, 2 [s. ἴασις 2]; Jos., Ant. 6, 151) ἐὰν όμολογῶμεν τὰς ἁμαρτίας ἡμῶν if we confess our sins 1 J 1: 9 (cf. Appian, Liby. 79 §369 όμολογοῦντες ἁμαρτεῖν; Sir 4: 26). S. on ἐξομολογέω 2a.—FSteinleitner, Die Beicht '13, 109 (inscr. fr. Sardis). S. on ἐξομολογέω 2a.

4. declare (publicly), acknowledge, confess, also confess that one is someth. όμολογήσω αὐτοῖς ὅτι (w. dir. disc.

foll.) I will say to them plainly Mt 7: 23. W. inf. foll. (X., Mem. 2, 3, 9; Jos., Ant. 9, 254) θεὸν όμολογοῦσιν εἰδέναι they claim to know God Tit 1: 16 (opp. ἀρν.). όμολογοῦσιν τὰ ἀμφότερα they acknowledge all of them Ac 23: 8.—Esp. of confessing Christ, or the teaching of his church; w. double acc. (Bl-D. §157, 2; 416, 3; Rob. 480. —Jos., Ant. 5, 52) ἐὰν όμολογήσῃς κύριον Ἰησοῦν if you confess Jesus as Lord Ro 10: 9. αὐτὸν όμ. Χριστόν confess that he is the Messiah J 9: 22. όμ. αὐτὸν σαρκοφόρον ISm 5: 2. όμ. Ἰησοῦν Χριστὸν ἐν σαρκὶ ἐληλυθότα acknowledge that Jesus Christ has come in the flesh 1 J 4: 2 (in the text); cf. 2 J 7. W. acc. and inf. (Isocr., Or. 4, 100 p. 61D; Aelian, V.H. 1, 27) όμ. Ἰησοῦν Χρ. ἐν σαρκὶ ἐληλυθέναι Pol 7: 1a; 1 J 4: 2 v.l. όμ. τὴν εὐχαριστίαν σάρκα εἶναι τοῦ σωτῆρος ἡμῶν Ἰ. Χρ. ISm 7: 1. W. ὅτι foll. (Isocr., Or. 11, 5 p. 222D) όμ. ὅτι Ἰησοῦς ἐστιν ὁ υἱὸς τοῦ θεοῦ 1 J 4: 15. όμ. ὅτι κύριον ἔχετε Hs 9, 28, 7 (opp. ἀρν.). W. a single acc. of the pers. whom one confesses, or whom one declares to be someth. revealed by the context: όμ. τὸν υἱόν 1 J 2: 23 (opp. ἀρν.). μὴ όμ. τὸν Ἰησοῦν 4: 3 in the text (s. λύω 4, end). Cf. 2 Cl 3: 2a. τινὰ ἔν τινι someone by someth. ἐν τοῖς ἔργοις 4: 3; cf. 3: 4. ἐὰν όμολογήσωμεν δι' οὗ ἐσώθημεν if we confess him through whom we were saved 3: 3. The acc. (αὐτόν) is supplied fr. the context J 12: 42; cf. Hs 9, 28, 4.—W. acc. of the thing όμ. τὸ μαρτύριον τοῦ σταυροῦ Pol 7: 1b. όμ. τὴν καλὴν όμολογίαν 1 Ti 6: 12 (όμ. όμολογίαν = 'make a promise': Pla., Crito 52A; Jer 51: 25; but = 'bear testimony to a conviction': Philo, Mut. Nom. 57, Abr. 203).—Instead of the acc. of the pers. we may have ἔν τινι confess someone, an Aramaism (cf. Mlt.-H. 463f; Bl-D. §220, 2; EbNestle, ZNW 7, '06, 279f; 8, '07, 241; 9, '08, 253; FCBurkitt, Earliest Sources for the Life of Jesus '10, 19f). ὅστις όμολογήσει ἐν ἐμοὶ ἔμπροσθεν τῶν ἀνθρώπων whoever confesses me before men Mt 10: 32a; cf. Lk 12: 8a. But 2 Cl 3: 2 uses the acc. when it quotes this saying (s. above). Jesus' acknowledgment of the believer on the Judgment Day forms the counterpart to this confession: ἐν αὐτῷ Mt 10: 32b; Lk 12: 8b. αὐτόν 2 Cl 3: 2b (opp. ἀρν. in all these pass.—GBornkamm, D. Wort Jesu vom Bekennen [Mt 10: 32]: Pastoraltheologie 34, '39, 108–18). τὸ ὄνομα αὐτοῦ Rv 3: 5.—Abs. pass. στόματι όμολογεῖται with the mouth confession is made Ro 10: 10.

5. praise w. dat. (Bl-D. §187, 4; Rob. 541. In the LXX ἐξομολογεῖσθαι τῷ θεῷ. S. ἐξομολογέω 2c) καρπὸς χειλέων όμολογούντων τῷ ὀνόματι αὐτοῦ the fruit of lips that praise his name Hb 13: 15.—OMichel, TW V 199–220: όμολογέω and related words. M-M. B. 1267.*

όμολόγησις, ήσεως, ἡ (Diod. S. 17, 68, 4) confessing as an act (opp. ἄρνησις) Hs 9, 28, 7.*

όμολογία, ας, ἡ (Hdt., Thu.+; inscr., pap., LXX, Philo, Jos., Bell. 4, 92, Ant. 15, 52, C. Ap. 1, 89 al. Loanw. in rabb.) confession (όμολογέω 4).

1. act. confessing as an action ἡ ὑποταγὴ τῆς όμ. ὑμῶν εἰς τὸ εὐαγγέλιον the subjection of your confession to the gospel (= your confessing the gospel finds expression in obedient subjection to its requirements) 2 Cor 9: 13.

2. pass. confession, acknowledgment that one makes: Jesus as ἀρχιερεὺς τῆς όμ. ἡμῶν the high priest of whom our confession speaks Hb 3: 1. κρατεῖν τῆς όμ. hold fast (to) the confession 4: 14. κατέχειν τὴν όμ. τῆς ἐλπίδος ἀκλινῆ hold fast the confession of hope without wavering 10: 23. όμολογεῖν τὴν καλὴν όμ. make the good profession of faith 1 Ti 6: 12 (όμολογέω 4). Jesus, the first Christian martyr (s. μαρτυρέω 1d), bore witness or testified to the same good profession of faith vs. 13 (cf.

CHTurner, JTS 28, '27, 270-3).—ASeeberg, Der Katechismus der Urchristenheit '03, 143; 172; 186; PFeine, D. Gestalt d. apostolischen Glaubensbekenntnisses in d. Zeit des NTs '25; EvDobschütz, D. Apostolicum in bibl.-theol. Beleuchtung '32; GBornkamm, Ὁμολογία: Her. 71, '36, 377-93, also ThBl 21, '42, 56-66 (Hb); AMHunter, Paul and his Predecessors '40; PCarrington, The Primitive Christian Catechism '40; OCullmann, Les premières confessions de foi chrétiennes '43; VHNeufeld, The Earliest Christian Confessions '63; HvCampenhausen, Das Bekenntnis im Urchristentum, ZNW 63, '72, 210-53. M-M.*

ὁμολογουμένως adv. (Thu.+; pap., 4 Macc) *confessedly, undeniably, most certainly* (so Thu. 6, 90, 3; X., An. 2, 6, 1; Pla., Menex. 243c; Diod. S. 9, 11, 2; 13, 27, 4; Epict. 1, 4, 7; Vett. Val. 168, 17; UPZ 161, 65 [119 bc]; 162 V, 32; 4 Macc 6: 31; 7: 16; 16: 1; Ep. Arist. 24 [s. p. xxix Wendl.]; Jos., Ant. 1, 180; 2, 229.—Crönert 241) 1 Ti 3: 16; Dg 5: 4. M-M.*

ὁμονοέω (Thu.+; Dio Chrys. 4, 42; 11[12], 74; Epict. 2, 20, 31; 2, 22, 24; inscr.; Sb 4827, 5; LXX; Ep. Arist. 185; Jos., Ant. 12, 283, C. Ap. 2, 294) *be in agreement, live in harmony* ὁμ. ἐν ἀγάπῃ κτλ. 1 Cl 62: 2.*

ὁμόνοια, ας, ἡ (Thu.+; Diod. S. 12, 75, 3; Epict. 4, 5, 35; Plut., Ages. 5, 5; Dio Chrys. 21[38] περὶ ὁμονοίας al.; Ael. Aristid. 23 and 24 K.=42 and 44 D.: περὶ ὁμονοίας; inscr.; late pap.; LXX; Ps.-Phoc. 74; 219; Philo; Jos., Bell. 2, 345, Ant. 13, 67, C. Ap. 2, 179; Test. Jos. 17, 3; Sib. Or. 3, 375. Loanw. in rabb.) *oneness of mind, unanimity, concord, harmony* (w. ἀγάπη) IEph 4: 1. W. εἰρήνη (q.v., 1b) 1 Cl 60: 4; 63: 2; 65: 1; w. still other sim. concepts 21: 1; 61: 1. W. πίστις and ἀγάπη IPhld 11: 2; w. still other Christian virtues Hm 8: 9; ἐνδύσασθαι τὴν ὁμ. *put on harmony* i.e. *be in agreement* 1 Cl 30: 3. ἡ ὁμ. ὑμῶν τῆς πίστεως *your unanimity in the faith* IEph 13: 1; ἐν ὁμ. *harmoniously, in agreement* (Ps 54: 15; 82: 6; Wsd 18: 9) 1 Cl 9: 4; 11: 2; 20: 3; 34: 7 (ἐν ὁμ. ἐπὶ τὸ αὐτό as Ps 82: 6). ἐν ὁμ. καὶ εἰρήνη 20: 10; cf. vs. 11. ἀγάπη πάντα ποιεῖ ἐν ὁμ. *love does everything in harmony* 49: 5. Hence ποιεῖν τι ἐν ὁμ. ἀγάπης *do someth. in loving harmony* 50: 5. διαμένετε ἐν τῇ ὁμ. ὑμῶν *continue in your (present) unanimity* ITr 12: 2. ἐν ὁμ. θεοῦ *in godly harmony* (i.e., h. brought about by God) IMg 6: 1; 15; IPhld inscr. σύμφωνοι ὄντες ἐν ὁμ. *being harmoniously in concord* IEph 4: 2 (cf. Philo, Mut. Nom. 200 τὸ σύμφωνον τῆς ὁμονοίας).—Personified as a virtue Hs 9, 15, 2 (cf. the goddess Ὁμόνοια: Apollon. Rhod. 2, 718; Nicol. Dam.: 90 fgm. 130, 69 Jac.; Paus. 5, 14, 9; Charito 3, 2, 16; CIG 4342, 3; Dit., Or. 479, 4; 11; 536, 6, Syll.³ Index III p. 179b).—HKramer, Quid valeat ὁμόνοια in litteris Graecis, Diss. Gött. '15.*

ὁμόσε adv. (Hom.+; pap.) *to one and the same place*, also for ὁμοῦ=*together* (Polyb. 6, 7, 5 al.; Vett. Val. index; PGiess. 4, 6 [II ad]; Jos., Ant. 12, 292.—Bl-D. §103; Rob. 299f) ὁμόσε ὄντων αὐτῶν Ac 20: 18 D.*

ὁμότεχνος, ον (since Hdt. 2, 89; Appian, Bell. Civ. 4, 27 §119; Lucian; Alciphr. 3, 25, 4; Philostrat., Vi. Soph. 1, 9 p. 11, 27; Ps.-Phoc. 88; Jos., Ant. 8, 334; Paton and Hicks, Inscr. of Cos 1891, 324) *practicing the same trade* Ac 18: 3. M-M.*

ὁμοῦ adv. (Hom.+; inscr. [Sb 293 Ptolemaic times]; pap., LXX, En., Joseph.; Test. Napht. 5: 3; Sib. Or. 3, 538; loanw. in rabb.) *together*.
1. *in the same place* ἦσαν ὁμ. Σίμων Πέτρος καὶ Θωμᾶς . . . *Simon Peter, Thomas . . . were together* J 21:

2. ἦσαν πάντες ὁμ. ἐπὶ τὸ αὐτό *they were all together in one place* Ac 2: 1 (πάντες ὁμ. as Jos., Ant. 7, 276). ἐστάθησαν ὁμ. *they had stood together* Hs 9, 4, 1.
2. *at the same time* (as), *in company* (*with*) ἔτρεχον οἱ δύο ὁμ. *the two were running together* J 20: 4 (cf. Test. Napht. 5: 3). τὰ δύο ὁμ. *these two things at the same time* IMg 5: 1. πάντες ὁμ. εὐφρανθήσονται *they will all rejoice together* Hv 3, 4, 2; cf. GP 8: 32 (cf. En. 6, 5; Jos., Ant. 7, 276 ὁμοῦ πάντες μιᾷ γνώμῃ). ἵνα ὁ σπείρων ὁμ. χαίρῃ καὶ ὁ θερίζων *so that the sower and the reaper may rejoice together* J 4: 36 (the double ptc. as Jos., Bell. 6, 271). πάντα ὁμ. καλά ἐστιν *all things together are good* IPhld 9: 2. ἐβάσταζον ὁμ. *they carried together* Hs 9, 3, 5. M-M.*

ὁμόφρων, ον (Hom.+; Plut., Mor. 432c; Dit., Or. 515, 4; Epigr. Gr. 493, 5f; Ps.-Phoc. 30) *like-minded, united in spirit, harmonious* (w. συμπαθής et al.) 1 Pt 3: 8 (Strabo 6, 3, 3 ὁμόφρονας ὡς ἂν ἀλλήλων ἀδελφούς). M-M.*

ὁμόφυλος, ον (Eur., Pla. X.+; pap.; Jos., Ant. 17, 313) *belonging to the same tribe*, subst. ὁ ὁμ. *the fellow-tribesman* (Eth. Epic. col. 20, 19; Alciphr. 1, 10, 5; 2 Macc 4: 10; 3 Macc 3: 21; Philo; Jos., Ant. 17, 285) 1 Cl 4: 10.*

ὁμοφωνία, ας, ἡ (Aristot., Pol. 2, 5; Philo, Conf. Lingu. 6) *harmony* (Ecphantus in Stob. 4, 7, 64) 1 Cl 51: 2.*

ὄμφαξ, ακος (Hom.+; inscr., LXX, ἡ and later also ὁ (e.g. Plut., Mor. 138e; 648f; Jer 38: 30; Ezk 18: 4 v.l.) *unripe grape* (fr. a quot. of unknown origin) 1 Cl 23: 4= 2 Cl 11: 3.*

ὅμως adv. (Hom.+; inscr., pap., LXX; Jos., Bell. 6, 385, Ant. 15, 151) *all the same, nevertheless, yet* strengthened ὅμ. μέντοι (s. μέντοι 2) J 12: 42.—Paul's use of the word, in the two passages in which it occurs in his letters, is peculiar, yet analogous to this: ὅμως τὰ ἄψυχα φωνὴν διδόντα . . . ἐὰν διαστολὴν τοῖς φθόγγοις μὴ δῷ, πῶς γνωσθήσεται . . . 1 Cor 14: 7 and ὅμως ἀνθρώπου κεκυρωμένην διαθήκην οὐδεὶς ἀθετεῖ Gal 3: 15. As a rule these passages are explained on the basis of 'trajection' or displacement of ὅμως, retaining the mng. 'nevertheless'; so for Gal 3: 15 the transl. would be 'even though it involves only a man's last will and testament, nevertheless no one annuls it' (so, gener., EDBurton, ICC, Gal '20, 178f; cf. passages like X., Cyr. 5, 1, 26 [Kühner-G. II p. 85f]). But since ὁμ. introduces a comparison both times in Paul (οὕτως follows it in 1 Cor 14: 9), we would perh. do better (with Bl-D. §450, 2) to consider the possibility that ὅμ. was influenced by the older ὁμῶς 'equally, likewise'. In that case the transl. would be greatly simplified, and we could render ὅμ. simply *likewise, also* (JoachJeremias, ZNW 52, '61, 127f agrees). M-M.*

ὀναίμην s. ὀνίνημι.

ὄναρ, τό (Hom.+; Herodas 1, 11; Philo; Jos., Bell. 2, 112, Ant. 2, 63; 10, 195; but only in nom. and acc. sing. *dream*, in our lit. only Mt chapters 1, 2, 27, and in the expr. κατ' ὄναρ *in a dream* (rejected by Photius, Lex. p. 149, 25f as a barbarism [Lob., Phryn. p. 422ff], but attested fr. the time of Conon [I bc/I ad]: 26 fgm. 1, 35, 3 Jac., Apollo gives orders; Strabo 4, 1, 4; Anth. Pal. 11, 263, 1; Diog. L. 10, 32; Eunap. 55; CIG 4331 χρηματισθεὶς κατὰ ὄναρ= 'after an oracle had been given me in a dream'.—Also Dit., Syll.³ 1147; 1148/9; Inschr. v. Pergamum 357, 8 [ESchweizer, Gramm. der perg. Inschr. 1898, 157]; IG XII 1, 979, 4f, but here w. the mng. 'as a result of a dream' [Dssm., NB 81–BS 253], as Paus. Attic. λ, 28) Mt 1: 20; 2:

12f, 19, 22; 27: 19.—ELEhrlich, D. Traum im AT '53, D. Traum im Talmud: ZNW 47, '56, 133–45; AWikenhauser, Pisciculi=Antike u. Christentum, Erg.-Bd. I '39, 320–33; AOepke, TW V 220–38. M-M. B. 269.*

ὀνάριον, ου, τό (Diphilus Com. [IV/III BC] 89 K.; Machon [III BC] in Athen. 13 p. 582c; Epict. 2, 24, 18; 4, 1, 79; pap.) lit. little donkey, but in many cases plainly a dim. in form only (of ὄνος), donkey (Celsus 4, 43; Vi. Aesopi Ic. 33 p. 304, 1; 4; 9; POxy. 63, 11; hence the possibility of a double dim. μικρὸν ὀναρίδιον PRyl. 239, 21) J 12: 14. M-M.*

ὀνειδίζω impf. ὠνείδιζον; 1 aor. ὠνείδισα (Hom.+; BGU 1024 VII, 21; PGiess. 40 II, 5; LXX, Philo, Joseph., Test. 12 Patr.).
   1. reproach, revile, heap insults upon w. acc. of the pers. affected (trag.; Pla., Apol. 30E; Lucian, Tox. 61; Ps 41: 11; 54: 13 al. LXX; Jos., Ant. 14, 430; 18, 360) of the reviling of Jesus Mk 15: 32; cf. Ro 15: 3 (Ps 68: 10) and of Jesus' disciples Mt 5: 11; Lk 6: 22. W. double acc. (Soph., Oed. Col. 1002 ὀν. τινὰ τοιαῦτα; Ael. Aristid. 28, 155 K.=49 p. 542 D.; Heliod. 7, 27, 5) τὸ αὐτὸ καὶ οἱ λῃσταὶ ὠνείδιζον αὐτόν the robbers also reviled him in the same way Mt 27: 44.—Pass. εἰ ὀνειδίζεσθε ἐν ὀνόματι Χριστοῦ if you are (being) reviled for the name of Christ 1 Pt 4: 14.—Only as v.l. in the two foll. pass.: εἰς τοῦτο κοπιῶμεν καὶ ὀνειδιζόμεθα it is for this (i.e., what precedes) that we toil and suffer reproach 1 Ti 4: 10 (the text has ἀγωνιζόμεθα). εἰς τί ὠνείδισάς με; why have you reproached me? or what have you reproached me for? (ὀν. τινὰ εἴς τι as Appian, Bell. Civ. 2, 104 §430 ὠνείδισεν ἐς δειλίαν=he reproached him for cowardice; 5, 54 §224; 5, 96 §400; Jos., Bell. 1, 237) Mk 15: 34 D and Macarius Magnes 1, 12 (the text has ἐγκατέλιπες. Cf. Harnack, SAB '01, 262ff=Studien I '31, 98ff; JSundwall, D. Zusammensetzung des Mk '34, 83).—A special kind of reproach is the manifestation of displeasure or regret which too often accompanies the giving of a gift (cf. Plut., Mor. 64A; Sextus 339 ὁ διδοὺς μετ᾽ ὀνείδους ὑβρίζει; Sir 20: 15; 41: 25.—ὀν. can also mean charge or reproach someone with someth., with the purpose of obtaining someth. from him, e.g., Maximus Tyr. 5, 7h τῷ θεῷ the building of a temple); God does not do this Js 1: 5.
   2. reproach justifiably, w. acc. of the pers. (Pr 25: 8; Philo, Fuga 30; Jos., Ant. 4, 189) and ὅτι foll. to give the reason for the reproach Mt 11: 20. W. acc. of the pers. and λέγων foll. w. dir. discourse (cf. BGU 1141, 23 [14 BC] ὀνειδίζει με λέγων) GP 4: 13. W. acc. of the thing censured (Isocr., Or. 15, 318 p. 345A; Herodian 3, 8, 6; Wsd 2: 12; Jos., Ant. 10, 139) τὴν ἀπιστίαν αὐτῶν καὶ σκληροκαρδίαν Mk 16: 14.—JSchneider, TW V 238–42: ὄνειδος and related words. M-M.*

ὀνειδισμός, οῦ, ὁ (Dionys. Hal.; Plut., Artax. 22, 12; Vett. Val. 65, 7; 73, 10; LXX; En. 103, 4; Jos., Ant. 19, 319; Test. 12 Patr. Late word: Lob., Phryn. p. 511f) reproach, reviling, disgrace, insult εἰς ὀν. ἐμπίπτειν fall into disgrace 1 Ti 3: 7.—Hb speaks of the ὀν. τοῦ Χριστοῦ and holds that even Moses took upon himself the reproach of Christ 11: 26, and he calls upon the believers: ἐξερχώμεθα πρὸς αὐτὸν ... τὸν ὀν. αὐτοῦ φέροντες 13: 13 (ὀν. φέρειν as Ezk 34: 29; Test. Reub. 4: 7).—Pl. (Test. Reub. 4: 2, Judah 23: 3) οἱ ὀν. reproaches, insults Ro 15: 3 (Ps 68: 10; s. ὀνειδίζω 1). W. θλίψεις: ὀνειδισμοῖς καὶ θλίψεσιν θεατριζόμενοι exposed as a public spectacle to insults and persecutions Hb 10: 33.*

ὄνειδος, ους, τό (Hom.+; Diod. S. 1, 93, 1; Maspéro 97 II, 76; LXX; Ep. Arist. 249; Philo; Jos., C. Ap. 1, 285 al.;

Sib. Or. 3, 607; Test. Reub. 6: 3) disgrace, reproach, insult ἀφελεῖν ὄν. μου ἐν ἀνθρώποις take away my disgrace among men Lk 1: 25 (cf. Gen 30: 23).—Object of reproach (Ps.-Callisth. 2, 18, 4) ὄν. ἀνθρώπων καὶ ἐξουθένημα λαοῦ 1 Cl 16: 15 (Ps 21: 7). B. 1187.*

Ὀνήσιμος, ου, ὁ Onesimus, lit. 'useful' (s. the play on words in Phlm 11), a name freq. found (inscr., pap.: reff. in Thieme 40; Preisigke, Namenbuch '22 and in the lit. below), esp. for slaves (Menand., Epitr. 1 al.; Galen, De Optima Doctr. 1 p. 82 JMarquardt [1884] Ὀν. ὁ Πλουτάρχου δοῦλος; Lghtf., St. Paul's Ep. to the Col. and to Phlm. p. 308f; Hatch 146; Zahn, Einleitung I³ 325).
   1. A slave of Philemon, in whose interest Paul wrote Phlm. Phlm 10; subscr.; πιστὸς καὶ ἀγαπητὸς ἀδελφός Col 4: 9. Cf. Col subscr.—ATRobertson, Exp. 8th Ser. XIX '20, 29ff; ERGoodenough, HTR 22, '29, 181–3; PNHarrison, ATR 32, '50, 268–93.
   2. An Onesimus appears as bishop of Ephesus in IEph 1: 3; 2: 1; 6: 2; CIG 2983 attests the name for this city (cf. EJGdspd., Introd. to the NT '37, 121f and ref. there to JKnox). M-M.*

Ὀνησίφορος, ου, ὁ (inscr.; Acta Apost. Apocr. [s. indices Lips.-Bonnet]) Onesiphorus 2 Ti 1: 16; 4: 19.—NMPlum, Teol. Tidsskrift 3, R. 10, '19, 193–200. M-M.*

ὀνικός, ή, όν (Dit., Or. 629, 30; PSI 527, 2 [III BC]; BGU 912, 24 [33 AD] τὰ ὀνικὰ κτήνη; PGenève 23, 4 [70 AD]) pertaining to a donkey, in our lit. only in the combination μύλος ὀν. a mill-stone worked by donkey-power (s. μύλος 2) Mt 18: 6; Mk 9: 42; Lk 17: 2 t.r. (or should we think not so much of the animal as of the upper millstone, the one that moves, which was called ὄνος ἀλέτης [X., An. 1, 5, 5; Alexis Com. [IV BC], fgm. 13 K.; Herodas 6, 83; Dialekt-Inschr. 4992a II, 7 Crete; Ael. Dion. o, 23: it is said of Aristot. that he also applied this term to the lower, stationary millstone]?). M-M.*

ὀνίνημι (Hom.+; Jos., Ant. 16, 242) in our lit. only mid. (as Sir 30: 2; Philo, Agr. 126), and, in fact, in the 2 aor. opt. (Audollent, Defix. Tab. 92, 3 [III BC] ὄναιντο; Epigr. Gr. 502, 27) ὀναίμην as a formula may I have joy or profit or benefit, may I enjoy w. gen. of the pers. or thing that is the source of the joy (Eur., Hec. 978 ὀναίμην τοῦ παρόντος; Aristoph., Thesm. 469 οὕτως ὀναίμην τῶν τέκνων; Lucian, Philops. 27; Philostrat., Vi. Apoll. 4, 16 p. 135, 3) ἐγώ σου ὀναίμην ἐν κυρίῳ let me have some benefit from you in the Lord Phlm 20. ὀναίμην ὑμῶν διὰ παντός may I have joy in you continually IEph 2: 2; IPol 6: 2. ὀν. ὑμῶν κατὰ πάντα let me have joy of you in all respects IMg 12. ὀν. τῶν θηρίων may I enjoy the wild animals IRo 5: 2; οὗ ἐγὼ ὀν. IMg 2; οὗ ὀν. ἐν θεῷ IPol 1: 1. M-M.*

ὄνομα, ατος, τό (Hom.+; inscr., pap., LXX, En., Ep. Arist., Philo, Joseph., Test. 12 Patr.).
   I. name, of proper names—1. gener. τῶν ἀποστόλων τὰ ὀν. ἐστιν ταῦτα Mt 10: 2; cf. Rv 21: 14. τῶν παρθένων τὰ ὀν. Hs 9, 15, 1. τὸ ὄν. τοῦ πατρός Lk 1: 59. ὄνομά μοι, sc. ἐστίν, my name is (Od. 9, 366) Mk 5: 9b. τί ὄν. σοι; what is your name? vs. 9a; w. copula Lk 8: 30.—The expressions ᾧ (ἧ) ὄνομα, οὗ τὸ ὄνομα, καὶ τὸ ὄνομα αὐτοῦ (αὐτῆς), ὄνομα αὐτῷ (parenthetic) are almost always without the copula (Bl-D. §128, 3; Rob. 395): ᾧ (ἧ) ὄνομα (Sb 7573, 13 [116 AD]) Lk 1: 26, 27a; 2: 25; 8: 41; 24: 13, 18 v.l.; Ac 13: 6.—οὗ τὸ ὄν. (without a verb as BGU 344, 1) Mk 14: 32. Cf. ὧν τὰ ὀνόματα ἐν βίβλῳ ζωῆς Phil 4: 3 (ὧν τὰ ὀν. is a formula [Dssm., LO 95–LAE 121]. S. esp. BGU 432 II, 3 ὧν τὰ ὀν. τῷ βιβλιδίῳ δεδήλωται).—καὶ τὸ ὄν. αὐτῆς ... Lk 1: 5b.

570

καὶ τὸ ὄν. τῆς παρθένου Μαριάμ vs. 27b.—ὄνομα αὐτῷ (Demosth. 32, 11 Ἀριστοφῶν ὄνομ' αὐτῷ; Dionys. Hal. 8, 89, 4; Aelian, Nat. An. 8, 2 γυνὴ . . . Ἡρακλῆις ὄνομα αὐτῇ; LXX) J 1: 6; 3: 1. ὁ καθήμενος ἐπάνω αὐτοῦ (i.e. τοῦ ἵππου), ὄνομα αὐτῷ (ὁ) θάνατος Rv 6: 8; cf. 9: 11a.—W. the copula ἦν δὲ ὄν. τῷ δούλῳ Μάλχος J 18: 10 (POxy. 465, 12 ὁ δὲ κραταιὸς αὐτοῦ, ὄνομα αὐτῷ ἐστιν Νεβῦ, μηνύει; Jos., Ant. 19, 332). ἄγγελος . . . , οὗ τὸ ὄνομά ἐστιν Θεγρί Hv 4, 2, 4.—The dat. is quite freq. ὀνόματι named, by name (X., Hell. 1, 6, 29 Σάμιος ὀνόματι Ἱππεύς; Tob 6: 11 BA; 4 Macc 5: 4; Bl-D. §160; 197; Rob. 487) ἄνθρωπον ὄν. Σίμωνα Mt 27: 32; cf. Mk 5: 22; Lk 1: 5a; 5: 27; 10: 38; 16: 20; 23: 50; 24: 18; Ac 5: 1, 34; 8: 9; 9: 10–12, 33, 36; 10: 1; 11: 28; 12: 13; 16: 1, 14; 17: 34; 18: 2, 7, 24; 19: 24; 20: 9; 21: 10; 27: 1; 28: 7; MPol 4. Also the acc. τοὔνομα (on the crasis s. Bl-D. §18; Mlt.-H. 63; FPreisigke, Griech. Urkunden des ägypt. Mus. zu Kairo ['11] 2, 6 γυνὴ Ταμοῦνις τοὔνομα; Diod. S. 2, 45, 4 πόλιν τοὔνομα Θ.; Lucian, Dial. Deor. 3; Philo, Leg. All. 1, 68; Jos., Ant. 7, 344, Vi. 382) named, by name (the acc. is class., also 2 Macc 12: 13.—Bl-D. §160; Rob. 487) Mt 27: 57.

2. used w. verbs—a. as their obj.: ὄν. ἔχειν bear the name or as name, be named ὄν. ἔχει Ἀπολλύων Rv 9: 11b (in this case the name Ἀ. stands independently in the nom.; Bl-D. §143; Rob. 458). καλεῖν τὸ ὄν. τινος w. the name foll. in the acc. (after the Hebr.; Bl-D. §157, 2; Rob. 459) καλέσεις τὸ ὄν. αὐτοῦ Ἰησοῦν you are to name him Jesus Mt 1: 21; Lk 1: 31.—Mt 1: 25. καλέσεις τὸ ὄν. αὐτοῦ Ἰωάννην Lk 1: 13. καλέσουσιν τὸ ὄν. αὐτοῦ Ἐμμανουήλ Mt 1: 23 (Is 7: 14). Pass. w. the name in the nom. ἐκλήθη τὸ ὄν. αὐτοῦ Ἰησοῦς Lk 2: 21; cf. Rv 19: 13. Also τὸ ὄν. τοῦ ἀστέρος λέγεται ὁ Ἄψινθος Rv 8: 11.— ἐπιθεῖναι ὄνομά τινι w. acc. of the name Mk 3: 16f; cf. B 12: 8f; κληρονομεῖν ὄν. receive a name Hb 1: 4=1 Cl 36: 2. κληροῦσθαι τὸ αὐτὸ ὄν. obtain the same name (s. κληρόω 2) MPol 6: 2.—τὰ ὀν. ὑμῶν ἐγγέγραπται ἐν τοῖς οὐρανοῖς Lk 10: 20.—Rv 13: 8; 17: 8. ἐξαλείψω τὸ ὄν. αὐτῶν 1 Cl 53: 3 (Dt 9: 14); Rv 3: 5a; s. ἐξαλείφω 1b.

b. in another way: ὃς καλεῖται τῷ ὀνόματι τούτῳ who is so named Lk 1: 61. ἀνὴρ ὀνόματι καλούμενος Ζακχαῖος a man whose name was Zacchaeus 19: 2. καλεῖν τι (i.e. παιδίον) ἐπὶ τῷ ὀνόματί τινος name someone after someone 1: 59. This brings us to the

3. use with prepositions: ἐξ ὀνόματος (Ctesias, Ind. p. 105 M.; Diod. S. 13, 15, 1; 37, 15, 2; Appian, Mithrid. 59, §243, Bell. Civ. 3, 21 §77; 4, 73 §310; PGM 4, 2973; Jos., Ant. 2, 275) by name, individually, one by one (so that no one is lost in the crowd) ἐξ ὀν. πάντας ζήτει IPol 4: 2. ἀσπάζομαι πάντας ἐξ ὀνόματος 8: 2. πάντες ἐξ ὀν. συνέρχεσθε (parallel to κατ' ἄνδρα) IEph 20: 2.—κατ' ὄνομα by name, individually (Diod. S. 16, 44, 2; Gen 25: 13; Ep. Arist. 247; Jos., Bell. 7, 14) J 10: 3 (animals called individually by name: Ps.-Aristot., Mirabil. 118.—HAlmqvist, Plut. u. das NT '46, 74). Esp. in greetings (BGU 27, 18 [II AD] ἀσπάζομαι πάντας τοὺς φιλοῦντάς σε κατ' ὄνομα; POxy. 1070, 46; pap. in Dssm., LO 160/1 l. 14f [LAE 193, l. 15, note 21]) 3 J 15; ISm 13: 2b. ῥάβδους ἐπιγεγραμμένας ἐκάστης φυλῆς κατ' ὄνομα staffs, each one inscribed with the name of a tribe 1 Cl 43: 2b.

4. in combination w. God and Jesus. On the significance of the Divine Name in history of religions cf. FGiesebrecht, Die atl. Schätzung des Gottesnamens '01; Bousset, Rel.³ 309ff; ADieterich, Eine Mithrasliturgie '03, 110ff; FCConybeare, JQR 8, 1896; 9, 1897, esp. 9, 581ff; JBoehmer, Das bibl. 'im Namen' 1898, BFChTh V 6, '01, 49ff; Studierstube 2, '04, 324ff; 388ff; 452ff; 516ff; 580ff; BJacob, Im Namen Gottes '03; WHeitmüller, 'Im Namen

Jesu' '03; WBrandt, ThT 25, 1891, 565ff; 26, 1892, 193ff; 38, '04, 355ff; RHirzel, Der Name: Abh. d. Sächs. Ges. d. Wiss. 36, 2, '18; Schürer III⁴ 409ff; HWObbink, De magische beteekinis van den naam inzonderheit in het oude Egypte '25; OGrether, Name u. Wort Gottes im AT '34. —The belief in the efficacy of the name is extremely old; its origin goes back to the most ancient times and the most primitive forms of intellectual and religious life. It has exhibited an extraordinary vitality. The period of our lit. also sees—within as well as without the new religious community—in the name someth. real, a piece of the very nature of the personality whom it designates, that partakes in his qualities and his powers. In accordance w. this, names, esp. holy names, are revered and used in customary practices, ritual, religion and superstition. In Judaism the greatest reverence was paid to the holy name of God and to its numerous paraphrases or substitutes; the names of angels and patriarchs occupied a secondary place. The syncretistic paganism of the period revered the names of gods, demons and heroes, or even magic words that made no sense at all, but had a mysterious sound. The Christians revere and use the name of God and, above all, the name of Jesus.—The names of God and Jesus

a. in combination w. attributes διαφορώτερον ὄν. a more excellent name Hb 1: 4=1 Cl 36: 2 (διάφορος 2). ἅγιον τὸ ὄν. αὐτοῦ Lk 1: 49 (cf. Ps 110: 9; Lev 18: 21; 22: 2; PGM 3, 570; 627; 4, 1005; 3071; 5, 77; 13, 561 μέγα κ. ἅγιον). τὸ μεγαλοπρεπὲς καὶ ἅγιον ὄν. αὐτοῦ 1 Cl 64; τὸ μέγα καὶ ἔνδοξον ὄν. Hv 4, 1, 3; 4, 2, 4 (on ἔνδοξον ὄν. cf. EPeterson, Εἶς θεός '26, 282.—ὄν. μέγα κ. ἅγ. κ. ἔνδ.: PGM 13, 183f; 504f). τὸ μέγα καὶ θαυμαστὸν καὶ ἔνδοξον ὄν. Hs 9, 18, 5; τὸ πανάγιον καὶ ἔνδοξον ὄν. 1 Cl 58: 1a; τοῦ παντοκράτορος καὶ ἐνδόξου ὄν. Hv 3, 3, 5; τὸ πανάρετον ὄν. 1 Cl 45: 7; τὸ παντοκρατορικὸν καὶ πανάρετον ὄν. 60: 4; τὸ ὁσιώτατον τῆς μεγαλωσύνης αὐτοῦ ὄν. 58: 1b. τὸ ὄν. μου θαυμαστὸν ἐν τοῖς ἔθνεσι D 14: 3 (cf. Mal 1: 14). The words ὄν. θεοπρεπέστατον IMg 1: 2 are difficult to interpret (s. Hdb. ad loc.).

b. in combination w. verbs: ἁγιάζειν τὸ ὄν. Mt 6: 9; Lk 11: 2; D 8: 2 (ἁγιάζω 3). βλασφημεῖν (q.v. 2bβ) τὸ ὄν. Rv 13: 6; 16: 9; εἰς τὸ ὄν. τοῦ θεοῦ Hs 6, 2, 3; pass. βλασφημεῖται τὸ ὄν. (Is 52: 5) Ro 2: 24; 2 Cl 13: 1f, 4; ITr 8: 2. βλασφημίας ἐπιφέρεσθαι τῷ ὄν. κυρίου bring blasphemy upon the name of the Lord 1 Cl 47: 7. βεβηλοῦν τὸ ὄν. Hs 8, 6, 2 (s. βεβηλόω). ἀπαγγελῶ τὸ ὄνομα τ. ἀδελφοῖς μου Hb 2: 12 (cf. Ps 21: 23). ὅπως διαγγελῇ τὸ ὄν. μου ἐν πάσῃ τῇ γῇ Ro 9: 17 (Ex 9: 16). δοξάζειν τὸ ὄν. (σου, τοῦ κυρίου, τοῦ θεοῦ etc.) Rv 15: 4; 1 Cl 43: 6; IPhld 10: 1; Hv 2, 1, 2; 3, 4, 3; 4, 1, 3; s 9, 18, 5 (cf. δοξάζω 1). ὅπως ἐνδοξασθῇ τὸ ὄν. τοῦ κυρίου ἡμῶν Ἰησοῦ 2 Th 1: 12. ἐλπίζειν τῷ ὄν. Mt 12: 21 (v.l. ἐν τῷ ὄν.; the pass. on which it is based, Is 42: 4, has ἐπὶ τῷ ὄν.). ἐπικαλεῖσθαι τὸ ὄν. κυρίου (or αὐτοῦ, σου etc., w. ref. to God or Christ) call on the name of the Lord Ac 2: 21 (Jo 3: 5); 9: 14, 21; 22: 16; Ro 10: 13 (Jo 3: 5); 1 Cor 1: 2. ψυχὴ ἐπικεκλημένη τὸ μεγαλοπρεπὲς καὶ ἅγιον ὄν. αὐτοῦ a soul that calls upon his exalted and holy name 1 Cl 64.—Pass. πάντα τὰ ἔθνη ἐφ' οὓς ἐπικέκληται τὸ ὄν. μου ἐπ' αὐτούς Ac 15: 17 (Am 9: 12). τὸ καλὸν ὄν. τὸ ἐπικληθὲν ἐφ' ὑμᾶς Js 2: 7 (on καλὸν ὄν. cf. Sb 343, 9 and the Pompeian graffito in Dssm., LO 237 [LAE 276]). πάντες οἱ ἐπικαλούμενοι τῷ ὄν. αὐτοῦ all those who are called by his name Hs 9, 14, 3; cf. οἱ κεκλημένοι τῷ ὄν. κυρίου those who are called by the name of the Lord s 8, 1, 1. ἐπαισχύνεσθαι τὸ ὄν. κυρίου τὸ ἐπικληθὲν ἐπ' αὐτούς be ashamed of the name that is named over them Hs 8, 6, 4. ὁμολογεῖν τῷ ὄν. αὐτοῦ praise his name Hb 13: 15. ὀνομάζειν τὸ ὄν. κυρίου 2 Ti 2: 19 (Is 26: 13). ψάλλειν τῷ ὀν. σου Ro 15: 9 (Ps 17: 50). οὐ μὴ λάβῃς ἐπὶ ματαίῳ τὸ ὄν. κυρίου B 19: 5 (Ex 20: 7; Dt 5: 11).—Although in the preceding examples the name is oft. practically inseparable fr. the being that bears it, this is perh. even more true of the foll. cases, in which the name appears nearly as the representative of the Godhead, as a tangible manifestation of his nature (Quint. Smyrn. 9, 465 Polidarius, when healing, calls on οὔνομα πατρὸς ἑοῖο 'the name of his father' [Asclepius]; Dt 18: 7; 3 Km 8: 16; Ps 68: 37; Zech 13: 2 ἐξολεθρεύσω τὰ ὀν. τῶν εἰδώλων; Zeph 1: 4): the 'name' of God is ἀρχέγονον πάσης κτίσεως 1 Cl 59: 3. Sim. τὸ ὄν. τοῦ υἱοῦ τοῦ θεοῦ μέγα ἐστὶ καὶ τὸν κόσμον ὅλον βαστάζει Hs 9, 14, 5. λατρεύειν τῷ παναρέτῳ ὀν. αὐτοῦ worship his most excellent name 1 Cl 45: 7. ὑπακούειν τῷ παναγίῳ καὶ ἐνδόξῳ ὀν. αὐτοῦ be obedient to his most holy and glorious name 58: 1a. ὑπήκοον γενέσθαι τῷ παντοκρατορικῷ καὶ παναρέτῳ ὀν. 60: 4. κηρύσσειν τὸ ὄν. τοῦ υἱοῦ τοῦ θεοῦ Hs 9, 16, 5. ἐπιγινώσκειν τὸ ὄν. τοῦ υἱοῦ τοῦ θεοῦ s 9, 16, 7. φοβεῖσθαι τὸ ὄν. σου Rv 11: 18. φανεροῦν τινι τὸ ὄν. σου J 17: 6. γνωρίζειν τινὶ τὸ ὄν. σου vs. 26. πιστεύειν τῷ ὀν. τοῦ υἱοῦ αὐτοῦ believe in the name of his son 1 J 3: 23. Also πιστεύειν εἰς τὸ ὄν. (s. 1 4cβ below and cf. πιστεύω 2aβ).—Of the name of Christian borne by the members of the Church: κρατεῖς τὸ ὄν. μου you cling to my name Rv 2: 13. The same mng. also holds for the expressions: λαμβάνειν τὸ ὄν. τοῦ υἱοῦ αὐτοῦ Hs 9, 12, 4; 8; 9, 13, 2a; 7. τοῦ βαστάσαι τὸ ὄν. μου ἐνώπιον ἐθνῶν to bear my name before (the) Gentiles Ac 9: 15. τὸ ὄν. ἡδέως βαστάζειν bear the name gladly Hs 8, 10, 3; cf. 9, 28, 5b. τὸ ὄν. τοῦ υἱοῦ τοῦ θεοῦ φορεῖν s 9, 13, 3; 9, 14, 5f; 9, 15, 2; cf. 9, 13, 2b. The Christian receives this name at his baptism: πρὶν φορέσαι τὸν ἄνθρωπον τὸ ὄν. τοῦ υἱοῦ τοῦ θεοῦ νεκρός ἐστιν before a man bears the name of God's Son (which is given him at baptism), he is dead s 9, 16, 3. Of hypocrites and false teachers ὄν. μὲν ἔχουσιν, ἀπὸ δὲ τῆς πίστεως κενοί εἰσιν they have the (Christian) name, but are devoid of faith s 9, 19, 2. Of Christians in appearance only ἐν ὑποκρίσει φέροντες τὸ ὄν. τοῦ κυρίου who bear the Lord's name in hypocrisy Pol 6: 3. δόλῳ πονηρῷ τὸ ὄν. περιφέρειν carry the name about in wicked deceit (evidently of wandering preachers) IEph 7: 1. τὸ ὄν. ἐπαισχύνονται τοῦ κυρίου αὐτῶν they are ashamed of their Lord's name Hs 9, 21, 3. More fully: ἐπαισχύνονται τὸ ὄν. αὐτοῦ φορεῖν 9, 14, 6.

c. used w. prepositions—a. w. διά and the gen. διὰ τοῦ ὀνόματός μου πιστεύειν PK 3 p. 15 l. 12; σωθῆναι διὰ τοῦ μεγάλου καὶ ἐνδόξου ὀν. be saved through the great and glorious name Hv 4, 2, 4. εἰς τὴν βασιλείαν τοῦ θεοῦ εἰσελθεῖν διὰ τοῦ ὀν. τοῦ υἱοῦ (τοῦ θεοῦ) s 9, 12, 5. ἄφεσιν ἁμαρτιῶν λαβεῖν διὰ τοῦ ὀν. αὐτοῦ Ac 10: 43. σημεῖα . . . γίνεσθαι διὰ τοῦ ὀν. . . . Ἰησοῦ by the power of the name 4: 30. Differently παρακαλεῖν τινα διὰ τοῦ ὀν. τοῦ κυρίου appeal to someone by the name (=while calling on the name) of the Lord 1 Cor 1: 10.—W. διά and the acc. μισούμενοι . . . διὰ τὸ ὄν. μου hated on account of my name (i.e., because you bear it) Mt 10: 22; 24: 9; Mk 13: 13; Lk 21: 17. ποιεῖν τι εἴς τινα διὰ τὸ ὄν. μου J 15: 21. ἀφέωνται ὑμῖν αἱ ἁμαρτίαι διὰ τὸ ὄν. αὐτοῦ your sins are forgiven on account of his name 1 J 2: 12. βαστάζειν διὰ τὸ ὄν. μου bear (hardship) for my name's sake Rv 2: 3 (cf. βαστάζω 2bβ). πάσχειν διὰ τὸ ὄν. (also w. a gen. like αὐτοῦ) Pol 8: 2; Hv 3, 2, 1b; s 9, 28, 3.

β. w. εἰς: somet. evidently as a rendering of the rabb. בשם with regard to, in thinking of δέχεσθαί τινα εἰς ὄν. Ἰ. Χρ. receive someone in deference to Jesus Christ IRo 9: 3. δύο ἢ τρεῖς συνηγμένοι εἰς τὸ ἐμὸν ὄν. two or three

gathered and thinking of me, i.e., so that I am the reason for their assembling Mt 18: 20; here, however, the other mng. (s. below) has had some influence: 'while naming' or 'calling on my name'. τῆς ἀγάπης ἧς ἐνεδείξασθε εἰς τὸ ὄν. αὐτοῦ (i.e. θεοῦ) Hb 6: 10 is either the love that you have shown with regard to him, i.e. for his sake, or we have here the frequently attested (s. Dssm. B 143ff, NB 25, LO 97f [BS 146f; 197]; LAE 121]; Heitmüller, op. cit. 100ff; FPreisigke, Girowesen im griech. Ägypt. '10, 149ff. On the LXX cf. Heitmüller 110f; JPsichari, Essai sur le Grec de la Septante 1898, 202f) formula of Hellenistic legal and commercial language: εἰς (τὸ) ὄνομά τινος to the name= to the account (over which the name stands). Then the deeds of love, although shown to men, are dedicated to God.—The concept of dedication is also highly significant, in all probability, for the understanding of the expr. βαπτίζειν εἰς (τὸ) ὄν. τινος. Through baptism εἰς (τὸ) ὄν. τ. the one who is baptized becomes the possession of and comes under the protection of the one whose name he bears; he is under the control of the effective power of the name and the One who bears the name, i.e., he is dedicated to them. An additional factor, to a degree, may be the sense of εἰς τὸ ὄν.='with mention of the name' (cf. Herodian 2, 2, 10; 2, 13, 2 ὀμνύναι εἰς τὸ ὄν. τινος; Cyranides p. 57, 1 εἰς ὄνομα τινος; 60, 18=εἰς τὸ ὄν. τ.; 62, 13. Another ex. in Heitmüller 107): Mt 28: 19; Ac 8: 16; 19: 5; D 7: 1, (3); 9: 5; Hv 3, 7, 3; cf. 1 Cor 1: 13, 15. S. βαπτίζω 2bβ and Silva New, Beginn. I 5, '33, 121-40.— πιστεύειν εἰς τὸ ὄν. τινος believe in the name of someone i.e., have confidence that he bears his name rightfully, that he really is what his name (rather in the sense of a title; cf. Phil 2: 9) declares that he is J 1: 12; 2: 23; 3: 18; 1 J 5: 13.

γ. with ἐν: ἐν ὀνόματι of God or Jesus means in the great majority of cases with mention of the name, while naming or calling on the name (LXX; no corresponding use has been found in secular Gk.—Heitmüller p. 13ff, esp. 44; 49). In many pass. it seems to be a formula. ἐν τῷ ὀνόματι Ἰησοῦ ἐκβάλλειν δαιμόνια Mk 9: 38; 16: 17; Lk 9: 49. τὰ δαιμόνια ὑποτάσσεται ἡμῖν ἐν τῷ ὀν. σου the demons are subject to us at the mention of your name 10: 17. ποιεῖν τι ἐν τῷ ὀνόματι Ac 4: 7; cf. Col 3: 17. Perh. J 10: 25 (but s. below). ἐν τῷ ὀν. Ἰησοῦ . . . οὗτος παρέστηκεν ὑγιής Ac 4: 10. ὄν. . . . ἐν ᾧ δεῖ σωθῆναι ἡμᾶς vs. 12. παραγγέλλω σοι ἐν τῷ ὀν. Ἰ. Χρ. 16: 18; cf. 2 Th 3: 6; IPol 5: 1. σοὶ λέγω ἐν τῷ ὀν. τοῦ κυρίου Ac 14: 10 D. Peter, in performing a healing, says ἐν τῷ ὀν. Ἰησοῦ Χρ. περιπάτει 3: 6 (s. Heitmüller 60). The elders are to anoint the sick w. oil ἐν τῷ ὀν. τοῦ κυρίου while calling on the name of the Lord Js 5: 14.—Of the prophets λαλεῖν ἐν τῷ ὀν. κυρίου 5: 10. παρρησιάζεσθαι ἐν τῷ ὀν. Ἰησοῦ speak out boldly in proclaiming the name of Jesus Ac 9: 27f. βαπτίζεσθαι ἐν τῷ ὀν. Ἰ. Χ. be baptized or have oneself baptized while naming the name of Jesus Christ Ac 2: 38 v.l.; 10: 48. αἰτεῖν τὸν πατέρα ἐν τῷ ὀν. μου (=Ἰησοῦ) ask the Father, using my name J 15: 16; cf. 14: 13, 14; 16: 24, 26. W. the latter pass. belongs vs. 23 (ὁ πατήρ) δώσει ὑμῖν ἐν τῷ ὀν. μου (the Father) will give you, when you mention my name. τὸ πνεῦμα ὃ πέμψει ὁ πατὴρ ἐν τῷ ὀν. μου the Spirit, whom the Father will send when my name is used 14: 26. To thank God ἐν ὀν. Ἰησοῦ Χρ. while naming the name of Jesus Christ Eph 5: 20. ἵνα ἐν τῷ ὀν. Ἰησοῦ πᾶν γόνυ κάμψῃ that when the name of Jesus is mentioned every knee should bow Phil 2: 10. χαίρετε, υἱοί, ἐν ὀν. κυρίου greetings, my sons, as we call on the Lord's name B 1: 1. ὁ ἐρχόμενος ἐν ὀν. κυρίου whoever comes, naming the Lord's name (in order thereby to show that he is a Christian) D 12: 1. ἀσπάζεσθαι ἐν ὀν. Ἰ. Χρ. *greet, while naming the name of J. Chr.* w. acc. of the pers. or thing greeted IRo inscr.; ISm 12: 2. Receive fellow church members ἐν ὀν. θεοῦ IEph 1: 3. συναχθῆναι ἐν τῷ ὀν. τοῦ κυρίου Ἰ. *I. meet and call on the name of the Lord Jesus*=as a Christian church 1 Cor 5: 4. μόνον ἐν τῷ ὀν. Ἰ. Χρ. *only (it is to be) while calling on the name of J. Chr.* ISm 4: 2.—Not far removed fr. these are the places where we render ἐν τῷ ὀν. with *through* or *by the name* (s. ἐν III 1a); the effect brought about by the name is caused by the utterance of the name ἀπελούσασθε, ἡγιάσθητε, ἐδικαιώθητε ἐν τῷ ὀν. τοῦ κυρίου Ἰ. Χρ. 1 Cor 6: 11. ζωὴν ἔχειν ἐν τῷ ὀν. αὐτοῦ (=Ἰησοῦ) J 20: 31. τηρεῖν τινα ἐν τῷ ὀν. (θεοῦ) 17: 11f.—ἐν τῷ ὀν. *at the command (of), commissioned by* ἔργα ποιεῖν ἐν τῷ ὀν. τοῦ πατρός J 10: 25 (but s. above). ἔρχεσθαι ἐν τῷ ὀν. τοῦ πατρός 5: 43a; in contrast ἔρχ. ἐν τῷ ὀν. τῷ ἰδίῳ vs. 43b. εὐλογημένος ὁ ἐρχόμενος ἐν ὀν. κυρίου 12: 13 (Ps 117: 26). The Ps-passage prob. has the same sense (despite Heitmüller 53f) in Mt 21: 9; 23: 39; Mk 11: 9; Lk 13: 35; 19: 38.— OMerlier, Ὄνομα et ἐν ὀνόματι dans le quatr. Év.: Rev. des Études grecques 47, '34, 180-204; RGBratcher, The Bible Translator 14, '63, 72-80.

δ. w. ἕνεκα (and the other forms of this word; s. ἕνεκα): of persecutions for one's Christian faith ἀπάγεσθαι ἐπὶ βασιλεῖς ἕνεκεν τοῦ ὀν. μου Lk 21: 12. πάσχειν or ὑποφέρειν εἵνεκα τοῦ ὀνόματος Hv 3, 1, 9; 3, 2, 1; s 9, 28, 5. ἕνεκεν τοῦ ὀν. (τοῦ) κυρίου v 3, 5, 2; s 9, 28, 6. ἀφιέναι οἰκίας . . . ἕνεκεν τοῦ ἐμοῦ ὀν. *for my name's sake* Mt 19: 29. ἔκτισας τὰ πάντα ἕνεκεν τοῦ ὀν. σου *thou didst create all things for thy name's sake,* i.e. that God's name might be praised for the benefits that the works of creation bring to mankind D 10: 3.

ε. w. ἐπί and the dat.: ἐπὶ τῷ ὀν. τινος *when someone's name is mentioned* or *called upon,* or *mentioning someone's name* (LXX; cf. Heitmüller 19ff; 43ff; s. also 47ff; 52ff; 87ff) in the NT only of the name of Jesus, and only in the synoptics and Ac ἐλεύσονται ἐπὶ τῷ ὀν. μου *they will come using my name* Mt 24: 5; Mk 13: 6; Lk 21: 8. κηρύσσειν ἐπὶ τῷ ὀν. αὐτοῦ μετάνοιαν 24: 47. λαλεῖν ἐπὶ τῷ ὀν. τούτῳ *to speak using this name* Ac 4: 17; 5: 40. διδάσκειν 4: 18; 5: 28. ποιεῖν δύναμιν ἐπὶ τῷ ὀν. μου Mk 9: 39. ἐπὶ τῷ ὀν. σου ἐκβάλλειν δαιμόνια Lk 9: 49 v.l. Of the (spiritual) temple of God: οἰκοδομηθήσεται ναὸς θεοῦ ἐνδόξως ἐπὶ τῷ ὀν. κυρίου *the temple of God will be gloriously built with the use of the Lord's name* B 16: 6f, 8 (quot. of uncertain orig.). βαπτίζεσθαι ἐπὶ τῷ ὀν. Ἰ. Χρ. Ac 2: 38. Baptism is also referred to in καλεῖσθαι ἐπὶ τῷ ὀν. τοῦ υἱοῦ τοῦ θεοῦ *receive a name when the name of God's son is named* Hs 9, 17, 4. The words δέχεσθαι (παιδίον) ἐπὶ τῷ ὀν. μου can also be classed here *receive (a child) when my name is confessed, when I am called upon* Mt 18: 5; Mk 9: 37; Lk 9: 48 (cf. Heitmüller 64); but s. also II below.—ἐπί w. acc.: πεποιθέναι ἐπὶ τὸ ὁσιώτατον τῆς μεγαλωσύνης αὐτοῦ ὀν. *have confidence in his most sacred and majestic name* 1 Cl 58: 1b; ἐλπίζειν ἐπὶ τὸ ὀν. *hope in the name* (of the Lord) B 16: 8b.

ζ. w. περί and the gen.: εὐαγγελίζεσθαι περὶ τοῦ ὀν. Ἰ. Χ. *bring the good news about the name of J. Chr.* Ac 8: 12.

η. w. πρός and acc.: πρὸς τὸ ὀν. Ἰησοῦ . . . πολλὰ ἐναντία πρᾶξαι *do many things in opposing the name of Jesus* Ac 26: 9.

θ. w. ὑπέρ and gen.: ὑπὲρ τοῦ ὀν. (Ἰησοῦ) ἀτιμασθῆναι Ac 5: 41. πάσχειν 9: 16; Hs 9, 28, 2. Cf. Ac 15: 26; 21: 13. The activity of the apostles takes place ὑπὲρ τοῦ ὀν. αὐτοῦ *to the honor of his (Jesus') name* Ro 1: 5. Cf. 3 J

7. Of the eucharistic thanksgiving in the prayer at the Lord's Supper εὐχαριστεῖν ὑπὲρ τοῦ ἁγίου ὀν. σου, οὗ κατεσκήνωσας ἐν ταῖς καρδίαις ἡμῶν *for thy holy name, which thou didst cause to dwell in our hearts* D 10: 2.

d. ὄνομα w. ref. to God or Christ not infreq. stands quite alone, simply *the Name:* Ac 5: 41; 3 J 7; 2 Cl 13: 1, 4; IEph 3: 1; 7: 1; IPhld 10: 1; Hv 3, 2, 1; s 8, 10, 3; 9, 13, 2; 9, 28, 3; 5.

II. *title, category* (cf. Cass. Dio 38, 44; 42, 24 καὶ ὅτι πολλῷ πλείω ἔν τε τῷ σχήματι καὶ ἐν τῷ ὀνόματι τῷ τῆς στρατηγίας ὢν καταπράξειν ἤλπιζε; inscr.: Sb 7541, 5 [II AD] Νύμφη ὄνομ' ἐστί σοι; POxy. 37 I, 17 [49 AD] βούλεται ὀνόματι ἐλευθέρου τὸ σωμάτιον ἀπενέγκασθαι; Jos., Ant. 12, 154 φερνῆς ὀνόματι; 11, 40. Other exx. in Heitmüller 50); the possibility of understanding ὄν. as *category* made it easier for the Greeks to take over the rabb. שֵׁם לְ (s. I 4cβ above) in the sense *with regard to a particular characteristic,* then simply *with regard to, for the sake of* ὁ δεχόμενος προφήτην εἰς ὄνομα προφήτου *whoever receives a prophet within the category 'prophet'* i.e., because he is a prophet, *as a prophet* Mt 10: 41a; cf. vss. 41b, 42.—ὃς ἂν ποτίσῃ ὑμᾶς ἐν ὀνόματι, ὅτι Χριστοῦ ἐστε *whoever gives you a drink under the category that you belong to Christ* i.e., *in your capacity as a follower of Christ* Mk 9: 41. εἰ ὀνειδίζεσθε ἐν ὀν. Χριστοῦ *if you are reviled for the sake of Christ* 1 Pt 4: 14. δοξαζέτω τὸν θεὸν ἐν τῷ ὀν. τούτῳ *let him praise God in this capacity* (=ὡς Χριστιανός) vs. 16. δέδεμαι ἐν τῷ ὀν. *I am imprisoned for the sake of the Name* IEph 3: 1.—δέχεσθαι (παιδίον) ἐπὶ τῷ ὀν. μου *for my (name's) sake* Mt 18: 5; Mk 9: 37; Lk 9: 48 (cf. Heitmüller 113. But s. I 4cε above).

III. *person* (Phalaris, Ep. 128; POxy. 1188, 8 [13 AD]; BGU 113, 11; Jos., Ant. 14, 22; other exx. in Dssm., NB 24f [BS 196f]; LXX) τὸ ποθητόν μοι ὄν. *my dear friend:* Alce ISm 13: 2; IPol 8: 3; Crocus IRo 10: 1. Pl. (PThéad. 41, 10; PSI 27, 22; Num 1: 18 al.) *people* Ac 1: 15; Rv 3: 4. ὀνόματα ἀνθρώπων 11: 13 (cf. Ael. Aristid. 50, 72 K.=26 p. 523 D.: ὀνόματα δέκα ἀνδρῶν). This is prob. the place for περὶ λόγου καὶ ὀνομάτων καὶ νόμου *about teaching and persons and (the) law* Ac 18: 15.

IV. *the (well-known) name, reputation, fame* (Hom.+; 1 Ch 14: 17; 1 Macc 8: 12) φανερὸν ἐγένετο τὸ ὀν. αὐτοῦ *his fame was widespread* Mk 6: 14. ὀν. ἔχειν (Pla., Apol. 38c, Ep. 2 p. 312c) w. ὅτι foll. *have the reputation of* Rv 3: 1.

V. *office* (POxy. 58, 6) στασιαζουσῶν τ. φυλῶν, ὁποία αὐτῶν εἴη τῷ ἐνδόξῳ ὀνόματι κεκοσμημένη *when the tribes were quarreling as to which one of them was to be adorned with that glorious office* 1 Cl 43: 2. τὸ ὄνομα τῆς ἐπισκοπῆς *the office of bishop* 44: 1.—HBietenhard, TW V 242-83: ὄνομα and related words. M-M. B. 1263f.

ὀνομάζω 1 aor. ὠνόμασα, pass. ὠνομάσθην (Hom.+; inscr., pap., LXX, Ep. Arist., Philo, Joseph., Test. 12 Patr.) *to name.*

1. *give a name, call, name* w. double acc. (Aelian, N.A. 12, 2; Wsd 2: 13; Philo, Gig. 6 al.) οὓς ἀποστόλους ὠνόμασεν *to whom he gave the name 'apostles'* Mk 3: 14 v.l.; Lk 6: 13. ὃν ὠνόμασεν Πέτρον *whom he named Peter* vs. 14 (cf. Jos., Ant. 1, 213 ὃν Ἴσακον ὠνόμασε.— Olympiodorus, Life of Plato p. 1 Westerm.: the man whose name was formerly Aristocles μετωνομάσθη Πλάτων by his teacher; the reason for this is then given). Passive w. nom. (Diod. S. 17, 87, 2 ὠνομάζετο Ἐμβύσαρος; Jos., Vi. 3) ὠνομάσθη τὸ ὄνομα Ἰ. Lk 2: 21 D. τὶς ἀδελφὸς ὀνομαζόμενος *one who is called a brother, a*

so-called brother 1 Cor 5: 11 (cf. 3 Macc 7: 17). ἐξ οὗ (i.e. τοῦ πατρός) πᾶσα πατριά...ὀνομάζεται from whom every family...receives its name Eph 3: 15 (for ὀνομάζειν ἐκ cf. Il. 10, 68; for ὀνομάζεσθαι ἐκ X., Mem. 4, 5, 12).

2. name a name, use a name or word πορνεία...μηδὲ ὀνομαζέσθω ἐν ὑμῖν sexual vice...is not even to be mentioned among you (much less is it actually to be practiced) Eph 5: 3. ὀν. τὸ ὄνομα κυρίου name the name of the Lord (almost='call on') 2 Ti 2: 19 (cf. Is 26: 13; Jer 20: 9). πᾶν ὄνομα ὀνομαζόμενον every name (of a supernatural being) that is named (i.e. called upon) Eph 1: 21. ὀν. τὸ ὄνομα τοῦ κυρίου Ἰησοῦ ἐπί τινα pronounce the name of the Lord Jesus over someone (to heal him) Ac 19: 13 (cf. Jer 32: 29).—Mention by name PK 4 p. 15, 32.

3. The pass. be named in the sense be known (cf. Esth 9: 4; 1 Macc 3: 9; 14: 10; Ep. Arist. 124) οὐχ ὅπου ὠνομάσθη Χριστός not where Christ is already known Ro 15: 20.—1 Cor 5: 1 t.r. M-M.*

ὄνος, ου (Hom.+; inscr., pap., LXX, Philo; Jos., Ant. 1, 225, Vi. 119; loanw. in rabb.), ὁ and ἡ donkey (male or female), ass, she-ass πῶλος ὄνου a donkey's colt J 12: 15. W. πῶλος Mt 21: 2 (Iambl. Erot. p. 222, 38 εὑρόντες ὄνους δύο), 5, 7 (KPieper, Zum Einzug Jesu in Jerusalem: BZ 11, '13, 397–402; FVogel, Mt 21: 1–11: Blätter für d. Bayerische Gymnasialschulwesen 59, '23, 212f; ELittmann, ZNW 34, '35, 28; CWFSmith, The Horse and the Ass in the Bible: ATR 27, '45, 86–97; W-S. §27, 3c). W. βοῦς (Is 1: 3) Lk 13: 15; 14: 5 t.r. ἐν ὄν. καθίσαι τινά seat someone on a donkey MPol 8: 1.—OMichel, TW V 285–7. M-M. B. 172.*

ὄντως adv. of the ptc. ὤν (Eur., X., Pla.+; inscr., pap., LXX, Philo, Joseph.; Test. Jos. 13: 9; loanw. in rabb.) really, certainly, in truth.

1. lit., as adv. (PGiess. 22, 6; Num 22: 37; Jer 3: 23; Jos., Bell. 1, 68) Lk 23: 47; 24: 34; J 8: 36; 1 Cor 14: 25; Gal 3: 21; PK 4 p. 16, 5. εἶχον τὸν Ἰωάννην ὄν. ὅτι προφήτης ἦν they held that John was really a prophet Mk 11: 32.

2. used attributively (Pla., Phaedr. 260A, Clit. 409E; Dit., Syll.³ 893B, 8f τὸν ὄν. Ἡρακλείδην; Strassb. pap. 53 in Novae Comoed. fgm. ed. OSchröder=Kl. T. 135 p. 47, 14 ὄν. θεός; Sb 3924, 39; Philo, Poster. Cai. 167; Jos., Ant. 15, 63 οἱ ὄν. βασιλεῖς) ἡ ὄν. χήρα the real widow (in contrast to one so called, who has relatives, or is still of marriageable age, or, as some hold, has been married several times) 1 Ti 5: 3, 5, 16. ἡ ὄν. ζωή real, true life 6: 19. Opp. ὁ ὄν. θάνατος Dg 10: 7. οἱ ὄν. ἀποφεύγοντες 2 Pt 2: 18 t.r. M-M.*

ὀξίζω 1 aor. ὤξισα (Soranus p. 69, 25; 70, 14; Diosc. 1, 115, 2; 5, 6, 14; Paradoxogr. Flor. 20; Geopon. 5, 29, 4; 7, 15, 6) become sour, taste of vinegar of half-empty wine jars ὀξίζουσι they turn sour Hm 12, 5, 3b. Therefore their owner fears μήποτε ὤξισαν that they have become sour m 12, 5, 3a.*

ὄξος, ους, τό (since Solon 26, 7 Diehl², Aeschyl., Hippocr.; pap., LXX; Philo, Aet. M. 113) sour wine, wine vinegar; it relieved thirst more effectively than water and, because it was cheaper than regular wine, it was a favorite beverage of the lower ranks of society and of those in moderate circumstances (Athen. 4 p. 173E; Plut., Cato Major 1, 13; Ruth 2: 14), esp. of soldiers (PLond. 1245, 9). Given to Jesus on the cross Mt 27: 48; Mk 15: 36; Lk 23: 36; J 19: 29f. In the latter pass. (s. vs. 28) scripture is fulfilled (prob. Ps 68: 22 ἐπότισάν με ὄξος). This act is interpreted

as being due to the malice of the Jews who committed it, and it is expanded to an offering of gall and vinegar (cf. Ps 68: 22) in GP 5: 16; B 7: 5 (both ποτίζειν χολὴν μετὰ ὄξους), 3. Betw. 7: 3 and 5 B quotes, as proof that vinegar was given, an otherwise unknown prophetic pass. that directs the priests to eat the goat's ἔντερον ἄπλυτον μετὰ ὄξους (s. ἔντερον) 7: 4. W. οἶνος (PLond. 856, 28; 1159, 49) and mixed w. it Hm 10, 3, 3.—Heidland, TW V 288f. M-M. B. 383.*

ὀξύπτερος, ον (Aesop, Fab. 8 Halm) swift-winged ὁ ὀξ. hawk (Cyranides p. 95, 27) B 10: 1, 4.*

ὀξύς, εῖα, ύ—1. sharp (so Hom.+; LXX; Ep. Arist. 60; 276; Philo; Jos., Ant. 14, 422; Test. Jud. 1: 4) ῥομφαία a sharp sword (Ezk 5: 1) Rv 1: 16; 2: 12; 19: 15. δρέπανον a sharp sickle 14: 14, 17f.

2. quick, swift (trag., Hdt.+; POxy. 900, 7; 1412, 18 ὀξέως; LXX, Philo; Jos., Ant. 5, 261) w. aor. inf. (Ael. Aristid. 34 p. 665 D.: τὰ βέλτιστα πρᾶξαι ὀ.) ὀξεῖς οἱ πόδες αὐτῶν ἐκχέαι αἷμα their feet are swift when it comes to shedding blood Ro 3: 15 (Ps 13: 3). M-M. B. 1034; 1069.*

ὀξυχολέω 1 aor. ptc. ὀξυχολήσας be irritable, easily moved to anger ὁ ἄνθρ. ὁ ὀξυχολήσας the man who is easily moved to anger Hm 10, 2, 3.*

ὀξυχολία, ας, ἡ (Cat. Cod. Astr. XII 143, 16; Christian wr.) irritability, bad temper Hm 5, 1, 3; 6f; 5, 2, 1; 4; 10, 2, 3. ἀπέχεσθαι ἀπὸ τῆς ὀξ. m 5, 2, 8a; ἀντιστῆναι τῇ ὀξ. resist bad temper 5, 2, 8b. ὀξ. προσπίπτει τινὶ irritability comes over someone 6, 2, 5. ἐὰν ὀξ. τις προσέλθῃ if bad temper enters in 5, 1, 3. Called a sister of λύπη and of διψυχία 10, 1, 1f. ἡ ὀξ. λυπεῖ τὸ πνεῦμα bad temper makes the Spirit sad 10, 2, 4. Personified among the vices s 9, 15, 3.*

ὀξύχολος, ον (the adv. in Soph., Ant. 955, the adj. Solon 1, 26 Diehl²; Anth. Pal. 9, 127, 4) irritable, irascible, bad-tempered w. πικρός and ἄφρων Hm 6, 2, 4. Subst. (cf. Lucian, Fugit. 19 τὸ ὀξύχολον=ἡ ὀξυχολία) ὁ ὀξ. the irascible, bad-tempered man m 5, 2, 7; s 6, 5, 5.*

ὀπή, ῆς, ἡ (Aristoph.+; LXX, Philo; Jos., Ant. 9, 163) opening, hole w. gen. (Herodas 2, 42; Ex 33: 22 ὀπ. τῆς πέτρας; Ob 3) τῆς γῆς (Alciphr. 2, 1, 2) in the ground Hb 11: 38. Abs. (Aesop, Fab. 353 P.=Babr. 112 Cr. of a mousehole) of the opening out of which a spring flows Js 3: 11. B. 909.*

ὄπισθεν adv. (Hom.+ [ὄπιθεν; cf. Kühner-Bl. II 309f]; inscr., pap., LXX, Joseph., Test. 12 Patr., Sib. Or. 3, 445).

1. as adv.—a. from behind (Appian, Syr. 24 §119; 63 §334, Bell. Civ. 4, 55 §239) Mt 9: 20; Mk 5: 27; Lk 8: 44.—b. behind opp. πρόσθεν (q.v. 1a and cf. Hes., Shield 132f πρόσθεν—ὄπισθε; Jos., Ant. 13, 30 ἔμπροσθεν αὐτῶν...ὄπισθεν) Rv 4: 6. Of a scroll w. writing on it, opp. ἔσωθεν inside and on the back, i.e. on the recto and verso 5: 1 (cf. PTebt. 58 recto, 37 [111 BC] τἀπίλοιπα ὀπείσωι='the rest is on the back'; ostracon of the Deissmann collection in PMMeyer, Griech. Texte '16, 107ff, no. 61, 15 [III BC] ὀπίσω='turn'; PGM 12, 207; 276).

2. as improper prep. w. the gen. (Hom.+; Dit., Syll.³ 46, 65; 969, 5f; PGM 4, 1230 ὄπισθεν αὐτοῦ σταθείς; LXX)—a. of place behind, after someone (Menand., Kolax 47 J. ὄπισθ' ἐβάδιζέ μου; Bl-D. §215, 1; Rob. 645) κράζειν ὀπ. τινος cry out after someone Mt 15: 23. ἤκουσα...ὀπ. μου I heard behind me Rv 1: 10 v.l.

φέρειν (τι) ὄπ. τινος *carry (someth.) behind someone* Lk 23: 26.

b. of time *after someone* or *someth.* B 4: 4 (Da 7: 24). M-M.*

ὀπίσω adv. (Hom. [ὀπίσσω]+; inscr., pap., LXX, Philo, Joseph.).

1. used as adv., of place—**a.** in answer to the quest. 'where?' *behind*, in our lit. only w. the art. τὸ ὀπ.: εἰς τοὐπίσω *back* (Pla., Phaedr. 254B, Rep. 528A; Lucian, De Merc. Cond. 21; Dionys. Byz. 53 p. 21, 16 RGüngerich ['27]; Jos., Ant. 7, 15) ἀφορμᾶν *start back* 1 Cl 25: 4. Mostly pl. τὰ ὀπ. *what lies behind* (ἐκ τῶν ὀπίσω: PPetr. III 23 [246 BC]; BGU 1002, 16) symbolically, of a foot-race: the part of the course which has already been covered Phil 3: 13. εἰς τὰ ὀπ. (1 Macc 9: 47; Philo, Leg. All. 2, 99 [=Gen 49: 17]): ἀπέρχεσθαι *shrink back* J 18: 6; fig. *draw back* 6: 66. στρέφεσθαι *turn back, turn around* 20: 14 (Antimachus Coloph. [V/IV BC] ed. BWyss '36, fgm. 60 στρέφεσθαι εἰς τοὐπίσω; cf. Ps 113: 3). Also ἐπιστρέφεσθαι Hv 4, 3, 7 (cf. 4 Km 20: 10). ἐπιστρέφειν *return* (home) Mt 24: 18; Mk 13: 16; Lk 17: 31. βλέπειν *look back(wards)* (cf. Plut., Nic. 14, 2 ὀπίσω βλ.; Artem. 1, 36 p. 37, 23 τὰ ὀπίσω βλέπειν; Gen 19: 17, 26) as a symbol Lk 9: 62. *Cast backward=reject* 1 Cl 35: 8 (Ps 49: 17).

b. in answer to the quest. 'whither', 'where to?' *back, behind* (Lucian, Dea Syr. 36; Appian, Maced. 18 §3, Mithrid. 104 §489; Polyaenus 7, 27, 1; Gen 24: 5; 3 Km 18: 37; Jos., Ant. 6, 15) στῆναι ὀπ. παρὰ τ. πόδας αὐτοῦ *come and stand behind him at his feet* Lk 7: 38. ὀπίσω τὰς χεῖρας ποιεῖν *put one's hands behind one* MPol 14: 1.

2. as improper prep. w. gen. (POxy. 43 B IV, 3 ὀπίσω Καπιτωλείου; LXX)—**a.** of place—**a.** *behind* (Dit., Or. 56, 62 [237 BC] ταύτης δ' ὀπίσω=behind this one; Ps.-Lucian, Asin. 17; 29; Chio, Ep. 4, 3; SSol 2: 9.—Gen 19: 6) ἤκουσα ὀπ. μου *I heard behind me* Rv 1: 10. τὰ ὀ. σου Hs 9, 2, 7.—ὕπαγε ὀπ. μου *get behind me! get out of my sight!* Mt 4: 10 t.r.; 16: 23; Mk 8: 33 (CHDodd, JTS 5, '54, 246f); Lk 4: 8 t.r. (cf. 4 Km 9: 19).—VEHarlow, Jesus' Jerusalem Expedition '36, 20-37: Ὀπίσω μου, esp. 31f.

β. *after* (Ex 15: 20; 2 Km 3: 16) Lk 19: 14. ὀπ. τῆς γυναικός *after the woman* Rv 12: 15. ἔρχεσθαι ὀπ. τινός *come after someone, follow someone* (at the same time fig. in the sense 'be an adherent') Mt 16: 24; Mk 8: 34; Lk 9: 23; 14: 27. Also ἀκολουθεῖν (q.v. 2.—Gulin [μιμητής 1]) Mt 10: 38; Mk 8: 34 v.l. ἀπέρχεσθαι Mk 1: 20; J 12: 19. πορεύεσθαι ὀπ. τινός Lk 21: 8. The two latter verbs are also combined w. ὀπίσω τινός in our lit. in another connection: ἀπέρχεσθαι ὀπ. σαρκὸς ἑτέρας *go after strange flesh=indulge in unnatural lust* by the Sodomites Jd 7. The parallel pass. 2 Pt 2: 10, on the other hand, has ὀπ. σαρκὸς ἐν ἐπιθυμίᾳ μιασμοῦ πορεύεσθαι, where the σάρξ seems rather to be the power of the defiling desire, to which (σάρξ) the sinners have pledged allegiance. Cf. Hv 3, 7, 3.—δεῦτε ὀπ. μου *come, follow me* (s. δεῦτε 2) Mt 4: 19; Mk 1: 17. ἀποσπᾶν τινα ὀπ. τινός (s. ἀποσπάω 2) Ac 20: 30. ἀφιστάναι λαὸν ὀπ. αὐτοῦ (s. ἀφίστημι 1) 5: 37. ἐκτρέπεσθαι ὀπ. τοῦ σατανᾶ (s. ἐκτρέπω) 1 Ti 5: 15. θαυμάζεσθαι ὀπ. τινός (s. θαυμάζω 2) Rv 13: 3.

b. of time *after* (3 Km 1: 6, 24; Eccl 10: 14) ἔρχεσθαι ὀπ. τινός Mt 3: 11; Mk 1: 7; J 1: 15, 27, 30 (CLindeboom, 'Die na mij komt, is voor mij geworden': Geref. Theol. Tijdschr. 16, '16, 438-46; differently ['a follower of mine'] KGrobel, JBL 60, '41, 397-401).—HSeesemann, TW V 289-92. M-M.*

ὁπλή, ῆς, ἡ (Hom.+; LXX; Ep. Arist. 150) *hoof,* includ-ing the split hoof of cattle (Hom. Hymns, Merc. 77; Hes., Works 491; Pind., Pyth. 4, 126; Hdt. 2, 71; Dit., Syll.³ 1026, 19 [IV/III BC]) ἐκφέρειν ὁπλάς *grow hoofs* 1 Cl 52: 2 (Ps 68: 32).*

ὁπλίζω 1 aor. mid. ὡπλισάμην (Hom.+; Sym. Jer 52: 25; Jos., Vi. 45; Sib. Or. 2, 119) *equip, arm,* mid. *arm oneself,* in our lit. only fig. τὶ *with someth.* τὴν αὐτὴν ἔννοιαν *arm oneself with the same insight* 1 Pt 4: 1 (cf. Soph., Electra 996 τοιοῦτον θράσος αὐτή θ' ὁπλίζει; Anth. Pal. 5, 92 ὥπλισμαι πρὸς Ἔρωτα περὶ στέρνοισι λογισμόν; Jos., Ant. 6, 187 τ. θεὸν ὥπλισμαι). Also w. the dat. τινί *with someth.* (Eur., Andr. 1118; X., Cyr. 6, 4, 4; Cornutus 31 p. 63, 17) τοῖς ὅπλοις τῆς δικαιοσύνης Pol 4: 1. M-M.*

ὅπλον, ου, τό (Hom.+; inscr., pap., LXX, Ep. Arist., Philo, Joseph.)—1. *tool* ὅπλα ἀδικίας *tools of wickedness,* i.e. tools for doing what is wicked Ro 6: 13a. Opp. ὅπλα δικαιοσύνης vs. 13b. But mng. 2 is also poss.; it is found in all the other pass. of our lit., and specif. in Paul.

2. *weapon*—**a.** lit., pl. (Jos., Vi. 99 ἧκον μεθ' ὅπλων) J 18: 3. Riders μετὰ τῶν συνήθων αὐτοῖς ὅπλων *with their usual arms* MPol 7: 1. Sing. τίθησιν Μωϋσῆς ἐν ὅπλον *Moses placed one weapon=shield* (so as early as Hdt.; Diod. S. 17, 21, 2; 17, 43, 9 [interchanged with ἀσπίδες 8]; 17, 57, 2; Sb 7247, 24 [296 AD]; Test. Levi 5: 3 ὅπλον καὶ ῥομφαίαν) *on the other one,* to stand on them and gain a better view of the battlefield B 12: 2.

b. symbol., pl. of a Christian's life as a battle against evil τὰ ὅπ. τῆς στρατείας ἡμῶν οὐ σαρκικά *the weapons of my warfare are not physical* 2 Cor 10: 4. ἐνδύσασθαι τὰ ὅπ. τοῦ φωτός *put on the weapons of light* Ro 13: 12. τὰ ὅπ. τῆς δικαιοσύνης τὰ δεξιὰ καὶ ἀριστερά *the weapons of righteousness for offense and defense* (s. ἀριστερός) 2 Cor 6: 7. ὁπλίζεσθαι τοῖς ὅπλοις τῆς δικαιοσύνης Pol 4: 1 (s. ὁπλίζω). Of evil desire: φοβουμένη τὰ ὅπ. σου (*your weapons,* i.e. those of the Christian who is equipped for the good fight) Hm 12, 2, 4. Of baptism: τὸ βάπτισμα ὑμῶν μενέτω ὡς ὅπλα *let baptism remain as your arms* ('remain' in contrast to the deserter, who throws his weapons away) IPol 6: 2.—AOepke and KGKuhn, TW V 292-315: ὅπλον and related words. M-M. B. 1383.*

ὁπόθεν adv. (Hom.+; not LXX) *where,* lit. 'from where' Papias 3.*

ὁποῖος, οἵα, οἷον (Hom.+; inscr., pap.; 2 Macc 11: 37) correlative pron. *of what sort, as* τοιοῦτος, ὅπ. (X., Cyr. 1, 6, 36; Ael. Aristid. 45, 1 K.=p. 81 D.; Jos., Ant. 7, 385) Ac 26: 29; cf. Hm 11: 15. Used as a pron. in indirect questions (class.; cf. Bl-D. §300, 1; Rob. 732) τὸ ἔργον ὅπ. ἐστιν *what sort of work* (each has done) 1 Cor 3: 13. ὅπ. εἴσοδον ἔσχομεν πρὸς ὑμᾶς *what sort of welcome we had among you* 1 Th 1: 9. ἐπελάθετο ὁποῖος ἦν *he forgets what sort of person he is* Js 1: 24. Almost equal to the relative 1 Cl 43: 2. ὁποῖοί ποτε ἦσαν οὐδέν μοι διαφέρει *it makes no difference to me what sort of people they were* Gal 2: 6 (s. Bl-D. §303; Rob. 732 and cf. VWeber, Erklärung von Gal 2: 6a: Der Katholik 80, '00, 481-99). M-M.*

ὁπόσος, η, ον (Hom.+; inscr.; PHal. 1, 206; BGU 1074, 6; Jos., Ant. 16, 351; 17, 30; Sib. Or. 3, 480) *how great, how much* neut. ὁπόσον (Dit., Syll.³ 400, 18) *how much* ὁπ. δίκαιός ἐστιν *how righteous he is* GP 8: 28 in the text (ms.: οτιποσον).*

ὁπόταν temporal particle (Pind.+ [Hom. separates it ὁπότ' ἄν; Dit., Syll.³ 344, 75; pap.; Job 29: 22; Jos., Ant. 6, 166; 16, 387 al.; Sib. Or. 5, 464) *whenever* εἶτα, ὁπόταν καθεῖλεν *then, whenever he let* (his hands) *drop* B 12: 2 (cf. Bl-D. §381; Rob. 971; Reinhold p. 108).*

ὁπότε temporal particle (Hom. +; inscr., pap., LXX; Jos., Ant. 15, 33; 17, 2 al.) *when* w. ind., w. ref. to concrete events in the past (Hom.; POxy. 243, 10; PRyl. 245, 3; Tob 7: 11S) B 12: 9; Lk 6: 3 (v.l. ὅτε).—Bl-D. §455, 1; Rob. 971. M-M.*

ὅπου particle denoting place (Hom. +; inscr., pap., LXX, En., Ep. Arist., Joseph.), that can also take on causal and temporal mng.

1. lit., part. denoting place—**a.** *where*—α. used in connection w. a designation of place, w. ind. foll. Mt 6: 19f; 13: 5; 28: 6; Mk 2: 4b; 4: 5; 9: 48; 16: 6; Lk 12: 33; J 1: 28; 4: 20, 46; 7: 42 al.; Ac 17: 1; Rv 11: 8; 20: 10 (here the verb is supplied fr. the context). πρὸς Καϊάφαν, ὅπου οἱ γραμματεῖς συνήχθησαν *to Caiaphas,* i.e. *to his palace, where the scribes were gathered* Mt 26: 57. παρ' ὑμῖν ὅπ. Rv 2: 13b; οὗτοι . . . ὅπου σπείρεται ὁ λόγος *those . . . in whom (=in whose hearts) the word is sown* Mk 4: 15. Looking toward an ἐκεῖ (Jos., C. Ap. 1, 32) Mt 6: 21; Lk 12: 34; 17: 37; J 12: 26.—Not infreq. ὅπ. is related to an ἐκεῖ that is omitted but is easily supplied (ἐκεῖ) ὅπ. (*there*) *where* (Maximus Tyr. 31, 5b) Mt 25: 24, 26; Mk 2: 4a; 13: 14; J 3: 8; 14: 3; 17: 24; 20: 12, 19; Ro 15: 20; Rv 2: 13a; (*thither*) *where* Mk 5: 40; 6: 55; J 6: 62; 7: 34, 36; 11: 32; 18: 1.—On the pleonastic use of the pers. pron. after ὅπου cf. Bl-D. §297; Rob. 683; 722f: ὅπ. ἡ γυνὴ κάθηται ἐπ' αὐτῶν Rv 17: 9. Corresp. ὅπου . . . ἐκεῖ (שָׁם . . . אֲשֶׁר‎) 12: 6, 14. Cf. Mk 6: 55 t.r.

β. ὅπ. ἄν w. the impf. expresses repetition in past time *whenever* Mk 6: 56 (cf. Bl-D. §367; Rob. 969; 972f).

γ. the subjunctive is used in a final relative clause ποῦ ἐστιν τὸ κατάλυμα ὅπου τὸ πάσχα φάγω; Mk 14: 14b; Lk 22: 11 (cf. Bl-D. §378; Rob. 969).

δ. ὅπου ἄν (or ἐάν) w. subj. *wherever, whenever* (Dit., Syll.³ 1218, 23; PEleph. 1, 5 [311/10 bc]; POxy. 484, 20; 1639, 20) w. the aor. subj. Mt 26: 13; Mk 6: 10; 9: 18; 14: 9 (cf. KBeyer, Semitische Syntax im NT, '62, 196), 14a. W. the pres. subj. (and ἐκεῖ to correspond) Mt 24: 28.

b. *where* w. motion implied (*whither*) (Soph., Trach. 40; X., An. 2, 4, 19, Cyr. 8, 3, 23 al. in codices; Epict. 4, 7, 14; Jos., Ant. 16, 325).

α. w. ind. foll., related to a 'there (thither)' to be supplied *where* (Ostrak. II 1162, 5 ὅπου θέλει) J 8: 21f; 13: 33, 36; 14: 4; 21: 18; Js 3: 4.

β. ὅπου ἄν (or ἐάν) w. pres. subj. *wherever* (POxy. 728, 11. W. aor. subj. Ruth 1: 16; Tob 13: 5 S; Jos., Ant. 6, 77) Mt 8: 19; Lk 9: 57; Rv 14: 4.

2. fig.—**a.** giving the more immediate circumstances or the presupposition (X., Cyr. 6, 1, 7) ὅπου οὐκ ἔνι Ἕλλην καὶ Ἰουδαῖος *where* (i.e., under the presupposition given by the idea of the 'new man') *there is no* (longer) *Gentile and Jew* Col 3: 11. Or ὅπου introduces a subordinate clause that indicates the circumstances which have as their result what is said in the main clause following it (cf. Pr 26: 20; Ep. Arist. 149): ὅπ. διαθήκη, θάνατον ἀνάγκη φέρεσθαι τοῦ διαθεμένου *where there is a will, the death of the one who made it must be established* Hb 9: 16. ὅπ. ἄφεσις τούτων, οὐκέτι κτλ. 10: 18. The main clause can use ἐκεῖ to refer back to the ὅπ. of the subord. clause *where . . . , there* Js 3: 16.—ὅπου ἄγγελοι οὐ φέρουσιν κρίσιν *where* (i.e. in a situation in which) *angels pronounce no judgment* 2 Pt 2: 11.

b. causal *in so far as, since* (Hdt. 1, 68 al.; Thu. 8, 96, 2; Charito 5, 6, 10; 4 Macc 2: 14; somet. also in the combination ὅπου γε as Dionys. Hal., Comp. Verb. 4; Jos., C. Ap. 2, 154) 1 Cor 3: 3; 1 Cl 43: 1; B 16: 6. M-M.

ὀπτάνομαι (a new present formed fr. the aor. pass. ὤφθην 'I let myself be seen', 'I appeared' [cf. Bl-D. §101 p. 47 under ὁράω; Mlt.-H. 214; 382]. This form is found UPZ 62, 32 [161/0 bc]; PTebt. 24, 5 [117 bc]; PGM 4, 3033; Herm Wr. 3, 2; 3 Km 8: 8; Tob 12: 19 BA.—St BPsaltes, Gramm. der Byz. Chroniken '13, 242) *appear* τινί *to someone* (Bl-D. §191, 1; 313; Rob. 820) of the risen Christ Ac 1: 3.—HJCadbury, JBL 44, '25, 218f. M-M.*

ὀπτασία, ας, ἡ (Anth. Pal. 6, 210, 6; LXX; Hesychius; Leontios 8 p. 16, 12=vision, phantom [s. also the word-list on p. 182a])—1. *a vision,* of that which the Deity permits a human being to see, either of his own Divine Being, or of someth. else usu. hidden fr. men (Theod. Da 9: 23; 10: 1, 7f; Psellus p. 132, 19 of a supernatural phenomenon) ὀπτασίαι (w. ἀποκαλύψεις) κυρίου *visions of the Lord* 2 Cor 12: 1 (ELombard, Les extases et les souffrances de l'apôtre Paul. Essai d'une interprétation de II Cor 12: 1–10: RThPh 36, '03, 450–500). οὐράνιος ὀπ. Ac 26: 19. ὀπτασίαν ὁρᾶν *see a vision* (Pel.-Leg. 18, 17) Lk 1: 22. W. the gen. of what is seen: ὀπ. ἀγγέλων ὁρᾶν *see a vision of angels* 24: 23. ἡ φανερωθεῖσα ὀπ. *the vision that appeared* MPol 12: 3.

2. of the state of being in which a pers. finds himself when he has a vision ἐν ὀπτασίᾳ *in a trance* MPol 5: 2.*

ὀπτάω (Hom. +; PSI 402, 5 [III bc]; PLond. 131, 115; LXX; Jos., Ant. 1, 197; 3, 255) *bake* (so Hdt. 8, 137; X., An. 5, 4, 29 ἄρτους ὀπτῶντες) MPol 15: 2.*

ὀπτός, ή, όν (Hom. +; pap.; Ex 12: 8, 9; Jos., Ant. 3, 255) *roasted, baked, broiled* ἰχθὺς ὀπ. *broiled fish* (Hippocr., Aff. 52 vol. VI p. 264 L. ἰχθύες ὀπτοί; Plut., Mor. 353D; Zen.-P. 59066, 13; 16 [III bc]; PGiess. 93, 6 [II ad]) Lk 24: 42.—S. the lit. on μελίσσιος. M-M.*

ὀπώρα, ας, ἡ properly *the time* beginning w. the rising of the star Sirius (in July), corresp. to late summer and early fall, when fruit ripens (so Hom. +); then the *fruit* itself (so trag., X., Pla. +; POxy. 298, 38 [I ad]; PGM 5, 231; Jer 31: 32; 47: 10, 12; Philo, Agr. 15; Jos., Bell. 3, 49. Loanw. in rabb.) ἡ ὀπ. σου τῆς ἐπιθυμίας τῆς ψυχῆς *the fruit for which your soul longed* Rv 18: 14. M-M. B. 375.*

ὅπως (Hom. +; inscr., pap., LXX, En., Ep. Arist., Joseph., Test. 12 Patr.).

1. as an adv. *how, in what way* (Bl-D. §300, 1; Rob. 985) w. the aor. ind. (Jos., Bell. 1, 6; 17) ὅπως τε παρέδωκαν αὐτὸν οἱ ἀρχιερεῖς Lk 24: 20; w. the pres. ind. (Pherecrates Com. [V bc], fgm. 45 K.) ὅπως κολάζονται 2 Cl 17: 7. But here the mng. of ὅπως prob. shows a development analogous to that of πῶς in colloq. usage, which comes to resemble ὡς (so Lk 24: 20 D)=ὅτι=*that* (X., Hier. 9, 1; Diod. S. 11, 46, 3; Lucian, Dial. Deor. 6, 2; BGU 846, 16 [II ad] γνοῦναι, ὅπως ὀφείλω='to know that I owe'; Dssm., LO 155, 26 [LAE 179, 28]; Bl-D. §396; cf. Rob. 1045).

2. as a conjunction, w. the subjunctive, predom. the aor. (the fut. ind. [as early as Homer and oft. in class. times: Andocides 1, 43; Demosth. 19, 316; Herodas 7, 90; Meisterhans³-Schw. 255, 32; Nicol. Dam.: 90 fgm. 16 p. 398, 5 Jac.; Hero Alex. I 368, 23 ὅπ. κινήσει; Jos., Ant. 11, 101] is given in several places as v.l. [e.g. Mt 26: 59], but prob. should be changed everywhere to the aor. subj.).

a. to indicate purpose (*in order*) *that,* neg. ὅπ. μή *in order that . . . not* (Bl-D. §369; Rob. 985–7).

α. without ἄν (this is the rule) after a pres. Mt 5: 45 (imper.); 6: 2, 5; Hb 9: 15; 1 Pt 2: 9; 2 Cl 9: 6. After a perf. Ac 9: 17; Hb 2: 9; Lk 16: 26 (w. μή). After the impf. Ac 9: 24. After the aor. vss. 2, 12; 20: 16 (w. μή); 25: 26; Ro 9:

17a, b (Ex 9: 16); 1 Cor 1: 29 (w. μή); Gal 1: 4; 1 Cl 10: 2; 35: 4; after the aor. imper. Mt 2: 8; 5: 16; 6: 4, 18 (w. μή); Ac 23: 15, 23; 2 Cor 8: 11 (here γένηται or ᾖ is to be supplied as the predicate of the ὅπως-clause). After the plpf. J 11: 57 (ὅπως is found only here in J, prob. for variety's sake, since ἵνα is used a few words before). After the fut. Mt 23: 35. In accord w. God's purpose as revealed in Scripture, an event can be presented w. the formula (this or that has happened) ὅπ. πληρωθῇ τὸ ῥηθὲν διὰ τ. προφητῶν (and sim. exprs.) Mt 2: 23; 8: 17; 12: 17 t.r.; 13: 35.—Alternating w. ἵνα (s. also J 11: 57 above) 2 Cor 8: 14; Lk 16: 27f (the ἵνα-clause gives the content of the plea; the ὅπως-clause gives the purpose of the gift requested); 2 Th 1: 11f (the ἵνα-clause gives the content, the ὅπως-clause the purpose of the prayer).

β. with ἄν and the aor. subj. (Bl-D. §369, 5; Rdm.² 194; Rob. 986; EHermann, Die Nebensätze in d. griech. Dialekten '12, 276f; JKnuenz, De enuntiatis Graecorum finalibus '13, 13ff; 26ff; Meisterhans³-Schw. 254; Mayser II 1 p. 254f.—X., Cyr. 8, 3, 6 ἐπιμεληθῆναι ὅπως ἂν οὕτω γένηται; Pla., Gorg. 523D; PSI 435, 19 [258 BC]; 438, 19; PMagd. 23, 7; LXX) Mt 6: 5 v.l.; Lk 2: 35; Ac 3: 20; 15: 17 (Am 9: 12 v.l.); Ro 3: 4 (Ps 50: 6).

b. more and more replacing the inf. after verbs of asking *that* (Bl-D. §392, 1) αἰτέομαι (Jos., Ant. 19, 288) Ac 25: 3. δέομαι (Ps.-Aeschines, Ep. 3, 1; Jos., Ant. 7, 191; 9, 9) Mt 9: 38; Lk 10: 2; Ac 8: 24 (w. μή). ἐρωτάω (PTebt. 409, 4ff [5 AD]) Lk 7: 3; 11: 37; Ac 23: 20. παρακαλέω (Jos., Ant. 8, 143) Mt 8: 34 (v.l. ἵνα). προσεύχομαι (cf. PGM 3, 107; Jon 1: 6; Jos., Ant. 11, 17) Ac 8: 15; Js 5: 16. So perh. also Phlm 6, where ὅπ. could be thought of as depending on προσεύχομαι derived in sense fr. vs. 4, unless ὅπως here=ὥστε (Archimed. I p. 16, 18 Heiberg ὅπως γένηται τὸ ἐπίταγμα al.).—Likew. after verbs of deciding (LXX) συμβούλιον λαμβάνειν ὅπ. *resolve to* Mt 12: 14; 22: 15 (D πῶς), where many scholars prefer the transl. *consult with a view to.* Also συμβούλιον διδόναι ὅπ. Mk 3: 6. M-M.

ὅραμα, ατος, τό (X.+; inscr., pap., LXX) in our lit. of supernatural visions, whether the pers. who has the vision be asleep or awake.

1. *vision* (acc. to Artem. 1, 2 p. 5, 19 ὅραμα is someth. that can actually be seen, in contrast to 5, 17 φάντασμα= a figment of the imagination; PGdspd. 3, 5 [III BC]; UPZ 78, 37 [159 BC] τὸ ὅραμα τοῦτο ὃ τεθέαμαι; Ex 3: 3; Dt 4: 34; Da 7: 1; En. 99, 8; Test. Levi 8: 1 εἶδον ὅραμα; 9: 2) of the Transfiguration Mt 17: 9. Of the appearing of God in the burning bush Ac 7: 31. Cf. Ac 10: 17, 19; 11: 5; 12: 9; 16: 9f (Appian, Bell. Civ. 4, 134 §565 Brutus, when he was about to cross over ἐκ τῆς Ἀσίας ἐς τὴν Εὐρώπην ... νυκτός has a vision. A φάσμα—not a human being, not a god, but a δαίμων κακός—stands at his side and speaks to him); Hv 4, 2, 2. ἐπιδεικνύναι τινὶ ὅραμα *show someone a vision* 3, 2, 3. δεικνύναι τινὶ ὁράματα (w. ἀποκαλύψεις) 4, 1, 3. ἀποκαλύπτειν τὰ ὁράματα *reveal the visions* (it is not clear, even in the original, whether this is to be understood of the visions themselves or of the interpretation of their mng.) 3, 4, 3.

2. the act by which the recipient of the vision is granted a vision, or the state of being in which he receives his vision (Dit., Syll.³ 1128 καθ' ὅραμα; LXX) of the Lord: εἰπεῖν ἐν νυκτὶ δι' ὁράματος *say at night in a vision* Ac 18: 9. ἐν ὁράματι (Gen 15: 1; 46: 2 εἶπεν ὁ θεὸς ἐν ὁρ. τῆς νυκτός; Da 7: 13) εἶδεν ἐν ὁρ. ἄγγελον (cf. Test. Jud. 3: 10) Ac 10: 3. Cf. 9: 10, 12 t.r. βλέπειν ἐν ὁρ. τῆς νυκτός Hv 3, 10, 6; apocr. gosp.-fgm. in POxy. 1224 fgm. 2 recto II, 3 (=Kl. T. 8³, p. 26, 10) Ἰησ. ἐν ὁράματι λέγει. Cf. ὅρασις 3, ὄναρ and πνεῦμα 6f. M-M.*

ὅρασις, εως, ἡ (Aristot.+; inscr., pap., LXX, En.; Ep. Arist. 142; Philo, Test. 12 Patr.).

1. *organ of sight, eye* (mostly pl. 'eyes' Diod. S. 2, 6, 10; Plut., Mor. 88D; PGM 13, 582. But also the sing. ὅρασις Diod. S. 3, 37, 9; 5, 43, 1; Proclus on Pla., Cratyl. p. 7, 25 Pasqu.), and hence *sight, appearance, face* (Ramsay, Phrygia I 2 653 no. 564 εἰς ὅρασιν καὶ εἰς ὅλον τὸ σῶμα; PGM 4, 308; 5, 147; Sir 11: 2; 25: 17; 3 Macc 5: 33) fig., of mental and spiritual perception ἀχλύος γέμοντες ἐν τῇ ὁράσει *with the eyes full of mistiness* 2 Cl 1: 6.

2. *that which is seen*—a. *appearance* (Philo Mech. 51, 10; 62, 23; Ezk 1: 5; 1 Km 16: 12) ὅμοιος ὁράσει λίθῳ ἰάσπιδι *like jasper in appearance* Rv 4: 3a; cf. b.

b. *spectacle* ἔσονται εἰς ὁρ. πάσῃ σαρκί *they will be a spectacle for all flesh* (Is 66: 24) 2 Cl 7: 6; 17: 5.

3. of supernatural vision (in this case the distinction made betw. ὅραμα 1 and 2 cannot be carried through w. certainty, so that mng. 1 will certainly predominate.— Critodemus, an astrologer of Hellenistic times, wrote a book entitled Ὅρασις in the form of a vision [Vett. Val. 150, 11; 329, 18f]; Herm. Wr. 1, 30 ἀληθινὴ ὁρ.; Tob 12: 19; Zech 10: 2; Pel.-Leg. 18, 20) *vision* (cf. Da 7: 1 Theod.) ἰδεῖν τι ἐν τῇ ὁρ. Rv 9: 17. ὅρασιν ἰδεῖν or ὁρᾶν Ac 2: 17 (Jo 3: 1); Hv 2, 4, 2. Of the visions of Hermas Hv 2, 1, 1; 3, 10, 3ff; 3, 11, 2; 4; 3, 12, 1; 3, 13, 1; 4, 1, 1. Titles Hv 2; 3; 4. M-M.*

ὁρατός, ή, όν (Hippocr., Pla.+; PGrenf. 1 no. 47, 14; LXX) verbal adj. of ὁράω *visible* (w. ἀόρατος; cf. Philo, Op. M. 12, Migr. Abr. 183 ἀόρατος ὡς ἂν ὁρ. ὤν; Test. Reub. 6: 12) σῶμα Dg 6: 4. ἄρχοντες ISm 6: 1. Of Christ ὁ ἀόρατος, ὁ δι' ἡμᾶς ὁρ. IPol 3: 2. τὰ ὁρατά (Ps.-Clem., Hom. 2, 7): τὰ ὁρ. καὶ τὰ ἀόρατα *things visible and invisible* Col 1: 16; cf. ITr 5: 2; IRo 5: 3. M-M.*

ὁράω (Hom.+; inscr., pap., LXX, En., Ep. Arist., Philo, Joseph., Test. 12 Patr.) impf. 3 pl. ἑώρων (J 6: 2; but ἐθεώρουν v.l.); pf. ἑώρακα and ἑόρακα (s. Bl-D. §68; W-S. §12, 2), 3 pl. ἑώρακαν beside ἑωράκασιν (W-S. §13, 15; Mlt.-H. 221); plpf. ἑωράκειν (Hv 2, 1, 3); fut. ὄψομαι, 2 sing. ὄψῃ (W-S. §13, 18); 1 aor. pass. ὤφθην; 1 fut. pass. ὀφθήσομαι; pf. pass. 3 sing. ὦπται (Ex 4: 1, 5; Hv 3, 1, 2). In Byz. times there was an aor. mid. ὠψάμην (Lob. on Phryn. p. 734). There is a subjunctive form corresponding to this in one place in the NT, though not without a v.l.; it is ὄψησθε (v.l. ὄψεσθε) Lk 13: 28. The functions of the aor. active are taken over by εἶδον and the forms belonging to it (s. εἶδον). βλέπω is used for the pres. and impf., for the most part. On the use of ὁράω and βλέπω s. Reinhold p. 95ff.

1. trans.—a. *see, catch sight of, notice* of sense perception—α. w. acc. of the pers. Mt 28: 7, 10; Mk 16: 7; Lk 16: 23; J 8: 57; 9: 37; 14: 9; 16: 16f, 19, 22; 20: 18, 25, 29; 1 J 4: 20a; Rv 1: 7. ὃν οὐδεὶς ἑώρακεν πώποτε (s. PGM 5, 101f of Osiris ὃν οὐδεὶς εἶδε πώποτε) J 1: 18; cf. 6: 46a, b; 1 J 4: 20b (on seeing God and its impossibility for mortal man s. WGrafBaudissin, 'Gott schauen' in d. atl. Rel.: ARW 18, '15, 173-239; RBultmann, ZNW 29, '30, 169-92; EFascher: Marb. Theol. Studien '31, 1, 41-77).—Also of the perception of personal beings that become visible in a supernatural manner (UPZ 78, 8 [159 BC] of a dream in the Serapeum ὁρῶ τ. διδύμας; 69, 6), of the vision of Christ that Paul had 1 Cor 9: 1. The acc. is to be supplied fr. the context Hb 11: 27; 1 Pt 1: 8. W. acc. of the ptc. (Bl-D. §416, 1; Rob. 1123.—UPZ 69, 6 [152 BC] ὁρῶ ἐν τῷ ὕπνῳ τὸν Μενέδημον ἀντικείμενον ἡμῖν; Ex 2: 11, 13; Philo, Leg. All. 3, 38) ὄψονται τὸν υἱὸν τοῦ ἀνθρώπου ἐρχόμενον Mt 24: 30; Mk 13: 26; Lk 21: 27. ὄψεσθε τὸν υἱὸν τοῦ ἀνθρώπου καθήμενον Mk 14: 62

(NPerrin, The End-product of the Christian Pesher Trad., NTS 12, '66, 150-5).—*Visit* (1 Km 20: 29) ὄψομαι ὑμᾶς Hb 13: 23.

β. w. acc. of the thing ὀπτασίαν ὁρ. *see a vision* (cf. ὀπτασία 1.—Dit., Syll.³ 1169, 6; UPZ 68, 6 [152 bc] ἐνύπνια ὁρῶ πονηρά) Lk 1: 22; 24: 23. ὁράσεις Ac 2: 17 (Jo 3: 1). ταῦτα Lk 23: 49. πάντα J 4: 45. σημεῖα 6: 2 (θεωρέω v.l.). Cf. also Hv 3, 2, 4. W. acc. of the ptc. (Dit., Syll.³ 685, 75; 1169, 15; Ex 33: 10) τὸν οὐρανὸν ἀνεῳγότα J 1: 51.—Hv 3, 8, 9. W. attraction of the relative ὧν = τούτων ἅ Lk 9: 36; Ac 22: 15. The attraction is hard to explain in μάρτυρα ὧν τε εἶδές με ὧν τε ὀφθήσομαί σοι a *witness to the things in which you saw me and to those in which I shall appear to you* Ac 26: 16b (the text is prob. not in order; s. MDibelius, Aufs. z. AG ed. HGreeven '51, 83). Of God τ. πάντα ὁρᾷ PK 2 p. 13, 24.—ὁρ. is a favorite word w. J, when he speaks of that which the preëxistent Son saw when he was with the Father (JSchneider, D. Christusschau des Joh.-ev. '35; differently LBrun, D. Gottesschau des joh. Christus: Symb. Osl. 5, '27, 1–22) ὃ ἑώρακεν J 3: 32; cf. vs. 11. ἃ ἑώρακα παρὰ τῷ πατρί 8: 38 (since this deals w. witness and speaking, the 'perceiving' could be thought of as 'hearing'. Cf. Diod. S. 13, 28, 5 ὁρᾷς; = do you hear [the outcry]?; schol. on Nicander, Ther. 165 ὁρῶ οἷα λέγεις; Polyaenus 7, 14, 2; Ex 20: 18 λαὸς ἑώρα τὴν φωνήν, 22; Dt 4: 9; also Philo, Migr. Abr. 47; Sib. Or. 8, 125 βρυγμὸν ὁρ.). Of that which the apostolic witnesses saw of Christ 1 J 1: 1–3. Abs. ὁ ἑωρακὼς *the eye-witness* J 19: 35.

γ. ὁρ. τὸ πρόσωπόν τινος as a periphrasis for *see someone* (cf. Gen 43: 3, 5; 46: 30) Ac 20: 25; Col 2: 1. ὁρ. τὸ πρόσωπον τοῦ θεοῦ (=רָאָה אֶת־פְּנֵי) Rv 22: 4 (πρόσωπον 1b). ὁρ. τὴν δόξαν τοῦ θεοῦ (=רָאָה אֶת־כְּבוֹד יי) *see the majesty of God* (Is 66: 18f) J 11: 40. Simply ὁρ. τὸν θεόν *see God* Mt 5: 8. ὀψόμεθα αὐτὸν καθώς ἐστιν 1 J 3: 2 (Maximus Tyr. 11, 11a τὸ μὲν ὅλον ὄψει τ. θεὸν τότε, ἐπειδὰν πρὸς αὐτὸν καλῇ). ὁρ. τὸν κύριον Hb 12: 14.—On ἃ ἑόρακεν ἐμβατεύων Col 2: 18 cf. ἐμβατεύω.

δ. pass. *become visible, appear* (Ael. Aristid. 51, 22 K. = 27 p. 539 D.: ὤφθη τοιάδε; LXX) abs. Rv 11: 19; 12: 1, 3. τινί *to someone* Ac 2: 3. ὅραμα διὰ νυκτὸς τ. Παύλῳ ὤφθη *a vision appeared to Paul at night* 16: 9 (Jos., Ant. 2, 70 τὰ διὰ νυκτὸς ὀφθέντα)—Of persons who appear in a natural way (Appian, Syr. 21 §96 ὤφθησαν = they made an appearance, Bell. Civ. 2, 130 §542; UPZ 145, 5 [164 bc]; 3 Km 3: 16 ὤφθησαν δύο γυναῖκες τῷ βασιλεῖ) (Μωϋσῆς) ὤφθη αὐτοῖς Ac 7: 26. Mostly of beings that make their appearance in a supernatural manner, almost always w. dat. of the pers. to whom they appear: God (Gen 12: 7; 17: 1; PGM 4, 3090 ἕως ὁ θεός σου ὀφθῇ) Ac 7: 2. Angels (Ex 3: 2; Judg 6: 12) Lk 1: 11; 22: 43 (LBrun, ZNW 32, '33, 265–76); Ac 7: 30, 35. Moses and Elijah Mt 17: 3; Mk 9: 4; Lk 9: 31 (without the dat. in this pass.: ὀφθέντες ἐν δόξῃ). The risen Christ Lk 24: 34; Ac 9: 17; 13: 31; 26: 16a; 1 Cor 15: 5–8 (cf. POxy. I, 3; JoachJeremias, Unknown Sayings of Jesus, tr. Fuller '57, 69–71); 1 Ti 3: 16 (ὤφθη ἀγγέλοις—the triumphant Christ appears to the angelic powers); Hb 9: 28 (Christ at his Second Coming).—οὐκ ἔτι σοι ὀφθήσεται *it will be seen by you no longer* (of evil desire) Hm 12, 2, 4 (Antig. Car. 11 ὁρᾶται = there is; Aristot. in Apollon. Paradox. 39 ὄφις ὤφθη = there was a snake).

b. *experience, witness* (cf. POxy. 120, 4 τινὰ ὁρῶντα ἑαυτὸν ἐν δυστυχίᾳ) Lk 17: 22 (s. εἶδον 5). ζωήν J 3: 36 (cf. Lycophron, Al. 1019 βίον; Ps 88: 49 θάνατον). μεῖζον τούτων 1: 50. ὄψεται πᾶσα σὰρξ τὸ σωτήριον τοῦ θεοῦ Lk 3: 6 (Is 40: 5).

c. fig. of mental and spiritual perception (Polystrat. p. 5

ὁρ. τῷ λογισμῷ; Simplicius In Epict. p. 110, 47 Düb. τὸ ἀληθές).

a. *notice, recognize, understand* w. the acc. of the ptc. (Diod. S. 2, 16, 5; 4, 40, 2; Appian, Syr. 14 §55, Bell. Civ. 2, 14 §50; PHib. 44, 4 [253 bc] ὁρῶντες δέ σε καταραθυμοῦντα; 4 Macc 4: 24; 9: 30; Jos., Vi. 373 ὄντα με ὁρ.) εἰς χολὴν πικρίας . . . ὁρῶ σε ὄντα *I perceive that you have fallen into the gall of bitterness* (i.e. *bitter jealousy*) Ac 8: 23. οὔπω ὁρῶμεν αὐτῷ τὰ πάντα ὑποτεταγμένα *we do not yet see everything subjected to him* Hb 2: 8; Dg 1. W. ὅτι foll. (M. Ant. 9, 27, 2; Philo, Migr. Abr. 46) Js 2: 24; 1 Cl 12: 8; 23: 4; 44: 6. W. indir. quest. foll. 1 Cl 16: 17; 41: 4; 50: 1; B 15: 8; Dg 7: 8. W. direct discourse foll. ὁρᾶτε 1 Cl 4: 7.

β. (mentally) *look at or upon* ὄψονται οἷς οὐκ ἀνηγγέλη περὶ αὐτοῦ *they who have never been told of him* (=Christ) *shall look upon him* Ro 15: 21 (Is 52: 15).—*Consider* ὅρα τοῦ ἀγγέλου τῆς πονηρίας τὰ ἔργα Hm 6, 2, 4.—*Become conscious of* ὁ κακοποιῶν οὐχ ἑώρακεν τ. θεόν 3 J 11. Cf. 1 J 3: 6.

2. intr.—a. *look* εἴς τινα *on* or *at someone* (Il. 24, 633; Od. 20, 373) J 19: 37 (s. ἐκκεντέω).

b. *see to, take care*—a. σὺ ὄψῃ *see to that yourself!* *that is your affair!* Mt 27: 4; cf. vs. 24; Ac 18: 15 (on this Latinism = videris s. DCHesseling in Bl-D. §362 w. app.; Rob. 109f). Imper. followed by imperatival fut. ὅρα ποιήσεις πάντα *see to it that you do everything* Hb 8: 5 (Ex 25: 40; cf. 4: 21). Foll. by indir. quest. (Ael. Aristid. 45 p. 121 D.: ὅρα τί ποιεῖς) ὅρα τί μέλλεις ποιεῖν take care what you are doing Ac 22: 26 D. t.r.

β. *be on one's guard* intr. by μή and the aor. subj. (Diod. S. 27, 17, 3 ὁρᾶτε μήποτε ποιήσωμεν; Epict., Ench. 19, 2; Lucian, Dial. Deor. 8, 2; BGU 37, 5 [50 ad]; POxy. 532, 15 ὅρα μὴ ἄλλως πράξῃς; 531, 9 ὅρα μηδενὶ ἀνθρώπων προσκρούσῃς.—Bl-D. §364, 3) Mt 8: 4; 18: 10; Mk 1: 44; 1 Th 5: 15; 1 Cl 21: 1; D 6: 1.—W. μή and imper. (Bl-D. §461, 1; Rob. 996) Mt 9: 30; 24: 6.—Elliptically (Bl-D. §480, 5; Rob. 949) ὅρα μή (sc. ποιήσῃς) *take care! don't do that!* Rv 19: 10; 22: 9.—Used w. ἀπό τινος *look out for someth.* (Bl-D. §149 w. app.; Rob. 472) ὁρᾶτε καὶ προσέχετε ἀπὸ τῆς ζύμης τῶν Φαρισαίων *look out* (*for*) *and be on your guard against the yeast of the Pharisees* Mt 16: 6. ὁρᾶτε, βλέπετε ἀπὸ τῆς ζύμης τῶν Φαρ. Mk 8: 15. ὁρᾶτε καὶ φυλάσσεσθε ἀπὸ πάσης πλεονεξίας Lk 12: 15.—WMichaelis, TW V 315–81: ὁράω and related words. M-M. B. 1042.

ὄργανον, ου, τό (Soph., Pla.+; pap., LXX; Ep. Arist. 101; Philo; Jos., Bell. 2, 230) *tool* τὰ ὀρ. τοῦ διαβόλου *the tools of the devil* 2 Cl 18: 2. Fig. of the animals in the arena as the tools through which the martyr becomes a perfect sacrifice to God IRo 4: 2.—Also of the material of which someth. is made (e.g. wood for a building: Pla., Leg. 3 p. 678d; Ps.-Aristot., Mirabilia 108) τὰ πρὸς τὴν πυρὰν ἡρμοσμένα ὀρ. MPol 13: 3 (*wooden instruments* is also possible.—s. ἁρμόζω 2 and cf. for ἠρμ. ὀρ. 2 Km 6: 5, 14). B. 586. *

ὀργή, ῆς, ἡ (Hes.+) *anger, indignation, wrath* (so trag., Hdt.+; inscr., pap., LXX, En., Ep. Arist., Philo, Joseph., Test. 12 Patr.).

1. as a human emotion GP 12: 50 (s. φλέγω 2). W. πικρία and θυμός Eph 4: 31; cf. Col 3: 8 (on the relationship betw. ὀργή and θυμός, which are oft. combined in the LXX as well, s. Zeno in Diog. L. 7, 113; Chrysipp. [Stoic. III fgm. 395]; Philod., De Ira p. 91 W.). W. διαλογισμοί 1 Ti 2: 8. W. μερισμός IPhld 8: 1. ἡ ἀθέμιτος τοῦ ζήλους ὀρ. *the lawless anger caused by*

jealousy 1 Cl 63: 2. ἀπέχεσθαι πάσης ὀρ. *refrain from all anger* Pol 6: 1. μετ᾽ ὀργῆς *angrily* (Pla., Apol. 34c; Esth 8: 12x; 3 Macc 6: 23) Mk 3: 5; βραδὺς εἰς ὀρ. *slow to be angry* Js 1: 19 (Aristoxenus, fgm. 56 Socrates is called τραχὺς εἰς ὀργήν). ἐλέγχετε ἀλλήλους μὴ ἐν ὀρ. *correct one another, not in anger* D 15: 3 (ἐν ὀργῇ Is 58: 13; Da 3: 13 Theod.). Anger ἄφρονα ἀναιρεῖ 1 Cl 39: 7 (Job 5: 2); leads to murder D 3: 2. δικαιοσύνην θεοῦ οὐκ ἐργάζεται Js 1: 20; originates in θυμός and results in μῆνις Hm 5, 2, 4.—Pl. *outbursts of anger* (Pla., Euthyphro 7ʙ ἐχθρὰ καὶ ὀργαί, Rep. 6 p. 493ᴀ; Maximus Tyr. 27, 6b; 2 Macc 4: 25, 40; Jos., Vi. 266) 1 Cl 13: 1; IEph 10: 2 (Bl-D. §142; W-S. §27, 4d). JStelzenberger, D. Beziehgen der frühchristl. Sittenlehre zur Ethik der Stoa '33, 250ff.

2. of the wrath of God (Parmeniscus [III/II ʙᴄ]) in the schol. on Eur., Medea 264 Schw. τῆς θεᾶς ὀργή; Diod. S. 5, 55, 6 διὰ τὴν ὀργήν of Aphrodite; Philostrat., Vi. Apoll. 6, 29; Dit., Syll.³ 1237, 5 ἕξει ὀργὴν μεγάλην τοῦ μεγάλου Διός, Or. 383, 210 [I ʙᴄ]; LXX; En. 106, 15; Philo, Somn. 2, 179, Mos. 1, 6; Sib. Or. 4, 162; 5, 75f; Test. Reub. 4: 4. Oft. Jos., e.g. Ant. 3, 321; 11, 127.—Ep. Arist. 254 θεὸς χωρὶς ὀργῆς ἁπάσης) as the divine reaction toward evil; it is thought of not so much as an emotion as in terms of the outcome of an angry frame of mind (*judgment*), already well known to OT history, where it somet. runs its course in the present, but more oft. is to be expected in the future, as God's final reckoning w. evil (ὀρ. is a legitimate feeling on the part of a judge; cf. RHirzel, Themis '07, 416; Pohlenz [s. below] 15, 3; Synes. Ep. 2 p. 158ʙ).

a. of the past and pres.: of the judgment upon the desert generation ὤμοσα ἐν τῇ ὀργῇ μου (Ps 94: 11) Hb 3: 11; 4: 3. Of the Jews in the pres. ἔφθασεν ἐπ᾽ αὐτοὺς ἡ ὀρ. *the wrath* (ὀργή abs.= ὀρ. θεοῦ also Ro 12: 19—AvanVeldhuizen, 'Geeft den toorn plaats' [Ro 12: 19]: ThSt 25, '07, 44 to 46; 13: 4; 1 Th 1: 10. Likew. Jos., Ant. 11, 141) *has come upon them* 1 Th 2: 16 (on 1 Th 2: 13-16 s. BPearson, HTR 64, '71, 79-94; Test. Levi 6: 11). Of God's wrath against sin in the pres. ἀποκαλύπτεται ὀρ. θεοῦ ἐπὶ πᾶσαν ἀσέβειαν Ro 1: 18 (JYCampbell, ET 50, '39, 229-33; SSchultz, ThZ 14, '58, 161-73). Of God's wrath against evildoers as revealed in the judgments of earthly gov. authorities 13: 4f (here ὀρ. could also be *punishment*, as Demosth. 21, 43). *The wrath of God remains* like an incubus upon the one who does not believe in the Son J 3: 36 (for ἡ ὀρ. μένει cf. Wsd 18: 20). Of the Lord's wrath against renegade Christians Hv 3, 6, 1. The Lord can ἀποστρέψαι τὴν ὀρ. αὐτοῦ ἀπό τινος *turn away his wrath from someone* (ἀποστρέφω 1aβ) Hv 4, 2, 6.—Of the wrath of God's angel of repentance Hm 12, 4, 1.

b. of God's future judgment ἔσται ὀρ. τῷ λαῷ τούτῳ Lk 21: 23; ἡ μέλλουσα ὀρ. Mt 3: 7; Lk 3: 7; IEph 11: 1. ἡ ὀρ. ἡ ἐρχομένη 1 Th 1: 10; cf. Eph 5: 6; Col 3: 6. σωθησόμεθα ἀπὸ τῆς ὀρ. Ro 5: 9. οὐκ ἔθετο ἡμᾶς ὁ θεὸς εἰς ὀρ. *God has not destined us for wrathful judgment* 1 Th 5: 9. θησαυρίζειν ἑαυτῷ ὀργήν (s. θησαυρίζω 2b and Epist. Claud. p. 8 Lösch [= PLond. 1912] ταμιευόμενος ἐμαυτῷ ὀργήν) Ro 2: 5a. This stored-up wrath will break out ἐν ἡμέρᾳ ὀργῆς (s. ἡμέρα 3bβ) vs. 5b. Elsewhere, too, the portrayal of the wrath of God in Paul is predom. eschatological: ὀρ. καὶ θυμός (s. θυμός 2) Ro 2: 8 (cf. IQS 4, 12); cf. 1 Cl 50: 4; δότε τόπον τῇ ὀρ. Ro 12: 19 (s. 2a above; τόπος 2c). Cf. 9: 22a. ἐπιφέρειν τὴν ὀργήν *inflict punishment* 3: 5 (s. 13: 4f under a above). Men are τέκνα φύσει ὀργῆς *by nature children of wrath*, i.e. subject to divine wrath Eph 2: 3 (JMehlman, Natura Filii Irae etc. '57). Cf. σκεύη ὀργῆς κατηρτισμένα εἰς ἀπώλειαν *objects of wrath prepared for destruction* Ro 9: 22b. Of the

law: ὀργὴν κατεργάζεται *it brings* (only) *wrath* 4: 15.— In Rv the concept is also thought of in eschatological terms 6: 16; 11: 18. ἡ ἡμέρα ἡ μεγάλη τῆς ὀρ. αὐτῶν *the great day of their* (God's and the Lamb's) *wrath* (s. above) 6: 17. On τὸ ποτήριον τῆς ὀρ. αὐτοῦ *the cup of his wrath* 14: 10 and οἶνος τοῦ θυμοῦ τῆς ὀρ. τοῦ θεοῦ 16: 19; 19: 15, cf. θυμός 1 and 2 (ATHanson, The Wrath of the Lamb, '57, 159-80).—ARitschl, Rechtfertigung u. Versöhnung II⁴ '00, 119-56; MPohlenz, Vom Zorne Gottes '09; GPWetter, D. Vergeltungsgedanke bei Pls '12; GBornkamm, D. Offenbarung des Zornes Gottes (Ro 1-3): ZNW 34, '35, 239-62; ASchlatter, Gottes Gerechtigkeit '35, 48ff; GHCMacGregor, NTS 7, '61, 101-9; JHempel, Gottes Selbstbeherrschung, H-WHertzberg Festschr., '65, 56-66; GStählin et al., TW V 382-448: ὀργή and related words. Cf. also κρίσις, end: Braun 41ff and Filson. M-M. B. 1134.*

ὀργίζω (the act. in Aristoph., X., Pla.+; Job 12: 6 v.l.; Pr 16: 30 v.l.) in our lit. only pass. (Soph., Thu.+; Dit., Syll.³ 1170, 5; UPZ 144, 3 [II ʙᴄ]; LXX, En., Philo, Joseph., Test. 12 Patr.) **ὀργίζομαι** 1 aor. ὠργίσθην, ptc. ὀργισθείς *be angry* foll. by dat. of the pers. (Diod. S. 10, 7, 4; Ael. Aristid. 38 p. 721 D.; Ps 84: 6; Is 12: 1; En. 18, 16; Jos., Ant. 4, 130; 16, 263) Mt 5: 22. Foll. by dat. of the pers. and ὅτι *be angry at someone because* Hv 1, 1, 6 (for ὅτι cf. Arrian, Anab. 4, 23, 5; 3 Km 11: 9). ὀρ. τινὶ ἕνεκά τινος *at someone because of someth.* (Jos., Ant. 12, 221) v 1, 3, 1a. διά τι ibid. b (cf. X., An. 1, 2, 26). ἐπί τινι *be angry at* or *with someone* (Andoc. 5, 10; Lysias 28, 2; Num 31: 14; Test. Sim. 2: 11) Rv 12: 17 (Bl-D. §196; cf. Rob. 605). Abs. (X., Hell. 4, 8, 30; Aelian, V.H. 12, 54; Jos., Ant. 6, 222) Mt 18: 34; 22: 7; Mk 1: 41 v.l. (for σπλαγχνισθείς).—On the v.l. ὀργισθείς s. CHTurner, JTS 28, '27, 145-58) Lk 14: 21; 15: 28; Rv 11: 18 (cf. Ps 98: 1). ὀργίζεσθε καὶ μὴ ἁμαρτάνετε (Ps 4: 5) *be angry, but do not sin* Eph 4: 26. M-M.*

ὀργίλος, η, ον (Hippocr.; Pla., Rep. 2 p. 405ᴄ; 411ʙ; X., De Re Equ. 9, 7; Aristot., Eth. Nic. 2, 7, 10; 4, 11 οἱ ὀργίλοι ταχέως ὀργίζονται καὶ οἷς οὐ δεῖ καὶ ἐφ᾽ οἷς οὐ δεῖ καὶ μᾶλλον ἢ δεῖ; Herodian 4, 9, 3; Ps 17: 49; Pr 21: 19; 22: 24; 29: 22; Jos., Ant. 19, 19) *inclined to anger, quick-tempered* (w. αὐθάδης et al.) Tit 1: 7. μὴ γίνου ὀρ. D 3: 2. M-M.*

ὀργίλως adv. (Demosth. 21, 215 al.; 4 Macc 8: 9) *angrily* Hm 12, 4, 1.*

ὀργυιά (or ὄργυια, but in the pl. prob. ὀργυιαί; s. Kühner-Bl. I 392f; W-S. §6, 7a; Mlt.-H. 58.—Hom., Hdt.+; inscr.; POxy. 669, 39; Jos., Bell. 1, 411), ἆς, ἡ *fathom* (properly the distance measured by a man's arms stretched out horizontally, reckoned at six feet=1.85 meters) as a nautical t.t., used to measure the depth of water (Diod. S. 3, 40, 3) Ac 27: 28a, b. M-M.*

ὀρέγω (the act. Hom.+ *reach, stretch out*) in our lit. only mid. **ὀρέγομαι** (Hom.+, lit. *stretch oneself, reach out one's hand*), and fig. *aspire to, strive for, desire* w. gen. of the thing (Thu. 2, 65, 10; X., Mem. 1, 2, 15; Pla., Rep. 6 p. 485ᴅ, Leg. 7 p. 807ᴄ; Polyb. 5, 104, 7; Diod. S. 4, 40, 5 δόξης ὀρεγόμενος= eager for glory; Plut., Phoc. 17, 1, Sol. 29, 4; Lucian, Bis Accus. 29; Epict. 2, 1, 10; 3, 26, 13. Oft. Philo; Jos., Vi. 70.—Bl-D. §171, 1; Rob. 508) ἐπισκοπῆς ὀρ. *aspire to the office of bishop* 1 Ti 3: 1 (on the combination of ὀρέγομαι and ἐπιθυμέω cf. Ep. Arist. 211). κρείττονος *long for a better* (home) Hb 11: 16. ἧ φιλαργυρίας ἧς τινες ὀρεγόμενοι 1 Ti 6: 10 is a condensed expr.; it is the ἀργύριον rather than the φιλαργυρία that is desired. M-M.*

ὀρεινός, ή, όν hilly, mountainous (so Hdt.+; inscr., pap., LXX, Ep. Arist., Philo, Joseph.) ἡ ὀρεινή (sc. χώρα, which is added in Hdt. 1, 110; X., Cyr. 1, 3, 3; Dit., Syll.³ 633, 78.—ἡ ὀρεινή alone e.g. in Aristot., H.A. 5, 28, 4 and oft. in LXX; Philo, Aet. M. 63) hill country, mountainous region πορεύεσθαι εἰς τὴν ὀρ. go into the hill country Lk 1: 39 (cf. Jos., Bell. 4, 451). ἐν ὅλῃ τῇ ὀρ. τῆς Ἰουδαίας in all the hill country of Judaea vs. 65 (Jos., Ant. 5, 128 ὀρ. τῆς Χαναναίας; 12, 7 ἀπὸ τ. ὀρεινῆς Ἰουδαίας). M-M.*

ὄρεξις, εως, ἡ longing, desire (Pla.+; LXX); in its only occurrence in our lit. it is used in an unfavorable sense (Democr., fgm. 219; Epicurus p. 161, 26 Us.; Sir 23: 6; Lucian, Tyr. 4 τὰς τῶν ἡδονῶν ὀρέξεις χαλιναγωγεῖν; Herodian 3, 13, 6; Herm. Wr. 12, 4; Philo.—Of sexual desire Jos., Ant. 7, 169; Ps.-Clem., Hom. 3, 68) οἱ ἄρσενες . . . ἐξεκαύθησαν ἐν τῇ ὀρ. αὐτῶν εἰς ἀλλήλους the men . . . were inflamed with (their) desire for each other Ro 1: 27. M-M.*

ὀρθοποδέω (ὀρθόπους Soph.+; cf. Nicander, Alexiph. 419 [II BC] ὀρθόποδες βαίνοντες.—ὀρθοποδία='progress': Papiri della Univers. di Milano, ed. AVogliano no. 24, 8 [117 AD]) walk straight, upright, fig. act rightly, be straightforward ὀρθοποδεῖν πρὸς τὴν ἀλήθειαν τοῦ εὐαγγελίου be straightforward about the truth of the gospel Gal 2: 14 (cf. Dit., Or. I, 48, 9 μὴ ὀρθῶς ἀναστρεφομένους). But perh. progress, advance in the direction of the truth (CHRoberts, JTS 40, '39, 55f. Also JGWinter, HTR 34, '41, 161f, after an unpubl. pap. in the Michigan collection [no. 337—III AD] ὀρθοποδεῖ τὸ παιδίον. 'the child is getting on, growing up').—GDKilpatrick, NT Studien f. RBultmann '54, 269–74 ('they were not on the right road toward the truth of the gospel'; good survey). M-M.*

ὀρθός, ή, όν (Hom.+; inscr., pap., LXX, Ep. Arist., Philo, Joseph., Test. 12 Patr.) superl. ὀρθότατος (Epil Mosq 1).

1. lit.—a. straight up, upright (Hom.+; inscr., pap., LXX; Jos., Ant. 20, 67) ἀνάστηθι ἐπὶ τ. πόδας σου ὀρθός stand upright on your feet Ac 14: 10. αἱ τρίχες μου ὀρθαί my hair stood on end Hv 3, 1, 5 (Ael. Aristid. 48, 33 K.=24 p. 474 D.: τρίχες ὀρθαί).

b. straight, in a straight line (Hes.+; LXX) τροχιαὶ ὀρ. Hb 12: 13 (Pr 4: 26). Of a way (class.; Pr 12: 15; 16: 25; Philo; Jos., Ant. 6, 13) in symbolic usage (Aesop, Fab. 287 P.=Babr. 8 Cr. [a road]; Philo, Fuga 131 al.) ὀρ. ὁδὸν ἔχειν have a straight path Hm 6, 1, 2a. τῇ ὀρ. ὁδῷ πορεύεσθαι walk in the straight path 6, 1, 2b; cf. 4.

2. fig. correct, true (Pind., Hdt.+; LXX; Ep. Arist. 244) συγγράμματα κάλλιστα καὶ ὀρθότατα Epil Mosq 1. γνώμῃ ὀ. IEph 1: 1 v.l. M-M. B. 896.*

ὀρθοτομέω found elsewh. independently of the NT only Pr 3: 6; 11: 5, where it is used w. ὁδούς and plainly means 'cut a path in a straight direction' or 'cut a road across country (that is forested or otherwise difficult to pass through) in a straight direction', so that the traveler may go directly to his destination (cf. Thu. 2, 100, 2 ὁδοὺς εὐθείας ἔτεμε; Hdt. 4, 136 τετμημένη ὁδός; Pla., Leg. 7 p. 810E; Plut., Galba 24, 7; Jos., C. Ap. 1, 309). Then ὀρθοτομεῖν τὸν λόγον τῆς ἀληθείας would perh. mean guide the word of truth along a straight path (like a road that goes straight to its goal), without being turned aside by wordy debates or impious talk 2 Ti 2: 15. For such other mngs. as teach the

word aright, expound it soundly, shape rightly, and preach fearlessly, s. M-M.*

ὀρθόω 1 aor. ὤρθωσα (Hom.+; LXX, Philo) set upright σταυρόν GP 4: 11 (cf. of a mast, Lucian, Catapl. 1; ξύλον=a cross, Esth 7: 9).*

ὀρθρίζω (so in LXX and NT; Moeris p. 272 ὀρθρεύει Ἀττικῶς. ὀρθρίζει Ἑλληνικῶς) impf. ὤρθριζον be up or get up very early in the morning (Ex 24: 4; 4 Km 6: 15; SSol 7: 13) ὁ λαὸς ὤρθριζεν πρὸς αὐτὸν ἐν τῷ ἱερῷ ἀκούειν αὐτοῦ the people used to get up very early in the morning (to come) to him in the temple and hear him Lk 21: 38 (ὀρ. πρός τινα also means gener. seek someone diligently: Job 8: 5; Ps 77: 34; Sir 4: 12; Wsd 6: 14; Test. Jos. 3: 6). M-M.*

ὀρθρινός, ή, όν (late substitute for ὄρθριος [Anecd. Gr. p. 54, 7; Lob., Phryn. p. 51], almost only in poets [Arat. 948; Posidippus Epigrammaticus [III BC] in Athen. 13, 69 p. 596D; several times Anth. Pal.]; LXX) early in the morning γυναῖκες . . . γενόμεναι ὀρθριναὶ ἐπὶ τὸ μνημεῖον Lk 24: 22. τί ὀρ. ὧδε ἐλήλυθας; why have you come here so early? Hs 5, 1, 1.—Rv 22: 16 t.r. M-M.*

ὄρθριος, ία, ιον (Hom. Hymns+; pap., LXX; Jos., Ant. 5, 330; 7, 195) early in the morning Lk 24: 22 t.r. (s. ὀρθρινός). M-M.*

ὄρθρος, ου, ὁ (Hes.+; pap., LXX; En. 100, 2; Joseph.; Test. Jos. 8: 1) dawn, early morning ὄρθρου βαθέως very early in the morning Lk 24: 1 (s. βαθύς 2 and cf. Heraclit. Sto. 16 p. 24, 16; 68 p. 88, 16; Polyaenus 4, 9, 1 ὄρθρος ἦν βαθύς). ὄρθρου early in the morning (Hes., Op. 577; Diod. S. 14, 104, 1; PFlor. 305, 11; LXX; Jos., Ant. 11, 37) J 8: 2. ὄρθρου τῆς κυριακῆς on Sunday at dawn GP 12: 50. ὑπὸ τὸν ὄρ. about daybreak (Cass. Dio 76, 17; PFay. 108, 10; Jos., Ant. 8, 382) Ac 5: 21. M-M. B. 993.*

ὀρθῶς adv. (Hes., Aeschyl., Hdt.+; inscr., pap., LXX, Ep. Arist., Philo; Jos., Ant. 1, 251; Test. 12 Patr.) rightly, correctly λαλεῖν speak intelligibly=normally Mk 7: 35. ὀρ. προσφέρειν, διαιρεῖν offer rightly, divide rightly 1 Cl 4: 4 (after Gen 4: 7; cf. διαιρέω). δουλεύειν αὐτῷ (=τῷ θεῷ) ὀρ. serve God in the right way=κατὰ τὸ θέλημα αὐτοῦ Hm 12, 6, 2. τελεῖν τὴν διακονίαν τοῦ κυρίου ὀρ. perform the service of the Lord properly s 2: 7; ἐργάζεσθαι ὀρ. act rightly s 8, 11, 4 (cf. ὀρ. ποιεῖν: Dit., Syll.³ 116, 10; 780, 37; PEleph. 9, 3; 1 Macc 11: 43; ὀρ. πράσσειν: Jos., Vi. 298). ὀρ. κρίνειν judge, decide correctly Lk 7: 43 (cf. Wsd 6: 4; Ps.-Clem., Hom. 10, 9.—Diod. S. 18, 56, 3 ὀρθῶς γινώσκειν=think rightly). ὀρ. ἀποκρίνεσθαι answer correctly (Herm. Wr. 13, 3) 10: 28. ὀρ. λέγειν καὶ διδάσκειν 20: 21 (cf. Aristoxenus, fgm. 33 p. 18, 2 ὀρθῶς λέγουσιν; Alex. Aphr., An. II 1 p. 20, 29 ὀρθῶς λέγειν=teach rightly. Of Cercidas [III BC] in Diehl², fgm. 11a, 4 ὀρθῶς λέγει που Κερκίδας; Dt 5: 28). ὀρ. διδάσκεσθαι be properly taught Dg 11: 2. ἀγαπᾶν ὀρ. love (someone) in the right way 12: 1. ὀρ. ἀπέχεσθαί τινος be right in abstaining from someth. 4: 6. M-M.*

ὀρίζω 1 aor. ὥρισα, pass. ptc. ὁρισθείς; pf. pass. ptc. ὡρισμένος (Aeschyl., Hdt.+; inscr., pap., LXX, En. 98, 5; Ep. Arist. 157; Philo; Jos., Ant. 8, 188).

1. determine, appoint, fix, set—a. someth.—a. expressed by the acc. προφήτης ὁρίζων τράπεζαν a prophet who orders a meal (cf. τράπεζα 3) D 11: 9.—Of time (Pla., Leg. 9 p. 864E; Demosth. 36, 26 ὁ νόμος τὸν χρόνον ὥρισεν; Epict., Ench. 51, 1; PFlor. 61, 45 [85 AD]; Jos., C. Ap. 1, 230; more freq. pass., s. below) ἡμέραν Hb 4: 7. ὀρ. προστεταγμένους καιρούς set appointed times Ac 17: 26;

pass. (Dit., Syll.³ 495, 171; PFay. 11, 16 [c. 115 BC]; PAmh. 50, 15; PTebt. 327, 12 al.) ὡρισμένοι καιροί (Diod. S. 1, 41, 7; cf. 16, 29, 2; Jos., Ant. 6, 78) *appointed times* 1 Cl 40: 2. ὡρισμένης τῆς ἡμέρας ταύτης *after this day has been fixed* Hv 2, 2, 5 (Diod. S. 2, 59, 5; 20, 110, 1 ὡρισμένη ἡμέρα; Herodian 1, 10, 5 ὡρισμένης ἡμέρας; Pollux 1, 67).—ὁ ὡρισμένος τόπος *the appointed place* B 19: 1. οἱ ὡρισμένοι νόμοι *the established laws* Dg 5: 10. ὁ ὡρισμένος τῆς λειτουργίας κανών *the established limits of (one's) ministry* 1 Cl 41: 1. ἡ ὡρισμένη βουλή *the definite plan* Ac 2: 23.—Subst. (cf. Dit., Syll.³ 905, 14 τῶν ὁρισθέντων ἄγνοια) κατὰ τὸ ὡρισμένον *in accordance with the* (divine) *decree* Lk 22: 22.

β. by an inf. (Appian, Bell. Civ. 5, 3 §12 ἀντιδοῦναι= to give as recompense; Bl-D. §392, 1a) ὥρισαν ... πέμψαι *they determined* (perh. *set apart*; so Field, Notes 119f and TGillieson, ET 56, '44/'45, 110) ... *to send* Ac 11: 29; by an indirect quest. 1 Cl 40: 3.

b. of persons *appoint, designate, declare:* God judges the world ἐν ἀνδρὶ ᾧ ὥρισεν *through a man whom he has appointed* Ac 17: 31. Pass. ὁ ὡρισμένος ὑπὸ τοῦ θεοῦ κριτής *the one appointed by God as judge* 10: 42. Of bishops οἱ κατὰ τὰ πέρατα ὁρισθέντες *those who are appointed in distant lands* IEph 3: 2. W. double acc. *declare someone to be someth.* (Meleag. in Anth. Pal. 12, 158, 7 σὲ γὰρ θεὸν ὥρισε δαίμων) pass. τοῦ ὁρισθέντος υἱοῦ θεοῦ ἐν δυνάμει *who has been declared to be the powerful son of God* Ro 1: 4.

2. *set limits to, define, explain* (a concept) (X. et al. in act. and mid.) περί τινος *give an explanation concerning someth.* B 12: 1. τὸ ὕδωρ καὶ τὸν σταυρὸν ἐπὶ τὸ αὐτὸ ὥρισεν *he defined the water and the cross together* (i.e. in the section on the tree by the streams of water Ps 1: 3) 11: 8. KLSchmidt, TW V 453-4. M-M.*

ὅριον, ου, τό (Soph., Thu.+; inscr., pap., LXX) *boundary;* mostly, in our lit. exclusively, pl. *boundaries=region, district* (Gen 10: 19; Ex 10: 4, al. in LXX) Mt 8: 34; 15: 22; Mk 5: 17; Ac 13: 50. ἐν ὁρ. Ζαβουλὼν καὶ Νεφθαλίμ *in the region of Zebulun and Naphtali* Mt 4: 13. τὰ ὅρ. Μαγαδάν 15: 39. τὰ ὅρ. τῆς Ἰουδαίας 19: 1; Mk 10: 1 (Jos., C. Ap. 1, 251 τὰ ὅρ. τῆς Συρίας). Of the region around a city (Jos., Ant. 6, 191) τὰ ὅρ. Τύρου (καὶ Σιδῶνος) 7: 24; cf. vs. 31a. ἀπὸ τῶν ὁρ. ἐκείνων *from that district* Mt 15: 22. ἀνὰ μέσον τῶν ὁρ. Δεκαπόλεως *through the region of the Decapolis* Mk 7: 31b. ἐν Βηθλέεμ καὶ ἐν πᾶσι τοῖς ὁρ. αὐτῆς *in Bethlehem and all the region around it* Mt 2: 16. ἔστησεν ἐθνῶν *he established the regions* (perh. *boundaries) for the nations* 1 Cl 29: 2 (Dt 32: 8).—The mng. *boundaries* is certain in ὅρια πατέρων παρορίζειν *transgress the boundaries set by the fathers* Dg 11: 5. M-M. B. 1311f.*

ὁρισμός, οῦ, ὁ (Hippocr.+; pap., LXX; Philo, Leg. All. 2, 63) lit. *marking out by boundaries*, then *a fixed course.* Heavenly bodies ἐξελίσουσιν τοὺς ἐπιτεταγμένους αὐτοῖς ὁρ. *roll on through their appointed courses* 1 Cl 20: 3.*

ὁρκίζω (in the sense 'cause someone to swear' X.+; inscr., pap., LXX; Jos., Ant. 18, 124) *adjure, implore* (so pap.; Jos., Vi. 258; LXX) τινὰ κατά τινος *someone by someone* (PGM 3, 36f; 4, 289; 7, 242 ὁρκίζω σε, δαίμων, κατὰ τῶν ὀνομάτων σου; 3 Km 2: 43; 2 Ch 36: 13.—Audollent, Defix. Tab. p. 473ff) Mt 26: 63 D. αὐτὸν ὁρ. κατὰ τοῦ κυρίου w. ἵνα foll. Hs 9, 10, 5. Also w. double acc. (Orph. Fgm. coll. OKern '22, p. 313 no. 299 οὐρανὸν ὁρκίζω σε; lead tablet fr. Hadrumetum in Dssm., B 28 [BS 274] ὁρκίζω σε, δαιμόνιον πνεῦμα, τὸν θεὸν τοῦ

Ἀβρααν κτλ.; PGM 4, 3045; Bl-D. §149; Rob. 483f) ὁρ. σε τὸν θεόν *I implore you by God* w. μή foll. Mk 5: 7. ὁρ. ὑμᾶς τὸν Ἰησοῦν Ac 19: 13 (cf. PGM 4, 3019 ὁρκίζω σε κατὰ τοῦ τῶν Ἑβραίων Ἰησοῦ). W. double acc. and foll. by acc. and inf. (Bl-D. §392, 1d; Rob. 1085) 1 Th 5: 27 t.r. M-M. B. 1437.*

ὅρκιον, ου, τό (Hom.+; Dit., Or. 453, 25 [39/5 BC], Syll.³ 581, 91 al.; Philo, Conf. Lingu. 43; Sib. Or. 3, 654) *oath, vow, pledge* ὅρκια πίστεως *pledges of faith* Dg 11: 5.*

ὅρκος, ου, ὁ (Hom.+; inscr., pap., LXX, Ep. Arist., Philo, Joseph.) *oath* Hb 6: 16. ὅρκον ὀμνύειν *swear an oath* (Hyperid. 5, 1; Lucian, Dial. Mer. 2, 1; PHal. 1, 226; 230 ὁμόσας τὸν ὅρκον) Js 5: 12 (Delphic commands: Dit., Syll.³ 1268 I, 8 [III BC] ὅρκῳ μὴ χρῶ). ὅρκῳ ὀμνύειν τινί *swear to someone with an oath* (Test. Judah 22: 3) Ac 2: 30. ὁρ. ὃν ὤμοσεν πρὸς Ἀβραάμ Lk 1: 73 (cf. Dit., Or. 266, 19 ὅρκος ὃν ὤμοσεν Παράνομος; for the foll. inf. w. the art. cf. Pel.-Leg. p. 13, 9 ἐν ὅρκῳ εἶχεν τοῦ μὴ γεύσασθαί τι). ὁρ. ψευδής *a false oath* B 2: 8 (Zech 8: 17). ἀποδιδόναι τῷ κυρίῳ τοὺς ὅρκους *perform oaths to the Lord* Mt 5: 33 (s. ἀποδίδωμι 1. But ἀποδοῦναί τινι ὅρκον also means 'give an oath': Demosth. 19, 318; Aeschin. 3, 74; Dit., Syll.³ 150, 15). μεσιτεύειν ὅρκῳ *guarantee by means of an oath* Hb 6: 17. μεθ᾽ ὅρκου *with an oath* (PRev. 42, 17 [258 BC] μεθ᾽ ὅρκου; Lev 5: 4; Num 30: 11; Cornutus 24 p. 46, 8 μεθ᾽ ὅρκων) Mt 14: 7; 26: 72; 1 Cl 8: 2.—Pl., even when basically only one oath is involved (cf. X., Hell. 5, 4, 54; Diod. S. 4, 46, 4; 17, 84, 1; Polyaenus 2, 19; Athen. 13 p. 557A; 2 Macc 4: 34; 7: 24; 14: 32; Ep. Arist. 126; Jos., Ant. 3, 272; 7, 294) διὰ τοὺς ὅρκους *because of his oath* Mt 14: 9; Mk 6: 26.—Lit. on ὀμνύω. JSchneider, TW V 458-67. M-M. B. 1438.*

ὀρκωμοσία, ας, ἡ (Doric.—Pollux 1, 38; 1 Esdr 8: 90; Ezk 17: 18f; Jos., Ant. 16, 163.—Bl-D. §2; 119, 3; cf. Mlt.-H. 338f; EFraenkel, Geschichte der griech. Nomina agentis auf -τήρ, -τωρ, -της I '10, 200) *oath, taking an oath* Hb 7: 20f, 28. M-M.*

ὁρμάω 1 aor. ὥρμησα; in our lit. used only intr. (so Hom.+; Dit., Syll.³ 709, 19 [c. 107 BC]; PStrassb. 100, 17 [II BC]; PTebt. 48, 24; LXX, Philo, Joseph.) *set out, rush* (*headlong*) of a herd ὁρ. κατὰ τοῦ κρημνοῦ εἰς τὴν θάλασσαν *rush down the slope into the lake* Mt 8: 32; Mk 5: 13; Lk 8: 33 (cf. POxy. 901, 6 of two swine τὴν ὁρμὴν ποιούμενοι). Of a crowd of people ὥρμησαν εἰς τὸ θέατρον *they rushed into the theater* Ac 19: 29 (cf. Jos., Ant. 11, 147). ὁρ. ἐπί τινα *rush at, fall upon someone* (X., An. 4, 3, 31; Alciphr. 3, 7, 3; 3, 18, 2; 2 Macc 12: 32; Jos., Ant. 12, 270, Vi. 245; Test. Jud. 7: 5) 7: 57. M-M.*

ὁρμή, ῆς, ἡ (Hom.+; inscr., pap., LXX, Ep. Arist., Philo, Joseph., Sib. Or. 5, 9) *impulse, inclination, desire* (so Hom.+; PGrenf. II 78, 15; 3 Macc 1: 16) of the pilot of a ship ὅπου ἡ ὁρ. τοῦ εὐθύνοντος βούλεται *wherever the impulse of the steersman leads him* Js 3: 4. καταδιαιρεῖν τι πρὸς τὰς αὐτῶν ὁρμάς *make a distinction betw. some things in accord with their (own) inclinations* Dg 4: 5. ἐγένετο ὁρ. τῶν ἐθνῶν *an attempt was made by the Gentiles* foll. by aor. inf. Ac 14: 5 (cf. Jos., Ant. 9, 161 ὁρμὴ ἀνακαινίσαι and 15, 52 ὁρ. ἐγένετο).—GBertram, TW V 468-75: ὁρμή *and related words.* M-M.*

ὅρμημα, ατος, τό (Hom.+; Plut., LXX) *violent rush, onset* ὁρμήματι βληθήσεται Βαβυλών *Babylon will be thrown down with violence* Rv 18: 21. M-M.*

ὄρνεον, ου, τό (Hom.+; IG IV² 1, 93, 17 [III/IV AD]; PPetr. III 71 [III BC]; PRyl. 98[a], 9; PLond. 1259, 16;

LXX; Philo; Jos., Ant. 1, 184; 3, 25; 18, 195) *bird* Rv 19: 17, 21. πᾶν ὄρ. ἀκάθαρτον καὶ μεμισημένον *every bird that is unclean and detestable* (for relig. reasons, e.g. the owl, heron, pelican, great horned owl) 18: 2 (cf. Dt 14: 11 πᾶν ὄρνεον καθαρόν). Of the phoenix 1 Cl 25: 2; 26: 1. Pl., of various unclean birds (cf. Dt 14: 11ff) B 10: 4. W. κτῆνος Hs 9, 1, 8. M-M.*

ὄρνιξ (so as nom., Athen. 9 p. 374D; Herodian Gramm. I p. 44, 7 L.; PZen. [ed. CCEdgar, Cairo] 375, 1. The dat. pl. ὄρνιξι also PLond. 131 recto, 125; 202 al. [78/9 AD]; cf. Mayser 531.—On this Doric form s. Kühner-Bl. I 510; Thumb 90f; APF 4, '08, 490; Crönert 174, 5; FRobert, Les noms des Oiseaux en grec ancien, Diss. Basel '11, 17; Bl-D. §47, 4) Lk 13: 34 Tdf. (acc. to אD) for the Att. ὄρνις. W-S. §9, 10; Mlt.-H. 130f; 133. M-M.*

ὄρνις, ιθος, ὁ and ἡ (Hom.+; pap.; LXX in one place [Thackeray p. 152f]; Philo; Jos., Bell. 2, 289 [ὄρνεις], C. Ap. 1, 203f [τὸν ὄρνιθα], Ant. 18, 185 [τὸν ὄρνιν]; Sib. Or. 2, 208 [ὄρνεις]) *bird,* specif. *cock* or *hen* (Aeschyl.+; X., An. 4, 5, 25; Polyb. 12, 26, 1 al.; Tit. Asiae Min. II 1, '20, 245, 8; pap.); the actions of the mother bird or specif. of the hen as a symbol of protecting care Mt 23: 37; Lk 13: 34. M-M. B. 175.*

ὀροθεσία, ας, ἡ (Inschr. v. Priene 42 II, 8 [133 BC] δικαίαν εἶναι ἔκριναν τὴν Ῥωδίων κρίσιν τε καὶ ὀροθεσίαν; BGU 889, 17 [II AD].—Bl-D. §119, 3; Mlt.-H. 340) *fixed boundary,* of God: ὁρίσας . . . τὰς ὀροθεσίας τῆς κατοικίας αὐτῶν (=τ. ἀνθρώπων) *he determined the boundaries of their habitation* Ac 17: 26 (cf. HJCadbury, JBL 44, '25, 219-21, 'fixed the term of residence'.—MDibelius, S. Hdlbg. Ak. d. W. 1938/9 2. Abh. p. 7f; 15: 'limited areas to be colonized'; WEltester, RBultmann-Festschr., '54, 209ff). M-M.*

ὄρος, ους, τό (Hom.+; inscr., pap., LXX, En., Ep. Arist., Philo, Joseph., Test. 12 Patr.) pl. τὰ ὄρη; gen., uncontracted ὀρέων (as early as X., An. 1, 2, 21 [Kühner-Bl. I 432]; Dit., Syll.³ 646, 18 [170 BC]; LXX [Thackeray 151; Helbing 41f]; Ep. Arist. 119. Not in Joseph., as it seems—he has ὀρῶν someth. like 600 times.—ESchweizer, Gramm. d. perg. Inschr. 1898, 153; Bl-D. §48; Mlt.-H. 139) Rv 6: 15; 1 Cl; Hermas (Reinhold 52); *mountain, hill* w. βουνός Lk 3: 5 (Is 40: 4); 23: 30 (Hos 10: 8). W. πέτρα Rv 6: 16; cf. vs. 15. W. πεδίον (Dit., Syll.³ 888, 120f) Hs 8, 1, 1; 8, 3, 2. W. νῆσος Rv 6: 14; 16: 20. As the scene of outstanding events and as places of solitude (PTebt. 383, 61 [46 AD] ὄρος denotes 'desert'; Dio Chrys. 19[36], 40 Ζωροάστρης withdraws fr. among men and lives ἐν ὄρει; Herm. Wr. 13 inscr. Hermes teaches his son Tat ἐν ὄρει) mountains play a large part in the gospels and in the apocalypses: Jesus preaches and heals on 'the' mountain Mt 5: 1 (HBCarré, JBL 42, '23, 39-48.—On the Sermon on the Mount cf. GHeinrici, Beiträge II 1899; III '05; JMüller, D. Bergpredigt '06; KFProost, De Bergrede '14; HWeinel, D. Bergpr. '20; KBornhäuser, D. Bergpr. '23, ²'27; PFiebig, Jesu Bergpr. '24; GerhKittel, D. Bergpr. u. d. Ethik d. Judentums: ZsystTh 2, '25, 555-94; ASteinmann, D. Bergpr. '26; AAhlberg, Bergpredikans etik '30; MMeinertz, Z. Ethik d. Bergpr.: JMausbach-Festschr. '31, 21-32; HHuber, D. Bergpredigt '32; RSeeberg, Z. Ethik der Bergpr. '34; JSchneider, D. Sinn d. Bergpr. '36; ADLindsay, The Moral Teaching of Jesus '37; MDibelius, The Sermon on the Mount '40; ThSoiron, D. Bergpr. Jesu '41; DFAndrews, The Sermon on the Mount '42; HPreisker, D. Ethos des Urchristentums² '49; HWindisch, D. Mng. of the Sermon on the Mount [tr. Gilmour] '51; WmManson, Jesus the Messiah '52, 77-93; TWManson,

The Sayings of Jesus '54; GBornkamm, Jesus v. Naz. '56, 92-100, 201-4 [Engl. transl. by JMRobinson et al. '60, 100-9, 221-5]; JoachJeremias, Die Bergpredigt '59; JDupont, Les Béatitudes, I rev. ed. '58; II, '69; WD Davies, The Setting of the Sermon on the Mount, '64; JManek, NovT 9, '67, 124-31.—On the site of the Sermon, CKopp, The Holy Places of the Gosp., '63, 204-13); 8: 1; 15: 29; calls the twelve Mk 3: 13; performs great miracles J 6: 3; prays Mt 14: 23; Mk 6: 46; Lk 6: 12; 9: 28; AP 2: 4. On an ὄρος ὑψηλόν (Lucian, Charon 2) he is transfigured Mt 17: 1; Mk 9: 2 and tempted Mt 4: 8; the risen Christ shows himself on a mountain (cf. Herm. Wr. 13, 1) Mt 28: 16. Jesus is taken away by the Holy Spirit εἰς τὸ ὄρος τὸ μέγα τὸ Θαβώρ GH 5; likew. the author of Rv ἐπὶ ὄρος μέγα κ. ὑψηλόν Rv 21: 10. From the top of one mountain the angel of repentance shows Hermas twelve other mountains Hs 9, 1, 4; 7ff. On the use of the mt. in apocalyptic lang. cf. also Rv 8: 8; 17: 9 (ἑπτὰ ὄ. as En. 24, 2). JohJeremias, D. Gottesberg '19; RFrieling, D. hl. Berg im A u. NT '30.—Of the mt. to which Abraham brought his son, to sacrifice him there 1 Cl 10: 7 (cf. Gen 22: 2). Esp. of Sinai τὸ ὄρος Σινά (LXX.—τὸ Σιναῖον ὄ. Jos., Ant. 2, 283f) Ac 7: 30, 38; Gal 4: 24f; B 11: 3 (cf. Is 16: 1); 14: 2 (cf. Ex 31: 18); 15: 1; also without mention of the name: Hb 8: 5 (Ex 25: 40); 12: 20 (cf. Ex 19: 13); 1 Cl 53: 2; B 4: 7. Of the hill of Zion (Σιών) Hb 12: 22; Rv 14: 1. τὸ ὄρ. τῶν ἐλαιῶν *the Mount of Olives* (s. ἐλαία 1) Mt 21: 1; 26: 30; Mk 14: 26; Lk 19: 37; 22: 39; J 8: 1 al. τὸ ὄρ. τὸ καλούμενον ἐλαιών Lk 19: 29; 21: 37; Ac 1: 12 (s. ἐλαιών). Of Mt. Gerizim (without mention of the name) J 4: 20f (cf. Jos., Ant. 12, 10; 13, 74).—πόλις ἐπάνω ὄρους κειμένη *a city located on a hill* Mt 5: 14 (cf. Jos., Ant. 13, 203 πόλις ἐπ' ὄρους κειμένη). Also πόλις οἰκοδομημένη ἐπ' ἄκρον ὄρους ὑψηλοῦ LJ 1: 7 (Stephan. Byz. s.v. Ἀστέριον says this city was so named ὅτι ἐφ' ὑψηλοῦ ὄρους κειμένη τοῖς πόρρωθεν ὡς ἀστὴρ φαίνεται).—Pl. τὰ ὄρη *hills, mountains, hilly* or *mountainous country* (somet. the sing. also means *hill-country* [Diod. S. 20, 58, 2 an ὄρος ὑψηλὸν that extends for 200 stades, roughly 21 miles; Polyaenus 4, 2, 4 al. sing.=hill-country; Tob 5: 6 S]) as a place for pasture Mt 18: 12.—Mk 5: 11; Lk 8: 32. As a remote place (s. above; also Dio Chrys. 4, 4; Πράξεις Παύλου p. 5, 18 ed. CSchmidt '36) w. ἐρημίαι Hb 11: 38. As a place for graves (cf. POxy. 274, 27 [I AD]; PRyl. 153, 5; PGrenf. II 77, 22: the grave-digger is to bring a corpse εἰς τὸ ὄρος for burial) Mk 5: 5. Because of their isolation an ideal refuge for fugitives (Appian, Bell. Civ. 4, 30 §130 ἐς ὄρος ἔφυγεν=to the hill-country; 1 Macc 9: 40) φεύγειν εἰς τὰ ὄρ. (Plut., Mor. 869B οἱ ἄνθρωποι καταφυγόντες εἰς τὰ ὄρη διεσώθησαν; Jos., Bell. 1, 36, Ant. 14, 418) Mt 24: 16; Mk 13: 14; Lk 21: 21.—Proverbially ὄρη μεθιστάνειν *remove mountains* i.e., do something that seems impossible 1 Cor 13: 2; cf. Mt 17: 20; 21: 21; Mk 11: 23. Of God: μεθιστάνει τοὺς οὐρανοὺς καὶ τὰ ὄρη καὶ τοὺς βουνοὺς καὶ τὰς θαλάσσας *he is moving from their places the heavens and mountains and hills and seas* Hv 1, 3, 4 (cf. Is 54: 10 and a similar combination PGM 13, 874 αἱ πέτραι κ. τὰ ὄρη κ. ἡ θάλασσα κτλ.).—WFoerster, TW V 475-86. M-M. B. 23.

ὄρος, ου, ὁ (Hom.+; inscr., pap., LXX; Ep. Arist. 211; Philo; Jos., Ant. 1, 62 al.; Test. 12 Patr.) *boundary, limit* of space τ. θάλασσαν ἰδίοις ὅροις ἐνέκλεισεν Dg 7: 2 (Arrian, Anab. 5, 26, 2 τῆς γῆς ὅρους ὁ θεὸς ἐποίησε). Of time ὁ ὅρος τῶν ἐτῶν *ending* of Mk in the Freer ms. 7.*

ὀρύσσω 1 aor. ὤρυξα; 2 aor. pass. ὠρύγην (Hs 9, 6, 7; cf. Dit., Or. 672, 7; 673, 6 ὠρύγη; POxy. 121, 8 ὀρυγῆναι; Ps 93: 13; En. 98, 13; Joseph.).

1. *dig (up)* τὶ *someth.* γῆν (cf. Pla., Euthyd. 288E; Achmes 94, 14) *to hide someth.* Mt 25: 18. Pass. ὠρύγη τὸ πεδίον *the plain was dug up and there were found* . . . Hs 9, 6, 7.

2. *dig out, prepare by digging* τὶ *someth.* (X., Cyr. 7, 3, 5; Diod. S. 1, 50, 5; Gen 26: 21, 25; Jos., Ant. 8, 341; Test. Zeb. 2: 7) ληνόν *a wine-press* Mt 21: 33. Also ὑπολήνιον Mk 12: 1 (cf. Is 5: 2). βόθρον θανάτου *a pit of death* B 11: 2 (cf. Jer 2: 13 and for ὀρ. βόθρ. Eccl 10: 8; Pr 26: 27).

3. *dig (a hole)* (X., Oec. 19, 2) ἐν τῇ γῇ (i.e. *to hide* τὸ ἐν τάλαντον) Mt 25: 18 t.r. M-M. B. 497.*

ὀρφανός, ή, όν *orphaned*—1. lit. = *deprived of one's parents* (so Hom.+; inscr., pap., LXX, Philo; Jos., Ant. 18, 314 al.), used so in our lit. only as a subst. (as Pla., Leg. 6 p. 766c; 11 p. 926c, al.; pap., LXX) in sing. and pl. *orphan(s)*, mostly grouped w. χήρα (or χήραι) as typically in need of protection (Liban., Or. 62 p. 379, 2 F. χήρας οἰκτείρων, ὀρφανοὺς ἐλεῶν; Maspéro 6r, 2; 2 Macc 3: 10; more commonly in the sing. in LXX fr. Ex 22: 22 on, πᾶσαν χήραν κ. ὀρφανόν) Mk 12: 40 v.l. ἐπισκέπτεσθαι ὀρφανοὺς καὶ χήρας Js 1: 27; Hs 1: 8. διαρπάζειν χηρῶν καὶ ὀρφανῶν τὴν ζωήν *rob widows and orphans of their living* s 9, 26, 2. κατεσθίειν τὰς οἰκίας τῶν χηρῶν καὶ ὀρφανῶν Mk 12: 40 v.l.; νουθετεῖν τὰς χήρας καὶ τοὺς ὀρ. *instruct the widows and orphans* Hv 2, 4, 3. W. χήραι and ὑστερούμενοι m 8: 10; in the sing. s 5, 3, 7. W. χήρα and πένης Pol 6: 1. W. χήρα and others in need of help ISm 6: 2. Collectively κρίνειν ὀρφανῷ *see to it that justice is done (to) the orphan* 1 Cl 8: 4 (Is 1: 17). χήρᾳ καὶ ὀρφανῷ προσέχειν *be concerned about (the) widow and orphan* B 20: 2.

2. fig., when Jesus says to his disciples that upon his departure οὐκ ἀφήσω ὑμᾶς ὀρφανούς *I will not leave you orphaned* (or [as] *orphans*) J 14: 18 (for this usage s. Pla., Phaedo 65 p. 116A, where the feelings of Socrates' friends are described thus: ἀτεχνῶς ἡγούμενοι ὥσπερ πατρὸς στερηθέντες διάξειν ὀρφανοὶ τὸν ἔπειτα βίον. Sim. the followers of Peregrinus in Lucian, M. Peregr. 6. Cf. Epict. 3, 24, 14; 15). M-M. B. 130.*

ὀρχέομαι mid. dep., impf. ὠρχούμην; 1 aor. ὠρχησάμην (Hom.+; LXX; Jos., Ant. 7, 87) *dance* of actual dancing Mt 14: 6; Mk 6: 22 (on the dancing of Herodias' daughter: GDalman, Pj 14, '18, 44–6 and s.v. Ἰωάννης 1.—F Weege, D. Tanz in d. Antike '26); Hs 9, 11, 5. Of children at play (w. αὐλεῖν; cf. Aesop, Fab. 27 H. ὅτε μὲν ηὔλουν, οὐκ ὠρχεῖσθε) Mt 11: 17; Lk 7: 32. M-M. B. 689.*

ὅς, ἥ, ὅ—I. relative pron. *who, which, what, that* (Hom.+; inscr., pap., LXX, En., Ep. Arist., Philo, Joseph.). On its use s. Bl-D. §293–7; 377–80; W-S. §24; Rob. 711–26, and for class. Gk. Kühner-G. II p. 399ff.

1. As a general rule, the relative pron. agrees in gender and number w. the noun or pron. to which it refers (i.e., its antecedent); its case is determined by the verb, noun, or prep. that governs it: ὁ ἀστήρ, ὃν εἶδον Mt 2: 9. ὁ Ἰησοῦς, ὃν ἐγὼ καταγγέλλω ὑμῖν Ac 17: 3. Ἰουδαῖον, ᾧ (sc. ἦν) ὄνομα Βαριησοῦς 13: 6. ὁ Ἰουδαῖος . . . , οὗ ὁ ἔπαινος Ro 2: 29. Ἰσραηλίτης, ἐν ᾧ δόλος οὐκ ἔστιν J 1: 47. οὗτος, περὶ οὗ ἀκούω τοιαῦτα Lk 9: 9 and very oft.

2. A demonstrative pron. is freq. concealed within the relative pron.:—a. in such a way that both pronouns stand in the same case: ὅς *the one who* ὃς οὐ λαμβάνει Mt 10: 38.—Mk 9: 40. οὗ *of the one whose* J 18: 26. ᾧ *to the one to whom* Ro 6: 16. ὃν *the one whom* (or someth. sim.) Mk 15: 12; J 1: 45. οἷς *to those for whom* Mt 20: 23. οὓς *those whom* Mk 3: 13; J 5: 21. ὅ *that which, what* Mt 10: 27.—If a prep. governs the relative, it belongs either to the (omitted) demonstr. pron. alone: παρ' ὅ Ro 12: 3; Gal 1:

8. ὑπὲρ ὅ (ἅ) 1 Cor 10: 13; 2 Cor 12: 6; Phlm 21. πρὸς ἅ 2 Cor 5: 10. εἰς ὅν J 6: 29, or it must be added to both pronouns: ἐν ᾧ *in that in which* 2 Cor 11: 12; 1 Pt 2: 12; 3: 16 (these passages in 1 Pt may be classed under I 11c also). ἐν οἷς Phil 4: 11. ὑπὲρ οὗ *because of that for which* 1 Cor 10: 30. ἀφ' ὧν *from the persons from whom* 2 Cor 2: 3.— The much disputed pass. ἑταῖρε, ἐφ' ὃ πάρει; Mt 26: 50 would belong here if we were to supply the words necessary to make it read about as follows: *friend,* (are you misusing the kiss) *for that* (purpose) *for which you are here?* (Wlh.; EKlostermann) or thus: *in connection with that* (=the purposes), *for which* (=for the realization of which) *you have appeared* (do you kiss me)? (Rdm.[2] 78). *Friend, are you here for this purpose?* FRehkopf, ZNW 52, '61, 109–15. But s. bβ and 9b below.

b. But the two pronouns can also stand in different cases; in such instances the demonstr. pron. is nearly always in the nom. or acc.

α. in the nom. οὗ *one whose* Ac 13: 25. ὧν *those whose* Ro 4: 7 (Ps 31: 1). ᾧ *the one to* or *for whom* Lk 7: 43; 2 Pt 1: 9. οἷς *those to whom* Mt 19: 11; Ro 15: 21 (Is 52: 15). ὅ *that* (nom.) *which* (acc.) Mt 13: 12; 25: 29; 26: 13; Mk 11: 23; Lk 12: 3. Likew. ἅ Lk 12: 20. ὃν *he whom* J 3: 34; 4: 18; Ac 10: 21. ἐφ' ὅν *the one about whom* Hb 7: 13.

β. in the acc. ὧν *the things of which* J 13: 29. ᾧ *the one (in) whom* 2 Ti 1: 12. So also w. a prep.: ἐν ᾧ *anything by which* Ro 14: 21. ἐν οἷς *things in which* 2 Pt 2: 12. ἐφ' ὅ *that upon which* Lk 5: 25. περὶ ὧν *the things of which* Ac 24: 13. ἐφ' οἷς *from the things of which* Ro 6: 21 (this passage is perh. a commercial metaphor). εἰς ὅν *the one in whom* Ro 10: 14a.—So Mt 26: 50 (s. 2a above), if the words to be supplied are about as follows: *friend,* (do that) *for which you have come!* (so ESchwartz, ByzZ 25, '25, 154f; ECEOwen, JTS 29, '28, 384–6; WSpiegelberg, ZNW 28, '29, 341–3; FZorell, Verb. Domini 9, '29, 112–16; sim. PMaas, Byz.-Neugriech. Jahrb. 8, '31, 99; 9, '32, 64; WEltester: OCullmann-Festschr., '62, 70–91; FWDanker, FWGingrich-Festschr., '72, 104f n. 6 reads ἐφ' ᾧ πάρει as a commercial idiom w. the colloq. sense 'what deal did you make?' [s. 11d, Ro 5: 12]. S. Jos., Bell. 2, 615 on πάρειμι 1a).

γ. Only in isolated instances does the demonstr. pron. to be supplied stand in another case: οὗ=τούτῳ, οὗ *in him of whom* Ro 10: 14b. παρ' ὧν=τούτοις, παρ' ὧν Lk 6: 34.

3. Constructions peculiar in some respect—a. The pleonastic use of the pers. pron. after ὅς (Mlt. 94f; Bl-D. §297) γυνὴ ἧς εἶχεν τὸ θυγάτριον αὐτῆς Mk 7: 25 is found as early as class. Gk. (Hyperid., Euxen. 3 ὧν . . . τούτων.—Kühner-G. II 433f), is not unknown in later Gk. (POxy. 117, 15), but above all is suggested by the Semitic languages (LXX; Thackeray 46; JTHudson, ET 53, '41/'42, 266f); the omission of αὐτῆς in אD is in line w. Gk. usage. οὗ τὸ πτύον ἐν τῇ χειρὶ αὐτοῦ Mt 3: 12; Lk 3: 17. οὗ . . . τῶν ὑποδημάτων αὐτοῦ Mk 1: 7; Lk 3: 16. οὗ τῷ μώλωπι αὐτοῦ 1 Pt 2: 24 v.l. In a quot. ἐφ' οὓς ἐπικέκληται . . . ἐπ' αὐτούς Ac 15: 17=Am 9: 12. οὗ ἡ πνοὴ αὐτοῦ 1 Cl 21: 9. Esp. freq. in Rv: 3: 8; 7: 2, 9; 9: 11 v.l.; 13: 8, 12; 20: 8.

b. constructions 'ad sensum'—a. a relative in the sing. refers to someth. in the pl. οὐρανοῖς . . . , ἐξ οὗ (οὐρανοῦ) Phil 3: 20.

β. a relative in the pl. refers to a sing. (Jdth 4: 8 γερουσία, οἵ) πλῆθος πολύ . . . , οἳ ἦλθον Lk 6: 17f. κατὰ πόλιν πᾶσαν, ἐν αἷς Ac 15: 36. Cf. ἤδη δευτέραν ἐπιστολήν, ἐν αἷς (i.e. ἐν ταῖς δυσὶν ἐπιστ.) 2 Pt 3: 1.

γ. the relative conforms to the natural gender rather than the grammatical gender of its antecedent noun τέκνα μου, οὕς Gal 4: 19; cf. 2 J 1; Phlm 10. ἔθνη, οἵ Ac 15: 17 (Am 9: 12); cf. 26: 17. παιδάριον, ὅς J 6: 9. θηρίον, ὅς Rv 13: 14. ὀνόματα, οἵ 3: 4 v.l. γενεᾶς σκολιᾶς, ἐν οἷς Phil 2: 15. W. ref. to Christ, τὴν κεφαλήν, ἐξ οὗ Col 2: 19.

4. Attraction (or assimilation) of the relative. Just as in class. Gk., inscr., pap., LXX, the simple relative ὅς, ἥ, ὅ is somet. attracted to the case of its antecedent, even though the relationship of the relative within its own clause would demand a different case.

a. In most cases it is the acc. of the rel. that is attracted to the gen. or dat. of the antecedent: περὶ πράγματος οὗ ἐὰν αἰτήσωνται Mt 18: 19. τῆς διαθήκης ἧς ὁ θεὸς διέθετο Ac 3: 25. Cf. Mt 24: 50b; Mk 7: 13; Lk 2: 20; 3: 19; 5: 9; 9: 43; 15: 16; J 4: 14; 7: 31; 15: 20; 17: 5; 21: 10; Ac 1: 1; 2: 22; 22: 10; 1 Cor 6: 19; 2 Cor 1: 6; 10: 8, 13; Eph 2: 10; 2 Th 1: 4; Jd 15 al.—The antecedent can also be a demonstr. pron. that is understood, not expressed (s. 2 above), that would stand in the gen. or dat.; the acc. of a relative pron. can be attracted to this gen. or dat. οὐδὲν ὧν ἑωρακαν is really οὐδὲν τούτων ἃ ἑωρακαν Lk 9: 36; ἃ takes on the case of τούτων which, in turn, is omitted (as early as class.).—23: 14, 41; Ac 8: 24; 21: 19, 24; 22: 15; 25: 11; 26: 16; Ro 15: 18; 1 Cor 7: 1; Eph 3: 20; Hb 5: 8. ὧν=τούτων, οὕς J 17: 9; 2 Cor 12: 17. οἷς=τούτοις, ἃ Lk 24: 25.

b. The dat. of the relative is less frequently attracted (Bl-D. §294, 2; Rob. 717) ἕως τῆς ἡμέρας ἧς (=ῇ) ἀνελήμφθη Ac 1: 22 (cf. Lev 23: 15; 25: 50; Bar 1: 19); Eph 1: 6; 4: 1; 1 Ti 4: 6 v.l.; κατέναντι οὗ ἐπίστευσεν θεοῦ= κατέν. τοῦ θεοῦ ῷ ἐπίστ. Ro 4: 17. διὰ τῆς παρακλήσεως ἧς παρακαλούμεθα 2 Cor 1: 4.

c. In relative clauses that consist of subject, predicate, and copula, the relative pron. somet. agrees in gender and number not w. the noun to which it refers, but w. the predicate if it is the subj. and, conversely, w. the subj. if it is the pred. of its own clause: πνεύματι..., ὅς ἐστιν ἀρραβών Eph 1: 14. τῷ σπέρματί σου, ὅς ἐστιν Χριστός Gal 3: 16. τὴν μάχαιραν τοῦ πνεύματος, ὅ ἐστιν ῥῆμα θεοῦ Eph 6: 17.—Rv 4: 5; 5: 8.

d. Inverse attraction occurs when the relative pronoun attracts its antecedent to its own case (as early as class.; cf. Kühner-G. II 413; Bl-D. §295; Rob. 717f) τὸν ἄρτον ὃν κλῶμεν, οὐχὶ κοινωνία... ἐστιν; ὁ ἄρτος ὅν.. 1 Cor 10: 16. λίθον, ὃν ἀπεδοκίμασαν... οὗτος ἐγενήθη (Ps 117: 22) Mt 21: 42; Mk 12: 10; Lk 20: 17; 1 Pt 2: 7 v.l.—παντὶ ῷ ἐδόθη πολύ, πολὺ ζητηθήσεται παρ' αὐτοῦ Lk 12: 48. ὅρκον, ὃν ὤμοσεν (=μνησθῆναι ὅρκου ὅν) 1: 73 (s. W-S. §24, 7 note). τοὺς λίθους, οὓς εἶδες, ἀποβεβλημένοι οὗτοι...ἐφόρεσαν Hs 9, 13, 3. Cf. 1 J 2: 25.

e. Attraction can, as in class. times (Thu. 2, 70, 5), fail to take place when the relative clause is more distinctly separated fr. its antecedent by additional modifiers of the noun and by the importance attaching to the content of the relative clause itself (Bl-D. §294, 1; Rob. 714f): τῆς σκηνῆς τῆς ἀληθινῆς, ἣν ἔπηξεν ὁ κύριος, οὐκ ἄνθρωπος Hb 8: 2. But cf. also Mk 13: 19; J 2: 22; 4: 5; Ac 8: 32; 1 Ti 4: 3; Tit 1: 2; Phlm 10; Hb 9: 7; Rv 1: 20.

5. The noun which is the antecedent of a relative clause can be incorporated into the latter—**a.** without abbreviating the constr. and without attraction of the case: ῇ οὐ δοκεῖτε ὥρᾳ=τῇ ὥρᾳ ῇ οὐ δοκ. Mt 24: 44. Cf. Lk 12: 40; 17: 29, 30. ἃ ἡτοίμασαν ἀρώματα 24: 1. ὃ ἐποίησεν σημεῖον J 6: 14. ὃ θέλω ἀγαθόν Ro 7: 19.

b. w. abbreviation, in that a prep. normally used twice is used only once: ἐν ῷ κρίματι κρίνετε κριθήσεσθε=ἐν τῷ κρίματι, ἐν ῷ κρίνετε, κριθήσεσθε Mt 7: 2a. Cf. vs. 2b;

Mk 4: 24. ἐν ῷ ἦν τόπῳ=ἐν τῷ τόπῳ ἐν ῷ ἦν J 11: 6. καθ' ὃν τρόπον=κατὰ τὸν τρόπον, καθ' ὅν Ac 15: 11.

c. w. a change in case, due mostly to attraction—**a.** of the relative pron. περὶ πάντων ὧν ἐποίησεν πονηρῶν= περὶ πάντων πονηρῶν, ἃ ἐπ. Lk 3: 19. περὶ πασῶν ὧν εἶδον δυνάμεων=περὶ πασῶν δυνάμεων, ἃς εἶδον 19: 37. αἰτίαν...ὧν ἐγὼ ὑπενόουν πονηρῶν Ac 25: 18.— The dat. of the relative is also attracted to other cases: ἄχρι ἧς ἡμέρας=ἄχρι τῆς ἡμέρας, ῇ Mt 24: 38; Lk 1: 20; 17: 27; Ac 1: 2. ἀφ' ἧς ἡμέρας Col 1: 6, 9.

β. of the noun to which the rel. refers: ὃν ἐγὼ ἀπεκεφάλισα Ἰωάννην, οὗτος ἠγέρθη=Ἰωάννης ὃν κτλ. Mk 6: 16. εἰς ὃν παρεδόθητε τύπον διδαχῆς=τῷ τύπῳ τῆς διδαχῆς εἰς ὃν παρεδόθητε Ro 6: 17.

d. The analysis is doubtful in passages like περὶ ὧν κατηχήθης λόγων=περὶ τῶν λόγων οὓς κατηχήθης or τῶν λόγων, περὶ ὧν κατηχήθης Lk 1: 4. ἄγοντες παρ' ῷ ξενισθῶμεν Μνάσωνι Ac 21: 16 must acc. to the sense=ἄγοντες πρὸς Μνάσωνα, ἵνα ξενισθῶμεν παρ' αὐτῷ. Cf. Bl-D. §294, 5 app.; Rob. 719.

6. The prep. can be omitted before the relative pron. if it has already been used before the antecedent noun: ἐν παντὶ χρόνῳ ῷ (=ἐν ῷ) Ac 1: 21. εἰς τὸ ἔργον ὅ (=εἰς ὅ) 13: 2. ἀπὸ πάντων ὧν (=ἀφ' ὧν) vs. 38. Cf. 26: 2. ἐν τῷ ποτηρίῳ ῷ (=ἐν ῷ) Rv 18: 6.

7. The neut. is employed—**a.** in explanations, esp. of foreign words and of allegories: ὅ ἐστιν *which* or *that is, which means*: βασιλεὺς Σαλήμ, ὅ ἐστιν βασιλεὺς εἰρήνης Hb 7: 2; cf. Mt 27: 33; Mk 3: 17; 7: 11, 34; 15: 42. Also ὅ ἐστιν μεθερμηνευόμενον Mt 1: 23; Mk 5: 41; Ac 4: 36. Cf. J 1: 38, 41f. ὅ ἐστιν μεθερμηνευόμενος κρανίου τόπος Mk 15: 22 (v.l. μεθερμηνευόμενον). τόπος, ὃ λέγεται Ἑβραϊστὶ Γολγοθά J 19: 17.—S. also αὐλῆς, ὅ ἐστιν πραιτώριον Mk 15: 16. λεπτὰ δύο, ὅ ἐστιν κοδράντης 12: 42. τοῦ σώματος αὐτοῦ, ὅ ἐστιν ἡ ἐκκλησία Col 1: 24. πλεονέκτης ὅ ἐστιν εἰδωλολάτρης Eph 5: 5. τὴν ἀγάπην ὅ ἐστιν σύνδεσμος τῆς τελειότητος Col 3: 14.—Bl-D. §132, 2.

b. when the relative pron. looks back upon a whole clause: τοῦτον τ. Ἰησοῦν ἀνέστησεν ὁ θεός, οὗ πάντες ἡμεῖς ἐσμεν μάρτυρες Ac 2: 32; cf. 3: 15; 11: 30; 26: 9f; Gal 2: 10; Col 1: 29; 1 Pt 2: 8; Rv 21: 8.

c. ὅ is to be understood as an obj. acc. and gains its content fr. what immediately follows in these places (cf. W-S. §24, 9; Rob. 715): ὃ ἀπέθανεν, τῇ ἁμαρτίᾳ ἀπέθανεν ἐφάπαξ=τὸν θάνατον, ὃν ἀπέθανεν κτλ. *what he died,* i.e. the death he suffered, *he suffered for sin* Ro 6: 10a; cf. b. ὃ νῦν ζῶ ἐν σαρκί *the life that I now live in the flesh* Gal 2: 20.

8. The relative is used w. consecutive or final mng. (result or purpose): τίς ἔγνω νοῦν κυρίου, ὃς συμβιβάσει αὐτόν; *who has known the mind of the Lord, so that he could instruct him?* 1 Cor 2: 16 (cf. Is 40: 13). ἄξιός ἐστιν ῷ παρέξῃ τοῦτο *he is worthy that you should grant him this* Lk 7: 4. ἀποστέλλω τὸν ἄγγελόν μου..., ὃς κατασκευάσει Mt 11: 10. ἔπεμψα Τιμόθεον..., ὃς ὑμᾶς ἀναμνήσει 1 Cor 4: 17.

9. taking the place of the interrogative pron.:—**a.** in indirect questions (Soph., Oed. R. 1068; Thu. 1, 136, 4; Attic inscr. of 411 BC in Meisterhans³-Schw.; pap. [Witkowski 30, 7]; oft. Joseph. [Schmidt 369]) ὃ ἐγὼ ποιῶ *what I am doing* J 13: 7. ἃ λέγουσιν 1 Ti 1: 7.—J 18: 21.

b. NT philology overwhelmingly rejects the proposition that ὅς is used in direct questions (Mlt. 93; Bl-D. §300, 2; Radermacher² 78; PMaas [see I 2bβ above]). An unambiguous example of it is yet to be found. Even the inscr. on a goblet in Dssm., LO 100ff [LAE 125–31], ET 33, '22,

584

491-3 leaves room for doubt. For this reason the translation of ἐφ' ὃ πάρει Mt 26: 50 as 'what are you here for?' (so Gdspd., Probs. 41-43; similarly, as early as Luther, later Dssm.; JPWilson, ET 41, '30, 334) is scarcely tenable.—Rob. 725 doubts the interrogative here, but Moulton-Turner, Syntax '63, p. 50 inclines toward it.—See also I 2a, b, β above.

10. combined w. particles—**a.** with ἄν (ἐάν), s. ἄν.—**b.** with γέ (s. γέ 2 and cf. PFlor. 370, 9) Ro 8: 32.—**c.** w. δήποτε *whatever* J 5: 4 (the rdg. varies betw. οἵῳ and ᾧ, δηποτοῦν and δήποτε).—**d.** w. καί *who also* Mk 3: 19; Lk 6: 13f; 7: 49 al.—**e.** with περ=ὅσπερ, ἥπερ, ὅπερ (Jos., Ant. 2, 277, Vi. 95) *just the one who* Mk 15: 6 t.r. ὅπερ *which indeed* GOxy 35; ISm 4: 1. πάντα ἅπερ *whatever* GP 11: 45.

11. used w. prepositions (s. also above: 2a; 2bβ; 5b, c, d; 6, and cf. Johannessohn 382f [index]), whereby a kind of conjunction is formed:

a. with ἀντί: ἀνθ' ὧν (s. ἀντί 3) *because* Lk 1: 20; 19: 44; Ac 12: 23; 2 Th 2: 10; *therefore* Lk 12: 3.

b. w. εἰς: εἰς ὅ *to this end* 2 Th 1: 11.—**c.** with ἐν: ἐν οἷς connects w. the situation described in what precedes *under which circumstances=under these circumstances, in the situation created by what precedes* Lk 12: 1; Ac 24: 18 t.r.; 26: 12. So also perh. ἐν ᾧ 1 Pt 1: 6; 2: 12; 3: 16, 19; 4: 4. S. also ἐν IV 6 and I 2a above.

d. w. ἐπί: ἐφ' ᾧ=ἐπὶ τούτῳ ὅτι *for the reason that, because* Ro 5: 12 (lit. on ἁμαρτία 3); 2 Cor 5: 4; Phil 3: 12; *for* 4: 10.—A commercial metaphor may find expression in the first 3 passages cited here; s. ἐπί II 1bγ, end.

e. οὗ χάριν *therefore* Lk 7: 47.—**f.** in indications of time: ἀφ' ἧς (s. ἀπό II 2c and cf. BGU 252, 9 [98 AD]) *from the time when; since* Lk 7: 45; Ac 24: 11; 2 Pt 3: 4; Hs 8, 6, 6; *as soon as, after* s 8, 1, 4.—ἀφ' οὗ (s. ἀπό II 2c) *when once, since* Lk 13: 25; 24: 21; Rv 16: 18. ἄχρι οὗ (s. ἄχρι 2a) *until (the time when)* Ro 11: 25; 1 Cor 11: 26; Gal 3: 19 v.l. Also ἕως οὗ *until* Mt 1: 25; 13: 33; 14: 22; 17: 9; Lk 13: 21; D 11: 6 al. μέχρις οὗ *until* Mk 13: 30; Gal 4: 19.—On the gen. οὗ as an adv. of place s. it as a separate entry.

II. Demonstrative pron. *this (one)* (Hom.+; class. prose [Kühner-G. II 227ff]; pap., LXX).

1. ὃς δέ *but he* (Ps.-Lucian, Philopatris 22; PRyl. 144, 14 [38 AD]) Mk 15: 23; J 5: 11. Mostly

2. ὃς μέν ... ὃς δέ *the one ... the other* (Hippocr.+; very oft. in later wr.; POxy. 1189, 7 [c. 117 AD]; Sib. Or. 3, 654) the masc. in var. cases of sing. and pl. Mt 22: 5; Lk 23: 33; Ac 27: 44; Ro 14: 5; 1 Cor 11: 21; 2 Cor 2: 16; Jd 22f. ὁ μέν ... ὁ δέ *this ... that* Ro 9: 21. ἃ μέν ... ἃ δέ (Lucian, Rhet. Praec. 15) *some ... others* 2 Ti 2: 20. ὃς μέν ... ὃς δέ ... ὃς δέ Mt 21: 35; 25: 15 (Lucian, Tim. 57 διδοὺς ... ᾧ μὲν πέντε δραχμάς, ᾧ δὲ μνᾶν, ᾧ δὲ ἡμιτάλαντον). ὃ μέν ... ὃ δέ ... ὃ δέ Mt 13: 8b, 23. ᾧ μέν ... ἄλλῳ δέ ... ἑτέρῳ (ἄλλῳ δέ is then repeated five times, and before the last one there is a second ἑτέρῳ) 1 Cor 12: 8-10. ὃ μέν ... καὶ ἄλλο κτλ. Mk 4: 4. ὃ μέν καὶ ἕτερον (repeated several times) Lk 8: 5. ἃ μέν ... ἄλλα δέ (repeated several times) Mt 13: 4-8a. In anacoluthon οὓς μέν without οὓς δέ 1 Cor 12: 28. ὃς μέν ... ὁ δέ ἀσθενῶν Ro 14: 2.—Bl-D. §250. MBlack, An Aramaic Approach³, '67, 100f. M-M.

ὁσάκις adv. (in Hom. ὁσσάκι; in the form ὁσάκις Lysias, Pla., X.+; inscr., pap.; Jos., Vi. 160) *as often as* w. ἐάν (Dit., Syll.³ 972, 124; BGU 1115, 22 [13 BC]; PHamb. 37, 3; PGiess. 12, 5) 1 Cor 11: 25f; Rv 11: 6. M-M.*

ὅσγε for ὅς γε s. ὅς I 10b. M-M.

ὅσιος, ία, ον (Aeschyl., Hdt.+; inscr., pap., LXX, En., Ep. Arist., Philo, Joseph., Test. 12 Patr., Sib. Or. 3, 735 [the noun ὁσίη is found as early as Hom.]. Mostly of three endings, but -ος, ον Pla., Leg. 8 p. 831D; Dionys. Hal. 5, 71; 1 Ti 2: 8. Bl-D. §59, 2; Mlt.-H. 157). Superl. ὁσιώτατος (Pla.; Dit., Or. 718, 1; Philo) 1 Cl 58: 1.

1. adj.—**a.** of men *devout, pious, pleasing to God, holy* w. δίκαιος (cf. Pla., Leg. 2 p. 663B, Gorg. 507B; Polyb. 22, 10, 8 παραβῆναι καὶ τὰ πρὸς τοὺς ἀνθρώπους δίκαια καὶ τὰ πρὸς τ. θεοὺς ὅσια; Dit., Syll.³ 800, 20f: ἀναστρέφεται πρός τε θεοὺς καὶ πάντας ἀνθρώπους ὁσίως κ. δικαίως; En. 104, 12; Jos., Ant. 9, 35; Test. Gad 5: 4, Benj. 3: 1) 2 Cl 15: 3 and still other virtues Tit 1: 8. ἔργα ὅσια κ. δίκαια (Jos., Ant. 8, 245) 2 Cl 6: 9. δίκαιον κ. ὅσιον w. acc. and inf. foll. 1 Cl 14: 1. W. ἄμωμος ἐν ὁσ. κ. ἀμώμῳ προθέσει δουλεύειν τῷ θεῷ *serve God with a holy and blameless purpose* 1 Cl 45: 7. ἄνδρες 45: 3. ὁσ. βουλή 2: 3.—ὅσιοι χεῖρες (Aeschyl., Choëph. 378; Soph., Oed. Col. 470: 'consecrated', 'ceremonially pure') 1 Ti 2: 8 transferred to the religio-ethical field (Philip of Perg. [II AD]: 95 fgm. 1 Jac. writes ὁσίῃ χειρί).—The word was prob. used in the cultic sense in the mysteries (ERohde, Psyche³ '03 I 288, 1): Aristoph., Ran. 335 ὅσιοι μύσται. The mystae of the Orphic Mysteries are called οἱ ὅσιοι: Pla., Rep. 2 p. 363C; Orph., Hymn. 84, 3 Qu.; cf. Ps.-Pla., Axioch. 371D. Sim. the Essenes are called ὅσιοι in Philo, Omn. Prob. Liber 91; cf. 75 ὁσιότης; PPar. 68c, 14 ὅσιοι Ἰουδαῖοι (s. Dssm., B 62, 4 [BS 68, 2]); PGM 5, 417 of a worshiper of Hermes.

b. of God (Orph., Hymn. 77, 2, Arg. 27; CIG 3594; 3830; Dt 32: 4; Ps 144: 17) *holy* μόνος ὅσιος Rv 15: 4. ἡ ὁσ. παιδεία *holy* (i.e. *divine*) *discipline* 1 Cl 56: 16. τὸ ὁσιώτατον ὄνομα *most holy name* 58: 1.—Also of Christ, the Heavenly High Priest (w. ἄκακος) Hb 7: 26.

2. subst.—**a.** τὰ ὅσια (*divine decrees* in contrast to τὰ δίκαια, *human statutes*: Pla., Polit. 301D; X., Hell. 4, 1, 33 al.—Wsd 6: 10; Jos., Ant. 8, 115) δώσω ὑμῖν τὰ ὅσ. Δαυὶδ τὰ πιστά *I will grant you the sure decrees of God relating to David* Ac 13: 34. This quot. fr. Is 55: 3 is evidently meant to show that the quot. fr. Ps 15: 10, which follows immediately, could not refer to the Psalmist David, but to Christ alone. The promises to David have solemnly been transferred to 'you'. However, David himself served not you, but his own generation (vs. 36). So the promises of God refer not to him, but to his Messianic Descendant. —ὅσια *holy acts* (ὀφείλω 2aα) 2 Cl 1: 3.

b. ὁ ὅσιος of God Rv 16: 5. Of Christ ὁ ὅσιός σου (after Ps 15: 10) Ac 2: 27; 13: 35.—Lit. s.v. ἅγιος. JohannaCh Bolkestein, Ὅσιος en Εὐσεβής, Diss. Amsterdam '36; JAMontgomery, HTR 32, '39, 97-102; MvanderValk, Z. Worte ὅσιος: Mnemosyne 10, '41; Dodd 62-4; FHauck, TW V 488-92: ὅσιος and related words. M-M. B. 1475. *

ὁσιότης, τητος, ἡ (X., Pla., Isocr. et al.; Epict. 3, 26, 32 δικαιοσύνη καὶ ὁσ.; inscr.; UPZ 33, 10 [162/1 BC]; 36, 13; LXX; En. 102, 5; Ep. Arist. 18 ἐν ὁσ.; Philo, Abr. 208 ὁσ. μὲν πρὸς θεόν, δικαιοσύνη δὲ πρὸς ἀνθρώπους, Spec. Leg. 1, 304, Virt. 47 δικ. καὶ ὁσ.; Jos., Ant. 19, 300) *devoutness, piety, holiness* of life ἐν ὁσ. καὶ δικαιοσύνῃ Lk 1: 75; 1 Cl 48: 4. Of the new man: he is created in the likeness of God ἐν δικαιοσύνῃ καὶ ὁσ. τῆς ἀληθείας *in true righteousness and holiness* Eph 4: 24. ἐν ὁσ. ψυχῆς 1 Cl 29: 1 (cf. Philo, Abr. 198). ἐν ὁσ. καρδίας (3 Km 9: 4; Dt 9: 5) 32: 4; 60: 2. M-M.*

ὁσίως adv. (Eur., X., Pla.+; inscr., pap., LXX; Ep. Arist. 306; 310; Philo, Aet. M. 10 εὐσεβῶς κ. ὁσ.) *devoutly, in a manner pleasing to God, in a holy manner*

1 Cl 21: 8. δουλεύειν τῷ θεῷ 26: 1. ἐπικαλεῖσθαι θεόν 60: 4 (acc. to the Lat., Syr. and Coptic versions; the word is lacking in the only Gk. ms. that includes this pass.). θεῷ ὀσ. εὐαρεστεῖν 62: 2. τὴν ἀγάπην ... ὀσ. παρέχειν τινί 21: 7. ὀσ. πολιτεύσασθαι 6: 1. W. δικαίως (s. ὅσιος 1a and δικαίως 1b): PK 2 p. 15, 2; ἀναστρέφεσθαι 2 Cl 5: 6. W. δικ. and ἀμέμπτως: γενέσθαι (cf. 1 Cl 40: 3) 1 Th 2: 10. ἀμέμπτως καὶ ὀσ. προσφέρειν τὰ δῶρα 1 Cl 44: 4. M-M.*

ὀσμή, ῆς, ἡ (trag., Thu.+; PGM 13, 365; LXX, En., Philo; Jos., Ant. 2, 297; Test. 12 Patr.; Sib. Or. 3, 462) and **ὀδμή** (Hom. +; later prose [s. L-S-J s.v. ὀσμή]; Phryn. p. 89 L.; in our lit. only Papias 3) *fragrance, odor*.

1. lit.—a. of a pleasant odor: of ointment J 12: 3 (cf. Achilles Tat. 2, 38, 3 ὀσμή of the fragrance of ointment and Plut., Alex. 20, 13 ὀδώδει ὑπ' ἀρωμάτων καὶ μύρων ὁ οἶκος).

b. of an unpleasant odor (Tob 6: 17 S; 8: 3; Job 6: 7) Papias 3 (ὀδμή).

2. fig. (Porphyr., Adv. Christ. [ABA 1916] 69, 20 speaks of the ὀσμή τῆς λέξεως, the [evil] odor [ὀσμή= stench; s. Artem. below] of the saying J 6: 53) ἡ ὀσμή τῆς γνώσεως αὐτοῦ *the fragrance of the knowledge of him* (=of God) 2 Cor 2: 14. This fragrance is spread throughout the world by the apostolic preaching and works οἷς μὲν ὀσμή ἐκ θανάτου εἰς θάνατον, οἷς δὲ ὀσμή ἐκ ζωῆς εἰς ζωήν vs. 16 (s. on εὐωδία). ἀπὸ τῆς ὀσμῆς ἐλεγχθή-σεσθε *you will be convicted* (or *tested*) *by the odor* (whether you have been corrupted or not; Artem. 1, 51 τὰ κρυπτὰ ἐλέγχει διὰ τ. ὀσμήν) IMg 10: 2. ὀσμή εὐωδίας (Gen 8: 21; Ex 29: 18; Lev 1: 9, 13 al.) *fragrant offering* fig., in relation to the Philippians' gift Phil 4: 18, to Jesus' sacrifice of himself Eph 5: 2, to a heart full of praise B 2: 10. M-M. B. 1022f.*

ὅσος, η, ον (Hom.+; inscr., pap., LXX, En., Ep. Arist., Philo, Joseph.) correlative w. πόσος, τοσοῦτος (Jos., Ant. 1, 318) *as great, how great; as far, how far; as long, how long; as much, how much*.

1. of space and time: τὸ μῆκος αὐτῆς (τοσοῦτόν ἐστιν), ὅσον τὸ πλάτος *its length is as great as its breadth* Rv 21: 16.—ἐφ' ὅσ. χρόνον *as long as* (UPZ 160, 12 [119 BC]) Ro 7: 1; 1 Cor 7: 39; Gal 4: 1. Also ἐφ' ὅσον (X., Cyr. 5, 5, 8; Polyaenus 4, 7, 10; UPZ 162 I, 23 [117 BC]; Jos., Ant. 13, 359) Mt 9: 15; 2 Pt 1: 13. ὅσ. χρόνον (X., Cyr. 5, 3, 25; Josh 4: 14) Mk 2: 19. ἔτι μικρὸν ὅσον ὅσον (Bl-D. §304 w. app.; Rob. 733; JWackernagel, Glotta 4, '13, 244f; OLagercrantz, Eranos 18, '18, 53ff) *in a very little while* Hb 10: 37; 1 Cl 50: 4 (both after Is 26: 20). ὅσον ὅσον *a short distance* (for ὅσον doubled s. Aristoph., Vesp. 213; Leonidas: Anth. Pal. 7, 472, 3; Hesychius 1421) Lk 5: 3 D.

2. of quantity and number: *how much* (*many*), *as much* (*many*) *as* (Aelian, V.H. 1, 4) ὅσον ἤθελον *as much as they wanted* J 6: 11 (Appian, Bell. Civ. 4, 11 §173 ὅσον ἐβούλετο).—W. πάντες (ἅπαντες) *all who* (Jos., Ant. 18, 370) ἅπαντες ὅσοι *all who* Lk 4: 40; J 10: 8; Ac 3: 24; 5: 36f. πάντα ὅσα *everything that* (Job 1: 12; Philo, Op. M. 40; Jos., Ant. 10, 35) Mt 13: 46; 18: 25; 28: 20; Mk 6: 30a; 11: 24; 12: 44; Lk 18: 12, 22.—Even without πάντες, ὅσοι has the mng. *all that* (Jos., Ant. 12, 399) οἱ πιστοὶ ὅσοι συνῆλθαν τῷ Πέτρῳ *all the believers who came with Peter* Ac 10: 45. ἱμάτια ὅσα *all the garments that* 9: 39. ὅσα κακὰ ἐποίησεν *all the harm that he has done* vs. 13. ὅσοι ..., αὐτοῖς *all who ..., to them* J 1: 12. ὅσοι ..., ἐπ' αὐτούς Gal 6: 16. ὅσοι ..., οὗτοι *all who ..., (these)* (Herm. Wr. 4, 4) Ro 8: 14; Gal 6: 12. ὅσα ..., ταῦτα Phil 4: 8 (for ὅσα repeated six times cf. Liban., Or.

20 p. 443, 1, where ὅσοι is repeated three times. Also Appian, Liby. 117 §554 ὅσα περιττὰ καὶ μάταια καὶ τρυφερὰ ἦν). W. οὗτοι preceding Hb 2: 15.—Abs. ὅσοι *all those who* Mt 14: 36; Mk 3: 10; Ac 4: 6, 34; 13: 48; Ro 2: 12a, b; 6: 3 al. ὅσα *everything that, whatever* Mt 17: 12; Mk 3: 8; 5: 19f; 9: 13; 10: 21; Lk 8: 39a, b; Ac 14: 27; 2 Ti 1: 18 al. W. ἄν (ἐάν) making the expr. more general *all those who, whoever,* lit. *as many as ever* (pap., LXX) ὅσοι w. ind. foll. Mk 6: 56; w. subjunctive foll. Mt 22: 9; Lk 9: 5; Ac 2: 39. ὅσα ἐάν (PGM 12, 71 ὅσα ἐὰν θέλω) Mt 18: 18a, b, or ἄν J 11: 22. Likew. πάντα ὅσα ἐάν (or ἄν) w. subj. foll. Mt 7: 12; 21: 22; 23: 3 (s. on this HGrimme, BZ 23, '35, 171–9); Ac 3: 22.

3. of measure and degree: ὅσον ..., μᾶλλον περισσότερον *as much as ..., so much the more* Mk 7: 36; cf. Hs 9, 1, 8. ὅσον ..., πλειόνως *the more ..., the more* IEph 6: 1. πλείονος ..., καθ' ὅσον πλείονα *as much more ... as* Hb 3: 3. καθ' ὅσον ..., κατὰ τοσοῦτο *to the degree that ..., to the same degree* 7: 20, 22. καθ' ὅσον ..., οὕτως *just as ..., so* 9: 27f. τοσούτῳ ..., ὅσῳ *(by) as much ..., as* 1: 4. τοσούτῳ μᾶλλον, ὅσῳ *all the more, as* 10: 25 (s. τοσοῦτος 2bγ). Without τοσούτῳ *to the degree that* (Polyb. 4, 42, 5; Plut., Alex. M. 5, 5) 8: 6. ὅσα ... τοσοῦτον *to the degree that ... to the same degree* Rv 18: 7. ὅσον *as far as* B 19: 8; D 12: 2. On ἐφ' ὅσον s. ἐπί III 3. M-M.

ὅσπερ s. ὅς I 10e. M-M.

ὀστέον, ου (Hom.+, and again in Hellenistic times, e.g. Plut., Pyrrh. 3, 6) pl. ὀστέα (Dit., Syll.³ 624, 7.—Lk 24: 39); gen. ὀστέων (Soph., Trach. 769; Pla., Phaedo 47 p. 98c and D; Dionys. Hal. 13, 4, 4; Jos., Bell. 6, 304.—Mt 23: 27; Hb 11: 22; Eph 5: 30 v.l.; 1 Cl 6: 3b [Gen 2: 23]; IRo 5: 3) and contracted ὀστοῦν, οῦ, τό (Att.; J 19: 36 [Ex 12: 46; Num 9: 12]; 1 Cl 6: 3a [Gen 2: 23]). Pl. ὀστᾶ (Diod. S. 22, 12; Epict. 4, 7, 32; Dit., Or. 599, 1; PLond. 1170 verso, 486; PGM 5, 460; Jos., Ant. 5, 125; 8, 232.— 1 Cl 18: 8 [Ps 50: 10]; 25: 3; MPol 18: 1) cf. Bl-D. §45; Mlt.-H. 121. The LXX uses the contracted forms in nom. and acc., the uncontracted in gen. and dat. (Thackeray 144) *bone*; of the above-mentioned places the following are of interest as far as content is concerned σὰρξ καὶ ὀστέα *flesh and bone* Lk 24: 39; Eph 5: 30 v.l. (cf. Od. 11, 219; Epict. 4, 7, 32 οὐ σὰρξ οὐδ' ὀστᾶ; Gen 29: 14; Judg 9: 2; 2 Km 5: 1; Mi 3: 2). σκορπισμοὶ ὀστέων *scattering(s) of bones* (in connection w. violent destruction of the human body) IRo 5: 3 (influenced by Ps 21: 15). ὀστᾶ τεταπεινωμένα *battered bones* 1 Cl 18: 8 (Ps 50: 10). M-M. B. 207.*

ὅστις, ἥτις, ὅ τι (Hom.+; inscr., pap., LXX, En., Ep. Arist.; Jos., Ant. 17, 7 al.—On the orthography of ὅ τι cf. Mlt.-H. 179), in our lit. as well as in the pap. occurring usu. in the nom.

1. generically or generalizing: *whoever, every one who*
a. w. pres. ind. foll. Mt 5: 39; 13: 12a, b; Mk 4: 20; 8: 34 v.l.; Lk 14: 27; Gal 5: 4. Pleonastically πᾶς ὅστις Mt 7: 24.

b. w. the aor. ind. Ro 11: 4; Rv 1: 7; 20: 4. πᾶς ὅστις Mt 19: 29.

c. w. fut. ind. Mt 5: 41; 18: 4; 23: 12a, b; πᾶς ὅστις 10: 32.—d. w. aor. subj. Mt 10: 33 v.l.; Js 2: 10. But s. on this Bl-D. §380, 4; Rob. 959; Kühner-G. II 426, 1.

e. w. ἄν (ἐάν), by which the indefiniteness of the expr. is heightened;—α. w. the pres. subj. J 2: 5; 1 Cor 16: 2; Gal 5: 10; Col 3: 17 (πᾶν ὅ τι ἐάν).—β. w. the aor. subj. Mt 10: 33 (s. 1d above); 12: 50; Lk 10: 35; J 14: 13; 15: 16; Ac 3: 23.

2. qualitatively—a. to indicate that persons (or things) belong to a certain class (*such a one*) *who* ἡγούμενος, ὅστις ποιμανεῖ *a leader who will shepherd* Mt 2: 6. εὐνοῦχοι οἵτινες 19: 12a, b, c; γεωργοὶ οἵτινες 21: 41. παρθένοι, αἵτινες 25: 1. τινὲς τῶν ὧδε ἑστώτων, οἵτινες 16: 28; Mk 9: 1.

b. to emphasize a characteristic quality, by which a preceding statement is to be confirmed *who* (*to be sure, by his very nature*), *in so far as* προσέχετε ἀπὸ τῶν ψευδοπροφητῶν οἵτινες ἔρχονται ἐν ἐνδύμασι προβάτων *beware of the false prophets, who come in sheep's clothing* Mt 7: 15. βαπτισθῆναι τούτους οἵτινες τὸ πνεῦμα ἔλαβον *who* (*indeed*) Ac 10: 47. οἵτινες ἐδέξαντο τὸν λόγον *in so far as they received the word* 17: 11. οἵτινες μετήλλαξαν *since indeed they had exchanged* Ro 1: 25; cf. vs. 32; 2: 15; 6: 2. ἀσπάσασθε Μαρίαν ἥτις *remember me to Mary, who certainly* 16: 6; cf. vss. 4, 7, 12. ψευδαδέλφους, οἵτινες παρεισῆλθον *false brethren, the kind who sneaked in* Gal 2: 4. Cf. Phil 2: 20; Eph 4: 19; 1 Ti 1: 4; Tit 1: 11 al. in Paul (Bl-D. §293, 4 w. app.; Rob. 728); Hb 8: 5; 10: 11; 13: 7. Sim. Ἀβραάμ, ὅστις ἀπέθανεν *who died, as you know* J 8: 53. φονεῖς ἐγένεσθε, οἵτινες ἐλάβετε . . . *who, to be sure, received* . . . Ac 7: 53. ἐπιθυμίαι, αἵτινες στρατεύονται κατὰ τῆς ψυχῆς 1 Pt 2: 11. οἵτινες οὐκ ἔγνωσαν *who, to be sure, have not learned* Rv 2: 24.—Yet many of the passages already mentioned may be classed under the following head (3), and some that are classed there may fit better in this one (2).

3. Quite oft. ὅστις takes the place of the simple rel. ὅς, ἥ, ὅ; this occurs rarely in class. usage (but s. Hdt. 4, 8, 1 and oft.; Thu. 6, 3, 1; Demosth. 38, 6; 17; Kühner-G. II 399f), but much more freq. in later Gk. (W-S. §24, 14d; Bl-D. §293; Mlt. 91f; Rdm.² 75; 77; 226; StBPsaltes, Grammat. d. Byz. Chroniken '13, 198; POxy. 110, 3; PFay. 108, 7 [both II ᴀᴅ]; Mayser II 3, 57. On the LXX cf. Thackeray 192), esp. in the Lucan writings; to explain a word or a thing εἰς πόλιν Δαυὶδ ἥτις καλεῖται Βηθλέεμ Lk 2: 4 (Hdt. 2, 99 πόλιν ἥτις νῦν Μέμφις καλέεται). τὴν χώραν τ. Γερασ. ἥτις ἐστὶν ἀντιπέρα τ. Γαλιλαίας 8: 26. ἄνδρες δύο. . .οἵτινες ἦσαν Μωϋσῆς κ. Ἠλίας 9: 30. Cf. 12: 1; Ac 16: 12; Hb 9: 2, 9; Rv 11: 8. τῇ δὲ ἐπαύριον ἥτις ἐστὶν μετὰ τὴν παρασκευήν Mt 27: 62 (POxy. 110, 3 αὔριον ἥτις ἐστὶν ιε΄). τὸν Βαραββᾶν ὅστις ἦν. . .βληθεὶς ἐν τῇ φυλακῇ Lk 23: 19. μετὰ τῶν στασιαστῶν δεδεμένος οἵτινες. . .φόνον πεποιήκεισαν Mk 15: 7. οἰκοδεσπότης ὅστις ἐφύτευσεν ἀμπελῶνα Mt 21: 33. οἰκοδεσπότης ὅστις ἐξῆλθεν 20: 1. Cf. 27: 55; Lk 7: 39; 8: 43; Ac 8: 15; 11: 20, 28; 12: 10; 13: 43; 17: 10; 21: 4; 23: 14, 21, 33; 24: 1; 28: 18; 2 Ti 2: 18. βλέπειν τὴν φωνὴν ἥτις ἐλάλει Rv 1: 12. τὴν γυναῖκα ἥτις ἔτεκεν 12: 13.

4. The use of ὅ τι as an interrogative word in the NT is doubtful, since all the passages where this use might occur are text-critically uncertain (against this PKatz, ThLZ 82, '57, 114).

a. In an indir. quest. λαληθήσεταί σοι ὅ τι σε δεῖ ποιεῖν Ac 9: 6 is well attested by ℵABC but despite that is rejected by Bl-D. §300, 1 app., though not by Rob. 730f.

b. As far as the dir. quest. is concerned ὅ τι (N. ὅτι) μετὰ τῶν τελωνῶν. . .ἐσθίει; *why does he eat with tax-collectors?* Mk 2: 16 is the reading only of BL (the t.r. reads τί ὅτι w. AC et al.; ℵD have διὰ τί or διατί instead of ὅ τι). Better attested and prob. to be understood as abbreviation of τί ὅ τι (Bl-D. §300, 2; Rob. 730) is the ὅ τι of Mk 9: 11, 28 (on this pass. cf. Field, Notes 33; Mlt.-Turner 49; MBlack, An Aramaic Approach³, '67, 119–212).—ὅτι = 'why' in indir. questions Thu. 1, 90; Jos.,

Ant. 6, 236; 12, 213; Gen 18: 13 A; Black, 119, cites Turner, JTS 27, '25, 58ff in support of this usage in Mk 8: 16f; 14: 60).

5. On τὴν ἀρχὴν ὅ τι καὶ λαλῶ ὑμῖν J 8: 25 cf. ἀρχή 1b, end.—Bl-D. §300, 2; Rob. 730.

6. The prepositional phrases ἀφ᾽ ὅτου (Diod. S. 2, 31, 9) Lk 13: 25 D, ἕως ὅτου (s. ἕως II 1bβ and γ; PGenève 56, 19) and μέχρις ὅτου (s. μέχρι 2) are fixed expressions. —HJCadbury, The Relative Pronouns in Acts and Elsewhere: JBL 42, '23, 150ff; LRydbeck, Fachprosa, '67, 98–118. M-M.

ὀστράκινος, η, ον (Hippocr.+; PLond. 1177, 75; 92; POxy. 1648, 63; LXX) *made of earth* or *clay* used w. σκεῦος (PLond. 77, 22; Lev 6: 21; 11: 33 al. Cf. Epict. 3, 9, 18) *earthen(ware) vessels* (w. those made of other materials) 2 Ti 2: 20. As a symbol, denoting breakableness ἔχειν τὸν θησαυρὸν ἐν ὀσ. σκεύεσιν 2 Cor 4: 7 (cf. Artem. 5, 25 εἶναι ἐν ὀστρακίνῳ σκεύει).—Of idols made of clay θεοί . . . ὀστράκινοι Dg 2: 7 (Sib. Or. 5, 495; cf. En. 99, 7). M-M.*

ὄστρακον, ου, τό (Hom. Hymns+; Dit., Syll.³ 1168, 82; 86 [IV ʙᴄ]; POxy. 234 II, 3; 1450, 4; Ostraka II 1152, 5; LXX; Philo, Somn. 2, 57) *baked clay, pottery* of pagan gods ὁ δὲ ὄστρακον *another is a piece of pottery* Dg 2: 2. Collectively ὀσ. λεπτόν *little pieces of broken pottery* Hs 9, 10, 1 (differently EJGoodspeed, JBL 73, '54, 85f).*

ὄσφρησις, εως, ἡ *sense of smell* (Pla., Phaedo 111ʙ al.; Philo; Test. Reub. 2: 5) or the organ of smell, *the nose* (sing. Ptolem., Apotel. 3, 15, 5; M. Ant. 10, 35, 2 w. ἀκοή = 'ear'; Diog. L. 6, 39 as a saying of Diogenes the Cynic; PRyl. 63, 5 [III ᴀᴅ] γλῶσσα ὄσφρησις ἀκοή) 1 Cor 12: 17 (ἀκοή 1a, c). M-M. B. 1022f.*

ὀσφῦς (on the accent cf. Bl-D. §13; Mlt.-H. 141f), ύος, ἡ (Aeschyl., Hdt.+; inscr., pap., LXX, Jos., Ant. 8, 217= 3 Km 12: 10).

1. *waist, loins* as the place where a belt or girdle is worn (4 Km 1: 8) Mt 3: 4; Mk 1: 6. Since the garment was worn ungirded about the house, girding denotes preparation for activity, esp. for a journey; freq. used in symbolic lang.: περιζώννυσθαι τὴν ὀσ. *have a belt around one's waist* (Jer 1: 17) Eph 6: 14; cf. Lk 12: 35 (cf. Ex 12: 11). Also ἀναζώννυσθαι τὰς ὀσ. 1 Pt 1: 13, where the gen. τῆς διανοίας shows the highly symbolic character of the expr. The gen. is lacking Pol 2: 1.

2. *the loins* as the place of the reproductive organs, in line w. the Hebr. phrase יָצָא מֵחֲלָצָיו פ' (cf. Gen 35: 11; 2 Ch 6: 9): ἐξέρχεσθαι ἐκ τῆς ὀσ. τινός *come forth from someone's loins= be someone's son or descendant* Hb 7: 5. ἐν τῇ ὀσ. τινὸς εἶναι vs. 10. καρπὸς τῆς ὀσ. τινός *the fruit of someone's loins= someone's descendants* Ac 2: 30 (cf. Ps 131: 11 v.l. [ARahlfs, Psalmi cum Odis '31].—καρπὸς ὀσφύος also Theodor. Prodr. 6, 370 H. Cf. Psellus p. 61, 33 τῆς βασιλείου ὀσφύος=of royal descent). The loins are prob. also thought of as an inmost source of power in αἱ ὀσ. ὑμῶν μὴ ἐκλυέσθωσαν *do not let your loins become powerless* D 16: 1 (cf. Test. Napht. 2: 8 ὀσφ. εἰς ἰσχύν). M-M.*

ὅταν (since Hom. who, however, always separates it [ὅτ᾽ ἄν]; inscr., pap., LXX, En., Ep. Arist., Philo, Joseph., Test. 12 Patr.) temporal particle *at the time that, whenever, when* of an action that is conditional, possible, and, in many instances, repeated.

1. w. the subj., in which case ὅτ. oft. approaches the mng. of ἐάν, since the time-reference also indicates the conditions under which the action of the main clause takes place (Kühner-G. II p. 447f). 1 J 2: 28 the mss. vary betw. ὅτ. and ἐάν (as e.g. also Judg 6: 3).

a. w. the pres. subj., when the action of the subordinate clause is contemporaneous w. that of the main clause. Preferably of (regularly) repeated action *whenever, as often as, every time that* (PFay. 109, 1 ὅταν θέλῃς = 'every time that you want'; likew. POxy. 1676, 26. Cf. ἄν 3a) ὅταν ποιῇς ἐλεημοσύνην Mt 6: 2; cf. 5f, 16; 10: 23; Mk 13: 11. ὅταν θέλητε 14: 7.—Lk 12: 11; 14: 12f al. W. τότε foll. *whenever . . . , then* (Hero Alex. III p. 214, 5) ὅταν ἀσθενῶ, τότε δυνατός εἰμι 2 Cor 12: 10. Also without the idea of repetition *when* 1 Th 5: 3.—Looking back upon a preceding time-reference ἕως τῆς ἡμέρας ἐκείνης ὅταν πίνω Mt 26: 29; Mk 14: 25.

b. w. the aor. subj., when the action of the subordinate clause precedes that of the main clause (PLeipz. 104, 16 [96/95 BC]; PRyl. 233, 2; Is 28: 19; 57: 13): ὅταν ὀνειδίσωσιν *when they (have) revile(d)* Mt 5: 11. Cf. 12: 43 (cf. KBeyer, Semitische Syntax im NT, '62, 285f); 13: 32; 23: 15; 24: 32f; Mk 4: 15f, 31f; 13: 28; Lk 6: 22, 26 and oft. W. τότε foll. *when* (someth. has happened), *then* (Sir 18: 7; Jos., Bell. 6, 287, Ant. 10, 213) Mt 24: 15f; 25: 31; Mk 13: 14; Lk 5: 35 (different in the parallels Mt 9: 15; Mk 2: 20, where ἡμέραι ὅταν *days when* belong together and τότε is connected w. καί); 21: 20; J 8: 28; 1 Cor 15: 28, 54; Col 3: 4.

2. w. the ind. (on this post-class. use s. Bl-D. §382, 4; Rob. 972f).

a. w. fut. ind. (1 Km 10: 7; Sib. Or. 4, 70; 11, 219) *when* 2 Cl 12: 2 (GEg 2a, b has the aor. subj. in the corresponding pass.); 17: 6; B 15: 5 (cf. Reinhold 108); Lk 13: 28 v.l. (for ὄψησθε). *Whenever* Rv 4: 9.

b. w. pres. ind. (Strabo 12, 27 p. 555 ὅταν δείκνυται; Ps.-Lucian, Philop. 26; PHamb. 70, 19 ὅταν τὸν λόγον δίδομεν; Ps 47: 4 v.l. [ARahlfs, Psalmi cum Odis '31]; Philo, Poster. Cai. 15 v.l.—ADebrunner, Glotta 11, '20, 26f) Mk 11: 25 (in addition to στήκετε, στήκητε and στῆτε are also found in the mss.). As a v.l. in Lk 11: 2; J 7: 27.—ὅταν βλέπετε *since you see* B 4: 14 (cf. Reinhold 108f).

c. w. impf. ind. (Polyb. 4, 32, 5f ὅταν . . . ἦσαν; inscr. in Ramsay, Phrygia I 2, 477 no. 343, 8; Gen 38: 9; 1 Km 17: 34; Ps 119: 7; Da 3: 7 Theod. v.l.) ὅταν αὐτὸν ἐθεώρουν Mk 3: 11.

d. w. aor. ind., in place of ὅτε *when* (Ex 16: 3; Ps 118: 32) Rv 8: 1 (v.l. ὅτε); *whenever* (Ex 17: 11; Num 11: 9) ὅταν ὀψὲ ἐγένετο, ἐξεπορεύοντο ἔξω τῆς πόλεως Mk 11: 19 (s. Bl-D. §367. Differently Mlt. 248); Hs 9, 4, 5; 9, 17, 3.

e. w. the plpf. ind. *as soon as* Hs 9, 1, 6. M-M.

ὅτε (Hom. +; inscr., pap., LXX, En., Ep. Arist., Joseph., Test. 12 Patr.) temporal particle.

1. lit., as a conjunction *when, while, as long as*, always w. the ind.—a. impf. Mk 14: 12; Ac 12: 6; 22: 20; *as long as, while* Mk 15: 41; J 21: 18; Ro 6: 20; 7: 5; 1 Cor 12: 2; 13: 11a; Hv 3, 6, 7 al.

b. predom. w. the aor. (Bl-D. §382, 1; Rob. 971) Mt 9: 25; 13: 48; 21: 34; Mk 1: 32; 4: 10; Lk 2: 21, 42; 15: 30; J 1: 19; 2: 22; Ac 1: 13; 8: 39; Gal 1: 15; 2: 11; Tit 3: 4; Hb 7: 10. ὅτε ἐπιστεύσαμεν *when we first believed* Ro 13: 11 al.—W. τότε foll. (Jos., C. Ap. 1, 127) Mt 13: 26; 21: 1; J 12: 16. Mt not infreq. has the transitional formula καὶ ἐγένετο ὅτε in narrative passages *and (it came about that) when . . .* (4 Km 14: 5) 7: 28; 11: 1; 13: 53; 19: 1; 26: 1.

c. perf. ὅτε γέγονα ἀνήρ *when I became a man* 1 Cor 13: 11b.—d. pres. *while* Hb 9: 17. W. historical pres. Mk 11: 1.

2. as a substitute for a relative pron. after a noun denoting time—a. w. the ind.—α. fut. ἐλεύσονται ἡμέραι ὅτε ἐπιθυμήσετε (*the*) *days will come, in which you will desire* Lk 17: 22. ἐν ἡμέρᾳ ὅτε κρινεῖ ὁ θεός Ro 2: 16 v.l. ἔρχεται ὥρα, ὅτε . . . προσκυνήσετε J 4: 21. Cf. vs. 23; 5: 25; 16: 25. καιρὸς ὅτε 2 Ti 4: 3.—β. pres. ἔρχεται νὺξ ὅτε οὐδεὶς δύναται ἐργάζεσθαι J 9: 4.

b. w. the aor. subj. (ὅτε w. subj. Hom. + in epic [Sib. Or. 8, 50] and lyric poetry; but also Vett. Val. 106, 36 ὅτε ἄρξηται) ἕως ἥξει ὅτε εἴπητε *until the time comes when you say* Lk 13: 35 (text uncertain; cf. Bl-D. §382, 2; Rob. 971f). M-M.

ὅτε adv. (Hom. +; inscr.) ὁτὲ μὲν . . . ὁτὲ δὲ . . . *now . . . now . . .* (Aristot., Pol. 2, 2, 16; Parthenius 27, 2; Dio Chrys. 50[67], 5; Polyaenus 5, 22, 4; Dit., Syll.³ 679, 83f) B 2: 4f (on the text s. Hdb. ad loc.).*

ὅτι (Hom. +; inscr., pap., LXX, En., Ep. Arist., Philo, Joseph., Test. 12 Patr.) conjunction (Bl-D. §396f; 408; 416; 470, 1 al.; Rob. 1032-6, al. [s. index]; HPernot, Études sur la langue des Évang. '27, 41ff) originally the neuter of ὅστις.

1. *that*—a. as a substitute for the epexegetical inf. (acc. w. inf.) after a preceding demonstrative (Bl-D. §394; cf. Rob. 1034) αὕτη δέ ἐστιν ἡ κρίσις, ὅτι τὸ φῶς ἐλήλυθεν *the judgment consists in this, that the light has come* J 3: 19. ἔστιν αὕτη ἡ ἀγγελία . . . , ὅτι ὁ θεὸς φῶς ἐστιν 1 J 1: 5. Cf. 3: 16; 4: 9, 10. ἐν τούτῳ . . . , ὅτι ἐκ τοῦ πνεύματος αὐτοῦ δέδωκεν ἡμῖν vs. 13; 5: 11. περὶ τούτου . . . ὅτι *about this . . . , that* J 16: 19. In ἔχω κατὰ σοῦ ὅτι . . . Rv 2: 4, ὅτι is epexegetical to a τοῦτο that remains unexpressed. Cf. vs. 6.

b. after verbs that denote mental or sense perception, or the transmission of such perception, or an act of the mind, to indicate the content of what is said, etc.

α. after verbs of saying, indicating, etc.: ἀπαγγέλλω, ἀποκρίνομαι, δείκνυμι, δῆλόν (ἐστιν), διδάσκω, εἶπον, ἐμφανίζω, λέγω, μαρτυρέω, ὁμολογέω, φημί etc.; s. the entries in question. Likew. after verbs of swearing, affirming and corresponding formulae: μαρτύρομαι Ac 20: 26; Gal 5: 3. μάρτυρα τὸν θεὸν ἐπικαλοῦμαι 2 Cor 1: 23. ὀμνύω Rv 10: 6. Cf. the sim. exprs. πιστὸς ὁ θεός 2 Cor 1: 18. ἰδοὺ ἐνώπιον τοῦ θεοῦ Gal 1: 20.—2 Cor 11: 10. Cf. also φάσις . . . ὅτι Ac 21: 31. αἱ γραφαὶ ὅτι *the Scriptures* (which say) *that* Mt 26: 54.—On 1 J 2: 12-14 s. BNoack, NTS 6, '60, 236-41.

β. after verbs that denote sense perception ἀκούω, θεάομαι, θεωρέω (q.v. 1); s. these entries.

γ. after verbs that denote mental perception ἀγνοέω, ἀναγινώσκω, βλέπω (perceive), γινώσκω, γνωστόν ἐστιν, ἐπιγινώσκω, ἐπίσταμαι, θεωρέω (q.v. 2a), καταλαμβάνω, μιμνῄσκομαι, μνημονεύω, νοέω, οἶδα, ὁράω (q.v. 1ca), συνίημι, ὑπομιμνῄσκω; s. these entries.

δ. after verbs of thinking, judging, believing, hoping: δοκέω (q.v. 1d), ἐλπίζω (q.v. 2; 3), κρίνω, λογίζομαι, νομίζω (q.v. 2), οἶμαι, πέπεισμαι, πέποιθα, πιστεύω (q.v. 1aβ), ὑπολαμβάνω; s. these entries. εἶχον τὸν Ἰωάννην ὅτι προφήτης ἦν *they held that John was a prophet* Mk 11: 32 (cf. Bl-D. §330; 397; 2; Rob. 1029; 1034).

ε. after verbs that denote an emotion and its expression ἀγανακτέω, ἐξομολογέομαι, ἐπαινέω, εὐχαριστέω, θαυμάζω, μέλει μοι, συγχαίρω, χαίρω, χάριν ἔχω τινί; s. these entries.

ζ. Very oft. the subj. of the ὅτι-clause is drawn into the main clause, and becomes the object of the latter: ἐπεγίνωσκον αὐτοὺς ὅτι (= ὅτι αὐτοὶ) σὺν τῷ Ἰησοῦ ἦσαν

Ac 4: 13. οἴδατε τὴν οἰκίαν Στεφανᾶ ὅτι (=ὅτι ἡ οἰκία
Σ.) ἐστὶν ἀπαρχή 1 Cor 16: 15. Cf. Mt 25: 24; Mk 12: 34;
J 8: 54; 9: 8; Ac 3: 10; 1 Cor 3: 20 (Ps 93: 11); 1 Th 2: 1; Rv
17: 8. Somet. the subj. is repeated by a demonstrative
pron. in the ὅτι-clause: ἐκήρυσσεν τὸν Ἰησοῦν ὅτι οὗτός
ἐστιν ὁ υἱὸς τοῦ θεοῦ Ac 9: 20.—Pass. εἰ Χριστὸς
κηρύσσεται ὅτι ἐκ νεκρῶν ἐγήγερται=εἰ κηρύσσεται
ὅτι Χρ. ἐκ νεκ. ἐγ. 1 Cor 15: 12.

c. Ellipses τί ὅτι; what (is it) that? why? Lk 2: 49; Ac 5:
4, 9; Mk 2: 16 v.l.—οὐχ ὅτι (= οὐ λέγω ὅτι) not that, not
as if J 6: 46; 7: 22; 2 Cor 1: 24; 3: 5; Phil 3: 12; 4: 11; 2 Th
3: 9 (so μὴ ὅτι PLond. 42, 43 [168 BC]).—οὐχ οἷον ὅτι Ro
9: 6 s. οἷος.—ὅτι alone is used for εἰς ἐκεῖνο ὅτι with
regard to the fact that, in consideration of the fact that
(Gen 40: 15; Ruth 2: 13) ποταπός ἐστιν οὗτος ὅτι; what
sort of man is this, (in consideration of the fact) that? Mt
8: 27 (but it is possible that in this and sim. passages the
causal force of ὅτι [s. 3 below] comes to the fore). τίς ὁ
λόγος οὗτος ὅτι; Lk 4: 36. Cf. 16: 3; Mk 4: 41; J 2: 18; 8:
22; 9: 17; 11: 47; 16: 9-11.—ὅτι=ἐν τούτῳ ὅτι in that Ro
5: 8. ὅτι=περὶ τούτου ὅτι concerning this, that Mt 16: 8;
Mk 8: 17.—On ὅτι=why? Mk 9: 11, 28 s. ὅστις 4.

d. Special uses—α. ὅτι w. acc. and inf. after θεωρεῖν
Ac 27: 10 (on the mingling of constructions cf. POxy. 237
V, 8 δηλῶν ὅτι . . . δεῖσθαι τὸ πρᾶγμα; Ep. Arist. 125;
schol. on Clem. of Alex., Protr. p. 296, 11f Stäh.—Bl-D.
§397, 6; Rob. 1036; Rdm.² 195; MArnim, De Philonis
Byzantii dicendi genere, Diss. Greifswald '12, 88 [but s. on
this Rdm.² 196, 1]). Less irregular is καὶ ὅτι w. a finite
verb as the second member dependent on παρακαλεῖν
after the inf. ἐμμένειν Ac 14: 22.—S. also 2, end, below
and cf. HJCadbury, JBL 48, '29, 412-25.

β. ὡς ὅτι is found three times in Pauline letters and
simply means 'that' in the later vernacular (exx. in Mlt.
212; Bl-D. §396 w. app.; Rob. 1033). But the subjective
mng. of ὡς must be conceded for the NT, since the Vulgate
renders it twice w. 'quasi' and the third time (2 Cor 5: 19)
w. 'quoniam quidem': δι' ἐπιστολῆς . . . , ὡς ὅτι ἐνέστηκεν ἡ ἡμέρα τοῦ κυρίου by a letter . . . (of such
content) that (in the opinion of its writer) the day of the
Lord is (now) here 2 Th 2: 2. Paul says ironically: κατὰ
ἀτιμίαν λέγω, ὡς ὅτι ἡμεῖς ἠσθενήκαμεν I must confess
to my shame that we have conducted ourselves as weak-
lings (as I must concede when I compare my conduct w.
the violent treatment you have had fr. others [vs. 20])
2 Cor 11: 21. Likew. 5: 19; we are a new creation in Christ
(vs. 17). This does not alter the fact that everything has its
origin in God, who reconciled us w. himself through Christ
(vs. 18), ὡς ὅτι θεὸς ἦν ἐν Χριστῷ κόσμον καταλλάσσων ἑαυτῷ that is (acc. to Paul's own conviction), (that) it
was God who was reconciling the world to himself in
Christ.

γ. consecutive ὅτι so that (Pel.-Leg. p. 20 τί διδοῖς τοῖς
ἀμνοῖς σου ὅτι ζωὴν αἰώνιον ἔχουσιν; Acta Christophori p. 68, 18 Usener τοιοῦτοι γάρ εἰσιν οἱ θεοὶ ὑμῶν,
ὅτι ὑπὸ γυναικὸς ἐκινήθησαν; Gen 20: 9; Judg 14: 3;
1 Km 20: 1; 3 Km 18: 9) ποῦ οὗτος μέλλει πορεύεσθαι,
ὅτι ἡμεῖς οὐχ εὑρήσομεν αὐτόν; J 7: 35. τί γέγονεν
ὅτι . . . ; what has happened, so that (=to bring it about
that) . . . ? 14: 22 (so Rob. 1001; differently Rdm.² 196
and Bl-D. §480, 6 app.). This is prob. also the place for
οὐδὲν εἰσηνέγκαμεν εἰς τὸν κόσμον, ὅτι οὐδὲ ἐξενεγ-
κεῖν τι δυνάμεθα we have brought nothing into the world,
so that (as a result) we can take nothing out of it 1 Ti 6: 7.
τί ἐστιν ἄνθρωπος, ὅτι μιμνῄσκῃ αὐτοῦ; Hb 2: 6 (Ps 8:
5).

2. to introduce direct discourse. In this case it is not to
be rendered into English, but to be represented by quo-

tation marks (ὅτι recitativum.—Bl-D. §397, 5; 470, 1;
EKieckers, IndogF 35, '15, 21ff; Rob. 1027f. As early as
class. Gk. [Pla., Apol. 23 p. 34 D.—Kühner-G. II p. 367];
Arrian, Alex. An. 2, 12, 4; 2, 26, 4; 4, 8, 9; Epict. 1, 9, 16;
Philostrat., Vi. Apoll. 1, 38 p. 40; POxy. 744, 11 [1 BC];
119, 10; 1064, 5; LXX; Jos., Ant. 11, 5; 18, 326, Vi. 55)
ὑμεῖς λέγετε ὅτι 'βλασφημεῖς' ὅτι εἶπον J 10: 36.
ὁμολογήσω αὐτοῖς ὅτι 'οὐδέποτε ἔγνων ὑμᾶς' Mt 7: 23.
So after var. verbs of saying as direct discourse: Mt 26:
72-5; 27: 43; Mk 1: 37; 2: 16; 5: 28; 12: 29; 13: 6
(JSundwall, Om bruket av ὅτι recit. i Mk: Eranos 31, '33,
73-81; MZerwick, Untersuchgen z. Mk-Stil '37, 39-48);
Lk 1: 25, 61 (PWinter, HTR 48, '55, 213-16); 4: 41a; 5:
26; 15: 27a; J 1: 20, 32; 4: 17; 6: 42; 16: 17; Ac 5: 23; 15:
1; Ro 3: 8 (Bl-D. §470, 1 app.; Rob. 1033; AFridrichsen,
ZNW 34, '35, 306-8); 2 Th 3: 10; 1 J 4: 20 al. Scripture
quotations are also introduced in this way (Appian, Bell.
Civ. 62 §260 a saying of Caesar in direct discourse is
introduced by ὅτι): Μωϋσῆς ἔγραψεν ἡμῖν ὅτι 'ἐάν τινος
κτλ.' Mk 12: 19.—Mt 2: 23; 21: 16; Lk 2: 23; J 10: 34; Ro
8: 36; 1 Cor 14: 21; Hb 11: 18.—On ὅτι foll. by the acc.
and inf. in direct discourse Lk 4: 43 cf. 1da above.

3. as a causal conjunction—a. subordinating because,
since ὅτι ἑώρακάς με, πεπίστευκας J 20: 29.—Mt 2: 18
(Jer 38: 15); 5: 3ff; 13: 16; Mk 1: 34; 5: 9; Lk 4: 41b; 5:
20ff; 8: 30; 10: 13; 11: 42ff; 13: 2b; 15: 27b; perh. 18: 9
(TWManson, The Sayings of Jesus '54, 309); 19: 17; J 1:
30, 50a; 2: 25; 3: 18; 5: 27; 9: 16, 22; Ro 6: 15; 1 Cor 12:
15f. On 1 J 2: 12-14 cf. BNoack, NTS 6, '60, 236-41
(opposes causal mng.).—Used w. demonstr. and interrog.
pronouns διὰ τοῦτο . . . ὅτι for this reason . . . , (namely)
that J 8: 47; 10: 17; 12: 39; 1 J 3: 1 al. διὰ τί; ὅτι . . . why?
because . . . Ro 9: 32; 2 Cor 11: 11. χάριν τίνος; ὅτι . . .
for what reason? because . . . 1 J 3: 12. Foll. by διὰ τοῦτο
because . . . for this reason J 15: 19. οὐχ ὅτι . . . ἀλλ' ὅτι
not because . . . but because 6: 26; 12: 6.

b. The subordination is oft. so loose that the transl. for
recommends itself (Bl-D. §456, 1; Rob. 962f). Naturally
the line betw. the two groups cannot be drawn with
certainty: Mt 7: 13; 11: 29; Lk 7: 47; 9: 12; 13: 31; 16: 24;
J 1: 16f; 9: 16; 1 Cor 1: 25; 4: 9; 10: 17; 2 Cor 4: 6; 7: 8, 14;
1 J 3: 14.—MBlack, An Aramaic Approach³, '67, 70ff.
M-M and suppl.

ὅτου gen. sing. masc. and neut. of ὅστις (q.v. 6).

οὗ really the gen. of ὅς, became an adv. of place (Aeschyl.
+; inscr., pap., LXX, En., Ep. Arist., Philo, Joseph.).

1. where—a. lit., of place.—α. οὗ . . . , ἐκεῖ where
. . . , there Mt 18: 20; Ro 9: 26. Without ἐκεῖ IPhld 8: 1.

β. mostly after a noun that denotes a locality, in place of
the relative pron., in, at, or on which (Jos., Ant. 8, 349) εἰς
Ναζαρά, οὗ ἦν τεθραμμένος Lk 4: 16. Cf. vs. 17; 23: 53;
Ac 1: 13; 2: 2; 7: 29; 12: 12; 16: 13 al.—The place in
which: ἐπάνω οὗ ἦν τὸ παιδίον Mt 2: 9 (cf. X., An. 1, 7, 6
μέχρι οὗ διὰ καῦμα οὐ δύνανται οἰκεῖν).

b. fig., indicating not the actual place, but the circumstances, someth. like (in a situation) where (Jos., Ant. 2,
272) οὗ δὲ οὐκ ἔστιν νόμος οὐδὲ παράβασις where no law
exists, there is no transgression, either Ro 4: 15. Cf. 5: 20.
οὗ δὲ τὸ πνεῦμα κυρίου ἐλευθερία 2 Cor 3: 17.

2. where, to which, (whither) (Dialekt-Inschr. 1758, 8;
1766, 7 [both Delphi]; Dit., Syll.³ 374, 25; Bar 2, 4, 13;
Ep. Arist. 269) εἰς πᾶσαν πόλιν . . . οὗ ἤμελλεν αὐτὸς
ἔρχεσθαι into every city where he was about to come Lk
10: 1. ἐπορεύθησαν . . . εἰς τὸ ὄρος οὗ ἐτάξατο αὐτοῖς ὁ
Ἰησοῦς to the mountain to which Jesus had directed them
(to go) Mt 28: 16. εἰς τὴν κώμην οὗ ἐπορεύοντο Lk 24:

28.—οὖ ἐάν w. the pres. subj. of future time (IG IV² 1, 68, 71; 73 [302 BC]; PSI 902, 4 [I AD]) ἄπειμι οὖ ἐὰν βούλησθε 1 Cl 54: 2. οὖ ἐὰν πορεύωμαι 1 Cor 16: 6. M-M.

οὐ (Hom.+; inscr., pap., LXX, En., Ep. Arist., Philo, Joseph., Test. 12 Patr., Sib. Or.) objective negative adv., denying the reality of an alleged fact; in the NT used w. the ind. (μή serves as the neg. for the other moods, including inf. and ptc.—w. certain exceptions, which will be discussed below. Cf. Bl-D. §426; Rob. 1168f; Mlt.-Turner 281f). Before vowels w. the smooth breathing it takes the form οὐκ; before those w. the rough breathing it is οὐχ; in the mss. this rule is freq. disregarded (W-S. §5, 10b, c; Bl-D. §14 w. app.; Rob. 224). On its use s. Bl-D. §426-33; Rdm.² p. 210ff; Rob. 1155-66.

1. οὐ w. an accent is the neg. answer *no* Mt 13: 29; J 1: 21; 7: 12; 21: 5. ἤτω ὑμῶν τὸ οὖ οὖ *let your 'no' be 'no'* Js 5: 12. Doubled for emphasis (s. ναί 5.—οὖ οὖ Nicetas Eugen. 5, 76 H. Likew. μὴ μή=no, no! [Herodas 3, 71; Meleager (I BC) in Anth. Pal. 12, 80, 3; Psellus p. 268, 15 μὴ μὴ μάγιστρε]) Mt 5: 37; 2 Cor 1: 17ff.

2. used to negative single words or clauses (class.; s. Kühner-G. II p. 182) *not*.

a. οὐ πᾶς *not every one* Mt 7: 21. οὐ πάντες 19: 11; Ro 9: 6; 10: 16. πάντες οὐ κοιμηθησόμεθα *we shall not all fall asleep* 1 Cor 15: 51 (cf. JHBurn, ET, '26, 236f; POppenheim, ThQ 112, '31, 92-135; AVaccari, Biblica 13, '32, 73-6; Bl-D. §433, 2 app.; Rob. 753). Likew. transposed διατί πάντες οὐ μετενόησαν; *why have not all repented?* Hs 8, 6, 2. οὐ πᾶσα σάρξ 1 Cor 15: 39. οὐ πάντως Ro 3: 9; 1 Cor 5: 10.—καλέσω τὸν οὐ λαόν μου λαόν μου *those who were not my people I will call my people* Ro 9: 25a (Hos 2: 25b); cf. 1 Pt 2: 10. οὐκ ἔθνος *no nation at all* Ro 10: 19 (Dt 32: 21).

b. freq. in litotes (cf. Lysias 13, 62 εἰ μὲν οὐ πολλοὶ ἦσαν) οὐ πολλοί, πολλαί J 2: 12; Ac 1: 5 (οὐ μετὰ πολλὰς ἡμέρας=μετ' οὐ πολλ. ἡμ. Cf. οὐκ ἐξ ὄντων= ἐξ οὐκ ὄντων 2 Macc 7: 28). οὐκ ὀλίγος, ὀλίγη, ὀλίγοι, ὀλίγαι Ac 17: 4, 12; 19: 23f; 27: 20. οὐκ ἄσημος 21: 39. οὐχ ἁγνῶς Phil 1: 17. οὐ μετρίως Ac 20: 12. οὐκ ἐκ μέτρου J 3: 34. μετ' οὐ πολύ *soon (afterward)* Ac 27: 14. S. also d below.

c. *not* in a contrast τῷ κυρίῳ καὶ οὐκ ἀνθρώποις Col 3: 23. τρέχω ὡς οὐκ ἀδήλως 1 Cor 9: 26.

d. as a periphrasis for some concepts expressed by verbs: οὐκ ἀγνοεῖν *know quite well* 2 Cor 2: 11. οὐκ ἐᾶν *prevent* Ac 16: 7; 19: 30. οὐ θέλειν *refuse* 2 Th 3: 10. οὐ πταίειν Js 3: 2. οὐχ ὑπακούειν *be disobedient* 2 Th 3: 14. οὐ φιλεῖν 1 Cor 16: 22.

3. From 2 above are derived the points under which, contrary to the rule given above, the neg. used w. the ptc. is somet. οὐ. In addition, it is poss. that in individual cases class. influence is still at work.—Bl-D. §430 w. app.; Mlt. 231f (w. pap. exx.); Rdm.² 212; Mlt.-Turner 284f.

a. to negative a single concept: πράγματα οὐ βλεπόμενα *things not seen* Hb 11: 1. οὐχ ὁ τυχὼν *extraordinary* Ac 19: 11; 28: 2 (cf. Com. Att. Fgm. III 442 no. 178 οὐδὲ τοῖς τυχοῦσι). θλιβόμενοι ἀλλ' οὐ στενοχωρούμενοι 2 Cor 4: 8; cf. vs. 9.

b. in strong emphasis or contrast: ἄνθρωπον οὐκ ἐνδεδυμένον ἔνδυμα γάμου (emphasizing the fact that his dress was improper) Mt 22: 11. οὐ προσδεξάμενοι τὴν ἀπολύτρωσιν (emphasizing the great heroism of their act) Hb 11: 35. In clear emphasis οὐ βλέπων Lk 6: 42. οὐκ ἰδόντες 1 Pt 1: 8. οὐκ ὄντος αὐτῷ τέκνου Ac 7: 5.—Contrast: Ac 28: 19. τότε μὲν οὐκ εἰδότες θεὸν...νῦν δέ Gal 4: 8. καὶ οὐ introducing a contrast is also used w. the ptc. καὶ οὐκ ἐν σαρκὶ πεποιθότες Phil 3: 3. καὶ οὐ

κρατῶν Col 2: 19. ὁ μισθωτὸς καὶ οὐκ ὢν ποιμήν J 10: 12.

c. In quotations fr. the LXX in the NT we notice the tendency of the OT translators regularly to render לֹא w. the ptc. by οὐ: ἡ οὐ τίκτουσα, ἡ οὐκ ὠδίνουσα Gal 4: 27 (Is 54: 1). τὴν οὐκ ἠγαπημένην Ro 9: 25b (Hos 2: 25a). οἱ οὐκ ἠλεημένοι 1 Pt 2: 10 (Hos 1: 6).

d. τὰ οὐκ ἀνήκοντα Eph 5: 4 t.r. is presumably a mingling of τὰ μὴ ἀνήκοντα and (the rdg. in the text itself) ἃ οὐκ ἀνῆκεν (as early as 𝔓⁴⁶).

4. οὐ in main clauses—**a.** simple statements w. the indic. οὐκ ἐγίνωσκεν αὐτήν Mt 1: 25. οὐ δύνασθε θεῷ δουλεύειν καὶ μαμωνᾷ 6: 24. οὐκ ἤφιεν λαλεῖν τὰ δαιμόνια Mk 1: 34. οὐκ ἦν αὐτοῖς τέκνον Lk 1: 7. οὐχ ὑμῶν ἐστιν Ac 1: 7. οὐ γὰρ ἐπαισχύνομαι τὸ εὐαγγέλιον Ro 1: 16 and very oft.

b. used to negative the prohibitive future (Hebr. לֹא w. the impf.—Synes., Ep. 67 p. 211B οὐκ ἀγνοήσεις) οὐ φονεύσεις Mt 5: 21; cf. vs. 27; Mt 19: 18; Ro 7: 7; 13: 9 (all commandments fr. the Decalogue: Ex 20: 13-17; Dt 5: 17-21). Also οὐκ ἐπιορκήσεις Mt 5: 33. οὐκ ἐκπειράσεις κύριον Lk 4: 12 (Dt 6: 16); Ac 23: 5 (Ex 22: 27); 1 Cor 9: 9 (Dt 25: 4).—Mt 6: 5.

c. in direct questions, when an affirmative answer is expected (Bl-D. §427, 2; Rob. 917): οὐκ ἀκούεις, πόσα σου καταμαρτυροῦσιν; *you hear, do you not...?* Mt 27: 13. οὐχ ὑμεῖς μᾶλλον διαφέρετε αὐτῶν; 6: 26. Cf. vs. 30. ὁ διδάσκαλος ὑμῶν οὐ τελεῖ δίδραχμα; *your teacher pays the two-drachma tax, does he not?* Mt 17: 24.—Mk 6: 3; 7: 18; 12: 24; Lk 11: 40; J 4: 35; 6: 70; 7: 25; Ac 9: 21 and oft. οὐ μέλει σοι ὅτι ἀπολλύμεθα; *does it make no difference to you that we are perishing?* Mk 4: 38.—The second pers. of the fut. indic. w. οὐ, as an impatient question, functions as an imperative οὐ παύσῃ; =παῦσαι! *will you not stop?= stop!* Ac 13: 10.

5. οὐ in subordinate clauses—**a.** in relative clauses w. indic. (in the NT, under this hypothesis, μή is found in such clauses only Tit 1: 11; 2 Pt 1: 9; 1 J 4: 3 [but cf. Bl-D. §428, 4 w. app. and cf. Rob. 1158]; Ac 15: 29 D; Col 2: 18 v.l.): Mt 10: 38; 12: 2; Mk 4: 25 (s. 2d above); Lk 6: 2; J 6: 64; Ro 15: 21 (Is 52: 15); Gal 3: 10 (Dt 27: 26) al.

b. in declarative clauses w. ὅτι, likew. in temporal and causal clauses w. indic.: ὅτι οὐ J 5: 42; 1 Th 2: 1. ὁ ἀρνούμενος ὅτι Ἰησοῦς οὐκ ἔστιν ὁ Χριστός 1 J 2: 22 (on the negative here s. ἀρνέομαι 2).—ἐπεὶ οὐ Lk 1: 34. ὅτε οὐ 2 Ti 4: 3.—εἰ οὐ w. indic.: εἰ οὐ δώσει αὐτῷ Lk 11: 8. εἰ ἐν τῷ ἀλλοτρίῳ πιστοὶ οὐκ ἐγένεσθε 16: 12; Mk 11: 26; Lk 18: 4; J 1: 25; 10: 37; Ro 8: 9b; 11: 21; Hb 12: 25.— Once actually in a contrary to fact condition: καλὸν ἦν αὐτῷ εἰ οὐκ ἐγεννήθη Mt 26: 24=Mk 14: 21 (Bl-D. §428, 2; Rob. 1160; Mlt.-Turner 284).

6. in combination w. other negatives—**a.** strengthening the negation (Mel. Chor. Adesp., fgm. no. 11 EDiehl² ['42] οὐ μήποτε τὰν ἀρετὰν ἀλλάξομαι ἀντ' ἀδίκου κέρδεος) Mt 22: 16; Mk 5: 37; Lk 4: 2; 23: 53 (οὐκ ἦν οὐδεὶς οὔπω); J 6: 63; 11: 49; 12: 19; 15: 5; Ac 8: 39; 2 Cor 11: 9. οὐ μηκέτι (s. μηκέτι 6a) Mt 21: 19.

b. destroying the force of the negation (class.): Ac 4: 20; 1 Cor 12: 15 (Bl-D. §431, 1; Rob. 1164).—In questions, if the verb itself is already negatived (by οὐ), the negation can be invalidated by the interrogative particle μή (s. μή C 1), which expects the answer 'no', so that the stage is set for an affirmative answer (Aesop, Fab. 404 H. μὴ οὐκ ἔστι χλόη; = certainly there is grass, is there not?) μὴ οὐκ ἤκουσαν; *surely they have heard, have they not?* Ro 10: 18; cf. vs. 19. μὴ οὐκ ἔχομεν ἐξουσίαν; *we have the right, do we not?* 1 Cor 9: 4; cf. vs. 5. μὴ οἰκίας οὐκ ἔχετε; *you have houses, do you not?* 11: 22.

c. On the combination of οὐ and μή s. μή D.

d. The combining of οὐδέ and οὐ μή to form οὐδ' οὐ μή instead of οὐδὲ μή is unclassical (Bl-D. §431, 3 w. app.; Rob. 1175; Mlt.-Turner 286.—Prayer to the god Socnopaeus: Wilcken, Chrest. 122, 2ff εἰ οὐ δίδοταί μοι συμβιῶσαι Ταπεθεῦτι Μαρρείους οὐδ' οὐ μὴ γένηται ἄλλου γυνή [Rdm.² 211f]; LXX) Mt 24: 21. οὐ μή σε ἀνῶ οὐδ' οὐ μή σε ἐγκαταλίπω Hb 13: 5 (Dt 31: 6 A, 8 A οὐδ οὐ μή; 1 Ch 28: 20 A).—οὐδὲν . . . οὐ μὴ ἀδικήσει instead of οὐδὲν . . . μή . . . Lk 10: 19. οὐδὲν οὐ μὴ λήψῃ Hm 9: 5.

7. w. one of two clauses that are either coordinate or contrasted.

a. οὐ . . . ἀλλά s. ἀλλά 1a, b.—1 Th 2: 4 the οὐ w. the ptc. is prob. to be explained under this head (s. 3 above).

b. οὐ . . . , . . . δέ Ac 12: 9, 14; Hb 4: 13, 15.—c. . . . , ἀλλ' οὐ looking back upon a 'to be sure' 1 Cor 10: 5, 23.—d. οὐ μόνον, ἀλλὰ (καί) s. μόνος 2c.—e. οὐ . . . εἰ μή s. εἰ VI 8. M-M.

οὐά (Tdf. οὐᾶ; cf. Proleg. p. 101) interjection denoting amazement (Epict. 3, 23, 24 εἰπέ μοι 'οὐά' καὶ 'θαυμαστῶς'; 32; 3, 22, 34; Cass. Dio 63, 20.—Kühner-Bl. II p. 252) aha! As an expression of scornful wonder Mk 15: 29. Cf. Mt 11: 26 v.l. M-M.*

οὐαί interjection denoting pain or displeasure woe, alas! (LXX, En. But also Epict. 3, 19, 1; ibid. and 3, 22, 32 οὐαί μοι; Vi. Aesopi W c. 37 οὐαὶ τῇ ἀτυχίᾳ; POxy. 413, 184f οὐαί σοι, ταλαίπωρε . . . οὐαί σοι· οὐαί μοι. Bl-D. §4, 2a. Loanw. in rabb.).

1. as an exclamation—a. w. dat. of the pers. or thing concerning whom (which) the pain is expressed (s. above; oft. LXX. Cf. Jos., Bell. 6, 306 αἰαὶ Ἱεροσολύμοις) οὐαί σοι Χοραζίν, οὐαί σοι Βηθσαϊδά(ν) Mt 11: 21; Lk 10: 13 (cf. Jer 13: 27).—Mt 18: 7b; 23: 13-16, 23, 25, 27, 29; 24: 19; 26: 24; Mk 13: 17; 14: 21; Lk 21: 23; 22: 22; 1 Cl 46: 8 (Mt 26: 24); Hv 4, 2, 6; D 1: 5; GP 7: 25.—Doubled for emphasis (Am 5: 16).—Procop. Soph., Ep. 36 and 62 ἰοὺ ἰού=alas, alas!): three times w. dat. foll. Rv 8: 13 t.r.—οὐαὶ δι' οὗ ἔρχεται (=τούτῳ δι' οὗ ἐρχ.) Lk 17: 1; cf. 2 Cl 13: 2; ITr 8: 2.—W. ὅτι foll. to give the reason Lk 6: 24f; 11: 42-4, 47, 52; also vs. 46, only w. the difference that here οὐαί follows: ὑμῖν τοῖς νομικοῖς οὐαί, ὅτι. Cf. Jd 11; 2 Cl 17: 5; B 6: 2, 7 (Is 3: 9).—W. the prep. ἀπό foll., also to give the reason: οὐαὶ τῷ κόσμῳ ἀπὸ τῶν σκανδάλων Mt 18: 7a; w. ὅταν foll. Lk 6: 26.—The transition to the next group is marked by: οὐαὶ ὑμῖν, οἱ ἐμπεπλησμένοι vs. 25a.

b. w. the nom. and article as a voc.: οὐαὶ οἱ γελῶντες νῦν Lk 6: 25b (cf. Am 5: 18; Hab 2: 6, 12; Zeph 2: 5). οὐαὶ οὐαὶ ἡ πόλις ἡ μεγάλη Rv 18: 10, 16, 19. οὐαὶ οἱ συνετοί B 4: 11 (Is 5: 21). Also without the art. οὐαὶ τυφλοὶ μὴ ὁρῶντες GOxy 31f (JoachJeremias, Unknown Sayings of Jesus, tr. Fuller '57, 36-9, 48).

c. w. acc. of the pers. (Bl-D. §190, 2; Rob. 1193) Rv 12: 12. οὐαί repeated three times 8: 13 (the reason for the 'woe' is introduced by ἐκ).

2. as a subst. (Ezk 2: 10; 7: 26; Kephal. I 105, 3) indecl. (Bl-D. §58; Rob. 302) οὐαί μοί ἐστιν 1 Cor 9: 16 (cf. Hos 9: 12). As a fem. ἡ οὐαί woe, calamity Rv 9: 12a; 11: 14a, b. Pl. ἔρχεται ἔτι δύο οὐαί 9: 12b (the lack of agreement in number [Bl-D. §136, 5] as Hes., Theog. 321 τῆς δ' [of the Chimaera] ἦν τρεῖς κεφαλαί. The schol. on Hes. explains this characteristic as Doric). M-M.*

Οὐαλέριος, ου, ὁ Valerius; freq. found as the name of a Roman gens (Diod. S. 11, 41, 1; 11, 60, 1; 13, 76, 1; 16, 46, 1). Valerius w. the cognomen Bito 1 Cl 65: 1.*

οὐδαμῶς adv. (Aeschyl., Hdt.+; Dit., Syll.³ 679, 80;

PTebt. 24, 53 [117 BC]; 27, 41; 58, 4; Sb 4426, 12; 4512, 76; LXX; Philo; Jos., Ant. 1, 303; 15, 158) by no means Mt 2: 6. M-M.*

οὐδέ negative conjunction (Hom.+; inscr., pap., LXX, En., Ep. Arist., Philo, Joseph., Test. 12 Patr.).

1. and not, nor joins neg. sentences or clauses to others of the same kind. After οὐ: κλέπται οὐ διορύσσουσιν οὐδὲ κλέπτουσιν Mt 6: 20. Cf. vs. 28; 5: 15; 7: 18; 10: 24; 25: 13; Mk 4: 22; Lk 6: 43f; 12: 24, 27 𝔓⁴⁵ 𝔓⁷⁵ et al.; J 6: 24; Ac 2: 27 (Ps 15: 10); Ro 2: 28; Gal 1: 1; 3: 28a, b; 1 Th 5: 5; Hb 9: 25; 1 Pt 2: 22 (cf. Is 53: 9); Rv 21: 23. οὐ . . . οὐδὲ . . . οὐδέ Mt 6: 26; J 1: 13, 25; 1 Th 2: 3. After οὔπω Mt 16: 9; Mk 8: 17. After οὐδείς Mt 9: 17; 11: 27; 22: 46; Rv 5: 3 (οὐδείς . . . οὐδὲ οὐδέ). ἵνα μή . . . οὐδὲ 9: 4.—οὐδὲ γάρ for . . . not J 8: 42; Ac 4: 12, 34; Ro 8: 7. οὐδὲ γάρ . . . οὐδένα for . . . not . . . anyone J 5: 22. οὐδὲ μὴ πέσῃ (cf. Is 49: 10 A) Rv 7: 16.

2. also not, not either, neither ἐὰν μὴ ἀφῆτε . . . , οὐδὲ ὁ πατὴρ ὑμῶν ἀφήσει τὰ παραπτώματα ὑμῶν if you do not forgive . . . , your Father will not forgive your transgressions (either) Mt 6: 15. Cf. 21: 27; 25: 45; Mk 16: 13; Lk 16: 31; J 15: 4; Ro 4: 15; 11: 21; 1 Cor 15: 13, 16. οὐδὲ γὰρ ἐγὼ . . . παρέλαβον αὐτὸ οὔτε (v.l. οὐδέ) . . . for I did not receive it . . . nor . . . Gal 1: 12. ἀλλ' οὐδέ and neither Lk 23: 15.

3. not even, Lat. ne . . . quidem (Bl-D. §445, 2; Rob. 1185; Libanius, Or. 11 p. 439, 14 F. οὐδὲ συγγνώμη= not even forbearance) οὐδὲ Σολομὼν περιεβάλετο ὡς ἓν τούτων not even Solomon was dressed like one of them Mt 6: 29. Cf. Lk 7: 9; 12: 26; J 21: 25; 1 Cor 5: 1. οὐδ' ἄν (X., Cyr. 8, 3, 3; Herodian 2, 8, 2) Hb 8: 4. οὐδ' οὕτως not even then 1 Cor 14: 21. οὐδείς . . . οὐδὲ . . . οὐδὲ . . . no one . . . not even . . . and not even . . . Mt 24: 36; Mk 13: 32. οὐδὲ τὴν γραφὴν ταύτην ἀνέγνωτε; have you never (even) read this passage of Scripture? Mk 12: 10. Cf. Lk 6: 3. Likew. in other questions Lk 23: 40; 1 Cor 11: 14.—καὶ οὐδέ Mk 6: 31. καὶ οὐδὲ ἀλύσει (οὐκέτι οὐδεὶς ἐδύνατο αὐτὸν δῆσαι) 5: 3.—ἀλλ' οὐδέ but not even Ac 19: 2; 1 Cor 3: 2; 4: 3; Gal 2: 3.—οὐδὲ εἷς not even one (X., Mem. 3, 5, 21; Dionys. Hal. 1, 73; Nicol. Dam.: 90 fgm. 103m, 2 Jac. οὐδὲ εἷς κλέπτει; 2 Km 13: 30; Philo, Rer. Div. Her. 66; Jos., C. Ap. 1, 66; 2, 141.—Bl-D. §302, 2; Rob. 751) Mt 27: 14; J 1: 3; Ac 4: 32; Ro 3: 10 (s. below). —After οὐ, strengthening it (Appian, Liby. 90 §424 οὐ γὰρ οὐδὲ δίδοτε=you do not even allow) οὐκ ἤθελεν οὐδὲ τοὺς ὀφθαλμοὺς ἐπᾶραι he would not even raise his eyes Lk 18: 13; cf. Ac 7: 5; Ro 3: 10 (s. above).—GValley, Üb. d. Sprachgebr. des Longus, Diss. Ups. '26, 36-44: on οὔτε and οὐδέ in later times. M-M.

οὐδείς, οὐδεμία, οὐδέν (Hom.+; inscr., pap., LXX, Ep. Arist., Philo, Joseph.—The forms οὐθείς [Hs 9, 5, 6], οὐθέν [Lk 23: 14; Ac 15: 9; 19: 27; 26: 26; 1 Cor 13: 2; Hm 4, 2, 1], οὐθενός [Lk 22: 35; Ac 20: 33 v.l.; 2 Cor 11: 9] appear freq. since Aristotle in lit. [Jos., Ant. 5, 250; 6, 47 al.], in inscr. [Meisterhans³-Schw. 258f], and in pap. [Mayser 181f], though they are even older [PStrassb. II 125, 4—c. 400 BC]; on them cf. Bl-D. §33 w. app.; W-S. §5, 27f and note 42; Mlt.-H. 111f; JWackernagel, Hellenistica '07, 23.—The LXX usage in Thackeray p. 58-62).

1. as an adj. no οὐδεὶς προφήτης Lk 4: 24. Cf. 16: 13. παροιμία οὐδεμία J 16: 29. Cf. 18: 38; Ac 25: 18; 27: 22. οὐδὲν εἴδωλον 1 Cor 8: 4a. Cf. J 10: 41. οὐδεὶς ἄλλος (UPZ 71, 15 [152 BC]) 15: 24.—οὐδεμία ἐκκλησία . . . εἰ μὴ ὑμεῖς Phil 4: 15.—W. other negatives: οὐ . . . οὐδεμίαν δύναμιν Mk 6: 5.

2. as a subst.—a. οὐδείς no one, nobody Mt 6: 24; 8: 10; 9: 16; Mk 2: 21f; 5: 4; 7: 24; Lk 5: 36f, 39; J 1: 18

(οὐδεὶς πώποτε as PGM 5, 102 Osiris, ὃν οὐδεὶς εἶδε πώποτε; Jos., C. Ap. 2, 124); Ro 14: 7b; 1 Cor 2: 11; 3: 11 and oft.—W. the partitive gen. (Epict. 4, 1, 3 οὐδεὶς τ. φαύλων; Jos., Ant. 3, 321 οὐδεὶς τ. ἱερέων) οὐδεὶς ἀνθρώπων *no one at all* Mk 11: 2. Cf. Lk 14: 24. οὐδεὶς τ. ἀνακειμένων J 13: 28. τῶν λοιπῶν οὐδεὶς *none of the others* Ac 5: 13. οὐδ. ὑμῶν 27: 34 (Diod. S. 14, 65, 2 οὐδεὶς ἡμῶν). Cf. Ro. 14: 7a. Instead of the part. gen. we may have ἐκ (Jos., Bell. 7, 398) Lk 1: 61; J 7: 19; 16: 5.—οὐδεὶς . . . εἰ μή *no one . . . except* Mt 11: 27; 17: 8; Mk 10: 18; Lk 10: 22; 18: 19; J 14: 6; 1 Cor 1: 14; 8: 4b; Rv 2: 17; 14: 3; 19: 12. οὐδεὶς ἐξ αὐτῶν ἀπώλετο εἰ μή J 17: 12.—Also οὐδεὶς . . . ἐὰν μή J 3: 2; 6: 44, 65. Used w. other negatives (Appian, Samn. 11 §4 οὐδένα λαβεῖν οὐδέν, οὔτε . . . οὔτε=nobody accepted anything, neither . . . nor) οὐ . . . οὐδείς (Appian, Bell. Civ. 1, 19 §80=nobody; Diog. L. 1, 53) Mt 22: 16; Mk 3: 27; 5: 37; 12: 14; Lk 8: 43; J 8: 15; 18: 31; Ac 4: 12; 1 Cor 6: 5. οὓς δέδωκάς μοι οὐκ ἀπώλεσα ἐξ αὐτῶν οὐδέ J 18: 9. οὐκέτι . . . οὐδείς Mk 9: 8. οὐδεὶς οὔπω *no one yet* Lk 23: 53 (v.l. οὐδέπω); οὐδεὶς οὔπω ἀνθρώπων Mk 11: 2. οὐδέπω οὐδείς J 19: 41; Ac 8: 16. οὐδεὶς οὐκέτι Mk 12: 34; Rv 18: 11. οὐδὲ ἀλύσει οὐκέτι οὐδείς Mk 5: 3.—οὐδενὶ οὐδέν 16: 8 (Appian, Liby. 128 §613 οὐδὲν οὐδείς=no one [set fire to] anything [ruling out all exceptions]). Cf. Lk 9: 36. οὐδὲ . . . οὐδείς J 5: 22.

b. οὐδέν *nothing*—**α.** lit. οὐδὲν ἀδυνατήσει ὑμῖν Mt 17: 20. Cf. 10: 26; 26: 62; 27: 12; Mk 7: 15. Foll. by partitive gen. Lk 9: 36b; 18: 34; Ac 18: 17. Foll. by εἰ μή *nothing but* Mt 5: 13; 21: 19; Mk 9: 29; 11: 13. οὐδὲν ἐκτὸς ὧν *nothing but what* Ac 26: 22. Used w. other negatives: οὐ . . . οὐδέν Mk 14: 60f; 15: 4; Lk 4: 2; J 3: 27; 5: 30; 9: 33; 11: 49. οὐ . . . οὐδενὶ τούτων 1 Cor 9: 15a. οὐ . . . οὐδέν, ἂν (=ἐὰν) μή J 5: 19. οὐκέτι . . . οὐδέν Mk 7: 12; 15: 5; Lk 20: 40. οὐδὲν ὑμᾶς οὐ μὴ ἀδικήσει Lk 10: 19 (cf. ἀδικέω 2b).

β. non-literally *worthless, meaningless, invalid* (X., Cyr. 6, 2, 8; Diod. S. 14, 35, 5; Dio Chrys. 4, 60; 15[32], 101 οὐδέν ἐστι=it means nothing, is unimportant) ὃς ἂν ὀμόσῃ ἐν τ. ναῷ, οὐδέν ἐστιν *whoever swears by the temple, (his oath) is worthless* Mt 23: 16, 18. Cf. J 8: 54; 1 Cor 7: 19a, b. εἰ καὶ οὐδέν εἰμι 2 Cor 12: 11b. οὐθέν εἰμι 1 Cor 13: 2 (on the neut. referring to a masc. subj. cf. Bl-D. §131; Rob. 751).—Ac 21: 24; 25: 11.—γενέσθαι εἰς οὐδέν 5: 36. εἰς οὐθὲν λογισθῆναι 19: 27. Antonym τις 1bζ.

γ. the acc. οὐδέν *in no respect, in no way* (Dio Chrys. 52[69], 6.—Bl-D. §154; 160; Rob. 751) οὐδὲν διαφέρει he *is different in no respect* Gal 4: 1. οὐθὲν διέκρινεν Ac 15: 9. Ἰουδαίους οὐδὲν ἠδίκηκα 25: 10; cf. Gal 4: 12. οὐδὲν ὑστέρησα 2 Cor 12: 11a. οὐδὲν ὠφελοῦμαι 1 Cor 13: 3. ἡ σὰρξ οὐκ ὠφελεῖ οὐδέν J 6: 63. οὐδὲν οὐδενὸς χρῄζει εἰ μή he needs nothing at all, except 1 Cl 52: 1. οὐδέν μοι διαφέρει Gal 2: 6 cf. διαφέρω 2c.—W. the same mng. ἐν οὐδενί Phil 1: 20.—Somet. the later usage οὐδέν=οὐ (Aristoph., Eccl. 644; Dionys. Hal. [Rdm.² 32, 5]; Epict. 4, 10, 36; POxy. 1683, 13; BGU 948, 13) suggests itself, e.g. Ac 18: 17; Rv 3: 17. M-M.

οὐδέποτε adv. (Hom.+; Epict.; Dit., Syll.³ 800, 29 οὐδέποτε μὴ λειφθῇ; PHib. 78, 5 [244/43 BC]; POxy. 1062, 11 [II AD]; LXX; Ep. Arist. 226; Philo, Op. M. 12; Joseph.) *never*, w. pres. 1 Cor 13: 8; Hb 10: 1, 11; Hs 4: 5. W. a past tense (Diod. S. 14, 6, 1; Appian, Bell. Civ. 2, 139 §578; Jos., Bell. 5, 399, Ant. 13, 311) Mt 7: 23; 9: 33; Mk 2: 12; Lk 15: 29a, b; J 7: 46; Ac 10: 14; 11: 8; 14: 8; IRo 3: 1; Hm 3: 3f; s 8, 10, 3; D 16: 4. W. fut. Mt 26: 33; Hm 4, 1, 1.—In questions: οὐδέποτε ἀνέγνωτε . . .; *have you never read . . . ?* Mt 21: 16, 42; Mk 2: 25. M-M.*

οὐδέπω adv. (Aeschyl., Pla.+; POxy. 275, 8 [66 AD]; 273, 13; PRyl. 178, 7; Ex 9: 30; Jos., Bell. 2, 138, Ant. 14, 350) *not yet* J 7: 8 𝔓⁶⁶, 39 (v.l. οὔπω); 20: 9; Hm 3: 3. οὐ . . . οὐδεὶς οὐδέπω *no one ever* Lk 23: 53 v.l. (for οὔπω). οὐδέπω οὐδείς (Jos., Ant. 6, 91) J 19: 41; cf. Ac 8: 16. M-M.*

οὐθείς s. οὐδείς. M-M.

οὐκέτι adv. (Hom.+; inscr., pap., LXX, En.; Ep. Arist. 231; Joseph.) *no more, no longer, no further.*

1. lit., of time (Jos., Ant. 7, 16) οὐκέτι εἰμὶ ἄξιος κληθῆναι υἱός σου Lk 15: 19, 21.—Mt 19: 6; Mk 10: 8; J 4: 42; 6: 66; 11: 54; 15: 15; Ro 6: 9b; Gal 2: 20; Eph 2: 19; Phlm 16; Rv 10: 6.—*Never. . . again* (Jos., Ant. 6, 156; Artem. 3, 13 ἀθάνατοι οἱ ἀποθανόντες, ἐπεὶ μηκέτι τεθνήξονται) Χριστὸς ἐγερθείς. . . οὐκέτι ἀποθνήσκει Ro 6: 9a. Cf. Ac 20: 25, 38; 2 Cor 1: 23.—W. the pres., of an event in the very near fut.: ὁ κόσμος με οὐκέτι θεωρεῖ *the world will see me no longer* J 14: 19; 16: 10, 16; 17: 11.—Used w. another negative: οὐ . . . οὐκέτι (Zeph 3: 15; En. 100, 5) Ac 8: 39. οὐδὲ . . . οὐκέτι Mt 22: 46. οὐδὲ . . . οὐκέτι οὐδείς Mk 5: 3. οὐκέτι οὐ 7: 12; 15: 5; Lk 20: 40. οὐκέτι οὐδείς (UPZ 42, 30 [162 BC]) Mk 9: 8. οὐδεὶς οὐκέτι 12: 34; Rv 18: 11. οὐκέτι οὐ μή *never again* (Am 9: 15) Mk 14: 25; Lk 22: 16; Rv 18: 14. οὐκέτι. . . οὐκέτι *no longer. . . no longer* B 8: 2 (Polyaenus 1, 41, 2 οὐκέτι three times).

2. In Paul there is found a usage that takes οὐκέτι not temporally, but logically (Melissus [V BC] B 9, Vorsokrat.⁵ I 275 εἰ . . . οὐκέτι ἓν εἴη, cf. B 7, 2 p. 270; Empedocles B 17, 31, I 317 εἴτε . . . οὐκέτ' ἂν ἦσαν; Ocellus c. 2 Harder; Ps.-Aristot., de Melisso etc. [ed. HDiels, ABA 1900] 1, 4; schol. on Apollon. Rhod. 2, 498–527a [p. 168, 23] οὐκέτι δὲ καὶ θυγάτηρ αὐτοῦ ἦν=then, accordingly, she was not his daughter) *then* (accordingly) *not* εἰ δὲ χάριτι οὐκέτι ἐξ ἔργων *if by grace, then not by deeds* Ro 11: 6a. Cf. 7: 20; 14: 15; Gal 3: 18. Likew. νυνὶ οὐκέτι Ro 7: 17. M-M.

οὐκοῦν adv. (trag., Pla., X.+; 4 Km 5: 23 v.l.)—1. inferential *therefore, so, accordingly* (Jos., C. Ap. 1, 171; 2, 226) B 5: 3, 11, 12; 6: 16; 7: 1, 10; 9: 4; 15: 4; Dg 2: 9; Hs 9, 28, 6.

2. interrogative, when the question has inferential force (Menand., Epitr. 144; 336 J; Epict. 1, 7, 6; 8; 2, 24, 3 al.; PHib. 12, 4 [III BC]), *so then* οὐκοῦν βασιλεὺς εἶ σύ; *so you are a king?* J 18: 37 (cf. Bl-D. §451, 1 w. app.; Rob. 1175; Kühner-G. II p. 163f). M-M.*

Οὐλαμμαούς Lk 24: 13 D for Ἐμμαοῦς of the text; influenced by the earlier name of Bethel, Gen 28: 19 (s. Rahlfs' ed. '26, 36).*

οὖλος, η, ον (Hom.+) *curly* of hair (Plut., Cim. 5, 3 οὔλῃ τριχί; Achilles Tat. 1, 4, 3; En. 106, 2; Sib. Or. 13, 105) AP 3: 10.*

οὐμενοῦν (οὐ μὲν οὖν) adv. (Aristoph., Pla. et al.) *not at all, by no means* (expressing a strongly negative answer to a question) Dg 7: 4.*

οὐ μή s. μή D.

οὖν (Hom.+; inscr., pap., LXX, En., Ep. Arist., Philo, Joseph., Test. 12 Patr.) a particle, never found at the beginning of a sentence. In our lit. it is an inferential and then mainly a transitional conjunction (so Hdt.+ [Kühner-G. II p. 326].—Bl-D. §451, 1 w. app.; Rob. 1191f; Mlt.-Turner 337f). Its mng. varies w. the context, and at times it may be left untranslated.

1. inferential, denoting that what it introduces is the result of or an inference fr. what precedes *so, therefore, consequently, accordingly, then.*

a. in declarative sentences Mt 1: 17; 7: 24; Lk 3: 9; 11: 35; J 6: 13; Ac 1: 21; 5: 41; Ro 5: 1; 6: 4; 11: 5; 13: 10; 16: 19; 1 Cor 4: 16; 7: 26; 2 Cor 3: 12; Eph 4: 1, 17; Phil 2: 28; 1 Pt 2: 7; 3 J 8 al.

b. in commands and invitations ποιήσατε οὖν καρπὸν ἄξιον τῆς μετανοίας Mt 3: 8 (s. also 3 below). ἔσεσθε οὖν ὑμεῖς τέλειοι 5: 48. μὴ οὖν φοβεῖσθε 10: 31. προσερχώμεθα οὖν μετὰ παρρησίας Hb 4: 16. Cf. Mt 6: 8, 9, 31; 9: 38; Mk 10: 9; 13: 35; Lk 8: 18; 10: 2, 40; Ac 2: 36; 3: 19; 8: 22; Ro 6: 12 (WNauck, Das οὖν- paräneticum, ZNW 49, '58, 134f); 1 Cor 10: 31; 2 Cor 7: 1; Gal 5: 1; Phil 2: 29; Col 2: 16 al. νῦν οὖν πορεύεσθε ἐν εἰρήνῃ Ac 16: 36.

c. in questions:—**α.** in real questions θέλεις οὖν; *do you want, then?* Mt 13: 28. σὺ οὖν εἶ; *are you, then?* Lk 22: 70. Cf. J 18: 39. νόμον οὖν καταργοῦμεν; μὴ γένοιτο Ro 3: 31. Cf. Gal 3: 21.—1 Cor 6: 15. τί οὖν; *why then?* (Menand., Her. 40, Epitr. 96 J.; Dio Chrys. 2, 9) Mt 17: 10; cf. 19: 7; J 1: 25; *what then?* (Menand., Epitr. 9, Per. 321) Mt 27: 22; Mk 15: 12; Lk 3: 10; 20: 15, 17; J 6: 30b. τίς οὖν; (Menand., Epitr. 4) Lk 7: 42. διὰ τί οὖν οὐκ ἐπιστεύσατε; Mt 21: 25; Mk 11: 31. πῶς οὖν; (Menand., Epitr. 224) Mt 22: 43; J 9: 19; Ro 4: 10. πότε οὖν; Lk 21: 7. πόθεν οὖν; Mt 13: 27, 56; J 4: 11. ποῦ οὖν; Ro 3: 27; Gal 4: 15.

β. Certain formulas are favorite expressions, esp. in Paul: τί οὖν; *what, then, are we to conclude?* (Dio Chrys. 14[31], 55; 60; 17[34], 28; Jos., Bell. 2, 364) J 1: 21; Ro 3: 9; 6: 15; 11: 7. τί οὖν ἐστιν; *what, then, is to be done?* Ac 21: 22; 1 Cor 14: 15, 26. τί οὖν ἐστιν Ἀπολλῶς; *what is Apollos, really?* 3: 5 (s. 3 below). τί οὖν φημι; 1 Cor 10: 19. τί οὖν ἐροῦμεν; *what, then, are we to say?* Ro 6: 1; 7: 7; 9: 14, 30. τί οὖν ἐροῦμεν πρὸς ταῦτα; 8: 31. τί οὖν ὁ νόμος; Gal 3: 19.

γ. in rhetorical questions πόσῳ οὖν διαφέρει ἄνθρωπος προβάτου *how much more, then, is a man worth than a sheep?* Mt 12: 12. πῶς οὖν σταθήσεται ἡ βασιλεία αὐτοῦ; *how then will his kingdom endure?* vs. 26.—26: 54; Lk 7: 31; Ro 10: 14 (s. also 4 below).

2. In historical narrative οὖν serves—**a.** to resume a subject once more after an interruption *so, as has been said* ἔλεγεν οὖν τοῖς ἐκπορευομένοις Lk 3: 7 (connecting w. vs. 3). Cf. 19: 12; J 4: 6, 28; Ac 8: 25; 12: 5.—Cf. 1 Cor 8: 4 (reaching back to vs. 1); 11: 20.

b. to indicate a transition to someth. new. So esp. in the Fourth Gospel *now, then* J 1: 22; 2: 18, 20; 3: 25; 4: 33, 46; 5: 10, 19; 6: 60, 67; 7: 25, 28, 33, 35, 40; 8: 13, 21, 22, 25, 31, 57; 9: 7f, 10, 16 and oft.; Ac 25: 1 al.

c. to indicate a response (HEDana and JRMantey, Manual Grammar of the Gk. NT '27, p. 254) where the transl. *in reply, in turn* (Ex 8: 6) is poss. J 4: 9, 48; 6: 53 al.

3. It may be that some traces of the class. usage in which οὖν is emphatic, = *certainly, really, to be sure* etc. (s. L-S-J s.v. 1) remain in the pap. (e.g. PLond. 28, 4 [c. 162 BC]; PTebt. 33, 2) and in the NT (so M-M., s.v. 3 and Dana and Mantey, op. cit. p. 255f) Mt 3: 8 (s. also 1b above), 10; J 20: 30; *of course* Ac 26: 9; 1 Cor 3: 5 (s. also 1cβ above) al.

4. οὖν seems also to be used adversatively ('slightly adversative sense'—M-M., s.v. 4, w. ref. to PTebt. 37, 15 [73 BC]; so also Dana and Mantey, op. cit. p. 256f; but cf. also Bl-D. §451, 1 app.) in some NT pass., e.g. J 9: 18; Ac 23: 21; 25: 4; 28: 5; Ro 10: 14 (s. 1cγ above), in the sense *but, however.*—JRMantey, Newly Discovered Mngs. for οὖν: Exp. 8th Ser. XXII '21, 205-14.

5. used w. other particles: ἄρα οὖν s. ἄρα 4. ἐὰν οὖν Mt 5: 19, 23; 24: 26; J 6: 62; 2 Ti 2: 21; Js 4: 4; Rv 3: 3b. ἐάν τε οὖν Ro 14: 8. εἰ οὖν s. εἰ VI 10. εἰ μὲν οὖν s. εἰ VI 6. εἴτε οὖν . . . εἴτε 1 Cor 10: 31; 15: 11. ἐπεὶ οὖν s. ἐπεί 2. μὲν οὖν . . . δέ (Jos., Ant. 13, 76f) Mk 16: 19f; Lk 3: 18f; J 19: 24f; Ac 8: 4f; 11: 19f; 1 Cor 9: 25.—Also without the δέ denoting contrast (Jos., Ant. 19, 337) Ac 1: 6, 18; 2: 41; 5: 41; 8: 25 al. νῦν οὖν Ac 10: 33b; 23: 15; also 15: 10 (s. νῦν 2).—ὅταν οὖν Mt 6: 2; 21: 40; 24: 15. ὅτε οὖν J 2: 22; 4: 45; 6: 24; 13: 12, 31; 19: 6, 8, 30; 21: 15. τότε οὖν 11: 14; 19: 1, 16; 20: 8. ὡς οὖν (Jos., Ant. 6, 145, Vi. 292) 4: 1, 40; 11: 6; 18: 6; 20: 11; 21: 9. ὥσπερ οὖν Mt 13: 40. M-M.

οὔπω adv. of time (Hom.+; pap., LXX, Philo, Joseph.) *not yet* Mt 24: 6; Mk 13: 7; J 2: 4; 6: 17; 7: 6, 8a (v.l. for οὐκ), b, 30, 39a (Aesop, Fab. 466 P. οἶνος γὰρ οὔπω ἦν [people still drank nectar]), b v.l. (for οὐδέπω); 8: 20, 57; 11: 30; 20: 17; 1 Cor 3: 2; 8: 2; Phil 3: 13 (v.l. οὐ); Hb 2: 8; 12: 4; 1 J 3: 2; Rv 17: 10, 12; IEph 3: 1; Hv 3, 9, 5; s 9, 5, 2. οὐδεὶς οὔπω *no one ever* (Maximus Tyr. 39, 3i) Mk 11: 2 (οὔπω is lacking in t.r.); Lk 23: 53 (v.l. οὐδέπω). οὔπω (for οὐδέπω) . . . ἐπ' οὐδενί Ac 8: 16 t.r. In questions: Mt 16: 9; Mk 4: 40 v.l. (for πῶς οὐκ); 8: 17, 21. οὔπω γάρ introducing a digression (Jos., Bell. 1, 39; 6, 80) J 3: 24. M-M.*

οὐρά, ᾶς, ἡ (Hom.+; inscr., pap., LXX; Jos., Bell. 4, 6, Ant. 3, 228) *tail* Rv 9: 10 (of a scorpion as schol. on Nicander, Ther. 885; Sib. Or. 5, 525), 19a, b (cf. Ael. Dion. α, 109 ὄφις ὁ καὶ ἐπὶ τῆς οὐρᾶς κεφαλὴν ἔχων); 12: 4. M-M. B. 209.*

οὐράνιος, ον (Hom.+; inscr., pap., LXX, Philo, Joseph.—An adj. of two endings Bl-D. §59, 2; Mlt.-H. 157; Attic wr. predom. form the fem. in -ία) *heavenly, belonging to heaven, coming from* or *living in heaven* (Diod. S. 6, 2, 8 τοὺς οὐρανίους θεούς; Hymn to Anubis fr. Kios 1 p. 139 Peek; Suppl. Epigr. Gr. VIII 2 [117/8 AD] θεοῦ ἁγίου οὐρανίου; other exx. of οὐ. as a designation of pagan deities: Syria 6, '25, p. 355, 4; Philo, Omn. Prob. Lib. 130; Jos., C. Ap. 1, 254f τ. οὐρανίους θεούς; Sib. Or. 3, 19; 286 θεὸς οὐ.) ὁ πατὴρ ὑμῶν (or μου) ὁ οὐράνιος Mt 5: 48; 6: 14, 26, 32; 15: 13; 18: 35 (t.r. ἐπουράνιος); 23: 9; 1 Cor 15: 47 v.l. στρατιὰ οὐράνιος *the heavenly host* or *army* (= צְבָא הַשָּׁמַיִם 3 Km 22: 19 ἡ στρατιὰ τοῦ οὐρανοῦ) Lk 2: 13 (v.l. οὐρανοῦ). ἡ οὐράνιος ὀπτασία *the heavenly vision* Ac 26: 19. ἡ οὐράνιος βασιλεία=ἡ βασ. τῶν οὐρανῶν MPol 22: 3. M-M.*

οὐρανόθεν adv. of place (Hom., Hes.; Iambl., Vi. Pyth. 32, 216; PGM 2, 95; 4 Macc 4: 10; Philo, Somn. 1, 112; Sib. Or. 8, 341; cf. μακρόθεν.—Lob., Phryn. p. 93f) *from heaven* (Apollon. Rhod. 1, 547=from heaven [as the abode of the divine]) Ac 14: 17; 26: 13.*

οὐρανός, οῦ, ὁ (Hom.+; inscr., pap., LXX, En., Philo, Joseph., Test. 12 Patr., Sib. Or.) *heaven.*

1. as a part of the universe (so mostly in the sing.; cf. Bl-D. §141, 1 w. app.)—**a.** mentioned w. the earth—**α.** forming a unity w. it as the totality of creation (Pla., Euthyd. 296D οὐρανὸς καὶ γῆ; Gen 1: 1; 14: 19, 22; Tob 7: 17 BA; Jdth 9: 12; Bel 5; 1 Macc 2: 37 al.; PGM 13, 784 ὁ βασιλεύων τῶν οὐρανῶν κ. τῆς γῆς κ. πάντων τῶν ἐν αὐτοῖς ἐνδιατριβόντων) ὁ οὐρανὸς καὶ ἡ γῆ Mt 5: 18; 11: 25; 24: 35; Mk 13: 31; Lk 10: 21; 16: 17; 21: 33; Ac 4: 24; 14: 15; 17: 24 (on the absence of the art. s. Bl-D. §253, 3); Rv 14: 7; 20: 11; Dg 3: 4.

β. standing independently beside the earth or contrasted w. it: Mt 5: 34f; Ac 7: 49 (cf. on both Is 66: 1). ἐν (τῷ) οὐρανῷ καὶ ἐπὶ (τῆς) γῆς Mt 6: 10; 28: 18; Lk 11: 2 D t.r.; Rv 5: 13.—1 Cor 8: 5; Rv 5: 3; ISm 11: 2. τὸ πρόσωπον τ.

γῆς καὶ τ. οὐρανοῦ Lk 12: 56. Cf. Hb 12: 26 (Hg 2: 6); Js 5: 12.—τὰ ἔσχατα τ. γῆς as extreme contrast to heaven 1 Cl 28: 3. By God's creative word the heaven was fixed and the earth founded on the waters Hv 1, 3, 4. Neither heaven nor earth can be comprehended by human measure B 16: 2 (Is 40: 12). On ἀπ᾽ ἄκρου γῆς ἕως ἄκρου οὐρανοῦ Mk 13: 27 s. under ἄκρον. ὁ πρῶτος οὐρ. καὶ ἡ πρώτη γῆ will give way in the last times to the οὐρ. καινός and the γῆ καινή Rv 21: 1 (cf. Is 65: 17; 66: 22).

b. as the firmament or *sky* over the earth; out of reach for men Hm 11: 18. Hence ἕως οὐρανοῦ Mt 11: 23; Lk 10: 15 or εἰς τὸν οὐρ. Hv 4, 1, 5 as an expr. denoting a great height. Likew. ἀπὸ τ. γῆς ἕως τ. οὐρανοῦ 1 Cl 8: 3 (scripture quot. of unknown origin); GP 10: 40 (for a supernatural being walking on the earth and touching the sky w. his head, s. Il. 4, 443). Since the heaven extends over the whole earth, ὑπὸ τὸν οὐρ. *under* (*the*) *heaven*= *on earth, throughout the earth* (Pla., Tim. 23c, Ep. 7 p. 326c; UPZ 106, 14 [99 bc]; Eccl 1: 13; 3: 1) Ac 2: 5; 4: 12; Col 1: 23; Hs 9, 17, 4; m 12, 4, 2. ὑποκάτωθεν τοῦ οὐρανοῦ *throughout the earth* 1 Cl 53: 3 (Dt 9: 14). ἐκ τῆς (i.e. χώρας) ὑπὸ τὸν οὐρ. εἰς τὴν ὑπ᾽ οὐρανόν *from one place on earth to another* Lk 17: 24 (cf. Dt 29: 19; Bar 5: 3; 2 Macc 2: 18 ἐκ τῆς ὑπὸ τὸν οὐρ. εἰς τὸν ἅγιον τόπον).—In the last days there will appear τέρατα ἐν τ. οὐρανῷ ἄνω *wonders in the heaven above* Ac 2: 19 (Jo 3: 3 v.l.). σημεῖον ἐν τῷ οὐρ. Rv 12: 1, 3 (cf. Diod. S. 2, 30, 1 τὰ ἐν οὐρανῷ γινόμενα=what takes place in the heavens; Ael. Aristid. 50, 56 K.=26 p. 519 D., where the statue of Asclepius from Pergamum appears ἐν τῷ οὐρανῷ). The sky can even be rolled up; s. ἑλίσσω.—The rain falls fr. heaven (X., An. 4, 2, 2) and the heaven must *be closed* to bring about a drought Lk 4: 25.—Rv 11: 6; Js 5: 18 (cf. 2 Ch 6: 26; 7: 13; Sir 48: 3). Lightning also comes fr. heaven (Bacchylides 17, 55f ἀπ᾽ οὐρανοῦ . . . ἀστραπάν [=Attic -ήν]) Lk 10: 18. Likew. of other things that come down like rain to punish sinners: fire Lk 9: 54 (cf. 4 Km 1: 10); Rv 20: 9; fire and brimstone Lk 17: 29 (cf. Gen 19: 24); apocalyptic hail Rv 16: 21.

c. as the starry heaven IEph 19: 2. τὰ ἄστρα τοῦ οὐρ. (cf. ἄστρον and s. Eur., Phoen. 1; Diod. S. 6, 2, 2 ἥλιον κ. σελήνην κ. τὰ ἄλλα ἄστρα τὰ κατ᾽ οὐρανόν; Ael. Aristid. 43, 13 K.=1 p. 5 D.) Hb 11: 12. οἱ ἀστέρες τοῦ οὐρ. 1 Cl 32: 2 (Gen 22: 17); cf. 10: 6 (Gen 15: 5). In the time of tribulation at the end of the world the stars will fall fr. heaven Mt 24: 29a; Mk 13: 25a; Rv 6: 13; 12: 4. Cf. 8: 10; 9: 1. ἡ στρατιὰ τοῦ οὐρ. (s. οὐράνιος) *the host of heaven* of the stars, which the Israelites worshipped idolatrously Ac 7: 42 (worship of the στρατιὰ τοῦ οὐρ. in enmity to Yahweh also Jer 7: 18; 19: 13; Zeph 1: 5; 2 Ch 33: 3, 5). These are also meant by the δυνάμεις τῶν οὐρανῶν Mt 24: 29b; Lk 21: 26; cf. Mk 13: 25b (cf. δύναμις 5).

d. as the place of the atmosphere; the clouds hover in it, the νεφέλαι τοῦ οὐρ. (cf. νεφέλη) Mt 24: 30b; 26: 64; Mk 14: 62; D 16: 8. Likew. the birds, τὰ πετεινὰ τοῦ οὐρανοῦ (Gen 1: 26; Ps 8: 9; Jdth 11: 7; cf. Bar 3: 17) Mt 6: 26; 8: 20; 13: 32; Mk 4: 32; Lk 8: 5; 9: 58; Ac 10: 12; B 6: 12 (Gen 1: 26), 18; Hs 9, 24, 1.—πυρράζει ὁ οὐρανός Mt 16: 2, 3.—Is perhaps in connection w. τὸν σατανᾶν ἐκ τοῦ οὐρανοῦ πεσόντα Lk 10: 18 the atmosphere to be thought of as the abode of the evil spirits? On Satan as the ἄρχων τῆς ἐξουσίας τοῦ ἀέρος, s. ἀήρ. Cf. also the λεγόμενοι θεοὶ εἴτε ἐν οὐρ. εἴτε ἐπὶ γῆς 1 Cor 8: 5. In any case Rv 12: 7f speaks of the dragon and his angels as being in heaven.

e. The concept of more than one heaven (s. 1aα above; the idea is Jewish; but s. FTorm, ZNW 33, '34, 48–50, who refers to Anaximander and Aristot. Also Ps.-Apollod. 1, 6,

1, 2 ms. and Achilles Tat. 2, 36, 4 and 37, 2 ms. have οὐρανοί; Himerius, Or. 66 [=Or. 20], 4 οὐρανοί as the abode of the gods; also Hesychius Miles. [IV ad] c. 66 JFlach of the 'godless heathen' Tribonian.—Schlatter, Mt² p. 58 on 3: 2: 'The pl. οὐρανοί is found neither in Philo nor Joseph.' Cf. PKatz, Philo's Bible '50, 141–6) is also found in our lit. (s. 1c, end, above); it is not always possible to decide with certainty just where the idea is really alive and where it simply survives in a formula (in the Fourth Gosp. the pl. is entirely absent; Rv has it only 12: 12 [fr. LXX]. Eph always has the pl. In others the sing. and pl. are interchanged for no apparent reason [cf. Hb 9: 23 w. 24 or Hv 1, 1, 4 w. 1, 2, 1; also GP 10: 40f]): *the third heaven* (cf. Ps.-Lucian, Philopatris 12 ἐς τρίτον οὐρανὸν ἀεροβατήσας [s. on ἀνακαινίζω and πνεῦμα 8]; PSI 29, 2ff [IV ad?] ἐπικαλοῦμαί σε τὸν καθήμενον ἐν τῷ πρώτῳ οὐρανῷ . . . ἐν τῷ βʹ οὐρ. . . . ἐν τῷ γʹ οὐρ.; Simplicius In Epict. p. 100, 13 Düb. ὀκτὼ οὐρανοί; Test. Levi 3: 3. Combination of the third heaven and Paradise, Apoc. of Moses 37. S. on τρίτος 1) 2 Cor 12: 2 (s. JohJeremias, Der Gottesberg '19, 41ff; Ltzm., Hdb.⁴ '49, exc. on 2 Cor 12: 3f [lit.]). ὑπεράνω πάντων τῶν οὐρανῶν Eph 4: 10. τ. πάντα ἐν τ. οὐρανοῖς κ. ἐπὶ τ. γῆς Col 1: 16; cf. vs. 20. ἔργα τ. χειρῶν σού εἰσιν οἱ οὐρ. Hb 1: 10 (Ps 101: 26).—4: 14; 7: 26; 2 Pt 3: 5, 7, 10, 12f (of the heavens, their destruction in the final conflagration, and their replacement by the καινοὶ οὐρ.); 1 Cl 20: 1; 33: 3. τακήσονταί τινες τῶν οὐρανῶν 2 Cl 16: 3.

2. as the abode of the divine (the pl. is preferred for this mng.: Bl-D. §141, 1; Rob. 408)—a. as the dwelling-place (or throne) of God (Sappho, fgm. 56 D.²; Solon 1, 22 D.²; Hom. Hymn to Aphrodite 291 [all three οὐρ. in the sing. as the seat of the gods]; Pla., Phaedr. 246e ὁ μέγας ἐν οὐρανῷ Ζεύς; Ps.-Aristot., De Mundo 2, 2; 3, 4 ὁ οὐρ. as οἰκητήριον θεοῦ or θεῶν; Dio Chrys. 19[36], 22 θεῶν μακάρων κατ᾽ οὐρανόν; Artem. 2, 68 p. 159, 13 ὁ οὐρανὸς θεῶν ἐστιν οἶκος; Ael. Aristid. 43, 14 K.=1 p. 5 D.; Maximus Tyr. 11, 11b; inscr. from Saïttai in Lydia [δύναμις 6]; Isisaretal. v. Kyrene 8 P.—On the OT GWestphal, Jahwes Wohnstätten '08, 214–73) Mt 23: 22; Ac 7: 55f; Hb 8: 1; B 16: 2b (Is 66: 1); Dg 10: 7. ὁ θεὸς ὁ ἐν τοῖς οὐρ. Hv 1, 1, 6 (cf. Tob 5: 17 S). ὁ θεὸς τοῦ οὐρ. (Gen 24: 3) Rv 11: 13; 16: 11. ὁ κύριος ἐν οὐρανοῖς Eph 6: 9; cf. Col 4: 1. ὁ πατὴρ ὑμῶν (μου, ἡμῶν) ὁ ἐν (τοῖς) οὐρ. (silver tablet fr. Amisos: ARW 12, '09, 25 ἐγώ εἰμι ὁ μέγας ὁ ἐν οὐρανῷ καθήμενος) Mt 5: 16, 45; 6: 1, 9; 7: 11, 21b; 10: 33; 12: 50; 16: 17; 18: 10b, 14, 19; Mk 11: 25f; Lk 11: 2 v.l.; D 8: 2 (here the sing. ὁ ἐν τῷ οὐρ. Cf. PGM 12, 261 τῷ ἐν οὐρανῷ θεῷ). ὁ πατὴρ ὁ ἐξ οὐρανοῦ *the Father who* (gives) *from heaven* Lk 11: 13 (Jos., Ant. 9, 73 ἐκχέαι τὸν θεὸν ἐξ οὐρανοῦ). God dwells in τὰ ὕψη τῶν οὐρ. 1 Cl 36: 2. Therefore the one who prays looks up toward heaven: ἀναβλέπειν εἰς τὸν οὐρ. (s. ἀναβλέπω 1) Mt 14: 19; Mk 6: 41; 7: 34; Lk 9: 16; MPol 9: 2; 14: 1. ἀτενίσας εἰς τὸν οὐρ. εἶδεν δόξαν θεοῦ Ac 7: 55; ἐπάρας τ. ὀφθαλμοὺς αὐτοῦ εἰς τὸν οὐρ. J 17: 1.—The Spirit of God comes fr. (the open) heaven Mt 3: 16; Mk 1: 10; Lk 3: 21; J 1: 32; Ac 2: 2(-4); 1 Pt 1: 12. The voice of God resounds fr. it (Maximus Tyr. 35, 7b Διὸς ἐξ οὐρανοῦ μέγα βοῶντος, the words follow) Mt 3: 17; Mk 1: 11; Lk 3: 22; J 12: 28; Ac 11: 9; MPol 9: 1, and it is gener. the place where divine pronouncements have their beginning Ac 11: 5 and their end vs. 10. The ὀργὴ θεοῦ reveals itself fr. heaven Ro 1: 18 (s. Jos., Bell. 1, 630 τὸν ἀπ᾽ οὐρανοῦ δικαστήν). A σημεῖον ἐκ (ἀπο) τοῦ οὐρ. is a *sign given by God* Mt 16: 1; Mk 8: 11; Lk 11: 16; 21: 11.

b. Christ is ἐξ οὐρανοῦ *from heaven, of a heavenly nature* 1 Cor 15: 47 (s. ἄνθρωπος 2d. On this HAAKennedy, St. Paul and the Conception of the 'Heavenly Man':

Exp. 8th Ser. VII '13, 97–110; EAGraham, CQR 113, '32, 226) and *has come down from heaven* J 3: 13b, 31; 6: 38, 42, 50, as ὁ ἄρτος ἐκ τοῦ οὐρανοῦ (s. ἄρτος 2). Cf. Ro 10: 6. He returned to heaven (on the ascension cf. CHönn, Studien zur Geschichte der Hf. im klass. Altertum: Progr. Mannheim '10; FPfister, Der Reliquienkult im Altertum II '12, 480ff; HDiels, Himmels u. Höllenfahrten v. Homer bis Dante: NJklA 49, '22, 239–53; RHolland, Zur Typik der Hf.: ARW 23, '25, 207–20; JKroll, Gott u. Hölle '32, 533 [index: Ascensus]; WMichaelis, Zur Überl. der Hf.-geschichte: ThBl 4, '25, 101–9; AFridrichsen, D. Hf. bei Lk: ibid. 6, '27, 337–41; GBertram, Die Hf. Jesu vom Kreuz: Deissmann-Festschr. '27, 187–217 [UHolzmeister, ZkTh 55, '31, 44–82]; HSchlier, Christus u. d. Kirche im Eph '30, 1ff; VLarrañaga, L'Ascension de Notre-Seigneur dans le NT '38 [fr. Spanish]. S. also on ἀνάστασις, end, and on διά A II 1) to live there in glory: Mk 16: 19; Lk 24: 51 t.r.; Ac 1: 10f; 2: 34; 7: 55f; 9: 3; 22: 6; 1 Pt 3: 22; B 15: 9. The Christians await his coming again fr. heaven: Ac 1: 11; Phil 3: 20; 1 Th 1: 10; 4: 16; 2 Th 1: 7.—When the Messianic woes have come to an end, τότε φανήσεται τὸ σημεῖον τοῦ υἱοῦ τ. ἀνθρώπου ἐν οὐρανῷ *then the sign of the Son of Man (who is) in heaven will appear*; acc. to the context, the sign consists in this, that he appears visibly in heavenly glory Mt 24: 30.

c. as the abode of angels (Gen 21: 17; 22: 11; Ps.-Clem., Hom. 8, 12) Mt 18: 10a; 22: 30; 24: 36; 28: 2; Mk 12: 25; 13: 32; Lk 2: 15; 22: 43; J 1: 51; Gal 1: 8; Rv 10: 1; 18: 1; 19: 14; 20: 1. Cf. Eph 3: 15.

d. The Christian dead also dwell in heaven (cf. Dio Chrys. 23[40], 35 οὐρανοῦ καὶ τῶν ἐν αὐτῷ θείων κ. μακαρίων αἰώνιον τάξιν; Libanius, Or. 21 p. 459, 9 F. πόρρω τοῦ τὸν οὐρανὸν οἰκοῦντος χοροῦ; Oenomaus in Euseb., Pr. Ev. 5, 33, 5; 12; Artem. 2, 68 p. 160, 25 τὰς ψυχὰς ἀπαλλαγείσας τῶν σωμάτων εἰς τὸν οὐρανὸν ἀνιέναι τάχει χρωμένας ὑπερβάλλοντι; Himerius, Or. 8 [=23], 23: the demon of the dead holds the σῶμα of the dead person, τὴν ψυχὴν ὁ οὐρανός; Quintus Smyrn. 7, 88). Their life, τὸ ἀληθῶς ἐν οὐρανῷ ζῆν, stands in strong contrast to the ὄντως θάνατος, that leads to the everlasting fire Dg 10: 7b. Rhoda, who *greets* Hermas *from heaven* Hv 1, 1, 4, need not have died (s. MDibelius, Hdb. ad loc.), and still she shows us that heaven is open for the godly. Furthermore, the Christian's true citizenship is *in heaven* (s. πολίτευμα) Phil 3: 20; cf. Dg 5: 9. Their names are enrolled *in heaven* (s. βίβλος 2) Lk 10: 20; Hb 12: 23. In heaven there await them their glorified body 2 Cor 5: 1f, their reward Mt 5: 12; Lk 6: 23, their treasure Mt 6: 20; Lk 12: 33, the things they hoped for Col 1: 5, their inheritance 1 Pt 1: 4; it is a place of peace Lk 19: 38.—ἐκ τοῦ οὐρανοῦ the New Jerusalem (s. Ἱεροσόλυμα 2) will come down to earth Rv 3: 12; 21: 2, 10.

e. The concept of a heaven in which God, his attendant spirits, and the righteous dead abide, makes it easy to understand the taking over of certain OT expressions in which heaven is personified εὐφραίνεσθε οὐρανοί (cf. Is 44: 23; 49: 13) Rv 12: 12; cf. 18: 20; B 9: 3 (Is 1: 2); 11: 2 (Jer 2: 12); 1 Cl 27: 7 (Ps 18: 2).

3. fig., synonymous with God (s. βασιλεία 3.—Philippides Com. [IV/III bc] 27 νὴ τὸν οὐρανόν. Acc. to Clem. Alex., Protr. 5, 66, 4 Θεόφραστον πῇ [in some way] μὲν οὐρανόν, πῇ δὲ πνεῦμα τὸν θεὸν ὑπονοεῖ; Appian, Hann. 56 §233 σημεῖα ἐκ Διός [l. 14 Viereck-R.]=ἐξ οὐρανοῦ [l. 16]). ἁμαρτάνειν εἰς τὸν οὐρ. *sin against God* Lk 15: 18, 21. ἐξ οὐρανοῦ ἢ ἐξ ἀνθρώπων Mt 21: 25; Mk 11: 30f; Lk 20: 4f. βασιλεία τῶν οὐρ. in Mt=βασιλεία τοῦ θεοῦ 3: 2; 4: 17; 5: 3, 10, 19f; 7: 21; 8: 11; 10: 7; 11: 11f; 13: 11, 24, 31, 33, 33f, 44f, 47, 52; 16: 19; 18: 1, 3f, 23; 19: 12, 14, 23; 20: 1; 22: 2; 23: 13; 25: 1; J 3: 5 v.l.—

GvRad and HTraub, TW V 496ff: οὐρανός and related words. M-M. B. 53; 1484.

Οὐρβανός, οῦ, ὁ (lead tablet fr. Hadrumetum 13 [Dssm., B 29; 37;—BS 275; 283] τὸν Οὐρβανὸν ὃν ἔτεκεν Οὐρβανά; PSI 27, 7 al. The Lat. Urbanus in inscr. in HDessau, Inscriptiones Latinae no. 7566; 7986 and Lghtf., Phil p. 174) *Urbanus,* a man to whom a greeting is addressed, described as συνεργὸς ἡμῶν ἐν Χριστῷ Ro 16: 9. M-M.*

Οὐρίας, ου, ὁ (אוּרִיָּה) *Uriah,* husband of Bathsheba who, after his death, married David and bore Solomon to him (2 Km 11; 12: 24; Jos., Ant. 7, 131–41; 144; 146; 153f.—The name is also found elsewh. in the OT and Joseph. [gen. Οὐρία: Ant. 7, 141; 144]) ἡ τοῦ Οὐρίου the *wife of Uriah* Mt 1: 6.*

οὖς, ὠτός, τό (Hom.+; inscr., pap., LXX, Ep. Arist. 165, Philo, Joseph.) *ear.*

1. lit. Mk 7: 33. δεξιόν Lk 22: 50 (MRostovtzeff, ZNW 33, '34, 196–9 after PTebt. 793 XI, 1ff [183 bc] Ἡσίοδος . . . τὸν Δωρίωνος δεξιὸν ὦτα εἰς τέλος ἐξέτεμεν. Also Leo Gramm. 118, 10 IBekker [1842] ἀπετμήθη τὸ δεξιὸν ὦς [=οὖς]; cf. JWDoeve, Die Gefangennahme Jesu, Studia Evangelica 73, '59, 457–80: connects w. Am 3: 12; for another view s. SHall, ibid. 501f); 1 Cor 12: 16. ἃ οὖς οὐκ ἤκουσεν in the apocr. saying of unknown origin (s. Hdb. z. NT 6 [J]³ '33, 4f) 1 Cor 2: 9; 1 Cl 34: 8; 2 Cl 11: 7; MPol 2: 3. πρὸς τὸ οὖς λαλεῖν τι *say someth. into someone's ear,* i.e. *secretly* or *in confidence, whisper* (Plut., Demetr. 14, 3; Jos., Ant. 6, 165; cf. Diog. L. 9, 26 εἰπεῖν πρὸς τὸ οὖς) Lk 12: 3. εἰς τὸ οὖς ἀκούειν (Eur., Or. 616, Andr. 1091) Mt 10: 27. Differently λαλεῖν εἰς τὰ ὦτα τῶν ἁγίων, where there is no suggestion of secrecy (cf. 2 Km 3: 19) Hv 3, 8, 11; 4, 3, 6. ὦτα κυρίου εἰς δέησιν αὐτῶν *the ears of the Lord are open to their prayer* 1 Pt 3: 12; cf. 1 Cl 22: 6 (both Ps 33: 16). συνέχειν τὰ ὦτα αὐτῶν *hold their ears shut* Ac 7: 57. βύειν τὰ ὦτα *stop the ears* IEph 9: 1 (cf. βύω). εἰσέρχεσθαι εἰς τὰ ὦτά τινος *come to someone's ears* (Paroem. Gr.: Zenob. [II ad] 3, 49 εἰς θεῶν ὦτα ἦλθεν; Ps 17: 7) Js 5: 4 (cf. Is 5: 9); also γίνεσθαι Lk 1: 44. ἠκούσθη τι εἰς τὰ ὦτά τινος *someth. came to someone's ears* (Is 5: 9) Ac 11: 22. ἐν τοῖς ὠσί τινος *in someone's hearing* (Dt 5: 1; 2 Km 3: 19; Bar 1: 3f) Lk 4: 21. If Mt 13: 16 is to be interpreted fr. the vantage point of vs. 17, it belongs here. If, on the other hand, it is to be explained on the basis of what precedes, it belongs under 2.

2. transferred fr. sense perception to mental and spiritual understanding: τοῖς ὠσὶ βαρέως ἀκούειν *be hard of hearing*=comprehend slowly (or, rather, not at all) Mt 13: 15a; Ac 28: 27a (both Is 6: 10a); cf. Mt 13: 15b; Ac 28: 27b (both Is 6: 10b). θέσθε ὑμεῖς εἰς τὰ ὦτα ὑμῶν τοὺς λόγους τούτους *receive the following words into your ears,* i.e. *take* them *to heart* Lk 9: 44 (cf. Ex 17: 14 δὸς εἰς τὰ ὦτα Ἰησοῖ). ὦτα τοῦ μὴ ἀκούειν Ro 11: 8 (cf. Dt 29: 3). W. ἔχειν (Hermocles [IV/III bc] p. 174, 16 Coll. [= Athen. 6, 63 p. 253e] images of the gods οὐκ ἔχουσιν ὦτα) ὦτα ἔχοντες οὐκ ἀκούετε; Mk 8: 18 (cf. Jer 5: 21; Ezk 12: 2). ὁ ἔχων οὖς ἀκουσάτω Rv 2: 7, 11, 17, 29; 3: 6, 13, 22; cf. ὁ ἔχων ὦτα ἀκουέτω Mt 11: 15; 13: 9, 43. ὃς (εἴ τις) ἔχει ὦτα ἀκούειν ἀκουέτω Mk 4: 9, 23; 7: 16. ὁ ἔχων ὦτα ἀκούειν ἀκουέτω Lk 8: 8; 14: 35 (MDibelius, 'Wer Ohren hat zu hören, der höre': StKr 83, '10, 461–71. Cf. Heraclitus [Vorsokrat.⁵ 22b 34] ἀξύνετοι ἀκούσαντες κωφοῖσιν ἐοίκασιν). ἀπερίτμητοι καρδίαις καὶ τοῖς ὠσὶν *uncircumcised in hearts and ears* i.e., impervious to moral instruction Ac 7: 51 (ἀπερίτμητος 2). JHorst, TW V 543–58: οὖς and related words. M-M. B. 226.*

οὐσία, ας, ἡ *property, wealth* (so Eur., Hdt.+; inscr., pap.; Tob 14: 13 BA; 3 Macc 3: 28; Philo; Jos., Bell. 4, 241, Ant., 7, 114) Lk 15: 12f (Diog. L. 9, 35 three brothers, one of whom wishes to move to a distant land, divide the οὐσία among them).—HHBerger, Ousia in de dialogen van Plato, '61. M-M. B. 769.*

οὔτε adv. (Hom.+; inscr., pap., LXX, En., Ep. Arist., Philo, Joseph., Test. 12 Patr. In the mss. freq. exchanged w. οὐδέ. The latter is found beside οὔτε in the text or as v.l. Mk 5: 3; Lk 12: 26; 20: 36; J 1: 25; Ac 4: 12; 1 Cor 3: 2; Gal 1: 12; 1 Th 2: 3; Js 3: 12; Rv 5: 3, 4; 9: 20; 12: 8; 20: 4. Likew. in several places only οὐδέ is attested, where one should expect οὔτε: Rv 7: 16; 9: 4; 21: 23.—Mayser p. 177; Bl-D. §445, 1 app.; Valley s.v. οὐδέ, end.—Dit., Syll.³ 747, 27 [73 BC] οὔτε stands for οὐδέ; cf. Rv 12: 8; 20: 4; 7: 16; 5: 4) *and not.* οὔτε . . . οὔτε *neither . . . nor* (Jos., Ant. 3, 16; 15, 182) ὅπου οὔτε σὴς οὔτε βρῶσις ἀφανίζει Mt 6: 20. Cf. 22: 30; Mk 12: 25; 14: 68; Lk 12: 24, 27 (. . . οὐδὲ 𝔓⁴⁷𝔓⁷⁵ et al.); 14: 35; 20: 35; J 4: 21; 5: 37; 8: 19; 9: 3; Ac 2: 31; 15: 10; 19: 37; 28: 21; 1 Cor 3: 7; 8: 8; 11: 11; Gal 5: 6; 6: 15; Rv 3: 15f. οὔτε . . . οὔτε . . . οὔτε *neither . . . nor . . . nor* (Xenophon Eph. 335, 28-30 six members) Ac 25: 8; Ro 8: 38f (οὔτε ten times); 1 Cor 6: 9f (οὔτε seven times, continued and concluded by οὐ three times); 1 Th 2: 5f (οὔτε three times, then twice in a new series: οὔτε ἀφ᾽ ὑμῶν οὔτε ἀπ᾽ ἄλλων); Rv 9: 20.—οὔτε several times after οὐ vs. 21; before (and after) οὐ 21: 4. In Ac 24: 12f οὔτε three times *neither . . . nor . . . nor* is continued by οὐδέ *and . . . not at all.* οὐδὲ γὰρ . . . οὔτε *for . . . not, . . . nor* Gal 1: 12 (v.l. has οὐδέ twice). οὐκ ἀφεθήσεται αὐτῷ οὔτε ἐν τούτῳ τ. αἰῶνι οὔτε ἐν τ. μέλλοντι Mt 12: 32 (the second οὔτε here is perhaps felt as intensifying. Cf. Arrian, Anab. 7, 14, 3 οὔτε βασιλεῖ οὔτε Ἀλεξάνδρῳ=neither for a king nor especially for Alex.). οὐδεὶς ἄξιος εὑρέθη ἀνοῖξαι τὸ βιβλίον οὔτε βλέπειν αὐτό Rv 5: 4.—οὔτε . . . (very rare in class. Gk. [Kühner-G. II 291, 3a]. More freq. later: Plut., Mor. 1115B; Polyaenus 1, 30, 8; Lucian, Jupp. Trag. 5, Dial. Meretr. 2, 4 οὔτε πάντα ἡ Λεσβία, Δωρί, πρὸς σὲ ἐψεύσατο καὶ σὺ τἀληθῆ ἀπήγγελκας Μυρτίῳ; Aelian, N.A. 1, 57; 11, 9; Longus, Past. 1, 17; 4, 28; Jos., Bell. 2, 403; 463.—Bl-D. §445, 3 app.; cf. Rob. 1189) οὔτε ἄντλημα ἔχεις καὶ τὸ φρέαρ ἐστὶν βαθύ *you have no bucket, and the well is deep* J 4: 11. οὔτε αὐτὸς ἐπιδέχεται τοὺς ἀδελφοὺς καὶ τοὺς βουλομένους κωλύει 3 J 10.—Js 3: 12 οὔτε can scarcely be correct, and perh. the text is faulty (s. Bl-D. §445, 1 app.; cf. Rob. 1189). M-M.**

οὗτος, αὕτη, τοῦτο (Hom.+; inscr., pap., LXX, En., Ep. Arist., Philo, Joseph., Test. 12 Patr.) demonstrative pron., used as adj. and subst.: *this,* referring to someth. comparatively near at hand, just as ἐκεῖνος refers to someth. comparatively farther away; cf. Lk 18: 14; Js 4: 15; Hm 3: 5. On its use s. Bl-D. §290 al.; Rob. 697-706; Mlt.-Turner 192f.

1. subst.—a. gener.—α. w. ref. to someth. here and now, directing attention to it (Appian, Liby. 62 §276 οὗτος =this man here [referring to one who is present]. Cf. Pherecrates Com. 134 K. οὗτος πόθεν ἦλθες; =you there, where did you come from?) οὗτός ἐστιν ὁ υἱός μου Mt 3: 17; 17: 5; Mk 9: 7; Lk 7: 44ff; J 1: 15, 30; Ac 2: 15; 4: 10 (οὗτος). 2 Pt 1: 17 and oft. τοῦτό ἐστιν τὸ σῶμά μου *this is my body* Mt 26: 26; Mk 14: 22; Lk 22: 19; 1 Cor 11: 24. τοῦτό ἐστιν τὸ αἷμά μου Mt 26: 28; Mk 14: 24.—W. a connotation of contempt (Ael. Aristid. 53 p. 628 D.: ὦ οὗτος=O you poor fellow! Likew. Maximus Tyr. 37, 8d)

Lk 5: 21; 7: 39, 49; J 6: 42, 52. The contexts of Mt 13: 55f; Mk 6: 2f; J 7: 15 suggest a similar connotation.—W. a connotation of wonder or amazement Mt 21: 10; Ac 9: 21.

β. w. ref. to someth. that has immediately preceded *this one* (who has just been mentioned) Lk 1: 32; J 1: 2; 6: 71; 2 Ti 3: 6, 8; Jd 7.—At the beginning of a narrative concerning a pers. already mentioned Mt 3: 3; Lk 16: 1; J 1: 41; 3: 2; 12: 21; 21: 21a; Ac 21: 24.—Emphasizing a pers. already mentioned *this (very) one* J 9: 9; Ac 4: 10 (ἐν τούτῳ); 9: 20; 1 J 5: 6; 2 Pt 2: 17. καὶ τοῦτον ἐσταυρωμένον *and him as the crucified one* 1 Cor 2: 2. καὶ τούτους ἀποτρέπου *avoid such people* (as I have just described) 2 Ti 3: 5. καὶ οὗτος *this one* (just mentioned) *also* Hb 8: 3.

γ. w. ref. to a subject more remote in the paragraph, but closer to the main concept under discussion (W-S. §23, 2; Rob. 702f) Ac 4: 11; 7: 19; 2 J 7.

δ. w. ref. to what follows: w. a relative foll. οὗτος ὅς Lk 5: 21. οὗτοί εἰσιν οἵτινες 8: 15. οὗτοί εἰσιν οἱ ἐπὶ τὰ πετρώδη σπειρόμενοι, οἳ . . . *these are the ones sowed on the rocky ground, who . . .* Mk 4: 16. ταύτην . . . εἰς ἣν στῆτε 1 Pt 5: 12. οὗτοι . . . ὅπου Mk 4: 15 s. ὅπου 1aα.—W. ὅτι foll.: αὕτη ἐστὶν ἡ κρίσις, ὅτι J 3: 19; cf. 1 J 1: 5; 5: 11, 14.—W. ἵνα foll.: αὕτη ἐστὶν ἡ ἐντολὴ ἡ ἐμή, ἵνα J 15: 12; cf. 17: 3; 1 J 3: 11, 23; 5: 3; 2 J 6a, b. τοῦτό ἐστι τὸ ἔργον, τὸ θέλημα τοῦ θεοῦ, ἵνα J 6: 29, 39f.—W. inf. foll. Js 1: 27.—W. ptc. foll. οὗτος ὁ ἀνοίξας J 11: 37. οὗτοί εἰσιν οἱ τὸν λόγον ἀκούσαντες *these are the ones who have heard the word* Mk 4: 18. ἀδελφοί μου οὗτοί εἰσιν οἱ . . . ἀκούοντες καὶ ποιοῦντες Lk 8: 21.—W. subst. foll. αὕτη ἐστὶν ἡ νίκη . . . ἡ πίστις ἡμῶν 1 J 5: 4.

ε. Resuming someth. previously mentioned, w. special emphasis: a subst.: Μωϋσῆν, ὃν ἠρνήσαντο . . . τοῦτον ὁ θεὸς . . . *Moses, whom they rejected, . . . is the very one whom God* Ac 7: 35 (Ps.-Callisth. 2, 16, 10 Δαρεῖος . . . , οὗτος). τῶν ἀνδρῶν . . . ἕνα τούτων *of the men. . . one of these (very men)* Ac 1: 21f. οὐ τὰ τέκνα τ. σαρκὸς ταῦτα τέκνα τ. θεοῦ Ro 9: 8; cf. vs. 6. ἕκαστος ἐν τῇ κλήσει ᾗ ἐκλήθη, ἐν ταύτῃ μενέτω *in this (very one)* 1 Cor 7: 20. Cf. J 10: 25; Ac 2: 23; 4: 10; Ro 7: 10; Gal 3: 7.—A relative clause: ὃς ἂν ποιήσῃ καὶ διδάξῃ, οὗτος . . . Mt 5: 19.—Mk 3: 35; 6: 16; Lk 9: 24b, 26; J 3: 26; Ro 8: 30. δ. . . , τοῦτο Ac 3: 6; Ro 7: 15f, 19f; Gal 6: 7. ἅ . . . , ταῦτα J 8: 26; Gal 5: 17b; Phil 4: 9; 2 Ti 2: 2. ὅστις . . . , οὗτος Mt 18: 4. ἅτινα . . . , ταῦτα Phil 3: 7. ὅσοι . . . , οὗτοι Ro 8: 14; Gal 6: 12.—A ptc.: ὁ ὑπομείνας, οὗτος σωθήσεται Mt 10: 22.—13: 20, 22; 24: 13; 26: 23; Mk 12: 40; Lk 9: 48; J 6: 46; 15: 5; Ac 15: 38; 1 Cor 6: 4.—After εἴ τις Ro 8: 9; 1 Cor 3: 17; 8: 3; Js 1: 23; 3: 2.—ὅσα ἐστὶν ἀληθῆ, ὅσα σεμνά, ὅσα . . . (ὅσα six times altogether), εἴ τις ἀρετὴ καὶ εἴ τις ἔπαινος, ταῦτα λογίζεσθε Phil 4: 8.—After ἐάν τις J 9: 31. After ὅταν Ro 2: 14. After καθώς J 8: 28.—After the articular inf. εἰ τὸ ζῆν ἐν σαρκί, τοῦτο . . . Phil 1: 22.

ζ. used w. αὐτός: αὐτὸς οὗτος *he himself* Ac 25: 25. Pl. 24: 15, 20.

η. As a subject, the demonstr. can take on the gender of its predicate (W-S. §23, 5; Rob. 698): τὸ καλὸν σπέρμα, οὗτοί εἰσιν οἱ υἱοὶ τῆς βασιλείας Mt 13: 38. Cf. Lk 8: 14f.—Mt 7: 12; Lk 2: 12; 8: 11; 22: 53; J 1: 19; Ro 11: 27 (Is 59: 21); 1 Cor 9: 3; Gal 4: 24.

b. In particular, the neut. is used—α. w. ref. to what precedes: Lk 5: 6; J 6: 61; Ac 19: 17. As the obj. of a verb of saying (Jos., Vi. 291, Ant. 20, 123 al.) Lk 24: 40; J 6: 6; 7: 9; 8: 6; 12: 33; 18: 38 al.—Freq. w. prepositions (cf. Johannessohn 383 [index]): διὰ τοῦτο cf. διὰ B II 2. εἰς τοῦτο cf. εἰς 4f. ἐκ τούτου cf. ἐκ 3f (= 'for this reason' also PRyl. 81, 24). ἐν τούτῳ *for this reason* J 16: 30; Ac 24: 16;

1 Cor 4: 4; 2 Cor 5:2; *by this* 1 J 3: 19. ἐπὶ τούτῳ cf. ἐπί II 2. μετὰ τοῦτο cf. μετά B II 3. τούτου χάριν (PAmh. 130, 6 [I AD]) Eph 3: 14.—The pl. summarizes what precedes: Lk 8: 8; 11: 27; 24: 26; J 5: 34; 15: 11; 21: 24 and oft.—On Midrashic use in Ac, s. EEEllis, BRigaux-Festschr., '70, 303–12.

β. w. ref. to what follows, esp. before clauses that express a statement, purpose, result, or condition, which it introduces: τοῦτο λέγω w. direct discourse foll. *this is what I mean* Gal 3: 17; in ellipsis τοῦτο δέ *the point is this* 2 Cor 9: 6; w. ὅτι foll. 1 Cor 1: 12. τοῦτό φημι ὅτι 7: 29 t.r.; 15: 50. τοῦτο γινώσκειν, ὅτι Lk 10: 11; 12: 39; Ro 6: 6; 2 Ti 3: 1; 2 Pt 1: 20; 3: 3. λογίζῃ τοῦτο, ὅτι . . . ; Ro 2: 3; ὁμολογῶ τοῦτο, ὅτι Ac 24: 14. εἰδὼς τοῦτο, ὅτι *understanding this, that* 1 Ti 1: 9. τοῦτο ἔχεις, ὅτι Rv 2: 6.—W. ἵνα foll.: πόθεν μοι τοῦτο, ἵνα ἔλθῃ ἡ μήτηρ . . . ; Lk 1: 43. Cf. J 6: 29, 39.—W. a prep. ἐν τούτῳ, ὅτι Lk 10: 20; J 9: 30 (θ°° τοῦτο); 1 J 3: 16, 24; 4: 9, 10. περὶ τούτου, ὅτι J 16: 19. διὰ τοῦτο, ὅτι *for this reason, (namely) that* 5: 16, 18; 8: 47. εἰς τοῦτο, ἵνα J 18: 37; Ac 9: 21; Ro 14: 9; 2 Cor 2: 9 al. διὰ τοῦτο, ἵνα 13: 10; 1 Ti 1: 16; Phlm 15. ἐν τούτῳ, ἵνα J 15: 8; 1 J 4: 17. ἐν τούτῳ ἐὰν J 13: 35; 1 J 2: 3. ἐν τούτῳ, ὅταν 5: 2.—Before an inf. τοῦτο κέκρικεν . . . , τηρεῖν τὴν ἑαυτοῦ παρθένον 1 Cor 7: 37. Cf. 2 Cor 2: 1. Before an inf. w. acc. Eph 4: 17. Even introducing a foll. subst.: τοῦτο εὐχόμεθα, τὴν ὑμῶν κατάρτισιν 2 Cor 13: 9.—On αὐτὸ τοῦτο cf. αὐτός 1h.

γ. καὶ τοῦτο *and at that, and especially* (Bl-D. §290, 5; 442, 9; Rob. 1181f) Ro 13: 11; 1 Cor 6: 6, 8; Eph 2: 8. καὶ ταῦτα (class.; cf. Kühner-G. I 647) passing over fr. *and at that* to *although* (Jos., Ant. 2, 266) Hb 11: 12.

δ. indicating a correspondence: τοῦτο μὲν . . . τοῦτο δέ *sometimes . . . sometimes, not only . . . but also* (Att.) Hb 10: 33.

ε. τοῦτ' ἔστιν, τουτέστι[ν] (on the orthography cf. Bl-D. §12, 3; 17) *that is* or *means* (Bl-D. §132, 2; Rob. 705. Cf. also εἰμί II 3) Mt 27: 46; Mk 7: 2; Ac 1: 19; 19: 4; Ro 1: 12; 7: 18; 9: 8; 10: 6, 7, 8; Phlm 12. Hb 2: 14 al.

ζ. An unfavorable connotation (this tone is noticed by Ps.-Demetr. c. 289 in the Κρατερὸν τοῦτον [in Demetrius of Phalerum]) is assumed (after GBernhardy, Wissenschaftl. Syntax der griech. Sprache 1829, 281, by Heinrici; JWeiss; EFascher, V. Verstehen d. NT '30, 126 al. ad loc. Differently W-S. §23, 9; cf. Rob. 704) καὶ ταῦτά τινες ἦτε *and that is the sort of people you were, at least some of you* 1 Cor 6: 11.

2. as an adj.—**a.** coming before a subst. (or subst. expr.) with the article (Bl-D. §292; Rob. 700f) ἐν τούτῳ τῷ αἰῶνι Mt 12: 32. Cf. 16: 18; 20: 12; Mk 9: 29; Lk 7: 44; J 4: 15; Ac 1: 11; Ro 11: 24; 1 Ti 1: 18; Hb 7: 1; 1 J 4: 21; Rv 19: 9; 20: 14 al. W. a touch of contempt Lk 18: 11; cf. 14: 30; 15: 30.

b. following the subst. that has the art.: ἐκ τῶν λίθων τούτων Mt 3: 9. Cf. 5: 19; Mk 12: 16; Lk 11: 31; J 4: 13, 21; Ac 6: 13; Ro 15: 28; 1 Cor 1: 20; 2: 6; 11: 26; 2 Cor 4: 1, 7; 8: 6; 11: 10; Eph 3: 8; 5: 32; 2 Ti 2: 19; Rv 2: 24. (Freq. the position of οὗτος varies, somet. before, somet. after the noun, in the mss.; s. the apparatus in Tdf. on Mk 14: 30; J 4: 20; 6: 60; 7: 36; 9: 24; 21: 23 al.) Somet. another adj. stands w. the noun ἀπὸ τῆς γενεᾶς τῆς σκολιᾶς ταύτης Ac 2: 40. ἡ χήρα αὕτη ἡ πτωχή Lk 21: 3. Cf. πάντα τὰ ῥήματα ταῦτα 2: 19, 51 v.l.

c. When the art. is lacking there is no real connection betw. the demonstrative and the noun, but the one or the other belongs to the predicate (Bl-D. §292; Rob. 701f) ταύτην ἐποίησεν ἀρχὴν τῶν σημείων J 2: 11 (s. J 4: 54 below). τοῦτο ἀληθὲς εἴρηκας 4: 18.—So esp. in com-

bination w. numerical concepts; the noun without the art. is to be taken as part of the predicate: οὗτος μὴν ἕκτος ἐστίν *this is the sixth month* Lk 1: 36. αὕτη ἀπογραφὴ πρώτη ἐγένετο *this was the first census* 2: 2. τοῦτο πάλιν δεύτερον σημεῖον ἐποίησεν J 4: 54 (s. J 2: 11 above). τρίτην ταύτην ἡμέραν *this is the third day* Lk 24: 21 (Achilles Tat. 7, 11, 2 τρίτην ταύτην ἡμέραν γέγονεν ἀφανής; Menand., Epitr. 26f; Lucian, Dial. Mort. 13, 3). τοῦτο τρίτον ἐφανερώθη *this was the third time that he appeared* J 21: 14. τρίτον τοῦτο ἔρχομαι *this will be the third time that I am coming* 2 Cor 13: 1; cf. 12: 14 (cf. Hdt. 5, 76 τέταρτον δὴ τοῦτο; Gen 27: 36 δεύτερον τοῦτο.— Num 14: 22; Judg 16: 15).—More difficult: οὐ μετὰ πολλὰς ταύτας ἡμέρας *not many days from now* Ac 1: 5 (Alciphr. 1, 14, 2; Achilles Tat. 7, 14, 2 ὡς ὀλίγων πρὸ τούτων ἡμερῶν; POxy. 1121, 12 [295 AD]; Bl-D. §226 w. app.; Rob. 702). Most difficult of all περὶ μιᾶς ταύτης φωνῆς Ac 24: 21 (cf. POxy. 1152, 5 βόηθι ἡμῖν καὶ τούτῳ οἴκῳ. Bl-D. §292; Rob. 702). M-M.

οὕτω and **οὕτως** adv. (Hom.+; inscr., pap., LXX, Ep. Arist., Philo, Joseph., Test. 12 Patr.); the latter form is most used, before consonants as well as before vowels; the former (En. 98, 3 before a vowel; Ep. Arist. only before consonants) in the NT only Ac 23: 11; Phil 3: 17; Hb 12: 21; Rv 16: 18 w. really outstanding attestation; taken into the text by W-H. also Mt 3: 15; 7: 17; Mk 2: 7; Ac 13: 47; Ro 1: 15; 6: 19 (Bl-D. §21; Mlt-H. 112f; W-H. appendix 146f. Also in inscr. [cf. ENachmanson, Laute u. Formen der magn. Inschr. '03, 112], pap. [Mayser 242f; Crönert 142] and LXX [Thackeray p. 136] οὕτως is predominant) *in this manner, thus, so.*

1. referring to what precedes—**a.** w. a correlative word καθάπερ . . . οὕτως (cf. καθάπερ) (*just*) *as* . . . *so* Ro 12: 4f; 1 Cor 12: 12; 2 Cor 8: 11. καθὼς . . . οὕτως (*just*) *as*. . . *so* Lk 11: 30; 17: 26; J 3: 14; 12: 50; 14: 31; 15: 4; 2 Cor 1: 5; 10: 7; Col 3: 13; 1 Th 2: 4. ὡς. . . οὕτως *as*. . . *so* Ac 8: 32 (Is 53: 7); 23: 11; Ro 5: 15, 18; 1 Cor 7: 17a; 2 Cor 7: 14. ὥσπερ. . . οὕτως (Jos., Vi. 1) Mt 12: 40; 13: 40; Lk 17: 24; J 5: 21, 26; Ro 5: 12, 19, 21; 6: 4. καθ' ὅσον . . . οὕτως *as*. . . *so* Hb 9: 27f. ὃν τρόπον . . . οὕτως 2 Ti 3: 8.

b. w. ref. to what precedes, absolutely Mt 5: 19; 6: 30; Ro 11: 5; 1 Cor 8: 12 al. ταῦτα οὕτως *so much for that* B 17: 2. οὐδὲ οὕτως *not even thus* Mk 14: 59. Pointing the moral after figures of speech, parables, and examples (Aristot., Rhet. 1393b [II, 20]) Mt 5: 16; 12: 45; 13: 49; 18: 14; 20: 16; Lk 12: 21; 15: 7, 10; J 3: 8.—οὕτως can take on a specif. mng. fr. what precedes: *so shamelessly* J 18: 22; *so basely* 1 Cor 5: 3; *so intensely* (of love) Dg 10: 3; *unmarried* 1 Cor 7: 26, 40. ἐὰν ἀφῶμεν αὐτὸν οὕτως *if we let him (go on) this way* (performing miracle after miracle) J 11: 48. Cf. Ro 9: 20.—οὕτως καί Mt 17: 12; 18: 35; 24: 33; Mk 13: 29; Lk 17: 10. οὐχ οὕτως ἐστίν ἐν ὑμῖν *it is not so among you* Mt 20: 26; Mk 10: 43. Elliptically (Bl-D. §480, 5) ὑμεῖς οὐχ οὕτως *you (are) not (to act) in this way* Lk 22: 26 (ὑμεῖς δὲ μὴ οὕτως [v.l. οὕτως μὴ ποιεῖτε] Test. Napht. 3: 4). Summarizing a thought expressed in what precedes: Mt 11: 26; Ac 7: 8; 1 Cor 14: 25; 1 Th 4: 17; 2 Pt 1: 11.—Drawing an inference fr. what precedes *so, hence* (Horapollo 1, 34 οὕτω ὀνομασθήσεται; En. 98, 3) Ro 1: 15; 6: 11. οὕτως ὅτι *as it is, since* Rv 3: 16.—Introducing a question *so* Mt 26: 40; Mk 7: 18; J 18: 22 (s. also above); 1 Cor 6: 5.—Summarizing the content of a preceding participial constr. (class.; Jos., Bell. 2, 129; Bl-D. §425, 6) Ac 20: 11; 27: 17.—ὁ μὲν οὕτως, ὁ δὲ οὕτως *the one in one way, the other in another* 1 Cor 7: 7.

2. referring to what follows *in this way, as follows* J 21: 1. Of spoken or written words: what is so introduced follows immediately after οὕτως γέγραπται Mt 2: 5. Cf. 6: 9; Ac 7: 6; 13: 34, 47; Ro 10: 6; Hb 4: 4; w. ὅτι recit. Lk 19: 31; Ac 7: 6; 13: 34. W. inf. foll. (Gen 29: 26) 1 Pt 2: 15. Correlatively: οὕτως...καθώς Lk 24: 24; Ro 11: 26; Phil 3: 17. οὕτως...ὂν τρόπον Ac 1: 11; cf. 27: 25. οὕτως...ὡς *thus...as* (Jos., Ant. 12, 304) Mk 4: 26; J 7: 46; 1 Cor 3: 15; 4: 1; 9: 26a, b; Eph 5: 33; Js 2: 12. οὕτως...ὥστε (Hdt. 7, 174; Epict. 1, 11, 4; 4, 11, 19; Dit., Syll.³ 1169, 57 [w. aor. indic.]; Jos., Ant. 8, 206; 9, 255) J 3: 16 (cf. Bl-D. §391, 2 app.; Mlt. 209; Rob. 1000); Ac 14: 1. οὕτως... ἵνα: οὕτως τρέχετε ἵνα καταλάβητε 1 Cor 9: 24.

3. to denote degree, *so*, before adj. and adv. (class.) σεισμὸς οὕτω μέγας *an earthquake so great* Rv 16: 18. οὕτως ἀνόητοί ἐστε; Gal 3: 3 (s. ἀνόητος 1). οὕτως φοβερόν Hb 12: 21. —οὕτως ταχέως (Jos., Vi. 92) Gal 1: 6. —Before a verb *so intensely* (X., Cyr. 1, 3, 11) 1 J 4: 11.

4. οὕτως *without further ado, just, simply* (Soph., Phil. 1067 ἀλλ' οὕτως ἄπει; 'then will you go away without further ado?'; Ael. Aristid. 51, 49 K. = 27 p. 546 D.; Aesop, Fab. 308 P. = Babr. 48 Cr.; Jos., Ant. 14, 438) Ἰησοῦς...ἐκαθέζετο οὕτως ἐπὶ τῇ πηγῇ J 4: 6 (cf. Ammonius, Catena in ev. S. Ioa. p. 216, 21 Cramer τὸ δὲ 'οὕτως' ἀντὶ τοῦ 'ὡς ἀπλῶς' καὶ 'ὡς ἔτυχε'). Likew. 8: 59 t.r. and prob. ἀναπεσὼν ἐκεῖνος οὕτως ἐπὶ τὸ στῆθος τοῦ Ἰησοῦ J 13: 25 (but here οὕτως can also refer to what precedes *accordingly*=following Peter's nod).

5. used as an adj. (Bl-D. §434, 1 w. app.) ἡ γένεσις οὕτως ἦν (= τοιαύτη ἦν) Mt 1: 18.—19: 10; Ro 4: 18 (Gen 15: 5). Cf. Rv 9: 17.—Also subst. *something like this* as subj. Mt 9: 33; as obj. Mk 2: 12. οὕτως ποιεῖν τινι *do thus and so* or *for someone* Lk 1: 25; 2: 48. M-M.

οὐχ s. οὐ.

οὐχί (a strengthened form of οὐ. Hom. +; Attic wr.; Dit., Syll.³ 646, 41 [170 bc]; 834, 18; PSI 499, 4 [257/6 bc]; Zen.-P. 111 [= Sb 6994], 27; LXX; En.; Jos., Ant. 17, 312 al.) *not* (Bl-D. §432; 427, 2; Rob. 296; 917 al.).

1. as a simple negative (so in the pass. mentioned above) οὐχὶ πάντες καθαροί ἐστε J 13: 11; cf. vs. 10 (ἀλλ' οὐχὶ as Jos., Ant. 8, 279); 14: 22; 1 Cor 6: 1. οὐχὶ μή Lk 18: 30. οὐχὶ μᾶλλον *not rather* 1 Cor 5: 2. Foll. by ἀλλά *not...but* 10: 29; 2 Cor 10: 13 v.l. (for οὐκ); B 12: 10; IMg 3: 2.

2. as an answer: *no, by no means* w. ἀλλά foll. (X., Cyr. 1, 3, 4 codd.; Gen 18: 15; 19: 2; 42: 12) Lk 1: 60; 16: 30; J 9: 9; Ro 3: 27. οὐχί, λέγω ὑμῖν, ἀλλά *no, I tell you, but rather* Lk 12: 51; 13: 3, 5.

3. as an interrogative word in questions that expect an affirmative answer (X., Cyr. 8, 3, 46; PGrenf. I 1 I, 25 [II bc]; Gen 40: 8; Judg 4: 6) οὐχὶ καὶ οἱ τελῶναι τὸ αὐτὸ ποιοῦσιν; Mt 5: 46. Cf. vs. 47; 6: 25; 10: 29; Lk 6: 39; 12: 6; 15: 8; 17: 17 v.l. (for οὐχ); 24: 26; J 11: 9; Ro 3: 29; 1 Cor 1: 20; Hb 1: 14; 1 Cl 31: 2; D 1: 3. ἀλλ' οὐχὶ ἐρεῖ αὐτῷ...; *will he not rather say to him...?* Lk 17: 8. ἡ οὐχί...; 1 Cl 46: 6.—διὰ τί οὐχὶ μᾶλλον ἀδικεῖσθε; 1 Cor 6: 7a; cf. b. πῶς οὐχί...; (1 Esdr 4: 32) Ro 8: 32. M-M.

ὀφειλέτης, ου, ὁ (Soph. +; BGU 954, 22; En. 6, 3 ἐγὼ μόνος ὀφειλέτης ἁμαρτίας μεγάλης).

1. lit. *debtor* (Pla., Leg. 5 p. 736D; Plut. et al.) w. the amount of the debt given in the gen. ὀφ. μυρίων ταλάντων *who owed ten thousand talents* Mt 18: 24.

2. fig.—**a.** *debtor* πάντες ὀφειλέται ἐσμὲν ἁμαρτίας *we are all debtors in the matter of sin* Pol 6: 1.

b. *one who is obligated* to do someth. ὀφειλέτην εἶναι

be under obligation w. the gen. or dat. of the pers. or thing to whom (which) one is obligated (Bl-D. §190, 1 app.; Rob. 537 al.): w. the gen. of the pers. *obligated to someone* Ro 15: 27. W. the dat. of the pers. 1: 14; 8: 12. That which one is obligated to do stands in the gen. ὀφειλέται ἐσμὲν οὐ τ. σαρκὶ τοῦ κατὰ σάρκα ζῆν *we are under obligation, but not to the flesh, to live according to its demands* Ro 8: 12 (cf. Bl-D. §400, 2; Rob. 1076). The simple inf. (Soph., Aj. 590) is found instead of the articular inf. in the gen.: ὀφ. ἐστὶν ὅλον τὸν νόμον ποιῆσαι Gal 5: 3.

c. *one who is guilty* of a misdeed, *one who is culpable, at fault*—**α.** in relation to men, w. the gen. of the one against whom the misdeed was committed ἀφήκαμεν τοῖς ὀφ. ἡμῶν *we have forgiven our debtors, those who are guilty of sin against us* Mt 6: 12; cf. D 8: 2.

β. in relation to God, *sinner* (cf. Lk 13: 4 w. vs. 2 ἁμαρτωλοί) abs. ὅτι αὐτοὶ ὀφειλέται ἐγένοντο παρὰ πάντας τοὺς ἀνθρώπους *that they were sinners to a greater degree than all the other people* Lk 13: 4. M-M.*

ὀφειλή, ῆς, ἡ *debt*—**1.** lit. (so oft. in pap. and ostraca [since III bc]) Mt 18: 32.

2. fig.—**a.** gener. *obligation, duty, one's due* τὴν ὀφειλήν τινι ἀποδιδόναι *give someone his (her) due* of conjugal duties 1 Cor 7: 3. Pl., of taxes, etc. Ro 13: 7.

b. in a relig. sense: *debt, guilt* ἄφες ἡμῖν τὴν ὀφ. ἡμῶν *forgive us our debt* D 8: 2. M-M.*

ὀφείλημα, ατος, τό (Thu. +; inscr., pap., LXX)—**1.** *debt* = *what is owed, one's due* (Pla., Leg. 4 p. 717B; Aristot., Eth. Nic. 8, 15 p. 1162b, 28; 9, 2 p. 1165a, 3; Dit., Syll.³ 1108, 10 [III/II bc]; PHib. 42, 10 [262 bc]; PLond. 1203, 4; POxy. 494, 10 ὀφειλήματα; Dt 24: 10; 1 Esdr 3: 20; 1 Macc 15: 8) of wages for work done οὐ λογίζεται κατὰ χάριν ἀλλὰ κατὰ ὀφείλημα *it is considered not as a favor, but as his due* Ro 4: 4 (on the contrast χάρις—ὀφείλημα cf. Thu. 2, 40, 4 οὐκ ἐς χάριν, ἀλλ' ἐς ὀφείλημα).

2. in a relig. sense: *debt*=sin (as Aram. אוֹבָה in rabb. lit.; cf. MBlack, Aramaic Approach³, '67, 140) ἄφες ἡμῖν τὰ ὀφ. ἡμῶν *forgive us our debts* (= sins) Mt 6: 12 (the parallel Lk 11: 4 has τὰς ἁμαρτίας ἡμῶν). M-M.*

ὀφείλω impf. ὤφειλον (Hom. +; inscr., pap., LXX, Philo, Joseph.); our lit. has only the pres. and impf.; *owe, be indebted.*

1. lit., of financial debts: τινί τι *owe someth. to someone* Mt 18: 28a; Lk 16: 5. W. acc. of the debt (Appian, Bell. Civ. 2, 8 §26; Jos., Ant. 13, 56) Mt 18: 28b; Lk 7: 41; 16: 7; Phlm 18. τὸ ὀφειλόμενον *the sum that is owed* (X.; Pla.; PRainer 228, 5. In pap. the pl. is more freq. found in this mng.) Mt 18: 30. πᾶν τὸ ὀφ. αὐτῷ *the whole amount that he owed him* vs. 34.

2. fig.—**a.** gener.—**α.** *owe, be indebted* τινί τι *(to) someone (for) someth.* (Alciphr. 4, 13, 1 Νύμφαις θυσίαν ὀφ.; Jos., C. Ap. 2, 295) πόσα αὐτῷ ὀφείλομεν ὅσια; *for how many holy deeds are we indebted to him?* 2 Cl 1: 3. μηδενὶ μηδὲν ὀφείλετε εἰ μὴ τὸ ἀλλήλους ἀγαπᾶν *owe nothing to anyone except to love each other* Ro 13: 8 (AFridrichsen, StKr 102, '30, 294–7). τὴν ὀφειλομένην εὔνοιαν *the goodwill that one owes*, a euphemism for marital duties 1 Cor 7: 3 t.r. εἰς τὸν ὀφειλόμενον τόπον τῆς δόξης *to the glorious place that he deserved* 1 Cl 5: 4. εἰς τὸν ὀφειλόμενον αὐτοῖς τόπον εἰσὶ παρὰ τῷ κυρίῳ Pol 9: 2.—Subst. τὰ ὀφειλόμενα (s. 1 above) *duties, obligations* ποιεῖν fulfill GP 12: 53.

β. *be obligated*, w. inf. foll. *one must, one ought* (class.; inscr., pap.; 4 Macc 11: 15; 16: 19; Philo, Agr. 164, Spec. Leg. 1, 101; Test. Jos. 14: 6) ὃ ὠφείλομεν ποιῆσαι πεποιήκαμεν Lk 17: 10. κατὰ τ. νόμον ὀφείλει ἀποθανεῖν J 19: 7. Cf. 13: 14; Ro 15: 1, 27; 1 Cor 7: 36; 9: 10; 11: 10; Eph 5: 28; 2 Th 1: 3; 2: 13; Hb 2: 17; 5: 3, 12; 1 J 2: 6; 3: 16; 4: 11; 3 J 8; 1 Cl 38: 4; 40: 1; 48: 6; 51: 1; 2 Cl 4: 3; B 1: 7; 2: 1, 9f; 4: 6; 5: 3; 6: 18; 7: 1, 11; 13: 3; Pol 5: 1; 6: 2; Hs 8, 9, 4; 9, 13, 3; 9, 18, 2; 9, 28, 5. Negat. *one ought not, one must not* (Jos., Vi. 149) Ac 17: 29; 1 Cor 11: 7; 1 Cl 56: 2; Hm 4, 1, 3; 8; s 5, 4, 2; 9, 18, 1. Cf. 2 Cl 4: 3. οὐκ ὀφείλει τὰ τέκνα τ. γονεῦσι θησαυρίζειν *children are under no obligation to lay up money for their parents* 2 Cor 12: 14.—ἐπεὶ ὠφείλετε ἄρα ἐκ τοῦ κόσμου ἐξελθεῖν *then you would have to come out of the world altogether* 1 Cor 5: 10. ἐγὼ ὤφειλον ὑφ᾽ ὑμῶν συνίστασθαι *I ought to have been recommended by you* 2 Cor 12: 11 (Bl-D. §358, 1; Rob. 920).

b. Rabbinic usage has given rise to certain peculiarities **α.** ὀφ. used absolutely [חַיָּב]: ὀφείλει *he is obligated, bound* (by his oath) Mt 23: 16, 18.

β. *commit a sin* (s. ὀφείλημα 2; but cf. also Dit., Syll.ʼ 1042, 15 ἁμαρτίαν ὀφιλέτω Μηνὶ Τυράννῳ) w. dat. *against someone* ἀφίομεν παντὶ ὀφείλοντι ἡμῖν Lk 11: 4. FHauck, ὀφείλω etc.: TW V 559-65. M-M. B. 641.*

ὄφελον (prob. not the first pers. 2 aor. of ὀφείλω [ὤφελον] without the augment [so most scholars, incl. Mlt. 201, n. 1; Mlt.-H. 191], but a ptc., originally w. ἐστίν to be supplied [JWackernagel, Sprachl. Untersuchungen zu Homer '16, 199f; Bl-D. §67, 2; so also L-S-J s.v. ὀφείλω, end]. ὄφελον: Dit., Or. 315, 16 [164/3 BC]; Epict. 2, 18, 15 v.l. Sch.; 2, 22, 12 as a correction in ms. S; LXX; En. 104, 11) a fixed form, functioning as a particle to introduce unattainable wishes (Bl-D. §359, 1; Rob. 1003f) *O that, would that* w. the impf. to express present time (Epict. 2, 22, 12; Dio Chrys. 21[38], 47 vArnim [ed. Budé has ὤφελον]) Rv 3: 15; 2 Cor 11: 1. καὶ ὄφελον ἐμιμοῦντο ISm 12: 1. W. the opt. (Ps 118: 5) Rv 3: 15 t.r.—W. the aor. indic. to express past time (Epict. 2, 18, 15; Charito 4, 4, 2; Achilles Tat. 2, 24; 3, 5, 15, 5; Ex 16: 3; Num 14: 2; 20: 3) 1 Cor 4: 8.—W. the fut. indic. (acc. to Lucian, Soloec. 1, end, ὄφελον ... δυνήσῃ is a solecism) ὄφ. καὶ ἀποκόψονται Gal 5: 12 (s. ἀποκόπτω 2 and Bl-D. §384; Rob. 923). M-M.*

ὄφελος, ους, τό (Hom.+; Dit., Or. 519, 26 οὐδὲν ὄφελος ἡμεῖν; POxy. 118 verso, 30 οὐδὲν ὄφ.; 1468, 6; Job 15: 3; Jos., Ant. 17, 154) *benefit, good* τί τὸ ὄφ.; *what good does it do?* Js 2: 16 (Hierocles, Carm. Aur. 14 p. 451 M.; Philo, Migr. Abr. 55 τί γὰρ ὄ.;). W. ἐάν foll. (cf. Ael. Aristid. 53 p. 640 D.; M. J. Brutus, Ep. 4) vs. 14; 2 Cl 6: 2 (a saying of Jesus; in Mt 16: 26 τί ὠφεληθήσεται ἄνθρωπος, ἐάν ...;). τί μοι τὸ ὄφ.; *what good is it to me?* 1 Cor 15: 32. τί μοι ὄφελος ταῦτα ἑωρακότι καὶ μὴ γινώσκοντι ...; *how does it benefit me to have seen this and not to understand ...?* Hv 3, 3, 1 (τί μοι ὄφελος; Charito 7, 4, 10). M-M.*

ὀφθαλμοδουλία, ας, ἡ (Bl-D. §115, 1; cf. Mlt.-H. 271; FWGingrich, JBL 52, '33, 263; Achmes p. 18, 12 says of a slave κατ᾽ ὀφθαλμὸν δουλεύειν) *eye-service*, i.e. service that is performed only to attract attention (CFDMoule, ET 59, '47/'48, 250), not for its own sake nor to please God or one's own conscience (s. Theodoret III p. 437 Schulze on Eph 6: 6f ὀφθαλμοδουλείαν δὲ καλεῖ τὴν οὐκ ἐξ εἰλικρινοῦς καρδίας προσφερομένην θεραπείαν, ἀλλὰ τῷ σχήματι κεχρωσμένην) κατ᾽ ὀφθαλμοδουλίαν Eph 6: 6. Pl., of more than one occurrence of this kind of service ἐν ὀφθαλμοδουλίαις Col 3: 22.*

ὀφθαλμός, οῦ, ὁ (Hom.+; inscr., pap., LXX, En., Ep. Arist., Philo, Joseph., Test. 12 Patr.) *eye.*

1. lit., as an organ of sense perception Mt 5: 29, 38 (Ex 21: 24; s. DDaube, JTS 45, '44, 177-89.—The principle ἐάν τίς τινος ὀφθαλμὸν ἐκκόψῃ, ἀντεκκόπτεσθαι τὸν ἐκείνου in early Gk. legislation in Diod. S. 12, 17, 4; Diog. L. 1, 57 [Solon]); 6: 22; 7: 3ff (s. δοκός); Mk 9: 47; Lk 6: 41f; 11: 34; J 9: 6; 1 Cor 12: 16f; Rv 1: 14; 2: 18; 7: 17; 19: 12; 21: 4; 1 Cl 10: 4 (Gen 13: 14) and oft. More than two eyes in the same creature (Artem. 1, 26 p. 28, 13ff) Rv 4: 6, 8 (after Ezk 1: 18; 10: 12); 5: 6 (cf. Lucian, Dial. Deor. 3 and 20, 8: Argus w. the many eyes, who sees w. his whole body, and never sleeps).—εἶδον οἱ ὀφ. μου (cf. Sir 16: 5) Lk 2: 30; cf. 4: 20; 10: 23; 1 Cor 2: 9 (= 1 Cl 34: 8; 2 Cl 11: 7; MPol 2: 3. On possible Gnostic associations s. UWilcken, Weisheit u. Torheit, '59, 77-80 and Hippolytus 5, 26, 16); Rv 1: 7.—ἰδεῖν τοῖς ὀφ. Dg 2: 1 (Philo, Sacr. Abel. 24). ὃ ἑωράκαμεν τοῖς ὀφ. ἡμῶν 1 J 1: 1 (cf. Zech 9: 8 A). ὀφ. πονηρός *an evil eye* i.e., one that looks w. envy or jealousy upon other people (Sir 14: 10; Maximus Tyr. 20: 7b) Mt 6: 23 (opp. ἁπλοῦς; s. this entry, the lit. s.v. λύχνος 2 and πονηρός 1aα, and also PFiebig, Das Wort Jesu v. Auge: StKr 89, '16, 499-507; CEdlund, Das Auge der Einfalt: Acta Sem. Neot. Upsal. 19, '52; HJCadbury, HTR 47, '54, 69-74). Cf. 20: 15. By metonymy for *envy, malice* Mk 7: 22 (but the mng. *stinginess, love for one's own possessions* is upheld for all the NT pass. w. ὀφ. πον. by CJCadoux, ET 53, '41/'42, 354f, esp. for Mt 20: 15, and w. ref. to Dt 15: 9 al. *Envy,* etc. is preferred by CRSmith, ibid. 181f; 54, '42/'43, 26 and JDPercy, ibid. 26f).—ἐν ῥιπῇ ὀφθαλμοῦ *in the twinkling of an eye* 1 Cor 15: 52. ἀγαπήσεις ὡς κόρην τοῦ ὀφ. σου *you are to love as the apple of your eye* B 19: 9 (s. κόρη).—Used w. verbs: αἴρω ἄνω (αἴρω 1b). ἀνοίγω (ἀνοίγω 1eβ). ἐξαιρέω (q.v. 1). ἐξορύσσω (q.v.). ἐπαίρω (q.v. 1). κρατέω (q.v. 2d). ὑπολαμβάνειν τινὰ ἀπὸ τῶν ὀφ. τινός *take someone up out of sight of someone* Ac 1: 9.—ἡ ἐπιθυμία τῶν ὀφθαλμῶν 1 J 2: 16 (Maximus Tyr. 19, 2 l m the ἐπιθυμία goes through the ὀφθαλμοί). ὀφθαλμοὶ μεστοὶ μοιχαλίδος 2 Pt 2: 14 (s. μεστός 2b).—It is characteristic of the OT (but s. also Hes., Op. 265 πάντα ἰδὼν Διὸς ὀφθαλμός; Polyb. 23, 10, 3 Δίκης ὀφ.; Aristaen., Ep. 1, 19 at the beginning, the pl. of the eyes of Tyche. ὄμματα is also found of a divinity: Alciphr. 3, 8, 2; 4, 9, 4) to speak anthropomorphically of the eyes of God Hb 4: 13; 1 Pt 3: 12; 1 Cl 22: 6 (the last two Ps 33: 16).

2. transferred fr. sense perception to mental and spiritual understanding: ὀφθαλμοὺς ἔχοντες οὐ βλέπετε Mk 8: 18.—Mt 13: 15b; J 12: 40b; Ac 28: 27b (all three Is 6: 10); Mt 13: 16. ἔδωκεν αὐτοῖς ὁ θεὸς ὀφθαλμοὺς τοῦ μὴ βλέπειν *the kind of eyes with which they do not see* (cf. Bl-D. §393, 6; 400, 2; Rob. 1061; 1076) Ro 11: 8 (cf. Dt 29: 3). οἱ ὀφ. τῆς καρδίας *the eyes of the heart* (s. καρδία 1bβ and cf. Herm. Wr. 7, 1 ἀναβλέψαντες τοῖς τῆς καρδίας ὀφθαλμοῖς; 10, 4 ὁ τοῦ νοῦ ὀφθαλμός.—Sir 17: 8) Eph 1: 18; 1 Cl 36: 2; 59: 3; MPol 2: 3. Cf. also the entries καμμύω, σκοτίζω, τυφλόω.—W. a prep.: ἀπέναντι τῶν ὀφ. τινος s. ἀπέναντι 1b. ἐκρύβη ἀπὸ ὀφθαλμῶν σου *it is hidden from the eyes of your mind* Lk 19: 42 (cf. Sir 17: 15). ἐν ὀφθαλμοῖς (LXX; cf. Thackeray 43): ἔστιν θαυμαστὴ ἐν ὀφθαλμοῖς ἡμῶν *it is marvelous in our sight* (= in our judgment; but Lucian, Tox. 39 ἐν ὀφθαλμοῖς ἡμῶν means 'before our eyes'. Likew. Apollon. Rhod. 4, 1619 τέρας ἐν ὀφθαλμοῖσιν ἰδόντες = gaze with their eyes on the portent; Diod. S. 3, 18, 5 ἐν ὀφθαλμοῖς = before their eyes) Mt 21: 42; Mk 12: 11 (both Ps 117: 23). κατ᾽ ὀφθαλμούς τινος *before someone's eyes, in someone's sight* (2 Km 12: 11; 4 Km 25: 7; Jer 35: 5; Ezk 20: 14, 22, 41; 21: 11; 22: 16; 36: 23) οἷς κατ᾽ ὀφθαλμοὺς Ἰ. Χριστὸς προεγράφη *before whose eyes Jesus Christ* *was portrayed* Gal 3: 1. πρὸ ὀφθαλμῶν *before* (*someone's*) *eyes* (Hyperid. 6, 17; Dit., Syll.³ 495, 120 [c. 230 BC]; BGU 362 V, 8; LXX; Ep. Arist. 284): πρὸ ὀφθαλμῶν λαμβάνειν (Polyb.; Diod. S. 26, 16b [cf. FKrebs, Die Präp. bei Polyb. 1882, 38]; 2 Macc 8: 17; 3 Macc 4: 4) *place before one's eyes* 1 Cl 5: 3. πρὸ ὀφθαλμῶν ἔχειν (Lucian, Tyrannicida 7; Dit., Or. 210, 8; PGiess. 67, 10) *keep one's eyes on* someth. MPol 2: 3. πρὸ ὀφθαλμῶν τινος εἶναι (Dt 11: 18) *be before someone's eyes* 1 Cl 2: 1; 39: 3 (Job 4: 16). M.-M. B. 225.

ὀφθείς, ὀφθήσομαι s. ὁράω.

ὄφις, εως, ὁ (Hom.+; Dit., Syll.³ 1168, 113 of the snake that functioned in healings in the temple of Asclepius at Epidaurus; PGM 8, 11; 13, 261; 881; LXX; Philo; Jos., Bell. 5, 108, Ant. 1, 41; 2, 287) *snake, serpent.*

1. lit. Mt 7: 10 (s. BHjerl-Hansen, RB 55, '48, 195-8); Mk 16: 18; Lk 11: 11; 1 Cor 10: 9 (Diod. S. 5, 58, 4 ὑπὸ τῶν ὄφεων διαφθαρῆναι); Rv 9: 19 (cf. Achilles Tat. 1, 3, 4 ὄφεις καὶ σκορπίοι). ὄφεις καὶ κόμαι (Procop. Soph., Ep. 136; Sb 6584, 6; Cat. Cod. Astr. VII 177, 21; Dt 8: 15; Philo, Praem. 90) Lk 10: 19. Symbol of cleverness (cf. Gen 3: 1; symbol of another kind Hyperides, fgm. 80) Mt 10: 16; IPol 2: 2. Of the brass serpent in the desert (Num 21: 6-9; Wsd 16: 5f) χαλκοῦς ὄφ. (Num 21: 9; cf. 4 Km 18: 4) B 12: 6. This serpent, raised aloft, as a type of Jesus J 3: 14; B 12: 5-7 (a typological evaluation of Num 21: 6-9 also in Philo, Leg. All. 2, 77ff, Agr. 95.—Appian, Mithrid. 77 §335 tells of a χαλκοῦς ὄφις in memory of Philoctetes; Diod. S. 2, 9, 5 of ὄφεις ἀργυροί on the temple of Zeus in Babylon).

2. fig., of depraved men (cf. Sib. Or. 5, 29 of Nero) ὄφεις γεννήματα ἐχιδνῶν Mt 23: 33.

3. as a symbolic figure, frequent in mythology (Apollon. Rhod. 4, 128 the dragon guarding the golden fleece; 4, 1434 the Lernaean Hydra.—WGrafBaudissin, Studien zur semitischen Religionsgesch. I 1876, 257ff, RE V 1898, 3ff; XVII '06, 580ff; HGunkel, Schöpfung u. Chaos 1895, 29ff; 320ff; JGFrazer, The Golden Bough³ IV 1, '19, 80ff; Pauly-W. 2nd Series II 1, 508f; EKüster, D. Schlange in der griech. Kunst u. Religion '13; EUlback, The Serpent in Myth and Scripture: Bibliotheca Sacra 90, '33, 449-55; PGM 4, 1638 the sun-god as ὁ μέγας ὄφις), as a designation for the devil (s. δράκων) Rv 12: 14f; Dg 12: 3, 6, 8 (here in vs. 6 the serpent of Paradise is clearly the devil). ὁ ὄφ. ὁ ἀρχαῖος (s. ἀρχαῖος 1) Rv 12: 9; 20: 2. In speaking of the serpent that seduced Eve, Paul evidently has the devil in mind 2 Cor 11: 3 (cf. 4 Macc 18: 8.—Ltzm. and Windisch on 2 Cor 11: 3; Dibelius, Geisterwelt 50f; SReinach, La Femme et la Serpent: L'Anthropologie 35, '05, 178ff). JFichtner and WFoerster, TW V 566-82. M.-M. B. 194.*

ὀφλισκάνω (Aeschyl., Hdt.+; inscr., pap.) w. the rare and unclassical 1 aor. ὤφλησα (Lysias 13, 65 ms.; Hippocr., Ep. 27 ed. Littré IX p. 426; Ael. Aristid. [s. below]) *become a debtor* w. acc. *incur the charge of, become guilty of a thing* (Soph., Oed. R. 512 κακίαν; Eur., Heracl. 985 δειλίαν, Ion 443 ἀνομίαν; Ael. Aristid. 39 p. 732 D.: αἰσχύνην ὀφλῆσαι; Philo, Agr. 93 γέλωτα ὀφ.=be laughed at) συμφέρει ἡμῖν ὀφλῆσαι μεγίστην ἁμαρτίαν ἔμπροσθεν τοῦ θεοῦ καὶ μή *it is better for us to become guilty of the greatest sin before God, than* GP 11: 48.*

ὀφρῦς (on the accent s. Mlt.-H. 141f), ύος, ἡ lit. *eyebrow* (so Hom.+; PPetr. I 11, 17 [220 BC]; PFay. 107, 15; Lev 14: 9; Ep. Arist. 98; Philo), then *brow, edge* of a cliff or hill (Il. 20, 151; Polyb. 7, 6, 3; Diod. S. 22, 13, 4; Plut.,

Numa 10, 8; Strabo 5, 3, 7; PAmh. 68, 9; 34 [I AD]) ἤγαγον αὐτὸν ἕως ὀφρύος τοῦ ὄρους *they led him to the brow of the hill* Lk 4: 29. On the situation cf. MBrückner, Pj 7, '11, 82. M.-M. B. 219.*

ὀχετός, οῦ, ὁ (Pind. +; Sym.) *canal, water-course* (Hdt. +; inscr., pap.; Philo, Leg. All. 1, 13, Poster. Cai. 50), then *drain, sewer* (Antonin. Liberal. 24, 3; Herodian 5, 8, 9; 7, 7, 3; Acta S. Apollonii §21a Klette); so Mk 7: 19 D (for ἀφεδρῶνα [q.v.]). The mng. *intestinal canal* (quotable since Hippocr.; X., Mem. 1, 4, 6) is not applicable here because of the proximity of κοιλία. M.-M.*

ὀχλέω (Aeschyl., Hdt.+; inscr., pap., ostraca, LXX) *trouble, disturb* (so mostly) pass. (Jos., Ant. 6, 217, Vi. 275 [ὀχ. ὑπό τινος]) ὀχλούμενος ὑπὸ πνευμάτων ἀκαθάρτων *tormented by unclean spirits* Ac 5: 16. Cf. Lk 6: 18 t.r. (Tob 6: 8 BA ἐάν τινα ὀχλῇ δαιμόνιον ἢ πνεῦμα πονηρόν; Act. Thom. 12 ὑπὸ δαιμονίων ὀχλούμενοι). M.-M.*

ὀχλοποιέω 1 aor. ptc. ὀχλοποιήσας (not found elsewh. But cf. Hippocr., Mul. 1, 14 ed. Littré VIII p. 52 ὄχλον ποιέει) *form a mob* Ac 17: 5.*

ὄχλος, ου, ὁ (Pind., Hdt. +; inscr., pap., LXX, Ep. Arist., Philo, Joseph.; loanw. in rabb.—In the NT only in the gospels, Ac, and Rv).

1. *crowd, throng,* (*multitude*) of people Mt 9: 23, 25; 15: 35; Mk 2: 4 (s. DDaube, ET 50, '38, 138f); 3: 9; Lk 5: 1; J 5: 13; 6: 22; Ac 14: 14; 21: 34f and oft. τὶς ἐκ τοῦ ὄχλου *someone from the crowd* Lk 12: 13; cf. 11: 27. ἀνὴρ ἀπὸ τοῦ ὄχ. 9: 38. τινὲς τῶν Φαρισαίων ἀπὸ τοῦ ὄχλου *some of the Pharisees in the crowd* 19: 39. ἀπὸ τοῦ ὄχλου *away from the crowd* Mk 7: 17, 33. οὐκ ἠδύνατο ἀπὸ τοῦ ὄχλου *he could not because of the crowd* Lk 19: 3 (s. ἀπό V 1). οὐ μετὰ ὄχλου *without a crowd* (present) Ac 24: 18 (cf. vs. 12). This is equivalent in mng. to ἄτερ ὄχλου (s. ἄτερ) *when there was no crowd present* Lk 22: 6 (cf. WLarfeld, Die ntl. Evangelien nach ihrer Eigenart '25, 190), unless ὄχ. means *disturbance* (Hdt. +) here (so Gdspd.).—πᾶς ὁ ὄχλος (Aelian, V.H. 2, 6) *the whole crowd, all the people* Mt 2: 2b; Mk 2: 13; 4: 1b; 9: 15; Lk 13: 17; Ac 21: 27; MPol 9: 2; 16: 1.—πολὺς ὄχ. (Jos., Vi. 133; 277) Mt 14: 14; Mk 6: 34. ὄχ. πολύς (Cebes 1, 2; IG IV² 1, 123, 25; several times LXX) Mt 20: 29; Mk 5: 21, 24; 9: 14; Lk 8: 4; J 6: 2. ὁ πολὺς ὄχ. Mk 12: 37. ὁ ὄχ. πολύς J 12: 9, 12.—ὄχ. ἱκανός *a considerable throng* Mk 10: 46; Lk 7: 12; Ac 11: 24, 26; cf. 19: 26. ὄχ. τοσοῦτος Mt 15: 33. ὁ πλεῖστος ὄχ. *the great throng* or *greater part of the crowd* (the verb in the pl. with a collective noun as Memnon [I BC/I AD]: 434 fgm. 1, 28, 6 Jac. εἷλον . . . ἡ Ῥωμαίων δύναμις. Cf. Bl-D. §134, 1) 21: 8. Cf. Mk 4: 1a. τὸ πλεῖον μέρος τοῦ ὄχ. *the greater part of the throng* Hs 8, 1, 16; τὸ πλῆθος τοῦ ὄχ. 9, 4, 4; αἱ μυριάδες τοῦ ὄχ. *the crowd in myriads* Lk 12: 1.—The pl. is common in Mt, Lk, and Ac (acc. to later usage: X., Mem. 3, 7, 5; Dionys. Hal.; Ael. Aristid. 34, 47 K.=50 p. 564 D.; Jos., Ant. 6, 25 al.) οἱ ὄχλοι *the crowds, the people* (the latter plainly Posidon.: 87 fgm. 36, 51 Jac. συλλαλήσαντες αὐτοῖς οἱ ὄχ.; Diod. S. 1, 36, 10; 1, 83, 8 ἐν ταῖς τῶν ὄχλων ψυχαῖς; 1, 72, 5 μυριάδες τῶν ὄχλων; 4, 42, 3; 14, 7, 2 ὄχλων πλῆθος=a crowd of people; 36, 15, 2 οἱ κατὰ τὴν πόλιν ὄχλοι=the people in the city; Artem. 1, 51 p. 49, 2; Ps.-Aeschines, Ep. 10, 4 ἡμεῖς ἅμα τ. ἄλλοις ὄχλοις; Ps.-Demetr., Form. Ep. p. 7, 11; Dit., Or. 383, 151 [I BC]; Jos., Ant. 9, 3) Mt 5: 1; 7: 28; 9: 8, 33, 36 and oft. Lk 3: 7, 10; 4: 42; 5: 3; 8: 42, 45 and oft. Ac 8: 6; 13: 45; 14: 11, 13, 18f; 17: 13. Mk only 6: 33 t.r. J only 7: 12a (v.l. ἐν τῷ ὄχλῳ). MPol

13: 1. Without the art. Mk 10: 1. ὄχ. πολλοί (s. πολύς I 1aβ) Mt 4: 25; 8: 1; 13: 2a; 15: 30; 19: 2; Lk 5: 15. 14: 25. πάντες οἱ ὄχ. Mt 12: 23.—A linguistic parallel to the pl. ὄχλοι and a parallel in content to the scene in Mk 15: 15 (ὁ Πιλᾶτος βουλόμενος τῷ ὄχλῳ τὸ ἱκανὸν ποιῆσαι ἀπέλυσεν αὐτοῖς τὸν Βαραββᾶν καὶ παρέδωκεν τὸν Ἰησοῦν φραγελλώσας ἵνα σταυρωθῇ) is offered by PFlor. 61, 59ff [85 AD], where, according to the court record, G. Septimius Vegetus says to a certain Phibion: ἄξιος μὲν ἦς μαστιγωθῆναι . . . χαρίζομαι δέ σε τοῖς ὄχλοις (cf. Dssm., LO 229 [LAE 266f], and on the favor of the ὄχλοι PGM 36, 275).

2. the (common) people, populace (PJoüon, Rech de Sc rel 27, '37, 618f) in contrast to the rulers: Mt 14: 5; 15: 10; 21: 26; Mk 11: 18; 12: 12. Likew. the pl. οἱ ὄχ. (Ep. Arist. 271) Mt 21: 46. The lower classes (X., Cyr. 2, 2, 21, Hier. 2, 3 al.) ἐπίστασις ὄχλου a disturbance among the people Ac 24: 12. Contemptuously rabble J 7: 49 (Bultmann ad loc. [w. lit.]).

3. a large number, (company) w. gen. (Eur., Iph. A. 191 ἵππων al.; Jos., Ant. 3, 66) ὄχ. τελωνῶν a crowd of tax-collectors Lk 5: 29. ὄχ. μαθητῶν 6: 17. ὄχ. ὀνομάτων Ac 1: 15. ὄχ. τῶν ἱερέων 6: 7.

4. the pl. ὄχλοι as a synonym beside λαοί and ἔθνη Rv 17: 15 (cf. Da 3: 4). RMeyer and PKatz, TW V 582-90. M-M. B. 929.

Ὀχοζίας, ου, ὁ (אֲחַזְיָה) Ahaziah, a Hebrew king (4 Km 8: 24; 9: 16; 2 Ch 22: 1; Joseph.) in the genealogy of Jesus Mt 1: 8 v.l.; Lk 3: 23ff D.*

ὀχυρός, ά, όν (Hes.+; LXX; Jos., Ant. 11, 89; Test. Jud. 9: 4) strong, firm, sturdy μακροθυμία Hm 5, 2, 3.*

ὀχύρωμα, ατος, τό stronghold, fortress, also prison (in the literal sense since X., Hell. 3, 2, 3; Dit., Syll.³ 502, 39 [III BC], Or. 455, 14 [39 BC]; PPetr. II 13[3], 2 [III BC]; PStrassb. 85, 23; LXX; Jos., Ant. 13, 27) fig. (Hybreas [I BC] in Seneca Rhet., Suas. 4, 5; Pr 21: 22 καθεῖλεν τὸ ὀχύρωμα ἐφ' ᾧ ἐπεποίθεισαν; 10: 29 ὀχύρωμα ὁσίου φόβος κυρίου) of spiritual weapons; they are δυνατά . . . πρὸς καθαίρεσιν ὀχυρωμάτων powerful . . . to tear down fortresses, i.e., to destroy λογισμοί, sophistries, and everything that opposes the γνῶσις θεοῦ 2 Cor 10: 4 (cf. Philo, Conf. Lingu. 129; 130 τὴν τοῦ ὀχ. τούτου καθαίρεσιν). M-M.*

ὀψάριον, ου, τό dim. of ὄψον (Hom.+; Tob 2: 2 BA; 7: 8 BA)='cooked food' eaten w. bread. ὀψάριον also has this mng. (PRyl. 229, 21; s. below). As food eaten w. bread ὀψάριον can mean 'tidbit' in general (so Tob 2: 2 S; Plut., De Sanit. Tuenda 7 p. 126A; Philemo Com. fgm. 98, 5 K.; POxy. 531, 18; PFay. 119, 31) or specif. fish (cf. Num 11: 22 πᾶν τὸ ὄψος τῆς θαλάσσης; Iambl., Vi. Pyth. 21, 98 θαλασσίων ὄψων.—Suidas: ὀψάριον· τὸ ἰχθύδιον. This mng. of ὀψάριον is found in: several comic wr. in Athen. 9, 35 p. 385f; Lucian, Jupp. Conf. 4; Cyranides p. 109, 4; 5; Griech. Dialekt-Inschr. 4706, 191 [Thera]; Dit., Or. 484, 12; 16; BGU 1095, 16 [57 AD] λαγύνιον ταριχηροῦ [=ῶν] ὀψαρίων=preserved fish; PLond. 483, 77 ὀψάρια ἐκ τῶν παντοίων ὑδάτων. In Mod. Gk. ψάρι=fish). It has the latter mng. in our lit., where it occurs only in the Fourth Gosp.: δύο ὀψάρια J 6: 9 (the synoptic parallels have δύο ἰχθύας: Mt 14: 17, 19; Mk 6: 38, 41; Lk 9: 13, 16. Cf. PRyl. 229, 21 [38 AD] τ. ἄρτους κ. τὸ ὀψάριον); vs. 11; 21: 9f, 13.—JEKalitsunakis, ᾿Οψον und ὀψάριον: PKretschmer-Festschr. '26, 96-106. M-EBoismard, RB 54, '47, 478 n. 2. M-M. B. 184.*

ὀψέ adv. (Hom.+; pap., LXX, Philo, Joseph.; Sib. Or. 5,

51)—1. late w. gen. ὀψὲ τῆς ὥρας at a late hour (Demosth. 21, 84; Charito 1, 14, 5; UPZ 6, 15 [163 BC]; Jos., Ant. 16, 218) MPol 7: 1.

2. late in the day, i.e. in the evening Mk 13: 35. ὀψὲ οὔσης τῆς ὥρας (cf. Bl-D. §129) 11: 11 (v.l. ὀψίας). As a predicate (Bl-D. §434, 1; cf. Rob. 973) ὅταν ὀψὲ ἐγένετο when it became evening, when evening came 11: 19.— Used almost like an indecl. subst. (Thu. 3, 108, 3 al. ἐς ὀψέ) μέχρις ὀψέ until evening Hs 9, 11, 1; also ἕως ὀψέ (PLond. 1177, 66 [113 AD]) 9, 11, 2.

3. used as an improper prep. w. gen. after ὀψὲ σαββάτων after the Sabbath Mt 28: 1 (Aelian, V.H. 2, 23; Polyaenus 5, 2, 5 ὀψὲ τῆς ὥρας=later than the hour [decided upon]; Philostrat., Vi. Apoll. 4, 18 p. 138, 8 ὀψὲ μυστηρίων; 6, 10 p. 213, 24 ὀψὲ τούτων, Her. 12 p. 190, 10 ὀψὲ τῆς μάχης.—Bl-D. §164, 4; Rob. 645f; ETobac, Revue d'Hist. eccl. 20, '24, 239-43; JMaiworm, ThGl 27, '35, 210-16; Gdspd., Probs. 43-5; JMGrintz, JBL 79, '60, 32-47). M-M. B. 961.*

ὀψία, ας, ἡ s. ὄψιος 2.

ὄψιμος, ον (Hom.+; pap., LXX) late in the season ὑετὸς ὄψιμος (w. πρόϊμος, as Dt 11: 14; Jer 5: 24 al.) late rain (in the spring; the early rain came in the fall; s. Dalman, Arbeit I 122ff; 302ff al.) Js 5: 7 t.r. The text has the subst. (ὁ) ὄψιμος in the same mng. S. πρόϊμος. M-M.*

ὄψιος, α, ον late—1. adj. (Pind.+; Thu. 8, 26, 1; PTebt. 304, 5 ὀψίας τῆς ὥρας γενομένης; BGU 380, 3) ὀψίας ἤδη οὔσης τῆς ὥρας since the hour was already late Mk 11: 11 v.l. (s. ὀψέ 2).

2. In our lit. mostly subst. ἡ ὀψία (sc. ὥρα; Bl-D. §241, 3) evening (Ael. Aristid. 48, 50 K.=24 p. 478 D.; POxy. 475, 16 [182 AD] ὀψίας 'in the evening'; 528, 5 καθ' ἑκάστης ἡμέρας καὶ ὀψίας; PGM 1, 69; Jdth 13: 1 ὡς ὀψία ἐγένετο) usu. in the combination ὀψίας δὲ γενομένης when evening came (Syntipas p. 49, 11; Jos., Ant. 5, 7) Mt 8: 16; 14: 15, 23; 20: 8; 26: 20; 27: 57; Mk 1: 32 (the expr. ὀψ. γενομένης, ὅτε ἔδυσεν ὁ ἥλ. is like Herm. Wr. 1, 29); Hs 9, 11, 6. ὀψίας γενομένης in the evening Mt 16: 2; Mk 4: 35; 6: 47; 14: 17. ἤδη ὀψ. γενομένης 15: 42. Also οὔσης ὀψίας (Jos., Ant. 5, 140) J 20: 19. ὡς ὀψ. ἐγένετο (s. Jdth above) 6: 16. The context oft. makes it easier to decide just what time is meant, whether before or after sundown. M-M. B. 997.*

ὄψις, εως, ἡ (Hom.+; inscr., pap., LXX, En., Ep. Arist.; Philo, Joseph., Test. 12 Patr.).

1. seeing, sight (Paus. 3, 14, 4 ὄψις ὀνείρατος=the seeing of a dream; PFay. 133, 11; Jos., Ant. 3, 38) ἡ ὄψις ὑμῶν the sight of you B 1: 3 (cf. Arrian, Anab. 6, 26, 3 ἐν ὄψει πάντων; Wsd 15: 5 ὧν ὄψις).

2. outward appearance, aspect (Thu. 6, 46, 3; Timaeus Hist. [IV/III BC] 566 fgm. 13b Jac.; Diod. S. 4, 54, 5; Appian, Liby. 96 §454; Polyaenus 7, 6, 6; Gen 24: 16; Ep. Arist. 77) τὴν ὄψιν νεωτέραν ἔχειν look younger Hv 3, 10, 4; 3, 12, 1. ἀνήρ τις ἔνδοξος τῇ ὄψει a man of splendid appearance 5: 1 (cf. Dit., Syll.³ 1169, 30 ἔδοξε τὰν ὄψιν εὐπρεπὴς ἀνήρ). Perh. Rv 1: 16 (s. 3 below).— κατ᾽ ὄψιν κρίνειν judge by the outward appearance J 7: 24 (cf. Lysias, Orat. 16, 19 p. 147 οὐκ ἀξιῶ ἀπ᾽ ὄψεως, ὦ βουλή, οὔτε φιλεῖν οὔτε μισεῖν οὐδένα, ἀλλ᾽ ἐκ τῶν ἔργων σκοπεῖν; POxy. 37 II, 3; 1 Km 16: 7; Jos., Bell. 3, 79).

3. face, countenance (Pla., Phaedr. 254B; Phlegon: 257 fgm. 36, 1, 3 Jac.; Diog. L. 6, 91f; PGiess. 22, 5; PAmh. 141, 12; BGU 451, 13; PGM 4, 746; 774; Jos., Ant. 6, 189) J 11: 44; AP 3: 7a; τὸ κάλλος τῆς ὄψ. AP 3: 7b. Perh. Rv

1:16 (s. 2 above). Of the face of God (cf. POxy. 1380, 127 of Isis τὴν ἐν Λήθῃ ἱλαρὰν ὄψιν; BGU 162, 4; 8 ὄψις θεοῦ Σοκνοπαίου; 590, 19) 1 Cl 36: 2.—Also the pl. αἱ ὄψεις, chiefly *the eyes* (Pla., Theaet. p. 156в; Musonius p. 106, 8 H.; Vett. Val. 228, 6; 268, 1; 279, 30; POxy. 911, 6; Tob 14: 2 BA), prob. means more gener. *face* (Jos., Ant. 12, 81; Test. Reub. 5: 5) ἐνέπτυον αὐτοῦ ταῖς ὄψεσι GP 3: 9. M-M.*

ὄψομαι s. ὁράω.

ὀψώνιον, ου, τό (since Menand., fgm. 1051; freq. used fr. Polyb. on, in sing. and pl.; oft. in inscr.; pap.; ostraca; only three times in LXX, all pl. The Atticists rejected it [Lob., Phryn. p. 420]).
   1. *ration-*(*money*) paid to a soldier, then *pay, wages* (this mng. is predom. throughout, and is the only one in the LXX; Ep. Arist. 20; 22=Jos., Ant. 12, 28 [pl.]. Somet. it is extended to mean *wages, pay, salary* gener., even for other than military services).

   a. lit. ἀρκεῖσθε τ. ὀψωνίοις ὑμῶν (said by J. the Baptist to the στρατευόμενοι) Lk 3: 14. στρατεύεσθαι ἰδίοις ὀψωνίοις serve as a soldier at one's own expense 1 Cor 9: 7.
   b. symbolically of the Christians as soldiers (on the Christian life as military service s. πανοπλία 2), whose wages are paid by the heavenly General: ἀρέσκετε ᾦ στρατεύεσθε, ἀφ᾽ οὗ καὶ τὰ ὀψώνια κομίζεσθε IPol 6: 2.—The military viewpoint seems to pass over into a more general one in λαβὼν ὀψώνιον πρὸς τὴν ὑμῶν διακονίαν *accepting support so that I might serve you* 2 Cor 11: 8 (on λαμβάνειν ὀψώνιον cf. Polyb. 6, 39, 12; Dit., Or. 266, 7 [III вс]; PPetr. II 13[17], 6 [258-3 вс]; PLond. 23[a], 26; POxy. 744, 7).—Ro 6: 23 is still further fr. the military scene, and it is prob. better to class it under the foll.
   2. *compensation* (Inschr. von Priene 121, 34 [I вс], public services χωρὶς ὀψωνίων; 109, 94; 106 [II вс] ἄτερ ὀψωνίου) τὰ ὀψώνια τ. ἀμαρτίας θάνατος *the compensation paid by sin* (for services rendered to it) *is death* Ro 6: 23. HWHeidland, TW V, 591f. M-M.*

Π

παγιδεύω 1 aor. subj. παγιδεύσω (LXX) a hunting term (Eccl 9: 12) *set a snare* or *trap, entrap* fig. (1 Km 28: 9; Test. Jos. 7: 1) ὅπως αὐτὸν παγιδεύσωσιν ἐν λόγῳ *in order that they might entrap him with something that he said* (s. λόγος 1αγ) Mt 22: 15 (cf. Graec. Venet. Pr 6: 2 τοῖς λόγοις. Also in the same, Dt 7: 25; 12: 30). M-M.*

παγίς, ίδος, ἡ (Aristoph.+; pap., LXX; En. 103, 8) *trap, snare*—1. lit. (Aristoph., Aves 527, Ranae 115; Anth. Pal. 6, 109; Pr 6: 5; 7: 23; Eccl 9: 12) ὡς π. *like a trap,* i.e. unexpectedly Lk 21: 35. As a piece of equipment for a bird-catcher (Aesop, Fab. 323 P.=152 Babr.) Mt 10: 29 v.l.
   2. fig. (Aristoph.+; LXX), of things that bring danger or death, suddenly and unexpectedly γενηθήτω ἡ τράπεζα αὐτῶν εἰς παγίδα *let their table become a snare* (to them) Ro 11: 9 (Ps 68: 23). παγὶς θανάτου *a deadly snare* (Tob 14: 10a; Ps 17: 6): of being double-tongued D 2: 4; B 19: 7 Funk; of the mouth gener. B 19: 8 (cf. Pr 11: 9; 18: 7). ἐμπίπτειν εἰς παγίδα *fall into the snare* (Tob 14: 10b; Pr 12: 13; Sir 9: 3): abs. εἰς πειρασμὸν καὶ παγίδα καὶ ἐπιθυμίας 1 Ti 6: 9. τοῦ διαβόλου 3: 7. ἀνανήφω ἐκ τῆς διαβόλου παγίδος 2 Ti 2: 26; cf. the entry ἀνανήφω.—IScheftelowitz, Das Schlingen u. Netzmotiv '12. JSchneider, TW V 593-6. M-M.*

πάγκαρπος, ον (Pind.+; Ps.-Pla., Axioch. 13 p. 371c; Ep. Arist. 63) *bearing much fruit* π. ξύλον *a tree laden with fruit* fig. Dg 12: 1.*

πάγος s. Ἄρειος πάγος. M-M.

παθεῖν, παθών s. πάσχω.

πάθημα, ατος, τό (Soph., Hdt.+; Philo, Joseph.)—1. *that which is suffered or endured, suffering, misfortune,* in our lit. almost always in pl. (which is also predom. in secular wr.: Plut., Mor. 360D; Appian, Bell. Civ. 2, 64 §269; 4, 1 §2; Jos., Ant. 2, 299) τὰ π. τοῦ νῦν καιροῦ *what we suffer at the present time* Ro 8: 18.—2 Cor 1: 6f (on παθ. . . . πάσχειν cf. Lamellae Aur. Orphicae ed. AOlivieri '15 p. 16, 4 [IV/III вс]). τὰ παθήματα ὑπὲρ ὑμῶν *the sufferings* (that I, Paul, am enduring) *for you* (the Colossians) Col 1: 24 (JSchneider [s. below] 54-61; JSchmid, BZ 21, '33, 330-44; GKittel, ZsystTh 18, '41, 186-91;

SHanson, The Unity of the Church, '46, 119f). W. διωγμοί 2 Ti 3: 11. ἄθλησις παθημάτων *a struggle w. suffering* Hb 10: 32. Of the sufferings of persecuted Christians gener. 1 Pt 5: 9; ISm 5: 1.—Of the sufferings of Christ Hb 2: 10. They are ever before the eyes of the Christians 1 Cl 2: 1. τὰ παθήματα τοῦ Χριστοῦ *Christ's sufferings* 2 Cor 1: 5; 1 Pt 4: 13; 5: 1 (θεοῦ P⁷²). παθήματα αὐτοῦ (=τοῦ Χρ.) Phil 3: 10. τὰ εἰς Χριστὸν παθήματα *the sufferings of Christ* 1 Pt 1: 11 (s. εἰς 4h; CAScott, Exp. 6th Ser. XII '05, 234-40). The suffering Christian stands in close relation to the suffering Christ. He suffers as Christ did, or for Christ's sake, or in mystic unity w. Christ. Cf. ASteubing, Der paul. Begriff 'Christusleiden', Diss. Heidelb. '05; TrSchmidt, Der Leib Christi '19, 210ff; RPaulus, Das Christusproblem der Gegenwart '22, 24f; RLiechtenhan, ZThK 32, '22, 368-99; OSchmitz, Das Lebensgefühl d. Pls, '22, 50ff, 105ff; JSchneider, D. Passionsmystik des Pls '29; ASchweitzer, D. Mystik des Ap. Pls '30, 141-58 (The Mysticism of Paul the Ap., tr. WMontgomery '31, 141-59); BAhern, CBQ 22, '60, 1-32, al.—The sing. (Arrian, Anab. 4, 22, 2=suffering, misfortune; 6, 11, 2; 3 of the wounding of Alexander) only Hb 2: 9 of Christ διὰ τὸ πάθημα τοῦ θανάτου (epexegetic gen.) *because of the death he suffered.*
   2. *passion* (like πάθος, but less frequently than the latter. Pla., Phaedo 79D al.; Aristot. [HBonitz, Index Aristot. 1870, 554]; Plut., Pomp. 8, 6) in a bad sense (Plut., Mor. 1128E) in our lit. only in Paul and only in the pl. τὰ π. τῶν ἀμαρτιῶν (*the*) *sinful passions* Ro 7: 5. W. ἐπιθυμίαι Gal 5: 24. M-M. B. 1089f.*

παθητός, ή, όν (Aristot.+) verbal adj. fr. πάσχω (Bl-D. §65, 3; Rob. 1097) *subject to suffering* (Plut., Mor. 765в; 1026D, Pelop. 16, 5, Numa 8, 7, oft. in contrast to ἀπαθής; Herm. Wr. 6, 2a, b; 10, 17; Sallust. 4 p. 8, 7; Philo, Spec. Leg. 3, 180) of the Messiah Ac 26: 23. Opp. ἀπαθής (s. above, also Proclus, Theol. 80 p. 74, 32) IEph 7: 2; IPol 3: 2. M-M.*

πάθος, ους, τό (trag., Hdt.+; inscr., pap., LXX, Philo, Joseph., Test. 12 Patr.)—1. *that which is endured or experienced, suffering* (trag., Hdt.+; Diod. S. 1, 97, 4 τὰ πάθη τῶν θεῶν [various painful experiences of the gods: the battle against the Titans, etc.]; Jos., Ant. 15, 57; 16,

315), so in our lit. only in Ign., but freq. in his wr., and always in the sing., w. ref. to the physical sufferings of Christ. The same things are true also of the only place in which πάθος in this sense is found elsewh., namely B 6: 7. IEph 20: 1; IMg 5: 2; ITr inscr.; 11: 2; IPhld 9: 2. τὸ θεομακάριστον π. ISm 1: 2. τὸ π. τοῦ θεοῦ μου IRo 6: 3. By his own baptism and by his suffering Christ consecrated the baptismal water for the Christians IEph 18: 2. ἀγαλλιᾶσθαι ἐν τῷ π. τοῦ κυρίου rejoice in the Passion of the Lord IPhld inscr. μετανοεῖν εἰς τὸ π. change the mind about the suffering ISm 5: 3. Of the church ἐκλελεγμένη ἐν πάθει ἀληθινῷ chosen by the real Passion IEph inscr. Used beside ἀνάστασις, so that it is equivalent to θάνατος (Appian, Bell. Civ. 1, 28 §129 the death of Nonius; 1, 38 §169 of Drusus; 5, 59 §250. S. πάσχω 3aa) IMg 11: ISm 7: 2; 12: 2. τῷ π. συγκατατίθεσθαι agree with, have a share in the Passion (of Christ) IPhld 3: 3.

2. *passion* (Pla.+, oft. 4 Macc; Philo; Jos., C. Ap. 1, 214), esp. of a sexual nature (Pla.; PMich 149 VI, 30 [II AD] π. αἰσχρόν; Ps.-Phoc. 194; Jos., Ant. 2, 53) ἐν πάθει ἐπιθυμίας in *lustful passion* 1 Th 4: 5. Abs. (w. other vices, some of which are also sexual in character) Col 3: 5. Of an adulterous woman: ἐπιμένειν τῷ π. τούτῳ *persist in this passion* Hm 4, 1, 6. Pl. πάθη ἀτιμίας *disgraceful passions* Ro 1: 26.—Also of the passion of anger Hs 6, 5, 5.—S. on πάσχω, end. M-M. B. 1089f.*

παιδαγωγός, οῦ, ὁ (since Eur.; Hdt. 8, 75; Plut.; inscr. [reff. in Dit., Syll.³ 1253 n. 1]; pap., Philo; Jos., Ant. 1, 56; 18, 202, Vi. 429. Common as a loanw. in rabb. [SKrauss, Griech. u. lat. Lehnwörter im Talmud usw. II 1899, 421]) *attendant (slave), custodian, guide*, lit. 'boy-leader', the man, usu. a slave (Plut., Mor. 4A, B), whose duty it was to conduct the boy or youth (Plut., Mor. 439F) to and from school and to superintend his conduct gener.; he was not a 'teacher' (despite the present mng. of the derivative 'pedagogue' [cf. Murray, New (Oxford) Engl. Dict. s.v. 1a as opposed to 2]; παιδαγωγός and διδάσκαλος are differentiated: X., De Rep. Lac. 3, 2; Pla., Lys. 208c [JSCallaway, JBL 67, '48, 353-5]; Diog. L. 3, 92; Philo, Leg. ad Gai. 53). When the young man became of age the π. was no longer needed (cf. JMarquardt²-AMau, D. Privatleben der Römer 1886, 114; WABecker-HGöll, Charikles II³ 1878, 46ff [Eng. transl. FMetcalfe, 1889, 226f]; ABaumeister, Denkmäler d. klass. Altertums 1885-88 II, 1125f). As a pers. to whom respect is due, beside the father (as Plut., Lyc. 17, 1) 1 Cor 4: 15. The law as a π. (so Plut., Mor. 645B, ς τοῦ νόμου καθάπερ παιδαγωγοῦ). Paul evaluates the Mosaic law as a παιδ. εἰς Χριστόν Gal 3: 24. Humankind remains under its authority, ὑπὸ παιδαγωγόν vs. 25, until God declares, by sending his Son, that it has come of age.—ESchuppe: Pauly-W. 18, part 2, 2375-85. M-M.*

παιδάριον, ου, τό (Aristoph., Pla.+; inscr., pap., LXX; Jos., Ant. 17, 13) dim. of παῖς.
1. *little boy, boy, child* (even a female: Hyperid., fgm. 164; Menand., fgm. 428)—a. playing about Mt 11: 16 t.r.
b. *a youth*, who is no longer a child (Gen 37: 30 cf. w. vs. 2; Tob 6: 3; Proseuche Aseneth 27 Batiffol 1889/90 of Benjamin, aged nineteen); so perh. J 6: 9. But this pass. could also belong under
2. *young slave* (Callixenus [III BC]: 627 fgm. 2 p. 173, 14 Jac.; X., Ag. 1, 21; Diog. L. 6, 52. Oft. pap. 1 Km 25: 5; Ruth 2: 5, 9) MPol 6: 1; 7: 1. M-M.*

παιδεία, ας, ἡ (Aeschyl., Thu.+; inscr., pap., LXX, Ep. Arist., Philo, Joseph.).
1. act. *upbringing, training, instruction*, in our lit.

chiefly as it is attained by *discipline, correction* (LXX), of the holy *discipline* of a fatherly God 1 Cl 56: 16. πᾶσα παιδεία *all discipline* Hb 12: 11. τὰ λόγια τῆς παιδείας τοῦ θεοῦ *the oracles of God's teaching* 1 Cl 62: 3. ἐκτρέφειν τινὰ ἐν π. καὶ νουθεσίᾳ κυρίου *bring someone up in the discipline and instruction of the Lord* (= Christian disc. and instr.) Eph 6: 4. μισεῖν παιδείαν *hate discipline* 1 Cl 35: 8 (Ps 49: 17; cf. Pr 5: 12). ὀλιγωρεῖν παιδείας κυρίου Hb 12: 5 (Pr 3: 11). ἀναλαμβάνειν παιδείαν *accept correction* (cf. λαμβάνειν παιδείαν Pr 8: 10; Jer 39: 33; 42: 13) 1 Cl 56: 2. παιδεύειν τινὰ παιδείαν (X., Cyr. 8, 3, 37; Aeschines, Or. 3, 148; Ps.-Demosth. 35, 42. S. also παιδεύω 2a): παιδεύειν τινὰ τὴν π. τοῦ φόβου τοῦ θεοῦ *bring someone up with a training that leads to the fear of God* 21: 6= Pol 4: 2. παιδεύειν παιδείᾳ (Pla., Leg. 5 p. 741A; X., Cyr. 1, 1, 6): παιδεύεσθαι παιδείᾳ δικαίᾳ *be corrected with just discipline* Hv 2, 3, 1. παραδίδοσθαί τινι εἰς ἀγαθὴν π. *be handed over to someone for good instruction* Hs 6, 3, 6. τῆς ἐν Χριστῷ παιδείας μεταλαμβάνειν *share in a Christian upbringing* 1 Cl 21: 8. ὠφέλιμος πρὸς παιδείαν τὴν ἐν δικαιοσύνῃ *useful for training in righteousness* 2 Ti 3: 16. Of discipline by God (Cyrill. Scyth. p. 38, 8; 23): χωρὶς παιδείας εἶναι *be* (left) *without* (divine) *discipline* Hb 12: 8. εἰς παιδείαν ὑπομένετε *you must endure* (your trials) *as* (divine) *discipline* vs. 7 (GBornkamm, Sohnschaft u. Leiden, '60, 188-98). π. εἰρήνης ἡμῶν ἐπ' αὐτόν *the chastisement that brought peace to us came upon him* 1 Cl 16: 5 (Is 53: 5).

2. pass., *the result of the upbringing, the state of being trained, etc., training* (Diod. S. 12, 13, 4; 12, 20, 1; Dit., Or. 504, 8 ἐπὶ παιδείᾳ τε καὶ τῇ ἄλλῃ ἀρετῇ; Sir 1: 27; Jos., Vi. 196; 359, C. Ap. 1, 73) μὴ ἔχειν παιδείαν *have no training* Hv 3, 9, 10. The word could have this mng. in some of the places dealt w. under 1.—WJaeger, Paideia I-III '34-'47 (Engl. tr. by GHighet, '39-'44); HvArnim, Leb. u. Werke des Dio v. Prusa mit e. Einleitung: Sophistik, Rhetorik, Philosophie in ihrem Kampf um d. Jugendbildung 1898; GBertram, Der Begriff d. Erziehung in d. griech. Bibel: Imago Dei (GKrüger-Festschr.) '32, 33-52; WJentzsch, Urchristl. Erziehungsdenken '51. M-M.*

παιδευτής, οῦ, ὁ (Pla.+; inscr.; Sb 5941, 2; LXX) *instructor, teacher* (Pla., Leg. 7 p. 811D; Plut., Lyc. 12, 4, Camill. 10, 3, De Liber. Educ. p. 4c; Diog. L. 7, 7; inscr.; Sir 37: 19; 4 Macc 5: 34; Philo, Omn. Prob. Lib. 143) π. ἀφρόνων Ro 2: 20.—Somet. the emphasis is upon the idea of correcting or disciplining *corrector, one who disciplines* (s. παιδεύω 2 and cf. Hos 5: 2; PsSol 8, 29) Hb 12: 9. M-M.*

παιδεύω impf. ἐπαίδευον; 1 aor. ἐπαίδευσα, pass. ἐπαιδεύθην; pf. pass. ptc. πεπαιδευμένος.
1. *bring up, instruct, train, educate* (trag.+; Pla.; X.; inscr., pap., Ep. Arist., Philo; Jos., C. Ap. 1, 22 γράμμασιν ἐπαιδεύθησαν) ἐπαιδεύθη Μωϋσῆς πάσῃ σοφίᾳ Αἰγυπτίων *Moses was educated in all the culture of the Egyptians* Ac 7: 22. πεπαιδευμένος κατὰ ἀκρίβειαν τοῦ πατρῴου νόμου *educated strictly according to the law of our fathers* 22: 3 (cf. Jos., Bell. 7, 343). CBurchard, ZNW 61, '70, 168f would put a comma after πεπαιδ.
2. *practice discipline*—a. *correct, give guidance* (LXX) τινά (to) *someone* (Aelian, V.H. 1, 34) τοὺς ἀντιδιατιθεμένους 2 Ti 2: 25. τοὺς ἐκλεκτούς, ἀλλήλους Hv 3, 9, 10. δι' οὗ ἡμᾶς ἐπαίδευσας *through whom* (i.e. Christ) *thou* (i.e. God) *hast led us to the right way* 1 Cl 59: 3. παιδευθῆναι παιδείᾳ δικαίᾳ Hv 2, 3, 1. παιδεύειν τὴν παιδείαν (Ammonius, Vi. Aristot. p. 10, 20 Westerm. S.

also παιδεία 1) 1 Cl 21: 6=Pol 4: 2. W. ἵνα foll. *lead to* Tit 2: 12.

b. *discipline* w. punishment—**α.** mostly of divine discipline (Cyrill. Scyth. p. 37, 23; 73, 3 παιδευόμενος ὑπὸ τοῦ δαίμονος; LXX) Hb 12: 6; 1 Cl 56: 4 (both Pr 3: 12). W. ἐλέγχειν (Ps 6: 2; 37: 2) 1 Cl 56: 5 (Ps 140: 5); Rv 3: 19 (cf. Pr 3: 12 w. v.l.). παιδεύων ἐπαίδευσέν με ὁ κύριος 1 Cl 56: 3 (Ps 117: 18). Cf. also Hb 12: 10b.—Pass. (Laud. Therap. 19 τὸ σῶμα παιδεύεται= is disciplined [by God]) 1 Cor 11: 32; 2 Cor 6: 9; 1 Cl 56: 16. παιδευθῆναι εἰς μετάνοιαν *accept correction so as to repent* 57: 1. Wholesome discipline can be exerted even through Satan; pass. w. inf. foll. (Bl-D. §392, 2) 1 Ti 1: 20.

β. of discipline by human fathers (Pr 19: 18; 28: 17a; 29: 17) Hb 12: 7, 10a.—**γ.**= *discipline by whipping* or *scourging* (Vi. Aesopi I c. 61; 3 Km 12: 11, 14; 2 Ch 10: 11, 14) Lk 23: 16, 22 (ANSherwin-White, Rom. Society and Rom. Law in the NT, '63, 27f). παιδεύω and related words: GBertram, TW V 596-624. M-M. B. 1446f.*

παιδιόθεν adv. *from childhood* ἐκ π. (Gen 47: 3 A; Sb 5294, 8 [III AD]; Martyr. Petri et Pauli 39.—Bl-D. §104, 3 w. app.; Rdm.² 32; Mlt.-H. 164) Mk 9: 21.—MLejeune, Les adverbes grecs en -θεν '39. S. παιδόθεν. M-M.*

παιδίον, ου, τό (Hdt., Aristoph.+; inscr., pap., LXX, En.; Ep. Arist. 248; Philo; Jos., Ant. 2, 219 al.) dim. of παῖς (Bl-D. §111, 3; Mlt.-H. 345).

1. *very young child, infant*, used of boys and girls. Of a new-born child (Diod. S. 4, 20, 3) Lk 2: 21 v.l. (eight days old, as Gen 17: 12); J 16: 21. Infants are fed honey, then milk B 6: 17 (cf. Diod. S. 5, 70, 3 αὗται [αἱ Νύμφαι] δὲ μέλι καὶ γάλα μίσγουσαι τὸ παιδίον [τὸν Δία] ἔθρεψαν. —HUsener [on γάλα 2]). Those who are born again have ὡς παιδίων τὴν ψυχήν *a soul like that of new-born children* B 6: 11.—Mt 2: 8, 9, 11, 13f, 20f; Lk 1: 59, 66, 76, 80; 2: 17, 27, 40; Hb 11: 23 (cf. Ex 2: 2f).

2. *child*—**a.** w. ref. to age: Mt 18: 2, 4f; Mk 9: 36f; 10: 15; Lk 9: 47f; 18: 17; 1 Cl 16: 3 (Is 53: 2). Pl. Mt 11: 16; 19: 13f; Mk 7: 28; 10: 13f; Lk 7: 32; 18: 16 (on Mk 10: 14, 15 and parallels cf. JBlinzler, Klerusblatt '44, 90-6). γυναῖκες καὶ παιδία (Num 14: 3; Jdth 7: 23; 4 Macc 4: 9; cf. Jos., Bell. 4, 115) Mt 14: 21; 15: 38. παιδία . . . πατέρες . . . νεανίσκοι 1 J 2: 14.—B 8: 1a, b. Of girls Mk 5: 39-41; 7: 30.

b. w. ref. to relationship; the father is indicated by a gen. (μου; cf. Epict. 4, 1, 141 σου) J 4: 49. Pl. Lk 11: 7. The child indicated by a gen., w. the father ὁ πατὴρ τοῦ παιδίου Mk 9: 24.

3. fig.—**a.** w. ref. to the intellect: παιδία ταῖς φρεσίν *children as far as the mind is concerned* 1 Cor 14: 20.—W. ref. to their attitude toward the truth (Artem. 2, 69 p. 162, 7: τὰ παιδία ἀληθῆ λέγει· οὐδέπω γὰρ οἶδε ψεύδεσθαι καὶ ἐξαπατᾶν) Mt 18: 3.

b. of the children of God Hb 2: 13f (vs. 13 after Is 8: 18, but understood in a NT sense).

c. as a form of familiar address on the part of a respected pers., who feels himself on terms of fatherly intimacy w. those whom he addresses (Cornutus 1 p. 1, 1 ὦ π.; Athen. 13, 47 p. 584c) 1 J 2: 18; 3: 7 v.l. Used by the risen Christ in addressing his disciples J 21: 5. M-M. B. 92.*

παιδίσκη, ης, ἡ dim. of παῖς *girl*, in our lit. always of the servant class *maid, servant-girl, female slave* (so Hdt.+; pap., LXX; Philo, Congr. Erud. Gr. 1=Gen 16: 1 [PKatz, Philo's Bible '50, 36]; Jos., Ant. 18, 40; Test. 12 Patr.) Mt 26: 69; Mk 14: 66, 69; Lk 22: 56; Ac 12: 13; 16: 16, 19 D. ἡ π. ἡ θυρωρός *the maid who kept the door* J 18: 17. W.

παῖς (Lev 25: 44; Dt 12: 12, 18; Pel-Leg. 12, 24f) Lk 12: 45. W. δοῦλος (2 Esdr[Ezra] 2: 65; Eccl 2:7) B 19: 7; D 4: 10; also of God's maidservants 1 Cl 60: 2. In contrast to ἐλευθέρα of Hagar Gal 4: 22f (Gen 16: 1ff; Philo, Leg. All. 3, 244); w. a turn in the direction of a more profound sense vss. 30a, b (=Gen 21: 10a, b), 31.—JWackernagel, Glotta 2, '09, 1-8; 218f; 315. M-M.*

παιδόθεν adv. (Ibycus [VI BC] 1, 10 Bergk [=ed. Diehl² 6, 12 v.l.]; Ps.-Lucian, Philopatr. 19; Themist., Or. 25 p. 310D) *from childhood* ἐκ π. (Laud. Therap. E, l. 8) Mk 9: 21 v.l. S. παιδιόθεν.*

παιδοφθορέω fut. παιδοφθορήσω (Christian usage: Justin., Dial. 95, 1; Tatian 8, 1) *commit sodomy, be a practicing homosexual*, lit. *corrupt boys* B 19: 4; D 2: 2.*

παιδοφθόρος, ου, ὁ (Physiogn. I 327, 16; Test. Levi 17: 11) *a practicing homosexual, pederast*, lit. *corrupter of boys* B 10: 6.*

παίζω (Hom.+; Epigr. Gr. 362, 5; BGU 1024 VII, 26; PGM 7, 428; LXX; Ep. Arist. 284; Philo; Jos., Bell. 4, 157) *play, amuse oneself, dance* (w. πίνειν Ion of Chios [V BC], Eleg. 1, 16; 2, 7 Diehl²; Appian, Syr. 26 §125 παίζοντας καὶ μεθύοντας) 1 Cor 10: 7 (Ex 32: 6). π. μετά τινος *play with someone* (Gen 21: 9; 26: 8) Hs 9, 11, 4f. παίζω and related words: GBertram, TW V 625-35. M-M.*

παῖς, παιδός, ὁ or ἡ (Hom.+; inscr., pap., LXX, Ep. Arist., Philo, Joseph., Test. 12 Patr., Sib. Or.) *child*.

1. ὁ παῖς—**a.** w. ref. to a relation betw. one human being and another—**α.** fr. the viewpoint of age *boy, youth* (Hom.+; inscr., pap., LXX; Philo, Op. M. 105; Jos., Ant. 12, 210) Mt 17: 18; Lk 9: 42; Ac 20: 12. Ἰησοῦς ὁ παῖς Lk 2: 43.—Pl. (as בַּיָּא a loanw. in rabb.) Mt 2: 16; 21: 15; B 8: 3f.—ἐκ παιδός *from childhood* (Diod. S. 1, 54, 5; 1, 73, 9; 1, 92, 5; 19, 40, 2 al. Simplicius in Epict. p. 129, 26 Düb.) Mk 9: 21 D.

β. fr. the viewpoint of descent *son* (Hom.+; Diod. S. 20, 22, 1 οἱ παῖδες αὐτοῦ; inscr., pap., LXX; Jos., Bell. 4, 646, Ant. 20, 140 al.) ὁ παῖς αὐτοῦ J 4: 51 (=υἱός vss. 46f, 50; υἱός 𝔓⁶⁶ et al. in vs. 51). This sense is also poss. in Mt 8: 6, 8, 13, but these pass. prob. belong to the foll.

γ. fr. the viewpoint of social position *servant, slave* (since Hipponax [VI BC] 16 D.²; Aeschyl., Cho. 652. Also HUsener, Epicurea 1887 p. 168, 10; Plut., Alcib. 4, 5, Mor. 65C; 70E; Dit., Syll.³ 96, 26. Oft. pap. and LXX. Jos., Ant. 18, 192, Vi. 223.—Even an especially trusted servant is termed ὁ παῖς: Diod. S. 15, 87, 6 Epaminondas' armor-bearer; Appian, Iber. 27 §107 Scipio's groom; Gen 24: 2ff Abraham's chief servant, vs. 5 ὁ παῖς) Lk 7: 7 (=δοῦλος vss. 2f, 10); 15: 26. W. παιδίσκη (q.v.) 12: 45.—Of those at a ruler's court οἱ παῖδες *courtiers, attendants* (Diod. S. 17, 36, 5; Gen 41: 10, 37f; 1 Km 16: 17; Jer 43: 31; 44: 2; 1 Macc 1: 6, 8) Mt 14: 2.

b. in relation to God—**α.** men as God's *servants, slaves* (Ael. Aristid. 45 p. 152 D.: θεῶν παῖδες [or 'sons of gods' as Polyb. 3, 47, 8; Charito 2, 1, 5 and Diog. L. 9, 72]; LXX; Jos., Ant. 10, 215) Israel (Is 41: 8f) Lk 1: 54. David (Ps 17: 1; Is 37: 35) 1: 69; Ac 4: 25; D 9: 2a.

β. angels as servants of God κατὰ παίδων αὐτοῦ οὐ πιστεύει *he does not trust his servants* 1 Cl 39: 4 (Job 4: 18).

γ. of Christ in his relation to God. In this connection it has the mng. *servant*, because of the identification of the 'servant of God' of certain OT pass. w. the Messiah (Is 52: 13 et al.) Mt 12: 18 (cf. Is 42: 1); B 6: 1; 9: 2 (on the last two cf. Is 50: 10). So prob. also D 9: 2b (because of the immediate proximity of Δαβὶδ ὁ παῖς σου 9: 2a); 9: 3; 10: 2f.—In other places the mng. *son* is certainly to be preferred (παῖς was so understood in secular Gk., when it expressed a relationship to a divinity: Il. 2, 205 Κρόνου παῖς; Sappho 1, 2 Diehl; Alcaeus 1; Bacchylides 17, 70 Minos, a παῖς of Zeus; Hermocles [IV/III BC] p. 174 Coll. =Athen. 6, 63 p. 253D: Demetrius Poliorcetes as π. Ποσειδῶνος θεοῦ; Diod. S. 17, 51, 1 the god Ammon has his prophet address Alexander thus χαῖρε, ὦ παῖ; what follows makes it clear that procreation is meant; Plut., Mor. 180D; Maximus Tyr. 14, 1d; Paus. 2, 10, 3 Ἄρατος Ἀσκληπιοῦ π.; Diogenes, Ep. 36, 1; Philostrat., Vi. Apoll. 7, 24 p. 279, 4; Porphyr., Vi. Plot. 23; Iambl., Vi. Pyth. 2, 10; IG IV² 128, 50 [280 BC] and oft.; Sb 8314, 9 Hermes conducts the dead man to the Elysian fields ἅμα παισὶ θεῶν. S. above 1ba the παῖδες θεῶν. Cf. also Herm. Wr. 13, 2 ὁ γεννώμενος θεοῦ θεὸς παῖς; 13, 4; 14; Rtzst., Poim. 223f.—Celsus 7, 9) παῖς αὐτοῦ ὁ μονογενὴς Ἰησοῦς Χρ. MPol 20: 2. God as ὁ τοῦ ἀγαπητοῦ κ. εὐλογητοῦ παιδὸς Ἰησοῦ Χρ. πατήρ 14: 1. Corresp. Christ as God's ἀγαπητὸς παῖς 14: 3; Dg 8: 11. The same is true of the other pass. in Dg 8: 9; 9: 1.—In the case of the rest of the pass. it is hardly poss. to decide which mng. is better: Ac 3: 13, 26; 4: 27, 30 (unless the παῖς σου thy *servant* of 4: 25 should demand the same transl. for the other pass. as well; JEMénard, CBQ 19, '57, 83–92 [Acts]); 1 Cl 59: 2–4 (but here the word ἠγαπημένος repeated in vss. 2 and 3 [cf. a magical pap. of c. 300 AD in ThSchermann, TU 34, 2b, '09, 3: Christ as ἠγαπημένος παῖς] could suggest the transl. *son*).—WBousset, Kyrios Christos² '21, 56f; AvHarnack, Die Bezeichnung Jesu als 'Knecht Gottes' u. ihre Geschichte in d. alten Kirche: SAB '26, 212–38; JoachJeremias, ZNW 34, '35, 115–23; KFEuler, D. Verkündigung v. leidenden Gottesknecht aus Jes 53 in d. griech. Bibel '34; PSeidelin, D. ʼEbed J. u. d. Messiasgestalt im Jesajatargum: ZNW 35, '36, 194–231; HWWolff, Jes 53 im Urchristent. '50²; EAMcDowell, Son of Man and Suffering Servant '44; ELohmeyer, Gottesknecht u. Davidssohn '45, esp. 2–8; TNicklin, Gospel Gleanings '50, 268f; OCullmann, Dieu Vivant 16, '50, 17–34; HHegermann, Jes 53 in Hexapla, Targum u. Peschitta '54; ELohse, Märtyrer u. Gottesknecht '55; WGrundmann, Sohn Gottes: ZNW 47, '56, 113–33; OCullmann, Die Christologie des NT '57; JLPrice, Interpretation 12, '58, 28–38 (Synoptics); MornaD Hooker, Jesus and the Servant '59; BvanIersel, 'D. Sohn' in d. synopt. Jesusworten, '61, 52–65 (bibliog.); HOrlinsky, The So-called Suffering Servant in Isaiah 53, '64 (cf. review in CBQ 27, '66, 147); EKränkl, Jesus der Knecht Gottes, '72 (Acts); FWDanker, Luke '76, 70–88. παῖς θεοῦ TW V 653–713 by WZimmerli and JoachJeremias.

2. ἡ παῖς *girl* (Pind., fgm. 122, 7 ὦ παῖδες=girls!; Hyperid., fgm. 144; Phalaris, Ep. 142, 1; Charito 1, 8, 2; Philostrat., Her. 19, 11 p. 204, 31; Gen 24: 28; 34: 12; Jos., Ant. 1, 254; 5, 266 al.) Lk 8: 51. ἡ παῖς (*my*) *child* (nom. w. art. for voc.; cf. Bl-D. §147, 3; Rob. 465f; 769) vs. 54. παῖς and related words: AOepke, WZimmerli and JoachJeremias TW V 636–713; the same authors: The Servant of God (tr. HKnight), '65=Studies in Bibl. Theol. 20. M-M. B. 87f.*

παίω 1 aor. ἔπαισα (Aeschyl., Hdt.+; pap., LXX)—**1.** lit. *strike, hit* w. acc. of the pers. (Philostrat., Vi. Soph. 2, 10, 6; PSI 168, 15 [II BC] ἔπαισάν με; 2 Km 14: 6; Jos., Bell. 2, 176) Mt 26: 68; Lk 22: 64. W. weapons *strike, wound* τινά (X., Cyr. 8, 5, 12; Diod. S. 11, 69, 5 παίει τῷ ξίφει τὸν Ἀρταξέρξην; 2 Km 20: 10; Jos., Ant. 4, 153)

Mk 14: 47; J 18: 10. Of scorpions *sting* (Aelian, N.A. 10, 23; Ael. Dion. ε, 8) w. acc. of the pers. Rv 9: 5.

2. fig., of divine punishment (in quotations fr. Job in 1 Cl) ἔπαισεν αὐτοὺς σητὸς τρόπον 1 Cl 39: 5 (Job 4: 19). Abs. ἔπαισεν, καὶ αἱ χεῖρες αὐτοῦ ἰάσαντο 56: 7 (Job 5: 18). M-M. B. 553.*

Πακατιανός, ή, όν *Pacatian, in Pacatia* a later (post-Constantine) name for a part of Phrygia, used in the subscription to 1 Ti (from 47 Tdf. [=1908 Gregory= Oᵖ¹⁰³ vSoden] al. KL have Καπατιάνης for it. Still other forms of the word are attested). The capital of this district was Laodicea where, acc. to the subscr., 1 Ti was written.*

πάλαι adv. denoting past time (Hom.+; inscr., pap., LXX)—**1.** designating a point of time in the past *long ago, formerly* (Philo, Sacr. Abel. 134 πάλαι, νῦν, αὖθις, ἀεί; Jos., Ant. 16, 40 π.—νῦν) πάλαι ἂν μετενόησαν they *would have repented long ago* Mt 11: 21; Lk 10: 13; Hb 1: 1. ταῦτα πάλαι ἠκούσαμεν these things we heard long ago 2 Cl 11: 2 (prophetic quot. of unknown origin). ἐκεῖνοι οἱ π. ἠρνημένοι those who denied in time past Hs 9, 26, 6. ἄνθρωποι οἱ π. προγεγραμμένοι Jd 4 (mng. 2a is also poss.). αἱ π. ἁμαρτίαι the former sins, sins committed in time past 2 Pt 1: 9 (cf. Appian, Bell. Civ. 4, 124 §521 ὁ πάλαι Καῖσαρ; BGU 747, 9 [II AD] οἱ πάλαι στρατιῶται). οἱ π. θεῖοι ἄγγελοι angels who were originally holy Papias 4.

2. covering a period of time, looking back fr. the present to a point of time in the past.

a. *for a long time* (Pla., Phaedo 8 p. 63D; Esth 3: 13g; Jos., Ant. 11, 32, Vi. 226) πάλαι δοκεῖτε *you imagine all along* 2 Cor 12: 19 (v.l. πάλιν). Perh. Jd 4 (s. 1 above) and Mk 6: 47 t.r. (s. 'b' below).

b. *already* (Appian, Syr. 66 §348) Mk 6: 47 v.l. (looks back to the moment of departure.—Mng. a is also poss.). εἰ πάλαι ἀπέθανεν (looks back to the moment of crucifixion) *whether he was already dead* Mk 15: 44 (v.l. ἤδη). πάλαι and related words: HSeesemann, TW V 713–17. M-M.*

παλαιός, ά, όν (Hom.+; inscr., pap., LXX, Philo; Jos., Bell. 4, 388, Ant. 10, 44, Vi. 192; loanw. in rabb.) *old*= in existence for a long time, oft. w. the connotation of being antiquated or outworn (so Soph., Oed. R. 290; Lysias, fgm. 6 Thalh.; Diod. S. 3, 46, 4).

1. lit. PK 2 p. 15, 7. μυθεύματα IMg 8: 1. βασιλεία IEph 19: 3. διαθήκη 2 Cor 3: 14 (s. διαθήκη 2). ἐντολὴ (ἡ) π. 1 J 2: 7a, b (cf. Pla., Leg. 1 p. 636B π. νόμιμον; 2 p. 659B, Lys. 6, 51; PGiess. 4, 9 [118 AD] παλαιὸν πρόσταγμα). οἶνος (opp. νέος) Lk 5: 39a, b (Od. 2, 340; Diod. S. 2, 14, 4; Lucian, De Merc. Cond. 26; PSI 191, 2; 193, 3). ἱμάτιον Mt 9: 16; Mk 2: 21a; Lk 5: 36a; w. ἱμάτιον to be supplied, ibid. b. ἀσκοί (Josh 9: 4) Mt 9: 17; Mk 2: 22; Lk 5: 37. Of the old rock, which is interpreted to mean Christ in Hermas s 9, 2, 2; 9, 12, 1. Of the υἱὸς τοῦ θεοῦ himself 9, 12, 2. Of the Logos οὗτος ὁ ἀπ' ἀρχῆς, ὁ καινὸς φανεὶς καὶ παλαιὸς εὑρεθεὶς καὶ πάντοτε νέος ἐν ἁγίων καρδίαις γεννώμενος Dg 11: 4 (καινός and π. contrasted as Hdt. 9, 26).—Subst. (Hippocr., Ep. 12, 5) τὸ καινὸν τοῦ παλαιοῦ the new from the old Mk 2: 21b. παλαιά (opp. καινά: Hdt. 9, 27 παλαιὰ κ. καινὰ λέγειν; Socrat., Ep. 28[30], 9; Procop. Soph., Ep. 122 μίγνυσι παλαιὰ καινοῖς) Mt 13: 52.

2. fig. ὁ π. ἄνθρωπος the old (i.e. earlier, unregenerate) *man* (ἄνθρωπος 2cβ) Ro 6: 6; Eph 4: 22; Col 3: 9. ἡ π. ζύμη the old yeast (s. ζύμη 2) 1 Cor 5: 7f (opp. νέον φύραμα). π. πράγματα old (i.e. Jewish) *ways of life* (παλ. πράγματα oft. in Vett. Val.; s. index) IMg 9: 1 (opp.

καινότης ἐλπίδος).—OLinton, 'Gammalt' och 'nytt':
Svensk Ex. Årsbok 5, '40, 43–55. M-M. B. 958.*

παλαιότης, ητος, ἡ (Eur., Aeschin., Pla. et al.) *age,
obsoleteness* δουλεύειν ... παλαιότητι γράμματος *serve
the old letter* (of the law; opp. καινότης πνεύματος) Ro 7:
6.*

παλαιόω pf. πεπαλαίωκα; 1 aor. pass. ἐπαλαιώθην
(Pla.+; pap., LXX; outside the Bible only in the pass.).
 1. act. (La 3: 4; Is 65: 22; Da 7: 25 Theod.) *make old,
declare* or *treat as obsolete* τὴν πρώτην (i.e. διαθήκην)
treat the first covenant as obsolete Hb 8: 13a.
 2. pass. *become old* (oft. w. the connotation of becoming useless: Pla., Symp. 208B; Diog. L. 7, 159; Sb
5827, 11 [69 BC]; APF 2, '03, 441 no. 55, 4 τείχη παλαιω-
θέντα 'walls that have become ruinous'; LXX; En. 104, 2;
Philo, Sobr. 56) βαλλάντια μὴ παλαιούμενα *purses that
do not wear out* Lk 12: 33. ὡς ἱμάτιον παλαιοῦσθαι (Dt
29: 4; Josh 9: 5; 2 Esdr 19 [Neh 9]: 21; Sir 14: 17; Is 51: 6)
Hb 1: 11 (Ps 101: 27); B 6: 2 (Is 50: 9). ζύμη παλαιω-
θεῖσα *yeast that has become old* (cf. 1 Cor 5: 7) IMg 10: 2.
παλαιοῦσθαι ταῖς λύπαις *be made old by sorrows* Hv 3,
11, 3. τὸ παλαιούμενον (w. γηράσκον) *what has become
obsolete* Hb 8: 13b (inscr. [218 BC]; ΕΛΛΗΝΙΚΑ 7, '34 p.
179, 14 παλαιούμενα = things that have become useless).
M-M.*

πάλη, ης, ἡ (Hom.+; inscr.; Sb 678, 6) *struggle*, lit.
'wrestling'; the opponent is introduced by πρός w. the acc.
against (Philo, Sobr. 65 πρὸς πάθη π.). Fig. (Longus 3,
19, 2 of love) of the Christians' struggle against the powers
of darkness Eph 6: 12. M-M.*

παλιγγενεσία, ας, ἡ (acc. to Plut., Mor. 722D the word
was first used by Democritus; elsewh. it is found first in
Neanthes [200 BC]: 84 fgm. 33 Jac.; Memnon [I BC/I AD]:
434 fgm. 1, 40, 2 Jac.; Cicero, Ad Attic. 6, 6, also a t.t. of
the Pythagoreans and Stoics [EZeller, Philosophie der
Griechen I⁵ 1892, 442; III 1⁴ '02, 158; HDiels, Doxographi
Graeci 1879, p. 469, 11ff], as well as of the Mysteries of
Dionysus [Orph. Fragmente 205 p. 225 OKern '22] and of
Osiris [Plut., De ει apud Delph. 9 p. 389A, De Isid. et
Osir. 35 p. 364F; 72 p. 379E, De Def. Orac. 51 p. 438D, De
Esu Carn. 1, 7 p. 996c; 2, 4 p. 998c. Cf. Lucian, Encom.
Musc. 7]. It is found in the Herm. Wr. [3, 3; 13, 1 ὁ τῆς
παλιγγενεσίας λόγος; 13, 3 al.—JKroll, Die Lehren des
Hermes Trismegistos '14, 360ff; Prümm 559–61]; Fluchtaf. 4, 18 ὁ θεὸς ὁ τῆς παλιγγενεσίας Θωβαρραβαυ;
PLond. 878 δῶρον παλιγγενεσίας; Philo, Cher. 114,
Poster. Caini 124, Leg. ad Gai. 325; Jos., Ant. 11, 66)
rebirth, regeneration.
 1. of the world—a. after the Deluge (so Philo, Mos. 2,
65, while the idea of the παλιγγενεσία of the κόσμος is
gener. Stoic and originated w. the Pythagoreans: M.Ant.
11, 1, 3; Philo, Aet. M. 47; 76) Νῶε παλ. κόσμῳ ἐκήρυξεν 1 Cl 9: 4.
 b. eschatol., of the renewing of the world in the time of
the Messiah (Schürer II⁴ 636ff; Bousset, Rel.³ 280ff) ἐν τῇ
παλ. *in the new* (Messianic) *age* or *world* Mt 19: 28.
 2. of the rebirth of a redeemed person (cf. Heraclit., Ep.
4, 4 ἐκ παλιγγενεσίας ἀναβιῶναι; Herm. Wr., loc. cit.
and PGM 4, 718 where the initiate calls himself πάλιν
γενόμενος): λουτρὸν παλιγγενεσίας καὶ ἀνακαινώσεως πνεύματος ἁγίου *bath of regeneration and renewal
by the Holy Spirit* Tit 3: 5 (MDibelius, Hdb., exc. ad loc.;
EGSelwyn, 1 Pt '46, 306f; ADNock, JBL 52, '33, 132f).—
PGennrich, Die Lehre v. d. Wiedergeburt in dogmen-
geschichtl. und religionsgeschichtl. Beleuchtung '07;

AvHarnack, Die Terminologie der Wiedergeburt: TU 42,
3, '18, p. 97–143; ADieterich, Eine Mithrasliturgie '03,
157ff; Rtzst., Mysterienrel.³ indices; HRWilloughby,
Pagan Regeneration '29; VJacono, La παλιγγενεσία in
S. Paolo e nel ambiente pagano: Biblica 15, '34, 369–98;
JDey, Παλιγγενεσια (on Tit 3: 5) '37; JYsebaert, Gk.
Baptismal Terminology, '62, 90ff; FBüchsel, TW I 685–8.
M-M.*

πάλιν adv. (Hom.+; inscr., pap., LXX, En., Ep. Arist.,
Philo, Joseph., Test. 12 Patr. On the spelling s. Bl-D. §20,
end; Mlt.-H. 113).
 1. *back*—a. w. verbs of going, sending, turning, calling
etc. πάλιν ἄγειν *go back, return* J 11: 7. ἀναβαίνειν Gal
2: 1. ἀναχωρεῖν J 6: 15. ἀποστέλλειν *send back* Mk 11:
3. διαπερᾶν 5: 21. ἔρχεσθαι (Jos., Ant. 2, 106; 11, 243)
Mt 26: 43; Mk 11: 27; J 4: 46; 2 Cor 1: 16. ἀπέρχεσθαι
Mk 14: 39; J 4: 3. εἰσέρχεσθαι Mk 2: 1. ἐξέρχεσθαι 7:
31. ἐπιστρέφειν *turn back* Gal 4: 9a. παραγίνεσθαι J 8:
2, etc. πάλιν λαβεῖν *take back* (X., An. 4, 2, 13) J 10:
17f. παραλαβὼν πάλιν τοὺς δώδεκα *he brought the
twelve back* (after he had been separated fr. them for a
time, and had preceded them) Mk 10: 32. ἀνεσπάσθη
πάλιν ἅπαντα εἰς τ. οὐρανόν *everything was drawn back
into heaven* Ac 11: 10.—ἡ ἐμὴ παρουσία πάλιν πρὸς
ὑμᾶς *my return to you* Phil 1: 26.—Also pleonastically w.
verbs that already include the concept 'back' (Eur., Ep. 1,
1 ἀναπέμπω πάλιν) πάλιν ἀνακάμπτειν (Bacchylides
17, 81f πάλιν ἀνακαμπτετ'; Synes., Kingship p. 29B) Ac
18: 21. πάλιν ὑποστρέφειν Gal 1: 17 (s. Bl-D. §484; cf.
Rob. 1205).
 b. In expressions that denote a falling back into a
previous state or a return to a previous activity. In Engl.
mostly *again*. εἰ ἃ κατέλυσα ταῦτα πάλιν οἰκοδομῶ Gal
2: 18. ἵνα πάλιν ἐπὶ τὸ αὐτὸ ἦτε 1 Cor 7: 5. διψήσει
πάλιν J 4: 13. πάλιν εἰς φόβον Ro 8: 15. Cf. 11: 23; Gal
5: 1; Phil 2: 28; Hb 5: 12; 6: 6; 2 Pt 2: 20.
 2. *again, once more, anew* when someone repeats
someth. he has already done (Jos., Ant. 12, 109), or an
event takes place in the same (or a similar) manner as
before, or a state of being recurs in the same (or nearly the
same) way as at first (Dicaearch., fgm. 34 W. Pythagoras
flees first to Καυλωνία...ἐκεῖθεν δὲ πάλιν εἰς Λο-
κρούς). πάλιν παραλαμβάνει αὐτὸν ὁ διάβολος εἰς ὄρος
Mt 4: 8 (cf. vs. 5). πάλιν ἐξελθών 20: 5 (cf. vs. 3).—21:
36 (cf. vs. 34); 26: 44 (cf. vs. 42), 72; 27: 50; Mk 2: 13; 3: 1;
4: 1. πάλιν πολλοῦ ὄχλου ὄντος 8: 1 (cf. 6: 34).—8: 25;
10: 1, 24; Lk 23: 20 (cf. vs. 13); J 1: 35 (cf. vs. 29); 8: 8;
20: 26; Ac 17: 32; Gal 1: 9; Phil 4: 4; Js 5: 18; Hv 3, 1, 5
al.—Somet. w. additions which, in part, define πάλιν
more exactly: πάλ. δεύτερον (cf. P. Argentor. Gr. 53, 5:
Kl. T. 135 p. 47 τὸ δεύτερον πάλιν) J 21: 16. πάλ. ἐκ
δευτέρου (Ctesias, Pers. 31; Maspéro 24, 12) Mt 26: 42; Ac
10: 15. Also pleonastically πάλ. ἄνωθεν Gal 4: 9b (s.
ἄνωθεν 3). πάλιν ἐξ ἀρχῆς (Mnesimachus Com. [IV BC]
4, 24 (Diod. S. 17, 37, 5) B 16: 8.—εἰς τὸ πάλιν = πάλιν
2 Cor 13: 2 (on this s. WSchmid, Der Attizismus 1887–
1897, I 129; II 129; III 282; IV 455; 625).
 3. *furthermore, thereupon* connecting things that are
similar (Ps.-Pla., Eryx. 11 p. 397A καὶ π. with a series of
examples): very oft. in a series of quotations fr. scripture
(cf. Diod. S. 37, 30, 2 καὶ πάλιν...καὶ...followed both
times by a poetic quotation; a third one had preceded it.
All three deal with riches as the highest good and probably
come from a collection of quotations; Ps.-Demetr. c. 184
καὶ πάλιν...καὶ π. with one quotation each. Cf. also
Diod. S. 1, 96, 6; Diog. L. 2, 18; 3, 16; Athen. 4, 17 p.
140c; 14 p. 634D; Plut., Mor. 361A καὶ πάλιν...καὶ

. . . ; a quotation follows both times) J 12: 39; 19: 37; Ro 15: 10-12; 1 Cor 3: 20; Hb 1: 5; 2: 13a, b; 4: 5; 10: 30; 1 Cl 10: 4; 15: 3f; 16: 15; 17: 6; 26: 3; B 2: 7; 3: 1; 6: 2, 4, 6, 14, 16 and oft. In a series of parables (Simplicius In Epict. p. 111, 13-34 Düb., connects by means of π. two stories that are along the same lines as the Good Samaritan and the Pharisee and the publican; Kephal. I 76, 34; 77, 8 [a series of proverbs]) Lk 13: 20 (cf. vs. 18). Also a favorite expr. when a speaker takes up a formula previously used and continues: πάλιν ἠκούσατε Mt 5: 33 (cf. vs. 27). πάλιν ὁμοία ἐστὶν ἡ βασιλεία 13: 45 (cf. vs. 44), 47.—18: 19 (cf. vs. 18); 19: 24 (cf. vs. 23).

4. *on the other hand, in turn* (Pla., Gorg. 482ᴅ; Theocr. 12, 14; Polyb. 10, 9, 1; Diod. S. 4, 46, 3; Charito 7, 6, 9; Wsd 13: 8; 16: 23; 2 Macc 15: 39) πάλιν γέγραπται *on the other hand, it is written* Mt 4: 7. πάλ. Ἀνδρέας *Andrew in turn* J 12: 22 t.r.—1 Cor 12: 21. τοῦτο λογιζέσθω πάλ. ἐφ' ἑαυτοῦ *let him remind himself, on the other hand* 2 Cor 10: 7; *on the other hand* Lk 6: 43; 1 J 2: 8.

5. A special difficulty is presented by Mk 15: 13, where the first outcry of the crowd is reported w. the words οἱ δὲ πάλιν ἔκραξεν. Is it simply a connective (so δὲ πάλιν Ps.-Callisth. 2, 21, 22; POxy. 1676, 20 ἀλλὰ καὶ λυπούμαι πάλιν ὅτι ἐκτός μου εἶ)? Is it because a different source is here used? Or is the meaning *they shouted back?* (so Gdspd.) cf. 1a. Or is this really a second outcry, and is the first one hidden behind vs. 11? Acc. to the parallel Mt 27: 21f, which actually mentions several outcries, one after the other, the first one may have been: τὸν Βαραββᾶν. The πάλιν of J 18: 40 is also hard to explain (Bultmann 502; 509, 3). Could there be a connection here betw. Mk and J?—Another possibility would be to classify Mk 15: 13 and Js 18: 40 under 4 above, with the meaning *in turn* (Aristoph., Acharn. 342 et al.; s. L-S-J). On a poss. Aram. background s. JTHudson, ET 53, '41/'42, 267f; Mlt.-H. 446; Mlt.-Turner 229; MBlack, An Aramaic Approach³, '67, 112f. M-M. B. 989.

παλινγενεσία s. παλιγγενεσία.

παμβότανον, ου, τό all the herbage π. τοῦ ἀγροῦ *all the plants of the field* 1 Cl 56: 14 (Job 5: 25).*

παμμεγέθης, ες (Pla., X. et al.; Polyb. 5, 59, 4; Lucian, Charon 20; Herm. Wr. 2, 4a; Dit., Or. 619, 6; Ps 67: 31 Sym.; Philo; Jos., Ant. 15, 364) superl. παμμεγεθέστατος (Suidas on Γολιάθης) *infinitely great, transcendent* τὸ παμμεγεθέστατον κράτος (of God.—π. is a divine attribute also in Aberciusinschr. 14: ἰχθὺς π.) 1 Cl 33: 3. Subst. τὸ παμμέγεθες *by far the greatest* 33: 4 (on κατὰ διάνοιαν here s. διάνοια 3).*

παμπληθεί adv. (Cass. Dio 75, 9, 1) *all together* ἀνέκραγον παμπληθεί Lk 23: 18.*

παμπληθής, ές (X.+; Diod. S. 4, 33, 5 and 6; 14, 13, 4; Plut., Sull. 35, 1; 2 Macc 10: 24; Ep. Arist. 90; Philo; Jos., Bell. 3, 69, Ant. 14, 461) *in full abundance, a vast amount of* τὴν π. τροφήν 1 Cl 20: 4.*

πάμπολυς, παμπόλλη, πάμπολυ (Aristoph., Pla.+; Plut.; inscr.; BGU 731 II, 8 [II ᴀᴅ]; 836, 3; POxy. 718, 11; Sym.; Philo, Aet. M. 119; Jos., Bell. 4, 529, Ant. 7, 106, C. Ap. 1, 107) *very great* π. ὄχλος (used w. πλῆθος: Pla., Leg. 3 p. 677ᴇ; Paradoxogr. Flor. 39; Dit., Syll.³ 1169, 45f) Mk 8: 1 t.r. M-M.*

Παμφυλία, ας, ἡ (Strabo 14, 3, 1; Appian, Mithrid. 56 §226; Cass. Dio 69, 14; Philo, Leg. ad Gai. 281; Joseph.

[Niese index]; inscr.; 1 Macc 15: 23.—On the use of the art. s. Bl-D. §261, 6 app.) *Pamphylia*, a province in the southern part of Asia Minor, along the Mediterranean seacoast. Visited by Paul several times. Ac 2: 10; 13: 13; 14: 24; 15: 38; 16: 6 v.l.; 27: 5 (cf. Jos., Ant. 2, 348 Παμφύλιον πέλαγος).—KGrafLanckoroński, Städte Pamphyliens u. Pisidiens 1890/92; OBenndorf and GNiemann, Reisen in Lykien u. Karien 1884.*

πανάγιος, ον (Iambl., in Nicomach. p. 126, 23 Pistelli; 4 Macc 7: 4; 14: 7) *all-holy* ὁ π. of God 1 Cl 35: 3. τὸ π. ὄνομα 58: 1.*

πανάρετος, ον (Philod., Rhet. 2, 203 Sudh.; Lucian, Philops. 6; Philo, Migr. Abr. 95; Dit., Or. 583, 8; Sb 330; 331) *most excellent, most* (lit. *all*) *virtuous* ὄνομα (of God) 1 Cl 45: 7; 60: 4 (w. παντοκρατορικός). πίστις 1: 2 (w. βέβαιος). πολιτεία 2: 8 (w. σεβάσμιος). Of the wisdom of God, speaking in the book of Proverbs: 1 Cl 57: 3.*

πανδοκεῖον s. πανδοχεῖον.

πανδοκεύς s. πανδοχεύς.

πανδοχεῖον, ου, τό (Strabo 5, 3, 9; 12, 8, 17; Epict., Ench. 11; Philostrat., Vi. Apoll. 4, 39 p. 157, 28; Test. Jud. 12: 1; PSI 99, 3.—The older form πανδοκεῖον in Aristoph., Ran. 550, but also in Theophr., Char. 11, 2; Polyb. 2, 15, 5; Epict. 2, 23, 36; 4, 5, 15; Plut., Crass. 22, 4; Palaeph. 45; Aelian, V.H. 14, 14; Polyaenus 4, 2, 3; inscr. [ENachmanson, Laute u. Formen der magn. Inschr. '04, 81]. Phrynichus rejects the form with χ, p. 307 Lob. Cf. Bl-D. §33; Mlt.-H. 108. Though lacking in Philo and Joseph., the word was taken over by the Jews as a loanw. [Billerb. II 183; Dalman, Gramm.² 187] and has survived to the pres. day in Arabic) *inn*, where a traveler may find a night's lodging Lk 10: 34; UGosp 1. 35=AHuck⁹-HLietzmann, Synopse '36, p. 37 note (Eng. transl., Gospel Parallels, ed. Cadbury et al. '49, p. 32 note). AHug, Pauly-W. 36, 3, '49, 520-9. M-M.*

πανδοχεύς, έως, ὁ (Polyb. 2, 15, 6 and Plut., Mor. 130ᴇ in mss.; Iambl., Vi. Pyth. 33, 238 [LDeubner, SAB '39 XIX p. 15]. The Att. πανδοκεύς in Pla., Leg. 11 p. 918ʙ et al.; Epict. 1, 24, 14; Polyb. [Büttner-W.] and Plut. [Paton-Wegehaupt '25], loc. cit. in the text. Taken over by the Jews [Billerb. II 183f], but not found in Philo and Joseph. —Bl-D. §33; Mlt.-H. 108) *inn-keeper* Lk 10: 35. M-M.*

πανήγυρις, εως, ἡ (Pind., Hdt.+; inscr., pap., LXX; Philo, In Flacc. 118; Jos., Bell. 5, 230, Ant. 2, 45) *festal gathering* (w. ἐκκλησία) Hb 12: 22. M-M.*

πανθαμάρτητος, ον *altogether sinful;* subst. pl. *men steeped in sin* B 20: 2; D 5: 2.*

πανθαμαρτωλός, όν *utterly sinful* 2 Cl 18: 2.*

πανοικεί or **πανοικί** (Tdf., W-H., N. have the former spelling, Lachm. and Tregelles the latter; it is hardly poss. to decide which is right. S. Kühner-Bl. II p. 303; Bl-D. §23; Mlt.-H. 279) adv. (Ps.-Pla., Eryx. 392c; PRyl. 434, 12; PIand. 8, 15; PFay. 129, 9; 130, 20; Ex 1: 1 v.l.; Philo, De Jos. 251, Mos. 1, 5; Jos., Ant. 4, 300; 5, 11) *with one's whole household* Ac 16: 34; MPol 20: 2. M-M.*

πανοπλία, ας, ἡ (Hdt., Aristoph.+; Polyb. 3, 62, 5; 4, 56, 3; Diod. S. 20, 84, 3; inscr., LXX) *full armor* of a heavy-armed soldier, *panoply*.

1. lit. (2 Km 2: 21; 2 Macc 3: 25; Jos., Bell. 2, 649, Ant. 7, 104; 20, 110) Lk 11: 22 (on vss. 21f cf. 4 Macc 3: 12 Α τὰς πανοπλίας καθωπλίσαντο [s. SLegasse, NovT 5, '62, 5-9]).

2. IPol 6: 2 marks a transition in the direction of a non-literal mng.; here endurance is compared with πανοπλία in a context that uses many concepts fr. the life of a soldier, and specif. mentions separate parts of his equipment. Purely metaphoric is πανοπλία τοῦ θεοῦ Eph 6: 11, 13 (fig. use of πανοπλία also Wsd 5: 17; Sir 46: 6; Philo, Somn. 1, 103; 108). On ἀναλαβεῖν τὴν πανοπλίαν vs. 13 cf. ἀναλαμβάνω 2.—On the 'military service' and 'warfare' of the Christian cf. AHarnack, Militia Christi '05; MMeinertz, D. Ap. Pls und d. Kampf: Internat. Monatsschr. 11, '17, 1115-50; MDibelius, Hdb. exc. on Eph 6: 10 and 1 Ti 1: 18; AVitti, Militum Christi Regis arma iuxta S. Paulum: Verbum Domini 7, '27, 310-18; Cumont³ '31, XIIf; 207f; HEmonds: Hlg. Überliefg. (ed. by OCasel) '38, 21-50 (anc. philos.); EFavier, L'armure du soldat de dieu d'après s. Paul '38; CLBond, Winning w. God (on Eph 6: 10-18) '40; AOepke and KGKuhn, TW V 295-301. M-M. B. 1398.*

πανουργία, ας, ἡ (Aeschyl., X., Pla.+; Polyb. 29, 8, 8; Plut., Mor. 91ʙ [w. ἀπάτη]; Herodian 2, 9, 11 [w. δόλος]; Dit., Or. 515, 47 [w. κακουργία]; POxy. 237 VIII, 12 [II ᴀᴅ]; LXX; Philo; Jos., Bell. 4, 503 al.; Test. 12 Patr.) quite predom., and in our lit. exclusively, in an unfavorable sense (evil) *cunning, craftiness, trickery,* lit. 'readiness to do anything' Lk 20: 23; 1 Cor 3: 19 (in Job 5: 12, 13, which is basic to this pass., vs. 12 has the adj. πανοῦργος); 2 Cor 4: 2; 11: 3 (in Gen 3: 1 Aq. and Sym. have the adj. πανοῦργος); Eph 4: 14. πανουργία and -ος: OBauernfeind, TW V 719-23. M-M.*

πανοῦργος, ον (trag., Pla.+; first, and in general predom., in a bad sense—so also Philo; Jos., Bell. 1, 223; later—Aristot.+ occasionally, also LXX—in a good sense as well) in our lit. never without an unfavorable connotation *clever, crafty, sly* lit. 'ready to do anything'. Paul says, taking up an expr. used by his opponents, ὑπάρχων πανοῦργος *crafty fellow that I am* 2 Cor 12: 16. Hermas is called πανοῦργος (w. αὐθάδης), because he is *crafty* enough to want to pry into secret things Hv 3, 3, 1; s 5, 5, 1. M-M.*

πανούργως adv. (Aristoph., Equ. 317; Pla., Soph. 239c et al.; Sb 8026, 14; Ps 82: 4 Sym.; Philo, Poster. Cai. 82) *deceitfully* πάντοτε πανούργως ἐλάλησα μετὰ πάντων Hm 3: 3 (on the play on words cf. Bl-D. §488, 1; Rob. 1201).*

πανπληθεί (so Tdf., W-H.) s. παμπληθεί. M-M.

πανπληθής s. παμπληθής.

πάνσεμνος, ον (Lucian, Vit. Auct. 26, Anach. 9) *greatly revered* πνεῦμα Hv 1, 2, 4 (the text is not certain; s. MDibelius ad loc.).*

πανταχῇ (for the spelling cf. Bl-D. §26 app.; Mlt.-H. 84; Meisterhans³-Schw. p. 145) adv. (Hdt.+; Pla., Ep. 7 p. 335c πάντως π.; inscr., pap., LXX; Jos., Ant. 14, 149) *everywhere* πάντας π. διδάσκων *who is teaching everyone everywhere* Ac 21: 28. μετὰ πάντων π. τῶν κεκλημένων *with all those everywhere who are called* 1 Cl 65: 2. M-M.*

πανταχόθεν adv. (Hdt., Thu., Pla.; Diod. S. 17, 82, 3; Strabo 8, 6, 15; Jos., Ant. 4, 133; 12, 353; inscr., pap.; 4 Macc 13: 1; 15: 32) *from every direction* Mk 1: 45 t.r. (for πάντοθεν). M-M.*

πανταχοῦ adv. (Soph., Thu.+; pap.; Is 42: 22; Jos., Bell. 1, 165, Ant. 14, 137).
   1. *everywhere* (so almost always) Mk 16: 20; Lk 9: 6; Ac 28: 22; 1 Cl 41: 2. πάντῃ τε καὶ π. *in every way and*

everywhere (Bl-D. §103; cf. Rob. 300) Ac 24: 3. Used in consonance w. πᾶς (Bl-D. §488, 1a; Dio Chrys. 11[12], 19; Philo, Aet. M. 68; Jos., Bell. 5, 310, Ant. 17, 143) ἀπαγγέλλει... πάντας π. μετανοεῖν 17: 30. π. ἐν πάσῃ ἐκκλησίᾳ 1 Cor 4: 17.
   2. *in all directions* (Aristoph., Lys. 1230; Lucian, Bis Accus. 27) Mk 1: 28. M-M.*

παντελής, ές (trag., Hdt.+; inscr., pap.; 3 Macc 7: 16) (*quite*) *complete, perfect, absolute* εἰς τὸ π. for the adv. παντελῶς (Philo, Joseph., Aelian). It can mean
   1. the same thing as παντελῶς, i.e. *completely, fully, wholly.* The Armen. version understands σῴζειν εἰς τὸ π. δύναται Hb 7: 25 in this sense; so also many more recent interpreters, such as Bengel, Bleek, Riggenbach. μὴ δυναμένη ἀνακῦψαι εἰς τὸ π. Lk 13: 11 is also understood in this sense by many: *she could not fully straighten herself* (RSV; εἰς τὸ π. in this mng. Aelian, N.A. 17, 27; Cyranides 57, 4; Philo, Leg. ad Gai. 144; Jos., Ant. 1, 267; 3, 264; 274; 6, 30; 7, 325).
   2. *at all;* so Lk 13: 11, if εἰς τὸ π. is taken w. μὴ δυναμένη instead of w. ἀνακῦψαι *she could not straighten herself up at all* (Gdspd.; so the Vulg., but the ancient Syriac gospel transl. [both Sinaitic and Curetonian] permits both this sense and mng. 1.—Ael. Aristid. 26, 72 K.=14 p. 351 D.: παράδειγμα εἰς τὸ π. οὐκ ἔχει).
   3. of time: *forever, for all time* (Aelian, V.H. 7, 2; 12, 20 [parall. to διὰ τέλους]; Dit., Or. 642, 2 εἰς τὸ παντελὲς αἰώνιον τειμήν; PLond. 1164f, 11. Perh. Jos., Ant. 3, 274); Hb 7: 25 is understood in this sense by the Vulg., Syr. and Copt. versions, and many moderns, including Rohr, Windisch, Strathmann⁴ '47, RSV. M-M.*

παντελῶς adv. (trag., Hdt.+; Polyb., Epict., inscr., pap.; 2 Macc; Ep. Arist., Philo; Jos., Ant. 4, 121) *fully, completely, altogether* in answers (cf. Pla., Rep. 2 p. 379ʙ.; 3 p. 401ᴀ; 6 p. 485ᴅ al.) οὐ παντελῶς *not at all; by no means* (Lucian, Catapl. 4) Hs 7: 4.*

παντεπόπτης, ου, ὁ *one who sees all, all-seeing* (Sb 4127, 18 Ἥλιον τὸν παντεπόπτην δεσπότην; Vett. Val. 1, 4; 331, 20 [Ἥλιος]; magical pap. [ThSchermann, Griech. Zauberpap. '09, 28f]; 2 Macc 9: 5; Ps.-Clem., Hom. 4, 14; 23; 5, 27; 8, 19; Sib. Or., fgm. 1, 4 v.l.—The Greeks call Zeus ὁ πανόπτης or παντόπτης) of God ὁ π. δεσπότης 1 Cl 55: 6. ὁ π. θεός 64; Pol 7: 2.*

πάντῃ (on its spelling s. Mlt.-H. p. 84; Bl-D. §26 app.) adv. (Hom.+; inscr., pap.; Sir 50: 22; 3 Macc 4: 1; Jos., Ant. 14, 183) *altogether* π. τε καὶ πανταχοῦ *in every way and everywhere* (Bl.-D. §103; Rob. 300) Ac 24: 3. M-M.*

πάντοθεν adv. (Hom.+; inscr., pap., LXX, En., Ep. Arist.; Jos., Ant. 14, 442) *from all directions* Mk 1: 45; Lk 19: 43; Hb 9: 4 (here we say *on all sides, entirely;* cf. PAmh. 51, 27 [88 ʙᴄ]; 3 Macc 3: 25; Ep. Arist. 69; 115; 142; esp. 57; Jos., Bell. 4, 587). M-M.*

παντοκρατορικός, όν (formed fr. παντοκράτωρ as a result of the feeling that this noun, since it denotes an agent [cf. EFraenkel, Geschichte der griech. Nomina agentis auf -τήρ, -τωρ, -της '10/'12], can not be used w. a neuter [s. παντοκράτωρ]) *almighty* in relation to God τὸ π. βούλημα αὐτοῦ 1 Cl 8: 5. τῷ παντοκρατορικῷ (conjecture for the παντοκράτορι of the ms.) καὶ παναρέτῳ ὀνόματί σου 60: 4.*

παντοκράτωρ, ορος, ὁ (Anth. Graec. IV p. 151 no. 169 Jacobs; Porphyr., Philos. Ex. Orac. ed. GWolff 1856, p. 145 l. 157 = Theosophien 27 p. 174, 4; CIG 2569, 12; Sb 4127, 19 of the Egypt. sun-god Mandulis; PGM 7, 668 Hermes; likew. Epigr. Gr. 815; PMich. 155, 3 [II ᴀᴅ];

PLeipz. 40 II, 13; PGM 4, 272; 969; HGraillot, Les Dieux tout-puissants, Cybèle et Attis: Rev. archéol. 58, '04 I 331ff; Cumont³ 230f.—Much more freq. in Jewish [LXX, Ep. Arist., Philo; Sib. Or. 1, 66, fgm. 1, 8.—Not in Joseph.] and Christian wr.) the *Almighty, All-Powerful, Omnipotent (One)* only of God (as transl. of צְבָאוֹת and שַׁדַּי) π. θεός (3 Macc 6: 2) 1 Cl inscr. ὁ π. θεός (2 Macc 8: 18) 2: 3; 32: 4; 62: 2; ὁ θεὸς ὁ π. Rv 16: 14; 19: 15; θεός π. (Jer 3: 19) Pol inscr. ὁ π. καὶ παντοκτίστης καὶ ἀόρατος θεός Dg 7: 2; κύριος π. (oft. LXX) 2 Cor 6: 18. ὁ κύριος ὁ π. (Zeph 2: 10) Hs 5, 7, 4 v.l. (ὁ κύριος ὁ θεὸς ὁ π. (=אֱלֹהֵי צְבָאוֹת .—Hos 12: 6; Am 3: 13; 4: 13; 5: 14) Rv 1: 8; 4: 8; 11: 17; 15: 3; 16: 7; 21: 22; MPol 14: 1; κύριος ὁ θεὸς ἡμῶν ὁ π. Rv 19: 6; ὁ θεὸς καὶ πατὴρ π. MPol 19: 2. God is addressed in the eucharistic prayer as δέσποτα π. D 10: 3 (cf. 3 Macc 2: 2 μόναρχε παντοκράτωρ).—νουθέτημα παντοκράτορος 1 Cl 56: 6 (Job 5: 17).—We find the gen. and dat. (sing.), which is the same in all genders, used w. the neut. ὄνομα. This becomes possible (s. παντοκρατορικός) because of the fact that God's name is almost equivalent to God himself (s. ὄνομα 4). τῷ ῥήματι τοῦ παντοκράτορος καὶ ἐνδόξου ὀνόματος Hv 3, 3, 5. The ms. rdg. τῷ παντοκράτορι καὶ παναρέτῳ ὀνόματί σου 1 Cl 60: 4 (s. παντοκρατορικός) is more difficult, since here the name and God are separated by σου.—FKattenbusch, Das apostolische Symbol II '00, 520ff; Dodd 19; HHommel, ThLZ 79, '54, 283f. Pantokrator: Theologia Viatorum 5, '53/'54; OMontevecchi, Studi in Onore di ACalderini e RParibeni II, '56, 401–32. M-M.*

παντοκτίστης, ου, ὁ *creator of the universe* w. παντοκράτωρ Dg 7: 2.*

πάντοτε adv. of time (Hellenist. and Mod. Gk.; Dionys. Hal.+; Peripl. Eryth. c. 29; Epict., Ench. 14, 1; Dio Chrys. 15[32], 37; Herodian 3, 9, 8; Artem. 4, 20; Plut.; Athen.; Diog. L.; Dit., Or. 458, 76 [I bc], Syll.³ 814, 37 [67 ad]; BGU 1123, 8 [I bc]; PGiess. 17, 4; 72, 11 [II ad]; Wsd 11: 21; 19: 18; Jos., Bell. 3, 42; Test. 12 Patr.—The Atticists preferred ἑκάστοτε, διαπαντός, or ἀεί [Phryn. 103 Lob.]) *always, at all times* Mt 26: 11a, b; Mk 14: 7a, b; Lk 15: 31; 18: 1; J 6: 34; 7: 6 (seven times in J); Ro 1: 10; 1 Cor 1: 4; 15: 58; 2 Cor 2: 14 (27 times in Paul); Hb 7: 25 (not found in Ac and Cath. Epistles; Bl-D. §105; cf. Rob. 300); Dg 11: 4; IEph 4: 2; Hv 1, 1, 7 (17 times in Hermas). M-M. B. 984.

πάντως adv. (Hom.+; inscr., pap., LXX, Philo, Joseph.; loanw. in rabb.).

1. *by all means, certainly, probably, doubtless* (Pla., Gorg. 527a; Herodas 7, 89; Diod. S. 20, 29, 3; Ps.-Demetr. 84; Ps.-Callisth. 2, 32, 3; Dit., Syll.³ 762, 30; BGU 248, 12; PFlor. 262, 11; POxy. 1676, 15; Tob. 14: 8 BA; 2 Macc 3: 13; Jos., Vi. 48, C. Ap. 2, 140) πάντως φονεύς ἐστιν ὁ ἄνθρωπος οὗτος Ac 28: 4. πάντως ἐρεῖτέ μοι Lk 4: 23. Cf. Ac 18: 21 t.r.; 21: 22 (on all these except Ac 18: 21 t.r. see 3 below). ἢ δι' ἡμᾶς πάντως λέγει; *or is he* (not) *certainly speaking in our interest?* 1 Cor 9: 10. πάντως διὰ πειρασμόν τινα. . .βραδύτερον λαμβάνεις *surely it is on account of some temptation. . .that you receive slowly* Hm 9: 7. πάντως θέλει ὁ δεσπότης *by all means the Master wishes* s 9, 9, 4. Cf. 7: 5.

2. *altogether, above all* Hs 1: 5; B 1: 4.—3. *of course* Hs 5, 7, 4 v.l.; 7: 4 (but *perhaps* [Lat. fortasse in both Hs passages] acc. to HJCadbury, JBL 44, '25, 223ff who suggests the same transl. for Lk 4: 23; Ac 21: 22; 28: 4; s. 1 above).

4. *at least* ἵνα πάντως τινὰς σώσω *in order to save at least some* 1 Cor 9: 22 (though *by [any and] all means* is also poss. here).

5. w. a negative—a. *not at all* (Theognis 305 Diehl οἱ κακοὶ οὐ πάντως κακοὶ ἐκ γαστρὸς γεγόνασι) πάντως οὐκ ἦν θέλημα *he was quite unwilling* 1 Cor 16: 12. Cf. Dg 9: 1. Also in answer to a question *not at all* (so PVat. A, 15= Witkowski² p. 65) Ro 3: 9 (the text is not certain; cf. Bl-D. §433, 2; Rob. 423).

b. *by no means* (Bl-D. §433, 2 and 3 with ref. to Ps.-Clem., Hom. 4, 8; 19, 9; 20, 5) 1 Cor 5: 10. M-M.*

πάνυ adv. of πᾶς (Aeschyl., Thu.+; inscr., pap., 2 Macc, Philo, Joseph.) *altogether, very.*

1. used w. verbs (Aeschyl.+; Dit., Syll.³ 798, 5; PGenève 74, 23; PFlor. 252, 12; Test. Gad 1: 5) π. σωφρονεῖν *show good sense in all respects* 1 Cl 1: 3.

2. w. adjectives (Aeschyl. +; Dit., Syll.³ 890, 15; PHib. 27, 19 [III bc]; 2 Macc 15: 17; Philo, Aet. M.; Jos., Bell. 3, 367; Test. Jos. 9: 5) πάνυ ἱλαρός *very well pleased* Hs 6, 1, 6.

3. w. adv. (Aristoph., X. et al.; 2 Macc 9: 6; 12: 43; 13: 8; Jos., Vi. 91) π. σαφῶς καὶ ἐπιμελῶς Dg 1.*

παρά (Hom.+; inscr., pap., LXX, Ep. Arist., Philo, Joseph., Test. 12 Patr., Sib. Or. On elision cf. Bl-D. §17 w. app.; Rob. 208) prep. w. three cases (Kühner-G. §440; Bl-D. §236–8; Rob. 612–16. Further lit. s.v. ἀνά, beg.; also HRau, De Praepositionis παρά usu: GCurtius, Studien usw. III 1870).

I. W. gen. which nearly always, as in class. Gk., denotes a pers., and indicates that someth. proceeds fr. this pers. (Hs 2: 3 is an exception): *from (the side of).*

1. w. the local sense preserved, used w. verbs of coming, going, sending, originating, going out, etc. (Lucian, Demon. 13 ἀπιὼν παρ' αὐτοῦ) ἐκπορεύεσθαι J 15: 26b. ἐξέρχεσθαι 16: 27; 17: 8; Lk 2: 1; 6: 19. ἔρχεσθαι 8: 49. παραγίνεσθαι Mk 14: 43. πέμπειν τινὰ παρά τινος J 15: 26a. εἶναι παρά τινος *be from someone* (cf. Job 21: 2, 9) J 6: 46; 7: 29; 9: 16, 33; 17: 7.

2. to denote the one who originates or directs (Appian, Bell. Civ. 4, 100 §420 παρὰ τ. θεῶν) παρὰ κυρίου ἐγένετο αὕτη *this was the Lord's doing* Mt 21: 42; Mk 12: 11 (both Ps 117: 23). W. a double negative: οὐκ ἀδυνατήσει παρὰ τ. θεοῦ πᾶν ῥῆμα (s. ἀδυνατέω) Lk 1: 37. τὰ λελαλημένα αὐτῇ παρὰ κυρίου *what was said to her* (by the angel) *at the Lord's command* vs. 45. ἀπεσταλμένος παρὰ θεοῦ John the Baptist was not, like Jesus, sent out fr. the very presence of God, but one whose coming was brought about by God J 1: 6 (cf. 2 Macc 11: 17). παρ' ἑαυτῆς φέρει καρπὸν καὶ παρὰ τῆς πτελέας *it* (i.e. the vine) *bears fruit which comes both from itself and from the elm* Hs 2: 3.

3. gener. denoting the point fr. which an action originates—a. after verbs of asking, demanding αἰτεῖν and αἰτεῖσθαι (cf. X., An. 1, 3, 16, Hell. 3, 1, 4; Dit., Syll.³ 785, 9f; PFay. 121, 12ff; Tob 4: 19 BA al.; LXX; Jos., Ant. 15, 92) Mt 20: 20 v.l. (for ἀπ' αὐτοῦ); J 4: 9; Ac 3: 2; 9: 2; Js 1: 5; 1 J 5: 15 v.l. (for ἀπ' αὐτοῦ); 1 Cl 36: 4 (Ps 2: 8); Hm 9: 2, 4; Dg 1. ζητεῖν (Tob 4: 18; Sir 7: 4; cf. 1 Macc 7: 13) Mk 8: 11; Lk 11: 16; 12: 48.

b. after verbs of taking, accepting, receiving λαμβάνειν (class.; Appian, Mithrid. 88 §397; Dit., Syll.³ 546 B, 23 [III bc]; Jdth 12: 15; Sus 55 Theod.; 1 Macc 8: 8; 11: 34; 4 Macc 12: 11) Mk 12: 2; Lk 6: 34; J 5: 34, 41, 44; 10: 18; Ac 2: 33; 3: 5; 17: 9; 20: 24; 26: 10 (Jos., Ant. 14, 167 λαβὼν ἐξουσίαν παρὰ σου [= τ. ἀρχιερέως], 11, 169); Js 1: 7; 2 Pt 1: 17; 2 J 4; Rv 2: 28; Hs 1: 8; 8, 3, 5. ἀπολαμβάνειν (Dit., Syll.³ 150, 20 [IV bc]; 4 Macc 18: 23) Hv 5: 7. παραλαμβάνειν (Hdt. et al.; oft. inscr.; POxy. 504, 14 al. in pap.) Gal 1: 12; 1 Th 2: 13; 4: 1; 2 Th 3: 6.

δέχεσθαι (Thu. 1, 20, 1 al.; 1 Macc 15: 20) Ac 22: 5; Phil 4: 18a. κομίζεσθαι (Dit., Syll.³ 244 I, 5ff [IV BC]; Gen 38: 20; 2 Macc 7: 11) Eph 6: 8. εὑρεῖν (Dit., Syll.³ 537, 69; 1099, 25. Cf. εὑρίσκω 3, end) 2 Ti 1: 18. ἔχειν τι παρά τινος have received someth. fr. someone (1 Esdr 6: 5) Ac 9: 14; cf. Hv 3, 9, 8. γίνεταί μοί τι παρά τινος I receive someth. from someone (Att.) Mt 18: 19. ἔσται μεθ᾽ ἡμῶν χάρις . . . παρὰ θεοῦ πατρὸς καὶ παρὰ Ἰησοῦ 2 J 3 (cf. X., An. 7, 2, 25). οἱ πιστευθέντες παρὰ θεοῦ ἔργον those who were entrusted by God with a task 1 Cl 43: 1 (cf. Polyb. 3, 69, 1; Dit., Syll.³ 1207, 12f). παρὰ τοῦ κυρίου πλουτίζεσθαι receive one's wealth fr. the Lord Hs 2: 10. —Sim. in the case of a purchase the seller is introduced by παρά: buy fr. someone ἀγοράζειν (s. ἀγοράζω 1, end) Rv 3: 18. ὠνεῖσθαι Ac 7: 16. ἄρτον φαγεῖν παρά τινος let oneself be supported by someone 2 Th 3: 8.

c. after verbs of learning, coming to know, hearing, asking ἀκούειν (cf. ἀκούω 1bβ and 2) J 1: 40; 6: 45; 7: 51; 8: 26, 40; 15: 15; Ac 10: 22; 28: 22; 2 Ti 1: 13; 2: 2. ἀκριβοῦν Mt 2: 7, 16. ἐξακριβάζεσθαι Hm 4, 2, 3. ἐπιγινώσκειν Ac 24: 8. μανθάνειν (since Aeschyl., Ag. 858; Jos., C. Ap. 2, 176; Sir 8: 8f; 2 Macc 7: 2 v.l.; 3 Macc 1: 1) 2 Ti 3: 14. πυνθάνεσθαι (Hdt. 3, 68; X., Cyr. 1, 6, 23; Pla., Rep. 5 p. 476E; Dit., Syll.³ 1169, 30; 2 Ch 32: 31) Mt 2: 4; J 4: 52 (without παρά 𝔓⁷⁵ B); B 13: 2 (Gen 25: 22).

4. adj. ὁ, ἡ, τὸ παρά τινος made, given etc. by someone
a. w. a noun (functioning as a gen.: Pla., Symp. 197E ὁ παρά τινος λόγος 'the expression made by someone'; X., Hell. 3, 1, 6 δῶρον παρὰ βασιλέως, Mem. 2, 2, 12 ἡ παρά τινος εὔνοια, Cyr. 5, 5, 13 τὸ παρ᾽ ἐμοῦ ἀδίκημα 'the crime committed by me'; Polyb. 3, 69, 3 ἡ παρ᾽ αὐτοῦ σωτηρία; Dit., Syll.³ 543, 25; Ex 4: 20; 14: 13; Philo, Plant. 14; Jos., Ant. 12, 400) ἡ παρ᾽ ἐμοῦ διαθήκη Ro 11: 27 (Is 59: 21). —Ac 26: 12 t.r.; 22 t.r.
b. subst. —α. τὰ παρά τινος what someone gives, someone's gifts (X., Mem. 3, 11, 13; Jos., Bell. 2, 124, Ant. 8, 175) Lk 10: 7; Phil 4: 18b. τὰ παρ᾽ αὐτῆς her property, what she had Mk 5: 26 (cf. Inschr. v. Priene 111, 177).
β. οἱ παρά τινος someone's envoys (class.; Bl-D. §237, 2) οἱ παρὰ τοῦ βασιλέως (1 Macc 2: 15; 1 Esdr 1: 15) 1 Cl 12: 4.—The Koine also uses this expr. to denote others who are intimately connected w. someone, e.g. family, relatives (PGrenf. II 36, 9 [II BC]; POxy. 805 [I BC]; 298, 37 [I AD]; PRainer 179, 16; 187, 7; Sb 5238, 19 [I AD]; Sus 33; 1 Macc 13: 52; Jos., Ant. 1, 193. Further exx. fr. pap. in Mlt. 106f; Rossberg [s. ἀνά, beg.] 52) Mk 3: 21 (cf. ChBruston et PFarel: Revue de Théol. et des Quest. rel. 18, '09, 82-93; AWabnitz, ibid. 221-5; SMonteil, ibid. 19, '10, 317-25; JHMoulton, Mk 3: 21: ET 20, '09, 476; GHartmann, Mk 3: 20f: BZ 11, '13, 248-79; FZorell, Zu Mk 3: 20, 21: ZkTh 37, '13, 695-7; JEBelser, Zu Mk 3: 20f: ThQ 98, '16, 401-18; Rdm.² 141; 227.—S. also on ἐξίστημι).

II. W. the dat. (nearly always of the pers.) it denotes nearness in space at or by (the side of), beside, near, with, acc. to the standpoint fr. which the relationship is viewed.
1. lit. —a. near, beside—α. w. things (Synes., Ep. 126 p. 262A; Epigr. Gr. 703, 1; POxy. 120, 23; 2 Km 10: 8; 11: 9; Jos., Ant. 1, 196) εἱστήκεισαν παρὰ τῷ σταυρῷ J 19: 25. κεῖσθαι παρὰ τῷ πύργῳ Hv 3, 5, 5.
β. w. persons ἔστησεν αὐτὸ παρ᾽ ἑαυτῷ he had him (i.e. the child) stand by his side Lk 9: 47.
b. in someone's house, city, company etc.—a. house: ἀριστᾶν Lk 11: 37. καταλύειν 19: 7 (Pla., Gorg. 447B; Demosth. 18, 82). μένειν (Jos., Ant. 1, 298; 299) J 1: 39; Ac 9: 43; 18: 3; 21: 8. ξενίζεσθαι 10: 6; 21: 16 (ξενίζω 1). So prob. also ἕκαστος παρ᾽ ἑαυτῷ each one at home 1 Cor

16: 2 (cf. Philo, Cher. 48 παρ᾽ ἑαυτοῖς, Leg. ad Gai. 271). ὃν ἀπέλιπον ἐν Τρῳάδι παρὰ Κάρπῳ 2 Ti 4: 13.
β. city: Rv 2: 13. So prob. also ἦσαν παρ᾽ ἡμῖν ἑπτὰ ἀδελφοί Mt 22: 25.—J 4: 40; Col 4: 16 (where the church at Laodicea is contrasted w. the one at Col.).
γ. other uses: παρὰ Ἰουδαίοις among the Jews Mt 28: 15. παρ᾽ αὐτοῖς ἐπιμεῖναι remain with them Ac 28: 14; cf. 21: 7. οἱ παρ᾽ ὑμῖν πρεσβύτεροι the elders among you 1 Cl 1: 3.—παρὰ τῷ πατρί with (of spatial proximity) the Father Mt 6: 1; J 8: 38a; cf. 17: 5 (Synes., Kingship 29 p. 31D: philosophy has her abode παρὰ τῷ θεῷ and if the world refuses to receive her when she descends to earth, μένει παρὰ τῷ πατρί. Of Jesus: παρ᾽ ὑμῖν μένων while I was with you (on earth) J 14: 25. Of the Spirit: παρ᾽ ὑμῖν μένει vs. 17. Of the Father and Son in their relation to the true Christian: μονὴν παρ᾽ αὐτῷ ποιησόμεθα we will take up our abode with him vs. 23.
2. fig. παρά τινι—a. before someone's judgment seat (Demosth. 18, 13 εἰς κρίσιν καθιστάναι παρά τινι; Appian, Maced. 11 §8 παρ᾽ ὑμῖν ἐς κρίσιν) 2 Pt 2: 11. Closely related is
b. in the sight or judgment of someone (Soph., Hdt.; PSI 435, 19 [258 BC] παρὰ τῷ βασιλεῖ) παρὰ τῷ θεῷ: δίκαιος παρὰ τῷ θεῷ righteous in the sight of God Ro 2: 13 (cf. Job 9: 2; Jos., Ant. 6, 205).—Cf. 1 Cor 3: 19; Gal 3: 11; 2 Th 1: 6; Js 1: 27; 1 Pt 2: 4; 2 Pt 3: 8. θυσία δεκτὴ παρὰ τῷ θεῷ Hs 5, 3, 8. ἔνδοξος παρὰ τῷ θεῷ m 2: 6; s 5, 3, 3; 8, 10, 1; 9, 27, 3; 9, 28, 3; 9, 29, 3.—9, 7, 6.—Acc. to the judgment of men (Jos., Ant. 7, 84) Hs 8, 9, 1. τί ἄπιστον κρίνεται παρ᾽ ὑμῖν; Ac 26: 8. ἵνα μὴ ἦτε παρ᾽ ἑαυτοῖς φρόνιμοι Ro 11: 25 v.l.; cf. 12: 16 (s. Pr 3: 7 μὴ ἴσθι φρόνιμος παρὰ σεαυτῷ).—'In the judgment' passes over into a simpler with (Himerius, Or. 8 [= 23], 10 παρὰ θεοῖς = with the gods) εὑρεῖν χάριν παρά τινι find favor with someone (Ex 33: 16; cf. Num 11: 15) Lk 1: 30; Hs 5, 2, 10. τοῦτο χάρις παρὰ θεῷ 1 Pt 2: 20. χάριν ἔχειν (Ex 33: 12) m 5, 1, 5. προέκοπτεν ἐν τῇ χάριτι παρὰ θεῷ καὶ ἀνθρώποις Lk 2: 52. τί ταπεινοφροσύνη παρὰ θεῷ ἰσχύει, τί ἀγάπη ἁγνὴ παρὰ θεῷ δύναται how strong humility is before God, what pure love before God can do 1 Cl 21: 8.
c. almost equivalent to the dat. (Ps 75: 13): δυνατόν or ἀδύνατον παρά τινι possible or impossible for someone Mt 19: 26a, b; Mk 10: 27a, b, c; Lk 1: 37 t.r.; 18: 27a, b; 1 Cl 27: 2.—AFridrichsen, Symb. Osl. 14, '35, 44-6.
d. (οὐκ) ἔστιν τι παρά τινι someth. is (not) with or in someone, someone has someth. (nothing) to do w. someth. (Demosth. 18, 277 εἰ ἔστι καὶ παρ᾽ ἐμοί τις ἐμπειρία; Gen 24: 25; Job 12: 13; Ps 129: 4 παρὰ σοὶ ὁ ἱλασμός ἐστιν) οὐκ ἔστιν προσωπολημψία παρά τ. θεῷ Ro 2: 11. Cf. 9: 14; Eph 6: 9; Js 1: 17. Sim. Mt 8: 10; 2 Cor 1: 17.
e. παρ᾽ ἑαυτοῖς among themselves (Philo, Cher. 48) διαλογίζεσθαι Mt 21: 25 v.l. (cf. Demosth. 10, 17 γιγνώσκειν παρ᾽ αὐτῷ; Epict., Ench. 48, 2).—In ἐν τούτῳ μενέτω παρὰ θεῷ 1 Cor 7: 24, the mng. of παρὰ θεῷ is not certain: let him remain in that position (to which he was called) before God; it is prob. meant to remind the Christian of the One fr. whom he received a call to his earthly occupation, whatever it may be, and before whom therefore he cannot even have the appearance of inferiority (inscr.: Wilcken, Chrest. 4, 4 [13 BC] παρὰ τῷ κυρίῳ Ἑρμῇ = 'before, in the sight of'; Sb 7616 [II AD] τὸ προσκύνημά σου ποιῶ παρὰ τῷ κυρίῳ Σαράπι = 'before the Lord S.'; 7661, 3 [c. 100 AD]; 7932, 7992, 6 [letter II/III AD]).
III. W. acc. of the pers. or the thing—1. of space (w. no difference whether it answers the question 'where?' or 'whither?' S. Bl-D. §236, 1; Rob. 615).

a. *by, along* περιπατεῖν παρὰ τὴν θάλασσαν (Pla., Gorg. 511ε. Cf. Dit., Syll.³ 1182; Jos., Ant. 2, 81) Mt 4: 18; cf. Mk 1: 16.

b. *at the edge* or *to the edge of*—**α.** παρὰ (τὴν) θάλασσαν *by the sea* (or *lake*), *at the shore* Mt 13: 1; Mk 4: 1; 5: 21; Ac 10: 6, 32; cf. Lk 5: 1, 2. παρὰ τὴν ὁδόν *by the side of the road* (X., An. 1, 2, 13; Plut., Lysander 29, 4 a tomb παρὰ τ. ὁδόν = beside the road) Mt 20: 30; Mk 10: 46; Lk 18: 35 (but *on the road* is also poss. in these three places; s. d below).

β. παρὰ τὴν θάλασσαν *to* (*the side of*) *the sea* (*lake*) Mt 15: 29; Mk 2: 13. παρὰ ποταμόν *to the river* Ac 16: 13.

c. gener. *near, at* παρὰ τοὺς πόδας τινός *at someone's feet* (sit, fall, place etc.) Mt 15: 30; Lk 7: 38; 8: 35, 41; 10: 39 t.r.; 17: 16; Ac 4: 35, 37 v.l.; 5: 2; 7: 58; 22: 3 (cf. ET 30, '19, 39f). παρὰ τὸν πύργον *beside the tower* Hs 9, 4, 8; 9, 6, 5; 8; 9, 7, 1; 9, 11, 6.—παρὰ τὴν ἰτέαν 8, 1, 2.

d. *on* παρὰ τὴν ὁδόν *on the road* (w. motion implied; Aesop, Fab. 226 P. = 420 H.: πεσὼν παρὰ τὴν ὁδόν; Phot., Bibl. 94 p. 74b on Iambl. Erot. [Hercher I p. 222, 22] πίπτουσι παρὰ τὴν ὁδόν) Mt 13: 4, 19; Mk 4: 4; Lk 8: 5; *on the road* (w. no motion implied; Theophr., Hist. Pl. 6, 6, 10: the crocus likes to be trodden under foot, διὸ καὶ παρὰ τὰς ὁδοὺς κάλλιστος; Phot. p. 222, 29 H. [s. above]) Mk 4: 15; Lk 8: 12. Perh. also Mt 20: 30; Mk 10: 46; Lk 18: 35 (s. ba above).—παρὰ τὸ χεῖλος τῆς θαλάσσης *on the seashore* Hb 11: 12.

2. of time (Lucian, Catapl. 24 παρὰ τ. βίον = during his life; POxy. 472, 10) παρ' ἐνιαυτόν *from year to year* (Plut., Cleom. 15, 1. Cf. ἐνιαυτός 1) B 10: 7.

3. in a comparative sense: *in comparison to, more than, beyond* ἁμαρτωλοί, ὀφειλέται π. πάντας Lk 13: 2, 4 (PSI 317, 6 [95 AD] παρὰ πάντας; Jos., C. Ap. 2, 234 παρὰ τ. ἄλλους ἅπαντας). κρίνειν ἡμέραν παρ' ἡμέραν (s. κρίνω 1) Ro 14: 5. π. πᾶσαν τὴν γῆν B 11: 9 (prophetic quot. of unknown orig.). π. πάντα τὰ πνεύματα *more than all other spirits* Hm 10, 1, 2. ἐλαττοῦν τινα π. τινα *make someone inferior to someone* Hb 2: 7, 9 (s. ἐλαττόω 1 and cf. PGrenf. I 42, 12 [II BC] ἐλαττουμένων ἡμῶν παρὰ τοὺς δεῖνα). εἶδος δὲ ἐκεῖνον π. τὸ εἶδος τῶν ἀνθρώπων (s. ἐκλείπω) 1 Cl 16: 3.—After a comp. (Thu. 1, 23, 3) Lk 3: 13; Hb 1: 4; 3: 3; 9: 23; 11: 4; 12: 24; B 4: 5 (cf. Da 7: 7); Hv 3, 12, 1; s 9, 18, 2.—When a comparison is made, one member of it may receive so little attention as to pass fr. consideration entirely, so that 'more than' becomes *instead of, rather than, to the exclusion of* (Plut., Mor. 984c; PsSol 9: 9; Ep. Arist. 134) λατρεύειν τῇ κτίσει παρὰ τὸν κτίσαντα *serve the creation rather than the Creator* Ro 1: 25 (cf. Ep. Arist. 139: the Jews worship τὸν μόνον θεὸν παρ' ὅλην τὴν κτίσιν). δεδικαιωμένος παρ' ἐκεῖνον *justified rather than the other* Lk 18: 14. ἔχρισέν σε . . . παρὰ τοὺς μετόχους *he has anointed thee and not thy comrades* Hb 1: 9 (Ps 44: 8). ὑπερφρονεῖν παρ' ὃ δεῖ φρονεῖν Ro 12: 3 (Plut., Mor. 83ϝ παρ' ὃ δεῖ). παρὰ καιρὸν ἡλικίας Hb 11: 11 (Plut., Rom. 25, 6 παρ' ἡλικίαν. Cf. ἡλικία 1ca).—παρὰ δύναμιν *beyond their means* (s. δύναμις 2) 2 Cor 8: 3.—After ἄλλος (Pla., Lach. 178β, Leg. 3 p. 693β; X., Hell. 1, 5, 5; Demosth. 18, 235) *another than* 1 Cor 3: 11.

4. παρὰ μικρόν *except for a little, almost* (s. μικρός 3a) Hs 8, 1, 14. Likew. παρά τι (cf. Vett. Val. 228, 6) Lk 5: 7 D; Hs 9, 19, 3.

5. causal *because of* (Pind., Olymp. 2, 65; Demosth. 4, 11; 9, 2; PRyl. 243, 6; POxy. 1420, 7) παρὰ τό w. acc. foll. *because* (Dit., Syll.³ 495, 130; UPZ 7, 13 [163 BC] παρὰ τὸ Ἕλληνά με εἶναι.—Mayser II 1, '26, 331; Gen 29: 20; Ex 14: 11) 1 Cl 39: 5f (Job 4: 20f). π. τοῦτο *because of this* (Kühner-G. I 513, 3; Synes., Ep. 44 p. 185A; 57 p. 192D)

ITr 5: 2; IRo 5: 1 (quot. fr. 1 Cor 4: 4, where Paul has ἐν τούτῳ). οὐ παρὰ τοῦτο οὐ (double neg. as a strengthened affirmative) *not for that reason any the less* 1 Cor 12: 15f.

6. adversative *against, contrary to* (class.; inscr., pap., LXX) π. τὴν διδαχήν Ro 16: 17. παρ' ἐλπίδα *against hope* (s. ἐλπίς 1) in a play on words w. ἐπ' ἐλπίδι 4: 18. π. φύσιν (Thu. 6, 17, 1; Pla., Rep. 5 p. 466D) 1: 26; 11: 24. π. τὸν νόμον (X., Mem. 1, 1, 18 παρὰ τοὺς νόμους; PMagd. 16, 5 [222 BC] παρὰ τοὺς νόμους; Jos., C. Ap. 2, 233) Ac 18: 13. παρ' ὅ *contrary to that which* Gal 1: 8f.

7. subtracting *less* (Hdt. 9, 33; Plut., Caesar 30, 5; Jos., Ant. 4, 176; POxy. 264, 4 [I AD]) τεσσεράκοντα π. μίαν *forty less one* = thirty-nine (i.e. lashes) 2 Cor 11: 24 (cf. Makkoth 3, 10 p. 369ff; SKrauss: Die Mischna IV 4; 5, '33).—On παρ' αὐτά ITr 11: 1 cf. παραυτά.—HRiesenfeld, TW V 724–33. M-M.

παραβαίνω 2 aor. παρέβην (Hom. +; inscr., pap., LXX, En., Ep. Arist., Philo, Joseph.).

1. intr. *go aside* fig. ἐκ τῆς ὁδοῦ *deviate from the way* 1 Cl 53: 2 (Ex 32: 8; Dt 9: 12). *Turn aside* fr. an office ἀποστολή, ἀφ' ἧς παρέβη Ἰούδας Ac 1: 25 (on the constr. w. ἀπό cf. Dt 9: 16; 17: 20).

2. trans. *transgress, break*—**a.** w. acc. τι *someth.* (Aeschyl. +; Thu. 4, 97, 2; oft. in inscr., pap., LXX) τὸν νόμον (Eur., Ion 231; Pla., Crito 53ε; Sir 19: 24; 1 Esdr 8: 24, 84; 3 Macc 7: 12; Jos., C. Ap. 2, 176; Sib. Or. 3, 599f) Hs 8, 3, 5. τὴν ἐντολὴν τοῦ θεοῦ (Epict. 3, 5, 8; Tob 4: 5; 4 Macc 13: 15; 16: 24) Mt 15: 3. τὴν παράδοσιν vs. 2.

b. abs. (w. 'commandments' to be supplied) παρέβησαν *they became transgressors* B 9: 4. Ptc. ὁ παραβαίνων *the transgressor* 2 J 9 t.r. (Aristot., Pol. 1325b; pl.: POxy. 34 III, 12 [II AD]; Sir 40: 14; Philo, Mos. 2, 49; Jos., C. Ap. 2, 215).—παραβαίνω and related words: JSchneider, TW V 733–41. M-M.*

παραβάλλω fut. παραβαλῶ; 2 aor. παρέβαλον (Hom. +; inscr., pap., LXX, Ep. Arist., Philo, Joseph.).

1. trans.—**a.** *throw to*, esp. of throwing fodder to animals (Il. 5, 369 al.; Pla., Phaedr. 247ε; Cass. Dio 59, 14) of the martyrs: τούτοις (i.e. τοῖς θηρίοις) σε παραβαλῶ MPol 11: 1. Pass. (cf. παραβληθῆναι τοῖς θηρίοις: Cass. Dio 59, 10; Athen. 3 p. 84ε) Dg 7: 7.

b. *give up* (Aristoph. et al.; Polyb. 40, 4, 2; POxy. 533, 13 [II AD]; Ep. Arist. 281.—Likew. the mid.) κινδύνῳ ἑαυτόν *expose oneself to danger* 1 Cl 55: 6.

c. *compare* (Hdt. +; PFlor. 312, 8 [I AD]; Philo, Leg. All. 3, 249 al.; Jos., C. Ap. 2, 150; 279) ἐν (instrumental) ποίᾳ παραβολῇ παραβάλωμεν αὐτήν; *what parable can we use in comparing it* (i.e. the Kgdm. of God)? Mk 4: 30 t.r.

2. intr. *approach, come near* to someone or someth. (Pla. et al.; oft. pap.; w. εἰς Polyb. 12, 5, 1; 16, 37, 7; 21, 8, 13; Diod. S. 1, 46, 7; 8; Plut., Demetr. 39, 2; PRyl. 153, 5), specif. as a t.t. in seaman's speech *come near by ship, cross over* (Hdt. 7, 179; Ep. Phil. in Demosth. 12, 16; Jos., Ant. 18, 161 εἰς Ποτιόλους παραβαλών) παρεβάλομεν εἰς Σάμον Ac 20: 15. M-M.*

παράβασις, εως, ἡ (Strabo et al.; pap., LXX, En., Philo, Joseph., Test. 12 Patr.) *overstepping, transgression* w. objective gen. (Plut., Mor. p. 122D, Ages. et Pomp. 1, 5; 2 Macc 15: 10) ἡ π. τοῦ νόμου *the violation of the law* (Porphyr., Abst. 2, 61 Nauck ἡ τοῦ νόμου παράβασις; Alex. Aphr., An. Mant. II p. 158, 37 δικαίων π. = violation of the laws.—Philo, Somn. 2, 123; Jos., Ant. 8, 129 τ. νομίμων π.; 13, 69 ἡ τ. νόμου π. 18, 263; 340) Ro 2: 23. W. the subjective gen. (Wsd 14: 31) ἡ π. Ἀδάμ *Adam's transgression* 5: 14. ἡ π. αὐτῶν B 12: 5b. Pl. αἱ π.

τοῦ οἴκου σου *the transgressions of your family* Hv 2, 3, 1. Abs. (Plut., Mor. p. 209A; 746C; Ps 100: 3; 4 Km 2: 24 v.l.; En. 98, 5) Ro 4: 15; Hb 9: 15; B 12: 5a. W. παρακοή Hb 2: 2. Among many other vices in a catalogue of vices B 20: 1. ἐν π. γίνεσθαι *become a transgressor* 1 Ti 2: 14. τῶν παραβάσεων χάριν *because of transgressions* i.e. to make them poss. and numerous Gal 3: 19. M-M.*

παραβάτης, ου, ὁ (in secular wr. mostly a warrior beside the charioteer, or a certain kind of foot-soldier) in our lit. only *transgressor* (so Aeschyl., Eum. 553 παρβάτης; παραβ. so Pythag., Ep. 3, 7 παραβάται τᾶν ὁμολογιᾶν γινόμεθα; Polemo [Macrobius, Saturnalia 5, 19, 29] π. θεῶν; Suidas on Ἀμάχιος; Sym.) (τοῦ) νόμου Ro 2: 25, 27; Js 2: 11; Lk 6: 5 D. Abs. *sinner* (Ps.-Clem., Hom. 3, 39) Gal 2: 18 (WMundle, ZNW 23, '24, 152f); Js 2: 9. M-M.*

παραβιάζομαι mid. dep.; 1 aor. παρεβιασάμην (Epicurea p. 36, 5 Us.; Polyb., Plut. et al.; LXX; s. Anz 359f) *use force* to accomplish someth. (Polyb. 24, 8, 3; Philo, Congr. Erud. Grat. 125; Jos., C. Ap. 2, 233); w. acc. ('do violence to' Plut., Mor. 19F μύθους, Cleom. 16, 2 τ. Ἀχαιούς; Gen 19: 9) *urge strongly, prevail upon* Lk 24: 29; Ac 16: 15. Foll. by acc. and inf. ὁ παραβιασάμενος ἑαυτόν τε καί τινας προσελθεῖν ἑκοντάς *the one who prevailed upon himself and others to come forward of their own free will* MPol 4. M-M.*

παραβλέπω (Aristoph.+; LXX; Philo, Virt. 173) *overlook, neglect, despise* (Polyb. 6, 46, 6 τὰς διαφοράς; Sir 38: 9) τινά *someone* of needy persons, widows and orphans Hs 1: 8.*

παραβολεύομαι (Sb 7562 [II AD]) 1 aor. παρεβολευσάμην *expose to danger, risk* (Inscr. Orae Sept. Ponti Euxin. I 21, 26–8 Latyschev: ἀλλὰ καὶ [μέχρι] περάτων γῆς ἐμαρτυρήθη τοὺς ὑπὲρ φιλίας κινδύνους μέχρι Σεβαστῶν συμμαχίᾳ παραβολευσάμενος = 'but also to the ends of the earth witness was borne to him that in the interests of friendship he exposed himself to dangers by his aid in [legal] strife, [taking his clients' cases] even up to the emperors'. Dssm., LO 69 [LAE 84]) τινί *someth.* (on the dat. s. Mlt. 64 and cf. παραβάλλεσθαι τοῖς ὅλοις 'risk everything' Polyb. 2, 26, 3; 3, 94, 4) τῇ ψυχῇ *one's life* (cf. Diod. S. 3, 36, 4 ταῖς ψυχαῖς παραβάλλεσθαι; Dit., Syll.³ 762, 39 ψυχῇ καὶ σώματι παραβαλλόμενος) Phil 2: 30. M-M.*

παραβολή, ῆς, ἡ (Pla., Isocr.+; inscr., pap., LXX. —JWackernagel, Parabola: IndogF 31, '12/'13, 262–7) *comparison.*

1. *type, figure* παραβολὴ εἰς τὸν καιρὸν τὸν ἐνεστηκότα *a symbol (pointing) to the present age* Hb 9: 9. ἐν παραβολῇ *as a type* (of the violent death and of the resurrection of Christ) 11: 19. λέγει ὁ προφήτης παραβολὴν κυρίου B 6: 10, where the mng. may be *the prophet is uttering a parable of the Lord* (Gdspd.), or *the prophet speaks of the Lord in figurative language* (Kleist), or *the prophet speaks in figurative language given him by the Lord.* W. αἴνιγμα PK 4 p. 15, 31. The things of the present or future cannot be understood by the ordinary Christian διὰ τὸ ἐν παραβολαῖς κεῖσθαι *because they are expressed in figures* B 17: 2.

2. In the synoptics the word denotes a characteristic form of the teaching of Jesus (in Mt 17 times, in Mk 13 times, in Lk 18 times) *parable, illustration* (cf. Euclides [400 BC] who, acc. to Diog. L. 2, 107, rejected ὁ διὰ παραβολῆς λόγος; Aristot., Rhet. 2, 20, 2ff; Περὶ ὕψους 37; Vi. Aesopi II p. 307, 15; Biogr. p. 87 Ὁμήρου

παραβολαί; Philo, Conf. Lingu. 99; Jos., Ant. 8, 44. The Gk. OT also used παραβολή for various words and expressions that involve comparison, even riddles [cf. Jülicher—s. 2 below— I² 32–40].—En. 1, 2; 3). A parable is a short discourse that makes a comparison; it often expresses a (single) complete thought. The evangelists considered that it needed interpretation because it sometimes presented teaching in obscure fashion. λέγειν, εἰπεῖν παραβολήν: Lk 13: 6; 16: 19 D; 19: 11. τινί to *someone* 4: 23 (here and in the next passage π.= *proverb*, quoted by Jesus); 6: 39; 18: 1; 21: 29. πρός τινα to *someone* 5: 36; 12: 16, 41; 14: 7; 15: 3; 18: 9; 20: 9; *with reference to someone* Mk 12: 12; Lk 20: 19. παραβολὴν λαλεῖν τινι Mt 13: 33. παραβολὴν παρατιθέναι τινί *put a parable before someone* vss. 24, 31. τελεῖν τὰς παραβολάς *finish the parables* vs. 53. διασαφεῖν τινι τὴν παραβολήν vs. 36. φράζειν τινὶ τὴν παρ. *explain the parable* ibid. v.l.; 15: 15. ἀκούειν Mt 13: 18; 21: 33, 45. γνῶναι and εἰδέναι *understand* Mk 4: 13b et al. μαθεῖν τὴν παρ. ἀπό τινος *learn the parable from someth.* Mt 24: 32; Mk 13: 28; (ἐπ)ερωτᾶν τινα τὴν παρ. *ask someone the mng. of the parable* Mk 7: 17; cf. 4: 10. Also ἐπερωτᾶν τινα περὶ τῆς παρ. 7: 17 t.r.; ἐπηρώτων αὐτὸν τίς εἴη ἡ παρ. *they asked him what the parable meant* Lk 8: 9; the answer to it: ἔστιν δὲ αὕτη ἡ παρ. *but the parable means this* vs. 11.—παραβολαῖς λαλεῖν τινί τι Mk 4: 33. W. the gen. of that which forms the subj. of the parable ἡ παρ. τοῦ σπείραντος Mt 13: 18. τῶν ζιζανίων vs. 36.—W. a prep. εἶπεν διὰ παραβολῆς Lk 8: 4.—χωρὶς παραβολῆς οὐδὲν ἐλάλει αὐτοῖς Mt 13: 34b; Mk 4: 34.—Mostly ἐν: τιθέναι τὴν βασιλείαν τοῦ θεοῦ ἐν παραβολῇ *present the Kgdm. of God in a parable* vs. 30. ἐν παραβολαῖς λαλεῖν τινι Mt 13: 10, 13; Mk 12: 1. ἐν παραβολαῖς λέγειν τινί Mt 22: 1; Mk 3: 23. λαλεῖν τινι τι ἐν παραβολαῖς Mt 13: 3, 34a. διδάσκειν τινά τι ἐν παραβολαῖς Mk 4: 2. ἀνοίξω ἐν παραβολαῖς τὸ στόμα μου Mt 13: 35 (Ps 77: 2). γίνεταί τινί τι ἐν παραβολαῖς *someth. comes to someone in the form of parables* Mk 4: 11; cf. Lk 8: 10.—AJülicher, Die Gleichnisreden Jesu I² 1899; II 1899 [the older lit. is given here I 203–322]; GHeinrici, RE VI 688–703, XXIII 561f; ChABugge, Die Hauptparabeln Jesu '03; PFiebig, Altjüdische Gleichnisse und d. Gleichnisse Jesu '04, D. Gleichnisse Jesu im Lichte der rabb. Gleich. '12, D. Erzählungsstil der Ev. '25; LFonck, Die Parabeln des Herrn³ '09 (w. much lit. on the individual parables), The Parables of the Gospel³ '18; JKögel, BFChTh XIX 6, '15; MMeinertz, Die Gleichnisse Jesu '16; 4'48; HWeinel, Die Gleichnisse Jesu⁵ '29; RBultmann, D. Geschichte der synoptischen Tradition² '31, 179–222; MDibelius, D. Formgeschichte des Ev.² '33; EBuonaiuti, Le parabole di Gesù: Religio 10–13, '34–'37; WOEoesterly, The Gospel Parables in the Light of their Jewish Background '36; EWechssler, Hellas im Ev. '36, 267–85; CHDodd, The Parables of the Kgdm.³ '36; BTD Smith, The Par. of the Syn. Gosp. '37; WMichaelis, Es ging e. Sämann aus. zu säen '38; OAPiper, The Understanding of the Syn. Par.: Evangelical Quarterly 14, '42, 42–53; ChMasson, Les Paraboles de Marc IV '45; Joach Jeremias, D. Gleichn. Jesu⁴ '56 (Eng. transl. '55); ELinnemann, Jesus of the Parables, tr. JSturdy, '66; AWeiser, D. Knechtsgleichnisse der synopt. Evv. '71; JKingsbury, The Parables of Jesus in Mt 13, '69; FWDanker, Fresh Persp. on Mt, CTM 41, '70, 478–90; JKingsbury, ibid. 42, '71, 579–96; TWManson, The Teaching of Jesus, '55, 57–86.

3. Apart fr. the syn. gospels, παρ. is found in our lit. freq. in Hermas who, however, is not independent of the synoptic tradition. But Hermas uses παρ. only once to designate a real illustrative (double) parable, in m 11: 18.

Elsewh παρ. is for Hermas an enigmatic presentation that is somet. seen in a vision, somet. expressed in words, but in any case is in need of detailed interpretation: w. gen. of the content (s. 2 above) τοῦ πύργου *about the tower* Hv 3, 3, 2. τοῦ ἀγροῦ *about the field* s 5, 4, 1. τῶν ὀρέων s 9, 29, 4. δηλοῦν τὴν παραβολήν s 5, 4, 1. ἀκούειν τὴν παραβολήν v 3, 3, 2; 3, 12, 1; s 5, 2, 1. παραβολὰς λαλεῖν τινι s 5, 4, 2a. τὰ ῥήματα τὰ λεγόμενα διὰ παραβολῶν 5, 4, 3b; γράφειν τὰς παρ. v 5: 5f; s 9, 1, 1; συνιέναι τὰς παρ. m 10, 1, 3. γινώσκειν s 5, 3, 1a; 9, 5, 5. νοεῖν m 10, 1, 4; s 5, 3, 1b. ἐπιλύειν τινί παρ. s 5, 3, 1c; 5, 4, 2b; 3a. συντελεῖν s 9, 29, 4. ἡ ἐπίλυσις τῆς παρ. *explanation, interpretation of the parable* s 5, 6, 8; αἱ ἐπιλύσεις τῶν παρ. s 5, 5, 1. ὁ υἱὸς τοῦ θεοῦ εἰς δούλου τρόπον κεῖται ἐν τῇ παρ. *the Son of God appears in the parable as a slave* s 5, 5, 5. ἡ παρ. εἰς τοὺς δούλους τοῦ θεοῦ κεῖται *the par. refers to the slaves of God* s 2: 4.—S. also the headings to the various parts of the third division of Hermas (the Parables) and on Hermas gener. cf. Jülicher, op. cit. I 204-9.—FHauck, TW V 741-59. M-M. B. 1262.*

παραβουλεύομαι 1 aor. παρεβουλευσάμην (Cat. Cod. Astr. XII 188, 27; Hesychius, prob. w. ref. to Phil 2: 30) *be careless* τινί *in relation to someth.* τῇ ψυχῇ *have no concern for one's life* Phil 2: 30 t.r.*

παραβύω 1 aor. παρέβυσα (Hippocr. et al.) *plunge into* π. ξιφίδιον *plunge a dagger into* (*a body*) MPol 16: 1 (Lucian, Toxar. 58 παραβύειν ἐς τὴν πλευρὰν τὸν ἀκινάκην).*

παραγγελία, ας, ἡ (X.+; Diod. S. 4, 12, 3; pap., Philo, In Flacc. 141; Jos., Ant. 16, 241) *order, command, precept, advice* παραγγελίαν λαμβάνειν *receive an order* Ac 16: 24; 1 Cl 42: 3. παραγγελίᾳ παραγγέλλειν τινί (Bl-D. §198, 6; Rdm.² 128; Rob. 531) foll. by μή and the inf. *give someone strict orders* Ac 5: 28. Of apostolic instructions παραγγελίας διδόναι τινί 1 Th 4: 2; παρατίθεσθαί τινι 1 Ti 1: 18. As instruction it is almost= *preaching* vs. 5.—GMilligan, St. Paul's Epistles to the Thess. '08 p. 47. M-M.*

παραγγέλλω impf. παρήγγελλον; 1 aor. παρήγγειλα (Aeschyl., Hdt.+; inscr., pap., LXX, Philo, Joseph., Test. 12 Patr.) *give orders, command, instruct, direct* of all kinds of persons in authority, worldly rulers, Jesus, the apostles. Abs. παραγγέλλων *in giving my instructions* 1 Cor 11: 17. W. the pres. inf. foll. Ac 15: 5. W. the acc. and aor. inf. foll. 1 Ti 6: 13f. τί *direct, urge, insist on* (Philo, Spec. Leg. 3, 80) 2 Th 3: 4; 1 Ti 4: 11; 5: 7. τινί (Jos., Ant. 2, 311) *direct, command someone* καθὼς ὑμῖν παρηγγείλαμεν 1 Th 4: 11. Pass. τὰ παρηγγελμένα τινί *what someone was told* (to do) short ending of Mk; τινί w. λέγων and dir. discourse foll. Mt 10: 5. τινί τι w. ὅτι and dir. disc. foll. 2 Th 3: 10.—τινί w. aor. inf. foll. (Philo, Poster. Cai. 29; Jos., C. Ap. 1, 244) Mt 15: 35; Mk 8: 6; Lk 8: 29; Ac 10: 42; 16: 18 (cf. Mlt. 119). τινί w. pres. inf. foll. (1 Km 23: 8) Ac 16: 23; 23: 30; 1 Cl 1: 3; IPol 5: 1. παραγγέλλειν w. an inf. and μή comes to mean *forbid to do someth.*: π. τινί w. aor. inf. Lk 5: 14; 8: 56; without the dat., which is easily supplied fr. the context Ac 23: 22. π. τινί w. pres. inf. (cf. an inscr. fr. Dionysopolis [Ramsay, ET 14, '03, 159] παραγγέλλω πᾶσι, μὴ καταφρονεῖν τοῦ θεοῦ; Philo, Leg. All. 1, 98) Lk 9: 21; Ac 1: 4 (for the transition from indirect discourse to direct cf. Arrian, Anab. 5, 11, 4: Alexander παρηγγέλλετο Κρατέρῳ μὴ διαβαίνειν τὸν πόρον . . . ἣν Πῶρος ἐπ᾽ ἐμὲ ἄγῃ [the last clause is spoken by Alexander]); 1 Ti 1: 3; 6: 17; without dat. (Jos., Ant. 19, 311) 1 Cl 27: 2, which can

be supplied fr. the context Ac 4: 18; 5: 40. παραγγελίᾳ παρηγγείλαμεν ὑμῖν μὴ διδάσκειν vs. 28.—τινί w. acc. and 1 aor. inf. foll. 1 Cor 7: 10; 1 Ti 6: 13f v.l. (παραγγέλλω σοι); the pres. inf. Ac 17: 30 t.r.; 23: 30 v.l.; 2 Th 3: 6.—W. ἵνα foll. (s. ἵνα II 1aδ) 2 Th 3: 12. παρήγγειλεν αὐτοῖς ἵνα μηδὲν αἴρωσιν *he forbade them to take anything* Mk 6: 8. OSchmitz, TW V 759-62. M-M.*

παράγγελμα, ατος, τό (Aeschyl., Thu.+; Dit., Syll.³ 985, 12; 34; PAmh. 50, 5; PLond. 904, 36; PGM 4, 749; 1 Km 22: 14; Philo; Jos., Ant. 16, 43, C. Ap. 1, 178) *order, direction, instruction, precept*, esp. of the edict of a ruler (Jos., Bell. 6, 383) 1 Cl 13: 3 (w. ἐντολή). ποιεῖν τὰ τοῦ Χριστοῦ π. *follow the precepts of Christ* 49: 1. M-M.*

παραγίνομαι impf. 3 pl. παρεγίνοντο; 2 aor. παρεγενόμην; plpf. 3 sing. παραγεγόνει (Hom.+; inscr., pap., LXX, Ep. Arist., Philo, Joseph.).

1. *come, arrive, be present* (Aristoph., Hdt.+; inscr., pap., LXX) foll. by εἰς and the acc. of place (Hdt.; POxy. 743, 23 [2 вс]; PRyl. 232, 3; Ex 16: 35; Josh 24: 11; Philo, Mos. 1, 86) Mt 2: 1; J 8: 2; Ac 9: 26; 13: 14 (w. ἀπὸ τ. Πέργης; cf. Jos., Ant. 18, 110); 15: 4. Also ἐν w. the dat. of place (POxy. 1185, 26; BGU 286, 6) Ac 9: 26 v.l.; ITr 1: 1. Foll. by ἐπί τινα *come against someone*, mostly w. hostile purpose (Thu. 2, 95, 3; 2 Macc 4: 34; 8: 16; 11: 2; 12: 6; 15: 24.—ἐπί III 1aε) Lk 22: 52. Foll. by πρός τινα (Lucian, Philops. 6; Zen.-P. 59 214, 5 [254 вс] πρὸς ἡμᾶς; PSI 341, 4; PEleph. 9, 4; Ex 2: 18; Judg 8: 15; Jos., Ant. 6, 131) Lk 7: 4, 20; 8: 19; 22: 52 v.l.; Ac 20: 18. φίλος παρεγένετο ἐξ ὁδοῦ πρός με Lk 11: 6 (παραγίνεσθαι ἐκ as Dit., Syll.³ 663, 4; PMagd. 1, 10 [III вс]; Gen 35: 9; 1 Macc 5: 14; Jos., Vi. 248 ἐκ τῆς ὁδοῦ παρεγενόμην). παραγίνεται ὁ Ἰησοῦς ἀπὸ τῆς Γαλιλαίας ἐπὶ τὸν Ἰορδάνην πρὸς τὸν Ἰωάννην Mt 3: 13 (π. ἐπί w. acc. of place as Dit., Syll.³ 474, 10; 633, 85; Sb 3925, 4; Jdth 6: 11; 14: 13; Bel 15). π. ἀπὸ τ. ἀληθείας *proceed from the truth* Papias 2: 3. Absol. Mk 14: 43; Lk 14: 21; 19: 16; J 3: 23; Ac 21f, 25; 9: 39; 10: 33; 11: 23; 14: 27; 17: 10; 18: 27; 21: 18; 23: 16, 35; 24: 17, 24; 25: 7; 28: 21; 1 Cor 16: 3; 1 Cl 12: 6; IRo 6: 2; Hs 9, 5, 7. Somet. the coming has rather the sense

2. *appear, make a public appearance*, of J. the Baptist Mt 3: 1. Of Jesus, w. inf. of purpose foll. (cf. 1 Macc 4: 46) Lk 12: 51. Χριστὸς παραγενόμενος ἀρχιερεύς Hb 9: 11.

3. *stand by, come to the aid of* (trag.; Thu. 3, 54, 4; Pla., Rep. 2 p. 368в) οὐδείς μοι παρεγένετο 2 Ti 4: 16. M-M.*

παράγω impf. παρῆγον (Pind., Hdt.+; inscr., pap., LXX, Joseph.).

1. trans.—a. act. (BGU 1139, 19 [5 вс]; 1 Km 16: 9f; Jos., Ant. 5, 97; 20, 200) *bring in, introduce* παράγουσι φόβους ἀνθρωπίνους 2 Cl 10: 3 (s. φόβος 2aα).

b. pass. *be brought past, pass away, disappear* (cf. 2 Esdr [Ezra] 9: 2 παρήχθη σπέρμα τὸ ἅγιον ἡ σκοτία παράγεται *the darkness is passing away* 1 J 2: 8; cf. vs. 17.

2. intr.—a. *pass by*—α. lit. (Polyb. 5, 18, 4; Appian, Bell. Civ. 2, 62 §259 θεοῦ παράγοντος=as though a god passed by [and struck Labienus with blindness]; Coll. Alex. Lyr. Adesp. 37, 25 ἐὰν . . . μνήματα κωφὰ παράγῃς; Menand., Epitr. 188; 194, Dyscol. 556 al.; CIG 2129, 2; PTebt. 17, 4; 2 Km 15: 18; Ps 128: 8; 3 Macc 6: 16) Mt 20: 30; Mk 2: 14; 15: 21; J 9: 1. π. παρὰ τὴν θάλασσαν *pass by along the lake* Mk 1: 16. Cf. ELohmeyer, 'Und Jesus ging vorüber': NThT 23, '34, 206-24.—β. fig. *pass away* (Ps 143: 4) 1 Cor 7: 31.

b. *go away* παρῆγεν οὕτως *so he went away* J 8: 59 t.r. (for the t.r., the παράγων of 9: 1 [s. 2aα above] belongs here). ἐκεῖθεν Mt 9: 9, 27. M-M.*

παραδειγματίζω 1 aor. inf. παραδειγματίσαι (Polyb. et al.; LXX. Mostly= 'make a public example of' by punishment [Polyb. 2, 60, 7; 29, 19, 5; LXX]; then also without the idea of punishment) *expose, make an example of* (Plut., Mor. 520b) τινά *someone* Mt 1: 19 t.r. (s. δειγματίζω); *hold up to contempt* w. ἀνασταυροῦν Hb 6: 6. M-M.*

παράδεισος, ου, ὁ (Old Persian pairidaêza='enclosure'; Hebr. פַּרְדֵּס. In Gk. since X.; inscr., pap., LXX, En., Philo; Jos., Bell. 4, 467, Ant. 7, 347; 12, 233; Sib. Or.) in our lit. not of any formal garden or park, but only *paradise*.
1. of the garden of Eden (Gen 2f; Philo; Jos., Ant. 1, 37; Sib. Or. 1, 24; 26; 30), lit. Dg 12: 3, and in the same connection fig., of those who love God, οἱ γενόμενοι παράδεισος τρυφῆς, in so far as they allow fruit-laden trees to grow up within them 12: 1 (cf. PsSol 14: 3; Gen 3: 24).
2. a place of blessedness above the earth (ὁ παράδεισος τῆς δικαιοσύνης appears as such En. 32, 3; cf. 20, 7; Test. Levi 18: 10; Sib. Or. fgm. 3, 48 and other passages in the OT Pseudepigrapha not preserved in Gk., as well as other sources in the lit. given below.—Dssm., B 146 [BS 148]) Lk 23: 43 (JPWeisengoff, Eccl. Review 103, '40, 163-7). More fully ὁ π. τοῦ θεοῦ (Gen 13: 10; Ez 28: 13; 31: 8; PGM 4, 3027 ἐν τῷ ἁγίῳ ἑαυτοῦ [= τ. θεοῦ] παραδείσῳ) Rv 2: 7. ἁρπάζεσθαι εἰς τὸν π. *be caught up into Paradise* 2 Cor 12: 4.—S. on οὐρανός 1e and τρίτος 1. Further, Bousset, Rel.³ 282ff; 488ff; PVolz, D. Eschatologie der jüd. Gemeinde im ntl. Zeitalter '34, 417f; Billerb. IV 1118-65; Windisch on 2 Cor 12: 4; AWabnitz, Le Paradis du Hadès: Rev. de Théol. et des Quest. rel. 19, '10, 328-31; 410-14; 20, '11, 130-8; JoachJeremias, TW V 763-71. M-M.*

παραδέχομαι fut. παραδέξομαι; 1 aor. παρεδεξάμην, pass. παρεδέχθην; 1 fut. pass. παραδεχθήσομαι (Hom. +; inscr., pap., LXX, En., Ep. Arist., Philo, Joseph.) *accept, receive.*
1. w. a thing as obj. in the acc. *accept, acknowledge* (*as correct*) (Epict. 3, 12, 15; BGU 1119, 54 [I AD] τὴν συντίμησιν; PRyl. 229, 16; PFay. 125, 10; Ex 23: 1; 3 Macc 7: 12) τὸν λόγον Mk 4: 20 (Diocles 112 p. 163, 18 παραδ. τὸν λόγον; Plut., Mor. 47ε; Philo, Leg. All. 3, 199). ἔθη Ac 16: 21. μαρτυρίαν 22: 18. κατηγορίαν 1 Ti 5: 19 (Sextus 259 διαβολὰς κατὰ φιλοσόφου μὴ παραδέχου). *Receive false teachings* IEph 9: 1. (Opp. παραιτεῖσθαι) τὰ κτισθέντα Dg 4: 2.
2. w. a pers. as obj. in the acc. (POxy. 492, 8; 14; 1676, 28; BGU 27: 10; Jos., C. Ap. 2, 256; 258) *receive, accept* heretics ISm 4: 1. θεὸν τὸν παραδεχόμενον ἡμᾶς (w. καλεῖν) 2 Cl 16: 1. Pass. (2 Macc 4: 22 Cod. V) Ac 15: 4. *Take back* a wife who was dismissed for adultery Hm 4, 1, 8a; pass. 4, 1, 7; 8b. Of a citizen who wishes to return to his home city after living in a strange land, pass. s 1: 5.— Corresp. to רָצָה *receive favorably*= love (Pr 3: 12) Hb 12: 6; 1 Cl 56: 4. M-M.*

παραδιατριβή, ῆς, ἡ *useless occupation* pl. 1 Ti 6: 5 t.r. M-M.*

παραδίδωμι (Pind., Hdt.+; inscr., pap., LXX, En., Ep. Arist., Philo, Joseph., Test. 12 Patr.) pres. subj. 3 sing. παραδιδῷ and παραδιδοῖ 1 Cor 15: 24 (Bl-D. §95, 2; Mlt.-H. 204); impf. 3 sing. παρεδίδου Ac 8: 3; 1 Pt 2: 23,

pl. παρεδίδουν Ac 16: 4 v.l.; 27: 1 and παρεδίδοσαν 16: 4 (Bl-D. §94, 1 app.; Mlt.-H. 202); fut. παραδώσω; 1 aor. παρέδωκα; 2 aor. indic. παρέδοσαν Lk 1: 2; 2 aor. subj. 3 sing. παραδῷ and παραδοῖ Mk 4: 29; 14: 10, 11; J 13: 2 (Bl-D. §95, 2; Mlt.-H. 210f), imper. παράδος, ptc. παραδούς; pf. παραδέδωκα, ptc. παραδεδωκώς Ac 15: 26; plpf. 3 pl. παραδεδώκεισαν Mk 15: 10 (on the absence of augment cf. Bl-D. §66, 1; Mlt.-H. 190). Pass.; impf. 3 sing. παρεδίδετο 1 Cor 11: 23b (-δίδοτο is also attested; Bl-D. §94, 1; Mlt.-H. 206), perf. 3 sing. παραδέδοται Lk 4: 6, ptc. παραδεδομένος Ac 14: 26; 1 aor. παρεδόθην; 1 fut. παραδοθήσομαι.

1. *hand over, give (over), deliver, entrust*—**a.** a thing τινί τι (Jos., Ant. 4, 83) τάλαντά μοι Mt 25: 20, 22. αὐτοῖς τὰ ὑπάρχοντα αὐτοῦ vs. 14. ὑμῖν τὴν γῆν 1 Cl 12: 5. τινὶ τὴν κτίσιν Hv 3, 4, 1; λίθους s 9, 7, 1; ἀμπελῶνα s 5, 6, 2. Also in the sense *give back, restore, give up* (X., Hell. 2, 3, 7 τινί τι) αὐτῷ τὴν παρακαταθήκην ἣν ἔλαβον Hm 3: 2.—Pass. w. the thing easily supplied fr. the context ἐμοὶ παραδέδοται Lk 4: 6.—παρέδωκεν τὸ πνεῦμα J 19: 30 needs no dat. *he gave up his spirit* voluntarily. ἄνθρωποι παραδεδωκότες τὰς ψυχὰς αὐτῶν ὑπὲρ τοῦ ὀνόματος τοῦ κυρίου *men who have risked* (*pledged* Field, Notes 124) *their lives for the name of the Lord* Ac 15: 26. καὶ ἐὰν παραδῶ τὸ σῶμά μου ἵνα καυθήσομαι *and if I give up my body to be burned* 1 Cor 13: 3 (Maximus Tyr. 1, 9i τῇ Αἴτνῃ αὐτοῦ παραδοὺς σῶμα; Syntipas p. 60, 11 πυρὶ σεαυτὴν παραδίδως). ὅταν παραδιδοῖ τ. βασιλείαν τῷ θεῷ *when he* (i.e. Christ) *delivers the kingship to God* 15: 24.

b. *hand over, turn over, give up* a person (as a t.t. of police and courts 'hand over into (the) custody (of)' Dit., Or. 669, 15; PHib. 92, 11; 17; PLille 3, 59 [both III BC]; PTebt. 38, 6 [II BC] al.) τινά *someone* Mt 10: 19; 24: 10; 27: 18; Mk 13: 11; Ac 3: 13. Pass. Mt 4: 12; Mk 1: 14; Lk 21: 16. τινά τινι Mt 5: 25 (fr. one official to another, as UPZ 124, 19f [II BC]); 18: 34; 27: 2; Mk 10: 33b; cf. 15: 1; Lk 12: 58; 20: 20; J 18: 30, 35; Ac 27: 1; 28: 16 v.l.; Hs 7: 5; 9, 10, 6; Pass. Lk 18: 32; J 18: 36; Hv 5: 3f; m 4, 4, 3; s 6, 3, 6b; 9, 11, 2; 9, 13, 9; 9, 20, 4; 9, 21, 4. τὸν Ἰησοῦν παρέδωκεν τῷ θελήματι αὐτῶν Lk 23: 25.—Esp. of the betrayal of Jesus by Judas, w. acc. and dat. ἐγὼ ὑμῖν παραδώσω αὐτόν Mt 26: 15. Cf. Mk 14: 10; Lk 22: 4, 6; J 19: 11. Pass. Mt 20: 18; Mk 10: 33a. Without a dat. Mt 10: 4; 26: 16, 21, 23; Mk 3: 19; 14: 11, 18; Lk 22: 48; J 6: 64, 71; 12: 4; 13: 21. Pass. Mt 26: 24; Mk 14: 21; Lk 22: 22; 1 Cor 11: 23b (to be sure, it is not certain that when Paul uses such terms as 'handing over', 'delivering up', 'arrest' [so clearly Posidon.: 87 fgm. 36, 50 Jac. παραδοθείς] he is thinking of the betrayal by Judas; cf. Ac 3: 13 παρεδώκατε). ὁ παραδιδοὺς αὐτόν (παραδιδούς με) *his* (*my*) *betrayer* Mt 26: 25, 46, 48; Mk 14: 42, 44; Lk 22: 21; J 13: 11; 18: 2, 5. Cf. Mt 27: 3, 4; J 21: 20.—τινὰ εἰς χεῖρας τινος *deliver someone into someone's hands* (a Semitic construction, but paralleled in Lat., cf. Livy 26, 12, 11; Dt 1: 27; Jer 33: 24; Jdth 6: 10; 1 Macc 4: 30; 1 Esdr 1: 50. Pass. Jer 39: 4, 36, 43; Sir 11: 6; Da 11: 11; cf. Jos., Ant. 2, 20) Ac 21: 11. Pass. Mt 17: 22; 26: 45; Mk 9: 31; 14: 41; Lk 9: 44; 24: 7 (NPerrin, JoachJeremias-Festschr., '70, 204-12); Ac 28: 17. ἡ γῆ παραδοθήσεται εἰς χεῖρας αὐτοῦ D 16: 4b. Also ἐν χειρί τινος (Judg 7: 9; 2 Esdr [Ezra] 9: 7; cf. 2 Ch 36: 17; 1 Macc 5: 50) 1 Cl 55: 5b.—W. indication of the goal, or of the purpose for which someone is handed over: in the inf. (Jos., Bell. 1, 655) παραδιδόναι τινά τινι φυλάσσειν αὐτόν *hand someone over to someone to guard him* (X., An. 4, 6, 1) Ac 12: 4. W. local εἰς (Dit., Or. 669, 15 εἰς τὸ πρακτόρειόν τινας παρέδοσαν; PGiess. 84 II, 18 [II AD] εἰς τ. φυλακήν): εἰς συνέδρια *hand over to the local courts* Mt 10: 17; Mk 13: 9. εἰς τὰς συναγωγὰς καὶ φυλακάς *hand someone over to the synagogues and prisons* Lk 21: 12. εἰς φυλακήν *put in prison* Ac 8: 3; cf. 22: 4. Also εἰς δεσμωτήριον (of a place of punishment outside the present visible world: cf. PGM 4, 1245ff ἔξελθε, δαῖμον, . . . παραδίδωμί σε εἰς τὸ μέλαν χάος ἐν ταῖς ἀπωλείαις) Hs 9, 28, 7. ἑαυτοὺς εἰς δεσμά *give oneself up to imprisonment* 1 Cl 55: 2a. W. final εἰς (En. 97, 10 εἰς κατάραν μεγάλην παρα[δο]θή-σεσθε): ἑαυτοὺς εἰς δουλείαν *give oneself up to slavery* 55: 2b. εἰς τὸ σταυρωθῆναι *hand over to be crucified* Mt 26: 2. εἰς τὸ ἐμπαῖξαι κτλ. 20: 19. εἰς θλῖψιν 24: 9. εἰς κρίμα θανάτου Lk 24: 20. εἰς κρίσιν 2 Pt 2: 4. εἰς θάνατον *hand over to death* (POxy. 471, 107 [II AD]; Mt 10: 21 (Joach Jeremias, Unknown Sayings of Jesus, tr. Fuller '57, 68 n. 3); Mk 13: 12; Hm 12, 1, 2f; pass.: ending of Mk in the Freer ms. 9; 2 Cor 4: 11; 1 Cl 16: 13 (Is 53: 12); B 12: 2; Hs 9, 23, 5. π. ἑαυτὸν εἰς θάνατον *give oneself up to death* 1 Cl 55: 1; fig. *hand oneself over to death* Hs 6, 5, 4. εἰς θλῖψιν θανάτου παραδίδοσθαι *be handed over to the affliction of death* B 12: 5. π. τὴν σάρκα εἰς καταφθοράν *give up his flesh to corruption* 5: 1.—ἵνα stands for final εἰς: τὸν Ἰησοῦν παρέδωκεν ἵνα σταυρωθῇ *he handed Jesus over to be crucified* Mt 27: 26; Mk 15: 15; cf. J 19: 16.—π. alone w. the mng. *hand over to suffering, death, punishment,* esp. in relation to Christ: κύριος παρέδωκεν αὐτὸν ὑπὲρ τῶν ἁμαρτιῶν ἡμῶν 1 Cl 16: 7 (cf. Is 53: 6). —Ro 8: 32. Pass. 4: 25; cf. B 16: 5. π. ἑαυτὸν ὑπέρ τινος Gal 2: 20; Eph 5: 25. παρέδωκεν ἑαυτὸν ὑπὲρ ἡμῶν προσφορὰν καὶ θυσίαν τῷ θεῷ *he gave himself to God for us as a sacrifice and an offering* vs. 2.—π. τινὰ τῷ σατανᾷ εἰς ὄλεθρον τῆς σαρκός *hand someone over to Satan for the destruction of his physical body* 1 Cor 5: 5. οὓς παρέδωκα τῷ σατανᾷ, ἵνα *whom I have turned over to Satan, in order that* 1 Ti 1: 20 (cf. the exorcism PGM 5, 334ff νεκυδαίμων, . . . παραδίδωμί σοι τὸν δεῖνα, ὅπως . . . and s. the lit. s.v. ὄλεθρος; also ChBruston, L'abandon du pécheur à Satan: Rev. de Théol. et des Quest. rel. 21, '12, 450–8; KLatte, Heiliges Recht '20; LBrun, Segen u. Fluch im Urchr. '32, 106ff). The angel of repentance says: ἐμοὶ παραδίδονται εἰς ἀγαθὴν παιδείαν *they are turned over to me for good instruction* Hs 6, 3, 6a (Demetr. Phaler. [IV/III BC] fgm. 164 FWehrli '49: Demosthenes παραδίδωσι ἑαυτὸν τῷ Ἀνδρονίκῳ to be initiated into dramatic art).—ἑαυτοὺς παρέδωκαν τῇ ἀσελγείᾳ *they gave themselves over to debauchery* Eph 4: 19. ταῖς ἐπιθυμίαις τ. αἰῶνος τούτου Hs 6, 2, 3. ταῖς τρυφαῖς καὶ ἀπάταις 6, 2, 4. παρεδώκατε ἑαυτοὺς εἰς τὰς ἀκηδίας Hv 3, 11, 3 (s. ἀκηδία). Of a God who punishes evil-doers: παρέδωκεν αὐτοὺς εἰς ἀκαθαρσίαν *he abandoned them to impurity* Ro 1: 24 (for the thought cf. IQH 2, 16–19. See also EKlostermann, ZNW 32, '33, 1–6 [retribution]). εἰς πάθη ἀτιμίας *to disgraceful passions* vs. 26. εἰς ἀδόκιμον νοῦν vs. 28. παρέδωκεν αὐτοὺς λατρεύειν τῇ στρατιᾷ τοῦ οὐρανοῦ Ac 7: 42. God, the All-Gracious One, is the subject of the extraordinary (s. lit. on διδαχή 2) expression εἰς ὃν παρεδόθητε τύπον διδαχῆς = τῷ τύπῳ δ. εἰς ὃν π. (obedient) *to the form of teaching, for the learning of which you were given over* i.e. by God Ro 6: 17 (cf. the inscr. fr. Transjordania in Nabatean times NGG Phil.-hist. Kl. Fachgr. V n.s. I, 1, '36, p. 3, 1 Abedrapsas thanks his paternal god: παρεδόθην εἰς μάθησιν τέχνης = 'I was apprenticed to learn a trade'. AFridrichsen, Con. Neot. 7, '42, 6–8; FWBeare, NTS 5, '59, 206–10; UBorse, BZ 12, '68, 95–103; FWDanker, FWGingrich-Festschr., '72, 94).

2. *give over, commend, commit* w. dat. (cf. PFlor. 309, 5 σιωπῇ παραδ. 'hand over to forgetfulness') παραδί-

δοσθαι τῇ χάριτι τοῦ κυρίου ὑπό τινος *be commended by someone to the grace of the Lord* Ac 15: 40. Ἀντιόχεια, ὅθεν ἦσαν παραδεδομένοι τῇ χάριτι τοῦ θεοῦ εἰς τὸ ἔργον *from which* (city they had gone out) *commended to the grace of God for the work* 14: 26.—παρεδίδου τῷ κρίνοντι *he committed his cause to the one who judges* 1 Pt 2: 23.

3. of oral or written tradition *hand down, pass on, transmit, relate, teach* (Theognis 1, 28f passes on what he himself learned as παῖς, ἀπὸ τῶν ἀγαθῶν; Pla., Phil. 16c, Ep. 12 p. 359D μῦθον; Demosth. 23, 65; Polyb. 7, 1, 1; 10, 28, 3; Diod. S. 12, 13, 2 π. τινί τι pass on someth. to future generations εἰς ἅπαντα τὸν αἰῶνα; Plut., Nic. 1, 5; Herm. Wr. 13, 15; Jos., C. Ap. 1, 60 τὴν κατὰ νόμους παραδεδομένην εὐσέβειαν; PMagd. 33, 5 of a report to the police concerning the facts in a case) Lk 1: 2. παραδόσεις Mk 7: 13 (of the tradition of the Pharisees, as Jos., Ant. 13, 297; cf. the rabbinic term מָסַר); 1 Cor 11: 2. ἔθη Ac 6: 14. ὁ ἡμῖν παραδοθεὶς λόγος *the teaching handed down to us* Pol 7: 2. ἡ παραδοθεῖσα αὐτοῖς ἁγία ἐντολή 2 Pt 2: 21. ἡ παραδοθεῖσα τοῖς ἁγίοις πίστις Jd 3. τὰ παραδοθέντα (Philo, Fuga 200) Dg 11: 1. παρεδίδοσαν αὐτοῖς φυλάσσειν τὰ δόγματα *they handed down to them the decisions to observe* Ac 16: 4.—(In contrast to παραλαμβάνειν [the same contrast in Diod. S. 1, 91, 4; 3, 65, 6; 5, 2, 3; PHermopol. 119 III, 22; BGU 1018, 24; PThéad. 8, 25]) *pass on* 1 Cor 11: 23a; 15: 3; Epil Mosq 1. W. a connotation of wonder and mystery (of mysteries and ceremonies: Theo Smyrn., Expos. Rer. Math. p. 14 Hiller τελετὰς παραδιδόναι; Diod. S. 5, 48, 4 μυστηρίων τελετὴ παραδοθεῖσα; Strabo 10, 3, 7; Wsd 14: 15 μυστήρια καὶ τελετάς. Cf. Herm. Wr. 13, 1 παλιγγενεσίαν; PGM 4, 475) πάντα (πᾶς 2aδ) μοι παρεδόθη ὑπό τ. πατρός μου Mt 11: 27; Lk 10: 22 (cf. Herm. Wr. 1, 32 πάτερ. . .παρέδωκας αὐτῷ [ὁ σὸς ἄνθρωπος is meant] τὴν πᾶσαν ἐξουσίαν; in Vett. Val. 221, 23 astrology is ὑπὸ θεοῦ παραδεδομένη τ. ἀνθρώποις.—For lit. on the saying of Jesus s. under υἱός 2b).—S. on παράδοσις, end.

4. *allow, permit* (Hdt. 5, 67; 7, 18 [subj. ὁ θεός]; X., An. 6, 6, 34 [οἱ θεοί]; Isocr. 5, 118 [οἱ καιροί]; Polyb. 22, 24, 9 τῆς ὥρας παραδιδούσης) ὅταν παραδοῖ ὁ καρπός *when the* (condition of the) *crop permits* Mk 4: 29.—On the whole word: WPopkes, Christus Traditus, '67. M-M. **

παράδοξος, ον (X., Pla.+; inscr., pap., LXX, Ep. Arist. 175; Philo; Jos., C. Ap. 1, 53 al. Loanw. in rabb.) *contrary to opinion* or *expectation, strange, wonderful, remarkable.* κατάστασις τῆς πολιτείας Dg 5: 4. σημεῖον 1 Cl 25: 1. Subst. in pl. παράδοξα *wonderful things* (Lucian, Somn. 14; Aelian, V.H. 13, 33; Celsus 1, 6; Philo, Mos. 1, 212; Jos., Bell. 4, 238) Lk 5: 26.—OWeinreich, Antike Heilungswunder '09, 198f. M-M.*

παράδοσις, εως, ἡ (Thu.+; inscr., pap., LXX, Philo, Joseph.) *handing down* or *over.*

1. = *betrayal, arrest* (Diod. S. 11, 33, 4) UGosp 29.—**2.** *tradition,* of teachings, commandments, narratives et al., first in the act. sense (Pla., Leg. 7 p. 803A; Ps.-Pla., Def. 416; Epict. 2, 23, 40; Philo, Ebr. 120; Jos., Vi. 361), but in our lit. only pass., of that which is handed down (Dit., Syll.³ 704E, 12 εἰσαγαγὼν τὴν τῶν μυστηρίων παράδοσιν; Herm. Wr. 13, 22b τῆς παλιγγενεσίας τὴν παράδοσιν): of the tradition preserved by the scribes and Pharisees. They themselves called it ἡ παράδοσις τῶν πρεσβυτέρων Mt 15: 2; Mk 7: 5; cf. vs. 3. In conversation w. them Jesus calls it παράδοσις ὑμῶν Mt 15: 3, 6; Mk 7: 9, 13 or even ἡ παράδοσις τῶν ἀνθρώπων vs. 8. Paul uses the latter term to characterize the Colossian heresy

Col 2: 8. In looking back upon his Jewish past he calls himself a ζηλωτὴς τῶν πατρικῶν παραδόσεων Gal 1: 14 (cf. Jos., Ant. 13, 297 τὰ ἐκ παραδόσεως τῶν πατέρων; 408. By this is meant the tradition of the rabbis ['fathers'; cf. Pirqe Aboth], accepted by the Pharisees but rejected by the Sadducees). Of Christian teaching ὁ τῆς π. ἡμῶν κανών 1 Cl 7: 2. Of Paul's teaching 2 Th 3: 6 (used w. παραλαμβάνειν). ἀποστόλων π. Dg 11: 6. Pl. of individual teachings 1 Cor 11: 2 (w. παραδιδόναι); 2 Th 2: 15 (cf. ASeeberg, D. Katechismus d. Urchristenheit '03, 1ff; 41f).—WGKümmel, Jesus u. d. jüd. Traditionsgedanke: ZNW 33, '34, 105–30; ADeneffe, D. Traditionsbegriff '31, 1ff; JRanft, D. Ursprung des kath. Traditionsprinzips '31; LGoppelt, Tradition nach Paulus, Kerygma u. Dogma 4, '58, 213–33; BGerhardsson, Memory and Manuscript, etc. '61 (rabb. Judaism and Early Christianity); PFannon, The Infl. of Trad. in St. Paul, TU 102, '68, 292–307. M-M.*

παραζηλόω fut. παραζηλώσω; 1 aor. παρεζήλωσα (Hesychius= παροξύνω) *provoke to jealousy, make jealous* (LXX) τινὰ ἐπί τινι *someone of someone* Ro 10: 19 (Dt 32: 21). τινά *someone* (3 Km 14: 22; Sir 30: 3) 11: 11. τὴν σάρκα (*brothers in the*) *flesh* vs. 14. It is this mng., rather than a more general one such as *make angry*, that we have 1 Cor 10: 22 ἢ παραζηλοῦμεν τ. κύριον or *shall we provoke the Lord to jealousy?* i.e., by being untrue to him and turning to demons. M-M.*

παραθαλάσσιος, ία (Bl-D. §59, 1; Mlt.-H. 158), ον (Hdt.+; inscr., LXX.—Bl-D. §123, 1; Mlt.-H. 320) (*located*) *by the sea* or *lake* of places (Hdt. 7, 109; Polyb. 1, 20, 6; 22, 11, 4; Ezk 25: 9; 1 Macc 7: 1; 11: 8; 2 Macc 8: 11; Jos., Bell. 1, 257) Καφαρναούμ ἡ παραθαλασσία Mt 4: 13; cf. Lk 4: 31 D. M-M.*

παραθαρσύνω (Thu. 4, 115, 1; Diod. S. 14, 115, 3; Plut., Fab. 17, 7, Crass. 27, 1; Herodian 3, 12, 4; 4 Macc 13: 8; Jos., Ant. 12, 290; 14, 440. The later Attic wr. have παραθαρρύνω) *encourage, embolden*, w. acc. of the pers. to be encouraged (X., An. 3, 1, 39; 4 Macc 13: 8; Jos., Ant. 12, 305) AP 2: 5.*

παραθεωρέω (X.+) *overlook, leave unnoticed, neglect* (so Hero Alex. I p. 410, 5; Diod. S. 40, 5; Dionys. Hal., De Isae. 18; Sb 1161, 38f [57/6 BC]= Wilcken, Chrest. 70, 24; BGU 1786, 5 [50 BC]) τινά *someone* pass. Ac 6: 1. M-M.*

παραθήκη, ης, ἡ (Hdt.+; Plato Comicus [V/IV BC], fgm. 158 K.; Polyb. 33, 6, 4; 9; Sext. Emp., Hyp. 3, 25, 189; Vett. Val. 39, 16; 67, 24; inscr., pap., LXX; Ps.-Phoc. 135.—Instead of this Attic prose has παρακαταθήκη; cf. Phryn. p. 312 Lob.; Nägeli 27) *deposit, property entrusted to another* fig. (so as early as Hdt. 9, 45 ἔπεα; also Sextus 21, the soul), in our lit. only in the pastorals and always used w. φυλάσσειν, of the spiritual heritage entrusted to the orthodox Christian. τὴν π. φυλάσσειν *guard what has been entrusted* (acc. to CSpicq, S. Paul et la loi des dépôts: RB 40, '31, 481–502, a legal t.t.) 1 Ti 6: 20; 2 Ti 1: 12, 14 (in the first and last passages the t.r. has παρακαταθήκη, q.v.). JRanft, art. 'Depositum' in RAC III, 778–84; RLeonhard, art. 'Depositum', Pauly-W. V 1, 233–6; WBarclay, ET 69, '58, 324–7. M-M.*

παράθου, παραθῶσιν s. παρατίθημι.

παραινέω impf. παρῄνουν (Pind., Hdt.+; inscr., pap., LXX, Philo, Joseph.; Test. Gad 6: 1) *advise, recommend, urge* τινά (instead of the class. dat.; cf. Bl-D. §152, 3; Rob. 475; and s. Ps.-Callisth. 3, 4, 16 παρῄνουν τὸν Ἀλέξανδρον οἱ Μακεδόνες; IG I² 7, 51, 11 [III AD] al.) w. inf. foll. (Jos., Bell. 5, 87f, Ant. 1, 201.—Bl-D. §392, 1d;

409, 5; Rdm.² 121; 226) Ac 27: 22. Abs. (Dit., Syll.³ 89, 40) w. direct disc. foll. IMg 6: 1; foll. by λέγων αὐτοῖς and direct disc. Ac 27: 9 (on the impf. παρῄνει cf. Bl-D. §328). τινί τι *recommend someth. to someone* (Oenomaus in Euseb., Pr. Ev. 5, 25, 1; Philo, Poster. Cai. 13) ISm 4: 1. τί (Chio, Ep. 16, 1 παρῄνουν ταῦτα) Lk 3: 18 D.—KWeidinger, Die Haustafeln: Ein Stück urchristlicher Paränese, '28. M-M.*

παραιτέομαι mid. dep.; imper. παραιτοῦ; impf. παρῃτούμην; 1 aor. παρῃτησάμην; pf. pass. ptc. παρῃτημένος (Pind., Hdt.+; inscr., pap., LXX; En. 106, 7; Ep. Arist., Philo, Joseph., Test. 12 Patr.).
1. *ask for, request* (for oneself), also in the sense *intercede for* τινά *someone* (Polyb. 4, 51, 1; Plut., Demetr. 9, 8, Thes. 19, 9. Cf. BGU 625, 7) δέσμιον Mk 15: 6 (Appian, Bell. Civ. 2, 24 §91 Σκαῦρον τοῦ πλήθους παραιτουμένου= the crowd interceded for Scaurus).—If π. is used in connection w. an invitation, it takes on the mng. *excuse* (Polyb. 5, 27, 3) pass. ἔχε με παρῃτημένον *consider me excused* (cf. ἔχω I 5) Lk 14: 18b, 19; as a reflexive *excuse oneself* (Jos., Ant. 7, 175; 12, 197) vs. 18a (for the various excuses used for declining an invitation, cf. Aristot., fgm. 554 [VRose 1886]=Paus. Att., τ. 37: 1: my wife is sick; 2: the ship is not ready to sail).
2. *decline* (Diod. S. 13, 80, 2 abs.)—a. w. acc. of the pers. *reject, refuse someone* or *refuse to do someth. to someone* (Ep. Arist. 184; Philo, Det. Pot. Ins. 38; Jos., Ant. 7, 167) Hb 12: 25a, b (to hear someone). νεωτέρας χήρας παραιτοῦ *refuse* (*to enroll*) *widows who are younger* (than 60 years of age), when they apply for help 1 Ti 5: 11. αἱρετικὸν ἄνθρωπον παραιτοῦ Tit 3: 10; but here perh. the word has the sense *discharge, dismiss, drive out* (cf. Diog. L. 6, 82 οἰκέτην; Plut., Mor. 206A γυναῖκα).
b. w. acc. of the thing *reject, avoid* (Pind., Nem. 10, 30 χάριν; Epict. 2, 16, 42; PLond. 1231, 3 [II AD]; Philo, Poster. Cai. 2 τὴν Ἐπικούρειον ἀσέβειαν; Jos., Ant. 3, 212; 5, 237) Dg 4: 2; 6: 10. γραώδεις μύθους παραιτοῦ 1 Ti 4: 7. ζητήσεις παραιτοῦ 2 Ti 2: 23 (cf. Herm. Wr. in Stob. I 277, 21 W.=p. 432, 20 Sc. τὰς πρὸς τοὺς πολλοὺς ὁμιλίας παραιτοῦ).—οὐ παραιτοῦμαι τὸ ἀποθανεῖν *I am not trying to escape death* Ac 25: 11 (cf. Jos., Vi. 141).
c. foll. by inf. w. the neg. μή (Thu. 5, 63, 3; cf. Bl-D. §429; Rob. 1094) παρῃτήσαντο μὴ προστεθῆναι αὐτοῖς λόγον *they begged that no further message be given them* Hb 12: 19 (μή is omitted in the v.l.). M-M.*

παρακαθέζομαι mid. dep.; 1 aor. pass. ptc. παρακαθεσθείς (Aristoph., Pla., X.+) *sit beside* (Jos., Ant. 8, 241) παρακαθεζόμενοι *as they sat beside* (him) MPol 8: 2. The aor. pass. w. reflexive mng. (as Jos., Ant. 6, 235) *have seated oneself beside, have taken one's place beside* ἣ καὶ παρακαθεσθεῖσα πρὸς τοὺς πόδας τοῦ κυρίου ἤκουεν τὸν λόγον αὐτοῦ *who, after she had taken her place at the Lord's feet, kept listening to what he said* Lk 10: 39. W. dat. of the pers. beside whom one sits down (Charito 3, 3, 17; Jos., Ant. 6, 235 αὐτῷ; 16, 50) GP 12: 53. M-M.*

παρακάθημαι (Aristoph., Thu.+; inscr., pap., LXX) *sit beside* τινί (so mostly; the acc. is rare) *sit beside someone* Hs 5, 1, 1; 6, 1, 2.*

παρακαθίζω (Pla.+, mostly in the mid., as Jos., Ant. 19, 264) in our lit. only in act. *sit down beside* τινί *someone* (Diod. S. 23, 9, 5; Plut., Mar. 17, 3, Cleom. 37, 16, Mor. p. 58D; Job 2: 13) Hv 5: 2. πρὸς τοὺς πόδας τινός Lk 10: 39 t.r.*

παρακαθίστημι (Isocr.+; inscr., pap.; 2 Macc 12: 3; Jos., Ant. 14, 438) *place* or *station beside* φύλακας Dg 2: 7

(cf. Diod. S. 4, 63, 3 φύλακας; Demosth. 4, 25; Plut., Fab. 7, 4 φυλακήν).*

παρακαλέω impf. παρεκάλουν; 1 aor. παρεκάλεσα. Pass.: pf. παρακέκλημαι; 1 aor. παρεκλήθην; 1 fut. παρακληθήσομαι (Aeschyl., Hdt.+; inscr., pap., LXX, Ep. Arist., Philo, Joseph., Test. 12 Patr.).

1. *call to one's side, summon*—a. τινά w. inf. foll., to indicate the purpose of the call; so perh. παρεκάλεσα ὑμᾶς ἰδεῖν *I have summoned you to see you* Ac 28: 20 (but s. 3 below).

b. *invite* τινά w. inf. foll. (this can be supplied fr. context) παρεκάλει αὐτὸν εἰσελθεῖν εἰς τὸν οἶκον Lk 8: 41. παρεκάλει αὐτόν (i.e. εἰσελθεῖν) 15: 28 (but s. 5 below). παρεκάλεσεν τὸν Φίλιππον καθίσαι Ac 8: 31 (cf. Jos., Ant. 12, 172). The content of the invitation follows in direct discourse 9: 38; introduced by λέγουσα 16: 15. Cf. ἀνὴρ Μακεδών τις ἦν παρακαλῶν αὐτὸν καὶ λέγων . . . βοήθησον ἡμῖν vs. 9. Pass., w. inf. foll. παρακληθέντες δειπνῆσαι *when you are invited to dine* Mt 20: 28 D= Agr 22.

c. *summon to one's aid, call upon for help* (Hdt.+) so esp. of God, upon whom one calls in time of need (Thu. 1, 118, 3; Pla., Leg. 2 p. 666в; 11 p. 917в; X., Hell. 2, 4, 17; Epict. 3, 21, 12; Jos., Ant. 6, 25; Dit., Syll.³ 1170, 30f in an account of a healing: περὶ τούτου παρεκάλεσα τὸν θεόν. Cf. the restoration in the pap. letter of Zoilus, servant of Serapis, in Dssm., LO 121, 11 [LAE 153, 4]; POxy. 1070, 8) τινά: τὸν πατέρα μου Mt 26: 53. ὑπὲρ τούτου τὸν κύριον παρεκάλεσα, ἵνα 2 Cor 12: 8.

2. *appeal to, urge, exhort, encourage* (X. et al.; LXX) w. acc. of the pers. Ac 16: 40; 2 Cor 10: 1; 1 Th 2: 12 (but s. 5 below); 5: 11; Hb 3: 13; ITr 12: 2; IRo 7: 2. The acc. is found in the immediate context Ac 20: 1; 1 Ti 5: 1 (but s. 5 below). Pass. 1 Cor 14: 31. τινὰ λόγῳ πολλῷ *someone with many words* Ac 20: 2; also τινὰ διὰ λόγου πολλοῦ 15: 32. τινὰ δι᾽ ὀλίγων γραμμάτων IPol 7: 3. W. acc. of the pers. and direct discourse 1 Cor 4: 16; 1 Th 5: 14; Hb 13: 22; 1 Pt 5: 1; direct discourse introduced by λέγων (Bl-D. §420) Ac 2: 40. W. acc. of the pers. and inf. foll. (Dit., Syll.³ 695, 43 [129 вс]) 11: 23; 27: 33f; Ro 12: 1 (EKäsemann, Gottesdienst im Alltag, '60 [Beih. ZNW], 165–71); 15: 30; 16: 17; 2 Cor 2: 8; 6: 1; Eph 4: 1; Phil 4: 2; Tit 2: 6; 1 Pt 2: 11 (ELohse, ZNW 45, '54, 68–89); Jd 3 (the acc. is found in the immediate context, as Philo, Poster Cai. 138); ITr 6: 1; IPhld 8: 2; IPol 1: 2a; Pol 9: 1 al. W. the inf. (acc. in the context), continued by καὶ ὅτι (cf. Bl-D. §397, 6; Rob. 1047) Ac 14: 22. W. acc. of the pers. and ἵνα foll. (PRyl. 229, 17 [38 AD]; Ep. Arist. 318; Jos., Ant. 14, 168.—Bl-D. §392, 1c; Rob. 1046) 1 Cor 1: 10; 16: 15f; 2 Cor 8: 6; 1 Th 4: 1 (π. w. ἐρωτάω as BGU 1141, 10; POxy. 294, 29) 2 Th 3: 12; Hm 12, 3, 2. The ἵνα-clause expresses not the content of the appeal, as in the pass. referred to above, but its aim: πάντας παρακαλεῖν, ἵνα σώζωνται IPol 1: 2b.—Without the acc. of the pers.: w. direct discourse foll. ὡς τοῦ θεοῦ παρακαλοῦντος δι᾽ ἡμῶν· δεόμεθα κτλ. *since God as it were makes his appeal through us: 'We beg' etc.* 2 Cor 5: 20; w. inf. foll. 1 Ti 2: 1. Abs. Ro 12: 8 (mng. 4 is also poss.); 2 Ti 4: 2; Tit 1: 9; Hb 10: 25; 1 Pt 5: 12 (w. ἐπιμαρτυρεῖν); B 19: 10.—W. acc. of the thing *impress upon someone, urge, exhort* πολλὰ ἕτερα Lk 3: 18. ταῦτα δίδασκε καὶ παρακάλει 1 Ti 6: 2. ταῦτα λάλει καὶ παρακάλει καὶ ἔλεγχε Tit 2: 15. In the case of several of the passages dealt with in this section, it is poss. that they would better be classed under

3. *request, implore, appeal to, entreat* (H. Gk.: Polyb., Diod. S., Epict., Plut., inscr., pap., LXX, Ep. Arist., Philo; Jos., Ant. 6, 143; 11, 338) w. acc. of the pers. Mt 8:

5; 18: 32; Mk 1: 40; 2 Cor 12: 18. πολλά *implore urgently* (4 Macc 10: 1) Mk 5: 23. τινὰ περί τινος *someone concerning someone* or *for someone* Phlm 10 (for the constr. w. περί cf. POxy. 1070, 8). Acc. w. direct discourse foll. (s. BGU 846, 10 παρακαλῶ σαι [= σε], μήτηρ· διαλλάγηθί μοι; PGiess. 12, 4), introduced w. λέγων: Mt 8: 31; 18: 29; Mk 5: 12; Lk 7: 4 (v.l. ἠρώτων). W. acc. of the pers. and inf. foll. (PTebt. 12, 21 [II вс]; 1 Macc 9: 35; Jos., Ant. 6, 25) Mk 5: 17; cf. Ac 19: 31. Pass. Ac 28: 14. W. acc. of the pers. (easily supplied fr. the context, if not expressed) and ὅπως foll. (Plut., Demetr. 38, 11; Dit., Syll.³ 563, 4; 577, 44f [200/199 вс]; UPZ 109, 9 [98 вс]; PFlor. 303, 3; 4 Macc 4: 11; Jos., Ant. 13, 76) Mt 8: 34 (v.l. ἵνα); Ac 25: 2; IEph 3: 2. W. acc. of the pers. and ἵνα foll. (Epict. 2, 7, 11; PRyl. 229, 17; Ep. Arist. 318.—Bl-D. §392, 1c; Rob. 1046) Mt 14: 36; Mk 5: 18; 6: 56; 7: 32; 8: 22; Lk 8: 31f; 2 Cor 5: 5. πολλά τινα, ἵνα *beg someone earnestly to* (cf. Test. Napht. 9: 1) Mk 5: 10; 1 Cor 16: 12. W. acc. of the pers. and μή w. subj. foll. IRo 4: 1. W. acc. and inf. foll. Ac 24: 4; pass. 13: 42. Foll. by the subst. inf. w. acc. (Bl-D. §400, 7; 409, 5; Rob. 1068; 1085) Ac 21: 12. παρεκάλεσα ὑμᾶς ἰδεῖν *I have requested to be permitted to see you* 28: 20 (but s. 1a above). Abs., but in such a way that the acc. is easily restored fr. the context Phlm 9.

4. *comfort, encourage, cheer up* (Plut., Otho 16, 2; Gen 37: 35; Ps 118: 50; Job 4: 3) w. acc. of the pers. (Sir 48: 24; Jos., Bell. 1, 667; Test. Reub. 4: 4) 2 Cor 1: 4b; 7: 6a; 1 Cl 59: 4; B 14: 9 (Is 61: 2); Hm 8: 10. παρακαλεῖν τινα ἔν τινι *comfort someone with someth.* 2 Cor 7: 6b. π. τινα ἐπί τινι *comfort someone w. regard to someth.* 1: 4a. π. τινα ὑπέρ τινος *encourage someone in someth.* 1 Th 3: 2. παρακαλεῖτε ἀλλήλους ἐν τοῖς λόγοις τούτοις *comfort one another w. these words* 4: 18.—Pass. *be comforted, receive comfort* through words, or a favorable change in the situation Mt 5: 4; Lk 16: 25; Ac 20: 12; 2 Cor 1: 6; 7: 13; 13: 11; *let oneself be comforted* Mt 2: 18 (Jer 38: 15 v.l.). παρεκλήθημεν ἐφ᾽ ὑμῖν *we have been comforted concerning you* 1 Th 3: 7. ἐν τῇ παρακλήσει ᾗ παρεκλήθη ἐφ᾽ ὑμῖν 2 Cor 7: 7. διὰ τῆς παρακλήσεως, ἧς (on attraction, for ᾗ, cf. Bl-D. §294, 2; Rob. 716) παρακαλούμεθα αὐτοί *by the comfort with which we ourselves are comforted* 1: 4c.—W. acc. of the thing τὰς καρδίας Eph 6: 22; Col 4: 8; 2 Th 2: 17; pass. Col 2: 2.—Abs. 2 Cor 2: 7; Ro 12: 8 (but s. 2 above). παρακαλεῖν ἐν τῇ διδασκαλίᾳ *encourage* (others) *with the teaching* Tit 1: 9.

5. In several places it is poss. that παρ. can mean *try to console* or *conciliate, speak to in a friendly manner, apologize to* (cf. 2 Macc 13: 23) Lk 15: 28 (but s. 1b); Ac 16: 39; 1 Cor 4: 13; 1 Th 2: 12 (s. 2 above); 1 Ti 5: 1 (s. 2 above).—OSchmitz and GStählin, TW V 771–98. M-M.

παρακαλύπτω pf. pass. ptc. παρακεκαλυμμένος (Pla., Plut., LXX, Philo) *hide, conceal* fig. (as Ezk 22: 26; Philo, Decal. 91 τ. ἀλήθειαν) ἦν παρακεκαλυμμένον ἀπ᾽ αὐτῶν *it was hidden from them* Lk 9: 45 (Bl-D. §155, 3). M-M.*

παρακαταθήκη, ης, ἡ (Hdt.+. This is the real Attic form [cf. παραθήκη], but is also found in Aristot., Eth. Nicom. 5, 8, 5 p. 1135b, 4; Polyb. 5, 74, 5; Diod. S. 4, 58, 6; 15, 76, 1; Plut., Anton. 21, 4; Aelian, V.H. 4, 1; Vett. Val. p. 60, 21; Philo; Jos., Bell. 3, 372, Ant. 4, 285; inscr., pap., LXX) *deposit* 1 Ti 6: 20; 2 Ti 1: 14, both t.r. (for παραθήκην. Used w. φυλάσσω as Socrat., Ep. 28, 6); Hm 3: 2. M-M.*

παράκειμαι (X., Pla.; pap., LXX, Ep. Arist., Philo) *be at hand, ready* (so Hom. et al.) in our lit. only twice in Ro 7, w. dat. of the pers. (Περὶ ὕψους p. 6, 10 V.; Lucian, De Merc. Cond. 26; PSI 542, 12 [III вс] ἐμοὶ οὔπω παράκειται κέρμα= 'I do not yet have any money at hand') vss. 18, 21.—JDMDerrett, Law in the NT, '70 (lit. p. 30, n. 1). M-M.*

παρακέκλημαι, παρακληθῶ s. παρακαλέω.

παρακελεύω 1 aor. παρεκέλευσα (as a mid. dep. Hdt.+; pap.; Pr 9: 16; Ep. Arist., Philo; Jos., Ant. 12, 300.—The act. Hippocr.+; Plut., Mor. 195A; Appian, Bell. Civ. 5, 89 §372; 4 Macc 5: 2) *encourage, exhort* τινά someone (Polyb. 16, 20, 8) IMg 14.*

παράκλησις, εως, ἡ (Thu.+; inscr., pap., LXX).
1. *encouragement, exhortation* (Thu. 8, 92, 11; Ps.-Pla., Def. 415E; Polyb. 1, 67, 10; 1, 72, 4; 22, 7, 2; Diod. S. 15, 56, 2; 2 Macc 7: 24; Philo, Vi. Cont. 12; Jos., Vi. 87) 1 Th 2: 3; 1 Ti 4: 13; Hb 12: 5. W. οἰκοδομή: λαλεῖν παράκλησιν *speak words of exhortation* 1 Cor 14: 3. παράκλησις ἐν Χριστῷ *Christian exhortation* Phil 2: 1 (mng. 3 is also poss.). Likew. interpretation varies betw. 1 and 3 for Ro 12: 8 (s. παρακαλέω 2 and 4).—2 Cor 8: 17 could stand under 1, but prob. may better be classed w. 2. λόγος τῆς π. *word of exhortation* (cf. 2 Macc 15: 11 ἡ ἐν τοῖς λόγοις παράκλησις; 7: 24; Dio Chrys. 1, 9) Hb 13: 22; cf. Ac 13: 15. ἰσχυρὰν παράκλησιν ἔχειν *be greatly encouraged* Hb 6: 18.
2. *appeal, request* (Strabo 13, 1, 1; Appian, Liby. 51 §221; PTebt. 392, 26; 36 [II AD]; PLond. 1164d, 10; in pap. VI AD oft. w. δέησις; 1 Macc 10: 24; Jos., Ant. 3, 22) μετὰ πολλῆς π. δεόμενοι *beg earnestly* 2 Cor 8: 4 (μετὰ παρακλήσεως as Astrampsychus p. 28 Dek. 53, 5). παράκλησιν ἐδέξατο *he has accepted (my) appeal* vs. 17 (Jos., Vi. 193; s. 1 above).
3. *comfort, consolation* (Epict. 3, 23, 28; Dio Chrys. 80[30], 6; Phalaris, Ep. 103, 1; Jer 16: 7; Hos 13: 14; Na 3: 7; Job 21: 2) Ac 9: 31; 2 Cor 1: 4-7; 7: 4, 13; Phil 2: 1 (s. 1 above); Phlm 7. παράκλησις αἰωνία *everlasting=inexhaustible comfort* 2 Th 2: 16. ἡ π. τῶν γραφῶν *the consolation that the scriptures give* Ro 15: 4 (cf. 1 Macc 12: 9 παράκλησιν ἔχοντες τὰ βιβλία τὰ ἅγια). ὁ θεὸς τῆς π. vs. 5; cf. 2 Cor 1: 3. Of comforting circumstances, events, etc. Lk 6: 24; Ac 15: 31; 2 Cor 7: 7.—In the eschatol. sense (Ps.-Clem., Hom. 3, 26 ἐν τῷ μέλλοντι αἰῶνι) προσδεχόμενος π. τοῦ Ἰσραήλ *looking for the consolation of Israel* (i.e. Messianic salvation; cf. Is 40: 1; 61: 2) Lk 2: 25 (cf. Dalman, Worte 89f; Billerb. II 124-6. —In later times the Jews occasionally called the Messiah himself מְנַחֵם= 'comforter'; cf. Billerb. I 66; Bousset, Rel.³ 227).—Ac 4: 36 The name Barnabas is translated υἱὸς παρακλήσεως (s. the entry Βαρναβᾶς and cf. also Dalman, Gramm.², 178, 4). M-M.*

παράκλητος, ου, ὁ originally meant in the passive sense (BGU 601, 12 [II AD] παράκλητος δέδωκα αὐτῷ= 'when I was asked I gave to him', but π. is restored from πάρακλος, and the restoration is uncertain), 'one who is called to someone's aid'. Accordingly the Latin translators commonly rendered it, in its NT occurrences, with 'advocatus' (Tertullian, Prax. 9; Cyprian, De Domin. Orat. 3, Epist. 55, 18; Novatian, De Trin. 28; 29; Hilary, De Trin. 8, 19; Lucifer, De S. Athanas. 2, 26; Augustine, C. Faust. 13, 17, Tract. in Joh. 94; Tractatus Orig. 20 p. 212, 13 Batiffol. Likew. many Bible mss.: acemq J 14: 16; amq 14: 26; eqr 15: 26; emq 16: 7. Euseb., H.E. 5, 1, 10 παράκλητος=advocatus, Rufinus. Field, Notes 102f). But the technical mng. 'lawyer', 'attorney' is rare (e.g. Bion of Borysthenes [III BC] in Diog. L. 4, 50). In the few places where the word is found in pre-Christian and extra-Christian lit. it has for the most part a more general

mng.: *one who appears in another's behalf, mediator, intercessor, helper* (Demosth. 19, 1; Dionys. Hal. 11, 37, 1; Heraclit. Sto. 59 p. 80, 19; Cass. Dio 46, 20, 1; POxy. 2725, 10 [71 AD]). The pass. idea of παρακεκλῆσθαι retreated into the background, and the active idea of παρακαλεῖν took its place (on the justification for equating παράκλητος with παρακαλῶν s. Kühner-Bl. II 289). So the Jews adopted it as a loanw. (פְּרַקְלִיט. Pirqe Aboth 4, 11.—SKrauss, Griech. u. latein. Lehnwörter in Talmud, Midrasch u. Targum 1898/99 I 210; II 496; Dalman, Gramm.² 185; Billerb. II 560-2). In Job 16: 2 Aq. and Theod. translate מְנַחֲמִים (=comforters) as παράκλητοι; LXX has παρακλήτορες. In Philo our word somet. means 'intercessor' (De Jos. 239, Vi. Mos. 2, 134, Spec. Leg. 1, 237, Exsecr. 166, Adv. Flacc. 13; 22), somet. 'adviser', 'helper' (Op. M. 23; 165). The Gk. interpreters of John's gosp. understood it in the active sense= παρακαλῶν or παρακλήτωρ (Euseb., Theol. Eccl. 3, 5, 11 p. 161, 26 Kl.; Theodore of Mopsuestia in the comm. on John p. 307f Chabot; Ammonius in the Corderius-Catena 365), and so did Ephraem the Syrian (Evang. Concord. Expos., ed. Aucher-Moesinger 1876, 225=RHarris, Fragments of the Comm. of Ephrem S. 1895, 86). In our lit. the act. sense *helper, intercessor* is suitable in all occurrences of the word (so Gdspd., Probs. 110f). τίς ἡμῶν παράκλητος ἔσται; 2 Cl 6: 9. πλουσίων παράκλητοι *advocates of the rich* B 20: 2; D 5: 2.—In 1 J 2: 1 (as Acta Jo. in a damaged fragment: POxy. 850, 10) Christ is designated as παράκλητος: παράκλητον ἔχομεν πρὸς τὸν πατέρα Ἰησοῦν Χριστὸν δίκαιον *we have Jesus Christ the righteous one, who intercedes for us*. The same title is implied for Christ by the ἄλλος παράκλητος of J 14: 16. It is only the Holy Spirit that is expressly called παρ.=*Helper* in the Fourth Gosp.: 14: 16, 26; 15: 26; 16: 7.—HUsener, Archiv für lat. Lexikographie 2, 1885, 230ff; HSasse, Der Paraklet im J: ZNW 24, '25, 260-77; HWindisch, Johannes u. die Synoptiker '26, 147f, Die fünf joh. Parakletsprüche: Jülicher-Festschr. '27, 110-37; RAsting, 'Parakleten' i Johannesevangeliet: Teologi og Kirkeliv. Avh. etc. '31, 85-98; SMowinckel, D. Vorstellungen d. Spätjudentums v. Hl. Geist als Fürsprecher u. d. joh. Paraklet: ZNW 32, '33, 97-130 (supported now by IQS 3, 24f; IQM 17, 6-8); JMusger, Dicta Christi de Paracleto '38; EPercy, Untersuchgen, üb. den Ursprung d. joh. Theol. '39; Bultmann, J '40, 437-40; NJohansson, Parakletoi: Vorstellgen. v. Fürsprechern f. d. Menschen vor Gott in d. atl. Rel., im Spätjudent. u. Urchristent. '40.; NHSnaith, ET 57, '45, 47-50 (*Convincer*); WFHoward, Christianity acc. to St. John '47, 71-80; WMichaelis, Con. Neot. 11, '47, 147-62; GBornkamm, RBultmann-Festschr. '49, 12-35; CKBarrett, JTS n. s. 1, '50, 8-15; JGDavies, ibid. 4, '53, 35-8; TPreiss, Life in Christ, '54, 19-25; OBetz, Der Paraklet, '63; MMiguens, El Paraclito (reviewed CBQ 26, '64, 115f); GJohnston, The Spirit-Paraclete in J, '70; REBrown, The Paraclete in Modern Research, TU 102, '68, 158-65.—JBehm, TW V 798-812. M-M.*

παρακοή, ῆς, ἡ (Pla., Ep. 7 p. 341B; Galen: CMG V 4, 2 p. 178, 14, Suppl. III p. 30, 2) *unwillingness to hear, disobedience* (so Ps.-Clem., Hom. 2, 31; Synes., Ep. 67; Syntipas p. 97, 2; Photius, Bibl. p. 503, 5; PLond. 1345, 36; 1393, 51 [both VIII AD]) Ro 5: 19; 2 Cor 10: 6; Dg 12: 2. W. παράβασις Hb 2: 2. M-M.*

παρακολουθέω fut. παρακολουθήσω; 1 aor. παρηκολούθησα; pf. παρηκολούθηκα (Aristoph., X., Pla.+; inscr., pap., 2 Macc, Philo, Joseph.) *follow* in our lit. only fig.
1. *follow, accompany, attend* w. dat. of the pers. (τύχη ἡμῖν π. Demosth. 42, 21; Plut., Mor. 207E; πυρετοί μοι

π. Demosth. 54, 11; βλάβη μοι π. PReinach 18, 15 [II BC]; 19, 12; PTebt. 28, 2; PStrassb. 22, 20. Cf. 2 Macc 8: 11; Philo, Sacr. Abel. 70) σημεῖα τοῖς πιστεύσασιν ταῦτα παρακολουθήσει these signs will attend those who have come to believe Mk 16: 17 (v.l. ἀκολουθήσει). π. τοῖς πρεσβυτέροις, τῷ κυρίῳ of direct discipleship Papias 2: 4, 15.

2. follow with the mind, understand, make one's own (Demosth. et al.; esp. a t.t. of the Stoics) w. dat. of the thing (Polyb. 3, 32, 2; Epict. 1, 6, 13; Vett. Val. 276, 23; Dit., Syll.³ 718, 9 [c. 100 BC]), but also follow faithfully, follow as a rule (Dit., Syll.³ 885, 32 π. τῇ περὶ τὸ θεῖον τῆς πόλεως θεραπείᾳ; PTebt. 124, 4 [I BC] τῇ αὐτῶν π. πίστει; 2 Macc 9: 27 π. τῇ ἐμῇ προαιρέσει) διδασκαλίᾳ 1 Ti 4: 6; 2 Ti 3: 10.

3. follow a thing, trace or investigate a thing w. dat. of the thing (Demosth. 18, 172; 19, 257; UPZ 71, 20 [152 BC] τῇ ἀληθείᾳ; Jos., C. Ap. 1, 53; 218) ἐμοὶ παρηκολουθηκότι ἄνωθεν πᾶσιν ἀκριβῶς to me having investigated everything carefully from the beginning Lk 1: 3 (cf. HJCadbury, Beginn. vol. 2, 501f and Exp. 8th ser., 144, '22, 401-20: having been familiar with, and M-M.; JH Ropes, JTS 25, '24, 67-71.—GHWhitaker, Exp. 8th ser. 118['20] 262-72; 119['20] 380-4; 121['21] 239ff; BW Bacon, Le témoignage de Luc sur lui-même: RHPhr 8, '28, 209-26. S. also s.v. ἀνατάσσομαι). M-M.*

παρακούω fut. παρακούσομαι; 1 aor. παρήκουσα (Aristoph., Hdt.+; inscr., pap., LXX, Philo, Joseph.).

1. hear what is not intended for one's ears, overhear (Aristoph., Frogs 750; Pla., Euthyd. 300D) τὶ someth. Ἰησοῦς π. τὸν λόγον Jesus overheard what was said Mk 5: 36. But perh. the next mng. is also poss.

2. pay no attention to, ignore τὶ someth. (Plut., Philop. 16, 1 καὶ παριδεῖν τι καὶ παρακοῦσαι τῶν ἁμαρτανομένων, De Curios. 14 p. 522B ἔνια παρακοῦσαι κ. παριδεῖν) Jesus ignored what they said (s. 1 above).

3. refuse to listen to, disobey w. gen. of the pers. or thing (Polyb. 24, 9, 1; Epict. 2, 15, 4 τῶν λόγων; Lucian, Prometh. 2; PHib. 170 [247 BC] ἡμῶν; Esth 3: 8; Jos., Ant. 1, 190; 6, 141) Mt 18: 17a, b. τῶν ἐντολῶν (Tob 3: 4; cf. UPZ 110, 130 [164 BC]) 2 Cl 3: 4; 6: 7. Abs. (Test. Dan 2: 3) 2 Cl 15: 5; Hv 4, 2, 6. M-M.*

παρακύπτω 1 aor. παρέκυψα (Aristoph., Hippocr.+; pap., LXX, En., Philo) bend over (to see someth. better. Field, Notes 80f).

1. lit. (Phlegon: 257 fgm. 36, 1, 3 Jac.; POxy. 475, 23 [II AD]; LXX) εἰς τὸ μνημεῖον she stooped to look into the tomb J 20: 11 (on π. εἰς τι cf. Lucian, Tim. 13; Pr 7: 6; Sir 21: 23). ἐκεῖ GP 13: 55. Abs. (Epict. 1, 1, 16; Aesop, Fab. 145 P.=251 H.) παρακύψας βλέπει Lk 24: 12; J 20: 5. Cf. GP 13: 56.

2. fig. look (in) εἴς τι into someth. (Philo, Leg. ad Gai. 56) εἰς νόμον τέλειον Js 1: 25 (here the expr. is suggested by the figure of the man who looks at himself in a mirror vss. 23f). Of the angels (cf. En. 9, 1), who strive to παρακύπτειν into the gospel of the suffering and glorified Christ, either: gain a clear glance, or: steal a glance at it (so POxy. loc. cit.; cf. Demosth. 4, 24) 1 Pt 1: 12. M-M.*

παραλαμβάνω (Eur., Hdt.+ inscr., pap., LXX, Ep. Arist., Philo, Joseph.) fut. παραλήμψομαι (on the spelling with μ cf. Mayser p. 194f; Thackeray p. 108ff; Bl-D. §101 p. 46; Mlt.-H. 246f; Reinhold 46f; WSchulze, Orthographica 1894.—On the mid. s. Bl-D. §77; Rob. 356); 2 aor. παρέλαβον, 3 pl. παρελάβοσαν 2 Th 3: 6 v.l. (Bl-D. §84, 2; Mlt.-H. 209); 1 fut. pass. παραλημφθήσομαι Lk 17: 34f.

1. take (to oneself), take with or along w. acc. of the pers. (Gen 47: 2; 2 Macc 5: 5; Jos., Vi. 66) Mt 2: 13f, 20f; 17: 1; 26: 37; Mk 4: 36; 5: 40; 9: 2; Lk 9: 28; Ac 15: 39; 16: 33; 21: 24, 26, 32 (v.l. λαβών); 23: 18; GOxy 7; Hs 6, 3, 3. παραλαμβάνει ἕτερα πνεύματα ἑπτά he brings along seven other spirits to help him Lk 11: 26 (Menand., Col. 109 ἐξήκονθ᾽ ἑταίρους παραλαβών). Pass. (Diod. S. 2, 40, 2) εἷς παραλαμβάνεται καὶ εἷς ἀφίεται the one is taken (by the angels), the other is left Mt 24: 40; cf. vs. 41; Lk 17: 34f. π. τινὰ μεθ᾽ ἑαυτοῦ (μετὰ σοῦ, μετ᾽ αὐτοῦ. Cf. Gen 22: 3) Mt 12: 45; 18: 16; Mk 14: 33. W. acc. of the pers., and w. the goal indicated by εἰς take (along) to, into (Aelian, V.H. 2, 18; Num 23: 27) Mt 4: 5, 8; 27: 27. παραλήμψομαι ὑμᾶς πρὸς ἐμαυτόν I will take you to myself J 14: 3 (cf. Dssm., LO 144 [LAE 166]; with me to my home ALHumphries, ET 53, '41/'42, 356). π. τινὰ κατ᾽ ἰδίαν take someone aside Mt 20: 17. Also without κατ᾽ ἰδίαν w. the same purpose of private instruction Mk 10: 32; Lk 9: 10 (here κατ᾽ ἰδίαν does not belong grammatically with παραλ.); 18: 31.—Of one's wife: take her into one's home Mt 1: 20, 24 (cf. Hdt. 4, 155; Lucian, Toxar. 24; SSol 8: 2; Jos., Ant. 1, 302; 17, 9).—Take into custody, arrest Ac 16: 35 D. Pass., GP 1: 2 (if it is correctly restored).

2. take over, receive—a. τινά someone, a prisoner J 19: 16b (cf. παρέδωκεν ibid. a.—Both verbs in this sense in Appian, Bell. Civ. 6, 76 §310f).

b. τὶ someth.—α. τὴν διακονίαν Col 4: 17 (Dit., Syll.³ 663, 12 [c. 200 BC] the office of priest). τὶ ἀπό τινος Hs 6, 2, 6.

β. βασιλείαν ἀσάλευτον receive a kingship that cannot be shaken Hb 12: 28 (βασ. π.: Hdt. 2, 120; Dit., Or. 54, 5ff [III BC]; 56, 6; 90, 1; 8; 47; 2 Macc 10: 11; Da 6: 1, 29; Jos., Ant. 15, 16, C. Ap. 1, 145. Of the ἅγιοι ὑψίστου Da 7: 18).

γ. of a mental or spiritual heritage (Hdt., Isocr., Pla. et al., esp. of mysteries and ceremonies that one receives by tradition [s. παραδίδωμι 3]: Theo. Smyrn., Expos. Rer. Math. p. 14 Hiller τελετὰς παραλ. Cf. Plut., Demetr. 26, 1; Porphyr., Abst. 4, 16; Herm. Wr. 1, 26b; CIA III 173; also the rabbinic term קִבֵּל) τὶ someth. 1 Cor 15: 3 (w. παραδίδωμι, as Jos., Ant. 19, 31). B 19: 11; D 4: 13. παρ᾽ ὃ παρελάβετε (=παρὰ τοῦτο ὃ) Gal 1: 9. τὰ νόμιμα τοῦ θεοῦ Hv 1, 3, 4. τὸ πνεῦμα τὸ ἅγιον s 9, 25, 2. ἃ παρέλαβον κρατεῖν things that have come down to them to observe Mk 7: 4. τὶ παρά τινος (Pla., Lach. 197D, Euthyd. 304C σοφίαν παρά τινος. The constr. w. παρά is common in inscr. and pap.; cf. Philo, Cher. 68) Gal 1: 12; 1 Th 2: 13; 2 Th 3: 6 (παράδοσιν παραλ.). παρελάβετε παρ᾽ ἡμῶν τὸ πῶς δεῖ περιπατεῖν you have learned from us how you ought to walk 1 Th 4: 1. ὡς παρέλαβεν παρὰ τοῦ ἁγίου Epil Mosq 1 (w. παραδίδωμι). παρέλαβον ἀπὸ τοῦ κυρίου, ὃ καὶ παρέδωκα ὑμῖν 1 Cor 11: 23 (s. ἀπό V 4).—παραλ. τὸν Χριστὸν Ἰησ. accept Christ Jesus, i.e. the proclamation of him as Lord Col 2: 6.

3. Somet. the emphasis lies not so much on receiving or taking over, as on the fact that the word implies agreement or approval

a. w. regard to persons: οἱ ἴδιοι αὐτὸν οὐ παρέλαβον his own people did not accept him J 1: 11.

b. w. regard to teaching and preaching accept: τὸ εὐαγγέλιον ὃ εὐηγγελισάμην ὑμῖν ὃ καὶ παρελάβετε 1 Cor 15: 1. ἃ καὶ ἐμάθετε καὶ παρελάβετε Phil 4: 9. M-M.*

παραλέγομαι impf. παρελεγόμην nautical t.t. sail past, coast along (Strabo 13, 1, 22) w. acc. of the place that one sails past (Hanno [IV BC], Periplus 11: CMüller, Geogr.

Gr. Min. I [1855] p. 9; Diod. S. 13, 3, 3 τὴν Ἰταλίαν; 14, 55, 2) αὐτήν Ac 27: 8. τὴν Κρήτην vs. 13. M-M.*

παραλείπω 2 aor. παρέλιπον; pf. παραλέλοιπα *leave to one side, neglect*, then esp. in speech or writing *leave out, omit* (Eur., Hel. 773; 976; Thu. 2, 51, 1; Pla., Meno 97в; Strabo 1, 1, 23; Plut., Mor. 114в) τὶ someth. (Diod. S. 3, 66, 5; Jos., Ant. 1, 17, Vi. 261) B 17: 1; Papias 2: 15.*

παραλημφθήσομαι s. παραλαμβάνω.

παράλιος, ον (Aeschyl.+; inscr., LXX; Philo, Agr. 81; Joseph.—Also of three endings: Sib. Or. 3, 493) (*located*) *by the sea* subst. ἡ παράλιος, sc. χώρα (Jos., C. Ap. 1, 60) *the seacoast* (Polyb. 3, 39, 3; Diod. S. 3, 15, 41; Arrian, Anab. 1, 24, 3; 2, 1, 1; Dt 33: 19; Jos., Bell. 1, 409; Test. Zeb. 5: 5 w. v.l.—ἡ παραλία as early as Hdt. 7, 185 and predom. in Polyb.; Diod. S. 20, 47, 2; Arrian, Anab. 3, 22, 4; 6, 15, 4; LXX; Jos., Ant. 12, 292) ἀπὸ τῆς παραλίου Τύρου καὶ Σιδῶνος *from the seacoast district of Tyre and Sidon* Lk 6: 17 (cf. Diod. S. 11, 14, 5 ἡ παράλιος τ. Ἀττικῆς; Jos., C. Ap. 1, 61 ἡ παράλιος τ. Φοινίκης). M-M. B. 32.*

παραλλαγή, ῆς, ἡ (Aeschyl., Pla.+; 4 Km 9: 20; Ep. Arist. 75. Rarely as an astronom. t.t. [Cat. Cod. Astr. VIII 3, 113]) *change, variation* Js 1: 17. M-M.*

παραλλάσσω pf. pass. ptc. παρηλλαγμένος (trag., Hdt.+; PHib. 27, 50 [III вс]; Sb 4947, 4; LXX) *change* παρηλλαγμένος *strange, extraordinary, peculiar* (Polyb. 2, 29, 1; 3, 55, 1; Diod. S. 14, 70, 4; 17, 90, 1; Plut., Thes. 34, 3, Them. 24, 3; Lucian, Dial. Deor. 10, 2; Philo, Poster. Cai. 9) διάλεκτος παρηλλαγμένη *a peculiar language* Dg 5: 2.*

παραλογίζομαι mid. dep.; 1 aor. παρελογισάμην (Isocr., Demosth.+; inscr., pap., LXX).
1. w. acc. of the pers. (Aeschin. et al.; Epict. 2, 20, 7; Dio Chrys. 10[11], 108; PMagd. 29, 5 [III вс]; PAmh. 35, 12; LXX; Jos., Ant. 11, 275) *deceive, delude* Col 2: 4; IMg 3: 2. ἑαυτόν *deceive oneself* Js 1: 22.
2. w. acc. of the thing *reckon fraudulently, defraud*, perh. *distort* (Dit., Or. 665, 15 of costs fraudulently reckoned; Gen 31: 41 τὸν μισθόν) τὰς ἐντολὰς Ἰησοῦ Χριστοῦ 2 Cl 17: 6. M-M.*

παραλόγως adv. (Thu., Aristot.+; Dit., Or. 665, 33; Jos., Bell. 4, 49) *in an unreasonable manner* (Polyb. 1, 74, 14; Celsus 5, 14) Dg 11: 1.*

παραλυτικός, ή, όν (Diosc. 1, 16; Vett. Val. 110, 34; 127, 21; Hippiatr. I 433, 6) *lame* only subst. (ὁ) π. *the lame person, paralytic* (Rufus [II ad] in Oribas. 8, 39, 8; Geopon. 8, 11) Mt 4: 24; 8: 6; 9: 2a, b, 6; Mk 2: 3-5, 9f; Lk 5: 24 v.l.; J 5: 3 D.—PWSchmidt, Die Geschichte Jesu II '04, 205ff; 261. M-M.*

παράλυτος, ον *lame* (Artem. 4, 67 p. 244, 2), only subst. ὁ π. *the paralytic* (Artem. 4, 67 p. 244, 4) Mk 2: 9 D.*

παραλύω pf. pass. ptc. παραλελυμένος (Eur., Hdt.+; inscr., pap., LXX; Philo, Det. Pot. Ins. 168; Jos., Bell. 3, 386) *undo, weaken, disable* (Hdt.+.—Diod. S. 20, 72, 2 παραλελυμένος by old age) τὰ παραλελυμένα γόνατα *the weakened knees* Hb 12: 12 (Is 35: 3; Sir 25: 23; cf. PsSol 8: 5.—Diod. S. 18, 31, 4 παραλελυμένος of a man who was lamed by a blow at the back of the knee). ἄνθρωπος ὃς ἦν παραλελυμένος Lk 5: 18; Ac 9: 33 (Artem. 5, 51 ἐνόσησε κ. παρελύθη; 1, 50 p. 48, 11). Subst. ὁ παραλελυμένος *the paralytic* Lk 5: 24 (v.l. τῷ παραλυτικῷ); Ac 8: 7. M-M.*

παραμένω fut. παραμενῶ; 1 aor. παρέμεινα, imper. παράμεινον (Hom.+; inscr., pap., LXX; En. 97, 10; Jos., Ant. 11, 309) *remain, stay* (at someone's side).
1. lit. *remain, stay* (*on*)—**a.** abs. εὔχομαι παραμεῖναι αὐτόν *I wish him to stay on* IEph 2: 1 (cf. FPreisigke, Griech. Urkunden d. ägypt. Mus. in Kairo '11 no. 15, 9).
b. w. dat. of the pers. *stay* or *remain with someone* (Hom.+; Dit., Syll.³ 1209, 24f; 1210, 7f; PPetr. III 2, 21 [III вс]; PTebt. 384, 21; 32; POxy. 725, 43f; Gen 44: 33) μενῶ καὶ παραμενῶ πᾶσιν ὑμῖν *I will remain and continue with you all* Phil 1: 25 (παραμ. has the sense remain alive, go on living Hdt. 1, 30; Dio Chrys. 3, 124; Artem. 2, 27; 67. For the sense *serve* in Phil 1: 25 s. 2 below). παρέμειναν τὰ πνεύματα αὐτοῖς *the spirits remained with them* Hs 9, 15, 6.—W. a prep.: παραμ. πρός τινα *stay with someone* 1 Cor 16: 6 v.l. παραμ. εἰς ζωὴν αἰώνιον *endure to eternal life* Hv 2, 3, 2.
2. *continue in an occupation* or *office* (Diod. S. 2, 29, 5) abs., of the priests in the earthly sanctuary, who are prevented by death fr. remaining in office Hb 7: 23 (cf. Jos., Ant. 9, 273). Of the one who has concerned himself w. the perfect law Js 1: 25 (perh. w. the connotation of *serving*; s. Vitelli on PFlor. 44, 19 and M-M.).—*Continue* in a state of being or quality παραμένουσα πραεῖα καὶ ἡσύχιος *it remains meek and quiet* Hm 5, 2, 3. παράμεινον ταπεινοφρονῶν *continue to be humble-minded* s 7: 6. M-M.*

παράμονος, ον—1. of things or circumstances *lasting, constant, enduring* (Ps.-Plut., Consol. ad Apollon. 26 p. 114ϝ πένθος; Vett. Val. p. 292, 30; Geopon. 1, 12, 5) δόξα (w. ἄτρεπτος) IEph inscr.; (w. αἰώνιος) χαρά IPhld inscr.; ἀφροσύνη Hs 6, 5, 2.
2. of pers. (Hesychius=καρτερός) *steadfast, constant* in our lit. in an unfavorable sense *stubborn, persistent* Hs 5, 5, 1. W. the dat. of that in which someone is persistent παράμονοι ταῖς καταλαλιαῖς αὐτῶν *stubborn slanderers* s 9, 23, 3.*

παραμυθέομαι mid. dep. (Hom.+; inscr., pap.; 2 Macc 15: 9; Jos., Bell. 1, 627, Ant. 6, 38) *encourage, cheer up* τινά *someone* (Thu. 2, 44, 1 al.) 1 Th 2: 12. τοὺς ὀλιγοψύχους 5: 14 (Arrian, Anab. 4, 9, 7 consolation for Alexander when he was depressed).—Esp. in connection w. death or other tragic events *console, comfort* w. acc. of the pers. (Thu. 2, 44, 1 al.; Ps.-Plut., Consol. ad Apollon. 104c; Dit., Syll.³ 796в, 13; 39f; 889, 20; IG V 2 no. 517, 13.—KBuresch, Consolationum a Graecis Romanisque scriptarum historia critica: Leipz. Studien z. klass. Phil. 9, 1886; FWDanker, Threnetic Penetration in Aeschylus and Sophocles, Diss. Chicago, '63) J 11: 31. τινὰ περί τινος *console someone concerning someone* vs. 19.—PJoüon, Rech de Sc rel 28, '38, 311-14. GStählin, TW V 815-22. M-M.*

παραμυθία, ας, ἡ (Pla.+; inscr., pap., LXX) *encouragement*, esp. *comfort, consolation* (Ps.-Pla., Axioch. 365а; Dio Chrys. 77 [27], 9 [the philosopher is sought out as a comforter]; Lucian, Dial. Mort. 15, 3; Aelian, V.H. 12, 1 end; Dit., Syll.³ 796в, 44; PFlor. 382, 65; Sb 4313, 11; Wsd 19: 12; Philo, Mos. 1, 137; Jos., Bell. 3, 194, Ant. 20, 94) λαλεῖν παραμυθίαν (w. οἰκοδομή, παράκλησις) 1 Cor 14: 3. M-M.*

παραμύθιον, ου, τό *encouragement*, esp. as *consolation, means of consolation, alleviation* (Soph., El. 129; Thu. 5, 103, 1; Appian, Mithrid. 28 §110 πενίας τὴν σοφίαν ἔθεντο παραμύθιον='they used philosophy [only] as a means of consoling themselves for their poverty', or 'to alleviate their poverty'; Epigr. Gr. 951, 4; PFlor. 332, 19; Wsd 3: 18; Philo, Praem. 72; Jos., Bell. 6, 183; 7, 392) εἴ τι π. ἀγάπης *if there is any solace afforded by love* Phil 2: 1. M-M.*

παράνοια, ας, ἡ (Aeschyl., Hippocr.+; Plut., Cato Min. 68, 6; Ps.-Lucian, Macrob. 24; Philo, Cher. 69 al.) *madness, foolishness* 2 Pt 2: 16 v.l. (Vulg. has 'vesania', w. the same mng.).*

παρανομέω (Hdt.+; inscr., pap., LXX, Philo; Jos., Bell. 2, 317; 7, 34, Ant. 11, 149; Test. 12 Patr.) *break the law, act contrary to the law* abs. (Thu. 3, 67, 5; Pla., Rep. 1 p. 338ε; Dit., Syll.³ 218, 21f; POxy. 1106, 9; LXX) παρανομῶν κελεύεις *in violation of the law you order* Ac 23: 3. οἱ παρανομοῦντες *those who violate the law, the evil-doers* (Diod. S. 1, 75, 2; Artem. 1, 54 p. 51, 21; Ps 25: 4; 74: 5; Philo, Spec. Leg. 1, 155) 1 Cl 14: 4 (cf. Ps. 36: 38). M-M.*

παρανομία, ας, ἡ (Thu.+; Diod. S. 20, 101, 2 [punished by a god]; PSI 222, 6; BGU 389, 8; POxy. 1119, 8; 10; 18; LXX; Philo; Jos., Bell. 1, 226, Ant. 3, 314; Test. 12 Patr.) *lawlessness, evil-doing* ἔλεγξιν ἔχειν ἰδίας π. *be rebuked for his evil-doing* 2 Pt 2: 16. M-M.*

παράνομος, ον (trag., Thu.+; inscr., pap., LXX, Ep. Arist. 240; Philo; Jos., Ant. 18, 38, Vi. 26; 80) *contrary to the law, lawless.* In our lit. only of pers., and subst. in pl. οἱ παράνομοι *the evil-doers* (Menand., Per. 66; Socrat., Ep. 28, 6; Job 27: 7; Ps 36: 38; Pr 2: 22 al.) 1 Cl 45: 4 (w. ἄνομοι, ἀνόσιοι); Hs 8, 7, 6 (w. διχοστάται).*

παραπικραίνω 1 aor. παρεπίκρανα, pass. παρεπικράν-θην (LXX, Philo, Hesychius).
1. w. acc. of the pers. *embitter, make angry, provoke* (oft. LXX w. an acc. referring to God. Also Philo, Somn. 2, 177 παραπικραίνειν καὶ παροργίζειν θεόν). Pass. *become embittered, be made angry* (La 1: 20 v.l.; Philo, Leg. All. 3, 114) Hs 7: 2f.
2. also without an acc., almost like an intransitive *be disobedient, rebellious* (toward God; cf. Dt 31: 27; Ps 67: 7; 105: 7; Ezk 3: 9; 12: 9 al.) Hb 3: 16 (KJV, Moffatt *provoke*). M-M.*

παραπικρασμός, οῦ, ὁ (1 Km 15: 23 Aq.; Job 7: 11 Sym.; Pr 17: 11 Theod.; Achmes 238, 5) *embitterment,* then *revolt, rebellion against God* (s. παραπικραίνω 2) ἐν τῷ π. *in the rebellion* (referring to the story of the Exodus, e.g. Ex 15: 23; 17: 7; Num 14; 20: 2-5) Hb 3: 8, 15 (both Ps 94: 8).—EbNestle, ET 21, '10, 94. M-M.*

παραπίπτω 2 aor. παρέπεσον, 1 pl. παρεπέσαμεν (Bl-D. §81, 3; cf. Mlt.-H. 208f) (trag., Hdt.+; pap., LXX; Jos., Ant. 19, 285. In the pap. mostly=become lost) *fall beside, go astray, miss* (Polyb. 3, 54, 5 τῆς ὁδοῦ; fig. 12, 12, 2 τῆς ἀληθείας; 8, 11, 8 τοῦ καθήκοντος) abs. (X., Hell. 1, 6, 4; Polyb. 18, 36, 6=make a mistake) *fall away, commit apostasy* (Wsd 6: 9; 12: 2; Ezk 22: 4) Hb 6: 6 (s. KBornhäuser, Empfänger u. Verf. des Hb '32). Also w. acc. of the inner content (cognate; Bl-D. §154; Rob. 477f) ὅσα παρεπέσαμεν *whatever sins we have committed* 1 Cl 51: 1. M-M.*

παραπλέω 1 aor. inf. παραπλεῦσαι *sail past* (so Thu. 2, 25 end; X., An. 6, 2, 1, Hell. 1, 3, 3; Pla., Phaedr. 259ᴀ; Jos., Bell. 1, 456.—The word is found in the sense 'steer toward' Thu.+, also Wilcken, Chrest. 1 II, 2 [c. 246 ʙᴄ]) w. acc. of the place (Diod. S. 3, 40, 1 π. τοὺς τόπους=sail past the places 3, 45, 1) τὴν Ἔφεσον *sail past Ephesus* Ac 20: 16. M-M.*

παραπλήσιος, ία, ιον (Hdt.+; PTebt. 5, 240 [II ʙᴄ]; 27, 72 [II ʙᴄ]; PSI 491, 13; Ep. Arist.; Philo, Aet. M. 23; 90; Jos., Bell. 3, 82; 6, 388, Ant. 13, 63.—Also of two endings, as Polyb. 9, 41, 2; 18, 54, 2) *coming near, resembling, similar* (w. ὅμοιος, as Demosth. 19, 196 παρ. τούτῳ κ. ὅμοιον) ὅσα τούτοις π. Hm 6, 2, 5 (Polyb. 3, 111, 11 ταῦτα κ. τούτοις παραπλήσια). Neut. used as an adv. (Thu. 7, 19, 2; Polyb. 3, 33, 7; 4, 40, 10; PTebt. 5, 71 [II ʙᴄ]='similarly') ἠσθένησεν παραπλήσιον θανάτῳ *he was so ill that he nearly died* Phil 2: 27 (v.l. θανάτου. Polyb. 1, 23, 6; LRydbeck, Fachprosa '67, 46-50.—Bl-D. §184; Rob. 646. Cf. PMich. 149, 4, 27 [II ᴀᴅ] παραπλήσιον νεκρῷ). M-M.*

παραπλησίως adv. (Hdt.+) *similarly, likewise* Hb 2: 14. The word does not show clearly just how far the similarity goes. But it is used in situations where no differentiation is intended, in the sense *in just the same way* (Hdt. 3, 104; Diod. S. 1, 55, 5; 4, 48, 3; 5, 45, 5; Dio Chrys. 67[17], 3; Maximus Tyr. 7, 2a; Philostrat., Vi. Apoll. 4, 18 p. 138, 21; Jos., Vi. 187, 233. Cf. Philo, Rer. Div. Her. 151 τὸ παραπλήσιον, Abr. 162; Arrian, Exped. 7, 1, 6 of Alexander the Great ἄνθρωπος ὢν παραπλήσιος τοῖς ἄλλοις). M-M.*

παραποιέω pf. pass. ptc. παραπεποιημένος (Thu.+) *imitate, falsify, counterfeit* (Philostrat., Vi. Apoll. 2, 30 p. 72, 12) παραπεποιημένος (w. ἄδικος) *falsified* 1 Cl 45: 3.*

παραπόλλυμι *destroy,* mid. **παραπόλλυμαι** 2 aor. subj. παραπόλωμαι *perish, be lost* (so Aristoph.+; Lucian, Nigrin. 13; PSI 606, 3 [III ʙᴄ]; BGU 388 II, 10; POxy. 705, 73; Philo, Ebr. 14; Jos., Ant. 11, 293) 2 Cl 17: 1.*

παραπορεύομαι mid. dep.; impf. παρεπορευόμην (Aristot.+; pap., LXX).
1. *go* or *pass by* (Polyb. 10, 29, 4; 10, 30, 9 al.; PPetr. II 13, 5, 3 [III ʙᴄ]; PSI 354, 13; LXX) abs. Mt 27: 39; Mk 11: 20; 15: 29.
2. *go* (*through*) (Dt 2: 14, 18; Josh 15: 6) w. διά and the gen. (Dt 2: 4; Zeph 2: 15 v.l.) διὰ τῶν σπορίμων *go through the grain-fields* 2: 23. διὰ τῆς Γαλιλαίας 9: 30. M-M.*

παράπτωμα, ατος, τό (Polyb.+; Diod. S. 19, 100, 3; PTebt. 5, 91 [118 ʙᴄ]; LXX) *false step, transgression, sin* (Polyb. 9, 10, 6; LXX).
1. of transgressions against men Mt 6: 14, 15a v.l.; 18: 35 t.r.
2. as a rule of sins against God—a. sing.—α. of Adam's one transgression (Wsd 10: 1) Ro 5: 15a, b, 17f.— προλαμβάνεσθαι ἔν τινι π. *be detected in some trespass* Gal 6: 1. οἱ ἔν τινι π. ὑπάρχοντες *those who are involved in any transgression* 1 Cl 56: 1. ἐλέγχειν τινὰ ἐπὶ παραπτώματι *rebuke someone for a transgression* B 19: 4 (s. D 4: 3 below). W. πειρασμός Hm 9: 7.
β. collectively ἵνα πλεονάσῃ τὸ π. Ro 5: 20. Of 'the' sin of Israel, i.e. unbelief 11: 11f.
b. mostly pl. Mt 6: 15b; Mk 11: 25, 26; Ro 4: 25; 5: 16; 2 Cor 5: 19; Eph 1: 7; 2: 5; Col 2: 13a, b; Js 5: 16 t.r.; 1 Cl 2: 6; 51: 3; 60: 1; Hm 4, 4, 4; D 4: 3 (s. 2aα above), 14; 14: 1. παραπτώματα κ. ἁμαρτίαι Eph 2: 1. M-M.*

παράπτωσις, εως, ἡ (Aristot.+) *misstep, transgression, sin* (Polyb. 15, 23, 5 al.) abs. (Polyb. 16, 20, 5; Jer 22: 21) 1 Cl 59: 1.*

παραρρέω (Soph., X., Pla.+; LXX) 2 aor. pass. subj. παραρυῶ (Pr 3: 21; Plut., Mor. 754ᴀ.—W-S. §5, 26b;

Rob. 212) *flow by, slip away* fig. *be washed away, drift away* μήποτε παραρυῶμεν *lest we drift away* Hb 2: 1 (CSpicq, L'Epître aux Hébreux, II '35, 25 disclaims a nautical metaphor, but s. EHilgert, The Ship and Related Symbols in the NT, '62, 133f). M-M.*

παράσημον, ου, τό s. παράσημος 2.

παράσημος, ον (trag.+; Philo; cf. Jos., Ant. 18, 241)
1. *extraordinary, peculiar* βίος Dg 5: 2.
2. *distinguished, marked* ἐν πλοίῳ...'Αλεξανδρινῷ παρασήμῳ Διοσκούροις *in an Alexandrian ship that was marked by the Dioscuri* i.e., that had the Dioscuri (twin sons of Zeus, Castor and Pollux) as its insignia Ac 28: 11 (on the dat. cf. Plut., Mor. p. 823в ἐπιφθόνοις παράση-μος=making oneself noticed by hateful deeds). Yet it is hard to escape the suspicion that the text here, as so oft. in Ac, is damaged, and that it originally contained the noun τὸ παράσημον *emblem, insignia* situated on both sides of the prow of a ship (Plut., Mor. 162A τῆς νεὼς τὸ παράσημον; PLond. 256a, 2; PTebt. 486; Wilcken, Chrest. 248, 19; Sb 423, 5. Note esp. CIL 3=ILS 4395 [22 AD] navis parasemo sopharia=a ship with sopharia as insignia. LCasson, Ships and Seamanship in the Ancient World, '71, 344f. —Bl-D. §198, 7 app.; M-M. (dat. absolute).*

παρασκευάζω fut. mid. παρασκευάσομαι; pf. mid. and pass. παρεσκεύασμαι (trag., Hdt.+; inscr., pap., LXX, Ep. Arist., Philo, Joseph.) *prepare*.
1. act., abs. (sc. τὸ δεῖπνον, which is used w. the verb Hdt. 9, 82; Athen. 4, 15 p. 138c; Jos., Ant. 1, 269; 7, 347; cf. also παρασκ. συμπόσιον Hdt. 9, 15; 2 Macc 2: 27) Ac 10: 10. π. ἑαυτὸν εἴς τι *prepare oneself for someth.* (Horapollo 1, 11 p. 17) 1 Pt 2: 8 v.l.
2. mid. *prepare* (oneself) εἰς πόλεμον (Diod. S. 18, 2, 4; Jer 6: 4; 27: 42.—Hdt. 3, 105; 9, 96; 99 παρασκευά-ζεσθαι ἐς μάχην, ἐς ναυμαχίην, ἐς πολιορκίην; Appian, Bell. Civ. 2, 105 §434 ἐς μάχην; Brutus, Ep. 29) 1 Cor 14: 8. Perf. *be ready* 2 Cor 9: 2f. M-M.*

παρασκευή, ῆς, ἡ (trag., Hdt.+; inscr., pap., LXX, Ep. Arist., Philo, Joseph.) lit. *preparation* (Polyaenus 7, 21, 6 τοῦ δείπνου; 7, 27, 3 πολέμου), in our lit. only of a definite day, as the *day of preparation* for a festival; acc. to Jewish usage (Jos., Ant. 16, 163; Synes., Ep. 4 p. 161D) it was Friday, on which day everything had to be prepared for the Sabbath, when no work was permitted Mt 27: 62 (CCTorrey, ZAW 65, '53, 242=JBL 50, '31, 234 n. 3, 'sunset'. Against Torrey, SZeitlin, JBL 51, '32, 263–71); Mk 15: 42; J 19: 31. ἡμέρα παρασκευῆς Lk 23: 54 (v.l. ἡμ. προσαββάτου, cf. Mk 15: 42). παρασκευὴ τῶν Ἰου-δαίων J 19: 42. παρασκευὴ τοῦ πάσχα *day of preparation for the Passover* (or *Friday of Passover Week*) vs. 14. For the Christians as well παρασκευή served to designate the sixth day of the week (ESchürer, ZNW 6, '05, 10; 11f) *Friday* MPol 7: 1, and so in Mod. Gk. For Christians it is a fast day, as the day of Jesus' death D 8: 1.—M-M. B. 1008.*

παραστάτις, ιδος, ἡ (Soph., X. et al.; inscr., Philo) fem. of παραστάτης a (female) *helper* Ro 16: 2 v.l.*

παρασχών s. παρέχω.

παράταξις, εως, ἡ (Aeschin., Isocr., Demosth.+; inscr., pap., LXX; Jos., Vi. 341 al.).
1. *array, procession* (lit. of soldiers: Lat. agmen. As a military term Diod. S. 1, 18, 5) π. ἀνδρῶν Hs 9, 6, 1.—2. pl. (w. ἀγροί and οἰκοδομαί) παρατάξεις πολυτελεῖς *costly establishments* or *furnishings* Hs 1: 1. (W. ὁ πλού-

τος ὑμῶν) αἱ παρατάξεις πᾶσαι *all your furnishings*, perh. even more gener. *all your possessions* 1: 8.*

παρατείνω 1 aor. παρέτεινα (Hdt.+; pap., LXX, Philo; Jos., Ant. 1, 105 χρόνον) *extend, prolong* τὸν λόγον *the speech* Ac 20: 7 (Aristot., Poet. 17, 5 p. 1455b, 2 λόγους; 9, 4 p. 1451b, 38 μῦθον). M-M.*

παρατηρέω impf. παρετήρουν, mid. παρετηρούμην; 1 aor. παρετήρησα (X.+; pap., LXX, Ep. Arist.; Philo, Sacr. Abel. 98; Joseph.) *watch closely, observe carefully* (act. and mid. are used side by side w. the same mng.; Bl-D. §316, 1; cf. Rob. 804-6).
1. *watch* someone to see what he does (X., Mem. 3, 14, 4 w. indirect question foll.). Fr. the context this can take on the mng. *watch maliciously, lie in wait for*.
a. τινά *someone*—α. act. (Polyb. 11, 9, 9; UPZ 64, 9 [156 BC]; Sus 16 Theod.) foll. by indirect question Mk 3: 2; Lk 6: 7 t.r.—β. mid. (Ps 36: 12) Lk 14: 1. W. indirect question foll. 6: 7.
b. abs. (Vett. Val. 205, 13) *watch one's opportunity* (Field, Notes 74) Lk 20: 20 (v.l. ἀποχωρήσαντες).
2. *watch, guard* τὰς πύλας *the gates*—a. act. Ac 9: 24 t.r.—b. mid. Ac 9: 24.
3. *observe* religiously, mid. w. acc. (Cass. Dio 53, 10, 3 ὅσα προστάττουσιν οἱ νόμοι; Ep. Arist. 246.—Pass. Jos., C. Ap. 2, 282) ἡμέρας καὶ μῆνας καὶ καιρούς Gal 4: 10 (cf. the act. Jos., Ant. 3, 91 παρατηρεῖν τὰς ἑβδο-μάδας; 14, 264 παρατηρεῖν τὴν τῶν σαββάτων ἡμέραν; 11, 294). The use of the verb in LJ 2: 6 seems to belong here also, but the badly damaged state of the text permits no certainty in interpretation. M-M.*

παρατήρησις, εως, ἡ (since Pythag., Ep. 5, 1; Polyb., inscr.; Aq. Ex 12: 42).
1. *observation* (Polyb. 16, 22, 8; Diod. S. 1, 9, 6; 1, 28, 1 [both τῶν ἄστρων]; 5, 31, 3 [observ. of the future by certain signs]; Περὶ ὕψους 23, 2 [observ. in the field of language]; Epict. 3, 16, 15; Plut., Mor. 266B; M.Ant. 3, 4, 1; Proclus on Pla., Cratyl. p. 40, 2 Pasqu.; medical wr. of the observ. of symptoms [Heraclit. Sto. 14, p. 22, 10; Hobart 153]; IG IV² 1, 687, 14 [II AD]; Jos., Bell. 1, 570) μετὰ παρατηρήσεως *with observation* (schol. on Soph., Ant. 637 p. 249 Papag.) οὐκ ἔρχεται ἡ βασιλεία τοῦ θεοῦ μετὰ παρατηρήσεως *the Kingdom of God is not coming with observation* i.e., in such a way that its rise can be observed Lk 17: 20 (HJAllen, Exp. 9th ser. IV '25, 59-61; s. also under ἐντός, esp. BNoack '48; AStrobel, ZNW 49, '58, 157-96, after AMerx, Die 4 kanonischen Evangelien II, 2, '05, 345: cf. Ex 12: 42).
2. *observance* of legal prescriptions (Jos., Ant. 8, 96 παρατήρησις τῶν νομίμων), esp. of festivals Dg 4: 5 (παρατηρέω 3). M-M.*

παρατίθημι (Hom.+; inscr., pap., LXX; Ep. Arist. 255; Joseph.; Test. 12 Patr.) fut. παραθήσω; 1 aor. παρέθηκα; 2 aor. subj. παραθῶ, inf. παραθεῖναι Mk 8: 7 t.r.; Lk 9: 16; 2 aor. mid. παρεθέμην, imper. παράθου 2 Ti 2: 2; 1 aor. pass. παρετέθην *place beside, place before*.
1. act.—a. of food *set before* (Hom.+; LXX; Abercius-inschr. 13 τροφήν) τινί *someone* (Gen 18: 8) Mk 6: 41; 8: 6b; Lk 9: 16. τι *someth.* (Gen 43: 31) Mk 8: 7. τινί τι *someth. to someone* (Theophr., Char. 10; 30 ἄρτους ἱκανούς; Gen 24: 33; 2 Km 12: 20) Lk 11: 6. Abs. Mk 8: 6a; π. τράπεζαν *set food* before the one who is being entertained (Od. 5, 92; 21, 29; Jos., Ant. 6, 338) Ac 16: 34. Pass. αὐτοῖς ἐκέλευσεν παρατεθῆναι φαγεῖν κ. πιεῖν MPol 7: 2. τὰ παρατιθέμενα *the food that is served* or *set before* (X., Cyr. 2, 1, 30; Aristot., Pol. 1, 6; Bel 21; cf. 18;

Pr 23: 1) τὰ παρατιθέμενα ὑμῖν Lk 10: 8; cf. the sing. 1 Cor 10: 27.

b. *put before* in teaching τὶ someth. (X., Cyr. 1, 6, 14; Lucian, Rhet. Praec. 9 παραδείγματα al.; Ex 19: 7; 21: 1) παραβολὴν παρέθηκεν αὐτοῖς Mt 13: 24, 31.—c. do βλάβην τινί ITr 5: 1.

2. mid.—a. *set, spread* τράπεζαν (Diod. S. 34+35, fgm. 2, 35; Jos., Bell. 7, 264) Dg 5: 7.

b. *give over, entrust, commend* (Ps.-X., Rep. Ath. [the Old Oligarch] 2, 16; Polyb. 33, 12, 3; Plut., Num. 9, 10; oft. pap.; Tob 1: 14; 4: 1, 20; 1 Macc 9: 35).

a. τί τινι *entrust* someth. *to someone* ᾧ παρέθεντο πολύ Lk 12: 48. For safekeeping or transmission to others 1 Ti 1: 18; 2 Ti 2: 2.

β. τινά τινι *entrust someone to the care* or *protection of someone* (Diod. S. 16, 2, 2; 17, 23, 5; PGiess. 88, 5 Ἀπολλωνοῦν παρατίθεμαί σοι; PSI 96, 2; Tob 10: 13; Jos., Ant. 7, 387) Hs 9, 10, 6. Of divine protection παρέθεντο αὐτοὺς τῷ κυρίῳ Ac 14: 23; cf. 20: 32. Sim. εἰς χεῖράς σου παρατίθεμαι τὸ πνεῦμά μου Lk 23: 46 (cf. Ps 30: 6.—With this saying of Jesus cf. the subject matter of Ps.-Callisth. 3, 30, 15: in the face of death, Alexander prays: 'ὦ Ζεῦ, δέχου κἀμέ'); cf. 1 Pt 4: 19 and GDalman, Jesus-Jeshua [tr. PLevertoff], '29, 209f.

c. *demonstrate, point out* (POxy. 33 vers. III, 12; Jos., Vi. 6) διανοίγων καὶ παρατιθέμενος ὅτι Ac 17: 3.—28: 23 v.l. M-M.*

παρατυγχάνω (Hom.+; inscr., pap.; Jos., Ant. 3, 100) *happen to be near* or *present* (PTebt. 703, 242 [III BC]; POxy. 113, 14; 76, 11; Jos., Ant. 2, 226; 17, 37 al.) ὁ παρατυγχάνων *anyone who comes by* (Polyb. 10, 15, 4) pl. οἱ παρατυγχάνοντες *those who happened to be there* Ac 17: 17. M-M.*

παραυτά adv. (Aeschyl., Demosth.+; Vett. Val. 152, 10; PTebt. 13, 15 [II BC]; PLeipz. 36, 6; PGM 4, 2071 al. in pap.) *on the spot, at once* ITr 11: 1.—KSKontos in Ἀθηνᾶ 6, 1894, 369.*

παραυτίκα adv. (trag., Hdt.+; Dit., Syll.³ 495, 62; 68; oft. pap.; Tob. 4: 14; Ps 69: 4; Jos., Ant. 9, 147; 12, 138; Sib. Or. 13, 143. On the spelling s. Bl-D. §12, 3 app.; Rob. 297) *on the spot, immediately, for the present* used w. the art. preceding, as an adj. (Thu. 8, 82, 1 τὴν παραυτίκα ἐλπίδα; X., Cyr. 2, 2, 24 αἱ π. ἡδοναί; Pla., Phaedr. 239A τὸ π. ἡδύ; Appian, Bell. Civ. 3, 127 §531 ἡ π. ὀργή= the anger of the moment; Philo, Praem. 103; POxy. 1381, 191f τ. π. καιρόν) τὸ π. ἐλαφρὸν τῆς θλίψεως *slight momentary trouble* 2 Cor 4: 17. M-M.*

παραφέρω (trag., Hdt.+; inscr., pap., LXX; Ep. Arist. 316; Joseph.) impf. παρέφερον; 2 aor. παρήνεγκον, inf. παρενέγκαι Lk 22: 42 v.l. (cf. Bl-D. §81, 2; cf. Mlt.-H. 211). Pass.: 1 aor. παρηνέχθην; pf. ptc. παρενηνεγμένος Hs 9, 4, 6. *Carry beside* or *to the side.*

1. *bring up* (pap.; Judg 6: 5 A; Jos., Ant. 7, 168) λίθους Hv 3, 2, 5; 3, 4, 2; s 9, 4, 4; 8a. Pass. s 9, 4, 5f; 8b.

2. *take* or *carry away*—a. lit. (of being carried off by the force of the wind or a stream of water: Diod. S. 18, 35, 6; Plut., Timol. 28, 9; Lucian, Hermot. 86; M. Ant. 4, 43; 12, 14) Pass. νεφέλαι ὑπὸ ἀνέμων παραφερόμεναι Jd 12.

b. fig. *lead* or *carry away* fr. the path of truth (Pla., Phaedr. 265B; Plut., Timol. 6, 1) pass. *be carried away* διδαχαῖς ποικίλαις (instrum. dat.) μὴ παραφέρεσθε Hb 13: 9.

c. *take away, remove* (Theophr., C. Pl. 2, 9, 9) τὶ ἀπό τινος someth. *from someone* παρένεγκε τὸ ποτήριον τοῦτο ἀπ' ἐμοῦ *remove this cup from me* Mk 14: 36; Lk 22: 42. M-M.*

παραφρονέω (Aeschyl., Hdt.+; Diod. S. 16, 78, 5; Wilcken, Chrest. 14 III, 14; Zech 7: 11) *be beside oneself, conduct oneself in an irrational manner* (Aristoxenus, fgm. 35 a disgrace for an old man) παραφρονῶν λαλῶ *I am talking as if I were beside myself* or *irrational* 2 Cor 11: 23. M-M.*

παραφρονία, ας, ἡ (hapax legomenon) *madness, insanity* of Balaam 2 Pt 2: 16. M-M.*

παραφροσύνη, ης, ἡ (Hippocr., Pla., Plut., Philo; Jos., Ant. 19, 284) *madness, insanity* 2 Pt 2: 16 v.l.*

παραφυάδιον, ου, τό (Hesychius s.v. ἑρμαῖ; Sib. Or. 3, 396–400) dim. of παραφυάς (q.v.) *a little offshoot* μικρὸν κέρας παραφυάδιον *a little horn as an offshoot* B 4: 5 (cf. Da 7: 8).*

παραφυάς, άδος, ἡ (Hippocr., Aristot. et al.; LXX; En. 26, 1) *offshoot, side growth.*

1. lit. (Theophr., H. Pl. 2, 2, 4; Nicander, fgm. 80 π. of the palm tree; Philo, Plant. 4) Hs 8, 1, 17f; 8, 2, 1f; 8, 3, 7; 8, 4, 6; 8, 5, 2; 5f.

2. fig. (Aristot., Eth. Nic. 1, 4 p. 1096 al.; 4 Macc 1: 28) of sectarians who, as side growths of the plant created by God, can bear nothing but death-dealing fruit ITr 11: 1.*

παραχαράσσω (fig.='counterfeit', 'debase' Plut., Mor. 332B; Lucian, Demon. 5; Herm. Wr. 488, 12 Sc.; Philo, Omn. Prob. Lib. 4 v.l.; Jos., Bell. 1, 529, Ant. 15, 315; Third Corinthians 3: 3.—Maspéro 353, 20) *debase* or *counterfeit* (money) lit. (Dio Chrys. 14[31], 24 οἱ παραχαράττοντες τὸ νόμισμα; Cecaumenus p. 51, 22) Hs 1: 11.*

παραχειμάζω fut. παραχειμάσω; 1 aor. παρεχείμασα; pf. ptc. παρακεχειμακώς (since Hyperid., fgm. 260; Demosth.; Polyb. 2, 64, 1; Diod. S. 19, 34, 8; Plut., Sertor. 3, 5; Cass. Dio 40, 4; Dit., Or. 544, 30) *winter, spend the winter* abs. Ac 27: 12. W. the place given: πρὸς ὑμᾶς 1 Cor 16: 6. ἐκεῖ Tit 3: 12; of a ship ἐν τῇ νήσῳ Ac 28: 11. M-M.*

παραχειμασία, ας, ἡ (Polyb. 3, 34, 6; 3, 35, 1; Diod. S. 19, 68, 5; Jos., Ant. 14, 195; Dit., Syll.³ 762, 16 [48 BC]) *wintering* ἀνεύθετος πρὸς παραχειμασίαν *not suitable for wintering* Ac 27: 12. M-M.*

παραχέω inf. παραχέειν; impf. παρέχεον (Hdt.+; PMagd. 33, 2 [III BC]) *pour near* or on ὕδωρ (Plut., Mor. 235A) w. dat. *pour water on* someth. Hs 8, 2, 7f.*

παραχράομαι 1 aor. παρεχρησάμην (Hdt.+; PRyl. 144, 17 [I AD]) *misuse* (Arist. in Plut., Mor. 527A) w. dat. of the thing αὐτῇ (of human σάρξ) Hs 5, 7, 2 (cf. Polyb. 13, 4, 5 τῷ σώματι). Abs. *misuse it* (Philo, De Jos. 144) 1 Cor 7: 31 v.l.*

παραχρῆμα adv. (Hdt., Thu., Aristoph.+; inscr., pap., LXX; Ep. Arist. 22; Jos., Bell. 4, 377, Ant. 15, 65. On the spelling cf. Bl-D. §12, 3; Rob. 297; on its use §102, 2 app.; Rob. 550) *at once, immediately* Mt 21: 19f. Elsewh. in the NT only in Lk and Ac: Lk 1: 64; 4: 39; 5: 25; 8: 44, 47, 55; 13: 13; 18: 43; 19: 11; 22: 60; Ac 3: 7; 5: 10; 12: 23; 13: 11; 16: 26, 33; 22: 29 v.l.—B 12: 7; MPol 13: 1. Pleonastically εὐθέως παραχρῆμα (class.; PStrassb. 35, 17 εὐθὺς καὶ παραχρῆμα) Ac 14: 10 D (Bl-D. §484 app.; cf. Rob. 1205).—DDaube, The Sudden in Scripture '64, 38–46 (but s. LRydbeck, Fachprosa, '67, 174–6). See εὐθέως. M-M.*

πάρδαλις, εως, ἡ (Hom.+; Herm. Wr. 510, 2 Sc.; PGM 7, 783; LXX, Philo; Jos., Ant. 12, 146; Test. 12 Patr.; Sib.

Or. 3, 737; 789; loanw. in rabb.) *leopard*; an apocalyptic θηρίον ὅμοιον παρδάλει Rv 13: 2 (cf. Da 7: 6). M-M.*

παρέβην s. παραβαίνω.

παρεγγυάω 1 aor. παρηγγύησα (trag., Hdt.+; pap.; not LXX) *command* (so X.+) Papias 4.*

παρεδρεύω (Eur.+; inscr., pap.; Pr 1: 21; 8: 3; Ep. Arist. 81) *sit beside, wait on,* then *apply oneself to, concern oneself with* τινι *someth.* (Athen. 7 p. 283c οἱ ταῖς κητείαις παρεδρεύοντες ἄνδρες) of the Jews π. ἄστροις καὶ σελήνῃ *watch the stars and moon closely* Dg 4: 5. τῷ θυσιαστηρίῳ π. *serve regularly at the altar* i.e. do the work of a priest (παρεδρεύω in cultic use Diod. S. 4, 3, 3 π. τῷ θεῷ; Vett. Val. 210, 3 ἐν ἱεροῖς τόποις ἢ ναοῖς παρεδρεύειν; Dit., Syll.³ 633, 20 [180 BC] τοῦ ταμίου τοῦ παρεδρεύοντος ἐν τῷ ἱερῷ θυσίας ποιήσασθαι; 695, 27f; παρεδρευέτωσαν ἐν τῷ ἱερῷ τὴν ἐπιβάλλουσαν τιμὴν καὶ παρεδρείαν ποιούμεναι τῆς θεοῦ) 1 Cor 9: 13. M-M.*

πάρεδρος, ον (Pind.+; Wsd 6: 14; 9: 4) *sitting beside* subst. **πάρεδρος, ου, ὁ** *attendant, assistant* (Hdt.+; inscr.; PGM 1, 54; 96; 4, 1841; 1850; 7, 884 al.) of the believers θεοῦ (οἰκονόμοι καὶ) πάρεδροι (καὶ ὑπηρέται) IPol 6: 1 (Sextus 230a the pious man as πάρεδρος θεῷ; cf. PGM 4, 1347 supernatural beings as πάρεδροι τοῦ μεγάλου θεοῦ; Ael. Aristid. 37, 5 K.=2 p. 14 D.: Athena as π. of Zeus; Philo, Spec. Leg. 4, 201).*

παρεῖδον s. παροράω.

παρειμένος s. παρίημι.

πάρειμι (fr. εἰμί) ptc. παρών; impf. 3 pl. παρῆσαν; fut. 3 sing. παρέσται Rv 17: 8.—(Hom.+; inscr., pap., LXX, En., Ep. Arist., Philo, Joseph.).

1. *be present*—a. of pers. J 11: 28; Rv 17: 8; GP 10: 38. ἰδοὺ πάρειμι *here I am* (En. 106, 8) 2 Cl 15: 3; B 3: 5 (both Is 58: 9). παρών (opp. ἀπών; Wsd 11: 11; 14: 17) *(being) present* (Himerius, Or. 44 [=Or. 8], 1 παρὼν μόνῳ τῷ σώματι) 1 Cor 5: 3a, b; 2 Cor 10: 2, 11; 13: 2, 10; ISm 9: 2; IRo 7: 2; IMg 15: 1. ἀκούσας αὐτοὺς παρόντας *when he heard that they were present* MPol 7: 2. μηδεὶς τῶν παρόντων ὑμῶν *none of you who are present* IRo 7: 1.—W. a prep.: ἐνώπιον τοῦ θεοῦ πάρεσμεν *we are here in the presence of God* Ac 10: 33. ἐπὶ σοῦ παρεῖναι *be here before you* 24: 19. π. πρός τινα *be present with someone* (UPZ 71, 18 [152 BC]) 2 Cor 11: 9; Gal 4: 18, 20. οἱ παρόντες *those (who were) present* (Appian, Hann. 39 §166; Dit., Syll.³ 665, 38; 1044, 43 τῶν τε παρόντων καὶ τῶν ἀπόντων; 1047, 19; 3 Macc 1: 13) MPol 9: 1.—The pres. 'be here' can take on the perfect sense *have come* (Bl-D. §322; Rob. 881; cf. 1 Macc 12: 42 v.l., 45; 2 Macc 3: 9; Jos., Ant. 3, 84 πάρεστι εἰς, Vi. 115) τίς ἡ αἰτία δι' ἣν πάρεστε; *why have you come?* Ac 10: 21. οὗτοι καὶ ἐνθάδε πάρεισιν *these men have come here too* 17: 6. πάρεστιν ἀπ' ἀγροῦ *has come from the country* Lk 11: 6 D.—Hv 5: 3; s 7: 1. On ἑταῖρε, ἐφ' ὃ πάρει (Jos., Bell. 2, 615 John ἐφ' ὃ παρῆν διεπράττετο) Mt 26: 50 cf. ὅς I 2bβ. παρὼν ἤγειρεν αὐτούς *he came and raised them from the dead* IMg 9: 3.—The impf. παρῆν *he had come,* or *he came* (Diod. S. 19, 59, 1 παρῆν=he came) Hs 9, 11, 8. Pl. παρῆσαν *they had come, they came* Lk 13: 1 (Diod. S. 17, 8, 2 παρῆσαν=they came; Plut., Mor. 509c; an indication of time w. π. by means of ἐν in X., Cyr. 1, 2, 4); πρός τινα (Jos., Ant. 14, 451) Ac 12: 20.

b. of impersonals: τοῦ εὐαγγελίου τοῦ παρόντος εἰς ὑμᾶς *of the gospel that has come to you* Col 1: 6 (π. εἰς as X., An. 1, 2, 2; Jos., Ant. 1, 285; 337). Of time (Hdt.+; Dit., Syll.³ 700, 10 ἐν τῷ παρόντι καιρῷ; La 4: 18 πάρεστιν ὁ καιρὸς ἡμῶν; Hab 3: 2) ὁ καιρὸς πάρεστιν *the time has come* J 7: 6. ἡ καταστροφὴ πάρεστιν 1 Cl 57: 4 (Pr 1: 27). τὸ παρόν *the present* (Hdt.+; inscr., pap.; 3 Macc 5: 17; Philo, Spec. Leg. 2, 175) πρὸς τὸ παρόν *for the present, for the moment* (Thu. 2, 22, 1; 3, 40, 7; Pla., Leg. 5 p. 736a; Lucian, Epist. Sat. 2, 28; Cass. Dio 41, 15; Herodian 1, 3, 5; PGiess. 47, 15; Sb 5113, 28; Jos., Ant. 6, 69) Hb 12: 11. κατὰ τὸ π. (Diod. S. 15, 47, 4; Dit., Syll.³ 814, 46f; PTebt. 28, 9; POxy. 711, 2; 3 Macc 3: 11) *for the present* MPol 20: 1. τὰ παρόντα *the present situation* (Hdt. 1, 113; Pla., Theaet. 186a; Philo, Spec. Leg. 1, 334; PYale 42, 34) ἐν τοῖς παροῦσιν *under the present circumstances* B 1: 8.

2. πάρεστίν τί μοι *someth. is at my disposal, I have someth.* (trag., Hdt.+; Wsd 11: 21) ᾧ μὴ πάρεστιν ταῦτα 2 Pt 1: 9. ἡ παροῦσα ἀλήθεια *the truth that you have* vs. 12. τὰ παρόντα *what one has, one's possessions* (X., Symp. 4, 42 οἷς τὰ παρόντα ἀρκεῖ, Cyr. 8, 4, 6, An. 7, 7, 36. Further exx. under ἀρκέω 2) Hb 13: 5. M-M.*

παρεισάγω fut. παρεισάξω (Isocr.+; Polyb. 3, 63, 2; UPZ 162 VIII, 4 [117 BC]; Ep. Arist. 20) *bring in,* w. the connotation that it is done *secretly* or *maliciously* (Polyb. 1, 18, 3; 2, 7, 8; Diod. S. 12, 41, 4 οἱ προδόται τοὺς στρατιώτας παρεισαγαγόντες ἐντὸς τῶν τειχῶν κυρίους τῆς πόλεως ἐποίησαν), but also without such connotation (Diod. S. 1, 96, 5 of the introduction of Egyptian doctrines into Greece; Heraclit. Sto. 30 p. 45, 7; 43 p. 64, 17) of false teachers οἵτινες παρεισάξουσιν αἱρέσεις ἀπωλείας *who will bring in destructive opinions* 2 Pt 2: 1 (of heretics also, Hegesippus in Euseb., H.E. 4, 22, 5; Hippolytus, Refut. 5, 17 end; 7, 29 beg.). M-M.*

παρείσακτος, ον (Strabo 17, 1, 8 p. 794 as the nickname of Ptolemy XI. In some mss. the prologue of Sir is called πρόλογος παρείσακτος ἀδήλου. Hesychius=ἀλλότριος) *secretly brought in, smuggled in, sneaked in* παρείσακτοι ψευδάδελφοι of Judaizers who, as Paul felt, had come into Gentile Christian congregations in a dishonorable fashion, in order to spy on them Gal 2: 4. Cf. WSchmithals, D. Häretiker in Galatien: ZNW 47, '56, 25–67.*

παρεισδύ(ν)ω (mostly in the mid., Hippocr.+; Plut., Herodian, Philo) *slip in stealthily, sneak in* (Plut., Agis 3, 1, Mor. 216b; in the same sense Jos., Bell. 1, 468 παραδύνομαι) Jd 4. The form παρεισεδύησαν in Nestle's text is 2 aor. pass. w. intrans. mng. (cf. W-S. §13, 11; Bl-D. §76, 2; Rob. 1214 s.v. δύνω; Helbing p. 96f). Beside this the act. παρεισέδυσαν is attested; the first pers. sing. of this could be either the 1 aor. παρεισέδυσα or the 2 aor. παρεισέδυν (cf. δύνω). M-M.*

παρείσδυσις, εως, ἡ *slipping in* stealthily, *sneaking in* (Theophr., C. Pl. 1, 7, 1; Chrysippus: Stoic. III 199; Plut., Mor. 476c; 879e) ὁ πονηρὸς παρείσδυσιν πλάνης ποιήσας ἐν ἡμῖν *the evil one, having caused error to creep in among us* B 2: 10. παρείσδυσιν ἔχειν (Vett. Val. 345, 8) *have opportunity to slip in, find a loophole* ἵνα μὴ σχῇ παρείσδυσιν ὁ μέλας 4: 9 (cf. PStrassb. 22, 30 [I AD] οὐδεμίαν παρείσδυσιν ἔχεις). M-M. s.v. -δύω.*

παρεισενέγκας s. παρεισφέρω.

παρεισέρχομαι mid. dep.; 2 aor. παρεισῆλθον (Epicurus +; Diod. S. 17, 105, 1; Vett. Val. 357, 9; Sb 5761, 3 [91–96 AD]).

1. *slip in, come in* as a side issue, of the law, which has no primary place in the Divine Plan Ro 5: 20.

2. *slip in* w. unworthy motives, *sneak in* (Polyb. 1, 7, 3; 1, 8, 4; 2, 55, 3; Plut., Popl. 17, 2; Lucian, Dial. Mer. 12,

3; Ps.-Lucian, Asin. 15 εἰ λύκος παρεισέλθοι; Philo, Op.
M. 150, Abr. 96; Test. Jud. 16: 2) of the Judaizing false
brethren Gal 2: 4. M-M.*

παρεισφέρω Hellenistic aor. παρεισήνεγκα (Bl-D. §81,
2; Rob. 338) (Demosth. et al.; PTebt. 38, 12; 14 [113 BC])
apply, bring to bear σπουδήν *make an effort* 2 Pt 1: 5
(σπουδὴν εἰσφέρειν is a favorite expr. in the Koine: Dit.,
Syll.³ [index s.v. σπουδή]; Jos., Ant. 20, 204). M-M.*

παρεκβαίνω (Hes.+; Dit., Or. 573, 17) *go beyond,
transgress* only fig. τὶ *someth.* (Ep. Arist. 112) τὸν
ὡρισμένον τῆς λειτουργίας κανόνα 1 Cl 41: 1. Of the sea
οὐ παρεκβαίνει τὰ περιτεθειμένα αὐτῇ κλεῖθρα 20: 6.*

παρέκβασις, εως, ἡ (Theophr., Aristot. et al.; Jos., C.
Ap. 1, 57; 183, Vi. 367) *deviation* fr. a prescribed course
1 Cl 20: 3.*

παρεκτός adv.—1. used as an adv. *besides, outside* χωρὶς
τῶν π. (sc. γινομένων) *apart from what I leave unmen-
tioned* or *what is external* (i.e. sufferings, etc.) 2 Cor 11:
28.
2. as (improper) prep. w. gen. *apart from, except for*
(Dositheus 45, 3 παρεκτὸς ἐμοῦ, Lat. praeter me; Cyrill.
Scyth. p. 34, 4 π. σαββάτου=except on the Sabbath;
Geopon. 13, 15, 7; Etym. Magn. p. 652, 18; Test. Zeb. 1:
4; Aq. Dt 1: 36) Mt 5: 32; 19: 9 v.l. (AOtto, Die Eheschdg.
im Mt '39; KStaab, D. Unauflöslichkeit d. Ehe u. d. sog.
'Ehebruchsklauseln' b. Mt 5: 32 u. 19: 9: EdEichmann-
Festschr. '40, 435-52, ZkTh 67, '43, 36-44. S. also
πορνεία 1); Ac 26: 29. π. θεοῦ *without God, leading away
from God* D 6: 1. M-M.*

παρεκφέρω (Plut., Mor. 102c; Dit., Syll.³ 834, 18) *bring*
to a place λίθους Hs 9, 4, 8.*

παρεμβάλλω fut. παρεμβαλῶ (Aristoph., Demosth.+;
pap., LXX; Jos., C. Ap. 1, 229).
1. The word is used freq. (even in the LXX) as a military
t.t., but w. var. mngs. παρεμβαλοῦσιν οἱ ἐχθροί σου
χάρακά σοι *your enemies will throw up a palisade against
you* Lk 19: 43 (acc. to אL. But AB have περιβαλοῦσιν; D
has βαλοῦσιν ἐπὶ σέ).
2. fig., of anger παρεμβάλλει ἑαυτὴν εἰς τὴν καρδίαν
it insinuates itself into the heart Hm 5, 2, 2. M-M.*

παρεμβολή, ῆς, ἡ (Aeschin.+). Mostly used as a military
t.t. (Polyb. et al.; inscr., pap., LXX; En. 1, 4; Test. 12
Patr.); so always in our lit.
1. *a* (fortified) *camp* (Polyb. 3, 75, 5; 9; Diod. S. 13, 87,
2; 15, 84, 1 al.; Dit., Syll.³ 700, 20; POxy. 736; LXX; Jos.,
Ant. 6, 110; 20, 152) ἡ παρεμβολὴ τῶν ἀλλοφύλων 1 Cl
55: 4 (cf. ἀλλόφυλος). Of the Israelite camp (LXX) ἔξω
τῆς παρεμβολῆς (Ex 29: 14.—Lev 4: 12, 21; 10: 4f al.) Hb
13: 11; 1 Cl 4: 11.—To the ἔξω τῆς π. Hb 13: 11, vs. 13
adds the appeal ἐξερχώμεθα ἔξω τῆς π., giving as a
reason that we have no 'lasting city' here. In this pass. the
words ἔξω τῆς π. seem to refer to separation fr. worldly
things in general (cf. Philo, Gig. 54 Μωϋσῆς ἔξω τῆς
παρεμβολῆς καὶ τοῦ σωματικοῦ παντὸς στρατοπέδου
πήξας τὴν ἑαυτοῦ σκηνήν); but cf. GABarton, JBL 57,
'38, 204f, Rome.—HKoester, HTR 55, '62, 299-315. Of
Jerusalem Hb 13: 12 v.l. (for πύλης).—ἡ παρεμβολὴ τῶν
ἁγίων Rv 20: 9 is also to be understood fr. the OT use of
the word.
2. of the *barracks* or *headquarters* of the Roman troops
in Jerusalem Ac 21: 34, 37; 22: 24; 23: 10, 16, 32. Also of
the barracks in Rome where the soldiers who accompanied
Paul were quartered Ac 28: 16 v.l.
3. *an army* in battle array, *battle line* (Polyb.; Aelian,

V.H. 14, 46; Ex 14: 19f; Judg 4: 16; 8: 11; 1 Km 14: 16)
Hb 11: 34.—FCFensham, 'Camp' in the NT and Mil-
hamah, Rev. de Qumran 4, '63, 557-62. M-M.*

παρεμπλέκω (Diphilus the physician [III BC] in Athen. 2,
49 p. 57c; Hero Alex. I p. 20, 11; Oribasius, Ecl. 40: CMG
VI 2, 2 p. 202, 7 π. τῷ ποτῷ τὴν τροφήν; schol. on Pind.,
Eustath., Prooem. 9; PTurin 8, 28 [116 BC]) med. t.t. *mix,
mingle, blend with* of false teachers ἑαυτοῖς παρεμπλέ-
κουσιν Ἰησοῦν Χριστόν *they mingle Jesus Christ with
themselves* (=*their teaching*) ITr 6: 2.*

παρέμπτωσις, εως, ἡ (Aristot.+) *intrusion, insidious
plot* διά τινας παρεμπτώσεις 1 Cl 51: 1 (the word is not
found in the Gk. ms. trad., but Clem. Alex. has it, Strom.
4, 113, 1, in a paraphrase of our pass., and the Lat. and
Copt. versions of 1 Cl agree w. him).*

παρεμφέρω (Galen, Vett. Val. in various mngs.) *bring* Hs
9, 4, 8 v.l. (for παρεκ-).*

παρένεγκε s. παραφέρω.

παρενθυμέομαι 1 aor. pass. παρενεθυμήθην (M. Ant. 5,
5, 5; 6, 20, 2; Iambl., In Nicom. p. 83, 15 Pistelli; Tituli
As. Minor. II 1 [ed. EKalinka '20] 245, 13; POxford [ed.
EPWegener '42] 3, 12 [142 AD]; Sb 7404, 39 [II AD]; Philo)
disregard, neglect, forget τὶ *someth.* (Philo, Spec. Leg. 4,
53) of commands Hm 5, 2, 8 (τὴν ἐντολὴν ταύτην); 12,
3, 6 (ταύτας, i.e. ἐντολάς). Referring to a good thought
(τὸ καλόν) and w. αὐτό to be supplied *make light of* s 5, 2,
7. W. ref. to the sins of the members of Hermas' family, w.
αὐτάς to be supplied v 2, 3, 1.*

παρενοχλέω (Hippocr.+; inscr., pap., LXX) *cause difficulty* (*for*), *trouble, annoy* w. dat. of the pers. (Polyb. 1,
8, 1; Plut., Timol. 3, 1; Epict. 1, 9, 23; PGenève 31, 4;
LXX) Ac 15: 19. M-M.*

παρεπιδημέω 1 aor. ptc. παρεπιδημήσας (Polyb. 27, 6,
3; Diod. S. 1, 83, 8; 19, 61, 1; Aelian, V.H. 8, 7 p. 90, 29;
inscr.; PPetr. II 13, 19 [258-53 BC]; UPZ 196 I, 13; 19 [119
BC]; Ep. Arist. 110; Philo, Conf. Lingu. 76, Agr. 65) *stay
for a short time in a strange place, visit* πρός τινα (*with*)
someone 1 Cl 1: 2.*

παρεπίδημος, ον (Polyb. 32, 6, 4; Athen. 5 p. 196A; Dit.,
Or. 383, 150; PPetr. I 19, 22 [225 BC]; III 7, 15; LXX.—
Dssm., B 146f [BS 149]) *staying* for a while in a strange
place, *sojourning* in our lit. subst. ὁ παρεπίδημος *stranger, exile, sojourner, resident alien* of the Christians, who
are not at home in this world ἐκλεκτοὶ π. *chosen exiles*
1 Pt 1: 1. (w. πάροικοι [cf. Gen 23: 4; Ps 38: 13) 2: 11. (W.
ξένοι) π. ἐπὶ τῆς γῆς *exiles on the earth* Hb 11: 13 (cf.
Ps.-Pla., Axioch. 365B παρεπιδημία τίς ἐστιν ὁ βίος.—
MMeister, De Axiocho Dial., Diss. Breslau '15, 86ff).
M-M.*

παρέρχομαι mid. dep.; fut. παρελεύσομαι; 2 aor.
παρῆλθον, imper. in H.Gk. παρελθάτω Mt 26: 39 (Bl-D.
§81, 3; Mlt.-H. 209); pf. παρελήλυθα (Hom.+; inscr.,
pap., LXX, Ep. Arist., Philo, Joseph., Test. 12 Patr.).
1. *go by, pass by*—a. lit.—α. of persons, w. acc. *someone* or *someth.* (Aelian, V.H. 2, 35; Lucian, De Merc.
Cond. 15) an animal Hv 4, 1, 9; 4, 2, 1. Of Jesus and his
disciples on the lake: ἤθελεν παρελθεῖν αὐτούς Mk 6: 48
(cf. HWindisch, NThT 9, '20, 298-308; GAvdBerghv
Eysinga, ibid. 15, '26, 221-9 al.; Lohmeyer s.v. παράγω
2aα). διὰ τῆς ὁδοῦ ἐκείνης *pass by along that road* Mt 8:
28 (constr. w. διά as PAmh. 154, 2; Num 20: 17; Josh 24:
17). παρὰ τὴν λίμνην GEb 2. τὸν τόπον Papias 3. Absol.
(X., An. 2, 4, 25) Lk 18: 37; 1 Cl 14: 5 (Ps 36: 36).

β. of time: *pass* (Soph., Hdt.+; inscr., pap., LXX) ἡ ὥρα ἤδη παρῆλθεν *the time is already past* Mt 14: 15. Of a definite period of time (SSol 2: 11 ὁ χειμὼν π.; Jos., Ant. 15, 408) διὰ τὸ τὴν νηστείαν ἤδη παρεληλυθέναι *because the fast was already over* Ac 27: 9. ὁ παρεληλυθὼς χρόνος *the time that is past* 1 Pt 4: 3 (cf. Isocr. 4, 167 χρόνος . . . ἱκανὸς γὰρ ὁ παρεληλυθώς, ἐν ᾧ τί τῶν δεινῶν οὐ γέγονεν; PMagd. 25, 3 παρεληλυθότος τοῦ χρόνου). τὰ παρεληλυθότα (beside τὰ ἐνεστῶτα and τὰ μέλλοντα; cf. Herm. Wr. 424, 10ff Sc.; Demosth. 4, 2; Jos., Ant. 10, 210) *things past, the past* (Demosth. 18, 191; Sir 42: 19; Philo, Spec. Leg. 1, 334, Leg. All. 2, 42) B 1: 7; 5: 3.

b. fig.—**α.** *pass away, come to an end, disappear* (Demosth. 18, 188 κίνδυνον παρελθεῖν; Theocr. 27, 8; Ps 89: 6; Wsd 2: 4; 5: 9; Da 7: 14 Theod.) of men ὡς ἄνθος χόρτου παρελεύσεται Js 1: 10. ὁ οὐρανὸς καὶ ἡ γῆ Mt 5: 18a; 24: 35a; Mk 13: 31a; Lk 16: 17; 21: 33a; cf. 2 Pt 3: 10; Rv 21: 1 t.r. ὁ κόσμος οὗτος D 10: 6. ἡ γενεὰ αὕτη Mt 24: 34; Mk 13: 30; Lk 21: 32. αἱ γενεαὶ πᾶσαι 1 Cl 50: 3. ἡ ὀργή vs. 4 (Is 26: 20). τὰ ἀρχαῖα παρῆλθεν 2 Cor 5: 17.— *Pass away* in the sense *lose force, become invalid* (Ps 148: 6; Esth 10: 3b τῶν λόγων τούτων· οὐδὲ παρῆλθεν ἀπ' αὐτῶν λόγος) οἱ λόγοι μου οὐ μὴ παρέλθωσιν (or οὐ [μὴ] παρελεύσονται) Mt 24: 35b; Mk 13: 31b; Lk 21: 33b. ἰῶτα ἓν ἢ μία κεραία οὐ μὴ παρέλθῃ ἀπὸ τοῦ νόμου Mt 5: 18b. οὐδὲν μὴ παρέλθῃ τῶν δεδογματισμένων ὑπ' αὐτοῦ 1 Cl 27: 5.

β. *pass by, transgress, neglect, disobey* τὶ someth. Hes., Theog. 613; Lysias 6, 52 τὸν νόμον; Demosth. 37, 37; Dionys. Hal. 1, 58; Dt 17: 2; Jer 41: 18; Jdth 11: 10; 1 Macc 2: 22; Jos., Ant. 14, 67) Lk 11: 42; 15: 29.

γ. of suffering or misfortune: *pass without touching* (Jos., Ant. 5, 31) ἀπό τινος *from someone* (for the constr. w. ἀπό cf. 2 Ch 9: 2) Mt 26: 39; Mk 14: 35. Abs. Mt 26: 42.

δ. *get by unnoticed, escape* (Theognis 419; Sir 42: 20) Hs 8, 2, 5a, b.

2. *go through, pass through* (Appian, Bell. Civ. 5, 68 §288 ὁ Ἀντώνιος μόλις παρῆλθεν = Antony made his way through [to the Forum] with difficulty; 1 Macc 5: 48 διελεύσομαι εἰς τὴν γῆν σου, τοῦ ἀπελθεῖν εἰς τὴν γῆν ἡμῶν· καὶ οὐδεὶς κακοποιήσει ὑμᾶς, πλὴν τοῖς ποσὶν παρελευσόμεθα) παρελθόντες τὴν Μυσίαν κατέβησαν εἰς Τρῳάδα Ac 16: 8 (lack of knowledge of this mng., and recognition of the fact that passing by is impossible in this case, gave rise to the v.l. διελθόντες D); cf. 17: 15 D.

3. *come to, come here, come* (trag., Hdt.+; inscr., pap., LXX, Ep. Arist. 176; Philo; Jos., Bell. 3, 347, Ant. 1, 337) Lk 12: 37; 17: 7; Ac 24: 7 t.r. M-M.*

πάρεσις, εως, ἡ (Hippocr.+; BGU 624, 21 [cf. Dssm., NB 94–BS 266]; Philo; Jos., Ant. 11, 236) *passing over, letting go unpunished* (Dionys. Hal. 7, 37 ὁλοσχερῆ πάρεσιν οὐχ εὕροντο, τὴν δὲ εἰς χρόνον ἀναβολὴν ἔλαβον; Dio Chrys. 80[30], 19 πάρεσίν τινα ἔχειν κτ. θεοῦ.—Corresp. the verb παριέναι means 'leave unpunished': X., Hipp. 7, 10; Dionys. Hal. 2, 35; Sir 23: 2; Jos., Ant. 15, 48 παρῆκεν τὴν ἁμαρτίαν.—The verb is also used of 'remitting' debts and other obligations: Phalaris, Ep. 81, 1 χρημάτων; Dit., Syll.³ 742, 33; 39, Or. 669, 50.—JMCreed, JTS 41, '40, 28–30; SLyonnet, Biblica 38, '57, 35–61) διὰ τὴν π. τῶν προγεγονότων ἁμαρτημάτων Ro 3: 25.—WGKümmel, Πάρεσις u. ἔνδειξις: ZThK 49, '52, 154–67. See s.v. ἔνδειξις. M-M.*

παρέχω impf. παρεῖχον, 3 pl. παρεῖχαν Ac 28: 2 W-H. (H.Gk.; cf. Bl-D. §82 app.; Mlt.-H. 194); fut. παρέξω; 2

aor. παρέσχον; pf. παρέσχηκα. Mid.: impf. παρειχόμην; fut., 2 sing. παρέξῃ (Hom. +; inscr., pap., LXX, Ep. Arist., Philo, Joseph., Test. 12 Patr.).

1. act.—**a.** *give up, offer, present* (schol. on Nicander, Alexiph. 204 παρέχειν πίνειν = offer to drink) τί τινι *someth. to someone* τὴν σιαγόνα Lk 6: 29. τὸν πλοῦτον Hs 2: 7.

b. *grant, show* τινί τι someth. *to someone* (Vi. Aesopi I c. 124 οὐδὲν αὐτῷ παρεῖχον; Aesop, Fab. 396 P. = 170 H.; Jos., Ant. 2, 329; 11, 2) Dg 12: 1. ἀγάπην 1 Cl 21: 7. φιλανθρωπίαν Ac 28: 2. πλέον anything greater IRo 2: 2. Of God (Appian, Bell. Civ. 3, 65 §265 ἦν οἱ θεοὶ παρέχωσιν εὐπραγεῖν; Alex. Aphr., Quaest. 1, 14 Bruns) ἡμῖν πάντα 1 Ti 6: 17; cf. Dg 8: 11. ὧν (attraction of the rel. fr. ἅ) τοῖς οἰομένοις διδόναι παρέχει αὐτός *which he himself supplies to those who think they are giving* Dg 3: 4. πίστιν παρασχὼν πᾶσιν Ac 17: 31 s. on πίστις 1c.—Without a dat. (Pind., Paeanes 4, 24 μοῖσαν) νοῦν *grant understanding* Dg 11: 5. ἡσυχίαν Ac 22: 2 (cf. Jos., Ant. 5, 235). δεῖγμά τινος Dg 3: 3 (s. δεῖγμα 2 and 1).—Without the acc., which is to be supplied fr. the context Dg 3: 5; ISm 11: 3.—W. dat. and inf. foll. MPol 18: 2.

c. *cause, bring about* τινί τι someth. *for someone* (Hdt. 1, 177 πόνον; Socrat., Ep. 14, 1 κακά; Arrian, Anab. 2, 21, 3 φόβον; Ep. Arist. 96 ἔκπληξιν ἡμῖν π.; Jos., Ant. 18, 175 ὄχλον [= annoyance] μοι π.) κόπους *cause trouble* (s. κόπος 1) Mt 26: 10; Mk 14: 6; Lk 11: 7; 18: 5 (κόπον, as Sir 29: 4); Gal 6: 17 (κόπους μοι μηδεὶς παρεχέτω in connection w. PGM 14b [ἐάν μοι ὁ δεῖνα κόπους παράσχῃ] is taken as a formula of adjuration by Dssm., B 262ff [BS 352–60], LO 256 [LAE 301]); Hv 3, 3, 2 (περί τινος *about someth.*). χαρὰν ἡμῖν π. *give us joy* 1 Cl 63: 2. ἐργασίαν πολλήν *bring great gain* Ac 16: 16 (Jos., Ant. 15, 332 πλείστην ἐργασίαν παρασχόν).—Without the dat. (s. ref. to Hdt. above.—Sir 29: 4 v.l.) Hm 11: 20. ξενισμόν *cause astonishment* IEph 19: 2. ἐκζητήσεις *give rise to speculations* 1 Ti 1: 4.

2. mid. (Bl-D. §316, 3; Rob. 810)—**a.** ἑαυτόν τι *show oneself to be someth.* (X., Cyr. 8, 1, 39; Dit., Syll.³ 333, 10f [306 BC]; 442, 8f; 620, 5f; 748, 31f; 1068, 6f; 1104, 18f; UPZ 144, 15 [164/3 BC]; POxy. 281, 13; PRainer 27, 14.—Dssm., NB 81f [BS 254]; Thieme 24; Rouffiac 52. In class. Gk. the act. would be used, as it is Jos., C. Ap. 2, 156) σεαυτὸν παρεχόμενος τύπον Tit 2: 7.

b. *grant* τινί τι someth. *to someone* (Diod. S. 20, 62, 1 παρείχετο τοῖς ἐμπόροις τὴν ἀσφάλειαν; Jos., Ant. 9, 255; cf. τὰ ἑαυτῶν δίκαια παρέσχοντο = they submitted their claims: letter of MAurelius l. 33 in ZPE 8, '71, 170f) τὸ δίκαιον καὶ τὴν ἰσότητα *what is just and fair* Col 4: 1. ἄξιός ἐστιν ᾧ παρέξῃ τοῦτο *he deserves that you grant him this* Lk 7: 4. *Offer* 1 Cl 20: 10.

c. *get for oneself,* among others τοῖς τεχνίταις ἐργασίαν Ac 19: 24. M-M.*

παρηγορία, ας, ἡ (Aeschyl.+; 4 Macc 5: 12; 6: 1) *comfort* (Aeschyl., Ag. 95; Plut., Per. 34, 3, Mor. 599B; Vett. Val. 183, 9f; 209, 25; Philo, Deus Imm. 65, Somn. 1, 112; Jos., Ant. 4, 195; Epigr. Gr. 204, 12 [I BC]) of pers. ἐγενήθησάν μοι παρηγορία *they have become a comfort to me* Col 4: 11. M-M.*

παρθενία, ας, ἡ (Sappho, Pind., trag.+; Plut.; Aelian, V.H. 13, 1 p. 143, 17; inscr., pap., LXX, Philo; Jos., Ant. 4, 248 al.) *virginity* as a state of being (Callim., Hymn. 3, 6 of Artemis: παρθενίη αἰώνιος; Aristocritus [III BC]: 493, fgm. 5 Jac. of Hestia; Diod. S. 5, 3, 4) ἡ π. Μαρίας IEph 19: 1. Of the time of virginity ἀπὸ τῆς π. αὐτῆς Lk 2: 36

(ἀπό II 2a. Also ἐκ παρθενίας in Charito 3, 7, 5; cf. cum quo vixit ab virginitate sua ad finem vitae suae, CIL 10, 3720). M-M.*

παρθένος, ου, ἡ and ὁ (Hom.+; inscr., pap., LXX; En. 98, 2; Philo; Jos., Ant. 4, 244, Vi. 414; Sib. Or. 3, 357).

1. *virgin* Mt 25: 1, 7, 11; 1 Cor 7: 25 (FStrobel, NovT 2, '58, 199–227), 28, 34; Pol 5: 3; Hv 4, 2, 1; s 9, 1, 2; 9, 2, 3; 5; 9, 3, 2; 4f; 9, 4, 3; 5f; 8 al. After Is 7: 14 (הָעַלְמָה הָרָה; on this ASchulz, BZ 23, '35, 229–41; WHBrownlee, The Mng. of Qumran for the Bible, esp. Is, '64, 274–81) Mt 1: 23 (cf. Menand., Sicyonius 372f παρθένος γ᾽ ἔτι, ἄπειρος ἀνδρός). Of Mary also Lk 1: 27a, b; ISm 1: 1 and prob. Dg 12: 8 (the idea that the spirit of a god could father a child by a woman, specifically a virgin, was not foreign to Egyptian religion: Plut., Numa 4, 6, Mor. 718B; Philo, Cher. 43–50 [on this ENorden, D. Geburt des Kindes 78–90]. Cf. further the lit. on Ἰωσήφ 4 and OBardenhewer, Mariä Verkündigung '05; EPetersen, Die wunderbare Geburt des Heilandes '09; HUsener, Das Weihnachtsfest² '11; ASteinmann, D. jungfräul. Geburt des Herrn³ '26, D. Jungfrauengeburt u. die vergl. Religionsgeschichte '19; GHBox, The Virgin Birth of Jesus '16; OECrain, The Credibility of the Virgin Birth '25; JG Machen, The Virgin Birth of Christ² '32 [on this FKattenbusch, StKr 102, '30, 454–74]; EWorcester, Studies in the Birth of Our Lord '32; KLSchmidt, D. jungfrl. Geb. J. Chr.: ThBl 14, '35, 289–97; FXSteinmetzer, Empfangen v. Hl. Geist '38; RGBratcher, Bible Translator 9, '58, 98–125 [Heb., LXX, Mt]; TBoslooper, The Virg. Birth '62; Hv Campenhausen, D. Jungfrauengeburt in d. Theol. d. alten Kirche '62.—RJCooke, Did Paul Know the Virg. Birth? '27; PRBotz, D. Jungfrausch. Mariens im NT u. in der nachap. Zeit, Diss. Tüb. '34; DEdwards, The Virg. Birth in History and Faith '43.—Clemen² 114–21; ENorden, D. Geburt des Kindes² '31; MDibelius, Jungfrauensohn u. Krippenkind '32. As a contrast to Dibelius' Hellenistic emphasis cf. OMichel and OBetz, Beih. ZNW 26, '60, 3–23, who stress Qumran parallels.). Of the daughters of Philip παρθένοι προφητεύουσαι Ac 21: 9. Of the virgins who were admitted to the church office of 'widows' ISm 13: 1 (cf. AJülicher, PM 22, '18, 111f. Differently LZscharnack, Der Dienst der Frau '02, 105ff).—On 1 Cor 7: 36–8 cf. γαμίζω 1 and s. also PKetter, Trierer Theol. Ztschr. 56, '47, 175–82 (παρθ. often means [virgin] daughter: Apollon. Rhod. 2, 86 παρθ. Ἀλήτεω and the scholion on this has the following note: παρθένον ἀντὶ τοῦ θυγατέρα; Lycophron vss. 1141, 1175; Diod. S. 8, 6, 2; 16, 55, 3; 20, 84, 3 [pl. beside υἱοί]. Likewise Theod. Prodr. 1, 293 H. τὴν σὴν παρθένον='your virgin daughter'; in 3, 332 τ. ἑαυτοῦ παρθένον refers to one's 'sweetheart'; likew. 6, 466, as well as the fact that παρθ. can mean simply 'girl' [e.g., Paus. 8, 20, 4]). RHSeboldt, Spiritual Marriage in the Early Church, CTM 30, '59, 103–19; 176–86.—The Christian Church as παρθένος ἁγνή (ἁγνός 1) 2 Cor 11: 2 (on this subj. s. FCConybeare, Die jungfräul. Kirche u. die jungfräul. Mutter: ARW 8, '05, 373ff; 9, '06, 73ff; Cumont³ 283, 33).

2. Also used of men who have had no intercourse w. women; in this case it is masc. gender *chaste man* (CIG IV 8784b; Proseuche Asenath 6 and 8 Batiffol uses π. of Joseph; Pel.-Leg. 27, 1 uses it of Abel; Suidas of Abel and Melchizedek; Nonnus of the apostle John, who is also called 'virgo' in the Monarchian Prologues [Kl. T. 1² '08, p. 13, 13]) Rv 14: 4.—JMFord, The Mng. of 'Virgin', NTS 12, '66, 293–9; GDelling, TW V 824–35. M-M. B. 90.**

Πάρθοι, ων, οἱ (since Hdt. 3, 93; Dit., Or. 544, 32;

Joseph. index; Sib. Or., index of names) *Parthians* (successors to the Persians. Parthia was southeast of the Caspian, but in NT times its empire extended to the Euphrates) Ac 2: 9 (Ps.-Callisth. 2, 4, 9 . . . Πάρθων καὶ Ἐλυμαίων καὶ Βαβυλωνίων καὶ τῶν κατὰ τὴν Μεσοποταμίαν . . . χώραν. Cf. 1, 2, 2 Σκύθαι καὶ Ἄραβες καὶ . . . ; 14 names in all).—Lit. in Schürer I⁴ 447, 44; JABrinkman, CBQ 25, '63, 418–27.*

παρίημι 2 aor. inf. παρεῖναι; pf. pass. ptc. παρειμένος (Hom.+; inscr., pap., LXX, Ep. Arist., Philo, Joseph.).

1. *leave undone, neglect* (Pind., Hdt.+; 4 Macc 5: 29) τὶ someth. (Jos., Bell. 2, 202, Ant. 8, 218) ταῦτα ἔδει ποιῆσαι κἀκεῖνα μὴ παρεῖναι Lk 11: 42.

2. *let fall at the side, slacken, weaken* pf. pass. ptc.—a. *weakened, listless, drooping* (Eur.+; Pla., Leg. 11 p. 931D; Diod. S. 14, 105, 2 τὰ σώματα παρειμένοι; Ps.-Plut., Consol. ad Apollon. 1 p. 102A; LXX; Philo, In Flacc. 10 διανοίας παρειμένης; Jos., Ant. 6, 35) παρειμέναι χεῖρες (Sir 2: 12; cf. Jos., Ant. 13, 343; Cornutus 16 p. 23, 18): w. παραλελυμένα γόνατα (as Is 35: 3; Sir 25: 23) Hb 12: 12.

b. *careless, indolent* w. νωθρός (as Sir 4: 29) 1 Cl 34: 1. (W. ἀργός) π. ἐπὶ πᾶν ἔργον ἀγαθόν *careless in every good work* 34: 4. M-M.*

παριστάνω s. παρίστημι.

παρίστημι and **παριστάνω** (Hom.+; the later form παριστάνω, which is the only one found in our lit. [Ro 6: 13, 16] Polyb.+; Epict. 3, 22, 87; Dit., Syll.³ 589, 46 [196 BC]; 814, 36 [67 AD]; 1109, 76.—Bl-D. §93; Mlt.-H. 202) fut. παραστήσω; 1 aor. παρέστησα; 2 aor. παρέστην; pf. παρέστηκα, ptc. παρεστηκώς or παρεστώς; plpf. παρειστήκειν; 1 fut. mid. παραστήσομαι; 1 aor. pass. παρεστάθην.

1. trans. (pres., impf., fut., 1 aor. act.)—a. *place beside, put at someone's disposal* τινά or τί τινι *someone or someth. to someone* (Socrates of Rhodes [I BC] in Athen. 4 p. 148B; Lucian, D. Mar. 6, 2) παραστήσει μοι λεγιῶνας Mt 26: 53. τὶ someth. (cf. 2 Macc 12: 3 v.l. σκάφη) κτήνη *provide riding animals* Ac 23: 24. Here belongs παραστήσατε ἑαυτοὺς τῷ θεῷ *put yourselves at God's disposal* Ro 6: 13b. W. dat. and double acc. (of the obj. and the pred.) ᾧ παριστάνετε ἑαυτοὺς δούλους (εἰς ὑπακοήν) *to whomever you yield yourselves as slaves (to obey him;* w. acc., followed by εἰς=to or for [s. MTreu, Alkaios '52, p. 12]) vs. 16; μηδὲ παριστάνετε τὰ μέλη ὑμῶν ὅπλα ἀδικίας τῇ ἁμαρτίᾳ vs. 13a; cf. vs. 19a, b.

b. *present, represent*—a. lit. τινά τινι *someone to someone* παρέστησαν τὸν Παῦλον αὐτῷ Ac 23: 33. παρθένον ἁγνὴν παραστῆσαι τῷ Χριστῷ 2 Cor 11: 2. Of the 'presentation' of Jesus in the Temple Lk 2: 22 (Billerb. II 120–3. Cf. also Olympiodorus, Life of Plato, ed. AWestermann 1850 p. 1: of Plato, said to be of supernatural origin λαβόντες οἱ γονεῖς βρέφος ὄντα τεθείκασιν ἐν τῷ Ὑμηττῷ βουλόμενοι ὑπὲρ αὐτοῦ τοῖς ἐκεῖ θεοῖς . . . θῦσαι). W. dat. of the pers., acc. of the obj., and pred. acc. οἷς παρέστησεν ἑαυτὸν ζῶντα *to whom he presented himself alive* Ac 1: 3; without a dat., which is supplied fr. the context παρέστησεν αὐτὴν ζῶσαν 9: 41.

β. fig. παραστήσω σε κατὰ πρόσωπόν σου *I will show you to yourself, face to face* 1 Cl 35: 10 (Ps 49: 21).

c. 'present' becomes almost equivalent to *make, render* (Plut., Mor. 676C [ἡ πίσσα] τὸν οἶνον εὔποτον παρίστησι] ἵνα παραστήσῃ αὐτὸς ἑαυτῷ ἔνδοξον τὴν ἐκκλησίαν *that he might render the church glorious* before him Eph 5: 27. σπούδασον σεαυτὸν δόκιμον παραστῆσαι τῷ θεῷ 2 Ti 2: 15. παραστῆσαι ὑμᾶς ἁγίους κατενώπιον αὐτοῦ to make you holy before him Col 1: 22. ἵνα παραστήσωμεν πάντα ἄνθρωπον τέλειον ἐν Χριστῷ that we may make everyone complete in Christ vs. 28.

d. as a t.t. in the language of sacrifice offer, bring, present (παριστάναι θυσίαν, θύματα etc.: Epici p. 19; Polyb. 16, 25, 7; Diod. S. 3, 72, 1; Lucian, De Sacrific. 13; Jos., Bell. 2, 89, Ant. 4, 113; Dit., Syll.³ 589, 46 [196 BC]; 694, 49; 736, 70, Or. 456, 20; 764, 23; 38. The mid. is also used in this way since X., An. 6, 1, 22) fig. παραστῆσαι τὰ σώματα θυσίαν ζῶσαν offer the bodies as a living sacrifice Ro 12: 1.

e. as a legal t.t. bring before (a judge) (Sb 4512, 82 [II BC]; Dit., Or. 669, 49; BGU 163, 3; 341, 14; 747 II, 26; 759, 22; 1139, 18). Some would prefer to understand 1 Cor 8: 8 in this sense: βρῶμα ἡμᾶς οὐ παραστήσει τῷ θεῷ food will not bring us before (the judgment seat of) God. Likew. ἡμᾶς ἐγερεῖ καὶ παραστήσει σὺν ὑμῖν he will raise us and bring us, together with you, before him (= before his judgment seat) 2 Cor 4: 14. But the forensic mng. is not certain in either of these places, and the sense is prob. bring before God= bring close to God (cf. Rtzst., ZNW 13, '12, 19f).

f. prove, demonstrate (Lysias 12, 51; X., Oec. 13, 1; Epict. 2, 23, 47; 2, 26, 4; Jos., Ant. 4, 47, Vi. 27; PLeipz. 64, 34) οὐδὲ παραστῆσαι δύνανταί σοι περὶ ὧν νυνὶ κατηγοροῦσίν μου nor can they prove to you the accusations they are now making against me Ac 24: 13.—The 1 aor. pass. Hs 8, 4, 1 occupies a peculiar middle ground betw. 1 and 2: κἀγὼ παρεστάθην αὐτῷ and I was placed beside him= took my place beside him.

2. intrans. (mid., and perf., plpf., 2 aor. act.)—a. pres., fut., aor.—α. approach, come τινί (to) someone (Philo, De Jos. 94) Ac 9: 39; 27: 23 (Plut., Lysander 20, 7 αὐτῷ κατὰ τοὺς ὕπνους παραστῆναι τὸν Ἄμμωνα).—Also as a t.t. of legal usage (s. 1e above.—Charito 6, 6, 4 παρέστην δικαστηρίῳ) Καίσαρί σε δεῖ παραστῆναι you must stand before the Emperor (as judge) Ac 27: 24; cf. 2 Ti subscr. πάντες παραστησόμεθα τῷ βήματι τοῦ θεοῦ Ro 14: 10. πάντας δεῖ παραστῆναι τῷ βήματι τοῦ Χριστοῦ Pol 6: 2 (τοῦ Χριστοῦ is the rdg. of the t.r. in Ro 14: 10).

β. of appearing with hostile intent, (Appian, Illyr. 17 §51) abs. παρέστησαν οἱ βασιλεῖς τῆς γῆς Ac 4: 26 (Ps 2: 2).

γ. come to the aid of, help, stand by τινί someone (Hom.+; X., Cyr. 5, 3, 19 al.; Mitteis, Chrest. 372 VI, 7; 12; Jos., Bell. 2, 245; Sib. Or. 8, 407) Ro 16: 2. ὁ κύριός μοι παρέστη 2 Ti 4: 17 (cf. PHermopol. 125B, 8 [III AD] θεὸς παρίσταταί σοι; Jos., Ant. 1, 341; Sib. Or. 3, 705).

b. perf. and plpf.—α. of personal beings stand (near or by), be present τινί (with) someone (LXX; Jos., Bell. 2, 281) Ac 1: 10; 1 Cl 34: 6 (Da 7: 10 Theod.). ἐνώπιόν τινος stand before someone (1 Km 16: 21) οὗτος παρέστηκεν ἐνώπιον ὑμῶν ὑγιής Ac 4: 10.—Mostly in the ptc.: modifying a noun and followed by an indication of place: ὁ κεντυρίων ὁ παρεστηκὼς ἐξ ἐναντίας αὐτοῦ Mk 15: 39 (cf. 1 Macc 11: 68 S). Γαβριὴλ ὁ παρεστηκὼς ἐνώπιον τοῦ θεοῦ Lk 1: 19 (cf. Jdth 4: 14; Tob 12: 15 S). Without indication of place (Diod. S. 17, 66, 7 παρεστὼς Φιλώτας =Philotas, who stood nearby; Diog. L. 2, 102; Abercius-inschr. 17; Ep. Arist. 19) εἷς παρεστηκὼς τῶν ὑπηρετῶν one of the servants who was standing by J 18: 22. ἰδὼν τὸν μαθητὴν παρεστῶτα when he saw the disciple standing near 19: 26. (ἄγγελοι) λειτουργοῦσιν παρεστῶτες 1 Cl 34: 5. παρεστὼς ὁ κύριος MPol 2: 2. οἱ παρεστῶτες

αὐτῷ those standing near him Ac 23: 2.—Subst. οἱ παρεστηκότες (PPetr. II 4, 6, 13 [III BC]) or οἱ παρεστῶτες (Diog. L. 9, 27) the bystanders, the spectators, those present Mk 14: 47, 69f; 15: 35 (v.l. ἑστηκότων); Lk 19: 24; Ac 23: 2ℵ, 4; in vs. 2 the more widely attested rdg., found in Nestle's text, adds a dat.: τοῖς παρεστῶσιν αὐτῷ (cf. POxy. 1204, 13 ὁ παρεστώς σοι).

β. of a point of time be here, have come (Il. 16, 853; Demosth. 18, 90) παρέστηκεν ὁ θερισμός the time for the harvest is here Mk 4: 29.

γ. as an agricultural t.t. (cf. Dit., Or. 56, 68 ὅταν ὁ πρώϊμος σπόρος παραστῇ; PLille 8, 5) someth. like be fully grown σταφυλὴ παρεστηκυῖα a ripe grape (in contrast to ὄμφαξ) 1 Cl 23: 4=2 Cl 11: 3 (quot. of unknown orig.). BReicke and GBertram, TW V 835–40. M-M.*

Παρμενᾶς, ᾶ, ὁ acc. -ᾶν (Sb 2489) Parmenas (short form of Παρμενίδης, Παρμενίων, Παρμενίσκος etc.—Bl-D. §125, 1; Rob. 173) one of the seven 'deacons' in Jerusalem Ac 6: 5. M-M.*

παροδεύω 1 aor. ptc. παροδεύσας (Theocr. 23, 47; Heraclit. Sto. 68, p. 88, 6; Plut., Mor. 973D; Lucian, Scyth. 10; Dit., Or. 544, 32; Epigr. Gr. 810, 11; PMich. 149, 12, 21; Wsd; Jos., Bell. 5, 426, Ant. 19, 331) pass, pass by ἔγνων παροδεύσαντάς τινας ἐκεῖθεν I learned to know certain people who had passed by on their way from that place IEph 9: 1. Subst. (Anton. Lib. 23, 6) ὡς παροδεύοντα as one who is passing by IRo 9: 3.*

παρόδιος, ον (Hyperid., fgm. 261; Plut., Mor. 521D al.; PTebt. 45, 22; 47, 14 [113 BC]) staying (somewhere) in the course of a journey; subst. ὁ π. one who is travelling by (otherw. παροδίτης or πάροδος.—Thackeray, The LXX and Jewish Worship '21, 26–8) D 12: 2.*

πάροδος, ου, ἡ (Thu.+; inscr., pap., LXX, Ep. Arist.; Philo, Praem. 112; Joseph.).

1. passage, thoroughfare (X., An. 4, 7, 4 al.; Diod. S. 20, 23, 2; Ep. Arist. 118; Jos., Ant. 14, 46) πάροδός ἐστε τῶν . . . you are the highway for those . . . IEph 12: 2. ἡ πάροδος μετὰ τῶν ἀγγέλων the way to the angels Hv 2, 2, 7; s 9, 25, 2.

2. passing by ἐν π. (Thu. 1, 126, 11; Polyb. 5, 68, 8; Cicero, Ad Att. 5, 20, 2; Lucian, Dial. Deor. 24, 2; PSI 354, 8; PLond. 1041, 2; Jos., Ant. 14, 38) ἰδεῖν τινα see someone in passing 1 Cor 16: 7. M-M.*

παροικέω 1 aor. παρῴκησα (Thu.+; inscr., pap., LXX, Philo; Jos., Ant. 1, 121).

1. In LXX mostly of strangers, who live in a place without holding citizenship (so also PSI 677, 2 [III BC]; Diod. S. 13, 47, 4). Also of persons who live as strangers on earth, far fr. their heavenly home (Philo, Cher. 120, Rer. Div. Her. 267 al.).

a. inhabit (a place) as a stranger w. acc. of the place (Isocr. 4, 162; Gen 17: 8; Ex 6: 4) 1 Cl inscr. a, b; MPol inscr. a.—In Lk 24: 18 we prob. have a rhetorical use σὺ μόνος παροικεῖς Ἰερουσαλήμ; someth. like are you the only one so strange in Jerusalem? But s. 2 below.—Prob. Pol inscr. belongs here too, since Φιλίπποις is certainly to be changed to Φιλίππους w. Lghtf. and Bihlmeyer (π. w. dat. means live beside, be a neighbor: Thu. 1, 71, 2; 3, 93, 2; Plut., Mor. 4A; Lucian, Catapl. 16; Philo, Sacr. Abel. 44; Dit., Or. 666, 13 [I AD]).

b. live as a stranger, w. ἐν (Gen 20: 1; 21: 34; 26: 3 al.; Philo, Conf. Lingu. 78) Lk 24: 18 t.r.; MPol inscr. b. Χριστιανοὶ παροικοῦσιν ἐν φθαρτοῖς Dg 6: 8.—c. migrate w. εἰς to Hb 11: 9.

2. also simply *inhabit*, *live in* without the connotation of being strange (Ps.-Scylax, Peripl. §93 at the beg. [ed. BFabricius 1878] π. τὰ ἔξω τῆς Σύρτιδος; Sus 28 LXX) perh. Lk 24: 18 (s. 1a[b] above). M-M.*

παροικία, ας, ἡ (PdeLabriolle, Paroecia: Rech de Sc rel 18, '28, 60–72).

1. *the stay* or *sojourn* of one who is not a citizen *in a strange place*, also the *foreign country* itself.

a. lit. (2 Esdr [Ezra] 8: 35; prol. to Sir l. 34; 3 Macc 7: 19) of the stay of the Israelites in Egypt (Wsd 19: 10) ἐν τῇ παροικίᾳ ἐν γῇ Αἰγύπτου Ac 13: 17.

b. fig., of the Christian's earthly life, far fr. his heavenly home (Ps 118: 54; 119: 5. Cf. παροικέω 1) ὁ τῆς π. ὑμῶν χρόνος *the time of your stay here in a strange land* 1 Pt 1: 17. καταλείπειν τὴν π. τοῦ κόσμου τούτου *give up their stay in the strange land of this world* 2 Cl 5: 1 (cf. CIG 9474; IG Sic. It. 531, 7 τούτου τοῦ βίου τὴν παροικίαν; Philo, Conf. Lingu. 80 ἡ ἐν σώματι παροικία).

2. *congregation, parish* (which is derived fr. π.) in so far as it represents a community of such 'strangers' (Euseb., H.E. 4, 23, 5 Sch. τῇ ἐκκλησίᾳ τῇ παροικούσῃ Γόρτυναν ἅμα ταῖς λοιπαῖς κατὰ Κρήτην παροικίαις; Irenaeus in Euseb. 5, 24, 14; Apollonius in Euseb. 5, 18, 9. παροικία means a community of persons in PsSol 17: 17) MPol inscr. M-M.*

πάροικος, ον (Aeschyl., Thu.+) *strange*, in our lit. almost always subst. **πάροικος, ου, ὁ** *stranger, alien*, one who lives in a place that is not his home (oft. inscr. [Dit., Or. and Syll.³ indices; Dssm., NB 54–BS 227f]; LXX; Philo, Cher. 121; Jos., Ant. 8, 59).

1. lit., w. the place indicated by ἐν Ac 7: 6 (adj., after Gen 15: 13), 29 (cf. Ex 2: 22 πάροικός εἰμι ἐν, γῇ ἀλλοτρίᾳ).

2. fig., of the Christians, whose real home is in heaven Dg 5: 5. W. ξένοι (this combination twice in Diod. S. 20, 84, 2) Eph 2: 19. W. παρεπίδημοι 1 Pt 2: 11. KLSchmidt, Israels Stellung zu d. Fremdlingen u. Beisassen usw.: Judaica 1, '46, 269–96.—KL and MASchmidt and R Meyer, πάροικος and related words: TW V 840–52. M-M.*

παροιμία, ας, ἡ—**1.** *proverb, maxim* (so Aeschyl.+; Socrat., Ep. 36 παροιμίαι κ. παραβολαί; Sir 6: 35; Philo, Abr. 235, Vi. Mos. 1, 156; 2, 29, Exsecr. 150) τὸ τῆς παροιμίας (Lucian, Dial. Mort. 6, 2; 8, 1) *what the proverb says* 2 Pt 2: 22.—LBieler, Die Namen d. Sprichworts in den klass. Sprachen: RhM n.s. 85, '36, 240–7; GDalman, Jesus (Engl. transl.) '29, 223–36.

2. in Johannine usage *dark saying, figure* of speech, in which esp. lofty ideas are concealed (Suidas: παροιμία = λόγος ἀπόκρυφος; Sir 39: 3 ἀπόκρυφα παροιμιῶν ἐκζητήσει. Acc. to 47: 17 ἑρμηνεία belongs to the παροιμίαι) J 10: 6; 16: 25, 6, 29.—JQuasten, CBQ 10, '48, 8f; FHauck, TW V 852–5. M-M.*

πάροινος, ον (Lysias 4, 8; Menand., Per. 444; Diog. L. 1, 92; Lucian, Tim. 55; Test. Jud. 14: 4; of people in all these exx.) *drunken, addicted to wine* 1 Ti 3: 3; Tit 1: 7. M-M.*

παροίχομαι mid. dep.; pf. ptc. παρῳχημένος *pass by, be gone of time* (Hom.+; Dionys. Hal. 11, 5 χρόνος; Dit., Syll.³ 885, 5 διὰ τῶν παρῳχημένων χρόνων; PRainer 10, 6; PRyl. 153, 35; Jos., Ant. 8, 301) ἐν ταῖς παρῳχημέναις γενεαῖς Ac 14: 16. M-M.*

παρομοιάζω (only Christian wr.) *be like* τινί someth. Mt 23: 27 (v.l. ὁμοιάζετε). M-M.*

παρόμοιος, (α), ον (Hdt.+) *like, similar* παρόμοια τοι-

αῦτα πολλὰ ποιεῖτε *you do many such things* Mk 7: 8 t.r., 13. M-M.*

παρόν, τό s. πάρειμι 1b.

παροξύνω impf. pass. παρωξυνόμην (trag., Thu.; Dit., Or. 48, 15; BGU 588, 7; LXX) *urge on, stimulate,* esp. *provoke to wrath, irritate* (Eur., Thu. et al.; LXX, Philo, Joseph., Test. 12 Patr.) pass. *become irritated, angry* (Thu. 6, 56, 2 et al.; M. Ant. 9, 42, 7; Arrian, Anab. 4, 4, 2; Sb 8852, 15 [III BC] παροξυνόμενοι οἱ νεώτεροι; Hos 8: 5; Zech 10: 3; Jos., Bell. 2, 8, Ant. 7, 33) of love 1 Cor 13: 5. παρωξύνετο τὸ πνεῦμα αὐτοῦ ἐν αὐτῷ *his spirit was aroused within him* (by anger, grief, or a desire to convert them) Ac 17: 16. M-M.*

παροξυσμός, οῦ, ὁ (Demosth. et al.; LXX)—**1.** *stirring, up, provoking* (so the verb παροξύνω in act. and pass.; X., Mem. 3, 3, 13 πρὸς τὰ καλά, Oec. 13, 9; Isocr., Ad Demonic. 46) εἰς π. ἀγάπης *for encouragement in love,* i.e. *to encourage someone in love* Hb 10: 24.

2. in an unfavorable sense *irritation, sharp disagreement* (Demosth. 45, 14; Ael. Aristid. 37 p. 709 D.; 52 p. 600; Dt 29: 27; Jer 39: 37) ἐγένετο π. *a sharp disagreement arose* Ac 15: 39.

3. *attack of fever,* esp. at its high point; *paroxysm* (Hippocr., Aph. 1, 11; 12; 2, 13; Galen XIII p. 210; Artem. 3, 56; PTebt. 272, 6.—Hobart 233) IPol 2: 1. M-M.*

παροράω 2 aor. παρεῖδον (X., Pla.+; inscr., pap., LXX) *overlook, take no notice of* (Aristot. et al.; BGU 1140, 23 [I BC]; Wsd 11: 23 παρορᾷς ἁμαρτήματα ἀνθρώπων εἰς μετάνοιαν; Philo, Rer. Div. Her. 109) Ac 17: 30 D.*

παροργίζω Att. fut. παροργιῶ; 1 aor. παρώργισα *make angry* (so in the pass. in Theophr., H. Pl. 9, 16, 6; Strabo 7, 2, 1; Dit., Or. 610, 4) τινά *someone* (LXX; Philo, Somn. 2, 177; Test. Levi 3: 10) Ro 10: 19 (Dt 32: 21); Eph 6: 4; Col 3: 21 v.l.; Hv 3, 6. 1. M-M.*

παροργισμός, οῦ, ὁ (LXX mostly act. 'provoking to anger': 3 Km 15: 30; 4 Km 23: 26 or 'an action that calls forth anger' in someone: 2 Esdr 19 [Neh 9]: 18) pass. *angry mood, anger* (Jer 21: 5 w. θυμός and ὀργή) Eph 4: 26 (cf. the Pythagorean saying Plut., Mor. 488B, C; also IQS 5, 26–6, 1; CD 9, 6–8). M-M.*

παρορίζω *overstep, transgress* (a boundary) (so Ammianus Epigr. [II AD]: Anth. Pal. 11, 209, 1; Anecd. Gr. p. 293, 16. As 'move the boundary' Inschr. v. Priene 37, 142 [II BC]; BGU 616, 4; PTebt. 410, 5 [I AD]) pass. οἷς (by whom) ὅρια παρορίζεται Dg 11: 5.*

παροτρύνω 1 aor. παρώτρυνα *arouse, incite, encourage* τινά *someone* (Pind., Ol. 3, 38; Lucian, Tox. 35, Deor. Concil. 4; Ael. Aristid. 53 p. 633 D.; Jos., Ant. 7, 118) Ac 13: 50. M-M.*

παρουσία, ας, ἡ (trag., Thu.+; inscr., pap., LXX)—**1.** *presence* (Aeschyl.+; Herm. Wr. 1, 22; Dit., Or. 640, 7, Syll.³ 730, 14) 1 Cor 16: 17; Phil 2: 12 (opp. ἀπουσία). ἡ π. τοῦ σώματος ἀσθενής *his bodily presence is weak* i.e., when he is present in person, he shows himself weak 2 Cor 10: 10.—Of God (Jos., Ant. 3, 80; 203; 9, 55) τῆς παρουσίας αὐτοῦ δείγματα *the proofs of his presence* Dg 7: 9 (cf. Diod. S. 3, 66, 3 σημεῖα τῆς παρουσίας τοῦ θεοῦ; 4, 24, 1).

2. *coming, advent* as the first stage in presence (Soph., El. 1104; Eur., Alc. 209; Thu. 1, 128, 5. Elsewh. mostly in later wr.: Polyb. 22, 10, 14; Diod. S. 15, 32, 2; 19, 64, 6;

Dionys. Hal. 1, 45, 4; inscr., pap.; Jdth 10: 18; 2 Macc 8: 12; 15: 21; 3 Macc 3: 17; Jos., Bell. 4, 345, Vi. 90).

a. of human beings, in the usual sense 2 Cor 7: 6f. ἡ ἐμὴ π. πάλιν πρὸς ὑμᾶς my coming to you again, my return to you Phil 1: 26.—RWFunk, JKnox-Festschr., '67, 249-68.

b. in a special technical sense (differently JFWalvoord, Biblioth. Sacra 101, '44, 283-9 on παρ., ἀποκάλυψις, ἐπιφάνεια) of Christ (and the Antichrist). The use of π. as a t.t. has developed in two directions. On the one hand the word served as a cult expr. for the coming of a hidden divinity, who makes his presence felt by a revelation of his power, or whose presence is celebrated in the cult (Diod. S. 3, 65, 1 ἡ τοῦ θεοῦ π. of Dionysus upon earth; 4, 3, 3; Ael. Aristid. 48, 30; 31 K.=24 p. 473 D.; Porphyr., Philos. Ex Orac. Haur. II p. 148 Wolff; Iambl., Myst. 2, 8; 3, 11; 5, 21; Jos., Ant. 3, 80; 203; 9, 55; report of a healing fr. Epidaurus: Dit., Syll.³ 1169, 34).—On the other hand, π. became the official term for a visit of a person of high rank, esp. of kings and emperors visiting a province (Polyb. 18, 48, 4; CIG 4896, 8f; Dit., Syll.³ 495, 85f; 741, 21; 30; UPZ 42, 18 [162 bc]; PTebt. 48, 14; 116, 57 [both II bc]; Ostraka II 1372; 1481.—Wilcken, Ostraka I 274ff; Dssm., LO 314ff [LAE 372ff]; MDibelius, Hdb. exc. after the expl. of 1 Th 2: 20). These two technical expressions can approach each other closely in mng., can shade off into one another, or even coincide (Inschr. von Tegea: Bull. de corr. hell. 25, '01 p. 275 ἔτους ξθ' ἀπὸ τῆς θεοῦ Ἀδριανοῦ τὸ πρῶτον ἰς τὴν Ἑλλάδα παρουσίας).— Herm. Wr. 1, 26 uses π. of the advent of the pilgrim in the eighth sphere.

α. of Christ, and nearly always of his Messianic Advent in glory to judge the world at the end of this age: Mt 24: 3 (PLSchoonheim, Een semasiolog. onderzoek van π. '53); 1 Cor 1: 8 v.l.; 15: 23; 2 Th 2: 8; 2 Pt 3: 4; 1 J 2: 28; Dg 7: 6; Hs 5, 5, 3. ἡ π. τοῦ υἱοῦ τ. ἀνθρώπου Mt 24: 27, 37, 39. ἡ π. τοῦ κυρίου 1 Th 4: 15; Js 5: 7f. ἡ π. τοῦ κυρίου ἡμῶν Ἰησοῦ 1 Th 3: 13; cf. 2: 19. ἡ π. τοῦ κυρίου ἡμῶν Ἰησοῦ Χριστοῦ 5: 23; 2 Th 2: 1; 2 Pt 1: 16 (δύναμις w. παρουσία as Jos., Ant. 9, 55; cf. Ael. Aristid. 48, 30 K. [both passages also b above]).—This explains the expr. ἡ π. τῆς τοῦ θεοῦ ἡμέρας the coming of the Day of God 2 Pt 3: 12. —EvDobschütz, Zur Eschatologie der Ev.: StKr 84, '11, 1-20; FTillmann, D. Wiederkunft Christi nach den paulin. Briefen '09; FGuntermann, D. Eschatol. des hl. Pls '32; BBrinkmann, D. Lehre v. d. Parusie b. hl. Pls u. im Hen.: Biblica 13, '32, 315-34; 418-34; EHaack, E. exeg.-dogm. Studie z. Eschatol. über 1 Th 4: 13-18: ZsystTh 15, '38, 544-69; OCullmann, Le retour de Christ, ²'45; WGKümmel, Verheissg. u. Erfüllg. ²'53; TFGlasson, The Second Advent '45; AFeuillet, CHDodd-Festschr. '56 (Mt and Js).—On delay of the Parousia WMichaelis, Wikenhauser-Festschr. '53, 107-23; EGrässer, D. Problem der Parousieverzögerung (synopt. and Ac), '57.— JATRobinson, Jesus and His Coming, '57.

β. in our lit. prob. only in a few late pass. of Jesus' advent in the Incarnation (so Test. Levi 8: 15, Jud. 22: 2; Justin, Apol. I 52, 3, Dial. 14, 8; 40, 4; 118, 2 ἐν τῇ πάλιν παρουσίᾳ; Ps.-Clem., Hom. 2, 52; 8, 5) τὴν παρουσίαν τοῦ σωτῆρος, κυρίου ἡμῶν Ἰησοῦ Χριστοῦ, τὸ πάθος αὐτοῦ καὶ τὴν ἀνάστασιν IPhld 9: 2; PK 4 p. 15, 33. But 2 Pt 1: 16 (s. α above) can hardly be classed here.

γ. Mng. α gave rise to an opposing use of π. to designate the coming of the Antichrist (s. ἄνομος 4) in the last times οὗ ἐστιν ἡ π. κατ' ἐνέργειαν τοῦ σατανᾶ whose coming results from Satan's power 2 Th 2: 9. AOepke, TW V, 856-69 (w. πάρειμι). M-M.*

παροψίς, ίδος, ἡ (since Magnes Com. [V bc] 2; Phere-

crates Com. [V bc] 147; X., Cyr. 1, 3, 4 in the sense 'side-dish' [food]) dish (=vessel. Antiphanes+; Plut., Mor. 828a; Epict. 2, 20, 30; Artem. 1, 74 p. 67, 6; Alciphr. 2, 17, 3; BGU 781, 2; 6; 14 [I ad]. This mng. is rejected by the Atticists: Phryn. p. 176 L.; Moeris p. 297 et al.) Mt 23: 25, 26 v.l. M-M.*

παρρησία, ας, ἡ (Eur., Pla.+; Stob., Flor. III 13 p. 453 H. [a collection of sayings περὶ παρρησίας]; inscr., pap., LXX, Ep. Arist., Philo, Joseph., Test. 12 Patr.; loanw. in rabb.—On the spelling s. Bl-D. §11, 1 app.; Mlt.-H. 101).

1. outspokenness, frankness, plainness of speech, that conceals nothing and passes over nothing (Demosth. 6, 31 τἀληθῆ μετὰ παρρησίας ἐρῶ πρὸς ὑμᾶς καὶ οὐκ ἀποκρύψομαι; Diod. S. 4, 74, 2; 12, 63, 2; Pr 1: 20; a slave does not have such a privilege: Eur., Phoen., 390-2) παρρησίᾳ plainly, openly (Ep. Arist. 125) Mk 8: 32; J 7: 13; 10: 24; 11: 14; 16: 25 (opp. ἐν παροιμίαις.—On the subject matter cf. Artem. 4, 71 οἱ θεοὶ πάντως μὲν ἀληθῆ λέγουσιν, ἀλλὰ ποτὲ μὲν ἁπλῶς λέγουσι, ποτὲ δὲ αἰνίσσονται=the gods always speak the truth, but sometimes in simplicity, sometimes in riddles), 29 t.r. (opp. παροιμία); Dg 11: 2. Also ἐν παρρησίᾳ J 16: 29. μετὰ παρρησίας (s. Demosth. above; Ael. Aristid. 30 p. 571 D.; Appian, Bell. Civ. 3, §15 λέγω μετὰ π.; 3 Macc 4: 1; 7: 12; Philo; Jos., Ant. 6, 256) plainly, confidently Ac 2: 29 μετὰ παρρησίας ἄκουε MPol 10: 1. This is also the place for πολλῇ παρρησίᾳ χρώμεθα (opp. Moses' veiling of his face) 2 Cor 3: 12 (παρρησίᾳ χράομαι as Appian, Maced. 11 §3; Cass. Dio 62, 13; Philo, De Jos. 107; Jos., Ant. 2, 116).—RMPope, ET 21, '10, 236-8; HWindisch, exc. on 2 Cor 3: 12.

2. 'Openness' somet. develops into openness to the public, before whom speaking and actions take place (Philo, Spec. Leg. 1, 321 τοῖς τὰ κοινωφελῆ δρῶσιν ἔστω παρρησία) παρρησίᾳ in public, publicly J 7: 26; 11: 54; 18: 20. δειγματίζειν ἐν παρρησίᾳ make a public example of Col 2: 15. ἐν παρρησίᾳ εἶναι to be known publicly J 7: 4 (opp. ἐν κρυπτῷ). This is prob. also the place for παρρησίᾳ Ac 14: 19 v.l. and μετὰ πάσης παρρησίας ἀκωλύτως quite openly and unhindered Ac 28: 31. Also ἐν πάσῃ παρρησίᾳ Phil 1: 20.

3. courage, confidence, boldness, fearlessness, esp. in the presence of persons of high rank.

a. in association with men (Socrat., Ep. 1, 12; Cass. Dio 62, 13; Ep. Arist. 125 παρρησίᾳ; Philo, De Jos. 107; 222, Rer. Div. Her. 5f; Jos., Ant. 9, 226; 15, 37; Test. Reub. 4, 2f. Cf. also Dit., Or. 323, 10; POxy. 1100, 15; PGM 12, 187; OEger, Rechtsgeschichtliches zum NT: Rektoratsprogr. Basel '19, 41f) Ac 4: 13. πολλή μοι παρρησία πρὸς ὑμᾶς (sc. ἐστιν and cf. Diod. S. 14, 65, 4 πρὸς τύραννον π.) 2 Cor 7: 4 (but mng. 2 is also poss.: I am perfectly frank with you, NEB). πολλὴν παρρησίαν ἔχων ἐπιτάσσειν σοι Phlm 8 (π. ἔχω as Dio Chrys. 26[43], 7). ἐν παρρησίᾳ fearlessly Eph 6: 19 (DSmolders, L'audace de l'apôtre: Collectanea Mechlinensia 43, '58, 16-30; 117-33). μετὰ παρρησίας (Aristoxenus, fgm. 32; Appian, Bell. Civ. 5, 42 §178; Jos., Ant. 6, 256; Ps.-Clem., Hom. 1, 11; 5, 18) Ac 2: 29 (cf. Chio 16, 7 ἀνέξῃ γὰρ μετὰ παρρησίας μοῦ λέγοντος); 4: 31; 1 Cl 34: 1. μετὰ παρρησίας πάσης (Jos., Ant. 16, 379) Ac 4: 29; 6: 10 D; 16: 4 D.

b. in relation to God (Job 27: 10; Philo, Rer. Div. Her. 5-7; Jos., Ant. 5, 38) w. προσαγωγή Eph 3: 12. Here joyousness, confidence is the result or the accompaniment of faith, as 1 Ti 3: 13; Hb 10: 35. W. καύχημα 3: 6; 1 Cl 34: 5. παρρησίαν ἔχειν πρὸς τὸν θεόν (Jos., Ant. 2, 52) 1 J 3: 21; cf. 5: 14. μετὰ παρρησίας with joyful heart Hb 4: 16; 2 Cl 15: 3. ἀλήθεια ἐν παρρησίᾳ 1 Cl 35: 2.

ἔχοντες παρρησίαν εἰς τὴν εἴσοδον τῶν ἁγίων *since we have confidence to enter the sanctuary* Hb 10: 19.—W. expressly eschatol. coloring (as Wsd 5: 1) παρρησίαν ἔχειν 1 J 2: 28 (opp. αἰσχύνεσθαι); 4: 17.—EPeterson, Z. Bedeutungsgesch. v. π.: RSeeberg-Festschr. I '29, 283–97; WCvUnnik, The Christian's Freedom of Speech: Bulletin of JRylands Library, '62, 466–88; HJBCombrink, Parresia in Handelinge: Nederduits Gereformeerde Teologiese Tydskrif, '75, 56–63; HSchlier, TW V, 869–84. M-M.*

παρρησιάζομαι mid. dep. (Pla.+; LXX, Philo) impf. ἐπαρρησιαζόμην; fut. παρρησιάσομαι; 1 aor. ἐπαρρησιασάμην (on the augment s. Bl-D. §69, 4 app.; Mlt.-H. 192, n. 3).

1. *speak freely, openly, fearlessly, express oneself freely* abs. (X., Ages. 11, 5; Aeschines 1, 172; 2, 70; Diod. S. 14, 7, 6; Jos., Ant. 16, 377) Ac 18: 26; 19: 8; likew. in the ptc. w. a verb of saying foll. (Appian, Bell. Civ. 1, 56 §247 παρρησιαζόμενον καὶ λέγοντα) παρρησιασάμενοι εἶπαν 13: 46.—26: 26. π. πρός τινα *speak freely to* or *with someone* (X., Cyr. 5, 3, 8; Diod. S. 23, 12, 1; Lucian, Adv. Indoctum 30) 1 Cl 53: 5. W. ἐν the reason for the παρρησία is given, and at the same time the object of the free speech: π. ἐν τῷ ὀνόματι Ἰησοῦ Ac 9: 27; cf. vs. 28; Eph 6: 20. Likew. w. ἐπί and dat. (Phalaris, Ep. 139 ἐπ' αὐτοῖς π.—Bl-D. §235, 2) π. ἐπὶ τῷ κυρίῳ Ac 14: 3.

2. When used w. the inf. π. gains (on the analogy of τολμᾶν, cf. Bl-D. §392, 3) the sense *have the courage, venture* 1 Th 2: 2 (so w. the ptc., Ps.-Clem., Hom. 4, 17).

3. The quot. fr. Ps 11: 6: παρρησιάσομαι ἐν αὐτῷ is unique, someth. like *I will deal openly* (or *boldly*) *with him* 1 Cl 15: 7. M-M.*

πᾶς, πᾶσα, πᾶν gen. παντός, πάσης, παντός (dat. pl. πᾶσι and πᾶσιν vary considerably in the mss.; s. W-S. §5, 28; cf. Rob. 219–21) (Hom.+; inscr., pap., LXX, En., Ep. Arist., Philo, Joseph., Test. 12 Patr.).

1. adj., used w. a noun—a. w. the noun in the sing. without the art.—α. emphasizing the individual members of the class denoted by the noun *every, each, any,* scarcely different in mng. fr. the pl. 'all': πᾶν δένδρον Mt 3: 10; Lk 3: 9. πᾶσα φυτεία Mt 15: 13. πᾶσα φάραγξ, πᾶν ὄρος Lk 3: 5 (Is 40: 4). πᾶς τόπος 4: 37. πᾶς ἄνθρωπος J 1: 9; 2: 10; Ro 3: 4 (Ps 115: 2); Gal 5: 3; Col 1: 28a, b, d; Js 1: 19. πᾶν ἔθνος Ac 17: 26a. πᾶσα ψυχή (Pla., Phaedr. 249ε) 2: 43; 3: 23 (cf. Lev 23: 29); Ro 2: 9. πᾶσα ἡμέρα Ac 5: 42; 17: 17. πᾶν σάββατον 18: 4. πᾶσα ἀρχὴ καὶ πᾶσα ἐξουσία 1 Cor 15: 24. πᾶσα συνείδησις 2 Cor 4: 2. πᾶς ἅγιος Phil 4: 21. πᾶς οἶκος Hb 3: 4. πᾶσα ἀντιλογία 7: 7. πᾶσα παιδεία *all discipline* 12: 11. πᾶς ὀφθαλμός Rv 1: 7a. πᾶν κτίσμα 5: 13a.—Mt 23: 35; Lk 2: 23 (Ex 13: 2); 4: 13; 21: 36; 2 Th 2: 4 (Da 11: 36). πᾶσα κτίσις *every creature* Col 1: 15; ἐν πάσῃ κτίσει *to every creature* vs. 23. πᾶσα γραφή 2 Ti 3: 16 (cf. γραφή 2a).—In the OT, also En. (1, 9) and Test. Gad 7: 2, but not in Ep. Arist., Philo, nor Joseph., is πᾶσα σάρξ (בָּל־בָּשָׂר) *all flesh* Lk 3: 6 (Is 40: 5). Mostly w. a neg. (so also En. 14, 21; 17, 6) οὐ (or μὴ) . . . πᾶσα σάρξ *no flesh = no one* Mt 24: 22; Mk 13: 20; Ro 3: 20; 1 Cor 1: 29; Gal 2: 16. Other sim. neg. expressions are also Hebraistic (cf. Bl-D. §302, 1; Mlt.-H. 433f) οὐ . . . πᾶν ῥῆμα *not a thing, nothing* Lk 1: 37 (cf. PRyl. 113, 12f [133 AD] μὴ . . . πᾶν πρᾶγμα). οὐδέποτε ἔφαγον πᾶν κοινόν *I have never eaten anything common* Ac 10: 14. Cf. Rv 7: 1, 16; 9: 4; 21: 27. Also in reverse order, πᾶς . . . οὐ or μή (Ex 12: 16; Sir 8: 19; 10: 6, but s. also GMLee, ET 63, '51f, 156) 18: 22; Eph 4: 29; 5: 5; 2 Pt 1: 20; 1 J 2: 21; 3: 15b.—Only rarely is a ptc. used w. πᾶς in this way: παντὸς ἀκούοντος *when anyone hears* Mt 13: 19. παντὶ ὀφείλοντι Lk 11: 4 (Mlt.-Turner 196f).

β. including everything belonging, in kind, to the class designated by the noun *every kind of, all sorts of,* for the words παντοδαπός and παντοῖος, which are lacking in our lit.: πᾶσα νόσος καὶ πᾶσα μαλακία Mt 4: 23. γέμουσιν πάσης ἀκαθαρσίας *they are full of all kinds of uncleanness* 23: 27. πᾶσα ἐξουσία 28: 18. ἀπὸ παντὸς ἔθνους *from every kind of nation* Ac 2: 5. Cf. 7: 22; 13: 10a, b; Ro 1: 18, 29. πᾶσα ἐπιθυμία (evil) *desire of every kind* 7: 8. ἐν παντὶ λόγῳ καὶ πάσῃ γνώσει 1 Cor 1: 5b. πᾶν ἁμάρτημα *every kind of sin* 6: 18. Cf. 2 Cor 7: 1; 9: 8b, c; 10: 5a, b; Eph 1: 3, 8, 21a; 4: 19; 5: 3; Phil 1: 9; 2 Th 2: 17. πᾶν ἔργον ἀγαθόν Tit 1: 16; 3: 1. Cf. 2: 14; Hb 13: 21. πᾶσα δόσις, πᾶν δώρημα Js 1: 17 (W-S. §20, 11b). Cf. vs. 21; 1 Pt 2: 1a, b; Rv 8: 7 al.

γ. *every, any and every, just any, any at all* μὴ παντὶ πνεύματι πιστεύετε *do not believe just any spirit* 1 J 4: 1. περιφερόμενοι παντὶ ἀνέμῳ τῆς διδασκαλίας Eph 4: 14. περὶ παντὸς πράγματος *about anything* Mt 18: 19. κατὰ πᾶσαν αἰτίαν *for any reason at all* 19: 3. Cf. 4: 4=Lk 4: 4 t.r. (Dt 8: 3); Mt 12: 31; 2 Cor 1: 4b (on ἐπὶ πάσῃ τῇ θλίψει ἡμῶν vs. 4a see 1cβ below).

δ. to denote the highest degree *full, greatest, all* (Pla., Rep. 9 p. 575A; Demosth. 18, 279 al.; LXX) μετὰ παρρησίας πάσης Ac 4: 29. ἐν πάσῃ ἀσφαλείᾳ 5: 23. πάσῃ συνειδήσει ἀγαθῇ *in all good conscience* 23: 1. Cf. 17: 11; 24: 3; 2 Cor 9: 8b; 12: 12; Eph 4: 2. ἐν πάσῃ προσκαρτερήσει *with the greatest perseverance* 6: 18c. Cf. Phil 1: 20; 2: 29; Col 1: 11a, b; 1 Ti 2: 2b, 11; 3: 4; 4: 9; 5: 2; Tit 2: 15; Js 1: 2; 2 Pt 1: 5; Jd 3 al. ἀσκεῖν πᾶσαν ὑπομονήν *practice patient endurance to the limit* Pol 9: 1 (Kleist).

ε. *all, the whole* before proper names, mostly geographic (X., Hell. 4, 8, 28 προστάται πάσης Λέσβου ἔσονται al.; LXX) πᾶσα Ἱεροσόλυμα Mt 2: 3 (s. Ἱερ.). πᾶς Ἰσραήλ (3 Km 8: 65; 11: 16; 1 Esdr 1: 19; 5: 45, 58; Jdth 15: 14) Ro 11: 26 (cf. W-S. §20, 11a and b; Rob. 772). The OT is also the source of πᾶς οἶκος Ἰσραήλ (1 Km 7: 2, 3) Ac 2: 36 and, in subject matter, ἐπὶ παντὸς προσώπου τῆς γῆς 17: 26b (but Gen 2: 6 has πᾶν τὸ πρόσωπον τῆς γῆς, and 7: 23; 11: 4, 8, 9 ἐπὶ προσώπου [or πρόσωπον] πάσης τῆς γῆς).—Perh. πᾶσα οἰκοδομή Eph 2: 21 (cf. W-S. §20: 11b; Rob. 772; Mlt.-Turner 199f; MDibelius, Hdb. ad loc.; M. Ant. 6, 36, 1; Dit., Or. 383, 86ff).

b. w. a noun in the pl., without the art. πάντες ἄνθρωποι *all men, everyone* (Lysias 12, 60; Andoc. 3, 25; X., Cyr. 7, 5, 52, Mem. 4, 4, 19; Demosth. 8, 5; 18, 72) Ac 22: 15; Ro 5: 12a, 18a, b; 12: 17, 18; 1 Cor 7: 7; 15: 19; 2 Cor 3: 2; Phil 4: 5; 1 Th 2: 15; 1 Ti 2: 4; 4: 10; Tit 2: 11. πάντες ἄγγελοι θεοῦ Hb 1: 6 (Dt 32: 43. Cf. Demosth. 18, 294 πάντες θεοί).

c. w. a noun in the sing., w. the art.—a. *the whole, all* (the), preceding a noun that has the art.: πᾶσα ἡ Ἰουδαία καὶ πᾶσα ἡ περίχωρος Mt 3: 5. πᾶσα ἡ ἀγέλη *the whole herd* 8: 32. Cf. vs. 34; 13: 2; 21: 10; 27: 25, 45; Mk 2: 13; 4: 1. πᾶσα ἡ ἀλήθεια 5: 33. πᾶσα ἡ κτίσις *the whole creation* Mk 16: 15; Ro 8: 22. Cf. Lk 1: 10; 2: 1, 10; Ac 3: 9, 11; 5: 21; 15: 12. πᾶς ὁ κόσμος Ro 3: 19b; Col 1: 6. πᾶν τὸ σπέρμα Ro 4: 16. πᾶσα ἡ γῆ 9: 17 (Ex 9: 16); Lk 4: 25. πᾶσα ἡ γνῶσις, πᾶσα ἡ πίστις 1 Cor 13: 2b, c. πᾶν τὸ πλήρωμα Eph 3: 19; Col 1: 19; 2: 9. πᾶν τὸ σῶμα Eph 4: 16; Col 2: 19. Cf. Hb 9: 19b, c.—W. a demonstrative pron. πᾶς ὁ λαὸς οὗτος *all these people* Lk 9: 13. πᾶσα ἡ ὀφειλὴ ἐκείνη Mt 18: 32.—Following the noun that has the article: τὴν κρίσιν πᾶσαν *the whole matter of judgment* J 5: 22. εἰς τὴν ἀλήθειαν πᾶσαν *into truth in all its outreach* 16: 13. τὴν ἐξουσίαν . . . πᾶσαν Rv 13: 12.

β. *all* ἐπὶ πάσῃ τῇ θλίψει ἡμῶν *in all our trouble* 2 Cor 1: 4a (on ἐν πάσῃ θλίψει vs. 4b s. 1aγ above); 7: 4;

1 Th 3: 7. ἐπὶ πάσῃ τῇ μνείᾳ ὑμῶν *in all remembrance of you* Phil 1: 3. πᾶσαν τὴν μέριμναν ὑμῶν *all your care* 1 Pt 5: 7.

γ. Oft. πᾶς ὁ, πᾶσα ἡ, πᾶν τό is used w. a ptc. *every one who, whoever* πᾶς ὁ (Soph., Aj. 152; Demosth. 23, 97; Sir 22: 2, 26; 1 Macc 1: 52; 2: 27) πᾶς ὁ ὀργιζόμενος Mt 5: 22. Cf. vs. 28, 32; 7: 8, 26 (= πᾶς ὅστις vs. 24; s. γ below); Lk 6: 47; 11: 10; 14: 11; 16: 18; 18: 14; 19: 26; J 3: 8, 15f, 20; 4: 13; 6: 40; 8: 34; 18: 37; Ac 10: 43b; 13: 39; Ro 2: 1, 10; 10: 4, 11; 1 Cor 9: 25; Gal 3: 13; 2 Ti 2: 19; Hb 5: 13; 1 J 2: 23, 29 al.; 2 J 9; Rv 22: 18.—πᾶν τό *everything that* (1 Macc 10: 41): πᾶν τὸ εἰσπορευόμενον Mt 15: 17; Mk 7: 18. πᾶν τὸ ὀφειλόμενον Mt 18: 34. πᾶν τὸ πωλούμενον 1 Cor 10: 25; cf. vs. 27. πᾶν τὸ φανερούμενον Eph 5: 14. πᾶν τὸ γεγεννημένον 1 J 5: 4.—An equivalent of this expr. is πᾶς ὅς (or ὅστις), πᾶν ὅ *every one who, whatever* (s. γ above and cf. Bl-D. §293, 1; 413, 2; Rob. 727; 957), masc.: Mt 7: 24; 10: 32; 19: 29; Lk 12: 8, 10 (RHolst, ZNW 63, '72, 122-4), 48; 14: 33; Ac 2: 21 (πᾶς ὃς ἐάν, after Jo 2: 32); Ro 10: 13 (πᾶς ὃς ἄν, after Jo 3: 5); Gal 3: 10. Neut. (Jdth 12: 14.—Jos., Ant. 5, 211 πᾶν ὅ=πάντες οἵ): J 6: 37, 39; 17: 2b; Ro 14: 23 (ὃν ἄν); Col 3: 17 (πᾶν ὅτι ἐάν).

d. w. a noun in the pl., w. the art. *all*—**a.** w. substantives: πᾶσαι αἱ γενεαί Mt 1: 17; Lk 1: 48; Eph 3: 21. πάντας τοὺς ἀρχιερεῖς Mt 2: 4. Cf. vs. 16; 4: 8; 11: 13; Mk 4: 13, 31f; 6: 33; Lk 1: 6; 2: 51; 6: 26; J 18: 20; Ac 1: 18; 3: 18; 10: 12, 43a; 14: 16; Ro 1: 5; 15: 11 (Ps 116: 1); 16: 4; 1 Cor 12: 26a, b; 2 Cor 8: 18; 11: 28; Eph 4: 10; 6: 16b; Col 2: 13; 1 Ti 6: 10; Hb 4: 4 (Gen 2: 2); 9: 21; Js 1: 8; Rv 1: 7b; 7: 11; 15: 4 al.—Used w. a demonstr. pron.: πᾶσαι αἱ παρθένοι ἐκεῖναι Mt 25: 7. πάντας τοὺς λόγους τούτους 26: 1. πάντα τὰ ῥήματα ταῦτα Lk 1: 65; 2: 19.—Somet. following the noun: τὰς πόλεις πάσας Mt 9: 35; Ac 8: 40. οἱ μαθηταὶ πάντες *the disciples, one and all* Mt 26: 56. αἱ θύραι πᾶσαι Ac 16: 26a. Cf. Ro 16: 16; 1 Cor 7: 17; 13: 2a; 15: 7; 16: 20; 1 Th 5: 26; 2 Ti 4: 21; Rv 8: 3. οἱ Ἱεροσολυμῖται πάντες Mk 1: 5.—On the position of ἐκεῖνος, ἕνεκα, πᾶς cf. NTurner, Vetus T V '55, 208-13.

β. w. participles πάντες οἱ: πάντες οἱ κακῶς ἔχοντες Mt 4: 24. πάντες οἱ κοπιῶντες 11: 28; cf. 21: 12; 26: 52; Lk 1: 66; 2: 47; 13: 17; Ac 1: 19; 2: 44; 4: 16; 5: 5, 11; 6: 15; 9: 14; 28: 30; Ro 1: 7; 4: 11; 1 Cor 1: 2; Eph 6: 24; 1 Th 1: 7; 2 Th 1: 10; 2 Ti 3: 12; 4: 8; Hb 5: 9; 13: 24; 2 J 1; Rv 13: 8; 18: 24. Following the ptc. οἱ κατοικοῦντες πάντες Ac 2: 14. ἐν τοῖς ἡγιασμένοις πᾶσιν 20: 32.—πάντα τά: πάντα τὰ γενόμενα Mt 18: 31. πάντα τὰ ὑπάρχοντα 24: 47; Lk 12: 44; 1 Cor 13: 3. Cf. Lk 17: 10; 18: 31; 21: 36; J 18: 4; Ac 10: 33b. Used w. a demonstr. pron.: περὶ πάντων τῶν συμβεβηκότων τούτων Lk 24: 14. Following: τὰ γινόμενα πάντα 9: 7.

γ. prepositional expressions, w. which ὄντες (ὄντα) is to be supplied: πάντες οἱ ἐν τῇ οἰκίᾳ Mt 5: 15; Ac 16: 32. πάντες οἱ σὺν αὐτῷ Lk 5: 9. πάντες οἱ ἐν τοῖς μνημείοις J 5: 28. πάντες οἱ εἰς μακράν Ac 2: 39. Cf. 5: 17. πάντες οἱ ἐξ Ἰσραήλ Ro 9: 6. Cf. 2 Ti 1: 15; 1 Pt 5: 14. πάντα τὰ ἐν αὐτοῖς Ac 4: 24; 14: 15 (Ex 20: 11); cf. 17: 24. Following: οἱ μετ᾽ ἐμοῦ πάντες Tit 3: 15a.

e. π. used w. pronouns.—**a.** w. personal pronouns: πάντες ἡμεῖς *we all* Ac 2: 32; 10: 33a; 26: 14; 28: 2; Ro 4: 16b. πάντες ὑμεῖς Mt 23: 8; 26: 31; Lk 9: 48; Ac 4: 10a; 22: 3; Ro 1: 8; 15: 33; 2 Cor 7: 15; Gal 3: 28; Phil 1: 4, 7a, b, 8; 1 Th 1: 2; 2 Th 3: 16c, 18; Tit 3: 15b; Hb 13: 25. πάντες αὐτοί Ac 4: 33; 19: 17b; 20: 36. Following the pron.: ἡμεῖς πάντες J 1: 16; Ro 8: 32a; 2 Cor 3: 18; Eph 2: 3. ὑμεῖς πάντες Ac 20: 25. αὐτοὶ πάντες Mt 12: 15; 1 Cor 15: 10. W. art. οἱ πάντες ἡμεῖς 2 Cor 5: 10.

β. w. a demonstr. pron.: πάντες οὗτοι *these all, all these* Ac 2: 7. Mostly following the pron.: οὗτοι πάντες 1: 14; 17: 7; Hb 11: 13, 39. πάντα ταῦτα Mt 6: 32; 24: 8; Lk 7: 18; Ac 24: 8; 1 Cor 12: 11; Col 3: 14; 1 Th 4: 6. ταῦτα πάντα Mt 4: 9; 6: 33; 13: 34, 51; Lk 12: 30; Ac 7: 50; Ro 8: 37; 2 Pt 3: 11.

γ. πάντες ὅσοι, πάντα ὅσα *all who, everything that,* masc.: Lk 4: 40 v.l. (for ἅπαντες); J 10: 8. Neut. (Philo, Aet. M. 15; 28; Jos., Ant. 8, 242) Mk 7: 12; 13: 46; 18: 25; 21: 22; Mk 11: 24; 12: 44b; Lk 18: 12, 22; J 10: 41.

f. πᾶς and πάντες stand attributively betw. art. and noun, when the noun is regarded as a whole, in contrast to its individual parts (cf. Kühner-G. I 632f).

a. sing. (Thu. 2, 7, 2 ὁ πᾶς ἀριθμός='the whole number'; 8, 93, 2 τὸ πᾶν πλῆθος; X., Mem. 1, 2, 8 εἰς τὸν πάντα βίον; Pla., Gorg. 470E ἡ πᾶσα εὐδαιμονία; 2 Macc 2: 17; 3 Macc 1: 29; 6: 14; 4 Macc 3: 8) ὁ πᾶς νόμος *the whole law* Gal 5: 14. τὸν πάντα χρόνον Ac 20: 18.

β. pl. (X., An. 5, 6, 7 οἱ πάντες ἄνθρωποι; Pla., Theaet. 204A τὰ πάντα μέρη) αἱ πᾶσαι ψυχαί *all the souls* Ac 27: 37. οἱ κατὰ τὰ ἔθνη πάντες Ἰουδαῖοι 21: 21. οἱ σὺν ἐμοὶ πάντες ἅγιοι Ro 16: 15. οἱ σὺν ἐμοὶ πάντες ἀδελφοί Gal 1: 2.—W. numerals (Hdt. 7, 4; Thu. 1, 60, 1) οἱ πάντες ἄνδρες ὡσεὶ δώδεκα *the whole number of the men was about twelve* Ac 19: 7.—JMBover, Uso del adjetivo singular πᾶς en San Pablo: Biblica 19, '38, 411-34.

2. subst.—**a.** without the art.—**a.** πᾶς *everyone without exception* Lk 16: 16.—**β.** πᾶν, w. prep.: διὰ παντός s. διά A II 1a. ἐν παντί *in every respect* or *way, in everything* (Pla., Symp. 194A; X., Hell. 5, 4, 29; Dit., Syll.³ 1169, 27; Sir 18: 27; 4 Macc 8: 3) πλουτίζεσθαι 1 Cor 1: 5; 2 Cor 9: 11. Cf. 2 Cor 4: 8; 7: 5, 11, 16; 8: 7; 9: 8b; 11: 6a, 9; Eph 5: 24; Phil 4: 6; 1 Th 5: 18.

γ. πάντες, πᾶσαι *all, everyone* (even when only two are involved=both: Appian, Bell. Civ. 2, 27 §105 [Caesar and Pompey] Mt 10: 22; 14: 20; 15: 37; 21: 26; 26: 27; Mk 1: 37; 5: 20; Lk 1: 63 and oft. πάντες ἥμαρτον Ro 5: 12 (on the sinfulness of πάντες cf. the saying of Bias s.v. πολύς I 2aα; FWDanker, Ro 5: 12, Sin under Law, NTS 14, '68, 430, n. 1).—οὐ πάντες *not everyone* Mt 19: 11. Cf. J 13: 10; Ro 10: 16.—πάντων as partitive and comparative gen. ὕστερον πάντων *last of all* Mt 22: 27; cf. Mk 12: 22, 43. Even in ref. to a fem. (Thu. 4, 52, 3; Aristoph., Av. 472) ἐντολὴ πρώτη πάντων Mk 12: 28 (but cf. Bl-D. §164, 1).

δ. πάντα *all things, everything.* In the absolute sense (Chrysippus in Stob., Ecl. 1, 1, 26 p. 31 W.; Ps.-Aristot., De Mundo 6; M. Ant. 4, 23; Ael. Aristid. 43, 9 K.=1 p. 3 D.: ἀρχὴ ἀπάντων Ζεύς τε καὶ ἐκ Διὸς πάντα; Herm. Wr. 5, 10; Hymn to Selene in PGM 4, 2838f ἐκ σέο γὰρ πάντ᾽ ἐστὶ καὶ εἰς σ᾽, αἰώνιε, πάντα τελευτᾷ [s. 2bβ below]; PGM 5, 139) Mt 11: 27=Lk 10: 22 (cf. the lit. on this pass. s.v. υἱός 2b. At present the word πάντα is understood for the most part not of power [so most recently Bousset, Schlatter; also Arvedson 154], but of knowledge and teaching: HHoltzmann, PSchmiedel, JWeiss, Norden, Zahn, Harnack, Wlh., EKlostermann, OHoltzmann, Schniewind); J 1: 3; 3: 35; 21: 17; 1 Cor 2: 10; 15: 27a (Ps 8: 7), b, 28c, d (πάντα ἐν πᾶσιν w. a somewhat different coloring: Dio Chrys. 54[71], 1) Eph 1: 22a (Ps 8: 7); Rv 21: 5. Here we may class ὁ ὢν ἐπὶ πάντων θεός (cf. Aristobulus in Euseb., Pr. Ev. 8, 10, 10; 13, 12, 4 ἐπὶ πάντων εἶναι τ. θεόν; Porphyr., Vi. Plot. 23 τῷ ἐπὶ πᾶσι θεῷ) *God, who rules over all* Ro 9: 5 (θεός 2).—Of a 'whole' that is implied fr. the context: πάντα ἀποδώσω σοι Mt 18: 26. Cf. 22: 4; Mk 4: 34; Lk 1: 3; Ro

8: 28 (s. Black s.v. συνεργέω); 2 Cor 6: 10; Gal 4: 1; Phil
2: 14; 1 Th 5: 21; 2 Ti 2: 10; Tit 1: 15; 1 J 2: 27. πάντα
ὑμῶν ἐστιν *everything is yours, belongs to you* 1 Cor 3: 21,
cf. 22 (Plut., Cic. 25, 4 πάντα τοῦ σοφοῦ εἶναι; Diog. L.
6, 72). πάντα ὑμῶν *everything you do* 16: 14. πρῶτον
πάντων 1 Ti 2: 1. πάντα four times as anaphora (rhetorical repetition) 1 Cor 13: 7 (cf. Libanius, Or. 3 p. 275, 4
πάντα φθεγγόμενοι, πάντα ἐργαζόμενοι, πάντα χαρι-
ζόμενοι).—The acc. of specification stands almost in the
sense of an adv. (Bl-D. §154; Rob. 487) πάντα *in all
respects, in every way, altogether* (Hom.+; Aelian, V.H.
12, 25; Jos., Ant. 9, 166; Sib. Or. 3, 205) Ac 20: 35 (perh.
always, as Ps.-Lucian, Asin. 22 p. 590); 1 Cor 9: 25b.
πάντα πᾶσιν ἀρέσκω (s. ἀρέσκω 1) 10: 33; 11: 2. Cf.
KGrobel, JBL 66, '47, 366 and s. τὰ πάντα in 2bβ below.
—W. a prep.: εἰς πάντα *in all respects, in every way* (Pla.,
Charm. 6 p. 158Α, Leg. 5 p. 738Α; Appian, Iber. 17 §64,
Bell. Civ. 4, 92 §385; BGU 798, 7) 2 Cor 2: 9. ἐν πᾶσιν *in
all respects, in every way* (PGiess. 69, 8; Appian, Bell. Civ.
2, 112 §467 [here ἐν ἅπασιν=in all respects]) 1 Ti 3: 11;
2 Ti 2: 7; 4: 5; Tit 2: 9, 10b; Hb 13: 4, 18; 1 Pt 4: 11. Perh.
also Eph 1: 23b. ἐν πᾶσι τούτοις *in* (or *besides*) *all this*
(Sir 48: 15; Job 2: 10; 12: 9) Lk 16: 26. κατὰ πάντα, s.
κατά II 6. περὶ πάντων *in every way* (Wilcken, Chrest. 6,
9; Sib. Or. 1, 198) 3 J 2. πρὸ πάντων *above all, especially*
(PReinach 18: 27 [II BC]; BGU 811, 3; PAmh. 135, 2) Js 5:
12; 1 Pt 4: 8.

b. w. the art.—**α.** οἱ πάντες *all* (*of them*) (*in contrast to
a part*) Ro 11: 32a, b; 1 Cor 9: 22 (cf. HChadwick, NTS 1,
'55, 261-75); Phil 2: 21. (*We, they*) *all* Mk 14: 64; 1 Cor
10: 17; 2 Cor 5: 14b. μέχρι καταντήσωμεν οἱ πάντες
until we all attain Eph 4: 13.

β. τὰ πάντα. In the abs. sense of the whole of creation
all things, the universe (Pla., Ep. 6 p. 323D τῶν πάντων
θεός; hymn to Selene in EAbel, Orphica [1885] 294, 36 εἰς
σὲ τὰ πάντα τελευτᾷ [s. 2aδ above]; Herm. Wr. 13, 17 τ.
κτίσαντα τὰ πάντα; Philo, Spec. Leg. 1, 208, Rer. Div.
Her. 36, Somn. 1, 241; PGM 1, 212 κύριε τῶν πάντων; 4,
3077) Ro 11: 36 (Musaeus in Diog. L. 1, 3 ἐξ ἑνὸς τὰ
πάντα γίνεσθαι καὶ εἰς ταὐτὸν ἀναλύεσθαι. Cf. Norden, Agn. Th. 240-50); 1 Cor 8: 6a, b; 15: 28a, b; Eph 3:
9; 4: 10b; Phil 3: 21; Col 1: 16a, b, 17b (HHegermann, D.
Vorstellung vom Schöpfungsmittler etc., TU 82, '61,
88ff); Hb 1: 3; 2: 10a, b; Rv 4: 11; 1 Cl 34: 2; PK 2 p. 13
(four times).—In the relative sense, indicated by the
context, *everything* (Κυπρ. I p. 42 no. 29 τὰς στοὰς καὶ
τὰ ἐν αὐταῖς πάντα; PGiess. 2, 14 [II BC] in a bill: τὰ π.
='everything taken together') ἐν παραβολαῖς τὰ πάντα
γίνεται *everything* (=all the preaching) *is in parables* Mk
4: 11. Cf. Ac 17: 25b; Ro 8: 32b. Of everything in heaven
and earth that is in need of uniting and redeeming Eph 1:
10 (EugWalter, Christus u. d. Kosmos [Eph 1: 10] '48);
Col 1: 20. τὰ πάντα *they all* (of the members of the body)
1 Cor 12: 19. The neut. is also used of persons: Gal 3: 22;
cf. 1 Ti 6: 13 (here including humankind and everything
else that possesses life).—As acc. of specification, almost
like an adv.: τὰ πάντα *in all respects* (Appian, Prooem. c.
6 §23) Eph 4: 15 (s. πάντα 2aδ above).—As a summation
of what precedes *all this* (Zen.-P. 59 741, 16; 59 742, 22;
BGU 1509 [all III BC]) 2 Cor 4: 15; Phil 3: 8b; Col 3: 8.—
Furthermore, πάντες can also have the limited sense
nearly all (Xenophon Eph. 2, 13, 4 πάντας ἀπέκτεινεν,
ὀλίγους δὲ καὶ ζῶντας ἔλαβε. μόνος δὲ ὁ Ἱππόθοος
ἠδυνήθη διαφυγεῖν).—Mlt.-Turner 199-201; BReicke,
TW V 885-95. B. 919.

πάσχα, τό indecl. (Aram. פַּסְחָא or פַּסְכָא for Hebr. פֶּסַח.—
LXX, Philo, Joseph.) *the Passover*.

1. A Jewish festival, celebrated on the 14th of the month
Nisan, and continuing into the early hours of the 15th
(Jos., Ant. 3, 284f). This was followed immediately by the
Feast of Unleavened Bread (Mazzoth; ἄζυμος 1b) on the
15th to 21st. Popular usage merged the two festivals and
treated them as a unity, as they were for practical purposes
(s. Lk 22: 1 and Mk 14: 12 below.—So also Philo and
Joseph.: Grace Amadon, ATR 27, '45, 109-15). τὸ π. *the
Passover* (*Festival*) Mk 14: 1; J 2: 23; 11: 55b; 12: 1; 18:
39; Ac 12: 4. τοῦτο τὸ π. *on this Passover* GEb 6b (a
rewording of Lk 22: 15 fr. the Encratite point of view). τὸ
π. τῶν Ἰουδαίων J 2: 13; 11: 55a. τὸ π., ἡ ἑορτὴ τῶν
Ἰουδαίων 6: 4; ἡ ἑορτὴ τοῦ π. Lk 2: 41; J 13: 1.
παρασκευὴ τοῦ π. (s. παρασκευή) J 19: 14. ἡ ἑορτὴ τῶν
ἀζύμων ἡ λεγομένη πάσχα Lk 22: 1 (Jos., Ant. 14, 21
τῆς τῶν ἀζύμων ἑορτῆς, ἣν πάσχα λέγομεν; 17, 213;
18, 29, Bell. 2, 10. HSchürmann, Der Paschamahlbericht,
Lk 22: 7-14, 15-18, '53). τὸ π. γίνεται *the Passover is
being celebrated* Mt 26: 2.

2. *the Paschal lamb* θύειν τὸ π. (זֶבַח הַפֶּסַח.—Ex 12:
21; Dt 16: 2, 6; 2 Esdr [Ezra] 6: 20) *kill the Passover lamb*
Mk 14: 12a; Lk 22: 7; fig. of Christ and his bloody death
1 Cor 5: 7 (ELohse, Märtyrer u. Gottesknecht, '55, 141-6).
φαγεῖν τὸ π. (אָכַל הַפֶּסַח.—2 Ch 30: 18 [φασεκ]; 2 Esdr
[Ezra] 6: 21) *eat the Passover* Mt 26: 17; Mk 14: 12b, 14;
Lk 22: 11, 15; J 18: 28; GEb 6a (here the word ἑτοιμάζειν
is found, taken fr. Passover terminology [s. 3], but π. still
retains its specific sense 'Paschal lamb').—For lit. s.
ἐσθίω 1a.

3. *the Passover meal* ἑτοιμάζειν τὸ π. *prepare the
Passover meal* Mt 26: 19; Mk 14: 16; Lk 22: 8, 13, ποιεῖν
τὸ π. (oft. LXX) *hold* or *celebrate the Passover* Mt 26: 18;
Hb 11: 28.

4. in later Christian usage *the Easter festival* τὸ κυρίου
π. Dg 12: 9.—GBeer, Pesachim '12 (p. 1, 1 lit.); Elbogen[3]
'31; HGuthe, Z. Passah der jüd. Religionsgem.: StKr
96/97, '25, 144-71; Billerb. IV '28, 41-76: D. Passamahl;
JoachJeremias, D. Passahfeier der Samaritaner '32, D.
Abendmahlsworte Jesu[2] '49, [3]'60; Eng. tr., The Eucha-
ristic Words of Jesus, OEhrhardt '55, 86-184, also [3] tr.
NPerrin, '64; Dalman, Jesus 80-160; JPedersen, Passah-
fest u. Passahlegende: ZAW 52, '34, 161-75; PJHeawood,
ET 53, '41/'42, 295-7; FBussby, ibid. 59, '47/'48, 194f;
GWalther, Jesus, d. Passalamm '50; ESchweizer, ThLZ
79, '54, 577-91; AJaubert, La date de la Cène '57;
JBSegal, The Hebrew Passover to AD 70, '63; HGrass,
Ostergeschehen u. Osterberichte, [2]'62; NFüglister, Die
Heilsbedeutung des Pascha, '63; ERuckstuhl, Die Chro-
nologie des letzten Mahles usw., '63 (Eng. tr. VJDrapela,
'65); RLeDéaut, La nuit pascale, '63; JvGoudoever, Studia
Evangelica III, '64, 254-9. The work of AJaubert above
has been transl. as The Date of the Last Supper by
IRafferty, '65; Jaubert's thesis rejected by EKutsch, Vetus
T 11, '61, 39-47.—JoachJeremias, TW V 895-903. M-M.*

πάσχω (Hom.+; inscr., pap., LXX; Ep. Arist. 214;
Philo, Joseph., Test. 12 Patr.) fut. 3 sing. παθεῖται (2 Cl
7: 5 cod. A; C has πείσεται. Cf. Reinhold p. 74; Bl-D.
§74, 3); 2 aor. ἔπαθον, pf. πέπονθα, ptc. πεπονθώς;
experience, be treated (π. expresses the passive idea
corresponding to the active idea in ποιέω) of everything
that befalls a person, whether good or ill. Yet its usage
developed in such a way that π. came to be used less and
less frequently in a good sense, and never without some
clear indication, at least fr. the context, that the good
sense is meant. In our lit. it is found

1. only once of pleasant experiences *experience* (Antiphanes 252, 2b ἀγαθὸν πάσχει; Diod. S. 20, 102, 2 εὖ

πάσχειν; Dionys. Hal. 7, 51; Plut., Mor. 1110D; Arrian, Ind. 34, 1, Peripl. 2, 4; Jos., Ant. 3, 312; POxy. 1855, 8; 10; 14 πάσχω ἀπόκρισιν of favorable information) τοσαῦτα ἐπάθετε εἰκῇ; have you had such remarkable experiences in vain? Gal 3: 4 (Procop. Soph., Ep. 18 τοσοῦτον παθών; Ps.-Aristot., Mirabilia 112 τὸ αὐτὸ πάσχει=he experiences the same thing.—Differently Zahn et al.; in their opinion this pass. belongs to 3b; in support of their view s. τοσαῦτα παθών Ep. 56 of Apollonius of Tyana [Philostrat. I 359, 16]).

2. Likew. there is only one place in which π. has a neutral mng. Even here the addition of κακῶς gives it an unfavorable connotation: κακῶς πάσχειν be badly off, in an evil plight (Hom+; Hdt. 3, 146 et al.; Wsd 18: 19; Philo, In Flacc. 124, Spec. Leg. 4, 3) Mt 17: 15 v.l.

3. In all other places, as always in LXX, in an unfavorable sense suffer, endure.

a. suffer—α. abs. (also in the sense suffer death, be killed, [have to] die: Appian, Bell. Civ. 1, 70 §321; 3, 87 §359; Arrian, Anab. 6, 10, 3; Paroem. Gr.: Zenob. 4, 60 the crow ἔπαθε from the scorpion's poison; Herodian 1, 17, 7; sim. Callinus [VII BC], fgm. 1, 17 D.² ἤν τι πάθῃ= if he fell; Demosth. 4, 11f; Strato of Lamps. in Diog. L. 5, 61 ἐάν τι πάσχω='if anything happens to me'. Diod. S. 13, 98, 2; Lucian, Dial. Mer. 8, 3; Iambl., Vi. Pyth. 33, 238; Jos., Ant. 15, 65; 18, 352; Ramsay, Phryg. I 2 p. 391 no. 254) πρὸ τοῦ με παθεῖν before I suffer Lk 22: 15. Cf. 24: 46; Ac 1: 3; 3: 18; 17: 3; 1 Cor 12: 26; Hb 2: 18 (on ἐν ᾧ s. ἐν IV 6d); 9: 26; 1 Pt 2: 20, 23; 3: 17; B 17: 2a. The expr. γῆ πάσχουσα B 6: 9 seems to transfer the philosoph. concept of suffering matter to the γῆ (Hefele, Hilgenfeld, Veil); earth capable of suffering (Gdspd.), earth capable of being molded into a human being (Kleist, note ad loc.).

β. w. additions: ὑπό τινος at the hands of someone denotes the one who caused the suffering (Antipho Rhet., fgm. 34; Ael. Aristid. 45 p. 134 D.; PAmh. 78, 4; Jos., Bell. 5, 19, Ant. 10, 92; Bl-D. §315) Mt 17: 12 (s. also b below). Also ὑπὸ χειρός τινος B 5: 5b. ὑπέρ τινος for someone or someth. (Appian, Bell. Civ. 1, 15 §63 π. ὑπέρ τινος=suffer for someone) Phil 1: 29; 2 Th 1: 5; 1 Pt 2: 21 (περί τινος 𝔓⁷² al.), ὑπὲρ τ. ὀνόματος τοῦ υἱοῦ τοῦ θεοῦ Hs 9, 28, 2a. ὑπὲρ τοῦ νόμου 8, 3, 6. ὑπὲρ τῆς σωτηρίας, ὑπὲρ ἁμαρτωλῶν MPol 17: 2a. ὑπὲρ τῶν ἁμαρτιῶν ἡμῶν ISm 7: 1. Also περί τινος (Nicol. Dam.: 90 fgm. 130, 29 p. 415, 29 Jac. περὶ τῶν διαδόχων αὐτοῦ ἅπαν . . . παθεῖν) περὶ ἁμαρτιῶν 1 Pt 3: 18 v.l.; περὶ τῆς ψυχῆς ἡμῶν B 5: 5a. διά w. acc. for the sake of: διὰ δικαιοσύνην 1 Pt 3: 14. διὰ τὸ ὄνομα (αὐτοῦ) Pol 8: 2; Hv 3, 2, 1; s 9, 28, 3. δι' ἡμᾶς B 7: 2b. διὰ τοὺς οἱ Hs 9, 28, 6a. εἵνεκα or ἔνεκεν τοῦ ὀνόματος v 3, 1, 9; 3, 5, 2; s 9, 28, 5; 6b. κατὰ τὸ θέλημα τοῦ θεοῦ 1 Pt 4: 19. ἔξω τῆς πύλης Hb 13: 12. ἐπὶ ξύλου on the tree B 5: 13b.—Used w. an instrumental dat.: αἰκίαις καὶ βασάνοις π. 1 Cl 6: 1. πολλαῖς πράξεσι Hs 6, 3, 4. W. dat. to denote manner 1 Pt 4: 1a, b (in b the t.r. has ἐν σαρκί).—Used w. an adverb: ἀδίκως 1 Pt 2: 19. ἀληθῶς ISm 2b. δικαίως (Test. Sim. 4: 3) Hs 6, 3, 6a. ἡδέως 8, 10, 4. προθύμως 9, 28, 2b; 4. οὕτω GP 4: 13; B 5: 13a. ὀλίγον (s. ὀλίγος 3a) 1 Pt 5: 10. τὸ δοκεῖν (δοκέω 2a) in semblance, seemingly ITr 10; ISm 2c.—ὡς φονεύς undergo punishment (cf. Dit., Syll.³ 1016, 7 π. ὡς ἱερόσυλος) as a murderer 1 Pt 4: 15.

b. endure, undergo τι someth. παθήματα π. endure sufferings 2 Cor 1: 6 (ὧν by attraction of the rel. fr. ἅ). αἰκίσματα 1 Cl 6: 2. πολλὰ π. (Jos., Ant. 13, 268; 403) Mt 27: 19; Mk 8: 31; 9: 12; Lk 9: 22 (s. further below); 17: 25; B 7: 11. τὰ ὅμοιά τινι the same things as someone GOxy 3. οὐδὲν κακόν suffer no harm Ac 28: 5. οὐδὲν τῶν

πονηρῶν Hs 6, 3, 6b. ὡς οὐδὲν πεπονθώς as if nothing had happened to him MPol 8: 3. ταῦτα Lk 13: 2; 24: 26; 2 Ti 1: 12; 1 Cl 45: 5. τί παθεῖται; what will he have to endure? 2 Cl 7: 5 (πάσχειν τι=endure punishment, as Pla., Leg. 10, 1 p. 885 AB). μὴ φοβοῦ ἃ μέλλεις πάσχειν do not be afraid of what you are about to undergo Rv 2: 10. W. attraction ἔμαθεν ἀφ' ὧν ἔπαθεν τὴν ὑπακοήν= ἔμαθεν τὴν ὑπακοὴν ἀπὸ τούτων ἃ ἔπαθεν he learned obedience from what he endured Hb 5: 8. π. τι ὑπό τινος endure someth. at someone's hands (X., Hiero 7, 8, Symp. 1, 9; Jos., Ant. 7, 209; 12, 401; s. 3aβ above) Mk 5: 26; 1 Th 2: 14; B 7: 5. Also π. τι ἀπό τινος (Dio Chrys. 67[17], 11; Lucian, Dial. Deor. 6, 4) Mt 16: 21; perh. Lk 9: 22. π. τι ἕνεκά τινος endure someth. for someone's sake 2 Cl 1: 2. Also π. τι διά τινα ISm 2a. ὅσα δεῖ αὐτὸν ὑπὲρ τοῦ ὀνόματός μου παθεῖν Ac 9: 16 (π. τι ὑπέρ τινος as Jos., Ant. 13, 199).—WWichmann, D. Leidenstheologie, e. Form der Leidensdeutung im Spätjudentum '30; HVondran, D. Leidensgedanke im Spiegel d. Selbstbewusstseins Jesu: NKZ 43, '32, 257-75; RLiechtenhan, D. Überwindung d. Leidens b. Pls. u. in d. zeitgen. Stoa: ZThK n.s. 3, '22, 368-99; WMichaelis, Herkunft u. Bed. des Ausdrucks 'Leiden u. Sterben J. Chr.' '45; HRiesenfeld, Jésus Transfiguré, '47, 314-17 (Le Messie Souffrant . . .); ELohse, Märtyrer u. Gottesknecht (Sühntod Jesu Christi), '55; EGüttgemanns, D. leidende Apostel, '66.—KH Schelkle, Die Passion Jesu etc., '49.—WMichaelis, πάσχω and related words (incl. -παθ-): TW V 903-39. M-M.**

Πάταρα, ων, τά neut. pl. Patara (Hdt. 1, 182; Strabo 14, 3, 3; Dit., Or. 441, 209; Sib. Or. 3, 441; 4, 112.—On the spelling s. Bl-D. §42, 3 app.; Rob. 183) a city in Lycia, on the southwest coast of Asia Minor. Paul stopped there on his journey fr. Corinth to Jerusalem Ac 21: 1.*

πατάσσω fut. πατάξω; 1 aor. ἐπάταξα (Hom.+; inscr., pap., LXX; Jos., C. Ap. 1, 203 [Hecataeus]; Test. Levi) strike, hit.

1. lit.—a. of a light blow or push τι someth. (Aesop, Fab. 246 P. τὸ στῆθος) τὴν πλευράν τινος strike someone's side in order to waken him Ac 12: 7. Abs., but w. the acc. easily supplied fr. the context, of touching w. a staff Hs 9, 6, 4.

b. of a heavy blow; w. acc. of the pers. (Demosth. 21, 33 τὸν ἄρχοντα; Appian, Bell. Civ. 2, 17 §64 δᾳδοῦχον ἐπάταξε ξίφει) π. τὸν δοῦλον Mt 26: 51; Lk 22: 50. Abs. strike ἐν μαχαίρῃ Lk 22: 49.

c. specif. strike down, slay τινά someone (PHal. 1, 196; UPZ 19, 8 [159 BC]; BGU 1024 III, 17) Mt 26: 31; Mk 14: 27; B 5: 12 (all three after Zech 13: 7; for the subject-matter s. Jos., Ant. 8, 404); Ac 7: 24 (Ex 2: 12).

2. fig., of heavenly beings; here it cannot be determined whether any actual touching or striking is involved, nor how far it goes (cf. Gen 8: 21; Ex 9: 15; 12: 23; Num 14: 12; Dt 28: 22; 4 Km 6: 18; 2 Macc 9: 5 and oft. in LXX; cf. also Dit., Syll.³ 1240, 11; PHamb. 22, 7) ἐπάταξεν αὐτὸν ἄγγελος κυρίου an angel of the Lord struck him Ac 12: 23. Used w. instrumental ἐν and dat.: of the two witnesses π. τὴν γῆν ἐν πάσῃ πληγῇ Rv 11: 6 (PGM 12, 368 θεόν, τὸν πατάξαντα γῆν; 2 Macc 9: 5 π. πληγῇ). Of the Logos as Judge of the World ἐν αὐτῇ (i.e. the ῥομφαία proceeding fr. his mouth) π. τὰ ἔθνη 19: 15. M-M.*

πατέω fut. πατήσω; 1 aor. pass. ἐπατήθην (Hom.+; pap., LXX; En. 1, 4; Philo) tread (on) w. the feet.

1. trans.—a. lit.—α. tread τι someth. (Herodas 8, 74) τὴν ληνόν (s. ληνός) Rv 19: 15; pass. 14: 20. Of a stone ὁ πατούμενος what is trodden under foot Dg 2: 2.

β. *set foot on, tread* of a place (Aeschyl. +; LXX) τὴν αὐλήν *the court* B 2: 5 (Is 1: 12). τὸ ἁγνευτήριον GOxy 12; τὸ ἱερόν ibid. 17; 20.

γ. *tread on, trample* (Iambl., Vi. Pyth. 31, 193) of the undisciplined swarming of a victorious army through a conquered city. Its heedlessness, which acknowledges no limits, causes π. to take on the concepts 'mistreat, abuse' (so πατέω in Plut., Tim. 14, 2; Lucian, Lexiph. 10 al.; Philo, In Flacc. 65) and 'tread contemptuously under foot' (s. 1b below). In Heliod. 4, 19, 8 π. πόλιν actually means *plunder a city.* τὴν πόλιν πατήσουσιν Rv 11: 2; pass. (Jos., Bell. 4, 171 πατούμενα τὰ ἅγια) Lk 21: 24 (ὑπὸ ἐθνῶν).

b. fig. *trample in contempt* or *disdain* (Il. 4, 157 ὅρκια; Soph., Aj. 1335, Antig. 745 al.; Herodian 8, 5, 9; Jos., Bell. 4, 258 τ. νόμους) τὸ τῆς αἰσχύνης ἔνδυμα πατεῖν *despise* (= throw away w. disdain) *the garment of shame* (s. αἰσχύνη 1) GEg 2.

2. intr. *walk, tread* (since Pind., Pyth. 2, 157) πατεῖν ἐπάνω ὄφεων Lk 10: 19 (ἐπάνω 2a and cf. Test. Levi 18: 12.—Diod. S. 3, 50, 2f speaks of the danger of death in πατεῖν on ὄφεις). HSeesemann, TW V 940-6. M-M.*

πατήρ, πατρός, ὁ (Hom. +; inscr., pap., LXX, En., Ep. Arist., Philo, Joseph., Test. 12 Patr.) voc. πάτερ; for this the nom. w. the art. ὁ πατήρ Mt 11: 26; Mk 14: 36; Lk 10: 21b; Ro 8: 15; Gal 4: 6.—πατήρ without the art. for the voc., in J 17: 11 B, 21 BD, 24 and 25 AB is regarded by Bl-D. §147, 3 app. as a scribal error (but as early as II AD BGU 423, 11 has κύριέ μου πατήρ. Perh. even PPar. 51, 36 [159 BC]). Cf. also W-S. §29, 4b and Mlt.-H. 136; *father.*

1. lit.—**a.** of the immediate (male) ancestor Mt 2: 22; 4: 21f; 8: 21; 10: 21; Mk 5: 40; 15: 21; Lk 1: 17 (after Mal 3: 23); J 4: 53; Ac 7: 14; 1 Cor 5: 1; B 13: 5 al. οἱ τῆς σαρκὸς ἡμῶν πατέρες *our physical fathers* Hb 12: 9a.—οἱ πατέρες *parents* (Pla., Leg. 6 p. 772b; Dionys. Hal. 2, 26; Diod. S. 21, 17, 2; Xenophon Eph. 1, 11; 3, 3; Epigr. Gr. 227) Hb 11: 23.—Eph 6: 4; Col 3: 21 (Apollon. Rhod. 4, 1089 of parents who are inclined to become λίην δύσζηλοι toward their children).

b. gener. *forefather, ancestor, progenitor*: of Abraham (Jos., Ant. 14, 255 Ἀ., πάντων Ἑβραίων πατήρ) Mt 3: 9; Lk 1: 73; 16: 24; J 8: 39, 53, 56; Ac 7: 2b. Of Isaac Ro 9: 10. Jacob J 4: 12. David Mk 11: 10; Lk 1: 32. οἱ πατέρες *the forefathers, ancestors* (Hom. +; oft. LXX; Jos., Ant. 13, 297) Mt 23: 30, 32; Lk 1: 55; 6: 23, 26; 11: 47f; J 4: 20; 6: 31; Ac 3: 13, 25; Hb 1: 1; 8: 9 (Jer 38: 32); B 2: 7 (Jer 7: 22); 5: 7; 14: 1; PK 2 p. 15, 6 (Jer 38: 32).

2. fig.—**a.** of spiritual fatherhood (Epict. 3, 22, 81f: the Cynic superintends the upbringing of all men as their πατήρ; Procop. Soph., Ep. 13; Ael. Aristid. 47 p. 425 D.: Pla. as τῶν ῥητόρων π. καὶ διδάσκαλος; Aristoxenus, fgm. 18: Epaminondas is the ἀκροατής of the Pythagorean Lysis and calls him πατήρ; Philostrat., Vi. Soph. 1, 8 p. 10, 4 the διδάσκαλος as πατήρ) ἐὰν μυρίους παιδαγωγοὺς ἔχητε ἐν Χριστῷ, ἀλλ' οὐ πολλοὺς πατέρας 1 Cor 4: 15 (on the subject matter ADieterich, Mithraslit. '03, 52; 146f; 151; Rtzst., Mysterienrel.³ 40: 'he [the "mystes"] by these teachings becomes the father of the novice. We find undoubted examples of πατήρ as a title in the Isis cult in Delos, in the Phrygian mystery communities, in the Mithras cult, in the worshippers of the θεὸς ὕψιστος and elsewh.').

b. as an honorary title or a form of respectful address (Diod. S. 21, 12, 2; 5; Ps.-Callisth. 1, 14, 2 πάτερ; 4 Km 2: 12; 6: 21; 13: 14; Jos., Ant. 12, 148; 13, 127. Also PGenève 52, 1; 5 κυρίῳ καὶ πατρὶ Ἀμινναίῳ Ἀλύπιος;

UPZ 65, 3 [154 BC]; 70, 2; BGU 164, 2; POxy. 1296, 15; 18; 1592, 3; 5; 1665, 2) Mt 23: 9a; specif. in addressing the members of the High Council Ac 7: 2a; cf. 22: 1.

c. as a designation of the older male members of a church (as respectful address by younger people to their elders Hom. +. S. also b above) 1 J 2: 13, 14b.

d. in some places the πατέρες are to be understood as the generation(s) of deceased Christians 2 Pt 3: 4; 1 Cl 23: 3=2 Cl 11: 2 (an apocryphal saying, at any rate interpreted in this way by the Christian writers). Christians of an earlier generation could also be meant in 1 Cl 30: 7; 60: 4; 62: 2; 2 Cl 19: 4. Yet it is poss. that these refer to

e. the great religious heroes of the OT, who are 'fathers' even to the Gentile Christians, the 'true Israel'. In 1 Cor 10: 1 Paul calls the desert generation of Israelites οἱ πατέρες ἡμῶν (the 'philosophers' of earlier times are so called in Kleopatra 114f). Likew. Ro 4: 12b Abraham ὁ πατὴρ ἡμῶν (on this s. f below). The latter is also referred to Js 2: 21; 1 Cl 31: 2; likew. the patriarch Jacob 4: 8.

f. the fatherhood can also consist in the fact that the one who is called 'father' is the prototype of a group or the founder of a class of persons (cf. Pla., Menex. 240E οὐ μόνον τῶν σωμάτων τῶν ἡμετέρων πατέρας ἀλλὰ καὶ τῆς ἐλευθερίας; 1 Macc 2: 54). Abraham who, when he was still uncircumcised, received the promise because of his faith, and then received circumcision to seal it, became thereby πατὴρ πάντων τῶν πιστευόντων δι' ἀκροβυστίας *father of all those who believe, though they are uncircumcised* Ro 4: 11 and likew. πατὴρ περιτομῆς *father of those who are circumcised* vs. 12a, in so far as they are not only circumcised physically, but are like the patriarch in faith as well. Cf. 4: 16, 17 (Gen 17: 5).

3. of God—**a.** as the originator and ruler (Pind., Ol. 2, 17 Χρόνος ὁ πάντων π.; Pla., Tim. 28c; 37c; Stoa: Epict. 1, 3, 1; Diog. L. 7, 147; Maximus Tyr. 2, 10a; Galen XIX p. 179 K. ὁ τῶν ὅλων πατὴρ ἐν θεοῖς; Job 38: 28; Mal 2: 10; Philo, Spec. Leg. 1, 96 τῷ τοῦ κόσμου πατρί; 2, 6 τὸν ποιητὴν καὶ πατέρα τῶν ὅλων, Ebr. 30; 81, Virt. 34; 64; 179; 214; Jos., Ant. 1, 20 πάντων πατήρ; 230; 2, 152; 7, 380 πατέρα τε καὶ γένεσιν τῶν ὅλων; Herm. Wr. 1, 21 ὁ πατὴρ ὅλων . . . ὁ θεὸς κ. πατήρ; 30 al., also p. 476, 23 Sc. δεσπότης καὶ πατὴρ καὶ ποιητής; PGM 4, 1170; 1182) ὁ πατὴρ τῶν φώτων *the father of the heavenly bodies* Js 1: 17 (cf. Apc. Mosis 36 [MCeriani, Monumenta Sacra et Profanà V 1, 1868] ἐνώπιον τοῦ φωτὸς τῶν ὅλων, τοῦ πατρὸς τῶν φώτων; 38).

b. as ὁ πατὴρ τῶν πνευμάτων Hb 12: 9b (cf. Num 16: 22; 27: 16 and in En. the fixed phrase 'Lord of the spirits').

c. as Father of mankind (since Hom. Ζεύς is called πατήρ or πατὴρ ἀνδρῶν τε θεῶν τε; Diod. S. 57, 2, 4 πατέρα δὲ [αὐτὸν προσαγορευθῆναι] διὰ τὴν φροντίδα καὶ τὴν εὔνοιαν τὴν εἰς ἅπαντας, ἔτι δὲ καὶ τὸ δοκεῖν ὥσπερ ἀρχηγὸν εἶναι τοῦ γένους τῶν ἀνθρώπων; Dio Chrys. 36[53], 12 Zeus as π. τῶν ἀνθρώπων, not only because of his position as ruler, but also because of his love and care [ἀγαπῶν κ. προνοῶν]. Cf. Plut., Mor. 167D; Jos., Ant. 4, 262 πατὴρ τοῦ παντὸς ἀνθρώπων γένους. In the OT God is called 'Father' in the first place to indicate his relationship to the Israelite nation as a whole, or to the king as the embodiment of the nation. Only in late writers is God called the Father of the pious Jew as an individual: Sir 23: 1, 4; Tob 13: 4; Wsd 2: 16; 14: 3; 3 Macc 5: 7.—Bousset, Rel.³ 377ff; EDBurton, ICC Gal '21, 384-92; RGyllenberg, Gott d. Vater im AT u. in d. Predigt Jesu: Studia Orient. I '25, 51-60; JLeipoldt, D. Gotteserlebnis Jesu '27; ALWilliams, 'My Father' in Jewish Thought of the First Century: JTS 31, '30, 42-7;

TWManson, The Teaching of Jesus, '55, 89-115; HW Montefiore, NTS 3, '56/'57, 31-46 [synoptics]; BIersel, 'D. Sohn' in den synopt. Ev., '61, 92-116).

α. as a saying of Jesus ὁ πατήρ σου Mt 6: 4, 6b, 18b. ὁ πατὴρ ὑμῶν Mt 6: 15; 10: 20, 29; 23: 9b; Lk 6: 36; 12: 30, 32; J 20: 17c. ὁ πατὴρ αὐτῶν=τῶν δικαίων) Mt 13: 43. ὁ πατὴρ ὑμῶν ὁ ἐν (τοῖς) οὐρανοῖς (the synagogue also spoke of God as 'Father in Heaven'; Bousset, Rel.³ 378) Mt 5: 16, 45; 6: 1; 7: 11; Mk 11: 25. ὁ πατὴρ ὑμῶν ὁ οὐράνιος Mt 5: 48; 6: 14, 26, 32. Cf. 23: 9b. ὁ πατὴρ ὁ ἐξ οὐρανοῦ Lk 11: 13. ὁ πατήρ σου ὁ ἐν τῷ κρυπτῷ (or κρυφαίῳ) Mt 6: 6a, 18a.—For the evangelist the words πάτερ ἡμῶν ὁ ἐν τοῖς οὐρανοῖς Mt 6: 9 refer only to the relation betw. God and men, though Jesus perh. included himself in this part of the prayer. The same is true of πάτερ ἁγιασθήτω τὸ ὄνομά σου Lk 11: 2 (for invocation in prayer cf. Simonides, fgm. 13, 20 Ζεῦ πάτερ).—ELohmeyer, D. Vaterunser erkl. '46 (Eng. tr. JBowden, '65); TWManson, The Sayings of Jesus, '54, 165-71; EGraesser, Das Problem der Parusieverzögerung in den synopt. Ev. usw., Beih. ZNW 22, '57, 95-113; AHamman, La Prière I, Le NT, '59, 94-134; JoachJeremias, Das Vaterunser im Lichte der neueren Forschung, '62 (Eng. tr., The Lord's Prayer, JReumann, '64); WMarchel, Abba, Père! La Prière, '63.

β. as said by Christians (Sextus 59=222; 225 God as π. of the pious. The servant of Serapis addresses God in this way: Sb 1046; 3731, 7) in introductions of letters ἀπὸ θεοῦ πατρὸς ἡμῶν: Ro 1: 7; 1 Cor 1: 3; 2 Cor 1: 2; Gal 1: 3, cf. vs. 4; Eph 1: 2; Phil 1: 2; Col 1: 2; Phlm 3; the word ἡμῶν is lacking 2 Th 1: 2 (where a v.l. adds it); 1 Ti 1: 2; 2 Ti 1: 2; Tit 1: 4; 2 J 3a (here b shows plainly that it is not 'our' father, but the Father of Jesus Christ who is meant).— πατὴρ ἡμῶν also Phil 4: 20; 1 Th 1: 3; 3: 11, 13; 2 Th 2: 16; D 8: 2; 9: 2f. τὸν ἐπιεικῆ καὶ εὔσπλαγχνον πατέρα ἡμῶν 1 Cl 29: 1. Likew. we have the Father of the believers Ro 8: 15; 2 Cor 1: 3b (ὁ πατὴρ τῶν οἰκτιρμῶν; cf. οἰκτιρμός); 6: 18 (cf. 2 Km 7: 14); Gal 4: 6; Eph 4: 6 (πατὴρ πάντων, as Herm. Wr. 5, 10); 1 Pt 1: 17. ὁ οἰκτίρμων καὶ εὐεργετικὸς πατήρ 1 Cl 23: 1. Cf. 8: 3 (perh. fr. an unknown apocryphal book). πάτερ ἅγιε D 10: 2 (cf. 8: 2; 9: 2f).

γ. as said by Jews ἕνα πατέρα ἔχομεν τὸν θεόν J 8: 41b. Cf. vs. 42.

d. as Father of Jesus Christ—**a.** in Jesus' witness concerning himself ὁ πατήρ μου Mt 11: 27a; 20: 23; 25: 34; 26: 29, 39, 42, 53; Lk 2: 49 (see ὁ II 7 and Gdspd., Probs. 81-3); 10: 22a; 22: 29; 24: 49; J 2: 16; 5: 17, 43; 6: 40 and oft. in J; Rv 2: 28; 3: 5, 21. ἡ βασιλεία τοῦ πατρός μου 2 Cl 12: 6 in an apocryphal saying of Jesus. ὁ πατήρ μου ὁ ἐν (τοῖς) οὐρανοῖς Mt 7: 21; 10: 32, 33; 12: 50; 16: 17; 18: 10, 19. ὁ πατήρ μου ὁ οὐράνιος 15: 13; 18: 35. Jesus calls himself the Son of Man, who will come ἐν τῇ δόξῃ τοῦ πατρὸς αὐτοῦ 16: 27; Mk 8: 38. Abs. ὁ πατήρ, πάτερ Mt 11: 25, 26; Mk 14: 36; Lk 10: 21a, b; 22: 42; 23: 34, 46 (all voc.); J 4: 21, 23a, b; 5: 36a, b, 37, 45; 6: 27, 37, 45, 46a, 65 and oft. in J. Father and Son stand side by side or in contrast Mt 11: 27b, c; 24: 36; 28: 19; Mk 13: 32; Lk 10: 22b, c; J 5: 19-23, 26; 1 J 1: 3; 2: 22-4; 2 J 9; B 12: 8. WFLofthouse, Vater u. Sohn im J: ThBl 11, '32, 290-300.

β. in the confession of the Christians π. τοῦ κυρίου ἡμῶν Ἰησοῦ Χριστοῦ Ro 15: 6; 2 Cor 1: 3a; Eph 1: 3; Col 1: 3; 1 Pt 1: 3. π. τοῦ κυρίου Ἰησοῦ 2 Cor 11: 31. Cf. 1 Cor 15: 24; Hb 1: 5 (2 Km 7: 14); Rv 1: 6; 1 Cl 7: 4; IEph 2: 1; ITr inscr. 12: 2; MPol 14: 1.

e. Oft. God is simply called (ὁ) πατήρ (the) Father (on the presence or absence of the art. cf. Bl-D. §257, 3 w. app.; Rob. 795) Eph 2: 18; 3: 14; 5: 20; 6: 23; 1 J 1: 2; 2: 1, 15; 3: 1; B 14: 6; Hv 3, 9, 10; IEph 3: 2; 4: 2; IMg 13: 2;

ITr 13: 3; IRo 2: 2; 3: 3; 7: 2; 8: 2; IPhld 9: 1; ISm 3: 3; 7: 1; 8: 1; D 1: 5; Dg 12: 9; MPol 22: 3. θεὸς π. Gal 1: 1 (on Ἰ. Χρ. καὶ θεὸς πατήρ cf. Diod. S. 4, 11, 1: Heracles must obey τῷ Διὶ καὶ πατρί; Oenomaus in Euseb., Pr. Ev. 5, 35, 3 Λοξίας [=Apollo] καὶ Ζεὺς πατήρ); Phil 2: 11; Col 3: 17; 1 Th 1: 1; 2 Pt 1: 17; Jd 1; IEph inscr. a; ISm inscr.; IPol inscr.; MPol inscr. ὁ θεὸς καὶ π. Js 1: 27; MPol 22: 1; ὁ κύριος καὶ π. Js 3: 9.—Attributes are also ascribed to the πατήρ (Zoroaster acc. to Philo Bybl. in Euseb., Pr. Ev. 1, 10, 52: God is π. εὐνομίας κ. δικαιοσύνης) ὁ πατὴρ τῆς δόξης Eph 1: 17. πατὴρ ὕψιστος IRo inscr. ὁ θεὸς καὶ πατὴρ παντοκράτωρ MPol 19: 2.

4. of Christ, in a statement which, to be sure, is half comparison ὡς πατὴρ υἱοὺς ἡμᾶς προσηγόρευσεν as a father he called us (his) sons 2 Cl 1: 4 (cf. Ps.-Clem., Hom. 3, 19).

5. of the devil—**a.** as father of the Jews J 8: 44a, b.— **b.** as father of lies (Celsus 2, 47 as π. τῆς κακίας) vs. 44c (on πατήρ in the sense of 'originator' cf. Caecil. Calact., fgm. 127 ὁ π. τοῦ λόγου=the author of the book). On the view that in 44a and c there might be a statement about the father of the devil cf. Hdb.³ ad loc. (NDahl, EHaenchen-Festschr. '64, 70-84 [Cain]).—πατήρ and related words: GSchrenk and GQuell, TW V 946-1024. M-M. B. 103.

Πάτμος, ου, ὁ (Thu. 3, 33, 3; Strabo 10, 5, 13; Pliny, H.N. 4, 23; CIG 2261; 2262; Dit., Syll.³ 1068, 2) *Patmos*, a small rocky island in the Aegean Sea, famous for the tradition that John had his 'revelation' here Rv 1: 9. His exile to Patmos (cf. Artem. 5, 21 εἰς νῆσον κατεδικάσθη) is an old tradition: Clem. Alex., Quis Div. Salv. 42; Origen, In Matth. vol. 16, 6; Euseb., H.E. 3, 18, 1-3; Tertullian, De Praescr. Haer. 36. Cf. JFrings, D. Patmosexil des Ap. Joh. nach Apk 1: 9: ThQ 104, '23, 23-30 and commentaries ad loc. *

πατραλῷας s. πατρολῷας.

πατριά, ᾶς, ἡ (Hdt. +; Dialekt-Inschr. 5501, 7 [Miletus]; Jos., Ant. 7, 365; 11, 68; LXX)—**1.** *family, clan, relationship* (so, as subdivision of the φυλή Tob 5: 12; Jdth 8: 2, 18 al. LXX; Jos., Ant. 6, 51) ἐξ οἴκου καὶ πατριᾶς Δαυίδ *from the house and family of David* Lk 2: 4.

2. more inclusively *people, nation;* αἱ πατριαὶ τῶν ἐθνῶν Ps 21: 28; 1 Ch 16: 28) πᾶσαι αἱ πατριαὶ τῆς γῆς Ac 3: 25.

3. *a division of a nation* (Hdt. 1, 200 al.; Dit., Syll.³ 438a, 26; 2, 60) ἐξ οὗ (i.e. τοῦ πατρός) πᾶσα πατριὰ ἐν οὐρανοῖς καὶ ἐπὶ γῆς ὀνομάζεται *from whom every family in heaven and on earth receives its name* Eph 3: 15 (on the idea of families of angels cf. En. 69, 4; 71, 1; 106, 5).—On this and the following entry see JWackernagel, Kl. Schr. 468-93: Über einige lat. u. griech. Ableitungen aus den Verwandschaftswörtern. M-M. *

πατριάρχης, ου, ὁ (LXX) *father of a nation, patriarch* of the Hebr. patriarchs, so of Abraham (cf. 4 Macc 7: 19) Hb 7: 4. Of the 12 sons of Jacob Ac 7: 8f; *ancestor* of David 2: 29. M-M. *

πατρικός, ή, όν (since Soph., Ichneutae [POxy. 9, 40f col. 3, 12]; Thu.; inscr., pap., LXX, Philo; Jos., C. Ap. 1, 109; Wackernagel, Kl. Schr. 480) *derived from* or *handed down by one's father, paternal* (Cratinus Com. 116 ἐν πατρικοῖσι νόμοις) αἱ πατρικαί μου παραδόσεις *the traditions of my forefathers*, prob. of the traditions of his father's house, adhering strictly to the law Gal 1: 14. M-M. *

πατρίς, ίδος, ἡ (really fem. of πάτριος 'of one's fathers', but used as subst. even in Hom. So also inscr., pap., LXX, Ep. Arist. 102; Philo, Joseph.).

1. *fatherland, homeland* (Hom. +; 2 Macc 8: 21; 13: 14; Philo; Jos., Bell. 1, 246, Ant. 19, 233) Dg 5: 5. Of Galilee as Jesus' homeland J 4: 44. Fig., of the heavenly home (cf. Ael. Aristid. 43, 18 K.=1 p. 7 D.: τὴν πρώτην πατρίδα τὴν οὐράνιον; Anaxagoras in Diog. L. 2, 7; Epict. 2, 23, 38; Philo, Agr. 65) Hb 11: 14. ἀγάπη τῆς πατρίδος *love of one's country* 1 Cl 55: 5.
2. *home town, one's own part of the country* (oft. inscr., pap.; Appian, Bell. Civ. 1, 48 §207; 210; Phlegon: 257 fgm. 36, 3, 14 Jac.; Herodian 3, 1, 1; Philo, Leg. ad Gai. 278; Jos., Ant. 6, 67; 10, 114) Mt 13: 54; Mk 6: 1; Lk 2: 3 D; 4: 23; Ac 18: 25 D, 27 D. As a proverb: οὐκ ἔστιν προφήτης ἄτιμος εἰ μὴ ἐν τῇ πατρίδι αὐτοῦ (Dio Chrys. 30[47], 6 πᾶσι τοῖς φιλοσόφοις χαλεπὸς ἐν τῇ πατρίδι ὁ βίος; Ep. 44 of Apollonius of Tyana [Philostrat. I 354, 12] ἡ πατρὶς ἀγνοεῖ; Epict. 3, 16, 11 the philosopher avoids his πατρίς) Mk 6: 4; cf. Mt 13: 57; Lk 4: 24; LJ 1: 6. Also J 4: 44; s. 1 above. M-M. B. 1303.*

Πατροβᾶς, ᾶ, ὁ (CIG 6864.—Short form of Πατρόβιος.—Bl-D. §125; Rob. 173) *Patrobas* recipient of a greeting Ro 16: 14. M-M.*

πατρολῴας, ου, ὁ (Aristoph., Pla. +; Jos., Ant. 16, 356. On the formation of the word see s.v. μητρολῴας) *one who kills one's father, a patricide* (w. μητρολῴας) 1 Ti 1: 9 (M. Ant. 6, 34 in a list of the grossest sins). M-M.*

πατροπαράδοτος, ον *inherited, handed down from one's father* or *forefathers* (Dionys. Hal. 5, 48; Diod. S. 4, 8, 5 [εὐσέβεια]; 15, 74, 5 [εὔνοια]; 17, 4, 1; Dit., Or. 331, 49; PGM 33, 23) ἡ ματαία ἀναστροφὴ π. *the futile way of life inherited from your forefathers* 1 Pt 1: 18 (WCvUnnik, The Critique of Paganism in 1 Pt 1: 18, Neotestamentica et Semitica [MBlack-Festschr.], '69, 129–42). M-M.*

πατρώνυμος, ον *named after the father* (Quarterly of Dept. of Antiquities in Palestine 1, '31, 155 [Gaza, III AD]) IRo inscr. (on the subject matter perh. one might cf. Eph 3: 14f; s. Lghtf. on IRo inscr.), where God the Father is meant.*

πατρῷος, α, ον (since Hom. [πατρώϊος]; inscr., pap., LXX, Philo, Joseph.) *paternal, belonging to one's father, inherited* or *coming from one's father* (or *forefathers*) ὁ πατρῷος νόμος Ac 22: 3 (Aelian, V.H. 6, 10; 3 Macc 1: 23; 4 Macc 16: 16; Jos., Ant. 13, 54 v.l.) τὰ ἔθη τὰ πατρῷα 28: 17 (Aelian, V.H. 7, 19 v.l.; Justin, Dial. c. Tr. 63 end). ὁ π. θεός (Aeschyl. + oft., in sing. and pl.—Dit., Or. 194, 6 τὰ τῶν μεγίστων καὶ πατρῴων θεῶν ἱερά; 654, 8, Syll.³ 711 L, 13 τὸν πατρῷον Ἀπόλλω; PLond. 973b, 6; POxy. 483, 24; 715, 28; PHermopol. 125 B, 7 ὁ πατρῷος ἡμῶν θεὸς Ἑρμῆς; 4 Macc 12: 17; Ezech. Trag. in Euseb., Pr. Ev. 9, 29, 14 p. 444D; Jos., Ant. 9, 256) *the God of my forefathers* Ac 24: 14. M-M.*

Παῦλος, ου, ὁ *Paul,* a Roman surname (never a praenomen), found in lit. (e.g., Diod. S. 14, 44, 1; 15, 76, 1), inscr., pap.—**1.** Sergius Paulus s. Σέργιος.
2. Paul, the apostle of Jesus Christ; fr. the beginning he bore the Jewish name Saul as well as the Graeco-Roman Paul (differently e.g. HDessau, Her 45, '10, 347–68 and EMeyer III 197; s. GHHarrer, HTR 33, '40, 19–33.—Σαούλ 2 and Σαῦλος), prob. born in Tarsus (s. Ταρσός), at any rate brought up there (but cf. WCvUnnik, Tarsus or Jerusalem, '62), born a Roman citizen. He was rabbinically trained, but was not untouched by the syncretistic thought-world in which he lived. At first he was a zealous Pharisee and as such a vehement foe of the Christians, but was converted by a vision of Christ (OKietzig, D. Bekehrg.

d. Pls '32; EPfaff, Die Bekehrg. d. hl. Pls in d. Exegese des 20. Jahrh. '42; CBurchard, Der Dreizehnte Zeuge, '70, 126 n. 278 [lit. since '54]). Most prominent of the apostles to the Gentiles. As such he worked in Nabataean Arabia, Syria, and Cilicia, traveled through Cyprus, Asia Minor, Macedonia, and Greece, and planned a missionary journey via Italy to Spain (s. Σπανία). He was prevented fr. carrying out this plan (at least at this time) by his subsequent arrest in Jerusalem and the lawsuit connected w. it (NGVeldhoen, Het Proces van den Ap. Pls '24; ESpringer, D. Proz. des Ap. Pls: PJ 218, '29, 182–96; HJCadbury, Roman Law and the Trial of Paul: Beginn. I 5, '33, 297–338). He reached Rome only as a prisoner (on the journey FLDavies, St. Paul's Voyage to Rome '31), and was martyred there. Ac chapters 9 and 13–28; Ro 1: 1; 1 Cor 1: 1, 12f; 3: 4f, 22; 16: 21; 2 Cor 1: 1; 10: 1; Gal 1: 1; 5: 2; Eph 1: 1; 3: 1; Phil 1: 1; Col 1: 1, 23; 4: 18; 1 Th 1: 1; 2: 18; 2 Th 1: 1; 3: 17; 1 Ti 1: 1; 2 Ti 1: 1; Tit 1: 1; Phlm 1, 9, 19; 2 Pt 3: 15; Pol 9: 1; (11: 2, 3). ὁ μακάριος Π. ὁ ἀπόστολος 1 Cl 47: 1. Π. ὁ ἡγιασμένος, ὁ μεμαρτυρημένος, ἀξιομακάριστος IEph 12: 2. ὁ μακάριος καὶ ἔνδοξος Π. Pol 3: 2. Mentioned w. Peter 1 Cl 5: 5; IRo 4: 3.—CClemen, Paulus '04, where the older lit. is given. More recent lit. in RBultmann, Theol. Rundschau n.s. 6, '34, 229–46; 8, '36, 1–22; WNLyons and MMParvis, NT Literature 1943–5, '48, 225–39; GBornkamm, RGG³ V, '61, 189f.—Fr. the recent works: ADeissmann, Pls² '25 [Eng. tr. WEWilson '26]; EvDobschütz, Der Ap. Pls I '26; LMurillo, Paulus '26; KPieper, Pls., Seine missionarische Persönlichkeit u. Wirksamkeit²˒³ '29; EBaumann, Der hl. Pls '27; PFeine, Der Ap. Pls '27; RLiechtenhan, Pls '28; HLietzmann, Gesch. d. Alten Kirche I '32, 102–31; JSStewart, A Man in Christ '36; CAAScott, St. Paul, the Man and the Teacher '36; ADNock, St. Paul '38; TR Glover, Paul of Tarsus '38; CYver, S. Paul '39; VGrønbech, Paulus '40; WvLoewenich, Pls '40; DWRiddle, Paul, Man of Conflict '40; EBuonaiuti, San Paolo '41; JMBover, San Pablo '41; EBAllo, Paul '42; JKlausner, Fr. Jesus to Paul '43; EJGoodspeed, Paul '47; JKnox, Chapters in a Life of Paul '50; MDibelius, Paulus '51; ²'56, with WGKümmel (Eng. tr. FClarke '53); EFascher, Pauly-W. Suppl. VIII 431–66, '57.—FPrat, La théologie de S. Paul '24f (Eng. tr. JLStoddard '57); CAAScott, Christianity Acc. to St. Paul '28; OMoe, Apostolen Pls' Forkyndelse og Laere '28; AKristoffersen, Åpenbaringstanke og misjonsforkynnelse hos Pls, Diss. Upps. '38; RGuardini, Jes. Chr. I (in Paul) '40; ChGuignebert, Le Christ '43, 3 (Paulinisme).—A Schweitzer, D. Mystik des Ap. Pls '30 (Eng. tr. WMontgomery '31); MGoguel, La Mystique Paulin.: RHPhr 11, '31, 185–210; MDibelius, Pls u. d. Mystik '41; AFaux, L' Orphisme et St. Paul: Rev. d'Hist. eccl. 27, '31, 245–92; 751–91; HWindisch, Pls u. Christus, E. bibl.-rel. gesch. Vergleich '34.—EEidem, Det kristna Livet enligt Pls I '27; MSEnslin, The Ethics of Paul '30; LHMarshall, The Challenge of NT Ethics '46; DWhiteley, The Theol. of St. Paul, '64.—AFPuukko, Pls u. d. Judentum: Studia Orientalia 2, '28, 1–86; HWindisch, Pls u. d. Judentum '35; NMånsson, Paul and the Jews '47; WLKnox, St. Paul and the Church of the Gentiles '39.—ASteinmann, Z. Werdegang des Pls. Die Jugendzeit in Tarsus '28; EBarnikol, D. vorchristl. u. früchristl. Zeit des Pls '29; AOepke, Probleme d. vorchristl. Zeit des Pls: StKr 105, '33, 387–424; GBornkamm, D. Ende des Gesetzes, Paulusstudien '52.— WKümmel, Jes. u. Pls: ThBl 19, '40, 209–31; ASchlatter, Jes. u. Pls '40; WDDavies, Paul and Rabbinic Judaism ²'67; ²'55.—GRicciotti, Paul the Apostle (Eng. transl. AIZizzamia) '53; JNSevenster, Paul and Seneca, '61; H-JSchoeps, Paulus '59 (Engl. transl. HKnight, '61);

BMMetzger, Index to Periodical Lit. on Paul '60; Wv Loewenich, Paul: His Life and Works (transl. GEHarris), '60; WSchmithals, Paul and James (transl. DMBarton), '65; EGüttgemanns, D. Leidende Apostel, '66; HBraun, Qumran u. d. NT '66, 165-80. M-M.*

παύω (Hom.+; inscr., pap., LXX, Philo, Joseph., Test. 12 Patr.) 1 aor. ἔπαυσα, imper. 3 sing. παυσάτω. Mid.: impf. ἐπαυόμην; fut. παύσομαι; 1 aor. ἐπαυσάμην, imper. παῦσαι; pf. πέπαυμαι. Pass.: 2 aor. inf. παῆναι (Hv 1, 3, 3; 3, 9, 1.—Reinhold p. 78; StBPsaltes, Gramm. der Byz. Chroniken '13, 225; Bl-D. §76, 1; 78; W-S. §13, 9).
1. act. *stop, cause to stop, quiet, relieve* (Jos., Ant. 20, 117 στάσιν, Vi. 173) τὶ ἀπό τινος *hinder, keep someth. from someth.* τὴν γλῶσσαν ἀπὸ κακοῦ *keep the tongue from evil* 1 Pt 3: 10; 1 Cl 22: 3 (both Ps 33: 14). *Relieve, cure* (Dit., Syll.³ 1168, 72) τί τινι *someth. with someth.* τοὺς παροξυσμοὺς ἐμβροχαῖς IPol 2: 1.
2. mid. *stop* (oneself), *cease* (on the syntax cf. DCHesseling, ByzZ 20, '11, 147ff) w. pres. act. ptc. foll. (Hom. +; Gen 11: 8 al.; Philo, Leg. All. 3, 131; Jos., Ant. 3, 223, Vi. 298) ἐπαύσατο λαλῶν (Gen 18: 33; Num 16: 31; Judg 15: 17 B) *he stopped speaking* Lk 5: 4. μετ᾿ ἐμοῦ λαλοῦσα Hv 3, 10, 1. ἐπαυσάμην ἐρωτῶν *I stopped asking* v 3, 8, 1; cf. v 3, 1, 6. π. τύπτων τινά *stop beating someone* Ac 21: 32. ἀναβαίνων Hs 9, 4, 4a.—οὐ π. foll. by pres. act. ptc. *not to stop doing someth., do someth. without ceasing* (X., Cyr. 1, 4, 2; Herodian 1, 6, 2; Philostrat., V.S. 2, 1, 6 οὐκ ἐπαύσαντο μισοῦντες; Jos., Ant. 9, 255) διδάσκων Ac 5: 42. λαλῶν 6: 13. διαστρέφων 13: 10. νουθετῶν 20: 31. εὐχαριστῶν Eph 1: 16. Followed by the pres. mid. ptc. (cf. Himerius, Or. 74 [=Or. 24], 5 μὴ παύονται ἐργαζόμενοι). προσευχόμενος Col 1: 9. αἰτούμενος Hv 3, 3, 2. Foll. by pres. pass. ptc. (Antiphon 5, 50 Thalheim; Pla., Rep. 9 p. 583D) ἐπεὶ οὐκ ἂν ἐπαύσαντο προσφερόμεναι (i.e. αἱ θυσίαι); *otherwise would they not have ceased to be offered?* Hb 10: 2.—W. gen. of the thing (Hom.+; Ex 32: 12; Philo, Dec. 97; Jos., Ant. 7, 144) *cease from, have done with someth.* τῶν ἀρχαίων ὑποδειγμάτων *leave the old examples,* i.e., mention no more 1 Cl 5: 1. πέπαυται ἁμαρτίας *he has done with sin* 1 Pt 4: 1. W. gen. of the inf. (Jos., Ant. 3, 218) π. τοῦ θύειν GEb 5. π. ἀπό τινος *cease from, leave* (Ps 36: 8) ἀπὸ τῶν πονηριῶν 1 Cl 8: 4 (Is 1: 16). ἀπὸ τῆς πονηρίας Hv 3, 9, 1. π. ἀφ᾿ ὑμῶν ἡ ὀργή *the wrath will cease from you* GEb 5.—Abs. *stop, cease, have finished, be at an end* (Hom.+; Ep. Arist. 293; Sib. Or. 5, 458) of Jesus at prayer ὡς ἐπαύσατο *when he stopped* Lk 11: 1. ἐπαύσαντο οἱ οἰκοδομοῦντες μικρόν *the builders stopped for a little while* Hs 9, 4, 4b. οὐ παύσεται ὁ ζητῶν, ἕως ἂν εὕρῃ (for the constr. cf. Sir 23: 17) *the one who seeks will not give up until he has found* GH 27; cf. LJ 2: 2. Of the raging wind and waves ἐπαύσαντο *they stopped* Lk 8: 24 (cf. Od. 12, 168; Hdt. 7, 193; Arrian, Ind. 22, 1 ὁ ἄνεμος ἐπαύσατο). Of an uproar Ac 20: 1. Of speaking in tongues, which will come to an end 1 Cor 13: 8. Also of time *elapse, come to an end* (Herodian 1, 16, 2; PGrenf. II 69, 21 τῆς πεπαυμένης τριετηρίδος) τῆς ἑορτῆς παυσαμένης *since the festival was over* GP 14: 58. μετὰ τὸ παῆναι αὐτῆς τὰ ῥήματα ταῦτα *after these words of hers had come to an end* Hv 1, 3, 3. M-M. B. 981.*

Πάφος, ου, ἡ (Hom.+; inscr.; Sib. Or. 4, 128; 5, 451) *Paphos,* a city on the west coast of Cyprus, seat of the Rom. proconsul. Paul visited the city on his so-called first missionary journey Ac 13: 6, 13.—Lit. s.v. Κύπρος and JHS 9, 1889, 158ff.*

παχύνω 1 aor. pass. ἐπαχύνθην (Aeschyl., Hippocr.+;

PTebt. 273, 31; Philo, Aet. M. 103) in our lit. only in OT quotations.
1. lit. *make fat, well-nourished* (Pla., X. et al.). Pass. *become fat* (X., Conv. 2, 17; Plut., Sol. 20, 8; LXX) ἔφαγεν καὶ ἔπιεν καὶ ἐπλατύνθη καὶ ἐπαχύνθη 1 Cl 3: 1 (Dt 32: 15).
2. fig. *make impervious* (orig. to water), *make gross, dull* (Plut., Mor. 995D τὰς ψυχάς; Philostrat., Vi. Apoll. 1, 8 νοῦν). Pass. *become dull* (Herm. Wr. in Stob.=508, 32 Sc. of the ψυχή; Sib. Or. 7, 106; Synes., Dreams 6 p. 136D; 137A 'become dull' [of eyes]) ἐπαχύνθη ἡ καρδία τοῦ λαοῦ τούτου Mt 13: 15; Ac 28: 27 (both Is 6: 10). KL and MASchmidt: παχύνω, πωρόω etc., TW V 1024-32. M-M. B. 887.*

πεδάω pf. pass. ptc. πεπεδημένος (Hom.+; LXX) *bind the feet with fetters,* then gener. *bind, fetter, shackle* (En. 21, 4; Philo, Aet. M. 129; Sib. Or. 1, 371) B 14: 7 (here the word πεπεδημένους, which occurs in sim. LXX passages [e.g. Ps 67: 7 ἐξάγων πεπεδημένους] has come into the context of Is 42: 7).*

πέδη, ης, ἡ (Hom.+; PSI 406, 24; PGM 5, 488; LXX; Jos., Ant. 19, 295) *fetter, shackle* in pl. w. ἀλύσεις (ἄλυσις 1) Mk 5: 4a, b; Lk 8: 29. M-M.*

πεδινός, ή, όν (Hdt.+; LXX) *flat, level* either as opposed to 'steep', 'uneven' (Aristot., Probl. 5, 1; Cass. Dio 68, 16; Dt 4: 43; Jos., Ant. 13, 217) or in contrast to 'high', 'elevated' (Aristot., Hist. An. 9, 32; Jer 17: 26; Ep. Arist. 107) τόπος π. *a level place* Lk 6: 17. M-M. B. 893.*

πεδίον, ου, τό (Hom.+; inscr., pap., LXX; Ep. Arist. 23; Philo, Det. Pot. Ins. 1; Jos., Ant. 5, 63, Vi. 207; Test. 12 Patr.; Sib. Or. 2, 337) *level place, plain, field* Hs 6, 1, 5; 7: 1; 8, 4, 2; 9, 1, 4; 9, 2, 1; 9, 6, 6f; 9, 9, 4; 9, 29, 4; 9, 30, 1. πεδία καὶ ὄρη *plains and mountains* Hs 8, 1, 1; 8, 3, 2.—1 Cl 4: 6a, b (Gen 4: 8a, b). B. 26.*

πεζεύω *travel by land* in contrast to a sea-journey (so X., An. 5, 5, 4; Polyb. 16, 29, 11; 10, 48, 6; Plut., Cato Maj. 9, 4 al.; Dit., Or. 199, 14; PBrem. 15, 22; Philo, Ebr. 158 πεζ. κ. πλεῖν) Ac 20: 13. But the orig. mng. *travel on foot* is not impossible here (Aristot., De Part. An. 3, 6; cf. Jos., Ant. 13, 208; Sib. Or. 4, 78). M-M.*

πεζῇ adv. (Hdt.+; PTebt. 5, 28; PSI 446, 13; 2 Km 15: 17. On the spelling s. Bl-D. §26 app.; Mlt.-H. 163) *by land* (opp. ἐν πλοίῳ.—So since Hdt., Thu.; Sb 7600, 10 [16 AD]; Jos., Bell. 4, 659; orig. 'on foot') Mt 14: 13 (v.l. πεζοί); Mk 6: 33. M-M.*

πεζός, ή, όν (Hom.+; inscr., pap., LXX) *going by land* (Hom.+; Jos., Bell. 3, 8) (opp. ἐν πλοίῳ, as Pind., Pyth. 10, 29 ναυσί) Mt 14: 13 v.l. πεζοὺς πέμπειν *send messengers* (who travel on the highway) IPol 8: 1. M-M.*

πειθαρχέω 1 aor. ptc. πειθαρχήσας (Soph., Hdt.+; M.Ant. 5, 9; inscr., pap., LXX. Oft. in Philo; Jos., Bell. 1, 454, C. Ap. 2, 293 τ. νόμοις) *obey* θεῷ Ac 5: 29 (cf. Pla., Apol. 17 p. 29D πείσομαι μᾶλλον τῷ θεῷ ἢ ὑμῖν; Socrat., Ep. 1, 7 ᾧ [=τ. θεῷ] πειστέον μᾶλλον; Jos., Ant. 17, 159), 32. τῷ λόγῳ τῆς δικαιοσύνης *obey the word of righteousness* Pol 9: 1. ἔδει μέν... πειθαρχήσαντάς μοι μὴ ἀνάγεσθαι *you ought to have followed my advice and not to have sailed* Ac 27: 21 (cf. Polyb. 3, 4, 3.—On the subject matter cf. the unavailing protest of the passenger Ael. Aristid. 48, 47f K.=24 p. 483 D.). Fig. of the heavenly bodies that obey the Creator Dg 7: 2. Abs. (as Dit., Or. 483, 70f) *be obedient* Tit 3: 1 (w. ἀρχαῖς ἐξουσίαις ὑποτάσσεσθαι).—ENachmanson, D. Konstruktionen v. πειθαρχεῖν in d. κοινή: Eranos 10, '10, 201-3. M-M.*

πειθός, ή, όν persuasive ἐν πειθοῖς σοφίας λόγοις in persuasive words of wisdom 1 Cor 2: 4. The word is found nowhere but here; its attestation is extremely good (as early as 𝔓⁴⁶), though it is in a context that is subject to considerable variation in detail (the situation is well reviewed in Ltzm., Hdb. ad loc.). The word is formed quite in accordance w. Gk. usage (cf. φειδός 'sparing' fr. φείδομαι), and the Gk. Fathers let it pass without comment (so Ltzm., Bachmann, Sickenberger, HermvSoden; Mlt.-H. 78). Despite this at the present time many (e.g. Heinrici, Schmiedel, JWeiss) reject this word because of its rarity and prefer the explanation that it originated in dittography of the σ (or perh. an error in hearing the passage dictated): ἐν πειθοῖ σοφίας, s. πειθώ; Bl-D. §47, 4; 112 app.; W-S. §16, 3 n. 20; Rob. 157; GZuntz, The Text of the Epistles '53, 23-5.—Rdm.² p. 63 takes πειθοῖς as a rare genitive formation from πειθώ, influenced by the dat. πειθοῖ; the mng. then would be 'words of persuasion from wisdom (herself)'. M-M.*

πειθώ, οῦς, ἡ persuasiveness, (the gift or art of) persuasion (Aeschyl., Thu.+; Ps.-Phoc. 78; Philo; Jos., Bell. 2, 8, C. Ap. 2, 186; 223) ἐν πειθοῖ σοφίας (without λόγοις, which is lacking as early as 𝔓⁴⁶; cf. JWeiss ad loc.) with the persuasiveness of wisdom 1 Cor 2: 4 (in case this rdg. is the correct one; s. πειθός. On the 'persuasive power' of words cf. Περὶ ὕψους 17, 1 πειθὼ τῶν λόγων; Philo, Virt. 217 τοῖς λόγοις πειθώ; Jos., Ant. 2, 272). M-M. s.v. πειθός.*

πείθω (Hom.+; inscr., pap., LXX, Ep. Arist., Philo, Joseph., Test. 12 Patr.) impf. ἔπειθον; fut. πείσω; 1 aor. ἔπεισα, imper. πεῖσον; 2 pf. πέποιθα, plpf. ἐπεποίθειν Lk 11: 22; impf. mid. and pass. ἐπειθόμην. Pass.: pf. πέπεισμαι; 1 aor. ἐπείσθην; 1 fut. πεισθήσομαι.

1. act., except for 2 perf. and plpf.—a. convince w. acc. of the pers. (X., Mem. 1, 2, 45 al.) ISm 5: 1. ἔπειθεν Ἰουδαίους καὶ Ἕλληνας he tried to convince Jews and Gentiles Ac 18: 4. πείθων αὐτοὺς περὶ τοῦ Ἰησοῦ trying to convince them about Jesus 28: 23 (π. τινὰ περί τινος as Jos., C. Ap. 2, 153). Without acc. πείθων περὶ τῆς βασιλείας 19: 8; the two last-named passages have the acc. of the thing as v.l.: τὰ περὶ τοῦ Ἰησοῦ or τῆς βασιλείας (on the acc. of the thing cf. Hdt. 1, 163; Pla., Apol. 27 p. 37A). Abs. (Jos., Vi. 19) πείθων, οὐ βιαζόμενος convincing, not compelling Dg 7: 4.—Also of convincing someone of the correctness of the objectionable teachings, almost=mislead (Ps.-Clem., Hom. 1, 22) Ac 19: 26. τινά τινι someone with someth. Hs 8, 6, 5.

b. persuade, appeal to, also in a bad sense cajole, mislead (so Jos., C. Ap. 2, 201) τινά someone ἀνθρώπους (Ael. Aristid. 34, 19 K.=50 p. 552 D.) 2 Cor 5: 11; perh. also Gal 1: 10 (but s. 1c below). Cf. MPol 3; 8: 2, 3. τινά w. inf. foll. (X., An. 1, 3, 19; Polyb. 4, 64, 2; Diod. S. 12, 39, 2; 17, 15, 5; Herodian 2, 4, 2; Jos., Ant. 8, 256) Ac 13: 43; MPol 4; 5: 1. ἔπειθεν (sc. αὐτὸν) ἀρνεῖσθαι he tried to induce him to deny 9: 2. Perh. this is the place for the textually uncertain and obscure pass. Ac 26: 28 ἐν ὀλίγῳ με πείθεις Χριστιανὸν ποιῆσαι (so אB et al.). In EHLP and most minuscules this difficult wording is simplified by replacing ποιῆσαι with γενέσθαι in a short time you are persuading (or trying to persuade) me to become a Christian (cf. Jos., Vi. 151 πρὸς ὀλίγον ἐπείθοντο= 'they were nearly persuaded'), prob. meant ironically. The other rdg. is prob. to be understood as a combination of the two expressions 'in a short time you are persuading me to become a Christian' and 'in a short time you will make me

a Christian', so that the sense is someth. like you are in a hurry to persuade me and make a Christian of me (so Gdspd., Probs. 137f. S. the lit. s.v. ὀλίγος 3b and under 3a below, also AFridrichsen, Symb. Osl. 14, '35, 49-52. Con. Neot. 3, '39, 13-16 [on the last cf. PBenoit, RB 53, '46, 303]; DCHesseling, Neophilol. 20, '37, 129-34; JE Harry, ATR 28, '46, 135f; EHaenchen, AG '56 ad loc.). Instead of the inf. we have ἵνα (Plut., Mor. 181A πείθωμεν ἵνα μείνῃ) Mt 27: 20 (Bl-D. §392, 1e; Rob. 993).

c. win over, strive to please (X., Cyr. 6, 1, 34; 2 Macc 4: 45) Ac 12: 20. τοὺς ὄχλους 14: 19. So perh. also Gal 1: 10 (s. 1b above.—π. τὸν θεόν=persuade God: Jos., Ant. 4, 123; 8, 256; Ps.-Clem., Hom. 3, 64).

d. conciliate, pacify, set at ease or rest (Hom.+) τὸν δῆμον (cf. X., Hell. 1, 7, 7 τοιαῦτα λέγοντες ἔπειθον τὸν δῆμον) MPol 10: 2. τὴν καρδίαν ἡμῶν 1 J 3: 19 (but the text is not in good order). Conciliate, satisfy Mt 28: 14 (unless π. ἀργυρίῳ bribe is meant: schol. on Pla. 18B; 2 Macc 10: 20; Jos., Ant. 14, 281; 490).

2. The 2 pf. (w. plpf.) has pres. mng. (Bl-D. §341; Rob. 881)—a. depend on, trust in, put one's confidence in w. dat. of the pers. or thing (Hom.+; 4 Km 18: 20; Pr 14: 16; 28: 26; Sir 32: 24; Wsd 14: 29; Is 28: 17) τίνι θεῷ (in) which God Dg 1 (here πέπ. w. dat. almost=believe in, a sense which πέπ. also approximates in the LXX; cf. Jos., Ant. 7, 122). τοῖς δεσμοῖς μου Phil 1: 14. τῇ ὑπακοῇ σου Phlm 21. ἐπί τινι (in) someone or someth. (PSI 646, 3 ἐπὶ σοὶ πεποιθώς; LXX; Sib. Or. 3, 545; Syntipas p. 52, 5) Mt 27: 43 v.l.; Mk 10: 24 v.l.; Lk 11: 22; 2 Cor 1: 9; Hb 2: 13 (Is 8: 17); B 9: 4; 1 Cl 57: 7; w. ὅτι foll. (Syntipas p. 32, 6; 35, 7) Lk 18: 9. ἐπί τινα (Ps 117: 8; Acta Christophori [ed. HUsener 1886] 68, 10) Mt 27: 43; 1 Cl 60: 1, cf. 58: 1; Hm 9: 6; s 9, 18, 5; w. ὅτι foll. 2 Cor 2: 3; 2 Th 3: 4. ἔν τινι (Jdth 2: 5) (in) someone or someth. Phil 3: 3f; w. ὅτι foll. 2: 24. εἴς τινα (Wsd 16: 24 v.l.) w. ὅτι foll. Gal 5: 10.

b. be convinced, be sure, certain foll. by acc. and inf. Ro 2: 19. W. ὅτι foll. Hb 13: 18 t.r. πεποιθὼς αὐτὸ τοῦτο ὅτι being sure of this very thing, that Phil 1: 6. τοῦτο πεποιθὼς οἶδα ὅτι convinced of this, I know that 1: 25. εἴ τις πέποιθεν ἑαυτῷ Χριστοῦ εἶναι if anyone is convinced in his own mind that he belongs to Christ 2 Cor 10: 7 (cf. BGU 1141, 17 [14 BC] πέποιθα γὰρ ἐμαυτῷ).

3. pass., except for the pf.—a. be persuaded, be convinced, come to believe, believe abs. (Pr 26: 25) Lk 16: 31; Ac 17: 4; Hb 11: 13 t.r. μὴ πειθομένου αὐτοῦ since he would not be persuaded Ac 21: 14. W. dat. of the thing by which one is convinced (opp. ἀπιστεῖν) τοῖς λεγομένοις (Hdt. 2, 146; Jos., Bell. 7, 415) 28: 24. πείθομαι I believe w. ὅτι foll. Hb 13: 18; Hs 8, 11, 2. Ac 26: 28 (s. 1b above), construed w. the inf., would belong here if the rdg. of A should prove to be right: ἐν ὀλίγῳ με πείθῃ Χριστιανὸν ποιῆσαι in too short a time you believe you are making a Christian of me (so Bachmann, Blass). οὐ πείθομαι w. acc. and inf. I cannot believe Ac 26: 26.

b. obey, follow w. dat. of the pers. or thing (Hom.+; Diod. S. 4, 31, 5 τῷ χρησμῷ=the oracle; Maximus Tyr. 23, 2d τῷ θεῷ; 36, 6g τ. νόμῳ τοῦ Διός; Appian, Iber. 19 §73 θεῷ; pap.; 4 Macc 10: 13; 15: 10; 18: 1) Ro 2: 8 (opp. ἀπειθεῖν, as Himerius, Or. 69 [= Or. 22], 7); Gal 3: 1 t.r.; 5: 7; Hb 13: 17; Js 3: 3; 2 Cl 17: 5; Dg 5: 10; IRo 7: 2a, b; Hm 12, 3, 3; s 8, 9, 3.

c. Some passages stand betw. a and b and permit either transl., w. dat. be persuaded by someone, take someone's advice or obey, follow someone Ac 5: 36f, 39; 23: 21; 27: 11 (objection of a passenger, to which the crew paid no attention, and suffered harm as a result: Chio, Ep. 4, 1 οἱ δ' οὐκ ἐπείθοντο).

4. perf. pass. πέπεισμαι be convinced, certain (Pla.+; pap., LXX) πεπεισμένος τοῦτο convinced of this B 1: 4.

πέπεισμαί τι περί τινος *be convinced of someth. concerning someone* Hb 6: 9. περί τινος *be sure of a thing* IPol 2: 3. Foll. by acc. and inf. (Diod. S. 12, 20, 2 πεπεῖσθαι θεοὺς εἶναι; PPetr. II 11, 4 [III BC]; Ep. Arist. 5) Lk 20: 6. W. περί τινος and acc. w. inf.: περὶ ὧν πέπεισμαι ὑμᾶς οὕτως ἔχειν *concerning this I am certain that it is so with you* ITr 3: 2. W. ὅτι foll. (X., Oec. 15, 8) Ro 8: 38; 14: 14 (w. οἶδα); 2 Ti 1: 5, 12; Pol 9: 2. πέπεισμαι περὶ ὑμῶν ὅτι Ro 15: 14.—RBultmann, TW VI 1-12. M-M. B. 1206; 1339.*

Πειλᾶτος s. Πιλᾶτος. M-M.

πεῖν s. πίνω.

πεινάω (Hom.+; PFlor. 61, 54; LXX; Philo, Joseph.) fut. πεινάσω; 1 aor. ἐπείνασα (on the forms in α, which our lit. shares w. the LXX, in contrast to class. Gk., s. Bl-D. §70, 2; 88; Mlt.-H. 195; 253) *hunger, be hungry.*

1. lit. Mt 4: 2; 12: 1, 3; 21: 18; 25: 35, 37, 42, 44; Mk 2: 25; 11: 12; Lk 4: 2; 6: 3, 25; Ro 12: 20 (Pr 25: 21); 1 Cor 11: 34; B 10: 3. Opp. μεθύειν 1 Cor 11: 21. Opp. χορτάζεσθαι Phil 4: 12. ὁ πεινῶν, οἱ πεινῶντες *he who is hungry, those who are hungry* Lk 1: 53 (cf. Ps 106: 9); 6: 21; 1 Cl 59: 4; B 3: 3 (Is 58: 7), 5 (Is 58: 10); Hv 3, 9, 5. W. διψᾶν (διψάω 1) 1 Cor 4: 11; Rv 7: 16 (Is 49: 10); ISm 6: 2.

2. fig. *hunger for someth. = desire someth. strongly* (X., Pla.+, but w. gen. of the thing. For the acc. cf. διψάω 3 and Zosimus: Hermet. IV p. 111, 3 πεῖν τὴν σὴν ψυχήν) w. acc. of the thing the Mt 5: 6 (w. διψᾶν, as Plut., Mor. 460B; Jer 38: 25). Of the longing for spiritual food J 6: 35 (also w. διψᾶν). Goppelt, TW VI 12-22. M-M.*

πεῖρα, ας, ἡ (Pind.+; inscr., pap., LXX)—1. act. *attempt, trial, experiment* (Jos., C. Ap. 2, 183) πεῖραν λαμβάνειν *make an attempt* or *make trial of* (trag.+; POxy. 1681, 10; Dt 28: 56) τινός *someone* or *someth.* (X., Cyr. 6, 1, 54, Mem. 1, 4, 18; Pla., Protag. 342A, Gorg. 448A; Polyb. 2, 32, 5; Jos., Ant. 8, 166; Suppl. Epigr. Gr. VIII 574, 21 [III AD]; UPZ 110, 129 [164 BC]) ἧς πεῖραν λαβόντες *when they attempted (to do) it* Hb 11: 29. On θεοῦ ζῶντος πεῖραν ἀθλῶμεν 2 Cl 20: 2 cf. ἀθλέω.

2. pass. *experience* won by attempting someth. (X. et al.; Inschr. v. Magn. 115, 21; Philo; Test. Gad 5: 2 ἐκ πείρας) πεῖράν τινος λαμβάνειν *have experience with* or simply *experience someth.* (Polyb. 6, 3, 1; 28, 9, 7; Diod. S. 12, 24, 4 τὴν θυγατέρα ἀπέκτεινεν, ἵνα μὴ τῆς ὕβρεως λάβῃ πεῖραν; Vett. Val. 74, 23; 82, 1; 84, 28 al.; Jos., Ant. 2, 60, Vi. 160) μαστίγων πεῖραν ἔλαβον *they experienced scourgings* Hb 11: 36. HSeesemann, TW VI 23-37. M-M.*

πειράζω impf. ἐπείραζον; fut. πειράσω; 1 aor. ἐπείρασα, mid. 2 pers. sing. ἐπειράσω. Pass.: 1 aor. ἐπειράσθην; pf. ptc. πεπειρασμένος (Hom., then Apollon. Rhod. 1, 495; 3, 10. In prose since Philo Mech. 50, 34; 51, 9; also Polyb.; Plut., Cleom. 7, 3, Mor. 230A; Vett. Val. 17, 6; schol. on Aristoph., Pl. 575; PSI 927, 25 [II AD]; LXX, Joseph.—Bl-D. §101 p. 47; Mlt.-H. 387 n. 1; 404).

1. *try, attempt* w. inf. foll. (Polyb. 2, 6, 9; Dt 4: 34.—Bl-D. §392, 1a) Ac 9: 26; 16: 7; 24: 6; Hs 8, 2, 7. Foll. by acc. w. inf. IMg 7: 1.

2. *try, make trial of, put to the test,* to discover what kind of a pers. someone is—**a.** gener. τινά *someone* (Epict. 1, 9, 29; Ps 25: 2) ἑαυτοὺς πειράζετε εἰ ἐστὲ ἐν τῇ πίστει 2 Cor 13: 5 (π. εἰ as Jos., Bell. 4, 340). ἐπείρασας τοὺς λέγοντας ἑαυτοὺς ἀποστόλους Rv 2: 2. προφήτην οὐ πειράσετε οὐδὲ διακρινεῖτε D 11: 7.

b. in a good sense of God or Christ, who put men to the test (Ps.-Apollod. 3, 7; 7, 4 Zeus puts τὴν ἀσέβειαν of

certain people to the test), so that they may prove themselves true J 6: 6; Hb 11: 17 (Abraham, as Gen 22: 1). Also of painful trials sent by God (Ex 20: 20; Dt 8: 2 v.l.; Judg 2: 22; Wsd 3: 5; 11: 9; Jdth 8, 25f) 1 Cor 10: 13; Hb 2: 18a, b; 4: 15; 11: 37 (lacking in 𝔓⁴⁶, Pesh., several minuscules and Fathers); Rv 3: 10 (SBrown, JBL 85, '66, 308-14 π. = *afflict*). Likew. of the measures taken by the angel of repentance Hs 7: 1.

c. in a bad sense, in order to bring out someth. to be used against the one who is being 'tried.' Jesus was so treated by his opponents Mt 16: 1; 19: 3; 22: 18, 35; Mk 8: 11; 10: 2; 12: 15; Lk 11: 16; 20: 23 t.r.; J 8: 6.

d. in a bad sense also of enticement to sin, *tempt* Gal 6: 1; Js 1: 13a (s. ἀπό V 6), b, 14. Above all the devil works in this way; hence he is directly called ὁ πειράζων *the tempter* Mt 4: 3; 1 Th 3: 5b. He tempts men 1 Cor 7: 5; 1 Th 3: 5a; Rv 2: 10. But he also makes bold to tempt Jesus Mt 4: 1; Mk 1: 13; Lk 4: 2. On the temptation of Jesus (s. also Hb 2: 18a; 4: 15; 2b above) cf. HWillrich, ZNW 4, '03, 349f; KBornhäuser, Die Versuchungen Jesu nach d. Hb: MKähler-Festschr. '05, 69-86; on this Windisch, Hb² '31, 38 exc. on Hb 4: 15; AHarnack, Sprüche u. Reden Jesu '07, 32-7; FSpitta, Zur Gesch. u. Lit. des Urchristentums III 2, '07, 1-108; AMeyer, Die evangel. Berichte üb. d. Vers. Christi: HBlümner-Festschr. '14, 434-68; DVölter, NThT 6, '17, 348-65; EBöklen, ZNW 18, '18, 244-8; PKetter, D. Versuchg. Jesu '18; BViolet, D. Aufbau d. Versuchungsgeschichte Jesu: Harnack-Ehrung '21, 14-21; NFreese, D. Versuchg. Jesu nach den Synopt., Diss. Halle '22, D. Versuchlichkeit Jesu: StKr 96/7, '25, 313-18; SEitrem-AFridrichsen, D. Versuchg. Christi '24; Clemen² '24, 214-18; HJVogels, D. Versuchungen Jesu: BZ 17, '26, 238-55; SelmaHirsch [s. on βαπτίζω 2a]; HThielicke, Jes. Chr. am Scheideweg '38; PSeidelin, Dt. Theol. 6, '39, 127-39; HPHoughton, On the Temptations of Christ and Zarathustra: ATR 26, '44, 166-75; EFascher, Jesus u. d. Satan '49; RSchnackenburg, ThQ 132, '52, 297-326; K-PKöppen, Die Auslegung der Versuchungsgeschichte usw. '61; EBest, The Temptation and the Passion (Mk), '65; JDupont, RB 73, '66, 30-76.

e. The Bible (but s. the Pythia in Hdt. 6, 86, 3 τὸ πειρηθῆναι τοῦ θεοῦ κ. τὸ ποιῆσαι ἴσον δύνασθαι) also speaks of a trial of God by men. Their intent is to put him to the test, to discover whether he really can do a certain thing, esp. whether he notices sin and is able to punish it (Ex 17: 2, 7; Num 14: 22; Is 7: 12; Ps 77: 41, 56; Wsd 1: 2 al.) 1 Cor 10: 9; Hb 3: 9 (Ps 94: 9). τὸ πνεῦμα κυρίου Ac 5: 9. In Ac 15: 10 the πειράζειν τὸν θεόν consists in the fact that after God has clearly made his will known by granting the Spirit to the Gentiles (vs. 8), some doubt him and make trial of him to see whether he really will make his will operative.—ASommer, D. Begriff d. Versuchung im AT u. Judentum, Diss. Breslau '35. HSeesemann, TW VI 23-37. Cf. πειράω. M-M. B. 652f.*

πειρασμός, οῦ, ὁ (in extra-Biblical usage only Diosc., Mat. Med. Praef. 5; Cyranides; Syntipas [s. 2b].—LXX).

1. *test, trial* (Sir 6: 7; 27: 5, 7) πρὸς πειρασμόν *to test you* 1 Pt 4: 12. διὰ πειρασμόν τινα *because you are being tried in some way* Hm 9: 7. Perh. Js 1: 2 and 1 Pt 1: 6 also belong here.

2. *temptation, enticement* to sin—**a.** act. *tempting* συντελέσας πάντα πειρασμὸν ὁ διάβολος *when the devil had exhausted every way of tempting* Lk 4: 13.

b. pass. *being tempted* Js 1: 12. *Temptation,* fr. without or fr. within, that can be an occasion of sin to a person (Sir 33: 1; 44: 20; 1 Macc 2: 52) μὴ εἰσενέγκῃς ἡμᾶς εἰς πειρασμόν Mt 6: 13; Lk 11: 4; D 8: 2; cf. Pol 7:

2.—KKnoke, Der ursprüngl. Sinn der sechsten Bitte: NKZ 18, '07, 200-20; AHarnack, Zur sechsten Bitte des Vaterunsers: SAB '07, 942-7; AKleber, CBQ 3, '41, 317-20; GBVerity, ET 58, '46/'47, 221f; FCGrant, Introd. to NT Thought, '50, 208.—(εἰσ-)έρχεσθαι εἰς πειρασμόν Mt 26: 41; Mk 14: 38 (JoachJeremias, Unknown Sayings of Jesus, tr. Fuller '57, p. 59 n. 1 and s. the agraphon fr. Tertullian, pp. 57-9;) Lk 22: 40 (HNBate, JTS 36, '35, 76f), 46. ἐμπίπτειν εἰς πειρασμόν 1 Ti 6: 9. ἐν καιρῷ πειρασμοῦ in a time of temptation Lk 8: 13. ἡ ὥρα τοῦ π. Rv 3: 10. ἐκ πειρασμοῦ ῥύεσθαι 2 Pt 2: 9. Cf. also Ac 15: 26 D; 1 Cor 10: 13a, b; 2 Cl 18: 2.—Also in the pl. temptations (Cyranides p. 40, 24 πειρασμοὶ ἐν γῇ κ. θαλάσσῃ; Syntipas p. 124, 18; Test. Jos. 2, 7) Lk 22: 28. μετὰ ταπεινοφροσύνης καὶ δακρύων καὶ πειρασμῶν Ac 20: 19. ἐν ποικίλοις πειρασμοῖς 1 Pt 1: 6; cf. Js 1: 2 (trial is also possible in the last two passages).—2 Pt 2: 9 v.l.— On the difficult saying τὸν πειρασμὸν ὑμῶν ἐν τῇ σαρκί μου οὐκ ἐξουθενήσατε Gal 4: 14 s. on ἐξουθενέω 1 and 2 and cf. JdeZwaan, ZNW 10, '09, 246-50.

3. in the sense of πειράζω 2e testing of God by men (cf. Dt 6: 16; 9: 22) Hb 3: 8 where vs. 9 shows that it is God who is being tested, and not the Israelites (Ps 94: 8f).— HJKorn, ΠΕΙΡΑΣΜΟΣ. Die Versuchg. des Gläubigen in der griech. Bibel, '37; MEAndrews, Peirasmos, A Study in Form-Criticism, ATR 24, '42, 229-44; KGKuhn, πειρασμός im NT, ZThK 49, '52, 200-22, New Light on Temptation, etc., in The Scrolls and the NT, ed. Stendahl, '57, 94-113. M-M.*

πειράω in our lit. only πειράομαι (Hom. +; inscr., pap., LXX, Ep. Arist., Philo, Joseph.) as a mid., in one place perh. as pass.: impf. 3 sing. ἐπειρᾶτο; pf. ptc. πεπειρα-μένος.

1. try, attempt, endeavor w. inf. foll. (Hom. +; inscr., pap., 2 Macc 2: 23; 10: 12; 3 Macc 2: 32; 4 Macc 12: 2; Ep. Arist. 297; Philo, Sacr. Abel. 123; Jos., C. Ap. 1, 70; 2, 283) Ἰουδαῖοί με ἐπειρῶντο διαχειρίσασθαι Ac 26: 21. Cf. 9: 26 t.r.; 2 Cl 17: 3; MPol 13: 2.

2. The sense of the wording is difficult in Hb 4: 15 t.r., which describes Christ as πεπειραμένος κατὰ πάντα. Starting fr. the mng. 'put someone or someth. to the test, in order to know him or it better', the mid. can= go through an experience and learn someth. by it (Aesop, Fab. 105 H.) and the perf. mid. = have experienced, know from experience, know (Hes., Hdt. +; X., Hiero 1, 2; 2, 6; Pla., Ep. 6 p. 323A). For our pass. this would result in the mng. who was experienced in all respects. The pass. sense tried, tested, tempted is hardly in accord w. Gk. usage. Cf. πειράζω 2b and d ad loc. M-M. B. 652f.*

πεισμονή, ῆς ἡ (Apollon. Dysc. = Gramm. Gr. II 2 p. 429, 9 U.; 299, 17; Eustathius on Hom. several times; Justin, Apol. I 53, 1; Irenaeus 4, 33, 7 al. in Church Fathers) persuasion (Apollon.; Justin, loc. cit.; PLond. 1674, 36 [VI AD]) οὐ πεισμονῆς τὸ ἔργον, ἀλλὰ μεγέθους ἐστὶν ὁ Χριστιανισμός Christianity is not a matter of persuasiveness, but of (true) greatness IRo 3: 3. ἡ π. οὐκ ἐκ τοῦ καλοῦντος that persuasion, that draws you away fr. the truth, does not come from him who calls you Gal 5: 8 (EDBurton, ICC Gal '20, 282f). Bl-D. §488, 1b app. favor the mng. 'obedience' (Folgsamkeit) here (also §109, 6), but must depart fr. the Gk. text as handed down by the great majority of witnesses. M-M.*

πέλαγος, ους, τό (Hom. +; Dit., Or. 74, 3; IG XII 2, 119; 2 Macc 5: 21; Ep. Arist. 214; Philo; Joseph.; Test. Napht. 6: 5; loanw. in rabb.).

1. the open sea, the depths (of the sea) (Aristot., Probl.

Sect. 23 Quaest. 3 p. 931b, 14f. ἐν τῷ λιμένι ὀλίγη ἐστὶν ἡ θάλασσα, ἐν δὲ τῷ πελάγει βαθεῖα; Jos., Bell. 1, 409) τὸ πέλαγος τῆς θαλάσσης (Apollon. Rhod. 2, 608. Cf. also Eur., Tro. 88 πέλαγος Αἰγαίας ἁλός. Hesychius: πέλαγος . . . βυθός, πλάτος θαλάσσης): ἐν τῷ π. τῆς θαλάσσης in the open (deep) sea Mt 18: 6 (Jos., C. Ap. 1, 307 of lepers ἵνα καθῶσιν εἰς τὸ πέλαγος). M-M.*

2. sea, mostly of an independent part of the whole (Aeschyl. +; Diod. S. 4, 77, 6 τὸ πέλ. Ἰκάριον; Philo, Op. M. 63; Jos., Ant. 2, 348) τὸ π. τὸ κατὰ τὴν Κιλικίαν the sea along the coast of Cilicia Ac 27: 5. M-M.*

πέλας adv. (Hom. +) near ὁ π. the neighbor (so Alcaeus 137 D.²; trag., Hdt.; Sextus 17; POxy. 79 II, 9; Pr 27: 2) MPol 1: 2 (after Phil 2: 4 where, however, it reads τὰ ἑτέρων instead of τὸ κατὰ τοῦ πέλας).*

πελεκίζω pf. pass. ptc. πεπελεκισμένος behead (with an ax—πέλεκυς) (Polyb. 1, 7, 12; 11, 30, 2; Diod. S. 19, 101, 3; Strabo 16, 2, 18; Plut., Ant. 36, 4; Jos., Ant. 20, 117; loanw. in rabb.) Rv 20: 4. M-M. B. 561.*

πεμπταῖος, α, ον, (Hom. +; pap.; Ep. Arist. 175) on the fifth day ἤλθομεν πεμπταῖοι we came in five days Ac 20: 6 D (Diod. S. 14, 103, 2 π. = 'on the fifth day'; Arrian, Anab. 1, 29, 1 ἀφικνεῖται πεμπταῖος).*

πέμπτος, η, ον (Hom. +; inscr., pap., LXX; Ep. Arist. 48; Philo, Joseph., Test. 12 Patr.) fifth Rv 6: 9; 9: 1; 16: 10; 21: 20; Hv 3, 1, 2; s 9, 1, 7; 9, 22, 1. ἡ πέμπτη, i.e. ἡμέρα the fifth day (Hes., Aristoph. +; Jos., Vi. 47) σαββάτων πέμπτῃ on the fifth day of the week i.e. on Thursday acc. to the Judaeo-Christian reckoning D 8: 1. M-M.*

πέμπω fut. πέμψω; 1 aor. ἔπεμψα; pf. πέπομφα (IEph 17: 2); 1 aor. pass. ἐπέμφθην (Hom. +; inscr., pap., LXX, Ep. Arist., Joseph., Test. 12 Patr.) send.

1. human beings and other beings of a personal character τινὰ someone J 1: 22; 13: 16; 20: 21b; Phil 2: 23, 28; ISm 11: 3. δοῦλον Lk 20: 11; cf. vs. 12f. τ. ἀδελφούς 2 Cor 9: 3. ἄνδρας πιστούς 1 Cl 63: 3. ὑπηρέτην Dg 7: 2. ἐπισκόπους IPhld 10: 2. W. double acc. π. τινὰ κατάσκοπον send someone out as a spy B 12: 9; w. acc. of a ptc. π. τινὰ κρίνοντα send someone as a judge Dg 7: 6. π. τινὰ πρεσβεύσοντα send someone to be a representative Pol 13: 1. W. the destination indicated, in which case the acc. can be omitted as self-evident, like the Engl. 'send to someone' = 'send a messenger to someone': π. (τινὰ) εἰς τι send (someone) to, into (X., Hell. 7, 4, 39; Jos., C. Ap. 1, 271 εἰς Ἱεροσ.) Mt 2: 8; Lk 15: 15; 16: 27; Ac 10: 5, 32 (without acc.); 15: 22; IEph 6: 1. W. the point of departure and the destination given ἀπὸ τῆς Μιλήτου εἰς Ἔφεσον Ac 20: 17 (without acc.). W. indication of the pers. to whom someone is sent π. (τινὰ) πρός τινα send (someone) to someone (X., Cyr. 1, 5, 4; Diod. S. 20, 72, 1 π. τινὰ εἰς Συρακούσας πρὸς τ. ἀδελφόν; PHib. 127 descr. 3 [III BC] π. τινὰ πρός τινα; Sb 6769, 5; 2 Esdr [Ezra] 5: 17; Manetho in Jos., C. Ap. 1, 241) Lk 7: 19 (αὐτούς them is supplied by the immediate context); Ac 10: 33 (without acc.); 15: 25; 19: 31 (without acc.); 23: 30 (the acc. αὐτόν him is supplied by the context.—S. further below, where this pass. is cited again); Eph 6: 22; Phil 2: 25; Col 4: 8; Tit 3: 12 (ἔπεμψεν 𝔓⁷⁵ et al.). In several of these places π. is used w. another verb that tells the purpose of the sending. This verb can be in the ptc.: ἔπεμψεν λέγων he sent to ask (cf. Gen 38: 25; 2 Km 14: 32; Jos., C. Ap. 1, 262) Lk 7: 19; cf. vs. 6. Or the verb w. π. is in a finite mood and π. stands in the ptc. (Appian, Bell. Civ. 5, 9 §34 πέμψας ἀνεῖλε = he sent and had [her] put to death; 5, 118 §489

ἤρετο πέμπων = he sent and asked; Gen 27: 42; Jos., Ant. 7, 149) πέμψαντες παρεκάλουν *they sent and advised* Ac 19: 31; cf. πέμψας ἀπεκεφάλισεν *he sent and had* (John) *beheaded* Mt 14: 10.—22: 7. Differently πέμψας αὐτοὺς εἶπεν *he sent them and said* Mt 2: 8. W. indication of the one who is to receive someone, in the dat. π. τινά τινι *send someone to someone* 1 Cor 4: 17; Phil 2: 19.—π. διά τινος could come fr. the OT (= שָׁלַח בְּיַד 1 Km 16: 20; 2 Km 11: 14; 3 Km 2: 25) and could have given rise to the expr. πέμψας διὰ τῶν μαθητῶν εἶπεν αὐτῷ *he sent word by his disciples and said to him* Mt 11: 2 (yet a similar expr. is found in Appian, Mithrid. 108 §516 ἔπεμπεν δι᾽ εὐνούχων.—With the v.l. ὁ ᾿Ιω. πέμψας δύο τῶν μαθητῶν αὐτοῦ εἶπεν αὐτῷ= 'sent two of his disciples and had them say to him' cf. Appian, Bell. Civ. 1, 96 §449 πέμψας τινὰς ὁ Πομπήιος συνέλαβεν [Κάρβωνα]= Pompey sent certain men and had Carbo taken into custody). W. purpose indicated by the inf. Lk 15: 15; 1 Cor 16: 3; cf. also J 1: 33; Rv 22: 16. Subst. inf. w. εἰς 1 Th 3: 2, 5. By εἰς (Appian, Mithrid. 108 §516 ἔπεμπεν τὰς θυγατέρας ἐς γάμους= in order to marry them [to Scythian princes]) εἰς αὐτὸ τοῦτο *for this very purpose* Eph 6: 22; Col 4: 8. εἰς ἐκδίκησιν κακοποιῶν 1 Pt 2: 14. W. εἰς twice: εἰς θεοῦ τιμὴν εἰς Σμύρναν IEph 21: 1. W. purpose indicated by ἵνα Lk 16: 24.—Esp. of sending forth of God's representatives (Aberciusinschr. 7; Philosophenspr. p. 497, 8 Mullach I 1860, the wise man is ἀποσταλείς, his πέμψας is God) Moses 1 Cl 17: 5; Elijah Lk 4: 26. The angel of repentance Hs 8, 11, 1. Above all the Father sends the Son (upon the earth) Ro 8: 3; IMg 8: 2. πέμψω τὸν υἱόν μου τὸν ἀγαπητόν Lk 20: 13 (cf. Hdt. 1, 119, 2f ἦν οἱ παῖς εἷς μοῦνος ... τοῦτον ἐκπέμπει ... ἐς ᾿Αστυάγεος ... ᾿Αστυάγης σφάξας αὐτόν). John's gospel is dominated by the thought that Jesus is sent by God fr. heaven (s. Hdb. exc. on J 3: 17) 4: 34; 5: 23f, 30, 37; 6: 38f, 44; 7: 16, 28, 33; 8: 16, 18, 26, 29; 9: 4; 12: 44f, 49; 13: 20; 14: 24; 15: 21; 16: 5. Jesus, or God in his name, will send the Paraclete or Holy Spirit J 14: 26; 15: 26 (ὃν ἐγὼ πέμψω ὑμῖν παρὰ τοῦ πατρός); 16: 7. Sim. πέμπει αὐτοῖς ὁ θεὸς ἐνέργειαν πλάνης *God sends them a deluding influence* 2 Th 2: 11.—The idea of moving from one place to another, which is inherent in 'sending', can retreat into the background, so that π. takes on the mng. *instruct, commission, appoint*: ὁ πέμψας με βαπτίζειν ἐν ὕδατι J 1: 33. Cf. 7: 18 and the pass. 1 Pt 2: 14. Elsewh., too, π. takes on a particular mng. fr. the context: πέμψον ἡμᾶς εἰς τοὺς χοίρους *let us go among the swine* Mk 5: 12. Of one under arrest: *have him transported* to his destination Ac 25: 25, 27; cf. 23: 30.—Abs. οἱ πεμφθέντες *those who were sent* Lk 7: 10.—In several of the places already mentioned (Ac 23: 30; Eph 6: 22; Phil 2: 28; Col 4: 8) ἔπεμψα is an epistolary aorist (Thu. 1, 129, 3; Chio, Ep. 15, 3 ἔπεμψα δὲ τὸ ἀντίγραφον; POxy. 937, 21.—Bl-D. §334; Rob. 845f).

    2. things: τινί τι *send someth. to someone* Rv 11: 10; Hv 2, 4, 3a; s 5, 2, 9; 5, 5, 3. The thing that is the object of the sending can remain unmentioned if it is easily supplied fr. the context πέμψον ταῖς ἑπτὰ ἐκκλησίαις, εἰς ῎Εφεσον καὶ εἰς ... *send* (the book) *to the seven churches, to Ephesus and to* ... Rv 1: 11. πέμψει Κλήμης εἰς τὰς ἔξω πόλεις *Clement is to send* (*it*= his copy or rescripts of it) *to the cities abroad* Hv 2, 4, 3b. ὥρισαν εἰς διακονίαν πέμψαι τοῖς ἀδελφοῖς *they decided to send* (someth.) *to the brethren for their support* Ac 11: 29. εἰς τὴν χρείαν μοι ἐπέμψατε *you have sent me* (what was necessary) *to satisfy my needs* Phil 4: 16.—On π. τὸ δρέπανον Rv 14: 15, 18 s. δρέπανον.—π. abs. means *send, write a document, letter, etc.* (Ps.-Callisth. 3, 18, 4; PGiess. 13, 5 [II

AD] ᾿Αρσινόη μοι ἔπεμψε περὶ τῶν δύο ταλάντων; 17, 8; 13; 27, 8 οὗ ἕνεκα πρὸς σὲ ἔπεμψα ἵνα ἐπιγνῶ; 81, 6; 14 πέμψον μοι οὖν περὶ τῆς σωτηρίας σου and oft. in pap.) ἐσπούδασα κατὰ μικρὸν ὑμῖν πέμπειν *I have taken pains to write to you briefly* B 1: 5.—KHRengstorf, TW I 397-405. M-M. **

πένης, ητος (Soph., Hdt.+; Jos., Ant. 14, 31) *poor, needy* in our lit. only subst. ὁ π. *the poor man* (Pla., X. et al.; PRyl. 62, 11; PReinach 47, 11; LXX; Ep. Arist., Philo; Jos., Bell. 4, 379, Ant. 7, 149; Test. 12 Patr.) 2 Cor 9: 9 (Ps 111: 9); 1 Cl 15: 6 (Ps 11: 6. On the juxtaposition here and elsewhere in the LXX of πένης and πτωχός Aristoph., Plut. 553 πτωχοῦ βίος ζῆν ἐστι μηδὲν ἔχοντα, τοῦ δὲ πένητος ζῆν φειδόμενον καὶ τοῖς ἔργοις προσέχοντα. Ammonius Gr. [100 AD] p. 108 Valck.; PFlor. 296, 18). Opp. ὁ πλούσιος (X., An. 7, 7, 28; Pla., Prot. 319D; Plut., Pericl. 7, 3; PSI 120, 47; 2 Km 12: 1; 1 Esdr 3: 19; Pr 23: 4; Ep. Arist. 249; Test. Reub. 4: 7) Hs 2: 5ff; B 20: 2; D 5: 2. W. χήρα, ὀρφανός Pol 6: 1.—JHemelrijk, Πενία en Πλοῦτος, Diss. Utrecht '25; JJvanManen, Πενία en Πλοῦτος in de periode na Alexander, Diss. Utrecht '31; FHauck, TW VI 37-40. M-M. B. 782.*

πενθερά, ᾶς, ἡ (Demosth.+; inscr., pap., LXX; Jos., Ant. 5, 323) *mother-in-law* Mt 8: 14; Mk 1: 30; Lk 4: 38. W. νύμφη (Mi 7: 6) Mt 10: 35; Lk 12: 53. M-M. B. 124.*

πενθερός, οῦ, ὁ (Hom.+; inscr., pap., LXX; Jos., Ant. 13, 120; 14, 71; Test. Jud. 13: 4) *father-in-law* J 18: 13. M-M. B. 124.*

πενθέω fut. πενθήσω; 1 aor. ἐπένθησα (Hom.+; LXX; Philo; Jos., Ant. 17, 206; Test. 12 Patr.).
    1. intr. *be sad, grieve, mourn* (Hom.+; Dit., Syll.³ 1219, 5; 8; POxy. 528, 9; LXX in most occurrences) in contrast to joy, inward and outward Mt 9: 15. παρακαλέσαι πάντας τοὺς πενθοῦντας B 14: 9 (Is 61: 2). Of sorrow for sins one has committed 1 Cor 5: 2 (in the OT of sorrow for the sins of others: 1 Esdr 8: 69; 9: 2; 2 Esdr [Ezra] 10: 6. Test. Reub. 1: 10 has πενθῶν ἐπὶ τῇ ἁμαρτίᾳ μου, but this has no counterpart in the LXX). Also, the πενθοῦντες Mt 5: 4 (al. 5) mourn not for their own sins, but because of the power of the wicked, who oppress the righteous. W. κλαίειν (POxy. 528, 9; 2 Km 19: 2; 2 Esdr 18 [Neh 8]: 9) Mk 16: 10; Lk 6: 25; Js 4: 9; Rv 18: 15, 19; GP 7: 27. π. ἐπί τινι *mourn over someth.* ἐπὶ τοῖς παραπτώμασιν τῶν πλησίον ἐπενθεῖτε 1 Cl 2: 6 (cf. Aeschines 3, 211; Epict. 3, 3, 15; 1 Esdr 8: 69 ἐμοῦ πενθοῦντος ἐπὶ τῇ ἀνομίᾳ; 2 Esdr [Ezra] 10: 6). ἐπί τινα *over someone* (2 Ch 35: 24) Rv 18: 11.
    2. trans. (Bl-D. §148, 2; Rob. 475) *mourn over* w. acc. of the pers. (Hom.+; Lysias 2, 66; Lucian, Dial. Deor. 14, 1; Gen 37: 34; 50: 3; 1 Esdr 1: 30; Bel 40; 1 Macc 12: 52; 13: 26; Jos., Bell. 2, 1) 2 Cor 12: 21. M-M.*

πένθος, ους, τό (Hom.+; inscr., pap., LXX, Philo; Jos., Ant. 12, 285; 15, 57; Test. 12 Patr.) *grief, sadness, mourning* (opp. ὁ γέλως) Js 4: 9. (W. θάνατος and λιμός) Rv 18: 8. (W. κραυγή and πόνος) 21: 4. (W. βασανισμός) 18: 7a. π. ἰδεῖν *see, have, experience sorrow* 18: 7b. Pl. (Ptolem., Apotel. 2, 9, 5; in contrast to ἑορταί=joyful feasts, as Philo, Exsecr. 171) *times of mourning* Dg 4: 5. RBultmann, TW VI 40-4. M-M. B. 1118.*

πενιχρός, ά, όν (Hom.+; Plut., Pyrrh. 34, 1, Mor. 242B; Vett. Val. 166, 18; PPetr. III 36a, 6; BGU 1024 VIII, 12; Ex 22: 24; Pr 28: 15; 29: 7; Philo, Somn. 2, 213; Jos., Bell. 4, 207, Ant. 13, 72) *poor, needy* χήρα π. Lk 21: 2. M-M.*

πεντάκις adv. *five times* (Pind.+; inscr., pap.; 4 Km 13: 19) 2 Cor 11: 24.*

πεντακισχίλιοι, αι, α (Hdt., Pla. et al.; inscr., LXX; Ep. Arist. 82; Jos., Bell. 1, 172, Ant. 11, 16, Vi. 212) *five thousand* Mt 14: 21; 16: 9; Mk 6: 44; 8: 19; Lk 9: 14; J 6: 10.—GerhKittel, Rabbinica: Arbeiten z. Religionsgesch. herausgeg. v. JLeipoldt I 3, '20, 39ff.*

πεντακόσιοι, αι, α (Hom.+; inscr.; PRyl. 129, 13; LXX; Ep. Arist. 104; Jos., Bell. 2, 477, Ant. 11, 16; Test. Jud. 9: 8) *five hundred* Lk 7: 41; 1 Cor 15: 6; 1 Cl 25: 2. M-M.*

πεντακοσιοστός, ή, όν (Aristoph., Lysias et al.; Philo, Mos. 1, 316) *five hundredth* ἔτος 1 Cl 25: 5.*

πέντε indecl. (Hom.+; pap., LXX, Ep. Arist., Philo, Joseph., Test. 12 Patr.) *five* Mt 14: 17, 19; 16: 9 and oft. πέντε ἄνδρας ἔσχες J 4: 18 (acc. to Lycophron vs. 143; 146ff Helen had five husbands).—GerhKittel (under πεντακισχίλιοι) and EHommel, ZNW 23, '24, 305–10. M-M.

πεντεκαιδέκατος, η, ον (Aristot.; Diod. S. 12, 81, 5; Plut., Mor. 1084D; inscr.; PAmh. 131, 7; LXX; Jos., Bell. 5, 282; 7, 401, Ant. 15, 89) *fifteenth* Lk 3: 1. M-M.*

πεντήκοντα indecl. (Hom.+; pap., LXX, Ep. Arist.; Jos., Bell. 4, 482, Ant. 11, 15) *fifty* Lk 7: 41; 16: 6; J 8: 57; 21: 11; Ac 13: 20. ὡσεὶ ἀνὰ πεντήκοντα Lk 9: 14 s. ἀνά 2. κατὰ π. Mk 6: 40 s. κατά II 3a. M-M.*

πεντηκόνταρχος, ου, ὁ (Ps.-X., Rep. Athen. 1, 2 al.; pap., LXX) *commander of 50 men, lieutenant* 1 Cl 37: 3.*

πεντηκοστή, ῆς, ἡ (the subst. fem. of πεντηκοστός *fiftieth* [this Pla.+; LXX], found in Hyperides, fgm. 106; Andoc. 1, 133; Demosth. 14, 27 al., also in inscr. and ostraca as t.t. in taxation ἡ πεντηκοστή [i.e. μερίς] 'the fiftieth part'=two per cent) in our lit. *Pentecost* (really ἡ π. ἡμέρα, because it means the festival celebrated on the fiftieth day after Passover [= חַג שָׁבֻעֹת 'feast of weeks' Dt 16:10]; rabb. חַג חֲמִשִׁים יוֹם 'feast of 50 days'.—Tob 2: 1; 2 Macc 12: 32; Philo, Decal. 160, Spec. Leg. 2, 176; Jos., Ant. 3, 252; 13, 252; 14, 337; 17, 254, Bell. 1, 253; 2, 42; 6, 299) ἕως τῆς π. *until Pentecost* 1 Cor 16: 8. ἡ ἡμέρα τῆς π. *the Day of Pentecost* Ac 2: 1; 20: 16.—WHRoscher, Die Zahl 50: Abh. der Sächs. Ges. d. Wiss. XXXIII, 5, '17; Billerb. II 597ff; CRErdman, The Mng. of Pentecost: Bibl. Review 15, '30, 491–508; KLake, Gift of the Spirit on the Day of Pentecost: Beginn. I 5, '33, 111–21; NAdler, D. erste chr. Pfingstfest '38. Lohse, TW VI 44–53; EHaenchen, AG '56, 133ff. M-M.*

πέπειρος, ον (Soph.+) *ripe* (Theophr., C. Pl. 3, 6, 9; Artem. 2, 25) τὸ πέπειρον *ripeness* (Herm. Wr. 1, 17: Rtzst., Poim. 333) εἰς πέπειρον καταντᾶν *come to ripeness of the fruit of the vine* (cf. Gen 40: 10) 1 Cl 23: 4.*

πέποιθα s. πείθω.

πεποίθησις, εως, ἡ (a word of later Gk. rejected by Phryn. p. 294 L.: LXX only 4 Km 18: 19, somewhat more freq. in the other Gk. translations of the OT; Philo, Virt. 226; Jos., Ant. 1, 73; 3, 45; 10, 16; 11, 299; Philod., Περὶ παρρησίας p. 22 Ol.; Hermogenes, De Ideis 1, 9 p. 265 Rabe; 2, 7 p. 355; Sext. Emp., Hypotyp. 1, 14, 60; 23, 197; Syntipas p. 125, 12 ἡ ἐπὶ τ. θεῷ π.; Simplicius In Epict., Ench. 79 p. 329; Eustath., In Od. p. 114; 717) *trust, confidence.*

1. *of trust or confidence in others.* In men, abs. 2 Cor 1: 15. Esp. of trust in God (occasionally almost=*faith*) μετ' εὐσεβοῦς πεποιθήσεως *with devout confidence* 1 Cl 2: 3.

ἐν π. πίστεως ἀγαθῆς 26: 1; πίστις ἐν π. 35: 2; cf. 45: 8; ἔχειν προσαγωγὴν ἐν π. *have access* (to God) *in confidence* Eph 3: 12.—W. prep.: π. εἰς τινα *trust, confidence in someone* 2 Cor 8: 22. Also ἔν τινι: ἔχειν πεποίθησιν ἐν σαρκί *put one's trust in physical matters* Phil 3: 4.

2. *of trust or confidence in oneself* θαρρῆσαι τῇ πεποιθήσει *be bold with confidence* (in his position as an apostle) 2 Cor 10: 2. πεποίθησιν τοιαύτην ἔχομεν διὰ τοῦ Χριστοῦ πρὸς τὸν θεόν such (as explained in what precedes) *is the self-confidence we have through Christ toward God* (who, acc. to what follows, is the real basis for the apostle's self-confidence) 3: 4. ἡ κενὴ π. *vain self-confidence* Hs 9, 22, 3.

3. *confidence* in the outcome of affairs μετὰ πεποιθήσεως *with confidence* 1 Cl 31: 3. ποίᾳ πεποιθήσει εἰσελευσόμεθα εἰς τὸ βασίλειον; *what basis for confidence* (= prospect) *do we have for getting into the Kingdom?* 2 Cl 6: 9. M-M.*

πέπονθα s. πάσχω.

πέπρακα s. πιπράσκω.

πέπτωκα s. πίπτω.

πέπωκα s. πίνω.

περ enclitic particle, w. intensive and extensive force (Bl-D. §107; Rob. 1153); s. the words compounded w. it: διόπερ, ἐάνπερ (s. ἐάν I 3c), εἴπερ (s. εἰ VI 11), ἐπειδήπερ, ἐπείπερ, ἤπερ (s. ἤ 2eβ), καθάπερ, καίπερ, ὅσπερ (s. ὅς I 10e), ὥσπερ (ὡσπερεί).

Πέραια, ας, s. πέραν 2c.

περαιτέρω (Aeschyl., Thu.+; Jos., Bell. 4, 107, Ant. 18, 301; 19, 141; BGU 372 II, 12 [154 AD]) adv. of περαίτερος, α, ον, the comp. of πέρα: *further, beyond* εἰ δέ τι π. ἐπιζητεῖτε *if there is anything further that you want to know* (cf. Pla., Phaedo 107B οὐδὲν ζητήσετε περαιτέρω) Ac 19: 39. M-M.*

πέραν adv. of place (Hom. [πέρην]+; inscr., pap., LXX) *on the other side.*

1. used as adv., and subst. w. the art. τὸ πέραν *the shore* or *land on the other side* (X., An. 4, 3, 11; Sb 7252, 19) εἰς τὸ πέραν (Pla.; Polyb.; Dit., Syll.³ 495, 84; 619, 27; 709, 6; BGU 1022, 25; 1 Macc 9: 48) Mt 8: 18, 28; 14: 22; 16: 5; Mk 4: 35; 5: 21; 6: 45; 8: 13.

2. as improper prep. w. gen. (Bl-D. §184; Rob. 646)—a. answering the question 'whither?' ἀπῆλθεν ὁ Ἰησοῦς πέραν τῆς θαλάσσης *Jesus went away to the other side of the lake* J 6: 1. ἤρχοντο πέραν τ. θαλάσσης εἰς Καφαρναούμ vs. 17. Cf. 10: 40; 18: 1.

b. answering the question 'where?' ταῦτα ἐν Βηθανίᾳ ἐγένετο πέραν τοῦ Ἰορδάνου *this took place in Bethany on the other side of the Jordan* J 1: 28 (PParker, JBL 74, '55, 257–61 [not 'beyond'=west, but 'across from'=east]). τὰ ὅρια τῆς Ἰουδαίας πέραν τοῦ Ἰορδάνου Mt 19: 1. Cf. J 3: 26; 6: 22, 25.—πέραν w. gen. can also be used w. the art. as a subst. (X., An. 3, 5, 2 εἰς τὸ πέραν τοῦ ποταμοῦ; Jos., Ant. 7, 198) ἦλθον εἰς τὸ πέραν τῆς θαλάσσης *they came to the* (land on the) *other side of the lake* Mk 5: 1. Cf. Lk 8: 22.

c. In a number of places πέραν τοῦ Ἰορδάνου (Is 8: 23; cf. Jos., Ant. 12, 222) functions as an indecl. name for the territory on the other (eastern) side of the Jordan, i.e. *Peraea* (Περαία, ας [oft. in Joseph.] is found in our lit. only as v.l.: Lk 6: 17.—The expression is by no means limited to Palestine. ἐν τῇ περαίᾳ in Appian, Bell. Civ. 2,

42 §168 refers to the land on the other side of the river. In addition, the region of the Carian mainland opposite the island of Rhodes was called Peraea: Appian, op. cit. 4, 72 §305; also Livy 32, 33; 33, 18). ἀπὸ τ. Γαλιλαίας καὶ Ἰουδαίας καὶ πέραν τοῦ Ἰορδάνου *from Galilee and Judaea and Peraea* Mt 4: 25. ἀπὸ τῆς Ἰδουμαίας καὶ πέραν τοῦ Ἰορδάνου Mk 3: 8. Cf. Mt 4: 15 (Is 8: 23); Mk 10: 1 (here the t.r. has διὰ τοῦ πέραν τοῦ Ἰορδάνου). — Meistermann (Καφαρναούμ, end) 93ff. M-M.*

πέρας, ατος, τό (Aeschyl. +; inscr., pap., LXX, En., Ep. Arist., Philo, Joseph.) *end, limit, boundary.*

1. of place, pl. τὰ πέρατα *the ends, limits* τῆς γῆς *of the earth* (Alcaeus [c. 600 bc] 50, 1 Diehl; Thu. 1, 69, 5; X., Ages. 9, 4; Inscr. Orae Sept. Ponti Euxini I 21, 26 Latyschev μέχρι περάτων γῆς; Ps 2: 8; 21: 28; Da 4: 21; En. 1, 5; 31, 2; Philo; Jos., Bell. 4, 262; Test. Napht. 6: 7) Mt 12: 42; Lk 11: 31 (on both these passages cf. Apollon. Rhod. 2, 165 ἐκ περάτων); Ac 13: 33 D (Ps 2: 8); 1 Cl 36: 4 (Ps 2: 8); IRo 6: 1; Hs 8, 3, 2; D 9: 4. τὰ πέρατα τῆς οἰκουμένης (Diod. S. 3, 53, 1 τὰ πέρατα τῆς οἰκουμένης; 1, 19, 6 τὸ πέρας τῆς οἰκ.; Jos., Ant. 8, 116) Ro 10: 18 (Ps 18: 5). Also τὰ πέρατα abs. in the same sense (Vett. Val. 226, 18; Philo, Leg. ad Gai. 18; 173; Ps 64: 9) οἱ ἐπίσκοποι, οἱ κατὰ τὰ πέρατα ὁρισθέντες *the bishops who are appointed in the most distant lands* IEph 3: 2.—JGeyer, Vetus T 20, '70, 87–90, replying to MTreves, ibid. 19, '69, 235.

2. of ceasing, bringing to an end: *end, conclusion* (Aeschyl., Pers. 632 τῶν κακῶν; Demosth. 18, 97 πέρας τοῦ βίου ὁ θάνατος; Polyb. 5, 31, 2; 7, 5, 5; Epict. 3, 26, 37; 4, 1, 106; Dit., Or. 669, 40; PGiess. 25, 7; BGU 1019, 7; POxy. 237 VIII, 16; 1 Esdr 9: 17; 2 Macc 5: 8; 3 Macc 5: 5; Philo, Op. M. 150 al.; Jos., Bell. 7, 157, Ant. 7, 374) πάσης ἀντιλογίας πέρας (as) *an end to all disputing* Hb 6: 16. Cf. IRo 1: 2 v.l. Funk.

3. as adv. πέρας *finally, in conclusion, further(more)* (since Aeschin. 1, 61; Polyb. 2, 55, 6; Alciphr. 4, 17, 3; Manetho in Jos., C. Ap. 1, 77; Jos., Bell. 7, 393, Ant. 16, 352) B 5: 8; 10: 2; 12: 6; 15: 6, 8; 16: 3; MPol 15: 1. M-M.*

Πέργαμος, ου, ἡ (X., Hell. 3, 1, 6; Paus. 7, 16, 1) or **Πέργαμον, ου, τό** (Polyb. 4, 48, 11; Diod. S. 28, 5; Strabo 13, 4, 1; 2; Appian, Mithrid. 52 §210; Jos., Bell. 1, 425 τὸ κατὰ Μυσίαν Πέργαμον.—In the NT, as in many other cases [e.g. Dit., Or. ind. II p. 595a] the gender cannot be determined) *Pergamus* or *Pergamum*, an important city in Mysia, in northwest Asia Minor. It was the center of several cults: Zeus Soter, Asclepius Soter and Athena Nicephorus had famous temples here. It was also a center of the imperial cult; as early as 29 bc the provincial assembly erected a sanctuary to Augustus and Roma. Christians seem to have been persecuted here at an early date (s. Ἀντίπας). Rv 1: 11; 2: 12.—Altertümer von Pergamon I-VIII 1885–1930; of this vol. VIII = D. Inschr. v. P. edited by MFränkel 1890/95; EPontremoli and MCollignon, Pergame '00; VSchultze, Altchristliche Städte u. Landschaften II 2, '26; AvSalis, D. Altar v. P. '12. M-M.*

Πέργη, ης, ἡ (Callim., Hymn to Diana 187; Strabo 14, 4, 2; Philostrat., V.S. 2, 6; inscr.; coins) *Perga*, a city in Pamphylia, near the south coast of Asia Minor. Visited by Paul on his so-called first missionary journey Ac 13: 14; 14: 25. Π. τῆς Παμφυλίας 13: 13.—WRuge, Pauly-W. XIX 1, '37, 694–704.*

περί (Hom. +; inscr., pap., LXX, En., Ep. Arist., Philo, Joseph., Test. 12 Patr., Sib. Or.) prep. w. gen. and acc., in

our lit. not (Bl-D. §203; Rob. 617) w. dat.—See the lit. s.v. ἀνά, beg.

1. w. the gen. to denote the object or pers. to which (whom) an action refers or relates—a. after verbs that denote an oral or written expression or its reception, a mental action, knowing, thinking, recognizing, etc. *about, concerning*; s. the entries ἀκούω (1c; 3c), ἀναγγέλλω (2, end), ἀπαγγέλλω (1), ἀπολογέομαι, γνωρίζω (1), γογγύζω, γράφω (2d), δηλόω, διαβεβαιόομαι, διαλέγομαι (1), διδάσκω (2c), διηγέομαι, εἶπον (1). ἐντέλλω, ἐπιστέλλω, κατηχέω, λαλέω (2aδ), λέγω (I 4); λόγον αἰτεῖν, ἀποδιδόναι, διδόναι, ποιεῖσθαι (s. λόγος 2a); μαρτυρέω (1a), μνημονεύω (1c), ὁμιλέω, πυνθάνομαι, προκαταγγέλλω, προφητεύω, ὑπομιμνήσκω, χρηματίζομαι, ἀγνοέω (1), ἀπορέω, ἐπινοέω, ἐπίσταμαι (2), οἶδα (1h), πέπεισμαι (s. πείθω 4), πιστεύω (1aβ). Also used w. the substantives belonging to these verbs or verbs w. similar mngs.: ἀπολογία (2a), γογγυσμός (2). διήγησις, εὐαγγέλιον, ἦχος (2), πρόφασις, φήμη; s. these entries. γινώσκω J 7: 17. συμφωνέω Mt 18: 19. τί ὑμῖν δοκεῖ περὶ τοῦ Χριστοῦ; *what do you think of the Christ?* 22: 42.

b. after verbs that express considering, asking, examining, charging, judging, censuring, punishing, praising etc. *on account of, because of, for, concerning.* S. the entries ἀποστοματίζω, ἀπορέω, διαπορέω, ἐγκαλέω, εἶδον 4 *deliberate concerning*, ἐκζητέω (1), ἐλέγχω (2 and 3), ἐξετάζω (1a), ἐπιζητέω (1b), ἐρωτάω (1), ζητέω (1c), κατηγορέω, παραμυθέομαι.—διαλογίζομαι Lk 3: 15. κρίνω J 8: 26. λιθάζω 10: 33. θεὸν αἰνέω Lk 19: 37. περὶ οὗ ... οἱ κατήγοροι οὐδεμίαν αἰτίαν ἔφερον *his accusers brought no charge of this kind* Ac 25: 18 (BWeiss, Preuschen take περὶ οὗ w. σταθέντες, which immediately follows it, and understand it to mean 'around him', 'near him' [περί τινος in this sense IG XIV 2508, 4]).—S. also the entry ζήτημα.

c. after verbs that denote emotion. S. the entries ἀγανακτέω, θαυμάζω (1aβ), καυχάομαι, σπλαγχνίζομαι.

d. after verbs of caring (for). S. the entries μέλει (2), μεριμνάω, προβλέπω.

e. after other verbs and expressions, mostly *with regard to, with reference to, in relation to*, w. *respect to* εὐλογεῖν Hb 11: 20. ἀναβαίνειν περὶ τοῦ ζητήματος *go up in relation to the question* Ac 15: 2. ἐντολὰς λαμβάνειν Col 4: 10. ἐξουσίαν ἔχειν 1 Cor 7: 37 (s. ἐξουσία 1). περὶ πάντων σε εὐοδοῦσθαι *be well off in all respects* 3 J 2 (περὶ π. = 'in all resp.': Pla., Gorg. 23 p. 467D.—Others take it as 'above all'; cf. Il. 1, 287; 21, 566).

f. w. certain verbs and nouns such as 'ask', 'pray', 'prayer' etc. περί introduces the pers. or thing in whose interest the petition is made. Thus it takes the place of ὑπέρ (Bl-D. §229, 1; Rob. 618; WSchulze, Zeitschr. für vergl. Sprachforschung 44, '11, 359: Callim., Epigr. 55, 3.—Dit., Syll.³ 1170, 30 περὶ τούτου παρεκάλεσα τὸν θεόν; POxy. 1298, 4; 1494, 6; Ep. Arist. 273) *for.* S. the entries δέομαι (4), δέησις, ἐρωτάω (2), παρακαλέω (3). προσεύχεσθαι (Gen 20: 7; 1 Km 7: 5; 2 Macc 1: 6; 15: 14) Lk 6: 28; Col 1: 3 (v.l. ὑπέρ); 4: 3; 1 Th 5: 25; 2 Th 1: 11; 3: 1; Hb 13: 18. προσευχὴ γίνεται Ac 12: 5. Παῦλος ἐσταυρώθη περὶ ὑμῶν; 1 Cor 1: 13 v.l. (for ὑπέρ). τὸ αἶμα τὸ περὶ πολλῶν ἐκχυννόμενον Mt 26: 28 (cf. Nicol. Dam.: 90 fgm. 730, 29 p. 415, 29 Jac. περὶ τῶν διαδόχων αὐτοῦ ἅπαν ... παθεῖν. ἀγῶνα ἔχω περὶ ὑμῶν Col 2: 1 t.r. (for ὑπέρ).

g. when used w. ἁμαρτία the word 'for' has the sense *to take away, to atone for* περὶ ἁμαρτίας (Num 8: 8) Ro 8: 3 (differently TCThornton, JTS 22, '71, 515–17). Ἰ. Χρ. τοῦ δόντος ἑαυτὸν περὶ τῶν ἁμαρτιῶν ἡμῶν Gal 1: 4 v.l. (for ὑπέρ). περὶ ἁμαρτιῶν ἀπέθανεν 1 Pt 3: 18. Cf. Hb 5: 3c.

προσφορὰ περὶ ἁμαρτίας 10: 18. θυσία περὶ ἁμαρτιῶν vs. 26. εἰσφέρεται τὸ αἷμα περὶ ἁμαρτίας 13: 11. τὸ περὶ τῆς ἁμαρτίας (i.e. προσφερόμενον) the sin-offering (Lev 6: 23; 14: 19) Hb 10: 6, 8 (both Ps 39: 7).

h. περί τινος abs. at the beginning of a sentence concerning, with reference to (Dit., Syll.[3] 736, 1; PEleph. 13, 4f; BGU 246, 13; 17; 1097, 5 [c. 50 AD]; 1095, 9 [57 AD]) περὶ ὧν (=περὶ τούτων ἃ) ἐγράψατε concerning the things that you wrote (to me) 1 Cor 7: 1 (s. γράφω 2d). Cf. 8: 1; 16: 1, 12. In other, seemingly similar, places it is to be connected w. the verb that follows: Mt 22: 31; 24: 36; Mk 12: 26; 13: 32; 1 Cor 7: 25; 8: 4; 12: 1; 2 Cor 9: 1; 1 Th 4: 9; 5: 1.

i. w. the art. τὰ περί τινος what concerns someone or someth., his or its circumstances, situation, condition (X., An. 2, 5, 37 ὅπως μάθοι τὰ περὶ Προξένου; Sir 19: 30) τὰ περὶ (τοῦ) Ἰησοῦ the reports about Jesus, concerning his miracles Mk 5: 27; of Jesus' passion experiences Lk 24: 19; of the preaching about Jesus Ac 18: 25; cf. 28: 31. τὰ περὶ ἑαυτοῦ (αὐτοῦ, ἐμοῦ, ἐμαυτοῦ, ἡμῶν, ὑμῶν) Lk 24: 27; Ac 23: 11, 15; 24: 10; 28: 15; Eph 6: 22; Phil 1: 27; 2: 19f; Col 4: 8.—τὰ περὶ τῆς βασιλείας τοῦ θεοῦ the things concerning the Kgdm. of God Ac 1: 3; 19: 8 v.l. (the text omits the art.). τὰ περὶ τῆς ὁδοῦ 24: 22 (ὁδός 2c).

2. w. the acc.—a. of place around, about, near—α. (all) around ἕως ὅτου σκάψω περὶ αὐτήν until I dig (all) around it Lk 13: 8. περιαστράψαι φῶς περὶ ἐμέ Ac 22: 6b.

β. of a part of the body around which someth. goes: (Heraclid. Pont. fgm. 55 W. περὶ τὸ μέτωπον) a belt περὶ τὴν ὀσφύν around the waist Mt 3: 4; Mk 1: 6; cf. Rv 15: 6. A millstone περίκειται περὶ τὸν τράχηλον Mk 9: 42; Lk 17: 2; cf. Mt 18: 6.

γ. of nearby places: αἱ περὶ αὐτὰς πόλεις the towns near them (Sodom and Gomorrah) Jd 7. τὰ περὶ τὸν τόπον the region around the place Ac 28: 7 (Diod. S. 1, 50, 6 τὰ π. τὴν Μέμφιν; Strabo 12, 7, 3). Without the art. περὶ Τύρον καὶ Σιδῶνα the neighborhood of T. and S. Mk 3: 8.

δ. of persons who are standing, sitting, working or staying close to someone ὄχλον περὶ αὐτόν Mt 8: 18; cf. Mk 9: 14. τοὺς περὶ αὐτὸν κύκλῳ καθημένους Mk 3: 34; cf. vs. 32. οἱ περὶ αὐτόν those about him, his followers Mk 4: 10; Lk 22: 49. The central person in the group can be included: οἱ περὶ Παῦλον Paul and his companions Ac 13: 13; 21: 8 t.r. οἱ περὶ (τὸν) Πέτρον Peter and those with him short ending of Mark; ISm 3: 2; cf. GH 22 (class.; Diod. S. 11, 40, 3; 11, 61, 3 οἱ περὶ τὸν Κίμωνα=Cimon and his men; inscr., pap.; 2 Macc 1: 33; 8: 30; 4 Macc 2: 19; Jos., Bell. 5, 10, Ant. 18, 354 al.; Bl-D. §228; Rob. 620). οἱ περὶ τὸν κεντυρίωνα the centurion and his men GP 11: 45. πρὸς τὰς περὶ Μάρθαν καὶ Μαριάμ J 11: 19 v.l. prob. means only the two sisters to Martha and Mary (cf. Phalaris, Ep. 136; Polyb. 4, 36, 6; 21, 11, 2; Diod. S. 1, 16, 1; 1, 37, 3; 16, 85, 2 οἱ περὶ Χάρητα καὶ Λυσικλέα=Chares and Lysicles [are made generals]; Plut., Tiber. Gracch. 2, 3 οἱ περὶ Δροῦσον=Δροῦσος, Pyrrh. 20, 1 οἱ περὶ Γάϊον Φαβρίκιον=Γάϊος Φαβρίκιος; Diog. L. 2, 43 οἱ περὶ Αἰσχύλον=Aeschylus; 2, 105; Ep. Arist. 51; Philo, Vi. Cont. 15; Jos., Ant. 13, 187; 15, 370, C. Ap. 1, 17). οἱ περὶ τὸν Παῦλον Ac 27: 1a v.l.=Παῦλος 1b.

b. of time about, near (class.; PGenève 17, 10; PGiess. 70, 7; Gen 15: 12; Ex 11: 4) περὶ τρίτην ὥραν (Appian, Bell. Civ. 2, 45 §182; Jos., Vi. 239; cf. 243; PSI 184, 5 χθὲς περὶ ἕκτην ὥραν) about the third hour Mt 20: 3. Likew. w. the hour given vs. 5f, 9; 27: 46; Ac 10: 3 (ὡσεὶ περὶ ὥραν ἐνάτην), 9; cf. Mk 6: 48; Ac 22: 6a.

c. of being occupied with περισπᾶσθαι (q.v. 2), θορυβάζεσθαι περί τι Lk 10: 40f. οἱ π. τὰ τοιαῦτα ἐργάται the workers who were occupied with such things (s. ἐργάτης 1a) Ac 19: 25.

d. with regard or respect to (Diod. S. 2, 18, 2 ἡ περὶ αὐτὴν ἀρετή=her valor; Lucian, Vit. Auct. 17, οἱ περὶ μοιχείαν νόμοι; Jos., Ant. 5, 259) ἀστοχεῖν 1 Ti 6: 21; 2 Ti 2: 18. ναυαγεῖν 1 Ti 1: 19. νοσεῖν have a morbid craving for someth. (s. νοσέω) 6: 4. περὶ πάντα in all respects Tit 2: 7.—Pol 4: 3. On 2 Cl 17: 2 s. ἀνάγω 4.— τὰ περὶ ἐμέ my situation, how I am getting along (Menand., Sam. 278; UPZ 68, 6 [152 BC] τὰ περὶ Ἀπολλώνιον; Jos., Ant. 2, 60) Phil 2: 23. αἱ π. τὰ λοιπὰ ἐπιθυμίαι desires for other things Mk 4: 19. HRiesenfeld, TW VI 53–6. M-M.

περιάγω impf. περιῆγον (Eur., Hdt.+; inscr., pap., LXX, Philo)—1. trans. lead around (Eur., Hdt.+; inscr., LXX, Joseph.) τινά take someone about or along with oneself, have someone with oneself (constantly) or accompany oneself (X., Cyr. 2, 2, 28; Demosth. 36, 45 τρεῖς παῖδας ἀκολούθους π.; Diod. S. 2, 38, 6 γυναικῶν πλῆθος περιάγειν; 17, 77, 6 codd. τὰς παλλακίδας= 'the concubines') ἀδελφὴν γυναῖκα π. take about a sister (i.e., a Christian woman) as wife 1 Cor 9: 5 (Diog. L. 6, 97 Crates the Cynic takes his like-minded wife with him on his philosophical journeys).

2. intr. go around, go about (Cebes 6, 3 codd.; rare in this sense, but s. L-S-J (lex.) s.v. II [Bl-D. §150 app.; 308; Rob. 477].—Intr. also Is 28: 27) perh. go around κύκλῳ τοῦ πύργου Hs 9, 11, 4. Go about of a blind man feeling his way Ac 13: 11. W. the place given: of wanderings go about ἐν ὅλῃ τῇ Γαλιλαίᾳ Mt 4: 23. W. acc. of the district travelled through (Zen.-P. 59 033, 3 [257 BC] π. πάντας τοὺς παραδείσους) τὰς πόλεις πάσας in all the cities 9: 35. τὰς κώμας κύκλῳ in the nearby villages Mk 6: 6. τὴν θάλασσαν καὶ τὴν ξηράν travel about on sea and land Mt 23: 15. M-M.*

περιαιρέω 2 aor. inf. περιελεῖν, ptc. περιελών; impf. pass. 3 sing. περιῃρεῖτο (Hom.+; pap., LXX).

1. lit. take away someth. that is found around someth. (τείχη: Hdt. 3, 159; 6, 46; Thu. 1, 108, 3; δέρματα σωμάτων Pla., Polit. 288ε; τὸν χιτῶνα Aristot., H.A. 5, 32), also gener. take away (PTebt. 5, 146; 165 [118 BC]; Jos., Bell. 1, 179, Ant. 20, 212) περιαιρεῖται τὸ κάλυμμα the veil is removed 2 Cor 3: 16 (cf. Ex 34: 34). τὰς ἀγκύρας περιελόντες they cast off or slipped the anchors (on both sides of the ship) Ac 27: 40.—In Ac 28: 13 περιελόντες abs. is a v.l. But this rdg. cannot be correct, even if τὰς ἀγκύρας is supplied (s. Blass ad loc.).

2. take away, remove (Ex 8: 4, 27) ἁμαρτίας 1 Ti (the 'removal' of sin by God is also mentioned) 1 Ch 21: 8; Zeph 3: 11, 15. Cf. Zen.-P. 59 147, 3 [256 BC] π.=cancel an entry, a right, and for the fig. use also M. Ant. 12, 2 τὸν πολὺν περισπασμὸν σεαυτοῦ περιαιρήσεις; Alciphr. 2, 25, 2 φόβον; Diog. L. 6, 7: to make it unnecessary to unlearn [anything]). Pass. περιῃρεῖτο ἐλπὶς πᾶσα all hope was gradually abandoned (impf.) Ac 27: 20. M-M.*

περιάπτω 1 aor. ptc. περιάψας (Pind.+; PTebt. 735, 11 [II BC]; 3 Macc 3: 7; Ep. Arist. 159; Philo; Jos., Ant. 12, 260) kindle πῦρ (Phalaris, Ep. 122, 2 Herch. v.l.) Lk 22: 55. M-M.*

περιαστράπτω 1 aor. περιήστραψα (Galen: CMG V 9, 1 p. 392, 2; 4 Macc 4: 10; Christian wr., as well as Rhet. Gr. I 616, 1).

1. trans. shine around τινά someone Ac 9: 3; 22: 6 D.

2. intr. shine (around) (Psellus p. 37, 19) περί τινα around someone 22: 6. M-M.*

περιβάλλω fut. περιβαλῶ; 2 aor. περιέβαλον, imper. περίβαλε, inf. περιβαλεῖν; 2 aor. mid. περιεβαλόμην; fut. mid. περιβαλοῦμαι; pf. pass. ptc. περιβεβλημένος (Hom.+; inscr., pap., LXX, Ep. Arist., Joseph., Test. 12 Patr.) *throw, lay,* or *put around.*

1. lit.—a. of an encircled city (περιβ. of the walling of a city by its inhabitants: Aelian, V.H. 6, 12; Palaeph. 17; Dit., Syll.³ 344, 14; Pr 28: 4. Of a piece of ground that is fenced in: POxy. 707, 32) περιβαλοῦσιν οἱ ἐχθροί σου χάρακά σοι *throw up an embankment around you* Lk 19: 43 v.l. (cf. Nearchus of Crete [c. 300 BC]: 133 fgm. 1, 33, 10 Jac.; Arrian, Anab. 5, 23, 6 Ἀλέξανδρος χάρακι περιβάλλει τ. πόλιν; Ezk 4: 2).

b. esp. of articles of clothing *put on*—a. τί τινι *someth. on someone* (Test. Levi 8: 7; cf. Plut., Popl. 5, 3 ἱμάτια τοῖς τραχήλοις; Ps.-Clem., Hom. 8, 22); hence (or fr. δ below) the mid. περιβάλλομαί τι *put someth. on* (oneself) (Hom.+; 1 Km 28: 8; 4 Km 19: 1; Jon 3: 8; Is 37: 1) τί περιβαλώμεθα; Mt 6: 31. Cf. Ac 12: 8; Rv 19: 8. περιβέβλημαί τι *have put someth. on, wear* as a garment (EpJer 11; Da 12: 6f; Jos., Ant. 8, 207) νεανίσκον περιβεβλημένον στολὴν λευκήν Mk 16: 5 (Lucian, Philops. 25 of a messenger from heaven: νεανίας λευκὸν ἱμάτιον περιβεβλημένος. Cf. Rv 7: 9, 13; 11: 3; 17: 4; 18: 16; 19: 13; GP 13: 55. ἄγγελον περιβεβλημένον νεφέλην Rv 10: 1. γυνὴ περιβεβλημένη τὸν ἥλιον 12: 1. περιβεβλημένος σινδόνα ἐπὶ γυμνοῦ *who wore* (nothing but) *a linen cloth on his naked body* Mk 14: 51.

β. τινά τινι *clothe someone in someth.* (Eur.+) περιβεβλημένη πορφυρᾷ καὶ κοκκίνῳ Rv 17: 4 t.r. (cf. Pla., Critias 116c περιβεβλημένος περιβόλῳ χρυσῷ; 3 Km 11: 29).

γ. περιβάλλεσθαι ἔν τινι *clothe oneself in* or *with someth.* (Dt 22: 12; 1 Ch 21: 16; Ps 44: 10, 14) Rv 3: 5; 4: 4.

δ. w. a double acc. τινά τι *put someth. on someone* (Ezk 27: 7.—Bl-D. §155, 5; Rob. 483) ἱμάτιον πορφυροῦν περιέβαλον αὐτόν J 19: 2. Cf. GP 3: 7. The acc. of the pers. is easily supplied Lk 23: 11.

ε. with no mention of the garment περιβάλλω τινά *clothe someone* (Ezk 18: 7, 16) Mt 25: 36, 43; B 3: 3 (Is 58: 7); w. the acc. supplied Mt 25: 38. Mid. περιβάλλομαι *dress oneself* (Hg 1: 6; Lev 13: 45) Mt 6: 29; Lk 12: 27; Rv 3: 18.

2. fig. of plunging someone into torture, involving him in misfortunes (Eur.+; PSI 330, 7 [258/7 BC]; 3 Macc 6: 26 τοὺς . . . περιέβαλεν αἰκίαις; Jos., Ant. 2, 276; cf. Ep. Arist. 208; 167) τοὺς δουλεύοντας τῷ θεῷ αἰκίαν περιβαλεῖν 1 Cl 45: 7. M-M.*

περιβλέπω (Soph., X., Pla.+; BGU 1097, 3; LXX; Jos., Bell. 1, 627 al.) in our lit. only mid. περιβλέπομαι (Polyb.; Περὶ ὕψους 55, 18 V. al.; LXX; Test. Jos. 7: 1. Cf. Bl-D. §316, 1; Rob. 809; 813) impf. 3 sing. περιεβλέπετο; 1 aor. ptc. περιβλεψάμενος.

1. *look around (at)* abs. (Diod. S. 16, 32, 2; Plut., Cato Min. 37; 8; Ex 2: 12; 3 Km 21: 40) Mk 9: 8; 10: 23. W. final inf. foll. (Bl-D. §392, 3; cf. Rob. 989f) περιεβλέπετο ἰδεῖν *he looked* (or *kept looking*) *around to see* Mk 5: 32. W. acc. of the pers. (Polyb. 9, 17, 6; Job 7: 8) περιβλεψάμενος τοὺς περὶ αὐτὸν κύκλῳ καθημένους *he looked around at those* etc. Mk 3: 34. Cf. vs. 5; Lk 6: 10. περιβλεψάμενος πάντα *when he had looked around at everything* Mk 11: 11.

2. w. loss of the literal mng. *look for, hunt* (w. acc. Epict. 3, 22, 65; M. Ant. 7, 55; Lucian, Vit. Auct. 12) περιβλέπονται τίνα ἐκδύσωσιν *they are looking for someone to plunder* B 10: 4. M-M.*

περιβόητος, ον (Soph., Thu.+) *well known, far famed, celebrated* (so Demosth. 34, 29; Menand., fgm. 402, 3; Plut., Ages. 24, 5, Themist. 15, 4; 2 Macc 2: 22; Philo, Mos. 2, 284 εὐσέβεια; Jos., Ant. 6, 165, C. Ap. 1, 315) φιλαδελφία 1 Cl 47: 5. (W. σεμνός and πᾶσιν ἀνθρώποις ἀξιαγάπητος) ὄνομα 1: 1.*

περιβόλαιον, ου, τό (Eur.+; PStrassb. 91, 9 [I BC]; LXX; En. 14, 20; Ep. Arist. 158) *covering, wrap, cloak, robe* of an article of clothing (Diod. S. 36, 2, 4; Dionys. Hal. 3, 61, 1; PStrassb. [s. above]; Dt 22: 12; Is 50: 3) someth. like a *cloak* or *mantle* ὡσεὶ π. ἑλίσσειν *roll up as a cloak* Hb 1: 12 (Ps 101: 27). ἡ κόμη ἀντὶ περιβολαίου δέδοται αὐτῇ *her* (the woman's) *hair is given to her as a covering* 1 Cor 11: 15 (cf. OMotta, ET 44, '33, 139–41 and s. on κατακαλύπτω, end). M-M.*

περιγίνομαι (Hom.+; inscr., pap., LXX; En. 102, 6; Philo, Op. M. 155; Test. 12 Patr.) *become master of, overcome* w. gen. (Hdt., Aristoph.+; Aelian, V.H. 1, 3; Vett. Val. p. 38, 20; 4 Macc 13: 3; Jos., Ant. 7, 165) Hv 1, 3, 2.*

περιδέω plpf. pass. 3 sing. περιεδέδετο (Hdt., Aristoph. +; Dit., Syll.³ 1168, 62) *bind* or *wrap around τί τινι someth. w. someth.* (Plut., Mor. 825E; Job 12: 18) ἡ ὄψις αὐτοῦ σουδαρίῳ π. *his face was wrapped in a cloth* J 11: 44. M-M.*

περιελαύνω impf. περιήλαυνον (since Hom. [where it is found in tmesis]; pap.; Jos., Bell., 3, 17; 4, 115) *drive about* of livestock (Palaeph. p. 26, 9; PTebt. 53, 18 [II BC]) ὧδε κἀκεῖσε περιήλαυνεν αὐτά (i.e. τὰ πρόβατα) *he was driving them about, here and there* Hs 6, 2, 7.*

περιελεῖν, -ών s. περιαιρέω.

περιεργάζομαι mid. dep. (Hdt.+; inscr., pap., LXX, Test. 12 Patr.) *do someth. unnecessary* or *useless, be a busybody* (Hdt. 3, 46; Pla., Apol. 3 p. 19B; Demosth. 26, 15; 32, 28; Polyb. 18, 51, 2; IG III 1, 74, 14ff; PLond. 1912, 58ff [=HIBell, Jews and Christians in Egypt '24]; Sir 3: 23; Ep. Arist. 315; Philo, In Flacc. 5; Jos., Ant. 12, 112. W. πολυπραγμονέω e.g. Aelian, V.H. 12, 1; Dit., Syll.³ 1042, 15) abs. (in a play on words w. ἐργάζεσθαι, as Demosth., Phil. 4, 72 ἐργάζῃ καὶ περιεργάζῃ) 2 Th 3: 11. Also *concern oneself* (Himerius, Or. 64 [= Or. 18], 3) περί τινος *about someth.* περὶ τῶν λοιπῶν μὴ περιεργάζου *do not concern yourself about the rest* Hs 9, 2, 7. M-M.*

περίεργος, ον (Lysias+; Menand., Epitr. fgm. 2, 45 J.; Philo, Joseph.)—1. of persons *paying attention to things that do not concern one, meddlesome, curious,* subst. *a busybody* (X., Mem. 1, 3, 1; Epict. 3, 1, 21; Herodian 4, 12, 3; POsl. 49, 7 [c. 100 AD]; Jos., C. Ap. 1, 16; Test. Iss. 3: 3) 1 Ti 5: 13 (w. φλύαρος). περίεργος εἶ περὶ τοιούτων πραγμάτων *you are inquisitive about such things* Hv 4, 3, 1.

2. of things *belonging to magic* (cf. Plut., Alex. 2, 5; Vett. Val. index; Aristaenet., Ep. 2, 18, 2; Dssm., B p. 5, 5 [BS 323, 5]; περιεργάζεσθαι in this sense: PGM 12, 404) τὰ περίεργα πράσσειν *practice magic* Ac 19: 19. M-M.*

περιέρχομαι 2 aor. περιῆλθον (Hom.+; inscr., pap., LXX; Jos., Vi. 397 al.) w. a personal subj. *go around* GP 5: 18; *go from place to place* (Cornutus 31 p. 63, 16) of wandering exorcists Ac 19: 13. π. ἐν μηλωταῖς *wander about in sheepskins* Hb 11: 37. W. acc. of the place (X., Ages. 9, 3 πᾶσαν γῆν; Pla., Phaedo 112D; PGenève 49, 8;

POxy. 1033, 12; Job 1: 7; Jos., Ant. 9, 2) π. ὅλην τὴν νῆσον Ac 13: 6 D. π. τὰς οἰκίας go about from house to house 1 Ti 5: 13 (cf. Appian, Mithrid. 59 §242 τὰς σκηνὰς περιῄει=he ran about from tent to tent; POxy. 1033, 12 περιερχόμενοι τὴν πόλιν; Job 2: 9d οἰκίαν ἐξ οἰκίας περιερχομένη). Of the passengers on a ship περιελθόν-τες we sailed around, made a circuit (along the east coast of Sicily) Ac 28: 13 (but s. EHaenchen, AG ad loc. On the v.l. περιελόντες s. περιαιρέω). M-M.*

περιέχω 2 aor. περιέσχον (Hom.+; inscr., pap., LXX, Ep. Arist., Philo, Joseph.)—1. surround, encircle—a. lit.
   α. of things, one of which surrounds the other (Pla. et al.; Dit., Syll.³ 685, 75; 1169, 20 τόπον κύκλῳ πέτραις περιεχόμενον; Job 30: 18) of water τὴν γῆν flow around the earth 1 Cl 33: 3.
   β. of persons, encircle w. hostile intent (Hdt.+; oft. LXX) περιέσχεν με συναγωγὴ πονηρευομένων B 6: 6 (Ps 21: 17).
   b. fig., of circumstances, emotions, moods, that seize, come upon or befall someone w. acc. of the pers. (PTebt. 44, 8 [114 BC] χάριν τῆς περιεχούσης με ἀρρωστίας; 2 Macc 4: 16; 3 Macc 5: 6; Jos., Bell. 4, 585; 6, 182) θάμβος περιέσχεν αὐτὸν amazement seized him, i.e. he was amazed Lk 5: 9 (cf. Da 7: 28 ἐκστάσει περιειχόμην).
   2. contain of a document—a. trans., w. acc. (Diod. S. 2, 1, 1; Plut., Demosth. 1, 7; Jos., C. Ap. 1, 39; 2, 37; 276; Dit., Syll.³ 683, 12f [140 BC] ἐπιστολὰν περιέχουσαν τὰν κρίσιν; BGU 1047 III, 11; PGiess. 57, 1) ἐπιστολὴν περιέχουσαν τάδε Ac 15: 23 D. ἐπιστολὴν περιέχουσαν τὸν τύπον τοῦτον 23: 25 t.r. Cf. Pol 13: 2.
   b. intr. (Dit., Syll.³ 685 [139 BC], 21 καθότι τὰ γράμματα περιέχει; 41; 730, 31 [I BC]; 820, 11; POxy. 95, 33 [95 BC]; BGU 19, 10 περιέχων οὕτως; 191, 8; 10; 1 Macc 15: 2; 2 Macc 11: 16 τὸν τρόπον τοῦτον=οὕτως 2 Macc 11: 22; Test. Levi 10: 5) περιέχει ἐν γραφῇ it stands or says in the scripture 1 Pt 2: 6 (ἐν as Jos., Ant. 11, 104; the quot. foll. as Dit., Syll.³ 685, 51).—Bl-D. §308; Rob. 800. M-M.*

περιζώννυμι and **περιζωννύω** 1 fut. mid. περιζώσομαι; 1 aor. mid. περιεζωσάμην, imper. περίζωσαι; pf. pass. ptc. περιεζωσμένος (since Theopompus [s. 2 below] and Aristoph; LXX) gird about.
   1. act. (Jos., Ant. 6, 184) w. double acc. gird someone (about) with someth. (Ps 17: 33, 40; 29: 12; Sir 45: 7). The pass. w. acc. of the thing can be understood as a development of this be girded with someth. (Diod. S. 1, 72, 2 σινδόνας; 4 Km 3: 21 ζώνην; PGM 5, 157 ὄφιν) περιε-ζωσμένον χρυσᾶν with a gold belt around him Rv 1: 13; cf. 15: 6 (but s. 2b below). Certainly pass. in the abs. ἔστωσαν ὑμῶν αἱ ὀσφύες περιεζωσμέναι let your waists or loins be well-girt Lk 12: 35 (Ex 12: 11; Philo, Sacr. Abel. 63). The abs. perf. ptc. can also be understood as a pass. in Hv 3, 8, 4; s 8, 4, 2; 9, 9, 5 and περιεζωσμέναι εὐπρεπῶς 9, 2, 4 (s. εὐπρεπῶς). But the passages in Rv and Hermas can also be taken as
   2. mid. gird oneself (since the comic wr. Theopompus [V BC], fgm. 37 K.: περιζωσάμενος ᾧαν [sheepskin]; oft. LXX).
   a. abs. (Polyb. 30, 13, 10; Paus. 1, 44, 1; Ps 92: 1; Jo 1: 13; 1 Macc 3: 58) Lk 12: 37; 17: 8; Ac 12: 8 t.r.
   b. w. acc. of the thing girded about one gird oneself w. someth., bind someth. about oneself (Theopompus [s. above]; Aristoph., Pax 670; Plut., Rom. 16, 4, Coriol. 9, 3; 2 Km 3: 31; Is 3: 24; Jer 4: 8; Jos., Ant. 11, 177) περίζωσαι ὠμόλινον Hs 8, 4, 1a; cf. b. This may also be the place for Rv 1: 13; 15: 6 (s. 1 above).

c. w. acc. of the part of the body that is girded τὴν ὀσφῦν (Jer 1: 17; Is 32: 11) gird one's waist; that with which one is girded is added w. ἐν (1 Ch 15: 27), fig. περιζωσάμενοι τὴν ὀσφὺν ἐν ἀληθείᾳ after you have girded your waists with truth Eph 6: 14. M-M.*

περίθεσις, εως, ἡ (Arrian, Anab. 7, 22; Sext. Emp., Pyrrh. 3, 15; Jos., Ant. 19, 30; Sym. Ps 31: 9) putting around, putting on π. χρυσίων the putting on or wearing of gold ornaments 1 Pt 3: 3.*

περιΐστημι 2 aor. περιέστην; pf. ptc. περιεστώς; pres. mid. imper. 2 sing. περιΐστασο (W-S. §15; Bl-D. §93; Mlt.-H. 207) (Hom.+; inscr., pap., LXX).
   1. act. place around (Jos., Bell. 3, 148)—a. 2 aor. stand around abs. Ac 25: 7 t.r. W. acc. of the pers. (Appian, Hann. 28 §118 περιστάντες τὸ βουλευτήριον=they stood about the Senate-house; Jos., Ant. 7, 16; 13, 169) περιέ-στησαν αὐτὸν οἱ Ἰουδαῖοι the Jews stood around him 25: 7.
   b. pf. stand around (2 Km 13: 31; Jdth 5: 22; Jos., Vi. 109) ὁ ὄχλος ὁ περιεστώς the crowd standing by (Appian, Hann. 19 §84 ἡ στρατιὰ περιεστῶσα) J 11: 42. οἱ π. the bystanders MPol 2: 2.
   2. mid. go around so as to avoid, avoid, shun (Philod., Rhet. I 384 S. τὰς ἁμαρτίας; M. Ant. 3, 4, 2; Sext. Emp., Math. 11, 93; Lucian, Herm. 86 κύνας; Diog. L. 9, 14; Iambl., Vi. Pyth. 31, 189 τὸ παράνομον; Philo, Ebr. 205; Jos., Bell. 2, 135, Ant. 1, 45; 10, 210) τὶ someth. τὰς κενοφωνίας 2 Ti 2: 16. μάχας νομικάς Tit 3: 9. M-M.*

περικαθαίρω (Pla.+; Phlegon: 257 fgm. 36, 1, 11 Jac. [περικαθαίρεσθαι=have oneself purified by rites of propitiation]; LXX; Philo, Plant. 112) purify completely περικαθαίρων (w. οἰωνοσκόπος, ἐπαοιδός, μαθηματι-κός) one who performs purificatory rites of propitiatory magic for gain, magician D 3: 4 (s. WLKnox, JTS 40, '39, 146–9, who proposes the transl. 'the one who performs circumcision').*

περικάθαρμα, ατος, τό fr. περικαθαίρω='cleanse all around' or 'on all sides'; that which is removed as a result of a thorough cleansing, i.e. dirt, refuse, off-scouring, also as a designation of the 'off-scouring' of mankind (Epict. 3, 22, 78; Vi. Aesopi I c. 14; cf. IQH 5, 21). Since purifica-tion is achieved by the removal of the περικάθαρμα, the word can take on the mng. propitiatory offering, ransom (Pr 21: 18). ὡς περικαθάρματα τοῦ κόσμου ἐγενήθημεν we have become like the off-scourings of the world or, since it is pl. in contrast to the foll. περίψημα, it is prob. better to transl. scapegoats for the world 1 Cor 4: 13. Cf. περίψημα and κάθαρμα.—FrHauck, TW III 434. M-M.*

περικαθίζω (Diod. S. 20, 103, 5 Fischer v.l.; Wilcken, Chrest. 11 B. Fr. a, 10 [123 BC]; Jos., Ant. 13, 151; Test. Jud. 9: 4, but mostly in a hostile sense= 'besiege') sit around (Maximus Tyr. 21, 6d περικαθίσαντες ἐν κύκλῳ τῇ πυρᾷ) Lk 22: 55 D. M-M.*

περικαλύπτω 1 aor. ptc. περικαλύψας; pf. pass. ptc. περικεκαλυμμένος (Hom.+; LXX; En. 13, 9 τὴν ὄψιν; Philo, Leg. All. 2, 62; Jos., Bell. 2, 148) cover, conceal τὶ someth. (3 Km 7: 5) περικαλύπτειν αὐτοῦ τὸ πρόσωπον Mk 14: 65 (s. on προφητεύω 2); shortened περικαλύ-ψαντες αὐτόν Lk 22: 64. Pass. ἡ κιβωτὸς περικεκαλυμ-μένη πάντοθεν χρυσίῳ the ark, covered on all sides with gold Hb 9: 4 (cf. Ex 28: 20).*

περίκειμαι mid. dep. (Hom.+; inscr., pap., LXX; Philo, Mos. 2, 182)—1. lie or be placed around—a. lit. περίκεῖται μύλος ὀνικὸς περὶ τὸν τράχηλον αὐτοῦ a mill-stone is hung about his neck Mk 9: 42; cf. Lk 17: 2.

b. fig., of a crowd of people surrounding someone (Herodian 7, 9, 1 τὸ περικείμενον πλῆθος) τοσοῦτον ἔχοντες περικείμενον ἡμῖν νέφος μαρτύρων Hb 12: 1 (s. νέφος).

2. περίκειμαί τι (for περιτέθειμαί τι as pass. of περιτίθημί τινί τι put someth. on someone) wear someth., have someth. on.

a. lit. (Hdt. 1, 171; Dionys. Hal. 2, 19; Strabo 15, 3, 15; Plut., Arat. 17, 6; Polyaenus 1, 20, 2; Herodian 2, 13, 8 ἐσθῆτας στρατιωτικάς; Dit., Or. 56, 66; EpJer 23; Jos., Ant. 14, 173, Vi. 334.—Bl-D. §159, 4; Rob. 485) δέρμα λευκόν wear a white (goat)skin Hv 5: 1; cf. s 6, 2, 5. Of fetters (4 Macc 12: 2 τὰ δεσμά) τὴν ἅλυσιν ταύτην περίκειμαι I am bearing this chain Ac 28: 20.

b. fig. (Sib. Or. 5, 228) νέφος be clothed in or surrounded by a cloud 2 Cl 1: 6b.—ἀσθένειαν be subject to weakness Hb 5: 2 (cf. Theocr. 23, 14 ὕβριν). ἀμαύρωσιν 2 Cl 1: 6a.

3. In τοῦ κλήρου, οὖ περίκειμαι ἐπιτυχεῖν ITr 12: 3 the text can hardly be in good order, and it is only w. reservations that the transl. the lot which is incumbent upon me to obtain (Gdspd.) is suggested (cf. Hdb. ad loc.; IAHeikel, StKr 106, '35, 317). M-M.*

περικεφαλαία, ας, ἡ (Aeneas Tact. 1376; Philo Mech. 93, 46; Polyb. 3, 71, 4; 6, 23, 8; Diod. S. 14, 43, 2; Dit., Syll.³ 958, 29 [III BC]; PPetr. III 140a [III BC]; LXX; Jos., Ant. 6, 184) helmet in our lit. only in a figure of speech, in which Christian virtues are compared to pieces of armor ἡ πίστις ὡς περικεφαλαία IPol 6: 2. ἡ π. τοῦ σωτηρίου the helmet of salvation Eph 6: 17 (after Is 59: 17). Sim. ἐνδυσάμενοι περικεφαλαίαν ἐλπίδα σωτηρίας 1 Th 5: 8. M-M. B. 1401.*

περικόπτω 2 aor. pass. περιεκόπην, ptc. περικοπείς (Thu.+; pap.) in our lit. only in Hermas in the allegory of the tower; pass.

1. hew all around (Plut., Mor. 74D) Hs 9, 7, 5.—**2.** cut away, take away τὶ someth. (Pla., Rep. 7 p. 519A al.) ὅταν περικοπῇ αὐτῶν ὁ πλοῦτος when the wealth is cut off from them (i.e. fr. the stones, which represent a class of people) Hv 3, 6, 6 (for the fig. use cf. Diod. S. 20, 77, 3 of hopes that were cut off; Porphyr., Antr. Nymph. c. 34 ὅπως τὰ ἐπίβουλα τῆς ψυχῆς αὐτοῦ περικόψῃ; Sb 6787, 23 [257 BC] of plundering property; Philo, Cher. 95).*

περικρατής, ές having power, being in command (Simias [III BC] 1, 11 [ed. HFränckel '15=Coll. p. 109]) τινός (Ps.-Callisth. 2, 4, 3; Sus 39 Theod. Λ ἐκείνου οὐκ ἠδυνήθημεν περικρατεῖς γενέσθαι) over or of a thing ἰσχύσαμεν μόλις περικρατεῖς γενέσθαι τῆς σκάφης we were scarcely able to get the boat under control Ac 27: 16. M-M.*

περικρύβω (κρύβω is a new formation in H. Gk. fr. the Hellenistic aor. ἐκρύβην. Kühner-Bl. II p. 467; Bl-D. §73; Mlt.-H. 245; Thackeray §19, 3 p. 227; Lob. on Phryn. p. 317.—The compound verb in Lucian, D. Mort. 10, 8; Eunap., Hist. Fgm. 55 p. 248f [LDindorf, Hist. Gr. Min. I 1870]; mid., Diog. L. 6, 61) impf. περιέκρυβον hide, conceal (entirely) περιέκρυβεν ἑαυτήν she kept herself hidden Lk 1: 24. M-M. s.v. -κρύπτω.*

περικυκλόω fut. περικυκλώσω (Hdt., Aristoph.+; Jos., Ant. 8, 282, mostly used in the mid. In the act. in Aristot., H.A. 4, 8 p. 533b, 11; Appian, Bell. Civ. 4, 55 §238; PLond. 681, 9; LXX; En. 24, 3; Philo, Leg. All. 1, 68) surround, encircle w. acc. of a beleaguered city (Josh 6: 13; 4 Km 6: 14) Lk 19: 43. M-M.*

περιλάμπω 1 aor. περιέλαμψα (Diod. S. 3, 69, 3; Lucian et al.) in our lit. only trans. shine around τινά someone (Plut., Artax. 13, 1 φωτὶ πολλῷ περιλαμπόμενος; Appian, Bell. Civ. 5, 117 §486) Lk 2: 9; Ac 26: 13. τί someth. (Plut., Cic. 35, 5 τὴν ἀγοράν; Synes., Calvit. 11 p. 74D; Philo, Somn. 1, 90; Jos., Bell. 6, 290) τὸν τόπον GEb 3.*

περιλείπομαι occurs only in pass. (Hom. [in tmesis]+; Eur.; Pla.; IG XII 3, 326, 24; Dit., Syll.³ 852, 46; BGU 1132, 12 [13 BC]; PSI 409, 12; 571, 14; LXX) remain, be left behind of pers. (Eur., Hel. 426; Plut., Ages. 22, 8; Herodian 2, 1, 7; PGiess. 82, 23 ἡμᾶς τοὺς ἔτι περιλειπομένους; 4 Macc 12: 6; 13: 18; Jos., C. Ap. 1, 35) 1 Th 4: 15, 17. Cf. AvVeldhuizen, ThSt 29, '11, 101–6; JoachJeremias, Unknown Sayings of Jesus, tr. Fuller '57, 64–7. M-M.*

περιλείχω (Aristoph.+) lick all around, lick off Lk 16: 21 v.l. (Hippiatr. I 251, 19 ἐν αὐτῇ τῇ γλώσσῃ περιλείχων τὰ ἕλκη).*

περίλυπος, ον (Hippocr.; Isocr.; Aristot., Eth. Nic. 4, 7 p. 1124a, 16; Plut.; LXX) very sad, deeply grieved περίλυπον γενέσθαι (Isocr. 1, 42; Plut., Mor. 634C; Da 2: 12) Mk 6: 26; Lk 18: 23; 1 Cl 4: 4 (Gen 4: 6). περίλυπός ἐστιν ἡ ψυχή μου (cf. Plut., Mor. 1101E; Ps 41: 6, 12; 42: 5) Mt 26: 38; Mk 14: 34 (JHéring, Cullmann-Festschr. '62, 64–9 [Gethsemane]). π. εἶναι περί τινος be very unhappy about someth. Hv 3, 10, 6 (here π. is further strengthened by λίαν).*

περιμένω 1 aor. περιέμεινα, imper. περίμεινον (Soph., Hdt.+; pap., LXX, Joseph.) wait for w. acc. τινά someone (Aristoph., Plut. 643; Thu. 5, 64, 4; X., An. 2, 1, 3; 2, 4, 1; POxy. 1762, 10; PGiess. 73, 4; Wsd 8: 12; Jos., Ant. 12, 193) Hs 9, 11, 1. τὶ someth. (Pla., Phaedo 63 p. 115A, Ep. 7 p. 327E; Gen 49: 18; Jos., Ant. 1, 219; 2, 69, Vi. 176) Ac 1: 4. Foll. by ἵνα wait to MPol 1: 2. Abs. wait (Appian, Syr. 9 §35; Jos., Ant. 6, 100) Ac 10: 24 D. M-M.*

πέριξ adv. (Aeschyl., Hdt.+; Jos., Ant. 11, 19 τὰ π. ἔθνη; Dit., Syll.³ 880, 43f ἐκ τῶν π. κωμῶν; PSI 317, 5) (all) around αἱ π. πόλεις the cities in the vicinity Ac 5: 16 (as Dio Chrys. 17[34], 27; Jos., Bell. 4, 241, Vi. 81). M-M.*

περιοικέω live around, in the neighborhood of w. acc. of the pers. (Hdt. 5, 78; Aristoph., Equ. 853; Jos., Bell. 1, 63) οἱ περιοικοῦντες αὐτούς their neighbors Lk 1: 65.*

περίοικος, ον living around, in the neighborhood; subst. in pl. οἱ περίοικοι the neighbors (Hdt. 1, 175; 4, 161; Thu. 1, 101, 2; Jos., Vi. 78, Ant. 16, 272; Dt 1: 7) Lk 1: 58 (w. συγγενεῖς).*

περιούσιος, ον chosen, especial (PGenève 11, 17 the married man is called ὁ περιούσιος 'the chosen one'. Herm. Wr. 1, 19: Rtzst., Poim. 334; LXX) λαὸς π., a transl. of עַם סְגֻלָּה Ex 19: 5; 23: 22 (here only in the LXX); Dt 7: 6; 14: 2 (λ. π. ἀπὸ πάντων τῶν ἐθνῶν or παρὰ πάντα τὰ ἔθνη); 26: 18; following these, Tit 2: 14; 1 Cl 64 a chosen people (Bl-D. §113, 1; Mlt.-H. 322; Lghtf., On a Fresh Revision of the Engl. NT 1891, 260ff). M-M.*

περιοχή, ῆς, ἡ (Theophr.+; Herm. Wr. 8, 5; pap., LXX; Philo, Aet. M. 4; Jos., Bell. 5, 169; 203) ἡ π. τῆς γραφῆς Ac 8: 32 can mean either

1. content or wording of the scripture passage (περιοχή in this sense, schol. on Thu. 1, 131 ἡ περ. τῶν γραμμάτων; schol. on Apollon. Rhod. 4 superscr. Cf. also Suidas s.v. Ὅμηρος Σέλλιος)—or

2. *the portion of scripture* (Dionys. Hal., de Thu. c. 25; Cicero, Ad Attic. 13, 25, 3).—Blass on Ac 8: 32. M-M.*

περιπατέω impf. περιεπάτουν; fut. περιπατήσω; 1 aor. περιεπάτησα; plpf. 3 sing. περι(ε)πεπατήκει (Ac 14: 8 v.l.; on augm. in the plpf. s. Bl-D. §66, 1; Mlt.-H. 190f) (Aristoph., X., Pla.+; inscr., pap., LXX, En., Ep. Arist., Philo, Joseph.) *go about, walk around.*

1. lit.—a. *go about, walk around* w. an indication of the place where one walks about (Demosth. 54, 7 ἐν ἀγορᾷ; Jos., C. Ap. 2, 117 ἐπὶ τῆς γῆς) ἐν τριβόλοις γυμνοῖς ποσὶ περιπατεῖν *walk among thistles barefoot* Hs 9, 20, 3. In several places one might almost translate *stay, spend some time, be,* though without the idea of remaining on the same spot (Chio, Ep. 13, 1 ἐν τῷ Ὠιδείῳ; 2 Km 11: 2; Da 3: 92 of the men in the fiery furnace; 4: 29; En. 17, 6; Jos., Ant. 7, 130): ἐν τῷ ἱερῷ (Cebes 1, 1.—Diog. L. in the temple of Asclepius) Mk 11: 27; J 10: 23; GOxy 9. ἐν τῇ Γαλιλαίᾳ J 7: 1a; cf. b. ὁ περιπατῶν ἐν μέσῳ τῶν ἑπτὰ λυχνιῶν Rv 2: 1. π. ἐν τοῖς Ἰουδαίοις *appear among the Jews* J 11: 54. ἐν τούτῳ τῷ κόσμῳ Papias 3.

b. *go about* w. indication of the way one is clothed ἐν στολαῖς Mk 12: 38; Lk 20: 46. ἐν λευκοῖς *clothed in white* Rv 3: 4 (Epict. 3, 22, 10 ἐν κοκκίνοις περιπ.). ἐν δέρμασιν αἰγείοις 1 Cl 17: 1.

c. gener. *walk, go* π. διὰ τοῦ φωτός *walk in the light* Rv 21: 24. π. εἰς τὸν ἀγρόν (*go for a*) *walk in the country* Hs 2: 1. ἐπὶ τῆς θαλάσσης (ἐπὶ I 1aa and cf. Job 9: 8.—GBertram, Le chemin sur les eaux: Congr. d'Hist. du Christ. I '28, 137–66) Mt 14: 26; Mk 6: 48f; J 6: 19. ἐπὶ τὴν θάλασσαν Mt 14: 25; J 6: 19ᵛ·ˡ·ᵃⁱ⁷⁵. ἐπὶ τὰ ὕδατα vs. 29 (ἐπὶ III 1aa). παρὰ τὴν θάλασσαν 4: 18 (παρά III 1a). π. μετά τινος *go about* w. *someone* J 6: 66; *walk with someone* Hs 9, 6, 2a; 9, 10, 1. π. περί τι *walk around someth.* s 9, 12, 7; also κύκλῳ τινός s 9, 6, 2b. μετά τινος κύκλῳ τινός π. *walk with someone around someth.* s 9, 11, 5. π. ἐπάνω *walk over* Lk 11: 44 (ἐπάνω 1a). More closely defined ὁμαλῶς π. καὶ ἀπροσκόπως Hm 6, 1, 4. γυμνὸν π. *go naked* Rv 16: 15. μόνον π. *walk alone* Hv 4, 1, 3 (cf. Jos., C. Ap. 1, 281). περιπάτεις ὅπου ἤθελες *you used to go where you pleased* J 21: 18 (En. 17, 6 ὅπου πᾶσα σὰρξ οὐ περιπατεῖ).—Abs. *walk (about)* (Diocles 141 p. 180, 19f; Diod. S. 1, 70, 10; Ep. Arist. 175) Mt 9: 5; 11: 5; 15: 31; Mk 2: 9; 5: 42; 8: 24; Lk 5: 23; 7: 22; J 5: 8f, 11f; 11: 9f; Ac 3: 6, 8a, b, 9, 12; 14: 8, 10; 1 Pt 5: 8; Rv 9: 20 (cf. Ps 113: 15); Hv 2, 1, 3; (*go for a*) *walk, be out walking* Mk 16: 12; Lk 24: 17; *walk by* J 1: 36. περιπατῶν ἀφύπνωσα *as I walked along I fell asleep* Hv 1, 1, 3. περιπατῶν ἀνεμνήσθην *as I was walking along I remembered* 2, 1, 1.

d. symbolically, and far on the way toward the non-literal use of the word: doubters are περιπατοῦντες ἐν ταῖς ἀνοδίαις Hv 3, 7, 1. Esp. in John: περιπατεῖν ἐν τῇ σκοτίᾳ J 8: 12; 12: 35b; 1 J 2: 11; cf. 1: 6. Corresp. ἐν τῷ φωτί vs. 7; ἐν αὐτῇ (=ἐν τῇ ὁδῷ τοῦ φωτός) B 19: 1 (but it may also refer to ἡ γνῶσις; then the pass. would belong under 2aδ below). Abs. περιπατεῖτε ὡς τὸ φῶς ἔχετε *walk while you have the light* J 12: 35a.

2. fig.—a. of the *walk of life* (Philod., περὶ παρρ. p. 12 Ol.; Epict. 1, 18, 20; Simplicius in Epict. p. 125, 52 Düb. Esp. acc. to OT models: 4 Km 20: 3 ἐν ἀληθείᾳ; Pr 8: 20 ἐν ὁδοῖς δικαιοσύνης.—Eccl 11: 9). In the NT this use of the word is decidedly Pauline (the pastoral epp. do not have the word at all); elsewh. it is reasonably common only in the two small Johannine letters, *live, conduct oneself, walk,* always more exactly defined.

α. by an adv. ἀξίως τινός Eph 4: 1; Col 1: 10; 1 Th 2: 12; Pol 5: 1. ἀτάκτως 2 Th 3: 6, 11. εὐσχημόνως Ro 13: 13; 1 Th 4: 12.

β. by the dat. to denote attendant circumstance, kind, and manner (Test. Iss. 5: 8 ἁπλότητι.—Bl-D. §198, 5; cf. Rob. 528–32) κώμοις καὶ μέθαις Ro 13: 13. τοῖς ἔθεσιν Ac 21: 21; cf. 15: 1 D; πνεύματι π. Gal 5: 16. τῷ αὐτῷ πνεύματι 2 Cor 12: 18.

γ. by a comparison ἕκαστον ὡς κέκληκεν ὁ θεός, οὕτως περιπατείτω 1 Cor 7: 17. περιπατεῖν καθὼς τὰ ἔθνη περιπατεῖ Eph 4: 17; ὡς τέκνα φωτός 5: 8.—Phil 3: 17; 1 J 2: 6. The comparison is implied fr. the context (ὡς ἐχθροὶ τοῦ σταυροῦ τοῦ Χριστοῦ) Phil 3: 18.—πῶς (καθὼς) περιπατεῖτε Eph 5: 15; 1 Th 4: 1a, b.

δ. by a prepositional expr. The state in which one lives or ought to live is designated by ἐν: pl. in sins Eph 2: 2; Col 3: 7; in good deeds Eph 2: 10; in the ordinances of the Lord B 21: 1 (Philo, Congr. Erud. Gr. 87 π. ἐν ταῖς τοῦ θεοῦ κρίσεσι κ. προστάξεσιν). Cf. Hb 13: 9. Sing. ἐν καινότητι ζωῆς Ro 6: 4. ἐν πανουργίᾳ 2 Cor 4: 2. ἐν ἀγάπῃ Eph 5: 2. ἐν σοφίᾳ Col 4: 5. ἐν (τῇ) ἀληθείᾳ 2 J 4; 3 J 3f; ἐν ἀκεραιοσύνῃ B 10: 4; cf. 19: 1 (s. 1d above). ἐν ἀλλοτρίᾳ γνώμῃ IPhld 3: 3. ἐν ἀμώμῳ ... συνειδήσει Pol 5: 3. ἐν αὐτῇ (=ἐν τῇ ἐντολῇ) 2 J 6b, ἐν αὐτῷ (=ἐν τῷ κυρίῳ) Col 2: 6.—The norm of conduct is designated by κατά w. acc. (s. κατά II 5bβ) κατὰ ἄνθρωπον *like ordinary* (unregenerate) *men* 1 Cor 3: 3. κατὰ σάρκα *according to the flesh, on the physical level* Ro 8: 4; 2 Cor 10: 2. κατὰ ἀγάπην Ro 14: 15. κατὰ τὴν παράδοσιν τῶν πρεσβυτέρων Mk 7: 5. κατὰ τὰς ἐντολὰς αὐτοῦ 2 J 6a.—BSEaston, NT Ethical Lists: JBL 51, '32, 1–12; SWibbing, D. Tugend- u. Lasterkataloge im NT, '59; EKamlach, Die Form der katalogischen Paränese im NT, '64; HBraun, Qumran u. das NT II, '66, 286–301.

b. rarely of physical life gener.: ἐν τούτῳ τῷ κόσμῳ περιπατεῖν B 10: 11. ἐν σαρκὶ 2 Cor 10: 3. διὰ πίστεως περιπατοῦμεν, οὐ διὰ εἴδους 5: 7. M-M. B. 690.*

περιπείρω 1 aor. περιέπειρα *pierce through, impale* (lit. in Diod. S.; Lucian; Plut., C. Gracch. 17, 5 κεφαλὴ περιπεπαρμένη δόρατι; Philo; Jos., Bell. 3, 296) fig. ἑαυτὸν π. ὀδύναις πολλαῖς *pierce oneself through with many a pang* 1 Ti 6: 10 (Philo, In Flacc. 1 ἀθρόους ἀνηκέστοις περιέπειρε κακοῖς). M-M.*

περίπικρος, ον (Philod., Ira p. 6 Wilke; Vi. Aesopi I c. 38 and other later wr.) *very bitter* fig., of a glance βλέμμα π. *a very bitter look* Hs 6, 2, 5.*

περιπίπτω 2 aor. περιέπεσον (trag., Hdt.+; inscr., pap., LXX, Philo, Joseph.) *fall in with, encounter, fall into* esp. misfortunes; w. dat. answering the quest. 'whither'? (Bl-D. §202 app.; cf. Rob. 528f).

1. lit. λῃσταῖς *fall among* or *into the hands of robbers* Lk 10: 30 (Diod. S. 14, 93, 4 λῃσταῖς περιέπεσον; Conon [I BC/I AD]: 26 fgm. 1, 22 Jac. λῃσταῖς περιπ.; Diog. L. 4, 50 λῃσταῖς περιέπεσε; Artem. 3, 65; cf. 1, 5; 2, 22; Simplicius In Epict. p. 111, 13 Düb. δύο εἰς Δελφοὺς ἀπιόντες λῃσταῖς περιεπεπτώκασι). εἰς τόπον διθάλασσον *strike a reef* Ac 27: 41.

2. fig. (as oft. since Hdt. 6, 106, 2; Thu. 8, 27, 3 κινδύνῳ. Also in inscr., pap., LXX; Philo, Leg. All. 2, 77; Jos., Ant. 10, 25; 20, 48; Test. Dan 4: 5) πειρασμοῖς ποικίλοις *become involved in various trials* Js 1: 2. αἰκίαις π. *suffer tortures* 1 Cl 51: 2 (Diod. S. 1, 74, 7 περιπίπτει τιμωρίαις=he incurs [lit. falls into] punishment). M-M.*

περιπλέκω impf. περιέπλεκον (Hom.+; LXX; Philo, Poster. Cai. 156) *weave* or *twine around* fig. (schol. on Soph., Ant. 244 p. 230 Papag. τὸν λόγον) of the tongue περιέπλεκεν δολιότητα (s. δολιότης) 1 Cl 35: 8 (Ps 49: 19).—Perh. the pass. *embrace* τινί *someone* (Hom.+; Jos., Ant. 8, 7) is to be read in Hs 9, 11, 4a, b.*

περιποιέω (Hdt.+; inscr., pap., LXX; Ep. Arist. 121) in our lit. only mid. (Thu.+; LXX, Joseph.) fut. περιποιήσομαι; 1 aor. περιεποιησάμην.

1. *save* or *preserve* (*for oneself*) τὶ someth. τὴν ψυχήν *preserve one's own life* Lk 17: 33 (cf. X., Cyr. 4, 4, 10 τὰς ψυχάς=his life).

2. *acquire, obtain, gain for oneself* (Thu. 1, 9, 2; X., Mem. 2, 7, 3; Polyb. 3, 6, 13; 24, 9, 6; Is 43: 21; Jos., Bell. 1, 180) τὸν αἰῶνα τοῦτον Hv 1, 1, 8. τὴν ἐκκλησίαν τοῦ θεοῦ, ἣν περιεποιήσατο διὰ τοῦ αἵματος τοῦ ἰδίου Ac 20: 28 (s. EHaenchen, AG, ad loc.).—Oft. w. a reflexive pron. pleonastically added (X., An. 5, 6, 17 ἑαυτῷ δύναμιν περιποιήσασθαι. Demosth. 19, 240; Pr 7: 4) βαθμὸν ἑαυτοῖς καλὸν περιποιοῦνται 1 Ti 3: 13. Cf. ἑαυτῷ μέγα κλέος 1 Cl 54: 3. σεαυτῷ ζωήν Hm 3: 5. ἑαυτῷ τιμήν 4, 4, 2. θάνατον ἑαυτοῖς s 6, 5, 7c. Also without an acc., which is easily supplied ἑαυτοῖς π. *enrich oneself* Hs 9, 26, 2.

3. *bring* (*about*) τινί τι someth. *for someone* (Aristot., Pol. 3, 16; PAmh. 34d, 2 [II BC] πλεῖόν τι περιποιούμενοι τῷ βασιλεῖ; 2 Macc 15: 21; Jos., Ant. 14, 386.— Mayser II 1, '26 p. 101) αὕτη ἡ τρυφὴ ζωὴν περιποιεῖται τῷ ἀνθρώπῳ Hs 6, 5, 7a. τιμωρίας αὐτοῖς περιποιοῦνται ibid. b. σεαυτῷ π. δόξαν s 5, 3, 3. M-M.*

περιποίησις, εως, ἡ (since Ps.-Pla., Defin. 451c; PTebt. 317, 26 [174/5 AD]; PReinach. 52, 2).

1. *keeping safe, preserving, saving* (s. περιποιέω 1. So Ps.-Pla., loc. cit. σωτηρία· π. ἀβλαβής; 2 Ch 14: 12; Test. Zeb. 2: 8) εἰς π. ψυχῆς Hb 10: 39 (opp. εἰς ἀπώλειαν).

2. *gaining, obtaining* (περιποιέω 2) w. obj. gen. foll. (Alex. Aphr., An. Mant. p. 164, 17 Bruns [1887]) 1 Th 5: 9; 2 Th 2: 14.

3. *possessing, possession, property* (PTebt. loc. cit.) λαὸς εἰς περιποίησιν *a people that has become* (*God's own*) *possession* 1 Pt 2: 9 (cf. Mal 3: 17). ἀπολύτρωσις τῆς π. Eph 1: 14 (s. ἀπολύτρωσις 2a). M-M.*

περίπτωσις, εως, ἡ (Stoic. II p. 29; Ammonius Gr. [100 AD] p. 60 Valck.: 'misfortune'; M. Ant. 6, 41, 1 π. τοῦ κακοῦ al.) *experience*, in this case an unpleasant one, *calamity* (w. συμφορά) 1 Cl 1: 1.*

περι(ρ)ραίνω (Aristoph.+; inscr.; Lev; Num; Philo; Jos., Ant. 9, 123; 13, 243) pf. pass. ptc. περιρεραμμένος (on the reduplication s. Kühner-Bl. II p. 23; Bl-D. §68; Rob. 211f) *sprinkle around, on all sides* (Diogenes the Cynic is of the opinion [Diog. L. 6, 42] that no matter how extensive the περι(ρ)ραίνειν, it is impossible to get rid of the ἁμαρτήματα) ἱμάτιον περιρεραμμένον αἵματι *a robe sprinkled on all sides with blood* Rv 19: 13 v.l. (for βεβαμμένον; other vv.ll. ῥεραντισμένον, περιρεραντισμένον, ἐρραμμένον). M-M.*

περι(ρ)ρήγνυμι (Aeschyl.+) 1 aor. ptc. περιρήξας (t.r. περιρρήξας, s. Bl-D. §11, 1) *tear off* (all around) τὶ someth., esp. clothes (Aeschyl., Sept. 329; Demosth. 19, 197 τὸν χιτωνίσκον; Polyb. 15, 33, 4; Diod. S. 17, 35, 7; 2 Macc 4: 38 τοὺς χιτῶνας; Philo, De Jos. 16 [mid.]; cf. Jos., Bell. 2, 601, Ant. 6, 357) περιρήξαντες αὐτῶν τὰ ἱμάτια Ac 16: 22. M-M.*

περισπάω (Eur., X.+; inscr., pap., LXX, Joseph.; s. Phryn. p. 415 L.) in our lit. only pass.; impf. 3 sing. περιεσπᾶτο.

1. *be pulled* or *dragged away* (the act. in Polyb., Diod. S., Dionys. Hal., Plut. et al. The pass. Cebes 33, 3; PTebt. 124, 39 [I BC] εἰς ἑτέρας λειτουργίας; Jos., Ant. 5, 46) περισπώμενος ὧδε κἀκεῖσε ἀπὸ τῶν πνευμάτων τῶν

πονηρῶν Hm 5, 2, 7 (on the constr. w. ἀπό cf. Epict. 1, 8, 5). Closely related to it is mng.

2. *become* or *be distracted, quite busy, overburdened* (Polyb. 4, 10, 3; Diod. S. 2, 29, 5; Epict. 3, 9, 19; Jos., Bell. 1, 232 al.; UPZ 59, 30 [168 BC]; PTebt. 37, 15 [I BC]; POxy. 743, 36 [I BC]) περί τι *with* or *by someth.* (Polyb. 3, 105, 1; Diod. S. 1, 74) περὶ πολλὴν διακονίαν Lk 10: 40. περὶ τὸν πλοῦτον Hs 2: 5. περὶ τὰς πράξεις 4: 5. M-M. and suppl.*

περισσεία, ας, ἡ (Herodian, Gr. I 291, 9 al.; schol. on Nicander, Ther. 266) *surplus, abundance* (IG V 1, 550 π. χρημάτων; VII 3221 ἐκ τῆς περισσήας; inscr. fr. Syria: Bull. de corr. hell. 21, 1897 p. 65. In LXX only several times in Eccl.—Dssm., LO 66 [LAE 80]) ἡ π. τῆς χάριτος Ro 5: 17. ἡ π. τῆς χαρᾶς 2 Cor 8: 2. μεγαλυνθῆναι εἰς π. *be greatly enlarged* 10: 15. π. κακίας *all the evil prevailing* (*around you*) Js 1: 21. M-M.*

περίσσευμα, ατος, τό—**1.** *abundance, fulness* (Eratosth. [III BC], Cat. 44 Olivieri; Plut., Mor. 310c; 962F.—The LXX of Eccl 2: 15 has the word in line 6, but this line is lacking in the Hebr. text, and hence is prob. a Christian addition: AHMcNeile, An Introd. to Eccl '04, 157; PKatz, ThLZ 63, '38, 34) 2 Cor 8: 14a, b (opp. ὑστέρημα). ἐκ (τοῦ) περισσεύματος (τῆς) καρδίας *from the abundance of the heart, what the heart is full of* Mt 12: 34; Lk 6: 45.

2. *what remains, scraps* (Artem. 3, 52) περισσεύματα κλασμάτων *pieces that were left* Mk 8: 8.*

περισσεύω impf. ἐπερίσσευον; fut. περισσεύσω; 1 aor. ἐπερίσσευσα (on the augment Bl-D. §69, 4 app.; Mlt.-H. 192); 1 fut. pass. περισσευθήσομαι (Hes., Thu.+; inscr., pap., LXX, Philo, Joseph.).

1. intr.—**a.** of things—**α.** *be more than enough, be left over* (Dit., Syll.³ 672, 19 [II BC]; Theophil. in Alex. Polyhist.: Euseb., Pr. Ev. 9, 34, 19; Jos., Ant. 3, 229, Vi. 333) τὰ περισσεύσαντα κλάσματα J 6: 12. ὁ χρόνος ὁ περισσεύων εἰς τὴν παρουσίαν αὐτοῦ *the time that remains before his coming* Hs 5, 5, 3. οἱ περισσεύοντες *the others, the remainder* 9, 8, 7; w. gen. οἱ π. αὐτῶν vs. 4; strengthened οἱ λοιποὶ οἱ περισσεύσαντες 9, 9, 4. τὸ περισσεῦον *what was left over* τῶν κλασμάτων Mt 14: 20; 15: 37 (cf. Jos., Ant. 13, 55). περισσεύει μοί τι *I leave someth.* (cf. Tob 4: 16) J 6: 13. τὸ περισσεῦσαν αὐτοῖς κλασμάτων *what they left in the way of fragments* Lk 9: 17.

β. *be present in abundance* (X., Cyr. 6, 2, 30; PFlor. 242, 2; PLond. 418, 4 ἵνα περισσεύῃ ὁ φόβος τοῦ θεοῦ ἐν σοί) 2 Cor 1: 5b; Phil 1: 26. ἐὰν μὴ περισσεύσῃ ὑμῶν ἡ δικαιοσύνη πλεῖον τῶν γραμματέων *unless your righteousness greatly surpasses that of the scribes* Mt 5: 20 (for the omission of 'that' in the Gk. text cf. Maximus Tyr. 15, 8d: their life is different in no respect σκωλήκων=fr. 'that' of the worms). περισσεύει τί τινι (cf. Thu. 2, 65, 13) *someone has someth. in abundance* (Tob 4: 16) ISm 9: 2. τὸ περισσεῦον τινι (opp. ὑστέρησις) *someone's abundance* Mk 12: 44. (Opp. ὑστέρημα) Lk 21: 4. ἐν τῷ περισσεύειν τινι *in this, namely that one has an abundance* 12: 15. περισσεύει τι εἴς τινα someth. *comes* or *is available to someone in great abundance*: ἡ χάρις τοῦ θεοῦ εἰς τοὺς πολλοὺς ἐπερίσσευσεν Ro 5: 15. περισσεύει τὰ παθήματα τοῦ Χριστοῦ εἰς ἡμᾶς *we share abundantly in Christ's sufferings* 2 Cor 1: 5a.

γ. *be extremely rich* or *abundant, overflow* 2 Cor 9: 12. εἰ ἡ ἀλήθεια τοῦ θεοῦ ἐν τῷ ἐμῷ ψεύσματι ἐπερίσσευσεν εἰς τὴν δόξαν αὐτου *if by my falsehood the truthfulness of God has shown itself to be supremely great, to his glory* Ro 3: 7. The thing in which the wealth consists is added in the dat. (Philistion [IV BC] in Athen. 3, 83 p. 115E πάσαις τ. ἀρεταῖς περιττεύει) π. δόξῃ *be extremely rich in glory* 2 Cor 3: 9 (t.r. ἐν δόξῃ). In oxymoron ἡ πτωχεία αὐτῶν ἐπερίσσευσεν εἰς τὸ πλοῦτος τῆς ἁπλότητος αὐτῶν *their poverty has overflowed into the wealth of their liberality* 8: 2.

δ. *grow* αἱ ἐκκλησίαι ἐπερίσσευον τῷ ἀριθμῷ καθ' ἡμέραν Ac 16: 5. ἵνα ἡ ἀγάπη ὑμῶν ἔτι μᾶλλον καὶ μᾶλλον περισσεύῃ ἐν ἐπιγνώσει Phil 1: 9.

b. *of persons*—**α.** *have an abundance, abound, be rich* τινός *of* or *in someth.* (Bl-D. §172; Rob. 510) ἄρτων Lk 15: 17 v.l. (the text has the mid. περισσεύονται [in case it should be pass., s. 2b below], but that is prob. not orig.; cf. Jülicher, Gleichn. 346). παντὸς χαρίσματος IPol 2: 2. Also ἔν τινι Dg 5: 13 (opp. ὑστερεῖσθαι). ἐν τῇ ἐλπίδι Ro 15: 13. Abs. (opp. ὑστερεῖσθαι) περισσεύομεν *we have more* (divine approval) 1 Cor 8: 8. ζητεῖτε ἵνα περισσεύητε *strive to excel* 14: 12. Cf. Phil 4: 12a (opp. ταπεινοῦσθαι), b (opp. ὑστερεῖσθαι). ἀπέχω πάντα καὶ περισσεύω *I have received full payment, and have more than enough* vs. 18. εἰς πᾶν ἔργον *have ample means for every enterprise* 2 Cor 9: 8b.

β. *be outstanding, be prominent, excel* (1 Macc 3: 30) ἔν τινι *in someth.* ἐν τῷ ἔργῳ τοῦ κυρίου 1 Cor 15: 58. Cf. 2 Cor 8: 7a, b; Col 2: 7. Abs. w. μᾶλλον added *progress more and more* 1 Th 4: 1, 10.

2. trans. (Athen. 2 p. 42B) *cause to abound, make extremely rich*—**a.** *of things,* that one greatly increases τὴν εὐχαριστίαν 2 Cor 4: 15. τὶ εἴς τινα *grant someth. to someone richly* 9: 8a; Eph 1: 8 (ἧς by attraction of the relat. for ἥν). Pass. w. dat. of the pers. δοθήσεται αὐτῷ καὶ περισσευθήσεται *to him* (more) *will be given, and he will have a great abundance* Mt 13: 12. Cf. 25: 29.

b. *of persons who receive someth. in great abundance* ὑμᾶς ὁ κύριος περισσεύσαι τῇ ἀγάπῃ *may the Lord cause you to abound in love* 1 Th 3: 12. πόσοι μίσθιοι περισσεύονται ἄρτων Lk 15: 17 *how many day laborers get more than enough bread* (s. 1bα above).—FHauck, TW VI 58-63. M-M.*

περισσός, ή, όν (Hes., Hdt.+; inscr., pap., LXX, En., Ep. Arist., Philo, Joseph.) *exceeding the usual number or size.*

1. *extraordinary, remarkable,* of that which is not usually encountered among men (Pla., Apol. 20c οὐδὲν τῶν ἄλλων περισσὸν πραγματεύεσθαι; BGU 417, 22 περισσόν ποιήσω=I am going to do someth. extraordinary; En. 102, 7) τί περισσὸν ποιεῖτε; *what are you doing that is remarkable?* Mt 5: 47 (cf. Plut., Mor. 233A τί οὖν μέγα ποιεῖς; what, then, are you doing that is so great?—ELombard, L'Ordinaire et l'Extraordinaire [Mt 5: 47]: RThPh 15, '27, 169-86). Subst. τὸ περισσόν *the advantage* (WSchubart, Der Gnomon des Idios Logos '19, 102 [II AD]) τὸ π. τοῦ Ἰουδαίου *the advantage of the Jew* Ro 3: 1. LCerfaux, Le privilège d'Israël sel. s. Paul: Ephem. theol. Lov. 17, '40, 5-26.

2. *abundant, profuse*—**a.** *going beyond what is necessary* περισσὸν ἔχειν *have* (someth.) *in abundance* J 10: 10 (cf. X., Oec. 20, 1 οἱ μὲν περισσὰ ἔχουσιν, οἱ δὲ οὐδὲ τὰ ἀναγκαῖα δύνανται πορίζεσθαι; Plut., Mor. 523D). περισσότερον J 10: 10 𝔓75.

b. *superfluous, unnecessary* (trag.+; cf. 2 Macc 12: 44) περισσόν μοί ἐστιν τὸ γράφειν ὑμῖν *it is unnecessary for me to write to you* 2 Cor 9: 1 (Wilcken, Chrest. 238 II, 4 περισσὸν ἡγοῦμαι διεξοδέστερον ὑμῖν γράφειν). περισσὸν ἡγοῦμαι *I consider it superfluous* (Appian, Prooem. c. 13 §50; Jos., Ant. 3, 215; cf. Philo, Agr. 59) Dg 2: 10. W. ἄχρηστος 4: 2.

3. *in the comparative sense;* περισσός together w. its adv. and comp. is a colloquial substitute for μᾶλλον, μάλιστα as well as for πλείων, πλεῖστος (Bl-D. §60, 3; Rob. 279; KKrumbacher, ByzZ 17, '08, 233). τὸ περισσὸν τούτων *whatever is more than this, whatever goes beyond this* Mt 5: 37 (on the gen. s. Bl-D. §185, 1; Rob. 660).—ἐκ περισσοῦ (Περὶ ὕψους 34, 2; Vi. Aesopi I c. 43; Dositheus 40, 4; Da 3: 22 Theod.) Mk 6: 51 s. ἐκ 6c and λίαν 1. M-M.*

περισσότερος, τέρα, ον comp. of περισσός (Hdt.+; PFlor. 127, 22; Da 4: 36 Theod. μεγαλωσύνη περισσοτέρα) *greater, more.*

1. used w. a subst. ἀγαθά 1 Cl 61: 3 (s. ἀγαθός 2bα). τιμή 1 Cor 12: 23a, 24; Hm 4, 4, 2. δόξα s 5, 3, 3. κρίμα *more severe punishment* Mt 23: 13 v.l.; Mk 12: 40; Lk 20: 47. εὐσχημοσύνη 1 Cor 12: 23b. λύπη *excessive sorrow* 2 Cor 2: 7.

2. περισσότερον *even more* (=more than the πολύ that was entrusted to him) Lk 12: 48. W. gen. of comparison περισσότερον αὐτῶν ἐκοπίασα 1 Cor 15: 10.—περισσότερόν τι *someth. more* or *further* (Lucian, Tyrannicida 3) Lk 12: 4 (s. on this KKöhler, ZNW 18, '18, 140f); 2 Cor 10: 8. W. gen. of comparison (Jos., Ant. 5, 23; 8, 410) περισσότερόν ἐστιν πάντων τῶν ὁλοκαυτωμάτων *is much more than all whole burnt offerings* Mk 12: 33. περισσότερον προφήτου Mt 11: 9; Lk 7: 26 might be taken as a neut. *someth. greater than a prophet.* But it may be understood as a masc. *one who is more than a prophet* (cf. Plut., Mor. 57F περιττότερος φρονήσει; Sym. Gen 49: 3 οὐκ ἔσῃ περισσότερος).

3. the neut. sing. as adv. (Hdt. 2, 129 al.; Vett. Val. p. 74, 6; PFlor. 127, 22; BGU 380, 10; PGM 13, 12) ζωὴν π. ἔχωσιν J 10: 10 𝔓75. π. ἐπιδεῖξαι *point out even more clearly* Hb 6: 17. π. ἔτι κατάδηλόν ἐστιν *it is even more evident* 7: 15. Strengthened *so much more* Mk 7: 36. M-M. s.v. περισσός. B. 924.*

περισσοτέρως adv. (Diod. S. 13, 108; Athen. 5 p. 192F; PGiess. 25, 12 [II AD]).

1. comp. (*even*) *more* Mk 15: 14 t.r.; *to a much greater degree, far more, far greater* (than Paul's opponents) 2 Cor 11: 23; (than those of his own age) Gal 1: 14. (Opp. ἧσσον) 2 Cor 12: 15 (ἀγαπάω 1aα). Intensifying *so much* (*the*) *more* Phil 1: 14; Hb 2: 1; 13: 19.

2. elative *especially* 2 Cor 1: 12; 2: 4; 7: 15; (*all*) *the more* 1 Th 2: 17. Strengthened περισσοτέρως μᾶλλον *even much more* 2 Cor 7: 13. M-M.*

περισσῶς adv. *exceedingly, beyond measure, very* (Eur., Hdt.+; Polyb. 1, 29, 7; 32, 15, 4; Athen. 11 p. 501D; PTebt. 488; LXX; Theod.; Philo, Det. Pot. Ins. 15 al.; Jos., Ant. 1, 258) Ac 26: 11.—Comp. *even more, even more* περισσῶς ἔκραζον *they cried out even louder* Mt 27: 23; cf. Mk 15: 14. π. ἐξεπλήσσοντο *they were even more astounded* 10: 26. M-M.*

περιστέλλω fut. περιστελῶ (Hom.+; Herm. Wr. 492, 21 Sc.; PGM 4, 3138; LXX; Jos., Ant. 19, 237, C. Ap. 2, 269) *surround, clothe* τινά *someone* (Diod. S. 19, 11, 7 τὸν ἄνδρα περιέστειλεν; Jos., Ant. 17, 59) B 3: 4 (Is 58: 8).*

περιστερά, ᾶς, ἡ (Hdt., Aristoph.+; inscr., pap., LXX; Ep. Arist. 145; Philo; Jos., Ant. 1, 184; 3, 230) *pigeon, dove* used for sacrifice, hence sold in the temple Mt 21: 12; Mk 11: 15; J 2: 14, 16. Dalman, Arbeit VII (s. οἰκία 1).—On the δύο νοσσοὶ περιστερῶν Lk 2: 24 s. on νοσσός. The dove which, fr. the viewpoint of natural science in ancient times, has no bile, was for the early

Christians the symbol of all kinds of virtues (cf. WBauer, D. Leben Jesu '09, 117): ἀκέραιοι ὡς αἱ περιστεραί Mt 10: 16; cf. IPol 2: 2. Hence the Holy Spirit, in appearing at Jesus' baptism, took the form of a dove (WTelfer, The Form of a Dove: JTS 29, '28, 238-42; LEKeck, NTS 17, '70/'71, 41-67 'dove-like descent' Mt 3: 16; Mk 1: 10; Lk 3: 22; J 1: 32; GEb 3.—HUsener, Das Weihnachtsfest² '11, 56ff; HGressmann, Die Sage v. d. Taufe Jesu und d. vorderoriental. Taubengöttin: ARW 20, '20/'21, 1-40; 323-59.—In MPol 16: 1 Wordsworth has inserted περὶ στύρακα 'around the sword-handle' by conjecture and thereby gained undeserved approval. The Gk. mss. have περιστερὰ καί (but s. JAKleist, tr. '48, note ad loc.). The concept of the dove as representing the soul underlies this (cf., in a way, Quint. Symyrn. 8, 202f ψυχὴ δι' ἕλκεος ἐξεποτήθη ἐκ μελέων=the soul flew out of his body through the wound).—GWeicker, D. Seelenvogel '02, 26f; HGünter, Die christl. Legende des Abenlandes '10, 13; 45; 86; 142; 148; 191; FSühling, D. Taube als. relig. Symbol im christl. Altertum '30; HGreeven, TW VI '56, 63-72. M-M.*

περιτειχίζω 1 aor. περιετείχισα; pf. pass. περιετείχισμαι (Thu., Aristoph.+; pap., LXX; Jos., Bell. 6, 323) *surround with a wall.*
1. lit., of a city περιτετειχισμένη κύκλῳ *walled around* Hs 9, 12, 5 (BGU 993 III, 1 [II BC] τόπος περιτετειχισμένος).
2. fig. *surrounded* τούτοις (i.e. ἀγγέλοις) περιτετείχισται ὁ κύριος s 9, 12, 6. Of the sea of flames coming fr. the pyre κύκλῳ περιετείχισε τὸ σῶμα τοῦ μάρτυρος *completely surrounded the martyr's body* MPol 15: 2 (w. κύκλῳ as Thu. 2, 78).*

περιτέμνω 2 aor. περιέτεμον. Pass.: pf. ptc. περιτετμημένος; 1 aor. περιετμήθην (Hom.+) *cut (off) around,* in our lit. and the LXX, somet. fig., only in the sense *circumcise* the foreskin (so somet. as act., somet. as mid. ['circumcise oneself'], since Hdt. 2, 36, 2; 2, 104, 1 [of the Egyptians and several other peoples], also Diod. S. 1, 28, 3; 1, 55, 5; 3, 32, 4 [Egyptians, Colchians, Ἰουδαῖοι]; Ptolemaeus, περὶ Ἡρῴδου [I AD]: 199 fgm. 1 Jac.; Strabo 17, 2, 5; Philo Bybl. [c. 100 AD] in Euseb., Pr. Ev. 1, 10, 33; Sallust. 9 p. 18, 17; PLond. 24, 3 [163 BC]; PTebt. 291, 33; 292, 7; 20; 293, 12; 14; 19; Wilcken, Chrest. 77 I, 11; III, 11; Philo Alex.; Joseph.; Test. Levi 6: 3) in our lit. prob. only in act. and pass.
1. lit., w. acc. of the pers. Lk 1: 59; 2: 21; J 7: 22; Ac 7: 8; 15: 5; 16: 3; 21: 21; B 9: 8 (Gen 17: 23ff). Pass. *be circumcised, have oneself circumcised* (Bl-D. §314 app.) Ac 15: 1, 24 t.r.; 1 Cor 7: 18b; Gal 2: 3 (Ptolemaeus, περὶ Ἡρῴδου τ. βασιλέως: no. 199 Jac. [I AD] Ἰδουμαῖοι ἀναγκασθέντες περιτέμνεσθαι. S. SBelkin, JBL 54, '35, 43-7); 5: 2f; 6: 12, 13b. οἱ περιτεμνόμενοι *those who have themselves circumcised* vs. 13a. περιτετμημένος *circumcised, in the state of being circumcised* 1 Cor 7: 18a; Gal 6: 13a v.l.
2. fig.—**a.** of baptism περιετμήθητε περιτομῇ ἀχειροποιήτῳ Col 2: 11 (OCullmann, D. Tauflehre des NT '48, 50-63).
b. Barnabas maintains strongly that the scripture does not require a physical circumcision: περιτέμεσθε ἡμῶν τὴν καρδίαν 9: 1a. The κύριος says περιτμήθητε τὰς καρδίας ὑμῶν vs. 1b. Obviously Jer 4: 4 (cf. Dt 10: 16) is meant; B comes closer to it in περιτμήθητε τῷ κυρίῳ ὑμῶν *let yourselves be circumcised for your Lord* 9: 5a, and in the explanation of it περιτμήθητε τὸ σκληρὸν τῆς καρδίας ὑμῶν vs. 5b. What is true of the heart is also true of the ears περιέτεμεν ἡμῶν τὰς ἀκοάς 9: 4. Cf. 10: 12. In 9: 6 it

is acknowledged that circumcision is somet. justified thus: περιτέτμηται ὁ λαὸς εἰς σφραγῖδα, and it is explained that Ἀβραὰμ ἐν πνεύματι προβλέψας εἰς τὸν Ἰησοῦν περιέτεμεν vs. 7.—Schürer I (Eng. tr. rev. ed.) '73, 536ff; Dssm., B 149ff [BS 151-3]; UWilcken, HGunkel and PWendland, APF 2, '03, 4-31; WOtto, Priester u. Tempel im hellenist. Ägypten I '05, 213ff; JCMatthes, De Besnijdenis: Teylers Theol. Tijdschrift 6, '08, 163-91; FJDölger, Sphragis '11, 51ff; Billerb. IV '28, 23-40; FBryk, D. Beschneidung b. Mann u. Weib '31. JMSasson, JBL 85, '66, 473-76.—RMeyer, TW VI 72-83. M-M.*

περιτίθημι 1 aor. περιέθηκα; 2 aor. imper. 2 pl. περίθετε, ptc. περιθείς. Pass.: impf. περιετιθέμην; pf. ptc. περιτεθειμένος; 1 aor. περιετέθην (Hom. [in tmesis]+; inscr., pap., LXX; En. 98, 2; Philo, Joseph.).
1. *put* or *place around, on* τί τινι someth. *around* someone or *someth.* φραγμὸν αὐτῷ (=τῷ ἀμπελῶνι) περιέθηκεν *a fence around a vineyard* Mt 21: 33; Mk 12: 1 (the dat. is to be supplied here, as Is 5: 2.—Dit., Syll.³ 898, 7f. τὸν περίβολον ὃν περιέθηκε τῷ τεμένει). αὐτῷ περιετίθετο τὰ ὄργανα *the wooden instruments* (or *firewood*) *were placed around him* MPol 13: 3 (Appian, Iber. §132 ξύλα περιθέντες αὐτῇ. Likew. Appian, Mithrid. 108 §512 ξύλα περιθέντες in order to ignite someth.). The bars or limits set for the sea 1 Cl 20: 6 (cf. Job 38: 10). σπόγγον καλάμῳ *put a sponge on a reed* Mt 27: 48; Mk 15: 36; cf. J 19: 29. *Put* or *lay* pieces of clothing *around, on* someone (Herodian 3, 7, 5 χλαμύδα; Dit., Or. 383, 137; PSI 64, 17 [I BC]; Job 39: 20; Jos., Ant. 6, 184; Test. Levi 8: 5, 6) χλαμύδα περιέθηκαν αὐτῷ Mt 27: 28. Esp. of headbands, wreaths etc. (Ps.-Pla., Alcib. 2 p. 151A στέφανόν τινι. Several times LXX; Philo, Mos. 2, 243) Mk 15: 17. κρεῖττον ἦν αὐτῷ περιτεθῆναι μύλον 1 Cl 46: 8.—Var. prep. constrs. take the place of the dat.: π. τὸ ἔριον ἐπὶ ξύλον *put the wool on a stick* B 8: 1 (cf. Gen 41: 42). π. τὸ ἔριον περὶ τὴν κεφαλήν 7: 8 (a quot. that cannot be identified w. certainty.—On π. περὶ τὴν κεφ. cf. Pla., Rep. 3 p. 406D).
2. fig. *put on* or *around* τί τινι=*invest someone w. someth., grant, bestow someth. to* or *on someone* (Hdt.+; Dit., Syll.³ 985, 50; LXX; Philo, Aet. M. 41) τιμήν π. w. the dat. *show honor* (Dit., Or. 331, 23; BGU 1141, 19 [14 BC]; Esth 1: 20. Cf. also Thu. 6, 89, 2 ἀτιμίαν τινὶ π.) 1 Cor 12: 23. περιθεὶς τὴν εὐπρέπειαν τῇ κτίσει αὐτοῦ Hv 1, 3, 4. M-M.*

περιτομή, ῆς, ἡ *circumcision* of the foreskin (Agatharchides [II BC] 61; Timagenes [I BC]: 88 fgm. 5 Jac.; Strabo 16, 2, 37 [in the pl.]; PTebt. 314, 5 [II AD]; Gen 17: 13; Ex 4: 25f; Artapanus [II BC] in Euseb., Pr. Ev. 9, 27, 10; Philo, Spec. Leg. 1, 8; 9; Jos., Ant. 1, 192; 214 [here in pl.], C. Ap. 2, 137; 143; Test. Levi 6: 6).
1. *circumcision* as a religious rite, lit., J 7: 22. διαθήκη περιτομῆς *covenant* or *decree of circumcision* Ac 7: 8. εἰ περιτομὴν ἔτι κηρύσσω Gal 5: 11.—B 9: 4a, 7. Cf. Phil 3: 5 (s. ὀκταήμερος); Dg 4: 1 which, however, can also be classed under
2. pass. *the state of having been circumcised*=τὸ περιτετμῆσθαι (Diod. S. 3, 32, 4; Jos., Ant. 12, 241, C. Ap. 2, 137) Ro 2: 25a, b, 26; 3: 1; 1 Cor 7: 19; Gal 5: 6; 6: 15. ἡ ἐν τῷ φανερῷ ἐν σαρκὶ περιτομή Ro 2: 28. διὰ περιτομῆς vs. 27 (s. διά A III 1c). περιτομὴν ἔχειν IPhld 6: 1. περιτομὴν λαμβάνειν J 7: 23. εἶναι ἐν περιτομῇ Ro 4: 10a; cf. b, where ὄντι is to be supplied. On vs. 11 cf. σημεῖον 1. οἱ Αἰγύπτιοι ἐν π. εἰσιν B 9: 6.
3. fig., of spiritual circumcision (cf. περιτέμνω 2) περιτομή…οὐ σαρκὸς…B 9: 4b. περιτομὴ καρδίας (s. περιτέμνω 2b) Ro 2: 29 (cf. Ode of Solomon 11, 1f).

περιτομὴ ἀχειροποίητος Col 2: 11a=περ. τοῦ Χριστοῦ b, by which baptism is meant (s. vs. 12).

4. abstr. for concr. (cf. e.g., Appian, Bell. Civ. 3, 61 §249 ἐπεξέρχεσθαι τὸν φόνον=proceed against the murder [i.e., the murderers]) those who are circumcised **a.** lit., of the Jews Ro 3: 30; 4: 9; Col 3: 11 (opp. ἀκροβυστία='Gentiles' in all three).—Ro 4: 12a; 15: 8; Gal 2: 7–9. οἱ λεγόμενοι ἀκροβυστία ὑπὸ τῆς λεγομένης περιτομῆς ἐν σαρκὶ χειροποιήτου those who are called the 'uncircumcision' by the so-called circumcision (whose circumcision is) a purely physical one (and is) made by hands Eph 2: 11. οἱ οὐκ ἐκ περιτομῆς μόνον who not only belong to the 'circumcised' Ro 4: 12b.—οἱ ἐκ περιτομῆς πιστοί those of the 'circumcised' who believe=the Jewish Christians Ac 10: 45. Likew. οἱ ἐκ περιτομῆς (ὄντες) 11: 2; Gal 2: 12; Col 4: 11; Tit 1: 10. EEEllis, TU 102, '68, 390–99.
b. fig. of the Christians (as the truly circumcised people of the promise) ἡμεῖς ἐσμεν ἡ περιτομή Phil 3: 3.—For lit. s. under περιτέμνω. M-M.*

περιτρέπω (Lysias, Pla. et al.; Wsd 5: 23; Philo) turn from one state to its opposite τινὰ εἴς τι (BGU 1831, 8 [51 BC] εἰς ἄπορον; Vett. Val. 250, 9f; Jos., Ant. 9, 72 τοὺς παρόντας εἰς χαρὰν περιέτρεψε.—Niese reads the simplex in 2, 293) τὰ πολλά σε γράμματα εἰς μανίαν περιτρέπει Ac 26: 24 (s. μανία and cf. the expression εἰς μανίαν περιτρέπειν in Lucian, Abdic. 30 and Vi. Aesopi I c. 55). M-M.*

περιτρέχω impf. περιέτρεχον; 2 aor. περιέδραμον, ptc. περιδραμών (Hom.+).
1. run or move around w. the acc. of the thing or pers. one moves around (Hdt. 8, 128; Aristoph., Ran. 193 τὴν λίμνην κύκλῳ; Athen. 5 p. 208Β; PFlor. 120, 7) ἄγγελοι περιέτρεχον αὐτοὺς ἐκεῖσε angels were moving about them there AP 5: 18. ὧδε κἀκεῖσε περιτρ. κύκλῳ τῆς πύλης run here and there around the gate Hs 9, 3, 1.
2. run about, go about in (Cebes 14, 1; Am 8: 12; Jer 5: 1 ἐν ταῖς ὁδοῖς) w. acc. (Aristoph., Thesmoph. 657 τὴν πύκνα πᾶσαν) ὅλην τὴν χώραν Mk 6: 55. ἐν τοῖς προβάτοις π. run about among the sheep Hs 6, 1, 6. M-M.*

περιφέρω carry about, carry here and there—**1.** lit., w. acc. (Eur., Pla.+; Plut., Mor. 331C; Dit., Syll.³ 1169, 65f, a spearhead in the face; Josh 24: 33a; 2 Macc 7: 27) the sick Mk 6: 55. τὰ δεσμά the chains IEph 11: 2; cf. IMg 1: 2; ITr 12: 2. τὴν νέκρωσιν τοῦ Ἰησοῦ ἐν τῷ σώματι π. 2 Cor 4: 10 (s. νέκρωσις 1).
2. fig. (Epict. 2, 8, 12 θεὸν π.=carry God about within oneself; 2, 16, 33; Philo, Omnis Prob. Lib. 117 τὴν ἀρετήν; POxy. 1664, 7 a dear person in one's heart) τὸ ὄνομα carry the name (of Christ, or of a Christian) about (prob. as wandering preachers) IEph 7: 1. The pass., fig. (Jos., Ant. 19, 46 διὰ λογισμῶν περιφερόμενος) περιφερόμενοι παντὶ ἀνέμῳ τῆς διδασκαλίας carried here and there by (any and) every wind of doctrine Eph 4: 14 (or does περιφέρεσθαι mean turn around here, and is the idea of a weathervane in the background?); cf. Hb 13: 9 v.l. M-M.*

περιφρονέω disregard, look down on, despise (so since Thu. 1, 25, 4; POxy. 71 II, 16; Jos., Ant. 4, 260) w. gen. (Ps.-Pla., Axioch. 372A τοῦ ζῆν; Plut., Thes. 1, 5, Per. 31, 1, Mor. 762E; 4 Macc 6: 9; 7: 16; 14: 1) Tit 2: 15. M-M.*

περιχαρής, ές (Soph., Hdt.+; 3 Macc 5: 44; Philo, Rer. Div. Her. 3; Jos., Ant. 7, 206) very glad π. γενέσθαι (Diod. S. 20, 76, 6 π. γενόμενος; Charito 6, 5, 1; Ael. Aristid. 50, 50 K.=26 p. 517 D.; Job 3: 22; 29: 22; Jos.,

Ant. 1, 284; 16, 358; PSI 887, 5 [VI AD]) Hv 3, 12, 2; foll. by the inf. in the gen. v 3, 8, 1.*

περίχωρος, ον neighboring (Gen 19: 28) quite predom. used as a subst. (οἱ περίχωροι 'the neighbors' Demosth. 19, 266; Plut., Cat. Maj. 25, 3, Eum. 15, 13; Aelian, N.A. 10, 46; Cass. Dio 36, 33) ἡ π. (sc. γῆ; Bl-D. §241, 1) region around, neighborhood (LXX, which also has τὸ περίχωρον and τὰ περίχωρα. Loanw. in rabb.) Mt 14: 35; Mk 6: 55 t.r.; Lk 4: 14, 37; 7: 17; Ac 14: 6; 1 Cl 11: 1; GP 9: 34. Used w. gen.: of a river, whose neighboring region to the right and left is designated as ἡ π.: ἡ π. τοῦ Ἰορδάνου (Gen 13: 10f) Mt 3: 5 (s. below); Lk 3: 3. ἡ περίχωρος τῶν Γερασηνῶν the Gerasenes and the people living around them Lk 8: 37. ὅλη ἡ π. τῆς Γαλιλαίας Mk 1: 28 is either epexegetic gen. the whole region around, that is, Galilee or the region around Galilee (Mt understands it so, and 4: 24 inserted ὅλη ἡ Συρία for it). By metonymy for the inhabitants Mt 3: 5. M-M.*

περίψημα, ατος, τό (Vi. Aesopi I c. 35; from περιψάω= 'wipe all around, wipe clean') that which is removed by the process of cleansing, dirt, off-scouring (Sym. Jer 22: 28) πάντων περίψημα the off-scouring of all things 1 Cor 4: 13. But reflection on the fact that the removal of the περίψ. cleanses the thing or the pers. to which (whom) it was attached, has given the word the further mng. ransom, scapegoat, sacrifice (cf. Tob 5: 19. Hesychius equates it w. περικατάμαγμα and ἀντίλυτρα, ἀντίψυχα. Photius p. 425, 3 explains περίψ. w. ἀπολύτρωσις and then continues, referring to the custom of making a human sacrifice every year for the benefit of the rest of the people [s. on this Ltzm. and JWeiss on 1 Cor 4: 13]: οὕτως ἐπέλεγον τῷ κατ' ἐνιαυτὸν ἐμβαλλομένῳ τῇ θαλάσσῃ νεανίᾳ ἐπ' ἀπαλλαγῇ τῶν συνεχόντων κακῶν· περίψημα ἡμῶν γενοῦ· ἤτοι σωτηρία καὶ ἀπολύτρωσις. καὶ οὕτως ἐνέβαλον τῇ θαλάσσῃ ὡσανεὶ τῷ Ποσειδῶνι θυσίαν ἀποτίννυντες). But it must also be observed in this connection that περίψ. had become more and more a term of polite self-depreciation, common enough in every-day speech (Dionys. of Alex. in Euseb., H.E. 7, 22, 7 τὸ δημῶδες ῥῆμα. S. also the grave-inscription [in WThieling, D. Hellenismus in Kleinafrika '11, p. 34] in which a wife says w. reference to her deceased husband ἐγώ σου περίψημα τῆς καλῆς ψυχῆς); the sense would then be someth. like most humble servant. So certainly in περίψ. τοῦ σταυροῦ IEph 18: 1. But prob. also 8: 1; B 4: 9; 6: 5 (s. HVeil: EHennecke, Hdb. zu den ntl. Apokryphen '04, 218).—GStählin, TW VI 83–92. M-M.*

περπερεύομαι (M. Ant. 5, 5, 4; Etym. Mag. p. 665, 37; Hesychius=κατεπαίρομαι. The compound ἐμπερπερεύομαι is more common: Epict. 2, 1, 34; Cicero, Ad Attic. 1, 14, 4) behave as a πέρπερος ('braggart, wind-bag': Polyb. 32, 2, 5; 39, 1, 2; Epict. 3, 2, 14), boast, brag 1 Cor 13: 4. M-M.*

Περσίς, ίδος, ἡ (Palest. inscr.: IPPeters and HThiersch, Painted Tombs of Marissa '05, nos. 38 and 41 [II BC]; esp. for female slaves: BGU 895, 29; 31 [II AD]; IG VII 2074; CIL V 4455) Persis, recipient of a greeting Ro 16: 12. M-M.*

πέρυσι before vowels πέρυσιν Hv 2, 1, 3 (on the ν cf. Lex. Rhet. in RReitzenstein, Index Lect. Rostock 1892/93 p. 6; Bl-D. §20 w. app.—Mlt.-H. 279) adv. of time (Simonides +) last year, a year ago (Aristoph., Pla. et al.; Plut., Mor. 155F; Philostrat., Her. 33 p. 139, 14 K.; inscr., pap.) Hv 2, 1, 1; 3. ἀπὸ π. (BGU 531 II, 1 [70–80 AD]; Dssm., NB 48f [BS 221]) a year ago, since last year 2 Cor 8: 10; 9: 2. M-M.*

περυσινός, ή, όν (Aristoph., Pla., X.+; PSI 560, 8 [III BC]; PTebt. 112, 19 [II BC]; al. in pap.) *of last year* ἡ περυσινὴ ὅρασις *the vision of the previous year* Hv 2, 1, 1; cf. 3, 10, 3. M-M. s.v. πέρυσι.*

πεσεῖν, -ών, πεσοῦμαι s. πίπτω.

πετάομαι (doubtful form for the older πέτομαι [q.v.].—Lob. on Phryn. p. 581; Bl-D. §101 p. 47; Helbing p. 83f; Reinhold p. 100.—The act. πετάω='fly' in Achmes 236, 6. πετάομαι in Aristot., Metaph. 1009b, 38 [WChrist '38] v.l.; Syntipas 79, 28 v.l.) in our lit. only in Rv, and in the pres. ptc. πετώμενος, as the rdg. of the t.r. in 4: 7; 8: 13; 14: 6; 19: 17.*

πετεινόν, οῦ, τό subst. neut. of πετεινός, ή, όν (Theognis, trag., Hdt. et al.; Jos., Ant. 2, 245; 3, 137; Test. Levi 9: 13) *bird* B 11: 3 (Is 16: 2). Mostly pl. (Hdt.; Ostraka II 1523 [127 BC]; LXX; En. 7, 5; Jos., Ant. 8, 40; Sib. Or. 3, 224) Mt 13: 4; Mk 4: 4; Lk 12: 24. W. κτήνη (Gen 8: 17; Lev 7: 26) Hs 9, 1, 8; 9, 24, 1. W. τετράποδα, ἑρπετά Ac 10: 12; Ro 1: 23. W. τετράποδα, θηρία, ἑρπετά (Herm. Wr. 1, 11b) Ac 11: 6; w. still others PK 2 p. 14, 17. W. θηρία, ἑρπετά, ἐνάλια Js 3: 7. W. θηρία, ἰχθύες B 6: 12, 18 (cf. ἑρπετόν on these combinations). τὰ π. τοῦ οὐρανοῦ (s. οὐρανός 1d) *the birds of the air* Mt 6: 26; 8: 20; 13: 32 (cf. IQH 8, 9); Mk 4: 32; Lk 8: 5; 9: 58; 13: 19; Ac 10: 12; 11: 6; B 6: 12 (Gen 1: 28), 18; Hs 9, 24, 1. Of birds of prey B 10: 10. M-M.*

πέτομαι (Hom.+; inscr., pap., LXX; Philo, Gig. 6; Hecataeus in Jos., C. Ap. 1, 203. S. on πετάομαι) *fly* Rv 4: 7; 8: 13; 12: 14; 14: 6; 19: 17. M-M. B. 682.*

πέτρα, ας, ἡ (Hom. [πέτρη]+; inscr., pap., LXX, Philo; Jos., Bell. 6, 410, Ant. 6, 114; Test. 12 Patr.; loanw. in rabb.).
1. *rock*—a. lit., of the rock in which a tomb is hewn (s. λατομέω 1) Mt 27: 60; Mk 15: 46. The rocks split apart during an earthquake Mt 27: 51 (cf. PGM 12, 242). αἱ πέτραι w. τὰ ὄρη (PGM 13, 872; all the elements are in disorder) Rv 6: 16; likew. vs. 15, where πέτρα rather takes on the mng. *rocky grotto* (as Il. 2, 88; 4, 107; Soph., Phil. 16 al.; Judg 15: 13; 1 Km 13: 6; Is 2: 10; Pr 30: 26. Cf. Diod. S. 5, 39, 5 ἐν ταῖς κοίλαις πέτραις καὶ σπηλαίοις). πέτρα *rocky ground* Lk 8: 6, 13 (Maximus Tyr. 20, 9g ἐπὶ πετρῶν σπείρεις; Pla., Leg. 8 p. 838E; Ael. Aristid. 46 p. 302 D.; PSI 433, 6 [260 BC] οὐκ ἐφυτεύθη ἐπὶ τῆς πέτρας). It forms a suitable foundation for the building of a house Mt 7: 24f; Lk 6: 48a, b t.r.—Used w. an adj.: of Sinai π. ἔρημος *a barren rock* B 11: 3 (Is 16: 1). στερεὰ πέτρα 5: 14; 6: 3 (both Is 50: 7). π. ἰσχυρά 11: 4 (Is 33: 16). π. ἀκίνητος IPol 1: 1.—The rock in the vision of Hermas Hs 9, 2, 1f; 9, 3, 1; 9, 4, 2; 9, 5, 3; 9, 9, 7; 9, 12, 1 (the interpretation); 9, 13, 5; 9, 14, 4.—The rock at various places in the desert fr. which Moses drew water by striking it (Ex 17: 6; Num 20: 8ff; Ps 77: 15f, 20; Philo, Mos. 1, 210; Jos., Ant. 3, 86.—Apollon. Rhod. 4, 1444-46: Heracles, when thirsty, struck a πέτρη at the suggestion of a divinity, and a great stream of water gushed forth at once. Paul calls it πνευματικὴ πέτρα 1 Cor 10: 4a and identifies it w. the preëxistent Christ vs. 4b (EEEllis, JBL 76, '57, 53-6; Philo, Leg. All. 2, 86 πέτρα=σοφία, Det. Pot. Ins. 118=λόγος θεῖος).
b. in a play on words w. the name Πέτρος (GGander, RThPh n.s. 29, '41, 5-29). The apostle so named, or the affirmation he has just made, is the rock upon which Christ will build his church (for the figure s. Od. 17, 463.—Arrian, Anab. 4, 18, 4ff; 4, 21, 1ff; 4, 28, 1ff πέτρα is a rocky district [so also Antig. Car. 165] as the foun-

dation of an impregnable position or a rocky fortress; 4, 28, 1; 2 this kind of a πέτρα could not be conquered even by Heracles.—Diod. S. 19, 95, 2 and 4; 19, 96, 1; 19, 97, 1 and 2; 19, 98, 1 al. ἡ πέτρα [always with the article] is the rock [Petra] that keeps the Nabataeans safe from all enemy attacks; Stephan. Byz. s.v. Στάσις: πόλις ἐπὶ πέτρης μεγάλης of a city that cannot be taken) Mt 16: 18 (cf. ADell, ZNW 15, '14, 1-49; 17, '16, 27-32; OImmisch, ibid. 17, '16, 18-26; Harnack, SAB '18, 637-54; '27, 139-52; RBultmann, ZNW 19, '20, 165-74, ThBl 20, '41, 265-79; FKattenbusch, Der Quellort der Kirchenidee: Festgabe für Harnack '21, 143-72, Der Spruch über Pt. u. d. Kirche bei Mt: StKr 94, '22, 96-131; SEuringer, D. Locus Classicus des Primates: AEhrhard-Festschr. '22, 141-79; HDieckmann, Die Verfassung der Urkirche '23; JoachJeremias, Ἄγγελος II '26, 108-17; ECaspar, Primatus Petri '27; KGGoetz, Pt. als Gründer u. Oberhaupt der Kirche '27; JGeiselmann, D. petrin. Primat (Mt 16: 17ff) '27; BBartmann, ThGl 20, '28, 1-17; HKoch, Cathedra Petri '30; TEngert, 'Tu es Pt': Ricerche relig. 6, '30, 222-60; FXSeppelt, Gesch. d. Papsttums I '31, 9-46; JTurmel, La papauté '33, 101ff; VBurch, JBL 52, '33, 147-52; JHaller, D. Papsttum I '34, 1-31; ACCotter, CBQ 4, '42, 304-10; WGKümmel, Kirchenbegr. u. Gesch.-bewusstsein in d. Urgem. u. b. Jesus: Symb. Bibl. Ups. 1, '43; OJFSeitz, JBL 69, '50, 329-40. OCullmann, TWManson mem. vol., '59, 94-105; OBetz, ZNW 48, '57, 49-77; cf. IQH 6, 26-8; HClavier, Bultmann-Festschr., '54, 94-107.—OCullmann, TW VI '56, 94-9: πέτρα. S. also the lit. under Πέτρος, end).
2. *stone* (in an OT quot., where πέτρα is used in parallelism w. λίθος) π. σκανδάλου Ro 9: 33; 1 Pt 2: 8 (both Is 8: 14). M-M. B. 51.*

Πέτρος, ου, ὁ (ὁ πέτρος='stone' Hom.+; Jos., Bell. 3, 240, Ant. 7, 142.—Π. as a name can scarcely be pre-Christian, as AMerx, D. vier kanon. Ev. II 1, '02, 160ff, referring to Jos., Ant. 18, 156 [Niese did not accept the v.l. Πέτρος for Πρῶτος], would have it. S. on the other hand ADell [πέτρα 1b] esp. 14-17. Fr. the beginning it was prob. thought of as the Gk. equivalent of the Aram. כֵּיפָא=Κηφᾶς: J 1: 42; cf. Mt 16: 18 and JWackernagel, Syntax II² '28, 14f, perh. formed on the analogy of the Gk. male proper name Πέτρων: UPZ 149, 8 [III BC]; 135 [78 BC]; Plut., Mor. 422D.—A Gentile named Πέτρος in Damasc., Vi. Isid. 59. S. also the Praeses Arabiae of 278/79 AD Aurelius P.: Publ. Princeton Univ. Arch. Expedition to Syria III A, '13, 4 no. 546) *Peter*, surname of the head of the circle of Twelve Disciples, whose name was orig. Simon. His father was a certain John (s. Ἰωάννης 4) or Jonah (s. Ἰωνᾶς 2). Acc. to J 1: 44 he himself was from Bethsaida, but, at any rate, when he met Jesus he lived in Capernaum (Mk 1: 21, 29). Fr. that city he and his brother Andrew made their living as fishermen (Mk 1: 16). He was married (Mk 1: 30; cf. 1 Cor 9: 5), but left his home and occupation, when Jesus called, to follow him (Mk 1: 18; 10: 28). He belonged to the three or four most intimate of the Master's companions (Mk 5: 37; 9: 2; 13: 3; 14: 33). He stands at the head of the lists of the apostles (Mt 10: 2; Mk 3: 16; Lk 6: 14; Ac 1: 13). Not all the problems connected w. the conferring of the name Cephas-Peter upon Simon (s. Σίμων 1) have yet been solved (the giving of a new name and the reason for it: Plato [s. ὀνομάζω 1] and Theophrastus [Prolegom. 1 in CFHermann, Pla. VI 196 Θεόφραστος, Τύρταμος καλούμενος πάλαι, διὰ τὸ θεῖον τῆς φράσεως Θ. μετεκλήθη]; CRoth, Simon-Peter HTR 54, '61, 91-7). He was at least not always a model of rock-like (πέτρος is a symbol of imperturbability Soph., Oed. Rex 334; Eur., Med. 28 al.) firmness (cf. Gethsemane, the denial, the unsuccessful attempt at walking on the water; his conduct at Antioch Gal 2: 11ff which, however, is fr. time to time referred to another Cephas; cf. KLake, HTR 14, '21, 95ff; AMVöllmecke, Jahrbuch d. Missionshauses St. Gabriel 2, '25, 69-104; 3, '26, 31-75; DWRiddle, JBL 59, '40, 169-80; NHuffman, ibid. 64, '45, 205f; PGaechter, ZkTh 72, '50, 177-212). Despite all this he was the leader of Jesus' disciples, was spokesman for the Twelve (e.g. Mt 18: 21; 19: 27; Mk 8: 27ff; Lk 12: 41; 18: 28) and for the three who were closest to Jesus (Mk 9: 5); he was recognized as leader even by those on the outside (Mt 17: 24). He is especially prominent in the scene pictured by Mt 16: 17-19. Only in the Fourth Gospel does Peter have a place less prominent than another, in this case the 'disciple whom Jesus loved' (s. Hdb. exc. on J 13: 23). In connection w. the miraculous events after Jesus' death (on this ELohmeyer, Galiläa u. Jerusalem '36; WMichaelis, D. Erscheinungen d. Auferstandenen '44; MWerner, D. ntl. Berichte üb. d. Erscheinungen d. Auferstandenen: Schweiz. Theol. Umschau '44) Pt. played a unique role (1 Cor 15: 5; Lk 24: 34; Mk 16: 7). He was one of the pillars of the early church (Gal 2: 9). Three years after Paul was converted, on his first journey to Jerusalem as a Christian, he established a significant contact w. Peter (Gal 1: 18). At least until the time of the Apostolic Council (Gal 2: 1-10[?]; Ac 15: 7) he was the head of the early church. He was also active as a missionary to the Jews (Gal 2: 8; 1 Cor 9: 5.—MGoguel, L'apôtre Pierre a-t-il joué un rôle personnel dans les crises de Grèce et de Galatie?: RHPhr 14, '34, 461-500). In 1 Pt 1: 1 and 2 Pt 1: 1 he appears as author of an epistle. It is very probable that he died at Rome under Nero, about 64 AD.—In the NT he is somet. called (s. this; in Ac 15: 14 and 2 Pt 1: 1 more exactly Συμεών = שִׁמְעוֹן); except for Gal 2: 7f Paul always calls him Κηφᾶς (q.v.). Both names Σίμων Π. Mt 16: 16; Lk 5: 8; J 1: 40; 6: 8, 68; 13: 6, 9, 24, 36; 18: 10, 15, 25; 20: 2, 6; 21: 2f, 7b, 11, 15. Σίμων ὁ λεγόμενος Π. Mt 4: 18; 10: 2. Σίμων ὁ ἐπικαλούμενος Π. Ac 10: 18; 11: 13. Σίμων ὃς ἐπικαλεῖται Π. 10: 5, 32.—Outside the NT it is found in our lit. GEb 2; GP 14: 60 (Σίμων Πέτρος); 1 Cl 5: 4 (Paul follows in 5: 5); 2 Cl 5: 3f (a piece fr. an apocr. gosp.); IRo 4: 3 (Πέτρος καὶ Παῦλος); ISm 3: 2= GHeb 22; Papias 2: 4 (w. other disciples), 15 (w. Mark as his ἑρμηνευτής).—Zahn, Einl. II §38-44; KErbes, Petrus nicht in Rom, sondern in Jerusalem gestorben: ZKG 22, '01, 1ff; 161ff (against him AKneller, ZkTh 26, '02, 33ff; 225ff; 351ff); PWSchmiedel, War der Ap. Petrus in Rom?: PM 13, '09, 59-81; HLietzmann, Petrus u. Pls in Rom² '27; GEsser, Der hl. Ap. Petrus '02; CGuignebert, La primauté de St. Pierre et la venue de Pierre à Rome '09; FJFoakes-Jackson, Peter, Prince of Apostles '27; HDannenbauer, D. röm. Pt-Legende: Hist. Ztschr. 146, '32, 239-62; 159, '38, 81-8; KHeussi, War Pt. in Rom? '36, War Pt. wirklich röm. Märtyrer? '37, Neues z. Pt.-frage '39, ThLZ 77, '52, 67-72; HLietzmann, Pt. röm. Märt.: SAB '36, XXIX; DFRobinson, JBL 64, '45, 255-67; HSchmutz, Pt. war dennoch in Rom: Benedikt. Monatsschr. 22, '46, 128-41; EFascher, Pauly-W. XIX '38, 1335-61.—On Mt 16: 17-19 s., in addition to the lit. on κλείς and πέτρα 1b: JSchnitzer, Hat Jesus das Papsttum gestiftet? '10, Das Papsttum eine Stiftung Jesu? '10; FTillmann, Jesus u. das Papsttum '10; AKneller, ZkTh 44, '20, 147-69; OLinton, D. Problem der Urkirche '32, 157-83; KPieper, Jes. u. d. Kirche '32; AEhrhard, Urkirche u. Frühkatholizismus I 1, '36.—JMunck, Pt. u. Pls

in der Offenb. Joh. '50 (Rv 11: 3-13).—OCullmann, Petrus², '60 (Eng. transl. Peter, FVFilson², '62), L'apôtre Pierre: NT Essays (TWManson memorial vol.), '59, 94-105; OKarrer, Peter and the Church: an examination of the Cullmann thesis, '63; RTO'Callaghan, Vatican Excavations and the Tomb of Peter: Bibl. Archeologist 16, '53, 70-87; AvGerkan, D. Forschung nach dem Grab Petri, ZNW 44, '52/'53, 196-205, Zu den Problemen des Petrusgrabes: Jahrb. f. Antike u. Christent. '58, 79-93; GF Snyder, Bibl. Archaeologist 32, '69, 2-24; JGwynGriffiths, Hibbert Journal 55, '56/'57, 140-9; TDBarnes, JTS 21, '70, 175-9; GSchulze-Kadelbach, D. Stellung des P. in der Urchristenheit: ThLZ 81, '56, 1-18 (lit.); PGaechter, Petrus u. seine Zeit, '58; EKirschbaum, The Tombs of St. Peter and St. Paul (transl. JMurray) '59; EHaenchen, Petrus-Probleme, NTS 7, '60/'61, 187-97; SAgourides, Πέτρος καὶ Ἰωάννης ἐν τῷ τετάρτῳ Εὐαγγελίῳ, Thessalonike, '66; DGewalt, Petrus, Diss. Hdlbg, '66; RBrown, KDonfried, JReumann edd., Peter in the NT, '73.—OCullmann, TW VI, '56, 99-112. M-M.

πετρώδης, ες (Soph. +) rocky, stony (so Hippocr., Aristot.; Jos., Bell. 7, 166, Vi. 187) subst. τὸ πετρῶδες Mk 4: 5 and τὰ πετρώδη (Aristot., Hist. An. 5, 17) Mt 13: 5, 20; Mk 4: 16 rocky ground, over which a thin layer of soil is spread (ὅπου οὐκ εἶχεν γῆν πολλήν). GDalman, Pj 22, '26, 124ff.*

Πετρώνιος, ου, ὁ rather freq. name (cf. e.g. Dit., Or. 538, 4; pap.; Philo, Leg. ad Gai. 209; Jos., Ant. 15, 307) Petronius, the centurion who commanded the guard at the grave GP 8: 31.—LVaganay, L'Évang. de Pierre '30, 283f.*

πεφίμωσο s. φιμόω.

πήγανον, ου, τό (Aristoph. +; Theophr., Hist. Pl. 1, 3, 4; Diosc. 3, 45 al.; POxy. 1675, 4; PTebt. 273 introd.; CWessely, Stud. z. Paläographie u. Papyruskunde 20['21], 27, 5; Jos., Bell. 7, 178; loanw. in rabb.) rue (ruta graveolens), mentioned among the garden herbs that are tithed Lk 11: 42 (the parallel Mt 23: 23 has ἄνηθον, hence EbNestle, ZNW 7, '06, 260f suspects an interchange of שַׁבְרָא and שִׁבַּתְּא). Acc. to the Mishna (Shebi'ith IX 1; cf. Billerb. II 189) it was not necessary to tithe it.—RStrömberg, Griech. Pflanzennamen '40, 144; EEFBishop, ET 59, '47/'48, 81; DCorrens, ΧΑΡΙΣ ΚΑΙ ΣΟΦΙΑ (KRengstorf-Festschr.), '64, 110-2. M-M.*

πηγή, ῆς, ἡ (Hom. +; inscr., pap., LXX; Ep. Arist. 89; Philo, Joseph.; Sib. Or. 2, 318; loanw. in rabb.) spring of water, fountain.

1. lit. Js 3: 11, 12 t.r.; Hs 9, 1, 8; 9, 25, 1. (αἱ) πηγαὶ (τῶν) ὑδάτων (the) springs of water (cf. Lev 11: 36; Num 33: 9; 3 Km 18: 5; Jdth 7: 7; Ps 17: 16; Jos., Ant. 2, 294) Rv 8: 10; 14: 7; 16: 4. ἀέναοι πηγαί everflowing springs 1 Cl 20: 10 (ἀέναος 1). As typical of sinners πηγαὶ ἄνυδροι (s. ἄνυδρος) 2 Pt 2: 17. Of a specific well (called φρέαρ in J 4: 11f; cf. Mod. Gk. πηγάδι='well'.—WRHutton, ET 57, '45/'46, 27) π. τοῦ Ἰακώβ, at the foot of Mt Gerizim (on the location of Jacob's well s. Dalman, Orte³ 226ff) J 4: 6a; cf. b (Paus. 8, 23, 4 ὀλίγον ὑπὲρ τ. πόλιν π. ἐστιν καὶ ἐπὶ τῇ π. . . .).—ἡ πηγὴ τοῦ αἵματος αὐτῆς (Lev 12: 7) Mk 5: 29 (Alex. Aphr., An. p. 40, 2 Bruns πηγὴ τ. αἵματος. Cf. πηγὴ δακρύων: Soph., Ant. 803; Charito 1, 3, 6; 2, 3, 6; 6, 7, 10; Achilles Tat. 7, 4, 6).

2. Quite symbolic (s. Hdb. exc. on J 4: 14 and cf. Dio Chrys. 15[32], 15 τὸ σῷζον [ὕδωρ] ἄνωθέν ποθεν ἐκ δαιμονίου τινὸς πηγῆς κάτεισι. In schol. on Pla. 611c

ἀθάνατος πηγή is a spring whose water bestows immortality) is its usage in some NT pass.: ἡ πηγὴ τοῦ ὕδατος τῆς ζωῆς *the spring of the water of life* Rv 21: 6; in the pl. ζωῆς πηγαὶ ὑδάτων 7: 17; πηγὴ ὕδατος ἀλλομένου εἰς ζωὴν αἰώνιον *a spring of water welling up for eternal life* J 4: 14 (Essenes apply this figure to the Torah, e.g., CD 6, 4; also s. Hdb. ad loc.).

3. fig., of the place of origin or the cause of a full abundance of someth. (Pind.+; Epict. 3, 1, 18 Apollo as πηγὴ τῆς ἀληθείας [πηγὴ ἀληθ. also in Himerius, Or. 48 [Or. 14], 35; Maximus Tyr. 12, 6c; 13, 9c; Philo, Mos. 1, 84) πηγὴ ζωῆς *source of life* (Pr 10: 11; 13: 14; 14: 27) of God B 11: 2 (Jer 2: 13 and 17: 13. Cf. Ps 35: 10); cf. B 1: 3 Funk.—WMichaelis, TW VI 112-17. M-M. B. 44.*

πήγνυμι 1 aor. ἔπηξα, ptc. πήξας (Hom.+; inscr., pap., LXX, Philo, Joseph.; Sib. Or. 5, 210).

1. *make firm, fix* of God's creative activity (Ps.-Lucian, Philopatr. 17 [θεὸς] γῆν ἐφ᾽ ὕδατος ἔπηξεν) τὸν οὐρανόν *the heaven* Hv 1, 3, 4 (cf. Is 42: 5). Pass., of milk *curdle* (Aristot., Part. An. 3, 15 p. 676a, 14 γάλα πήγνυται; Cyranides p. 63, 13) AP fgm. 2 p. 12, 24f.

2. *put together, build* σκηνήν *pitch a tent* (Pla., Leg. 7 p. 817c; Polyb. 6, 27, 2; 6 al.; Gen 26: 25; 31: 25; Num 24: 6; Judg 4: 11; Jos., Ant. 3, 247) GP 8: 33. Of the tabernacle (Ex 33: 7; 38: 26; Josh 18: 1; Philo, Leg. All. 2, 54) *set up* Hb 8: 2. M-M.*

πηδάλιον, ου, τό (Hom.+; POxy. 1449, 14; 1650, 11) *steering paddle, rudder* Js 3: 4 (w. χαλινός vs. 3; cf. the combination of rudder and bridle Plut., Mor. 33F καθάπερ ἱππεὺς διὰ χαλινοῦ καὶ [διὰ] πηδαλίου κυβερνήτης [HAlmqvist, Plut. u. das NT '46, 132f]; cf. Aristot., Mech. 5, 850b). Pl. (as PLond. 1164h, 8) Ac 27: 40, since each ship had two rudders, connected by a crossbar and operated by one man. M-M. B. 734.*

πηδάω (Hom.+; LXX; Philo, In Flacc. 162) *leap, spring* of a bolt of fire (Pla., Ep. 7 p. 341c) ἀπό τινος *from someone* AP fgm. 1 p. 12, 15. B. 688.*

πηλίκος, η, ον (Pla.+; LXX; Ep. Arist. 52; Jos., Ant. 13, 1) correlative pron. *how large?* but in our lit., in both places where it occurs, in an exclamation (for class. ἠλίκος; cf. Bl-D. §304; Rob. 741).

1. lit. ἴδετε πηλίκοις ὑμῖν γράμμασιν ἔγραψα *see with what large letters I am writing to you* Gal 6: 11 (Dssm., B 264 [BS 358]. Against him KLClarke, ET 24, '13, 285 and JSClemens, ibid. 380.—CStarcke, D. Rhetorik des Ap. Pls im Gal u. die 'πηλίκα γράμματα': Progr. Stargard i. P. '11).

2. fig. *how great* of Melchizedek θεωρεῖτε πηλίκος οὗτος *consider how great this man must have been* Hb 7: 4. M-M.*

πήλινος, η, ον (Demosth.+; PPetr. III 48, 9 [241 BC]; LXX; Sib. Or. 3, 589) *made of clay* οἰκίας π. *houses of clay* 1 Cl 39: 5 (Job 4: 19).*

πηλός, οῦ, ὁ (Aeschyl., Hdt.+; Dit., Or. 483, 61; PRainer 232, 17; POxy. 1450, 4; LXX, Philo, Joseph.).

1. *clay*—a. used in making pottery (trag.+; Polyb. 15, 35, 2 [the potter deals with ὁ τροχός=potter's wheel and ὁ πηλός]; Is 29: 16; 41: 25; Jer 18: 6; Sir 33: 13) Ro 9: 21 (cf. esp. Wsd 15: 7).—In a comparison that has allegorical traits mankind is called πηλὸς εἰς τὴν χεῖρα τοῦ τεχνίτου 2 Cl 8: 2 (=ἐν τῇ χειρί, s. εἰς 9a).

b. Like the pliable material which the artist uses (Jos., C. Ap. 2, 252), clay is also the material fr. which man is made (cf. Aristoph., Av. 686 πηλοῦ πλάσματα of men; Herodas 2, 28f; Epict. 4, 11, 27; Lucian, Prometh. 13;

Themist., Or. 32 after Aesop; Job 10: 9) 1 Cl 39: 5 (Job 4: 19).

2. *mud, mire* (Pla., Parm. 130c π. καὶ ῥύπος; Plut., Marius 16, 7, Mor. 993E; 1059F οἱ πηλὸν ἢ κονιορτὸν ἐπὶ τοῦ σώματος ἔχοντες), esp. of the soft mass produced when the ground is wet, e.g. on the roads (Aeneas Tact. 1421; Herodas 1, 14; Arrian, Anab. 5, 15, 2; 2 Km 22: 43; Zech 9: 3; 10: 5; Jos., Ant. 1, 244). Jesus ἔπτυσεν χαμαὶ καὶ ἐποίησεν πηλὸν ἐκ τοῦ πτύσματος J 9: 6a (π. ποιεῖν like Charito 1, 3, 2); cf. b, 11, 14, 15. For the use of πηλός in the healing art of ancient times, even on the part of benevolent divinities s. Hdb. ad loc. and KHRengstorf, Die Anfänge der Auseinandersetzung zw. Christusglaube u. Asklepiosfrömmigkeit '53, p. 39f, note 61, also TW VI '56, 118f. M-M. B. 20.*

πήρα, ας, ἡ (Hom.+; Jdth 10: 5; 13: 10, 15; Joseph.; Sib. Or. 6, 15) *knapsack, traveler's bag* which Jesus' disciples were directed not to take w. them when they were sent out, since it was not absolutely necessary (s. on ὑπόδημα) Mt 10: 10; Mk 6: 8; Lk 9: 3; 10: 4; 22: 35; cf. vs. 36. But perh. this pass. has in mind the more specialized mng. *beggar's bag* (Diog. L. 6, 33; Gk. inscr. fr. Syria: Bull. de corr. hell. 21, 1897 p. 60; PGM 4, 2381; 2400. Cf. Const. Apost. 3, 6. Such a bag was part of a Cynic itinerant preacher's equipment [PWendland, D. hellenist.-röm. Kultur²,³ '12, 84. Crates the Cynic wrote a piece entitled Πήρα: HDiels, Poetae Philosophi '02 fgm. 4 p. 218. Cf. Dio Chrys. 49(66), 21; Lucian, Dial. Mort. 1, 3; Alciphr. 3, 19, 5].— Acc. to Diog. L. 6, 13 Antisthenes the Cynic was the first one to fold his cloak double [so he could sleep on it]—6, 22—and take a staff and πήρα with him—Dssm., LO 87 [LAE 108ff]; SKrauss, Ἄγγελος I '25, 96ff; KHRengstorf, Jebamot '29, 214f).—Such a bag was also used by shepherds (Ammon. Gramm. [I/II AD], Diff. 112 πήρα . . . φέρουσιν οἱ ποιμένες; Longus 1, 13, 1; 3, 15, 3; Aesop 31b H.; Babr. 86, 2; Jos., Ant. 6, 185 π. ποιμενική; s. the statue of the Good Shepherd in the Lateran) Hv 5: 1; s 6, 2, 5; 9, 10, 5.—WMichaelis, TW VI 119-21. M-M.*

πηρός, ά, όν (Hom.+; pap., Philo; Sib. Or. 3, 793) *maimed, disabled, weakened* in any part of the body, w. ref. to the eyes *blind* (Appian, Samn. 9 §5; Aesop, Fab. 37 P.=57 H.), fig. (Philo, Somn. 1, 27 πρὸς αἴσθησιν πηροί; Ps.-Lucian, Am. 46 πηροὶ οἱ τῆς διανοίας λογισμοί) πηροὶ τῇ διανοίᾳ *blind in mind* 2 Cl 1: 6.*

πηρόω (Aristoph., Hippocr.+; Job 17: 7 v.l.; 4 Macc 18: 21; Philo; Jos., C. Ap. 2, 15) *disable, maim* in our lit. in several places as v.l. for πωρόω (the witnesses also vary in the same way in Job 17: 7) ἐπήρωσεν αὐτῶν τὴν καρδίαν J 12: 40 v.l. Pass. (M. Ant. 5, 8, 13) Mk 8: 17 v.l. οἱ λοιποὶ ἐπηρώθησαν Ro 11: 7 v.l. (here the mng. is surely to *blind*, which πηρόω signifies as early as Aristot., Hist. An. 620a, 1 and Ephorus [IV BC]: 70, fgm. 1 Jac.; likew. schol. on Apollon. Rhod. 2, introd. and 2, 182). On Ac 5: 3 v.l. see πληρόω 1a.*

πήρωσις, εως, ἡ (since Democr. 296; Hippocr.; Maximus Tyr. 29, 2f; Dt 28: 28 Aq.; Philo; Jos., Ant. 1, 267) *disabling,* esp. also *shortsightedness, blindness* (Dio Chrys. 47[64], 6; Artem. 2, 36 p. 134, 28 ὀφθαλμῶν π.; Lucian, Dom. 29) fig. (Manetho 4, 518 π. ψυχῆς; Philo, Ebr. 160, Omn. Prob. Lib. 55 λογισμοῦ π.) π. τῆς καρδίας Mk 3: 5 v.l. (s. πώρωσις).*

πηχυαῖος, α, ον (Hdt.+; inscr.) *a cubit* (about 18 inches) *long* of sticks Hs 8, 1, 2.*

πῆχυς, εως, ὁ (Hom.+; inscr., pap., LXX, Ep. Arist.) gen. pl. πηχῶν (Hellenistic: Polyb.; Diod. S.; Hero Alex.;

Plut.; Dit., Syll.³ 1231, 14; pap. [Mayser p. 267]; LXX [cf. Thackeray p. 151, 21]; En. 7, 2; Jos., Bell. 6, 166, C. Ap. 2, 119; Sib. Or. 5, 57.—Phryn. p. 245 L.; Dssm., B 152 [BS 153f]; Bl-D. §48; Mlt.-H. 140f) orig. *forearm*, then *cubit* or *ell* as a measure of length (about 18 inches, or .462 of a meter.—KFHermann, Lehrb. der griech. Antiquitäten IV³ 1882, 438ff; FHultsch, APF 3, '06, 438ff) Rv 21: 17 (Lucian's marvelous city [Ver. Hist. 2, 11] is measured not by the ordinary human cubit, but by the πῆχυς βασιλικός). ὡς ἀπὸ πηχῶν διακοσίων *about a hundred yards away* (s. ἀπό III) J 21: 8. προσθεῖναι πῆχυν (Epicharmus in Diog. L. 3, 11): προσθεῖναι ἐπὶ τὴν ἡλικίαν αὐτοῦ π. (ἕνα) *add a single hour to his life* (s. ἡλικία 1a and cf. Mimnermus 2, 3 Diehl² πήχυιον ἐπὶ χρόνον= 'for only a cubit of time'. This is a small matter, but a πῆχυς of bodily stature is monstrously large. Alcaeus, fgm. 50 D.² gives the measurement of an enormous giant as less than 5 cubits) Mt 6: 27; Lk 12: 25 (Damasc., Vi. Isid. 166 of spiritual growth: αὔξεσθαι κατὰ πῆχυν; Epict. 3, 2, 10 γέγονέ σου τὸ ψυχάριον ἀντὶ δακτυλιαίου δίπηχυ= your little soul, as long as a finger, has become two cubits in length [because you were praised]). M-M. B. 236f.*

πιάζω (Alcman 28 D.²; Theocr. 4, 35; Sethianische Verfluchungstafeln 49, 58; 59 Wünsch [1898]; POxy. 812, 5 [5 BC]; PHamb. 6, 16; LXX [cf. Thackeray 282.—Bl-D. §29, 2; 101 p. 48; Mlt.-H. 69; 254; 405]; Test. Napht. 5: 2, 3) Doric and colloq. for Attic πιέζω (cf. Thumb 67 note) 1 aor. ἐπίασα, pass. ἐπιάσθην, only in the sense *take hold of, seize, grasp.*
1. neutral *take (hold of)* τινὰ τῆς χειρός *someone by the hand* Ac 3: 7 (cf. Theocr. 4, 35 τὸν ταῦρον ὁπλᾶς).
2. w. hostile intent—**a.** of men *seize, arrest, take into custody* (cf. BGU 325, 2 λῃστοπιαστής) τινά *someone* (PGM 5, 172 κλέπτην) J 7: 30, 32, 44; 8: 20; 10: 39; 11: 57; UGosp 18; 2 Cor 11: 32. ὃν πιάσας ἔθετο εἰς φυλακήν Ac 12: 4.
b. of animals *catch* (SSol 2: 15) of fish (PLond. II p. 328, 76) J 21: 3, 10. Pass. ἐπιάσθη τὸ θηρίον Rv 19: 20. M-M. B. 575; 744.*

πίε, πιεῖν, πίεσαι s. πίνω.

πιέζω pf. pass. ptc. πεπιεσμένος (Hom.+; Hero Alex. I p. 58, 4; Dit., Syll.³ 904, 7; pap.; Mi 6: 15 πιέσεις ἐλαίαν; Philo, Migr. Abr. 157, Aet. M. 129; Jos., Ant. 17, 28. Cf. πιάζω) *press* μέτρον πεπιεσμένον *a measure that is pressed down* Lk 6: 38. M-M. B. 575; 744.*

πιθανολογία, ας, ἡ *persuasive speech, art of persuasion* (so Pla., Theaet. 162E) in an unfavorable sense in its only occurrence in our lit. ἐν πιθανολογίᾳ *by plausible* (but false) *arguments* Col 2: 4 (cf. PLeipz. 40 III, 7 διὰ πιθανολογίας). M-M.*

πίθηκος, ου, ὁ (Aristoph., Pla.+; Lucian, Philops. 5; Plut., Mor. 52B; pap. [Sb 2009]; 2 Ch 9: 21; Jos., Ant. 8, 181) *ape* PK 2 p. 14, 20.*

πιθός the spelling preferred by W-H. for πειθός (q.v.).

πικραίνω fut. πικρανῶ; 1 aor. pass. ἐπικράνθην *make bitter*—1. lit. (Hippocr. et al.) πικρανεῖ σου τὴν κοιλίαν (κοιλία 1) Rv 10: 9. Pass., of the stomach ἐπικράνθη ἡ κοιλία vs. 10. Of someth. that has been swallowed: (τὰ ὕδατα) ἐπικράνθησαν 8: 11 (prob. not of οἱ ἄνθρωποι, who were 'made bitter'= poisoned). Of honey when wormwood is mixed w. it Hm 5, 1, 5.
2. fig. *make bitter, embitter* (Pla.+; LXX) pass. *become bitter* or *embittered* abs. (Demosth., Ep. 1, 6; Ep.

---

6 of Apollonius of Tyana: Philostrat. I 346, 19; Is 14: 9; Philo, Mos. 1, 302) Hm 10, 2, 3. π. πρός τινα *be embittered against someone* Col 3: 19 (πρός τινα as Lynceus in Athen. 6 p. 242B). M-M.*

πικρία, ας, ἡ (Demosth., Aristot.+; pap., LXX) *bitterness*—1. lit. (Theophr., C. Pl. 6, 10, 7; Plut., Mor. 897A), but used symbolically, of a βοτάνη πικρίαν ἔχουσα *a plant that has a bitter taste* GEg 1d (Diog. L. 9, 80 πικρός is 'inedible' in contrast to ἐδώδιμος. Likew. Jos., Ant. 3, 30 πικρία= 'inedibility'). A reprehensible pers. is called χολὴ πικρίας= χολὴ πικρά (on the close connection of χολή w. πικρία s. Vett. Val. 249, 16; Dt 29: 17; La 3: 19; Test. Napht. 2: 8) *bitter gall* Ac 8: 23. ῥίζα πικρίας *a bitter root*, a root that bears bitter fruit Hb 12: 15 (cf. Dt 29: 17; Hippocr., Ep. 16, 4 τ. πικρὴν ῥίζαν ἐκκόψαι).
2. fig. *bitterness, animosity, anger, harshness* (Demosth.+; Bion of Borysthenes [III BC] in Diog. L. 4, 46 [of the inhuman cruelty of a slaveholder]; LXX, Philo); it arises from ὀξυχολία Hm 5, 2, 4; 5, 2, 8; 6, 2, 5. ἐν π. γίνεσθαι *become embittered* m 5, 2, 2. ἐπιτάσσειν τινὶ ἐν π. *give an order to someone harshly* B 19: 7; cf. D 4: 10. W. θυμός, ὀργή al. (cf. Philo, Ebr. 223; Jos., Ant. 17, 148) in a list of vices Eph 4: 31. τὸ στόμα ἀρᾶς καὶ πικρίας γέμει *the mouth is full of curses and of bitter words* Ro 3: 14 (Ps 13: 3; cf. 9: 28. π. γέμειν as Philo, Migr. Abr. 36). M-M.*

πικρός, ά, όν (Hom.+; pap., LXX, Test. 12 Patr.) *bitter*
1. lit. (opp. γλυκύς; cf. Pla., Theaet. 166E πικρῷ γλυκὺ μεμιγμένον; Pr 27: 7) of water that is not potable (as Appian, Iber. 88, 385; Ex 15: 23; Philo, Rer. Div. Her. 208; Jos., Bell. 4, 476; 7, 186 [opp. γλυκύς]) Js 3: 11 (τὸν θυμόν 𝔓⁷⁴).
2. fig. *bitter, embittered, harsh* ζῆλον π. ἔχειν ἐν τῇ καρδίᾳ *have bitter jealousy in one's heart* Js 3: 14. Of ὀξυχολία (πικρία 2) Hm 5, 1, 6. Of the commandments of the devil m 12, 4, 6. Of persons (trag. et al.; Diod. S. 14, 65, 4 π. τύραννος; Aelian, fgm. 74 p. 222, 27; 103 p. 235, 24; Alciphr. 1, 15, 5; Philo, Omn. Prob. Lib. 106; Jos., C. Ap. 2, 277) *harsh* (w. ὀξύχολος and ἄφρων) m 6, 2, 4; (w. ἄσπλαγχνος) s 6, 3, 2. Of patience μηδὲν ἐν ἑαυτῇ ἔχουσα πικρόν *it has no bitterness in it* m 5, 2, 3.—WMichaelis, TW VI 122-7: πικρός and related words. M-M. B. 1033.*

πικρῶς adv. (Aeschyl.+; pap., LXX) *bitterly*, fig. (Diod. S. 3, 71, 3 of the painful oppression of Cronus' rule; Appian, Liby. 100 §472 π. κολάζειν= punish severely; Jos., Ant. 9, 118 βλασφημεῖν) κλαίειν (Is 22: 4; 33: 7) *weep bitterly* Mt 26: 75; Lk 22: 62. M-M.*

Πιλᾶτος, ου, ὁ (on the form Πειλᾶτος, which is preferred by Tdf. and W-H., s. Tdf., Proleg. 84f; W-H., app. 155. On the use of the art. w. it W-S. §18, 6d) *Pilate* (Pontius P.), procurator of Judaea 26-36 AD (s. PLHedley, JTS 35, '34, 56f). He played the decisive role in Jesus' trial and gave the order for his crucifixion. Mt 27: 2ff; Mk 15: 1ff; Lk 3: 1; 13: 1 (this is the only place in our lit. where a detail is given fr. his life outside the Passion Narrative. SEJohnson, ATR 17, '35, 91-5; JBlinzler, NovT 2, '58, 24-49); 23: 1ff; J 18: 29ff; 19: 1ff; Ac 3: 13; 4: 27; 13: 28, 29 D; 1 Ti 6: 13 (s. μαρτυρέω 1d); IMg 11; ITr 9: 1; ISm 1: 2; GP 1: 1; 2: 3-5; 8: 29, 31; 11: 43, 45f, 49.—Non-Christian sources, esp. Tacitus, Ann. 15, 44; Philo, Leg. ad Gai. 299-305 based on a letter of Agrippa I; Jos., Bell. 2, 169-77, Ant. 18, 35; 55-64; 85-9; 177.—Schürer I⁴ 487ff; HPeter, Pontius Pilatus: NJklA 19, '07, 1-40; KKastner, Jesus vor Pilatus '12; MDibelius, 'Herodes u. Pilatus': ZNW 16, '15, 113-26; BSEaston, The Trial of Jesus: AJTh

19, '15, 430-52; RWHusband, The Prosecution of Jesus '16; FDoerr (attorney), Der Prozess Jesu in rechtsgesch. Beleuchtung '20; GBertram, Die Leidensgesch. Jesu u. der Christuskult '22, 62-72; GLippert (attorney), Pil. als Richter '23; PRoué, Le procès de Jésus '24; GRosadi, D. Prozess Jesu '26, Il processo di Gesù[14] '33; GAicher, D. Proz. Jesu '29; MRadin, The Trial of Jes. of Naz. '31; SLiberty, The Importance of P.P. in Creed and Gosp.: JTS 45, '44, 38-56; JBlinzler, D. Prozess Jesu '51, Münchener Theol. Ztschr. 5, '54, 171-84.—On Pilate's wife: E Fascher, ThLZ 72, '47, 201-4; AOepke, ibid. 73, '48, 743-6.—S. also s.v. ἀποκτείνω 1a, and Feigel, Weidel and Finegan s.v. Ἰούδας 6.—EStauffer, Zur Münzprägung u. Judenpolitik des Pontius Pilatus: La Nouvelle Clio 9, '50, 495-514; EBammell, Syrian Coinage and Pilate: Journ. of Jewish Studies 2, '51, 108-10. M-M. s.v. Πειλ.*

πίμπλημι 1 aor. ἔπλησα. Pass.: 1 aor. ἐπλήσθην; 1 fut. πλησθήσομαι (Hom.+; pap., LXX, En., Joseph.; Sib. Or. 3, 311.—On the spelling Bl-D. §93; 101; Thackeray p. 110; Mlt.-H. 106).
1. *fill, fulfill*—**a.** lit.—**α.** of external, perceptible things τὶ *someth.* Lk 5: 7 τὶ τινος *someth. with someth.* (Hom.+; PLond. 453, 6; LXX) a sponge w. vinegar Mt 27: 48; Mk 15: 36 D; J 19: 29 t.r. Pass. (Jos., Ant. 3, 299) ἐπλήσθη ὁ νυμφὼν ἀνακειμένων Mt 22: 10. ἐπλήσθη ἡ πόλις τῆς συγχύσεως Ac 19: 29.—ἡ οἰκία ἐπλήσθη ἐκ τῆς ὀσμῆς J 12: 3 v.l. (Hom. Hymns, Dem. 280 αὐγῆς ἐπλήσθη δόμος).
β. of man's inner life (Hom.+; Diod. S. 15, 37, 2 φρονήματος [with enthusiasm] ἐπίμπλαντο; PGM 13, 234 πλησθεὶς τῆς θεοσοφίας; LXX) pass. ἐπλήσθησαν φόβου (Appian, Bell. Civ. 4, 48 §204) Lk 5: 26; ἀνοίας 6: 11; θάμβους καὶ ἐκστάσεως Ac 3: 10; ζήλου 5: 17; 13: 45; θυμοῦ (Da 3: 19) Lk 4: 28. Of the Holy Spirit (cf. Sir 48: 12a; Pr 15: 4.—Dio Chrys. 55[72], 12 the Pythia is ἐμπιμπλαμένη τοῦ πνεύματος): πνεύματος ἁγίου πλησθήσεται Lk 1: 15; cf. vs. 41, 67; Ac 2: 4; 4: 8, 31; 9: 17; 13: 9.
b. fig.—**α.** of prophecies, pass. *be fulfilled* Lk 1: 20 v.l.; 21: 22.—**β.** of a period of time that passes or comes to an end, pass. ἐπλήσθησαν αἱ ἡμέραι *the days came to an end* Lk 1: 23. A gen. added denotes the event that follows upon the expiration of the time: ἐπλήσθη ὁ χρόνος τοῦ τεκεῖν αὐτήν *the time for her to be delivered came to an end* Lk 1: 57. Cf. 2: 6, 21, 22.
γ. ἐπλήσθησαν αἱ ἀνομίαι αὐτῶν *the measure of their iniquities has become full* Hv 2, 2, 2.
2. *satiate* pass. *be satiated, have one's fill* τινός *with or of someth.* (Soph., Ant. 121; Epigram of Ptolemaeus: Anth. Pal. 9, 577 πίμπλαμαι ἀμβροσίης) τῆς ἀσεβείας 1 Cl 57: 6 (Pr 1: 31).—GDelling, TW VI 127-34: πίμπλημι and related words. M-M.*

πίμπρημι pass.: πίμπραμαι, inf. πίμπρασθαι; 1 aor. ptc. πρησθείς (Hom.+; inscr., LXX.—On the spelling s. Bl-D. §93; 101; Mlt.-H. 106; Thackeray p. 110) a medical term (Hobart 50), but by no means confined to that profession. The pass. means either
1. *burn with fever* (Pherecrates Com. [V BC], fgm. 80, 4 Kock; Dit., Syll.³ 1179, 15 [cf. note 6]; 1180, 3) or
2. *become distended, swell up* (Hippocr. et al.; Dit., Syll.³ 1169, 123; Num 5: 21, 27; Jos., Ant. 3, 271. Field, Notes 149). Of Judas, Papias 3. Either mng. is poss. in προσεδόκων αὐτὸν μέλλειν πίμπρασθαι Ac 28: 6. M-M. B. 75.*

πινακίδιον, ου, τό (Hippocr., Aristot. et al.) dim. of

πίναξ *little* (wooden) *tablet*, esp. of a writing-tablet for notes (Epict. 3, 22, 74; Sym. Ezk 9: 2) Lk 1: 63. M-M.*

πινακίς, ίδος, ἡ *little* (wooden) *writing tablet* (Macho [III BC] in Athen. 13 p. 582c al.; WSchubart, Der Gnomon d. Idios Logos '19 [= BGU V] 36; PRyl. 144, 19 [38 AD]; Sym. Ezk 9: 11; Artapanus in Euseb., Pr. Ev. 9, 27, 26) Lk 1: 63 v.l. S. πινακίδιον.*

πίναξ, ακος, ἡ (Hom.+; inscr., pap.) *platter, dish* (Hom.+; BGU 781 V, 16; CWessely, Stud. z. Paläographie u. Papyruskunde 20['21] 67, 22; Jos., Bell. 5, 562, Ant. 8, 91; loanw. in rabb.) ἐπὶ πίνακι *on a platter* (s. φέρω 4aa) Mt 14: 8, 11; Mk 6: 25, 28. W. ποτήριον Lk 11: 39. M-M. B. 345; 599.*

πίνω (Hom.+; inscr., pap., LXX; En. 102, 9 φαγεῖν κ. πεῖν; Philo, Joseph., Test. 12 Patr.; Sib. Or. 4, 26 al.) impf. ἔπινον; fut. πίομαι (Bl-D. §74, 2; 77; Rob. 354), 2 sing. πίεσαι (Ruth 2: 9; Bl-D. §87; Thackeray p. 218; 282; Rob. 340; Mlt.-H. 198); 2 aor. ἔπιον (on ἔπιαν 1 Cor 10: 4 D cf. Bl-D. §81, 3 app.; Mlt.-H. 208), imper. πίε, πιέτω, inf. πιεῖν (contracted πεῖν [πῖν]; cf. Bl-D. §101 p. 48; §31, 2; Rob. 72; 204; Mayser 365; Thackeray p. 63f; W-H., app. 170); perf. πέπωκα (W-S. §13, 15; Bl-D. §83, 1) *drink*.
1. lit., w. acc. of the thing Mt 6: 25; 26: 29b; Mk 16: 18; Lk 1: 15 (cf. Dt 29: 5); 5: 39; 12: 29; J 6: 53f, 56 (cf. the picture in Jos., Bell. 5, 344 ἐσθίειν . . . καὶ τὸ τῆς πόλεως αἷμα πίνειν; Ro 14: 21 (Is 22: 13) al. τί πίωμεν; *what will we have to drink?* Mt 6: 31. ἐσθίειν καὶ πίνειν τὰ παρά τινος *eat and drink what someone sets before one* Lk 10: 7. Foll. by ἀπό τινος *drink* (of) *someth.* (Ctesias in Sotion [I/II AD], fgm. 17 in the Παραδοξογρ. p. 183-91 Westerm. π. ἀπ᾽ αὐτῆς [a spring]; Ael. Aristid. 39, 4 K.=18 p. 409 D.; Jer 28: 7) 22: 18. μηδεὶς φαγέτω μηδὲ πιέτω ἀπὸ τῆς εὐχαριστίας D 9: 5. Foll. by ἔκ τινος (of) *someth.* (Gen 9: 21; Syntipas p. 43, 15 ἐκ τοῦ δηλητηρίου πίομαι) Mt 26: 29a; Mk 14: 25a; J 4: 13f. Foll. by acc. of the vessel fr. which one drinks, in which case the vessel and its contents are identified (ποτήριον 1) ποτήριον κυρίου πίνειν 1 Cor 10: 21; cf. 11: 26f. The vessel can also be introduced by ἐκ (Hipponax [VI BC] 16 and 17 D.²; Aristoph., Equ. 1289; Pla., Rep. 417A; X., An. 6, 1, 4 ἐκ ποτηρίων; Dit., Syll.³ 1168, 80) ἐκ τοῦ ποτηρίου πινέτω (s. 2 Km 12: 3) 1 Cor 11: 28; cf. Mt 26: 27; Mk 14: 23. Likew. ἐξ αὐτοῦ (=ἐκ τοῦ φρέατος.—Paus. Attic. κ, 56 κρήνη, ἐξ ἧς ἔπινον; Num 21: 22; Philo, Deus Imm. 155) *from it* J 4: 12. ἐκ πέτρας 1 Cor 10: 4b.—On the acc. κρίμα ἑαυτῷ ἐσθίει καὶ πίνει 11: 29b cf. κρίμα 4b.—Abs. Mt 27: 34b. W. ἐσθίειν 11: 18f; Lk 5: 33; 12: 19, 45 and oft. τρώγειν καὶ π. Mt 24: 38. ἐσθίειν καὶ π. μετά τινος *eat and drink w. someone* Mt 24: 49; Mk 2: 16 v.l.; Lk 5: 30. δοῦναί τινι πιεῖν (τι) *give someone someth. to drink* (numerous exx. of δοῦναι πιεῖν in ADKnox and WHeadlam, Herodas '22 p. 55f; Jos., Ant. 2, 64) Mt 27: 34a; Mk 15: 23 t.r.; J 4: 7 (δὸς πεῖν as POxy. 1088, 55 [I AD] and Cyranides p. 49, 16. Cf. Lamellae Aur. Orphicae ed. AOlivieri '15 p. 12 σοι δώσουσι πιεῖν θείης ἀπὸ κρήνης [IV/III BC]), 10. πῶς παρ᾽ ἐμοῦ πεῖν αἰτεῖς; *how can you ask me for a drink?* vs. 9.
2. fig.—**a.** of the earth: γῆ ἡ πιοῦσα τὸν ὑετόν Hb 6: 7 (this figure and corresp. exprs. trag.+; cf. Hdt. 3, 117; 4, 198; Anacreontea 21, 1; Dt 11: 11; Sib. Or. 3, 696).
b. of persons—**a.** π. τὸ ποτήριον w. added words that make the sense clear *drink the cup*=submit to a severe trial, or death (ποτήριον 2) Mt 20: 22f; Mk 10: 38f; J 18: 11; cf. Mt 26: 42 (for the fig. use cf. Herodas 1, 25 π.

ἐκ καινῆς=from the new cup. Then, as Mt 20: 22f; Mk 10: 38f of those who suffer the same fate: Aristoph., Eq. 1289 οὔποτ᾽ἐκ ταὐτοῦ μεθ᾽ ἡμῶν πίεται ποτηρίου= he will never drink from the same cup as we do; Libanius, Ep. 355, 4 F. μνήμη τῶν ἐκ ταὐτοῦ κρατῆρος πεπωκότων). Sim. πίεται ἐκ τοῦ οἴνου τοῦ θυμοῦ τοῦ θεοῦ Rv 14: 10; cf. 18: 3 (θυμός 1; 2).

β. In J, Jesus calls those who are thirsty to him, that they may drink the water he gives them and never thirst again (cf. Lucian, Dial. Deor. 4, 5 πίνειν τῆς ἀθανασίας) J 4: 14 (s. 1 above); 7: 37.—LGoppelt, TW VI 135-60: πίνω and related words. M-M. B. 331.

Πιόνιος, ου, ὁ *Pionius*, one of those who gathered and edited accounts of Polycarp's martyrdom MPol 22: 3; Epil Mosq 4.—PCorssen, ZNW 5, '04, 266ff; ESchwartz, De Pionio et Polycarpo, Progr. Göttingen '05.*

πιότης, τητος, ἡ (Hippocr.; LXX, Philo) *fatness, richness* of plants (Theophr., H. Pl. 9, 1, 3; Jos., Bell. 3, 516) ἡ ῥίζα τῆς πιότητος *the rich root* of the cultivated olive tree (cf. Test. Levi 8: 8; Judg 9: 9) Ro 11: 17. M-M.*

πιπράσκω (Aeschyl., Hdt.+; inscr., pap., LXX; Ep. Arist. 22; Philo, De Jos. 15; 16; Jos., Ant. 12, 169; Test. 12 Patr.—Bl-D. §101 p. 48; cf. Mlt.-H. 254) impf. ἐπίπρασκον; pf. πέπρακα (Mt 13: 46 and Hv 1, 1, 1 it has aorist mng.; cf. Bl-D. §343, 1; Rob. 900). Pass.: pf. ptc. πεπραμένος; 1 aor. ἐπράθην; *sell*, w. acc. of the thing Mt 13: 46; Ac 2: 45. Pass. 4: 34; 5: 4. W. gen. of the price (Isaeus 7, 31; Lysias 18: 20; Dt 21: 14) Mt 26: 9; J 12: 5; πραθῆναι ἐπάνω δηναρίων τριακοσίων Mk 14: 5 (cf. ἐπάνω 1b). W. acc. of the pers. *sell someone* (as a slave) Hv 1, 1, 1. Pass. Mt 18: 25. As a symbol (Ps.-Demosth. 17, 13 τοῖς πεπρακόσιν ἑαυτοὺς εἰς τἀναντία='to those who have sold themselves to what is opposed' [to their country's interests]) of a man who is sold as a slave to sin πεπραμένος ὑπὸ τὴν ἁμαρτίαν Ro 7: 14 (sim. 3 Km 20: 25; 4 Km 17: 17; 1 Macc 1: 15 ἐπράθησαν ποιῆσαι πονηρόν). M-M.*

πίπτω (Hom.+; inscr., pap., LXX, Philo, Joseph., Test. 12 Patr.) impf. ἔπιπτον; fut. πεσοῦμαι (Bl-D. §77; Rob. 356); 2 aor. ἔπεσον and ἔπεσα (Bl-D. §81, 3; Mlt.-H. 208; W-H., app. p. 164; Tdf., Prol. p. 123); pf. πέπτωκα, 2 sing. πέπτωκες Rv 2: 5 (Bl-D. §83, 2; Mlt.-H. 221), 3 pl. πέπτωκαν Rv 18: 3 v.l. (W-S. §13, 15; Mlt.-H. 221); *fall*, the passive of the idea conveyed in βάλλω.

1. lit.—a. *fall (down)* from a higher point, w. the 'point from which' designated by ἀπό (Hom.+) ἀπὸ τῆς τραπέζης *from the table* Mt 15: 27; Lk 16: 21. ἀπὸ τοῦ οὐρανοῦ Mt 24: 29. ἀπὸ τῆς κεφαλῆς Ac 27: 34 t.r. (of the falling out of hair, as Synes., Calv. 1, p. 63в). The direction or destination of the fall is expressed by an adv. ἀπὸ τοῦ τριστέγου κάτω *down from the third story* Ac 20: 9. ἀπὸ τοῦ κεράμου χαμαί *from the roof to the ground* Hm 11: 20. ἔκ τινος *from someth.*: ἐκ τοῦ οὐρανοῦ (Sallust. 4 p. 8, 19; Job 1: 16; 3 Km 18: 38.—Sib. Or. 5, 72 ἐξ ἄστρων) Mk 13: 25; of lightning (Ps.-Plut., Hom. 111 εἰ ἐκπίπτοι ἡ ἀστράπη; Ps.-Clem., Hom. 9, 5; 6) Lk 10: 18 (Lycophron, vs. 363 of the image of the goddess ἐξ οὐρανοῦ πεσοῦσα. Cf. σατάν; *be thrown* is also possible here); Rv 8: 10a; the destination is added ἐκ τοῦ οὐρανοῦ εἰς τὴν γῆν 9: 1 (Ps.-Callisth. 2, 10, 10 ἐξ οὐρανοῦ εἰς τὸ ἔδαφος πεπτωκότες). W. only the destination given ἐν μέσῳ τῶν ἀκανθῶν *among the thorns* Lk 8: 7. ἐπί τι *on someth.* Rv 8: 10b. ἐπὶ τὴν γῆν (Aeschyl., Ag. 1019; Am 3: 5) Mt 10: 29 (with the v.l. εἰς παγίδα cf. Am 3: 5 and Aesop, Fab. 193 P.=340 H. of a bird: ἐμπίπτειν εἰς τοὺς

βρόχους); 13: 8; Hm 11: 21 (here the 'place from which' is designated by an adv.: ἄνωθεν).—ἐπὶ τὰ πετρώδη Mt 13: 5; cf. Mk 4: 5 (ἐπί III 1aβ). ἐπὶ τὰς ἀκάνθας Mt 13: 7 (ἐπί III 1aγ). A man falls down ἐπὶ τὸν λίθον *on the stone* Mt 21: 44a; Lk 20: 18a. Conversely the stone falls on the man Mt 21: 44b; Lk 20: 18b. Likew. ἐπί τινα 23: 30; Rv 6: 16 (cf. on both Hos 10: 8). εἰς τι (Hes., Op. 620) εἰς τὴν γῆν (Phlegon: 257 fgm. 36, 1, 5 Jac. πίπτειν εἰς τὴν γῆν) Mk 4: 8; Lk 8: 8; J 12: 24; Rv 6: 13; 1 Cl 24: 5. εἰς τὴν ὁδόν Hv 3, 7, 1. εἰς βόθυνον Mt 15: 14; cf. Lk 14: 5. εἰς τὰς ἀκάνθας Mk 4: 7; Lk 8: 14. εἰς τὸ πῦρ Hv 3, 7, 2. παρά τι *on someth.* παρὰ τὴν ὁδόν (Iambl. Erot. p. 222, 22) Mt 13: 4; Mk 4: 4; Lk 8: 5. ἐγγύς τινος *near someth.* ἐγγὺς (τῶν) ὑδάτων Hv 3, 2, 9; 3, 7, 3.

b. of someth. that, until recently, has been standing (upright) *fall (down)*, *fall to pieces*—a. of persons—א. *fall to the ground, fall down (violently)* εἰς τὸ πῦρ καὶ εἰς τὸ ὕδωρ Mt 17: 15 (but HZimmern, Die Keilinschriften u. d. AT³ '03, 366; 363f, and JWeiss ad loc. take the falling into fire and water to mean fever and chills). ἐπὶ τῆς γῆς (Sib. Or. 4, 110; 5, 100) Mk 9: 20 (π. under the infl. of a demon, as Jos., Ant. 8, 47). ἐπὶ τὴν γῆν (Sib. Or. 4, 110 v.l.) Ac 9: 4; cf. 22: 7 (s. ἔδαφος). χαμαί (Job 1: 20; Philo, Agr. 74) J 18: 6. ἔπεσα πρὸς τοὺς πόδας αὐτοῦ ὡς νεκρός Rv 1: 17. Abs. *fall down* GP 5: 18 v.l. *Fall dead* (Paradox. Vat. 37 Keller πίπτει) Ac 5: 5, 10; 1 Cor 10: 8 (cf. Ex 32: 28); Hb 3: 17 (Num 14: 29). Specifically *fall* in battle (Ael. Aristid. 46 p. 233 D.; Appian, Hann. 56 §236; Jos., Vi. 341; 354) Lk 21: 24 (cf. στόμα 2 and Sir 28: 18).

ב. *fall down, throw oneself to the ground* as a sign of devotion, before high-ranking persons or divine beings, esp. when one approaches w. a petition (LXX), abs. Mt 2: 11; 4: 9; 18: 26, 29; Rv 5: 14; 19: 4; 22: 8 (in all these places [except Mt 18: 29] π. is closely connected w. προσκυνεῖν [as Jos., Ant. 10, 213 after Da 3: 5]. Sim. in many of the places already mentioned). W. var. words added (Jos., Ant. 10, 11 πεσὼν ἐπὶ πρόσωπον τ. θεὸν ἱκέτευε; Gen 17: 3, 17; Num 14: 5) ἐπὶ πρόσωπον (αὐτοῦ, αὐτῶν) Mt 17: 6; 26: 39; Lk 5: 12; 17: 16 (ἐπὶ πρόσωπον παρὰ τοὺς πόδας αὐτοῦ); 1 Cor 14: 25; ἐπὶ τὰ πρόσωπα αὐτῶν Rv 7: 11; 11: 16; ἐπὶ τῆς γῆς Mk 14: 35. Further, the one to whom devotion is given can be added in var. ways: ἐνώπιόν τινος (cf. 2 Km 3: 34) Rv 4: 10; 5: 8; 7: 11. ἔμπροσθεν τῶν ποδῶν τινος 19: 10. εἰς τοὺς πόδας τινός (Diog. L. 2, 79) Mt 18: 29 t.r.; J 11: 32 t.r. ἐπὶ τοὺς πόδας Ac 10: 25 (v.l. adds αὐτοῦ). παρὰ τοὺς πόδας τινός Lk 8: 41; 17: 16 (s. above). πρὸς τοὺς πόδας τινός Mk 5: 22; J 11: 32; Hv 3, 2, 3.

β. of things, esp. structures *fall, fall to pieces, collapse, go down* (Appian, Iber. 54 §228; Jos., C. Ap. 1, 192, Ant. 16, 18) of the σκηνὴ Δαυίδ (σκηνή, end) Ac 15: 16 (Am 9: 11). Of a house *fall (in)* (Diod. S. 11, 63, 2 τῶν οἰκιῶν πιπτουσῶν; Dio Chrys. 6, 61; 30[47], 25; Aristeas Hist. in Euseb., Pr. Ev. 9, 25, 3; Job 1: 19) Mt 7: 25, 27; Lk 6: 49 t.r. (Diod. S. 15, 12, 2 τῶν οἰκιῶν πιπτουσῶν because of the influx of the ποταμός). τὰ τείχη Ἰεριχὼ ἔπεσαν Hb 11: 30 (cf. Josh 6: 5, 20.—Appian, Bell. Civ. 1, 112 §524; Ael. Aristid. 25, 42 K.=43 p. 813 D.: τὰ τείχη π.). ἐφ᾽ οὓς ἔπεσεν ὁ πύργος *upon whom the tower fell* Lk 13: 4 (of a πύργος X., Hell. 5, 2, 5; Arrian, Anab. 6, 7, 5; Polyaenus 6, 50; Jos., Bell. 5, 292; Sib. Or. 11, 12.—π. ἐπί τινα Job 1: 19). οἶκος ἐπὶ οἶκον πίπτει *house falls upon house* 11: 17 (Jülicher, Gleichn. 221f). Of a city (Oenomaus in Euseb., Pr. Ev. 5, 25, 6) LJ 1: 7; cf. Rv 11: 13; 16: 19.

2. fig. and symbol.—a. of persons—a. *fall, be destroyed* ἔπεσεν ἔπεσεν Βαβυλών (cf. Is 21: 9; Jer 28:

8.—Repetition of the verb for emphasis as Sappho, fgm. 131 D.² οὐκέτι ἴξω, οὐκέτι ἴξω; Aristoph., Equ. 247; M. Ant. 5, 7; Ps.-Libanius, Char. Ep. p. 33, 5 ἐρῶ, ἐρῶ. This is to remove all possibility of doubt, as Theod. Prodr. 5, 66 εἶδον, εἶδον='I have really seen'; Theocr. 14, 24 ἔστι Λύκος, Λύκος ἐστί=it really is a wolf) Rv 14: 8; 18: 2.

β. *fall* in the relig. or moral sense, *be completely ruined* (Polyb. 1, 35, 5; Diod. S. 13, 37, 5; Pr 11: 28; Sir 1: 30; 2: 7; Test. Gad 4: 3)=fall from a state of grace Ro 11: 11 (fig. w. πταίω [q.v. 1]), 22; Hb 4: 11 (perh. w. ref. to the final judgment). Also in a less severe sense=*go astray morally* τοὺς πεπτωκότας ἔγειρον 1 Cl 59: 4.—In a play on words 'stand and fall' (cf. Pr 24: 16) Ro 14: 4; 1 Cor 10: 12; 2 Cl 2: 6. μνημόνευε πόθεν πέπτωκες *remember (the heights) from which you have fallen* Rv 2: 5.

γ. ὑπὸ κρίσιν π. *fall under condemnation* Js 5: 12 (on π. ὑπό τι cf. Diod. S. 4, 17, 5 π. ὑπ' ἐξουσίαν; Herodian 1, 4, 2; 2 Km 22: 39).

δ. *fall, perish* (Philo, Aet. M. 128) πίπτοντος τοῦ Ἰσραήλ B 12: 5. οἱ πέντε ἔπεσαν *the five have perished, disappeared, passed from the scene* Rv 17: 10 (cf. also π.='die' Job 14: 10).

b. of things—α. ὁ ἥλιος π. ἐπί τινα *the (heat of the) sun falls upon someone* Rv 7: 16 (Maximus Tyr. 4, 1a ἡλίου φῶς πίπτον εἰς γῆν; Alex. Aphr., An. Mant. p. 146, 9 Br. τὸ φῶς ἐπὶ πάντα πίπτει).

β. ὁ κλῆρος π. ἐπί τινα (κλῆρος 1) Ac 1: 26.—γ. *come (upon)* ἐπί τινα *someone* ἀχλὺς καὶ σκότος Ac 13: 11. φόβος Rv 11: 11 t.r.

δ. *become invalid, come to an end, fail* (Pla., Euthyphr. 14D; Philostrat., Ep. 9) Lk 16: 17 (cf. Josh 23: 14 v.l.; Ruth 3: 18); 1 Cor 13: 8.—WMichaelis, TW VI 161-74: πίπτω and related words. M-M. B. 671.*

Πισιδία, ας, ἡ (Strabo 12, 8, 14 Ἀντιόχεια ἡ πρὸς Πισιδίᾳ; Ptolemaeus 5, 4, 11; 5, 5, 4; Dit., Or. 535, 5 al. in inscr.) *Pisidia*, a mountainous region in central Asia Minor, west of the Taurus Mts., traversed by Paul, Ac 14: 24. Ἀντιόχεια τῆς Πισ. Ac 13: 14 t.r.—Zahn, Einl.³ I 130ff; VSchultze, Altchristl. Städte und Landschaften II 2, '26. S. also on Παμφυλία.*

Πισίδιος, ία, ιον *Pisidian* εἰς Ἀντιόχειαν τὴν Πισιδίαν Ac 13: 14. Since, however, the adj. Πισίδιος is found nowhere else (s. also FBlass ad loc.), and 'Pisidian' is rather expressed by Πισιδικός, ή, όν (Diod. S. 18, 25, 6; 18, 44, 1; 18, 45, 3; Strabo), this reading must probably be abandoned in favor of the v.l. (D, t.r.) εἰς Ἀντιόχειαν τῆς Πισιδίας. M-M.*

πιστεύω (trag.+; inscr., pap., LXX, En., Ep. Arist., Philo, Joseph., Test. 12 Patr.) impf. ἐπίστευον; 1 aor. ἐπίστευσα; pf. πεπίστευκα; plpf. πεπιστεύκειν Ac 14: 23 (on the omission of the augment s. Bl-D. §66, 1; Mlt.-H. 190). Pass.: pf. πεπίστευμαι; 1 aor. ἐπιστεύθην (the word does not occur in Phlm, 2 Pt, 2 and 3 J, Rv, MPol, or D. On the other hand it is a special favorite of J and 1 J, where it is found 96 times and six times respectively; πίστις is not found in the gospel at all, and occurs in 1 J only once, 5: 4. Our lit. uses it quite predominantly in the relig. sense, or at least w. relig. coloring).

1. *believe*—a. *believe (in) someth., be convinced of someth.*, w. that which one believes (in) added—α. in the acc. of the thing (Soph., Oed. Rex 646 τάδε; Aristot., Analyt. Pr. 2, 23 p. 68b, 13 ἅπαντα; PSI 494, 14 μηθέν; UPZ 70, 29 [152/1 BC] π. τὰ ἐνύπνια) ἡ ἀγάπη πάντα πιστεύει 1 Cor 13: 7. πεπιστεύκαμεν τὴν ἀγάπην *we believe in the love* 1 J 4: 16. πιστεύεις τοῦτο; J 11: 26b. Cf. Ac 13: 41 (Hab 1: 5). Pass. ἐπιστεύθη τὸ μαρτύριον

ἡμῶν *our testimony was believed* 2 Th 1: 10b (cf. Aristot., Eth. Nic. 10, 2 p. 1172b, 15 ἐπιστεύοντο οἱ λόγοι; Gen 42: 20).

β. by means of a ὅτι-clause *believe that* (Plut., Mor. 210D; Aelian, V.H. 1, 16 p. 8, 9; Herm. Wr. 4, 4; Porphyr., Ad Marcellam 24; PLond. 897, 12 [I AD]; Tob 10: 8 S; Job 9: 16; 15: 31; 39: 12; La 4: 12; 4 Macc 7: 19) μακαρία ἡ πιστεύσασα ὅτι ἔσται τελείωσις Lk 1: 45 (ὅτι here may=*for*: s. ὅτι 3b).—Mk 11: 23; cf. vs. 24; J 8: 24 (ὅτι ἐγώ εἰμι as Is 43: 10); 11: 27, 42; 13: 19; 14: 10; 16: 27, 30; 17: 8, 21; 20: 31a; Ac 9: 26; Ro 6: 8; 10: 9; 1 Th 4: 14; Hb 11: 6; Js 2: 19a; 1 J 5: 1, 5; Hv 3, 8, 4; 4, 2, 4; m 1: 1; 6, 2, 10b; s 2: 5.—π. περί τινος ὅτι *believe concerning someone that* J 9: 18 (M. Ant. 1, 15, 5 πιστεύειν περὶ ὧν λέγοι ὅτι οὕτως φρονεῖ='believe, w. respect to what he says, that he thinks in this way'.—π. περί τινος as Plut., Lyc. 19, 4; Jos., Ant. 14, 267).

γ. by the acc. and inf. (pres. Pla., Gorg. 524A; PTebt. 314, 3 [II AD]; 4 Macc 5: 25; Jos., C. Ap. 2, 160) πιστεύω τὸν υἱὸν τοῦ θεοῦ εἶναι τὸν Ἰησοῦν Ac 8: 37b.—IRo 10: 2.—By the inf. (Thu 2, 22, 1; Job 15: 22) πιστεύομεν σωθῆναι Ac 15: 11.—By the acc. and ptc. ἐν σαρκὶ αὐτὸν πιστεύω ὄντα *I believe that he was in the flesh* ISm 3: 1.

δ. by means of the dat. of the thing *give credence to, believe* (Aeschyl., Pers. 786 θεῶν θεσφάτοισιν; Soph., Phil. 1374 τοῖς ἐμοῖς λόγοις, El. 886; Pla., Phaedo 88C, Leg. 7 p. 798D; Polyb. 5, 42, 9; 9, 33, 1; Herodian 7, 5, 5 ἐλπίδι κρείττονι; BGU 674, 6 τῷ λόγῳ; 2 Ch 9: 6 τοῖς λόγοις; Ps 105: 24; Pr 14: 15; Sir 19: 15; En. 104, 13 ταῖς βίβλοις; Philo, Leg. All. 3, 229 τοῖς κενοῖς λογισμοῖς, Virt. 68 the sayings of God; Jos., C. Ap. 2, 286, Ant. 10, 39 τ. λόγοις) οὐκ ἐπίστευσας τοῖς λόγοις μου Lk 1: 20. τῇ γραφῇ καὶ τῷ λόγῳ J 2: 22. Cf. 4: 50; 5: 47a, b. τοῖς γεγραμμένοις Ac 24: 14 (Diod. S. 16, 52, 7 πιστεύσαντες τοῖς γεγραμμένοις). τῇ ἐπαγγελίᾳ τοῦ θεοῦ 2 Cl 11: 1 (Diod. S. 1, 53, 10 τῇ τοῦ προρρήσει πιστεύειν; 19, 90, 3). τῷ ψεύδει, τῇ ἀληθείᾳ 2 Th 2: 11, 12. τῇ καταλαλιᾷ Hm 2: 2. τῇ ἀκοῇ ἡμῶν (Is 53: 1; cf. Jos., C. Ap. 2, 14 π. ἀκοῇ πρεσβυτέρων) J 12: 38; Ro 10: 16; 1 Cl 16: 3. τοῖς ἔργοις J 10: 38b (=their testimony); Hm 6, 2, 10a (that they are good and must be followed).—Pass. ἐπιστεύθη τῷ λόγῳ μου *they believed my word* Hm 3: 3.

ε. w. prepositional expressions: εἰς Ro 4: 18, if εἰς τὸ γενέσθαι αὐτόν here is dependent on ἐπίστευσεν. πιστεύειν εἰς τὴν μαρτυρίαν *believe in the witness* 1 J 5: 10c. ὁ Χριστιανισμὸς οὐκ εἰς Ἰουδαϊσμὸν ἐπίστευσεν *Christianity did not believe in Judaism* (s. Hdb. ad loc.) I Mg 10: 3a; cf. b (Χριστιανισμόν, εἰς ὃν πᾶσα γλῶσσα πιστεύσασα). On πιστεύειν εἰς τὸ ὄνομά τινος s. 2aβ below. πιστεύετε ἐν τῷ εὐαγγελίῳ *believe in the gospel* (so Ps 105: 12 ἐπίστευσαν ἐν τοῖς λόγοις αὐτοῦ). Rather in the sense 'put one's trust in' Sir 32: 21 μὴ πιστεύσῃς ἐν ὁδῷ ἀπροσκόπῳ. Cf. Bl-D. §187, 6 w. app.; Rob. 540. ALoisy, Les Évangiles synopt. I '07, 430; 434; Wlh., JWeiss, PDausch, EKlostermann, JSchniewind ad loc.) Mk 1: 15 (Hofmann understands it as 'on the basis of', Wohlenberg 'bei'; Lohmeyer is undecided; Dssm. and Mlt. 67f 'in the sphere of'; s. p. 235). ἐν τούτῳ *by this* J 16: 30.—ἐπί τινι: πιστεύειν ἐπὶ πᾶσιν οἷς ἐλάλησαν οἱ προφῆται Lk 24: 25.

b. w. the pers. to whom one *gives credence* or whom one *believes*, in the dat. (Demosth. 18, 10; Aristot., Rhet. 2, 14 p. 1390a, 32; Polyb. 15, 26, 6 τοῖς εἰδόσι τὴν ἀλήθειαν; Herodian 2, 1, 10; PHib. 72, 18; POxy. 898, 29; PTebt. 418, 15; Ex 4: 1, 5; 3 Km 10: 7; 2 Ch 32: 15; Tob 2: 14; Jer 47: 14; Philo, Praem. 49) τοῖς θεασαμένοις αὐτὸν ἐγηγερμένον οὐκ ἐπίστευσαν *they did not believe those who saw him after he was raised from the dead* Mk 16: 14. Cf.

Mt 21: 25, 32a, b, c; Mk 11: 31; 16: 13; Lk 20: 5; J 5: 46a; Ac 8: 12; 26: 27a (τ. προφήταις as Jos., Ant. 11, 96); 1 J 4: 1; Hm 6, 1, 2a, b.—Also of Jesus and God whom one *believes*, in that he accepts their disclosures without doubt or contradiction: Jesus: Mt 27: 42 t.r.; J 5: 38, 46b; 6: 30; 8: 45, 46; 10: 37, 38a. God: J 5: 24; Ro 4: 3 (Gen 15: 6), 17 (κατέναντι οὗ ἐπίστευσεν θεοῦ=κατέναντι θεοῦ ᾧ ἐπίστευσεν); Gal 3: 6; Js 2: 23; 1 Cl 10: 6 (all three Gen 15: 6). ὁ μὴ πιστεύων τῷ θεῷ ψεύστην πεποίηκεν αὐτόν 1 J 5: 10b.

c. w. pers. and thing added π. τινί τι *believe someone with regard to someth.* (X., Apol. 15 μηδὲ ταῦτα εἰκῇ πιστεύσητε τῷ θεῷ) Hm 6, 2, 6.—W. dat. of the pers. and ὅτι foll.: πιστεύετέ μοι ὅτι ἐγὼ ἐν τῷ πατρί J 14: 11a. Cf. 4: 21; Ac 27: 25.

d. abs. (in which case the context supplies the obj., etc.) ἐάν τις ὑμῖν εἴπῃ· ἰδοὺ ὧδε ὁ Χριστός, μὴ πιστεύσητε *do not believe* (him or it [the statement]) Mt 24: 23; cf. vs. 26; Mk 13: 21; Lk 22: 67; J 3: 12a, b; 10: 25f; 12: 47 t.r.; 14: 29; 16: 31; 19: 35; 20: 8, 25, 29a, b (πιστεύσαντες *those who have nevertheless believed* [it=the fact of the Resurrection]); Ac 4: 4; 26: 27b; 1 Cor 11: 18 (πιστεύω I *believe* [it=that there are divisions among you]); 15: 11; Js 2: 19b (*even the demons believe this*); Jd 5. Pass. καρδίᾳ πιστεύεται *with* (or *in*) *the heart men believe* (it=that Jesus was raised fr. the dead) Ro 10: 10.

e. *believe*= *let oneself be influenced* κατά τινος *against someone* Pol 6: 1.

f. πιστεύομαι I *am believed, I enjoy confidence* (X., An. 7, 6, 33; Diod. S. 5, 80, 4 τοῖς μάλιστα πιστευομένοις ἐπηκολουθήσαμεν; 17, 32, 1; 1 Km 27: 12; Jos., Ant. 10, 114; PGM 12, 279 πιστευθήσῃ= you will be believed) of Eve παρθένος πιστεύεται *men believe that she is a virgin* Dg 12: 8, or perh. *a virgin is entrusted* (to someone without fear). Cf. 3 below.

2. *believe* (*in*), *trust* of relig. belief in a special sense, as faith in the Divinity that lays special emphasis on trust in his power and his nearness to help, in addition to being convinced that he exists and that his revelations or disclosures are true. In our lit. God and Christ are objects of this faith. The obj. is

a. given—α. in the dat. (cf. Soph., Philoct. 1374 θεοῖς πιστ.; X., Mem. 1, 1, 5; Ps.-Pla., Epinom. 980c πιστεύσας τοῖς θεοῖς εὔχου; Ptolem. Lagi [300 bc]: 138 fgm. 8 Jac.; Maximus Tyr. 3, 8k τῷ Ἀπόλλωνι; Epict., App. E, 10 p. 488 Sch. θεῷ; Himerius, Or. 8 [=23], 18 πῶς Διονύσῳ πιστεύσω; how can I trust D.?; UPZ 144, 12 [164 bc] τ. θεοῖς; Jdth 14: 10; Wsd 16: 26; 4 Macc 7: 21 al. in LXX; Philo, Leg. All. 3, 229 πιστεύειν θεῷ, Rer. Div. Her. 92 μόνῳ θεῷ, Op. M. 45, Sacr. Abel. 70 τῷ σωτῆρι θεῷ, Abr. 269, Mos. 1, 225, Virt. 216 [on faith in Philo cf. Bousset, Rel.³ 446ff; EHatch, Essays in Biblical Gk. 1889, 83ff; ASchlatter, D. Glaube im NT⁴ '27; EBréhier, Les idées philosophiques et religieuses de Philon d'Alexandrie '08, ²'25; HWindisch, Die Frömmigkeit Philos '09, 23ff; HAWolfson, Philo '47 I, 143-56, esp. II, 215-8]; Jos., Ant. 2, 117; 333; 3, 309; 20, 48, Bell. 3, 387 [cf. ASchlatter, D. Theol. d. Judentums nach d. Bericht des Jos. '32, 104ff]). Some of the passages referred to in 1b above, end, are repeated, since they may be classified here or there w. equal justification. Of God: π. τῷ θεῷ Ac 16: 34; 13: 12 D; Tit 3: 8; PK 4 p. 16, 2; B 16: 7; Hm 12, 6, 2; s 5, 1, 5. Cf. m 1: 2. τῷ κυρίῳ (Sir 11: 21; 2: 8) v 4, 2, 6. οἱ πιστεύσαντες τῷ κυρίῳ διὰ τοῦ υἱοῦ αὐτοῦ s 9, 13, 5. τῷ θεῷ w. ὅτι foll. m 9: 7; cf. s 1: 7.—Of Christ: Mt 27: 42 t.r. (for ἐπ' αὐτόν); J 6: 30 (σοί=vs. 29 εἰς ὃν ἀπέστειλεν ἐκεῖνος); J 8: 31 (αὐτῷ=vs. 30 εἰς αὐτόν, but see Mlt. 67f); Ac 5: 14; 18: 8a (both τῷ κυρίῳ); Ro 10: 14b (οὗ οὐκ

ἤκουσαν=τούτῳ [about equivalent to εἰς τοῦτον; cf. vs. 14a] οὗ οὐκ ἤκ.); 2 Ti 1: 12; ITr 9: 2.—Pass. *be believed in* (X., Cyr. 4, 2, 8; 6, 1, 39; Pla., Lach. 181ʙ; Ps.-Demosth. 58, 44 al.; 1 Km 27: 12. Cf. Bl-D. §312, 1; cf. Rob. 815f) ἐπιστεύθη ἐν κόσμῳ 1 Ti 3: 16.—π. τῷ ὀνόματι τοῦ υἱοῦ *believe in the name of the Son*, i.e. believe in the Son and accept what his name proclaims him to be 1 J 3: 23.

β. w. εἰς (cf. Hippolyt., Elench. 6, 19, 7 W. οἱ εἰς τὸν Σίμωνα καὶ τὴν Ἑλένην πεπιστευκότες) God (BGU 874, 11 π. εἰς τὸν θεόν): J 12: 44b; 14: 1a (cf. ET 21, '10, 53-7; 68-70; 138f); 1 Pt 1: 21 t.r.—Pol 2: 1.—Christ: Mt 18: 6; Mk 9: 42 t.r.; J 2: 11; 3: 15 t.r., 16, 18a, 36; 4: 39; 6: 29, 35, 40, 47 t.r.; 7: 5, 31, 38f, 48; 8: 30; 9: 35f; 10: 42; 11: 25, 26a, 45, 48; 12: 11, 36 (εἰς τὸ φῶς), 37, 42, 44a, 46; 14: 1b, 12; 16: 9; 17: 20; Ac 10: 43; 14: 23; 18: 8 D; 19: 4; Ro 10: 14a; Gal 2: 16; Phil 1: 29; 1 Pt 1: 8; 1 J 5: 10a; Hs 8, 3, 2.—εἰς τὸ ὄνομα Ἰησοῦ (or αὐτοῦ, etc.) J 1: 12; 2: 23; 3: 18c; 1 J 5: 13 (cf. ὄνομα I 4b and s. 2aα above, end). π. εἰς τὸν θάνατον αὐτοῦ ITr 2: 1. π. εἰς τὸ αἷμα Χριστοῦ ISm 6: 1.

γ. w. ἐπί and the dat., of God Ac 11: 17 D. Of Christ: Mt 27: 42 v.l.; J 3: 15 v.l.; Ro 9: 33; 10: 11; 1 Pt 2: 6 (the last three Is 28: 16 אAQ); 1 Ti 1: 16.

δ. w. ἐπί and the acc. (Wsd 12: 2) of God: Ac 16: 34 D; Ro 4: 5, 24; PK 3 p. 15, 12. Of Christ: Mt 27: 42; J 3: 15 v.l.; Ac 9: 42; 11: 17; 16: 31; 22: 19.

ε. π. ἔν τινι *believe in someone* (Jer 12: 6; Da 6: 24 Theod.; Ps 77: 22) is not found in our lit. at all, except J 3: 15 (B, al.; Nestle); Eph 1: 13 if ἐν ᾧ is connected w. πιστεύσαντες; it is possible to hold that π. stands abs. both times. But s. 1aε above π. ἐν τῷ εὐαγγελίῳ Mk 1: 15.

b. not expressed at all (Aristot., Rhet. 2, 17 p. 1391b, 1ff; Plut., Mor. 170ꜰ; Porphyr., Ad Marcellam 24 πιστεῦσαι δεῖ, ὅτι [=because] μόνη σωτηρία ἡ πρὸς τὸν θεὸν ἐπιστροφή; Herm. Wr. 9, 10a, b ἐπίστευσε καὶ ἐν τῇ καλῇ πίστει ἐπανεπαύσατο; cf. 1, 32 πιστεύω καὶ μαρτυρῶ=Pap. Berol. 9795 [RReitzenstein, Studien z. antiken Synkretismus '26, p. 161, 2]; Num 20: 12; Ps 115: 1; Is 7: 9; Sir 2: 13; 1 Macc 2: 59; Philo, Rer. Div. Her. 14; 101, Deus Imm. 4, Mut. Nom. 178) Mk 15: 32; 16: 16f; Lk 8: 12f; J 1: 7, 50; 3: 15, 18b; 4: 41f, 48, 53; 5: 44; 6: 36, 47, 64a, b, perh. 69 (MSEnslin, The Perf. Tense in the Fourth Gosp.: JBL 55, '36, 121-31, esp. 128); 9: 38; 10: 26; 11: 15, 40; 12: 39; 20: 31b; Ac 4: 4; 8: 13, 37a; 11: 21; 13: 12, 39, 48; 14: 1; 15: 5, 7; 17: 12, 34; 18: 8b, 27; 19: 2; 21: 25; Ro 1: 16; 3: 22; 4: 11; 10: 4; 13: 11; 15: 13; 1 Cor 1: 21; 3: 5; 15: 2; Gal 3: 22; Eph 1: 13, 19; 1 Th 2: 10, 13; Hb 4: 3; 1 Pt 2: 7; 1 Cl 12: 7; 2 Cl 17: 3; 20: 2; B 9: 4; 11: 11; ISm 3: 2; Hs 8, 10, 3; 9, 17, 4; 9, 22, 3. τὸ πιστεύειν *faith* IMg 9: 2. ἐν ἀγάπῃ πιστεύειν IPhld 9: 2.—The participles in the var. tenses are also used almost subst.: (οἱ) πιστεύοντες (*the*) *believers*, (*the*) *Christians* Ac 2: 44 t.r.; Ro 3: 22; 1 Cor 14: 22a, b (opp. οἱ ἄπιστοι); 1 Th 1: 7; Hs 8, 3, 3. (οἱ) πιστεύσαντες (*those*) *who became Christians*, (*the*) *Christians, believers* Ac 2: 44; 4: 32; 2 Th 1: 10a; 2 Cl 2: 3; Hs 9, 19, 1. οἱ πεπιστευκότες *those who became* (and remained) *believers* Ac 19: 18; 21: 20.—οἱ μέλλοντες πιστεύειν *future believers* 1 Cl 42: 4; Hm 4, 3, 3a. οἱ νῦν πιστεύσαντες *those who have just come to believe* ibid. b.

c. A special kind of this faith is the confidence that God or Christ is in a position to help the suppliant out of his distress, *have confidence* (some of the passages already mentioned might just as well be classified here) abs. ὡς ἐπίστευσας γενηθήτω σοι *may it be done to you in accordance with the confidence you have* Mt 8: 13. ὅσα ἂν αἰτήσητε πιστεύοντες *whatever you pray for with confi-*

dence 21: 22. Cf. Mk 5: 36; 9: 23f; Lk 8: 50; 2 Cor 4: 13a (Ps 115: 1), b. W. ὅτι foll.: πιστεύετε ὅτι δύναμαι τοῦτο ποιῆσαι; *do you have confidence that I am able to do this?* Mt 9: 28.—Mk 11: 23.

3. *entrust* τινί τι *someth. to someone* (X., Mem. 4, 4, 17; Plut., Mor. 519E; Athen. 8 p. 341A; Lucian, Dial. Deor. 25, 1; Dit., Syll.² 845, 7, cf. for numerous other examples index VI p. 384b. Cf. Wsd 14: 5; 1 Macc 8: 16; 4 Macc 4: 7; Jos., Bell. 4, 492) τὸ ἀληθινὸν τίς ὑμῖν πιστεύσει; Lk 16: 11. αὑτόν τινι *trust oneself to someone* (Lysias 30, 7; Brutus, Ep. 25; Plut., Mor. 181D ἀνδρὶ μᾶλλον ἀγαθῷ πιστεύσας ἑαυτὸν ἢ ὀχυρῷ τόπῳ; Ep. Arist. 270; Jos., Ant. 12, 396) J 2: 24 (EStauffer, CHDodd-Festschr., '56, 281–99.—Diod. S. 34+35 fgm. 39a οὐ τοῖς τυχοῦσι φίλοις ἑαυτὸν ἐπίστευσεν= he did not trust himself to casual friends).—Pass. πιστεύομαί τι *I am entrusted with someth.* (Pla., Ep. 1 p. 309A; Polyb. 8, 17, 5; 31, 26, 7; Diod. S. 20, 19, 2; Appian, Bell. Civ. 2, 136 §568 ἃ ἐπιστεύθην; inscr., pap.; Jos., Bell. 5, 567, Vi. 137. Cf. Esth 8: 12e.—Dssm., LO 320f [LAE 379]). ἐπιστεύθησαν τὰ λόγια τοῦ θεοῦ Ro 3: 2. πεπίστευμαι τὸ εὐαγγέλιον Gal 2: 7 (PGM 13, 140 ὁ ὑπό σου πάντα πιστευθείς; 446); cf. 1 Th 2: 4; 1 Ti 1: 11.—Tit 1: 3. οἰκονομίαν πεπίστευμαι 1 Cor 9: 17; cf. Dg 7: 1. S. also 7: 2; IMg 6: 1; IPhld 9: 1a, b. πιστεύομαί τι παρά τινος *I am entrusted by someone with someth.* (Polyb. 3, 69, 1; Jos., Bell. 1, 667): οἱ πιστευθέντες παρὰ θεοῦ ἔργον τοιοῦτο 1 Cl 43: 1.

4. A unique use is found in ὃς μὲν πιστεύει φαγεῖν πάντα, someth. like *the one trusts himself to eat anything* Ro 14: 2 (a combination of two ideas: 'he is so strong in the faith' and: 'he is convinced that he may'. Cf. Ltzm., Hdb. ad loc.). Another possibility is the sense *think* or *consider* (*possible*), in Ro 14: 2 perh. *holds everything possible*; cf. J 9: 18 οὐκ ἐπίστευσαν *they refused to entertain the possibility*, and Ac 9: 26.—For lit. s. πίστις, end. M-M. **

πιστικός, ή, όν (since Pla., Gorg. 455A) only as modifying νάρδος, w. πολυτελής or πολύτιμος Mk 14: 3; J 12: 3; variously interpreted.

1. In later writers π. means that which belongs to πίστις, *faithful, trustworthy* (Artem. 2, 32; Vett. Val. p. 10, 14; pap. 'trusted man'; Celsus 1, 39 λόγος πιστικός). Fr. this as a basis the word has been interpreted to mean *genuine, unadulterated* (Euseb., Dem. Ev. 9, 8, 9 τοῦ πιστικοῦ τῆς καινῆς διαθήκης κράματος. Given as a possibility by Theophyl. Sim., s. 3 below. Cf. Bl-D. §113, 2; Mlt.-H. 379f).

2. The derivation fr. πίνω (so L-S-J), w. the sense *drinkable, liquid*, is very improbable.

3. It is more nearly poss. that π. is derived from a name of some kind (Theophyl. Sim. [Patr. Gr. 123, 645B] πιστικὴν νάρδον νοεῖ ἤτοι εἶδος νάρδου οὕτω λεγόμενον πιστικὴν ἢ τὴν ἄδολον νάρδον); e.g., it may be the Gk. form of the Lat. spicatum (Galen XII 604 K. τὰ πολυτελῆ μύρα τῶν πλουσίων γυναικῶν ἃ καλοῦσιν αὗται σπίκατα.—EbNestle, ZNW 3, '02, 169ff), or it may be derived fr. πιστάκια 'pistachio tree' (AMerx on Mk 14: 3; MBlack, An Aramaic Approach³, '67, 223–5)) or the East-Indian piçita, the name of the plant Nardostachys Jatamansi.—UvWilamowitz, Reden u. Vorträge² '02, 204; ANJannaris, CIR 16, '02, 9; RKöbert, Biblica 29, '48, 279–81. W-S. §16, 3b note 24. Cf. also νάρδος. M-M. *

πίστις, εως, ἡ (Hes., Hdt.+; inscr., pap., LXX; Ep. Arist. 37; Philo, Joseph.) *faith, trust.*

1. that which causes trust and faith—**a.** *faithfulness, reliability* (X., An. 1, 6, 3; 3, 3, 4; Aristot., Eth. Eud. 7, 2

p. 1237b, 12; Polyb. 7, 12, 9; 38, 1, 8 al.; Herodian 2, 14, 4 al.; Dit., Syll.³ 675, 22, Or. 557, 16; PTebt. 27, 6; 51 [II BC]; POxy. 494, 9; 705, 32; Ps 32: 4; Pr 12: 22; Jos., Ant. 2, 61; Test. Ash. 7: 7) w. κρίσις and ἔλεος Mt 23: 23. (Opp. ἀπιστία as Hes., Op. 370) τὴν πίστιν τοῦ θεοῦ καταργεῖν *nullify the faithfulness of God* (cf. Ps 32: 4; Hos 2: 22) Ro 3: 3. πᾶσαν π. ἐνδείκνυσθαι ἀγαθήν *show all good faith(fulness)* Tit 2: 10 (cf. BGU 314, 19 μετὰ πίστεως ἀγαθῆς). W. other virtues Gal 5: 22 (on πίστις, πραΰτης cf. Sir 45: 4; 1: 27). W. ὑπομονή 2 Th 1: 4. τὴν πίστιν τετήρηκα *I have remained faithful* or *loyal* (πίστιν τηρεῖν as Polyb. 6, 56, 13; 10, 37, 5; Jos., Bell. 2, 121; 6, 345; Dit., Or. 339, 46f; Gk. Inscr. Brit. Mus. III 587b, 5f [Dssm., LO 262-LAE 309, esp. note 3]) 2 Ti 4: 7, though this would be classified by some under 3 below. S. also 1c below.

b. *solemn promise, oath, troth* (X., Cyr. 7, 1, 44; 8, 8, 3, Hell. 1, 3, 12; Diod. S. 14, 9, 7; Appian, Bell. Civ. 4, 86 §362 μεγάλας πίστεις ἔδωκεν= solemn assurances; 3 Macc 3: 10; Jos., Ant. 12, 382) τὴν πρώτην πίστιν ἠθέτησαν 1 Ti 5: 12 (s. also ἀθετέω 1a and cf. CIA App. [Wünsch, Praef. p. xv] of a woman who πρώτη ἠθέτησεν τὴν πίστιν to her husband).

c. *proof, pledge* (Pla., Phaedo 70B; Isocr. 3, 8; Aristot., Rhet. 1, 1; 3, 13; Epicurus in Diog. L. 10, 63; 85; πίστις βεβαία= dependable proof; Polyb. 3, 100, 3; Περὶ ὕψους p. 24, 11 V.; Epict. 1, 28, 3; Appian, Bell. Civ. 4, 119 §500; Jos., Ant. 15, 69) πίστιν παρασχὼν πᾶσιν ἀναστήσας αὐτόν *(God has appointed the Man Jesus to be Judge of the world, and) he has furnished proof* (of his fitness for this office) *to all men by raising him* (on πίστιν παρέχειν cf. Jos., Ant. 2, 218 πίστιν παρεῖχε; 15, 260; Polyb. 2, 52, 4 πίστιν παρέσχετο= gave a pledge, security) Ac 17: 31 (others would class it under 2da below). JMTBarton, Biblica 40, '59, 878–84: π. in 2 Ti 4: 7= *bond deposited by an athlete. But see 3 below.—WSchmitz, 'Η Πίστις in den Papyri, Diss. Cologne, '64.

2. *trust, confidence, faith* in the active sense= 'believing', in relig. usage (Soph. Oed. R. 1445 νῦν γ' ἂν τῷ θεῷ πίστιν φέροις; Pla., Leg. 12 p. 966D, E; Plut., Mor. 402E; 756B; Dio Chrys. 3, 51 παρὰ θεῶν τιμή κ. πίστις; Ael. Aristid. 13 p. 226 D.: πίστιν ἐν τ. θεοῖς ἔχειν; Ep. 33 of Apollonius of Tyana [Philostrat. I 352, 14]; Herm. Wr. 9, 10 ἐπίστευσε καὶ ἐν τῇ καλῇ πίστει ἐπανεπαύσατο; Porphyr., Ad Marcellam 21 τῆς βεβαίας πίστεως, τὸ μεμαθηκέναι, ὅτι ὑπὸ τοῦ θεοῦ προνοεῖται πάντα. The divinity Πίστις in Plut., Num. 16, 1 and in magic [exx. in Rtzst., Mysterienrel.³ 234f, among them Aberciusinschrift 12; PGM 4, 1014 ἀλήθεια καὶ πίστις; 12, 228]; Wsd 3: 14; 4 Macc 15: 24; 16: 22; 17: 2; Philo, Abr. 270; 271; 273, Mut. Nom. 182, Migr. Abr. 43f, Conf. Lingu. 31, Poster. Cai. 13 [on faith in Philo s. the lit. given under πιστεύω 2aa]; Jos., C. Ap. 2, 163; 169), in our lit. directed toward God and Christ, their revelations, teachings, promises, their power and readiness to aid.

a. God: πίστις θεοῦ (cf. Jos., Ap. 2, 218, Ant. 17, 179) *faith, trust, confidence in God* Mk 11: 22; cf. Ac 19: 20 D; 1 Cl 3: 4; 27: 3. π. θείου πνεύματος *faith in the Divine Spirit* Hm 11: 9. ἡ π. τοῦ κυρίου s 6, 3, 6. π. (καὶ ἐλπὶς) εἰς θεόν 1 Pt 1: 21. π. ἐπὶ θεόν Hb 6: 1. ἡ πίστις ἡ πρὸς τὸν θεόν 1 Th 1: 8 (on the constr. w. πρὸς τ. θ. cf. Philo, Abr. 268; 271; 273).—πίστις can also be characterized as faith in God by the context, without the addition of specific words; so in connection w. OT personalities: Abraham Ro 4: 5, 9, 11–13, 16, 19f (s. also 2da below); 1 Cl 10: 7; 31: 2; of Rahab 12: 1, 8; of Esther 55: 6 (ἡ τελεία κατὰ πίστιν). The OT heroes of faith Hb 11: 4–33, 39.—But in Hb it is also true that God is specifically the object of the Christian's faith, and Christ 12: 2 is ὁ τῆς πίστεως ἀρχηγὸς καὶ τελειώτης. Cf. 10: 38; 11: 3; 13: 7. (On faith in Hb s. Schlatter, Der Glaube im NT⁴ '27, 520ff; BHeigl, Verfasser u. Adresse des Hb '05, 109–18; GHoennicke, Die sittl. Anschauungen des Hb: ZWTh 45, '02, 26ff; Windisch, Hdb. exc. on Hb 11; Riggenbach and Michel on Hb 11; Strathmann on 10: 38. Cf. ὑπόστασις, end.)—ἐὰν ἔχητε πίστιν Mt 17: 20. Opp. doubt 21: 21. αἰτείν ἐν πίστει μηδὲν διακρινόμενος Js 1: 6. ἡ εὐχὴ τῆς πίστεως 5: 15 (εὐχή 1). ἡ πίστις τῆς ἐνεργείας τοῦ θεοῦ τοῦ ἐγείραντος αὐτὸν ἐκ νεκρῶν *faith in the working of God, who raised him from the dead* Col 2: 12.

b. Christ—**α.** of belief and trust in the Lord's help in physical and spiritual distress; oft. in the synopt. gospels: Mt 8: 10; 9: 2, 22, 29 (κατὰ τὴν πίστιν ὑμῶν); 15: 28; Mk 2: 5; 4: 40; 5: 34; 10: 52; Lk 5: 20; 7: 9, 50; 8: 25, 48; 17: 19; 18: 42.—Cf. also ἔχει πίστιν τοῦ σωθῆναι (the lame man) *had faith that he would be cured* Ac 14: 9.

β. The faith is clearly designated as faith in Christ by the addition of certain words. By the obj. gen. πίστις Ἰησοῦ Χριστοῦ *faith in Jesus Christ* (and sim. exprs.) Ro 3: 22, 26; Gal 2: 16a, b, 20; 3: 22; Eph 3: 12; Phil 3: 9a; Js 2: 1; Rv 14: 12; cf. 2: 13 (ἡ πίστις μου= *faith in me*, the Son of Man); IMg 1: 1. (The πίστις Χριστοῦ in Paul is taken as a subj. gen. by JHaussleiter, Der Glaube Jesu Christi 1891, Was versteht Paulus unter christlichem Glauben?: Greifswalder Studien für HCremer 1895, 161–82 and GottfrKittel, StKr 79, '06, 419ff. Cf. also Schläger, ZNW 7, '06, 356–8.—ADeissmann, most recently Paulus² '25, 125f [Paul, tr. WEWilson, '26, 162ff], speaks of the mystical gen., 'faith in Christ'. Likew. HEWeber, Die Formel 'in Christo Jesu': NKZ 31, '20, 213ff, esp. 231, 3; WWeber, Christusmystik '24, 82. S. also LAlbrecht, Der Glaube Jesu Christi '21; OSchmitz, Die Christusgemeinschaft des Pls im Lichte seines Genetivgebr. '24, 91–134; OHoltzmann, D. Glaube an Jes.: Stromata '30, 11–25; GMTaylor, JBL 85, '66, 58–76: the passages in Gal= Christ's reliability as a trustee).—By prepositional phrases: πίστις εἰς Χριστόν (and sim. exprs.) *faith in Christ* Ac 20: 21; 24: 24; 26: 18; Col 2: 5.—Also πίστις ἐν Χριστῷ (and sim.) Gal 3: 26; Eph 1: 15; Col 1: 4; 1 Ti 3: 13; 2 Ti 3: 15; 1 Cl 22: 1. In ἱλαστήριον διὰ πίστεως ἐν τῷ αὐτοῦ αἵματι Ro 3: 25, ἐν κτλ. prob. goes not w. πίστις, but w. ἱλαστήριον (cf. Ltzm., Hdb. ad loc.; W-S. §20, 5d).—πίστις, ἣν ἔχεις πρὸς τ. κύριον Ἰησοῦν Phlm 5.—πίστις διὰ τοῦ κυρίου ἡμῶν Ἰ. Χριστοῦ Ac 20: 21 D; cf. ἡ πίστις ἡ δι' αὐτοῦ 3: 16b (cf. 1 Pt 1: 21).—Jesus Christ is called ἡ τελεία πίστις ISm 10: 2.

c. The πίστις can also be characterized by an objective gen. of the thing: ἡ πίστις τοῦ ὀνόματος αὐτοῦ *faith in his* (Jesus') *name* Ac 3: 16a. ἡ πίστις τοῦ εὐαγγελίου Phil 1: 27. εὐαγγελίων πίστις Dg 11: 6. πίστις ἀληθείας 2 Th 2: 13.

d. πίστις is found mostly without an obj., *faith*—**α.** as true piety, genuine religion (Sextus 7a and 7), which for our lit. means being a Christian: Lk 18: 8 (s. on this Jülicher, Gleichn. 288); 22: 32; Ac 6: 5= vs. 8 t.r.; cf. 11: 24.—6: 7; 13: 8; 14: 22; 15: 9; 16: 5; Ro 1: 5, 8, 12, 17a, b (ἐκ πίστεως εἰς πίστιν does not mean a gradation [as, in a way, Appian, Mithrid. 40 §154: Sulla came upon ἕτερον ὅμοιον ἐξ ἑτέρου= one wall, i.e., fortification, after another similar one] or a transition from one kind to another [Himerius, Or.= Ecl. 10, 6 ἐκ ᾠδῆς εἰς ᾠδὴν ἄλλην μετέβαλον= they changed from one kind of song to another], it merely expresses in a rhetorical way the thought that πίστις is the beginning and the end; cf. Ltzm., Hdb. ad loc., and a grave-inscr. [ADNock, Sallust. p. xxxiii 94] ἐκ γῆς εἰς γῆν ὁ βίος οὗτος= 'dust is the

beginning and the end of human life'.—AFridrichsen, Coniect. Neot. 12, '48, 54); 17c (here and in Gal 3: 11 the LXX of Hab 2: 4 is not followed literally, since it has ἐκ πίστεώς μου= 'as a result of my faithfulness'; even in Hb 10: 38, where μου does occur, it goes w. δίκαιος, not w. πίστεως); Ro 3: 27f (Luther's addition of the word 'alone' in vs. 28 is hard to contest from the viewpoint of language. Cf., e.g., Diog. L. 9, 6: Heraclitus wrote his work in very obscure language ὅπως οἱ δυνάμενοι προσίοιεν αὐτῷ= in order that only the capable might approach it), 30f; 4: 5–20 (s. also 2a above); 5: 1f; 9: 30, 32; 10: 6, 17; 11: 20 (opp. ἀπιστία); 12: 3, 6; 14: 1, 23a, b (but s. ε below); 16: 26; 1 Cor 2: 5; 15: 14, 17; 16: 13; 2 Cor 1: 24a, b; 4: 13; 10: 15; 13: 5; Gal 3: 7–26; 5: 5, 6 (cf. ἐνεργέω 1b); 6: 10 (οἱ οἰκεῖοι τῆς πίστεως, s. οἰκεῖος 2); Eph 2: 8; 3: 17; 4: 5, 13; 6: 16; Phil 1: 25 (χαρὰ τῆς πίστεως); 2: 17; 3: 9b; Col 1: 23; 2: 7; 1 Th 3: 2, 5, 7, 10; 2 Th 1: 3, 11; 3: 2; 1 Ti 1: 2, 4, 5 (π. ἀνυπόκριτος), 19a, b; 4: 1; 5: 8; 6: 10, 12, 21 (but s. 3 below); 2 Ti 1: 5 (ἀνυπόκριτος π.); 2: 18; 3: 8; Tit 1: 1, 4, 13; 3: 15; Phlm 6 (s. κοινωνία 4); Hb 6: 12; 10: 22, 39 (opp. ὑποστολή); Js 1: 3; 2: 5; 1 Pt 1: 5, 7, 9; 5: 9; 2 Pt 1: 1; 1 J 5: 4; 1 Cl 1: 2 (ἡ πανάρετος κ. βεβαία π.); ISm 1: 1 (ἀκίνητος π.); Hm 5, 2, 1; 12, 5, 4 (both πλήρης ἐν τῇ πίστει *full of faith*); 5, 2, 3 (π. ὁλόκληρος); 9: 6 (ὁλοτελὴς ἐν τ. π.), 7 (opp. διψυχία), 12 (π. ἡ ἔχουσα δύναμιν); 12, 6, 1; s 9, 19, 2 (ἀπὸ τῆς π. κενοί); 9, 26, 8 (κολοβοὶ ἀπὸ τῆς π. αὐτῶν).—τὸ ῥῆμα τ. πίστεως Ro 10: 8. οἱ λόγοι τῆς π. 1 Ti 4: 6. τὸ μυστήριον τῆς π. 3: 9. ὁ θεὸς ἤνοιξεν τοῖς ἔθνεσιν θύραν πίστεως *God has opened the door of faith to the Gentiles*, i.e. opened the way for them to embrace the true religion, Christianity Ac 14: 27 (cf. also θύρα 2c). ἀκοὴ πίστεως Gal 3: 2, 5 (cf. ἀκοή 2b). (τὸ) ἔργον (τῆς) π. 1 Th 1: 3; 2 Th 1: 11 (cf. ἔργον 1b). οἱ ἐκ πίστεως *the men of faith* (cf. ἐκ 3d) Gal 3: 7, 9.—If Christianity is essentially faith, then π. in relation to it can mean simply *religion* (cf. Dit., Syll.³ 932, 7 [II/I BC]) νῦν εὐαγγελίζεται τὴν πίστιν ἣν ποτε ἐπόρθει Gal 1: 23 (s. 3 below). Perh. also Ro 1: 5.

β. Hb 11: 1 defines πίστις as ἐλπιζομένων ὑπόστασις, πραγμάτων ἔλεγχος οὐ βλεπομένων *the assurance of what we hope for, the proving of* (or *a conviction about*) *what we cannot see* (s. 2a above). Paul contrasts walking διὰ εἴδους (εἶδος 3) as the lower degree, with διὰ πίστεως περιπατεῖν 2 Cor 5: 7 (cf. KDeissner, Pls. u. die Mystik seiner Zeit² '21, 101ff). On the other hand πίστις is on a higher level than merely listening to Christian preaching Hb 4: 2.

γ. πίστις abs., as a Christian virtue, is often coupled w. others of the same kind, esp. oft. w. ἀγάπη: 1 Th 3: 6; 5: 8; 1 Ti 1: 14; 2 Ti 1: 13; Phlm 5; B 11: 8; IEph 1: 1; 9: 1; 14: 1; 20: 1; IMg 1: 2; 13: 1; ISm inscr.; 6: 1; 13: 2. W. ἀγάπη and other concepts of a sim. nature 2 Cor 8: 7; Gal 5: 22; Eph 6: 23; 1 Ti 2: 15; 4: 12; 6: 11; 2 Ti 2: 22; 3: 10; Tit 2: 2; Rv 2: 19; IPhld 11: 2; Pol 4: 2; Hm 8: 9; cf. v 3, 8, 2–5. The triad πίστις, ἐλπίς, ἀγάπη 1 Cor 13: 13; cf. also Col 1: 4f; 1 Th 1: 3; 5: 8; B 1: 4 (on this triad see s.v. ἀγάπη I 1a). W. ἐλπίς only (cf. 1 Pt 1: 21) 1 Cl 58: 2. The ζωῆς ἐλπίς is called ἀρχὴ καὶ τέλος πίστεως ἡμῶν B 1: 6.—W. ἀλήθεια 1 Ti 2: 7; 1 Cl 60: 4. W. δικαιοσύνη Pol 9: 2. W. ὑπομονή Rv 13: 10; w. ὑπομ. and other concepts 2 Pt 1: 5f; Pol 13: 2 (cf. also the following passages already referred to in this section: 1 Ti 6: 11; 2 Ti 3: 10; Tit 2: 2 and Js 1: 3 [a above]). W. γνῶσις et al. 2 Pt 1: 5f [s. above]; D 10: 2. ἵνα μετὰ τῆς πίστεως ὑμῶν τελείαν ἔχητε τὴν γνῶσιν B 1: 5. W. φόβος and ἐγκράτεια Hm 6, 1, 1.

δ. *faith* as recognition and acceptance of Christian teaching as such. This point of view calls for ἔργα as well as the kind of πίστις that represents only one side of true piety: Js 2: 14a, b, 17, 18a, b, c, 20, 22a, b, 24, 26 (ἔργον 1a); Hv 3, 6, 5; s 8, 9, 1a, b.

ε. Ro 14: 22 and 23 π. gains fr. the context the mng. *freedom* or *strength in faith, conviction* (s. Ltzm., Hdb. ad loc.).

ζ. In addition to the πίστις that every Christian possesses (s. 2da above) Paul speaks of a special gift of faith that is the possession of a select few 1 Cor 12: 9. In this category he understands π. as an unquestioning belief in God's power to aid men with miracles, the faith that 'moves mountains' 13: 2 (cf. Mt 17: 20.—21: 21; s. 2a above). This special kind of faith is what the disciples had in mind when they asked πρόσθες ἡμῖν πίστιν Lk 17: 5; cf. vs. 6.

3. That which is believed, *body of faith* or *belief, doctrine* (Diod. S. 1, 23, 8 ἰσχυρὰν πίστιν καὶ ἀμετάθετον=an article of faith that was firm and unshakable [concerning Orpheus and Dionysus]). So clearly Jd 3 (τῇ ἅπαξ παραδοθείσῃ τοῖς ἁγίοις πίστει), 20 (τῇ ἁγιωτάτῃ ὑμῶν πίστει.—ἅγιος 1aα). πίστις θεοῦ=that which, acc. to God's will, is to be believed IEph 16: 2.—This objectivizing of the πίστις-concept is found as early as Paul: Ro 1: 5; Gal 1: 23 (s. 2da, end, above) and perh. Gal 3: 23-5 (s. Ltzm., Hdb. ad loc.). ASeeberg, D. Katechismus der Urchristenheit '03, 110f, understands 1 Ti 1: 19; 4: 1, 6; 6: 10, cf. 21; 2 Ti 2: 18 in this manner. Ro 12: 6 and 2 Ti 4: 7 are also interpreted in this way by many; perh. 1 Ti 6: 21 belongs here.—EDBurton, ICC Gal '21, 475-86; ASchlatter, D. Glaube im NT⁴ '27; APott, Das Hoffen im NT in seiner Beziehung zum Glauben '15; ANairne, The Faith of the NT '20; RGyllenberg, Pistis '22; WGKümmel, D. Glaube im NT: ThBl 16, '38, 209-21; Dodd 65-8; TFTorrance, ET 68, '57, 111-4; CFDMoule, ibid. 157.—Synoptics: TShearer, ET 69, '57, 3-6.—Esp. for Paul: BBartmann, Pls, die Grundzüge seiner Lehre u. die moderne Religionsgeschichte '14; WMorgan, The Religion and Theology of Paul '17; WHPHatch, The Pauline Idea of Faith in its Relation to Jewish and Hellenistic Religion '17; Ltzm., Hdb. exc. after Ro 4: 25; FKnoke, Der christl. Glaube nach Pls '22; ERohde, Gottesglaube u. Kyriosglaube bei Pls: ZNW 22, '23, 43-57; EWissmann, Das Verh. v. πίστις und Christusfrömmigkeit bei Pls '26; MDibelius, Glaube u. Mystik b. Pls: Neue Jahrb. f. Wissensch. u. Jugendbildg. 7, '31, 683-99; WMundle, D. Glaubensbegriff des Pls '32 (p. xi-xvi extensive bibliog.); RGyllenberg, Glaube b. Pls: ZsystTh 13, '37, 612-30; MHansen, Om Trosbegrebet hos Pls '37; LHMarshall, Challenge of NT Ethics, '47, 270-7; 298-300; RBultmann, Theologie des NT '48, 310-26 (Engl. transl. KGrobel I '51, 314-30; for the Johannines II, 70-92, '55); MOMassinger, Bibliotheca Sacra 107, '50, 181-94 et al. S. also δικαιοσύνη 3, end.—For the Fourth Gosp.: JOBuswell, The Ethics of 'Believe' in the Fourth Gospel: Bibl. Sacra 80, '23, 28-37; JHuby, De la connaissance de foi chez S. Jean: Rech de Sc rel 21, '31, 385-421; RSchnackenburg, D. Glaube im 4. Ev., Diss. Breslau '37; WHPHatch, The Idea of Faith in Christ. Lit. fr. the Death of St. Paul to the Close of the Second Century '26.—EGraesser, D. Glaube im Hebräerbrief '65.—ABaumeister, D. Ethik des Pastor Hermae, '12, 61-140.—ESeidl, π. in d. griech. Lit. (to Peripatetics), Diss. Innsbruck, '53; HLjungman, Pistis, '64; DLührmann, Pistis im Judent., ZNW 64, '73, 19-38. On faith in late Judaism s. Bousset, Rel.³ 534a (index). On the 'Hellenistic concept πίστις' Rtzsch., Mysterienrel.³ 234-6.—On the whole word RBultmann and AWeiser, TW VI '56, 174-230: πίστις and related words. M-M.**

πιστός, ή, όν (Hom.+; inscr., pap., LXX, Ep. Arist., Philo, Joseph.).

1. pass. *trustworthy, faithful, dependable, inspiring trust* or *faith* (Hom.+).

a. of pers.—α. of human beings (and Christ) δοῦλος (1 Km 22: 14; 2 Macc 1: 2; Jos., Ant. 6, 256; Dit., Syll.³ 910 A, 5 [Christian]; PLond. 251, 14 [IV AD] δούλους πιστοὺς καὶ ἀδράστους): δοῦλε ἀγαθὲ καὶ πιστέ Mt 25: 21a, 23a; cf. 24: 45; Hs 5, 2, 2. οἰκονόμος Lk 12: 42; 1 Cor 4: 2. μάρτυς (Pind., Pyth. 1, 88; 12, 27; Pr 14: 5, 25; Ps 88: 38; Jer 49: 5; Philo, Sacr. Abel. 17) ὁ μάρτυς μου ὁ πιστός μου Rv 2: 13 (μάρτυς 3); in this 'book of martyrs' Christ is ὁ μάρτυς ὁ πιστὸς (καὶ ὁ ἀληθινός) 1: 5; 3: 14; cf. 19: 11 (the combination of ἀληθινός and πιστός in the last two passages is like 3 Macc 2: 11). Cf. Rv 17: 14. πιστὸς ἀρχιερεύς *a faithful* or *reliable high priest* Hb 2: 17 (of Christ); cf. 3: 2 (ἀρχιερέα...πιστὸν ὄντα τῷ ποιήσαντι αὐτόν). σύμβουλοι πιστοί B 21: 4. πιστοὶ ἄνθρωποι *reliable men* 2 Ti 2: 2 (cf. Is 8: 2; sing. Tob 5: 3 S; 10: 6 S). Paul honors his co-workers w. π. as a designation: Timothy 1 Cor 4: 17. Tychicus Eph 6: 21; Col 4: 7 (both πιστὸς διάκονος ἐν κυρίῳ). Onesimus Col 4: 9. Epaphras 1: 7 (πιστὸς ὑπὲρ ὑμῶν διάκονος τοῦ Χριστοῦ). Cf. 1 Pt 5: 12 (διὰ Σιλουανοῦ τ. πιστοῦ ἀδελφοῦ). —Moses was πιστὸς ἐν ὅλῳ τῷ οἴκῳ αὐτοῦ Hb 3: 5 (Num 12: 7). πιστόν τινα ἡγεῖσθαι *consider someone trustworthy* (Aristoph., Plut. 27) 1 Ti 1: 12 (cf. Hb 11: 11; s. β below); s. PK 3 p. 15, 18. γίνου πιστός (γίνομαι II 1 and cf. Jos., Vi. 110, Ant. 19, 317) Rv 2: 10.—πιστὸς ἔν τινι *faithful, reliable, trustworthy in someth.* (Test. Jos. 9: 2 π. ἐν σωφροσύνῃ) ἐν τῷ ἀδίκῳ μαμωνᾷ *in the things of the unrighteous Mammon* Lk 16: 11. ἐν τῷ ἀλλοτρίῳ *in connection with what belongs to someone else* vs. 12. ὁ π. ἐν ἐλαχίστῳ καὶ ἐν πολλῷ π. ἐστιν *he who is trustworthy in a very small matter is also trustworthy in a large one* vs. 10; 2 Cl 8: 5; cf. Lk 19: 17. π. ἐν πᾶσιν *trustworthy in every respect* 1 Ti 3: 11. Also ἐπί τι *in (connection w.) someth.* Mt 25: 21b, 23b.—When Paul explains in 1 Cor 7: 25 that the Lord graciously granted him the privilege of being πιστός, and uses this as a basis for his claim to be heard w. respect, πιστός can hardly mean 'believing' (s. 2 below); the apostle rather feels that in a special sense he has been called and commissioned because of the confidence God has in him (πιστός is almost like a title= 'trusted man, commissioner', oft. in inscr.: PhLeBas-WHWaddington, Voyage III 1870, 2022a; 2029; 2034; 2045f; 2127f; 2130; 2219; 2238-40; 2243; 2394.—Corresp. πίστις= 'position of trust': Achilles Tat. 8, 15, 1 οἱ ἄρχοντες οἱ ταύτην ἔχοντες τὴν πίστιν).

β. of God as the One in whom we can have full confidence (Pind., Nem. 10, 54; Dt 7: 9; 32: 4; Is 49: 7; Philo, Rer. Div. Her. 93, Sacr. Abel. 93, Leg. All. 3, 204) 1 Cor 1: 9; 10: 13; 2 Cor 1: 18; 1 Th 5: 24; Hb 10: 23; 11: 11; 1 Pt 4: 19; 1 J 1: 9; 1 Cl 60: 1; ITr 13: 3. π. ἐν ταῖς ἐπαγγελίαις 1 Cl 27: 1 (cf. Ps 144: 13a πιστὸς κύριος ἐν τοῖς λόγοις αὐτοῦ). πιστός ἐστιν ὁ ἐπαγγειλάμενος *he is trustworthy, who has promised* 2 Cl 11: 6.—Also of the 'Lord' (Christ), who is spoken of in the same way as God 2 Th 3: 3; 2 Ti 2: 13.

b. of things, esp. of words (Hdt. 8, 83; Pla., Tim. 49B; Aristot., Rhet. 2, 1 p. 1377b, 23; Polyb. 3, 9, 4; 15, 7, 1; Plut., Mor. 160E; Cass. Dio 37, 35; Jos., Ant. 19, 132; Aberciusinschr. 6 γράμματα πιστά [of a divine teacher]) πιστὸς ὁ λόγος (Dionys. Hal. 3, 23, 17; Dio Chrys. 28[45], 3) *it is a trustworthy saying* 1 Ti 1: 15; 3: 1; 4: 9; 2 Ti 2: 11; Tit 3: 8; cf. 1: 9 (JMBover, Biblica 19, '38, 74-9). οἱ λόγοι πιστοὶ καὶ ἀληθινοί Rv 21: 5; 22: 6. Opp. ψευδής Hm 3:

5a, b. On τὰ ὅσια, Δαυὶδ τὰ πιστά Ac 13: 34 cf. ὅσιος 2a.—Of water *dependable* (i.e. not likely to dry up suddenly; cf. Dt 28: 59 νόσοι πισταί), *unfailing, plentiful* B 11: 5 (Is 33: 16). πιστὸν ποιεῖν τι *act loyally* 3 J 5.

2. act. *trusting, cherishing faith* or *trust* (Aeschyl., Pers. 55, Prom. 916; Soph., Oed. Col. 1031; Pla., Leg. 7 p. 824; Cass. Dio 37, 12, 1) also *believing, full of faith, faithful* (cf. POxy. 1380, 152 ὁρῶσί σε [=Isis] οἱ κατὰ τὸ πιστὸν ἐπικαλούμενοι [on this s. AMFestugière, RB 41, '32, 257–61]; Sextus 1; 8; Wsd 3: 9; Sir 1: 14, 24 v.l.; Ps 100: 6; Sib. Or. 3, 69; 724) of OT worthies: Abraham (who is oft. called πιστός; cf. Philo, Post. Cai. 173 Ἀβρ. ὁ πιστὸς ἐπώνυμος; 2 Macc 1: 2; 1 Macc 2: 52; Sir 44: 20) Gal 3: 9; 1 Cl 10: 1; (Noah) 9: 4; (Moses) 17: 5; 43: 1 (both Num 12: 7) and cf. 1aα above (Hb 3: 5). Of believers in contrast to doubters Hm 11: 1a, b. Of belief in the resurrection of Jesus μὴ γίνου ἄπιστος ἀλλὰ πιστός J 20: 27. Of one who confesses the Christian faith *believing* or *a believer in the Lord, in Christ, in God* πιστ. τῷ κυρίῳ Ac 16: 15. Also π. ἐν κυρίῳ Hm 4, 1, 4. π. ἐν Χριστῷ Ἰησοῦ Eph 1: 1. πιστοὶ ἀδελφοὶ ἐν Χρ. Col 1: 2. δι' αὐτοῦ (=Χριστοῦ) πιστοὶ (πιστεύοντες 𝔓⁷² et al.) εἰς θεόν 1 Pt 1: 21.—The abs. πιστός also means *believing (in Christ), a (Christian) believer* and is used both as adj. and as subst. Ac 16: 1; 2 Cor 6: 15; 1 Ti 4: 10; 5: 16; 6: 2a, b; Tit 1: 6; 1 Cl 48: 5; 62: 3; 63: 3; Hm 9: 9; s 8, 7, 4; 8, 9, 1; 8, 10, 1; 9, 22, 1. οἱ πιστοί *the believers=the Christians* Ac 12: 3 D; 1 Ti 4: 3, 12; IEph 21: 2; IMg 5: 2 (opp. οἱ ἄπιστοι); MPol 12: 3; 13: 2. οἱ ἅγιοι καὶ πιστοὶ αὐτοῦ ISm 1: 2. οἱ ἐκ περιτομῆς πιστοί *the Jewish Christians* Ac 10: 45. Without the art. Dg 11: 2, 5. νέοι ἐν τῇ πίστει καὶ πιστοί *young in the faith, but nevertheless believers* Hv 3, 5, 4.—πιστὸς εἶναι *be a believer* IRo 3: 2. ἐὰν ᾖ τις πιστότατος ἀνήρ *even though a man is a firm believer* Hm 6, 2, 7.—LPFoley, CBQ 1 '39, 163–5. M-M. B. 1167.*

πιστόω 1 aor. pass. ἐπιστώθην (Hom.+; inscr., LXX, Ep. Arist., Philo; Jos., Bell. 4, 213, Ant. 15, 85.—Apart fr. our lit. mostly mid., rarely pass., and act. only Thu. 4, 88; 2 Km 7: 25; 1 Ch 17: 14; 2 Macc 7: 24; 12: 25; Philo, Leg. All. 3, 206) in our lit. only pass., and 1 aor.

1. *show oneself faithful* ἔν τινι *prove oneself faithful to someth.* 1 Cl 15: 4 (Ps 77: 37).

2. *feel confidence, be convinced* (so the 1 aor. pass. Od. 21, 218; Soph., Oed. Col. 1039; Ep. Arist. 91) σὺ μένε ἐν οἷς (=τούτοις, ἃ) ἔμαθες καὶ ἐπιστώθης *but you must stand by what you have learned and become convinced of* 2 Ti 3: 14. πιστωθέντες ἐν τῷ λόγῳ τοῦ θεοῦ (w. πληροφορηθέντες διὰ τῆς ἀναστάσεως τοῦ κυρίου Ἰ. Χρ.) *full of faith in* or *by the word of God* 1 Cl 42: 3. M-M.*

πιστῶς adv. (since Antipho Or. 2, 47; inscr.; pap.; 4 Km 16: 2; Jos., C. Ap. 2, 44) *faithfully* στηρίζεσθαι 1 Cl 35: 5. φυλάσσειν Dg 7: 2.*

πίων, πῖον gen. πίονος (Hom.+; LXX; Philo, Aet. M. 100; Jos., Bell. 4, 468; Sib. Or. 3, 639) *fat* θυσία MPol 14: 2 (w. προσδεκτή).*

πλανάω fut. πλανήσω; 1 aor. ἐπλάνησα. Pass.: perf. πεπλάνημαι; 1 aor. ἐπλανήθην (Hom., Aeschyl., Hdt.+; inscr., pap., LXX, En., Philo, Joseph., Test. 12 Patr.; Sib. Or. 3, 721).

1. act.—a. *lead astray, cause to wander* τινά *someone* (Aeschyl., Prom. 573; Hdt. 4, 128 et al.) as a symbol π. τινὰ ἀπὸ τῆς ὁδοῦ *cause someone to wander from the right way* D 6: 1 (for πλ. ἀπὸ τ. ὁδοῦ cf. Dt 11: 28; Wsd 5: 6).

b. fig. *mislead, deceive* τινά *someone* (Pla., Prot. 356D, Leg. 655D al.; pap., LXX) Mt 24: 4f, 11, 24; Mk 13: 5f; J 7: 12; 1 J 2: 26; 3: 7; Rv 2: 20; 12: 9; 13: 14; 19: 20; 20: 3, 8, 10; IMg 3: 2; IPhld 7: 1a. π. ἑαυτόν *deceive oneself* 1 J 1: 8. Abs. 2 Ti 3: 13a.—S. 2cδ below.

2. pass. *go astray, be misled, wander about*—a. lit. (since Il. 23, 321; Gen 37: 15; Jos., Bell. 7, 160) ἐπὶ ἐρημίαις πλανώμενοι Hb 11: 38. Of sheep who have become lost (Ps 118: 176) Mt 18: 12a, b, 13. ὡς πρόβατα πλανώμενα 1 Pt 2: 25 t.r.

b. as a symbol, of men who had strayed fr. the right way, ὡς πρόβατα πλανώμενοι 1 Pt 2: 25. ὡς πρόβατα ἐπλανήθημεν 1 Cl 16: 6a (Is 53: 6a; cf. also Ps 118: 176). καταλείποντες εὐθεῖαν ὁδὸν ἐπλανήθησαν 2 Pt 2: 15. ἄνθρωπος τῇ ὁδῷ αὐτοῦ ἐπλανήθη *everyone went astray in his (own) path* 1 Cl 16: 6b (Is 53: 6b). πλανῶνται καὶ ταλαιπωροῦσιν περιπατοῦντες ἐν ταῖς ἀνοδίαις *they wander about and are miserable as they go through trackless country* Hv 3, 7, 1 (ἐν as Lucian, Calumn. 1 ἐν σκότῳ; Hb 11: 38 v.l.).

c. fig., without preserving the symbolism—α. *go astray, be misled, deluded* (Cebes 6, 3; 24, 2) Tit 3: 3 (Dio Chrys. 4, 115 πλανῶνται... δεδουλωμέναι ἡδοναῖς) Hb 5: 2; 1 Cl 39: 7 (Job 5: 2); 59: 4; 2 Cl 15: 1 (of the ψυχή as Pr 13: 9a; Wsd 17: 1); B 2: 9; 16: 1. πλανῶνται τῇ καρδίᾳ *their minds are going astray* Hb 3: 10 (Ps 94: 10).

β. *wander away* ἀπὸ τῆς ἀληθείας Js 5: 19 (cf. Wsd 5: 6).—γ. *be mistaken* in one's judgment, *deceive oneself* (Isocr., Ep. 6, 10 al.; Jos., Bell. 1, 209, Ant. 10, 19; PFlor. 61, 16; 2 Macc 7: 18) Mt 22: 29; Mk 12: 24; Hv 2, 4, 1. πολὺ πλανᾶσθε *you are very much mistaken* Mk 12: 27. μὴ πλανᾶσθε *make no mistake* (Epict. 4, 6, 23) 1 Cor 6: 9; Gal 6: 7; Js 1: 16. ἐν πᾶσιν πεπλανήμεθα *we are wholly mistaken* B 15: 6 (cf. Hero Alex. III p. 214, 2 ἐν μηδενὶ πλανᾶσθαι).

δ. as the pass. of 1b: *be deceived, be misled* πλανῶντες καὶ πλανώμενοι *deceivers* (of others) *and* (themselves) *deceived* 2 Ti 3: 13 (cf. Herm. Wr. 16, 16 ὁ πλανώμενος κ. πλανῶν).—*Let oneself be misled, deceived* (Bel 7 Theod.) Mt 24: 24 v.l.; Lk 21: 8; J 7: 47; Rv 18: 23. μὴ πλανᾶσθε 1 Cor 15: 33; IEph 16: 1; IMg 8: 1; IPhld 3: 3. μηδεὶς πλανάσθω IEph 5: 2; ISm 6: 1. τὸ πνεῦμα οὐ πλανᾶται *the Spirit is not led into error* IPhld 7: 1b. ὑπὸ τοῦ ὄφεως πλανᾶται *he is deceived by the serpent* or *he lets himself be misled by the serpent* Dg 12: 6 (UPZ 70, 28 [152/1 BC] πλανώμενοι ὑπὸ τ. θεῶν; Alex. Aphr., Fat. 12 p. 180, 25 Br. ὑπὸ τ. φύσεως).—HBraun, TW VI 230–54: πλανάω and related words. M-M.*

πλάνη, ης, ἡ (Aeschyl., Hdt.+; BGU 1208, 6 [27/6 BC]; LXX; En. 99, 7; Philo; Jos., Ant. 4, 276; Test. 12 Patr.) *wandering, roaming*, in our lit. only fig. of *wandering* fr. the path of truth, *error, delusion, deceit, deception* to which one is subject (Pla. et al., also Diod. S. 2, 18, 8; Herm. Wr. 1, 28 οἱ συνοδεύσαντες τῇ πλάνῃ; Tob 5: 14 BA; Pr 14: 8; Jer 23: 17) Mt 27: 64. Of a false concept of God, the idolatry of the heathen (Wsd 12: 24) Ro 1: 27; cf. τερατεία καὶ πλάνη τῶν γοήτων Dg 8: 4 (Jos., Ant. 2, 286 κατὰ γοητείαν κ. πλάνην).—Eph 4: 14 (s. μεθοδεία); 1 Th 2: 3; 2 Th 2: 11 (opp. ἀλήθεια vs. 10). ἡ τῶν ἀθέσμων πλ. *the error of unprincipled men* 2 Pt 3: 17; τῶν ἁμαρτωλῶν B 12: 10. Cf. IEph 10: 2. ἡ τῆς πλ. ἀνομία B 14: 5 (ἀνομία 1). ἡ πλ. τοῦ νῦν καιροῦ 4: 1. παρείσδυσιν πλάνης ποιεῖν 2: 10 (s. παρείσδυσις). W. ἀπάτη Dg 10: 7. W. ἀπώλεια 2 Cl 1: 7. ἡ κενὴ ματαιολογία καὶ ἡ τῶν πολλῶν πλάνη Pol 2: 1. μῦθος καὶ πλάνη *a myth and a delusion* 2 Cl 13: 3. οἱ ἐν πλάνῃ ἀναστρεφόμενοι 2 Pt 2: 18. τὸ πνεῦμα τῆς πλάνης

(Test. 12 Patr.—Opp. to τὸ πνεῦμα τῆς ἀληθείας: Test. Judah 20: 1) *the spirit of error* 1 J 4: 6. ἐκ πλάνης ὁδοῦ αὐτοῦ Js 5: 20 (ὁδός 2b). τῇ πλάνῃ τοῦ Βαλαὰμ μισθοῦ ἐξεχύθησαν *for gain they have wholly given themselves up to Balaam's error* Jd 11 (s. μισθός 1 and ἐκχέω 3).— πλάνη τοῦ ὄφεως Dg 12: 3 is prob. not act., meaning deceiving by the serpent, but the deceit or error originated by it; cf. 12: 8. M-M. B. 1185.*

πλάνης, ητος, ὁ (Soph.+; X., Mem. 4, 7, 5; Dio Chrys. 30[47], 8; Vett. Val. 64, 6; Philo; loanw. in rabb.) Jd 13 v.l. The word is equivalent in mng. to πλανήτης, q.v.*

πλανήτης, ου, ὁ (Soph.+; Vett. Val. 65, 4; Hos 9: 17; Jos., Ant. 3, 145) *wanderer, roamer* used as subst. and adj. in our lit. only in the combination ἀστέρες πλανῆται (Aristot., Meteor. 1, 6; Plut., Mor. 604Α; 905cf; Ps.-Lucian. Astrol. 14, Salt. 7 al.; PGM 7, 513, mostly of the planets) *wandering stars* Jd 13 (the v.l. πλάνητες [s. πλάνης] is by no means rare in secular writers in just this combination).—S. ἀστήρ, end. M-M.*

πλάνος, ον (trag.+; LXX, Philo, Joseph.) in our lit. only in the mng. *leading astray, deceitful.*
1. adj. (so Menand., fgm. 288; Theocr. 21, 43; Moschus 1, 28; 5, 10; Jos., Bell. 2, 259) πνεύματα πλάνα *deceitful spirits* 1 Ti 4: 1.
2. subst. ὁ πλάνος *deceiver, impostor* (Diod. S. 34+35, fgm. 2, 14; Vett. Val. 74, 18; Ps.-Clem., Hom. 4, 2) of Jesus Mt 27: 63 (cf. Test. Levi 16: 3). W. ὁ ἀντίχριστος 2 J 7b; pl. ibid. a. ὡς πλάνοι καὶ ἀληθεῖς *considered impostors, and (yet are) true* 2 Cor 6: 8. M-M.*

πλάξ, πλακός, ἡ (Pind.+; inscr., pap., LXX, En., Test. 12 Patr.) *flat stone, tablet, table* in our lit. of the tables of the law (LXX; Philo, Migr. Abr. 85; Jos., Ant. 3, 90; Sib. Or. 3, 257; on the custom of putting inscriptions on πλάκες of stone cf. Wilcken, Chrest. 54, 1ff [III BC]; Dit., Or. 672, 12) Β 14: 2 (cf. Ex 31: 18; 34: 4). πλάκες λίθιναι γεγραμμέναι τῷ δακτύλῳ τῆς χειρὸς τοῦ κυρίου 4: 7 (Ex 31: 18). αἱ πλάκες τῆς διαθήκης (διαθήκη 3) Hb 9: 4. Thrown to the ground and broken in pieces by Moses (Ex 32: 19; Dt 9: 17) Β 4: 8; 14: 3. Paul speaks, w. Ex 32: 16; 34: 1 in mind and alluding to Ezk 11: 19; 36: 26, of an ἐπιστολή...ἐγγεγραμμένη οὐκ ἐν πλαξὶν λιθίναις ἀλλ' ἐν πλαξὶν καρδίαις (the t.r. has the easier καρδίας) σαρκίναις 2 Cor 3: 3 (cf. Theodor. Prod. 8, 353 Hercher ζωγραφεῖν πρὸς καρδίας πινακίῳ). M-M.*

πλάσις, εως, ἡ (Theophr.+; pap.) *formation, molding, creation* (w. gen. Polyb. 6, 53, 5; Plut., Cic. 4, 4; PSI 712, 5 πλάσις ὀπτῆς πλίνθου; π. τῶν ἀνθρώπων Third Corinthians 1: 13) ἡ π. τοῦ Ἀδάμ Β 6: 9. δευτέρα π. of the spiritual new creation through Christ vs. 13.*

πλάσμα, ατος, τό (Aristoph., Pla.+; PGM 4, 212; 304; 5, 378; LXX; En. 104, 10; Philo; Jos., C. Ap. 1, 254; 2, 122; Third Corinthians 3: 12) *that which is formed or molded, image, figure* μὴ ἐρεῖ τὸ πλάσμα τῷ πλάσαντι; *can what is molded say to its molder?* Ro 9: 20 (Is 29: 16; Ro 9: 21 proceeds to mention κεραμεὺς τοῦ πηλοῦ; cf. Aristoph., Av. 686 πλάσματα πηλοῦ). The account of the creation (Gen 1: 26) is interpreted w. ref. to regeneration, and the Christians speak of themselves as τὸ καλὸν π. ἡμῶν *our beautiful creation* Β 6: 12. The words φθορεῖς πλάσματος θεοῦ Β 20: 2 need not be understood fr. this as a background; as the parallel D 5: 2 shows, it comes fr. a different complex of ideas. Beside φονεῖς τέκνων it means perh. *those who destroy what God has formed* in the womb, by abortion (but s. φθορεύς). M-M.*

πλάσσω 1 aor. ἔπλασα; pf. ptc. πεπλακώς; 1 aor. pass. ἐπλάσθην (Hes.+; inscr. [e.g. Isishymn. v. Andros 94]; pap., LXX; En. 104, 10; Philo; Jos., C. Ap. 1, 293; Sib. Or. 4, 6) *form, mold.*
1. lit.—a. of the manufacture of certain objects Ro 9: 20 (cf. πλάσμα); Dg 2: 3.
b. esp. of God's creative activity in forming man (cf. Semonides of Amorgos 7, 21 of a woman as obj. πλάσαντες γηίην Ὀλύμπιοι; Babrius 66, 2f πλάσσασθαι ἄνθρωπον ἐκ γῆς. Cf. Cornutus 18 p. 31, 20).—Artem. 3, 17 it is said of Prometheus πλ. τοὺς ἀνθρώπους.
α. of Adam (Gen 2: 7f, 15; cf. 2 Macc 7: 23; Philo, Op. M. 137; Jos., Ant. 1, 32; Sib. Or. 3, 24) ἄνθρωπον ταῖς ἱεραῖς χερσὶν ἔπλασεν *he formed man with his holy hands* 1 Cl 33: 4. Pass. 1 Ti 2: 13 (also Eve).
β. In Adam men were created of whom it is said οὕς (i.e. the men) ἐκ τῆς ἰδίας εἰκόνος ἔπλασεν *whom he formed in his own image* Dg 10: 2 (Himerius, Or. 64 [=Or. 18], 4 πλ. of the forming of figures by the sculptor).
γ. of mankind gener., with no special ref. to Adam (oft. LXX; Third Corinthians 3: 7) 1 Cl 38: 3; Β 19: 2. Specif. the heart of man was formed by God Β 2: 10 (cf. Ps 32: 15).
2. fig., of mental things, in the difficult pass. δεῖξαι αὐτῷ φῶς καὶ πλάσαι τῇ συνέσει *show him light and form him with understanding* (?) 1 Cl 16: 12 (Is 53: 11 LXX, without support in the orig. text as handed down to us.—For the figurative meaning cf. Pla., Rep. 377c πλάττειν τὰς ψυχάς [through education], Leg. 671c παιδεύειν καὶ πλάττειν; Theocr. 7, 44).—HBraun, TW VI 254-63: πλάσσω and related words. M-M. B. 617.*

πλαστός, ή, όν (Hes.+) *made up, fabricated, false* (so since Eur., Bacch. 218; Hdt. 1, 68; Lycophron v. 432 ἐν πλασταῖς γραφαῖς, also PSI 494, 13 [III BC]; POxy. 237 VIII, 14 [II AD]; Philo, Somn. 2, 140; Jos., Vi. 177; 337) π. λόγοι 2 Pt 2: 3 (Ael. Aristid. 36, 91 K. =48 p. 474 D.: ὁ λόγος πέπλασται). M-M.*

πλατεῖα, ας, ἡ (really the fem. of πλατύς, w. ὁδός to be supplied: Sext. Emp., Pyrrh. 1, 188 ὅταν λέγωμεν πλατεῖαν, δυνάμει λέγομεν πλατεῖαν ὁδόν) *wide road, street* (Ps.-Eur., Rhes. 283; Diod. S. 12, 10, 7; 17, 52, 3; Plut., Dio 46, 2, Thes. 27, 4; Dit., Or. 491, 9; Lyc. inscr. [Hauser 96]; pap., LXX; Jos., Bell. 1, 425, Ant. 16, 148; loanw. in rabb.) Mt 12: 19 (Is 42: 2); Mk 6: 56 v.l.; Lk 10: 10; 13: 26; Ac 5: 15 (Maximus Tyr. 6, 2 people put their sick out in the street so that passersby can advise them or influence them for good); Rv 11: 8; 21: 21; 22: 2. W. ῥύμη (Tob 13: 17, 18 BA; Is 15: 3) Lk 14: 21. ἐν ταῖς γωνίαις τῶν π. at or *on the street-corners* Mt 6: 5. M-M. B. 720.*

πλάτος, ους, τό (Hdt.+; inscr., pap., LXX; En. 21, 7; Ep. Arist., Philo; Jos., Bell. 7, 312, Ant. 8, 65, C. Ap. 2, 119.—ὁ πλάτος only as an oversight Eph 3: 18 𝔓⁴⁶) *breadth, width.*
1. lit., w. τὸ μῆκος Rv 21: 16a as well as τὸ μῆκος and τὸ ὕψος vs. 16b. On τὸ πλάτος καὶ μῆκος καὶ ὕψος καὶ βάθος Eph 3: 18 cf. βάθος 1.—τὸ πλάτος τῆς γῆς Rv 20: 9 comes fr. the OT (Da 12: 2 LXX. Cf. Hab 1: 6; Sir 1: 3). But the sense is not clear. *Breadth=the broad plain of the earth* is perh. meant to provide room for the countless enemies of God vs. 8, but the 'going up' is better suited to Satan (vs. 7) who has recently been freed, and who comes up again fr. the abyss (vs. 3).
2. The fig. sense (cf. Procop. Soph., Ep. 65; Nicetas Eugen. 2, 10 H. καρδίας πλάτος) is given the word in the OT expr. (cf. Pr 7: 3; 22: 20; 3: 3 A) τὰ δικαιώματα τοῦ κυρίου ἐπὶ τὰ πλάτη τῆς καρδίας ὑμῶν ἐγέγραπτο *the*

ordinances of the Lord had been written on the (broad) *tables of your heart* 1 Cl 2: 8. M-M.*

πλατύνω pass.: pf. 3 sing. πεπλάτυνται; 1 aor. ἐπλατύνθην (X.+; inscr., LXX; Jos., Ant. 9, 206) *make broad, enlarge.*
1. lit. τὶ someth. τὰ φυλακτήρια Mt 23: 5 (s. φυλακτήριον). Pass. (w. παχύνεσθαι. S. παχύνω 1) *be enlarged* 1 Cl 3: 1 (Dt 32: 15).
2. fig. ἡ καρδία ἡμῶν πεπλάτυνται *my heart is open wide* 2 Cor 6: 11 (the expr. also occurs Dt 6: 12 v.l.; 11: 16; Ps 118: 32. Cf. Epict., fgm. Stob. 60 τὰς ψυχὰς αὔξειν) πλατύνθητε καὶ ὑμεῖς *you must open your hearts* (wide), *too* vs. 13. M-M.*

πλατύς, εῖα, ύ (Hom.+; inscr., pap., LXX, Philo, Joseph.) *broad, wide* Mt 7: 13 of a road, in case the correct rdg. is πλατεῖα καὶ εὐρύχωρος ἡ ὁδός (cf. X., Cyr. 1, 6, 43 ἢ στενὰς ἢ πλατείας ὁδούς; Arrian, Anab. 1, 1, 8 ὁδὸς πλατεῖα; Dit., Syll.³ 57, 25 [V BC]; 313, 19f; Jos., Bell. 6, 149), of a gate if the rdg. is πλατεῖα ἡ πύλη καὶ ... (cf. Plut., Caes. 33, 1 πλατεῖαι πύλαι; PFlor. 333, 11 μέχρι πλατείας πύλης; Jos., Bell. 3, 81). M-M. B. 885.*

πλατυσμός, οῦ, ὁ (Diosc. 5, 6 al.; LXX; Philo, Somn. 2, 36).—1. *extension, enlargement, expansion* (schol. on Pind., Eustath., Prooem. 4) of a church (w. δόξα) 1 Cl 3: 1.—2. *broad space, extent* (2 Km 22: 20; Ps 17: 20; 118: 45) Hm 5, 2, 3 (εὐθηνέω 2).*

πλέγμα, ατος, τό *anything entwined, woven, braided* (of the most diverse kinds, since Eur., Pla., X.; Is 28: 5 Aq. and Theod.; Philo; Jos., Ant. 2, 220. Cf. πλέκω) of hair 1 Ti 2: 9.*

πλείων, πλειόνως, πλεῖστος s. πολύς II and III. M-M.

πλέκω 1 aor. ἔπλεξα; pf. pass. ptc. πεπλεγμένος (Hom.+; POsl. 159, 10; 19 [III AD]; LXX; Ep. Arist. 70; Philo, Aet. M. 105; Jos., Ant. 3, 170) *weave, plait* στέφανον a wreath (Epici p. 23, Cypria fgm. 4, 2; Pind.+) Mk 15: 17. τὶ ἔκ τινος (Alciphr. 2, 35, 1; Paus. 2, 35, 5 στεφ. ἐκ) Mt 27: 29; J 19: 2; pass. AP 3: 10. M-M. B. 622.*

πλέον s. πολύς II (πλείων).

πλεονάζω 1 aor. ἐπλεόνασα (Thu., Hippocr.+; inscr., pap., LXX; Ep. Arist. 295 [conject. by Wendl.]).
1. intr. (Thu.+)—a. *be or become more, be or become great, be present in abundance, grow, increase* (Strabo 4, 1, 13; Appian, Bell. Civ. 5, 89 §370; Ael. Aristid. 33 p. 616 D.; schol. on Nicander, Ther. 553; 2 Ch 24: 11; Philo, Rer. Div. Her. 245; Jos., Ant. 19, 319) 2 Pt 1: 8. *Increase* in number, *multiply* Dg 6: 9; cf. 7: 8. Of sin (cf. Sir 23: 3 ὅπως μὴ αἱ ἁμαρτίαι μου πλεονάσωσι) Ro 5: 20a (cf. Philistion [IV BC] 4 p. 110, 8 Wellmann [s. Diocles] ἐπειδὰν πλεονάσῃ τὸ θερμόν), b. Of grace 6: 1; 2 Cor 4: 15. Of love 2 Th 1: 3. ἐπιζητῶ τὸν καρπὸν τὸν πλεονάζοντα *I seek the fruit that increases* Phil 4: 17.
b. *have more than is necessary, have too much* (Diod. S. 2, 54, 7; 11, 59, 4; 19, 81, 3; Appian, Bell. Civ. 4, 108 §454 of legions with more than the usual number of men) 2 Cor 8: 15 (Ex 16: 18).
2. trans.—a. *increase, bring forth in abundance* τὶ someth. (Ps 70: 21; Jos., Ant. 1, 32) τὸ στόμα σου ἐπλεόνασεν κακίαν 1 Cl 35: 8 (Ps 49: 19).
b. *cause to increase, become rich* τινά τινι someone in someth. (w. περισσεύειν) ὑμᾶς ὁ κύριος πλεονάσαι τῇ ἀγάπῃ *may the Lord cause you to increase in love* 1 Th 3: 12.—GDelling, TW VI 263-6. M-M.*

πλεονεκτέω 1 aor. ἐπλεονέκτησα, pass. ἐπλεονεκτήθην (since Hdt. 8, 112; inscr., pap., LXX; Ep. Arist. 270; Philo; Jos., Bell. 6, 79, Ant. 1, 66; 2, 260 al.; Test. 12 Patr.; predom. intr., cf. Bl-D. §148, 1; Mlt. 65). In our lit. only trans.
1. *take advantage of, outwit, defraud, cheat* τινά *someone* (Dionys. Hal. 9, 7; Dio Chrys. 67[17], 8 τὸν ἀδελφόν; Plut., Marc. 29, 7; Ps.-Lucian, Amor. 27).
a. of men, who take advantage of others 2 Cor 7: 2 (w. ἀδικεῖν and φθείρειν); 12: 18. πλ. τινὰ διά τινος *take advantage of someone through someone* vs. 17. πλ. τινὰ ἐν τῷ πράγματι 1 Th 4: 6 (s. πρᾶγμα).
b. of Satan, pass. (Demosth. 41, 25 πλεονεκτεῖσθαι χιλίαις δραχμαῖς; Dit., Or. 484, 27 πλεονεκτεῖσθαι τοὺς ὀλίγους ὑπ' αὐτῶν ἀνθρώπους) ἵνα μὴ πλεονεκτηθῶμεν ὑπὸ τοῦ σατανᾶ *that we may not be outwitted by Satan* 2 Cor 2: 11 ('robbed' by Satan of a member of our group: BNoack, Satanas u. Soteria '48, 98f).
2. *increase the number of* τὶ someth. (Maspéro 3, 9 πλεονεκτῆσαι τὰ πράγματα) of the hare κατ' ἐνιαυτὸν πλ. τὴν ἀφόδευσιν B 10: 6 (cf. ἀφόδευσις). M-M.*

πλεονέκτης, ου, ὁ (since Hdt. [7, 158 adj.]; PMagd. 5, 7 [221 BC]; Sir 14: 9; Philo, Mos. 1, 56) *one who is greedy for gain, a covetous person,* whose ways are judged to be extremely sinful by the Christians and many others (s. πλεονεξία and JWeiss on 1 Cor 5: 11). Among the sinners of the 'two ways' B 19: 6; D 2: 6. Also elsewh. w. those who are burdened w. serious vices (as M. Ant. 11, 18, 6; Philo, Sacr. Abel. 32) 1 Cor 5: 10f; 6: 10; Eph 5: 5 (here characterized as εἰδωλολάτρης; s. on πλεονεξία); Hs 6, 5, 5 (Thu. 1, 40, 1; X., Mem. 1, 2, 12 [both w. βίαιος]; 1, 5, 3, Cyr. 1, 6, 27 [w. κλέπτης and ἅρπαξ]; Aristot., Eth. Nicom. 5, 2 [w. ὁ παράνομος and ὁ ἄνισος]; Diod. S. 20, 106, 4; Plut., Ages. 20, 6 [w. ἐν ταῖς ἐξουσίαις πονηρός], Mor. 57c [w. κακοῦργος]; Vett. Val. 42, 28 [w. ἀλλοτρίων ἐπιθυμητής]). M-M.*

πλεονεξία, ας, ἡ *greediness, insatiableness, avarice, covetousness,* lit. 'a desire to have more' (so Hdt., Thu.+; Aristoxenus, fgm. 50 p. 23, 36ff [πλ. as the vice pure and simple]; Diod. S. 21, 1, 4 [πλ. as the μητρόπολις τῶν ἀδικημάτων]; Musonius 72, 9; 90, 10 H.; Dio Chrys., Or. 67[17] περὶ πλεονεξίας: ὁ μέγιστον κακῶν αἴτιον; 7 μέγιστον κακόν; Ael. Aristid. 39 p. 733 D.: πλ. is among the three most disgraceful things; Herm. Wr. 13, 7; pap., LXX; Ep. Arist. 277; Philo, Spec. Leg. 1, 173, Praem. 15 al.; Test. 12 Patr.; Jos., Bell. 7, 256, Ant. 3, 67; 7, 37 al.) B 10: 4; w. other vices (as Diod. S. 13, 30, 4 in catalogues of vices. On these s. AVögtle, Die Tugend- u. Lasterkataloge im NT '36) Ro 1: 29; 1 Cl 35: 5; B 20: 1; D 5: 1; Pol 2: 2; Hm 6, 2, 5; 8: 5. Used w. ἀκαθαρσία Eph 4: 19; 5: 3. Characterized as εἰδωλολατρία, Col 3: 5 (s. εἰδωλολατρία, πλεονέκτης and cf. Test. Judah 19: 1. Chaeremon the Stoic, Nero's teacher, in Porphyr., Abst. 4, 6 contrasts πλεονεξία with θεία γνῶσις). Of false teachers 2 Pt 2: 3, 14 (s. γυμνάζω, end). πρόφασις πλεονεξίας (subj. gen.) *pretext for avarice* 1 Th 2: 5 (cf. Philostrat. I 362, 14 πρόσχημα τ. πλεονεξίας). φυλάσσεσθαι ἀπὸ πάσης πλ. *guard against every form of greed* Lk 12: 15.—The pl. of the individual expressions of greed (Bl-D. §142.—X., Cyr. 1, 6, 29; Plut., Pomp. 39, 6; 2 Macc 4: 50; Philo, Agr. 83, Vi. Cont. 70; Jos., Ant. 17, 253) Mk 7: 22.—In 2 Cor 9: 5 the context calls for the pregnant mng. *a gift that is grudgingly granted by avarice* (εὐλογία 5); *extortion* (Plummer, ICC ad loc.).—WBSedgwick, ET 36, '25, 478f; TWManson, JTS 44, '43, 86f; EKlaar, Πλεονεξία, -έκτης, -εκτεῖν ThZ 10, '54, 395-7; GDelling, TW VI 266-74: πλεονεκτέω and related words. M-M.*

πλευρά, ᾶς, ἡ (Hom.+; inscr., pap., LXX, Philo; Jos.,
Bell. 1, 332; 5, 64, Ant. 15, 403) *side,* mostly of the human
body Mt 27: 49 v.l.; J 19: 34 (on both s. *νύσσω*); 20: 20,
25, 27; Ac 12: 7 (s. *πατάσσω* 1a).—Of the flat side of a
stone Hs 9, 4, 1. M-M. B. 862.*

πλέω impf. 1 pl. *ἐπλέομεν* (Hom.+; inscr., pap., LXX;
Philo, Ebr. 158; Joseph.; Sib. Or. 4, 78) *travel by sea, sail*
abs. (X., An. 5, 1, 4; Herodian 8, 2, 3) Lk 8: 23; Ac 27: 24.
W. the destination given (X., Hell. 1, 1, 8; Jos., Ant. 18,
111 *εἰς τὴν Ῥώμην) εἰς Συρίαν* 21: 3. *εἰς τὴν Ἰταλίαν*
27: 6. *εἰς τοὺς κατὰ τὴν Ἀσίαν τόπους* vs. 2. W. the
point of departure given as well as the destination (Appian,
Liby. 113 §535 *ἀπὸ Σικελίας ἐς Ἰτύκην* [Utica]) *ἀπὸ
Τρῳάδος εἰς Νεάπολιν* IPol 8: 1. *πᾶς ὁ ἐπὶ τόπον πλέων*
Rv 18: 17 is uncertain in mng. and the rdg. varies. The
majority prefer to interpret it as *every one who sails along
the coast* (de Wette, HHoltzmann, Bousset, more recently
Lohmeyer, Hadorn, Behm, IRohr. For *πλ. ἐπί* w. acc. of
the place cf. Thu. 1, 53, 2; 4 Macc 7: 3. In Philosophenspr.
p. 489, 28 Mull. we have *πλέοντες παρὰ τόπον.* On the
v.l. *ὁ ἐπὶ τῶν πλοίων πλέων* cf. Lucian, Ver. Hist. 1, 34;
Dit., Syll.³ 409, 5f *ἔπλευσεν ἐπὶ τῶν νεῶν.* Ms. 469 has
ἐπὶ πόντον, partially supported by Primasius' 'super
mare'. Cf. EbNestle, Einführung in das Griech. NT³ '09,
182; AFridrichsen, K. Hum. Vetensk.-Samf. i Upps.
Årsb. '43, 31 note *ὁ ἐπίτοπον πλέων*=one who sails
occasionally, a passenger.—S. also IHeikel, StKr 106,
'34/'35, 317). M-M. B. 680f.*

πληγή, ῆς, ἡ (Hom.+; inscr., pap., LXX) *blow, stroke*
1. lit. (Diod. S. 4, 43, 3 [blow of a whip]; Jos., Vi. 335)
Lk 12: 48 (on the omission of *πληγάς* with *πολλάς,
ὀλίγας* vs. 47f, s. *δέρω* and cf. Pla., Leg. 9 p. 854D; 879E;
Demosth. 19, 197; Herodas 3, 77; 5, 33; Diod. S. 36, 8, 3
τρίτην [i.e., *πληγὴν*] *λαβών*; Bl-D. §241, 6; Rob. 653);
2 Cor 6: 5; 11: 23. *ἐπιθεῖναί τινι πληγάς (ἐπιτίθημι*
1aβ) Ac 16: 23; cf. Lk 10: 30.
2. *wound, bruise* as the result of a blow (Diod. S. 15, 55,
4; Nicol. Dam.: 90 fgm. 130, 26 p. 410, 24 Jac.; Appian,
Iber. 74 §314 al.; schol. on Pla., Rep. 566A; Jos., Ant. 7,
128; 10, 77) Ac 16: 33 (Appian, Bell. Civ. 2, 26 §98 *πλ.*=
weal, scar caused by being beaten with rods). *ἡ πλ. τῆς
μαχαίρης* the sword-wound (cf. Philosophenspr. p. 496,
151 Mull. *ξίφους πληγή*) Rv 13: 14 (*πλ.* alone=fatal
wound: Diod. S. 16, 12, 3; Jos., Ant. 9, 121.—*πλ. ἔχειν*:
Anaxandrides Com. 72). *ἡ πλ. τοῦ θανάτου mortal wound*
(cf. Lucian, Dial. Deor. 14, 2; Plut., Anton. 76, 10 *πλ.
εὐθυθάνατος*) vss. 3, 12. The sing. collectively *ἡ πληγή
wounding*=*wounds* B 5: 12; 7: 2.
3. fig. *blow* in the sense 'a blow of fate', etc. (Aeschyl.
+; Polyb. 14, 9, 6; Appian, Bell. Civ. 3, 72 §295; LXX;
En. 10, 7; Philo, Joseph.) *plague, misfortune* (sent by God:
Διὸς πλ. Aeschyl., Ag. 367; Soph., Aj. 137. *πληγαὶ θεοῦ*
Plut., Mor. 168C.—Ex 11: 1 and oft.; Jos., Bell. 1, 373,
Ant. 6, 94; Test. 12 Patr.; Sib. Or. 3, 306; 519) Rv 9: 18,
20; 11: 6; 15: 1, 6, 8; 16: 9, 21a, b; 18: 4, 8; 21: 9; 22: 18.
Of the suffering Servant of God *ἐν πληγῇ εἶναι be struck
down with misfortune* 1 Cl 16: 3, 4 (Is 53: 3, 4); *καθαρίσαι
αὐτὸν τῆς πλ. free him from misfortune* vs. 10 (Is 53: 10).
M-M. B. 305.*

πλῆθος, ους, τό (Hom.+; inscr., pap., LXX, Ep. Arist.,
Philo, Joseph., Test. 12 Patr.—In our lit. it is lacking in
Mt, the Pauline epp., the catholic epp. [except Js and
1 Pt], Rv, and D [B has it only in a quot. fr. the OT]; in the
NT the large majority of occurrences are in Lk and Ac).
1. *quantity* or *number* *καθὼς τὰ ἄστρα τοῦ οὐρανοῦ τῷ*

πλήθει Hb 11: 12 (cf. Josh 11: 4; Da 3: 36 v.l.—S. also
Hdt. 6, 44 al.).
2. concrete: *large number, multitude*—a. of things, w.
gen. (Diod. S. 15, 3, 3 *σίτου*; 15, 9, 3; Polyaenus 8, 28,
Exc. 15, 9; Suppl. Epigr. Gr. VIII 467, 15f [217 BC] *πολὺ
πλ. χρυσίου κτλ.) πλ. ἰχθύων* (Eparchides [III BC]: 437
fgm. 1 Jac.; Diod. S. 3, 44, 8; 5, 19, 4) *πολύ* Lk 5: 6; cf. J
21: 6. *πλ. ἁμαρτιῶν a host of sins* (cf. Sir 5: 6; Ezk 28:
17f; Jos., Ant. 12, 167) Js 5: 20; 1 Pt 4: 8; 1 Cl 49: 5; 2 Cl
16: 4. *φρυγάνων πλ. a bundle of sticks* Ac 28: 3. *πλ.
αἵματος a great quantity of blood* MPol 16: 1. *πλ. τῶν
θυσιῶν* B 2: 5 (Is 1: 11). *τὸ πλ. τῶν οἰκτιρμῶν σου the
abundance of thy compassion* 1 Cl 18: 2 (Ps 50: 3). *τὸ πλ.
τῶν σχισμάτων the large number of cracks* Hs 9, 8, 3.
b. of persons—α. gener. *crowd (of people), throng,
host,* also specif. a disorganized crowd (as Maximus Tyr.
39, 2e; h) *πολὺ πλ.* Mk 3: 7f. W. gen. of the pers. (Jos.,
Bell. 7, 35, Ant. 18, 61; Diod. S. 15, 14, 4 *στρατιωτῶν*;
Cebes 1, 3 *γυναικῶν*; Appian, Bell. Civ. 1, 81 §370
στρατιᾶς πολὺ πλ.=a large number of military men)
πλῆθος πολὺ τοῦ λαοῦ a great throng of people Lk 6: 17;
23: 27 (a *πλ.* at an execution Jos., Ant. 19, 270). *τὸ πλ.
τοῦ λαοῦ* Ac 21: 36 (*πλῆθος . . . κράζοντες* is constructio
ad sensum as Diod. S. 13, 111, 1 *συνέδριον . . . λέγοντες;* Polyb. 18, 9, 9 *σύγκλητος . . . ἐκεῖνοι* and similar
expressions). *τὸ πλ. τοῦ ὄχλου* Hs 9, 4, 4. *πλ. τῶν
ἀσθενούντων a large number of sick people* J 5: 3.
Ἑλλήνων πολὺ πλ. Ac 14: 1; 17: 4. *πλῆθός τι ἀνδρῶν a
large number of* (other) *men* Hs 9, 3, 1 (Diod. S. 15, 76, 2
and Appian, Iber. 59 §248 *πλ. ἀνδρῶν,* Bell. Civ. 2, 67
§276 *πολὺ πλ. ἀνδρῶν). πολὺ πλ. ἐκλεκτῶν* 1 Cl 6: 1.—
Of angels *πλ. στρατιᾶς οὐρανίου a throng of the heavenly
army* Lk 2: 13 (*πλ.* of military men Diod. S. 20, 50, 6;
Appian, Bell. Civ. 1, 81 §370 *στρατιᾶς πλ.*; Jos., Ant. 14,
482). *τὸ πᾶν πλ. τῶν ἀγγέλων αὐτοῦ* 1 Cl 34: 5.—Pl.
(cf. Socrat., Ep. 1, 2; Diod. S. 1, 64, 5; 1, 85, 2; Appian,
Bell. Civ. 2, 120 §503; 2 Macc 12: 27; 3 Macc 5: 24; Ep.
Arist. 15; 21. S. Mayser II 1, '26, 38f) *πλήθη ἀνδρῶν
large numbers of men* Ac 5: 14.
β. a (stated) *meeting, assembly ἐσχίσθη τὸ πλ.* Ac 23:
7. *πᾶν τὸ πλ.* MPol 3. *ἅπαν τὸ πλ. αὐτῶν* Lk 23: 1 (the
verb is in the pl. as Polyaenus 7, 1; 8, 46; Xenophon Eph.
1, 3, 1 *ἦλθον ἅπαν τὸ πλῆθος.* Cf. Herodian 8, 7, 8 *ὁ
δῆμος ὑπεδέχοντο).*
γ. *people, populace, population* (Diod. S. 5, 15, 2;
Appian, Samn. 4 §14; Dit., Syll.³ 581, 95 [c. 200 BC] *τὸ
πλῆθος τὸ Ῥοδίων;* 695, 20 [II BC] *τὸ πλ. τὸ Μαγνήτων;* IG XII 1, 846, 10; 847, 14 [cf. Dit., op. cit. 765 note
5]; 1 Macc 8: 20; 2 Macc 11: 16; Ep. Arist. 308, the last
three: *τὸ πλ. τῶν Ἰουδαίων;* Jos., Vi. 198 *τὸ πλ. τῶν
Γαλιλαίων) τὸ πλῆθος the populace* abs. (as Polyaenus 8,
47; 50) Ac 2: 6; 1 Cl 53: 5 (= *ὁ λαὸς* vss. 3, 4). *ὅλον τὸ πλ.*
Ac 14: 7 D. W. gen. *τὸ πλ. τῆς πόλεως* (Sir 7: 7) Ac 14: 4.
τὸ πλ. τῶν πέριξ πόλεων 5: 16. *ἅπαν τὸ πλ. τῆς
περιχώρου* Lk 8: 37. *ἅπαν τὸ πλ. τῶν Ἰουδαίων* Ac 25:
24; cf. MPol 12: 2.
δ. in the usage of relig. communities as a t.t. for the
whole body of their members, *fellowship, community,
church* (cf. IQS 5, 2; 9; 22; 6, 19; IG XII 1, 155, 6; 156, 5;
Dit., Syll.³ 1023, 16f *τὸ πλῆθος τῶν μετεχόντων τοῦ
ἱεροῦ;* Lucian, Syr. Dea 50) abs. *τὸ πλ. the community,
the church* Ac 15: 30; 19: 9; 21: 22 v.l.; 1 Cl 54: 2; ISm 8:
2; Hm 11: 9. *πᾶν τὸ πλ. the whole community, group* Ac
6: 5; 15: 12. Also *τὸ πᾶν πλ.* IMg 6: 1. *τὸ ἐν θεῷ πλ.* ITr
8: 2. W. gen. *τὸ πᾶν πλ. ὑμῶν* 1: 1. *πᾶν τὸ πλ. τοῦ λαοῦ*
Lk 1: 10. *ἅπαν τὸ πλ. τῶν μαθητῶν the whole community of his disciples* Lk 19: 37; cf. Ac 6: 2. *τὸ πλ. τῶν*

πιστευσάντων 4: 32.—Dssm., NB 59f [BS 232f]. GDelling, TW VI 274–82: πλῆθος and πληθύνω. M-M. B. 929.*

πληθύνω fut. πληθυνῶ; 1 aor. opt. 3 sing. πληθύναι (Gen 28: 3; 2 Cor 9: 10 t.r.). Pass.: impf. ἐπληθυνόμην; 1 aor. ἐπληθύνθην (Aeschyl.+; LXX; Jos., C. Ap. 2, 139 al.; Test. 12 Patr.).
1. trans.—a. act. *increase, multiply* (En. 16, 3), in our lit. always of God: τὶ someth. τὸν σπόρον ὑμῶν 2 Cor 9: 10. ἔθνη 1 Cl 59: 3. Of God's promise to Abraham πληθύνων πληθυνῶ σε *I will surely multiply you* Hb 6: 14 (Gen 22: 17). κύριος ἐπλήθυνεν αὐτοὺς ἐν τοῖς κόποις τῶν χειρῶν αὐτῶν *the Lord has given them abundance in the works of their hands* Hs 9, 24, 3. ὁ θεὸς κτίσας τὰ ὄντα καὶ πληθύνας καὶ αὐξήσας v 1, 1, 6.
b. pass. *be multiplied, grow, increase* (En. 5, 5; 9) in number ἐπληθύνετο ὁ ἀριθμὸς τῶν μαθητῶν Ac 6: 7. ηὔξησεν ὁ λαὸς καὶ ἐπληθύνθη 7: 17 (cf. Ex 1: 7).—9: 31; D 16: 3. αὐξάνεσθε καὶ πληθύνεσθε (Gen 1: 28. Cf. Sib. Or. 1, 57; Herm. Wr. 3, 3 εἰς τὸ αὐξάνεσθαι ἐν αὐξήσει καὶ πληθύνεσθαι ἐν πλήθει) 1 Cl 33: 6; B 6: 12; cf. vs. 18.—Of the growth of Christian preaching, expressed in the number of converts ὁ λόγος τοῦ κυρίου ηὔξανεν καὶ ἐπληθύνετο Ac 12: 24. Of the spread of godlessness τὸ πληθυνθῆναι τὴν ἀνομίαν Mt 24: 12. As a formula in devout wishes (cf. Da 4: 1 Theod., 37c; 6: 26 Theod.) χάρις ὑμῖν καὶ εἰρήνη πληθυνθείη *may grace and peace be yours in ever greater measure* 1 Pt 1: 2; 2 Pt 1: 2. Cf. Jd 2; 1 Cl inscr.; Pol inscr.; MPol inscr. Cf. also Dg 11: 5.
2. intr. (Herodian 3, 8, 8; Jos., Bell. 5, 338; Ex 1: 20; Sir 16: 2; 23: 3; 1 Macc 1: 9. Cf. Anz 296f; Thackeray 282) *grow, increase* πληθυνόντων τ. μαθητῶν *when the disciples were increasing (in number)* Ac 6: 1; 19: 20 D. M-M.*

πλήκτης, ου, ὁ (Aristot., Eth. Eud. 2, 3; Plut., Dio 30, 4, Marcell. 1, 2; Diog. L. 6, 38; Sym. Ps 34: 15) *pugnacious man, bully* in a list of qualities for a bishop 1 Ti 3: 3; Tit 1: 7.*

πλημμέλεια, ας, ἡ (Democr., Pla.+; LXX) *fault, error, sin* (lit. 'false note' in music) (Aristot. 1251a, 31 ἀσέβεια ἢ περὶ θεοὺς πλ.; Jos., C. Ap. 2, 250) θυσίαι περὶ ἁμαρτίας καὶ πλημμελείας *sin and trespass offerings* (LXX, esp. Lev 7: 37) 1 Cl 41: 2. Pl. (Plut., Mor. 168D ἁμαρτίαι κ. πλημμέλειαι; Philo, Mos. 2, 230; Jos., Bell. 5, 392) 60: 1 (w. ἀνομίαι, ἀδικίαι, παραπτώματα).—Dodd 76.*

πλήμμυρα, ης (on the form of the gen. s. Bl-D. §43, 1; Mlt.-H. 118; on the spelling Mlt.-H. 101; 274), ἡ (Dionys. Hal. 1, 71; Crinagoras no. 33, 1; Plut., Rom. 3, 6, Caes. 38, 4, Mor. 897 B and C; Arrian, Ind. 21, 3; 6; POxy. 1409, 17; Job 40: 23 ἐὰν γένηται πλήμμυρα; Philo, Op. M. 58, Leg. All. 1, 34, Abr. 92, Mos. 1, 202; 2, 195) *high water, flood* πλημμύρης γενομένης Lk 6: 48.—The spelling with one μ, which belongs to the older period of the language, is found in mss. D W 𝔓75 et al. On this see Mlt.-H. p. 101; 274f; JWackernagel, Kl. Schr. '53, 1164, 1. M-M.*

πλήν—1. adv. used as conjunction (trag.+; inscr., pap., LXX, Ep. Arist., Philo, Joseph.), coming at the beginning of a sentence or clause.
a. adversative *but*: μὲν—πλήν (*indeed*)—*but* (cf. Bl-D. §447, 6; Rob. 1187) Lk 22: 22.
b. *only, nevertheless, however, but* (πλήν is the real colloq. word for this idea [Schmid I 133]), so in the First and Third Gospels (Bl-D. §449, 1 w. app.—Cf. L-S-J s.v.

B III 2) πλὴν λέγω ὑμῖν *nevertheless I tell you* Mt 11: 22, 24 (ἀμὴν λέγω ὑμῖν in the corresp. pass. Mt 10: 15); 26: 64 (Mt 17: 12 λέγω δὲ ὑμῖν; Mk 9: 13 ἀλλὰ λέγω ὑμῖν). πλὴν οὐαί Mt 18: 7; cf. Lk 17: 1 οὐαὶ δὲ (πλὴν οὐαί 𝔓75 et al.). πλὴν οὐχ ὡς ἐγὼ θέλω, ἀλλ' ὡς σύ Mt 26: 39; cf. Lk 22: 42 (Mk 14: 36 ἀλλ' οὐ τί ἐγὼ θέλω).—Lk 6: 24, 35; 10: 11, 14, 20; 11: 41; 13: 33; 18: 8; 19: 27; 22: 21.—Also looking back at a neg.: μὴ κλαίετε ἐπ' ἐμέ, πλὴν ἐφ' ἑαυτὰς κλαίετε *do not weep for me, but* (*rather*) *weep for yourselves* Lk 23: 28. μὴ ζητεῖτε . . . πλὴν ζητεῖτε 12: (29–)31.
c. *only, in any case, however, but,* breaking off a discussion and emphasizing what is important (UPZ 110, 207 [164 BC]; Sb 6994, 28; Bl-D. §449, 2; Rob. 1187; s. L-S-J loc. cit.), so in Paul 1 Cor 11: 11; Eph 5: 33; Phil 3: 16; 4: 14. Perh. 1: 18 τί γάρ; πλὴν ὅτι . . . *what then? In any case . . .* (but the text is not certain; s. also d); Rv 2: 25.
d. πλὴν ὅτι *except that* (class.; Hero Alex. I p. 188, 1; Dionys. Hal., Comp. Verb. 14, end; Plut., Cato Maj. 23, 6) Ac 20: 23. Perh. also Phil 1: 18 (s. c above) τί γὰρ πλὴν ὅτι . . . ; *what then will come of it, except that . . . ?*
e. breaking off and passing to a new subject *only, however* (exx. in L-S-J πλήν B III 2.—Polyb. 2, 17, 1; Plut., Pericl. 34, 1 begin new sections with πλήν) πλὴν ἰδοὺ ἡ χεὶρ κτλ. *but here is* (*my betrayer's*) *hand* with mine on the table (the narration passes from the institution of the Lord's Supper to a prediction of the betrayal) Lk 22: 21.
2. improper prep. w. gen. *except* (since Od. 8, 207; inscr., pap., LXX [Johannessohn 342–4]; Bl-D. §216, 2; Rob. 646) mostly after neg. statements: Mk 12: 32 (οὐκ ἄλλος πλήν as Jos., Ant. 1, 182); J 8: 10 t.r.; Ac 15: 28; 20: 23; 27: 22. After a positive statement (Thu. 4, 54, 2; X., An. 2, 4, 27; Appian, Liby. 14 §59; Jos., Ant. 12, 422 ἔφυγον πάντες πλὴν ὀκτακοσίων) Ac 8: 1. M-M.**

πλήρης, ες (Aeschyl., Hdt.+; inscr., pap., LXX, En., Philo; Jos., Vi. 165 al.).
1. *filled, full*—a. of things—a. τινός *with* or *of someth.* (Diod. S. 2, 4, 2 λίμνη πλήρης ἰχθύων; Appian, Hann. 15 §66; PSI 422, 14 [III BC] ἡ γῆ ῥηγμῶν [fissures] πλ. ἐστίν; Num 7: 26; Dt 6: 11; Diog. L. 6, 37 πάντα ἐστὶ αὐτοῦ [= θεοῦ] πλήρη) baskets κλασμάτων πλ. *full of pieces* Mk 8: 19; cf. 6: 43 t.r. A vineyard βοτανῶν πλ. *full of weeds* Hs 5, 2, 3. Of a mountain ἀκανθῶν καὶ τριβόλων πλ. s 9, 1, 5; πηγῶν πλ. vs. 8. Trees καρπῶν πλ. s 9, 28, 1. πλήρης πᾶσα ἡ κτίσις τ. δόξης αὐτοῦ 1 Cl 34: 6 (Is 6: 3). εἰς συναγωγὴν πλήρη ἀνδρῶν δικαίων Hm 11: 14.
β. abs. ἑπτὰ σπυρίδες πλήρεις Mt 15: 37; cf. 14: 20. Of jars Hm 12, 5, 3a, b.—ἐκ πλήρους (Dit., Syll.³ 1104, 20 ἐποίησεν ἐκ πλήρους τὰ δίκαια; PTebt. 106, 20 [II BC]; 281, 22; BGU 584, 6 and oft. in pap. = 'in [the] full [amount]'. Acc. to CHTurner, JTS 21, '20 p. 198, 1 this is a Latinism for 'in pleno') *in full, in all fulness* τι ἐκ πλ. Hv 2, 2, 6.
b. of persons, w. gen. ἀνὴρ πλήρης λέπρας Lk 5: 12 (= all covered w. it, as 4 Km 7: 15; Is 1: 15). Mostly *full of* a power, gift, feeling, characteristic quality, etc. (class.; Jos., Vi. 192 πλ. συνέσεως; LXX.—Procop. Soph., Ep. 68 πλ. τοῦ θεοῦ) πλ. πνεύματος ἁγίου Lk 4: 1; Ac 7: 55. πλ. πνεύματος ἁγίου καὶ πίστεως 11: 24; cf. 6: 5. πλ. πνεύματος καὶ σοφίας vs. 3. πλ. χάριτος καὶ ἀληθείας J 1: 14 (s. at the end of this entry). πλ. χάριτος καὶ δυνάμεως Ac 6: 8. πλ. τῆς χάριτος τοῦ θεοῦ MPol 7: 2. πλ. ἔργων ἀγαθῶν *rich in good deeds* Ac 9: 36. πάσης

κακίας πλ. 1 Cl 45: 7 (Maximus Tyr. 34, 3a πλ. κακῶν. Similarly Appian, Bell. Civ. 3, 19 §69, who calls the murderers of Caesar φόνου πλήρεις). πλ. παντὸς δόλου Ac 13: 10 (πλήρης δόλου Sir 1: 30; 19: 26; Jer 5: 27). γενόμενοι πλήρεις θυμοῦ 19: 28 (cf. Petosiris, fgm. 21, l. 29 πλῆρες τὸ ἀγαθὸν γενήσεται). πλ. ἁμαρτιῶν (cf. Is 1: 4) Hs 9, 23, 4. πλ. πάσης ἀπλότητος Hv 1, 2, 4.—Of a heart (cf. 2 Ch 15: 17; 1 Esdr 1: 21) πλ. εἰδωλολατρίας B 16: 7.—Surfeited (with) πλ. εἰμὶ ὁλοκαυτωμάτων I am surfeited with whole burnt offerings B 2: 5 (Is 1: 11).

2. complete, w. nothing lacking, full, in full (Hdt. et al.; LXX) μισθὸς πλ. (X., An. 7, 5, 5; Ruth 2: 12. πλ. is a favorite word in the pap. for a sum that is complete) 2 J 8. πλ. σῖτος fully ripened grain (cf. the 'fully developed' στάχυες Gen 41: 7, 22, 24) Mk 4: 28. νηστεία πλ. a complete fast Hs 5, 1, 3. πλ. πνεύματος ἔκχυσις a full outpouring of the Spirit 1 Cl 2: 2.—Of persons who are complete in a certain respect or who possess someth. fully πλ. ἔν τινι· ἐν τούτοις πλ. 2 Cl 16: 4. πλ. ἐν τῇ πίστει Hm 5, 2, 1; 12, 5, 4.—In some of the passages already mentioned πλήρης is indecl., though never without v.l., and almost only when it is used w. a gen. In Nestle's text τὴν δόξαν αὐτοῦ ... πλήρης (referring to αὐτοῦ) χάριτος καὶ ἀληθείας J 1: 14 (cf. CHTurner, JTS 1, '00, 120ff; 561f). It is found as a v.l. in Mk 8: 19; Ac 6: 3, 5; 19: 28, and without a gen. 2 J 8. Examples of this use of πλήρης are found fr. the second century BC, and fr. the first century AD on it is frequently found in colloq. H.Gk.: PLeid. C II, 14 (160 BC). Wooden tablet fr. Egypt fr. the time of Augustus in Revue Archéol. 29, 1875, 233f= Sb 3553, 7; BGU 707, 15; POxy. 237 IV, 14 (all three II AD); Wilcken, Chrest. 499, 9 (II/III AD); En. 21, 7. S. the exx. in Crönert 179, 4 and cf. also Mayser 63f (w. lit.); 297; Dssm., LO 99f (LAE 125ff); Thackeray 176f; Reinhold 53; Bl-D. §137, 1 w. app.; Mlt. 50; Rob. 275f.—GDelling, TW VI 283-309: πλήρης and related words. M-M. B. 931.*

πληροφορέω 1 aor. imper. πληροφόρησον, inf. πληροφορῆσαι. Pass.: 1 aor. inf. πληροφορηθῆναι, ptc. πληροφορηθείς; pf. πεπληροφόρημαι, ptc. πεπληροφορημένος (Ctesias, fgm. 29, 39; elsewh. since LXX Eccl 8: 11; Test. Abr. [NTS 1, '54/'55, 223]; BGU 665 II, 2 [I AD]; APF 5, '13, 383 no. 69B, 5 [I/II AD]; BGU 747 I, 22 [139 AD]; PAmh. 66 II, 42; POxy. 509, 10 [both II AD]; Vett. Val. 43, 18; 226, 20.—Dssm., LO 67f [LAE 82f]).

1. fill (completely), fulfill, a synonym of πληρόω, which occasionally appears as v.l. for it. In our lit. only fig.

a. w. a thing as obj. τὶ someth., adding to someth. that which it lacks, someth. like fill out, complement, aid τὸν πλοῦτον Hs 2: 8a. τὰς ψυχάς 8b.—τὴν διακονίαν σου πληροφόρησον fulfill your ministry 2 Ti 4: 5. Also the pass. ἵνα δι' ἐμοῦ τὸ κήρυγμα πληροφορηθῇ vs. 17.—Of a request that is fulfilled Hm 9: 2 (the pap. use the word mainly in the sense 'fully satisfy a demand').—Accomplish τὰ πεπληροφορημένα ἐν ἡμῖν πράγματα the things that have been accomplished among us Lk 1: 1 (cf. M-JLagrange, Le sens de Luc 1: 1 d'après les papyrus: Bull. d'ancienne Litt. et Arch. chrét. 2, '12, 96-100; OAPiper, Union Sem. Rev. 57, '45, 15-25: Lk [and Ac] as 'fulfilment' of the OT.—S. also the lit. given s.v. παρακολουθέω, end). Some (e.g. KHRengstorf, Das NT Deutsch '37 ad loc.) would here transl. on which there is full conviction among us, and put the pass. under 2.

b. of pers. πεπληροφορημένος τινός filled w. someth. ἀγάπης love 1 Cl 54: 1 (w. εὔσπλαγχνος). Perh. also ἔν τινι (πληρόω 1b) πεπληροφορημένοι ἐν παντὶ θελήματι τ. θεοῦ full of everything that is (in accord with) God's will Col 4: 12 (s. also 2 below).

2. convince fully (Act. Phil. 9 p. 5, 20B; Ps.-Clem., Hom. 1, 20 al.) pass. be fully convinced, assured, certain (cf. Test. Gad 2: 4 ἐπληροφορήθημεν τῆς ἀναιρέσεως αὐτοῦ='we were quite filled w. the intention to kill him'. —Hegesippus in Euseb., H.E. 2, 23, 14; Martyr. Pionii 4, 17) foll. by ὅτι be fully convinced that (Ps.-Clem., Hom. p. 9, 22 Lag.) Ro 4: 21; IMg 8: 2. Have perfect faith (i.e. limited by no doubt at all) εἰς τὸν κύριον in the Lord ISm 1: 1. ἔν τινι in someth. IMg 11; IPhld inscr.—Abs. (in case ἐν παντὶ κτλ. [s. 1b above] belongs to σταθῆτε) be fully assured τέλειοι καὶ πεπληροφορημένοι Col 4: 12 (but in that case it may also mean here complete, finished). πληροφορηθέντες διὰ τῆς ἀναστάσεως τοῦ κυρίου be fully assured by the Lord's resurrection 1 Cl 42: 3. ἕκαστος ἐν τῷ ἰδίῳ νοΐ πληροφορείσθω every one must be fully convinced in his own mind Ro 14: 5.—Ltzm., Hdb. on Ro 4: 21. M-M. and suppl.*

πληροφορία, ας, ἡ full assurance, certainty (PGiess. 87, 25 [II AD]; Rhet. Gr. VII 108, 3; Hesychius= βεβαιότης. S. πληροφορέω 2); this mng. is poss. in the word's occurrences in our lit. πλοῦτος τῆς πληροφορίας τῆς συνέσεως a wealth of assurance, such as understanding brings Col 2: 2. ἐν ... πλ. πολλῇ with full conviction 1 Th 1: 5. ἐν πλ. τῆς ἐλπίδος Hb 6: 11. πλ. πίστεως 10: 22. πλ. πνεύματος ἁγίου the assurance that the Holy Spirit gives 1 Cl 42: 3. But at least in Col 2: 2; Hb 6: 11; 10: 22; 1 Cl 42: 3 the mng. fulness is also poss. Likew. Ro 15: 29 D* G. M-M.*

πληρόω impf. 3 sing. ἐπλήρου; fut. πληρώσω; 1 aor. ἐπλήρωσα; pf. πεπλήρωκα; plpf. 3 sing. πεπληρώκει (on the omission of the augm. Bl-D. §66, 1; Mlt.-H. 190). Pass.: impf. ἐπληρούμην; pf. πεπλήρωμαι; plpf. 3 sing. πεπλήρωτο (cf. Bl-D. §66, 1; Mlt.-H. 190); 1 aor. ἐπληρώθην; 1 fut. πληρωθήσομαι (Aeschyl., Hdt.+; inscr., pap., LXX, En., Ep. Arist., Philo, Joseph., Test. 12 Patr., Sib. Or.).

1. make full, fill (full)—a. of things τὶ someth. τὴν γῆν B 6: 12 (Gen 1: 28; cf. Ocellus [II BC] c. 46 Harder ['26] τὸν πλείονα τῆς γῆς τόπον πληροῦσθαι with their descendants). The marks left by stones Hs 9, 10, 2. Pass., of a net ἐπληρώθη Mt 13: 48. πᾶσα φάραγξ πληρωθήσεται Lk 3: 5 (Is 40: 4). ὀθόνη πλοίου ὑπὸ πνεύματος πληρουμένη a ship's sail filled out by the wind MPol 15: 2.—τόπον πληρῶσαι fill a space Hs 9, 7, 5.—Also of sounds and odors (as well as light: schol. on Pla. 914B) ἦχος ἐπλήρωσεν τὸν οἶκον a sound filled the house Ac 2: 2 (Diod. S. 11, 24, 4 αἱ οἰκίαι πένθους ἐπληροῦντο=with cries of grief). ἡ οἰκία ἐπληρώθη ἐκ τῆς ὀσμῆς the house was filled with the fragrance J 12: 3 (cf. Diod. S. 4, 64, 1 τὴν οἰκίαν πληρῶσαί ἀτυχημάτων; Ael. Aristid. 36, 84 K.=48 p. 471 D.: ὅταν οἴκημα πληρωθῇ).—Also in other ways of the filling of impers. objects with real but intangible things or qualities: τὸ πρόσωπον αὐτοῦ (i.e. of the martyr Polycarp) χάριτος ἐπληροῦτο MPol 12: 1 (χάρις 1 and 4). πεπληρώκατε τὴν Ἰερουσαλὴμ τῆς διδαχῆς ὑμῶν you have filled Jerusalem with your teaching Ac 5: 28. ὑμεῖς πληρώσατε (aor. imper. as a rhetor. demand; B has πληρώσετε; D has ἐπληρώσατε) τὸ μέτρον τῶν πατέρων ὑμῶν of filling the measure of sins (cf. Da 8: 23) Mt 23: 32; cf. ἐπεὶ πεπλήρωτο ἡ ἡμετέρα ἀδικία Dg 9: 2. θεὸς πληρώσει πᾶσαν χρείαν ὑμῶν Phil 4: 19 (cf. Thu. 1, 70, 7). πλ. τὴν καρδίαν τινός fill someone's heart, i.e., take full possession of it (cf. Eccl 9: 3) ἡ λύπη πεπλήρωκεν ὑμῶν τ. καρδίαν J 16: 6. διὰ τί ἐπλήρωσεν ὁ σατανᾶς τ. καρδίαν σου; Ac 5: 3 (Ad'Alès, Rech de Sc rel 24, '34, 199f; 474f prefers the v.l. ἐπήρωσεν. Against him LSt.-Paul Girard, Mém. de l'inst. franç. du Caire 67, '37,

309–12). ὁ ψευδοπροφήτης πληροῖ τὰς ψυχὰς αὐτῶν Hm 11: 2.—Of Christ, who passed through all the cosmic spheres ἵνα πληρώσῃ τὰ πάντα Eph 4: 10 (cf. Jer 23: 24; Philo, Leg. All. 3, 4 πάντα πεπλήρωκεν ὁ θεός, Vita Mos. 2, 238, Conf. Lingu. 136). The mid. in the sense of the act. (Bl-D. §316, 1; Rob. 805f. Cf. X., Hell. 6, 2, 14; 35 al.; Plut., Alc. 35, 6) τὸ πλήρωμα τοῦ τὰ πάντα ἐν πᾶσιν πληρουμένου Eph 1: 23 (πλήρωμα 2).

b. of persons *fill* w. powers, qualities, etc. τινά *someone* ὁ ἄγγελος τοῦ προφητικοῦ πνεύματος πληροῖ τὸν ἄνθρωπον Hm 11: 9a. τινά τινος *someone with someth.* (Bl-D. §172 w. app.; Rob. 510) πληρώσεις με εὐφροσύνης Ac 2: 28 (Ps 15: 11). Cf. Ro 15: 13. τινά τινι *someone with someth.* (Bl-D. §195, 2) ὁ διάβολος πληροῖ αὐτὸν τῷ αὐτοῦ πνεύματι Hm 11: 3.—Mostly pass., in pres., impf., fut., aor. *become filled* or *full*; in the perf. *have been filled*, *be full*: w. gen. of the thing (Diod. S. 20, 21, 3 τῶν βασιλείων πεπληρωμένων φόνων =when the palace was full of murderous deeds; Diog. L. 5, 42 τὸ πάσης ἀρετῆς πεπληρῶσθαι) Lk 2: 40 v.l.; Ac 13: 52 (Jos., Ant. 15, 421 ἐπληρώθη χαρᾶς); Ro 15: 14; 2 Ti 1: 4; Dg 10: 3; IRo inscr.; GOxy 40f.—W. dat. of the thing (Aeschyl., Sept. 464 al.; Parthenius 10, 4 ἄχει ἐπληρώθη; 2 Macc 7: 21; 3 Macc 4: 16; 5: 30. Cf. BGU 1108, 12 [I BC]) Lk 2: 40; Ro 1: 29; 2 Cor 7: 4; Hm 5, 2, 7; 11: 9b.—W. acc. of the thing (the pap. use the act. and pass. w. the acc. of the thing in the sense 'settle in full by [paying or delivering] someth.': PLond. 243, 11; 251, 30; POxy. 1133, 8; 1134, 6; PFlor. 27, 3 al.; Bl-D. §159, 1; Rob. 510) πεπληρωμένοι καρπὸν δικαιοσύνης Phil 1: 11. Cf. Col 1: 9.—W. ἐν and dat. of the thing ἐν πνεύματι *with the Spirit* Eph 5: 18. ἐν πίστει καὶ ἀγάπῃ ISm inscr. Cf. Col 4: 12 t.r., in case ἐν κτλ. here belongs to πεπληρωμένοι (s. πληροφορέω 1b); however, mng. 3 is also poss. ἐστὲ ἐν αὐτῷ πεπληρωμένοι Col 2: 10 is prob. different, meaning not 'with him', but *in him* or *through him.*—Abs. Eph 3: 19 (εἰς denotes the goal; s. πλήρωμα 3b). πεπλήρωμαι *I am well supplied* Phil 4: 18 (cf. Diod. S. 14, 62, 5 πληροῦν τινα=supply someone fully).

2. of time, *fill (up), complete* a period of time, *reach its end* (Pla., Leg. 9 p. 866A, Tim. 39D; Plut., Lucull. 35, 8; POxy. 275, 24 [66 AD] μέχρι τοῦ τὸν χρόνον πληρωθῆναι; 491, 6; PTebt. 374, 10; BGU 1047 III, 12 al. in pap.; Gen 25: 24; 29: 21; Lev 8: 33; 12: 4; 25: 30; Num 6: 5; Tob 10: 1; 1 Macc 3: 49 al.; Jos., Ant. 4, 78; 6, 49) in our lit. only pass. (Ps.-Callisth. 3, 17, 39; 41 πεπλήρωται τὰ τῆς ζωῆς ἔτη) πεπλήρωται ὁ καιρός Mk 1: 15; cf. J 7: 8. χρόνος instead of καιρός Hs 6, 5, 2; cf. πληρωθέντος τοῦ χρόνου *when the time has elapsed* 1 Cl 25: 2. πεπλήρωνται αἱ ἡμέραι *the days are over, have come to an end* Hv 2, 2, 5.—Ac 9: 23. ending of Mk in the Freer ms. 6f. πληρωθέντων ἐτῶν τεσσεράκοντα *when forty years had passed* Ac 7: 30.—24: 27; 1 Cl 25: 5. ὡς ἐπληροῦτο αὐτῷ τεσσαρακονταετὴς χρόνος *when he had become 40 years old* Ac 7: 23 (PFlor. 382, 6; 11 ἑβδομήκοντα ἔτη ἐπλήρωσας).

3. *bring* someth. *to completion, finish* someth. already begun (X., Hell. 4, 8, 16; Herodian 1, 5, 8; Olympiodorus, Life of Plato p. 2 Westerm.: the hymn that was begun; Himerius, Or. 6[2], 14 πληρῶσαι τὴν ἐπιθυμίαν=fully gratify the desire, in that the Persians wished to incorporate into their great empire a small piece of the west, i.e., Greece) τὸ εὐαγγέλιον τοῦ Χριστοῦ *bring (the preaching of) the gospel to completion* by proclaiming it in the most remote areas Ro 15: 19; sim. πλ. τ. λόγον τοῦ θεοῦ Col 1: 25. πληρώσατέ μου τ. χαράν Phil 2: 2. Cf. 2 Th 1: 11.—Pass. 2 Cor 10: 6; Col 4: 12 t.r. (s. 1b above). ὁ πᾶς νόμος ἐν ἑνὶ λόγῳ πεπλήρωται Gal 5: 14 because of its past tense is prob. to be translated *the whole law has*

found its full expression in a single word (but perh. this passage belongs under 4b). οὐχ εὕρηκά σου ἔργα πεπληρωμένα Rv 3: 2. Johannine usage speaks of *joy that is made complete* (the act. in Phil 2: 2, s. above) J 3: 29; 15: 11; 16: 24; 17: 13; 1 J 1: 4; 2 J 12.

4. *fulfill*, by deeds, a prophecy, an obligation, a promise, a law, a request, a purpose, a desire, a hope, a duty, a fate, a destiny, etc. (Pla., Gorg. 63 p. 507E ἐπιθυμίας; Herodian 2, 7, 6 ὑποσχέσεις; Epict. 2, 9, 3; 8 ἐπαγγελίαν; Plut., Cic. 17, 5 τὸ χρεών [=destiny]; Procop. Soph., Ep. 68 τ. ἐλπίδας; Spartan inscr. in Annual of the Brit. School of Athens 12, '05/'06, p. 452 [I AD] τὰ εἰθισμένα; pap., LXX; Philo, Praem. 83 τὰς θείας παραινέσεις μὴ κενὰς ἀπολιπεῖν τῶν οἰκείων πράξεων, ἀλλὰ πληρῶσαι τοὺς λόγους ἔργοις ἐπαινετοῖς; Jos., Ant. 5, 145; 14, 486).

a. of the fulfilment of divine predictions or promises. The word stands almost always in the passive *be fulfilled* (Polyaenus 1, 18 τοῦ λογίου πεπληρωμένου; Alex. Aphr., Fat. 31, II 2 p. 202, 21 ὅπως πληρωθῇ τὸ τῆς εἱμαρμένης δρᾶμα; 3 Km 2: 27; Ps.-Clem., Hom. 8, 4) and refers mostly to the Scripture and its words: τοῦτο γέγονεν ἵνα πληρωθῇ τὸ ῥηθὲν ὑπὸ κυρίου διὰ τοῦ προφήτου (cf. 2 Ch 36: 21) Mt 1: 22; cf. 2: 15, 17, 23; 4: 14; 8: 17; 12: 17; 13: 35; 21: 4; 26: 54, 56; 27: 9 (PNepper-Christensen) D. Mt-evangelium, '58, 136–62); Mk 14: 49; 15: 28; Lk 1: 20; 4: 21; 21: 22 t.r.; 24: 44; J 12: 38; 13: 18; 15: 25; 17: 12; 19: 24, 36; Ac 1: 16 (cf. Test. Napht. 7: 1 δεῖ ταῦτα πληρωθῆναι); Js 2: 23. A vision MPol 12: 3.—The OT type *finds its fulfilment* in the antitype Lk 22: 16 (cf. MBlack, ET 57, '45/'46, 25f, An Aramaic Approach², '67, 229–36). At times one of Jesus' predictions is fulfilled: J 18: 9, 32. The act. *bring to fulfilment,* partly of God, who brings his prophecies to fulfilment Ac 3: 18; MPol 14: 2, partly of men who, by what they do, help to bring the divine prophecies to realization (Vi. Thu. I 8 οὗτος ἐπλήρωσε τὰ μεμαντευμένα) Ac 13: 27. Jesus himself *fulfills* his destiny by dying, as God's messengers Moses and Elijah foretell Lk 9: 31.—GP 5: 17.

b. a prayer (Charito 8, 1, 9 πεπληρώκασιν οἱ θεοὶ τὰς εὐχάς; Aristaen., Ep. 1, 16 the god πεπλήρωκε τ. εὐχήν [= prayer]; Inscr. Brit. Mus. 894) πληρῶσαί μου τὴν αἴτησιν *answer my prayer* ITr 13: 3 (cf. Ps 19: 5). A command(ment) (Herodian 3, 11, 4 τὰς ἐντολάς; POxy. 1252A, 9 πλήρωσον τὸ κεκελευσμένον; 1 Macc 2: 55; Sib. Or. 3, 246) πεπλήρωκεν ἐντολὴν δικαιοσύνης Pol 3: 3. νόμον (Ps.-Demetr., Form. Ep. p. 12, 9; cf. Hdt. 1, 199 ἐκπλῆσαι τὸν νόμον) Ro 13: 8; pass. Gal 5: 14 (but s. 3 above and cf. Aeschyl., Ag. 313). τὸ δικαίωμα τοῦ νόμου Ro 8: 4. πᾶσαν δικαιοσύνην (cf. 4 Macc 12: 14 πλ. τὴν εὐσέβειαν) Mt 3: 15 (cf. AFridrichsen: Congr. d'Hist. du Christ. I '28, 167–77; OEissfeldt, ZNW 61, '70, 209–15 and s. βαπτίζω 2a, end); pass. ISm 1: 1 (cf. δικαιοσύνη 2a). Also ἐστὶ πρέπον πληρωθῆναι πάντα *it is fitting that all things should be fulfilled* GEb 3 (cf. APF 3, '06, 370 II, 7 [II AD] ἕως ἅπαντα τὰ κατ' ἐμὲ πεπληρωθῶσαι).—A duty or office βλέπε τὴν διακονίαν . . . ἵνα αὐτὴν πληροῖς *pay attention to your duty . . . and perform it* Col 4: 17 (cf. CIG 2336 πλ. πᾶσαν ἀρχὴν κ. λειτουργίαν; PFlor. 382, 40 πληρῶσαι τὴν λειτουργίαν).—LRobert, Nouvelles Inscr. de Sardes, 1, '64, 39, n. 5.—Abs., in the broadest sense and in contrast to καταλύειν (s. καταλύω 1c): οὐκ ἦλθον καταλῦσαι ἀλλὰ πληρῶσαι Mt 5: 17; depending on how one prefers to interpret the context, πληρόω is understood here either as *fulfill*= do, carry out, or as *bring to full expression*= show it forth in its true mng., or as *fill up*= complete (s. AKlöpper, ZWTh 39, 1896, 1ff; AHarnack, Aus Wissenschaft u. Leben II '11, 225ff, SAB '12, 184ff; JHänel, Der Schriftbegriff Jesu

'19, 155ff; Dalman, Jesus 56-66 *confirm*; WHPHatch, ATR 18, '36, 129-40; HLjungman, D. Gesetz Erfüllen, '54; WGKümmel, Verheissung u. Erfüllung³, '56; JO Rourke, The Fulfilment Texts in Mt, CBQ 24, '62, 394-403).

5. *complete, finish, bring to an end* (1 Macc 4: 19) πάντα τὰ ῥήματα Lk 7: 1. τὴν διακονίαν Ac 12: 25. τὸν δρόμον 13: 25; cf. the abs. ἕως πληρώσωσιν *until they should complete (their course)* Rv 6: 11 v.l. (s. 6 below). τὸ ἔργον Ac 14: 26. τὴν εὐχήν MPol 15: 1. τὰ κυνηγέσια 12: 2 (another possibility here is the quite rare [Hdt. 2, 7 al.] intrans. sense *be complete, be at an end*). Pass. *be accomplished, be finished, at an end* (Ps.-Callisth. 1, 24, 9 as a saying of Philip as he lay dying: ἐμοῦ τὸ πεπρωμένον πεπλήρωται=my destiny has been fulfilled) ὡς ἐπληρώθη ταῦτα Ac 19: 21. ἄχρι οὗ πληρωθῶσιν καιροὶ ἐθνῶν Lk 21: 24. αἱ ἀποκαλύψεις αὗται τέλος ἔχουσιν· πεπληρωμέναι γάρ εἰσιν *these revelations have attained their purpose, for they are completed* Hv 3, 3, 2.

6. *complete a number*, pass. *have the number made complete* (since Hdt. 7, 29) ἕως πληρωθῶσιν οἱ σύνδουλοι Rv 6: 11 (s. 5 above).—CFDMoule, Fulfilment Words in the NT, NTS 14, '68, 293-320. M-M.*

πλήρωμα, ατος, τό (Eur., Hdt.+; inscr., pap., LXX, Philo).

1. *that which fills*—**a.** *that which fills (up), content(s)* (Eur., Ion 1051 κρατήρων πληρώματα; Hippocr., Aër. 7 τὸ πλ. τῆς γαστρός. Esp. oft. of the crew or cargo of ships since Thu. 7, 12, 3; 14, 1) ἡ γῆ καὶ τὸ πλ. αὐτῆς *the earth and everything that is in it* 1 Cor 10: 26; 1 Cl 54: 3 (both Ps 23: 1). ἦραν κλάσματα δώδεκα κοφίνων πληρώματα *they gathered (enough) pieces to fill twelve baskets, twelve basketfuls of pieces* Mk 6: 43; cf. 8: 20 (s. Eccl 4: 6; cf. EFFBishop, ET 60, '48, 192f).

b. *that which makes someth. full* or *complete, supplement, complement* (Appian, Mithr. 47 §185 τὰ τῶν γυναικῶν πάντα ἐς τὸ πλήρωμα τῶν δισχιλίων ταλάντων συνέφερον) lit. of the *patch* on a garment Mt 9: 16; Mk 2: 21 (FCSynge, ET 56, '44/'45, 26f).—Fig., perh., of the church which, as the body, is τὸ πλ., the *complement* of Christ, who is the head Eph 1: 23 (so Chrysostom. The word could be understood in a similar sense Pla., Rep. 2 p. 371 E πλ. πόλεώς εἰσι καὶ μισθωτοί). Much more probably the Eph passage belongs under

2. *that which is full of someth.* (Lucian, Ver. Hist. 2, 37; 38 and Polyaenus 3, 9, 55 the manned and loaded ship itself [s. 1a above]; Philo, Praem. 65 γενομένη πλ. ἀρετῶν ἡ ψυχή . . . οὐδὲν ἐν ἑαυτῇ καταλιποῦσα κενόν; Herm. Wr. 12, 15 God is called πλήρωμα τῆς ζωῆς; 6, 4 ὁ κόσμος πλήρωμά ἐστι τῆς κακίας, ὁ δὲ θεὸς τοῦ ἀγαθοῦ; 16, 3 τ. πάντων τὸ πλ. ἕν ἐστι.—Rtzst., Poim. 25, 1) *(that) which is full of him who* etc. (so as early as Severian of Gabala [KStaab, Pls-Kommentare '33, 307] and Theodoret, who consider that it is God who fills the church.—Cf. CLMitton, ET 59, '47/'48, 325; 60, '48/'49, 320f; CFDMoule, ibid. 53 and Col and Phil '57, 164-9).

3. *that which is brought to fulness* or *completion*—**a.** *full number* (Hdt. 8, 43; 45 of ships; Aristot., Pol. 2, 7, 22 of citizens) τὸ πλ. τῶν ἐθνῶν Ro 11: 25 (cf. Ael. Aristid. 13 p. 262 D: πλήρωμα ἔθνους. For 11: 12, which is also classed here by many, s. 4 below).

b. *sum total, fulness*, even *(super)abundance* (Diod. S. 2, 12, 2 καθάπερ ἔκ τινος πηγῆς μεγάλης ἀκέραιον διαμένει τὸ πλήρωμα=as if from a great source the abundance [of bitumen] remains undiminished) τινός *of someth.* πλ. εὐλογίας Χριστοῦ *the fulness of Christ's blessing* Ro 15: 29. πᾶν τὸ πλ. τῆς θεότητος *the full*

measure of deity (s. θεότης) Col 2: 9; without the gen., but in the same sense 1: 19.—W. gen. to denote the one who possesses the fulness: θεοῦ πατρὸς πλ. IEph inscr. (s. Hdb. ad loc.). εἰς πᾶν τὸ πλ. τοῦ θεοῦ *that you may be filled with all the fulness of God* Eph 3: 19 (s. πληρόω 1b). Of Christ: ἐκ τοῦ πληρώματος αὐτοῦ J 1: 16 (s. Bultmann 51, 7).—Abs. ἀσπάζομαι ἐν τῷ πληρώματι *I greet in the fulness* of the Christian spirit ITr inscr.—On εἰς μέτρον ἡλικίας τοῦ πληρώματος τοῦ Χριστοῦ Eph 4: 13 s. μέτρον 2b.

4. *fulfilling, fulfilment* (= πλήρωσις, as Eur., Tro. 824; Philo, Abr. 268 π. ἐλπίδων) τὸ πλήρωμα αὐτῶν *their* (the Jews') *fulfilling* (the divine demand) Ro 11: 12 (opp. παράπτωμα and ἥττημα). But this pass. is considered by many to belong under 3 above. πλ. νόμου ἡ ἀγάπη 13: 10.

5. *the state of being full, fulness* of time (πλήρωμα 2) τὸ πλήρωμα τοῦ χρόνου Gal 4: 4 (cf. American Studies in Papyri VI, 587, 34 [24/25 AD], '70 τοῦ δὲ χρόνου πληρωθέντος). τὸ πλ. τῶν καιρῶν Eph 1: 10.—Lghtf., Col and Phlm 255-71; ARobinson, Eph '04, 255ff; HMaVallisoleto, Christi 'Pleroma' iuxta Pli conceptionem: Verbum Domini 14, '34, 49-55; FRMontgomery-Hitchcock, The Pleroma of Christ: Church Quart. Review 125, '37, 1-18; JGewiess: MMeinertz-Festschr. '51, 128-41; PBenoit, RB 63, '56, 5-44 (prison epp.); AFeuillet, Nouvelle Revue Theol. (Tournai) 88, '56, 449-72; 593-610 (Eph 1: 23); GMünderlein NTS 8, '62, 264-76 (Col 1: 19); HSchlier, D. Brief an die Epheser⁴, '63, 96-9. M-M.*

πλήσας, πλησθείς s. πίμπλημι.

πλησίον (in form, the neut. of πλησίος, α, ον, an adj. that goes back to Hom.) adv. (Hom.+; inscr., pap., LXX, En., Philo, Joseph., Test. 12 Patr.).

1. as adv. *near, close by*—**a.** abs. (Diod. S. 11, 4, 1 πλησίον εἶναι; Dionys. Byz. §102; Dit., Syll.³ 344, 83; 888, 127; Wilcken, Chrest. 11, 6; 2 Macc 6: 11) πλ. ἑκάτερον πεφύτευται *they were planted close to each other* Dg 12: 4.

b. subst. ὁ πλησίον *the neighbor, the one who is near* or *close by, the fellow man* (Theognis et al.; X., Mem. 3, 14, 4; Pla., Theaet. 174в ὁ πλησίον καὶ ὁ γείτων; Polyb. 12, 25, 5); Plut., Mor. 40c; 57D; Ael. Aristid. 23, 28 K.=42 p. 777 D. al.; Epict. 4, 13, 2; 9; M. Ant. 4: 18 al.; Ps.-Lucian, Philopatr. 16 ἐὰν κτάνῃς τὸν πλησίον, θανατωθήσῃ παρὰ τ. δίκης; LXX; En. 99, 15; Philo, Virt. 116; Jos., Bell. 7, 260) with and without gen., of a fellow-countryman Ac 7: 27 (cf. Ex 2: 13). Of fellow-Christians Ro 15: 2; Eph 4: 25 (Zech 8: 16); Js 4: 12; 1 Cl 38: 1; Dg 10: 6; IMg 6: 2; ITr 8: 2; Pol 3: 3. In the teaching about the Two Ways: B 19: 3, 5f, 8; D 1: 2 (cf. Lev 19: 18); 2: 2 (cf. Ex 20: 17), vs. 6. Quite freq. as a quot. from or in close connection with the OT: B 2: 8 (Zech 8: 17). Esp. oft. the passage involved is Lev 19: 18 (Philosophenspr. p. 489, 27 M. warns against λυπεῖν τὸν πλησίον) Mt 5: 43 (here the NT introduces the contrast ὁ πλησίον–ὁ ἐχθρός); 19: 19; 22: 39; Mk 12: 31, 33; Lk 10: 27; Ro 13: 9; cf. vs. 10; Gal 5: 14; Js 2: 8. Without the art., as pred. (cf. Bl-D. §266; Rob. 547 and SSol 5: 16) καὶ τίς ἐστιν μου πλησίον; *and who is my neighbor?* Lk 10: 29; cf. vs. 36. —Pl. οἱ πλησίον (Alex. Aphr., An. Mant. p. 162, 19 Br.) of fellow Christians 1 Cl 2: 6; 51: 2; Dg 10: 5.—Billerb. I 353-68, Nathanael 34, '18, 12ff; JChrGspann, Die Nächstenliebe im NT: Der Katholik 87, '07, 376-91; MRade, Der Nächste: Jülicher-Festschr. '27, 70-9; RBultmann, Aimer son prochain: RHPhr 10, '30, 222-41; EFuchs, ThBl 11, '32, 129-40; HWeinel, D. Nächstenliebe: Arch. f. d. gesamte Psychol. 86, '33, 247-60; ATNikolainen, D.

Nächste als rel. Frage im NT '37 (cf. Theol. Fennica 1, '39, 13–22); HPreisker, D. Ethos des Urchristentums '49, 68–81; JBowman, ET 59, '47/'48, 151–3; 248f.—HGreeven, TW VI, '56, 309–16.

2. as an improper prep. w. gen. (Hom. +; Dionys. Hal. 9, 35, 2; 4; Plut., Mor. 148E πλ. τοῦ ἀνδρός; inscr., pap., LXX; Ep. Arist. 181; Jos., Ant. 5, 225; 13, 333 al.) *near, close to someth.* πλ. τοῦ χωρίου (Menand., Epitr. 25 πλ. τῶν χωρίων) J 4: 5. πλ. τοῦ τόπου ἐκείνου AP 11: 26. πλ. ἐκείνων 13: 28.—ANissen, Gott u. der Nächste im Antiken Judentum, '74. M-M. B. 867.*

πλησμονή, ῆς, ἡ (Eur., Pla., X. +; Plut., LXX, Philo; Jos., Ant. 11, 34) *satiety* esp. w. food and drink, but also w. other types of enjoyment, *satisfaction, gratification* (cf. Ps.-Clem., Hom. 8, 15 πρὸς τὴν ἑαυτῶν πλησμονήν). In our lit. the word is found only Col 2: 23 in a difficult saying (Theodore of Mops. I 296 Swete) πρὸς πλησμονὴν τ. σαρκός. The Gk. exegetes understood this to mean *for the gratification of physical needs.* But σάρξ, acc. to vs. 18, is surely to be taken in a bad sense, and the transl. should be *for the indulgence of the flesh.*—BGHall, ET 36, '25, 285; PLHedley, ZNW 27, '28, 211–16; GBornkamm, ThLZ 73, '48, 18. M-M.*

πλήσσω impf. ἔπλησσον; 2 aor. pass. ἐπλήγην (Hom. +; inscr., pap., LXX, Philo; Jos., Bell. 1, 662; 6, 138, Ant. 8, 389; Sib. Or. 5, 530) *strike.*
1. lit., of flames of fire (Lucian, Jupp. Conf. 15 of lightning) τινὰ κατὰ τῶν ὀφθαλμῶν (κατά I 1b) AP 11: 26.
2. fig., of 'blows' that come to persons or things (Ex 9: 31f; Ps 101: 5; Test. Reub. 1: 7 ἔπληξέ με πληγῇ μεγάλῃ); pass. (Diod. S. 17, 117, 2 ὑπό τινος πληγῆς πεπληγμένος; Ael. Aristid. 13 p. 206 D.: ἐκ θεοῦ πληγείς; Ep. Arist. 313 ὑπὸ τ. θεοῦ) of heavenly bodies, which lose one third of their light as the result of a blow Rv 8: 12. M-M.*

πλοιάριον, ου, τό (Aristoph., X. +; Diod. S. 14, 30; Zen.-P. 39 [= Sb 6745], 3 [253/2 BC]; BGU 812, 5; PGenève 14, 8; Ostraka II 1051, 4) dim. of πλοῖον, *small ship, boat, skiff* Mk 3: 9 (πλοῖον is used for the same kind of vessel 4: 1; hence it is prob. no longer thought of as a dim.; this is plainly the case in Ael. Aristid. 50, 35 K. = 26 p. 512 D., where there are nothing but πλοιάρια in the harbor); 4: 36 t.r.; Lk 5: 2 (πλοῖα 𝔓⁷⁵ et al.); J 6: 22, 23 (v.l. πλοῖα), 24. οἱ μαθηταὶ τῷ πλοιαρίῳ (comitative-instrum. dat.; cf. Kühner-G. I 430ff. Loc., perh. instrum.: Rob. 520f; 533) 21: 8. M-M.*

πλοῖον, ου, τό (Aeschyl., Hdt. +; esp. freq. in later times, when ναῦς [in our lit. only Ac 27: 41; on the differentiation s. Didymus p. 321 MSchmidt] became rare; inscr., pap., LXX; En. 101, 4; Ep. Arist. 214; Joseph.; Test. Napht. 6: 2f) *ship* of any kind, though esp. a merchant ship.
1. of rather large sea-faring ships Ac 20: 13, 38; 21: 2f, 6; 27: 2–44 (on vs. 44 s. FZorell, BZ 9, '11, 159f); 28: 11; Js 3: 4; Rv 8: 9; 18: 19.
2. *boat* of the small fishing vessels on Lake Gennesaret (Jos., Vi. 163; 165) Mt 4: 21f; Mk 1: 19f; Lk 5: 2 (v.l.) f, 7; J 6: 19, 21a, b, 23 (𝔓⁷⁵ B al.); ἐμβαίνειν εἰς πλ. *get into a boat* Mt 9: 1; 13: 2; Mk 4: 1; Lk 8: 22, 37. ἐμβαίνειν εἰς τὸ πλ. Mt 14: 22 (v.l. without τό); 15: 39; Mk 5: 18; 8: 10; J 21: 3; ἀναβαίνειν εἰς τὸ πλ. Mt 14: 32; Mk 6: 51. συνεισέρχεσθαι εἰς τὸ πλ. J 6: 22. ἐξέρχεσθαι ἐκ τοῦ πλ. *get out of the boat* Mk 6: 54. κατάγειν τὰ πλ. ἐπὶ τὴν γῆν (s. κατάγω) Lk 5: 11.
3. quite gener. ὀθόνη πλοίου *the sail of a ship* MPol 15:

2.—EHilgert, The Ship and Related Symbols in the NT, '60. M-M. B. 727; 729.

πλόκαμος, ου, ὁ (Hom. +) *braid* or *lock of hair* predom. of women (so in pl. since Il. 14, 176; also 3 Macc 1: 4) AP 9: 24.*

πλοκή, ῆς, ἡ (Eur., Pla. +; pap.; Ex 28: 14; Ep. Arist.) *braiding, braid* ὁ ἐκ πλοκῆς τριχῶν κόσμος 1 Pt 3: 3 v.l.*

πλόος (Hom. +) or contracted **πλοῦς** (Att.; inscr., pap., Wsd 14: 1; Philo, Joseph.), ὁ orig. belonging to the second declension. In Hellenistic times it passed over to the third decl. and is declined like βοῦς (cf. Bl-D. §52; W-S. §8, 11, end; Mlt.-H. 127; 142. Our lit.—i.e., Ac—has the gen. πλοός (Peripl. Eryth. c. 61; Xenophon Eph. 1, 14; 5, 12; Dit., Or. 572, 21 [c. 200 AD]) and the acc. πλοῦν (Jos., Bell. 2, 40, Ant. 8, 181); *voyage, navigation* (so Hom. +) Ac 27: 9f. τὸν πλ. διανύειν (s. διανύω 1) 21: 7. M-M.*

πλούσιος, ια, ιον (Hes., Hdt. +; inscr., pap., LXX, Ep. Arist., Philo; Jos., Bell. 4, 414, Ant. 6, 295) *rich, wealthy.*
1. lit., of earthly possessions ἄνθρωπος πλ. *a rich man* (i.e. one who does not need to work for a living) Mt 27: 57; Lk 12: 16; cf. 16: 1, 19 (here, in 𝔓⁷⁵, the rich man's name is given as νευης, q.v. as a separate entry); 18: 23; 19: 2. γείτονες πλ. *wealthy neighbors* 14: 12.—Subst. ὁ πλ. *the rich man* (oft. in contrast to the poor.—Cf. PHFurfey, CBQ 5, '43, 241–63) Lk 16: 21f; Js 1: 10f; 1 Cl 13: 1 (Jer 9: 22); 38: 2; Hs 2: 5–7 (vs. 4 εἰς πτωχὸν καὶ πλούσιον the art. is omitted after the prep.). Pl. οἱ πλ. (Menand., fgm. 281, 1) Lk 6: 24; 21: 1; 1 Ti 6: 17; Js 2: 6; 5: 1; Rv 6: 15; 13: 16; 1 Cl 16: 10 (Is 53: 9); Hs 2: 8; 9, 20, 1f. Without the art. πλούσιος *a rich man* Mt 19: 23f; Mk 10: 25; Lk 18: 25 (cf. Sextus 193 χαλεπόν ἐστιν πλουτοῦντα σωθῆναι). Pl. Mk 12: 41; B 20: 2; D 5: 2.—For lit. s. under πλοῦτος 1.
2. fig. (Menand., fgm. 1094 and Ep. Arist. 15 πλουσία ψυχή) *rich ἔν τινι in someth.* of God ἐν ἐλέει Eph 2: 4; of men ἐν πίστει Js 2: 5. πλ. τῷ πνεύματι (analogous, but not in contrast to πτωχὸς τῷ πνεύματι Mt 5: 3) *rich in the Spirit* B 19: 2. Abs., of those who are rich in a relig. sense Rv 2: 9; 3: 17. Of the preëxistent Christ δι᾽ ὑμᾶς ἐπτώχευσεν πλούσιος ὤν *for your sake he became poor, though he was rich* 2 Cor 8: 9. ἀπὸ τοῦ πλουσίου τῆς ἀγάπης κυρίου *from the Lord, who is rich in love* B 1: 3 (on the text which, perhaps, is damaged, s. Windisch, Hdb. ad loc.). The text is also uncertain in vs. 2, where μεγάλων ὄντων καὶ πλουσίων τῶν τοῦ θεοῦ δικαιωμάτων εἰς ὑμᾶς is prob. to be rendered: *since the righteous deeds of God toward you are great and generous.* M-M.*

πλουσίως adv. (since Eur.; Hdt. 2, 44; Dit., Or. 767, 18; Philo) *richly, abundantly* ἐκχέειν Tit 3: 6. ἐνοικεῖν Col 3: 16. ἐπιχορηγεῖν 2 Pt 1: 11. μανθάνειν B 9: 7. παρέχειν 1 Ti 6: 17. Comp. πλουσιώτερον (X., Oec. 9, 13) *more richly, more abundantly* (w. ὑψηλότερον) B 1: 7. M-M.*

πλουτέω 1 aor. ἐπλούτησα; pf. πεπλούτηκα (Hes., Hdt. +; Dit., Syll.³ 1268, 30; PGiess. 13, 19; LXX, En., Philo, Joseph., Test. 12 Patr.) *be rich;* aor. *become rich;* pf. *have become rich.*
1. lit., abs. (Artem. 4, 59; En. 97, 8 πλούτῳ πεπλουτήκαμεν; Philo, Virt. 166; Jos., Ant. 4: 14) Lk 1: 53; 1 Ti 6: 9; 2 Cl 20: 1; Dg 10: 5; Hv 3, 6, 7; AP 15: 30. οἱ πλουτοῦντες ἐν τούτῳ τῷ αἰῶνι *those who have riches in this age* Hv 3, 6, 6.—Aor. Hs 8, 9, 1. The source fr. which the wealth comes is indicated by ἀπό τινος (Aristoph., Plut. 569; Lucian, Dial. Deor. 16, 1; Sir 11: 18) οἱ ἔμποροι

οἱ πλουτήσαντες ἀπ' αὐτῆς Rv 18: 15. Also ἔκ τινος (Lysias 32, 25) vss. 3, 19.

2. fig. *be rich ἔν τινι in someth.* (Synes., Ep. 130 p. 265B; Ode of Solomon 11, 9) *ἐν ἔργοις καλοῖς* 1 Ti 6: 18. *ἐν ἐντεύξει* Hs 2: 7. *εἰς θεὸν πλ. be rich in God* or *toward God,* in any case, in the things that are worthy in the sight of God Lk 12: 21. The εἰς-constr. in Ro 10: 12 is different: *κύριος πλουτῶν εἰς πάντας the Lord, who is rich* (and *generous*) *toward all,* i.e., who gives of his wealth generously to all (Philostrat., Vi. Apoll. 4, 8 p. 129, 16 εἰς τὸ κοινόν).—Abs., of being rich in a relig. sense 1 Cor 4: 8; 2 Cor 8: 9 (τῇ ἐκείνου πτωχείᾳ is dat. of instrument or of cause); Rv 3: 18. Pf. πλούσιός εἰμι καὶ πεπλούτηκα vs. 17 (cf. also Hos 12: 9). M-M.*

πλουτίζω 1 aor. ἐπλούτισα, pass. ἐπλουτίσθην (Aeschyl., X. +; inscr., LXX; Anz 297) *make rich.*

1. lit. *τινά someone* (Gen 14: 23; Sir 11: 21; Jos., Ant. 17, 147) Hs 1: 9. Abs. (w. πτωχίζω) of God 1 Cl 59: 3 (cf. 1 Km 2: 7). Pass. παρὰ τοῦ κυρίου πλουτίζεσθαι *receive one's riches from the Lord* Hs 2: 10.

2. fig., of spiritual riches *τινά someone,* of the apostle Paul, to whom alone the pl. prob. refers in ὡς πτωχοὶ πολλοὺς πλουτίζοντες *as poor, though making many rich* 2 Cor 6: 10; cf. of the Christians πτωχεύουσι καὶ πλουτίζουσι πολλούς Dg 5: 13. Pass. ὁ υἱός, δι' οὗ πλουτίζεται ἡ ἐκκλησία 11: 5. πλουτίζεσθαι ἔν τινι *be made rich in someth. ἐν παντί in everything* 1 Cor 1: 5; it is resumed w. ἐν παντὶ λόγῳ and given content. The ἐν αὐτῷ in the same verse denotes that this rich possession is dependent upon a close relationship to Christ. ἐν παντὶ πλουτιζόμενοι εἰς πᾶσαν ἁπλότητα *being made rich in every way for every* (*demonstration of*) *generosity* i.e. so that you might demonstrate generosity in every way 2 Cor 9: 11. M-M.*

πλοῦτος, ου, ὁ (Hom. +; inscr., pap., LXX; En. 97, 10; 100, 6; Ep. Arist. 321; Philo; Jos., C. Ap. 2, 186 al.; Test. Benj. 6: 3); Paul, who also uses the masc., on eight occasions (2 Cor 8: 2; Eph 1: 7; 2: 7; 3: 8, 16; Phil 4: 19; Col 1: 27; 2: 2) has in the nom. and acc. the neuter τὸ πλοῦτος (Act. Phil. 109 p. 42, 5 B.; Is 29: 2 [acc. to SA; cf. Thackeray 159]); s. Tdf., Proleg. 118; W-H., App. 158; Bl-D. §51, 2 app.; Mlt.-H. 127; *wealth, riches.*

1. lit., of the possession of many earthly goods Mt 13: 22; Mk 4: 19; Lk 8: 14; 1 Ti 6: 17; Js 5: 2; Rv 18: 17; 1 Cl 13: 1 (Jer 9: 22); Hv 3, 6, 5b; 6b; m 10, 1, 4; s 1: 8; 2: 5, 7f; AP 15: 30. Leading souls (astray) Hv 3, 6, 6a. πλ. τοῦ αἰῶνος τούτου v 3, 6, 5a. πολυτέλεια πλούτου m 8: 3; 12, 2, 1. γαυριᾶν ἐν τῷ πλούτῳ *glory in wealth* Hv 1, 1, 8. Also γαυροῦσθαι ἐν τῷ πλ. 3, 9, 6.—OSchilling, Reichtum u. Eigentum in der altkirchl. Lit. '08 (p. ix–xii for lit.); ETroeltsch, D. Soziallehren der christl. Kirchen u. Gruppen '12; MWeber, D. Wirtschaftsethik der Weltreligionen: Archiv f. Sozialwissensch. 44, '18, 52ff; F Hauck, Die Stellung des Urchristentums zu Arbeit u. Geld '21; ELohmeyer, Soziale Fragen im Urchristentum '21; HGreeven, D. Hauptproblem der Sozialethik in der neueren Stoa u. im Urchristentum '35 (slavery, property, marriage); KBornhäuser, D. Christ u. s. Habe nach dem NT '36; HvCampenhausen, D. Askese im Urchristentum '49. Cf. πτωχός 1a.

2. fig. *a wealth* or *abundance* of someth., w. gen. of the thing (Pla., Euthyphr. 12A π. τῆς σοφίας) τῆς ἁπλότητος 2 Cor 8: 2. τῆς δόξης Ro 9: 23; Eph 1: 18; 3: 16; Col 1: 27. τῆς πληροφορίας 2: 2. τῆς χάριτος Eph 1: 7; 2: 7. τῆς χρηστότητος Ro 2: 4 (Simplicius In Epict. p. 12, 7 πλοῦτος τῆς αὐτοῦ [God] ἀγαθότητος). The gen. in Ro 11: 12, πλ. κόσμου, πλ. ἐθνῶν are different: (*an*) *abun-*

dance (*of benefits*) *for the world, for the Gentiles.* Of that which God or Christ possesses in boundless abundance: βάθος πλούτου vs. 33 (s. βάθος 2 and cf. Jos., Bell. 6, 442 ὁ πλοῦτος ὁ βαθύς).—Phil 4: 19.—Eph 3: 8; Rv 5: 12 (w. δύναμις, σοφία, ἰσχύς, τιμή, δόξα, εὐλογία. Cf. Crantor [IV/III BC]: Fgm. Phil. Gr. III 148 Mullach πλοῦτος κ. δόξα; Diod. S. 4, 74, 1 πλ. κ. δόξα).—μείζονα πλ. ἡγησάμενος τῶν Αἰγύπτου θησαυρῶν τὸν ὀνειδισμὸν τοῦ Χριστοῦ *he considered the reproach suffered on behalf of the Christ to be greater wealth than the treasures of Egypt* Hb 11: 26.—For lit. s. on πένης. Also FHauck and WKasch, TW VI 316–30: πλοῦτος and related words. M-M. B. 772.*

πλύνω impf. ἔπλυνον; fut. πλυνῶ; 1 aor. ἔπλυνα, imper. πλῦνον (Hom. +; Dit., Or. 483, 169 ἱμάτια; PStrassb. 91, 8; PSI 599, 7; PLond. 1695, 18; LXX; Philo, Leg. All. 3, 144; 147) *wash.*

1. lit. *τὶ someth. τὰ δίκτυα wash the nets* Lk 5: 2. Washing of clothes as a symbol of cleansing fr. sins ἔπλυναν τὰς στολὰς αὐτῶν Rv 7: 14 (on πλύνειν τ. στολ., at times w. ἔν τινι, cf. Gen 49: 11.—Appian, Samn. 7 §6 of a defiled garment ἐκπλυνεῖτε τοῦτο αἵματι πολλῷ = you will wash this out with a great deal of blood); cf. 22: 14. This affords an easy transition to

2. fig. in the sense *free from* (Artem. 2, 4) i.e. from the impurity of sin; the original mng. of πλ., however, is still felt. πλῦνόν με ἀπὸ τῆς ἀνομίας μου 1 Cl 18: 3 (Ps 50: 4) and in the continuation of the quot. πλυνεῖς με vs. 7 (Ps 50: 9). M-M. B. 579.*

πνεῦμα, ατος, τό (Aeschyl., Pre-Socr., Hdt. +; inscr., pap., LXX, En., Ep. Arist., Philo, Joseph., Test. 12 Patr., Sib. Or. On the history of the word s. Rtzst., Mysterienrel.³ 308ff).

1. *blowing, breathing* (even the glowing exhalations of a volcanic crater: Diod. S. 5, 7, 3)—**a.** *wind* (Aeschyl. +; LXX, Ep. Arist., Philo; Jos., Ant. 2, 343; 349; Sib. Or. 8, 297) τὸ πνεῦμα πνεῖ *the wind blows* J 3: 8a (EpJer 60 πνεῦμα ἐν πάσῃ χώρᾳ πνεῖ. But cf. TMDonn, ET 66, '54f, 32). ὀθόνη πλοίου ὑπὸ πνεύματος πληρουμένη MPol 15: 2. Of God ὁ ποιῶν τοὺς ἀγγέλους αὐτοῦ πνεύματα *who makes his angels winds* Hb 1: 7; 1 Cl 36: 3 (both Ps 103: 4).

b. *the breathing out of air, blowing, breath* (Aeschyl. +; Pla., Tim. 79B; LXX) ὁ ἄνομος, ὃν ὁ κύριος Ἰησοῦς ἀνελεῖ τῷ πνεύματι τοῦ στόματος αὐτοῦ 2 Th 2: 8 (cf. Is 11: 4; Ps 32: 6).

2. *breath, (life-)spirit, soul,* that which gives life to the body (Aeschyl. +; Polyb. 31, 10, 4; Ps.-Aristot., De Mundo 4 p. 394b, 8ff; PHib. 5, 54 [III BC]; PGM 4, 538; 658; 2499; LXX; Sib. Or. 4, 46) ἀφιέναι τὸ πνεῦμα *give up one's spirit, breathe one's last* (Eur., Hec. 571; Porphyr., Vi. Plotini c. 2) Mt 27: 50. J says for this παραδιδόναι τὸ πν. 19: 30. Of the return of the (*life-*)*spirit* of a deceased person into her dead body ἐπέστρεψεν τὸ πν. αὐτῆς Lk 8: 55 (cf. Jdg 15: 19). εἰς χεῖράς σου παρατίθεμαι τὸ πν. μου *into thy hands I entrust my spirit* 23: 46 (Ps 30: 6). κύριε Ἰησοῦ, δέξαι τὸ πνεῦμά μου Ac 7: 59 (on the pneuma flying upward after death cf. Epicharm. in HDiels, Fragm. der Vorsokrat.⁵ I '34 no. 23 [=⁴ 13], B 9 and 22; Eur., Suppl. 533 πνεῦμα μὲν πρὸς αἰθέρα, τὸ σῶμα δ' ἐς γῆν; PGM 1, 177ff τελευτήσαντός σου τὸ σῶμα περιστελεῖ, σοῦ δὲ τὸ πνεῦμα...εἰς ἀέρα ἄξει σὺν αὐτῷ). τὸ σῶμα χωρὶς πν. νεκρόν ἐστιν Js 2: 26. πν./εισθεν ἐκ τ. θεοῦ εἰσῆλθεν ἐν αὐτοῖς (i.e. the prophet-witnesses who have been martyred) Rv 11: 11 (cf. Ezk 37: 10 v.l. εἰσῆλθεν εἰς αὐτοὺς πνεῦμα ζωῆς; 5). Of the *spirit* that animated the image of the beast, and enabled it to speak and to have Christians put to death 13: 15.—After a person's death, his πν. lives on as an independent being, in heaven πνεύματα δικαίων τετελειωμένων Hb 12: 23 (cf. Da 3: 86 εὐλογεῖτε, πνεύματα καὶ ψυχαὶ δικαίων, τὸν κύριον). According to non-biblical sources, the πν. are in the underworld (cf. En. 22: 3-13; Sib. Or. 7, 127) or in the air (PGM 1, 178), where evil spirits can prevent them from ascending higher (s. ἀήρ). τοῖς ἐν φυλακῇ πνεύμασιν πορευθεὶς ἐκήρυξεν 1 Pt 3: 19 belongs here if it refers to Jesus' preaching to the spirits of the dead in hell (so Usteri, BWeiss, Kühl, HermvSoden, Windisch, Bigg, HHoltzmann [Ntl. Theologie² II '11, 358f], Vrede, Feine, JA McCulloch [The Harrowing of Hell, '30] et al.), whether it be when he descended into Hades, or when he returned to heaven (so RBultmann, Bekenntnis u. Liedfragmente im 1 Pt: Con. Neot. 11, '47, 1-14).—CClemen, Niedergefahren zu den Toten '00; JTurmel, La Descente du Christ aux enfers '05; JMonnier, La Descente aux enfers '06; HHoltzmann, ARW 11, '08, 285-97; KGschwind, Die Niederfahrt Christi in die Unterwelt '11; DPlooij, De Descensus in 1 Pt 3: 19 en 4: 6: ThT 47, '13, 145-62; JHBernard, The Descent into Hades a Christian Baptism (on 1 Pt 3: 19ff): Exp. VIII 11, '16, 241-74; CSchmidt, Gespräche Jesu mit seinen Jüngern: TU 43, '19, 452ff; JFrings, BZ 17, '26, 75-88; JKroll, Gott u. Hölle '32; RGanschinietz, Katabasis: Pauly-W. X 2, '19, 2359-449; Clemen² 89-96; WBieder, Die Vorstellung v. d. Höllenfahrt Jesu Chr. '49; SEJohnson, JBL 79, '60, 48-51; WDalton, Christ's Proclamation to the Spirits, '65. S. also the lit. in Windisch, Hdb.² '30, exc. on 1 Pt 3: 20; EGSelwyn, The First Ep. of St. Peter '46 and 4c below.— This is prob. also the place for θανατωθεὶς μὲν σαρκὶ ζωοποιηθεὶς δὲ πνεύματι· ἐν ᾧ καί ... 1 Pt 3: 18f (𝔓⁷² reads πνεύματι instead of πνεύμασιν in vs. 19, evidently in ref. to the manner of Jesus' movement); πνεῦμα is that part of Christ which, in contrast to σάρξ, did not pass away in death, but survived as an individual entity after death; cf. ἐν IV 6e. Likew. the contrast κατὰ σάρκα—κατὰ πνεῦμα Ro 1: 3f. Cf. 1 Ti 3: 16.

3. the spirit as a part of the human personality—a. when used with σάρξ, the flesh, it denotes the immaterial part 2 Cor 7: 1; Col 2: 5. Flesh and spirit= the whole personality, in its outer and inner aspects, oft. in Ign.: IMg 1: 2; 13: 1a; ITr inscr.; 12: 1; IRo inscr.; ISm 1: 1; IPol 5: 1.—In the same sense beside σῶμα, the body (Simplicius In Epict. p. 50, 1; Ps.-Phoc. 106f; PGM 1, 178) 1 Cor 5: 3-5; 7: 34.—The inner life of man is divided into ψυχὴ καὶ πνεῦμα (cf. Ps.-Pla., Axioch. 10 p. 370c τὶ θεῖον ὄντως ἐνῆν πνεῦμα τῇ ψυχῇ=a divine spirit was actually in the soul; Wsd 15: 11; Jos., Ant. 1, 34. S. also Herm. Wr. 10, 13; 16f; PGM 4, 627; 630) Hb 4: 12. Cf. Phil 1: 27. τὸ πνεῦμα καὶ ἡ ψυχὴ καὶ τὸ σῶμα 1 Th 5: 23 (s. GMilligan, Thess. '08, 78f; EvDobschütz in Meyer X⁷ '09, 230ff; EDBurton, Spirit, Soul, and Flesh '18; AMFestugière, La Trichotomie des 1 Th 5: 23 et la Philos. gr.: Rech de Sc rel 20, '30, 385-415; ChMasson, RThPh 33, '45, 97-102; FCGrant, An Introd. to NT Thought '50, 161-6).

b. as the source and seat of insight, feeling, and will, gener. as the representative part of the inner life of man (cf. PGM 4, 627; 3 Km 20: 5; Sir 9: 9 al.) ἐπιγνοὺς ὁ Ἰησοῦς τῷ πν. αὐτοῦ Mk 2: 8. ἀναστενάξας τῷ πν. αὐτοῦ λέγει 8: 12 (s. ἀναστενάζω). ἠγαλλίασεν τὸ πν. μου Lk 1: 47 (in parallelism w. ψυχή vs. 46, as Sir 9: 9). ἠγαλλίασατο τῷ πν. 10: 21 t.r.; Ἰησοῦς ἐνεβριμήσατο τῷ πν. J 11: 33 (s. ἐμβριμάομαι); Ἰησ. ἐταράχθη τῷ πν. 13: 21. παρωξύνετο τὸ πν. αὐτοῦ ἐν αὐτῷ Ac 17: 16; ζέων τῷ πν. 18: 25 (s. ζέω). τὸ παιδίον ἐκραταιοῦτο πνεύματι Lk 1: 80; 2: 40 t.r.; ἔθετο ὁ Παῦλος ἐν τῷ πν.

Ac 19: 21. προσκυνήσουσιν τῷ πατρὶ ἐν πνεύματι of the spiritual, i.e. the pure, inner worship of God, that has nothing to do w. holy times, places, appurtenances, or ceremonies J 4: 23; cf. vs. 24b. πν. συντετριμμένον (Ps 50: 19) 1 Cl 18: 17; 52: 4.—2 Cl 20: 4; Hv 3, 12, 2; 3, 13, 2.—This usage is also found in Paul. His conviction (s. 5 below) that the Christian possesses the (divine) πνεῦμα and thus is different fr. all other men, leads him to choose this word in preference to others, in order to characterize the inner being of the believer gener. ᾧ λατρεύω ἐν τῷ πν. μου Ro 1: 9. οὐκ ἔσχηκα ἄνεσιν τῷ πν. μου 2 Cor 2: 13. Cf. 7: 13. As a matter of fact, it can mean simply a person's very self, or ego: τὸ πνεῦμα συμμαρτυρεῖ τῷ πνεύματι ἡμῶν the Spirit (of God) bears witness to our very self Ro 8: 16 (cf. PGM 12, 327 ἠκούσθη μου τὸ πνεῦμα ὑπὸ πνεύματος οὐρανοῦ). ἀνέπαυσαν τὸ ἐμὸν πν. καὶ τὸ ὑμῶν they have refreshed both me and you 1 Cor 16: 18. ἡ χάρις τοῦ κυρίου ἡμῶν Ἰ. Χρ. μετὰ τοῦ πν. (ὑμῶν) Gal 6: 18; Phil 4: 23; Phlm 25. Cf. 2 Ti 4: 22. Likew. in Ign. τὸ ἐμὸν πν. my (unworthy) self IEph 18: 1; IRo 9: 3; cf. 1 Cor 2: 11a.—Only a part of the inner life, i.e. that which concerns the will, is meant in τὸ μὲν πνεῦμα πρόθυμον, ἡ δὲ σὰρξ ἀσθενής Mt 26: 41; Mk 14: 38; Pol 7: 2. That which is inferior, anxiety, fear of suffering, etc. is attributed to the σάρξ.—The mng. of the expr. οἱ πτωχοὶ τῷ πνεύματι Mt 5: 3 is difficult to determine w. certainty (it has a secular counterpart in Pla., Ep. 7 p. 335A πένης ἀνὴρ τὴν ψυχήν. The dat. as τῇ ψυχῇ M. Ant. 6, 52; 8, 51). The sense is prob. those who are poor in their inner life, because they do not have a Pharisaic pride in their own spiritual riches (cf. AKlöpper, Über den Sinn u. die ursprgl. Form der ersten Seligpreisung der Bergpredigt bei Mt: ZWTh 37, 1894, 175-91; RKabisch, Die erste Seligpreisung: StKr 69, 1896, 195-215; KKöhler, Die ursprgl. Form der Seligpreisungen: StKr 91, '18, 157-92; JBoehmer, De Schatkamer 17, '23, 11-16, Teol. Tidsskrift [Copenhagen] 4, '24, 195-207, JBL 45, '26, 298-304; WMMacgregor, ET 39, '28, 293-7; VMacchioro, Journ. of Rel. 12, '32, 40-9; EEvans, Theology 47, '44, 55-60; HLeisegang, Pneuma Hagion '22, 134ff).

c. spiritual state, state of mind, disposition ἐν ἀγάπῃ πνεύματί τε πραΰτητος with love and a gentle spirit 1 Cor 4: 21; cf. Gal 6: 1. τὸ πν. τοῦ νοὸς ὑμῶν Eph 4: 23 (cf. νοῦς 3a). ἐν τῷ ἀφθάρτῳ τοῦ ἡσυχίου πνεύματος with the imperishable (gift) of a quiet disposition 1 Pt 3: 4.

4. a spirit as an independent being, in contrast to a being that can be perceived by the physical senses (ELangton, Good and Evil Spirits '42).

a. God himself: πνεῦμα ὁ θεός J 4: 24a (on God as a Spirit, esp. in the Stoa, s. MPohlenz, D. Stoa '48/'49. Hdb. ad loc. Also Celsus 6, 71 [Stoic]; Herm. Wr. 18, 3 ἀκάματον μέν ἐστι πνεῦμα ὁ θεός).

b. good, or at least not expressly evil spirits or spirit-beings (cf. CIG III 5858b δαίμονες καὶ πνεύματα; Proclus on Pla., Cratyl. p. 69, 6; 12 Pasqu.; En. 15, 4; 6; 8; 10; PGM 3, 8 ἐπικαλοῦμαί σε, ἱερὸν πνεῦμα; 4, 1448; 3080; 12, 249) πνεῦμα w. ἄγγελος (cf. Jos., Ant. 4, 108; Ps.-Clem., Hom. 3, 33; 8, 12) Ac 23: 8f. God is ὁ παντὸς πνεύματος κτίστης καὶ ἐπίσκοπος 1 Cl 59: 3b.—Pl., God the μόνος εὐεργέτης πνευμάτων 1 Cl 59: 3a. Cf. 64 (s. on this Num 16: 22; 27: 16. Prayers for vengeance fr. Rheneia [Dssm., LO 351-5 (LAE 423ff]=Dit., Syll.³ 1181, 2] τὸν θεὸν τὸν κύριον τῶν πνευμάτων; PGM 5, 467 θεὸς θεῶν, ὁ κύριος τῶν πν.; sim. the magic pap.: PWarr. 21, 24; 26 [III AD]); the πατὴρ τῶν πνευμάτων Hb 12: 9. The intermediary beings that serve God are called λειτουργικὰ πνεύματα Hb 1: 14. In Rv we read of the ἑπτὰ πνεύματα (τοῦ θεοῦ) 1: 4; 3: 1; 4: 5; 5: 6; cf. ASkrinjar, Biblica 16, '35, 1-24; 113-40.—*Ghost* Lk 24: 37, 39.

c. evil *spirits* (PGM 13, 798; 36, 160), esp. in the accounts of healings in the Synoptics: (τὸ) πνεῦμα (τὸ) ἀκάθαρτον Mt 12: 43; Mk 1: 23, 26; 3: 30; 5: 2, 8; 7: 25; 9: 25a; Lk 8: 29; 9: 42; 11: 24; Rv 18: 2. Pl. (Test. Benj. 5: 2) Mt 10: 1; Mk 1: 27; 3: 11; 5: 13; 6: 7; Lk 4: 36; 6: 18; Ac 5: 16; 8: 7; Rv 16: 13; ending of Mk in the Freer ms. 3.—τὸ πν. τὸ πονηρόν Ac 19: 15f. Pl. (En. 99, 7; Test. Sim. 4: 9; 6: 6, Judah 16: 1) Lk 7: 21; 8: 2; Ac 19: 12f.—πν. ἄλαλον Mk 9: 17; cf. vs. 25b (s. ἄλαλος). πν. πύθων Ac 16: 16 (s. πύθων). πν. ἀσθενείας Lk 13: 11. Cf. 1 Ti 4: 1b. πνεῦμα δαιμονίου ἀκαθάρτου (s. δαιμόνιον 2) 4: 33. πνεύματα δαιμονίων Rv 16: 14 (on the combination of πν. and δαιμ. cf. the love spell Sb 4324, 16f τὰ πνεύματα τῶν δαιμόνων τούτων).—Abs. *demon* Mk 9: 20; Lk 9: 39; Ac 16: 18. Pl. Mt 8: 16; 12: 45; Lk 10: 20; 11: 26.—1 Pt 3: 19 (s. 2 above) belongs here if the πνεύματα refer to demonic powers, evil spirits, fallen angels (so FSpitta, Christi Predigt an die Geister 1890; HGunkel, Zum religionsgesch. Verständnis des NT '03, 72f; WBousset, most recently ZNW 19, '20, 50-66; Rtzst., Herr der Grösse '19, 25ff; Knopf, Windisch, FHauck ad loc.; BReicke, The Disobedient Spirits and Christian Baptism '46, esp. 54-6, 69).—Hermas also has the concept of evil spirits that lead an independent existence, and live and reign within the inner life of a pers.; the Holy Spirit, who also lives or would live there, is forced out by them (cf. Test. Dan 4) Hm 5, 1, 2-4; 5, 2, 5-8; 10, 1, 2. τὸ πν. τὸ ἅγιον—ἕτερον πονηρὸν πν. m 5, 1, 2. These πνεύματα are ὀξυχολία m 5, 1, 3; 5, 2, 8 (τὸ πονηρότατον πν.); 10, 1, 2; διψυχία m 9: 11 (ἐπίγειον πν. ἐστι παρὰ τοῦ διαβόλου); 10, 1, 2; λύπη m 10, 1, 2 (πάντων τῶν πνευμάτων πονηροτέρα) and other vices. On the complicated pneuma-concept of the Mandates of Hermas cf. MDibelius, Hdb. exc. after Hm 5, 2, 7.

5. *the spirit* as that which differentiates God fr. everything that is not God, as the divine power that produces all divine existence, as the divine element in which all divine life is carried on, as the bearer of every application of the divine will. All those who belong to God possess or receive this spirit and hence have a share in his life. This spirit also serves to distinguish the Christians fr. all unbelievers (cf. PGM 4, 1121ff, where the spirit enters a man and, in accordance w. God's will, separates him fr. himself, i.e. fr. the purely human part of his nature).

a. the Spirit of God, of the Lord (= God) etc. (LXX; Ps.-Phoc. 106; Philo; Joseph. [s. c below]; Sib. Or. 3, 701; Test. Sim. 4: 4. Cf. Plut., Numa 4, 6 πνεῦμα θεοῦ, capable of begetting children) τὸ πν. τοῦ θεοῦ 1 Cor 2: 11b, 14; 3: 16; 6: 11; 1 J 4: 2a; τὸ τοῦ θεοῦ πν. 1 Pt 4: 14. τὸ πν. τὸ ἐκ τοῦ θεοῦ 1 Cor 2: 12b. τὸ πν. κυρίου Ac 5: 9; B 6: 14; 9: 2. τὸ πνεῦμά μου or αὐτοῦ: Mt 12: 18 (Is 42: 1); Ac 2: 17f (Jo 3: 1f.—Cf. IQS iv, 21); 1 Cor 2: 10a t.r.; Eph 3: 16; 1 Th 4: 8 (where τὸ ἅγιον is added); 1 J 4: 13.—τὸ πν. τοῦ πατρὸς ὑμῶν Mt 10: 20. τὸ πν. τοῦ ἐγείραντος τὸν Ἰησοῦν Ro 8: 11a.—Without the art. πν. θεοῦ *the Spirit of God* Mt 3: 16; 12: 28; Ro 8: 9b, 14; 1 Cor 7: 40; 12: 3a; 2 Cor 3: 3 (πν. θεοῦ ζῶντος); Phil 3: 3. πν. κυρίου Lk 4: 18 (Is 61: 1); Ac 8: 39 (like J 3: 8; 20: 22; Ac 2: 4, this pass. belongs on the border-line betw. the mngs. 'wind' and 'spirit' [Diod. S. 3, 60, 3 Ἕσπερον ἐξαίφνης ὑπὸ πνευμάτων συναρπαγέντα μεγάλων ἄφαντον γενέσθαι]). Cf. HLeisegang, Der Hl. Geist I 1, '19, 19ff; OCullmann, Theol. Zeitschr. 4, '48, 364); 1 Cl 21: 2.

b. the Spirit of Christ, of the Lord (= Christ) etc. τὸ πν.

Ἰησοῦ Ac 16: 7. (τὸ) πν. Χριστοῦ Ro 8: 9c; 1 Pt 1: 11. τὸ πν. Ἰησ. Χριστοῦ Phil 1: 19. τὸ πν. κυρίου 2 Cor 3: 17b (JHermann, Kyrios und Pneuma, '61). τὸ πν. τοῦ υἱοῦ αὐτοῦ (= θεοῦ) Gal 4: 6. As possessor of the divine Spirit, and at the same time controlling its distribution among men, Christ is called κύριος πνεύματος *Lord of the Spirit* 2 Cor 3: 18 (cf. Windisch ad loc.); but many prefer to transl. *from the Lord who is the Spirit.*—CFDMoule, OCullmann-Festschr., '72, 231-7.

c. Because of his heavenly origin and nature this Spirit is called (*the*) *Holy Spirit* (cf. PGM 4, 510 ἵνα πνεύσῃ ἐν ἐμοὶ τὸ ἱερὸν πνεῦμα.—Neither Philo nor Josephus called the Spirit πν. ἅγιον; the former used θεῖον or θεοῦ πν., the latter πν. θεῖον: Ant. 4, 118; 8, 408; 10, 239).

α. w. the art. τὸ πνεῦμα τὸ ἅγιον (Is 63: 10f; Ps 50: 13; 142: 10 v.l.; cf. Sus 45 Theod.) Mt 12: 32 = Mk 3: 29 (= Lk 12: 10 [τὸ ἅγιον πνεῦμα]. On the 'sin against the Holy Spirit' cf. HLeisegang, Pneuma Hagion '22, 96-112; AFridrichsen, Le péché contre le Saint-Esprit: RHPhr 3, '23, 367-72); Mk 12: 36; 13: 11; Lk 2: 26; 3: 22; 10: 21; J 14: 26; Ac 1: 16; 2: 33; 5: 3, 32; 7: 51; 8: 18 t.r.; 10: 44, 47; 11: 15; 13: 2; 15: 8, 28; 19: 6; 20: 23, 28; 21: 11; 28: 25; Eph 1: 13 (τὸ πν. τῆς ἐπαγγελίας τὸ ἅγιον); 4: 30 (τὸ πν. τὸ ἅγιον τοῦ θεοῦ); Hb 3: 7; 9: 8; 10: 15; 1 Cl 13: 1; 16: 2; 18: 11 (Ps 50: 13); 22: 1; IEph 9: 1; Hs 5, 5, 2; 5, 6, 5-7 (on the relationship of the Holy Spirit to the Son in Hermas cf. ALink, Christi Person u. Werk im Hirten des Hermas 1886; JvWalter, ZNW 14, '13, 133-44; MDibelius, Hdb. exc. after Hs 5, 6, 8 p. 572-6).—τὸ ἅγιον πνεῦμα (Wsd 9: 17) Mt 28: 19; Lk 12: 10 (s. above), 12; Ac 1: 8; 2: 38 (epexegetic gen.); 4: 31; 9: 31; 10: 45; 13: 4; 16: 6; 1 Cor 6: 19; 2 Cor 13: 13; 1 J 5: 7 t.r. As the mother of Jesus GH 5 (HLeisegang, Pneuma Hagion '22, 64ff; Selma Hirsch, D. Vorstellg. v. e. weibl. πνεῦμα ἁγ. im NT u. in d. ältesten christl. Lit. '27. Also WBousset, Hauptprobleme der Gnosis '07, 9ff).

β. without the art. (cf. Bl-D. §257, 2; Rob. 761; 795) πνεῦμα ἅγιον (PGM 3, 289; Da 5: 12 LXX. S. also Theod. Da 4: 8, 9, 18 θεοῦ πνεῦμα ἅγιον or πνεῦμα θεοῦ ἅγιον) Mk 1: 8; Lk 1: 15, 35, 41, 67; 2: 25; 4: 1; 11: 13; J 20: 22 (Cassien, La pentecôte johannique [J 20: 19-23] '39.—Cf. also IQS iv, 20f); Ac 2: 4a; 4: 8; 7: 55; 8: 15, 17, 19; 9: 17; 10: 38; 11: 24; 13: 9; 19: 2a, b; Hb 2: 4; 6: 4; 1 Pt 1: 12; 1 Cl 2: 2.—So oft. in combination w. a prep.: διὰ πνεύματος ἁγίου Ac 1: 2; 4: 25; Ro 5: 5; 2 Ti 1: 14; 1 Cl 8: 1 (cf. διὰ πν. αἰωνίου Hb 9: 14). ἐκ πνεύματος ἁγίου (Euseb., Pr. Ev. 3, 12, 3 of the Egyptians: ἐκ τ. πνεύματος οἴονται συλλαμβάνειν τὸν γῦπα. Here πνεῦμα = 'wind'; s. Horapollo 1, 11 p. 14f. The same of other birds since Aristot.—On the neut. πνεῦμα as a masc. principle cf. Aristoxenus, fgm. 13 of the two original principles: πατέρα μὲν φῶς, μητέρα δὲ σκότος) Mt 1: 18, 20; IEph 18: 2. ἐν πνεύματι ἁγίῳ (PsSol 17: 37) Mt 3: 11; Mk 1: 8 v.l.; Lk 3: 16; J 1: 33b; Ac 1: 5 (cf. IQS 3, 7f); 11: 16; Ro 9: 1; 14: 17; 15: 16; 1 Cor 12: 3b; 2 Cor 6: 6; 1 Th 1: 5; 1 Pt 1: 12 (without ἐν 𝔓72 et al.); Jd 20. ὑπὸ πνεύματος ἁγίου 2 Pt 1: 21. Cf. ἐν δυνάμει πνεύματος ἁγίου Ro 15: 13, 19 (v.l.). μετὰ χαρᾶς πνεύματος ἁγίου 1 Th 1: 6. διὰ ἀνακαινώσεως πνεύματος ἁγίου Tit 3: 5.

d. abs.—**α.** w. the art. τὸ πνεῦμα. In this connection the art. is perh. used anaphorically at times, w. the second mention of a word (s. Bl-D. §252; Rob. 762); perh. Mt 12: 31 (looking back to vs. 28 πν. θεοῦ); Mk 1: 10, 12 (cf. vs. 8 πν. ἁγίου); Lk 4: 1b, 14 (cf. vs. 1a); Ac 2: 4b (cf. a).—As a rule it is not possible to assume that anaphora is present: Mt 4: 1; J 1: 32, 33a; 3: 6a, 8b, 34; 7: 39a; Ac 8: 29; 10: 19; 11: 12, 28; 19: 1 D; 20: 3 D, 22; 21: 4; Ro 8: 23 (ἀπαρχή 2, end), 26a, 27; 12: 11; 15: 30; 2 Cor 1: 22 and 5: 5 (s. ἀρραβών); 12: 18 (τῷ αὐτῷ πν.); Gal 3: 2, 5, 14 (ἐπαγγελία 2b); Eph 4: 3 (gen. of the author); 6: 17 (perh. epexegetic gen.); 1 Ti 4: 1a; Js 4: 5; 1 J 3: 24; 5: 6a, b (אA et al. add καὶ πνεύματος to the words δι' ὕδατος κ. αἵματος at the beg. of the verse; this is approved by HermvSoden, Moffatt, Vogels, Merk, and w. reservations by CHDodd, The Joh. Epistles '46, TWManson, JTS 48, '47, 25–33), 8; Rv 2: 7, 11, 17, 29; 3: 6, 13, 22; 14: 13; 22: 17; B 19: 2, 7= D 4: 10 (s. ἑτοιμάζω 2). ἐν τῷ πνεύματι (lead) by the Spirit Lk 2: 27.—Paul equates this Spirit of God, known to every Christian, with Christ ὁ κύριος τὸ πνεῦμά ἐστιν 2 Cor 3: 17a (UHolzmeister, 2 Cor 3: 17 Dominus autem Spiritus est '08; JBNisius, Zur Erklärung v. 2 Cor 3: 16ff: ZkTh 40, '16, 617–75; JKögel, Ὁ κύριος τὸ πνεῦμά ἐστιν: ASchlatter-Festschr. '22, 35–46; Ch Guignebert, Congr. d'Hist. du Christ. II '28, 7–22; E Fuchs, Christus u. d. Geist b. Pls '32; HMHughes, ET 45, '34, 235f; CLattey, Verb. Dom. 20, '40, 187–9; DRGriffiths ET 55, '43, 81–3; HIngo, Kyrios und Pneuma, '61 [Paul]); JDDunn, JTS 21, '70, 309–20).

β. without the art. πνεῦμα B 1: 3. κοινωνία πνεύματος Phil 2: 1 (κοινωνία 1 and 2). πνεύματι in the Spirit or through the Spirit Gal 3: 3; 5: 5, 16, 18; 1 Pt 4: 6. εἰ ζῶμεν πνεύματι, πνεύματι καὶ στοιχῶμεν if we live by the Spirit, let us also walk by the Spirit Gal 5: 25. Freq. used w. a prep.: διὰ πνεύματος 1 Pt 1: 22 t.r. ἐξ (ὕδατος καὶ) πνεύματος J 3: 5. ἐν πνεύματι in, by, through the Spirit Mt 22: 43; Eph 2: 22; 3: 5; 5: 18; 6: 18; Col 1: 8 (ἀγάπη ἐν πνεύματι love called forth by the Spirit); B 9: 7. κατὰ πνεῦμα Ro 8: 4f; Gal 4: 29. ἐν ἁγιασμῷ πνεύματος 2 Th 2: 13; 1 Pt 1: 2 (s. ἁγιασμός).—In neg. expressions: οὔπω ἦν πνεῦμα the Spirit had not yet come J 7: 39b. ψυχικοὶ πνεῦμα μὴ ἔχοντες worldly men, who do not have the Spirit Jd 19.—ἓν πνεῦμα one and the same Spirit 1 Cor 12: 13; Eph 2: 18; 4: 4; one (in) Spirit 1 Cor 6: 17.

e. The Spirit is more closely defined by a gen. of the thing: τὸ πν. τῆς ἀληθείας (Test. Judah 20: 5) J 14: 17; 15: 26; 16: 13 (in these three places the Spirit of Truth is the Paraclete promised by Jesus upon his departure); 1 J 4: 6 (opp. τὸ πνεῦμα τῆς πλάνης, as Test. Jud. 20: 1; cf. IQS 4, 23); τὸ τῆς δόξης πν. 1 Pt 4: 14. τὸ πν. τῆς ζωῆς the Spirit of Life Ro 8: 2. τὸ πν. τῆς πίστεως 2 Cor 4: 13. πν. σοφίας καὶ ἀποκαλύψεως Eph 1: 17. πν. υἱοθεσίας Ro 8: 15b (opp. πν. δουλείας vs. 15a). πν. δυνάμεως καὶ ἀγάπης καὶ σωφρονισμοῦ 2 Ti 1: 7 (opp. πν. δειλίας). τὸ πν. τῆς χάριτος (s. Test. Jud. 24: 2) Hb 10: 29 (Zech 12: 10); cf. 1 Cl 46: 6.

f. Of Christ: (ἐγένετο) ὁ ἔσχατος Ἀδὰμ εἰς πνεῦμα ζωοποιοῦν 1 Cor 15: 45. The scripture pass. upon which the first part of this verse is based is Gen 2: 7, where Wsd 15: 11 also substitutes the words πνεῦμα ζωτικόν for πνοὴν ζωῆς. Cf. on the other hand Philo, Leg. All. 1, 42 and s. the lit. s.v. Ἀδάμ ad loc.

g. The (divine) Pneuma stands in contrast to everything that characterizes this age or the finite world gener.: οὐ τὸ πν. τοῦ κόσμου ἀλλὰ τὸ πν. τὸ ἐκ τοῦ θεοῦ 1 Cor 2: 12; cf. Eph 2: 2; 1 Ti 4: 1a, b.

α. in contrast to σάρξ, which is more closely connected w. sin than any other earthly material: J 3: 6; Ro 8: 4–6, 9a, 13; Gal 3: 3; 5: 17a, b; 6: 8. Cf. B 10: 9. πᾶσα ἐπιθυμία κατὰ τοῦ πνεύματος στρατεύεται Pol 5: 3.

β. in contrast to the σῶμα (= σάρξ) Ro 8: 10 and to the σάρξ (= σῶμα, as many hold) J 6: 63a (for τὸ πν. ἐστιν τὸ ζωοποιοῦν cf. Philo, Op. Mund. 30; Herm. Wr. in Cyrill., C. Jul. I 556c= 542, 24 Sc. the pneuma τὰ πάντα ζωοποιεῖ καὶ τρέφει. S. also f above). Cf. Ro 8: 11b.

γ. in contrast to γράμμα, which is the characteristic quality of God's older declaration of his will in the law: Ro 2: 29; 7: 6; 2 Cor 3: 6a, b, 8 (cf. vs. 7).—δ. in contrast to the wisdom of men 1 Cor 2: 13.

6. The Divine Spirit reveals his presence in the persons whom he fills, in various ways (cf. HPreisker, Geist u. Leben '33).

a. πνεῦμα is accompanied by another noun, which characterizes the working of the Spirit more definitely: πνεῦμα καὶ δύναμις Spirit and power Lk 1: 17; 1 Cor 2: 4. Cf. Ac 10: 38; 1 Th 1: 5. πνεῦμα καὶ ζωή J 6: 63b. πνεῦμα κ. σοφία Ac 6: 3; cf. vs. 10 (cf. Test. Reub. 2: 6 πνεῦμα λαλίας). πίστις κ. πνεῦμα ἅγιον 6: 5. χαρὰ καὶ πνεῦμα ἅγ. 13: 52.

b. Unless he is frustrated by man in his natural condition, the Spirit produces a spiritual type of conduct Gal 5: 16, 25 and produces the καρπὸς τοῦ πνεύματος vs. 22 (s. Vögtle under πλεονεξία).

c. The Spirit inspires the men of God B 12: 2; 13: 5, above all, in their capacity as proclaimers of a divine revelation (Strabo 9, 3, 5 the πνεῦμα ἐνθουσιαστικόν, that inspired the Pythia; Περὶ ὕψους 13, 2; 33, 5 of the divine πν. that impels prophets and poets to express themselves; schol. on Pla. 856E of the μάντις: ἄνωθεν λαμβάνειν τὸ πνεῦμα καὶ πληροῦσθαι τοῦ θεοῦ; Aristobulus in Euseb., Pr. Ev. 8, 10, 4 τὸ θεῖον πν., καθ' ὃ καὶ προφήτης ἀνακεκήρυκται. Cf. Marinus, Vi. Procli 23 of Proclus: οὐ γὰρ ἄνευ θείας ἐπινοίας...διαλέγεσθαι). προφητεία came into being only as ὑπὸ πνεύματος ἁγίου φερόμενοι ἐλάλησαν ἀπὸ θεοῦ ἄνθρωποι 2 Pt 1: 21; cf. Ac 15: 29 v.l. Cf. 1 Cl 8: 1. David Mt 22: 43; Mk 12: 36; cf. Ac 1: 16; 4: 25. Isaiah Ac 28: 25. Moses B 10: 2, 9; the Spirit was also active in giving the tables of the law to Moses 14: 2. Christ himself spoke in the OT διὰ τοῦ πνεύματος τοῦ ἁγίου 1 Cl 22: 1. The ἱεραὶ γραφαί are called αἱ διὰ τοῦ πν. τοῦ ἁγίου 45: 2.—The Christian prophet Agabus also ἐσήμαινεν διὰ τοῦ πν. Ac 11: 28; cf. Ac 21: 11. Likew. Ign. IPhld 7: 2. In general the Spirit reveals the most profound secrets to those who believe 1 Cor 2: 10a, b.—1 Cl claims to be written διὰ τοῦ ἁγ. πν. 63: 2.

d. The Spirit of God, being one, shows the variety and richness of his life in the different kinds of spiritual gifts which are granted to certain Christians 1 Cor 12: 4, 7, 11; cf. vs. 13a, b.—Vss. 8–10 enumerate the individual gifts of the Spirit, using various prepositions: διὰ τοῦ πν. vs. 8 a; κατὰ τὸ πν. vs. 8b; ἐν τῷ πν. vs. 9a, b. τὸ πν. μὴ σβέννυτε do not quench the Spirit 1 Th 5: 19 refers to the gift of prophecy, acc. to vs. 20.—The use of the pl. πνεύματα is explained in 1 Cor 14: 12 by the varied nature of the Spirit's working, and in vs. 32 by the number of persons who possess the prophetic spirit; on the latter cf. Rv 22: 6 and 19: 10.

e. One special type of spiritual gift is represented by ecstatic speaking. Of those who 'speak in tongues' that no earthly person can understand, and do so under the influence of the Pneuma: πνεύματι λαλεῖ μυστήρια 1 Cor 14: 2. Cf. vss. 14–6 and s. νοῦς 1. τὸ πνεῦμα ὑπερεντυγχάνει στεναγμοῖς ἀλαλήτοις Ro 8: 26b. Of speech that is ecstatic, but expressed in words that can be understood λαλεῖν ἐν πνεύματι D 11: 7, 8; cf. vs. 9 (on the subject-matter 1 Cor 12: 3; Jos., Ant. 4, 118f). Of the state of mind of the seer of the Apocalypse: ἐν πνεύματι Rv 17: 3; 21: 10; γενέσθαι ἐν πν. 1: 10; 4: 2 (cf. γίνομαι II 4a, ἐν I 5d and EMoering, StKr 92, '20, 148–54). On the Spirit at Pentecost Ac 2: 4 cf. KLake: Beginn. I 5, '33, 111–21.

f. The Spirit leads and directs Christian missionaries in their journeys (Aelian, N.A. 11, 16 the young women are led blindfolded to the cave of the holy serpent; they are guided by a πνεῦμα θεῖον) Ac 16: 6, 7 (by dreams, among other methods; cf. vs. 9f and s. Marinus, Vi. Procli 27: Proclus ἔφασκεν προθυμηθῆναι μὲν πολλάκις γράψαι, κωλυθῆναι δὲ ἐναργῶς ἔκ τινων ἐνυπνίων).

7. Only rarely do we read in our lit. of persons who are possessed by a spirit that is not fr. God: *πν. ἕτερον a different* (kind of) *spirit* 2 Cor 11: 4. Cf. 2 Th 2: 2; 1 J 4: 1–3. Because there are persons activated by such spirits, it is necessary to test the var. kinds of *spirits* (the same problem Artem. 3, 20 περὶ διαφορᾶς μάντεων, οἷς δεῖ προσέχειν καὶ οἷς μή) 1 Cor 12: 10; 1 J 4: 1b. ὁ διάβολος πληροῖ αὐτὸν αὐτοῦ πν. Hm 11: 3. Also οὐκ οἴδατε ποίου πνεύματός ἐστε Lk 9: 55 v.l. distinguishes betw. the spirit shown by Jesus' disciples, and another kind of spirit.— Even more rarely God gives a spirit that is not his own; so (in a quot. fr. Is 29: 10) a πνεῦμα κατανύξεως Ro 11: 8.

8. *The Spirit* appears as an independent personality in formulas that became more and more fixed and distinct (cf. Ps.-Lucian, Philopatr. 12 θεόν, υἱὸν πατρός, πνεῦμα ἐκ πατρὸς ἐκπορευόμενον ἓν ἐκ τριῶν καὶ ἐξ ἑνὸς τρία, ταῦτα νόμιζε Ζῆνα, τόνδ' ἡγοῦ θεόν. The whole context is influenced by Christianity): βαπτίζοντες αὐτοὺς εἰς τὸ ὄνομα τοῦ πατρὸς καὶ τοῦ υἱοῦ καὶ τοῦ ἁγίου πνεύματος Mt 28: 19 (on the text s. βαπτίζω 2bβ; on the subject-matter GWalther, Die Entstehung des Taufsymbols aus dem Taufritus: StKr 95, '24, 256ff; D 7: 1, 3. Cf. 2 Cor 13: 13; 1 Cl 58: 2; IEph 9: 1; IMg 13: 1b, 2; MPol 14: 3; 22: 1, 3; Epil Mosq 4. On this s. HUsener, Dreiheit: RhM 58, '03, 1ff; 161ff; 321ff; esp. 36ff; EvDobschütz, Zwei- u. dreigliedrige Formeln: JBL 50, '31, 116–47 (also Heinrici-Festschr. '14, 92–100); Norden, Agn. Th. 228ff; JMMainz, Die Bed. der Dreizahl im Judentum '22; Clemen² 125–8; NSöderblom, Vater, Sohn u. Geist '09; DNielsen, Der dreieinige Gott I '22; GKrüger, Das Dogma v. der Drei-einigkeit '05, 46ff; AHarnack, Entstehung u. Entwicklung der Kirchenverfassung '10, 187ff; JHaussleiter, Trinita-rischer Glaube u. Christusbekenntnis in der alten Kirche: BFChTh XXV 4, '20; JLebreton, Histoire du dogme de la Trinité I: Les origines⁶ '27; RBlümel, Pls u. d. dreieinige Gott '29.—On the whole word FRüsche, D. Seelenpneuma '33; HLeisegang, Der Hl. Geist I 1, '19; EDBurton, ICC Gal. '21, 486–95; PVolz, Der Geist Gottes u. d. verwand-ten Erscheinungen im AT '10; JHehn, Zum Problem des Geistes im alten Orient u. im AT: ZAW n.s. 2, '25, 210–25; SLinder, Studier till Gamla Testamentets föreställ-ningar om anden '26; AMarmorstein, Der Hl. Geist in der rabb. Legende: ARW 28, '30, 286–303; NHSnaith, The Distinctive Ideas of the OT '46, 229–37; FWDillistone, Bibl. Doctrine of the Holy Spirit: Theology Today 3, '46/'47, 486–97; TNicklin, Gospel Gleanings '50, 341–6; ESchweizer, CHDodd-Festschr., '56, 482–508; DLys, Rûach, Le Souffle dans l'AT, '62; DHill, Gk. Words and Hebr. Mngs. '67, 202–93.—HGunkel, Die Wirkungen des Hl. Geistes² 1899; HWeinel, Die Wirkungen des Geistes u. der Geister im nachap. Zeitalter 1899; EWWinstanley, The Spirit in the NT '08; HBSwete, The Holy Spirit in the NT '09, The Holy Spirit in the Ancient Church '12; EFScott, The Spirit in the NT '23; FBüchsel, Der Geist Gottes im NT '26; EvDobschütz, Der Geistbesitz des Christen im Urchristentum: Monatsschr. für Pastoral-theol. 20, '24, 228ff; FJBadcock, 'The Spirit' and Spirit in the NT: ET 45, '34, 218–21; RBultmann, Theologie des NT '48, 151–62 (Eng. transl. KGrobel, '51, I 153–64); ESchweizer, Geist u. Gemeinde im NT '52, Interpretation 6, '52, 259–78.—WTosetti, Der Hl. Geist als göttliche

Pers. in den Evangelien '18; HLeisegang, Pneuma Hagion. Der Ursprung des Geistbegriffs der syn. Ev. aus der griech. Mystik '22; AFrövig, Das Sendungsbewusstsein Jesu u. der Geist '24; HWindisch, Jes. u. d. Geist nach syn. Überl.: Studies in Early Christianity, presented to FCPorter and BWBacon '28, 209–36; FCSynge, The Holy Spirit in the Gospels and Acts: ChQR 120, '35, 205–17; CKBarrett, The Holy Spirit and the Gospel Trad. '47.— ESokolowski, Die Begriffe Geist u. Leben bei Pls '03; KDeissner, Auferstehungshoffnung u. Pneumagedanke bei Pls '12; GVos, The Eschatological Aspect of the Pauline Conception of the Spirit: Bibl. and Theol. Studies by the Faculty of Princeton Theol. Sem. '12, 209–59; HBertrams, Das Wesen des Geistes nach d. Anschauung des Ap. Pls '13; WReinhard, Das Wirken des Hl. Geistes im Menschen nach den Briefen des Ap. Pls '18; HRHoyle, The Holy Spirit in St. Paul '28; PGächter, Z. Pneuma-begriff des hl. Pls: ZkTh 53, '29, 345–408; ASchweitzer, D. Mystik des Ap. Pls '30, 159–74 al. [Mysticism of Paul the Apostle, tr. WMontgomery '31, 160–76 al.]; E-BAllo, Sagesse et Pneuma dans la prem. épître aux Cor: RB 43, '34, 321–46; Ltzm., Hdb. exc. after Ro 8: 11; Synge [s. above], the Spirit in the Paul. Ep.: ChQR 119, '35, 79–93; NAWaaning, Onderzoek naar het gebruik van πνεῦμα bij Pls, Diss. Amsterd. '39; RJewett, Paul's Anthropological Terms, '71, 167–200.—HvBaer, Der Hl. Geist in den Lukasschriften '26; MGoguel, La Notion joh. de l'Esprit '02; JGSimpson, The Holy Spirit in the Fourth Gospel: Exp., 9th Ser. IV '25, 292–9; HWindisch, Jes. u. d. Geist im J.: Amicitiae Corolla (RHarris-Festschr.) '33, 303–18; WFLofthouse, The Holy Spirit in Ac and J: ET 52, '40/'41, 334–6; CKBarrett, The Holy Spirit in the Fourth Gospel: JTS 1 new series, '50, 1–15; FJCrump, Pneuma in the Gospels, Diss. Catholic Univ. of America, '54; GWH Lampe, Studies in the Gospels (RHLightfoot memorial vol.) '55, 159–200; NQHamilton, The Holy Spirit and Eschatology in Paul, '57; WDDavies, Paul and the Dead Sea Scrolls: Flesh and Spirit, in The Scrolls and the NT, ed. KStendahl, '57, 157–82.—GJohnston, 'Spirit' and 'Holy Spirit' in the Qumran Lit., in NT Sidelights (AC Purdy-Festschr.) '60, 27–42; JPryke, 'Spirit' and 'Flesh' in Qumran and NT, Revue de Qumran 5, '65, 346–60; HBraun, Qumran und d. NT II, '66, 150–64; DHill, Greek Words and Hebrew Meanings, '67, 202–93; WBieder, Pneumatolog. Aspekte im Hb, OCullmann-Festschr. '72, 251–9.—HKleinknecht, ESchweizer et al., TW VI 330–453: πνεῦμα and related words. M-M. B. 260; 1087.**

πνευματικός, ή, όν (Pre-Socr. +, mostly in the sense 'pertaining to the wind or breath'; Strabo 1, 3, 5; Cleomedes [II AD] 1, 8 p. 84, 22 HZiegler 1891; Vett. Val. p. 1, 11; 231, 20; PGM 5, 25; Philo) predom. in Paul in our lit. (elsewh. only 1 Pt, 2 Cl, B, Ign., D) *pertaining to the spirit, spiritual.*

1. referring to the inner life of a human being (s. πνεῦμα 3.—Plut., Mor. 129c πν. stands in contrast to σωματικόν; Hierocles 27 p. 483 τὸ πνευματικὸν τῆς ψυχῆς ὄχημα=the spiritual vehicle of the soul; cf. also Philo, Rer. Div. Her. 242); so perh. IPol 1: 2 (cf. ἐπιμέλεια); 2: 2; IMg 13: 2; ISm 12: 2; 13: 2. But mng. 2 is not imposs.

2. In the great majority of cases it refers to the divine πνεῦμα (s. πνεῦμα 5); *caused by* or *filled with the* (divine) *Spirit, pertaining* or *corresponding to the* (divine) *Spirit* (Philo, Abr. 113; PGM 4, 1778; Zosimus [2aγ below, end]).

a. adj.—**α.** of Jesus; in his preëxistence 2 Cl 14: 2. σαρκικός τε καὶ πνευματικός *of flesh and* (at the same time) *of spirit* IEph 7: 2. Of the δεύτερος ἄνθρωπος 1 Cor 15: 47 𝔓⁴⁶.

β. as a rule it is used of impersonal things: the law given by God Ro 7: 14. χάρισμα πν. 1: 11. τῆς δωρεᾶς πνευματικῆς χάριν B 1: 2 (s. δωρεά). εὐλογία πν. Eph 1: 3 (s. εὐλογία 3bα). ᾠδαὶ πν. *spiritual songs* 5: 19; Col 3: 16. σύνεσις πν. *understanding given by the Spirit* 1: 9. The Christians are to let themselves be built up into an οἶκος πν. 1 Pt 2: 5a and they are to bring πν. θυσίαι vs. 5b (EGSelwyn, 1 Pt, '46 p. 281-5). Using the same figure, B 16: 10 characterizes the believer as πν. ναός. Ign. calls his bonds πν. μαργαρῖται IEph 11: 2; *the fellowship that binds him to the Ephesian bishop is* συνήθεια οὐκ ἀνθρωπίνη ἀλλὰ πνευματική 5: 1; the presbytery he calls ἀξιόπλοκος πνευματικὸς στέφανος *a worthily woven spiritual wreath* IMg 13: 1.—Of the Lord's Supper and its OT counterpart: πνευματικὸν βρῶμα 1 Cor 10: 3 and πν. πόμα vs. 4a, the former in the manna granted fr. heaven (cf. βρῶμα 1), the latter in the water ἐκ πν. πέτρας vs. 4b (s. πέτρα 1a). πνευματικὴ τροφὴ καὶ (πνευματικὸν is supplied) ποτόν D 10: 3.—That which belongs to the supernatural order of being is described as πν.: accordingly, the resurrection body is a σῶμα πν. (the expr.: Kleopatra p. 24 l. 24) 1 Cor 15: 44a; cf. vs. 44b. Of the preëxistent church 2 Cl 14: 1, 2, 3.

γ. ὁ πνευματικός (w. ἄνθρωπος to be supplied) 1 Cor 2: 15 stands in contrast to ψυχικὸς ἄνθρωπος of vs. 14. The latter is a person who has nothing more than an ordinary human soul; the former possesses the divine πνεῦμα, not beside his natural human soul, but in place of it; this enables him to penetrate the divine mysteries. This treatment of ψυχή and πνεῦμα in contrast to each other is also found in Hellenistic mysticism (s. Rtzst., Mysterienrel.³ 70f; 325ff; 333ff; JWeiss, exc. on 1 Cor 15: 44a. Cf. Zosimus in MBerthelot, Collection des anciens Alchimistes grecs 1887 II 230 οὐ δεῖ τὸν πνευματικὸν ἄνθρωπον τὸν ἐπιγνόντα ἑαυτὸν κτλ.=Hermetica IV p. 105, 25 Sc.; also p. 107, 7.—HFMüller, Plotinos u. der Ap. Pls: Her. 54, '19, 109f).

b. subst.—**α.** neut. τὰ πνευματικά *spiritual things* or *matters* (in contrast to τὰ σαρκικά *earthly things*) Ro 15: 27; 1 Cor 9: 11; it is characteristic of the orthodox people, as τὰ σαρκ. is of the heretics IEph 8: 2 (s. β below).—τὰ πν. *spiritual gifts* 1 Cor 12: 1 (the gen. here may also be masc. those who possess spiritual gifts); 14: 1. In πνευματικοῖς πνευματικὰ συνκρίνοντες 1 Cor 2: 13 the dat. is either to be taken as a neut. (Lghtf., BWeiss, Bachmann, Ltzm., Rtzst. op. cit. 336, H-DWendland) or as a masc. (Schmiedel, Heinrici, JWeiss, Sickenberger); s. συγκρίνω and πνευματικῶς 2.—τὸ πνευματικόν (in contrast to τὸ ψυχικόν [s. 2aγ above]) 1 Cor 15: 46.

β. masc. (ὁ) πνευματικός *possessing the Spirit, the one who possesses the Spirit* (w. προφήτης) 1 Cor 14: 37. (οἱ) πνευματικοί *(the) spirit-filled people* 3: 1 (opp. σάρκινοι and νήπιοι ἐν Χριστῷ); Gal 6: 1; B 4, 11; IEph 8: 2 (of the orthodox people in contrast to the σαρκικοί, the heretics; s. 2bα above). Perh. also 1 Cor 2: 13 (s. 2bα above) and 12: 1 (2bα).

3. *pertaining to* (evil) *spirits* (s. πνεῦμα 4c) subst. τὰ πνευματικὰ τῆς πονηρίας *the spirit-forces of evil* Eph 6: 12. M-M.*

πνευματικῶς adv. (Hermogenes [II AD], Inv. 4, 1 in the sense 'in one breath'—s. L-S-J) *spiritually, in a spiritual manner, in a manner caused by* or *filled with the Spirit.*

1. w. ref. to the inner life of a man (s. πνευματικός 1) μένετε ἐν Ἰησοῦ Χριστῷ σαρκικῶς καὶ πνευματικῶς *remain in Jesus Christ both in body and in spirit, i.e. w.*

---

one's whole personality (s. πνεῦμα 3a) IEph 10: 3. On the other hand μετὰ τὴν ἀνάστασιν συνέφαγεν αὐτοῖς ὡς σαρκικὸς καίπερ πνευματικῶς ἡνωμένος τῷ πατρί ISm 3: 3 at least marks the transition to

2. w. ref. to the divine πνεῦμα (s. πνευματικός 2) πνευματικῶς ἀνακρίνεται *it must be examined in a manner consistent with the* (divine) *Spirit* 1 Cor 2: 14.— Vs. 13 (s. πνευματικός 2bα) has πνευματικῶς as a v.l. for πνευματικοῖς. It is said of Paul when he wrote 1 Cor that πνευματικῶς ἐπέστειλεν ὑμῖν *full of the* (divine) *Spirit he wrote to you* 1 Cl 47: 3.—This is also the place for ἥτις (i.e. the city of Jerusalem) καλεῖται πνευματικῶς Σόδομα Rv 11: 8: if one follows the *spiritual* (the opp. is σαρκικῶς Justin, Dial. 14) understanding of scripture (cf. Is 1: 9f), Jerusalem lies concealed beneath the name Sodom.*

πνευματοφόρος, ον (on similar formations s. Hdb. Ergänzungsband 189-91 on θεοφόρος) *bearing the* (divine) *Spirit* within oneself, subst. (Herm. Wr. 13, 19) *a bearer of the Spirit* of Christian prophets Hm 11: 16 (adj. of OT prophets Hos 9: 7; Zeph 3: 4).*

πνέω 1 aor. ἔπνευσα (Hom.+; pap., LXX, Philo, Joseph.)—**1.** abs.—**a.** *blow* of the wind (Hom.+; Ptolem., Apotel. 1, 11, 4 οἱ πνέοντες ἄνεμοι; PHib. 27, 59; Sir 43: 20; EpJer 60; Jos., Bell. 7, 318, Ant. 7, 76; Sib. Or. 5, 375) Mt 7: 25, 27; Lk 12: 55; J 3: 8 (Diod. S. 24, 1, 2 πνεύματος πνεύσαντος=when a wind blew); 6: 18; Rv 7: 1. τῷ ἀνέμῳ ἐπιδόντες τῷ πνέοντι Ac 27: 15 v.l.— Subst. ἡ πνέουσα (sc. αὔρα; this word is added by Arrian, Peripl. 3, 2) *the wind that was blowing* (Lucian [ἐπιδίδωμι 2]) Ac 27: 40.

b. *breathe out, give forth an odor* ὡς λιβανωτοῦ πνέοντος MPol 15: 2.

2. w. acc. (Hom.+; schol. on Nicander, Ther. 308 δυσωδίαν πνέοντες; 2 Macc 9: 7; En. 29, 2) *breathe something* (*out*). The anointing of Jesus had for its purpose ἵνα πνέῃ τῇ ἐκκλησίᾳ ἀφθαρσίαν *that he might breathe immortality upon* and therefore *into the church* IEph 17: 1 (on πνέω τινί τι='instill someth. into someone' cf. Ps.-Clem., Hom. 4, 19). M-M. B. 260; 684.*

πνίγω impf. ἔπνιγον; 1 aor. ἔπνιξα (trag., Hdt.+; Lind. Tempelchr. B, 111; PTebt. 278, 40; 1 Km 16: 14f; Jos., Bell. 2, 327, Ant. 10, 121).

1. lit.—**a.** *choke, strangle* (since Sophron Com. [V BC] 68; Pla., Gorg. 522A; cf. Vett. Val. 127, 1; 1 Km 16: 14) κρατήσας αὐτὸν ἔπνιγεν *he seized him and tried* (conative impf.) *to strangle him* Mt 18: 28 (Lucian, Dial. Mort. 22, 2 uses the synonym ἄγχω for the treatment of a debtor).

b. Anger chokes out the Holy Spirit within the human personality: τὸ πνεῦμα τὸ ἅγιον . . . πνίγεται ὑπὸ τοῦ πονηροῦ πνεύματος Hm 5, 1, 3 (cf. 1 Km 16: 14f).

c. of weeds in relation to the good seed *choke* (X., Oec. 17, 14) Mt 13: 7 v.l. ὁ ἀμπελὼν μὴ ἔχων βοτάνας πνιγούσας αὐτόν *the vineyard without the weeds that were choking it* Hs 5, 2, 4b; cf. ibid. a.

d. pass. *be choked*, intr. *choke* (Themistocl., Ep. 12), *drown* (X., An. 5, 7, 25; Plut., Mor. 599B; Jos., Ant. 10, 121; 20, 248) Mk 5: 13.

2. fig. (Lysippus Com. [V BC], fgm. 7, 9 [I p. 702 Kock] πνίγομαι ἐπ' αὐτοῖς=I choke with disgust at them) πνίγεσθαι ὑπὸ τῶν πράξεων *be choked by one's work* Hs 9, 20, 2. M-M.*

πνικτός, ή, όν (in secular Gk. only w. another mng.: Pherecrates Com. [V BC] 175 and Alexis Com. 124, 2= 'steamed, stewed, baked'; Galen VI p. 707, 1 al. It is restored in an inscr. fr. the Asclepiaeum on Cos A 26f; 41 by RHerzog: ARW 10, '07, 402; 408f.—Not in LXX nor in Hellenistic Jewish wr.) in Ac it plainly means *strangled, choked to death* (so also Ps.-Clem., Hom. 7, 8; 8, 19) of animals killed without having the blood drained fr. them, whose flesh the Jews were forbidden to eat (Lev 17: 13f. In this connection Philo, Spec. Leg. 4, 122 opposes those who are ἄγχοντες and ἀποπνίγοντες animals.—Hierocles, Carm. Aur. 26 p. 480 M. the Pythagorean dietary laws forbid τῶν ἀθύτων σαρκῶν μετάληψις= of meat fr. animals that have not been properly slaughtered) Ac 15: 20, 29; 21: 25 (D omits it in all three places).—On the questions raised by this word cf. Harnack, SAB 1899, 150ff (=Studien I 1f) and w. another result in: Die Apostelgeschichte '08, 189ff and Neue Untersuchungen zur AG '11, 22ff; GResch, D. Aposteldekret: TU n.s. XIII, '05; ASeeberg, Die beiden Wege u. d. Aposteldekret '06; HvanOort, ThT 40, '06, 97ff; HCoppieters, RB 4, '07, 31ff; 218ff; WSanday, The Apostolic Decree, Acts 15: 20-9: Theol. Studien, ThZahn dargebr. '08, 317-38, The Text of the Apost. Decr.: Exp. 8th Ser. VI '13, 289-305; HDiehl, ZNW 10, '09, 277-96; KLake, ChQR 71, '11, 345ff, Jew. Stud. in Mem. of IAbrahams '27, 244ff, Beginn. I 5, '33, note 16, esp. p. 206ff; KSix, Das Aposteldekret '12; FDibelius, StKr 87, '14, 618ff; AWikenhauser, Die AG '21, 213ff; LBrun, Apostelkonzil u. Aposteldekret: Norsk Teol. Tidsskrift 21, '20, 1-52; JHRopes, The Text of Acts (=Beginn. I 3) '26, 265ff; HLietzmann, Amicitiae Corolla '33, 203-11; HWaitz, D. Problem des sog. Aposteldekrets: ZKG 55, '36, 227-63; MDibelius, D. Apostelkonzil: ThLZ 72, '47, 193-8; OCullmann, Petrus '52, 47ff; WGKümmel, KKundsin-Festschr. '53, 83ff; EHaenchen, Ac '56, 395-419. M.-M.*

πνοή, ῆς, ἡ—1. *wind* (Hom.+; Job 37: 10; Sib. Or. 5, 375 [πνοιή]) πν. βιαία *a strong wind* Ac 2: 2.

2. *breath* (trag.+; LXX) with ζωή (cf. Gen 2: 7; 7: 22; Philo, Spec. Leg. 4, 123 πνοὴ ζωῆς and Pr 24: 12 ὁ πλάσας πνοὴν πᾶσιν) Ac 17: 25 (cf. TCMitchell, The OT Usage of NᵉSama, Vetus T 11, '61, 177-87). Abstr. for concr. πᾶσα πν. *everything that breathes* (Ps 150: 6) Pol 2: 1. It passes over to the mng. πνεῦμα (PGM 12, 331; 333) of God's πνοή 1 Cl 21: 9 (Knopf, Hdb. ad loc.); 57: 3 (Pr 1: 23). M.-M. B. 260.*

ποδαπός s. ποταπός.

ποδήρης, ες *reaching to the feet* (Aeschyl.+; LXX; Ep. Arist. 96; Philo, Fuga 185) subst. ὁ ποδ. (sc. χιτών; used w. χιτών X., Cyr. 6, 4, 2; Paus. 5, 19, 6; Ex 29: 5; Jos., Ant. 3, 153. Without χιτ. Appian, Liby. 66, §296; Ex 25: 7; 28: 4; Ezk 9: 3; Ep. Arist. 96; Philo, Leg. All. 2, 56; Jos., Bell. 5, 231; Test. Levi 8: 2) *a robe reaching to the feet* Rv 1: 13; B 7: 9. M.-M.*

ποδονιπτήρ, ῆρος, ὁ (Stesichorus in Athen. 10 p. 451ᴅ; Plut., Mor. 151ᴇ; Phryn. p. 689 L.) *basin for washing the feet* J 13: 5 𝔓⁶⁶ (ed. VMartin, Geneva '56). More commonly found in the spelling ποδανιπτήρ (Hdt. 2, 172; Aristot., Pol. 1, 12 al.; Dialekt-Inschr. 3340, 33 [Argolis]; Dit., Syll.³ 1169, 33 [III вс]).*

πόθεν interrog. adv. (Hom.+; inscr., pap., LXX) *from where, from which, whence?* in direct and indir. questions.

1. locally *from what place? from where?* (Hom.+; Gen 16: 8; 29: 4; Tob 7: 3; Jos., Ant. 9, 211; 11, 210) Mt 15: 33; Mk 8: 4 (QQuesnell, The Mind of Mark '69, 164-8); Lk 13: 25, 27; J 3: 8 and sim. IPhld 7: 1 (cf. EvdGoltz, Ign. v. Ant. 1894, 134-6); J 4: 11; 8: 14a, b (πόθεν ἦλθον καὶ ποῦ ὑπάγω. Cf. GPWetter, Eine gnost. Formel im vierten Ev.:

ZNW 18, '18, 49-63); 9: 29f; 19: 9; Rv 7: 13.—As a symbol μνημόνευε πόθεν πέπτωκες *remember from what* (state) *you have fallen* Rv 2: 5. γινώσκομεν πόθεν ἐλυτρώθημεν *we realize from what* (state) *we have been redeemed* B 14: 7.

2. of origin *from what source? brought about* or *given by whom? born of whom?* (Hom. +; Jos., Vi. 334) Mt 13: 27, 54, 56; 21: 25; Mk 6: 2; Lk 20: 7; J 2: 9; Js 4: 1a, b; 2 Cl 1: 2; 4: 5; B 10: 12; IEph 19: 2. πόθεν ἐστίν J 7: 27a, b could be interpreted in accordance w. 6: 42, and then would mean *of what kind of parents he was born.* But a more general sense is also poss.

3. of cause or reason *how, why, in what way?* (Aeschyl. +) Mk 12: 37. In a question expressing surprise (Att.; Jer 15: 18) Lk 1: 43 (πόθεν ἐμοί Plut., Mor. 526ғ); J 1: 48; 6: 5 (Field, Notes 91 'with what'). M.-M.*

ποθέω 1 aor. ἐπόθησα (Hom. +; LXX) *desire, wish (for), be anxious, strive after* τὶ someth. (Philo, De Jos. 90 ἀλήθειαν; Jos., Ant. 2, 65; Test. Iss. 2: 5; Sib. Or. 5, 420) Dg 10: 1; D 4: 3 Lake. Foll. by the aor. inf. (Philo, Fuga 8 μαθεῖν; Jos., Vi. 204) B 16: 10; Dg 3: 1. τὰ παρὰ θεῷ ποθούμενα *what is desirable in the sight of God* 12: 8.*

ποθητός, ή, όν (Aelian, N.A. 7, 3; Alciphr. 3, 39, 2; IG VII 3434; Ramsay, Phrygia I 2 p. 386 l. 3 τέκνα π.) *longed-for,* (dearly) *beloved* IRo 10: 1; ISm 13: 2; IPol 8: 3.*

πόθος, ου, ὁ (Hom.+; Philo; Jos., Ant. 12, 242; 15, 18) *longing, wish, desire* ἀκόρεστος π. εἰς ἀγαθοποιίαν *an insatiable longing to do good* 1 Cl 2: 2 (π. εἰς like Aq. Ps 9: 24; Sib. Or. 2, 112).*

ποῖ interrog. adv. (Theognis+; Celsus 6, 11; Jos., Ant. 1, 197; 16, 373) *where? whither?* 1 Cl 28: 4.*

ποία, ας, ἡ (Doric form, quotable since Pind., also Dit., Syll.³ 1169, 121 [III вс]; Mal 3: 2 v.l.; Jer 2: 22 v.l. for Att. πόα, Ion. and epic ποίη. Cf. Lob., Phryn. p. 496) *grass, herb, weed*; this mng. was formerly assumed at times for Js 4: 14 (Exp. 7th Ser. X, 566); it is better taken as the fem. of ποῖος. M.-M.*

ποιέω impf. ἐποίουν; fut. ποιήσω; 1 aor. ἐποίησα; pf. πεποίηκα; plpf. πεποιήκειν Mk 15: 7 (as Inschr. v. Magn. 93b, 24; on the omission of the augment s. Bl-D. §66, 1; Mlt.-H. 190). Mid.: impf. ἐποιούμην; 1 aor. ἐποιησάμην; pf. πεποίημαι 1 Cl 1: 1. Pass. (has disappeared almost entirely; Bl-D. §315) pf. ptc. πεποιημένος Hb 12: 27; 1 fut. ποιηθήσομαι (Hom.+; inscr., pap., LXX, En., Ep. Arist., Philo, Joseph., Test. 12 Patr., Sib. Or.).

I. active—1. *do, make—a.* of external things *make, manufacture, produce* τὶ someth. (Gen 6: 14ff; 33: 17 al.).

a. of human activity: σκεῦος 2 Cl 8: 2. χιτῶνας, ἱμάτια Ac 9: 39. εἰκόνα Rv 13: 14b. θεούς *make gods* Ac 7: 40 (Ex 32: 1). ναοὺς ἀργυροῦς 19: 24. ἀνθρακιάν J 18: 18. τέσσερα μέρη 19: 23 (s. μέρος 1). πηλόν 9: 11, 14. σκηνὰς *pitch tents, build huts* (1 Ch 15: 1; 2 Esdr 18 [Neh 8]: 16f; Jdth 8: 5; Jos., Ant. 3, 79) Mt 17: 4; Mk 9: 5; Lk 9: 33.—Used w. prepositional expressions ποιῆσαι αὐτὴν (i.e. τὴν σκηνὴν τοῦ μαρτυρίου) κατὰ τὸν τύπον *to make it* (the tent of testimony) *according to the model* (Ex 25: 40) Ac 7: 44; cf. Hb 8: 5. ποιεῖν τι ἔκ τινος *make someth. from* or *out of someth.* (i.e. fr. a certain material; Hdt. 2, 96; cf. X., An. 4, 5, 14; Theophr., Hist. Pl. 4, 2, 5; Ex 20: 24f; 28: 15; 29: 2) J 2: 15; 9: 6; Ro 9: 21.

β. of God's creative activity *create* (Hes., Op. 109; Heraclitus, fgm. 30 κόσμον οὔτε τις θεῶν οὔτε ἀνθρώπων ἐποίησεν, ἀλλ᾿ ἦν ἀεὶ καὶ ἔστιν καὶ ἔσται; Pla., Tim. 76c ὁ ποιῶν 'the Creator'; Epict. 1, 6, 5; 1, 14, 10; 2, 8, 19 σε ὁ Ζεὺς πεποίηκε; 4, 1, 102; 107; 4, 7, 6 ὁ θεὸς πάντα πεποίηκεν; Ael. Aristid. 43, 7 K.=1 p. 2 D.: Ζεὺς τὰ πάντα ἐποίησεν; Herm. Wr. 4, 1. In LXX oft. for בָּרָא, also Wsd 1: 13; 9: 9; Sir 7: 30; 32: 13; Tob 8: 6; Jdth 8: 14; Bar 3: 35; 4: 7; 2 Macc 7: 28; Aristobulus in Euseb., Pr. Ev. 13, 12, 12; Philo, Sacr. Abel. 65 and oft.; Sib. Or. 3, 28 and fgm. 3, 3; 16) w. acc. ἡ χείρ μου ἐποίησεν ταῦτα πάντα Ac 7: 50 (Is 66: 2). τοὺς αἰῶνας Hb 1: 2 (s. αἰών 3). τὸν κόσμον (Epict. 4, 7, 6 ὁ θεὸς πάντα πεποίηκεν τὰ ἐν τῷ κόσμῳ καὶ αὐτὸν τὸν κόσμον ὅλον; Sallust. 5 p. 10, 29; Wsd 9: 9) Ac 17: 24. τὸν οὐρανὸν καὶ τὴν γῆν (cf. Ael. Aristid. 43, 7 K.=1 p. 2 D.; Gen 1: 1; Ex 20: 11; Ps 120: 2; 145: 6; Is 37: 16; Jer 39: 17 al.; Jos., C. Ap. 2, 121) Ac 4: 24; 14: 15b; cf. Rv 14: 7. τὰ πάντα PK 2 p. 13, 26 (s. Ael. Aristid. β above). Lk 11: 40 is classed here by many. Of the relation of Jesus to God Ἰησοῦν, πιστὸν ὄντα τῷ ποιήσαντι αὐτόν Hb 3: 2 (cf. Is 17: 7).—W. a second acc., that of the predicate (PSI 435, 19 [258 BC] ὅπως ἂν ὁ Σάραπις πολλῷ σὲ μείζω ποιήσῃ) ἄρσεν καὶ θῆλυ ἐποίησεν αὐτούς he created them male and female Mt 19: 4b; Mk 10: 6 (both Gen 1: 27c).—Pass. Hb 12: 27.—ὁ ποιήσας the Creator Mt 19: 4a v.l.

b. of actions that one undertakes, of events or states of being that one brings about *do, cause, bring about, accomplish, prepare* etc.

α. ἔργα π. *do deeds*, also in sing.: τὰ ἔργα τοῦ Ἀβραὰμ π. *do as Abraham did* J 8: 39. τὰ ἔργα τοῦ πατρὸς ὑμῶν vs. 41; cf. 10: 37. τὰ πρῶτα ἔργα Rv 2: 5. ἔργον *commit a deed* 1 Cor 5: 2 v.l. ἔργον ποίησον εὐαγγελιστοῦ 2 Ti 4: 5 (s. ἔργον 2).—ἔργον or ἔργα somet. refer to miraculous *deeds*: ἓν ἔργον ἐποίησα *I have done just one* (miraculous) *deed* J 7: 21. Pl. 14: 12a; cf. b, c. This illustrates the transition to

β. *do, perform* miracles δυνάμεις Mt 7: 22; 13: 58; Ac 19: 11; sing. Mk 6: 5; 9: 39. θαυμάσια Mt 21: 15 (cf. Sir 31: 9). σημεῖα (Ex 4: 17) J 2: 23; 3: 2; 7: 31; 9: 16; 11: 47b; 20: 30; Rv 13: 13a; 16: 14; 19: 20. Sing. J 6: 30; 10: 41. τέρατα καὶ σημεῖα Ac 6: 8; 7: 36. ὅσα Mk 3: 8; 6: 30; Lk 9: 10.—Ac 10: 39; 14: 11.

γ. of conditions *bring about*, etc.: εἰρήνην *make, establish peace* Eph 2: 15; Js 3: 18 (cf. 2 Macc 1: 4). τὴν ἔκβασιν *provide a way out* 1 Cor 10: 13 (on the foll. gen. of the inf. w. the art. s. Bl-D. §400, 2; Rob. 1067). ἐπίστασιν ὄχλου *cause a disturbance among the people* Ac 24: 12. τὰ σκάνδαλα *create difficulties* Ro 16: 17.— W. the dat. of advantage ἐποίουν χαρὰν τοῖς ἀδελφοῖς *they brought joy to the brethren* Ac 15: 3.

δ. used w. a noun as a periphrasis for a simple verb of doing (s. II 1.—ποιέω in such combinations as early as Inschr. v. Priene 8, 63 [c. 328 BC], also Plut., Crass. 13, 6; s. ἑορτή, end) διαθήκην π. Hb 8: 9 (Jer 38: 32 cod. Q; cf. Is 28: 15). π. τὴν ἐκδίκησιν Lk 18: 7f; cf. Ac 7: 24 (s. ἐκδίκησις). ἐνέδραν 25: 3. κοπετόν 8: 2. κρίσιν (q.v. 1aα and β) J 5: 27; Jd 15. λύτρωσιν Lk 1: 68. ὁδὸν ποιεῖν (v.l. ὁδοποιεῖν) Mk 2: 23 (ὁδός 1b). π. (τὸν) πόλεμον (μετά τινος) *wage war* (*on someone*) Rv 11: 7; 12: 17; 13: 7 (Da 7: 8 LXX; 7: 21 Theod.; Gen 14: 2). πρόθεσιν Eph 3: 11; συμβούλιον π. Mk 3: 6 v.l.; 15: 1 v.l. συστροφήν Ac 23: 12; cf. vs. 13. φόνον Mk 15: 7 (cf. Dt 22: 8; Callinicus, Vi. Hyp. 98, 21 Bonn).—τὸ ἱκανὸν ποιεῖν τινι s. ἱκανός 1c.

ε. what is done is indicated by the neut. of an adj. or pron.: τὸ ἀγαθὸν π. *do what is good* Ro 13: 3; τὰ ἀγαθὰ π. J 5: 29; ἀγαθὸν π. *do good* Mk 3: 4; 1 Pt 3: 11 (Ps 33: 15). τὸ καλὸν Ro 7: 21; 2 Cor 13: 7b; Gal 6: 9. τὰ καλὰ (καὶ εὐάρεστα ἐνώπιον αὐτοῦ) 1 Cl 21: 1. καλόν Js 4: 17.

τὸ κακόν Ro 13: 4. τὰ κακά 3: 8. κακόν 2 Cor 13: 7a (κακὸν μηδέν; cf. Dit., Syll.³ 1175, 20 κακόν τι ποιῆσαι). κακά 1 Pt 3: 12 (Ps 33: 17). τὰ ἀρεστὰ αὐτῷ (=τῷ θεῷ) J 8: 29; cf. Hb 13: 21b; 1 J 3: 22. πάντα 1 Cor 9: 23; 10: 31b; IEph 15: 3.—ὅ Mt 26: 13; Mk 14: 9; J 13: 7, 27a. τοῦτο Mt 13: 28; Mk 5: 32; Lk 5: 6; J 14: 13, 14 v.l.; Ro 7: 15f, 20 (cf. Epict. 2, 26, 4 ὃ θέλει οὐ ποιεῖ καὶ ὃ μὴ θέλει ποιεῖ); 1 Cor 11: 24f (the specific sense 'sacrifice' in this passage is opposed by TKAbbott [JBL 9, 1890, 137–52], but favored by FMozley [ET 7, 1896, 370–86], AAndersen [D. Abendmahl in d. ersten zwei Jahrh. '04], and KG Goetz [D. Abendmahlsfrage² '07]). αὐτὸ τοῦτο Gal 2: 10. ταῦτα Mt 21: 23; 23: 23; Gal 5: 17; 2 Pt 1: 10b. αὐτά J 13: 17; Ro 1: 32; 2: 3. τὸ αὐτό Mt 5: 46, 47b.—τί ποιήσω; Mk 10: 17; cf. J 18: 35. τί ἀγαθὸν ποιήσω; Mt 19: 16. τί κακὸν ἐποίησεν; Mt 27: 23; Lk 23: 22; Mk 15: 14. τί περισσὸν ποιεῖτε; Mt 5: 47a. τί ποιεῖτε τοῦτο; *what is this that you are doing?* or *why are doing this?* Mk 11: 3 (cf. Bl-D. §299, 1; Rob. 736; 738). τί ταῦτα ποιεῖτε; Ac 14: 15a (as Demosth. 55, 5). τί σὺ ὧδε ποιεῖς; Hv 1, 1, 5. W. ptc. foll. (Bl-D. §414, 5; Rob. 1121) τί ποιεῖτε λύοντες; *what are you doing, untying?* Mk 11: 5. τί ποιεῖτε κλαίοντες; *what are you doing, weeping?* or *what do you mean by weeping?* Ac 21: 13. τί ποιήσουσιν οἱ βαπτιζόμενοι; *what are they to do, who have themselves baptized?* 1 Cor 15: 29.—A statement of what is to be done follows in an indirect question ὃ ποιεῖς ποίησον *do what you must do* J 13: 27 (as Epict. 3, 21, 24 ποίει ἃ ποιεῖς; 3, 23, 1; 4, 9, 18).

ζ. of meals or banquets, and of festivities of which a banquet is the principal part *give* ἄριστον Lk 14: 12. δεῖπνον (q.v. 2) Mk 6: 21; Lk 14: 12, 16; J 12: 2; Hs 5, 2, 9. δοχήν (s. δοχή) Lk 5: 29; 14: 13. γάμους (s. γάμος 1a) Mt 22: 2.—*Keep, celebrate* (PFay. 117, 12) the Passover (feast) Mt 26: 18; Hb 11: 28 (s. πάσχα 3). Also in connection w. τὴν ἑορτὴν ποιῆσαι Ac 18: 21 D the Passover is surely meant. But π. is also used of festivals in general (cf. X., Hell. 4, 5, 2 ποιεῖν Ἴσθμια; 7, 4, 28 τὰ Ὀλύμπια).

η. of the natural processes of growth; in plant life *send out, produce, bear, yield* καρπόν, καρπούς (Aristot., Plant. 1, 4 p. 819b, 31; 2, 10 p. 829a, 41; LXX [καρπός 1a]) Mt 3: 10; 7: 17a, b, 18 v.l., 19; 13: 26; Lk 3: 9; 6: 43a, b; 8: 8; 13: 9; Rv 22: 2; also as a symbol Mt 3: 8; 21: 43; Lk 3: 8. κλάδους Mk 4: 32. ἐλαίας Js 3: 12a (cf. Jos., Ant. 11, 50 ἄμπελοι, αἳ ποιοῦσιν τὸν οἶνον). π. ὕδωρ *produce water* vs. 12b (but s. ἁλυκός).—Of capital yielding a return ἡ μνᾶ ἐποίησεν πέντε μνᾶς *the mina has made five minas* Lk 19: 18. Also of the person who operates w. the capital *make money* (Ps.-Demosth. 10, 76; Polyb. 2, 62, 12) ἐποίησεν ἄλλα πέντε τάλαντα Mt 25: 16 v.l.

θ. The result of the action is indicated by the acc. and inf.; *make* (*to*), *cause* (*someone*) *to, bring it about that* (Hom.+; inscr. [s. Dit., Syll.³ IV p. 510a index]; pap., LXX) ποιεῖ αὐτὴν μοιχευθῆναι Mt 5: 32. ποιήσω ὑμᾶς γενέσθαι ἀλεεῖς ἀνθρώπων Mk 1: 17. Cf. 7: 37b; Lk 5: 34 (*force someone to fast*); J 6: 10; Ac 17: 26; Rv 13: 13b.—ἵνα takes the place of the inf.: ποιήσω αὐτοὺς ἵνα ἥξουσιν Rv 3: 9; cf. 13: 12b, 16. ἵνα without acc. J 11: 37; Col 4: 16; Rv 13: 15.—ἡμῖν ὡς πεποιηκόσιν τοῦ περιπατεῖν αὐτόν *us, as though we had caused him to walk* Ac 3: 12.

ι. w. a double accusative, of the obj. and the pred. (class.; LXX), *make someone* or *someth.* (into) *someth.* The predicate acc. is a noun: ποιήσω ὑμᾶς ἀλεεῖς ἀνθρώπων Mt 4: 19. ὑμεῖς αὐτὸν (i.e. τὸν οἶκον τοῦ θεοῦ) ποιεῖτε σπήλαιον λῃστῶν 21: 13; Mk 11: 17; Lk 19: 46. Cf. Mt 23: 15b; J 2: 16; 4: 46, 54; cf. 2: 11; Ac 2: 36; 2 Cor

5: 21; Hb 1: 7 (Ps 103: 4); Rv 1: 6; 3: 12 al. ποιήσόν με ὡς ἕνα τ. μισθίων σου Lk 15: 19, 21 v.l. (cf. Gen 45: 8; 48: 20 and Bl-D. §453, 4; Rob. 481). If the obj. acc. is missing, it may be supplied fr. the context as self-evident ἁρπάζειν αὐτὸν ἵνα ποιήσωσιν βασιλέα take him by force, in order to make (him) king J 6: 15.—1 Cor 6: 15. *Claim that someone is someth., pretend that someone is someth.* J 8: 53; 10: 33; 19: 7, 12; 1 J 1: 10; 5: 10.—The predicate acc. is an adj.: εὐθείας ποιεῖτε τὰς τρίβους (Is 40: 3) *make the paths straight* Mt 3: 3; Mk 1: 3; Lk 3: 4. τρίχα λευκὴν π. Mt 5: 36. Cf. 12: 16; 20: 12b; 26: 73; 28: 14; Mk 3: 12; J 5: 11, 15; 7: 23; 16: 2; Ac 7: 19; Eph 2: 14 (ὁ ποιήσας τὰ ἀμφότερα ἕν); Rv 12: 15; 21: 5. ἴσον ἑαυτὸν ποιῶν τῷ θεῷ (thereby) *declaring that he was equal to God* or *making himself equal to God* J 5: 18.

c. *do, keep, carry out, practice, commit*—**α.** *do, keep* the will or law obediently τὸ θέλημα τοῦ θεοῦ al. (θέλημα 1cγ) Mt 7: 21; 12: 50; Mk 3: 35; J 4: 34; 6: 38; 7: 17; 9: 31; Eph 6: 6; Hb 10: 7, 9 (both Ps 39: 9), 36; 13: 21; 1 J 2: 17; Pol 2: 2; τὰ θελήματα Mk 3: 35 v.l.; Ac 13: 22; Eb Ev 4. π. τὰ θελήματα τῆς σαρκός Eph 2: 3. Cf. Mt 21: 31.—π. τὸν νόμον J 7: 19; Gal 5: 3; cf. Mt 5: 19; Ro 2: 14; Gal 3: 10 (Dt 27: 26); vs. 12 (cf. Lev 18: 5).—Mt 7: 24, 26; Lk 6: 46; J 2: 5; 8: 44.—ἐξουσίαν ποιεῖν *exercise authority* Rv 13: 12a.

β. *do, practice* virtues: π. τὴν ἀλήθειαν (ἀλήθεια 2b) *live the truth* J 3: 21 (cf. IQS 1, 5 al.); 1 J 1: 6. (τὴν) δικαιοσύνην (δικαιοσύνη 2b) 1 J 2: 29; 3: 7, 10; Rv 22: 11; 2 Cl 4: 2; 11: 7. Differently Mt 6: 1 (δικαιοσύνη 2a), which belongs with ποιεῖν ἐλεημοσύνην vs. 2a, 3a (s. ἐλεημοσύνη). π. χρηστότητα Ro 3: 12 (Ps 13: 1, 3; 52: 4 v.l.). π. ἔλεος *show mercy* Js 2: 13; μετά τινος *to someone* Lk 1: 72; 10: 37a (s. ἔλεος 1 and μετά II 1cγ).

γ. *do, commit, be guilty of* sins and vices (τὴν) ἀμαρτίαν (ἀμαρτία 1) J 8: 34; 2 Cor 11: 7; 1 Pt 2: 22; 1 J 3: 4a, 8, 9; pl. Js 5: 15. ἀμάρτημα (q.v.) 1 Cor 6: 18. (τὴν) ἀνομίαν (ἀνομία 2) Mt 13: 41; 1 J 3: 4b; 1 Cl 16: 10 (Is 53: 9). βδέλυγμα καὶ ψεῦδος Rv 21: 27. τὰ μὴ καθήκοντα Ro 1: 28. ὃ οὐκ ἔξεστιν Mk 2: 24; cf. Mt 12: 2.

d. π. τι *do someth.*, w. some indication of the pers. (or thing) with whom someth. is done; the action may result to the advantage or disadvantage of this person:

α. neutral π. τί τινα *do someth. with someone* (double acc. as Demosth. 23, 194 τί ποιεῖν ἀγαθὸν τὴν πόλιν) τί ποιήσω Ἰησοῦν; *what shall I do with Jesus?* Mt 27: 22. Also τί ποιήσεις τὸν ἀγρόν; *what will you do with the land?* Hs 1: 4. Cf. Mk 15: 12.—Bl-D. §157, 1; Rob. 484. —Neutral is also the expr. π. τί τινι *do someth. to someone* J 9: 26; 12: 16; 13: 12; Ac 4: 16. Likew. the passive form of the familiar saying of Jesus ὡς ποιεῖτε, οὕτω ποιηθήσεται ὑμῖν *as you do* (whether it be good or ill), *it will be done to you* 1 Cl 13: 2.

β. to his advantage: π. τί τινι (Diod. S. 18, 51, 3): ὅσα ἐὰν θέλητε ἵνα ποιῶσιν ὑμῖν οἱ ἄνθρωποι Mt 7: 12a. τί θέλετε ποιήσω ὑμῖν; *what do you want me to do for you?* Mt 20: 32.—25: 40; cf. vs. 45; Mk 5: 19f; 7: 12; 10: 35f, 51; Lk 1: 49 (ἐποίησέν μοι μεγάλα ὁ δυνατός); 8: 39a, b; J 13: 15a.—π. τι εἴς τινα 1 Th 4: 10. π. τι μετά τινος Ac 14: 27; 15: 4 (on the constr. w. μετά s. I 1cβ above and cf. BGU 798, 7; 948, 8).

γ. to his disadvantage: π. τί τινι (Gen 20: 9) τί ποιήσει τοῖς γεωργοῖς; *what will he do to the vine-dressers?* Mt 21: 40.—Mk 9: 13; Lk 6: 11; 20: 15; Ac 9: 13; Hb 13: 6 (Ps 117: 6).—π. τι εἴς τινα (PSI 64, 20; 22 [I BC] μηδὲ ποιήσειν εἰς σὲ φάρμακα) J 15: 21. π. τι ἔν τινι Mt 17: 12; Lk 23: 31.

e. specialized expressions—**α.** *get* or *gain* someth. for

oneself, *provide oneself* with someth. ποιήσατε ἑαυτοῖς βαλλάντια Lk 12: 33; φίλους 16: 9 (cf. X., An. 5, 5, 12 φίλον ποιεῖσθαί τινα).—Without a dat. Ἰησοῦς μαθητὰς ποιεῖ *Jesus was gaining disciples* J 4: 1.

β. *assume, suppose, take as an example* (class.) w. double acc. (Pla., Theaet. 197D) ποιήσατε τὸ δένδρον καλόν *suppose the tree is good* Mt 12: 33a; cf. b.

γ. ἔξω ποιεῖν τινα *take someone out(side)* (colloq. *put out*; cf. X., Cyr. 4, 1, 3 ἔξω βελῶν ποιεῖν='put outside bowshot') Ac 5: 34.

δ. w. an acc. of time *spend, stay* (Anth. 11, 330; PSI 362, 15 [251/0 BC]; UPZ 70, 21; PFlor. 137, 7 [III AD] ἡμέραν, ἣν ποιεῖ ἐκεῖ; PGenève 54, 18 τρεῖς ἡμέρας; Pr 13: 23; Tob. 10: 7 BA; Jos., Ant. 6, 18 μῆνας τέσσαρας. Demosth. 19, 163 and Pla., Phileb. 50D are wrongly cited in this connection, as shown by WSchulze, Graeca Latina '01, 23f) χρόνον (Dionys. Hal. 4, 66) Ac 15: 33; 18: 23. μῆνας τρεῖς 20: 3. νυχθήμερον 2 Cor 11: 25. ἐνιαυτόν Js 4: 13.

2. *do, act, proceed*—**a.** The manner of the action is more definitely indicated by means of an adv. (Jos., C. Ap. 2, 51).

α. καλῶς ποιεῖν *do good* or *well* Mt 12: 12; 1 Cor 7: 37, 38a; κρεῖσσον π. 7: 38b; Js 2: 8 (s. γ below), 19; φρονίμως π. *act wisely* Lk 16: 8; π. οὕτως *do so* (Charito 8, 6, 4 ποιήσομεν οὕτως=this is the way we will proceed) Mt 24: 46; Lk 9: 15; 12: 43; J 14: 31 (καθὼς . . . οὕτως π.); Ac 12: 8; 1 Cor 16: 1; Js 2: 12; B 12: 7. π. ὡσαύτως *proceed in the same way* Mt 20: 5; ὁμοίως π. Lk 3: 11; 10: 37b. ὥσπερ οἱ ὑποκριταὶ ποιοῦσιν *as the hypocrites do* Mt 6: 2b. καλῶς ποιεῖτε 1 Th 5: 11.—ποιεῖν foll. by a clause beginning w. ὡς: ἐποίησεν ὡς προσέταξεν *he did as he* (the angel) *had ordered* Mt 1: 24; cf. 26: 19. Or the clause begins w. καθὼς Mt 21: 6; J 13: 15b.

β. w. dat. ἐποίησαν αὐτοῖς ὡσαύτως *they treated them in the same way* Mt 21: 36. οὕτως μοι πεποίηκεν κύριος *the Lord has dealt thus with me* Lk 1: 25; cf. 2: 48; Mt 18: 35. εὖ ποιεῖν τινι Mk 14: 7. καλῶς π. τινι Mt 5: 44 t.r.; Lk 6: 27. ὁμοίως π. τινι 6: 31b.—[ποιεῖν] καθὼς ἐποίει αὐτοῖς [*to do*] *as he was accustomed to do for them* Mk 15: 8.

γ. καλῶς ποιεῖν w. ptc. foll. *do well if, do well to,* as a formula somet.=*please* (s. καλῶς 4a and cf. Dit., Syll.³ 561, 6f καλῶς ποιήσειν τοὺς πολίτας προσδεξαμένους; UPZ 110, 11 [164 BC]; POxy. 300, 5 [I AD]; 525, 7; Hdt. 5, 24 εὖ ἐποίησας ἀφικόμενος; Dit., Syll.³ 598E, 8f) Ac 10: 33; Phil 4: 14; 2 Pt 1: 19; *please* 3 J 6; GEg 1b.—Sim. καλῶς ποιεῖν, εἰ . . . Js 2: 8 (cf. PPetr. II 11[1], 1 καλῶς ποιεῖς εἰ ἔρρωσαι).

b. The manner of the action is more definitely indicated by a prepositional expr.—**α.** ποιεῖν κατά τι *do* or *act in accordance w. someth.* (Dit., Syll.³ 915, 13 π. κατὰ τὰς συνθήκας; 1016, 6; PLille 4, 6; 22 [III BC]; BGU 998 II, 12 [II BC] π. κατὰ τὰ προγεγραμμένα) κατὰ τὰ ἔργα αὐτῶν *as they do* Mt 23: 3b.—Lk 2: 27. Also π. πρός τι: πρὸς τὸ θέλημα 12: 47.

β. w. dat. κατὰ τὰ αὐτὰ ἐποίουν τοῖς προφήταις οἱ πατέρες αὐτῶν Lk 6: 23; cf. vs. 26.

c. abs. *work, be active* (X., An. 1, 5, 8; Ruth 2: 19) w. acc. of time (Socrat., Ep. 14, 8 ποιήσας ἡμέρας τριάκοντα) μίαν ὥραν ἐποίησαν *they have worked for only one hour* Mt 20: 12a. ποιῆσαι μῆνας *be active for months* Rv 13: 5.—Somet. it is not a general action or activity that is meant, but the doing of someth. quite definite. The acc. belonging to it is easily supplied fr. the context: λέγουσιν καὶ οὐ ποιοῦσιν *they say* (it), *but do not do* or *keep* (it) Mt 23: 3c (the contrast is not betw. speaking [λαλεῖν] and acting in general).—2 Cor 8: 10f; 1 Th 5: 24.

II. middle *make* or *do someth. for oneself* or *of oneself*
1. mostly as a periphrasis of the simple verbal idea (s. I 1bδ above) ἀναβολὴν ποιεῖσθαι Ac 25: 17 (s. ἀναβολή). ἐκβολὴν ποιεῖσθαι 27: 18 (s. ἐκβολή); αὔξησιν π. Eph 4: 16; δέησιν or δεήσεις π. Lk 5: 33; Phil 1: 4; 1 Ti 2: 1 (s. δέησις). διαλογισμοὺς π. 1 Cl 21: 3; τὴν ἔνωσιν π. IPol 5: 2; ἐπιστροφὴν π. 1 Cl 1: 1 (ἐπιστροφή 1); καθαρισμὸν π. Hb 1: 3 (καθαρισμός 2). κοινωνίαν Ro 15: 26. κοπετόν Ac 8: 2 t.r. λόγον (Isocr., Ep. 2, 2) 1: 1a; 11: 2 D; 20: 24 v.l. (on these three passages s. λόγος: 1aζ; 1aγ and 1aa, end). μνείαν Ro 1: 9; Eph 1: 16; 1 Th 1: 2; Phlm 4 (μνεία 2). μνήμην 2 Pt 1: 15 (s. μνήμη 1). μονήν J 14: 23 (μονή 1). νουθέτησιν 1 Cl 56: 2. ὁμιλίαν IPol 5: 1 (ὁμιλία 2). πορείαν π. (= πορεύεσθαι; cf. X., An. 5, 6, 11, Cyr. 5, 2, 31; Plut., Mor. 571E; Jos., Vi. 57; 2 Macc 3: 8; 12: 10) Lk 13: 22. πρόνοιαν π. *make provision, care* (Isocr. 4, 2 and 136; Demosth., Prooem. 16; Ps.-Demosth. 47, 80; Polyb. 4, 6, 11; Dion. Hal. 5, 46; Aelian, V.H. 12, 56. Oft. in inscr. and pap.; Da 6: 19 προν. ποιούμενος αὐτοῦ; Jos., Bell. 4, 317, C. Ap. 1, 9) Ro 13: 14. προσκλίσεις π. 1 Cl 47: 3; σπουδὴν π. *be eager* or *anxious* (Hdt. 1, 4; 5, 30 πᾶσαν σπουδὴν ποιεύμενος; 9, 8; Pla., Euthyd. 304E, Leg. 1, 628E; Isocr. 5, 45 πᾶσαν τὴν σπ. περὶ τούτου ποιεῖσθαι; Polyb. 1, 46, 2 al.; Diod. S. 1, 75, 1; Plut., Mor. p. 4E; Dit., Syll.³ 539A, 15f; 545, 14 τὴν πᾶσαν σπ. ποιούμενος; PHib. 71, 9 [III BC] τ. πᾶσαν σπ. ποιῆσαι; 44, 8) Jd 3. συνελεύσεις ποιεῖσθαι *come together, meet* 1 Cl 20: 10. συνωμοσίαν ποιεῖσθαι *form a conspiracy* (Polyb. 1, 70, 6; Herodian 7, 4, 3; Dit., Syll.³ 526, 16) Ac 23: 13.
2. w. double acc., of the obj. and pred. (Lucian, Prom. es in Verb. 6 p. 34 σεμνοτάτας ἐποιεῖτο τὰς συνουσίας; Dialekt-Inschr. 4629 II, 22; 25 [Laconia]; Jos., Ant. 2, 263; s. I 1bι above) βεβαίαν τὴν κλῆσιν ποιεῖσθαι *make the calling certain* 2 Pt 1: 10.—HBraun, TW VI 456–83: ποιέω and related words. M-M. B. 538.

ποίημα, ατος, τό (Hdt.+; Dit., Syll.³ 532, 5; LXX) *what is made, work, creation* in our lit. only of the works of divine creation (Aesop, Fab. 444 P.=142 H. ποιήματα; Ps 142: 5; Philo, Det. Pot. Ins. 125 θεοῦ ποιήματα. Cf. Aelian, N.A. 1, 53 π. Προμηθέως; Alex. Aphr., An. Mant. II 1 p. 112, 1 of the creations of Nus) τὰ ἀόρατα αὐτοῦ τοῖς ποιήμασι νοούμενα καθορᾶται *his (God's) invisible nature is perceived with the mind's eye by the things he has created* Ro 1: 20 (on this s. the lit. under ἀόρατος and γνωστός 2). Of the Christians αὐτοῦ ἐσμεν π. *we are his creation*, i.e. *he has made us what we are* Eph 2: 10. M-M.*

ποίησις, εως, ἡ (Hdt.+; inscr., pap., LXX)—1. *doing, working* (Pla., Soph. 266b θείας ἔργα ποιήσεως, Charm. 163E; Jos., Ant. 17, 94) μακάριος ἐν τῇ ποιήσει αὐτοῦ ἔσται *he will be blessed in his doing* Js 1: 25. Of God: ποίησις χειρῶν αὐτοῦ 1 Cl 27: 7 (Ps 18: 2).
2. *work, creation* of the artist (Aristoph., Pla.+; Ep. Arist. 57; Jos., C. Ap. 1, 12), in our lit. of the Divine Artist (Proclus on Pla., Cratylus p. 21, 18f Pasqu.): God is merciful ἐπὶ τῇ τῶν ποίησιν αὐτοῦ (Da 9: 14 Theod.) Hm 4, 3, 5; 9: 3. M-M.*

ποιητής, οῦ, ὁ—1. *one who does someth., maker*, then specif. *poet* (so Aristoph., Ran. 96; 1030; Pla., Phaedo 61B al.; oft. inscr. [Dit., Syll.³ IV 510b index, Or. II 694b ind.]; PHermopol. 125B, 6; POsl. 189, 13 [III AD]; Ep. Arist. 31; Philo; Jos., Ant. 12, 38; 110 al.) Ac 17: 28.
2. *one who does someth. prescribed, a doer* w. obj. gen. (cf. 1 Macc 2: 67) Ro 2: 13; Js 4: 11. (Opp. ἀκροατής) π. λόγου 1: 22f. π. ἔργου *a doer that acts* (opp.: a forgetful hearer) vs. 25. M-M. B. 1299.*

ποικιλία, ας, ἡ (Pla., X.+; inscr., PTebt. 703, 93 [III BC]; LXX; Ep. Arist. 56; Philo) *many-colored appearance, variety, diversity* τῶν ὀρέων ἡ π. Hs 9, 18, 5. Pl. (Isocr. 5, 27) αἱ ποικιλίαι τοῦ νοὸς τῶν ἐθνῶν *the diversity of mental attitudes among the nations* 9, 17, 2. αἱ ποικιλίαι τῶν λίθων *the various appearances of the stones* 9, 6, 4.*

ποικίλος, η, ον (Hom.+; inscr., pap., LXX)—1. *of various kinds, diversified, manifold* (Pind.+; 2 Macc 15: 21; Ep. Arist. 78; Philo; Jos., Bell. 3, 393, Ant. 10, 142) ἄνθη (Ps.-Pla., Axioch. 13 p. 371c) AP 3: 10. ἀρνήσεις Hs 8, 8, 4. ἀσθένειαι s 6, 3, 4c. βάσανοι *many, various kinds of torments* Mt 4: 24; Hs 6, 3, 4b; of torture MPol 2: 4. βοτάναι Hm 10, 1, 5. δυνάμεις Hb 2: 4. ἔθνη Hs 9, 17, 2b; ἐπιθυμίαι 2 Ti 3: 6; cf. Tit 3: 3. ἰδέαι Hs 9, 17, 1. καρποί 9, 28, 3; Dg 12: 1. νόσοι (Philo, Omn. Prob. Lib. 58 νοσήματα) Mt 4: 24; Mk 1: 34; Lk 4: 40. ὄρη Hs 9, 17, 2a, c, 3. πειρασμοί Js 1: 2; 1 Pt 1: 6 (πολλοῖς 𝔓⁷²). πονηρίαι Hs 9, 18, 3. πραγματεῖαι (cf. Philo, In Flacc. 3) s 9, 20, 1. τιμωρίαι s 6, 3, 3; 4a. τρυφαί m 6, 2, 5. π. χάρις θεοῦ *the grace of God, that manifests itself in various ways* 1 Pt 4: 10. χρόαι Hs 9, 4, 5a, c. W. ξένος: διδαχαί Hb 13: 9 (s. also 3 below). W. πολύς (Diod. S. 5, 62, 1 πολλοὶ κ. ποικίλοι λόγοι=many and varied reports; 17, 13, 1; Maximus Tyr. 11, 11e; Ps.-Plut., Hom. 122) Hm 4, 2, 3; s 9, 20, 2. ἐν πάσαις θλίψεσι π. *in all kinds of afflictions* s 7: 4.
2. *many-colored, variegated* (Hom.+; Polyaenus 6, 1, 4; Lucian, Deor. Conc. 10; PGM 4, 2709; LXX [Gen 37: 3 al.]; Jos., Ant. 11, 235; Test. Zeb. 1: 3). This mng. is to be preferred in οἱ λίθοι οἱ π. *the many-colored stones* (IG IV² 1, 106 I, 96; 113 [IV BC]) Hs 9, 4, 5b.
3. also in the sense of fault-finding *ambiguous, crafty, sly, deceitful* of persons, ways of thinking, words, actions (Hes.+; trag.; Pind., Nem. 5, 52 βουλεύματα; Aristoph., Thesm. 438 λόγοι; Polyb. 8, 18, 4 Κρὴς ὑπάρχων καὶ φύσει ποικίλος) Hb 13: 9 (s. also 1 above). M-M.*

ποιμαίνω fut. ποιμανῶ; 1 aor. ἐποίμανα Ps 77: 72, imper. 2 pl. ποιμάνατε 1 Pt 5: 2 (Hom.+; inscr., pap., LXX, Philo, Joseph., Test. 12 Patr.) *herd, tend, (lead to) pasture.*
1. lit., w. acc. (Jos., Ant. 2, 264) π. ποίμνην *tend a flock* 1 Cor 9: 7. Abs. (Jos., Ant. 1, 309) δοῦλος ποιμαίνων *a slave tending sheep* Lk 17: 7.—Dalman (under ἀμφιβάλλω).
2. fig., of activity that protects, rules, governs, fosters
a. in the sense 'lead', 'guide', 'rule' (Eur., fgm. 744 στρατόν; Ps.-Lucian, Amor. 54 τ. ἀμαθεῖς).
α. w. the symbol prominently in mind: of the direction of a congregation ποιμαίνειν τὸ ποίμνιον τοῦ θεοῦ *tend God's flock* 1 Pt 5: 2 (PsSol 17: 40 ποιμαίνων τὸ ποίμνιον κυρίου ἐν πίστει κ. δικαιοσύνῃ). ποίμαινε τὰ προβάτιά μου J 21: 16.
β. w. the symbol retreating into the background (cf. 1 Ch 11: 2; Mi 7: 14; Jer 23: 2): of the administration of a congregation ποιμ. τὴν ἐκκλησίαν τοῦ θεοῦ Ac 20: 28.— Of the Messiah ποιμανεῖ τὸν λαόν μου Ἰσραήλ (cf. 2 Km 5: 2; 7: 7.—Himerius, Or. 39 [= Or. 5], 8 Ἀττικὴ Μοῦσα ποιμαίνει τὴν πόλιν, i.e., Thessalonica) Mt 2: 6. Of death: θάνατος ποιμανεῖ αὐτούς 1 Cl 51: 4 (Ps 48: 15). The latter pass. forms a transition to several others in which
γ. the activity as 'shepherd' has destructive results (cf. Jer 22: 22 and s. ELohmeyer, Hdb. on Rv 2: 27) ποιμανεῖ αὐτοὺς ἐν ῥάβδῳ σιδηρᾷ (after Ps 2: 9) Rv 2: 27; 12: 5; 19: 15 (cf. Heraclitus fgm. 11 πᾶν ἑρπετὸν πληγῇ νέμεται =everything that creeps is shepherded by a blow [from God]. Pla., Critias 109B alludes to this).

b. *protect, care for, nurture* (Aeschyl., Eumen. 91 ἱκέτην; Pla., Lys. 209Α τὸ σῶμα) αὐτούς Rv 7: 17 (cf. Ps 22: 1; Ezk 34: 23). π. ἑαυτόν *look after oneself* i.e. care for oneself alone (cf. Ezk 34: 2) Jd 12. M-M. B. 146.*

ποιμενικός, ή, όν (Pla.+; poets since Theocr. 1, 23. In prose: Maximus Tyr. 20, 6b; 38, 2a; Philostrat., Imag. 2, 18 p. 370, 9; LXX; Philo; Jos., Ant. 6, 185) *pertaining to a shepherd* (Vi. Aesopi W c. 75 τὸ ποιμενικὸν σχῆμα) σχήματι ποιμενικῷ *in the garb of a shepherd* Hv 5: 1.*

ποιμήν, ένος, ὁ (Hom.+; pap., LXX; Philo; Jos., Ant. 8, 404 al.) *shepherd, sheep-herder.*

1. lit. Mt 9: 36=Mk 6: 34 (Num 27: 17); Mt 25: 32. Of the shepherds at Jesus' birth Lk 2: 8, 15, 18, 20 (cf. HGressmann, Das Weihnachtsevangelium '14 [on this CClemen, StKr 89, '16, 237-52]; JGeffcken, D. Hirten auf dem Felde: Her. 49, '14, 321-51 [against him JKroll, Her. 50, '15, 137ff]; Clemen² '24, 195; 203ff; IHarrie, Die Anbetung der Hirten: ARW 23, '25, 369-82; RBultmann, Gesch. d. syn. Trad.² '31, 323-6; GErdmann, D. Vorgesch. d. Lk u. Mt '32; ADeissmann, D. Anbetung d. Hirten u. d. Anbetung d. Weisen: Lutherring 16, '35, 377-82).—Used as a symbol: πατάξω τὸν ποιμένα, καὶ διασκορπισθήσονται τὰ πρόβατα τῆς ποίμνης (cf. Zech 13: 7) Mt 26: 31 (𝔓³⁷ D t.r. have the more correct form διασκορπισθήσεται); Mk 14: 27; B 5: 12. Of Christ in an extended allegory J 10: 2, 7 (𝔓⁷⁵ al.), 16; (opp. ὁ μισθωτός) vs. 12; ὁ ποιμὴν ὁ καλός vs. 11a, b, 14 (Maximus Tyr. 6, 7d Cyrus is called ποιμὴν ἀγαθός, because he protects the Persian 'flock' fr. the barbarian 'wolves').

2. fig. (Diog. L. 9, 40 Democritus is called ποιμὴν [=guardian] μύθων)—a. esp. freq. in Hermas—a. as the angel of repentance and bearer of a revelation (MDibelius, Der Offenbarungsträger im 'Hirten' des H.: Harnack-Ehrung '21, 105-18; Rtzst., Erlösungsmyst. '21, 149) Hv 5: 3, 8; s 2: 1; 5, 1, 1; 8, 1, 4; 18; 8, 2, 5f; 8; 8, 4, 1; 8, 5, 1; 6; 8, 6, 1; 9, 1, 1; 9, 2, 6; 9, 5, 2; 7; 9, 7, 1; 3f; 9, 8, 1; 9, 9, 5-7; 9, 10, 1; 4; 6; 9, 11, 1; 8.

β. in the vision of the shepherds Hs 6, 1, 5f; 6, 2, 1; 5f; 6, 3, 2; 7: 1.

b. of those who lead the Christian churches—a. God (Philo, Agr. 51; Aberciusinschr. 3 π. ἁγνός) IRo 9: 1.

β. Christ τὸν ποιμένα τῶν προβάτων τὸν μέγαν Hb 13: 20 (RGyllenberg, D. Christol. des Hb: Ztschr. f. syst. Theol. 11, '34, 662-90). τὸν ποιμένα καὶ ἐπίσκοπον τῶν ψυχῶν ὑμῶν 1 Pt 2: 25 (cf. Philo, Mut. Nom. 116 of the θεῖος λόγος; Ezk 34: 23). ποιμ. τῆς ἐκκλησίας MPol 19: 2. S. above 1, end, and Hdb. exc. after J 10: 21; Bultmann 276-93; JQuasten, Hlg. Überliefg. (edited by OCasel) '38, 51-8 (Hellenistic and early Christian); WJost, Poimen. D. Bild v. Hirten in d. bibl. Überl. u. s. christol. Bed., Diss. Giessen '39; ThKKempf, Christus der Hirt '42; VMuller, Prehistory of the Good Shepherd: Jour. of Near East. Stud. 3, '44, 87-90.

γ. of human leaders (on 'shepherds' as the founders and temporary thiasarchs [leaders] of Gk. religious guilds s. EMaass, Orpheus 1895, 181; Himerius, Or. 54 [=Or. 15] when greeting his newly arrived students, compares the teachers to shepherds [ἀγελάρχαι] and the pupils to the flock [ἀγέλη alternating with ποίμνιον §2]. S. also Jer 2: 8; 3: 15; Ezk 34: 2) *pastor* Eph 4: 11 (w. other church leaders). ὅπου ὁ ποιμήν (i.e. the bishop) ἐστιν, ἐκεῖ ὡς πρόβατα ἀκολουθεῖτε IPhld 2: 1. Cf. also IRo 9: 1 (Ign. as 'shepherd' of the Syrian church).—EHatch-AHarnack, D. Gesellschaftsverf. der christl. Kirchen im Altertum 1883, 230; HBruders, D. Verfassung der Kirche bis zum Jahr 175 n. Chr. '04, 190f; 371f; Harnack, D. Mission⁴ I '23, 350f; NCavatassi, De Munere Pastoris in

NT: Verb. Domini 29, '51, 215-27; 275-85.—On the whole word JoachJeremias, TW VI 484-501: ποιμήν and related words. M-M. B. 149.*

ποίμνη, ης, ἡ (Hom.+; PAmh. 127, 39; Gen 32: 17; Philo; Jos., Ant. 6, 295; Test. Gad) *flock,* esp. of sheep (Diod. S. 4, 26, 2 ποίμνας προβάτων; 5, 65, 2; 20, 8, 4) Lk 2: 8; 1 Cor 9: 7b. ποιμαίνειν ποίμνην vs. 7a.—As a symbol: w. ref. to Jesus' disciples Mt 26: 31; B 5: 12 (both=Zech 13: 7 A); to the church and to Jesus as its head μία ποίμνη εἷς ποιμήν J 10: 16 (Maximus Tyr. 35, 2g ἐν ἀγέλῃ μιᾷ ὑπὸ ποιμένι ἑνί; Philo, Agr. 51 God as ποιμήν leads the whole world as ποίμνη). M-M.*

ποίμνιον, ου, τό (Soph., Hdt.+; PRyl. 114, 20; LXX; Philo) *flock,* esp. of sheep (Ps.-Apollod., Epit. 7, 5, 8; Tzetzes on Lycophron 344; Ep. Arist. 170; Jos., Ant. 8, 404; 18, 316; Test. 12 Patr.).

1. lit. MPol 14: 1.—2. fig. (Hippocr., Ep. 1, 2; Themist., Or. 23 p. 289)—a. in the vision of the shepherds (ποιμήν 2aβ) Hs 6, 1, 6.

b. of the Christian church (as of the people of Israel in the OT: Jer 13: 17 τὸ π. κυρίου; Zech 10: 3 al.) Ac 20: 28f; 1 Pt 5: 3. τὸ π. τοῦ θεοῦ vs. 2. τὸ π. τοῦ Χριστοῦ 1 Cl 44: 3; 54: 2; 57: 2; cf. 16: 1. Of Jesus' disciples (Liban., Or. 58, 36 of a sophist's pupils; Himerius, Or. 54 [=Or. 15], 2 of the hearers) τὸ μικρὸν π. (nom. w. art. for voc. Bl-D. §147 app.; Rob. 465) Lk 12: 32. M-M.*

ποῖος, α, ον (Hom.+; inscr., pap., LXX; Jos., Bell. 7, 265f al.) interrog. pron., in direct and indir. interrog. sentences.

1. *of what kind?*—a. used w. a noun (Bl-D. §298, 2; cf. Rob. 740)—a. beside τίς (Hdt. 7, 21, 1; Herodas 6, 74f; Maximus Tyr. 33, 5a τίνα καὶ ποῖον τύραννον; PTebt. 25, 18 [117 BC]; BGU 619, 8) εἰς τίνα ἢ ποῖον καιρόν *to what time or what kind of time* 1 Pt 1: 11 (cf. UPZ 65, 52 [154 BC] ἀπὸ ποίου χρόνου=since what time). ποῖον οἶκον . . . ἢ τίς τόπος . . . ; Ac 7: 49; B 16: 2 (both Is 66: 1; s. ed. JZiegler).

β. in a direct question (3 Km 22: 24) διὰ ποίου νόμου; *by what kind of law?* Ro 3: 27. ποίῳ σώματι; *with what kind of a body?* 1 Cor 15: 35. ποῖον κλέος; ironically *what kind of credit?* 1 Pt 2: 20; sim. ποία ὑμῖν χάρις ἐστίν; Lk 6: 32, 33, 34; cf. D 1: 3.—1 Cl 28: 2; 2 Cl 1: 5; Hs 9: 1, 2, 1; m 12, 1, 3a; s 6, 5, 5.—For Js 4: 14 see γ below.

γ. in an indir. quest. (Archimed. II 416, 6 Heib. ποῖαι γωνίαι) ποίῳ θανάτῳ (by) *what sort of death* J 12: 33; 18: 32; 21: 19.—Lk 9: 55 v.l.; Js 4: 14 (this is possibly to be taken as a direct quest.; s. Windisch ad loc.); 1 Cl 38: 3a; Hm 4, 2, 3; 12, 1, 3b.

b. without a noun ποῖοι καὶ τίνες 1 Cl 38: 3b.

2. (=τίς) *which, what?*—a. w. a noun—a. in a dir. question (Theopomp. [IV BC]: 115 fgm. 263a Jac.; 2 Km 15: 2; 3 Km 13: 12; Jon 1: 8; Jos., Ant. 15, 137) ποία ἐντολή; *which commandment?* Mt 22: 36; cf. Mk 12: 28; J 10: 32. ποίῳ τρόπῳ; *in what way?* Hv 1, 1, 7.

β. in an indir. quest. (Aeschin., In Ctesiph. c. 24; Tob 5: 9) Mt 24: 42f; Lk 12: 39; Rv 3: 3. ἐκ ποίας ἐπαρχίας ἐστίν Ac 23: 34.—Hv 4, 3, 7.

γ. In some cases π. takes the place of the gen. of the interrog. τίς (in dir. as well as indir. questions. Cf. Charito 4, 4, 3 Blake ποίᾳ δυνάμει πεποιθώς;) ἐν ποίᾳ δυνάμει ἢ ἐν ποίῳ ὀνόματι; *by whose power or by whose name?* Ac 4: 7. ἐν ποίᾳ ἐξουσίᾳ(;) Mt 21: 23, 24, 27; Mk 11: 28, 29, 33; Lk 20: 2, 8.

b. without a noun—a. which can, however, be supplied fr. the context (Jos., C. Ap. 1, 254 ποίους;): ποίας (i.e. ἐντολάς) Mt 19: 18. ποῖα; (i.e. γενόμενα) Lk 24: 19.

β. gen. of place, w. ellipsis (Bl-D. §186, 1; Mlt. 73) ποίας (i.e. ὁδοῦ) *by what way* Lk 5: 19. M-M.**

πολεμέω fut. πολεμήσω; 1 aor. ἐπολέμησα; 1 fut. pass. πολεμηθήσομαι (Soph., Hdt.+; inscr., pap., LXX, Philo, Joseph., Test. 12 Patr.).

1. lit.—**a.** act. *make war, fight* μετά τινος *on* or *with (against) someone* (μετά A II 3a) Rv 12: 7a; 13: 4; 17: 14. π. μετά τινος ἐν τῇ ῥομφαίᾳ *war against someone with the sword* 2: 16 (for πολ. ἐν τῇ ῥομφ. cf. 1 Macc 3: 12). πολ. κατά τινος *war against someone* Rv 12: 7a t.r. Abs. 12: 7b; (w. κρίνειν) 19: 11. διὰ τὸ πολεμεῖν αὐτούς *because they went to war* B 16: 4.

b. pass. *be warred upon, be fought against* ὑπό τινος (Demosth. 9, 9; Jos., Ant. 9, 255) B 12: 2a. Abs. (Thu. 1, 68, 3; X., Hell. 7, 4, 20) ibid. b.

2. fig., of the hostile attitude of the Jews toward the Christians ὑπὸ Ἰουδαίων ὡς ἀλλόφυλοι πολεμοῦνται Dg 5: 17 (of perpetrating hostile actions Vi. Aesopi I c. 127; Jos., Vi. 244); Gal 1: 13 G, 23 G.—The impenitent Jews εἰς τὸν αἰῶνα πολεμηθήσονται B 12: 2c. Of the disputes of the Christians among themselves Js 4: 2 (Diod. S. 13, 84, 4; Sb 4317, 12).—τὸ ζῆλος ἐμὲ πολεμεῖ *the passionate desire* (for martyrdom) *is pressing me hard* ITr 4: 2 (the acc. as Dinarchus 1, 36; Diod. S. 2, 37, 3; Charito 7, 5, 3).—Of the hostile attitude of the σάρξ toward the ψυχή Dg 6: 5 (Herm. Wr. 392, 3 Sc. of the ψυχή: αὐτὴν ἑαυτῇ πολεμῆσαι δεῖ). M-M. B. 1370.*

πόλεμος, ου, ὁ (Hom.+; inscr., pap., LXX; Ep. Arist. 273; Philo, Joseph.; Test. 12 Patr.; Sib. Or. 5, 13; loanw. in rabb.).

1. lit. *armed conflict*—**a.** *war* Hb 11: 34. πόλεμοι καὶ ἀκοαὶ πολέμων *wars and rumors of wars* Mt 24: 6; Mk 13: 7. W. ἀκαταστασίαι Lk 21: 9. W. λιμός 1 Cl 56: 9 (Job 5: 20). συμβαλεῖν τινι εἰς πόλεμον *make war on someone* Lk 14: 31 (συμβάλλω 1b). ποιεῖν πόλεμον μετά τινος (s. μετά A II 3a) Rv 11: 7; 12: 17; 13: 7 (Da 7: 21 Theod.); 19: 19. AFridrichsen, Krig och fred i Nya Testamentet '40.

b. of a single engagement *battle, fight* (Hom., Hes.; Diod. S. 22, 13, 5; Appian, Bell. Civ. 3, 67 §278; Polyaenus, Exc. 13, 3; 9; 3 Km 22: 34; 1 Macc 4: 13; 10: 78; Jos., Bell. 3, 189) παρασκευάζεσθαι εἰς π. *prepare for battle* 1 Cor 14: 8. Of horses (Dio Chrys. 46[63], 4) ἑτοιμάζεσθαι εἰς π. *be made ready for battle* Rv 9: 7. τρέχειν εἰς π. *rush into battle* vs. 9. Cf. 12: 7; 16: 14; 20: 8.

2. fig. *strife, conflict, quarrel* (since Soph., El. 218; Pla. [e.g. Phaedo 66c]; Epict. 3, 20, 18; Philo, Praem. 91, Gig. 51; Test. Gad 5: 1) of earthly and heavenly powers IEph 13: 2 (opp. εἰρήνη).—Of the situation in Corinth 1 Cl 3: 2; 46: 5. Pl. (w. μάχαι; cf. Dio Chrys. 11[12], 78; Himerius, Or. [Ecl.] 3, 7) Js 4: 1. M-M. B. 1374.*

πολιά, ᾶς, ἡ (fem. subst. of the adj. [in use since Hom.] πολιός, ά, όν 'gray') *old age* (Cornutus 23 p. 44, 19; Lucian, Philops. 23; Ps.-Lucian, Amor. 12; Themist. p. 163D; 182B; LXX; Philo, Spec. Leg. 2, 238) ἀγαθή πολ. (cf. Judg 8: 32 A πολιὰ ἀγαθή) MPol 13: 2 v.l. (for πολιτεία).*

πολιορκία, ας, ἡ (Hdt.+; inscr.; Sb 3776, 4 [I BC]; LXX; Jos., Bell. 3, 183, Vi. 329; Test. Jud. 23: 3) *siege,* later also *distress, tribulation* (Plut., Sulla 25, 4 Z. v.l.) w. θλῖψις 1 Cl 57: 4 (Pr 1: 27).*

πόλις, εως, ἡ (Hom.+; inscr., pap., LXX, Ep. Arist., Philo, Joseph., Test. 12 Patr., Sib. Or.) *city, city-state.*

1. lit. Mt 5: 14; Lk 10: 8, 10. Pl. Mt 11: 20; Lk 5: 12; 19: 17, 19. ἡ πόλις *the city* designated in the context Mt 8: 33;

21: 17f; 26: 18; Mk 11: 19; 14: 13, 16; Lk 4: 29a; 7: 12a, b; J 4: 8, 28, 30; Ac 8: 9; 14: 4; Rv 11: 13; B 16: 5. Likew. αἱ πόλεις Ac 16: 4. ἡ πόλις *the city* can also be *the capital city, the main city* (Mayser II 2 p. 28; Jos., C. Ap. 2, 125) Ac 8: 5; cf. Mk 5: 14 (s. vs. 1); Lk 8: 27 (s. vs. 26). ἡ πόλις ἐκείνη Mt 10: 14f; Lk 9: 5; 10: 12; 18: 3; J 4: 39; Ac 8: 8; Hs 9, 12, 5b. ἡ πόλ. αὕτη Mt 10: 23a; Ac 4: 27; 18: 10; 22: 3; Hs 1: 3. ἔν τινι πόλει *in a certain city* Lk 18: 2; cf. Hs 9, 12, 5a. εἰς τήνδε τὴν πόλιν Js 4: 13 (s. ὅδε 3). πᾶσα πόλις Lk 10: 1. αἱ πόλεις πᾶσαι Mt 9: 35; Ac 8: 40; cf. Mk 6: 33.—πόλις (πόλεις) beside κώμη (κῶμαι) Mt 9: 35; 10: 11; Lk 8: 1; 13: 22. W. κῶμαι and ἀγροί Mk 6: 56. ἡ πόλις καὶ οἱ ἀγροί 5: 14; Lk 8: 34. W. τόπος 10: 1. In contrast to the open plain or the desert, where no cities are found Mt 14: 13; Mk 1: 45; 2 Cor 11: 26; to the interior of a building Ac 12: 10.—Used w. the gen.: to denote the region in which it is located πόλ. τῆς Γαλιλαίας Lk 1: 26; 4: 31. πόλ. Ἰούδα (Ἰούδας 1c) 1: 39. Cf. J 4: 5; Ac 14: 6; 21: 39; to denote the inhabitants (Diod. S. 34 and 35 fgm. 23 ἡ τῶν Γαλατῶν πόλις; Jos., Ant. 1, 200) ἡ πόλ. Δαμασκηνῶν 2 Cor 11: 32. π. Σαμαριτῶν Mt 10: 5; Lk 9: 52 v.l. Cf. 23: 51; Ac 19: 35; Epil Mosq 3. αἱ πόλεις τοῦ Ἰσραήλ *the cities in which the people of Israel live* Mt 10: 23b (Ἰσραήλ 2).—Rv 16: 19b. ἡ πόλ. αὐτῶν Mt 22: 7; Lk 4: 29b.—2: 39. Also w. the gen. sing. πόλ. Δαυίδ *city of David* Lk 2: 4b, 11; ἡ ἑαυτοῦ πόλ. *his own city* vs. 3.—J 1: 44. Also ἡ ἰδία πόλ. (s. ἴδιος 2) Mt 9: 1; Hs 1: 2b (symbol., s. 2 below). Pl. 1 Cl 55: 1. The πόλεις ἴδιαι of the Christians Dg 5: 2 are those inhabited by them alone; they are contrasted w. πόλεις Ἑλληνίδες Greek cities (cf. Dit., Syll.³ 761, 15 [48/7 BC]; 909, 2), π. βάρβαροι Dg 5: 4.—π. μεγάλαι great cities 1 Cl 6: 4. In Rv ἡ πόλ. ἡ μεγάλη is almost always 'Babylon' (s. Βαβυλών) 16: 19a; 17: 18; 18: 16, 18f, 21; ἡ πόλις ἡ μεγάλη, Βαβυλὼν ἡ πόλις ἡ ἰσχυρά 18: 10. On the other hand ἡ πόλ. ἡ μεγάλη 11: 8 is clearly Jerusalem (as Sib. Or. 5, 154; 226). Elsewh. Jerus. is called ἡ πόλ. ἡ ἠγαπημένη 20: 9; ἡ ἁγία πόλ. Mt 4: 5; 27: 53; Rv 11: 2 (ἅγιος 1aa); πόλ. τοῦ μεγάλου βασιλέως *the city of the Great King* Mt 5: 35 (βασιλεύς 2b).—The name of the city that goes w. πόλις stands either in the epexegetic gen. (class.) πόλις Θυατίρων Ac 16: 14; πόλεις Σοδόμων καὶ Γομόρρας 2 Pt 2: 6 or in the case in which πόλις itself is found, ἐν πόλει Ἰόππῃ Ac 11: 5.—27: 8. A special place is necessary for the uses w. indecl. place names Lk 2: 4a, 39. πόλις λεγομένη or καλουμένη w. the name following Mt 2: 23; Lk 7: 11; 9: 10. Cf. J 11: 54.—ἀπὸ πόλεως εἰς πόλιν (Aesop, Fab. 228 P. μεταβαίνουσιν ἀπὸ πόλεως εἰς πόλιν) Mt 23: 34. κατὰ τὴν πόλιν (anywhere) *in the city* Ac 24: 12. Cf. Lk 8: 39 (κατά II 1a). κατὰ πόλιν *from city to city* IRo 9: 3; pl. Lk 13: 22; *in every city* (Appian, Bell. Civ. 1, 39 §177) Ac 15: 21, 36 (κατὰ πόλιν πᾶσαν); 20: 23; Tit 1: 5 (Diod. S. 5, 78, 2 Crete has, indeed, 'not a few' cities). Cf. Lk 8: 1, 4 (κατά II 1d). αἱ ἔξω πόλεις Ac 26: 11 (ἔξω 1aγ). αἱ πέριξ πόλεις 5: 16 (s. πέριξ). αἱ περὶ αὐτὰς (i.e. Sodom and Gomorrah) πόλεις Jd 7. πρὸ τ. πόλεως (Jos., Bell. 1, 234, Ant. 10, 44) Ac 14: 13.

2. of the heavenly city, the New Jerusalem (Bousset, Rel.³ 283ff; RKnopf, GHeinrici-Festschr. '14, 213-19; McQueen, Exp. 9th ser. II '24, 220-6; FDijkema, NThT 15, '26, 25-43) Hb 11: 10, 16. πόλ. θεοῦ ζῶντος 12: 22 (Sib. Or. 5, 250 θεοῦ π. of Jerus.). ἡ μέλλουσα (opp. οὐ . . . μένουσα πόλις) 13: 14. Esp. in Rv: ἡ πόλις ἡ ἁγία Ἰερουσαλήμ (καινή) 21: 2, 10 (CBouma, Geref. Theol. Tijdschr. 36, '36, 91-8). Further vss. 14-16, 18f, 21, 23; 22: 14, 19; also 3: 12. (S. Lucian's description of the wonder-city in Ver. Hist. 2, 11f: ἡ πόλις πᾶσα χρυσῆ, τὸ τεῖχος σμαράγδινον. πύλαι . . . ἑπτά, πᾶσαι μονό-

ξυλοι κινναμώμιναι . . . γῆ ἐλεφαντίνη . . . ναοὶ βη-
ρύλλου λίθου . . . βωμοὶ . . . ἀμεθύστινοι . . . ποταμὸς
μύρου τοῦ καλλίστου . . . οἶκοι ὑάλινοι . . . οὐδὲ νὺξ
οὐδὲ ἡμέρα).—Hs 1: 1, 2.

3. fig., *city* for its inhabitants (X., Cyr. 1, 4, 25;
Herodian 3, 2, 7; Jos., Ant. 5, 357) Lk 4: 43; Ac 14: 21; 16:
20 (cf. Jos., Bell. 7, 41). πᾶσα ἡ πόλις (Diod. S. 18, 70, 2;
Appian, Numid. 1) Mt 8: 34; 21: 10 (w. λέγουσα foll.); Ac
13: 44; ὅλη ἡ π. (Diod. S. 10, 3, 2) Mk 1: 33; Ac 21: 30.
πόλις μερισθεῖσα καθ' ἑαυτῆς Mt 12: 25.—HStrathmann, TW VI 516-35: πόλις and related words. M-M.
B. 1308.

πολιτάρχης, ου, ὁ *civic magistrate, politarch.* A number
of politarchs (five or six in Thessalonica) formed the city
council in Macedonian cities, and occasionally in others
(cf. EDBurton, The Politarchs in Macedonia and Elsewhere: AJTh 2, 1898, 598-632 w. exx. fr. the inscr.; s. also
Dit., Syll.³ 700, 1; 48 [the Maced. city of Letae, 118/17
BC]; POxy. 745, 4 [I BC/I AD]; Sb 5765, 7) specif. in
Thessalonica (CIG II 1967; Bull. de corr. hell. 18, 1894,
420; 21, 1897, 161 al.) Ac 17: 6, 8. M-M.*

πολιτεία, ας, ἡ (Hdt.+; inscr., pap.; 2, 3, 4 Macc;
Philo, Joseph.)—1. *citizenship* (Hdt. 9, 34; X., Hell. 1, 1,
26; 1, 2, 10; 4, 4, 6; Polyb. 6, 2, 12; Diod. S. 14, 8, 3; 14,
17, 3; Kyr.-Inschr. l. 57; 59; Gnomon [=BGU V 1] 47;
3 Macc 3: 21, 23; Jos., Ant. 12, 119) lit. of Roman
citizenship (Dio Chrys. 24[41], 2 Ῥωμαίων π.; Ael.
Aristid. 30, 10 K.=10 p. 117 D.; IG IV² 1, 84, 33 [40/42
AD]; Jos., Bell. 1, 194 and Vi 423 π. Ῥωμαίων.—WM
Ramsay, The Social Basis of Roman Power in Asia Minor
'41) πολιτείαν ἐκτησάμην Ac 22: 28.—In a fig. sense,
this transl. is poss. (EHaupt, PEwald, Henle, Lueken et
al.) for Eph 2: 12, but not very probable (s. 2 below).

2. *commonwealth, state, body politic* (Thu. 1, 127, 3;
Pla., Rep. 10 p. 619c; Diod. S. 5, 45, 3; Appian, Bell. Civ.
2, 19 §68) ἀπηλλοτριωμένοι τ. πολιτείας τοῦ Ἰσραήλ
alienated from the commonwealth of Israel Eph 2: 12 (so
HermvSoden, Klöpper, Belser, Meinertz, MDibelius, RSV
et al.; s. 1 above).

3. *way of life, conduct* (Athen. 1 p. 19A; Herm. Wr. in
Stob. p. 486, 24 Sc. ἡ τῶν ἀνθρώπων ἄγριος πολιτεία;
Ps.-Liban., Charact. Ep. p. 34, 2; 47, 8; 10; Biogr. p. 261)
Dg 5: 4; ἀγαθῇ πολ. MPol 13: 2; ἡ ἀπ' ἀρχῆς ἀνεπί-
ληπτος πολ. 17: 1; ἡ πανάρετος καὶ σεβάσμιος πολ.
1 Cl 2: 8. οἱ πολιτευόμενοι τὴν ἀμεταμέλητον πολι-
τείαν τοῦ θεοῦ *those who follow God's way of life, that
brings no regrets* 54: 4 (πολιτεύεσθαι πολιτείαν in Nicol.
Dam.: 90 fgm. 126 Jac. and in the Synagogue inscr. fr.
Stobi [c. 100 AD] l. 6f: ZNW 32, '33, 93f). M-M.*

πολίτευμα, ατος, τό (Pla.+; inscr., pap.) *commonwealth,
state* (so Polyb. 1, 13, 12; 35, 5; Diod. S. 19, 75, 4; inscr.;
2 Macc 12: 7; Jos., Ant. 1, 13, C. Ap. 2, 257; fig. Philo,
Agr. 81 τῷ τῆς ἀρετῆς ἐγγεγραμμέναι πολιτεύματι,
Conf. Lingu. 78 πατρίδα τὸν οὐράνιον χῶρον ἐν ᾧ
πολιτεύονται.—Schürer III 71f; PCBöttger, ZNW 60,
'69, 244-53) ἡμῶν τὸ πολ. ἐν οὐρανοῖς ὑπάρχει *our
commonwealth is in heaven* Phil 3: 20 (πολίτευμα oft.
denotes a colony of foreigners or relocated veterans CIG
5361, III add. 5866c; PTebt. 32, 9; 17 [II BC]; Ep. Arist.
310. Cf. Dit., Or. 737, 2m; note 2 and the lit. in
MDibelius, Hdb. ad loc.; JdeZwaan, Philippenzen 3: 20
en de Κοινή: ThSt 31, '13, 298-300; LFuchs, D. Juden in
Ägypten '24, 89; MEngers, Πολίτευμα: Mnemosyne 54,
'26, 154-61; WRuppel, Politeuma: Philol. 82, '27, 268-
312; 433-52; EPeterson s.v. ἐκκλησία, end; 'Our home is
in heaven, and here on earth we are a colony of heavenly

citizens' MDibelius.—The sense seems to be more general
in Menand. Rhet. [II AD] III 421, 16 Spengel: the deceased, so the word of consolation goes, πολιτεύεται μετὰ
τῶν θεῶν; Hierocles, Carm. Aur. 3, 2 p. 424 Mullach:
angels convey the souls of the righteous πρὸς τὴν θείαν
πολιτείαν. Olympiodorus In Platonis Phaedonem, ed.
WNorvin '13 p. 122, 8 [on Pla., Phaedo p. 69c] of the
philosopher: συμπολιτεύεσθαι τοῖς θεοῖς καὶ συνοικονομεῖν). M-M.*

πολιτεύομαι (the mid., which is the only voice found in
our lit., since Thu., Aristoph.; inscr., pap., LXX) 1 aor.
ἐπολιτευσάμην, subj. 1 pl. πολιτευσώμεθα; pf. πεπο-
λίτευμαι.

1. *have one's citizenship* or *home* (Philo, Conf. Lingu.
78 [s. πολίτευμα]) of the Christians ἐν οὐρανῷ Dg 5: 9
(Himerius, Or. 8 [=23], 23 of a deceased person: μετὰ
θεῶν πολιτεύεσθαι).

2. *rule* or *govern the state* abs. (Thu. 2, 15, 1 al.; Jos.,
Ant. 14, 91 π. ἐν Ἱεροσ.) of God ἐν οὐρανοῖς πολιτεύεται *he rules in heaven* 10: 7.—Also of the work of church
officials 1 Cl 44: 6.

3. *live, conduct oneself, lead one's life* (UPZ 144, 14
[164/3 BC] ὁσίως κ. δικαίως; Hierocles, Carm. Aur. 11 p.
444 M.; Ps.-Liban., Charact. Ep. p. 31, 5 σεμνῶς; 34, 1;
2 Macc 6: 1; 11: 25; 3 Macc 3: 4; 4 Macc 2: 8 al.; Philo,
Virt. 161, Spec. Leg. 4, 226; Jos., Ant. 12, 142, Vi. 12)
καλῶς κ. ἀγνῶς Hs 5, 6, 6. ὁσίως 1 Cl 6: 1. ἀξίως τινός
Phil 1: 27 (RRBrewer, JBL 73, '54, 76-83: 'discharge your
obligations as citizens'); 1 Cl 21: 1; Pol 5: 2. μετὰ φόβου
καὶ ἀγάπης 1 Cl 51: 2. (W. πορεύεσθαι) πολιτεύεσθαι
κατὰ τὸ καθῆκον τῷ Χριστῷ 3: 4 (πολ. κατά τι as Dit.,
Syll.³ 618, 12 [188 BC]; 2 Macc 11: 25; 4 Macc 2: 23; Ep.
Arist. 31; Jos., Ant. 12, 142); π. πολιτείαν 54: 4 (πολιτεία 3). W. a double dat. συνειδήσει ἀγαθῇ πεπολί-
τευμαι τῷ θεῷ *I have lived my life with a clear conscience
before God* Ac 23: 1 (for the dat. τῷ θεῷ cf. PHib. 63, 10
[III BC] εἰ οὕτως πολιτευσόμεθα ἀλλήλοις). M-M.*

πολίτης, ου, ὁ (Hom.+; inscr., pap., LXX, Ep. Arist.,
Philo, Joseph.)—1. *citizen* of one who lives in or comes fr.
a city or country πόλεως Ac 21: 39. τῆς χώρας ἐκείνης Lk
15: 15. (Opp. ξένοι, as Philo, Poster. Cai. 109) Dg 5: 5.

2. *fellow-citizen, fellow-townsman* (Pla., Apol. 37c,
Prot. 339F; Diod. S. 11, 47, 3; 11, 62, 1 al.; Phlegon: 257
fgm. 36, 2, 4 Jac.; Appian, Bell. Civ. 4, 127 §531 al.; Chio,
Ep. 15, 1; Pr 11: 9; 24: 28; Jos., Ant. 1, 21, Vi. 274) Hb 8:
11 (Jer 38: 34). The (*fellow-*) *countrymen* or *subjects* of a
ruler are likew. so called (Jos., Ant. 12, 162) 1 Cl 55: 1. Cf.
Lk 19: 14. M-M.*

πολλά s. πολύς I 2b.

πολλάκις adv. (Hom.+; inscr., pap., LXX; Philo, Aet.
M. 42; Jos., Bell. 2, 310, C. Ap. 2, 175) *many times, often,
frequently* Mt 17: 15; Mk 5: 4; 9: 22; J 18: 2; Ac 26: 11; Ro
1: 13; 15: 22 v.l.; 2 Cor 11: 23, 26, 27a, b; Phil 3: 18;
2 Ti 1: 16; Hb 6: 7; 9: 25f; 10: 11; Hv 3, 1, 2. In paronomasia (Dio Chrys. 11[12], 50; 71; Theodor. Prodr. 6, 93 H.
πολλοὺς πολλαχοῦ κ. πολλάκις; Dit., Syll.³ 888, 138f
πολλοὶ πολλάκις στρατιῶται; Esth 8: 12e πολλάκις δὲ
καὶ πολλοὺς κτλ.; Jos., C. Ap. 2, 219; 231) ἐν πολλοῖς
πολλάκις *often in many ways* 2 Cor 8: 22 (πολύ and
πολλῇ follow in the same sentence). M-M. B. 986.*

πολλαπλασίων, ον, gen. ονος (Isocr. 15, 177; Archimed.
II 134, 13 Heib.; Polyb. 35, 4, 4; Philodem., Π. σημ. 9,
32; Plut., Mor. 215B; Ael. Aristid. 27, 20 K.=16 p. 390 D.
for class. πολλαπλάσιος [so Philo, Somn. 1, 53; Jos.,
Bell. 5, 553]) neut. pl. πολλαπλασίονα *many times as*

much, manifold λαμβάνειν (Jos., Bell. 1, 514; Test. Zeb. 6: 6) Mt 19: 29; Lk 18: 30.—ESchwyzer, Museum Helveticum 2, '45, 137–47. M-M.*

πολυαγάπητος, ον (Hesychius s.v. πολύθεστος) much-loved ὄνομα IEph 1: 1.*

Πολύβιος, ου, ὁ (Dit., Syll.³ 686; 1115, 30) Polybius, bishop of Tralles ITr 1: 1.*

πολυευσπλαγχνία, ας, ἡ richness in mercy π. τοῦ κυρίου Hs 8, 6, 1.*

πολυεύσπλαγχνος, ον rich in compassion of God Js 5: 11 v.l.; Hs 5, 4, 4.*

πολυεύτακτος, ον very well ordered or disciplined; subst. ὑμῶν τὸ π. τῆς κατὰ θεὸν ἀγάπης how well-ordered your God-like love is IMg 1: 1.*

Πολύκαρπος, ου, ὁ (references for the name in the Hdb. on Pol inscr.) Polycarp, bishop of Smyrna, acc. to tradition a pupil of John, whom as early a writer as Irenaeus (3, 3, 4) considered to be John the apostle. He died as a martyr, prob. Feb. 22, 156 AD (so ESchwartz, De Pionio et Polycarpo '05, Christl. und jüd. Ostertafeln: AGG n.s. VIII 6 ['05] 125ff). Other calculations conclude that the date is Feb. 23 of 155 or 166 AD (s. Harnack, Chronologie I 1897, 325ff; PCorssen, ZNW 3, '02, 61ff; NBonwetsch, RE XV '04, 535ff). We possess a letter to the Philippians written by him (Pol—Cf. PNHarrison, Polycarp's Two Epistles to the Philippians '36 [rich bibliogr.]); MPol is a contemporary report of his martyrdom. IEph 21: 1; IMg 15; IPol inscr.; 7: 2; 8: 2; Pol inscr.; MPol 1: 1 al.— RMGrant, Polycarp of Smyrna: ATR 28, '46, 137–48.

πολύλαλος, ον (Cleobulus [VI BC] in Stob. III p. 112, 3 H.; Ael. Dion. κ, 8; Vi. Aesopi I c. 26; schol. on Soph., Ant. 324 p. 234 Papag.; Plotinus 6, 2, 21; Sym. Job 11: 2) talkative, garrulous w. ἀναιδής Hm 11: 12. De Sande Bakhuizen suspects that πολύλαλοι was once read Js 3: 1 (Bl-D. §115, 1).*

πολυλογία, ας, ἡ (X., Cyr. 1, 4, 3; Pla., Leg. 1 p. 641E; Plut., Mor. 6c; 519c; Vett. Val. 108, 8; 23; Herm. Wr. 14, 5; Sextus 155; Pr 10: 19) much speaking, wordiness ἐν τῇ π. αὐτῶν with their many words Mt 6: 7; Lk 11: 2 D (Ael. Aristid. 45, 8 K.=8 p. 85 D.: θεοὺς ἄνευ μέτρων προσαγορεύοντες οὐκ αἰσχυνόμεθα). M-M.*

πολυμερῶς adv. (Diod. S. 5, 37, 2; Plut., Mor. 537D; several times in Vett. Val. [index III]; Jos., Ant. 12, 54) of πολυμερής, ές (Aristot.; Plut., Mor. 427B; 757D; PGM 13, 304; Wsd 7: 22) in many ways w. πολυτρόπως (the two words together also Maximus Tyr. 1, 2b; 11, 7a) Hb 1: 1 (on the alliteration cf. the beginning of Philo, περὶ μετανοίας). M-M.*

πολυπλήθεια, ας, ἡ (Hippocr. et al.; Περὶ ὕψους 32, 1 p. 56, 5 V.; Ps.-Plut., Hom. 85; Dit., Syll.³ 880, 40; 2 Macc 8: 16) large crowd Ac 14: 7 (in an addition in codex E; codex D has πλῆθος). τὴν π. (πολυπληθία is to be rejected, w. Lghtf., and πολυπλήθεια, which is also attested, is to be inserted) ὑμῶν ἀπείληφα I have received your whole (large) congregation IEph 1: 3.*

πολυπλοκία, ας, ἡ (Theognis 67) cunning, craftiness τοῦ διαβόλου Hm 4, 3, 4.*

πολυποίκιλος, ον (Eur. +) (very) many-sided (so Orph. Hymn., 6, 11; 61, 4 [λόγος]; Sib. Or. 8, 120 [ὀργή]) σοφία Eph 3: 10. M-M.*

πολύπους, ποδος, ὁ octopus (Hom. +; Ps.-Phoc. 49; Philo, Ebr. 172) w. sea-eel and cuttle-fish B 10: 5 (vGebhardt's edition has πώλυπα [s. πῶλυψ]. πολύποδα is also attested; Bihlmeyer ad loc.).*

πολυπραγμοσύνη, ης, ἡ (Thu., Aristoph. +, mostly in an unfavorable sense) inquisitiveness, meddlesomeness, fussiness, officiousness ἡ Ἰουδαίων πολυπρ. Dg 4: 6.*

πολυπράγμων, ον, gen. ονος (since Eupolis Com. [V BC] 222, Lysias, Aristoph.; Philo Bybl. [100 AD] in Euseb., Pr. Ev. 1, 9, 24; Philo Alex., Abr. 20, Spec. Leg. 1, 69; Jos., Ant. 15, 182) inquisitive π. ἄνθρωποι Dg 5: 3.*

πολύς, πολλή, πολύ, gen. **πολλοῦ, ῆς, οῦ** (Hom. +; inscr., pap., LXX, En., Ep. Arist., Philo, Joseph., Test. 12 Patr.).

I. positive much, many—1. adj., preceding or following a noun—a. used w. a noun (or ptc. or adj. used subst.) in the pl.

a. many, numerous δυνάμεις πολλαί many mighty deeds Mt 7: 22b. δαιμονιζόμενοι πολλοί 8: 16. Cf. vs. 30; 9: 10; 13: 17; 24: 11; 27: 52, 55; Mk 2: 15a; 6: 13; 12: 41; Lk 4: 25, 27; 7: 21b; 10: 24; J 10: 32; 14: 2; Ac 1: 3; 2: 43; 8: 7b; 14: 22; Ro 4: 17f (Gen 17: 5); 8: 29; 12: 4; 1 Cor 8: 5a, b; 11: 30; 12: 12a, 20; 1 Ti 6: 12; 2 Ti 2: 2; Hb 2: 10; 1 J 4: 1; 2 J 7; Rv 5: 11; 9: 9; 10: 11; 1 Cl 55: 3a, b. ἔτη πολλά many years: Lk 12: 19b (εἰς ἔτη π.); Ac 24: 10 (ἐκ π. ἐτῶν); Ro 15: 23 v.l. (ἀπὸ π. ἐτῶν).—αἱ ἁμαρτίαι αἱ πολλαί Lk 7: 47a. αἱ εὐεργεσίαι αἱ π. 1 Cl 21: 1.— πολλὰ καὶ βαρέα αἰτιώματα many serious charges Ac 25: 7 (cf. Ps.-Pla., Sisyph. 1 p. 387A πολλά τε καὶ καλὰ πράγματα; Bl-D. §442, 11; Rob. 655). πολλὰ καὶ ἄλλα σημεῖα J 20: 30 (on the form X., Hell. 5, 4, 1 πολλὰ μὲν οὖν κ. ἄλλα Ἑλληνικά; Dionys. Hal. 2, 67, 5; Ps.-Demetr. c. 142 πολλὰς κ. ἄλλας χάριτας; Jos., Ant. 3, 318. On the subject-matter Bultmann 540, 3; also Porphyr., Vi. Pyth. 28 after a miracle-story: μυρία δ' ἔτερα θαυμαστότερα κ. θειότερα περὶ τἀνδρὸς ... εἴρηται κτλ.).— ἄλλοι πολλοί many others IRo 10: 1. ἄλλαι πολλαί Mk 15: 41. ἄλλα πολλά (Jos., Bell. 6, 169, Ant. 9, 242) J 21: 25. ἔτεροι πολλοί Ac 15: 35. ἔτερα πολλά (Jos., Vi. 39) Lk 22: 65.—Predicative: πολλοί εἰσιν οἱ εἰσερχόμενοι Mt 7: 13.—Mk 5: 9; 6: 31; Gal 4: 27 (Is 54: 1).—οὐ πολλοί not many=(only) a few οὐ πολλαὶ ἡμέραι (Jos., Ant. 5, 328, Vi. 309) Lk 15: 13; J 2: 12; Ac 1: 5. οὐ πολλοὶ σοφοί not many wise (people) 1 Cor 1: 26a; cf. b, c. οὐ πολλοὶ πατέρες not many fathers 4: 15.

β. many, large, great, extensive, plentiful ὄχλοι πολλοί great crowds or probably better many people (as Diod. S. 20, 59, 2; Ps.-Clem., Hom. 10, 3. For the corresponding mng. of ὄχλοι s. ὄχλος 1) Mt 4: 25; 8: 1; 13: 2; 15: 30a; 19: 2; Lk 5: 15; 14: 25. κτήματα πολλά a great deal of property Mt 19: 22; Mk 10: 22 (cf. Da 11: 28 χρήματα π.). ὕδατα πολλά much water, many waters (Maximus Tyr. 21, 3g of the Nile ὁ πολὺς ποταμός, likew. Procop. Soph., Ep. 111) J 3: 23; Rv 1: 15; 14: 2; 17: 1; 19: 6b. θυμιάματα πολλά a great deal of incense 8: 3. τὰ πολλὰ γράμματα Ac 26: 24. πολλοὶ χρόνοι long periods of time (Plut., Thes. 6, 9). πολλοῖς χρόνοις for long periods of time (Dit., Syll.³ 836, 6; pap.) Lk 8: 29; 1 Cl 44: 3. ἐκ πολλῶν χρόνων (Diod. S. 3, 47, 8; Jos., Ant. 14, 110; 17, 204) 42: 5.

b. used w. a noun in the sing.—α. to denote quantity much, large, great πολὺς ἀριθμός Ac 11: 21. W. words that in themselves denote a plurality (Appian, Bell. Civ. 5, 80 §338 στρατὸς πολύς) πολὺς ὄχλος (s. ὄχ. 1) Mt 14: 14; 20: 29; 26: 47; Mk 5: 21, 24; 6: 34a; 8: 1; 9: 14; 12: 37 (ὁ π. ὄχ.); Lk 5: 29; 6: 17a; 8: 4; J 6: 2, 5 (for the expression ὁ πολύς

ὄχλος πολύς, in which π. follows the noun, J 12: 9, 12, cf. Arrian, Anab. 1, 9, 6 ὁ φόνος πολύς); Ac 6: 7; Rv 7: 9; 19: 1, 6. πολὺ πλῆθος (s. πλ. 2bα) Mk 3: 7f; Lk 5: 6; 6: 17f; 23: 27; Ac 14: 1; 17: 4; 1 Cl 6: 1. λαὸς πολύς *many people* Ac 18: 10. Of money and its value, also used symbolically μισθὸς πολύς Mt 5: 12; Lk 6: 23, 35 (all three predicative, as Gen 15: 1). ἐργασία π. Ac 16: 16. π. κεφάλαιον 22: 28.—Of things that occur in the mass or in large quantities (Diod. S. 3, 50, 1 πολλὴ ἄμπελος) γῆ πολλή Mt 13: 5; Mk 4: 5; θερισμὸς π. Mt 9: 37; Lk 10: 2 (both pred.). χόρτος π. J 6: 10; καρπὸς π. (Cyranides p. 121, 11) 12: 24; 15: 5, 8.—λόγος π. *a long speech* (Diod. S. 13, 1, 2) Ac 15: 32; 20: 2. περὶ οὗ πολὺς ἡμῖν ὁ λόγος *about this we have much to say* Hb 5: 11 (cf. Pla., Phaedo 115D).—Of time: πολὺς χρόνος *a long time* (Hom. +; Jos., Ant. 8, 342; 19, 28) J 5: 6 (cf. ἔχω I 2f); Hs 6, 4, 4 (pred.). μετὰ πολὺν χρόνον (Jos., Ant. 12, 324) Mt 25: 19. Differently ὥρα πολλή *late hour* (Polyb. 5, 8, 3; Dionys. Hal. 2, 54) Mk 6: 35a, b.

β. to denote degree *much, great, strong, severe, hard, deep, profound* (Diod. S. 13, 7, 4 πολὺς φόβος; schol. on Apollon. Rhod. 4, 57; 58 p. 265, 3 πολλὴ δικαιοσύνη; Eccl 5: 16 θυμός π.; Sir 15: 18 σοφία) ἀγάπη Eph 2: 4. ἀγών 1 Th 2: 2. ἄθλησις Hb 10: 32. ἁπλότης Hv 3, 9, 1. ἀσιτία Ac 27: 21. βία 24: 7 t.r. γογγυσμός J 7: 12. διακονία Lk 10: 40. δοκιμή 2 Cor 8: 2. δόξα Mt 24: 30; Hv 1, 3, 4; 2, 2, 6. δύναμις Mk 13: 26. ἐγκράτεια *strict self-control* Hv 2, 3, 2. εἰρήνη (Diod. S. 3, 64, 7; 11, 38, 1) Ac 24: 2. ἔλεος 1 Pt 1: 3. ἐπιθυμία 1 Th 2: 17. ζημία Ac 27: 10. ζήτησις 15: 7. θλῖψις 2 Cor 2: 4a; 1 Th 1: 6. καύχησις 2 Cor 7: 4b (pred.). μακροθυμία Ro 9: 22. ὀδυρμός Mt 2: 18. παράκλησις 2 Cor 8: 4. παρρησία (Wsd 5: 1) 3: 12; 7: 4a (pred.); 1 Ti 3: 13; Phlm 8. πεποίθησις 2 Cor 8: 22c. πλάνη 2 Cl 1: 7. πληροφορία 1 Th 1: 5. πόνος Col 4: 13. σιγή *a great hush* (X., Cyr. 7, 1, 25; Arrian, Anab. 5, 28, 4) Ac 21: 40. στάσις 23: 10. τρόμος 1 Cor 2: 3. φαντασία Ac 25: 23. χαρά 8: 8; Phlm 7.

2. subst.—a. πολλοί *many* i.e. persons—α. without the art. Mt 7: 22; 8: 11; 12: 15; 20: 28; 24: 5a, b; 26: 28; Mk 2: 2; 3: 10 (Mt 12: 15 has πάντας; other passages to be compared in this connection are Mk 10: 45=Mt 20: 28 πολλῶν and 1 Ti 2: 6 πάντων. Cf. the double tradition of the saying of Bias in Clem. of Alex., Strom. 1, 61, 3 πάντες ἄνθρωποι κακοί ἢ οἱ πλεῖστοι τ. ἀνθρώπων κακοί.—On Mk 10: 45 s. OCullmann, Theol. Ztschr. 4, '48, 471-3); 11: 8; Lk 1: 1 (cf. Herm. Wr. 11, 1, 1b and see JBauer, NovT 4, '60, 263-6), 14; J 2: 23; 8: 30; Ac 9: 42; Ro 16: 2; 2 Cor 11: 18; Gal 3: 16 (πολλοί=a plurality); Tit 1: 10; 2 Pt 2: 2. Opp. ὀλίγοι Mt 22: 14; 20: 16 v.l. (cf. Pla., Phaedo 69c ναρθηκοφόροι μὲν πολλοί, βάκχοι δέ τε παῦροι=the thyrsus-bearers [officials] are many, but the truly inspired are few)—W. a partitive gen. πολλοί τῶν Φαρισαίων Mt 3: 7. π. τῶν υἱῶν Ἰσραήλ Lk 1: 16. —J 4: 39; 12: 11; Ac 4: 4; 8: 7a; 13: 43; 18: 8; 19: 18; 2 Cor 12: 21; Rv 8: 11.—W. ἐκ and gen. (Jos., Ant. 11, 151) πολλοί ἐκ τῶν μαθητῶν J 6: 60, 66 v.l.—10: 20; 11: 19, 45; 12: 42; Ac 17: 12. ἐκ τοῦ ὄχλου πολλοί J 7: 31 (Appian, Iber. 78 §337 πολλοὶ ἐκ τοῦ πλήθους).

β. w. the art. οἱ πολλοί *the many,* of whatever appears in the context Mk 6: 2 (the many people who were present in the synagogue); 9: 26b (the whole *crowd*). Opp. ὁ εἷς Ro 5: 15a, c, 19a, b; *the many* who form the ἓν σῶμα *the one body* 12: 5; 1 Cor 10: 17. Paul pays attention to the interests of *the many* rather than to his own vs. 33 (cf. Jos., Ant. 3, 212).—*The majority, most* (X., An. 5, 6, 19; Appian, Maced. 7, Bell. Civ. 4, 73 §309; 2 Macc 1: 36; En.

104, 10; Jos., Ant. 17, 72) Mt 24: 12; Hb 12: 15. W. a connotation of disapproval *most people, the crowd* (Socrat., Ep. 6, 2; Dio Chrys. 15[32], 8; Epict. 1, 3, 4; 2, 1, 22 al.; Plut., Mor. 33A; 470b; Plotinus, Enn. 2, 9, 9; Philo, Rer. Div. Her. 42) 2 Cor 2: 17; Pol 2: 1; 7: 2.—JoachJeremias, The Eucharistic Words of Jesus³, tr. NPerrin, '66, 179-82; 226-31, and TW VI 536-45: πολλοί.

b. πολλά—a. *many things, much* without the art.: γράφειν *write at length* B 4: 9. διδάσκειν Mk 4: 2; 6: 34b. λαλεῖν Mt 13: 3. μηχανᾶσθαι MPol 3. πάσχειν (Pind., Ol. 13, 90 al.; Jos., Ant. 13, 268; 403) Mt 16: 21; Mk 5: 26a; 9: 12; Lk 9: 22; 17: 25; B 7: 5, 11. ποιεῖν Mk 6: 20 t.r. United w. another neut. by καί (Lucian, Icar. 20 πολλὰ κ. δεινά; Ael. Aristid. 46 p. 345 D.: πολλὰ κ. καλά; Ps.-Demetr., El. 70 πολλὰ κ. ἄλλα; likew. Appian, Bell. Civ. 5, 13 §53; Arrian, Anab. 6, 11, 2) πολλὰ κ. ἕτερα *many other things* Lk 3: 18. πολλὰ ἂν κ. ἄλλα εἰπεῖν ἔχοιμι Dg 2: 10 (Eur., Ep. 3, 2, πολλὰ κ. ἕτερα εἰπεῖν ἔχω; Diod. S. 17, 38, 3 πολλὰ δὲ καὶ ἄλλα... διαλεχθείς. ἐν πολλοῖς *in many ways* (Diod. S. 26, 1, 2; Dit., Or. 737, 7 [II BC]) 2 Cor 8: 22a. ἐπὶ πολλῶν (opp. ἐπὶ ὀλίγα) *over many things* Mt 25: 21, 23.—W. the art. (Pla., Apol. 1 p. 17A) τὰ πολλὰ πράσσειν *transact a great deal of business* Hs 4: 5b.

β. The acc. is used as an adv. *greatly, earnestly, strictly, loudly, often,* etc. (X., Cyr. 1, 5, 14; Diod. S. 13, 41, 5; Lucian, Dial. Deor. 19, 2; Aelian, V.H. 1, 23; 4 Km 10: 18; Is 23: 16; Jos., Ant. 14, 348) ἀλαλάζειν πολλά Mk 5: 38 (s. ἀλαλάζω). πολλὰ ἁμαρτάνειν Hs 4: 5c. π. ἀνακρίνειν Ac 28: 18 v.l. π. ἀπορεῖν Mk 6: 20 (Field, Notes 29). π. ἀσπάζεσθαι (ἀσπάζομαι 1) 1 Cor 16: 19. δεηθῆναι π. (Jos., Vi. 173; 343) Hs 5, 4, 1. διαστέλλεσθαι Mk 5: 43 (s. διαστέλλω). π. ἐπιτιμᾶν 3: 12. π. ἐρωτᾶν *earnestly pray* Hv 2, 2, 1. κατηγορεῖν π. Mk 15: 3 (s. κατηγορέω 1a). κηρύσσειν π. *talk freely* 1: 45. κλαίειν *bitterly* Ac 8: 24 D. κοπιᾶν (CIG IV 9552, 5...μοι πολλὰ ἐκοπίασεν, cf. Dssm., LO 266, 5 [LAE 317]) *work hard* Ro 16: 6, 12; 2 Cl 7: 1b. νηστεύειν π. *fast often* Mt 9: 14a v.l. παρακαλεῖν Mk 5: 10, 23; Ac 20: 1 D; 1 Cor 16: 12. π. πταίειν *make many mistakes* Js 3: 2. π. σπαράσσειν *convulse violently* Mk 9: 26a.—W. the art. ἐνεκοπτόμην τὰ πολλὰ *I have been hindered these many times* (cf. Ro 1: 13 πολλάκις) Ro 15: 22 (𝔓⁴⁶ BD have πολλάκις here too).

c. πολύ—a. *much* ᾧ ἐδόθη πολύ, πολὺ ζητηθήσεται παρ' αὐτοῦ, καὶ ᾧ παρέθεντο πολὺ κτλ. Lk 12: 48. Cf. 16: 10a, b; 2 Cl 8: 5; καρποφορεῖν π. *bear much fruit* Hs 2: 3. πολὺ κατὰ πάντα τρόπον *much in every way* Ro 3: 2 (Ael. Aristid. 34, 43 K.=50 p. 562 D. gives answer to a sim. quest. asked by himself: πολλὰ καὶ παντοῖα).—Is 5: 16.—As gen. of price πολλοῦ *for a large sum* of money (Menand., fgm. 197; PRyl. 244, 10) Mt 26: 9.—Of time: ἐπὶ πολύ (*for*) *a long time* (ἐπί III 2b) Ac 28: 6. μετ' οὐ πολύ *soon afterward* 27: 14 (μετά B II 3).—ἐπὶ πολύ *more than once, often* (Is 55: 7) Hm 4, 1, 8.—Before the comp. (class.; Bl-D. §246; Rob. 664) in the acc. πολὺ βέλτιον *much better* Hs 1: 9. π. ἐλάττων v 3, 7, 6. π. μᾶλλον *much more, to a much greater degree* (Dio Chrys. 2, 10; 17; 64 al.; Ael. Aristid. 34, 9 K.=50 p. 549 D.) Hb 12: 9, 25 (by means of a negative it acquires the mng. *much less.* Cf. Diod. S. 7, 14, 6 πολὺ μᾶλλον μή... =even much less); Dg 2: 7b. π. πλέον 2: 7a. π. σπουδαιότερος 2 Cor 8: 22b. Cf. 1 Pt 1: 7 t.r.; in the dat. of degree of difference πολλῷ μᾶλλον (Thu. 2, 51, 4; UPZ 42, 48 [162 BC]; Ep. Arist. 7; 24 al.; Sir prol. l. 14; Jos., Ant. 18, 184) Mt 6: 30; Mk 10: 48b; Lk 18: 39; Ro 5: 9f, 15b, 17; 1 Cor 12: 22; 2 Cor 3: 9, 11; Phil 2: 12. πολλῷ μᾶλλον κρεῖσσον 1: 23 (𝔓⁴⁶ without μᾶλλον). πολλῷ πλείους J 4: 41.—W. the art. τὸ πολύ (opp. τὸ ὀλίγον as X., An. 7, 7, 36) 2 Cor 8: 15 (cf. Ex 16: 18).

β. the acc. as adv. *greatly, very much, strongly* (Da 6: 15, 24 Theod.) ἀγαπᾶν πολύ *love greatly* Lk 7: 47b. κλαίειν π. *weep loudly* Rv 5: 4.—Mk 12: 27; Ac 18: 27.

d. πολύς (Diod. S. 14, 107, 4 πολὺς ἦν ἐπὶ τῇ τιμωρίᾳ =he was strongly inclined toward punishing) μὴ πολὺς ἐν ῥήμασιν γίνου *do not be profuse in speech, do not gossip* 1 Cl 30: 5 (Job 11: 3).

II. comparative **πλείων, πλεῖον** (18 times in the NT, 4 times in the Apost. Fathers) or **πλέον** (Lk 3: 13; J 21: 15; Ac 15: 28 and 14 times in the Apost. Fathers), **ονος**; pl. πλείονες, contracted πλείους, neut. πλείονα and πλείω (Bl-D. §30, 2; Mlt.-H. 82; Thackeray p. 81f; Mayser p. 68f) *more* (Hom.+; inscr., pap., LXX, Ep. Arist.).

1. adj.—a. w. a plural (Diod. S. 14, 6, 1 μισθοφόρους πλείους=many mercenaries) πλείονας πόνους (opp. οὐχ ἕνα οὐδὲ δύο) 1 Cl 5: 4. ἐπὶ ἡμέρας πλείους *for a (large) number of days, for many days* (Jos., Ant. 4, 277; cf. Theophr. in Apollon. Paradox. 29 πλείονας ἡμ.) Ac 13: 31.—21: 10 (Jos., Ant. 16, 15); 24: 17; 25: 14; 27: 20. οἱ μὲν πλείονές εἰσιν γεγονότες ἱερεῖς *the priests of former times existed in greater numbers* Hb 7: 23. ἑτέροις λόγοις πλείοσιν *in many more words* (than have been reported) Ac 2: 40. ταῦτα καὶ ἕτερα πλείονα MPol 12: 1.—W. a gen. of comparison ἄλλους δούλους πλείονας τῶν πρώτων *other slaves, more than* (he had sent) *at first* Mt 21: 36. πλείονα σημεῖα ὧν *more signs than those which* J 7: 31. Also w. ἤ: πλείονας μαθητὰς ἤ *more disciples than* 4: 1. After πλείονες(-α) before numerals the word for 'than' is omitted (Bl-D. §185, 4; Kühner-G. II 311; Rob. 666) ἐτῶν ἦν πλειόνων τεσσεράκοντα ὁ ἄνθρωπος *the man was more than 40 years old* Ac 4: 22. πλείους τεσσεράκοντα 23: 13, 21. Cf. 24: 11; 25: 6 (Jos., Ant. 6, 306 δέκα οὐ πλείους ἡμέρας).—The ref. is to degree in τὰ ἔργα σου τὰ ἔσχατα πλείονα τῶν πρώτων *your deeds, the latter of which are greater than the former* Rv 2: 19.

b. w. a singular καρπὸν πλείονα *more fruit* J 15: 2, 8 𝔓⁶⁶; Hs 5, 2, 4. τὸ πλεῖον μέρος τοῦ ὄχλου *the greater part of the throng* 8, 1, 16. ἐπὶ πλείονα χρόνον *for a longer time* (PTebt. 6, 31 [II BC]) Ac 18: 20. Foll. by gen. of comparison: πλείονα τιμήν *more honor* Hb 3: 3b.—IPol 1: 3a. Foll. by παρά τινα for comparison Hb 3: 3a; 11: 4; Hs 9, 18, 2. ὅσῳ πλείονος κατηξιώθημεν γνώσεως, τοσούτῳ μᾶλλον 1 Cl 41: 4.—τὸ πλεῖον μέρος as adv. acc. *for the greater part* Hv 3, 6, 4a.

2. subst.—a. (οἱ) πλείονες, (οἱ) πλείους—α. *the majority, most* (Diog. L. 1, 20; 22; Jos., Ant. 10, 114) Ac 19: 32; 27: 12. W. ἐξ: ἐξ ὧν οἱ πλείονες *most of whom* 1 Cor 15: 6. W. gen. and a neg. (litotes) οὐκ ἐν τ. πλείοσιν αὐτῶν ηὐδόκησεν ὁ θεὸς *God was pleased with only a few of them* 10: 5. This is perh. (s. γ below) the place for 1 Cor 9: 19; 2 Cor 2: 6; 9: 2. Phil 1: 14; MPol 5: 1.

β. (even) *more* πλείονες *in even greater numbers* Ac 28: 23. πολλῷ πλείους ἐπίστευσαν *many more came to believe* J 4: 41.—διὰ τῶν πλειόνων *to more and more people*= those who are still to be won for Christ 2 Cor 4: 15.

γ. In contrast to a minority οἱ πλείονες can gain the sense *the others, the rest* (so τὰ πλείονα Soph., Oed. Col. 36; τὸ πλέον Thu. 4, 30, 4; Jos., Ant. 12, 240; Bl-D. §244, 3 w. app.). So perh. (s. α above) ἵνα τ. πλείονας κερδήσω (opp. the apostle himself) 1 Cor 9: 19; 2 Cor 2: 6 (opp. the one who has been punished too severely.—In this case [s. α above] his punishment would have been determined by a

unanimous vote of the church, rather than by a majority). Cf. 9: 2; Phil 1: 14; MPol 5: 1.

b. πλείονα *more* Mt 20: 10 t.r.; *various things* Lk 11: 53. ἐκ τοῦ ἑνὸς πλείονα 1 Cl 24: 5.

c. πλεῖον, πλέον *more* τὸ πλεῖον *the greater sum* (cf. Diod. S. 1, 82, 2= the greater part; Ps 89: 10); Lk 7: 43. πλεῖον λαμβάνειν *receive a larger sum* Mt 20: 10. W. the partitive gen. ἐπὶ πλεῖον προκόψουσιν ἀσεβείας *they will arrive at an ever greater measure of godlessness*= become more and more deeply involved in godlessness 2 Ti 2: 16. W. a gen. of comparison πλεῖον τῆς τροφῆς *someth. greater (more important) than food* Mt 6: 25; Lk 12: 23. πλεῖον Ἰωνᾶ Mt 12: 41; cf. vs. 42; Lk 11: 31f. ἡ χήρα πλεῖον πάντων ἔβαλεν *the widow put in more than all the rest* Mk 12: 43; Lk 21: 3. μηδὲν πλέον *nothing more* (Jos., Bell. 1, 43); the words *than, except* following are expressed by παρά and the acc. Lk 3: 13 or by πλήν w. gen. Ac 15: 28.—The acc. is used as an adv. *more, in greater measure, to a greater degree* (Herm. Wr. 13, 21 Nock after the mss.) Lk 7: 42; IRo 1: 1; w. a gen. of comparison Mt 5: 20 (περισσεύω 1aβ); J 21: 15; IPol 5: 2 (cf. Ad'Alès, Rech de Sc rel 25, '35, 489–92). τριετίαν ἢ καὶ πλεῖον *for three years or even more* Ac 20: 18 D.— ἐπὶ πλεῖον *any farther* (of place) Ac 4: 17 (ἐπί III 1aα); (of time) *at length* Ac 20: 9 (ἐπί III 2b) or *any longer, too long* 24: 4; 1 Cl 55: 1 (ἐπί III 2b); *any more, even more* (ἐπί III 3) 2 Ti 3: 9; 1 Cl 18: 3 (Ps 50: 4). Strengthened πολὺ πλέον *much more, much rather* (4 Macc 1: 8; cf. X., An. 7, 5, 15; BGU 180, 12f [172 AD] πολλῷ πλεῖον) Dg 2: 7; 4: 5.—Also w. indications of number (s. 1a above) πλεῖον ἢ ἄρτοι πέντε Lk 9: 13 (the words πλ. ἤ outside the constr. as X., An. 1, 2, 11). In πλείω δώδεκα λεγιῶνας ἀγγέλων *more than twelve legions of angels* Mt 26: 53 the text is uncertain (Bl-D. §185, 4 app.; cf. Rob. 666).—The adv. can also be expressed by **πλειόνως** (Aeneas Tact. 237; Jos., Ant. 17, 2; Leontios 24, p. 52, 10) *more* ὅσον—πλειόνως *the more—the more* IEph 6: 1.

III. superlative **πλεῖστος, η, ον** (Hom.+; inscr., pap., LXX)—1. adj.—a. w. a plural *most* of αἱ πλεῖσται δυνάμεις Mt 11: 20.

b. w. the singular—α. superlative proper τὸ πλεῖστον μέρος *the greatest part* w. partitive gen. Hs 8, 2, 9; 9, 7, 4. As adv. acc. *for the greatest part* 8, 5, 6; 8, 10, 1 (s. μέρος 1d).

β. elative (cf. Mayser II 1, '26, 53) *very great, very large* (ὁ) πλεῖστος ὄχλος Mt 21: 8 (ὁ πλεῖστος ὄχλος could also be *the greatest part of the crowd*, as Thu. 7, 78, 2; Pla., Rep. 3 p. 397D); Mk 4: 1.

2. subst.—a. οἱ πλεῖστοι *the majority, most* Ac 19: 32 D.

b. the neut. acc. as adv. (sing. Hom.+; pl. Pind.+)— α. pl. πλεῖστα in the formula of greeting at the beginning of a letter πλεῖστα χαίρειν (POxy. 742; 744; 1061 [all three I BC] and fr. there on very oft. in pap.—Griech. Pap. ed. Ltzm.: Kl. Texte 14², '10, p. 4, 5, 6, 7 al.) *heartiest greeting(s)* IEph inscr.; IMg inscr.; ITr inscr.; IRo inscr.; ISm inscr.; IPol inscr.

β. sing. τὸ πλεῖστον *at the most* (Aristoph., Vesp. 260; Diod. S. 14, 71, 3 πεμπταῖοι ἢ τὸ πλ. ἑκταῖοι; POxy. 58, 17) κατὰ δύο ἢ τὸ πλ. τρεῖς (word for word like Περὶ ὕψους 32, 1) 1 Cor 14: 27. M-M. B. 922f.*

πολυσπλαγχνία, ας, ἡ *sympathy, compassion, mercy* as a divine attribute Hv 1, 3, 2; 2, 2, 8; 4, 2, 3; m 9: 2.*

πολύσπλαγχνος, ον *sympathetic, compassionate, merciful* (Clem. Alex., Quis Div. Salv. 39, 6; Act. Thom. 119) of God Js 5: 11; Hm 4, 3, 5; s 5, 7, 4.*

πολυτέλεια, ας, ἡ (Hdt.+; Diod. S. 5, 42, 6; inscr.; Ep. Arist. 80; Philo; Jos., Ant. 11, 200, C. Ap. 2, 234) *extravagance, luxury, richness* Hs 1: 10f. π. ἐδεσμάτων πολλῶν *luxury of many (kinds of) food(s)* Hm 6, 2, 5. π. πλούτου *extravagance of wealth* (i.e. such as wealth affords) m 8: 3; 12, 2, 1.*

πολυτελής, ές (Hdt.+; inscr., pap., LXX) (*very*) *expensive, costly* (so Thu.+; inscr., pap., LXX, Philo; Jos., C. Ap. 2, 191) of an ointment Mk 14: 3. Of clothing (X., An. 1, 5, 8; Diod. S. 4, 53, 3; 17, 35, 2; Polyaenus 6, 1, 4; Philo, Sacr. Abel. 21; Jos., Bell. 1, 605) 1 Ti 2: 9. Of stones (Diod. S. 1, 33, 3; 2, 16, 4; Dit., Or. 90, 34; 132, 8 [s. note 7]; Suppl. Epigr. Gr. VIII 467, 16 [217 Bc]; PGM 5, 239. So mostly LXX; En. 18, 6; Ep. Arist. 60 al.) λίθος π. B 6: 2 (Is 28: 16); pl. MPol 18: 1. παρατάξεις π. *costly establishments* (s. παράταξις 2) Hs 1: 1.—Symbolically, of true adornment ἐνώπιον τοῦ θεοῦ πολυτελές 1 Pt 3: 4. M-M.*

πολυτελῶς adv. (since Eupolis Com. 335 [V Bc]; Lysias 7, 31; Diod. S. 5, 41, 2; Dit., Or. 524, 7; Philo, Mos. 2, 95; Jos., Ant. 8, 95; 18, 92) *abundantly, lavishly* τὸ ἀγαθὸν π. ἐργάζεσθαι *do good lavishly* Hm 4, 2, 2.*

πολύτιμος, ον (Cornutus 16 p. 21, 16; Plut., Pomp. 5, 2; Alciphr. 3, 10, 4; Herodian 1, 17, 3; POxy. 1121, 20 [II AD]; PHermopol. 9, 7; Jos., Ant. 7, 161) *very precious, valuable* of a pearl Mt 13: 46. Of an ointment 26: 7 v.l.; J 12: 3. Comp. τὸ δοκίμιον τῆς πίστεως πολυτιμότερον χρυσίου *the genuineness* (δοκίμιον 2) *of* (your) *faith which is more precious than gold* 1 Pt 1: 7. M-M.*

πολυτρόπως adv. (Philo, Aet. M. 129; Geopon. 9, 11, 4; 4 Macc 3: 21 v.l.) fr. πολύτροπος (Hom.+; PFlor. 33, 15; Job 5: 13 v.l.; 4 Macc; Philo, Vi. Mos. 1, 117, Dec. 83; Jos., Ant. 10, 142) *in various ways* (w. πολυμερῶς, q.v.) Hb 1: 1. M-M.*

πόμα, ατος, τό (so Pind., Hdt. and later writers, also Epigr. Gr. 244, 10; LXX; Philo for class. πῶμα. Kühner-Bl. II p. 286) *a drink*—1. pl., of the usual things to drink (w. βρώματα; s. βρῶμα 1) Hb 9: 10.

2. symbolically (Ael. Aristid. 28, 114 K.=49 p. 528 D.: π. ἐξ Ἀπόλλωνος πηγῶν; Philo, Somn. 2, 248 θεῖον π.; Sib. Or. 5, 240) ἓν πόμα ἐποτίσθημεν 1 Cor 12: 13 v.l., prob. w. ref. to the Lord's Supper. The typological predecessor of the Lord's Supper in the OT is seen (beside manna as the πνευματικὸν βρῶμα) as τὸ πνευματικὸν πόμα *the spiritual drink* (fr. the spiritual rock that followed them) 1 Cor 10: 4. Ign. describes the joys of communion w. Christ that accompany martyrdom by means of expressions taken fr. the liturgy of the Eucharist, among them πόμα IRo 7: 3 (Hdb. ad loc.). M-M.*

πονέω (Pind.+ [the mid. as dep. as early as Hom.]; inscr., pap., LXX; Jos., Ant. 12, 240; 15, 33) *toil, be troubled* ἐπί τινι *about* or *in behalf of someone* ἐπὶ καταπονουμένῳ (s. καταπονέω) B 20: 2; D 5: 2. πονεῖ ἡ ψυχή μου ἐπὶ τοῖς υἱοῖς τῶν ἀνθρώπων LJ 1: 3 (of the ψυχή as Philo, Somn. 1, 255).*

πονηρεύομαι mid. dep.; fut. πονηρεύσομαι *be wicked* and *act wickedly* (Heraclit.+; Demosth. 19, 32; Menand., Epitr. 133; Plut., Pomp. 39, 5, Cic. 7, 4, Cato Maj. 9, 10; Ael. Aristid. 39 p. 745 D.; LXX; Philo, Spec. Leg. 2, 11; 4, 76; Jos., Ant. 15, 348; Test. 12 Patr.), *do wrong, commit sin* Hm 10, 3, 2a, b. Opp. ἀγαθοποιεῖν Hs 9, 18, 1f. π. εἴς τινα *act wickedly toward someone, do harm to someone* m 4, 3, 4; 9: 9; s 9, 22, 4. π. ἔν τινι (*commit*) *sin with*

someth. (Mi 3: 4): w. the tongue Hv 2, 2, 3. μηδὲν πονηρεύσῃ *you must do no evil* s 5, 1, 5. οἱ πονηρευόμενοι ποικίλαις πονηρίαις *doers of various kinds of wickedness*=*sinners of every description* 9, 18, 3.—The subst. ptc. in the pl. οἱ πονηρευόμενοι *the evil-doers, the sinners* (Dit., Or. 515, 58; LXX; Philo, Virt. 227) B 5: 13; 6: 6 (cf. on both Ps 21: 17).*

πονηρία, ας, ἡ (Soph., Hippocr.+) in our lit. only in the ethical sense *wickedness, baseness, maliciousness, sinfulness* (Soph.; Lysias 22, 16 et al.; Dit., Or. 519, 10; PLeipz. 119A, B I, 7; LXX; Philo, De Jos. 212; Jos., Ant. 10, 37; 13, 120; Test. 12 Patr.; loanw. in rabb.) Mt 22: 18; Hv 3, 5, 4; 3, 6, 1. W. ἁρπαγή Lk 11: 39; w. ἄνοια 2 Cl 13: 1; w. δολιότης Hs 8, 6, 2; w. κακία 1 Cor 5: 8. In the Lord's Prayer Mt 6: 13 v.l. In a catalogue of vices (s. Philo, Ebr. 223) Ro 1: 29; 1 Cl 35: 5. Cf. Hs 9, 15, 3, where Πονηρία and other vices are personified. πονηρία μεγάλη Hv 2, 2, 2a. Of children μὴ γινώσκοντα τὴν πονηρίαν τὴν ἀπολλύουσαν τὴν ζωήν *who know nothing of the wickedness that ruins the life* Hm 2: 1.—In the objective gen. κόλασις τῆς π. *punishment for wickedness* Hs 9, 18, 1; ὁ μισθὸς τῆς π. B 4: 12. In the gen. of quality (to be rendered as an adj.) ἡ ἐπιθυμία τῆς π. *evil desire* Hv 1, 1, 8; m 11: 2. συμφυρμοὶ πονηρίας v 2, 2, 2b. διδάσκαλοι πονηρίας *evil teachers* or obj. gen. *teachers of wickedness* s 9, 19, 2; τὰ πνευματικὰ τῆς π. Eph 6: 12 (cf. πνευματικός 3). ὁ ἄγγελος τῆς πονηρίας (opp. ἄγγ. τῆς δικαιοσύνης) Hm 6, 2, 1; 4f; 7; 9f (cf. IQS 3, 18f). πλείονα πονηρίαν ποιεῖν *act more wickedly* Hs 9, 18, 2.—The pl., of the various kinds of evil-mindedness and individual expressions of it (Demosth. 21, 19; Aristot. 1389a, 18; Jer 39: 32; Bl-D. §142; cf. Rob. 408) Mk 7: 22 (*malicious acts*); Ac 3: 26; 1 Cl 8: 4 (Is 1: 16); Hv 3, 7, 2; m 8: 3. αἱ π. ἐν ταῖς καρδίαις ἐμμένουσιν *wickedness remains in their hearts* Hv 3, 6, 3 (here the pl. could refer to the plurality of persons involved, since basically only one kind of wickedness is meant). On πονηρεύεσθαι ποικίλαις πονηρίαις s 9, 18, 3 cf. πονηρεύομαι.—S. also ἁγιάζω (4), ἀποβάλλω (1bα), ἀφαιρέω (1), κατισχύω (2), παύω (2). M-M.**

πονηρός, ά, όν (Hes., Thu.+; inscr., pap., LXX, En., Philo, Joseph., Test. 12 Patr.) comp. πονηρότερος Mt 12: 45; Lk 11: 26; superl. πονηρότατος (Diod. S. 14, 4, 2; Catal. of the Gk. and Lat. Pap. in the JRyl. Libr. III '38, no. 493, 89) Hm 3: 5.

1. adj.—a. in the physical sense—α. *in poor condition, sick* (Pla., Prot. 313A σῶμα; πονηρῶς ἔχειν 'be badly off', 'be ill' since Thu. 7, 83, 3) of the eye (cf. Pla., Hipp. Min. 374D πονηρία ὀφθαλμῶν) Mt 6: 23; Lk 11: 34 (Weizsäcker, BWeiss, HHoltzmann, Gdspd., RSV. But see s.v. ἁπλοῦς, λύχνος 2, ὀφθαλμός 1, also 1bβ below and the four articles ET 53, '42, 181f; 354f; 54, '42, 26; 26f).

β. *painful, virulent, serious* (since Theognis 274) ἕλκος *sore, ulcer* (Dt 28: 35; Job 2: 7) Rv 16: 2.

γ. *bad, spoiled, worthless* (X., Pla.+) καρποί (Ael. Aristid. 23, 57K. = 42 p. 787 D.) Mt 7: 17f (cf. Jer 24: 8 τὰ σῦκα τὰ πονηρά).

b. in the ethical sense *wicked, evil, bad, base, worthless, vicious, degenerate*—α. of persons (since trag. and Ps.-X., Rep. Ath. ['the Old Oligarch'] 1, 1; Is 9: 16; Sir 25: 16, 25; Philo, Joseph.) ὁ πον. ἄνθρωπος (Plut., Alcib. 13, 4; cf. Philo, Exsecr. 149; Jos., Ant. 7, 291) Mt 12: 35a; Lk 6: 45a (where ἄνθρωπος is to be supplied); cf. 2 Th 3: 2; 2 Ti 3: 13. δοῦλος πον. (Philemo Com. 167; Jos., Ant. 2, 55; 16, 296) Mt 18: 32; 25: 26; Lk 19: 22; ἄνδρες πον. Ac 17: 5;

γενεὰ πον. Mt 12: 39, 45b; 16: 4; Lk 11: 29.—Mt 12: 34. Men are called πονηροί in contrast to God Mt 7: 11; Lk 11: 13 (Iambl., Vi. Pyth. 18, 82 ἀληθέστατον . . . πονηροὶ οἱ ἄνθρωποι).—Of demons τὸ πνεῦμα τὸ πονηρόν (Cat. Cod. Astr. X 180, 16; 186, 4) Ac 19: 15f. Pl. (Cyranides p. 51, 14) Lk 7: 21; 8: 2; Ac 19: 12f. Of the *evil spirit* which contends w. the Holy Spirit for a place in the human soul (cf. 1 Km 16: 14-23) Hm 5, 1, 2; 3. ἄγγελος πον. B 9: 4 (Paus. Attic. τ, 18 πονηροὶ δαίμονες; Julian p. 371, 5; 11 Hertlein δαίμονες πονηροί; PLeipz. 34, 8 π. δαίμων). ὁ πονηρὸς ἄρχων 4: 13 (ἄρχων 3).

β. of things βουλή (Menand., Mon. 568) B 6: 7 (Is 3: 9); 19: 3; D 2: 6; Hv 1, 2, 4a (βουλή 2a). διαλογισμοί Mt 15: 19; Js 2: 4 (διαλογισμός 1). διδαχή Hm 6, 2, 7 (παντὶ ἔργῳ is dat. of disadvantage). δόλος (Dit., Syll.³ 693, 6 [129 BC]) IEph 7: 1. ἐπιθυμία (-αι: Dio Chrys. 4, 89) 2 Cl 16: 2; Hv 1, 1, 8b; 1, 2, 4c; s 6, 2, 1 and oft. ἔργον 2 Ti 4: 18; Hv 1, 2, 4b. ἔργα J 3: 19; 7: 7; Col 1: 21; 1 J 3: 12b; 2 J 11; Hv 3, 7, 6; 3, 8, 4 al. θησαυρός Mt 12: 35b; Lk 6: 45b (here θησ. is to be supplied fr. the context). καρδία (cf. Menand., fgm. 540, 8 ψυχή) 1 Cl 3: 4; καρδία πονηρὰ ἀπιστίας (gen of characteristic; cf. Bl-D. §165; definition Mlt. 74) Hb 3: 12. καταλαλιά Hm 2: 3. *Arrogant* καύχησις Js 4: 16; λόγοι π. *malicious words* (Menand., Mon. 542) 3 J 10. Of the ὁδὸς τοῦ θανάτου D 5: 1; cf. B 4: 10. ὀφθαλμὸς π. (ὀφθαλμός 1 and s. 1aa above) Mt 20: 15; Mk 7: 22. πρᾶγμα (Menand., Epitr. 673, fgm. 784) Hv 1, 1, 8a; ῥᾳδιούργημα π. Ac 18: 14. ῥῆμα π. *slanderous, evil word* (Dit., Syll.³ 1175, 16; Jdth 8: 8, 9) Mt 5: 11 t.r.; Hs 5, 3, 6; συνείδησις π. *evil, guilty conscience* Hb 10: 22; B 19: 12; D 4: 14; Hm 3: 4; ὑπόνοιαι π. 1 Ti 6: 4. Cf. Ac 25: 18 v.l. τὸ πονηρότατον ψεῦσμα *the most wicked sin of lying* Hm 3: 5. Of a Christian's name ἐκβάλλειν τὸ ὄνομα ὡς πονηρόν *spurn the name as vile* (i.e as held only by worthless persons) Lk 6: 22.—In the judgment of Christians a close connection w. sin is the chief characteristic of this age: ἐκ τοῦ αἰῶνος τοῦ ἐνεστῶτος πονηροῦ Gal 1: 4. Cf. αἱ ἡμέραι πονηραί εἰσιν Eph 5: 16.—B 2: 1. Sing. Eph 6: 13.

2. subst.—a. *wicked* or *evil-intentioned person, evil-doer* (Dt 21: 21; Esth 7: 6) ὁ πονηρός (the art. is generic) Mt 5: 39; 1 Cor 5: 13 (Dt 17: 7); B 19: 11 (but τὸ πον. Lake).—Pl. πονηροὶ καὶ ἀγαθοί (cf. Philo, Praem. 3; Jos., Ant. 6, 307; 8, 314 God ἀγαπᾷ τ. ἀγαθούς, μισεῖ δὲ τ. πονηρούς) Mt 5: 45; 22: 10. Opp. οἱ δίκαιοι 13: 49. W. οἱ ἀχάριστοι (s. ἀχάριστος. Also Lucian, Timon 48, perh. fr. comedy [III p. 654 Kock]) Lk 6: 35. W. ἁμαρτωλοί B 4: 2.

b. ὁ πονηρός *the evil one* = the devil (Third Corinthians 3: 15) Mt 13: 19; J 17: 15; Eph 6: 16; 1 J 2: 13f; 5: 18, 19 (κεῖμαι 2d); B 2: 10; 21: 3; MPol 17: 1. ἐκ τοῦ πονηροῦ εἶναι *be a child of the evil one* (ἐκ 3a, end) 1 J 3: 12a; cf. οἱ υἱοὶ τοῦ πονηροῦ Mt 13: 38, in case πον. is masc. here.—The gen. τοῦ πονηροῦ Mt 5: 37; 6: 13 can also be taken as masc. (it is so taken by Ps.-Clem., Hom. 3, 55 p. 51, 19; 21; Tertullian, Cyprian, Origen, Chrysostom; KAFFritzsche, JWeiss; more recently Schniewind on Mt 6: 13; Weymouth, Gdspd.;—it is taken as a neut. by Augustine: WMangold, De Ev. sec Mt 6: 13, 1886; BWeiss, Zahn, Wlh.; Harnack SAB '07, 944; EKlostermann, Dausch; PFiebig, D. Vaterunser '27, 92; Mft., RSV.) Lk 11: 4 t.r.; 2 Th 3: 3; D 8: 2. It is poss. that these passages belong under

c. τὸ πονηρόν (*that which is*) *evil* Lk 6: 45c; Ro 12: 9; 1 Th 5: 22 (εἶδος 2). πᾶν πον. *all kinds of evil* Mt 5: 11; ποιεῖν τὸ πονηρὸν ἔμπροσθεν τοῦ κυρίου (cf. Dt 17: 2; 4 Km 21: 2, 20) Hm 4, 2, 2; cf. Ac 5: 4 D; 1 Cl 18: 4 (Ps 50:

6). ἀγρυπνεῖν εἰς τὸ π. D 5: 2 and ἐπὶ τὸ π. B 20: 2 s. ἀγρυπνέω 2. ἐλάλησέν τι περὶ σοῦ πονηρόν Ac 28: 21.—Pl. *wicked thoughts, evil deeds* (Gen 6: 5; 8: 21) Mt 9: 4; 12: 35c; Mk 7: 23; Lk 3: 19; J 3: 20 𝔓⁶⁶ et al.; Ac 25: 18; 2 Cl 8: 2. δύο καὶ πονηρά *two evil things* B 11: 2 (Jer 2: 13 v.l.).—πονηρόν ἐστίν τινι *it is bad for someone* Hm 5, 1, 4.—S. Lofthouse s.v. κακός, end; WBrandt, ZNW 14, '13, 189ff. GHarder, TW VI 546-66: πονηρός and related words. M-M. **

πονηρόφρων, ον, gen. ονος *evil-minded* w. αὐθάδης D 3: 6 (the word is found only here and in Apost. Constit. 7, 7, which is dependent upon this pass.). *

πονηρῶς adv. (Thu., Aristoph. et al.) *basely, wickedly* w. ἀφρόνως Hv 5: 4. *

πόνος, ου, ὁ (Hom.+; inscr., pap., LXX)—1. (*hard*) *labor, toil* (Onesicritus [c. 310 BC]: 134 fgm. 17a Jac.: because of the ὕβρις of men, Zeus brought the utopian state of affairs in India to an end, and sent πόνος into the life of men; Ps 89: 10; Philo; Jos., Ant. 3, 49; 18, 244) πόνον ἔχειν ὑπέρ τινος Col 4: 13 (πόνον ἔχειν: Il. 15, 416; Hes., Shield 305; Paus. 4, 16, 3.—Theocr. 7, 139 has it in the sense 'take pains' with a ptc.). μετὰ πόνου *with difficulty, laboriously, painstakingly* (Pla., Soph. 230A μετὰ πολλοῦ πόνου) Dg 11: 8.

2. *pain, distress, affliction* (X., Mem. 2, 2, 5; Aelian, N.A. 7, 30 p. 190, 9; Dit., Syll.³ 708, 11; POxy. 234 II, 24; 37; Is 65: 14; Job 4: 5) w. πένθος and κραυγή Rv 21: 4. εἶναι ἐν πόνῳ (cf. Gen 34: 25) 1 Cl 16: 3f (Is 53: 4). ἀφαιρεῖν ἀπὸ τ. πόνου τῆς ψυχῆς (ἀφαιρέω 1.—πόνος τ. ψυχῆς: Maximus Tyr. 1, 4b) vs. 12 (Is 53: 10f). Of the Crucified One ὡς μηδὲ πόνον ἔχων *as though he felt no pain at all* GP 4: 10. Of a hailstone πῶς πόνον παρέχει *how much pain it causes, how much it hurts* Hm 11: 20. ἐκ τοῦ π. *in pain* (Appian, Iber. 97 §423) Rv 16: 10; pl. (Gen 41: 51; Jos., C. Ap. 2, 146; Test. Jud. 18: 4) ἐκ τῶν π. (Eur., fgm. 364 Nauck²) *because of their sufferings* vs. 11. πόνους ὑποφέρειν *undergo hardship* 1 Cl 5: 4.—HT Kuist, Biblical Review 16, '32, 415-20 (πόνος, μόχθος). M-M. B. 540. *

Ποντικός, ή, όν *from Pontus* (s. Πόντος) (Hdt.+) subst. (Socrat., Ep. 30, 14) of Aquila Π. τῷ γένει *a native of Pontus* Ac 18: 2. *

Πόντιος, ου, ὁ (Diod. S. 14, 116, 3; Plut.; Dit., Syll.³ 797, 2 [37 AD], Or. 656, 4) *Pontius,* the name of a Roman, originally Samnite gens, going as far back as the Samnite Wars (Cic., De Off. 2, 21, 75; Livy 9, 1), the nomen (middle, gentile, or tribal name) of Pilate (s. Πιλᾶτος) Mt 27: 2 v.l.; Lk 3: 1; Ac 4: 27; 1 Ti 6: 13. WSchulze, Zur Geschichte latein. Eigennamen: GGAbh. V 5, '04; JOllivier, Ponce Pilate et les Pontii: RB 5, 1896, 247-54; 594-600. *

πόντος, ου, ὁ (Hom.+; Arrian, Anab. 6, 19, 4; 5; Ex 15: 5) *the* (high) *sea* ὁ ἐπὶ πόντον πλέων Rv 18: 17 v.l. (cf. Diod. S. 20. 25, 2 οἱ πλέοντες τὸν Πόντον=those who sail the Pontus). *

Πόντος, ου, ὁ (Aeschyl., Hdt.+; Philo, Deus Imm. 174; Joseph.; inscr.) *Pontus,* orig. the name of a sea (the Euxine, or Black Sea), then the abbreviated designation of an empire founded by the Achaemenid Persians in northeast Asia Minor, extending fr. the Black Sea to the Caucasus. After Pompey's conquest a part of it was made a Roman province. Acc. to Appian, Mithrid. 15 §53 many Ἕλληνες had settled there. Ac 2: 9; 1 Pt 1: 1 (on the address Ps.-Callisth. 2, 11, 2, an encyclical letter of Alexander [s. Καππαδοκία]). JMarquardt, Römische Staatsverwaltung I² 1881, 349ff; EMeyer and Brandis, Pauly-W. III 507ff; VSchultze, Altchristl. Städte u. Landschaften II 1, '22.*

Πόπλιος, ου, ὁ (Diod. S. 11, 41, 1; 13, 7, 1; 14, 47, 1 al.; Plut.; Philo, Leg. ad Gai. 333; Jos., Ant. 14, 236; inscr., pap.) *Publius*, a Roman praenomen (first or personal name; cf. AWalde, Latein. etymolog. Wörterbuch² '10 s.v. poplicus; Bl-D. §41, 2; cf. Mlt.-H. 155). Ac 28: 7f mentions a Π. as πρῶτος τῆς νήσου for the island of Malta. The title is also attested elsewh. for Malta: IG XIV 601 Λ. Καστρίκιος Κυρ(είνᾳ) Προύδηνς ἱππεὺς Ῥω-μ(αίων), πρῶτος Μελιταίων καὶ πάτρων, ἄρξας καὶ ἀμφιπολεύσας θεῷ Αὐγούστῳ; CIL X 7495 municipi Melitensium primus omnium. As a rule it is taken for granted that it was a designation for the highest Roman official on the island (Felten, Belser, HHoltzmann, Wendt, Preuschen, Knopf, Hoennicke). More recently it has been thought to refer to any office that was non-Roman in origin (AMayr, Die Insel Malta im Altertum '09, 116; AWikenhauser, Die AG '21, 345f). M-M.*

πορεία, ας, ἡ (Aeschyl., X., Pla.+; inscr., pap., LXX) *going*—1. lit. *journey, trip* πορείαν ποιεῖσθαι (X., An. 5, 6, 11; Diod. S. 14, 39, 4; Cornutus 19 p. 33, 20; Plut., Mor. 162ꜰ; 2 Macc 3: 8; Jos., Ant. 7, 49; 14, 128) w. the destination given (Jos., Ant. 14, 358 εἰς Μ.) εἰς Ἱερο-σόλυμα Lk 13: 22. In the judgment of the majority (Herder, Mayor, HermvSoden, Spitta, Hollmann, Belser, Windisch, Meinertz; RSV et al.) Js 1: 11 also belongs here: ὁ πλούσιος ἐν ταῖς πορείαις αὐτοῦ *the rich man on his* (business) *journeys* or more gener. *in his undertakings* or *pursuits.* The pl. is a strong indication that this transl. is correct; nevertheless, the pl. may be thought of as parallel to vs. 8 ἐν τοῖς ὁδοῖς αὐτοῦ, so that we cannot finally exclude the sense

2. *way of life, conduct* (Pr 2: 7.—Of the 'way' that one should take: Socrat., Ep. 27, 5) Hs 5, 6, 6. κατευθύνοντες τὴν πορείαν αὐτῶν ἐν ὁσιότητι 1 Cl 48: 4. Cf. 62: 1 v.l. Funk. Fr. this point of view Js 1: 11 would be translated *in all his ways* (so Gebser, Weizsäcker, Beyschlag, Ropes, MDibelius, FHauck, JBPhillips). M-M.*

πορεύω (Pind.+) in our lit. only as mid. and pass. **πορεύομαι** (trag., Hdt.+; inscr., pap., LXX, En., Ep. Arist., Joseph., Test. 12 Patr.) impf. ἐπορευόμην; fut. πορεύσομαι; 1 aor. ἐπορεύθην; pf. ptc. πεπορευμένος. On the fut. mng. of the pres. s. Bl-D. §323, 3; Rob. 869. On the durative sense of the pres. imper. πορεύου in contrast to the aor. πορεύθητι s. Bl-D. §336, 1; cf. Rob. 855f; 890; *go, proceed, travel.*

1. lit., w. indication of the place from which: ἀπό τινος *begone, depart from someone* (X., An. 4, 4, 17) Mt 25: 41; Lk 4: 42b. ἐντεῦθεν 13: 31. ἐκεῖθεν Mt 19: 15. W. indication of the place to which: εἴς τι (X., Hell. 7, 4, 10; Is 22: 15 εἴς τι πρός τινα) *to, in, into, toward* Mt 2: 20; 17: 27; Mk 16: 12; Lk 1: 39; 4: 42a; 9: 56 (εἰς ἑτέραν κώμην, cf. Jos., Vi. 231); 22: 33 (εἰς φυλακήν); J 7: 35b; Ac 1: 11; 19: 21; 20: 1, 22 (πορεύομαι=*I am going, I am about to go*); 22: 5, 10; Ro 15: 24, 25 (*I am going, am about to go*); IPol 7: 2; 8: 2; Hv 1, 1, 3; 2, 1, 1. Of fish π. εἰς τὸ βάθος *dive into the depth* B 10: 10b. Also of passing into the beyond, in a good sense of Paul and Peter: π. εἰς τὸν ἅγιον τόπον 1 Cl 5: 7; εἰς τὸν ὀφειλόμενον (ὀφείλω 2aα) τόπον τῆς δόξης 5: 4 (so of Peter in Ac 12: 17: WMSmaltz, JBL 71, '52, 211-6), and in a bad sense of Judas the traitor εἰς τὸ τόπον τὸν ἴδιον Ac 1: 25. εἰς τὰ

ἔθνη *to the heathen* 18: 6. ἐπὶ Καίσαρα π. *go to Caesar, appear before the Emperor* (ἐπί III 1aγ) 25: 12. πρός τινα *to someone* (Soph., Ant. 892; Pla., Clit. p. 410c; Theophr., Char. 2, 1; Diog. L. 8, 43; Gen 26: 26) Mt 25: 9; 26: 14; Lk 11: 5; 15: 18; 16: 30; J 14: 12, 28; 16: 28 (in the three J pass. *I am about to go*); Ac 27: 3; 1 Cl 31: 4. σύν τινι *with someone* Lk 7: 6; Ac 10: 20; 26: 13; 1 Cor 16: 4b. ἐπί τι *after someth.* (ἐπί III 1aδ) Lk 15: 4; (*up*) *to someth.* (ἐπί III 1aβ) Mt 22: 9; Ac 8: 26; 9: 11, also ἕως ἐπί τι Ac 17: 14. W. ἕως and gen. of the place Ac 23: 23. W. διά and gen. of the place *through* (X., An. 4, 7, 15) Mt 12: 1; Mk 9: 30 v.l. ποῦ (instead of ποῖ) J 7: 35a. οὗ (instead of ὅποι, as 1 Macc 13: 20) Lk 24: 28a; 1 Cor 16: 6. π. τῇ ὁδῷ *go one's way, proceed on one's journey* 1 Cl 12: 4; also ἐπορεύετο τὴν ὁδὸν αὐτοῦ Ac 8: 39 (cf. Josh 3: 4; Jos., Ant. 1, 282). π. ἐν τῇ ὁδῷ *go along the road* Lk 9: 57; also π. κατὰ τὴν ὁδόν Ac 8: 36.—W. the purpose indicated by the inf. (Gen 37: 25) Lk 2: 3; 14: 19, 31; J 14: 2. Also ἵνα 11: 11.—Somet. the place fr. which or to which is easily supplied fr. the context: θέλετε πορεύεσθαι *you wish to go* (i.e. to the house of the non-Christian who has invited you) 1 Cor 10: 27. πορ. (i.e. εἰς Ἱερουσαλήμ) 16: 4a. πορ. (i.e. εἰς Δαμασκόν) Ac 22: 6.—The aor. ptc. of πορ. is oft. used pleonastically to enliven the narrative (Bl-D. §419, 2.—4 Km 5: 10; Josh 23: 16; Jos., Ant. 7, 318); in any case the idea of going or traveling is not emphasized Mt 9: 13; 11: 4; 18: 12; 21: 6; 22: 15; 25: 16; 27: 66; 28: 7; Mk 16: 10; Lk 7: 22; 9: 13; 13: 32; 14: 10 al.—Abs. (X., An. 5, 3, 2) ἐπορεύθησαν *they set out* Mt 2: 9. πορεύθητι καὶ πορεύεται *go, and he goes* (cf. PGM 1, 185 πορεύου καὶ ἀπελεύσεται) 8: 9; Lk 7: 8 (opp. ἔρχεσθαι, as Epict. 1, 25, 10 'Αγαμέμνων λέγει μοι 'πορεύου...' πορεύομαι. 'ἔρχου'. ἔρχομαι).—Lk 10: 37; *be on the way, be journeying* Lk 10: 38; 13: 33; Ac 9: 3.—ἔμπροσθέν τινος (UPZ 78, 15 [159 BC] ἔμπροσθεν αὐτῶν ἐπορευόμην; Josh 3: 6): ἔ. αὐτῶν πορεύεται *he goes in front of them* J 10: 4 (schol. on Apollon. Rhod. 1, 577 προπορεύεται ὁ ποιμήν); cf. B 11: 4 (Is 45: 2). μὴ πορευθῆτε ὀπίσω αὐτῶν *do not go after them* Lk 21: 8 (ὀπίσω 2aβ). προθύμως μετὰ σπουδῆς ἐπορεύετο *he walked on quickly and eagerly* MPol 8: 3.—πορεύου=go your way (Diog. L. 4, 11): πορεύου εἰς εἰρήνην Lk 7: 50; 8: 48 or ἐν εἰρήνῃ Ac 16: 36 s. εἰρήνη 2.

2. fig.—a. as a euphemism, *go to one's death* (cf. Lk 22: 33 εἰς θάνατον πορεύεσθαι), *die* Lk 22: 22.

b. πορ. ὀπίσω τινός in the sense 'seek a close relation with' (cf. Judg 2: 12; 3 Km 11: 10; Sir 46: 10) οἱ ὀπίσω σαρκὸς ἐν ἐπιθυμίᾳ μιασμοῦ πορευόμενοι *follow* (i.e. indulge) *their physical nature in desire that defiles* 2 Pt 2: 10. ὀπίσω τῶν ἐπιθυμιῶν Hv 3, 7, 3.

c. *conduct oneself, live, walk* (Soph., Oed. R. 884; LXX) w. ἔν τινι foll.: (En. 99, 10 ἐν ὁδοῖς δικαιοσύνης; Test. Reub. 1: 6; 4: 1 ἐν ἁπλότητι καρδίας, Iss. 3: 1, Ash. 4: 5) ἐν ὁδῷ θανάτου B 19: 2. ἐν ἀληθείᾳ (Tob 3: 5 BA; Pr 28: 6) Hm 3: 4. ἐν ἀκακίᾳ καὶ ἁπλότητι v 2, 3, 2. ἐν ἀσελγείαις κτλ. 1 Pt 4: 3. ἐν τῇ ἁγνότητι ταύτῃ Hm 4, 4, 4. ἐν ὁσιότητι 1 Cl 60: 2. ἐν ταῖς ἐντολαῖς τοῦ κυρίου (cf. Ps 118: 1 ἐν νόμῳ κυρίου) Lk 1: 6; cf. Pol 2: 2; 4: 1; Hs 6, 1, 1-4. ἐν τοῖς προστάγμασιν s 5, 1, 5.—κατά τι (Num 24: 1; Wsd 5: 4) κατὰ τὰς ἐπιθυμίας *according to the passions* 2 Pt 3: 3; Jd 16, 18.—τῇ ὀρθῇ ὁδῷ πορ. *follow the straight way* Hm 6, 1, 2 (on the dat. cf. Bl-D. §198, 5; Rob. 521 and Dit., Syll.³ 313, 20; LXX [reff. in MJohannessohn, Der Gebr. der Kasus in LXX, Diss. Berlin '10, 57f]). ταῖς ὁδοῖς αὐτῶν Ac 14: 16. τῇ ὁδῷ τοῦ Κάϊν Jd 11. τῷ φόβῳ τοῦ κυρίου *live in the fear of the Lord* Ac 9: 31.

d. of life gener. (Dio Chrys. 58[75], 1 διὰ τ. βίου); abs. πορευόμενοι *as they pass by* (Jülicher, Gleichn. 529) Lk 8:

14.—GDKilpatrick, JTS 48, '47, 61–3 (in synopt. gosp.). M-M.

πορθέω impf. ἐπόρθουν; 1 aor. ἐπόρθησα (Hom. +; Dit., Or. 201, 17; BGU 588, 3 πορθοῦντες ὑμᾶς; 4 Macc 4: 23; 11: 4; Jos., Bell. 4, 405, Ant. 10, 135 τὰ Ἱεροσόλυμα) *pillage, make havoc of, destroy, annihilate* τὶ someth. ἐπόρθουν αὐτήν (i.e. τὴν ἐκκλησίαν τοῦ θεοῦ) *I tried to destroy the church of God* Gal 1: 13. τὴν πίστιν ἥν ποτε ἐπόρθει *the faith which he once tried to destroy* vs. 23. τινά *someone* (Aeschyl. +; Diod. S. 11, 32, 1; s. BGU above) π. τοὺς ἐπικαλουμένους τὸ ὄνομα τοῦτο Ac 9: 21. —P-HMenoud, EHaenchen-Festschr., '64, 178–86 (Ac, Gal). M-M.*

πορία s. πορεία.

πορίζω (trag., Thu. +; inscr., pap., Wsd 15: 12) *procure, provide* ἑαυτῷ τὴν τροφήν *food for oneself* (Horapollo 1, 42 αἱ τροφαὶ πορίζονται; PGrenf. II 14a, 11 [III BC] πόρισόν μοι εἰς τὴν τροφήν; Aelian, V.H. 13, 26 and Jos., Ant. 8, 13 π. αὐτῷ τι) B 10: 4.*

πορισμός, οῦ, ὁ (Polyb. et al.; Wsd 13: 19; 14: 2; Ep. Arist. 111; Philo, Op. M. 128; Jos., Bell. 2, 603) *means of gain* (so Plut., Cato Maj. 25, 1 δυσὶ μόνοις πορισμοῖς, γεωργίᾳ καὶ φειδοῖ; Test. Iss. 4: 5 v.l.) 1 Ti 6: 5, 6. M-M.*

Πόρκιος, ου, ὁ (Polyb., Plut.; Jos., Ant. 20, 182) *Porcius*, name of a Roman gens to which, among others, the Catos belonged. Festus the procurator belonged to it (s. Φῆστος) Ac 24: 27.*

πορνεία, ας, ἡ (Demosth. +; LXX, Philo, Test. 12 Patr.) *prostitution, unchastity, fornication*, of every kind of unlawful sexual intercourse.
  1. lit. Ro 1: 29 t.r.; 1 Cor 5: 1a, b; 6: 13; Hm 4, 1, 1. W. ἀκαθαρσία 2 Cor 12: 21; Gal 5: 19; Eph 5: 3; Col 3: 5. Differentiated fr. μοιχεία (Philo, Mos. 1, 300) Mt 15: 19; Mk 7: 21 (WGabriel, Was ist 'porneia' im Sprachgebr. Jesu?: Ethik 7, '31, 106–9; 363–9); Hm 8: 3; D 5: 1 (the pl. denotes individual acts). On the other hand μοιχεία appears as πορνεία (cf. Sir 23: 23) Hm 4, 1, 5. Of the sexual unfaithfulness of a married woman Mt 5: 32; 19: 9 (most recently JSickenberger, ThQ 123, '42, 189–206, ZNW 42, '49, 202ff; KStaab [παρεκτός 2]; AAllgeier, Angelicum 20, '43, 128–42. Uniquely AFridrichsen, Sv. Exeg. Årsbok 9, '44, 54–8; AIsaksson, Marriage and Ministry in the New Temple, '65, 127–42 [lit.]). Caused by lust D 3: 3. διὰ τὰς πορνείας 1 Cor 7: 2 (the pl. points out the various factors that may bring about sexual immorality). BMalina, Does Porneia Mean 'Fornication'? NovT 14, '72, 10–17. φεύγειν τὴν π. 6: 18. Also ἀπέχεσθαι ἀπὸ τῆς π. 1 Th 4: 3 (cf. Tobit 4: 12). ἐκ π. γεννηθῆναι *be an illegitimate child, a bastard* (cf. Cephalio [II AD]: 93 fgm. 5 p. 444, 5 Jac. ἐγέννησε ἐκ πορ.; Gen 38: 24) J 8: 41. On ἀπέχεσθαι τῆς πορνείας καὶ πνικτοῦ Ac 15: 20 (cf. vs. 29; 21: 25) s. the lit. s.v. πνικτός and in BWBacon, The Apost. Decree against πορνεία: Exp. 8th Ser. VII '14, 40–61.
  2. fig., in accordance w. an OT symbol of apostasy fr. God, of idolatry; fr. the time of Hosea the relationship betw. God and his people was regarded as a marriage bond. This usage was more easily understandable because many pagan cults (Astarte, Isis, Cybele et al.) were connected w. sexual debauchery (cf. Hos 6: 10; Jer 3: 2, 9; 4 Km 9: 22) Rv 19: 2. μετανοῆσαι ἐκ τῆς π. αὐτῆς *repent of her immorality* 2: 21; cf. 9: 21. ὁ οἶνος τοῦ θυμοῦ τῆς π. *the wine of her passionate immorality* 14: 8; 18: 3 (on these passages s. θυμός 1 and 2). ὁ οἶνος τῆς π. 17: 2. τὰ ἀκάθαρτα τῆς π. vs. 4 (ἀκάθαρτος 2). M-M.*

πορνεύω fut. πορνεύσω; 1 aor. ἐπόρνευσα (Hdt. +; LXX, Test. 12 Patr.) *to prostitute, practice prostitution* or *sexual immorality* gener.
  1. lit. 1 Cor 10: 8a, b. Distinguished fr. μοιχεύειν 'commit adultery' D 2: 2; B 19: 4; Mk 10: 19 v.l. Regarded as a sin against one's own body 1 Cor 6: 18. W. φαγεῖν εἰδωλόθυτα 'eat meat offered to idols' Rv 2: 14, 20.
  2. fig. (Phalaris, Ep. 121, 1) in the sense 'practice idolatry' (πορνεία 2 and cf. Hos 9: 1; Jer 3: 6; Ezk 23: 19; 1 Ch 5: 25; Ps 72: 27; En. 8, 2) Rv 17: 2; 18: 3, 9. M-M.*

πόρνη, ης, ἡ (since Aristoph. and X., Mem. 1, 5, 4; PSI 352, 4 [254/3 BC]; POxy. 528, 18 [II AD]; BGU 1024 VI, 4; LXX, Philo. Loanw. in rabb.) *prostitute, harlot*.
  1. lit. (since Aristoph. 109 + 110, 26 D.²) Lk 15: 30 (cf. Pr 29: 3; Test. Levi 14: 5 μετὰ πορνῶν); 1 Cor 6: 15. Of Rahab (Josh 2: 1; 6: 17, 23, 25) Hb 11: 31; Js 2: 25; 1 Cl 12: 1 (a πόρνη rewarded for a rescue also in Neanthes [200 BC]: 84 fgm. 9 Jac.). W. tax-collectors as the lowest class of people, morally speaking Mt 21: 31f. W. flute-girls GOxy 36. κολλᾶσθαι τῇ π. *have to do with a prostitute* (Sir 19: 2) 1 Cor 6: 16.
  2. fig. (s. πορνεία 2 and πορνεύω 2; Is 1: 21; 23: 15f; Jer 3: 3; Ezk 16: 30f, 35) as the designation of a government that is hostile to God and his people Rv 17: 15f. ἡ πόρνη ἡ μεγάλη vs. 1; 19: 2. Βαβυλὼν (q.v.) ἡ μεγάλη ἡ μήτηρ τῶν πορνῶν 17: 5.—For the woman sitting on the beast cf. Cebes 5, 1, a beautifully adorned woman sitting on a throne. She is called 'Απάτη, ἡ ἐν τῇ χειρὶ ἔχει ποτήριόν τι, from which she gives men to drink (ποτίζει Cebes 5, 2 as Rv 14: 8), in order to lead them astray (πλανάω as Rv 18: 23).—FHauck and SSchulz, TW VI 579–95: πόρνη and related words. M-M. B. 1368.*

πόρνος, ου, ὁ (Aristoph., X. + in the sense 'male prostitute', etc.; Sir 23: 17; Philo, Leg. All. 8) in our lit. quite gener. *fornicator, one who practices sexual immorality* 1 Cor 5: 9, 11; Hb 12: 16. οἱ π. τοῦ κόσμου τούτου the (sexually) *immoral persons in this world* 1 Cor 5: 10. W. other sinners Eph 5: 5; 1 Ti 1: 10; Rv 21: 8; 22: 15. Differentiated fr. an adulterer 1 Cor 6: 9; Hb 13: 4. Excluded fr. the Kgdm. of God, w. others guilty of grave sins 1 Cor 6: 9 (= Pol 5: 3). M-M.*

πόρρω adv. (Pla., X. +; LXX; Ep. Arist. 31.—Thackeray p. 123; Bl-D. §34, 2) *far (away)*.
  1. used as an adv. 1 Cl 3: 4; Hv 3, 6, 1. π. εἶναι *be far away* (Bl-D. §434, 1; Rob. 546) Lk 14: 32. π. ἀπό (En. 32, 4; Jos., Vi. 281): π. γίνεσθαι ἀπό τινος *be or remain far from someone or someth.* fig. (cf. Bar 3: 21) 1 Cl 23: 3; 30: 3; 39: 9 (Job 5: 4). π. ἀπέχειν ἀπό τινος *be far removed fr. someone,* fig. Mt 15: 8; Mk 7: 6; 1 Cl 15: 2; 2 Cl 3: 5 (all four Is 29: 13).
  2. used as an improper prep. w. gen. (Isocr., Ep. 6, 13 κινδύνων π.; Περὶ ὕψους p. 34, 15 V.; Ael Aristid. 28, 103 K. = 49 p. 525 D.; π. θεῶν; Philo, Op. M. 63; Jos., Ant. 7, 71, Vi. 167) ὧν μακρὰν καὶ πόρρω πραΰτης B 20: 2.—As comp. of the adv. we have in the text of Lk 24: 28 πορρώτερον (Aristot. +), and as v.l. πορρωτέρω (X., Pla.; Jos., Bell. 4, 108, Vi. 326.—Thumb 77): πορρ. πορεύεσθαι *go farther.* M-M. B. 868.*

πόρρωθεν adv. (Pla. +; LXX; KDieterich, Untersuchungen zur Gesch. der griech. Sprache 1898, 183f) *from a distance* (Aeneas Tact. 540; 1199; Diod. S. 1, 83, 4; Jos., Bell. 3, 113; 4, 157, Ant. 3, 9) Hb 11: 13. W. substitution of one concept for another *from a distance = at a distance*

(Herodian 2, 6, 13 π. ἑστῶτες) οἳ ἔστησαν πόρρωθεν *who stood at a distance* (ἵστημι II 1a) Lk 17: 12 (Aesop, Fab. 1 P. = 5 H. πόρρωθεν στᾶσα). οἱ πόρρωθεν *those who are at a distance* (Jos., Bell. 3, 394) B 9: 1 (Is 33: 13). M-M.*

πορρώτερον and **πορρωτέρω** s. πόρρω, end.

πορφύρα, ας, ἡ (Aeschyl., Hdt. +; inscr., pap., LXX, Ep. Arist.; Philo, Congr. Erud. Gr. 117; Jos., Bell. 6, 390; Test. Levi 8: 7. Loanw. in rabb.) the purple fish (a shellfish, murex), then a purple dye obtained fr. it, finally the cloth, clothing, etc. In our lit. only in the last-named sense (so Aeschyl. +; Aristot., Polyb., Lucian; Jos., Ant. 8, 185; Ep. Arist. 320; LXX) *purple (cloth)* w. βύσσος (q.v.) Lk 16: 19. *Purple garment* (Appian, Liby. 66, 297) w. τὸ βύσσινον (s. βύσσινος and cf. Joseph and Aseneth 5, 6 πορφύρα ἐκ βύσσου χρυσοϋφής) Rv 18: 12. Cf. 17: 4 t.r. Of the red garment which the soldiers put on Jesus Mk 15: 17, 20; GP 3: 7 (Appian, Bell. Civ. 2, 150 the Roman soldier's cloak is called ἡ πορφύρα; cf. χλαμύς.—Dio Chrys. 4, 71 and Jos., Ant. 11, 256; 257 of a royal purple garment; cf. 1 Macc 10: 62).—Lit. s. on κόκκινος, also RGradwohl, Die Farben im AT, Beih. ZAW 83, '63, 66–73 and lit. M-M.*

πορφυρόπωλις, ιδος, ἡ (the fem., found in CIG 2519 [where it is restored, but is surely correct], and PFlor. 71, 641 [IV AD] of πορφυροπώλης, ου, ὁ [e.g. Inschr. v. Hierap. 156; Sb]=dealer in purple [woolen] cloth [cf. WASchmidt, Forschungen aus dem Gebiete des Altertums I 1842, 163ff]) *a (woman) dealer in purple cloth*, of Lydia of Thyatira (s. Θυάτιρα) at Philippi Ac 16: 14. M-M.*

πορφυροῦς, ᾶ, οῦν (the form preferred in Attic Gk., also in LXX, Joseph. [e.g. Bell. 7, 124, Ant. 10, 235; Schmidt 492] for the older [Hom. +; Dit., Syll.³ 999, 5; Sib. Or. 3, 659] πορφύρεος, έα, εον) *purple in color* ἱμάτιον πορφυροῦν (Diod. S. 2, 59, 4; Num 4: 14; EpJer 11; cf. PRyl. 151, 14 [40 AD] χιτῶνα πορφυροῦν) *a purple cloak* J 19: 2, 5. Subst. τὸ πορφυροῦν (i.e. ἱμάτιον) *purple clothing* w. κόκκινον (s. κόκκινον) Rv 17: 4; cf. 18: 16.—GEuler, πορφυροῦς, purpureus, Progr. Weilburg '07. M-M.*

ποσάκις adv. (Pla. +; POxy. 528, 24; LXX; Test. Jos. 3: 1) *how many times? how often?* Mt 18: 21; 23: 37; Lk 13: 34. M-M.*

πόσις, εως, ἡ (Hom. +; BGU 1191, 3 [I BC]; Theban Ostraca '13, no. 3, 1) in our lit. always w. βρῶσις (as Da 1: 10).
1. *drinking, the act of drinking* (Hdt. 1, 172; Pla., Leg. 1 p. 637D al.) lit. βρῶσις καὶ πόσις (βρῶσις 1) Ro 14: 17; Col 2: 16.
2. *a drink*, that which one drinks (Aeneas Tact. 589; Da 1: 10; Philo, Op. M. 38) of Jesus' blood ἀληθής ἐστιν πόσις J 6: 55. M-M.*

πόσος, η, ον (Aeschyl. +; inscr., pap., LXX, Joseph.) a correlative pron. in dir. and indir. questions.
1. *how great (?)* in the sing. Ac 22: 28 D (indir.); 1 Cl 56: 16 (indir.). Placed after the word τὸ σκότος πόσον; *how great must the darkness be?* Mt 6: 23. πόσ. χρόνος ἐστίν; *how long is it?* Mk 9: 21 (on πόσ. χρόν. cf. Soph., Oed. R. 558; Pla., Rep. 7 p. 546A). In an exclamation (Appian, Mithrid. 58 §237 πόσην ὠμότητα, πόσην ἀσέβειαν!—Bl-D. §304; Rob. 741) πόσην κατειργάσατο ὑμῖν σπουδήν *how much zeal it has called forth in you!* 2 Cor 7: 11. πόσῳ; *to what degree? how much?* πόσῳ διαφέρει ἄνθρωπος προβάτου; Mt 12: 12. W. a comp. foll. (Poly-

aenus 3, 9, 25 πόσῳ φοβερώτεροι;) πόσῳ δοκεῖτε χείρονος ἀξιωθήσεται τιμωρίας; *how much greater a punishment do you think one will deserve?* Hb 10: 29. πόσῳ μᾶλλον; *how much more?* (PFlor. 170, 8 [III AD] εἰ ... πόσῳ μᾶλλον = if ... how much more; Syntipas 19, 15; Jos., Bell. 2, 365; Diod. S. 1, 2, 2 [Loeb]) Mt 7: 11; 10: 25; Lk 11: 13; 12: 24, 28; J 13: 14 v.l.; Ro 11: 12, 24; Phlm 16; Hb 9: 14; B 19: 8; D 4: 8; IEph 5: 1f; 16: 2. πόσῳ μᾶλλον οὐ; *how much less?* (Ps.-Clem., Hom. 10, 20) 2 Cl 17: 1.—JBonsirven, Exégèse rabbinique et exégèse paulinienne '39; HMüller, Der rabbinische Qal-Wachomer-Schluss in paul. Typologie (Ro 5), ZNW 58, '67, 73–92.
2. *how much, how many(?)*—a. w. a noun in the pl. (Aeschin. 2, 95; X., Mem. 1, 2, 35; 2 Km 19: 35) πόσους ἄρτους ἔχετε; *how many loaves do you have?* Mt 15: 34; Mk 6: 38; 8: 5. Cf. Mt 16: 9, 10; Mk 8: 19, 20; Lk 15: 17 (exclam. like Ps 118: 84); Ac 21: 20 (Jos., Ant. 7, 318 πόσαι μυριάδες εἰσὶ τοῦ λαοῦ); 2 Cl 1: 3.
b. without a noun—α. in the pl. πόσοι *how many?* (Ps.-Clem., Hom. 9, 18; 10, 23) Hs 8, 6, 1.—πόσα; *how many things?* (Ps.-Clem., Hom. 9, 18) Mt 27: 13; Mk 15: 4.
β. in the sing. πόσον; *how much?* (BGU 893, 26 ἐπύθετο, πόσον ἔχει) πόσον ὀφείλεις; Lk 16: 5, 7. M-M.*

ποσότης, ητος, ἡ (Aristot., Metaph. 1028a, 19; Polyb. 16, 12, 10 al.; inscr., pap., Philo) *greatness in degree or number, quantity, amount* w. καλλονή 1 Cl 35: 3. συμψηφίζειν τὴν π. τῆς δαπάνης *estimate the amount of the cost* Hs 5, 3, 7.*

ποταμός, οῦ, ὁ (Hom. +; inscr., pap., LXX, En., Ep. Arist., Philo, Joseph., Sib. Or.) *river, stream.*
1. lit., of the Jordan (Jos., Ant. 20, 97, Vi. 399; Sib. Or. 6, 5) Mt 3: 6; Mk 1: 5. Of the Euphrates (s. Εὐφράτης) Rv 9: 14; 16: 12. Of the Tiber (Sib. Or. 5, 170) Hv 1, 1, 2a, b; on the other hand, the ποταμός of 1, 1, 3 cannot be identified (cf. Hdb. ad loc.). ἦν π. ἕλκων ἐκ δεξιῶν (ἕλκω 2) B 11: 10. Cf. Ac 16: 13; 2 Cor 11: 26; Rv 8: 10; 12: 15f; 16: 4.—Lk 6: 48 ὁ ποταμός means a river near the house in question. On the other hand, in the parallel Mt 7: 25, 27 οἱ ποταμοί are to be understood as the *mountain torrents* or *winter torrents* which arise in ravines after a heavy rain and carry everthing before them (so the pl. in Heraclit. Sto. 38 p. 55, 9; Quint. Smyrn. [400 AD] 8, 384; 14, 5). The *river of living water* in the heavenly Jerusalem Rv 22: 1; cf. vs. 2.
2. The pl. of large amounts of flowing water. Fig. ποταμοὶ ἐκ τῆς κοιλίας αὐτοῦ ῥεύσουσιν ὕδατος ζῶντος *streams of living water will flow from his* (the Redeemer's —s. κοιλία 3) *body* J 7: 38 (scripture quot. of unknown orig. Cf. Hdb. ad loc.; Bultmann 229, 2; LKöhler, Kleine Lichter '45, 39–41; CGoodwin, JBL 63, '54, 72f). M-M. B. 42.*

ποταμοφόρητος, ον (PAmh. 85, 16 [78 AD]; PTebt. 610; PStrassb. 5, 10; PFlor. 368, 12 al. in pap.) *swept away by a river, overwhelmed by a stream* ἵνα αὐτὴν π. ποιήσῃ *that he might sweep her away with the stream* i.e. drown her Rv 12: 15.—AWikenhauser, BZ 6, '08, 171; 7, '09, 48. M-M.*

ποταπός, ή, όν a substitute for the older ποδαπός (the latter occurs Aeschyl., X., Pla. +; Jos., Bell. 4, 169, Ant. 6, 345; so D Mk 13: 1; Lk 1: 29; 7: 39; s. Lob., Phryn. p. 56f), but only in the sense (quotable for ποδαπός Demosth. +) *of what sort* or *kind* (Dionys. Hal.; Lucian; Philo; Jos., Bell. 2, 32, C. Ap. 1, 255 al.; POxy. 1678, 16

[III AD]; Sus 54 LXX; Bl-D. §298, 3; Rob. 741) of persons Mt 8: 27; 2 Pt 3: 11; Hs 8, 6, 3. τίς καὶ ποταπὴ ἡ γυνή who and what kind of woman Lk 7: 39 (cf. Jos., Ant. 7, 72). ποταποὶ τὴν μορφήν what kind of form they have AP 2: 5.—Of things Lk 1: 29; Hv 3, 4, 3; s 4: 3; 6, 3, 4. Somet. the context calls for the mng. how great, how wonderful Mk 13: 1a, b; how glorious 1 J 3: 1.—In ποταπαί... εἰσὶν αἱ πονηρίαι; Hm 8: 3 ποταπαί is simply=τίνες: what are the vices? M-M.*

ποταπῶς adv. of ποταπός (q.v.) in what way, how Ac 20: 18 D.*

πότε interrog. adv. of time (Hom.+; inscr., pap., LXX; Jos., Vi. 374) when(?) predom. in direct questions, but also in indirect: Mt 24: 3 (perh. indir.); 25: 37-9, 44; Mk 13: 4 (perh. indir.), 33 (indir.), 35 (indir.); Lk 12: 36 (indir.); 17: 20 (indir.); 21: 7; J 6: 25; 2 Cl 12: 2 (indir.; apocryphal saying of Jesus); B 12: 1 (prophetic quot. of uncertain orig.); Hv 1, 1, 7; 3, 6, 6. Elliptic (indir.) εἴρηκεν πότε he has told (us) when (it will happen) B 6: 19. ἕως π.; (LXX.—Jos., Ant. 2, 309 ἄχρι π.) how long?, lit. until when? Mt 17: 17a, b; Mk 9: 19a, b; Lk 9: 41; J 10: 24; Rv 6: 10; Hv 3, 6, 5. ἀπὸ πότε since Mk 8: 2 D (Bl-D. §203). M-M.*

ποτέ enclitic particle (Hom.+; pap., LXX)—1. of time at some time or other of the past once, formerly (Jos., Bell. 7, 112) J 9: 13; Ro 7: 9; 11: 30; Gal 1: 13, 23; Eph 2: 2f al.— Of the future (Appian, Bell. Civ. 3, 63 §257=at last; Jos., Bell. 5, 19) σύ ποτε ἐπιστρέψας when once you (will) have turned Lk 22: 32.—ποτὲ μὲν—ποτὲ δέ now—now, at times—at times (X., Mem. 4, 2, 32; Pla., Theaet. 170c; Diod. S. 1, 32, 2; 2, 59, 5; Wsd 16: 18f) B 10: 7 (on ποτὲ —νῦν [νυνί] δέ, s. νῦν 1). On ἤδη ποτέ now at last Ro 1: 10; Phil 4: 10; 2 Cl 13: 1 s. ἤδη 1c.—After negatives ever οὐ...ποτέ not...ever, never 2 Pt 1: 21; IRo 2: 1. οὔτε... ποτέ...οὔτε 1 Th 2: 5; MPol 17: 2. οὐδεὶς ποτε Eph 5: 29 (X., Mem. 1, 4, 19 μηδέν ποτε) οὐ μὴ...ποτέ 2 Pt 1: 10. On μή ποτε s. μήποτε. In rhetorical questions that expect a neg. answer τίς... ποτέ; 1 Cor 9: 7. Cf. Hb 1: 5, 13.
2. indicating a supposition I presume ἐν τῇ φιλοξενίᾳ εὑρίσκεται ἀγαθοποίησις ποτε Hm 8: 10. Cf. s 5, 5, 4.
3. generalizing, after relatives ever ὅσοι ποτέ whatever, whoever Hs 9, 6, 7; 9, 28, 3. On ὁποῖοί ποτε ἦσαν Gal 2: 6 s. ὁποῖος and cf. Epict. 2, 20, 5 τίνες ποτέ;—οἱ Ἀκαδημαϊκοὺς αὐτοὺς λέγοντες=who were they then?— Those who call themselves Academics. M-M.

πότερος, α, ον (Hom.+) in out lit. (and in the LXX where, however, it is found only in Job; Thackeray p. 192) only in the fixed form πότερον as an interrog. word (Bl-D. §64, 6; 298, 1; Rob. 741; 1177) in a disjunctive question πότερον —ἤ whether—or whether (Pind.; X., Mem. 2, 7, 4; Appian, Bell. Civ. 3, 53 §220; Dit., Syll.³ 977, 24; 29 ἐπερωτᾷ πότερον—ἤ; 987, 14; 19; PTebt. 289, 6 [23 AD]; Job 7: 12; Jos., Ant. 6, 71, C. Ap. 2, 120) J 7: 17; B 19: 5; D 4: 4; Hs 9, 28, 4. M-M.*

ποτήριον, ου, τό (Alcaeus, Sappho, Hdt.+; inscr., pap., LXX; Ep. Arist. 293; Jos., Ant. 8, 48) cup, drinking-vessel.
1. lit. Mt 23: 25f; Mk 7: 4, 8 v.l.; Lk 11: 39. π. χρυσοῦν (Lind. Tempelchr. B, 42) Rv 17: 4. W. gen. of its contents: π. ὕδατος Mk 9: 41. π. ψυχροῦ a cup of cold water Mt 10: 42 (on the ellipsis cf. Bl-D. §241, 7; Rob. 1202). Oft. in the language of the Lord's Supper λαβὼν ποτήριον Mt 26: 27; Mk 14: 23; cf. Lk 22: 17, [20a]; 1 Cor 11: 25a; IPhld 4;

D 9: 2.—The cup stands, by metonymy, for what it contains (Pr 23: 31) [Lk 22: 20b]; 1 Cor 11: 25b, 26 (τὸ ποτ. corresponds to τὸν ἄρτον).—ἐκ τοῦ ποτηρίου πίνειν vs. 28 (Alcaeus 34 D.²). τὸ ποτήριον τῆς εὐλογίας (εὐλογία 4) 1 Cor 10: 16. W. gen. of the pers. who bestows the drink (τὸ) ποτήριον (τοῦ) κυρίου πίνειν vs. 21a; 11: 27. Opp. ποτήριον δαιμονίων 10: 21b (FJDölger, D. Kelch der Dämonen: Antike u. Christentum IV '34, 266-70).
2. fig. (in the OT ποτήριον is an expr. for destiny in both good and bad senses. On the concept of drinking a cup of suffering cf. Is 51: 17, 22; La 4: 21; Ps 10: 6; 74: 9. —WLotz, D. Sinnbild des Bechers: NKZ 28, '17, 396-407; F-JLeenhardt, Le Sacrement de la Sainte Cène '48, 43-5) of undergoing a violent death; first of Christ himself τὸ ποτήριον ὃ δέδωκέν μοιο πατήρ οὐ μὴ πίω αὐτό; shall I not drink the cup which the Father has given me? J 18: 11. Cf. Mt 20: 22; 26: 39, 42 t.r.; Mk 10: 38; 14: 36 (CEB Cranfield, ET 59, '47/'48, 137f; DDaube, A Prayer Pattern in Judaism, Studia Evangelica 73, '59, 539-45); Lk 22: 42. The martyrdom of a Christian is corresp. described as a λαβεῖν μέρος ἐν τῷ ποτηρίῳ τοῦ Χριστοῦ share in the cup of Christ MPol 14: 2. Cf. Mt 20: 23; Mk 10: 39 (s. on these pass. ESchwartz, Über den Tod der Söhne Zebedaei: GGAbh. n.s. VII 5, '04, NGG '07, 266ff, ZNW 11, '10, 89-104; FSpitta, ibid. 39-58; ChBruston, Revue de Théol. et des Quest. rel. 19, '10, 338-44, RHPhr 5, '25, 69-71; VWeber, Der Katholik 92, '12, 434-45; JHBernard, ET 39, '28, 456-8).—On τὸ ποτήριον τοῦ οἴνου τοῦ θυμοῦ τῆς ὀργῆς αὐτοῦ Rv 16: 19 cf. θυμός 1 and 2. On the pass. belonging w. it, i.e. Rv 14: 10; 18: 6 cf. κεράννυμι 1. M-M. B. 348.*

ποτίζω impf. ἐπότιζον; 1 aor. ἐπότισα; pf. πεπότικα. Pass.: impf. ἐποτιζόμην B 7: 3 (Hs 9, 1, 8; 9, 25, 1 are prob. mid., s. 4 below); 1 aor. ἐποτίσθην; pf. ptc. πεποτισμένος (Hippocr., X.+; inscr., pap., LXX, Philo) make it possible for someone or someth. to drink.
1. of persons give to drink τινά to someone Mt 25: 35, 37, 42; 27: 48; Mk 15: 36; Ro 12: 20 (Pr 25: 21). W. double acc. cause someone to drink someth., τινά τι π. give someone someth. to drink (Pla., Phaedr. 247E; Gen 19: 32; Judg 4: 19a; 1 Km 30: 11 al.; Bl-D. §155, 7; Rob. 484) water (ποτίζειν τινὰ ποτήριον as Jer 16: 7) Mt 10: 42; Mk 9: 41. χολὴν μετὰ ὄξους GP 5: 16; B 7: 5. As a symbol π. τινὰ γάλα give someone milk to drink 1 Cor 3: 2 (οὐ βρῶμα is added in zeugma; Bl-D. §479, 2; Rob. 1200f). Instead of the acc. of the thing we have ἔκ τινος Rv 14: 8 (symbol.). Pass. be given (someth.) to drink w. dat. of the thing (for the act. w. the dat. of the thing s. Dit., Or. 200, 16; Cebes 5, 2; 3 Macc 5: 2) ἐποτίζετο ὄξει καὶ χολῇ he was given vinegar and gall to drink B 7: 3. Also acc. of the thing (Bl-D. §159, 1; Rob. 485) symbol. (cf. e.g. Sir 15: 3; Is 29: 10) πάντες ἓν πνεῦμα ἐποτίσθημεν we have all been made to drink (or been imbued with) the same Spirit 1 Cor 12: 13.
2. of animals water (Diod. S. 19, 94, 9; Polyaenus 6, 4, 2; Dit., Or. 483, 169; oft. LXX) Lk 13: 15.—3. of plants water (X., Symp. 2, 25 al.; Ezk 17: 7; Kleopatra l. 93 τ. βοτάνας. The sense 'irrigate' a field, garden, etc. is much more common; oft. so in pap., LXX) τὰς ῥάβδους the sticks that have been planted Hs 8, 2, 9a. Pass. 8, 2, 9b (ὕδατι); 8, 3, 8. Abs., symbolically of the founding of a church, w. φυτεύειν (as Hs 8, 3, 8) 1 Cor 3: 6-8.
4. mid. water oneself, drink πᾶν γένος τῆς κτίσεως τοῦ κυρίου ἐποτίζοντο ἐκ τῶν πηγῶν Hs 9, 1, 8; cf. 9, 25, 1. M-M.*

Ποτίολοι, ων, οἱ (Strabo 5, 4, 6; Porphyr., Vi. Plot. 2; Jos., Ant. 18, 161, Vi. 16; inscr. [Dit., Or. II 595b index]; on the spelling cf. Bl-D. §41, 1; Mlt.-H. 76) *Puteoli,* a city on the Gulf of Naples in Italy. Paul landed there on his journey to Rome, and stayed for a week w. the Christians there Ac 28: 13. M-M.*

ποτόν, οὗ, τό (Hom.+; PSI 64, 21 [I вc]; PGiess. 19, 6; LXX, Philo; Jos.; Bell. 3, 183, Ant. 1, 245f; Sib. Or. 3, 746. Subst. neut. of ποτός, ή, όν=drinkable) *drink* w. τροφή (food and) *drink* (Longus 2, 7, 4; Jos., Ant. 7, 159) gener. D 10: 3a, then of the Eucharist πνευματικὴ τροφὴ καὶ ποτόν 3b. Pl. βρώματα καὶ ποτά (βρῶμα 1 and cf. PSI loc. cit. μήτε ἐν ποτοῖς μήτε ἐν βρωτοῖς; Ep. Arist. 128 al.) ITr 2: 3. Also σιτία καὶ ποτά (cf. Hdt. 5, 34, 1; X., An. 7, 1, 33; oft. Philo) Dg 6: 9.*

πότος, ου, ὁ (X., Pla. et al.; LXX; Ep. Arist. 262; Philo, Vi. Cont. 46; Jos., Ant. 5, 289; Test. Jud. 8: 2) *drinking,* esp. *a drinking party, carousal* pl. (Aristoph., Pla. et al.; Pr 23: 30) w. κῶμοι (q.v. and Synes., Providence 1, 14 p. 107c) 1 Pt 4: 3. M-M.*

ποῦ interrog. adv. of place (Hom.+; inscr., pap., LXX; Jos., Ant. 10, 156 al.; Sib. Or. 5, 67 al.).
1. *where(?), at which place(?)*—a. in direct questions Mt 2: 2; 26: 17; Mk 14: 12, 14; Lk 17: 17, 37; 22: 9, 11; J 1: 38; 7: 11; 8: 10, 19; 9: 12; 11: 34. In rhetorical questions that expect a neg. answer *where is?* (Il. 5, 171; Diod. S. 14, 67, 1 ποῦ . . . ; ποῦ . . . ; Lucian, Dial. Deor. 4, 4) Lk 8: 25; Ro 3: 27; 1 Cor 1: 20a, b, c (ποῦ in several direct questions consecutively as Libanius, Or. 61 p. 337, 18 F.); 12: 17a, b, 19; 15: 55a, b (Hos 13: 14a, b); Gal 4: 15; 1 Pt 4: 18 (Pr 11: 31); 2 Pt 3: 4.
b. in indir. questions instead of ὅπου w. indic. foll. (En. 12, 1b) Mt 2: 4; Mk 15: 47; J 1: 39; 11: 57; 20: 2, 13, 15; Rv 2: 13. W. subj. foll.: οὐκ ἔχειν ποῦ (Epict. 2, 4, 7) *have no place, have nowhere* Mt 8: 20; Lk 9: 58; 12: 17.
2. (for ποῖ, which is not found in Bibl. Gk.; s. it) *where(?), whither(?), to what place(?)* (Antiphon 2, 4, 8; X., Cyr. 1, 2, 16; Epict. [index Sch.]; Vett. Val. 137, 35; 341, 6; Alciphr. 4, 13, 2; Gen 16: 8; Judg 19: 17; Jdth 10: 12; 1 Macc 3: 50; En.—Kühner-G. I 545, 4; Bl-D. §103; Rob. 298; AMaidhof, Z. Begriffsbestimmung der Koine: Beiträge zur histor. Syntax der Griech. Sprache 20, '12, 298ff).
a. in direct questions (Cebes 6, 2; 20, 1; En. 102, 1) J 7: 35; 13: 36; 16: 5 (cf. the pagan amulet in ABarb, Der Österreich. Limes XVI 54f ποῦ ὑπάγεις; also Rtzst., ARW 24, '26, 176-8); 1 Cl 28: 2, 3 (Ps 138: 7), 4.
b. in indir. questions (En. 12, 1a) J 3: 8; 8: 14a, b; 12: 35; 14: 5; Hb 11: 8; 1 J 2: 11; IPhld 7: 1; Hm 12, 5, 4. M-M.**

πού enclitic adv. (Hom.+; pap., LXX)—1. of place *somewhere* w. quotations (Diod. S. 1, 12, 10 'the poet' [=Homer] says που κατὰ τὴν ποίησιν=somewhere in his poem. Of Cercidas [111 вc] [ed. Diehl² fgm. 11a, 4] ὀρθῶς λέγει που Κερκίδας [quot. follows]. Lucian, Ver. Hist. 2, 42 φησὶ γάρ που κἀκεῖνος [i.e. Antimachus IV вc], then a quot.; Appian, Bell. Civ. 1, 97 §452 [with a quot.]; Philo, Ebr. 61 εἶπε γάρ πού τις, and Gen 20: 12 follows) Plut., Mor. 553в) Hb 2: 6; 4: 4; 1 Cl 15: 2; 21: 2; 26: 2; 28: 2; 42: 5. Cf. Papias 2: 4.—After a neg.=*nowhere* Dg 5: 2.
2. indicating a supposition *about, approximately* w. numbers (Paus. 8, 11, 14 περὶ εἴκοσί που σταδίους; Aelian, V.H. 13, 4; Jos., C. Ap. 1, 104) Ro 4: 19.—On δή π., μή π. s. δήπου, μήπου. M-M.*

Πούδης, εντος, ὁ (BGU 455, 4 [I AD] al. in pap.; Jos., Bell. 6, 172) *Pudens,* Roman personal name (the *n* was lost, as on Rom. inscr., because it was nasalized in pronunciation: Bl-D. §41, 2; 54; cf. Mlt.-H. 134). An otherw. unknown Christian 2 Ti 4: 21 (the identification w. the husband of Claudia mentioned CIL VI 15066 is uncertain).—Lghtf., St. Clement I 1890, 76ff; GEdmundson, The Church in Rome '13, 244-9. M-M.*

πούς, ποδός, ὁ (Hom.+; inscr., pap., LXX, Ep. Arist., Philo; Jos., Bell. 1, 621, Ant. 18, 187; Sib. Or. 5, 264; Test. 12 Patr.) *foot.*
1. of persons or (rarely in our lit.) animals, or the strange creatures of Rv—a. lit. Mt 4: 6 (Ps 90: 12); 7: 6; Mk 9: 45a, b al. W. κεφαλή J 20: 12; 1 Cor 12: 21; 1 Cl 37: 5a, b. W. χείρ or χεῖρες (Ps 21: 17) Mt 18: 8a, b; 22: 13; Lk 24: 39, 40 v.l.; J 11: 44; 1 Cor 12: 15 (for the speculation by foot and hand concerning their relation to the whole body cf. Epict. 2, 10, 4). ὑποδήσασθαι τοὺς π. *put shoes on the feet* Eph 6: 15 (the whole expr. is symbolic here). Of listeners and pupils καθῆσθαι παρὰ τοὺς π. τινός *sit at someone's feet* Lk 8: 35; cf. 10: 39. W. at least more than half symbolic mng. ἀνατεθραμμένος παρὰ τοὺς πόδας Γαμαλιήλ Ac 22: 3 (schol. on Pla. 467в παρὰ πόδας τοῦ Σωκράτους). Also half symbolic (Synes., Ep. 17 p. 175c παρὰ πόδας ἀποδίδως τὴν χάριν) ἐτίθουν παρὰ τοὺς πόδας τῶν ἀποστόλων 4: 35; cf. vs. 37; 5: 2. πίπτειν (q.v. 1b⊃) εἰς τοὺς πόδας τινός Mt 18: 29 t.r.; J 11: 32 t.r.; ἔμπροσθεν τῶν ποδῶν τινος Rv 19: 10; ἐπὶ τοὺς πόδ. Ac 10: 25; παρὰ τοὺς π. τινός Lk 8: 41; 17: 16. πρὸς τοὺς π. τινός Mk 5: 22; 7: 25 (προσπίπτειν πρὸς κτλ.); J 11: 32; Ac 5: 10; 10: 25 D (the gen. is easily supplied); Rv 1: 17; Hv 3, 2, 3. προσπίπτειν πρὸς τοὺς π. τινι Ac 16: 29 D. προσκυνεῖν ἐνώπιον (or ἔμπροσθεν) τῶν ποδῶν τινος Rv 3: 9; 22: 8. To wash feet (Gen 18: 4; 19: 2) J 13: 5f, 8-10, 12, 14a, b (λούω 2aβ) 1 Ti 5: 10; cf. Lk 7: 44a.—Cf. HAlmqvist, Plutarch u. d. NT '46, 75. Anoint feet (Anaxandrides Com. [IV вc] 40 μύρῳ . . . ἀλείφει τ. πόδας Καλλιστράτου; Eubulus Com. [IV вc] 90, 5f) Lk 7: 46; cf. vs. 38c; J 12: 3a; cf. 11: 2. Kiss feet: Lk 7: 38c, 45.—In Rv 10: 1 πούς clearly means *leg* (cf. Lucian, Zeuxis 4, Pseudomant. 59 πούς μέχρι τοῦ βουβῶνος [groin]; Achilles Tat. 1, 1, 10; Aëtius p. 86, 2; PGiess. 43, 14; PFlor. 42, 9 and s. Charles, ICC ad loc.).
b. fig.: the one who is vanquished lies beneath the victor's feet (Diod. S. 17, 100, 8 ῥιφέντος ἐπὶ γῆν ἐπιβὰς ἐπὶ τὸν τράχηλον τῷ ποδί=[the victor] placed his foot on the neck of his foe, who had been thrown to the ground) τιθέναι τοὺς ἐχθροὺς ὑποκάτω τῶν ποδῶν σου Mt 22: 44; Mk 12: 36; here Ps 109: 1 is quoted; its wording acc. to the LXX is quoted more exactly as ὑποπόδιον τῶν ποδῶν σου Lk 20: 43; Ac 2: 35; Hb 1: 13; 10: 13; 1 Cl 36: 5; B 12: 10. For this in the same Ps.-quot. τιθ. ὑπὸ τοὺς πόδας (αὐτοῦ) 1 Cor 15: 25 (Plut., Mor. 1197c ὑπὸ πόδας τιθ.). πάντα ὑπέταξεν ὑπὸ τοὺς πόδας αὐτοῦ 1 Cor 15: 27; Eph 1: 22; these passages quote Ps 8: 7, the exact wording of which in the LXX appears in ὑποκάτω τῶν ποδῶν αὐτοῦ Hb 2: 8.—συντρίψει τὸν σατανᾶν ὑπὸ τοὺς πόδας ὑμῶν Ro 16: 20.—The earth as God's footstool (Is 66: 1) ὑποπόδιον τῶν ποδῶν αὐτοῦ (or, as LXX, μου) Mt 5: 35; Ac 7: 49; B 16: 2.—Acc. to a usage common also in the OT (Eur., Hipp. 661, Or. 1217) the feet represent the person who is in motion: οἱ πόδες τῶν θαψάντων *those who have buried* Ac 5: 9. ὀξεῖς οἱ πόδες αὐτῶν ἐκχέαι αἷμα *they are quick to shed blood* Ro 3: 15 (cf. Is 59: 7). τοῦ κατευθῦναι τοὺς πόδας ὑμῶν εἰς ὁδὸν εἰρήνης *to guide us in the way of peace* Lk 1: 79. Cf. Ro 10: 15 (cf. Is 52: 7).

2. of the legs of a couch (so Aristoph.+; Arrian, Anab. 6, 29, 5; Dit., Syll.³ 996, 9f; PLond. 402 II, 27; 30; POxy. 520, 17) Hv 3, 13, 3.

3. the *foot* as a measure of length (Hdt., also inscr., pap.) Hv 4, 1, 6; 4, 2, 1; cf. Ac 7: 5. KWeiss, TW VI 624–32. M-M. B. 243.

πρᾶγμα, ατος, τό (Pind., Hdt.+; inscr., pap., LXX, Ep. Arist., Philo, Joseph., Test. 12 Patr.).

1. *that which is done, deed, thing, event, occurrence* (Jos., Ant. 16, 376; Ps.-Clem., Hom. 9, 5) περὶ τῶν πεπληροφορημένων πραγμάτων *concerning the events that have come about* Lk 1: 1 (cf. Jos., Vi. 40 τ. ἱστορίαν τ. πραγμάτων τούτων ἀναγράφειν, C. Ap. 1, 47). τὸ πρᾶγμα τοῦτο *this deed* Ac 5: 4. ἁγνοὶ τῷ πράγματι *guiltless in the matter* under discussion 2 Cor 7: 11. διὰ δύο πραγμάτων ἀμεταθέτων *through two unchangeable things* (i.e. the promise and the oath) Hb 6: 18.

2. *that which is to be done, undertaking, occupation, task* (Appian, Mithrid. 103 §477 μεγάλα πράγματα= great undertakings; Lucian, Nav. 41; Eccl 3: 1) βιωτικὰ πράγματα *the tasks of every-day life* Hv 3, 11, 3; m 5, 2, 2. ἐν ᾧ ἂν ὑμῶν χρῇζῃ πράγματι *in whatever undertaking she may need you* Ro 16: 2. πλεονεκτεῖν ἐν τῷ πράγματι τὸν ἀδελφόν 1 Th 4: 6 (but s. 6 below). ἄξιον πρᾶγμα *a task that is worthy* ISm 11: 3.—3. *doing, deed, thing* IMg 5: 1; Hv 1, 2, 4.

4. gener. *thing, matter, affair* (Fgm. Iamb. Adesp. 12 Diehl οὐκ ἔστ᾽ ἐμὸν τὸ πρ.; Dio Chrys. 13[7], 53; 16[33], 36; 19[36], 18) περὶ παντὸς πράγματος *about anything at all* Mt 18: 19. Cf. Hb 10: 1; 11: 1 (ROPTaylor, ET 52, '40/'41, 256–9: 'affair'); Hv 3, 4, 1; m 9: 10; 10, 2, 3; s 5, 6, 6; 9, 29, 2. Pl. Hv 3, 3, 1; 4, 1, 4; 4, 3, 1. μέγα π. *something great* Hv 3, 2, 4; cf. s 9, 2, 5; πονηρὸν π. *an evil thing* Hv 1, 1, 8; s 5, 1, 5; 7: 5; πᾶν φαῦλον π. *every evil thing, everything that is evil* Js 3: 16. περιγίνεσθαι τοῦ π. *master the thing* Hv 1, 3, 2. τὰ πρ. *relationships, ways, circumstances* (Diod. S. 14, 97, 3; 19, 50, 2; 19, 52, 1; 6; Appian, Bell. Civ. 5, 3 §12; Artem. 4, 27; Jos., Bell. 4, 318) ἐν παλαιοῖς π. ἀναστραφῆναι *live in old, obsolete ways* IMg 9: 1. Also w. an unfavorable connotation *difficulties, troubles* (Soph., Aj. 314; X., An. 2, 1, 16; 7, 6, 24, Mem. 2, 7, 2; Socrat., Ep. 3; Diod. S. 13, 12, 1; 13, 97, 6; Jos., Ant. 13, 7) 1 Cl 1: 1 (s. ἐπιζητέω 1c).

5. *law-suit, dispute* (X., Mem. 2, 9, 1 al.; Polyaenus 6, 36; Kyr.-Inschr. l. 54; 67; 123. Oft. pap.; Jos., C. Ap. 2, 177) πρᾶγμα ἔχειν πρός τινα *have a law-suit with someone* (POxy. 743, 19 [I ʙᴄ]; 706, 4; BGU 22, 9) 1 Cor 6: 1 (LVischer, Die Auslegungsgeschichte von 1 Cor 6: 1–11, '55).

6. perh. as a euphemism for *illicit sexual conduct* 1 Th 4: 6. M-M and suppl. B. 634.*

πραγματεία, ας, ἡ (Hippocr., X., Pla.+; pap., LXX, Philo; Jos., Ant. 1, 5; 14, 218; loanw. in rabb.) *activity, occupation*, in our lit. only pl. *undertakings, business, affairs* Hm 10, 1, 4; s 9, 20, 1f. αἱ τοῦ βίου π. *the affairs of everyday* (civilian) *life* 2 Ti 2: 4 (Philo, Spec. Leg. 2, 65 αἱ περὶ βίον π.). π. πονηραί Hv 2, 3, 1. Under persecution, leading to denial of Christ v 3, 6, 5; s 8, 8, 2. Enticing people to lie m 3: 5. Separating fr. the saints s 8, 8, 1. M-M.*

πραγματεύομαι mid. dep.; 1 aor. ἐπραγματευσάμην (Hdt.+; inscr., pap., LXX, Philo; Jos., Bell. 2, 594, Ant. 4, 149; 16, 180 al.) *conduct* or *be engaged in a business* (so Plut., Sull. 17, 2, Cato Min. 59, 3; Zen.-P. 32 [= Sb 6738], 11 [255 ʙᴄ]; UPZ 106, 5 [99 ʙᴄ]; BGU 246, 8; PLond.

1674, 84; 1855, 3), also gener. *do business, trade* (Philo, In Flacc. 57) Lk 19: 13. M-M. B. 819.*

πραθείς, πραθῆναι s. πιπράσκω.

πραιτώριον, ου, τό (Lat. loanw.: praetorium. Attested in Gk. in inscr. and pap. Cf. CWessely, Wiener Studien 24, '02, 144; UWilcken, APF 2, '03, 138; 4, '08, 116; 121; Bl-D. §5, 1; Rob. 109) *the praetorium*, orig. the praetor's tent in camp, w. its surroundings. In the course of its history (sketched by MDibelius, exc. on Phil 1: 13) the word also came to designate the governor's official residence (IG XIV 2548 τοῦ ἡγεμονικοῦ πραιτωρίου; Dit., Syll.³ 880, 63; BGU 288, 14; POxy. 471, 110). This is the mng. of the word in the gospels Mt 27: 27; Mk 15: 16; J 18: 28a, b, 33; 19: 9. But it is a matter of dispute whether it refers to the Palace of Herod in the western part of the city (Schürer I⁴ 457 [Engl. tr. I, '73, 361]; REckardt, Das Praetorium des Pilatus: ZDPV 34, '11, 39–48. More recently EKlostermann, FHauck; JBlinzler, Der Prozess Jesu³, '60, 183–6) or to the fortress Antonia northwest of the temple area (so the later trad. and more recently, to some extent, ASchlatter; SMeistermann, Le Prétoire de Pilate et la forteresse Antonia '02; CSachsse, ZNW 19, '20, 34–8; CLattey, JTS 31, '30, 180–2). Cf. also Dalman, Orte³ 355–63; HVincent, L'Antonia et le Prétoire: RB 42, '33, 83–113, Autour du Prétoire: ibid. 46, '37, 563–70. In Caesarea, at any rate, the Palace of Herod served as the 'praetorium'. Paul was imprisoned ἐν τῷ πραιτωρίῳ τοῦ Ἡρῴδου Ac 23: 35. ELohmeyer (Phil '30, 3; 40f) places Phil 1: 13 here; this conclusion is variously regarded, depending on one's conception of the place where Paul was imprisoned. If the letter was written fr. Rome, the words ἐν ὅλῳ τῷ πραιτωρίῳ are best taken to mean *in the whole praetorian* (or *imperial*) *guard* (EHaupt, PEwald, FTillmann). If it belongs to a non-Roman imprisonment, τὸ πραιτώριον beside οἱ λοιποί includes those who live in the governor's palace (s. PFeine [s.v. Φίλιπποι] p. 72f; 88 and the other lit. given there). M-M.*

πράκτωρ, ορος, ὁ (Aeschyl.+; Is 3: 12) a t.t. designating certain officials, esp. tax-collectors and other finance officials (Antiphon+; inscr., pap. [Dssm., B 152–BS 154; BGU 530, 36 al.]. Also oft. Sb [word-list sect. 8 p. 339]). In Lk 12: 58a, b, the only place where it occurs in our lit., the word refers to a court functionary who is under the judge's orders, someth. like a *bailiff* or *constable*, who is in charge of the debtor's prison (πρακτόρειον: Dit., Or. 669, 15; 17. In UPZ 118, 15; 24 πρ. is the constable; it is his duty, after sentence is passed, to collect [by force, if necessary] debts, under orders fr. the judge. The τοῦ κριτηρίου ὑπηρέτης 'servant of the court' l. 18 is differentiated fr. him). M-M.*

πρᾶξις, εως, ἡ (Hom.+; inscr., pap., LXX, Ep. Arist., Philo, Joseph., Test. 12 Patr.).

1. *acting, activity, function* κατὰ τὴν πρᾶξιν αὐτοῦ *in accordance with his activity* or *what he did* Mt 16: 27. τὰ μέλη πάντα οὐ τὴν αὐτὴν ἔχει πρᾶξιν *the parts do not all have the same function* Ro 12: 4. ἐν πάσῃ πράξει αὐτοῦ Hm 5, 2, 7; cf. 7: 1; 10: 1.

2. *way of acting, course of action* αὕτη ἡ πρᾶξις ἐπὶ γυναικὶ καὶ ἀνδρὶ κεῖται *this is the proper course of action for the wife and for the husband* Hm 4, 1, 8; cf. 11.

3. *plan of action, undertaking* (Jos., Bell. 1, 230, Vi. 271) περὶ πράξεώς τινος *concerning any undertaking* Hm 11: 4.

4. *act, action, deed*—a. gener. (Diod. S. 10, 19, 5= deed) Hm 10, 2, 2; 10, 2, 4b. ἡ ἀγαθὴ πρᾶξις 1 Cl 30: 7.

μεγάλαι καὶ ἔνδοξοι πράξεις *great and glorious deeds* 19: 2.—This is also the place for the title of Ac πράξεις (ἀποστόλων); cf. 2 Ch 12: 15; 13: 22; 28: 26 and the transl. of Res Gestae Divi Augusti: Inscr. Rom. III 159 πράξεις τε καὶ δωρεαὶ Σεβαστοῦ Θεοῦ; Socrat., Ep. 28, 1 Ἀντίπατρος . . . γράφει τὰς Ἑλληνικὰς πράξεις; Diod. S. 3, 1, 1 of the first two books of Diodorus ἡ πρώτη contains the πράξεις τῶν βασιλέων; 16, 1, 1 πόλεων ἢ βασιλέων πράξεις=the story of cities or kings; Jos., Ant. 14, 68 οἱ τὰς κατὰ Πομπήιον πράξεις ἀναγράψαντες. Also the exx. in AWikenhauser, Die AG '21, 94-104: D. antike Praxeis-Lit. The sing., πρᾶξις (ἀποστόλων), which is also attested, views the deeds collectively, *work.* —For lit. on Ac s. EGrässer, Theolog. Rundschau 26, '60, 91-167.

b. *evil* or *disgraceful deed* (Polyb. 2, 7, 9; 2, 9, 2; 4, 71, 6; Diod. S. 3, 57, 4; 4, 49, 3; 4, 63, 4) Lk 23: 51; Hm 4, 2, 2. Pl. Ro 8: 13; Col 3: 9; Hm 4, 2, 1.—In Ac 19: 18, because of the context, it is poss. that πρᾶξις is specif. a t.t. for certain magical practices (PGM 4, 1227 πρᾶξις γενναία ἐκβάλλουσα δαίμονας. Cf. PGM 1, 276; 4, 159; 1317 and oft.; Ps.-Clem., Hom. 2, 26; Acta Pil. A 1, 1; πράσσειν='practice magic' PGM 3, 125).

5. *undertaking, business* (so Aesop, Fab. 236 P.=312 H.; very oft. in Vett. Val., s. index; PGM 4, 2366; loanw. in rabb.) pl. Hm 6, 2, 5; 10, 1, 4; s 6, 3, 5. αἱ βιωτικαὶ πρ. *the affairs of every-day living* Hv 1, 3, 1 (Lucian, Halc. 5 αἱ κατὰ τὸν βίον πρ.).

6. *state, condition, situation* (Pind., Hdt.+) τὴν πρᾶξιν, ἣν ἔχουσιν ἐν ἑαυτοῖς Hs 9, 26, 8; also in the pl. (Soph., Ant. 1305 κακαὶ πράξεις) ἀπὸ τῶν προτέρων αὐτοῦ πράξεων *from his former condition* Hv 3, 12, 2. ἑτέραις πολλαῖς πράξεσι πάσχοντες *suffering in many other situations* s 6, 3, 4. M-M.**

πρᾶος (without ι subscr.; s. W-S. §5, 11a; Mlt.-H. 84; Mayser 121) s. πραΰς.

πραότης s. πραΰτης.

πρασιά, ᾶς, ἡ (Hom. [πρασιή]+; PTebt. 703, 198 [III BC —πρασιά]; BGU 530, 27 [πρασεά]; Sir 24: 31) lit. *garden plot, garden bed* fig. πρασιαὶ πρασιαί *group by group,* picturing the groups of people contrasted w. the green grass Mk 6: 40 (on the distributive force of the repetition s. Bl-D. §493, 2; Mlt. 97; Rob. 673). M-M.*

πράσσω impf. ἔπρασσον; fut. πράξω; 1 aor. ἔπραξα; pf. πέπραχα. Pass.: 1 aor. ἐπράχθην; pf. ptc. πεπραγμένος (Hom.+ [the Attic form πράττω only Ac 17: 7 t.r.]; inscr., pap., LXX, Ep. Arist., Philo, Joseph., Test. 12 Patr.).

1. trans.—**a.** *do, accomplish* (oft. used without distinction betw. itself and ποιεῖν, as Diod. S. 16, 27, 1 ἔξεστιν αὐτῷ πράττειν ὃ βούλεται. Cf. Ro 1: 32; 2: 3; IMg 7: 1). τί *someth.* προσέχετε ἑαυτοῖς . . . τί μέλλετε πράσσειν Ac 5: 35; πάντα πρ. IMg 4; 6: 1; cf. 7: 1; ITr 2: 2 al. πρᾶξιν πράσσειν (s. also farther below) *do a deed, do someth.* Hs 5, 2, 11; τὰ πνευματικὰ πρ. *do spiritual things* IEph 8: 2a. ἄξια τῆς μετανοίας ἔργα πρ. *do deeds that are consistent with repentance, act in a manner consistent* etc. Ac 26: 20. τὴν δικαιοσύνην 2 Cl 19: 3 (cf. Xenophanes 1, 16 Diehl² τὰ δίκαια πρήσσειν). εἴτε ἀγαθὸν εἴτε φαῦλον 2 Cor 5: 10; cf. Ro 9: 11.—1 Cor 9: 17; Eph 6: 21; Phil 4: 9.—Pass. οὐκ ἔστιν ἐν γωνίᾳ πεπραγμένον τοῦτο Ac 26: 26.—Mostly of actions that are not praiseworthy *do, commit* τὶ *someth.* Lk 22: 23; 23: 15, 41a; Ro 1: 32a, b; 2: 1-3; 7: 15; 2 Cor 12: 21 (ἤ by attraction for ἥν); Gal 5: 21; 1 Cl 35: 6; 2 Cl 4: 5; 10: 5;

Hm 3: 3; D 1: 5 (περὶ ὧν=περὶ τούτων ἅ). τὸ ἔργον τοῦτο πρ. 1 Cor 5: 2 (Herodas 3, 62; cf. 82 ἔργα πράσσειν=commit evil deeds; τὸ ἔργον πρ. as Jos., Vi. 47). τὴν πολυτέλειαν τῶν ἐθνῶν πρ. Hs 1: 10; ἄτοπον τι πρ. Lk 23: 41b (ἄτοπος 2). (τὸ) κακόν (Pr 13: 10 κακά; Jos., Ant. 19, 193) Ro 7: 19; 13: 4. τὸ πονηρόν Hm 10, 2, 4. πονηρά 2 Cl 8: 2; 19: 2. πονηρὰ ἔργα Hs 6, 3, 5; cf. 6. πονηρίαν s 8, 8, 2. προπετές τι Ac 19: 36. (τὰ) φαῦλα J 3: 20; 5: 29. πρᾶξιν πράσσειν *commit a(n evil) deed* (πρᾶξις 4b) Hm 4, 2, 2; 10, 2, 3 (ἤ by attraction for ἥν); pl. Hs 8, 9, 4; 8, 10, 4. ἄλλα τινὰ πράσσοντες ἀνάξια θεοῦ *while doing certain other things unworthy of God* IEph 7: 1. ἄξιον θανάτου πράσσειν τι *do someth. worthy of death* Ac 25: 11, 25; 26: 31; pass. οὐδὲν ἄξιον θανάτου ἐστὶν πεπραγμένον αὐτῷ (*by him,* Bl-D. §191; Rob. 534; cf. Demosth. 29, 1 τὰ τούτῳ πεπραγμένα; Diod. S. 17, 1, 2; Appian, Bell. Civ. 3, 44 §180 τὰ Καίσαρι πεπραγμένα; Charito 2, 5, 8 πέπρακταί σοί τι δεινόν=a terrible deed has been committed by you; Syntipas p. 17, 1 τὰ πραχθέντα μοι; PTebt. 23, 8 [119 or 114 BC] πέπρακταί σοι; Jos., Ant. 14, 161 τὰ Ἡρῴδῃ πεπραγμένα. Other exx. in Mlt.-H. 459; Schmid IV 612) Lk 23: 15. πρὸς τὸ ὄνομα Ἰησοῦ πολλὰ ἐναντία πρᾶξαι Ac 26: 9 (ἐναντία πρ. as X., Cyr. 8, 7, 24). μηδὲν πράξῃς σεαυτῷ κακόν *do yourself no harm* 16: 28.—Ign. is fond of combinations w. κατά and the acc. μηδὲν κατ' ἐριθείαν πρ. IPhld 8: 2; κατὰ θεόν τι πρ. 4; κατὰ σάρκα τι πρ. *do someth. in the* (physical) *body* IEph 8: 2b; likew. 16: 2 *do someth. as a mortal man,* i.e. without sinning against the teaching of the church, as the false teachers do.—More in the sense *practice, busy oneself with, mind* τὶ *someth.* τὰ περίεργα *magic* Ac 19: 19. τὰ ἴδια one's *own affairs* 1 Th 4: 11 (ἴδιος 3 and Soph., El. 678 σὺ μὲν τὰ σαυτῆς πρᾶσσε; X., Mem. 2, 9, 1 τὰ ἑαυτοῦ πρ.). τὰ πολλὰ πρ. *busy oneself with many things* Hs 4: 5; νόμον πρ. *observe the law* Ro 2: 25.

b. of taxes, duties, interest *collect* (Hdt.+; Theophr., Char. 6, 10; inscr., pap., LXX; Jos., Ant. 9, 233 al.) τὶ *someth.* Lk 19: 23. W. a slight connotation in the direction of 'exhort' 3: 13 (cf. Dit., Or. 519, 22 τὰ μὴ ὀφειλόμενα αὐτοῖς παραπράσσουσιν).

2. intr.—**a.** *act* κατὰ ἄγνοιαν πρ. Ac 3: 17; ἀπέναντι τῶν δογμάτων πρ. *act contrary to the decrees* 17: 7. καθὰ πράσσομεν *in our actions* IMg 10: 1. εὖ πράσσειν *act rightly, do well* (cf. POxy. 1067, 3 [III AD] καλῶς πρ. and Appian, Hann. 2, §3 πρ. κακῶς) IEph 4: 2; ISm 11: 3; perh. also Ac 15: 29 (s. εὖ and b below).

b. *be, be situated* (Pind., Hdt.; pap.) εὖ πρ. *be well off* (cf. εὖ) so perh. Ac 15: 29 (s. 2a above). ἵνα εἰδῆτε . . . τί πράσσω *in order that you may know . . . how* (lit. 'in respect to what') *I am getting along* Eph 6: 21 (Soph., Oed. R. 74 τί πράσσει; Pla., Theaet. 174B; BGU 93, 32 δήλωσόν μοι, τί ἔπραξας; 821, 8; Jos., Ant. 6, 176; 19, 239).—CMaurer, TW VI 624-32: πρ. and related words. M-M. B. 537f.**

πραϋπάθεια, ας, ἡ (Philo, Abr. 213; Hesychius explains it by using the words ἡσυχία and πραΰτης as synonyms) *gentleness* 1 Ti 6: 11 (t.r. πραότητα); ITr 8: 1. On the spelling πραϋπαθία, which is poss., cf. κακοπάθεια, -ια Kühner-Bl. II 276, 1; so W-H. See also ADebrunner, Griech. Wortbildungslehre '17, §299. M-M.*

πραΰς, πραεῖα, πραΰ (Hom.+; Crinagoras [I BC/I AD] 8, 4, 46, 4; 51, 6 Rubensohn; PGM 4, 1046; LXX; Jos., Ant. 19, 330; Sib. Or. 4, 159 with v.l.) pl. πραεῖς (on πραΰς and πρᾶος Kühner-Bl. I 532f; Bl-D. §26 app.; Mlt.-H. 160; Thackeray 180f; Crönert 290, 2.—But in our lit.

πρᾶος [2 Macc 15: 12; Philo; Jos., C. Ap. 1, 267] occurs only Mt 11: 29 t.r.) *gentle, humble, considerate, meek* in the older favorable sense (cf. Murray, New [Oxford] Engl. Dict. s.v. 1b), *unassuming* D 3: 7a; Mt 21: 5 (Zech 9: 9). W. ταπεινός (Is 26: 6) Mt 11: 29 (ThHaering, Schlatter-Festschr. '22, 3-15; MRist, Journ. of Religion 15, '35, 63-77). W. ἡσύχιος (and occasionally other characteristics) 1 Pt 3: 4; 1 Cl 13: 4 (cf. Is 66: 2); B 19: 4; Hm 5, 2, 3; 6, 2, 3; 11: 8. Among the qualities required of church officials D 15: 1. πρὸς τὰς ὀργὰς αὐτῶν ὑμεῖς πραεῖς *gentle in the face of their wrath* IEph 10: 2 (cf. PLond. 1912 εἵνα [sic] Ἀλεξανδρεῖς πραέως καὶ φιλανθρόπως [sic] προσφέροντε [=προσφέρωνται] Ἰουδαίοις [letter of Claudius, 41 AD]).—οἱ πραεῖς (Ps 36: 11) Mt 5: 5 (WKLowther Clarke, Theology 47, '44, 131-3); D 3: 7b.—LHMarshall, Challenge of NT Ethics '47, 80ff; 300ff. M-M.*

πραΰτης, ητος, ἡ (Appian, Bell. Civ. 4, 123 §518 διὰ πραΰτητα; Aesop, Fab. 168 P.; CIG 2788; LXX [Thackeray p. 91; 181]; Sextus 545) and the class. (Thu.+; also Appian, Basil. 1 §5; PLond. 1912, 101 [41 AD]; Philo; Jos., Bell. 6, 383, Ant. 19, 334) πραότης, ητος, ἡ (so in Ign. and Hermas, while in the NT πραΰτης is the predom. form and πραότης appears as v.l. For the lit. s. πραΰς) *gentleness, humility, courtesy, considerateness, meekness* in the older favorable sense (s. πραΰς) w. ἐπιείκεια (Plut., Caesar 57, and, occasionally, other qualities, as Lucian, Somn. 10) 2 Cor 10: 1 (RLeivestad, NTS 12, '66, 156-64); 1 Cl 30: 8; Dg 7: 4; cf. Tit 3: 2; 1 Cl 21: 7. W. other virtues (Ps 44: 5) Gal 5: 23; Col 3: 12; Eph 4: 2; B 20: 2; D 5: 2; Hm 12, 3, 1. ἐν π. *with* or *in gentleness* (Sir 3: 17; 4: 8) 2 Ti 2: 25; IPol 2: 1; 6: 2; *with humility* Js 1: 21; 3: 13 (ἐν πραΰτητι σοφίας *in wise gentleness*. Cf. Appian, Bell. Civ. 3, 79 §323 ἐπὶ σοφίᾳ τε καὶ πραότητι); ἐν εἰρήνῃ καὶ π. 1 Cl 61: 2. Also μετὰ π. (so in PLond. above) 1 Pt 3: 16; Hm 5, 2, 6. As a characteristic of a bishop ITr 3: 2. The devil is thwarted by humility 4: 2. πνεῦμα πραΰτητος 1 Cor 4: 21; Gal 6: 1.—AvHarnack, 'Sanftmut, Huld und Demut' in der alten Kirche: JKaftan-Festschr. '20, 113ff; CSpicq, RB 54, '47, 321-39 (χρηστότης, πραΰτης, ἠπιότης, ἐπιείκεια).—FHauck and SSchulz, TW VI, 645-51. M-M.*

πρέπω (Hom.+) *be fitting, be seemly* or *suitable* (Pindar+; inscr., pap., LXX, Philo; Jos., C. Ap. 2, 143) impf. 3 sing. ἔπρεπεν.—τοιοῦτος ἡμῖν ἔπρεπεν ἀρχιερεύς *it was fitting that we should have such a high priest* Hb 7: 26. Cf. 1 Ti 2: 10; Tit 2: 1. μηδὲν ὑμῖν πρεπέτω *let nothing be pleasing to you* IEph 11: 2.—The impers. constr. πρέπει τινί *it is fitting for someone* (X., Hell. 4, 1, 37) καθὼς πρέπει ἁγίοις Eph 5: 3. ὡς πρέπει ἀγαπῶντι B 4: 9. W. dat. and inf. foll. (Charito 7, 6, 12; Philo, Leg. All. 1, 48 πρέπει τῷ θεῷ φυτεύειν) Hb 2: 10; IEph 4: 1; IMg 3: 1; ITr 12: 2; IPol 5: 2. W. inf. foll., in which case the dat. is to be supplied ISm 11: 2; IPol 7: 2.—πρέπον ἐστίν *it is fitting, proper, right* (POxy. 120, 24 ὡς πρέπον ἐστίν; 1 Macc 12: 11; 3 Macc 7: 13) w. dat. of the pers. and inf. foll. (Isocr., Ep. 5, 3) Mt 3: 15; IRo 10: 2; IPhld 10: 1. W. inf. foll. and dat. to be supplied IEph 2: 2; IMg 3: 2; 4: 1; ISm 7: 2. W. acc. and inf. foll. (Lysias 19, 59) 1 Cor 11: 13.—MPohlenz, Τὸ πρέπον: NGG '33, 53-92. M-M. B. 641.*

πρεσβεία, ας, ἡ *embassy*, abstract for concrete *ambassador, ambassadors* (Aristoph., X., Pla.+; inscr., pap.) π. ἀποστέλλειν (Dit., Syll.³ 412, 6 al. [index IV p. 526a]; cf. 2 Macc 4, 11; Philo, Leg. ad Gai. 239; Jos., Ant. 4, 296) Lk 14: 32; 19: 14. πρεσβεύειν θεοῦ πρεσβείαν *travel as*

an ambassador of God IPhld 10: 1 (πρεσβεύειν πρεσβείαν as Philo, Congr. Erud. Gr. 111). M-M.*

πρεσβευτής, οῦ, ὁ (Thu.+; Pla., inscr., pap.) *ambassador* cj. in place of πρεσβύτης (q.v.) Phlm 9.*

πρεσβεύω fut. πρεσβεύσω; 1 aor. ἐπρέσβευσα (trag., Hdt.+) *be an ambassador* or *envoy, travel* or *work as an ambassador* (so Aristoph., X., Pla.+; inscr., pap., Philo; Jos., Ant. 12, 163f, Vi. 65. Used esp. of the emperor's legates: Magie 89; Dssm., LO 320 [LAE 378f]) πέμπειν τινὰ πρεσβεύσοντα περί τινος *send someone as a representative for someone* Pol 13: 1. πρεσβεύειν θεοῦ πρεσβείαν IPhld 10: 1 s. πρεσβεία. Paul speaks of his apostolic work as ὑπὲρ Χριστοῦ πρεσβεύειν *work as an ambassador for Christ* 2 Cor 5: 20; cf. Eph 6: 20 (πρεσβεύειν ὑπέρ τινος: Dit., Or. 339, 6, Syll.³ 591, 5; 656, 19; 805, 7ff). M-M.*

πρεσβυτέριον, ου, τό *council of elders*—1. of the highest Jewish council in Jerusalem, in our lit. usu. called συνέδριον (Schürer II⁴ 245) τὸ πρεσβυτέριον τοῦ λαοῦ Lk 22: 66. ὁ ἀρχιερεὺς καὶ πᾶν τὸ πρ. Ac 22: 5.

2. as a Christian church council, including all the πρεσβύτεροι (s. πρεσβύτερος 2b), *presbytery*. So, except for 1 Ti 4: 14 (JoachJeremias, ZNW 48, '57, 127-32: 'honor' or 'privilege of an elder'; cf. Sus 50 [Theodotion] and rabb.), in our lit. only in Ign.: w. bishop and deacons IMg 13: 1; ITr 7: 2; IPhld 4; 7: 1; ISm 12: 2. W. the bishop IEph 2: 2; 20: 2; IMg 2; ITr 13: 2. Bishop and π. belong together as the strings to the harp IEph 4: 1. The π. is to be obeyed as the apostles ITr 2: 2; ISm 8: 1. The apostles are described as π. ἐκκλησίας IPhld 5: 1.*

πρεσβύτερος, α, ον (Hom.+; inscr., pap., LXX, Ep. Arist., Philo, Joseph. Comp. of πρέσβυς).

1. of age—a. of an individual person *older* of two ὁ υἱὸς ὁ π. (cf. Aelian, V.H. 9, 42) Lk 15: 25; of Manasseh (w. Ephraim) B 13: 5. In contrast to the younger generation οἱ πρεσβύτεροι *the older ones* J 8: 9. Opp. οἱ νεανίσκοι Ac 2: 17 (Jo 3: 1). Opp. νεώτεροι (s. νέος 2bβ) 1 Ti 5: 1 (similar advice, containing a contrast betw. πρ. and νεώτ., from inscr. and lit. in MDibelius, Hdb. ad loc.); 1 Pt 5: 5 (though here the πρεσβύτεροι are not only the older people, but at the same time, the 'elders'; s. 2b below). The same double mng. is found for πρεσβύτεροι in 1 Cl 1: 3 beside νέοι, while in 3: 3; 21: 6, beside the same word, the concept of being old is the dominant one (as Jos., C. Ap. 2, 206). On the disputed pass. Hv 3, 1, 8 (οἱ νεανίσκοι—οἱ πρεσβύτεροι) cf. MDibelius, Hdb. ad loc.—Fem. πρεσβυτέρα *old(er) woman* (opp. νεωτέρα, as Gen 19: 31) 1 Ti 5: 2.—With no ref. to younger persons, w. complete disappearance of the comparative mng.: πρεσβύτερος *an old man* (Jos., Ant. 13, 226; 292 [as a witness of events in the past, as Ps.-Pla., Virt. 3 p. 377B; 4 p. 377C]) Hv 3, 12, 2; cf. 3, 11, 3. The personified church is called λίαν πρεσβυτέρα *very old* Hv 3, 10, 3; cf. 3, 11, 2. She appears as ἡ πρ. *the elderly woman* Hv 2, 1, 3; 3, 1, 2; 3, 10, 6; 9 and has τὰς τρίχας πρεσβυτέρας *the hair of an old woman* v 3, 10, 4; 5; 3, 12, 1.

b. of a period of time (Petosiris, fgm. 3 and 4 mention οἱ πρεσβύτεροι and οἱ νεώτεροι. In both instances the context shows that the reference is to astrologers from earlier and more recent times) οἱ πρεσβύτεροι *the men of old, our ancestors* Hb 11: 2. ἡ παράδοσις τῶν πρεσβυτέρων *the tradition of the ancients* (cf. Iambl., Vi. Pyth. 35, 253 τῶν π. συγγράμματα) Mt 15: 2; Mk 7: 3, 5 (ELohse, D. Ordination im Spätjudentum u. NT, '51, 50-6: *scholars*).

2. as designation of an official (cf. Lat. senator) *elder, presbyter*—**a.** among the Jews (the congregation of a synagogue in Jerusalem used πρεσβύτεροι to denote its officers before 70 AD: Suppl. Epigr. Gr. VIII 170, 9; cf. Dssm., LO 378-80).

α. for members of local councils in individual cities (cf. Josh 20: 4; Ruth 4: 2; 2 Esdr [Ezra] 10: 14; Jdth 8: 10; 10: 6) Lk 7: 3; 1 Cl 55: 4.—Schürer II⁴ 224.

β. for members of a group in the Sanhedrin (Schürer II⁴ 251ff; JoachJeremias, Jerusalem z. Zt. Jesu II B 1: Die gesellschaftl. Oberschicht '29, 88ff). They are mentioned together w. (the) other groups: ἀρχιερεῖς (Ac 4: 5 has ἄρχοντες for this), γραμματεῖς, πρεσβύτεροι (the order is not always the same) Mt 16: 21; 26: 3 t.r.; 27: 41; Mk 8: 31; 11: 27; 14: 43, 53; 15: 1; Lk 9: 22; 20: 1.—Only ἀρχιερεῖς (Ac 4: 8 has for this ἄρχοντες τοῦ λαοῦ) and πρεσβύτεροι (τοῦ λαοῦ: cf. Ex 19: 7; Num 11: 16b, 24; 1 Macc 7: 33; 12: 35) Mt 21: 23; 26: 3, 47, 59 t.r.; 27: 1, 3, 12, 20; 28: (11), 12; Lk 22: 52 (here, as an exception, οἱ στρατηγοὶ τοῦ ἱεροῦ); Ac 4: 23; 23: 14; 25: 15; cf. 24: 1. Also οἱ πρεσβύτεροι καὶ οἱ ἱερεῖς GP 7: 25 (for this combination cf. Jos., Ant. 11, 83; 12, 406).—Only πρεσβύτεροι and γραμματεῖς Mt 26: 57; Ac 6: 12.—The use of πρεσβύτερος as a title among the Jews of the Diaspora appears quite late, except for the allusions in the LXX (cf. Schürer III⁴ 89f; Monumenta As. Min. antiqua III '31 [Cilicia] No. 344; 448 [cf. ZNW 31, '32, 313f]. Whether πρεσβύτερος is to be understood in the older Roman inscriptions [CII 378] as a title [so JBFrey, CII p. LXXXVI], remains doubtful).

b. among the Christians (for their use of the word as a title one must bear in mind not only the Jewish custom, but also its use as a t.t. among the ἔθνη, in connection w. associations of the 'old ones' [FPoland, Geschichte des griech. Vereinswesens '09, 98ff] and to designate civic as well as religious officials [Dssm., B 153ff [BS 154-7], NB 60ff [BS 233-5], LO 315, 5; HHausschildt, ZNW 4, '03, 235ff; MLStrack, ibid. 213ff; HLietzmann, ZWTh 55, '14, 116-32 [=Kl. Schr. I '58, 156-69]; MDibelius, exc. on 1 Ti 5: 17ff].—BGU 16, 6 [159 AD] πρεσβύτεροι ἱερεῖς θεοῦ Σοκνοπαίου; 347, 6; PWien Bosw. 1, 31 [87 AD].—The Engl. word 'priest' comes fr. πρεσβύτερος; later Christian usage is largely, if not entirely, responsible for this development; cf. Murray, New [Oxford] Engl. Dict. s.v. priest B).

α. Ac 11: 30; 14: 23; 15: 2, 4, 6, 22f; 16: 4 (in all the places in Ac 15 and 16 mention is made of οἱ ἀπόστολοι καὶ οἱ πρεσβύτεροι in the Jerusalem church); 20: 17; 21: 18; 1 Ti 5: 17, 19 (Nicol. Dam.: 90 fgm. 103a Jac. νεωτέρῳ πρεσβυτέρου καταμαρτυρεῖν οὐκ ἔξεστι); Tit 1: 5; Js 5: 14; 1 Pt 5: 1, 5 (s. 1a above); 1 Cl 44: 5; 47: 6; 54: 2; 57: 1. WWrede, Untersuchungen zum 1 Cl 1891, 8ff.—Acc. to 2 Cl 17: 3, 5 exhortation and preaching in the church services were among their duties.—In Ign. the πρεσβύτεροι come after the bishop, to whom they are subordinate IMg 2; 3: 1; 6: 1, or betw. the bishop and the deacons IPhld inscr.; 10: 2; IPol 6: 1, or the higher rank of the bishop in comparison to them is made plain in some other way ITr 3: 1; 12: 2 (s. πρεσβυτέριον 2).—Polycarp —no doubt as bishop—groups himself w. the presbyters in Pol inscr., and further takes the presence of presbyters in Philippi for granted (beside deacons, though no ἐπίσκοπος is mentioned; cf. Hdb. on Pol inscr.) Pol 5: 3.

β. Just how we are to understand the words ὁ πρεσβύτερος, applied to himself by the author of the two smallest Johannine letters 2 J 1; 3 J 1, remains in doubt. But in any case it is meant to indicate a position of great dignity *the elder.*—HWindisch, exc. on 3 J, end; ESchwartz, Über

den Tod der Söhne Zebedaei '04, 47; 51; HHWendt, ZNW 23, '24, 19; EKäsemann, ZThK 48, '51, 292-311.—ὁ πρ. and οἱ πρ. are mentioned by Papias in these much-discussed passages: 2: 3, 4, 5, 7, 14, 15. For some of the lit. s. the note on JAKleist's transl. '48, p. 207 n. 18.

γ. In Rv there are 24 elders sitting on thrones about the throne of God; they form a heavenly council of elders (cf. Is 24: 23) 4: 4, 10; 5: 5-14; 7: 11, 13; 11: 16; 14: 3; 19: 4. The elders have been understood as glorified human beings of some kind (so e.g. HHoltzmann, Swete, Schlatter, Lohmeyer, Rohr) or astral deities (or angels) (e.g. Spitta, Bousset, Calmes, Allo, Zahn, Hadorn, OHoltzmann, Behm; JMichl, D. 24 Ältesten in d. Apk. d. hl. J. '38); the number 24 has been referred to the following: the 24 priestly classes of the Jews (1 Ch 24: 7-18; Jos., Ant. 7, 365-7) whose heads were called 'elders' (Yoma 1, 5; Tamid 1, 1; Middoth 1, 8); the 24 stars which, according to Babylonian belief, stood half on the north and half on the south of the zodiac (Diod. S. 2, 31, 4; POsl. 4, 19: HGunkel, Z. religionsgesch. Verständnis des NT '03, 42f; Boll 35f); the 24 hours of the day, represented as old men w. shining garments and w. crowns (acc. to the Test. of Adam [ed. CBezold, ThNöldeke-Festschr. '06, 893-912]: JWellhausen, Analyse der Offb. Joh. '07, p. 9, 1; NMorosof, Offb. Joh. '12, 32); the 24 Yazatas in the state of the gods in heaven, acc. to Persian thought (Bousset). It is certainly an open question whether, or how far, the writer of Rv had any of these things in mind. —On the presbyters, and esp. on the question how ἐπίσκοπος and πρεσβύτερος were originally related to each other (a question which is raised particularly in the pastorals; cf. MDibelius, Hdb. exc. after 1 Ti 3: 7 section 2 [w. lit.] and before 5: 17), s. the lit. s.v. ἐπίσκοπος.—BSEaston, Pastoral Epistles '47, 188-97; WMichaelis, Das Ältestenamt '53; GBornkamm, πρεσβύτερος: TW VI 651-83. M-M. B. 1472. **

πρεσβύτης, ου, ὁ (Aeschyl., Hippocr.+; IG IV² 1, 123, 120; pap.; LXX; Jos., Bell. 1, 312) *old man, aged man* (Philo, Op. M. 105, after Hippocr.: a man of 50-56 years; Dio Chrys. 57[74], 10 πρεσβύτης immediately follows the series παῖς, μειράκιον νεανίσκος; Aristoxenus fgm. 35 has the steps νήπιος, παῖς, νεανίσκος, ἀνήρ, πρεσβύτης) Lk 1: 18; Tit 2: 2; Phlm 9 (where many accept Bentley's conjecture πρεσβευτής *ambassador*, i.e. of Christ: Lghtf.; W-H., app.; EHaupt; Lohmeyer; RSV; Gdspd., Probs. 185-7; against this point of view HermvSoden, MDibelius, Meinertz. On this pass. cf. also RSteck, PM 18, '14, 96-100; 192f; PSchmidt, ibid. 156-8.—Polyaenus 8, 9, 1 πρεσβύτης and πρεσβευτής are found as variants); MPol 7: 2 (used attributively w. ἀνήρ: πρ. ἀνήρ as Theophyl. Sim., Ep. 60); Hm 8: 10.—FBoll (s. νεανίας) 116f. M-M.*

πρεσβῦτις, ιδος, ἡ (Aeschyl., Pla.+; Diod. S. 4, 51, 1; 4 Macc 16: 14; Philo, Spec. Leg. 2, 33; Jos., Ant. 7, 142; 186) *old(er) woman, elderly lady* Tit 2: 3; Hv 1, 2, 2 (γυνὴ πρ., as Aeschines 3, 157). M-M.*

πρηνής, ές, gen. οῦς (Hom.+; PGM 4, 194; LXX.—X. has πρανής, which is found in later Attic usage beside πρηνής) *forward, prostrate, head first, headlong* πρηνὴς γενόμενος *falling headlong* Ac 1: 18 (Posid.: 87 fgm. 5 Jac. πρ. προσπεσών; Diod. S. 34+35, fgm. 28a πρηνὴς ἐπὶ τὴν γῆν; Appian, Celts 10 κατέπεσε πρηνής; Philo, Op. M. 157 πρηνὲς πεπτωκός; Jos., Bell. 1, 621 and Vi. 138 πρ. πεσών, Bell. 6, 64, Ant. 18, 59; Sib. Or. 4, 110). The mng. *swollen, distended* was first proposed by FH Chase, JTS 13, '12, 278-85; 415, and has been accepted by

Harnack, ThLZ 37, '12, 235-7; EbNestle, ZNW 19, '20, 179f; HHWendt and GHoennicke, ad loc.; JMoffatt, transl. '13; RHarris, AJTh 18, '14, 127-31; Gdspd., Probs. 123-6; L-S-J lex. gives it as a possibility s.v. πρανής; in this case it would be derived fr. the root πρη-, πίμπρημι (q.v.), which is linguistically possible. Other exx. of πρηνής in the sense 'swollen' are lacking, unless the word be given this mng. in Wsd 4: 19 (so Gdspd.).— Bursting as a result of a violent fall is also found Aesop, Fab. 177b H. κατακρημνισθεὶς διερράγη.—S. further Zahn, Forsch. VI '00, 126; 153-5; IX '16, 331-3; AD Knox, JTS 25, '24, 289f; HJCadbury, JBL 45, '26, 192f; KLake, Beginn. I 5, '33, 22-30; Beyer and Steinmann ad loc.; RSV. M-M.*

πρίζω ([Ps.-?] Pla., Theag. 124B; Diod. S. 3, 27, 3; 4, 76, 5; PHermopol. 28, 11 φοίνικες πεπρισμένοι; Am 1: 3; designated as unattic by Pollux 7, 114) or πρίω (trag., Thu. +) 1 aor. pass. ἐπρίσθην saw (in two) as a method of execution (Sus 59 Theod.); acc. to tradition (Martyr. of Is. 5, 2; 4; Justin, Dial. 120 et al.; MGaster and BHeller, Monatsschr. f. Gesch. u. Wissensch. des Judent. 80, '36, 32-44) Isaiah met his death in this manner, Hb 11: 37. M-M.*

πρίν (Hom. +; inscr., pap., LXX) lit. an adv. of time before, formerly; then a
1. temporal conjunction before (the ms. tradition oft. varies betw. πρίν, which is predom. Attic, and πρὶν ἤ [s. ἤ 2d], which is Ionic, and predominates in the Koine).
   a. w. the aor. subj. (Plut., Caes. 58, 2; Lucian, Ver. Hist. 2, 18) or opt. (Bl-D. §383, 3; Rob. 977) πρὶν ἀκουσθῶσι τὰ ῥήματα Hs 5, 7, 3. Lk 2: 26 is text-critically uncertain πρὶν ἢ ἂν ἴδῃ, but ἤ is omitted (cf. Kyr.-Inschr. l. 123 πρὶν ἄν w. aor. subj.) as well as ἄν in some mss., and א* has ἕως ἂν ἴδῃ. Likew. in 22: 34 ἕως, ἕως οὗ, ἕως ὅτου are also attested instead of πρὶν ἤ; the corrector has been at work in all these passages, so that the original rdg. can no longer be determined w. certainty.—Only once w. the opt., in indirect discourse after a past tense (Bl-D. §386, 4; Rob. 970) πρὶν ἢ ὁ κατηγορούμενος ἔχοι Ac 25: 16 (cf. Jos., Ant. 20, 210).
   b. foll. by the acc. and the aor. inf. (Bl-D. §395; Rob. 977.—Plut., Lysander 27, 1 πρὶν ἐπανελθεῖν τὸν Ἀγησίλαον; Lucian, Dial. Deor. 20, 16 πρίν; Jos., Ant. 11, 1 πρὶν ἤ) Mt 1: 18 (πρὶν ἤ); J 8: 58; Ac 7: 2 (πρὶν ἤ); 1 Cl 38: 3; Dg 2: 3 (πρὶν ἤ); 8: 1; Hs 9, 16, 3. Also of future things (Arrian, Ind. 24, 6 πρὶν ταχθῆναι τὴν φάλαγγα =before the phalanx will have been drawn up) πρὶν ἀλέκτορα φωνῆσαι before the cock will have crowed Mt 26: 34, 75; Mk 14: 30 (πρὶν ἤ), 72; Lk 22: 61. Cf. J 4: 49; Ac 2: 20 (Jo 3: 4); Hs 9, 26, 6.—Without the acc., which is understood fr. the context (Menand., Epitr. 47; 291; Diod. S. 13, 10, 1; 14, 52, 1; Chio, Ep. 4, 4; Ps.-Apollod. 3, 3, 2; Jos., Bell. 6, 213) J 14: 29; Hv 3, 1, 3.
2. (improper) prep. w. gen. before (since Pind., Pyth. 4, 43, also Plut., Mor. 883B; Arrian, Anab. 3, 18, 6; PGM 7, 418; 420 πρὶν ἡλίου ἀνατολῆς; En. 14, 6; Jos., Ant. 4, 269 πρὶν ἡλίου δυσμῶν; Sus 35a LXX=42 Theod.) πρὶν ἀλεκτοροφωνίας Mt 26: 34 v.l.; πρὶν Ἀβραὰμ ἐγὼ εἰμί J 8: 58 v.l.—Even πρίν w. the acc. occurs as v.l. πρὶν τὸ πάσχα J 11: 55 v.l. πρὶν σάββατον Mk 15: 42 v.l. (cf. Bl-D. §395 app.; JWackernagel, Syntax II² '28, 215).—AlTschuschke, De πρίν particulae apud scriptores aet. August. prosaicos usu, Diss. Bresl. '13. M-M.*

Πρίσκα (Πρῖσκα? s. Bl-D. §41, 3 app.; cf. Mlt.-H. 155) and its dim. Πρίσκιλλα, ης, ἡ (s. Preisigke, Namenbuch. A priestess of Zeus named Πρίσκιλλα is mentioned in an

honorary inscr. fr. the city of Olbasa: Ramsay, Phrygia I p. 309 no. 122) Prisca, Priscilla, wife of Aquila (s. Ἀκύλας and the lit. there), named before her husband in the majority of cases (Harnack [s.v. Ἀκ.] concludes fr. this that she was a more important pers. than her husband and that she may have played the major part in the writing of Hb: ZNW 1, '00, 16ff.—In Ramsay, op. cit. p. 637 no. 530 [70-80 AD] Julia Severa is named before her husband Tyrronius Rapon, prob. because she was of higher rank) Ac 18: 2, 18, 26. The forementioned passages have the name Πρίσκιλλα (likew. Ro 16: 3 t.r.; 1 Cor 16: 19 t.r.). On the other hand, Πρίσκα is the predominant form in the Pauline letters Ro 16: 3; 1 Cor 16: 19; 2 Ti 4: 19. M-M.*

πρίω s. πρίζω.

πρό prep. w. gen. (Hom. +; inscr., pap., LXX, Ep. Arist., Joseph., Test. 12 Patr., Sib. Or.—S. the lit. s.v. ἀνά, beg.) before.
1. of place before, in front of, at πρὸ τῆς θύρας at the door Ac 12: 6, 14; cf. 5: 23 t.r.; perh. J 10: 8 belongs here (Jesus is the door, vs. 7). πρὸ τῆς πόλεως (Jos., Bell. 1, 234, Ant. 10, 44): ὁ ἱερεὺς τοῦ Διὸς τοῦ ὄντος πρὸ τῆς πόλεως the priest of (the temple of) Zeus just outside the city (gate) 14: 13 (CIG 2963c τῆς μεγάλης Ἀρτέμιδος πρὸ πόλεως ἱερεῖς. Cf. the sim. inscriptions w. πρὸ πόλεως 2796; 3194; 3211; Bull. de corr. hell. 11, 1887 p. 464 no. 29 ὁ πρὸ πόλεως Ἀπόλλων [Thyatira]; ThWiegand, SAB '06, 259 Ἀσκληπιοῦ πρὸ πόλεως [Miletus]).—Symbolically ὁ κριτὴς πρὸ τῶν θυρῶν ἔστηκεν Js 5: 9. Fig.: πρὸ ὀφθαλμῶν ἔχειν, λαμβάνειν and πρὸ ὀφθαλμῶν τινος εἶναι; on these s. ὀφθαλμός 2.—πρὸ προσώπου τινός (= 'פ ׳ לִפְנֵי; cf. Johannessohn 184f) before someone Mt 11: 10; Mk 1: 2; Lk 7: 27 (on all three compare Mal 3: 1; Ex 23: 20); 1: 76 v.l.; 9: 52; 10: 1; 1 Cl 34: 3 (cf. Is 62: 11); IEph 15: 3. W. transition to a temporal mng. προκηρύξαντος Ἰωάννου πρὸ προσώπου τῆς εἰσόδου αὐτοῦ after John had preached as his forerunner before his (i.e. Jesus') appearance Ac 13: 24.
2. of time πρὸ τοῦ ἀρίστου before the meal (X., Cyr. 6, 2, 21) Lk 11: 38. πρὸ τοῦ βαπτίσματος D 7: 4a. πρὸ χειμῶνος 2 Ti 4: 21. πρὸ τοῦ πάσχα J 11: 55. πρὸ τῆς ἑορτῆς τοῦ πάσχα 13: 1. πρὸ τοῦ κατακλυσμοῦ Mt 24: 38. πρὸ καταβολῆς κόσμου J 17: 24; Eph 1: 4; 1 Pt 1: 20. πρὸ ἡλίου καὶ σελήνης 2 Cl 14: 1 (s. ἥλιος). πρὸ πάντων Col 1: 17; cf. πρὸ τούτων πάντων Lk 21: 12. πρὸ τῶν αἰώνων (Ps 54: 20) 1 Cor 2: 7; cf. IEph inscr.; IMg 6: 1. πρὸ χρόνων αἰωνίων 2 Ti 1: 9; Tit 1: 2. πρὸ παντὸς τοῦ αἰῶνος Jd 25. πρὸ καιροῦ before the proper time or the last times (καιρός 4; cf. Sir 51: 30; Theod. Prodr. 1, 281 H.) Mt 8: 29; 1 Cor 4: 5. π. τούτων τῶν ἡμερῶν Ac 5: 36; 21: 38; Hm 4, 3, 4. πρὸ ἐτῶν 2 Cor 12: 2. πρὸ τῆς μεταθέσεως Hb 11: 5. Latinizing (on the use of the Rom. calendar among the Gks. s. Hahn 245) πρὸ ἐννέα καλανδῶν Σεπτεμβρίων on August twenty-fourth IRo 10: 3. πρὸ ἑπτὰ καλανδῶν Μαρτίων on February twenty-third MPol 21 (cf. Inschr. v. Priene 105, 23 πρὸ ἐννέα καλανδῶν Ὀκτωβρίων).—On the expr. πρὸ ἐξ ἡμερῶν τοῦ πάσχα J 12: 1 s. ἡμέρα 2 and cf. Am 1: 1; 4: 7. πρὸ τριῶν ἡμερῶν τοῦ συλληφθῆναι αὐτὸν MPol 5: 2. πρὸ μιᾶς τῶν ἀζύμων one day before the feast of unleavened bread GP 2: 5 (Plut., Lucull. 27, 9 πρὸ μιᾶς νωνῶν Ὀκτωβρίων, Publicola 9, 8; Appian, Bell. Civ. 2, 115 §479 πρὸ μιᾶς τοῦδε τοῦ βουλευτηρίου). πρὸ μιᾶς (sc. ἡμέρας [Polyaenus 7, 10 πρὸ μιᾶς ἡμέρας]; cf. Lucian, Alex. 46; Dositheus 40, 2; PGM 13, 350) one day before D 7: 4b; the day before Hs 6, 5, 3.—LRydbeck, Fachprosa '67, 62-77; Mlt.-Turner 260.—W. the gen. of the personal pron. (PTebt. 61b, 384 [118/17 BC]) πρὸ ὑμῶν (Lev 18: 28) Mt 5:

12; cf. Ac 7: 4 D. πρὸ ἐμοῦ (1 Macc 15: 5) J 5: 7; 10: 8 (s. also 1 above); Ro 16: 7; Gal 1: 17. Cf. 1 Cl 19: 1.—πρὸ τοῦ w. acc. and inf. (Bl-D. §403; Rob. 1074f) πρὸ τοῦ ὑμᾶς αἰτῆσαι Mt 6: 8. Cf. Lk 2: 21; 22: 15; J 1: 48; 13: 19 (here the acc. is missing, but can easily be supplied); 17: 5; Ac 23: 15; Gal 2: 12; 3: 23; B 16: 7.

3. of precedence, rank, advantage (class.; pap.; Jos., Ant. 16, 187 πρὸ ἐκείνων) πρὸ παντός above all, especially Pol 5: 3. Also πρὸ πάντων (POxy. 292, 11; 294, 30) Js 5: 12; 1 Pt 4: 8; D 10: 4. M-M.**

προαγαπάω 1 aor. προηγάπησα love before, love first τινά someone Dg 10: 3.*

προάγω impf. προῆγον; fut. προάξω; 2 aor. προήγαγον (Hdt.+; inscr., pap., LXX, Ep. Arist., Joseph.).
1. trans. lead forward, lead or bring out τινά someone προαγαγὼν αὐτοὺς ἔξω after he had led them out Ac 16: 30 (Diod. S. 4, 44, 3 τῆς φυλακῆς προαγαγεῖν=lead out of the prison). αὐτοὺς προαγαγεῖν εἰς τὸν δῆμον 17: 5 (Jos., Ant. 16, 320 εἰς τὸ πλῆθος). Cf. 12: 6 (Jos., Ant. 2, 105 al.).—In the language of the law-court bring before (Jos., Bell. 1, 539, Ant. 16, 393.—ἐπί 1 1aδ) Ac 25: 26.
2. intr. go before, lead the way, precede—a. in place τινά go before someone (2 Macc 10: 1; Bl-D. §150; Rob. 477) Mt 2: 9; 21: 9. Abs. (Diod. S. 17, 19, 1 προῆγε=he pushed on; Jos., Bell. 1, 673, Ant. 14, 388) Mt 21: 9 t.r.; Mk 11: 9 (opp. ἀκολουθεῖν); Lk 18: 39. Walk ahead of those who are going slowly and w. hesitation ἦν προάγων αὐτοὺς ὁ Ἰησοῦς . . . οἱ δὲ ἀκολουθοῦντες Mk 10: 32. κατὰ πόλιν με προῆγον they went before me from city to city IRo 9: 3.—As a symbol πᾶς ὁ προάγων καὶ μὴ μένων ἐν τῇ διδαχῇ anyone who goes too far and does not remain in the teaching 2 J 9. Of πίστις (cf. Aberciusinschr. 12 πίστις προῆγε), which is followed by ἐλπίς (ἐπακολου-θεῖν), προαγούσης τῆς ἀγάπης love leads the way Pol 3: 3.
b. in time go or come before someone w. acc. of the pers. προάγειν αὐτὸν εἰς τὸ πέραν go before him to the other shore Mt 14: 22. προάξω ὑμᾶς εἰς τὴν Γαλιλαίαν I will go before you to Galilee 26: 32; Mk 14: 28 (CFEvans, JTS 5, '54, 3-18); cf. Mt 28: 7; Mk 16: 7. Without the acc. (which can be supplied fr. the ἕως-clause [cf. Dit., Syll.³ 684, 25]) προάγειν εἰς τὸ πέραν πρὸς Βηθσαϊδάν Mk 6: 45. οἱ τελῶναι προάγουσιν ὑμᾶς εἰς τὴν βασιλείαν τοῦ θεοῦ the tax-collectors will get into the kingdom of God before you Mt 21: 31. Symbolically of sins προάγουσαι εἰς κρίσιν they go before (the sinners) to judgment 1 Ti 5: 24 (Oenomaus in Euseb., Pr. Ev. 5, 24, 1 εἰς τ. κρίσιν προάγειν='come before the court').—πάντα τὰ προά-γοντα everything that had gone before MPol 1: 1. κατὰ τὰς προαγούσας προφητείας in accordance with the prophecies that were made long ago 1 Ti 1: 18 (IG XII 3, 247 τὰ προάγοντα ψαφίσματα; PFlor. 198, 7 [III AD] κατὰ τὸ προάγον ἔθος; POxy. 42, 3 ἡ πανήγυρις προά-γουσα). ἀθέτησις προαγούσης ἐντολῆς Hb 7: 18 (ἀθέ-τησις 1). M-M.*

προαδικέω (since Aeschin. and Menand., Her. Pr. 7; Diod. S. 4, 53, 1; 13, 30, 2; Plut., Dio 47, 8, Mor. 1090E; Wsd 18: 2; Philo, Mos. 1, 303) be first in wrong-doing, injure beforehand. It appears in a mutilated context at the beginning of GOxy, where its meaning cannot be deter-mined w. certainty.*

προαθλέω pf. ptc. προηθληκώς (schol. on Pind., Ol. 8, 71) contest in former times of the martyrs of earlier ages (opp. οἱ μέλλοντες) MPol 18: 2.*

προαιρέω (Hdt., Aristoph.+; inscr., pap., LXX) 2 aor.

προεῖλον; 2 aor. mid. προειλόμην, 3 pl. προείλαντο (Bl-D. §80; 81, 3; cf. Mlt.-H. 212; Dit., Or. 383, 46 [I BC] προειλάμην); pf. mid. προήρημαι, ptc. προῃρημένος.
1. act. bring or take out (Aristoph., Thu.+; PTebt. 112, 31 [II BC]; PFay. 119, 21; Jdth 13: 15) τὶ someth. 1 Cl 43: 5.
2. mid. choose (for oneself), prefer (X., Pla.+; inscr., pap., LXX, Ep. Arist., Philo, Joseph.) τὸν φόβον τοῦ κυρίου οὐ προείλαντο they did not choose the fear of the Lord 1 Cl 57: 5 (Pr 1: 29). πρ. τι μᾶλλον ἤ τι prefer one thing to another (X., Mem. 2, 1, 2) 2 Cl 10: 3. Undertake, determine, decide, make up one's mind (Pla. et al.; Diod. S. 2, 54; inscr., pap.; Pr 21: 25; 2 Macc 6: 9; 3 Macc 2: 30; 7: 2; Ep. Arist. 33; 45 al.) w. inf. foll. (Diod. S. 3, 55, 3; Ael. Aristid. 38 p. 721 D.; Philo, Mos. 1, 325; Jos., C. Ap. 1, 257, Vi. 103) IMg 1: 1. Abs. (Demosth. 18, 190) καθὼς προῄρηται τῇ καρδίᾳ as he has made up his mind 2 Cor 9: 7. M-M.*

προαιτιάομαι mid. dep.; 1 aor. προῃτιασάμην accuse beforehand followed by the acc. and inf. (Bl-D. §397, 3; Rob. 1036) προῃτιασάμεθα we (=I) have already charged that Ro 3: 9. M-M.*

προακούω 1 aor. προήκουσα (Hdt.+; Philo, Ebr. 160) hear beforehand τὶ someth. (Nicol. Dam. 90 fgm. 66, 24 Jac. τὶ παρά τινος) ἐλπίδα ἣν προηκούσατε what you hope for (ἐλπίς 4), about which you have heard before (i.e. before you receive it or before you received this letter) Col 1: 5 (Diod. S. 16, 66, 4 Τιμολέων προακηκοὼς ἦν= he had heard before it happened; 19, 38, 6 πρ. τὸ μέλλον; Jos., Ant. 8, 301 Βασάνης προακηκοὼς τὰ μέλλοντα αὐτῷ συμβήσεσθαι).*

προαμαρτάνω pf. ptc. προημαρτηκώς (Dit., Or. 751, 10 [II BC] w. μετανοεῖν; Herodian 3, 14, 4; Jos., Bell. 1, 481; Justin, Apol. I 61, 10) sin beforehand πολλοὺς τῶν προημαρτηκότων (prob. for πολλοὺς τοὺς προημαρτη-κότας, Ltzm. ad loc.) many who sinned before 2 Cor 12: 21; cf. 13: 2. M-M.*

προαύλιον, ου, τό (Themist., Or. 33 p. 443, 13 symb. τὸ π. τοῦ λόγου) the place in front of the house, forecourt, gateway (Pollux 1, 77; 9, 16; Suidas) Mk 14: 68.*

προβαίνω 2 aor. προέβην, ptc. προβάς; pf. ptc. προβε-βηκώς (Hom.+; pap., LXX; En. 22, 5; Joseph.) go ahead, go on, advance.
1. lit. go on (X., Ages. 6, 7; Herodian 7, 12, 4) ὀλίγον a little (distance) Mk 1: 19. Also μικρόν Hv 4, 1, 5; s 6, 2, 5. ἐκεῖθεν Mt 4: 21.
2. fig. προβεβηκέναι ἐν ταῖς ἡμέραις be advanced in years Lk 1: 7, 18; cf. 2: 36 (ἡμέρα, end; also Lysias 24: 16 προβεβηκὼς τῇ ἡλικίᾳ; Diod. S. 12, 18, 1; 13, 89, 2; UPZ 161, 61 [119 BC] π. τοῖς ἔτεσιν; Mitteis, Chrest. 31 VII, 29 [116 BC]; Jos., Vi. 266, Ant. 7, 182). M-M.*

προβάλλω impf. προέβαλον; 2 aor. προέβαλον (Hom. +; inscr., pap., LXX; Ep. Arist. 212; Philo, Joseph.) throw or put before.
1. put forward, cause to come forward (cf. Jos., Bell. 4, 230) τινά someone (Demosth. 18, 149; Vi. Aesopi I 85 push someone forward to speak in the theater; 86) Ac 19: 33. τὴν γλῶσσαν πρ. thrust out the tongue (schol. on Nicander, Ther. 206 πρ. τ. γλ. of a serpent thrusting out its tongue; 2 Macc 7: 10) Hv 4, 1, 9.
2. of plants put out foliage or fruit (w. acc. Epict. 1, 15, 7 τὸν καρπόν; likew. Jos., Ant. 4, 226. Cf. SSol 2: 13 Aq.) abs. (though D et al. add τὸν καρπὸν αὐτῶν) ὅταν προβάλωσιν ἤδη when they (i.e. the trees) put out (their leaves) Lk 21: 30. M-M.*

προβάς s. προβαίνω.

προβατικός, ή, όν *pertaining to* (*a*) *sheep* (PGoodspeed 30, 6, 5; 31, 9 al. [II AD]; 2 Esdr [s. below]) ἡ προβατική (sc. πύλη, as Vita Polyc. per Pionium ed. Lghtf. 3 on ἐπὶ τὴν καλουμένην Ἐφεσιακήν [after c. 20]. The Christian POxy. 1151 [V AD]=PGM II p. 192 and the ostrakon 3 p. 210 add κολυμβήθρα: sheep pool) *sheep gate*, a gate in the north city wall of Jerusalem ([ἡ] πύλη ἡ προβατική 2 Esdr 13 [Neh 3]: 1, 32; 22 [Neh 12]: 39; s. HGuthe, RE VIII 680, 24ff) J 5: 2 (s. Hdb. ad loc. and on Βηθζαθά; also JoachJeremias, D. Wiederentdeckung v. Bethesda '49). M-M.*

προβάτιον, ου, τό (Aristoph., Pla.+; Plut., Fab. 1, 4; PTebt. 793, 1; 28 [183 BC]) dim. of πρόβατον; *lamb*, though it is oft. used without dim. sense=*sheep* (Menand., Her. 26; Plut., Popl. 11, 4 Z. v.l., interchanged w. πρόβατον; Philostrat., Her. p. 133, 5; Celsus 4, 43) J 21: 16f (for the juxtaposition of βόσκειν, ἀρνία, ποιμαίνειν and πρόβατα cf. Inschr. v. Priene 362, 17f [IV BC] φέρειν τοὺς τὰ πρόβατα βόσκοντας ἀπὸ τῆς ποίμνης ἄρνα). 10: 3 𝔓⁶⁶.*

πρόβατον, ου, τό (Hom.+; inscr., pap., LXX; Ep. Arist. 93; Philo; Jos., Ant. 6, 295; 18, 317; Test. 12 Patr.) *sheep* (cf. on this mng. Wilcken, Ostraka I 286; Bl-D. §126, 1aα; L-S-J lex. s.v. I. The more general senses 'cattle' or 'small cattle' scarcely merit serious attention for our lit., though they are barely poss. in certain passages).

1. lit. Mt 12: 11f; 18: 12; Lk 15: 4, 6 (on this parable: GONordberg, Svensk exeg. Årsbok 1, '37, 55–63); Rv 18: 13. As a sacrificial animal 1 Cl 4: 1 (Gen 4: 4); J 2: 14f. πρόβατα σφαγῆς *sheep to be slaughtered* Ro 8: 36 (Ps 43: 23). Defenseless in the midst of wolves Mt 10: 16. In danger without a shepherd Mt 9: 36; Mk 6: 34 (both Num 27: 17; cf. Ezk 34: 5 and Jdth 11: 19); Mt 26: 31; Mk 14: 27; B 5: 12 (the three last Zech 13: 7); 1 Cl 16: 6f (Is 53: 6f); B 5: 2 (Is 53: 7). ἐν ἐνδύμασι προβάτων (cf. ἔνδυμα 2. Proverbia Aesopi 123 P. κρύπτειν τὸν λύκον προβάτου δορᾷ) Mt 7: 15. The firstfruits of the sheep belong to the prophets D 13: 3. Jesus ὡς πρόβατον ἐπὶ σφαγὴν ἤχθη . . . ἄφωνος (after Is 53: 7) Ac 8: 32 (cf. Vi. Aesopi I c. 48 a dispute over the question: διὰ τί τὸ πρόβατον ἐπὶ θυσίαν ἀγόμενον οὐ κέκραγεν).

2. The lit. usage passes over to the non-literal, or the sheep appear for the most part as symbols of certain people: in the great allegory of the Good Shepherd and the sheep J 10: 1–16, 26f (in vs. 3 𝔓⁶⁶ reads προβάτια). Jesus is ὁ ποιμὴν τῶν προβάτων ὁ μέγας Hb 13: 20. Cf. 1 Pt 2: 25. The bishop is the shepherd, the church members the sheep IPhld 2: 1. Cf. J 21: 16 v.l., 17 v.l. (Porphyr., Adv. Chr. fgm. 26: the ἀρνία are the catechumens, but the πρόβατα are οἱ πιστοὶ εἰς τὸ τῆς τελετώσεως προβάντες μυστήριον). The Christians are called πρόβατα τῆς νομῆς σου (= God's) 1 Cl 59: 4 (cf. Ps 78: 13; 94: 7; 99: 3); B 16: 5 (En. 89, 56; 66f). In the last times under the influence of lying prophets τὰ πρόβατα will be turned εἰς λύκους D 16: 3. At the Last Judgment men will be divided as the shepherd separates τὰ πρόβατα from οἱ ἔριφοι (Mt 25: 32f.—S. ἔριφος. PAmh. 73, 6 [129/30 AD] differentiates πρόβ. and αἶγες), and the πρόβατα, representing those blessed by the Father, will stand at the right hand of the Son of Man vs. 33 (HGraffmann, D. Gericht nach d. Werken im Mt: KBarth-Festschr. '36, 124–36). Jesus knows that he is sent Mt 15: 24, and sends his disciples 10: 6 πρὸς τὰ πρόβατα τὰ ἀπολωλότα οἴκου Ἰσραήλ.—In Hermas sheep appear (w. shepherds) as symbolic of all kinds of persons Hs 6, 1, 5f; 6, 2, 3f; 6f; 6, 3, 2; 9, 1, 9; 9, 27, 1. M-M. B. 144.*

προβεβηκώς s. προβαίνω.

προβιβάζω 1 aor. προεβίβασα, pass. ptc. προβιβασθείς *bring forward, cause to come forward* (Soph., Oed. Col. 180) ἐκ τοῦ ὄχλου προεβίβασαν Ἀλέξανδρον *they made Alexander come out from the crowd* Ac 19: 33 t.r. ἡ δὲ προβιβασθεῖσα ὑπὸ τῆς μητρός *but she, put forward by her mother* Mt 14: 8 (here many prefer the mng. 'incite, urge on [beforehand], prompt'. But προβιβ. εἴς τι in places like X., Mem. 1, 5, 1 εἰς ἐγκράτειαν, Pla., Prot. 328B εἰς ἀρετήν, Musonius p. 60, 5 H. νέους εἰς φιλοσοφίαν means 'lead on to', 'train in'. It would be better to refer to the LXX, where the word='instruct, teach, inculcate': Ex 35: 34; Dt 6: 7). M-M.*

προβλέπω impf. προέβλεπον; 1 aor. προέβλεψα (Dionys. Hal. 11, 20; somet. in Vett. Val. [index]; Epigr. Gr. 326; Ps 36: 13) *see beforehand, foresee* ὦν (=τούτων, οὓς) προέβλεπεν τὸ πνεῦμα κυρίου B 6: 14. ἐν πνεύματι προβλέψας εἰς τὸν Ἰησοῦν *looking forward in the spirit to Jesus* 9: 7. προβλέψας, ὡς *foreseeing that* 3: 6. Mid. τὶ περί τινος *select* or *provide someth. for someone* Hb 11: 40. M-M.*

προγενής, ές gen. οὖς *born in early times, primeval* comp. προγενέστερος, α, ον *older* (Hom.+; Theodot. [II BC] in Euseb., Pr. Ev. 9, 22, 3) τινός *than someth.* of the Son of God πάσης τῆς κτίσεως αὐτοῦ προγενέστερος *older than his whole creation* Hs 9, 12, 2.*

προγίνομαι pf. ptc. προγεγονώς (Hom.+) *originate, be born earlier in time, happen* or *be done before* (Hdt.+; inscr., pap., LXX) τὰ προγεγονότα ἁμαρτήματα *the sins that were committed in former times*, i.e. when God showed forbearance Ro 3: 25 (schol. on Apollon. Rhod. 4, 411–13 τὰ προγεγενημένα ἁμαρτήματα; Diod. S. 19, 1, 3 τὰ προγεγενημένα ἀδικήματα. Cf. X., Mem. 2, 7, 9 τ. προγεγονυῖαν χάριν). τὰ προγεγονότα πονηρά Hv 1, 3, 1. ὁ προγεγονώς *the former one* (i.e. the Phoenix), *predecessor* 1 Cl 25: 3. M-M.*

προγινώσκω 2 aor. προέγνων, ptc. προγνούς; pf. pass. ptc. προεγνωσμένος (Eur., X., Pla.+; BGU 1141, 39 [14 BC]; Wsd) *know beforehand, in advance, have foreknowledge (of)* τὶ *someth.* (Philo, Somn. 1, 2; Jos., Vi. 106) affliction Hs 7: 5. Abs. (Jos., Ant. 2, 86) προγινώσκοντες *since you know this* (i.e. what the context makes clear) *in advance* 2 Pt 3: 17. Of God (Alex. Aphr., An. p. 1, 7 Br. τὰ μέλλοντα, Fat. 30 p. 200, 29) πάντα Hm 4, 3, 4. *Choose beforehand* τινά *someone* Ro 8: 29. τὸν λαὸν αὐτοῦ 11: 2 (EWeber, D. Problem der Heilsgesch. nach Ro 9–11, '11; ThHoppe, D. Idee d. Heilsgesch. b. Pls '26; FWMaier, Israel in d. Heilsgesch. nach Ro 9–11, '29; EvDobschütz, Prädestination: StKr 106, '35, 9–19; JMunck, Christus u. Israel: Ro 9–11, '56; EDinkler, Prädestination bei Paulus, GDehn-Festschr., '57, 61–102. S. also on προορίζω). Pass. of Christ προεγνωσμένος πρὸ καταβολῆς κόσμου 1 Pt 1: 20.—*Know from time past* (Jos., Bell. 6, 8) προγινώσκοντές με ἄνωθεν Ac 26: 5. M-M.*

πρόγλωσσος, ον (Ptolem., Apotel. 3, 14, 31 Boll-B.; Polemo Physiognom. 37 Förster et al.) *hasty in speech, talkative* B 19: 8.*

πρόγνωσις, εως, ἡ (Hippocr.+ as a medical t.t.; Plut., Mor. 399D; 982C; Phlegon of Tralles [time of Hadrian] in Orig., C. Cels. 2, 14; Lucian, Alex. 8; Vett. Val. 220, 9; 221, 25; 355, 9; Jos., Ant. 15, 373 πρόγνωσιν ἐκ θεοῦ τῶν μελλόντων ἔχων; 17, 43; PGM 7, 294; Jdth 11: 19) *foreknowledge* πρ. λαμβάνειν τελείαν *receive exact foreknowledge* 1 Cl 44: 2. Of God's omniscient wisdom and intention (so Alex. Aphr., Fat. 30 p. 200, 31 Br.; Proverbia Aesopi 131 P.; Jdth 9: 6) w. βουλή Ac 2: 23. κατὰ πρόγνωσιν θεοῦ πατρός *according to the predestination of God the Father* 1 Pt 1: 2 (WFArndt, Theological Monthly 9, '29, 41-3). M-M.*

προγνώστης, ου, ὁ (PGM 5, 410) *one who knows someth. beforehand* of God (Justin, Apol. I 44, 11, Dial. 16, 3; 23: 2; Theophil., Ad Autolyc. 2, 15.—Of Apollo: Tatian, Orat. ad Graec. 19 p. 21, 21 Schwartz) πρ. τῶν πάντων *one who knows everything beforehand* 2 Cl 9: 9.*

πρόγονος, ον (Hom.+) *born early* or *before* in our lit. only subst. in the pl. οἱ πρόγονοι (Pind.+; inscr., pap., LXX; Ep. Arist. 19; Philo; Jos., Ant. 12, 150, C. Ap. 2, 157) *parents, forefathers, ancestors* 1 Ti 5: 4. ἀπὸ προγόνων *from my ancestors=as my ancestors did* (Dit., Or. 485, 3; 529, 1; Inschr. v. Magn. 163, 2; 164, 3) 2 Ti 1: 3. M-M. B. 119.*

προγράφω 1 aor. προέγραψα. Pass.: 2 aor. προεγράφην; pf. ptc. προγεγραμμένος (Aristoph., Thu.+; inscr., pap., LXX, Joseph.).

1. *write before(hand)*—a. in the same document in which the word is found (so oft. pap.) καθὼς προέγραψα *as I have written above* Eph 3: 3 (Inschr. v. Sinuri no. 46, 17 LRobert '45 καθότι προγέγραπται). τὰ προγεγραμμένα *what I have written above* (PPetr. III p. 179 [III BC]; BGU 1107, 30; 1131, 55 al.) Hv 4, 3, 6. ὁ προγεγραμμένος, τὸ προγεγραμμένον *the person* or *thing mentioned above* (POxford [ed. EPWegener '42] 8, 13 [104/5 AD] ὁ πρ. μου ἀνήρ; 10, 10; 16) τὰ προγεγραμμένα πρόσωπα *the persons mentioned above* IMg 6: 1 (cf. also Da 3: 3). τὸ πρ. (ἀντίγραφον) *the afore-mentioned copy* MPol 22: 3.

b. What is written before, is found in an older document (by another author, as well; cf. Ps.-Clem., Hom. p. 12, 31 Lag.) ὅσα προεγράφη *what was written in earlier times* (in the γραφή) Ro 15: 4.—εἴς τι *mark out, designate for someth.* (Appian, Bell. Civ. 4, 1 §2 τ. ἐχθροὺς ἐς θάνατον πρ.) of false teachers: οἱ πάλαι προγεγραμμένοι εἰς τοῦτο τὸ κρίμα *who for a long time have been marked out* (or *written about*) *for this judgment* (described in what follows) Jd 4.

2. *show forth* or *portray publicly, proclaim* or *placard in public* (γράφω='draw, paint' Hdt., Aristoph.+; here and there in Pla.; Jos., C. Ap. 2, 252; PGM 2, 47; 36, 265.—PGM 2, 60 προγράφω of a figure 'drawn above') οἷς κατ' ὀφθαλμοὺς Ἰ. Χρ. προεγράφη ἐσταυρωμένος *before whose eyes Jesus Christ was portrayed on the cross* Gal 3: 1 (many would prefer to transl. *placard publicly, set forth in a public proclamation* so that all may read: Aristoph., Demosth.+; Plut., Demetr. 46, 10, Mor. 408D; IG X 4, 24; PFlor. 99, 11).—GSchrenk, TW I 771f. M-M.*

πρόδηλος, ον (Soph., Hdt.+; inscr.; POxy. 237 VII, 9; LXX; Ep. Arist. 133; Philo, Gig. 39; Jos., Vi. 22; 217, Sib. Or. 5, 37) *clear, evident, known to all* 1 Ti 5: 24f; 1 Cl 51: 3. προδήλων ἡμῖν ὄντων τούτων *since this is quite plain to us* 40: 1. πρόδηλον ποιεῖν foll. by ὅτι *reveal, make clear* 11: 1; 12: 7. πρόδηλον (sc. ἐστίν) foll. by ὅτι *it is known to all* (X., Hell. 6, 4, 9; Hero Alex. III p. 312, 17) Hb 7: 14 (Bl-D. §397, 4; Rob. 1034). M-M.*

προδηλόω 1 aor. προεδήλωσα; pf. pass. ptc. προδεδηλωμένος (Thu. 6, 34, 7; inscr., pap.; 3 Macc 4: 14; Philo, Decal. 45; 50) *reveal, make known beforehand* τί *someth.* (Diod. S. 20, 37, 1; Plut., Pomp. 32, 6; Jos., Bell. 2, 629) τὴν θλῖψιν Hs 7: 5. Pass. οἱ προδεδηλωμένοι πατέρες

the fathers, whom we have previously mentioned (cf. IG XII 7, 239, 23; 3 Macc 4: 14) 1 Cl 62: 2.*

προδημιουργέω 1 aor. προεδημιούργησα (Philoponus [VI AD], Generat. Anim. 61, 14 Hayduck) *create beforehand* 1 Cl 33: 3.*

προδίδωμι 1 aor. προέδωκα; 2 aor. ptc. προδούς—1. *give in advance* (X.; Aristot.; Polyb. 8, 18, 7; inscr., pap.) τινί *to someone* Ro 11: 35 (Job 41: 3; cf. Is 40: 14 v.l., which is taken from Ro 11: 35).

2. *hand over, betray* (Aeschyl., Hdt.+; inscr.; PThéad. 17, 16; LXX; Jos., Bell. 2, 594; 4, 228, C. Ap. 2, 263) τινά *someone* Mk 14: 10 D. Of betrayal in persecutions MPol 4 v.l. Funk; 6: 1f; Hv 2, 2, 2a, b. M-M.*

προδότης, ου, ὁ (Aeschyl., Hdt.+; 2 and 3 Macc; Ep. Arist. 270; Philo, Leg. All. 2, 10, Spec. Leg. 3, 164; Jos., Bell. 3, 354, Vi. 133) *traitor, betrayer* in a catalogue of vices 2 Ti 3: 4. W. φονεύς Ac 7: 52. W. blasphemers Hs 9, 19, 3b. W. apostates and blasphemers (for the gen. cf. Diod. S. 11, 3, 1 τῆς ἐλευθερίας; cf. Sextus 365 προδότης θεοῦ) προδόται τῆς ἐκκλησίας Hs 8, 6, 4 or προδόται τῶν δούλων τοῦ θεοῦ 9, 19, 1; cf. 3a. ἤκουσαν προδόται γονέων *they were called* or *were known to be betrayers of their parents* Hv 2, 2, 2. Of Judas Lk 6: 16 (πρ. γίν. as Diod. S. 8, 6, 3; Jos., Ant. 19, 61; on the betrayer s. the lit. s.v. Ἰούδας 6). M-M.*

πρόδρομος, ον *going* (lit. *running*) *before*, also subst. (Aeschyl., Hdt.+; Ael. Aristid. 38, 21 K.=7 p. 78 D.; inscr. fr. Delos [Bull. de corr. hell. 29, '05 p. 448, 7]; LXX) of Jesus, who entered the Holy of Holies as the *forerunner* of his followers Hb 6: 20. M-M.*

προεῖδον s. προοράω.

πρόειμι ptc. προών (from εἰμί. Cf. Il. 1, 70 τά τ' ἐόντα τά τ' ἐσσόμενα πρό τ' ἐόντα; Hes., Theog. 32 τά τ' ἐσσόμενα πρό τ' ἐόντα and later wr.; pap., Ep. Arist.) *be preëxistent* (Herm. Wr. 422, 25 Sc. ὁ προὼν θεός) of the Holy Spirit Hs 5, 6, 5.*

προεῖπον defective verb, used as 2 aor. of προλέγω; fut. προερῶ (M-M.); pf. προείρηκα; pf. pass. ptc. προειρημένος (Hom. [in tmesis], Hdt., Pla.+; inscr., pap., LXX, Ep. Arist., Joseph.). On προεῖπον and προεῖπα Bl-D. §81, 1; Mlt.-H. 208. *Foretell, tell before(hand)*.

1. *foretell, tell* or *proclaim beforehand* of prophetic utterances concerning future events and circumstances, of a scripture pass. (Jos., Bell. 6, 109) τὴν γραφήν, ἣν προεῖπεν τὸ πνεῦμα τὸ ἅγιον Ac 1: 16. τινί τι *tell someone someth. beforehand* (Dio Chrys. 28[45], 4 τ. θεοῦ προειπόντος τ. ἡγεμονίαν αὐτῷ; Philostrat., Vi. Soph. 2, 11, 3 πρ. αὐτῷ ταῦτα. Cf. Ael. Aristid. 46 p. 191 D.: ὁ θεὸς πρ. τῇ μητρί . . .) Mk 13: 23; cf. Mt 24: 25, where the context supplies the acc. Pass. (Jos., Ant. 2, 17 τὰ προειρημένα) τὰ ῥήματα τὰ προειρημένα ὑπὸ τῶν ἀποστόλων Jd 17; cf. 2 Pt 3: 2; 1 Cl 58: 1. W. a quot. foll. καθὼς προείρηκεν Ἠσαΐας (Is 1: 9 follows) Ro 9: 29.

2. *the aor.* or *pf. in contrast to the present*—a. *have said someth. before* or *previously* (Appian, Samn. 10 §11 προεῖπε Κινέας=Cineas had said previously) w. ref. to a previous visit (cf., in a way, Sb 8247, 17 [I AD] ἐν τῇ παρεμβολῇ εἶπα ὑμῖν καὶ νῦν τὸ αὐτὸ λέγω) ὡς προειρήκαμεν καὶ ἄρτι πάλιν λέγω Gal 1: 9. καθὼς προείπαμεν ὑμῖν *as we have told you before* 1 Th 4: 6. W. ὅτι foll. προλέγω ὑμῖν, καθὼς προεῖπον Gal 5: 21. προείρηκα καὶ προλέγω 2 Cor 13: 2. In the four last passages πρ. connotes warning. μετὰ τὸ προειρηκέναι (i.e. τὸ πνεῦμα τὸ ἅγιον) is followed by Jer 38: 33, and in such a

way that λέγει κύριος (in the LXX φησὶν κύριος) introduces the main clause *after he* (the Holy Spirit) *said . . . , the Lord said* (as follows) Hb 10: 15 t.r. Of the act of baptism ταῦτα πάντα προειπόντες βαπτίσατε *after you have repeated all these things* (the prescribed admonitions), *baptize* D 7: 1.
b. *have already said* (in the same document), *have mentioned previously* (Appian, Syr. 66, §349 προεῖπον= I have mentioned earlier; Artem. 4, 69; oft. pap.) προείρηκα ὅτι *I have already said* 2 Cor 7: 3 (cf. 3: 2; 6: 12). Tautologically προειρήκαμεν ἐπάνω B 6: 18 (cf. vs. 12). Pass. καθὼς προείρηται (cf. Diod. S. 2, 32, 5 and PTebt. 27, 74 [II BC] καθότι προείρηται) Hb 4: 7 (cf. 3: 15).— The pf. pass. ptc. *already mentioned, aforementioned* (Polyb. 1, 20, 7; 3, 51, 8 al.; Diod. S. 4, 66, 1; 11, 20, 3 al.; Ps.-Demetr. c. 264; 288; 2 Macc 3: 28; 4: 1; 3 Macc 6: 35b; Jos., Vi. 45) with and without a name 1 Cl 41: 2; 43: 1; 44: 2; Dg 3: 2; Hm 9: 4; 10, 1, 5; s 6, 5, 7; 8, 11, 3; 9, 29, 3; D 11: 1. M-M.*

προείρηκα, προείρημαι s. προεῖπον.

προελπίζω pf. προήλπικα (Posidippus [III BC] in Athen. 9 p. 377c; Simplicius In Epict. p. 29, 51) *hope before, be the first to hope* ἐν τῷ Χριστῷ Eph 1: 12 (if ἡμεῖς here refers to the Jewish Christians, as most scholars [fr. Chrysostom to MDibelius[2] '27; this interpr. opposed by EPercy, D. Probleme der Kolosser u. Epheserbriefe, '46, 266f] prefer to take it, then προ would suggest 'before the Gentiles' or even 'before Christ appeared'. If the ἡμεῖς are the Christians as a whole [EHaupt; PEwald; Meinertz; HRendtorff; HGreeven in Dibelius[3] '53], then προ looks forward to the fulfilment of the hope in the future).*

προενάρχομαι 1 aor. προενηρξάμην (hapax legomenon) *begin (beforehand)* so that the beginning lies in the past as contrasted w. the present τί *someth.* 2 Cor 8: 10 (where προ is explained by ἀπὸ πέρυσι, and νυνί vs. 11 forms the contrast). Abs. (opp. ἐπιτελεῖν) vs. 6.*

προεξομολογέομαι 1 aor. προεξωμολογησάμην (an emendation by AvHarnack; see the apparatus in Funk) *confess (one's sins) beforehand* D 14: 1 (i.e. before the Lord's Supper; the ms. has προσεξομολογησάμενοι [= at the same time confessing your sins]).*

προεπαγγέλλω (the act. in Cass. Dio) 1 aor. mid. προεπηγγειλάμην in our lit. only mid. and pass. *promise before(hand), previously* (so mid. in Cass. Dio 42, 32; 46, 40) τί *someth.* Ro 1: 2. Pf. pass. ptc. (Inschr. v. Priene 11, 71 [84 BC] τὰ προεπηγγελμένα) ἡ προεπηγγελμένη εὐλογία *the bountiful gift which was (previously) promised* 2 Cor 9: 5. M-M.*

προεπικαλέω Pol 3: 1 v.l.; s. προεπιλακτίζω.*

προεπιλακτίζω 1 aor. mid. προεπελακτισάμην. The word προεπελακτίσασθε= 'you have forced me' Pol 3: 1 is Zahn's restoration of the text on the basis of four different Gk. readings that are alike in that they yield no sense. Until now the word is not attested lexically; neither is ἐπιλακτίζειν or προλακτίζειν. The form προεπεκαλέσασθε, preferred by Lghtf., Funk, Hilgenfeld, Krüger, Bihlmeyer means *you have invited*, but it has no more lexical attestation than Zahn's conjecture. But ἐπικαλεῖν and προκαλεῖν were in current use and the 'provocastis' of the Latin version seems to presuppose it.*

προέρχομαι dep.; impf. προηρχόμην; 2 aor. προῆλθον; fut. προελεύσομαι (Hdt.+; inscr., pap., LXX; Ep. Arist. 235 π. εἰς= 'go over to'; Philo, Joseph.).

1. *go forward, advance, proceed* w. acc. of the degree or the way (Pla., Rep. 1 p. 328ε; 10 p. 616β ὁδόν) μικρόν *a little* (Plut., Thes. 11, 1; cf. Jos., Vi. 304 π. ὀλίγον) Mt 26: 39 (v.l. προσελθών); Mk 14: 35 (v.l. προσελθών). ῥύμην μίαν *go along one street* or *go one block farther* Ac 12: 10. πρ. ὡσεὶ πόδας λ' Hv 4, 2, 1.—Of time *advance, come on* (Iambl., Vi. Pyth. 35, 251) τὸ κυρίου πάσχα προέρχεται Dg 12: 9.

2. *go before* as forerunner or leader προελεύσεται (v.l. προσελεύσεται) ἐνώπιον αὐτοῦ Lk 1: 17 (cf. Gen 33: 3, 14). W. acc. of the pers. (Plut., Brut. 25, 4 ὁ Βροῦτος πολὺ προῆλθε τοὺς κομίζοντας τὸ ἄριστον=Brutus went before the bearers) Ἰούδας προήρχετο αὐτούς Lk 22: 47; the t.r. has αὐτῶν for this (for the gen. cf. X., Cyr. 2, 2, 7; Jdth 2: 19).

3. *come* or *go before* someone, *go on before* or *ahead* (cf. Sir 32: 10) abs. (Herodian 1, 5, 2) Ac 20: 5 (v.l. προσελθόντες). πρ. ἐπὶ τὸ πλοῖον *go on board the ship beforehand* vs. 13 (v.l. προσελθόντες). πρ. εἰς ὑμᾶς *go on to you before (me)* 2 Cor 9: 5. οἱ προελθόντες με ἀπὸ Συρίας εἰς Ῥώμην *those who have gone before me from Syria to Rome* IRo 10: 2; cf. εἰς κόσμον προέλθῃ Third Corinthians 3: 6.—*Arrive at a place before* τινά *someone* προῆλθον αὐτούς Mk 6: 33.

4. *come out, proceed* (2 Macc 4: 34; Philo, Op. M. 161; Jos., Bell. 4, 651)—**a.** of human beings, abs. *come out of the house* (Ps.-Lucian, De Asin. 47; POxy. 472, 5 [II AD]) Ac 12: 13 v.l. (for προσῆλθεν).
b. of Christ *come forth, proceed* ἀπό *from* (π. ἀπό as 2 Macc 10: 27 v.l.) ἀφ' ἑνὸς πατρός IMg 7: 2. ἀπὸ σιγῆς 8: 2 (Proclus on Pla., Cratyl. p. 67, 9 Pasqu.: God ἀπ' ἄλλου προῆλθεν; 100, 6). M-M.*

προετοιμάζω 1 aor. προητοίμασα, mid. προητοιμασάμην (Hdt.+; Wsd 9: 8; Is 28: 24; Philo, Op. M. 77; Jos., Ant. 17, 121) *prepare beforehand*; the act. is used in our lit. only of God; τί *someth.* τὰς εὐεργεσίας αὐτοῦ 1 Cl 38: 3. W. indication of the goal: ἃ προητοίμασεν εἰς δόξαν Ro 9: 23. οἷς (by attraction for ἃ) προητοίμασεν ὁ θεὸς ἵνα Eph 2: 10. The martyr speaks of himself as a sacrifice prepared by God acc. to his good pleasure. In this sense the context fills out the expr. καθὼς προητοίμασας MPol 14: 2.—1 Cl 33: 3 Funk; IEph 9: 1 v.l. Funk.—Mid. *prepare oneself* w. μετανοεῖν Hv 4, 2, 5.*

προευαγγελίζομαι 1 aor. προευηγγελισάμην *proclaim good news in advance* (schol. on Soph., Trach. 335 p. 299 Papag.; Philo, Op. M. 34, Mut. Nom. 158) τινί *to someone*, foll. by direct discourse introduced by ὅτι Gal 3: 8. M-M.*

προέχω (Hom.+; pap.; Job 27: 6 Swete v.l.)—**1.** act., intr. *jut out, excel, be first* (Jos., C. Ap. 2, 186) w. gen. of the thing that is exceeded (Memnon [I BC/I AD]: 434 fgm. 1, 34, 7 Jac.; Cebes 34, 1; Dio Chrys. 44[61], 11; Ael. Aristid. 30 p. 581 D.; Ep. Arist. 235) πάντων προέχουσα ἐπιθυμία *above all there is (the) desire* Hm 12, 2, 1.

2. mid. In Ro 3: 9, which is text-critically uncertain, the mid. either has the same mng. as the act. (the act. is so used in X., Cyr. 2, 1, 16; Jos., Ant. 7, 237) *have an advantage* (Vulgate)—a mng. not found elsewh. for the mid.—or its customary sense *hold someth. before oneself for protection* (so also En. 99, 3). In that case, if the 'we' in προεχόμεθα refers to the Jews, then the οὐ πάντως that follows vigorously rejects the idea that they possess anything that might shield them fr. God's wrath. However, if the 'we' in 9a must of necessity be the same as in 9b, i.e. Paul himself, he is still dealing w. the opponents whom he has in mind in vss. 7, 8, and he asks ironically: *am I* *protecting myself?, am I making excuses?* He is able to answer this question w. a flat 'no', since his explanation in vs. 9b is no less clear and decisive than his earlier statements (for προέχεσθαι='put up as a defense' cf. Soph., Ant. 80; Thu. 1, 140, 4). S. 3 below.

3. pass. It is also poss. to take προεχόμεθα Ro 3: 9 as a pass., meaning *are we excelled?*, then *are we in a worse position (than they)?* (so Field, Notes 152f; Gdspd.; RSV mg.; Plut., Mor. 1038D οὐθὲν π. ὑπὸ τοῦ Διός). M-M.*

προηγέομαι mid. dep.; fut. προηγήσομαι (Hdt., Aristoph.+; inscr., pap., LXX; Philo, Op. M. 28) *go before and show the way* τινός (to) someone (X., Hipparch. 5, 4; 2 Macc 11: 8) symbolically *of righteousness that goes before the good man to judgment* B 4: 12. *Preside* (Dit., Syll.³ 1109, 87; PLeipz. 63, 6) οἱ προηγούμενοι *the officials* (cf. Dt 20: 9; 1 Esdr 5: 8f; 9: 12 [τοῦ πλήθους]) of the Christian churches 1 Cl 21: 6. More definitely οἱ πρ. τῆς ἐκκλησίας Hv 2, 2, 6. W. πρωτοκαθεδρῖται 3, 9, 7. The difficult passage τῇ τιμῇ ἀλλήλους προηγούμενοι Ro 12: 10 is understood by the versions (It., Vulg., Syr., Armen.) to mean *try to outdo one another in showing respect.* Others would take ἡγεῖσθαι=*consider, esteem* and prefer the sense *consider better, esteem more highly* for προηγ.: *as far as honor is concerned, let each one esteem the other more highly* (than himself); cf. Bl-D. §150 app. M-M.*

πρόθεσις, εως, ἡ—1. *setting forth, putting out, presentation* (Pla.+; inscr.; Sb 5252 [pap. of 65 AD regarding the farming out of the fees fr. a temple of Isis: l. 19 φαγεῖν ἐκθέτου οὔσης τῆς προθέσεως]. On the relig. use of the verb προτίθημι in Diocles [Athen. 3, 110b] cf. Dssm., B 155f [BS 157]; on πρόθεσις τ. ἄρτων s. UPZ 149, 21, vol. I p. 638–40) of the *sacred bread*, lit. *loaves of presentation* οἱ ἄρτοι τῆς προθέσεως (ἄρτος 1b) Mt 12: 4; Mk 2: 26; Lk 6: 4 (all three 1 Km 21: 7). ἡ πρ. τῶν ἄρτων in a concrete usage, the furniture for the presentation of the bread, *the table for the sacred bread*, despite the presence of τράπεζα in the immediate context, with which it is identical (cf. Ex 25: 23–30; Lev 24: 6) Hb 9: 2. Some exegetes here take π. in the abstract sense= presentation of the showbread.

2. *plan, purpose, resolve, will* (Aristot.+; Polyb. 1, 26, 1 and oft.; Plut., Mor. 960F; inscr., pap.; 2 and 3 Macc; Ep. Arist., Philo; Jos., Ant. 18, 272; 19, 190).

a. of men 2 Ti 3: 10 (here perh. w. a turn toward the mng. *way of thinking*; cf. Polyb. 4, 73, 2 ἡ πρ., ἣν ἔχει πρός τινα). ὁσία καὶ ἄμωμος πρ. 1 Cl 45: 7. ἡ πρ. τῆς καρδίας *purpose of heart*, i.e. *devotion* Ac 11: 23. τῆς πρ. κρατεῖν *obtain one's purpose* 27: 13. κατὰ πρόθεσιν *according to the purpose* (Polyb.; PTebt. 27, 81 [II BC]; 3 Macc 5: 29; Ep. Arist. 199) w. gen. κατὰ πρόθεσιν εὐνουχίας *in accordance with the resolve to remain unmarried* Agr 18.

b. of the divine purpose (s. lit. s.v. προγινώσκω) οἱ κατὰ πρόθεσιν κλητοὶ ὄντες *those who are called in accordance with his purpose* Ro 8: 28 (ECBlackman, ET 50, '39, 378f). ἡ κατ' ἐκλογὴν πρόθεσις τοῦ θεοῦ *God's purpose of (s)election* 9: 11. κατὰ πρόθεσιν (Philo, Mos. 2, 61) *according to the design* Eph 1: 11. Cf. 2 Ti 1: 9. κατὰ πρόθεσιν τῶν αἰώνων *according to the eternal purpose* Eph 3: 11 (cf. αἰών 1b). M-M. B. 1240f.*

προθεσμία, ας, ἡ (Lysias, Pla.+; inscr. [e.g. the inscr. in JZingerle, Hlg. Recht: Jahreshefte des Österr. Arch. Instit. 23, '26, col. 23f οὐκ ἐτήρησε τὴν προθεσμίαν τῆς θεοῦ]; pap. [e.g., POxy. 2732, 19 (154 AD); 2754, 6 (III AD) πάλαι τοῦ διαλογισμοῦ τὴν προθεσμίαν εἰδότες=having

known long ago the time fixed for the circuit court]; Sym.; Philo; Jos., Bell. 2, 633, Ant. 12, 201. Loanw. in rabb.— Subst. fem. of προθέσμιος, α, ον; ἡμέρα is to be supplied) *appointed day, fixed* or *limited time*, of the day when a son reaches his majority ἄχρι τῆς προθεσμίας τοῦ πατρός *until the time set by the father* Gal 4: 2. It is uncertain whether Paul is referring here to certain legal measures which gave the father the right to fix the date when his son would come of age, or whether he is rounding out his comparison w. details that occur to him at the moment, as he so oft. does (though there was a προθεσμία τοῦ πατρός for the coming of age of mankind in general; the parallel phrase, τὸ πλήρωμα τοῦ χρόνου, vs. 4 is used oft. in the pap. of contractual termination; see s.v. πληρόω 2).— Lghtf. and Zahn ad loc. M-M.*

προθυμία, ας, ἡ (Hom.+; inscr., pap.; Sir 45: 23; Ep. Arist., Philo, Joseph.) *willingness, readiness, good will* 2 Cor 8: 19; 9: 2; Dg 1. W. ἐκτένεια 1 Cl 33: 1; ἐν ἀγαθῇ πρ. 2: 3. μετὰ πάσης προθυμίας (as Hdt. 4, 98; Pla., Rep. 412E; Philo, Abr. 246; Jos., Ant. 15, 124; Dit., Syll.³ 532, 6f; Inschr. v. Magn. 97, 74; Inscr. fr. Gerasa [CHKraeling, Gerasa '38] no. 192; Dit., Or. 229, 98) Ac 17: 11 here w. emphasis on *goodwill* and absence of prejudice (FWDanker, NTS 10, '64, 366f). εἰ ἡ πρ. πρόκειται *if willingness is present*, i.e. *if a man is willing* 2 Cor 8: 12. προθυμίαν ἔχειν *have zeal* (Hdt. et al.) Hs 5, 3, 4b; foll. by gen. *for someth.* 5, 3, 4a. ἡ προθυμία τοῦ θέλειν (as Pla., Leg. 3 p. 697D) 2 Cor 8: 11. M-M.*

πρόθυμος, ον (Soph., Hdt.+; inscr., pap., LXX; Ep. Arist. 94; Philo, Joseph.) *ready, willing, eager* of the spirit (opp. ἡ σὰρξ ἀσθενής) Mt 26: 41; Mk 14: 38=Pol 7: 2. πρ. εἴς τι (Thu. et al.; Dit., Or. 221, 61; Hab 1: 8) *prompt in someth.* 1 Cl 34: 2. πρόθυμον εἶναι w. inf. foll. Hm 12, 5, 1. Gener. *willing, eager* w. ἱλαρός Hs 9, 2, 4.—The subst. neut. τὸ πρόθυμον *desire, eagerness* (Eur., Med. 178; Thu. 3, 82, 8; Pla., Leg. 9 p. 859B; Herodian 8, 3, 5; Jos., Ant. 4, 42; 213; 3 Macc 5: 26) τὸ κατ' ἐμὲ πρόθυμον *my eagerness* (κατά II 7b) Ro 1: 15. M-M.*

προθύμως adv. (Aeschyl., Hdt.+; inscr., pap., LXX, Philo; Jos., Ant. 12, 133; 18, 374) *willingly, eagerly, freely* opp. αἰσχροκερδῶς 1 Pt 5: 2. μάλιστα προθύμως *with the greatest eagerness* MPol 13: 1. *Readily* πάσχειν Hs 9, 28, 2; 4. *Eagerly* MPol 8: 3. M-M.*

προϊδών s. προοράω.

προΐημι fut. mid. προήσομαι (Hom.+; inscr., pap., LXX, Philo, Joseph.) in our lit. only mid. *bring forth, express* (Demosth. 19, 118 ῥῆμα; Ps.-Pla., Tim. Locr. p. 100C λόγον; Jos., C. Ap. 1, 43 ῥῆμα) τινί τι *someth. to someone* (Alciphr. 3, 18, 3) προήσομαι ὑμῖν ἐμῆς πνοῆς ῥῆσιν 1 Cl 57: 3 (Pr 1: 23).*

πρόϊμος, ον (this is most likely the correct form of the word, derived as it is fr. πρό; its opp. is ὄψιμος 'late in the year'. The spelling πρώϊμος [X., Oec. 17, 4 al.; Dit., Or. 56, 68 πρώϊμος σπόρος—III BC; PTebt. 27, 25; 76—113 BC] derives it fr. πρωΐ and clearly confuses it w. πρωϊνός [opp. ἑσπερινός]. The LXX keeps the two forms carefully separate [Thackeray p. 90].—Bl-D. §35, 1; Mlt.-H. 73). The subst. (cf. Bl-D. §241, 5) πρόϊμος Js 5: 7 (opp. ὄψιμος) is usu. understood to mean *early rain* in line w. the t.r., which adds ὑετός (Hollmann, Windisch, MDibelius, Meinertz, OHoltzmann, FHauck, w. ref. to Dt 11: 14; Hos 6: 3; Jo 2: 23; Zech 10: 1; Jer 5: 24. So Engl. transl.). Others think of the *early crops* (Spitta, Belser; cf. Petosiris, fgm. 6, l. 45 πρώϊμοι καρποί; Geopon. 1, 12, 32 οἱ πρώϊμοι καρποὶ κ. οἱ ὄψιμοι).—In B 3: 4, τότε ῥαγήσεται πρόϊμον τὸ φῶς σου is quoted fr. Is 58: 8. The LXX might better have translated the Hebr. orig. w. πρωϊνός. But it seems likely that the translator meant 'early'=soon. M-M.*

προϊνός Rv 2: 28 v.l.; 22: 16 v.l. is prob. a faulty spelling of πρωϊνός (q.v.).*

προΐστημι 2 aor. inf. προστῆναι; pf. 3 pl. προεστᾶσιν (Dg 5: 3); (Hom.+; inscr., pap., LXX, Joseph.). In our lit. only intr. (pres. and impf. mid., also 2 aor., pf., plpf.).
1. *be at the head (of), rule, direct* w. gen. of the pers. or the thing (Hdt., Thu. et al.; inscr., pap.; Am 6: 10; 1 Macc 5: 19) *manage, conduct* τοῦ ἰδίου οἴκου 1 Ti 3: 4f. τέκνων, οἴκων vs. 12. Of officials and administrators in the church (cf. Diod. S. 40, 3, 4 of suitable men δυνησομένους τοῦ σύμπαντος ἔθνους [Jewish people] προΐστασθαι; Jos., Ant. 8, 300 πρ. τοῦ πλήθους, Vi. 168). So perh. (s. 2 below) οἱ προϊστάμενοι ὑμῶν 1 Th 5: 12 and the abs. ὁ προϊστάμενος (cf. Jos., Vi. 93) Ro 12: 8 (s. 2 below). Certainly οἱ καλῶς προεστῶτες πρεσβύτεροι 1 Ti 5: 17 (s. Nicol. Dam.: fgm. 130, 28 p. 414, 2 Jac. τοῦ κοινοῦ προεστῶτες τῆς πολιτείας). οἱ πρεσβύτεροι οἱ προϊστάμενοι τῆς ἐκκλησίας Hv 2, 4, 3.—HGreeven, ZNW 44, '52/'53, 31–41.
2. *be concerned about, care for, give aid* (Demosth. 4, 46; Epict. 3, 24, 3; PFay. 13, 5; PTebt. 326, 11 τοῦ παιδίου; BGU 1105, 6; Ep. Arist. 182; Jos., Ant. 14, 196 τ. ἀδικουμένων) w. gen. δόγματος ἀνθρωπίνου Dg 5: 3. So perh. (s. 1 above) οἱ προϊστάμενοι ὑμῶν (betw. κοπιῶντες and νουθετοῦντες) 1 Th 5: 12 and ὁ προϊστάμενος (betw. μεταδιδούς and ἐλεῶν) Ro 12: 8 (cf. vDobschütz on 1 Th 5: 12 and the exc. after vs. 13. Against him vHarnack, ZNW 27, '28, 7–10). *Busy oneself with, engage in* w. gen. (Soph., Elect. 980 φόνου; Athen. 13 p. 612A τέχνης; Ep. 53 of Apollonius of Tyana [Philostrat. I 358, 8] προϊστάμενοι φιλοσοφίας; Pr 26: 17; Jos., Ant. 5, 90) καλῶν ἔργων Tit 3: 8, 14. M-M.*

προκάθημαι (Hdt.+; inscr.) *preside (over), lead* (Pla.+; Polyb. 12, 16, 6; Plut., Rom. 14, 5; Cass. Dio 49, 40 al.; Dit., Syll.³ 663, 12 [c. 200 вс] προκαθήμενος ταῖς θεραπείαις; UPZ 110, 165 [164 вс]; 1 Esdr)
1. lit. of the bishop IMg 6: 1. Of the other church officials beside the bishop οἱ προκαθήμενοι *the leaders* 6: 2. Of the Roman church προκάθηται ἐν τόπῳ (s. τύπος, end) χωρίου Ῥωμαίων *it holds the presidency in the land of the Romans* IRo inscr. a (s. on this Lghtf. and Hdb. ad loc.; Harnack, SAB 1896, 111–31; JChapman, Rev. Bénéd. 13, 1896, 385ff; FXFunk, Kirchengeschichtl. Abhandlungen u. Untersuchungen I 1897, 1–23; HAchelis, Das Christentum in den ersten drei Jahrhunderten '12, I 210ff).
2. fig., of the Roman church προκαθημένη τῆς ἀγάπης *preëminent in love* IRo inscr. b (cf. AJülicher, GGA 1898, 4).*

προκαλέω mostly mid. (Hom.+; inscr., pap.; 2 Macc 8: 11; Jos., Ant. 7, 315; 18, 369) *provoke, challenge* τινά someone Gal 5: 26 (Diod. S. 4, 17, 4 προκαλεῖσθαί τινα εἰς μάχην; Arrian, Cyneg. 16, 1; Lucian, Conv. 20 ἐς ἀγῶνα προκαλέσασθαι αὐτόν). M-M.*

προκαταγγέλλω 1 aor. προκατήγγειλα; pf. pass. ptc. προκατηγγελμένος (Jos., Ant. 1, 219; 2, 218) *announce beforehand, foretell* of prophetic utterance τὶ someth. (Jos., Ant. 10, 67) Ac 3: 24 t.r. Acc. of the thing foll. by the aor. inf. (Bl-D. §350; 397, 3; Rob. 1036) 3: 18. περὶ τινος *give information concerning someth. beforehand,* i.e. *foretell someth.* 7: 52. Pass. 2 Cor 9: 5 t.r. M-M.*

προκαταρτίζω 1 aor. subj. προκαταρτίσω (Hippocr.+) *get ready* or *arrange for in advance* τὶ someth. (Suppl. Epigr. Gr. IV 449, 13 [II вс] λίθους) 2 Cor 9: 5.*

προκατέχω (Hom. Hymns, Thu.+; pap.; Jos., Bell. 4, 503) *gain possession of* or *occupy previously* τὶ someth. fig. (cf. Polyb. 8, 33, 3 προκατέχεσθαι τῇ πρὸς Ῥωμαίους εὐνοίᾳ; 27, 4, 9) ἀπὸ τῶν προκατεχόντων σου τὴν διάνοιαν λογισμῶν Dg 2: 1. The word is also found Ro 3: 9 DG προκατέχομεν περισσόν; *do we have a previous advantage?*

πρόκειμαι (Hom.+; inscr., pap., LXX, Ep. Arist., Philo, Joseph.) defective dep. *be set before.*
1. *be exposed* to public view (of corpses lying in state Aeschyl., Sept. 965 al.) of Sodom and Gomorrha πρόκεινται δεῖγμα *they are exhibited as a(n)* (horrible) *example* Jd 7 (cf. Jos., Bell. 6, 103 καλὸν ὑπόδειγμα πρόκειται).
2. *lie before, be present* (Ps.-Clem., Hom. 3, 51) ἡ προθυμία πρόκειται *willingness is present* 2 Cor 8: 12. ἀντὶ τῆς προκειμένης αὐτῷ χαρᾶς instead of (ἀντὶ 1) the joy that was set before him, i.e. was within his grasp, he endured the cross Hb 12: 2 (ERiggenbach; JBNisius, Zur Erklärung v. Hb 12: 2: BZ 14, '17, 44–61); s. also 3 below. ἡ προκειμένη ἐλπίς the hope that is set before 6: 18 (cf. Jos., Ant. 1, 14 εὐδαιμονία πρόκειται τινι παρὰ θεοῦ). πρόκειται *it lies before (us),* i.e. *that is the question at issue* (Diod. S. 8, 11, 4; Περὶ ὕψους p. 4, 11; 31, 22 V.) IPhld 8: 2.
3. of a goal or destination, w. dat. of the pers. *lie* or *be set before someone* (Ael. Aristid. 31, 2 K.=11 p. 127 D.: μητρὶ πένθος πρόκειται) ὁ προκείμενος ἡμῖν σκοπός *the goal that is set before us* 1 Cl 63: 1 (s. σκοπός). ὁ προκείμενος ἡμῖν ἀγών (s. ἀγών 1) Hb 12: 1. Without a dat. (Diod. S. 4, 42, 7) IMg 5: 1. τὸ προκείμενον ζῆν *the life that is set before* (you) IEph 17: 1.—Also *be in prospect* (Jos., Ant. 1, 14; 8, 208.—Diod. S. 15, 60, 1 [a prize] and Περὶ ὕψους p. 66, 20 V. of wages that have been allowed); so perh. (s. 2 above) Hb 12: 2: *for* (ἀντὶ 3) *the joy that was in prospect for him* (so Windisch², Strathmann; cf. Moffatt; RSV). M-M.*

προκηρύσσω 1 aor. ptc. προκηρύξας; pf. pass. ptc. προκεκηρυγμένος (since Soph.; X., De Rep. Lac. 11, 2; inscr., pap., Philo, Joseph.) *proclaim publicly;* in our lit. the prefix προ- obviously gives the word the sense *proclaim beforehand* (Lucian, Tyrannic. 9; Alex. Aphr., An. p. 1, 6 Br.; Jos., Bell. 6, 385) τὶ someth. of John the Baptist βάπτισμα μετανοίας Ac 13: 24. Of the OT prophets (Jos., Ant. 10, 79 Ἱερεμίας τὰ μέλλοντα τῇ πόλει προεκήρυξε) τὴν ἔλευσιν τοῦ κυρίου Pol 6: 3. Pass. Ac 3: 20 t.r. M-M.*

προκοιμάομαι pf. pass. ptc. προκεκοιμημένος *fall asleep before, earlier* (Cat. Cod. Astr. VIII 3, 110; Leontios 45 p. 94, 18) Hs 9, 16, 5f.*

προκοπή, ῆς, ἡ (Polyb.+; Bion in Diog. L. 4, 50; Posidonius in Diog. L. 7, 91; Diod. S. 16, 6, 3; Epict. [index Sch.]; Dit., Or. 627, 2; PRyl. 233, 16; PGiess. 27, 7; Sir 51: 17; 2 Macc 8: 8; Ep. Arist. 242; Philo; Jos., Ant. 4, 59; Test. 12 Patr.; loanw. in rabb. Rejected by the Atticists: Phryn. p. 85 Lob.) *progress, advancement, furtherance* Phil 1: 25; 1 Ti 4: 15. εἰς πρ. τινος ἔρχεσθαι *tend to advance someth.* Phil 1: 12. M-M.*

προκόπτω (Eur., Hdt.+) in our lit. only intr. *go forward, make progress, prosper* (Polyb. et al.; inscr., pap., Philo, Joseph.) impf. προέκοπτον; fut. προκόψω; 1 aor. προέκοψα.

1. of time *be advanced, be far gone* (Charito 2, 3, 9; Appian, Bell. Civ. 2, 78 §325 ἡ ἡμέρα προύκοπτεν) ἡ νὺξ προέκοψεν (Jos., Bell. 4, 298) Ro 13: 12.
2. *progress, advance* in what is good or in what is bad τινί *in someth.* (Diod. S. 11, 87, 5; Dit., Syll.³ 708, 18 [II BC] ἡλικίᾳ προκόπτων; Philo, Sacr. Abel. 7) Lk 2: 52 v.l. Also ἔν τινι (Diod. S. 17, 69, 4; Epict. 2, 17, 4; Lucian, Hermot. 63; M. Ant. 1, 17, 8; Vett. Val. 60, 15; 19) Lk 2: 52. ἐν τῷ Ἰουδαϊσμῷ Gal 1: 14. ἐν ταῖς ἐντολαῖς 2 Cl 17: 3; ἐπὶ πλεῖον πρ. (Diod. S. 14, 98, 3) *make further progress* 2 Ti 3: 9; w. gen. foll. (Ael. Aristid. 46 p. 405 D. τ. σοφίας) ἐπὶ πλεῖον πρ. ἀσεβείας 2: 16 (cf. Jos., Ant. 20, 205). πρ. ἐπὶ τὸ χεῖρον *go on from bad to worse* 3: 13 (Paroem. Gr.: Zenob. 3, 82 τῶν ἐπὶ τὸ χεῖρον προκοπτόντων; Jos., Bell. 6, 1 τὰ πάθη προύκοπτεν καθ' ἡμέραν ἐπὶ τὸ χεῖρον, Ant. 4, 59; 18, 340; Test. Jud. 21: 8 v.l. ἐπὶ τὸ κακόν; schol. on Soph., El. 875 p. 142 Papag. ἐπὶ τὸ βέλτιον). M-M.*

πρόκριμα, ατος, τό (as a legal t.t. IG V [1], 21 II, 7 [II BC]; Mitteis, Chrest. 88 II, 30) *prejudgment, discrimination* χωρὶς πρ. (PFlor. 68, 13; 16f three times) 1 Ti 5: 21. M-M.*

προκρίνω pf. pass. προκέκριμαι (Eur., Hdt.; inscr., pap., Wsd 7: 8) *prefer* τινός *to someth.* (Herm. Wr. 4, 8a) pass. *be preferred* (Arrian, Anab. 1, 16, 4; Wilcken, Chrest. 27, 6 [II AD] προκρίνονται παντὸς οὑτινοσοῦν οἱ νόμοι; Philo, Cher. 46; Jos., Ant. 11, 196; 18, 46) of faith and love ὧν οὐδὲν προκέκριται *to which nothing is preferred* or *superior* ISm 6: 1 (Diog. L. 1, 82 Βίας προκεκριμένος τῶν ἑπτά = Bias, who surpassed the others of the seven [wise men]); cf. IMg 1: 2.*

προκυρόω pf. pass. ptc. προκεκυρωμένος *make valid* or *ratify previously* (Suppl. Epigr. Gr. III 674A, 28 [II BC]) διαθήκη προκεκυρωμένη ὑπὸ τοῦ θεοῦ *a will* or *covenant* (διαθήκη 1) *previously ratified by God* Gal 3: 17.*

προλαμβάνω 2 aor. προέλαβον; 1 aor. pass. προελήμφθην (on the spelling s. Bl-D. §101 p. 46; Mlt.-H. 246f) (trag., Hdt.+; inscr., pap., LXX, Ep. Arist., Philo, Joseph., Sib. Or. 3, 569) *take before(hand)*.
1. in uses where the temporal force of προ- is still felt
a. πρ. τι *do someth. before the usual time, anticipate someth.* (cf. Theophr., Hist. Pl. 8, 1, 4 πρ. ταῖς εὐδίαις τὴν αὔξησιν 'begin the growth beforehand in favorable weather'; IG Sic. It. 2014, 1; Philo, Somn. 1, 2) w. inf. foll. (Jos., Ant. 6, 305; Bl-D. §392, 2; Rob. 1120) προέλαβεν μυρίσαι τὸ σῶμά μου *she had anointed my body beforehand* Mk 14: 8.
b. *take it upon oneself, undertake* (in the sense 'anticipate mentally' in Polyb., Plut.; Ep. Arist. 206; w. inf. foll. Hippocr., Ep. 27, 41) προέλαβον παρακαλεῖν ὑμᾶς IEph 3: 2.
2. in uses where the temporal sense of προ- is felt very little, if at all—**a.** *take, get* of a meal (Dit., Syll.³ 1170, 7; 9; 15 of the taking of food [ἄρτον, γάλα et al.] in the temple of Asclepius in Epidaurus. Cf. also vWilamowitz in note 4 to the inscr.) ἕκαστος τὸ ἴδιον δεῖπνον προλαμβάνει ἐν τῷ φαγεῖν *in eating, everyone takes his own supper* 1 Cor 11: 21 (s. ἴδιος 1aβ).
b. *detect, overtake, surprise* τινά *someone* pass. (POxy. 928, 8; Wsd 17: 16) ἐὰν προλημφθῇ ἄνθρωπος ἔν τινι παραπτώματι Gal 6: 1. Cf. Field, Notes 190; JDRobb, ET 57, '45/'46, 222. M-M.*

προλέγω pf. pass. 3 sing. προλέλεκται (Aeschyl., Hdt. +; inscr.; Is 41: 26; Ep. Arist. 8).
1. *tell beforehand* or *in advance* of the event (Demetr. of Phal. [300 BC]: 228 fgm. 39 Jac. τὶς θεῶν αὐτοῖς προύλεγε τὸ μέλλον; Apollon. Paradox. 3 τὰ μέλλοντα; Jos., Ant. 7, 226; cf. προεῖπον 1) w. ὅτι foll. (Pla., Rep. 1 p. 337A) 2 Cor 13: 2; Gal 5: 21 (corresponding to the words προλέγω καθὼς προεῖπον, Appian, Bell. Civ. 2, 139 §579 has the doublet προλέγομεν ... καὶ προεροῦμεν); 1 Th 3: 4 (in the above-mentioned passage from Appian, Brutus says προλέγομεν 'we', as Paul says προελέγομεν). Of a prophetic saying προλέγει ἡμῖν (a quot. fr. Is follows) 1 Cl 34: 3 (Appian, Bell. Civ. 1, 71 §326 the priests in charge of the sacrifices foretell what is to happen).
2. pf. pass. *be said above* (προεῖπον 2b) ὡς προλέλεκται *as has been stated above* (Ps.-Demetr., Eloc. 89) Epil Mosq 4. M-M.*

προμαρτύρομαι mid. dep. (PLond. 1356, 32 [710 AD]) *bear witness to beforehand, predict* τὶ *someth.* 1 Pt 1: 11 (the form in the v.l., προμαρτυρέομαι, is found PLond. 1343, 27 [709 AD]). M-M.*

προμελετάω (Aristoph.; Ps.-X., Rep. Ath. 1, 20; Pla. et al.; Philo, Fuga 36) *practice beforehand, prepare* (t.t. for practicing a speech Aristoph., Eccl. 116) w. inf. foll. (Bl-D. §392, 2) πρ. ἀπολογηθῆναι *prepare one's defense* (in court) Lk 21: 14.*

προμεριμνάω *concern oneself* or *be anxious beforehand* w. indir. quest. foll. Mk 13: 11.*

προνηστεύω 1 aor. προενήστευσα (Hdt. 2, 40; Hippocr. ed. Littré VII p. 412; VIII 178) *fast beforehand* D 7: 4.*

προνοέω (Hom.+; inscr., pap., LXX) *think of beforehand, take care*—**1.** *care for, provide for* τινός *someone* or *someth.* (X.+; Maximus Tyr. 5, 4c [προνοεῖ ὁ θεὸς τοῦ ὅλου]; inscr., pap.; Wsd 13: 16; Philo, Virt. 216) τῶν ἰδίων καὶ μάλιστα οἰκείων *his own people and especially the members of his family* 1 Ti 5: 8 (Horapollo 2, 108 ὑπὸ τ. οἰκείων προνοούμενος); the mid. in the same sense (Horap., loc. cit. προνοούμενος ἑαυτοῦ) ibid. v.l.
2. *take thought for, take into consideration, have regard for* w. gen. foll. (Jos., Ant. 1, 53 ἀρετῆς) ἁγνείας Pol 5: 3. τοῦ καλοῦ ἐνώπιον θεοῦ Pol 6: 1. W. acc. καλὰ ἐνώπιον κυρίου (cf. Pr 3: 4 for this and Pol 6: 1) 2 Cor 8: 21. Foll. by πῶς *so that* D 12: 4.—The mid. in the same sense (Thu.+; inscr., pap., LXX, Philo; Jos., Ant. 9, 3; 19, 309 al.), w. acc. (X., Mem. 4, 3, 12) καλὰ ἐνώπιον πάντων ἀνθρώπων Ro 12: 17; cf. 2 Cor 8: 21 v.l. M-M.*

πρόνοια, ας, ἡ (Aeschyl., Hdt.+; inscr., pap., LXX, Ep. Arist., Philo, Joseph.) *foresight*.
1. of God *providence, forethought* (trag.; Hdt. 3, 108, 1; X., Mem. 1, 4, 6; 4, 3, 6; Pla., Tim. 30B; 44C; Polyb. 23, 17, 10; Posidonius fr. Diog. L. 7, 138; Diod. S. 1, 1, 3; 3, 57, 5; 4, 47, 1 θεῶν πρόνοια al.; Diog. L. 3, 24; Plut., Mor. 425F; 436D; Achilles Tat. 7, 10, 1; Herm. Wr. 1, 19; 12, 14; 21; in Stob. p. 514, 24; 516, 5 Sc. ἡ ἄνω πρόνοια; p. 418, 28 Sc.; Dit., Syll.³ 700, 29 [117 BC] μετὰ τῆς τῶν θεῶν προνοίας; POsl. 148 [II/I BC] τῇ τ. θεῶν προνοίᾳ; POxy. 1682, 6; Wsd; 3 and 4 Macc; Ep. Arist. 201. Philo wrote a work entitled Περὶ προνοίας [Euseb., H.E. 2, 18, 6, Praep. Ev. 7, 20, 9; 8, 13, 7]; Jos., Bell. 3, 391; 7, 453, Ant. 2, 60; 349 al.; Sib. Or. 5, 227; 323; Third Corinthians 3: 19) 1 Cl 24: 5. W. σοφία (Ael. Aristid. 36, 123 K.= 48 p. 488 D.) Hv 1, 3, 4.
2. of men *foresight, care* Ac 24: 2. πρόνοιαν ποιεῖσθαι τινος *make provision for someth., be concerned for* or *about someth.* (Demosth.; Polyb.; Dionys. Hal. 10, 1; Plut.; Dit., Syll.³ 734, 5 τὰς εὐσεβείας and oft. [s. index]; POxy. 899, 17; PFlor. 2, 207; PLond. 1912 [letter of

Claudius], 103 [41 AD] and oft.; Da 6: 19; Ep. Arist. 80; Jos., C. Ap. 1, 9, Vi. 62) τῆς σαρκὸς πρόνοιαν μὴ ποιεῖσθε εἰς ἐπιθυμίας Ro 13: 14 (Philo, Ebr. 87 σαρκῶν ποιεῖσθαι πρόνοιαν). ἐνὸς ἐποιήσατο πρ. Papias 2: 15.—JAmann, D. Zeusrede d. Ail. Arist. '31, 73ff. M-M.*

προοδοιπορέω 1 aor. ptc. προοδοιπορήσας (Lucian, Hermot. 27; Diog. L. 7, 176; Jos., Ant. 3, 2) travel or go on before euphemist. for die before now οἱ προοδοιπορήσαντες πρεσβύτεροι 1 Cl 44: 5.*

προοδοιπόρος, ον (late and rare; s. Hesychius s.v. ὀδουρός) going before, subst. ὁ, ἡ προοδοιπόρος of vice as (ἡ) προοδοιπόρος τῶν ἁμαρτιῶν ἡμῶν the forerunner of our sins 2 Cl 10: 1.*

πρόοιδα (Hdt.+; Epict. 2, 10, 5; PSI 349, 8 [III BC]; Wsd 19: 1; 4 Macc 4: 25) defective perf. w. pres. mng., ptc. προειδώς; plpf. προῄδειν know beforehand, previously τὶ someth. (Menand., Per. 222 J; Polyb. 5, 13, 5 τὸ μέλλον; Herodian 7, 1, 9) Ac 2: 31 v.l.; IPhld 7: 2 v.l. (s. Bihlmeyer ad loc.). Foll. by acc. and inf. 1 Cl 43: 6.*

προοράω (Hdt.+; inscr., pap., LXX, Philo, Joseph.) 2 aor. προεῖδον (Hom.+); pf. προεώρακα; impf. mid. προορώμην (on this form Bl-D. §66, 2 app.; Mlt.-H. 190).
1. see previously looking back fr. the present (Hdt.; Aristot.) ἦσαν προεωρακότες Τρόφιμον ἐν τῇ πόλει σὺν αὐτῷ they had previously seen Trophimus in the city with him Ac 21: 29.
2. foresee, see in advance w. an eye to the future τὶ (X., Cyr. 2, 4, 21 τοῦτο προϊδὼν ὡς; Jos., Ant. 10, 142) ITr 8: 1. W. ὅτι foll. Gal 3: 8. Abs. (Jos., Bell. 2, 619) προϊδὼν ἐλάλησεν Ac 2: 31.
3. mid. see before one, have before one's eyes w. acc. (Menand., Per. 12 J; Dit., Syll.³ 569, 13; UPZ 42, 22 [162 BC]; Philo) τινά someone προορώμην τὸν κύριον ἐνώπιόν μου Ac 2: 25 (Ps 15: 8). M-M.*

προορίζω 1 aor. προώρισα, pass. προωρίσθην (Demosth. 31, 4 codd.; Heliod. 7, 24, 4; Sopater Rhet. [V AD]: Rhet. Gr. V p. 152, 20. Pap. fr. VI AD in secular usage) decide upon beforehand, predestine of God τινά someone Ro 8: 30. Foll. by inf. Ac 4: 28. W. final εἰς foll.: τὶ someth. 1 Cor 2: 7; τινά someone Eph 1: 5. τινά τι someone as someth., to be someth. Ro 8: 29. Pass. w. inf. foll. IEph inscr. Foll. by εἰς τὸ εἶναι Eph 1: 11(12).—RLiechtenhan, D. göttl. Vorherbestimmung bei Pls u. in d. Posidonianischen Philosophie '22; HBraun, Qumran u. d. NT II, '66, 243–50. S. also s.v. προγινώσκω.*

προπάσχω 2 aor. προέπαθον (Soph., Hdt.+; Appian, Liby. 51 §223; 52 §225; Jos., Vi. 250) suffer previously προπαθόντες after we had already suffered 1 Th 2: 2. M-M.*

προπάτωρ, ορος, ὁ (Pind., Hdt.+; Cass. Dio 44, 37; Lucian, Alex. 43; Ps.-Plut., Consol. ad Apoll. 10 p. 106F; Dit., Or. 446, 3; PGiess. 25, 16 [II AD]; 3 Macc 2: 21 [of God]; Philo, Op. M. 145; Jos., Ant. 4, 26; 19, 123) forefather of Abraham (Jos., Bell. 5, 380) Ro 4: 1 (the Cynics call Diogenes προπάτωρ: ADieterich, E. Mithrasliturgie '03, p. 161, 1). M-M.*

προπέμπω impf. προέπεμπον; 1 aor. προέπεμψα, pass. προεπέμφθην (Hom.+; inscr., pap., LXX).
1. accompany, escort (Soph., Hdt.+; PFlor. 206, 2; LXX; Jos., Bell. 2, 631, Ant. 20, 50) προέπεμπον αὐτὸν εἰς τὸ πλοῖον they accompanied him to the ship Ac 20: 38. ἕως ἔξω τῆς πόλεως escort outside the city 21: 5.
2. help on one's journey with food, money, by arranging

for companions, means of travel, etc., send on one's way (1 Macc 12: 4; 1 Esdr 4: 47; Ep. Arist. 172) τινά someone 1 Cor 16: 11. W. δέχεσθαι Pol 1: 1. σπουδαίως Tit 3: 13. ἀξίως τοῦ θεοῦ 3 J 6. W. the destination given οὗ ἐὰν πορεύωμαι 1 Cor 16: 6. Pass. w. ὑπό τινος Ac 15: 3. Also w. the destination: εἰς τὴν Ἰουδαίαν 2 Cor 1: 16; ἐκεῖ Ro 15: 24. M-M.*

προπετής, ές gen. οῦς (Pind.+) in our lit. only fig. rash, reckless, thoughtless (Isocr., Pla.; Appian, Bell. Civ. 3, 43 §176; et al.; Pr 10: 14; 13: 3; Sir 9: 18; Jos., Ant. 5, 106, Vi. 170) 2 Ti 3: 4. W. αὐθάδης 1 Cl 1: 1. μηδὲν π. πράσσειν do nothing rash Ac 19: 36 (schol. on Soph., Aj. 32 p. 5 Papag. μὴ προπετές τι πράσσειν; Menand., 439 προπετὲς ποιεῖν μηδέ; 441 τὶ πράξω προπετές; Jos., Ant. 15, 82). M-M.*

προπορεύομαι fut. προπορεύσομαι (X.+; POxy. 1144, 3; 5; 9 [I/II AD]; LXX) go on before τινός someone (Aristot. 844b, 5; LXX) Ac 7: 40 (Ex 32: 1, 23). ἐνώπιόν τινος Lk 1: 76 shows the influence of OT usage, though the v.l. πρὸ προσώπου τινός is also found in the LXX.—The fig. προπορεύσεται ἔμπροσθέν σου ἡ δικαιοσύνη Β 3: 4 (Is 58: 8) also has an OT background (but cf. X., Cyr. 4, 2, 23 πορεύεσθε ἔμπροσθεν). M-M.*

πρός prep. w. gen., dat., or acc. (s. the lit. s.v. ἀνά, beg.) (Hom.+; inscr., pap., LXX, En., Ep. Arist., Philo, Joseph., Test. 12 Patr.).

I. w. the gen. to the advantage of, advantageous for (Thu. 3, 59, 1 οὐ πρὸς τῆς ὑμετέρας δόξης τάδε; Hdt. 1, 75; Dionys. Hal. 10, 30, 5; Diod. S. 18, 50, 5; Lucian, Dial. Deor. 20, 3; Bl-D. §240; Rob. 623f) οἱ πρ. ζωῆς μαζοὶ the life-giving breasts 1 Cl 20: 10. πρ. τῆς σωτηρίας necessary for safety Ac 27: 34 (πρὸς τῆς σ. as Jos., Ant. 16, 313).*

II. w. the dat.—1. of place near, at, by (Hom.+; LXX; Jos., Ant. 8, 349; 381) Mk 5: 11; around Rv 1: 13. πρ. τῇ θύρᾳ ἑστηκέναι stand at the door (Menand., fgm. 420, 1; 830 K.) J 18: 16; cf. 20: 11. ἐγγίζοντος αὐτοῦ πρ. τῇ καταβάσει τοῦ ὄρους when he came close to the slope of the mountain Lk 19: 37 (s. κατάβασις). πρ. τῇ κεφαλῇ, τοῖς ποσίν at the head, at the feet J 20: 12. τὰ πρ. ταῖς ῥίζαις the parts near the roots Hs 9, 1, 6; 9, 21, 1. In geographical designations Μαγνησία ἡ πρ. Μαιάνδρῳ Magnesia on the Maeander IMg inscr.
2. in addition to (Hom.+; Polyb., inscr.) πρὸς τούτοις (Dit., Syll.³ 495, 105; 685, 70; 100; 796B, 30; 888, 35 al.; UPZ 26, 18; 25 [163 BC]; 2 Macc 4: 9; 5: 23; 9: 17, 25; 14: 4, esp. 12: 2; Philo, Aet. M. 67 al.) 1 Cl 17: 1.*

III. w. the acc.—1. of place toward(s), to w. acc. of the place, the pers., or the thing, after verbs—a. of going; cf. ἄγω 5, ἀναβαίνω 1aa, ἀνακάμπτω 1a, ἀπέρχομαι 2, διαβαίνω, διαπεράω, εἴσειμι, εἰσέρχομαι 1c, ἐκπορεύομαι 1c, ἐπισυνάγομαι Mk 1: 33, ἔρχομαι I 1aβ, ἥκω 1b et al.—προσαγωγή πρὸς τὸν πατέρα Eph 2: 18. εἴσοδος 1 Th 1: 9a.
b. verbs of sending; cf. ἀναπέμπω Lk 23: 7, 15; Ac 25: 21, ἀποστέλλω 1ba, πέμπω.
c. of motion gener.; cf. βληθῆναι (βάλλω 1b), ἐπιστρέφω 1ba, β, 2b, κεῖμαι 1, πίπτω 1aℵ and ℶ, προσκολλάω 1, προσκόπτω 1a, προσπίπτω.
d. of leading, guiding; cf. ἄγω 1a, ἀπάγω 2a and 4, ἕλκω J 12: 32, κατασύρω, etc.
e. of saying, speaking; cf. ἀποκρίνομαι 1, δημηγορέω Ac 12: 21, εἶπον 1, λαλέω 2aδ and 2b, λέγω I 1a, 3 et al. Hebraistically λαλεῖν στόμα πρὸς στόμα speak face to face (Jer 39: 4) 2 J 12b; 3 J 14 (cf. PGM 1, 39 τὸ στόμα πρὸς τὸ στόμα). πρὸς ἀλλήλους to one another, with each

other, among themselves: s. ἀντιβάλλω, διαλαλέω, διαλέγομαι Mk 9: 34, διαλογίζομαι 8: 16; Lk 20: 14, εἶπον 24: 32; J 16: 17; 19: 24, λαλέω, λέγω et al. πρὸς ἑαυτούς *to themselves, to each other*: s. διαλογίζομαι 1, εἶπον Mk 12: 7; J 7: 35, λέγω (Ps.-Callisth. 2, 15, 7 πρὸς ἑαυτὸν ἔλεγεν) Mk 10: 26; 16: 3. διαθήκην ὁ θεὸς διέθετο πρὸς τοὺς πατέρας ὑμῶν, λέγων πρὸς Ἀβραάμ *God made a covenant with your fathers, when he said to Abraham* Ac 3: 25 (διατίθημι 1). ὅρκον ὀμνύναι πρ. τινα (ὀμνύω, end) Lk 1: 73.

f. *of asking, praying* δέομαι Ac 8: 24. εὔχομαι (cf. 2 Macc 9: 13) 2 Cor 13: 7. προσεύχομαι (cf. 1 Km 12: 19; 2 Esdr 12 [Neh 2]: 4; 2 Macc 2: 10) Hv 1, 1, 9. γνωρίζεσθαι πρὸς τὸν θεόν Phil 4: 6 (γνωρίζω 1).—Also after nouns like δέησις, λόγος et al. Ro 10: 1; 15: 30; 2 Cor 1: 18 al.

2. *of time*—a. *denoting approach toward* (X., Pla. et al.) πρὸς ἑσπέραν *toward evening* Lk 24: 29 (s. ἑσπέρα).

b. *of the duration of a period of time for* πρὸς καιρόν *for a time, for a while* (καιρός 1) Lk 8: 13; 1 Cor 7: 5. πρὸς καιρὸν ὥρας (καιρός 1) 1 Th 2: 17. πρὸς ὥραν *for an hour*, i.e. *for a short time* J 5: 35; 2 Cor 7: 8; Gal 2: 5a; Phlm 15; MPol 11: 2. πρὸς ὀλίγας ἡμέρας Hb 12: 10. Also πρὸς ὀλίγον Js 4: 14 (ὀλίγος 3b). πρὸς τὸ παρόν *for the present* Hb 12: 11 (πάρειμι 1b).

3. *of the goal aimed at or striven toward*—a. *with conscious purpose for, for the purpose of, on behalf of* οὗτος ἦν ὁ πρὸς τὴν ἐλεημοσύνην καθήμενος *this was the one who sat (and begged) for alms* Ac 3: 10. πρὸς τὴν ἔνδειξιν τῆς δικαιοσύνης αὐτοῦ Ro 3: 26. τοῦτο πρὸς τὸ ὑμῶν αὐτῶν σύμφορον λέγω 1 Cor 7: 35a; cf. b. ἐγράφη πρὸς νουθεσίαν ἡμῶν 10: 11. Cf. Ro 15: 2; 1 Cor 6: 5; 2 Cor 4: 6; 7: 3; 11: 8; Eph 4: 12.—W. the acc. of the inf. (Polyb. 1, 48, 5; PRyl. 69, 16; BGU 226, 22; Jer 34: 10; 2 Macc 4: 45; Jos., Ant. 14, 170; 15, 148 al.) πρὸς τὸ θεαθῆναι τοῖς ἀνθρώποις *in order to be seen by men* Mt 23: 5; cf. 6: 1. πρὸς τὸ κατακαῦσαι αὐτά 13: 30. πρὸς τὸ ἐνταφιάσαι με 26: 12. πρὸς τὸ ἀποπλανᾶν εἰ δυνατὸν τοὺς ἐκλεκτούς Mk 13: 22. πρὸς τὸ μὴ ἀτενίσαι υἱοὺς Ἰσραήλ 2 Cor 3: 13. Cf. Eph 6: 11a; 1 Th 2: 9; 2 Th 3: 8; Js 3: 3 t.r.

b. *of the result that follows a set of circumstances* (*so that*) πάντα πρὸς οἰκοδομὴν γινέσθω *everything is to be done in such a way that it contributes to edification* 1 Cor 14: 26; cf. vs. 12; Col 2: 23 (but see 4a below); 1 Ti 4: 7. ὁ βλέπων γυναῖκα πρὸς τὸ ἐπιθυμῆσαι αὐτήν *the one who looks at a woman in such a way that desire for her is aroused in him* Mt 5: 28. λευκαί εἰσιν πρὸς θερισμόν *they* (the fields) *are white, so that the harvest may begin* J 4: 35. αὕτη ἡ ἀσθένεια οὐκ ἔστιν πρὸς θάνατον *this disease is not of the kind that will lead to death* 11: 4. Cf. ἁμαρτία πρὸς θάνατον 1 J 5: 16f.

c. gener. *of purpose, destiny* (Jos., Bell. 4, 573 τὸ πρ. σωτηρίαν φάρμακον) τῷ θεῷ πρὸς δόξαν *for the glory of God* 2 Cor 1: 20 (on πρὸς δόξαν cf. Dit., Syll.³ 456, 15; 704E, 21; 3 Macc 2: 9). τῇ πυρώσει πρὸς πειρασμὸν ὑμῖν γινομένῃ 1 Pt 4: 12.—After adjectives and participles *for* ἀγαθὸς πρὸς οἰκοδομήν Eph 4: 29 (ἀγ. 1aβ). ἀδόκιμος Tit 1: 16. ἀνεύθετος πρὸς παραχειμασίαν Ac 27: 12. γεγυμνασμένος Hb 5: 14. δυνατός 2 Cor 10: 4. ἐξηρτισμένος 2 Ti 3: 17. ἕτοιμος (q.v. 2) Tit 3: 1; 1 Pt 3: 15. ἱκανός (q.v. 2) 2 Cor 2: 16. ὠφέλιμος 1 Ti 4: 8a, b; 2 Ti 3: 16.

4. *denoting a hostile or friendly relationship*—a. *hostile against, with* after verbs of disputing, etc.; cf. ἀνταγωνίζομαι, γογγύζω, διακρίνομαι (διακρίνω 2a), διαλέγομαι 1, πικραίνομαι (s. πικραίνω 2), στασιάζω, ἔστην (ἵστημι II 1c). ἐστίν τινι ἡ πάλη πρός Eph 6: 12. ἔχειν τι πρός τινα *have anything* (*to bring up*) *against someone*

Ac 24: 19. μομφὴν ἔχειν πρός τινα Col 3: 13. πρᾶγμα ἔχειν πρός τινα 1 Cor 6: 1 (πρᾶγμα 5). ἐγένετο γογγυσμὸς τῶν Ἑλληνιστῶν πρὸς τοὺς Ἑβραίους Ac 6: 1. τὸ στόμα ἡμῶν ἀνέῳγεν πρὸς ὑμᾶς 2 Cor 6: 11 (ἀνοίγω 2). ἐν ἔχθρᾳ ὄντες πρὸς αὐτούς Lk 23: 12. βλασφημίαι πρὸς τὸν θεόν Rv 13: 6. ἀσύμφωνοι πρ. ἀλλήλους *unable to agree among themselves* Ac 28: 25; cf. the parallel structure in Col 2: 23.

b. *friendly to, toward, with, before* ἐργάζεσθαι τὸ ἀγαθόν Gal 6: 10a, b (ἐργάζομαι 2a). μακροθυμεῖν 1 Th 5: 14. εἰρήνην ἔχειν πρ. τὸν θεόν Ro 5: 1 (s. εἰρήνη 3). παρρησίαν ἔχειν πρὸς τ. θεόν 1 J 3: 21; cf. 5: 14. πίστιν ἔχειν πρὸς τ. κύριον Ἰ. Phlm 5. πεποίθησιν ἔχειν πρὸς τ. θεόν 2 Cor 3: 4. ἔχειν χάριν πρ. ὅλον τὸν λαόν Ac 2: 47 (FPCheetham, ET 74, '63, 214f). πραΰτητα ἐνδείκνυσθαι Tit 3: 2. ἐν σοφίᾳ περιπατεῖν Col 4: 5. ἤπιον εἶναι πρὸς πάντας 2 Ti 2: 24.—After substantives πίστις 1 Th 1: 8 (cf. 4 Macc 15: 24). παρρησία 2 Cor 7: 4. κοινωνία 6: 14. συμφώνησις vs. 15 (cf. Is 7: 2).

5. *to indicate a connection*—a. *with reference to* (Ocellus Luc. c. 42 πρὸς ἡμᾶς = with reference to us) ἔγνωσαν ὅτι πρὸς αὐτοὺς τὴν παραβολὴν εἶπεν *they recognized that he had spoken the parable with reference to them* Mk 12: 12; Lk 20: 19; cf. 12: 41. ἔλεγεν παραβολὴν πρὸς τὸ δεῖν προσεύχεσθαι *he told them a parable about the need of praying* 18: 1. οὐδεὶς ἔγνω πρὸς τί εἶπεν αὐτῷ *nobody understood with respect to what* (= *why*) *he said* (*this*) *to him* J 13: 28. πρὸς τὴν σκληροκαρδίαν ὑμῶν *with reference to* (i.e. *because of*) *your perversity* Mt 19: 8; Mk 10: 5. Cf. Ro 10: 21a; Hb 1: 7f. οὐκ ἀπεκρίθη αὐτῷ πρὸς οὐδὲ ἓν ῥῆμα *he did not answer him a single word with reference to anything* Mt 27: 14 (s. ἀποκρίνομαι 1). ἀνταποκριθῆναι πρὸς ταῦτα Lk 14: 6 (s. ἀνταποκρίνομαι). ἀπρόσκοπον συνείδησιν ἔχειν πρὸς τὸν θεόν *have a clear conscience with respect to God* Ac 24: 16.

b. *as far as—is concerned, with regard to* (Maximus Tyr. 31, 3b) πρὸς τὴν πληροφορίαν τῆς ἐλπίδος Hb 6: 11. συνιστάνοντες ἑαυτοὺς πρὸς πᾶσαν συνείδησιν ἀνθρώπων *we are recommending ourselves as far as every human conscience is concerned* = *to every human conscience* (πρός w. acc. also stands simply for the dative; s. Mayser II 2 p. 359) 2 Cor 4: 2. τὰ πρὸς τὸν θεόν *that which concerns God* or as adverbial acc. *with reference to what concerns God* (Soph., Phil. 1441; X., De Rep. Lac. 13, 11; Ps.-Isocr. 1, 13 εὐσεβεῖν τὰ πρὸς τ. θεούς; Dit., Syll.³ 204, 51f; 306, 38; Wilcken, Chrest. 109, 3 εὐσεβὴς τὰ πρὸς θεούς; Ex 4: 16; 18: 19; Jos., Ant. 9, 236) Ro 15: 17; Hb 2: 17; 5: 1. τὰ πρός τι *that which belongs to someth.; that which is necessary for someth.* (Plut., Mor. 109B; Jos., Ant. 12, 405 τὰ πρὸς τὴν μάχην; 14, 27) τὰ πρὸς ἀπαρτισμόν Lk 14: 28 t.r. τὰ πρὸς εἰρήνην (Test. Jud. 9) vs. 32; *what makes for peace* 19: 42. Cf. Ac 28: 10; 2 Pt 1: 3.

c. *elliptically* τί πρὸς ἡμᾶς (sc. ἐστιν); *what is that to us?* Mt 27: 4. τί πρὸς σέ; *how does it concern you?* J 21: 22f (cf. Epict. 4, 1, 10 τί τοῦτο πρὸς σέ; Plut., Mor. 986B; Vi. Aesopi I c. 14 p. 265, 4 τί πρὸς ἐμέ;).

d. *in accordance with* ὀρθοποδεῖν πρὸς τὴν ἀλήθειαν Gal 2: 14. πρὸς τὸ κένωμα *in accordance with the emptiness* Hm 11: 3. πρὸς τὸ θέλημα *in accordance w. the will* Lk 12: 47; Hs 9, 5, 2. πρὸς ἃ ἔπραξεν 2 Cor 5: 10. πρὸς ὅ Eph 3: 4.—*In comparison with, to be compared to* (Pind., Hdt.+; Ps.-Pla., Alcyon c. 3 πρὸς τὸν πάντα αἰῶνα = [life is short] *in comparison to all eternity*; Sir 25: 19) ἄξια πρός Ro 8: 18 (RLeaney, ET 64, '52f; 92 interprets Col 2: 23 in the light of this usage). Cf. IMg 12.

e. *expressing purpose* πρὸς τό w. inf. *in order to, for the purpose of* Mk 13: 22; Ac 3: 19.

6. adverbial expressions (cf. πρὸς ὀργήν=ὀργίλως Soph., Elect. 369; Jos., Bell. 2, 534. πρὸς βίαν=βιαίως Aeschyl., Prom. 210, 355, Eum. 5; Menand., Sam. 214; Philo, Spec. Leg. 3, 3. πρὸς ἡδονήν Jos., Ant. 7, 195; 12, 398) πρὸς φθόνον prob.=φθονερῶς jealously Js 4: 5 (s. φθόνος, where the lit. is given).

7. by, at, near πρός τινα εἶναι be (in company) with someone Mt 13: 56; Mk 6: 3; 9: 19a; 14: 49; Lk 9: 41; J 1: 1f; 1 Th 3: 4; 2 Th 2: 5; 3: 10; 1 J 1: 2. διαμένειν Ac 10: 48 D; Gal 2: 5b. ἐπιμένειν 1: 18; 1 Cor 16: 7. καταμένειν 16: 6. μένειν Ac 18: 3 D. παρεῖναι 12: 20; 2 Cor 11: 9; Gal 4: 18, 20; cf. παρουσία πρὸς ὑμᾶς Phil 1: 26. παρεπιδημεῖν 1 Cl 1: 2. πρὸς σὲ ποιῶ τὸ πάσχα Mt 26: 18b. Cf. also 2 Cor 1: 12; 7: 12; 12: 21; 2 Th 3: 1; Phlm 13; 1 J 2: 1; Hm 11: 9b.—πρὸς ἑαυτούς among or to themselves Mk 9: 10 (in case πρὸς ἑ. belongs w. τὸν λόγον ἐκράτησαν; Bl-D. §239, 1 app.). πρὸς ἑαυτὸν προσηύχετο he uttered a prayer to himself Lk 18: 11. Cf. 24: 12.—δεδεμένον πρὸς θύραν tied at a door Mk 11: 4. πρὸς τ. θάλασσαν by the sea-side Mk 4: 1b. On πρὸς τὸ φῶς at the fire Mk 14: 54; Lk 22: 56 cf. Bl-D. §239, 3; Rob. 625 (perh. w. the idea of turning toward the fire; cf. also 4 Km 23: 3). πρὸς ἓν τῶν ὀρέων on one of the mountains 1 Cl 10: 7. τὰ πρὸς τὴν θύραν the place near the door Mk 2: 2. πρὸς γράμμα letter by letter Hv 2, 1, 4. M-M.

προσάββατον, ου, τό (Jdth 8: 6; Ps 91: 1 S; Ps 92: 1; Bull. de l'Inst. franç. d'Archéol. orient. 30, '31, p. 4–6) the day before the Sabbath, i.e. Friday, used to explain the word παρασκευή Mk 15: 42. Also in the fgm. of the Diatessaron fr. Dura (CHKraeling, A Gk. Fgm. of Tatian's Diatessaron fr. Dura: Studies and Documents [ed. KLake and Silva Lake] III '35=AHuck⁹-HLietzmann, Synopse '36, 206 [Eng. transl., Gospel Parallels '49, 184]) l. 6. M-M.*

προσαγορεύω 1 aor. προσηγόρευσα, pass. προσηγορεύθην—1. greet (Aeschyl., Hdt.+; Dit., Or. 771, 48; oft. in pap.) τινά someone MPol 20: 2a, b.
2. call, name, designate (X., Pla.+; inscr., pap., LXX) w. double acc. of the obj. and predicate (X., Mem. 3, 2, 1; Plut., Aem. 8, 3; inscr.; Wsd 14: 22; 2 Macc 1: 36) of God υἱοὺς ἡμᾶς προσηγόρευσεν he called us sons 2 Cl 1: 4. Pass. (Pla. et al.; Diod. S. 1, 4, 7; 13, 98, 3; 40, 3, 3; 1 Macc 14: 40; 2 Macc 4: 7; 14: 37; Philo, Agr. 66, Abrah. 121, Mos. 2, 109; 112; Jos., Bell. 3, 35, Ant. 15, 293, C. Ap. 1, 250) Hb 5: 10. Of Abraham φίλος προσηγορεύθη τοῦ θεοῦ 1 Cl 17: 2; cf. 10: 1 (s. Ἀβραάμ and φίλος 2aα). M-M.*

προσάγω 2 aor. προσήγαγον, imper. προσάγαγε, inf. προσαγαγεῖν. Pass.: impf. προσηγόμην; 1 aor. προσήχθην (Hom.+; inscr., pap., LXX, Ep. Arist., Philo, Joseph., Test. 12 Patr.).
1. trans. bring (forward)—a. lit. τινά someone Ac 12: 6 v.l.; B 13: 5a. Pass. MPol 9: 1f. προσάγαγε ὧδε τὸν υἱόν Lk 9: 41. W. the acc. to be supplied Ἰωσὴφ προσήγαγεν (αὐτόν) εἰς . . . B 13: 5b (π. τινα εἴς τι Herodian 1, 5, 1). τινά τινι bring someone to someone Ac 16: 20; B 13: 4 (Gen 48: 9); pass. Mt 18: 24.
b. fig.—α. of Christ, who brings men to God (X., Cyr. 1, 3, 8 of admission to an audience with the Great King) ἵνα ὑμᾶς προσαγάγῃ τῷ θεῷ 1 Pt 3: 18 (Jos., Ant. 14, 272 the mid. has the mng. 'negotiate peace', 'reconcile').
β. as a t.t. of sacrificial procedure (Hdt. 3, 24 et al.; LXX; Ep. Arist. 45 π. θυσίας) bring, present of Isaac προσήγετο θυσία 1 Cl 31: 3. τὴν θρησκείαν πρ. αὐτῷ (=τῷ θεῷ) offer (cultic) worship to God Dg 3: 2 (cf. Tob 12: 12).
2. intr. come near, approach (Theocr. et al.; Plut., Mor.

800A, Pomp. 46, 1; Dit., Syll.³ 1042, 2f; PTebt. 47, 15; Josh 3: 9; 1 Km 9: 18; 3 Km 18: 30a, b; Sir 12: 13; 2 Macc 6: 19; Ep. Arist. 59; Jos., Ant. 6, 52.—Anz 335).
a. lit. ὑπενόουν προσάγειν τινὰ αὐτοῖς χώραν they suspected that land was near (lit. 'approaching them') Ac 27: 27.
b. fig., of men approaching God B 2: 9. προσάγειν τῷ φόβῳ αὐτοῦ (=τοῦ θεοῦ) approach (the fear of) God 1: 7, unless πρ. here means bring an offering (so Lghtf. et al.). M-M.

προσαγωγή, ῆς, ἡ (Hdt.+; inscr., pap., Ep. Arist. 42) intr. approach, access (the intr. mng. is certain in Polyb. 10, 1, 6; Plut., Aem. Paul. 13, 3) abs. Eph 3: 12. εἴς τι to someth. Ro 5: 2. πρός τινα to someone Eph 2: 18. M-M.*

προσαιτέω (Pind.+; PSI 349, 6) abs. beg (Aristoph., X., Pla.+; Plut., Mor. 471A, 1058D; Job 27: 14) Mk 10: 46 t.r.; Lk 18: 35 t.r.; J 9: 8. M-M.*

προσαίτης, ου, ὁ (Plut., Mor. 294A; Diog. L. 6, 56; Lucian, Navig. 24) beggar Mk 10: 46; J 9: 8.*

προσαναβαίνω 2 aor. προσανέβην, imper. προσανάβηθι (since Plato Com. [V/IV BC], fgm. 79 K.; X.; pap., LXX) go up, move up ἀνώτερον move up (higher) to one of the places of honor at the table Lk 14: 10. M-M.*

προσαναλαμβάνω (Polyb. et al.; Diod. S. 13, 3, 3; pap.) take in besides, welcome πάντας ἡμᾶς us all to the fire Ac 28: 2 v.l.*

προσαναλίσκω or **προσαναλόω** 1 aor. ptc. προσαναλώσας (Kühner-Bl. II p. 367. X., Pla.+; Dit., Syll.³ 497, 7) spend lavishly (in addition) τί τινι someth. on someth. or someone (Diog. L. 6, 98; Cass. Dio 43, 18; cf. Philo, Agr. 5 τὶ ὑπέρ τινος) ἰατροῖς προσαναλώσασα ὅλον τὸν βίον who had spent all her property on physicians Lk 8: 43 v.l. M-M.*

προσαναπληρόω 1 aor. προσανεπλήρωσα (Aristot.; Diod. S. 5, 71, 1; 14, 2, 4; Athen. 14 p. 654D; Wsd 19: 4; Philo, Praem. 103. The mid. as early as Pla., Meno 84D) fill up or replenish besides τὶ someth. τὰ ὑστερήματά (or τὸ ὑστέρημά) τινος supply someone's wants 2 Cor 9: 12; 11: 9 (schol. on Soph., El. 32 p. 100 Papag.: διὰ τ. διηγήσεως ταύτης τὸ λεῖπον τ. ἱστορίας προσανεπλήρωσεν ἡμῖν). M-M.*

προσανατίθημι 2 aor. mid. προσανεθέμην (X.+; inscr.; PTebt. 99, 5 [II BC]) in our lit. only mid.—1. add or contribute τινί τι someth. to someone (cf. X., Mem. 2, 1, 8) Gal 2: 6. Another possibility is simply lay before, submit (Vi. Aesopi W c. 37 αὐτῷ προσανάθου τὸ ζήτημα= submit the question to him; c. 83–5).
2. τινί consult with someone (Clearchus, fgm. 76b ὀνειροκρίτῃ; Chrysipp.: Stoic. II 344; Diod. S. 17, 116, 4 τοῖς μάντεσι; Lucian, Jupp. Tragoed. 1) Gal 1: 16. M-M.*

προσανέχω (Polyb.; Jos., Bell. 4, 84, Ant. 1, 15) rise up toward τινί someone (Synes., Ep. 82 p. 229A τῷ θεῷ) Ac 27: 27 v.l. M-M.*

προσαπειλέω 1 aor. mid. ptc. προσαπειλησάμενος (Demosth. 21, 93; Synes., Ep. 47 p. 186D; Sir 13: 3 v.l.; Jos., Ant. 14, 170) threaten further or in addition Ac 4: 21.*

προσαχέω (Doric form for προσηχέω [Plut. et al.]; cf. Mlt.-H. 71) resound of the surf, indicating that land is near by Ac 27: 27 v.l.; s. προσάγω 2a. M-M.*

προσβιάζομαι mid. dep.; fut. προσβιάσομαι; 1 aor. ptc. προσβιασάμενος (Aristoph., Pla.) *compel, use force* in our lit. only of the conduct of a martyr in the arena toward animals which show no inclination to attack him; abs. προσβιάσομαι *I will use force* IRo 5: 2. προσβιασάμενος *by force* MPol 3.*

προσβλέπω *look upon, look at*—1. w. the acc. (Aeschyl., Pla., X.+; Vett. Val. 114, 25; Dit., Syll.³ 1168, 44; Philo, Op. M. 152) τὸν ἐπίσκοπον ὡς αὐτὸν τὸν κύριον προσβλέπειν *look upon the bishop as the Lord himself* IEph 6: 1.

2. w. the dat. (X., Symp. 3, 14; Plut., Cato Min. 65, 11; Lucian, Alex. 42, Dial. Mer. 11, 4; Philo, Abr. 76) *look at* τοῖς ἁγίοις σκεύεσιν GOxy 29.*

προσδαπανάω 1 aor. προσεδαπάνησα *spend in addition* (Lucian, Epist. Sat. 4, 39; Dit., Syll.³ 661, 10; 691, 8f; Inschr. v. Priene 118, 11) Lk 10: 35. M-M.*

προσδεκτός, ή, όν (Pr 11: 20; 16: 15; Wsd 9: 12) *acceptable* ἐνώπιον τοῦ ποιήσαντος ἡμᾶς 1 Cl 7: 3. θυσία MPol 14: 2. ἔντευξις Hs 2: 6.*

προσδέομαι (Hdt.+) pass. dep. *need in addition* or *further* (so Thu.+; inscr., pap.; Pr 12: 9; Sir; Jos., Ant. 7, 340—but the force of προσ- is no longer felt e.g. in Epict. 1, 16, 1; Dit., Syll.³ 313, 11 [IV BC]; UPZ 110, 154 [164 BC]; PTebt. 59, 8 [99 BC]) w. gen. of what is needed (Thu. 2, 41, 4 al.; Ep. Arist. 11; 113) Dg 3: 4a. Of God, who has need of nothing 3: 5; Ac 17: 25; cf. Dg 3: 3, 4b (προσδέομαι in this sense of God in Pla., Tim. 34B; Aristot., Eth. Eud. 7, 12; 'Onatas' the Pythagorean in Stob., Ecl. 1, 1, 39 vol. I 49, 20 W. [Norden, Agn. Th. 14]; Philo, Op. M. 13; 46). M-M.*

προσδέχομαι (Hom.+; inscr., pap., LXX) mid. dep.; impf. προσεδεχόμην; 1 aor. προσεδεξάμην, pass. προσεδέχθην.
1. *take up, receive, welcome* (Aeschyl., Hdt.+; Ep. Arist. 257)—a. w. acc. of the pers. (Pla., Leg. 4 p. 708A; Jos., Ant. 6, 255; Test. Levi 16: 5) ἁμαρτωλούς Lk 15: 2. τινὰ ἐν κυρίῳ *welcome someone in the Lord*, i.e. as a Christian brother or sister (cf. 1 Ch 12: 19) Ro 16: 2; Phil 2: 29. ἵνα ἡμᾶς προσδέξηται ὡς υἱούς 2 Cl 9: 10 (Diod. S. 17, 37, 4 Ἀλέξανδρον ὡς θεὸν προσεδέξαντο). Pass. MPol 14: 2.
b. w. acc. of the thing (Jos., Ant. 14, 30) *receive* οἱ δὲ ὡς περὶ βρώσεως προσεδέξαντο (i.e. τὰ δόγματα) *they took (the decrees) as if they really dealt with food* B 10: 9.—*Receive willingly, put up with* (Hdt.+; cf. Pla., Phileb. 15B ὄλεθρον) τὴν ἁρπαγὴν τῶν ὑπαρχόντων Hb 10: 34. τὰ ἐνεργήματα ὡς ἀγαθά B 19: 6; D 3: 10.—W. a negative *refuse to accept, reject* (Jos., Ant. 6, 42) τὸ βάπτισμα B 11: 1. τὴν ἀπολύτρωσιν Hb 11: 35 (ἀπολύτρωσις 1).
2. *wait for, expect* (Hom.+; Jos., Ant. 14, 451)—a. w. acc. of the pers. (X., Cyr. 4, 5, 22) Lk 1: 21 D; Ac 10: 24 D. τὸν κύριον Lk 12: 36.
b. w. acc. of the thing (X., Hiero 1, 18, Apol. Socr. 33; Herodian 3, 1, 1; Dit., Syll.³ 1268 [Praecepta Delphica III BC] II 21 καιρὸν προσδέχου=wait for the [right] time) τὴν βασιλείαν τοῦ θεοῦ Mk 15: 43; Lk 23: 51. λύτρωσιν Ἰερουσαλήμ 2: 38. παράκλησιν τοῦ Ἰσραήλ vs. 25. τὴν ἐπαγγελίαν (ἐπαγγελία 1) Ac 23: 21. ἐλπίδα *wait for a hope* Tit 2: 13 (cf. Job 2: 9a); *anticipate* (the realization of) Ac 24: 15. τὸ ἔλεος τοῦ κυρίου Jd 21. τὴν ἐσχάτην ἡμέραν Hv 3, 12, 2; cf. 3, 13, 2. ἀφθαρσίαν Dg 6: 8.
c. abs. *wait* ἡμέραν ἐξ ἡμέρας *wait day after day* 2 Cl 11: 2 (prophetic saying of unknown origin). M-M.*

προσδέω 1 aor. προσέδησα *tie, bind*—1. lit. (Hdt.; Diod. S. 17, 41; Lucian, Dial. Deor. 6, 5; Ps.-Lucian, Asinus 38; Plut., Pericl. 28, 2; Dit., Syll.³ 1169, 41; 4 Macc 9: 26) τινά MPol 14: 1.
2. fig., pass. (Jos., Ant. 5, 135 ἡδονῇ προσδεδεμένοι) *be bound securely* τινί *to someone* 1 Cl 27: 1.*

προσδηλόω fut. προσδηλώσω (Aristot., Anal. Post. 2, 7 p. 92b, 23) *explain further* (in a second letter) IEph 20: 1 (w. a rel. clause foll.).*

προσδίδωμι (trag., Isocr., X.+; inscr., pap., LXX) *give (over)* Lk 24: 30 D.*

προσδοκάω impf. προσεδόκων, pass. προσεδοκώμην; 1 aor. προσεδόκησα (Aeschyl., Hdt.+; pap., LXX, Philo, Joseph.) *wait for, look for, expect*, in hope, in fear, or in a neutral state of mind.
1. w. acc. of the pers. (Jos., Bell. 5, 403) Mt 11: 3; Lk 1: 21; 7: 19f; 8: 40; Ac 10: 24; 1 Cl 23: 5 (Mal 3: 1); IMg 9: 3; IPol 3: 2.
2. w. acc. of the thing (La 2: 16; Ps 118: 166; Philo; Jos., Bell. 5, 528 φαῦλον, Ant. 7, 114 τὰ βελτίω) 2 Pt 3: 12–14; Dg 8: 11; 12: 6; Hv 3, 11, 3. Pass. (Appian, Illyr. 17 §51 προσδοκωμένου τοῦ πολέμου=since the war was to be expected) θάνατος προσεδοκᾶτο *death was to be expected* Dg 9: 2 (Achilles Tat. 3, 2, 1 τ. θάνατον πρ.).
3. abs., though the obj. is to be supplied fr. the context (Himerius, Or. 62 [Or. 16], 8; Philo, Leg. All. 2, 43) Mt 24: 50; Lk 3: 15; 12: 46; Ac 27: 33; 28: 6b.
4. foll. by acc. and inf. (Appian, Bell. Civ. 4, 51 §220; 2 Macc 12: 44; Jos., Ant. 5, 340; 7, 213) Ac 28: 6a.—5. w. inf. foll. (Jos., Ant. 15, 358) Ac 3: 5; Dg 4: 6; Hs 1: 2 (Bl-D. §350; 397, 2; Rob. 1036). M-M.*

προσδοκία, ας, ἡ (Thu., X., Pla. et al.; pap., LXX, Philo, Jos., Ant. 15, 58 al.) *expectation* w. obj. gen. (cf. for the obj. gen. and use w. φόβος Plut., Anton. 75, 4 φόβος καὶ προσδοκία τοῦ μέλλοντος, Demetr. 15, 4; Philo, Abr. 14; Jos., Ant. 3, 219 κακοῦ πρ.) τῶν ἐπερχομένων Lk 21: 26. W. subj. gen. πρ. τοῦ λαοῦ Ac 12: 11. M-M.*

προσδραμών s. προστρέχω.

προσεάω (PLond. 1790, 7) *permit to go farther* τινά *someone* Ac 27: 7. M-M.*

προσεγγίζω 1 aor. προσήγγισα *approach, come near* (Polyb. 38, 7, 4; Diod. S. 3, 16, 4; Hero Alex. III p. 218, 22; Leonidas of Tarentum [300 BC]: Anth. 7, 442, 6; LXX; Test. 12 Patr.) Mk 2: 4 t.r.; Ac 27: 27 v.l.; εἰς τὴν Καισάρειαν 10: 25 D.*

προσεδρεύω (Eur.+; 1 Macc 11: 40) *attend, serve, wait upon*, lit. 'sit near' w. dat. (Aristot., Pol. 8, 4, 4 p. 1338b, 25; Demosth. 1, 18; Diod. S. 5, 46, 3 πρ. ταῖς τῶν θεῶν θεραπείαις; Ael. Aristid. 48, 9 K.=24 p. 467 D.: τ. θεῷ. Also inscr., pap.; Jos., C. Ap. 1, 30 τῇ θεραπείᾳ τοῦ θεοῦ; Archäolog.-epigr. Mitteilungen aus Österreich 6, 1882 p. 23 no. 46: an association of Σαραπιασταί has as officials οἱ προσεδρεύοντες τῷ ἱερῷ) τῷ θυσιαστηρίῳ 1 Cor 9: 13 t.r.*

I. πρόσειμι (from εἰμί. Aeschyl., X., Pla.+; inscr., pap.; Sir 13: 24 v.l.; Jos., C. Ap. 1, 61) *belong to, be present* τινί *(with) someone, be an attribute* or *custom of someone* (Nicolaus Com. 1, 41 πάντα πρόσεστί μοι; Herodas 1, 19; Diog. L. 2, 37; Dio, Ep. 2 τὰ προσόντα αὐτῷ) βία οὐ πρόσεστι τῷ θεῷ Dg 7: 4.*

II. πρόσειμι (from εἶμι. Hom.+; inscr., pap.; 4 Macc; Jos., Bell. 2, 324) *approach, come forward* MPol 4.*

προσενήνοχα s. προσφέρω.

προσεξομολογέομαι D 14: 1 s. προεξομολογέομαι.*

προσεργάζομαι 1 aor. προσηργασάμην or προσειργασάμην—Bl-D. §67, 3 w. app.; cf. Mlt.-H. 189f (Eur., Hdt. +; pap.) make more, earn in addition (X., Hell. 3, 1, 28; Zen.-PCairo 509, 13) ἡ μνᾶ σου δέκα προσηργάσατο μνᾶς your mina has made ten minas more Lk 19: 16. M-M.*

προσέρχομαι mid. dep. (Aeschyl., Hdt.+; inscr., pap., LXX, En., Ep. Arist., Philo, Joseph., Test. 12 Patr.) impf. προσηρχόμην; fut. προσελεύσομαι; 2 aor. προσῆλθον (also προσῆλθα Bl-D. §81, 3 w. app.; cf. Mlt.-H. 208); pf. προσελήλυθα; come or go to, approach.

1. lit. (esp. oft. in Mt, about 50 times) w. dat. of the pers. (X., Cyr. 1, 4, 27; Aelian, V.H. 9, 3, end; En. 14, 25; Jos., Ant. 12, 19) Mt 5: 1; 8: 5; 9: 14 al.; Lk 23: 52; J 12: 21; Ac 9: 1; 18: 2; MPol 16: 1. W. dat. of the place (Herodian 2, 6, 5) Hb 12: 18, 22. Abs. Mt 4: 11; Lk 9: 42; Ac 8: 29; 20: 5 v.l. (s. ChMaurer, ThZ, 3, '47, 321–37). MPol 4. The ptc. is freq. used w. verbs denoting an activity, to enliven the narrative προσελθὼν εἶπεν (cf. BGU 587, 2 [II BC]; Jos., Ant. 9, 194) Mt 4: 3; 8: 19; 18: 21; cf. 13: 10; 15: 12; 25: 20, 22, 24; Mk 6: 35; 14: 45; Lk 9: 12. πρ. προσεκύνει Mt 8: 2; 9: 18. πρ. ἔπεσεν 26: 39 v.l.; cf. Mk 14: 35 v.l., et al. Foll. by inf. denoting purpose (1 Macc 2: 23) προσῆλθον οἱ μαθηταὶ αὐτοῦ ἐπιδεῖξαι his disciples came up to show Mt 24: 1. προσερχομένου αὐτοῦ κατανοῆσαι Ac 7: 31. Cf. 12: 13.

2. fig.—a. of coming to, approaching a deity (Cass. Dio 56, 9, 2 τοῖς θεοῖς προσερχώμεθα) PGiess. 20, 24= Wilcken, Chrest. no. 94; Jer 7: 16; Sir 1: 28 μὴ προσέλθῃς αὐτῷ [=τῷ κυρίῳ] ἐν καρδίᾳ δισσῇ; Philo, Plant. 64, Deus Imm. 8) πρ. τῷ θεῷ Hb 7: 25; 11: 6; cf. 1 Cl 23: 1; 29: 1. W. dat. of the place τῷ θρόνῳ τῆς χάριτος Hb 4: 16. Also abs. προσέρχεσθαι means come to God 10: 1, 22 (πρ. in Hb may connote 'appear in court': POxy. 40, 4 [II/III AD]; 2783, 25 [III AD]; PRyl. 234, 6 [II AD]). This prob. furnishes the clue to the abs. πυκνότερον προσερχόμενοι 2 Cl 17: 3.—To Jesus 1 Pt 2: 3 (of proselytes, FWDanker, ZNW 58, '67, 95f; w. πρός as Lucian, Ver. Hist. 2, 28; Ex 34: 32; Josh 14: 6).

b. turn to or occupy oneself with a thing (Diod. S. 1, 95, 1 τοῖς νόμοις; Plut., Cato Min. 12, 2; Epict. 4, 11, 24; pap.; Sir 4: 15 v.l.; 6: 19, 26; Philo, Agr. 123, Migr. Abr. 86 ἀρετῇ; PYale 83, 15) οὐ προσελεύσῃ ἐπὶ προσευχήν σου D 4: 14.—Also in the sense agree with, accede to εἴ τις μὴ προσέρχεται ὑγιαίνουσιν λόγοις 1 Ti 6: 3 (v.l. προσέχεται, q.v.). πρ. τῷ θελήματι αὐτοῦ (=τοῦ θεοῦ) 1 Cl 33: 8.

c. also of inanimate things (Soph. et al.; cf. Eur., Or. 859 προσῆλθεν ἐλπίς; BGU 614, 21) πρ. τινί someth. comes upon or over someone φρίκη μοι προσῆλθεν Hv 3, 1, 5. ὑμῖν ἰσχυρότης 3, 12, 3. Without a dat., which is easily supplied fr. the context m 5, 1, 3. M-M.

προσευχή, ῆς, ἡ—1. prayer (pagan pap. BGU 1080, 4 [III AD] κατὰ τὰς κοινὰς ἡμῶν εὐχὰς καὶ προσευχάς; LXX, Philo; Jos., Bell. 5, 388, perh. C. Ap. 2, 10 and Ant. 14, 258; Test. 12 Patr.) IEph 1: 2; 5: 2; 10: 2; 11: 2; IPhld 5: 1; ISm 11: 1, 3. αἱ πρ. τῶν ἁγίων Rv 5: 8; 8: 3f.—1 Pt 3: 7. W. δέησις Ac 1: 14 t.r.; Eph 6: 18; Phil 4: 6; IMg 7: 1; cf. 1 Ti 2: 1; 5: 5 (s. δέησις). W. εὐχαριστία ISm 7: 1. W. ἐλεημοσύναι Ac 10: 4; διὰ τὴν πρ. IPol 7: 1; διὰ τῶν πρ. Phlm 22; ἐν (τῇ) πρ. through prayer Mk 9: 29; IEph 20: 1; IPhld 8: 2; in prayer IRo 9: 1; ἐν ταῖς πρ. in the prayers IMg 14: 1; ITr 13: 1; Col 4: 12. W. the same mng. ἐπὶ τῶν

πρ. Ro 1: 10; Eph 1: 16; 1 Th 1: 2; Phlm 4; κατὰ τὴν πρ. IPhld 10: 1. ἡ πρ. τοῦ θεοῦ prayer to God Lk 6: 12. Also πρ. γινομένη πρὸς τὸν θεόν Ac 12: 5 (π. πρός as Ps 68: 14). W. νηστεία Mt 17: 21; Mk 9: 29 v.l. Fasting called better than prayer 2 Cl 16: 4a. Prayer fr. a good conscience saves fr. death, ibid. b; drives out demons Mk 9: 29. τὰς πρ. ἀναφέρειν πρὸς τὸν θεόν (s. ἀναφέρω 2) 2 Cl 2: 2; προσκαρτερεῖν τῇ πρ. Ac 1: 14; Ro 12: 12; Col 4: 2; cf. Ac 2: 42; 6: 4 (w. τῇ διακονίᾳ). σχολάζειν τῇ πρ. 1 Cor 7: 5 (on prayer and abstinence s. Test. Napht. 8: 8); cf. IPol 1: 3. νήφειν εἰς προσευχάς 1 Pt 4: 7; καταπαύειν τὴν πρ. MPol 8: 1; αἰτεῖν ἐν τῇ πρ. Mt 21: 22. προσευχῇ προσεύχεσθαι pray earnestly Js 5: 17. In a kneeling position or prone on the ground; hence ἀναστὰς ἀπὸ τῆς πρ. Lk 22: 45; ἐγείρεσθαι ἀπὸ τῆς πρ. Hv 2, 1, 3; εἰσηκούσθη ἡ πρ. Ac 10: 31. Public, communal prayer ἡ μετ' ἀλλήλων πρ. ITr 12: 2. αἱ πρ. ὑπέρ τινος πρὸς τὸν θεόν intercessions to God on behalf of someone Ro 15: 30; ὥρα τῆς πρ. Ac 3: 1 (s. ἔνατος and the lit. there.—On a fixed time for prayer s. Marinus, Vi. Procli 24 καιρὸς τῶν εὐχῶν; also 22, end). οἶκος προσευχῆς (=בֵּית־תְּפִלָּה Is 56: 7) house of prayer Mt 21: 13; Mk 11: 17; Lk 19: 46. On προσέρχεσθαι ἐπὶ προσευχήν D 4: 14 s. προσεύχομαι 2b. Cf. B 19: 12.—For lit. s. προσεύχομαι, end.

2. place of (or for) prayer, chapel Ac 16: 13, 16. Esp. used among Jews, this word is nearly always equivalent to συναγωγή (q.v. and cf. SKrauss, Pauly-W. 2. R. IV, '32, 1287f). But many consider that the πρ. in Ac 16: 13, 16 was not a regular synagogue because it was attended only by women (vs. 13), and because the word συν. is freq. used elsewh. in Ac (e. g. 17: 1, 10, 17); the πρ. in our passage may have been an informal meeting place, perh. in the open air. S. the handbooks.—In the rare cases in which a pagan place of prayer is called πρ., Jewish influence is almost always poss. (reff. fr. lit., inscr. and pap. in Schürer II⁴ 499f; 517f; Mayser I 3² '36 p. 19. Cf. also 3 Macc 7: 20 al.; Suppl. Epigr. Gr. VIII 366 [II BC]; Dssm., NB 49f [BS 222f]; MLStrack, APF 2, '03, 541f; Elbogen² 445; 448; 452; SZarb, De Judaeorum προσευχή in Act. 16: 13, 16: Angelicum 5, '28, 91–108; also συναγωγή 2). But such infl. must be excluded in the case of the inscr. fr. Epidaurus of IV BC (IG IV² 1, 106 I, 27), where the Doric form of προσευχή occurs in the sense 'place of prayer': ποτευχὰ καὶ βωμός. Hence it is also improbable in Inscr. Or. Sept. Pont. Eux., ed. BLatyschev I 98, 7 and in Artem. 3, 53 p. 188, 27; 189, 2.—MHengel, Proseuche u. Synagoge, KGKuhn-Festschr., '71, 157–84. M-M.*

προσεύχομαι impf. προσηυχόμην; fut. προσεύξομαι; 1 aor. προσηυξάμην (on the augment s. W-H., App. 162; Tdf., Prol. 121; Bl-D. §67, 1 app.; Mlt.-H. 191f) mid. dep. pray (Aeschyl., Hdt.+; Zen.-P. 7 [=Sb 6713], 10 [257 BC]; Sb 3740 [I AD] Ἄττηος προσεύχεται τοῖς ἐν Ἀβύδῳ θεοῖς; LXX, Philo, Joseph., Test. 12 Patr.) abs. (Demochares [300 BC]: 75 fgm. 2 Jac.; Dio Chrys. 35[52], 1) Mt 6: 5–7; 14: 23; 26: 36; Mk 1: 35; 6: 46; Lk 1: 10; 5: 16; Ac 1: 24; 6: 6; 1 Cor 11: 4f; 14: 14b; Js 5: 13, 18; MPol 5: 2; 12: 3; Hv 1, 1, 4; 3, 1, 6; s 9, 11, 7a; D 8: 2. Followed by a prayer introduced by λέγων (Is 44: 17) Mt 26: 42; Lk 22: 41; cf. Mt 26: 39; Lk 11: 2 (on the Lord's Prayer cf. TWManson, The Sayings of Jesus '54, 165–71; EGrässer, D. Problem der Parusieverzögerung, '57, 95–113). W. dat. of the pers. to whom the prayer is addressed (so predom. in secular usage; cf. Bl-D. §187, 4; cf. Rob. 538) πρ. τῷ θεῷ pray to God (Diod. S. 13, 16, 7 τοῖς θεοῖς; Charito 3, 10, 6 θεῷ; Athen. 13, 32 p. 573D τῇ θεῷ; Philostrat., Vi. Apollon. 5, 28 p. 186, 9 πρ. τοῖς θεοῖς; Jos., Ant. 10, 252; cf. 256) 1 Cor 11: 13; τῷ κυρίῳ πρ. (Test. Jos. 3: 3; 7: 4)

Hv 1, 1, 3; 2, 1, 2; τῷ πατρὶ πρ. Mt 6: 6b. Also πρὸς τὸν θεόν (LXX) Hv 1, 1, 9. W. dat. of manner πρ. γλώσσῃ, τῷ πνεύματι, τῷ νοΐ pray in a tongue, in the spirit, with the understanding 1 Cor 14: 14a, 15; ἐν πνεύματι πρ. Eph 6: 18; cf. Jd 20; προσευχῇ πρ. pray earnestly Js 5: 17. ἀδιαλείπτως 1 Th 5: 17; IEph 10: 1; Hs 9, 11, 7b. ἀδεῶς MPol 7: 2a. πρ. ὑπέρ τινος pray for someone or someth. (Philostrat., Vi. Apoll. 8, 26 p. 340, 5; LXX) Mt 5: 44; Col 1: 9; IEph 10: 1; 21: 2; ISm 4: 1; D 1: 3. Also πρ. περί τινος (LXX; s. περί 1f) Lk 6: 28; Col 1: 3; 1 Th 5: 25; Hb 13: 18; ITr 12: 3; MPol 5: 1; D 2: 7. Foll. by ἵνα (Bl-D. §392, 1c) Mt 24: 20; 26: 41; Mk 13: 18; 14: 38. τοῦτο πρ. ἵνα Phil 1: 9. περί τινος ἵνα Col 4: 3; 2 Th 1: 11; 3: 1. περί τινος ὅπως Ac 8: 15. ὑπέρ τινος ὅπως Js 5: 16. Foll. by the gen. of the inf. w. the art. (Bl-D. §400, 7; Rob. 1094) τοῦ μὴ βρέξαι Js 5: 17. πρ. ἐπί τινα (ἐπί III 1aζ) vs. 14 (cf. Marinus, Vi. Procli 20b: Proclus, on his death-bed, has his friends recite hymns to him). W. acc. foll., which refers to the content or manner of the prayer (Philostrat., Vi. Apoll. 6, 18 p. 229, 32) ταῦτα πρ. Lk 18: 11. μακρὰ πρ. make long prayers Mk 12: 40; Lk 20: 47.— W. the acc. of the thing prayed for πρ. τι pray for someth. (X., Hell. 3, 2, 22 νίκην) Mk 11: 24; Ro 8: 26 (on the ability of the ordinary person to pray cf. Philosophenspr. p. 497, 7 μόνος ὁ σοφὸς εἰδὼς εὔχεσθαι=only the wise man knows how to pray).—FHeiler, Das Gebet[5] '23 (lit.); FJDölger, Sol Salutis: Gebet u. Gesang im christl. Altert.[2] '25 (material fr. history of religions); JDöller, Das G. im AT in rel.-gesch. Beleuchtung '14; AGreiff, Das G. im AT '15; JHempel, G. u. Frömmigkeit im AT '22, Gott u. Mensch im AT[2] '36; Elbogen[2] 353ff; 498ff.—EvdGoltz, Das G. in der ältesten Christenheit '01; IRohr, Das G. im NT '24; JMarty, La Prière dans le NT: RHPhr 10, '30, 90-8; JMNielen, G. u. Gottesdienst im NT '37; HGreeven, G. u. Eschatologie im NT '31. LRuppoldt, D. Theol. Grundlage des Bittgebetes im NT, Diss. Leipzig '53; AHamman, La Prière, I (NT), '59.—JoachJeremias, D. Gebetsleben Jesu: ZNW 25, '26, 123-40; AJuncker, Das G. bei Pls '05, Die Ethik des Ap. Pls II '19, 55-72; CSchneider, Ἄγγελος IV '32, 11-47 (Paul); EOrphal, Das Plsgebet '33; J-AEschlimann, La Prière dans S. Paul '34; GHarder, Pls u. d. Gebet '36; AKlawek, Das G. zu Jesus '21; AFrövig, D. Anbetung Christi im NT: Tidskr. for Teol. og Kirke 1, '30, 26-44; EDelay, A qui s'adresse la prière chr.? RThPh 37, '49, 189-201.—OHoltzmann, Die tägl. Gebetsstunden im Judentum u. Urchristentum: ZNW 12, '11, 90-107. HWagenvoort, Orare: Precari: Verbum, HWObbink-Festschr., '64, 101-11 (prayer among the Romans). On the whole subject JHerrmann and HGreeven, TW II 774-808. M-M. B. 1471.

προσέχω impf. προσεῖχον; 2 aor. προσέσχον (1 Cl 4: 2 =Gen 4: 5); pf. προσέσχηκα (Aeschyl., Hdt.+; inscr., pap., LXX, Philo, Joseph., Test. 12 Patr.).

1. act. turn one's mind to (so in the phrase πρ. τὸν νοῦν τινι Aristoph.+, but also freq. without τὸν νοῦν X.+, likew. Wsd 8: 12; 1 Macc 7: 11; 4 Macc 1: 1).

a. pay attention to, give heed to, follow—α. w. dat. of the pers. (Polyb. 6, 37, 7; Cass. Dio 58, 23, 2; Diog. L. 1, 49; Jos., Bell. 1, 32, Ant. 8, 34; 264) τῷ ἐπισκόπῳ IPhld 7: 1; IPol 6: 1. τοῖς προφήταις ISm 7: 2. Cf. Ac 8: 10f. πρ. τοῖς φυσιοῦσίν με pay heed to those who puff me up ITr 4: 1. πρ. πνεύμασι πλάνοις 1 Ti 4: 1.

β. w. dat. of the thing (Mnesimachus Com. [IV BC] 4, 21 πρόσεχ' οἷς φράζω; Plut., Is. et Os. 29 p. 362B; PPetr. II 20 II, 1 τῇ ἐπιστολῇ; 1 Macc 7: 11; Jos., Ant. 8, 241 τ. λόγοις; Test. Zeb. 1: 2) πρ. τοῖς λεγομένοις ὑπὸ τοῦ Φιλίππου pay attention to what was said by Philip Ac 8: 6

(λέγω I 10); cf. 16: 14. πρ. μύθοις (Ps.-Plut., Pro Nobilitate 21, end τοῖς Αἰσωπικοῖς μύθοις προσέχοντες) 1 Ti 1: 4; Tit 1: 14.—Hb 2: 1; 2 Pt 1: 19. ἐμαῖς βουλαῖς 1 Cl 57: 5 (Pr 1: 30); cf. 57: 4 (Pr 1: 24; w. the dat. τοῖς λόγοις to be supplied).—1 Cl 2: 1; 2 Cl 19: 1; MPol 2: 3. (τούτοις) ἃ ἐνετείλατο προσέχετε B 7: 6.

γ. abs. pay attention, be alert, notice (Demosth. 21, 8; Diod. S. 20, 21, 2 οὐδεὶς προσεῖχεν; PMagd. 22, 5 [221 BC]; Sir 13: 13) 2 Cl 17: 3; B 4: 9; 7: 9. προσέχετε ἀκριβῶς pay close attention 7: 4. Foll. by indir. question: πῶς 7: 7. τί 15: 4. προσέχετε ἵνα see to it that 16: 8.— προσέχετε as v.l. for προσεύχεσθε Mt 5: 44.

δ. ἐπὶ ταῖς θυσίαις αὐτοῦ οὐ προσέσχεν he (God) took no notice of his (Cain's) sacrifices 1 Cl 4: 2 (Gen 4: 5).

b. be concerned about, care for, pay attention to w. dat. χήρᾳ, ὀρφανῷ B 20: 2. προσέχετε ἑαυτοῖς καὶ παντὶ τῷ ποιμνίῳ Ac 20: 28 (Sb IV, 7353, 9 [200 AD]).—προσέχειν ἑαυτῷ be careful, be on one's guard (Plut., Mor. 150B νήφων καὶ προσέχων ἑαυτῷ; Gen 24: 6; Ex 10: 28; 34: 12; Dt 4: 9; 6: 12 al.) Lk 17: 3; B 4: 6. W. inf. foll. 2: 1. προσέχετε ἑαυτοῖς ἐπὶ τοῖς ἀνθρώποις τούτοις τί μέλλετε πράσσειν take care what you propose to do with these men Ac 5: 35 (on the function of ἐπί here, see ἐπί II 1bδ). Foll. by μήποτε take care that . . . not Lk 21: 34. Foll. by ἀπό τινος beware of, be on one's guard against someth. (Test. Levi 9: 9, Dan 6: 1.—Bl-D. §149 app.; Rob. 577) 12: 1.—The reflexive pron. can also be omitted (cf. UPZ 69, 7 [152 BC] προσέχω μή; 2 Ch 25: 16; Sir 13: 8) προσέχωμεν μήποτε B 4: 14. προσέχετε μήπως GOxy 2 (JoachJeremias, Unknown Sayings of Jesus, tr. Fuller, '57, 93f). προσέχειν ἀπό τινος beware of someone or someth. (Sir 6: 13; 11: 33; 17: 14; 18: 27; Syntipas p. 94, 28 πρόσεχε ἀπὸ τῶν πολιτῶν) Mt 7: 15; 10: 17; 16: 6, 11f; Lk 20: 46; D 6: 3; 12: 5. Foll. by μή and the inf. take care not Mt 6: 1.

c. occupy oneself with, devote or apply oneself to w. dat. (Hdt.+; Demosth. 1, 6 τῷ πολέμῳ; Herodian 2, 11, 3 γεωργίᾳ καὶ εἰρήνῃ; POxy. 531, 11 [II AD] τοῖς βιβλίοις σου) τῇ ἀναγνώσει κτλ. 1 Ti 4: 13. τῷ θυσιαστηρίῳ officiate at the altar Hb 7: 13. οἴνῳ πολλῷ πρ. be addicted to much wine 1 Ti 3: 8 (Polyaenus, Strateg. 8, 56 τρυφῇ καὶ μέθῃ).

2. mid. cling τινί to someth. (lit. and fig. trag., Hdt.+) εἴ τις μὴ προσέχεται ὑγιαίνουσιν λόγοις 1 Ti 6: 3 v.l. M-M.*

προσήκω fut. προσήξω (Aeschyl., Thu.+; inscr., pap., LXX; Ep. Arist. 29; Philo; Jos., Bell. 7, 450).

1. lit. come to, approach w. dat. of the pers. (Dio Chrys. 65[15], 2) IRo 9: 3.—ἐπὶ προσευχήν come to prayer B 19: 12.

2. be fitting, suitable, proper, be one's duty (trag., Thu. et al.; Jos., Ant. 13, 432 τὰ μὴ προσήκοντα) κατὰ τὸ προσῆκον as is fitting (Plut., Mor. 122A; Dit., Or. 90, 18 [196 BC]; Maspéro 167, 16) MPol 10: 2.*

προσηλόω 1 aor. προσήλωσα (Pla.+; inscr.; 3 Macc 4: 9; Philo, De Prov. in Euseb., Pr. Ev. 8, 14, 24; Jos., Ant. 5, 208) nail (fast) τί τινι someth. to someth. (Diod. S. 4, 47, 5) a bond to the cross Col 2: 14 (cf. Dibelius, Lohmeyer ad loc.; FJDölger, Die Sonne der Gerechtigkeit und d. Schwarze '18, 129ff.—πρ. σταυρῷ='crucify' Diod. S. 2, 18, 1; Artem. 2, 56; Jos., Bell. 2, 308; Galen, De Usu Part. II 214, 8 Helmr.). Nail the condemned man fast to the pyre MPol 13: 3 (the more general sense 'fasten' [Jos., Bell. 5, 232] is excluded by the specific mention of nails). Perh. it is used in the sense chain fast (Lucian, Promth. 2 κατάκλειε καὶ προσήλου, Dial. Deor. 1, 1). M-M.*

προσήλυτος, ου, ὁ *proselyte*, i.e. 'one who has come over' (fr. paganism to Judaism), *convert* (so Gdspd., Probs. 36f), a designation for a Gentile won for Judaism by Jewish missionary efforts, who became a Jew by undergoing circumcision (the word is found in Apollon. Rhod. 1, 834 [μετοίκους καὶ προσηλύτους] and in the LXX. Plainly in a technical sense in Philo; cf. Spec. Leg. 1, 51 τούτους δὲ καλεῖ προσηλύτους ἀπὸ τοῦ προσεληλυθέναι καινῇ καὶ φιλοθέῳ πολιτείᾳ; Sb 1742 Σάρρα προσήλυτος. Roman grave inscriptions also contain 'proselytus' or 'proselyta' [Schürer III⁴ 168, 54].—Perh. πρ. was used as a t.t. in the Isis cult [=Lat. 'advena' in Apuleius, Metam. 11, 26; cf. Rtzst., Mysterienrel.³ 193]). W. Ἰουδαῖοι Ac 2: 11. Of Nicolaus of Antioch 6: 5. Of Jewish efforts to proselytize Mt 23: 15. They are to be differentiated fr. the σεβόμενοι τὸν θεόν, who had obligated themselves only to follow certain commandments; in a mixed expr. Ac 13: 43 speaks of σεβόμενοι πρ.—ABertholet, Die Stellung der Israeliten u. der Juden zu den Fremden 1896, 257ff; KAxenfeld, Die jüd. Propaganda als Vorläuferin der urchristl. Mission: Missionswissenschaftl. Studien für GWarneck '04, 1–80; ILevi, Le Prosélytisme juif: Rev. des Études juives 50, '05, 1ff; 51, '06, 1ff; 53, '07, 56ff; Schürer III⁴ 150ff; HGressmann, ZMR 39, '24, 10ff; 169ff; MMeinertz, Jesus u. die Heidenmission² '25; Bousset, Rel.³ 76ff; Billerb. I 924ff; II 715ff; Harnack, Mission I⁴ '23, 1–23 (Eng. tr., JMoffatt², '08, 1–23); GRosen, Juden u. Phönizier '29; GFMoore, Judaism I, '27, 323–53; FMDerwacter, Preparing the Way for Paul '30; HLietzmann, Gesch. d. Alten Kirche 1, '32, 68–101; CSchneider, Ntl. Zeitgeschichte '34, 173–5; HPreisker, Ntl. Zeitgesch. '37, 290–3; BJBamberger, Proselytism in the Talmudic Period '39; WGBraude, Jewish Proselyting in the First Five Centuries of the Common Era '40; SLieberman, Greek in Jewish Palestine '42: Gentiles and Semi-Proselytes, 68–90; JKlausner, From Jesus to Paul (tr. WFStinespring) '43, 31–49; EM Simon, Verus Israel '48; ELerle, Proselytenwerbung u. Urchristentum '60; SZeitlin, Proselytes and Proselytism, etc.: HAWolfson-Festschr. '65, 871–81.—KGKuhn, TW VI 727–45.—S. also lit. s.v. σέβω. M-M.*

προσηνῶς (Theophr.; Diod. S. 5, 44, 6 et al.) adv. of προσηνής, ές (Pind., Hdt.+; Dit., Syll.³ 783, 29; Pr 25: 25; Philo; Jos., Bell. 3, 507) *kindly, gently, lovingly* w. ἠπίως of God (Orph. Hymns 2, 5; 40, 12; 60, 7 Qu. use the adj. to characterize goddesses) 1 Cl 23: 1.*

πρόσθεν adv. (Hom.+; inscr., pap.; Jos., Ant. 14, 370; 463; Sib. Or. 3, 391) in our lit. only of time *earlier, former* ὁ πρόσθεν χρόνος *the former time* (X.; Dit., Syll.³ 85, 11; 136, 6; 165, 13) Dg 9: 1, 6.*

πρόσθεσις, εως, ἡ (Thu.+; inscr., pap., LXX, Philo, in every case in a different sense than in the NT, such as 'application', etc.; e.g. Polyaenus 2, 3, 8 πρόσθεσις τοῦ θεοῦ='God's help') ἄρτοι τῆς προσθέσεως (for προθέσεως) Mt 12: 4 D=Mk 2: 26 D=Lk 6: 4 D.*

πρόσκαιρος, ον (Strabo 7, 3, 11; Ael. Aristid. 46 p. 218 D. al.; Dit., Or. 669, 14 [I AD], Syll.³ 1109, 44; pap.; 4 Macc 15: 2, 8, 23; Jos., Bell. 5, 66, Ant. 2, 51) *lasting only for a time, temporary, transitory* (Appian, Bell. Civ. 5, 43, §179) opp. αἰώνιος (Dionys. Hal., Ars Rhet. 7, 4; 6 ἀθάνατος; Cass. Dio 12 fgm. 46, 1 ἀΐδιος) of the things in the visible world 2 Cor 4: 18 (Ps.-Clem., Hom. 2, 15 ὁ μὲν παρὼν κόσμος πρόσκαιρος, ὁ δὲ ἐσόμενος ἀΐδιος; Pel.-Leg. p. 12, 26; Joseph and Aseneth 12, 12 ἰδοὺ γὰρ πάντα τὰ χρήματα τοῦ πατρός μου Πεντεφρῆ πρόσκαιρά εἰσι)

κ. ἀφανῆ, τὰ δὲ δώματα τῆς κληρονομίας σου, κύριε, ἄφθαρτά εἰσι κ. αἰώνια). πρ. ἀπόλαυσις (s. ἀπόλαυσις) Hb 11: 25. Of persecutions τὸ πῦρ τὸ πρ. Dg 10: 8. Of a pers.: πρ. ἐστιν *he lasts only a little while* (Dalman, Pj 22, '26, 125f) Mt 13: 21; Mk 4: 17. M-M.*

προσκαλέω (Soph., X., Pla.+; inscr., pap., LXX) in secular Gk. predom., in LXX and our lit. exclusively mid.; 1 aor. προσεκαλεσάμην; pf. προσκέκλημαι; *summon*.
  1. lit.—a. *summon, call on, call to oneself, invite* τινά someone (Gen 28: 1; Esth 4: 5; Sir 13: 9; Ep. Arist. 182; Jos., Ant. 1, 271, Vi. 110; Test. Reub. 4: 9) Mt 10: 1; 15: 10; Mk 3: 13, 23; 6: 7; 7: 14; 15: 44; Lk 7: 18; 15: 26; Ac 6: 2; 23: 17f, 23; Js 5: 14; Hv 1, 4, 2; s 5, 2, 2; 6; 9, 7, 1; 9, 10, 6.
  b. as a legal t.t. (so Aristoph., Lysias+; pap.) *call in, summon* Ac 5: 40. Perh. Mt 18: 32.
  2. fig., of a divine call—a. *call (to) God or Christ, to faith*, etc. Ac 2: 39 (cf. Jo 3: 5). πρ. διὰ τοῦ πνεύματος τοῦ ἁγίου *call through the Holy Spirit* (i.e. through inspired scripture) 1 Cl 22: 1. Of Christ δι' οὗ (i.e. τοῦ σταυροῦ) ἐν τῷ πάθει αὐτοῦ προσκαλεῖται ὑμᾶς *by which* (i.e. the cross) *in his suffering he calls you* ITr 11: 2.
  b. *call to a special task or office* εἰς τὸ ἔργον ὅ (=εἰς ὅ) προσκέκλημαι αὐτούς Ac 13: 2. τινά foll. by the inf. εὐαγγελίσασθαι 16: 10. M-M.

προσκαρτερέω (Demosth.+; Dit., Syll.³ 717, 84, Or. 383, 130; 168 al.; pap., LXX; Jos., Bell. 6, 27) *adhere to, persist in*.
  1. w. dat. of the pers. *attach oneself to, wait on, be faithful to someone* (Ps.-Demosth. 59, 120; Polyb. 23, 5, 3; Diog. L. 8, 11, 14; PGiess. 79 II, 9 [II AD]; PLond. 196, 3) Ac 8: 13; 10: 7. Of a boat, that *always stands ready for someone* Mk 3: 9.
  2. w. dat. of the thing—a. *busy oneself with, be busily engaged in, be devoted to* (τῇ πολιορκίᾳ Polyb. 1, 55, 4; Diod. S. 14, 87, 5; ταῖς θήραις Diod. S. 3, 17, 1; τῇ καθέδρᾳ Jos., Ant. 5, 130; τῇ γεωργίᾳ PAmh. 65, 3; BGU 372 II, 15; PLond. 904, 27.—POxy. 530, 9; PHamb. 34, 9 [all the pap. II AD]) τῇ προσευχῇ Ac 1: 14; Ro 12: 12; Col 4: 2; cf. Ac 6: 4. νηστείαις Pol 7: 2.—Instead of the dat. εἴς τι Ro 13: 6.
  b. *hold fast to someth., continue* or *persevere in someth.* (Polyb. 1, 59, 12 τῇ ἐπιμελείᾳ) τῇ διδαχῇ κτλ. (Posidon.: 87 fgm. 36, 48 Jac. τοῖς λόγοις=the teaching) Ac 2: 42 (mng. 2a is also poss.). τῇ ἐλπίδι Pol 8: 1.
  3. foll. by local ἐν *spend much time in* (Sus 6 Theod. ἐν τῇ οἰκίᾳ) ἐν τῷ ἱερῷ Ac 2: 46. On προσκαρτερέω in Ac s. ESchürer, SAB 1897, 214f.—On the whole word W Grundmann, TW III 620–2. M-M.*

προσκαρτέρησις, εως, ἡ (Philod., Rhet. I 11 S.; Inscr. Antiqu. Orae Septentr. Ponti Eux. ed. Latyschev II 1890 no. 52; 53 [both end of I AD]; ELHicks, JTS 10, '09, 571f; Dssm., LO 80 [LAE 100f]) *perseverance, patience* Eph 6: 18. M-M.*

πρόσκειμαι (Hom.+; inscr., pap., LXX; Jos., Bell. 2, 450; 542, Ant. 17, 225) defective dep.; w. dat. of the thing *be involved* or *absorbed in, be devoted to* (Soph., Ajax 406; Thales in Diog. L. 1, 44; Paus. 4, 9, 3 μαντικῇ; Thu. 7, 50, 4 and Plut., Nic. 4, 1 θειασμῷ; Jos., Ant. 12, 363) Hm 10, 1, 4.*

προσκεφάλαιον, ου, τό *pillow* (Aristoph., Hippocr.+; Diod. S. 13, 84, 6; Diog. L. 4, 37; pap.; 1 Esdr 3: 8; Ezk 13: 18, 20) MPol 5: 2; 12: 3. Perh. the word has this mng. in Mk 4: 38 as well. But here the mng. sailor's *cushion* is just as likely (Cratinus Com. [V BC] 269; Dit., Syll.³ 736, 23 [92 BC]). M-M.*

προσκληρόω 1 aor. pass. *προσεκληρώθην* (Plut., Mor. 738D; Ps.-Lucian, Amor. 3) *allot, assign* pass. *be attached to, join* w. dat. *someone* (cf. Dit., Or. 257, 5 [109 BC] τῷ πατρὶ ἡμῶν προσκληθέντας [s. Dittenberger's note]; UPZ 144, 18 [II BC]; Philo, Sacr. Abel. 6, Exsecr. 162, Leg. ad Gai. 3; 68 τῶν μὲν τούτῳ τῶν δὲ ἐκείνῳ προσκληρουμένων; Jos., Bell. 2, 567) Ac 17: 4. M-M.*

πρόσκλησις s. *πρόσκλισις*. M-M.

προσκλίνω 1 aor. pass. *προσεκλίθην* (Hom.+; inscr.; Jos., Ant. 5, 193) *cause to lean against* pass. intr. *incline toward* w. dat. of the pers. *attach oneself to, join someone* (Sext. Emp., Math. 7, 324; schol. on Aristoph., Plut. 1027 τοῖς δικαίοις προσεκλίθη; 2 Macc 14: 24) Ac 5: 36; 1 Cl 47: 4; 63: 1. M-M.*

πρόσκλισις, εως, ἡ (Polyb. 5, 51, 8; 6, 10, 10; Diod. S. 3, 27, 2; Diog. L., Prooem. 20 al.) *inclination,* in our lit. only in an unfavorable sense κατὰ πρόσκλισιν *in a spirit of partiality* 1 Ti 5: 21 (v.l., as Ep. Arist. 5, πρόσκλησιν *summons, invitation*); cf. 1 Cl 21: 7. δίχα προσκλίσεως ἀνθρωπίνης *free from human partisanship* 50: 2. προσκλίσεις ποιεῖσθαι *engage in partisan strife* 1 Cl 47: 3; cf. 4. M-M.*

προσκολλάω 1 fut. pass. *προσκολληθήσομαι*; in our lit. only pass.; fig. *adhere closely to, be faithfully devoted to, join τινί someone* (Pla., Phaedo 82E, Leg. 5 p. 728B; Sir 6: 34; 13: 16) Ac 5: 36 t.r.—Of the attachment felt by a husband for his wife (after Gen 2: 24) τῇ γυναικί (LXX v.l.) Mt 19: 5 v.l.; πρὸς τὴν γυν. (LXX, text; Philo, Leg. All. 2, 49) Mk 10: 7 t.r.; Eph 5: 31 (of a wife in relation to her husband POxy. 1901, 26; 41; 43; 63). M-M.*

πρόσκομμα, ατος, τό (Plut., Mor. 1048c; Athen. 3 p. 97F; LXX) *stumbling, offense.*
1. the *stumbling* itself—**a.** λίθος προσκόμματος *a stone that causes men to stumble* (Sir 31: 7 ξύλον προσκόμματος; Is 8: 14 λίθου πρόσκομμα) symbolically, of Christ Ro 9: 32f; 1 Pt 2: 8.—**b.** fig. διὰ προσκόμματος ἐσθίειν Ro 14: 20 (διά A III 1c).
2. *the opportunity to take offense* or *to make a misstep*
a. lit. *obstacle, hindrance* of a rough road ἔχει ἀνοδίας καὶ προσκόμματα πολλά Hm 6, 1, 3.
b. fig. τιθέναι πρόσκομμα τῷ ἀδελφῷ *give the brother an occasion to take offense, put an obstacle in the brother's way* Ro 14: 13 (w. σκάνδαλον). βλέπετε μή πως ἡ ἐξουσία ὑμῶν πρόσκομμα γένηται τοῖς ἀσθενέσιν *take care that your freedom does not somehow become a hindrance to the weak,* or *cause the weak to stumble* 1 Cor 8: 9. σεμνότης, ἐν ᾗ οὐδὲν πρόσκομμά ἐστιν πονηρὸν reverence, *in which there is no evil cause for offense* Hm 2: 4.—JLindblom, Z. Begriff 'Anstoss' im NT: Strena Philologica Upsaliensis '22, 1-6. Cf. σκανδαλίζω, end.*

προσκοπή, ῆς, ἡ (Polyb.)=πρόσκομμα 2b (q.v.) *an occasion for taking offense* or *for making a misstep,* fig. διδόναι προσκοπήν 2 Cor 6: 3.*

προσκόπτω 1 aor. *προσέκοψα* (Aristoph., X.+; Dit., Syll.³ 985, 41; pap., LXX; En. 15, 11).
1. lit.—**a.** trans. *strike τὶ someth.* (*against*) (Aristoph., Vesp. 275 πρ. τὸν δάκτυλον ἐν τῷ σκότῳ) πρός τι *against someth.* πρὸς λίθον τὸν πόδα σου (Ps 90: 12) Mt 4: 6; Lk 4: 11 (in symbolic usage).
b. intr. *beat against, stumble* (of the blind Tobit, Tob

11: 10; Pr 3: 23; Jer 13: 16) ἐάν τις περιπατῇ ἐν τῇ ἡμέρᾳ, οὐ προσκόπτει J 11: 9; cf. vs. 10. Of winds προσέκοψαν τῇ οἰκίᾳ *they beat against the house* Mt 7: 27 (preferred to προσέπεσαν for vs. 25 by JPWilson, ET 57, '45, 138).
2. fig.—**a.** *take offense at, feel repugnance for, reject* (Polyb. 1, 31, 7; 5, 7, 5; 6, 6, 3; 6; Diod. S. 4, 61, 7 p. 306 Vogel διὰ τὴν ὑπερβολὴν τῆς λύπης προσκόψαντα τῷ ζῆν; 17, 30, 4; Epict. 1, 28, 10; 3, 22, 89; M. Ant. 6, 20; 10, 30) in a quite non-literal use προσέκοψαν τῷ λίθῳ τοῦ προσκόμματος (πρόσκομμα 1. προσκόπτω of 'striking one's foot against a stone' Vi. Aesopi I c. 66) Ro 9: 32; cf. 1 Pt 2: 8 (cf. also Diod. S. 15, 6, 3 προσκόπτειν τοῖς ῥηθεῖσι=take offense at the words). ἔν τινι Ro 14: 21 (on πρ. ἐν cf. Sir 32: 20).
b. *give offense* (Polyb. 5, 49, 5; 7, 5, 6; Epict. 4, 11, 33; Sir 31: 17) w. dat. of the pers. (Posidippus Com., fgm. 36 K. προσέκοψε τῷ ἀνθρώπῳ; Diod. S. 6, 7, 6 Διί; 17, 77, 7 al.; Aesop, Fab. 417b H. πρ. ἀνθρώποις) μᾶλλον ἀνθρώποις προσκόψωμεν ἢ τῷ θεῷ 1 Cl 21: 5.—Lit. s.v. πρόσκομμα, end. M-M.*

προσκυλίω 1 aor. *προσεκύλισα* (Aristoph., Vesp. 202 al.; Polyaenus 2, 31,·3) *roll (up to) τὶ someth.* λίθον τῇ θύρᾳ *a stone to the opening* Mt 27: 60; also ἐπὶ τὴν θ. Mk 15: 46; Lk 23: 53 v.l.*

προσκυνέω impf. *προσεκύνουν*; fut. *προσκυνήσω*; 1 aor. *προσεκύνησα* (trag., Hdt.+; inscr., pap., LXX; En. 10, 21; Ep. Arist., Philo, Joseph., Test. 12 Patr.) used to designate the custom of prostrating oneself before a person and kissing his feet, the hem of his garment, the ground, etc.; the Persians did this in the presence of their deified king, and the Greeks before a divinity or someth. holy; (*fall down and*) *worship, do obeisance to, prostrate oneself before, do reverence to, welcome respectfully,* in Attic Gk., and later (e.g. Appian, Mithrid. 104 §489), used w. the acc. (so Mt 4: 10 and Lk 4: 8 [Dt 6: 13 v.l.]; J 4: 22a, b, 23b, 24a v.l.; Rv 9: 20.—Gen 37: 9; Ex 11: 8; Judg 7: 15 A; Ep. Arist. 137; 138; Philo; Jos., C. Ap. 1, 239, Ant. 2, 13; 7, 250); beside it the Koine uses the dat. (Phryn. p. 463 L.; JWittmann, Sprachl. Untersuchungen zu Cosmas Indicopl., Diss. Munich '13, 16; KWolf, Studien z. Sprache des Malalas II, Diss. Munich '12, 34; Bl-D. §151, 2; Rob. 455; 476f); the LXX and our lit. prefer the dat. (s. also Ep. Arist. 135; Jos., Ant. 6, 55.—6, 154 πρ. τῷ θεῷ immediately after τὸν θεὸν πρ.). This reverence or worship is paid
1. to human beings who, however, are to be recognized by this act as belonging to a superhuman realm (Appian, Mithrid. 104 §489: Pompey; Galen, Protr. 5 p. 12, 2ff John: Socrates, Homer, Hippocrates, Plato): to a king (so Hdt.+; cf. 2 Km 18: 28; 24: 20; 3 Km 1: 16, 53. On proskynesis in the Hellenistic ruler cults s. LRTaylor, JHS 47, '27, 53ff, The Divinity of the Rom. Emperor '31, esp. 256-66; against him WWTarn, Alexander the Great II, '50, 347-73) ὁ δοῦλος προσεκύνει αὐτῷ Mt 18: 26 (of a female slave toward her κύριος PGiess. 17, 11f=Wilcken, Chrest. 481; cf. Jos., Ant. 2, 11); to Peter fr. Cornelius Ac 10: 25 (cf. Apollonius [c. 197 AD] in Euseb., H.E. 5, 18, 6).—The church at Philadelphia προσκυνήσουσιν ἐνώπιον τῶν ποδῶν σου Rv 3: 9 (on πρ. ἐνώπιόν τινος cf. Ps 21: 28; 85: 9; Is 66: 23).
2. to God (Aeschyl.+; X., An. 3, 2, 9; 13; Pla., Rep. 3 p. 398A; Polyb. 18, 37, 10; Plut., Pomp. 14, 4; Lucian, Pisc. 21 τῇ θεῷ; PGM 4, 649. Of various divinities in the inscr. [cf. Dit., Or. II 700a index VIII; Sb 7911ff]; PFlor. 332, 11 θεούς; LXX; Philo, Gig. 54 τὸν θεόν al.; Jos., Ant. 6, 154; 20, 164 al.).

a. of the God worshipped by monotheists (Christians, Jews, Samaritans) κύριον τὸν θεόν σου προσκυνήσεις (Dt 6: 13 v.l.) Mt 4: 10; Lk 4: 8. πρ. τῷ πατρί J 4: 21, 23a; cf. b. τῷ θεῷ (Jos., Ant. 6, 55; 9, 267) Rv 19: 4 (w. πίπτειν), 10b. Cf. Hb 1: 6 (Dt 32: 43 LXX). τῷ ζῶντι Rv 4: 10. τῷ ποιήσαντι τὸν οὐρανόν 14: 7. πεσὼν ἐπὶ πρόσωπον προσκυνήσει τῷ θεῷ he will fall down and worship God (s. 2 Km 9: 6) 1 Cor 14: 25; cf. Rv 7: 11; 11: 16. ἐνώπιόν σου (s. 1, end) 15: 4. Abs. (Dit., Syll.³ 1173, 2; PTebt. 416, 7; LXX) J 4: 20a, b, 24a, b; Ac 8: 27. Used w. ἀναβαίνειν (UPZ 62, 33 [161 BC] ἐὰν ἀναβῶ κἀγὼ προσκυνῆσαι; Jos., Ant. 20, 164) J 12: 20; Ac 24: 11; cf. Rv 11: 1. W. πίπτειν (s. Jos., Ant. 8, 119) Rv 5: 14. προσεκύνησεν ἐπὶ τὸ ἄκρον τῆς ῥάβδου αὐτοῦ he bowed in worship (or prayed) over the head of his staff Hb 11: 21 (Gen 47: 31).

b. of the idol-worship of polytheism (LXX) προσκυνεῖν τοῖς νεκροῖς θεοῖς 2 Cl 3: 1 or λίθους καὶ ξύλα κτλ. 1: 6 (cf. Ep. Arist. 135 . . . οἷς πρ.). Cf. Ac 7: 43; Dg 2: 5. τὰ ὑφ' ὑμῶν προσκυνούμενα the things that are worshipped by you 2: 4. Abs., w. θύειν MPol 12: 2.

3. to the devil and Satanic beings Mt 4: 9; Lk 4: 7 (on πρ. ἐνώπιον ἐμοῦ s. 1 above). τὰ δαιμόνια Rv 9: 20. τῷ δράκοντι 13: 4a. τῷ θηρίῳ 13: 4b. τὸ θηρίον vss. 8; 12; 20: 4. τῇ εἰκόνι (Da 3: 5 al.) τοῦ θηρίου 13: 15; cf. 16: 2; 19: 20. τὸ θηρίον καὶ τ. εἰκόνα αὐτοῦ 14: 9, 11. Cf. θηρίον 1b; also PTouilleux, L'Apocalypse et les cultes de Domitien et de Cybèle '35.—**4.** to angels Rv 22: 8; cf. 19: 10a.

5. to Jesus, who is revered and worshipped as Messianic King and Divine Helper: Mt 2: 2, 8, 11.—8: 2; 9: 18; 14: 33; 15: 25; J 9: 38.—Mt 20: 20. The demons ask a favor of him Mk 5: 6.—Mock worship on the part of soldiers 15: 19 (στέφανος 1).—The Risen Lord is esp. the object of worship: Mt 28: 9, 17; Lk 24: 52 𝔓⁷⁵ et al. Likewise the exalted Christ MPol 17: 3.—Lit. s.v. προσεύχομαι, end; Bolkestein [δεισιδαιμονία, end] 23ff; JHorst, Proskynein: Z. Anbetung im Urchristentum nach ihrer religionsgesch. Eigenart '32; BertheMMarti, Proskynesis and adorare: Language 12, '36, 272–82; BReicke, Some Reflections on Worship in the NT: TWManson mem. vol. '59, 194–209. M-M. B. 1469.*

προσκυνητής, οῦ, ὁ (pre-Christian Syrian inscr. in Dit., Or. 262, 21 [Dssm., LO 79f–LAE 99]; Byz. pap.) worshiper ἀληθινοὶ πρ. J 4: 23. M-M.*

προσλαλέω 1 aor. προσελάλησα speak to or with, address τινί (Antiphanes Com. 218, 3 Kock; Heniochus Com. 4, 3; cf. Ex 4: 16; Wsd 13: 17; Jos., Bell. 1, 444) Ac 13: 43; IEph 3: 1; IMg 1: 1; IPol 5: 1. Abs. (Theophr., Char. 7, 5; pap.) Ac 28: 20. M-M.*

προσλαμβάνω 2 aor. προσέλαβον; pf. προσείληφα; 2 aor. mid. προσελαβόμην (Aeschyl., Hdt.+; inscr., pap., LXX; Ep. Arist. 2; Joseph.).
1. act.—**a.** take, partake of food (X., Mem. 3, 14, 4 ἄρτον) w. the partitive gen. Ac 27: 34 t.r.
b. take advantage of (Demosth. 2, 7 τὴν ἄνοιαν) τὴν νεωτερικὴν τάξιν the youthful appearance (of the bishop) IMg 3: 1.
2. mid.—**a.** take aside τινά someone Mt 16: 22; Mk 8: 32. So prob. also Ac 18: 26: Priscilla and Aquila take Apollos aside to teach him undisturbed.
b. receive or accept in one's society, in(to) one's home or circle of acquaintances τινά someone (2 Macc 10: 15) of one Christian receiving another Ro 14: 1; 15: 7a. Of God or Christ accepting the believer (cf. Charito 8, 2, 13 θεῶν προσλαμβανομένων) 14: 3; 15: 7b; 1 Cl 49: 6 (cf. Ps 26: 10; 64: 5; 72: 24).—Ac 28: 2; Phlm 12 t.r.; 17 (PTebt. 61a,

2 [II BC] πρ. εἰς τὴν κατοικίαν; BGU 1141, 37 [14 BC] προσελαβόμην αὐτὸν εἰς οἶκον παρ' ἐμέ).
c. take along w. oneself as companion or helper (PFay. 12, 10 [103 BC] πρ. συνεργὸν Ἀμμώνιον; PAmh. 100, 4; POxy. 71 II, 9 προσελαβόμην ἐμαυτῇ εἰς βοήθειαν Σεκοῦνδον; 2 Macc 8: 1; Jos., Ant. 18, 4, C. Ap. 1, 241) ἄνδρας τινὰς πονηρούς Ac 17: 5.
d. take of food μηθέν Ac 27: 33. W. partitive gen. τροφῆς vs. 36 (s. Ps.-Clem., Hom. 3, 21). M-M.*

προσλέγω (Hom.+, but almost always in the mid. The act. is found now and then in the pap. [Mayser 494]) answer, reply w. dat. of the pers., and foll. by direct discourse introduced by ὅτι, ending of Mark in the Freer Ms. 6.*

πρόσλημψις or **πρόσληψις** (t.r.; Bl-D. §101 s.v. λαμβάνειν; likew. Mlt.-H. 247), εως, ἡ (Pla.+; PTebt. 64b, 6; 72, 246 [II BC]; Jos., Ant. 18, 353) acceptance (by God) Ro 11: 15.*

προσμένω 1 aor. προσέμεινα (Pind., Hdt.+; inscr.; UPZ 60, 16 [168 BC]; LXX; Jos., Vi. 62; 63; Sib. Or. 5, 131).
1. remain or stay with τινί someone or someth.—**a.** lit. Mt 15: 32; Mk 8: 2.—**β.** fig. τῷ κυρίῳ remain true to the Lord Ac 11: 23 (Jos., Ant. 14, 20 τῷ Ἀριστοβούλῳ).
b. w. dat. of the thing continue in ταῖς δεήσεσιν 1 Ti 5: 5. τῇ χάριτι τοῦ θεοῦ Ac 13: 43. τῇ προθέσει τῆς καρδίας πρ. ἐν τῷ κυρίῳ 11: 23 v.l.
2. remain longer, further (Herodas 8, 3) ἡμέρας ἱκανάς Ac 18: 18. ἐν Ἐφέσῳ 1 Ti 1: 3. M-M.*

προσομιλέω 1 aor. inf. προσομιλῆσαι (Eur., Thu.+) speak to, converse with τινί someone (Theognis 1, 31 κακοῖσι μὴ προσομίλει ἀνδράσιν; Pla., Gorg. 502E; Vett. Val. 353, 1; Philo, Agr. 60) of communication by letter IEph 9: 2.*

προσονομάζω (since Hdt. 2, 52; Plut., Alex. 54, 6, Thes. 36, 6; Cass. Dio 57, 5; 59, 4; Diog. L. 2, 85; 3, 50; 7, 135; 147; Dit., Or. 56, 22; 24 [III BC] ἢ προσονομασθήσεται πέμπτη φυλή; 90, 39; 2 Macc 6: 2; Ep. Arist.; Philo, Abr. 57) name pass. be named, be called 1 Cl 25: 2.*

προσορμίζω 1 aor. pass. προσωρμίσθην (Hdt.+; inscr., pap.); the act., which is rare, means 'bring a ship into harbor', the middle (Philo, Agr. 64, cf. Somn. 2, 143) or passive (Arrian, Anab. 6, 4, 6; 20, 7; Aelian, V.H. 8, 5; Cass. Dio 41, 48; 64, 1) aorist come into (the) harbor, come to anchor Mk 6: 53. M-M.*

προσοφείλω (Thu.+; inscr., pap.) owe besides, though it is oft. scarcely poss. to find any special force in the prep. and to differentiate the compound fr. the simple verb τινί τι someth. to someone (PHib. 63, 14 ὃ προσοφείλεις μοι) σεαυτόν μοι προσοφείλεις you owe me your very self (besides) Phlm 19. M-M.*

προσοχθίζω 1 aor. προσώχθισα be angry, offended, provoked (LXX; Test. Jud. 18: 5; Sib. Or. 3, 272) w. dat. of the pers. at someone (Cass. Dio 7, 21, 3; Test. Dan 5: 4) Hb 3: 17. W. dat. of the thing (Sib. Or. 3, 272) τῇ γενεᾷ ταύτῃ vs. 10 (Ps 94: 10). Abs. Hs 9, 7, 6. M-M.*

πρόσοψις, εως, ἡ appearance (so pass. Pind.+; Polyb. 9, 41, 2; Diod. S. 1, 91, 6; 13, 27, 6; Lucian, Tim. 41; Epigr. Gr. 376, 8; LXX; Ep. Arist. 59) Hs 9, 1, 10.*

προσπαίω 1 aor. προσέπαισα (Soph., fgm. 310 v.l.; schol. on Aeschyl., Prom. 885) strike or beat against τινί someth. substituted by Lachmann for προσέπεσαν in Mt

7: 25; favored by SANaber, Mnemosyne 9, 1881, 276 and EbNestle, ZNW 9, '08, 252f. Bl-D. §202 app. M-M.*

πρόσπεινος, ον (Demosthenes Ophthalmicus [I AD] in Aëtius p. 74, 26 εἰ πρόσπεινοι γένωνται) *hungry* πρόσπεινον γενέσθαι *become hungry* Ac 10: 10. M-M.*

προσπήγνυμι 1 aor. προσέπηξα (Eur., fgm. 679 Nauck²; Philo Mech. 74, 10; Cass. Dio 40, 9; 63, 2) *fix or fasten to*, abs. *nail to* (*the cross*) Ac 2: 23.*

προσπίπτω impf. προσέπιπτον; aor. προσέπεσον or προσέπεσα—Bl-D. §81, 3 w. app.; Mlt.-H. 208 (Hom.+; pap., LXX; Ep. Arist. 180; Philo, Joseph.).
1. *fall down before* or *at the feet of* (Soph.+) w. dat. of the pers. *someone* (Pla., Ep. 7 p. 349A; Polyb. 10, 18, 7; Plut., Marc. 23, 2, Pyrrh. 3, 4; PPetr. II 1, 4 [III BC]; Ps 94: 6; Jos., Bell. 3, 201; 454) Mk 3: 11; 5: 33; Lk 8: 28, 47; Ac 16: 29; GEb 3.—Before God τῷ δεσπότῃ 1 Cl 48: 1; abs. 9: 1.—πρ. τοῖς γόνασίν τινος *fall at someone's feet* (Eur., Or. 1332 al.; Plut., Pomp. 5, 2, Mor. 1117B; Charito 3, 2, 1; Achilles Tat. 5, 17, 3; Jos., Ant. 19, 234) Lk 5: 8, unless the ref. here is to the *clasping* of a person's knees by a suppliant, as perh. in the Eur. pass. above (cf. L-S-J lex. s.v. γόνυ I 1, but also s.v. προσπίπτω 3). πρὸς τοὺς πόδας τινός (Esth 8: 3; cf. Ex 4: 25 and Zen.-P. 59 210, 1 [254 BC] πρὸς τὰ γόνατα) Mk 7: 25.
2. *fall upon, strike against* (cf. Thu. 3, 103, 2 et al.; Appian, Bell. Civ. 4, 113 §472; Arrian, Anab. 3, 13, 6; Sir 25: 21; Pr 25: 20; Jos., Bell. 4, 343) τινί *someth.* of the winds (Ael. Aristid. 36, 8 K.=48 p. 440 D.) that *beat upon* a house w. great force Mt 7: 25 (s. προσπαίω and προσκόπτω 1b).—*Come* (*suddenly*) *upon* ὀξυχολία προσπίπτει τινί *bad temper comes over someone* Hm 6, 2, 5 (Menand., Epitr. 497 J. χολὴ μέλαινα πρ.). M-M.*

προσποιέω 1 aor. mid. προσεποιησάμην (Eur., Hdt.+; pap., LXX) in our lit. only mid.
1. *make* or *act as though, pretend* (Thu., Pla. et al.; Diod. S. 1, 94, 1; 15, 46, 2; Plut., Timol. 5, 2; Aelian, V.H. 8, 5; Zen.-P. 59 534, 44; 61 [III BC]; Philo, In Flacc. 40; 98; Jos., C. Ap. 1, 5, Vi. 319; Test. Jud. 7: 2) w. inf. foll. (so mostly in the passages cited, also Jos., Ant. 13, 102; Test. Jos. 3, 7) προσεποιήσατο πορρώτερον πορεύεσθαι *he made as though he were going farther* Lk 24: 28. προσποιεῖ ἀγνοεῖν με *you are pretending that you do not know me* MPol 10: 1.
2. *take notice* (*of*) abs. (Zeno the Eleatic in Diog. L. 9, 29 ἐὰν μὴ προσποιῶμαι=if I do not notice [it].—The thing that one notices is added in the acc.: Diog. L. 1, 20 τί; Job 19: 14 με) μὴ προσποιούμενος *taking no notice* J 8: 6 v.l. M-M.*

προσπορεύομαι dep. (Aristot., Polyb.; Dit., Syll.³ 344, 112; PEleph. 18, 5 [223/2 BC]; PMagd. 27, 6; PAmh. 33, 17; UPZ 79, 3 [159 BC] προσπορεύεταί μοι; LXX) *come up to, approach* τινί Mk 10: 35. M-M.*

προσρήσσω (on the relationship betw. ῥήσσω and ῥήγνυμι s. EFraenkel, Gesch. der griech. Nomina agentis II '12, 40f; Bl-D. §101 under ῥηγνύναι; Mlt.-H. 403) 1 aor. προσέρηξα (on the form w. -ρρ- s. W-S. §5, 26b; Mlt.-H. 193).
1. trans. *break to pieces, shatter* (Jos., Ant. 6, 182; 9, 91) pass. (schol. on Soph., Trach. 821 Papag.) w. dat. of the thing *be broken* or *wrecked on* or *against someth.* (M. Ant. 4, 49, 1 ἄκρα, ᾗ τὰ κύματα προσρήσσεται; Etym. Mag. p. 703, 20 προσρησσομένου τῇ γῇ ὕδατος) ἵνα μὴ προσρησσώμεθα τῷ ἐκείνων νόμῳ *that we might not be wrecked on their law* B 3: 6.

2. intr., w. dat. of the thing *burst upon someth.* προσέρηξεν ὁ ποταμὸς τῇ οἰκίᾳ Lk 6: 48; cf. vs. 49; Mt 7: 27 v.l. M-M.*

πρόσταγμα, ατος, τό (Pla. +; inscr., pap., LXX, En., Ep. Arist., Philo; Jos., Ant. 11, 220; loanw. in rabb.) *order, command(ment), injunction,* in our lit. only of divine precepts (πρόσταγμα of a divine command: Dio Chrys. 16[33], 9; Ael. Aristid. 48, 51 K.=24 p. 478 D.; Ptolem., Apotel. 1, 3, 6 θεῖον πρ.; Dit., Syll.³ 1127, 8; 1129; 1131; 1138; IG XI 1263; Zen.-P. 7 [=Sb 6713], 19 [257 BC] τὰ ὑπὸ τοῦ θεοῦ προστάγματα; Sb 685 [II BC] τοῦ θεοῦ πρόσταγμα ἔχων; UPZ 20, 27; PGM 5, 138; 13, 268; LXX; En. 18, 15; Ep. Arist. 279; Philo; Jos., C. Ap. 2, 231 τὰ τοῦ νόμου πρ., Ant. 2, 291 θεοῦ πρ.) Dg 12: 5. Elsewh. always pl. 1 Cl 20: 5. τὰ ἄμωμα πρ. αὐτοῦ 37: 1; τὰ λαϊκὰ πρ. *rules for laymen* 40: 5. W. δικαιώματα 2: 8; 58: 2. τὰ πρ. τοῦ θεοῦ ποιεῖν *keep the commandments of God* 50: 5. πορεύεσθαι ἐν τοῖς πρ. αὐτοῦ Hs 5, 1, 5. ἐν τοῖς νομίμοις τῶν προσταγμάτων αὐτοῦ πορεύεσθαι *walk according to the laws of his commandments* 1 Cl 3: 4. ὑπακούειν τοῖς πρ. *obey the instructions* 2 Cl 19: 3.*

προστάσσω 1 aor. προσέταξα. Pass.: pf. προστέταγμαι, ptc. προστεταγμένος; 1 aor. προσετάχθην; 2 aor. προσετάγην (Aeschyl., Hdt.+; inscr., pap., LXX, Ep. Arist., Philo, Joseph.; Sib. Or. 3, 258) *command, order* w. dat. of the pers. Mt 1: 24; 21: 6 v.l. W. acc. of the thing *order, prescribe someth.* Mt 8: 4; Mk 1: 44; PK 4 p. 16, 5. πρ. τὰ περί τινος *give orders concerning someone* Hs 7: 1. τινί τι pass. Ac 10: 33 (cf. Dit., Or. 664, 15 τὰ ὑπ' ἐμοῦ προσταχθέντα). τοῖς ἱερεῦσιν τόπος προστέτακται *an office is assigned to the priests* 1 Cl 40: 5. Foll. by the acc. and inf. (Eur., X.; PTebt. 7, 1; 1 Esdr 8: 10; 3 Macc 7: 8; Philo, Spec. Leg. 2, 130; Jos., Ant. 10, 213) Ac 10: 48; 1 Cl 20: 11. Pass., w. inf. foll. (Jos., Bell. 1, 488) Hm 4, 1, 10. ποιεῖν τὰ προστασσόμενα ὑπὸ τοῦ πλήθους 1 Cl 54: 2. Abs. καθὼς προσέταξεν (cf. Gen 47: 11; Jos., Ant. 8, 267) Lk 5: 14; Hs 7: 5; cf. IPol 8: 1. (οἱ) προστεταγμένοι καιροί (*the*) *fixed times* Ac 17: 26; 1 Cl 40: 4 (καιρός 3, end.—Jos., Ant. 3, 30 τὸ προστεταγμένον μέτρον). M-M.*

προστάτης, ου, ὁ (Aeschyl., Hdt.+; inscr., pap., LXX; Ep. Arist. 111; Jos., Bell. 1, 385) *defender, guardian,* of gods (Soph., Oed. Rex 881, Trach. 208; Cornutus 27 p. 51, 15 πρ. κ. σωτήρ; Heraclit. Sto. 11 p. 18, 9; 38 p. 55, 11; Ael. Aristid. 28, 156 K.=49 p. 542 D.; 33, 2 K.=51 p. 572 D.; Ἀσκληπιὸς πρ. ἡμέτερος; schol. on Pind., Isthm. 1, 11c πρ. ὁ θεός; Jos., Ant. 7, 380) of Christ, in each case w. ἀρχιερεύς, 1 Cl 64. πρ. καὶ βοηθός 36: 1. προστάτης τῶν ψυχῶν ἡμῶν 61: 3.*

προστάτις, ιδος, ἡ (Cornutus 20 p. 37, 20; Lucian, Bis Accus. 29 θεὰ προστάτις ἑαυτῶν; Cass. Dio 42, 39 al.; PGM 36, 338) *protectress, patroness, helper* προστάτις πολλῶν ἐγενήθη καὶ ἐμοῦ αὐτοῦ *she has been of great assistance to many, including myself* Ro 16: 2 (Ltzm., Hdb. ad loc. The masc. προστάτης took on a technical sense and is found w. this mng. in Jewish [Schürer III⁴, 89] as well as in pagan [Dit., Or. 209, Syll.³ 1109, 13; CIG I, 126; GHeinrici, ZWTh 19, 1876, 516ff.—EZiebarth, Das griech. Vereinswesen 1896, index s.v.; WOtto, Priester u. Tempel im hellenist. Ägypten II '08 p. 75, 1] religious circles). M-M.*

προστίθημι (Hom.+; inscr., pap., LXX, Ep. Arist., Philo, Joseph., Test. 12 Patr.) impf. 3 sing. προσετίθει Ac 2: 47; fut. προσθήσω; 1 aor. προσέθηκα; 2 aor. subj.

προσθῶ, imper. πρόσθες, inf. προσθεῖναι, ptc. προσθείς; 2 aor. mid. προσεθέμην. Pass.: impf. 3 pl. προσετίθεντο; 1 aor. προσετέθην; 1 fut. προστεθήσομαι.

1. *add, put to*—a. of things that are added to someth. already present: abs. (opp. ἀφαιρεῖν; cf. Isocr. 12, 264; Pla., Leg. 5 p. 742ɒ al.; Epict. 1, 6, 10; Dt 4: 2; 13: 1) *add* (*someth.*) B 19: 11; D 4: 13. Pass. Mk 4: 24. τὶ *someth.* Hs 5, 3, 3; D 11: 2. Of the addition of a word, sentence, etc. (Demosth. et al.; Mitteis, Chrest. 372 v., 11 [the statement follows in direct discourse]; PStrassb. 41, 21) 1 Cl 8: 2; of an addition to a written document (Ep. Arist. 26; Jos., Ant. 1, 17) ῥήματα Hv 2, 4, 2. Pass. (ὁ νόμος) προσετέθη (*the law*) *was added* to the promise Gal 3: 19.—π. λόγον τινί *speak a further message* to someone (Dionys. Hal. 6, 88, 3; 8, 9, 1) Hb 12: 19 (παραιτέομαι 2c).—τί τινι *someth. to someth.* ταῖς ἁμαρτίαις αὐτῶν τὰς ἀσελγείας Hv 2, 2, 2.—It is oft. used w. the dat. alone, fr. which the acc. is easily supplied. In these cases it may be translated *add to, increase* πρ. ταῖς ἁμαρτίαις ὑμῶν Hv 5: 7; cf. m 4, 3, 7; 12, 6, 2; s 6, 1, 4; 6, 2, 3; 8, 11, 3. προσθεῖναι τῷ δρόμῳ σου *to press on in your course* IPol 1: 2.—τὶ ἐπὶ τι *someth. to someth.* (4 Km 20: 6) Mt 6: 27; Lk 12: 25. τὶ ἐπί τινι (Sir 3: 27) προσέθηκεν καὶ τοῦτο ἐπὶ πᾶσιν *he added this to all* (*his*) *other* (*misdeeds*) 3: 20 (Bl-D. §461, 2; Rob. 605).

b. of persons who are added to a group already existing, or who are attached to an individual, to whom they henceforth belong: *add, associate* (Diod. S. 5, 45, 3) πρ. τινὰ τῇ ἐκκλησίᾳ Ac 2: 47 t.r. The same dat. is to be supplied in the text which is preferred by the critical editions in this pass.; likew. vs. 41 and 5: 14 (if τῷ κυρίῳ is to be taken w. πιστεύοντες here, another dat. is to be supplied w. προσετίθεντο).—προστίθεσθαι τῷ κυρίῳ *be brought to the Lord* 11: 24. Also 5: 14 (s. above), in case τῷ κυρ. here belongs w. προσετίθ. (προστίθεσθαι hardly means 'attach oneself to' as in Demosth. 18, 39 al.; 1 Macc 2: 43; Jos., Vi. 87, 123).—Of one deceased πρ. πρὸς τοὺς πατέρας αὐτοῦ *be gathered to his forefathers* (Judg 2: 10; 4 Km 22: 20; 1 Macc 2: 69) Ac 13: 36.

c. In accordance w. Hebr. usage (but s. Helbing p. IV, contradicted by AWifstrand, Svensk Teol. Kvartalskrift 16, '40, 257) the adverbs *again, further* and sim. expressions are paraphrased w. πρ. (Bl-D. §392, 2; 419, 4; 435a w. app.; Mlt.-H. 445f.) προσθεὶς εἶπεν παραβολήν *again he told a parable,* or *he proceeded to tell a parable* Lk 19: 11 (Gen 38: 5 προσθεῖσα ἔτεκεν υἱόν). οὐ μὴ προσθῶ πεῖν *I shall never again drink* Mk 14: 25 v.l. προσθήσω τοῦ ἐπερωτῆσαι Hm 4, 3, 1. It is usu. found in the mid. w. the inf. foll. (Gen 8: 12; Ex 9: 34 Φαραὼ προσέθετο τοῦ ἁμαρτάνειν; 1 Km 18: 29) Lk 20: 11f. προσέθετο συλλαβεῖν καὶ Πέτρον *he proceeded to have Peter arrested* Ac 12: 3. Cf. 1 Cl 12: 7; B 2: 5 (Is 1: 13).

2. *provide, give, grant, do* (X., Cyr. 2, 18 τὰς τιμὰς ἑκάστῳ; PRyl. 153, 27) τινί τι *someth. to someone* πρόσθες ἡμῖν πίστιν *grant us faith* Lk 17: 5. W. dat. of the thing προσέθηκε τῷ ἀμπελῶνι ἔργον καλόν *he did good work in the vineyard* Hs 5, 2, 7.—Pass. ταῦτα προστεθήσεται ὑμῖν Mt 6: 33; Lk 12: 31. Cf. Agr 10a, b (JoachJeremias, The Unknown Sayings of Jesus, tr. Fuller, '57, 87-9). M-M.*

πρόστιμον, ου, τό *penalty* (Hippocr.; Polyb. 1, 17, 11; Diod. S. 1, 65, 3; Lucian, Anach. 21; Plut., Solon 23, 2; inscr., pap.; 2 Macc 7: 36; Jos., Ant. 4, 248) θάνατον τὸ πρόστιμον ἔχειν *incur the death penalty* 1 Cl 41: 3.*

προστρέχω 2 aor. προσέδραμον (Aristoph., X., Pla.+; POxy. 247, 12 [non-literal]; LXX; Jos., Ant. 7, 249, Vi.

140) *run up* (*to*); except for the v.l. J 20: 16, it is used in our lit. only in the ptc., combined w. another verb (Menand., Per. 35 J; Num 11: 27; Tob 11: 9 BA; Jos., Bell. 1, 662; Test. Napht. 5: 2) προστρέχοντες ἠσπάζοντο αὐτόν Mk 9: 15. Cf. 10: 17; Ac 8: 30; Hs 9, 6, 2. M-M.*

προσφάγιον, ου, τό *a relish* eaten w. bread (Proverbia Aesopi 98 P. πρ. beside ἄρτος; POxy. 498, 33; 39 ἄρτον ἕνα καὶ προσφάγιον; 736, 46; 89; 739, 7; 10; 12; 14; BGU 916, 22; PGrenf. II 77, 21; Dit., Or. 484, 26. Acc. to Moeris and Hesychius it=ὄψον. But the latter word, as well as its dim. ὀψάριον [q.v.], is oft. simply='fish'), *fish* μή τι προσφάγιον ἔχετε; *you have no fish, have you?* J 21: 5. M-M.*

πρόσφατος, ον (Hom.+) *new, recent* (Aeschyl.+; Inscr., Gr. 1501, 24 [103/2 ʙᴄ]; POxy. 1088, 25; LXX; Jos., Ant. 1, 264. Cf. Phryn. p. 374 L.) Hs 9, 2, 2 (opp. παλαιός). Also in the sense 'not previously existing' (cf. Eccl 1: 9 οὐκ ἔστιν πᾶν πρόσφατον ὑπὸ τὸν ἥλιον; Ps 80: 10) ὁδός Hb 10: 20. M-M.*

προσφάτως adv., of time *recently* (Macho [III ʙᴄ] in Athen. 13 p. 581ᴇ; Polyb. 3, 37, 11; Alciphr. 4, 14, 2; Dit., Or. 315, 23 [164/3 ʙᴄ] ἐληλυθότι προσφάτως; UPZ 144, 10 [164 ʙᴄ]; LXX; Ep. Arist. 5; Jos., Bell. 1, 127, Ant. 10, 264) in our lit. used w. ἐληλυθὼς ἀπό Ac 18: 2; MPol 4. M-M.*

προσφέρω impf. προσέφερον; aor. προσήνεγκον and προσήνεγκα (cf. Bl-D. §81, 2 w. app.; Rob. 338; 363); pf. προσενήνοχα Hb 11: 17; 1 aor. pass. προσηνέχθην (Pind.+; inscr., pap., LXX, Ep. Arist., Philo, Joseph., Test. 12 Patr.).

1. act. and pass. *bring* (*to*)—a. w. acc. of the pers. τινά τινι *bring someone to someone,* sick people to Jesus or his disciples Mt 4: 24; 8: 16; 9: 2, 32; 12: 22 v.l. (for the pass.); 14: 35; 17: 16. The acc. is lacking but easily supplied Mk 2: 4. Children to Jesus Mk 10: 13a; cf. b v.l.; Lk 18: 15. Pass. Mt 19: 13. *Bring someone before* a judge, king, etc. Lk 23: 14; cf. 12: 11 t.r. Pass. Mt 18: 24 v.l.

b. w. acc. of the thing *bring* (*to*), *offer* τί τινι *someth.* (*to*) *someone* προσήνεγκαν αὐτῷ δηνάριον Mt 22: 19. Cf. Ac 8: 18; 1 Cl 43: 2. Without a dat., which is supplied by the context Mt 25: 20; Hs 8, 1, 12.—Esp. *bring someone* someth. *to drink* (Menand., Georg. 61 J. φαγεῖν πρ.; Jos., Bell. 1, 488, Ant. 4, 72 οἶνον προσφέρεσθαι='take wine', Vi. 225) ὄξος προσφέροντες αὐτῷ Lk 23: 36. Cf. σπόγγον μεστὸν τοῦ ὄξους ... προσήνεγκαν αὐτοῦ τῷ στόματι *they held a sponge full of vinegar to his mouth* J 19: 29.

2. *bring, offer, present* of offerings, gifts etc. (Simplicius In Epict. p. 93, 41 Düb. τὰς ἀπαρχάς [τῷ θεῷ]; oft. LXX; Jos., Bell. 3, 353, Ant. 3, 231).

a. lit. τὶ *someth.* with or without the dat. of the pers. δῶρον, δῶρα (Jos., Ant. 6, 67), of the gifts brought by the Magi Mt 2: 11 (cf. Ps 71: 10); of sacrificial gifts 5: 23f; 8: 4; Hb 8: 3f; 9: 9 (pass.). θυσίαν, θυσίας (Ep. Arist. 170b; Jos., Ant. 8, 118) Hb 11: 4; D 14: 3 (cf. Mal 1: 11+vs. 13 v.l.).—Hb 10: 11; cf. vss. 1, 2 (pass.); PK 2 p. 14, 21. σφάγια καὶ θυσίας προσηνέγκατέ μοι Ac 7: 42 (Am 5: 25). προσενέγκαι μοι ὁλοκαυτώματα καὶ θυσίας B 2: 7 (Jer 7: 22f). Cf. 7: 6 (cf. Lev 16: 7, 9); 8: 1.—τινά *someone* of the offering up of Isaac προσενήνοχεν (the pf. to denote what 'stands written'; cf. Mlt. 129; 142; 238) Ἀβραὰμ τὸν Ἰσαὰκ καὶ τὸν μονογενῆ προσέφερεν (impf., in a conative sense, because the sacrifice was not actually made) Hb 11: 17. Cf. Ἰσαὰκ προσενεχθεὶς ἐπὶ τὸ θυσιαστήριον B 7: 3b (on ἐπὶ τὸ θυσ. cf. 1 Esdr 8:

15). Of Jesus ἑαυτὸν πρ. Hb 7: 27 v.l.; cf. 9: 14 (τῷ θεῷ);
vs. 25. πρ. αὐτὸν ἐπὶ τὴν σφαγήν B 8: 2b. Pass. ὁ
Χριστὸς προσενεχθείς Hb 9: 28; here the purpose is
indicated by εἰς τό w. the inf. foll. Elsewh. the purpose is
expressed by means of other preps.: πρ. (τι) περί τινος
(Lev 16: 9; Job 1: 5) Mk 1: 44; cf. Lk 5: 14. περὶ ἑαυτοῦ
προσφέρειν περὶ ἁμαρτιῶν Hb 5: 3. Also ὑπέρ τινος
(1 Macc 7: 33) Hb 5: 1; 9: 7; 10: 12; B 7: 5. Pass. Ac 21:
26; B 7: 4 ('scripture' quot. of unknown origin). W. double
acc. offer someone or someth. as a θυσίαν sacrifice 1 Cl
10: 7; B 7: 3a (w. ὑπέρ τινος). πρ. τινί sacrifice to
someone Dg 3: 3. Abs. make an offering, sacrifice B 8: 2a.
ὀρθῶς 1 Cl 4: 4 (Gen 4: 7). αἷς δοκεῖτε τιμαῖς προσφέρειν by the honors which you think you offer (them) Dg 2:
8. Pass. 1 Cl 41: 2b. The pres. ptc. used as a subst. τὸ
προσφερόμενον the offering 41: 2c.—NHSnaith, The
Sin-Offering and Guilt-Offering, Vetus T 15, '65, 73–80.
   b. fig. (cf. BGU 1024 VII, 25 of a poor girl ζῶσα
προσεφέρετο τοῖς βουλομένοις ὡς νεκρά='she offered
herself') the killing of Christians will be considered by the
Jews as λατρείαν προσφέρειν τῷ θεῷ J 16: 2 (s. on
ἀποκτείνω 1a). δεήσεις καὶ ἱκετηρίας πρ. πρὸς (τὸν
θεόν) Hb 5: 7 (Achilles Tat. 7: 1 προσφέρειν δέησιν; Jos.,
Bell. 3, 353 προσφέρει τῷ θεῷ εὐχήν).—ἁμαρτίαν 1 Cl
47: 4 Funk; δῶρα 1 Cl 44: 4.
   3. pass. meet, deal with w. dat. of the pers. (so oft.
Thu.+; Diod. S. 14, 90, 3; Aelian, V.H. 12, 27; Herodian
1, 13, 7; Philo, Ebr. 69, De Jos. 47; Jos., Bell. 7, 254; 263;
Dit., Or. 456, 64, Syll.³ 807, 13 [54 AD]; PLond. 1912, 65
[41 AD]) ὡς υἱοῖς ὑμῖν προσφέρεται ὁ θεός Hb 12: 7.
M-M.*

προσφεύγω 2 aor. προσέφυγον; pf. προσπέφευγα
(Plut., Pomp. 46, 7, Cic. 3, 5; Herodian 3, 9, 2; PMagd.
13, 13 [III BC]; BGU 180, 16; POxy. 488, 23; Sym.; Philo,
Det. Pot. Ins. 62; Jos., Ant. 1, 311, Vi. 154) flee for refuge
τινί to someth. or someone (Cornutus 20 p. 38, 8) 1 Cl 20:
11; IPhld 5: 1.*

προσφιλής, ές (Aeschyl., Hdt.+; inscr., pap., LXX act.
and pass.) in our lit. only pass. pleasing, agreeable, lovely,
amiable (so also Diod. S. 5, 39, 4; Dit., Or. 331, 9; PSI
361, 9 [251/0 BC]; BGU 1043, 24; Sir 4: 7; 20: 13) abs. Phil
4: 8. λόγῳ πρ. pleasing to the λόγος Dg 1: 2 (Diod. S. 2,
49, 2; 6, 7, 6 τ. θεοῖς; Dio Chrys. 16[33], 28 τοῖς θεοῖς;
70[20], 21 τῇ θεῷ; Jos., Ant. 1, 258; 17, 149). M-M.*

προσφορά, ᾶς, ἡ (Soph.+; pap., LXX; Ep. Arist. 170;
Joseph.)—1. the act of bringing, presenting, offering
(Pla., Aristot., Polyb.), in our lit. in fig. and literal uses
sacrificing, offering (Sir 46: 16 προσφορὰ ἀρνός) foll. by
the obj. gen. διὰ τῆς προσφορᾶς τοῦ σώματος Ἰησοῦ
through the offering of Jesus' body in sacrifice Hb 10: 10.
Cf. vss. 14, 18 (s. Windisch, Hdb., exc. on Hb 10: 18).
προσφορὰς ποιεῖν have sacrifices made Ac 24: 17; 1 Cl
40: 4. W. λειτουργίαι vs. 2. ἀνθρωποποίητος πρ. an
offering made by man B 2: 6 (mng. 2 is also poss.).
   2. that which is brought, gift (Theophr., Char. 30, 19)
in our lit. in fig. and literal use offering (Sir 14: 11; 34: 18,
19 al.; Test. Levi 14: 5) w. ὁλοκαύτωμα MPol 14: 1. W.
θυσία Eph 5: 2; Hb 10: 5 (Ps 39: 7). W. θυσίαι, ὁλοκαυτώματα κτλ. (cf. Da 3: 38; Jos., Ant. 11, 77) vs. 8 (Ps 39:
7); B 2: 4; ἀνθρωποποίητος προσφορά a sacrifice made
by man vs. 6 (mng. 1 is also poss.; s. above). προσηνέχθη
ἡ προσφορά Ac 21: 26 (προσφέρω 2a). Jesus is called ὁ
ἀρχιερεὺς τῶν προσφορῶν ἡμῶν the High Priest of our
offerings in that he brings the prayers of the Christians into
God's presence 1 Cl 36: 1. ἡ προσφορὰ τῶν ἐθνῶν the

offering that consists of the Gentiles (who have become
Christian) Ro 15: 16. M-M.*

προσφωνέω impf. προσεφώνουν; 1 aor. προσεφώνησα
(Hom.+; inscr., pap., LXX; Ep. Arist. 306; Joseph.).
   1. call out, address (Hom.+, as a rule w. acc. of the
pers.) w. dat. of the pers. (Diod. S. 4, 48, 1; Diog. L. 7, 7;
PPetr. II 38b, 3 [242 BC]; PTebt. 27, 109; Wilcken, Chrest.
27 verso, 15) Mt 11: 16; Lk 7: 32; 23: 20. τῇ Ἑβραΐδι
διαλέκτῳ προσεφώνει αὐτοῖς Ac 22: 2; without the dat.
of the pers., ibid. D; 21: 40. Likew. abs. Lk 23: 20 t.r.
   2. call to oneself τινά someone (Jos., Ant. 7, 156) Lk 6:
13 (D ἐφώνησεν); 13: 12; Ac 11: 2 D. M-M.*

προσχαίρω (Plut., Ant. 29, 4; Pr 8: 30) be glad Mk 9: 15
v.l.*

πρόσχυσις, εως, ἡ (Justin, Apol. II 12, 5; Ps.-Clem.,
Hom. 2, 44. From προσχέω [Ex 24: 6; 29: 21 al.])
pouring, sprinkling, spreading ἡ πρόσχυσις τοῦ αἵματος
the sprinkling of the blood (on the doorposts) Hb 11: 28
(cf. Ex 12: 22).*

προσψαύω (Pind.+; Jos., Bell. 7, 348) touch τινί
someth. (Herophil. [300 BC] in Galen II p. 570, 12 K.) ἑνὶ
τῶν δακτύλων ὑμῶν οὐ προσψαύετε τοῖς φορτίοις you
do not touch the burdens with one of your fingers Lk 11:
46.*

προσωπολημπτέω (this word and the two words following, which are closely related, have so far been found
only in Christian writers. They are based upon the πρόσωπον λαμβάνειν of the LXX, which is in turn is modelled
on the Hebr. [s. πρόσωπον 1b, end]. On the spelling with
or without μ s. λαμβάνω, beg.) show partiality Js 2: 9.
M-M.*

προσωπολήμπτης, ου, ὁ (s. προσωπολημπτέω.—Leontios 4 p. 10, 14 uses προσωπολήπτης [which is, in the
final analysis, a biblical word] apart from a scriptural
context, as an element of popular speech) one who shows
partiality of God οὐκ ἔστιν πρ. he is not one to show
partiality Ac 10: 34.*

προσωπολημψία, ας, ἡ (s. προσωπολημπτέω) partiality
named as a sin, w. other sins Pol 6: 1. Not found in God Ro
2: 11; Eph 6: 9; Col 3: 25. Pl. τὴν πίστιν ἔχειν ἐν
προσωπολημψίαις hold the faith while showing partiality
Js 2: 1 (Gdspd., Probs. 142f).*

πρόσωπον, ου, τό (Hom.+; inscr., pap., LXX, En., Ep.
Arist., Philo, Joseph., Test. 12 Patr.; Sib. Or. 3, 549; 557;
679 [all three w. ref. to the face of God]).
   1. face, countenance—a. lit. Mt 6: 16f; 17: 2; Mk 14:
65; Lk 9: 29 (s. εἶδος 1); Ac 6: 15a, b (Charito 2, 2, 2
θαυμάζουσι τὸ πρόσωπον ὡς θεῖον; Damasc., Vi. Isid.
80 Πρόκλος ἐθαύμαζε τὸ Ἰσιδώρου πρόσωπον, ὡς
ἔνθεον ἦν; Marinus, Vi. Procli 23); 2 Cor 3: 7 bis, 13
(JMorgenstern, Moses with the Shining Face: Hebr. Union
Coll. Annual 2, '25, 1–28); cf. vs. 18; 4: 6; in the last two
passages, however, there is a transition from the face of
Moses to a symbolic use of πρ. (s. 1cγ below); Rv 4: 7; 9:
7a, b; 10: 1; MPol 12: 1; Hv 3, 10, 1. ἐμβριθεῖ τῷ πρ.
MPol 9: 2 (s. ἐμβριθής). πρόσωπον τῆς γενέσεως αὐτοῦ
the face he was born with Js 1: 23 (γένεσις 2). ἐμπτύειν
εἰς τὸ πρ. τινος spit in someone's face (s. ἐμπτύω) Mt 26:
67. εἰς πρ. δέρειν τινά strike someone in the face 2 Cor 11:
20. συνέπεσεν τὸ πρόσωπον αὐτοῦ his face fell or
became distorted 1 Cl 4: 3; cf. vs. 4 (Gen 4: 6 and 5).
πίπτειν ἐπὶ (τὸ; the art. is usu. lacking; Bl-D. §255, 4;
259, 1; cf. Rob. 792) πρ. αὐτοῦ fall on one's face as a sign

of devotion (= נָפַל עַל פְּנֵי; cf. Gen 17: 3; Ruth 2: 10) Mt 17: 6; 26: 39; Rv 7: 11; 11: 16. Without αὐτοῦ (Gen 17: 17; Num 14: 5; Jos., Ant. 10, 11) Lk 5: 12; 17: 16; 1 Cor 14: 25.

b. fig., in all kinds of more or less symbolic expressions which, in large part, represent OT usage, and in which the face is oft. to be taken as the seat of the faculty of seeing. βλέπειν πρόσωπον πρὸς πρόσωπον to see face to face 1 Cor 13: 12 (cf. Gen 32: 31 [Jos., Ant. 1, 334 θεοῦ πρόσωπον]; Judg 6: 22. Cf. HRiesenfeld, Coniect. Neot. V '41, 19; 21f [abstracts of four articles]). κλίνειν τὸ πρ. εἰς τὴν γῆν Lk 24: 5 (κλίνω 1a). πρ. κυρίου ἐπὶ ποιοῦντας κακά 1 Pt 3: 12; 1 Cl 22: 6 (both Ps 33: 17). ἐπίφανον τὸ πρ. σου ἐφ᾽ ἡμᾶς (ἐπιφαίνω 1a) 60: 3 (cf. Num 6: 25). ἐμφανισθῆναι τῷ προσώπῳ τοῦ θεοῦ (ἐμφανίζω 1a) Hb 9: 24. βλέπειν τὸ πρ. τινος, i.e. of God (βλέπω 1a, ὁράω 1aγ and cf. JBoehmer, Gottes Angesicht: BFChTh 12, '08, 321–47; EGGulin, D. Antlitz Jahwes im AT: Annal. Acad. Scient. Fenn. 17, 3, '23; FNötscher, 'Das Anges. Gottes schauen' nach bibl. u. babylon. Auffassung '24) Mt 18: 10; cf. Rv 22: 4. ὁρᾶν, ἰδεῖν or θεωρεῖν τὸ πρ. τινος see someone's face, i.e. see someone (present) in person (UPZ 70, 5 [152/1 BC] οὐκ ἂν με ἴδες τὸ πρόσωπον. Cf. Gen 32: 21; 43: 3, 5; 46: 30 al.) Ac 20: 25, 38; 1 Th 2: 17b; 3: 10; IRo 1: 1; cf. IPol 1: 1. τὸ πρόσωπόν μου ἐν σαρκί Col 2: 1. τῷ προσώπῳ ἀγνοούμενος unknown by face, i.e. personally Gal 1: 22 (ἀγνοέω 2). ἀπορφανισθέντες ἀφ᾽ ὑμῶν προσώπῳ οὐ καρδίᾳ (dat. of specification) orphaned by separation from you in person, not in heart or outwardly, not inwardly 1 Th 2: 17a. ἐκζητεῖν τὰ πρόσωπα τῶν ἁγίων (ἐκζητέω 1) B 19: 10; D 4: 2. ἀποστρέφειν τὸ πρ. ἀπό τινος (ἀποστρέφω 1aa) 1 Cl 18: 9 (Ps 50: 11); 16: 3 (Is 53: 3).—τὸ πρόσωπον στηρίζειν (s. on στηρίζω 1 and cf. SAntoniades, Neotestamentica: Neophilologus 14, '29, 129–35) Lk 9: 51. τὸ πρ. αὐτοῦ ἦν πορευόμενον εἰς Ἰερουσαλήμ his face was set toward Jerusalem vs. 53 (cf. 2 Km 17: 11).—θαυμάζειν πρόσωπον flatter Jd 16 (s. θαυμάζω 1ba). λαμβάνειν πρόσωπον (= נָשָׂא פָנִים. Cf. Sir 4: 22; 35: 13; 1 Esdr 4: 39. Cf. Thackeray p. 43f; Bl-D. p. 4 [Engl. transl. Funk p. 3] note 5; Rob. 94) show partiality or favoritism, lit. 'lift up the face' Lk 20: 21; B 19: 4; D 4: 3. λαμβ. πρόσωπόν τινος (cf. Mal 1: 8) Gal 2: 6.

c. governed by prepositions, in usages where πρ., in many cases, can no longer be translated—α. ἀπὸ προσώπου τινός from the presence of someone (Vi. Aesopi W c. 104 v.l. ἐπιστολὴ ὡς ἐκ προσώπου τοῦ Αἰσώπου) Ac 3: 20; (away) from someone or someth. (Ctesias, Pers. 2 φυγεῖν ἀπὸ προσώπου Κύρου; Herodas 8, 59 ἔρρ᾽ ἐκ προσώπου = get out of my sight; LXX) 5: 41; 7: 45; 2 Th 1: 9; Rv 6: 16 (Is 2: 10, 19, 21); 12: 14; 20: 11 (cf. Ex 14: 25; Josh 10: 11; Sir 21: 2; 1 Macc 5: 34 and oft.) 1 Cl 4: 8 (s. ἀποδιδράσκω), 10 (s. the passages cited for Rv 20: 11 above); 18: 11 (Ps 50: 13; ἀπο[ρ]ρίπτω 1b); 28: 3 (Ps 138: 7).

β. εἰς πρόσωπον: (Aesop, Fab. 302 P. εἰς Ζηνὸς πρόσωπον ἔρχεσθαι = before the face of Zeus) εἰς πρόσωπον τῶν ἐκκλησιῶν before (lit. 'in the face of') the churches 2 Cor 8: 24. τὰ φαινόμενά σου εἰς πρόσωπον what meets your eye, i.e. the visible world IPol 2: 2. βλέπειν εἰς πρόσωπόν τινος Mt 22: 16; Mk 12: 14 (s. βλέπω 5). To one's face Hv 3, 6, 3 (cf. POxy. 903, 2; BGU 909, 12).

γ. ἐν προσώπῳ (Maximus Tyr. 38, 1a) ἐν προσώπῳ Χριστοῦ before the face of Christ that looks down with approval 2 Cor 2: 10 (cf. Pr 8: 30; Sir 35: 4), or as the representative of Christ (NEB); differently 4: 6 on the face of Christ (s. 1a above).

δ. κατὰ πρόσωπον face to face, (present) in person (Polyb. 24, 15, 2; Diod. S. 19, 46, 2; Plut., Caesar 17, 8; Inschr. v. Magn. 93b, 11; Inschr. v. Priene 41, 6; Dit., Or. 441, 66 [81 BC]; PLond. 479, 6; POxy. 1071, 1) B 15: 1. (Opp. ἀπών) 2 Cor 10: 1. Παῦλος, ὃς γενόμενος ἐν ὑμῖν κατὰ πρόσωπον Pol 3: 2. πρὶν ἢ ὁ κατηγορούμενος κατὰ πρόσωπον ἔχοι τοὺς κατηγόρους Ac 25: 16. κατὰ πρόσωπον αὐτῷ ἀντέστην I opposed him to his face Gal 2: 11 (cf. Diod. S. 40, 5a of an accusation κατὰ πρόσωπον; 2 Macc 7: 6; Jos., Ant. 5, 46; 13, 278).—κατὰ πρόσωπον with partiality, in favoritism B 19: 7; D 4: 10.—τὰ κατὰ πρόσωπον what is before your eyes 2 Cor 10: 7.—Used w. the gen. like a prep. (PPetr. III 1 II, 8 κατὰ πρόσωπον τοῦ ἱεροῦ; LXX; Jos., Ant. 3, 144; 9, 8) κατὰ πρ. τινος before or in the presence of someone (Jos., Ant. 11, 235) Lk 2: 31; Ac 3: 13; 16: 9 D.

ε. μετὰ προσώπου: πληρώσεις με εὐφροσύνης μετὰ τοῦ προσώπου σου Ac 2: 28 (Ps 15: 11); μετὰ Α II 1cγ.

ζ. πρὸ προσώπου τινός (LXX; cf. Johannessohn 184–6) before someone Mt 11: 10; Mk 1: 2; Lk 7: 27 (on all three cf. Mal 3: 1).—Lk 1: 76 v.l. (cf. Ex 32: 34); 9: 52 (cf. Ex 23: 20); 10: 1; 1 Cl 24: 3 (cf. Is 62: 11).—πρὸ προσώπου τῆς εἰσόδου αὐτοῦ Ac 13: 24 (εἴσοδος 1).

d. external things, appearance opp. καρδία (1 Km 16: 7) 2 Cor 5: 12. ἡ εὐπρέπεια τοῦ προσώπου αὐτοῦ (i.e. of grass and flowers) Js 1: 11. Of the appearance of the sky Mt 16: 3; cf. Lk 12: 56 (cf. Ps 103: 30).

e. face = surface πρόσωπον τῆς γῆς (Gen 2: 6; 7: 23; 11: 4, 8 al.) Lk 21: 35; Ac 17: 26; B 11: 7 (Ps 1: 4). B 6: 9 prob. belongs here also.

2. person (Polyb. 5, 107, 3; 8, 13, 5; 12, 27, 10; 27, 7, 4; Diod. S. 37, 12, 1; Plut., Mor. 509B; Epict. 1, 2, 7; Vett. Val. cf. index; POxy. 1672, 4 [37–41 AD] ξένοις προσώποις = 'to strangers'; 237 VII, 34; PRyl. 28, 88. Cf. Phryn. p. 379, also Lob. p. 380; KPraechter, Philol. 63, '04, 155f) ὀλίγα πρόσωπα a few persons 1 Cl 1: 1; ἐν ἢ δύο πρ. 47: 6. τὰ προγεγραμμένα πρ. the persons mentioned above IMg 6: 1. Furthermore, this is surely the place for ἐκ πολλῶν προσώπων by many persons 2 Cor 1: 11 (Luther, Schmiedel, Ltzm., Windisch, RSV et al.; 'face' is preferred by Heinrici, Kühl, Bachmann, Plummer.—With this expr. cf. Diod. S. 15, 38, 4 ἐκ τρίτου προσώπου = [claims were raised] by a third 'party', i.e., Thebes, against Sparta and Athens).—SSchlossmann, Persona u. Πρόσωπον im röm. Recht u. christl. Dogma '06; RHirzel, Die Person; Begriff u. Name derselben im Altertum: SB der Bayer. Ak. d. W. '14, Heft 10; HRheinfelder, Das Wort 'Persona'; Gesch. seiner Bed. '28; FAltheim, Persona: ARW 27, '29, 35–52; ELohse, TW VI 769–81. M-M. and suppl. B. 216. **

προτάσσω (Aeschyl. +; Thu. 3, 52; inscr., pap.; Jos., Ant. 2, 340) fix, determine, allot (beforehand) (Soph., Trach. 164; Aristot., Probl. 30, 11; 2 Macc 8: 36) προτεταγμένοι καιροί t.r. instead of προστετ. κ. Ac 17: 26 (s. προστάσσω, end). M-M. *

προτείνω 1 aor. προέτεινα (trag., Hdt. +; inscr., pap.; LXX nearly always in 2 Macc and always of stretching out the hands; Ep. Arist. 179; Philo; Jos., Vi. 30) stretch out, spread out a criminal who is to be flogged ὡς προέτειναν αὐτὸν τοῖς ἱμᾶσιν Ac 22: 25; the transl. depends on one's understanding of the dat.; s. ἱμάς. M-M. *

πρότερος, α, ον (Hom. +; inscr., pap., LXX) comp. of πρό—1. of time earlier—a. adj. (Hom. +; inscr., pap., LXX; Jos., C. Ap. 2, 1) former, earlier ἡ πρ. ἀναστροφή Eph 4: 22. τὰ πρ. ἁμαρτήματα 2 Cl 13: 1; Hm 12, 6, 2; s

9, 23, 5. ἡ πρ. ἁμαρτία m 4, 1, 11; pl. Hv 2, 3, 1; m 4, 3, 3; s 6, 1, 4; 8, 11, 3; αἱ ἁμαρτίαι αἱ πρ. m 4, 3, 1. τὰ πρ. ἀγνοήματα Hs 5, 7, 3f. τὰ πρ. παραπτώματα m 4, 4, 4. ἡ πρ. ὅρασις v 4, 1, 1. αἱ πρ. λύπαι 3, 13, 2. τὰ πρ. ὁράματα 4, 2, 2. τὰ πρ. χαλεπά Hv 1, 4, 2. οἱ πρ. χρόνοι s 9, 20, 4. ἡ ζωὴ ἡ πρ. s 9, 16, 2.

b. the neut. πρότερον as adv. *earlier, formerly, in former times* (Pind., Hdt.+; inscr., pap., LXX, Ep. Arist.; Jos., Ant. 19, 201 al.).

α. without the art.; opp. νῦν (Ael. Aristid. 33, 16 K.=51 p. 576 D.; Procop. Soph., Ep. 88) νῦν καὶ οὐ πρότερον *now and not in former times* Dg 1. πρότερον—ἔπειτα (Ps.-Clem., Hom. 7, 6. Cf. Artem. 2, 39 p. 144, 27f πρότερον—εἶτα) Hb 7: 27. Oft. the time which is later than the one designated by πρ. is not expressed, but is understood fr. the context *earlier, beforehand, previously* (oft. Pind., Hdt.+) J 7: 50𝔓⁷⁵ et al., 51 t.r.; 2 Cor 1: 15; 1 Ti 1: 13 t.r.; Hb 4: 6.

β. w. the art., used as a subst. οἱ πρότερον *the former ones* (Hero Alex. I p. 338, 3) Hs 9, 4, 3.—As an adj. (Hdt. 6, 87; Aristoph., Equ. 1355; Diod. S. 17, 69, 3) αἱ πρότερον ἡμέραι Hb 10: 32. αἱ πρ. ἐπιθυμίαι 1 Pt 1: 14.—As an adv. τὸ πρότερον *before, once, formerly* (X., Mem. 3, 8, 1; Menand., Dyscolus 15; Hero Alex. I p. 190, 19; Jos., Ant. 20, 173) J 6: 62; 7: 50𝔓⁶⁶ et al.; 9: 8; 1 Ti 1: 13; Hv 3, 3, 5. *The first time* Hv 3, 12, 1; s 9, 1, 3. So prob. also Gal 4: 13. But naturally the transl. *once* is also poss., and fr. a lexical point of view it is not poss. to establish the thesis that Paul wished to differentiate betw. a later visit and an earlier one.

2. of rank *superior, preferable, more prominent* (Pla., Lach. 183ʙ πρότεροι ἡμῶν; Aristot. p. 14b, 5ff εἰώθασι δὲ καὶ οἱ πολλοὶ τοὺς ἐντιμοτέρους καὶ μᾶλλον ἀγαπωμένους ὑπ' αὐτῶν προτέρους φάσκειν εἶναι; Wsd 7: 29) ἄλλοι σου πρότεροί εἰσιν *others are superior to you* Hv 3, 4, 3. M-M.**

προτίθημι 2 aor. subj. προθῶ; 2 aor. mid. προεθέμην (Hom.+; inscr., pap., LXX, Joseph.).

1. act. *set before* τινί *someone as a task* or *duty* (Soph., Ant. 216; Hdt. 3, 38; 9, 27) ἐὰν σὺ σεαυτῷ προθῇς ὅτι Hm 12, 3, 5.

2. mid.—**a.** *display publicly* (Appian, Bell. Civ. 3, 26 §101) of Christ ὃν προέθετο ὁ θεὸς ἱλαστήριον Ro 3: 25 (s. ἱλαστήριον). But the act., at least, seems to have had the mng. *offer* as well (cf. Dit., Syll.³ 708, 15 w. the editor's note 5; 714, 16-18, and M-M.; also ZPE 3, '68, 166 n. 9).

b. *plan, propose, intend* τὶ *someth.* (Pla., Phaedr. 259ᴅ; Polyb. 6, 12, 8; Jos., Vi. 290) Eph 1: 9. W. inf. foll. (Pla., Rep. 1 p. 352ᴅ, Leg. 1 p. 638ᴄ; Polyb. 8, 13, 3; 11, 7, 3; Jos., C. Ap. 2, 287, Ant. 18, 286; 19, 37) Ro 1: 13 (Bl-D. §392, 1a). ὁ καιρὸς ὃν θεὸς προέθετο φανερῶσαι . . . *the time that God had appointed to reveal* . . . Dg 9: 2. M-M.*

προτρέπω in our lit. only mid. (this Hom.+; inscr., pap., LXX, Philo, Joseph.) 1 aor. προετρεψάμην; *urge (on), encourage, impel, persuade* (Soph.+) τινά *someone* w. inf. foll. (Hyperid. 6, 24; UPZ 110, 165 [164 ʙᴄ]; PRyl. 77, 48; BGU 164, 17; 450, 15; 2 Macc 11: 7; Jos., Ant. 12, 166) 1 Cl 34: 4. Abs. (Jos., Ant. 5, 171; 7, 262) Ac 18: 27. M-M.*

προτρέχω 2 aor. προέδραμον (Antiphon+; LXX) *run ahead* J 20: 4 (cf. X., An. 1, 5, 2 προδραμόντες . . . πολὺ γὰρ τῶν ἵππων ἔτρεχον θᾶττον); Ac 10: 25 D. πρ. εἰς τὸ ἔμπροσθεν *run on ahead* Lk 19: 4 (s. ἔμπροσθεν 1a

and cf. Tob 11: 3; Job 41: 14 v.l.; *progress* Third Corinthians 3: 2).*

προϋπάρχω impf. προϋπῆρχον intr. *exist before* (so Thu.+; Diod. S. 16, 82, 6; inscr., pap.; Job 42: 18; Philo, Op. M. 130; Jos., Ant. 1, 290) w. ptc. foll. (Bl-D. §414, 1; Rob. 1121) προϋπῆρχεν μαγεύων *he had practiced magic* Ac 8: 9 (Jos., Ant. 4, 125 ἅ τε καὶ προϋπῆρξεν ἐν τοῖς ἔμπροσθεν χρόνοις γενόμενα τοῖς ἀνθρώποις). προϋπῆρχον ἐν ἔχθρᾳ ὄντες Lk 23: 12 (cf. Diod. S. 19, 7, 2 διὰ τὰς προϋπαρχούσας ἔχθρας; Vett. Val. 283, 24 διὰ τὴν προϋπάρχουσαν ἔχθραν). M-M.*

προφανερόω 1 aor. προεφανέρωσα, pass. προεφανερώθην *reveal beforehand* or *in advance* τὸ πάθος pass. B 6: 7. τινὶ περί τινος *reveal someth. to someone in advance* 3: 6. Without the dat., which is to be supplied fr. the context 11: 1. τί τινι *someth. to someone* 7: 1. Abs. (w. προετοιμάζειν and followed by πληροῦν, the 'fulfilling' of the revelation) MPol 14: 2.*

πρόφασις, εως, ἡ (Hom+)—**1.** *actual motive* or *reason, valid excuse* (Pind., Thu.+; Dit., Syll.³ 888, 137; PLeipz. 64, 8 διὰ τὴν πρόφασιν ταύτην='for this reason'; Philo; Jos., Ant. 13, 427, Vi. 167; Test. Jos. 8: 5) πρ. ἔχειν περί τινος *have a valid excuse for someth.* J 15: 22.

2. *falsely alleged motive, pretext, ostensible reason, excuse* (Hom.+; Dit., Or. 669, 15 προφάσει='under the pretext'; pap., LXX, Philo; Jos., Bell. 2, 348, Vi. 79; 282) προφάσει *with false motives* (opp. ἀληθείᾳ, Thu. 6, 33, 2; cf. Arrian, Anab. 1, 25, 3.—In reality they have other interests) Phil 1: 18. *For a pretext, for appearance' sake* (as if they felt an inner need) Mt 23: 14 v.l.; Mk 12: 40; Lk 20: 47 (JDerrett, NovT 14, '72, 1-9: a display of piety to secure confidence in them). προφάσει ὡς *under the pretext that, pretending that* (Philip in Demosth. 18, 77 πρόφασιν ὡς w. ptc.) Ac 27: 30. ἐν πρ. πλεονεξίας *with a pretext for* (satisfying) *greed* 1 Th 2: 5.—KDeichgräber, Πρόφασις: Quellen u. Stud. z. Gesch. der Naturwissenschaften u. d. Med. III Heft 4, '33; LPearson, Prophasis and Aitia: Trans. and Proc. of the Amer. Phil. Ass'n, 83, '52, 205-23. M-M.*

προφέρω (Hom.+; inscr., pap., LXX) *bring out, produce* (Appian, Syr. 59 §309; Jos., Bell. 1, 671) τὶ ἔκ τινος (Alciphr. 4, 13, 15; Pr 10: 13) Lk 6: 45a, b. M-M.*

προφητεία, ας, ἡ (Lucian, Alex. 40; 60; Heliod. 1, 22, 7; 1, 33, 2; 2, 27, 1; Ps.-Callisth. 2, 1, 3 [office of a prophet]; CIG 2880, 4-6; 2881, 4; 5; Dit., Or. 494, 8f; PTebt. 294, 8; 295, 10; LXX, Philo, Joseph.) *prophecy.*

1. *prophetic activity* αἱ ἡμέραι τῆς προφητείας αὐτῶν Rv 11: 6. μισθοὺς λαμβάνει τῆς προφητείας αὐτοῦ *he accepts pay for his activity as prophet* Hm 11: 12.

2. *the gift of prophecy, of prophesying* of Rahab 1 Cl 12: 8. Of Christians Ro 12: 6; 1 Cor 12: 10; 13: 2, 8 v.l.; 14: 22. The pl. of various kinds and grades of prophetic gifts 13: 8; 1 Th 5: 20 (here mng. 3b is also poss.). τὸ πνεῦμα τῆς πρ. *the spirit of prophecy* Rv 19: 10.

3. *the utterance of the prophet, prophetic word, prophecy* (Jos., Ant. 9, 119)—**a.** of OT prophecies ἡ προφητεία Ἡσαΐου Mt 13: 14. αἱ προφητεῖαι beside ὁ νόμος Μωσέως (Μωϋσέως is better; s. Bihlmeyer XXXVI) ISm 5: 1. Gener. of OT sayings 2 Pt 1: 20f (but 𝔓⁷² appears to distinguish prophecy and OT writing: προφητεία καὶ γραφή); B 13: 4 (Gen 48: 11).

b. of utterances by Christian prophets ἐν προφητείᾳ *in the form of a prophetic saying* 1 Cor 14: 6; 1 Th 5: 20 (s. 2 above); 1 Ti 1: 18; 4: 14. οἱ λόγοι τῆς πρ. *the words of the* *prophecy* Rv 1: 3. οἱ λόγοι τῆς πρ. τοῦ βιβλίου τούτου *the words of prophecy in this book* 22: 7, 10, 18. οἱ λόγ. τοῦ βιβλίου τῆς προφ. ταύτης *the words of this book of prophecy* vs. 19. M-M.*

προφητεύω impf. ἐπροφήτευον; fut. προφητεύσω; 1 aor. ἐπροφήτευσα (on the augment s. Bl-D. §69, 4 app.; Mlt.-H. 192); (Pind., Hdt.+; Diod. S. 17, 51, 1; Ps.-Aristot., De Mundo 1 p. 391a, 16 ἡ ψυχὴ θείω ψυχῆς ὄμματι τὰ θεῖα καταλαβοῦσα τοῖς τε ἀνθρώποις προφητεύουσα; Plut., Mor. 412в; Lucian, V.H. 2, 33; Herodian 5, 5, 10; Dit., Or. 473, 2; 530, 9; Gnomon [=BGU V] 93; LXX, Philo, Joseph., Test. 12 Patr., Sib. Or.) *prophesy.*
  1. *proclaim a divine revelation* abs. (Diod. S. 17, 51, 1; Jos., Ant. 5, 348) οὐ τῷ σῷ ὀνόματι ἐπροφητεύσαμεν; Mt 7: 22 (cf. Jer 34: 15).—Ac 2: 17f (Jo 3: 1); 19: 6; 21: 9; 1 Cor 11: 4f (w. προσεύχεσθαι); 13: 9; 14: 1, 3-5, 24, 31, 39; Rv 11: 3; B 16: 9; Hm 11: 12. Of sayings fr. scripture B 9: 2; Hv 2, 3, 4 (the quot. here fr. the book of Eldad and Modat has no bearing on the future. Naturally that does not exclude the possibility that these 'prophets' practiced their art in the sense of mng. 3 below).
  2. *prophetically reveal* what is hidden, of the scornful challenge to Jesus προφήτευσον ἡμῖν, Χριστέ, τίς ἐστιν ὁ παίσας σε; Mt 26: 68; cf. Mk 14: 65; Lk 22: 64 (cf. the mocking of Eunus the soothsayer in Diod. S. 24, 2 [GRudberg, ZNW 24, '25, 307-9] and WCvanUnnik, ZNW 29, '30, 310f; PBenoit, OCullmann-Festschr., '62, 92-110). Of Christian pseudoprophets Hm 11: 13.
  3. *foretell the future, prophesy* (Sib. Or. 3, 163; 699 al.), of prophets and men of God in times past: Mt 11: 13. πρ. περί τινος *prophesy about someone* or *someth.* (2 Ch 18: 7) Mt 15: 7; Mk 7: 6; 1 Pt 1: 10. πρ. εἴς τινα *prophesy with reference to someone* B 5: 6. Also πρ. ἐπί τινι 5: 13. Foll. by direct discourse 12: 10. ἐπροφήτευσεν λέγων, foll. by dir. disc. Lk 1: 67 (John the Baptist's father); also τινί *to someone* Jd 14 (Enoch). Of the high priest (cf. Jos., Bell. 1, 68f= Ant. 13, 299f; s. also 282f; CHDodd, OCullmann-Festschr., '62, 134-43.—According to Diod. S. 40, 3, 5; 6 the Jews considered the ἀρχιερεύς to be an ἄγγελος τῶν τοῦ θεοῦ προσταγμάτων. Whatever is revealed to him he communicates to the people in their assemblies [κατὰ τὰς ἐκκλησίας] J 11: 51 (w. ὅτι foll.). Of the writer of Rv πρ. ἐπὶ λαοῖς Rv 10: 11. M-M.*

προφήτης, ου, ὁ (Pind., Hdt.+; inscr., pap., LXX, Philo, Joseph., Test. 12 Patr.; Sib. Or. 3, 582; 781; 5, 239. Exx. in Fascher, in the work mentioned at the end) *prophet* as proclaimer and interpreter of the divine revelation (among pagans e.g. Plato Com. [V/IV вс] 184 [Orpheus]; Ephor. [IV вс]: 70 fgm. 206 Jac. of Ammon, likew. Diod. S. 17, 51, 1; Plut., Numa 9, 8 the pontifex maximus as ἐξηγητὴς κ. προφήτης; Dio Chrys. 19[36], 42 πρ. τῶν Μουσῶν; Ael. Aristid. 45, 4 K.=8 p. 83 D.: προφήται τῶν θεῶν; 45, 7 K.= p. 84 D.; 46 p. 159 D.: οἱ πρ. κ. οἱ ἱερεῖς, likew. Himerius, Or. 8 [Or. 23], 11; Alciphr. 4, 19, 9 Διονύσου πρ.; Himerius, Or. 38 [Or. 4], 9 Socrates as Μουσῶν καὶ Ἑρμοῦ προφήτης, Or. 48 [Or. 14], 8 προφῆται of the Egyptians; PGM 3, 256).
  1. of prophets and prophetic personalities in the OT (cf. GHölscher, Die Profeten v. Israel '14; BDuhm, Israels Propheten² '22; HGunkel, Die Proph. '17; LDürr, Wollen u. Wirken der atl. Proph. '26; JSeverijn, Het Profetisme '26; HWHertzberg, Prophet u. Gott '23; JHempel, Gott u. Mensch im AT² '36, 95-162). Some are mentioned by name: Jeremiah the prophet Mt 2: 17; 27: 9. Isaiah the prophet 3: 3; 4: 14; 8: 17; Lk 3: 4; J 1: 23; 12: 38; Ac 28: 25

al. Joel Ac 2: 16. Jonah Mt 12: 39. Daniel Mt 24: 15. Elijah, Elisha, Ezekiel 1 Cl 17: 1. Elisha Lk 4: 27. Samuel Ac 13: 20; cf. 3: 24. David Ac 2: 30 (JAFitzmyer, CBQ 34, '72, 332-9). Even Balaam 2 Pt 2: 16.—Somet. the identity of *the prophet* is known only fr. the context, or the reader is simply expected to know who is meant, as the Gk. writer says ὁ ποιητής, feeling sure that he will be understood correctly (Antig. Car. 7 [Hom. Hymn to Hermes]; Diod. S. 1, 12, 9; 3, 66, 3 al. [Homer]; schol. on Nicander, Ther. 452; Ps.-Dicaearchus p. 147 F. [Il. 2, 684]; Steph. Byz. s.v. Χαλκίς [Il. 2, 537]): Mt 1: 22 (Isaiah); 2: 5 (Micah), 15 (Hosea); 21: 4 (Zechariah); Ac 7: 48 (Isaiah). Cf. B 6: 2, 4, 6f, 10, 13; 11: 2, 4, 9; 14: 2, 7-9.—The pl. οἱ προφῆται brings *the prophets* together under one category: Mt 2: 23; 5: 12; 16: 14; Mk 6: 15b; Lk 1: 70; 6: 23; 13: 28; J 1: 45 (w. Moses); 8: 52f; Ac 3: 21; 7: 52; 10: 43; Ro 1: 2; 1 Th 2: 15; Hb 11: 32 (w. David and Samuel); Js 5: 10; 1 Pt 1: 10 (classed under 5 below by EGSelwyn, 1 Pt '46, ad loc. and 259-68); 2 Pt 3: 2; 1 Cl 43: 1 (Μωϋσῆς καὶ οἱ λοιποὶ πρ.); B 1: 7; IMg 9: 3; IPhld 5: 2; οἱ θειότατοι πρ. IMg 8: 2; οἱ ἀγαπητοὶ πρ. IPhld 9: 2. οἱ ἀρχαῖοι πρ. (Jos., Ant. 12, 413) D 11: 11b.—The prophet also stands for his book ἀνεγίνωσκεν τ. προφήτην Ἡσαΐαν Ac 8: 28, 30; cf. Mk 1: 2. λέγει (κύριος) ἐν τῷ προφήτῃ B 7: 4. ἐν ἄλλῳ πρ. λέγει 11: 6. Cf. 6: 14; 12: 4 and 1. Pl. of the prophets as a division of scripture: οἱ προφῆται καὶ ὁ νόμος (s. 2 Macc 15: 9) Mt 11: 13. Cf. Lk 16: 16; Ac 13: 15; 24: 14; Ro 3: 21; Dg 11: 6. Μωϋσῆς κ. οἱ πρ. Lk 16: 29, 31. Cf. 24: 27; Ac 28: 23. πάντα τὰ γεγραμμένα ἐν τῷ νόμῳ Μωϋσέως καὶ τοῖς προφήταις καὶ ψαλμοῖς Lk 24: 44. Now and then οἱ προφῆται alone may mean all scripture Lk 24: 25; J 6: 45 (cf. JHänel, Der Schriftbegriff Jesu '19, 21); Hb 1: 1 (cf. CBüchel, Der Hb u. das AT: StKr 79, '06, 508-91).—οἱ πρ. Mt 5: 17; 7: 12; 22: 40 (all three w. ὁ νόμος) unmistakably refers to the contents of the prophetic books.
  2. John the Baptist is also called a prophet Mt 14: 5; 21: 26; Mk 11: 32; Lk 1: 76 (προφήτης ὑψίστου; cf. Dit., Or. 756, 2 τὸν προφήτην τοῦ ἁγιωτάτου θεοῦ ὑψίστου); 20: 6, but Jesus declared that he was higher than the prophets Mt 11: 9; Lk 7: 26.
  3. Jesus appears as a prophet (FGils, Jésus prophète [synoptics], '57 [lit.]) οὗτός ἐστιν ὁ προφήτης Ἰησοῦς Mt 21: 11. Cf. vs. 46; Mk 6: 15a; Lk 7: 16 (πρ. μέγας), 39; 13: 33; 24: 19; J 7: 52. This proverb is applied to him: οὐκ ἔστιν προφήτης ἄτιμος εἰ μὴ ἐν τῇ πατρίδι αὐτοῦ Mt 13: 57; Mk 6: 4; cf. Lk 4: 24; J 4: 44; LJ 1: 6 (EPreuschen, Das Wort v. verachteten Proph.: ZNW 17, '16, 33-48). He was also taken to be one of the ancient prophets come to life again: Mt 16: 14; Mk 8: 28. πρ. τις τῶν ἀρχαίων Lk 9: 8, 19.—In Ac 3: 22f and 7: 37 (cf. IQS 9, 11), Dt 18: 15, 19 is interpreted w. ref. to the Messiah and hence to Jesus (HJSchoeps, Theol. u. Geschichte des Judenchristentums '49, 87-98).—For J, Jesus is ὁ προφήτης *the Prophet* 6: 14; 7: 40, also 4: 19; 9: 17, a title of honor which is disclaimed by the Baptist 1: 21, 25 (s. exc. in the Hdb. on J 1: 21; HAFischel, JBL 65, '46, 157-74). Cf. also Lk 7: 39 v.l.—RMeyer, Der Proph. aus Galiläa '40; PEDavies, Jesus and the Role of the Prophet: JBL 64, '45, 241-54; AJBHiggins, Jesus as Proph.: ET 57, '45/'46, 292-4; FWYoung, Jesus the Proph.: JBL 68, '49, 285-99.— RSchnackenburg, D. Erwartung des 'Propheten' nach dem NT u. Qumran: Studia Evangelica '59, 622, n. 1; HBraun, Qumran u. das NT, I, '66, 100-06.
  4. also in other senses, without excluding the actual prophets, of men who proclaim the divine message w. special preparation and w. a special mission (1 Macc 4: 46; 14: 41): Mt 11: 9 and parallels (s. 2 above); 13: 57 and

parall. (s. 3 above); 23: 30, 37; Lk 10: 24 (on προφῆται καὶ βασιλεῖς cf. Boll 136–42); 13: 33f; Ac 7: 52. The two prophets of God in the last times Rv 11: 10 (s. μάρτυς 2c and Πέτρος, end). In several of the passages already mentioned (1 Th 2: 15; Mt 23: 30, 37; Lk 13: 34; Ac 7: 52) or still to be mentioned (Mt 23: 34; Lk 11: 49 [OJFSeitz, TU 102, '68, 236–40]) various Jews are murderers of the prophets (cf. 3 Km 19: 10, 14; Jos., Ant. 9, 265).—HJSchoeps, D. jüd. Prophetenmorde '43.—Jesus also sends to his own people προφήτας καὶ σοφούς Mt 23: 34 or πρ. κ. ἀποστόλους Lk 11: 49; cf. also Mt 10: 41 (πρ. beside δίκαιος, as 13: 17). This brings us to the

5. Christians, who are endowed w. the gift of προφητεία Ac 15: 32; 1 Cor 14: 29, 32, 37; Rv 22: 6, 9; D 10: 7; 13: 1, 3f, 6. W. ἀπόστολοι (Celsus 2, 20) Lk 11: 49; Eph 2: 20 (though here the ref. could be to the OT prophets, as is surely the case in Pol 6: 3. Acc. to PJoüon, Rech de Sc rel 15, '25, 534f, τῶν ἀπ. καὶ πρ. in Eph 2: 20 refer to the same persons); 3: 5; D 11: 3. πρ. stands betw. ἀπόστολοι and διδάσκαλοι 1 Cor 12: 28f; cf. Eph 4: 11. W. διδάσκαλοι Ac 13: 1; D 15: 1f. W. ἅγιοι and ἀπόστολοι Rv 18: 20. W. ἅγιοι 11: 18; 16: 6; 18: 24. Prophets foretell future events (cf. Pla., Charm. 173c προφῆται τῶν μελλόντων) Ac 11: 27(f); 21: 10(ff). True and false prophets: τὸν προφήτην καὶ τὸν ψευδοπροφήτην Hm 11: 7; cf. vss. 9 and 15 (the rest of this 'mandate' also deals w. this subj.); D 11: 7–11.—Harnack, Lehre der Zwölf Apostel 1884, 93ff; 119ff, Mission⁴ I '23, 344f; 362ff; Rtzst., Mysterienrel.³ 236–40; s. EGSelwyn on 1 Pt 1: 10 in 1 above; HGreeven, Propheten, Lehrer, Vorsteher b. Pls: ZNW 44, '52/'53, 3–15.

6. Only in one place in our lit. is a pagan called a 'prophet', i.e. the poet whose description of the Cretans is referred to in Tit 1: 12: ἴδιος αὐτῶν προφήτης their (the Cretans') own prophet (s. ἀργός 2).—EFascher, Προφήτης. Eine sprach- und religionsgeschichtliche Untersuchung '27.—GFriedrich et al., TW VI 781–863: πρ. and related words. M-M.

προφητικός, ή, όν (Lucian, Alex. 60; Philo, Migr. Abr. 84 al.; PGM 1, 278; 4, 933) prophetic γραφαὶ πρ. the writings of the prophets=the OT Ro 16: 26 (cf. Act. Phil. 77 p. 30, 6 B.). ὁ πρ. λόγος (Philo, Plant. 117) 2 Pt 1: 19; 2 Cl 11: 2 (the origin of the prophetic word that follows is unknown). ὁ ἄγγελος τοῦ πρ. πνεύματος Hm 11: 9 (πρ. πνεῦμα, as Philo, Fuga 186). Of Polycarp διδάσκαλος ἀποστολικὸς καὶ προφητικός MPol 16: 2.*

προφητικῶς adv. prophetically εἰπεῖν speak prophetically (followed by direct discourse) MPol 12: 3.*

προφῆτις, ιδος, ἡ (Eur., Pla.+; Diod. S. 14, 13, 3 [Pythia]; inscr.: CIG 3796; Inschr. v. Magn. 122d, 3 [in case it is correctly restored]; LXX; Philo; Jos., Ant. 10, 59; Sib. Or. 3, 818; Sextus 441) prophetess, fem. of προφήτης Lk 2: 36. Of the Jezebel who was misleading the church at Thyatira ἡ λέγουσα ἑαυτὴν προφῆτιν who calls herself a prophetess Rv 2: 20 (cf. Ἰεζάβελ and the lit. there). M-M.*

προφθάνω 1 aor. προέφθασα (Aeschyl., Pla.+; Plut., Mor. 806F; pap., LXX)—1. come before, anticipate w. acc. and ptc. foll. (Aristoph., Eccl. 884; Bl-D. §414, 4; Rob. 1120; φθάνω w. the ptc.: Ep. Arist. 137) προέφθασεν αὐτὸν λέγων he spoke to him first Mt 17: 25.

2. do before or previously w. inf. foll. (Bl-D. §392, 2; Rob. 1120) ἐὰν προφθάσῃ εἰς τὴν κάμινον αὐτὸ βαλεῖν if he has previously (=already) put it into the furnace 2 Cl 8: 2. M-M.*

προφυλάσσω (Hom. Hymns, Hdt.+; Dit., Syll.³ 730, 15) guard, protect (beforehand) τινά someone ITr 8: 1. πρ. τινὰ ἀπό τινος someone against someone ISm 4: 1 (on ἀπό τινος cf. 2 Km 22: 24).—Mid. be on one's guard (Hdt., Thu. et al.; 2 Km 22: 24; Sib. Or. 3, 733) w. μή and inf. IMg 11 (though because of the analogy of the two passages mentioned above the mid. here could have act. mng. [Diogenianus the Epicurean—II AD—in Euseb., Pr. Ev. 4, 3, 7 end, twice, and Philo, Cher. 34 the mid. means 'ward someth. off'']; Rdm.³ 79).*

προχειρίζω in our lit., as mostly, only as mid. dep. προχειρίζομαι 1 aor. προεχειρισάμην; pass. pf. ptc. προκεχειρισμένος choose for oneself, select, appoint τινά someone (Isocr.+; Polyb. 2, 43, 1; 6, 58, 3; Dionys. Hal., De Orat. Ant. 4; Plut., Galba 8, 3, Caesar 58, 8; Lucian, Tox. 10; Dit., Syll.³ 873, 14f, Or. 339, 46; 50; pap.; 2 Macc 3: 7; 8: 9) foll. by an inf. of purpose Ac 22: 14. W. double acc. of the obj. and the pred. (Polyb. 1, 11, 3; Diod. S. 12, 27, 1; PLond. 2710 r., 5; Ex 4: 13) προχειρίσασθαί σε ὑπηρέτην 26: 16. Pass. (προκεχειρισμένος as UPZ 117 II, 4 [II BC]; BGU 1198, 2 [I BC]; PFay. 14, 1) τὸν προκεχειρισμένον ὑμῖν Χριστὸν Ἰησοῦν Christ Jesus, who was appointed for you or Jesus who was appointed (or destined) to be your Messiah Ac 3: 20 (the dat. like Josh 3: 12). M-M.*

προχειροτονέω pf. pass. ptc. προκεχειροτονημένος choose or appoint beforehand (so Pla., Leg. 6 p. 765B; c al.; Cass. Dio 50, 4; BGU 1191, 6 [I BC] τῷ προκεχειροτονημένῳ) Ac 10: 41. M-M.*

Πρόχορος, ου, ὁ (found in later Gk.) Prochorus, one of the seven 'deacons' in the church at Jerusalem Ac 6: 5.*

προχωρέω (Soph., Hdt.+; inscr., pap.) go forward, advance fig. of things turn out well, succeed w. dat. of the pers. for whom someth. goes well (Hdt. 5, 62; Thu. 4, 73, 4; Lucian, Icar. 10; PLond. 358, 13 [II AD] προχωρεῖν αὐτοῖς τὰ ἄνομα; Jos., Vi. 122) οὐδὲν αὐτοῖς ὅλως προχωρεῖ nothing at all turns out well for them Hs 6, 3, 5.*

πρύμνα, ης, ἡ (Hom.+; pap.) the stern (of a ship) ἦν ἐν τῇ πρύμνῃ καθεύδων he was in the stern sleeping Mk 4: 38.—Ac 27: 29 (WStammler, AG 27 in nautischer Beleuchtung usw., '31, 3–15; against him FFBruce, Acts, '51, 463), 41 (w. πρῷρα as X., An. 5, 8, 20; Ael. Aristid. 44, 13 K.=17 p. 405 D.). M-M.*

πρωΐ adv. of time (Hom.+—in Attic writers as πρῴ; pap., LXX; Jos., Vi. 91, Ant. 3, 307) early, early in the morning Mt 16: 3; 21: 18; Mk 1: 35; 11: 20; 16: 9; Hs 9, 11, 2 (opp. ὀψέ). As the fourth watch of the night (after ὀψὲ ἢ μεσονύκτιον ἢ ἀλεκτοροφωνίας) it is the time fr. three to six o'clock Mk 13: 35. εὐθὺς πρ. as soon as morning came 15: 1. ἅμα πρ. (ἅμα 2, end) Mt 20: 1; λίαν πρ. w. dat., of the day very early Mk 16: 2. ἀπὸ πρ. ἕως ἑσπέρας from morning till evening Ac 28: 23 (cf. Jos., Ant. 13, 97). πρωῒ σκοτίας ἔτι οὔσης J 20: 1. ἦν πρ. it was early in the morning (Bl-D. §129; 434, 1) 18: 28. τὸ πρωΐ is likew. an adv. (PSI 402, 10 [III BC] τὸ πρωΐ εὐθέως; LXX; Test. Napht. 1: 3; Bl-D. §160; 161, 3) Ac 5: 21 D. ἐπὶ τὸ πρωΐ toward morning Mk 15: 1 t.r.; for this another v.l. has ἐπὶ τῷ πρ. M-M. B. 960.*

πρωΐα, ας, ἡ (Diod. S.; CIG 1122, 16; BGU 1206, 20 [28 BC]; PLond. 131, 16; 401; 1177, 66 ἀπὸ πρωΐας ἕως ὀψέ; LXX; Ep. Arist. 304; Philo, Vi. Cont. 89; Jos., Ant. 7, 164.—Really the fem. of πρώϊος [Hom.+], sc. ὥρα) (early) morning πρωΐας γενομένης when it was morning (Syntipas p. 49, 17; 53, 6) Mt 27: 1; 1 Cl 43: 5. Cf. J 18: 28 t.r.; 21: 4. Gen. of time πρωΐας (early) in the morning Mt 21: 18 t.r.; GP 9: 34. M-M. B. 994.*

πρωΐθεν adv. of time (LXX; Herodian, Gr. I 501, 9) from morning, though the ending -θεν has lost its force and become meaningless (Bl-D. §104, 2; Rob. 300; MLejeune, Les adverbes grecs en -θεν '39), so that ἀπό can be used before it (Georg. Monach. 179, 16 de Boor 1892) ἀπὸ πρ. ἕως ἑσπέρας 1 Cl 39: 5 (Job 4: 20).*

πρώϊμος s. πρόϊμος.

πρωϊνός, ή, όν (Zen.-P. ed. CCEdgar II '26, no. 59 207, 36 [III BC]; Babrius, Fab. 124, 17 Crus. w. the v.l. προϊνῶν fr. cod. V.; Plut., Mor. 726E; Athen. 1, 19 p. 11c; LXX) early, belonging to the morning ὁ ἀστὴρ ὁ πρ. the morning star, Venus Rv 2: 28; 22: 16. M-M.*

πρῷρα (Hom.+; PSI 382, 2 [III BC]; Zen.-P. 9 [=Sb 6715], 15 [257 BC]. On the ι subscript Bl-D. §26 app.; Mlt.-H. 84), ης (PGM 8, 40; Bl-D. §43, 1; Mlt.-H. 118), ἡ, the forepart, bow or prow of a ship Ac 27: 30, 41 (s. πρύμνα). M-M.*

πρωτεῖος, α, ον of the first quality or rank (BGU 950, 4; PLond. 1764, 7; Sym.) the neut. subst. in the pl. (Ael. Aristid. 38 p. 720 D.; Stephan. Byz. s.v. Ἰδουμαῖοι; Sb 6997, 28; PSI 716, 14 where, unfortunately, the text breaks off after τὰ πρωτεῖα. The sing. is found Epigr. Gr. 560, 3 [I AD]; Jos., Vi. 37; Proclus, Theol. 98 p. 88, 24) περὶ πρωτείων for the first places, about preëminence Hs 8, 7, 4; 6.*

πρωτεύω (Pla., X.+; inscr., pap., LXX) be first, have first place ἵνα γένηται ἐν πᾶσιν αὐτὸς πρωτεύων that he might come to have first place in everything Col 1: 18 (ἐν πᾶσιν like Plut., Mor. 9B. The pres. ptc. like PLeipz. 40 II, 16; POxy. 1983, 2; 2 Macc 6: 18; 13: 15; Ep. Arist. 275; Jos., Ant. 9, 167; 20, 182). M-M.*

πρωτοκαθεδρία, ας, ἡ (schol. on Eur., Orest. 93; Theophanes Conf. 163, 26 de Boor) place of honor, best seat desired by the Pharisees in the synagogue Mt 23: 6; Mk 12: 39; Lk 11: 43; 20: 46. Likew. by the false prophet θέλει πρωτοκαθεδρίαν ἔχειν Hm 11: 12.*

πρωτοκαθεδρίτης, ου, ὁ (only in Christian writers) the one who occupies a seat of honor (w. οἱ προηγούμενοι) of the church leaders Hv 3, 9, 7.*

πρωτοκλισία, ας, ἡ (inscr. fr. Delos [II BC]: JHS 54, '34, 142; Suidas) the place of honor at a dinner, beside the master of the house or the host Mt 23: 6; Mk 12: 39; Lk 14: 7f; 20: 46. M-M.*

πρωτόμαρτυς, υρος, ὁ first martyr of Stephen Ac 22: 20 v.l. (cf. Πράξεις Παύλου p. 235 Lips. v.l. in the fem. of Thecla).*

πρῶτος, η, ον (Hom.+; inscr., pap., LXX, Ep. Arist., Philo, Joseph., Test. 12 Patr.; Sib. Or. 7, 1; 2; loanw. in rabb. Superlative of πρό).

1. πρῶτος first of several, but also when only two persons or things are involved (= πρότερος; exx. in Hdb. on J 1: 15; Rdm.² 71f; Thackeray 183; s. also Mlt. 79; 245; Bl-D. §62; Rob. 516; 662; and cf. Mt 21: 31 t.r.).

a. of time first, earliest, earlier adj. ἀπὸ τῆς πρώτης ἡμέρας ἄχρι τοῦ νῦν Phil 1: 5; cf. Ac 20: 18 (on the absence of the art. [also Phil 1: 5 t.r.] cf. Bl-D. §256; Rob. 793). ἡ πρώτη ἀπολογία 2 Ti 4: 16 (MMeinertz, Worauf

bezieht sich die πρώτη ἀπολογία 2 Ti 4: 16?: Biblica 4, '23, 390–4). ἡ πρ. διαθήκη Hb 9: 15. τὰ πρῶτα ἔργα Rv 2: 5. ἡ ἀνάστασις ἡ πρώτη 20: 5f. ἡ πρώτη ὅρασις Hv 3, 10, 3; 3, 11, 2; 4. ἡ ἐκκλησία ἡ πρ. 2 Cl 14: 1.—Subst. τὰ πρ.—τὰ ἔσχατα (Job 8: 7): γίνεται τὰ ἔσχατα χείρονα τῶν πρώτων Mt 12: 45; cf. Lk 11: 26; 2 Pt 2: 20. οἱ πρῶτοι (those who came earlier, as Artem. 2, 9 p. 93, 19 those who appeared earlier) Mt 20: 10; cf. vs. 8. ἀπέστειλεν ἄλλους δούλους πλείονας τῶν πρώτων 21: 36. Cf. 27: 64. πρῶτος ἐξ ἀναστάσεως νεκρῶν the first to rise from the dead Ac 26: 23. ὁ πρῶτος the first one J 5: 4; 1 Cor 14: 30. On the self-designation of the Risen Lord ὁ πρ. καὶ ὁ ἔσχατος Rv 1: 17; 2: 8; 22: 13 cf. ἔσχατος 3b (πρ. of God: Is 44: 6; 48: 12).—As a predicate adj., where an adv. can be used in English (Bl-D. §243; Rob. 657), as the first one=first ἦλθεν πρῶτος he was the first one to come= he came first J 20: 4; cf. vs. 8. πρῶτος Μωϋσῆς λέγει Ro 10: 19. Ἀβραὰμ πρῶτος περιτομὴν δούς Abraham was the first to practice circumcision B 9: 7. οἱ ἄγγελοι οἱ πρῶτοι κτισθέντες the angels who were created first Hv 3, 4, 1; s 5, 5, 3.—1 Ti 2: 13; 1 J 4: 19.—ἐν ἐμοὶ πρώτῳ in me as the first 1 Ti 1: 16.—Used w. a gen. of comparison (Manetho 1, 329; Athen. 14, 28 p. 630c codd.) πρῶτός μου ἦν he was earlier than I= before me J 1: 15, 30 (PGM 13, 543 σοῦ πρῶτός εἰμι.—Also Ep. 12 of Apollonius of Tyana: Philostrat. I p. 348, 30 τὸ τῇ τάξει δεύτερον οὐδέποτε τῇ φύσει πρῶτον). So perh. also ἐμὲ πρῶτον ὑμῶν μεμίσηκεν 15: 18 (s. 2a below) and πάντων πρώτη ἐκτίσθη Hv 2, 4, 1.—As a rule the later element, that follows the first or earlier one, is of the same general nature as the first one. But it can also be someth. quite different, even its exact opposite: τὴν πρώτην πίστιν ἠθέτησαν 1 Ti 5: 12. τὴν ἀγάπην σου τὴν πρώτην ἀφῆκες Rv 2: 4.—Used elliptically ἡ πρώτη (i.e. ἡμέρα) τῶν ἀζύμων Mt 26: 17. πρώτη σαββάτου on the first day of the week Mk 16: 9. In some of the passages mentioned above the idea of sequence could be predom.

b. of number or sequence (the area within which this mng. is valid cannot be marked off w. certainty from the area of mng. a) Mt 21: 28; 22: 25; Mk 12: 20; Lk 14: 18; 16: 5; 19: 16; 20: 29 J 19: 32; Ac 12: 10; 13: 33 v.l.; Rv 4: 7; 8: 7; 21: 19; Hs 9, 1, 5. τὸ πρῶτον—τὸ δεύτερον (Alex. Aphr., An. p. 28, 9 Br.) Hb 10: 9. On πρώτη τῆς μερίδος Μακεδονίας πόλις Ac 16: 12 cf. μερίς 1.—Since πρῶτος can stand for πρότερος (s. 1 above, beg.; cf. Mlt.-Turner 32), it by no means follows from τὸν μὲν πρῶτον λόγον Ac 1: 1 that the writer of the Third Gospel and of Ac must have planned to write a third book (Zahn, NKZ 28, '17, 373ff, Comm. '19, 16ff holds that he planned to write a third volume; against this view cf. EJGoodspeed, Introd. to the NT '37, 189f.—Athenaeus 15 p. 701c mentions the first of Clearchus' two books on proverbs with the words ἐν τῷ προτέρῳ περὶ παροιμιῶν, but 10 p. 457c with ἐν τῷ πρώτῳ περὶ παροιμιῶν. Diod. S. 1, 42, 1 the first half of a two-part work is called ἡ πρώτη βίβλος and 3, 1, 1 mentions a division into πρώτη and δευτέρα βίβ. In 13, 103, 3 the designation for the first of two works varies between ἡ πρώτη σύνταξις and ἡ προτέρα σ. Cf. E Haenchen, AG '56, 107).—πρῶτος is also used without any thought that the series must continue: τὸν πρῶτον ἰχθύν the very first fish Mt 17: 27. αὕτη ἀπογραφὴ πρώτη ἐγένετο Lk 2: 2, likewise, does not look forward in the direction of additional censuses, but back to a time when there were none at all (Ael. Aristid. 13 p. 227 D. παράκλησις αὕτη [= 'challenge to a sea-fight'] πρώτη ἐγένετο).—τὰ τείχη τὰ πρῶτα Hs 8, 6, 6 does not contrast the 'first walls' w. other walls; rather it distinguishes the only walls in the picture (Hs 8, 7, 3; 8, 8, 3) as one edifice, from the tower as the other edifice.

c. of rank or degree *first, foremost, most important, most prominent*—**a.** of things (Ocellus [II BC] c. 56 Harder ['26] πρώτη κ. μεγίστη φυλακή; Ael. Aristid. 23, 43 K.=42 p. 783 D.: πόλεις; Ezk 27: 22) ἡ μεγάλη καὶ πρώτη ἐντολή Mt 22: 38; cf. Mk 12: 29. ἐντολὴ πρώτη πάντων vs. 28 (OHLehmann, TU 73, '59, 557-61 [rabb.]; CBurchard, ZNW 61, '70, cites Joseph and Aseneth, 15, 10; 18, 5). Without superl. force ἐντολὴ πρώτη ἐν ἐπαγγελίᾳ *a commandment of the greatest importance, with a promise attached* Eph 6: 2 (the usual transl. 'first commandment w. a promise' loses sight of the fact that Ex 20: 4-6=Dt 5: 8-10 has an implied promise of the same kind as the one in Ex 20: 12=Dt 5: 16. πρ. here is best taken in the same sense as in Mk 12: 28f above). στολὴν τὴν πρώτην *the best robe* Lk 15: 22.—ἐν πρώτοις *among the first= most important things*, i.e. *as of first importance* 1 Cor 15: 3 (Pla., Pol. 522c ὃ καὶ παντὶ ἐν πρώτοις ἀνάγκη μανθάνειν; Epict., Ench. 20; Wilcken, Chrest. 14 II, 9 ἐν πρώτοις ἐρωτῶ σε; Josh 9: 2d).

β. of persons (Dio Chrys. 19[36], 35 πρ. καὶ μέγιστος θεός; Jos., Ant. 15, 398) ὃς ἂν θέλῃ ἐν ὑμῖν εἶναι πρῶτος *whoever wishes to be the first among you* Mt 20: 27; Mk 10: 44; cf. 9: 35. πρῶτος Σίμων Mt 10: 2 is not meant to indicate the position of Simon in the list, since no other numbers follow, but to single him out as the *most prominent* one of the twelve. W. gen. ὦν (=τῶν ἁμαρτωλῶν) πρῶτός εἰμι 1 Ti 1: 15. Pl. (οἱ) πρῶτοι in contrast to (οἱ) ἔσχατοι Mt 19: 30; 20: 16; Mk 9: 35; 10: 31; Lk 13: 30; LJ 2: 4 (cf. Sallust. 9 p. 16, 21f τοῖς ἐσχάτοις—τοῖς πρώτοις.—ἔσχατος 2).—οἱ πρῶτοι *the most prominent men, the leading men* w. gen. of the place (Jos., Ant. 7, 230 τῆς χώρας) οἱ πρ. τῆς Γαλιλαίας Mk 6: 21; cf. Ac 13: 50, or of the group (Strabo 13, 2, 3 οἱ πρ. τῶν φίλων; Jos., Ant. 20, 180) οἱ πρ. τοῦ λαοῦ (Jos., Ant. 11, 141) Lk 19: 47; cf. Ac 25: 2; 28: 17. On ὁ πρῶτος τῆς νήσου vs. 7 (cf. inscr.: Ramsay, Phrygia p. 642 no. 535 ὁ πρῶτος ἐν τῇ πόλει; p. 660 no. 616) cf. Πόπλιος.

d. of space *outer, anterior* σκηνὴ ἡ πρώτη *the outer tent*, i.e. the holy place Hb 9: 2; cf. vss. 6, 8.

2. the neut. πρῶτον as adv.—**a.** of time *first, in the first place, before, earlier, to begin with* (Peripl. Eryth. c. 4; Charito 8, 2, 4) πρῶτον πάντων *first of all* Hv 5: 5a. ἐπίτρεψόν μοι πρῶτον ἀπελθεῖν καὶ θάψαι *let me first go and bury* Mt 8: 21. συλλέξατε πρῶτον τὰ ζιζάνια *gather the weeds first* 13: 30. Cf. 17: 10, 11 t.r.; Mk 7: 27; 9: 11f; 13: 10; Lk 9: 59, 61; 12: 1 (*first* Jesus speaks to his disciples, and only then [vs. 15] to the people. If one prefers to take πρ. w. what follows, as is poss., it has mng. c); 14: 28, 31; J 7: 51; 18: 13; Ac 26: 20; Ro 15: 24 al. in NT; B 15: 7; Hv 3, 1, 8; 3, 6, 7; 3, 8, 11; 5: 5b. τότε πρῶτον *then for the first time* Ac 11: 26 D. πρῶτον . . . καὶ τότε *first . . . and then* (Sir 11: 7; 18, 187) Mt 5: 24; 7: 5; 12: 29; Mk 3: 27; Lk 6: 42; IEph 7: 2. τότε is correlative w. πρῶτον without καί J 2: 10 v.l. Likew. πρῶτον—εἶτα (εἶτεν) *first—then* (εἶτα 1) Mk 4: 28; 1 Ti 3: 10; B 6: 17. πρῶτον—ἔπειτα (ἔπειτα 2a) 1 Cor 15: 46; 1 Th 4: 16. πρῶτον—μετὰ ταῦτα Mk 16: 9, s. 12. πρῶτον—εἶτα—μετὰ ταῦτα 1 Cl 23: 4; 2 Cl 11: 3 (in both cases the same prophetic saying of unknown origin). πρῶτον—ἐν τῷ δευτέρῳ Ac 7: 12.—Pleonastically πρῶτον πρὸ τοῦ ἀρίστου Lk 11: 38.—W. gen. (Charito 5, 4, 9 cod. πρῶτον τ. λόγων=before it comes to words) ἐμὲ πρῶτον ὑμῶν μεμίσηκεν *it hated me before* (*it hated*) *you* J 15: 18 (but s. 1a above).—W. the art. τὸ πρῶτον (Hom.+; Jos., Ant. 8, 402; 14, 205) *the first time* J 10: 40;

19: 39; *at first* (Diod. S. 1, 85, 2; Jos., Ant. 2, 340) 12: 16; 2 Cl 9: 5. τὰ πρῶτα (Hom.+; Appian, Syr. 15 §64; Ps.-Phoc. 8) *the first time, at first* MPol 8: 2.

b. of sequence in enumerations (not always clearly distinguished fr. mng. a) *first* πρῶτον ἀποστόλους, δεύτερον προφήτας, τρίτον . . . 1 Cor 12: 28 (Wilcken, Chrest. 20 II, 10ff [II AD] τὸ πρ. . . . τὸ δεύτερον . . . τὸ τρίτον. Without the art. 480, 12ff [II AD]; Diod. S. 36, 7, 3). Cf. Hb 7: 2; Js 3: 17.—Not infrequently Paul begins w. πρῶτον μέν without continuing the series, at least in form (Bl-D. §447, 4 w. app.; Rob. 1152. On πρ. without continuation cf. Plut., Mor. 87B; Jos., Ant. 1, 182) Ro 1: 8; 3: 2; 1 Cor 11: 18. Cf. also 2 Cl 3: 1.

c. of degree *in the first place, above all, especially* (Jos., Ant. 10, 213) ζητεῖτε πρῶτον τὴν βασιλείαν Mt 6: 33. Ἰουδαίῳ τε πρῶτον καὶ Ἕλληνι Ro 1: 16; cf. 2: 9f.— Ac 3: 26; 2 Pt 1: 20; 3: 3. Of the Macedonian Christians ἑαυτοὺς ἔδωκαν πρῶτον τῷ κυρίῳ καὶ ἡμῖν *they gave themselves first of all to the Lord, and* (*then*) *to us* 2 Cor 8: 5. παρακαλῶ πρῶτον πάντων *first of all I urge* 1 Ti 2: 1. M-M. B. 939.

πρωτοστάτης, ου, ὁ (Thu.+; Job 15: 24) *leader, ringleader* πρ. τῆς τῶν Ναζωραίων αἱρέσεως Ac 24: 5. M-M.*

πρωτοτόκια, ων, τά (Bl-D. §120, 1; Mlt.-H. 279) *the birthright* of the first-born son, *right of primogeniture* (Gen 27: 36; Philo, Leg. All. 2, 47, Sacr. Abel. 120 al. in the Esau story) Ἠσαῦ ἀντὶ βρώσεως μιᾶς ἀπέδοτο τὰ πρωτοτόκια ἑαυτοῦ *Esau sold his birthright for a single meal* Hb 12: 16 (Gen 25: 33).*

πρωτότοκος, ον (Sb 6647 [5 BC; s. WMichaelis below p. 314f]; Epigr. Gr. 460, 4; 730, 3; PLeipz. 28, 16; PGM 36, 312; Anth. 8, 34; 9, 213; LXX; Philo, Cher. 54 al.; Jos., Ant. 4, 71; Sib. Or. 3, 627) *first-born.*

1. lit. ὁ υἱὸς ὁ πρ. (PLeipz. loc. cit. υἱὸν γνήσιον καὶ πρωτότοκον; Gen 25: 25 al. LXX) Mt 1: 25 t.r.; Lk 2: 7; cf. B 13: 5 (Gen 48: 18). τὰ πρ. *the first-born*= all the first-born (τὰ πρ. Ex 22: 28; Num 18: 15 al.) Hb 11: 28 (cf. Ex 11: 5). τὰ πρ. τῶν προβάτων *the first-born of the sheep* 1 Cl 4: 1 (Gen 4: 4).

2. fig.—**a.** of Christ, as the first-born of a new humanity which is to be glorified, as its exalted Lord is glorified πρωτότοκος ἐν πολλοῖς ἀδελφοῖς Ro 8: 29. Also simply πρωτότοκος Hb 1: 6; cf. Rv 2: 8 v.l. This expr., which is admirably suited to describe Jesus as the one coming forth fr. God to found the new community of saints, is also used in some instances where it is uncertain whether the force of the element -τοκος is still felt at all (s. the originally pagan Naassene psalm in Hippol., Elench. 5, 10, 1) (ὁ) πρ. (ἐκ) τῶν νεκρῶν Col 1: 18; Rv 1: 5. πρ. πάσης κτίσεως Col 1: 15 (JGewiess, Christus u. d. Heil nach d. Kol. Diss. Breslau '32; EACerny, Firstborn of Every Creature [Col 1: 15]: Diss., Baltimore '38; Romualdus, Studia Cath. 18, '42, 155-71; WMichaelis, D. Beitrag d. LXX zur Bedeutungsgeschichte von πρ.: ADebrunner-Festschr. '54, 313-20, ZsystTh 23, '54, 137-57; AWArgyle, ET 66, '54, 61f, cf. 124f, 318f; NKehl, D. Christushymnus im Kol., '67, 82-98).

b. of men—**a.** of the 'just men made perfect' (cf. Ex 4: 22) ἐκκλησία πρωτοτόκων Hb 12: 23.

β. The confirmed heretic is a πρωτότοκος τοῦ Σατανᾶ Pol 7: 1 (NADahl, D. Erstgeborene Satans u. d. Vater des Teufels: EHaenchen-Festschr., '64, 70-84). Specif. of Marcion acc. to a saying of Polycarp, Epil Mosq 2 (cf. Irenaeus 3, 3, 4); s. also the corresp. Hebr. expr. in

HZucker, Studien z. jüd. Selbstverwaltg. im Altert. '36, 135. M-M.*

πρώτως adv. (Aristot. et al.; Dit., Or. 602, 4; UPZ 110, 81 [164 вс]; POxy. 1023, 3f [II AD]; 1267, 10; Ep. Arist. 4) *for the first time* (so Polyb. 6, 5, 10; Diod. S. 4, 24, 1; Inschr. v. Priene 117, 39; Dit., Syll.³ 797, 16; PRyl. 235, 11; Jos., Bell. 2, 25. Cf. Lob., Phryn. p. 311f; Crönert 193; Bl-D. §102, 5; Mlt.-H. 163) Ac 11: 26 (v.l. πρῶτον). M-M.*

πταίω 1 aor. ἔπταισα (Pind.+; inscr., pap., LXX, Ep. Arist., Philo, Joseph.) in our lit. only intr. *stumble, trip* (X., An. 4, 2, 3 πρὸς τὰς πέτρας; Polyb. 31, 11, 5 πρὸς τὸν λίθον; Jos., Bell. 6, 64 πρὸς πέτρᾳ), and in the fig. sense (as Aeschyl., Hdt.+).

1. in usages in which the lit. sense is clearly discernible. Abs. (Maximus Tyr. 34, 2e) μὴ ἔπταισαν ἵνα πέσωσιν; *they did not stumble so as to fall into ruin, did they?* Ro 11: 11. The 'stumbling' means *to make a mistake, go astray, sin* (Pla., Theaet. 160Dal.; abs. Arrian, Anab. 4, 9, 6; M. Ant. 7, 22 ἴδιον ἀνθρώπου φιλεῖν καὶ τοὺς πταίοντας; POxy. 1165, 11 εἴτε ἔπταισαν εἴτε οὐκ ἔπταισαν='whether they have committed an error or not'; Dt 7: 25; Ep. Arist. 239; Philo, Leg. All. 3, 66) ὅσα παρεπέσαμεν καὶ ἐπταίσαμεν 1 Cl 51: 1. πολλὰ πταίομεν *we commit many sins* Js 3: 2a. πτ. ἐν ἑνί *sin in one respect* 2: 10. ἐν λόγῳ *in what one says* 3: 2b.

2. *be ruined, be lost* (Hdt. 9, 101; Aristot., Rhet. 3 al.; Diod. S. 15, 33, 1 et al.; Philo, De Jos. 144; Jos., Ant. 7, 75; 14, 434) of the loss of salvation 2 Pt 1: 10. But mng. 1 is also poss. M-M.*

πτελέα, ας, ἡ (Hom. [πτελέη]+; Sym. Is 41: 19) *elm tree* as a support for vines Hs 2: 1ff.*

πτέρνα, ης, ἡ (Hom.+; LXX; Jos., Ant. 1, 258 [after Gen 25: 26]; Sib. Or. 1, 63. Cf. Bl-D. §43, 2) *heel* ἐπαίρειν τὴν π. ἐπί τινα *raise one's heel against someone* for a malicious kick J 13: 18 (w. some relation to a form of Ps 40: 10 which, in the LXX, ends w. ἐπ' ἐμὲ πτερνισμόν).*

πτεροφυέω (*get* or) *grow feathers* or *wings* (Plut., Mor. 751F of Eros; Lucian, Icar. 10; Olympiodorus, Life of Plato p. 2 Westermann; Horapollo 1, 55; Is 40: 31.—In fig. sense as early as Pla.) 1 Cl 25: 3.*

πτερύγιον, ου, τό (Aristot.+; Aeneas Tact. 1440; inscr., LXX) dim. of πτέρυξ 'wing'; it serves to designate the tip or extremity of anything *end, edge* τὸ πτερύγιον τοῦ ἱεροῦ someth. like *the pinnacle* or *summit of the temple* Mt 4: 5; Lk 4: 9 (also in Hegesippus: Euseb., H.E. 2, 23, 11. Rufinus has for this 'excelsus locus pinnae templi'.—Cf. Theod. Da 9: 27 [reading of a doublet; s. ed. JZiegler '54 p. 191] and M-JLagrange, RB 39, '30, 190). JoachJeremias, ZDPV 59, '36, 195-208 proposes: 'the lintel or super-structure of a gate of the temple.' But for Greeks the word for this that was most easily understood would be ὑπέρθυρον (Parmenides [VI/V вс], fgm. 1, 12 [28 B Diels]; Hdt. 1, 179; Herodas 2, 65; Artem. 2, 10 p. 97, 26; 4, 42 p. 226, 8.—Jos., Bell. 5, 201 in a description of the Jerus. temple). M-M.*

πτέρυξ, υγος, ἡ (Hom.+; Dit., Syll.³ 1167, 1-5; POxy. 738, 10; LXX; Jos., Ant. 8, 72) *wing*, of birds Mt 23: 37; Lk 13: 34; Rv 12: 14 (Test. Napht. 5: 6 πτ. ἀετοῦ). The four strange creatures of the Apocalypse have six wings apiece (cf. Is 6: 2) Rv 4: 8. Of the apocalyptic locusts ἡ φωνὴ τῶν πτ. *the noise of the wings* 9: 9. M-M. B. 245.*

πτερωτός, (ή), όν (Aeschyl., Hdt.+; LXX) *feathered, winged*; subst. τὰ πτερωτά *winged creatures, birds* (Aeschyl., Suppl. 510; Eur., Hel. 747.—Ps 77: 27 and 148: 10 in the expr. πετεινὰ πτερωτά, πετεινά is clearly the subst. The masc. οἱ πτερωτοί occurs in the same sense: Eur., Bacch. 257) ἐκτείνεται δίκτυα πτερωτοῖς B 5: 4 (Pr 1: 17).*

πτηνός, (ή), όν (Pind.+) *feathered, winged*; subst. τὰ πτηνά *the birds* (Aeschyl., Pla.+; Aq. Job 5: 7; Ep. Arist. 145; 146; 147; Philo; Sib. Or. 3, 370) 1 Cor 15: 39. M-M.*

πτοέω 1 aor. pass. ἐπτοήθην (Hom.+; LXX) *terrify, frighten*; pass. *be terrified, be alarmed, frightened, startled* (Polyb. 8, 19, 2; 31, 11, 4; Diod. S. 17, 102, 3 πτοηθέντες; LXX; Jos., Bell. 1, 591; 4, 108; Test. Jos. 2: 5; PGM 4, 3093; 13, 199; 765) Lk 12: 4 𝔓⁴⁵; 21: 9. W. ἔμφοβοι γενόμενοι 24: 37 (cf. En. 21, 9 φοβεῖσθαι κ. πτ.); for this passage cf. also the variants θροηθέντες 𝔓⁷⁵ et al.; φοβηθέντες ℵW. M-M.*

πτόησις, εως, ἡ (Pla.+; LXX)—1. act., the act of *terrifying, intimidation*—2. pass. *fear, terror* (Philo, Rer. Div. Her. 251, end). In μὴ φοβούμεναι μηδεμίαν πτόησιν 1 Pt 3: 6 (Pr 3: 25) both mngs. are poss. In the case of mng. 2 πτόησιν would be acc. of the inner obj. *

Πτολεμαΐς, ΐδος, ἡ (on the spelling s. Bl-D. §15; 30, 1; 34, 6; Mlt.-H. 81) *Ptolemais*, a Phoenician seaport city (Polyb. 5, 61f; 71; Strabo 2, 5, 39; also 1 and 2 Macc; Ep. Arist. 115; Joseph.) Ac 21: 7.—Schürer II⁴ 141ff (lit.).*

πτύον, ου, τό (Hom.+; Artem. 2, 24 p. 117, 28; PFay. 120, 5 [c. 100 AD]; Sym. Is 30: 24) *winnowing shovel*, a fork-like shovel, with which the threshed grain was thrown into the wind; thus the chaff was separated fr. the grain Mt 3: 12; Lk 3: 17.—S. Dalman s.v. ἀλοάω. M-M. B. 500.*

πτύρω *frighten, scare*, almost always pass. *be frightened, terrified, let oneself be intimidated* (since Hippocr., Mul. Morb. 1, 25; Ps.-Pla., Axioch. 370A; Philo Bybl. [I/II AD] in Euseb., Pr. Ev. 1, 10, 4; Plut., Mor. 800c; M. Ant. 8, 45, 2) μὴ πτυρόμενοι ἐν μηδενὶ ὑπὸ τῶν ἀντικειμένων *in no way intimidated by your opponents* Phil 1: 28. M-M.*

πτύσμα, ατος, τό (Hippocr.+; Polyb. 8, 12, 5; Sib. Or. 1, 365; Pollux 2, 103) *saliva, spit(tle)* used by Jesus in the healing of a blind man J 9: 6.—On this subj. s. EKlostermann, Hdb., exc. on Mk 7: 33; Billerb. II 15ff; AJacoby, ZNW 10, '09, 185-94; OWeinreich, Antike Heilungswunder '09, 97f; FJDölger, D. Exorzismus im altchr. Taufritual '09, 118ff; 130ff; JJHess, ZAW 35, '15, 130f; SEitrem, Some Notes on Demonology in the NT, Symb. Osl. 12, '50, 46-9. M-M.*

πτύσσω 1 aor. ἔπτυξα (Hom.+) *fold up* (Jos., Ant. 10, 16 ἐπιστολάς; 15, 171. Of the folding of a document PGenève 10, 17 [IV AD]; Sb 5174, 23; 5175, 24) πτύξας τὸ βιβλίον *after he had rolled up the scroll* Lk 4: 20. M-M. B. 544.*

πτύω 1 aor. ἔπτυσα (Hom.+; Num 12: 14; Sir 28: 12) *spit, spit out* χαμαί *on the ground* J 9: 6. πτύσας εἰς τὰ ὄμματα αὐτοῦ *when he had spit on his eyes* Mk 8: 23 (Jos., Ant. 5, 335 πτ. εἰς τὸ πρόσωπον). Abs. 7: 33.—Lit. s.v. πτύσμα. M-M. B. 264.*

πτῶμα, ατος, τό (Aeschyl.+; LXX, Philo, Joseph.; Sib. Or. 3, 183; 5, 457; loanw. in rabb.) *that which has fallen,* (*dead*) *body, corpse*, esp. of one killed by violence (used w. νεκροῦ or the gen. of a name as early as trag. Without them in Polyb. 15, 14, 2; Plut., Alex. 33, 8; Vett. Val. 275, 19; Herodian 7, 9, 7; Jos., Bell. 5, 570, Ant. 7, 16 al.; Dit., Syll.³ 700, 17 [118 bc]; Epigr. Gr. 326, 5; LXX) Mt 14: 12; 24: 28 (gathering-point for vultures as Cornutus 21 p. 41, 15f); Mk 6: 29; 15: 45; Rv 11: 8f (τὸ πτῶμα αὐτῶν in vss. 8 and 9a, τὰ πτώματα αὐτῶν 9b).—Mt 14: 12 and Mk 15: 45 have as v.l. σῶμα, a more dignified word. M-M. B. 290.*

πτῶσις, εως, ἡ (Pla.+; LXX; Jos., Ant. 17, 71) *falling, fall* (Diod. S. 5, 31, 3; Lucian, Anach. 28) lit. of the *fall* or *collapse* of a house (Manetho, Apot. 4, 617) Mt 7: 27. Fig. (Petosiris, fgm. 6 l. 96=downfall, destruction, i.e., of the barbarians; Diogenian. Ep., 8, 2; oft. LXX; En. 100, 6) οὗτος κεῖται εἰς πτῶσιν καὶ ἀνάστασιν πολλῶν *he is destined to cause the fall and rise of many* Lk 2: 34 (cf. 1QH 2, 8–10).*

πτωχεία, ας, ἡ (Hdt., Aristoph.+; PGenève 14, 23; LXX, Test. 12 Patr.) (*extreme*) *poverty*, lit. 'beggarliness'; lit., w. θλῖψις Rv 2: 9. ἡ κατὰ βάθους πτ. (βάθος 2) 2 Cor 8: 2. Paradoxically τῇ πτ. τινὸς πλουτῆσαι *become rich through someone's poverty* vs. 9. In LJ 1: 4 the word πτωχία occurs, but the context is lost. M-M.*

πτωχεύω 1 aor. ἐπτώχευσα (='beg' Hom.+; LXX) *be or become* (*extremely*) *poor* (Aristot., Rhet. 27 in contrast to πλουτεῖν; Antiphanes Com. 322 Kock; Ps.-Pla., Eryx. 394b) in our lit. only figuratively, of Christ ἐπτώχευσεν πλούσιος ὤν *he became poor* (ingressive aor. as Tob 4: 21; Bl-D. §331; Rob. 834) 2 Cor 8: 9. Of the Christians πτωχεύουσι καὶ πλουτίζουσι πολλούς Dg 5: 13. ὁ πλούσιος τὰ πρὸς τὸν κύριον πτωχεύει Hs 2: 5.*

πτωχίζω *make* (*extremely*) *poor* opp. πλουτίζειν 1 Cl 59: 3 (cf. 1 Km 2: 7).*

πτωχός, ή, όν (Hom.+; PPetr. III 36a, 17f; 140a, 1; LXX; Philo in Euseb., Pr. Ev. 8, 7, 6; Joseph., Test. 12 Patr.).

1. orig. *begging* (s. on πένης for a differentiation betw. the two words; note that they are synonymous in Ps 55: 1; 69: 6 al.), *dependent on others for support*, but also simply *poor* (as Mod. Gk. φτωχός)—a. quite literally χήρα πτωχή Mk 12: 42; cf. vs. 43; Lk 21: 3. Mostly as subst. (Jos., Bell. 5, 570) opp. ὁ πλούσιος (Pla., Theaet. 24 p. 175a; Maximus Tyr. 1, 9a) Lk 6: 20 (cf. vs. 24); Rv 13: 16; 1 Cl 38: 2; Hs 2: 4.—Mt 26: 11; Mk 14: 7; Lk 14: 13, 21; 16: 20, 22; J 12: 6, 8; Ro 15: 26 (οἱ πτ. τῶν ἁγίων τῶν ἐν Ἰερουσαλήμ, part. gen. On the other hand πτωχοί [in the sense of b, below]=ἅγιοι: KHoll, SAB '21, 937–9 and Ltzm., exc. on Ro 15: 25); 2 Cor 6: 10 (in a play on words w. πλουτίζειν); Gal 2: 10; Js 2: 2f, 6; B 20: 2; D 5: 2. οἱ πτ. τῷ κόσμῳ *those who are poor in the world's estimation* Js 2: 5 (opp. πλούσιοι ἐν πίστει). διδόναι (τοῖς) πτ. Mt 19: 21; Mk 10: 21; Lk 19: 8; cf. 18: 22; J 13: 29; D 13: 4. Pass. Mt 26: 9; Mk 14: 5; J 12: 5.

b. at times the ref. is not only to the unfavorable circumstances of these people from an economic point of view; the thought is also that since they are oppressed and disillusioned they are in special need of God's help, and may be expected to receive it shortly (LXX; HBruppacher, D. Beurteilung d. Armut im AT '24; WSattler, D. Anawim im Zeitalter Jes. Chr.: Jülicher-Festschr. '27, 1–15; A Meyer, D. Rätsel des Jk '30, 146ff; HBirkeland, 'Ani u. 'anāw in den Psalmen '33; LHMarshall, Challenge of NT Ethics '47, 76f; KSchubert, The Dead Sea Community '59,

85–8; 137–9; AGelin, The Poor of Yahweh, '64; FWDanker, The Literary Unity of Mk 14: 1–25, JBL 85, '66, 467–72. S. on πλοῦτος 1). The gospel is preached to them (Is 61: 1) Mt 11: 5; Lk 4: 18; 7: 22; 1 Cl 52: 2 (Ps 68: 33); Pol 2: 3 (εἶπεν ὁ κύριος διδάσκων).

c. expressly fig. οἱ πτωχοὶ τῷ πνεύματι Mt 5: 3 (s. πνεῦμα 3b and Gdspd., Probs. 16f; MHFranzmann, CTM 18, '47, 889ff; EBest, NTS 7, '60/'61, 255–8; SLégasse, NTS 8, '61/'62, 336–45 (Qumran); HBraun, Qumran u. d. NT I, '66, 13; LEKeck, The Poor among the Saints in Jewish Christianity and Qumran, ZNW 57, '66, 54–78). The angel of the church at Laodicea, who says of himself πλούσιός εἰμι καὶ πεπλούτηκα, is termed πτωχός Rv 3: 17. In 1 Cl 15: 6, Ps 11: 6 is quoted w. ref. to the situation in the Corinthian church.

2. *poor, miserable, beggarly, impotent* (Dionys. Hal., Comp. Verb. 4 νοήματα) of the στοιχεῖα (w. ἀσθενής) Gal 4: 9. Of the grace of God πτωχὴ οὐκ ἐγενήθη 1 Cor 15: 10 D.—FHauck and EBammel, TW VI 885–915. M-M. B. 782; 784.*

πτωχότης, ητος, ἡ *poverty* (Griech. . . . Ostraka der . . . Bibl. zu Strassburg, ed. PViereck '23, 794) Hv 3, 12, 2.*

πυγμή, ῆς, ἡ—1. *fist* (so Eur., Hippocr.+; PPetr. III 22 (e) 2 [III bc]; LXX) in a difficult pass. ἐὰν μὴ πυγμῇ νίψωνται τὰς χεῖρας lit. *unless they wash their hands with* (*the*) *fist* Mk 7: 3 (where the v.l. πυκνά [s. πυκνός] is substituted for π. in א and acc. to the Vulgate [crebro], Goth., and Copt., thus alleviating the difficulty. Itala codex d has 'primo' [on this and other Itala readings s. AJülicher, Itala II '40, p. 59]). This procedure is variously described and interpreted as a washing: 'in which one clenched fist is turned about in the hollow of the other hand', or 'up to the elbow' or 'the wrist', or 'with a handful' of water. FSchulthess, ZNW 21, '22, 232f thinks of it simply as a rubbing w. the dry hand.—Palladius, Hist. Laus. 55 νίψασθαι τὰς χεῖρας καὶ τοὺς πόδας πυγμῇ ὕδατι ψυχροτάτῳ. CCTorrey, ZAW 65, '53, 233f. —For lit. s. βαπτίζω 1.—Field, Notes 30f; Gdspd., Probs. 59f; MBlack, Aramaic Approach², '53, 8f; PR Weis, NTS 3, '56/'57, 233–6 (Aramaic); SMReynolds, JBL 85, '66, 87f (with cupped hands; against him MHengel, ZNW 60, '69, 182–98; reply by Reynolds ibid. 62, '71, 295f).

2. *fist-fight, boxing* (Hom.+; inscr.) more generally (Jos., Ant. 14, 210) ἐν μέσῳ τῆς πυγμῆς *in the midst of the fight* B 12: 2. M-M.*

πυθόμενος, -εσθαι s. πυνθάνομαι.

πύθων, ωνος, ὁ *the Python*, acc. to Strabo 9, 3, 12 the serpent or dragon that guarded the Delphic oracle; it lived at the foot of Mt. Parnassus, and was slain by Apollo. Later the word came to designate a *spirit of divination*, then also a ventriloquist, who was believed to have such a spirit dwelling in his (or her) belly (Plut., De Def. Orac. 9, p. 414e τοὺς ἐγγαστριμύθους νῦν πύθωνας προσαγορευομένους. Sim., Erotiani Vocum Hippocr. Coll. fgm. 21 p. 105, 20 Nachmanson ['18]; Hesychius and Suidas on ἐγγαστρίμυθος, also L-S-J lex. on the same word.— Suidas on Πύθωνος: δαιμονίου μαντικοῦ. τὰς τε πνεύματι Πύθωνος ἐνθουσιώσας καὶ φαντασίαν κινήσεως παρεχομένας τῇ τοῦ δαιμονίου περιφορᾷ ἠξίου τὸ ἐσόμενον προαγορεῦσαι; Ps.-Clem., Hom. 9, 16 καὶ πύθωνες μαντεύονται, ἀλλ' ὑφ' ἡμῶν ὡς δαίμονες ὁρκιζόμενοι φυγαδεύονται; Syntipas p. 62, 6; 15; 63, 4 πύθωνος πνεῦμα. So as loanw. in rabb.—On the difference betw. ancient and modern ideas of ventriloquism, s. A-JFestugière, RB 54, '47, 133 and cf. Murray, New [Oxford] Engl. Dict. s.v. ventriloquist) πνεῦμα πύθωνα *a spirit of divination* or *prophecy* (in apposition like ἄνθρωπος βασιλεύς Ac 16: 16 (the t.r. has πνεῦμα πύθωνος= 'the spirit of a ventriloquist').—WEbstein, D. Medizin im NT u. im Talmud '03; JTambornino, De Antiquorum Daemonismo '09; FJDölger, Der Exorzismus im altchristl. Taufritual '09; AWikenhauser, Die AG '21, 401ff; TK Oesterreich, D. Besessenheit '21, esp. 319-30. M-M.*

πυκνός, ή, όν *frequent, numerous* (so as early as Od. 14, 36; 3 Macc 1: 28; Ep. Arist. 90; Jos., Ant. 13, 139) ἀσθένειαι 1 Ti 5: 23.—Neut. pl. as adv. *often, frequently* (Hom. +; X., An. 5, 9, 8, De Rep. Lac. 12, 5; Pla., Rep. 6 p. 501B; Plut., Mor. 228D) Mt 9: 14 v.l. (for πολλά); Mk 7: 3 v.l. (s. πυγμή); Lk 5: 33.—Neut. of the comp. πυκνότερον as adv. *more often, more frequently* and in an elative sense *very often, quite frequently* (Pla., Demosth. et al.; PTebt. 41, 3 [II BC]; POxy. 717, 16; 3 Macc 4: 12) also *as often as possible* (POxy. 805 [25 BC] ἀξιῶ δὲ ἀντιφωνεῖν μοι πυκνότερον; PGM 13, 58; 430; Ep. Arist. 318; Bl-D. §244, 1 app.; Rob. 665) Ac 24: 26; 2 Cl 17: 3; IEph 13: 1a; IPol 4: 2 (Clidemus [350 BC] no. 323 fgm. 7 Jac. of the Athenians: συνήεσαν εἰς τὴν Πύκνα ὀνομασθεῖσαν διὰ τὸ τὴν συνοίκησιν πυκνουμένην εἶναι). M-M. B. 888; 986.*

πυκνῶς adv. (posthomeric [Hom. has πυκινῶς]) *frequently, often* (Ps.-X., Cyneg. 6, 22; Plut., Mor. 229E; Jos., Ant. 7, 22; PGM 4, 2569; 2639) IEph 13: 1b; Hm 11: 4; D 16: 2.*

πυκτεύω (X., Pla. +; Dio Chrys. 14[31], 156; Epigr. Gr. 291, 1) *fight with fists, box* symbolically 1 Cor 9: 26. M-M.*

πύλη, ης, ἡ (Hom. +; inscr., pap., LXX; Ep. Arist. 158; Joseph.; Test. 12 Patr.; Sib. Or.; loanw. in rabb.) *gate, door.*

1. lit., of the gates of cities (X., Mem. 3, 9, 7; Maximus Tyr. 15, 3a; Polyaenus 7, 13; Jos., Vi. 108) Lk 7: 12; Ac 9: 24 (a situation as in Appian, Bell. Civ. 4, 12 §48 αἱ πύλαι κατείχοντο in the hunt for proscribed men). ἔξω τῆς πύλης *outside the gate, outside the city* 16: 13; Hb 13: 12 (crucifixion outside the city was the usual practice: Artem. 2, 53 p. 152, 17). Of a gate of the temple in Jerusalem ἡ ὡραία πύλη Ac 3: 10 (s. on ὡραῖος). The prison has τὴν πύλην τὴν σιδηρᾶν 12: 10 (cf. Jos., Bell. 7, 245). πύλας χαλκᾶς συντρίψω B 11: 4 (Ps 106: 16). In the vision of the rock w. a gate(way) Hs 9, 2, 2f; 9, 3, 1f; 4; 9, 4, 1f; 5f; 8; 9, 5, 3; 9, 6, 7; 9, 12, 1-6; 9, 13, 6; 9, 14, 4; 9, 15, 5. On the πύλαι ᾅδου Mt 16: 18 s. ᾅδης 1 and cf. the lit. s.v. κλείς 1 and πέτρα 1b, also JHBernard, The Gates of Hades: Exp. 8th ser. XI '16, 401-9; REppel, Aux sources de la tradition Chrétienne: MGoguel-Festschr. '50, 71-3; OBetz, ZNW 48, '57, 49-77 (Qumran; cf. IQH 6, 24).

2. fig. and symbolically, of the στενὴ πύλη that leads into life Mt 7: 13a, 14 (Sib. Or. 2, 150 π. ζωῆς); cf. also vs. 13b; Lk 13: 24 t.r. (cf. Cebes 15, 1-3 the difficult road and the narrow gate, which afford an ἀνάβασις στενὴ πάνυ to the ἀληθινὴ παιδεία). π. δικαιοσύνης *the gate of righteousness* 1 Cl 48: 2a; cf. b (Ps 117: 19). Also ἡ ἐν δικαιοσύνη (πύλη) vs. 4b. This gate is also called ἡ πύλη τοῦ κυρίου *the gate to the Lord* (or *of the Lord*) vs. 3 (Ps 117: 20). πολλῶν πυλῶν ἀνεῳγυιῶν *since many gates are open* vs. 4a. M-M. B. 466.*

πυλών, ῶνος, ὁ (Polyb.; Diod. S. 13, 75, 7; Cebes 1, 2 al.; inscr., pap., LXX, Joseph.; Test. Zeb. 3: 6. Loanw. in rabb.).

1. *gate*, esp. of the large gate at the entrance of temples and palaces (Ps.-Aristot., De Mundo 6, 8; Plut., Tim. 12, 9; inscr., LXX; Jos., Bell. 1, 617), at the palace of the rich man Lk 16: 20. Of the gates of the heavenly Jerusalem (Berosus in Jos., C. Ap. 1, 140 of the magnificent city gates of Babylon; Cephalio [II AD]: 93 fgm. 5 p. 444, 23 Jac., of Thebes πόλιν μεγάλην πάνυ, δωδεκάπυλον) οἱ πυλῶνες αὐτῆς οὐ μὴ κλεισθῶσιν Rv 21: 25; cf. vss. 12a, b, 13a, b, c, d, 15, 21a, b; 22: 14. Of the gates of a temple or of a city Ac 14: 13.

2. *gateway, portal, vestibule* (Lucian, Nigr. 23) ἡ θύρα τοῦ πυλῶνος (Jos., Bell. 5, 202 δύο ἑκάστου πυλῶνος θύραι) Ac 12: 13. Cf. vs. 14a, b; 10: 17.

3. *gateway, entrance* separated fr. the house by a court (Inscr. Or. Sept. Pont. Eux. I² 32B, 48 [III BC]; Polyb. 2, 9, 3; 4, 18, 2; Diod. S. 1, 47, 1; Ps.-Aristot., De Mundo 6). Peter leaves (ἐξελθόντα) the court (vs. 69) and enters εἰς τὸν πυλῶνα Mt 26: 71, and finally leaves it (vs. 75). M-M.*

πυνθάνομαι mid. dep. (Hom. +; inscr., pap., LXX, Ep. Arist., Philo, Joseph.) impf. ἐπυνθανόμην; 2 aor. ἐπυθόμην (on the use of the two tenses s. Bl-D. §328 app.).

1. *inquire, ask, seek to learn* παρά τινος B 13: 2 (Gen 25: 22). τὶ παρά τινος (Pla., Gorg. 455c; Dit., Syll.³ 1169, 30; 2 Ch 32: 31; Jos., C. Ap. 1, 6) J 4: 52 (ἐκείνην 𝔓⁷⁵ B). τὶ ἀκριβέστερον πυνθάνεσθαι περὶ αὐτοῦ Ac 23: 20 (π. περί τινος as X., An. 5, 5, 25; PHib. 72, 11; POxy. 930, 12; 1064, 4; Esth 6: 4.—π. ἀκριβέστερον as PPetr. II 16, 13 [III BC]). π. (καὶ λέγειν) foll. by dir. quest. Ac 17: 19 D. Foll. by indir. quest. (Pla., Soph. 216D; 2 Macc 3: 9; Jos., Ant. 8, 331 πυθ. τίς εἴη; BGU 893, 26 ἐπύθετο, πόσον ἔχει; POxy. 1063, 6) Lk 15: 26; 18: 36; J 13: 24 𝔓⁶⁶ et al.; Ac 21: 33. π. εἰ w. indic. foll. *inquire whether*. . . 10: 18 (cf. 2 Macc 3: 9; Jos., Ant. 10, 259). π. παρά τινος w. indir. quest. foll. (Lucian, Nigr. 1; Jos., Vi. 258, Ant. 16, 328) Mt 2: 4. Foll. by a dir. quest. (Plut., Demetr. 27, 9) Ac 4: 7; 10: 29; 23: 19.

2. *learn* by inquiry w. ὅτι foll. (X., An. 6, 3, 23; PHamb. 27, 7 [III BC] πυνθανόμενος αὐτοῦ, ὅτι ἀπῆλθεν) Ac 23: 34. π. περί τινος (Appian, Bell. Civ. 4, 123 §515 περὶ τοῦ λιμοῦ) foll. by indir. quest. Dg 1. M-M.*

πυξίς, ίδος, ἡ *box* made of boxwood, then any kind of box, esp. as a container for medicine (Lucian, Philops. 21; Galen XIII 743 K.; Jos., Bell. 1, 598; BGU 1300, 8 [III/II BC]; PRyl. 125, 26f [I AD]; Sb 4324, 17) of a container for poison (as Jos., Bell. 1, 598, Ant. 17, 77) Hv 3, 9, 7.*

πύον, ου, τό (Hippocr. +; Antig. Car. 117) *pus* AP 16: 31.*

πῦρ, ός, τό (Hom. +; inscr., pap., LXX, En., Ep. Arist., Philo, Joseph., Test. 12 Patr.) *fire.*

1. lit.—a. of earthly fire, as an important element in creation Dg 7: 2.—Mt 17: 15; Mk 9: 22; Ac 28: 5; Js 5: 3 (cf. 4 Macc 15: 15); ITr 2: 3. Melting lead 2 Cl 16: 3. Necessary for forging metals Dg 2: 3. Testing precious metals for purity 1 Pt 1: 7; Hv 4, 3, 4; cf. the metaphor Rv 3: 18. For ἄνθρακες πυρός Ro 12: 20 s. ἄνθραξ. For κάμινος (τοῦ) πυρός 1 Cl 45: 7; 2 Cl 8: 2 s. κάμινος. For βάλλειν εἰς (τὸ) π. s. βάλλω 1b.—περιάπτειν πῦρ *kindle a fire* Lk 22: 55. κατακαίειν τι πυρί *burn someth. (up) with fire* pass. Mt 13: 40; τινὰ ἐν πυρί Rv 17: 16 (v.l. without ἐν). Pass. 18: 8. ὑπὸ πυρὸς κατακαίεσθαι MPol 5: 2 (κατακαίω, end). πῦρ καιόμενον 11: 2b (καίω 1a).

πυρὶ καίεσθαι Hb 12: 18; Rv 8: 8 (καίω 1a). Fire is used in comparisons γλῶσσαι ὡσεὶ πυρός Ac 2: 3 (Ezek. Trag. in Euseb., Pr. Ev. 9, 29, 14 ἀπ' οὐρανοῦ φέγγος ὡς πυρὸς ὤφθη ἡμῖν). φλὸξ πυρός *a flame of fire* (Ex 3: 2; Is 29: 6): ὀφθαλμοὶ ὡς φλὸξ πυρός Rv 1: 14; cf. 2: 18; 19: 12.—Of the Christian worker who has built poorly in the congregation it is said σωθήσεται ὡς διὰ πυρός *he will be saved as if through (the) fire,* i.e. like a person who must pass through a wall of fire to escape fr. a burning house (Crates, Ep. 6 κἂν διὰ πυρός; Jos., Ant. 17, 264 διὰ τοῦ πυρός; Diod. S. 1, 57, 7; 8 διὰ τοῦ φλογὸς . . . σωθείς from a burning tent) 1 Cor 3: 15 (s. σῴζω 3). Cf. Jd 23 (ἁρπάζω 2a).—Of the torture of a martyr by fire IRo 5: 3; ISm 4: 2; MPol 2: 3; 11: 2a; 13: 3; 15: 1f; 16: 1; 17: 2. Cf. Hb 11: 34.

b. of fire that is heavenly in origin and nature (cf. Diod. S. 4, 2, 3 of the 'fire' of lightning, accompanying the appearance of Zeus; 16, 63, 3 τὸ θεῖον πῦρ): an angel appears to Moses ἐν φλογὶ πυρὸς βάτου *in the flame of a burning thorn-bush* Ac 7: 30 (cf. Ex 3: 2; PKatz, ZNW 46, '55, 133-8). God makes τοὺς λειτουργοὺς αὐτοῦ πυρὸς φλόγα (cf. Ps 103: 4, esp. in the v.l. [ARahlfs, Psalmi cum Odis '31]) Hb 1: 7; 1 Cl 36: 3. Corresp., there burn before the heavenly throne seven λαμπάδες πυρός Rv 4: 5 and the 'strong angel' 10: 1 has πόδες ὡς στῦλοι πυρός. Fire appears mostly as a means used by God to execute punishment: in the past, in the case of Sodom ἔβρεξεν πῦρ καὶ θεῖον ἀπ' οὐρανοῦ Lk 17: 29 (Gen 19: 24; cf. 1QH 3, 31). Cf. Lk 9: 54 (4 Km 1: 10, 12; Jos., Ant. 9, 23 πῦρ ἀπ' οὐρανοῦ πεσόν). Quite predom. in connection w. the Last Judgment: the end of the world δι' αἵματος καὶ πυρός Hv 4, 3, 3; cf. Ac 2: 19 (Jo 3: 3. Also Sib. Or. 4, 173; 5, 376f); Rv 8: 7. The Judgment Day ἐν πυρὶ ἀποκαλύπτεται makes its appearance with fire 1 Cor 3: 13a; cf. b (JGnilka, Ist 1 Cor 3: 10-15 . . . Fegfeuer?, '55); 2 Pt 3: 7. When Jesus comes again he will reveal himself w. his angels ἐν πυρὶ φλογός (cf. Sir 45: 19) 2 Th 1: 8. Oft. in Rv: fire is cast fr. heaven upon the earth 8: 5; 13: 13; 20: 9 (καταβαίνω 1b). It proceeds fr. the mouths of God's two witnesses 11: 5 and fr. the mouths of the demonic horses 9: 17f. Cf. 16: 8. For πυρὸς ζῆλος ἐσθίειν μέλλοντος τ. ὑπεναντίους Hb 10: 27 s. ζῆλος 1, end.—The fire w. which God punishes sinners οὐ σβέννυται (cf. Is 66: 24) Mk 9: 48; 2 Cl 7: 6; 17: 5. Hence it is called (cf. PGM 5, 147 τὸ πῦρ τὸ ἀθάνατον) (τὸ) πῦρ (τὸ) αἰώνιον (4 Macc 12: 12; Test. Zeb. 10: 3) Mt 18: 8; 25: 41; Jd 7; Dg 10: 7 (opp. τὸ πῦρ τὸ πρόσκαιρον 10: 8). πῦρ ἄσβεστον (ἄσβεστος 1) Mt 3: 12; Mk 9: 43, 45 t.r.; Lk 3: 17; 2 Cl 17: 7; IEph 16: 2. It burns in the γέεννα (τοῦ) πυρός (s. γέεννα and cf. En. 10, 13 τὸ χάος τοῦ πυρός) Mt 5: 22; 18: 9 (cf. 1QS 2, 7f); Mk 9: 47 t.r.; 2 Cl 5: 4 (a saying of Jesus not recorded elsewhere). ἡ λίμνη τοῦ πυρός (καὶ θείου) Rv 19: 20; 20: 10, 14a, b, 15 (cf. Joseph and Aseneth 12, 10 ἄβυσσον τοῦ πυρός); cf. 21: 8; 14: 10, 18; 15: 2. The fiery place of punishment as ἡ κάμινος τοῦ πυρός Mt 13: 42, 50. The fire of hell is also meant in certain parables and allegories, in which trees and vines represent persons worthy of punishment Mt 3: 10; 7: 19; Lk 3: 9; J 15: 6. The one whose coming was proclaimed by John the Baptist βαπτίσει ἐν πνεύματι ἁγίῳ καὶ πυρί; whether πῦρ in Mt 3: 11; Lk 3: 16 refers to the receiving of the Holy Spirit (esp. in Lk 3: 16) or to the fire of divine judgment is debatable; for association of πῦρ with πνεῦμα cf. Ac 2: 3f; Third Corinthians 3: 13 (βαπτίζω 3b). As Lord of Judgment God is called πῦρ καταναλίσκον Hb 12: 29 (Dt 4: 24; 9: 3.—Mesomedes calls Isis πῦρ τέλεον ἄρρητον [Isishymn. p. 145, 14 Peek]).—Of a different

kind is the pagan idea that fire is to be worshipped as a god (Maximus Tyr. 2, 4b of the Persians: πῦρ δέσποτα; Theosophien 14 p. 170, 11 τὸ πῦρ ἀληθῶς θεός) Dg 8: 2.

2. fig. (Charito 2, 4, 7 πῦρ εἰς τ. ψυχήν; Ael. Aristid. 28, 110 K.=49 p. 527 D.: τὸ ἱερὸν κ. θεῖον πῦρ τὸ ἐκ Διός; Aristaen., Ep. 2, 5; PGrenf. I=Coll. p. 177 l. 15 [II BC] of the fire of love) ἡ γλῶσσα πῦρ Js 3: 6, cf. 5 (γλῶσσα 1a). The saying of Jesus πῦρ ἦλθον βαλεῖν ἐπὶ τὴν γῆν Lk 12: 49 seems, in the context where it is now found, to refer to the fire of discord (s. vss. 51-3). πῦρ is also taken as fig. in Agr 3, the sense of which, however, cannot be determined w. certainty (s. JoachJeremias, Unknown Sayings of Jesus, tr. Fuller, '57, 54-6) ὁ ἐγγύς μου ἐγγὺς τοῦ πυρός. ὁ δὲ μακρὰν ἀπ' ἐμοῦ μακρὰν ἀπὸ τῆς βασιλείας (s. ἐγγύς 3. ἐγγὺς εἶναι τοῦ πυρός as someth. dangerous also Charito 6, 3, 9). On the difficult pass. πᾶς πυρὶ ἁλισθήσεται Mk 9: 49 and its variants s. ἁλίζω and cf., in addition to ἅλας 2, NDColeman, JTS 24, '23, 381-96, ET 48, '37, 360-2; PHaupt, Salted with Fire: AJPh 45, '24, 242-5; AFridrichsen, Würzung durch Feuer: Symb. Osl. 4, '26, 36-8; JdeZwaan, Met vuur gezouten worden, Mc 9: 49: NThSt 11, '28, 179-82; RHarris, ET 48, '37, 185f; SEitrem, Opferritus u. Voropfer der Griechen u. Römer '15, 309-44. JBBauer, ThZ 15, '59, 446-50; HZimmermann (Mk 9: 49), ThQ 139, '59, 28-39; TJBaarda (Mk 9: 49), NTS 5, '59, 318-21.—F Lang, TW VI 927-53: πῦρ and related words. M-M. B. 71.**

πυρά, ᾶς, ἡ (Hom.+; PGM 4, 32; LXX; Philo, Conf. Lingu. 157; Sib. Or. 8, 494) in our lit. only of a *pile of combustible* or even of *burning material, a fire* ἅπτειν πυράν (Hdt. 1, 86; 2 Macc 10: 36) Ac 28: 2; cf. Lk 22: 55 v.l.; Ac 28: 3.—Of a *pyre* on which someone is burned (of Croesus: Hdt. 1, 86, 2ff; Ep. 56 of Apollonius of Tyana [Philostrat. I 359, 13]; of Calanus, the wise man of India: Arrian, Anab. 7, 3, 4ff) of a martyr MPol 13: 2f.*

πύργος, ου, ὁ (Hom.+ [a Nordic loanw.: PKretschmer, Glotta 22, '34, 100ff]; inscr., pap., LXX, Philo; Jos., Bell. 5, 144; 147; 151, Ant. 18, 147 al.; Test. 12 Patr.; Sib. Or. 11, 10; 12. Loanw. in rabb.).

1. *tower* ὁ πύργος ἐν τῷ Σιλωάμ Lk 13: 4 (Demetr. of Kallatis [200 BC]: 85 fgm. 6 Jac. πεσόντος τοῦ πύργου πεσεῖν κ. αὐτάς [=25 girls]). Of towers such as are built in a vineyard for watchmen (BGU 650, 8 [60/61 AD]; Is 5: 2) Mt 21: 33; Mk 12: 1; perh. also Lk 14: 28 (but s. 2 below and cf. C-HHunzinger, ZNW Beiheft 26, '60, 211-17 [Gospel of Thomas]).—B 16: 5 (scripture quot., presumably fr. En. 89, 56). In Hermas the church is symbolically pictured as a tower (cf. Sib. Or. 5, 424) Hv 3; 4, 3, 4; s 8 and 9 (149 times).

2. *farm building* (cf. FPreisigke, Her. 54, '19, 93; EMeyer, Her. 55, '20, 100; AAlt, ibid. 334-6; JHasebroek, Her. 57, '22, 621-3; PMMeyer, Ztschr. für vergleichende Rechtswissenschaft 40, '22, 207. Rejected by WCrönert, Gnomon 4, '28, 80) so prob. Lk 14: 28 (but s. 1 above). M-M.*

πυρέσσω (Eur., Hippocr.+; Epict. [s. index Sch.]; M. Ant. 8, 15; Diog. L. 6, 1, 6; Jos., Vi. 404; POsl. 95, 20 [96 AD]; 152, 4) *suffer with a fever* Mt 8: 14; Mk 1: 30. M-M.*

πυρετός, οῦ, ὁ *fever* ([Il. 22, 31]; Aristoph.; Hippocr.; Dit., Syll.³ 1239, 20; 1240, 12; Audollent, Defix. Tab. 74, 6; BGU 956, 2; POxy. 924, 6; 1151, 35; Dt 28: 22; Philo; Jos., Vi. 48) Lk 4: 39. ἀφῆκεν αὐτὴν (αὐτὸν) ὁ πυρετός Mt 8: 15; Mk 1: 31; J 4: 52. In the two passages foll. πυρ.

is used w. συνέχεσθαι (cf. Diod. S. 36, 13, 3 παραχρῆμα πυρετῷ συνεσχέθη; Jos., Ant. 13, 398 πυρετῷ συσχεθείς; POxy. 986, 33 ὄντα πυρετίοις συνεχόμενον), pl. (Demosth. et al.; Hippocr.: CMG I 1 p. 40, 1; 50, 6; w. δυσεντερία p. 57, 27f; 60, 27) πυρετοῖς καὶ δυσεντερίῳ συνεχόμενον Ac 28: 8. συνεχομένη πυρετῷ μεγάλῳ suffering with a severe attack of fever Lk 4: 38 (cf. Diod. S. 32, 10, 3 τῶν πυρετῶν μεγάλων συνεπιγινομένων; Galen, De Diff. Febr. 1, 1 vol. VII 275 Kühn σύνηθες τοῖς ἰατροῖς ὀνομάζειν τὸν μέγαν τε καὶ μικρὸν πυρετόν; Alexander of Aphrodisias, De Febribus Libell. 31 [JLIdeler, Physici et Medici Graeci Minores I 1841, 105f] μικρούς τε καὶ μεγάλους ὀνομάζομεν πυρετούς; Aulus Cornel. Celsus 4, 14 magnae febres.—S. on this JSchuster, M.D., BZ 13, '15, 338ff; HJCadbury, JBL 45, '26, 194f; 203; 207 note); GDunst, ZPE 3, '68, 148-53 (fever-cult). M-M.*

πύρινος, η, ον fiery, the color of fire (Aristot.+; Epigr. Gr. 987 [95 AD]; PTebt. 1, 16 [I BC]; BGU 590, 1; PGM 4, 589; Sir 48: 9 ἐν ἅρματι ἵππων πυρίνων; Ezk 28: 14, 16; En. 14, 11) ἀκρίδες πύριναι fiery locusts Hv 4, 1, 6. Spectral riders wear θώρακας πυρίνους Rv 9: 17 (Sib. Or. 3, 673 ῥομφαῖαι πύριναι). M-M.*

πυρκαϊά, ᾶς, ἡ (Hom.+; trag., Hdt., Aristot.) funeral pyre MPol 13: 2 v.l. Funk (for πυρά).*

πυροειδής, ές (Pla., Leg. 10 p. 895c et al.); Cleanthes: Stoic. fgm. 506) the color of fire, red as fire= bright red (w. αἱματώδης, q.v.) Hv 4, 1, 10; 4, 3, 3.—S. αἷμα 3.*

πυρόω pf. pass. ptc. πεπυρωμένος; 1 aor. ἐπυρώθην (Pind.+; inscr., LXX, Philo) set on fire, burn up, in our lit. only pass. (Ps.-Pla., Axioch. 372A of tortures in Tartarus; Philo).
1. burn—a. lit., of the fiery end of the world οὐρανοὶ πυρούμενοι λυθήσονται 2 Pt 3: 12. Symbolically τὰ βέλη τὰ πεπυρωμένα (cf. βέλος) Eph 6: 16 (cf. Cicero, Tusc. Disp. 5, 27, 76).
b. fig. (act. Cornutus 25 p. 47, 11 πυροῦν τ. ψυχάς; pass., Horapollo 1, 22 ἡ καρδία πυροῦται) burn, be inflamed w. sympathy, readiness to aid, or indignation 2 Cor 11: 29 (cf. 2 Macc 4: 38; 10: 35; 14: 45; 3 Macc 4: 2; Philo, Leg. All. 1, 84 πεπύρωται ἐν εὐχαριστίᾳ θεοῦ. So prob. also the Jewish-Gk. inscr. fr. Tell el Yehudieh ed. Ltzm. [ZNW 22, '23, 282] 18, 5 πατὴρ καὶ μήτηρ οἱ πυρώμενοι='father and mother, who are burning w. grief'; Ltzm. thinks of the burning of the dead, referring to 20, 4 where, however, the act. is used); burn with sexual desire 1 Cor 7: 9 (cf. Anacreontea 11, 15 Preis.: Ἔρως εὐθέως με πύρωσον; PGM 4, 2931 βάλε πυρσὸν ἔρωτα; 36, 111; 200 πυρουμένη; PBerlin 9909, 48; Hos 7: 4; Sir 23: 17; SDGordon, ET 21, '10, 478f).
2. make red hot, cause to glow, heat thoroughly (Lucian, Alex. 21 βελόνην) of metals πεπυρωμένον σίδηρον AP 13: 28. By such heating precious metals are tested and refined (Job 22: 25; Ps 11: 7; 65: 10; Pr 10: 20) Rv 1: 15 (πεπυρωμένης is one of the linguistic peculiarities of Rv [s. καὶ ἔχων which follows soon thereafter]. All the variant readings here are simply corrections. FRehkopf, Joach Jeremias-Festschr., '70, 214-19; 3: 18; MPol 15: 2.—Hv 4, 3, 4 makes a comparison betw. the refining influence of fire on metals and the effect that fiery trials have in removing impurities from Christians. M-M.*

πυρράζω (only in Byzantine writers [Psaltes 332]; LXX has πυρρίζω) be (fiery) red of the color of the morning or evening sky Mt 16: 2f. M-M.*

πυρρός, ά, όν (Aeschyl., Hdt.+; inscr., pap., LXX; En. 18, 7. On the double ρ cf. Bl-D. §34, 2; Mlt.-H. 101) red (as fire) as the apocalyptic color of a horse (Theocr. 15, 53, of a fox standing on its hind legs) Rv 6: 4 (τὸ λευκόν, μέλαν, ἐρυθρόν, χλωρόν are the four basic colors [Theophr., Sens. 13, 73-5]. In Rv, prob. because of the influence of the ἵππος πυρρός of Zech 1: 8 and 6: 2, the word ἐρ. has been changed to its practical equivalent πυρρ.—Cf. Petosiris, fgm. 12 l. 25f: μέλας . . . λοιμὸν [better λιμὸν acc. to l. 187] ποιεῖ, χλωρὸς δὲ νόσους, πυρρὸς δὲ πόλεμον καὶ σφαγάς. RGradwohl, D. Farben im AT, Beih. ZAW 83, '63, 8). Of a dragon Rv 12: 3 (in Diod. S. 1, 88, 4 π. is the color of Typhon, the enemy of the gods. Cf. also Phlegon: 257 fgm. 36, 3, 11 Jac. ὑπὸ λύκου πυρροῦ εὐμεγέθους καταβρωθῆναι). Symbolically of sins πυρρότεραι κόκκου redder than scarlet 1 Cl 8: 3 (quot. of unknown orig.).—For lit. s. αἷμα 3. M-M.*

Πύρρος, ου, ὁ (Gk. lit.; inscr., pap.) Pyrrhus, father of Sopater of Beroea; Sop. accompanied Paul when he took the collection to Jerusalem Ac 20: 4. M-M.*

πύρωσις, εως, ἡ (Aristot., Theophr. et al.; PGM 2, 110; Am 4: 9)—1. lit., pass. the process of burning (Jos., Ant. 1, 203) τὸν καπνὸν τῆς πυρώσεως αὐτῆς Rv 18: 9, 18.
2. fig. ἡ π. τῆς δοκιμασίας the fiery test D 16: 5. π. πρὸς πειρασμὸν γινομένη fiery ordeal to test you 1 Pt 4: 12 (cf. the πύρωσις for testing metals Pr 27: 21). M-M.*

πωλέω impf. ἐπώλουν; 1 aor. ἐπώλησα (Eur., Hdt.+; inscr., pap., LXX; Jos., Vi. 296 al.; Test. 12 Patr.) sell τὶ someth. Mt 13: 44; 19: 21; 21: 12b (on πωλεῖν in the ἱερόν cf. Leges Graecorum Sacrae II 88, 31 LZiehen ['06]; Mk 10: 21; 11: 15b; Lk 12: 33; 18: 22 (PRyl. 113, 8 πάντα τὰ ἐμαυτοῦ πωλήσας); 22: 36; J 2: 14, 16; Ac 5: 1. The obj. is to be supplied 4: 34, 37.—Pass. be offered for sale, be sold (Artem. 4, 15) πᾶν τὸ ἐν μακέλλῳ πωλούμενον 1 Cor 10: 25. W. gen. of price (X., Mem. 1, 2, 36; PPetr. II 38(b), 2 [243 BC] τὸ ἔλαιον πωλεῖσθαι τιμῆς . . . ; Jos., Vi. 75.—Bl-D. §179, 1; Rob. 510f) Mt 10: 29; Lk 12: 6. Abs. (opp. ἀγοράζειν; s. ἀγοράζω 1) Lk 17: 28; Rv 13: 17. οἱ πωλοῦντες the sellers, dealers Mt 25: 9; Lk 19: 45. W. οἱ ἀγοράζοντες (cf. Is 24: 2) Mt 21: 12a; Mk 11: 15a. On ascetic practices, s. HvCampenhausen, Tradition and Life in the Church, '68, 90-122. M-M.*

πῶλος, ου, ὁ (Hom.+; inscr., pap., LXX) the colt of a horse (Hom.+; besides, it refers to a horse that is old enough to use: Hipponax 41 Diehl; Anacr. 88 D.; X., De Re Equ. 1, 6 al.; PGM 2, 95), but also young animal, in our lit. only ass's foal, young donkey (Geopon. 16, 21, 6; PLille 8, 9 [III BC]; BGU 373, 7; Gen 32: 15; 49: 11a, b) Mt 21: 2, 7; Mk 11: 2, 4f, 7; Lk 19: 30, 33a, b, 35. W. ref. to Zech 9: 9; Mt 21: 5; J 12: 15.—But since the publication of this entry in his fourth ed., WBauer has made more extensive researches, publ. in JBL 72, '53, 220-9: The 'Colt' of Palm Sunday (Der Palmesel); the German original in WBauer, Aufsätze u. kleine Schriften, ed. G Strecker, '67, 109-20. Here he shows that π. in Gk. lit. fr. Homer down means young animal when another animal is named in its context (e.g. the donkey in the exx. fr. Geopon., PLille and BGU above), but simply horse (not colt) when no other animal is so found. W. this as a background Bauer prefers horse for the passages in Mk and Lk.—See PNepper-Christensen, Das Mt-evangelium, '58, 143-8; HWKuhn, Das Reittier Jesu usw., ZNW 50, '59, 82-91; OMichel, Einzugsgeschichte, NTS 6, '59/'60, 81f, TW VI, 959-61: πῶλος.—S. also the lit. s.v. ὄνος. M-M. B. 171.*

πῶλυψ, ποs, ὁ *octopus* (so Epicharmus in Athen. 7 p. 323ꜰ; Diphilus Siphnius [III ʙᴄ] ibid. 8 p. 356ᴇ) B 10: 5; s. πολύπους.*

πώποτε adv. (Hom.+; inscr., pap., LXX, Joseph.) *ever, at any time* Dg 8: 11; MPol 8: 1. Usu. used w. a neg. As a rule the verb w. it stands in a past tense *never, not ever* οὐδεὶς πώποτε *no one ever* (X., An. 1, 6, 11; Jos., C. Ap. 2, 124, Ant. 17, 310) Lk 19: 30; J 1: 18 (Galen II p. 66 K. μηδ' ἑωρακέναι πώποτε; PGM 5, 102 Osiris, ὃν οὐδεὶς εἶδε πώποτε); 8: 33; 1 J 4: 12. Cf. J 5: 37.—Only rarely of the future (Batr. 178; 1 Km 25: 28; PGM 4, 291) οὐ μὴ διψήσει πώποτε *he will never thirst again* J 6: 35. M-M.*

πωρόω 1 aor. ἐπώρωσα; pf. πεπώρωκα J 12: 40 t.r. Pass.: 1 aor. ἐπωρώθην; pf. ptc. πεπωρωμένος (Hippocr., Aristot.+; Job 17: 7 [of the eyes=become dim]) *harden, petrify*, in our lit. only fig., mostly of hearts τὴν καρδίαν τινός *make dull* or *obtuse* or *blind* J 12: 40 (ἐπήρωσεν 𝔓⁶⁶ 𝔓⁷⁵ et al.); pass. ἦν αὐτῶν ἡ καρδία πεπωρωμένη Mk 6: 52; cf. 8: 17; Hm 4, 2, 1; 12, 4, 4.—Of the νοήματα 2 Cor 3: 14. Of persons themselves Ro 11: 7.—Zahn on Ro, exc. III p. 618-20; Windisch on 2 Cor 3: 14; KLSchmidt, on KLSchmidt, Verstockung des Menschen durch Gott: ThZ 1, '45, 1-17. M-M.*

πώρωσις, εως, ἡ (Hippocr., Galen; on the history of the word s. JARobinson, JTS 3, '02, 81-93, Eph '04, 264ff) *hardening, dulling* in our lit. only fig. (Test. Levi 13: 7 πώρωσις ἁμαρτίας) *dullness, insensibility, obstinacy* ἡ π. τῆς καρδίας (s. πωρόω and LCerfaux, Muséon 59, '46, 267-79) Mk 3: 5; Eph 4: 18. π. τῷ Ἰσραὴλ γέγονεν *insensibility has come over Israel* Ro 11: 25. M-M.*

πῶs interrog. particle (Hom.+; inscr., pap., LXX, En., Ep. Arist., Philo, Joseph., Test. 12 Patr.) *how? in what way?*—1. in direct questions—a. to determine how someth. has come to be, how someth. is happening, or should happen; w. indic. *how? in what?* πῶς ἔσται τοῦτο; Lk 1: 34. πῶς ἀναγινώσκεις; 10: 26; cf. Mk 12: 26. πῶς οὖν ἠνεῴχθησάν σου οἱ ὀφθαλμοί; J 9: 10.—3: 4, 9; 9: 19 (π. οὖν), 26; Ro 4: 10 (π. οὖν); 1 Cor 15: 35 (cf. 1 Ch 13: 12); B 5: 5 (π. οὖν); IEph 19: 2 (π. οὖν); Hm 3: 3 (π. οὖν). W. the special mng. *with what right? in what sense?* πῶς λέγουσιν οἱ γραμματεῖς ὅτι ὁ Χριστὸς υἱὸς Δαυὶδ ἐστιν; Mk 12: 35.—Mt 22: 43 (π. οὖν), 45; Lk 20: 41, 44 (cf. Gen 39: 9); J 12: 34.—γέγραπται Mk 9: 12.

b. in questions indicating surprise *how is it (possible) that? I do not understand how* (Manetho in Jos., C. Ap. 259 a series of questions expressing surprise, introduced again and again by πῶς; Lucian, Deor. Conc. 10 πῶς φέρεις;) πῶς παρ' ἐμοῦ πεῖν αἰτεῖς; J 4: 9.—7: 15; Ac 2: 8; Gal 4: 9. W. a neg. πῶς οὐ νοεῖτε; *how is it possible that you do not understand?* Mt 16: 11; Mk 8: 21 v.l. πῶς οὐκ ἔχετε πίστιν; *how is it that you have no faith?* Mk 4: 40.—8: 21 t.r.; Mt 21: 20; Lk 12: 56.

c. in questions denoting disapproval or rejection *with what right? how dare you?* πῶς ἐρεῖς τῷ ἀδελφῷ σου; Mt 7: 4 (πῶς ἐρεῖς as Jer 2: 23). πῶς εἰσῆλθες ὧδε; *how is it that you are bold enough to come in here?* 22: 12. πῶς σὺ λέγεις; *how can you say?* (cf. Job 33: 12) J 14: 9.—Lk 6: 42; *what does he mean by saying?* J 6: 42; 8: 33; 1 Cor 15: 12; Gal 2: 14.

d. in rhetorical questions that call an assumption into question or reject it altogether *how (could or should)?=by no means, it is impossible that* (Job 25: 4) πῶς (οὖν) σταθήσεται ἡ βασιλεία αὐτοῦ; Mt 12: 26; Lk 11: 18. Cf.

Mt 12: 29, 34; Mk 3: 23; 4: 13; J 3: 12; 5: 44, 47; 6: 52; 9: 16; 14: 5 (KBeyer, Semitische Syntax im NT, '62, 94f). ἐπεὶ πῶς κρινεῖ ὁ θεὸς τὸν κόσμον; *otherwise* (i.e. if he were unjust) *it would be impossible for God to judge the world* Ro 3: 6. Cf. 6: 2; 1 Cor 14: 7, 9, 16; 1 Ti 3: 5; Hb 2: 3; 1 J 3: 17; 4: 20 t.r.; MPol 9: 3; Hv 3, 9, 10.—If πῶς is accompanied by a neg., the 'impossible' becomes *most surely, most certainly* (Hyperid. 3, 35; 5, 15; Pr 15: 11 πῶς οὐχί; Ep. Arist. 149; Jos., C. Ap. 1, 256) πῶς οὐχὶ τὰ πάντα ἡμῖν χαρίσεται; Ro 8: 32.—2 Cor 3: 8.—As an exceptional case the opt. w. ἄν (potential; cf. Bl-D. §385, 1; Rob. 938; 1021f and Ael. Aristid. 29 p. 557 D.) πῶς γὰρ ἂν δυναίμην;=it is impossible for me to do so Ac 8: 31 (cf. Gen 44: 8; Dt 28: 67; Sir 25: 3).

e. in questions of deliberation w. a deliberative subjunctive (Bl-D. §366, 1; Rob. 934f.—Epict. 4, 1, 100; 2 Km 23: 3; Sir 49: 11; Ps.-Clem., Hom. 19, 2) πῶς οὖν πληρωθῶσιν αἱ γραφαί; Mt 26: 54. πῶς ὁμοιώσωμεν τὴν βασιλείαν; *what comparison can we find for the Kingdom?* Mk 4: 30. πῶς φύγητε; *how are you to escape?*=you will not escape at all Mt 23: 33. πῶς οὖν w. subj. Ro 10: 14a, foll. by πῶς δέ and the subj. three times in vss. 14b, c, 15.—Hs 5, 7, 3.

2. in indirect questions—a. w. indic. after verbs of knowing, saying, asking etc. ἀκούειν B 7: 3. ἀπαγγέλλειν Lk 8: 36; 1 Th 1: 9. βλέπειν 1 Cor 3: 10; Eph 5: 15. διηγεῖσθαι Mk 5: 16; Ac 9: 27a, b; 12: 17. εἰδέναι (X., Mem. 1, 2, 36) J 9: 21; Col 4: 6; 2 Th 3: 7. ἐπέχειν Lk 14: 7. ἐπιδεικνύειν B 6: 13. ἐπισκέπτεσθαι Ac 15: 36. ἐπίστασθαι 20: 18. ἐρωτᾶν J 9: 15. θεωρεῖν Mk 12: 41. καταμαθεῖν Mt 6: 28 (on π. αὐξάνουσιν here s. PKatz, JTS 5, '54; 207-9); ISm 6: 2. κατανοεῖν Lk 12: 27; 1 Cl 24: 1; 37: 2. μνημονεύειν Rv 3: 3. νοεῖν 1 Cl 19: 3. ὁρᾶν 50: 1.—The addition of an article gives the indir. question the value of a noun παρελάβετε τὸ πῶς δεῖ ὑμᾶς περιπατεῖν 1 Th 4: 1 (s. also 2b below).—In some of the passages given under 2a πῶς could have the same mng. as ὅτι *that*, in accordance w. the tendency in later Gk. (Epict.; M. Ant. 9, 40; Jos., Ant. 12, 205; BGU 37, 6 [50 ᴀᴅ]; PRyl. 235, 6 ἐθαύμασα δὲ πῶς οὐκ ἐδήλωσάς μοι. Cf. GNHatzidakis, Einl. in die neugriech. Gramm. 1892, 19; Rdm.² 196; Bl-D. §396; Rob. 1032). That is clearly the mng. in Mt 12: 4; Mk 2: 26; Ac 11: 13; B 11: 1; 14: 6; 1 Cl 34: 5.

b. w. deliberative subjunctive μὴ μεριμνήσητε πῶς ἢ τί λαλήσητε Mt 10: 19.—Mk 11: 18; 14: 1, 11; Lk 12: 11. μεριμνᾷ πῶς ἀρέσῃ 1 Cor 7: 32, 33, 34 (t.r. has the fut. in Mk 11: 18 and 1 Cor 7: 32-4; cf. Herodian 5, 4, 9 ἠγνόουν, πῶς χρήσονται τῷ πράγματι). In this case, too, the article can be added (s. 2a above) Lk 22: 2, 4; Ac 4: 21.

3. in exclamations *how . . . !* (X., An. 6, 5, 19 al.; Epict. 1, 16, 13; 4, 1, 115; 116, Ench. 24, 3 πῶς ἄνισοί ἐστε καὶ ἀγνώμονες; M. Ant. 6, 27.—Bl-D. §436; Rob. 302; OLagercrantz, Eranos 18, '18, 26ff; KRupprecht, Philol. 80, '24, 207) πῶς δύσκολόν ἐστιν Mk 10: 24; cf. vs. 23; Lk 18: 24. πῶς συνέχομαι 12: 50. πῶς ἐφίλει αὐτόν J 11: 36.—Hm 11: 20; 12, 4, 2. JBauer, Pōs in der gr. Bibel, NovT 2, '57, 81-91. M-M.**

πῶs enclitic particle (Hom.+; inscr., pap., LXX, Jos., C. Ap. 2, 24) *somehow, in some way, perhaps* ἐάν πως (cf. Dit., Syll.³ 364, 24 [III ʙᴄ]; 3 Km 18: 5) ISm 4: 1. W. a neg. οὐδ' ἄν πως οἱ ἄνθρωποι ἐσώθησαν *men could in no way have been saved* B 5: 10.—In combination w. εἰ and μή s. εἰ VI 12 (also Jos., Bell. 6, 442, Ant. 2, 159) and μήπως. M-M.*

P

ρ′ as a numeral=100 (Jos., C. Ap. 2, 134) Hv 4, 1, 6.*

'Ραάβ (רָחָב) ἡ indecl. (LXX.—In Joseph. 'Ραάβη [v.l. 'Ραχάβη], ης [Ant. 5, 8]) Rahab, a harlot in Jericho who, acc. to Josh 2, saved the Israelite spies by hiding them. For this reason she was spared when the city was taken (Josh 6: 17, 25). Mentioned as a model of righteousness by faith and of hospitality Hb 11: 31; Js 2: 25; 1 Cl 12: 1, 3. FWYoung, JBL 67, '48, 339-45. S. also 'Ραχάβ (Bl-D. §39, 3; Mlt.-H. 109).*

ῥαββί (also ῥαββεί; on the interchange of ει and ι s. Bl-D. §38 app.; W-S. §5, 13a; cf. Mlt.-H. 76f.—EbNestle, ZNW 7, '06, 184) rabbi from רַב 'lord, master', רַבִּי 'my lord', properly a form of address, and so throughout our lit., then an honorary title for outstanding teachers of the law Mt 23: 7f (here, too, ῥαββί is a form of address). Of John the Baptist, whom his disciples addressed in this manner J 3: 26. Otherw. always of Jesus: Mt 26: 25, 49; Mk 9: 5; 10: 51 v.l.; 11: 21; 14: 45; J 1: 49; 4: 31; 6: 25; 9: 2; 11: 8. κύριε ῥ. Mk 10: 51 D; cf. the apocryphal gospel fgm. ZNW 22, '23, 153f. With the transl. διδάσκαλε, which paraphrases the sense J 1: 38; cf. 3: 2.—Schürer II⁴375f; The Jewish Encyclopedia X '05, 294ff; Dalman, Worte 272-80; ThReinach, Revue des Études juives 48, '04, 191-6 (inscr. fr. Cyprus: εὐχὴ ῥαββὶ 'Αττικοῦ); Billerb. I 916f. M-M.*

ῥαββουνί (also written ῥαββουνεί, ῥαββονί, ῥαββονεί, s. on ῥαββί), properly a heightened form of רַבָּן and beside it רַבּוֹן, w. suffix רַבּוּנִי or רַבּוֹנִי my Lord, my Master. Jesus is so addressed in Mk 10: 51 and J 20: 16; in the latter pass. διδάσκαλε is added as a transl.—E Kautzsch, Grammatik des Bibl.-Aramäischen 1884, 10; Dalman, Gramm.² §35, 2, Worte 267; 279, Jesus 12; Schürer II⁴ 377; Billerb. II 25; PKahle, The Cairo Geniza '47, 129 (exx. fr. Jewish sources); WFAlbright, Recent Discoveries in Palestine and J, in CHDodd-Festschr. '56, 158 ('my dear [or] little master').*

ῥαβδίζω (since Pherecrates Com. [V BC] 50; Aristoph.; Theophr.; PRyl. 148, 20; LXX) 1 aor. pass. ἐραβδίσθην (on the quest. whether to spell it ἐρ- or ἐρρ- s. Bl-D. §11, 1; Mlt.-H. 101f; 192f) beat with a rod (Aristoph., Lys. 587; Diod. S. 19, 101, 3) of the punishment known in Lat. as verberatio; Paul suffered it three times acc. to 2 Cor 11: 25; in his case it was prob. a punishment prescribed by city magistrates, cf. Ac 16: 22.—ThMommsen, ZNW 2, '01, p. 89, 1. M-M.*

ῥαβδίον, ου, τό (Theophr. et al.; Ezk 21: 26 v.l.) dim. of ῥάβδος stick, twig Hs 8, 1, 2f; 8, 2, 9.*

ῥάβδος, ου, ἡ (Hom.+; inscr.; PSI 168, 16; PTebt. 44, 20; LXX; Philo; Jos., Bell. 2, 365f, Ant. 5, 284) rod, staff, stick gener. Rv 11: 1; 52 times in Hb. Of the test involving the rods (Num 17) 1 Cl 43: 2-5; Hb 9: 4 (Num 17: 23). Of the shepherd's staff (Mi 7: 14) Hv 5: 1; s 6, 2, 5. Symbolically ποιμαίνειν τινὰ ἐν ῥ. σιδηρᾷ (ποιμαίνω 2aγ and cf. PGM 36, 109) Rv 2: 27; 12: 5; 19: 15. Of a traveler's staff (lit. s.v. ὑπόδημα) Mt 10: 10; Mk 6: 8; Lk 9: 3. Of the ruler's staff, the scepter (Pind., Ol. 9, 50; LXX) Hb 1: 8 (Ps 44: 7). Of a 'magic' wand (Lucian, Dial. Deor. 7, 4, Dial. Mort. 23, 3) Hv 3, 2, 4; s 9, 6, 3. Of a stick as a means of punishment (Pla., Leg. 3 p. 700c; Plut., Mor. 268D; 693F; Ex 21: 20; Is 10: 24) ἐν ῥάβδῳ ἔρχεσθαι (opp. ἐν ἀγάπῃ) come with a stick 1 Cor 4: 21

(cf. ἐν 1 4cβ). ῥάβδοι πυρός fiery rods AP 19: 33. Of an old man's staff Hb 11: 21 (Gen 47: 31). M-M.**

ῥαβδοῦχος, ου, ὁ (Aristoph., Thu.+; inscr., pap.) orig. 'staff-bearer', then of the Roman lictor (Polyb.+; Diod. S. 5, 40, 1; Plut., Mor. 280A διὰ τί λικτώρεις τοὺς ῥαβδούχους ὀνομάζουσι; Herodian 7, 8, 5.—Joseph. does not have the word, but ῥάβδοι in Bell. 2, 365f prob. refers to the fasces or bundles of sticks carried by the lictors), roughly equiv. to constable, policeman. The στρατηγοί (q.v.) of Philippi had two lictors in attendance on them (JMarquardt, Röm. Staatsverwaltung I² 1881 p. 175, 7) Ac 16: 35, 38. M-M.*

ῥαβιθά. In Mk 5: 41 codex D reads ραββι θαβιτα; this is meant for ῥαβιθά, the fem. of râbiâ, girl; accordingly ῥ. = ταλιθά, which is read by the majority of witnesses.— Wlh. ad loc.; FSchultess, ZNW 21, '22, 243 note.*

'Ραγαύ (רְעוּ), ὁ indecl. (LXX.—In Jos., Ant. 1, 148 v.l. 'Ράγαους) Reu, son of Peleg and father of Serug (Gen 11: 18-21), in the genealogy of Jesus Lk 3: 35.*

ῥαδιούργημα, ατος, τό (Dionys. Hal. 1, 77; Plut., Pyrrh. 6, 7, Mor. 860D; Ps.-Lucian, Calumn. 20) prank, roguish trick, but also of more serious misdeeds, knavery, crime (Oenomaus in Euseb., Pr. Ev. 5, 26, 2) ῥ. πονηρόν a serious piece of villainy Ac 18: 14 (w. ἀδίκημα).*

ῥαδιουργία, ας, ἡ (X.+) frivolity, but then a somewhat mild expr. for wickedness, villainy, deceit, fraud, unscrupulousness (Polyb. 12, 10, 5; Diod. S. 5, 11, 1; Plut., Cato Min. 16, 3; PMagd. 35, 11 [216 BC]; BGU 226, 14 [99 AD]; POxy. 237 VIII, 15; PStrassb. 40, 30; Philo, Cher. 80) w. δόλος Ac 13: 10.—AWikenhauser, BZ 8, '10, 273. M-M.*

ῥᾳδίως adv. (Att. [Hom.+ in the form ῥηιδίως]; Dit., Or. 508, 8; PPetr. II 11, 1; 4; PGiess. 47, 26; POxy. 471, 54; Philo; Jos., Bell. 3, 99; 6, 157, Ant. 11, 240) easily Hv 4, 1, 2; Papias 3.*

ῥαθυμέω (X., Pla.+; Dit., Or. 521, 15; pap., LXX; Philo, Migr. Abr. 133; Jos., Ant. 14, 166), better **ῥᾳθυμέω** (Zen.-P. 83 [=Sb 6789], 6; PHib. 46, 12 [III BC]) 1 aor. ἐραθύμησα be unconcerned, be idle, relax Hv 1, 3, 2.*

ῥαίνω 1 aor. ἔρρανα (Hom.+; inscr.; pap. [Sb 8000, 17—III AD]; LXX; Jos., Ant. 3, 205; 242; 4, 79; 81) sprinkle τι someth. ῥ. ὕδωρ sprinkle water (Ezk 36: 25) in cleaning a place Hs 9, 10, 3. Pass. Rv 19: 13 v.l. (Lucian, Anach. 11 αἵματι ῥαινόμενος).*

ῥακά (also written ῥαχά; so as an uncomplimentary, perh. foul epithet in a Zenon pap. of 257 BC: Sb 7638, 7 'Αντίοχον τὸν ῥαχᾶν [s. on this ECColwell, JBL 53, '34, 351-4; Gdspd., Probs. 20-3; MSmith, JBL 64, 1945, 502f]) Mt 5: 22, a term of abuse, as a rule derived fr. the Aramaic רֵיקָא or רֵיקָה 'empty one', found (Billerb. I 278f) in the Talmud (EKautzsch, Gramm. des Biblisch-Aramäischen 1884, 10; Dalman, Gramm.² 173f; SIFeigin, Journ. of Near Eastern Stud. 2, '43, 195f; Mlt.-H. 152 w. note 3) fool, empty-head. Doubt as to the correctness of this derivation is expressed by Wlh. and Zahn ad loc.; FSchultess, ZNW 21, '22, 241-3. Among the ancient interpreters, the Gk. Onomastica, Jerome, Hilary, and the Opus Imperfectum p. 62 (Migne, Gr. 56, 690) take ῥ. as=κενός=Lat. vacuus=empty-head, numbskull, fool,

Chrysostom says (VII p. 214 Montf.): τὸ δὲ ρακὰ οὐ μεγάλης ἐστὶν ὕβρεως ρῆμα . . . ἀντὶ τοῦ σύ. The same thing in somewhat different words in Basilius, Regulae 51 p. 432c: τί ἐστί ρακά; ἐπιχώριον ρῆμα ἠπιωτέρας ὕβρεως, πρὸς τοὺς οἰκειοτέρους λαμβανόμενον. Sim., Hecataeus (in Plut., Mor. 354D) explains the name Ammon as coming fr. a form of address common among the Egyptians: προσκλητικὴν εἶναι τὴν φωνήν.—SKrauss, OLZ 22, '19, 63; JLeipoldt, CQR 92, '21, 38; FBussby, ET 74, '64, 26. S. the lit. s.v. μωρός. M-M.*

ρἀκος, ους, τό—1. *tattered garment, rag* (Hom.+; POxy. 117, 14; Is 64: 5) ρἀκη ρυπαρά *filthy rags* (Cebes 10, 1; Plut., Mor. 168D) AP 15: 30.
2. *piece of cloth, patch* (Hdt. 7, 76; Hippocr. et al.; Artem. 1, 13; PGM 4, 1082; 3192; 7, 208; 359; Jer 45: 11; Jos., Ant. 6, 289) ἐπίβλημα ρἀκους ἀγνάφου *a patch made of a piece of new cloth* Mt 9: 16; Mk 2: 21 (RRLewis, ET 45, '34, 185). M-M. B. 398.*

Ῥαμά (רָמָה), ἡ indecl. (Judg 19: 13; 3 Km 15: 17.—Jos., Ant. 8, 303f has Ἀρμαθών, ῶνος) *Rama*, a city in the tribe of Benjamin, about six miles north of Jerusalem Mt 2: 18 (Jer 38: 15). Buhl, Geogr. 172; Dalman, Orte⁾ 29.*

ραντίζω (Ael. Dion. π. 40 ἐρραντισμένος αἵματι; Athen. 12 p. 521A; Lev 6: 20; 4 Km 9: 33.—Thumb 223) fut. ραντιῶ; 1 aor. ἐράντισα (on the quest. whether to spell it w. one ρ or two s. Bl-D. §11, 1; Mlt.-H. 101f); pf. pass. ptc. ρεραντισμένος (Bl-D. §68; Mlt.-H. 100; Kühner-Bl. I p. 278, 5).
1. *(be)sprinkle* w. acc., of the rite of purification (Num 19) τὸν λαὸν ἐράντισεν *he sprinkled the people* Hb 9: 19. Cf. B 8: 1 and, without the acc. (supplied fr. the context) 8: 3f. τί τινι *someth. w. someth.* Hb 9: 21. ραντιεῖς με ὑσσώπῳ 1 Cl 18: 7 (Ps 50: 9).—Pass. (s. above) ἱμάτιον ρεραντισμένον αἵματι *a garment sprinkled with blood* Rv 19: 13 v.l. (for βεβαμμένον; there are also other variants). The act. is also used of liquids and of other things that *sprinkle someone* Hb 9: 13.
2. The mid. is found in our lit. w. the mng. *cleanse, purify*—a. *cleanse* or *wash oneself* ἐὰν μὴ ραντίσωνται οὐκ ἐσθίουσιν Mk 7: 4 (v.l. βαπτίσωνται; s. βαπτίζω 1).
b. *purify someth. for oneself*, fig. ρεραντισμένοι τὰς καρδίας ἀπὸ συνειδήσεως πονηρᾶς *after we have purified our hearts of an evil conscience* Hb 10: 22. M-M.*

ραντισμα, ατος, τό (Vett. Val. 110, 17) *sprinkling* ἐν τῷ αἵματι τοῦ ραντίσματος αὐτοῦ *by his sprinkled blood* B 5: 1.*

ραντισμός, οῦ, ὁ (LXX) *sprinkling*. The blood of Jesus is called αἷμα ραντισμοῦ *blood of sprinkling*, i.e. *blood that is sprinkled* for atonement Hb 12: 24 (cf. Num 19: 9 al. ὕδωρ ραντισμοῦ). The Christians are destined by God's choice εἰς ραντισμὸν αἵματος Ἰησοῦ Χρ. *to be sprinkled with the blood of Christ* and thus have their sins expiated 1 Pt 1: 2. M-M.*

ραπίζω (since Xenophanes in Diog. L. 8, 36; Hdt.; LXX) fut. ραπίσω; 1 aor. ἐράπισα (on the spelling w. one ρ or two cf. Bl-D. §11, 1; Mlt.-H. 101f) lit., and almost always in secular authors *strike with a club* or *rod*; the abs. ἐράπισαν Mt 26: 67 could have this mng. But in the other places in our lit. the sense is clearly *strike with the open hand*, esp. in the face, *slap* (Suidas: ραπίσαι: πατάσσειν τὴν γνάθον ἀπλῇ τῇ χειρί.—Hyperid., fgm. 97 and Plut., Mor. 713C) ρ. τινὰ ἐπὶ κόρρης; Achilles Tat. 2, 24;

5, 23; 6, 20 κατὰ κόρρης; Jos., Ant. 8, 408 in retelling the story of 3 Km 22: 24 uses ραπίζειν instead of πατάσσειν ἐπὶ τὴν σιαγόνα; 1 Esdr 4: 30; Hos 11: 4 ρ. ἐπὶ τὰς σιαγόνας; Phryn. p. 175) ρ. τινὰ εἰς τὴν σιαγόνα αὐτοῦ *slap someone on the cheek* Mt 5: 39 (s. σιαγών). Also τὰς σιαγόνας τινὸς ρ. GP 3: 9. M-M.*

ράπισμα, ατος, τό lit. *a blow with a club, rod*, or *whip* (Antiphanes in Athen. 14 p. 623B; Lucian, Dial. Mer. 8, 2) so perh. οἱ ὑπηρέται ραπίσμασιν αὐτὸν ἔλαβον Mk 14: 65 (cf. λαμβάνω 1ea). But even here it may have the mng. that is certain for the other passages in our lit., *a slap in the face* (s. ραπίζω and cf. ράπισμα Ael. Dion. ε, 55 [ράπισμα τὸ ἐπὶ τῆς γνάθου]; Alciphr. 3, 3, 2; schol. on Pla. 508D, also Anth. Pal. 5, 289 [VI AD] ρ. ἀμφὶ πρόσωπα; Act. Jo. 90 p. 195f B.) διδόναι ράπισμά τινι *give someone a slap in the face* J 18: 22 (but s. Field, Notes 105f); pl. 19: 3. ἐὰν τίς σοι δῷ ράπισμα εἰς τὴν δεξιὰν σιαγόνα D 1: 4. τιθέναι τὰς σιαγόνας εἰς ραπίσματα *offer the cheeks to slaps* B 5: 14 (Is 50: 6).—PBenoit, Les Outrages à Jésus Prophète, OCullmann-Festschr., '62, 92–110. M-M.*

ράσσω (Demosth. 54, 8; Achilles Tat. 5, 23, 5; LXX) *strike, dash, throw down* τινά *someone* Mk 9: 18 D (for ρήσσω, q.v. 2a).*

ραφίς, ίδος, ἡ *needle*, esp. one used for sewing (Hippocr., Morb. 2, 66 al.; POxy. 736, 75) τρῆμα ραφίδος *the eye of a needle* Mt 19: 24. Also τρυμαλιὰ ρα. Mk 10: 25; Lk 18: 25 t.r.—See s.v. βελόνη, also Field, Notes 196; PSMinear, JBL 61, '42, 157–69. M-M. B. 412.*

ραχά s. ρακά.

Ῥαχάβ (רָחָב) ἡ indecl. *Rahab* (s. Ῥαάβ.—Jos., Ant. 5, 8; 11; 15 al. has beside Ῥαάβη, ης [Ant. 5, 8], the v.l. Ῥαχάβη), in the genealogy of Jesus Mt 1: 5, wife of Salmon and mother of Boaz.—S. on Θαμάρ.*

ραχή, ἡ s. ράχος.

Ῥαχήλ (רָחֵל), ἡ indecl. (LXX, Philo, Test. 12 Patr.—Joseph. has Ῥάχηλα, ας [Ant. 1, 301]) *Rachel*, Jacob's wife Mt 2: 18 (Jer 38: 15).*

ραχία, ας, ἡ name of a berry-bush, perh. *the blackberry* ἐπὶ φρύγανον τὸ λεγόμενον ρ. *on a bush called the blackberry* B 7: 8 (but s. the textual tradition in Bihlmeyer).*

ράχος (ραχός?), ου, ἡ *thorn-bush* (since Hdt. [7, 142 ρηχός]; inscr.: Leges Graecorum Sacrae II 153 [III BC] LZiehen ['06]; BGU 1466, 4 [I BC]), name of a bush bearing sweet fruits, perh. *the blackberry* (cf. ραχία, w. which the text of Gebh.-Harn.-Zahn interchanges it as an equivalent. Bihlmeyer has ραχή in both places) B 7: 8 (JRHarris, On the Locality of Pseudo-Barnabas, JBL 9, 1890, 60–70).*

Ῥεβέκκα, ας (רִבְקָה), ἡ (declined in LXX, Philo, and Joseph.) *Rebecca*, wife of Isaac Ro 9: 10; B 13: 2 (Gen 25: 21), 3.*

ρέδη, ης, ἡ (acc. to Quintilian 1, 5, 57 orig. a Celtic word [s. also Caesar, Bell. Gall. 1, 51; 6, 30]. It came into Gk. lit. by way of Lat. authors [in the form 'reda' or 'raeda' in Cicero; Horace, Sat. 1, 5, 86; 2, 6, 42; Suetonius, Jul. 57 al.]. S. on it, as well as on the spelling ραίδη, Bl-D. §5, 1d; 41, 1; Mlt.-H. 81; 155; Hahn 263, 5 [lit.]) *a (four-wheeled) carriage* Rv 18: 13 (v.l. ραίδη). M-M.*

Ῥεμφάν, Ῥεφάν s. Ῥομφά.

Ῥέος, ου, ὁ *Rheus* (s. Hdb. on IPhld 11: 1), surnamed Agathopus (s. Ἀγαθόπους) IPhld 11: 1; ISm 10: 1.*

ῥεριμμένος s. ῥίπτω.

ῥέω (Hom.+; inscr., pap., LXX, Philo; Jos., Bell. 6, 105 μνήμη ῥέουσα δι᾽ αἰῶνος; Sib. Or. 3, 54) fut. ῥεύσω (Bl-D. §77; Rob. 355).
    1. *flow* symbolically, of the Redeemer ποταμοὶ ἐκ τ. κοιλίας αὐτοῦ ῥεύσουσιν ὕδατος ζῶντος J 7: 38 (Hdb. ad loc., and s. κοιλία 3).
    2. fig. *(over)flow with, have more than enough of* τὶ someth. γῆ ῥέουσα γάλα καὶ μέλι *a land flowing w. milk and honey* (LXX) B 6: 8, 10, 13 (for a more detailed treatment of this pass. s. Windisch, Hdb. on B 6: 8.—Cf. also γάλα 1). M-M. B. 677.*

Ῥήγιον, ου, τό (Aeschyl., Hdt.+; inscr.; Philo, Aet. M. 139; Jos., Ant. 19, 205) *Rhegium*, a city and promontory in Bruttium, at the 'toe' of Italy, opposite the Sicilian city of Messina Ac 28: 13. M-M.*

ῥῆγμα, ατος, τό (since Archippus Com. [V/IV BC], fgm. 38; Hippocr.; pap., LXX; Jos., Bell. 6, 337) *wreck, ruin, collapse*, lit. 'breaking' τῆς οἰκίας (this mng. is not found elsewh.; but the pl. w. ref. to bldgs.: Polyb. 13, 6, 8; PSI 456, 11 τοῦ πύργου ῥήγματα; Am 6: 11 v.l. πατάξει τὸν οἶκον ῥήγμασιν.—PLond. 131 recto, 45; 60 [78/9 AD] uses the word of a break in a dam on the Nile, i.e. of damage by water) Lk 6: 49. M-M.*

ῥήγνυμι Mt 9: 17 and its by-form ῥήσσω Mt 9: 17 D; Lk 5: 6 v.l.; fut. ῥήξω; 1 aor. ἔρ(ρ)ηξα, imper. ῥῆξον; 2 fut. pass. ῥαγήσομαι (Hom.+; LXX).
    1. *tear (in pieces), break, burst* τινά or τὶ someone or someth. (Jos., Ant. 5, 310) of wine τοὺς ἀσκούς *burst the wine-skins* (Alex. Aphr., An. Mant. 124, 20 Br.) Mk 2: 22; Lk 5: 37; cf. Hm 11: 3. Pass. *be torn, burst* (Diod. S. 3, 34, 2; Test. Jud. 2: 6; PGM 4, 361; 2674; 13, 264) Mt 9: 17. ὥστε τὰ δίκτυα ῥήσσεσθαι Lk 5: 6 D. Of rabid animals *tear in pieces* w. their teeth μήποτε ῥήξωσιν ὑμᾶς Mt 7: 6 (Aesop, Fab. 408 H. of a swine: τοῖς ὀδοῦσιν ἀναρρήξειν τὴν κύνα).
    2. *tear* or *break loose, let loose, break out in* (Hdt. 2, 2 and Aelian, fgm. 41 p. 203, 2 φωνήν; Plut., Pericl. 36, 7 κλαυθμόν; LXX; Philo, Conf. Lingu. 194. Cf. also Ps.-Oppian, Cyneg. 1, 226 PBoudreaux [1908] ῥῆξόν ποτε δεσμὰ σιωπῆς) ῥῆξον καὶ βόησον *break forth and cry aloud* (Is 54: 1) Gal 4: 27; 2 Cl 2: 1.—Pass. *break forth* (PPetr. II 23, 1, 12 [III BC] ὕδωρ ἐρράγη; Sib. Or. 4, 53) of light B 3: 4 (Is 58: 8).—S. also ῥήσσω. M-M.*

ῥηθείς s. εἶπον.

ῥῆμα, ατος, τό (Pind., Hdt.+; inscr., pap., LXX, En. 14, 7; Philo; Jos., Bell. 6, 172, Ant. 16, 306 al.; Test. 12 Patr. —On the mng. of the word s. ADebrunner, TW IV 74f).
    1. *that which is said, word, saying, expression* τὰ ῥήματα *the words* (opp. τὰ ἔργα) 2 Cl 13: 3; Hs 9, 21, 2; cf. Ac 16: 38. πᾶν ῥῆμα *every word* B 11: 8. πᾶν ῥῆμα ἀργόν Mt 12: 36. πᾶν ῥ. πονηρόν Hs 5, 3, 6; οὐδὲ ἕν ῥ. *not even one word* Mt 27: 14; cf. ῥῆμα ἕν Ac 28: 25.—Lk 2: 17, 50; 20: 26; 1 Cl 27: 7 (Ps 18: 3). φωνὴ ῥημάτων *the sound of words, a voice whose words* Hb 12: 19; αἰσχρὸν ῥ. Hv 1, 1, 7. ὡσεὶ λῆρος τὰ ῥ. Lk 24: 11. ἄρρητα ῥήματα (s. ἄρρητος) 2 Cor 12: 4. ῥ. ἔκφρικτα Hv 1, 3, 3b. ῥ. ἀληθῆ m 11: 3; δεινὰ ῥ. MPol 8: 3. ῥ. βλάσφημα Ac 6: 11. ῥῆμα, ῥήματα ἀκούειν B 16: 10; Hv 1, 1, 6; 4, 1, 7; 4, 2, 6 al. τὰ

προειρημένα ῥ. (s. προεῖπον 1) 2 Pt 3: 2; cf. Jd 17; Hm 9: 4. πολὺν ἐν ῥήμασιν γενέσθαι *be profuse in speech, be too talkative* 1 Cl 30: 5 (Job 11: 3).—τὸ ῥ., τὰ ῥ. oft. takes a special significance fr. the context: *prophecy, prediction* Mt 26: 75; Mk 9: 32; 14: 72; Lk 1: 38; 2: 29; 9: 45a, b; 18: 34; 22: 61 v.l.; Ac 11: 16; MPol 16: 2. *Word of scripture* 2 Cl 15: 4.—*Command(ment), order, direction* Lk 5: 5; esp. of God (Dt 1: 26) 3: 2; Hb 11: 3; 1 Cl 10: 1; ῥ. τῆς δυνάμεως αὐτοῦ Hb 1: 3. τὸ ἰσχυρὸν ῥ. *the mighty creative word* Hv 1, 3, 4; cf. 3, 3, 5. διὰ ῥήματος Χριστοῦ Ro 10: 17.—*Threat* λαλεῖν ῥήματα κατά τινος *make threats against someth.* Ac 6: 13.—τὰ ῥ. *speech, sermon, proclamation* πάντα τὰ ῥ. αὐτοῦ *everything he had to say* Lk 7: 1. ἐνωτίσασθε τὰ ῥήματά μου *pay attention to what I am proclaiming* Ac 2: 14.—10: 44; J 8: 20. τὰ ῥήματα αὐτῶν *their preaching* Ro 10: 18 (Ps 18: 5).—Of the words of (Christian) teaching or of divine understanding πῶς τοῖς ἐμοῖς ῥήμασιν πιστεύσετε; J 5: 47. Cf. 6: 63; 10: 21; 12: 47f; 14: 10; 15: 7; 17: 8; Lk 24: 8; Ac 10: 22. ῥήματα ζωῆς αἰωνίου J 6: 68. τὰ ῥήματα τῆς ζωῆς ταύτης Ac 5: 20. ῥήματα ἀληθείας κ. σωφροσύνης 26: 25. ῥήματα ἐν οἷς σωθήσῃ 11: 14. τὰ ῥ. τοῦ θεοῦ (Sextus 4, 39 ῥήματα θεοῦ; Marinus, Vi. Procli 32 θεῖα ῥ.) J 3: 34; 8: 47. ἐπὶ παντὶ ῥήματι ἐκπορευομένῳ διὰ στόματος θεοῦ (Dt 8: 3) Mt 4: 4. τὰ ῥήματα τοῦ κυρίου τὰ λεγόμενα διὰ παραβολῶν *the Lord's teachings which were expressed in the form of parables* Hs 5, 4, 3. διάσταλμα ῥήματος *the special meaning of the teaching* B 10: 11. Gener. the sing. brings together all the divine teachings as a unified whole, w. some such mng. as *gospel*, or *confession*. ἐγγύς σου τὸ ῥῆμά ἐστιν Ro 10: 8a, 9 v.l. (Dt 30: 14). MJSuggs, 'The Word is Near You' Ro 10: 6-10, JKnox-Festschr. '67, 289-312. Cf. Eph 5: 26. τὸ ῥῆμα τὸ εὐαγγελισθὲν εἰς ὑμᾶς 1 Pt 1: 25b. W. objective gen. τὸ ῥῆμα τῆς πίστεως Ro 10: 8b. W. subjective gen. ῥῆμα θεοῦ Eph 6: 17; Hb 6: 5. τὸ ῥ. κυρίου 1 Pt 1: 25a (cf. Is 40: 8).—GKittel, D. Wort Gottes im NT: Pastoralblätter für Predigt usw. 80, '37/'38, 345-55.
    2. after the Hebrew *thing, object, matter, event* οὐκ ἀδυνατήσει παρὰ τοῦ θεοῦ πᾶν ῥῆμα *nothing will be impossible with God* Lk 1: 37 (Gen 18: 14). ἐπὶ στόματος δύο μαρτύρων σταθῇ πᾶν ῥῆμα Mt 18: 16; 2 Cor 13: 1 (both Dt 19: 15). Cf. sing. Lk 2: 15 (cf. 1 Km 4: 16); Ac 10: 37. Pl. Lk 1: 65; 2: 19, 51; Ac 5: 32; 13: 42.—ERepo, Der Begriff Rhema im Bibelgriechischen: I Rhema in der LXX, II Rhema im NT, Diss. Helsinki '51, '54; adversely reviewed by GZuntz, L'Antiquité Classique 22, '53, 106-12. M-M. B. 1262.**

Ῥησά, ὁ indecl. *Rhesa*, in the genealogy of Jesus Lk 3: 27 (GKuhn, ZNW 22, '23, 212).*

ῥῆσις, εως, ἡ (Hom.+; pap. [e.g. Kl.T. 135 p. 47, 8]; LXX, Philo; Sib. Or. 5, 258) *word, expression* ἐμῆς πνοῆς ῥῆσις (πνοή 2) 1 Cl 57: 3 (Pr 1: 23).*

ῥήσσω—1. by-form of ῥήγνυμι, q.v.—2. epic ῥήσσω (s. προσρήσσω and the lit. there)=Att. ῥάττω *throw down, dash to the ground* (Artem. 1, 60; Wsd 4: 19) τινά someone—a. lit., of an evil spirit's treatment of its victim Mk 9: 18; Lk 9: 42.—b. fig., of the devil, who tries *to cause the righteous man to fall* Hm 11: 3.*

ῥήτωρ, ορος, ὁ *public speaker, orator* (since Soph.; Thu. 8, 1, 1; inscr., pap.; Philo, Vi. Cont. 31; Jos., Ant. 17, 226; 19, 208), then specif. *a speaker in court, advocate, attorney* (Dio Chrys. 59[76], 4; POxy. 37 I, 4 [49 AD]; 237 VII, 25; BGU 969 I, 8; 15 al. in pap.; Preisigke, Fachw. '15) Ac 24: 1. M-M.*

ῥητῶς adv. *expressly, explicitly* (Aristot. 1017b, 1; 3; Stoic. III 219, 45; Polyb. 3, 23, 5; Plut., Brut. 29, 4; Diog. L. 8, 71; Dit., Or. 515, 39, Syll.³ 685, 77; 83; UPZ 110, 62 [164 BC]; POxy. 237 VII, 7; Philo, Leg. All. 1, 60 al.; Jos., Ant. 1, 24, C. Ap. 1, 83) τὸ πνεῦμα ῥητῶς λέγει 1 Ti 4: 1. M-M.*

ῥίζα, ης, ἡ (Hom.+; inscr., pap., LXX, Philo; Jos., Ant. 3, 174 al.).
1. *root*—a. lit. Mt 3: 10; Lk 3: 9; Hs 9, 1, 6; 9, 21, 1. ἐκ ῥιζῶν *to its roots, root and branch* (Heraclid. Pont., fgm. 50 W.; Plut., Pomp. 21, 3; Job 31: 12; Polyaenus 2, 1, 10; Aesop, Fab. 70 P.) Mk 11: 20. ῥίζαν ἔχειν have (*deep*) *root*(*s*) Mt 13: 6; Mk 4: 6 (Theophr., Hist. Pl. 6, 6, 7 πολλὴν ἔχουσα ῥίζαν).
b. symbolically and fig. (LXX; oft. Philo; Sib. Or. 3, 396): in the parable οὐκ ἔχειν ῥίζαν (ἐν ἑαυτῷ) *have no firm root* and hence be easily inclined to fall away Mt 13: 21; Mk 4: 17; Lk 8: 13.—In Paul's figure of the olive tree, its root and branches Ro 11: 16–18. On ῥίζας βάλλειν 1 Cl 39: 8 (Job 5: 3) s. βάλλω 2c.—Of the beginnings fr. which someth. grows (Socrat., Ep. 14, 2; Herm. Wr. 4, 10): a family or nation (Ael. Aristid. 30, 16 K.=10 p. 120 D.; Dit., Or. 383, 30f [I BC] ἐμοῦ γένους ῥίζα) ἐκκόπτειν ἐκ ῥιζῶν *root out, destroy root and branch* B 12: 9. ῥίζα πικρίας Hb 12: 15 (πικρία 1). ῥ. πάντων τῶν κακῶν 1 Ti 6: 10 (cf. Constantin. Manasseh 2, 9 H.: φθόνος ἡ ῥίζα τῶν κακῶν; Himerius, Ecl. 32, 5 W.: παιδεία ῥίζα τῶν ἀγαθῶν). τῆς πίστεως ῥ. Pol 1: 2 (cf. Epicurus in Athen. 12, 67 p. 546f [HUsener, Epicurea 1887 p. 278, 10] ἀρχὴ καὶ ῥίζα παντὸς ἀγαθοῦ; Plut., Mor. p. 4B πηγὴ καὶ ῥίζα καλοκἀγαθίας; Sir 1: 6, 20 ῥ. σοφίας; Wsd 15: 3 ῥ. ἀθανασίας).
2. *shoot* or *scion* growing fr. the root, symbolically *descendant* (Diod. S. 26, 16a μηδὲ ῥίζαν ἀπολιπεῖν συγγενείας=not a single scion of the family should survive; Ps.-Apollod. 2, 1, 4, 2 Ἀγήνωρ τῆς μεγάλης ῥίζης ἐγένετο γενεάρχης=the progenitor of the strong offshoot; Sir 40: 15; 1 Macc 1: 10) of the Messiah ἡ ῥίζα τοῦ Ἰεσσαί *the Scion from Jesse* Ro 15: 12 (Is 11: 10); ἡ ῥίζα Δαυίδ (cf. Sir 47: 22) Rv 5: 5; cf. 22: 16. ὡς ῥίζα ἐν γῇ διψώσῃ 1 Cl 16: 3 (Is 53: 2).
3. Hs 9, 30, 1f speaks of the ῥίζαι τοῦ ὄρους (of a mountain, hill, etc. as its foot: Aeschyl., Prom. 365 [pl.]; Polyb. 2, 66, 10; Diod. S. 20, 41, 3; Plut., Sulla 16, 1). M-M. B. 523.*

ῥιζόω (Hom.+; LXX, Philo) pf. pass. ptc. ἐρριζωμένος (w. double ρ; cf. W-S. §5, 26b) *cause to take root,* mostly fig., *fix firmly, put on a firm foundation* (Hom.+) pass. *be* or *become firmly rooted* or *fixed* (Pla., Ep. 7 p. 336B ἐξ ἀμαθίας πάντα κακὰ ἐρρίζωται; Sext. Emp., Math. 1, 271; Epigr. Gr. 1078, 7 of a bridge αἰώνιος ἐρρίζωται) ἐρριζωμένοι· ἐν ἀγάπῃ Eph 3: 17, ἐν κυρίῳ Col 2: 7 (Nicander, Ther. 183 ῥιζοῦσθαι ἐν=be firmly rooted in; Philosophenspr. p. 499, 38 Mull. ῥιζωθέντες ἐκ θεοῦ). M-M.*

ῥιπή, ῆς, ἡ (Hom.+; Philo, Somn. 2, 125, Aet. M. 20; Sib. Or. 5, 464) *throwing, rapid movement,* e.g. of the eyes; the 'casting' of a glance takes an extremely short time: ἐν ῥιπῇ ὀφθαλμοῦ *in the twinkling of an eye* 1 Cor 15: 52 (Billerb. II, 156).*

ῥιπίζω (Aristoph. et al.) *blow here and there, toss* of the wind (Da 2: 35; Ep. Arist. 70), that sets a wave in motion on the water, pass. (Philo, Aet. M. 125 πρὸς ἀνέμων ῥιπίζεται τὸ ὕδωρ; a quot. in Dio Chrys. 15[32], 23 δῆμος ἄστατον κακὸν καὶ θαλάσσῃ πανθ' ὅμοιον ὑπ' ἀνέμου

ῥιπίζεται; Cass. Dio 70, 4 ῥιπιζομένη ἄχνη. Cf. also Epict., fgm. F 2 p. 487 Sch.) ὁ διακρινόμενος ἔοικεν κλύδωνι θαλάσσης ἀνεμιζομένῳ καὶ ῥιπιζομένῳ Js 1: 6. M-M.*

ῥίπτω and ῥιπτέω the latter Demosth. 19, 231; Dio Chrys. 3, 15; Ac 22: 23; Hv 3, 5, 5 (the word is found Hom.+; inscr., pap., LXX; En. 21, 3; Joseph. [ῥίπτω Bell. 1, 150, Ant. 16, 248.—ῥιπτέω Ant. 2, 206; 14, 70]; Sib. Or. 3, 103; 5, 233) impf. ἐ(ρ)ρίπτουν; 1 aor. ἔ(ρ)ριψα, imper. ῥῖψον; pf. pass. ptc. ἐ(ρ)ριμμένος (on the doubling of the ρ s. W-S. §5, 26b; Bl-D. §11, 1; Mlt.-H. 101f).
1. *throw* in a manner suited to each special situation: *throw away* (Achilles Tat. 2, 11, 5) Μωϋσῆς ἔ(ρ)ριψεν ἐκ τῶν χειρῶν τὰς πλάκας B 14: 3 (Ex 32: 19; Dt 9: 17); cf. 4: 8. ῥ. τι μακρὰν ἀπό τινος *throw someth. far away from someth.* Hv 3, 2, 7; s 9, 7, 2. Pass. Hv 3, 2, 9; 3, 6, 1; 3, 7, 1.—*Throw* into the sea, fr. a ship (Charito 3, 5, 5; Achilles Tat. 3, 2, 9) Ac 27: 19, 29; fr. dry land, pass. εἰς τὴν θάλασσαν Lk 17: 2 (ῥ. εἰς as Polyaenus 8, 48; schol. on Nicander, Ther. 825 [ῥ. εἰς τὴν θαλ.]; Gen 37: 20; Ex 1: 22; Test. Zeb. 2: 7).—ῥίψας τὰ ἀργύρια εἰς τὸν ναόν Mt 27: 5 (Diod. S. 27, 4, 8 the temple-robbers, suffering an attack of conscience ἐρρίπτουν τὰ χρήματα; Appian, Bell. Civ. 2, 23 §86 Πτολεμαίου τὰ χρήματα ῥίψαντος εἰς τὴν θάλασσαν; Ps.-Anacharsis, Ep. 6 ῥίψας τὸ ἀργύριον).—*Throw off* clothing (Aristoph., Eccl. 529; Pla., Rep. 5 p. 474A τὰ ἱμάτια) Ac 22: 23 (s. Field, Notes 136).—*Throw down* to the floor τινά someone Lk 4: 35.—*Expose* new-born infants (Apollod. [II BC]: 244 fgm. 110a Jac.; Diod. S. 2, 58, 5; Epict. 1, 23, 10; Aelian, V.H. 2, 7; cf. Wsd 11: 14; Sib. Or. 2, 282) Dg 5: 6.
2. w. no connotation of violence *put* or *lay down* (Demosth. 19, 231; Crinagoras 2, 1; Gen 21: 15; 2 Macc 3: 15) ἔ(ρ)ριψαν αὐτοὺς (the sick people) παρὰ τοὺς πόδας αὐτοῦ Mt 15: 30. Pass.: pf. ptc. *lying down, lying on the ground* or *floor* (X., Mem. 3, 1, 7; Polyb. 5, 48, 2; Plut., Galba 28, 1; Epict. 3, 26, 6 χαμαὶ ἐρριμμένοι; Charito 2, 7, 4 ἐρρ. ὑπὸ λύπης; 3 Km 13: 24; Jer 14: 16; 1 Macc 11: 4; Jos., Ant. 3, 7; 6, 362) the vine, without the support of the elm tree, is ἐ(ρ)ριμμένη χαμαί Hs 2: 3; cf. 4. Of the crowds of people ἦσαν ἐσκυλμένοι καὶ ἐ(ρ)ριμμένοι ὡσεὶ πρόβατα μὴ ἔχοντα ποιμένα Mt 9: 36 (of animals lying on the ground Heraclit. Sto. 14 p. 22, 20 τὰ ἐπὶ γῆς ἐρριμμένα ζῷα; Eutecnius 4 p. 42, 25). M-M. B. 673.*

ῥίς, ῥινός, ἡ (Hom.+; pap. fr. III BC; LXX) *nose;* pl. *nostrils,* i.e. *nose* (so Hom.+) Papias 3.*

ῥιψοκινδύνως (Appian, Bell. Civ. 1, 103 §482; POxy. 2131, 16 [III AD]) adv. of ῥιψοκίνδυνος (the adj. as early as X., Mem. 1, 3, 10; Vett. Val. 17, 27; BGU 909, 15; PFlor. 36, 2; PSI 686, 5; Philo, Agr. 167; Jos., Bell. 7, 77) *rashly, recklessly, in a foolhardy manner* 1 Cl 14: 2.*

Ῥοβοάμ (רְחַבְעָם), ὁ indecl. (3 Km 12; 1 Ch 3: 10.—Joseph. has Ῥοβόαμος, ου [Ant. 8, 212]) *Rehoboam,* son and successor of Solomon; in the genealogy of Jesus Mt 1: 7a, b; Lk 3: 23ff D.*

Ῥόδη, ης, ἡ (in myths and comedy [Menand., fgm. 245, 6; 546, 5; Philemo Com., fgm. 84]; Longus 4, 36, 3; 4, 37, 2; Sb 392 [III BC]; inscr.) *Rhoda*—1. a maidservant Ac 12: 13 (Dalman, Arbeit I 365).—2. Hermas' owner Hv 1, 1, 1. M-M.*

ῥόδον, ου, τό (Hom. Hymns+; Lucian, Nigrin. 32; inscr.: Bull. de corr. Hell. 10, 461, 101 [364 BC]; Sb 7541, 10 [II AD]; PIand. 66, 7; Sb 1080; a Jewish-Gk. inscr. fr. Tell el

Yehudieh: ZNW 22, '23, 282 no. 19, 7; LXX) *rose* ἐρυθρότερος παντὸς ῥ. AP 3: 8 (cf. En. 106, 2; 10). B. 527.*

'Ρόδος, ου, ἡ (Hom.+; inscr.; 1 Macc 15: 23; Philo, Aet. M. 120; Joseph.; Sib. Or. 3, 444) *Rhodes,* an island off the southwest point of Asia Minor; its main city bears the same name. Ac 21: 1.—FHillervGaertringen, Pauly-W., Suppl. V '31, 731–840.*

ῥοιζηδόν adv. (Lycophron 66; Nicander, Theriaca 556; Polyaenus, Exc. 18, 5; Geopon. 15, 2, 34) *with a hissing* or *crackling sound, w. a roar, w. great suddenness* 2 Pt 3: 10. M-M.*

ῥοῖζος, ου, ὁ and ἡ (Hom.+; Isishymn. v. Andr. 150 Peek [I BC]; PGM 2, 96; LXX; Philo, Aet. M. 128; Sib. Or. 3, 304) *the noise made by someth.* passing swiftly through the air ῥοίζῳ *with a rush* (Cornutus 1 p. 2, 14; Plut., Demetr. 21, 13; Longus 2, 10, 2; 2 Macc 9: 7; Jos., Bell. 3, 243.—233 and 488 of the irresistible rush of an attack) Hv 4, 1, 8 (Apollon. Rhod. 4, 129: the dragon who is guarding the golden fleece ῥοίζει πελώριον=hisses mightily; the noun follows in 138: ῥοίζῳ=[frightened] by a hissing).*

'Ρομφά, ὁ indecl. (the form of the word differs considerably in the mss.: 'Ραιφαν, 'Ρεμφαν, 'Ρομφαν, 'Ρεμφα, 'Ρομφα, 'Ρεφαν, and the mss. of the LXX are not in full agreement ['Ραιφαν, 'Ρεμφαν. S. ed. JZiegler '43]) *Rephan, Rompha,* a pagan deity worshiped by some Israelites, put by the LXX in Am 5: 26 in the place of כִּיּוּן (=Saturn); this is quoted in Ac 7: 43.—WGrafBaudissin, RE XVI '05, 636–49 (lit.). M-M.*

ῥομφαία, ας, ἡ a large and broad *sword,* used by barbaric peoples, esp. the Thracians (Phylarch. [III BC]: 81 fgm. 57 Jac.; Plut., Aemil. 18, 5; Hesychius; Suidas). In our lit. simply *sword* (so also LXX; Jos., Bell. 6, 289, Ant. 6, 254; 7, 299; Test. 12 Patr.; Sib. Or. 3, 673 al.—In Philo always of the angel's flaming sword after Gen 3: 24) Lk 21: 24 D; Rv 2: 16; 6: 8; 19: 15, 21. ῥ. δίστομος καὶ ὀξεῖα *a sharp and double-edged sword* Rv 2: 12; cf. 1: 16. φείδεσθαι τῆς ψυχῆς τινος ἀπὸ ῥ. *spare someone's life from the sword* (so that he may die on the cross) B 5: 13 (Ps 21: 21). Symbolically for pain or anguish (cf. Sib. Or. 5, 260 v.l.) τὴν ψυχὴν διελεύσεται ῥομφαία Lk 2: 35 (ῥ. διελεύσ. symb. as Sib. Or. 3, 316; cf. Ezk 14: 17.—Artem. 1, 41 p. 39, 19 τιτρώσκεσθαι κατὰ τὸ στῆθος means 'receive sad news'). M-M.*

ῥοπή, ῆς, ἡ (Aeschyl., Pla.+; Herodas 7, 33; Vett. Val. 301, 1; Dit., Syll.³ 761, 5 [48/7 BC]; UPZ 110, 73 [164 BC]; PTebt. 27, 79; LXX; Philo; Jos., Bell. 3, 396; 4, 367; 5, 88 al.) *downward movement* (esp. of a scale-pan), *inclination* ἐν ῥ. ὀφθαλμοῦ *in the twinkling of an eye* 1 Cor 15: 52 D al. (ῥοπή, though without ὀφθαλμοῦ=moment, orig. 'decisive moment': Diod. S. 13, 23, 2; 13, 24, 6 [ῥ. καιροῦ]; 20, 34, 2; Plut., Ages. 33, 3; Wsd 18: 12 πρὸς μίαν ῥοπήν; 3 Macc 5: 49 ὑστάτη βίου ῥοπή; Ep. Arist. 90). M-M.*

'Ρουβήν (רְאוּבֵן), ὁ indecl. (LXX, Philo; Test. 12 Patr. ['Ρουβήμ].—Joseph. has 'Ρουβῆλος, ου [Ant. 1, 307]) *Reuben,* oldest son of Jacob and Leah (Gen 29: 32) Rv 7: 5.*

'Ρούθ (רוּת), ἡ indecl. (LXX.—Joseph. has 'Ρούθη) *Ruth,* a Moabitess, heroine of the OT book of the same name. In the genealogy of Jesus as wife of Boaz Mt 1: 5.—S. on Θαμάρ.*

'Ρούφος, ου, ὁ a Latin name found freq. even in its Greek spelling (Diod. S. 11, 60, 1; 14, 107, 1; Ael. Aristid. 48, 15 K.=24 p. 469 D.; Joseph., index; inscr., pap.) *Rufus.* 1. son of Simon of Cyrene and brother of Alexander Mk 15: 21.—2. recipient of a greeting Ro 16: 13.—3. a martyr w. Ignatius and Zosimus Pol 9: 1 (cf. Euseb., H.E. 3, 36, 13 and s. Lghtf. ad loc.). M-M.*

ῥύμη, ης, ἡ (Thu., Aristoph.+, in the sense 'swing, rush'; Philo; Jos., Ant. 7, 239) in later Gk. *narrow street, lane, alley* (Polyb. 6, 29, 1 al.; oft. in pap. since PPetr. II 17, 2, 19 [III BC]; also LXX; Sib. Or. 3, 364) Ac 12: 10. W. συναγωγαί Mt 6: 2. W. πλατεῖαι (Is 15: 3; Tob 13: 18 and 17 BA) Lk 14: 21. Provided w. a name (cf. the Alexandrian pap. in APF 5, '13, 37, 1, fr. Augustan times Εὐδαίμων ἐν τῇ Εὐδαίμονος λεγομένῃ ῥύμῃ) Ac 9: 11. M-M. B. 720.*

ῥύομαι mid. dep. (Hom.+; inscr., pap., LXX, Philo; Jos., Bell. 3, 103; 6, 120; Test. 12 Patr.—Anz 275f; FHChase, The Lord's Prayer in the Early Church: Texts and Studies I 3, 1891, 71ff) fut. ῥύσομαι; 1 aor. ἐ(ρ)ρυσάμην, imper. ῥῦσαι Mt 6: 13, pass. ἐ(ρ)ρύσθην (on the spelling w. one ρ or two s. Bl-D. §11, 1; 101 p. 48; Mlt.-H. 101f; 193) *save, rescue, deliver, preserve* τινά someone Mt 27: 43 t.r. (Ps 21: 9); 2 Pt 2: 7; 1 Cl 8: 4 (Is 1: 17); 16: 16 (Ps 21: 9); 22: 8 (Ps 33: 20) v.l. Funk; 55: 6; 2 Cl 6: 8 (Ezk 14: 18). τινὰ ἀπό τινος *rescue, save, deliver,* or *preserve someone fr. someone* or *someth.* (Bl-D. §180; cf. Rob. 517f.—Pr 2: 12; Is 25: 4; Ezk 37: 23; 1 Macc 12: 15; Test. Reub. 4: 10; Sib. Or. 2, 344) Mt 6: 13; Lk 11: 4 t.r. (on the subject matter cf. Carm. Aur. v. 61 [Hierocl. 25 p. 474 Mull.] Ζεῦ πάτερ, ἦ πολλῶν κε κακῶν λύσειας ἅπαντας); 2 Ti 4: 18; 1 Cl 60: 3b; D 8: 2; 10: 5. Pass. Ac 5: 15 E; Ro 15: 31; 2 Th 3: 2; 1 Cl 60: 3a. Also τινὰ ἔκ τινος (Anacreon 111 Diehl; Hdt. 5, 49; Diod. S. 12, 53, 1; hymn to Isis: Suppl. Epigr. Gr. VIII 548, 27 [I BC]; PBad. 48, 3 [126 BC] ἐκ πολεμίων; LXX; Jos., Ant. 12, 407; Test. Sim. 2: 8.—Aristoxenus, fgm. 113 ῥύεσθαι καὶ ἐρύεσθαι διαφορὰν ἔχει πρὸς ἄλληλα. τὸ μὲν γὰρ ῥύεσθαι ἐκ θανάτου ἕλκειν, τὸ δὲ ἐρύεσθαι φυλάττειν) 2 Ti 3: 11; from death (Sib. Or. 2, 81) 2 Cor 1: 10a; 1 Cl 56: 9 (Job 5: 20); 2 Cl 16: 4 (w. acc. to be supplied); fr. the power of darkness Col 1: 13; fr. the wrath to come 1 Th 1: 10; fr. blood-guiltiness 1 Cl 18: 14 (Ps 50: 16); fr. all afflictions 22: 7 (Ps 33: 18); fr. eternal punishment 2 Cl 6: 7; fr. temptation 2 Pt 2: 9. τίς με ῥύσεται ἐκ τοῦ σώματος τοῦ θανάτου τούτου; *who will set me free from this body of death?* Ro 7: 24. Pass. ῥυσθῆναι ἐκ χειρός τινος *be rescued from someone's power* Lk 1: 74 (cf. Jos., Vi. 83, Ant. 7, 151; Third Corinthians 1: 8). ἐκ στόματος λέοντος *be saved from the jaws of the lion* 2 Ti 4: 17. ῥ. τινά τινι *save someone by someth.* (Diod. S. 13, 64, 6 ἐρρύσατο χρήμασι τὴν ἰδίαν ψυχήν=his life by means of money) 2 Cl 6: 9. Also ῥ. τινα διά τινος 1 Cl 55: 1. Abs. Mt 27: 43 (for a 'divine' rescue of a θεοσεβής fr. extreme danger cf. Croesus on the pyre Hdt. 1, 86, 2: Κῦρος βουλόμενος εἰδέναι εἴ τίς μιν δαιμόνων ῥύσεται τοῦ μὴ ζῶντα κατακαυθῆναι. Cf. also Ps 21: 9); 2 Cor 1: 10b. ὁ ῥυόμενος *the Deliverer* Ro 11: 26 (Is 59: 20); 1 Cl 35: 11 (Ps 49: 22). ῥυσθείητε ἀπὸ τούτων ἁπάντων *may you be delivered from all these* (men or sins) D 5: 2. M-M.*

ῥυπαίνω 1 aor. pass. ἐ(ρ)ρυπάνθην (since Pherecrates Com. [V BC] 228; X.) *befoul, soil, (make) dirty* fig. (Aristot.+; Dionys. Hal. 11, 5; Vett. Val. 116, 8; Herm. Wr. 9, 5; Philo, Det. Pot. Ins. 20; Jos., C. Ap. 1, 220) *defile, pollute* pass. (Sotacus in Apollon. Paradox. 36; Plut., Mor. 85ϝ) ὁ ῥυπαρὸς ῥυπανθήτω ἔτι *let him who is* defiled continue to be defiled or be defiled more and more Rv 22: 11. M-M.*

ῥυπαρεύω (hapax legomenon) befoul, defile Rv 22: 11 v.l.*

ῥυπαρία, ας, ἡ (since Critias [V BC] in Pollux 3, 116) dirt, filth, fig., in the ethical field moral uncleanness, vulgarity (Pel.-Leg. p. 6, 30 ἀφῆκεν ἐν τῷ ὕδατι πᾶσαν αὐτῆς τὴν ῥυπαρίαν), esp. sordid avarice, greediness (Teles p. 33, 4; 37, 5 H.; Plut., Mor. 60D; Cass. Dio 74, 5, 7) w. κακία Js 1: 21. M-M.*

ῥυπαρός, ά, όν (Teleclides Com. [V BC], fgm. 3; Hippocr. et al.; pap.; LXX) dirty.
1. lit., Hs 9, 7, 6. Of clothes (Plut., Phoc. 18, 4; Cass. Dio 65, 20; Artem. 2, 3 p. 88, 23; Aelian, V.H. 14, 10; PGiess. 76, 2f [II AD]; Zech 3: 3f; Sib. Or. 5, 188; Jos., Ant. 7, 267 ῥυπαρὰν τὴν ἐσθῆτα) ἐσθής Js 2: 2. ῥάκη ῥ. filthy rags (s. ῥάκος 1) AP 15: 30. In a symbolic expr., occasioned by the proximity of ῥύπος: ἡμέραι ῥ. foul days B 8: 6.
2. fig., in a moral sense unclean, defiled (Dionys. Hal. et al. use the word for 'sordidly avaricious'; cf. Vett. Val. 104, 5; 117, 10; Test. Judah 14: 3 διαλογισμοὶ ῥ.) Rv 22: 11; IEph 16: 2. M-M. B. 1081.*

ῥύπος, ου, ὁ (Hom.+; LXX) dirt—1. lit., of a greasy, viscous juice (e.g. ear-wax, Artem. 1, 24; PGM 36, 332) ῥ. ὑσσώπου the foul or dark juice of the hyssop B 8: 6 (but JAKleist, transl. '48, p. 175 note 97, refers it to the mixture of water and heifer's ashes sprinkled by means of hyssop) σαρκὸς ἀπόθεσις ῥύπου removing of dirt from the body 1 Pt 3: 21 (on the gen. s. W-S. §30, 12f).
2. fig. (M. Ant. 7, 47 ὁ ῥύπος τοῦ χαμαὶ βίου; Is 4: 4), in an ethical sense uncleanness καθαρὸς ἀπὸ ῥύπου 1 Cl 17: 4 (Job 14: 4; the Job pass. also in Philo, Mut. Nom. 48). W. ἁμαρτίαι B 11: 11. M-M.*

ῥυπόω 1 aor. imper. 3 sing. ῥυπωσάτω (Od. 6, 59; schol. on Apollon. Rhod. 2, 301–2a; Themist., Or. 7 p. 112, 6; Achmes 63, 8; 118, 2; Pel.-Leg. 9, 9; Pollux 4, 180; Philo, fgm. 9 RHarris) (make) dirty, soil fig. defile, pollute Rv 22: 11 t.r. (s. ῥυπαίνω, ῥυπαρεύω). M-M.*

ῥύσις, εως, ἡ (Hippocr., Pla.+; pap.; En. 26, 2; Philo; Sib. Or. 1, 315) flowing, flow ῥ. αἵματος flow of blood (Lev 15: 25; medical wr. [Hobart 15]; Diod. S. 5, 31, 3; Aelian, V.H. 6, 6 p. 79, 17; Vett. Val. 282, 30 αἵματος πολλὴν ῥύσιν), of a hemorrhage fr. which a woman suffered Mk 5: 25; Lk 8: 43f. M-M.*

ῥυτίς, ίδος, ἡ (Aristoph., Pla.+; Plut., Mor. 789D; Lu-

cian) wrinkle symbolically, of the church μὴ ἔχουσα σπίλον ἢ ῥυτίδα Eph 5: 27. M-M.*

Ῥωμαϊκός, ή, όν (Polyb.+; Arrian, Peripl. 10, 1 τὰ Ῥωμαϊκὰ γράμματα=the Latin letter; inscr., pap., Philo, Joseph.) Roman, Latin Lk 23: 38 t.r. M-M.*

Ῥωμαῖος, α, ον Roman subst. ὁ Ῥ. (Polyb.+; inscr., pap., 1 and 2 Macc, Philo, Joseph., Sib. Or.) the Roman, the Roman citizen, pl. the Romans as a people or Roman citizens in the pl. J 11: 48 (Appian, Bell. Civ. 2, 26 §98 Ῥωμαίων πολῖται and Ῥωμαῖοι alternate); Ac 2: 10; 16: 21, 37f; 22: 25–7, 29; 23: 27 (on Rom. citizenship s. FSchulz, Rom. Registry of Births, Journ. of Rom. Studies 32, '42, 78–91; 33, '43, 55–64); 25: 16; 28: 17 (on Ac 16: 37f; 22: 25 cf. μαστίζω). Phlm subscr. In the sense Roman Christians Ro inscr. χωρίον Ῥωμαίων IRo inscr. (cf. Hdb. ad loc.). ἡ Ῥωμαίων πόλις Rome (Jos., C. Ap. 1, 66, Ant. 19, 7) Epil Mosq 3.*

Ῥωμαϊστί adv. in (the) Latin (language) (Diosc. I 115, 5; Epict. 1, 17, 16; Jos., Ant. 14, 191 ἑλληνιστὶ καὶ ῥωμαϊστί) J 19: 20.—Subscr. after Mk in minuscule 13 et al. (the Ferrar group. K and SLake, Studies and Documents XI '41, p. 116) ἐγράφη ῥωμαϊστὶ ἐν Ῥώμῃ. M-M.*

Ῥώμη, ης, ἡ (Aristot., Polyb. et al.; inscr., 1 Macc, Philo, Joseph., Sib. Or.) Rome Ac 18: 2; 19: 21; 23: 11; 28: 14, 16; Ro 1: 7 (where the words ἐν Ῥ. are missing in many mss.; s. Ltzm., Hdb. exc. on Ro 1: 7; Zahn, comm., exc. I p. 615; Harnack, ZNW 3, '02, 83ff; RSteinmetz, ZNW 9, '08, 177ff), 15 (here, too, the words ἐν Ῥώμῃ are omitted in a few isolated mss.); 2 Ti 1: 17; 1 Cl inscr.; IEph 1: 2; 21: 2; IRo 5: 1; 10: 2; Epil Mosq 1; Hv 1, 1, 1. Also 1 Pt 5: 13 v.l. and the subscr. of Gal, Eph, Phil, Col, 2 Th, 2 Ti, Phlm, Hb.*

ῥώννυμι pf. pass. ἔρρωμαι be strong (so since Eur., Thu.; also LXX) perf. pass. imper. ἔρρωσο, ἔρρωσθε (always w. double ρ: Bl-D. §11, 1; Mlt.-H. 101f; ῥώννυμι was obsolete in NT times) farewell, goodbye in the conclusions of letters (Hippocr., X., Pla.+; inscr. [Dit., Syll.³ IV p. 549b index]; pap. [very oft.; cf. FXJExler, The Form of the Ancient Gk. Letter '23, 74ff; HLietzmann, Kl. Texte 14,² '10, nos. 3; 4; 6; 7; 8 al.] 2 Macc 11: 21, 33; 3 Macc 7: 9; Ep. Arist. 40; 46; Jos., Vi. 227; 365) Ac 15: 29; 23: 30 t.r.; IEph 21: 2; IMg 15; ITr 13: 2; IRo 10: 3; IPhld 11: 2; ISm 13: 1f; IPol 8: 3b (in Ign. the greeting is combined w. various additions fr. Christian usage). Periphrastically ἐρρῶσθαι ὑμᾶς εὔχομαι (oft. pap.) IPol 8: 3a; MPol 22: 1. M-M. and suppl.*

Σ

σαβαχθάνι (Tdf., W-H. σαβαχθανεί) Aram. שְׁבַקְתַּנִי instead of the Hebr. עֲזַבְתָּנִי Ps 22: 2; fr. שְׁבַק forsake: thou hast forsaken me Mt 27: 46; Mk 15: 34.—EKautzsch, Gramm. des Bibl.-Aram. 1884, 11; Dalman, Gramm.² 147 note 4; 156; 221, Jesus '22, 185f; DSidersky, Rev. de l'Hist. des Rel. 103, '31, 151–4. On the accent s. Wlh. on Mk 15: 34.*

Σαβαώθ indecl. Sabaoth (LXX; Sib. Or.; PGM 4, 1235; 15, 14; 18a, 1; 35, 20; Fluchtaf. 2; 3, 27; 4, 15) Greek transcription of צְבָאוֹת, pl. of צָבָא=army, in a name

applied to God κύριος Σ.= יהוה צְבָאוֹת Yahweh or Lord of the Armies, Lord of Hosts (on the mng. EKautzsch, RE XXI '08, 620–7 [lit.]; here 626f a short treatment of the usage in the LXX. Also XXIV '13, 661f. More exact information in Thackeray 9. PKatz, Philo's Bible, 146–9) Ro 9: 29 (Is 1: 9); 1 Cl 34: 6 (Is 6: 3); Js 5: 4. M-M.*

σαββατίζω 1 aor. ἐσαββάτισα (LXX; Byz. chron. in Psaltes p. 329) keep the Sabbath ἐὰν μὴ σαββατίσητε τὸ σάββατον, οὐκ ὄψεσθε τὸν πατέρα LJ 1: 2 (LEWright, JBL 65, '46, 180). On the other hand, the Jews who have become Christians give up the celebration of the Sabbath in favor of the Lord's Day, Sunday IMg 9: 1.*

σαββατισμός, οῦ, ὁ (Plut., Mor. 166A) *Sabbath rest, Sabbath observance* fig. Hb 4: 9 (CKBarrett, CHDodd-Festschr., '56, 371f [eschat.]).—S. on κατάπαυσις. M-M.*

σάββατον, ου, τό (שַׁבָּת) dat. pl. σάββασιν (Meleager [I BC]: Anth. Pal. 5, 160; 1 Macc 2: 38; Jos., Vi. 279, Ant. 16, 163) always in NT except that a v.l. at Mt 12: 1 and 12 acc. to B has σαββάτοις (so usu. LXX [Thackeray 35]; Jos., Bell. 1, 146, Ant. 3, 294. Cf. W-S. §8, 12; Bl-D. §52; Mlt.-H. 128; MBlack, BRigaux-Festschr., '70, 60f).—The word is found Plut. et al.; pap., LXX; En. 10, 17; Philo, Joseph.

1. *Sabbath,* the seventh day of the week in the Jewish calendar, marked by rest fr. work and by special religious ceremonies.

a. sing. (τὸ) σάββατον (Neptunianus [I AD] ed. W Gemoll, Progr. Striegau 1884, 53; LXX; Philo, Cher. 87; Jos., Ant. 3, 143; 255) Mt 12: 8; Mk 2: 27f (Alex. Aphr., Eth. Probl. 10, II 2 p. 130, 34ff ὁ ἄνθρωπος τῶν ἀρετῶν χάριν, ἀλλ' οὐκ ἔμπαλιν [=vice versa]); 6: 2; 15: 42 v.l.; 16: 1; Lk 6: 5; 23: 54; J 5: 9f; 9: 14; B 15: 1a; GP 2: 5 al. ἁγιάζειν τὸ σ. B 15: 1b (cf. 2 Esdr 23 [Neh 13]: 22). βεβηλοῦν τὸ σ. Mt 12: 5b; λύειν τὸ σ. J 5: 18 (s. λύω). τηρεῖν τὸ σ. 9: 16. σαββατίζειν τὸ σ. (cf. Lev 23: 32) LJ 1: 2. φυλάσσειν τὸ σ. (cf. Ex 31: 13f; Lev 19: 3) B 15: 2, cf. 3. *On the Sabbath* (cf. Bl-D. §200, 3; Rob. 523): ἐν τῷ σαββάτῳ (2 Esdr 23 [Neh 13]: 15a, 16) Lk 6: 7; J 19: 31a; ἐν σαββάτῳ (2 Esdr 20: 32b [Neh 10: 31b]) Mt 12: 2; Lk 6: 1; J 5: 16; 7: 22f; τῷ σαββάτῳ Lk 6: 5 D (JoachJeremias, Unknown Sayings of Jesus, tr. Fuller, '57, 49-54); 6: 9; 13: 14a, 15; 14: 3; σαββάτῳ (Jos., Bell. 2, 456) Mt 24: 20 (s. Boll 134, 1); Lk 14: 1; J 6: 59 v.l.; ἐν ἑτέρῳ σ. Lk 6: 6; τῷ ἐρχομένῳ σ. Ac 13: 44; ἐν τῇ ἡμέρᾳ τοῦ σ. (cf. Jer 17: 21f) Lk 14: 5 t.r.; ἐν ἡμέρᾳ τοῦ σ. (2 Esdr 20: 32a [Neh 10: 31a]; 23 [Neh 13]: 15b; cf. Cyranides p. 79, 11 ἐν ἡμ. σαββάτου) Lk 14: 5; τῇ ἡμέρᾳ τοῦ σ. Lk 13: 14b, 16. In the acc. of duration of time (Bl-D. §161, 2) τὸ σάββατον *throughout the Sabbath* Lk 23: 56. κατὰ πᾶν σ. (on) *every Sabbath* Ac 13: 27; 15: 21; 18: 4; εἰς τὸ μεταξὺ σ. *on the following Sabbath* Ac 13: 42. ἡ ἡμέρα πρὸ σαββάτου Lk 23: 54 D.—σάββατον μέγα *Great Sabbath* MPol 8: 1; 21: 1; cf. J 19: 31b (s. ESchwartz, Christl. u. jüd. Ostertafeln: AGG VIII 6, '05, 127). σ. τὸ λεγόμενον πρῶτον *the so-called first Sabbath* PK 2, p. 14, 28.—On σαββάτου ὁδός a *Sabbath day's journey* Ac 1: 12 cf. ὁδός 1.

b. pl.—α. of more than one Sabbath (2 Ch 31: 3; Ezk 46: 3; Jos., Ant. 13, 252) σάββατα τρία Ac 17: 2; B 15: 8a (Is 1: 13), b.

β. τὰ σάββατα for a single Sabbath day (Zen.-P. Cairo 762, 6 [III BC]; Plut., Mor. 169c; 671E τὴν τῶν σαββάτων ἑορτήν; 672A; Ex 20: 10; Lev 23: 32 al.; Philo, Abr. 28 τὴν ἑβδόμην, ἣν Ἑβραῖοι σάββατα καλοῦσιν; Jos., Ant. 1, 33; 3, 237; 12, 259; 276.—Bl-D. §141, 3 w. app.; Rob. 408; ESchwyzer, Ztschr. f. vergleich. Sprachforschung 62, '35, 1-16; ASchlatter, Mt '29, 393) ὀψὲ σαββάτων Mt 28: 1a (s. ὀψέ 3). Also prob. Col 2: 16. ἡ ἡμέρα τῶν σαββάτων (Ex 20: 8; 35: 3; Dt 5: 12; Jer 17: 21f; Jos., Ant. 12, 274) Lk 4: 16; Ac 13: 14; 16: 13; Dg 4: 3. (ἐν) τοῖς σάββασιν *on the Sabbath* (Jos., Vi. 279 τοῖς σάββασιν, Ant. 13, 252 v.l. ἐν τοῖς σάββασιν) Mt 12: 1, 5, 10-12; Mk 1: 21: 2: 23, 24; 3: 2, 4; Lk 4: 31; 6: 2; 13: 10. ἡ περὶ τὰ σάββατα δεισιδαιμονία *superstitious veneration of the Sabbath* Dg 4: 1 (only extreme danger to human life can cause the Sabbath law to be suspended: Synes., Ep. 4 p.

162B, c). τὰ σάββατα the *Sabbath feasts* B 2: 5 (Is 1: 13).—JMeinhold, Sabbat u. Woche im AT '05, Sabbat u. Sonntag '09; JHehn, Siebenzahl u. Sabbat bei den Babyloniern u. im AT '07, Der israelit. Sabbat '09, Zur Sabbatfrage: BZ 14, '17, 198-213; EMahler, Der Sabbat: ZDMG 62, '08, 33-79, Handbuch der jüd. Chronologie '16; GBeer, Schabbath '08; WNowack, Schabbat '24; MWolff, Het ordeel der helleensch-romeinsche schrijvers over. . . den Sabbath: ThT 44, '10, 162-72; ELohse, Jesu Worte über den Sabbat, Beih. ZNW 26, '60, 79-89. S. also κυριακός, end.

2. *week*—a. sing. δὶς τοῦ σαββάτου *two days* (in) a *week* Lk 18: 12. πρώτῃ σαββάτου *on the first day of the week* (Sunday) Mk 16: 9. κατὰ μίαν σαββάτου *every Sunday* 1 Cor 16: 2. πρωΐ μιᾶς σαββάτου *early on Sunday morning* Mk 16: 2 D.

b. pl. (ἡ) μία (τῶν) σαββάτων (i.e. ἡμέρα) *the first day of the week* Mt 28: 1b (s. Dalman, Gramm. 247; SKrauss, Talm. Archäologie II '11, 428f; PGardner-Smith, JTS 27, '26, 179-81); Mk 16: 2; Lk 24: 1; J 20: 1, 19; Ac 20: 7; 1 Cor 16: 2 t.r. The Jews fast δευτέρᾳ σαββάτων καὶ πέμπτῃ *on the second and fifth days of the week* (Monday and Thursday) D 8: 1 (s. νηστεύω and the lit. there).— ESchürer, Die siebentägige Woche im Gebr. der christl. Kirche der ersten Jahrhunderte: ZNW 6, '05, 1-66; FH Colson, The Week '26; FBoll, Hebdomas: Pauly-W. VII 2, '12, 2547-8; RNorth, The Derivation of 'Sabbath', Biblica 36, '55, 182-201; WRordorf, Sunday, tr. AGraham, '68.—ELohse, TW VII 1-35: σάβ. and παρασκευή. M-M. B. 1005.*

σαγήνη, ης, ἡ (Plut., Mor. 169c; Lucian, Pisc. 51, Tim. 22; Artem. 2, 14, p. 107, 13; Ael. Aristid. 13 p. 200 D.; Aelian, H.A. 11, 12; LXX) a large *dragnet* σαγήνῃ βληθείσῃ εἰς τὴν θάλασσαν Mt 13: 47 (βάλλειν σαγ. as Babrius, Fab. 4, 1; 9, 6). S. ἀμφιβάλλω. M-M.*

Σαδδουκαῖος, ου, ὁ *the Sadducee,* always pl. οἱ Σαδδουκαῖοι *the Sadducees* members of a Jewish party in Jerusalem in the time of Jesus and the apostles (s. Joseph.: the passages are printed in Schürer II⁴ 449-52; on pp. 452-4 the evidence fr. the Mishna is added). Ac 5: 17 mentions them as equivalent to the High Priest and his adherents. Acc. to Mt 22: 23; Mk 12: 18; Lk 20: 27; Ac 23: 8 they denied the resurrection of the dead. Cf. also Mt 3: 7; 16: 1, 6, 11f; 22: 34; Ac 4: 1; 23: 6f. Many questions concerning the origin, name, and character of the Sadducees cannot yet be satisfactorily answered.—Wlh., Pharisäer u. die Sadd. 1874; GHölscher, Der Sadduzäismus '06; Schürer II⁴ '07, 475ff; RLeszynsky, Die Sadduzäer '12; BDEerdmans, Farizeën en Saduceën: ThT 48, '14, 1-16; MH Segall, Pharisees and Sadducees: Exp. 8th Ser. XIII '17, 81ff; GHBox, Who Were the Sadducees in the NT: ibid. 401ff; XVI '18, 55ff; EMeyer II '21, 290ff; JWLightley, Jewish Sects and Parties in the Time of Jesus '23; HRasp, Fl. Joseph. u. die jüd. Religionsparteien: ZNW 23, '24, 27-47; JoachJeremias, Jerusalem z. Zeit Jesu II '24/'29; Billerb. IV '28, 334-52: D. Pharis. u. d. Sadd. in d. altjüd. Lit.; TWManson, Sadducee and Pharisee—the Origin and Significance of the Names: Bull. of the JRylands Library 22, '38, 144-59; WStrawson, Jesus and the Future Life '59, 203-20; JLeMoyne, Les Sadducéens, '72.—RMeyer, TW VII 35-54.*

Σαδώκ (צָדוֹק), ὁ indecl., freq. in the OT (Joseph. has Σάδωκος, ου [Ant. 7, 201]) *Zadok,* in the genealogy of Jesus Mt 1: 14a, b; Lk 3: 23ff D.*

σαίνω at first, of dogs, *wag the tail* (Hom. +), hence *fawn upon, flatter* (so trag. +; Antig. Car. 172 σαίνειν φιλοφρόνως; Jos., Bell. 6, 336). It is in this direction that many prefer to take the mng. of the pass. in the only place in our lit. where the word occurs, 1 Th 3: 3 τὸ μηδένα σαίνεσθαι (ἐν ταῖς θλίψεσιν ταύταις) *so that no one might be deceived* (PSchmidt, Schmiedel, Wohlenberg, GMilligan, CBWilliams, Frame ad loc., also Zahn, Einl.³ I 158f). However, a more suitable mng. is the one preferred without exception by the ancient versions and the Gk. interpreters *move, disturb, agitate* (Soph., Ant. 1214 παιδός με σαίνει φθόγγος; Diog. L. 8, 41 οἱ σαινόμενοι τοῖς λεγομένοις ἐδάκρυον.—In Stoic. III 231, 8f σαίνεσθαι is='be carried away w. someth.'), *so that no one might be shaken* or *disturbed* (Bornemann, vDobschütz [p. 133f note 3 the material necessary for understanding the word is brought together], MDibelius, Steinmann, Oepke ad loc., RSV; HChadwick, JTS n.s. 1, '50, 156ff). On the construction s. Bl-D. §399, 3 app.; Rob. 1059 and cf. also EbNestle, ZNW 7, '06, 361f; GMercati, ZNW 8, '07, 242; RPerdelwitz, StKr 86, '13, 613ff; ADKnox, JTS 25, '24, 290f; RStJParry, ibid. 405; IAHeikel, StKr 106, '35, 316. M-M.*

σάκκος, ου, ὁ (Hdt., Aristoph. +; inscr., pap., LXX, Joseph., Test. 12 Patr.—Semit. loanw.: HLewy, Die semit. Lehnwörter im Griech. 1895, 87 [cf. שַׂק]. On the quest. whether to spell it w. one κ or two s. Mayser 215) *sack, sackcloth* ὠμόλινον ἐκ σάκκου γεγονός *a rough linen towel made of (a) sack(cloth)* Hs 8, 4, 1. The fabric from which a sack is made is usu. dark in color ἁμάρτιαι μελανώτεραι σάκκου 1 Cl 8: 3 (quot. of unknown orig.). μέλας ὡς σάκκος τρίχινος Rv 6: 12 (cf. Is 50: 3). Hence *sackcloth* is esp. suited to be worn as a mourning garment (LXX; Jos., Bell. 2, 237, Ant. 5, 37 al.) περιβεβλημένοι σάκκους Rv 11: 3 (cf. 4 Km 19: 2; Is 37: 2 and s. περιβάλλω 1ba). W. σποδός (Esth 4: 2f; Jos., Ant. 20, 123; Test. Jos. 15: 2) ἐν σ. καὶ σποδῷ καθῆσθαι *sit in sackcloth and ashes* Lk 10: 13. ἐν σ. καὶ σποδῷ μετανοεῖν Mt 11: 21. ἐπὶ σ. καὶ σποδοῦ κόπτεσθαι (κόπτω 2) B 7: 5. καὶ σάκκον ἐνδύσησθε καὶ σποδὸν ὑποστρώσητε 3: 2 (Is 58: 5).—Menand., fgm. 544 Kock, of Syrian penitents, who have sinned against the goddess: ἔλαβον σακίον, εἶτ' εἰς τὴν ὁδὸν ἐκάθισαν αὑτοὺς ἐπὶ κόπρου, καὶ τὴν θεὸν ἐξιλάσαντο τῷ ταπεινοῦσθαι σφόδρα; Plut., Superst. 7 p. 168D: ἔξω κάθηται σακκίον ἔχων καὶ περιεζωσμένος ῥάκεσι ῥυπαροῖς, πολλάκις δὲ γυμνὸς ἐν πηλῷ κυλινδούμενος ἐξαγορεύει τινὰς ἁμαρτίας—ὡς τόδε φαγόντος ἢ πιόντος ἢ βαδίσαντος ὁδόν, ἣν οὐκ εἴα τὸ δαιμόνιον. On the rags of a penitent cf. ἐν ἱεροῖς ῥακενδύταις Hermes Trismeg., Cat. Cod. Astr. VIII 4 p. 148, 2; 165, 16. M-M.*

Σαλά (שֶׁלַח) ὁ indecl. *Shelah*, in Luke's genealogy of Jesus.
1. son of Nahshon and father of Boaz Lk 3: 32; here the t.r. has Σαλμών (Mt 1: 4f; 1 Ch 2: 11; cf. Ruth 4: 20f).—EbNestle, Sala, Salma, Salmon: ZNW 11, '10, 242f.
2. son of Cainan and father of Eber (Gen 10: 24; 11: 13–15; 1 Ch 1: 18 A) Lk 3: 35.*

Σαλαθιήλ (שְׁאַלְתִּיאֵל), ὁ indecl. (LXX.—Jos., Ant. 11, 73 Σαλαθίηλος) *Shealtiel, Salathiel*, father of Zerubbabel (1 Ch 3: 19; 2 Esdr [Ezra] 3: 2; 5: 2; 22 [Neh 12]: 1; Hg 1: 1); in the genealogy of Jesus Mt 1: 12 he is a son of Jechoniah (1 Ch 3: 17), in Lk 3: 27 a son of Neri.*

Σαλαμίς, ῖνος, ἡ (on the v.l. Σαλαμίνη cf. Bl-D. §57 w. app.; Mlt.-H. 128) *Salamis*, a large city on the east coast of the island of Cyprus (Aeschyl., Hdt. et al.; inscr.; Sib. Or. 4, 128; 5, 452 πόλις μεγάλη) visited by Paul on his 'first' missionary journey Ac 13: 5.—S. the lit. on Κύπρος. M-M.*

σαλεύω 1 aor. ἐσάλευσα. Pass.: pf. ptc. σεσαλευμένος; 1 aor. ἐσαλεύθην; 1 fut. σαλευθήσομαι (Aeschyl., Pla., X. +; Dit., Or. 515, 47; pap., LXX; En. 101, 4; Philo; Jos., Bell. 2, 636, Ant. 8, 136 al.; Sib. Or. 3, 675) in our lit. only trans. *shake, cause to move to and fro, cause to waver* or *totter*, pass. *be shaken, be made to waver* or *totter*.
1. lit. (Diod. S. 12, 47, 2 τ. τείχη) οἰκίαν *shake a house* (a flood: Sb 8267, 8 [5 BC]) Lk 6: 48. τὴν γῆν Hb 12: 26.—Pass. κάλαμος ὑπὸ ἀνέμου σαλευόμενος *a reed driven to and fro by the wind* (Appian, Bell. Civ. 4, 28 §120 [pass. of a swaying reed]; cf. Is 7: 2; Jos., Ant. 4, 51 ἐξ ἀνέμου σαλευόμενον κῦρα) Mt 11: 7; Lk 7: 24. Cf. Rv 6: 13 v.l. Of a house ἐσαλεύθη ὁ τόπος *the place shook*, lit. *was shaken* (cf. Ps 17: 8) Ac 4: 31 (cf. Lucian, Necyom. 10 ἅπαντα ἐκεῖνα ἐσαλεύετο.—σαλεύεσθαι as a sign of Divine Presence Jos., Ant. 7, 76f). Of foundations shaking in an earthquake (cf. Ps 81: 5) 16: 26. αἱ δυνάμεις τῶν οὐρανῶν σαλευθήσονται *the armies of heaven will be shaken* Mt 24: 29; Lk 21: 26; cf. Mk 13: 25 (PJoüon, Rech de Sc rel 29, '39, 114f). Also of the heavens *moving* in orderly fashion at God's command οἱ οὐρανοὶ σαλευόμενοι 1 Cl 20: 1. μέτρον σεσαλευμένον *a measure that is shaken together* Lk 6: 38.
2. fig. (Appian, Iber. 102 §442 of wavering in loyalty) ἵνα μὴ σαλευθῶ *that I may not be shaken* or *disturbed* Ac 2: 25 (Ps 15: 8); *incite* 17: 13. σαλευθῆναι ἀπὸ τοῦ νοός (Theodor. Prodr. 4, 319 H. τὸν νοῦν σαλευθείς) 2 Th 2: 2.—τὰ σαλευόμενα *that which is* or *can be shaken* Hb 12: 27a forms a contrast (cf. Philo, Leg. All. 38) to τὰ μὴ σαλευόμενα *that which is not* (and *cannot be*) *shaken* vs. 27b; the former is the heaven and earth of the world as it now exists (vs. 26), the latter the coming Kingdom (vs. 28). M-M. B. 675.*

Σαλήμ (שָׁלֵם), ἡ (LXX; Philo.—Jos., Ant, 1, 180 has Σόλυμα, also indecl.) *Salem*. Hb 7: 1f, following Gen 14: 18, calls Melchizedek βασιλεὺς Σαλήμ and interprets it as 'King of peace' (cf. Philo, Leg. All. 3, 79 Μελχισέδεκ βασιλέα τῆς εἰρήνης—Σαλὴμ τοῦτο γὰρ ἑρμηνεύεται).—S. on Μελχισέδεκ and Erbes s.v. Βηθανία 2.

Σαλίμ, τό indecl. *Salim*. John baptized ἐν Αἰνὼν ἐγγὺς τοῦ Σαλίμ J 3: 23. Acc. to Euseb., Onom. p. 40, 1 this place lay eight Roman miles south of Scythopolis in northern Samaria (so Lagrange and Abel; s. Αἰνών). Today there is a place called Salim about 3½ mi. (6 km.) east of Shechem; it is mentioned in Epiph., Haer. 55, 2 (this one is preferred by WFAlbright, HTR 17, '24, 193f). Cf. in addition to Αἰνών also EbNestle, ZDPV 30, '07, 210ff; BWBacon, Biblical World 33, '09, 223ff; KKundsin, Topolog. Überlieferungsstoffe im J '25. Erbes s.v. Βηθανία 2.*

Σαλμών (שַׂלְמוֹן), ὁ indecl. *Salmon*, son of Nahshon and father of Boaz (1 Ch 2: 11; cf. Ruth 4: 20f [Σαλμάν; but A reads Σαλμών]), in the genealogy of Jesus Mt 1: 4f; Lk 3: 32 t.r. (cf. Σαλά 1).*

Σαλμώνη, ης, ἡ (this form of the name is found only in our passage. Elsewh. it is called Σαλμώνιον, Σαμώνιον, Σαμμώνιον, Σαλμωνίς; see the exx. in JWeiss, RE XI 89, 14ff) *Salmone*, a promontory on the northeast corner of Crete Ac 27: 7.*

σάλος, ου, ὁ *rolling* or *tossing motion, surge,* esp. of the *waves* in a rough sea (trag.; Plut., Lucull. 10, 3; Lucian, Tox. 19, Hermot. 28; Jon 1: 15; Ps 88: 10.—Philo, Sacr. Abel. 13 al. as a symbol w. κλύδων. As a symb. also Jos., Ant. 14, 376), but also of an earthquake (Eur., Iph. Taur. 46; Is 24: 20 v.l.; Jos., Ant. 4, 51); however, the former is more probable in Lk 21: 25. M-M.*

σάλπιγξ, ιγγος, ἡ (Hom.+; Epigr. Gr. 1049, 7; PHermopol. 121, 10; LXX; Philo; Jos., Bell. 3, 89, Ant. 7, 359; loanw. in rabb.) *trumpet*.
1. the instrument itself 1 Cor 14: 8; Hb 12: 19 (cf. Ex 19: 16); Rv 1: 10; 4: 1; 8: 2, 6, 13; 9: 14; D 16: 6; Epil Mosq 3. μετὰ σάλπιγγος φωνῆς μεγάλης *with a loud trumpet-call* Mt 24: 31 t.r. (s. φωνή 1).
2. the sound made or signal given by the instrument *trumpet-call,* (*sound of the*) *trumpet* (Aristoph., Ach. 1001; X., R. Equ. 9, 11, Hipp. 3, 12; Aristot., Rhet. 3, 6; Polyb. 4, 13, 1; Ael. Aristid. 34, 22 K.=50 p. 554 D.; τῇ πρώτῃ σ.) μετὰ σάλπιγγος μεγάλης *with a loud trumpet-call* Mt 24: 31. ἐν τῇ ἐσχάτῃ σάλπιγγι *at the sound of the last trumpet* 1 Cor 15: 52. ἐν σάλπιγγι θεοῦ (καταβήσεται ἀπ' οὐρανοῦ) *at the call of the trumpet sounded by God's command* 1 Th 4: 16. M-M.*

σαλπίζω (Hom.+; LXX; Philo, Spec. Leg. 2, 188; Jos., Ant. 5, 23) fut. σαλπίσω (Lob. on Phryn. p. 191); 1 aor. ἐσάλπισα (Aelian, V.H. 1, 26; LXX; Jos., Ant. 7, 279.—On both forms s. Bl-D. §71; Mlt.-H. 257) *sound the trumpet, trumpet* (*forth*) Rv 8: 6-13; 9: 1, 13; 10: 7; 11: 15.—Impers. (X., An. 1, 2, 17) σαλπίσει *the trumpet will sound* 1 Cor 15: 52 (Bl-D. §129; Rob. 392). It is prob. to be taken symbolically (cf. Ps.-Lucian, Ocypus v. 114 ἀλέκτωρ ἡμέραν ἐσάλπισεν; Achilles Tat. 8, 10, 10 ὑπὸ σάλπιγγι . . . μοιχεύεται; M. Ant. 5, 6 ἄνθρωπος εὖ ποιήσας οὐκ ἐπιβοᾶται; Synesius, To Paeonius 1 p. 308A τὸ κηρύττειν ἑαυτὸν καὶ πάντα ποιεῖν ὑπὲρ ἐπιδείξεως οὐ σοφίας ἀλλὰ σοφιστοῦ ἐστί=to trumpet one's own achievements and do everything for the sake of publicity is not the part of wisdom, but of sophistry) in μὴ σαλπίσῃς ἔμπροσθέν σου *you must not sound a trumpet before you* Mt 6: 2 (it is taken non-symbolically by EKlostermann ad loc.; ABüchler, JTS 10, '09, 266ff). M-M.*

σαλπιστής, οῦ, ὁ (a later form for the older σαλπι(γ)κτής.—Theophr., Char. 25; Polyb. 1, 45, 13; Dionys. Hal. 4, 17, 3; 4, 18, 3; Charito 8, 2, 6 al.; Dit., Syll.³ 1058, 4; 1059 II, 20; Sb 4591, 3.—WGRutherford, The New Phrynichus 1881, 279) *trumpeter* Rv 18: 22. M-M.*

Σαλώμη, ης, ἡ (Suppl. Epigr. Gr. VIII 197 [I AD; Jerusalem]; Joseph. index and cf. Bl-D. §53, 3; Mlt.-H. 144) *Salome,* one of the Galilean women who followed Jesus Mk 15: 40; 16: 1; in case it is permissible to combine Mk 15: 40 w. its parallel Mt 27: 56, where the name does not occur, she was the wife of Zebedee and mother of James and John. (The daughter of Herodias mentioned but not named in Mk 6: 22ff; Mt 14: 6ff was also called Salome, cf. Jos., Ant. 18, 136.—HDaffner, Salome, '12; WSpeyer, D. Tod der Salome, Jahrb. f. Antike u. Christent. 10, '67, 176-80).*

Σαλωμών (LXX; s. Thackeray 165; Christian magical pap. 17, 10 ed. Preisigke II p. 206) Ac 7: 47 Tdf. s. Σολομών.*

Σαμάρεια, ας, ἡ (to be spelled and accented on the analogy of Ἀλεξάνδρεια etc.; cf. Bl-D. §38 app., but also Rob. 197; Mlt.-H. 147) *Samaria* (the Gk. form of the name in Polyb. 5, 71, 11; Strabo 16, 2, 34; Diod. S. 19, 93, 7; Pliny 5, 13, 17; Joseph. index; LXX), orig. the name of the city (Hebr. שֹׁמְרוֹן, Aram. שָׁמְרַיִן), though not so in our lit., then transferred to the whole province which, in NT times, included the region fr. the Plain of Jezreel southward to the border of Judaea. J 4: 4 (Jos., Vi. 269 ἔδει δι' ἐκείνης [=τ. Σαμαρείας] πορεύεσθαι, Ant. 20, 118), 5; Ac 8: 9, 14. W. Judaea 1: 8; 8: 1; w. Judaea and Galilee 9: 31; w. Galilee Lk 17: 11; w. Phoenicia Ac 15: 3. γυνὴ ἐκ τῆς Σαμαρείας a Samaritan woman J 4: 7. ἡ πόλις τῆς Σαμαρείας *the* (main) *city of Samaria* (cf. πόλις 1), i.e. the city of Samaria which, since the time of Herod the Great, was known as Sebaste Ac 8: 5 (on this s. JBoehmer, ZNW 9, '08, 216-18).—GHölscher, Palästina in der persischen u. hellenist. Zeit '03; Baedeker, Palästina u. Syrien⁷ '10; HGuthe, RE XVII '06, 419ff; XXIV '13, 448f; Schürer⁴ index; LHaefeli, Gesch. der Landschaft Sam. von 722 BC bis 67 AD '22; AParrot, Samaria, trans. SHHooke, '58. M-M.*

Σαμαρία s. Σαμάρεια.

Σαμαρίτης, ου, ὁ (Joseph. index; Damasc., Vi. Isid. 141. For the spelling s. Bl-D. §38 app.; Rob. 197.—Stephan. Byz. s.v. Ὠρεός requires Σαμαρείτης and refers s.v. Σαμάρεια to a certain Antiochus as authority.—Appian, Bell. Civ. 5, 75 §319 has the form Σαμαρεύς, έως; Ἰδουμαίων καὶ Σαμαρέων) a *Samaritan* Lk 17: 16. Main character in the well-known parable (on this EBuonaiuti, Religio 11, '35, 117-25; JCGordon, ET 56, '45, 302-4; FJLeenhardt, Aux sources de la tradition chrétienne [MGoguel-Festschr.] '50, 132-8; BGerhardsson, Con. Neot. 16, '58; JDerrett, Law in the NT, '70, 208-27; s. παραβολή 2, end) Lk 10: 33. Pl. J 4: 39f. Avoided by the Jews vs. 9 (cf. Sir 50: 25f; Jos., Ant. 18, 30; 20, 118, Bell. 2, 232f), also despised by them 8: 48. πόλις Σαμαριτῶν Mt 10: 5; κώμη Σ. Lk 9: 52; cf. Ac 8: 25.—Lit. s.v. Σαμάρεια, also EKautzsch, RE XVII '06, 428ff; JAMontgomery, The Samaritans '07; JEHThomson, The Samaritans '19; MGaster, The Samaritans '25; Lightley (Σαδδουκαῖος, end); Billerb. I 538-60; KBornhäuser, ZsystTh 9, '32, 552-66; JoachJeremias, Jerusalem z. Zeit Jesu II B '29-'37, 224ff: Die Samaritaner; MSEnslin, Lk and the Samaritans: HTR 36, '43, 278-97; JBowman, Samaritan Studies: Bulletin of the JRylands Library 40, '58, 298-329. M-M.*

Σαμαρῖτις, ιδος, ἡ (1 Macc 10: 30; 11: 28; Ep. Arist. 107; Jos., Bell. 3, 48 al.; IG III 2892) fem. of Σαμαρίτης adj. and subst., *Samaritan* (fem.) ἡ γυνὴ ἡ Σαμαρῖτις *the Samaritan woman* J 4: 9a; cf. b.*

Σαμοθράκη, ης, ἡ (oft. in lit. and inscr.) *Samothrace,* an island in the northern part of the Aegean Sea Ac 16: 11. M-M.*

Σάμος, ου, ἡ (Hom.+; oft. in inscr.; 1 Macc 15: 23; Sib. Or. 3, 363) *Samos,* an island off the west coast of Asia Minor, opposite the promontory of Mycale, not far fr. Ephesus. Landing-place for ships on the voyage fr. the Hellespont to Syria (Jos., Ant. 16, 23; 62) Ac 20: 15.—CCurtius, Urkunden zur Gesch. von Samos 1873, Inschriften u. Studien zur Geschichte von S. 1877.*

Σαμουήλ (שְׁמוּאֵל), ὁ indecl. *Samuel* (1 Km 1: 1-25: 1, 28; Jer 15: 1; Ps 98: 6; 1 Ch 6: 13, 18; 9: 22; 1 Esdr 1: 18 ἀπὸ τῶν χρόνων Σαμουὴλ τοῦ προφήτου; Sir 46: 13; Philo.—Joseph. has Σαμούηλος, ου [Ant. 6, 51]; cf. Ep. Arist. 50; Preisigke, Namenbuch); in our lit. he brings the period of the Judges to an end Ac 13: 20, and begins the line of the prophets 3: 24. περὶ Δαυὶδ τε καὶ Σαμουὴλ καὶ τῶν προφητῶν Hb 11: 32. M-M.*

Σαμφουρειν indecl. ἀπῆλθεν εἰς τ. χώραν Σαμφουρειν (= Sepphoris) ἐγγὺς τῆς ἐρήμου εἰς Ἐφράιμ λεγομένην πόλιν J 11: 54 D. S. the commentaries.*

Σαμψών (שִׁמְשׁוֹן), ὁ indecl. Samson, a Judge in Israel (Judg 13–16.—Jos., Ant. 5, 290–318 has Σαμψών, ῶνος [297]) Hb 11: 32 (Bl-D. §39, 5; 8 app.; Mlt.-H. 103).*

σανδάλιον, ου, τό (Hdt.+; Diod. S. 5, 46, 2; Lucian, Herod. 5; LXX w. the same mng. as in our lit.) dim. of σάνδαλον (Hom. Hymns+; Jos., Ant. 4, 256; loanw. in rabb.) sandal, a sole made of leather or wood with an upper part, held on the foot by means of thongs. ὑπόδησαι τὰ σανδάλιά σου put on your sandals Ac 12: 8. ὑποδεδεμένος σανδάλια with (nothing but) sandals on one's feet Mk 6: 9. M-M.*

σανίς, ίδος, ἡ (Hom.+; inscr.; PFlor. 69, 21; SSol 8: 9; Ezk 27: 5; Philo, De Prov.: Euseb., Pr. Ev. 8, 14, 26; Jos., Ant. 8, 134 al.) board, plank; beside τὰ ἀπὸ τοῦ πλοίου, the pieces of wreckage fr. the ship, the σανίδες of Ac 27: 44 are perh. boards or planks that were used to hold the cargo of grain in place (Breusing 203). M-M.*

Σαούλ (שָׁאוּל), ὁ indecl. Saul—1. son of Kish; first king of Israel (1 Km 9ff; 1 Ch 8: 33; 1 Macc 4: 30; Philo, Migr. Abr. 196.—Joseph. has Σάουλος, ου [Ant. 6, 74].—Bl-D. §53, 2 w. app.; Mlt.-H. 144) Ac 13: 21; 1 Cl 4: 13.

2. Jewish name of the Apostle Paul (cf. Παῦλος 2). Ac, which is the only book in our lit. that uses the name Saul for the apostle, has it mostly in its Gk. form (s. Σαῦλος). The OT Σαούλ is found only in the account of his conversion, and as a voc. 9: 4, 17; 22: 7, 13; 26: 14 (cf. Test. Levi 2: 6 the call of the angel fr. the opened heavens: Λευί, Λευί, εἴσελθε).*

σαπρός, ά, όν (Hipponax [VI BC], Aristoph., Hippocr.+; Dit., Syll.² 587, 24; pap.) decayed, rotten.

1. lit., of spoiled fish (Antiphanes in Athen. 6 p. 225F) Mt 13: 48. Of plants and their products (Aristoph., Theophr. et al.; PFay. 119, 4; 6): of decayed trees Mt 7: 17f; 12: 33a; Lk 6: 43b. Of rotten fruits (Theophr., H.Pl. 4, 14, 10 olives; PFlor. 176, 9 figs) Mt 12: 33b; Lk 6: 43a; of grapes that lie on the ground and rot Hs 2: 4. Of stones λίθοι σ. stones that are unsound or crumbling Hs 9, 5, 2. But in 9, 6, 4 the transition to the more general mng. unusable, unfit, bad (Herodas 2, 23 worn-out shoes; PLond. 356, 11 [I AD]) is complete; this mng. also recommends itself for some of the passages dealt w. above (e.g., do 'rotten' fish swim into a net, and do 'rotten' trees bear any fruit at all?).

2. fig. bad, evil, unwholesome (Menand., Mon. 722; Epict. 3, 22, 61 σαπρὰ δόγματα; Sb 5761, 23 [I AD] σ. ὄνομα; PSI 717, 4 [II AD] ἐὰν κατ᾽ ἐμοῦ καταψηφίσηταί τι σαπρόν; 312, 13 [IV AD] οὐδὲν σαπρὸν ποιήσει) λόγος σαπρός an evil word, evil speech Eph 4: 29 (cf. M. Ant. 11, 15 ὡς σαπρὸς ὁ λέγων).—CLindhagen, Die Wurzel ΣΑΠ im AT u. NT: Upps. Univ. Årsskr. 5, ’50, 27–53. M-M.*

Σάπφιρα (Aram. שַׁפִּירָא. On the spelling and accentuation cf. Bl-D. §38 app.; 39, 7 app.; 40 app.; Mlt.-H. 145; M-M. Both Aramaic and Gk. forms are found on the recently discovered ossuaries near Jerusalem: Suppl. Epigr. Gr. VIII 201 [I BC/I AD]; 184 [I AD]; HJCadbury, Amicitiae Corolla [RHarris-Festschr.] ’33, 54f), gen. ης, dat. ῃ, ἡ (on its declension s. Bl-D. §43, 1; Mlt.-H. 118)

Sapphira, wife of Ἀνανίας (q.v. 2 and the lit. s.v. κοινός 1a. PHMenoud, La mort d’An. et de Saph.: Aux sources de la tradition chrét. [MGoguel-Festschr.] ’50, 146–54) Ac 5: 1. M-M.*

σάπφιρος, ου, ἡ (Semitic loanw., Hebr. סַפִּיר.—Theophr., Lap. 1, 8; 4, 23; 6, 37; Diosc. 5, 157; Aelian, V.H. 14, 34; PGM 3, 515; LXX; En. 18, 8 [σάφφ-]; Jos., Bell. 5, 234, Ant. 3, 168) the sapphire, a blue, transparent precious stone (though the ancients prob. understood the σα. to be the lapis lazuli) Rv 21: 19 (cf. Tob 13: 17; Is 54: 11).—RGradwohl, D. Farben im AT Beih. ZAW 83, ’63, 33f; other lit. s.v. ἀμέθυστος. M-M.*

σαργάνη, ης, ἡ (Aeschyl.+, in the sense 'plait, braid') basket (so Aeneas Tact. 1348; Timocl. [IV BC] in Athen. 8 p. 339E; 9 p. 407E; Lucian, Lexiph. 6; BGU 417, 14; PFlor. 269, 7; PStrassb. 37, 13) 2 Cor 11: 33, where it is 'clearly a rope-basket', B. 623.—FJAHort, JTS 10, ’09, 567ff (κόφινος, σφυρίς, σαργάνη).—MSchnebel, D. Landwirtsch. im hellenist. Ägypt. I ’25, 280f. M-M. B., s. above.*

Σάρδεις, εων, αἱ (this spelling of the name Aeschyl., Thu.+; inscr.; Sib. Or. 5, 289) Sardis, the ancient capital city of Lydia, in western Asia Minor Rv 1: 11; 3: 1, 4.—Ramsay, Letters ’05. Its inscriptions are found in Sardis: Publications of the American Soc. for the Excav. of Sardis VII ’32. Apollonius of Tyana wrote letters τοῖς ἐν Σάρδεσιν (nos. 38; 75f) and τοῖς Σαρδιανοῖς (56): Philostrat. I p. 353; 359; 366; SEJohnson, Christianity in Sardis, HRWilloughby-Festschr. ’61, 81–90.*

σάρδινος, ου, ὁ (Anecdot. Gr. Ox. ed. Cramer IV [1837] 229) late form of σάρδιον Rv 4: 3 t.r.; s. σάρδιον.*

σάρδιον, ου, τό (Aristoph.+; Pla., Phaedo 110D; Theophr., Lap. 1, 8; 4, 23; Diod. S. 3, 53, 6; Dit., Syll.² 588, 3; PHolm. 3, 36; LXX; Jos., Bell. 5, 234) carnelian, sard(ius), a reddish precious stone Rv 4: 3 (t.r. σαρδίνῳ); 21: 20.—Lit. s.v. ἀμέθυστος. M-M.*

σαρδόνυξ, υχος, ὁ (Plut., Mor. 1160F; 1163A; Cyranides p. 34, 2; Jos., Bell. 5, 233, Ant. 3, 165 al.) the sardonyx, a precious stone, a variety of agate Rv 21: 20.—Lit. s.v. ἀμέθυστος. M-M.*

Σάρεπτα (צָרְפַת. On the spelling s. Bl-D. §39, 2 app.; Mlt.-H. 147), ων (declinable in this way at least Ob 20; cf. Bl-D. §56, 2 app.; Mlt.-H. 147), τά Zarephath, a city on the Phoenician coast betw. Tyre and Sidon (Jos., Ant. 8, 320), where Elijah lived during the famine. Σ. τῆς Σιδωνίας (as 3 Km 17: 9 in this same account) Lk 4: 26.*

σαρκικός, ή, όν (Aristot., H. Anim. 10, 2 p. 635a, 11 ed. LDittmeyer ’07 v.l. acc. to mss.; a verse, perh. by Sotades Lyr. [III BC] 19, p. 244 Coll.; Maximus Tyr. 11, 10e v.l. [for σάρκινος].—σαρκικός means 'belonging to the σάρξ' [opp. πνευματικός], 'fleshly'; on the other hand, σάρκινος is 'consisting' or 'composed of flesh', 'fleshy'. Our lit., or at least its copyists, did not observe this distinction in all occurrences of the word. The forms are interchanged in the tradition. Bl-D. §113, 2 w. app.; Rob. 158f) fleshly, in the manner of the flesh, carnal (in older usage).

1. belonging to the order of earthly things, material τὰ σαρκικά Ro 15: 27; 1 Cor 9: 11. Ign. is fond of using σαρκ. in contrast w. πνευματικός: ἀγάπη σαρκική τε καὶ πνευματική ISm 13: 2; cf. ἑνότης 12: 2. ἕνωσις IMg 13: 2. ἐπιμέλεια IPol 1: 2.

2. consisting of flesh, the earthly material: Polycarp is σαρκικὸς καὶ πνευματικός IPol 2: 2. Jesus is called

σαρκικός τε καὶ πνευματικός, γεννητὸς καὶ ἀγέννητος IEph 7: 2. The Risen Lord συνέφαγεν αὐτοῖς (i.e. the disciples) ὡς σαρκικός *he ate with them as a being made of flesh* ISm 3: 3 (cf. ἐγείρειν σαρκικούς Third Corinthians 3: 6).

3. *belonging to the realm of the flesh* in so far as it is weak, sinful, and transitory, and in these respects is the opp. of the spirit (Anth. Pal. 1, 107): (ἄνθρωποι) σ. 1 Cor 3: 4 t.r.; ὅπλα 2 Cor 10: 4. σοφία 1: 12. αἱ σαρκικαὶ ἐπιθυμίαι 1 Pt 2: 11; αἱ σαρκικαὶ καὶ σωματικαὶ ἐπιθυμίαι D 1: 4. Of immature Christians σαρκικοί ἐστε 1 Cor 3: 3a, b. Of heretics in contrast to orthodox believers οἱ σαρκικοὶ τὰ πνευματικὰ πράσσειν οὐ δύνανται, οὐδὲ οἱ πνευματικοὶ τὰ σαρκικά IEph 8: 2.—In addition, σαρκικός is found as a v.l. (while σάρκινος is in the text, as Maximus Tyr. 11, 10f; Philo, Sacr. Abel. 63) in Ro 7: 14; 1 Cor 3: 1; Hb 7: 16; in all three places the v.l. is the rdg. of the t.r. M-M.*

σαρκικῶς adv. *in the flesh, acc. to the flesh* w. πνευματικῶς IEph 10: 3 (σαρκικός 1).*

σάρκινος, η, ον (since Eupolis Com. [V BC] 387; Pla.; PLond. 1177, 169; 172 [II AD]; LXX, En., Philo.—Cf. with σαρκικός).
1. *fleshy, (made) of flesh* (Theocr., Id. 21, 66; Maximus Tyr. 17, 3f σῶμα; Artem. 2, 35 p. 132, 27) καρδία *a heart of flesh* (opp. λιθίνη), i.e. a heart capable of feeling B 6: 14 (Ezk 11: 19; 36: 26); cf. 2 Cor 3: 3.
2. *fleshly, belonging to the realm of the flesh* in so far as it is weak, sinful, and transitory, *carnal* (in older usage) (Epict., App. D, 4 [p. 479f Sch.] εὐχόμενος θεοῖς αἴτει τὰ θεῖα, ὧν οὐδὲν σάρκινον κ. γήινον ψαύει πάθος; Maximus Tyr. 11, 10f; 29, 7g; Cass. Dio 38, 21, 3; Philo, Sacr. Abel. 63) νόμος ἐντολῆς σαρκίνης (opp. ζωῆς) Hb 7: 16. Of men (Hipparchus the Pythagorean in Stob. IV 980, 15 H. θνατοὶ κ. σάρκινοι; Iambl., Protr. 20 p. 104, 10 Pistelli; Sib. Or., fgm. 1, 1) 1 Cor 3: 1 (opp. πνευματικός); cf. Ro 7: 14.—σάρκινος as v.l. (for σαρκικός) 2 Cor 1: 12. M-M.*

σαρκίον, ου, τό dim. of σάρξ *piece of flesh* (Hippocr. et al.), of the whole *body* (Plut., Brut. 8, 3; M. Ant. 2, 2, 1; 2) κοινωνῆσαι τῷ ἁγίῳ (κοινωνέω 1ba) MPol 17: 1.*

σαρκοφάγος, ον (Aristot. et al.; cf. Ep. Arist. 146; Sib. Or. 2, 236) *flesh-eating* θηρία λεπτὰ σ. of worms AP fgm. 2, p. 12, 27.*

σαρκοφόρος, ον (Nicetas Eugen. 3, 319 Hercher; of men Sib. Or. 8, 222; of Christ 1, 325; Clem. of Alex., Strom. 5, 34, 1) *flesh-bearing* of Christ's appearing in true human form ὁμολογεῖν αὐτὸν (=κύριον) σαρκοφόρον confess *that he was clothed in flesh* (adj. or subst.) ISm 5: 2.*

σάρξ, σαρκός, ἡ (Hom.+; inscr., pap., LXX, En., Ep. Arist., Philo, Joseph., Test. 12 Patr.; Sib. Or. 6, 3) *flesh*.
1. lit., of the material that covers the bones of a human or animal body 1 Cor 15: 39a, b, c, d; Hv 3, 10, 4; 3, 12, 1. The pl. (which denotes flesh in the mass [Lucian, Dial. Mort. 10, 5], while the sing. rather denotes the substance. —Herodas 4, 61; Gen 40: 19; 1 Km 17: 44; 4 Km 9: 36; Philo) Lk 24: 39 v.l.; Rv 19: 18, 21 (Quint. Smyrn. 11, 245: the σάρκες of the slain are food for the birds); B 10: 4; symbolically Rv 17: 16. It decays 1 Cl 25: 3. Normally gives forth an evil odor when burned MPol 15: 2. W. bones (cf. ὀστέον) 1 Cl 6: 3 (Gen 2: 23); Lk 24: 39; Eph 5: 30 v.l. (symbol.). Paul speaks of his illness as a σκόλοψ τῇ σαρκί (s. σκόλοψ) 2 Cor 12: 7. ἡ ἐν σαρκὶ περιτομή *the physical circumcision* Ro 2: 28; cf. Eph 2: 11b; Col 2: 13 (ἀκρο-

βυστία 2); Gal 6: 13 (ἡ σάρξ=the flesh that is circumcised); B 9: 4. Symbolically: the corrosion on the precious metals of the rich φάγεται τὰς σάρκας ὑμῶν ὡς πῦρ Js 5: 3.—Of the flesh as physically attractive: ὀπίσω σαρκὸς ἑτέρας *after other kinds of flesh* Jd 7. Cf. 2 Pt 2: 10.—Ign. describes the elements of the Eucharist as σάρξ (or αἷμα) Ἰησοῦ Χριστοῦ IRo 7: 3; IPhld 4; ISm 7: 1. Also J 6: 51–6 urges that one must eat the flesh of the Son of Man (and drink his blood) (ThPhilips, Die Verheissung der hl. Eucharistie nach Joh. '22; Bultmann 161f; 174–7; AWikenhauser '48, 105f).—His anti-Docetic position also leads Ign. to use the concept 'flesh (and blood) of Christ' in other contexts as well ITr 8: 1; IPhld 5: 1.
2. *the body* itself, viewed as substance (Aeschyl., Sept. 622: opp. νοῦς; Ex 30: 32; 4 Km 6: 30; w. καρδία or ψυχή Alex. Aphr., An. p. 98, 7–10 Br.; Ps 37: 8; 62: 2; Eccl 2: 3; Ezk 11: 19; 44: 7 al.; Jos., Bell. 6, 47, Ant. 19, 325) οὔτε ἡ σάρξ αὐτοῦ εἶδεν διαφθοράν Ac 2: 31. W. ψυχή 1 Cl 49: 6. W. καρδία Ac 2: 26 (Ps 15: 9).—Eph 5: 29. ἑόρακαν τὸ πρόσωπόν μου ἐν σαρκί *they have seen me face to face* Col 2: 1. Opp. πνεῦμα (PGM 5, 460 ἐπικαλοῦμαί σε τὸν κτίσαντα πᾶσαν σάρκα κ. πᾶν πνεῦμα) 1 Cor 5: 5; 2 Cor 7: 1; Col 2: 5; 1 Pt 4: 6; Hm 3: 1; 10, 2, 6; also in relation to Christ (though this is disputed) J 6: 63; Hs 5, 6, 5–7. Cf. 1 Ti 3: 16.—ἀσθένεια τῆς σαρκός *bodily illness* Gal 4: 13; cf. vs. 14. ἀσθενὴς τῇ σαρκί *weak in the body* Hs 9, 1, 2. ὁ ἀλγῶν σάρκα *the one who is ill in body* B 8: 6. πάσχειν σαρκί 1 Pt 4: 1b. ἡ τῆς σαρκὸς καθαρότης *the purity of the body* Hb 9: 13 (opp. καθαρίζειν τὴν συνείδησιν v. 14). σαρκὸς ἀπόθεσις ῥύπου 1 Pt 3: 21 (s. ῥύπος). Cf. 2 Cor 7: 5. The σάρξ is raised fr. the dead 1 Cl 26: 3; 2 Cl 9: 1. Of the body of Christ during his earthly ministry Eph 2: 14 (JHAHart, The Enmity in His Flesh: Exp. 6th Ser. III '01, 135–41); Hb 10: 20; 1 Pt 3: 18; 4: 1a; 1 J 4: 2; 2 J 7; B 5: 1, 10f; 6: 7, 9; 7: 5; 12: 10; IEph 7: 2; Pol 7: 1. Married couples form μία σάρξ (Gen 2: 24. —GAicher, Mann u. Weib ein Fleisch: BZ 5, '07, 159–65) Mt 19: 5f; Mk 10: 8a, b; 1 Cor 6: 16; Eph 5: 31 (on these passages, TABurkill, ZNW 62, '71, 115–20). δικαιώματα σαρκός behind 'all sorts of ceremonial washings' there are *regulations that concern the physical body* Hb 9: 10.
3. *a man of flesh and blood* ὁ λόγος σὰρξ ἐγένετο J 1: 14 (RSeeberg, Festgabe AvHarnack dargebracht '21, 263–81.—Artem. 2, 35 p. 132, 27 ἐὰν σάρκινοι οἱ θεοὶ φαίνωνται; Synes., Dio 6 p. 45B). πᾶσα σάρξ *every person, everyone* (LXX for כָּל־בָּשָׂר, s. πᾶς 1aa) Lk 3: 6 (Is 40: 5); J 17: 2; Ac 2: 17 (Jo 3: 1); 1 Pt 1: 24 (Is 40: 6); 1 Cl 59: 3; 64; 2 Cl 7: 6; 17: 5 (the last two Is 66: 24). οὐ πᾶσα σάρξ *no person, nobody* (En. 14, 21 end.—W-S. §26, 10a; Bl-D. §275, 4; 302, 1; Rob. 752) Mt 24: 22; Mk 13: 20; Ro 3: 20 (cf. Ps 142: 2 πᾶς ζῶν); 1 Cor 1: 29 (μή); Gal 2: 16. σὰρξ καὶ αἷμα (cf. Sir 17: 31; Philo, Quis Rer. Div. Her. 57) *a human being* in contrast to God and other supernatural beings Mt 16: 17; Gal 1: 16; Eph 6: 12 (here vice versa, αἷ. καὶ σ.). Because they are the opposites of the divine nature σὰρξ καὶ αἷμα βασιλείαν θεοῦ κληρονομῆσαι οὐ δύναται 1 Cor 15: 50 (JoachJeremias, NTS 2, '56, 151–9).
4. *human* or *mortal nature, earthly descent* Ἀβραὰμ τὸν προπάτορα ἡμῶν κατὰ σάρκα Ro 4: 1. οἱ συγγενεῖς μου κατὰ σάρκα 9: 3. τοὺς τῆς σαρκὸς ἡμῶν πατέρας Hb 12: 9. τὸν Ἰσραὴλ κατὰ σάρκα *the earthly Israel* 1 Cor 10: 18 (opp. τὸν Ἰσραὴλ τοῦ θεοῦ Gal 6: 16). Of natural descent τὰ τέκνα τῆς σαρκός *children by natural descent* Ro 9: 8 (opp. τὰ τέκνα τῆς ἐπαγγελίας). ὁ μὲν ἐκ τῆς παιδίσκης κατὰ σάρκα γεγέννηται Gal 4: 23; cf. vs. 29. μου τὴν σάρκα *my fellow countrymen* Ro 11: 14 (cf. Gen 37: 27).—Of Christ's physical nature Ro 8: 3c; Hb 5: 7.

Christ is descended fr. the patriarchs and fr. David (τὸ) κατὰ σάρκα *according to the human side of his nature, as far as his physical descent is concerned* Ro 1: 3 (JDDunn, Jesus—Flesh and Spirit [Ro 1: 3f], JTS 24, '73, 40-68); 9: 5; 1 Cl 32: 2; IEph 20: 2. On ὑποτάγητε τῷ ἐπισκόπῳ ὡς ὁ Χριστὸς τῷ πατρὶ κατὰ σάρκα IMg 13: 2 cf. Hdb. ad loc. and MRackl, Die Christologie des hl. Ignatius v. Ant. '14, 228.—τὰ παιδία κεκοινώνηκεν αἵματος καὶ σαρκός *the children share mortal nature* Hb 2: 14.

5. *corporeality, physical limitation(s), life here on earth* θλῖψιν τῇ σαρκὶ ἕξουσιν 1 Cor 7: 28. Cf. 2 Cor 4: 11; Col 1: 24. Of Christ τὸ σῶμα τῆς σαρκὸς αὐτοῦ *his body with its physical limitations* Col 1: 22; cf. 2: 11—s. 7 below (cf. En. 102, 5 τὸ σῶμα τῆς σαρκὸς ὑμῶν; IQ p Hab 9, 2).— Of human life: ἀποδημεῖν τῆς σαρκός MPol 2: 2 (s. ἀποδημέω). ἐπιμένειν τῇ σαρκί Phil 1: 24. ζῆν ἐν σαρκί vs. 22; Gal 2: 20. ἐν σ. περιπατεῖν 2 Cor 10: 3a. ἐν σ. τυγχάνειν Dg 5: 8a. τὸν ἐπίλοιπον ἐν σαρκὶ χρόνον 1 Pt 4: 2. ἡ ἐπιδημία τῆς σαρκὸς ταύτης *our sojourn in life* 2 Cl 5: 5. ἐν τῇ σαρκί *in our earthly life* 8: 2.

6. *the external* or *outward side of life,* as it appears to the eye of an unregenerate person, that which is natural or earthly σοφοὶ κατὰ σάρκα *wise (people) according to human standards* 1 Cor 1: 26. καυχᾶσθαι κατὰ (τὴν) σάρκα *boast of one's outward circumstances,* i.e. descent, manner of life, etc. (cf. vs. 22) 2 Cor 11: 18. κατὰ σάρκα Χριστόν *Christ from a human point of view* or *as far as externals are concerned* 5: 16b, cf. a (κατά II 5bβ and 7a; also VWeber, BZ 2, '04, 178-88; HWindisch, exc. ad loc.; Rtzst., Mysterienrel.[3], 374-6; FCPorter, Does Paul Claim to Have Known the Historical Jesus [2 Cor 5: 16]?: JBL 47, '28, 257-75; RAMoxon, CQR 108, '29, 320-8). οἱ κατὰ σάρκα κύριοι *those who, according to human standards, are masters* Eph 6: 5; Col 3: 22. ὑμεῖς κατὰ τὴν σ. κρίνετε *you judge by outward things, by externals* J 8: 15. Of the route that one takes in his earthly life ἡ ὁδὸς ἡ κατὰ σάρκα IRo 9: 3.—ἐν σαρκὶ πεποιθέναι *place one's trust in earthly things* or *physical advantages* Phil 3: 3f. εὐπροσωπῆσαι ἐν σαρκί Gal 6: 12. Onesimus is a beloved brother to Philemon καὶ ἐν σαρκὶ καὶ ἐν κυρίῳ *both as a man* (in the external relationship betw. master and slave) *and as a Christian* Phlm 16. ὑμῶν δὲ ἐν σαρκὶ ἐπισκόπῳ IEph 1: 3 (cf. IMg 3: 2).

7. In Paul's thought esp., the *flesh* is the willing instrument of sin, and is subject to sin to such a degree that wherever flesh is, all forms of sin are likew. present, and no good thing can live in the σάρξ Ro 7: 18 (cf. Philo, Gig. 29 αἴτιον δὲ τῆς ἀνεπιστημοσύνης μέγιστον ἡ σὰρξ καὶ ἡ πρὸς σάρκα οἰκείωσις; Sextus 317 ἀγαθὸν ἐν σαρκὶ μὴ ἐπιζήτει. The OT lays no stress on a necessary relationship betw. flesh as a substance, and sin. But for Epicurus the σάρξ is the bearer of sinful feelings and desires as well as the means of sensual enjoyment: Ep. in Plut., Mor. 135c; 1087β; F; 1089ε; 1096c αἱ τῆς σαρκὸς ἐπιθυμίαι. Also Diog. L. 10, 145. Likew. Plut. himself: Mor. 101β ταῖς τῆς σαρκὸς ἡδοναῖς; 672ε; 688D; 734A; Ps.-Plut., Consol. ad Apollon. 13 p. 107F σαρκὶ καὶ τοῖς πάθεσι ταύτης; Maximus Tyr. 33, 7a. Cf. 4 Macc 7: 18 τὰ τῆς σαρκὸς πάθη; Philo, Deus Imm. 143 σαρκὸς ἡδονή, Gig. 29; Test. Judah 19: 4, Zeb. 9: 7); Ro 6: 19; 7: 25 (opp. νοῦς); 8: 3a, 4-9, 12f; Gal 5: 13, 24; Col 2: 23; Jd 23; Dg 6: 5 (opp. ψυχή, as Plut., Mor. 101β). Opp. τὸ πνεῦμα Ro 8: 4, 5, 6, 9, 13; Gal 3: 3; 5: 16, 17a, b; 6: 8a, b; J 3: 6; B 10: 9. τὸ μὲν πνεῦμα πρόθυμον, ἡ δὲ σὰρξ ἀσθενής Mt 26: 41; Mk 14: 38; Pol 7: 2. σὰρξ ἀμαρτίας *sinful flesh* 3b. ἐπιθυμία (τῆς) σαρκός (cf. Maximus Tyr. 20, 9f σαρκῶν ... ἐπιθυμίας) Gal 5: 16; 1 J 2: 16; B 10: 9. Pl.

Eph 2: 3a, cf. b; 2 Pt 2: 18; cf. Ro 13: 14. τὰ ἔργα τῆς σαρκός Gal 5: 19 (s. Vögtle on πλεονεξία). τὰ θελήματα τῆς σαρκός Eph 2: 3b. ὁ νοῦς τῆς σαρκός Col 2: 18. τὸ σῶμα τῆς σαρκός *the body of (sinful) flesh* 2: 11; cf. 1: 22 —s. 5 above (cf. Sir 23: 17 σῶμα σαρκὸς αὐτοῦ; En. 102, 5 τῷ σώματι τῆς σαρκὸς ὑμῶν). τὰ τῆς σαρκός *what pertains to (sinful) flesh* Ro 8: 5b. ἐν (τῇ) σαρκὶ εἶναι *be in an unregenerate* (and sinful) *state* Ro 7: 5; 8: 8f. τὰ ἔθνη ἐν σαρκί Eph 2: 11a. κατὰ σάρκα εἶναι Ro 8: 5a; ζῆν vs. 12b; 13; Dg 5: 8b; περιπατεῖν Ro 8: 4; 2 Cor 10: 2; βουλεύεσθαι 2 Cor 1: 17; στρατεύεσθαι 10: 3b; cf. IRo 8: 3 (opp. κατὰ γνώμην θεοῦ).

8. The σάρξ is the source of the sexual urge, without any suggestion of sinfulness connected w. it ἐκ θελήματος σαρκὸς ἐγεννήθησαν J 1: 13.—HWindisch, Taufe u. Sünde '08; EDBurton, ICC Gal. '20, 492-5; WSchauf, Sarx '24; WBieder, Auferstehung des Fleisches od. des Leibes?, ThZ 1, '45, 105-20. W. special ref. to Paul: Ltzm., Hdb. exc. on Ro 7: 14 and 8: 11; Lohmeyer (ἀμαρτία 3); EKäsemann, Leib u. Leib Christi '33; RM Grant, ATR 22, '40, 199-203; RBultmann, Theologie des NTs '48, 228-49 (Engl. tr. by KGrobel, '51 I, 227-59); LHMarshall, Challenge of NT Ethics, '47, 267-70; E Schweizer, Die hellenist. Komponente im NT sarx-Begriff, ZNW 48, '57, 237-53; two in KStendahl, The Scrolls and the NT, '57: KGKuhn, 94-113; WDDavies, 157-82; JPryke, 'Spirit' and 'Flesh' in Qumran and NT, Revue de Qumran 5, '65, 346-60; DLys, La chair dans l'AT, '67; ASand, D. Begriff 'Fleisch', '67 (Paul); RJewett, Paul's Anthropological Terms, '71, 49-166. On Ign.: CCRichardson, The Christianity of Ign. of Ant. '35, esp. 49; 61. S. also the lit. s.v. πνεῦμα, end.—ESchweizer, FBaumgärtel, RMeyer, TW VII 98-151. M-M. B. 202.**

σάρος, ου, ὁ (a rare masc. [Hesychius] for the usual neut. σάρον. The gender cannot be determined in Dit., Syll.[3] 1169, 48 σάρῳ τινὶ ἀποκαθαίρειν and Anth. Pal. 11, 207, 4 σάρον acc.) *broom* Hs 9, 10, 3.*

Σαρούχ t.r. for Σερούχ (q.v.).

σαρόω (later form for σαίρω; disapproved by Phryn., see Lobeck) 1 aor. ἐσάρωσα. Pass.: 1 aor. ἐσαρώθην; pf. ptc. σεσαρωμένος *sweep (clean)* (so Artem. 2, 33; Apollon. Dysc. p. 253, 7; Geopon. 14, 6, 5; PGiess. 11, 19 [II AD]) τὶ *someth.* Lk 15: 8. Pass. (cf. Sb 8000, 17 [III AD] συνσαρωθῆναι καὶ ρανθῆναι τὸν οἶκον) Mt 12: 44; Lk 11: 25; Hs 9, 10, 2. Abs. Hs 9, 10, 3. M-M. B. 580.*

Σάρρα, ας (שָׂרָה Gen 17: 15), ἡ (declined as in LXX, Philo, Joseph.; Bl-D. §40 app.; Mlt.-H. 144) *Sarah,* wife of Abraham, mother of Isaac Ro 4: 19; 9: 9 (cf. Gen 18: 10); Hb 11: 11; 1 Pt 3: 6. M-M.*

Σαρων, ωνος, ὁ (שָׁרוֹן Is 33: 9.—The accent cannot be determined, though it was probably on the second syllable, as in Hebr. Further, it is not impossible that the form is indecl. Bl-D. §56, 2 app.; Mlt.-H. 149) *Sharon,* a plain along the coast of Palestine fr. Joppa to Caesarea. Ac 9: 35.*

σατάν, ὁ indecl. and **σατανᾶς, ᾶ, ὁ** (the former=Hebr. שָׂטָן 3 Km 11: 14, the latter Sir 21: 27, also Test. 12 Patr., =Aram. סָטָנָא; the gen. σατανός Lk 11: 18 𝔓[75]) lit. *the adversary,* in our lit. only the *Adversary* in a very special sense, the enemy of God and all of those who belong to God, simply *Satan* (on the concept of Satan cf. the lit. s.v. διάβολος 2), almost always w. the art. (Bl-D. §254, 1), without it only Mk 3: 23; Lk 22: 3; 2 Cor 12: 7.—Mt 4: 10

(here, as well as in the two passages at the very end of this entry, without the art. and in the voc.); Mk 1: 13; 3: 26; Lk 11: 18; 22: 31. W. διάβολος of the same being Rv 20: 2; cf. 2: 9f; Pol 7: 1. The Antichrist appears κατ' ἐνέργειαν τοῦ σατανᾶ 2 Th 2: 9. He incites men to evil Mk 4: 15; Ac 5: 3; 1 Cor 7: 5; 2 Cor 2: 11; Rv 12: 9. Esp. did he instigate Judas' evil deed by entering into the traitor Lk 22: 3; J 13: 27. Causing sickness Lk 13: 16 (s. δέω 1b, end). Hence driven out in healings Mt 12: 26; Mk 3: 23. Hindering the apostle in his work 1 Th 2: 18 (cf. Julian., Ep. 40[68] p. 46, 19 Bidez-Cumont εἰ μή τι δαιμόνιον γένοιτο κώλυμα). Causing false beliefs to arise 1 Ti 5: 15; hence the one who denies the resurrection and judgment is called πρωτότοκος τοῦ σ. Pol 7: 1; Polycarp uses the same expr. in speaking of Marcion, Epil Mosq 2. Persecutions of Christians are also inspired by Satan Rv 2: 13a, b (on the θρόνος τοῦ σ. cf. θρόνος 1e); hence the Jews who were hostile to the Christians are called συναγωγὴ τοῦ σ. Rv 2: 9; 3: 9. God will crush him Ro 16: 20. Jesus saw Satan fallen (or falling) fr. heaven Lk 10: 18 (FSpitta, ZNW 9, '08, 160-3; CAWebster, ET 57, '45/'46, 52f; πεσ. is timeless and means 'I watched him fall'). Imprisoned, but freed again after the millennium Rv 20: 7. ὁ σ. μετασχηματίζεται εἰς ἄγγελον φωτός Satan disguises himself as an angel of light 2 Cor 11: 14 (s. μετασχηματίζω; on the subject s. Windisch ad loc.). ἄγγελος σατανᾶ 2 Cor 12: 7; ἄγγελοι τοῦ σ. B 18: 1 (ἄγγελος 2c). αἱ δυνάμεις τοῦ σ. IEph 13: 1 (δύναμις 6). τὰ βαθέα τοῦ σ. Rv 2: 24 (s. βαθύς 2). ἡ ἐξουσία τοῦ σ. the power of Satan Ac 26: 18; ending of Mk in the Freer ms. l. 7 (ἐξουσία 2); cf. l. 2. παραδοῦναί τινα τῷ σ. 1 Cor 5: 5 (s. ὄλεθρος); 1 Ti 1: 20 (cf. on both passages παραδίδωμι 1b).—In Mt 16: 23; Mk 8: 33 Peter is called Satan by Jesus, because his attempt to turn the Master aside fr. his God-given duty to suffer for mankind has made him a tempter of a diabolical sort, who might thwart the divine plan of salvation.—BNoack, Satanás u. Soteria '48. M-M.*

σάτον, ου, τό (Aram. סָאתָא = Hebr. סְאָה.—Hg 2: 16; Jos., Ant. 9, 85 ἰσχύει τὸ σάτον μόδιον καὶ ἥμισυ Ἰταλικόν) *seah*, a Hebr. *measure* for grain, equivalent (s. Joseph. above) to a modius and a half, i.e. about a peck and a half (s. μόδιος). ἀλεύρου σάτα τρία *three measures of flour* Mt 13: 33; Lk 13: 21. On estimating the size of the measure cf. Billerb. I 669f. M-M.*

Σαῦλος, ου, ὁ *Saul*, Grecized form of שָׁאוּל (Joseph. mentions several Jews w. this name; s. index s.v. Σαοῦλος), the Jewish name of the Apostle Paul (s. Παῦλος 2 and Σαούλ) Ac 7: 58; 8: 1, 3; 9: 1, 8, 11, 22, 24; 11: 25, 30; 12: 25; 13: 1f, 7, 9; 22: 7 D (Σαῦλε); 26: 14 v.l. (Σαῦλε). M-M.*

σαφῶς adv. (Hom. [σαφέως] +; inscr., pap., LXX, Philo, Jos., Bell. 2, 104 σ. ἐπίσταμαι, Ant. 4, 41) *clearly, exactly, very well* εἰδέναι (Pla., Ep. 6 p. 323D, Ep. 7 p. 324A; Diod. S. 19, 9, 2; Appian, Bell. Civ. 3, 82 §335; Zen.-P. 59 110, 12 [257 BC]) 1 Cl 62: 3; PK 3 p. 15, 26. μανθάνειν (Menand., Epitr. 115; Wilcken, Chrest. 6, 4) Dg 11: 2. (W. ἐπιμελῶς) πυνθάνεσθαι (Menand., Epitr. 493) Dg 1.*

σβέννυμι fut. σβέσω; 1 aor. ἔσβεσα, inf. σβέσαι Eph 6: 16; 1 fut. pass. σβεσθήσομαι (Hom. +; Sb 7033, 46; 67; LXX) *extinguish, put out* τὶ someth.
1. lit., fire (Jos., Bell. 7, 405) Hb 11: 34. Symbolically, fiery arrows Eph 6: 16; a smoldering wick Mt 12: 20 (Is 42: 3). Pass. *be extinguished, be put out, go out* (Artem. 2, 9;

Pr 13: 9; Philo, Leg. All. 1, 46; Test. Levi 4: 1) of lamps (cf. PGM 7, 364 σβέσας τὸν λύχνον; Musaeus v. 338) Mt 25: 8. Cf. D 16: 1. Of a pyre μετ' ὀλίγον σβεννύμενον MPol 11: 2. Of the fire of hell, that οὐ σβέννυται (Is 66: 24) Mk 9: 44 v.l., 46 v.l., 48; 2 Cl 7: 6; 17: 5; μηδέποτε σβεννύμενον πῦρ MPol 2: 3.
2. fig. *quench, stifle, suppress* (Il. 9, 678 χόλον; Pla., Leg. 8 p. 835D ὕβριν; 10 p. 888A τὸν θυμόν; Herm. Wr. 12, 6; SSol 8: 7 τὴν ἀγάπην; 4 Macc 16: 4 τὰ πάθη; Jos., Bell. 6, 31 τ. χαράν, Ant. 11, 40) τὸ πνεῦμα μὴ σβέννυτε 1 Th 5: 19 (Plut., Mor. 402B τοῦ πνεύματος ἀπεσβεσμένου; Ps.-Plut., Hom. 127 τὸ πνεῦμα τὸ κατασβεννύμενον). M-M.*

σεαυτοῦ (not σαυτοῦ [so Jos., Ant. 18, 336], Bl-D. §31, 1; Mlt.-H. 180f; Rob. 287), ῆς (Alcaeus [c. 600 BC] +; pap., LXX, En., Ep. Arist.) reflexive pron. of the second pers. sing. (Kühner-Bl. I 596ff; Bl-D. §283; Rob. 687-90) used only in the gen., dat., and acc. (on the replacement of σεαυτοῦ by ἑαυτοῦ s. ἑαυτοῦ 2) *yourself*.
1. gen. Mt 18: 16 v.l.; J 1: 22; 8: 13; 2 Ti 4: 11; Hv 3, 6, 7; m 1: 2.—2. dat. J 17: 5; Ac 9: 34; 16: 28; Ro 2: 5; Hm 3: 5; 9: 1b; 12, 3, 5f.
3. acc. Mt 4: 6; 8: 4; Mk 1: 44; Lk 5: 14; Ro 2: 21; Gal 6: 1; 1 Ti 4: 16b; B 19: 3; Dg 2: 1; Hm 9: 8.—On the quot. fr. Lev 19: 18: Mt 19: 19; 22: 39; Mk 12: 31; Lk 10: 27; D 1: 2, cf. Appian, Bell. Civ. 3, 75 §305: Pansa says to Octavian ἐγὼ τῷ σῷ πατρὶ φίλος ἦν ὡς ἐμαυτῷ; Vi. Aesopi W c. 31 ed. Perry: θέλω (see θέλω 4b= love) αὐτὴν (his wife) ὡς ἐμαυτόν= ed. Eberh. I c. 8 p. 247, 1 ταύτην ὡς ἐμαυτὸν στέργω. M-M.

σεβάζομαι dep. (Hom. +) 1 aor. ἐσεβάσθην= σέβομαι *worship, show reverence to* (Orph., Argon. 550; oracular saying in Euseb., Pr. Ev. 9, 10, 4 σεβαζόμενοι θεὸν ἁγνῶς; Apol. of Aristid. 12, 7 p. 29, 11 Hennecke, of certain pagans ἐσεβάσθησαν πρόβατον. Cf. Hos 10: 5 Aq.) 1 aor. pass. in act. sense (Sib. Or. 5, 405; 8, 46; s. Aristid. above) ἐσεβάσθησαν καὶ ἐλάτρευσαν τῇ κτίσει παρὰ τὸν κτίσαντα Ro 1: 25. M-M.*

σέβασμα, ατος, τό *an object of worship, sanctuary* (so Dionys. Hal. 1, 30; Wsd 14: 20; 15: 17; Bel 27 Theod.; Jos., Ant. 18, 344; Sib. Or. 8, 57; Ps.-Clem., Hom. 10, 21; 22) w. θεός 2 Th 2: 4. Pl. Ac 17: 23. M-M.*

σεβάσμιος, ον (Plut.; Vett. Val. 221, 23; Lucian; Herodian; Jos., Bell. 4, 164, Ant. 18, 349; inscr.; oft. used w. ὅρκος in the pap.) *worthy of veneration, honorable* (w. πανάρετος) πολιτεία 1 Cl 2: 8.*

σεβαστός, ή, όν (Dionys. Hal. 2, 75; Dit., Syll.³ 820, 6; pap., Philo, Joseph.; loanw. in rabb.) *revered, worthy of reverence, august*, as a transl. of Lat. Augustus and designation of the Roman emperor (Paus. 3, 11, 4 τὸ δὲ ὄνομα εἶναι τούτῳ Αὔγουστος, ὃ κατὰ γλῶσσαν δύναται τὴν Ἑλλήνων σεβαστός; Strabo 3, 3, 8; 12, 13, 14; Lucian, Herodian, Philo; Jos., Ant. 16, 173 al.; CIA III 63 [27 BC] ἱερεὺς θεᾶς Ῥώμης καὶ Σεβαστοῦ σωτῆρος; IG XII 3, 174 [6 BC]; pap.—EBréhier, ByzZ 15, '06, 161f; 164f; Hahn 116f; Dssm., LO 306 [LAE 358ff]; HDieckmann, Kaisernamen u. Kaiserbez. bei Lukas: ZkTh 43, '19, 213-34; Gdspd., Probs. 136f) ὁ Σεβαστός *His Majesty the Emperor* Ac 25: 21, 25 (of Nero).—In σπεῖρα Σεβαστή 27: 1 (cf. Dit., Or. 421, Σεβαστή is likew. an exact transl. of Lat. Augusta, an honorary title freq. given to auxiliary troops (Ptolem. renders it Σεβαστή in connection w. three legions that bore it: 2, 3, 30; 2, 9, 18; 4, 3, 30) *imperial cohort*. On the other hand, σπεῖρα Σεβαστή cannot be regarded as equivalent to σπεῖρα Σεβαστη-νῶν.—For lit. s. on ἑκατοντάρχης. M-M.*

σέβω—1. act. (Pind.+) *worship* (X., Mem. 4, 4, 19 θεοὺς σέβειν; Epict. 3, 7, 26 θεὸν σέβειν; POxy. 1464, 5; Philo, Virt. 34) θεὸν σέβειν Dg 3: 2; cf. 2: 7. Elsewh. always
  2. mid. (Hom.+; inscr., pap., LXX) *worship*—a. the Deity (Pind.+; Pla., Phaedr. 251A ὡς θεὸν σέβεται, Leg. 11 p. 917B; X., Hell. 3, 4, 18; Diod. S. 1, 35, 6; 2, 59, 2 θεούς; Plut., Is. et Osir. 44 σεβόμενοι τὸν "Ανουβιν; Dit., Syll.³ 611, 24 τοὺς θεούς; 557, 7 [207/6 BC] οἱ σεβόμενοι Ἀπόλλωνα; 559, 6; 560, 17; PTebt. 59, 10 [I BC] σέβε-σθαι τὸ ἱερόν; LXX; Ep. Arist. 16 al.; Jos., Ant. 9, 205 εἴδωλα; 8, 192 θεούς; Sib. Or., fgm. 1, 15; 3, 28; 30; Test. Jos. 4, 6) w. the acc. of that which is worshipped Mt 15: 9; Mk 7: 7 (both Is 29: 13); Ac 18: 13; 19: 27; PK 2 four times, once w. the acc. expressed.—σεβόμενοι τὸν θεόν *God-fearers, worshippers of God* is a term applied to pagans who accepted the ethical monotheism of Judaism and attended the synagogue, but who did not obligate themselves to keep the whole Jewish law; in particular, the males did not submit to circumcision (Jos., Ant. 14, 110 πάντων τῶν κατὰ τὴν οἰκουμένην Ἰουδαίων καὶ σεβο-μένων τὸν θεόν.—JBernays, Gesammelte Abhandlungen 1885 II 71-80; EvDobschütz, RE XVI 120f; Schürer III⁴ 174f, Die Juden im Bosporanischen Reiche u. die Genos-senschaften der σεβόμενοι θεὸν ὕψιστον: SAB 1897, 200-25; FCumont, Hypsistos: Suppl. à la Revue de l'in-struction publ. en Belgique 1897; Dssm., LO 391f [LAE 451f]; GFMoore, Judaism I, '27, 323-53; JKlausner, From Jesus to Paul, tr. WFStinespring, '43, 31-49). In our lit. it is limited to Ac, where the expr. takes various forms: σεβ. τὸν θεόν 16: 14; 18: 7. Simply σεβ. 13: 50; 17: 4, 17. Once σεβόμενοι προσήλυτοι 13: 43. S. also s.v. φοβέω 2a and προσήλυτος.—Of the worship of Christ by the faithful MPol 17: 2b; cf. a.
  b. of a reverent attitude toward human beings *show reverence* or *respect for* (Aeschyl.+; X., Cyr. 8, 8, 1 Κῦρον ὡς πατέρα, Hell. 7, 3, 12; Pla., Leg. 7 p. 813D; Polyb. 6, 39, 7; Chilo in Stob. III 116, 7 H. πρεσβύτερον σέβου; PSI 361, 9 [III BC] ὅσοι αὐτὸν σέβονται πρεσβύτας σέβεσθαι Hm 8: 10.—WFoerster, TW VII 168-95: σέβο-μαι and many related words. M-M. B. 1469.*

Σεγρί Hv 4, 2, 4 v.l. Lake for Θεγρί.*

σειρά, ᾶς, ἡ (Hom. [σειρή]+; Dit., Syll.² 588, 200; LXX; Jos., Ant. 3, 170) fr. the beginning w. the mng. *cord* or *rope* and *chain*; σειραῖς ζόφου *with chains of hell* (ζόφος 2. Cf. also Wsd 17: 16 μιᾷ ἁλύσει σκότους ἐδέθησαν; Pythag. in Diog. L. 8, 31: the ψυχαὶ ἀκάθαρτοι after their separation from the σῶμα are bound in hell by the Erinyes ἐν ἀρρήκτοις δεσμοῖς) is the rdg. of 𝔓⁷² KLP, Vulg., Syr., Boh. in 2 Pt 2: 4 (cf. σειρός and σιρός). M-M.*

σειρός: in 2 Pt 2: 4 ABC have σειροῖς, which is better spelled σιροῖς; s. σιρός. M-M.*

σεισμός, οῦ, ὁ *shaking*; of a *storm* on the sea, w. waves caused by high winds σεισμὸς μέγας ἐν τῇ θαλάσσῃ Mt 8: 24 (cf. vs. 26f where ἄνεμοι is found w. θάλ.; schol. on Pla. 25c τὸ τὸν σεισμὸν ποιοῦν πνεῦμα=ἄνεμος; Artem. 2, 38 σεισμὸς κ. ὄμβρος corresponds to 1, 73 p. 66, 7 χειμὼν κ. ὄμβ.; Diod. S. 26, 8 Rhodes is swallowed up by a σεισμός [as a result of a storm or earthquake at sea]; cf. σείω Maximus Tyr. 9, 6a; 11, 7h.—GBornkamm, D. Sturmstillg. im Mt: Jahrb. d. Theol. Schule Bethel '48, 49-54).—Mostly *earthquake* (Soph., Hdt.+; Diod. S. 25, 19 ed. Dindorf p. 351, l. 17 σεισμὸς ἐγένετο δεινός, ὡς

ὄρη διαστῆναι; Dit., Syll.³ 505; 1116, 6; LXX; Philo, Op. M. 59; Jos., Ant. 9, 225 σ. μέγας) Mt 27: 54; Ac 16: 35 D; Rv 11: 13b. Pl. in the account of the Messianic woes Mt 24: 7; Mk 13: 8; σεισμοὶ μεγάλοι Lk 21: 11 (cf. the σεισμοί seen in prospect Cat. Cod. Astr. VII 186, 8; 22; VIII 3, 174, 21; Boll 131). The σεισμός is accompanied by peals of thunder (Esth 1: 1d; cf. Is 29: 6) Rv 8: 5; 11: 19. σ. μέγας a severe earthquake (Lucian, M. Peregr. 39; Jer 10: 22; Ezk 38: 19) Mt 28: 2 (CAWebster, ET 42, '31, 381f); Ac 16: 26; Rv 6: 12; 11: 13a; 16: 18a, b. M-M.*

σείω fut. σείσω; 1 aor. pass. ἐσείσθην (Hom.+; pap., LXX, Philo; Jos., Ant. 4, 44) *shake, cause to quake, agitate.*
  1. lit. τὶ someth. τὴν γῆν, τὸν οὐρανόν Hb 12: 26 (Hg 2: 6.—Cf. X., Hell. 4, 7, 4 ἔσεισεν ὁ θεός). Pass. of the earth *be shaken, quake* (Apollon. Rhod. 3, 864 σείετο γαῖα; Dio Chrys. 46[63], 3; 80[30], 11; Judg 5: 4; 2 Km 22: 8; Ps 67: 9) Mt 27: 51; ἡ γῆ πᾶσα ἐσείσθη GP 6: 21 (cf. Jer 8: 16; En. 102, 2; Jos., Ant. 15, 121).—Ps.-Callisth. 1, 12, 9: when Alexander touched the earth, σεισμὸς ἐγέ-νετο, ὥστε τὸν πάντα κόσμον συγκινηθῆναι). Pass., of a tree that is shaken by the wind (cf. Sib. Or. 8, 297) Rv 6: 13.
  2. fig. *stir up, set in motion*; pass. *be stirred* of a city, as a result of a striking event Mt 21: 10. Of mental agitation (Philostrat., Vi. Soph. 2, 1, 11 ἐσείσθη τ. καρδίαν; Philo) *tremble* 28: 4. M-M. B. 675.*

Σεκοῦνδος (Σέκουνδος is also permissible; Bl-D. §41, 3; cf. Mlt.-H. 59) a name of Latin origin (in the Gk. form e.g. Dit., Or. 481, 4, Syll.³ 1063, 3; pap.), ου, ὁ *Secundus* of Thessalonica Ac 20: 4. M-M.*

Σελεύκεια, ας, ἡ (Tdf., W-H. accent Σελευκία) *Seleucia*, the port city of Antioch in Syria (mentioned in Polyb. 5, 58, 4; Strabo 7, 5, 8 al.; inscr.; 1 Macc 11: 8; Jos., Ant. 13, 221-3, C. Ap. 1, 207) Ac 13: 4.*

σελήνη, ης, ἡ (Hom.+; inscr., pap., LXX, Philo; Jos., Ant. 1, 31 al.; Test. 12 Patr.) *moon* PK 2 p. 14, 27 (twice). W. sun and stars (X., Mem. 4, 3, 4; Dit., Syll.³ 1267, 18f; Jo 2: 10; 4: 15; EpJer 59; Test. Napht. 3: 2) Lk 21: 25; 1 Cor 15: 41; Rv 6: 12f; 1 Cl 20: 3; B 15: 5; Dg 7: 2; IEph 19: 2. W. the sun (oft. in LXX) Rv 12: 1; 21: 23; 2 Cl 14: 1 (cf. ἥλιος, end). W. the stars (Ps 8: 4) Dg 4: 5. Darkened in the time of tribulation (cf. Is 13: 10; Ezk 32: 7; Jo 2: 10; 4: 15) Mt 24: 29; Mk 13: 24; changed to blood Ac 2: 20 (Jo 3: 4); cf. Rv 6: 12.—WGrafBaudissin, RE XIII 337-49; ORühle, RGG IV '30, 161-7 (lit.). M-M. B. 55.*

σεληνιάζομαι (Lucian; Vett. Val. 113, 10; Cat. Cod. Astr. VIII 1 p. 199, 7; Manetho, Apotel. 4, 81; 217, in both cases the act. as v.l.) *be moon-struck* (here connected w. epilepsy) Mt 17: 15. W. δαιμονίζεσθαι 4: 24.—JWeiss, RE IV 412, 25ff. M-M.*

Σεμεΐν (v.l. Σεμεΐ, Σεμεεί, Σεμεΐν), ὁ indecl. (שִׁמְעִי, freq. in the OT: Ex 6: 17; Num 3: 18; 2 Km 16: 5ff.—Joseph. has var. forms [s. index s.v. Σαμούις]) *Semein*, in the genealogy of Jesus Lk 3: 26.*

σεμίδαλις, εως, ἡ (since Hermippus Com. [V BC] 63, 22; Hippocr.; BGU 1067, 15; POxy. 736, 82; PSI 580, 3; LXX; Ep. Arist. 92; Philo; Jos., Ant. 1, 197; 3, 235; loanw. in rabb., and prob. orig. a Semit. word—s. L-S-J lex., s.v.) *fine flour*, the finest grade of wheat flour B 2: 5 (Is 1: 13). W. oil and grain Rv 18: 13. M-M.*

σεμνός, ή, όν (Hom. Hymns+; inscr., pap., LXX, Ep. Arist., Philo, Joseph.).

1. of persons—a. human beings *worthy of respect* or *honor, noble, dignified, serious* of deacons 1 Ti 3: 8. Of the aged men Tit 2: 2. Of the women (cf. X., Mem. 1, 2, 24 and the inscr. in Ramsay, Phrygia II p. 656 no. 590) 1 Ti 3: 11. W. δίκαιος (Jos., Bell. 4, 319) and other good qualities Hs 8, 3, 8.

b. supernatural beings *worthy of reverence, august, sublime, holy* (fr. the beginning an epithet of divinities; cf. also Sb 4094, 8 [I AD] ἡ σεμνὴ Ἴσις) ὁ σεμνότατος ἄγγελος the most reverend angel (of repentance) Hv 5: 2 (Suppl. Epigr. Gr. VIII 550, 2 [I BC] Ἴσι σεμνοτάτη); m 5, 1, 7.

2. of characteristics, states of being, and things *honorable, worthy, venerable, holy, above reproach* (Maximus Tyr. 3, 5c νόμοι; Jos., C. Ap. 2, 221) Phil 4: 8 (Lucian, Enc. Patr. 1 ὅσα σεμνὰ κ. θεῖα; cf. Cicero, Tusc. Disp. 5, 23[67]). ἔργα (Philo, Sacr. Abel. 49) Hv 3, 8, 7 (w. ἀγνά [as Ep. Arist. 31] and θεῖα). ἐπιθυμία m 12, 1, 1 (w. ἀγαθή; cf. Sib. Or. 5, 262). ἀγωγή 1 Cl 48: 1 (w. ἀγνή). συνείδησις 1: 3b (w. ἄμωμος and ἀγνή). κανών 7: 2 (w. εὐκλεής). ὄνομα (2 Macc 8: 15; Philo, Dec. 136) 1: 1 (w. περιβόητον and ἀξιαγάπητον). πνεῦμα Hm 3: 4 (w. ἀληθές). κλῆσις (Philo, Leg. ad Gai. 163) m 4, 3, 6 (w. μεγάλη).

3. the neut. as subst. (Demosth. 21, 126; BGU 1024 VIII, 7; Philo) τὸ σεμνὸν τῆς φιλαδελφίας ὑμῶν the worthy character of your brotherly love 1 Cl 47: 5. Pl. (Menand., Mon. 336; Polyb. 15, 7, 6 τὰ σ. καὶ καλά; Philo, Aet. M. 77) μέτρια καὶ σεμνὰ νοεῖν have moderate and seemly thoughts 1 Cl 1: 3a. M-M.*

σεμνότης, τητος, ἡ (Eur., X., Pla.+; Dit., Syll.³ 807, 8, Or. 567, 19; Ep. Arist. 5; 171; Philo).

1. of men *reverence, dignity, seriousness, respectfulness, holiness, probity* (Diod. S. 17, 34, 6; Philo; Jos., Vi. 258 μετὰ πάσης σ.) 1 Ti 3: 4; 1 Cl 41: 1; Hm 4, 1, 3. W. εὐσέβεια 1 Ti 2: 2. W. ἁγνεία Hm 4, 4, 3; s 5, 6, 5. W. ἁγνεία and other virtues m 6, 2, 3. W. other καλὰ ἔργα Tit 2: 7. Loved by the Lord Hm 5, 2, 8; ἐνδύσασθαι τὴν σ. m 2: 4. Personified w. other virtues v 3, 8, 5; 7, cf. 3, 9, 1.

2. of God *holiness* (cf. 2 Macc 3: 12; Philo, Spec. Leg. 2, 7; Jos., C. Ap. 1, 225) πορεύεσθαι κατὰ τὴν σ. τοῦ θεοῦ walk in accordance with the holiness of God Hv 3, 5, 1. M-M.*

σεμνῶς adv. (Aeschyl., X., Pla.+; inscr., pap.; 4 Macc 1: 17; Ep. Arist.; Philo, Op. M. 12) *reverently, honorably, worthily, in a manner above reproach* διακονεῖν κτλ. Hv 3, 5, 1; cf. s 9, 25, 2 (both w. ἀγνῶς). W. καλῶς (Alex. Aphr., Eth. Probl. 21 p. 142, 9 Br.) Hs 9, 1, 2. τὰ κατὰ τὸν οἶκον σεμνῶς οἰκουργεῖν 1 Cl 1: 3.*

Σεπτέμβριος, ου, ὁ *September,* also used as an adj. (Dionys. Hal. 9, 67 περὶ τὰς καλάνδας τοῦ Σεπτεμβρίου μηνός; 6, 48 καλάνδαις Σεπτεμβρίαις; Plut., Popl. 14, 6 εἰδοῖς Σεπτεμβρίαις. On the use of the Rom. calendar by Greeks s. Hahn 245) τῇ πρὸ ἐννέα καλανδῶν Σεπτεμβρίων on the twenty-fourth of August IRo 10: 3.*

Σέργιος, ου, ὁ *Sergius,* name of a Roman gens (in its Gk. form in Diod. S. 12, 24, 1; 12, 43, 1; 14, 19, 1; Dit., Syll.³ 646, 16; pap.). It has been established w. more or less certainty that the name of Sergius Paulus, proconsul of Cyprus, is found on several inscriptions (in Soli on the north coast of Cyprus: Inscr. Rom. III 930 [cf. Groag, Pauly-W. VI '09, 1781. Rejected by HDessau, ZNW 2, '01, p. 83, 3; here also on two doubtful passages in Pliny, Nat. Hist.]; terminal stone in the city of Rome CIL VI 31, 545

[cf. Mommsen, ZNW 2, '01, p. 83, 3]; two inscriptions fr. Pisidian Antioch [Ramsay, Bearing 150; 153f; GLCheesman, Journal of Roman Studies 3, '13, 262]) Ac 13: 7.—ThZahn, NKZ 15, '04, 23-41; 189-200; Ramsay, Bearing 150-72; Cheesman, loc. cit. 253-66; AWikenhauser, Die AG '21, 338-41; EHaenchen, AG 58f. M-M.*

Σερούχ (שְׂרוּג), ὁ indecl. (LXX.—Jos., Ant. 1, 148 has Σερούγος) *Serug,* son of Reu and father of Nahor (Gen 11: 20-3; 1 Ch 1: 26); in the genealogy of Jesus Lk 3: 35.*

Σήθ (שֵׁת), ὁ indecl. (LXX, Philo; Test. Benj. 10: 6.—Joseph. has Σῆθος, ου [Ant. 1, 68]) *Seth,* son of Adam and father of Enos (Gen 4: 25f; 5: 3-8; 1 Ch 1: 1; Sir 49: 16); in the genealogy of Jesus Lk 3: 38.*

σηκός, οῦ, ὁ (Hom.+; inscr., pap.; 2 Macc 14: 33; Sib. Or. 3, 266; 281) *pen, enclosure,* of birds *nest* (Aristot., H.A. 6, 8), also *burial-place, sepulcher* (Simonides in Diod. S. 11, 11, 6; also Diod. S. 17, 71, 7). In the σηκός which the bird Phoenix prepared for itself 1 Cl 25: 2f, the mngs. *nest* and *coffin* seem to merge.*

Σήμ (שֵׁם), ὁ indecl. (LXX; Philo.—Joseph. has Σῆμας, α [Ant. 1, 143]) *Shem,* son of Noah and father of Arphaxad (Gen 5: 32; 9: 26f; 10: 22; Sir 49: 16); in the genealogy of Jesus Lk 3: 36.*

σημαίνω (Hom.+; inscr., pap.) impf. ἐσήμαινον; 1 aor. ἐσήμανα (X., Hell. 1, 1, 2; BGU 1097, 17; Judg 7: 21; s. Bl-D. §72; Mlt.-H. 214f).

1. *make known, report, communicate* (trag., Hdt.+; inscr., pap., LXX, En., Ep. Arist.; Philo, Post. Cai. 155 al.; Jos., Vi. 206) τὶ someth. Ac 25: 27. τινί to someone (En. 106, 13; 107, 2) Rv 1: 1.

2. in relation to the future *indicate (beforehand), foretell* (Ezek. Trag. in Euseb., Pr. Ev. 9, 29, 6. Cf. Appian, Liby. 104 §491 προσημαίνειν τὰ μέλλοντα of divine prediction of the future) w. acc. and inf. foll. (Jos., Ant. 6, 50; cf. 8, 409) Ac 11: 28.—Also of speech that simply gives a vague indication of what is to happen (Heraclitus in Plut., De Pyth. Orac. 21 p. 404E w. ref. to the Delphic oracle οὔτε λέγει, οὔτε κρύπτει, ἀλλὰ σημαίνει; Epict. 1, 17, 18f; Jos., Ant. 7, 214; 10, 241) w. an indirect question foll. J 12: 33; 18: 32; 21: 19.—*Mean, signify* (Pla., Cratylus 393A; Aristot., Physics 213b, 30, Rhet. 32f; Dionys. Hal., Thucyd. 31) B 15: 4 Funk. M-M.*

σημεῖον, ου, τό (Aeschyl., Hdt.+; inscr., pap., LXX, Ep. Arist., Philo, Joseph., Sib. Or.; loanw. in rabb.) *sign.*

1. *the sign* or *distinguishing mark* by which someth. is known, *token, indication* (Diod. S. 3, 66, 3=evidences τῆς παρουσίας τοῦ θεοῦ; Cornutus 16 p. 21, 9.—Arrian, Anab. 6, 26, 4 of marks in the landscape showing direction). τοῦτο ὑμῖν σημεῖον this (will be) a sign for you Lk 2: 12 (cf. Is 37: 30). ὅ ἐστιν σ. ἐν πάσῃ ἐπιστολῇ this is the mark of genuineness in every letter 2 Th 3: 17 (Ps.-Pla., Ep. 13 p. 360A has at its beginning the words σύμβολον ὅτι παρ' ἐμοῦ ἐστιν). Of a *signal* previously agreed upon δοῦναί τινι σημεῖον (PFay. 128, 7 ἔδωκεν ἡμῖν σημεῖον='he gave us a signal'; Jos., Ant. 12, 404) Mt 26: 48; 1 Cl 12: 7.—*A sign* of things to come (Philo, Op. M. 58 σημεῖα μελλόντων; Jos., Bell. 6, 285; 296; 297) Mk 13: 4; Lk 21: 7. The event to be expected is added in the gen. τί τὸ σ. τῆς σῆς παρουσίας; Mt 24: 3. τὸ σ. τοῦ υἱοῦ τοῦ ἀνθρώπου by which one can mark the coming of the Son of Man vs. 30 (TFGlasson, JTS 15, '64, 299f [a military metaphor, 'standard'; cf. Is 18: 3; 1QM 3f]). τὰ σημεῖα τῶν καιρῶν the signs of the (end-) times (καιρός 4) Mt 16: 3.—*A sign* of warning (Plut., Caes.

63, 1; Sib. Or. 3, 457) 1 Cl 11: 2. Prob. in like manner αἱ γλῶσσαι εἰς σημεῖόν εἰσιν τοῖς ἀπίστοις *the tongues* (γλῶσσα 3) *serve as a (warning) sign to the unbelievers* 1 Cor 14: 22. Likew. the *sign of Jonah* (cf. Ἰωνᾶς 1) in the Third Gosp.: Lk 11: 29, 30. Here the Son of Man is to be a sign to his generation, as Jonah was to the Ninevites; cf. οὗτος κεῖται εἰς σημεῖον ἀντιλεγόμενον (s. ἀντιλέγω 2) 2: 34 (cf. Is 11: 12).—GRunze, Das Zeichen des Menschensohnes u. der Doppelsinn des Jonazeichens 1897 (against him PWSchmiedel, Lit. Centralblatt 48, 1897, 513-15; Runze again, ZWTh 41, 1898, 171-85; finally PWSchm. ibid. 514-25); PAsmussen, Protestantenblatt 37, '04, 375-8; SLTyson, Bibl. World 33, '09, 96-101; CRBowen, AJTh 20, '16, 414-21; JHMichael, JTS 21, '20, 146-59; JBonsirven, Rech de Sc rel 24, '34, 450-5; HM Gale, JBL 60, '41, 255-60; PSeidelin, Das Jonaszeichen, Studia Theologica 5, '51, 119-31; AVögtle, Wikenhauser-Festschr. '53, 230-77; OGlombitza, D. Zeichen des Jona, NTS 8, '62, 359-66. W.-S. §30, 10d.—In the OT circumcision is σημεῖον διαθήκης = a sign or token of belonging to the covenant (Gen 17: 11). For Paul this sign becomes a *mark*, or *seal* (so σημεῖον: BPGrenfell, Revenue-Laws of Ptolemy Philadelphus [1896] 26, 5 [III BC]; PReinach 9 introd. [II BC]; 35, 3; BGU 1064, 18) σημεῖον ἔλαβεν περιτομῆς σφραγῖδα *he received the mark of circumcision as a seal* Ro 4: 11. In the difficult pass. B 12: 5 ἐν σημείῳ is prob. best taken as *by a sign*; but it is poss. that the text is defective (cf. the interpretations, most recently Windisch, Hdb. ad loc.; RAKraft, Did. and Barnabas, '65, 119 note: 'standard, norm').—τὰ σημεῖα τοῦ ἀποστόλου 2 Cor 12: 12a belongs rather to the next category; *the signs of the* (true) *apostle* (cf. Dit., Syll.³ 831, 14 [117 AD] ἡγούμην σημεῖα ἀγαθῶν ἀνδρῶν) are, as is shown by the verb κατειργάσθη and what follows, the wonders or miracles performed by him.

2. *a sign consisting of a wonder or miracle*, an event that is contrary to the usual course of nature.

a. *miracle of divine origin*, performed by God himself, by Christ, or by men of God (cf. Diod. S. 5, 70, 4 πολλὰ σ. of the young Zeus; 16, 27, 2 ἐγένετο αὐτῷ σημεῖον ἐν τῷ ἱερῷ τοῦ Ἀπόλλωνος; Strabo 16, 2, 35 παρὰ τ. θεοῦ σ.; Appian, Ital. 8 §1 σημείων γενομένων ἐκ Διός, Hann. 56 §233; Dit., Syll.³ 709, 25 [c. 107 BC] διὰ τῶν ἐν τῷ ἱερῷ γενομένων σαμείων; PGM 1, 65; 74; Jos., Ant. 2, 274; 280): Mt 12: 38f; 16: 1 (σ. ἐκ τοῦ οὐρανοῦ), 4; Mk 8: 11 (σ. ἀπὸ τοῦ οὐρανοῦ, as Synes., Prov. 1, 7; cf. OLinton, The Demand for a Sign from Heaven, Studia Theologica 18, '64, 112-29), 12; 16: 17, 20; Lk 11: 16 (σ. ἐξ οὐρανοῦ), 29 (s. 1 above); 23: 8; J 2: 11, 18, 23; 3: 2; 4: 54; 6: 2, 14, 26, 30; 7: 31; 9: 16; 10: 41; 11: 47; 12: 18, 37; 20: 30 (on σημ. as a designation of Jesus' miracles in J s. Hdb. on J 2: 11 and 6: 26; JHBernard, ICC John '29, I introd. 176-86; CKBarrett, The Gosp. acc. to St. John, '55, 62-5); Ac 4: 16, 22 (τὸ σ. τῆς ἰάσεως the miracle of healing); 8: 6; 1 Cor 1: 22; Agr 9.—σημεῖα καὶ τέρατα (Polyb. 3, 112, 8 σημείων δὲ καὶ τεράτων πᾶν μὲν ἱερόν, πᾶσα δ' ἦν οἰκία πλήρης; Plut., Alex. 75, 1 [sing.]; Appian, Bell. Civ. 2, 36 §144 τέρατα καὶ σημεῖα οὐράνια; 4, 4 §14; Aelian, V.H. 12, 57; Philo, Mos. 1, 95, Aet. M. 2; Jos., Bell. 1, 28, Ant. 20, 168. Oft. in LXX: Ex 7: 3; Dt 4: 34; 6: 22; 7: 19 al.; Is 8: 18; 20: 3; Jer 39: 21; Wsd 8: 8; 10: 16) J 4: 48; Ac 2: 43; 4: 30; 5: 12; 6: 8; 7: 36; 14: 3; 15: 12; Ro 15: 19; Hb 2: 4; 1 Cl 51: 5; B 4: 14; 5: 8. δυνάμεις καὶ τέρατα κ. σημεῖα Ac 2: 22; 2 Cor 12: 12b. σημεῖα καὶ δυνάμεις Ac 8: 13.—1 Cl 25: 1; 2 Cl 15: 4. SVMcCasland, JBL 76, '57, 149-52; MWhittaker, Studia Evangelica 5, '68, 155-8.

b. *miracle of a demonic nature*, worked by Satan and his agents Rv 13: 13f; 16: 14; 19: 20. σημεῖα κ. τέρατα Mt

24: 24; Mk 13: 22 (GRBeasley-Murray, A Commentary on Mk 13, '57; EGrässer, D. Problem der Parusieverzögerung, '57, 152-70); 2 Th 2: 9; D 16: 4.

c. *terrifying appearances in the heavens*, never before seen, as *portents* of the last days Lk 21: 11, 25 (Appian, Bell. Civ. 4, 4 §14 σημεῖα πολλά around the sun); Ac 2: 19 (cf. Jo 3: 3); cf. D 16: 6. Of that which the seer of the Apocalypse sees ἐν τῷ οὐρανῷ Rv 12: 1, 3; 15: 1. Of the portentous signs in heaven and earth at the death of Jesus GP 8: 28 (cf. Da 6: 28 Theod. σημεῖα κ. τέρατα ἐν οὐρανῷ κ. ἐπὶ τῆς γῆς; Diod. S. 38+39 fgm. 5: at the end of each one of the eight ages ordained by God there is a σημεῖον ἐκ γῆς ἢ οὐρανοῦ θαυμάσιον).—On miracles cf. Dit., Syll.³ 1168-73; RLembert, Das Wunder bei Römern u. Griechen I '05; RReitzenstein, Hellenist. Wundererzählungen '06; OWeinreich, Antike Heilungswunder '09, Gebet u. Wunder: WSchmid-Festschr. '29, 169ff; PWendland, De Fabellis Antiquis earumque ad Christianos Propagatione '11; FKutsch, Attische Heilgötter u. Heilheroen '13; WAJayne, The Healing Gods of Ancient Civilizations '25; RHerzog, D. Wunderheilungen v. Epidaurus '31; PFiebig, Jüdische Wundergeschichten des ntl. Zeitalters '11; ASchlatter, Das Wunder in d. Synagoge '12.—RLehmann, Naturwissenschaft u. bibl. Wunderfrage '30; GNaumann, Die Wertschätzung des Wunders im NT '03; GTraub, Das Wunder im NT² '07; KBeth, Die Wunder Jesu '08; JMThompson, Miracles in the NT '11; LFonck, Die Wunder des Herrn im Ev.² '07; LFillion, Les miracles de Jésus-Christ '09/'10; PDausch, Die Wunder Jesu '12; SEitrem, Nordisk Tidskrift for Filologie 5, '19, 30-6; RBultmann, Die Gesch. der synopt. Tradition² '31, 223-60; RJelke, Die Wunder Jesu '22; GRHShafto, The Wonders of the Kingdom '24; JHBest, The Miracles of Christ in the Light of our Present Day Knowledge '37; TTorrance, Expository Studies in St. John's Miracles '38; ARichardson, The Miracle Stories of the Gospels '41; AFridrichsen, Le Problème du Miracle dans le Christianisme primitif: Études d'Hist. et de Phil. rel. XII '25; HSchlingensiepen, Die Wunder des NT '33; OPerels, D. Wunderüberlieferung der Synoptiker '34; PSaintyves, Essais de folklore biblique '23; GMarquardt, D. Wunderproblem in d. deutschen prot. Theologie der Gegenwart '33; GDelling, D. Verständnis des Wunders im NT, ZSystTh 24, '55, 265-80, Zur Beurteilung des Wunders durch d. Antike; Studien zum NT, '70, 53-71; SVMcCasland, Signs and Wonders, JBL 76, '57, 149-52; CKBarrett, The Gosp. acc. to John, '55, 62-5; JPCharlier, La notion de signe (sêmeion) dans J, Revue des sciences philos. et theol. 43, '59, 434-48; PRiga, Signs of Glory (J), Interpretation 17, '63, 402-24; HvanderLoos, The Miracles of Jesus, '65; WNicol, The Sēmeia in the Fourth Gosp., '72.—Esp. on the healing of demoniacs JWeiss, RE IV 408ff; JJaeger, Ist Jesus Christus ein Suggestionstherapeut gewesen? '18; KKnur, M.D., Christus medicus? '05; KDusberger, Bibel u. Kirche '51, 114-17 (Vorzeichen).—RMGrant, Miracle and Natural Law in Graeco-Roman and Early Christian Thought '52. S. also the lit. s.v. δαιμόνιον 2.—KHRengstorf, TW VII 199-268: σημεῖον and related words. M-M. B. 914. **

σημειόω (since Hippocr. V 672 L.; Theophr.; inscr., pap., Ps 4: 7; Ep. Arist., Philo) 1 aor. mid. ἐσημειωσάμην; usu., and in our lit. exclusively, in the mid.

1. *note down* (for oneself), *write* (Dit., Or. 629, 168 ὡς καὶ Κουρβούλων ὁ κράτιστος ἐσημειώσατο ἐν τῇ ἐπιστολῇ) τὶ someth. πάντα ἐν ταῖς ἱεραῖς βίβλοις 1 Cl 43: 1.—**2.** *mark, take special notice of* τινά someone 2 Th 3: 14. M-M. *

σημείωσις, εως, ἡ (Chairemon, fgm. 5, p. 32, 8; Plut., Mor. 961c; pap.; Ps 59: 6; Ep. Arist.) *sign, signal* εἰς σ. γίνεσθαί τινι serve as a (*sign of*) *warning to someone* 1 Cl 11: 2 (σημεῖον 1). M-M. s.v. σημειόω.*

σήμερον adv. of time (Hom.+ [the Attic τήμερον is not found in our lit.: Bl-D. §34, 1; Mlt.-H. 279]; inscr., pap., LXX; Ep. Arist. 180; Philo, Joseph., Test. 12 Patr.; loanw. in rabb.) *today* Mt 6: 11 (BMMetzger, How Many Times Does ἐπιούσιος Occur Outside the Lord's Prayer? ET 60, '57, 52–4; see ἐπιούσιος); 16: 3; 21: 28; Lk 4: 21; 23: 43 (= *before today is over* as Philostrat., Vi. Soph. 1, 25, 14); Ac 4: 9 and oft.; Lk 3: 22 v.l. (Ps 2: 7); cf. Hb 1: 5; 5: 5; 1 Cl 36: 4. Opp. αὔριον Js 4: 13. ἡ σήμερον ἡμέρα (Dio Chrys. 31[48], 3; Dit., Syll.³ 1181, 11=prayer for vengeance fr. Rheneia: Dssm., LO 351ff, esp. 357 [LAE 414ff]; LXX) *today, this very day:* Mt 28: 15 (μέχρι τῆς σ. ἡμέρας, as 1 Esdr 8: 74; Jos., Ant. 10, 265); Ac 20: 26 (ἐν τῇ σ. ἡμέρᾳ, as Phlegon: 257 fgm. 36, 3, 11 Jac.; Josh 5: 9; PGM 4, 1580; 1699; 2062; 5, 187; 194); Ro 11: 8 (ἕως τῆς σ. ἡμέρας, as UPZ 57, 3; Gen 19: 38 al.); 2 Cor 3: 14 (ἄχρι τῆς σ. ἡμέρας, as Jos., Ant. 7, 366). W. ellipsis (BGU 598, 6; POxy. 121, 6; LXX; Bl-D. §241, 2) ἡ σήμερον: Mt 11: 23; 28: 15 v.l. (both μέχρι τῆς σ. as Jos., Ant. 9, 28); 27: 8 (ἕως τῆς σ. as UPZ 5, 5 [163 BC]); Ac 19: 40 (περὶ τῆς σ.). —ἕως σ. 2 Cor 3: 15.—Since the Jews consider that the day begins at sun-down, the whole night belongs to one and the same 24-hour period: σ. ταύτῃ τῇ νυκτί *this very night* Mk 14: 30. Also simply σ. Mt 27: 19; Lk 2: 11; 22: 34.—σ. serves to denote a limited period of time (Appian, Liby. 112 §532): σήμερον—αὔριον= 'now—in a little while' Mt 6: 30; Lk 12: 28. The expr. σήμερον καὶ αὔριον καὶ τῇ τρίτῃ (or καὶ τῇ ἐχομένῃ) refers to a short period of time, the exact duration of which the speaker either cannot or does not wish to disclose Lk 13: 32f (JBlinzler, Klerusblatt '44, 381–3). On ἐχθὲς καὶ σήμερον Hb 13: 8 cf. ἐχθές. Looking fr. the present to the coming judgment ἄχρις οὗ τὸ σήμερον καλεῖται *as long as 'today' lasts* Hb 3: 13 (cf. Philo, Leg. All. 3, 25 ὁ αἰὼν ἅπας τῷ σήμερον παραμετρεῖται and s. καλέω 1aδ, end).—Cf. ABonhöffer, Epiktet u. das NT '11, 329f on σήμερον in the ethical teaching of Epict. M-M. B. 998.

σημικίνθιον s. σιμικίνθιον.

σηπία, ας, ἡ (Aristoph. et al.) *cuttle-fish, sepia* w. sea-lamprey and octopus B 10: 5 (cf. Lev 11: 10).*

σήπω 2 pf. σέσηπα (Hom.+; pap., LXX) *cause to rot* or *decay;* usu., and in our lit. exclusively, pass. *decay, rot* (Philo, Aet. M. 125; Jos., C. Ap. 2, 143), 2 pf. act. *be decayed* ξύλον σεσηπός *rotten wood* Dg 2: 2. σηπομένης τῆς σαρκός *as the flesh decays* 1 Cl 25: 3 (Cyranides p. 7, 21 ἐσέσηπτο ἡ σάρξ; Jos., Bell. 6, 164 σηπόμενον σῶμα). οὐ πάντα σηπόμενα; Dg 2: 4. Of a vine creeping along on the ground: σεσηπότα φέρειν *bear rotten fruit* Hs 2: 3. Of the treasures of the rich Js 5: 2. M-M.*

σηρικός s. σιρικός.

σής (since Pind., fgm. 222 Διὸς παῖς ὁ χρυσός. κεῖνον οὐ σὴς οὐδὲ κὶς δάπτει; LXX), σητός (so Aristot., H.A. 5, 32; Menand. et al.; LXX; Philo, Abr. 11.—The class. gen. is σεός cf. Kühner-Bl. I 510f), ὁ *the moth,* whose larvae eat clothing (Menand., fgm. 540, 5 Kock; Lucian, Ep. Sat. 1, 21 ἱμάτια ὑπὸ σητῶν διαβρωθέντα) Mt 6: 19f; Lk 12: 33. Being eaten by moths as a symbol of feebleness and destruction 1 Cl 39: 5 (Job 4: 19); B 6: 2 (Is 50: 9).—Worms, specific. wood-worms, seem to be meant (cf. Philo, Somn. 1, 77), since the σής is damaging sticks Hs 8, 1, 6f; 8, 4, 5; 8, 6, 4. M-M.*

σητόβρωτος, ον (Sb 7404, 28 [II AD]; Sib. Or. fgm. 3, 26; Hesychius) *motheaten* ἱμάτια (Job 13: 28) Js 5: 2. M-M.*

σθενόω fut. σθενώσω (Herodian Gramm. 449, 21; Rhet. Gr. VII 260, 20; Hesychius) *strengthen, make strong* 1 Pt 5: 10. M-M.*

σιαγών, όνος, ἡ (Soph., X., Pla.+; usu. in its orig. sense 'jaw, jawbone', so also LXX [e.g. Judg 15: 14–17] and Jos., Ant. 5, 300) *cheek* (so fr. III BC [s. L-S-J lex. s.v.], pap., LXX [e.g. Is 50: 6]) Mt 5: 39; Lk 6: 29; D 1: 4 (on the subject-matter JWeismann, ZNW 14, '13, 175f; JMoffatt, Exp. 8th. S. VII '14, 89; VIII '14, 188f; UHolzmeister, ZkTh 45, '21, 334ff; HEBryant, ET 48, '37, 236f); GP 3: 9. τιθέναι τὰς σ. εἰς ῥαπίσματα *give up one's cheeks to blows* B 5: 14 (Is 50: 6). M-M. B. 222.*

σιαίνομαι (Hippiatr. II 81, 5; POxy. 1837, 2 [VI AD]; 1849, 2; Byz. Chron. [Psaltes p. 333]) *be disturbed* or *annoyed* (the act.= 'cause annoyance' or 'loathing': schol. on Lucian p. 261, 22 Rabe) 1 Th 3: 3 v.l.—S. vDobschütz ad loc. and the lit. s.v. σαίνω. M-M.*

Σίβυλλα, ης, ἡ (Heraclitus and Eur.+; Sib. Or. 3, 815; 4, 22; Jos., Ant. 1, 118) *the Sibyl, prophetess* (WBousset, RE XVIII 265 [lit.]) Hv 2, 4, 1 (cf. MDibelius, Hdb. ad loc., Festgabe für AvHarnack '21, 118).*

σιγάω 1 aor. ἐσίγησα; pf. pass. ptc. σεσιγημένος—1. *intr. be silent, keep still* (Hom.+; Sb 7183, 5; LXX; Jos., Vi. 175, Ant. 19, 44) in the senses:
a. *say nothing, keep silent* (Pind., Nem. 5, 19 τὸ σιγᾶν πολλάκις ἐστὶ σοφώτατον ἀνθρώπῳ) Mk 14: 61 D; Lk 19: 40 D; 20: 26; Ac 12: 17; 15: 12; 1 Cor 14: 28. αἱ γυναῖκες ἐν τ. ἐκκλησίαις σιγάτωσαν vs. 34 (s. the lit. s.v. γυνή 1. Also RSeeberg, Aus Rel. u. Gesch., Ges. Aufs. I '06, 128–44; HHöpfl, Bened. Monatsschr. 14, '32, 63–77.—PWSchmiedel, JWeiss, WBousset ad loc., HWindisch [s. γυνή 1], RBultmann [ThBl 12, '33, 362] consider vs. 34f a secondary gloss); 1 Cl 35: 9 (Ps 49: 21); IEph 6: 1; 15: 1f (opp. λαλεῖν, as Alex. Aphr., Fat. 9 p. 175, 23 Br.); IPhld 1: 1 (opp. λαλεῖν).
b. *stop speaking, become silent* (Charito 5, 7, 8; Synes., Kingship 29 p. 32A; Sib. Or. 3, 473) Lk 18: 39; Ac 13: 41 D; 15: 13; 1 Cor 14: 30; MPol 7: 2.—c. *hold one's tongue, keep someth.* (a) *secret* Lk 9: 36.
2. *trans. keep secret, conceal* τὶ *someth.* (Pind.+; Charito 3, 10, 1; POxy. 471, 41 [II AD]) pass. μυστήριον χρόνοις αἰωνίοις σεσιγημένον *a secret that was concealed for long ages* Ro 16: 25. M-M. B. 1259.*

σιγή, ῆς, ἡ (Hom.+; Wsd 18: 14; 3 Macc 3: 23; Ep. Arist.; Jos., Vi. 417) *silence, quiet* in the sense of the absence of all noise, whether made by speaking or by anything else 1 Cl 21: 7. πολλῆς σιγῆς γενομένης *when they had become silent* Ac 21: 40 (likew. Ps.-Callisth. 2, 15, 6; without πολλῆς Arrian, Anab. 4, 12, 2; Vi. Aesopi W c. 87; Jos., Vi. 141, Ant. 5, 236); cf. Rv 8: 1 (Clemen² 391; WEBeet, ET 44, '33, 74–6). σιγὴν ἔχειν *be silent* (Appian, Hann. 14 §60; Arrian, Anab. 5, 1, 4; Paroem. Gr.: App. 3, 7) Hs 9, 11, 5. Christ is called αὐτοῦ (= τοῦ θεοῦ) λόγος, ἀπὸ σιγῆς προελθών *his Word, proceeding from silence* IMg 8: 2 (on the text and subj. matter cf. Hdb. ad loc.; H-WBartsch, Gnost. Gut u. Gemeindetradition b. Ign. v. Ant. '40. On the deity that is silence and that can be rightly worshiped only in silence, s. Mesomedes 1, 1–3, addressing the goddess: Ἀρχὰ καὶ πάντων γέννα, Πρεσβίστα κόσμου μᾶτερ Καὶ νὺξ καὶ φῶς καὶ σιγά; Porphyr., Abst. 2, 34 διὰ σιγῆς καθαρᾶς θρησκεύομεν [θεόν]; Sextus 578 τιμὴ μεγίστη θεῷ θεοῦ γνῶσις ἐν σιγῇ; PGM 4, 558ff λέγε·σιγή, σιγή, σιγή, σύμβολον θεοῦ ζῶντος ἀφθάρτου· φύλαξόν με, σιγή; 1782. Hermes in Iambl., De Myst. 8, 3 ὃ δὴ διὰ σιγῆς μόνης θεραπεύεται. Herm. Wr. 10, 5 ἡ γὰρ γνῶσις αὐτοῦ βαθεῖα σιωπή ἐστι. Martyr. Petri p. 96, 16ff Lips.— HKoch, Ps.-Dionys. Areop. '00, 128ff; OCasel, De Philosophorum Graecorum Silentio Mystico '19, Vom hl. Schweigen: Bened. Monatsschr. 3, '21, 417ff; GMensching, Das hl. Schweigen '26). M-M.*

σίδηρος, ου, ὁ (Hom.+; inscr., pap., LXX) *iron* Dg 2: 3. W. χαλκός (as Diod. S. 1, 33, 3; 2, 16, 4; Ep. Arist. 119; Philo, Aet. M. 20) Rv 18: 12; PK 2 p. 14, 14. Destroyed by rust Dg 2: 2. Symbolically for sword (Hom.+; Jos., Bell. 3, 364; 6, 273, Ant. 19, 148) 1 Cl 56: 9 (Job 5: 20). πεπυρωμένος σ. *red-hot iron* (Alex. Aphr., Quaest. 2, 17) AP 13: 28. M-M. B. 613.*

σιδηροῦς, ᾶ, οῦν (Hom.+ in the form σιδήρεος, while the Attic Gks. have the contracted form. The word is also found in inscr., pap., LXX; Philo, Op. M. 141; Joseph. [in both forms; cf. Schmidt 492]; Sib. Or. 3, 540) *(made of) iron* of a bar B 11: 4 (Is 45: 2). Of a prison door (s. πύλη 1) Ac 12: 10. Of breastplates Rv 9: 9. Symbolically='merciless' (Hom.+; cf. Περὶ ὕψους 13, 1 after Pla., Rep. 586A σιδηροῖς κέρασι) ῥάβδος σιδηρᾶ (after Ps 2: 9) Rv 2: 27; 12: 5; 19: 15 (ποιμαίνω 2aγ). M-M.*

Σιδών, ῶνος (צִידוֹן), ἡ (Hom.+; inscr., LXX; Philo, Leg. ad Gai. 337; Joseph.; Sib. Or. 14, 83) *Sidon*, an ancient Phoenician royal city, on the coast betw. Berytus (Beirut) and Tyre. Oft. combined w. Tyre, almost as a formula (Philostrat., Her. 1, 1; Jos., Ant. 8, 320; 15, 95) Mt 11: 21f; Mk 3: 8; Lk 6: 17; 10: 13f (written Σιδόνι vs. 13 𝔓⁷⁵). τὰ μέρη Τύρου καὶ Σιδῶνος *the region around Tyre and Sidon* Mt 15: 21; also τὰ ὅρια Τ. καὶ Σ. Mk 7: 24 v.l.; ἦλθεν διὰ Σιδῶνος εἰς *he went by way of Sidon to* . . . Mk 7: 31. Σάρεπτα τ. Σιδῶνος *Zarephath, which belongs to Sidon* Lk 4: 26 t.r. Visited by Paul on his journey to Rome Ac 27: 3.—FCEiselen, Sidon: Columbia Univ. Oriental Studies IV '07; HGuthe, RE XVIII 280ff; XXIV 503f. M-M.*

Σιδώνιος, ία, ιον (Soph., Hdt. et al.; inscr., LXX) *Sidonian, from Sidon*—1. ἡ Σ. (sc. χώρα) *the country around Sidon* (Od. 13, 285 [Σιδονία]; LXX) Σάρεπτα τῆς Σιδωνίας (3 Km 17: 9) *Zarephath in the region of Sidon* Lk 4: 26.

2. οἱ Σιδώνιοι (Od. 4, 84 al.; inscr.; Sib. Or. 3, 451; 5, 203 all write Σιδόνιος; but Dit., Syll.³ 185, 5 [376–360 BC]; 391, 2; 15; LXX; Jos. [index] Σιδώνιος) *the Sidonians* mentioned w. Tyrians (as Diod. S. 16, 41, 1; 1 Esdr 5: 53) Ac 12: 20 (Beginn. ad loc.).*

σικάριος, ου, ὁ (Lat. loanw., fr. sica='dagger'; cf. Bl-D. §5, 1; Mlt.-H. 347; Rob. 109, and the entry Ἰσκαριώθ.— The word is found several times in Joseph. [s. index].— σικάριον='dagger' POxy. 1294, 8 [II/III AD].—Also as a loanw. in the Talmud; cf. SKrauss, Griech. u. latein. Lehnwörter im Talmud usw. II 1899, 392) *sicarius* (pl. -ii), *dagger man, assassin*, name of the most fanatical group among the Jewish nationalists, quite hostile to Rome; they did not hesitate to assassinate their political opponents (Jos., Bell. 2, 254–7, Ant. 20, 186) Ac 21: 38.—Schürer I⁴ 575f, rev. ed. '73, 463; MHengel, Die Zeloten, '61, 47–54; M-M.*

σίκερα (Galen XIX 693 K. [though the tractate in question is strongly interpolated by Christians, acc. to PKatz]; Anecdota Astrologica [ALudwich, Maximi et Ammonis

Carmina 1877] p. 120, 23 οἶνος κ. σίκερα; LXX, Hesychius, Suidas) indecl. (Euseb., Pr. Ev. 6, 10, 14 has σίκερος as a gen.—Also 8 the verb σικερατίζω), τό (Aram. שִׁכְרָא =Hebr. שֵׁכָר; Is 5: 11, 22; 24: 9 make it certain that the gender is neut. Cf. Bl-D. §58; Rob. 105. Orig. Akkadian; cf. HZimmern, Akkad. Lehnwörter '15, 39) *strong drink*, which prob. could include wine (Num 28: 7), but as a rule was differentiated fr. wine and mentioned w. it (Lev 10: 9; Num 6: 3; Dt 29: 5; Is 29: 9; Test. Reub. 1: 10. The Akkadian šikaru='barley beer') Lk 1: 15 (cf. Judg 13: 4 A). M-M.*

Σίλας, α or Σιλᾶς, ᾶ (still other spellings are attested for the NT; s. Bl-D. §53, 2 app.; 125, 2), ὁ (several times in Joseph. as a Semitic name; Dit., Or. 604, 4; Inscr. Rom. III 817, 1. Evidently=שְׁאִילָא, the Aram. form [in Palmyrene inscriptions] of שָׁאוּל *Saul) Silas*. This name, which occurs only in Ac, is borne by a respected member of the church at Jerusalem who was prophetically gifted 15: 22, 27; he was sent to Antioch and stayed there vss. 32, 34; later he accompanied Paul on his so-called 'second' missionary journey 15: 40–18: 5 (mentioned nine times). Despite CWeizsäcker, Das apost. Zeitalter² 1892, 247 et al., incl. LRadermacher, ZNW 25, '26, 295, it is hardly to be doubted that this Silas is the same pers. as the Σιλουανός who is mentioned in Paul and 1 Pt. See the next entry and cf. AStegmann, Silvanus als Missionär u. 'Hagiograph' '17. S. also s.v. Ἰωάν(ν)ης 6. M-M.*

Σιλουανός, οῦ, ὁ (Diod. S. 11, 27, 1, a Σ. as contemporary with the battle of Salamis [480 BC]; Dit., Or. 533, 50 [time of Augustus] and later inscr. and pap.; Jos., Ant. 20: 14; in rabbinic lit. סִילְוָנִי) *Silvanus*; surely the same man who appears in Ac as Σίλας (q.v.). Either he had two names (like Paul), one Semit. and one Lat. (Zahn), or Σιλουανός is the Lat. form of the same name that is Grecized in Σίλας (Bl-D. §125, 2; Mlt.-H. 109f; 146). 2 Cor 1: 19 (here 𝔓⁴⁶ and other representatives of the v.l. have the form Σιλβανός, which is also found Diod. S. 11, 41, 1); 1 Th 1: 1; 2 Th 1: 1 (s. also the subscr. of 2 Th); 1 Pt 5: 12 (this pass. has given rise to the conclusion that Silvanus was somehow or other [as translator? In Sb 8246, 38 Germanus speaks before the court δι' Ἀνουβίωνος ἑρμηνεύοντος] connected w. the writing of 1 Pt; e.g., Zahn [Einleitung II³ 10f], GWohlenberg [NKZ 24, '13, 742–62], WBornemann [Der erste Petrusbrief—eine Taufrede des Silvanus?: ZNW 19, '20, 143ff], Harnack [Mission I⁴ '23, 85], LRadermacher [Der 1 Pt u. Silvanus: ZNW 25, '26, 287ff]; EGSelwyn, 1 Pt '46, 9–17 but s. WGKümmel [Introd. NT; tr. HCKee, '75, 416–25]). M-M.*

Σιλωάμ (שִׁלֹחַ), ὁ indecl. (masc.: Is 8: 6 τὸ ὕδωρ τοῦ Σιλωάμ; 2 Esdr 13: 15 S κολυμβήθρα τοῦ Σιλωάμ; but fem.: Jos., Bell. 5, 505 τὴν Σιλωάμ.—Elsewh. Jos. usu. has declinable forms: τοῦ Σιλωᾶ Bell. 2, 340; 6, 363; ἡ Σιλωά, ᾶς, ᾷ, άν 5, 140; 145 [τὴν Σιλωάν πηγήν]; 252, 410; 6, 401.—Bl-D. §56, 4; cf. Rob. 95) *Siloam*, name of a system of water supply in Jerusalem, through which the water of the spring Gihon became available for the Fortress of David. ἡ κολυμβήθρα τοῦ Σ. *the pool of Siloam* was prob. the basin into which the water was conducted J 9: 7; cf. vs. 11.—Vincent-Abel, Jérus.: (s. Ἱεροσόλυμα 1b) II chap. 34 §2; GDalman, Jerus. u. s. Gelände '30, 386 (Sachreg.); CKopp, The Holy Places of the Gospels tr. RWalls, '63, 314–20.—ὁ πύργος ἐν τῷ Σ. *the tower near the pool of Siloam* Lk 13: 4. M-M.*

Σιμαίας, ου, ὁ שְׁמַעְיָה. The name is freq. in the OT, but the LXX always renders it differently from 2 Ti, even though the LXX does not always spell it in the same way; Schürer II⁴ 423, 24) *Simaias,* named in 2 Ti 4: 19 v.l. as the son of Aquila. *

σιμικίνθιον, ου, τό (Aesop fr. the Cod. Paris. 1277: ChRochefort, Notices et Extraits II 1789 p. 718 no. 18. Latin loanw.: semicinctium; Bl-D. §5, 1d; 41, 1; Rob. 109; 189; 192) *an apron,* such as is worn by workmen; w. σουδάριον Ac 19: 12. It is not certain just what is meant by this ref. Hesychius took it to be a *band* or *bandage* of some kind. Ammonius and Theophylact thought it was a *handkerchief,* but this does not accord well w. σουδάριον. Suidas combined the two ideas: φακιόλιον (towel) ἢ σουδάριον.—On the indirect mediation of miracle-working fr. one pers. to another s. FPfister, Der Reliquienkult im Altertum I '09, 331ff. M-M. *

Σίμων, ωνος, ὁ (שִׁמְעוֹן).—The name is found freq. among Greeks [Aristoph.+; inscr., pap. Cf. AFick²-FBechtel, Die griech. Personennamen 1894 p. 30; 251] and Jews [LXX; Ep. Arist. 47; 48; Joseph.; cf. GHölscher, ZAW Beihefte 41, '25, 150f; 155; MNoth, D. israelit. Personennamen '28, 38; Wuthnow 113; CRoth, Simon-Peter, HTR 54, '61, 91-7—first and second century].—On its declension s. Mlt.-H. 146) *Simon.*

1. surnamed Πέτρος=Κηφᾶς, most prominent of the twelve disciples Mt 4: 18; Mk 1: 16; Lk 4: 38 and oft. Cf. Πέτρος.

2. another of the twelve disciples, called ὁ Καναναῖος Mt 10: 4; Mk 3: 18, or (ὁ) ζηλωτής (cf. Καναναῖος) Lk 6: 15; Ac 1: 13; GEb 2 (the two Alexandrian Epicureans named Ptolemaeus are differentiated as ὁ μέλας καὶ ὁ λευκός).—KLake, HTR 10, '17, 57-63; JSHoyland, Simon the Zealot '30.—3. name of a brother of Jesus Mt 13: 55; Mk 6: 3.

4. *Simon* of Cyrene, who was pressed into service to carry Jesus' cross to the place of execution Mt 27: 32; Mk 15: 21; Lk 23: 26. There is little basis for the idea that this Simon was a Negro (s. Κυρήνη).—SReinach, S. de Cyrène: Cultes, Mythes et Religions IV '12, 181ff; on this JHalévy, Revue sémit. 20, '12, 314-19; ABKinsey, Simon the Crucifier and Symeon the Prophet: ET 35, '24, 84ff.—5. father of Judas Iscariot J 6: 71; 12: 4 t.r.; 13: 2, 26.

6. Σ. ὁ λεπρός *Simon the leper* owner of a house in Bethany on the Mount of Olives. Jesus paid him a visit fr. Jerusalem, and on this occasion the anointing of Jesus took place, acc. to the first two evangelists Mt 26: 6; Mk 14: 3.—CCTorrey, The Four Gospels '33, 296; ELittmann, ZNW 34, '35, 32.

7. name of a Pharisee who invited Jesus to his home and thereby gave a sinful woman the opportunity to anoint the Master Lk 7: 40, 43f.

8. a tanner in Joppa, w. whom Peter stayed for a while; fr. here he went to Caesarea to visit Cornelius Ac 9: 43; 10: 6, 17, 32b.

9. *Simon* the magician Ac 8: 9, 13, 18, 24. He is portrayed as a Samaritan who μαγεύων vs. 9 or ταῖς μαγείαις vs. 11 led his fellow-countrymen to believe that he was the 'Great Power of God'; the miracles of the apostles surprised and disturbed him to such a degree that he tried to buy the gift of imparting the Holy Spirit fr. them.—HWaitz, RE XVIII '06, 351ff; XXIV '13, 518ff (lit. in both vols.); KPieper, Die Simon-Magus Perikope '11; OWeinreich, ARW 18, '15, 21ff; Ramsay, Bearing 117ff; MLidzbarski, NGG '16, 86-93; EdeFaye, Gnostiques et Gnosticisme² '25, 216ff; 430f; CSchmidt, Studien zu d. Ps.-Clementinen '29, 47ff; RPCasey: Beginn. I 5, 151-63; ADNock, ibid. 164-88; L-HVincent, RB 45, '36,

221-32; HJSchoeps, Theol. u. Gesch. des Judenchristentums '49, 127-34; MSmith, Simon Magus in Ac 8: HA Wolfson-Festschr., '65, 735-49; JSelles-Dabadie, Recherches sur Simon le Mage, '69. M-M.

Σινά indecl. (סִינַי).—LXX Σινα: Ex 16: 1; Dt 33: 2; Judg 5: 5; Ps 67: 9; Sir 48: 7. τὸ ὄρος τὸ Σινα: Ex 19: 11, 20, 23; 24: 16. [τὸ] ὄρος Σινα: Ex 19: 16; Lev 7: 38; 25: 1; 26: 46; Num 3: 1; 2 Esdr 19 [Neh 9]: 13; Sib. Or. 3, 256. τὸ Σιν' ὄρος: En. 1, 4.—Joseph. has Σίναιον ὄρος) *Sinai,* name of a rocky mountain on the peninsula named after it. Mountain on which the law was given: Ac 7: 30 (on ἡ ἔρημος τοῦ ὄρους Σινά cf. ἡ ἔρημος [τοῦ] Σ. Ex 19: 1, 2; Num 33: 15, 16 al.), 38; B 11: 3; 14: 2 (cf. Ex 31: 18); 15: 1. On Gal 4: 24f cf. Ἀγάρ. Also SRiva, Il Sinai egizio e cristiano: Ricerche Religiose 9, '33, 12-31.—Mlt.-H. 148. *

σίναπι, εως, τό (Diocles 141 p. 184, 13; PTebt. 9, 13; 18 [III BC]; 11, 19 [II BC]; PFay. 122, 4; 12; 165; PFlor. 20, 21 al. in pap.) *mustard* κόκκος σινάπεως *mustard seed,* popularly viewed as the smallest of all seeds (cf. Antig. Car. 91 and likew. word for word Diod. S. 1, 35, 2 ὁ κροκόδειλος ἐξ ἐλαχίστου γίνεται μέγιστος) Mt 13: 31; 17: 20; Mk 4: 31; Lk 13: 19; 17: 6.—ILöw, D. Flora d. Juden I '28, 516-27. On the parable of the mustard seed s. in addition to the interpr. of the parables and of the synoptic gospels CRBowen, AJTh 22, '18, 562ff; FJehle, NKZ 34, '23, 713-19; KWClark, Class. Weekly 37, '43/'44, 81-3. M-M. *

σινδών, όνος, ἡ (trag., Hdt.+; IG IV² 1, 118, 70 and 71 [III BC]; Dit., Syll.² 754, 5; PPetr. I 12, 21 [III BC]; PTebt. 182; PPar. 18b, 10; LXX; Jos., Ant. 3, 153) *linen.*

1. of the linen cloth in which the body of Jesus was wrapped Mt 27: 59 (Vi. Aesopi I c. 112 σινδ. καθαράν of a linen garment for the king; PGM 13, 653 σινδ. καθ.; PJouon, Mt 27: 59 σινδῶν καθ.: Rech de Sc rel 24, '34, 93-5); Mk 15: 46; Lk 23: 53; GP 6: 24 (JBlinzler, 'Sindon' in Evangeliis, Verbum Domini 34, '56, 112f).

2. of the *tunic* or *shirt* (cf. Hdt. 2, 95) which was the only garment worn by the youth who tried to follow Jesus after Jesus' arrest, unless it was simply a sheet that he wrapped about his body (pap.) Mk 14: 51f (on περιβεβλημένος σινδόνα cf. 1 Macc 10: 64. For the sense 'in his tunic' Diog. L. 6, 90.—Appian, Iber. 35 §143: when an unexpected cry from a herald wakened them early in the morning, soldiers run out ἐν χιτῶσι μόνοις, without dressing fully). M-M. *

σινιάζω 1 aor. ἐσινίασα (a late word, for the earlier σήθω; found Syntipas p. 31, 14; 16; Byz. Chron. [Psaltes p. 332]; Hesychius; Suidas; Etym. Mag.; Bl-D. §108, 3; Mlt.-H. 405) *shake in a sieve, sift* symbolically ἐξητήσατο ὑμᾶς τοῦ σινιάσαι ὡς τὸν σῖτον Lk 22: 31 (for the idea cf. Synes., King. 20 p. 24D καθαρτέον τὸ στρατόπεδον, ὥστε θημῶνα πυρῶν).—CHPickar, CBQ 4, '42, 135; BNoack, Satanas u. Soteria '48, 101f. M-M. *

σιρικός, ή, όν (the spelling attested by the uncials [cf. Peripl. Eryth. c. 39, p. 13, 11; IG XIV 785, 4 σιρικοποιός] for the more usual σηρικός [='silken' Strabo 15, 1, 20; Plut., Mor. 396B; Cass. Dio 57, 15; Jos., Bell. 7, 126].—Bl-D. §41, 1; 42, 4; Mlt.-H. 72; 378; cf. Σῆρες 'Chinese'. Loanw. in rabb.) *silk(en)* subst. τὸ σιρικόν *silk* cloth or garments w. other costly materials Rv 18: 12. M-M. B. 403. *

σιρός, οῦ, ὁ (Eur., Demosth.+; Longus 1, 11, 2; Dit., Syll.³ 83, 10 οἰκοδομῆσαι σιρούς; PLond. 216, 11 [I AD]) *pit, cave* σιροῖς ζόφου 2 Pt 2: 4 א (cf. *σειρός*). On the rdg. of the t.r. cf. *σειρά*.—Field, Notes 241. M-M.*

σιτευτός, ή, όν *fattened* (X., An. 5, 4, 32; Polyb. 38, 8, 7; pap., LXX) ὁ μόσχος ὁ σιτευτός *the calf that has been fattened* (Athen. 9, 32 p. 384A; 14, 74 p. 657B; Judg 6: 28 A; Jer 26: 21) Lk 15: 23, 27, 30. M-M.*

σιτία, ας, ἡ (Christian wr.; Hesychius.—σιτεία=feeding, fattening is found as early as Zen.-P. 59 534, 1 [III BC]. Is this a different word, from σιτεύω=feed, fatten, or just another spelling?) (*a batch of*) *dough* (so Apophtheg. Patrum [c. VI AD]: Migne, Patr. Gr. LXV, 192A; 196B) σ. ποιεῖν D 13: 5.*

σιτίον, ου, τό (Hdt., Aristoph.+; PGiess. 19, 2; POxy. 1158, 11; Pr 30: 22; Philo; Joseph.) dim. of σῖτος; mostly, and in our lit. always in the pl. τὰ σιτία *food* (*made from grain*) (oft. in Hdt. et al.; pap.; Jos., Ant. 4, 270; 15, 300) Ac 7: 12. σιτία καὶ ποτά *food and drink* (s. ποτόν and cf. HMørland, Symb. Osl. 13, '34, 103; LDeubner, SAB '35, XIX, 71) Dg 6: 9. M-M. B. 329.*

σιτιστός, ή, όν *fattened* (Athen. 14 p. 656E ὄρνιθες; Jos., Ant. 8, 40 βόες; Sym. Ps 21: 13; Jer 46: 21) subst. τὰ σιτιστά *cattle that have been fattened* Mt 22: 4. M-M.*

σιτομέτριον, ου, τό *a measured allowance of grain* or *food, ration* (PPetr. II 33a, 5 [cf. Dssm., B 156, 5 (BS 158, 1); Mayser 431]; inscr. fr. Rhodiapolis in Lycia of 149 AD [RHeberdey, Opramoas 1897 p. 50 XIX A, 8; cf. Dssm., LO 82, 1 (LAE 104, 1)] σειτομέτριον; Rhet. Gr. VI 226, 29.—σιτομετρία is more common) διδόναι τὸ σ. *give out the food-allowance* Lk 12: 42. M-M.*

σῖτος, ου, ὁ (Hom.+; inscr., pap., LXX, Philo; Jos., Vi. 71) *wheat*, then *grain* gener. Mt 13: 25, 29 (weeds in it as Sib. Or. 1, 397); Lk 16: 7; J 12: 24; 1 Cor 15: 37; Rv 6: 6 (on this s. Diod. S. 14, 111, 1 as an indication of severe famine and rising prices πέντε μνῶν γενέσθαι τὸν μέδιμνον τοῦ σίτου; Jos., Ant. 14, 28); 18: 13. συνάγειν τὸν σ. εἰς τὴν ἀποθήκην Mt 3: 12; 13: 30; Lk 3: 17; cf. 12: 18. σινιάσαι τὸν σ. 22: 31. As a ship's cargo Ac 27: 38. σ. ὥριμος 1 Cl 56: 15 (Job 5: 26). For πλήρης σῖτος Mk 4: 28 cf. πλήρης 2.—Pl. τὰ σῖτα (Hdt.+; Philo, Det. Pot. Ins. 19 and LXX, where this form occurs in Job and Pr; however, the pl. is not found in any other book; cf. Thackeray 155.—Bl-D. §49, 3 w. app.; Mlt.-H. 122; 372) Ac 7: 12 t.r. Ignatius, in his fervent longing for martyrdom, uses this symbolic language: σῖτός εἰμι θεοῦ *I am God's wheat* and will be ground by the teeth of the wild beasts IRo 4: 1. M-M. B. 514.*

σίφων, ωνος, ὁ (since Hipponax [VI BC] 52 D.²; Eur., Hippocr.; PEleph. 5, 4 [III BC]; PLond. 1177, 129; loanw. in rabb.) *water-pump, fire-engine* (Hero Alex. I p. 18, 2; 28, 18 al.) Hm 11: 18.*

σιφωνίζω 1 aor. ἐσιφώνισα (Aristoph., Thesm. 557) *squirt* Hm 11: 18.*

Σιχάρ s. Συχάρ.

Σιών (ﬥﬡﬠ), ἡ indecl. (LXX; on the spelling cf. Bl-D. §38 app.; 56, 3; cf. Mlt.-H. 149) *Zion.*—**1.** of Mount Zion, a hill within the city of Jerusalem (Dalman, Pj 11, '15, 39ff. S. on Ἱεροσόλυμα 1) τὸ ὄρος Σιών, the place where the Lamb is standing w. his people Rv 14: 1. As a counterpart to Sinai (cf. Gal 4: 24–6; Ps.-Cyprian, De Montibus Sina et Sion: Cyprian III p. 104ff Hartel) Hb 12: 22. **2.** of the city of Jerusalem, in poetic usage (Jer 3: 14 et al.).—**a.** ἡ θυγάτηρ Σιών of the city of Jerus. and its

inhabitants (cf. θυγάτηρ 2e) Mt 21: 5; J 12: 15 (both Zech 9: 9; cf. Sib. Or. 324).

b. more gener. of the people of Israel, whose center is Jerus. Ro 9: 33; B 6: 2 (both Is 28: 16); Ro 11: 26 (Is 59: 20).—**c.** of the New Jerus. of Christianity 1 Pt 2: 6 (Is 28: 16). M-M.*

σιωπάω impf. ἐσιώπων; fut. σιωπήσω; 1 aor. ἐσιώπησα (Hom.+; pap., LXX, Philo; Jos., Vi. 195; 338) *be silent.*

1. *keep silent, say nothing, make no sound* Mt 26: 63 (Maximus Tyr. 3, 7e, Socr. before the jury. On the subject matter cf. Diog. L. 3, 19 Plato before the popular assembly on Aegina, on trial for his life: μηδ' ὁτιοῦν φθέγξασθαι = did not say a single word; Eur. in Plut., Mor. 532F); Mk 3: 4; 9: 34; 14: 61; Ac 18: 9 (opp. λαλεῖν as PGM 5, 292); IEph 15: 1 (opp. λαλεῖν); IRo 2: 1a; GP 4: 10. σ. περί τινος *be silent concerning someone* IEph 3: 2. σ. ἀπό τινος *be silent and leave someone alone* (Gdspd.) IRo 2: 1b.

2. *stop speaking, be* or *become quiet*—**a.** of persons (Menand., Georg. 54 J; Plut., Mor. 434F; Herm. Wr. 1, 16; Jos., Ant. 7, 378; Test. Jos. 9: 4) Mt 20: 31; Mk 10: 48; Lk 18: 39 t.r.; 19: 40; MPol 7: 3 Funk.—*Be silent* in the sense *lose the ability to speak* Lk 1: 20.

b. not of human beings: of swine B 10: 3 (opp. κραυγάζειν).—Symbolically, of the wind and waves in a storm Mk 4: 39 (cf. also the fig. Theocr., Idyll 2, 38 σιγᾷ πόντος). M-M. B. 1259.*

σιωπῇ dat. of σιωπή, ῆς, ἡ 'silence' (as a noun Soph., X.+; inscr., pap., LXX) as adv. (as early as Hom.; X., Cyr. 5, 3, 43; Ps.-Demosth. 48, 31; Dit., Syll.³ 1218, 11 [V BC]) *quietly, privately* J 11: 28 D.*

σκάμμα, ατος, τό (Pla.+) *that which is dug, trench*, then *arena* (surrounded by a trench, or dug up and covered w. sand; CIG 2758), a favorite in symbolic usage (Polyb. 38, 18, 5; Epict. 4, 8, 26) ἐν τῷ αὐτῷ σ. εἶναι *be in the same arena* 1 Cl 7: 1.*

σκανδαλίζω 1 aor. ἐσκανδάλισα. Pass.: pf. ptc. ἐσκανδαλισμένος; 1 aor. ἐσκανδαλίσθην; 1 fut. σκανδαλισθήσομαι (LXX; Aq.; Sym.; Theod. [but not in Ep. Arist., Philo, Joseph., Test. 12 Patr.]; Cat. Cod. Astr. X 67, 23; Christian authors).

1. *cause to be caught* or *to fall*, i.e. *cause to sin* (the sin may consist in a breach of the moral law, in unbelief, or in the acceptance of false teachings)—**a.** τινά *someone* (Mal 2: 8 Sym., Theod.; PsSol 16: 7 γυναικὸς σκανδαλιζούσης ἄφρονα; Hist. Laus. 5 p. 21 Butler σκανδαλίσαι ψυχήν) Mt 5: 29f; 18: 6, 8f; Mk 9: 42f, 45, 47; Lk 17: 2; 1 Cor 8: 13a, b; 1 Cl 46: 8.—Pass. *be led into sin* (Sir 23: 8; 32: 15; Act. Jo. 82 p. 192 B.) so perh. 2 Cor 11: 29 (s. 2 below).—The abs. pass. can also mean *let oneself be led into sin, fall away* (Passio Perpet. 20, 10 vGebh.; Martyr. Petri 3 p. 82, 22 Lips.) Mt 13: 21; 24: 10; Mk 4: 17; 14: 27, 29; J 16: 1; D 16: 5.—ἐσκανδαλισμένοι Hv 4, 1, 3; m 8: 10 are *people who have been led astray*, but who have not altogether fallen away fr. the faith.

b. σκανδαλίζεσθαι ἔν τινι (Sir 9: 5; 23: 8; 32: 15) *be led into sin, be repelled by someone, take offense at someone*, of Jesus: by refusing to believe in him or by becoming apostate fr. him a person falls into sin Mt 11: 6; 13: 57; 26: 31, 33 (cf. Ascensio Isaiae 3, 14 [PAmh. I p. 10f] δώδεκα οἱ μετ' αὐτοῦ ὑπ' αὐτοῦ σκανδαλισθήσονται); Mk 6: 3; Lk 7: 23. ἐν ᾧ ὁ ἀδελφὸς σκανδαλίζεται Ro 14: 21 t.r.

2. *give offense to, anger, shock* (Act. Jo. 56 p. 178B; Athanasius, Vita Anton. 81; Histor. Lausiaca 37 p. 115

σκανδαλίζω πολλούς; 46 p. 136) τινά someone Mt 17: 27 (JDMDerrett, NovT 6, '63, 1-15); J 6: 61. Pass. Mt 15: 12.—τίς σκανδαλίζεται; perh. who has any reason to take offense? 2 Cor 11: 29 (s. 1a above).—S. on σκάνδαλον, end. M-M.*

σκάνδαλον, ου, τό (secular pap.; PLond. 1338, 25; 1339, 10 [both 709 AD]; LXX; Aq.; Sym.; Theod. [but not in Ep. Arist., Philo, Joseph., Test. 12 Patr.], then Christian wr. Later word for σκανδάληθρον [Aristoph. et al.]; cf. Hesychius and Photius s.v.).

1. trap w. παγίς, used symbolically (Josh 23: 13; Ps 140: 9; 1 Macc 5: 4; Is 8: 14 Sym. and Theod.) Ro 11: 9 (Ps 68: 23).

2. temptation to sin, enticement to apostasy, false belief, etc. (Ezk 7: 19[Aq.; Sym.]; Wsd 14: 11) Mt 18: 7a, b, c; Lk 17: 1; B 4: 9. τὸ τέλειον σκ. the final temptation 4: 3. βαλεῖν σκάνδαλον ἐνώπιον τῶν υἱῶν Ἰσραήλ entice the sons of Israel to sin Rv 2: 14. σκάνδαλα ποιεῖν bring about temptations (to sin) Ro 16: 17. τιθέναι τινὶ σκάνδαλον put a temptation in someone's way 14: 13 (on τιθέναι σκ. cf. Jdth 5: 1); in place of the dat. κατά τινος 1 Cl 35: 8 (Ps 49: 20).—Also of persons (PsSol 4: 23; 1 Macc 5: 4): Jesus censures Peter, as Satan σκάνδαλον εἶ ἐμοῦ you are tempting me to sin Mt 16: 23. In ἀπεχόμενοι σκανδάλων καὶ τῶν ψευδαδέλφων κτλ. Pol 6: 3, σκ. is prob. best taken as one who tempts others to sin (cf. Pistis Sophia 105; 106 p. 173-5 CSchmidt ὡς σκάνδαλον καὶ ὡς παραβάτης; Act. Jo. 64 of a woman ἡ σκάνδαλον γενομένη ἀνδρί; 79).—To those who cannot come to a decision to believe on him, Jesus is a σκάνδαλον (σκανδαλίζω 1b). In line w. OT fig. language (Is 8: 14, where Aq., Sym., Theod.—in contrast to the LXX—have our word) Jesus is called πέτρα σκανδάλου Ro 9: 33; 1 Pt 2: 8 (on the relation of these two passages to each other cf. RHarris, Testimonies I '16, 18f; 26f).

3. that which gives offense or causes revulsion, that which arouses opposition, an object of anger or disapproval, stain etc. (Sir 7: 6; 27: 23) σκ. ἐν αὐτῷ οὐκ ἔστιν in him there is no stain or fault 1 J 2: 10 (cf. Jdth 5: 20). Of the cross ὅ ἐστιν σκάνδαλον τοῖς ἀπιστοῦσιν which is revolting to those who have no faith IEph 18: 1. The crucified Christ is a σκ. to the Jews 1 Cor 1: 23. τὸ σκάνδαλον τοῦ σταυροῦ the stumbling-block of the cross, i.e. that which, in the preaching about the cross, arouses opposition Gal 5: 11. συλλέξουσιν ἐκ τῆς βασιλείας αὐτοῦ πάντα τὰ σκ. they will gather out of his kingdom everything that is offensive Mt 13: 41 (this interpr., which refers τὰ σκ. to things, would correspond to the scripture passage basic to this one, i.e. Zeph 1: 3, where Sym. has our word in the combination τὰ σκάνδαλα σὺν [τοῖς] ἀσεβέσι. Nevertheless the fact that Mt continues w. καὶ τοὺς ποιοῦντας τὴν ἀνομίαν could require us to take τὰ σκ. to mean persons; s. 2 above).—WCAllen, Mk '15, 199ff; ASchmitz, Vom Wesen des Ärgernisses² '25; JLindblom, Skandalon: e. lexikal-exeget. Untersuchung '21 (s. also πρόσκομμα, end); GStählin, Skandalon '30; KSchilder, Over het 'Skandalon': Geref. Theol. Tijdschr. 32, '32, 49-67; 97-130; RAKnox, Trials of a Translator '49, 66-73; AHumbert, Biblica 35, '54, 1-28 (synoptics).—GStählin, TW VII 338-59. M-M.*

σκάπτω fut. σκάψω; 1 aor. ἔσκαψα. Pass.: pf. ptc. ἐσκαμμένος; 2 aor. ἐσκάφην (Hom. Hymns, Thu.+; inscr., pap.; Is 5: 6).

1. intr. dig (Aristoph. et al.; BGU 1119, 23 [I BC] σκάπτειν καὶ ποτίζειν) σκάπτειν οὐκ ἰσχύω Lk 16: 3 (cf. the proverbial expr. Aristoph., Av. 1432 σκάπτειν οὐκ ἐπίσταμαι and Galen, Protr. 13 p. 42, 1ff John ἰσχύς

enough to σκάπτειν. Digging is the hardest kind of work [Charito 8, 8, 2; Appian, Liby. 15 §61]; the uneducated workman must engage in it [Diog. L. 7, 169; Ps.-Phoc. 158]). σκ. καὶ βαθύνειν (s. βαθύνω) 6: 48 (Stephan. Byz. s.v. Ἄργιλος: σκάπτειν εἰς τὸ θεμελίους καταβαλέσθαι).—περὶ αὐτήν dig around it (the fig tree) 13: 8 (cf. Diod. S. 5, 41, 6 περισκαφείσης τ. γῆς ἀπὸ τῶν ῥιζῶν).

2. trans. dig (up), spade up τὶ someth. τὸν ἀμπελῶνα (Diod. S. 4, 31, 7; PLond. 163, 33 [I AD]) Hs 5, 2, 4. Pass. (Is 5: 6) 5, 2, 5; 5, 6, 2. M-M. B. 497.*

Σκαριώθ is the rdg. of D in Mk 3: 19; J 6: 71 and Σκαριώτης is the rdg. of D in Mt 10: 4; 26: 14; Mk 14: 10 for Ἰσκαριώθ (-ώτου), q.v.*

σκάφη, ης, ἡ (Aeschyl., Hdt.+; inscr., pap.; Bel LXX 33, Theod. 33; Jos., C. Ap. 2, 11 [a quot. fr. Apion w. σκάφη as fem. sing.]; loanw. in rabb.) (small) boat, skiff (so Soph.+; Polyb. 1, 23, 7; PGradenwitz [SA Heidelberg '14] 9, 5 [III BC]; BGU 1157, 8; 1179) of a ship's boat (ordinarily in tow, LCasson, Ships and Seamanship in the Ancient World, '71, 248f) Ac 27: 16, 30, 32. M-M. B. 730.*

σκελοκοπέω (hardly σκελοκοπάω) 1 aor. pass. ἐσκελοκοπήθην break the legs of someone (s. σκέλος) GP 4: 14.*

σκέλος, ους, τό (Hom.+; inscr., pap., LXX, Ep. Arist., Philo; Jos., Ant. 3, 271) leg καταγνύναι τὰ σ. break the legs, of the breaking of leg-bones as a punishment, known in Lat. as crurifragium. Orig. this was a separate form of capital punishment, comparable to torture on the wheel (s. κατάγνυμι and KKohler, Das Verbot d. Knochenzerbrechens: ARW 13, '10, 153f) Phlm subscr.—J 19: 31-3 it accompanied crucifixion, in order to hasten death (s. also Appian, Bell. Civ. 4, 44 §189 ἑνὸς τὸ σκέλος συντριβέντος = one [of the bearers] broke his leg).—GABarton, 'A Bone of Him Shall Not Be Broken' J 19: 36: JBL 49, '30, 13-19. M-M. B. 241.*

σκεπάζω 1 aor. ἐσκέπασα. Pass.: 1 aor. ἐσκεπάσθην; 1 fut. σκεπασθήσομαι (X., Aristot.; pap., LXX).

1. cover (Jos., Ant. 1, 44) τὶ someth. (X. et al.; Sib. Or. 3, 612) of a tree that covers the earth w. its shade Hs 8, 1, 1; 8, 3, 2; cf. 9, 27, 1. Pass. (cf. Philo, Leg. All. 2, 53) 8, 1, 2.

2. protect, shelter (PSI 440, 14 [III BC]; PTebt. 5, 60 [II BC]; PLond. 897, 6; LXX; Sib. Or. 3, 705) τινά someone of bishops σκ. τὰς χήρας τῇ διακονίᾳ shelter the widows by their ministry Hs 9, 27, 2 (a play on words w. σκεπάζω 9, 27, 1 [s. 1 above]). Pass. (PHib. 35, 10 [III BC]) 1 Cl 60: 3; Hs 9, 27, 3. σκ. ἀπὸ τῶν μελλόντων κριμάτων be protected from the judgments to come 1 Cl 28: 1. B. 849.*

σκέπασμα, ατος, τό (Pla.+) covering, of anything that serves as a cover and hence as a protection. Chiefly clothing (Aristot., Pol. 7, 17 p. 1336a, 17; Philo, Det. Pot. Ins. 19; Jos., Bell. 2, 129), but also house (Aristot., Metaph. 7 p. 168, 11 οἰκία σκέπασμα ἐκ πλίνθων κ. λίθων) w. διατροφή 1 Ti 6: 8. M-M.*

σκέπη, ης, ἡ (Hdt.+; inscr., pap., LXX; Ep. Arist. 140; Manetho in Jos., C. Ap. 1, 237; Jos., Ant. 1, 44) protection, shelter, shade afforded, e.g., by trees (cf. Diod. S. 5, 65, 1; Philo, Sacr. Abel. 25) Hs 8, 1, 1; 8, 3, 2; 9, 1, 9.*

Σκευᾶς, ᾶ, ὁ (Plut., Caes. 16, 2; Appian, Bell. Civ. 2, 60 §247 [a centurion: Lat. Scaeva]; Cass. Dio 56, 16, 1; CIG 2889; Bl-D. §125, 2) Sceva a high priest Ac 19: 14 (acc. to EHKase, Am. Hist. Review 43, '38, 437f a misunderstanding due to dittography). M-M.*

σκευή, ῆς, ἡ (Pind., Hdt.+; Philo; Jos., Bell. 3, 117, Ant. 4, 301; BGU 775, 6; 11) *equipment, (household) furnishings,* esp. of a *ship's gear* or *equipment* (Diod. S. 14, 79, 4; Appian, Bell. Civ. 5, 88 §367 [=τὰ σκεύη τὰ ἐν τῷ πλοίῳ Jon 1: 5]) ἡ σκευὴ τοῦ πλοίου of the equipment of a ship that can be dispensed w. Ac 27: 19 (acc. to ChVoigt, Die Romfahrt des Ap. Pls: Hansa 53, '16, 725-32 *the tackle* or *rigging of a ship;* so RSV et al.). M-M.*

σκεῦος, ους, τό (Aristoph., Thu.+; inscr., pap., LXX) —**1.** lit.—**a.** gener. *thing, object* used for any purpose at all (e.g., a table: Diod. S. 17, 66, 5) Mk 11: 16. σκεῦος ἐλεφάντινον or ἐκ ξύλου Rv 18: 12a, b. Pl. (Diod. S. 13, 12, 6) Dg 2: 2-4. Of all one has (Jos., Vi. 68; 69) τὰ σκεύη αὐτοῦ *his property* Lk 17: 31.—Mt 12: 29; Mk 3: 27 (both in allusion to Is 49: 24f).—By an added statement or through the context σκ. can become an object of a certain specific kind: τὰ σκεύη τῆς λειτουργίας *the equipment used in the services* Hb 9: 21 (cf. Jos., Bell. 6, 389 τὰ πρὸς τὰς ἱερουργίας σκεύη). Also τὰ ἅγια σκεύη GOxy 14; 21; 29f (Jos., Bell. 2, 321; cf. Plut., Mor. 812в σκεῦος ἱερόν; Philo, Mos. 2, 94 σκεύη ἱερά). τὸ σκεῦος Ac 27: 17 seems to be the *kedge* or *driving-anchor* (Breusing 177ff; Blass ad loc.; Voigt [s. σκευή]. Differently HBalmer, Die Romfahrt des Ap. Pls '05, 355ff. Cf. FBrannigan, ThGl 25, '33, 182-4; Zen.-P. 6 [=Sb 6712], 10 [258 вс] ἄνευ τῶν ἀναγκαίων σκευῶν πλεῖν τὰ πλοῖα. Pl. also X., Oec. 8, 11f and elsewh. of ship's gear; Arrian, Peripl. 5, 2 τὰ σκεύη τὰ ναυτικά. Engl. transl. have 'gear', 'sails'). Ac 10: 11, 16; 11: 5 represent a transitional stage on the way to sense b.

b. *vessel, jar, dish,* etc. (Aristoph., Thesm. 402; X., Mem. 1, 7, 5; Aelian, V.H. 12, 8; Herodian 6, 7, 7; LXX) Lk 8: 16; J 19: 29; 2 Ti 2: 20 (four kinds as Plut., Caes. 48, 7). τὸ κενὸν σκεῦος Hm 11: 13. ποιεῖν σκ. *make a vessel* 2 Cl 8: 2. τὰ σκεύη τὰ κεραμικά Rv 2: 27 (s. κεραμικός). σκ. εἰς τιμήν or εἰς ἀτιμίαν (s. τιμή 2b) Ro 9: 21; 2 Ti 2: 21 (the fig. sense makes itself felt in the latter pass.).

2. fig. (Polyb. 13, 5, 7 Δαμοκλῆς ὑπηρετικὸν ἦν σ.) for Christ Paul is a σκεῦος ἐκλογῆς *a chosen instrument* Ac 9: 15.—Of the body, in which the Spirit dwells (cf. Test. Napht. 8: 6 ὁ διάβολος οἰκειοῦται αὐτὸν ὡς ἴδιον σκεῦος and the magical prayer in FPradel, Griech. u. südital. Gebete '07, p. 9, 11f ἐξορκίζω σε ἐξελθεῖν ἀπὸ τοῦ σκεύους τούτου) Hm 5, 1, 2. Christ's body as τὸ σκ. τοῦ πνεύματος *the vessel of the Spirit* B 7: 3; 11: 9; cf. τὸ καλὸν σκεῦος 21: 8 (of the human body). On the human body as ὀστράκινα σκεύη 2 Cor 4: 7 cf. ὀστράκινος. Those who are lost are σκεύη ὀργῆς Ro 9: 22 (cf. Jer 27: 25.—But CHDodd, JTS 5, '54, 247f: *instruments of judgment),* those who are saved σκ. ἐλέους vs. 23.—1 Pt 3: 7 woman is called ἀσθενέστερον σκεῦος (ἀσθενής 1b). τὸ ἑαυτοῦ σκεῦος 1 Th 4: 4 from antiquity has been interpreted to mean *one's own body* (Theodoret, Calvin, Milligan, Schlatter, MDibelius; RAKnox, transl. '44; CCD transl. '41, mg.) or *one's own wife* (Theodore of Mopsuestia, Schmiedel, vDobschütz, Frame, Oepke; WVogel, ThBl 13, '34, 83-5; RSV et al.). The former interpr. is supported by the passages cited at the beg. of this section 2, and the latter is in accord w. rabb. usage (Billerb. III 632f. Cf. also κτάομαι 1.—So early a term as the Akkadian 'laḥanattu' combines the meanings (1) vessel, (2) harlot, darling [communication fr. LKoehler]).—Still another possibility for 1 Th 4: 4 is *membrum virile* (so Antistius [I ad] in Anthol. Plan. 4, 243; Aelian, N.A. 17, 11; cf. MPoole, Synopsis Criticorum Ali. Sacrae Script., 1669-76, IV, 2, col. 958; communication fr. WHPHatch,

'53). In this case κτᾶσθαι must mean someth. like 'gain control of', etc.—CMaurer, TW VII 359-68. M-M.*

σκηνή, ῆς, ἡ (trag., X., Pla.+; inscr., pap., LXX, Philo, Joseph.) *tent, booth,* also gener. *lodging, dwelling* of the tents of nomads (Gen 4: 20; 12: 8.—Dalman, Arbeit VI '39) Hb 11: 9. Of a soldier's tent σκηνὴν πηγνύναι *pitch a tent* (πήγνυμι 2) GP 8: 33. δίαιτα τῆς σκηνῆς (s. δίαιτα) 1 Cl 56: 13 (Job 5: 24). τρεῖς σκηναί in the account of the Transfiguration (w. ποιεῖν as Jos., Ant. 3, 79) Mt 17: 4; Mk 9: 5; Lk 9: 33 (lit. s.v. μεταμορφόω 1; esp. ELohmeyer, ZNW 21, '22, 191ff; HRiesenfeld, Jésus transfiguré '47, 146-205).—ἡ σκηνὴ τοῦ μαρτυρίου the *Tabernacle* or *Tent of Testimony* (Ex 27: 21; 29: 4; Lev 1: 1; Num 1: 1 and oft.) Ac 7: 44; 1 Cl 43: 2, 5. Also simply ἡ σκηνή (LXX; Jos., Ant. 20, 228) Hb 8: 5; 9: 21; 1 Cl 43: 3. οἱ τῇ σκ. λατρεύοντες Hb 13: 10 (s. on θυσιαστήριον 2d and OHoltzmann, ZNW 10, '09, 251-60). σκηνὴ ἡ πρώτη *the outer tent,* i.e. the Holy Place 9: 2; cf. vss. 6, 8 (πρῶτος 1d; Jos., C. Ap. 2, 12 has ἡ πρώτη σκηνή of the tabernacle in contrast to Solomon's temple). Hence σκηνὴ ἡ λεγομένη Ἅγια Ἁγίων *the Tabernacle* or *Tent that is called the Holy of Holies* vs. 3, ἡ δευτέρα (σκηνή) vs. 7. The earthly Tabernacle (cf. RKittel, RE XIX 33-42 and s. GABarton, JBL 57, '38, 197-201) corresponds in Hb to another σκηνή: Christ as High Priest, taking his own blood (rather than that of goats and calves), goes διὰ τῆς μείζονος καὶ τελειοτέρας σκηνῆς ἐφάπαξ εἰς τὰ ἅγια 9: 11f. He is τῶν ἁγίων λειτουργὸς καὶ τῆς σκηνῆς τῆς ἀληθινῆς 8: 2. Rv 15: 5 speaks of a ναὸς τῆς σκηνῆς τοῦ μαρτυρίου ἐν τῷ οὐρανῷ. God has his σκ.=*dwelling* in heaven 13: 6, and will some time have it among men 21: 3. αἱ αἰώνιοι σκηναί *the eternal dwellings* of the life to come Lk 16: 9 (RPautrel, 'Aeterna tabernacula' [Lk 16: 9]: Rech de Sc rel 30, '40, 307-27; LSEby, JBL 58, '39, p. xi).—ἡ σκηνὴ τοῦ Μολόχ of a portable sanctuary (cf. ἡ ἱερὰ σκηνή of the Carthaginians in Diod. S. 20, 65, 1) of Moloch (q.v.) Ac 7: 43 (Am 5: 26). ἡ σκηνὴ Δαυὶδ ἡ πεπτωκυῖα *David's fallen dwelling* of his ruined kingdom 15: 16 (Am 9: 11). Here σκηνή may perh. mean *king's tent* (Diod. S. 17, 36, 4. More precisely 5 ἡ τοῦ Δαρείου σκηνή; 17, 76, 6 ἡ βασιλικὴ σκηνή) *David's fallen royal tent.*—OScherling, De Vocis σκηνή Significatione et Usu, Diss. Marburg '08; HBornhäuser, Sukka '35, 126-8: Σκηνή u. verwandte Worte im NT. M-M. B. 461.*

σκηνοπηγία, ας, ἡ (Aristot., H.A. 9, 7 of the nest-building of swallows. Elsewh. only as a t.t. of Jewish religious lang.—σκανοπαγέομαι is found as a rel.-technical term in an inscr. of the island of Cos [II вс.—Dssm., LO 92f— LAE 92f]. On σκηνὴν πηγνύναι s. πήγνυμι 2) *the building of tents* or *booths,* as a name for the *Festival of Booths* or *Tabernacles* (σκ. in this sense, mostly w. ἑορτή: Dt 16: 16; 31: 10; Zech 14: 16, 18, 19; 1 Esdr 5: 50; 2 Macc 1: 9; Jos., Ant. 4, 209; 8, 100; 123; 11, 154; 13, 241; 372; 15, 50, Bell. 2, 515. Jewish inscr. fr. Berenice in the Cyrenaica CIG III 5361 [13 вс]=Schürer III⁴ 79, 20 l. 1f), a festival celebrated Tishri (roughly=October) 15-21, out of doors when poss., in booths made fr. branches of trees (חַג הַסֻּכּוֹת). Joseph. declares (Ant. 15, 50; cf. 8, 123) that it is the most important Jewish festival. J 5: 1 v.l.; 7: 2 (CWFSmith, NTS 9, '63, 130-46).—Billerb. II 774-812; HBornhäuser, Sukka '35, esp. pp. 34-9.—Demetrius of Scepsis in Athen. 4 p. 141 ef tells of the τῶν Καρνείων of the Spartans σκηναῖς ἔχοντες παραπλήσιόν τι. They put up for nine days 'something like a tent'. At times nine men eat together in them.—GWMacRae, The Mng. and

Evolution of the Feast of Tabernacles, CBQ 22, '60, 251-76. M-M.*

σκηνοποιός, οῦ, ὁ *tentmaker* (acc. to Pollux 7, 189 the Old Comedy used the word as a synonym for μηχανοποιός= either a 'stagehand' who moved stage properties [as Aristoph., Pax 174] or a 'manufacturer of stage properties'. In his fifth ed. WBauer, basing his judgment on the latter interpr. of the statement by Pollux, seems to give priority to the sense 'manufacturer of theatrical properties' for the word in Ac 18: 3. But it is improbable that either Aquila or Paul would, in the face of evident Jewish objection to theatrical productions [cf. Schürer II⁴, 1907, 60f], have practiced such a trade. Bauer also points out an apparent impediment to the rendering *tentmaker* in the fact that σκηνή appears freq. as the obj. of ποιέω in the sense 'pitch' or 'erect a tent' (s. ποιέω I 1aα; act. σκηνοποιέω Sym. Is 13: 20; 22: 15; mid. σκηνοποιέομαι Aristot., Meteor. 348b, 35; Clearch., fgm. 48 W.; Polyb. 14, 1, 7; Diod. S. 3, 27, 4; Ps.-Callisth. 2, 9, 8; σκηνοποιΐα Aeneas Tact. 8, 3; Polyb. 6, 28, 3; inscr., Rev. Arch. 3, '34, 40; and acc. to the text. trad. of Dt 31: 10 as an alternate expr. for σκηνοπηγία. Analogously σκηνοποιός would then mean 'one who pitches or erects tents'. However, those living in nomadic areas would not depend on specialists to help in a task that any Jew could learn on his own (cf. Mt 17: 4 par.). Moreover, it is clear from Ac 20: 34; 1 Cor 4: 12; 1 Th 2: 9; 2 Th 3: 8 that Paul's work was of a technical nature and was carried out in metropolitan areas. Therefore, w. respect to the semantic function of -ποιός compounds, it can be noted that the noun in such formations is viewed as the object of actual production (similarly the adjectival form σκηνοποιός Herm. Wr. 516, 10f=Stob. I, 464, 7ff is used to express production of a dwelling appropriate for the soul), and Ex 26: 1 offers clear evidence of use of the non-compounded σκηνή+ποιέω in the sense 'produce' or 'manufacture (not pitch) a tent'. The verb ἐπιτελεῖν Hb 8: 5 is not an alternate expr. for 'production' of a tent, but denotes 'completion' of a project, connoting a strong sense of religious commitment; see ἐπιτελέω 2. Early versions and patristic writers (s. the lit. below) display a variety of attempts to connote the particular skill (e.g., weaver of tent-cloth, leather-worker) that Paul brought to the making of his tents, but such interpretations appear to reflect awareness of local practices rather than semantic precision. Absence of any qualification in the NT, lack of unanimity in the tradition, and ambivalence in rabbinic writings respecting the religious and social status of specific crafts or occupations preclude certainty beyond the denotation *tentmaker*. Adding to the difficulty is the fact that σκηνοποιός is found only once in the Gk. Bible, and nowhere independently of it, except for the passages from Pollux and Herm. Wr. cited above. Synonym σκηνορράφος Aelian 2, 1; Bull. Inst. Arch. Bulg. 8, 69 (s. L-S-J Suppl. s.v.).—JWeiss, Das Urchristentum '17, 135; FWGrosheide, Παῦλος σκηνοποιός: ThSt 35, '17, 241f; Zahn, AG II 632, 10; 634; Billerb. II 745-7; Beginn. IV, 223; JoachJeremias, ZNW 30, '31, 299; WMichaelis, TW VII, 394-6. M-M.*

σκῆνος, ους, τό (Pre-Socr., Hippocr.+; inscr.; Wsd 9: 15) *tent, lodging* only fig. of the body (Democr. [Diels, Fgm. der Vorsokrat. index] et al.; Ps.-Pla., Axioch. 365ε; 366Α; Herm. Wr. 13, 12; 15; Achilles Tat. 2, 36, 3 τὸ οὐράνιον θνητῷ σκήνει δεδεμένον; CIG 1656 σκῆνος μὲν . . . , ψυχὴ δέ; 3123; 6309; PGM 1, 319; 4, 1951; 1970; Wsd 9: 15) εἶναι ἐν τῷ σ. *be in one's tent,* i.e. be physically alive 2 Cor 5: 4. ἡ ἐπίγειος ἡμῶν οἰκία τοῦ σ. *the earthly tent*

we live in vs. 1 (on the gen.-combination s. Bl-D. §168, 1; Rob. 498).—S. γυμνός 4, end. M-M.*

σκηνόω fut. σκηνώσω; 1 aor. ἐσκήνωσα (X., Pla. et al.; LXX; Jos., Vi. 244, Ant. 3, 293) *live, dwell* (X., Demosth. 54, 3; Dit., Syll.³ 344, 3; PSI 340, 10; 13 [III βϲ]; LXX) w. ἐν and the dat. of the place (X., An. 5, 5, 11; Zen.-P. 68[= Sb 6774], 7; Gen 13: 12) ἐν τ. οὐρανῷ Rv 13: 6; cf. 12: 12 ἐν ἡμῖν temporarily *among us* J 1: 14 (Diogenes, Ep. 37, 1 παρὰ τούτοις ἐσκήνωσα='I took up residence w. them'). μετ' αὐτῶν *with them* Rv 21: 3. ἐπ' αὐτούς *over* or *above them,* i.e. shelter them, of God (cf. σκηνή) 7: 15. M-M.*

σκήνωμα, ατος, τό (Eur., X.+; LXX; Jos., Ant. 11, 187) *tent,* gener. *dwelling, lodging,* in our lit. only in specialized mngs.

1. of the temple as God's *dwelling-place* (Paus. 3, 17, 6; LXX) Ac 7: 46 (after Ps 131: 5).

2. of the body (Ps.-Callisth. 1, 24, 11; Herm. Wr. in Stob., Flor. I 396, 1 W.=p. 476, 3 Sc.; PGM 19a, 49; Sextus 320; cf. σκῆνος) εἶναι ἐν τούτῳ τῷ σκ.=remain alive 2 Pt 1: 13; opp. ἡ ἀπόθεσις τοῦ σκ.=death vs. 14. ἡ ψυχὴ ἐν θνητῷ σκηνώματι κατοικεῖ Dg 6: 8 (Sext., loc. cit. τὸ σ. τῆς ψυχῆς). M-M.*

σκῆπτρον, ου, τό (Hom.+; inscr.; PGM 13, 182; 187; LXX)—1. *scepter* as a symbol of the power to rule (Jos., Ant. 17, 197) σκ. τῆς μεγαλωσύνης τοῦ θεοῦ *the scepter of the majesty of God* 1 Cl 16: 2 (cf. Esth 4: 17q; Ezekiel Trag. in Euseb., Pr. Ev. 9, 29, 5; Philo, Mut. Nom. 136; Sib. Or. 3, 49. The scepter of Zeus Pind., Pyth. 1, 10; Cornutus 9 p. 10, 10; Iambl., Vi. Pyth. 28, 155; that of Rhea Pind., Nem. 11, 4; that of Isis Is.-Aretal. of Cyrene [WPeek, Is.-Hymn. v. Andros '30, 129]; that of Selene PGM 4, 2843f.—FJMdeWaele, The Magic Staff or Rod in Graeco-Italian Antiquity '27, chap. 1).

2. *tribe* of the tribes of Israel (1 Km 2: 28; 9: 21; 3 Km 11: 31f, 35f al.; Jos., Ant. 6, 61; Test. Judah 25: 1, Napht. 5: 8) 1 Cl 32: 2.*

σκιά, ᾶς, ἡ (Hom.+; inscr., pap., LXX, Philo; Jos.; Bell. 2, 28 σκιά—σῶμα, Ant. 5, 238; 10, 29).

1. *shade, shadow*—a. lit. Mk 4: 32 (cf. Ezk 17: 23); Ac 5: 15.—b. fig. (s. σκότος 2b.—Jos., Bell. 1, 215) σκιὰ θανάτου *shadow of death* (Job 12: 22; Ps 22: 4; 43: 20; Jer 13: 16.—So also σκιά by itself of the shadow of death, which stands beside the old man: Herodas 1, 16) Mt 4: 16 (Is 9: 1); w. σκότος (Job 3: 5; Ps 106: 10) Lk 1: 79. For σκοτία 1 J 2: 8 A.

2. *shadow, foreshadowing* (in contrast to reality: Prodicus in X., Mem. 2, 1, 22; Achilles Tat. 1, 15, 6 τὸ ὕδωρ ἦν κάτοπτρον, ὡς δοκεῖν τὸ ἄλσος εἶναι διπλοῦν, τὸ μὲν τ. ἀληθείας, τὸ δὲ τ. σκιᾶς; Phalaris, Ep. 35 λόγος ἔργου σκ. Oft. in Philo: Somn. 1, 206, Plant. 27; Leg. All. 3, 102, Post. Caini 112) σκιὰ τῶν μελλόντων a *foreshadowing of what is to come* Col 2: 17 (opp. τὸ σῶμα, as Philo, Conf. Lingu. 190; Jos., Bell. 2, 28; Lucian, Hermot. 79). ὑπόδειγμα καὶ σκιὰ τῶν ἐπουρανίων Hb 8: 5 (Synes., Ep. 44 p. 182D τοῦ θείου σκ. τὸ ἀνθρώπινον). σκιά forms a contrast to εἰκών (s. εἰκών 2) 10: 1. M-M. B. 62.*

σκιρτάω 1 aor. ἐσκίρτησα (Hom.+; PGM 3, 200; LXX; Philo, Spec. Leg. 1, 304) *leap, spring about* as a sign of joy (Jer 27: 11; Mal 3: 20; Jos., Bell. 5, 120) Lk 6: 23. Of sheep gaily skipping about (cf. Dio Chrys. 69[19], 3; Longus 1, 9, 1; Theophyl. Sim., Ep. 29; Eutecnius 1 p. 18, 3) Hs 6, 1, 6; 6, 2, 3f; 6. ἐκκλησίας χάρις σκιρτᾷ Dg 11: 6.—Of the movements of a child in the womb (Gen 25: 22. Cf.

ENorden, Die Geburt des Kindes '24 p. 104, 1), which are taken as an expression of joy Lk 1: 41, 44. M-M.*

σκληροκαρδία, ας, ἡ (Biblical [Dt 10: 16; Jer 4: 4; Sir 16: 10; cf. En. 16, 3; Test. Sim. 6: 2; Philo, Spec. Leg. 1, 305] and ecclesiastical word.—Bl-D. §120, 4; Mlt.-H. 279) *hardness of heart, coldness, obstinacy, stubbornness* Mt 19: 8; Mk 10: 5; Hv 3, 7, 6; B 9: 5 Funk (Jer 4: 4). W. ἀπιστία Mk 16: 14.*

σκληρός, ά, όν (Hes., Hdt.+; inscr., pap., LXX, En., Ep. Arist., Philo, Joseph.) *hard* (to the touch), *rough.*
1. of things—a. lit. λίθοι *hard* (Dit., Or. 194, 28; Wsd 11: 4) Hs 9, 6, 8; 9, 8, 6a, b. ῥάβδος *rough*, of a knotty stick (cf. Pind., Olymp. 7, 29; Diogenes the Cynic [IV вc] in Diog. L. 6, 21 σκληρὸν ξύλον = a hard staff; Aelian, V.H. 10, 16) 6, 2, 5.
b. fig.: of words *hard, harsh, unpleasant* (Demetrius in Stob., Flor. 3, 8, 20 vol. III p. 345 H.; Diogenes, Ep. 21; Gen 21: 11; 42: 7; Dt 1: 17; En.) J 6: 60; Jd 15 (after En. 1, 9); cf. Hv 1, 4, 2 (w. χαλεπός). ἐντολαί *hard, difficult* (Diod. S. 14, 105, 2 σκ. πρόσταγμα; Porphyr., Vi. Pyth. 8 προστάγματα) Hm 12, 3, 4f; 12, 4, 4 (w. δύσβατος). ἄνεμοι *rough, strong* (Aelian, V.H. 9, 14; Pollux 1, 110; Procop., Bell. 3, 13, 5; Pr 27: 16) Js 3: 4.
2. of persons *hard, strict, harsh, cruel, merciless* (Soph., Pla.+; Dit., Or. 194, 14; 1 Km 25: 3; Is 19: 4; 48: 4; Ep. Arist. 289) Mt 25: 24. Of the devil Hm 12, 5, 1.
3. the neut.—a. subst. τὸ σκληρόν w. gen. (Polyb. 4, 21, 1; Jos., Ant. 16, 151 τὸ σκ. τοῦ τρόπου) τὸ σκ. τῆς καρδίας *the hardness of the heart* B 9: 5 (v.l. σκληροκαρδία, q.v.).
b. σκληρόν σοι (sc. ἐστίν) *it is hard for you* w. inf. foll. Ac 9: 5 t.r.; 26: 14.—On the history of the word s. KDieterich, RhM, n.s. 60, '05, 236ff; FWDanker, Hardness of Heart, CTM 44, '73, 89-100. M-M. B. 1064.*

σκληρότης, ητος, ἡ (Antipho, Pla.+; LXX, Philo; Jos., Ant. 3, 2) *hardness* (of heart), *stubbornness* as a human characteristic (Pla., Rep. 3 p. 410D; 10 p. 607B; Aristot., Poet. 15, 11; Dt 9: 27; Philo, Spec. Leg. 304) Ro 2: 5. Of the spirit of *harshness, roughness* w. which the Holy Spirit cannot live Hm 5, 2, 6 (cf. Antipho Or. 3, 3, 4 σκλ. τοῦ δαίμονος). M-M.*

σκληροτράχηλος, ον (Aesop 318 Halm; Physiogn. I 368, 4; LXX; En. 98, 11.—τράχηλος σκληρός: Hippocr., Coac. Progn. 2, 14, 256 ed. Littré V p. 640) *stiff-necked, stubborn* Ac 7: 51; 1 Cl 53: 3 (Dt 9: 13). M-M.*

σκληρύνω fut. σκληρυνῶ; 1 aor. ἐσκλήρυνα. Pass.: impf. ἐσκληρυνόμην; 1 aor. ἐσκληρύνθην (Hippocr.+; Aristot., Galen; PLeid. X II, 28; LXX) in our lit. only in fig. sense.
1. act. *harden* (LXX)—a. w. a human subject τί *something* τὴν καρδίαν 1 Cl 51: 3a; τὰς καρδίας (Ps 94: 8) Hb 3: 8, 15; 4: 7. τὸν τράχηλον σκλ. *stiffen the neck* B 9: 5 (Dt 10: 16).
b. w. God as subj. τινά *harden the heart of someone* (cf. Ex 7: 3; 9: 12 al.) Ro 9: 18. KLSchmidt, D. Verstockung des Menschen durch Gott: ThZ 1, '45, 1-17.
2. pass. *be* or *become hardened, harden oneself* (Sir 30: 12) ἐσκληρύνοντο Ac 19: 9; cf. Hb 3: 13. ἐσκληρύνθη ἡ καρδία (cf. Ex 8: 15; 9: 35) 1 Cl 51: 3b; cf. 5. M-M.*

σκολιός, ά, όν (Hom.+; Epigr. Gr. 244, 4; LXX, Joseph.; Sib. Or. 1, 124) *crooked*—1. lit. (opp. εὐθύς. Cf. Jos., Bell. 3, 118 τὰ σκολιὰ τῆς λεωφόρου [= highway] κατευθύνειν) ἔσται τὰ σκολιὰ εἰς εὐθείας Lk 3: 5 (cf. schol. on Nicander, Ther. 478 of the ὁδός in contrast to εὐθύς; Is 40:

4; 42: 16). Symbolically of τοῦ μέλανος ὁδός B 20: 1 (cf. Pr 21: 8; 28: 18).
2. fig. *crooked, unscrupulous, dishonest*, etc. (Hom.+; Dio Chrys. 58[75], 1 w. πονηρός; Lucian, Bis Accus. 16 ῥημάτια; LXX; Jos., C. Ap. 1, 179) γενεὰ σκ. (Dt 32: 5 γεν. σκ. καὶ διεστραμμένη; Ps 77: 8. Also Dionysius Perieg. [Geogr. Gr. Min. ed. CMüller II 186 p. 127 v. 392 σκολιὸν γένος) Ac 2: 40 (differently MWilcox, The Semitisms of Ac, '65, 30); Phil 2: 15. δεσπόται *harsh, unjust* 1 Pt 2: 18 (opp. ἀγαθοὶ κ. ἐπιεικεῖς).—σκολιόν τι *someth. wrong* 1 Cl 39: 4 (Job 4: 18). M-M. B. 897.*

σκολιότης, ητος, ἡ (Hippocr.+; LXX, Aq., Sym.) fig. (Aristaen., Ep. 1, 28) *crookedness, perversity, deceit* (Ezk 16: 5 τῇ σκολ. τῆς ψυχῆς σου) w. πονηρία Hv 3, 9, 1.*

σκόλοψ, οπος, ὁ (Hom.+; Artem.; PGM 36, 152; 270; LXX) *a* (pointed) *stake*, then *thorn, splinter*, etc., specif. of an injurious foreign body (Dit., Syll.³ 1168, 92; Num 33: 55 σκόλοπες ἐν τοῖς ὀφθαλμοῖς; Sext. Emp. in BGU 380, 8 τὸν πόδαν πονεῖς ἀπὸ σκολάπου; Aesop, Fab. 187 P.; 363 P. = Babrius no. 136, 19 Cr.; Artem. 3, 33; Cyranides p. 112, 24 a prescription for removing σκόλοπας κ. ἀκάνθας.—Field, Notes 187). Paul alludes to his illness (s. κολαφίζω 2 and cf. also EMMerrins, St. Paul's Thorn in the Flesh: Bibliotheca Sacra 64, '07, 661-92; ChBruston, L'Écharde de St. Paul: Rev. de Théol. et des Quest. rel. 21, '12, 441ff; PJöuon, Rech de Sc rel 15, '25, 532f; CHNash, Paul's 'Thorn in the Flesh': Review and Expositor 28, '31, 33-51; PHMenoud, Studia Paulina [JdeZwaan-Festschr.] '53, 163-71; HClavier, ibid. 66-82; TYMullins, JBL 76, '57, 299-303; AHisey and JSPBeck, Journ. of Bible and Religion 29, '61, 125-9; JJThierry, D. Dorn im Fleisch, NovT 5, '62, 301-10) in ἐδόθη μοι σκ. τῇ σαρκί *there was given me a thorn in the flesh* 2 Cor 12: 7. The fact that Celsus uses the word σκ. (2, 55; 68) w. evident scorn (Origen has σταυρός) to mean the cross of Jesus, can scarcely indicate that Paul is using it in that sense here, since he always says σταυρός elsewh. (against ASchlatter, Pls, d. Bote J. Chr. '34, 666). Lucian also, in M. Peregr. 13 p. 337, speaks contemptuously of the ἀνεσκολοπισμένος ἐκεῖνος σοφιστής. Cf. 11 p. 334 ἄνθρωπος ἀνασκολοπισθείς. A believer does not use that sort of language. M-M.*

σκοπέω (Hom.+; inscr., pap.; Esth 8: 12g; 2 Macc 4: 5; Philo, Joseph.—Bl-D. §101, p. 48; Mlt.-H. 258) *look* (out) *for, notice, keep one's eyes on* w. acc. of the pers. or thing *someone* or *someth.* (Jos., Ant. 12, 30) σκοπεῖτε τοὺς οὕτω περιπατοῦντας *notice those who conduct themselves thus*, i.e. in order to imitate them Phil 3: 17. σκοπεῖν τοὺς τὰς διχοστασίας ποιοῦντας *look out for those who cause divisions*, i.e. avoid them Ro 16: 17.—σκ. τὰ βλεπόμενα *keep one's eyes on what can be seen* 2 Cor 4: 18. τὰ ἑαυτῶν *look out for one's own interests* (Pla., Phaedr. 232D) Phil 2: 4. Also τὸ καθ' ἑαυτοῦ MPol 1: 2. τὸ κοινὸν τῆς ἐλπίδος 1: 2. ἑαυτόν foll. by μή *look to oneself, that . . . not* Gal 6: 1. σκόπει μὴ τὸ φῶς σκότος ἐστίν *consider whether the light be darkness* Lk 11: 35 (μή interrog. = Lat. 'num' because of the indic.; cf. Epict. 4, 5, 18 ὅρα μὴ Νερωνιανὸν ἔχει χαρακτῆρα). M-M.*

σκοπός, οῦ, ὁ (Hom.+; LXX) *goal, mark* (Hom.+; inscr., pap.; Job 16: 12; La 3: 12; Wsd 5: 12; Ep. Arist. 251; Jos., Ant. 16, 248) ὁ τῆς εἰρήνης σκ. 1 Cl 19: 2; ὁ προκείμενος ἡμῖν σκ. 63: 1 (Philo, Mos. 1, 48; Jos., Bell. 4, 555 σκοπὸς προύκειτο Ῥωμαίοις). κατὰ σκοπὸν διώκειν *press on toward the goal* (διώκω 1) Phil 3: 14. σκοπὸν τιθέναι *set a mark* (cf. Pla., Leg. 12 p. 961ε; Polyb. 7, 8, 9) 2 Cl 19: 1. M-M.*

σκορπίζω 1 aor. ἐσκόρπισα, pass. ἐσκορπίσθην—1. *scatter, disperse* (Hecataeus in Phryn. p. 218; Strabo 4, 4, 6; Ps.-Lucian, Asinus 32; Aelian, V.H. 13, 45; Jos., Ant. 16, 10; LXX) of a wolf τὰ πρόβατα σκορπίζει *he chases the sheep in all directions* J 10: 12. Opp. συνάγειν (Artem. 1, 56 p. 52, 17 συνάγει τοὺς ἐσκορπισμένους τὸ ὄργανον; Tob 13: 5 BA) ὁ μὴ συνάγων μετ᾽ ἐμοῦ σκορπίζει, prob. w. ref. to a flock rather than to a harvest Mt 12: 30; Lk 11: 23 (in Astrampsychus 40 Dek. 83, 8 and Cat. Cod. Astr. II 162 σκ.= 'squander'.—On the idea cf. Polyaenus 8, 23, 27: Καῖσαρ Πομπηΐου κηρύξαντος ἐχθρὰν καὶ τοῖς μηδετέρῳ προστιθεμένοις ἀντεκήρυξε καὶ φίλους ἡγήσεσθαι κατ᾽ ἴσον τοῖς ἑαυτῷ συμμαχήσασιν. In Lat. in Cicero: AFridrichsen, ZNW 13, '12, 273–80. Caesar's point of view resembles that of Mk 9: 40= Lk 9: 50). Pass. (Plut., Timol. 4, 2; Philo; Jos., Ant. 6, 116; 1 Macc 6: 54 ἐσκορπίσθησαν ἕκαστος εἰς τὸν τόπον αὐτοῦ) *be scattered* ἵνα σκορπισθῆτε ἕκαστος εἰς τὰ ἴδια J 16: 32.

2. *scatter abroad, distribute* (PLond. 131, 421 [I AD] of fertilizer that is spread over the whole field; PFlor. 175, 22 τὰ καμήλια ἐσκορπίσαμεν= 'we have distributed the camels in various places'; Jos., Ant. 16, 10) of God ἐσκόρπισεν, ἔδωκεν τοῖς πένησιν 2 Cor 9: 9 (Ps 111: 9). M-M.*

σκορπίος, ου, ὁ (Aeschyl., Pla.+; Sb 1209 ἐτελεύτησεν ὑπὸ σκορπίου; 1267, 7; LXX, Philo, Joseph.).

1. lit., *the scorpion,* a species of vermin (an arachnid, 4 to 5 inches long) common in southern latitudes, much feared because of its sting Rv 9: 3, 5, 10 (the κέντρον as Demosth. 25, 52). W. serpents (Dio Chrys. 57[74], 20; Sb 6584, 6; Dt 8: 15) Lk 10: 19; 11: 12 (s. ἀντί 1. HPegg, ET 38, '27, 468).

2. fig., as a type of extreme harmfulness, of prostitutes ἔνδοθεν πεπλήρωνται σκορπίων καὶ πάσης ἀδικίας GOxy 40 (as a symbol of evil persons in Ps.-Demosth. 25, 52; Artem. 2, 13 p. 107, 11 al. Cf. also Ezk 2: 6).—S. Eitrem, Der Sk. in Mythol. u. Religionsgesch.: Symb. Osl. 7, '28, 53–82. M-M.*

σκορπισμός, οῦ, ὁ (M. Ant. 7, 50, 2; Artem. 2, 30 p. 126, 13; Hippiatr. 70, 6 [of the dispersion of fever-heat]; Cat. Cod. Astr. VIII 1, p. 268, 26 σκ. χρημάτων; Aq., Sym., Theod. Jer 25: 34; PsSol 17: 18; Philo, Leg. All. 2, 86; Sib. Or. 3, 317) *scattering* σκ. ὀστέων *scattering* (=wrenching apart?) *of bones,* one of the many similar tortures accompanying martyrdom, in the unbridled imagination of Ign., IRo 5: 3.*

σκοτεινός, ή, όν (Aeschyl.+; Cebes 10, 1; Cornutus 17, p. 29, 14; UPZ 78, 19 [159 BC] εἰς σκοτινὸν τόπον; LXX; Jos., Bell. 1, 77, Ant. 2, 344.—W-H. σκοτινός) *dark* opp. φωτεινός (cf. X., Mem. 3, 10, 1; 4, 3, 4; Plut., Mor. 610ε; 953c; En. 22, 2): Mt 6: 23; Lk 11: 34, 36 (cf. Test. Benj. 4: 2 σκοτεινὸς ὀφθαλμός; Damasc., Vi. Isid. 92 τὸ σκ. τῶν ὀφθαλμῶν). Opp. φανερός *obscure* B 8: 7. θησαυροὶ σκ. *treasures that lie in darkness* 11: 4 (Is 45: 3). Of color ἔνδυμα *a dark garment* AP 6: 21. M-M.*

σκοτία, ας, ἡ (Apollon. Rhod. 4, 1698; Anth. 8, 187; 190; Sb 6648, 4; PGM 4, 2472; Job 28: 3; Mi 3: 6; Is 16: 3; Sib. Or. 5, 349) *darkness, gloom.*

1. lit. J 6: 17. σκοτίας ἔτι οὔσης *while it was still dark* 20: 1. Perh. 12: 35b (s. 2 below). Symbolically ἐν τῇ σκ. λέγειν (εἰπεῖν) τι *say someth. in the dark,* i.e. in secret

(opp. ἐν τῷ φωτί) Mt 10: 27; Lk 12: 3 (cf. HGrimme, BZ 23, '35, 258–60).

2. fig., of the darkening of the mind or spirit, of ignorance in moral and relig. matters Mt 4: 16 (cf. Is 9: 1). Esp. in Johannine usage as a category including everything that is at enmity w. God, earthly and demonic J 1: 5a, b; 8: 12; 12: 35a; perh. also b (s. 1 above), 46; 1 J 1: 5; 2: 8f, 11a, b, c.—HBakotin, De Notione Lucis et Tenebrarum in Ev. Jo. '43.*

σκοτίζω (since Polyb. 12, 15, 10; Test. 12 Patr. in act.), in our lit., as well as in LXX [it is not found in En., Ep. Arist., Philo, Joseph.], only pass. **σκοτίζομαι,** pass.: pf. ἐσκότισμαι; 1 aor. ἐσκοτίσθην *be* or *become dark, be darkened.*

1. lit. (Cleomedes [II AD] 2, 4 p. 188, 18; 24 [HZiegler 1891]) of the sun which, in times of tribulation, loses its radiance (Eccl 12: 2; Is 13: 10) Mt 24: 29; Mk 13: 24; cf. Rv 8: 12. Of the darkening of the sun at Jesus' death Lk 23: 45 t.r.

2. fig., of the organs of relig. and moral perception (Polyb. 12, 15, 10 Bütt.-W. v.l.=no. 566 fgm. 124b Jac. in the text [the pass. of moral darkening]; Plut., Mor. 1120ε; Test. Reub. 3: 8, Levi 14: 4, Gad 6: 2 τὸν νοῦν): among the heathen ἐσκοτίσθη ἡ ἀσύνετος αὐτῶν καρδία Ro 1: 21. σκοτισθήτωσαν οἱ ὀφθαλμοὶ αὐτῶν τοῦ μὴ βλέπειν 11: 10 (Ps 68: 24). σκοτίζεσθαι τὴν διάνοιαν *be darkened in one's understanding* 2 Cl 19: 2; cf. Eph 4: 18 t.r. M-M.*

σκότος, ους, τό (as a masc. word Hom.+ and so in the Attic writers [EFraenkel, Zeitschr. für vergleichende Sprachforschung 43, '10, 195ff; σκότος and φῶς], as well as Jos., Ant. 19, 216; 217; as a neut. Pind.+ and H.Gk. gener., also in LXX [Thackeray p. 159]; En., Philo; Jos., Bell. 6, 140, Ant. 1, 27; Test. 12 Patr.; PWarr. 21, 25; 30 [III AD].—Bl-D. §51, 2 w. app.; Mlt.-H. 127. Only in Hb 12: 18 does ὁ σκ. appear as a v.l. in the t.r.) *darkness, gloom.*

1. lit., of the darkness in the depths of the sea B 10: 10. Of dark clouds AP 10: 25. Of the darkening of the sun (σκότος at the death of Aeschyl., acc. to Aristoph.: Ael. Aristid. 32, 32 K.=12 p. 145 D. At the death of Alexander ἐγένετο σκότος: Ps.-Callisth. 3, 33, 26. Others HUsener, RhM n.s. 55, '00, 286f) Mt 27: 45; Mk 15: 33; Lk 23: 44; GP 5: 15; Ac 2: 20 (Jo 3: 4.—Here σκ. means 'bearer of darkness'; s. 2b below, end). Of the darkness of chaos (Gen 1: 2) 2 Cor 4: 6. Of the darkness of non-existence 1 Cl 38: 3 (Sb 8960, 19 [grave-epigram I BC] σκότους πύλας). Of the darkness of the place of punishment far removed fr. the Kingdom (Philo, Exsecr. 152 βαθὺ σκότος. Cf. Wsd 17: 20; PsSol 14: 9.—σκ. κ. βόρβορος await those who are untrue to the Eleusinian Mysteries, Ael. Aristid. 22, 10 K.=19 p. 421 D. Of the darkness of death and the underworld in Hom. and the trag. As the domain of evil spirits PGM 36, 138) τὸ σκ. τὸ ἐξώτερον *the darkness outside* Mt 8: 12; 22: 13; 25: 30 (with these three passages cf. Vi. Aesopi W c. 31, where Aesop advises a man: ῥῖψον αὐτὴν [his wife] εἰς τὸ σκότος.—ROPTaylor, Theology 33, '42, 277–83). Also ὁ ζόφος τοῦ σκότους (ζόφος 2) 2 Pt 2: 17; Jd 13.—Of the darkness in which the blind live (Soph., Oed. R. 419; Eur., Phoen. 377; 1534; Dt 28: 29) w. ἀχλύς (q.v. 1) Ac 13: 11.

2. fig.—a. of the state of being unknown τὰ κρυπτὰ τοῦ σκότους *the things that are hidden in darkness* and therefore are known to nobody 1 Cor 4: 5.

b. of religious and moral darkness, of darkening by sin, of the state of unbelievers and of the godless, opp. φῶς

(Herm. Wr. 7, 2a; Philo, Det. Pot. Ins. 101, Somn. 2, 39; Test. Levi 19: 1, Napht. 2: 10) Mt 4: 16 v.l. (Is 9: 1); Mt 6: 23b; J 3: 19; Ac 26: 18; Ro 2: 19; 2 Cor 6: 14; 1 Th 5: 4f; 1 Pt 2: 9; 1 J 1: 6; 1 Cl 59: 2; B 14: 7 (Is 42: 7); 18: 1. Opp. δικαιοσύνη 5: 4. Cf. 14: 5f. W. σκιὰ θανάτου (σκιά 1b) Lk 1: 79 (schol. on Soph., El. 1079 p. 149 P. ἐν σκότει γενέσθαι τ. θανάτου. For σκότος=darkness of death cf. Plut., Mor. 296AB, an oath 'by the σκότος near the oak tree, where the men of Priene had been killed in such great numbers').—Sins are τὰ ἔργα τοῦ σκότους Ro 13: 12; Eph 5: 11.—On ἡ ἐξουσία τοῦ σκότους Lk 22: 53; Col 1: 13 s. ἐξουσία 4b. On οἱ κοσμοκράτορες τοῦ σκότους τούτου Eph 6: 12 s. κοσμοκράτωρ.—In several places σκότος has the sense bearer or victim or instrument of darkness Mt 6: 23a; Lk 11: 35; Eph 5: 8 (cf. KGKuhn, NTS 7, '61, 339f [Qumran]). S. also 1 above. M-M. B. 61.*

σκοτόω (Soph., Hippocr., Pla.+; POxy. 1854, 3; LXX) pass.: pf. ptc. ἐσκοτωμένος; 1 aor. ἐσκοτώθην darken, in our lit. only pass. be or become darkened.
1. lit. ἐσκοτώθη ὁ ἥλιος καὶ ὁ ἀήρ Rv 9: 2 (cf. Job 3: 9). Of the kingdom of the 'Beast' 16: 10.
2. fig. (schol. on Nicander, Alexiphar. 27 τοῖς ἐσκοτωμένοις τῇ μέθῃ; Test. Dan 2: 4 σκ. τὴν διάνοιαν) διάνοια ἐσκοτωμένη darkened understanding 1 Cl 36: 2. ἐσκοτωμένος τῇ διανοίᾳ Eph 4: 18. M-M.*

σκύβαλον, ου, τό refuse, rubbish, leavings, dirt, dung (Plut. et al.; PSI 184, 7; PRyl. 149, 22; PFay. 119, 7; Sir 27: 4; Philo, Sacr. Abel. 109; 139; Jos., Bell. 5, 571; Sib. Or. 7, 58.—τὰ σκύβαλα specif. of human excrement: Artem. 1, 67 p. 61, 23; 2, 14 p. 108, 21; Jos., Bell. 5, 571 [cf. Epict., Fgm. Stob. 19 ἀποσκυβαλίζω].—MDibelius, Hdb. on Phil 3: 8) πάντα ἡγεῖσθαι σκύβαλα consider everything rubbish or dung Phil 3: 8. M-M.*

Σκύθης, ου, ὁ the Scythian, living in what is now southern Russia (Hes., Hdt.+; inscr., LXX, Philo, Joseph.), the barbarian or savage 'par excellence' (cf. Cicero, In Pis. 8, Nat. Deor. 2, 34; Seneca, In Troad. 1104; 2 Macc 4: 47; 3 Macc 7: 5) w. βάρβαρος (Philostrat., Ep. 5) Col 3: 11.— ThHermann, Barbar u. Sk.: ThBl 9, '30, 106; WLKnox, St. Paul and the Church of the Gentiles '39, 175 w. note 4. M-M.*

σκυθρωπός, (ή), όν (Aeschyl., Hippocr., X.+; PGM 13, 259; LXX, Philo; Jos., Ant. 6, 229; Test. Sim. 4: 1) with a sad, gloomy, or sullen look (X., Mem. 2, 7, 12; Menand., Epitr. 43 J; Jos., Bell. 1, 80) Mt 6: 16; Lk 24: 17. M-M.*

σκύλλω pf. pass. ptc. ἐσκυλμένος (Aeschyl.+; inscr., pap.) orig. 'flay, skin'.
1. weary, harass (Herodian 7, 3, 4; UPZ 110, 25 [164 BC] σκύλλεσθαι μὴ μετρίως; En. 104, 5) pass. ἐσκυλμένοι harassed Mt 9: 36.
2. act. trouble, bother, annoy τινά someone (PTebt. 421, 11; POxy. 295, 5; Sb 4317, 22) Mk 5: 35; Lk 8: 49.
3. pass. trouble oneself (POxy. 1669, 13 σκύληθι καὶ αὐτὸς ἐνθάδε; 123, 10; 941, 3) Lk 7: 6. M-M.*

σκῦλον, ου, τό (Soph., Thu.+; inscr., pap., LXX) usu., and in our lit. always, pl. τὰ σκῦλα=armor and weapons taken fr. the body of a slain enemy, then gener. booty, spoils (Dit., Syll.³ 61, 1 [V BC], Or. 332, 8; PHamb. 91, 4; Jos., Bell. 2, 464, Ant. 7, 161) μερίζειν σκῦλα divide the spoils 1 Cl 16: 13 (Is 53: 12). Also σκῦλα διαδιδόναι Lk 11: 22 (in apparent allusion to Is 49: 24f; cf. PsSol 5: 3; WGrundmann, Der Begriff der Kraft in der NTlichen

Gedankenwelt, '32, 49f; SLegasse, 'L'Homme Fort' [Lk 11: 21f], NovT 5, '62, 5–9). M-M. B. 1415.*

σκωληκόβρωτος, ον eaten by worms (used of plants Theophr., H. Pl. 3, 12, 6; 4, 11, 1, C. Pl. 5, 9, 1; PSI 490, 14 [III BC]. Not yet found as a medical t.t., but men are spoken of as being eaten by σκώληκες: Lucian, Alex. 59; 2 Macc 9: 9; Jos., Ant. 17, 169) Ac 12: 23 (for the subject-matter s. Jos., Ant. 19, 346–50 and cf. φθειρόβρωτος= 'eaten by lice' [Hesychius Miles. 40], as Plato acc. to Diog. L. 3, 40). M-M.*

σκώληξ, ηκος, ὁ (Hom.+; LXX; Jos., Ant. 3, 30) worm 1 Cl 25: 3 (on σκ. and the phoenix s. Artem. 4, 47 p. 229, 14); Papias 3. Symbol of insignificance and wretchedness (Maximus Tyr. 15, 8d; Lucian, Vit. Auct. 27) 1 Cl 16: 15 (Ps 21: 7; cf. Epict. 4, 1, 142). Acc. to Is 66: 24 a never-dying worm shall torment the damned (cf. Jdth 16: 17; Sir 7: 17) Mk 9: 44 v.l., 46 v.l., 48; 2 Cl 7: 6; 17: 5. Cf. the σκώληκες AP 10: 25 (s. on σκωληκόβρωτος). M-M. B. 194.*

σκωρία, ας, ἡ (Aristot.+; Strabo 9, 1, 23; Sym.) slag, dross, refuse produced when metal is smelted Hv 4, 3, 4.*

σμαράγδινος, η, ον (of) emerald (both='made of emerald' [Phylarchus—III BC—81 fgm. 41 Jac.; Lucian, Ver. Hist. 2, 11] and='emerald in color' [Eutecnius 2 p. 29, 30; PRainer 27, 8; PHamb. 10, 25]) ἶρις ὅμοιος ὁράσει σμαραγδίνῳ prob. should have λίθῳ supplied w. it a halo that was like an emerald in appearance Rv 4: 3. M-M.*

σμάραγδος, ου, ὁ (Hdt.+; inscr. fr. Delos: Bull. de corr. hell. 14, 1891, 402, 44 [279 BC]; PGM 5, 239; Jos., Bell. 5, 234, Ant. 3, 168; in the older period it was fem.; so also Theophr., Lap. 1, 4; 8; 6, 34; LXX. As a masc. first in Strabo 16, 4, 20; Philo, Mos. 2, 133; M. Ant. 7, 15; Lucian, Dom. 15) emerald, a bright green transparent precious stone Rv 21: 19 (cf. Tob 13: 17). Lit. s.v. ἀμέθυστος. M-M.*

σμῆγμα, ατος, τό (Plut.; Aëtius p. 14, 4; 16; schol. on Pla. 429E; 430B; pap.; Sus 17 Theod.) ointment, salve J 19: 39 v.l.*

σμήχω 1 aor. mid. ἐσμηξάμην (Hom.+) rub off, wash off, then gener. wash, cleanse τὶ someth. GOxy 37. Mid. wash oneself (Hippocr.; Jos., Bell. 2, 123 τὸ σῶμα) τὸ ἐκτὸς δέρμα ἐσμήξω you have washed your outer skin 35.*

σμίγμα, ατος, τό for μίγμα (q.v.) J 19: 39 v.l.*

σμύραινα, ης, ἡ (Aristot., Hist. An. 1, 5; 2, 13; 15; Nicander, Ther. 823) the sea eel, which the Jews were forbidden to eat B 10: 5 (cf. Lev 11: 10).*

σμύρνα, ης, ἡ (trag., Hdt.+; Dit., Or. 214, 58; POxy. 234 II; PGM 13, 20 al. [here mostly spelled ζμύρνα, in line w. the tendency for ζ to replace σ in pap. and inscr. after 329 BC: UPohle, D. Sprache des Redners Hypereides '28, 11f]; Greek Pap. Chiefly Ptolemaic ed. Grenfell 1896 no. 14, 9; 10; 18; 192, 11; 205, 11; Ps 44: 9; SSol 3: 6 σμ. καὶ λίβανον; Jos., Ant. 3, 197) myrrh, the resinous gum of the bush 'balsamodendron myrrha': w. incense and other aromatic substances (Diod. S. 5, 41, 4–6) 1 Cl 25: 2. W. gold and incense Mt 2: 11. W. aloes (s. ἀλόη) J 19: 39 (for embalming a corpse, as Hdt. 2, 40; 86; 3, 107; Theophr., Hist. Pl. 9, 3f).—ILöw, D. Flora d. Juden I '28, 305–11; RSteuer, Myrrhe u. Stakte '33; PGrassi, Aromi inutili: Religio 10, '34, 530–3. M-M.*

Σμύρνα, ης, ἡ (on the spelling Ζμύρνα s. that entry and cf. Tdf.⁸ on Rv 1: 11; Lghtf., Ign. II² 1889, 331 note; W-S. §5, 27d; Mlt. 45) *Smyrna* (Mimnermus, Hdt.+; inscr., Sib. Or.), a prosperous commercial city on the west coast of Asia Minor. Rv 1: 11; 2: 8; IEph 21: 1; IMg 15; ITr 1: 1; 12: 1; IRo 10: 1; ISm inscr.; MPol inscr.; 12: 2; 16: 2; 19: 1; Epil Mosq 3.—JWeiss, RE X 550, 29ff; Ramsay, Letters '05, chap. 19f; VSchultze, Altchristl. Städte u. Landschaften II 2, '26; CJCadoux, Ancient Smyrna '38. M-M.*

Σμυρναῖος, α, ον *coming from Smyrna* ὁ Σ. *the Smyrnaean* (Pind., Hdt.+; inscr.) pl. Rv 2: 8 t.r.; IMg 15; ITr 13: 1; IPhld 11: 2; ISm 13: 2; IPol inscr.*

σμυρνίζω (in the sense 'be like myrrh' Diosc., Mat. Med. 1, 66, 1 W.) perf. pass. ptc. ἐσμυρνισμένος *treat with myrrh* (cf. Cyranides p. 89, 13; 97, 20; PGM 36, 313; Cos. and Dam. 33, 115) ἐσμυρνισμένος οἶνος *wine flavored with myrrh* Mk 15: 23 (cf. Pliny, Nat. Hist. 14, 13 vina myrrhae odore condita; Charito 8, 1, 12 οἶνος κ. μύρα). The μυρσινίτης οἶνος (Diosc. 5, 37; Chio, Ep. 6), wine mixed with myrtle juice, was something different.*

Σόδομα, ων, τά (סְדֹם).—LXX [Thackeray 168]; Test. Napht. 4: 1; Philo; Jos., Ant. 1, 174; Strabo 16, 2, 44; Galen XI 694 K.) *Sodom,* the city which was destroyed by God w. fire and brimstone because of the sinfulness of its inhabitants (Gen 19: 24) Lk 17: 29; 1 Cl 11: 1. As an ex. of extraordinary sinfulness Mt 11: 23f; Lk 10: 12. As such, and as proof of the terrible power of God to punish, beside Gomorrha (cf. the inscr. fr. Pompeii, 'Sodoma Gomora': AMau, Pompeji² '08, 16) Mt 10: 15; Mk 6: 11 t.r.; Ro 9: 29 (Is 1: 9); 2 Pt 2: 6; Jd 7.—Jerusalem is called πνευματικῶς Σόδομα καὶ Αἴγυπτος Rv 11: 8 (cf. Sib. Or. 6, 21ff). M-M.*

Σολομών, ῶνος, ὁ (so predom. in NT and Joseph. [even in quotations fr. Dios (pre-Christian): C. Ap. 1, 114f and Menander of Ephesus (III BC): C. Ap. 1, 120]; Eupolemus the Jew [II BC] in Euseb., Pr. Ev. 9, 30, 8ff; Christian magical pap. 10, 30 [II 198 Pr.], rare in the LXX) and **Σολομῶν, ῶντος, ὁ** (Cass. Dio. 69, 14, 2 τὸ μνημεῖον τοῦ Σολομῶντος; Zosimus: Hermet. IV p. 111, 13; Ac 3: 11 and 5: 12 as στοὰ Σολομῶντος); only as v.l. the indecl. Σολομών Mt 1: 6 א and Σαλωμών Ac 7: 47 AC (the latter is the normal form in the LXX) or Σαλωμῶν א; cf. Tdf., Proleg. 104; 110; W-H., App. 158; Bl-D. §53, 1; 55, 2; Mlt.-H. 146f; Thackeray p. 165f (שְׁלֹמֹה) *Solomon,* son and successor of David, known for his love of splendor Mt 6: 29; Lk 12: 27 and for his wisdom Mt 12: 42a, b; Lk 11: 31a, b. Builder of the first temple in Jerusalem Ac 7: 47. There was also a colonnade named for him in Herod's temple J 10: 23; Ac 3: 11; 5: 12 (cf. Jos., Ant. 20, 221, Bell. 5, 185). In the genealogy of Jesus Mt 1: 6f. M-M.*

σορός, οῦ, ἡ (Hom.+; pap.) *coffin, bier* (so Hdt. 2, 78; Aristoph., Plut. 277 al.; Lucian, Hermot. 78; Dit., Or. 526, Syll.³ 1236, 5; PGM 4, 1424; 7, 236; Gen 50: 26; Test. Reub. 7: 2) Lk 7: 14. M-M.*

σός, σή, σόν (Hom.+; inscr., pap., LXX, Ep. Arist., Joseph., Sib. Or.—Bl-D. §285, 1; Rob. 288; 684) *possess. pron. of the second pers. sing. your, yours* (sing.); in older and formal usage *thy, thine.* It has more weight than the gen. σοῦ or σεαυτοῦ; it serves to emphasize or to contrast.

1. used w. nouns (Jos., Ant. 2, 67; Sib. Or. 6, 22) τὴν ἐν τῷ σῷ ὀφθαλμῷ δοκὸν οὐ κατανοεῖς; Mt 7: 3. Cf. vs. 22a, b, c; 13: 27; Mk 2: 18; J 4: 42; 18: 35; Ac 5: 4; 24: 2, 4; 1 Cor 8: 11; 14: 16; Phlm 14; 1 Cl 60: 2; Hs 1: 5.

2. subst.—a. masc. οἱ σοί *your own people* (Soph., Pla., X. +; oft. in pap.; Jos., Ant. 7, 218; 8, 54) Mk 5: 19.

b. neut. τὸ σόν *what is yours* (Soph., Pla.+) Mt 20: 14; 25: 25. Likew. the pl. τὰ σά (Hom.+; BGU 1040, 5; POxy. 903, 11) Lk 6: 30; J 17: 10b.—S. Kilpatrick, s.v. ἐμός, end. M-M.

σουδάριον, ου, τό (Lat. loanw.: sudarium [ESchwyzer, NJklA 7, '01, 242; Hahn 263, 2]; Pollux 7, 71; PRainer 27, 7f [190 AD]; 21, 19 [230 AD]; PGM 36, 269.—Also as a loanw. in Mishna and Talmud [SKrauss, Griech. u. lat. Lehnwörter im Talmud II 1899, 373; Schürer II⁴ 80]) *face-cloth* for wiping perspiration, corresp. somewhat to our *handkerchief* (cf. GustavMeyer, SAWien 132, 3, 1895, 62) Lk 19: 20; J 11: 44; 20: 7; Ac 19: 12. M-M.*

Σουσάννα, ης (this form of the gen. Sus 27; 28 Theod.) or **ας** (so Sus 30 LXX.—Thackeray 161), ἡ *Susanna* Lk 8: 3. M-M.*

σοφία, ας, ἡ (Hom.+; LXX, Ep. Arist., Philo, Joseph., Test. 12 Patr.) *wisdom.*

1. the natural *wisdom* that belongs to this world σοφία Αἰγυπτίων (Synes., Provid. 1, 1 p. 89A; Jos., Ant. 2, 286) Ac 7: 22 (on the subj. cf. Philo, Vita Mos. 1, 20ff; Schürer II⁴ 405). In contrast to God's wisdom and the wisdom that comes fr. God ἡ σοφία τῶν σοφῶν 1 Cor 1: 19 (Is 29: 14). ἡ σοφία τοῦ κόσμου (τούτου) vs. 20; 3: 19. σοφία τοῦ αἰῶνος τούτου 2: 6b. ἀνθρωπίνη σοφία 2: 13. σ. ἀνθρώπων vs. 5. Cf. 1: 21b, 22; 2: 1. σοφία λόγου *cleverness in speaking* 1: 17. On ἐν πειθοῖς σοφίας λόγοις 2: 4 cf. πειθός. σοφία σαρκική 2 Cor 1: 12. σ. ἐπίγειος, ψυχική, δαιμονιώδης Js 3: 15.—An advantage that is given to certain persons (like strength and riches) 1 Cl 13: 1 (Jer 9: 22); 32: 4; 38: 2. So perh. also 39: 6 (Job 4: 21); but mng. 2 is also poss.

2. the wisdom which God imparts to those who are close to him. Solomon (3 Km 5: 9; Pr 1: 2; Jos., Ant. 8, 168 σ. τοῦ Σ.) Mt 12: 42; Lk 11: 31; Stephen Ac 6: 10; Paul 2 Pt 3: 15; Pol 3: 2; to those believers who are called to account for their faith Lk 21: 15. The gift of unveiling secrets (2 Km 14: 20; Da 1: 17; 2: 30. Oenomaus in Euseb., Pr. Ev. 5, 27, 1 ἡ σοφία is necessary for the proper use of the oracles) Ac 7: 10; Rv 13: 18; 17: 9. Good judgment in the face of the demands made by human and specif. by the Christian life, (*practical*) *wisdom* Ac 6: 3; Col 4: 5; Js 1: 5; 3: 13, 17 (for the view that σ. in Js 1: 5; 3: 17 = πνεῦμα s. WBieder, ThZ 5, '49, 111). The apostle teaches men ἐν πάσῃ σοφίᾳ Col 1: 28, and the Christians are to do the same among themselves 3: 16 (ἐν πάσῃ σ. also Eph 1: 8; Col 1: 9).—W. φρόνησις (q.v. 2) Eph 1: 8. W. ἀποκάλυψις vs. 17. W. σύνεσις (Jos., Ant. 8, 49): σοφία καὶ σύνεσις πνευματική Col 1: 9. σοφία, σύνεσις, ἐπιστήμη, γνῶσις (cf. Philo, Gig. 27) B 2: 3; 21: 5. σοφία καὶ νοῦς τῶν κρυφίων αὐτοῦ *wisdom and understanding of his* (i.e. the Lord's) *secrets* 6: 10.—As a spiritual gift the λόγος σοφίας stands beside the λόγος γνώσεως 1 Cor 12: 8 (s. γνῶσις 2 and cf. Aesopica 213, 1 P.: Τύχη ἐχαρίσατο αὐτῷ λόγον σοφίας). Paul differentiates betw. his preaching to unbelievers and immature Christians and σοφίαν λαλεῖν ἐν τοῖς τελείοις 2: 6a; the latter he also calls λαλεῖν θεοῦ σοφίαν ἐν μυστηρίῳ *set forth the wisdom that comes fr. God as a mystery* vs. 7 (WBaird, Interpretation 13, '59, 425-32).—The false teachers of Colossae consider that their convictions are σοφία Col 2: 23.—JdeFinance, La σοφία chez St. Paul: Rech de Sc rel 25, '35, 385-417.

3. *wisdom* of Christ and of God—a. Christ: of Jesus as a boy (s. ἡλικία 1b) Lk 2: 40, 52. Of him as an adult Mt 13: 54; Mk 6: 2. Of the exalted Christ ἐν ᾧ εἰσιν πάντες οἱ θησαυροὶ τῆς σοφίας καὶ γνώσεως Col 2: 3.—Rv 5: 12. By metonymy Χρ. Ἰ., ὃς ἐγενήθη σοφία ἡμῖν ἀπὸ θεοῦ *Christ Jesus, who has become a source of wisdom from God for us* 1 Cor 1: 30.

b. *wisdom* of God (Diog. L. 1, 28 σοφίᾳ πρῶτον εἶναι τὸν θεόν): revealed in his creation and rule of the world 1 Cor 1: 21a, or in the measures intended to bring salvation to the believers Ro 11: 33 (w. γνῶσις); Eph 3: 10; Hv 1, 3, 4 (w. πρόνοια).—Rv 7: 12; 1 Cl 18: 6 (Ps 50: 8); B 16: 9 (cf. δικαίωμα 1). Christ is called θεοῦ σοφία *the embodiment of the wisdom of God* 1 Cor 1: 24 (Diog. L. 9, 50 Protagoras is called Σοφία.—Lucian in M. Peregr. 11 speaks ironically of the θαυμαστὴ σοφία τῶν Χριστιανῶν).—UWilckens, Weisheit u. Torheit (1 Cor 1 and 2), '59; FChrist, Jesus Sophia (synopt.), '70.

4. In several passages Wisdom is personified (Ael. Aristid. 45, 17 K. as a mediatrix betw. Sarapis and men; perh.= Isis; AHöfler, D. Sarapishymnus des Ail. Aristid. '35, 50; 53f). In connection w. Pr 1: 23-33: 1 Cl 57: 3 (λέγει ἡ πανάρετος σοφία), 5 (= Pr 1: 29); 58: 1. On ἐδικαιώθη ἡ σοφία κτλ. Mt 11: 19; Lk 7: 35 cf. δικαιόω 2 and Ps.-Pla., Eryx. 6 p. 394D ἡ σοφία καὶ τὰ ἔργα τὸ ἀπὸ ταύτης = wisdom and her fruits. ἡ σοφία τοῦ θεοῦ εἶπεν 11: 49 introduces a statement made by 'wisdom' ('wisdom' is variously explained in this connection; on the one hand, it is said to refer to the OT, or to an apocryphal book by this title; on the other hand Jesus is thought of as proclaiming a decree of divine wisdom, or Lk is thinking of wisdom that Jesus has communicated to them at an earlier time).—The older lit. is given in Schürer III⁴ 212, 12; EBréhier, Les idées philosophiques et religieuses de Philon d'Alexandrie '07, 115ff; JMeinhold, Die Weisheit Israels '08; GHoennicke, RE XXI '08, 64ff; HWindisch, Die göttl. Weisheit der Juden u. die paulin. Christologie: Heinrici-Festschr. '14, 220ff; PHeinisch, Die persönl. Weisheit des ATs in religionsgesch. Beleuchtung² '23; Bousset, Rel.³ 343ff; FAFerrari, Il Progresso religioso 8, '28, 241-53; MargTechert, La notion de la Sagesse dans les trois prem. siècles: Archiv. f. Gesch. d. Philos. n.s. 32, '30, 1-27; WLKnox, St. Paul and the Church of the Gentiles '39, 55-89; BRigaux, NTS 4, '57/'58, esp. 252-7 (Qumran); HConzelmann, Pls. u. die Weisheit, NTS 12, '66, 231-44; MJSuggs, Wisdom, Christology, and Law in Mt, '70.—UWilckens and GFohrer, TW VII 465-529: σοφία κτλ. M-M.*

σοφίζω impf. ἐσόφιζον; 1 aor. ἐσόφισα—1. act.—a. *make wise, teach, instruct* (pass. in Hes., also Diog. L. 5, 90; POxy. 1790, 23 [I BC]. Act., Ps 18: 8; 104: 22) τινά *someone* 2 Ti 3: 15; ISm 1: 1. τινὰ ἔν τινι *make someone wise in* or *for someth.* B 5: 3 (cf. the pass. w. ἔν τινι Sir 38: 31).

b. in a bad sense *deceive, mislead* (so the mid. elsewh.: Philo, Mut. Nom. 240; Jos., Bell. 4, 103) B 9: 4.

2. mid. *reason out, concoct subtly* or *slyly, devise craftily* (Hdt., X. et al.; PSI 452, 11; Jos., Bell. 3, 222), as it seems, GOxy 1 πάντα σοφίζεται *he reasons it all out quite subtly*. Pass. (Soph., Phil. 77; Demosth. 29, 28) σεσοφισμένοι μῦθοι 2 Pt 1: 16. M-M.*

σοφός, ή, όν (Pind., Hdt.+; LXX; Ep. Arist., Philo, Joseph.)—1. *clever, skilful, experienced* (Pind., Nem. 7, 25 κυβερνήτης) σ. ἀρχιτέκτων 1 Cor 3: 10 (Is 3: 3; cf. Il. 15, 412 σοφία τέκτονος; Eur., Alc. 348 σοφῇ χειρὶ τεκτόνων; Maximus Tyr. 6, 4d ὁ τέκτων σ.; Philo,

Somn. 2, 8). Cf. 6: 5. σοφὸς ἐν διακρίσει λόγων *skilful in the interpretation of discourse* 1 Cl 48: 5 (σ. ἐν as Maximus Tyr. 24, 6b).

2. *wise, learned* of human intelligence and education above the average, perh. related to philosophy (Pind. et al.; Jos., Bell. 6, 313): ὁ σοφός beside ὁ ἰσχυρός and ὁ πλούσιος 1 Cl 13: 1 (Jer 9: 22); 38: 2. Opp. ἀνόητος Ro 1: 14. The one who is wise acc. to worldly standards, the σοφὸς κατὰ σάρκα 1 Cor 1: 26, stands in contrast to God and his wisdom, which remains hidden for him Ro 1: 22 (Oenomaus in Euseb., Pr. Ev. 5, 34, 10 οἰομένους εἶναι σοφούς); 1 Cor 1: 19 (Is 29: 14), 20, 27; 3: 19 (cf. Job 5: 13), 20 (Ps 93: 11); IEph 18: 1. W. συνετός (Jos., Ant. 11, 57; 58) Mt 11: 25; Lk 10: 21 (GDKilpatrick, JTS 48, '47, 63f).

3. *wise* in that the wisdom is divine in nature and origin (opp. ἄσοφος) Eph 5: 15. (Opp. μωρός) 1 Cor 3: 18a, b. W. ἐπιστήμων (Philo, Migr. Abr. 58) Js 3: 13; B 6: 10. σοφὸς εἰς τὸ ἀγαθόν (opp. ἀκέραιος εἰς τὸ κακόν) Ro 16: 19. Jesus intends to send out προφήτας καὶ σοφοὺς κ. γραμματεῖς Mt 23: 34.

4. In the abs. sense God is called σοφός (Sir 1: 8; cf. 4 Macc 1: 12; Sib. Or. 5, 360.—Ael. Aristid. 46 p. 409 D.: σοφώτατον εἶναι θεὸν) μόνος σοφὸς θεός (Ps.-Phoc. 54 εἷς θεὸς σοφ.; Herm. Wr. 14, 3. Cf. GRudberg, Coniect. Neot. 7, '42, 12) Ro 16: 27; 1 Ti 1: 17 t.r.; Jd 25 t.r. Cf. 1 Cor 1: 25. ὁ σοφὸς ἐν τῷ κτίζειν 1 Cl 60: 1 (w. συνετὸς ἐν τῷ κτλ.). σοφῇ βουλῇ God's *wise counsel* Dg 8: 10. (On 3 and 4 cf. Sb 6307 [III BC] of Petosiris the astrologer: ἐν θεοῖς κείμενος, μετὰ σοφῶν σοφός). M-M. B. 1213.*

Σπανία, ας, ἡ (Diod. S. 5, 37, 2; Athen. 8 p. 330F; 13 p. 657F; pap. [CWessely, Wiener. Stud. 24, '02, 147]; 1 Macc 8: 3) *Spain,* the goal of a journey planned by Paul Ro 15: 24, 28 (EBarnikol, Spanienreise u. Römerbrief '34). That he reached Spain at some time is maintained w. more or less certainty by BWeiss, FSpitta (Zur Gesch. u. Lit. des Urchristentums I 1893, 1-108), Zahn (Einl. I³ '07 §33-7), Harnack (Mission I⁴ '23, 83), JFrey (Die zweimalige röm. Gefangenschaft u. das Todesjahr des Ap. Pls '00, Die letzten Lebensjahre des Pls '10), EDubowy (Klemens v. Rom über d. Reise Pauli nach Spanien '14), JWeiss (Das Urchristentum '17, 300), ADeissmann (Paulus² '25, 192= Paul '26, 248) et al.; on the other hand, it is denied by HHoltzmann, AHausrath, OPfleiderer, CWeizsäcker, AJülicher, PWendland (Die urchristl. Literaturformen '12, 366), FPfister (ZNW 14, '13, 216ff), EMeyer (III '23, 131f), FHielscher (Forschungen zur Geschichte des Ap. Pls '25), EvDobschütz (Der Ap. Pls I '26, 17) et al.; HLietzmann, Gesch. der Alten Kirche I '32, 111 and ADNock, St. Paul '38, 142-4 (Paulus '40, 112f) leave the question open. M-M.*

σπαράσσω 1 aor. ἐσπάραξα *tear, pull to and fro, convulse* (Aristoph., Ran. 424 τὰς γνάθους; Diod. S. 8, 32, 3 and 19, 34, 3 τὰς τρίχας; Jos., Ant. 11, 141 τὴν κεφαλήν; Charito 3, 10, 4 τὰς κόμας; Da 8: 7 ἐσπάραξεν αὐτὸν ἐπὶ τὴν γῆν.—The word in another sense goes back to Aeschyl.; also PPetr. II 17, 4, 2; 6; LXX, Philo) τινά *someone* (Aristoph., Acharn. 688 ἄνδρα σπαράττων καὶ ταράττων; Herodas 5, 57; cf. Jos., Ant. 13, 233) the unclean spirit convulses the person in whom it dwells (ἄνθρωπος σπαρατόμενος on an attack: Cyranides p. 59, 15) Mk 1: 26; 9: 20 v.l.; Lk 9: 39. W. the acc. of the pers. to be supplied Mk 9: 26. M-M. B. 566.*

σπαργανόω (Eur., Hippocr.+; Posidon.: 87 fgm. 58a Jac.; Plut.; Ps.-Apollod. 1, 1, 7; Job 38: 9; Ezk 16: 4) 1 aor. ἐσπαργάνωσα; pf. pass. ptc. ἐσπαργανωμένος (Cornutus 6 p. 7, 7) *wrap (up)* in σπάργανα=(*swaddling-)cloths τινά someone* Lk 2: 7. Pass. vs. 12 (cf. Gdspd., Probs. 73f). M-M.*

σπαρείς s. σπείρω.

σπαταλάω 1 aor. ἐσπατάλησα *live luxuriously* or *voluptuously, in indulgence* (Polyb. 36, 17, 7; Epigr. Gr. 646a, 5; Ezk 16: 49; Sir 21: 15) 1 Ti 5: 6; Js 5: 5; B 10: 3. Of sheep in rich pasture *be frisky* Hs 6, 1, 6; 6, 2, 6. M-M.*

σπάω (Hom.+; LXX; Philo) 1 aor. mid. ἐσπασάμην *draw, pull,* in our lit. (as almost always in the LXX) only mid. in the sense *draw a sword* (so Od. 22, 74; X., An. 7, 4, 16 al.) τὴν μάχαιραν (PTebt. 48, 19 [113 BC]; 1 Ch 21: 5; 1 Esdr 3: 22; Ps 151: 7; Jos., Vi. 303) Mk 14: 47; Ac 16: 27. M-M. B. 571.*

σπείρα (trag.+), ης (this form of the gen. in inscr. [Dit., Or. index VIII p. 704a]; BGU 462, 5 [150–156 AD]; 142, 10 [159 AD]; 26, 12; PRainer 18, 1; POxy. 477, 3 al.; Bl-D. §43, 1; Mlt.-H. 117f; Mayser 12, 4), ἡ a military t.t. (Polyb.+; inscr., pap.; 2 Macc 8: 23; 12: 20; Jdth 14: 11; Jos., Bell. 2, 318, Vi. 214). This is the Gk. word used to transl. the Lat. 'cohors' (Polyb. 11, 23, 1; inscr., pap. [cf. Sb, word-list 10 p. 345; Dit., loc. cit.]; also as loanw. in the Mishna: SKrauss, Griech. u. lat. Lehnwörter im Talmud II 1899, 408; 497], but also Lat. 'manipulus' (Polyb. 6, 24, 5; cf. 2, 3, 2; 3, 115, 12 al.; Dionys. Hal. 5, 42, 2; Strabo 12, 3, 18). In our lit. prob. always *cohort,* the tenth part of a legion (the σπ. thus normally had 600 men, but the number varied; cf. Jos., Bell. 3, 67). Mt 27: 27; Mk 15: 16; J 18: 3, 12; Ac 21: 31. On σπεῖρα ἡ καλουμένη Ἰταλική 10: 1 cf. Ἰταλικός, on σπεῖρα σεβαστή 27: 1 cf. σεβαστός and the lit. there. On the whole word cf. Schürer I rev. Eng. ed. '73, 363–5 and the lit. s.v. ἑκατοντάρχης. M-M.*

σπείρω 1 aor. ἔσπειρα. Pass.: 2 aor. ἐσπάρην; pf. ptc. ἐσπαρμένος (Hes., Hdt.+; inscr., pap., LXX, Philo; Jos., Ant. 12, 192; Sib. Or. 3, 148 al.).

1. *sow seed*—a. lit.—α. abs., opp. θερίζω Mt 6: 26; Lk 12: 24.—Mt 13: 3b, 4; Mk 4: 3b, 4; Lk 8: 5c. ὁ σπείρων a *sower* Mt 13: 3a (cf. Cicero, Tusc. Disp. 2, 5[13]); Mk 4: 3a; Lk 8: 5a; 2 Cor 9: 10 (Is 55: 10); 1 Cl 24: 5. Also ὁ σπείρας Mt 13: 18. On the sower in the parable: UHolzmeister, Verb. Dom. 22, '42, 8–12; KGrayston, ET 55, '44, 138f; SKFinlayson, ibid. 306f; DHaugg, ThQ 127, '47, 60–81; 166–204.

β. w. acc. of what is sown (X., Oec. 14, 5) 1 Cor 15: 36, 37a, b; (τὸ) καλὸν σπέρμα Mt 13: 24, 27, 37. τὸν σπόρον Lk 8: 5b. ζιζάνια Mt 13: 39. Pass. Mk 4: 32.

γ. w. indication of the place in which or on which someth. is sown (Pla., Leg. 8, 7 p. 838E εἰς πέτρας κ. λίθους σπ.) εἰς τὰς ἀκάνθας Mt 13: 22; Mk 4: 18. Also ἐπὶ τὰς ἀκ. 4: 18 v.l. ἐν τῷ ἀγρῷ *sow in the field* Mt 13: 24, 31. ἐπὶ τῆς γῆς Mk 4: 31. ἐπὶ τὰ πετρώδη 4: 16; Mt 13: 20. ἐπὶ τὴν καλὴν γῆν vs. 23; cf. Mk 4: 20. παρὰ τὴν ὁδόν Mt 13: 19b (GDalman, Viererlei Acker: Pj 22, '26, 120–32; gener. Dalman, Arbeit II: D. Ackerbau '32). But in these passages the lit. usage is already passing over into the metaphorical.

b. symbolically and metaphorically—α. in proverbial expressions based on the contrast θερίζειν—σπείρειν (cf. θερίζω 2a and ἐπί II 1bζ) of appropriating the fruits of another's labor, without doing any work θερίζων ὅπου οὐκ ἔσπειρας Mt 25: 24, 26. Cf. Lk 19: 21f. ἄλλος ἐστὶν ὁ σπείρων καὶ ἄλλος ὁ θερίζων J 4: 37. The harvest

corresponds to what is sown (Hes., fgm. 174 Rz. εἰ κακὰ σπείραις, κακὰ κέρδεά κ᾽ ἀμήσαιο) ὃ ἐὰν σπείρῃ ἄνθρωπος, τοῦτο καὶ θερίσει Gal 6: 7; cf. vs. 8a, b (here the 'field' is given w. εἰς τὴν σάρκα or τὸ πνεῦμα); 2 Cor 9: 6a, b.

β. The word of God, the gospel et al. are sown (Herm. Wr. 1, 29 ἔσπειρα αὐτοῖς τοὺς τῆς σοφίας λόγους) ὁ σπείρων τὸν λόγον σπείρει Mk 4: 14; cf. 15a, b; Mt 13: 19a; J 4: 36. τὰ πνευματικά 1 Cor 9: 11. The κακὴ διδαχή of the false teachers IEph 9: 1a, b.

γ. μὴ σπείρητε ἐπ᾽ ἀκάνθαις B 9: 5 (Jer 4: 3). καρπὸς δικαιοσύνης ἐν εἰρήνῃ σπείρεται τοῖς ποιοῦσιν εἰρήνην Js 3: 18 (σπ. καρπόν as Antiphanes 228, 4; Paus. 1, 14, 2).

δ. The body after burial is compared to a seed-grain, which rises fr. the earth. This is the background of the contrast σπείρειν—ἐγείρειν 1 Cor 15: 42–4.

2. *scatter, disperse* (Hdt. et al.) ἔσπαρται κατὰ πάντων τῶν τοῦ σώματος μελῶν ἡ ψυχή *the soul is spread throughout all the members of the body* Dg 6: 2. M-M. B. 505.*

σπεκουλάτωρ, ορος (t.r. ωρος), ὁ (Lat. loanw., 'speculator': PGoodspeed 30 VII, 31 [II AD]; POsl. 59, 9; POxy. 1193, 1; 1223, 21; Martyr. S. Dasii v. 303: Anal. Bolland. 16, 1897, 15, 5.—Also loanw. in the Mishna: SKrauss, Griech. u. lat. Lehnwörter usw. II 1899, 92; Billerb. II 12) lit. *spy, scout;* then *courier,* but also *executioner* (Seneca, Benef. 3, 25, Ira 1, 18, 4; Syntipas p. 61, 8; 71, 10; Martyr. Pauli 5 p. 115, 17 Lips.) Mk 6: 27.—Schürer I rev. Eng. ed. '73, 371, esp. notes 84 and 85. M-M.*

σπένδω (Hom.+; inscr., pap., LXX; Jos., Ant. 6, 22; Sib. Or. 7, 81) *offer a libation* or *drink-offering,* in our lit. only pass. and fig. (cf. Philo, Ebr. 152 νοῦν σπένδεσθαι θεῷ) of the apostle who is about *to be offered up,* to shed his blood as a sacrifice 2 Ti 4: 6; Phil 2: 17 (cf. θυσία 1; 2b and ChBruston, RThPh 42, '09, 196–228.—In the Apollonaretal., Berl. Gr. Pap. 11 517 [II AD]: Her. 55, '20, 188–95 l. 26, the putting to death of a prophet of Apollo who was true to his god appears as a σπονδή). M-M.*

σπέρμα, ατος, τό (Hom.+; pap., LXX, En., Philo, Joseph., Test. 12 Patr.) *seed.*

1. lit.—a. of the seeds of plants pl. *seeds* 1 Cl 24: 5; (*kinds of*) *seeds* Mt 13: 32; Mk 4: 31; 1 Cor 15: 38 (MEDahl, The Resurrection of the Body [1 Cor 15], '62, 121–5). Sing., collective (POsl. 32, 15 [1 AD] τὸ εἰς τ. γῆν σπέρμα) Mt 13: 24, 27, 37f; 2 Cor 9: 10 (Is 55: 10).

b. of the male seed or semen (Pind. et al.), so perh. Hb 11: 11 (cf. καταβολή 2 and s. 2b below, also Cadbury [αἷμα 1a]) and J 7: 42; Ro 1: 3; 2 Ti 2: 8; IEph 18: 2; IRo 7: 3 (s. also 2b below on these passages).

2. fig.—a. of a few *survivors,* fr. whom a new generation will arise (cf. Wsd 14: 6; 1 Esdr 8: 85; Jos., Ant. 11, 144; 12, 303; cf. also Pla., Tim. 23C; Phlegon: 257 fgm. 36, 2, 3 v. 21 Jac. ὅ τί που καὶ σπέρμα λίποιτο) Ro 9: 29 (Is 1: 9).

b. *descendants, children, posterity* (in Pind. and trag., but mostly of an individual descendant; Pla., Leg. 9 p. 853C ἄνθρωποί τε καὶ ἀνθρώπων σπέρμασιν νομοθετοῦμεν. The pl. also 4 Macc 18: 1; Ps.-Phoc. 18; Jos., Ant. 8, 200) in our lit. (as well as Aeschyl.; Soph., Trach. 1147; Eur., Med. 669 and, above all, LXX) collective τῷ Ἀβραὰμ καὶ τῷ σπέρματι αὐτοῦ Lk 1: 55. Cf. J 8: 33, 37; Ac 7: 5, 6 (Gen 15: 13); 13: 23; Ro 4: 13; 11: 1; 2 Cor 11: 22; Hb 2: 16; 11: 18 (Gen 21: 12); 1 Cl 10: 4–6 (Gen 13: 15f; 15: 5); 16: 11 (Is 53: 10); 32: 2 (cf. Gen 22: 17); 56: 14 (Job 5: 25); B 3: 3 (Is 58: 7); Hv 2, 2, 2; s 9, 24, 4.—ἀνιστάναι σπ. τινί *raise up children for someone* Mt 22: 24 (cf.

ἀνίστημι 1b and Dt 25: 5). Also ἐξανιστάναι σπ. Mk 12: 19; Lk 20: 28 (cf. ἐξανίστημι 1). ἔχειν σπ. Mt 22: 25; ἀφιέναι σπ. Mk 12: 20, 22. Also καταλείπειν σπ. vs. 21.—Hb 11: 11 may belong here (cf. καταβολή 1 and s. 1b above); ἐκ (τοῦ) σπέρματος Δαυίδ w. ref. to Jesus may be classed here w. considerable certainty (cf. Ps 88: 5 and s. 1b above) J 7: 42; Ro 1: 3; 2 Ti 2: 8; IEph 18: 2; IRo 7: 3. —σπ. is also used w. ref. to the spiritual sons of Abraham, i.e., those who have faith like his Ro 4: 16, 18 (Gen 15: 5); 9: 8; cf. vs. 7a, b (Gen 21: 12); Gal 3: 29.—It is contrary to normal OT usage (for, even if Gen 4: 25; 1 Km 1: 11 σπέρμα is used w. ref. to a single individual, he stands as the representative of all the descendants) when one person, i.e. the Messiah, is called σπέρμα and thus is exalted above the mass of Abraham's descendants. In Ac 3: 25 the promise of Gen 22: 18 is referred to him. Esp. Gal 3: 16, 19 (EDBurton, ICC Gal. '21, 505-10).—In Rv 12: 17 the Christians are called οἱ λοιποὶ τοῦ σπέρματος αὐτῆς *the rest* (in addition to the son just born to her) *of her* (the heavenly woman's) *children*.

c. the seed of God (acc. to BWeiss=the word of God; acc. to EHaupt, Westcott, HHoltzmann, OBaumgarten, OHoltzmann, HHWendt, FHauck=the beginning or germ of a new life, planted in us by the Spirit of God; acc. to HWindisch and ThHaering, who are uncertain=word or spirit; acc. to WWrede=the grace that makes us holy; RSV et al. *nature*), that dwells in the one who is γεγεννημένος ἐκ τοῦ θεοῦ (γεννάω 1bβ), and makes it 'impossible for him to sin' 1 J 3: 9 (cf. Epict. 1, 13, 3: the slave has, just as you do, τὸν Δία πρόγονον, ὥσπερ υἱὸς ἐκ τῶν αὐτῶν σπερμάτων γέγονεν; Herm. Wr. 9, 3; 4a; 6 ἀπό τ. θεοῦ λαβὼν τὰ σπέρματα; Philo, Ebr. 30 τὰ τοῦ θεοῦ σπέρματα al.; Synes., Ep. 151 p. 289B τὸ σπ. τὸ θεῖον.—Musonius p. 8, 1 ἀρετῆς σπ. Maximus Tyr. 10, 4g σπ. ψυχῆς. As early as Pind., Pyth. 3, 15 σπέρμα θεοῦ καθαρόν). M-M. B. 505.*

σπερμολόγος, ον lit. *picking up seeds* (of birds, Alex. of Myndos [I AD] in Athen. 9, 39 p. 388A; Plut., Demetr. 28, 5) subst. of a kind of bird, the *rook* (Aristoph.; Aristot.; Lynceus fr. Samos [280 BC] in Athen. 8, 32 p. 344c), used non-literally of persons *gossip, chatterer, babbler, one who makes his living by picking up scraps, a rag-picker* (so Gdspd., Probs. 132f, and cf. the ref. to Eustath. below.— Demosth. 18, 127 σπερμολ. περίτριμμα ἀγορᾶς; Dionys. Hal. 19, 5, 3 [=17, 8]; Eustath. on Od. 5, 490 σπερμολόγοι· οἱ περὶ τὰ ἐμπόρια καὶ ἀγορὰς διατρίβοντες διὰ τὸ ἀναλέγεσθαι τὰ ἐκ τῶν φορτίων ἀπορρέοντα καὶ διὰ ζῆν ἐκ τούτων; Philo, Leg. ad Gai. 203) Ac 17: 18 (Norden, Agn. Th. 333; Beginn. IV, 211). M-M.*

σπεύδω impf. ἔσπευδον; 1 aor. ἔσπευσα (Hom.+; inscr., pap., LXX)—1. intr.—a. *hurry, make haste* w. inf. foll. (Diod. S. 12, 68, 3 ἔσπευδεν κύριος γενέσθαι= hastened to become master [of a city]; Pr 28: 22.—Bl-D. §392, 1a; cf. Rob. 1077f) Ac 20: 16; 1 Cl 33: 1; MPol 6: 2. Foll. by acc. w. inf. Hs 9, 3, 2. Abs. (PTebt. 19, 8 [114 BC]; Jos., Vi. 89) σπεῦσον καὶ ἔξελθε *make haste and go out, leave as quickly as possible* Ac 22: 18. In asyndeton σπεῦσον κατάβηθι Lk 19: 5 D. In the ptc. w. a finite verb (1 Km 4: 14, 16; Jos., Bell. 1, 222) ἦλθαν σπεύσαντες 2: 16. σπεύσας κατέβη 19: 6. σπεύσας κατάβηθι vs. 5.

b. *go in haste, hasten* πρός τινα *to someone* (Herm. Wr. 4, 8b; Jos., Ant. 7, 222; cf. Philo, Aet. M. 30) πρὸς Πιλᾶτον GP 11: 45.

c. *be zealous, exert oneself, be industrious* σπεύσῃ τοῖς ἔργοις αὐτοῦ B 19: 1.

2. trans. *hasten* (POxy. 121, 12 [III AD] σπεῦσον τοῦτο.

—Sir 36: 7 καιρόν) or *strive for* (Od. 19, 137; Pind., Pyth. 3, 109 βίον ἀθάνατον; Hdt. 1, 38; Thu. 5, 16, 1, also Is 16: 5 δικαιοσύνην) τὶ *someth.* τὴν παρουσίαν τῆς τοῦ θεοῦ ἡμέρας 2 Pt 3: 12. M-M. B. 971.*

σπήλαιον, ου, τό (Pla.+; Sb 5295, 7; LXX) *cave,* as a robbers' *den* (Jer 7: 11; cf. Jos., Ant. 14, 415; 421; Field, Notes 15); Mt 21: 13; Mk 11: 17; Lk 19: 46 (s. on ἱερόν 2); 2 Cl 14: 1. As a place of refuge (Cornutus 27 p. 50, 5; Jos., C. Ap. 1, 292; 300) B 11: 4 (Is 33: 16); Hb 11: 38; Rv 6: 15. Of tombs (Test. Reub. 7: 2) J 11: 38. M-M.*

σπιθαμή, ῆς, ἡ *span,* as a measure of distance= the space betw. the thumb and little finger of the hand when spread out, about nine inches (Hdt. 2, 106 al.; Diod. S. 3, 47, 2; pap., LXX) B 16: 2 (Is 40: 12). M-M.*

σπιλάς, άδος, ἡ used symbolically in Jd 12. The interpretation depends on which of two possible mngs. is preferred:

1. *a rock washed by the sea, a (hidden) reef* (Hom.+; Nicander, Alex. 290; Philostrat., Imag. 2, 13 p. 359, 19; Sb 6160, 1; Jos., Bell. 3, 420). Acc. to the Etymol. Magnum it is characteristic of the σπιλάδες that they cannot be seen, and hence a ship can be wrecked on them before any danger is suspected (αἱ ὑπὸ θάλασσαν κεκρυμμέναι πέτραι; Diod. S. 3, 44, 4 σπιλάδας ἐνθαλάττους). This type of interpr. is preferred by deWette, Mayor, Wordsworth, Chase, Weymouth, and conditionally by HermvSoden, Windisch, RSV (mg.).

2. *spot, stain* (Orpheus, Lithica 614 GHermann=620 Ch-ÉRuelle [1898]: the agate is said to be κατάστικτος σπιλάδεσσι='sprinkled w. spots'. Hesychius explains σπιλάδες in our pass. w. μεμιασμένοι. S. also the parall. 2 Pt 2: 13 s.v. σπίλος and Bl-D. §45 app.; Mlt.-H. 360f) so Spitta, BWeiss, Kühl, Bigg, Hollmann, Zahn, Wohlenberg, Vrede, Holtzmann, L-S-J lex., RSV (text), and conditionally HermvSoden, Windisch.—ADKnox, Σπιλάδες: JTS 14, '13, 547-9; 16, '15, 78 (dirty, foul wind); HSJones, ibid. 23, '22, 282f. M-M.*

σπίλος, ου, ὁ (Dionys. Hal. et al.—On the accent cf. Bl-D. §13; Mlt.-H. 57) *spot* (Jos., Bell. 1, 82, Ant. 13, 314) in Hermas in the allegory of the building of the tower, of certain stones, which represent people w. serious faults Hs 9, 6, 4; 9, 8, 7; 9, 26, 2. Fig. *stain, blemish* (Lysis in Iambl., Vi. Pyth. 17, 76 Deubner v.l.; Dionys. Hal. 4, 24, 6) 2 Pt 2: 13 (w. μῶμος). Of the church Eph 5: 27 (here, beside ῥυτίς, σπίλος means a spot on the body: Diosc. 1, 39; Artem. 5, 67; Ps.-Lucian, Amor. 15). M-M.*

σπιλόω pf. pass. ptc. ἐσπιλωμένος (Dionys. Hal. et al.; Wsd 15: 4; Test. Asher 2: 7) *stain, defile* in our lit. only symbolically (Dositheus 68: 3) Js 3: 6; Jd 23. M-M.*

σπλαγχνίζομαι (Pr 17: 5 A; Ex 2: 6 Cod. Venet.; 1 Km 23: 21; Ezk 24: 21 Sym.; Test. Zeb. 4: 6, 7, 8; PFlor. 296, 23 [VI AD].—The act.= Att. σπλαγχνεύω 2 Macc 6: 8; the pass. so on an inscr. fr. Cos [IV BC]: ABA '28, 6 p. 12 no. 4, 14) pass. dep., 1 aor. ἐσπλαγχνίσθην; 1 fut. σπλαγχνισθήσομαι *have pity, feel sympathy,* perh. τινός *with* or *for someone* (Bl-D. §176, 1 app.; Rob. 509) Mt 18: 27 (the constr. is in doubt; τοῦ δούλου should prob. rather be taken w. ὁ κύριος). Also ἐπί τινι (Bl-D. §235, 2 app.) Mt 14: 14; Mk 6: 34 t.r.; Lk 7: 13; Hs 9, 14, 3; ἐπί τινα (Bl-D. §233, 2; Test. Zeb. 7: 1) Mt 14: 14 t.r.; 15: 32; Mk 6: 34; 8: 2; 9: 22; Lk 7: 13 v.l.; Hv 3, 12, 3; m 4, 3, 5; 9: 3; s 6, 3, 2; 8, 6, 3. W. περί τινος (Bl-D. §229, 2) Mt 9: 36.—Abs. Mt 18: 27 (s. above); 20: 34; Mk 1: 41; Lk 10: 33; 15: 20; 2 Cl 1: 7; Hs 7: 4; 8, 11, 1. M-M.*

σπλάγχνον, ου, τό (Hom.+, almost always pl.; inscr., pap., LXX)—1. pl. σπλάγχνα, ων, τά—a. lit. *inward parts, entrails* (Hom.+; inscr.; PRyl. 63, 6; 2 Macc 9: 5f; 4 Macc 5: 30; 10: 8; Philo; Jos., Bell. 2, 612) Ac 1: 18 (Appian, Bell. Civ. 2, 99 §410 of Cato's suicide προπε-σόντων αὐτῷ τῶν σπλάγχνων).

b. fig., of the seat of the emotions, in our usage *heart* (Aeschyl.+; Pr 12: 10; Sir 30: 7; Jos., Bell. 4, 263; Test. Levi 4: 4 al. in the Test. 12 Patr.—On Engl. 'bowels' in this sense s. Murray, New Engl. [Oxford] Dict. s.v. bowel sb. 3). mostly as the seat and source of love (so Herodas 1, 57; Theocr. 7, 99; Dionys. Hal. 11, 35, 4), sympathy, and mercy σπλάγχνα ἐλέους *the merciful heart* (qualitative gen.; Test. Zeb. 7: 3; 8: 2) Lk 1: 78. Also σπλάγχνα οἰκτιρμοῦ Col 3: 12. σπλάγχνα καὶ οἰκτιρ-μοί *affection and sympathy* Phil 2: 1 (on the constr. s. Bl-D. §137, 2; Rob. 130). τὰ σπλ. αὐτοῦ εἰς ὑμᾶς ἐστιν *his heart goes out to you* 2 Cor 7: 15. ἐν τοῖς σπλ. ὑμῶν *in your own hearts* 6: 12. σπλάγχνα ἔχειν ἐπί τινα *have compassion for someone* 1 Cl 23: 1. κλείειν τὰ σπλάγχ-να αὐτοῦ ἀπό τινος *close one's heart to someone* in need 1 J 3: 17. ἀναπαύειν τὰ σπλ. τινός (ἀναπαύω 1) Phlm 20; pass., vs. 7.—On τοὺς λόγους αὐτοῦ ἐνεστερνισμέ-νοι ἦτε τοῖς σπλάγχνοις 1 Cl 2: 1 cf. ἐνστερνίζω.

c. of the feeling itself *love, affection* (Wsd 10: 5) τὰ σπλ., ἃ ἔχετε ἐν Χρ. 'Ι. IPhld 10: 1. ἐπιποθεῖν τινα ἐν σπλάγχνοις Χριστοῦ 'Ι. *long for someone with the affection of Christ Jesus* Phil 1: 8.—Love= the object of love (Artem. 1, 44; 5, 57) αὐτόν, τοῦτ'ἔστιν τὰ ἐμὰ σπλ. *him, my beloved* Phlm 12 (or in sense 1b *my very heart*).

2. sing. (Jos., Ant. 15, 359), fig. (so occasionally since Soph., Aj. 995; BGU 1139, 17 [5 BC]) *mercy, love* σπλάγχνον ἔχειν ἐπί τινα Hs 9, 24, 2. M-M. B. 1085f.*

σπόγγος, ου, ὁ (Hom.+; PSI 535, 20 [III BC]; 558, 7; loanw. in rabb.—On the spelling Bl-D. §34, 5; Mlt.-H. 109) *sponge* (Antig. Car. 158 σπόγγοις πρὸς ξύλοις δεδεμένοις=[water is brought up] by means of sponges tied to poles) Mt 27: 48; Mk 15: 36; J 19: 29. M-M.*

σποδός, οῦ, ἡ (Hom.+; inscr., LXX; Jos., Ant. 20, 89; 123) *ashes* w. γῆ as a designation for someth. transitory 1 Cl 17: 2 (Gen 18: 27). On its use w. σάκκος Mt 11: 21; Lk 10: 13; B 3: 2; 7: 5 s. σάκκος. The ashes of the red heifer (Num 19: 9; cf. IScheftelowitz, Das Opfer der Roten Kuh [Num 19]: ZAW 39, '24, 113-23) Hb 9: 13; B 8: 1. M-M.*

σπονδίζω (late form for σπένδω) 1 aor. pass. ἐσπον-δίσθην *pour out as an offering* pass. IRo 2: 2.*

σπορά, ᾶς, ἡ (Aeschyl.+; inscr., pap., LXX, Philo, Jo-seph.; Test. Reub. 2: 8) means as an activity *sowing* and fig. *procreation*, then *that which is sown* (Eur., Andr. 637; pap.; 1 Macc 10: 30; Jos., Ant. 2, 306), and it also comes to mean *seed* (Dit., Syll.³ 826c, 15 [117 BC] μήτε σπορῶν μήτε καρπῶν; Herm. Wr. 13: 2; PGM 1, 32; 13, 176), which is generally accepted for 1 Pt 1: 23 (cf. θεοῦ σπορά Ps.-Callisth. 1, 10; 13), though EGSelwyn, 1 Pt '46, 307 prefers *origin* or *sowing*. M-M.*

σπόριμος, ον (X.+; IG XII 3, 344; 345; pap., LXX) *sown*, subst. τὰ σπόριμα *standing grain, grain fields* (Ps.-Aeschines, Ep. 9, 1; Sib. Or. 8, 181; Geopon. 1, 12, 37; PLond. 413, 14f ἐπιδὴ τὰ δορκάδια ἀφανίζουσειν τὰ σπόριμα) Mt 12: 1; Mk 2: 23; Lk 6: 1.—BMurmelstein, Jesu Gang durch d. Saatfelder: Αγγελος III '30, 111-20. M-M.*

σπόρος, ου, ὁ—1. *sowing* (Hdt.+; inscr., pap.; Philo, Fuga 171; Jos., Ant. 18, 272) 1 Cl 24: 4.

2. *seed* (Apollon. Rhod. 3, 413; 498; Theocr. 25, 25; Diod. S. 5, 68, 2; Plut., Mor. 670в; pap., LXX; En. 10, 19; Philo) Mk 4: 27; Lk 8: 11. βάλλειν τὸν σπ. ἐπὶ τῆς γῆς Mk 4: 26. Also σπεῖραι τὸν σπ. (cf. Dt 11: 10) Lk 8: 5 (on the parable cf. GHarder, Theologia Viatorum, '48/'49, 51-70; JoachJeremias, NTS 13, '66, 48-53. On the philosopher as sower of seed, AHenrichs, ZPE 1, '67, 50-3). Cf. 2 Cor 9: 10a v.l.—Symbolically πληθυνεῖ τὸν σπόρον ὑμῶν *he will increase your store of seed* (i.e., your store of things to distribute to the needy) 2 Cor 9: 10b. M-M.*

σπουδάζω (Soph., X., Pla.+; inscr., pap., LXX, Philo, Joseph., Test. 12 Patr.) fut. σπουδάσω (Polyb. 3, 5, 8; Diod. S. 1, 58, 4; Ep. Arist. 10; Jos., Ant. 17, 203; Bl-D. §77; Mlt.-H. 259); 1 aor. ἐσπούδασα.

1. *hasten, hurry* w. inf. foll. (Jdth 13: 12 ἐσπούδασαν τοῦ καταβῆναι; Jos., Ant. 8, 202 σπ. καταλιπεῖν) 2 Ti 4: 9, 21; Tit 3: 12; IEph 1: 2. διὰ τὸ ἕκαστον σπουδάζειν, ὅστις ἅψηται *because each one hastened to touch* MPol 13: 2. But mng. 2 is also acceptable in all these places.

2. *be zealous* or *eager, take pains, make every effort* w. inf. foll. (X., Ap. 22; Diod. S. 1, 58, 4; Herodian 1, 1, 1; Jos., Ant. 17, 203, C. Ap. 1, 116; Test. Dan 6: 3, Napht. 3: 1) Gal 2: 10; Eph 4: 3; 1 Th 2: 17; 2 Ti 2: 15; Hb 4: 11; 2 Pt 1: 10; 3: 14; 2 Cl 10: 2; 18: 2; B 1: 5; 4: 9; 21: 9; IEph 5: 3; 10: 2; 13: 1; IMg 6: 1; 13: 1; IPhld 4. Foll. by acc. and inf. (BGU 1080, 14; PFlor. 89, 11; 13; 131) 2 Pt 1: 15. W. nom. and inf. (Epict. 2, 22, 34) IEph 10: 3.—Bl-D. §392, 1a; cf. Rob. 1077f. M-M.*

σπουδαῖος, α, ον (Pind., Hdt.+; inscr., pap.; Ezk 41: 25 [σπουδαῖα ξύλα]. Oft. Philo. Jos., Ant. 6, 296 v.l., C. Ap. 1, 214) *eager, zealous, earnest, diligent* ἔν τινι 2 Cor 8: 22a; σπ. εἴς τι *eagerly intent upon someth.* Hv 3, 1, 2. πλέον σπουδαῖος *even more diligent* IPol 3: 2.—Comp. σπουδαιότερος *very earnest* (Bl-D. §244, 2. Cf. Leges Graecorum Sacrae II [ed. LZiehen '06] 7, 34 [III AD] εὐσεβέστερος) 2 Cor 8: 17. πολὺ σπουδαιότερος *much more zealous* vs. 22b.—For 2 Ti 1: 17 t.r., s. on σπου-δαίως. M-M.*

σπουδαίως adv. (X., Pla., Aristot. et al.; PSI 742, 6; Wsd 2: 6; Joseph.)—1. *with haste* (Pollux 3, 149) comp. σπου-δαιοτέρως *with special urgency* Phil 2: 28.

2. *diligently, earnestly, zealously* (Diog. L. 6, 27; Jos., Ant. 8, 6; inscr.: Ramsay, Phrygia no. 480) 2 Ti 1: 17; Tit 3: 13. παρακαλεῖν σπ. *urge strongly* Lk 7: 4.—Comp. *very eagerly* σπουδαιότερον (Pla., Rep. 7 p. 536c; Jos., Ant. 16, 85) 2 Ti 1: 17 t.r.; σπουδαιοτέρως (Ps.-Plut., Nobil. 15, ed. Bern. VII 252, 15) ibid. v.l. M-M.*

σπουδή, ῆς, ἡ (Hom.+; inscr., pap., LXX, Ep. Arist., Philo, Joseph.; Sib. Or. 1, 90)—1. *haste, speed* μετὰ σπουδῆς *in haste, in a hurry* (Appian, Iber. 27 §105; 28 §110; Herodian 3, 4, 1; 6, 4, 3; PTebt. 315, 8 [II AD]; Ex 12: 11; Wsd 19: 2; Jos., Ant. 7, 223) Mk 6: 25; Lk 1: 39 (BHospodar, CBQ 18, '56, 14-18 ['seriously']); MPol 8: 3.

2. *eagerness, earnestness, diligence*, also *zeal* in matters of religion (Inschr. v. Magn. 53, 61; 85, 12; 16; cf. Thieme 31; Herm. Wr. 2, 17 σπουδὴ εὐσεβεστάτη; Jos., Ant. 13, 245) Ro 12: 11; 2 Cor 7: 11; 8: 7, 8 (subj. gen.). μετὰ σπουδῆς *diligently, attentively* (Polyb. 1, 27, 9; Ps.-Aristot., De Mundo 1; Dit., Syll.³ 611, 5; UPZ 110, 131 [164 BC]; 3 Macc 5: 24, 27; Philo; Jos., C. Ap. 2, 42) Dg 12: 1. Also ἐν σπ. Ro 12: 8. σπ. ὑπέρ τινος *good will toward, devotion for someone* (cf. Philo, Leg. ad Gai. 242) 2 Cor 7: 12; 8: 16. ἐνδείκνυσθαι σπουδὴν πρός τι *show earnestness in someth.* Hb 6: 11 (cf. Philo, Somn. 2, 67;

Jos., Ant. 12, 134). σπουδὴν πᾶσαν παρεισενέγκαντες ἐπιχορηγήσατε *make every effort to add* 2 Pt 1: 5 (πᾶσα σπ. as PTebt. I, 33, 18f; Philo, Leg. ad Gai. 338, Sacr. Abel. 68; Third Corinthians 1: 16). πᾶσαν σπ. ποιεῖσθαι (s. ποιέω II 1) *be very eager* w. inf. foll. (Philostrat., Ep. 1) Jd 3. σπουδὴ τοῦ συλληφθῆναι τοιοῦτον ἄνδρα MPol 7: 2. M-M.*

σπυρίς, ίδος, ἡ (Hdt., Aristoph. +; pap.; Philo, Spec. Leg. 3, 160; on the form σφυρίς, which is also attested [Mt 15: 37 D; 16: 10 BD; Mk 8: 8 אAD, 20 D; Ac 9: 25 אC] and which W-H. prefer, in contrast to Tdf., v. Soden and N., cf. Bl-D. §34, 5; Mlt.-H. 109; Mayser 173; Dssm., B 157, NB 13 [BS 158; 185]) *basket, hamper* Ac 9: 25. In connection w. the miracle of feeding (as a basket for edibles: Hdt. 5, 16; Epict. 4, 10, 21; Athen. 8 p. 365a) Mt 15: 37; 16: 10; Mk 8: 8, 20.—S. κόφινος. M-M. B. 623.*

σταγών, όνος, ἡ (Aeschyl., Hippocr. +; inscr., LXX) *drop* of water Hm 11: 20. M-M. B. 672.*

στάδιον, ου, τό (Jos., Ant. 15, 415) pl. τὰ στάδια J 6: 19 אD; Hv 4, 1, 2 and οἱ στάδιοι (both plurals also in Attic Gk.; cf. Kühner-Bl. I 500; Bl-D. §49, 3; Mlt.-H. 122; Mayser 289; Thackeray 155; Helbing 46f; Reinhold 53f) *stade, stadium*.
1. *stade* as a measure of distance (Hdt. et al.; inscr., pap.; Da 4: 12; 2 Macc; Ep. Arist.; Jos., Bell. 5, 192 ἐξ σταδίους; 7, 284, Ant. 18, 60)=600 Greek (625 Roman; c. 607 English) feet=185 meters. Mt 14: 24; Lk 24: 13 (for the v.l. in אΘ cf. Appian, Bell. Civ. 5, 35 §140 ἐξήκοντα καὶ ἑκατὸν σταδίους); J 6: 19; 11: 18; Rv 14: 20; 21: 16; Hv 4, 1, 2; 5.—S. ASegré, JBL 64, '45, 369-71.
2. *arena, stadium* (Pind. +; inscr., pap.; Philo, Op. M. 78; Jos., Bell. 2, 172, Vi. 331 τὸ στ.; loanw. in rabb.) on or in which the foot-races and other public athletic contests were held MPol 6: 2; 8: 3; 9: 1f; 12: 1. ἐν στ. τρέχειν *run in the race* 1 Cor 9: 24. ἔξω βάλλεσθαι τοῦ στ. *be expelled from the stadium* 2 Cl 7: 4 (s. μαστιγόω 1). M-M.*

στάζω 1 aor. ἔσταξα—1. trans. *cause to drop* (Hom. +; LXX) symbolically of God στ. τὴν δικαιοσύνην ἐπί τινα *instill righteousness into someone* Hv 3, 9, 1.
2. intr. *drip, trickle* (since trag.; Hdt. 6, 74; Hippocr.; LXX; Sib. Or. 5, 373) B 12: 1 (quot. of uncertain orig.). M-M.*

σταθμός, οῦ, ὁ (Hom. +; inscr., pap., LXX; Philo, Rer. Div. Her. 144; Test. Napht. 2: 3) the mng. in ἀνέμων σταθμοί 1 Cl 20: 10 is uncertain; it may be: *station* (?—so Polyaenus 5, 8, 1; Jos., Bell. 1, 308) or *weight* (?—so Jos., C. Ap. 2, 216; cf. Job 28: 25).*

στάμνος, ου (Aristoph. +; inscr., pap., LXX), ἡ (so in Attic Gk.; but ὁ in Doric and LXX: Bl-D. §49, 1; Thackeray p. 146; note on PHamb. 10, 35; Mlt.-H. 124) *jar*, in which the manna was kept (Ex 16: 33; Philo, Congr. Erud. Grat. 100) Hb 9: 4. M-M.*

στασιάζω 1 aor. ἐστασίασα (Aristoph., Hdt. +; inscr., LXX; Jos., Bell. 5, 248, Ant. 17, 277) *rebel* πρός τινα *against someone* (X., An. 6, 1, 29, Hell. 1, 1, 28; Pla., Rep. 8, p. 545d; 566a al.; cf. Jos., Ant. 1, 110; 13, 74) 1 Cl 4: 12; 46: 7; 47: 6; 51: 3. Abs. (Menand., Epitr. 641 J.; Diod. S. 18, 39, 3; Polyaenus 5, 26; 8, 23, 21; Oenomaus in Euseb., Pr. Ev. 5, 28, 8; Philo, Op. M. 33) 43: 2; 49: 5; 55: 1.*

στασιαστής, οῦ, ὁ (Diod. S. 10, 11, 1; Dionys. Hal. 6, 70, 1; Jos., Bell. 6, 157, Ant. 14, 8; PSI 442, 4 [III bc]) *rebel, revolutionary* Mk 15: 7. M-M.*

στάσις, εως, ἡ—1. *existence, continuance* στάσιν ἔχειν *be in existence, be standing* (Polyb. 5, 5, 3; Plut., Mor. 731b ἔχ. γένεσιν καὶ στάσιν) Hb 9: 8 (also poss. is *place, position* [Hdt. 9, 24 al.; Diod. S. 12, 72, 10; 13, 50, 9; LXX; En. 12: 4]).
2. *uprising, riot, revolt, rebellion* (since Alcaeus 46a, 1 D.[2] [ἀνέμων στάσις=tumult of the winds]; Aeschyl., Hdt.; Sb 6643, 18 [88 bc]; PLond. 1912, 73 [41 ad]; Philo, Jos., Ant. 20, 117; loanw. in rabb.) against the civil authority Mk 15: 7; Lk 23: 19 (of an uprising: Dio Chrys. 21[38], 14 γενομένης στάσεως), 25; Ac 19: 40. Against the leaders of a Christian congregation 1 Cl 1: 1. W. διχοστασία 51: 1. But it is difficult to differentiate in 1 Cl betw. this sense and the foll. one.
3. *strife, discord, disunion* (Diod. S. 12, 14, 3 στάσεις ἐν τ. οἰκίαις; Appian, Bell. Civ. 4, 45 §193 ἡ Καίσαρος κ. Ἀντωνίου στάσις; IG IV[2] 1, 687, 13; PStrassb. 20, 10; Jos., Ant. 18, 374 al.) 1 Cl 46: 9. W. ἔρις 3: 2; 14: 2 (στάσεις). W. ἔρις and σχίσματα 54: 2. W. σχίσμα 2: 6. W. ζήτησις Ac 15: 2. τὴν καταβολὴν τῆς στ. ποιεῖν *lay the foundation of the discord* 1 Cl 57: 1. ἡσυχάζειν τῆς ματαίας στ. *cease from that futile dissension* 63: 1. Specif. of a difference in opinion, *dispute* (Aeschyl., Pers. 738; Diog. L. 3, 51; Philo, Rer. Div. Her. 248; Jos., Vi. 143 γίνεται στ.) Ac 23: 7, 10 (Polyaenus, Exc. 40, 3 στάσεως γενομένης). κινεῖν στάσεις (t.r. στάσιν) τισί *create dissension among certain people* Ac 24: 5. M-M.*

στατήρ, ῆρος, ὁ (as the name of coins Aristoph., Hdt. +; inscr., pap., Aq., Sym., Jos., Ant. 7, 379; loanw. in rabb.) *the stater*, a silver coin=four drachmas, worth about eighty cents in normal value Mt 17: 27 (s. OLZ 40, '37, 665-70; JDMDerrett, Law in NT, '70, 248-52; NJMc Eleney, CBQ 38, '76, 178-92); 26: 15 v.l.—Lit. s.v. ἀργύριον 2c. M-M.*

Στάτιος, ου, ὁ *Statius*, a Roman name, Στάτιος Κοδρᾶτος, *Statius Quadratus*, proconsul of Asia at the time of Polycarp's martyrdom MPol 21. The time when he held office is variously estimated; s. on Πολύκαρπος.*

στατίων, ωνος (Lat. loanw. statio, found also in rabb., used w. various mngs. in Strabo 17, 3, 2 p. 826; inscr. [Dit., Or. index VIII p. 704b; Hahn 227, 14]; BGU 326 II, 10; PRyl. 78, 23; Wilcken, Ostraka I 294.—Cf. Dit., op. cit. 595 note 4; JSvennung, ZNW 32, '33, 294-308), ἡ and rarely ὁ (Dit. 755, 4) *post, station* στατίωνα ἔχειν=Lat. stationem habere *do guard duty, stand sentinel*; this became part of the ecclesiastical vocabulary and meant symbolically *keep a fast* (cf. Tertullian, Jejun. 13, Orat. 19, Fuga 1, Ad Uxorem 2, 4) Hs 5, 1, 1f.*

σταυρίσκω *crucify* τινά *someone* GP 2: 3.*

σταυρός, οῦ, ὁ *the cross* (Hom. + in the sense 'upright, pointed stake' or 'pale') in our lit. of the instrument by which the capital punishment of crucifixion was carried out (Diod. S. 2, 18, 1; Plut. et al.; Epict. 2, 2, 20; Diog. L. 6, 45; Philo, In Flacc. 84; Jos., Ant. 11, 261; 266f. S. also CSchneider, TW III 414, 4 and JJCollins, The Archeology of the Crucifixion, CBQ 1, '39, 154-9; JBlinzler, Der Prozess Jesu[3], '60, 278-81), a stake sunk into the earth in an upright position; a cross-piece was oft. (Artem. 2, 53) attached to its upper part, so that it was shaped like a T or thus †.—MHengel, Crucifixion '77.
1. lit., w. other means of execution (Diogenes, Ep. 28, 3) IRo 5: 3; Hv 3, 2, 1. Used in the case of Jesus Mt 27: 40, 42; Mk 15: 30, 32; J 19: 25, 31; Phil 2: 8; GP 4: 11; 10: 39, 42. ὑπομένειν σταυρόν *submit to the cross* Hb 12: 2. The condemned man himself carried his cross to the place of

execution (Plut., Mor. 554A ἕκαστος κακούργων ἐκφέρει τὸν αὑτοῦ σταυρόν; Charito 4, 2, 7 ἕκαστος τ. σταυρὸν ἔφερε; Artem. 2, 56.—Pauly-W. IV 1731) J 19: 17; in the synoptics Simon of Cyrene was made to carry the cross for Jesus (Σίμων 4) Mt 27: 32; Mk 15: 21; Lk 23: 26. An inscription on the cross indicated the reason for the execution J 19: 19 (s. τίτλος).—WMichaelis, Zeichen, Siegel, Kreuz, ThZ 12, '56, 505-25.

2. symbolically, of the suffering and death which the believer must take upon himself in following his Lord λαμβάνειν τὸν σταυρὸν αὐτοῦ Mt 10: 38. ἆραι τὸν στ. αὐτοῦ 16: 24; Mk 8: 34; 10: 21 t.r.; Lk 9: 23. βαστάζειν τὸν στ. ἑαυτοῦ 14: 27 (cf. on these parallel passages AFridrichsen, Festskrift for Lyder Brun '22, 17-34.—EDinkler, Jesu Wort v. Kreuztragen: Bultmann-Festschr. '54, 110-29).

3. the cross of Christ as one of the most important elements of Christian religion and preaching: w. death and resurrection IPhld 8: 2 and other details of his life PK 4 p. 15, 33. For the Jews a σκάνδαλον Gal 5: 11; cf. IEph 18: 1. Hence an occasion for persecution Gal 6: 12 (τῷ σταυρῷ because of the cross; dat. of cause, s. ἀπιστία 2b). For Paul, on the other hand, it was his only reason for boasting vs. 14. ὁ λόγος ὁ τοῦ σταυροῦ the message of the cross 1 Cor 1: 18, w. its mysterious, paradoxical character, is necessarily foolishness to unbelievers. For this reason any attempt to present this message in the form of worldly wisdom would rob the σταυρὸς τοῦ Χριστοῦ of its true content vs. 17. τὸ μαρτύριον τοῦ σταυροῦ is the testimony rendered by the Passion to the fact of Christ's bodily existence Pol 7: 1.—Christ's death on the cross brings salvation Eph 2: 16; Col 2: 14. εἰρηνοποιεῖν διὰ τοῦ αἵματος τοῦ σταυροῦ αὐτοῦ make peace through his blood shed on the cross 1: 20 (cf. W-S. §30, 12c; Rob. 226). Hence we may ἐπὶ τὸν σταυρὸν ἐλπίζειν B 11: 8b. Paul knows of baptized Christians whom he feels constrained to call ἐχθροὶ τοῦ σταυροῦ τοῦ Χριστοῦ because of their manner of life Phil 3: 18. On the other hand Ign. speaks of blameless Christians ὥσπερ καθηλωμένους ἐν τῷ σταυρῷ τοῦ κυρίου Ἰησοῦ Χρ. σαρκί τε καὶ πνεύματι as if nailed to the cross of the Lord Jesus Christ both in the flesh and in the spirit ISm 1: 1. In the symbolic language of Ign. the cross is called ἡ μηχανὴ Ἰησοῦ Χρ. IEph 9: 1 (s. HSchlier, Relgesch. Untersuchungen zu d. Ign.-briefen '29, 110-24), and the orthodox believers are the κλάδοι τοῦ σταυροῦ branches of the cross ITr 11: 2.—B seeks to show in several passages that acc. to the scriptures it was necessary for the Messiah to die on the cross: 8: 1 (the ξύλον that plays a part in connection w. the red heifer, Num 19: 6, is ὁ τύπος ὁ τοῦ σταυροῦ); 9: 8 (in the case of the 318 servants of Abraham Gen 14: 14 the number 300 [represented by the numerical value of the letter T] points to the cross; cf. Lucian, Jud. Voc. 12: the letter tau has the form of the σταυρός); 11: 1, 8a (the ξύλον of Ps 1: 3); 12: 1 (scripture quot. of uncertain origin), 2.—WWoodSeymour, The Cross in Tradition, History and Art 1898 (here, p. xx-xxx, lit.); HFulda, D. Kreuz u. Kreuzigung 1879; VSchultze, RE XI 90ff; HFHitzig, Pauly-W. IV '01, 1728-31; PWSchmidt, Die Geschichte Jesu II '04, 386ff; 409ff; UHolzmeister, Crux Domini '34; GWiencke, Pls über Jesu Tod '39; HWSchmidt, D. Kreuz Christi bei Paulus: ZsystTh 21, '50, 145-59; VTaylor, The Cross of Christ, '56; LMorris, The Cross in the NT, '65.—Joh Schneider, TW VII 572-84. M-M. B. 902f.*

σταυρόω (in the sense 'fence w. stakes' Thu.+) fut. σταυρώσω; 1 aor. ἐσταύρωσα. Pass.: pf. ἐσταύρωμαι; 1 aor. ἐσταυρώθην nail to the cross, crucify (Polyb. 1, 86, 4;

Diod. S. 16, 61, 2; Epict. 2, 2, 20; Artem. 2, 53; 4, 49; Esth 7: 9; 8: 12 r; Jos., Ant. 2, 77; 17, 295).

1. lit. τινά someone w. ref. to Jesus' crucifixion Mt 20: 19; 23: 34; 26: 2; 27: 22f, 26, 31, 35, 38; 28: 5; Mk 15: 13ff, 20, 24f, 27; 16: 6; Lk 23: 21, 23, 33; 24: 7, 20; J 19: 6a, b (the doubling of the imperative as Anaxarchus [IV BC] in Diog. L. 9, 59 πτίσσε, πτίσσε=pound, pound away [in a mortar]), c, 10, 15f, 18, 20, 23, 41; Ac 2: 36; 4: 10; 13: 29 D; 1 Cor 2: 8; 2 Cor 13: 4; Rv 11: 8; B 7: 3, 9; 12: 1; IEph 16: 2; GP 4: 10; 12: 52. Χριστὸς ἐσταυρωμένος 1 Cor 1: 23; cf. 2: 2; Gal 3: 1. Also simply ὁ ἐσταυρωμένος MPol 17: 2. ὁ σταυρωθείς GP 13: 56. ἀληθῶς ἐσταυρώθη he was truly crucified (in contrast to the Docetic view that the Passion was unreal) ITr 9: 1. μὴ Παῦλος ἐσταυρώθη ὑπὲρ ὑμῶν; 1 Cor 1: 13.—On the crucifixion of Jesus cf. Feigel, Weidel, and Finegan s.v. Ἰούδας 6; also EBickermann, Utilitas Crucis: Rev. de l'Hist. des Rel. 112, '35, 169-241.

2. fig. οἱ τοῦ Χριστοῦ Ἰ. τὴν σάρκα ἐσταύρωσαν those who belong to Christ Jesus have crucified the flesh w. its sinful desires Gal 5: 24. Pass.: of the cross of Christ, δι' οὗ ἐμοὶ κόσμος ἐσταύρωται κἀγὼ κόσμῳ through which the world has been crucified to me, and I (have been crucified) to it, the believer who is inseparably united to his Lord has died on the cross to the kind of life that belongs to this world Gal 6: 14. ὁ ἐμὸς ἔρως ἐσταύρωται my desire (for worldly things) has been crucified IRo 7: 2. M-M.*

σταφυλή, ῆς, ἡ (Hom.+; inscr., pap., LXX) (a bunch of) grapes Mt 7: 16; Lk 6: 44 (w. σῦκον as Epict. 3, 24, 86; 91; Jos., Bell. 3, 519); Rv 14: 18. στ. παρεστηκυῖα a bunch of ripe grapes (παρίστημι 2bγ) 1 Cl 23: 4=2 Cl 11: 3 (quot. of unknown origin). M-M. B. 378.*

στάχυς, υος, ὁ—1. head or ear (of grain) (Hom.+; inscr., pap., LXX; Ep. Arist. 63; Philo, Aet. M. 98; Jos., Bell. 2, 112, Ant. 5, 213 al.) Mk 4: 28a, b. τίλλειν (τοὺς) στάχυας pick (the) heads of wheat 2: 23; Mt 12: 1; cf. Lk 6: 1.

2. νάρδου στάχυς (Geopon. 7, 13, 1)=ναρδοστάχυς (spike)nard flower (shaped like a head of grain) AP 3: 10. M-M.*

Στάχυς, υος, ὁ (several times in Zen.-P. [III BC]; Wilcken, Chrest. 10, 14 [131/0 BC]; IG III 1080, 37; 1095, 19; XII 3, 624; 749; Inschr. v. Magn. 119, 25; CIL VI 8607) Stachys, recipient of a greeting Ro 16: 9. M-M.*

στέαρ, ατος, τό (Hom.+; pap., LXX, Philo) fat 1 Cl 4: 1 (Gen 4: 4). B 2: 5 (Is 1: 11).*

στέγη, ης, ἡ (Aeschyl., Hdt.+; inscr., pap., LXX; En. 14, 17; Jos., Ant. 8, 67f; loanw. in rabb.) roof Mk 2: 4 (on uncovering the roof cf. Jos., Ant. 14, 459 and FSchulthess, ZNW 21, '22, 220; Hedwig Jahnow, ibid. 24, '25, 155ff [cf. JDMDerrett, Law in the NT, '70, sv, n. 1]; against Jahnow: SKrauss, ibid. 25, '26, 307ff; LFonck, Biblica 6, '25, 450-4 and PGvanSlogteren, NThT 14, '25, 361-5. Cf. also CCMcCown, JBL 58, '39, 213-16). On εἰσέρχεσθαι ὑπὸ τὴν στ. (τινός) Mt 8: 8; Lk 7: 6 s. εἰσέρχομαι 1g. M-M. B. 473.*

στέγος, ους, τό (Aeschyl.+; inscr.; EpJer 9 v.l.) roof (Diod. S. 19, 45, 7; Jos., Ant. 7, 130 al.) συνάξεις τοὺς σοὺς ὑπὸ τὸ στέγος σου you are to gather your people under your roof 1 Cl 12: 6.*

στέγω (Aeschyl.+; inscr., pap.)—1. cover, pass over in silence, keep confidential (Eur., Electra 273 τἀμὰ ἔπη; Thu. 6, 72, 5; Polyb. 8, 14, 5 τὸν λόγον; Sir 8: 17; Jos., Vi. 225; Field, Notes 177f), so perh. ἡ ἀγάπη πάντα στέγει 1 Cor 13: 7 of love that throws a cloak of silence over what is displeasing in another person (Harnack, SAB '11, 147; but s. 2 below).

2. *bear, stand, endure* (Aeschyl.+; Polyb.; Diod. S.; Plut.; Dit., Syll.³ 700, 23; Philo, In Flacc. 64 στέγειν τὰς ἐνδείας) τὶ someth. πάντα 1 Cor 9: 12; perh. (s. 1 above) 13: 7 (GHWhitaker, 'Love Springs No Leak': Exp. 8th Ser. XXI '21, 126ff). Abs. (PGrenf. I 1, 18 [II bc]; POxy. 1775, 10 καὶ ἔστεξα, ἕως ἔλθῃς) μηκέτι στέγων *since I could not bear it any longer* 1 Th 3: 5; cf. vs. 1.—WKasch, TW VII, 585-7. M-M. B. 849.*

στεῖρα, ας, ἡ (Hom.+; Isishymnus v. Andros 82 Peek; Philo; LXX adj. and subst.) *barren, incapable of bearing children* Lk 1: 7, 36; 23: 29; Gal 4: 27 (Is 54: 1); Hb 11: 11 𝔓⁴⁶ D; 2 Cl 2: 1 (Is 54: 1); B 13: 2 (Gen 25: 21). M-M.*

στέλλω (Hom.+ in the sense 'make ready, send', etc.; inscr., pap., LXX, Philo; Jos., Ant. 2, 43) in our lit., as well as in LXX, only mid.

1. *keep away, stand aloof* ἀπό τινος (Polyb. 8, 22, 4; cf. Mal 2: 5) *from someone* 2 Th 3: 6.

2. *avoid, try to avoid* (Hippocr., π. ἀρχ. ἰητρ. 5 Heib. acc. to codd. οὔτ' ἂν ἀπόσχοιντο οὐδενός, ὧν ἐπιθυμέουσιν οὐδὲ στείλαιντο='not keep away from . . . nor avoid it'; Suppl. Epigr. Gr. II 615 στέλλεο Περσεφόνας ζᾶλον. Mal 2: 5 uses στ. as a parallel to φοβεῖσθαι, which corresponds to Hesychius: στέλλεται· φοβεῖται) στελλόμενοι τοῦτο, μή τις *avoiding* or *trying to avoid this, lest someone* 2 Cor 8: 20 (so It., Vulg., Goth., Chrys., Luther, Calvin and many in later times).—KHRengstorf, TW VII, 588-99: στέλλω and related words. M-M.*

στέμμα, ατος, τό (Hom.+; inscr., pap.) *wreath* or *garland of flowers* (but wool was also necessary for religious purposes: Herodas 8, 11) Ac 14: 13 (Inscr. of Cos [s. ἀγαθός 1ba] no. 37, 29-31: ἱερεύς . . . βοῦς . . . στέμμα in a sacrifice to Zeus; s. Field, Notes 122). M-M.*

στεναγμός, οῦ, ὁ (Pind.+; Sb 4949, 12; 5716, 12; PGM 4, 1406; 7, 768; LXX; En. 9, 10; Jos., Bell. 6, 272; Test. Jos.) *sigh, groan,* coll. *groaning* Ac 7: 34 (cf. Ex 2: 24 [like this Philo, Leg. All. 3, 211]; 6: 5) 1 Cl 15: 6 (Ps 11: 6); Hv 3, 9, 6. Pl. (Diod. S. 3, 29, 7 στεναγμοὶ μεγάλοι) στεναγμοὶ ἀλάλητοι (cf. ἀλάλητος) Ro 8: 26 (WBieder, ThZ 4, '48, 31-3; JSchniewind, Nachgelassene Reden, '52, 81-103; ADietzel, ThZ 13, '57, 12-32 [Hodayoth]; EKäsemann, EHaenchen-Festschr., '64, 142-55; MDibelius, Formgeschichte des Evangeliums⁵, '66, 82f). M-M.*

στενάζω fut. στενάξω; 1 aor. ἐστέναξα (trag., Demosth.+; Sb 2134, 14; LXX; En. 12, 6; Philo; Test. Jos. 7: 1) *sigh, groan* because of an undesirable circumstance (Herm. Wr. in Stob. I 395, 5 W.=474, 22 Sc.) 2 Cor 5: 2 (ἐν τούτῳ=in this earthly body), 4; Hb 13: 17; MPol 2: 2; 9: 2; Hv 3, 9, 6, στ. ἐν ἑαυτῷ *sigh to oneself* Ro 8: 23 (cf. Lycophron 1462f στ. ἐν καρδίᾳ). στ. κατά τινος *groan against, complain of someone* Js 5: 9.—In connection w. a healing, prob. as an expr. of power ready to act Mk 7: 34 (cf. PGM 13, 945). M-M. B. 1131.*

στενός, ή, όν (Aeschyl., Hdt.+; inscr., pap., LXX; Ep. Arist. 118; Jos., Bell. 1, 41) *narrow* πύλη (q.v. 2) Mt 7: 13f. θύρα (Arrian, Anab. 6, 29, 5 of the θυρὶς στενή in the grave of Cyrus ὡς μόλις ἂν εἶναι ἑνὶ ἀνδρὶ οὐ μεγάλῳ πολλὰ κακοπαθοῦντι παρελθεῖν) Lk 13: 24. στ. ὁδός (Nicol. Dam.: 90 fgm. 66, 38 Jac.; Diod. S. 20, 29, 7; Maximus Tyr. 39, 3n μία [ὁδὸs] στενὴ κ. τραχεῖα κ. οὐ πολλοῖς πάνυ ὁδεύσιμος; Appian, Syr. 43 §225; Arrian, Anab. 2, 11, 3; 3, 18, 4; Jos., Ant. 19, 116) Mt 7: 14 v.l. M-M. B. 886.*

στενοχωρέω (since Macho [III bc]; pap., though intr.) trans. *crowd, cramp, confine, restrict* (Diod. S. 20, 29, 7); Lucian, Nigr. 13, Tox. 29 al.; LXX) fig., pass. *be confined, restricted* (Herm. Wr. 2, 11; schol. on Eur., Med. 57 στενοχωρεῖσθαι τῷ κακῷ; Is 28: 20; Jos., Bell. 4, 163) οὐ στενοχωρεῖσθε ἐν ἡμῖν, στενοχωρεῖσθε δὲ ἐν τοῖς σπλάγχνοις ὑμῶν *you are not restricted in us* (i.e. in the open heart of the apostle; cf. vs. 11), *but rather in your own hearts* 2 Cor 6: 12. As the higher degree beside θλίβεσθαι (Epict. 1, 25, 28) θλιβόμενοι ἀλλ' οὐ στενοχωρούμενοι *hard pressed, but not crushed* 4: 8. Of the Holy Spirit, when anger moves into a person whom he indwells: στενοχωρεῖται *he is distressed* Hm 5, 1, 3. Of the hardships that the slaves of God, in contrast to the unrighteous, must undergo 2 Cl 20: 1. M-M.*

στενοχωρία, ας, ἡ (in the lit. sense, 'narrowness', Thu.+) fig. *distress, difficulty, anguish, trouble* (Polyb. 1, 67, 1; Petosiris, fgm. 7 l. 22 [w. πόλεμος]; Plut., Mor. 182b; Artem. 3, 14; Aelian, V.H. 2, 41; Cass. Dio 39, 34; Cat. Cod. Astr. VII 169, 21; Sir 10: 26; 1 Macc 2: 53; 3 Macc 2: 10; En. 98, 10) w. θλῖψις (Artem. 1, 68; 82; 2, 3 al.; Dt 28: 53; 55; 57; Is 8: 22; 30: 6; Esth 1: 1g; PLond. 1677, 11 [VI ad]. Cf. Epict. 1, 25, 26 στενοχωρία . . . θλίβειν) Ro 2: 9; 8: 35. W. λύπη Hv 4, 3, 4; m 10, 2, 6. Pl. *difficulties* (oft. Artem.; 1 Macc 13: 3; Cat. Cod. Astr. VIII 1 p. 165, 2) 2 Cor 6: 4; 12: 10. M-M.*

στέργω (Aeschyl., Hdt. +; inscr., pap.; Sir 27: 17; Philo; Jos., Bell. 1, 596, Ant. 8, 249; Sib. Or. 4, 25) *love, feel affection for* τινά someone, of the love of a wife for her husband (Theocr. 17, 130) 1 Cl 1: 3; Pol 4: 2. BBWarfield, The Terminology of Love in the NT, PTR 16, '18, 1-45; 153-203. B. 1110.*

στερεός, ά, όν (Hom.+; inscr., pap., LXX, Ep. Arist., Philo, Joseph.)—1. lit. *firm, hard, solid, strong* θεμέλιος 2 Ti 2: 19. πέτρα (PPetr. II 4, 1, 3 [III bc]; LXX; En. 26, 5) B 5: 14; 6: 3 (both Is 50: 7). (Opp. γάλα) στερεὰ τροφή *solid food* (Theophr., C. Pl. 3, 16; Diod. S. 2, 4, 5; Epict. 2, 16, 39; Lucian, Lexiph. 23) Hb 5: 12, 14.

2. fig., of human character (Hom.+) *steadfast, firm* (Diog. L. 2, 132 of athletes; Quint. Smyrn. [c. 400 ad] 5, 597; 9, 508 Zimmermann [1891] στερεῇ φρενί='w. steadfast mind') στερεοὶ τῇ πίστει 1 Pt 5: 9 (ἑδραῖοι 𝔓⁷²). M-M.*

στερεόω 1 aor. ἐστερέωσα. Pass.: impf. ἐστερεούμην; 1 aor. ἐστερεώθην (X.+; LXX; En. 103, 15) *make strong, make firm.*

1. lit., of impotent limbs, pass. *become strong, be strengthened* ἐστερεώθησαν αἱ βάσεις αὐτοῦ Ac 3: 7 (X., De Re Equ. 4, 3 τοὺς πόδας; Hippocr., Epid. 2, 3, 17 ed. Littré V p. 118 τὰ ὀστέα; Hippiatr. II 82, 1). On the basis of this passage the act. is used in referring to the same act of healing τοῦτον ἐστερέωσεν τὸ ὄνομα *the name* (of Christ) *has made this man strong* vs. 16.

2. fig. (1 Km 2: 1 ἡ καρδία), pass. αἱ ἐκκλησίαι ἐστερεοῦντο τῇ πίστει *the churches were continually* (impf.) *being strengthened in the faith* Ac 16: 5. M-M.*

στερέω 1 aor. ἐστέρησα (Hom.+; pap., LXX; Jos., C. Ap. 2, 277, Ant. 16, 93) *deprive* τινά τινος *someone of a thing* B 13: 4 (Gen 48: 11).*

στερέωμα, ατος, τό (Aristot.+; Polemo, Decl. I, 45 p. 16, 8 [support]; Herm. Wr. 514, 12 Sc.; PGM 4, 1210; Fluchtaf. 4, 22; LXX).

1. *the solid part, firmament,* of the sky (Gen 1: 6ff; En. 18, 2; Philo, Op. M. 36; Test. Napht. 3: 4; Audollent, Defix. Tab. 242, 8 [III ad]) 1 Cl 27: 7 (Ps 18: 2).

2. *firmness, steadfastness* τῆς πίστεως Col 2: 5 (cf. 1 Macc 9: 14 [military sense]). M-M.*

Στεφανᾶς, ᾶ, ὁ (CIG II 3378; Sb 361, 10 [in the gen. Στεφανᾶτος].—Short form of Στεφανηφόρος? or a development of Στέφανος? Bl-D. §125, 1; Rob. 173; 255; W-S. §16, 9; AFick²-FBechtel, Griech. Personennamen 1894, 253f) *Stephanas,* a member of the church at Corinth who, w. his household, was baptized by Paul himself 1 Cor 1: 16 as the 'firstfruits of Achaia' 16: 15. Acc. to vs. 17 he was w. Fortunatus and Achaicus in Paul's company at Ephesus. S. also 1 Cor subscr. and Third Corinthians 1: 1. M-M.*

Στέφανος, ου, ὁ (since Andocides 1, 18 and Demosth.; inscr., pap.: Jos., Bell. 2, 228) a name freq. found, *Stephen,* one of the seven 'deacons' in Jerusalem. Ac relates that he performed miracles and became esp. prominent as a preacher. Religious differences w. certain Jews brought him before the Sanhedrin, where he made a long speech; he was thereupon stoned to death in an outbreak of mob violence, and became the first Christian martyr. Ac 6: 5, 8f; 7: 1 D, 59; 8: 2; 11: 19; 22: 20.—KPahncke, StKr 85, '12, 1–38; WMundle, ZNW 20, '21, 133–47; EMeyer III 154ff; JHRopes, StKr 102, '30, 307–15; AFridrichsen, Le Monde oriental 25, '32, 44–52; RSchumacher, Der Diakon Stephanus '10; MSimon, St. Stephen and the Hellenists in the Primitive Church, '58; JBihler, D. Stephanusgeschichte usw., '63; CKBarrett, Stephen and the Son of Man, EHaenchen-Festschr., '64, 32–8; MHScharlemann, Stephen, a Singular Saint, '68 (lit.). M-M.*

στέφανος, ου, ὁ (Hom. +; inscr., pap., LXX, Ep. Arist., Philo; Jos., Bell. 7, 14 al.; Test. 12 Patr.) *wreath, crown.*
1. lit., made of palm branches Hs 8, 2, 1a, b. Jesus' 'crown of thorns' Mt 27: 29; Mk 15: 17; J 19: 2, 5; GP 3: 8 (on the crowning w. thorns and mocking of Jesus cf. FCumont, Anal. Boll. 16, 1897, 3ff; LParmentier, Le roi des Saturnales: Rev. de Philol., n.s. 21, 1897, 143ff; PWendland, Jesus als Saturnalienkönig: Her. 33, 1898, 175–9; WRPaton, ZNW 2, '01, 339–41; SReinach, Le roi supplicié: L'Anthropologie 33, '02, 621ff; HReich, D. König m. der Dornenkrone '05 [= NJklA 13, '04, 705–33]; HVollmer, ZNW 6, '05, 194–8, 8, '07, 320f; Jesus u. das Sacäenopfer '05; KLübeck, Die Dornenkrönung Christi '06; JGeffcken, Her. 41, '06, 220–9; KKastner, Christi Dornenkrönung u. Verspottung durch die röm. Soldateska: BZ 6, '08, 378–92, ibid. 9, '11, 56; ThBirt, PJ 137, '09, 92–104; HAllroggen, Die Verspottung Christi: ThGl 1, '09, 689–708; HZimmern, Zum Streit um die Christusmythe '10, 38ff, Verh. d. Sächs. Ges. d. W., phil.-hist. Kl. 70, 5, '18, Pauly-W. second series II 1, 208; LRadermacher, ARW 28, '30, 31–5; RDelbrueck, Antiquarisches zu den Verspottungen Jesu: ZNW 41, '42, 124–45). The wreath for the winner of an athletic contest (Aelian, V.H. 9, 31) 1 Cor 9: 25; as a symbol of the heavenly reward 2 Cl 7: 3.—In Rv the (golden) crown is worn by beings of high rank (divine beings w. a golden crown: PGM 4, 698; 1027; the high priest w. the στ. χρύσεος: Jos., Ant. 3, 172; the king 17, 197): by the 24 elders 4: 4, 10 (perh. the gold crowns or wreaths of the 24 elders simply belong to the usual equipment of those who accompany a divinity. Cf., in a way, Athen. 5 p. 197ғ the triumphal procession of Dionysus with 40 σάτυροι wearing golden wreaths; also the whole fantastic procession here described); also by the Son of Man 14: 14 (who, however, in 19: 12 wears the real head-dress of the ruler [s. διάδημα]. But cf. 2 Km 12: 30; 1 Ch 20: 2; SSol 3: 11); s. also 6: 2; 9: 7; 12: 1 (στεφ. ἀστέρων δώδεκα, cf. Boll. 99).—Ign. uses as a symbol of

the presbytery the words ἀξιόπλοκος πνευματικὸς στέφανος *a worthily-woven spiritual wreath* IMg 13: 1.
2. fig., though the imagery of the wreath becomes less and less distinct (Lycurgus 50 Bl.; Ael. Aristid. 27, 36 K.=16 p. 397 D.: τῶν ἀθανάτων στ.; PSI 405, 3 [III ʙᴄ]).
a. *prize, reward,* w. obj. gen. τ. δικαιοσύνης *for righteousness* (cf. δικαιοσύνη 2b) 2 Ti 4: 8. W. epexegetical gen. (this is the sense of στ. δικαιοσύνης Ep. Arist. 280; Test. Levi 8: 2) ὁ στέφ. τῆς ζωῆς (cf. ζωή end) Js 1: 12; Rv 2: 10; cf. 3: 11; ὁ τῆς ἀφθαρσίας στ. MPol 17: 1; 19: 2; ὁ ἀμαράντινος τῆς δόξης στ. 1 Pt 5: 4 (cf. Jer 13: 18 στ. δόξης; La 2: 15; cf. IQS 4, 7; IQH 9, 25).
b. that which serves as someone's *adornment, pride* (Epigr. ed. DBMonro [1896] 13, 1 ἀνδρὸς μὲν στέφανος παῖδες; Eur., Iphig. Aul. 193 Αἴας τᾶς Σαλαμῖνος στέφ.; Pr 12: 4; 17: 6.—Expr. denoting tender love: HSwoboda et al., Denkmäler aus Lykaonien etc. 1935 p. 78, no. 168) of the Philippians χαρὰ καὶ στέφανός μου Phil 4: 1. (χαρὰ ἢ) στέφανος καυχήσεως *prize to be proud of* (Gdspd.) (cf. Pr 16: 31) 1 Th 2: 19.—JKöchling, De Coronarum apud Antiquos Vi atque Usu '14; LDeubner, D. Bedeutg. des Kranzes im klass. Altertum: ARW 30, '33, 70–104 (lit.); KBaus, D. Kranz in Antike u. Christent. '40; WGrundmann, TW VII, 615–35. M-M.*

στεφανόω 1 aor. ἐστεφάνωσα. Pass.: 1 aor. ἐστεφανώθην; pf. ptc. ἐστεφανωμένος (Hom.+; inscr., pap., LXX; Philo; Jos., C. Ap. 2, 256 al.; Sib. Or. 1, 12) *wreathe, crown.*
1. lit. τινά *someone* (Diod. S. 20, 94, 5) Hs 8, 2, 1. The winner in an athletic contest, pass. (Pind., Ol. 4, 11; Hdt. 8, 59; Zen.-P. Cairo 60, 7 [257 ʙᴄ]) 2 Ti 2: 5; 2 Cl 7: 1; cf. 7: 2, 3 (where 2 Cl passes over to the crowning of the victor in the immortal contest. Cf. the hymn to Serapis IG XI 4, 1299 l. 9f [c. 200 ʙᴄ] διὰ τὴν εὐσέβειαν ἐστεφανώθη ὑπὸ τοῦ θεοῦ). Hs 8, 3, 6; 8, 4, 6. Pregnant constr. στεφανωθεὶς κατ' αὐτῆς *crowned as victor* (in the struggle) *against it* (i.e., evil desire) Hm 12, 2, 5.—One of the two goats on the great Day of Atonement (Lev 16: 5ff) is called ἐστεφανωμένος and is taken to be a type of Christ B 7: 9.
2. fig. *honor, reward, crown* (Pind., Eur.+—Cebes 22, 1 στ. δυνάμει; 23, 4) δόξῃ καὶ τιμῇ ἐστεφάνωσας αὐτόν Hb 2: 7 (Ps 8: 6); cf. vs. 9 (Windisch, Hdb. ad loc. [lit.]). Of Polycarp the martyr ἐστεφανωμένος τὸν τῆς ἀφθαρσίας στέφανον MPol 17: 1 (Diod. S. 16, 13, 1 στεφάνοις ἐστεφανωμένους). Cf. 2 Cl 20: 2. M-M.*

στῆθος, ους, τό (Hom.+; inscr., pap., LXX; Ep. Arist. 97; Philo; Jos., Ant. 3, 154; Sib. Or. 5, 265) *chest, breast* Rv 15: 6; Hv 1, 4, 2. ἀναπεσεῖν ἐπὶ τὸ στ. τινος (ἀναπίπτειν 2) J 13: 25; 21: 20. τύπτειν τὸ στῆθος (αὐτοῦ) *beat one's breast* as a sign of grief Lk 18: 13 (t.r. εἰς τὸ στῆθος); 23: 48. Also κόπτεσθαι τὸ στ. (κόπτω 2) GP 8: 28. As the seat of the inner life (as early as Alcaeus [VII/VI ʙᴄ] p. 6, l. 3 [new-found fgm., since '41: ed. MTreu, Alkaios '52]; Iambl., Vi. Pyth. 35, 252) 2 Cl 19: 2. M-M. B. 247.*

στήκω (found first in the NT; in the LXX only as an untrustworthy v.l. [ADebrunner, GGA '26, 146f], but also occurs Epigr. Gr. 970; Hippiatr. 69, 2 and 4 p. 269, 16; 270, 16; PGM 4, 923; 36, 273. A new formation fr. ἕστηκα, the perf. of ἵστημι, and used beside it; cf. Bl-D. §73; Mlt.-H. 220; 259.—ἑστηκεν J 8: 44 is prob. the perf. of ἵστημι, whether written ἕστ. or ἔστ.; cf. EAbbott, The Authorship of the 4th Gosp. and Other Critical Essays, 1888, 286–93; Bl-D. §14; 73; 97, 1; differently Rob. 224, after W-H.; cf. Mlt.-H. 100. In Rv 12: 4 the impf. ἔστηκεν is prob. to be preferred to the perf. ἔστ.).

1. lit. *stand* Mk 11: 25; ἔξω στ. *stand outside* 3: 31. μέσος ὑμῶν στήκει *there is one standing in your midst* J 1: 26. ὁ δράκων ἔστηκεν ἐνώπιον τῆς γυναικός Rv 12: 4 v.l. (s. above).

2. fig. *stand firm, be steadfast* ἔν τινι *in someth.*: ἐν τῇ πίστει 1 Cor 16: 13. ἐν κυρίῳ Phil 4: 1; 1 Th 3: 8. ἐν ἑνὶ πνεύματι *in one spirit* Phil 1: 27. τῷ ἰδίῳ κυρίῳ στήκειν ἢ πίπτειν *stand or fall to the advantage or disadvantage of his own master or to be his own master's concern whether he stands or falls* Ro 14: 4. Abs. 2 Th 2: 15; Gal 5: 1 ('in freedom' is to be supplied).—WGrundmann, TW VII 635-52: στήκω and ἵστημι. M-M.*

στήλη, ης, ἡ (Hom.+; inscr., pap., LXX, Philo; Jos., Ant. 14, 188; loanw. in rabb.) *pillar,* w. τάφοι νεκρῶν *tombstones* (στ. has had this mng. Hom.+) IPhld 6: 1. στ. ἁλός *a pillar of salt* (Gen 19: 26) 1 Cl 11: 2.*

στηριγμός, οῦ, ὁ (Aristot.+ in the sense 'standing still') *firmness* fig. τοῦ στ. ἐκπίπτειν *lose one's firm hold* 2 Pt 3: 17. M-M.*

στηρίζω (Hom.+; Dit., Or. 612, 8; 769, 11; PSI 452, 3; LXX; Philo, Op. M. 84; Jos., Ant. 10, 269 [text acc. to Chrysost.]; Sib. Or. 3, 27) fut. στηρίξω (beside στηρίσω Bl-D. §71; Mlt.-H. 259; Rob. 1219 and στηριῶ [s. Ezk 14: 8; Sir 6: 37]); 1 aor. ἐστήριξα and ἐστήρισα (Bl-D. §71; Mlt.-H. and Rob. as above). Pass.; perf. ἐστήριγμαι; 1 aor. ἐστηρίχθην; *set up, fix (firmly), establish, support.*

1. lit. τὶ *someth.* τοὺς οὐρανούς 1 Cl 33: 3 (στ. of the creation of the world: Arat., Phaen. 10; Orphica, fgm. 170, 3). Pass., of a city *be well established* LJ 1: 7. Of a chasm ἐστήρικται *has been fixed* Lk 16: 26 (cf. Gen 28: 12 κλίμαξ ἐστηριγμένη; En. 24, 2). Hebraistically (=אֶל פָּנִים שִׂים) στηρίζειν τὸ πρόσωπον *set one's face* (Ezk 6: 2; 13: 17; 14: 8; 15: 7) to denote firmness of purpose (cf. Jer 21: 10) foll. by the gen. of the inf. w. the art. (Bl-D. §400, 7; Rob. 1068) Lk 9: 51 (s. πρόσωπον 1b and on 9: 51-19: 27 HConzelmann, The Theology of St. Luke, tr. GBuswell, '60, esp. 60-73).

2. fig. *confirm, establish, strengthen* (Apollon. Rhod. 4, 816 hatred; Appian, Bell. Civ. 1, 98 τὴν ἀρχήν; Ps 50: 14; Sir 3: 9; 1 Macc 14: 14) w. acc. οὐ τὰ ἑστῶτα στηρίζειν ἀλλὰ τὰ πίπτοντα 2 Cl 2: 6 (cf. Sir 13: 21).—Lk 22: 32; Ac 18: 23; Ro 16: 25; 1 Th 3: 2; 2 Th 3: 3; 1 Pt 5: 10; Rv 3: 2. Pass. Ro 1: 11. τὴν καρδίαν τινός (Judg 19: 5, 8; Sir 6: 37; 22: 16) Js 5: 8; w. a second acc. στ. ὑμῶν τὰς καρδίας ἀμέμπτους 1 Th 3: 13 (cf. Rtzst., Erlösungsmyst. 147, 3). τινὰ ἔν τινι *someone in someth.* 2 Th 2: 17; IPhld inscr. Pass. 2 Pt 1: 12. τινά τινι *strengthen someone w. someth.* 1 Cl 18: 12 (Ps 50: 14). τινὶ στ. ἑαυτὸν εἴς τι *strengthen oneself w. someth.* 13: 3; *in order to do someth.* 13: 3. τινὶ *establish (someth.) by someth.* 8: 5. ἐὰν ἐστηριγμένη ᾖ ἡ διάνοια ἡμῶν πιστῶς πρὸς τὸν θεόν *if our mind is firmly fixed on God in faith* 35: 5. ἐγὼ ὑπὸ κίνδυνον, ὑμεῖς ἐστηριγμένοι *I am in danger, you are secure* IEph 12: 1. M-M.*

στιβάζω (exx. in WCrönert, GGA '09, 656) *store (up)* εἰς ἀποθήκην οἶνον *wine in the cellar* Hm 11: 15.*

στιβαρός, ά, όν (Hom.+; Isishymnus v. Andros 170; Ezk 3: 6; Jos., Bell. 6, 161; 293; Sib. Or. 3, 39) *stout, sturdy* (w. ἰσχυρός) δύναμις Hm 5, 2, 3.*

στιβάς, άδος, ἡ (Eur., Hdt.+; inscr., pap., of a kind of bed or mattress made of straw, rushes, reeds, leaves etc.) in the only place where it occurs in our lit. (it is lacking in LXX, Ep. Arist., and Philo, but is a loanw. in rabb.) it obviously means *leaves, leafy branches* Mk 11: 8 (on the spelling στοιβάς in the t.r. cf. W-S. §5, 16; Mlt.-H. 76). M-M.*

στίγμα, ατος, τό (Hdt.+; Dit., Syll.³ 1168, 48; SSol 1: 11) *mark, brand* (not only did the master put a στίγμα on his slave [Porphyr., Vi. Pyth. 15; Ps.-Phoc. 225.—Diod. S. 34+35 fgm. 2, 32 expresses this with τὰ στίγματα and 34+35, fgm. 2, 1 with the sing. στιγμή], but religious tattooing also played a great role in antiquity: Hdt. 2, 113 στίγματα ἱερά; Lucian, Syr. Dea 59 στιγματηφορεῖν in honor of the goddess.—Dssm., B 265f [BS 349-52]; WHeitmüller, Heinrici-Festschr. '14, 47; FJDölger, Sphragis '11, 39ff, Antike u. Christentum I '29, 66ff; II '30, 102ff; III '32, 257ff) τὰ στ. τοῦ Ἰησοῦ ἐν τῷ σώματί μου βαστάζω *I bear on my body the marks of Jesus* Gal 6: 17 (Lucian, Catapl. 28: the whole [ὅλος] man is covered with στίγματα; cf. Third Corinthians 3: 35). Paul is most likely alluding to the wounds and scars which he received in the service of Jesus (Plut., Mor. 566F and Hierocles, Carm. Aur. 11 p. 445 Mull. στίγματα are the scars left by the divine rod of discipline).—JHMoulton, ET 21, '10, 283f; TWCrafer, The Stoning of St. Paul at Lystra and the Epistle to the Galatians: Exp. 8th Ser. VI '13, 375-84; OSchmitz, Die Christus-Gemeinschaft des Pls im Lichte seines Genetivgebrauchs '24, 185ff; UWilcken, Deissmann-Festschr. '27, 8f; OHoltzmann, ZNW 30, '31, 82f against EHirsch, ibid. 29, '30, 196f; EGüttgemanns, D. leidende Apostel, '66, 126-35; HWindisch, Pls u. Christus '34, 187; 251f; OBetz, TW VII, 657-64. M-M.*

στιγμή, ῆς, ἡ first *point* (Aristot.+), then of someth. quite insignificant (Demosth. et al.), finally specif. of time, *a moment* (Plut.; M. Ant. 2, 17; Vett. Val. 131, 4; 239, 11 ἐν στιγμῇ; Is 29: 5; 2 Macc 9: 11), more fully στιγμὴ χρόνου (Plut., Mor. 13B; Ps.-Plut., Cons. ad Apollon. 104B from Demetr. Phaler., fgm. 79 [ed. FWehrli '49]) Lk 4: 5. M-M.*

στίλβω *shine, be radiant* of garments (Hom.+; Pla., Phaedo 59 p. 110D. In LXX almost always of the radiance of stars or the luster of metals) at the Transfiguration Mk 9: 3 (cf. Hippiatr. I 287, 16 ὀφθαλμοὶ γίνονται στίλβοντες; Odes of Solomon 11, 14). Of a gate ἔστιλβεν ὑπὲρ τὸν ἥλιον Hs 9, 2, 2 (cf. Charito 1, 1, 5 στίλβων ὥσπερ ἀστήρ). M-M.*

στοά, ᾶς, ἡ (Aristoph., Hdt.+; inscr., pap., LXX, Joseph.; loanw. in rabb.) (*roofed*) *colonnade* or *cloister, portico* J 5: 2 (Callicrates-Menecles [before 86 BC]: 370 fgm. 1 Jac. κύκλῳ τοῦ λιμένος στοαὶ πέντε). ἡ στοὰ τοῦ Σολομῶνος (cf. Nicol. Dam.: 90 fgm. 130, 82 Jac. ἡ Πομπηίου στοά) J 10: 23 (Ps.-Pla., Eryx. 1 p. 392A περιπατοῦντες ἐν τῇ στοᾷ τοῦ Διός); cf. Ac 3: 11; 5: 12 (s. Σολομών, end). M-M.*

στοιβάς s. στιβάς.

Στοϊκός (the form Στωϊκός, which is also attested, is more correct, but not necessarily the original one [cf. Bl-D. §35, 1; Mlt.-H. 73 prefers Στω- as the orig.]), ή, όν *Stoic* (Dionys. Hal., Comp. Verb. 2 p. 7, 3 Us.-Rad.; Diog. L. 4, 67; Philo; Jos., Vi. 12) Στοϊκοὶ φιλόσοφοι, mentioned beside Epicureans Ac 17: 18. MPohlenz, Die Stoa '48; '49; WBarclay, ET 72, '61, 5 articles passim, 164-294. M-M.*

στοιχεῖον, ου, τό (Aristoph., X., Pla.+; BGU 959, 2; LXX, Philo, Joseph.) in our lit. only pl.

1. *elements (of learning), fundamental principles* (X., Mem. 2, 1, 1; Isocr. 2, 16; Plut., Lib. Educ. 16, 2) or even

letters of the alphabet, ABC's (Pla.+) τὰ στ. τῆς ἀρχῆς τῶν λογίων τοῦ θεοῦ the very elements of the truths of God Hb 5: 12. This mng. is also poss. for the passages in Gal and Col; s. 3 below.

2. elemental substances, the basic elements fr. which everything in the natural world is made, and of which it is composed (Pla.+; PGM 4, 440; Wsd 7: 17; 19: 18; 4 Macc 12: 13), to disappear in the world conflagration at the end of time 2 Pt 3: 10, 12 (lit. s.v. καυσόω). The four elements of the world (earth, air, fire, water) Hv 3, 13, 3 (cf. Diog. L. 7, 137 [Zeno the Stoic] ἔστι δὲ στοιχεῖον, ἐξ οὗ πρῶτου γίνεται τὰ γινόμενα καὶ εἰς ὃ ἔσχατον ἀναλύεται . . . τὸ πῦρ, τὸ ὕδωρ, ὁ ἀήρ, ἡ γῆ; Plut., Mor. 875c; Philo, Cher. 127 τὰ τέσσαρα στοιχεῖα; Jos., Ant. 3, 183.—JKroll, Die Lehren des Hermes Trismegistos '14, 178ff). πῦρ . . . ὕδωρ . . . ἄλλο τι τῶν στοιχείων Dg 8: 2; cf. 7: 2.

3. The mng. of στ. in τὰ στοιχεῖα τοῦ κόσμου Gal 4: 3; Col 2: 8, 20 (for the expr. στοιχ. τ. κόσμου cf. Sib. Or. 2, 206; 3, 80f; 8, 337) and τὰ ἀσθενῆ καὶ πτωχὰ στοιχεῖα Gal 4: 9 is much disputed. For a survey s. EDBurton, ICC Gal '21, 510-18. Some (e.g. Burton, Gdspd.) prefer to take it in sense 1 above, as referring to the elementary forms of religion, Jewish and Gentile, which have been superseded by the new revelation in Christ (so also WL Knox, St. Paul and the Church of the Gentiles '39, 108f; RMGrant, HTR 39, '46, 71-3; AWCramer, Stoicheia Tou Kosmou, '61 [the unregenerate tendencies within men]).—Others (e.g. WBauer, Mft., RSV) hold that the ref. is to the elemental spirits which the syncretistic religious tendencies of later antiquity associated w. the physical elements (Herm. Wr. Κόρη κόσμου in Stob. I 409 W.= St. 486ff, esp. 486, 23; 25; 490, 14: the στοιχεῖα, fire, air, water, earth, complain to the god who is over all; Orph. Hymn. 5, 4; 66, 4 Qu.; Ps.-Callisth. 1, 3 [s. below Pfister p. 416f]; Simplicius In Aristot. De Caelo 1, 3 p. 107, 15 Heiberg.—MDibelius, Geisterwelt 78ff; 228ff, Hdb. z. NT² exc. on Col 2: 8; ELohmeyer, Col '30, 4-8; 103-5; FPfister, Die στοιχεῖα τοῦ κόσμου in den Briefen des Ap. Pls: Philol. 69, '10, 411-27; GHCMacgregor: ACPurdy-Festschr., '60, 88-104); they were somet. worshipped as divinities (Vett. Val. 293, 27; Philo, Vita Cont. 3 τοὺς τὰ στοιχεῖα τιμῶντας, γῆν, ὕδωρ, ἀέρα, πῦρ. Cf. Diels [s. below] 45ff). It is not always easy to differentiate betw. this sense and the next, since heavenly bodies were also regarded as personal beings and given divine honors.

4. heavenly bodies (Diog. L. 6, 102 τὰ δώδεκα στοιχεῖα of the signs of the zodiac; POsl. 4, 18 δώδεκα στ. τοῦ οὐρανοῦ; Ps.-Callisth. 13, 1.—PGM 4, 1303 the 'bear' is called a στοιχεῖον ἄφθαρτον.—Rtzst., Poim. 69ff, Herr der Grösse 13ff; Diels [s. below] 53f; JvanWageningen, Τὰ στοιχεῖα τοῦ κόσμου: ThSt 35, '17, 1-6; FHColson, The Week '26, 95ff) Dg 7: 2.—Cf. also HDiels, Elementum 1899; ABonhöffer, Epiktet u. das NT '11, 130ff; OLagercrantz, Elementum '11 (p. 41 στοιχεῖα τοῦ κόσμου = θεμέλια τοῦ κόσμου); BSEaston, The Pauline Theol. and Hellenism: AJTh 21, '17, 358-82; KDieterich, Hellenist. Volksreligion u. byz.-neugriech. Volksglaube: Ἄγγελος I '25, 2-23; GKurze, D. στοιχεῖα τοῦ κόσμου Gal 4 and Col 2: BZ 15, '27, 335; WHPHatch, Τὰ στοιχεῖα in Paul and Bardaisân: JTS 28, '27, 181f; JHuby, Στοιχεῖα dans Bardesane et dans St. Paul: Biblica 15, '34, 365-8; LEScheu, Die 'Weltelemente' beim Ap. Pls (Gal 4: 3, 9 and Col 2: 8, 20): Diss., Cath. Univ., Washington '34; BReicke, JBL 70, '51, 259-76 (Gal 4: 1-11); WHBrownlee, Messianic Motifs of Qumran and the NT, NTS 3, '56/'57, 195-210.—GDelling, TW VII, 666-87: στοιχεῖον and related words. M-M. B. 1501.*

στοιχέω fut. στοιχήσω (X.+; inscr., pap.; Eccl 11: 6) orig. 'be drawn up in line', in our lit. only fig. be in line with, stand beside a pers. or thing, hold to, agree with, follow w. dat. (Polyb. 28, 5, 6; Dionys. Hal. 6, 65; Dit., Or. 339, 51 [II AD], Syll.³ 685, 18; 734, 6; Inscr. Gr. 544, 14 βουλόμενος στοιχεῖν τοῖς πρασσομένοις; pap. not until Byz. times) ὅσοι τῷ κανόνι τούτῳ στοιχήσουσιν all those who will follow this rule Gal 6: 16; cf. Phil 3: 16 t.r.; στ. τῷ λόγῳ Ἰησοῦ Χρ. MPol 22: 1. πνεύματι στ. follow the Spirit Gal 5: 25. εἰς ὃ ἐφθάσαμεν τῷ αὐτῷ στ. we must hold on to what we have attained Phil 3: 16. στ. τοῖς ἴχνεσίν τινος follow in someone's footsteps (s. ἴχνος) Ro 4: 12.—Abs. (so perh. Dit., Or. 308, 21) στοιχεῖς φυλάσσων τὸν νόμον Ac 21: 24 (the ptc. tells what it is that Paul adheres to). M-M.*

στοῖχος, ου, ὁ (Hdt.+; inscr.; POxy. 1119, 12; Philo, Op. M. 141; Jos., Ant. 15, 413) row, course of masonry (so Dit., Syll.³ 970, 11) Hs 9, 4, 3.*

στολή, ῆς, ἡ robe (trag., X., Pla.+) esp. a long, flowing robe (Dit., Syll.³ 1025, 10; Zen.-P. 9 [= Sb 6715], 32 [258 bc]; 44 [= Sb 6750], 4 al. in pap.; Ex 28: 2; 2 Ch 18: 9; Esth 6: 8 al. in LXX; Ep. Arist. 319f; Philo; Jos., Ant. 20, 7, Vi. 334; Test. 12 Patr.; loanw. in rabb.) Lk 15: 22 (πρῶτος 1ca); Rv 7: 14; 22: 14 (on the symbolic use in both these places cf. πλύνω 1). στολὴ λευκή (PGiess. 20, 17) as worn by angels Mk 16: 5 and by glorified believers Rv 6: 11; 7: 9, 13. στ. λαμπροτάτη GP 13: 55 (cf. the priest's sacred robe Dit., Syll.³ 1025, 10). Of the scribes ἐν στολαῖς περιπατεῖν walk about in long robes (M. Ant. 1, 7, 4 ἐν στολίῳ [v.l. στολῇ] περιπατεῖν) Mk 12: 38; Lk 20: 46 (of priests' vestments Philo, Leg. ad Gai. 296; Jos., Ant. 3, 151; 11, 80).—KHRengstorf, OMichel-Festschr., '63, 383-404. M-M.*

στόμα, ατος, τό (Hom.+; inscr., pap., LXX, En., Ep. Arist., Philo; Jos., Ant. 12, 38 al.; Test. 12 Patr.; Sib. Or. 3, 725; 4, 2; loanw. in rabb.).

1. mouth—a. of humans or of beings whose appearance resembles that of humans: Mt 15: 11a, 17; J 19: 29; Ac 11: 8; 23: 2; 2 Th 2: 8 (cf. Is 11: 4; Ps 32: 6); Rv 11: 5.—Used in symbolic speech Rv 1: 16; 2: 16; 3: 16; 10: 9f (cf. Ezk 3: 1ff); 19: 15, 21.—As an organ of speech Mt 15: 11b, 18 (cf. Num 32: 24); 21: 16 (Ps 8: 3); Lk 4: 22; 11: 54; Ro 10: 8 (Dt 30: 14); Eph 4: 29; Js 3: 10 (cf. Aesop, Fab. 35 P. = 64 H.: ἐκ τοῦ αὐτοῦ στόματος τὸ θερμὸν καὶ τὸ ψυχρὸν ἐξιεῖς = out of the same mouth you send forth warm and cold [of the person who blows in his hands to warm them, and on his food to cool it off]); 1 Cl 15: 3 (Ps 61: 5), 4 (Ps 77: 36); 2 Cl 9: 10; B 11: 8; Hm 3: 1. ἀπόθεσθε αἰσχρολογίαν ἐκ τοῦ στόματος ὑμῶν put away evil speech from your mouth Col 3: 8. ἀκούειν τι ἐκ τοῦ στόματός τινος Ac 22: 14; 2 Cl 13: 3; B 16: 10; ἀκ. ἀπὸ τοῦ στ. τινος (Polyaenus 8, 36 ἀπὸ στόματος τῆς ἀδελφῆς) Lk 22: 71; ἀκ. τι διὰ τοῦ στ. τινος Ac 1: 4 D; 15: 7.—ἀνεῴχθη τὸ στ. αὐτοῦ (of a dumb man) his mouth was opened (Wsd 10: 21) Lk 1: 64. ἀνοίγειν τὸ στόμα τινός open someone's mouth for him and cause him to speak 1 Cl 18: 15 (cf. Ps 50: 17). ἀνοίγειν τὸ (ἑαυτοῦ) στόμα open one's (own) mouth to speak (cf. ἀνοίγω 1ea) Mt 5: 2; 13: 35 (Ps 77: 2); Ac 8: 35; 10: 34; 18: 14; GEb 2. οὐκ ἀνοίγει τὸ στ. αὐτοῦ = he is silent Ac 8: 32; 1 Cl 16: 7 (both Is 53: 7). For ἄνοιξις τοῦ στόματος Eph 6: 19 cf. ἄνοιξις. On στόμα πρὸς στόμα λαλεῖν speak face to face 2 J 12; 3 J 14 cf. πρός III 1e. On ἵνα πᾶν στ. φραγῇ Ro 3: 19 cf. φράσσω.—There is no δόλος or ψεῦδος in the mouth of the upright Rv 14: 5; 1 Cl 50: 6 (Ps 31: 2); 1 Cl 16: 10; Pol 8: 1.—στόμα stands for the person

in his capacity as speaker (3 Km 17: 24; 22: 22; 2 Ch 36: 21f): ἐκ τοῦ περισσεύματος τῆς καρδίας τὸ στόμα λαλεῖ Mt 12: 34 (καρδία—στ. as Test. Napht. 2). διὰ στόματός τινος by (the lips of) someone Lk 1: 70; Ac 1: 16; 3: 18, 21.—By metonymy for that which the mouth utters ἐπὶ στόματος δύο μαρτύρων (Dt 19: 15) Mt 18: 16; 2 Cor 13: 1. ἐκ τοῦ στόματός σου κρινῶ σε Lk 19: 22.— ἐν ἑνὶ στόματι with one voice (ἐν στόμα Aristoph., Equ. 670; Pla., Rep. 364A, Laws 1 p. 634E; Ael. Aristid. 51, 40 K. = I p. 544 D.; PGiess. 36, 12 [161 BC] αἱ τέτταρες λέγουσαι ἐξ ἑνὸς στόματος; Pla., Rep. 364A) Ro 15: 6; cf. 1 Cl 34: 7.—ἐγὼ δώσω ὑμῖν στόμα καὶ σοφίαν I will give you eloquence and wisdom Lk 21: 15.

b. of God (Dexippus of Athens [III AD]: 100 fgm. 1, 7 Jac. ἡ τοῦ θεοῦ μαρτυρία διὰ στόματος; Theognis 18 Diehl) Mt 4: 4 (Dt 8: 3); 1 Cl 8: 4 (Is 1, 20).

c. of animals and animal-like beings mouth, jaws of a fish (PGM 5, 280ff) Mt 17: 27. Of horses Js 3: 3; cf. Rv 9: 17-9; a weasel B 10: 8; lion (Judg 14: 8) Hb 11: 33; Rv 13: 2, symbolically 2 Ti 4: 17; an apocalyptic monster (Diod. S. 3, 70, 4 the Aegis: ἐκ τοῦ στόματος ἐκβάλλον φλόγα) Rv 12: 15, 16b; 16: 13a, b, c; Hv 4, 1, 6; 4, 2, 4 (cf. Da 6: 22 Theod.).

d. of the earth in which a fissure is opened (cf. Gen 4: 11) ἤνοιξεν ἡ γῆ τὸ στόμα αὐτῆς Rv 12: 16a.

2. The sword, like the jaws of a wild animal, devours people; hence acc. to OT usage (but s. Philostrat., Her. 19, 4 στ. τῆς αἰχμῆς; Quint. Smyrn. 1, 194; 813 and on μάχαιρα 1; cf. also στ. = 'point' of a sword Hom. +) στόμα μαχαίρης the edge of the sword (Josh 19: 48; Sir 28: 18; cf. also μάχαιρα 1, end) Lk 21: 24; Hb 11: 34. M-M. B. 228; esp. 860.

στόμαχος, ου, ὁ (Hom. +, orig. mng. 'throat'; Philo; Test. Napht. 2: 8; loanw. in rabb.) stomach (so Plut., Mor. 698A, B; Epict. 2, 20, 33; Athen. 3 p. 79E; PGM 13, 830) 1 Ti 5: 23. M-M. *

στραγγαλιά, ᾶς, ἡ (Ptolem., Apotel. 4, 9, 10 Boll-B.; Hippiatr. 51, 3; 4, vol. I 228, 9; 229, 7; LXX) knot διαλύειν στραγγαλιὰς βιαίων συναλλαγμάτων untie the knots of forced agreements B 3: 3 (Is 58: 6). *

στραγγαλόω 1 aor. pass. ἐστραγγαλώθην (Philo Mech. 57, 42; Alex. Aphr., Probl. 1, 76 Ideler) strangle (Tob 2: 3 BA), pass., also intrans. choke 1Tr 5: 1. *

στρατεία, ας, ἡ (Aeschyl., Hdt. +; inscr., pap., LXX; Jos., Bell. 3, 445, Ant. 16, 343. On the spelling s. Dssm., NB 9f [BS 181f]; Bl-D. §23; Mlt.-H. 78) expedition, campaign fig. (Epict. 3, 24, 34 στρατεία τίς ἐστιν ὁ βίος ἑκάστου; Maximus Tyr. 13, 4d) τὰ ὅπλα τῆς στρατείας ἡμῶν the weapons we use in our warfare 2 Cor 10: 4 (v.l. στρατιας is itacism: W-S. §5 A. 31). στρατεύεσθαι τὴν καλὴν στρατείαν fight the good fight 1 Ti 1: 18 (for στρατεύεσθαι στρ. cf. Isaeus 10, 25; Aeschin. 2, 169; Plut., Mor. 204A; Epict. 2, 14, 17; Dit., Syll.³ 346, 55; 4 Macc 9: 24; Philo, Leg. All. 3, 14).—On the Christian life as military service cf. πανοπλία 2. M-M. *

στράτευμα, ατος, τό army (so trag., Hdt. +; inscr., pap., LXX; Ep. Arist. 37; Philo; Jos., Bell. 3, 162, Ant. 4, 94) sing. Rv 19: 19b. Pl. 19: 14, 19a.—Of a smaller detachment of soldiers, sing. Ac 23: 10, 27.—τὰ στρατεύματα the troops (4 Macc 5: 1; Jos., Ant. 13, 131. Cf. AWVerrall, JTS 10, '09, 340f) Mt 22: 7 (MBlack, An Aramaic Approach³, '67, 128); Lk 23: 11; Rv 9: 16. M-M. B. 1377. *

στρατεύω mostly (Aeschyl., Hdt. +; inscr., pap., LXX),

in our lit. always, a mid. dep. **στρατεύομαι** 1 aor. ἐστρατευσάμην do military service, serve in the army.

1. lit. (X., Mem. 1, 6, 9; BGU 1097, 8 [I AD]; Jos., Bell. 2, 520, Ant. 17, 270, Vi. 346) 2 Ti 2: 4; 1 Cl 37: 2. στ. ἰδίοις ὀψωνίοις serve as a soldier at one's own expense 1 Cor 9: 7. στρατευόμενοι soldiers (Thu. 8, 65, 3; Plut., Mor. 274A; Appian, Bell. Civ. 3, 41 §168; 3, 90 §371; Sb 8008, 49 [261 BC]) Lk 3: 14 (SVMcCasland, JBL 62, '43, 59-71).

2. fig. (Lucian, Vit. Auct. 8 ἐπὶ τὰς ἡδονάς) of Christians 1 Cl 37: 1; IPol 6: 2; of the apostle's activity 2 Cor 10: 3. On στρατεύεσθαι τὴν καλὴν στρατείαν 1 Ti 1: 18 cf. στρατεία. Of the struggles of the passions within the human soul Js 4: 1; 1 Pt 2: 11; Pol 5: 3.—OBauernfeind, TW VII, 701-13: στρατεύομαι and related words. M-M.*

στρατηγός, οῦ, ὁ (Aeschyl., Hdt. +; inscr., pap., LXX; Ep. Arist. 280; Philo, Joseph.; loanw. in rabb. Orig. 'general').

1. praetor, chief magistrate pl. of the highest officials of the Roman colony of Philippi. This title was not quite officially correct, since these men were properly termed 'duoviri', but it occurs several times in inscr. as a popular designation for them (JWeiss, RE XII '03, p. 39, 39f.— στρατηγοί governed Pergamum [Jos., Ant. 14, 247] and Sardis [14, 259]) Ac 16: 20, 22, 35f, 38.—Mommsen, Röm. Geschichte V 274ff; JMarquardt, Staatsverw. I² 1881, 316ff; Ramsay, JTS 1, '00, 114-16; FHaverfield, ibid. 434f; Zahn, Einl.³ I 378ff; AWikenhauser, Die AG '21, 346f.

2. ὁ στρατηγὸς τοῦ ἱεροῦ the captain of the temple Ac 4: 1; 5: 24. Also simply ὁ στρατηγός (Jos., Bell. 6, 294, Ant. 20, 131) vs. 26. In the pl. (LXX; s. Schürer II⁴ 321, 14) στρατηγοί (τοῦ ἱεροῦ) Lk 22: 4, 52.—Schürer II⁴ 320-2 and s. EBriess, Wiener Studien 34, '12, 356f (CIG 3151 στ. ἐπὶ τοῦ ἱεροῦ). M-M. B. 1381f.*

στρατιά, ᾶς, ἡ—**1.** army (so Pind., Hdt. +; inscr., pap., LXX, Philo; Jos., Bell. 7, 31, Ant. 14, 271. Loanw. in rabb.) of Pharaoh's army 1 Cl 51: 5 (cf. Ex 14: 4, 9, 17).— στρατιὰ οὐράνιος the heavenly army of angels (cf. 3 Km 22: 19; 2 Esdr 19 [Neh 9]: 6.—Pla., Phaedr. 246E στρατιὰ θεῶν τε καὶ δαιμόνων) Lk 2: 13 (for the constr. ad sensum πλῆθος στρατιᾶς . . . αἰνούντων cf. Appian, Bell. Civ. 5, 64 §272 ὁ στρατὸς αἰσθανόμενοι εἵλοντο). ἡ στρατιὰ τοῦ οὐρανοῦ the host of heaven of the heavenly bodies (cf. Ps.-Demetr. c. 91 after an ancient lyric poet ἄστρων στρατόν; Maximus Tyr. 13, 6e; 2 Ch 33: 3, 5; Jer 8: 2; PGM 35, 13) Ac 7: 42.

2. occasionally (poets, pap.) in the same sense as στρατεία (q.v.) 2 Cor 10: 4 v.l. M-M.*

στρατιώτης, ου, ὁ (Aristoph., Hdt. +; inscr., pap., LXX, Ep. Arist.; Jos., Bell. 1, 338, Ant. 5, 218 al. Loanw. in rabb.) soldier.

1. lit. Mt 8: 9; 27: 27; 28: 12; Mk 15: 16; Lk 7: 8; J 19: 2; Ac 10: 7; GP 8: 30-2 al.

2. fig. στ. Χριστοῦ Ἰησοῦ a soldier of Christ Jesus 2 Ti 2: 3 (on the idea cf. the lit. s.v. πανοπλία 2 and s. PGM 4, 193). M-M. B. 1380.

στρατιωτικός, ή, όν (X., Pla. +; inscr., pap., Ep. Arist.; Philo, Virt. 23; Jos., Bell. 1, 340) belonging to or composed of soldiers στρατιωτικὸν τάγμα a detachment of soldiers 1Ro 5: 1.*

στρατολογέω 1 aor. ἐστρατολόγησα gather an army, enlist soldiers (Diod. S. 12, 67, 5; 14, 54, 6; Dionys. Hal. 11, 24; Plut., Caesar 35, 1; Jos., Bell. 5, 380) ὁ στρατολογήσας the one who enlisted (him) 2 Ti 2: 4. M-M.*

στρατοπεδάρχης (Dionys. Hal. 10, 36; Lucian, Hist. 22; Vett. Val. 76, 13; Jos., Bell. 2, 531; 6, 238; Dit., Or. 605, 3; Mitteis, Chrest. 87, 5 [II AD]) t.r. or **στρατοπέδαρχος** v.l., ου, ὁ *military commander, commandant of a camp* Ac 28: 16. On the subject-matter s. Mommsen and Harnack, SAB 1895, 491ff; Zahn, Einl.³ I 392ff; Hitzig, Pauly-W. IV '01, 1896ff; AWikenhauser, Die AG '21, 358f. M-M.*

στρατόπεδον, ου, τό (Aeschyl., Hdt.+; inscr., LXX, Philo, Joseph.) lit. *camp* (Jos., Vi. 398), then *body of troops, army* (Eur., Hdt.+; inscr., LXX; Ep. Arist. 20; Jos., Ant. 14, 271), even specif. *legion* (Polyb. 1, 16, 2; 1, 26, 6; 6, 20ff; 27ff; BGU 362 XI, 15 [III AD].—Hahn 46) Lk 21: 20. M-M. B. 1377.*

στρεβλός, ή, όν (Aristoph., Hippocr.+; LXX) *crooked* of the way of unrighteousness Hm 6, 1, 2f. Of persons *perverted* (Eupolis Com. [V BC] 182) 1 Cl 46: 3 (Ps 17: 27). B. 897.*

στρεβλόω imper. 2 sing. **στρέβλου** (Hdt., Aristoph.+; pap., LXX) *twist, wrench*—1. *torture, torment* (so very oft., incl. BGU 195, 13 [II AD]; 4 Macc; Jos., Bell. 7, 373) fig. (Diod. S. 16, 61, 3 tortured by anxiety) μὴ στρέβλου σεαυτόν *do not trouble yourself* (with the solving of a riddle, as Vi. Aesopi W c. 78) Hs 9, 2, 7.

2. *twist, distort* (2 Km 22: 27) τὶ someth., so that a false mng. results (Numenius of Apamea, περὶ τῆς τῶν Ἀκαδημαϊκῶν πρὸς Πλάτωνα διαστάσεως 1, 1 ed. KSGuthrie [1917] p. 63) 2 Pt 3: 16. M-M.*

στρέφω 1 aor. ἔστρεψα; 2 aor. pass. ἐστράφην (Hom.+; pap., LXX; Jos., Bell. 5, 200, Ant. 6, 153, Vi. 400).

1. act.—a. trans.—α. *turn* (Sib. Or. 5, 497 στ. ψυχάς) τί τινι someth. to someone Mt 5: 39; D 1: 4.—So perh. also in a non-literal sense ἔστρεψεν ὁ θεός *God turned the Israelites toward the heavenly bodies, so that they were to serve them as their gods* Ac 7: 42 (cf. 3 Km 18: 37 σὺ ἔστρεψας τὴν καρδίαν τοῦ λαοῦ τούτου ὀπίσω. But s. 1b below).

β. *turn, change* τὶ εἰς τι someth. into someth. ὕδατα εἰς αἷμα Rv 11: 6 (cf. Ps 113: 8; 29: 12). Pass. *be changed, be turned* (1 Km 10: 6 εἰς ἄνδρα ἄλλον) στραφήσονται τὰ πρόβατα εἰς λύκους D 16: 3a. ἡ ἀγάπη στραφήσεται εἰς μῖσος D 16: 3b (cf. La 5: 15; 1 Macc 1: 39, 40).

γ. *bring back, return* τὶ someth. τὰ τριάκοντα ἀργύρια Mt 27: 3.

b. intr. *turn (away)* (X., An. 4, 3, 26; 32, Ages. 2, 3) so perh. ἔστρεψεν ὁ θεός *God turned away* from them Ac 7: 42 (s. 1aα above).

2. pass., w. reflexive mng.—a. *turn around, turn toward*—α. lit. στραφείς foll. by a finite verb *he turned (around) and . . .* (X., Cyr. 3, 3, 63). The purpose of the turning can be to attack someone Mt 7: 6, or a desire to see or speak w. someone 9: 22 (cf. Wilcken, Chrest. 20 I, 6 στραφεὶς καὶ ἰδὼν Ἡλιόδωρον εἶπεν); 16: 23; Lk 7: 9; 9: 55; 14: 25; 22: 61; J 1: 38; 20: 16; MPol 5: 2. στρ. πρός w. acc. *turn to* or *toward* (schol. on Nicander, Ther. 677 πρὸς ἥλιον στρέφεσθαι of the heliotrope): στραφεὶς πρός τινα foll. by a finite verb Lk 7: 44; 10: 22 t.r., 23; 23: 28. στρ. εἰς τὰ ὀπίσω *turn around* J 20: 14 (cf. X., De Re Equ. 7, 12 στρέφεσθαι εἰς τὰ δεξιά).

β. fig. στρεφόμεθα εἰς τὰ ἔθνη *we turn to the Gentiles* Ac 13: 46. ἐστράφησαν ἐν ταῖς καρδίαις αὐτῶν εἰς Αἴγυπτον *in their hearts they turned back to Egypt* 7: 39.

b. *turn, change* inwardly, *be converted* (Sib. Or. 3, 625) Mt 18: 3 (JDupont, MBlack-Festschr., '69, 50–60); J 12: 40 (Is 6: 9.—Field, Notes 99). Also *turn to* someth. evil, *be perverted* D 11: 2.—GBertram, TW VII 714–29: στρέφω and related words. M-M. B. 666.*

στρηνιάω 1 aor. ἐστρηνίασα (Antiphanes in Athen. 3 p. 127D; Diphilus in Bekker, Anecdot. p. 113, 25; PMMeyer, Griech. Texte aus Ägypten '16 no. 20, 23; Sym. Is 61: 6; POxy. 2783, 24 of bulls running wild) *live in luxury, live sensually* Rv 18: 7. W. πορνεύειν vs. 9. M-M.*

στρῆνος, ους, τό (in Nicostratus [IV BC]: Com. Att. fgm. p. 230 no. 42 Kock; Lycophron 438 al.; also 4 Km 19: 28 in a different sense) *sensuality, luxury* (Palladas [VI AD]: Anth. Pal. 7, 686) ἡ δύναμις τοῦ στρήνους (δύναμις 5) Rv 18: 3. M-M.*

στρογγύλος, η, ον (Aristoph., Thu., X., Pla.+; inscr., pap., LXX; Philo, Leg. All. 3, 57 [opp. τετράγωνος]) *round* of stones (X., De Re Equ. 4, 4; Cebes 18, 1 [opp. τετράγωνος]) Hv 3, 2, 8; 3, 6, 5f; s 9, 6, 7f (opp. τετράγωνος); 9, 9, 1; 2 (opp. τετρ.); 9, 29, 4a, b; 9, 30, 4. B. 904.*

στρουθίον, ου, τό (Aristot. et al.; LXX; Jos., Bell. 5, 467) dim. of στρουθός *sparrow* as an example of an article that has little value Mt 10: 29, 31; Lk 12: 6f. But Vi. Aesopi I c. 26 expresses the opinion that the στρουθία πολλοῦ πωλεῖται (s. Perry's note and the saying of Aesop there).—Dssm., LO 234f (LAE 272ff); HGrimme, BZ 23, '35, 260–2. M-M.*

στρωννύω=στρώννυμι impf. ἐστρώννυον; 1 aor. ἔστρωσα; pf. pass. ptc. ἐστρωμένος (Bl-D. §92; Rob. 318.—Hom. [στορέννυμι, στόρνυμι], Aeschyl., X., Pla.; inscr., pap., LXX, Joseph.; Sib. Or. 5, 438) *spread (out)* τὶ someth. ἱμάτια κτλ. ἐν τῇ ὁδῷ Mt 21: 8a, b; also εἰς τὴν ὁδόν Mk 11: 8 (for the idea cf. 4 Km 9: 13; Jos., Ant. 9, 111 ὑπεστρώννυεν αὐτῷ τὸ ἱμάτιον). χιτῶνας χαμαί Hs 9, 11, 7. στρῶσον σεαυτῷ (i.e. τὴν κλίνην; στρ. is used w. this acc. in Eur., Pla., and Nicol. Dam.: 90 fgm. 44, 2 Jac.; Diod. S. 8, 32, 2; Dit., Syll.³ 687, 16; 1022, 1f τὴν κλίνην στρῶσαι τῷ Πλούτωνι. Cf. Ezk 23: 41; Jos., Ant. 7, 231 κλίνας ἐστρωμένας) *make your own bed* Ac 9: 34. ἀνάγαιον ἐστρωμένον may be a *paved upper room* (στρ. has this mng. in an inscr. APF 2, '03, 570 no. 150. So Luther to Zahn.—Jos., Ant. 8, 134 ἐστρωμένος means 'floored' or 'panelled'). Others prefer to take it as referring to a room *furnished* w. carpets or couches for the guests to recline on as they ate (EKlostermann, ELohmeyer; Field, Notes 39; somewhat as Plut., Artax. 22, 10; Artem. 2, 57 codd. Also Diod. S. 21, 12, 4; IG II 622 ἔστρωσεν refers to a couch at a meal; Dalman, Arbeit VII 185. Eng. transl. gener. prefer this sense.—PGM 1, 107 χώρημα στρῶσαι means to prepare a room for a banquet) Mk 14: 15; Lk 22: 12. M-M. B. 573.*

στυγητός, ή, όν (Aeschyl., Prom. 592; Philo, Dec. 131; Heliod. 5, 29, 4) *hated, hateful* Tit 3: 3; 1 Cl 35: 6; 45: 7. M-M.*

στυγνάζω 1 aor. ἐστύγνασα—1. *be shocked, appalled* (Ezk 27: 35; 28: 19; 32: 10 ἐπί τινα) so perh. στυγνάσας ἐπὶ τῷ λόγῳ Mk 10: 22 (s. 2a below).

2. *be* or *become gloomy, dark*—a. of a man whose appearance shows that he is sad or gloomy (PGM 13, 177; 494; schol. on Aeschyl., Pers. 470; schol. on Soph., Ant. 526; schol. on Apollon. Rhod. 2, 862f; Eustathius Macrembolita [c. 900 AD] 4, 1, 2 Hilberg 1876; Nicetas Eugen. 6, 286 H.) ἐπί τινι *at someth.*, so perh. Mk 10: 22 (s. 1 above).

b. of the appearance of the sky (s. στυγνός: Heraclit. Sto. 39 p. 56, 18) Mt 16: 3 (Cat. Cod. Astr. XI 2 p. 179, 19 is dependent on this). M-M.*

στυγνός, ή, όν *gloomy, sad* (so since Aeschyl.; X., An. 2, 6, 9. Also PSI 28, 1 στυγνοῦ σκότους; LXX; Jos., Ant. 19, 318) Hv 1, 2, 3.*

στῦλος, ου, ὁ (Aeschyl., Hdt.+; inscr., pap., LXX; Jos., Ant. 13, 211. On the accent s. KHALipsius, Gramm. Untersuchungen 1863 p. 43) *pillar, column* lit. στῦλοι πυρός (En. 18, 11; 21, 7; the sing. Ex 13: 21f; 14: 24) Rv 10: 1. Symbolically (Philo, Migr. Abr. 124) ποιήσω αὐτὸν στ. ἐν τῷ ναῷ τοῦ θεοῦ *I will make him a pillar in the temple of God* 3: 12 (στῦλοι in the temple 3 Km 7: 3= Jos., Ant. 8, 77). Hence fig. of the leaders of the Jerusalem church: James, Cephas, John Gal 2: 9 (cf. Eur., Iph. Taur. 57 στῦλοι οἴκων εἰσὶ παῖδες ἄρσενες. Vi. Aesopi I c. 106 Aesop is called ὁ κίων [pillar] τῆς βασιλείας. Cf. CKBarrett, Studia Paulina '53, 1–19; RAnnand, ET 67, '56, 178 ['the markers' in a racecourse]). In 1 Cl 5: 2 the term is applied to the apostles and other leaders of the primitive church.—The church is στῦλος καὶ ἐδραίωμα τῆς ἀληθείας *support* (στ. is also used in this general sense Sir 24: 4; 36: 24) *and foundation of the truth* 1 Ti 3: 15. M-M.*

στύραξ, ακος, ὁ (X., Pla.+) lit. the spike at the butt end of a spear-shaft, then the *shaft, spear* itself; περὶ στύρακα MPol 16: 1 as a conjecture instead of the ms. rdg. περιστερὰ καί (s. περιστερά, end).*

Στωϊκός s. Στοϊκός. M-M.

σύ (Hom.+; inscr., pap., LXX, En., Ep. Arist., Philo, Joseph., Sib. Or.) personal pron. of the second pers. σοῦ (σου), σοί (σοι), σέ (σε); pl. ὑμεῖς, ὑμῶν, ὑμῖν, ὑμᾶς: *you* (older and more formal sing. *thou*).

1. the nominative—a. in contrast to another pers. ἐγώ —σύ Mt 3: 14; 26: 39; Mk 14: 36; J 13: 7; Js 2: 18; cf. Lk 17: 8. σὺ—ἕτερος Mt 11: 3. πᾶς ἄνθρωπος—σύ J 2: 10. Μωϋσῆς—σὺ οὖν 8: 5. οὐδεὶς—σύ 3: 2 and oft. αὐτοὶ—σύ Hb 1: 11 (Ps 101: 27). ἐγώ—ὑμεῖς or vice versa J 7: 34, 36; 8: 15, 22f; 13: 15; 15: 5 al.; Gal 4: 12. ὑμεῖς—ἡμεῖς or vice versa J 4: 22; 1 Cor 4: 10a, b, c; 2 Cor 13: 9.—The contrast is evident fr. the context: Mt 6: 6, 17; Ro 2: 3. ὑμεῖς Mt 5: 48; 6: 9, 26b.—On σὺ λέγεις Mt 27: 11; Mk 15: 2; Lk 23: 3 cf. λέγω II 1e.

b. for emphasis before a voc. σὺ Βηθλεέμ Mt 2: 6 (Mi 5: 1). σὺ παιδίον (Lucian, Dial. Deor. 2, 1) Lk 1: 76. σὺ κύριε Ac 1: 24. σὺ δὲ ὦ ἄνθρωπε θεοῦ 1 Ti 6: 11. ὑμεῖς οἱ Φαρισαῖοι Lk 11: 39.

c. used w. a noun or ptc., by which the pron. is more exactly defined σὺ Ἰουδαῖος ὤν *you as a Jew* J 4: 9; cf. Gal 2: 14. ὑμεῖς πονηροὶ ὄντες Mt 7: 11.—Esp. emphasizing the subj.: σὺ τρίς με ἀπαρνήσῃ *you are the very one who will deny me three times* Mk 14: 30. δότε αὐτοῖς ὑμεῖς φαγεῖν *you yourselves are to give them someth. to eat* Mt 14: 16. Cf. J 13: 6; 17: 8; 20: 15. εὐλογημένη σὺ ἐν γυναιξὶν Lk 1: 42. σὺ μόνος παροικεῖς 24: 18. So freq. w. forms of εἰμί: σὺ εἶ ὁ Χριστός Mt 16: 16. σὺ εἶ Πέτρος vs. 18. σὺ εἶ ὁ βασιλεὺς τῶν Ἰουδαίων; 27: 11. καὶ σύ *you, too* 26: 69, 73; Lk 19: 19; 22: 58; Gal 6: 1. καὶ ὑμεῖς Mt 7: 12; 15: 3, 16; Lk 17: 10. σὺ δέ *but you* Lk 9: 60; Ro 11: 17; 2 Ti 3: 10. ὑμεῖς δέ Mt 21: 13; Js 2: 6.

d. pleonastically added to forms that are clear enough by themselves (Semitism? Cf. Bl-D. §277, 2; cf. Mlt.-H. 431f) σὺ τί λέγεις Mk 14: 68. μὴ φοβεῖσθε ὑμεῖς Mt 28: 5. μὴ ἀνελεῖν με σὺ θέλεις; Ac 7: 28 (Ex 2: 14). ὑμεῖς Mt 5: 13f.

2. The accented forms are used in the oblique cases of the sing. when emphasis is to be laid on the pron. or when a contrast is intended σοῦ δὲ αὐτῆς τὴν ψυχήν Lk 2: 35. οὐ σὺ ῥίζαν βαστάζεις ἀλλὰ ἡ ῥίζα σέ Ro 11: 18. καὶ σέ

Phil 4: 3. The accented forms also appear without special emphasis when used w. prepositions (Bl-D. §279; Mlt.-H. 180) ἐν σοί Mt 6: 23. ἐπὶ σέ Lk 1: 35. μετὰ σοῦ vs. 28. σὺν σοί Mt 26: 35 (but πρός σε Mt 14: 28; 25: 39; cf. ἐγώ).

3. σου and ὑμῶν as substitutes for the possessive pron. (as well as for the gen. of the reflexives σεαυτοῦ and ὑμῶν αὐτῶν) come after the word they modify: τὴν γυναῖκά σου Mt 1: 20. τὸν πόδα σου 4: 6 (Ps 90: 12). ἡ πίστις ὑμῶν Ro 1: 8; τὰ μέλη ὑμῶν 6: 19; or before the word they modify: ἀρόν σου τὴν κλίνην Mt 9: 6. ἀφέωνταί σου αἱ ἁμαρτίαι Lk 7: 48. μηδείς σου τῆς νεότητος καταφρονείτω 1 Ti 4: 12; or betw. the noun and the art.: διὰ τῆς ὑμῶν δεήσεως Phil 1: 19. εἰς τὴν ὑμῶν προκοπήν vs. 25. —On τί ἐμοὶ καὶ σοί; cf. ἐγώ, end; on τί ἡμῖν κ. σοί; cf. τίς 1bε. M-M.

συγγένεια, ας, ἡ (Eur., Thu.+; inscr., pap., LXX; Ep. Arist. 241; Philo; Jos., Bell. 7, 204 ἐκ μεγάλης σ., Ant. 1, 165) *relationship, kinship,* concr. the *relatives* (Eur., Pla.+; LXX) Lk 1: 61; Ac 7: 3; 1 Cl 10: 2f (the two last Gen 12: 1); Ac 7: 14 (Diod. S. 16, 52, 3 μετεπέμψατο ἀμφοτέρους μεθ' ὅλης τῆς συγγενείας; 34+35 fgm. 23). M-M.*

συγγενεῦσιν s. the following entry.

συγγενής, ές *related, akin to* (Pind., Thu.+; inscr., pap., LXX, Philo, Joseph.) in our lit. only subst. In the sing. masc. (Jos., Vi. 177) J 18: 26 and fem. (Menand., fgm. 929 K.; Jos., Ant. 8, 249) Lk 1: 36 t.r. Predom. pl. οἱ συγγενεῖς (the dat. of this form, made on the analogy of γονεῖς—γονεῦσιν, is συγγενεῦσιν [a Pisidian inscr.: JHS 22, '02, p. 358 no. 118; 1 Macc 10: 89 v.l.] Mk 6: 4; Lk 2: 44 [both passages have συγγενέσιν as v.l., like Diod. S. 1, 92, 1; Dit., Or. 177, 7 (97/6 bc); UPZ 161, 21 (119 bc); PTebt. 61, 79; 1 Macc 10: 89, text; Jos., Vi. 81, Ant. 16, 382]; Bl-D. §47, 4 w. app.; Mlt.-H. 138; Thackeray 153) Lk 2: 44; 21: 16. W. a gen. (Bl-D. §194, 2) Mk 6: 4; Lk 1: 58; 14: 12; Ac 10: 24.—In the broader sense *fellow-countryman, fellow-citizen* of members of the same nation (Jos., Bell. 7, 262, Ant. 12, 338) οἱ συγγενεῖς μου κατὰ σάρκα Ro 9: 3; cf. 16: 7, 11, 21. M-M. B. 132.*

συγγενικός, ή, όν (Hippocr., Aristot.+; inscr.) *related, kindred, of the same kind* (Diog. L. 10, 129 [Epicurus]; Plut., Mor. 561B, Pericl. 22, 4, Themist. 5, 2; Vett. Val. index; Herm. Wr. 440, 6 Sc.; Ep. Arist. 147; Philo) τὸ συγγενικὸν ἔργον *the task so well suited to you* IEph 1: 1.*

συγγενίς, ίδος, ἡ (Plut., Mor. 267D; Charito 5, 3, 7; Suppl. Epigr. Gr. IV 452, 4; Bull. de corr. hell. 24 ['00] 340, 17; OBenndorf-GNiemann, Reisen I 1884 no. 53 E, 3; Dit., Or. index VIII [of cities]; PAmh. 78, 9 [II AD]; Mitteis, Chrest. 123, 9; StBPsaltes, Gramm. der byz. Chroniken '13, 152), a peculiar fem. of συγγενής, rejected by the Atticists (Ps.-Herodian in Lob., Phryn. p. 451f): ἡ σ. the *(female) relative, kinswoman* Lk 1: 36.— Bl-D. §59, 3 w. app.; Mlt.-H. 131. M-M.*

συγγινώσκω 2 aor. συνέγνων (trag., Hdt.+; inscr., pap., LXX; Jos., C. Ap. 1, 218) *think with (someone), have the same opinion, purpose,* or *wish, agree* (Hdt. et al.; BGU 341, 4; 432 III, 8) w. dat. of the pers., esp. of understanding and forbearance for someone (Simonides, fgm. 13, 20f Ζεῦ . . . ὅτι θαρσαλέον ἔπος εὔχομαι . . . , σύγγνωθί μοι= because I am using a bold word in my prayer, grant me your understanding; Philo, Mos. 1, 173; Jos., Vi. 103; Test. Sim. 3, 6) σύγγνωτέ μοι *agree with* *me, understand my position* IRo 6: 2.—Another possibility is *forgive* or *pardon me* (Soph.+; Mod. Gk.).*

συγγνώμη, ης, ἡ (Soph., Hdt.+; inscr., pap., LXX, Ep. Arist., Philo; Jos., Vi. 227) *concession, indulgence, pardon* συγγνώμην ἔχειν *pardon, be indulgent to* τινί *someone* (Soph., Hdt.+; Zen.-P. 81 [= Sb 6787], 36 [257 BC] συγγνώμην ἡμῖν ἔχων; without dat., Himerius, Or. 36, 17 [= Ecl. 36, 14]; Sir Prol. l. 18 and 3: 13; Ep. Arist. 295) συγγνώμην μοι ἔχετε IRo 5: 3. τοῦτο λέγω κατὰ συγγνώμην οὐ κατ' ἐπιταγήν *I say this as a concession* (to meet you half way), *not as a command* 1 Cor 7: 6. M-M.*

συγγνωμονέω *make allowance for, pardon* w. dat. (Sext. Emp., Math. 1, 126; Athen. 4 p. 177D; 4 Macc 5: 13; Jos., Ant. 11, 144) *pardon* τινί *someone* (Ps.-Callisth. 1, 40, 5 συγγνωμονέω ὡς θεὸς ἀνθρώποις) ITr 5: 1.*

σύγγραμμα, ατος, τό (Hdt.+) *writing, book, work* (X., Mem. 2, 1, 21; 4, 2, 10; Pla., Ep. 2 p. 314c; Philo, Vi. Cont. 29; Jos., C. Ap. 1, 44; 2, 288) Epil Mosq 1a, b, 3, 4.*

συγγραφή, ῆς, ἡ (Heraclitus, fgm. 129; Hdt.+; inscr., pap., LXX; Jos., C. Ap. 1, 129) *document, contract* (Thu.+; oft. in inscr., pap.) ἄδικον συγγραφὴν διασπᾶν *tear up an unjust contract* B 3: 3 (Is 58: 6).*

συγγράφω 1 aor. mid. συνεγραψάμην (Hdt.+; inscr., pap.) *write down, compose* mid. Papias 2: 16.*

συγκάθημαι (Hdt.+; Sb 6796, 98 [Zen.-P. 258/7 BC]; Jos., Ant. 16, 362) *sit with* τινί *someone* (Wilcken, Chrest. 14 II, 5; 13 [I AD] συγκαθημένων αὐτῷ [τῷ Καίσαρι] συγκλητικῶν) ὁ βασιλεὺς ... καὶ οἱ συγκαθήμενοι αὐτοῖς Ac 26: 30. Also μετά τινος (Ps 100: 6) Mk 14: 54. M-M.*

συγκαθίζω 1 aor. συνεκάθισα—1. trans. *cause to sit down with* ἡμᾶς ... συνεκάθισεν ἐν τοῖς ἐπουρανίοις he (God) *made us sit down with* (Christ) *in heaven* Eph 2: 6.
2. intr. *sit down with others* (Gen 15: 11; Ex 18: 13; 1 Esdr 9: 6. The mid. so X.+) Lk 22: 55.*

συγκακοπαθέω 1 aor. imper. συγκακοπάθησον (schol. on Eur., Hecub. 203) *suffer together with someone* abs. συγκακοπάθησον ὡς καλὸς στρατιώτης *suffer hardship* (with me) *as a good soldier* 2 Ti 2: 3. συγκακοπάθησον τῷ εὐαγγελίῳ (dat. of advantage) *join with* (me, the apostle in prison) *in suffering for the gospel* 1: 8.*

συγκακουχέομαι (hapax legomenon) *suffer* or *be mistreated with someone else* τῷ λαῷ τοῦ θεοῦ *with God's people* Hb 11: 25. M-M.*

συγκαλέω 1 aor. συνεκάλεσα, mid. συνεκαλεσάμην *call together*—1. act. (Hom.+; Dit., Syll.³ 1185, 15; PLond. 1711, 53; LXX; Jos., Ant. 7, 363; 18, 279) foll. by acc. (Arrian, An. Alex. 6, 22, 2 σ. τὸ πλῆθος) Mk 15: 16; Lk 15: 6, 9; Ac 5: 21; 1 Cl 43: 5.
2. mid. (Hdt. 2, 160; 2 Macc 15: 31) *call to one's side, summon* (Bl-D. §316, 1) foll. by the acc. Lk 9: 1; 15: 6 v.l., 9 t.r.; 23: 13; Ac 5: 21 D; 10: 24; 13: 7 D; 28: 17; Hs 5, 2, 11. M-M.*

συγκαλύπτω pf. pass. ptc. συγκεκαλυμμένος (Hom.+; Dit., Syll.³ 1170, 6; BGU 1816, 19 [I BC]; PGM 36, 270; 272; LXX; Jos., Ant. 9, 209; Test. Napht. 9: 2) *cover* (completely), *conceal* (opp. ἀποκαλύπτω) pass. Lk 12: 2. M-M.*

συγκάμπτω 1 aor. συνέκαμψα (Hippocr., X., Pla.+;

Dit., Syll.³ 1168, 28 συγκάμψας τὰν χῆρα; LXX) (cause to) *bend* τὸν νῶτον αὐτῶν σύγκαμψον *cause their back(s) to bend* Ro 11: 10 (Ps 68: 24). M-M.*

συγκαταβαίνω 2 aor. ptc. συγκαταβάς *go down with someone* fr. a high place to a lower one (Aeschyl., Thu.+; LXX; Philo, Abr. 105; Jos., Bell. 6, 132), fr. Jerusalem to Caesarea by the sea Ac 25: 5. M-M.*

συγκατάθεσις, εως, ἡ (= 'approval, assent': Polyb. 2, 58, 11; 21, 26, 16; Dionys. Hal. 8, 79; Epict. and oft.; incl. Dit., Or. 448, 32; pap.; Philo, Poster. Cai. 175) *agreement, union* (of a decision arrived at by a group, an agreement BGU 194, 11; 19; PGenève 42, 21; PFlor. 58, 8 al.) τίς σ. ναῷ θεοῦ μετὰ εἰδώλων; *what agreement is there betw. the temple of God and idols?* 2 Cor 6: 16. M-M.*

συγκατανεύω 1 aor. συγκατένευσα *agree, consent* by a nod (Polyb. 3, 52, 6; 7, 4, 9 al.; Jos., Vi. 22; 124. Abs., Anth. Pal. 5, 286, 8) Ac 18: 27 D.*

συγκατατάσσω 1 aor. inf. συγκατατάξαι (X.+; inscr.) *set down* (= *write*) *along with* τινί *someth.* Papias 2: 3.*

συγκατατίθημι nearly always, and in our lit. and the LXX always, mid. συγκατατίθεμαι (Isaeus, Demosth.+; Dit., Syll.³ 742, 52f, Or. 437, 43; pap.; Ex 23: 1, 32; Sus 20 Theod.) *agree with, consent to* (lit. 'put down the same vote as') τινί *something* (Demosth. 18, 166; Epict. 1, 28, 4; 2, 8, 24; Jos., Ant. 8, 166; 20, 13 τ. γνώμῃ) Lk 23: 51 (the rdg. varies betw. the pres. and the perf. ptc.); Ac 4: 18 D; 15: 12 D; *find oneself in agreement* τινί *with someth.* IPhld 3: 3. M-M.*

συγκαταψηφίζομαι 1 aor. pass. συγκατεψηφίσθην (found only in one other place, Plut., Them. 21, 7, where it is a mid. dep. = 'join in a vote of condemnation') pass. *be chosen* (by a vote) *together with*, then more gener. *be added* μετὰ τῶν ἕνδεκα ἀποστόλων *to the eleven apostles* Ac 1: 26. M-M.*

σύγκειμαι (Soph., Hdt.+; Dit., Syll.³ 633, 25 [180 BC]; pap., LXX; Jos., C. Ap. 1, 112; 198) *recline together* (Soph., Aj. 1309) for συνανάκειμαι (q.v.) Mt 9: 10 D.*

συγκεράννυμι (Aeschyl., Hdt.+; Dit., Syll.³ 783, 32; LXX, Philo) 1 aor. συνεκέρασα; pf. pass. ptc. συγκερασμένος Hb 4: 2 or συγκεκραμένος t.r. (Bl-D. §101 p. 46; Mlt.-H. 243); plpf. 3 sing. συνεκέρατο AP 3: 9; *mix* (together), *blend, unite.*
1. lit., pass., of colors AP 3: 9.—2. fig. (Maximus Tyr. 16, 4f of the powers granted the soul by God) τὸ σῶμα *compose the body* (by unifying its members so as to form one organism) 1 Cor 12: 24. συγκεράσαι ὑμῶν τὴν φρόνησιν ἐπὶ τὸ αὐτό *unite your wisdom harmoniously* Hv 3, 9, 8. οὐκ ὠφέλησεν ὁ λόγος τῆς ἀκοῆς ἐκείνους μὴ συγκεκερασμένος τῇ πίστει τοῖς ἀκούσασιν *the word which they heard did not benefit them, because it was not united by faith* (dat. of instrum.; cf. Bl-D. §202 app.) *with the hearers* Hb 4: 2. Instead of the sing. συγκεκερασμένος (as in א, 𝔓⁴⁶ 𝔓¹³ ABCD have the acc. pl. συγκεκερασμένους, prob. = (those) *who were not united with those who heard it in faith.* (Libanius, Ep. 571 t. X 536 F. συγκεράννυ τῷ νεανίσκῳ σαυτόν). M-M.*

συγκινέω 1 aor. συνεκίνησα; impf. pass. συνεκινούμην *set in motion* pass. *be set in motion* (Herm. Wr. 2, 6b; Epict. Ench. 33, 10) τὰ πάντα συνεκινεῖτο *everything was set in commotion* IEph 19: 3 (cf. Philo, Dec. 44 πάντα συγκεκινῆσθαι). τινά *arouse someone* Ac 6: 12. M-M.*

συγκλάω fut. συγκλάσω (Aristoph., Pla.+; PAmsterdam 1, 8 [455 AD]: PGroninganae, Verh. Kon. Akad. v. Wetensch. '33; LXX) *shatter* τὶ *someth.* bars B 11: 4 (Is 45: 2).*

συγκλεισμός, οῦ, ὁ (pap., LXX) *confinement, encirclement* (Ezk 4: 3, 7, 8; 5: 2; 1 Macc 6: 21) ἐν συγκλεισμῷ οὔσης τῆς πόλεως *when the city was being besieged* 1 Cl 55: 4; cf. vs. 5.*

συγκλείω 1 aor. συνέκλεισα (Eur., Hdt.+; inscr., pap., LXX; Jos., Vi. 74, Ant. 12, 328) *close up together, hem in, enclose.*
   1. lit. τὶ *someth.* fish in a net (Aristot., Hist. An. 533b, 26; Ael. Aristid. 32 p. 606 D.) Lk 5: 6.
   2. fig. *confine, imprison* τινὰ εἴς τι (Polyb. 3, 63, 3 εἰς ἀγῶνα; Diod. S. 19, 19, 8 εἰς τοιαύτην ἀμηχανίαν συγκλεισθείς Ἀντίγονος μετεμέλετο; Herm. Wr. 500, 8 Sc.; Ps 30: 9 οὐ συνέκλεισάς με εἰς χεῖρας ἐχθροῦ, 77: 50 τὰ κτήνη εἰς θάνατον συνέκλεισεν. Cf. in the literal sense PFay. 12, 17 [II BC] συνκλείσαντές με εἰς τὴν οἰκίαν) of God συνέκλεισεν τοὺς πάντας εἰς ἀπείθειαν *he has imprisoned them all in disobedience,* i.e. put them under compulsion to be disobedient or given them over to disobedience Ro 11: 32. τὶ ὑπό τι: συνέκλεισεν ἡ γραφὴ τὰ πάντα ὑπὸ ἁμαρτίαν *the Scripture* (i.e. God's will as expressed in the Scripture) *has imprisoned everything under the power of sin* Gal 3: 22; cf. vs. 23. M-M.*

συγκληρονόμος, ον *inheriting together with,* mostly subst. (Philo, Ad Gai. 67; inscr. [The Coll. of Ancient Gk. Inscr. in the Brit. Mus. III no. 633 p. 249: Ephesus; inscr. on a sarcophagus fr. Thessalonica: Mitteil. des Deutsch. Arch. Instit. Ath., Abt. 21, 1896, 98; Suppl. Epigr. Gr. VIII 91, 3 [II AD] ἀδελφὸς καὶ σ.]; PLond. 1686, 35 and other pap. of Byz. times) Eph 3: 6. Foll. by objective gen. of the thing Hb 11: 9; 1 Pt 3: 7. Foll. by gen. of the pers. w. whom one is inheriting σ. Χριστοῦ *fellow-heir with Christ* Ro 8: 17. W. dat. of the pers. w. whom one inherits Hs 5, 2, 7f; 11. M-M.*

συγκοιμάομαι pass. dep. (Aeschyl.+) 1 aor. pass. συνεκοιμήθην *sleep with* τινί *someone* of sexual intercourse (trag., Hdt.; En. 9, 8) AP 17: 32. Before συνεγείρεσθε and after συμπάσχετε, συγκοιμᾶσθε is prob. a euphemism *suffer together, die together, rise together* IPol 6: 1 (on the series of compounds w. σύν, among them συγκοιμ., cf. Epict. 2, 22, 13).*

συγκοινωνέω 1 aor. συνεκοινώνησα (Hippocr.+)—1. *participate in* with someone, *be connected* τινί *with someth.* (Herm. Wr. 1, 28 τῇ ἀγνοίᾳ; w. gen. of the thing Demosth. 57, 2; τινί τινος='w. someone in someth.' Cass. Dio 37, 41; 77, 16) in the sense of actually taking part Eph 5: 11; Rv 18: 4. In the sense of taking a sympathetic interest Phil 4: 14.
   2. *share* τί τινι *someth.* w. *someone* συγκοινωνεῖν πάντα τῷ ἀδελφῷ *share everything with one's brother* D 4: 8.*

συγκοινωνός, οῦ, ὁ *participant, partner* (PBilabel 19, 2 [110 AD]; Maspéro 158, 11 of business partners οἱ συγκοινωνοί μου) w. gen. of the thing in which one shares (Stephan. of Athens, in Hippocr. 1, 76 Dietz [1834] συγκοινωνὸς τῆς βασιλείας μου) Ro 11: 17. ἵνα συγκ. αὐτοῦ (i.e. τοῦ εὐαγγελίου) γένωμαι *that I might jointly share in it* (i.e., in the benefits promised by the gospel; differently EMolland, D. paul. Euangelion '34, 53f: 'fellow-worker in the gospel [Mitarbeiter des Evan.]') 1 Cor 9: 23. συγκοινωνοί μου τῆς χάριτος *sharers of the same*

grace as myself Phil 1: 7. Also συγκ. τινος ἔν τινι *sharer with someone in someth.* Rv 1: 9.—MPol 17: 3 Funk v.l. M-M.*

συγκομίζω 1 aor. συνεκόμισα, pass. συνεκομίσθην—
   1. *bring in* of the harvest (so Hdt.+, in the act. [cf. also Jos., Ant. 14, 472], and the mid. X.+, oft. in pap.) pass. θημωνιὰ ἅλωνος καθ' ὥραν συγκομισθεῖσα *a heap of sheaves on the threshing-floor, brought in* (to the barn) *at the right time* 1 Cl 56: 15 (Job 5: 26).
   2. *bury* (Soph., Aj. 1048; Plut., Sulla 38, 5) τινά *someone* Ac 8: 2. M-M.*

συγκοπή, ῆς, ἡ (Dionys. Hal., Comp. Verb. 15; 22; Peripl. Eryth. c. 6; Plut.; POxy. 1654, 6 [II AD]) *cutting to pieces, mangling* σ. μελῶν IRo 5: 3.*

συγκοπιάω (schol. on Eur., Hecuba 862; Suppl. Epigr. Gr. VI 473 [IV AD]) *labor together* τινί *with someone* τῷ πνεύματι *with the Spirit* Hs 5, 6, 6. συγκοπιᾶτε ἀλλήλοις *unite your efforts* IPol 6: 1.*

συγκόπτω fut. συγκόψω; 2 aor. pass. συνεκόπην (Eur., Hdt.+; inscr., pap., LXX; Sib. Or. 3, 188; 613) *break up, break to pieces.*
   1. lit. (X., Cyr. 6, 4, 3; PSI 630, 20; 4 Km 24: 13) stones Hv 3, 6, 1.—2. fig. *destroy* (Lucian, Cal. 1) τὴν δύναμιν τοῦ διαβόλου *break the power of the devil* Hm 12, 6, 4. Pass., of a depressed frame of mind *be overcome* ἀπὸ τῆς λύπης *by grief* Hv 5: 4.*

σύγκρασις, εως, ἡ (Eur., Pla.+; Cornutus 8 p. 8, 15; Vett. Val.; Herm. Wr. 11, 7; PGM 7, 512; Ezk 22: 19) *mixture, blending* 1 Cl 37: 4.*

συγκρατέω fut. συγκρατήσω; 1 aor. pass. συνεκρατήθην (Plut. et al.; Sym. Ps 16: 5; Jos., Ant. 8, 67) *hold together* w. acc. (Anaximenes [VI BC] 2 Diels: ἡ ψυχὴ συγκρατεῖ ἡμᾶς) Hs 9, 7, 5. *Surround* and protect τὸν λαόν Hs 5, 5, 3; cf. 9, 12, 8.—*Support, hold upright* (cf. Aretaeus, 1, 5; 7; 40, 29 Hude ὕπνος συγκ. τὰ μέλεα; Geopon., Prooem. 6) pass., of a sick man ἵνα συγκρατηθῇ ἡ ἀσθένεια τοῦ σώματος αὐτοῦ *that his weak body might find support* Hv 3, 11, 4.*

συγκρίνω 1 aor. συνέκρινα (since Epicharmus [V BC] in Plut., Mor. 110A; inscr., pap., LXX).
   1. *bring together, combine* (Epicharmus+; Pla.; Aristot., Metaph. 1, 4 p. 985a, 24) so perh. πνευματικοῖς (neut.) πνευματικὰ συγκρίνοντες *giving spiritual truth a spiritual form* (Gdspd., Lghtf., BWeiss, Bousset) 1 Cor 2: 13 (s. 2b and 3 below).
   2. *compare* (Aristot.+; Polyb., Diod. S., Dionys. Hal., Epict., Philo; Jos., Ant. 5, 77 al.)—a. τινά τινι *someone with someone* (Diod. S. 4, 44, 6; cf. CIG 5002 ὁ ἱερεὺς . . ., πατὴρ τῶν ἱερέων, ᾧ οὐδεὶς τῶν ἱερέων συγκρίνεται; Philo, Ebr. 45) ἑαυτόν τινι *oneself with someone* (Plut., G. Gracch. 4, 6) 2 Cor 10: 12a, b.
   b. 1 Cor 2: 13 (s. 1 above and 3 below) may also be classified here: *comparing the spiritual gifts and revelations* (which we already possess) *with the spiritual gifts and revelations* (which we are to receive, and judging them thereby; cf. Maximus Tyr. 6, 4a)—so Rtzst., Mysterienrel.³ 336; Ltzm., Hdb. ad loc.; Field, Notes 168.
   3. *explain, interpret* (Polyb. 14, 3, 7; Gen 40: 8, 16, 22; 41: 12f, 15; Da 5: 12 Theod.) πνευματικοῖς (masc.) πνευματικὰ συγκρίνοντες *interpreting spiritual truths to those who possess the Spirit* 1 Cor 2: 13 (s. 1 and 2b above) —so RSV text, PWSchmiedel, Heinrici, JSickenberger.— FBlass and JWeiss propose emendation of the text. M-M.*

συγκύπτω (Hdt., Aristoph. +; LXX) *be bent over* (Sir 12: 11; 19: 26; Celsus 4, 36) of a woman possessed by a spirit of illness ἦν συγκύπτουσα *she was bent double* Lk 13: 11.*

συγκυρία, ας, ἡ (Hippocr.: CMG I 1 p. 42, 16; Sym. 1 Km 6: 9; Hesychius) *coincidence, chance* κατὰ συγκυρίαν *by coincidence* (Eustath., In Il. 3, 23 p. 376, 11) Lk 10: 31 (συγτυχείαν = συντυχείαν 𝔓⁷⁵ᶜ; τύχᾳ D). M-M.*

συγχαίρω impf. συνέχαιρον; fut. συγχαρήσομαι; aor. συνεχάρην (Aeschyl., X. +; inscr., pap., LXX).
1. *rejoice with, feel joy with* τινί *someone* (Aristot., Eth. Nic. 1166a, 8; UPZ 148, 3 [II вс]; BGU 1080, 2; Philo, Det. Pot. Ins. 124) Lk 1: 58; Phil 2: 17f (s. also 2 below); ITr 1: 1. συνεχάρην ὑμῖν μεγάλως *I rejoiced with you from the bottom of my heart* Pol 1: 1. τινί foll. by ὅτι *rejoice w. someone because* (Socrat., Ep. 33, 2; PLond. 43, 3f [II AD]) Lk 15: 6, 9. Without dat., which is easily supplied (X., Hiero 5, 4) 1 Cor 12: 26 (symbolically: the 'parts' stand for the believers).—τινί *over* or *because of someth.* (Herm. Wr. 1, 26.—In this case the compound has the same mng. as the simple verb, as Jos., Ant. 15, 210 [opp. ἄχθεσθαι]) οὐ χαίρει ἐπὶ τῇ ἀδικίᾳ, συγχαίρει δὲ τῇ ἀληθείᾳ *it does not rejoice over injustice, but rejoices in the truth* 1 Cor 13: 6 (EFranz, ThLZ 87, '62, 795-8). Cf. Hs 8, 2, 7.
2. *congratulate* τινί *someone* (Aeschin. 2, 45 w. ὅτι foll.; Polyb. 29, 7, 4; 30, 10, 1 al.; Diod. S. 22, 13, 7; Plut., Mor. 231в; PTebt. 424, 5; cf. Jos., Ant. 8, 50) B 1: 3; IEph 9: 2; IPhld 10: 1; ISm 11: 2; Hs 5, 2, 6.—Lk 1: 58 and Phil 2: 17f could perh. be classed here as well. M-M.*

συγχέω (Hom. +; inscr., PGM 4, 3101; LXX, Philo, Joseph.), and beside it the Hellenistic συγχύν(ν)ω (Bl-D. §73; 101; Mlt.-H. 195; 214f; 265; W-S. §15; Thackeray §19, 2; 24) Ac 21: 31 συγχύννεται, v.l. συγχύνεται; Hv 5: 5 συγχύνου; impf. συνέχεον Ac 21: 27 (cf. W-S. §13, 13 note 13) aor. συνέχυννεν; 1 aor. συνέχεα Ac 21: 27 v.l. Pass.: pf. συγκέχυμαι; 1 aor. συνεχύθην; lit. 'pour together', then *confuse, confound, trouble, stir up* w. acc. (Eunap., Vi. Soph. p. 44 Boiss. ἅπαντα; Philo, Mut. Nom. 72 τ. ψυχήν, Spec. Leg. 1, 328 πάντα; Jos., Ant. 11, 140) πάντα τὸν ὄχλον Ac 21: 27. Pass. *be in confusion* (PGM 13, 874) 19: 29 D, 32. ὅλη συγχύννεται Ἱερουσαλήμ 21: 31.—*Confound, throw into consternation* w. acc. Ac 9: 22. Pass. *be amazed, surprised, excited, agitated* (Diod. S. 4, 62, 3 συνεχύθη τὴν ψυχήν = he became distraught in spirit; Phlegon: 257 fgm. 36, 1, 5 Jac.; Achilles Tat. 5, 17, 7; 1 Km 7: 10; Jo 2: 1; Jos., Bell. 2, 230, Ant. 8, 199; 12, 317) 2: 6; Hv 5: 4f; m 12, 4, 1f. M-M.*

συγχράομαι mid. dep. (Polyb. +; inscr., pap.) inf. συγχρᾶσθαι IMg 3: 1—1. *make use of* w. dat. of the thing that one makes use of (Polyb. 1, 8, 1; Epict. 1, 16, 10; 2, 19, 1; Ep. Arist. 162; 266 al.; Dit., Syll.³ 685, 45; BGU 1187, 22 [I вс]), also in the sense *take advantage of* τῇ ἡλικίᾳ τοῦ ἐπισκόπου *the bishop's youth* IMg 3: 1.
2. *have dealings with, associate on friendly terms with* τινί *someone* (Ps.-Demetr., Eloc. c. 281; Diogenes Oenoand. [II AD], fgm. 64 W.; Ps.-Callisth. 2, 19, 3 συγχρησάμενός μοι = 'associating with me'; Ps.-Clem., Hom. 9, 22) οὐ συγχρῶνται Ἰουδαῖοι Σαμαρίταις (s. Σαμαρίτης) J 4: 9 (DDaube, JBL 69, '50, 137-47 prefers 'use [vessels for food and drink] together' and discusses the pass. fr. Diogenes Oenoand., also IMg 3: 1). M-M.*

συγχρωτίζομαι (Hecato on Zeno the Stoic in Diog. L. 7, 2; Herm. Wr. 10, 17) *be in defiling contact with, defile by touching* τινός Dg 12: 8.*

συγχύν(ν)ω s. συγχέω. M-M.

σύγχυσις, εως, ἡ (Eur., Thu. +; Jos., Bell. 4, 129, Ant. 16, 75; inscr., pap., LXX) *confusion, tumult* (Diod. S. 1, 75, 2; 20, 9, 5 συγχύσεως τὴν πόλιν ἐχούσης; Chio, Ep. 1; Philo; Jos., Bell. 2, 294 σύγχυσις εἶχεν τὸν δῆμον; 4, 125; Sib. Or. 8, 81) ἐπλήσθη ἡ πόλις τῆς συγχύσεως Ac 19: 29.*

συγχωρέω (trag., Hdt. +; inscr., pap., LXX)—1. *yield* τινί *to someone* (Thu. 1, 140, 5 al.) IMg 3: 1.
2. *grant, permit* τινί (to) *someone* (Bel 26; Jos., Ant. 3, 277) w. dat. and inf. (X., Cyr. 6, 3, 20; Diod. S. 38+39 fgm. 8, 1; Appian, Bell. Civ. 5, 62 §260; Jos., Ant. 11, 6) mid. Ac 21: 39 D. Pass. (Herm. Wr. 1, 13a) pf. συγκεχώρηται *it is granted* Dg 8: 6.*

συζάω (Aeschyl., Pla. et al.; Ep. Arist., Philo) fut. συζήσω (on the spelling συνζάω s. Bl-D. §19, 2 app.; Rob. 217; W-S. §5, 25) *live with* τινί *someone* (Demosth. 19, 69; Epigr. Gr. 1085, 2; Ep. Arist. 130) of living with a sinner Hm 4, 1, 9. Of the believer's life w. the exalted Lord Ro 6: 8 (s. σύμφυτος). Also μετά τινος (Demosth. 18, 314 v.l.; Plut., Pyrrh. 20, 4; Aristot., Eth. Nic. 8, 3 p. 1156a, 27 μετ᾽ ἀλλήλων) of living w. one's wife Hm 4, 1, 4f; w. heathen s 8, 9, 1; 3. Abs. (w. συναποθνῄσκειν as Athen. 6, 54 p. 249в τούτους [the bodyguards] οἱ βασιλεῖς ἔχουσι συζῶντας καὶ συναποθνῄσκοντας): the Corinthians have a place in Paul's heart εἰς τὸ συναποθανεῖν καὶ συζῆν *to live together and die together* 2 Cor 7: 3. The Christians die and live w. their Lord 2 Ti 2: 11. M-M.*

συζεύγνυμι 1 aor. συνέζευξα lit. *yoke together* (X., Cyr. 2, 2, 26), then gener. *join together, pair* (PGiess. 34, 3; Ezk 1: 11; Philo), specif. of matrimony (Eur. +; cf. X., Oec. 7, 30 νόμος συζευγνὺς ἄνδρα καὶ γυναῖκα; Aristot., H.A. 7, 6; Jos., Ant. 6, 309; PLond. 1727, 9) ὃ οὖν ὁ θεὸς συνέζευξεν Mt 19: 6; Mk 10: 9 (cf. the pagan counterpart in Nicetas Eugen. 3, 12; 7, 265 Hercher: two lovers οὓς θεὸς [a god] συνῆψε, τίς διασπάσοι;). M-M.*

συζητέω impf. συνεζήτουν (Pla. +; 2 Esdr 12: 4 v.l.)—
1. *discuss, carry on a discussion* περί τινος *about someth.* B 4: 10. Foll. by indir. question Mk 9: 10. Abs. 1: 27. ὁμιλεῖν καὶ συζητεῖν Lk 24: 15.
2. *dispute, debate, argue* τινί *with someone* (American Studies in Pap. 6, '70, 581, 9 ἀλλὰ καὶ συνζητήσαντό[ς] μου αὐτῶν περὶ τούτων [ca. 126-8 AD]; POxy. 532, 17; 1673, 20 [II AD] Mk 8: 11; 9: 14 t.r.; Ac 6: 9. Also πρός τινα Mk 9: 14, 16; Lk 22: 23 (w. τό and indir. quest.); Ac 9: 29. Abs. (Cyranides p. 10, 22) Mk 12: 28. συζητοῦντες ἀποθνῄσκουσιν *they are perishing while they dispute* ISm 7: 1.
3. *reflect, meditate* (in solitude) περί τινος Hs 6, 1, 1 (NT never has περί τινος w. συζητέω). Foll. by ὅτι 2: 1. M-M.*

συζήτησις, εως, ἡ (Cicero, Ad Fam. 16, 21, 4; Philo, Det. Pot. Ins. 1, Leg. All. 3, 131, Op. M. 54 v.l.) *dispute, discussion* (collection of Epicurean sayings: CBailey, Epicurus '26 p. 116, fgm. 74) Ac 15: 2 t.r., 7 t.r. πολλὴν ἔχοντες ἐν ἑαυτοῖς συζήτησιν *disputing vigorously among themselves* 28: 29 t.r. M-M.*

συζητητής, οῦ, ὁ (hapax legomenon) *disputant, debater* (s. συζήτησις and συζητέω 2) 1 Cor 1: 20 (= IEph 18: 1).*

σύζυγος, ον (Aeschyl. +; Aq. Ezk 23: 21). The corresp. subst. σύζυγος, ου, ὁ has not yet been found as a proper name (AFick²-FBechtel, Die griech. Personennamen 1894,

132), but only as a compound common noun (= 'brother', Eur., Tro. 1001;= 'comrade, companion' Eur., Iph. T. 250; Aristoph., Plut. 945; Anth. 8, 145; Magnet. Graffiti ed. Kern 321; 328 [I AD] σύζυγοι Βαίβιος Κάλλιπος; Herm. Wr. 6, 1b. In the same sense as Lat. commilito ['fellow-soldier'] of gladiators, each one of whom is his opponent's σύζυγος: RHerzog, Koische Forschungen u. Funde 1899 no. 133; CIG 4175.—Thieme 32) γνήσιε σύζυγε true comrade, lit. 'yoke-fellow' Phil 4: 3. It is no longer possible to determine w. certainty just whom the apostle has in mind (MDibelius; FTillmann.—Epaphroditus has been conjectured by some fr. Victorinus to Lghtf. and Zahn. JoachJeremias, NT Essays [TWManson memorial vol.] '59, 136–43, esp. 140 [Silas]). Since ἡ σύζυγος= 'wife' (Eur., Alc. 314; 342; Anth. 8, 161, 6; 164, 2; Syntipas p. 16, 9; 18, 6; Test. Reub. 4: 1), some have thought that Paul's wife is meant (since Clem. Alex., Strom. 3, 53, 1; Origen, Comm. in Ep. ad Rom. 1, 1). Lohmeyer considers it to mean a 'brother in suffering' who is sharing Paul's imprisonment. Finally, the idea that σ. is a proper name enjoys considerable support (RALipsius, EHaupt, PEwald, KBarth, GHeinzelmann, W-H. mg.). M-M.*

συζωοποιέω 1 aor. συνεζωοποίησα (only in Christian writers) *make alive together with someone* ἡμᾶς τῷ Χριστῷ *us together w. Christ* Eph 2: 5. ὑμᾶς σὺν αὐτῷ *you together w. him* (=Christ) Col 2: 13. The ref. is to people who were dead in their sins, but through union w. Christ have been made alive by God together w. him.*

συκάμινος, ου, ἡ (Theophr.; Phaenias in Athen. 2 p. 51ε; Diod. S. 1, 34, 8; Strabo 17, 2, 4; Diosc. 1, 23; inscr. fr. Sinuri [ed. LRobert '45] no. 47a, 13; BGU 492, 7; 9; PTebt. 343, 86 al. In LXX for שִׁקְמָה, the sycamore.—HLewy, Die semit. Fremdwörter bei den Griechen 1895, 23) *the mulberry tree,* which is evidently differentiated fr. the sycamore (s. συκομορέα) in Lk 17: 6 (cf. 19: 4), as well as in the ancient versions.—On the two kinds of trees, and on the question whether Lk may not have differentiated betw. them, cf. Löw (s. συκῆ; here also SKlein) I 266–74. M-M.*

συκῆ, ῆς, ἡ (Hom.+; inscr., pap., LXX; Jos., Bell. 3, 517, Ant. 5, 236f) *the fig tree,* much cultivated because of its sweet fruit, also growing wild Mt 24: 32; Mk 13: 28; Lk 13: 6f; 21: 29; J 1: 48, 50; Js 3: 12; Rv 6: 13 (cf. Is 34: 4). Jesus curses a fig tree Mt 21: 19–21; Mk 11: 13, 20f; s. WHvan deSandeBakhuyzen, NThT 7, '18, 330–8; FJFvanHasselt, NThSt 8, '25, 225–7; SHirsch, NThT 27, '38, 140–51; AdeQRobin, NTS 8, '61/'62, 276–81 (Mi 7: 1–6); H-WBartsch, ZNW 53, '62, 256–60.—On the fig tree s. HGraf zu Solms-Laubach, Die Herkunft usw. des gewöhnlichen Feigenbaums 1882; FGoldmann, La Figue en Palestine à l'époque de la Mišna '11; SKlein, Weinstock, Feigenbaum u. Sykomore in Palästina: Festschr. für ASchwarz '17; ILöw, D. Flora der Juden I '28, 224–54; WRauh u. HReznik, SBHdlbg. math.-nat. '51, Abh. 3, 164–74; CHHunzinger, TW VII, 751–9. M-M.*

συκομορέα, ας, ἡ (Hippiatr. II 165, 16; Geopon. 10, 3, 7. —Bl-D. §25; 45; Mlt.-H. 81. L. writes it συκομωρέα) *the fig-mulberry tree, sycamore fig* (s. συκάμινος) Lk 19: 4.—Cf. Löw (s. συκῆ) I 274–80. M-M.*

σῦκον, ου, τό (Hom.+; inscr., pap., LXX; Jos., Bell. 3, 519, Vi. 14) *the fig,* fruit of the fig tree (s. συκῆ), esp. *ripe fig* Mt 7: 16; Mk 11: 13; Lk 6: 44; Js 3: 12. M-M. B. 378.*

συκοφαντέω 1 aor. ἐσυκοφάντησα (Aristoph., X., Pla. +; pap., LXX, Philo; Jos., Bell. 1, 11, Ant. 10, 114, Vi. 52; Sib. Or. 2, 73).

1. *accuse falsely, slander,* then gener. *annoy, harass, oppress, blackmail* τινά *someone* (Pr 14: 31; 22: 16 πένητα; 28: 3 πτωχούς) w. διασείω (q.v. and cf. in addition Antipho, Or. 6, 43; UPZ 113, 9f [156 BC]; PTebt. 43, 26 συκοφαντηθῶμεν and 36 συκοφαντίας τε καὶ διασισμοῦ χάριν) Lk 3: 14.

2. *extort* (Lysias 26, 24 τὶ παρά τινος) εἴ τινός τι ἐσυκοφάντησα *if I have extorted anything from anyone* Lk 19: 8.—EbNestle, Sykophantia im bibl. Griech.: ZNW 4, '03, 271f.—On the derivation of the word s. L-S-J s.v. M-M.*

συλαγωγέω *carry off as booty* or *as a captive, rob* τινά *someone* (Heliod. 10, 35 p. 307, 32 Bekker οὗτός ἐστιν ὁ τὴν ἐμὴν θυγατέρα συλαγωγήσας; Aristaen. 2, 22 Hercher) fig. of carrying someone away fr. the truth into the slavery of error Col 2: 8. M-M.*

συλάω 1 aor. ἐσύλησα (Hom.+; inscr., pap.; EpJer 17; Jos., C. Ap. 2, 263) *rob* τινά *someone* as a highly fig. expr. for Paul's procedure in accepting financial support fr. certain sources ἄλλας ἐκκλησίας ἐσύλησα *I robbed other churches* and thus obtained the money that enabled me to serve you free of charge 2 Cor 11: 8. M-M.*

συλλαβή, ῆς, ἡ (Aeschyl.) *syllable* (Pla., Demosth. et al.; Philo, Poster. Cai. 94) Hv 2, 1, 4 (Porphyr., Vi. Plot. 8 ἔγραψε οὔτε εἰς κάλλος ἀποτυπούμενος τὰ γράμματα οὔτε εὐσήμως τὰς συλλαβὰς διαιρῶν). M-M.*

συλλαλέω impf. συνελάλουν; 1 aor. συνελάλησα (Polyb.; Dit., Or. 229, 23; pap., LXX) *talk* or *converse with, discuss with* τινί *someone* (Polyb. 4, 22, 8; PHib. 66, 4 [III BC]; PRainer 18, 23; Ex 34: 35; Pr 6: 22; Is 7: 6) Mk 9: 4; Lk 9: 30; 22: 4. Also μετά τινος Mt 17: 3; Ac 18: 12 D; 25: 12. συνελάλουν πρὸς ἀλλήλους λέγοντες Lk 4: 36. M-M.*

συλλαμβάνω fut. συλλήμψομαι (for the spelling cf. s.v. λαμβάνω); 2 aor. συνέλαβον, mid. συνελαβόμην; pf. συνείληφα; 1 aor. pass. συνελήμφθην (Aeschyl., Hdt. +; inscr., pap., LXX, Philo, Joseph., Test. 12 Patr.).

1. act. (w. fut. mid.)—a. *seize, grasp, apprehend*—α. of the taking of prisoners into custody τινά *arrest someone* (Soph., Thu.+; Dit., Syll.³ 700, 30; PHib. 54, 20; POxy. 283, 12 al.; LXX; Jos., Bell. 2, 292, Ant. 15, 124) Mt 26: 55; Mk 14: 48; Lk 22: 54; J 18: 12; Ac 1: 16; 12: 3; 1 Cl 12: 2a. Pass. Ac 23: 27; 1 Cl 12: 2b; MPol 5: 2; 7: 2; 9: 1; 21.

β. of animals *catch* (Dio Chrys. 25[42], 3; Aelian, H.A. 1, 2; Philo, Omn. Prob. Lib. 147) Lk 5: 9 (cf. ἄγρα).

b. *conceive* in the sexual sense, of the woman (Aristot., H.A. 7, 1 p. 582a, 19, Gen. An. 1, 19 p. 727b, 8; Plut., Mor. 829B; Lucian, Sacrif. 5; LXX; cf. Ep. Arist. 165) abs. *become pregnant* (Gen 4: 1; 30: 7 al.) Lk 1: 24; B 13: 2; AP 11: 26 mg. as restored by Dieterich et al. Also συλλ. ἐν γαστρί (Hippocr., Aph. 5, 46 ed. Littré IV 548, Mul. 1, 75 vol. VIII 162. Cf. Gen 25: 21) Lk 1: 31. Pass. ἐν ἀνομίαις συνελήμφθην 1 Cl 18: 5 (Ps 50: 7).—W. the acc. of the child to be born (Lucian, V. Hist. 1, 22; LXX) Lk 1: 36. Pass. πρὸ τοῦ συλλημφθῆναι αὐτὸν ἐν τῇ κοιλίᾳ *before he was conceived in the womb* 2: 21.—Symbolically (cf. Περὶ ὕψους 14, 3 τὰ συλλαμβανόμενα ὑπὸ τῆς ψυχῆς; Ps 7: 15; Test. Benj. 7: 2 συλλαμβάνει ἡ διάνοια διὰ τοῦ Βελιάρ; Philo) ἡ ἐπιθυμία συλλαβοῦσα τίκτει ἁμαρτίαν Js 1: 15.

c. *take hold of together*, then *support, aid, help* (Aeschyl. +) w. dat. of the one to whom help is given (Eur., Med. 812; Hdt. 6, 125; Pla., Leg. 10 p. 905c; POxy. 935, 3; 8 συλλαμβάνουσι ἡμῖν οἱ θεοί; 1064, 7; Jos., Ant. 12, 240) συλλάβωμεν ἑαυτοῖς *let us help each other* 2 Cl 17: 2.

2. mid.—a. *seize, arrest* Ac 26: 21; MPol 6: 1.—b. *come to the aid of, help, assist* (Soph., Phil 282; Pla., Theag. 129ε; Diod. S. 11, 40, 1; Jos., Ant. 4, 198; 7, 341 τῷ παιδί; PGiess. 25, 4 συλλαμβανόμενός μοι; PTebt. 448 συλλαβὼν αὐτῷ) τινί *someone* Lk 5: 7 (βοηθεῖν v.l.); Phil 4: 3. M-M.*

συλλέγω fut. συλλέξω; 1 aor. συνέλεξα (Hom. +; inscr., pap., LXX; Jos., Vi. 119, Ant. 5, 240 τὸν καρπόν; Sib. Or. 8, 55) *collect, gather* (*in*), *pick* τὶ *someth.* weeds Mt 13: 28–30. Pass. vs. 40. The place to which what is gathered is taken is indicated by εἰς vs. 48; the place fr. which it is removed is indicated by ἐκ vs. 41 (σκάνδαλον 3). Hence also ἐξ ἀκανθῶν συλλ. Lk 6: 44; also ἀπὸ ἀκανθῶν Mt 7: 16. M-M.*

συλλογίζομαι 1 aor. συνελογισάμην (Hdt. +; inscr., pap., LXX) *reason, discuss, debate* (Pla., Demosth., Polyb.; Is 43: 18; Philo, Leg. All. 2, 99; Jos., Bell. 1, 560; 4, 125) πρὸς ἑαυτόν *to oneself* (Plut., Pomp. 60, 3) or pl. *among themselves* Lk 20: 5. M-M.*

συλλυπέω trans. *hurt* or *grieve with* or *at the same time* pass. *be grieved with, feel sympathy* (Hdt. +; Diod. S. 4, 11, 2; Is 51: 19); in συλλυπούμενος ἐπὶ τῇ πωρώσει τῆς καρδίας αὐτῶν Mk 3: 5 the prep. surely has no other force than to strengthen the simple verb *deeply grieved at the hardening of their heart.* *

συμβαίνω (Aeschyl., Hdt. +) impf. συνέβαινον; fut. συμβήσομαι; 2 aor. συνέβην; pf. συμβέβηκα; *meet, happen, come about* (trag., Hdt. +; inscr., pap., LXX, Ep. Arist., Philo, Joseph.) συμβαίνει τί τινι (trag., Thu. et al.; Test. Sim. 2: 13) Mk 10: 32 (w. ref. to death: last will and testament of Aristot. in Diog. L. 5, 11; 12); Ac 20: 19; 1 Cor 10: 11; 1 Pt 4: 12; 2 Pt 2: 22; 1 Cl 23: 3 (scripture quot. of unknown origin); B 19: 6; D 3: 10. οὕτως συμβαίνει πᾶσι Hm 5, 2, 7. καθὼς φρονοῦσιν καὶ συμβήσεται αὐτοῖς *as they hold their opinions, so it shall turn out for them* ISm 2. W. inf. foll. (Hdt. 6, 103 al.; inscr.; POxy. 491, 10) Hv 3, 7, 6. συνέβη foll. by acc. and inf. (Hdt. 7, 166 al.; Dit., Syll.³ 535, 5; 685, 36f; 1 Esdr 1: 23; Jos., Ant. 9, 185) συνέβη βαστάζεσθαι αὐτὸν ὑπὸ τῶν στρατιωτῶν Ac 21: 35; Papias 4; (Bl-D. §393, 5; 408; Rob. 392; 1043).—τὸ συμβεβηκός τινι *what has happened to someone* (Sus 26 Theod.; Jos., Vi. 51) Ac 3: 10. Sing., without the dat. τὸ συμβάν *what had happened* (Epict. 3, 24, 13; Appian, Hann. 36 §154; Agatharchides in Jos., C. Ap. 1, 211; cf. Jos., Ant. 13, 413 τὰ ξυμβάντα) GP 14: 59. Pl. τὰ συμβεβηκότα *the things that had happened* (Isocr. 5, 18; 1 Macc 4: 26; Ep. Arist.; Jos., Bell. 4, 43, Ant. 13, 194) Lk 24: 14. M-M.*

συμβάλλω impf. συνέβαλλον; 2 aor. συνέβαλον, mid. συνεβαλόμην; pf. συμβέβληκα (Hom. +; inscr., pap., LXX).

1. act.—a. trans.—α. *converse, confer* (w. λόγους added Eur., Iphig. Aul. 830; without λ. Plut., Mor. 222c) τινί *with someone* (Epict. 4, 12, 7; Iambl., Vi. Pyth. 2, 12; PFay. 129, 2) Ac 17: 18. πρὸς ἀλλήλους 4: 15.

β. *consider, ponder, draw conclusions about* (Pla., Crat. 384ᴀ μαντείαν; Philo, In Flacc. 139; Jos., Ant. 2, 72

συμβαλὼν τῷ λογισμῷ τὸ ὄναρ) τὰ ῥήματα συμβάλλουσα ἐν τῇ καρδίᾳ αὐτῆς Lk 2: 19 (cf. the colloquial 'get it all together').

γ. *compare* (Hdt. +; pap.; Sir 22: 1f; Jos., Ant. 1, 105) τινά τινι *someone with someth.* ἑαυτὸν ξύλῳ 1 Cl 23: 4= 2 Cl 11: 3 (quot. of unknown orig.).

b. intr. *meet, fall in with* (Hom. +; pap.) τινί *someone* (on a journey; cf. Jos., Ant. 1, 219; 2, 184) Ac 20: 14. Cf. MPol 8: 1.—Mostly in a hostile sense τινί *engage, fight someone* (Polyb. 1, 9, 7; 3, 111, 1 al.; Wilcken, Chrest. 16, 6; 1 Macc 4: 34; 2 Macc 8: 23; 14: 17) εἰς πόλεμον *meet someone in battle, wage war on someone* Lk 14: 31 (cf. εἰς μάχην Polyb. 3, 56, 6; Jos., Bell. 1, 191, Ant. 12, 342; πρὸς μάχην Polyb. 10, 37, 4).—*Quarrel* or *dispute* τινί *with someone* (PSI 93, 4 συνέβαλον τοῖς ἐπιτρόποις) συμβάλλειν αὐτῷ περὶ πλειόνων *quarrel with him about many things* Lk 11: 53 v.l.

2. mid. *help, be of assistance* (Philo, Migr. Abr. 219) τινί (*to*) *someone* (Pla.; Demosth. 21, 133; Antipho 5, 79 p. 138, 37 πολλὰ συμβ. τοῖς βουλομένοις; Polyb. 2, 13, 1; Epict. 3, 22, 78 πλείονά τινι σ.; PLond. 1915, 13; Wsd 5: 8; Jos., Ant. 12, 312) Apollos συνεβάλετο πολὺ τοῖς πεπιστευκόσιν Ac 18: 27. M-M.*

συμβασιλεύω fut. συμβασιλεύσω (Polyb. 30, 2, 4; Dionys. Hal., Strabo; Lucian, Dial. Deor. 16, 2; Plut., Lyc. 5, 5, Num. 3, 6, Anton. 54, 4; 1 Esdr 8: 26 v.l.) *rule* (*as king*) *with someone* fig. of the eschatological situation when the Christians are to share the kingship w. their royal Lord 2 Ti 2: 12; Pol 5: 2. Paul ironically states that the Corinthians have achieved kingship; he wishes they had achieved it because then he would be reigning with them; actually he was still leading a miserable life (cf. vs. 9) 1 Cor 4: 8. M-M.*

συμβιβάζω fut. συμβιβάσω; 1 aor. συνεβίβασα, pass. ptc. συμβιβασθείς (Hdt. +; inscr., LXX).

1. *bring together, unite*—a. lit., of the body, which is *held together* by sinews, ligaments, joints τὸ σῶμα συμβιβαζόμενον διὰ πάσης ἁφῆς Eph 4: 16 (GHWhitaker, JTS 31, '30, 48f; cf. Col 2: 19.

b. fig. *unite, knit together* (Hdt. 1, 74; Thu. 2, 29, 6; Pla., Prot. 337ε) pass. συμβιβασθέντες ἐν ἀγάπῃ Col 2: 2 (so Lghtf., Klöpper, EHaupt, Lueken, Meinertz, H Rendtorff, Lohmeyer, Abbott, Peake, Gdspd., RSV. But s. 4 below).

2. *conclude, infer* (Pla., Hipp. Min. 369ᴅ, Rep. 6 p. 504ᴀ) Ac 16: 10 (w. ὅτι foll.).—3. *demonstrate, prove* (Aristot., Top. 7, 5 p. 150a, 36 [ὅτι]; 8, 3 p. 154b, 27; 8, 11 p. 157b, 37; Iambl., Vi. Pyth. 13, 60) συμβιβάζων ὅτι οὗτός ἐστιν ὁ Χριστός Ac 9: 22.

4. *instruct, teach, advise* τινά *someone* (LXX) 1 Cor 2: 16 (Is 40: 13f); Ac 19: 33 (where, however, the rdg. is not certain).—Some (e.g. MDibelius, Mft.) classify Col 2: 2 here (s. 1b above). M-M.*

σύμβιος, ον *living together* (Aristot. +; Philo, Poster. Cai. 78) subst. *companion*, then esp. ὁ, ἡ σ. *husband, wife* (inscr. and oft. in pap.) IPol 5: 1; Hv 2, 2, 3.*

συμβουλεύω 1 aor. συνεβούλευσα (Theognis, trag., Hdt. +; inscr., pap., LXX)—1. act. *advise, give advice to* τινί *someone* (Ex 18: 19; Jos., C. Ap. 1, 309a) J 18: 14. τινί τι *advise someone* (*to do*) *someth.* (Hdt. 7, 237 al.; 3 Km 1: 12 συμβουλεύσω σοι συμβουλίαν) MPol 8: 2. W. dat. and inf. foll. (Hdt. +; BGU 1097, 8 [I ᴀᴅ]; 4 Macc 8: 29; Jos., Ant. 12, 384) Rv 3: 18. Abs. (Diog. L. 1, 92a; Jos., Bell. 2, 345) 2 Cl 15: 1.

2. mid.—a. *consult, plot* (Jos., Ant. 8, 379; Test. Jud. 13: 4) w. ἵνα foll. Mt 26: 4; J 11: 53 t.r. Foll. by inf. of purpose Ac 9: 23.

b. *meditate on, consider* (PPetr. II 13, 6, 13; PSI 236, 30) τὶ someth. Hv 1, 2, 2. M-M.*

συμβουλή, ῆς, ἡ *advice, counsel* (Hdt. 1, 157 al.; Philo, Fuga 24; Jos., Ant. 19, 192) δέχεσθαι σ. *accept advice* 1 Cl 58: 2.*

συμβουλία, ας, ἡ *advice, counsel* (Hdt.+; inscr., pap., LXX, Philo; Jos., Ant. 5, 336; 8, 277 al.) συμβουλίαν ποιεῖσθαι περί τινος *give advice about someth.* (Diod. S. 12, 17, 2) 2 Cl 15: 1. γνώμης ἀγαθῆς λαμβάνειν συμβουλίαν *accept well-meant advice* B 21: 2 (cf. Vi. Aesopi I c. 26 συμβ. λαμβάνειν).*

συμβούλιον, ου, τό (Plut., Cass. Dio et al.; inscr. [since II bc]; pap.—Dssm., NB 65 [BS 238])—**1.** (*consultation and its result*): *plan, purpose* σ. λαμβάνειν a Latinism= consilium capere (Bl-D. §5, 3b, cf. a; Rob. 109.—Jos., Ant. 6, 38 βουλὰς λ.) *form a plan, decide, consult, plot* Mt 12: 14; 22: 15; 27: 1, 7; 28: 12. In the same sense σ. διδόναι (s. IAHeikel, StKr 106, ʼ35, 314) Mk 3: 6. σ. ἑτοιμάζειν *reach a decision* 15: 1 (in both Mk-passages συμβούλιον ποιεῖν is found as a v.l., mng. *hold a consultation*).

2. *council session, meeting* (Plut., Rom. 14, 3, Luc. 26, 4; BGU 288, 14 [II ad]; 511 I, 20; PRyl. 75, 29) συμβούλιον ἄγειν *convene a council* IPol 7: 2.

3. *council* as a body (inscr., pap.; 4 Macc 17: 17; Jos., Ant. 14, 192; 16, 163.—Mommsen, Röm. Staatsrecht[3] 1887 I 307ff; II 249; Schürer I rev. Eng. ed. ʼ73, 370 note 80 [sources and lit.]) Φῆστος συλλαλήσας μετὰ τοῦ συμβουλίου Ac 25: 12. M-M.*

σύμβουλος, ου, ὁ (trag., Hdt.+; Dit., Syll.[3] 496, 16; PPetr. II 13, 6, 11 [III bc]; LXX; Ep. Arist. 264; Philo; Jos., Ant. 14, 183; 17, 108, C. Ap. 2, 156; 158; 160) *adviser, counsellor* Ro 11: 34 (Is 40: 13); B 21: 4; Dg 9: 6; Hs 5, 2, 6; 5, 4, 1; 5, 5, 3; 5, 6, 4; 7; 9, 12, 2. M-M.*

Συμεών, ὁ indecl. Semitic (שִׁמְעוֹן) name (for which the similar-sounding genuine Gk. name Σίμων [q.v.] is sometimes substituted; Bl-D. §53, 2d app.; Mlt.-H. 146.— LXX, Philo, Test. 12 Patr. In Joseph. Συμεών, ῶνος: Bell. 4, 159, Ant. 12, 265; Preisigke, Namenbuch) *Symeon, Simeon.*

1. son of Jacob (Gen 29: 33.—49: 5; Jdth 9: 2; 4 Macc 2: 19). Ancestor of the tribe of the same name (Jdth 6: 15) Rv 7: 7.

2. in the genealogy of Jesus Lk 3: 30.—**3.** a devout old man in Jerusalem 2: 25, 34.

4. *Simeon* surnamed Niger, named w. other teachers and prophets of the church at Antioch Ac 13: 1.

5. The original name of the apostle Peter (cf. Σίμων 1) is occasionally written in this way Ac 15: 14. Συμεὼν (𝔓[72] et al. Σίμων) Πέτρος 2 Pt 1: 1. M-M.*

συμμαθητής, οῦ, ὁ (Pla., Euthyd. 1 p. 272c; Anaxippus Com. [IV bc] 1, 2 vol. III p. 296 K.; Diog. L. 6, 2; Ps.-Callisth. 1, 13, 5; Pollux 6, 159) *fellow-pupil, fellow-disciple* J 11: 16; MPol 17: 3. M-M.*

συμμαρτυρέω (Soph., Thu.+) *testify* or *bear witness with* (Plut., Thes. et Romul. 6, 5, Mor. 64c; BGU 86, 40 [II ad] al.), then also gener. *confirm, testify in support of someone* or *someth.* (as early as Solon 24, 3 D.[2] the prefix συν- has in the highest degree the effect of strengthening. Likewise trag.+; Pla., Hipp. Major 282b συμμαρτυρῆσαι

δέ σοι ἔχω ὅτι ἀληθῆ λέγεις; X., Hell. 7, 1, 35 συνεμαρτύρει αὐτῷ ταῦτα πάντα; 3, 3, 2; Jos., Ant. 19, 154. Without dat. and w. ὅτι foll. Plut., Mor. 724d) συμμαρτυρούσης αὐτῶν τῆς συνειδήσεως Ro 2: 15. συμμαρτυρούσης μοι τῆς συνειδήσεώς μου . . . ὅτι 9: 1 (on the witness of the conscience Jos., C. Ap. 2, 218). τὸ πνεῦμα συμμαρτυρεῖ τῷ πνεύματι ἡμῶν ὅτι 8: 16.—The mid. Rv 22: 18 t.r. M-M.*

συμμαχέω *fight at someone's side, be an ally,* also gener. *help, assist* (Aeschyl., Hdt.+; inscr.; POxy. 705, 33; LXX; Jos., C. Ap. 1, 236 σ. τινί, Ant. 1, 313) τὰ συμμαχοῦντα ἡμῖν (w. βοηθοί) B 2: 2.*

συμμείγνυμι 2 aor. pass. ptc. συμμιγείς (Hom. [συμμίσγω]+; inscr., pap., LXX) *mix together* pass. *join with* of sexual union (Hdt. 4, 114; Pla., Symp. 207b, Laws 930d) AP 9: 24.*

συμμερίζω (Diod. S.; Dionys. Hal.; Diog. L. et al.) mid. **συμμερίζομαι** (Inschr. v. Hierap. 336, 11; Eutecnius 2 p. 23, 12) *share with* τινί *someone* or *someth.* (Pr 29: 24 v.l. ὃς συμμερίζεται κλέπτῃ; Philopon. in Aristot., De An. p. 417, 35 Hayduck) τῷ θυσιαστηρίῳ συμμερίζονται *they share with the altar* in the things sacrificed on it 1 Cor 9: 13. M-M.*

συμμέτοχος, ον (Aristot., Plant. 1, 1; Jos., Bell. 1, 486 συμμέτοχοι τοῦ σκέμματος αὐτῷ; PLond. 1733, 52) *sharing with someone* τινός *in someth.* Eph 3: 6. συμμέτοχοι αὐτῶν *sharing with them, casting one's lot with them* 5: 7. M-M.*

συμμιμητής, οῦ, ὁ *fellow-imitator* w. obj. gen. foll. συμμιμηταί μου γίνεσθε *join* (w. the others) *in following my example* Phil 3: 17. M-M.*

συμμορφίζω (only in Christian wr.) *grant* or *invest with the same form* pass. συμμορφίζεσθαί τινι *be conformed to, take on the same form as* τῷ θανάτῳ αὐτοῦ= the form that he (Christ) took on through his death Phil 3: 10. M-M.*

σύμμορφος, ον (Ps.-Lucian, Amor. 39 al.) *having the same form, similar in form* τινός *as* or *to someth.* (Bl-D. §182, 1; Rob. 504; 528) σύμμ. τῆς εἰκόνος τοῦ υἱοῦ αὐτοῦ *like his Son in form* or *appearance* Ro 8: 29 (JKürzinger, BZ 2, ʼ58, 294–99). Also w. the dat. (Nicander [II bc], Ther. 321 ed. OSchneider [1856]; Heraclit. Sto. 77 p. 102, 12 σ. τρισὶ θεοῖς of Agamemnon; Bl-D. §194, 2; Rob. 528) σύμμ. τῷ σώματι τῆς δόξης αὐτοῦ Phil 3: 21.*

συμμορφόω *give the same form* pass. *take on the same form* (Libanius, Descript. 30, 5 vol. VIII 542, 10 F.; Menand. Protector [VI ad]: Historici Gr. Min. ed. LDind. II 1871 p. 67, 8) Phil 3: 10 t.r.*

συμμύστης, ου, ὁ *one who has been initiated into the same mysteries, fellow-initiate* (IG XII 8, 173, 13 [66 bc]; Dit., Or. 541, 9 οἱ τῶν τῆς θεοῦ μυστηρίων συμμύσται; PGM 4, 732; 12, 94.—FPoland, Gesch. d. griech. Vereinswesens ʼ09, 39), fig. of the Christians in Ephesus Παύλου συμμύσται *fellow-initiates of Paul* IEph 12: 2. Cf. the apostolic church discipline in AHilgenfeld, NT Extra Canonem Receptum[2] IV 1884 p. 117, 7: the presbyters are the συμμύσται of the bishop; Origen, Hom. 7, 2 in Lev., Hom. 7 in Jos.*

συμπαθέω 1 aor. συνεπάθησα *sympathize with, have* or *show sympathy with* (Isocr. et al.; Plut., Timol. 14, 1; 4 Macc 13: 23; Jos., Ant. 16, 404; Sib. Or. 11, 58; Test.

Sim. 3: 6) w. dat. of the pers. or thing that is the obj. of the sympathy (Isocr. 4, 112 v.l.; Dionys. Hal. 10, 6 τῷ ἀνδρί; Plut., Marcell. 16, 1, Mor. 90ϝ; Philo, Spec. Leg. 2, 115; Test. Benj. 4: 4; 4 Macc 5: 25) w. dat. of the thing ταῖς ἀσθενείαις ἡμῶν Hb 4: 15 (cf. Philistion [Comic. Att. Fgm. II no. 230 Kock] ἐκ τοῦ παθεῖν γίγνωσκε καὶ τὸ συμπαθεῖν· καὶ σοὶ γὰρ ἄλλος συμπαθήσεται παθών); 10: 34 t.r. (δεσμοῖς); w. dat. of the pers., ibid. in the crit. texts (δεσμίοις); IRo 6: 3.—WBurkert, Zum altgriech. Mitleidsbegriff, Diss. Erlangen '55, 63-6. M-M.*

συμπαθής, ές (Aristot. et al.; CIG 9438; Dit., Or. 456, 66; LXX, Philo) *sympathetic* (Polyb. 2, 56, 7; 8, 22, 9; Plut., Eum. 18, 5, Mor. 536Α; Jos., Ant. 19, 330) 1 Pt 3: 8. M-M.*

συμπαραγίνομαι mid. dep.; 2 aor. συμπαρεγενόμην.—
1. *come together* (Hdt. et al.; PSI 502, 24 [III ʙᴄ]; Ps 82: 9) ἐπὶ τὴν θεωρίαν ταύτην *for this spectacle* Lk 23: 48.
2. *come to the aid of* (Thu. 2, 82; 6, 92, 5) τινί *someone* 2 Ti 4: 16 t.r. (for παρεγένετο). M-M.*

συμπαρακαλέω (X., Pla.+) *encourage together* (Polyb. 5, 83, 3) pass. συμπαρακληθῆναι ἐν ὑμῖν *receive encouragement* or *comfort together with you* Ro 1: 12.*

συμπαραλαμβάνω 2 aor. συμπαρέλαβον (Pla.+; pap., LXX) *take along* (with oneself) τινά *someone* (PLond. 358, 6; BGU 226, 12; Job 1: 4; 3 Macc 1: 1; Jos., Ant. 9, 7) Ac 12: 25; 15: 37f; Gal 2: 1. M-M.*

συμπαραμένω fut. συμπαραμενῶ (Thu. et al.; PSI 64, 3 [I ʙᴄ]; Ps 71: 5) *stay with* (τινί *someone*) *to help* (Thu. 6, 89, 4; Dit., Syll.³ 567 A, 12f) πᾶσιν ὑμῖν Phil 1: 25 t.r.*

συμπάρειμι *be present* (at the same time) (X., Lac. 2, 2 al.; inscr., pap., LXX) τινί *with someone* (Dit., Syll.³ 685, 28 [139 ʙᴄ]; PSI 439, 29; Jos., Ant. 10, 239) Ac 25: 24; *be present (together) with* τινί *someone* (Jos., Ant. 11, 322) ITr 12: 1. M-M.*

σύμπας, ασα, αν (Hom.+; inscr., pap., LXX; En. 102, 2 ἡ γῆ σύμπασα; Ep. Arist. 16; Philo; Jos., Bell. 2, 307, C. Ap. 2, 190) *all (together), whole* ὁ σύμπας κόσμος 1 Cl 19: 2. τὰ σύμπαντα Β 15: 4.*

συμπάσχω 2 aor. συνέπαθον *suffer with*, also *suffer the same thing as* (Pla., Charm. 169c) w. the dat. (Epict. 1, 14, 2; IG XIV 2124, 3 [c. 200 ᴀᴅ]; POxy. 904, 7 ἅμα μοι συνπαθεῖν; Herm. Wr. 494, 1 Sc.; Philo, De Prov. in Euseb., Pr. Ev. 8, 14, 23; Test. Zeb. 7: 5. So also in the sense *have sympathy*: Polyb.; Diod. S. 17, 36, 3 τοῖς ἠτυχηκόσιν; Plut.) αὐτῷ (= Ἰησοῦ Χριστῷ) ISm 4: 2; cf. Pol 9: 2. Abs., but also of suffering w. Christ Ro 8: 17. —συμπάσχει πάντα τὰ μέλη w. one part of the body that suffers 1 Cor 12: 26 (Diod. S. 18, 42, 4 συμπασχόν-των ἁπάντων τῶν μελῶν=all the members [of the σῶμα] are involved in suffering [or exertion] together; Diog. L. 2, 94 τὴν ψυχὴν συμπαθεῖν τῷ σώματι. Cf. Maximus Tyr. 28, 2c; Alex. Aphr., An. p. 100, 3 Br. πάντα τὰ μόρια ἀλλήλοις ἐστὶν ἐν τῷ σώματι συμ-παθῆ; Philo, Spec. Leg. 3, 194; Plut., Solon 18, 6 τ. πολίτας ὥσπερ ἑνὸς σώματος μέρη συναισθάνεσθαι κ. συναλγεῖν ἀλλήλοις).—Rather w. the mng. *have sympathy* IRo 6: 3. συμπάσχειν ἀλλήλοις 2 Cl 4: 3; IPol 6: 1. M-M.*

συμπέμπω 1 aor. συνέπεμψα (Pind., Hdt.+; inscr., pap.; Jos., C. Ap. 1, 48) *send (with)* or *at the same time* τινά τινι *someone with someone* (Hdt. et al.; Zen.-P. Cairo 59 230, 4 [253 ʙᴄ]; Wilcken, Chrest. 11A, 47 [123

ʙᴄ]) 2 Cor 8: 22. Also τινὰ μετά τινος (cf. X., Hell. 1, 4, 21) vs. 18. M-M.*

συμπεριέχω (Dionys. Hal. 3, 43) *surround* or *stand around (together)* w. κύκλῳ added Lk 12: 1 D.*

συμπεριλαμβάνω 2 aor. ptc. συμπεριλαβών (Pla., Aristot.+; inscr., pap., Ezk 5: 3; Jos., C. Ap. 2, 32) *embrace, throw one's arms around* w. acc. to be supplied Ac 20: 10 (like X., An. 7, 4, 10 περιλαβὼν τὸν παῖδα). M-M.*

συμπίνω 2 aor. συνέπιον (Hdt., Aristoph.+; Esth 7: 1 συμπιεῖν τῇ βασιλίσσῃ; Jos., Vi. 224 ἡμῖν) *drink with* (beside συνεσθίειν as Dit., Syll.³ 1179, 18f) τινί *someone* Ac 10: 41; ISm 3: 3. M-M.*

συμπίπτω 2 aor. συνέπεσον (Hom.+; inscr., pap., LXX, Joseph., Test. 12 Patr.) *fall together*—1. lit. *fall in, collapse* (trag.; Thu. 8, 41, 2; Diod. S. 19, 45, 2 houses as a result of a downfall of rain and hail; Jos., Bell. 1, 331 οἶκος; Dit., Or. 595, 15; 28; PMagd. 9, 3; POxy. 75, 27 al. in pap.; Sb 5109, 2 [I ᴀᴅ] οἰκίας συμπεπτωκυίας) Lk 6: 49.
2. fig.—a. of a person's mental state (1 Macc 6: 10 συνπέπτωκα τῇ καρδίᾳ ἀπὸ τῆς μερίμνης; Test. Zeb. 10: 1) *collapse* fr. fright MPol 12: 1.
b. in OT expressions συνέπεσεν τὸ πρόσωπον *his countenance fell, has become distorted* 1 Cl 4: 3, 4 (Gen 4: 5 [συνέπεσεν τῷ προσώπῳ], 6; cf. Test. Jos. 7: 2). M-M.*

συμπληρόω impf. pass. συνεπληρούμην (Hdt.+; inscr., pap., Philo, Joseph.) *fill completely*; pass. *become quite full*.
1. lit., of a ship (cf. Arrian, Anab. 1, 19, 10; Menand. Ephes. in Jos., Ant. 9, 285) that is being filled w. water in a storm συνεπληροῦντο *they were being swamped* Lk 8: 23.
2. fig., of time *fulfill, approach, come* (πληρόω 2.— Herodian 7, 4, 1; BGU 1122, 22 [13 ʙᴄ] ἐπὶ τοῦ συμπλη-ρωθῆναι τοῦτον [τὸν χρόνον]; Jer 25: 12 v.l.; Jos., Ant. 4, 176) ἐν τῷ συμπληροῦσθαι τὰς ἡμέρας τῆς ἀναλήμψεως *since the days of his* ἀνάλημψις (q.v.) *were approaching* Lk 9: 51. ἐν τῷ συνπληροῦσθαι τὴν ἡμέραν τῆς πεντη-κοστῆς *when the day of Pentecost had come* Ac 2: 1 (s. JHRopes, HTR 16, '23, 168–75). M-M.*

συμπλοκή, ῆς, ἡ (Pla. et al.; inscr.; Philo, Rer. Div. Her. 198; Jos., Bell. 4, 423) *(lustful) embrace, intercourse* (Pla., Symp. 191c; Aristot., H.A. 5, 5; Cornutus 24 p. 45, 9) μιαραὶ κ. ἄναγναι συμπλοκαί 1 Cl 30: 1 (cf. Achilles Tat. 7, 5, 4 μεμιασμένας συμπλοκάς).*

συμπνέω (Aeschyl.+; pap.; lit. 'breathe with') *agree, coincide, coalesce* (Polyb. 30, 2, 8 συμπ. καὶ μιᾷ γνώμῃ χρῆσθαι; Plut.; Herodian; Herm. Wr. 10, 17; BGU 1024, 8, 20; Philo, Conf. Lingu. 69; Jos., Ant. 7, 105) 1 Cl 37: 5.*

συμπνίγω impf. συνέπνιγον; 1 aor. συνέπνιξα (Jos., Ant. 12, 275 v.l.)—1. *(crowd together and) choke*, of plants whose food and light is cut off by weeds (Theophr., C. Pl. 6, 11, 6 δένδρα συμπνιγόμενα) Mk 4: 7. Symbol-ically in the interpr. of the parable τὸν λόγον Mt 13: 22; Mk 4: 19. Pass. Lk 8: 14.
2. as a hyperbolic expr. for *crowd around, press upon*, someth. like *almost crush* (Gdspd.) οἱ ὄχλοι συνέπνιγον αὐτόν Lk 8: 42. ἀλλήλους 12: 1 D.*

συμπολιτεύομαι 1 aor. συνεπολιτευσάμην *be a fellow-citizen, live in the same state* (Thu. et al. in the act. The mid. in Aeschin. 1, 17; Isocr. 3, 4; 5, 20 al.; Epict. 3, 22, 99; inscr., pap.) τινί *of* or *as someone* (Diod. S. 5, 58, 2; Dit., Or. 504, 6 συνπεπολιτευμένος ἡμεῖν; Jos., Ant. 19, 306) MPol 22: 2; Epil Mosq. 1.*

συμπολίτης, ου, ὁ (Eur., Her. 826; Aelian, V.H. 3, 44; Jos., Ant. 19, 175; IG XIV 1878; pap.) *fellow-citizen* fig. The Gentiles, when they accept the faith, become συμπολῖται τῶν ἁγίων *fellow-citizens of the saints* who, as Christians, are citizens of the Kingdom of God Eph 2: 19. M-M.*

συμπορεύομαι impf. συνεπορευόμην—1. *go (along) with* (Eur.; Pla.; PSI 353, 13 [III BC]; LXX) τινί *someone* (Pla., Phaedr. 249c; Zen.-P. 42 [=Sb 6748], 2 [253/2 BC]; Tob 5: 3, 9) Lk 7: 11; 14: 25; 24: 15.

2. *come together, flock* (Polyb. 5, 6, 1 πρός τινα; 6, 16, 4 al.; Plut., Eum. 13, 8; inscr.; Dt 31: 11; Job 1: 4 πρὸς ἀλλήλους) πρός τινα *to someone* Mk 10: 1. M-M.*

συμποσία, ας, ἡ (Pind.+; 3 Macc 5: 15, 16, 17; 7: 20) *a common meal* Mk 6: 39 D.*

συμπόσιον, ου, τό (Theognis+ =drinking-party, banquet [so Philo, Op. M. 78; Jos., Ant. 8, 137; 12, 231]; X.+ also= hall where a drinking-party or banquet is held; also pap., LXX in both mngs.) *a party* or *group* of people eating together (so Plut., Mor. 157D; 704D) repeated, in a distributive sense (Bl-D. §493, 2 and app.; Mlt. 97): συμπόσια συμπόσια *in parties* Mk 6: 39 (cf. πρασιά). M-M.*

συμπρεσβύτερος, ου, ὁ (only in Christian sources [Suppl. Epigr. Gr. VI 347, 2]. But συμπρεσβευτής='fellow-ambassador' not infreq. in lit. and inscr.; likew. the pl. συμπρέσβεις w. the same mng. [Thu. 1, 90, 5; 1, 91, 3; Jos., Vi. 62; 73]) *fellow-presbyter* or *-elder* (πρεσβύτερος 1a) 1 Pt 5: 1. M-M.*

συμφέρω impf. συνέφερον; 1 aor. συνήνεγκα, ptc. συνενέγκας (Hom. [mid.]+; Aeschyl., Hdt.+; inscr., pap., LXX, Ep. Arist., Philo, Joseph., Test. 12 Patr.).

1. *bring together* τὶ someth. (cf. X., An. 6, 4, 9; Jos., Bell. 5, 262, Ant. 16, 45) Ac 19: 19.

2. *help, confer a benefit, be advantageous* or *profitable* or *useful* (Jos., Ant. 1, 162)—**a.** impers. συμφέρει τι someth. *is good (for someone* or *someth.), someth. is useful* or *helpful* 1 Cor 6: 12; 10: 23. οὐ συμφέρει μοι 2 Cor 12: 1 t.r. (s. Windisch on this pass., which has prob. been damaged textually). συμφέρει τί τινι (Soph.+; Pr 19: 10; Sir 30: 19; 37: 28 οὐ πάντα πᾶσιν συμφέρει) 2 Cor 8: 10; IRo 5: 3. συμφέρει τινί foll. by inf. (Epict. 2, 22, 20; Esth 3: 8) GP 11: 48; ISm 7: 1. συμφ. τινί foll. by ἵνα (Bl-D. §393, 1; Rob. 992; POxy. 1220, 19) Mt 5: 29f (foll. by καὶ μή to denote, by way of contrast, what is not advantageous; here and elsewh. it is well translated *it is better . . . than*) Mt 18: 6; J 11: 50 (foll. by καὶ μή); 16: 7. οὐ συμφέρει γαμῆσαι *it is better not to marry* Mt 19: 10 (Polyaenus 3, 9, 2 διώκειν οὐ συμφέρει). W. acc. and inf. (cf. Ep. Arist. 25) συμφέρει ἕνα ἄνθρωπον ἀποθανεῖν J 18: 14.

b. ptc. συμφέρων *profitable*, etc.—**α.** τὰ συμφέροντα *what is good for you* Ac 20: 20 (Pla., Rep. 1 p. 341E; Philo; Jos., Bell. 2, 502, Vi. 370; 3 Macc 6: 24)—**β.** σοὶ συμφέρον ἐστί w. inf. foll. Hs 7: 5. οὐ συμφέρον (sc. ἐστίν) *there is nothing to be gained by it* 2 Cor 12: 1 (cf. Thu. 3, 44, 2).

γ. subst. τὸ συμφέρον *profit, advantage* (Soph.+; inscr.; 2 Macc 11: 15; 4 Macc 5: 11; Philo; Jos., Ant. 12, 54; 13, 152, τὸ αὐτοῦ σ. 14, 174) τὸ ἐμαυτοῦ συμφέρον 1 Cor 10: 33 t.r. τὸ κοινῇ συμφέρον *the common good* (cf. τὸ δημοσίᾳ συμφέρον POxy. 1409, 11; Ocellus [II BC] 48 Harder ['26] τὸ σ. τῷ κοινῷ) B 4: 10. πρὸς τὸ συμφέρον (τινός) *for* (someone's) *advantage* 1 Cor 7: 35 t.r.; 12: 7 (Aeneas Tact. 469; schol. on Pind., Isth. 1, 15b; cf. Jos., Ant. 15, 22). Also ἐπὶ τὸ συμφέρον Hb 12: 10 (cf. Appian, Liby. 89 §420 ἐπὶ συμφέροντι κοινῷ, Syr. 41 §217; Jos., Bell. 1, 558 and Vi. 48 ἐπὶ συμφέροντι). M-M.*

σύμφημι (trag., X., Pla.+) *agree* σύμφημι τῷ νόμῳ ὅτι καλός *I agree with the law* (and thus bear witness) *that it is good* Ro 7: 16 (σ. ὅτι: Pla., Phaedo 9 p. 64B).*

συμφορά, ᾶς, ἡ *misfortune, calamity, disaster* (so in sing. and pl. Pind., Hdt.+; inscr., pap., LXX; Philo, Spec. Leg. 4, 179; Jos., Bell. 2, 411, Ant. 10, 106 al.). Pl. w. περιπτώσεις 1 Cl 1: 1. B. 1096.*

σύμφορος, ον *beneficial, advantageous, profitable* (Hes., Hdt.+; inscr.; POxy. 1676, 25 τὸ σύνφορόν σοι ποίει; 2 Macc 4: 5) τινί *to* or *for someone* Hv 1, 3, 3; 5: 5; s 6, 1, 3; 6, 5, 7. Comp. (Epict. 1, 28, 7; Jos., C. Ap. 2, 294) συμφορώτερόν ἐστι w. inf. foll. Hm 6, 1, 4.—Subst. τὸ σύμφορον *benefit, advantage* (Thu. 5, 98. The pl. τὰ σύμφορα is more freq. Soph.+) τό τινος σύμφορον 1 Cor 7: 35; 10: 33. M-M.*

συμφορτίζω *burden together with others* συμφορτιζόμενος τῷ θανάτῳ αὐτοῦ *burdened* (together w. him) *by his death* Phil 3: 10 v.l.*

συμφυλέτης, ου, ὁ (pagan inscr. IG XII 2, 505, 18 [II BC]; Dox. Gr. 655, 8; Rhet. Gr. VII 49, 22; Isocr. 12, 145 Bl. v.l.; Herodian Gr., Philetaerus [in the edition of Moeris by JPierson] p. 475; Hesychius) *fellow-countryman, compatriot* 1 Th 2: 14. M-M.*

συμφυρμός, οῦ, ὁ (hapax legomenon.—συμφύρομαι Eur.+; Jos., Bell. 2, 150) *mixing, mingling* of sexual intercourse (w. ἀσέλγειαι) συμφυρμοὶ πονηρίας *wicked immorality* Hv 2, 2, 2.*

σύμφυτος, ον (Pind.+; pap., LXX, Philo; Jos., C. Ap. 1, 42, but mostly= 'innate' or someth. sim.) *grown together* (Aristot., Hist. Anim. 5, 32 p. 557b, 18, Topica 7, 6 p. 145b, 3; 13) τινί with someth. (Antipho; POxy. 1364, 44f) fig. σύμφυτοι γεγόναμεν τῷ ὁμοιώματι τοῦ θανάτου αὐτοῦ Ro 6: 5 (ὁμοίωμα 1.—Cf. Dio Chrys. 11[12], 28 of the men of primitive times in their relationship to the divinity: οὐ μακρὰν τ. θείου. . .ἀλλὰ ἐν αὐτῷ μέσῳ πεφυκότες μᾶλλον δὲ συμπεφυκότες ἐκείνῳ). SStricker, D. Mysteriengedanke des hl. Pls nach Rö 6: 2–11: Liturgisches Leben 1, '34, 285–96; OKuss, D. Römerbrief I, '63, 299f; see also the comm. by OMoe² '48; ANygren '51; CEBCranfield '75. M-M.*

συμφύω 2 aor. pass. ptc. συμφυείς (trans. in Pla. et al.; intr. in Hippocr., Plato et al., incl. Wsd 13: 13; Philo, Dec. 87; Jos., Bell. 6, 155, Ant. 8, 63 [συμφυέντες]) pass. intr. *grow up with* someth. Lk 8: 7. M-M.*

συμφωνέω fut. συμφωνήσω; 1 aor. συνεφώνησα, pass. συνεφωνήθην (Pla., Aristot.+; inscr., pap., LXX, Philo; Jos., Ant. 10, 106, C. Ap. 2, 181).

1. of things—**a.** *fit (in) with, match (with), agree with* (Pla., Aristot.+) w. dat. τούτῳ συμφωνοῦσιν οἱ λόγοι τῶν προφητῶν *with this* (i.e. w. God's call to the Gentiles) *the words of the prophets agree* Ac 15: 15 (cf. Jos., Ant. 1, 107; 15, 174). τῷ παλαιῷ οὐ συμφωνήσει τὸ ἐπίβλημα Lk 5: 36. (λίθοι) μὴ συμφωνοῦντες τοῖς ἑτέροις λίθοις Hs 9, 6, 4.

b. *fit together* συμφωνοῦσιν αἱ ἁρμογαί *the joints* (of the stones) *fit together* Hv 3, 5, 1c. συμφ. ταῖς ἁρμογαῖς αὐτῶν *they fit together at their joints* 3, 5, 1a. συμφ. ταῖς ἁρμογαῖς αὐτῶν μετὰ τῶν ἑτέρων λίθων 3, 5, 2; cf. 3, 2, 6.

c. *harmonize* (in sound) συμφωνοῦσιν ἀλλήλοις of jars that knock against each other Hm 11: 13.

2. of persons—**a.** *be in agreement, in harmony* (Pla., Aristot. +; Strabo 12, 3, 25) ἑαυτοῖς συνεφώνησαν *they were in agreement with each other* Hv 3, 5, 1b.—*Be of one mind, agree* (Diod. S. 12, 25, 3; 4 Km 12: 9; Jos., C. Ap. 1, 17; 2, 255 τινὶ περί τινος ἐὰν δύο συμφωνήσουσιν περὶ πράγματος Mt 18: 19. Impers. passive συνεφωνήθη ὑμῖν πειρᾶσαι *did you agree to test?*, lit. 'was it agreed by you to test?' Ac 5: 9 (Bl-D. §202 app.; 409, 3 app.; cf. Lat. convenit inter vos; Rob. 1084). Of a business arrangement (oft. pap.) συμφωνήσας μετὰ τῶν ἐργατῶν ἐκ δηναρίου *he came to an agreement* or *he settled with the workmen for a denarius* Mt 20: 2. Also prob. οὐχὶ δηναρίου (gen. of price) συνεφώνησάς μοι; vs. 13. But in the latter pass. the mng. may also be

b. *be in agreement* τινί *with someone.* M-M.*

συμφώνησις, εως, ἡ (Anecd. Gr. Oxon. ed. JACramer IV [1837] p. 326, 12) *agreement* τινὸς πρός τινα *of someone with someone* 2 Cor 6: 15. M-M.*

συμφωνία, ας, ἡ (Pla. +; pap., LXX; Ep. Arist. 302; Philo; Jos., C. Ap. 2, 170; 179) in our lit. only in one pass., as a term dealing w. music Lk 15: 25. It is variously interpreted:

1. *music* produced by several instruments (Paradoxogr. Flor. 43), also *band, orchestra* (PFlor. 74, 5; 18; POxy. 1275, 9; 12; 24 συμφωνία αὐλητῶν καὶ μουσικῶν).

2. a single instrument (Polyb. 26, 1, 4 μετὰ κερατίου καὶ συμφωνίας; Athen. 13 p. 594Ε χορῷ μεγάλῳ κ. παντοίοις ὀργάνοις κ. συμφωνίαις; Da 3: 5, 15 v.l. Loanw. in rabb. w. the mng. 'double flute' [Billerb. IV 396, 400]). Acc. to PBarry, JBL 23, '04, 180ff; 27, '08, 99ff a kind of *bagpipe*. Against this GFMoore, ibid. 24, '05, 166ff. M-M.*

σύμφωνος, ον (Hom. Hymns, Pla. +; inscr., pap., 4 Macc)—**1.** *harmonious* in symbolic usage IEph 4: 1, 2; 5: 1.

2. *agreeing* (Ep. Arist. 302; Jos., C. Ap. 2, 169, Ant. 15, 408); subst. τὸ σύμφωνον *agreement* (Philo) ἐκ συμφώνου *by agreement* (PLond. 334, 19; PHamb. 15, 8; P Strassb. 14, 13; BGU 446, 13 al. in pap.) 1 Cor 7: 5. M-M.*

συμψέλιον, ου, τό (POxy. 921; Sb 4292, 4. Written σεμψέλλιον: PGrenf. II 111, 37; CWessely, Wiener Studien 24, '02, 99f. Lat. loanw. = 'subsellium'. Loanw. in rabb.) *bench* Hv 3, 1, 4; 7; 3, 2, 4; 3, 10, 1; 5; 3, 13, 3; m 11: 1.*

συμψηφίζω (as a mid. Aristoph., X. +) in our lit. act. (as PGM 13, 348) 1 aor. συνεψήφισα *count up, compute* τί *someth.* τὰς τιμὰς αὐτῶν *the price of them* (= the books) Ac 19: 19. τὴν ποσότητα τῆς δαπάνης *count up the amount of the cost* Hs 5, 3, 7. τὰς ὥρας *count the hours* v 3, 1, 4.—The pass. (cf. Appian, Bell. Civ. 3, 22 §83; Sb 7378, 9 [II AD]; Jer 30: 14 AQ) συνεψηφίσθη μετὰ τ. ἀποστόλων *he was counted as one of the apostles* Ac 1: 26 D (verbs compounded w. σύν are oft. used w. μετά in the LXX: Johannessohn 205). M-M.*

σύμψυχος, ον *harmonious, united in spirit* (so in Polemo, Decl. 2, 54 p. 34, 19) w. τὸ ἓν φρονῶν Phil 2: 2 (but

AFridrichsen, Philol. Wochenschr. 58, '38, 910–12 *wholeheartedly*). M-M.*

σύν (the Koine knows nothing of the Attic form ξύν; Bl-D. §34, 4; Rob. 626) prep. w. dat. (Hom. +; inscr., pap., LXX, En., Ep. Arist., Joseph., Test. 12 Patr.—For lit. s. on ἀνά and μετά, beg.; Tycho Mommsen esp. p. 395ff; Bl-D. 221 w. app.; Rob. 626–8) *with.*

1. w. the dat. of the pers. to denote accompaniment and association—**a.** *be, remain, stand,* etc., *with someone* ἀνακεῖσθαι σύν τινι J 12: 2. διατρίβειν Ac 14: 28. τὸν ἄνθρωπον σὺν αὐτοῖς ἑστῶτα Ac 4: 14. μένειν Lk 1: 56; 24: 29 (here alternating w. μένειν μετά τινος as its equivalent).

b. *go, travel,* etc. *with someone* ἔρχεσθαι σύν τινι *go with, accompany someone* (Jos., Vi. 65) J 21: 3; Ac 11: 12; *come with someone* 2 Cor 9: 4. ἀπέρχεσθαι Ac 5: 26. εἰσέρχεσθαι (X., Cyr. 3, 3, 13) Lk 8: 51; Ac 3: 8. ἐξέρχεσθαι J 18: 1; Ac 10: 23; 14: 20. συνέρχεσθαι 21: 16. πορεύεσθαι Lk 7: 6; Ac 10: 20.

c. In the case of εἶναι σύν τινι the emphasis is sometimes purely on *being together,* and somet. upon accompaniment: *be with someone* (X., An. 1, 8, 26; Alexandrian graffito, prob. fr. imperial times [Dssm., LO 257, 4—LAE 303, 1] εὔχομαι κἀγὼ ἐν τάχυ σὺν σοί εἶναι [addressed to a deceased person]) Lk 24: 44 (ἔτι ὢν σὺν ὑμῖν as 4 Macc 18: 10); Phil 1: 23 (Quint. Smyrn. 7, 698 of Achilles ἐστὶ σὺν ἀθανάτοισι); Col 2: 5; w. indication of the place ἐν τῷ ὄρει 2 Pt 1: 18. *Accompany, follow someone* Lk 7: 12. *Be someone's companion* or *disciple* 8: 38; 22: 56; Ac 4: 13; *be among someone's attendants* 13: 7. ἐσχίσθη τὸ πλῆθος καὶ οἱ μὲν ἦσαν σὺν τοῖς Ἰουδαίοις, οἱ δὲ σὺν τοῖς ἀποστόλοις 14: 4 (cf. X., Cyr. 7, 5, 77). οἱ σύν τινι ὄντες *someone's comrades, companions, attendants* Mk 2: 26; Ac 22: 9. Without ὄντες (X., An. 2, 2, 1; UPZ 160, 9 [119 BC]; Jos., Vi. 196, Ant. 11, 105; 12, 393) Lk 5: 9; 8: 45 v.l.; 9: 32; 24: 10 (αἱ σὺν αὐταῖς); 24: 33; Ac 5: 17. In the sing. Τίτος ὁ σὺν ἐμοί Gal 2: 3.—With a subst. (POxy. 242, 33; BGU 1028, 19) οἱ σὺν αὐτῷ τεχνῖται *his fellow-craftsmen* Ac 19: 38. οἱ σὺν αὐτοῖς ἀδελφοί Ro 16: 14; cf. Gal 1: 2; Ro 16: 15; Phil 4: 21; MPol 12: 3.

d. γενέσθαι σύν τινι *join someone* Lk 2: 13 (γίνομαι I 4cζ). καθῆσαι σύν τινι *sit beside someone* Ac 8: 31.

2. *do* or *experience someth.* *with someone*—**a.** do: Ἀνανίας σὺν Σαπφίρῃ ἐπώλησεν κτῆμα Ac 5: 1. ἐπίστευσεν σὺν τῷ οἴκῳ αὐτοῦ 18: 8. προσεύχεσθαι 20: 36. ἁγνίσθητι σὺν αὐτοῖς 21: 24.—Phil 2: 22.

b. *experience, suffer:* σύν τινι ἀποθανεῖν Mt 26: 35. ἀναιρεθῆναι Lk 23: 32. σταυρωθῆναι Mt 27: 38; cf. vs. 44. Cf. Ac 8: 20; 1 Cor 11: 32. οἱ ἐκ πίστεως εὐλογοῦνται σὺν τῷ πιστῷ Ἀβραάμ Gal 3: 9. ἡ ζωὴ ὑμῶν κέκρυπται σὺν τῷ Χριστῷ ἐν τῷ θεῷ Col 3: 3.—In mystic union w. Christ the Christian comes to ἀποθανεῖν σὺν Χριστῷ Ro 6: 8; Col 2: 20 and to ζῆν σὺν αὐτῷ 2 Cor 13: 4; cf. 1 Th 5: 10 (ELohmeyer, Σὺν Χριστῷ: Deissmann-Festschr. '27, 218–57; JDupont, Σὺν Χριστῷ . . . suivant St. Paul; 1ère partie—la vie future '52).

c. To the personal obj. acc. of the verb in the act., σύν adds other persons who are undergoing the same experience *at the same time with,* just as (Philochorus [IV/III BC]: no. 328 fgm. 7a Jac. ὥπλιζε σὺν τοῖς ἄρρεσι τὰς θηλείας) σὺν αὐτῷ σταυροῦσιν δύο λῃστάς Mk 15: 27. ὁ βεβαιῶν ἡμᾶς σὺν ὑμῖν 2 Cor 1: 21. ἡμᾶς σὺν Ἰησοῦ ἐγερεῖ 4: 14. Cf. Col 2: 13; 1 Th 4: 14.

3. to denote help (X., Cyr. 5, 4, 37 ἢν οἱ θεοὶ σὺν ἡμῖν ὦσιν, An. 3, 1, 21; [the expr. σὺν θεῷ, PGrenf. II 73, 16 ὅταν ἔλθῃ σὺν θεῷ; POxy. 1220, 23 et al. (cf. Pind., Ol.

10, 105[115] σὺν Κυπρογενεῖ) is not semantically parallel; cf. BRRees, Journ. of Egypt. Arch. 36, '50, 94f]; Jos., Ant. 11, 259 θεὸς σὺν αὐτῷ) ἡ χάρις τοῦ θεοῦ (ἡ) σὺν ἐμοί God's grace, that came to my aid 1 Cor 15: 10.

4. combining persons and things—a. *with, at the same time as* τὸ ἐμὸν σὺν τόκῳ *my money with interest* Mt 25: 27 (POsl. 40, 7 [150 AD] κεφάλαιον σὺν τ. τόκοις). αὐτὸν σὺν τῷ κλινιδίῳ Lk 5: 19. σὺν αὐτῷ τὰ πάντα Ro 8: 32. σὺν τῷ πειρασμῷ καὶ τὴν ἔκβασιν 1 Cor 10: 13.

b. somet. σύν is nearly equivalent to καί (Ostraka 1535, 5 [II BC] τοῖς συνστρατιώταις σὺν Πλάτωνι; Johannessohn 207) (*together*) *with* οἱ γραμματεῖς σὺν τοῖς πρεσβυτέροις Lk 20: 1. Πέτρος σὺν τῷ Ἰωάννῃ Ac 3: 4. Cf. Lk 23: 11; Ac 2: 14; 10: 2; 14: 5; 23: 15; Eph 3: 18; Phil 1: 1 (cf. POxy. 1293, 3 [117-38 AD]); 1 Cl 65: 1; IPol 8: 2. τὴν σάρκα σὺν τοῖς παθήμασιν Gal 5: 24. Cf. Eph 4: 31; Js 1: 11.

5. when a new factor is introduced *besides, in addition to* (Jos., Ant. 17, 171) σὺν πᾶσιν τούτοις *beside all this, in addition to* or *apart from all this* (cf. σὺν τούτοις= 'apart fr. this': Galen, CMG V 9, 1 p. 381, 2; Proseuche Aseneth 11 Bat.; 3 Macc 1: 22) Lk 24: 21.—6. in combination w. ἅμα (ἅμα 2) 1 Th 4: 17; 5: 10.—BMcGrath, CBQ 14, '52, 219-26: 'Syn'-Words in Paul; OGert, D. mit. *syn*-verbundenen Formulierungen in paul. Schrifttum, Diss. Berlin, '52; WGrundmann, TW VII, 766-98: σύν and μετά w. gen. M-M.

συνάγω (Hom.+; inscr., pap., LXX, Ep. Arist., Philo, Joseph., Test. 12 Patr.) fut. συνάξω; 1 aor. inf. συνάξαι Lk 3: 17 v.l. (JHMoulton, Cambridge Bibl. Essays '09, 485f); 2 aor. συνήγαγον. Pass.: pf. ptc. συνηγμένος; 1 aor. συνήχθην; 1 fut. συναχθήσομαι.

1. *gather (in)* things: J 15: 6. κλάσματα 6: 12f. ξύλα MPol 13: 1. Of fish of every kind, which the net *gathers up* when it is cast Mt 13: 47. Of the fragments of a ms. that is wearing out MPol 22: 3a; Epil Mosq 4a. Of field crops (Ex 23: 10; Lev 25: 3) Mt 25: 24, 26; cf. pass. (Jos., Ant. 5, 242) D 9: 4a. W. indication of the destination εἴς τι (Diod. S. 19, 100, 2 τ. ἀσφαλτον σ. εἴς τινα τόπον) εἰς τὴν ἀποθήκην Mt 3: 12; 6: 26; 13: 30; Lk 3: 17. ποῦ 12: 17. ἐκεῖ vs. 18. συνάγειν πάντα Lk 15: 13 *gather everything together*, perh. in the sense or w. the connotation *turn everything into cash* (cf. Plut., Cato Min. 6, 7 κληρονομίαν εἰς ἀργύριον συναγαγών).—Symbolically συνάγειν μετά τινος *join with someone in gathering* (opp. σκορπίζω, q.v. 1) Mt 12: 30; Lk 11: 23. συνάγειν καρπὸν εἰς ζωὴν αἰώνιον J 4: 36. Of sheep, metaph. 10: 16 𝔓⁶⁶.

2. *bring* or *call together, gather* a number of persons (1 Km 5: 11; Jos., C. Ap. 1, 234) πάντας οὓς εὗρον Mt 22: 10. πάντας τοὺς ἀρχιερεῖς 2: 4 (Appian, Bell. Civ. 4, 4 §15: in view of frightening signs ἡ βουλὴ μάντεις συνῆγεν). πάντα τὰ ἔθνη 2 Cl 17: 4; (Is 66: 18). συνέδριον (Diod. S. 17, 4, 2 συνέδριον συναγαγών, likew. 17, 30, 1.—Cf. Ex 3: 16 τ. γερουσίαν, likew. Jos., Ant. 5, 332) J 11: 47. τὸ πλῆθος (Jos., Ant. 3, 188) Ac 15: 30. τὴν ἐκκλησίαν (Aeneas Tact. 431; Lucian, Jupp. Trag. 15) 14: 27; cf. D 10: 5. συναάξεις πάντας τοὺς σοὺς ὑπὸ τὸ στέγος σου 1 Cl 12: 6. Foll. by εἰς to indicate the place (X., Ages. 1, 25; Jos., Vi. 280 τὸ πλῆθος εἰς τὴν προσευχήν) εἰς τὸν τόπον Rv 16: 16 (Diod. S. 17, 20, 1 συνήγαγεν εἰς ἕνα τόπον τοὺς ἀρίστους; 13, 49, 3). εἰς ἕν J 11: 52 (cf. εἰς 2a); to indicate the purpose (Dionys. Hal. 2, 45 ὅπως εἰς φιλίαν συναξουσι τὰ ἔθνη; Jos., C. Ap. 1, 111) εἰς τὸν πόλεμον Rv 16: 14; 20: 8. Cf. 13: 1 v.l. ἐπί τινα Mt 27: 27. ἵνα κἀμὲ συναγάγῃ ὁ κύριος Ἰ. Χρ. μετὰ τῶν ἐκλεκτῶν *that the Lord Jesus Christ may*

gather me also with the elect MPol 22: 3b; Epil Mosq 4b.—Pass., either in the passive sense *be gathered* or *brought together* συναχθήσονται ἔμπροσθεν αὐτοῦ πάντα τὰ ἔθνη Mt 25: 32. συναχθήτω σου ἡ ἐκκλησία ἀπὸ τῶν περάτων τῆς γῆς εἰς τὴν σὴν βασιλείαν D 9: 4b; or in the reflexive sense *gather, come together, assemble* (Gen 29: 8; Dt 33: 5; Esth 9: 18; Test. Reub. 1: 2) Mt 22: 41; 27: 17; Mk 2: 2; MPol 18: 2; D 14: 1; 16: 2. The subj. can also be a collective word συνήχθη τὸ πρεσβυτέριον Lk 22: 66; ἡ πόλις Ac 13: 44. More closely defined: as to place εἴς τι Mt 26: 3; Ac 4: 5 v.l. εἰς τὸ δεῖπνον Rv 19: 17. ἔν τινι: Ac 4: 5 text, 31. ἐν τῇ ἐκκλησίᾳ *with the church* 11: 26. ἐὰν ἦτε μετ' ἐμοῦ συνηγμένοι ἐν τῷ κόλπῳ μου *if you are gathered with me in my bosom* 2 Cl 4: 5 (a saying of the Lord, of unknown origin). παρά τινι *with someone* Ac 21: 18 D. πρός τινα *to* or *with someone* (Test. Benj. 10: 11) Mt 13: 2; 27: 62; Mk 4: 1; 6: 30; 7: 1. πρὸς ἀλλήλους GP 8: 28. ἐπί τινα *with* or *around someone* Mk 5: 21; *against someone* (Gen 34: 30; Josh 10: 6; Hos 10: 10) Ac 4: 27 (=κατά τινος vs. 26 after Ps 2: 2). ἐπὶ τὴν ζωήν *into life* 2 Cl 17: 3. ἐπὶ τὸ αὐτό (s. αὐτός 4b and ἐπί III 1aζ) Mt 22: 34; Ac 4: 26 (Ps 2: 2); 1 Cl 34: 7. σύν τινι (Mi 2: 12) 1 Cor 5: 4. συναχθέντες μετὰ τῶν πρεσβυτέρων Mt 28: 12; also of an individual pers. συνήχθη Ἰησοῦς μετὰ τῶν μαθητῶν αὐτοῦ J 18: 2 (HReynen, BZ 5, '61, 86-90 'stay'). W. an adv. of place οὗ Mt 18: 20; Ac 20: 8; ὅπου Mt 26: 57; J 20: 19 t.r.; ἐκεῖ (Test. Benj. 9: 2; Jos., Ant. 6, 23) Mt 24: 28; Lk 17: 37 t.r.; J 18: 2. Foll. by inf. of purpose Ac 13: 44; 15: 6; 20: 7; Rv 19: 19.

3. *bring together, reconcile* (Demosth. et al.; Herodian 3, 13, 5; 4, 3, 4; 9) μαχομένους συναγαγών B 19: 12.

4. *lead* or *bring (to)* (Hom.+) pass. πᾶσα γλῶσσα εἰς θεὸν συνήχθη IMg 10: 3.—5. *invite* or *receive as a guest* (w. εἰς τὴν οἰκίαν or εἰς τὸν οἶκον added Judg 19: 18; 2 Km 11: 27; Dt 22: 2. Cf. also Gen 29: 22; Achilles Tat. 3, 8, 3) Mt 25: 35, 38, 43.

6. intr. (so, but w. a different mng., Theocr. 22, 82; Polyb. 11, 18, 4 [both= meet in hostile fashion]) *advance, move* (Aelian, V.H. 3, 9 συνάγοντος τοῦ πολέμου) σύναγε ἔτι ἄνω *move farther up* Mt 20: 28 D= Agr 22.—On Dg 12: 9 s. καιρός, end (cf. Jos., C. Ap. 1, 126 συνάγεται πᾶς ὁ χρόνος). M-M.*

συναγωγή, ῆς, ἡ (Thu.+; inscr., pap., LXX)—1. *gathering-place, place where someth. collects* of the basins in which water is gathered at the creation (Gen 1: 9; cf. Jos., Ant. 15, 346 σ. ὑδάτων) 1 Cl 20: 6.

2. *place of assembly* (Cybele-inscr. [Bilderatlas z. Religionsgesch. 9-11, '26 p. xix no. 154] ἐν τῇ τοῦ Διὸς συναγωγῇ; Sb 4981, 6.—On συναγωγή as a room for meetings cf. συνέδρια of the meeting-houses of the Pythagoreans Polyb. 2, 39, 1)—a. of the Jewish *synagogue* (it is used for a place of assembly for Jews in Philo, Omn. Prob. Lib. 81 [w. ref. to the Essenes]; Jos., Bell. 2, 285; 289; 7, 44, Ant. 19, 300; 305; CIG 9894; 9904; Bull. de corr. hell. 21, 1897 p. 47; Συναγωγὴ Ἑβραίων in Corinth [s. Κόρινθος, end], in Rome [CIG IV 9909] and Lydia [JKeil and AvPremerstein, Bericht über e. dritte Reise in Lyd.: Denkschr. d. Ak. Wien 57, '14, p. 32ff no. 42].—Av Harnack, Mission⁴ II '24, p. 568, 2; GKittel, ThLZ 69, '44, 11f); people came to the συν. to worship God Mt 4: 23; 6: 2, 5; 9: 35; 12: 9; 13: 54; Mk 1: 39; 3: 1; 6: 2; Lk 4: 15; 6: 6; J 18: 20. In the same buildings court was also held and punishment was inflicted: Mt 10: 17; 23: 34; Mk 13: 9; Lk 12: 11; 21: 12; Ac 22: 19; 26: 11. Synagogues are also mentioned as existing in Antioch in Pisidia 13: 14; Athens 17: 17; Beroea vs. 10; Damascus 9: 20; Ephesus 18: 19;

Capernaum Mk 1: 21; Lk 4: 33; 7: 5; J 6: 59 (HKohl and CWatzinger, Antike Synagogen in Galiläa '16; HVincent, RB 30, '21, 438ff; 532ff; GOrfali, Capharnaum et ses ruines '22); Corinth Ac 18: 4; Ephesus 19: 8 (s. above); Nazareth Lk 4: 16; Salamis on the island of Cyprus Ac 13: 5; Thessalonica 17: 1.—ELSukenik, Ancient Synagogues in Palestine and Greece '34.—On the relationship betw. συναγωγή and προσευχή (q.v. 2) cf. SKrauss, Synagogale Altertümer '22, 11; Pauly-W. second ser. IV '32, 1284-1316; ERivkin, AHSilver-Festschr., '63, 350-54.—AWGroenman, De Oorsprong der Joodsche Synagoge: NThT 8, '19, 43-87; 137-88; HLStrack, RE XIX 221-6; Elbogen[2] 444ff; 571ff; Billerb. IV 115-52 (the syn. as an institution), 153-88 (the syn. services); GDalman, Jesus-Jeshua (tr. PLevertoff) '29, 38-55; SSafrai, MStern et al., The Jewish People in the 1st Century II, '77, 908-44.

b. a Christian assembly-place can also be meant in Js 2: 2 (so LRost, Pj 29, '33, 53-66, esp. 54f). εἰς σ. πλήρη ἀνδρῶν Hm 11: 14 (cf. the superscription on a Marcionite assembly-place near Damascus συναγωγὴ Μαρκιωνιστῶν [Dit., Or. 608, 1 fr. 318/19 AD]; Harnack, SAB '15, 754ff). S. 5 below.

3. (the congregation of a) synagogue (references for this usage in Schürer[4] II 504f; III 81ff; EPeterson, Byz.-Neugriech. Jahrbücher 2, '21, 208) Ac 6: 9 (Schürer II[4] 87); 9: 2.

4. The Jews who are hostile to the Christians are called (instead of συναγωγὴ κυρίου: Num 16: 3; 20: 4; 27: 17; Josh 22: 16; Ps 73: 2) συναγωγὴ τοῦ σατανᾶ synagogue of Satan Rv 2: 9; 3: 9.

5. a meeting for worship, of the Jews λυθείσης τῆς συναγωγῆς Ac 13: 43 (cf. λύω 3).—Transferred to meetings of Christian congregations (cf. Test. Benj. 11: 2, 3) ἐὰν εἰσέλθῃ εἰς συναγωγὴν ὑμῶν Js 2: 2 (this is the preferred interpr.: HermvSoden, Ropes, Meinertz, F Hauck. S. 2b above). συναγωγὴ ἀνδρῶν δικαίων Hm 11: 9, 13, cf. 14. πυκνότερον συναγωγαὶ γινέσθωσαν meetings (of the congregation) should be held more often IPol 4: 2. (συναγ. is also found outside Jewish and Christian circles for periodic meetings; cf. the exx. in MDibelius, Jakobus '21 p. 124, 1. Also Philo Bybl. in Euseb., Pr. Ev. 1, 10, 52 Ζωροάστρης ἐν τῇ ἱερᾷ συναγωγῇ τῶν Περσικῶν φησι; Dit., Or. 737, 1 [II BC] σ. ἐν τῷ Ἀπολλωνείῳ; PLond. 2710r., 12: HTR 29, '36, 40; 51.—Sb 8267, 3 [5 BC] honorary inscr. of a pagan συν.= association. W. ref. to the imperial cult BGU 1137, 2 [6 BC]). On the Christian use of the word cf. also ADeissmann, Die Urgeschichte des Christentums im Lichte der Sprachforschung '10, 35f.

6. of any group of people: band, gang σ. πονηρευομένων (Ps 21: 17) B 5: 13; 6: 6.—WSchrage, TW VII, 798-850: συναγωγή and related words. M-M.

συναγωνίζομαι mid. dep.; 1 aor. συνηγωνισάμην (Thu.+; inscr.; Test. Ash. 6: 2) fight or contend along with τινί someone, then also gener. help, assist someone (Demosth. 21, 190; Dit., Syll.[3] 651, 14 τοῖς πρεσβευταῖς συναγωνιζόμενος ἐκτενῶς; Philo, Spec. Leg. 4, 179; Jos., Ant. 12, 18; 17, 220; noun in POxy. 1676, 36f [III AD]: 'fellow-worker') Ro 15: 30. M-M.*

συναθλέω (Diod. S. 3, 4, 1='help') 1 aor. συνήθλησα contend or struggle along with τινί someone ἐν τῷ εὐαγγελίῳ συνήθλησάν μοι they fought at my side in (spreading) the gospel Phil 4: 3. τῇ πίστει (dat. of advantage) τοῦ εὐαγγελίου for the faith of the gospel 1: 27. Abs. IPol 6: 1.*

συναθροίζω 1 aor. συνήθροισα. Pass.: 1 aor. συνηθροί-

σθην; pf. ptc. συνηθροισμένος (Thu. et al.; inscr.; POxy. 1253, 5; LXX).

1. gather, bring together w. acc. of the pers. (cf. 2 Km 2: 30; Jos., Bell. 4, 645) Ac 19: 25. Pass. be gathered, meet (X., An. 6, 5, 30; Antig. Car. 173; Josh 22: 12; 1 Km 8: 4; Jo 4: 11; Jos., Bell. 5, 533, C. Ap. 1, 308) Lk 24: 33 t.r.; Ac 12: 12; hold meetings for purposes of worship IMg 4 (cf. Ex 35: 1; Jos., Bell. 2, 289 εἰς τὴν συναγωγήν, Ant. 3, 84).

2. unite with, be joined to w. dat. τοῖς ἀνδράσιν συνηθροίσθη πολὺ πλῆθος ἐκλεκτῶν 1 Cl 6: 1. M-M.*

συναινέω 1 aor. συνήνεσα (Aeschyl., Hdt.+; inscr., pap., 3 Macc) agree with, be in accord with τινί someone (Ep. Arist. 226; cf. Philo, Op. M. 2; Jos., Ant. 3, 192) IEph 11: 2 (συνήνεσαν is read by Lghtf., Funk, Hilgenfeld, GKrüger, Bihlmeyer; on the other hand Zahn [also Forschungen VI '00 p. 191, 1] prefers συνῆσαν, though it is less well attested).*

συναίρω 1 aor. inf. συνᾶραι (Hom.+; Ex 23: 5 v.l.; Jos., Ant. 12, 286) συναίρειν λόγον settle accounts (in act. and mid. [Bl-D. §310, 1; Mlt. 160]; PFay. 109, 6 [I AD]; BGU 775, 19; POxy. 113, 27. Now and then in the expr. παντὸς λόγου συνηρμένου='when accounts have been settled in full': PFlor. 372, 14 al.) μετά τινος with someone (PLond. 131, 194 [I AD]) Mt 18: 23; 25: 19. Without λόγον, which is supplied by the preceding verse, 18: 24. On the legal principles involved s. RSugranyes de Franch, Études sur le droit Palestinien à l'époque évangélique '46. M-M.*

συναιχμάλωτος, ου, ὁ (Ps.-Lucian, Asinus 27; Theodor. Prodr. 7, 256 Hercher; Nicetas Eugen. 9, 46; 81) fellow-prisoner Ro 16: 7; Col 4: 10; Phlm 23. M-M.*

συνακολουθέω impf. συνηκολούθουν; 1 aor. συνηκολούθησα (Thu., Aristoph.+; PTebt. 39, 14 [II BC]; 2 Macc 2: 4, 6; Philo, Omn. Prob. Lib. 94; Jos., Ant. 6, 365) follow, accompany someone w. dat. of the pers. who is followed (X., Cyr. 8, 7, 5; Diod. S. 14, 39, 5 συνακολούθουν αὐτοῖς) Mk 5: 37 t.r.; 14: 51; Lk 23: 49 (here 'follow' has the connotation of being a disciple, as Philostrat., Vi. Apoll. 8, 19 p. 335, 32; cf. ἐκολουθέω 3); J 13: 36 v.l. A Diatessaron fgm. fr. Dura (s. on προσάββατον) l. 2. W. μετά τινος instead of the dat. (Isocr. 4, 146: Diod. S. 13, 62, 5) Mk 5: 37. M-M.*

συναλίζω; in the difficult passage συναλιζόμενος παρήγγειλεν αὐτοῖς Ac 1: 4, the word is variously understood:

1. συνἄλίζω eat (salt) with (cf. ἅλς) so the Lat., Syr., Copt. and the other ancient versions, Ephraem (AMerck, Der neuentdeckte Komm. des hl. Ephraem zur AG: ZkTh 48, '24, 228), Chrysost., Overbeck; PFeine, Eine vorkanonische Überl. des Lukas 1891, 160; Felten; AHilgenfeld, ZWTh 38, 1895, 74; BWeiss, Blass, Preuschen; CRBowen, ZNW 13, '12, 247-59 (= Studies in the NT, ed. RJHutcheon '36, 89-109); Wendt, Zahn, Jacquier, JMoffatt; Gdspd., Probs. 122f; EGill, Rev. and Expos. 36, '39, 197f 'salt covenant'; L-S-J; OCullmann, Urchristentum u. Gottesdienst '44, 15; EFFBishop, ET 56, '44/'45, 220; PBenoit, RB 56, '49, 191 note 3; EHaenchen, AG. The objections to this point of view are that it fits rather poorly into the context, and the circumstance that this mng., strictly speaking, is not found elsewh. (Manetho, Apotel. 5, 339 and Ps.-Clem., Hom. p. 11, 12; 134, 19 Lag. it does not necessarily refer to table fellowship. Yet Libanius V 246, 13 F. ἁλῶν κοινωνεῖν=τραπέζης κ.); and Ac 10: 41 appears to echo 1: 4.

2. συναλίζω *bring together, assemble,* pass. *come together* (both Hdt. +; the pass. also Petosiris, fgm. 33, 1. 6 [Πετόσειρις as an ἀνὴρ παντοίαις τάξεσι θεῶν τε καὶ ἀγγέλων συναλισθείς] and Jos., Bell. 3, 429, the act. Ant. 8, 105) so Weizsäcker; WBrandt, Die evangel. Gesch. 1893 p. 371, 1; Field, Notes 110f ('as he was assembling w. them'); HHoltzmann, Knopf; WHPHatch, JBL 30, '11, 123-8; ASteinmann, OHoltzmann. The objections to this are the singular number (IAHeikel, StKr 106, '35, 315 proposes συναλιζομένοις) and the pres. tense of συναλιζόμενος (a linguistic counterpart may perh. be found in the sing. pres. in Ocellus [II BC] c. 15 Harder ['26] πῦρ εἰς ἓν συνερχόμενον).

3. The difficulties in 1 and 2 have led some to resort to the expedient of finding in συναλιζόμενος simply another spelling of συναυλιζόμενος, which is actually the reading of several minuscules here (the same variation in X., Cyr. 1, 2, 15 and Ps.-Clem., Hom. p. 11, 12). συναυλίζομαι dep., lit. *spend the night with,* then also gener. *be with, stay with* (Babrius, Fab. 106, 6; Pr 22: 24; Synes., Kingship 19 p. 21 D; Achmes 109, 18). So HJCadbury, JBL 45, '26, 310-17; KLake; RSV text. Cf. CFDMoule, NTS 4, '57/'58, 58-61; MWilcox, The Semitisms of Ac, '65, 106-9.—On the whole question cf. also CCTorrey, The Composition and Date of Acts '16, 23f. M-M.*

συναλίσκομαι (Plut. +; Aelian, N.A. 11, 12; Diog. L. 2, 105) pass. *be taken captive together* Ac 1: 4 D.*

συνάλλαγμα, ατος, τό (Hippocr. +) *contract, agreement* (Demosth., Aristot. +; inscr., pap.; 1 Macc 13: 42; Jos., Ant. 16, 45) βίαια συναλλάγματα *extorted contracts* B 3: 3 (Is 58: 6).*

συναλλάσσω impf. συνήλλασσον (Aeschyl. +; inscr., pap.) *reconcile* (Thu. +) τινά *someone* συνήλλασσεν αὐτοὺς εἰς εἰρήνην *he tried* (conative impf., as Diod. S. 20, 37, 3 προῆγεν = she wanted to set out; 20, 71, 1 ἠνάγκαζε = he wanted to compel) *to reconcile them, so that they would be peaceful* Ac 7: 26. M-M.*

συναναβαίνω 2 aor. συνανέβην *come* or *go up with* (Hdt. +; LXX) τινί *with someone* (PTebt. 21, 11 [115 BC]; Ex 12: 38) w. the destination given (Ps.-Lucian, Charid. 24 εἰς Ἴλιον σ. τοῖς Ἀχαιοῖς) εἰς Ἱεροσόλυμα Mk 15: 41; w. place fr. which and place to which ἀπὸ τῆς Γαλιλαίας εἰς Ἱερουσαλήμ Ac 13: 31. Instead of the dat. μετά τινος (Dit., Or. 632, 2 [II AD] μετ᾽ αὐτοῦ; LXX) Hs 9, 16, 7. M-M.*

συνανάκειμαι impf. συνανεκείμην *recline at table with, eat with* (3 Macc 5: 39) τινί *with someone* Mt 9: 10; Mk 2: 15; Lk 14: 10. οἱ συνανακείμενοι *the guests* Mt 14: 9; Mk 6: 22, 26 t.r.; Lk 7: 49; 14: 15; J 12: 2 t.r.*

συναναμείγνυμι *mix up together* (Hippocr.; Athen. 5 p. 177B) pass. *mingle* or *associate with* w. dat. of the pers. (Clearchus [IV/III BC] in Athen. 6 p. 256A; Plut., Philop. 21, 8; Hos 7: 8, cf. Ezk 20: 18; Philo, Mos. 1, 278; Jos., Ant. 20, 165) 1 Cor 5: 9; 2 Th 3: 14. Abs. 1 Cor 5: 11. M-M.*

συναναπαύομαι 1 aor. συνανεπαυσάμην *rest* or *find rest (with)* τινί *someone, in someone's company* Ro 15: 32 (elsewh. only lit. = 'lie down, sleep w. somebody' [Arrian, Cyneg. 9, 2], esp. of married couples [Dionys. Hal.; Plut.].—Is 11: 6). M-M.*

συναναστρέφω in our lit. only pass.
συναναστρέφομαι (Jos., Bell. 5, 58; Test. Napht. 4: 2) *associate, go about* τινί *with someone* (Agatharchides [II

BC]: 86 fgm. 12 Jac.; Diod. S. 3, 58, 3; Epict. 3, 13, 5; Dit., Syll.³ 534, 8 [218/17 BC]; Sir 41: 5; Jos., Ant. 20, 206) Ac 10: 41 D (the dat. is to be supplied).*

συναναφύρω 1 aor. pass. συνανεφύρην (Lucian; Galen: CMG V 9, 1 p. 193, 6; Proclus on Pla., Tim. III p. 49, 13 Diehl; PHolm. 26, 39; Ezk 22: 6) *knead together* fig. *entangle, involve* pass. ταῖς πραγματείαις σου συνανεφύρης ταῖς πονηραῖς *you have involved yourself in your wicked affairs* Hv 2, 3, 1 (the dat. as Lucian, Ep. Sat. 2, 28).*

συναναχέω (Heliod. [III AD]) *pour on together with* v.l. 𝔓⁷⁴ Ac 11: 26.*

συναντάω fut. συναντήσω; 1 aor. συνήντησα *meet*—1. lit. (Hom. +; inscr., pap., LXX) τινί *someone* (X., An. 7, 2, 5; Diod. S. 3, 65, 1; PLille 6, 6 [III BC]; 1 Macc 5: 25; Jos., Ant. 8, 331) Lk 9: 18 v.l., 37; 22: 10; Ac 10: 25; Hb 7: 1, 10; Epil Mosq 2. Abs. (Jos., Bell. 5, 40) ISm 4: 1 (sc. αὐτοῖς).

2. fig., of events (PSI 392, 1 [242/1 BC]; Plut., Sulla 2, 7; Ex 5: 3; Job 30: 26; Test. Levi 1: 1.—The mid. is also used in this way: Polyb. 22, 7, 14; Eccl 2: 14; 9: 11) τὰ ἐν αὐτῇ συναντήσοντα ἐμοὶ μὴ εἰδὼς *without knowing what will happen to me there* Ac 20: 22. M-M.*

συνάντησις, εως, ἡ (Eur., Hippocr. et al.; pap.) *meeting* εἰς συνάντησίν τινι *to meet someone* (Ps.-Callisth. 3, 25, 5 σοι εἰς συνάντησιν; oft. LXX w. dat. and also gen.—Johannessohn 295f) Mt 8: 34 t.r.; J 12: 13 v.l. M-M.*

συναντιλαμβάνομαι 2 aor. συναντελαβόμην (Diod. S. 14, 8, 2; Dit., Syll.³ 412, 7 [270 BC], Or. 267, 26; PHib. 82, 18 [perh. 238 BC]; PSI 329, 6; 591, 12; LXX; Jos., Ant. 4, 198 [replaced by Niese w. συλλαμβάνομαι].—Dssm., LO 68 [LAE 87f]) *take part with* (Ep. Arist. 123), gener. *help, come to the aid of* τινί *someone* (Ex 18: 22; Ps 88: 22) Lk 10: 40. τὸ πνεῦμα συναντιλαμβάνεται τῇ ἀσθενείᾳ ἡμῶν *the Spirit helps us in our weakness* Ro 8: 26 (v.l. τῆς ἀσθενείας; Bl-D. §170, 3; Rob. 529; 573). M-M.*

συναπάγω 1 aor. pass. συναπήχθην (X., pap.; Ex 14: 6) in our lit. only pass. and fig. (Zosimus, Hist. 5, 6, 9 αὐτὴ ἡ Σπάρτη συναπήγετο τῇ κοινῇ τῆς Ἑλλάδος ἁλώσει) *lead away* or *carry off with.* Pass. *be led* or *carried away* τινί *by someth.* (instrum. dat.) or *to someth.* (cf. Kühner-G. I p. 407) Gal 2: 13; 2 Pt 3: 17. τοῖς ταπεινοῖς συναπαγόμενοι Ro 12: 16 may be taken to refer to things *accommodate yourself to humble ways* (Weymouth) in contrast to τὰ ὑψηλὰ φρονοῦντες (so, gener., BWeiss, RALipsius, Lietzmann, Kühl, Sickenberger, OHoltzmann, Althaus, Gdspd., WGBallantine, RSV mg.) or to people *associate with humble folk* (Moffatt; so, gener., the ancient versions and Chrysostom; Hilgenfeld, Zahn; KThieme, ZNW 8, '07, 23ff; Lagrange; RSV text = 20th Cent.). The two interpretations are connected in so far as the form is taken to be neuter, but referring to persons (so FSpitta, Zur Gesch. u. Lit. des Urchristentums III 1, '01, 113; Jülicher. Cf. the ambiguous transl. of Weizsäcker: 'sich heruntergeben zur Niedrigkeit', or the sim. Confraternity of Christian Doctrine transl. '41: 'condescend to the lowly'. S. also PBerlin 9734 of Tyche: τὰ ταπεινὰ πολλάκις εἰς ὕψος ἐξαίρεας).—AFridrichsen, Horae Soederblom. I 1, '44, 32. M-M.*

συναποθνῄσκω 2 aor. συναπέθανον (Hdt. +; Diod. S. 19, 34, 1 [of the burning of widows in India]; Sir 19: 10; Philo, Spec. Leg. 1, 108) *die with* τινί *someone* (Clearch., fgm. 28; Diod. S. 18, 41, 3 αὐτῷ; Περὶ ὕψους 44, 2; Polyaenus 8, 39; Charito 4, 2, 14; Hierocles 11 p. 445 μὴ συναποθνῄσκειν τῷ σώματι τὴν ψυχήν) Mk 14: 31. Abs. (opp. συζῆν as Nicol. Dam.: 90 fgm. 80 Jac.) 2 Cor 7: 3; 2 Ti 2: 11 (dying and living with Christ).—FOlivier, Συναποθνῄσκω: RThPh 17, '29, 103-33; WTHahn, D. Mitsterben u. Mitauferstehen mit Chr. bei Pls '37. M-M.*

συναπόλλυμι (act. Thu.+; LXX; Jos., Ant. 1, 199) fut. mid. συναπολοῦμαι; 2 aor. συναπωλόμην destroy with. Mid. be destroyed, perish with (Hdt.+; POxy. 486, 35 [131 AD]; LXX; Jos., Ant. 19, 144) w. dat. (Hdt. 7, 221 al.; Plut., Phoc. 36, 3; Philo, Mut. Nom. 80) Hb 11: 31; B 21: 3. Also μετά τινος with someth. 21: 1 (cf. Gen 18: 23). M-M.*

συναποστέλλω 1 aor. συναπέστειλα (Thu.+; inscr., pap., LXX) send at the same time, send with τινά someone (Zen.-P. [PMich. 45= Sb 6798] l. 25 [256 BC]) 2 Cor 12: 18. M-M.*

συναριθμέω pf. pass. ptc. συνηριθμημένος (Isaeus, Pla.+; POxy. 1208, 17; Ex 12: 4) count, number with or together (Aristot., Eth. 1, 5; 2, 3; Plut., Mor. 1018F; Philo, Mos. 1, 278) ἔν τινι (Plut., Brut. 29, 10) ἐν τῷ εὐαγγελίῳ IPhld 5: 2.*

συναρμόζω (or συναρμόττω; Pind., Thu.+; inscr., pap.; Ep. Arist. 71; Jos., Bell. 7, 307, C. Ap. 2, 173) pf. pass. συνήρμοσμαι; 1 aor. pass. συνηρμόσθην. 1. fit in (with) συνηρμόσθησαν εἰς τὴν οἰκοδομὴν τοῦ πύργου Hs 9, 16, 7.—2. be associated τινί with someone pass. (Dit., Syll.³ 783, 30 συνηρμόσθη αὐτῷ γυνή; BGU 1103, 23; 1104, 24; PSI 166, 17) τὸ πρεσβυτέριον συνήρμοσται τῷ ἐπισκόπῳ IEph 4: 1, though in this context mng. 3 is also poss.—3. attune (so the pass., X., Symp. 3, 1); s. 2 above.*

συναρμολογέω (only in Christian writers) fit or join together pass. of a building Eph 2: 21. Of the body (s. συμβιβάζω 1a) 4: 16. M-M.*

συναρπάζω 1 aor. συνήρπασα; plpf. συνηρπάκειν; 1 aor. pass. συνηρπάσθην (trag., X.+; pap., LXX, Philo, Joseph.) seize by violence, drag away τινά someone (Soph. et al.; Diod. S. 37, 27, 2; Dio Chrys. 5, 15; PSI 353, 12 [III BC]) Ac 6: 12; 19: 29. Of a demoniac who is seized by an unclean spirit Lk 8: 29. Pass. (Diod. S. 20, 29, 11; Philo, Plant. 39; Jos., Ant. 7, 177 συναρπαγεὶς ὑπὸ τ. πάθους) of a ship that was caught, torn away by the wind Ac 27: 15. M-M.*

συναυλίζομαι s. συναλίζω 3.

συναυξάνω (X.+; inscr., pap., LXX; Jos., Ant. 14, 116) pass. (X., Cyr. 8, 7, 6; Plut., Numa 5, 3; Philo, Aet. M. 103; Jos., Ant. 1, 32) grow together, grow side by side Mt 13: 30. M-M.*

συνβ- s. συμβ-.

συνγ- s. συγγ-.

σύνδενδρος, ον (Timaeus Hist. [IV/III BC]: no. 566 fgm. 57 Jac.; Polyb. 12, 4, 2; Diod. S. 5, 65, 1; Sb 4483, 6; Ep. Arist. 112) covered with trees, forested ὄρος Hs 9, 1, 10.*

σύνδεσμος, ου, ὁ (Eur., Thu.+; LXX; Jos., Ant. 3, 120) and τὸ σύνδεσμον B 3: 3 (the pl. σύνδεσμα is found occasionally beside σύνδεσμοι) that which binds together. 1. bond that holds someth. together—a. lit. (Appian, Bell. Civ. 4, 115 §483 οἱ σύνδεσμοι of the fastenings that hold the various ships together; Herm. Wr. 1, 18; Ep. Arist. 85= 'fastening') of the sinews of the body (Eur., Hipp. 199 al.) w. ἁφή Col 2: 19.

b. fig. σύνδ. τῆς εἰρήνης the bond of peace, i.e. that consists in peace (epexegetic gen.; Plut., Numa 6, 4 σύνδεσμος εὐνοίας κ. φιλίας; W-S. §30, 9b) Eph 4: 3. Love is σύνδεσμος τῆς τελειότητος the bond that unites all the virtues (which otherwise have no unity) in perfect harmony or the bond of perfect unity for the church Col 3: 14 (cf. Simplicius In Epict. p. 89, 15 Düb. οἱ Πυθαγόρειοι ... τὴν φιλίαν ... σύνδεσμον πασῶν τ. ἀρετῶν ἔλεγον; Pla., Polit. 310A.—Cf. also Pla., Leg. 21, 5 p. 921C of the law: τῆς πόλεως σ.).—On σύνδεσμος as a philos. concept: WJaeger, Nemesios v. Emesa '13, 96-137. KReinhardt, Kosmos u. Sympathie '26; AFridrichsen, Serta Rudbergiana '31, 26, Symb. Osl. 19, '39, 41-5; GRudberg, Con. Neot. 3, '39, 19-21. 2. the bond that hinders, fetter only fig. σύνδεσμος ἀδικίας (Is 58: 6) fetter that consists in unrighteousness Ac 8: 23 (s. also 3 below); B 3: 3, 5 (in the two last-named passages Is 58: 6 and 9 are quoted in context). 3. that which is held together by a bond, bundle (so Ac 8: 23 Mft., Gdspd. et al.; s. 2 above), band, college (Herodian 4, 12, 6 ὁ σ. τῶν ἐπιστολῶν) σ. ἀποστόλων ITr 3: 1. M-M.*

συνδέω pf. pass. ptc. συνδεδεμένος (Hom.+; pap., LXX; En. 101, 6) bind someone or put someone in chains with (Jos., Ant. 2, 70 δοῦλος συνδεδεμένος τῷ οἰνοχόῳ; 18, 196) ὡς συνδεδεμένοι as (though you were) fellow-prisoners Hb 13: 3. But σ. can also mean simply bind, imprison, so that the force of συν- is no longer felt (Nicol. Dam.: 90 fgm. 4 p. 332, 19 Jac.; Aristaen., Ep. 2, 2, 2 p. 171 [end] Herch.). M-M.*

συνδιδασκαλίτης, ου, ὁ (hapax legomenon) apparently in the mng. fellow-pupil, fellow-disciple IEph 3: 1 (s. Hdb. ad loc.).*

συνδοξάζω 1 aor. συνεδόξασα, pass. συνεδοξάσθην (Aristot. et al.)—1. (cf. δόξα 3) join w. others in praising τὶ someth. ISm 11: 3.—2. (cf. δόξα 1) pass. be glorified with someone, share in someone's glory Ro 8: 17.*

σύνδουλος, ου, ὁ (Eur., Lysias+; BGU 1141, 20 [13 BC]; PLond. 1213a, 4; PLeipz. 40 II, 3; 2 Esdr; Jos., Ant. 11, 118. Other reff. in Herodas ed. ADKnox and WHeadlam '22 p. 252f) fellow-slave. 1. lit. (e.g. Herodas 5, 56) Mt 24: 49; Hs 5, 2, 9f.—2. w. ref. to the relationship betw. the oriental court official and his ruler (s. δοῦλος 2) Mt 18: 28f, 31, 33. 3. w. ref. to a relationship to the heavenly κύριος. Paul and Ign. designate certain Christians as their σύνδουλοι: Col 1: 7; 4: 7 (σύνδουλος ἐν κυρίῳ); IEph 2: 1; IMg 2; IPhld 4; ISm 12: 2 (in the last two passages there are no names mentioned, as in the others; the 'deacons' are called σ.). In Rv 6: 11 σύνδουλος also has the sense 'fellow-Christian'. 4. In Rv the revealing angel calls himself the fellow-slave of the seer and his brothers 19: 10; 22: 9. M-M.*

συνδρομή, ῆς, ἡ running together, forming of a mob (Cephisodorus [V/IV BC] in Aristot., Rhet. 3, 10 p. 1411a, 29; Polyb. 1, 69, 11; Diod. S. 3, 71, 3; 15, 90, 2; 3 Macc 3: 8) ἐγένετο σ. τοῦ λαοῦ the people rushed together Ac 21: 30 (Polyb. 1, 67, 2; Jdth 10: 18 ἐγένετο συνδρομή). M-M.*

συνεγείρω 1 aor. συνήγειρα, pass. συνηγέρθην (= 'assist someone in lifting up' Ex 23: 5; 4 Macc 2: 14; Ps.-Phoc. 140) cause someone to awaken or to rise up with another (cf. Ps.-Plut., Consol. ad Apollon. 117C τὰς λύπας καὶ τοὺς θρήνους συνεγείρειν. Pass., Ael. Aristid.

48, 43 K.=24 p. 476D; Is 14: 9 συνηγέρθησάν σοι πάντες).

1. lit., pass. συνεγείρεσθε *awaken* or *rise up together* IPol 6: 1.—2. fig., of participating in the resurrection of Jesus; the believer, in mystic union w. him, could experience this ὁ θεὸς . . . ἡμᾶς συνήγειρεν Eph 2: 6.—Pass. συνηγέρθητε τῷ Χριστῷ Col 3: 1. ἐν ᾧ συνηγέρθητε 2: 12. *

συνέδριον, ου, τό (Hdt.+; inscr., pap., LXX; Ep. Arist. 301; Philo, Joseph.—Schürer II⁴ 243, 14).

1. gener. *council* (Posidon.: 87 fgm. 71 Jac.; Diod. S. 15, 28, 4; συνέδριον ἐν Ἀθήναις συνεδρεύειν; 19, 46, 4; Ael. Aristid. 13 p. 286 D.; Jos., Ant. 20, 200, Vi. 368), transferred by Ign. to the Christian situation. The presbyters (cf. CIG 3417 the civic συνέδριον τῶν πρεσβυτέρων in Philadelphia; CCurtius, Her. 4, 1870: inscr. fr. Ephesus nos. 11 and 13 p. 199; 203; 224) are to take the place of the συνέδριον τῶν ἀποστόλων *the council of the apostles* in the esteem of the church IMg 6: 1. They are called συνέδριον θεοῦ ITr 3: 1. συνέδριον τοῦ ἐπισκόπου IPhld 8: 1.

2. quite predom. *the high council, Sanhedrin* (Joseph. [Schürer 245, 18]; Hebraized in the Mishna סַנְהֶדְרִין); in Roman times this was the highest indigenous governing body in Judaea, composed of high priests (ἀρχιερεύς 1), elders, and scholars (scribes), and meeting under the presidency of the ruling high priest. This body was the ultimate authority not only in religious matters, but in legal and governmental affairs as well, in so far as it did not encroach on the authority of the Roman procurator. The latter, e.g., had to confirm any death sentences passed by the council. (Schürer II⁴ 237-67; MWolff, De Samenstelling en het Karakter van het groote συνέδριον te Jeruzalem voor het jaar 70 n. Chr.: ThT 51, '17, 299-320; SBHoenig, The Great Sanhedrin, '53.—On the jurisdiction of the council in capital cases s. ἀποκτείνω 1 [J 18: 31]. Also KKastner, Jes. vor d. Hoh. Rat '30; MDibelius, ZNW 30, '31, 193-201; JLengle, Z. Prozess Jesu: Her. 70, '35, 312-21; EBickermann, Rev. de l'Hist. des Rel. 112, '35, 169-241; ESpringer, PJ 229, '35, 135-50; JBlinzler, D. Prozess Jesu '51 [much lit.], ²'55, Eng. transl., The Trial of Jesus, I and FMcHugh, '59, ³'60; JoachJeremias, ZNW 43, '50/'51, 145-50; PWinter, On the Trial of Jesus, in Studia Judaica, vol. I, '61.—SZeitlin, Who Crucified Jesus? '42; on this s. CBQ 5, '43, 232-4; ibid. 6, '44, 104-10; 230-5; SZeitlin, The Political Synedrion and the Religious Sanhedrin, '45. Against him HAWolfson, Jewish Quarterly Review 36, '46, 303-6; cf. Zeitlin, ibid. 307-15; JDerrett, Law in the NT, '70, 389-460; DCatchpole, The Problem of the Historicity of the Sanhedrin Trial: CFD Moule-Festschr. '70, 47-65.—On Jesus before the council cf. also Feigel, Weidel, Finegan s.v. Ἰούδας 6). Mt 5: 22 (RAGuelich, ZNW 64, '73, 43ff); 26: 59; Mk 14: 55; 15: 1; Lk 22: 66 (perh.; s. below); Ac 5: 21, 27, 34, 41; 6: 12, 15; 22: 30; 23: 1, 6, 15, 20, 28; 24: 20.—Also of an official session of the members of this council συνήγαγον οἱ ἀρχιερεῖς καὶ οἱ Φαρισαῖοι συνέδριον *the high priests and the Pharisees called a meeting of the council* J 11: 47 (Diod. S. 13, 111, 1 συναγαγὼν συνέδριον).—Of the room where the council met (Dit., Syll.³ 243 D, 47; 249 II, 77f; 252, 71; POxy. 717, 6; 11 [II BC]; BGU 540, 25) Ac 4: 15; perh. (s. above) Lk 22: 66 (GSchneider, Verleugnung usw. [Lk 22: 54-71], '69).

3. *local council,* as it existed in individual cities pl. Mt 10: 17; Mk 13: 9.—ELohse, TW VII, 858-69. M-M. *

συνέδριος Ac 5: 35 D, prob. an error, caused by the presence of συνέδριον in vs. 34, for

σύνεδρος, ου, ὁ (Hdt.+; Diod. S. 16, 60, 1; 36, 7, 4; Arrian, Tact. 27, 4; inscr., LXX; Philo, Sobr. 19; Jos., Ant. 14, 172) *member of a council.* *

συνείδησις, εως, ἡ—1. *consciousness* (Democr., fgm. 297 σ. τῆς κακοπραγμοσύνης; Chrysipp. in Diog. L. 7, 85 τὴν ταύτης συνείδησιν; Eccl 10: 20; Sir 42: 18 v.l.; Jos., Ant. 16, 212) w. obj. gen. συνείδησις ἁμαρτιῶν *consciousness of sin* Hb 10: 2 (Diod. S. 4, 65, 7 διὰ τὴν συνείδησιν τοῦ μύσους; Philo, Det. Pot. Ins. 146 οἱ συνειδήσει τῶν οἰκείων ἀδικημάτων ἐλεγχόμενοι, Virt. 124 σ. ἁμαρτημάτων). συνείδησις θεοῦ *consciousness, spiritual awareness of God* 1 Pt 2: 19 (s. EGSelwyn, 1 Pt '46, 176-8). Opp. σ. τοῦ εἰδώλου *the consciousness that this is an idol* 1 Cor 8: 7a, t.r. (but συνηθείᾳ is the correct rdg.).

2. *moral consciousness, conscience* (Menand., Monost. 597 ἅπασιν ἡμῖν ἡ συνείδησις θεός comes close to this mng.; cf. 654; Dionys. Hal., Jud. Thuc. 8 μιαίνειν τὴν ἑαυτοῦ συνείδησιν; Heraclit. Sto., 37 p. 54, 8 σ. ἁμαρτόντος ἀνθρώπου; Ps.-Lucian, Amor. 49 οὐδεμιᾶς ἀπρεποῦς συνειδήσεως παροικούσης; Hierocles, In Carm. Aur. 14 p. 451 Mull.; Stob., Flor. 3, 24 [I 601ff H.] quotes sayings of Bias and Periander on ὀρθὴ or ἀγαθὴ συνείδησις; PRyl. 116, 9 [II AD] θλιβομένη τῇ συνειδήσει περὶ ὧν ἐνοσφίσατο; Mitteis, Chrest. 88, 35 [II AD]; BGU 1024 III, 7; PFlor. 338, 17 [III AD] συνειδήσει= conscientiously; Wsd 17: 10; Jos., Ant. 16, 103 κατὰ συνείδησιν ἀτοπωτέραν; Test. Reub. 4: 3) w. subj. gen. Ro 2: 15; 9: 1; 1 Cor 10: 29a; 2 Cor 1: 12; 4: 2; 5: 11; Hb 9: 14 al.; ἡ ἰδία σ. 1 Ti 4: 2. Opp. ἄλλη σ. *another's scruples* 1 Cor 10: 29b; διὰ τὴν σ. *for conscience' sake* (cf. Dit., Or. 484, 37 διὰ τὸ συνειδός; Ps.-Dio Chrys. 20[37], 35) Ro 13: 5; 1 Cor 10: 25, 27f; τὸ μαρτύριον τῆς σ. 2 Cor 1: 12, cf. σ. as the subj. of μαρτυρεῖν Ro 9: 1; cf. 2: 15, or of ἐλέγχειν J 8: 9 v.l. (s. ἐλέγχω 2). W. attributes: σ. ἀγαθή *a good conscience* (cf. Herodian 6, 3, 4; PReinach s.v. καλός 1b) Ac 23: 1; 1 Ti 1: 5; 1 Pt 3: 21; ἔχειν ἀγαθὴν σ. 1 Ti 1: 19; 1 Pt 3: 16. Also ἐν ἀγαθῇ σ. ὑπάρχειν 1 Cl 41: 1. ἐν ἀμώμῳ καὶ ἁγνῇ συνειδήσει περιπατεῖν Pol 5: 3; cf. 1 Cl 1: 3. σ. ἀσθενής *a weak conscience,* one that cannot come to a decision 1 Cor 8: 7; cf. vss. 10, 12. σ. ἀπρόσκοπος Ac 24: 16; καθαρὰ σ. 1 Ti 3: 9; 2 Ti 1: 3; 1 Cl 45: 7; καθαρὸς τῇ σ. ITr 7: 2; καλὴ σ. Hb 13: 18; 2 Cl 16: 4. σ. πονηρά *a bad conscience* or *a consciousness of guilt* (s. καρδία 1bδ) Hb 10: 22; D 4: 14; B 19: 12; Hm 3: 4. ἡ σ. μολύνεται 1 Cor 8: 7. μιαίνεται Tit 1: 15 (s. Dionys. Hal. above). καθαριεῖ τ. συνείδησιν ἡμῶν ἀπὸ νεκρῶν ἔργων Hb 9: 14. κατὰ συνείδησιν (s. on this Vett. Val. 210, 1) τελειῶσαί τινα vs. 9.

3. *conscientiousness* (late pap.) μετὰ συνειδήσεως *conscientiously* 1 Cl 2: 4; ἐν ὁμονοίᾳ συναχθέντες τῇ σ. *assembled in concord, with full consciousness of our duty* 1 Cl 34: 7.—MKähler, Das Gewissen I 1, 1878, RE VI 1899, 646ff; RSteinmetz, Das Gewissen bei Pls '11; M Pohlenz, GGA '13, 642ff, Die Stoa '48; '49 (index), ZNW 42, '49, 77-9; HBöhlig, Das Gewissen bei Seneka u. Pls: StKr 87, '14, 1-24; FTillmann, Zur Geschichte des Begriffs 'Gewissen' bis zu den paulin. Briefen: SMerkle-Festschr. '22, 336-47; FZucker, Syneidesis-Conscientia '28; ThSchneider, D. paulin. Begriff d. Gewissens (Syneidesis): Bonner Zeitschr. f. Theol. u. Seelsorge 6, '29, 193-211, D. Quellen d. paul. Gewissensbegr.: ibid. 7, '30, 97-112; BSnell, Gnomon 6, '30, 21ff; MDibelius, Hdb.² '31 exc. on 1 Ti 1: 5; HOsborne, Σύνεσις and σ.: CIR 45, '31, 8-10, Συνείδησις: JTS 32, '31, 167-79; GRudberg, JAEklund-Festschr. '33, 165ff; Gertrud Jung, Συνείδησις, Conscientia, Bewusstsein: Archiv f. d. gesamte Psychologie 89, '34, 525-40; WJAalders, Het Geweten, '35;

CSpicq, La conscience dans le NT: RB 47, '38, 50–80; BReicke, The Disobedient Spirits and Christian Baptism '46, 174–82; JDupont, Studia Hellenistica 5, '48, 119–53; HClavier, Συν., une pierre de touche de l'Hellénisme paulinien, announced in Studia Paulina [JdeZwaan-Festschr.] '53, p. 80 n. 1; CAPierce, Conscience in the NT, '55; BReicke, ThZ 12, '56, 157–61, esp. 159; PDelhaye, Studia Montis Regii (Montreal) 4, '61, 229–51; JStelzenberger, Syneidesis im NT, '61; MargThrall, NTS 14, '67/'68, 118–25; BFHarris, Westminster Theol. Journal 24, '62, 173–86; RJewett, Paul's Anthropological Terms, '71, 402–46. M-M.*

συνεῖδον s. συνοράω.

συνειδός, τό s. σύνοιδα 2.

I. σύνειμι (fr. εἰμί) impf. 3 sing. συνῆν be with (Hom.+; inscr., pap., LXX, Ep. Arist.) τινί someone (trag., Thu. et al.; Jos., Ant. 3, 75) Lk 9: 18; Ac 22: 11; IEph 11: 2. M-M.*

II. σύνειμι (fr. εἶμι) come together (Hom.+; inscr.; Jos., Ant. 4, 203.—In late pap. as an accounting expr.) συνιόντος ὄχλου εἶπεν when a crowd gathered, he said Lk 8: 4 (cf. Jos., Vi. 9). M-M.*

συνεισέρχομαι 2 aor. συνεισῆλθον (Eur., Thu.+; BGU 388 II, 26; LXX; Jos., Ant. 9, 133 εἰς) enter with, go in(to) with τινί someone εἴς τι (into) someth. (Eur., Hel. 1083 ἐς οἴκους τινί; Appian, Iber. 43 §176 συνεισῆλθεν αὐτοῖς ἐς τὸ στρατόπεδον) J 6: 22; 18: 15; Mk 6: 33 v.l. M-M.*

συνέκδημος, ου, ὁ (Diod. S.; Plut., Otho 5, 2, Mor. 100F; Palaeph., 45 p. 67, 7; Jos., Vi. 79; Dit., Syll.³ 1052, 9) traveling companion Ac 19: 29; 2 Cor 8: 19. M-M.*

συνεκλεκτός, ή, όν chosen together with someone understood, only fem. and subst. ἡ ἐν Βαβυλῶνι συνεκλεκτή 1 Pt 5: 13. No individual lady is meant, least of all Peter's wife, but rather a congregation w. whom Peter is staying. Cf. Βαβυλών. M-M.*

συνεκπορεύομαι (Polyb. 6, 32, 5; Judg 11: 3 A; 13: 25 B) go out with someone understood Ac 3: 11 D.*

συνελαύνω 1 aor. συνήλασα (Hom.+; pap.; 2 Macc; Jos., Bell. 2, 526; 4, 567, Ant. 2, 249; 5, 162 [all four times w. εἰς and the local acc.]) drive, force, bring εἴς τι to someth. (Aelian, V.H. 4, 15 εἰς τὸν τῆς σοφίας ἔρωτα; Sb 5357, 13 σ. τινὰ πρὸς εὐγνωμοσύνην = make someone reasonable) Ac 7: 26 t.r.*

συνέλευσις, εως ἡ (Plut., Ptolemaeus et al.; PSI 450, 10; Judg 9: 46 B; Jos., Ant. 3, 118) meeting, coming together, also of sexual intercourse (Vett. Val. 47, 8) 1 Cl 20: 10.*

συνεξέρχομαι 2 aor. συνεξῆλθον go out with τινί someone (Eur., Hdt., Thu.+; BGU 380, 13; Jdth 2: 20) 1 Cl 11: 2.*

συνεπέρχομαι 2 aor. συνεπῆλθον come together against, attack together (Quint. Smyrn. 2, 302; Dit., Syll.³ 700, 22 [117 BC]; PLeipz. 40 II, 5; 17) συνεπελθόντες when they closed in on him MPol 7: 1.*

συνεπιμαρτυρέω testify at the same time (Petosiris, fgm. 21 l. 58; Polyb. 25, 6, 4; Ps.-Aristot., De Mundo 6; Sext. Emp., Math. 8, 323; Athen. 13 p. 595E; Ep. Arist. 191; Philo, Mos. 2, 123) w. ὅτι 1 Cl 23: 5. τινί by means of someth. Hb 2: 4, to someth. 1 Cl 43: 1. M-M.*

συνεπίσκοπος, ου, ὁ fellow-bishop Phil 1: 1 v.l.*

συνεπιτίθημι mostly, as in its only occurrence in our lit., mid. **συνεπιτίθεμαι** 2 aor. συνεπεθέμην join w. others in an attack on pers. or things (Thu., Isaeus, X.; Polyb., Diod. S., Plut.; Dt 32: 27; Jos., Ant. 10, 116) abs. Ac 24: 9. M-M.*

συνέπομαι mid. dep.; impf. συνειπόμην (Hom.+; POxy. 1415, 8; 2 and 3 Macc) accompany τινί someone (Jos., Ant. 13, 21; Test. Jud. 3: 10) Ac 20: 4. M-M.*

συνεργέω impf. συνήργουν; 1 aor. συνήργησα (Eur., X.+; inscr., pap., LXX, Philo; Jos., Bell. 6, 38, Ant. 1, 156; Test. 12 Patr.) work (together) with, cooperate (with), help abs. τοῦ κυρίου συνεργοῦντος (PAmh. 152, 5 τοῦ θεοῦ συνεργήσαντος) Mk 16: 20. παντὶ τῷ συνεργοῦντι to everyone who helps (such people as Stephanas) in the work 1 Cor 16: 16. With συνεργοῦντες 2 Cor 6: 1 either θεῷ (Hofmann, Windisch, Sickenberger, RSV) or ὑμῖν (Chrysost., Bengel, Schmiedel, Bachmann) can be supplied. σ. ἐν παντὶ πράγματι be helpful in every respect Hs 5, 6, 6. W. the dat. of the person or thing that is helped (X., Mem. 4, 3, 12; Diod. S. 4, 25, 4 σ. ταῖς ἐπιθυμίαις = assist [him] in his wishes; Dit., Or. 45, 11 [III BC]; PSI 376, 4 [250 BC]; 1 Macc 12: 1; Test. Reub. 3: 6, Iss. 3: 7 ὁ θεός): βλέπεις ὅτι ἡ πίστις συνήργει τοῖς ἔργοις αὐτοῦ you see that faith worked with (and thereby aided) his good deeds Js 2: 22. W. the goal indicated by εἰς (Epict. 1, 9, 26; Appian, Syr. 59 §309 ἐς τὸν θάνατον σ., Bell. Civ. 5, 90 §378; Philo, Agr. 13; Test. Gad 4: 7 εἰς θάνατον, εἰς σωτηρίαν): in τοῖς ἀγαπῶσιν τὸν θεὸν πάντα συνεργεῖ εἰς ἀγαθόν Ro 8: 28, σ. means help (or work with) someone to obtain someth. or bring someth. about (IG II and III ed. min. 654, 15 σ. εἰς τ. ἐλευθερίαν τῇ πόλει; Plut., Eroticus 23 p. 769D οὕτως ἡ φύσις γυναικὶ πρὸς εὔνοιαν ἀνδρὸς μεγάλα συνήργησεν. Cf. Polyb. 11, 9, 1). Then the subj. will be either πάντα everything helps (or works with or for) those who love God to obtain what is good (Vulg., Zahn, Sickenberger, Althaus, RSV mg.), or ὁ θεός, which is actually read after συνεργεῖ in good and very ancient mss. (𝔓⁴⁶ BA; Orig. For ἡμῖν συνεργεῖν of the gods: X., Mem. 4, 3, 12; but s. MBlack, The Interpr. of Ro 8: 28, OCullmann-Festschr., '62, 166–72); in the latter case πάντα is acc. of specification (πᾶς 2aδ) in everything God helps (or works for or with) those who love him to obtain what is good (so RSV text; Syr., Copt., BWeiss, RALipsius, Jülicher, Kühl, Ltzm.; Gdspd., Probs. 148–50.—This would correspond exactly to Alex. Aphr., Fat. 31 p. 203, 8 Br. acc. to cod. Η εἰς ἀγαθὸν οὐδὲν ὁ Πύθιος τῷ Λαΐῳ συνεργεῖ = in no respect does Apollo work w. Laius for good, or help L. to obtain what is good). For the idea cf. Herm. Wr. 9, 4b πάντα γὰρ τῷ τοιούτῳ (= θεοσεβεῖ), κἂν τοῖς ἄλλοις τὰ κακά, ἀγαθά ἐστι; Plotin. 4, 3, 16, 21. JBBauer, ZNW 50, '59, 106–12. M-M.*

συνεργός, όν (Pind., Thu.+; inscr., pap.; 2 Macc 8: 7) working together with, helping, also subst., as always in our lit. helper, fellow-worker (Philo; Jos., Bell. 2, 102, Ant. 7, 346; Polyb. 31, 24, 10). Paul refers to those who helped him in spreading the gospel as his fellow-workers (subjective gen.) Ro 16: 3, 9, 21; Phil 2: 25; 4: 3; 1 Th 3: 2 t.r.; Phlm 1, 24. Instead of the gen. there may be an indication of the field in which the coöperation took place εἰς in (Alex. Aphr., An. Mant. p. 167, 9 Br.) συνεργοὶ εἰς τὴν βασιλείαν τοῦ θεοῦ co-workers in the Kingdom of God Col 4: 11. εἰς ὑμᾶς συνεργός fellow-worker among you 2 Cor 8: 23. συνεργὸς τοῦ θεοῦ ἐν τῷ εὐαγγελίῳ God's helper in the gospel 1 Th 3: 2. συνεργοί ἐσμεν τῆς χαρᾶς ὑμῶν we are working with you to bring you joy 2 Cor 1: 24 (on the gen. cf. X., Cyr. 2, 4, 10; 3, 3, 10 συνεργοὺς τοῦ κοινοῦ ἀγαθοῦ). W. the dat. of that which is assisted (Eur., Thu.+) ἵνα συνεργοὶ γινώμεθα τῇ ἀληθείᾳ that we may be helpers of the truth 3 J 8 (σ. γίνεσθαί τινι as UPZ 146, 3 [II BC]). In θεοῦ ἐσμεν συνεργοί 1 Cor 3: 9 the συν- refers either to communion w. God we are fellow-workers with God or to the community of teachers at Corinth we are fellow-laborers in the service of God (so VPFurnish, JBL 80, '61, 364–70). M-M.*

συνέρχομαι (since Il. 10, 224 [in tmesis]; inscr., pap., LXX, Ep. Arist., Philo, Joseph., Test. 12 Patr.) impf. συνηρχόμην; fut. συνελεύσομαι; 2 aor. συνῆλθον (συν-ῆλθα Bl-D. §81, 3 w. app.; Mlt.-H. 208); pf. ptc. συν-εληλυθώς; plpf. 3 pl. συνεληλύθεισαν.

1. come together—a. lit. assemble, gather συνέρχεται ὁ ὄχλος Mk 3: 20. συνέρχονται πάντες οἱ ἀρχιερεῖς 14: 53.—Ac 1: 6 (s. Bl-D. §251; Rob. 695); 2: 6, 37 D; 5: 16; 10: 27; 16: 13; 19: 32; 21: 22 v.l.; 22: 30; 28: 17; 1 Cor 14: 26. W. the addition of εἰς w. the acc. of place (Pla., Leg. 6, 13 p. 767c; Diod. S. 13, 100, 7 συνῆλθον εἰς Ἔφεσον; Zech 8: 21) Ac 5: 16 v.l.; ἐν w. the dat. of place (POxy. 1187, 6) ἐν ἐκκλησίᾳ 1 Cor 11: 18; αὐτοῦ Mk 6: 33 v.l.; ὅπου J 18: 20; ἐπὶ τὸ αὐτό (cf. αὐτός 4b; σ. ἐπὶ τὸ αὐτό Josh 9: 2; Syntipas p. 75, 16) 1 Cor 11: 20; 14: 23; B 4: 10. Foll. by the dat. come together with someone, assemble at someone's house (PTebt. 34, 4 [I BC] συν-ελθεῖν Ὥρῳ; Jos., Bell. 2, 411) Mk 14: 53 t.r.; D 14: 2. πρός τινα come together to (meet) someone (Ex 32: 26) Mk 6: 33 t.r. Foll. by an inf. of purpose Lk 5: 15; by εἰς denoting purpose 1 Cor 11: 33; IEph 13: 1. εἰς can also introduce a result that was not intended οὐκ εἰς τὸ κρεῖσσον ἀλλὰ εἰς τὸ ἧσσον συνέρχεσθε you hold your meetings in such a way that they turn out not to your advantage, but to your disadvantage 1 Cor 11: 17. εἰς κρίμα vs. 34 (on the solemnity of the celebration cf. the schol. on Aristoph., Pax 967f: to the question 'τίς τῇδε;' the group answers 'πολλοὶ κἀγαθοί'. τοῦτο δὲ ἐποίουν οἱ σπένδοντες, ἵνα οἱ συνειδότες τι ἑαυτοῖς ἄτοπον ἐκχωροῖεν τ. σπονδῶν). W. indication of the nature and manner of the meeting συνέρχεσθε ἐν μιᾷ πίστει IEph 20: 2.

b. of coming together in a sexual sense (X., Mem. 2, 2, 4; Diod. S. 3, 58, 4; Ps.-Apollod. 1, 3, 3; Philo, Virt. 40; 111; Jos., Ant. 7, 168; 213) ἐπὶ τὸ αὐτό σ. 1 Cor 7: 5 t.r. In πρὶν ἢ συνελθεῖν αὐτούς Mt 1: 18 domestic and marital relations are combined. (In the marriage contracts in the pap. πρὸς γάμον τινὶ συνελθεῖν means 'marry'. Also without πρὸς γάμον: BGU 970, 13 [II AD] συνηρχόμην τῷ προγεγραμμένῳ μου ἀνδρί).

2. come, go, or travel (together) with someone (BGU 380, 13; 596, 4 [84 AD]) τινί (Ep. Arist. 35; Jos., Ant. 9, 33) τοὺς συνελθόντας αὐτῷ Ἰουδαίους J 11: 33. ἦσαν συνεληλυθυῖαι ἐκ τῆς Γαλιλαίας αὐτῷ Lk 23: 55. Cf. Ac 1: 21; 9: 39; 10: 23, 45; 11: 12. σ. τινι εἰς τὸ ἔργον 15: 38. σύν τινι instead of the dat. alone 21: 16. συνελθόντων ἐνθάδε prob. means (because of συνκαταβάντες 25: 5) they came back here with (me) 25: 17. M-M.*

συνεσθίω impf. συνήσθιον; 2 aor. συνέφαγον (Pla.+; Plut., Lucian; Dit., Syll.³ 1179; LXX) eat with τινί someone (Pla., Leg. 9 p. 881D; Epict., Ench. 36; Ps 100: 5) Lk 15: 2; Ac 11: 3; 1 Cor 5: 11; UGosp 34 (= Huck⁹-L. Synopse p. 37 note= Gospel Parallels '49, p. 32 note); w. συμπίνειν (as Polyaenus 6, 24; Dit., loc. cit.) Ac 10: 41; ISm 3: 3. Instead of the dat. μετά τινος (cf. Ex 18: 12; Aristoph., Acharn. 277 ξυμπίνειν μετά τινος) Gal 2: 12. VParkin, Studia Evangelica III, '64, 250–53. M-M.*

συνευρυθμίζω pf. pass. 3 sing. συνευρύθμισται bring into harmony with συνευρύθμισται ταῖς ἐντολαῖς ὡς

σύνεσις, εως, ἡ (Hom.+)—1. the faculty of comprehension, intelligence, acuteness, shrewdness (Pind.+; Dit., Or. 323, 6 [II BC] συνέσει κ. παιδείᾳ προάγων; LXX, Philo; Jos., C. Ap. 2, 125; Test. Jud. 14: 7; Sib. Or. 8, 452) Lk 2: 47 (s. Jos., Vi. 8f); D 12: 4. ἡ σύνεσις τῶν συνετῶν 1 Cor 1: 19 (Is 29: 14). W. σοφία (Aristot., Eth. Nic. 1, 13, 20; Diod. S. 9, 3, 3; Dt 4: 6) 1 Cl 32: 4. The whole field of the inner life is covered by the expr. ἐξ ὅλης τῆς καρδίας καὶ ἐξ ὅλης τῆς συνέσεως καὶ ἐξ ὅλης τῆς ἰσχύος Mk 12: 33.

2. insight, understanding in the religio-ethical realm (IG IV² 1, 86, 18) such as God grants to his own (LXX; Test. Reub. 6: 4, Levi 18: 7; Sib. Or. 2, 29): w. σοφία, ἐπιστήμη, γνῶσις B 2: 3; 21: 5 (cf. Ex 31: 3; 35: 31; Sir 1: 19). (W. σοφία as Jos., Ant. 8, 24) σύνεσις πνευματική Col 1: 9. (W. ἐπίγνωσις τ. μυστηρίου τοῦ θεοῦ) πλοῦτος τῆς πληροφορίας τῆς συνέσεως 2: 2. Personified w. other godly virtues Hs 9, 15, 2. Where the Lord dwells there is σύνεσις πολλή m 10, 1, 6. σύνεσις ἔν τινι insight into, understanding of someth. Eph 3: 4; 2 Ti 2: 7. —σύνεσιν αἰτεῖσθαι IPol 1: 3; Hs 5, 4, 3f. σύνεσιν διδόναι 2 Ti 2: 7; Hm 4, 2, 2a. σ. λαμβάνειν (Aristot., Eth. Nic. 1161b, 26) Hs 9, 2, 6. σ. ἔχειν (Hdt. 2, 5) s 9, 22, 2b; 3; D 12: 1. ἀπέστη ἀπ' αὐτῶν ἡ σύνεσις understanding has departed from them Hs 9, 22, 2a. ἐν τῇ συνέσει in the correct (God-given, comprehending the true mng.) understanding B 10: 1. συνέσει 1 Cl 16: 12 (Is 53: 11). Repentance is σύν. Hm 4, 2, 2b, c, d.

3. the wisdom of the creator 1 Cl 33: 3; Hv 1, 3, 4. M-M.*

συνεστώς s. συνίστημι.

συνετίζω 1 aor. imper. συνέτισον (Rhet. Gr. I 584, 30; LXX) cause to understand τινά someone (Test. Levi 4: 5; 9: 8; Hesychius; Suidas) Hm 4, 2, 1. Pass. be given insight Dg 12: 9.*

συνετός, ή, όν intelligent, sagacious, wise, with good sense (Theognis, Pind.+; LXX; Ep. Arist. 148; Philo, Joseph.) ἀνὴρ σ. Ac 13: 7. συνετὸν εἶναι Hm 12, 1, 2; s 5, 5, 4; 9, 2, 6. W. μακρόθυμος m 5, 1, 1. (οἱ) συνετοί (w. σοφοί; s. σοφός 2) Mt 11: 25; Lk 10: 21. ἡ σύνεσις τῶν συνετῶν 1 Cor 1: 19 (Is 29: 14.—Cf. Maximus Tyr. 16, 4c συνετὰ συνετοῖς). οἱ συνετοὶ ἑαυτοῖς those who are wise in their own sight (w. ἐνώπιον ἑαυτῶν ἐπιστήμονες) B 4: 11 (cf. Is 5: 21). οἱ λεγόμενοι σ. IEph 18: 1. Of the Creator συνετὸς ἔν τινι understanding in someth. (w. σοφὸς ἔν τινι) 1 Cl 60: 1. M-M.*

συνευδοκέω 1 aor. συνηυδόκησα (Polyb. 32, 6, 9; Diod. S.; Dit., Syll.³ 712, 46; pap.; 1 and 2 Macc) agree with, approve of, consent to, sympathize with w. dat. of the pers. (BGU 834, 24 [II AD]) approve of someone Ro 1: 32 (as Test. Ash. 6: 2); 1 Cl 35: 6. W. dat. of the thing approve of, give approval to (BGU 1130, 3 [I BC]; POxy. 504, 32; PGenève 11, 3 al.; 1 Macc 1: 57; 2 Macc 11: 24) Lk 11: 48; Ac 8: 1; Dg 9: 1. Abs. (Polyb. 23, 4, 13; Diod. S. 4, 24, 1; 11, 57, 5; BGU 1129, 6; 2 Macc 11: 35) Ac 22: 20. συνευδοκησάσης τῆς ἐκκλησίας πάσης with the consent of the whole church 1 Cl 44: 3. W. the inf. foll. be willing to do someth. (PMich. 202, 12 [105 AD]) 1 Cor 7: 12f. W. dat. of the pers., foll. by the acc. and inf. Hs 5, 2, 11. ταύτῃ τῇ γνώμῃ ὁ υἱὸς τοῦ δεσπότου συνηυδόκησεν αὐτῷ, ἵνα the son of the master agreed with him in this decision, namely that 5, 2, 8 (on the text, which may be damaged, s. MDibelius, Hdb. ad loc.). M-M.*

χορδαῖς κιθάρα *he is attuned to the* (divine) *commandments as the lyre to the strings* IPhld 1: 2.*

συνευφραίνομαι *rejoice* (*together*) *with* (Ps.-Dionys. Hal., A. Rh. 2, 5; Ael. Aristid. 42, 9 K.=6 p. 68 D.; Pollux 5, 129; Pr 5: 18; Philo, Conf. Lingu. 6) w. dat. foll. (Demosth. 18, 217; Herodian 2, 8, 9) B 2: 3.*

συνευωχέομαι pass. *feast together* (Aristot., Eth. Eud. 7, 12, 14 p. 1245b; Posidonius in Athen. 4 p. 152в; Philo, Spec. Leg. 4, 119 al.) Jd 12. τινί *with someone* (Lucian, V. Hist. 2, 15, Ep. Sat. 4, 36 al.; Jos., Ant. 1, 92; 4, 203; BGU 596, 10 [I AD] ὅπως συνευωχηθῇς ἡμῖν; PGM 4, 3150) 2 Pt 2: 13. M-M.*

συνέφαγον s. συνεσθίω.

συνεφίστημι 2 aor. συνεπέστην (Thu.+) mid. and 2 aor. act. intr. *rise up together, join in an attack* κατά τινος *against* or *upon someone* Ac 16: 22.*

συνέχω fut. συνέξω; 2 aor. συνέσχον; impf. pass. συνειχόμην (Hom.+; inscr., pap., LXX, Ep. Arist., Philo, Test. 12 Patr.).
1. *hold together, sustain* τὶ someth. (Ael. Aristid. 43, 16 K.=1 p. 6 D.; τὰ πάντα σ.; PTebt. 410, 11. Cf. IG XIV 1018 to Attis συνέχοντι τὸ πᾶν [s. CWeyman, BZ 14, '17, 17f]; PGM 13, 843. Other exx. in Cumont³ 230, 57; Wsd 1: 7; Aristobulus in Euseb., Pr. Ev. 13, 12; Philo; Jos., C. Ap. 2, 208) συνέχει αὐτὴ (i.e. ἡ ψυχή) τὸ σῶμα Dg 6: 7. Pass. 1 Cl 20: 5.
2. *close by holding* (*together*), *stop* trans., *shut* (στόμα Ps 68: 16; Is 52: 15. The heavens, so that there is no rain Dt 11: 17; 3 Km 8: 35) συνέσχον τὰ ὦτα αὐτῶν Ac 7: 57.
3. *press hard, crowd* τινά *someone* Lk 8: 45. Of a city (2 Macc 9: 2) οἱ ἐχθροί σου συνέξουσίν σε πάντοθεν 19: 43.—4. *hold in custody* (Lucian, Tox. 39; PMagd. 42, 7; PLille 7, 15 [III BC]) Lk 22: 63.
5. of untoward circumstances *seize, attack, distress, torment* τινά *someone* τὰ συνέχοντά με *that which distresses me* IRo 6: 3. Mostly pass. (Aeschyl., Hdt.+) *be tormented by, suffer from* τινί *someth.* of sickness (Pla. et al.; Dit., Syll.³ 1169, 50 ἀγρυπνίαις συνεχόμενος; POxy. 896, 34 πυραιτίοις συνεχόμενος) νόσοις καὶ βασάνοις Mt 4: 24. πυρετῷ (Hippiatr. I 6, 23; Jos., Ant. 13, 398; s. also πυρετός) Lk 4: 38. πυρετοῖς καὶ δυσεντερίῳ Ac 28: 8. Of unpleasant emotional states (Diod. S. 29, 25 λύπῃ; Aelian, V.H. 14, 22 ὀδυρμῷ; Ps.-Plut., De Fluv. 2, 1; 7, 5; 17, 3; 19, 1) φόβῳ μεγάλῳ συνείχοντο *they were seized with terror* Lk 8: 37 (cf. Job 3: 24).—Without the dat. (Leontios 16 p. 33, 13 συνεχόμενος=tormented) πῶς συνέχομαι *how great is my distress, what vexation I must endure* 12: 50. The apostle, torn betw. conflicting emotions, says συνέχομαι ἐκ τῶν δύο *I am hard pressed* (to choose) *between the two* Phil 1: 23.
6. συνέχομαί τινι *I am occupied with* or *absorbed in* someth. (Herodian 1, 17, 9 ἡδοναῖς; Diog. L. 7, 185 γέλωτι; Wsd 17: 19) συνείχετο τῷ λόγῳ (Paul) *was wholly absorbed in preaching* Ac 18: 5 (EHenschel, Theologia Viatorum 2, '50, 213-15) in contrast to the activity cited in vs. 3.—Arrian, Anab. 7, 21, 5 ἐν τῷδε τῷ πόνῳ ξυνείχοντο=they were intensively engaged in this difficult task).
7. *urge on, impel* τινά *someone* ἡ ἀγάπη συνέχει ἡμᾶς 2 Cor 5: 14 (so Bachmann, Belser, Sickenberger, Lietzmann, Windisch, OHoltzmann, 20th Cent. But *hold within bounds, control* Klöpper, Schmiedel, BWeiss, Kühl, Bousset, H-DWendland, RSV. Heinrici leaves the choice open betw. the two. *Include, embrace* GSHendry,

ET 59, '47/'48, 82). Pass. συνείχετο τῷ πνεύματι ὁ Παῦλος Ac 18: 5 t.r. M-M.*

συνεχῶς adv. of time (Hes.+; inscr., pap., Ep. Arist. 78 al.; Philo; Jos., Vi. 20, Ant. 19, 318; Test. 12 Patr.) *continually, unremittingly* ἐκζητεῖν B 21: 8.*

συνζ- s. συζ-.

συνήγορος, ου, ὁ (Aeschyl., Demosth.+; inscr., PAmh. 23, 15; 24 [II BC]; POxy. 1479, 5; Philo, Conf. Lingu. 121; loanw. in rabb.) *advocate* in the sense of *attorney* (Diod. S. 1, 76, 1; Philo, Vi. Cont. 44) ISm 5: 1.*

συνήδομαι pass. dep. (Soph., X.+; Dio Chrys. 3, 103; Dit., Syll.³ [index]; Philo, Conf. Lingu. 7; Jos., Bell. 4, 656, Ant. 8, 386; POxy. 1663a, 4 τινι='rejoice with someone') συνήδομαι τῷ νόμῳ I (*joyfully*) *agree with the law* Ro 7: 22 (cf. Simplicius In Epict. p. 53, 5 Düb. τ. ἐπιτάγμασι σ.). M-M.*

συνήθεια, ας, ἡ—1. *friendship, fellowship, intimacy* (Isocr., Aeschin. et al.; inscr., pap.) πρός τινα *with someone* (Polyb. 1, 43, 4; 31, 14, 3; Plut., Crass. 3, 6; PAmh. 145, 10; Jos., Ant. 15, 97) IEph 5: 1 (συνήθειαν ἔχ. πρός τινα also Vett. Val. 228, 23).
2. *habit, custom, being* or *becoming accustomed* (Hom. Hymns; Pla.; inscr., pap., 4 Macc; Philo, Spec. Leg. 3, 35 al.; Joseph.; so as loanw. in rabb.).
a. subjectively *being* or *becoming accustomed* τῇ συνηθείᾳ ἕως ἄρτι τοῦ εἰδώλου (obj. gen. as Dit., Syll.³ 888, 154 διὰ τὴν συνήθειαν τῆς τοιαύτης ἐνοχλήσεως.—τῇ σ. is dat. of cause; s. on ἀπιστία 2b) *through being accustomed to idols in former times* 1 Cor 8: 7.
b. objectively *custom, habit, usage* (Jos., Ant. 10, 72) Dg 2: 1. συνήθειαν ἔχειν (PFlor. 210, 15) 1 Cor 11: 16; w. inf. foll. Hm 5, 2, 6. ἔστιν συνήθειά τινι w. ἵνα foll. J 18: 39. M-M.*

συνήθης, ες (Hes.+) *habitual, customary, usual* (Soph., Thu.+; inscr., pap., Sym., Philo; Jos., Ant. 6, 339; 12, 300) μετὰ τῶν συνήθων αὐτοῖς ὅπλων *with the weapons that they usually carried* MPol 7: 1 (Callisth. 124 fgm. 14a Jac. μετὰ τῆς συνήθους στολῆς). σύνηθές ἐστί τινι *it is someone's custom* (Eur., Alc. 40) ὅπερ ἦν σύνηθες αὐτῷ 5: 1.*

συνῆκα s. συνίημι.

συνηλικιώτης, ου, ὁ (CIG III 4929; Alciphr. 1, 15, 1; Ps.-Callisth. 1, 36, 3; in Diod. S. 1, 53, 10 and Dionys. Hal. 10, 49, 2 the best witnesses have ἡλικιώτης) *a person of one's own age, a contemporary* Gal 1: 14. M-M.*

συνθάπτω 2 aor. pass. συνετάφην *bury* (*together*) *with* (Aeschyl., Hdt.+; PEleph. 2, 12; Jos., Ant. 10, 48) pass. *be buried with* τινί *someone* (Hdt. 5, 5 συνθάπτεται τῷ ἀνδρί; Charito 6, 2, 9), in our lit. only fig. (Lycurgus, Or. in Leocr. 50 συνετάφη τοῖς τούτων σώμασιν ἡ τῶν Ἑλλήνων ἐλευθερία) of the believer's being buried together w. his Lord in baptism συνταφέντες αὐτῷ (=τῷ Χριστῷ) ἐν τῷ βαπτίσματι Col 2: 12 (cf. Diod. S. 18, 22, 7 ἐν ταῖς οἰκίαις συνετάφησαν τοῖς οἰκείοις=they were buried in the houses together with their relatives). διὰ τοῦ βαπτίσματος Ro 6: 4 (s. σύμφυτος.—EStommel, 'Begraben mit Chr.' [Rö 6: 4]: Röm. Quartalschr. 49, '54, 1-20). M-M.*

σύνθεσις, εως, ἡ (Pla. et al.; inscr., pap., LXX, Philo; Jos., Ant. 14, 173) *placing together, combination*, of clothing σύνθεσις ἱματίων *a collection* (=a suit) of *clothing* (POxy. 496, 4 [II AD] al. Cf. συνθεσίδιον = garment PGiess. 21, 8 [II AD]) Hs 6, 1, 5.*

συνθλάω 1 fut. pass. συνθλασθήσομαι (Alexis in Athen. 11 p. 466E; Eratosth. p. 13, 18; Diod. S. 2, 57, 2; Manetho 5, 201; Plut., Artax. 19, 9; Inscr. Gr. 817, 21 [IV BC]; LXX) *crush* (*together*), *dash to pieces* pass., abs. (Aristot., Probl. 1, 38 p. 863b, 13) Mt 21: 44 (RSwaeles, NTS 6, '60, 310–13); Lk 20: 18. M-M.*

συνθλίβω impf. συνέθλιβον (Pla. +; Strabo, Plut.; Philo, Aet. M. 110; Joseph.; LXX) *press together, press upon* τινά *someone*, of a crowd of people Mk 5: 24, 31 (cf. Appian, Mithrid. 81 §365 συνθλιβεὶς ἐν πλήθει; Jos., Bell. 3, 393 τ. πλήθους συνθλιβομένου περὶ τῷ στρατηγῷ).*

συνθραύω (Eur., X. +; inscr.; Sym. Eccl 12: 6) *break in pieces* pass., of pers. who become unnerved *be broken to pieces*, intr. *be broken, shattered* Hm 11: 14 (cf. 11: 13 σκεῦος θραύεται).*

συνθρύπτω (Hippiatr. II 106, 4f.—HJCadbury, JBL 52, '33, 61) *break in pieces* (Jos., Ant. 10, 207) fig. τὴν καρδίαν τινός *break someone's heart* Ac 21: 13. M-M.*

συνίημι (Hom. +; pap., LXX; Ep. Arist. 200; Philo, Aet. M. 27; Jos., Ant. 7, 186 al.; Test. 12 Patr.); the NT has only one quite certain ex. of the conjugation in -μι: the inf. συνιέναι Ac 7: 25a. In all the other cases the ms. tradition is divided: 3 pl. συνιᾶσιν 2 Cor 10: 12 (cf. Windisch ad loc.); inf. συνιέναι Lk 24: 45; ptc. συνιείς, -έντος Mt 13: 19, 23; Eph 5: 17 t.r. Beside it συνίω Hm 4, 2, 1; 10, 1, 3; 3 pl. συνίουσιν Mt 13: 13; 2 Cor 10: 12 t.r.; Hm 10, 1, 5; 6a (the accentuation συνιοῦσιν is wrong; cf. W-S. §14, 16; Mlt.-H. 60). Imperative σύνιε Hm 6, 2, 3; s 5, 5, 1; 9, 12, 1. Ptc. συνίων Mt 13: 23 t.r.; Mk 4: 9 v.l. a; Ro 3: 11; B 12: 10 (not συνιῶν or συνιών; cf. W-S. loc. cit.). Either the -μι form or the -ω form could supply the 2 pl. indic. or imper. συνίετε Mt 15: 10; Mk 8: 17, 21; Eph 5: 17, the 3 sing. imper. συνιέτω Mk 4: 9 v.l. b and, depending on the way the form is accented, the foll. subjunctive forms: 3 pl. συνιῶσιν (συνιῶσιν or συνίωσιν) Mk 4: 12; Lk 8: 10; cf. συνιῶμεν B 10: 12b. συνιῆτε B 6: 5.—Fut. συνήσω; 1 aor. συνῆκα 2 Cor. subj. συνῆτε, συνῶσιν, imper. 2 pl. σύνετε.—Bl-D. §94, 2 w. app.; Mlt.-H. 202–7; 325; Reinhold p. 94; Mayser 354, 2; Crönert 258; WSchmid, Der Attizismus II 1889, 26; Thackeray 250f; Rob. 314f; *understand, comprehend, gain (an) insight into* τὶ *someth.* (Pind., Hdt. +; Jos., Ant. 1, 255 τὴν γνώμην τ. θεοῦ) Mt 13: 51; Lk 2: 50; 18: 34; 24: 45; Ac 13: 27 D; 1 Cl 35: 11 (Ps 49: 22); B 10: 12b; 12: 10; Hm 4, 2, 1; 6, 2; 10, 1, 3; s 5, 5, 1. W. ὅτι foll. (Herodian 4, 15, 6; Jos., C. Ap. 1, 319; Test. Levi 8: 18) Mt 16: 12; 17: 13; Ac 7: 25a; B 14: 3; Hm 4, 2, 2; s 5, 4, 1. W. indir. quest. foll. Eph 5: 17. σ. ἐπί τινι *understand with regard to, gain an insight (into someth.)* (revealed by the context) ἐπὶ τοῖς ἄρτοις *in connection with the loaves* i.e. in the miraculous feeding *gain an insight* into the omnipotence of Jesus Mk 6: 52. ἐπὶ τῷ πλούτῳ αὐτοῦ *understand in connection with his wealth* what the Christian's duty is Hs 2: 7. Abs., but w. the obj. easily supplied fr. the context Mt 13: 13f (Is 6: 9), 19, 23; 15: 10 (Eupolis Com. [V BC] 357, 1 ἀκούετε κ. ξυνίετε); Mk 4: 12 (Is 6: 9); 7: 14; 8: 17, 21; Lk 8: 10 (Is 6: 9); Ac 7: 25b; 28: 26 (Is 6: 9); Ro 3: 11 (cf. Ps 13: 2); Is 52: 15); B 4: 6, 8; 5: 5; 10: 12a; Hm 6, 2, 3; 10, 1, 6a; s 2: 10; 9, 12, 1. συνιέναι τῇ καρδίᾳ (dat. of instr.; cf. καρδία 1bβ) Mt 13: 15; Ac 28: 27 (both Is 6: 10).—2 Cor 10: 12 (and 13) the text is in

doubt and the words οὐ συνιᾶσιν. ἡμεῖς δέ are omitted by many, w. DG It. Ambrosiaster 109 (recently by Holsten, Schmiedel, Bousset, Windisch, Mft.; JHennig, CBQ 8, '46, 332–43; Bl-D. §416, 2; EbNestle⁴-vDobschütz, Einführung in das Griechische NT '23, 30). If the words are allowed to stand, since they occur in the best witnesses, incl. 𝔓⁴⁶ (w. Hofmann, Klöpper, Heinrici, Schlatter, Bachmann, Lietzmann, Sickenberger, Gdspd., RSV), the two preceding participles indicate the ways in which the ignorance of those people is expressed.—HConzelmann, TW VII, 886–94: συνίημι and related words. M-M. B. 1207.*

συνίστημι (Hom. +; inscr., pap., LXX, En., Ep. Arist., Philo, Joseph.) Ro 3: 5; 5: 8; 16: 1; 2 Cor 4: 2 v.l.; 6: 4 v.l.; 10: 18b; Gal 2: 18 t.r. Beside it **συνιστάνω** (Polyb. 4, 82, 5; 31, 29, 8; Jos., Bell. 1, 15, Ant. 6, 272.—ESchweizer, Gramm. der pergam. Inschr. 1898, 177; ENachmanson, Laute u. Formen der magn. Inschr. '03, 157; KDieterich, Untersuchungen 1898, 218; Bl-D. §93; W-S. §14, 14; Rob. 315f) 2 Cor 3: 1; 4: 2; 6: 4; 10: 12, 18a; Gal 2: 18 and **συνιστάω** 2 Cor 4: 2 t.r.; 6: 4 t.r.; 10: 18 t.r.—1 aor. συνέστησα; pf. συνέστηκα, ptc. συνεστώς; 1 aor. mid. συνεστησάμην; 1 aor. pass. ptc. συσταθείς.

I. *transitive*—1. *act.* and *pass.*—a. *bring together, unite, collect* pass. of the water of the boundless sea συσταθὲν εἰς τὰς συναγωγάς *collected in its gathering-places* 1 Cl 20: 6.

b. *present, introduce* or *recommend someone to some-one else* (X., Pla.; PHamb. 27, 3; PHib. 65, 3; POxy. 292, 6; PGiess. 71, 4 al.; 1 Macc 12: 43; 2 Macc 4: 24; 9: 25; Jos., Ant. 16, 85) τινά τινι (re)commend *someone to someone* (PSI 589, 14 [III BC] σύστησόν με Σώσῳ) ὑμῖν Φοίβην Ro 16: 1 (in a letter, as Chio, Ep. 8 ὅπως αὐτὸν συστήσαιμί σοι). In a bad sense ἑαυτοὺς συνιστάνομεν ὑμῖν 2 Cor 5: 12. τινά *someone* ὃν ὁ κύριος συνίστησιν 10: 18b. σ. ἑαυτούς in a good sense (ὡς θεοῦ διάκονοι) 6: 4; in a bad sense (s. above) 3: 1; 10: 12, 18a (ἑαυτόν). συνιστάνοντες ἑαυτοὺς πρὸς πᾶσαν συνείδησιν ἀνθρώπων *we commend ourselves to every human conscience* 4: 2 (σ. πρός w. acc. as PMich. 210, 4 [c. 200 AD]). Pass. συνίστασθαι ὑπό τινος *be recommended by someone* (Epict. 3, 23, 22; PPetr. II 2, 4, 4 [III BC]) 12: 11.

c. *demonstrate, show, bring out* τὶ *someth.* (Polyb. 4, 5, 6 εὔνοιαν) Ro 3: 5. συνίστησιν τὴν ἑαυτοῦ ἀγάπην εἰς ἡμᾶς ὁ θεός 5: 8. Difficult and perh. due to a damaged text (Bl-D. §197) is the constr. w. acc. and inf. (cf. Diod. S. 14, 45, 4) συνεστήσατε ἑαυτοὺς ἁγνοὺς εἶναι τῷ πράγματι 2 Cor 7: 11. W. a double acc. (Diod. S. 13, 91, 4; Sus 61 Theod.; Philo, Rer. Div. Her. 258 συνίστησιν αὐτὸν προφήτην [so in the mss.]; Jos., Ant. 7, 49) παραβάτην ἐμαυτὸν συνιστάνω *I demonstrate that I am a wrong-doer* Gal 2: 18 (WMundle, ZNW 23, '24, 152f).

2. *mid. put together, constitute, establish, prepare* τὶ *someth.* (Pla. et al.; pap.) of God's creative activity (Lucian, Hermot. 20 Ἥφαιστος ἄνθρωπον συνεστήσατο; En. 101, 6; Philo, Leg. All. 3, 10 θεὸν τὸν τὰ ὅλα συστησάμενον ἐκ μὴ ὄντων; Jos., Ant. 12, 22 τὸν ἅπαντα συστησάμενον θεόν) ἐν λόγῳ συνεστήσατο τὰ πάντα 1 Cl 27: 4 (Herm. Wr. 1, 31 ἅγιος εἶ, ὁ λόγῳ συστησάμενος τὰ ὄντα).

II. *intransitive*, in our lit. the pres. mid. and perf. act.

1. *stand with* or *by* (1 Km 17: 26) τινί *someone* Lk 9: 32 (οἱ συνεστῶτες as Apollon. Paradox. 5).

2. *be composed* or *compounded, consist* ἔκ τινος *of someth.* (Pla., X. et al.; Herm. Wr. 13, 2; Jos., Vi. 35) ἡ μῆνις ἐκ τοσούτων κακῶν συνισταμένη Hm 5, 2, 4.

3. *continue, endure, exist, hold together* (Ep. Arist. 154 τὸ ζῆν διὰ τῆς τροφῆς συνεστάναι) γῆ ἐξ ὕδατος καὶ δι' ὕδατος συνεστῶσα 2 Pt 3: 5 (here and in the next pass. the mngs. II 2 and 3 are prob. blended. Cf. also Philo, Plant. 6). τὰ πάντα ἐν αὐτῷ συνέστηκεν Col 1: 17 (cf. Pla., Rep. 7 p. 530A, Tim. 61A; Aristot.; Philo, Rer. Div. Her. 58; PGM 4, 1769 τὰ πάντα συνέστηκεν); SHanson, The Unity of the Church in the NT '46, 112.—RAWard, Aristotelian Terms in the NT: Baptist Quarterly 11, '45, 398–403 (συνίστημι). M-M.*

συνκ- s. συγκ-.

συνλ- s. συλλ-.

συνμ- s. συμμ-.

συνοδεύω 1 aor. συνώδευσα *go with* τινί *someone*—1. lit. *travel with* τινί (Plut., Mor. 609D; Lucian, Peregr. 24; Vett. Val. 248, 7; Herodian 4, 7, 6; Achilles Tat. 7, 3, 7; Tob 5: 17 S; Jos., Ant. 1, 226) Ac 9: 7. Restored in UGosp 33f (=Huck⁹-L. Synopse p. 37 note=Gospel Parallels '49, 32 note).
2. fig. (Alex. Aphr., An. p. 80, 11, Fat. c. 6 p. 169, 22 Br.; Herm. Wr. 1, 28 οἱ συνοδεύσαντες τῇ πλάνῃ; Wsd 6: 23) of the Lord ἐμοὶ συνώδευσεν ἐν ὁδῷ δικαιοσύνης *he was my traveling companion in the way of righteousness* B 1: 4. M-M.*

συνοδία, ας, ἡ *caravan, group of travelers* (so Strabo 4, 6, 6; 11, 14, 4; Epict. 4, 1, 91; Dit., Or. 633, 1; 638, 7; 646, 6; Jos., Bell. 2, 587, Ant. 6, 243; loanw. in rabb.—2 Esdr 17 [Neh 7]: 5, 64 συνοδία means 'family') Lk 2: 44. M-M.*

σύνοδος, ου, ὁ *traveling companion, fellow-traveler* (Manetho, Ap. 5, 58; Epict. 4, 1, 97; Anth. Pal. 7, 635, 2) fig. of people who are traveling the same way (here the way of love, commanded by God) IEph 9: 2 (cf. 9: 1). M-M.*

σύνοιδα (Aeschyl., Hdt.+; inscr., pap., LXX, Philo, Joseph.) defective verb, perf. w. pres. mng.; ptc., fem. gen. sing. συνειδυίης (for the form cf. BGU 55; 77 εἰδυίης; Ex 8: 17, 20; 1 Km 25: 20; Tdf., Prol. 117; W-H., App. 156).
1. *share knowledge with, be implicated* (Soph.+; BPGrenfell, Revenue Laws of Ptolemy Philadelphus [1896] 8, 1; 21, 9; PPetr. III 36a, 9 [III BC]; BGU 1141, 50; PFlor. 373, 6) Ac 5: 2 (Jos., Ant. 13, 424 ξυνῄδει ἡ γυνὴ μόνη; 16, 330).
2. σύνοιδα ἐμαυτῷ *I know with myself,* i.e. *I am conscious* (Eur., Hdt. et al.; Diod. S. 4, 38, 3 συνειδυῖα ἑαυτῇ τὴν ἁμαρτίαν=being conscious of her error; Dit., Syll.³ 983, 6f; POxy. 898, 20; Job 27: 6) w. ὅτι foll. B 1: 4. οὐδὲν ἐμαυτῷ σύνοιδα 1 Cor 4: 4 (cf. Polyb. 4, 86 διὰ τὸ μηδὲν αὐτοῖς συνειδέναι; Demosth., Ep. 2, 15; Diod. S. 17, 106, 2 πολλοὶ συνειδότες ἑαυτοῖς ὕβρεις).—τὸ συνειδός (since Demosth. 18, 110) *consciousness* in which the subject imparts information to himself, *conscience* (Plut., Mor. 85C; 556A; Epict. 3, 22, 94; Charito 3, 4, 13; Appian, Bell. Civ. 1, 82 §373 τὸ συνειδὸς τῶν ἄλλων χεῖρον=worse than that of the others; 5, 16 §67 τὸ σ., that punishes the guilty; Philo, Spec. Leg. 1, 235 ὑπὸ τοῦ συνειδότος ἐλεγχόμενος; 4, 6; 40, Op. M. 128; Jos., C. Ap. 2, 218, Bell. 1, 453; 2, 582, Ant. 1, 47; 13, 316; 16, 102 ἐκ τοῦ συνειδότος='fr. a consciousness of guilt, fr. a bad conscience'; Dit., Or. 484, 37; POxy. 532, 23 [II AD]) ἐκ συνειδότος *because of the witness of my own conscience* ISm 11: 1.—S. on συνείδησις, end; also CMaurer, TW VII, 897–918: σύνοιδα and συνείδησις. M-M.*

συνοικέω *live with* τινί *someone* (since Hipponax [VI BC] 20 Diehl² and Aeschyl.) of man and wife (Hdt. et al.; Dit., Or. 771, 28; pap., LXX; Jos., Ant. 4, 247; 8, 191; cf. Philo, Sacr. Abel. 20) 1 Pt 3: 7. M-M.*

συνοικοδομέω 1 aor. pass. συνῳκοδομήθην (Thu.+; Dit., Syll.³ 913, 16; POxy. 1648, 60; 1 Esdr 5: 65) *build together with,* in our lit. only symbolically and exclusively pass. (both as Philo, Praem. 120).
1. of the various parts of a structure, fr. which the latter is *built up* (together) (Περὶ ὕψους 10, 7) Eph 2: 22.
2. *be built in* (Thu. 1, 93, 5 λίθοι; Diod. S. 13, 82, 3 συνῳκοδομοῦντο οἱ κίονες τοῖς τοίχοις) Hs 9, 16, 7. M-M.*

συνομιλέω *talk, converse with* (Cebes 13, 1; Jos., Bell. 5, 533; BGU 401, 15) τινί *someone* Ac 10: 27; *live with* τινί (Antiochus of Athens [II AD]: Cat. Cod. Astr. VII 109, 30) 1 Pt 3: 7 v.l. M-M.*

συνομορέω (elsewh. only in Byz. writers; the simple verb w. the same mng. in Plut.; Herodian 6, 7, 2; inscr., pap., LXX) *border on, be next (door) to* τινί *someth.* Ac 18: 7. M-M.*

συνοράω 2 aor. συνεῖδον (X., Pla.+; inscr., pap., LXX) in our lit. only of mental seeing *perceive, become aware of, realize* (Polyb. 1, 4, 6; 3, 6, 9 al.; Plut., Themist. 7, 3 τὸν κίνδυνον; Dit., Syll.³ 495, 54; PReinach 18, 17; 19, 12; BGU 1139, 13 [I BC]; 2 Macc 4: 41; 14: 26, 30; 3 Macc 5: 50; Ep. Arist. 56; Philo, Sacr. Abel. 76, Somn. 1, 94; Jos., Bell. 4, 338, C. Ap. 2, 153) συνιδόντες κατέφυγον *when they became aware of (it) they fled* Ac 14: 6. συνιδών *when he realized (this)* 12: 12 (Field, Notes 120).*

συνορία, ας, ἡ (Peripl. Eryth. c. 65; Dit., Or. 168, 18 [II BC]; 206, 3; pap.) *neighboring country* Mt 4: 24 v.l.*

συνοχή, ῆς, ἡ (Hom.+; LXX; Ep. Arist. 61; Jos., Ant. 8, 65)—1. *prison* (PLond. 354, 24 [10 BC]) ἐν σ. γενόμενος *when he is put into prison* D 1: 5 (in the pl. the word means *bonds, fetters* Manetho, Ap. 1, 313 al., several times in Vett. Val. index).
2. *distress, dismay, anguish* (Artem. 2, 3 p. 88, 14; Astrampsychus p. 24 Dek. 42, 8; p. 26 Dek. 48, 10; BGU 1821, 21 and 28 [50 BC]; PLond. 122, 35 [IV AD]; Cat. Cod. Astr. VIII 1 p. 267, 5; Job 30: 3; Aq. Ps. 24: 17) Lk 21: 25. (W. θλῖψις) συνοχὴ καρδίας *anguish of heart* 2 Cor 2: 4. M-M.*

συνπ- s. συμπ-.

συνρ- s. συρρ-.

συνσ- s. συσσ-.

συνσπ- s. συσπ-.

συνστ- s. συστ-.

σύνταξις, εως, ἡ (Thu., X., Pla.+) *complete exposition* (Aristot., Polyb. et al.) Papias 2: 15 (HARigg, Jr., NovT 1, '56, 161–83: 'any special arrangement').*

συνταράσσω 1 aor. συνετάραξα (Hom. [in tmesis]+) *throw into confusion, disturb* (Hdt., Thu. et al.; Pla., Leg. 7 p. 798A συνταραχθεὶς ὑπὸ νόσων; Dit., Or. 669, 41 [I AD]; LXX; Test. Jud. 14: 3) Lk 9: 42 D.*

συντάσσω 1 aor. συνέταξα (Hdt.+; Jos., Ant. 3, 213; 7, 305 al.) *order, direct, prescribe* (X., Cyr. 8, 6, 8; Polyb. 3, 50, 9; inscr., pap., LXX) τινί *(for) someone* (Zen.-P. 10 [=Sb 6716], 2 [258/7 BC] Ἀμύντου μοι συντάσσοντος)

Mt 21:6 (προστάσσω v.l., cf. 1:24); 26:19; 27:10 (cf. Ex 37:20; 40:19; Num 27:11 al.; RPesch, Eine ATliche Ausführungsformel im Mt, BZ 10, '66, 220-45). M-M.*

συνταφείς s. συνθάπτω.

συντέλεια, ας, ἡ (Pla., Demosth. et al.; inscr., pap., LXX; En. 106, 18; Aristob. in Euseb., Pr. Ev. 8, 10, 9; Jos., Ant. 15, 389; 20, 262) *completion, close, end* (Polyb. 1, 3, 3; 1, 4, 3 al.; Dit., Syll.³ 695, 13 [II BC]; POxy. 1270, 42 [II AD] σ. τοῦ ἔτους; LXX) συντέλεια (τοῦ) αἰῶνος *the end of the* (present; αἰών 2a) *age* (Test. Benj. 11: 3) Mt 13: 39f, 49; 24: 3; 28: 20. τοῦ αἰῶνος τούτου *of this age* 13: 40 t.r. τῶν αἰώνων *of the ages* (Test. Levi 10: 2) Hb 9: 26. τῶν καιρῶν (Da 9: 27) Hv 3, 8, 9. τοῦ κόσμου Mt 13: 49 D. ἐπ' ἐσχάτων τῶν ἡμερῶν τῆς συντελείας *in the last days of the consummation* (of the age) Hs 9, 12, 3 (cf. Test. Zeb. 9: 9 καιρὸς συντελείας). M-M.*

συντελέω fut. συντελέσω. Pass.: 1 aor. συνετελέσθην; 1 fut. συντελεσθήσομαι (Thu.+; inscr., pap., LXX, En., Ep. Arist., Philo, Joseph., Test. 12 Patr.).

1. *bring to an end, complete, finish, close* τὶ someth. (Diod. S. 1, 3, 2; Philo, Ebr. 53; Jos., Ant. 15, 269) Hs 8, 11, 1; 9, 7, 1; 9, 29, 4. πάντα πειρασμόν Lk 4: 13. A teaching, a speech, λόγους Mt 7: 28 t.r. τὰς ἐντολάς Hm 12, 3, 2. Abs., though the obj. is to be supplied fr. the context B 15: 3f (Gen 2: 2). Pass., of the building of a tower (cf. PSI 407, 2 [III BC] ἐπειδή σοι [=by you] τὰ ἔργα [s. ἔργον 3] συντετέλεσται; Berosus in Jos., C. Ap. 1, 140) Hv 3, 4, 2; 3, 8, 9; s 9, 5, 2.—Of time *come to an end, be over* (Dt 34: 8; Job 1: 5; Tob 10: 7) Lk 2: 21 D; 4: 2; Ac 21: 27; B 16: 6 (quot. of uncertain origin). Perh. this is the place for ὅταν μέλλῃ ταῦτα συντελεῖσθαι πάντα *when all this* (cf. vs. 2) *is to come to an end* Mk 13: 4 (s. 2 below).

2. *carry out, fulfill, accomplish* τὶ someth. (Polyb. 4, 81, 3; Diod. S. 4, 53, 2 συντελέσαι τὴν ὑπόσχεσιν=keep one's word; Phlegon: 257 fgm. 36, 1, 11 perform an act of expiation; Jos., Bell. 7, 392) τὰ γεγραμμένα Hs 5, 3, 7. Of God λόγον *carry out* (his) *word, bring* (his) *word to accomplishment* (cf. Sb 717, 2, 25 [217 BC] εὐχαριστῶν τοῖς θεοῖς ἐπὶ τῷ συντελέσαι αὐτοὺς ἃ ἐπηγγείλαντο αὐτῷ; Polystrat. p. 10 τ. θεὸν συντελεῖν ταῦτα κατὰ βούλησιν; La 2: 17; the magical inscr. fr. Ashmunên published by the Soc. Ital. per la Ricerca dei Papiri Greci in Egitto in the Omaggio for the conference of class. philologians April 1911 no. 5, 40 ναὶ κύριε βασιλεῦ χθονίων θεῶν συντέλεσον τὰ ἐγγεγραμμένα τῷ πεδάλῳ τούτῳ; PGM 3, 121; 57, 2) Ro 9: 28 (Is 10: 22). συντελέσω διαθήκην καινήν *I will bring a new covenant to accomplishment* Hb 8: 8 (cf. Jer 38[31]: 31 διαθήσομαι; 41[34]: 8, 15); possibly simply *I will establish a new covenant* (σ.='make' X., Cyr. 6, 1, 50; Demosth. 21, 22).—Perh. Mk 13: 4 (s. 1 above), in case it is to be translated *when all this is to be accomplished* (Diod. S. 2, 30, 1 everything is accomplished by a decision of the gods.—In 17, 1, 2 συντελεῖσθαι is simply=happen). Cf. B 12: 1 (prophetic saying of unknown origin). πρᾶξις συντελεῖται *a course of action finds application* Hm 4, 1, 11 (Diod. S. 26, 7 συνετελέσατο πρᾶξιν=he perpetrated a[n impious] deed).

3. pass. *give out* of the exhaustion of a supply συνετελέσθη ὁ οἶνος τοῦ γάμου J 2: 3 v.l. (the act.='blot out, destroy' Jer 14: 12; Ezk 7: 15; Test. Levi 5: 4; corresp. the pass. Jer 14: 15; 16: 4; Test. Dan 6: 4). M-M.*

συντέμνω pf. συντέτμηκα, pass. ptc. συντετμημένος *cut short, shorten, limit* (Aeschyl., Thu.+; LXX) of time

(Philippides [Com. Att. III 308 Kock] 25 [IV/III BC] ὁ τὸν ἐνιαυτὸν συντεμὼν εἰς μῆν' ἕνα; Da 5: 26-8 LXX; 9: 24 Theod.; Jos., Ant. 1, 152) τοὺς καιρούς B 4: 3. A passage not only of uncertain interpretation, but fraught w. textual difficulties as well, is λόγον συντελῶν καὶ συντέμνων ποιήσει ὁ κύριος Ro 9: 28 (Is 10: 22b-23; these two compounds of συν- are also combined in Da 5: 26-8 LXX; sim. Da 9: 24 Theod.) *the Lord will act by accomplishing* (συντελέω 2) *his word and by shortening* or *cutting off*; in this case the shortening is thought of as referring either to God's promise to Israel, which will be fulfilled only to a limited degree (RALipsius, BWeiss), or to the Israelite nation, which is to enter into salvation trimmed and cut down, as a (vs. 27) 'remnant' (Jülicher, Sickenberger). Others take it to mean: *The Lord will act by closing the account and shortening* (*the time*), i.e. he will not prolong indefinitely the period of his long-suffering (Zahn; sim. also Hofmann and Althaus; cf. the RSV 'the Lord will execute his sentence w. rigor and dispatch'.—Mnesimachus [Com. Att. II 436 Kock] 3, 4 [IV BC] σύντεμνε= 'make it short, come to the point'; Musonius p. 87, 6 ἵνα συντεμὼν εἴπω='in short'; Psellus p. 232, 31 συντεμὼν τὸν λόγον=I will speak concisely; Philostrat., Vi. Apollon. 7, 14 p. 268, 16 λόγους ξυντεμεῖν πάντας='bring the speech to a sudden close'). M-M.*

συντεχνίτης, ου, ὁ (pap. fr. VI AD on) *one who follows the same trade* ἄνδρες συντεχνῖται *fellow-craftsmen* Ac 19: 25 D.*

συντηρέω impf. συνετήρουν; fut. συντηρήσω (Aristot. et al.; inscr., pap., LXX, Ep. Arist., Joseph.).

1. *protect, defend* against harm or ruin τινά someone (PTebt. 416, 14) Mk 6: 20; Hm 5, 1, 7; s 5, 6, 2. Pass. (IG XII 5, 860, 44 [I BC]; Jos., Bell. 1, 184) *be saved, preserved* (opp. ἀπόλλυσθαι) Mt 9: 17; Lk 5: 38 t.r.

2. *keep in mind, be concerned about* τὶ someth (Polyb. 4, 60, 10; inscr., pap., LXX) ἀδελφότητα Hm 8: 10.

3. *hold* or *treasure up* (in one's memory) (Sir 39: 2; Da 7: 28 Theod. τὸ ῥῆμα ἐν τῇ καρδίᾳ μου; sim. Test. Levi 6: 2.—Polyb. 30, 30, 5 the word means 'keep to oneself, conceal', as perh. also Jos., Bell. 2, 142) συνετήρει (διετήρει 2: 51) τὰ ῥήματα Lk 2: 19 (Da 7: 28 Theod.; Syntipas p. 102, 1; 104, 9 συνετήρουν ἐν τῇ καρδίᾳ πάντα); BFMeyer, CBQ 26, '64, 31-49. M-M.*

συντίθημι 2 aor. mid. συνεθέμην; plpf. συνετεθείμην (Hom.+; inscr., pap., LXX; Ep. Arist. 136; Philo, Aet. M. 28 al.; Jos., Bell. 7, 312, Ant. 17, 38).

1. act. and pass. *put* or *place with* σκεῦος κενὸν μετὰ τῶν κενῶν συντιθέμενον *an empty vessel placed beside the* (other) *empty* vessels (in such a way that it knocks against them) Hm 11: 13 (cf. X., Cyr. 8, 5, 4; POxy. 1631, 17).

2. mid.—a. *agree*—a. w. someone (Hdt. et al.) συνέθεντο αὐτῷ ἀργύριον δοῦναι where, no matter how the dat. is construed, the sense is *they came to an agreement with him, to pay him money* Lk 22: 5.

β. among themselves, *decide* (Jos., Vi. 196; Test. Zeb. 1: 6) foll. by the articular inf. in the gen. (Bl-D. §400, 7; Rob. 1068; Test. Jos. 6: 9) Ac 23: 20. W. ἵνα foll. J 9: 22.

b. *consent* (Lysias+; Dionys. Hal., Isocr. 18; Paus. 4, 15, 2; PSI 484, 2 [III BC]; 524, 4) Ac 24: 9 t.r. M-M.*

σύντομος, ον (Aeschyl., Hdt.+; pap., LXX; Jos., Bell. 4, 228) *cut short, short, brief*, then also *short and to the point* (Aeschin., Or. 2, 51 Bl.; Philo, Praem. 50), *close at hand, ready* (of Nemesis, Anth. 12, 12, 2.—Jos., Bell. 4, 227) εὔχομαι (τὰ θηρία) σύντομά μοι εὑρεθῆναι *I pray that* *they* (the beasts) *might show themselves ready for me* IRo 5: 2.*

συντόμως adv. (Aeschyl., Hippocr.+; inscr., pap., LXX, Joseph.; Test. Jos. 7: 1. Loanw. in rabb.)—1. *in a short time, promptly, readily* (Aeschyl., Hippocr.+; pap.; Pr 13: 23; 3 Macc 5: 25; Jos., Ant. 2, 315) 2 Cl 20: 4; IRo 5: 2; alternative short ending of Mk.

2. of discourse *briefly, concisely* (Aeschyl., Isocr.; cf. Jos., C. Ap. 1, 3; 29) IMg 14. ἀκοῦσαί τινος συντόμως *give someone a hearing briefly* (i.e. someone who promises to speak briefly and to the point) Ac 24: 4. M-M.*

σύντονος, ον *stretched tight, intense, vehement* (trag.+; Philo, Joseph.) the neut. as subst. τὸ σύντονον *intense desire, zeal* (Philo, Leg. ad Gai. τὸ σ. τῆς σπουδῆς) ὑμῶν τὸ σύντονον τῆς ἀληθείας *your intense desire for the truth* IPol 7: 3.—The neut. of the comp. as adv. (Aristot., Pol. 5, 8, 2; Plut., Cato Maj. 21, 5; Jos., Bell. 1, 274; 3, 13) συντονώτερον γράφειν *write more sharply* ITr 3: 3.*

συντρέχω 2 aor. συνέδραμον (Hom., Aeschyl., Hdt.+; pap., LXX; Philo, Aet. M. 103; Joseph., Test. 12 Patr.) *run together.*

1. *of a number of persons who run to a place and gather there* (X. et al.; Wilcken, Chrest. 20 III, 8; LXX πρός τινα (Diod. S. 19, 13, 7 πρὸς ἀλλήλους; Plut., Alc. 32, 3, Mar. 29, 10, Pomp. 60, 5; Charito 5, 9, 5; Jos., Bell. 1, 250) Ac 3: 11 (Jos., Ant. 7, 257 ἅπαντα τὸν λαὸν συνδραμεῖν πρὸς αὐτόν). ἐκεῖ (Diod. S. 20, 96, 4) Mk 6: 33. εἰς ναόν IMg 7: 2 (cf. Jdth 6: 16; Archilochus, fgm. 54 Diehl²; Posidon.: 87 fgm. 36, 51 Jac.; Diod. S. 4, 42, 3 εἰς ἐκκλησίαν).

2. *run (together) with someone* (Appian, Bell. Civ. 2, 49 §200), in our lit. only fig., of close association *go with* τινί *someone* 1 Cl 35: 8 (Ps 49: 18). Also μετά τινος B 4: 2. εἴς τι *to denote the common goal* (Himerius, Or. [Ecl. 10, 3 fig.) συντρέχειν εἰς τὴν αὐτὴν τῆς ἀσωτίας ἀνάχυσιν *plunge with (them) into the same stream of debauchery* 1 Pt 4: 4.

3. *agree with, be in harmony with* (Aeschyl.+) τινί someth. (Soph., Trach. 880; Mitteis, Chrest. 96, 11 τούτῳ τῷ λόγῳ) τῇ γνώμῃ τοῦ θεοῦ IEph 3: 2; cf. 4: 1. With other συν- compounds IPol 6: 1. M-M.*

συντριβή, ῆς, ἡ (Vett. Val. 74, 4; Heliod. 10, 28; Sb 5763, 42; LXX) *rubbing away, crushing, destruction* of Christ, who is put in place like a firm stone εἰς συντριβήν to destroy those who dash against (= take offense at) him B 6: 2 ('polishing' JAKleist, transl. '48, p. 172 n. 59).*

συντρίβω fut. συντρίψω; 1 aor. συνέτριψα. Pass.: perf. inf. συντετρῖφθαι, ptc. συντετριμμένος; 2 aor. συνετρίβην; 2 fut. συντριβήσομαι (Eur., Thu.+; inscr., pap., LXX; En. 103, 10; Test. 12 Patr.) *shatter, smash, crush.*

1. lit.—a. of things (Diod. S. 14, 58, 3; 15, 86, 2; Arrian, Anab. 6, 9, 4) ἀλάβαστρον *break an alabaster flask* Mk 14: 3. πύλας χαλκᾶς *shatter gates of brass* (cf. PTebt. 45, 21 [113 bc]) B 11: 4 (Is 45: 2). Pass. (cf. Diod. S. 4, 62, 3 συντριβῆναι of a wagon; Jos., Bell. 1, 43; 90) of a reed *be bent* Mt 12: 20 (cf. Is 42: 3). Of fetters *be broken* Mk 5: 4. Of bones *be broken* (Hippocr., Ep. 22, 3 ὀστέων συντριβομένων; Himerius, Or. 69 [=Or. 22], 5 of Ibycus' broken hand; Stephan. Byz. s.v. Ἀμαζόνες: σ. τὰ μέλη of people) J 19: 36 (Ps 33: 21.—Cf. σκέλος, end). Of the tables of the law (Ex 32: 19; Dt 9: 17) B 14: 3; cf. 4: 8. Vessels (Ael. Aristid. 19, 7 K.=41 p. 765 D.; Aesop, Fab. 190 H. τὰ σκεύη συνέτριψε; Dit., Syll.³ 1168, 82)

are broken Rv 2: 27 (cf. Ps 2: 9) or *break* (intr.) 2 Cl 8: 2. Of waves *be dashed into foam* 1 Cl 20: 7 (Job 38: 11).

b. of persons *mistreat, beat someone severely* (Eur.+), also *wear out, bruise* (PPetr. II 4, 3, 5; PLeipz. 38, 17) Lk 9: 39. Of enemies *annihilate, crush* (Polyb. 5, 47, 1; 1 Macc 3: 22 al.) ὁ θεὸς συντρίψει τὸν σατανᾶν Ro 16: 20.

2. fig. of mental and emotional states (συντριβῆναι τῇ διανοίᾳ Polyb. 21, 13, 2; 30, 32, 11; Diod. S. 4, 66, 4 ταῖς ἐλπίσιν=their hopes were shattered; τοῖς φρονήμασιν Diod. S. 11, 78, 4.—Plut., Mor. 47A; 165B; LXX) καρδία συντετριμμένη (καρδία 1bϵ) 1 Cl 18: 17b; B 2: 10 (both Ps 50: 19b). πνεῦμα συντετριμμένον 1 Cl 18: 17a; 52: 4 (both Ps 50: 19a). οἱ συντετριμμένοι τὴν καρδίαν (Is 61: 1; cf. Ps 33: 19; 146: 3) Lk 4: 18 t.r.; B 14: 9. M-M.*

σύντριμμα, ατος, τό (Aristot.+; LXX) *destruction, ruin* Ro 3: 16 (Is 59: 7; Ps 13: 3). M-M.*

σύντροφος, ον *nourished* or *brought up together with,* also *familiar, on friendly terms* (trag., Hdt.+), subst. ὁ σ. *foster-brother, companion* (from one's youth), *intimate friend* τινός *of someone* (σύντροφος τοῦ βασιλέως Polyb. 5, 9, 4; Diod. S. 1, 53, 5; 1, 54, 5; Dit., Or. 247, 2; 323, 2 al. Cf. Aelian, V.H. 12, 26; POxy. 1034, 2; 7; 2 Macc 9: 29; Jos., Bell. 1, 215, Ant. 14, 183) Ac 13: 1 (s. Μαναήν. —A Cilician inscr. in Monum. As. Min. Ant. III '31 no. 62 [I bc] mentions Hermias as the σύντρ.='intimate friend' of the Seleucid King Philip II). M-M. B. 1346.*

συντυγχάνω 2 aor. συνέτυχον (trag.+; inscr., pap.; 2 Macc 8: 14; Ep. Arist.; Joseph.) *come together with, meet, join* (trag., Hdt.+; Jos., Ant. 1, 219; 15, 187; pap.) Lk 8: 19; GOxy 11. Without the dat., which is to be supplied Ac 11: 26 D. M-M.*

Συντύχη, ης, ἡ *Syntyche* (reff., esp. fr. inscr., in Zahn, Einl. I 379), a Christian woman in Philippi Phil 4: 2. M-M.*

συντυχία, ας, ἡ (lyric poets, Hdt.+) *chance, incident* Lk 10: 31 𝔓⁷⁵ (spelled -εία), as v.l. for συγκυρία.*

συνυποκρίνομαι dep.; 1 aor. συνυπεκρίθην (Polyb. 3, 92, 5 al.; Plut., Marius 14, 14; 17, 5; Ep. Arist. 267) *join in pretending* or *playing a part, join in playing the hypocrite* w. dat. of the pers. whom one joins in hypocrisy Gal 2: 13. M-M.*

συνυπουργέω (Hippocr.; Lucian, Bis Acc. 17) *join in helping, co-operate with* τινί *by means of someth.* συνυπουργούντων ὑμῶν ὑπὲρ ἡμῶν τῇ δεήσει *while you join in helping us through your prayers* 2 Cor 1: 11.*

συνφ- s. συμφ-.

συνχ- s. συγχ-.

συνψ- s. συμψ-.

συνωδίνω (Eur., Hel. 727; Aelian, N. An. 3, 45 p. 78, 5 after Aristot.; Porphyr., Abst. 3, 10) *be in travail with* or more gener. *suffer agony together* Ro 8: 22 (on στενάζειν and the ὠδῖνες of the κτίσις cf. Heraclit. Sto. c. 39 p. 58, 9 ἐπειδὰν ἡ μεμυκυῖα γῆ τὰς κυοφορουμένας ἔνδον ὠδῖνας ἐκφήνῃ='when [after the winter's cold] the groaning earth gives birth in travail to what has been formed within her').—Diod. S. 5, 5, 1 quotes the tragic poet Carcinus: all Sicily, filled with fire from Aetna, groaned [στενάξαι] over the loss of Persephone.*

συνωμοσία, ας, ἡ *conspiracy, plot* (Thu., Aristoph. et al.; inscr.; Sym. Ezk 22: 25; Jos., Ant. 15, 288; 16, 111) συνωμοσίαν ποιεῖσθαι *form a conspiracy* (Polyb. 1, 70, 6; Diod. S. 3, 57, 5; Herodian 7, 4, 3) Ac 23: 13. M-M. B. 1363.*

Σύρα, ας, ἡ *the Syrian woman* (Aristoph. +) Mk 7: 26 v.l. (s. Συροφοινίκισσα).*

Συράκουσαι, ῶν, αἱ (Pind., Hdt. +; inscr. in var. spellings) *Syracuse,* a city on the east coast of Sicily Ac 28: 12. M-M.*

Συρία, ας, ἡ (Aeschyl., Hdt. +; inscr., LXX; Ep. Arist. 22; Philo, Joseph.; Sib. Or. 12, 102 [elsewh. Συρίη; s. the index of names]. Cf. Bl-D. §261, 6 app.) *Syria,* the part of Western Asia that is bounded on the north by the Taurus Mts., on the east by the lands of the Euphrates, on the south by Palestine, on the west by the Mediterranean Sea. In 64 BC it became a Roman province; its capital was Antioch. Mt 4: 24; Ac 18: 18; 20: 3; 21: 3; IEph 1: 2; IRo 5: 1; 10: 2; ISm 11: 2; IPol 7: 2; 8: 2; IPhld 11: 1; Pol 13: 1. Mentioned beside Cilicia, its neighboring province in Asia Minor (X., An. 1, 4, 4; Diod. S. 16, 42, 1; 9 of the two neighboring satrapies of Persian times) Ac 15: 23, 41; Gal 1: 21. Ἀντιόχεια τῆς Σ. (cf. Ἀντιόχεια 1) ISm 11: 1; IPol 7: 1; IPhld 10: 1. The province was governed by an imperial legate (cf. ἡγεμονεύω and Κυρήνιος) Lk 2: 2. ἡ ἐκκλησία ἡ ἐν Συρίᾳ *the church in Syria* IEph 21: 2; IMg 14; ITr 13: 1; IRo 9: 1. Ignatius is ὁ ἐπίσκοπος Συρίας IRo 2: 2.—GBeer, RE XIX '07, 281–95 (lit.); RDussaud, Mission dans les régions désertiques de la Syrie moyenne '03, Topographie historique de la Syrie antique et médiévale '26; BMaisler, Untersuchungen z. alten Gesch. u. Ethnographie Syriens u. Palästinas I '29; KBaedeker, Palästina u. Syrien⁷ '10, Syrie-Palestine, Irâq, Transjordanie '32; LHaefeli, Syrien u. sein Libanon '26; UKahrstedt, Syr. Territorien in hellenist. Zeit '26. On the relig. situation cf. Schürer III⁴ 10f; Dussaud, Notes de Mythologie Syrienne '03–'05; FCumont, Études Syriennes '17, Religionen³ '31, 94–123; 253–77 (lit.); HPreisker, Ntl. Zeitgesch. '37, 146–57; Prümm 264–8; 651–4. S. also ChClermont-Ganneau, Recueil d'archéol. orientale, eight vols. 1888–1924. M-M.*

Σύρος, ου, ὁ *the Syrian* (Soph., Hdt. +; inscr., pap., Philo, Joseph.; Test. Napht. 5: 8; Sib. Or.) of Naaman, the Syrian army commander Lk 4: 27 (cf. 2 Kings 5). Circumcision practiced by the Syrians B 9: 6 (cf. Windisch, Hdb. ad loc.). M-M.*

Συροφοινίκισσα, ης, ἡ *the Syrophoenician woman* (the masc. Συροφοῖνιξ in Lucian, Concil. Deor. 4; Eunap., Vi. Soph. p. 98), an inhabitant of Syrophoenicia, a district which was so called because Phoenicia belonged to the province of Syria (cf. Diod. S. 19, 93, 7 ἡ Φοινίκη Συρία; Justin, Dial. 78 p. 305A Συροφοινίκη: EHonigmann, Pauly-W. 2nd series IV '32, 1788f), and could thus be differentiated fr. Libophoenicia around Carthage (Diod. S. 20, 55, 4 Λιβυφοίνικες; Strabo 17, 19) Mk 7: 26 (v.l. Συροφοίνισσα, Σύρα Φοινίκισσα; cf. Bl-D. §111, 1; Mlt.-H. 279; 349).—DSMargoliouth, The Syrophoenician Woman: Exp. 8th Ser. XXII '21, 1–10; AvanVeldhuizen, De Syrofenicische Vrouw: Op den Uitkijk 3, '26, 65ff; JIHalser, The Incident of the Syrophoenician Woman: ET 45, '34, 459–61; TBurkill, The Historical Devel. of the Story of the Syr. Woman, NovT 9, '67, 161–77; WStorch, BZ 14, '70, 256f. S. also on Χαναναῖος. M-M.*

συρρέω (X. +; pap.) *flow together* Papias 3.*

συρρήγνυμι (Hom. +; Jos., Bell. 1, 251; 3, 302; Sib. Or.

2, 201) intr. (Hdt. +; Jos., Bell. 1, 364) *dash* (*together*) τινί *upon someth.* Lk 6: 49 D.*

Σύρτις, εως, ἡ (Hdt. +) *the Syrtis;* name of two gulfs along the Libyan coast which, because of their shallowness and shifting sand-banks, were greatly feared by mariners (Apollon. Rhod. 4, 1235ff; Strabo 17, 3, 20; Dio Chrys. 5, 8–11; Jos., Bell. 2, 381). The Syrtis meant in Ac 27: 17 is the so-called Great one, toward Cyrenaica.*

σύρω impf. ἔσυρον (Aristot.; Theocr. et al.; pap., LXX, Joseph.) *drag, pull, draw, drag away* τὶ *someth.* (cf. PFlor. 158, 7 τὸ ταυρικὸν σύρει τὰ ξύλα) σύροντες τὸ δίκτυον *dragging in the net* J 21: 8 (σ. in catching fish: Plut., Mor. 977F). Of the dragon in heaven: ἡ οὐρὰ αὐτοῦ σύρει τὸ τρίτον τῶν ἀστέρων *his tail swept away a third of the stars* Rv 12: 4.—τινά *drag someone away* (*by force*) (Ps.-Theocr., Hymn to the Dead Adonis l. 12 [Bucoliques Grecs ed. ELegrand '25 vol. II p. 112] ἔσυρον αἰχμάλωτον; Epict. 1, 29, 16; 22; Jos., Bell. 1, 452; 2, 491, Ant. 20, 136.—4 Macc 6: 1 ἐπί τι) Ac 8: 3; GP 3: 7 (cf. Eutecnius 4 p. 41, 33 σύρειν αἰσχρῶς κατὰ γῆς). ἀδελφοὺς ἐπὶ τοὺς πολιτάρχας Ac 17: 6.—Of a (supposedly) lifeless human body (Herodian 1, 13, 6; 5, 8, 9) ἔσυρον ἔξω τῆς πόλεως 14: 19. S. κατασύρω. M-M.*

συσκέπτομαι impf. συνεσκεπτόμην (Sym. Ps 2: 2; 30: 14) *contemplate together, determine* τινί *with someone* (Herodian 1, 17, 7; Iambl., Protr. 21, 31 p. 123, 19 Pistelli) ἀλλήλοις GP 11: 43 (w. inf. foll.).*

συσπαράσσω 1 aor. συνεσπάραξα (Maximus Tyr. 7, 5e) *tear* (*to pieces*)*, pull about, convulse* τινά *someone,* of the demon, who so treats the person who is in his power Mk 9: 20; w. ῥήγνυμι Lk 9: 42.*

συσπάω (Pla. +; La 5: 10) *draw together, keep closed* τὰς χεῖρας πρὸς τὸ δοῦναι *clench one's fists when it comes to giving* (RKnopf D 4: 5) or *keep one's hands closed* (HWindisch B 19: 9) B 19: 9; D 4: 5. But since this expr. is contrasted w. ἐκτείνειν τὰς χεῖρας (cf. ἐκτείνω 1), it may be better to translate *pull back, pull in, retract* (cf. Lucian, Tim. 13 συσπ. τοὺς δακτύλους; Aristot., H.A. 2, 17 τ. γλῶτταν; 5, 20 τὴν κεφαλήν).*

σύσσημον, ου, τό (since Menand. [Per. 362 J.], as Phryn. p. 418 L. explains in rejecting the word; Diod. S., Strabo, Plut., LXX; loanw. in rabb.) *signal* previously agreed upon Mk 14: 44. *Sign, token, standard* αἴρειν σύσσημον (Aeneas Tact. 223; Diod. S. 11, 22, 1; 19, 30, 1; 20, 51, 1; Strabo 6, 3, 3; Is 49: 22) *raise a sign* ISm 1: 2 (Is 5: 26). M-M.*

σύσσωμος, ον (only in Christian writers) *belonging to the same body* w. συγκληρονόμος, συμμέτοχος τῆς ἐπαγγελίας Eph 3: 6.—EPreuschen, ZNW 1, '00, 85f. M-M.*

συστασιαστής, οῦ, ὁ (Jos., Ant. 14, 22) *fellow-insurrectionist* Mk 15: 7 t.r.*

σύστασις, εως, ἡ (Eur., Hdt. +; inscr., pap., LXX, Ep. Arist., Philo; Jos., Ant. 15, 194).

1. *gathering, union, association* (Appian, Bell. Civ. 5, 132, §547 συστάσεις=bands [of robbers]) αἱ συστάσεις αἱ ἀρχοντικαί (cf. ἀρχοντικός and ἄρχων 3) ITr 5: 2. On the basis of this pass. and the Lat. version θηρίων συστάσεις IRo 5: 3 can be taken to mean *packs of wild beasts.* But mng. 2 is also poss. here.—2. *encounter, struggle* (Eur., Hdt. +; Diod. S. 4, 16, 2): *struggles with wild beasts.*

3. *structure, constitution, nature* (Diod. S. 15, 32, 1; Alex. Aphr., An. p. 3, 19 Br.) τοῦ κόσμου (Cornutus 18 p. 32, 5; cf. Wsd 7: 17) 1 Cl 60: 1. Another possibility is *permanence, duration.* *

συστατικός, ή, όν (since Aristot. in Diog. L. 5, 18; pap.) *introducing, commendatory* συστατικὴ ἐπιστολή *a letter of recommendation* (Ammonius, Vi. Aristot. p. 11, 18 Westerm. συστατικαὶ ἐπ.) 2 Cor 3: 1 (Epict. 2, 3, 1 γράμματα παρ' αὐτοῦ λαβεῖν συστατικά; Diog. L. 8, 87; POxy. 1587, 20; PTebt. 315, 29 [II AD] ἔχει συστατικάς, i.e. ἐπιστολάς.—Models: Ps.-Demetr., Form. Ep. p. 3, 16ff; Ps.-Libanius, Charact. Ep. p. 22, 12ff; also p. 58). On this subject cf. Dssm., LO 137f (LAE 170-2); Windisch ad loc.; CWKeyes, The Gk. Letter of Introduction: AJPh 56, '35, 28ff. M-M*

συσταυρόω Pass.: pf. συνεσταύρωμαι; 1 aor. συνεσταυρώθην *crucify* (*together*) *with*, in our lit. only pass., of one who is nailed to the cross w. one or more persons. 1. lit. σύν τινι Mt 27: 44; Mk 15: 32. Also simply w. the dat. J 19: 32.—2. fig., of the crucifixion of a person when he becomes a Christian ὁ παλαιὸς ἡμῶν ἄνθρωπος συνεσταυρώθη Ro 6: 6. Χριστῷ συνεσταύρωμαι Gal 2: 19 (cf. GStaffelbach, D. Vereinigung mit Christus als Prinzip der Moral bei Pls, Diss. Freiburg, Switzerland, '32).*

συστέλλω 1 aor. συνέστειλα; pf. pass. ptc. συνεσταλμένος (Eur., Thu.+; inscr., pap., LXX, Philo, Joseph.). 1. *draw together, limit, shorten* (Hippocr.: CMG I 1 p. 53, 14; 85, 9; Isocr. 12, 230; X., Vect. 4, 3; Diod. S. 1, 41, 2; Cass. Dio 39, 37; Jos., Ant. 14, 74) of time ὁ καιρὸς συνεσταλμένος ἐστίν 1 Cor 7: 29, where it is not certain whether Paul has a divine act of shortening in mind (JWeiss), or whether there is no reference intended to a time that was originally longer (Diod. S. 4, 20, 1 τοῖς ὄγκοις συνεσταλμένοι=compact in body [of the Ligurians]). σ. τὰ ἱστία Ac 27: 15 v.l., see s.v. ἱστίον. 2. οἱ νεώτεροι συνέστειλαν αὐτόν Ac 5: 6, cf. 10 D, is variously interpreted. The possibilities are: a. *cover, wrap up* (Eur., Tro. 377; Lucian, Imag. 7; Achilles Tat. 8, 1, 5; Ps.-Callisth. 2, 22, 3 ὃν [=Darius when dying] τῇ χλαμύδι συστείλας). So the Syrian and Coptic versions; de Wette, BWeiss, Blass, Wendt, Preuschen, Hoennicke, ASteinmann, Beyer, Bauernfeind, RSV et al. Less probable is b. *pack* or *fold up, snatch up* (Psellus 50, 31 σ. τὰ παραπετάσματα=gather the curtains together). So the Armenian version and HAWMeyer, Overbeck, Weizsäcker, Zahn; or c. *take away, remove* (Philo, Leg. All. 3, 35). So the Vulgate, amoverunt. M-M.*

συστενάζω *lament* or *groan together* (*with*) (Eur., Ion 935 and Test. Iss. 17: 5 τινί 'with someone'.—Nicetas Eugen. 1, 342 H. without dat.) of creation *groan together* (w. συνωδίνειν, q.v. Also A-MDubarle, RSphth 38, '54, 445-65) Ro 8: 22.*

συστοιχέω of soldiers *stand in the same line*, hence in grammarians and in the Pythagorean tables of categories (in Aristot., Eth. Nic. 1, 4 p. 1906b, 6, Metaphys. 1, 5 p. 986a, 23) *correspond* (the members of the same categories in the tables συστοιχοῦσι, while members of opposite categories ἀντιστοιχοῦσι.—Ltzm., Hdb. on Gal 4: 25) w. the dat. Ἁγὰρ=Σινᾶ ὄρος ... συστοιχεῖ τῇ νῦν Ἰερουσαλήμ *corresponds to the present Jerusalem* Gal 4: 25. M-M.*

συστρατιώτης, ου, ὁ (X., Pla.+; BGU 814, 27 [soldier's

letter]; Ostraka II 1535 [II BC]; Jos., Ant. 4, 177) *comrade in arms, fellow-soldier*, in our lit. only fig. of those who devote themselves to the service of the gospel; as a term of honor (which in Polyaenus 8, 23, 22 makes the soldier equal to the commander-in-chief, and in Synes., Kingship 13 p. 12c makes the warrior equal to the king) applied to certain fellow-workers of Paul mentioned in Phil 2: 25; Phlm 2 (on the Christian life as military service cf. πανοπλία 2). M-M.*

συστρέφω 1 aor. συνέστρεψα (Aeschyl., Hdt.+; pap., LXX)—1. *gather up, bring together* τὶ someth. a bundle of sticks Ac 28: 3. τινάς *certain people* 17: 5 D (cf. Diod. S. 3, 35; Judg 12: 4 B; 2 Macc 14: 30; Jos., Ant. 18, 85). 2. *be gathered, gather, come together* (Hdt.+; En. 100, 4; Jos., Bell. 3, 302, Ant. 18, 351) Ac 10: 41 D*; 11: 28 D; 16: 39 D. So perh. also Mt 17: 22. Zahn suggests: 'while they were crowding' (around Jesus), and VEHarlow, Jesus' Jerusalem Expedition '36, 38-55 a 'half-military review'. M-M.*

συστροφή, ῆς, ἡ—1. *disorderly* or *seditious gathering, commotion* (Hdt. 7, 9; Polyb. 4, 34, 6; Jos., Bell. 4, 601) Ac 19: 40. ποιήσαντες συστροφὴν οἱ Ἰουδαῖοι *the Jews came together in a mob* 23: 12. But in the last pass. the word may also mean—2. *plot, conspiracy* (Am 7: 10 συστροφὰς ποιεῖται; Ps 63: 3). M-M.*

συσχηματίζω *form* or *mold after someth.* (Aristot., Top. 6, 14 p. 151b, 8 τὶ πρός τι; Plut., Mor. 83B) pass. *be formed like, be conformed to, be guided by* (Plut., Mor. 100F; Eunap., Vi. Soph. p. 111) w. the dat. of the thing to which one is conformed τῷ αἰῶνι τούτῳ Ro 12: 2. ταῖς ἐπιθυμίαις 1 Pt 1: 14. M-M.*

Συχάρ, ἡ indecl. *Sychar*, a city in Samaria, acc. to Jerome, Quaest. in Gen. 66, 6 and Epict. 108, 13, a corrupt form of Συχέμ (Sinaitic Syr. Shechim); s. the foll. entry. Many in recent times reject this conclusion, usu. in favor of identifying Sychar w. Askar (Samaritan Ischar) at the southeast foot of Mt. Ebal. Yet recent excavations seem to show that Jerome was right (s. RB 37, '28, 619). A place called Sichar or Suchar in the Babyl. Talmud (Baba Kamma 82b; Menachoth 64b) cannot be identified w. certainty. J 4: 5.—ESchwartz, NGG '08, 504f; Zahn, NKZ 19, '08, 207-18; JBoehmer, ZNW 9, '08, 218-23; KKundsin, Topolog. Überlieferungsstoffe im Joh. '25; CKopp, The Holy Places of the Gospels, tr. RWalls '63, 155-66.*

Συχέμ (םֶכְשׁ) indecl. *Shechem*—1. fem. (Συχέμ Test. Levi 5: 3=Σίκιμα Gen 48: 22; Josh 24: 32; Theodot. [II BC] in Euseb., Pr. Ev. 9, 22, 2; Joseph.), a city in Samaria. West of it Vespasian founded a new city, Flavia Neapolis (Euseb., Onom. p. 150, 1) Ac 7: 16a, b.—KBaedeker, Pal. u. Syr.⁷ '10, 203ff; FFörster, Sichem, s. Gesch. u. Bed., Diss. Lpz. '23; ESellin, most recently (earlier material in PThomsen, Palästina u. s. Kultur³ '31, 116): ZAW 50, '32, 303-8; PThomsen, Reallex. d. Vorgesch. XII '28, 74ff; ThBöhl, De opgraving van Sichem '27. 2. masc., son of Hamor (cf. Ἐμμώρ) Ἐμμὼρ τοῦ Συχέμ (cf. Gen 33: 19) *Hamor the father of Shechem* Ac 7: 16 D t.r. (in Jos., Ant. 1, 337f Συχέμμης). M-M.*

σφαγή, ῆς, ἡ (trag., X., Pla.+; LXX; Jos., Ant. 1, 102; 7, 39) *slaughter* πρόβατα σφαγῆς *sheep to be slaughtered* (cf. Zech 11: 4, 7) Ro 8: 36 (Ps 43: 23). προσφέρειν ἐπὶ τὴν σφαγήν *bring to be slain* B 8: 2. Pass. ἐπὶ σ. ἄγεσθαι Ac 8: 32; 1 Cl 16: 7; B 5: 2 (in each case Is 53: 7. Cf. Lucian, Dem. Enc. 40 the question βοῦν ἐπὶ σφαγὴν ἤγομεν; fig. w. ref. to Demosth.). ἡμέρα σφαγῆς *day of slaughter (Jer 12: 3; En. 16, 1; cf. Syntipas p. 13, 1 ἡμέρα . . . τ. σφαγῆς.—σφ.=massacre, blood-bath: Appian, Bell. Civ. 2, 24 §91) of the Day of Judgment (Beyschlag, Spitta, FHauck, Meinertz) or of a day of misfortune, when things turned out badly for the poor, but not for the rich (Windisch, MDibelius) Js 5: 5 (σφ. w. reference to humans: Diod. S. 13, 48, 1; 8).*

σφάγιον, ου, τό (Aeschyl., Hdt.+; LXX, Philo; Jos., Bell. 6, 434) victim to be sacrificed, offering pl. (w. θυσίαι) Ac 7: 42 (Am 5: 25).*

σφάζω fut. σφάξω; 1 aor. ἔσφαξα; pf. pass. ptc. ἐσφαγμένος (Hom.+ [Att. σφάττω; cf. Bl-D. §71; Mlt.-H. 404]; inscr., pap., LXX) to slaughter w. acc. ἀρνίον Rv 5: 6, 12; 13: 8 (in all these passages pass., ἀρνίον ἐσφαγμένον). Abs. B 8: 1. Of the killing of a person by violence (Pind.+) σφάζειν τινά butcher or murder someone (4 Km 10: 7; Jer 52: 10; Manetho in Jos., C. Ap. 1, 76) 1 J 3: 12; Rv 6: 4. Pass. (Hdt. 5, 5) 5: 9; 6: 9; 18: 24. κεφαλὴ ὡς ἐσφαγμένη εἰς θάνατον a head that seemed to be mortally wounded 13: 3. M-M.*

σφάλλω 2 fut. pass. σφαλήσομαι (Hom.+; LXX, Philo; Jos., Bell. 3, 479, Ant. 7, 264) pass. slip, stumble, fall lit. (Aristoph., Vesp. 1324; X., Lac. 5, 7; Diod. S. 3, 24, 3; Maximus Tyr. 21, 2b; 34, 2e; Dt 32: 35) Mt 15: 14 v.l.*

σφόδρα adv. (Pind., Hdt.+; inscr., pap., LXX, En., Joseph., Test. 12 Patr.) very (much), extremely, greatly used w. an adj. (Lucian, Nigr. 37; Zen.-P. 11 [=Sb 6717], 6 [257 BC]; En. 32, 3; Jos., Vi. 191) Mt 2: 10; 14: 30 v.l.; Mk 16: 4; Lk 18: 23; Rv 16: 21. Used w. verbs (Aeneas Tact. 1463; Test. Benj. 1, 5; Jos., Vi. 159 ἐταράχθην σφόδρα; Herm. Wr. 1, 1) φοβεῖσθαι σ. Mt 17: 6; 27: 54. λυπεῖσθαι σ. (1 Macc 14: 16) 17: 23; 18: 31; 26: 22. ἐκπλήττεσθαι 19: 25. πληθύνεσθαι Ac 6: 7. M-M.*

σφοδρῶς adv. (Hom.+; Aelian, N.A. 14, 26 p. 359, 23; Dit., Syll.³ 1169, 57; LXX; Jos., Ant. 13, 292 al.) very much, greatly, violently σ. χειμάζεσθαι be violently beaten by a storm Ac 27: 18 (cf. Jos., Ant. 14, 377 χειμῶνι σφοδρῷ περιπεσών).*

σφραγίζω 1 aor. ἐσφράγισα, mid. ἐσφραγισάμην. Pass.: pf. ptc. ἐσφραγισμένος; 1 aor. ἐσφραγίσθην (Aeschyl.+; inscr., pap., LXX, Philo, Joseph.) (provide with a) seal.

1. lit., w. the acc. of the obj. that is to be secured or fastened by the seal: of a stone, to prevent its being moved fr. position (Da 6: 18=Jos., Ant. 10, 258) Mt 27: 66 (but s. μετά A III 2). Likew. GP 9: 34, where the words μνημεῖον ἐσφραγισμένον refer back to the sealing of the stone used to close the tomb (8: 32f). In the case of a closed building, so that it cannot be opened (Bel 11; 14) τὰς κλεῖδας 1 Cl 43: 3. A bundle of rods, that were not to be disturbed 43: 2. Abs. ἐσφράγισεν ἐπάνω αὐτοῦ he sealed (the closed mouth of the abyss) over him Rv 20: 3.

2. fig.—a. seal up τὶ someth. in order to keep it secret (Solon in Stob., Flor. III p. 114, 8 H. τοὺς λόγους σιγῇ; Kleopatra l. 73 μυστήριον ἐσφραγισμένον; PTebt. 413, 6; Job 14: 17; 24: 16; Da 9: 24 Theod.; Da 12: 9 LXX) Rv 10: 4; 22: 10.

b. mark (with a seal) as a means of identification (Eur., Iph. T. 1372. In pap., of all kinds of animals), so that the mark which denotes ownership also carries w. it the protection of the owner: σφραγίσωμεν τοὺς δούλους τοῦ θεοῦ ἐπὶ τῶν μετώπων αὐτῶν Rv 7: 3 (marking w. a seal on the forehead in the cult of Mithra: Tertullian, Praescr. Haer. 40). Corresp. ἐσφραγισμένοι vs. 4a, b, 5, 8 (on the

concept of sealing eschatologically cf. Ezk 9: 4ff; Is 44: 5; PsSol 15: 6, 9; 4 Esdr 6: 5f; 8: 51ff. S. also LBrun, Übriggebliebene u. Märtyrer in Apk: StKr 102, '30, 215-31). This forms a basis for understanding the symbolic expr. which speaks of those who enter the Christian fellowship as being sealed with or by the Holy Spirit Eph 1: 13; cf. 4: 30. Sim. θεός, ὁ σφραγισάμενος ἡμᾶς καὶ δοὺς τὸν ἀρραβῶνα τοῦ πνεύματος ἐν ταῖς καρδίαις ἡμῶν 2 Cor 1: 22; but here σφ. obviously means more than just 'provide w. a mark of identification'. Rather it='endue with power from heaven', as plainly in J 6: 27 (s. σφραγίς 2a); but EDinkler, OCullmann-Festschr., '62, 183-8 associates 2 Cor 1: 22 w. baptism; cf. σφραγίς 2b.

c. attest, certify, acknowledge (as a seal does on a document: pap.; Jer 39: 10f; Esth 8: 8, 10.—Anth. Pal. 9, 236 ἐσφράγισαν ὅρκοι) w. ὅτι foll. J 3: 33.

d. σφραγισάμενος αὐτοῖς τὸν καρπὸν τοῦτον Ro 15: 28 is perh. to be understood fr. the practice of sealing sacks of grain (Dssm., NB 65f [BS 238f]). But the figure is perh. rather hard to maintain, since the 'fruit' must not only be sealed, but also forwarded to Jerusalem and delivered there. In any case the sense of the expr. is easier to understand in some such wording as this: when I have placed the sum that was collected safely (sealed) in their hands (cf. LRadermacher, ZNW 32, '33, 87-9; HW Bartsch, ZNW 63, '72, 95-107). M-M.*

σφραγίς, ῖδος, ἡ (trag., Hdt.+; inscr., pap., LXX, Philo; Jos., Ant. 15, 408; 18, 93 al.; loanw. in rabb.) seal, signet.

1. lit.—a. seal (GP 8: 33; 1 Cl 43: 5. In Rv a book w. seven seals 5: 1 (a last will and testament acc. to EHuschke, Das Buch mit sieben Siegeln 1860, Zahn, JWeiss; cf. JMarquardt, Römisches Privatleben² 1886, 805f; ThBirt, Die Buchrolle in der Kunst '07, 243.—On Rv 5f: WSattler, ZNW 20, '21, 231-40; 21, '22, 43-53; KathStaritz, ibid. 30, '31, 157-70; WSTaylor, JTS 31, '30, 266-71). λῦσαι τὰς σφραγῖδας Rv 5: 2, 5 t.r. (cf. λύω 1a). Also ἀνοῖξαι vs. 5, 9; 6: 1, 3, 5, 7, 9, 12 (Aeschyl., Eum. 828); 8: 1 (ἀνοίγω 1d).

b. the instrument with which one seals or stamps, signet (Aristot., Strabo et al., Appian, Liby. 32 §137; 104 §493, Bell. Civ. 2, 22 §82, pap., LXX) σφραγὶς θεοῦ Rv 7: 2.

c. the mark or impression of a seal (Hdt.+) Rv 9: 4 (cf. Martial 3, 21, of a slave 'fronte notata'). Symbolically ὁ θεμέλιος τοῦ θεοῦ ἔχων τὴν σφραγίδα ταύτην κτλ. God's foundation that bears the following mark=inscription . . . 2 Ti 2: 19.

d. sign or stamp of approval, certificate (cf. the Abercius Inscr. 9 λαὸς λαμπρὰν σφραγεῖδαν ἔχων and the Naassene hymn in Hippolytus, Ref. 5, 10, 2 σφραγῖδας ἔχων καταβήσομαι. Likew. the Books of Jeû and the Mandaean Writings. Mani, Kephal. (chapt.) I '39, p. 225, 13; 15; 18) Hs 8, 2, 2; 4.

2. fig.—a. that which confirms, attests, or authenticates w. the gen. of that which is confirmed or authenticated ἡ σφραγίς μου τῆς ἀποστολῆς ὑμεῖς ἐστε you are the certification of my apostleship 1 Cor 9: 2. σημεῖον ἔλαβεν περιτομῆς σφραγίδα τῆς δικαιοσύνης τῆς πίστεως he (Abraham) received the sign of circumcision as something that simply confirms the righteousness through faith that was already present Ro 4: 11. σφ. need be no more than a metaphor for attestation or confirmation in περιτέτμηται ὁ λαὸς εἰς σφραγῖδα B 9: 6.

b. as a term for baptism in 2 Cl and Hermas (Theognis 1, 19: the author's name, as a σφρηγίς, insures his work against all possibility of falsification): ἡ σφραγίς 2 Cl 7: 6; 8: 6; Hs 8, 6, 3; 9, 16, 3ff al. ἡ σφ. τοῦ υἱοῦ τοῦ θεοῦ Hs 9, 16, 3 (also Act. Thom. 131. Cf. ἡ σφ. τοῦ κυρίου Clem.

Alex., Quis Div. Salv. 42, 4. ἡ σφ. τοῦ Χριστοῦ Act. Phil. 134; ἡ ἐν Χριστῷ σφ. Act. Pauli et Thecl. 25; Mart. Thom. p. 291 B.). Used with the verbs διδόναι τινὶ (τὴν σφ.) Hs 9, 16, 5b (Act. Thom. 28; 49). λαμβάνειν 8, 6, 3; 9, 16, 3; 9, 17, 4. ἔχειν 9, 16, 5a; 7; κηρύσσειν 9, 16, 4b. τεθλακέναι 8, 6, 3. τηρεῖν 2 Cl 7: 6; 8: 6=τηρεῖν τὸ βάπτισμα 6: 9 (δέχεσθαι Act. Thom. 26; περιτιθέναι Celsus in Origen 2, 96f).—GAnrich, Das Antike Mysterienwesen 1894, 120ff; GWobbermin, Religionsgesch. Studien 1896, 144ff; ASeeberg, Der Katechismus der Urchristenheit '03, 232ff; FJDölger, Sphragis als Taufbez. '11, 49ff, Antike u. Christentum I '29, 88–91; AvStromberg, Studien zur Theorie u. Praxis der Taufe '13, 89ff; WHeitmüller, ΣΦΡΑΓΙΣ: Heinrici-Festschr. '14, 40ff; WBousset, Kyrios Christos² '21, 227ff; FPreisigke, Die Gotteskraft der frühchristl. Zeit '22, 25f; EMaass, Segnen, Weihen, Taufen: ARW 21, '22, 241ff; JYsebaert, Greek Baptismal Terminol., '62, 204f; GFitzer, TW VII, 939–54. M-M.*

σφυδρόν, οῦ, τό (PFlor. 391, 53; 56 [III AD]; Hesychius) *ankle* Ac 3: 7 (v.l. σφυρόν, q.v.). M-M.*

σφυρίς, ίδος, ἡ s. σπυρίς. M-M.

σφυροκοπέω (Philod., σημ. 2, 7 Gomp.; Judg 5: 26 B) *beat with a hammer* τὶ someth. of a smith τὸ ἔργον αὐτοῦ *his work* Hv 1, 3, 2.*

σφυρόν, οῦ, τό—**1.** *ankle* (Hom.+; Ep. Arist. 87; Jos., Ant. 3, 155; 7, 171).—**2.** *heel* (Eur., Alc. 586; Ps.-Oppian, Cyn. 3, 143); both are poss. in Ac 3: 7 t.r. Cf. σφυδρόν.*

σχεδόν adv. (Hom.+) *nearly, almost* (Soph., X., Pla.; inscr., pap.; 2 Macc 5: 2; 3 Macc 5: 14, 45; Ep. Arist., Philo) Ac 13: 44 (cf. Jos., Ant. 7, 20 πᾶσαν σχεδόν); 19: 26; Hb 9: 22 (cf. Jos., Ant. 1, 18 πάντα σχ.); B 16: 2; MPol 1: 1; 22: 3; Epil Mosq 4. M-M.*

σχῆμα, ατος, τό (fr. the same root as ἔχω. Aeschyl., Thu. +; inscr., pap.; Is 3: 17; Ep. Arist. 105; Philo; Jos., Bell. 7, 267, Ant. 3, 282; Test. 12 Patr. Loanw. in rabb.) *bearing, manner, deportment,* cf. Lat. 'habitus'.
1. of pers. *outward appearance, form, shape* Hv 5: 1 (Menyllus: 295 fgm. 2 Jac. Ἄρης ἐν σχήματι ποιμένος). σχήματι εὑρεθεὶς ὡς ἄνθρωπος Phil 2: 7 (cf. Lucian, Somn. 13 ἀφεὶς... τιμήν κ. δόξαν... κ. δύναμιν σχῆμα δουλοπρεπὲς ἀναλήψῃ; Jos., Ant. 10, 11 a king who exchanges his kingly robes for sackcloth and takes on a σχῆμα ταπεινόν. For the σχῆμα ταπεινόν cf. also Appian, Syr. 40 §206).
2. of things παράγει τὸ σχῆμα τοῦ κόσμου τούτου *this world in its present form is passing away* 1 Cor 7: 31 (Eur., Bacch. 832 τὸ σχ. τοῦ κόσμου; Philostrat., Vi. Apoll. 8, 7 p. 312, 9 τὸ σχ. τοῦ κόσμου τοῦδε; PGM 4, 1139 σχῆμα κόσμου). M-M. B. 874.*

σχίζω fut. σχίσω; 1 aor. ἔσχισα, pass. ἐσχίσθην (Hom. Hymns+; pap., LXX, Philo; Jos., Ant. 8, 207; 20, 97; Test. 12 Patr.) *split, divide, separate, tear apart, tear off.*
1. lit. τὶ someth.—**a.** act. τὸ ξύλον *split the wood* (Antig. Car. 142 ξύλον σχίσας; Paradoxogr. Flor. 9; Paroem. Gr.: Apostolius 7, 24a) LJ 1: 5 (cf. Eccl 10: 9, also Gen 22: 3; 1 Km 6: 14 and see ἐγείρω 1αγ). τὸ καινὸν σχίσει he will tear the new Lk 5: 36b. Cf. J 19: 24. ἐπίβλημα ἀπὸ ἱματίου σχ. *tear (off) a patch from a garment* Lk 5: 36a (cf. Jos., Ant, 8, 207).
b. pass. *be divided, be torn, be split* αἱ πέτραι ἐσχίσθησαν *the rocks were split* Mt 27: 51b (cf. Is 48: 21;

Test. Levi 4: 1; PTebt. 273, 43; 52 λίθος σχισθείς). Of the curtain in the temple (s. καταπέτασμα) ἐσχίσθη (it) *was torn* (cf. Anacr. 95b Diehl) Lk 23: 45; εἰς δύο (cf. schol. on Apollon. Rhod. 4, 282–91b p. 281, 10 W. σχίζεται εἰς δύο; Polyb. 2, 16, 11 εἰς δύο μέρη; PGM 13, 262 σχίσον εἰς δύο=in two) Mt 27: 51a; Mk 15: 38 (D+μέρη). Of a net J 21: 11. Of the dome of heaven Mk 1: 10 (Himerius, Or. [Ecl.] 32, 14 οὐρανὸν σχίσας for a divine announcement, to bring from the house of Zeus a pure soul, τῶν θείων φασμάτων παρ' ἡμᾶς τὴν οὐσίαν διαπορθμεύουσαν =who communicates to us the nature of the divine appearances).
2. fig.—**a.** act. *cause a division* or *schism* IPhld 3: 3 (cf. Dionys. Alex. in Euseb., H.E. 6, 45).
b. pass. *become divided, disunited* (X., Symp. 4, 59 ἐσχίσθησαν, καὶ οἱ μὲν..., οἱ δὲ) ἐσχίσθη τὸ πλῆθος Ac 14: 4; 23: 7 (cf. Diod. S. 12, 66, 2 τοῦ πλήθους σχιζομένου κατὰ τὴν αἵρεσιν; Celsus 3, 10; Ps.-Lucian, Asin. 54 εἰς δύο γνώμας). M-M. B. 564; 845.*

σχίσμα, ατος, τό *split, division*—**1.** lit. *tear, crack* (Aristot., H.A. 2, 1; Physiogn. I 372, 6; En. 1, 7) in a garment Mt 9: 16; Mk 2: 21; in a stone Hs 9, 8, 3.
2. fig. *division, dissension, schism* (PLond. 2710 r., 13 [=Sb 7835—I BC] the ἡγούμενος of the brotherhood of Zeus Hypsistos forbids σχίσματα most strictly; Cat. Cod. Astr. XI 2 p. 122, 24 πολέμους, φόνους, μάχας, σχίσματα) J 7: 43; 9: 16; 10: 19; 1 Cor 1: 10; 11: 18; 12: 25; 1 Cl 46: 9; 49: 5. W. στάσις 2: 6; w. στάσις, ἔρις 54: 2. ἔρεις, θυμοί, διχοστασίαι, σχίσματα, πόλεμος 46: 5. ποιεῖν σχίσμα *cause a division* D 4: 3; B 19: 12. σχίσματα ἐν ἑαυτοῖς ἐποίησαν *they brought about divisions* (of opinion) *in their own minds* (or *among themselves*; cf. ἑαυτοῦ 3) Hs 8, 9, 4. Cf. the agraphon from Justin, Trypho 35 quoted in JoachJeremias, Unknown Sayings of Jesus, tr. Fuller '57, 59–61: ἔσονται σχίσματα καὶ αἱρέσεις. M-M.*

σχισμή, ῆς, ἡ *crack, fissure* (Rhet. Gr. I 552, 4; LXX) in stones (cf. Is 2: 19, 21; Sib. Or. 3, 607) Hv 3, 2, 8; 3, 6, 3; s 9, 6, 4; 9, 8, 3f; 9, 23, 1–3; in sticks Hs 8, 1, 9f; 14; 8, 4, 6; 8, 5, 1; 4f; 8, 7, 1f; 4; 8, 10, 1; in a mountain (Jon 2: 6) s 9, 1, 7.*

σχοινίον, ου, τό (Hdt.+; inscr., pap., LXX; Jos., Ant. 8, 385; 19, 346) *rope* or *cord* made of rushes, then gener.; used to elevate someth. IEph 9: 1. Of the ropes that hold a ship's boat in place Ac 27: 32. Jesus uses them to make a whip J 2: 15. M-M. B. 549.*

σχοίνισμα, ατος, τό (LXX) *a piece of land* measured out by means of a measuring-line (σχοῖνος, σχοινίον), *allotment* (Hesychius; Etym. Mag. p. 740, 46) σχ. κληρονομίας αὐτοῦ *the allotment that he acquired* 1 Cl 29: 2 (Dt 32: 9).*

σχολάζω 1 aor. ἐσχόλασα (Aeschyl., Thu.+; inscr., pap., LXX, Philo) *have time* or *leisure.*
1. of persons τινί *for someone* or *someth.,* i.e. *busy oneself with, devote oneself to, give one's time to* (Lucian, V. Hist. 2, 15; Ps.-Lucian, Macrob. 4 φιλοσοφίᾳ; Epict. 2, 14, 28; Herodian 1, 8, 1 al.; Dit., Syll.³ 717, 34f [100 BC] τοῖς φιλοσόφοις, Or. 569, 23 θεῶν θρησκείᾳ; Sb 4284, 15 τῇ γῇ; PAmh. 82, 6 γεωργίᾳ; Philo, Spec. Leg. 3, 1 al.; Test. Jud. 20: 1) τῇ προσευχῇ 1 Cor 7: 5 (on this subj. s. Test. Napht. 8: 8); cf. IPol 1: 3. Χριστιανὸς θεῷ σχολάζει 7: 3 (cf. the pagan letter Sb 4515 οὐ μέλλω θεῷ σχολάζειν, εἰ μὴ πρότερον ἀπαρτίσω τὸν υἱόν μου).
2. of a place or house *be unoccupied, stand empty* (Plut., G. Gracch. 12, 6 τόπος; Julian, Caes. p. 316c

καθέδρα; Suppl. Epigr. Gr. XI 121, 13) of a house Mt 12: 44; Lk 11: 25 v.l. HSNyberg, Ntl. Sem. zu Uppsala 4, '36, 22-35, Con. Neot. 13, '49, 1-11. M-M.*

σχολή, ῆς, ἡ (Pind.+ in the sense 'leisure': inscr.. pap., LXX, Philo, Joseph., loanw. in rabb.) school of the place where teachers and pupils meet (Dionys. Hal., Isocr. 1, Demosth. 44; Plut., Mor. 42A; 519F; 605A; Epict. 1, 29, 34; Jos., C. Ap. 1, 53) Ac 19: 9. M-M. B. 1227.*

σχῶ s. ἔχω.

σῴζω fut. σώσω; 1 aor. ἔσωσα; pf. σέσωκα. Pass.: impf. ἐσῳζόμην; pf. 3 sing. σέσῳσται Ac 4: 9 (v.l. σέσωται. See UPZ 122, 18 [157 BC] σέσωμαι), ptc. σεσῳσμένος; 1 aor. ἐσώθην; 1 fut. σωθήσομαι (Hom.+; inscr., pap., LXX, En.; Ezek. Trag. in Euseb., Pr. Ev. 9, 29, 8; Ep. Arist., Philo, Joseph., Test. 12 Patr.; Sib. Or. 5, 230.—σῴζω [=σωΐζω] and the forms surely derived fr. it are to be written w. ι subscript. On the other hand, it is not possible to say how far the ι has spread fr. the present to the tenses formed fr. the root σω-. Kühner-Bl. II 544; Bl-D. §26 app.; Mlt.-H. 84; Mayser 134) save, keep from harm, preserve, rescue.

1. preserve or rescue fr. natural dangers and afflictions (X., An. 3, 2, 10 οἱ θεοί . . . ἱκανοί εἰσι κ. τοὺς μεγάλους ταχὺ μικροὺς ποιεῖν κ. τοὺς μικροὺς σῴζειν; Musonius p. 32, 10. Chio, Ep. 11; 12 θεοῦ σῴζοντος πλευσοῦμαι).

a. save from death (inscr. [I BC]: Sb 8138, 34 σῴζονθ' οὗτοι ἅπαντες who call upon Isis in the hour of death) τινά someone (Apollon. Rhod. 3, 323 θεός τις ἄμμ' [=ἡμᾶς] ἐσάωσεν from danger of death at sea; Diod. S. 11, 92, 3f) Mt 14: 30; 27: 40, 42, 49; Mk 15: 30f; Lk 23: 35a, b, 37, 39; 1 Cl 16: 16 (Ps 21: 9). Pass. Mt 24: 22; Mk 13: 20; J 11: 12 (ἐγερθήσεται 𝔓⁷⁵); Ac 27: 20, 31; 1 Cl 7: 6. Abs., w. acc. easily supplied Mt 8: 25. ψυχὴν σῶσαι save a life (Achilles Tat. 5, 22, 6; PTebt. 56, 11 [II BC] σῶσαι ψυχὰς πολλάς; Ep. Arist. 292; Jos., Ant. 11, 255) Mk 3: 4; Lk 6: 9; 21: 19 v.l. τὴν ψυχὴν αὐτοῦ σῶσαι save one's own life (Gen 19: 17; 1 Km 19: 11; Jer 31: 6) Mt 16: 25; Mk 8: 35a=Lk 9: 24a (on Mk 8: 35b=Lk 9: 24b s. 2aβ below); 17: 33 t.r. (PGM 5, 140 κύριε [a god] σῶσον ψυχήν).

b. w. ἔκ τινος bring out safely fr. a situation fraught w. mortal danger (X., An. 3, 2, 11; Dit., Syll.³ 1130, 1 ἐκ κινδύνων, Or. 69, 4; Jos., C. Ap. 1, 286) ἐκ γῆς Αἰγύπτου Jd 5. ἐκ Σοδόμων 1 Cl 11: 1 (Pla., Gorg. 511D ἐξ Αἰγίνης δεῦρο). ἐκ τῆς ὥρας ταύτης J 12: 27. ἐκ θανάτου from (the threat of) death (Hom.+; Pla., Gorg. 511c) Hb 5: 7.—Of the evil days of the last tribulation ἐν αἷς ἡμεῖς σωθησόμεθα B 8: 6; cf. 1 Cl 59: 4.

c. save or free from disease (Hippocr., Coac. 136 vol. 5 p. 612 L.; IG ed. min. II and III 1028, 89 [I BC]; Wilcken, Chrest. 68, 32 [132 BC]: gods bring healing) or from demonic possession τινά someone ἡ πίστις σου σέσωκέν σε Mt 9: 22a; Mk 5: 34; 10: 52; Lk 8: 48; 17: 19; 18: 42. Cf. Js 5: 15. Pass. be restored to health, get well (Ael. Aristid. 33, 9 K.=51 p. 573 D.) Mt 9: 21, 22b; Mk 5: 23, 28; 6: 56; Lk 8: 36; Ac 4: 9; 14: 9. Also of the restoration that comes about when death has already occurred Lk 8: 50.

d. keep, preserve in good condition (pap.) τὶ someth. (Eunap., Vi. Soph. p. 107: θειασμός) pass. τὴν κλῆσιν σῴζεσθαι Hs 8, 11, 1.

e. pass. thrive, prosper, get on well (Sib. Or. 5, 227) σῴζεσθαι ὅλον τὸ σῶμα 1 Cl 37: 5. As a form of address used in parting σῴζεσθε farewell, remain in good health B 21: 9.

2. save or preserve from eternal death, fr. judgment, and fr. all that might lead to such death, e.g. sin, also in a positive sense bring Messianic salvation, bring to salvation (LXX; Herm. Wr. 13, 19 σῴζειν='endow w. everlasting life'.—Of passing over into a state of salvation and a higher life: Cebes 3, 2; 4, 3; 14, 1).

a. act. τινά someone or τὶ someth.—α. of God and Christ. God: 1 Cor 1: 21; 2 Ti 1: 9; Tit 3: 5. The acc. is easily supplied Js 4: 12. ὁ θεὸς ὁ σῴζων Mt 16: 16 D.—Christ: Mt 18: 11; Lk 19: 10; 1J 2: 47; 1 Ti 1: 15; 2 Ti 4: 18 (εἰς 7); Hb 7: 25; MPol 9: 3. σώσει τὸν λαὸν αὐτοῦ ἀπὸ τῶν ἁμαρτιῶν αὐτῶν Mt 1: 21 (σ. ἀπό as Jos., Ant. 4, 128). The acc. is to be supplied 2 Cl 1: 7.

β. of persons who are mediators of the divine salvation: apostles Ro 11: 14; 1 Cor 9: 22; 1 Ti 4: 16b. The believing partner in a mixed marriage 1 Cor 7: 16a, b (JoachJeremias, Die missionarische Aufgabe in der Mischehe, Bultmann-Festschr., '54, 255-60). One Christian of another σώσει ψυχὴν αὐτοῦ ἐκ θανάτου Js 5: 20 (on σ. ἐκ θαν. s. 1b above). Cf. Jd 23. A man of himself 1 Ti 4: 16a or his life Mk 8: 35b=Lk 9: 24b (for Mk 8: 35a=Lk 9: 24a s. 1a above).

γ. of qualities, etc., that lead to salvation ἡ πίστις σου σέσωκέν σε Lk 7: 50 (s. 1c above). Cf. Js 1: 21; 2: 14; 1 Pt 3: 21; Hv 2, 3, 2.

b. pass. be saved, attain salvation Mt 10: 22; 19: 25; 24: 13; Mk 10: 26; 13: 13; 16: 16; Lk 8: 12; 18: 26; J 5: 34; 10: 9; Ac 2: 21 (Jo 3: 5); 15: 1; 16: 30f; Ro 10: 9, 13 (Jo 3: 5); 11: 26; 1 Cor 5: 5; 10: 33; 1 Th 2: 16; 2 Th 2: 10; 1 Ti 2: 4 (JTurmel, Rev. d'Hist. et de Littérature religieuses 5, '00, 385-415); 1 Pt 4: 18 (Pr 11: 31); 2 Cl 4: 2; 13: 1; IPhld 5: 2; Hs 9, 26, 6.—σωθῆναι διά τινος through someone (Ctesias in Ps.-Demetr., Eloc. c. 213 σὺ δι' ἐμὲ ἐσώθης; Herm. Wr. 1, 26b ὅπως τὸ γένος τῆς ἀνθρωπότητος διὰ σοῦ ὑπὸ θεοῦ σωθῇ) J 3: 17; 2 Cl 3: 3; through someth. Ac 15: 11; 1 Cor 15: 2; 1 Ti 2: 15 (διά A III 1d); Hv 3, 3, 5; 3, 8, 3 (here faith appears as a person, but still remains as a saving quality); 4, 2, 4. ἔν τινι in or through someone 1 Cl 38: 1; in or through someth. Ac 4: 12; 11: 14; Ro 5: 10. ὑπό τινος by someone (Herm. Wr. 9, 5 ὑπὸ τ. θεοῦ σ.; Philo, Leg. All. 2, 101 ὑπὸ θεοῦ σῴζεται) 2 Cl 8: 2. ἀπό τινος save oneself by turning away from Ac 2: 40 (on σ. ἀπό s. 2aα above). διά τινος ἀπό τινος through someone from someth. Ro 5: 9.—χάριτι by grace Eph 2: 5; Pol 1: 3. τῇ χάριτι διὰ πίστεως Eph 2: 8. τῇ ἐλπίδι ἐσώθημεν (only) in hope have we (thus far) been saved or it is by this hope that we have been saved Ro 8: 24.—οἱ σῳζόμενοι those who are to be or are being saved Lk 13: 23; Ac 2: 47 (BFMeyer, CBQ 27, '65, 37f: cf. Is 37: 2); 1 Cor 1: 18; 2 Cor 2: 15 (opp. οἱ ἀπολλύμενοι in the last two passages); 1 Cl 58: 2; MPol 17: 2.

3. Certain passages belong under 1 and 2 at the same time. They include Mk 8: 35=Lk 9: 24 (s. 1a and 2aβ above), already mentioned, and Lk 9: 56 t.r., where σῴζειν is used in contrast to destruction by fire fr. heaven, but also denotes the bestowing of salvation (cf. Cornutus 16 p. 21, 9f οὐ πρὸς τὸ βλάπτειν, ἀλλὰ πρὸς τὸ σῴζειν γέγονεν ὁ λόγος [='Ερμῆς]). In Ro 9: 27 τὸ ὑπόλειμμα σωθήσεται (Is 10: 22) the remnant that is to escape death is interpreted to mean the minority who are to receive the Messianic salvation. In 1 Cor 3: 15 escape fr. a burning house is a symbol for the attainment of eternal salvation (πῦρ 1a. Cf. also Cebes 3, 4 ἐὰν δέ τις γνῷ, ἡ ἀφροσύνη ἀπόλλυται, αὐτὸς δὲ σῴζεται).—WWagner, Über σῴζειν u. seine Derivata im NT: ZNW 6, '05, 205-35; J-BColon, La conception du Salut d'après les Év. syn.: Rev. des Sc. rel. 10, '30, 1-39; 189-217; 370-415; 11,

'31, 27-70; 193-223; 382-412; JNSevenster, Het verlossingsbegrip bij Philo. Vergeleken met de verlossingsgedachten van de syn. evangeliën '36; PSMinear, And Great Shall be your Reward '41; MGoguel, Les fondements de l'assurance du salut chez l'ap. Paul: RHPhr 17, '38, 105-44; WFoerster, TW VII, 966-1024: σῴζω, etc. M-M. B. 752.**

Σωκράτης, ους, ὁ *Socrates*, a name freq. found; a Christian in Corinth, who made a copy of the MPol: 22: 2. Epil Mosq 4 gives his name as Ἰσοκράτης.*

σῶμα, ατος, τό (Hom.+; inscr., pap., LXX, En., Ep. Arist., Philo, Joseph., Test. 12 Patr.) *body.*

1. *body* of man or animal—a. *dead body, corpse* (so always in Hom. and oft. later, e.g., Memnon: no. 434 fgm. 1, 3, 3 Jac. καίειν τὸ σ.=burn the corpse. Inscr., pap., LXX; Philo, Abr. 258; Jos., Bell. 6, 276, Ant. 18, 236) Mt 14: 12 t.r.; 27: 59; Mk 15: 45 t.r.; Lk 17: 37; Ac 9: 40; GP 2: 4. Pl. J 19: 31. W. gen. Mt 27: 58; Mk 15: 43; Lk 23: 52, 55; 24: 3, 23; J 19: 38a, b, 40; 20: 12; Jd 9; GP 2: 3. Pl. Mt 27: 52; Hb 13: 11.

b. *the living body* (Hes.+; inscr., pap., LXX) of animals Js 3: 3.—Mostly of human beings Mt 5: 29f; 6: 22f; 26: 12; Mk 5: 29; 14: 8; Lk 11: 34a, b, c; J 2: 21; Ro 1: 24; 1 Cor 5: 18a, b; IRo 5: 3. τὰ τοῦ σώματος *the parts of the body* 4: 2. Of women αἱ ἀσθενεῖς τῷ σώματι 1 Cl 6: 2; cf. Hv 3, 11, 4.—W. and in contrast to πνεῦμα (4 Macc 11: 11) Ro 8: 10, 13; 1 Cor 5: 3; 7: 34; Js 2: 26. W. and in contrast to ψυχή (Pla., Gorg. 47, 493A; Diod. S. 34+35 fgm. 2, 30; Appian, Bell. Civ. 5, 112 §467; Ael. Aristid. 45, 17f K.=8 p. 88f D.; Lucian, Imag. 23; PGM 7, 589; Wsd 1: 4; 8: 19f; 2 Macc 7: 37; 14: 38; 4 Macc 1: 28; Ep. Arist. 139; Philo; Jos., Bell. 3, 372-8; 6, 55) Mt 6: 25a, b; 10: 28a, b; Lk 12: 4 v.l., 22f; 2 Cl 5: 4 (a saying of Jesus, fr. an unknown source); 12: 4; MPol 14: 2. τὸ πνεῦμα καὶ ἡ ψυχὴ καὶ τὸ σῶμα (s. the Christian POxy. 1161, 6 [IV AD]) 1 Th 5: 23. W. and in contrast to its parts Ro 12: 4; 1 Cor 12: 12a, b, c (Ltzm. ad loc.), 14-20 (PMich. 149, 4, 26 [II AD] ἦπαρ . . . ὅλον τὸ σῶμα); Js 3: 3; 1 Cl 37: 5a, b, c. d. The body as the seat of the sexual function Ro 4: 19; 1 Cor 7: 4a, b (rights over the σῶμα of one's spouse as Artem. 1, 44 p. 42, 14f).—The body as the seat of mortal life εἶναι ἐν σώματι *be in the body=alive, subject to mortal ills* (Poryphr., Abst. 1, 38) Hb 13: 3. ἐνδημεῖν ἐν τῷ σώματι 2 Cor 5: 6 (s. ἐνδημέω). ἐκδημῆσαι ἐκ τοῦ σώματος vs. 8 (s. ἐκδημέω). διὰ τοῦ σώματος *during the time of one's mortal life* (cf. Lucian, Menipp. 11, end, Catapl. 23) vs. 10 (cf. κομίζω 2a, but s. also below in this section). Paul does not know whether, in a moment of religious ecstasy, he was ἐν σώματι or ἐκτὸς (χωρὶς) τοῦ σώματος 12: 2f (of Epimenides [Vorsokrat.⁵ I p. 29] it was said ὡς ἐξίοι ἡ ψυχὴ ὁπόσον ἤθελε καιρὸν καὶ πάλιν εἰσῄει ἐν τῷ σώματι; Clearchus, fgm. 7: καθάπερ ὁ Κλέαρχος ἐν τοῖς περὶ ὕπνου φησίν, περὶ τῆς ψυχῆς, ὡς ἄρα χωρίζεται τοῦ σώματος καὶ ὡς εἴσεισιν εἰς τὸ σῶμα καὶ ὡς χρῆται αὐτῷ οἷον καταγωγίῳ [a resting-place]. In fgm. 8 Clearchus tells about Cleonymus the Athenian, who seemed to be dead, but awakened after 3 days and thereupon reported everything that he had seen and heard ἐπειδὴ χωρὶς ἦν τοῦ σώματος. His soul is said finally to have arrived εἴς τινα χῶρον ἱερὸν τῆς Ἑστίας; Maximus Tyr. 38, 3a-f Ἀριστέας ἔφασκεν τὴν ψυχὴν αὐτῷ καταλιποῦσαν τὸ σῶμα in order to wander through the universe. He finds faith everywhere. Likew. 10, 2f. See also the story of Hermotimus in Apollon. Paradox. 3 as well as Lucian, Musc. Enc. [The Fly] 7.—On the two kinds

of supermundane vision [with or without the body] s. Proclus, In Pla. Rem Publ. II p. 121, 26ff Kroll: οἱ μὲν μετὰ τοῦ σώματος τῶν τοιούτων ἵστορες [=eyewitnesses]—like Ἐμπεδότιμος—, οἱ δὲ ἄνευ σώματος—like Κλεώνυμος. καὶ πλήρεις αἱ παραδόσεις τούτων). ἀπὼν τῷ σώματι (παρὼν δὲ τῷ πνεύματι) 1 Cor 5: 3. ἡ παρουσία τοῦ σώματος 2 Cor 10: 10 (παρουσία 1). The body is the instrument of human experience and suffering 4: 10a, b; Gal 6: 17; Phil 1: 20; the body is the organ of man's activity: δοξάσατε τὸν θεὸν ἐν τῷ σώματι ὑμῶν *glorify God through your body*, i.e. by leading a holy life 1 Cor 6: 20; cf. Ro 12: 1. This may be the place (s. above in the same section) for διὰ τοῦ σώματος 2 Cor 5: 10 which, in that case, would be taken in an instrumental sense *with* or *through the body* (cf. Pla., Phaedo 65A; Ps.-Pla., Axioch. 13 p. 371c; Aelian, Nat. Hist. 5, 26 τὰ διὰ τοῦ σώματος πραττόμενα). In some of the last-named passages (such as Ro 12: 1; Phil 1: 20, also Eph 5: 28; the last has a parallel in Plut., Mor. 142E—s. HAlmqvist, Plut. u. d. NT '46, 116f) the body is almost synonymous w. the whole personality (as Aeschin., Or. 2, 58; X., An. 1, 9, 12 τὰ ἑαυτῶν σώματα=themselves. Appian, Syr. 41 §218 παρεδίδου τὸ σῶμα τοῖς ἐθέλουσιν ἀπαγαγεῖν=[Epaminondas] gave himself up to those who wished to take him away, Mithr. 27 §107 ἐς τὸ σῶμα αὐτοῦ=against his person, Bell. Civ. 2, 106 §442 Caesar's person [σῶμα] is ἱερὸς καὶ ἄσυλος=sacred and inviolable; 3, 39 §157 ἔργον—σῶμα=course of action—person; Wilcken, Chrest. 55, 7 [III BC] ἑκάστου σώματος=for every person. See Wilcken's note).—Because it is subject to sin and death, man's mortal body is τὸ σῶμα τῆς σαρκός (σάρξ 7) Col 2: 11 is a σῶμα τῆς ἁμαρτίας Ro 6: 6 or τοῦ θανάτου 7: 24; cf. 8: 11. In fact, σῶμα can actually take the place of σάρξ 8: 13 (cf. Herm. Wr. 4, 6b ἐὰν μὴ πρῶτον τὸ σῶμα μισήσῃς, σεαυτὸν φιλῆσαι οὐ δύνασαι; 11, 21a). As a σῶμα τῆς ταπεινώσεως *lowly body* it stands in contrast to the σῶμα τῆς δόξης *glorious body* of the heavenly beings Phil 3: 21. In another pass. σῶμα ψυχικόν of mortal man is opposed to the σῶμα πνευματικόν after the resurrection 1 Cor 15: 44a, b, c.—Christ's earthly body, which was subject to death Ro 7: 4; Hb 10: 5 (Ps 39: 7 v.l.), 10; 1 Pt 2: 24; τὸ σῶμα τῆς σαρκὸς αὐτοῦ Col 1: 22. Esp. in the language of the Lord's Supper (opp. αἷμα) Mt 26: 26; Mk 14: 22; Lk 22: 19; 1 Cor 10: 16 (GBornkamm, NTS 2, '56, 202-6); 11: 24, 27, 29. S. the lit. s.v. ἀγάπη II and εὐχαριστία 3, also JBonsirven, Biblica 29, '48, 205-19.—ἓν σῶμα *a single body* 1 Cor 6: 16 (cf. Jos., Ant. 7, 66 Δαυίδης τὴν τε ἄνω πόλιν κ. τὴν ἄκραν συνάψας ἐποίησεν ἓν σῶμα; Artem. 3, 66 p. 196, 9; RKempthorne, NTS 14. '67/'68, 568-74).

2. pl. σώματα *slaves* (Herodas 2, 87 δοῦλα σώματα; Polyb. et al.; oft. Vett. Val.; inscr., pap.; Gen 36: 6; Tob 10: 10; Bel 32; 2 Macc 8: 11; Jos., Ant. 14, 321) Rv 18: 13.

3. In order to gain an answer to his own question ποίῳ σώματι ἔρχονται; (i.e. the dead after the resurrection) Paul speaks in 1 Cor 15: 35 of bodies of plants (which are different in kind fr. 'body' of the seed which is planted.—Maximus Tyr. 40, 60e makes a distinction betw. the σώματα of the plants, which grow old and pass away, and their σπέρματα, which endure.—σώματα of plants also in Apollon. Paradox. 7 [after Aristot.]) vs. 37f, and of σώματα ἐπουράνια of the heavenly bodies vs. 40 (cf. Ps.-Aristot., De Mundo 2, 2 the stars as σώματα θεῖα; Maximus Tyr. 21, 8b οὐρανὸς κ. τὰ ἐν αὐτῷ σώματα, acc. to 11, 12a οἱ ἀστέρες; 40, 4h; Sallust. 9 p. 18, 5).

4. of the body that casts a shadow, in contrast to the σκιά (q.v. 2) *the thing itself, the reality* Col 2: 17.

5. the Christian community, the church as a unified σῶμα (Περὶ ὕψους 10, 1 ἕν τι σῶμα of lively, well-organized speech; Polyaenus, Exc. 18, 4 of the phalanx; Libanius, Or. 1 p. 176, 25 F. τὸ τῆς πόλεως σ.; Plut., Lives I, 360c [Philopoemen 8, 2]), esp. as the body of Christ, which he fills or enlivens as its Spirit (in this case the head belongs with the body, as Appian, Bell. Civ. 3, 26 §101, where a severed head is differentiated from τὸ ἄλλο σῶμα=the rest of the body), or crowns as its Head (Hdt. 7, 140; Quint. Smyrn. 11, 58; Dit., Syll.³ 1169, 3; 15 κεφαλή w. σῶμα as someth. equally independent): οἱ πολλοὶ ἓν σῶμά ἐσμεν ἐν Χριστῷ Ro 12: 5. Cf. 1 Cor 10: 17; 12: 13, 27; Eph (s. Schlier s.v. ἐκκλησία 4d) 1: 23; 2: 16; 4: 12, 16; 5: 23, 30; Col 1: 18, 24; 2: 19; 3: 15; ISm 1: 2; Hs 9, 17, 5; 9, 18, 3f. ἐν σῶμα καὶ ἐν πνεῦμα Eph 4: 4; cf. Hs 9, 13, 5; 7 (Iambl., Vi. Pyth. 30, 167: all as ἓν σῶμα κ. μία ψυχή). διέλκομεν τὰ μέλη τοῦ Χριστοῦ καὶ στασιάζομεν πρὸς τὸ σῶμα τὸ ἴδιον 1 Cl 46: 7.—Traugott Schmidt, Der Leib Christi (σῶμα Χριστοῦ) '19; EKäsemann, Leib u. Leib Christi '33 (for a critique s. SHanson, Unity of the Church in NT '46, 113-16); ÉMersch, Le Corps mystique du Christ² '36; AWikenhauser, D. Kirche als d. myst. Leib Christi, nach d. Ap. Pls² '40; EPercy, D. Leib Christi in d. paulin. Homologumena u. Antilegomena '42; RHirzel, Die Person: SAMünchen '14 H. 10 p. 6-28 (semantic history of σῶμα); WLKnox, Parallels to the NT use of σῶμα: JTS 39, '38, 243-6; FWDillistone, How is the Church Christ's Body?, Theology Today 2, '45/'46, 56-68; WGoossens, L'Église corps de Christ d'après St. Paul² '49; CTCraig, Soma Christou: The Joy of Study '51, 73-85; JATRobinson, The Body: A Study in Pauline Theol. '52; RBultmann, Theol. of the NT, tr. KGrobel '51, 192-203; HClavier, CHDodd Festschr. '56, 342-62; CColpe, Zur Leib-Christi Vorstellung im Eph, '60, 172-87; KGrobel, Bultmann-Festschr. '54, 52-9; HHegermann, ThLZ 85, '60, 839-42; ESchweizer, ibid. 86, '61, 161-74; 241-56; JJMeuzelaar, D. Leib des Messias, '61; MEDahl, The Resurrection of the Body, '62; RJewett, Paul's Anthropological Terms, '71, 201-304.—ESchweizer, TW VII, 1024-91. M-M. B. 198.

σωματικός, ή, όν (Aristot. et al.; inscr., pap., 4 Macc) bodily, corporeal—1. being or consisting of a body, bodily (opp. ἀσώματος Ps.-Pla., Tim. Locr. 96A; Philo, Op. M. 16; 18) σωματικῷ εἴδει Lk 3: 22.
2. pertaining or referring to the body (Aristot. et al.; Herm. Wr. 1, 1; inscr., pap., Philo; Jos., Bell. 1, 430; 6, 55 σ. ἕξις) ἡ σωματικὴ γυμνασία 1 Ti 4: 8. (σαρκικαὶ καὶ) σωματικαὶ ἐπιθυμίαι D 1: 4 (Aristot., Eth. Nic. 7, 7 p. 1149b, 26 ἐπιθυμίαι καὶ ἡδοναί; 4 Macc 1: 32). M-M.*

σωματικῶς adv. (Plut., Mor. 424D; Vett. Val. 231, 2; 269, 28; Dit., Or. 664, 17; pap. [Sb 8748, 15—178 AD]; Philo, Rer. Div. Her. 84) bodily, corporeally of Christ ἐν αὐτῷ κατοικεῖ πᾶν τὸ πλήρωμα τῆς θεότητος σωματικῶς in him the whole fulness of Deity dwells bodily Col 2: 9 (prob. to be understood fr. 2: 17 [cf. σῶμα 4] as=in reality, not symbolically). M-M.*

σωμάτιον, ου, τό (Isocr. et al.; pap.) dim. of σῶμα; little body, esp. poor body (Socrat., Ep. 30, 1; 31; Epict. 1, 1, 10; 24; 1, 9, 2 al., s. the index of Schenkl's ed.; Lucian, Jupp. Trag. 41; Philo, Leg. ad Gai. 273)—1. lit., of the tortured body of a martyr MPol 17: 1.—2. fig., of the 'body' of a persecuted church ISm 11: 2 (for σωματεῖον 'corporate body', the rdg. of Lake's text, s. L-S-J).*

Σώπατρος, ου, ὁ (Athen.; Jos., Ant. 14, 241; inscr.) Sopater, son of Pyrrhus. S. was a Christian in Beroea and companion of Paul on his last journey to Jerusalem Ac 20: 4. His father's name is lacking in the t.r., and a v.l. gives the name itself as Σωσίπατρος (q.v.). M-M.*

σωρεύω fut. σωρεύσω; pf. pass. ptc. σεσωρευμένος (Aristot. +; Jdth 15: 11; Philo, De Prov. in Euseb., Pr. Ev. 8, 14, 62; Jos., Ant. 12, 211).
1. heap or pile (up) (Polyb.; Diod. S. 5, 46, 5 et al.; Jos., Bell. 4, 380; 6, 431) τὶ ἐπί τι someth. on someth. Ro 12: 20 (Pr 25: 22; cf. ἄνθραξ).
2. fill (a place) with (Polyb. 16, 8, 9; Maximus Tyr. 35, 3b; Herodian 4, 8, 9 βωμοὺς λιβάνῳ; 5, 5, 8) pass., fig. γυναικάρια σεσωρευμένα ἁμαρτίαις silly women, overwhelmed by their sins 2 Ti 3: 6. M-M.*

Σωσθένης, ους, ὁ (Diod. S., Diog. L.; Achilles Tat. 5, 17, 5 al.; inscr., pap.) Sosthenes.
1. leader of a synagogue in Corinth at the time of Paul's first missionary work in that city. He was beaten in the presence of Gallio the proconsul, but the account in Ac (18: 12-17) does not say why, 18: 17. From Theodoret to Zahn many scholars, not without good reason, have identified him with the foll.
2. Paul mentions a 'brother' Sosthenes in the salutation 1 Cor 1: 1, beside himself. Cf. subscr. He is known to the Corinthians, but need not have been a Corinthian himself, unless he is to be identified w. 1. M-M.*

Σωσίπατρος, ου, ὁ (Athen.; inscr., pap.; 2 Macc 12: 19, 24) Sosipater, designated as a συγγενής of Paul in Ro 16: 21, where he also sends greetings to the church. He is freq. considered to be the same man as Sopater of Beroea (s. Σώπατρος), e.g. by Zahn, Ltzm. Linguistically this is quite poss. M-M.*

σωτήρ, ῆρος, ὁ savior, deliverer, preserver, as a title of divinities Pind., Aeschyl. +; inscr., pap. Esp. was Asclepius, the god of healing, so called (Ael. Aristid. 42, 4 K. σ. τῶν ὅλων; Dit., Or. 332, 9 [138-133 BC], cf. note 8, Syll.³ 1112, 2; 1148); Celsus compares the cult of Ascl. w. the Christian worship of the Savior (Origen, C. Cels. 3, 3). Likew. divinities in the mystery religions, like Serapis and Isis (Σαράπιδι Ἴσιδι Σωτῆρσι: Dit., Or. 87; Sb 597 [both III BC]; Sb 169 [Ptolemaic times]; 596; CIG 4930b [I BC]), as well as Heracles (τῆς γῆς κ. τῶν ἀνθρώπων σ.: Dio Chrys. 1, 84) or Zeus (Ael. Aristid. 52 p. 608 D.: Ζεὺς ὁ σ.).—GAnrich, Das antike Mysterienwesen 1894, 47ff; GWobbermin, Religionsgesch. Studien 1896, 105ff.—The LXX has σωτήρ as a term for God, and so do Philo (s. MDibelius, Hdb., exc. on 2 Ti 1: 10) and Sib. Or. 1, 73; 3, 35; on the other hand, σ. is not so found in Ep. Arist., Test. 12 Patr., or Josephus (s. ASchlatter, Wie sprach Jos. von Gott? '10, 66).—At an early date σωτήρ was used as a title of honor for deserving men (cf. X., Hell. 4, 4, 6, Ages. 11, 13; Plut., Arat. 53, 4; Herodian 3, 12, 2.—Ps.-Lucian, Ocyp. 78 in an address to a physician [s. θεός 4a]; Jos., Vi. 244; 259 Josephus as εὐεργέτης καὶ σωτήρ of Galilee), and in inscr. and pap. we find it predicated of high-ranking officials and of persons in private life. This is never done in our lit. But elsewh. it is also applied to personalities who are active in the world's affairs, in order to remove them fr. the ranks of ordinary humankind and place them in a significantly higher position. So it is, e.g. when Epicurus is called σωτήρ by his followers (Philod.: Pap. Herc. 346, 4, 19 ὑμνεῖν τὸν σωτῆρα τὸν ἡμέτερον.—ARW 18, '30, 392-5; ChJensen, Ein neuer Brief Epikurs: GGAbh. III 5, '33, 80f). Of much greater import is the designation of the (deified) ruler as σ. (Ptolemy I Soter [323-285 BC] Πτολεμαῖος καὶ Βερενίκη θεοὶ Σωτῆρες:

APF 5, '13, 156; 1; cf. Sb 306 and oft. in later times, of the Roman emperors as well [Philo, In Flacc. 74; 126, Leg. ad Gai. 22; cf. Jos., Bell. 3, 459]).—PWendland, Σωτήρ: ZNW 5, '04, 335ff; Magie 67f; HLietzmann, Der Weltheiland '09; WOtto, Augustus Soter: Her. 45, '10, 448-60; FJDölger, Ichthys '10, 406-22; Dssm., LO 311f (LAE 368f); ELohmeyer, Christuskult u. Kaiserkult '19; Bousset, Kyrios Christos² '21, 241ff; EMeyer III 392ff; E-BAllo, Les dieux sauveurs du paganisme gréco-romain: RSphth 15, '26, 5-34; KBornhausen, Der Erlöser '27; HLinssen, θεος Σωτηρ, Diss. Bonn '29=Jahrb. f. Liturgiewiss. 8, '28, 1-75; AOxé, Σωτηρ b. den Römern: Wien. Stud. 48, '30, 38-61; WStaerk, Soter, I '33; II '38. Cf. also GertrudHerzog-Hauser, Soter . . . im altgriech. Epos '31; ADNock, s.v. εὐεργέτης.—CColpe, Die Religionsgeschichtliche Schule, '61 (critique of some of the lit. cited above).

1. of God ὁ θεὸς ὁ σωτήρ μου (Ps 24: 5; 26: 9; Mi 7: 7 al.) Lk 1: 47. θεὸς σ. ἡμῶν 1 Ti 1: 1; Jd 25. ὁ σ. ἡμῶν θεός 1 Ti 2: 3; Tit 1: 3; 2: 10; 3: 4. σ. πάντων ἀνθρώπων μάλιστα πιστῶν 1 Ti 4: 10 (cf. PPetr. III 20, I, 15 [246 BC] πάντων σωτῆρα and s. above Heracles as τῶν ἀνθρώπων σ. and in 2 below Serapis). ὁ τῶν ἀπηλπισμένων σωτήρ the Savior of those in despair 1 Cl 59: 3.

2. of Christ Lk 2: 11; Ac 13: 23; Phil 3: 20; Dg 9: 6; GOxy 12; [21]; 30. W. ἀρχηγός Ac 5: 31; 2 Cl 20: 5 (ἀρχηγὸς τῆς ἀφθαρσίας). σωτὴρ τοῦ σώματος Savior of the body (i.e. of his body, the church) Eph 5: 23. ὁ σωτὴρ τοῦ κόσμου (inscr.; cf. WWeber, Untersuchungen zur Gesch. des Kaisers Hadrianus '07, 225f; 222) J 4: 42; 1 J 4: 14. σ. τῶν ἀνθρώπων (Ael. Aristid. 45, 20 K. =8 p. 90 D. calls Serapis κηδεμόνα καὶ σωτῆρα πάντων ἀνθρώπων αὐτάρκη θεόν) GP 4: 13. ὁ σ. ἡμῶν Χρ. Ἰ. 2 Ti 1: 10; ISm 7: 1; w. Χρ. Ἰ. or Ἰ. Χρ. preceding Tit 1: 4; 3: 6; IEph 1: 1; IMg inscr.; Pol inscr. ὁ μέγας θεὸς καὶ σ. ἡμῶν Χρ. Ἰ. our great God and Savior Christ Jesus Tit 2: 13 (PLond. 604B, 118 τῷ μεγάλῳ θεῷ σωτῆρι). Cf. MDibelius, exc. after Tit 2: 14; HWindisch, Z. Christologie der Past.: ZNW 34, '35, 213-38.—ὁ σωτὴρ κύριος ἡμῶν Ἰ. Χρ. IPhld 9: 2. ὁ σ. τῶν ψυχῶν MPol 19: 2. ὁ θεὸς ἡμῶν καὶ σ. Ἰ. Χρ. 2 Pt 1: 1. ὁ κύριος (ἡμῶν) καὶ σ. Ἰ. Χρ. vs. 11; 2: 20; 3: 18; without any name (so ὁ σωτήρ [meaning Asclep.] Ael. Aristid. 47, 1 K.=23 p. 445 D.; 66 K.=p. 462 D.; 48, 7 K.=24 p. 466 D.) vs. 2. M-M.*

σωτηρία, ας, ἡ (trag., Hdt.+; inscr., pap., LXX, En., Ep. Arist., Philo, Joseph., Test. 12 Patr.) deliverance, preservation.

1. gener. of preservation in danger, deliverance fr. impending death, esp. on the sea (Diod. S. 3, 40, 1 λιμὴν σωτηρίας; 2 Macc 3: 32; Philo, Mos. 1, 317; Jos., Ant. 7, 5; 183) Ac 27: 34; Hb 11: 7. Of the deliverance of the Israelites fr. Egyptian bondage (Jos., Ant. 2, 331) Ac 7: 25 (διδόναι σωτηρίαν on the part of a deity: Menand., fgm. 292, 5). A transition to sense 2 is found in Lk 1: 71, where σωτηρία ἐξ ἐχθρῶν ἡμῶν deliverance from the hand of our enemies is expected (cf. Ps 105: 10).—1 Cl 39: 9 (Job 5: 4).

2. quite predom. salvation, which the true religion bestows (LXX. But likew. Herm. Wr. 7, 2; Ael. Aristid., Sacr. Serm. 3, 46 p. 424 Keil ἐγένετο φῶς παρὰ τῆς Ἴσιδος καὶ ἑτέρα ἀμύθητα φέροντα εἰς σωτηρίαν. The Hymn to Attis in Firmicus Maternus, De Errore Prof. Relig. 22, 1 Θαρρεῖτε μύσται τοῦ θεοῦ σεσωσμένου Ἔσται γὰρ ὑμῖν ἐκ πόνων σωτηρία [HHepding, Attis, seine Mythen u. sein Kult '03, 167]. The Lat. 'salus' in the description of the Isis ceremony in Apuleius corresponds to the Gk. σωτηρία [GAnrich, Das antike Mysterienwesen

1894, 47f; Rtzst., Mysterienrel.³ 39]). In our lit. this sense is found only in connection w. Jesus Christ as Savior. This salvation makes itself known and felt in the present, but it will be completely disclosed in the future. Opp. ἀπώλεια Phil 1: 28; θάνατος (cf. Damasc., Vi. Isid. 131: through Attis and the Mother of the Gods there comes ἡ ἐξ ᾅδου γεγονυῖα ἡμῶν σωτ.) 2 Cor 7: 10; ὀργή 1 Th 5: 9. W. ζωή 2 Cl 19: 1; ζωὴ αἰώνιος IEph 18: 1. σωτηρία αἰώνιος (Is 45: 17) Hb 5: 9; short ending of Mk; ἡ κοινὴ ἡμῶν σωτ. Jd 3 (Dit., Syll.³ 409, 33f ἀγωνιζόμενος ὑπὲρ τῆς κοινῆς σωτηρίας); σωτ. ψυχῶν salvation of souls 1 Pt 1: 9; cf. 10 (EGSelwyn, 1 Pt '46, 252f). σωτηρία ἡ τῶν ἐκλεκτῶν MPol 22: 1. ἡ τῶν σῳζομένων σωτ. 17: 2. κέρας σωτηρίας Lk 1: 69 s. κέρας 3. σωτηρίας as objective gen. dependent upon various nouns: γνῶσις σωτηρίας Lk 1: 77; ἐλπὶς σωτ. (cf. Philemo Com. 181 οἱ θεὸν σέβοντες ἐλπίδας καλὰς ἔχουσιν εἰς σωτηρίαν) 1 Th 5: 8; 2 Cl 1: 7; ἔνδειξις σωτ. Phil 1: 28 (opp. ἀπώλεια). τὸ εὐαγγέλιον τῆς σωτηρίας ὑμῶν Eph 1: 13. ὁ λόγος τῆς σωτηρίας ταύτης Ac 13: 26. ὁδὸς σωτηρίας way to salvation 16: 17; περιποίησις σωτ. 1 Th 5: 9. ἡμέρα σωτηρίας (quot. fr. Is 49: 8) of the day when the apostle calls them to salvation 2 Cor 6: 2a, b (cf. the mystery in Apuleius, Metam. 11, 5 'dies salutaris'='day of the initiation'). Christ is ὁ ἀρχηγὸς τῆς σωτ. Hb 2: 10 (ἀρχηγός 3). ὁ θεὸς τῆς σωτ. μου 1 Cl 18: 14 (Ps 50: 16). τοῦ θεοῦ ἡμῶν καὶ σωτηρος Ἰησοῦ Χριστοῦ 2 Pt 1: 2 𝔓⁷⁵.—Used w. verbs: ἔχειν σωτηρίαν Hv 2, 2, 5; 3, 6, 1; m 10, 2, 4; 12, 3, 6. κληρονομεῖν σωτηρίαν Hb 1: 14. τὴν ἑαυτοῦ σωτ. κατεργάζεσθαι Phil 2: 12 (κατεργάζομαι 2). σωτηρίας τυχεῖν τῆς ἐν Χριστῷ 2 Ti 2: 10 (τυχεῖν σωτηρίας: Diod. S. 11, 4, 4; 11, 9, 1). εἰς σωτηρίαν for salvation (i.e. to appropriate it for oneself or grant it to another) Ro 1: 16; 10: 1, 10; 2 Cor 7: 10; Phil 1: 19 (ἀποβαίνω 2); 2 Th 2: 13; 2 Ti 3: 15; 1 Pt 2: 2 τὰ ἀνήκοντα εἰς σωτηρίαν the things that pertain to salvation 1 Cl 45: 1; B 17: 1 (cf. Dit., Syll.³ 1157, 12f).—σωτηρία is plainly expected to be fully culminated w. the second coming of the Lord Ro 13: 11; Hb 9: 28; 1 Pt 1: 5. —(ἡ) σωτηρία without further qualification=(the) salvation is also found Lk 19: 9; J 4: 22 (ἡ σωτ. ἐκ τῶν Ἰουδαίων ἐστίν); Ac 4: 12 (cf. Jos., Ant. 3, 23 ἐν θεῷ εἶναι τ. σωτηρίαν αὐτοῦ καὶ οὐκ ἐν ἄλλῳ); Ro 11: 11; 2 Cor 1: 6; Hb 2: 3 (τηλικαύτη σωτ.); 6: 9. ἡ σωτ. ἡμῶν 2 Cl 1: 1; 17: 5; B 2: 10.—Christ died even for the salvation of the repentant Ninevites in the time of Jonah 1 Cl 7: 7; cf. vs. 4.—σωτηρία stands by metonymy for σωτήρ (in the quot. fr. Is 49: 6) τοῦ εἶναί σε εἰς σωτηρίαν ἕως ἐσχάτου τῆς γῆς Ac 13: 47; B 14: 8. On the other hand, for a circumstance favorable for our attainment of salvation ἡγεῖσθαί τι σωτηρίαν 2 Pt 3: 15.—In the three places in Rv in which σωτ. appears as part of a doxology we have a Hebraism (cf. Ps 3: 9 τοῦ κυρίου ἡ σωτηρία) 7: 10; 12: 10; 19: 1.—LHMarshall, Challenge of NT Ethics '47, 248-66; HHaerens, Studia Hellenistica 5, '48, 57-68; FJDölger, Antike u. Christentum 6, '50, 257-63. M-M.*

σωτήριος, ον (trag., Thu.+; inscr., pap., LXX, Philo, Joseph., Test. 12 Patr.) saving, delivering, preserving, bringing salvation.

1. as an adj. ἐπεφάνη ἡ χάρις τοῦ θεοῦ σωτήριος πᾶσιν ἀνθρώποις the grace of God has appeared, bringing salvation to all men (σ. τινι as Thu. 7, 64, 2 τοῖς ξύμπασι σωτήριος) Tit 2: 11.

2. subst., neut. τὸ σωτήριον means of deliverance, then also the deliverance itself (Aeschyl.+; Plut., Lucian; Herm. Wr. 10, 15 τοῦτο μόνον σωτήριον ἀνθρώπῳ ἐστίν, ἡ γνῶσις τοῦ θεοῦ; LXX; Jos., Bell. 3, 171; 6, 310

[τὰ σ. of God]), in our lit. of Messianic *salvation* and the one who mediates it. Dg 12: 9. W. gen. τὸ σωτ. τοῦ θεοῦ (Test. Sim. 7: 1; cf. Test. Dan 5: 10) Lk 3: 6 (Is 40: 5); Ac 28: 28; 1 Cl 35: 12 (Ps 49: 23); cf. 18: 12 (Ps 50: 14); περικεφαλαία τοῦ σωτ. Eph 6: 17 (Is 59: 17). θήσομαι ἐν σωτηρίῳ 1 Cl 15: 6 (v.l. σωτηρία.—Ps 11: 6 v.l.).—Also of the σωτήρ Himself εὕρομεν τὸ σωτήριον ἡμῶν Ἰησοῦν Χρ. 36: 1. εἶδον οἱ ὀφθαλμοί μου τὸ σωτήριόν σου Lk 2: 30.—ELohse, Passafest, '53, 50-6 ['peace-offering' in some LXX passages]. M-M.*

σωφρονέω 1 aor. ἐσωφρόνησα (trag., X., Pla.+; pap.) *be of sound mind.*
   1. of mental health (in contrast to μαίνεσθαι; Pla., Phaedr. 22 p. 244A, Rep. 331C; Ps.-Apollod. 3, 5, 1; 6; Philo, Cher. 69) *to be in one's right mind* of a demoniac who was healed Mk 5: 15; Lk 8: 35. Sim., 2 Cor 5: 13 (opp. ἐκστῆναι; cf. ἐξίστημι 2a).
   2. *be reasonable, sensible, serious, keep one's head* (X., Cyr. 3, 2, 4; Philo, Det. Pot. Ins. 114; Jos., Ant. 2, 296) Tit 2: 6. W. νήφειν 1 Pt 4: 7. Esp. of women *be chaste, virtuous* (Musonius p. 14, 12ff H.; Arrian, Anab. 4, 20, 2; Alciphr., 4, 17, 3; Jos., Ant. 18, 66.—σωφροσύνη 2) 1 Cl 1: 3; Pol 4: 3.—In contrast to ὑπερφρονεῖν and in a play on words w. it and w. φρονεῖν twice Ro 12: 3 (cf. Plut., Mor. 776D φρονεῖν κ. σωφ.; Socrat., Ep. 36 σωφρονέω—συσσωφρονέω). M-M.*

σωφρονίζω (Eur., Thu.+; Aq. Is 38: 16; Philo; Jos., Bell. 2, 493) *bring τινά someone to his senses* (Demosth. 25, 93; Dio Chrys. 17[34], 49; Maximus Tyr. 30, 5g; Wilcken, Chrest. 20 IV, 11; Jos., Bell. 3, 445; 4, 119), also simply *encourage, advise, urge* (cf. GAGerhard, Phoinix v. Kolophon '09, 35ff) w. acc. and inf. foll. ἵνα σωφρονίζωσιν τὰς νέας φιλάνδρους εἶναι Tit 2: 4. M-M.*

σωφρονισμός, οῦ, ὁ—1. in secular Gk. act. (=σωφρόνισις) *the teaching of morality, good judgment,* or *moderation; advice, improvement* (Strabo 1, 2, 3; Plut., Cato Maj. 5, 1, Mor. 653C; 961D; Appian, Liby. 65 §290; Philo, Leg. All. 3, 193; Jos., Bell. 2, 9, Ant. 17, 210); the Syriac version understands 2 Ti 1: 7 in this sense. But mng. 2 is prob. to be preferred here.
   2. (s. above) *moderation, self-discipline, prudence* (=σωφροσύνη. So the Vulgate. σωφρονισμός is used in someth. like this sense in Plut., Mor. 712C; Iambl., Vi. Pyth. 30, 174). M-M.*

σωφρόνως adv. (Aeschyl., Hdt.+; inscr.; Wsd 9: 11) *soberly, moderately, showing self-control* ζῆν (Strabo 16, 2, 35; Inschr. v. Magn. 162, 6 ζήσαντα σωφρόνως; Test. Judah 16: 3; Jos., Ant. 4, 248) w. δικαίως, εὐσεβῶς Tit 2: 12 (Ps.-Pla., Alcib. 1, 134D and Sextus 399 w. δικαίως).*

σωφροσύνη, ης, ἡ (Hom.+; inscr., pap., LXX [esp. 4 Macc]; Ep. Arist., Philo, Joseph., Test. 12 Patr.).
   1. *reasonableness, rationality, mental soundness* (in contrast to μανία X., Mem. 1, 1, 16; Pla., Prot. 323B) ἀληθείας καὶ σωφροσύνης ῥήματα *true and rational words* (opp. μαίνομαι) Ac 26: 25.
   2. *good judgment, moderation, self-control* (Pla., Rep. 4 p. 430E ἡ σωφροσύνη ἐστὶ καὶ ἡδονῶν τινων καὶ ἐπιθυμιῶν ἐγκράτεια, cf. Phaedo 68C, Symp. 196C; Aristot., Rhet. 1, 9, 9 σωφροσύνη δὲ ἀρετὴ δι᾽ ἣν πρὸς τὰς ἡδονὰς τοῦ σώματος οὕτως ἔχουσιν ὡς ὁ νόμος κελεύει, ἀκολασία δὲ τοὐναντίον, De Virt. et Vit. 2; Diog. L. 3, 91; 4 Macc 1: 3, 31; Philo; Jos., Ant. 2, 48, C. Ap. 2, 170 [w. other virtues]) w. ἁγνεία IEph 10: 3. W. still other virtues 1 Cl 64. W. ἐγκράτεια and other virtues 62: 2. Esp. as a feminine virtue *decency, chastity* (Diod. S. 3, 57, 3; Phalaris, Ep. 78, 1; Philo, Spec. Leg. 3, 51 w. αἰδώς; Jos., Ant. 18, 73; BGU 1024, 8; 15; grave inscr. APF 5, '13, 169 no. 24. S. σωφρονέω w. αἰδώς (X., Cyr. 8, 1, 30f and Philo, above) 1 Ti 2: 9. W. other virtues vs. 15.—TEBird, CBQ 2, '40, 259-63; AKollmann, Sophrosyne: Wiener Studien 59, '41, 12-34. M-M.*

σώφρων, ον, gen. **ονος** (Hom.+; inscr., pap., 4 Macc, Ep. Arist., Philo, Joseph., Test. 12 Patr.) *prudent, thoughtful, self-controlled* (Aristot., Eth. Nicom. 3, 15, end ἐπιθυμεῖ ὁ σώφρων ὧν δεῖ καὶ ὡς δεῖ καὶ ὅτε) w. πιστός 1 Cl 63: 3; w. other virtues Tit 2: 2. In the list of qualifications for a bishop 1 Ti 3: 2 (used w. κόσμιος as Lysias 21, 19; Pla., Gorg. 508A; Menand., Sam. 129; Lucian, Bis Accus. 17; Inschr. v. Magn. 162, 6); Tit 1: 8 (w. δίκαιος as Ep. Arist. 125).—Esp. of women *chaste, decent, modest* (Menand., fgm. 610. In inscr. on women's graves: Bull. de corr. hell. 22, 1898, 496; 23, 1899, 301; 25, '01, 88; Philo; Jos., Ant. 18, 180.—Dssm., LO 267 [LAE 315]. S. σωφρονέω 2 and σωφροσύνη 2) Tit 2: 5 (w. ἀγαθή as Jos., Ant. 6, 296).—ἡ σώφρων καὶ ἐπιεικὴς ἐν Χριστῷ εὐσέβεια 1 Cl 1: 2.—ULuck, TW VII, 1094-1102. M-M. B. 1213.*

T

τ′ as a numeral=300 (Sib. Or. 5, 21; 38; 42). Because of its form (T) a symbol of the cross B 9: 8 (cf. Lucian s.v. σταυρός, end); spelled out ταῦ, v.l.*

ταβέρναι, ῶν, αἱ (Lat. loanw.: tabernae; cf. GMeyer, Die lat. Lehnworte im Neugriech.: SAWien 132, vol. 1895, app. 3, p. 64) *tavern, shop, store,* as a place name Τρεῖς Ταβέρναι *Three Taverns,* a station on the Appian Way, located betw. Aricia and Appii Forum at the foot of the Alban Mount. It was 33 Roman miles fr. Rome (Cicero, Ad. Attic. 2, 10.—CIL IX 593; X p. 684). Ac 28: 15.*

Ταβιθά, ἡ indecl. (Aram. טְבִיתָא; cf. EKautzsch, Gramm. des Bibl.-Aram. 1884, 11; Dalman, Grammatik² 141) *Tabitha* (on this name in rabbin. lit. s. Billerb. II 694. Late pap. in Preisigke, Namenbuch), a Christian woman in Joppa Ac 9: 36, 40. Her name is interpreted in vs. 36 as Δορκάς (q.v.).—Mk 5: 41 W, for ταλιθά. M-M.*

Ταβώρ s. Θαβώρ.

ταγή, ῆς, ἡ (Aristoph.+; inscr., pap.) *order, decree* pl. (Suppl. Epigr. Gr. IV 467, 3 [263 AD]) 1 Cl 20: 8.*

τάγμα, ατος, τό (X., Pla.+; inscr., pap., LXX) *that which is ordered*—1. of a number of persons who belong together and are therefore arranged together *division, group.*
   a. military t.t. for bodies of troops in various numbers (since X., Mem. 3, 1, 11; Diod. S. 1, 86, 4; 20, 110, 4; Appian, Celt. 1 §7 τὰ τάγματα=the divisions of the army; Polyaenus 3, 13, 1; inscr., pap.; 2 Km 23: 13; Ep. Arist. 26; Jos., Bell. 4, 645, Ant. 20, 122 al. So as loanw. in rabb.) στρατιωτικὸν τάγμα (Diod. S. 17, 33, 1 τάγματα

τῶν στρατιωτῶν) *a detachment of soldiers* IRo 5: 1. Cf. 1 Cl 37: 3; because of the latter pass. 41: 1 is prob. to be classed here, too.

b. without any special military application *class, group* (Epicurus p. 24, 9 Us.; Sext. Emp., Math. 9, 54; inscr., pap.; Philo, Migr. Abr. 100; Jos., Bell. 2, 164 the Sadducees as a δεύτερον τάγμα; cf. 2, 122; 143 of the Essenes) Hs 8, 5, 1-6. τάγματα τάγματα *group by group, by groups* 8, 2, 8a; 8, 4, 2b, cf. 6. Likew. κατὰ τάγματα 8, 2, 8b.—Acc. to 1 Cor 15: 23f the gift of life is given to various ones in turn (cf. Arrian, Tact. 28, 2 ἐπειδὰν τάγμα τάγματι ἔπηται), and at various times. One view is that in this connection Paul distinguishes three groups: Christ, who already possesses life, the Christians, who will receive it at his second coming, and the rest of humanity (s. τέλος 2), who will receive it when death, as the last of God's enemies, is destroyed: ἕκαστος ἐν τῷ ἰδίῳ τάγματι (ζῳοποιηθήσεται)· ἀπαρχὴ Χριστός, ἔπειτα οἱ τοῦ Χριστοῦ ἐν τῇ παρουσίᾳ αὐτοῦ, εἶτα τὸ τέλος (JWeiss and Ltzm. ad loc. Cf. also JHéring, RHPhr 12, '32, 300-20; E-BAllo, RB 41, '32, 187-209).

2. *order, turn, arrangement* (Ps.-Pla., Def. 414E; Aristot., Pol. 4, 7[9], 3; Plut., Mor. 601A) κατὰ τὸ τάγμα ὡς *in the order in which* Hs 8, 4, 2a. M-M.*

τακήσομαι s. τήκω.

τακτός, ή, όν (since Thu. 4, 65, 1; pap.; Job 12: 5; Jos., Ant. 8, 396) *fixed, appointed* τακτὴ ἡμέρα (Polyb. 3, 34, 9; Dionys. Hal. 2, 74; PFlor. 133, 4 τὰς τακτὰς ἡμέρας) Ac 12: 21. M-M.*

ταλαιπωρέω impf. ἐταλαιπώρουν; 1 aor. ἐταλαιπώρησα—1. intr.—a. *endure sorrow* or *distress, be miserable* (Eur., Thu.+; LXX; Manetho in Jos., C. Ap. 1, 237; Sib. Or. 5, 75) 2 Cl 19: 4; Hv 3, 7, 1; s 6, 2, 7.

b. *be wretched* and, in giving expression to this feeling, *lament, complain* w. πενθεῖν, κλαίειν Js 4: 9.

2. trans. *torment, afflict* (Ps 16: 9; Is 33: 1) pass. *be tormented, afflicted* (Thu. 3, 3, 1 al.; Philo, In Flacc. 155; Jos., Ant. 2, 334; 5, 147 al.) Hs 6, 3, 1.*

ταλαιπωρία, ας, ἡ (Hdt.+; PTebt. 27, 40 [113 BC]; Libanius, Or. 50 p. 485, 19 F. [opp. ἀσέλγεια]; LXX; Philo; Jos., Bell. 7, 278, Ant. 2, 257) *wretchedness, distress, trouble, misery* Ro 3: 16 (Is 59: 7). ἡ ταλαιπωρία τῶν πτωχῶν 1 Cl 15: 6 (Ps 11: 6). Pl. *miseries* (Hdt. 6, 11; Diod. S. 1, 36, 5; Galen, Protr. 14 p. 46, 20 J; Ep. Arist. 15; Philo, Somn. 1, 174; Jos., Ant. 14, 379) Js 5: 1. M-M.*

ταλαίπωρος, ον (Pind.+; UPZ 110, 132 [164 BC]; APF 5, '13, 381 no. 56, 9 [I AD]; Sb 643, 8 [ostracon, Christian times]; LXX; Ep. Arist. 130; Philo; Jos., Ant. 11, 1; prayers for vengeance fr. Rheneia [Dssm., LO 352; 354; 356, LAE 413ff; Dit., Syll.³ 1181, 4f]) *miserable, wretched, distressed* w. ἐλεεινός and other adjs. Rv 3: 17. ταλαίπωρος ἐγὼ ἄνθρωπος *wretched man that I am* Ro 7: 24 (Epict. 1, 3, 5 τί γὰρ εἰμί; ταλαίπωρον ἀνθρωπάριον; ZPE 4, '69, 206: fgm. B 1, 5 of a romance ὦ ταλαίπωρε ἄνθρωπε [reconstr.]; ibid. line 9 ὁ μισητὸς ἔφη ἐγώ); cf. Hs 1: 3. In the latter pass. w. δίψυχος, and also of a doubter in the scripture quot. of uncertain origin 1 Cl 23: 3=2 Cl 11: 2; cf. 2 Cl 11: 1. Subst. (Demosth. 18, 121 ὦ ταλαίπωρε; likewise Diogenes the Cynic in Diog. L. 6, 66) οἱ ταλαίπωροι *the wretched men* (Epict. 3, 22, 44) B 16: 1.—Cf. Eranos 29, '32, 3; 4. M-M.*

ταλαντιαῖος, α, ον *weighing a talent* (so Aristot., Cael. 4, 4; Polyb. 9, 41, 8; Diod. S. 20, 87, 1; Jos., Bell. 5, 270. Cf.

Dit., Syll.³ 966, 44 note) χάλαζα μεγάλη ὡς ταλαντιαία *a severe hailstorm* with hailstones *weighing a talent* (the talent=125 librae, or Roman pounds of 12 ounces each) (*heavy as a hundred-weight* RSV) Rv 16: 21. M-M.*

τάλαντον, ου, τό *talent* (Hom.+), a measure of weight varying in size fr. about 58 to 80 lb. (26 to 36 kg.). Then a unit of coinage (lit., inscr., pap., LXX, Ep. Arist.; Jos., Bell. 5, 571, C. Ap. 2, 266; Test. Jos. 18: 3), whose value differed considerably in various times and places, but was always comparatively high; it varied also with the metal involved, which might be gold, silver, or copper. The (silver) talent of Aegina was worth about $1,625, the Attic talent of Solon about $1,080 in normal values (s. further any unabridged Engl. dict.). But, among others, there was also a Syrian talent=about $250. In our lit. only in Mt 18: 24; 25: 15-28 (JDerrett, Law in the NT '70, 17-47).—Lit. s.v. ἀργύριον 2c. M-M.*

ταλιθά Aram. טַלְיְתָא or טְלִיתָא, emphatic state of טַלְיָה (Dalman, Gramm.² 150) *girl, little girl* Mk 5: 41. S. ῥαβιθά.*

ταμεῖον, ου, τό (this contracted form of the older ταμιεῖον [q.v.] is found as early as the first cent. BC in inscr. [Dit., Syll.³ 783, 37] and pap. [BGU 1115, 41], but does not become very common until the beginning of our era. Cf. Plut., Mor. 9D; Babrius, Fab. 108, 2; LXX [Thackeray 63.—Rahlfs inserts the uncontracted form into the text every time the word is used]; En. 11: 1; Philo, Omn. Prob. Lib. 86. S. also Lob. on Phryn. p. 493; Mayser 92; Bl-D. §31, 2; Mlt. 44f; Mlt.-H. 89f; ENachmanson, Laute u. Formen d. magn. Inschr. '03, 71. In rabb. as loanw. טְמִין).

1. *storeroom* (the word has this sense Thu.+; oft. pap., LXX) w. ἀποθήκη Lk 12: 24.

2. gener. of rooms in the interior of a house *innermost, hidden*, or *secret room* (so X., Hell. 5, 4, 6 v.l.; Gen 43: 30; Ex 7: 28; SSol 1: 4 al. in LXX) Mt 6: 6 (Test. Jos. 3: 3). ἐν τοῖς ταμείοις *in one of the inner rooms* Mt 24: 26; Lk 12: 3. εἰς τὰ ταμεῖα 1 Cl 50: 4 (cf. Is 26: 20). M-M.*

ταμιεῖον, ου, τό (Thu.+; likew. in the older inscriptions and pap.; Ep. Arist. 111 [on this HGMeecham, The Letter of Aristeas '35, 79]; Jos., Bell. 2, 17, Ant. 8, 410; 18, 312; s. on ταμεῖον) *hidden, secret room* fig. τὰ ταμιεῖα τῆς γαστρός 1 Cl 21: 2 (Pr 20: 21). In the NT only Mt 24: 26 as a poorly attested v.l. (Bl-D. §31, 2 app.; Mlt.-H. 89). N. always prints the uncontracted form.*

τανῦν s. νῦν 3c.

τάξις, εως, ἡ (Aeschyl., Hdt.+; inscr., pap., LXX, Ep. Arist., Philo, Joseph., Test. 12 Patr.; loanw. in rabb.).

1. *fixed succession* or *order* (Epict. 3, 2, 2; Appian, Bell. Civ. 4, 22 §92; Test. Napht. 2: 8 ἐν τάξει) ἐν τῇ τάξει τῆς ἐφημερίας αὐτοῦ Lk 1: 8. Without ἐν: τάξει *in* (strict chronological) *order* Papias 2: 15, though JAKleist, transl. '48, 207f, note 19, prefers *verbatim*. HARigg, Jr., NovT 1, '56, 171: emends to τάχει=in a slipshod manner.

2. *(good) order* πάντα τάξει ποιεῖν 1 Cl 40: 1. κατὰ τάξιν *in order, in an orderly manner* (Lucian, Alex. 46; Alex. Aphr., Quaest. 1, 4, 1 p. 10, 17 Br.) 1 Cor 14: 40; Dg 8: 7.—Col 2: 5.—HvCampenhausen, Tradition and Life in the Church, '68, 123-40.

3. *position, post* (Hyperid. 3, 30; Demosth. 18, 258; Diod. S. 15, 64, 4; Epict. 1, 29, 39 [assigned by God]; Diog. L. 9, 21, end; 1 Esdr 1: 15; Jos., Vi. 397, Ant. 7, 36) εἰς τοσαύτην αὐτοὺς τάξιν ἔθετο ὁ θεός *God has ap-*

pointed them (i.e. the Christians) *to so great a position* Dg 6: 10.—*Administration* (of a position) Papias 4.

4. *nature, quality, manner, condition, appearance* (Polyb. 3, 20, 5; Diod. S. 1, 25, 5; Ep. Arist. 69 κρηπῖδος ἔχουσα τάξιν='it had the appearance of a shoe') ἡ νεωτερικὴ τάξις *the youthful nature* or *appearance* IMg 3: 1. Perh. it is in this way that Hb understood Ps 109: 4b, which he interprets to mean that Jesus was a high priest κατὰ τὴν τάξιν Μελχισέδεκ *according to the nature of= just like Melchizedek* 5: 6, 10; 6: 20; 7: 11a, 17, 21 t.r. In any case the reference is not only to the higher 'rank', but also to the entirely different nature of Melchizedek's priesthood as compared w. that of Aaron 7: 11b. (In Wilcken, Chrest. 81, 16; 19 al. in pap. τάξις='position of a priest'.) M-M.*

Ταουΐα, ας, ἡ *Tavia,* an otherw. unknown Christian woman in Smyrna ISm 13: 2 (Ταουΐα is the form of the name in the Gk. ms. and in the Lat. version. It is not found elsewh. But we find Ταουις as a woman's name PLond. 258, 184, and Ταουεις PLond. 257, 212; 245 as well as the Lat. masc. Tavius e.g. CIL III 6248.—The interpolated Gk. and the Armen. have Γαουΐα).*

ταπεινός, ή, όν (Pind., Aeschyl., Hdt.+; pap., LXX; En. 26, 4 [ὅρος]; Ep. Arist., Philo, Joseph., Test. 12 Patr.) *low,* in our lit. only in a fig. sense.

1. of position, power and esteem *of low position, poor, lowly, undistinguished, of no account* (Hdt. 7, 14; Pla., Phaedr. 257c; Isocr. 3, 42 al.; 1 Km 18: 23; Jos., Bell. 4, 365, Ant. 7, 95; 13, 415) ὁ ἀδελφὸς ὁ ταπ. (opp. πλούσιος) Js 1: 9.—Subst. (Philo, Poster. Cai. 109; Jos., Bell. 4, 319) B 3: 3. Pl. (Heraclides Pont., fgm. 55 W. ταπεινοί beside δοῦλοι; Diod. S. 14, 5, 4; Menand., Monost. 412; Ps.-Callisth. 2, 16, 10 of Fortune: ἡ τοὺς ταπεινοὺς ὑπεράνω νεφῶν τιθεῖ ἡ τοὺς ἀφ' ὕψους εἰς ζόφον κατήγαγεν; Zeph 2: 3; Is 11: 4; 14: 32) Lk 1: 52 (opp. δυνάσται). ὁ παρακαλῶν τοὺς ταπεινούς *who comforts the downhearted* 2 Cor 7: 6 (Is 49: 13). On τοῖς ταπεινοῖς συναπαγόμενοι Ro 12: 16 cf. συναπάγω. 1 Cl 59: 3f prob. belongs here (but s. 2b below); also B 14: 9 (Is 61: 1 v.l.).

2. of emotional states and ways of thinking—a. in a bad sense *pliant, subservient, abject* (X., Mem. 3, 10, 5; Pla., Leg. 6 p. 774c; Demochares [III bc]: 75 fgm. 1 Jac. αἰσχρὰ κ. ταπεινά; Cass. Dio 74, 5; POxy. 79 II, 2 [II ad]) in a judgment pronounced by Paul's opponents upon him κατὰ πρόσωπον ταπεινός 2 Cor 10: 1.

b. in a good sense *lowly, humble* (Aeschyl. +; Pla., Leg. 4 p. 716a; X., Ag. 11, 11; PGenève 14, 6; LXX; Ep. Arist. 263; Test. Gad 5: 3) ταπεινὸς τῇ καρδίᾳ (w. πραΰς, q.v.) Mt 11: 29. Subst. pl., opp. (οἱ) ὑψηλοί 1 Cl 59: 3 (but s. 1 above); B 19: 6; D 3: 9. Opp. ὑπερήφανοι (after Pr 3: 34) Js 4: 6; 1 Pt 5: 5; 1 Cl 30: 2. τὸ ταπεινὸν τῆς ψυχῆς *the humility of the soul* 55: 6. RLeivestad, ΤΑΠΕΙΝΟΣ- ΤΑΠΕΙΝΟΦΡΩΝ, NovT 8, '66, 36–47.—WGrundmann, TW VIII, 1–27: ταπ. and related words. M-M.*

ταπεινοφρονέω impf. ἐταπεινοφρόνουν; fut. ταπεινοφρονήσω; 1 aor. ἐταπεινοφρόνησα (Epict. 1, 9, 10 in a bad sense) *be humble-(minded), be modest, unassuming* (Ps 130: 2; Sib. Or. 8, 480; Rhet. Gr. I 624, 29) 1 Cl 13: 3; 48: 6; Hs 5, 3, 7; 7: 6. Opp. ἀλαζονεύεσθαι 1 Cl 2: 1; cf. 13: 1; 16: 2, 17; 17: 2; 19: 1 v.l.; 38: 2 Funk. Opp. ἐπαίρεσθαι 16: 1. W. ἐγκρατεύεσθαι 30: 3. ταπ. τὰ πρὸς τὸν θεόν *be humble toward God* 62: 2 (cf. ὁ ΙΙ 5 and s. Bl-D. §160; cf. Rob. 486f). ταπεινοφρονῆσαι ἐν πάσῃ πράξει αὐτοῦ *be humble in all that he does* Hs 7: 4.*

ταπεινοφρόνησις, εως, ἡ *humility* w. μακροθυμία Hs 8, 7, 6.*

ταπεινοφροσύνη, ης, ἡ (Epict. 3, 24, 56; Jos., Bell. 4, 494, both in a bad sense) in our lit. only in a good sense *humility, modesty* Phil 2: 3 (in the dat. of the motivating cause); 1 Pt 5: 5; 1 Cl 21: 8; Hs 5, 3, 7 (of the humility that expresses itself in fasting). W. ἐπιείκεια 1 Cl 56: 1; cf. 58: 2. W. ἐπιείκεια and πραΰτης 30: 8. W. πραΰτης, μακροθυμία and other virtues Col 3: 12; cf. 2: 23. μετὰ πάσης ταπ. *in all humility* Ac 20: 19; Eph 4: 2 (+καὶ πραΰτητος); without πάσης 1 Cl 31: 4; 44: 3. πᾶσα ἐρώτησις ταπεινοφροσύνης χρῄζει *every prayer requires humility* Hv 3, 10, 6. Humility can also be wrongly directed Col 2: 18, 23.—Lit. s.v. πραΰτης and ταπεινόω 2b. Also K Deissner, D. Idealbild d. stoischen Weisen '30; Vögtle (s.v. πλεονεξία) word-list; LGilen, Demut des Christen nach d. NT: Ztschr. f. Asz. u. Myst. 13, '38, 266–84; LHMarshall, Challenge of NT Ethics '47, 92–6; ADihle, Demut: RAC III '56, 735–78 [lit.].*

ταπεινόφρων, ον, gen. ονος (in Plut., Mor. 336e; 475e and Iambl., Protr. 21, 15 p. 115, 23 Pistelli='faint-hearted') in our lit. *humble* (Pr 29: 23) 1 Pt 3: 8 (t.r. φιλόφρονες); B 19: 3; Hm 11: 8 (w. πραΰς and other adjs.). πρὸς τὰς μεγαλορρημοσύνας αὐτῶν ὑμεῖς ταπεινόφρονες *you are to be humble in contrast to their boastfulness* IEph 10: 2 (w. πραεῖς).—Subst. ὁ ταπεινόφρων 1 Cl 38: 2. τὸ ταπεινόφρον *humility* 19: 1. S. Leivestad s.v. ταπεινός.*

ταπεινόω fut. ταπεινώσω; 1 aor. ἐταπείνωσα. Pass.: pf. ptc. τεταπεινωμένος; 1 aor. ἐταπεινώθην; 1 fut. ταπεινωθήσομαι (Hippocr.+; LXX; En. 106, 1; Ep. Arist. 257; Philo, Joseph.) *lower, make low.*

1. lit. (cf. Diod. S. 1, 36, 8; Bar 5: 7; En. 1, 6) ὄρος, βουνόν *level a mountain, hill* Lk 3: 5 (Is 40: 4).

2. fig.—a. *humble, humiliate* by assigning to a low(er) place or exposing to shame, w. acc. of the pers. or thing treated in this manner (Diod. S. 8, 25, 1) μὴ ταπεινώσῃ με ὁ θεὸς πρὸς ὑμᾶς *that God may not humiliate me before you* 2 Cor 12: 21. ταπ. ἑαυτόν *humble oneself* of Christ, who went voluntarily to his death Phil 2: 8 (cf. on the whole pass. the lit. s.v. ἁρπαγμός and κενόω 1; also KThieme, D. ταπεινοφροσύνη Phil 2 u. Ro 12: ZNW 8, '07, 9–33). Of Paul, who did not hesitate to work w. his hands *degrade* 2 Cor 11: 7. ὅστις ταπεινώσει ἑαυτὸν ὑψωθήσεται (ταπ.—ὑψόω: Chilo in Diog. L. 1, 69) Mt 23: 12b; cf. Lk 14: 11b; 18: 14b (s. also 2b below). Also the pass. (Hyperid. 6, 10; Jos., Ant. 18, 147) Mt 23: 12a; Lk 14: 11a; 18: 14a (cf. X., An. 6, 3, 18 θεὸς τοὺς μεγαληγορήσαντας ταπεινῶσαι βούλεται).—*Abase, confound, overthrow* (Diod. S. 13, 24, 6 Tyche [Fortune] ταπεινοῖ τοὺς ὑπερηφάνους; Cyranides p. 49, 12 ἐχθρούς) τοὺς ὑψηλούς 1 Cl 59: 3b; ὕβριν ὑπερηφάνων vs. 3a. Cf. B 4: 4f (Da 7: 24).—ταπεινόω can also refer to external losses, about='hold down, harm' (Petosiris, fgm. 6 l. 21 [act.] and 24 [pass.]).

b. *humble, make humble* in a good sense (Philod., περὶ κακιῶν col. 22, 3=p. 38 Jensen ἑαυτόν; Celsus 3, 62 αὐτόν) ὅστις ταπεινώσει ἑαυτὸν ὡς τὸ παιδίον τοῦτο Mt 18: 4. So perh. also 23: 12b; Lk 14: 11b; 18: 14b (s. 2a above). ταπεινοῦσθαι *humble oneself, become humble* (Menand., fgm. 544, 6 Kock τὴν θεὸν ἐξιλάσαντο τῷ ταπεινοῦσθαι σφόδρα; Sir 18: 21) ταπεινώθητε ἐνώπιον κυρίου Js 4: 10. ταπεινώθητε ὑπὸ τὴν χεῖρα τοῦ θεοῦ *bow down beneath the hand of God* (cf. Gen 16: 9) 1 Pt 5: 6. καρδία τεταπεινωμένη *a humbled heart* 1 Cl

18: 17 (Ps 50: 19). ψυχὴ τεταπεινωμένη B 3: 5 (Is 58: 10.
—Cf. Diod. S. 20, 53, 3 τῇ ψυχῇ ταπεινωθείς; 20, 77, 3
ἐταπεινώθη τὴν ψυχήν). Corresp. ὀστᾶ τεταπεινωμένα
1 Cl 18: 8 (Ps 50: 10).—KThieme, D. christl. Demut I
(history of the word, and humility in Jesus) '06; DFyffe,
ET 35, '24, 377-9. S. also πραΰτης, end.

c. In accordance w. OT usage, ταπεινοῦν τὴν ἑαυτοῦ
ψυχήν (Lev 16: 29, 31; 23: 27; Ps 34: 13; Is 58: 3 al.) or
ταπεινοῦσθαι (Sir 34: 26; 2 Esdr [Ezra] 8: 21. Cf. the
prayers for vengeance fr. Rheneia [Dssm., LO 353f, LAE
413ff=Dit., Syll.³ 1181, 11] θεὸς ᾧ πᾶσα ψυχὴ ταπει-
νοῦται. Cf. Dssm., LO 357f, LAE 419) means *discipline
oneself, fast* B 3: 1, 3 (Is 58: 5); Hm 4, 2, 2 (s. ταπεινοφροσύνη). οἶδα ταπεινοῦσθαι (opp. περισσεύειν) Phil 4:
12.—WCvanUnnik, Zur Bedeutung von ταπεινοῦν τὴν
ψυχήν bei den Apost. Vätern, ZNW 44, '52f, 250-5. On
the whole word: ESchweizer, Erniedrigung u. Erhöhung
bei Jesus u. s. Nachfolgern '55. M-M.*

ταπείνωσις, εως, ἡ (Pla., Aristot.+; Dit., Or. 383, 201 [I
BC]; LXX, Philo, Joseph., Test. 12 Patr.).
1. *humiliation* as an experience (Epict. 3, 22, 104; Jos.,
Bell. 2, 604, Ant. 2, 234; Test. Jud. 19: 2) Ac 8: 33; 1 Cl
16: 7 (both Is 53: 8). καυχάσθω ὁ πλούσιος ἐν τῇ
ταπεινώσει αὐτοῦ *let the rich man boast* (said in irony) *in
his (coming) humiliation* Js 1: 10 (BWeiss, Beyschlag,
Windisch, MDibelius, FHauck). In Diod. S. 11, 87, 2
ταπείνωσις is the *limitation* placed upon the financial
worth of a wealthy man. Petosiris, fgm. 6 lines 5; 11; 29
the word means the humiliation or depression caused by
severe external losses, someth. like a *breakdown.*
2. *humility, humble station, humiliation* as a state of
being (Diod. S. 2, 45, 2; Horapollo 1, 6) Hb 11: 20 D.
ἐπιβλέπειν ἐπὶ τὴν ταπ. τινος *look upon someone's
humble station* i.e. show concern for someone in her
humble station Lk 1: 48 (cf. 1 Km 1: 11; 9: 16; Ps 30: 8.—
HJToxopeüs, Lc. 1: 48a, ThT 45, '11, 389-94). τὸ σῶμα
τῆς ταπ. *the humble body* of the material body in contrast
to the glorified body Phil 3: 21.
3. *self-abasement, chastising* (ταπεινόω 2c) w. νηστεία (cf. Test. Jos. 10: 2) 1 Cl 53: 2; 55: 6. M-M.*

ταράσσω impf. ἐτάρασσον; 1 aor. ἐτάραξα. Pass.: impf.
ἐταρασσόμην; pf. τετάραγμαι, ptc. τεταραγμένος; 1
aor. ἐταράχθην (Hom.+; inscr., pap., LXX, Philo,
Joseph., Test. 12 Patr.; Sib. Or. fgm. 3, 10).
1. lit. *shake together, stir up* of water (Hom.+; Aesop
155 P.=274b Halm=160 Hausr.; Babrius 166, 5; Athen.
7, 52 p. 298c ταραττομένου τοῦ ὕδατος; Hos 6: 8; Is 24:
14; Ezk 32: 2, 13) J 5: 4 t.r.; pass. (Solon 11 Diehl²) *be
moved, be stirred* vss. 4 v.l., 7.
2. fig. *stir up, disturb, unsettle, throw into confusion*
(Aeschyl., Hdt.+; inscr., pap., LXX), in our lit. of mental
and spiritual agitation and confusion (Menand., Epitr.
547 J.; Philo, Conf. Lingu. 69), which can manifest
themselves in outward tumult τὸν ὄχλον Ac 17: 8; cf. vs.
13 (Hyperid. 1, 31, 8; POxy. 298, 27; PGiess. 40 II, 20
ταράσσουσι τὴν πόλιν). τὴν διάνοιάν τινος ταρ. 2 Cl
20: 1 (Epict., Ench. 28 τ. γνώμην σου). Of mental
confusion caused by false teachings ταρ. τινά Ac 15: 24
(w. λόγοις foll.); Gal 1: 7; 5: 10. Of Jesus in John's Gospel
ἐτάραξεν ἑαυτόν *he was troubled or agitated* J 11: 33 (s.
Hdb. ad loc.—Menand., Sam. 327 J. σαυτὸν ταράττεις;
M. Ant. 4, 26 σεαυτὸν μὴ τάρασσε).—Pass. *be troubled,
frightened, terrified* (Ps 47: 6; Is 8: 12; Jos., Ant. 7, 153;
12, 164) Mt 2: 3; 14: 26; Mk 6: 50; Lk 1: 12; 24: 38; MPol
5: 1; 12: 1; Hm 12, 4, 2. μηδὲ ταραχθῆτε *do not let
yourselves be intimidated* 1 Pt 3: 14 (Is 8: 12). ἡ ψυχή μου

τετάρακται J 12: 27 (cf. Diod. S. 17, 112, 4 Alexander
ἐταράττετο τὴν ψυχήν at the prediction of his death; Dio
Chrys. 23[40], 20 ταράξαι τὴν ψυχήν; Chio, Ep. 16, 7
ταράσσειν τὴν ψυχήν; Ps 6: 4; Test. Zeb. 8: 6, Dan 4:
7b); also ἡ καρδία 14: 1, 27 (cf. Ps 108: 22; 54: 5; Test.
Dan 4: 7a). ταραχθῆναι τῷ πνεύματι *be inwardly moved*
13: 21 (Ps.-Callisth. 2, 12, 5 ἐταράσσετο τῇ ψυχῇ).
M-M.*

ταραχή, ῆς, ἡ (Pind., Hdt.+; inscr., pap., LXX, Ep.
Arist., Philo, Joseph., Test. 12 Patr.; loanw. in rabb.) *a
disturbance of the usual order.*
1. lit. *the stirring up* of the water, which was usually
quiet J 5: 4 v.l.—2. fig.—a. *perplexity, disquietude* (Thu.,
Pla., LXX; Jos., Ant. 14, 273 w. φόβος) IEph 19: 2.
b. *disturbance, tumult, rebellion* (Hdt. et al.; Dit., Or.
90, 20; PAmh. 30, 10 [II BC]; Wilcken, Chrest. 167, 14 [II
BC]; 3 Macc 3: 24; Jos., Bell. 1, 216) pl. (Diod. S. 5, 40, 1
ταραχαί=confusion; Artem. 1, 17; 52 al.; Test. Dan 5: 2;
Jos., Vi. 103) Mk 13: 8 t.r. M-M.*

τάραχος, ου, ὁ (since Hippocr. I 604; VI 112 L.; X.; BGU
889, 23 [II AD]; LXX; Jos., Bell. 4, 495)=ταραχή.
1. *mental agitation, consternation* (X., An. 1, 8, 2;
Epicurus in Diog. L. 10, 77; 82 ἐν τ. ψυχαῖς; Aretaeus p.
142, 7) Ac 12: 18.—2. *disturbance, commotion* (Appian,
Bell. Civ. 5, 87 §365) 19: 23 (in both places τάραχος οὐκ
ὀλίγος. In the same sense Chio, Ep. 3, 2 πολὺς τάραχος).
M-M.*

Ταρσεύς, έως, ὁ (Apollodorus [II BC]: 244 fgm. 55 Jac.;
Strabo 14, 5, 14; Arrian, Anab. 2, 4, 7; Plut., Mar. 46, 2
al.; inscr.; 2 Macc 4: 30) (*a man) from Tarsus* of Paul, who
(Ac 22: 3) was born in Tarsus Ac 9: 11; 21: 39. M-M.*

Ταρσός, οῦ, ἡ (the sing. form of the name in Diod. S. 14,
20, 2; Strabo 14, 5, 9; Dio Chrys. 16[33], 17; 17[34], 46;
Arrian, Anab. 2, 4, 7; Joseph., inscr.) *Tarsus,* capital of
Cilicia in southeast Asia Minor (Diod. S., loc. cit., μεγίστη τῶν ἐν Κιλικίᾳ πόλεων) famous as a seat of Gk.
learning Ac 9: 30; 11: 25; 21: 39 D; 22: 3 (T. τῆς Κιλικίας
as Xenophon Eph. 2, 13, 5; Jos., Ant. 9, 208).—WMRamsay, The Cities of St. Paul '07, 85-244; HBöhlig, Die
Geisteskultur v. Tarsos '13; HSteinmann, Z. Werdegang
d. Pls. D. Jugendzeit in Tarsus '28; ACvanUnnik, Tarsus
or Jerusalem '52; also EHaenchen on Ac 22: 3 (p. 559, 5).
S. also s.v. Κιλικία.*

ταρταρόω 1 aor. ἐταρτάρωσα (Acusilaus Hist. [V BC] 8
ed. Jac. I p. 50; Philod., π. εὐσεβ. 32, 19 Gomp.; Jo.
Lydus, Men. 4, 158 p. 174, 26 W.; cf. Sext. Emp., Pyrrh.
Hypot. 3, 24, 210 ὁ Ζεὺς τὸν Κρόνον κατεταρτάρωσεν
[this compound several times in Ps.-Apollod.: 1, 1, 4; 1, 2,
1, 2; 1, 2, 3]. Tartarus, thought of by the Greeks as a
subterranean place lower than Hades where divine punishment was meted out, was so regarded in Jewish apocalyptic
as well: Job 41: 24; En. 20, 2; Philo, Exs. 152; Jos., C. Ap.
2, 240; Sib. Or. 2, 302; 4, 186) *hold captive in Tartarus*
2 Pt 2: 4. M-M.*

τάσσω 1 aor. ἔταξα, mid. ἐταξάμην; perf. τέταχα.
Pass.: pf. τέταγμαι, ptc. τεταγμένος (Pind., Aeschyl.,
Pre-Socr., Hdt.+; inscr., pap., LXX, En.; Aristobulus in
Euseb., Pr. Ev. 13, 12, 11; 12; Ezech. Trag. ibid. 9, 29, 8;
Ep. Arist., Philo, Joseph.; Test. 12 Patr.).
1. *place* or *station* a pers. or thing *in a fixed spot*—a.
appoint to or *establish in an office* pass. αἱ οὖσαι (ἐξουσίαι) ὑπὸ θεοῦ τεταγμέναι εἰσίν (*the authorities) who are
now in power are instituted by God* Ro 13: 1; cf. MPol 10:
2 (τάσσεσθαι ὑπό τινος as here, Eur., Iph. A. 1363; X..

An. 1, 6, 6; 2, 6, 13; Simplicius In Epict. p. 60, 19 Düb. τεταγμένοι ὑπὸ θεοῦ).

b. used w. a prep. τάσσειν τινὰ ἐπί τινος *put someone over* or *in charge of someone* or *someth.* (Polyb. 5, 65, 7; inscr.; Wilcken, Chrest. 11, 51 [II BC]; BPGrenfell, Revenue Laws of Ptolemy Philadelphus [1896] 51, 9 [III BC]) pass. (Arrian, Anab. 3, 6, 7 ἐπὶ τῶν χρημάτων=in charge of the finances; En. 20, 5; Jos., Ant. 2, 70; 7, 370) ἐφ᾽ ἧς (i.e. the way of light) εἰσὶν τεταγμένοι φωταγωγοὶ ἄγγελοι B 18: 1.—On ἄνθρωπος ὑπὸ ἐξουσίαν τασσόμενος Mt 8: 9 v.l.; Lk 7: 8 cf. ἐξουσία 4a (τάσσεσθαι ὑπό τινα 'be put under someone's command' Polyb. 3, 16, 3; 5, 65, 7; Diod. S. 2, 26, 8; 4, 9, 5; Dit., Or. 56, 13 [237 BC] τοῖς ὑπὸ τὴν βασιλείαν τασσομένοις).—τάσσειν τινὰ εἰς *assign someone to a (certain) classification*, used also w. an abstract noun (Pla., Rep. 2 p. 371c, Polit. 289E) pass. *belong to, be classed among those possessing* ὅσοι ἦσαν τεταγμένοι εἰς ζωὴν αἰώνιον Ac 13· 48.—τάσσειν ἑαυτὸν εἰς διακονίαν *devote oneself to a service* (cf. X., Mem. 2, 1, 11 εἰς τὴν δουλείαν ἐμαυτὸν τάττω; Pla., Rep. 2 p. 371c τάττειν ἑαυτὸν ἐπὶ τὴν διακονίαν ταύτην) 1 Cor 16: 15.

2. *order, fix, determine, appoint* (trag., Hdt.+; inscr., pap., LXX)—a. act. and pass., foll. by acc. w. inf. (X., An. 3, 1, 25) Ac 15: 2; 18: 2 v.l. περὶ πάντων ὧν τέτακταί σοι ποιῆσαι *concerning everything that you have been ordered to do* 22: 10 (cf. X., Resp. Lac. 11, 6). ὁ τεταγμένος ὑπ᾽ αὐτοῦ δρόμος *the course which has been fixed by him* (i.e. by God) 1 Cl 20: 2 (cf. Philo, Poster. Cai. 144, Rer. Div. Her. 97 τεταγμέναι περίοδοι ἀστέρων). κατὰ καιροὺς τεταγμένους *at appointed times* 40: 1 (cf. Polyb. 17, 1, 1).

b. mid.=act. (Hdt. et al.; 2 Km 20: 5) εἰς τὸ ὄρος οὗ ἐτάξατο αὐτοῖς ὁ Ἰησοῦς (i.e. πορεύεσθαι) Mt 28: 16. ταξάμενοι αὐτῷ ἡμέραν ἦλθον *they set a day for him and came* Ac 28: 23 (τασσ. ἡμέραν as Polyb. 18, 19, 1; Jos., Ant. 9, 136). GDelling, TW VIII, 27–49: τάσσω and related words. M-M.*

ταῦρος, ου, ὁ (Hom.+; inscr., pap., LXX, Philo, Joseph.) *bull, ox* as a sacrificial animal (Cornutus 22 p. 42, 12; Arrian., Anab. 1, 11, 6; Philo, Omn. Prob. Lib. 102; Jos., Ant. 13, 242) Ac 14: 13 (Diod. S. 16, 91, 3 ταῦρος ἐστεμμένος); Hb 9: 13; 10: 4; B 2: 5 (Is 1: 11). For great banquets Mt 22: 4. M-M. B. 154.*

ταὐτά=τὰ αὐτά, only as v.l. Lk 6: 23, 26; 17: 30; 1 Th 2: 14.—Bl-D. §18; Rob. 208; W-H., App. 145; HermvSoden, D. Schriften des NTs I 2, '11, 1380f.*

ταφή, ῆς, ἡ—1. *burial* (Soph.,Hdt.+; Dit., Or. 90, 32 [II BC]; PSI 328; 2; 5 [III BC]; PAmh. 125, 1; PTebt. 479 al.; LXX: Philo, Mos. 2, 283; Jos., Bell. 4, 317, Ant. 6, 292; 9, 182) αἰτεῖν τὸ σῶμα πρὸς ταφήν *ask for the corpse for burial* GP 2: 3 (Diod. S. 10, 29, 1 ἵνα λάβῃ τὸ σῶμα εἰς ταφήν). δώσω τοὺς πονηροὺς ἀντὶ τῆς ταφῆς αὐτοῦ *I will deliver up the wicked for his burial*, i.e. for putting him in the grave (parall. to θάνατος) 1 Cl 16: 10 (Is 53: 9).

2. *burial-place* (2 Ch 26: 23 ἡ τ. τῶν βασιλέων; Prinz Joachim-Ostraka edited by FPreisigke and WSpiegelberg '14, 2, 2; 3, 2 al.; 18, 11 [I BC] ταφὴ ἰβίων καὶ ἱεράκων ,α ='a burial-place for 1,000 mummies of ibises and falcons'. In the sense 'grave' oft. Hdt.+; Dt 34: 6) εἰς ταφὴν τοῖς ξένοις *as a burial ground for strangers* Mt 27: 7. M-M.*

τάφος, ου, ὁ (in Hom.='funeral rites') *grave, tomb* (Hes. +; inscr., pap., LXX; Philo, Mos. 2, 291; Jos., Ant. 9, 183; 14, 284).

1. lit. Mt 27: 61, 64, 66; 28: 1 (EBickermann, Das leere

Grab: ZNW 23, '24, 281–92; Guillaume Baldensperger, Le tombeau vide: RHPhr 12, '32, 413–33; 13, '33, 105–44; 14, '34, 97–125; ChMasson, Le tomb. v.: RThPh 32, '44, 161–74; HvCampenhausen, D. Ablauf der Osterereignisse u. das leere Grab '52; JSKennard, Jr., The Burial of Jesus: JBL 74, '55, 227–38; WNauck, ZNW 47, '56, 243–67; Finegan s.v. Ἰούδας 6; s. also ἀνάστασις 2, end and μνημεῖον 2.—An external parallel to the motif of the empty τάφος in Charito 3, 3, 1–4.—Phlegon: 257 fgm. 36, 1, 9 Jac.: in order to ascertain whether a resurrection from the dead had actually occurred, ὁ τάφος is opened and entered to see πότερον εἴη τὸ σῶμα ἐπὶ τῆς κλίνης ἢ κενὸν τόπον εὑρήσομεν); GP 6: 24; 8: 31; 9: 36f; 10: 39; 11: 45; 13: 55. οἱ τάφοι τῶν προφητῶν Mt 23: 29 (on the cult of graves and veneration of holy men among the Jews s. Billerb. I 937f; JoachJeremias, Heiligengräber in Jesu Umwelt '58). On τάφοι κεκονιαμένοι vs. 27; GNaass 6, cf. κονιάω. In the apocryphal gospel τάφ. κεκ. is used metaphorically. Likew. τάφοι νεκρῶν, ἐφ᾽ οἷς γέγραπται μόνον ὀνόματα ἀνθρώπων *graves of the dead, on which only the names of men are inscribed* IPhld 6: 1. ἔρχεσθαι ἐν τάφῳ *come to the grave* 1 Cl 56: 15 (Job 5: 26).

2. fig., of the dark place fr. which God introduces us into the world at birth 1 Cl 38: 3. Of the wild animals who are to be Ignatius' grave ἵνα μοι τάφος γένωνται (i.e. τὰ θηρία) IRo 4: 2 (Gorgias in Περὶ ὕψους 3, 2 calls vultures ἔμψυχοι τάφοι). Of sinful men τάφος ἀνεῳγμένος ὁ λάρυγξ (s. ἀνοίγω 1b and cf. Artem. 1, 80 p. 80, 27 τὸ στόμα τάφῳ ἔοικε) Ro 3: 13 (Ps 5: 10; 13: 3). M-M. B. 294.*

τάχα adv. (Hom.+) *perhaps, possibly, probably* (Aeschyl., Hdt. et al.; pap.. Wsd., quite predom. w. ἄν and the opt. Rarely, as in both NT passages, w. the indic. and without ἄν: Dio Chrys. 15[32], 33; Ps.-Demetr., El. c. 180; BGU 1040, 41 [II AD] τάχα δύνασαι; POxy. 40, 7; Wsd 13: 6 αὐτοὶ τάχα πλανῶνται; Philo, Aet. M. 54; Jos., Ant. 6, 33; 18, 277.—MArnim, De Philonis Byz. dicendi genere, Diss. Greifswald '12, 86; JScham, Der Optativgebrauch bei Klemens v. Alex. '13, 83; Bl-D. §385, 1) Ro 5 7; Phlm 15. M-M. B. 965.*

τάχειον (so e.g. POsl. 52, 15 [II AD]) defective spelling for τάχιον (ταχέως 2).

ταχέως adv. of ταχύς—1. positive ταχέως (Hom.+; pap., LXX)—a. *quickly, at once, without delay, soon* (Diod. S. 13, 106, 4; 17, 4, 6; En. 98, 16; Ep. Arist. 291; Jos., Bell. 7, 31; Ant. 9, 51) Lk 14: 21; 15: 22 D; 16: 6; J 11: 31; 1 Cor 4: 19; Phil 2: 19 (τ. πέμπ. as Plut., Mor. 612E), 24; 2 Ti 4: 9; B 3: 4.

b. also in an unfavorable sense *too quickly, too easily, hastily* (Pr 25: 8; Wsd 14: 28; Sib. Or. fgm. 1, 2) Gal 1: 6 (Third Corinthians 3: 2); 2 Th 2: 2; 1 Ti 5: 22; Pol 6: 1.

2. comp. τάχιον (Hippocr., Mul. Morb. 1, 2; Epicurus in Diog. L. 10, 98; Diod. S. 13, 106, 1; oft. in colloq. speech in general, incl. Jos., Bell. 5, 537, Ant. 2, 142 al.; inscr., pap.; Wsd 13: 9; 1 Macc 2: 40; Test. Iss. 6: 3. This form was rejected by the Atticists; the Attic form θᾶττον [also 2 Macc; Philo, Aet. M. 30; Jos., Ant. 12, 143—WSchmidt 505], which replaced the Homeric θᾶσσον, is found in our lit. only 1 Cl 65: 1a; MPol 13: 1.—Bl-D. §61, 1; 244, 1 w. app. 2; Mlt.-H. 164).

a. *more quickly, faster* Hb 13: 19. τάχ. τοῦ Πέτρου *faster than Peter* J 20: 4. The comparison is supplied fr. the context, *more quickly* (than the others), *be the first to . . .* MPol 13: 2. θᾶττον ἤ *more quickly than* 13: 1. *As quickly, as soon as possible* (Test. Iss. 6: 3; Ps.-Clem., Hom. 1, 14) 1 Cl 65: 1a (θᾶττον) and b (τάχιον); MPol 3.

b. without any suggestion of comparison *quickly, soon, without delay* (PGM 4, 1467 θᾶττον; Jos., Vi. 310 θᾶσσον) J 13: 27; 1 Ti 3: 14; Hb 13: 23; Hm 10, 1, 6.

3. superl. **τάχιστα** only once, in the expr. taken fr. the literary lang. (Bl-D. §60, 2; 244, 1; 453, 4; Rob. 488; 669. —Alcaeus 70, 15 D.[2]; Menand., Per. 287 J.; Arrian., Anab. 6, 2, 2; Ael. Aristid. 24, 26 K.=44 p. 833 D.; Dit., Syll.[3] 1168, 4 [IV bc]; PSI 360, 12 [252/1 bc]; 792, 10; 3 Macc 1: 8; Jos., Vi. 16) ὡς τάχιστα *as soon as possible* Ac 17: 15. M-M.*

ταχινός, ή, όν (Theocr.+; CIA III 1344, 3; Cat. Cod. Astr. I 137; LXX)—**1.** *quick, in haste* ταχινὸς γενέσθω Hs 9, 26, 6.

2. *coming soon, imminent, swift* 2 Pt 1: 14; 2: 1. ἡ μετάνοια αὐτῶν ταχινὴ ὀφείλει εἶναι *they must repent soon* Hs 8, 9, 4; cf. 9, 20, 4. M-M.*

τάχιον, τάχιστα s. ταχέως 2 and 3.

τάχος, ους, τό (Hom.+; inscr., pap., LXX) *speed, quickness, swiftness, haste* μετὰ τάχους *with speed* (Pla., Prot. 332b, Leg. 944c; POxy. 2107, 4 [III ad]) MPol 13: 1.— ἐν τάχει (Pind., Aeschyl.+; inscr., pap., LXX; Jos., Ant. 6, 163; 17, 83) *quickly, at once, without delay* Ac 10: 33 D; 12: 7; 17: 15 D; 22: 18; 1 Cl 48: 1; 63: 4; *soon, in a short time* Lk 18: 8; Ro 16: 20; 1 Ti 3: 14 v.l.; Rv 1: 1; 22: 6; 1 Cl 65: 1; *shortly* Ac 25: 4.—τάχει (Tetrast. Iamb. 2, 6, 1 p. 287; Sib. Or. 1, 205;—in Plut., Caes. 20, 4, Lys. 11, 2 w. the addition of πολλῷ, παντί) *quickly* Rv 2: 5 t.r. (אCAP et al.).—τὸ τάχος as acc. of specification, adverbially (*very*) *quickly, without delay* (PHib. 62, 13; PPetr. II 9, 2, 9; PSI 326, 12; 495, 17; 18 [all III bc]; LXX; Jos., Ant. 13, 8. Without the art. as early as Aeschyl.) 1 Cl 53: 2; B 4: 8; 14: 3 (w. all three cf. Ex 32: 7). M-M.*

ταχύνω almost always intr. (Aeschyl., X.+; LXX) *hasten, hurry* combined w. another verb by means of καί *hasten to do someth.* (Judg 13: 10) B 4: 3.*

ταχύς, εῖα, ύ (Hom.+; LXX)—**1.** adj. *quick, swift, speedy* ταχ. καρπός *fruit that ripens quickly* 2 Cl 20: 3. ταχὺς εἰς τὸ ἀκοῦσαι *quick to hear* Js 1: 19 (Lucian, Epigr. 18 ταχ. εἰς τὸ φαγεῖν; Sir 5: 11; Libanius, Or. 33 p. 186, 15 ἐν τῷ δῆσαι ταχύς, ἐν τῷ κρῖναι βραδύς).

2. mostly in the neut. sing. as adv. ταχύ (trag., Hdt.+; pap., LXX; En. 97, 10; Jos., Bell. 7, 394, Vi. 149).

a. *quickly, at a rapid rate* ταχὺ ἔφυγον Mk 16: 8 t.r.— Mt 28: 8.—**b.** *without delay, quickly, at once* (though it is not always poss. to make a clear distinction betw. this mng. and the one in c below) Mt 5: 25; 28: 7; Lk 15: 22; J 11: 29; Ac 14: 2 D; 1 Cl 23: 5a, b (Is 13: 22); 53: 2 (Ex 32: 8; Dt 9: 12); Hm 9: 7. This is prob. the place for the ἔρχεσθαι ταχύ of Rv: 2: 5 t.r. (many cursives and printed texts), 16; 3: 11; 11: 14; 22: 7, 12, 20 (P-ÉLangevin, Jésus Seigneur, '67, 209–35).

c. *in a short time, soon* (s. b above) Mk 9: 39 (*soon afterward*); Hv 3, 8, 9; m 12, 5, 3. This is also prob. the place for the μετανοεῖν ταχύ of Hs: 8, 7, 5; 8, 8, 3; 5; 8, 10, 1; 9, 19, 2; 9, 21, 4; 9, 23, 2. M-M.*

τέ (Hom.+; pap., LXX; En. 99, 7; Ep. Arist., Philo, Joseph., Sib. Or.) enclitic particle (in the NT never elided to τ'. In Mt three times, in Luke's gosp. nine times, in John's gosp. three times ['in each case open to doubt' Bl-D. §443, 1 app.], in Paul [quite predom. in Ro] someth. more than twenty times, scarcely less oft. in Hb, in 1 Cl forty-three times, in Dg seven times, in Js twice, once each in Jd, Rv, 2 Cl, B. It is not found at all in Mk, Gal, Col, 1 and 2 Th, 1 and 2 Ti, Tit, 1, 2 and 3 J; 1 and 2 Pt. By far

most freq. [about 150 times] in Ac. The ms. tradition oft. confuses τέ and δέ.—Bl-D. §443f w. app.; Rdm.[2] p. 5f, 37; Rob. index. p. 1285; Mlt.-Turner 338.

1. Used alone, mng. *and,* τέ connects—**a.** clauses, thereby indicating a close relationship betw. them (Bl-D. §443, 3) ἑτέροις τε λόγοις πλείοσιν διεμαρτύρατο *and likewise* . . . Ac 2: 40 (here D has the poorer rdg. δέ). κατενύγησαν τὴν καρδίαν, εἶπόν τε . . . , *and so they said* vs. 37.—J 4: 42; 6: 18; Ac 4: 33; 5: 19, 35; 6: 7, 12f al.; Ro 2: 19; Hb 12: 2; Jd 6.—The use of τέ to introduce a parenthesis is scarcely admissible; δέ is to be preferred: Ac 1: 15; 4: 13 (cf. Bl-D. §443, 1 app.; 447, 7).

b. more rarely it connects single concepts, parts of clauses, or words (cf. Kühner-G. II 241) ἐν ἀγάπῃ πνεύματί τε πραΰτητος 1 Cor 4: 21. θεοῦ ῥῆμα δυνάμεις τε μέλλοντος αἰῶνος Hb 6: 5. Cf. 9: 1. In this manner are connected: participles συναχθέντες συμβούλιόν τε λαβόντες Mt 28: 12. φοβούμενος τὸν θεὸν μαρτυρούμενός τε Ac 10: 22. Cf. Mt 27: 48; Ac 2: 33; 20: 11; 28: 23a; Hb 1: 3; 6: 4; infinitives ἁρπάσαι αὐτὸν ἐκ μέσου αὐτῶν ἄγειν τε Ac 23: 10. Cf. 11: 26; 24: 23; 27: 21b; Eph 3: 19.

2. τὲ—τὲ *as—so, not only—but also* connects sentences and parts of sentences that are closely related to each other (Kühner-G. II 243; Jos., Ant. 1, 92) μάρτυρα ὧν τε εἶδές με ὧν τε ὀφθήσομαί σοι Ac 26: 16. ἐάν τε γὰρ ζῶμεν, τῷ κυρίῳ ζῶμεν, ἐάν τε ἀποθνήσκωμεν, τῷ κυρίῳ ἀποθνήσκομεν *for just as when we live, we live to the Lord, so also when we die, we die to the Lord* Ro 14: 8a. ἐάν τε οὖν ζῶμεν ἐάν τε ἀποθνήσκωμεν, τοῦ κυρίου ἐσμέν so, *not only if we live, but also if we die* (i.e. *whether we live or die*) *we belong to the Lord* vs. 8b. Cf. Ac 2: 46; 17: 4; 26: 10.

3. w. the same mng. τὲ—καί (Jos., Bell. 2, 142, Ant. 1, 9) and τὲ καί—**a.** connecting concepts, usu. of the same kind or corresponding as opposites. In these uses τὲ καί can oft. be translated simply *and*: δῶρά τε καὶ θυσίας Hb 5: 1. δεήσεις τε καὶ ἱκετηρίας vs. 7. ὀνειδισμοῖς τε καὶ θλίψεσιν 10: 33. φόβητρά τε καὶ σημεῖα Lk 21: 11b. Cf. 22: 66; Ac 4: 27; 26: 3. ποιεῖν τε καὶ διδάσκειν Ac 1: 1. ἀσφαλῆ τε καὶ βεβαίαν Hb 6: 19. πάντη τε καὶ πανταχοῦ Ac 24: 3. ὑμῶν τε καὶ ἐμοῦ Ro 1: 12; cf. 1 Cor 1: 2 t.r. πονηρούς τε καὶ ἀγαθούς Mt 22: 10. ἄνδρες τε καὶ γυναῖκες Ac 8: 12; 9: 2; 22: 4. Ἰουδαίοις τε καὶ Ἕλλησιν 1 Cor 1: 24. μικρῷ τε καὶ μεγάλῳ Ac 26: 22a. When used w. a noun that has the art. τέ comes after the latter: ὅ τε στρατηγὸς . . . καὶ οἱ ἀρχιερεῖς Ac 5: 24; cf. Lk 23: 12; J 2: 15; Ac 8: 38; 17: 10; 27: 1; Hb 2: 11.—τέ can be followed by more than one καί (Libanius, Or. 2 p. 256, 6 F.) τήν τε Μαριὰμ καὶ τὸν Ἰωσὴφ καὶ τὸ βρέφος Lk 2: 16. ἐσθίειν τε καὶ πίνειν καὶ μεθύσκεσθαι 12: 45. Cf. Ac 1: 8, 13; Hb 2: 4; 9: 2.—In 1 Cor 1: 30 τὲ καί connects the second and third members of a series, and another καί joins the fourth one. Sim. Hb 11: 32. τὲ καί doubled Ἕλλησίν τε καὶ βαρβάροις, σοφοῖς τε καὶ ἀνοήτοις Ro 1: 14. θηρίων τε καὶ πετεινῶν ἑρπετῶν τε καὶ ἐναλίων Js 3: 7.—τὲ καί—τέ: ἐνώπιον ἐθνῶν τε καὶ βασιλέων υἱῶν τε Ἰσραήλ Ac 9: 15. Cf. 26: 10f. The τὲ καί . . . τὲ . . . καί of vs. 20 seems to be due to a textual error.

b. infrequently connecting whole sentences ἠνεῴχθησάν τε αἱ θύραι, καὶ πάντων τὰ δεσμὰ ἀνέθη Ac 16: 26 t.r. καὶ . . . , καὶ—τὲ . . . , καί 2: 2–4 t.r. τὲ . . . , καὶ . . . , καί 21: 30.—On εἴτε s. εἰ VI 13. On μήτε s. that entry. M-M.

τέγος, ους, τό (Hom. [Od.]+; Lucian; Aelian, N.A. 2, 48 p. 56, 11; Jos., Bell. 1, 337, Ant. 17, 71; Sib. Or. 3, 186) *roof*: ὑπὸ τὸ τέγος *under the roof* (lead, as Appian, Bell.

Civ. 4, 18 §70) 1 Cl 12: 6 (as the rdg. preferred to στέγος by Lghtf.—The same confusion of rdgs. in EpJer 9).*

τεθνάναι, τέθνηκα s. θνήσκω.

τεθραμμένος s. τρέφω.

τεῖχος, ους, τό (Hom.+; inscr., pap., LXX; En. 14, 9; Ep. Arist. 139; Philo, Aet. M. 129 al.; Jos., Vi. 156 al.; Test. 12 Patr.; Sib. Or. 3, 274; loanw. in rabb.) *wall,* esp. *city wall* Ac 9: 25; 2 Cor 11: 33 (διὰ τοῦ τείχους as Jos., Ant. 5, 15. Cf. Athen. 5 p. 214Α κατὰ τῶν τειχῶν καθιμήσαντας φεύγειν); Hb 11: 30; Rv 21: 12, 14f, 17–19. Pl. of several circular walls surrounding the tower in Hermas: Hs 8, 2, 5; 8, 6, 6; 8, 7, 3; 8, 8, 3. M-M. B. 472.*

τεκεῖν s. τίκτω.

τεκμήριον, ου, τό (Aeschyl., Hdt.+; inscr., pap., LXX, Philo, Joseph.) convincing, decisive *proof* (Diod. S. 17, 51, 3 τεκμήρια τῆς ἐκ τοῦ θεοῦ γενέσεως; Dit., Syll.³ 867, 37 μέγιστον τεκμήριον w. ref. to Artemis; 685, 84; PGiess. 39, 9) ἐν πολλοῖς τεκμηρίοις *by many convincing proofs* Ac 1: 3 (cf. Jos., Ant. 5, 39 διὰ πολλῶν τεκμηρίων.—τεκ. used w. παραστῆσαι Ant. 17, 128). M-M.*

τεκνίον, ου, τό (Epict. 3, 22, 78; Pal. Anth.; PFlor. 365, 15 [III AD]; POxy. 1766, 14) dim. of τέκνον; (*little*) *child,* voc. pl. τεκνία; in our lit. only in the voc. pl., used by Jesus in familiar, loving address to his disciples, or by a Christian apostle or teacher to his spiritual children τεκνία J 13: 33; 1 J 2: 12, 28; 3: 7, 18; 4: 4; 5: 21. τεκνία μου (Test. Reub. 1: 3 v.l.) Gal 4: 19 v.l.; 1 J 2: 1. M-M.*

τεκνογονέω (Philippus Epigr. [I AD]: Anth. Pal. 9, 22, 4 [of an animal]) *bear* or *beget children* (Appian., Basil. 1a §5; Achmes 63, 10) 1 Ti 5: 14; Dg 5: 6. M-M.*

τεκνογονία, ας, ἡ (Hippocr., Ep. 17, 21; Aristot., H.A. 7, 1, 8 p. 582a, 28; Stoic. III 158, 5; Galen: CMG V 9, 1 p. 27, 12) *the bearing of children* 1 Ti 2: 15 (RFalconer, JBL 60, '41, 375–9). M-M.*

τέκνον, ου, τό (Hom.+; inscr., pap., LXX, En., Ep. Arist., Philo, Joseph., Test. 12 Patr.) *child.*

1. lit.—**a.** *child* in relation to father and mother—**α.** without ref. to sex Mt 10: 21a (on the complete dissolution of family ties s. Lucian, Cal. 1); Mk 13: 12a; Lk 1: 7; Ac 7: 5; Rv 12: 4. Pl. Mt 7: 11; 10: 21b; 18: 25; 19: 29; 22: 24 (=σπέρμα, cf. Dt 25: 5f) but σπ. and τ. are contrasted Ro 9: 7; Mk 13: 12b; Lk 1: 17; 14: 26; 1 Cor 7: 14 (on the baptism of children s. HGWood, Enc. of Rel. and Ethics II '09, 392ff; JLeipoldt, D. urchr. Taufe '28, 73–8; AOepke, LIhmels-Festschr. '28, 84–100, ZNW 29, '30, 81–111 [against him HWindisch, ZNW 28, '29, 118–42]; JoachJeremias, Hat d. Urkirche d. Kindertaufe geübt? '38;² '49; also ZNW 40, '42, 243–5; AFrøvig, Tidsskr. f. Teol. og. K. 11, '40, 124–31; EMolland, Norsk Teol. T. 43, '42, 1–23; KBarth, Z. kirchl. Lehre v. d. Taufe² '43; F-JLeenhardt, Le Baptème chrétien '46; OCullmann, D. Tauflehre d. NT '48; P-HMenoud, Verbum Caro 2, '48, 15–26; HSchlier, ThLZ 72, '47, 321–6; GFleming, Baptism in the NT '49. Further WGKümmel, ThR 18, '50, 32–47): 2 Cor 12: 14a, b (as a symbol); 1 Th 2: 7 (symbol), 11 (symb.); 1 Ti 3: 4, 12; 5: 4 al. In the table of household duties (s. MDibelius Hdb. exc. after Col 4: 1; KWeidinger, Die Haustafeln '28) Eph 6: 1 (τὰ τέκνα voc.), 4; Col 3: 20 (τὰ τ. voc.), 21. In the case of φονεῖς τέκνων B 20: 2; D 5: 2, what follows shows that *murders* of their own *children* are meant.—The unborn embryo is also called τέκνον B 19: 5; D 2: 2 (like παιδίον: Hippocr., π. σαρκ. 6 vol. VIII 592 L.).

β. The sex of the child can be made clear by the context, *son* (Herodian 7, 10, 7; PGenève 74, 1ff; PAmh. 136, 1f; POxy. 930, 18; Jos., Ant. 14, 196) Mt 21: 28a; Phil 2: 22 (symbol); Rv 12: 5. The voc. τέκνον as an affectionate address to a son Mt 21: 28b; Lk 2: 48; 15: 31.

b. In a more general sense the pl. is used for *descendants, posterity* Ῥαχὴλ κλαίουσα τὰ τέκνα αὐτῆς Mt 2: 18 (cf. Jer 38: 15).—27: 25; Ac 2: 39; 13: 33. The rich man is addressed by his ancestor Abraham as τέκνον Lk 16: 25. τὰ τέκνα τῆς σαρκός *the physical descendants* Ro 9: 8a.

2. fig.—**a.** in the voc. gener. as a form of familiar address *my child, my son* (Herodian 1, 6, 4; Achilles Tat. 8, 4, 3. Directed to fully grown persons, Vi. Aesopi I c. 60, where a peasant addresses Aesop in this way) Mt 9: 2; Mk 2: 5.

b. of a spiritual child in relation to his master, apostle, or teacher (PGM 4, 475.—Eunap. p. 70 the sophist applies this term to his students) 2 Ti 1: 2; Phlm 10. τέκνον ἐν κυρίῳ 1 Cor 4: 17. τεκ. ἐν πίστει 1 Ti 1: 2. τεκ. κατὰ κοινὴν πίστιν Tit 1: 4. Pl. 1 Cor 4: 14; 2 Cor 6: 13; 3 J 4. In direct address (voc.): sing. (on dir. address in the sing. cf. Sir 2: 1 and oft.; Herm. Wr. 13, 2a, b; PGM 13, 226; 233; 742; 755.—S. also Norden, Agn. Th. 290f; Boll 138f): 1 Ti 1: 18; 2 Ti 2: 1; D 3: 1, 3–6; 4: 1. Pl.: Mk 10: 24; B 15: 4.—1 Cl 22: 1 understands the τέκνα of Ps 33: 12 as a word of Christ to the Christians. Cf. B 9: 3. The address in Gal 4: 19 is intended metaphorically for *children* for whom Paul is once more undergoing the pains of childbirth.—The adherents of false teachers are also called their τέκνα Rv 2: 23.

c. of the members of a church 2 J 1; 4; 13. In Hermas the venerable lady, who represents the church, addresses the believers as τέκνα Hv 3, 9, 1. In Gal 4: 31 οὐκ ἐσμὲν παιδίσκης τέκνα ἀλλὰ τῆς ἐλευθέρας is a fig. expr. for: 'we belong not to the OT community, but to the NT church'.

d. The parent-child relationship may involve simply an inner similarity of nature betw. the persons involved. In this sense there are children of Abraham Mt 3: 9; Lk 3: 8; J 8: 39; Ro 9: 7. True Christian women are children of Sarah 1 Pt 3: 6.

e. The believers are (τὰ) τέκνα (τοῦ) θεοῦ (cf. Is 63: 8; Wsd 16: 21; Sib. Or. 5, 202. On the subj. matter s. HHoltzmann, Ntl. Theologie I² '11, 54; Bousset, Rel.³ 377f; ADieterich, Mithrasliturgie '03, 141ff; Hdb. on J 1: 12; WGrundmann, Die Gotteskindschaft in d. Gesch. Jesu u. ihre relgesch. Voraussetzungen '38; WTwisselmann, D. Gotteskindsch. der Christen nach dem NT '39; SLegasse, Jésus et L'enfant [synopt.], '69), in Paul as those adopted by God Ro 8: 16f, 21; 9: 7, 8b (opp. σπέρμα); Phil 2: 15, s. also Eph 5: 1; in John as those begotten by God J 1: 12; 11: 52; 1 J 3: 1f, 10a; 5: 2. Corresp. τὰ τέκνα τοῦ διαβόλου 1 J 3: 10b (on this subj. s. Hdb. on J 8: 44).

f. Hebraistic expressions (Rdm.² p. 28; Mlt.-H. 441) are **α.** the designation of the inhabitants of a city as its τέκνα (Jo 2: 23; Zech 9: 13; Bar 4: 19, 21, 25 al.; 1 Macc 1: 38) Mt 23: 37; Lk 13: 34; 19: 44; Gal 4: 25.

β. its use w. abstract nouns τέκνα ἀγάπης B 9: 7; ἀγ. καὶ εἰρήνης 21: 9 (ἀγάπη I 2a). εὐφροσύνης 7: 1 (s. εὐφροσύνη). κατάρας 2 Pt 2: 14 (s. κατάρα). ὀργῆς Eph 2: 3 (Third Corinthians 3: 19 οὐ τέκνα δικαιοσύνης ἀλλὰ τέκνα ὀργῆς). ὑπακοῆς 1 Pt 1: 14. φωτός Eph 5: 8; cf. IPhld 2: 1. On the 'children of wisdom', i.e. those who attach themselves to her and let themselves be led by her Mt 11: 19 v.l.; Lk 7: 35 s. δικαιόω 2. M-M.

τεκνοτροφέω 1 aor. ἐτεκνοτρόφησα (since Aristot., H.A. 9, 40, 14 p. 625b, 20 [of the bee]; IG XII 5, 655, 8 [II/III

AD]) *bring up children*, i.e. care for them physically and spiritually (Epict. 1, 23, 3 after Epicurus) 1 Ti 5: 10. M-M.*

τεκνόω (since Hes., fgm. 138 R.; trag.; Phalaris, Ep. 103, 2; inscr., pap.) *beget* (Plut., Pericl. 24, 10; En. 15, 5; Jos., Ant. 1, 150; 2, 213), but *bear* (*a child*) (Jos., Ant. 4, 255) in Hb 11: 11 D.*

τέκτων, ονος, ὁ (Hom.+; pap., LXX; Jos., Ant. 15, 390; Sib. Or. 5, 404) *carpenter, wood-worker, builder* (acc. to Maximus Tyr. 15, 3c he makes ἄροτρα, acc. to Justin, Dial. 88 ἄροτρα καὶ ζυγά. Acc. to Epict. 1, 15, 2 he worked w. wood; acc. to Ael. Aristid. 46 p. 211 D. w. stone.—CCMcCown, ὁ τέκτων: Studies in Early Christ., ed. SJCase '28, 173–89). In Mt 13: 55 Jesus is called ὁ τοῦ τέκτονος υἱός, in Mk 6: 3 ὁ τέκτων (this difference may perh. be explained on the basis of a similar one having to do with Sophillus, the father of Sophocles. Aristoxenus, fgm. 115 calls him τέκτων, but the Vita Sophoclis I rejects this and will admit only that he may possibly have possessed τέκτονες as slaves).—HHöpfl, Nonne hic est fabri filius?: Biblica 4, '23, 41–55; ELombard, Charpentier ou maçon: RThPh '48, 4; EStauffer, Jeschua ben Mirjam (Mk 6: 3), MBlack-Festschr., '69, 119–28. M-M. B. 589.*

τέλειος, α, ον (Hom.+; inscr., pap., LXX; Ep. Arist. 15; Philo, Joseph.) *having attained the end* or *purpose, complete, perfect.*
    1. of things—a. in a good sense—α. adj. ἔργον Js 1: 4a (s. ἔργον 1b); cf. ISm 11: 2. δώρημα Js 1: 17 (s. δώρημα). νόμος vs. 25 (opp. the Mosaic law). ἀγάπη 1 J 4: 18. ἀνάλυσις 1 Cl 44: 5. γνῶσις 1 Cl 1: 2; B 1: 5. πρόγνωσις 1 Cl 44: 2. μνεία 56: 1. πίστις ISm 10: 2. χάρις 11: 1. νηστεία Hs 5, 3, 6. ναός B 4: 11. τελειοτέρα σκηνή (s. σκηνή) Hb 9: 11.
    β. subst. τὸ τέλειον *what is perfect* Ro 12: 2; perh. 1 Cor 13: 10 (opp. ἐκ μέρους. S. EHoffmann, Coniect. Neot. 3, '38, 28–31). ἐνάρετον καὶ τέλειον (someth.) *virtuous and perfect* IPhld 1: 2. W. the gen. τὸ τέλειον τῆς γνώσεως ἡμῶν *the full measure of our knowledge* B 13: 7. Pl. (Philo) τέλεια *what is perfect* ISm 11: 3b.
    b. in a bad sense—α. adj. ἁμαρτίαι B 8: 1; Hv 1, 2, 1. σκάνδαλον B 4: 3.—β. subst. τὸ τέλειον τῶν ἁμαρτιῶν *the full measure of the sins* 5: 11.
    2. of persons—a. of age *full-grown, mature, adult* (Aeschyl., Pla., X.+; inscr.; Philo; Jos., Ant. 19, 362).
    α. adj. ἀνὴρ τέλειος Eph 4: 13 (opp. νήπιοι, as Polyb. 5, 29, 2; Philo, Leg. All. 1, 94, Sobr. 9 νήπιον παιδίον πρὸς ἄνδρα τέλειον, Somn. 2, 10). μὴ παιδία γίνεσθε ταῖς φρεσίν, ἀλλὰ τῇ κακίᾳ νηπιάζετε, ταῖς δὲ φρεσὶν τέλειοι γίνεσθε 1 Cor 14: 20.
    β. subst. (Dio Chrys. 34[51], 8 οἱ τ.; Diogenes, Ep. 31, 3 οἱ τ.—οἱ παῖδες) τελείων ἐστὶν ἡ στερεὰ τροφή *solid food is* (only) *for adults* Hb 5: 14 (opp. νήπιος. οἱ τέλειοι 1 Cor 2: 6 is contrasted with νήπιοι 3: 1 by WBauer, Mündige u. Unmündige bei dem Ap. Paulus, Diss. Marburg, '02 (also Aufsätze u. Kleine Schriften, ed. GStrecker, '67, 124–30 et al.; cf. also GDelling, TW VIII 76–8.) But this may also be an example of
    b. τέλειος as a t.t. of the mystery religions, which refers to one initiated into the mystic rites (τελετή; s. τελειόω 3), *the initiate* (cf. Herm. Wr. 4, 4; Philod., Περὶ θεῶν 1, 24, 12 [ed. HDiels, ABA '15 p. 41; 93]; Iambl., Myst. 3, 7 p. 114 Parthey; Philo, Somn. 2, 234; Gnostics [WBousset Kyrios Christos² '21 p. 197, 1].—Rtzst., Mysterienrel.³ 133f; 338f; JWeiss, exc. after 1 Cor 3: 3, also p. xviiif, Das Urchristentum '17, 492; HAAKennedy, St. Paul and the Mystery Religions '13, 130ff; Clemen² 314). Phil 3: 15 and

Col 1: 28 also prob. belong here (s. MDibelius, Hdb. on both passages).—ChGuignebert, Quelques remarques sur la Perfection (τελείωσις) et ses voies dans le mystère paulinien: RHPhr 8, '28, 412–29; UWilckens, Weisheit u. Torheit, '59, 53–60 supports Reitzenstein against Bauer.
    c. of persons who are fully up to standard in a certain respect *perfect, complete, expert* (Tit. Asiae Minor. II 1, '20, no. 147, 4f ἰατρὸς τέλειος; ZPE 3, '68, 86: Didymus fgm. 281, 7 τέλειος γεώμετρος; Wsd 9: 6; 1 Ch 25: 8) τέλειος ἀθλητής IPol 1: 3. Esther is τελεία κατὰ πίστιν 1 Cl 55: 6. Jesus became τέλειος ἄνθρωπος *perfect man* ISm 4: 2.
    d. *perfect, fully developed* in a moral sense τέλειος ἀνήρ Js 3: 2 (s. RHöistad, Coniect. Neot. 9, '44, p. 22f). Mostly without a noun εἰ θέλεις τέλειος εἶναι Mt 19: 21 (EYarnold, TU 102, '68, 269–73). Cf. IEph 15: 2; D 1: 4; 6: 2. Pl. Mt 5: 48a; ISm 11: 3a. W. ὁλόκληροι Js 1: 4b. W. πεπληροφορημένοι Col 4: 12.
    e. God is termed τέλειος (Pind., Aeschyl.+; Theocr., Diod. S., Plut. et al.) Mt 5: 48b (cf. on this verse Hierocles 18 p. 459: the goal is τὴν πρὸς θεὸν ὁμοίωσιν κτήσασθαι [so oft. in Hierocles]; Marinus, Vi. Procli 18 ἵνα τὴν ὁμοίωσιν ἔχῃ πρὸς τὸν θεόν, ὅπερ τέλος ἐστὶ τὸ ἄριστον τῆς ψυχῆς).—RNFlew, The Idea of Perfection '34; FCGrant, The Earliest Gospel, '43; EFuchs, RBultmann-Festschr., '54 (Beih. ZNW 21), 130–6; PJDuPlessis, Teleios. The Idea of Perfection in the NT '59; KPrümm, Das NTliche Sprach- u. Begriffsproblem der Vollkommenheit, Biblica 44, '63, 76–92; AWikgren, Patterns of Perfection in Hb, NTS 6, '60, 159–67. M-M.*

τελειότης, ητος, ἡ *perfection, completeness* (Ps.-Pla., Def. 412B; Epict. 1, 4, 4; M. Ant. 5, 15, 2; PGM 7, 778; Wsd 6: 15; 12: 17; Philo) of love in its perfection 1 Cl 50: 1; 53: 5. Of *maturity* in contrast to the stage of elementary knowledge Hb 6: 1.—On σύνδεσμος τῆς τελειότητος Col 3: 14 s. σύνδεσμος 1b. M-M.*

τελειόω 1 aor. ἐτελείωσα; perf. τετελείωκα. Pass.: pf. τετελείωμαι; 1 aor. ἐτελειώθην; 1 fut. τελειωθήσομαι (Soph., Hdt.+; inscr., pap., LXX, Ep. Arist., Philo; Jos., Vi. 12 al. The form τελεόω. freq. in secular writers, occurs only Hb 10: 1 v.l.—Bl-D. §30, 2; Thackeray p. 82).
    1. *complete, bring to an end, finish, accomplish* (Dionys. Hal. 3, 69, 2 τῆς οἰκοδομῆς τὰ πολλὰ εἰργάσατο, οὐ μὴν ἐτελείωσε τὸ ἔργον; Polyb. 8, 36, 2; 2 Ch 8: 16; 2 Esdr 16 [Neh 6]: 3, 16) τὸ ἔργον J 4: 34; 17: 4; pl. 5: 36. πάντα 1 Cl 33: 6. τελειώσω τὸν δρόμον μου καὶ τὴν διακονίαν Ac 20: 24. ἁγνῶς τελειοῦν τὴν διακονίαν *complete the service as deacon in holiness* Hs 9, 26, 2. τὰς ἡμέρας *spend all the days* of the festival Lk 2: 43 (cf. Jos., Ant. 3, 201). Pass. ἵνα τελειωθῇ ἡ γραφή *in order that the scripture might receive its final fulfilment* J 19: 28 (perh. this belongs to 2c).—τελειῶσαί τινα *allow someone to reach his goal* (Hdt. 3, 86) pass. τῇ τρίτῃ τελειοῦμαι *on the third day I will reach my goal* Lk 13: 32 (hardly mid., 'bring to a close' [Iambl., Vi. Pyth. 158] w. 'my work' to be supplied. But s. 2d below).—This may also be the place for Hb 7: 19 (s. 2ea below); 11: 40 (s. 2d below).
    2. *bring to an end, bring to its goal* or *to accomplishment* in the sense of the overcoming or supplanting of an imperfect state of things by one that is free fr. objection.
    a. of Jesus: ἔπρεπεν αὐτῷ (i.e. τῷ θεῷ) διὰ παθημάτων τελειῶσαι (Ἰησοῦν) Hb 2: 10; pass., 5: 9; 7: 28. This is usu. understood to mean the *completion* and *perfection* of Jesus by the overcoming of earthly limitations (s. Windisch, Hdb. exc. on Hb 5: 9.—JKögel, Der Begriff τελειοῦν im Hb: MKähler-Festschr. '05, 35–68; OMichel,

D. Lehre von d. christl. Vollkommenheit nach d. Anschauung des Hb: StKr 106, '35, 333-55; FTorm, Om τελειοῦν i Hb: Sv. Ex. Årsb. 5, '40, 116-25; OMoe, ThZ 5, '49, 165ff). S. 3 below.

b. *bring to full measure, fill the measure of* τὶ someth. τὰς ἀποκαλύψεις καὶ τὰ ὁράματα Hv 4, 1, 3. ἐτελείωσαν κατὰ τῆς κεφαλῆς αὐτῶν τὰ ἁμαρτήματα GP 5: 17 (κατά I 2bγ).

c. *fulfill* of prophecies, promises, etc., which are not satisfied until they are fulfilled (τελείωσις 2.—Jos., Ant. 15, 4 θεοῦ τοὺς λόγους τελειώσαντος; Artem. 4, 47 p. 2; 228, 19 ἐλπίδας) ἡ πίστις πάντα ἐπαγγέλλεται, πάντα τελειοῖ Hm 9: 10; pass. *be fulfilled* ἐξαίφνης τελειωθήσεται τὸ βούλημα αὐτοῦ 1 Cl 23: 5.—MPol 16: 2a, b. The promises of the prophets find their fulfilment, by implication, in the gospel ISm 7: 2. This may be the place for J 19: 28 (so Bultmann.—S. 1 above).

d. *of the perfection* of just men who have gone on before, pass. (Wsd 4: 13; Philo, Leg. All. 3, 74 ὅταν τελειωθῇς καὶ βραβείων καὶ στεφάνων ἀξιωθῇς) πνεύματα δικαίων τετελειωμένων Hb 12: 23. So perh. also 11: 40 (s. 1 above) and Lk 13: 32 (s. 1 above).

e. *make perfect*—α. someone ὁ νόμος οὐδέποτε δύναται τοὺς προσερχομένους τελειῶσαι Hb 10: 1; likew. perh. (s. 1 above) 7: 19 (then οὐδέν would refer to mankind). κατὰ συνείδησιν τελειῶσαι τὸν λατρεύοντα 9: 9. Perh. 10: 14 (s. 3 below). Pass. *become perfect* (Zosimus: Hermet. IV p. 111, 15f) D 16: 2; ἔν τινι in someth. (Jos., Ant. 16, 6) ἐν (τῇ) ἀγάπῃ 1 J 4: 18; 1 Cl 49: 5; 50: 3. W. inf. foll. B 6: 19. ἵνα ὦσιν τετελειωμένοι εἰς ἕν *in order that they might attain perfect unity* J 17: 23.—Also in an unfavorable sense τελειωθῆναι τοῖς ἁμαρτήμασιν B 14: 5.—For Phil 3: 12 s. 3 below.

β. *someth.* The Lord is called upon, in the interest of his church τελειῶσαι αὐτὴν ἐν τῇ ἀγάπῃ σου D 10: 5. Pass. (Philo, Somn. 1, 131 ψυχὴ τελειωθεῖσα ἐν ἄθλοις ἀρετῶν) ἐκ τῶν ἔργων ἡ πίστις ἐτελειώθη *faith was perfected in good deeds* Js 2: 22. Of love 1 J 2: 5; 4: 12, 17. Cf. 2 Cor 12: 9 t.r.

3. As a term of the mystery religions *consecrate, initiate* pass. *be consecrated, become a* τέλειος (s. τέλειος 2b) Phil 3: 12 (though mng. 2eα is also poss.). Some of the Hb-passages (s. 2a; eα above) may belong here, esp. those in which a *consecration* of Jesus is mentioned 2: 10; 5: 9; 7: 28 (cf. ThHaering, Monatschr. für Pastoraltheol. 17, '21, 264-75. Against him ERiggenbach, NKZ 34, '23, 184-95 and Haering once more, ibid. 386-9.—EKaesemann, D. wand. Gsvolk '39, 82-90; GAvdBerghvEysinga, De Brief aan de Hebreën en de oudchristelijke Gnosis: NThT 28, '39, 301-30). M-M.*

τελείως adv. (this form in Isocr. 13, 18; Ps.-Pla., Def. 411 D; Aristot. et al.; Polyb. 6, 24, 7; Hero Alex. I p. 20, 25; PPetr. III p. 114 [III BC]; PFlor. 93, 27; LXX [Thackeray p. 82]; Philo) *fully, perfectly, completely, altogether* ἔχειν τὴν πίστιν IEph 14: 1. ἐλπίζειν 1 Pt 1: 13. λειτουργεῖν 1 Cl 9: 2. φεύγειν B 4: 1. μισεῖν τι 4: 10. φανεροῦσθαι Dg 9: 2. ἔργον ἀπαρτίζειν IEph 1: 1. ἀπαρνεῖσθαι ISm 5: 2. ἔχειν τελείως περί τινος *have received full enlightenment concerning someth.* B 10: 10. M-M. and suppl.*

τελείωσις, εως, ἡ (since Hippocr. VII 436; 448 L.; Epicurus p. 38, 5 Us.; Aristot.; inscr., pap., LXX, En., Ep. Arist.; Philo, Aet. M. 71; 99; Jos., Ant. 19, 199 in a different sense)—**1.** *perfection* (En. 25, 4) Hb 7: 11.—**2.** *fulfilment* of a promise (Jdth 10: 9; Philo, Mos. 2, 288.—τελειόω 2c) Lk 1: 45. M-M.*

τελειωτής, οῦ, ὁ (hapax legomenon) *perfecter* (opp. ἀρχηγός, q.v. 3) τῆς πίστεως Hb 12: 2 (AWikgren, NTS 6, '60, 159-67).*

τέλεον neut. acc. sing. of τέλεος (=τέλειος; cf. Sib. Or. 3, 117) used as an adv. (Περὶ ὕψους c. 41, 1; Ael. Aristid. 33 p. 635 D.; Lucian, Merc. Cond. 5; Appian, Bell. Civ. 1, 8 §34; BGU 903, 12 [II AD]; PFay. 106, 21; 3 Macc 1: 22; Jos., Bell. 4, 285) *fully, altogether, in the end* Dg 2: 5.*

τελεσφορέω (Theophr. et al.; 4 Macc 13: 20; Philo; Jos., Ant. 1, 140) *bear fruit to maturity* (Jülicher, Gleichn. 530.—Cf. Ocellus Luc. [II BC] c. 16 Harder ['26]; Epict. 4, 8, 36) Lk 8: 14, 15 v.l. M-M.*

τελευταῖος, α, ον (Aeschyl., Hdt.+; inscr., pap., LXX, Philo; Jos., Ant. 9, 265, C. Ap. 1, 278) *last* τελευταία ἡμέρα (Demosth. et al.; Epict. 2, 23, 21; IG IV² 1, 123, 128 [IV BC] ἐν ταῖς τελευταίαις ἀμέραις) τῶν ἀζύμων GP 14: 58.*

τελευτάω (Hom.+) fut. τελευτήσω; 1 aor. ἐτελεύτησα; perf. ptc. τετελευτηκώς; in our lit. only intr. *come to an end* (Aeschyl.+) Papias 4, and almost always=*die* (Aeschyl., Hdt.+; inscr., pap., LXX; En. 9, 10; Ep. Arist. 268; Philo, Joseph.—Bl-D. §480, 2) Mt 2: 19; 9: 18; 22: 25; Lk 7: 2; J 11: 39; Ac 2: 29; 7: 15; Hb 11: 22; 1 Cl 39: 6 (Job 4: 21 v.l.); Papias 3. Of the phoenix 1 Cl 25: 2f. After Is 66: 24 of the worm in hell: Mk 9: (44, 46), 48; 2 Cl 7: 6; 17: 5. θανάτῳ τελευτάτω *let him die the death=surely die* (=יוּמָת Ex 21: 17. But s. also schol. on Soph., Ajax 516 p. 46 Papag. τελευτᾶν θανάτῳ) Mt 15: 4 (cf. Ex 21: 16); Mk 7: 10. M-M.*

τελευτή, ῆς, ἡ *end,* a euphemism for *death* (Pind., Thu. +; pap., LXX, Philo; Jos., Ant. 8, 190; Test. 12 Patr.; Sib. Or. 3, 633. W. βιότοιο as early as Il. 7, 104) Mt 2: 15. M-M.*

τελέω fut. τελέσω; 1 aor. ἐτέλεσα; pf. τετέλεκα. Pass.: perf. τετέλεσμαι; 1 aor. ἐτελέσθην; 1 fut. τελεσθήσομαι (Hom.+; inscr., pap., LXX, Ep. Arist., Philo; Jos., Bell. 1, 609 al.; Sib. Or. 3, 758 al.).

1. *bring to an end, finish, complete* τὶ someth. ταῦτα Hs 8, 2, 5. τὸν δρόμον (Il. 23, 373; 768; Soph., El. 726) 2 Ti 4: 7. τοὺς λόγους τούτους Mt 7: 28; 19: 1; 26: 1. τὰς παραβολὰς ταύτας 13: 53. τὴν μαρτυρίαν Rv 11: 7. τὴν ἐξήγησιν Hv 3, 7, 4. τὰ γράμματα 2, 1, 4. τελέσας τὴν χαράκωσιν *when he had finished the fencing* Hs 5, 2, 3. τελεῖν πάντα τὰ κατὰ τὸν νόμον Lk 2: 39 (τελ. πάντα as Jos., Ant. 16, 318). τελ. τὰς πόλεις τοῦ Ἰσραήλ *finish* (*going through*) *the cities of Israel* Mt 10: 23 (on this pass. KWeiss, Exegetisches z. Irrtumslosigkeit u. Eschatologie Jesu Christi '16, 184-99; JDupont, NovT 2, '58, 228-44; AFeuillet, CBQ 23, '61, 182-98; MKünzi, Das Naherwartungslogion Mt 10: 23, '70 [history of interp.]). Foll. by a ptc. to designate what is finished (Bl-D. §414, 2; Rob. 1121; cf. Josh 3: 17) ἐτέλεσεν διατάσσων Mt 11: 1. Cf. Lk 7: 1 v.l.; Hv 1, 4, 1.—Pass. *be brought to an end, be finished, completed* of the building of the tower (cf. 2 Esdr [Ezra] 5: 16; 16 [Neh 6]: 15) Hv 3, 4, 1f; 3, 5, 5; 3, 9, 5; s 9, 5, 1; 9, 10, 2 (τὸ ἔργον). Of time *come to an end, be over* (Hom.+; Aristot., H.A. 7, 1 p. 580a, 14 ἐν τοῖς ἔτεσι τοῖς δὶς ἑπτὰ τετελεσμένοις; Lucian, Alex. 38) Lk 2: 6 D; Rv 20: 3, 5, 7. πάντα τετέλεσται J 19: 28 (GDalman, Jesus-Jeschua, 1922, 211-18 [Engl. transl. PLevertoff '29, same pages].—Diagoras of Melos in Sext. Emp., Adv. Math. 9, 55 κατὰ δαίμονα κ. τύχην πάντα τελεῖται= 'everything is accomplished acc. to the will of the god and of fate'; an anonymous writer of mimes [II AD] in OCrusius, Herondas⁵ [p. 110-16] l. 175 τοῦτο τετέλεσται); cf. τετέλεσται used absolutely in vs. 30 (if these two verses are to be taken as referring to the carrying out [s. 2 below] of divine ordinances contained in the Scriptures, cf. Diod. S. 20, 26, 2 τετελέσθαι τὸν χρησμόν=the oracle had been fulfilled; Ael. Aristid. 48, 7 K.=24 p. 467 D.: μέγας ὁ Ἀσκληπιός· τετέλεσται τὸ πρόσταγμα). Willibald Schmidt, De Ultimis Morientium Verbis, Diss. Marburg '14; OCullmann, ThZ 4, '48, 370, both chronological and theol. Diod. S. 15, 87, 6 reports the four last sayings of Epaminondas, two in indirect discourse and the other two in direct. S. also the last words of Philip s.v. πληρόω 5.—ἡ δύναμις ἐν ἀσθενείᾳ τελεῖται power finds its consummation or reaches perfection in (the presence of) weakness 2 Cor 12: 9. The passives in Rv 10: 7; 15: 1, 8; 17: 17 belong under 2 as well as under 1.

2. *carry out, accomplish, perform, fulfill, keep* τὶ *someth.* (Hom.+. Also rites, games, processions, etc., dedicated to a divinity or ordained by him: Eur., Bacch. 474 τὰ ἱερά; Pla., Laws 775A; X., Resp. Lac. 13, 5; Plut., Mor. 671 al.) τὸν νόμον *carry out the demands of, keep the law* Ro 2: 27; Js 2: 8. τὴν ἐντολήν Hs 5, 2, 4 (Jos., Bell. 2, 495 τὰς ἐντολάς). τὸ ἔργον (Theogn. 914; Apollon. Rhod. 4, 742; Sir 7: 25) Hs 2: 7a; 5, 2, 7. τὴν διακονίαν m 2: 6a, b; 12, 3, 3; s 2: 7b; pass. Hm 2: 6c. τὰς διακονίας Hs 1: 9. τὴν νηστείαν 5, 3, 8. ἐπιθυμίαν σαρκὸς τελεῖν *carry out what the flesh desires, satisfy one's physical desires* (Artem. 3, 22; Achilles Tat. 2, 13, 3 αὐτῷ τὴν ἐπιθυμίαν τελέσαι) Gal 5: 16. ὡς ἐτέλεσαν πάντα τὰ περὶ αὐτοῦ γεγραμμένα *when they had carried out everything that was written* (in the Scriptures) *concerning him* Ac 13: 29 (Appian, Bell. Civ. 3, 59 §243 τὸ κεκριμένον τ.=carry out what was decided upon). Pass. Lk 18: 31; 22: 37 (s. above 1, end). ἕως ὅτου τελεσθῇ *until it* (the baptism) *is accomplished* Lk 12: 50. ἵνα ὁ τύπος τελεσθῇ *in order that the type might be fulfilled* B 7: 3.

3. *pay* (class., pap.; Jos., Ant. 2, 192 al.) φόρους (Ps.-Pla., Alc. 1 p. 123a τὸν φόρον; Appian, Syr. 44 §231; PFay. 36, 14 [111/12 AD]; Philo, Agr. 58; Jos., Ant. 15, 106) Ro 13: 6. τὰ δίδραχμα Mt 17: 24. M-M. B. 797.*

τέλος, ους, τό (Hom.+; inscr., pap., LXX, Ep. Arist., Philo, Joseph., Test. 12 Patr.).

1. *end*—a. in the sense *termination, cessation* (Nicol. Dam.: 90 fgm. 130 §139 Jac. τέλος τ. Βίου Καίσαρος; Maximus Tyr. 13, 9d ἀπιστίας) τῆς βασιλείας αὐτοῦ οὐκ ἔσται τέλος Lk 1: 33. μήτε ἀρχὴν ἡμερῶν μήτε ζωῆς τέλος ἔχων Hb 7: 3. τὸ τέλος τοῦ καταργουμένου *the end of the fading* (splendor) 2 Cor 3: 13. τέλος νόμου Χριστός Ro 10: 4 (perh. 1c). πάντων τὸ τέλος ἤγγικεν *the end of all things is near* 1 Pt 4: 7. τὸ τ. Ἰερουσαλήμ GP 7: 25. τὸ τέλος κυρίου Js 5: 11 is oft. (fr. Augustine to ABischoff, ZNW 7, '06, 274-9) incorrectly taken to mean *the end*=the death (this is what τέλος means e.g. in Appian, Syr. 64 §342, Bell. Civ. 1, 107 §501; 3, 98 §408; Arrian, Anab. 3, 22, 2; 7, 24, 1) *of the Lord* Jesus (s. 1c below). τέλος ἔχειν *have an end, be at an end* (X., An. 6, 5, 2; Pla., Phaedr. 241D, Rep. 3 p. 392C; Diod. S. 14, 18, 8; 16, 91, 2) Mk 3: 26 (opp. στῆναι). The possibility of repenting ἔχει τέλος *is at an end* Hv 2, 2, 5. Of the consummation that comes to prophecies when they are fulfilled (Xenophon Eph. 5, 1, 13; Jos., Ant. 2, 73; 4, 125; 10, 35; Sib. Or. 3, 211): revelations Hv 3, 3, 2. So perh. τὸ περὶ ἐμοῦ τέλος ἔχει *the references* (in the Scriptures) *to me are being fulfilled* Lk 22: 37; also poss. is *my life's work is at an end* (cf. Diod. S. 20, 95, 1 τέλος ἔχειν of siege-machines, the construction of which entailed a great

deal of hard work: *be completed*; Plut., Mor. 615E; Jos., Vi. 154).

b. *the last part, close, conclusion* esp. of the last things, the final act in the cosmic drama (Sb 8422, 10 [7 BC] τοῦτο γάρ ἐστι τέλος) Mt 24: 6, 14; Mk 13: 7; Lk 21: 9; PK 2 p. 13, 22. Perh. 1 Cor 15: 24, if ἔσται is to be supplied w. εἶτα τὸ τέλος *then the end will come* (so JHéring, RHPhr 12, '33, 300-20; s. below, 1da and 2). ἔχει τέλος *the end is here* Hv 3, 8, 9. On τὰ τέλη τῶν αἰώνων 1 Cor 10: 11 cf. αἰών 2b and s. c and 3 below; also MMBogle, ET 67, '56, 246f: τ.='mystery'.—PVolz, D. Eschatologie d. jüd. Gemeinde im ntl. Zeitalter '34; Bousset, Rel.³ 202-301; EHaupt, Die eschatol. Aussagen Jesu in den synopt. Evangelien 1895; HBSharman, The Teaching of Jesus about the Future acc. to the Synopt. Gospels '09; FSpitta, Die grosse eschatol. Rede Jesu: StKr 82, '09, 348-401; EvDobschütz, The Eschatology of the Gospels '10, Zur Eschatol. der Ev.: StKr 84, '11, 1-20; PCorssen, Das apokalypt. Flugblatt in der synopt. Überl.: Wochenschr. für klass. Philol. 32, '15, nos. 30-1; 33-4; DVölter, Die eschat. Rede Jesu: SchThZ 32, '15, 180-202; KWeiss (s. τελέω 1); JWeiss, Das Urchristent. '17, 60-98; Joach Jeremias, Jesus als Weltvollender '30; WGKümmel, Die Eschatologie der Ev.: ThBl 15, '36, 225-41, Verheissg. u. Erfüllg. '45; CJCadoux, The Historic Mission of Jesus '41 (eschat. of the synoptics); HPreisker, Das Ethos des Urchristentums '49; AStrobel, Untersuchungen zum eschat. Verzögerungsproblem, '61. Billerb. IV 799-976. Cf. also ἀνάστασις 2b, end.—In contrast to ἀρχή: B 1: 6a, b; IEph 14: 1a, b; IMg 13: 1. Of God Rv 1: 8 t.r.; 21: 6; 22: 13 (ἀρχή 1d).

c. *end* or *goal* toward which a movement is being directed, *outcome* (Dio Chrys. 67[17], 3; Epict. 1, 30, 4; 3, 24, 7; Maximus Tyr. 20, 3b; Jos., Ant. 9, 73; Test. Ash. 1: 3) Mt 26: 58. τὸ τέλος κυρίου *the outcome which the Lord brought about* in the case of Job's trials Js 5: 11 (Diod. S. 20, 13, 3 τὸ δαιμόνιον τοῖς ὑπερηφάνως διαλογιζομένοις τὸ τέλος τῶν κατελπισθέντων εἰς τοὐναντίον μετατίθησιν=the divinity, in the case of the arrogant, turns the outcome of what they hoped for to the opposite. —On Js 5: 11 s. 1a above). τὸ τέλος τῆς παραγγελίας ἐστὶν ἀγάπη *the preaching has love as its aim* 1 Ti 1: 5 (τ.='goal' or 'purpose': Epict. 1, 20, 15; 4, 8, 12; Diog. L. 2, 87). Perh. this is the place for Ro 10: 4, in the sense that Christ is the goal and the termination of the law at the same time, somewhat in the sense of Gal 3: 24f (schol. on Pla., Leg. 625D τέλος τῶν νόμων=goal of the laws; Plut., Mor. 780E δίκη . . . νόμου τέλος ἐστί; FFlückiger, ThZ 11, '55, 153-7); s. 1a.—Esp. also of the final *goal* toward which men and things are striving, of the *outcome* or *destiny* which awaits them in accordance w. their nature (Aelian, V.H. 3, 43; Alciphr. 4, 7, 8; Procop. Soph., Ep. 154; Philo, Exs. 162, Virt. 182; Test. Ash. 6: 4) τὸ τέλος ἐκείνων θάνατος . . . τὸ τέλος ζωὴν αἰώνιον Ro 6: 21f. Cf. 2 Cor 11: 15; Phil 3: 19 (HKoester, NTS 8, '61/'62, 325f): perh. a play on a mystery term; 1 Pt 4: 17; Hb 6: 8. κομιζόμενοι τὸ τέλος τῆς πίστεως 1 Pt 1: 9. τέλος τὰ πράγματα ἔχει *all things have a goal or final destiny* (i.e. death or life) IMg 5: 1 (τέλος ἔχειν as Plut., Mor. 382E; Polyaenus 4, 2, 11 τέλος οὐκ ἔσχεν ἡ πρᾶξις=did not reach its goal; Jos., C. Ap. 2, 181, Ant. 17, 185.—Ael. Aristid. 52 p. 597 D.: τὸ τέλος πάντων πραγμάτων). εἰς τέλος εἶναι *be at=reach the goal* IRo 1: 1 (εἰς for ἐν; cf. εἰς 9).

d. adverbial expressions—a. adv. acc. τὸ τέλος *finally* (Pla. et al.; BGU 1024 VII, 23; Bl-D. §160; cf. Rob. 486-8.—The usual thing in this case is τέλος without the art.) 1 Pt 3: 8. εἶτα τὸ τέλος 1 Cor 15: 24 is classed here by Hofmann²; FCBurkitt, JTS 17, '16, 384f; KBarth, Die Auferstehung der Toten² '26, 96 (s. 1b above and 2 below).

β. *to the end, to the last*: ἄχρι τέλους Hb 6: 11; Rv 2: 26; ἕως τέλους (Da 6: 27 Theod.) 1 Cor 1: 8; 2 Cor 1: 13 (here, too, it means *to the end*=until the parousia [Windisch, Sickenberger, ASV '01] rather than 'fully' [Ltzm., Hdb.; RSV '46]); Hs 9, 27, 3; μέχρι τέλους (Phocylides [VI BC] 17 Diehl² ἐξ ἀρχῆς μέχρι τέλους; Charito 4, 7, 8; Appian, Mithrid. 112 §550; Polyaenus 4, 6, 11; POxy. 416, 3; PTebt. 420, 18; Wsd 16: 5; 19: 1; Jos., Vi. 406) Hb 3: 6, 14; Dg 10: 7. S. also εἰς τέλος (γ below).

γ. εἰς τέλος *in the end, finally* (Hdt. 3, 40 et al.; PTebt. 38, 11 [113 BC]; 49, 12; Gen 46: 4; Ps.-Clem., Hom. 18, 2) Lk 18: 5. σωθῆναι 2 Cl 19: 3.—*To the end, until the end* (Epict. 1, 7, 17; Jos., Ant. 19, 96) Mt 10: 22; 24: 13; Mk 13: 13; IEph 14: 2; IRo 10: 3.—*Forever, through all eternity* (Dionys. Hal. 13, 88, 3; Ps 9: 19; 76: 9; 1 Ch 28: 9; Da 3: 34) ἔφθασεν ἐπ᾽ αὐτοὺς ἡ ὀργὴ εἰς τέλος 1 Th 2: 16 (s. also below and cf. Test. Levi 6: 11). εἰς τέλος ἀπολέσαι τὴν ζωήν *lose one's life forever* Hs 8, 8, 5b.—*Decisively, extremely, fully, altogether* (Polyb. 1, 20, 7; 10; 12, 27, 3 and oft.; Diod. S. 18, 57, 1 ταπεινωθέντες εἰς τ.= ruined utterly; Lucian, Philop. 14; Appian, Bell. Mithr. 44 §174; Dit., Or. 90, 12 [II BC]; PTebt. 38, 11 [II BC]; 49, 11; 793 [s. οὖς]; Josh 8: 24; 2 Ch 12: 12; Ps 73: 1; Job 6: 9; PsSol 1: 1; Jos., Vi. 24; Diodorus on Ps 51: 7 Migne XXXIII p. 1589b εἰς τέλος τουτέστι παντελῶς) 1 Th 2: 16 (*forever* is also poss.; s. above); B 4: 6; 10: 5; 19: 11. ἱλαρὰ εἰς τέλος ἦν she was *quite cheerful* Hv 3, 10, 5. Cf. 3, 7, 2; m 12, 2, 3; s 6, 2, 3; 8, 6, 4; 8, 8, 2; 5a; 8, 9, 9, 14, 2.—For εἰς τέλος ἠγάπησεν αὐτούς J 13: 1 s. εἰς 3.

δ. ἐν τέλει *at the end* (opp. πρὸ αἰώνων IMg 6: 1.

2. *rest, remainder* (Aristot., De Gen. Anim. 1, 18 p. 725b, 8; Is 19: 15. Of a military formation Arrian, Tact. 10, 5; 18, 4), if τὸ τέλος 1 Cor 15: 24 is to be taken, w. JWeiss and Ltzm., of a third and last group (τάγμα 1b; s. 1b and 1da above).

3. *(indirect) tax, customs duties* (X., Pla. et al.; inscr., pap.; 1 Macc 10: 31; 11: 35; Jos., Ant. 12, 141) ἀποδιδόναι τὸ τέλος Ro 13: 7b; cf. a (w. φόρος as Appian, Sicil. 2, 6, Bell. Civ. 2, 13 §47; Vi. Aesopi W c. 92; Ps.-Clem., Hom. 10, 22). λαμβάνειν τέλη ἀπό τινος Mt 17: 25 (w. κῆνσος).—τὰ τέλη τ. αἰώνων 1 Cor 10: 11 is transl. the (spiritual) *revenues of the ages* by ASouter (Pocket Lex. of the NT '16, s.v. τέλος) and PMacpherson, ET 55, '43/'44, 222 (s. 1b above).—GDelling, TW VIII, 50–88: τέλος and related words, also ZNW 55, '64, 26–42=Studien zum NT, '70, 17–31. M-M. B. 802; 979.*

τελωνεῖον s. τελώνιον (now held itacistic spelling).

τελώνης, ου, ὁ (Aristoph., Aeschin.+; inscr., pap., ostraca; formed of τέλος+ὠνέομαι) *tax-collector, revenue officer* (s. τέλος 3; Gdspd., Probs. 28). The τελ. in the synoptics (the only part of our lit. where they are mentioned) are not the holders (Lat. *publicani*) of the 'tax-farming' contracts themselves, but subordinates (Lat. *portitores*) hired by them; the higher officials were usu. foreigners, but their underlings were taken fr. the native population as a rule. The prevailing system of tax collection afforded the collector many opportunities to exercise his greed and unfairness. Hence they were particularly hated and despised as a class (cf. these condemnatory judgments on the τελῶναι: Demochares [300 BC] 75 fgm. 4 Jac. τελ. βάναυσος; Xeno Com. vol. III p. 390 Kock πάντες τελῶναι ἅρπαγες; Herodas 6, 64; Diogenes, Ep. 36, 2; Lucian, Necyom. 11; Artem. 1, 23; 4, 42; 57; Ps.-

Dicaearchus p. 143, 7 Fuhr.; Iambl. Erot. 34; Cicero, De Off. 1, 150; UPZ 113, 9; 16 [156 BC]; Wilcken, Ostraka I 568f; PPrinceton Univ. II '36 no. 20, 1ff [on this OWReinmuth, Class. Philology 31, '36, 146–62]; Philo, Spec. Leg. 2, 93ff. Rabbinic material in Schürer I⁴ 479, 116; Billerb. I 377f). The strict Jew was further offended by the fact that the tax-collector had to maintain continual contact w. Gentiles in the course of his work; this rendered a Jewish tax-collector ceremonially unclean. The prevailing attitude is expressed in these combinations: τελῶναι καὶ ἁμαρτωλοί (s. on ἁμαρτωλός 2) Mt 9: 10f; 11: 19; Mk 2: 15, 16a, b (RPesch, BRigaux-Festschr., '70, 63–87); Lk 5: 30; 7: 34; 15: 1 (JoachJeremias, ZNW 30, '31, 293–300). ὁ ἐθνικὸς καὶ ὁ τελώνης Mt 18: 17. οἱ τελῶναι καὶ αἱ πόρναι 21: 31f. As typically selfish 5: 46.—Lk 3: 12 (Sb 8072, 6 [II AD] the prefect reprimands τελ. who demand τὰ μὴ ὀφιλόμενα αὐτοῖς); 5: 29; 7: 29. The Pharisee and the tax-collector Lk 18: 10f, 13. Μαθθαῖος ὁ τελώνης Mt 10: 3 (Jos., Bell. 2, 287 Ἰωάννης ὁ τελώνης). τελ. ὀνόματι Λευί Lk 5: 27 (cf. Λευί 4).—Schürer I rev. Eng. ed. '73, 372ff; JMarquardt, Staatsverw. II² 1884, 261ff; 289ff; AHJones, Studies in Rom. Gov't. and Law, '60, 101–14; JRDonahue, CBQ 33, '71, 39–61.—OMichel, TW VIII, 88–106. M-M.*

τελώνιον, ου, τό *revenue* or *tax office* (Posidippus Com. [III BC], fgm. 13; Strabo 16, 1, 27; Dit., Or. 496, 9; 525, 10; UPZ 112 VIII, 3 [203/2 BC]; Wilcken, Chrest. 223, 3) Mt 9: 9; Mk 2: 14; Lk 5: 27; GEb 2 (PPetr. II 11[2], 3 ἐπὶ τελώνιον). M-M.*

τέξομαι s. τίκτω.

τέρας, ατος, τό (Hom.+; LXX, Philo, Joseph.) *prodigy, portent, omen, wonder* in our lit. only pl. and combined w. σημεῖα; s. σημεῖον 2a, b, c, where all the passages containing τέρατα are given (Appian, Bell. Civ. 1, 83 §377 τέρατα πολλὰ ἐγίνοντο, i.e., terrifying portents caused by a divinity [τὸ δαιμόνιον, ὁ θεός] that foretell the destructive results of Sulla's campaign in Italy).—PStein, ΤΕΡΑΣ, Diss. Marburg '09. M-M.*

τερατεία, ας, ἡ (Aristoph., Isocr.+) *illusion, jugglery, untrustworthy talk* (Aristoph., Isocr.+; Polyb. 2, 17, 6; Diod. S. 4, 51, 3; Heraclit. Sto. 27 p. 42, 10; Jos., Bell. 1, 630) Dg 8: 4 (w. πλάνη).*

τέρμα, ατος, τό (Hom.+; Dialekt-Inschr. 711; PFay. 217 βίου τέρμα; Sb 5829, 12; 3 Km 7: 32; Wsd 12: 27; Sib. Or. 3, 756) *end, limit, boundary* (Hdt. 7, 54 ἐπὶ τέρμα τ. Εὐρώπης γίνεσθαι; Philostrat., Vi. Apoll. 5, 4; En. 106, 8; Philo, Mos. 1, 2 τὰ τ. γῆς τέρματα; Jos., Bell. 7, 284) τὸ τέρμα τῆς δύσεως *the farthest limits of the west* 1 Cl 5: 7 (the var. interpretations of the expr. are dealt w. by Dubowy [s.v. Σπανία] 17–79). On the question of Paul's journey to Spain s. the lit. s.v. Σπανία.*

τερπνός, ή, όν (Tyrtaeus [VII BC]+; LXX; Sib. Or. 4, 191) *delightful, pleasant, pleasing* 1 Cl 7: 3 (cf. Ps 132: 1). Subst. (τὸ τερπνόν Polyb. 1, 4, 11; Ep. Arist. 77; Jos., Ant. 19, 181; τὰ τ. Isocr. 1, 21; Philo, Somn. 2, 209) τὰ τερπνὰ τοῦ κόσμου *the delights* or *pleasures of the world* IRo 6: 1 (so Zahn, w. the Gk. witnesses to the uninterpolated text, though Lghtf., Funk, Hilgenfeld, GKrüger and Bihlmeyer w. the interpolated Gk. and the Lat. and Syr. versions prefer πέρατα).*

Τέρτιος, ου, ὁ (Gk. inscr. fr. I AD in GEdmundson, The Church in Rome '13 p. 22, 1) *Tertius,* a Christian brother helpful to Paul; in Ro 16: 22 he is ὁ γράψας τὴν ἐπιστολήν, and sends personal greetings to the church for which the letter is intended. Cf. Ro subscr. M-M.*

Τέρτουλλος, ου, ὁ (lit., inscr., coins) *Tertullus.* The name of the Roman eparch under whom Onesimus suffered martyrdom is spelled this way in Phlm subscr.*

Τέρτυλλος, ου, ὁ (CIG 3001; 4337; IG VII 4173; XIV 826, 44; CIL III 14 428; 14 447. On the spelling cf. WDittenberger, Her. 6, 1872, 293f; Bl-D. §41, 1) *Tertullus,* attorney for those who accused Paul before Felix the procurator Ac 24: 1f.—StLösch, D. Dankesrede des T.: ThQ 112, '31, 295–319. M-M.*

τεσσαράκοντα (Hom. +; Ep. Arist. 105; Jos., Ant. 11, 15 al.; Test. 12 Patr.; Sib. Or. 8, 148), though in the NT the oldest witnesses fr. 𝔓⁴⁶ on at 2 Cor 11: 24 have throughout the Ionic-Hellenistic form **τεσσεράκοντα** (so Dit., Syll.³ 344, 45 [c. 303 BC]; LXX in the uncials [Thackeray 62f; 73], but hardly in the autographs, since even in I AD the pap. almost never have τεσσεράκοντα; one exception is PSI 317, 4 [95 AD].—Bl-D. §29, 1; Mlt.-H. 66f; Tdf., Proleg. 80; W-H., App. 158) indecl. *forty,* often of days (Dicaearchus, fgm. 35b W. of Pythagoras: ἀποθανεῖν τετταράκοντα ἡμέρας ἀσιτήσαντα; Diod. S. 17, 111, 6 ἐν ἡμ. τεττ.; Jos., Ant. 18, 277; Procop., Bell. 6, 15, 7) Mt 4: 2a, b; Mk 1: 13; Lk 4: 2 (including the nights as Ps.-Callisth. 3, 26, 7 p. 127, 3); J 2: 20; Ac 1: 3 al. (eight times in all; PMenoud, OCullmann-Festschr., '62, 148–56); 2 Cor 11: 24 (cf. Jos., Ant. 4, 238; 248); Hb 3: 10 (Ps 94: 10), 17; Rv 7: 4 al. (six times); 1 Cl 53: 2a, b; B 4: 7a, b (Ex 34: 28); 14: 2 (cf. Ex 34: 28); Hs 9, 4, 3; 9, 5, 4; 9, 15, 4; 9, 16, 5 (in these Hermas passages 'forty' appears as a numeral: μ').—EKönig, Die Zahl 40 u. Verwandtes: ZDMG 61, '07, 913–17; WHRoscher, Die Zahl 40 im Glauben, Brauch u. Schrifttum der Semiten: Abh. der Sächs. Ges. d. W. 27, no. IV '08, Die Tessarakontaden: Ber. der Sächs. Ges. d. W. 61, '09, 21–206; KSchubert, The Dead Sea Community, tr. Doberstein '59 (symbolism of '40' in Qumran). M-M.

τεσσαρακονταετής, ές (Hes., Op. 441) or **τεσσερακονταετής** (Sb 8246, 9; 21 [340 AD]) see s.v. τεσσαράκοντα; on the accent s. ἑκατονταετής; *forty years (old)* τεσσ. χρόνος *a period of forty years* (Appian, Mithrid. 118 §583 τεσσ. χρ.; cf. διετὴς χρ.: Hdt. 2, 2; Jos., Ant. 2, 74) Ac 7: 23; 13: 18.*

τέσσαρες (Hom. +) neut. τέσσαρα or τέσσερα (the latter is practically never found in inscr. and pap. [Mayser p. 57 w. lit.; Rdm.² p. 43], but on the other hand is predom. in the LXX-mss.). Gen. τεσσάρων (Ep. Arist.; Jos., Vi. 75. —τὸ διὰ τεσσάρων as a musical expr.: Dionys. Hal., Comp. Verb. 11). Dat. τέσσαρσιν (Ac 11: 5 D τέτρασιν; Bl-D. §63, 1 app.). Acc. masc. τέσσαρας (τέσσαρες as acc. [pap., LXX; for both s. Thackeray 148f] is poorly attested for the NT [Bl-D. §46, 2; Mlt.-H. 130; 170]) *four* Mt 24: 31 (ἄνεμος 1); Mk 2: 3; 13: 27 (ἄνεμος 1); Lk 2: 37; J 11: 17; 19: 23; Ac 10: 11 al. (six times in all); Rv 4: 4a, b al. (29 times); Hv 1, 4, 1 al. (13 times); D 10: 5 (ἄνεμος 1). On τέσσερα ζῷα Rv 4: 6 cf. Lohmeyer ad loc.; FJDölger, Die Sonne der Gerechtigkeit u. der Schwarze '18. M-M.

τεσσαρεσκαιδέκατος, η, ον (Hippocr., Epid. 6, 3, 2 L.; Dit., Syll.³ 1112, 14; PEleph. 1, 1 [311 BC]; POsl. 40, 35 [150 AD]; LXX [cf. Thackeray 189]; Jos., Ant. 2, 311 al., C. Ap. 1, 159. The Ionic-Hellenistic form τεσσερεσκαιδέκατος Hdt. 1, 84; Dit., Syll.³ 633, 27 [c. 180 BC]; 1017, 10) *fourteenth* Ac 27: 27, 33. M-M.*

τεσσερ- s. τεσσαρ-.

τεταρταῖος, α, ον (Hippocr., Pla., X. +; Polyb. 3, 52, 2; Diod. S. 14, 29, 2; 17, 67, 1; Jos., Ant. 13, 398; Dit., Syll.³ 1239, 20; PTebt. 275, 21; POxy. 1151, 37) *happening on the fourth day* τεταρταῖός ἐστιν *he has been dead four days* (cf. X., An. 6, 4, 9 ἤδη γὰρ ἦσαν πεμπταῖοι=they had already been dead for five days) J 11: 39. M-M.*

τέταρτος, η, ον (Hom. +; inscr., pap., LXX; Ep. Arist. 48; Joseph.) *fourth* Mt 14: 25; Mk 6: 48; Ac 10: 30; Rv 4: 7 al.; B 4: 5 (Da 7: 7); Hs 9, 1, 6; 9, 15, 2f; 9, 21, 1. The subst. neut. τὸ τέταρτον (i.e. μέρος) *the fourth part, quarter* (Diod. S. 1, 50, 2; POxy. 611; 1102, 9; 1293, 25 [II AD]; Jos., Ant. 14, 203) τὸ τέταρτον τῆς γῆς Rv 6: 8. M-M.

τετραα- s. τετρα-.

τετράγωνος, ον (Hdt. +; inscr., pap., LXX, Philo; Jos., Ant. 3, 116; 12, 227; loanw. in rabb.) *(four)-square* of a city ἡ πόλις τετράγωνος κεῖται *the city is laid out as a square* Rv 21: 16 (Rome was originally built in this way acc. to Appian, Basil. 1a §9; Strabo 12, 4, 7 of Nicaea: ἔστι τῆς πόλεως ἑκκαιδεκαστάδιος ὁ περίβολος ἐν τετραγώνῳ σχήματι . . . τετράπυλος ἐν πεδίῳ κείμενος); but s. also below. Of stones that are to be used in a building (Appian, Mithrid. 30 §119; Arrian, Peripl. 2, 1; 1 Macc 10: 11 ed. Kappler v.l.; Jos., Ant. 20, 221) Hv 3, 2, 4; 3, 5, 1; s 9, 3, 3; 9, 6, 7f; 9, 9, 2; cf. v 3, 6, 6. *Shaped like a cube* of a tremendous rock Hs 9, 2, 1. Perh. Rv 21: 16 (s. above) also has this sense.—Subst. neut. τὸ τετράγωνον *rectangle, square* (Pla. et al.; Dit., Or. 90, 45 [II BC]; POxy. 669, 21) ἐν τετραγώνῳ *in a square* or *rectangle* Hv 3, 2, 5. M-M.*

τετράδιον, ου, τό (BGU 956, 3 [III AD]; POxy. 2156, 10) as a military t.t. (Philo, In Flacc. 111) *a detachment* or *squad* (so Gdspd., Probs. 131f) *of four soldiers,* one for each of the four night watches (cf. Vegetius, De Re Militari 3, 8 p. 84f Lang) τέσσαρσιν τετραδίοις στρατιωτῶν Ac 12: 4 (on the subj.-matter Philostrat., Vi. Apoll. 7, 31). M-M.*

τετρακισχίλιοι, αι, α (Hdt., Aristoph. +; LXX; Jos., Bell. 2, 501, Vi. 371) *four thousand* Mt 15: 38; 16: 10; Mk 8: 9, 20; Ac 21: 38. M-M.*

τετρακόσιοι, αι, α (Hdt. +; pap., LXX; Ep. Arist. 20; Jos., Bell. 5, 382, Ant. 11, 15; 18) *four hundred* Ac 5: 36; 7: 6 (Gen 15: 13.—The ἔτη τετρακόσια is a round number, not necessarily strictly exact; the same number is used in Appian, Bell. Civ. 1, 98 §459 to indicate approximately the period of time in which there had been no dictator); 13: 20; 21: 38 v.l.; Gal 3: 17. M-M.*

τετράμηνος, ον *lasting four months* (Thu. et al.; inscr., pap.), in the only occurrence in our lit. subst. (cf. Judg 19: 2 A; 20: 47 A; Bl-D. §241, 3 app.; Mlt.-H. 286) ἡ τετράμηνος (sc. ὥρα) *the period of four months, third of a year* (Dit., Syll.³ 410, 4 τὴν πρώτην τετράμηνον, 24 [274 BC]; 442, 3; 17; 645, 74; BGU 1118, 8; 1119, 17 [both I BC]) ἔτι τετράμηνός ἐστιν καί *four months more, then* J 4: 35. The t.r. has τὸ τετράμηνον in the same mng. (JMBover, Biblica 3, '22, 442ff). M-M.*

τετραπλοῦς, ῆ, οῦν (contracted fr. τετραπλόος, όη, όον. The word since X., An. 7, 6, 7; Jos., Ant. 7, 150 al.; as adv. 3 Km 6: 33) *four times, fourfold* ἀποδιδόναι τετραπλοῦν *pay back four times as much* Lk 19: 8 (cf. PSI 1055, 13 [III AD] τοῦ τετραπλοῦ μισθοῦ). M-M.*

τετράποδος, ον a by-form (since Polyb. 1, 29, 7) of τετράπους (q.v.) *four-footed* σὺν κτήνεσι τετραπόδοις PK 2 p. 14, 19.*

τετράπους, ουν, gen. ποδος *four-footed* (Hdt.+; inscr., pap.) in our lit. only subst. τὰ τετράποδα *four-footed animals, quadrupeds* (Thu. 2, 50, 1; PHib. 95, 8 [256 BC]; PStrassb. 5, 15; LXX; Philo, Gig. 31; Jos., Ant. 4, 70; Sib. Or. 3, 692) always w. πετεινά and ἑρπετά Ac 10: 12; Ro 1: 23.—Ac 11: 6 adds θηρία. M-M.*

τετραρχέω (Tdf., W-H., N. spell it τετρααρχέω; on this s. Bl-D. §124; Mlt.-H. 63 al.) *be tetrarch* (Jos., Bell. 3, 512 of Philip; Vita 52) Lk 3: 1 three times w. gen. of the region governed (Bl-D. §177; Rob. 510).—S. τετράρχης.*

τετράρχης, ου, ὁ (Tdf., W-H., N. spell it τετραάρχης; on this s. Bl-D. §124; Mlt.-H. 63 al.) *tetrarch* (Strabo; Joseph.; inscr.: s. the reff. in Schürer I⁴ 423, 12. Also Plut., Anton. 56, 7; 58, 11; Polyaenus 8, 39), orig. ruler of the fourth part of a region (Strabo 12, 5, 1 p. 567); later, when the orig. sense was wholly lost (Appian, Mithrid. 46 §178; 58 §236 there are more than four Galatian tetrarchs), title of a petty dependent prince, whose rank and authority were lower than those of a king. In our lit. Herod Antipas is given this title (as well as in the inscr. Dit., Or. 416, 3; 417, 4; Jos., Ant. 17, 188; 18, 102; 109; 122) Mt 14: 1; Lk 3: 19; 9: 7; Ac 13: 1; ISm 1: 2.—Schürer I⁴ 423f; BNiese, RhM n.s. 38, 1883, 583ff; EvDobschütz, RE XX '08, 627f; XXIV '13, 622. M-M.*

τετράς, άδος, ἡ *the number four* (Aristot., Philo), esp. *the fourth day* (Hes.+; inscr., pap., LXX of the fourth day of the month) *the fourth day of the week, Wednesday* τετράδα *on Wednesday* D 8: 1 (on the acc. in answer to the question 'when?' s. Bl-D. §161, 3; Rob. 470f).*

τεφρόω 1 aor. ἐτέφρωσα (Theophr. et al.; Philo, Ebr. 223 [of Sodom and Gomorrah]; Sib. Or. 5, 124) *cover with* or *reduce to ashes* πόλεις Σοδ. καὶ Γομ. 2 Pt 2: 6. M-M.*

τέχνη, ης, ἡ (Hom.+; inscr., pap., LXX, Ep. Arist., Philo; Jos., Ant. 1, 162, C. Ap. 2, 191 al.; Test. Napht. 8: 7; loanw. in rabb.) *skill, trade* Ac 17: 29; Rv 18: 22. Pl. Dg 2: 3. σκηνοποιὸς τῇ τ. α σκ. *by trade* Ac 18: 3. τέχνην ἔχειν *have and practice a skill* or *trade* (Eur., Suppl. 381; X., Mem. 3, 10, 1 al.) Hs 9, 9, 2; D 12: 4. M-M.*

τεχνίτης, ου, ὁ (X., Pla.; inscr., pap., LXX, Ep. Arist., Philo; Jos., Ant. 20, 219) *craftsman, artisan, designer* Dg 2: 3; D 12: 3. Of the silversmith Ac 19: 24, 25 v.l., 38. Of the potter 2 Cl 8: 2 (symbolically). πᾶς τεχνίτης πάσης τέχνης Rv 18: 22.—Of God (Dox. Gr. 280a, 7 [Anaxagoras]; Maximus Tyr. 13, 4c; 41, 4g; Herm. Wr. 486, 30 Sc. al.; Wsd 13: 1; Philo, Op. M. 135, Mut. Nom. 31 δημιούργημα τοῦ τῶν καλῶν καὶ ἀγαθῶν μόνων τεχνίτου) as the *architect* of the heavenly city (w. δημιουργός) Hb 11: 10. Of the holy Logos ὁ τεχνίτης καὶ δημιουργὸς τῶν ὅλων Dg 7: 2 (cf. Herm. Wr. 490, 34 Sc. ὁ τῶν συμπάντων κοσμοποιητὴς καὶ τεχνίτης).—HFWeiss, TU 97, '66, 52-5; s. also lit. s.v. δημιουργός. M-M.*

τηγανίζω (Posidippus Com. [III BC], fgm. 5; BGU 665, 3 [I AD]; 2 Macc 7: 5; Jos., Ant. 7, 167. Loanw. in rabb.) *fry in a pan,* pass. of those undergoing fiery torments in hell AP 20: 34.*

τήκω 2 fut. pass. τακήσομαι 2 Pt 3: 12 v.l.; 2 Cl 16: 3 (Hom.+; LXX; Jos., Bell. 5, 426; Sib. Or. 7, 77) *melt* (trans.); pass. *melt* (intr.), *be melted, dissolve* (Philo, Aet. M. 110 of the earth) of the στοιχεῖα et al. at the end of the

world (Is 34: 4 v.l. [quoted AP, fgm. 5]; En. 1, 6; Test. Levi 4: 1) 2 Pt 3: 12. τακήσονταί τινες τῶν οὐρανῶν καὶ πᾶσα ἡ γῆ ὡς μόλιβος ἐπὶ πυρὶ τηκόμενος 2 Cl 16: 3 (Apollon. Rhod. 4, 1680 τηκομένῳ μολίβῳ). πᾶσα δύναμις AP fgm. 5 (s. above). M-M.*

τηλαυγής, ές (Pind.+; LXX, Philo) lit. *far-shining;* then gener. *clear, plain;* neut. comp. as adv. τηλαυγέστερον (Diod. S. 1, 50, 1; Vett. Val. 54, 7f οἱ παλαιοὶ μυστικῶς καὶ σκοτεινῶς διέγραψαν, ἡμεῖς δὲ τηλαυγέστερον; Philo, Poster. Cai. 65) *more clearly* Hs 6, 5, 1 (s. also δηλαυγῶς).*

τηλαυγῶς adv. (Strabo 17, 1, 30; POxy. 886, 24 [III AD]; Philo, Congr. 24, 25) *(very) plainly, clearly* Mk 8: 25 (v.l. δηλαυγῶς, q.v.—Bl-D. §119, 4 app.; Rdm.² 37; cf. Mlt.-H. 283). M-M.*

τηλικοῦτος, αύτη, οῦτο (Aeschyl., X., Pla.+; inscr., pap., LXX) a demonstrative pron. correlative to ἡλίκος (as Diod. S. 10, 19, 5; Hero Alex. I p. 396, 26; 416, 1; Jos., Ant. 8, 208; 13, 5).—On the form of the neut. s. Bl-D. §64, 4; Rob. 290. For the use of the art. w. it Bl-D. §274; Rob. 771.

1. *so great, so large* of bodily size (Polyaenus 7, 35, 1) θηρίον Hv 4, 2, 3f. κῆτος 4, 1, 9. πλοῖα Js 3: 4.—2. *so great, so important, so mighty* etc. (Diod. S. 13, 41, 2 χειμών; Ep. Arist. 312; Jos., Bell. 4, 157 τὸ τηλικοῦτον [sic] ἀσέβημα 7, 393, Ant. 14, 352) σημεῖα καὶ τέρατα B 4: 14; 5: 8. σεισμός Rv 16: 18 (w. οὕτω μέγας pleonastically added). θόρυβος MPol 8: 3. θάνατος *so great a peril of death* (θάνατος 1c) 2 Cor 1: 10. σωτηρία Hb 2: 3. M-M.*

τημελέω (Eur., Pla.+; Sym. Ps 30: 4; Is 40: 11; Philo; Jos., Ant. 1, 252; 2, 79) *care for, look after* τινά *someone* (Eur., Iph. A. 731; Plut., Mor. 148D; Sext. Emp., Math. 1, 249) τὸν ἀσθενῆ 1 Cl 38: 2.*

τημελοῦχος, ον *care-taking, fostering* τημελοῦχος ἄγγελος *a guardian angel* AP, fgm. 1 and 2 (fr. Clem. Alex., Ecl. Proph. 41, 1; 48, 1 Stählin).*

τηνικαῦτα adv. *at that time, then* (Soph., Hdt.+; Ael. Aristid. 53 p. 624, 23 D.) Phlm subscr.*

τηρέω impf. ἐτήρουν; fut. τηρήσω; 1 aor. ἐτήρησα; pf. τετήρηκα, 3 pl. τετήρηκαν J 17: 6 (Bl-D. §83, 1; Mlt. 52f; Mlt.-H. 221). Pass.: impf. ἐτηρούμην; pf. τετήρημαι, 1 aor. ἐτηρήθην (Pind., Thu.+; inscr., pap., LXX, En., Ep. Arist. 263; Philo, Joseph., Test. 12 Patr.).

1. *keep watch over, guard* τινά, τὶ *someone, someth.* a prisoner (Thu. 4, 30, 4) Mt 27: 36, 54; Ac 16: 23; a building (cf. PPetr. II 37, 1, 19 [III BC] τηρεῖν τὸ χῶμα; PFlor. 388, 32; 1 Macc 4: 61; 6: 50) Hs 9, 6, 2; 7: 3. Pass. (Jos., Ant. 14, 366) Πέτρος ἐτηρεῖτο ἐν τῇ φυλακῇ Ac 12: 5. Cf. 24: 23; 25: 4, 21b. τηρεῖν τὴν φυλακὴν *guard the jail* 12: 6. Abs. *(keep) watch* (PSI 165, 4; 168, 9; 1 Esdr 4: 11; 2 Esdr [Ezra] 8: 29) MPol 17: 2. οἱ τηροῦντες *the guards* (SSol 3: 3) Mt 28: 4.

2. *keep, hold, reserve, preserve someone* or *someth.* (Aristoph., Pax 201)—a. for a definite purpose or a suitable time (Jos., Ant. 1, 97) τετήρηκας τὸν καλὸν οἶνον ἕως ἄρτι J 2: 10 (POxy. 1757, 23 τήρησόν μοι αὐτά, ἕως ἀναβῶ). Cf. 12: 7 (WKühne, StKr 98/99, '26, 476f). τηρηθῆναι αὐτὸν εἰς τὴν τοῦ Σεβαστοῦ διάγνωσιν Ac 25: 21a. κληρονομίαν τετηρημένην ἐν οὐρανοῖς εἰς ὑμᾶς (εἰς 4g) 1 Pt 1: 4.—2 Pt 2: 4 (cf. Test. Reub. 5: 5 εἰς κόλασιν αἰώνιον τετήρηται), 9, 17; 3: 7 (cf. Jos., Ant. 1,

97 τηρεῖσθαι κατακλυσμῷ); Jd 6b, 13; MPol 2: 3; 11: 2; 15: 1.

b. *keep,* etc. *unharmed* or *undisturbed* (Polyb. 6, 56, 13 one's word; Herodian 7, 9, 3) ὁ δὲ ἀγαπῶν με τηρηθήσεται ὑπὸ τοῦ πατρός μου J 14: 21 𝔓75. τὴν σφραγῖδα 2 Cl 7: 6. τὴν ἐκκλησίαν 14: 3a (opp. φθείρειν). τὴν σάρκα 14: 3b. τηρεῖ ἑαυτόν 1 J 5: 18 t.r. τηρεῖν τὴν ἑαυτοῦ παρθένον *keep his virgin inviolate* as such 1 Cor 7: 37 (Heraclit. Sto. 19 p. 30, 3; Achilles Tat. 8, 18, 2 παρθένον τὴν κόρην τετήρηκα. SBelkin, JBL 54, '35, 52 takes τηρ. here to mean *support* one's fiancée, without having marital relations.—On this subj. s. the lit. s.v. γαμίζω 1).—W. a second acc. (of the predicate, to denote the condition that is to remain unharmed. Cf. M. Ant. 6, 30 τήρησαι σεαυτὸν ἁπλοῦν; BGU 1141, 25 [13 BC] ἄμεμπτον ἐμαυτὸν ἐτήρησα; Wsd 10: 5) τὴν ἐντολὴν ἄσπιλον 1 Ti 6: 14. τὸ βάπτισμα ἁγνόν 2 Cl 6: 9. τὴν σφραγῖδα ὑγιῆ Hs 8, 6, 3. τὴν σάρκα ἁγνήν 2 Cl 8: 4, 6. τὴν σάρκα ὡς ναὸν θεοῦ IPhld 7: 2. σεαυτὸν ἁγνόν 1 Ti 5: 22.—2 Cor 11: 9; Js 1: 27. Pass. ὁλόκληρον ὑμῶν τὸ πνεῦμα τηρηθείη 1 Th 5: 23. τηρεῖν τινα ἔν τινι *keep someone (unharmed) by* or *through someth.* J 17: 11f. ἑαυτοὺς ἐν ἀγάπῃ θεοῦ τηρήσατε *keep yourselves from harm by making it possible for God to show his love for you in the future also* Jd 21. τοῖς Χριστῷ τετηρημένοις κλητοῖς *to those who have been called and who have been kept unharmed for Christ,* or in case the ἐν before θεῷ is to be repeated, *through Christ* Jd 1.

3. *keep*=*not lose* (as Diod. S. 17, 43, 9 τὰ ὅπλα, the shields) τὴν ἁγνείαν Hm 4, 4, 3. τὴν ἑνότητα τοῦ πνεύματος Eph 4: 3. τὴν πίστιν 2 Ti 4: 7 (cf. Diod. S. 19, 42, 5 τηρεῖν τὴν πίστιν; Brit. Mus. Inscr. III no. 587b, 5 ὅτι τὴν πίστιν ἐτήρησα; Jos., Bell. 2, 121, Ant. 15, 134). τὰ ἱμάτια αὐτοῦ Rv 16: 15 (or else he will have to go naked). αὐτόν (=τὸν θεόν) 1 J 5: 18. W. a neg.: *fail to hold fast*=*lose* through carelessness or *give up* through frivolity or a deficient understanding of the value of what one has τὶ *someth.* 2 Cl 8: 5 (a saying of Jesus whose literary source is unknown). τὴν ἑαυτῶν ἀρχήν (s. ἀρχή 4) Jd 6a.

4. *keep*=*protect* (Pind.+; En. 100, 5) τινὰ ἔκ τινος *someone from someone* or *someth.* J 17: 15; Rv 3: 10b (cf. Pr 7: 5 τηρεῖν τινα ἀπό τινος).

5. *keep, observe, fulfill, pay attention to,* esp. of law and teaching (LXX) τὶ *someth.* (Polyb. 1, 83, 5 legal customs; Herodian 6, 6, 1) Mt 23: 3; Ac 21: 25 t.r. τὸν νόμον (Achilles Tat. 8, 13, 4; Tob 14: 9; Test. Dan 5: 1.—τ. νόμους Jos., C. Ap. 2, 273) 15: 5; Js 2: 10; Hs 8, 3, 3-5. τὰ νόμιμα τοῦ θεοῦ Hv 1, 3, 4 (τηρ. τὰ νόμιμα as Jos., Ant. 8, 395; 9, 222). δικαιώματα κυρίου B 10: 11. πάντα ὅσα ἐνετειλάμην ὑμῖν Mt 28: 20. τὰς ἐντολάς (Ramsay, Phryg. I 2 p. 566f no. 467-9 [313/14 AD] τηρῶν ἐντολὰς ἀθανάτων, i.e., θεῶν; Sir 29: 1; Jos., Ant. 8, 120) 19: 17; J 14: 15, 21; 15: 10a, b; 1 J 2: 3f; 3: 22, 24; 5: 3; Rv 12: 17; 14: 12; Hm 7: 5; 12, 3, 4; 12, 6, 3; s 5, 1, 5; 5, 3, 3; 6, 1, 4. Pass. 5, 3, 5a. τὸ σάββατον *observe the Sabbath* J 9: 16. τὴν νηστείαν *keep the fast* Hs 5, 3, 5b; cf. 5, 3, 9. τὴν παράδοσιν (Jos., Vi. 361b) Mk 7: 9. τὸν λόγον J 8: 51f, 55; 14: 23; 15: 20a, b; 17: 6; Rv 3: 8. τὸν λόγον τῆς ὑπομονῆς μου vs. 10a. τοὺς λόγους (1 Km 15: 11) J 14: 24. τοὺς λόγους τῆς προφητείας Rv 22: 7, τοῦ βιβλίου τούτου vs. 9. τὰ ἐν τῇ προφητείᾳ γεγραμμένα 1: 3. ὁ τηρῶν τὰ ἔργα μου *he who takes my deeds to heart* Rv 2: 26. Abs., but w. the obj. easily supplied fr. the context τήρει *pay attention to it* 3: 3 (cf. Philo, Leg. All. 3, 184).—HRiesenfeld, TW VIII, 139-51: τηρέω and related words. M-M.*

τήρησις, εως, ἡ (Thu.+; inscr., pap., LXX; Jos., Ant. 17, 205)—**1.** *custody, imprisonment* (Jos., Ant. 16, 321)—**2.** *prison* (BGU 388 III, 7). Both mngs. are poss. (as Thu. 7, 86, 2; Jos., Ant. 18, 235) in ἔθεντο εἰς τήρησιν Ac 4: 3. ἔθεντο αὐτοὺς ἐν τηρήσει δημοσίᾳ 5: 18.

3. *keeping, observance* (Wsd 6: 18) ἐντολῶν (Sir 32: 23.—τῶν νόμων Hierocles, Carm. Aur. 2, 2 p. 422 M.) 1 Cor 7: 19. M-M.*

Τιβεριάς, άδος, ἡ (Josephus index) *Tiberias,* a city on the west shore of the Lake of Gennesaret, founded by Herod Antipas as the capital of his domain and named in honor of the Emperor Tiberius; J 6: 23. The Lake of Gennesaret (cf. EbNestle, Der Name des Sees Tiberias: ZDPV 35, '12, 48-50; JGDuncan, The Sea of Tiberias and its Environs: PEF 58, '26, 15-22; 65-74; RDMiddleton, Tiberias: ibid. 162f) is also called θάλασσα τῆς Τιβεριάδος (cf. Paus. 5, 7, 4 λίμνην Τιβεριάδα ὀνομαζομένην; Jos., Bell. 3, 57 Τιβεριὰς λίμνη; 4, 456 Τιβεριέων λίμνη; Sib. Or. 12, 104 Τιβεριάδος ἄλμη) J 21: 1, more fully θάλασσα τῆς Γαλιλαίας τῆς Τιβεριάδος 6: 1.—Baedeker, Palästina u. Syrien⁷ '10, 234f; Schürer II⁴ '07, 216-22; Dalman, Orte³ '24; MAvi-Yonah, The Foundation of Tiberias: Israel Exploration Journ. 1, '50f, 160-9.*

Τιβέριος, ου, ὁ *Tiberius* (the name is found Diod. S. 15, 51, 1: Τιβέριος Ἰούλιος a Rom. military tribune IV BC), a Roman emperor (he ruled fr. Aug. 19, 14 AD to March 16, 37 AD; mentioned in Philo and Joseph. Cf. Sib. Or. 5, 20-3) Lk 3: 1 places the first appearance of John the Baptist as a preacher in the fifteenth year of Tiberius' reign. On the chronological matters involved s. EMeyer I 46f; III 205f; CCichorius, ZNW 22, '23, 16ff; HDieckmann, Die effektive Mitregentschaft des T.: Klio 15, '19, 339-75, Das fünfzehnte Jahr des T.: BZ 16, '24, 54-65, Das fünfzehnte Jahr des Cäsar T.: Biblica 6, '25, 63-7; cf. Αὔγουστος. HDessau, Gesch. der röm. Kaiserzeit II 1, '26; GPBaker, Tib. Caesar '29; ECiaceri, Tiberio '34; CESmith, Tib. and the Rom. Empire '42.—On the chronology of the Life of Jesus gener.: OGerhardt, Grundzüge der Chronologie Jesu Christi '34; RHennig, D. Geburts- u. Todesjahr Jesu Christi '36. M-M.*

Τίβερις, εως or **ιδος, ὁ** acc. Τίβεριν (Polyb. 6, 55, 1; Strabo et al.; Sib. Or. 5, 170) *the Tiber* river Hv 1, 1, 2.*

τίθημι (Hom.+; inscr., pap., LXX, Ep. Arist., Philo, Joseph., Test. 12 Patr., Sib. Or.) and its by-form **τιθέω** (Hv 1, 1, 3 and 2, 1, 2 as historical present; Bl-D. §321 app.; cf. Rob. 318); impf. 3 sing. ἐτίθει, 3 pl. ἐτίθεσαν Mk 6: 56 and ἐτίθουν Ac 3: 2; 4: 35; Hv 3, 2, 7 (Bl-D. §94, 1 and app.; Mlt.-H. 202); fut. θήσω; 1 aor. ἔθηκα (Bl-D. §95, 1; Rob. 308; 310); 2 aor. subj. θῶ, 2 pl. imper. θέτε, inf. θεῖναι, ptc. θείς; pf. τέθεικα. Mid.: fut. θήσομαι; 2 aor. ἐθέμην. Pass.: pf. τέθειμαι, ptc. τεθειμένος (Nicol. Dam.: 90 fgm. 130, 18 p. 401, 3 Jac.) J 19: 41; Hs 9, 15, 4 (on the pf. cf. Bl-D. §97, 2); 1 aor. ἐτέθην.

I. active and passive—**1.** *put, place, lay*—**a.** gener.—**α.** w. acc. *lay (away), set up, put (away)* ποῦ τεθείκατε αὐτόν; *where have you laid him?* J 11: 34 (though as early as Hom. τιθέναι has the special sense *lay away, bury*); cf. Mk 16: 6; J 19: 42; 20: 2, 13, 15. Pass. Mk 15: 47; Lk 23: 55. ὅπου ἦν τεθείς GP 12: 51. λίθον Ro 9: 33 (Is 28: 16 ἐμβαλῶ); 1 Pt 2: 6. Pass. B 6: 2. θεμέλιον *lay a foundation* Lk 14: 29; 1 Cor 3: 10f (symbol.). ὑπόδειγμά τινος τιθ. *set up an example of someth.* 2 Pt 2: 6 (cf. Jos., Ant. 17, 313 παράδειγμα τῆς ἀρετῆς τιθέναι). Those persons are added, in the dat., to whose advantage or disadvantage the example is given: τιθέναι πρόσκομμα τῷ ἀδελφῷ Ro 14: 13 (πρόσκομμα 2b). σκοπὸν τοῖς νέοις θήσομεν 2 Cl 19: 1.—Of stones ἐξώτεροι ἐτέθησαν *they were placed on the outside* Hs 9, 8, 3; 5b (cf. a and c); 7. ἐν ἰσχύι τέθεικεν τὴν σάρκα αὐτοῦ κύριος *the Lord* (God) *has set his* (Christ's) *flesh in strength* B 6: 3a; cf. b (Is 50: 7).

β. w. the acc., oft. supplied fr. the context, and a prepositional expr. closely related to the verb (Herodas 4, 34 τιθέναι εἰς τοὺς λίθους ζοήν [sic]) εἰς κρύπτην *put someth. in a cellar* Lk 11: 33. εἰς μνημεῖον *lay in a tomb* Ac 13: 29; cf. Rv 11: 9. Of stones τιθ. εἰς τ. οἰκοδομήν *put into the building* Hv 3, 2, 7. Pass. Hs 9, 4, 5; 9, 6, 8; cf. 9, 5, 4. Opp. ἐκ τῆς οἰκοδομῆς ἐτέθησαν *they were put out of the building* 9, 8, 1. ἔμπροσθέν τινος GP 4: 12. ἔν τινι (Gen 50: 26; Jos., Ant. 14, 124): ἐν μνημείῳ Mt 27: 60; cf. Mk 6: 29; 15: 46 v.l.; Lk 23: 53; Ac 7: 16. Pass. J 19: 41.—Mk 6: 56; Ac 9: 37. ἐνώπιόν τινος (1 Km 10: 25) Lk 5: 18. ἐπί τινος (X., Cyr. 8, 8, 16; Ezk 40: 2; Jos., Ant. 6, 15) 8: 16b; J 19: 19; Ac 5: 15; Rv 10: 2; GP 3: 8; 6: 21; 12: 53. ἐπί τινι 8: 32. ἐπί τι (Ps 20: 4; 1 Km 6: 8) Mk 4: 21b; Lk 6: 48 (θεμέλιον; s. a above); 2 Cor 3: 13. Esp. τὰς χεῖρας ἐπί τι or ἐπί τινα (cf. Ps 138: 5) Mk 8: 25 v.l.; 10: 16; τὴν δεξιάν Rv 1: 17. θήσω τὸ πνεῦμά μου ἐπ' αὐτόν Mt 12: 18 (=ἔδωκα Is 42: 1; τ. τὸ πνεῦμα as Is 63: 11). παρά τι (Plut., Mor. 176ε; 3 Km 13: 31) Ac 4: 35, 37 v.l.; 5: 2. πρός τι 3: 2; 4: 37. ὑπό τι Mt 5: 15; Mk 4: 21; 1 Cor 15: 25. ὑποκάτω τινός (Jer 45: 12) Lk 8: 16a.—Mt 22: 44 (Ps 109: 1); Mk 12: 36.

b. special expressions—α. τιθέναι τὰ γόνατα (prob. a Latinism: genua ponere Ovid, Fasti 2, 438; Curt. 8, 7, 13; Bl-D. §5, 3b) *bend the knee, kneel down* Mk 15: 19; Lk 22: 41; Ac 7: 60; 9: 40; 20: 36; 21: 5; Hv 1, 1, 3; 2, 1, 2.

β. *place before someone, serve* (X., Mem. 3, 14, 1) οἶνον J 2: 10 (Bel 11 Theod. οἶνον θές).—γ. as a t.t. of commercial life *put aside, store up, deposit* (Demosth. 52, 3 ἀργύριον al.; Hyperid. 5, 4; Theocr., Epigr. 14, 2; Plut., Mor. 829b; pap.) opp. αἴρειν *you withdraw what you did not deposit* Lk 19: 21; cf. vs. 22. ἕκαστος παρ' ἑαυτῷ τιθέτω *each one is to put aside at home* 1 Cor 16: 2.

δ. in Joh. lit. *take off, remove* τὰ ἱμάτια (Hdt. 1, 10, 1 τ. τὰ εἵματα; cf. Herodas 5, 62; Plut., Alc. 8, 2; Jos., Bell. 1, 390 τ. τὸ διάδημα and s. ἱμάτιον 3) J 13: 4. τὴν (ἑαυτοῦ) ψυχὴν *give* (up) *one's life* 10: 11, 15 (δίδωμι𝔓45 66 et al.), 17, 18a, b (EFascher, Z. Auslegg. v. J 10: 17, 18: Deutsche Theol. '41, 37-66); 13: 37f; 15: 13; 1 J 3: 16a, b (Appian, Bell. Civ. 4, 68 §289 δεξιάς; Sib. Or. 5, 157 τ. is simply=δίδωμι).

ε. θέτε ἐν ταῖς καρδίαις w. inf. foll. *make up* (your) *minds* Lk 21: 14 (s. II 1c below).—ἐν τίνι παραβολῇ θῶμεν (τὴν βασιλείαν τοῦ θεοῦ); *in what figure of speech can we present* (the Kgdm. of God)? Mk 4: 30. τ. ἐπί τινος foll. by the acc. and inf. *ordain by means of someone that...* B 13: 6.—τὸ μέρος αὐτοῦ μετὰ τῶν ὑποκριτῶν θήσει (μέρος 2) Mt 24: 51; cf. Lk 12: 46.

ζ. of a law *establish, give* (τιθέναι νόμον since Soph., El. 580; the mid. τίθεσθαι νόμον since Hdt. 1, 29. Both oft. in Pla.; likew. Diod. S. 5, 83, 5, where the act. as well as the mid. is used of the law). The act. also Ep. Arist. 15; Jos., C. Ap. 1, 316, Ant. 16, 1. The mid. also Appian, Bell. Civ. 3, 55 §228; Jos., C. Ap. 1, 269; 2, 273) only in the pass. (as Pla., Leg. 4 p. 705d al.; Jos., C. Ap. 2, 184) ὁ νόμος ἐτέθη Gal 3: 19 D.

2. *make*—a. w. a double acc. of the obj. and of the pred. *make someone or someth. of someone* (Hom. +; X., Cyr. 4, 6, 3; Lucian, Dial. Marin. 14, 2; Aelian, V.H. 13, 6; Lev 26: 31; Is 5: 20; Wsd 10: 21; Jos., Ant. 11, 39).

α. *someone* ὃν ἔθηκεν κληρονόμον πάντων Hb 1: 2.

πατέρα πολλῶν ἐθνῶν τέθεικά σε Ro 4: 17 (Gen 17: 5). ἕως ἂν θῶ τοὺς ἐχθρούς σου ὑποπόδιον τῶν ποδῶν σου *until I make your enemies a footstool for your feet* (Ps 109: 1): Mt 22: 44 t.r.; Lk 20: 43; Ac 2: 35; Hb 1: 13. Pass. ἐτέθην ἐγὼ κῆρυξ 1 Ti 2: 7; 2 Ti 1: 11. Cf. Hb 10: 13 (on this expr. cf. Plut., Mor. 1097c [HAlmqvist, Pl. u. das NT '46, 104]).—β. *someth.* (Mimnermus 1, 10 D.[2] *cause someth. to become someth.* [adj.]: 'God has made old age vexatious') ἀδάπανον θήσω τὸ εὐαγγέλιον 1 Cor 9: 18.

b. τιθέναι τινὰ εἴς τι *make someone someth., destine or appoint someone to* or *for someth.* (cf. Ael. Aristid. 53 p. 636 D.: τοὺς οὐκ ὄντας νόμους εἰς νόμους τ.) τέθεικά σε εἰς φῶς ἐθνῶν Ac 13: 47 (Is 49: 6). εἰς κόλασιν 1 Cl 11: 1. Pass. 1 Pt 2: 8. Also τιθ. τινὰ ἵνα *appoint someone to* . . . J 15: 16.

II. middle, basically not different in mng. fr. the act. (Bl-D. §316, 1; cf. Rob. 804f).

1. *put, place, lay*—a. w. acc. *arrange, fix, establish, set* καιροὺς οὓς ὁ πατὴρ ἔθετο *times which the Father has fixed* Ac 1: 7. θέμενος ἐν ἡμῖν τὸν λόγον τῆς καταλλαγῆς *as he established among us the word of reconciliation* (=entrusted it *to us*; cf. Ps 104: 27 ἔθετο ἐν αὐτοῖς τ. λόγους) 2 Cor 5: 19. ὁ θεὸς ἔθετο τὰ μέλη *God has arranged the parts* of the body 1 Cor 12: 18.

b. τίθεσθαί τινα ἐν τηρήσει Ac 5: 18; ἐν (τῇ) φυλακῇ (Gen 41: 10; 42: 17) Mt 14: 3 t.r.; Ac 5: 25; εἰς φυλακήν (PPetr. II 5a, 3 [III bc]) 12: 4; εἰς τήρησιν (w. the acc. easily supplied) 4: 3. ἐν σωτηρίῳ *place in safety, cause to share salvation* (w. acc. to be supplied) 1 Cl 15: 6 (Ps 11: 6).

c. ἔθεντο ἐν τῇ καρδίᾳ αὐτῶν *they kept in mind* (the obj. acc. is supplied by the immediate context) Lk 1: 66 (1 Km 21: 13). The same expr.=*come to think of someth., contrive someth. in one's mind* 21: 14 t.r. (s. I 1be above); Ac 5: 4. Likew. ἔθετο ὁ Παῦλος ἐν τῷ πνεύματι w. inf. foll. *Paul resolved* 19: 21. θέσθε εἰς τὰ ὦτα ὑμῶν τοὺς λόγους τούτους Lk 9: 44.

2. *make*—a. w. acc. (Appian, Bell. Civ. 2, 106 §442 εὐχὰς τίθεσθαι=offer prayers) βουλήν *reach a decision* (βουλή 2) Ac 27: 12.

b. w. a double acc. *make someone someth.* (schol. on Pind., Ol. 1, 58b; 2 Macc 5: 21. S. also Tyrtaeus [VII bc] 8, 5 D.[2] of the man who is called upon to hate his own life [in battle]: ἀνὴρ ἐχθρὴν ψυχὴν θέμενος Ac 20: 28 (ChClaereboets, Biblica 24, '43, 370-87); 1 Cor 12: 28.

c. τινὰ εἴς τι *destine* or *appoint someone to* or *for someth.* 1 Th 5: 9; Dg 6: 10. W. acc. easily supplied 1 Ti 1: 12.—CMaurer, TW VIII, 152-70: τίθημι and related words. M.-M. B. 832.**

τίκτω fut. τέξομαι; 2 aor. ἔτεκον; 1 aor. pass. ἐτέχθην (Hom. +; inscr., pap., LXX, En., Ep. Arist., Philo, Joseph., Test. 12 Patr.) *bear, give birth* (to).

1. lit., w. acc. υἱόν, etc. (Jos., Ant. 1, 257) Mt 1: 21 (Ps.-Callisth. 1, 8 Philip learns in a dream: ἡ γυνή σου τέξει σοι υἱόν, ὃς κυριεύσει τ. κόσμον πάντα; Apollon. Rhod. 4, 802 according to a saying of Themis, it is destined that Thetis will παῖδα τεκεῖν who will tower over everything), 23 (Is 7: 14), 25; Lk 1: 31; 2: 7; Rv 12: 4b, 5, 13. Abs. J 16: 21; Gal 4: 27; 2 Cl 2: 1 (the last two Is 54: 1); Rv 12: 2, 4a; GEg 1b, c. ὁ χρόνος or αἱ ἡμέραι τοῦ τεκεῖν αὐτήν (acc. as subj.) Lk 1: 57; 2: 6. Pass. (Petosiris, fgm. 9 l. 93 ἐκ τῆς ἄχλυος [mist] τίκτονται σκώληκες) Mt 2: 2; Lk 2: 11.

2. symbolically, of the earth (Aeschyl., Cho. 127; Eur., Cycl. 333; Philo, Op. M. 132 γῆς τῆς πάντα τικτούσης) *bring forth* βοτάνην Hb 6: 7. Of desire συλλαβοῦσα

τίκτει (on this combination cf. Gen 4: 17, 25; 29: 35) ἁμαρτίαν Js 1: 15 (cf. Aeschyl., Ag. 764 φιλεῖ δὲ τίκτειν ὕβρις ὕβριν; Solon in Stob. III p. 114, 7 H. ἡδονὴ λύπην τ.; Pla., Symp. 212A ἀρετήν, Ep. 3 p. 315c ἡδονὴ ὕβριν τίκτουσα ἐν τῇ ψυχῇ. The symbolic use is a favorite w. Philo. Sib. Or. 3, 235 κακὰ τ.). M-M. B. 281.*

τίλλω impf. ἔτιλλον (Hom.+; pap., LXX) pluck, pick τὶ someth. (Diod. S. 5, 21, 5 τοὺς παλαιοὺς στάχυς τίλλειν; τιλλ. χόρτον: PFlor. 321, 47; 322, 20.—Philo, Leg. ad Gai. 223, De Jos. 16) στάχυας heads of wheat Mt 12: 1; Mk 2: 23; Lk 6: 1.—BCohen, The Rabb. Law Presupp. by Mt 12: 1 and Lk 6: 1: HTR 23, '30, 91f; Murmelstein (s. on σπόριμος). M-M.*

Τιμαῖος, ου, ὁ Timaeus Mk 10: 46 (s. Βαρτιμαῖος). M-M.*

τιμάω fut. τιμήσω; 1 aor. ἐτίμησα, mid. ἐτιμησάμην; perf. pass. τετίμημαι, ptc. τετιμημένος (Hom.+; inscr., pap., LXX, Ep. Arist., Philo, Joseph., Test. 12 Patr.).

1. set a price on, estimate, value (Thu. et al.; inscr.; PSI 382, 15 [I bc]; PFlor. 266, 6 al.) pass. τὴν τιμὴν τοῦ τετιμημένου (sc. ἀγροῦ or ἀνθρώπου, the latter referring to Judas) the price for the field or for the man whose price was set (τιμή 1) Mt 27: 9a. Mid. set a price on or estimate for oneself (Hdt.+; Wilcken, Chrest. 224a, 8; c, 8; 11 [III bc]; PHal. 1, 201; 205 al. in pap.; Lev 27: 8; Jos., Ant. 5, 79) ὃν ἐτιμήσαντο the one (=field or man) on which they had set a price vs. 9b.

2. honor, revere τινά someone God (X., Mem. 4, 3, 13; Diod. S. 6, 1, 4; 8 τοὺς θεούς; Strabo 16, 2, 35; Dio Chrys. 16[33], 45; 58[75], 8; Ael. Aristid. 13 p. 297 D.: πρὸ τῶν γονέων; Is 29: 13; Ep. Arist. 234; Philo; Jos., Ant. 9, 153; 256) Mt 15: 8; Mk 7: 6; 1 Cl 15: 2; 2 Cl 3: 5; cf. 3: 4.—J 5: 23b, d; 8: 49 (Jesus honors his Father).Christ J 5: 23b, c. On GP 3: 9 cf. τιμή 2a. Parents (Ex 20: 12) Mt 15: 4; 19: 19; Mk 7: 10; 10: 19; Lk 18: 20; Eph 6: 2. Cf. Mt 15: 6. Presbyters 1 Cl 21: 6. The bishop ISm 9: 1a. The teacher of the divine word D 4: 1. Those who are really widows 1 Ti 5: 3 (though the mng. of τιμή 2e may be influential here; cf. Sir 38: 1). πάντας (JPWilson, ET 54, '42/'43, 193f), τὸν βασιλέα 1 Pt 2: 17a, b. πολλαῖς τιμαῖς (τιμή 2a) Ac 28: 10; cf. GP 3: 9. Abs. Dg 5: 15.—Of God (Soph., fgm. 226 N. ὃν τιμᾷ θεός. Pass. 4 Macc 17: 20) or Christ: (show) honor (to) or reward the Christians (so Isocr. 9, 42; X., An. 1, 9, 14; 5, 8, 25, Cyr. 3, 3, 6; Diod. S. 2, 3, 2 τιμᾶν δώροις; 2, 6, 9; 14, 42, 1; 16, 13, 1; Ps.-Callisth. 2, 1, 2 τιμάω τινὰ χρυσῷ. Pass. Hdt. 7, 213; Lys. 12, 64; 19, 18; Diod. S. 15, 74, 1.—On the rewarding of pious persons by God: Ps.-Aristot., Mund. 6, 23 τιμᾶν; Simplicius In Epict. p. 79, 11 Düb. τιμᾶν κ. κολάζειν) J 12: 26; 1 Cl 59: 3; IPhld 11: 2; pass. ISm 9, 1b.—The officials of a congregation are called οἱ τετιμημένοι ὑμῶν (partitive gen.) the honorable men among you D 15: 2 (οἱ τετιμημένοι of persons in high standing: X., Cyr. 8, 3, 9). For ἡ αὐτοῖς τετιμημένη λειτουργία 1 Cl 44: 6 cf. λειτουργία 2. M-M.*

τιμή, ῆς, ἡ (Hom.+; inscr., pap., LXX, En., Ep. Arist., Philo, Joseph., Test. 12 Patr. Loanw. in rabb.).

1. price, value (Hdt. et al.; POxy. 1382, 18 [II ad]) συνεψήφισαν τὰς τιμὰς αὐτῶν (s. συμψηφίζω) Ac 19: 19. Also concrete the price received in selling someth. 5: 2. W. the gen. of that for which the price is paid (Is 55: 1; Jos., Vi. 153, Ant. 4, 284; Test. Zeb. 3: 2) ἡ τιμὴ τοῦ χωρίου the price paid for the piece of ground vs. 3. ἡ τιμὴ τοῦ τετιμημένου (τιμάω 1) Mt 27: 9. τιμὴ αἵματος the

money paid for a bloody deed (αἷμα 2a), blood money vs. 6. Pl. (Diod. S. 5, 71, 3; 6=prize, price, reward) τὰς τιμὰς τῶν πιπρασκομένων Ac 4: 34. τὰς τιμὰς αὐτῶν the prices that they received for themselves 1 Cl 55: 2.—W. the gen. of price ᾧ (by attr. of the rel. for ὅ) ὠνήσατο Ἀβραὰμ τιμῆς ἀργυρίου which Abraham had bought for a sum of silver Ac 7: 16. Abs. τιμῆς at or for a price, for cash (Hdt. 7, 119; PTebt. 5, 185; 194; 220 [118 bc]; BGU 1002, 13 δέδωκά σοι αὐτὰ τιμῆς.—Bl-D. §179, 1 app.; Rob. 510f; Dssm., LO 275f [LAE 323f]) ἠγοράσθητε τιμῆς 1 Cor 6: 20; 7: 23 (ἀγοράζω 2).—οὐκ ἐν τιμῇ τινι Col 2: 23 may be a Latinism (cf. Ovid, Fasti 5, 316 nec in pretio fertilis hortus; Livy 39, 6, 9; Seneca, Ep. 75, 11. See Lohmeyer ad loc.) are of no value (RSV). See also s.v. πλησμονή.—GBornkamm, ThLZ 73, '48, col. 18, 2 observes that τ. here has nothing to do with 'honor', as it does in the expr. ἐν τιμῇ εἶναι X., An. 2, 5, 38; Herodian 4, 2, 9; Arrian, Anab. 4, 21, 10; Lucian, De Merc. Cond. 17.

2. honor, reverence—a. act., the showing of honor, reverence, or respect as an action (X., Cyr. 1, 6, 11; Diod. S. 17, 76, 3; Herodian 4, 1, 5; 2 Macc 9: 21) 1 Ti 6: 1. ταύτῃ τῇ τιμῇ τιμήσωμεν τ. υἱὸν τοῦ θεοῦ GP 3: 9. So perh. τῇ τιμῇ ἀλλήλους προηγούμενοι Ro 12: 10 (s. προηγέομαι). Pl. οἱ πολλαῖς τιμαῖς ἐτίμησαν ἡμᾶς Ac 28: 10 (cf. Diod. S. 11, 38, 5 τιμαῖς ἐτίμησε τὸν Γέλωνα; Dit., Or. 51, 13 τοὺς τοιούτους τιμᾶν ταῖς πρεπούσαις τιμαῖς; Jos., Ant. 20, 68.—For the τιμαί that belong to the physician, cf. Sir 38: 1; s. e. below). Of the demonstrations of reverence that characterize pagan worship (Dit., Or. 56, 9 αἱ τιμαὶ τῶν θεῶν; Himerius, Or. 8 [=23], 11 ἡ θεῶν τιμή) Dg 2: 8; Jewish worship 3: 5a.

b. pass. the respect that one enjoys, honor as a possession. The believers are promised τιμή 1 Pt 2: 7 (it is given them w. Christ, the λίθος ἔντιμος vs. 6) but see 3 below; cf. IMg 15. τιμὴν ἔχειν be honored (Hdt. 1, 168) J 4: 44; Hb 3: 3. τιμήν τινι (ἀπο-)διδόναι Ro 13: 7; 1 Cor 12: 24; Rv 4: 9 (w. δόξαν). τιμήν τινι ἀπονέμειν 1 Pt 3: 7; 1 Cl 1: 3; MPol 10: 2. τιμήν τινι περιτιθέναι 1 Cor 12: 23. λαβεῖν τιμήν (w. δόξαν) 2 Pt 1: 17; (w. δόξαν and δύναμιν. Cf. FPfister, Philol. 84, '29, 1–9) Rv 4: 11; 5: 12 (w. δύναμις, as Plut., Mor. 421E: the divinity grants both of them if it is addressed by its various names). τ. τιμῆς μεταλαβεῖν Dg 3: 5b. ἑαυτῷ τιμὴν περιποιεῖσθαι Hm 4, 4, 2 (w. δόξαν).—εἰς τιμήν for honor=to be honored σκεῦος, a vessel that is honored (or dishonored) by the use to which it is put Ro 9: 21; 2 Ti 2: 20f. εἰς τιμήν τινος for someone's honor=that he might be honored (Cornutus 28 p. 55, 7 εἰς τιμὴν τῆς Δήμητρος; Dit., Or. 111, 26 εἰς τιμὴν Πτολεμαίου) IEph 2: 1; 21: 1, 2; IMg 3: 2; ITr 12: 2; ISm 11: 2; IPol 5: 2b; cf. a (εἰς τιμὴν τῆς σαρκὸς τοῦ κυρίου). On εἰς λόγον τιμῆς IPhld 11: 2 cf. λόγος 2c.—An outstanding feature of the use of τι., as already shown in several passages, is its combination w. δόξα (Dio Chrys. 4, 116; 27[44], 10; Appian, Bell. Civ. 3, 18 §68; Arrian, Ind. 11, 1; Jos., Ant. 12, 118; Plut., Mor. 486B): of earthly possessions τὴν δόξαν καὶ τὴν τιμὴν τῶν ἐθνῶν Rv 21: 26 (τιμή concr.=an object of value: Ezk 22: 25). Of the unique, God-given position of the ruler 1 Cl 61: 1, 2 (in the latter pass. w. ἐξουσία). Mostly of heavenly possessions: Ro 2: 7 (w. ἀφθαρσία), vs. 10 (w. εἰρήνη); 1 Pt 1: 7 (w. ἔπαινος); 1 Cl 45: 8. Christ is (acc. to Ps 8: 6) crowned w. δόξα and τιμή Hb 2: 7, 9. God is called (amid many other predicates) φῶς, τιμή, δόξα, ἰσχύς, ζωή Dg 9: 6.—Hence esp. in the doxological formulas (God as the recipient of τ.: Eur., Bacch. 323 θεῷ τιμὴν διδόναι; Paus. 9, 13, 2; Ps 28: 1 [w. δόξα]; 95[96]: 7 [w. δόξα];

τιμή — τίς

Philo; Jos., C. Ap. 2, 206) 1 Ti 1: 17 (w. δόξα); 6: 16 (w. κράτος αἰώνιον); w. δόξα and κράτος Jd 25 𝔓⁷² et al.; Rv 5: 13 (w. δόξα et al.); 7: 12 (w. δόξα et al.); 1 Cl 64 (w. δόξα et al.); 65: 2 (w. δόξα et al.); MPol 20: 2; 21 (both w. δόξα et al.).

c. as a state of being *respectability* (s. τίμιος 1c) 1 Th 4: 4 (w. ἁγιασμός).—**d.** *place of honor, (honorable) office* (Hom.+ [s. FBleek on Hb 5: 4]; pap. In Joseph. of the high-priestly office: Ant. 12: 42 Ἐλεαζάρῳ τῷ ἀρχιερεῖ ταύτην λαβόντι τὴν τιμήν; 157 and oft.) οὐχ ἑαυτῷ τις λαμβάνει τὴν τιμήν *no one takes the office of his own accord* Hb 5: 4.

e. *honorarium, compensation* (test. of Lycon [III bc] in Diog. L. 5, 72, a physician's honorarium; Sir 38: 1; s. 2a above), so perh. 1 Ti 5: 17 (MDibelius, Hdb. ad loc. and see s.v. διπλοῦς.—Mng. 2b is also poss. In that case cf. Ael. Aristid. 32, 3 K.=12 p. 134 D.: διπλῇ τιμῇ τιμῆσαι. —JoachJeremias combines both mngs.).—MGreindl (s. δόξα, end).

3. perh. *privilege* 1 Pt 2: 7 (FWDanker, ZNW 58, '67, 96).—JohSchneider, TW VIII 170–82: τιμή, etc. M-M. B. 825; 1143.*

τίμιος, α, ον (Hom.+; inscr., pap., LXX, Philo, Joseph.) *valuable, precious.*
1. of things (Herodas 4, 5 of altars)—**a.** *costly, precious* λίθος Rv 17: 4; 18: 12a, 16; 21: 19 (cf. Tob 13: 17 S). Superl. (Jos., Ant. 17, 225 φίλον τιμιώτατον) λίθος τιμιώτατος 21: 11. Pl. λίθοι τίμιοι 1 Cor 3: 12 (s. λίθος 1c and cf. the lit. s.v. ἀμέθυστος). ξύλον τιμιώτατον Rv 18: 12b. τίμια ἀρώματα MPol 15: 2.

b. *of great worth* or *value, precious* of the blood of Jesus τίμιον αἷμα 1 Pt 1: 19; τίμιον τῷ θεῷ *precious to God* 1 Cl 7: 4. τίμιος καρπὸς τῆς γῆς Js 5: 7. τὰ τίμια καὶ μέγιστα ἐπαγγέλματα 2 Pt 1: 4. Comp. τιμιώτερος w. gen. (Eur., Alc. 301; Menand., Mon. 482; 552): of the martyr's bones τιμιώτερα λίθων πολυτελῶν (Pr 3: 15) MPol 18: 1. Of the δοκίμιον τῆς πίστεως: πολὺ τιμιώτερον χρυσίου 1 Pt 1: 7 t.r. (on τιμιώτερον χρυσ. cf. Diog. L. 8, 42; Ep. Arist. 82; Philo, Sacr. Abel. 83, Det. Pot. Ins. 20; Theophyl. Sim., Ep. 81).

c. *held in honor, respected* (τιμή 2c) τίμιος ὁ γάμος Hb 13: 4.—**d.** For οὐδενὸς λόγου ποιοῦμαι τὴν ψυχὴν τιμίαν ἐμαυτῷ Ac 20: 24 cf. λόγος 1aa, end.

2. of pers. *held in honor* or *high regard, respected* (oft. in the salutations of pap.-letters) τινί *by someone* (Jos., Bell. 5, 527 τῷ δήμῳ τίμιος, Ant. 1, 273) Ac 5: 34; 17: 34 E. M-M.*

τιμιότης, ητος, ἡ (Aristot.+; in pap. as an honorary title) *costliness* abstract for concrete *abundance of costly things* Rv 18: 19. M-M.*

Τιμόθεος, ου, ὁ (freq. found Aristoph., X.+; inscr., pap., LXX; Jos., Ant. 12, 329–44) voc. Τιμόθεε 1 Ti 1: 18; 6: 20. *Timothy,* a friend, traveling companion and co-worker of Paul. Ac 16: 1ff tells us that he lived in Lycaonia, prob. in Lystra, and was born of a pagan father and a Jewish-Christian mother (named Eunice acc. to 2 Ti 1: 5). Paul had him circumcised before taking him on the great journey (2 Cor 1: 19; Ac 17: 14f; 18: 5), and used him permanently as an assistant (συνεργός Ro 16: 21). He is named as the 'co-writer' of six letters (2 Cor 1: 1; Phil 1: 1; Col 1: 1; 1 Th 1: 1; 2 Th 1: 1; Phlm 1). He was active in Thessalonica (1 Th 3: 2, 6; cf. the subscr. to 2 Th), Corinth (1 Cor 4: 17; 16: 10), and then again in Macedonia (Ac 19: 22) as a messenger of the great apostle. He also accompanied him on his last journey to Jerusalem (Ac 20: 4).

Later he shared Paul's imprisonment (cf. Phil 2: 19 and also the introductions of the imprisonment epistles except Eph). In 1 and 2 Ti he is mentioned in the salutations (1 Ti 1: 2; 2 Ti 1: 2) and also 1 Ti 1: 18; 6: 20 (s. above, beg.); 2 Ti subscr. Finally he appears once more in the NT, Hb 13: 23. He is mentioned nowhere else in our lit.—AJülicher, RE XIX '07, 781–8; FXPölzl, Die Mitarbeiter des Weltap. Pls '11, 136ff; EBRedlich, St. Paul and his Companions '13; WHadorn (s.v. ὑπηρέτης); JPAlexander, The Character of Tim.: ET 25, '14, 277–85 (against him GFindlay, ibid. 426); EFascher, Pauly-W. VI A '37, 1342–54. On the composition and language of the Pastorals s. PNHarrison, The Problem of the Pastoral Epistles '21; BSEaston, The Pastoral Epistles '47; comprehensive commentary by CSpicq '47; MDibelius and HConzelmann, The Pastoral Epistles (transl. PButtolph and AYarbro) '72. M-M.*

Τίμων, ωνος, ὁ (freq. in lit., inscr., pap.) *Timon,* one of the seven 'deacons' in Jerusalem Ac 6: 5. M-M.*

τιμωρέω 1 aor. pass. ἐτιμωρήθην (trag., Hdt.+; inscr., pap., LXX) *punish* τινά *someone, have someone punished* (Soph., Oed. Rex 107; Lysias 13, 41; 42; Jos., Ant. 2, 107; 7, 93; Test. Jos. 14: 1. But the mid. is much more widely used in this sense [it is the usual thing in Philo; Jos., Ant. 1, 195; 17, 211]) Ac 26: 11. τιμωρεῖν τινα δειναῖς τιμωρίαις *punish someone with terrible punishments* Hs 6, 3, 3. Pass. (X., An. 2, 5, 27; Pla., Gorg. 81 p. 525B; 2 Macc 7: 7; En. 22, 13) Ac 22: 5; Hs 6, 3, 4; 6, 5, 3f; 6. M-M.*

τιμωρητής, οῦ, ὁ (2 Macc 4: 16; Philo, Rer. Div. Her. 109; Maspéro 5, 16) *avenger, punisher* of the punishing angel ὁ ποιμὴν ὁ τιμωρητής Hs 7: 1. ὁ ἄγγελος ὁ τιμ. 7: 6 (cf. ὁ τιμωρὸς δαίμων Herm. Wr. 1, 23; Jo. Lydus, Mens. 90, 24 Wünsch).*

τιμωρία, ας, ἡ *punishment* (Aeschyl., Hdt.+; inscr., pap., LXX, Philo; Jos., Bel. 4, 365, Vi. 132; 335) in our lit. inflicted by God (Theopompus [IV bc]: 115 fgm. 253 Jac. παρὰ θεῶν τιμ.; Eth. Epic. col. 12, 7 τιμ. ἐκ θεῶν; Diod. S. 13, 21, 1 τιμ. παρὰ θεῶν; 16, 64, 1; Aesop, Fab. 1 P.= 5 H. ἐκ θεοῦ τιμ. Cf. Jos., Bell. 2, 155 τιμωρίαι ἀδιάλειπτοι) B 20: 1; Hs 6, 3, 2b; 6, 4, 4; 6, 5, 3a, b. πόσῳ δοκεῖτε χείρονος ἀξιωθήσεται τιμωρίας; *how much more severe a punishment, do you think, will be decreed for . . . ?* Hb 10: 29 (Diod. S. 4, 12, 7 ἕκαστος τιμωρίας ἠξιώθη=each one had punishment inflicted on him; 16, 31, 2; 16, 46, 3). Pl. (Pla., Ep. 7 p. 335A μεγίστας τ. [of God]; Diod. S. 1, 96, 5 τὰς τῶν ἀσεβῶν ἐν ᾅδου τιμωρίας; Plut., Mor. 566E [in the underworld]; LXX; Ep. Arist. 208; Philo; Jos., C. Ap. 2, 292; Test. Jos. 3: 1) Hs 6, 3, 3; 4a; b; 6, 5, 7; Papias 3. τιμωρίαν ὑπέχειν *undergo punishment* (schol. on Soph., Oed. Col. 1565 p. 460 Papag.) MPol 6: 2. ὁ ἄγγελος τῆς τιμωρίας *the punishing angel* (cf. τιμωρητής) Hs 6, 3, 2a; 7: 2. M-M.*

τίνω (Hom.+; PHamb. 22, 5) fut. τίσω (better τείσω: Kühner-Bl. II 552; Mayser 91, 2; Bl-D. §23; Mlt.-H. 261) *pay, undergo* δίκην *a penalty, be punished* (since Soph., Aj. 113; cf. δίκη 1; Pr 27: 12 ζημίαν τείσουσιν) 2 Th 1: 9; Hm 2: 5; s 9, 19, 3. M-M.*

τίς, τί gen. τίνος, dat. τίνι, acc. τίνα, τί (Hom.+; inscr., pap., LXX, En., Ep. Arist., Philo, Joseph., Sib. Or.) *interrogative pron.* in direct, indirect and rhetorical questions (W-S. §25, 1ff; Bl-D. §298f, al.; Rob. 735–40 al.) *who? which (one)? what?*

818

1. subst.—a. τίς;—**α.** *who? which one?* τίς ὑπέδειξεν
ὑμῖν; Mt 3: 7; Lk 3: 7. τίς ἐστιν ὁ παίσας σε; Mt 26: 68.
τίνος υἱός ἐστιν; *whose son is he?* 22: 42b. τίνα λέγουσιν οἱ ἄνθρωποι εἶναι τὸν υἱὸν τοῦ ἀνθρώπου; 16: 13.
Cf. Mk 11: 28; 12: 16; 16: 3; Lk 9: 9, 18; J 18: 4, 7 (cf. Jos.,
Ant. 9, 56).—Esp. in questions to which the answer
'nobody' is expected Ac 8: 33 (Is 53: 8); Ro 7: 24; 8: 33-5;
9: 19b; 10: 16 (Is 53: 1); 11: 34a, b (Is 40: 13a, b); 1 Cor 9:
7a, b, c; 2 Cor 11: 29a, b. Likew. τίς . . . εἰ μή; *who . . .
except (for), but?* Mk 2: 7; Lk 5: 21b; 1 J 2: 22; 5: 5. Pl.
ὑμεῖς δὲ τίνες ἐστέ; Ac 19: 15. Cf. 2 Ti 3: 14; Hb 3:
16-18; Rv 7: 13.—Foll. by the partitive gen. τίς τούτων
τῶν τριῶν; Lk 10: 36. τίνος ὑμῶν υἱός; 14: 5. τίνι τῶν
ἀγγέλων Hb 1: 5. τίνα τῶν προφητῶν; Ac 7: 52. Cf. Mt
22: 28; Mk 12: 23; Hb 1: 13 al. For the part. gen. τίς ἐξ
ὑμῶν; etc. Mt 6: 27; Lk 11: 5; 14: 28.—Mt 21: 31. τίνα
ἀπὸ τῶν δύο; Mt 27: 21.

β. *who?* in the sense *what sort of (a) person?* (=ποῖος;
cf. Ex 3: 11; Jdth 12: 14; Jos., Ant. 6, 298) τίς ἐστιν οὗτος
ὃς λαλεῖ βλασφημίας; Lk 5: 21a. Cf. 19: 3; J 8: 53; Ac
11: 17 (cf. 4 Km 8: 13); Ro 14: 4; 1 Cor 3: 5a, b t.r.; Js 4:
12. σὺ τίς εἶ; *(just) who are you? what sort of man are
you?* (Menand., Epitr. 174; Epict. 3, 1, 22; 23; Herm. Wr.
1, 2; Job 35: 2) J 1: 19; 8: 25; 21: 12.

γ. *which of two?* (=πότερος) Mt 27: 17; Lk 22: 27; J 9:
2.—**δ.** as a substitute for the rel. pron. (Callimachus
28[=30], 2; Ptolemaeus Euergetes in Athen. 10 p. 438ᴇ
τίνι ἡ τύχη δίδωσι, λαβέτω. Cf. BGU 665 III, 13 [I ᴀᴅ];
822, 4 [III ᴀᴅ] εὗρον γεωργόν, τίς αὐτὰ ἑλκύσῃ; Gen 38:
25; Lev 21: 17; Dt 29: 17; s. 1bζ below and cf. Kühner-G.
II 517f; OImmisch, Leipz. Studien z. klass. Philol. 10,
1887, 309ff; KBuresch, RhM n.s. 46, 1891, 231ff; Mlt. 21
n. 1; 93f; Rob. 737f; Dssm., LO 266, 5 [CIG 9552—LAE
313, 6]; Mayser II 1, '26, 80) τίνα με ὑπονοεῖτε εἶναι οὐκ
εἰμὶ ἐγώ Ac 13: 25 t.r. So also Js 3: 13, in case it is to be
punctuated τίς σοφὸς ἐν ὑμῖν, δειξάτω.

b. τί;—**α.** *what?* τί σοι δοκεῖ; Mt 17: 25a; cf. 18: 12;
21: 28. τί ποιήσει; vs. 40. Cf. Mk 9: 33; 10: 3, 17; Lk 10:
26; J 1: 22b; 18: 38; Ac 8: 36; Ro 10: 8; 1 Cor 4: 7b al.
τίνι; *to what (thing)?* Lk 13: 18a, b; 20.—W. prepositions: διὰ τί; *why? for what reason?* cf. διά B II 2. εἰς τί;
why? for what purpose? cf. εἰς 4f. ἐν τίνι; *with what?
through whom?* Mt 5: 13; 12: 27; Mk 9: 50; Lk 11: 19; 14:
34; Ac 4: 9. πρὸς τί; *why?* (X., Cyr. 6, 3, 20; 8, 4, 21) J 13:
28. χάριν τίνος; *why?* lit. 'because of what thing?' 1 J 3:
12.

β. *what sort of (a) thing?* (=ποῖον) τί ἐστιν τοῦτο;
what sort of thing is this? (Ps.-Lucian, Alcyon c. 1 τίς ἡ
φωνή; Ex 16: 15) Mk 1: 27. τί τὸ πλοῦτος *what sort of
wealth* Col 1: 27; cf. Eph 1: 19; 3: 18.

γ. *which of two?* (=πότερον. Pla., Phileb. 52ᴅ) Mt 9: 5;
23: 19; Mk 2: 9; Lk 5: 23; 1 Cor 4: 21; Phil 1: 22.

δ. τί as pred. can go w. a subject that is in the pl. (Pla.,
Theaet. 155ᴄ τί ἐστι ταῦτα; Lucian, Dial. Deor. 11, 1;
Synes., Prov. 2, 2 p. 118ᴮ; Laud. Therap. 18 τί μοι
ταῦτα; cf. Jos., Vi. 296 τί γεγόνασιν;) or that is not
neut. gender (Bl-D. §299, 1; 2; Rob. 736. Cf. X., Hell. 2,
3, 17 τί ἔσοιτο ἡ πολιτεία; Mem. 4, 2, 21): τί ἐστι
ἄνθρωπος; (Epict. 2, 5, 26; 2, 9, 2) Hb 2: 6 (Ps 8: 5).
ταῦτα τί ἐστιν εἰς τοσούτους; J 6: 9. ἐπυνθάνετο τί ἂν
εἴη ταῦτα Lk 15: 26. τί ἐσόμεθα 1 J 3: 2. τί ἄρα ὁ Πέτρος
ἐγένετο *what had become of Peter* Ac 12: 18. οὗτος δὲ τί
(ἔσται); *what about this man?* J 21: 21. This pass. forms a
transition to

ε. Elliptical expressions: τί οὖν; (X., Mem. 4, 2, 17;
Teles p. 25, 13; Diod. S. 13, 26, 1; Ael. Aristid. 28, 17
K.=49 p. 496 D.; schol. on Pind., Ol. 12, 20c; Jos., Bell.

2, 364.—1 Cor 14: 15, 26 the expr. is given more fully τί
οὖν ἐστιν; Ro 6: 1; 7: 7; 9: 14, 30 τί οὖν ἐροῦμεν; 1 Cor
10: 19 τί οὖν φημι;) J 1: 21; Ro 3: 9; 6: 15 (Seneca, Ep.
47, 15 also introduces an absurd inference w. 'quid ergo');
11: 7.—τί γάρ; *what, then,* is the situation? (Ps.-Pla.,
Eryx. 1 p. 392ᴮ; Diod. S. 34+35 fgm. 2, 38; Dio Chrys.
71[21], 16; Lucian, Tyrannic. 13) Ro 3: 3; *what does it
matter?* Phil 1: 18. Also τί γάρ μοι; w. inf. foll. *is it any
business of mine?* (Epict. 2, 17, 14; 3, 22, 66; Maximus
Tyr. 2, 10c) 1 Cor 5: 12.—On τί πρὸς ἡμᾶς (πρός σε), cf.
πρός III 5c. On τί ἐμοὶ καὶ σοί, s. ἐγώ, end; also Gdspd.,
Probs. 98-101; MSmith, JBL 64, '45, 512f; JLLilly, CBQ
8, '46, 52-7. τί ἡμῖν καὶ σοί; has the same mng.: Mt 8:
29; Mk 1: 24a; Lk 4: 34a (cf. Epict. 2, 19, 16; 2, 20, 11).—
τί ὅτι; =τί γέγονεν ὅτι; (cf. J 14: 22) *what* has happened
that?, why? (LXX) Mk 2: 16 t.r.; Lk 2: 49; Ac 5: 4, 9; Hs
9, 5, 2.—On ἵνα τί s. the entry ἱνατί.

ζ. τί as a substitute for the relative (Dit., Syll.³ 543, 12;
705, 56; 736, 50; s. 1aδ above) οὐ τί ἐγὼ θέλω ἀλλὰ τί σύ
Mk 14: 36. Cf. 4: 24; Lk 17: 8; Ac 13: 25. Pl. 1 Ti 1: 7.—
οὐκ ἔχουσιν τί φάγωσιν Mt 15: 32; Mk 8: 2 (cf. vs. 1) is
prob. to be understood as an indirect question='they do
not know what they are to eat' (W-S. §24, 17b).

c. Two interrog. pronouns stand together without a
conjunction (distributive; cf. Kühner-G. II 521f; Bl-D.
§298, 5 w. app.; Rob. 737) τίς τί ἄρῃ *what each one
should receive* Mk 15: 24. τίς τί διεπραγματεύσατο Lk
19: 15. Cf. Hv 3, 8, 6; m 6, 1, 1 (s. also Ael. Aristid. 31 p.
598 D.: τί τίς ἂν λέγοι; Ps.-Clem., Hom. 2, 33).

2. adj. τίνα *what (sort of)* μισθὸν ἔχετε; Mt 5: 46. τίς
βασιλεύς; Lk 14: 31. Cf. 15: 4, 8; J 2: 18; 18: 29; Ac 10:
29; 1 Cor 15: 2; 2 Cor 6: 14-16 (five times); 1 Th 4: 2 *What
sort of* Ac 7: 49 (=ποῖος Is 66: 1; cf. Ac 7: 49 D). τί
περισσόν; etc.: Mt 5: 47; 19: 16; 27: 23; 1 Pt 1: 11.

3. adv.—a. τί; *why?* (class., LXX) τί μεριμνᾶτε; *why
do you worry?* Mt 6: 28. Cf. 7: 3; 19: 17; Mk 2: 7a, 8; 4:
40; 11: 3; Lk 2: 48; 6: 46; 19: 33; 24: 38a; J 7: 19; 18: 23;
Ac 1: 11; 14: 15; 26: 8; 1 Cor 4: 7t; 10: 30; Col 2: 20. τί οὖν
ὁ νόμος; *why, then* does *the law exist?* Gal 3: 19. τί καί;
why, indeed? for what possible reason? 1 Cor 15: 29b, 30.

b. τί in an exclamation *how!* (transl. of Hebr. מָה; W-S.
§21, 4; Bl-D. §299, 4; Rob. 739; 1176; LXX [Ps 3: 2; SSol
1: 10; 7: 7; 2 Km 6: 20]; Basilius, Hexaëm. p. 8ʙ Migne τί
καλὴ ἡ τάξις [cf. JTrunk, De Basilio Magno sermonis
Attici imitatore: Wissensch. Beilage z. Jahresber. d.
Gymn. Ehingen a. D. '11, 36]) τί στενή Mt 7: 14 v.l.; τί
θέλω Lk 12: 49 (s. θέλω 1, end, and Black, Aramaic
Approach³, '67, 121-4). M-M.

τὶς, τὶ, gen. **τινός,** dat. **τινί,** acc. **τινά, τὶ** (Hom.+;
inscr., pap., LXX, En., Ep. Arist., Philo, Joseph.) enclitic, indefinite pronoun (W-S. §26, 1-4; Bl-D. §301 al.;
Rob. 741-4) *anyone, anything; someone, something; many
a one* or *thing.*

1. subst.—a. τὶς, τινές—**α.** *someone, anyone, somebody* Mt 12: 29, 47; Mk 8: 4; 9: 30; 11: 16; Lk 8: 46; 9: 57;
13: 6, 23; J 2: 25; 6: 46; Ac 5: 25; 17: 25; Ro 5: 7a, b; 1 Cor
15: 35; 2 Cor 11: 20 (five times); Hb 3: 4; Js 2: 18; 2 Pt 2:
19 al. Pl. τινές *some, a number of* (people—supplied as in
Appian, Hann. 47 §203 λαβών τινας=he received some,
i.e., people) Lk 13: 1; Ac 15: 1; Gal 2: 12; 2 Th 3: 11; *anyone* 2 Pt 3: 9b.—In contrast to a majority made evident by
the context *some* of those present (Appian, Bell. Civ. 1, 26
§119 ἔφερόν τινες) Mk 14: 65; J 13: 29a; of all (under
consideration) 1 Cor 8: 7; 9: 22.—W. the partitive gen.
(Diod. S. 2, 24, 4; Plut., Mor. 189ᴀ τῶν ἐχθρῶν τις;
Epict. 2, 14, 1 τὶς τῶν Ῥωμαϊκῶν) τὶς τῶν Φαρισαίων

(some)one of the Pharisees, a Pharisee Lk 7: 36. Cf. 11: 45; Ac 5: 15. τὶς ὑμῶν 1 Cor 6: 1. Pl. τινές τῶν γραμματέων *some (of the) scribes* Mt 9: 3. Cf. 12: 38; 28: 11; Mk 7: 1f; 12: 13; Lk 6: 2; Ac 10: 23; 12: 1; 17: 18a, 28; 1 Cor 10: 7–10 al.—Also τὶς ἐκ (Plut., Galba 27, 2; Appian, Bell. Civ. 3, 84 §343 τὶς ἐκ τῆς βουλῆς) τὶς ἐξ ὑμῶν Js 2: 16; Hb 3: 13. Pl. τινές ἐξ αὐτῶν (Jos., Bell. 1, 311) Lk 11: 15. Cf. J 6: 64; 7: 25, 44; 9: 16; 11: 37, 46; Ac 15: 24.—τὶς ἐν ὑμῖν *any one among you, any of you* Js 5: 13a, 14, 19. ἐν ὑμῖν τινες 1 Cor 15: 12.—ταῦτά τινες ἦτε *some of you were that sort of people* 6: 11 (οὗτος 1bζ). τινές described by a rel. clause (Dionysius Com. [IV BC] 11 εἰσίν τινες νῦν, οὕς . . .) Mk 9: 1.

β. τὶς *a certain man*, etc., of a definite pers. Lk 9: 49; 2 Cor 2: 5; 10: 7; 11: 21 (of an opponent as UPZ 146, 2 [II BC]; Sallust. 12 p. 24, 20; 24.—Artem. 4, 22 p. 214, 20ff τὶς . . . οὗ ἐγὼ καίπερ εὖ εἰδὼς τὸ ὄνομα οὐκ ἐπιμνησθήσομαι). Pl. τινές *certain people*, etc. (Crates, Ep. 32; Demosth. 25, 40, Ep. 3, 8; Diod. S. 15, 18, 1; Appian, Bell. Civ. 5, 112 §470 'certain' people who had conspired to cause trouble; Iambl., Myst. 1, 13 p. 43, 2 P.; Sallust. 4 p. 4, 28) Ro 3: 8; 1 Cor 4: 18; 15: 34; 2 Cor 3: 1; 1 Ti 1: 3, 19 al.; 2 Pt 3: 9a. W. the name added ἦν δέ τις ἀσθενῶν, Λάζαρος *there was a man who was ill, named L.* J 11: 1 (begins like a story that originally circulated independently. Cf. Alcman 84 Diehl² ἦσκέ [=ἦν] τις Καφεὺς ἀνάσσων=there was once someone, named Capheus, who ruled). The name is also added in Ac 18: 7. W. a subst. ptc. τινές εἰσι οἱ ταράσσοντες Gal 1: 7 (cf. Lysias 19, 57 εἰσί τινες οἱ προαναλίσκοντες).

γ. For εἷς τις cf. εἷς 3c. For εἴ τις cf. εἰ VII. ἐάν τις Mt 21: 3a; 24: 23; Mk 11: 3; Lk 16: 30; J 6: 51 al.; Ac 13: 41 (Hab 1: 5); 1 Cor 8: 10; 10: 28; Col 3: 13a; 1 Ti 1: 8; 2 Ti 2: 5; Js 2: 14; 1 J 2: 1, 15; 4: 20; Rv 3: 20; 22: 18f. ἐὰν μή τις *if someone . . . not* J 3: 3, 5; 15: 6; *if no one* Ac 8: 31. τὶς w. a neg. *no one, nobody* οὐ . . . τὶς J 10: 28. οὐδὲ . . . τὶς Mt 11: 27; 12: 19. οὔτε . . . τὶς Ac 28: 21. οὐ . . . ὑπό τινος 1 Cor 6: 12. μή τις *that no one* Mt 24: 4; Mk 13: 5; Ac 27: 42; 1 Cor 1: 15; 16: 11; 2 Cor 8: 20; 11: 16a; Eph 2: 9; 1 Th 5: 15; Hb 4: 11 al. πρὸς τὸ μή τινα 1 Th 2: 9. ὥστε μή . . . τινά Mt 8: 28.

δ. The ptc. that belongs directly w. the indef. pron. is added w. the art. πρός τινας τοὺς πεποιθότας *to some who put their trust* Lk 18: 9. Cf. 2 Cor 10: 2; Gal 1: 7; Col 2: 8. But it also stands without the art. . . . τινῶν λεγόντων Lk 21: 5. Cf. 1 Ti 6: 10, 21; Hb 10: 28.

ε. corresponding τὶς . . . ἕτερος δέ *someone . . . and another* 1 Cor 3: 4. τινές (μέν) . . . τινές (δέ) Lk 9: 7f; Phil 1: 15 (τινές μέν—τινές δέ as Diod. S. 12, 41, 6).

ζ. τὶς *a person of importance* εἶναί τις *to be a person of importance* (Eur., El. 939; Theocr. 11, 79; Herodas 6, 54; Epict. 3, 14, 2, Ench. 13; Lucian, Lexiph. 22, Adv. Indoct. 1; PGM 13, 288 ἐγώ εἰμί τις) λέγων εἶναί τινα ἑαυτόν Ac 5: 36; IEph 3: 1 (so also τὶ; s. 1bε below; antonym s.v. οὐδείς 2bβ).

η. *each one* καθὼς ἄξιός ἐστι τις κατοικεῖν *as each one deserves to dwell* Hs 8, 2, 5a. Cf. 8, 4, 2. Bl-D. §301, 2.

b. τὶ, τινά—a. *something, anything* ὁ ἀδελφός σου ἔχει τι κατὰ σοῦ Mt 5: 23. Cf. 20: 20; Mk 8: 23; 9: 22; 13: 15; Lk 7: 40; 11: 54; J 13: 29a; 1 Cor 10: 31 al.—W. partitive gen. (Diod. S. 20, 39, 3 τινα τῶν ἀφῃρπασμένων=some of what had been seized [by the enemy]) τὶ τῶν ὑπαρχόντων Ac 4: 32. Cf. Ro 15: 18; Eph 5: 27.

β. in negative statements *nothing* οὔτε . . . τὶ Ac 25: 8. οὐδὲ . . . τὶ 1 Ti 6: 7.—γ. τινὰ μέν . . . τινὰ δέ *some . . . others* (w. ref. to πρόβατα and hence neut.) Hs 6, 2, 2.—δ. On εἴ τι cf. εἰ VII.

ε. εἶναί τι *be* or *amount to someth.* Gal 2: 6; 1 Cor 3: 7. εἰ δοκεῖ τις εἶναί τι μηδὲν ὤν Gal 6: 3 (s. 1aζ above and cf. W.-S. §26, 3).

2. adj.—a. *some, any, a certain,* though oft. omitted in transl. into Engl.; used with—a. a subst. τὶς: ἱερεύς τις Lk 1: 5; 10: 31. ἀνήρ (a narrative begins in this way Syntipas p. 16, 4; 30, 3; 46, 16; 57, 1) Ac 3: 2; 8: 9a; 14: 8. ἄνθρωπος Mt 18: 12. κώμη Lk 17: 12. Cf. 7: 2, 41; 18: 2; J 4: 46; Ac 27: 8; Hb 4: 7.—τὶ: ὕδωρ Ac 8: 36. σκεῦος 10: 11.

β. a proper name (X., Hell. 5, 4, 3; Jos., Ant. 12, 160) Σίμωνά τινα *a certain Simon* Lk 23: 26; Ac 10: 5f; Mk 15: 21. Cf. Ac 21: 16; 22: 12; 25: 19b.

γ. an adj. or adjectival pron. μέγας Ac 8: 9b. ἕτερός τις vs. 34. τὶς ἄλλος 1 Cor 1: 16; Phil 3: 4. τινές ἄλλοι (Diod. S. 5, 81, 4 ἄλλοι τινές [τ. ποιητῶν]; Jos., Ant. 8, 248) Ac 15: 2. τὶ ἀγαθόν Ro 9: 11. ἀσφαλές τι Ac 25: 26. Cf. Hb 11: 40.—In neg. statements *no* Lk 11: 36; Js 5: 12.

b. serving to moderate or heighten—a. to moderate an expr. that is too definite (Diod. S. 1, 1, 3; Appian, Bell. Civ. 1, 15 §65 οἷά τινες δορυφόροι=as a kind of bodyguard) ἀπαρχήν τινα *a kind of first-fruits* Js 1: 18 (Appian, Bell. Civ. 3, 39 §162 τὶς μετάνοια=something like remorse; 3, 77 §314 συγγνώμη τις=some kind of pardon).—So perh. δύο τινὰς τῶν μαθητῶν *several disciples, perhaps two* Lk 7: 18 (cf. Appian, Bell. Civ. 2, 59 §245 δύο τινάς=a few [ships], about two; Jos., Ant. 16, 274). But the expr. in Ac 23: 23 τινὰς δύο τῶν ἑκατονταρχῶν certainly means two, who simply cannot be more closely defined (cf. W.-S. §26, 1b; Rob. 742; Mlt.-Turner 195).

β. w. adjectives of quality and quantity to heighten the rhetorical emphasis φοβερά τις ἐκδοχὴ κρίσεως Hb 10: 27. βραχύ τι (*only*) *a little* 2: 7, 9 (Ps 8: 6).

c. of an indefinite quantity that is nevertheless not without importance *some, considerable* χρόνον τινά (Diod. S. 13, 75, 6 μετὰ τινα χρόνον; Jos., Ant. 8, 398) Ac 18: 23; 1 Cor 16: 7. Cf. Ro 1: 11, 13. μέρος τι 1 Cor 11: 18.

d. τινές *several* (Appian, Bell. Civ. 2, 49 §202 ἱππεῖς τινες) ἡμέρας τινάς Ac 9: 19; 10: 48; 15: 36. γυναῖκές τινες Lk 8: 2. Cf. Ac 15: 2; 17: 5f al.—On its position in the sentence cf. W.-S. §26, 4; Bl-D. §473, 1; Rob. 743. M-M.

Τίτιος, ου, ὁ (CIL III 3053; 6010, 223; XII 4141; Jos., Ant. 16, 270) *Titius,* a σεβόμενος τὸν θεόν (σέβω 2a) in Corinth, whose surname was Justus Ac 18: 7 (v.l. Τίτος; the t.r. omits this half of the name entirely and has simply Ἰούστου).—EJGoodspeed, JBL 69, '50, 382f identifies Titius Justus w. Gaius (Γάϊος 3).*

τίτλος, ου, ὁ (Lat. loanw.=titulus: inscr. [Hahn 231, 10, w. lit.; Hatch 143f]; later pap.; Jer 21: 4 in Aq., Sym., Theod.) *inscription, notice* on the cross, which gave the reason for condemnation J 19: 19f (on this custom cf. Sueton., Calig. 32, Domit. 10; Cass. Dio 54, 8; also the letter of the churches at Lyons and Vienne: Euseb., H.E. 5, 1, 44). P-FRegard, Le titre de la Croix d'après les Év.: Rev. Archéol. 5. sér. 28, '28, 95–105. M-M.*

Τίτος, ου, ὁ (Polyb.; Diod. S. 11, 51, 1; 15, 23, 1; 16, 40, 1 et al.; inscr., pap.; Jos., Ant. 14, 229f) *Titus.*
1. friend and helper of Paul, mentioned in our lit. only in Paul's letters. As a Gentile Christian he accompanied Paul to the council at Jerusalem; Paul did not have him circumcised, though the Judaizers demanded that he do so Gal 2: 1, 3. Later he effected a reconciliation betw. Paul

and the Corinthian church when the latter seemed lost to the apostle, and he arranged for the collection. Cf. 2 Cor 2: 13; 7: 6, 13f; 8: 6, 16, 23; 12: 18; subscr.—2 Ti 4: 10 mentions a journey of Titus to Dalmatia. Acc. to Tit 1: 4 the apostle left him, his γνήσιον τέκνον, behind in Crete to organize the churches there (cf. vs. 5); title and subscr. —AJülicher, RE XIX '07, 798–800; CKBarrett, MBlack-Festschr., '69, 1–18. Lit. s.v. Τιμόθεος (Pölzl 103ff) and Ἰωάν(ν)ης 6.—2. surnamed Justus Ac 18: 7 v.l.; s. Τίτιος. M-M.*

τιτρώσκω pf. pass. ptc. τετρωμένος (Hom.+; inscr., LXX, Philo; Jos., Bell. 2, 526, Ant. 7, 128) *wound, injure, damage* fig. of damage to the inner life τετρωμένος κατὰ διάνοιαν *wounded in mind* (διάνοια 1) GP 7: 26 (cf. 2 Macc 3: 16 τιτρώσκεσθαι τὴν διάνοιαν; Diod. S. 17, 112 τετρωμένος τὴν ψυχήν; Herodian 1, 8, 7; Philo).*

τοί (Hom.+; LXX; Jos., Ant. 15, 374; 16, 319) enclitic particle emphasizing the reliability of a statement *let me tell you, surely,* in our lit. only in the transition formula πέρας γέ τοι *and furthermore, besides* (πέρας 3) B 5: 8; 10: 2; 12: 6; 15: 6, 8; 16: 3.—μέν τοι s. μέντοι.*

τοιγαροῦν (Soph., Hdt.+; PTebt. 315, 14 [II AD]; PGiess. 3, 7; Sb 6222, 12; LXX; En. 102, 9; Philo, Virt. 202; Jos., Bell. 4, 168, Ant. 10, 10, C. Ap. 2, 178) a particle introducing an inference *for that very reason, then, therefore* 1 Th 4: 8; 1 Cl 57: 4, 6 (Pr 1: 26, 31). In an exhortation (Achilles Tat. 7, 11, 3; Jos., C. Ap. 2, 201) Hb 12: 1 (here 𝔓⁴⁶ has τοίγαρ). M-M.*

τοίνυν (Pind., Hdt.+; inscr., pap.) inferential particle *hence, so, indeed,* as the second word in its clause (class.; POxy. 902, 10; 1252 verso, 18; Wsd 1: 11; Job 8: 13; 36: 14; En. 101, 1; Jos., Ant. 2, 67; 14, 32) 1 Cor 9: 26; Js 2: 24 t.r.; Dg 3: 2. Beginning its clause (Sext. Emp., Math. 8, 429; IG IV 620, 13; POxy. 940, 3; Is 3: 10; 5: 13; 27: 4; 33: 23) Lk 20: 25 (w. imper.); Hb 13: 13 (w. hortatory subj.); 1 Cl 15: 1 (w. hortatory subj.) M-M.*

τοιόσδε, άδε, όνδε (Hom., Hdt.+; 2 Macc 11: 27; 15: 12; Jos., Ant. 17, 142; 209) *such as this, of this kind,* referring to what follows and in the sense 'so unique' 2 Pt 1: 17. M-M. and suppl.*

τοιοῦτος, αύτη, οῦτον (this form of the neut. is predom. in Attic wr.; Jos., C. Ap. 1, 12; 2, 222; Mt 18: 5 v.l.; Ac 21: 25 D) and οὗτο (Zen.-P. Cairo 379, 8; 482, 13 [III BC]; POsl. 17, 9 [136 AD]; Mt 18: 5; 1 Cl 43: 1; Dg 5: 3) correlative adj. *of such a kind, such as this* (Hom.+; inscr., pap., LXX, En., Ep. Arist., Philo, Joseph.). 1. correlative οἷος ... τοιοῦτος (X., Mem. 2, 6, 12; Lucian, Dial. Deor. 4, 4; Sir 49: 14) 1 Cor 15: 48a, b; 2 Cor 10: 11b. τοιούτους ὁποῖος (Jos., Ant. 7, 385) Ac 26: 29.

2. adj.—a. used w. a noun—α. w. the art., mostly attributive ἐν τῶν τοιούτων παιδίων *one child like this* (as indicated in vs. 36) Mk 9: 37. τὸν τοιοῦτον ἄνθρωπον *such a man* 2 Cor 12: 3 (cf. vs. 2). τῆς τοιαύτης διακονίας IPhld 10: 2 (cf. vs. 1). οἱ τοιοῦτοι δίκαιοι 2 Cl 6: 9 (cf. vs. 8). Pred. αἱ δυνάμεις τοιαῦται *such are the miracles* Mk 6: 2. ἡ γνῶσις τοιαύτη *the knowledge is of this kind* (as is described in what follows) B 19: 1.

β. without the article ἐξουσίαν τοιαύτην *such power* Mt 9: 8.—18: 5; Mk 4: 33; J 9: 16; Ac 16: 24; 1 Cor 11: 16; 2 Cor 3: 4, 12; Hb 7: 26; 13: 16; Js 4: 16.

γ. τοι. can have its mng. made clear by a rel. clause τοιαύτη πορνεία ἥτις οὐδὲ ἐν τοῖς ἔθνεσιν (sc. ἀκούε-

ται) 1 Cor 5: 1. τοιοῦτος ἀρχιερεύς, ὅς Hb 8: 1 (Dio Chrys. 15[32], 7 χορὸς τοιοῦτος ..., ὅς). ἄνθρωποι τοιοῦτοι οἵτινες B 10: 3–5.

b. τοιοῦτος ὤν *since I am the sort of person* (who presumes to give you orders) Phlm 9 (foll. by ὡς=in my character as; Andoc., Alcibiades 16). ὁ πατὴρ τοιούτους ζητεῖ τοὺς προσκυνοῦντας αὐτόν *the Father seeks such people to worship him* J 4: 23 (double acc. as Vett. Val. 315, 20 τινὰς τοὺς τοιούτους; Jos., Ant. 12, 281). The pleonastic use of τοι. after a relative is due to Semitic infl. (Ex 9: 18, 24; 11: 6) θλῖψις οἵα οὐ γέγονεν τοιαύτη *tribulation such as has never been seen* Mk 13: 19.

3. subst.—a. quite predom. w. the art. (Bl-D. §274; Rob. 771)—α. of persons ὁ τοιοῦτος *such a person;* either in such a way that a definite individual with his special characteristics is thought of, or that any bearer of certain definite qualities is meant Ac 22: 22; 1 Cor 5: 5; 2 Cor 2: 6f; 10: 11a; 12: 2, 5; Gal 6: 1; Tit 3: 11. Pl. οἱ τοιοῦτοι (Aeschyl., Thu.+; Test. Ash. 2: 9; 4: 5) Mt 19: 14; Mk 10: 14; Lk 18: 16; Ro 16: 18; 1 Cor 7: 28; 16: 16 al.

β. of things τὰ τοιαῦτα *such* or *similar things, things like that* (X., Cyr. 1, 2, 2 a catalogue of vices concluding καὶ ... τἆλλα τὰ τοιαῦτα ὡσαύτως. Sim., Ael. Aristid. 37, 27 K.=2 p. 27 D.; Plut., Mor. 447A) Ac 19: 25; Ro 1: 32; 2: 2f; Gal 5: 21; Eph 5: 27. ἐν τοῖς τοιούτοις *in such cases, under such circumstances* (X., Cyr. 5, 4, 17) 1 Cor 7: 15.

b. without the art. τοιαῦτα *such things* (Socrat., Ep. 14, 6; Test. Napht. 9: 1) Lk 9: 9; 13: 2 𝔓⁷⁵ et al.; Hb 11: 14. M-M.

τοῖχος, ου, ὁ (Hom.+; inscr., pap., LXX; En. 14, 10; Ep. Arist. 90; Jos., Ant. 1, 78 al.; Sib. Or. 1, 223) *wall,* as a term of invective τοῖχε κεκονιαμένε *whitewashed wall* Ac 23: 3 (since RSmend, Ezech. 1880, Ezk 13: 10 is usu. compared here). M-M.*

τοκετός, οῦ, ὁ (Aristot. et al.; BGU 665 II, 10 [I AD]; Sb 5873, 4; LXX; Jos., Ant. 1, 213) *childbearing, giving birth* IEph 19: 1. Symbolically of the tortures of martyrdom ὁ τοκετός μοι ἐπίκειται *the pains of birth are upon me* IRo 6: 1.*

τόκος, ου, ὁ (Hom.+ in the sense 'offspring' etc.) *interest on money loaned* (Pind., Pla.+; inscr., pap., LXX, Philo; Jos., C. Ap. 2, 208) Mt 25: 27; Lk 19: 23. τόκοι τόκων *compound interest* (Aristoph., Nub. 1156 al.) AP 16: 31. —JHerrmann, Zinssätze usw. [Greco-Egypt. pap.], Journ. of Juristic Papyrology 14, '62, 23–31. M-M. B. 800.*

τόλμα, ης, ἡ (Pind., Hdt.+; Diod. S. 18, 25, 1; Dit., Syll.³ 709, 25 [107 BC]; POxy. 1119, 8; PFlor. 382, 48; LXX; Jos., Bell. 4, 424, Ant. 14, 474, Vi. 222; Sib. Or. 4, 154) *audacity* (w. θράσος [as Socrat., Ep. 14, 1], αὐθάδεια) 1 Cl 30: 8.*

τολμάω impf. ἐτόλμων; fut. τολμήσω; 1 aor. ἐτόλμησα (Hom.+; inscr., pap., LXX, Philo; Jos., Ant. 17, 258). 1. w. inf.—a. *dare, have the courage, be brave enough* ὑπὲρ τοῦ ἀγαθοῦ τάχα τις καὶ τολμᾷ ἀποθανεῖν Ro 5: 7 (on being willing to die for a good man cf. Ael. Aristid. 46 p. 346 D.; Vita Philonid. [s.v. τράχηλος]). Cf. Phil 1: 14. Mostly used w. a neg. (Jos., Ant. 20, 7 ἀντιλέγειν οὐκ ἐτόλμων) οὐδὲ ἐτόλμησέν τις ἐπερωτῆσαι Mt 22: 46. Cf. Mk 12: 34; Lk 20: 40; J 21: 12; Ac 5: 13. Μωϋσῆς οὐκ ἐτόλμα κατανοῆσαι *Moses did not venture to look at* (it) 7: 32.

b. *bring oneself, presume* (Theognis 1, 377 D.² Zeus brings something about; 'The Tragedy' in Simplicius In

Epict. p. 95, 42 τολμῶ κατειπεῖν=I do not hesitate to say plainly; 3 Macc 3: 21; Philo, Somn. 1, 54; Jos., C. Ap. 1, 318; Himerius, Or. 20, 3 λέγειν τ.) τολμᾷ τις ὑμῶν κρίνεσθαι ἐπὶ τῶν ἀδίκων; can any of you bring himself to go to law before the unrighteous? 1 Cor 6: 1 (κρίνω 4aβ). W. a neg. οὐ τολμήσω τι λαλεῖν Ro 15: 18. Cf. 2 Cor 10: 12; Jd 9.

2. abs. be courageous (Job 15: 12) ἐν ᾧ ἄν τις τολμᾷ, . . . τολμῶ κἀγώ whatever anyone else dares to do, . . . I can bring myself (to do the same) 2 Cor 11: 21. τολμῆσαι ἐπί τινα show courage or boldness toward or against someone (En. 7, 4) 10: 2. τολμήσας εἰσῆλθεν he summoned up courage and went in Mk 15: 43 (cf. Plut., Camillus 22, 6 τολμήσας παρέστη). M-M. B. 1149.*

τολμηρός, ά, όν (Eur., Thu.+; Sir 8: 15; 19: 3; Jos., Ant. 1, 113; 14, 165) bold, daring, audacious, adv. τολμηρῶς (Thu. 3, 74, 1; 83, 3 al.; Wilcken, Chrest. 461, 25 [III AD]). Comp. τολμηρότερος (Isocr. 14, 8 Bl. and oft.; Sir 19: 2; Philo, Op. M. 170), and its adverbs τολμηροτέρως Ro 15: 15 and τολμηρότερον (Thu. 4, 126, 4; Polyb. 1, 17, 7) Ro 15: 15 v.l., both=rather boldly.*

τολμητής, οῦ, ὁ (Thu. 1, 70, 3; Plut.; Lucian; Philo, De Jos. 222; Jos., Bell. 3, 475) bold, audacious man τολμηταὶ αὐθάδεις 2 Pt 2: 10. M-M.*

τομός, ή, όν (Soph., Pla.+) cutting, sharp comp. τομώτερος (PSI 624, 1 [III BC]) symbol. of the word of God Hb 4: 12 (for the symbol. usage s. Lucian, Tox. 11; Ps.-Phoc. 124 ὅπλον τοι λόγος ἀνδρὶ τομώτερόν ἐστι σιδήρου). M-M.*

τόνος, ου, ὁ (Aeschyl., Hdt.+; Philo; Jos., Bell. 6, 162) in our lit. only fig. tension, then force, lasting quality (Plut., Brut. 34, 3 τῆς ὀργῆς) ὁ φόβος αὐτοῦ τόνον οὐκ ἔχει Hm 12, 4, 7.*

τόξον, ου, τό (Hom.+; inscr., pap., LXX; Jos., Ant. 1, 103; Sib. Or. 3, 730) the bow as a weapon (Hecataeus in Jos., C. Ap. 1, 203; Test. Jud. 7: 5; 9: 3) Rv 6: 2. M-M. B. 1388.*

τοπάζιον, ου, τό (Athenodorus [I BC] in Clem. Alex., Protr. 4, 48, 5; Diod. S. 3, 39, 5; Strabo 16, 4, 6; Ex 28: 17; 36: 17; Job 28: 19; Ps 118: 127; Ezk 28: 13) topaz, a bright yellow, more or less transparent precious stone, in ancient times oft. made into seals and gems; though perh. it is the more valuable golden-yellow chrysolith that is meant Rv 21: 20.—For lit. see s.v. ἀμέθυστος. M-M.*

τοποθεσία, ας, ἡ (Diod. S., Ptolem. et al.; pap.) αἱ τοποθεσίαι αἱ ἀγγελικαί are either the ranks of the angels or the places where the angels live ITr 5: 2 (Vett. Val. 42, 12 of the arrangement of the heavenly bodies).*

τόπος, ου, ὁ (Aeschyl.+; inscr., pap., LXX, En., Ep. Arist., Philo; Jos., Vi. 241 al.; Test. 12 Patr.) place, position, region.

1. lit.—a. inhabited place, of a city, village, etc. (Manetho in Jos., C. Ap. 1, 238; Diod. S. 1, 15, 6; 2, 13, 6; 13, 64, 7; Jos., C. Ap. 1, 86; 2, 34) οἱ ἄνδρες τοῦ τόπου ἐκείνου (cf. Gen 29: 22) Mt 14: 35. Cf. Mk 6: 11; Lk 4: 37; 10: 1 (w. πόλις as 2 Ch 34: 6; Jos., C. Ap. 2, 115); Ac 16: 3; 27: 2; Rv 18: 17 (cf. πλέω). ἐν παντὶ τόπῳ everywhere that men or Christians live (cf. Diod. S. 13, 22, 3 εἰς πάντα τόπον; Mal 1: 11; Test. Dan 6: 7, and on the exaggeration in epistolary style PLond. 891, 9 ἡ εὐφημία σου περιεκύκλωσεν τ. κόσμον ὅλον) 1 Cor 1: 2; 2 Cor 2: 14; 1 Th 1: 8; 2 Th 3: 16 v.l.; MPol 19: 1. Also κατὰ πάντα τόπον MPol inscr. ἐν παντὶ τόπῳ καὶ χρόνῳ D

14: 3. This is perh. the place for τὸν τόπον καὶ τὸ ἔθνος J 11: 48 (the Sin. Syr. and Chrysost. vol. VIII 386E take τόπ. to mean Jerusalem [cf. 2 Macc 3: 2, 12]; but s. 1b below). εἰς ἕτερον τόπον to another place (Dio Chrys. 70[20], 2; Plut., Mor. 108D) Ac 12: 17. Cf. AFridrichsen, Kgl. Hum. Vetensk. Samf. i. Uppsala, Årsbok '43, 28–30.

b. inhabited space, place, building et al. (Diod. S. 20, 100, 4 τόποι=buildings; POsl. 55, 10 [c. 200 AD]; 1 Km 24: 23; 2 Ch 25: 10) Ac 4: 31 (Stephan. Byz. s.v. Τρεμιθοῦς: the τόπος quakes at the παρουσία of Aphrodite). Esp. of a temple (2 Macc 5: 17–20 [w. ἔθνος]; 10: 7; 3 Macc 1: 9a, b al.; Ep. Arist. 81) perh. J 11: 48 (s. 1a above; the same problem arises concerning τόπος PLond. 2710 r., 6: HTR 29, '36, 40; 45f.—τ. of a temple Wilcken, Chrest. 94, 20 [beg. II AD]; Jos., Ant. 16, 165); τόπος ἅγιος (cf. Is 60: 13; 2 Macc 1: 29; 2: 18; 8: 17) Mt 24: 15; Ac 6: 13; 21: 28b.

c. place, location (Diod. S. 2, 7, 5 τόπος τῆς πόλεως= the place on which the city stands) ἔρημος τόπος (ἔρημος 1a) Mt 14: 13; cf. vs. 15; Mk 1: 35; 6: 31f, 35; Lk 4: 42; 9: 12. Pl. Mk 1: 45. πεδινός Lk 6: 17. κρημνώδης Hv 1, 1, 3; s 6, 2, 6. καλός Hv 3, 1, 3b. τόπος τοῦ ἀγροῦ a place in the country 2, 1, 4; 3, 1, 3a. Cf. 2, 1, 1; s 6, 2, 4. On τόπος διθάλασσος Ac 27: 41 cf. διθάλασσος. τραχεῖς τόποι rocky places vs. 29. ὁ τόπος ὅπου the place where Mt 28: 6; Mk 16: 6; J 4: 20; 6: 23; 10: 40; 11: 30; 19: 20, 41. ὁ τόπος ἔνθα GP 13: 56. ὁ τόπος ἐφ' ᾧ ἕστηκας Ac 7: 33 (cf. Ex 3: 5). The dat. for εἰς w. acc. (Bl-D. §199) ποίῳ τόπῳ ἀπῆλθεν Hv 4, 3, 7. ἐν παντὶ τόπῳ in every place (in Jerusalem) 1 Cl 41: 2. Combined w. a name εἰς τόπον λεγόμενον Γολγοθᾶ Mt 27: 33a. ἐπὶ τὸν Γολγοθᾶν τόπον Mk 15: 22a.—Lk 23: 33; J 19: 13; Ac 27: 8; Rv 16: 16. W. gen.: κρανίου τόπος Mt 27: 33b; Mk 15: 22b; J 19: 17 (s. κρανίον). τόπος τῆς καταπαύσεως Ac 7: 49; B 16: 2 (both Is 66: 1; s. κατάπαυσις 1).—(Definite) place, (particular) spot, scene Lk 10: 32; 19: 5; 22: 40; J 5: 13; 6: 10.

d. pl. regions, districts (Diod. S. 4, 23, 2; 13, 109, 2; Artem. 2, 9 p. 92, 28; PHib. 66, 2; PTebt. 281, 12 al.; Ep. Arist. 22; Jos., C. Ap. 1, 9) ἄνυδροι τόποι Mt 12: 43; Lk 11: 24. οἱ ἀνατολικοὶ τόποι the east 1 Cl 25: 1. κατὰ τόπους in various regions (κατά II 1a) Mt 24: 7; Mk 13: 8; Lk 21: 11. εἰς τοὺς κατὰ τὴν Ἀσίαν τόπους Ac 27: 2 (Antig. Car. 172 εἰς τοὺς τόπους).

e. place, room to live, stay, sit etc. (UPZ 146, 31; 37 [II BC]) Rv 12: 14. ἔτι τόπος ἐστίν there is still room Lk 14: 22 (Epict. 2, 13, 10 ποῦ ἔτι τόπος; where is there still room?). οὐκ ἦν αὐτοῖς τόπος ἐν τῷ καταλύματι 2: 7. ἔχειν τόπον have (a) place Rv 12: 6; cf. IPhld 2: 2; Hv 3, 5, 5; 3, 7, 5; 3, 9, 5; m 12, 5, 4a, b. ἑτοιμάσαι τινὶ τόπον J 14: 2f (cf. Rv 12: 6). δὸς τούτῳ τόπον make room for this man Lk 14: 9a (Epict. 4, 1, 106 δὸς ἄλλοις τόπον= make room for others). ὁ ἔσχατος τόπος (ἔσχατος 1 and 2) vss. 9b and 10 (on τόπος='a place to sit' cf. Jos., Ant. 12, 210 οἱ τ. τόπους κατὰ τὴν ἀξίαν διανέμοντες; Epict. 1, 25, 27; Paus. Attic. α, 128 τόπος of a seat in the theater; Diog. L. 7, 22 ὁ τῶν πτωχῶν τόπ.=the place where the poor people sat [in the auditorium where Zeno the Stoic taught]; Eunap. p. 21; Inschr. v. Pergam. 618, cf. Dssm., NB 95 [BS 267]). ὁ τόπος αὐτῶν μετὰ τῶν ἀγγέλων ἐστίν their place is with the angels Hs 9, 27, 3. On ὁ ἀναπληρῶν τῶν τόπον τοῦ ἰδιώτου 1 Cor 14: 16 cf. ἀναπληρόω 4 (for τόπος='position' cf. Philo, Somn. 1, 238; Jos., Ant. 16, 190 ἀπολογουμένου τόπον λαμβάνων).

f. the place where someth. is found, or at least should or could be found; w. gen. of the thing in question ἀπόστρεψον τὴν μάχαιράν σου εἰς τὸν τόπον αὐτῆς Mt 26: 52 (w.

ref. to the sheath). ὁ τόπος τῶν ἥλων the place where the nails had been J 20: 25 (Theod. Prodr. 9, 174 'the mark' of scratch-wounds). ὁ τόπος αὐτῆς its place, of the lampstand's place Rv 2: 5. Cf. 6: 14. τόπος οὐχ εὑρέθη αὐτοῖς there was no longer any place for them (Da 2: 35 Theod.—Ps 131: 5) 20: 11; cf. 12: 8. Non-literal use οὐκ ἂν δευτέρας (sc. διαθήκης) ἐζητεῖτο τόπος there would have been no occasion sought for a second Hb 8: 7. On τὸν τῆς ὑπακοῆς τόπον ἀναπληρώσαντες 1 Cl 63: 1 cf. ἀναπληρόω 3.

g. Esp. of the place to which a person's final destiny brings him. Of the place of salvation (Tob 3: 6 ὁ αἰώνιος τόπος): 2 Cl 1: 2. πορεύεσθαι εἰς τὸν ὀφειλόμενον τόπον τῆς δόξης 1 Cl 5: 4. εἰς τὸν ὀφειλόμενον αὐτοῖς τόπον παρὰ τῷ κυρίῳ Pol 9: 2. ὁ ἅγιος τόπος 1 Cl 5: 7. Cf. 44: 5; B 19: 1.—ὁ ἴδιος τόπος can be neutral (PGM 4, 3123; Cyranides p. 120, 6), the place where one is destined to go IMg 5: 1. But the expr. can also gain its specif. mng. fr. the context. Of the place of torment or evil (Iambl., Vi. Pyth. 30. 178 ὁ τῶν ἀσεβῶν τ. Proclus on Pla., Cratylus p. 72, 7 Pasqu.) Ac 1: 25b; cf. Hs 9, 4, 7; 9, 5, 4; 9, 12, 4. W. gen. ὁ τόπος τῆς βασάνου Lk 16: 28.

2. in special mngs.—a. place, passage in a book (X., Mem. 2, 1, 20. Περὶ ὕψους p. 6, 17; 15, 10 V.; 1 Esdr 6: 22 v.l.; Philo, De Jos. 151; Jos., Ant. 14, 114) Lk 4: 17. Cf. 1 Cl 8: 4; 29: 3; 46: 3.

b. position, office (Diod. S. 1, 75, 4 in a judicial body; 19, 3, 1 of a chiliarch [commander of 1,000 men]; Ps.-Callisth. 2, 1, 5 the τόπος of the priest-prophetess; inscr. [ΕΛΛΗΝΙΚΑ 7, '34, p. 179 l. 50, 218 BC]; pap.; Dssm., NB 95 [BS 267]) λαβεῖν τὸν τόπον τῆς διακονίας Ac 1: 25a. For ἐκδίκει σου τὸν τόπον IPol 1: 2 cf. ἐκδικέω 3. τόπος μηδένα φυσιούτω let no one's high position make him proud (lit. puff him up) ISm 6: 1. τοῖς ἱερεῦσιν ἴδιος ὁ τόπος προστέτακται a special office has been assigned the priests 1 Cl 40: 5.—44: 5.

c. possibility, opportunity, chance w. gen. (Polyb. 1, 88, 2 τόπος ἐλέους; Heliod. 6, 13, 3 φυγῆς τόπος; 1 Macc 9: 45) τόπον ἀπολογίας λαβεῖν have an opportunity to defend oneself Ac 25: 16 (cf. Jos., Ant. 16, 258 μήτ' ἀπολογίας μήτ' ἐλέγχου τόπον ἐχόντων). μετανοίας τόπον εὑρεῖν Hb 12: 17; διδόναι (cf. Wsd 12: 10) 1 Cl 7: 5. In the latter pass. the persons to whom the opportunity is given are added in the dat. (cf. Plut., Mor. 62D; Wilcken, Chrest. 14 III, 15 [I AD] βασιλεῖ τόπον διδόναι =give a king an opportunity; Sir 4: 5). μηδὲ δίδοτε τόπον τῷ διαβόλῳ do not give the devil a chance to exert his influence Eph 4: 27. δότε τόπον τῇ ὀργῇ give the wrath (of God) an opportunity to work out its purpose Ro 12: 19 (on ὀργῇ διδόναι τόπον cf. Plut., De Cohib. Ira 14 p. 462B; cf. also δὸς τόπον νόμῳ Sir 19: 17. On Ro 12: 19 s. ERSmothers, CBQ 6, '44, 205-15, w. reff. there; Gdspd., Probs. 152-4). τόπον ἔχειν have opportunity (to do the work of an apostle) 15: 23.

d. ἐν τῷ τόπῳ οὗ ἐρρέθη αὐτοῖς . . . , ἐκεῖ κληθήσονται is prob. to be rendered instead of their being told . . . , there they shall be called Ro 9: 26 (cf. Hos 2: 1; Achmes 207, 17 ἐν τῷ τόπῳ ἐκείνῳ=instead of that). M-M.*

τοσοῦτος, αύτη, οῦτον (this form of the neut. is predom. in Attic Gr., also Appian, Bell. Civ. 3, 43 §177; Jos., C. Ap. 1, 226; 2, 176; Hb 7: 22 t.r.; 12: 1; 1 Cl 1: 1; MPol 2: 2; Hm 5, 1, 5) and οὗτον (Clearchus, fgm. 48 W.: Diod. S. 1, 58, 4; Zen.-P. Cairo 367, 38; Zen.-P. Mich. 28, 17 [III BC]; Hb 7: 22; 1 Cl 45: 7) correlative adj. (Hom.+; inscr.; pap., LXX, Ep. Arist.; Jos., Ant. 12, 395 [τ.–ὅσος] al.) so great, so large, so far, so much, so strong etc.

1. used w. a noun—a. sing.—α. of quantity ὁ τοσοῦτος πλοῦτος Rv 18: 17 (only here w. the art.; cf. Bl-D. §274; Rob. 771). τοσοῦτον μέλι so great a quantity of honey Hm 5, 1, 5. τοσαύτη ἔκρυσις Papias 3b. Of space μῆκος Rv 21: 16 t.r. Of time χρόνος (PLond. 42, 23 [168 BC]; POxy. 1481, 2; Jos., Bell. 1, 665; 2, 413; Dio Chrys. 74, 18b) so long J 14: 9; Hb 4: 7. τοσ. διαφορά so great a difference MPol 16: 1. Referring back to ὅσα: τοσοῦτον βασανισμόν Rv 18: 7.

β. of quality πίστις faith as strong as this Mt 8: 10; Lk 7: 9. ἔλεος 2 Cl 3: 1. ζωή 14: 5. χρηστότης 15: 5. σπουδή MPol 7: 2. τάχος 13: 1. W. ὥστε foll. (Ps.-Callisth. 3, 26, 7 p. 127, 6) τοσ. ἀπόνοια 1 Cl 46: 7. W. ὡς foll. as strong as MPol 15: 2; so strong that AP 5: 16. This is prob. the place for τοσοῦτον νέφος μαρτύρων so great a cloud of witnesses Hb 12: 1.

b. pl., of number so many ἄρτοι τοσοῦτοι Mt 15: 33 (w. ὥστε foll.). ἔτη Lk 15: 29. σημεῖα J 12: 37. Cf. 21: 11; 1 Cor 14: 10 (cf. τυγχάνω); Hs 6, 4, 4.

2. without a noun—a. pl.—α. τοσοῦτοι of number so many people J 6: 9.—β. τοσαῦτα of quantity so much (Socrat., Ep. 14, 6) Hv 2, 1, 3. ἡμαρτηκὼς τοσαῦτα since I have committed so many sins Hm 9: 1; such serious sins is also poss. In that case degree is meant, as in τοσαῦτα ἐπάθετε; have you had such remarkable experiences? Gal 3: 4 (πάσχω 1).

b. sing.—α. of price τοσούτου (gen. of price) for so much and no more Ac 5: 8a, b.—β. εἰς τοσοῦτο(ν) foll. by gen. and ὥστε to such a degree of (Andoc. 2, 7 Bl.: εἰς τοσοῦτον ἦλθον τῆς δυσδαιμονίας . . . , ὥστε; Pla., Apol. 13 p. 25E; Clearchus, fgm. 48; Jos., Bell. 4, 317 εἰς τοσ. ἀσεβείας, ὥστε, C. Ap. 1, 226) 1 Cl 1: 1; 45: 7; MPol 2: 2.

γ. correlative: τοσοῦτον–ὅσον as much–as Papias 2: 4. τοσούτῳ w. the comp., corresp. to ὅσῳ (by) so much (greater, more, etc.)–than or as (X., Mem. 1, 3, 13; Ael. Aristid. 23, 55 K.=42 p. 786 D.) Hb 1: 4; 10: 25 (τοσούτῳ μᾶλλον ὅσῳ as Ael. Aristid. 33 p. 616 D.; 46 p. 345; cf. X., Mem. 1, 4, 10); the more–the more 1 Cl 41: 4; 48: 6. καθ' ὅσον–κατὰ τοσοῦτο Hb 7: 20-2. τοσούτῳ ἥδιον– ἐπειδή all the more gladly–since 1 Cl 62: 3. τοσοῦτον– ὡς to such a degree–that Papias 3a. M-M.

τότε (Hom.+; inscr., pap., LXX, En., Ep. Arist., Joseph., Test. 12 Patr.) a correlative adv. of time, in the NT a special favorite of Mt, who uses it about 90 times (AH McNeile, Τότε in St. Matthew: JTS 12, '11, 127f). In Mk 6 times, Lk 15 times, Ac 21 times, J 10 times. It is lacking in Eph, Phil, Phlm, Pastorals, Js, 1 Pt, 1, 2, and 3 J, Jd, Rv.

1. at that time—a. of the past then (Jos., Ant. 7, 317; 15, 354) τότε ἐπληρώθη then was fulfilled Mt 2: 17; 27: 9. εἶχον τότε δέσμιον vs. 16. Cf. 3: 5. (Opp. νῦν) Gal 4: 8, 29; Hb 12: 26. ἀπὸ τότε from that time on (PLond. 1674, 21; 2 Esdr [Ezra] 5: 16b; Ps 92: 2) Mt 4: 17; 16: 21; 26: 16; Lk 16: 16 (cf. Bl-D. §459, 3). Used as an adj. w. the art. preceding (Appian, Bell. Civ. 4, 30 §128 ἡ τότε τύχη; Lucian, Imag. 17; Jos., Ant. 14, 481) ὁ τότε κόσμος the world at that time 2 Pt 3: 6 (PHamb. 21, 9 ὁ τότε καιρός).

b. of the fut. then (Socrat., Ep. 6, 10) τότε οἱ δίκαιοι ἐκλάμψουσιν Mt 13: 43. (Opp. ἄρτι) 1 Cor 13: 12a, b.—c. of any time at all that fulfils certain conditions ὅταν ἀσθενῶ, τότε δυνατός εἰμι 2 Cor 12: 10.

2. to introduce that which follows in time (not in accordance w. class. usage) then, thereupon (Bl-D. §459, 2) τότε Ἡρῴδης λάθρα καλέσας τοὺς μάγους then (after he had received an answer fr. the council) Herod secretly summoned the Magi Mt 2: 7. τότε (=after his baptism) ὁ

Ἰησοῦς ἀνήχθη εἰς τὴν ἔρημον 4: 1. Cf. 2: 16; 3: 13, 15; 4: 5, 10f; 8: 26; 12: 22; 25: 34–45 (five times); 26: 65 and very oft.; Lk 11: 26; 14: 21; 21: 10; 24: 45; Ac 1: 12; 4: 8; B 8: 1. καὶ τότε and then καὶ τότε ἐάν τις ὑμῖν εἴπῃ and then if anyone says to you Mk 13: 21.—Mt 7: 23; 16: 27; 24: 10, 14, 30a, b; Mk 13: 26f; Lk 21: 27; 1 Cor 4: 5; Gal 6: 4; 2 Th 2: 8; 2 Cl 16: 3. τότε οὖν (so) then (Test. Jud. 7: 5, Iss. 2: 1) J 11: 14; 19: 1, 16; 20: 8. εὐθέως τότε immediately thereafter Ac 17: 14.—W. correlatives: ὅτε (w. aor.)—τότε when (this or that happened)—(then) Mt 13: 26; 21: 1; J 12: 16; B 5: 9. Also ὡς (w. aor.)—τότε J 7: 10; 11: 6. ὅταν (w. aor. subj.)—τότε when (this or that happens)—(then) (Diod. S. 11, 40, 3 τότε—ὅταν [w. aor. subj.]=then—when) Mt 24: 16; 25: 31; Mk 13: 14; Lk 5: 35; 21: 20; J 8: 28; 1 Cor 15: 28, 54; 16: 2; Col 3: 4. ὅταν (w. pres. subj.)—τότε when—then (Jos., Bell. 6, 287) ὅταν λέγωσιν . . . τότε 1 Th 5: 3. In an enumeration πρῶτον—, καὶ τότε first—, and then Mt 5: 24; 7: 5; 12: 29; Mk 3: 27; Lk 6: 42; J 2: 10 t.r.; IEph 7: 2.—It is put pleonastically (cf. Vett. Val. 211, 8) after μετά and the acc. μετὰ τὸ ψωμίον, τότε after (he took) the piece of bread, (then) J 13: 27. Cf. Hv 2, 2, 4. Also after the ptc. διασωθέντες, τότε ἐπέγνωμεν Ac 28: 1. Likew. pleonastically 6: 11 D; 27: 21. M-M.

τοὐναντίον s. ἐναντίον 2.

τοὔνομα s. ὄνομα I 1, end.

τοὐπίσω=τὸ ὀπίσω; see ὀπίσω 1.

τουτέστιν s. εἰμί II 3 and on the spelling Bl-D. §12, 3; 17 app.; Rob. 207. M-M.

τράγος, ου, ὁ (Hom.+; inscr., pap., LXX, Philo; Jos., Ant. 2, 35) he-goat named w. others as a sacrificial animal Hb 9: 12f, 19; 10: 4; B 2: 5 (Is 1: 11). Used esp. on the Day of Atonement 7: 4 (prophetic saying of unknown origin), 6, 8, 10. M-M. B. 165.*

Τράλλεις, εων, αἱ (X., An. 1, 4, 8 al.; inscr. It occurs mostly in the pl. form [X.; Diod. S. 14, 36, 3; Jos., Ant. 14, 245; Dit., Or. 441, 162], though the sing. Τράλλις, ιος [epigram in Agathias Hist. p. 102, 15 Bonn.; Stephan. Byz. s.v.; Sib. Or. 3, 459; 5, 289] is not impossible) Tralles, a city in Caria (southwest Asia Minor), north of the Maeander River ITr inscr.—JWeiss, RE X 547; V Schultze, Altchristliche Städte und Landschaften II 2, '26.*

Τραλλιανός, οῦ, ὁ (Strabo 14, 1, 42; Appian, Mithr. 23; Polyaenus 7, 41; Jos., Ant. 14, 242; inscr. [Dit., Or. 498, 3, Syll.³ index p. 156; Inschr. v. Magn. index p. 204b]; correctly and predom. w. double λ) Trallian, from Tralles (s. Τράλλεις), of the ἀρχιερεύς Philip, under whom Polycarp suffered martyrdom MPol 21. S. also the title of ITr (Apollonius of Tyana wrote a letter Τραλλιανοῖς [no. 69]: Philostrat. I p. 364).*

τράπεζα, ης, ἡ (Hom.+; inscr., pap., LXX, Ep. Arist., Philo, Joseph., Test. 12 Patr.; Sib. Or. 5, 470; loanw. in rabb.) table
1. upon which someth. can be placed; of the table of showbread (cf. 1 Macc 1: 22 τρ. τῆς προθέσεως; Ex 25: 23–30; Jos., Bell. 5, 217) Hb 9: 2. Of the τράπεζα τοῦ θεοῦ in the tabernacle, upon which Moses laid the twelve rods 1 Cl 43: 2.
2. specif. the table upon which a meal is spread out (Hom.+; Jos., Ant. 8, 239) Mt 15: 27; Mk 7: 28; Lk 16: 21; 22: 21. Of the heavenly table at which the Messiah's

companions are to eat at the end of time vs. 30 (cf. JoachJeremias, Zöllner u. Sünder, ZNW 30, '31, 293–300). Also in γενηθήτω ἡ τράπεζα αὐτῶν εἰς παγίδα it is prob. (cf. Jos., Ant. 6, 363) this kind of table that is meant Ro 11: 9 (Ps 68: 23).—The contrast betw. τράπεζα κυρίου and τρ. δαιμονίων 1 Cor 10: 21 is explained by the custom of eating a cult meal in the temple of pagan divinities (POxy. 110 ἐρωτᾷ σε Χαιρήμων δειπνῆσαι εἰς κλείνην τοῦ κυρίου Σαράπιδος ἐν τῷ Σαραπείῳ αὔριον, ἥτις ἐστὶν ιε´ ἀπὸ ὥρας θ´; 523; POsl. 157 [all three II AD]; Jos., Ant. 18, 65. τράπεζα of the table of a divinity is found in such and similar connections Diod. S. 5, 46, 7 τρ. τοῦ θεοῦ; Dit., Syll.³ 1106, 99 ἐπὶ τὴν τράπεζαν τὴν τοῦ θεοῦ; 1022, 2; 1038, 11; 1042, 20; dedication inscr. III 1870, 1 no. 395, 17 Σαράπιδι καὶ Ἴσιδι τράπεζαν; POxy. 1755.—Ltzm., Hdb. exc. on 1 Cor 10: 21; HMischkowski, D. hl. Tische im Götterkultus d. Griech. u. Römer, Diss. Königsberg '17).
3. fig., of that which is upon the table, a meal, food (Eur., Alc. 2; Hdt. 1, 162; Pla., Rep. 3 p. 404D; Lucian, Dial. Mort. 9, 2; Athen. 1 p. 25E) παραθεῖναι τράπεζαν set food before someone (Thu. 1, 130; Charito 1, 13, 2; Aelian, V.H. 2, 17; Jos., Ant. 6, 338.—Ps 22: 5 ἑτοιμάζειν τρ.) Ac 16: 34; τράπ. κοινήν (κοινός 1a) Dg 5: 7. ὁρίζειν τράπεζαν order a meal D 11: 9. διακονεῖν τραπέζαις wait on tables, serve meals Ac 6: 2 (so ELohmeyer, JBL 56, '37, 231; 250f. But Field, Notes 113 [referring to Plut., Caesar 28, 4; 67, 1] and Gdspd., Probs. 126f [reff. to pap.] prefer sense 4 in this pass.).
4. the table on which the money-changers display their coins (Pla., Ap. 17c; cf. PEleph. 10, 2 [223/2 BC] the τραπεζῖται ἐν τοῖς ἱεροῖς) Mt 21: 12; Mk 11: 15; J 2: 15. Hence simply bank (Lysias, Isocr., Demosth. et al.; Ep. Arist.; Jos., Ant. 12, 28; inscr.; PEleph. 27, 23; POxy. 98 al. in pap. The Engl. 'bank' is the money-lender's 'bench'; cf. Murray, New [Oxford] Engl. Dict. s.v. bank sb.³) διδόναι τὸ ἀργύριον ἐπὶ τράπεζαν put the money in the bank to bear interest Lk 19: 23. M-M. B. 352 (meal); 483; 778 (bank).*

τραπεζίτης, ου, ὁ (Lysias, Demosth.; inscr., pap.; Ep. Arist. 26=Jos., Ant. 12, 32. Loanw. in rabb.) money-changer, banker Mt 25: 27. δόκιμος τραπεζίτης an experienced money-changer, who accepts no counterfeit money; fig. (on the subj. cf. Philo, Spec. Leg. 4, 77) of Christians γίνεσθε δόκιμοι τραπεζῖται Agr 11a, cf. b (Cebes 31, 3 μηδὲ γίνεσθαι ὁμοίους τοῖς κακοῖς τραπεζίταις). AResch, Agrapha² '06, 112–28; HJVogels, BZ 8, '10, 390; HJSchoeps, Theol. u. Gesch. des Judenchristentums '49, 151–5; JoachJeremias, Unknown Sayings of Jesus, tr. Fuller '57, 89–93.—Cf. PEleph. s.v. τράπεζα 4. M-M.*

τραῦμα, ατος, τό (Aeschyl., Hdt.+; inscr., pap., LXX; Jos., Bell. 1, 197, Ant. 4, 92 al.) a wound Lk 10: 34; IPol 2: 1. M-M. B. 304.*

τραυματίζω 1 aor. ἐτραυμάτισα, pass. ἐτραυματίσθην; perf. pass. ptc. τετραυματισμένος (Aeschyl., Hdt.+; pap., LXX; Jos., C. Ap. 2, 243) to wound Lk 20: 12; Ac 19: 16; 1 Cl 16: 5; B 5: 2 (the last two Is 53: 5). M-M.*

τραχηλίζω perf. pass. ptc. τετραχηλισμένος (Theophr., Teles et al. in a different mng. [twist the neck, etc.]; Philo, Cher. 78, Mos. 1, 297; Jos., Bell. 4, 375; PPetr. II 15[1]a, 2); in its only occurrence in our lit. πάντα γυμνὰ καὶ τετραχηλισμένα τοῖς ὀφθαλμοῖς Hb 4: 13 it must almost certainly mean everything is open and laid bare to the eyes (Hesychius explains τετραχηλισμένα with πεφανερωμένα, and as early as Oenomaus in Euseb., Pr. Ev. 5, 29, 5 we have μισθοῦ τραχηλίζειν='reveal' or 'open for a price').—WSWood, Exp. 9th Ser. III '25, 444–55; HW Montefiore, The Epistle to the Hebrews '64, 89 ('everything is naked and prostrate before . . . him'). M-M.*

τράχηλος, ου, ὁ (Eur., Hdt.+; inscr., pap., LXX; Jos., Ant. 3, 170 al.) *neck, throat* Mt 18: 6; Mk 9: 42; Lk 17: 2 (cf. Menand., fgm. 258 περὶ τὸν τρ. ἀλύσιον διδόναι). ἐπιπεσεῖν ἐπὶ τὸν τράχηλόν τινος *fall upon someone's neck, embrace someone* (ἐπιπίπτω 1b) Lk 15: 20; Ac 20: 37.—In symbolic usage: οἵτινες ὑπὲρ τῆς ψυχῆς μου τὸν ἑαυτῶν τράχηλον ὑπέθηκαν *who risked their necks for my life* Ro 16: 4 (cf. Vita Philonidis ed. Crönert [SAB '00, 951] ὑπὲρ[?] τοῦ μάλιστ' ἀγαπωμένου παραβάλοι ἂν ἑτοίμως τὸν τράχηλον. S. on this Dssm., LO 94f [LAE 117f]. Endangering the τράχηλος Diog. L. 4, 11). On the other hand ὑποθεῖναι τὸν τράχηλον 1 Cl 63: 1 *bow the neck* in obedience (cf. Epict. 4, 1, 77.—Sir 51: 26). Also κάμπτειν τὸν τράχ. B 3: 2 (Is 58: 5). Opp. τὸν τράχ. σκληρύνειν 9: 5 (Dt 10: 16). ἐπιθεῖναι ζυγὸν ἐπὶ τὸν τράχ. τινος Ac 15: 10. M-M. B. 232.*

τραχύς, εῖα, ύ (Hom.+; inscr., pap., LXX, En., Ep. Arist., Philo; Jos., Bell. 4, 5, Ant. 7, 239 al.) *rough, uneven* of a mountain (Herodian 6, 5, 5) Hs 9, 1, 7; 9, 22, 1. Of stones (Hom.+) 9, 6, 4; 9, 8, 6. τραχεῖς τόποι (schol. on Nicander, Ther. 143) Ac 27: 29. Of a road (Hyperid., fgm. 70, 3 J. τραχεῖα ὁδός; Pla., Rep. 1 p. 328ε ὁδὸς τραχεῖα; Cebes 15, 2; Jer 2: 25; Bar 4: 26) Hm 6, 1, 3f. ἡ τραχεῖα (X., An. 4, 6, 12; Lucian, Rhet. Praec. 3; sc. ὁδός) *the rough road* pl. Lk 3: 5 (Is 40: 4). M-M. B. 1066.*

Τραχωνῖτις, ιδος (Philo, Leg. ad Gai. 326; Joseph. index s.v. Τράχων) fem. of Τραχωνίτης, as Joseph. calls an inhabitant τοῦ Τράχωνος. The fem. is used abs. by Philo and Joseph. ἡ Τραχωνῖτις=(the) *Trachonitis.* This is the district south of Damascus, also called ὁ Τράχων by Josephus. In the only place where the word occurs in our lit. it is used as an adj. ἡ Τρ. χώρα *the region of Trachonitis* Φιλίππου τετραρχοῦντος τῆς Ἰτουραίας καὶ Τραχωνίτιδος χώρας Lk 3: 1.—GRindfleisch, Die Landschaft Haurān in röm. Zeit. u. in der Gegenwart: ZDPV 21, 1898, 1–46; Schürer I⁴ 426ff; HGuthe, RE XX 7f.*

τρεῖς, τρία gen. τριῶν, dat. τρισίν (Hom.+; inscr., pap., LXX, En., Ep. Arist., Philo, Joseph., Test. 12 Patr.) *three* Mt 12: 40 (Jon 2: 1); Mk 8: 2; Lk 1: 56; J 2: 19 al. τὰ τρία ταῦτα 1 Cor 13: 13 (cf. Philo, Det. Pot. Ins. 169 τὰ ἑπτὰ ταῦτα and several times τρία ταῦτα: Leg. All. 1, 93; 3, 249, Mos. 1, 224). τρεῖς εἰσιν οἱ μαρτυροῦντες *there are three that bear witness* 1 J 5: 7 (cf. Alexis, fgm. 271 τρεῖς δ' εἰσὶν αἱ κεκτημέναι).—On ἐν τρισὶν ἡμέραις (ἐν II 1a) and μετὰ τρεῖς ἡμέρας (μετὰ B II 1) cf. WBauer, M. Leben Jesu im Zeitalter d. ntl. Apokryphen '09, 253f. Both expressions together, evidently w. the same mng.: Sb 7696, 120f [250 AD]; on μετὰ τρ. ἡμ.='on the third day' s. Jos., Ant. 7, 280f; 8, 214 and 218.—For δύο ἢ τρεῖς s. δύο 1c.— See s.v. πνεῦμα 8 and cf. FGöbel, Formen u. Formeln der epischen Dreiheit in d. griech. Dichtung '35; FNötscher, Biblica 35, '54, 313–19; JBBauer, Biblica 39, '58, 354–8; JoachJeremias, KGKuhn-Festschr. '71, 221–9. M-M. B. 941ff.

Τρεῖς Ταβέρναι s. ταβέρναι.

τρέμω used only in the pres. and the impf. (Hom.+; PFay. 124, 27; PGM 12, 248f; Fluchtaf. 4, 44; LXX, En., Philo,

Joseph.) *tremble, quiver,* but also fig. *be afraid, fear, stand in awe of* (Jos., Bell. 1, 341; 6, 395) Lk 8: 47; Ac 9: 6 t.r. W. φοβεῖσθαι (Da 5: 19 Theod.; Philo, Leg. All. 3, 54) Mk 5: 33. W. θαμβεῖν Ac 9: 6 t.r. W. acc. *tremble at, stand in awe of* (trag. et al.; Herm. Wr. 1, 7) τὰ λόγια 1 Cl 13: 4 (Is 66: 2). τοὺς λόγους B 19: 4; D 3: 8. δόξας οὐ τρέμουσιν βλασφημοῦντες *they are not afraid to blaspheme glorious angels* 2 Pt 2: 10 (Bl-D. §415; Rob. 1121f). M-M.*

τρέπω 1 aor. ἔτρεψα (Hom.+; inscr., pap., LXX, Ep. Arist., Philo, Joseph.)—1. act. *turn, direct* τινὰ εἴς τι *turn* or *incline someone toward someth.* MPol 2: 4.

2. mid. *turn* (*oneself*) (Jos., C. Ap. 1, 25) w. indication of the place from which and of the goal (Socrat., Ep. 17, 2 οἱ νέοι εἰς ἀκρασίαν ἐτρέποντο; Appian, Bell. Civ. 2, 22 §83 ἐς ἁρπαγὰς ἐτράποντο=they turned to pillage; schol. on Nicander, Ther. 825 εἰς φυγὴν τρεπόμενοι; Ep. Arist. 245 τρέπεσθαι εἰς; likew. Jos., Ant. 18, 87) ἔνθεν εἰς βλασφημίαν τρέπονται *they turn from that* (i.e. fr. admiration) *to blasphemy* 2 Cl 13: 3. B. 666.*

τρέφω 1 aor. ἔθρεψα; pf. pass. ptc. τεθραμμένος (Hom. +; inscr., pap., LXX; Philo, Aet. M. 99; Joseph.).

1. *feed, nourish, support, provide with food* animals (X., Mem. 2, 9, 2) or men w. acc.: Mt 6: 26; 25: 37; Lk 12: 24; Rv 12: 6, 14 (pass.); B 10: 11. Occasionally also of plants (Il. 18, 57) ἡ πτελέα ὕδωρ ἔχουσα τρέφει τὴν ἄμπελον Hs 2: 8.—Of the mothers' breasts that *nurse* or *nourish* (cf. Od. 12, 134; Hdt. 1, 136; PRyl. 178, 5) Lk 23: 29 (abs.). ἐθρέψατε τὰς καρδίας ὑμῶν *you have fattened yourselves* by revelry Js 5: 5. In διὰ τὸ τρέφεσθαι αὐτῶν (i.e. the inhabitants of Tyre and Sidon) τὴν χώραν ἀπὸ τῆς βασιλικῆς, τρέφεσθαι can be either mid. or pass. *because their country supported itself* or *was supported* (by importing grain) *from the king's country* Ac 12: 20 (X., An. 7, 4, 11 has the mid. τρέφεσθαι ἐκ τῶν κωμῶν).

2. of children *rear, bring up, train* (Hom.+; 1 Macc 3: 33; 11: 39; Jos., Ant. 2, 209) τινά *someone* Hv 1, 1, 1. Pass. *grow up* (Aelian, V.H. 12, 1 p. 117, 2 H.; Jos., C. Ap. 1, 141) Ναζαρά, οὗ ἦν τεθραμμένος Lk 4: 16.— CMoussy, Recherches sur τρέφω et al., '69. M-M.*

τρέχω impf. ἔτρεχον; 2 aor. ἔδραμον (Hom.+; inscr., pap., LXX) *run*—1. lit. Mk 5: 6; J 20: 2, 4; GP 3: 6. δραμών w. finite verb foll. (Gen 24: 28; Jos., Bell. 6, 254; 294) Mt 27: 48; Mk 15: 36; Lk 15: 20. Foll. by inf. of purpose Mt 28: 8. The goal is indicated w. ἐπὶ and acc. (Alciphr. 3, 17; 2; 3, 40, 3) ἐπὶ λῃστὴν *advance against a robber* (in order to catch him) MPol 7: 1 (cf. Sus 38 Theod.; Test. Jud. 3: 1); ἐπὶ τὸ μνημεῖον Lk 24: 12 (cf. Gen 24: 20). W. εἰς: Ac 19: 28 D. τρ. εἰς πόλεμον *rush into battle* Rv 9: 9. Of foot-racing in the stadium 1 Cor 9: 24a, b.

2. fig.—a. using the foot-races in the stadium as a basis (on the use of such figures in the Cynic-Stoic diatribe s. PWendland, Die urchristl. Literaturformen: Hdb. I 3, '12 p. 357, 4) *exert oneself to the limit of one's powers in an attempt to go forward, strive to advance* Ro 9: 16 (the emphasis is entirely upon the effort which the person makes; cf. Anth. Pal. 11, 56 Düb. μὴ τρέχε, μὴ κοπία); 1 Cor 9: 24c, 26. μήπως εἰς κενὸν τρέχω ἢ ἔδραμον Gal 2: 2 (μήπως 2). Cf. Phil 2: 16=Pol 9: 2. On τρ. τὸν ἀγῶνα Hb 12: 1 s. ἀγών 1. ἐτρέχετε καλῶς *you were making such fine progress* Gal 5: 7 (cf. Philo, Leg. All. 3, 48 καλὸν δρόμον κ. ἄριστον ἀγώνισμα; Odes of Solomon 11: 3 ἔδραμον ὁδὸν ἀληθείας).

b. *proceed quickly and without hindrance* ἵνα ὁ λόγος τ. κυρίου τρέχῃ *that the word of the Lord might spread* *rapidly* 2 Th 3: 1 (cf. Ps 147: 4).—OBauernfeind, TW VIII, 225-35: τρέχω, δρόμος. M-M. B. 692.*

τρῆμα, ατος, τό (Aristoph., Hippocr., Pla.+; PRyl. 21 fgm. 3 II, 5 [I вc]; Ep. Arist. 61=Jos., Ant. 12, 66) *opening, hole* τρῆμα ῥαφίδος *eye of a needle* Mt 19: 24. Also τρῆμα βελόνης Lk 18: 25. S. the lit. under κάμηλος, κάμιλος, τρυμαλιά. M-M.*

τριάκοντα indecl. (Hom.+; inscr., pap., LXX, Ep. Arist.; Jos., Ant. 11, 15; Test. 12 Patr.; loanw. in rabb.) *thirty* Mt 13: 8; Mk 4: 8 (a thirty-fold yield of grain on the Tauric peninsula: Strabo 7, 4, 6 p. 311. For the yield of wheat fr. good soil cf. GDalman, Pj 22, '26, 129-31); Lk 3: 23 (Porphyr., Vi. Plot. 4 ὧν ἐτῶν τρ.); Hv 4, 2, 1 al. τριάκοντα πέντε (=λε´) *thirty-five* Hs 9, 4, 3; 9, 5, 4; 9, 15, 4. M-M.

τριακόσιοι, αι, α (Hom.+; inscr., pap., LXX; Jos., Bell. 1, 625, Ant. 11, 15) *three hundred* Mk 14: 5; J 12: 5; B 9: 8 (Gen 14: 14; Jos., Ant. 1, 178).*

τρίβολος, ου, ὁ (Alcaeus [600 вc] 100 Diehl; Aristoph., Theophr. et al.; inscr., pap., LXX; Philo, Somn. 2, 161) of prickly weeds, esp. *the thistle,* which grows in Palestine in great abundance and infinite variety. Pl. Hs 9, 20, 3. W. ἄκανθαι (Gen 3: 18; Hos 10: 8) Mt 7: 16; Hb 6: 8; Hs 6, 2, 6f; 9, 1, 5; 9, 20, 1.—ILöw, Aram. Pflanzennamen 1881 §302, D. Flora der Juden IV '34, 660 (index); LFonck, Streifzüge durch die bibl. Flora '00; FLundgreen, Die Pflanzen im NT: NKZ 28, '17, 828ff; GDalman, Pj 22, '26, 126ff (w. picture), Arbeit I 407, 2: blackberry bush. M-M.*

τριβολώδης, ες *full of thistles* Hs 6, 2, 6.*

τρίβος, ου, ἡ (Hom. Hymns, Hdt.+; inscr.: APF 1, '01, p. 221, 21; PRainer 42, 14; LXX; Jos., Ant. 15, 347) *a beaten* (τρίβω) *path,* and hence *a way that is familiar and well-worn* Hm 6, 1, 3. Also *path* gener. Mt 3: 3; Mk 1: 3; Lk 3: 4 (all three Is 40: 3; cf. also Sib. Or. 3, 777). Fig. τὰς τρίβους τῆς ζωῆς (cf. Pr 16: 17; Sib. Or. 3, 721) Hs 5, 6, 3. M-M.*

τριετία, ας, ἡ (Theophr.+; Plut., Lucian; Artem. 4, 1 p. 202, 9; Dit., Or. 669, 35; pap.; Jos., Ant. 19, 351) (*a period of*) *three years* Ac 20: 18 D, 31. M-M.*

τρίζω *cry shrilly, creak, gnash, grind* (intr. Hom., Hdt.+, also of teeth that grind [Epicharmus in Athen. 10 p. 411в]), trans. in the only place where it occurs in our lit. τρίζειν τοὺς ὀδόντας *gnash* or *grind the teeth* (Ps.-Callisth. 3, 22, 13 [twice]; Cyranides p. 46, 5) Mk 9: 18. Cf. Bl-D. §148, 1 app. M-M.*

τρίμηνος, ον (Soph.+) *of three months* as subst. ἡ τρίμηνος (Hdt. 2, 124; Aeschin. 3, 70; PLond. 18, 10 [161 вc]; PSI 689, 5; 30. Cf. Bl-D. §241, 3 app.: sc. περίοδος) or τὸ τρίμηνον (Polyb. 1, 38, 6; 5, 1, 12; Plut., Crass. 12, 3; Ptolem. 1, 8, 6.—Doubtful ἐν τριμήνῳ: Dit., Syll.³ 527, 114 [perh. 220 вc]; 1023, 31; διὰ τριμήνου PLond. 306, 22 [II AD]; LXX) (*a period of*) *three months* τρίμηνον (acc. in answer to the question, how long? 4 Km 24: 8; 2 Ch 36: 2.—Bl-D. §161, 2; Rob. 469-71) *for three months* Hb 11: 23. M-M.*

τρίς adv. (Hom.+; Ael. Aristid. 30, 23 K.=10 p. 122 D.: ὦ τρὶς εὐδαίμονες; inscr., LXX) *three times, thrice* Mt 26: 34, 75; Mk 14: 30, 72; Lk 22: 34, 61; J 13: 38; 2 Cor 11: 25a, b; 12: 8. ἐπὶ τρίς (CIG 1122, 9; PGM 36, 273=εἰς τρίς, found since Pind., Hdt., also Jos., Ant. 5, 348) *three*

times, in both places where it occurs in our lit. prob. = (*yet*) *a third time* (PHolm. 1, 18) Ac 10: 16; 11: 10. M-M.**

τρίστεγον, ου, τό *the third story* (Sym. Gen 6: 16.—Neut. of τρίστεγος='of three stories' [Dionys. Hal. 3, 68; Jos., Bell. 5, 220; pap.]) Ac 20: 9. M-M.*

τρισχίλιοι, αι, α (Hom.+; pap., LXX; En. 7, 2; Jos., Bell. 2, 500, Vi. 213; 233) *three thousand* Ac 2: 41 (on the number of those converted cf. Iambl., Vi. Pyth. §29 [LDeubner, SAB '35, XIX p. 54].—In case the numbers in Ac 2: 41 and 4: 4 originally referred to the same event or account of it, then cf. Appian, Bell. Civ. 3, 42 §173: some, on the one hand, say χίλιοι, the others τρισχίλιοι. διαφέρονται γὰρ περὶ τοῦ ἀριθμοῦ. Also 2, 70 §289f with the conclusion 'so inexact are the reports of numbers' in the tradition; 2, 82 §345f).*

τρίτος, η, ον (Hom.+; inscr., pap., LXX; Ep. Arist. 47; Philo; Jos., Vi. 205, Ant. 2, 105 τ. τρίτῃ τῶν ἡμερῶν; Test. 12 Patr.) *third.*

1. used as adj., w. a noun that can oft. be supplied fr. the context ἕως τρίτου οὐρανοῦ 2 Cor 12: 2 (IdeVuippens, Le Paradis terrestre au troisième ciel '25. Also EPeterson, ThLZ 52, '27, 78-80. Further lit. s.v. οὐρανός 1e). τὸ τρίτον ζῷον Rv 4: 7. Cf. 6: 5a, b; 8: 10a; 11: 14. τρίτον γένος PK 2 p. 15, 8 (s. γένος 3). (ἐν) τῇ τρίτῃ ἡμέρᾳ (Appian, Liby. 122 §578) Mt 16: 21; 17: 23; 20: 19; Lk 9: 22; 24: 7, 46; Ac 10: 40. τῇ ἡμέρᾳ τῇ τρίτῃ Lk 18: 33; J 2: 1; 1 Cor 15: 4. SVMcCasland, The Scripture Basis of 'On the Third Day': JBL 48, '29, 124-37; GMLandes, JBL 86, '67, 446-50 (Jonah). See s.v. τρεῖς.—ἕως τρίτης ἡμέρας Mt 27: 64. μετὰ τρίτην ἡμέραν *after three days* (Appian, Iber. 43 §177) Ac 10: 40 D. τρίτη ὥρα (=nine o'clock in the morning) 20: 3 or ὥρα τρίτη Mk 15: 25 (AMahoney, CBQ 28, '66, 292-9); Ac 2: 15. τρίτη ὥρα τῆς νυκτός (=nine o'clock at night) Ac 23: 23. ἐν τῇ τρ. φυλακῇ Lk 12: 38.—τρίτην ταύτην ἡμέραν (Lucian, Dial. Mort. 13, 3; Achilles Tat. 7, 11, 2; s. ἄγω 4) Lk 24: 21. ἄλλος ἄγγελος τρίτος Rv 14: 9.—The noun is supplied fr. the context (Diog. L. 2, 46 Ἀριστοτέλης ἐν τρίτῳ [i.e., book] περὶ ποιητικῆς) Mt 22: 26; Mk 12: 21; Lk 20: 12, 31; Rv 16: 4; 21: 19. τῇ τρίτῃ (sc. ἡμέρᾳ. Likew. τῇ τρίτῃ Dialekt-Inschr. p. 874,[n] 50b [Chios about 600 вc]; Demosth. [I AD] in Aëtius 186, 16; Arrian, Anab. 7, 11, 1. Cf. Jos., Vi. 229 εἰς τρίτην) Lk 13: 32 (looking toward the fut. after σήμερον and αὔριον=*the day after tomorrow;* cf. Epict. 4, 10, 31; 4, 12, 21; M. Ant. 4, 47.—With a look back at the past the third day would='the day before yesterday'. Cf. Ps.-Pla., Alcyon c. 3 ἑῴρας τρίτην ἡμέραν ὅσος ἦν ὁ χειμών=the day before yesterday you experienced how severe the storm was); Ac 27: 19.

2. as a subst. τὸ τρίτον (sc. μέρος; cf. Bl-D. §241, 7.— τὸ τρ. in this sense Diod. S. 17, 30, 3; Lucian, Tox. 46 τὸ τρ. τῆς ἀτιμίας; PFlor. 4, 17; 19; Wilcken, Chrest. 402 I, 18 τὸ νενομισμένον τρίτον=the third in accordance w. the law; Num 15: 6, 7) *the third part, one-third* foll. by partitive gen. (Appian, Illyr. 26 §75 τὸ τρ. τούτων) Rv 8: 7-12; 9: 15, 18; 12: 4.

3. adv. τὸ τρίτον *the third time* (Hom.+; PLeipz. 33 II, 15), τρίτον *a third time* (Aeschyl.+; Jos., Ant. 8, 371), both in the sense *for the third time* Mk 14: 41; Lk 23: 22; J 21: 17a, b. In the same mng. ἐκ τρίτου (Pla., Tim. 54в; Aelian, V.H. 14, 46) Mt 26: 44. τρίτον τοῦτο *now for the third time, this is the third time* J 21: 14; 2 Cor 12: 14; 13: 1. In enumerations (τὸ) τρίτον *in the third place* 1 Cor 12: 28; D 16: 6 (cf. Pla., Rep. 2 p. 358c; Plut., Mor. 459d;

Iambl., Vi. Pyth. 29, 165 πρῶτον ... δεύτερον ... τρίτον; 30, 171). M-M.**

τρίχινος, η, ον (X., Pla.+; pap., LXX) *made of hair* σάκκος (oft. pap., e.g. PSI 427, 3 [III BC]; PHamb. 10, 39) Rv 6: 12. M-M.*

τρόμος, ου, ὁ (Hom.+; PSI 135, 10; LXX; En.; Philo, Leg. ad Gai. 267; Test. 12 Patr.) *trembling, quivering* fr. fear, w. ἔκστασις Mk 16: 8. Mostly combined w. φόβος (as Gen 9: 2; Ex 15: 16; Dt 2: 25; 11: 25 al.; En. 13, 3) μετὰ φόβου καὶ τρόμου 2 Cor 7: 15; Eph 6: 5; Phil 2: 12 (s. κατεργάζομαι 2). ἐν φόβῳ καὶ ἐν τρόμῳ (cf. Is 19: 16; Ps 2: 11) 1 Cor 2: 3. ὁ φόβος καὶ ὁ τρόμος ὑμῶν ἐπέπεσεν τοῖς κατοικοῦσιν αὐτήν 1 Cl 12: 5 (cf. Ex 15: 16; Jdth 2: 28). τρόμος με ἔλαβεν Hv 3, 1, 5 (cf. Ex 15: 15; Is 33: 14). M-M. B. 1153.*

τροπή, ῆς, ἡ *turn, turning, turning around, return*—1. of the *solstice* (Hom.+; Dit., Syll.³ 1264, 5; PHib. 27, 120; 210 [III BC] ἡλίου τροπή; PRyl. 27; Sb 358, 6; Dt 33: 14; Wsd 7: 18), gener. of the *movements* of heavenly bodies fr. one place in the heavens or fr. one constellation to another (Pla., Tim. 39D; Aristot., H.A. 5, 9; Sext. Emp., Math. 5, 11; Philo, Agr. 51).

2. *turn(ing), variation, change* (Pla., Plut. et al.). In our lit. the word occurs only in τροπῆς ἀποσκίασμα Js 1: 17. Here the context (cf. φῶτα) suggests the astral mng. and, in case the text is in proper order (but s. JHRopes, MDibelius, FHauck, ASchlatter ad loc.; Gdspd., Probs. 189f.—אBP²³ and three minuscules have ἀποσκιάσματος, the more general sense is to be preferred to the more specialized (solstice); s. ἀποσκίασμα.—Yet this 'technical' sense can prob. not be sharply distinguished from the other sense *darkening, which has its basis in change.* That God, in contrast to all else, is unchangeable, was a truth often expressed in Hellenistic theol. (Herm. Wr. in Stob. I p. 277 Wachsm.=p. 432, 15 Sc. τί θεός; ἄτρεπτον ἀγαθόν. τί ἄνθρωπος; τρεπτὸν κακόν; Philo, Leg. All. 2, 89 πάντα τὰ ἄλλα τρέπεται, μόνος αὐτὸς [=θεός] ἄτρεπτός ἐστι; 33, Deus Imm. 22, Poster. Caini 19).—The transl. of τροπ. ἀποσκ. as 'shadow (=trace) of change', which has had some vogue fr. Oecumenius and Theophylact to HEwald et al., cannot be supported lexically. M-M.*

τρόπος, ου ὁ (Pind., Hdt.+; inscr., pap., LXX, En., Ep. Arist., Philo, Joseph., Test. 12 Patr.).

1. *manner, way, kind, guise* εἰς δούλου τρόπον κεῖσθαι *appear in the guise of* (=as) *a slave* (κεῖμαι 2c) Hs 5, 5, 5; 5, 6, 1.—ἐν παντὶ τρόπῳ *in every way* (3 Macc 7: 8 v.l.) 2 Th 3: 16. κατὰ πάντα τρόπον *in every way* or *respect* (X., An. 6, 30 al.; Num 18: 7; Ep. Arist. 215; Philo, Op. M. 10; Sib. Or. 3, 430) Ro 3: 2; IEph 2: 2; ITr 2: 3; ISm 10: 1; IPol 3: 2. μὴ ... κατὰ μηδένα τρόπον *by no means, not ... in any way* (*at all*) (Dit., Syll.³ 799, 20 μηδὲ ... κατὰ μηδένα τρόπον; 588, 44; PAmh. 35, 28; 3 Macc 4: 13b μὴ ... κατὰ μηδένα τρ.; 4 Macc 4: 24; 10: 7) 2 Th 2: 3. καθ᾽ ὃν τρόπον *in the same way as* (POxy. 237 VIII, 29 καθ᾽ ὃν ἔδει τρόπον; PRainer 5, 11; 9, 12; 10, 6; BGU 846, 12; 2 Macc 6: 20; 4 Macc 14: 17 v.l.) Ac 15: 11; 27: 25.—In the acc. (cf. Bl-D. §160 app.; MJohannessohn, Der Gebr. der Kasus in LXX, Diss. Berlin '10, 81f) τρόπον w. gen. *like* (Aeschyl., Hdt.+; Philo. Oft. w. animals: θηρίων τρόπον 2 Macc 5: 27; 3 Macc 4: 9; σκορπίου τρόπον 4 Macc 11: 10) σητὸς τρόπον 1 Cl 39: 5 (Job 4: 19). τὸν ὅμοιον τρόπον τούτοις *in the same way* or *just as they* Jd 7. ὃν τρόπον *in the manner in which*=(*just*)

as (X., Mem. 1, 2, 59, An. 6, 3, 1; Pla., Rep. 5 p. 466E; Diod. S. 3, 21, 1; Dit., Syll.³ 976, 35; 849, 13f; PLeipz. 41, 9; Gen 26: 29; Ex 14: 13; Dt 11: 25 and very oft. in LXX; Jos., Ant. 3, 50, Vi. 412b) Mt 23: 37; Lk 13: 34; Ac 7: 28 (Ex 2: 14); 1 Cl 4: 10 (Ex 2: 14); 2 Cl 9: 4; corresponding to οὕτως (Dit., Syll.³ 685, 51ff; Josh 10: 1; 11: 15; Is 10: 11; 62: 5; Ezk 12: 11 al.) Ac 1: 11; 2 Ti 3: 8; 2 Cl 8: 2; 12: 4. τίνα τρόπον; *in what manner? how?* (Aristoph., Nub. 170; Pla., Prot. 322C; Jos., C. Ap. 1, 315) 1 Cl 24: 4; 47: 2.—In the dat. (Bl-D. §198, 4; Rob. 487.—Jos., Ant. 5, 339) παντὶ τρόπῳ *in any and every way* (Aeschyl., Thu.+; X., Cyr. 2, 1, 13; Pla., Rep. 2 p. 368c; pap.; 1 Macc 14: 35; Jos., Ant. 17, 84) Phil 1: 18. ποίῳ τρόπῳ; (Aeschyl., Soph. et al.; Test. Jos. 7: 1) Hv 1, 1, 7. ποίοις τρόποις m 12, 3, 1.

2. *way of life, turn of mind, conduct, character* (Pind., Hdt.+; Inscr. Gr. 545, 7; pap., LXX; Jos., Ant. 12, 252; Sib. Or. 4, 35) Hv 1, 1, 2. ἀφιλάργυρος ὁ τρόπος Hb 13: 5 (X., Cyr. 8, 3, 49 τρόπος φιλέταιρος). Also pl. (Aeschyl. +; Appian, Bell. Civ. 4, 95 §398; Dit., Syll.³ 783, 11; IG XII 7, 408, 8; Ep. Arist. 144) *ways, customs, kind of life* ἔχειν τοὺς τρόπους κυρίου *have the ways that the Lord himself had* or *which the Lord requires of his own* D 11: 8. M-M. B. 656.*

τροποφορέω 1 aor. ἐτροποφόρησα *bear* or *put up with* (*someone's*) *manner, moods* etc. (so Cicero, Ad Att. 13, 29, 2; schol. on Aristoph., Ran. 1479) w. acc. of the pers. Ac 13: 18 (Dt 1: 31 v.l., though τροφοφορεῖν stands in the text there; it is a v.l. in Ac.—Bl-D. §119, 1; Mlt.-H. 390. Origen, In Matth. vol. 10, 14 p. 16, 16 Klostermann '35). M-M.*

τροφεύς, έως, ὁ (Aeschyl., Pla.+; Dit., Or. 148, 2 [II BC] al.; Jos., Ant. 9, 127) *nourisher* of God (Philo, Leg. All. 3, 177, Congr. Erud. Gr. 171; Herm. Wr. 16, 12 ὁ ἥλιος as σωτὴρ κ. τροφεύς; p. 390, 12 Sc. ὁ δημιουργός as πατὴρ κ. τροφεύς) Dg 9: 6.*

τροφή, ῆς, ἡ *nourishment, food* (so trag., Hdt., Hippocr., X., Pla. et al.; pap., LXX, Ep. Arist., Philo; Jos., Vi. 200; 242; Test. 12 Patr.).

1. lit. Mt 3: 4; 6: 25; 10: 10 (cf. HGrimme, BZ 23, '35, 254f); 24: 45 (for δοῦναι αὐτοῖς τ. τρ. ἐν καιρῷ cf. Ps 103: 27 with v.l.); Lk 12: 23; Ac 14: 17; 1 Cl 20: 4; B 10: 4; Dg 9: 6; Hv 3, 9, 3; D 13: 1f. W. ποτόν 10: 3. τροφὴν λαβεῖν *take nourishment* (Jos., C. Ap. 2, 230) Ac 9: 19; but *receive food* B 10: 11. τροφῆς μεταλαμβάνειν (μεταλαμβάνω 1) Ac 2: 46; 27: 33f; προσλαμβάνεσθαι vs. 36; κορεσθῆναι vs. 38. Pl. (Diod. S. 15, 36, 1; Appian, Bell. Civ. 4, 136 §576; Aelian, V.H. 12, 37 p. 132, 28 ἀπορία τροφῶν) of a rather large supply of food J 4: 8. τροφὴ φθορᾶς *perishable food* IRo 7: 3. ἡ ἐφήμερος τροφή Js 2: 15 (s. ἐφήμερος).

2. symbolically (Pythagorean saying: Wiener Stud. 8, 1886 p. 277 no, 99 τ. ψυχὴν τρέφειν τῇ ἀϊδίῳ τροφῇ; Philo, Fuga 137 ἡ οὐράνιος τροφή) of spiritual nourishment ἡ στερεὰ τροφή *solid food* (opp. γάλα) Hb 5: 12, 14 (cf. στερεός). ἡ χριστιανὴ τροφή (opp. the poisonous food of false teaching) ITr 6: 1. M-M. B. 329.*

Τρόφιμος, ου, ὁ (IG III 1026; 1062; 1095; 1119; 1144 al.; POxy. 1160, 2) *Trophimus,* a companion of Paul on his last journey to Jerusalem: T.'s home was in Ephesus Ac 20: 4; 21: 29.—2 Ti 4: 20. M-M.*

τροφός, οῦ, ἡ (Hom.+; inscr., pap., LXX, Philo; Jos., C. Ap. 1, 122; Sib. Or. 13, 43) *nurse* (X., Oec. 5, 17 [w. μήτηρ]; Ael. Aristid. 13 p. 163 D. [w. μήτηρ]. Pap. since

III BC; s. also Test. Napht. 1: 9), possibly *mother* (Lycophron 1284 Europa τροφὸς Σαρπηδόνος; Dionys. Byz. §2 μητέρα καὶ τροφόν of one and the same person; schol. on Pla. 112ε of Phaedra in her relationship to Hippolytus [as stepmother]) 1 Th 2: 7. M-M.*

τροφοφορέω 1 aor. ἐτροφοφόρησα *carry in one's arms*, i.e. *care for τινά someone* (tenderly) Ac 13: 18 v.l. (fr. Dt 1: 31 [s. τροποφορέω]. Cf. also 2 Macc 7: 27 and Macarius, Hom. 46, 3). S. Beginn. I, 4, 149. M-M.*

τροχιά, ᾶς, ἡ (as early as Philo Mech. 54, 41) *wheel-track, course, way* (Anth. Pal. 7, 478; 9, 418; Herodian Gr. I 301, 2; Pr 2: 15; 4: 11; 5: 6, 21; Hesychius; Suidas) τροχιὰς ὀρθὰς ποιεῖν *make straight paths* upon which one can advance quickly and in the right direction; symbolically of the moral life τροχιὰς ὀρθὰς ποιεῖτε τοῖς ποσὶν ὑμῶν Hb 12: 13 (Pr 4: 26).*

τροχός, οῦ, ὁ (Hom. +; pap., LXX, En.; Ps.-Phoc. 27 ὁ βίος τροχός; Philo; Sib. Or. 2, 295; loanw. in rabb.) *wheel*, in our lit. only in the expr. ὁ τροχὸς τῆς γενέσεως Js 3: 6. S. γένεσις 4 and cf. JStiglmayr, BZ 11, '13, 49-52 (against Stiglmayr JSchäfers, ThGl 5, '13, 836-9); V Burch, Exp. 8th Ser. XVI '18, 221ff; REisler, Orphisch-dionys. Mysteriengedanken in der christl. Antike: Vorträge der Bibl. Warburg II 2, '25, 86-92; GerhKittel, Die Probleme des palästin. Spätjudentums u. das Urchristentum '26, 141-68; GHRendall, The Epistle of St. James and Judaic Christianity '27, 59f; DSRobertson, ET 39, '28, 333; NMacnicol, ibid. 55, '43/'44, 51f; WBieder, ThZ 5, '49, 109f; Windisch, Hdb.² exc. on Js 3: 6; JMarty, L'épître de Jacques '35.—Or should the word be accented (ὁ) τρόχος (Soph., Hippocr. +. On the difference betw. the words s. Trypho Alex. [I BC]; fgm. 11 AvVelsen [1853]; s. L-S-J lex. s.v. τροχός; Diehl² accents the word thus in the passage Ps.-Phoc. 27 referred to above), and should the transl. be *course* or *round* of existence? M-M. B. 725.*

τρύβλιον, ου, τό (on the accent s. Tdf., Prol. 102) *bowl, dish* (Aristoph., Hippocr. +; Plut., Lucian; Aelian, V.H. 9, 37; LXX; Ep. Arist. 320; Jos., Ant. 3, 220; 12, 117; Test. Jos. 6: 2) ἐμβάπτειν μετά τινος τὴν χεῖρα ἐν τῷ τρυβλίῳ dip one's hand into the bowl together with *someone*=share one's meal w. someone Mt 26: 23; cf. Mk 14: 20. M-M.*

τρυγάω fut. τρυγήσω; 1 aor. ἐτρύγησα (Hom. +; pap., LXX) *gather ripe fruit, esp. pick (grapes)* w. acc. of the fruit (POsl. 21, 13 [71 AD]; Jos., Ant. 4, 227) Lk 6: 44; Rv 14: 18 (symbolic, as in the foll. places). τὸν τῆς ἀναστάσεως καρπὸν τρυγήσουσι 2 Cl 19: 3. Cf. also the textually uncertain (s. αἱρέω 1) pass. Dg 12: 8.—W. the acc. of that which bears the fruit *gather the fruit of* the vine (cf. X., Oec. 19, 19; Diod. S. 3, 62, 7; Lucian, Cat. 20 τὰς ἀμπέλους τρ.; Philostrat., Her. 1, 2) or the vineyard (s. ἄμπελος 1) Rv 14: 19 (cf. Procop. Soph., Ep. 11 χωρία τρ.). M-M.*

τρυγών, όνος, ἡ (Aristoph., Aristot., Theocr. +; Aelian, V.H. 1, 15; LXX; Ep. Arist. 145; Philo; Jos., Ant. 1, 184; 3, 230. Fr. τρύζω=coo) *turtledove*, as a sacrificial animal of poor people Lk 2: 24 (Lev 12: 8.—W. περιστερά Aëtius 42, 8; 20; 44, 22.—PGM 12, 31 τρυγόνα καὶ . . . νεοσσὰ δύο). M-M.*

τρυμαλιά, ᾶς, ἡ (Sotades in Plut., Mor. 11A; Aesop, Fab. 26 H. of the openings in a net; Judg 15: 11 B; Jer 13: 4; 16: 16) *hole* τρυμαλιὰ ῥαφίδος *eye of a needle* Mt 19: 24 v.l.; Mk 10: 25; Lk 18: 25 t.r.—See s.v. κάμηλος and κάμιλος.

—On the eye of a needle as a symbol of the smallest thing imaginable s. JNSepp, ZDPV 14, 1891, 30-4. M-M.*

τρῦπα (Ps.-Herodian, Epim. p. 89 ἡ τοῦ μυὸς τρῦπα; Syntipas p. 55, 25; 27) or **τρύπη** (Anth. 14, 62, 2; Theognost., Canon. p. 24, 24; Ps.-Herodian, Epim. p. 136), ης, ἡ *hole, opening* of the anus B 10: 6 (on the subj. cf. ἀφόδευσις).*

τρυπάω 1 aor. ἐτρύπησα (Hom. +; Hero Alex. I p. 4, 23; 36, 14; LXX) *make a hole in, bore through τὶ someth.* τὸν οὐρανόν *the sky* Hm 11: 18. τὸν λίθον 11: 20. B. 593.*

τρύπη, ης, ἡ s. τρῦπα.

τρύπημα, ατος, τό (Aristoph.; Aeneas Tact. 725 al.; Philo Mech. 57, 19; Hero Alex., Plut. et al.) *that which is bored, a hole* τρύπημα ῥαφίδος *eye of a needle* Mt 19: 24 v.l.*

Τρύφαινα, ης, ἡ *Tryphaena*, a Christian woman who receives a greeting Ro 16: 12. In the Gk. form this name in Lucian; Gk. inscr. from Cyprus: Κυπρ. I p. 50 no. 4, p. 91 no. 21; CIG 3092; as the name of a Jewess in a pap. of 72/3 AD (in Schürer III⁴ 46), also BGU 1105, 2-5; 1119, 7; 1162, 16, esp. as the name of the daughter of Polemon of Pontus (Dit., Syll.³ 798, 14; 17; 19; 799, 4; 29). Also Acta Pauli (et Theclae) 27ff p. 255, 3ff Lips. In its Lat. form CIL VI 15622-6; XII 3398; XIV 415; 734.—Mommsen, Ephemeris Epigraphica I 1872, 270ff; II 1875, 259ff; Lghtf., Phil 175f; Zahn, Einl.³ I 299. M-M.*

τρυφάω 1 aor. ἐτρύφησα (Eur., Isocr. +; Epigr. Gr. 362, 5; PLond. 973b, 13; 2 Esdr 19 [Neh 9]: 25; Is 66: 11; Sir 14: 4; Philo; Jos., Ant. 4, 167; 7, 133; Test. Jos. 9: 2) *lead a life of luxury* or *self-indulgence, revel, carouse* Js 5: 5; Hs 6, 4, 1f; 4a, b; 6, 5, 3-5. Fig. of revelling in the doing of good vs. 7.—Of animals *be contented, well-fed* (Philo, Dec. 117) Hs 6, 1, 6; 6, 2, 6 (though the sheep here represent luxury-loving people). M-M.*

τρυφερός, ά, όν (Eur., Thu. +; BGU 1080, 18; LXX; Philo, Somn. 2, 9; Sib. Or. 3, 527) *delicate, gentle, subdued* of the Holy Spirit Hm 5, 1, 3; 5, 2, 6. Of the ἄγγελος τῆς δικαιοσύνης 6, 2, 3. Of maidens Hs 9, 2, 5 (Charito 2, 2, 2; cf. Sus 31 where, however, the ref. is to a woman's voluptuousness).*

τρυφή, ῆς, ἡ (Eur., X., Pla. +; Dit., Syll.³, 888, 124; LXX) —**1.** *indulgence, revelling* (Sextus 73; Philo, Spec. Leg. 2, 240, Somn. 1, 123; Jos., Ant. 10, 193; 16, 301) 2 Pt 2: 13 (cf. Cicero, Pro Caelio 47); Hs 6, 4, 4a, b; 6, 5, 1; 3; 4; 5. τρυφὴ πονηρά Hm 8: 3. ἄγγελος τρυφῆς Hs 6, 2, 1. Pl. (Jos., Vi. 284) Hm 6, 2, 5; 11: 12; 12, 2, 1; s 6, 2, 2; 4; 6, 5, 6; 7c.—**2.** *luxury, splendor* (Ps.-Lucian, Amor. 3 ἐσθὴς μέχρι ποδῶν τὴν τρυφὴν καθειμένη) Lk 7: 25.

3. in a good sense *enjoyment, joy, delight* (Menand., Cith. fgm. 5, 2 J.; Suppl. Epigr. Gr. VIII 549, 28 bestowed by Isis; En. 14, 13; Philo, Cher. 12; Jos., C. Ap. 2, 228; Test. Jud. 25: 2) οἵαν τρυφὴν ἔχει ἡ μέλλουσα ἐπαγγελία *what enjoyment the promise of the future brings* 2 Cl 10: 4. παράδεισος τρυφῆς a *Paradise of delight* Dg 12: 1 (Gen 3: 23; Ode of Solomon 11: 24).—*Revelling* in the doing of good Hs 6, 5, 7b; ibid. a, the pl. M-M.*

Τρυφῶσα, ης, ἡ *Tryphosa*, a Christian woman, recipient of a greeting Ro 16: 12. The name is found in Gk. and Lat. inscr. (CIG II 2819; 2839; 3348; IG III 2880; IX 2, 766; XIV 2246; PhLeBas-WHWaddington, Voyage III 1870, 710.—CIL VI 4866; 15241; X 2551 al.). She is mentioned together w. Τρύφαινα (q.v.) and hence is regarded by many (e.g. Lghtf., Phil p. 175, 7) as her sister. M-M.*

Τρῳάς, άδος, ἡ *Troas*, *(the) Troad*, actually fem. of the noun Τρῶς and the adj. Τρῳός; a city and region in the northwest corner of Asia Minor, near the site of ancient Troy. So since Hom. Hymns and trag.; the trag. connect it with γῆ, as does Hdt. 5, 26 ἐν τῇ Τρῳάδι γῇ. But Hdt. also uses the word 5, 122 without any addition of the region in general, and the same is true of X.; Diod. S. 14, 38, 2 τὰς ἐν τῇ Τρῳάδι πόλεις; 14, 38, 3 several cities κατὰ τὴν Τρῳάδα; 17, 7, 10; 17, 17, 6 (cf. ἡ Ἰνδική Hdt. 3, 106=Ἰνδικὴ χώρη 3, 98). In a time when there were many cities named Ἀλεξάνδρεια the one located in the Troad was known as Ἀλεξάνδρεια [ἡ] Τρῳάς=the Trojan Alexandria (Polyb. 5, 111, 3; Strabo 13, 1, 1 p. 581; Dit., Or. 441, 165f [81 BC]). This city, as well as the region around it, was occasionally called Τρῳάς for short (Pauly-W. I col. 1396, 15f and 2d Series VII 1 col. 383f [WRuge]).—In our lit. Τρῳάς has the article in Paul in 2 Cor 2: 12 (Bl-D. §261, 4) and prob. means the region, which the apostle soon left (vs. 13) for Macedonia. Elsewhere the article is almost always omitted, as is usually the case w. place-names (Bl-D. §261, 1). In Ac 20: 6, the only exception, the use of the art. can be justified as a glance backward at the preceding verse, where T. almost certainly means the city. In vs. 6 ἡ T.=Troas, which was just mentioned.—The other passages are: Ac 16: 8, 11; 2 Ti 4: 13; IPhld 11: 2; ISm 12: 1 and the subscription at the end of this letter; IPol 8: 1.*

Τρωγύλλιον, ου, τό (Strabo, Ptolem. et al., in var. spellings; Bl-D. §42, 3 app.) *Trogyllium* a promontory and town south of Ephesus in Asia Minor. Acc. to Ac 20: 15 t.r. (ἐν Τρωγυλλίῳ; D has ἐν Τρωγυλίᾳ; others ἐν Τρωγυνλίῳ) Paul stayed there one night.*

τρώγω (Hom.+; Dit., Syll.³ 1171, 9; PGM 7, 177; Sb 5730, 5. Not found in LXX, Ep. Arist., Philo or Joseph. Bl-D. §101 s.v. ἐσθίειν; 169, 2; Rob. 351; JHaussleiter, Archiv für lat. Lexikographie 9, 1896, 300–2) *gnaw, nibble, munch, eat* (audibly), of animals (Hom.+) B 10: 3.—Of human beings (Hdt.+ and so in Mod. Gk.) τὶ someth. (Hdt. 1, 71 σῦκα; Aristoph., Equ. 1077) B 7: 8. ὁ τρώγων μου τὸν ἄρτον as a symbol of close comradeship (Polyb. 31, 23, 9 δύο τρώγομεν ἀδελφοί) J 13: 18 (cf. Ps 40: 10 ὁ ἐσθίων ἄρτους μου, which is the basis for this pass.). W. gen. (Athen. 8 p. 334b τῶν σύκων) Hs 5, 3, 7. Abs. B 10: 2. W. πίνειν (Demosth. 19, 197; Plut., Mor. 613B; 716E) Mt 24: 38. J uses it, in order to offset any Docetic tendencies to 'spiritualize' the concept so that nothing physical remains in it, in what many hold to be the language of the Lord's Supper ὁ τρώγων τοῦτον τὸν ἄρτον 6: 58. ὁ τρώγων με vs. 57. ὁ τρώγων μου τὴν σάρκα (w. πίνων μου τὸ αἷμα) vss. 54, 56. M-M. B. 327.*

τυγχάνω (Hom.+; inscr., pap., LXX, Ep. Arist., Philo, Joseph.) impf. ἐτύγχανον; fut. τεύξομαι; 2 aor. ἔτυχον; perf. (for Att. τετύχηκα; cf. Phryn. p. 395 Lob.) τέτευχα (Ion. [Hdt. and Hippocr.; cf. Kühner-Bl. II 556], then Aristot.+; Dit., Or. 194, 31 [42 BC]; pap. [Mayser I 2² '38, 151f]; LXX [Thackeray §24 p. 287]; Ep. Arist. 121; ENachmanson, Laute u. Formen der magn. Inschr. '03 p. 160, 1; Crönert 279; WSchmid, Attiz. I 1887, 86; IV 1897, 40; 600) Hb 8: 6 or in some editions v.l. τέτυχα (Diod. S. 12, 17, 99; Aesop 363 Halm [removed by correction]; Jos., Bell. 7, 130 [removed by correction]; Ep. Arist. 180 συντέτευχε); Bl-D. §101; W-S. §13, 2; Mlt.-H. 262.

1. *meet, attain, gain, find, experience* w. gen. of the pers. or thing that one meets, etc. (Hom.+) Lk 20: 35; Ac 24: 2; 26: 22; 27: 3; 2 Ti 2: 10 (Diod. S. 4, 48, 7 τετεύχασι

τῆς σωτηρίας. With the v.l. σωτηρίαν in mss. FG cf. Solon 24, 2 D.² τυγχ. τι); Hb 8: 6; 11: 35; 1 Cl 61: 2; 2 Cl 15: 5; Dg 2: 1; 9: 6; IEph 10: 1; IMg 1: 3; ISm 9: 2; 11: 3; IPol 4: 3; Hm 10, 1, 5; s 9, 26, 4.

2. intr. *happen, turn out*—a. *happen to be, find oneself* (X., Hell. 4, 3, 3) ἐν σαρκὶ τυγχάνειν Dg 5: 8; ἐπὶ γῆς 10: 7. ἀφέντες ἡμιθανῆ τυγχάνοντα *they left him for half-dead, as indeed he was* Lk 10: 30 t.r.

b. εἰ τύχοι as a formula *if it should turn out that way, perhaps* (Cleanthes, fgm. 529 vArnim=Sext. Emp., Math. 9, 89; Dionys. Hal. 4, 19; Hero Alex. III p. 220, 13; Dio Chrys. 16[33], 53; Philo [KReik, Der Opt. bei Polyb. u. Philo von Alex. '07, 154]; Bl-D. §385, 2) 1 Cor 15: 37 (cf. Plut., fgm. 104, ed. Sanbach, '67 πυροῦ τυχὸν ἢ κριθῆς= perhaps of wheat or barley); Dg 2: 3. In τοσαῦτα εἰ τύχοι γένη φωνῶν εἰσιν 1 Cor 14: 10, εἰ τύχ. is prob. meant to limit τοσαῦτα (Heinrici: JWeiss) *there are probably ever so many different languages* (Gdspd.—Nicol. Dam.: 90 fgm. 130, 110 Jac. καθ' ἣν τύχοι πρόφασιν ='under who knows what sort of pretext').

c. τυχόν, actually the acc. absolute of the neut. of the aor. ptc. (Bl-D. §424; Rob. 490) *if it turns out that way, perhaps, if possible* (X., An. 6, 1, 20; Ps.-Pla., Alcib. 2 p. 140A; 150c; Epict. 1, 11, 11; 2, 1, 1; 3, 21, 18 al.; letter [IV BC] in Dssm., LO 121 [LAE 151]; Dit., Syll.³ 1159, 5; Sib. Or. 5, 236) 1 Cor 16: 6; Lk 20: 13 D; Ac 12: 15 D.

d. ὁ τυχών the first one whom one happens to meet in the way (X., Pla. et al.; Philo, Op. M. 137), hence οὐχ ὁ τυχών *not the common* or *ordinary one* (Fgm. Com. Att. III 442 fgm. 178 Kock; Theophr., H. Pl. 8, 7, 2; Περὶ ὕψους 9 [of Moses]. Numerous other exx. fr. lit. in Wettstein on Ac 19: 11. Inscr. fr. Ptolemaic times: Bull. de corr. hell. 22, 1898 p. 89 θόρυβον οὐ τὸν τυχόντα παρέχοντες; Dit., Syll.³ 528, 10 [221/19 BC] ἀρωστίαις οὐ ταῖς τυχούσαις; BGU 36, 9; POxy. 899, 14; 3 Macc 3: 7; Jos., Ant. 2, 120; 6, 292) δυνάμεις οὐ τὰς τυχούσας *extraordinary miracles* Ac 19: 11. Cf. 28: 2; 1 Cl 14: 2. M-M. B. 658.*

τυμπανίζω 1 aor. pass. ἐτυμπανίσθην *torture with the τύμπανον*, a certain kind of instrument of torture (so Aristoph., Plut. 476 et al.; 2 Macc 6: 19, 28. S. L-S-J lex. s.v. τύμπανον II 1 and ἀποτυμπανίζω.—AKeramopoulos, Ὁ Ἀποτυμπανισμος '23), then *torment, torture* gener. (Aristot., Rhet. 2, 5; Plut., Mor. 60A; Lucian, Jupp. Trag. 19. The compound ἀποτυμπ. in the same sense Plut., Dio 28, 2; UPZ 119, 37 [156 BC]; 3 Macc 3: 27; Jos., C. Ap. 1, 148) pass. Hb 11: 35.—ECEOwen, JTS 30, '29, 259–66. M-M.*

τυπικῶς (Rufus [II AD] in Oribas. 8, 47, 11; schol. on Pind., Ol. 1, 118 v.l.) adv. of τυπικός (Plut., Mor. 442c) *typologically, as an example* or *warning*, in connection w. the typological interpr. of Scripture ταῦτα τυπικῶς συνέβαινεν ἐκείνοις 1 Cor 10: 11. M-M.*

τύπος, ου, ὁ (Aeschyl., Hdt.+; inscr.; pap., LXX, En., Ep. Arist., Philo, Joseph., Test. 12 Patr., Sib. Or.; loanw. in rabb.).

1. *visible impression* of a stroke or pressure, *mark, trace* (Posidon.: 169 fgm. 1 Jac.; Anth. Pal. 6, 57, 5 ὀδόντων; Athen. 13, 49 p. 585c τῶν πληγῶν; Diog. L. 7, 45; 50 of a seal-ring; Philo, Mos. 1, 119; Jos., Bell. 3, 420; PGM 4, 1429; 5, 307) τῶν ἥλων J 20: 25a, b v.l.—This may be the place for οἱ τύποι τῶν λίθων Hs 9, 10, 1f (cf. KLake, Apost. Fathers II, '17; MDibelius, Hdb. But s. 4 below).

2. *copy, image* (cf. Artem. 2, 85 the children are τύπ. of their parents) the master is a τύπος θεοῦ *image of God* to

the slave B 19: 7; D 4: 11. The bishop is τύπος τοῦ πατρός ITr 3: 1; cf. IMg 6: 1a, b (here, however, τύπον is Zahn's conjecture, favored by Lghtf., for τόπον, which is unanimously read by Gk. and Lat. mss., and which can be retained, with Funk, Hilgenfeld, Krüger, Bihlmeyer).

3. *that which is formed, an image or statue* of any kind of material (Hdt. 3, 88 τύπ. λίθινος. Of images of the gods Herodian 5, 5, 6; Jos., Ant. 1, 311 τ. τύπους τῶν θεῶν; 15, 329; Sib. Or. 3, 14) Ac 7: 43 (Am 5: 26).

4. *form, figure, pattern* (Aeschyl.+; Pla., Rep. 387c; 397c) ἐποίησεν ἡμᾶς ἄλλον τύπον *he has made us men of a different stamp* (Kleist) B 6: 11. τύπον διδαχῆς *pattern of teaching* Ro 6: 17 (cf. διδαχή 2; Iambl., Vi. Pyth. 23, 105 τὸν τύπον τῆς διδασκαλίας.—The use of τύπος for the imperial 'rescripts' [s. Dit., Or. 521, 5; cf. note 4, esp. the reff. for θεῖος τύπος] appears too late to merit serious consideration.—JKürzinger, Biblica 39, '58, 156–76; EKLee, NTS 8, '61/'62, 166–73 [*mold*]). Of the *form (of expression)* (Dionys. Hal., Ad Pomp. 4, 2 Rad.; PLeipz. 121, 28 [II AD]; POxy. 1460, 12), perh. better of the *content* (Iambl., Vi. Pyth. 35, 259 τύπος τ. γεγραμμένων; 3 Macc 3: 30; PFlor. 278 II, 20 [III AD] τῷ αὐτῷ τύπῳ κ. χρόνῳ=of the same content and date) γράψας ἐπιστολὴν ἔχουσαν τὸν τύπον τοῦτον Ac 23: 25 (Ep. Arist. 34 ἐπιστολὴ τὸν τύπον ἔχουσα τοῦτον).—On τοὺς τύπους τῶν λίθων ἀναπληροῦν Hs 9, 10, 1 cf. ἀναπληρόω 3. S. also 1 above.

5. *(arche)type, pattern, model* (Pla., Rep. 379A περὶ θεολογίας)—a. technically *model, pattern* (Diod. S. 14, 41, 4) Ac 7: 44; Hb 8: 5 (cf. on both Ex 25: 40).

b. in the moral life *example, pattern* (Dit., Or. 383, 212 [I BC] τ. εὐσεβείας; Sib. Or. 1, 380; in a bad sense 4 Macc 6: 19 ἀσεβείας τύπ.) τύπος γίνου τῶν πιστῶν 1 Ti 4: 12.—Phil 3: 17; 1 Th 1: 7; 2 Th 3: 9; Tit 2: 7; 1 Pt 5: 3; IMg 6: 2.—S. EGSelwyn, 1 Pt '46, 298f.

6. of the *types* given by God as an indication of the future, in the form of persons or things (cf. Philo, Op. M. 157); of Adam: τύπος τοῦ μέλλοντος ('Αδάμ) *a type of the Adam to come* (i.e. of Christ) Ro 5: 14. Cf. 1 Cor 10: 6, 11 t.r.; B 7: 3, 7, 10f; 8: 1; 12: 2, 5f, 10; 13: 5. Also of the pictorial *symbols* that Hermas sees, and their deeper meaning Hv 3, 11, 4. The vision serves εἰς τύπον τῆς θλίψεως τῆς ἐπερχομένης *as a symbol or foreshadowing of the tribulation to come* 4, 1, 1; cf. 4, 2, 5; 4, 3, 6. The two trees are to be εἰς τύπον τοῖς δούλοις τοῦ θεοῦ s 2: 2a; cf. b.—ἐν τύπῳ χωρίου Ῥωμαίων IRo inscr. is a conjecture by Zahn for ἐν τόπῳ χ. 'P., which is read by all mss. and makes good sense.—AvBlumenthal, Τύπος u. παράδειγμα: Her. 63, '28, 391–414; LGoppelt, Typos. D. typolog. Deutung des AT im Neuen '39; RBultmann, ThLZ 75, '50, cols. 205–12; AFridrichsen et al., The Root of the Vine (typology) '53; GLampe and KJWoollcombe, Essays in Typology, '57.—LGoppelt, TW VIII, 246–60: τύπος etc. M-M.*

τύπτω impf. ἔτυπτον (Hom.+; inscr., pap., LXX, Ep. Arist., Philo, Joseph., Test. Jos.—Defective, cf. Bl-D. §101; Mlt.-H. 262) *strike, beat*.

1. lit. τινά *someone* (Jos., Ant. 20, 206, Vi. 108; 233) Mt 24: 49; Lk 12: 45; Ac 18: 17; 21: 32; Tit 1: 11 v.l. Pass. Ac 23: 3b.—τὸ στόμα τινός *strike someone on the mouth* 23: 2. τὸ πρόσωπόν τινος *strike someone in the face* (Hermippus Com. [V BC] 80) Lk 22: 64 t.r.; αὐτοῦ τὴν κεφαλὴν καλάμῳ Mk 15: 19 (for the dat. cf. Diod. S. 15, 86, 2 ἀλλήλους τοῖς δόρασι; Quint. Smyrn. 1, 247). τινὰ ἐπὶ τὴν σιαγόνα *strike someone on the cheek* Lk 6: 29. εἰς τὴν κεφαλήν τινος Mt 27: 30. As a sign of contrition or

sorrow (cf. Arrian, Anab. 7, 24, 3 τύπτεσθαι τὰ στήθη; Jos., Ant. 7, 252) ἔτυπτεν τὸ στῆθος ἑαυτοῦ Lk 18: 13. τύπτοντες τὰ στήθη 23: 48. τύπτω κατά τι *strike on someth.* (schol. on Nicander, Alexiph. 456): κατὰ ἕνα λίθον ἔτυπτεν *he struck on each individual stone* Hs 9, 6, 3. Pass. of an anvil IPol 3: 1.

2. fig., misfortunes designated as blows coming fr. God (Ex 7: 27; 2 Km 24: 17; Ezk 7: 6; 2 Macc 3: 39; Ep. Arist. 192) Ac 23: 3a.—τύπ. τὴν συνείδησίν τινος *wound someone's conscience* 1 Cor 8: 12 (Il. 19, 125; Hdt. 3, 64 Καμβύσεα ἔτυψε ἡ ἀληθηΐη τῶν λόγων; 1 Km 1: 8). M-M. B. 552f.*

τυραννίς, ίδος, ἡ *despotic rule, tyranny* (so Archilochus [VII BC], Hdt.+; LXX, Philo; Jos., Bell. 4, 166, Ant. 1, 114, Vi. 260; Sib. Or. 3, 202) ἐπὶ τυραννίδι *in order to set up a tyranny* Dg 7: 3.*

τύραννος, ου, ὁ *despotic ruler, tyrant* (so Theognis, Hdt. +; inscr., pap., LXX; Ep. Arist. 289; Philo; Jos., Bell. 5, 439, C. Ap. 2, 241; loanw. in rabb.) MPol 2: 4 (Wilcken, Chrest. 20 II, 5: Appian calls the Emperor Commodus a 'tyrant', though the emperor, l. 6, wishes to be known as βασιλεύς). W. βασιλεύς (Memnon [I BC/I AD] no. 434 fgm. 1, 4, 6 Jac.; Wsd 12: 14; Philo; Jos., Ant. 11, 287; 18, 169) Ac 5: 39 D.*

Τύραννος, ου, ὁ (lit.; Joseph. [index]; inscr., pap.) *Tyrannus*, an Ephesian in whose hall (s. σχολή) Paul lectured. Whether this otherw. unknown man was himself a teacher of philosophy or rhetoric, or whether he simply owned the house in which the hall was situated, we do not know (acc. to Diog. L. 9, 54 Protagoras held his lectures in Athens ἐν τῇ Εὐριπίδου οἰκίᾳ or acc. to others ἐν τῇ Μεγακλείδου) Ac 19: 9. M-M.*

τυρβάζω (Soph.+) *trouble, stir up*, mid. or pass. *trouble oneself, be troubled* περί τι *with* or *about someth.* (Aristoph., Pax 1007) περὶ πολλά Lk 10: 41 t.r. (Nilus, Ep. 2, 258 μὴ ἄγαν τυρβάζου).*

Τύριος, ου, ὁ (Hdt. et al.; Joseph. [index]; inscr., LXX) *the Tyrian* (s. Τύρος; Sib. Or. 4, 90) Ac 12: 20, 22 D.*

Τύρος, ου, ἡ (Hdt. et al.; Joseph. [index], inscr., LXX, Sib. Or. 5, 455.—Heb. צֹר; Aram. מור) *Tyre*, a city in Phoenicia Ac 21: 3, 7. Named w. Sidon Mt 11: 21f; 15: 21; Mk 3: 8; 7: 24 (καὶ Σ. v.l.), 31; Lk 6: 17; 10: 13f.—WBFleming, The History of Tyre '15.*

τυφλός, ή, όν (Hom.+; inscr., pap., LXX, Philo, Joseph.) *blind*—1. lit. (34 times in the canonical gospels)—a. adj. —α. as attribute ἄνθρωπος τυφλός J 9: 1 (s. γενετή); τυφ. προσαίτης Mk 10: 46.—β. as predicate J 9: 18, 24; Ac 13: 11; Dg 2: 4 (almost word for word like Plut., Mor. 420B εἴδωλα κωφὰ κ. τυφλὰ κ. ἄψυχα). Mostly

b. subst. Mt 9: 27f; 11: 5; 20: 30; Mk 8: 22f (LSzimonidesz, D. Heilung des Blinden von Bethsaida u. Buddhas Gleichn. von den Blindgeborenen u. dem Elefanten: NThT 24, '35, 233–59); 10: 49, 51; Lk 7: 21f; J 5: 3; 10: 21; 11: 37 al. (on Mt 11: 5; Lk 7: 22 cf. also κωφός 2). On Mt 15: 14; Lk 6: 39 s. ὁδηγέω 1 and cf. Sext. Emp., Πρὸς Μαθημ. I, 31 ὡς οὐδὲ ὁ τυφλὸς τὸν τυφλὸν ὁδηγεῖν (sc. δύναται).

2. symbol. and fig., of mental and spiritual blindness (since Pind.; Soph., Oed. R. 371; Lucian, Vit. Auct. 18 τῆς ψυχῆς τὸν ὀφθαλμόν; Ps 145: 8; Philo; Jos., C. Ap. 2, 142 τυφλὸς τὸν νοῦν).

a. adj.—α. as attribute ὁδηγὸς τυφλός (cf. X., Mem. 1, 3, 4; Demetr. Phaler. [IV BC; ed. FWehrli '49], fgm. 121

οὐ μόνον τὸν πλοῦτον τυφλόν, ἀλλὰ καὶ τὴν ὁδηγοῦσαν αὐτὸν τύχην; Philo, Virt. 7) Mt 15: 14; 23: 16, 24. Φαρισαῖε τυφλέ vs. 26.—β. as a predicate J 9: 40f; 2 Pt 1: 9; Rv 3: 17. τυφλοί εἰσιν τῇ καρδίᾳ αὐτῶν LJ 1: 3.

b. subst. Mt 23: 17, 19; Ro 2: 19; B 14: 7 (Is 42: 7), 9 (Is 61: 1). οὐαὶ τυφλοὶ μὴ ὁρῶντες GOxy 31.—WSchrage, TW VIII, 270–94. M-M. B. 322.

τυφλόω 1 aor. ἐτύφλωσα; pf. τετύφλωκα (Pind., Hdt. +; Ramsay, Phrygia II p. 386 no. 232, 15; PLond. 1708, 84; LXX) *to blind, deprive of sight* in our lit. only symbol. (Is 42: 19) τετύφλωκεν αὐτῶν τοὺς ὀφθαλμούς (cf. Test. Dan 2: 4) J 12: 40; cf. Is 6: 10).—1 J 2: 11; or fig. τυφ. τὰ νοήματα 2 Cor 4: 4 (Pla., Phaedo 99E μὴ τὴν ψυχὴν τυφλωθείην; Herm. Wr. 478, 32 Sc.; Philo, Ebr. 108 διάνοιαν τυφλωθείς; Jos., Ant. 8, 30; Test. Sim. 2: 7 ὁ ἄρχων τῆς πλάνης ἐτύφλωσέ μου τὸν νοῦν). M-M.*

τῦφος, ους, τό for the usual (cf. ζῆλος, beg.) **τῦφος, ου, ὁ** *delusion, conceit, arrogance* (so Pla. et al.; Philo Bybl. [c. 100 AD] in Euseb., Pr. Ev. 1, 9, 26; Dio Chrys. 4, 6; Vett. Val. 4, 28; 150, 5; 3 Macc 3: 18; Philo; Sib. Or. 8, 8; 111) 1 Cl 13: 1.*

τυφόω pf. pass. τετύφωμαι; 1 aor. ἐτυφώθην *becloud, delude,* but only in a fig. sense and quite predom., in our lit. exclusively, in the pass. (Hippocr., Pla.) **τυφόομαι;** for our lit. the mngs. are surely
1. *be puffed up, conceited* (Strabo 15, 1, 5; Plut., Mor. 59A; Aelian, V.H. 3, 28; Diog. L. 6, 7; 26 al.; Philo, Congr. Erud. Gr. 128; Jos., Vi. 53) τυφωθείς (cf. Sext. Emp., Pyrrh. 3, 193) 1 Ti 3: 6. Cf. 2 Ti 3: 4. The ancient versions also understand τετύφωται μηδὲν ἐπιστάμενος 1 Ti 6: 4 in this sense, though this pass. may belong under mng. 2.
2. *be blinded, become foolish* (Hippocr. +) pf. pass. *be foolish, stupid* (Demosth. 9, 20; 19, 219 μαίνομαι καὶ τετύφωμαι; Polyb. 3, 81, 1 ἀγνοεῖ κ. τετύφωται; Dio

Chrys. 30[47], 18 ἢ ἐγὼ τετύφωμαι καὶ ἀνόητός εἰμι; Philo, Conf. Lingu. 106; Jos., C. Ap. 1, 15; 2, 255). M-M.*

τύφω (Eur., Hdt. +) *give off smoke* or *steam* pass. *smoke, smolder, glimmer* (Philostrat., Vi. Apoll. 5, 17 p. 177, 30; Jos., Bell. 6, 257) of a wick Mt 12: 20 (s. the lit. s.v. κάλαμος 1).*

τυφωνικός, ή, όν *like a whirlwind* ἄνεμος τυφωνικός *a typhoon, hurricane* Ac 27: 14 (Etym. Mag. p. 755, 11 τῶν τυφωνικῶν καλουμένων πνευμάτων; schol. on Soph., Ant. 418 p. 239 P. τὸν τυφώνιον ἄνεμον; Eustath. in Il. 2, 782 p. 345, 43).—Rdm.² 28f. M-M.*

τυχεῖν, τύχοι s. τυγχάνω.

τύχη, ης, ἡ (Hom. Hymns, Hdt. +; inscr., pap., LXX; Jos., Bell. 4, 365, C. Ap. 2, 130; 227) *fortune,* in our lit. only as v.l. in Lk 10: 31D *by chance,* and in the expr. ὀμνύναι τὴν Καίσαρος τύχην *swear by the Fortune of Caesar* (cf. Cass. Dio 44, 6; 50; 57, 8; Jos., Ant. 16, 344. Very oft. in pap., from POxy. 483, 21 [108 AD] on) MPol 9: 2; 10: 1. B. 1096.*

Τυχικός, οῦ, ὁ (inscr., e.g. nine times in those fr. Magnesia.—On the accent s. KHALipsius, Gramm. Untersuchungen über die biblische Gräz. 1863, 30; Tdf., Proleg. 103) *Tychicus,* a man fr. the province of Asia who accompanied Paul on his journey to Jerusalem w. the collection Ac 20: 4. In Eph 6: 21 he is called ὁ ἀγαπητὸς ἀδελφὸς καὶ πιστὸς διάκονος ἐν κυρίῳ, and in Col 4: 7 σύνδουλος is added to these. In both of these he is to report to the recipients of the letter concerning the apostle. In 2 Ti 4: 12 he is sent to Ephesus. In Tit 3: 12 it is proposed to send him or Artemas to Titus in Crete. S. also Eph subscr.; Col subscr. M-M.*

τυχόν adv. s. τυγχάνω 2c.

Υ

ὕαινα, ης, ἡ *the hyena* (so Hdt. +; Sir 13: 18; Jer 12: 9), named as an unclean animal whose flesh the Jews were not permitted to eat B 10: 7 (for the extraordinary interpr. represented here cf. Windisch ad loc. Also Diod. S. 32, 12, 2, a report from mythological writers who maintain concerning the hyena ἄρρενας ἅμα καὶ θηλείας ὑπάρχειν καὶ παρ' ἐνιαυτὸν ἀλλήλους ὀχεύειν; Aesop, Fab. 242; 243 P.=405; 406 H.; Cyranides p. 74, 14–16; Horapollo 2, 69).*

ὑακίνθινος, ίνη, ινον (Hom.+; PSI 183, 5; LXX; Philo, Spec. Leg. 1, 94; Jos., Ant. 3, 165) *hyacinth-colored,* i.e. dark blue (dark red?) w. πύρινος Rv 9: 17. M-M.*

ὑάκινθος, ου, ὁ (as early as Hom. as the name of a flower) *the jacinth* or *hyacinth* (Peripl. Eryth. c. 56 [gender undetermined]; Galen vol. XIII p. 970; Ptolem. 7, 4, 1; Heliod. 2, 30, 3 [in him clearly fem.]; Achilles Tat. 2, 11, 3 [gender undetermined].—In the LXX and in Philo and Joseph. [Ant. 3, 164] hyacinth-colored cloth is meant), a precious stone Rv 21: 20, perh. blue in color, someth. like the sapphire (but cf. vs. 19); on it s. Murray, New [Oxford] Engl. Dict. s.v. hyacinth 1a, b. It was often made into gems by the ancients (Pliny, Nat. Hist. 37, 9, 41f).—For lit. see s.v. ἀμέθυστος. M-M.*

ὑάλινος, η, ον (since Corinna [VI BC] 42 Diehl; Dit., Syll.³ 1106, 153; PPetr. III 42 H 7, 3 [III BC]; POxy. 1740, 30) *of glass, transparent as glass* Rv 4: 6; 15: 2a, b. M-M.*

ὕαλος, ου, ἡ (so since Hdt. 3, 24 [ὕελος]; Aristoph.; Pla.; PFay. 134, 4), rarely ὁ (Theophr., Lapid. 49 [ὕελ.]; Bl-D. §49, 1; Mlt.-H. 67; 124.—Job 28: 17 the gender cannot be determined) *glass, crystal* (w. χρυσίον; cf. Job 28: 17) ὕαλ. καθαρός Rv 21: 18. ὕαλ. διαυγής vs. 21. M-M. B. 620.*

ὑβρίζω 1 aor. ὕβρισα. Pass.: 1 aor. ὑβρίσθην; 1 fut. ὑβρισθήσομαι (Hom.+; inscr., pap., LXX, Philo, Joseph., Test. 12 Patr.) in our lit. only trans. *treat in an arrogant* or *spiteful manner, mistreat, scoff at, insult* (Aristot., De Rhet. 2, 2 ἔστιν ὕβρις τὸ πράττειν καὶ λέγειν ἐφ' οἷς αἰσχύνη ἐστὶ τῷ πάσχοντι) τινά *someone* (oft. in pap. [Mayser II 2 p. 303; reff. for the pass. also here]) *mistreat* Mt 22: 6 (w. ἀποκτείνω POxy. 903, 5f [IV AD]); Ac 14: 5. Pass. Lk 18: 32; 1 Th 2: 2; Tit 1: 11 v.l.; Dg 5: 15 (w. λοιδορεῖσθαι; cf. Dit., Syll.³ 1109, 74; 76; 78 [178 AD]; Test. Benj. 5: 4); Hs 6, 3, 4; *insult* (Jos., Ant. 4, 187) w. words ἡμᾶς ὑβρίζεις Lk 11: 45; by one's conduct *abuse, outrage someth.* τὴν σάρκα 2 Cl 14: 4a. τὴν ἐκκλησίαν 14: 4b (cf. Jos., Bell. 3, 371 [θεοῦ] τὸ δῶρον,

Ant. 9, 257 τὸν θεόν); *carry on presumptuously with* αὐτοὺς (χλευάζετε καὶ) ὑβρίζετε Dg 2: 7. M-M.*

ὕβρις, εως, ἡ (Hom.+; inscr., pap., LXX, Philo, Jos., Test. 12 Patr., Sib. Or.)—1. act. *insolence, arrogance* (Appian, Basil. 5 §2 καθ' ὕβριν=out of arrogance; Pr 11: 2; 29: 23; Is 9: 8; Philo, Spec. Leg. 3, 186; Jos., Ant. 6, 61) ὕβρ. ὑπερηφάνων 1 Cl 59: 3 (ὕβρ. w. ὑπερηφανία: Ael. Aristid. 28, 101 K.=49 p. 524 D.; Paroem. Gr.: Zenob. [II AD] 5, 44. Also ὑβριστικῶς κ. ὑπερηφάνως Diod. S. 16, 41, 2).

2. pass. *shame, insult, mistreatment* (PEleph. 1, 8 [311 BC] ἐφ' ὕβρει=for insult, for outrage; PMagd. 24 verso; Proseuche Aseneth 28 Batiffol; Philo, In Flacc. 58; Sib. Or. 3, 529; Celsus 4, 46) ὕβριν ὑποφέρειν Hm 8: 10. ὕβριν ποιεῖν τινι do harm to someone Hs 9, 11, 8. εἰς ὕβριν τo (someone's) *shame* Papias 3. Pl. *mistreatment* (Polyb. 6, 8, 5; 10, 37, 8; 11, 5, 7; Sb 5235, 12 [I AD] ὕβρεις καὶ πληγάς; PLond. 358, 8; Sir 10: 8; Sib. Or. 4, 164) 2 Cor 12: 10.

3. fig. *hardship, disaster, damage* caused by the elements (Pind., Pyth. 1, 140; Anth. Pal. 7, 291, 4 δείσασα θαλάττης ὕβριν; Jos., Ant. 3, 133 τὴν ἀπὸ τῶν ὄμβρων ὕβριν) w. ζημία Ac 27: 10 (μετὰ ὕβ. as Dit., Syll.³ 780, 18; 30; 3 Macc 3: 25; Jos., Ant. 1, 60), 21.—JJFraenkel, Hybris '42; GBertram, TW VIII, 295–307: ὕβρις, etc. M-M.*

ὑβριστής, οῦ, ὁ (Hom.+; LXX, Philo; Jos., Ant. 5, 339; Sib. Or. 2, 259) *a violent, insolent man* Ro 1: 30 (w. ὑπερήφανος in a catalogue of vices in Ps.-Dicaearchus p. 143 Fuhr. The same juxtaposition of ὑπερήφανος and ὑβριστής in Diod. S. 5, 55, 6 and Aristot., Rhet. 1390b, 33 [II, 16, 1]); 1 Ti 1: 13. M-M.*

ὑγεία this spelling for the older ὑγίεια appears in the pap. fr. II AD (POxy. 496, 10 [127 AD]; 497, 11; 715, 29; PTebt. 298, 77; PAmh. 132, 3; 18 [all II AD]), but also Dit., Syll.³ 810, 15 [55 AD].—Ep. Arist. 190; 237; 259; Test. Napht. 2: 8. Predom. in Philo. For the LXX s. Thackeray p. 63f.— ESchweizer, Gramm. der perg. Inschr. 1898, 101; ENachmanson, Laute u. Formen der magnet. Inschr. '03, 71; Crönert 34; Mayser I 92, 5; s. ὑγίεια.

ὑγιαίνω (Theognis, Hdt.+; inscr., pap., LXX, Philo, Joseph., Test. 12 Patr.) *be in good health, be healthy* or *sound.*

1. lit., of physical health Mt 8: 13 v.l.; Lk 5: 31 (Artem. 4, 22 οὐ τοῖς ὑγιαίνουσιν ἀλλὰ τοῖς κάμνουσιν δεῖ θεραπείων); 7: 10; 15: 27. As a formula in an epistolary greeting (e.g. Ltzm., Griech. Papyri² [=Kl. T. 14] '10 no. 1, 3 [=BGU 423]; 2, 3 [BGU 846]; 8, 3 [=BGU 27]; 9, 4 [=BGU 38] and oft. in pap.; cf. Ep. Arist. 41) 3 J 2.

2. fig., in the Pastoral Epistles w. ref. to Christian teaching: ὑγιαίνουσα διδασκαλία 1 Ti 1: 10; 2 Ti 4: 3; Tit 1: 9; 2: 1. ὑγιαίνοντες λόγοι 1 Ti 6: 3; 2 Ti 1: 13. ὑγιαίνειν (ἐν) τῇ πίστει Tit 1: 13; 2: 2 (on its use w. the dat. cf. Jos., C. Ap. 1, 222). S. λόγος ὑγιής Tit 2: 8 (ὑγιής 2). Thus, in accord w. prevailing usage, Christian teaching is designated as *correct* instruction, since it is reasonable and appeals to sound intelligence (Plut., Mor. 20F αὗται γάρ εἰσιν ὑγιαίνουσαι περὶ θεῶν δόξαι καὶ ἀληθεῖς; Philo, Abr. 223 al. τοὺς ὑγιαίνοντας λόγους; Jos., C. Ap. 1, 222 οἱ ὑγιαίνοντες τῇ κρίσει [opp. ἀνόητοι]. S. also ὑγιής 2).—MDibelius, Hdb. exc. on 1 Ti 1: 10. M-M.*

ὑγίεια, ας, ἡ (or Ion. ὑγιείη, Pind., Hdt.+; inscr., pap., LXX; Philo, Sacr. Abel. 39, Aet. M. 116.—For the spelling ὑγεία in 1 Cl 20: 10, s. that as a separate entry) *health* 1 Cl 61: 1; (w. ἀπόλαυσις) 20: 10.*

ὑγιής, ές acc. ὑγιῆ (Hom.+; inscr., pap., LXX, Philo, Joseph.) *healthy, sound.*

1. lit.—a. of persons Mt 15: 31; Ac 4: 10; or of their individual members (Dit., Syll.³ 1170, 26 ἡ χείρ) Mt 12: 13; Mk 3: 5 t.r.; Lk 6: 10 t.r. ὑγ. γίνεσθαι get well (Dit., Syll.³ 1168, 47; 94; 102; 1169, 18 [IV BC]) J 5: 4, 6 (s. Artem. 3, 39: no one says to a healthy man 'ὑγιανεῖς'= you will get well), 9, 14. ποιεῖν τινα ὑγιῆ *cure someone, restore someone to health* (X., Mem. 4, 2, 7) J 5: 11, 15; 7: 23. ἴσθι ὑγιὴς ἀπό... *be healed* (and free) *from*... Mk 5: 34.

b. of things *sound, undamaged* (Eur., Thu. et al.; inscr., pap.) of trees Hs 8, 1, 3f; 8, 3, 1. Of stones (Dit., Syll.³ 972, 32; 101) 9, 8, 3 (comparative); 5; 7.

2. fig. τηρεῖν ὑγιῆ i.e. τὴν σφραγῖδα *keep the seal* (=baptism) *unbroken* Hs 8, 6, 3.—λόγος ὑγιής *sound teaching* or *preaching* Tit 2: 8 (s. ὑγιαίνω 2 and cf. Musonius p. 6, 2 H.; Dio Chrys. 1, 49 ὑγ. λόγ.; Maximus Tyr. 16, 3f ἀλήθειάν γε καὶ ὑγιῆ λόγον; M. Ant. 8, 30 ὑγιὴς λόγος, also Epict. 1, 11, 28 ὑγιές ἐστι τὸ ὑπὸ τ. φιλοσόφων λεγόμενον; 1, 12, 5; 6; Dit., Syll.³ 983, 5 γνώμην ὑγ.; Epict. 3, 9, 5 ὑγιῆ δόγματα; Ep. Arist. 250; Philo, Spec. Leg. 2, 164 ὑγ. δόξα; Jos., Ant. 9, 118 μηδὲν ὑγιὲς φρονεῖν). M-M. B. 300.*

ὑγρός, ά, όν (Hom.+; inscr., pap., LXX; Sib. Or. 3, 144) *moist, pliant,* of fresh wood *green* (so ὑγρότης Theophr., H.Pl. 5, 9, 7; 8; Philostrat., Ep. 55 ὑγρός of fresh roses) Lk 23: 31 (opp. ξηρός as Dio Chrys. 80[30], 15 and oft. in Philo; Jos., Ant. 4, 267).—AJeremias, Hdb. der altoriental. Geisteskultur '13, 263ff (cult of Tammuz). M-M. B. 1074.*

ὑδρία, ας, ἡ *water jar* (so Diocles Com. [V BC] 1; Aristoph., Eccl. 678, Vesp. 926; Athen. 5 p. 199D; 11 p. 462B; inscr.; POxy. 502, 37; PSI 428, 89; Gen 24: 14ff; Jos., Ant. 8, 341) J 2: 6 (Synes., Ep. 126 p. 261 ὑδρία... κείσεται), 7; 4: 28. M-M. B. 347.*

ὑδροποτέω (opp. οἴνῳ διαχρῆσθαι Hdt. 1, 71; X., Cyr. 6, 2, 26; Pla., Rep. 8 p. 561c; Epict. 3, 13, 21, cf. 3, 14, 4; Aelian, V.H. 2, 38 μὴ ὁμιλεῖν οἴνῳ ἀλλὰ ὑδροποτεῖν; Lucian, Bis Accus. 16; Da 1: 12) *drink* (only) *water* of an abstemious way of life μηκέτι ὑδροπότει, ἀλλὰ οἴνῳ ὀλίγῳ χρῶ 1 Ti 5: 23. M-M.*

ὑδρωπικός, ή, όν *suffering from dropsy* (Hippocr.+ in medical [Hobart 24] and lay [HJCadbury, JBL 45, '26, 205; cf. ibid. 52, '33, 62f; e.g. also Περὶ ὕψους 3, 4; Ptolem., Apotel. 4, 9, 3; Proverbia Aesopi 95 P.; Diog. L. 4, 27; schol. on Nicander, Ther. 70 p. 10, 27] writers) ἄνθρωπός τις ἦν ὑδρωπικός Lk 14: 2. M-M.*

ὕδωρ, ατος, τό (Hom.+; inscr., pap., LXX, En., Ep. Arist., Philo, Joseph., Test. 12 Patr.; loanw. in rabb.) *water.*

1. lit., as an element Dg 8: 2 (στοιχεῖον 2). Of the ocean 1 Cl 33: 3; pl. Hv 1, 3, 4 (cf. Ps 135: 6, w. the sing. as v.l.). An earth (before the Deluge) formed ἐξ ὕδατος καὶ δι' ὕδατος 2 Pt 3: 5 (cf. HDiels, Doxographi Graeci 1879 p. 276, 12 [Θαλῆς] ἐξ ὕδατός φησι πάντα εἶναι καὶ εἰς ὕδωρ πάντα ἀναλύεσθαι; JChaine, Cosmogonie aquatique et conflagration finale d'après 2 Pt: RB 46, '37, 207–16. S. also Artem. 1, 77 p. 70, 6 al. ἐξ ὕδατος ἢ δι' ὕδατος). Of the waters of the Deluge 1 Pt 3: 20; 2 Pt 3: 6. σίφων ὕδατος *a water-pump* Hm 11: 18. κεράμιον ὕδατος *a water jar* (s. κεράμιον) Mk 14: 13; Lk 22: 10. ποτήριον ὕδατος (PGenève 51, 9) *a cup of water* Mk 9: 41. Water for washing Mt 27: 24; Lk 7: 44; J 13: 5. Cf. Hs 9, 10, 3. Water fr. a well J 4: 7; fr. a spring Js 3: 12 (γλυκὺ ὕδωρ; s.

γλυκύς, also Herm. Wr. 13, 17); of a stream Rv 16: 12.—τὸ ὕδωρ specif.=the river Mt 3: 16; Mk 1: 10; =the pool J 5: 3f, 7; =the lake Lk 8: 24, pl. Mt 8: 32; 14: 28f; =the spring, etc. pl. Rv 8: 11a, b. Cf. πηγαὶ (τῶν) ὑδάτων vs. 10; 14: 7; 16: 4; =the mountain torrent pl. Hv 1, 1, 3; of waters gener., or not more exactly defined Mt 17: 15. ὕδωρ τι Ac 8: 36a. Cf. vs. 38f. Pl. Mk 9: 22. ὕδατα πολλά (Ps 28: 3) J 3: 23; Rv 17: 1. φωνὴ ὑδάτων πολλῶν the sound of many waters (Ps 92: 4) 1: 15; 14: 2; 19: 6. χεόμενα ὕδατα water that is poured out GOxy 32f.—W. bread as that which is necessary to maintain life Hs 5, 3, 7. In contrast to wine J 2: 9. W. blood J 19: 34 (s. αἷμα 1a). Christ came δι᾽ ὕδατος καὶ αἵματος and ἐν τῷ ὕδατι καὶ ἐν τῷ αἵματι 1 J 5: 6a, b, c; cf. vs. 8 (s. διά A I 1, ἐν I 4cβ and ἔρχομαι I 1aη). Gener. of John's baptism by water (alone), opp. πνεῦμα Mt 3: 11; Mk 1: 8; Lk 3: 16; J 1: 33 (26, 31); Ac 1: 5; 11: 16. Of Christian baptism, the new birth ἐξ ὕδατος καὶ πνεύματος J 3: 5 (on the originality of the rdg. ὕδατος καί s. Hdb.³ ad loc.; Bultmann 98, 2), 8 v.l. Cf. Ac 10: 47. καθαρίσας τῷ λουτρῷ τοῦ ὕδατος ἐν ῥήματι Eph 5: 26. λελουσμένοι τὸ σῶμα ὕδατι καθαρῷ Hb 10: 22 (καθαρός 1). Even the OT points to the water of baptism B 11: 1a, b, 8a, b, which Christ has consecrated by his own baptism IEph 18: 2. The symbolic language of Hermas makes many allusions to the baptismal water: δι᾽ ὕδατος ἀναβαίνειν s 9, 16, 2. εἰς ὕδωρ καταβαίνειν m 4, 3, 1; s 9, 16, 6. The tower (=church) is built ἐπὶ ὑδάτων Hv 3, 2, 4; 3, 3, 5a, b, ὅτι ἡ ζωὴ ὑμῶν διὰ ὕδατος ἐσώθη καὶ σωθήσεται 3, 3, 5c. Acc. to D 7: 1, when at all poss., ὕδωρ ζῶν running water (ζάω 4a) is to be used in baptizing. Cf. 7: 2.

2. fig. the transition to this sense is marked by J 4: 10f, where (τὸ) ὕδωρ (τὸ) ζῶν (cf. 1QH 8, 7 and CD 6, 4; 3, 16) is partly spring water and partly a symbol of the benefits conferred by Jesus (OCullmann, ThZ 4, '48, 367f.—For the symbolic use cf. Sir 15: 3.—Cf. 1QH 8, 4). Cf. 7: 38; 4: 14a, b, c (cf. Sir 24: 21); IRo 7: 2 (cf. Anacreontea 12, 7 p. 9 Preisendanz λάλον ὕδωρ). ζωῆς (τῆς) ζωῆς water of life (cf. Hdb. z. NT exc. on J 4: 14; REisler, Orphisch-dionys. Mysteriengedanken in der christl. Antike: Vorträge der Bibl. Warburg II 2, '25, 139ff; Herm. Wr. 1, 29 ἐτράφησαν ἐκ τοῦ ἀμβροσίου ὕδατος) Rv 21: 6; 22: 1, 17. βεβάμμεθα ἐν ὕδασι ζωῆς GOxy 43f. ζωῆς πηγαὶ ὑδάτων springs of living water Rv 7: 17.—SEitrem, Opferritus u. Voropfer der Griechen u. Römer '15, 78ff, Beiträge z. griech. Religionsgesch. III '20, 1ff; MNinck, Die Bed. des Wassers im Kult u. Leben der Alten '21; ArchdaleAKing, Holy Water: A Short Account of the Use of Water for Ceremonial and Purificatory Purposes in Pagan, Jewish, and Christian Times '26; TCanaan, Water and the 'Water of Life' in Palest. Superstition: Journ. of the Palest. Orient. Soc. 9, '29, 57-69.—LGoppelt, TW VIII, 313-33. M-M. B. 35.

ὑετός, οῦ, ὁ (Hom.+; PPetr. II 49a, 13 [III BC]; LXX, Philo; Jos., Ant. 8, 106; 18, 285; Sib. Or. 3, 690) rain Ac 14: 17; 28: 2; Hb 6: 7; Js 5: 7 t.r., 18; Rv 11: 6. M-M. B. 68.*

υἱοθεσία, ας, ἡ (Diod. S. 31, 27, 2 ed. Dind. X 31, 13; Diog. L. 4, 53. Oft. inscr. [Dit., Syll.³ index; Dssm., NB 66f-BS 239; Rouffiac]; pap. [PLeipz. 28, 14; 17; 22 al.; POxy. 1206, 8; 14 al., both IV AD; Third Corinthians 3: 8; Preisigke, Fachwörter '15; PMMeyer, Jurist. Pap. '20 no. 10 introd. p. 22]) adoption (of children), lit. a legal t.t.; in our lit., i.e. in Paul, only in a religious sense.

1. of the acceptance of the nation of Israel as son of God (cf. Ex 4: 22; Is 1: 2 al. where, however, the word υἱοθ. is lacking; it is found nowhere in the LXX) Ro 9: 4.

2. of those who turn to Christianity and are accepted by God as his sons τὴν υἱοθεσίαν ἀπολαβεῖν Gal 4: 5. Cf. Eph 1: 5. The Spirit, whom the converts receive, works as πνεῦμα υἱοθεσίας Ro 8: 15 (opp. πν. δουλείας=such a spirit as is possessed by a slave, not by the son of the house). The believers enter into full enjoyment of their υἱοθεσία only when the time of fulfilment releases them fr. the earthly body vs. 23.—Harnack (s. παλιγγενεσία 2); TWhaling, Adoption: PTR 21, '23, 223-35; Astrid Wentzel, Her. 65, '30, 167-76; ADieterich, Eine Mithrasliturgie '03, 134-56; LHMarshall, Challenge of NT Ethics '47, 258f; WHRossell, JBL 71, '52, 233f; DJTheron, Evangelical Quarterly 28, '56, 6-14. M-M.*

υἱός, οῦ, ὁ (Hom.+; inscr., pap., LXX, En., Philo, Joseph., Test. 12 Patr.; loanw. in rabb.) son.

1. in the usual sense—a. quite literally—α. of the direct male issue of a person τέξεται υἱόν Mt 1: 21. Cf. vs. 23 (Is 7: 14) and 25; 10: 37 (w. θυγάτηρ); Mk 12: 6a; Lk 1: 13, 31, 57; 11: 11; 15: 11 (on this JEngel, Die Parabel v. Verlorenen Sohn: ThGl 18, '26, 54-64; MFrost, The Prodigal Son: Exp. 9th Ser. II '24, 56-60; EBuonaiuti, Religio 11, '35, 398-402); Ac 7: 29; Ro 9: 9 (cf. Gen 18: 10); Gal 4: 22 al. W. gen. Mt 7: 9; 20: 20f; 21: 37a, b; Mk 6: 3; 9: 17; Lk 3: 2; 4: 22; 15: 19; J 9: 19f; Ac 13: 21; 16: 1; 23: 16; Gal 4: 30a, b, c (Gen 21: 10a, b, c); Js 2: 21. Also ἐγὼ Φαρισαῖός εἰμι υἱὸς Φαρισαίων Ac 23: 6 is prob. a ref. to direct descent. μονογενὴς υἱός (s. μονογενής) Lk 7: 12. ὁ υἱὸς ὁ πρωτότοκος (πρωτότοκος 1) 2: 7.

β. of the immediate offspring of an animal (Ps 28: 1 υἱοὺς κριῶν; Sir 38: 25. So Lat. filius: Columella 6, 37, 4) ἐπὶ πῶλον υἱὸν ὑποζυγίου Mt 21: 5 (cf. Zech 9: 9 πῶλον νέον).

b. in a more extended sense—α. of one who is not a direct offspring descendant Ἰωσὴφ υἱὸς Δαυίδ Mt 1: 20 (cf. Jos., Ant. 11, 73); s. 2a below. υἱοὶ Ἰσραήλ (Ἰσραήλ 1) Mt 27: 9; Lk 1: 16; Ac 5: 21; 7: 23, 37; 9: 15; 10: 36; Ro 9: 27; 2 Cor 3: 7, 13; Hb 11: 22 al. οἱ υἱοὶ Λευί (Num 26: 57) Hb 7: 5. υἱὸς Ἀβραάμ Lk 19: 9. υἱοὶ Ἀδάμ 1 Cl 29: 2 (Dt 32: 8).

β. of one who is accepted or adopted as a son (Herodian 5, 7, 1; 4; 5) Ac 7: 21 (cf. Ex 2: 10).—J 19: 26.

c. fig.—α. of a pupil, follower, or one who is otherw. a spiritual son (Dit., Syll.³ 1169, 12 οἱ υἱοὶ τοῦ θεοῦ=the pupils and helpers [40] of Asclepius; sim. Maximus Tyr. 4, 2c.—For those who are heirs of guild-secrets or who are to perpetuate a skill of some kind, however, some combination w. παῖδες is the favorite designation. Pla., Rep. 3 p. 407Ε, Leg. 6 p. 769Β; Dionys. Hal., Comp. Verbi 22 p. 102, 4 Us.-Rdm. ['04] ῥητόρων παῖδες; Lucian, Anach. 19, Dial. Mort. 11, 1 Χαλδαίων π.=dream-interpreters, Dips. 5 ἰατρῶν π., Amor. 49; Himerius, Or. 48 [=Or. 14], 13 σοφῶν π.); the 'sons' of the Pharisees Mt 12: 27; Lk 11: 19. Peter says Μᾶρκος ὁ υἱός μου 1 Pt 5: 13 (cf. Μᾶρκος). As a familiar form of address by a spiritual father or teacher Hb 12: 5 (Pr 3: 11). υἱοὶ καὶ θυγατέρες B 1: 1.

β. of the individual members of a large and coherent group (cf. perh. the υἷες Ἀχαιῶν in Homer; also Dio Chrys. 71[21], 15; LXX) οἱ υἱοὶ τοῦ λαοῦ μου 1 Cl 8: 3 (scripture quot. of unknown origin). υἱοὶ γένους Ἀβραάμ Ac 13: 26. οἱ υἱοὶ τῶν ἀνθρώπων (Gen 11: 5; Ps 11: 2, 9; 44: 3; Test. Levi 3: 10, Zeb. 9: 7) the sons of men Mk 3: 28; Eph 3: 5; 1 Cl 61: 2 (of the earthly rulers in contrast to the heavenly king).

γ. of those who are bound to a personality by close, non-material ties; it is this personality that has promoted the relationship and given it its character: those who believe are υἱοὶ Ἀβραάμ, because Abr. was the first whose relationship to God was based on faith Gal 3: 7. In a special sense the devout, believers, are sons of God (cf. Dio Chrys. 58[75], 8 ὁ τοῦ Διὸς ὄντως υἱός; Epict. 1, 9, 6; 1, 3, 2; 1, 19, 9; Sextus 58; 60; 135; 376a; Dt 14: 1; Ps 28: 1; 72: 15; Is 43: 6 [w. θυγατέρες μου]; 45: 11; Wsd 2: 18; 5: 5; 12: 21 al.; Jdth 9: 4, 13; Esth 8: 12q; 3 Macc 6: 28; Sib. Or. 3, 702) Mt 5: 45; Lk 6: 35; Ro 8: 14, 19; 9: 26 (Hos 2: 1); 2 Cor 6: 18 (w. θυγατέρες); Gal 3: 26 (cf. PsSol 17: 27); 4: 6a, 7a, b (here the υἱός is the κληρονόμος and his opposite is the δοῦλος); Hb 2: 10 (JKögel, Der Sohn u. die Söhne: Eine exeget. Studie zu Hb 2: 5-18, '04); 12: 5-8 (in vs. 8 opp. νόθος, q.v.); Rv 21: 7; 2 Cl 1: 4; B 4: 9. Corresp. there are sons of the devil (on this subj. cf. Hdb. on J 8: 44) υἱὲ διαβόλου Ac 13: 10. οἱ υἱοὶ τοῦ πονηροῦ (masc.) Mt 13: 38b. In υἱοί ἐστε τῶν φονευσάντων τοὺς προφήτας Mt 23: 31 this mng. is prob. to be combined w. sense 1bα. On the view that υἱοὶ θεοῦ Mt 5: 9 (not the confirmation of an existing relationship, but a promise for the future. S. Köhler and Windisch below); Lk 20: 36 signifies angels (Ps 88: 7; θεῶν παῖδες as heavenly beings: Maximus Tyr. 11, 5a; 12a; 13, 6a.—Hierocles 3 p. 424 the ἄγγελοι are called θεῶν παῖδες) cf. KKöhler, StKr 91, '18, 198f; HWindisch, Friedensbringer-Gottessöhne: ZNW 24, '25, 240-60).

δ. υἱός w. gen. of the thing, to denote one who shares in this thing or who is worthy of it, or who stands in some other close relation to it, oft. made clear by the context; this constr. is prob. a Hebraism in the main (Bl-D. §162, 6; Mlt.-H. 441; Dssm., B p. 162-6 [BS 161-6]; Papers of the Amer. School of Class. Stud. at Athens II 1884, no. 2 υἱὸς πόλεως [time of Nero]; Inschr. v. Magn. 167, 5; 156, 12) οἱ υἱοὶ τοῦ αἰῶνος τούτου (αἰών 2a) Lk 16: 8a (opp. οἱ υἱοὶ τοῦ φωτός vs. 8b); 20: 34. τῆς ἀναστάσεως υἱοί (ἀνάστασις 2b) 20: 36b. υἱοὶ τῆς ἀνομίας 1; cf. CD 6, 15) Hv 3, 6, 1; AP 1: 3; τῆς ἀπειθείας (s. ἀπείθεια) Eph 2: 2; 5: 6; Col 3: 6 t.r.; τῆς ἀπωλείας AP 1: 2. ὁ υἱὸς τῆς ἀπωλείας of Judas the traitor J 17: 12 (cf. similar expressions in Eur., Hec. 425; Menand., Dyscolus 88f; FWDanker, NTS 7, '60/'61, 94), of the Antichrist 2 Th 2: 3. υἱοὶ τῆς βασιλείας (βασιλεία 3g) Mt 8: 12; 13: 38a. υἱοὶ βροντῆς Mk 3: 17 (s. Βοανηργές). υἱὸς γεέννης (s. γέεννα) Mt 23: 15; τ. διαθήκης (PsSol 17: 15) Ac 3: 25; εἰρήνης Lk 10: 6. υἱοὶ τοῦ νυμφῶνος (s. νυμφών) Mt 9: 15; Mk 2: 19; Lk 5: 34. υἱὸς παρακλήσεως Ac 4: 36 (s. Βαρναβᾶς). υἱοὶ (τοῦ) φωτός Lk 16: 8b (opp. υἱοὶ τοῦ αἰῶνος τούτου); J 12: 36. υἱοὶ φωτός ἐστε καὶ υἱοὶ ἡμέρας 1 Th 5: 5 (EBuonaiuti, 'Figli del giorno e della luce' [1 Th 5: 5]: Rivista storico-critica delle Scienze teol. 6, '10, 89-93).

2. in various combinations as a designation of the Messiah and a self-designation of Jesus—**a.** υἱὸς Δαυίδ *son of David* of the Messiah (PsSol 17: 21) Mt 22: 42-5; Mk 12: 35-7; Lk 20: 41-4; B 12: 10c. Specif. of Jesus as Messiah Mt 1: 1a; 9: 27; 12: 23; 15: 22; 20: 30f; 21: 9, 15; Mk 10: 47f; Lk 18: 38f.—WWrede, Jesus als Davidssohn: Vorträge u. Studien '07, 147-77; WBousset, Kyrios Christos² '21, 4, Rel.³ 226f; ELohmeyer, Gottesknecht u. Davidssohn '45, esp. 68; 72; 77; 84; TNicklin, Gospel Gleanings '50, 251-6; WMichaelis, Die Davidsohnschaft Jesu usw., in D. histor. Jesus u. d. kerygm. Christus, ed. Ristow and Matthiae, '61, 317-30; LRFisher, ECColwell-Festschr., '68, 82-97.

b. ὁ υἱὸς τοῦ θεοῦ, υἱὸς θεοῦ *(the) Son of God* (in Judaism this was at least not a frequently-used honorary title for the Messiah [Dalman, Worte 219-24 (Eng. tr. DM Kay, '02, 268-89); Bousset, Kyrios Christos² 53f; EHuntress, 'Son of God' in Jewish Writings Prior to the Christian Era: JBL 54, '35, 117-23]. In the pagan world, on the

other hand, sons of the gods in a special sense are not only known to myth and legend, but definite historical personalities are also designated as such. Among them are famous wise men such as Pythagoras and Plato [HUsener, Das Weihnachtsfest² '11, 71ff], the deified rulers, above all the Roman emperors since the time of Augustus [oft. in inscr. and pap.: Dssm., B 166f-BS 166f, LO 294f-LAE 346f; Thieme 33]. According to Memnon [I BC/I AD] no. 434 fgm. 1, 1, 1 Jac., Clearchus [IV BC] carried his boasting so far as Διὸς υἱὸν ἑαυτὸν ἀνειπεῖν. Also, persons who were active at that time as prophets and wonder-workers laid claim to the title υἱὸς τοῦ θεοῦ, e. g. the Samaritan Dositheus in Origen, C. Cels. VI 11 [cf. GPWetter, 'Der Sohn Gottes' '16; Hdb. exc. on J 1: 34]. S. also Clemen² 76ff; ENorden, Die Geburt des Kindes '24, 75; 91f; 132; 156f; EKlostermann, Hdb. exc. on Mk 1: 11 [⁴ '50]; M-JLagrange, Les origines du dogme paulinien de la divinité de Christ: RB 45, '36, 5-33; HPreisker, Ntl. Zeitgesch. '37, 187-208; HBraun, ZThK 54, '57, 353-64; ADNock, 'Son of God' in Paul. and Hellen. Thought, Gnomon 33, '61, 581-90 [=Essays on Religion and the Anc. World II, '72, 928-39]—originality in Paul's thought): Ps 2: 7 is applied to Jesus υἱός μου εἶ σύ, ἐγὼ σήμερον γεγέννηκά σε Lk 3: 22 v.l.; GEb 3; Ac 13: 33; Hb 1: 5a; 5: 5; 1 Cl 36: 4. Likew. Hos 11: 1 (w. significant changes): Mt 2: 15, and 2 Km 7: 14: Hb 1: 5b. The voice of God calls him ὁ υἱός μου ὁ ἀγαπητός (s. ἀγαπητός 1) at his baptism Mt 3: 17; Mk 1: 11; Lk 3: 22; GEb 3a, b and at the Transfiguration Mt 17: 5; Mk 9: 7; Lk 9: 35 (here instead of ἀγαπ.: ἐκλελεγμένος); 2 Pt 1: 17. Cf. J 1: 34. The angel at the Annunciation uses these expressions in referring to him: υἱὸς ὑψίστου Lk 1: 32 and υἱὸς θεοῦ vs. 35. The centurion refers to him at the crucifixion as υἱὸς θεοῦ Mt 27: 54; Mk 15: 39; GP 11: 45; cf. vs. 46 (CMann, ET 20, '09, 563f; JPobee, The Cry of the Centurion—A Cry of Defeat, CFDMoule-Festschr. '70, 91-102). The high priest asks εἰ σὺ εἶ ὁ Χριστὸς ὁ υἱὸς τοῦ θεοῦ Mt 26: 63. Jesus is asked to show that he is God's Son 27: 40, even to the devil 4: 3, 6; Lk 4: 3, 9. On the other hand, the demons do not doubt that he is the Son of God Mt 8: 29; Mk 3: 11; 5: 7; Lk 4: 41; 8: 28; and the disciples testify that he is Mt 14: 33; 16: 16. S. also Mk 1: 1 v.l. (SCELegg, Ev. Sec. Marc. '35).—Jesus also refers to himself as Son of God, though rarely apart fr. the Fourth Gosp.: Mt 28: 19 (the Risen Lord in the trinitarian baptismal formula); Mt 21: 37f=Mk 12: 6 (an allusion in the parable of the vinedressers); Mt 27: 43; Mk 13: 32; Rv 2: 18. The main pass. is the so-called Johannine verse in the synoptics Mt 11: 27=Lk 10: 22 (s. PWSchmiedel, PM 4, '00, 1-22; FCBurkitt, JTS 12, '11, 296f; HSchumacher, Die Selbstoffenbarung Jesu bei Mt 11: 27 [Lk 10: 22] '12 [lit.]; Norden, Agn. Th. 277-308; JWeiss, Heinrici-Festschr. '14, 120-9, Urchristentum '17, 87ff; Bousset, Kyrios Christos² '21, 45ff; EMeyer I 280ff; RBultmann, Gesch. d. synopt. Trad.² '31, 171f; MDibelius, Die Formgeschichte des Evangeliums² '33, 259; MRist, Is Mt 11: 25-30 a Primitive Baptismal Hymn?: Journ. of Religion 15, '35, 63-77; TArvedson, D. Mysterium Christi: E. Studie zu Mt 11: 25-30, '37; WDDavies, 'Knowledge' in the Dead Sea Scrolls and Mt 11: 25-30, HTR 45, '53, 113-39; WGrundmann, Sohn Gottes, ZNW 47, '56, 113-33; JBieneck, Sohn Gottes als Christusbez. der Synopt. '51; PWinter, Mt 11: 27 and Lk 10: 22, NovT 1, '56, 112-48; JJocz, Judaica 13, '57, 129-42; OMichel and OBetz, Von Gott Gezeugt, Beih. ZNW [Jeremias-Festschr.] 26, '60, 3-23 [Qumran]).—Apart fr. the synoptics, testimony to Jesus as the Son of God is found in many parts of our lit. Oft. in Paul: Ro 1: 3, 4, 9; 5: 3; 8: 3, 29,

32; 1 Cor 1: 9; 15: 28; 2 Cor 1: 19; Gal 1: 16; 2: 20; 4: 4; Eph 4: 13; Col 1: 13; 1 Th 1: 10. Cf. Ac 9: 20. In Hb: 1: 2, 8; 4: 14; 5: 8; 6: 6; 7: 3, 28; 10: 29. In greatest frequency in John (s. on this Herm. Wr. 1, 6 the Λόγος as υἱὸς θεοῦ. Likew. Philo, Agr. 51 πρωτόγονος υἱός, Conf. Lingu. 146 υἱὸς θεοῦ) J 1: 49; 3: 16-18 (s. μονογενής), 35f; 5: 19-26; 6: 40; 8: 35f; 10: 36; 11: 4, 27; 14: 13; 17: 1; 19: 7; 20: 31; 1 J 1: 3, 7; 2: 22-4; 3: 8, 23; 4: 9f, 14f; 5: 5, 9-13, 20; 2 J 3, 9.—B 5: 9, 11; 7: 2, 9; 12: 8; 15: 5; Dg 7: 4; 9: 2, 4; 10: 2 (τὸν υἱὸν αὐτοῦ τὸν μονογενῆ); IMg 8: 2; ISm 1: 1; MPol 17: 3; Hv 2, 2, 8; s 5, 2, 6 (ὁ υἱὸς αὐτοῦ ὁ ἀγαπητός); 8; 11; 5, 4, 1; 5, 5, 2; 3; 5; 5, 6, 1; 2; 4; 7 (on the Christology of the Shepherd s. Dibelius, Hdb. on Hs 5, also ALink and JvWalter [πνεῦμα 5cα]); s 8, 3, 2; 8, 11, 1. Cf. 9, 1, 1; 9, 12, 1ff.—In trinitarian formulas, in addition to Mt 28: 19, also IMg 13: 1; Epil Mosq 4; D 7: 1, 3.—The deceiver of the world appears w. signs and wonders ὡς υἱὸς θεοῦ D 16: 4.—EKühl, Das Selbstbewusstsein Jesu '07, 16-44; GVos, The Self-disclosure of Jesus '26.—EDBurton, ICC Gal '21, 404-17; TNicklin, Gospel Gleanings '50, 211-36; MHengel, The Son of God (tr. JBowden) '76.

c. ὁ υἱὸς τοῦ ἀνθρώπου the Son of Man, the Man (Jewish thought contemporary w. Jesus knows of a heavenly being looked upon as a 'Son of Man' or 'Man', who exercises Messianic functions such as judging the world [symbolic, pictorial passages in En. 46-8; 4 Esdr 13: 3, 51f.—Bousset, Rel.³ 352-5; NMessel, D. Menschensohn in d. Bilderreden d. Hen. '22; ESjöberg, Kenna 1 Henok och 4 Esra tanken på den lidande Människosonen? Sv. Ex. Årsb. 5, '40, 163-83, D. Menschensohn im äth. Hen. '46]. This concept is in some way connected w. Da 7: 13; acc. to some it derives its real content fr. an eschatological tradition that ultimately goes back to Iran [WBousset, Hauptprobleme der Gnosis '07, 160-223; Reitzenstein, Erlösungsmyst. 119ff, ZNW 20, '21, 18-22, Mysterienrel.³ 418ff; Clemen² 72ff; CHKraeling, Anthropos and Son of Man: A Study in the Religious Syncretism of the Hellenistic Orient '27]; acc. to this tradition the First Man was deified; he will return in the last times and usher in the Kingdom of God. In our lit. the title υἱὸς τοῦ ἀνθρώπου is found predom. in the gospels, where it occurs in the synoptics about 70 times (about half as oft. if parallels are excluded), and in J 12 times (for more exact figures s. EKlostermann, Hdb. exc. on Mk 8: 31). In every case the title is applied by Jesus to himself. Nowhere is it found in an address to him, in a saying or narrative about him: Mt 8: 20; 9: 6; 10: 23; 11: 19; 12: 8, 32, 40; 13: 37, 41; 16: 13, 27f; 17: 9, 12, 22; 18: 11 v.l.; 19: 28; 20: 18, 28; 24: 27, 30, 37, 39, 44; 25: 13 t.r., 31; 26: 2, 24a, b, 45, 64; Mk 2: 10, 28; 8: 31, 38; 9: 9, 12, 31; 10: 33, 45; 13: 26; 14: 21a, b, 41, 62; Lk 5: 24; 6: 5, 22; 7: 34; 9: 22, 26, 44, 56 t.r., 58; 11: 30; 12: 8, 10, 40; 17: 22, 24, 26, 30; 18: 8, 31; 19: 10; 21: 27, 36; 22: 22, 48, 69; 24: 7.—John (FWGrosheide, Τ ἱὸς τ. ἀνθρ. in het Evang. naar Joh.: ThSt 35, '17, 242-8; HDieckmann, D. Sohn des Menschen im J: Scholastik 2, '27, 229-47; HWindisch, ZNW 30, '31, 215-33; 31, '32, 199-204; WMichaelis, ThLZ 85, '60, 561-78 [Jesus' earthly presence]) 1: 51; 3: 13, 14; 5: 27 (BVawter, Ezekiel and John, CBQ 26, '64, 450-58); 6: 27, 53, 62; 8: 28; 9: 35; 12: 23, 34; 13: 31.—Outside the gospels: Ac 7: 56; Rv 1: 13; 14: 14 (both after Da 7: 13). The quot. fr. Ps 8: 5 in Hb 2: 6 prob. does not belong here, since there is no emphasis laid on υἱὸς ἀνθρώπου. In IEph 20: 2 Jesus is described acc. to both sides of his nature as υἱὸς ἀνθρώπου καὶ υἱὸς θεοῦ. Differently B 12: 10 Ἰησοῦς, οὐχὶ υἱὸς ἀνθρώπου ἀλλὰ υἱὸς τοῦ θεοῦ Jesus, not son of man but Son of God. —HLietzmann, Der Menschensohn 1896; Dalman, Worte 191-219 (Eng. tr. DMKay, '02, 234-67); Wlh., Einl.²

123-30; PFiebig, Der Menschensohn '01; NSchmidt, The Prophet of Nazareth '05, 94-134, Recent Study of the Term 'Son of Man': JBL 45, '26, 326-49; FTillmann, Der Menschensohn '07; EKühl, Das Selbstbewusstsein Jesu '07, 65ff; HHoltzmann, Das messianische Bewusstsein Jesu, '07, 49-75 (lit.), Ntl. Theologie² I '11, 313-35; FBard, D. Sohn d. Menschen '08; HGottsched, D. Menschensohn '08; EAAbbott, 'The Son of Man', etc., '10; EHertlein, Die Menschensohnfrage im letzten Stadium '11, ZNW 19, '20, 46-8; JMoffatt, The Theology of the Gospels '12, 150-63; WBousset, Kyrios Christos² '21, 5-22 (the titles of the works by Wernle and Althaus opposing his first edition ['13], as well as Bousset's answer, are found s.v. κύριος, end); DVölter, Jesus der Menschensohn '14, Die Menschensohnfrage neu untersucht '16; FSchulthess, ZNW 21, '22, 247-50; Rtzst., Herr der Grösse '19 (see also the works by the same author referred to above in this entry); EMeyer II 335ff; HGressmann, ZKG n.s. 4, '22, 170ff, D. Messias '29, 341ff; GDupont, Le Fils d'Homme '24; ASPeake, The Messiah and the Son of Man '24; MWagner, Der Menschensohn: NKZ 36, '25, 245-78; Guillaume Baldensperger, Le Fils d'Homme: RHPhr 5, '25, 262-73; WBleibtreu, Jesu Selbstbez. als der Menschensohn: StKr 98/99, '26, 164-211; AvGall, Βασιλεία τοῦ θεοῦ '26; OProcksch, D. Menschensohn als Gottessohn: Christentum u. Wissensch. 3, '27, 425-43; 473-81; CGMontefiore, The Synoptic Gospels² '27 I 64-80; ROtto, Reich Gottes u. Menschensohn '34, Engl. transl. The Kgdm. of God and the Son of Man, tr. Filson and Woolf² '43; EWechssler, Hellas im Ev. '36, 332ff; PParker, The Mng. of 'Son of Man': JBL 60, '41, 151-7; HBSharman, Son of Man and Kingdom of God '43; JYCampbell, The Origin and Mng. of the Term Son of Man: JTS 48, '47, 145-55; HRiesenfeld, Jésus Transfiguré '47, 307-13 (survey and lit.); TWManson, Coniect. Neot. 11, '47, 138-46 (Son of Man=Jesus and his disciples in Mk 2: 27f); GSDuncan, Jesus, Son of Man '47, 135-53 (survey); JBowman, ET 59, '47/'48, 283-8 (background); MBlack, ET 60, '48f, 11-15; 32-6; GAFKnight, Fr. Moses to Paul '49, 163-72 (survey); TNicklin, Gospel Gleanings '50, 237-50; TWManson [Da, En. and gospels], Bulletin of the JRylands Library 32, '50, 171-93; ThéoPreiss, Le Fils d'Homme: Études Théol. et Religieuses 26, no. 3, '51 and Life in Christ, '54, 43-60; SMowinckel, He That Cometh, tr. Anderson, '54, 346-450; GIber, Überlieferungsgesch. Unters. z. Begriff des Menschensohnes im NT, Diss. Heidelb. '53; ESjöberg, D. verborgene Menschensohn in den Ev. '55; WGrundmann, ZNW 47, '56, 113-33; HRiesenfeld, The Mythological Backgrd. of NT Christology, CHDodd-Festschr., '56, 81-95; PhVielhauer, Gottesreich u. Menschensohn in d. Verk. Jesu: GDehn-Festschr. '57, 51-79; EMSidebottom, The Son of Man in J, ET 68, '57, 231-5; 280-3; AJBHiggins, Son of Man-Forschung since (Manson's) 'The Teaching of Jesus'; NT Essays: TW Manson memorial vol. '59, 119-35; HETödt, D. Menschensohn in d. synopt. Überl. '59 (transl. Barton '65); JMuilenburg, JBL 79, '60, 197-209 (Da, En.); ESchweizer, JBL 79, '60, 119-29 and NTS 9, '63, 256-61; BMFv Iersel, 'Der Sohn' in den synopt. Jesusworten, '61 [community?]; MBlack, Bull. of the JRylands Libr. 45, '63, 305-18; FHBorsch, ATR 45, '63, 174-90; AJBHiggins, Jesus and the Son of Man, '64; RECFormesyn, NovT 8, '66, 1-35 [barnasha=I]; SSandmel, HSilver-Festschr., '63, 355-67; JoachJeremias, Die älteste Schicht der Menschensohn-Logien, ZNW 58, '67, 159-72; GVermes, MBlack, Aram. Approach³, '67, 310-30.—Various authors, TW VIII 334-492: υἱός, υἱὸς τ. ἀνθρώπου, υἱὸς Δαυίδ. M-M. B. 105.

ὕλη, ης, ἡ (Hom.+; inscr., pap., LXX, Philo, Joseph.; Sib. Or. 8, 378)—1. *wood,* both standing, as a *forest* (Hom.+; Jos., Ant. 18, 357; 366), and cut down, specif. *firewood, wood used for building* etc. (Hom.+; Jos., C. Ap. 1, 110) Js 3: 5 (cf. Sir 28: 10; Ps.-Phoc. 144).

2. *material, matter, stuff* (Hom.+; Jos., C. Ap. 2, 191) in our lit. only earthly, perishable, non-divine matter φθαρτὴ ὕλη (as Philo, Post. Cai. 165; Jos., Bell. 3, 372), fr. which idols are made (Maximus Tyr. 2, 3a) PK 2 p. 14, 15; Dg 2: 3. Men, too, are made of such material 1 Cl 38: 3 (Philo, Leg. All. 1, 83 ὕ. σωματική. Cf. Epict. 3, 7, 25 ἀνθρώπου ἡ ὕλη=τὰ σαρκίδια). W. the connotation of that which is sinful, hostile to God (as in Philo and Gnostic lit.) IRo 6: 2. M-M. B. 46.*

ὑμεῖς s. σύ.

Ὑμέναιος, ου, ὁ (esp. in mythol., also Dialekt-Inschr. 251, 5) *Hymenaeus,* handed over (w. Alexander) to Satan because of defection fr. the true faith 1 Ti 1: 20. Acc. to 2 Ti 2: 17 his error and that of Philetus consisted in maintaining that the resurrection had already taken place (cf. Acta Pauli [et Theclae] 14 p. 245 Lips.; Justin, Apol. I 26, 4 [of Menander]; Irenaeus 1, 23, 5). M-M.*

ὑμέτερος, α, ον (Hom.+; pap.; LXX quite rarely; not at all in Ep. Arist. and Test. 12 Patr. In Joseph. e.g. Ant. 16, 38 al.) possessive pron. of the second pers. pl. *your* (largely replaced by the gen. of the pers. pron.; Bl-D. §285, 1; Rob. 288), in our lit. only 15 times.

1. *belonging to* or *incumbent upon you* etc.; Lk 6: 20; J 8: 17 (ὑ. νόμος as Jos., Bell. 5, 402); Ac 27: 34; 2 Cor 8: 8; Gal 6: 13; 1 Cl 47: 7; 57: 4 (Pr 1: 26); MPol 13: 3. ὁ καιρὸς ὁ ὑμέτερος *your time*=the time for you to act J 7: 6. ὁ λόγος ὁ ὑμέτερος *your teaching* 15: 20. Perh. 1 Cor 16: 17 (s. 2 below).—Subst. τὸ ὑμέτερον (opp. τὸ ἀλλότριον) *your own property* Lk 16: 12 v.l. τὶς τῶν ὑμετέρων *one of your own number* ISm 11: 3.

2. for the obj. gen. (Thu. 1, 69, 5 αἱ ὑμέτεραι ἐλπίδες. W.-S. §22, 14b) τῷ ὑμετέρῳ ἐλέει *by the mercy shown to you* Ro 11: 31. νὴ τὴν ὑμετέραν καύχησιν ἣν ἔχω *by the pride that I have in you=as surely as I may boast about you* 1 Cor 15: 31. Perh. (s. 1 above) τὸ ὑμέτερον ὑστέρημα *that which is lacking in you* 16: 17.—S. GDKilpatrick s.v. ἐμός, end. M-M.*

ὑμνέω impf. ὕμνουν; fut. ὑμνήσω; 1 aor. ὕμνησα—1. trans. (Hes., Hdt.+; inscr.; PGM 13, 628; 637; 21, 19; LXX; Sib. Or. 5, 151) *sing the praise of, sing hymns of praise to* τινά *someone* God (Xenophanes [VI BC] 1, 13 Diehl² θεόν; X., Cyr. 8, 1, 23 θεόν; Dio Chrys. 80[30], 26; Alciphr. 4, 18, 16 Διόνυσον; Dit., Syll.³ 662, 10ff τοὺς θεοὺς ὕμνησεν; LXX; Philo, Leg. All. 2, 102 al.; Jos., Ant. 7, 80; 11, 80 τὸν θεόν) Ac 16: 25; Hb 2: 12 (Ps 21: 23).

2. intr. *sing (a hymn)* (Ps 64: 14; 1 Macc 13: 47; En. 27, 5; Jos., Ant. 12, 349; Test. Jos. 8: 5a) ὑμνήσαντες *after they had sung the hymn* (of the second part of the Hallel [Ps 113-18 Heb.], sung at the close of the Passover meal) Mt 26: 30 (EBammel, JTS 24, '73, 189 [𝔓⁶⁴]); Mk 14: 26.—GDelling, TW VIII, 492-506: ὑμνέω, ψάλλω, etc. M-M.*

ὕμνος, ου, ὁ *hymn* or *song* of praise (Hom.+), also in honor of a divinity (ὕμνος θεῶν Aeschyl., Cho. 475; Pla., Leg. 7 p. 801 D; Athen. 14 p. 627F.—Pla., Rep. 10 p. 607A; Athen. 1 p. 22B; 14 p. 626B; Arrian, Anab. 4, 11, 2; Dit., Syll.³ 449, 2 τοὺς ὕμνους τοῖς θεοῖς; 450, 4 θεῷ ὕμνον; 695, 29, Or. 56, 69; PGiess. 99, 8 [II AD]; POxy.

130, 21; RWünsch, Pauly-W. IX 1, 141f.—Ps 39: 4; Is 42: 10; 1 Macc 13: 51; Philo; Jos., Ant. 7, 305 [w. ᾠδαί] al.; Sib. Or. 3, 306; loanw. in rabb.) w. ψαλμοί (Jos., Ant. 12, 323), ᾠδαὶ πνευματικαί Eph 5: 19; Col 3: 16 (Diod. S. 5, 46, 3 ὕμνοι μετ' ᾠδῆς in praise of the πράξεις of the gods and of their εὐεργεσίαι εἰς ἀνθρώπους; Test. Gad 7: 2).—JKroll (s. ᾄδω); same author: Antike 2, '26, 258ff and Gnomon 5, '29, 30ff; JQuasten, Musik u. Gesang in d. Kulten der heidn. Antike u. christl. Frühzeit '30; Ruth EMessenger, Christ. Hymns of the First Three Cent.: Papers of the Hymn Soc. 9, '42, 1-27; GSchille, Früchristliche Hymnen, '62. M-M.*

ὑπάγω impf. ὑπῆγον (Hom.+, but predom. trans. [= 'bring under', etc.] in secular writers; so also Ex 14: 21). In our lit. (though not found at all in Ac, Paul, Hb; most frequently in John) only intr. (so Hdt., Eur., Aristoph.+; oft. pap.; JKalitsunakis, ByzZ 29, '29, 228ff) *go away, withdraw, go* (only the pres., mostly in the imper., and the impf. are found.—Bl-D. §101 p. 43 under ἄγειν; 308: it tends more and more to mean simply 'go' in colloq. speech; so in Mod. Gk.).

1. *go away* in the sense 'leave a person's presence' (Epict. 3, 23, 12) ὕπαγε σατανᾶ *be gone, Satan!* Mt 4: 10; combined w. ὀπίσω μου ibid. v.l.; 16: 23; Mk 8: 33; Lk 4: 8 t.r. ὑπάγετε ἀπ' ἐμοῦ 2 Cl 4: 5 (saying of Jesus, fr. an unknown source). μὴ καὶ ὑμεῖς θέλετε ὑπάγειν; *do you, too, want to go away* (fr. me)? J 6: 67.—ὕπαγε *go (away)* (PGM 4, 348; 371; 36, 354), esp. *go home* (Epict. 3, 22, 108) Mt 8: 13; 19: 21; 20: 14; Mk 2: 9 v.l.; 7: 29; 10: 52. On ὕπαγε εἰς εἰρήνην Mk 5: 34 or ὑπάγετε ἐν εἰρήνῃ Js 2: 16 cf. εἰρήνη 2. In other moods than the imper. in the general sense *go away* J 18: 8; Hs 8, 2, 5; 9, 10, 4; *go away* =leave Mk 6: 33. ὑπάγουσα λέγει *as she went she said* Hv 1, 4, 3. ἄφετε αὐτὸν ὑπάγειν *let him go* (prob.=go home) J 11: 44. Naturally the boundary betw. *go away* and *go* (elsewhere) is not fixed; cf. e.g. οἱ ἐρχόμενοι καὶ οἱ ὑπάγοντες *people coming and going* Mk 6: 31.

2. *go* (in a certain direction) w. the goal indicated by εἰς w. the acc. (Epict. 3, 22, 108; Suppl. Epigr. Gr. VIII 574, 19 [III AD]; PLond. 131, 155; 218 [I AD] al. in pap.) Mt 9: 6; 20: 4, 7; Mk 2: 11; 11: 2; 14: 13; Lk 19: 30; J 6: 21; 7: 3; 9: 11; 11: 31; Hv 4, 1, 2; s 8, 3, 6; 9, 11, 6. Also symbolically of stones that go into a building=are used in its construction Hv 3, 5, 1 and 3; 3, 6, 2; s 9, 3, 3f. Fig. εἰς αἰχμαλωσίαν ὑπάγειν *go into captivity* Rv 13: 10; εἰς ἀπώλειαν 17: 8, 11. ὑπάγετε εἰς τὴν πόλιν πρὸς τὸν δεῖνα Mt 26: 18; cf. Mk 5: 19 (ὑπάγειν πρός τινα as PTebt. 417, 4; 21). ὑπάγειν μετά τινος (PTebt. 422, 9 ὕπαγε μετὰ Μέλανος πρὸς Νεμεσᾶν) Mt 5: 41=D 1: 4; μετά τινος ἐπί τινα Lk 12: 58. ἐκεῖ J 11: 8. ποῦ (=ποῖ) 3: 8; cf. IPhld 7: 1; J 12: 35. ὅπου ἂν ὑπάγῃ Rv 14: 4 (cf. POxy. 1477, 2 ὅπου ὑπάγω; Test. Levi 13: 3 ὅπου ὑπάγει). W. inf. of purpose ὑπάγω ἁλιεύειν J 21: 3.—The imper. ὕπαγε, ὑπάγετε is followed by another imper., in the NT almost always without a connective (Epict. 3, 21, 6; 22, 5; 23, 12 al.; Vi. Aesopi W c. 44 ὕπαγε, δός) ὕπαγε ἔλεγξον Mt 18: 15; cf. 5: 24; 8: 4; 19: 21; 21: 28; 27: 65; 28: 10; Mk 1: 44; 6: 38; 10: 21; 16: 7; J 4: 16; 9: 7; Rv 10: 8. W. the conjunction καί (PTebt. 417, 5f [III AD] ὕπαγε καὶ εἴδε) ὑπάγετε καὶ ἐκχέετε 16: 1; cf. Hv 3, 1, 7; 4, 2, 5; s 8, 11, 1; 9, 10, 1.—Abs. *go* (the context supplies the destination) ὑπάγετε Mt 8: 32; cf. 13: 44; Lk 10: 3; J 15: 16. ἐν τῷ ὑπάγειν αὐτόν *as he was going* Lk 8: 42; cf. 17: 14.—J 12: 11 (𝔓⁶⁶ om. ὑπ.); Hv 3, 10, 2.

3. used esp. of Christ and his *going* to the Father, characteristically of J. ὑπάγω πρὸς τὸν πέμψαντά με J 7:

33; 16: 5a; πρὸς τὸν πατέρα vss. 10, 17. ἀπὸ θεοῦ ἐξῆλθεν καὶ πρὸς τὸν θεὸν ὑπάγει 13: 3. οἶδα πόθεν ἦλθον καὶ ποῦ ὑπάγω 8: 14a; cf. b (GPWetter, E. gnost. Formel im vierten Ev.: ZNW 18, '18, 49–63). ὅπου ἐγὼ ὑπάγω ὑμεῖς οὐ δύνασθε ἐλθεῖν vs. 21b, 22; 13: 33; cf. vs. 36b. Abs. ἐγὼ ὑπάγω I am taking my departure 8: 21a. ὑπάγω καὶ ἔρχομαι I am going away and returning again 14: 28. S. in addition 13: 36a; 14: 4, 5; 16: 5b; 1 J 2: 11.—ὁ υἱὸς τοῦ ἀνθρώπου ὑπάγει Mt 26: 24; Mk 14: 21 places less emphasis upon going to be w. God; it is rather a euphemism for death the Son of Man is to go away=he must die. M-M. B. 694.*

ὑπακοή, ῆς, ἡ (2 Km 22: 36; Test. Jud. 17: 3; pap. fr. VI AD, e.g. PStrassb. 40, 41)—1. obedience—a. gener., the obedience which every slave owes his master εἰς ὑπακοήν =εἰς τὸ ὑπακούειν to obey Ro 6: 16a.

b. predom. of obedience to God and his commands, abs. (opp. ἁμαρτία) Ro 6: 16b. Cf. 1 Cl 9: 3; 19: 1. δι᾽ ὑπακοῆς obediently, in obedience (toward God) 10: 2, 7. Of Christ's obedience Hb 5: 8.—W. subjective gen. of Christ's obedience to God Ro 5: 19 (opp. παρακοή); of men's obedience to the will of God as expressed in the gospel Ro 15: 18; 16: 19; of obedience to God's chosen representatives, the apostle and his emissaries 2 Cor 7: 15; 10: 6 (opp. παρακοή); Phlm 21.—W. the objective gen. ὑπ. τοῦ Χριστοῦ obedience to Christ 2 Cor 10: 5; 1 Pt 1: 2 (where Ἰησοῦ Χρ. goes w. ὑπακοήν). ὑπ. τῆς ἀληθείας vs. 22. Perh. εἰς ὑπακοὴν πίστεως Ro 1: 5; 16: 26 is to be taken in this sense to promote obedience to the message of faith. But it may be better to render it more generally with a view to (promoting) obedience which springs from faith (so GHParke-Taylor, ET 55, '44, 305f; gen. of source). On τέκνα ὑπακοῆς 1 Pt 1: 14 s. τέκνον 2fβ; on τὸν τῆς ὑπακοῆς τόπον ἀναπληροῦν 1 Cl 63: 1 s. ἀναπληρόω 3.—OKuss, D. Begriff des Gehorsams im NT: ThGl 27, '35, 695–702; HvCampenhausen, Recht u. Gehors. in d. ältest. Kirche: ThBl 20, '41, 279–95—2. (obedient) answer GP 10: 42. M-M.*

ὑπακούω impf. ὑπήκουον; fut. ὑπακούσομαι; 1 aor. ὑπήκουσα (Hom.+; inscr., pap., LXX; Ep. Arist. 44; Philo, Joseph., Test. 12 Patr.) listen to.

1. obey, follow, be subject to w. gen. of the pers. (Hdt. 3, 101 al.; so predom. in pap. and LXX; Test. Gad 8: 3) B 9: 1 (Ps 17: 45 v.l.; the text has μοι). W. dat. of the pers. (Thu., Aristoph. et al.; Philo, Mos. 1, 156; Jos., Ant. 13, 275; Test. Jud. 1: 4; 18: 6 θεῷ; in pap. and LXX the dat. is less freq. than the gen. Bl-D. §173, 3; 187, 6; cf. Rob. 507; 634): parents Eph 6: 1; Col 3: 20; masters Eph 6: 5; Col 3: 22; cf. Ro 6: 16; husband (cf. Philemo Com. 132 K. ἀγαθῆς γυναικός ἐστιν μὴ κρεῖττον᾽ εἶναι τὰνδρός, ἀλλ᾽ ὑπήκοον; Jos., C. Ap. 2, 201) 1 Pt 3: 6; bishop IEph 20: 2, cf. IMg 3: 2 v.l. Funk (Sb 7835, 10 [I BC] in the charter of the cult-brotherhood of Zeus Hypsistos: ὑπακούειν πάντας τοῦ ἡγουμένου); Christ Hb 5: 9 (cf. Ael. Aristid. 50, 86 K.=26 p. 527 D.: τῷ θεῷ; EKamlah, Die Form der katalogischen Paränese im NT, '64 [moral exhortation]). The pers. is supplied fr. the context (cf. PTebt. 24, 26; Ep. Arist. 44; 2 Ch 24: 19 v.l.) Phil 2: 12; 1 Cl 7: 6; 57: 4 (Pr 1: 24). ὑπακούσωμεν τῷ ὀνόματι αὐτοῦ 1 Cl 58: 1 marks the transition to the next usage (w. things).—W. dat. of the thing to which one is obedient or which one embraces in full surrender (cf. Athen. 6 p. 247D ὑπ. δείπνῳ=accept the invitation) ὑπακούειν τῇ πίστει Ac 6: 7; τῷ εὐαγγελίῳ Ro 10: 16; 2 Th 1: 8; τῷ λόγῳ ἡμῶν 2 Th 3: 14; τῇ βουλήσει αὐτοῦ (=τοῦ θεοῦ) 1 Cl 9: 1; 42: 4; τοῖς προστάγμασι 2 Cl 19: 3 (Aeschines 1,

49 and Dit., Syll.³ 785, 18 τ. νόμοις; Demosth. 18, 204; Jos., Ant. 3, 207 τ. λεγομένοις; 5, 198); ταῖς ἐπιθυμίαις αὐτοῦ (= τοῦ θνητοῦ σώματος ὑμῶν) Ro 6: 12. ὑπηκούσατε εἰς ὃν παρεδόθητε τύπον διδαχῆς vs. 17 (παραδίδωμι 1b, end).—Foll. by the inf. which shows what the obedience results in (Gen 39: 10) Ἀβραὰμ ὑπήκουσεν ἐξελθεῖν Abr. went out obediently Hb 11: 8.—Also of the enforced obedience of the demons ὑπακούουσιν αὐτῷ they are forced to obey him Mk 1: 27; of the elements Mt 8: 27 (OBetz, ZNW 48, '57, 49–77, esp. 70–2); Mk 4: 41; Lk 8: 25; of a tree that must yield to a higher power 17: 6 (cf. Hippocr., Epid. 3, 8; Galen VI 354 K., who speak of diseases that ὑπ.='must yield' to a remedy [dative]).

2. hear, grant one's request (of God Diod. S. 4, 34, 5 τοὺς ἀθανάτους ὑπακούσαντας; Vi. Aesopi I c. 5 of Isis; Is 65: 24; Jos., Ant. 14, 24.—X., Cyr. 8, 1, 18 of a judge who hears the plaintiff) 1 Cl 39: 7 (Job 5: 1).

3. technically of the door-keeper, whose duty it is to listen for the signals of those who wish to enter, and to admit them if they are entitled to do so, simply open or answer (the door) (Pla., Phaedo 59E ὁ θυρωρός, ὅσπερ εἰώθει ὑπακούειν, Crito 43A; X., Symp. 1, 11; Theophr., Char. 4, 9; 28, 3; Lucian, Icarom. 22 et al.) προσῆλθεν παιδίσκη ὑπακοῦσαι Ac 12: 13. M-M.*

ὑπαλείφω 1 aor. pass. ὑπηλείφθην (Aristoph., X.+) anoint (from below) fig. (Aristoph., Ach. 1029 εἰρήνη τινά) ἐμὲ ἔδει ὑφ᾽ ὑμῶν ὑπαλειφθῆναι πίστει I needed to be anointed by you with faith IEph 3: 1.*

ὕπανδρος, ον under the power of or subject to a man ἡ ὕπανδρος γυνή the married woman (Polyb. 10, 26, 3; Aelian, N.A. 3, 42 p. 77, 3; Artem. 1, 78 p. 74, 6; Athen. 9 p. 388C; Heliod. 10, 22; Num 5: 20, 29; Pr 6: 24, 29; Sir 9: 9; 41: 23) Ro 7: 2. M-M.*

ὑπαντάω impf. ὑπήντων; 1 aor. ὑπήντησα (Pind., X.+; inscr., pap., LXX) (come or go to) meet τινί someone (Appian, Bell. Civ. 4, 111 §406; 4, 134 §566; PStrassb. 101, 4 [I BC] ἡμῖν; Tob 7: 1 BA; Philo, Det. Pot. Ins. 135; Jos., Vi. 49, Ant. 2, 279) Mt 8: 28; 28: 9; Mk 5: 2; Lk 8: 27; 17: 12 v.l.; J 4: 51; 11: 20, 30; 12: 18; Ac 16: 16 (freq. interchanged in NT mss. w. ἀπαντάω, q.v.); MPol 8: 2; Hv 4, 2, 1.—Also in a hostile sense oppose (X.; Appian, Illyr. 23 §68; 26 §75; Bell. Civ. 4, 115 §480; Jos., Bell. 1, 177, Ant. 7, 128; Test. Benj. 2: 4) Lk 14: 31. M-M.*

ὑπάντησις, εως, ἡ coming to meet (Ptolem., Apotel. 3, 11, 16; 32; 4, 9, 1; Appian, Bell. c. 4, 6 §22; Jos., Bell. 7, 100, Ant. 11, 327; Dit., Syll.³ 798, 16; 23 [37 AD]) in our lit. only in the expr. εἰς ὑπάντησιν to meet τινί someone (Ps.-Callisth. p. 116, 23; PGiess. 74, 6 [II AD] εἰς ὑπάντησιν Οὐλπιανῷ [acc. to the rdg. recommended by FPreisigke, Wörterbuch s.v. and accepted by M-M.]; 1 Ch 14: 8 A; Pr 7: 15 B) Mt 8: 34; J 12: 13. Also τινός (Jdth 2: 6 S; 1 Macc 9: 39 S) Mt 25: 1.—NSvensson, Bull. de corr. hell. 50, '26, 527ff. M-M.*

ὕπαρξις, εως, ἡ (Aristot.+; Philo; Jos., Ant. 16, 48)—1. existence (Philodem, Piet. 114; Plut., Mor. 1067C et al.; Philo, Op. M. 170 θεοῦ) τὰ δοῦλα τ. ὑπάρξεως things that are subservient to (their) existence PK 2 p. 14, 16.

2. =τὰ ὑπάρχοντα that which one has, property, possession (Polyb. 2, 17, 11; Dionys. Hal. 5, 48; Diod. S. 20, 71, 1; Plut., Mor. 226C; Artem. 2, 24; POxy. 707, 15; 1274, 14; BGU 195, 22; PAmh. 80, 5 al.; 2 Ch 35: 7; Ps 77: 48; Pr 18: 11; 19: 14; Jer 9: 9; Test. Levi 17: 9) Hb 10: 34; Hs 1: 5. Pl. possessions, belongings (w. κτήματα) Ac 2: 45. (W. ἀγροί and οἰκήσεις) Hs 1: 4. M-M.*

ὑπάρχω impf. ὑπῆρχον (Hom.+; inscr., pap., LXX, En., Ep. Arist., Philo, Joseph., Test. 12 Patr., Sib. Or.).
1. *exist (really), be present, be at one's disposal* (Pind., Aeschyl., Hdt.+) μηδενὸς αἰτίου ὑπάρχοντος *since there is no good reason* Ac 19: 40. Cf. 27: 21; 28: 18; *be (found)* somewhere 4: 34; 10: 12; 17: 27; Phil 3: 20; 1 Cl 61: 2; Epil Mosq 3. ἀκούω σχίσματα ἐν ὑμῖν ὑπάρχειν *I hear that there are actually divisions among you* 1 Cor 11: 18. W. dat. of the pers. ὑπάρχει μοί τι *someth. is at my disposal, I have someth.* (X., An. 2, 2, 11; PMagd. 9, 2 [III BC] ὑπάρχει ἐμοὶ Ἰσιεῖον; Sir 20: 16; Jos., Ant. 7, 148) χρυσίον οὐχ ὑπάρχει μοι Ac 3: 6. Cf. 4: 37; 28: 7; 2 Pt 1: 8. τὰ ὑπάρχοντά τινι *what belongs to someone, someone's property, possessions, means* (Dit., Syll.³ 646, 25 [170 BC]; very oft. in pap. since PHib. 94, 2; 15; 95, 12 [III BC]; Tob 4: 7; Jos., Ant. 4, 261) Lk 8: 3; 12: 15; Ac 4: 32. Subst. in the same sense τὰ ὑπάρχοντά τινος (Dit., Syll.³ 611, 14; very oft. in pap. since PHib. 32, 5; 84, 9; PEleph. 2, 3 [III BC]; Gen 31: 18; Sir 41: 1; Tob 1: 20 BA) Mt 19: 21; 24: 47; 25: 14; Lk 11: 21; 12: 33, 44; 14: 33; 16: 1; 19: 8; 1 Cor 13: 3; Hb 10: 34.
2. as a widely used substitute in H.Gk. for εἶναι (Bl-D. §414, 1; cf. Rob. 1121) w. a predicate noun (Dit., Or. 383, 48 [I BC] ὅπως οὗτος ... ὑπάρχη καθιδρυμένος; Sib. Or. 3, 267, fgm. 1, 28) οὗτος ἄρχων τῆς συναγωγῆς ὑπῆρχεν Lk 8: 41. Cf. 9: 48; Ac 7: 55; 8: 16; 16: 3; 19: 36; 21: 20; 1 Cor 7: 26; 12: 22; Js 2: 15; 2 Pt 3: 11; 1 Cl 19: 3 and oft. Very freq. in the ptc. w. a predicate noun *who is, since he is,* etc. (Test. Sim. 4: 4 ἐλεήμων ὑπάρχων) οἱ Φαρισαῖοι φιλάργυροι ὑπάρχοντες Lk 16: 14. Cf. 11: 13; 23: 50; Ac 2: 30; 3: 2; 16: 20, 37; 17: 24, 29; 22: 3; 27: 12; Ro 4: 19; 1 Cor 11: 7; 2 Cor 8: 17; 12: 16; Gal 1: 14; 2: 14; 2 Pt 2: 19; 1 Cl 1: 1; 11: 1, 2; 25: 2; B 5: 10.—ὑπ. w. a prep. ἐν (Jer 4: 14; Philo, Leg. All. 1, 62; Jos., Ant. 7, 391): οἱ ἐν ἱματισμῷ ἐνδόξῳ ὑπάρχοντες Lk 7: 25; cf. 16: 23; Ac 5: 4; 14: 9 D; Phil 2: 6; 1 Cl 1: 3; 32: 2; 56: 1. τοῦτο πρὸς τῆς ὑμετέρας σωτηρίας ὑπάρχει Ac 27: 34 (s. πρός I). M-M.**

ὑπείκω (Hom.+) *yield,* fig. *give way, submit* to someone's authority (Hom.+; 4 Macc 6: 35) w. dat. of the pers. to whom one submits (Hom.; Pla., Leg. 4 p. 717D; Sextus 17; cf. Philo, Mos. 1, 156) Hb 13: 17. M-M.*

ὑπεναντίος, α, ον (Hes., Hdt.+) mostly *opposed, contrary, hostile* (Thu. 2, 2, 2; Pla., Theaet. 176A; Demosth. 24, 108 al.; inscr., pap.; Jos., C. Ap. 2, 180) τινί *against someone* Col 2: 14. Subst. ὁ ὑπεναντίος *the opponent* (X.; Polyb. 1, 11, 14; Plut., Thes. 13, 2; inscr.; POxy. 1151, 55; LXX; predom. in pl.) οἱ ὑπεναντίοι *the adversaries* (X., Cyr. 1, 6, 38) of God Hb 10: 27 (cf. Is 26: 11). M-M.*

ὑπενεγκεῖν s. ὑποφέρω.

ὑπεξέρχομαι 2 aor. ὑπεξῆλθον *go out quietly* or *secretly* (Pla. et al.; Plut., Lucullus 16, 7; Lucian, Dial. Mar. 2, 4; Cass. Dio 38, 17; Jos., Vi. 21, Ant. 14, 16) MPol 5: 1a. W. the destination given (Hdt. 8, 36 ἐς Ἄμφισσαν) εἰς ἀγρίδιον 5: 1b.*

ὑπέρ (Hom.+; inscr., pap., LXX, En., Ep. Arist., Philo, Joseph., Test. 12 Patr.) prep. w. gen. and acc. (lit. s.v. ἀνά, beg. In addition to this, for ὑπέρ: LWenger, Die Stellvertretung im Rechte der Papyri 1896; ATRobertson, The Use of ὑπέρ in Business Documents in the Papyri: Exp. 8th Ser. XVIII, '19, 321-7) *over, above,* in out lit. not in a local sense (not in the LXX either), only in non-literal senses. The mss. oft. fluctuate between ὑπέρ and περί; see 1f below.

1. w. gen.—a. *for, in behalf of, for the sake of someone* or *someth.*—α. after words that express a request, prayer, etc. After the verbs δέομαι (q.v. 3), εὔχομαι (q.v. 1), προσεύχομαι (q.v.), ἐντυγχάνω (q.v. 1a; cf. b), ὑπερεντυγχάνω (q.v.), λιτανεύω (q.v.) etc. After the nouns δέησις (q.v., end), προσευχή (q.v. 1). Cf. also 1 Ti 2: 1f.
β. after words and expressions that denote working, caring, concerning oneself about. After the verbs ἀγρυπνέω (q.v. 2), ἀγωνίζομαι (q.v. 2b), μεριμνάω (q.v. 2), πρεσβεύω (q.v.) etc. After the nouns ζῆλος (q.v. 1), σπουδή (q.v. 2), ἔχειν πόνον (πόνος 1). ὑπὲρ ὑμῶν διάκονος Col 1: 7.
γ. after expressions having to do w. sacrifice: ἁγιάζω (q.v. 2), ἁγνίζομαι (s. ἁγνίζω 2b). τὸ πάσχα ἡμῶν ὑπὲρ ἡμῶν ἐτύθη Χριστός 1 Cor 5: 7 t.r. ἕως οὗ προσηνέχθη ὑπὲρ ἑνὸς ἑκάστου αὐτῶν ἡ προσφορά Ac 21: 26 (προσφέρω 2a).—Eph 5: 2; Hb 9: 7.
δ. gener. εἶναι ὑπέρ τινος *be for someone, be on someone's side* (Pland. 16, 8 τὸ νόμιμον ὑπὲρ ἡμῶν ἐστιν.—Opp. εἶναι κατά τινος) Mk 9: 40; Lk 9: 50; Ro 8: 31.—ἐπιτρέπεταί σοι ὑπὲρ σεαυτοῦ λέγειν Ac 26: 1. ἵνα μὴ εἷς ὑπὲρ τοῦ ἑνὸς φυσιοῦσθε κατὰ τοῦ ἑτέρου 1 Cor 4: 6. Cf. 2 Cor 1: 11a, b; 5: 20b (δεόμεθα ὑπὲρ Χριστοῦ=*as helpers of Christ we beg you.* Also poss. is *we beg you by* or *in the name of Christ* [Apollon. Rhod. 3, 701 λίσσομ᾽ ὑπὲρ μακάρων=by the gods, in imitation of Il. 22, 338.—Theaetetus—III BC—: Anth. Pal. 7, 499, 2]). τοῦτο φρονεῖν ὑπὲρ πάντων ὑμῶν *to be thus minded in behalf of you all* Phil 1: 7 (perh. simply=*about;* s. 1f below); cf. 4: 10 (think of me=care for, be interested in me).
ε. after expressions of suffering, dying, devoting oneself, etc. ἀποθνῄσκειν ὑπέρ τινος *die for someone* or *someth.* (ἀποθνῄσκω 1aa; also Jos., Ant. 13, 6) J 11: 50-2; 18: 14; Ro 5: 7a, b. τὴν ψυχὴν αὐτοῦ τίθησιν ὑπέρ τινος (cf. Jos., Bell. 2, 201; Sir 29: 15) J 10: 11, 15; 13: 37f; 15: 13; 1 J 3: 16b.—Ro 16: 4; 2 Cor 12: 15; Eph 3: 1, 13; Col 1: 24a.—So esp. of the death of Christ (already referred to at least in part in some of the passages already mentioned. S. also above 1aγ and below 1c) *for, in behalf of* mankind, the world, etc.: Mk 14: 24; Lk 22: 19f; Ro 5: 6, 8; 8: 32; 14: 15; 1 Cor 1: 13 (where the expr. μὴ Παῦλος ἐσταυρώθη ὑπὲρ ὑμῶν; was chosen for no other reason than its ref. to the redeeming death of Christ); 11: 24; 15: 3; Gal 2: 20; 3: 13; Eph 5: 25; 1 Th 5: 10 t.r.; 1 Ti 2: 6; Tit 2: 14; Hb 2: 9; 6: 20; 1 Pt 2: 21 (περὶ 𝔓⁷² A); 3: 18; 1 J 3: 16a; MPol 17: 2a, b.—AMetzinger, Die Substitutionstheorie u. das atl. Opfer, Biblica 21, '40, 159-87, 247-72, 353-77; EHBlakeney, ET 55, '43/'44, 306.
b. w. gen. of the thing, in which case it must be variously translated ὑπὲρ (τῶν) ἁμαρτιῶν *in order to atone for (the) sins* or *to remove them* Gal 1: 4; Hb 5: 1b; 7: 27; 9: 7 (where ... τῶν ἀγνοημάτων); 10: 12; B 7: 3, 4 (prophetic saying of unknown origin), 5f.—ὑπὲρ τῆς τοῦ κόσμου ζωῆς *to bring life to the world* J 6: 51. ὑπὲρ τῆς δόξης τοῦ θεοῦ *to reveal the glory of God* 11: 4. ὑπὲρ τοῦ ὀνόματος αὐτοῦ (cf. Sb 7681, 7 [312 AD] ὑπὲρ τοῦ ὀνόματός μου=in behalf of) *to spread his name* Ro 1: 5; cf. 3 J 7. ὑπὲρ ἀληθείας θεοῦ=in order to show that God's promises are true Ro 15: 8. ὑπὲρ τῆς ὑμῶν παρακλήσεως *in order to comfort you* 2 Cor 1: 6a, b. Cf. 12: 19. ὑπὲρ τῆς πίστεως ὑμῶν *for the strengthening of your faith* 1 Th 3: 2.
c. *in place of, instead of, in the name of* (Eur.; Polyb. 3, 67, 7; Jos., C. Ap. 2, 142;—in pap. very oft. ὑπὲρ αὐτοῦ *to explain that the writer is writing 'as the representative of'* an illiterate pers.; Dssm. LO 285, 2 [LAE 335, 4]) ἵνα

ὑπὲρ σοῦ μοι διακονῇ Phlm 13. Somet. the mng. *in place of* merges w. *on behalf of*, *for the sake of* Ro 9: 3. οἱ βαπτιζόμενοι ὑπὲρ τῶν νεκρῶν 1 Cor 15: 29a is debated; cf. b (s. the lit. s.v. βαπτίζω 2bγ; also KBornhäuser, Die Furche 21, '34, 184–7). εἰς ὑπὲρ πάντων ἀπέθανεν 2 Cor 5: 14; cf. 15a, b, 21 (Eur., Alc. 701 κατθανεῖν ὑπέρ σου).

d. to denote the moving cause or the reason *because of*, *for the sake of*, *for* (Diod. S. 10, 21, 2 τὴν ὑπὲρ τῶν ἁμαρτημάτων τιμωρίαν; schol. on Pind., Ol. 6, 154b), w. verbs of suffering, giving the reason for it ὑπὲρ τοῦ ὀνόματος Ac 5: 41; 9: 16; 21: 13; ὑπὲρ Χριστοῦ Phil 1: 29a, b; cf. 2 Th 1: 5; ὑπὲρ θεοῦ ἀποθνήσκω IRo 4: 1. Likew. used w. nouns that denote suffering ὑπὲρ Χριστοῦ *for Christ's sake* 2 Cor 12: 10.—εὐχαριστεῖν ὑπέρ τινος *give thanks for someth.* 1 Cor 10: 30; Eph 5: 20; D 9: 2; 10: 2 (cf. Sb 3926, 12 [I BC] τὸ κατεσκευασμένον ὑπὲρ [=in gratefulness for] τῆς ἡμετέρας σωτηρίας Ἰσιδεῖον). δοξάζειν τὸν θεὸν ὑπέρ τινος *praise God for someth.* Ro 15: 9.—ὑπὲρ τούτου *with reference to someth.* (Synes., Ep. 67 p. 209c) 2 Cor 12: 8.

e. The mng. *above and beyond* is poss. in ὑπὲρ τῆς εὐδοκίας Phil 2: 13 (εὐδοκία 1).

f. *about*, *concerning* (about equivalent to περί [τινος], w. which it is freq. interchanged in the mss.; cf. Kühner-G. I p. 487 [w. class. exx.]. Also quite common in Polyb., Diod. S., Dionys. Hal., Joseph., inscr. and pap. [Schmidt 396]; Mlt. 105; Rdm.² p. 140; Johannessohn 216–21; LDeubner, Bemerkungen z. Text der Vita Pyth. des Iamblichos: SAB '35, XIX 27; 71), oft. at the same time in the sense 'in the interest of' or 'in behalf of' οὗτός ἐστιν ὑπὲρ οὗ ἐγὼ εἶπον J 1: 30 (t.r. περί). Ἡσαΐας κράζει ὑπὲρ τοῦ Ἰσραήλ Ro 9: 27 (v.l. περί). Cf. 2 Cor 1: 8 (v.l. περί); 5: 12; 7: 4, 14; 8: 24; 9: 2f; 12: 5a, b (in all the passages in 2 Cor except the first dependent on καυχάομαι, καύχημα, καύχησις); 2 Th 1: 4 (ἐγκαυχᾶσθαι). *With reference to* (Demosth. 21, 121) 2 Cor 8: 23; 2 Th 2: 1. ἡ ἐλπὶς ἡμῶν βεβαία ὑπὲρ ὑμῶν *our hope with reference to you is unshaken* 2 Cor 1: 7 (ἐλπὶς ὑ. τινος 'for someth.' Socrat., Ep. 6, 5).

2. w. the acc., in the sense of excelling, surpassing *over and above*, *beyond*, *more than* κεφαλὴ ὑπὲρ πάντα *the supreme Head* Eph 1: 22 (Appian, Bell. Civ. 5, 74 §314 ὑπὲρ ἅπαντα). ὑπὲρ δύναμιν *beyond one's strength* 2 Cor 1: 8; cf. 8: 3 t.r. (Dit., Or. II 767, 19f ὑπὲρ δύναμιν; Cyranides 63, 22 ὑπὲρ δύναμιν). Also ὑπὲρ ὃ δύνασθε 1 Cor 10: 13. μὴ ὑπὲρ ἃ γέγραπται *not* (to go) *beyond what is written* 1 Cor 4: 6 (s. WLütgert, Freiheitspredigt u. Schwarmgeister in Korinth '08, 97ff; ASchlatter, Die korinth. Theologie '14, 7ff; OLinton, StKr 102, '30, 425–37; LBrun, ibid. 103, '31, 453–6; PWallis, ThLZ 75, '50, 506–8; ALegault, NTS 18, '71/'72, 227–31). ὑπὲρ ἃ λέγω ποιήσεις *you will do even more than I ask* Phlm 21. ὑπέρ τι καὶ καθ' ὑπερβολὴν ὑπερευφραίνομαι *I feel an exceeding and overwhelming joy* B 1: 2.—After an adj. in comp. or superl. for ἤ *than*: mostly so after the comp. (Judg 11: 25 B; 15: 2 B; 18: 26 B; 3 Km 19: 4; Ps 18: 11; Hab 1: 8) τομώτερος ὑπὲρ πᾶσαν μάχαιραν Hb 4: 12. Cf. Lk 16: 8; J 12: 43 v.l.; MPol 18: 1. τοὺς ἀποστόλους ὄντας ὑπὲρ πᾶσαν ἁμαρτίαν ἀνομωτέρους *the apostles, who were more lawless than* (men who commit) *any and every sin* B 5: 9; rarely after the superl. γλυκυτάτη ὑπὲρ τὸ μέλι Hm 5, 1, 6. Likew. after verbs that express the idea of comparison ἡσσώθητε (= ἐγένεσθε ἥσσονες) ὑπὲρ τὰς λοιπὰς ἐκκλησίας; *were you treated worse than the other churches?* 2 Cor 12: 13.—'More than' also takes on the sense *more exalted* or *excellent* or *glorious than*; as the timeless one (ἄχρονος), Christ is called ὁ ὑπὲρ καιρόν

the one who is exalted beyond time IPol 3: 2. ὑπὲρ θάνατον *exalted above death* ISm 3: 2. οὐκ ἔστιν μαθητὴς ὑπὲρ τὸν διδάσκαλον *a disciple is not superior to his teacher* Mt 10: 24a; Lk 6: 40.—Mt 10: 24b; Ac 26: 13; Phil 2: 9. οὐκέτι ὡς δοῦλον ἀλλὰ ὑπὲρ δοῦλον *no longer as a slave, but as someth. better than a slave* Phlm 16. τῷ δυναμένῳ ὑπὲρ πάντα ποιῆσαι *to him who is able to do greater things than all* (we can ask or imagine) Eph 3: 20.—*More than* (Test. Gad 7: 1) ἀγαπᾶν ὑμᾶς ὑπὲρ τὴν ψυχήν μου B 1: 4; cf. 4: 6; 19: 5; D 2: 7. φιλεῖν Mt 10: 37a, b. ἀρέσει αὐτῷ ὑπὲρ μόσχον 1 Cl 52: 2 (Ps 68: 32). λάμπειν IEph 19: 2. προκόπτειν Gal 1: 14. στίλβειν Hs 9, 2, 2.

3. The adverbial use of ὑπέρ is, so far, almost unknown outside the NT (but cf. L-S-J s.v. ὑπέρ E; Ursing 49 cites fr. an Aesop-ms. ὅπερ ἔτι ὑπὲρ ἀπεδέξατο, where all the other mss. have μᾶλλον [Phil 3: 4 ἐγὼ μᾶλλον]. On the adverbial use of other prepositions s. Kühner-G. I p. 526f). διάκονοι Χριστοῦ εἰσιν; ὑπὲρ ἐγώ *are they servants of Christ? I am so even more* (than they) 2 Cor 11: 23 (W-H. accent ὕπερ). Wallis (s. 2 above) classes 1 Cor 4: 6 here.—On ὑπὲρ ἄγαν, ὑπὲρ ἐκεῖνα, ὑπὲρ ἐκπερισσοῦ, ὑπὲρ λίαν s. ὑπεράγαν, ὑπερέκεινα, ὑπερεκπερισσοῦ (-ῶς), ὑπερλίαν. M-M.

ὑπεραγάλλομαι dep. *rejoice* or *exult greatly* ὑπεραγαλλόμενος *with the highest joy* IPhld 5: 1.*

ὑπεράγαν adv. (ὑπέρ+ἄγαν: Strabo 3, 2, 9; Aelian, N.A. 3, 38; Vett. Val. p. 63, 5; Diog. L. 3, 26; 2 Macc 10: 34. Written separately as early as Eur., Med. 627.—Bl-D. §116, 3) *beyond measure* 1 Cl 56: 2.*

ὑπεραγαπάω 1 aor. ὑπερηγάπησα (Demosth. 23, 196; Aristot., Eth. Nic. 9, 7 p. 1168a, 1; Cass. Dio 77, 22, 1; Herodian 4, 7, 4; Aristaen., Ep. 1, 19; 2, 16 σε; Eunap. p. 67; Jos., Ant. 1, 222; 12, 195) *love most dearly* τινά *someone* (Plut., Ages. 35, 2; Ps.-Callisth. 2, 21, 2) B 5: 8.*

ὑπεραίρω (Aeschyl., Pla.+; inscr., pap., LXX, Ep. Arist.; Jos., C. Ap. 2, 223 in var. mngs.) in our lit. only ὑπεραίρομαι *rise up*, *exalt oneself*, *be elated* (Aristaen. 1, 17; Anth. Pal. 5, 299, 5; 2 Macc 5: 23 [w. dat.]) ἐπί w. acc. 2 Th 2: 4. Abs. 2 Cor 12: 7a, b (Byz. folk-song in Theophanes Conf. [VIII AD], Chron. 283, 19ff de Boor [cf. KKrumbacher, Byz. Lit.² 1897, 792] δὸς αὐτοῦ κατὰ κρανίου, ἵνα μὴ ὑπεραίρηται). M-M.*

ὑπέρακμος, ον (Soranus, Hesychius, Suidas) fr. ἀκμή= highest point or prime of a person's development (ἀκ. in this sense in Pla., Rep. 5 p. 460E; Philo, Leg. All. 1, 10) 1 Cor 7: 36. Depending on one's understanding of this pass. (cf. γαμίζω 1), it may apply either to the woman *past one's prime*, *past marriageable age*, *past the bloom of youth* (so Soranus p. 15, 8.—Diod. S. 32, 11, 1 speaks of the ἀκμὴ τῆς ἡλικίας of a woman and in 34+35 fgm. 2, 39 uses ἀκμή of the youthful bloom of a παρθένος.— Lycon [III BC] in Diog. L. 5, 65 commiserates the father of a παρθένος on the smallness of her dowry ἐκτρέχουσα [=goes beyond] τὸν ἀκμαῖον τῆς ἡλικίας καιρόν) or to the man (Diod. S. 32, 10, 2 ἀκμή; Ps.-Clem., Hom. p. 8, 17 Lag. ἀκμαία ἐπιθυμία; Syntipas p. 10, 14 uses ἀκμάζω in that way), in which case ὑπέρ is not to be understood in the temporal sense, but expresses intensification (cf. ὑπέρ 2. Diod. S. 36, 2, 3 ὁ ἔρως of a man in love ἤκμαζεν and became irresistible), *with strong passions*. M-M.*

ὑπεράνω adv. (Aristot.+; inscr., pap., LXX) (*high*) *above* as improper prep. w. gen. (Bl-D. §215, 2; Rob. 646f) of place (Archimed. II 318, 6 Heib.; Eratosth. p. 46, 7; Ocellus Luc. c. 36 ὑπ. σελήνης; Diod. S. 20, 23, 1; schol. on Apollon. Rhod. 2, 160b; Ezk 43: 15; Jos., Ant. 3, 154) Eph 4: 10; Hb 9: 5.—Of rank, power, etc. (Lucian, Demon. 3; Dt 28: 1; Philo, Conf. Lingu. 137; Test. Levi 3: 4) Eph 1: 21. M-M.*

ὑπερασπίζω (Gen 15: 1; 4 Km 19: 34; Pr 2: 7; Polyb. 6, 39, 6 al.; Dionys. Hal. 6, 12, 2; inscr.) *protect*, lit. 'hold a shield over' αὐτούς Js 1: 27 𝔓74.*

ὑπερασπισμός, οῦ, ὁ (LXX; see ὑπερασπίζω) *protection* 1 Cl 56: 16. B. -σις 1410.*

ὑπερασπιστής, οῦ, ὁ (LXX; Philo, Ebr. 111; Jo. Lydus, De Mag. 1, 46 p. 48, 22 W.; Hesychius, Suidas) *protector* 1 Cl 45: 7.*

ὑπεραυξάνω (in trans. sense Andoc.+) intr. (Callisth. in Stob. V p. 871, 2 H. = Ps.-Plut., Fluv. 6, 2) *grow wonderfully, increase abundantly* fig., of faith 2 Th 1: 3. M-M.*

ὑπερβαίνω (Hom.+; inscr., pap., LXX; Ep. Arist. 122; Philo, Joseph.)—1. lit. *go beyond* of the head of the risen Lord κεφαλὴν ὑπερβαίνουσαν τοὺς οὐρανούς *that reaches up above the heavens* GP 10: 40.

2. *overstep, transgress, break* (laws and commandments: Pind., Hdt.+), also abs. *trespass, sin* (Il. 9, 501; Pla., Rep. 2 p. 366a) w. πλεονεκτεῖν τὸν ἀδελφόν 1 Th 4: 6. M-M.*

ὑπερβαλλόντως (Pla., X.+; Dit., Syll.3 685, 36 [II bc]; PGM 4, 649; Job 15: 11) adv. of the pres. ptc. of ὑπερβάλλω: *exceedingly, immeasurably*, also comp. *surpassingly, to a much greater degree* (Philo, Plant. 126, Migr. Abr. 58) 2 Cor 11: 23. M-M.*

ὑπερβάλλω (Hom.+; inscr., pap., LXX) *go beyond, surpass, outdo* (Aeschyl., Pla., X.+; Philo, Mos. 2, 1; Jos., Ant. 2, 7; 8, 211) in an extraordinary constr. ἦν ὑπερβάλλων τὸ φῶς αὐτοῦ ὑπὲρ πάντα *it went far beyond them all as far as its light was concerned, it surpassed them all in light* IEph 19: 2.—The ptc. ὑπερβάλλων, ουσα, ον *surpassing, extraordinary, outstanding* (Aeschyl., Hdt.+; Artem. 4, 72 ὑπερβάλλουσα εὐδαιμονία; 2 Macc 4: 13; 7: 42; 3 Macc 2: 23; Ep. Arist. 84; Philo; Jos., Ant. 4, 14) μέγεθος (Philo, Deus Imm. 116) Eph 1: 19. πλοῦτος 2: 7. χάρις 2 Cor 9: 14. φιλανθρωπία Dg 9: 2. δόξα 2 Cor 3: 10. δωρεαί (cf. Philo, Migr. Abr. 106) 1 Cl 19: 2; 23: 2. Used w. the gen. of comparison (Alex. Aphr., An. Mant. p. 169, 17 Br. ὑπ. τούτων) ὑπερβάλλουσα τῆς γνώσεως ἀγάπη *a love that surpasses knowledge* Eph 3: 19. M-M.*

ὑπερβολή, ῆς, ἡ (since Hdt. 8, 112, 4; inscr., pap.) *excess, extraordinary quality* or *character* w. gen. of the thing (Diod. S. 4, 52, 2 εὐσεβείας ὑπερβολή; Epict. 4, 1, 17 ὑπ. τυραννίδος; Dio Chrys. 14[31], 117; 123; Philo; Jos., Bell. 6, 373, Ant. 1, 234; 13, 244) ἡ ὑπ. τῆς δυνάμεως *the extraordinary (quality of the) power* 2 Cor 4: 7. ἡ ὑπερβολὴ τῶν ἀποκαλύψεων *the extraordinary revelations* 12: 7. ἡ ὑπ. τῆς ἀγαθότητος 2 Cl 13: 4 (cf. Simplicius In Epict. p. 43, 9 Düb. ὑπ. τῆς θείας ἀγαθότητος; Ael. Aristid. 39 p. 743 D.: ὑπ. φαυλότητος).—καθ' ὑπερβολὴν *to an extraordinary degree, beyond measure, utterly* (Soph., Oed. R. 1195; Isocr. 5, 11; Polyb. 3, 92, 10; Diod. S. 2, 16, 2; 17, 47; 19, 86, 3; PTebt. 23, 4; 4, 25; PReinach 7, 4 [all three II bc]; 4 Macc 3: 18) w. verbs 2 Cor 1: 8 (w. ὑπὲρ δύναμιν); Gal 1: 13; B 1: 2; w. an adj.

καθ' ὑπ. ἁμαρτωλός *sinful in the extreme* Ro 7: 13; w. a noun as a kind of adj. ἔτι καθ' ὑπερβολὴν ὁδὸν δείκνυμι *I will show* (you) *a far better way* 1 Cor 12: 31; in a play on words beside εἰς ὑπερβολήν (Diod. S. 14, 48, 2; Aelian, Var. Hist. 12, 1; Vi. Aesopi III p. 309, 7), which means essentially the same thing *to excess*, etc. (Eur., Hipp. 939 al.; Lucian, Tox. 12; Diog. L. 2, 51), *beyond all measure and proportion* 2 Cor 4: 17. M-M.*

ὑπερδοξάζω (Suidas) *glory exceedingly, break out in rapturous praise* abs. IPol 1: 1.*

ὑπερεγώ is the way Lachmann writes ὑπὲρ ἐγώ 2 Cor 11: 23; s. ὑπέρ 3.

ὑπερεῖδον 2 aor. of ὑπεροράω (q.v.). M-M.

ὑπερέκεινα adv. (= ὑπέρ + ἐκεῖνα, cf. ἐπέκεινα. Thomas Mag. 155, 7 ἐπέκεινα ῥήτορες λέγουσιν . . . ὑπερέκεινα δὲ μόνοι οἱ σύρφακες [rabble].—Bl-D. §116, 3; Rob. 171; 297) *beyond* used w. gen. τὰ ὑπερέκεινα ὑμῶν (sc. μέρη) *the lands that lie beyond you* 2 Cor 10: 16 (Bl-D. §184; Rob. 647). M-M.*

ὑπερεκπερισσοῦ adv. (elsewh. only Da 3: 22 Complutensian and Aldine editions; Test. Jos. 17: 5.—Bl-D. §12 app.; 116, 3; Rob. 170f) *quite beyond all measure* (highest form of comparison imaginable) ὑπ. δεῖσθαι *pray as earnestly as possible* (to God) 1 Th 3: 10.—5: 13 v.l. (s. ὑπερεκπερισσῶς). W. gen. of comparison (Bl-D. §185, 1; Rob. 647) ὑπ. ὦν (= τούτων ἅ) *infinitely more than* Eph 3: 20. M-M.*

ὑπερεκπερισσῶς adv. *beyond all measure, most highly* w. ἡγέομαι (q.v. 2, end) 1 Th 5: 13 (v.l. ὑπερεκπερισσοῦ, q.v.).—Mk 7: 37 v.l.; 1 Cl 20: 11.*

ὑπερεκτείνω (Proclus, Theol. 59 p. 56, 35; Damasc., Princ. 284; Suidas) *stretch out beyond* ὑπερεκτείνομεν ἑαυτούς *we are overextending ourselves* (beyond the limits set by God) 2 Cor 10: 14.*

ὑπερεκχύν(ν)ω (= ὑπερεκχέω; s. ἐκχέω, beg.—The word is found Diod. S. 11, 89, 4; Aelian, N.A. 12, 41; Artem. 2, 27; Jo 2: 24; 4: 13; Pr 5: 16; Jos., Bell. 1, 407) *pour out over*, in our lit. only pass. (Hero Alex. I p. 26, 4; Philo, Ebr. 32) *overflow* ὑπερεκχυννόμενον Lk 6: 38. M-M.*

ὑπερεντυγχάνω (Clem. Alex., Paed. 1, 6, 47, 4 p. 118, 21f Stählin) *plead, intercede* Ro 8: 26; the t.r. adds ὑπὲρ ἡμῶν. M-M.*

ὑπερεπαινέω (Hdt., Aristoph.+) *praise highly* τὶ *someth.* (Aelian, V.H. 9, 30) IEph 6: 2.*

ὑπερευφραίνομαι (Arrian, Cyneg. 7, 2; Lucian, Icarom. 2; Ps.-Lucian, Amor. 5; Acta Pauli [et Theclae] 7 p. 241, 1 Lips.) *rejoice exceedingly* ἐπί τινι (Jos., Bell. 7, 14) B 1: 2.*

ὑπερευχαριστέω (PTebt. 12, 24 [118 bc] = 'be overjoyed'; Euseb., Martyr. Palaest. 11, 26) *give heartiest thanks* τινι *to someone* B 5: 3. M-M.*

ὑπερέχω fut. ὑπερέξω (Hom.+; inscr., pap., LXX; En. 24, 3; Philo; Jos., Ant. 6, 25) *rise above, surpass, excel*—1. lit. (Polyaenus 2, 2, 1) τὶ *someth* (3 Km 8: 8; Jos., Ant. 1, 89) ἀνὴρ ὑψηλός, ὥστε τὸν πύργον ὑπερέχειν Hs 9, 6, 1.

2. fig.—a. *have power over, be in authority* (over), *be highly placed* (οἱ ὑπερέχοντες = 'those in authority', 'superiors' Polyb. 28, 4, 9; 30, 4, 17; Herodian 4, 9, 2;

Artem. 2, 9 p. 92, 17; 2, 12 p. 102, 4; PGM 4, 2169; of kings Wsd 6: 5) βασιλεῖ ὡς ὑπερέχοντι 1 Pt 2: 13. ἐξουσίαι ὑπερέχουσαι *governing authorities* (Syntipas p. 127, 4) Ro 13: 1. οἱ ὑπερέχοντες *those who are in high position* (cf. Epict. 3, 4, 3; Diog. L. 6, 78; Philo, Agr. 121) B 21: 2, *those who are better off* (economically) Hv 3, 9, 5. ὑπερέξει λαὸς λαοῦ *one people shall rule over the other* B 13: 2 (Gen 25: 23).

b. *be better than, surpass, excel* w. gen. (Ps.-X., Cyneg. 1, 11; Pla., Menex. 237D; Demosth. 23, 206; Diod. S. 17, 77, 3; Zen.-P. 11 [= Sb 6717], 6 [257 BC]; Sir 33: 7; Test. Jud. 21: 4) ἀλλήλους ἡγούμενοι ὑπερέχοντας ἑαυτῶν *each one should consider the others better than himself* Phil 2: 3. W. the acc. (Eur., Hipp. 1365; X., Hell. 6, 1, 9; Da 5: 11) of some angels who are greater than others ὑπερέχοντες αὐτούς Hv 3, 4, 2. ἡ εἰρήνη τοῦ θεοῦ ἡ ὑπερέχουσα πάντα νοῦν Phil 4: 7 (νοῦς 1a). Abs. ὑπερέχων *more excellent, superior* Hs 9, 28, 3; 4.

c. The neut. of the pres. ptc. as subst. τὸ ὑπερέχον *the surpassing greatness* w. gen. τῆς γνώσεως *of personal acquaintance* (w. Christ; s. γνῶσις 2, end) Phil 3: 8. M-M.*

ὑπερηφανέω 1 aor. ὑπερηφάνησα—1. intr. *be proud, haughty* (so Hom. and later wr. as Polyb. 6, 10, 8; BGU 48, 19 [III AD]; 2 Esdr 19 [Neh 9]: 10; Jos., Bell. 3, 1, Ant. 4, 38) IEph 5: 3.

2. trans. *treat arrogantly* or *disdainfully, despise* w. acc. (Polyb. 5, 33, 8; Lucian, Nigr. 31; POxy. 1676, 10; PFlor. 367, 12 [both III AD]; 4 Macc 5: 21; Jos., Bell. 1, 344, Ant. 16, 194) δούλους IPol 4: 3. τὰ δεσμά μου ISm 10: 2.*

ὑπερηφανία, ας, ἡ (X., Pla. et al.; LXX; En. 5, 8; Ep. Arist. 262; 269; Philo, Virt. 171; Jos., Ant. 1, 195; 16, 4; Test. 12 Patr.; PGM 17a, 6) *arrogance, haughtiness, pride* w. ἀλαζονεία 1 Cl 16: 2. W. ἀλαζονεία and other vices 35: 5; Hm 6, 2, 5; D 5: 1. W. other vices (without ἀλαζ.) Mk 7: 22; B 20: 1; Hm 8: 3; βδελυκτὴ ὑπ. 1 Cl 30: 1. ὑπερηφανίαν μεγάλην ἐνδύσασθαι Hs 8, 9, 1. M-M.*

ὑπερήφανος, ον in our lit. only in an unfavorable sense (as Hes., Pla.+; Diod. S. 6, 7, 1–4 [a man who was ἀσεβής as well as ὑπ. is hated by Zeus, to whom he claims to be superior; cf. 13, 21, 4 τοὺς ὑπερηφανοῦντας παρὰ θεοῖς μισουμένους; 20, 13, 3; 23, 12, 1; 24, 9, 2]; UPZ 144, 50 [164 BC, of Nemesis, whom Zeus threatens]; POxy. 530, 28 [II AD]; LXX, Ep. Arist.; Jos., Ant. 4, 224) *arrogant, haughty, proud* Lk 1: 51 (on the διανοίᾳ καρδίας αὐτῶν s. διάνοια 2; PLSchoonheim, NovT 8, '66, 235–46); Ro 1: 30 (w. ἀλαζών as Jos., Bell. 6, 172; in a list of vices as Test. Levi 17: 11; see also s.v. ὑβριστής); 2 Ti 3: 2; D 2: 6. Opp. ταπεινός (after Pr 3: 34; cf. Ep. Arist. 263; Diod. S. 13, 24, 6 Tyche ταπεινοῖ τοὺς ὑπερηφάνους; Cleobulus of Lindos in Stob. III p. 114, 3f H.; Xenophon of Ephesus 1, 2, 1 the god Eros is inexorable toward the ὑπ.) Js 4: 6; 1 Pt 5: 5; 1 Cl 30: 2; cf. 59: 3; IEph 5: 3. ὑπ. αὐθάδεια 1 Cl 57: 2. οὐδὲν ὑπερήφανον (cf. Ep. Arist. 170) 49: 5. M-M. B. 1146.*

ὑπέρλαμπρος, ον *exceedingly bright* (of sound, Demosth. 18, 260. In the pap. the word is used as an honorary title) of light (Aristoph., Nub. 571 ἀκτῖνες) χῶρος ὑπέρλαμπρος τῷ φωτί AP 5: 15.*

ὑπερλίαν (Eustath. 1396, 42; 1184, 18) adv. (ὑπέρ+λίαν; Bl-D. §12 app.; 116, 3) *exceedingly, beyond measure*, as adj. οἱ ὑπερλίαν ἀπόστολοι the *super-apostles* 2 Cor 11: 5; 12: 11. These are either the original apostles (so the older interpr., FCBaur, Heinrici, HHoltzmann;

KHoll, SAB '21, 925; 936; EMeyer III 456; Rtzst., Mysterienrel.[3] 367ff; Schlatter; EKäsemann, ZNW 41, '42, 33–71) or, perh. w. more probability, the opponents of Paul in Corinth (OPfleiderer, Das Urchristentum[2] '02, I 127; Schmiedel, Ltzm., Sickenberger, Windisch, H-DWendland; RBultmann, Symb. Bibl. Ups. 9, '47, 23–30; WG Kümmel, Introd. to the NT, rev. ed. tr. HCKee, '73, 284–6). M-M.*

ὑπέρμαχος, ου, ὁ *champion, defender* (Archias [I BC]: Anth. Pal. 7, 147, 1; Inscr. Creticae I '35 XIX 3, 29 [II BC]; LXX, Philo) of God (2 Macc 14: 34; Philo, Abr. 232; Sib. Or. 3, 709) 1 Cl 45: 7.*

ὑπερνικάω (Hippocr., Hebd. 50 [WHRoscher '13]; Menand., Monost. 299 Meineke καλὸν τὸ νικᾶν, ὑπερνικᾶν δὲ σφαλερόν; Galen XIX 645 K.; Ps.-Libanius, Charact. Ep. p. 39, 24; Socrat., History of the Church 3, 21; Tactics of the Emperor Leo [Migne, P. Gr. CVII p. 669-1120] 14, 25 νικᾷ καὶ μὴ ὑπερνικᾷ; schol. on Eur., Hipp. 426 ὑπερνικάω as expl. for ἀμιλλάομαι; Hesychius; Ps 42: 1 Sym.; Da 6: 3 Theod.) as a heightened form of νικᾶν: ὑπερνικῶμεν *we are winning a most glorious victory* Ro 8: 37 (for the idea s. Epict. 1, 18, 22; Hermonax Delius [III or II BC] 2 p. 252 Coll.: νίκην κ. ὑπέρτερον εὖχος = victory and more than victory). M-M.*

ὑπέρογκος, ον (X., Pla.+; LXX, Philo; Jos., Bell. 3, 471; Test. Ash. 2: 8) *of excessive size, puffed up, swollen*, also *haughty, bombastic* (Plut., Mor. 1119B) of words (Arrian, Anab. 3, 10, 2; Aelian, fgm. 228; Ex 18: 22, 26; cf. Himerius, Or. 69 [= Or. 22], 2 γλῶσσα ὑπέρογκος) λαλεῖν ὑπέρογκα Jd 16 (cf. Da 11: 36 Theod.); cf. 2 Pt 2: 18. M-M.*

ὑπεροράω fut. ὑπερόψομαι; 2 aor. ὑπερεῖδον (q.v.) (Hdt., Thu.+; inscr., pap., LXX, Philo, Joseph.).

1. *disdain, despise* (Thu.+; PHamb. 23, 36; LXX) w. acc. (since Hdt. 5, 69; Lev 26: 37) τινά *someone* B 3: 3 (cf. the pass. on which this is based, Is 58: 7, where ὑπ. is also used, but is not trans.); D 15: 2. τὸν κόσμον Dg 1.

2. *overlook, disregard* (Aristoxenus [300 BC], fgm. 89 Wehrli ['45]; Dionys. Hal. 5, 52, 2; δέομαι μὴ ὑπεριδεῖν με: PPetr. II 32, 1, 31; PReinach 7, 26; PStrassb. 98, 5 [all III/II BC]; Josh 1: 5; Ps 9: 22; Philo, De Jos. 171; Jos., Bell. 2, 534, Ant. 6, 281; 14, 357) Ac 17: 30.*

ὑπεροχή, ῆς, ἡ *projection, prominence*, in our lit. only fig. (Pla.+; Polyb., Epict., Plut., inscr., pap. [Class. Philology 22, '27, p. 245 no. 191, 11; PGM 1, 215]; LXX, Ep. Arist.; Philo, Op. M. 109; Jos., Bell. 4, 171).

1. *abundance, superiority* ἦλθον οὐ καθ' ὑπεροχὴν λόγου ἢ σοφίας *I have not come as a superior person* (κατά to denote kind and manner: κατά II 5bβ.—καθ' ὑπεροχήν: Aristot., Hist. An. 1, 1, 4) *in speech or* (human) *wisdom* 1 Cor 2: 1 (cf. Eunap., Vi. Soph. p. 32 ὑπ. σοφίας; 50 λόγων ὑπ.). καθ' ὑπεροχὴν δοκοῦντες *being pre-eminent in reputation* 1 Cl 57: 2 (s. Jos., Ant. 9, 3).

2. *a place of prominence* or *authority* of prominent officials οἱ ἐν ὑπεροχῇ ὄντες (Polyb. 5, 41, 3; Inschr. v. Perg. 252, 19f; PTebt. 734, 24 [II BC]. Cf. 2 Macc 3: 11; Jos., Ant. 9, 3) 1 Ti 2: 2. M-M.*

ὑπερπερισσεύω 1 aor. ὑπερεπερίσσευσα—1. intr. *be present in* (greater) *abundance* (Moschio, De Pass. Mulier., ed. FODewez 1793 p. 6, 13) Ro 5: 20.

2. trans. *cause someone to overflow* w. someth. pass. *overflow* ὑπερπερισσεύομαι τῇ χαρᾷ (on the dat. s. Bl-D. §195, 2 app.) *I am overflowing with joy* 2 Cor 7: 4.*

ὑπερπερισσῶς adv. (Bl-D. §12 app.; 116, 3; Rob. 297) *beyond all measure* Mk 7: 37.*

ὑπερπλεονάζω 1 aor. ὑπερεπλεόνασα *be present in great abundance* (Hero Alex. I p. 76, 14; Vett. Val. 85, 17) 1 Ti 1: 14. Of a vessel *run over, overflow* Hm 5, 2, 5. M-M.*

ὑπερσπουδάζω pf. ptc. ὑπερεσπουδακώς *take great pains, be very eager* (Menand., Sam. 4 J.; Lucian, Anach. 9; Philostrat., Vi. Apoll. 5, 26; Jos., Ant. 15, 69 ὑπερεσπουδακώς) μανθάνειν *to learn* Dg 1.*

ὑπέρτατος, η, ον (Hom.+; PStrassb. 40, 41) superl. of ὑπέρ *uppermost, loftiest, supreme* (Aeschyl., Suppl. 672 of Zeus) God's ὑπερτάτη ὄψις 1 Cl 36: 2. τῇ ὑπερτάτῳ (here as an adj. of two terminations) αὐτοῦ (i.e. God's) βουλήσει 40: 3.*

ὑπερτίθημι 2 aor. mid. ὑπερεθέμην (Pind., Hdt. as act. and mid. [the latter is quite predom. in inscr., pap.; Philo, Op. M. 156; Jos., Vi. 239]) mid. *set aside, do away w.* τὶ someth. (Appian, Illyr. 15 §45; cf. Pr 15: 22) IMg 10: 2.*

ὑπερυψόω 1 aor. ὑπερύψωσα (LXX; Cat. Cod. Astr. XII 146, 31)—1. act. *raise* τινά *someone to the loftiest height* (Synes., Ep. 79 p. 225A) Phil 2: 9 (cf. Ps 96: 9).—2. mid. *raise oneself, rise* 1 Cl 14: 5 (Ps 36: 35).*

ὑπερφρονέω (Aeschyl., Hdt.+; 4 Macc; Ep. Arist. 122; Jos., Ant. 1, 194) *think too highly of oneself, be haughty* (Ael. Aristid. 50, 19 K.=26 p. 507 D.) Ro 12: 3 (in a play on words w. φρονεῖν. Cf. X., Mem. 4, 7, 6 παραφρονεῖν —φρονεῖν; Maximus Tyr. 18, 1c ἐσωφρόνει–ὑπερεφρόνει; Demetr. Phaler., fgm. 92 Wehrli ὑπερφρ.–καταφρ.). M-M.*

ὑπερῷον, ου, τό (Hom.+; Suppl. Epigr. Gr. 2, 754; BGU 999 I, 6 [99 BC]; PFlor. 285, 12; LXX; Jos., Vi. 146 al. Really the neut. subst. of ὑπερῷος [q.v.], sc. οἴκημα [Philo, Mos. 2, 60]) *upper story, room upstairs,* also of the tower-like room (עֲלִיָּה) built on the flat roof of the oriental house Ac 1: 13 (here, too, a private house is meant [differently BBThurston, ET 80, '68, 21f]); 9: 37, 39; 20: 8; 1 Cl 12: 3.—FLuckhard, D. Privathaus im ptolem. u. röm. Ägypt. '14, 72f. M-M.*

ὑπερῷος, (α), ον (Dionys. Hal., Plut. et al.; inscr., pap.; Ezk 42: 5; Philo, Mos. 2, 60; Jos., Bell. 5, 221) *upstairs, in the upper story, under the roof* δωμάτιον ὑπ. (s. δωμάτιον) MPol 7: 1.*

ὑπέχω 2 aor. ὑπέσχον (Hom.+; inscr., pap., LXX) in our lit. only as a legal t.t. δίκην ὑπέχειν *undergo punishment* (Soph.+ [δίκη 1]; PHal. 1, 163 [III BC]; PFay. 21, 25 [II AD] ὅπως τὴν προσήκουσαν δίκην ὑπόσχωσι; Wilcken, Chrest. 469, 10; Jos., C. Ap. 2, 194, Ant. 1, 99) Jd 7. Also ὑπ. τιμωρίαν MPol 6: 2 (cf. 2 Macc 4: 48 ζημίαν ὑπ.; Theophyl. Sim., Ep. 68 ὑπ. κόλασιν). M-M.*

ὑπήκοος, ον (Aeschyl., Hdt.; inscr., pap., LXX; Ep. Arist. 254; Philo, Joseph.) *obedient* Phil 2: 8. W. dat. (X., Cyr. 2, 4, 22, Hell. 6, 1, 7; Dit., Syll.³ 709, 13f; PPetr. III 53j, 10; PGM 5, 165 [the gen. is usual in secular writers]; Pr 4: 3; 13: 1; Philo, Op. M. 72) Ac 7: 39 (ὑπ. γενέσθαι as Jos., Ant. 2, 48); 1 Cl 10: 1; 13: 3; 14: 1; 60: 4; 63: 2. εἰς πάντα *in every respect* 2 Cor 2: 9. M-M. B. 1328.*

ὑπήνεγκα s. ὑποφέρω.

ὑπηρεσία, ας, ἡ (Thu., Aristoph.+; Ael. Aristid. 28, 81 K.=49 p. 518 D.: ἡ τῷ θεῷ ὑ.; Epict. 3, 24, 114: to God;

inscr., pap., LXX, Philo; Jos., Ant. 16, 184) *service, ministry* 1 Cl 17: 5; Dg 2: 2.*

ὑπηρετέω 1 aor. ὑπηρέτησα (trag., Hdt.+; inscr., pap., Wsd; Sir 39: 4; Ep. Arist., Philo, Joseph.; Test. Jos. 14: 3) *serve, render service, be helpful* w. dat. of the pers. (Hyperid. 3, 39; PSI 502, 30 [257 BC]) Ac 24: 23; Hm 8: 10; s 9, 10, 2. Δαυίδ ὑπηρετήσας τῇ τοῦ θεοῦ βουλῇ Ac 13: 36 (of obedience to God Aristaen., Ep. 1, 17 p. 148 H. ὑπ. θεῷ).—B 1: 5. ἐν λόγῳ θεοῦ ὑπηρετεῖ μοι *he is of service to me in the word of God* IPhld 11: 1. ὑπ. τί τινι *offer someth. (in helpfulness) to someone* (Epict. 4, 1, 37; Polyaenus 7, 23, 2; Lucian, Tim. 22; Jos., Ant. 14, 99) Dg 11: 1. W. dat. of the thing (Papyrus Revenue Laws of Ptolemy Philadelphus [ed. Grenfell 1896] 22, 1 [258 BC]) ταῖς χρείαις μου Ac 20: 34 (cf. Jos., Ant. 13, 225). M-M.*

ὑπηρέτης, ου, ὁ (Aeschyl., Hdt.+; inscr., pap., LXX, Ep. Arist., Philo, Joseph.; loanw. in rabb.) *servant, helper, assistant,* who serves a master or a superior (e.g. a physician's assistant: Hobart 88f; an adjutant: Arrian, Tact. 10, 4; 14, 4; the lictor beside the consul: Appian, Liby. 90 §424; the 20 senators with Pompey: Appian, Bell. Civ. 2, 18 §67; the priest's helpers: Diod. S. 1, 73, 3; the assistant to the ἡγούμενος of a cult-brotherhood: Sb 7835, 11 [I BC] Dg 7: 2. John (Mark) as ὑπ. of Paul and Barnabas Ac 13: 5 (BTHolmes, Luke's Description of John Mark: JBL 54, '35, 63–72; WHadorn, D. Gefährten u. Mitarbeiter des Pls: ASchlatter-Festschr. '22, 65–82; ROPTaylor, ET 54, '42/'43, 136–8). Of the servants of a board or court (Diod. S. 14, 5, 1f and Appian, Bell. Civ. 1, 31 §138 of servants of the court; Diod. S. 17, 30, 4 παρέδωκε τοῖς ὑπηρέταις ... ἀποκτεῖναι; Maximus Tyr. 3, 2b), of the Sanhedrin (Jos., Bell. 1, 655 παρέδωκεν τοῖς ὑ. ἀνελεῖν, Ant. 4, 37 πέμψας ὑ.; 16, 232) Mt 5: 25 (Ael. Aristid. 45 p. 68 D.: ὁ δικαστὴς παραδίδωσι τ. ὑπηρέταις); 26: 58; Mk 14: 54, 65; J 7: 32, 45f; 18: 3, 12, 22; 19: 6; Ac 5: 22, 26. W. δοῦλοι (as Pla., Polit. 289c) J 18: 18. Of a synagogue attendant (as prob. in the Roman-Jewish grave inscr.: RGarrucci, Dissertazioni archeologiche II 1865, p. 166 no. 22) Lk 4: 20 (ὑπ. as a title of cult officials: Thieme 33. Also Paus. 10, 5, 6 acc. to 'Musaeus': Pyrcon as Poseidon's ὑπηρέτης ἐς τὰ μαντεύματα; Dio Chrys. 19[36], 33 ὑπ. τῶν τελετῶν; PLond. 2710r., 11 [HTR 29, '36, p. 40; 50]). Of a king's retinue J 18: 36. The apostles as servants of Christ Ac 26: 16; 1 Cor 4: 1 (Epict. 3, 22, 82 the Cynic as ὑπ. τοῦ Διός; Galen, Protr. 5 p. 12, 5 J.: Socr., Hom. et al. as ὑπ. τοῦ θεοῦ; Pythagorean saying: Wien. Stud. 8, 1886, p. 278 no. 105 τὸν εὐεργετοῦντά σε εἰς ψυχὴν ὡς ὑπηρέτην θεοῦ μετὰ θεὸν τίμα; Sextus 319). Believers gener. as θεοῦ ὑπηρέται (w. οἰκονόμοι [as 1 Cor 4: 1] and πάρεδροι IPol 6: 1 (cf. PGM 59, 3; 5 (and Jos., Bell. 2, 321, Ant. 3, 16). Also w. the objective gen. of that to which the services are rendered (Appian, Bell. Civ. 3, 41 §169 τῆς πατρίδος ὑπ.; Wsd 6: 4) ὑπηρέται τοῦ λόγου *ministers of the word* Lk 1: 2. ἐκκλησίας θεοῦ ὑπηρέται *servants of the church of God* ITr 2: 3.—On the obscure οἱ τῶν ἐχθρῶν ὑπηρέται B 16: 4 cf. Windisch, Hdb. ad loc.—On the functions of the ὑπ. in Greco-Rom. Egypt, HKupiszewski and JModrzejewski, JJP vols. 11 and 12, '57/'58, 141–66.—KHRengstorf, TW VIII, 530–44. M-M. B. 1334.*

ὑπισχνέομαι mid. dep.; 2 aor. ὑπεσχόμην (Hom.+; inscr., pap., LXX, Philo; Jos., Ant. 11, 228, Vi. 111; Sib. Or. 3, 769) *promise* w. dat., foll. by the aor. inf. Pol 5: 2. B. 1272.*

ὕπνος, ου, ὁ (Hom.+; inscr.; Sb 4317, 3; LXX, En., Ep. Arist., Philo, Joseph., Test. 12 Patr.) *sleep* lit. Mt 1: 24 (a divine command in sleep, as e.g. Lind. Tempelchron. D, 68f; Diod. S. 1, 53, 9 Hephaestus κατ᾽ ὕπνον; 5, 51, 4); Lk 9: 32; J 11: 13; Ac 20: 9a, b. Also symbol. (oft. Philo) ἐξ ὕπνου ἐγερθῆναι *wake from sleep*, i.e. bid farewell to the works of darkness Ro 13: 11 (for ἐξ ὕπνου cf. Appian, Liby. 21 §88).—HBalz, TW VIII, 545-56: ὕπνος and related words. M-M. B. 268.*

ὑπνόω 1 aor. ὕπνωσα intr. *sleep, go to sleep* (Hippocr., Polyb. et al.; BGU 1141, 35 [14 BC]; LXX; En. 100, 5; Philo; Jos., Ant. 1, 208; Test. 12 Patr.) 1 Cl 26: 2 (Ps 3: 6).*

ὑπό (Hom.+; inscr., pap., LXX, En., Ep. Arist., Philo, Joseph., Test. 12 Patr.) prep. w. gen. and acc., in our lit. not (cf. Bl-D. §203; Rob. 634) w. dat. (Bl-D. §232; Rob. 633-6).—Lit. s.v. ἀνά, beg.
1. w. gen. (in our lit. as well as the LXX no longer in a local sense), denoting the agent or cause, *by*.
   a. w. the pass. of a verb—α. w. gen. of the pers. τὸ ῥηθὲν ὑπὸ κυρίου (cf. Gen 45: 27; Dit., Syll.³ 679, 85) Mt 1: 22 (Jos., Ant. 8, 223 ὑπὸ τοῦ θεοῦ διὰ τ. προφήτου); 2: 15. Cf. vs. 16; Mk 1: 13; Lk 2: 18; J 14: 21; Ac 4: 11; 1 Cor 1: 11; 2 Cor 1: 4; Gal 1: 11; Eph 2: 11; Phil 3: 12; 1 Th 1: 4; 1 Cl 12: 2; 2 Cl 1: 2; Hm 4, 3, 6 and oft. Also w. the pass. in the sense 'allow oneself to be . . . by' Mt 3: 6, 13; Mk 1: 5, 9.
   β. w. gen. of the thing (cf. X., An. 1, 5, 5 ὑπὸ λιμοῦ ἀπολέσθαι; Diod. S. 5, 54, 3 ὑπὸ σεισμῶν διεφθάρησαν; Nicol. Dam.: 90 fgm. 22 p. 342, 17 Jac. ὑπὸ φαρμακῶν διαφθαρείς; Appian, Liby. 35 §147 ὑπὸ τοῦ χειμῶνος κατήγοντο, Bell. Civ. 4, 123 §515; Longus 2, 18 a nose smashed ὑπὸ πληγῆς τινος; Herm. Wr. 10, 4b; UPZ 42, 9 [162 BC]) καλύπτεσθαι ὑπὸ τῶν κυμάτων Mt 8: 24. Cf. 11: 7; 14: 24; Lk 7: 24; 8: 14; Ac 27: 41; Ro 3: 21; 12: 21; 1 Cor 10: 29; 2 Cor 5: 4; Col 2: 18; Js 1: 14; 3: 4a, b; 2 Pt 2: 17; Jd 12; Rv 6: 13; Hm 10, 1, 4.
   b. w. verbs and verbal expressions that have a pass. sense πάσχειν ὑπό τινος (πάσχω 3aβ; b) Mt 17: 12; Mk 5: 26; 1 Th 2: 14a, b. ὑπὸ χειρὸς ἀνθρώπων παθεῖν B 5: 5. ἀπολέσθαι 1 Cor 10: 9f (Jos., Ant. 2, 300; cf. Sb 1209 Ἀπολλώνιος ἐτελεύτησεν ὑπὸ σκορπίου). ὑπομένειν ἀντιλογίαν Hb 12: 3. τεσσεράκοντα παρὰ μίαν λαβεῖν 2 Cor 11: 24. ὑπὸ τοῦ θεοῦ ἀναστάς *raised by God* Pol 9: 2. γίνεσθαι ὑπό τινος *be done by someone* (s. γίνομαι 2a) Lk 13: 17; 23: 8; Ac 20: 3; 26: 6; Eph 5: 12. Cf. Ac 23: 30 t.r. W. ὑπὸ γυναικός Hv 1, 2, 3 someth. like 'it was brought about' is to be supplied.
   c. w. nouns ἡ ἐπιτιμία ἡ ὑπὸ τῶν πλειόνων *the punishment at the hands of the majority* 2 Cor 2: 6 (cf. X., Cyr. 3, 3, 2 ἡ ὑπὸ πάντων τιμή; Dit., Syll.³ 1157, 10 διὰ τὰς εὐεργεσίας τὰς ὑπὸ τοῦ θεοῦ; Esth 1: 20 ὁ νόμος ὁ ὑπὸ τοῦ βασιλέως).
   d. When used w. an act., ὑπό introduces the one through whose agency the action expressed by the verb becomes poss. (Hdt. 9, 98; Pla., Phil. 66A ὑπ᾽ ἀγγέλων φράζειν='say through messengers'; cf. Herm. Wr. 9, 9 ὑπὸ δεισιδαιμονίας βλασφημεῖν) ἀποκτεῖναι ὑπὸ τῶν θηρίων Rv 6: 8. ὑπὸ ἀγγέλου βλέπεις *you see under the guidance of an angel* Hs 9, 1, 2b; cf. a and b Mayser II, 2, 511f; to the ref. there add PLeid. XI, 1, col. 1, 15.
2. w. acc.—a. of place *under, below*, in answer to the question 'whither?' or the question 'where?'
   α. answering the question 'whither?' ἔρχεσθαι 1 Cl 16: 17; Hs 8, 1, 1. εἰσέρχεσθαι ὑπὸ τὴν στέγην Mt 8: 8; Lk

7: 6. συνάγειν 1 Cl 12: 6. ἐπισυνάγειν Mt 23: 37; Lk 13: 34. τιθέναι Mt 5: 15; Mk 4: 21a, b; Lk 11: 33. κρύπτειν (cf. Job 20: 12) 1 Cl 12: 3. Also (*below*) at κάθου ὑπὸ τὸ ὑποπόδιόν μου Js 2: 3. ὑπὸ τοὺς πόδας *under the feet* (Hdt. 7, 88) 1 Cor 15: 25, 27; Eph 1: 22. ὁ θεὸς συντρίψει τὸν σατανᾶν ὑπὸ τοὺς πόδας ὑμῶν *God will crush Satan so that he will lie at your feet* Ro 16: 20.
   β. in answer to the question 'where?' (Il. 5, 267; Ael. Aristid. 39 p. 734 D.: τὰ ὑπὸ τὸν ἥλιον; Maximus Tyr. 35, 5b) Mk 4: 32. ὄντα ὑπὸ τὴν συκῆν J 1: 48. Cf. Ro 3: 13 (Ps 13: 3; 139: 4); 1 Cor 10: 1; Jd 6. ὑπὸ τὸν οὐρανόν *under heaven*=on earth Ac 4: 12; as adj. ὁ ὑπὸ τὸν οὐρανόν (*found*) *under heaven*=on earth (Demosth. 18, 270; UPZ 106, 14 [99 BC] τῶν ὑπὸ τὸν οὐρανὸν χωρῶν) 2: 5; Col 1: 23; Hm 12, 4, 2; ἡ ὑπὸ τὸν οὐρανόν (χώρα to be supplied. Cf. Ex 17: 14; Job 28: 24) Lk 17: 24a; cf. b. ὑπὸ ζυγὸν δοῦλοι (ζυγός 1) 1 Ti 6: 1.
   b. of power, rule, sovereignty, command, etc. *under* (Dit., Or. 56, 13 [237 BC] ὑπὸ τὴν βασιλείαν τασσόμενοι; PHib. 44, 2 [253 BC] al. in pap.) ἄνθρωπος ὑπὸ ἐξουσίαν τασσόμενος (ἐξουσία 4a) Lk 7: 8a; cf. Mt 8: 9a; Hs 1: 3 (Vett. Val. 209, 35 ὑπὸ ἑτέρων ἐξουσίαν ὄντας). ἔχων ὑπ᾽ ἐμαυτὸν στρατιώτας (Polyb. 4, 87, 9 Μεγαλέαν ὑφ᾽ αὑτῷ εἶχεν) Mt 8: 9b; Lk 7: 8b (Dit., Or. 86, 11 [III BC] οἱ ὑπ᾽ αὐτὸν τεταγμένοι στρατιῶται). ὑπό τινα εἶναι *be under someone's power* (Thu. 6, 86, 4; PSI 417, 36 [III BC] ὑπὸ τὸν ὅρκον εἶναι) Gal 3: 25; 4: 2; ὑφ᾽ ἁμαρτίαν Ro 3: 9; ὑπὸ νόμον 6: 14, 15 (both opp. ὑπὸ χάριν); 1 Cor 9: 20a, b, c, d; Gal 4: 21; 5: 18; ὑπὸ κατάραν 3: 10. ὑπὸ νόμον ἐφρουρούμεθα vs. 23. γενόμενος ὑπὸ νόμον Gal 4: 4 (γίνομαι II 4a and Thu. 1, 110, 2 Αἴγυπτος ὑπὸ βασιλέα ἐγένετο). ὑπὸ τὰ στοιχεῖα τοῦ κόσμου ἤμεθα δεδουλωμένοι vs. 3. συνέκλεισεν ἡ γραφὴ τὰ πάντα ὑπὸ ἁμαρτίαν 3: 22 (s. συγκλείω). πεπραμένος ὑπὸ τὴν ἁμαρτίαν Ro 7: 14. ταπεινώθητε ὑπὸ τὴν χεῖρα τοῦ θεοῦ 1 Pt 5: 6 (s. ταπεινόω 2b). οἱ ὑπὸ νόμον *those who are under (the power of) the law* Gal 4: 5 (cf. X., Cyr. 3, 3, 6 τινὰς τῶν ὑφ᾽ ἑαυτούς).
   c. of time (class.; PTebt. 50, 18 [112 BC]; Jos., Ant. 14, 420. In LXX and our lit. quite rare) ὑπὸ τὸν ὄρθρον *about daybreak* Ac 5: 21 (s. ὄρθρος).
   d. ὑφ᾽ ἕν at one stroke (Epict. 3, 22, 33; Wsd 12: 9) B 4: 4. ὑπὸ χεῖρα *continually* (see s.v. χείρ 2c) Hv 3, 10, 7; 5, 5; m 4, 3, 6.
   e. ὑπὸ τὰ ἴχνη IEph 12: 2 is translated *in the footsteps*. Can ὑπό mean this, someth. like Ezk 13: 8 (ed. JZiegler '52 v.l.), where it stands for עַל? On the other hand, if it='under', then τὰ ἴχνη would require a different interpretation. See ἴχνος 2. M-M.

ὑποβάλλω 2 aor. ὑπέβαλον (Hom.+; inscr., pap.; 1 Esdr 2: 14; Philo; Jos., C. Ap. 1, 154) *instigate* (*secretly*), *suborn* (Appian, Bell. Civ. 1, 74 §341 ὑπεβλήθησαν κατήγοροι; Test. Sim. 3: 3; Da 3: 9 Theod. v.l.—ὑπόβλητος='secretly instigated' Jos., Bell. 5, 439) τινά *someone* Ac 6: 11; MPol 17: 2a. ταῦτα ὑποβαλλόντων Ἰουδαίων (they said) *this because the Jews instigated them* 17: 2b. M-M.*

ὑπογραμμός, οῦ, ὁ lit. *model, pattern* to be copied in writing or drawing (2 Macc 2: 28; cf. ὑπογράφειν Pla., Protag. 326D), then *example* (Ps.-Clem., Hom. 4, 16; cf. Pla., Leg. 4 p. 711B πάντα ὑπογράφειν τῷ πράττειν) of Paul ὑπομονῆς γενόμενος μέγιστος ὑπο. 1 Cl 5: 7. Mostly of Christ 1 Pt 2: 21; 1 Cl 16: 17; 33: 8; τοῦτον ἡμῖν τὸν ὑπογραμμὸν ἔθηκε δι᾽ ἑαυτοῦ Pol 8: 2. M-M.*

ὑποδεής, ές inferior τὸ ὑποδεές τινος someone's modesty (w. τὸ ταπεινόφρον) 1 Cl 19: 1. In secular lit. (Hdt.+, likew. IG IV² 1, 91, 3 [III AD]; pap.) always in the comp. ὑποδεέστερος, α, ον, pl. οἱ ὑποδεέστεροι those who are inferior; so also Dg 10: 5.*

ὑπόδειγμα, ατος, τό (rejected by the Atticists in favor of παράδειγμα [Lob. on Phryn. p. 12]. It is found in X., Equ. 2, 2, b and Philo Mech. 69, 10, then fr. Polyb. on [exx. fr. lit. in FBleek, Hb II 1, 1836, 555]; Vett. Val.; Inschr. v. Priene 117, 57 [I BC]; Dit., Or. 383, 218; BGU 1141, 43 [I BC]; PFay. 122, 16; LXX; Ep. Arist. 143; Philo, Joseph.).
1. *example, model, pattern* (schol. on Nicander, Ther. 382=example) in a good sense as someth. that does or should spur one on to imitate it 1 Cl 5: 1a, b (τὰ γενναῖα ὑποδείγματα). 6: 1 (ὑπόδειγμα κάλλιστον.—Jos., Bell. 6, 103 καλὸν ὑπ.; Philo, Rer. Div. Her. 256); 46: 1; 55: 1; 63: 1. ὑπόδειγμα ἔδωκα ὑμῖν J 13: 15. W. gen. of the thing (Sir 44: 16; 2 Macc 6: 28, 31) Js 5: 10.—In ἵνα μὴ ἐν τῷ αὐτῷ τις ὑποδείγματι πέσῃ τῆς ἀπειθείας Hb 4: 11, ὑπόδειγμα refers not to an example of disobedience (as BGU 747 II, 14 [139 AD] ὑπόδιγμα τῆς ἀπειθίας), but to an example of falling into destruction as a result of disobedience. Cf. also ἀσεβείας ὑπ. Papias 3.—A warning *example* (Cornutus 27 p. 51, 16; Vi. Aesopi W c. 95 πρὸς ὑπόδειγμα=as a warning example; Jos., Bell. 2, 397) Sodom and Gomorrah are ὑπόδειγμα μελλόντων ἀσεβεῖν for the godless men of the future 2 Pt 2: 6 (εἰς τὸ δεῖγμα 𝔓⁷²).
2. *copy, imitation* ὑπόδειγμα καὶ σκιά Hb 8: 5 (suggestion EKLee, NTS 8, '61/'62, 167–9).—9: 23. PKatz, Biblica 33, '52, 525. M-M.*

ὑποδείκνυμι or -ύω fut. ὑποδείξω; 1 aor. ὑπέδειξα (Hdt., Thu.+; inscr., pap., LXX, En., Ep. Arist., Joseph., Test. 12 Patr., Sib. Or. 3, 555) *show, indicate.*
1. lit. τινί to someone ὑποδεικνύουσα αὐτοῖς ἐναλλάξ as she pointed in the wrong direction 1 Cl 12: 4. Also of the visions of the martyrs to whom the Lord has shown the eternal blessings that no earthly eye can behold, pass. MPol 2: 3.
2. fig. *show, give direction, prove, set forth* τὶ someth. (Jos., Ant. 2, 21) B 1: 8. Otherw. always w. dat. of the pers. τινί (to) someone; foll. by a rel. clause Ac 9: 16; foll. by an inf. *warn* Mt 3: 7; Lk 3: 7; foll. by ὅτι (Test. Napht. 8: 1; cf. Bl-D. §397, 4) Ac 20: 35 (πάντα='at every opportunity'); foll. by indirect question Lk 6: 47; 12: 5. M-M.*

ὑποδέχομαι mid. dep.; 1 aor. ὑπεδεξάμην; pf. ὑποδέδεγμαι (Hom.+; inscr., pap., LXX, Philo) *receive, welcome, entertain as a guest* τινά someone (POsl. 55, 8 [c. 200 AD]; Jos., Ant. 1, 180 al.) Lk 19: 6; Ac 17: 7; Js 2: 25; ISm 10: 1. τινὰ εἰς τὴν οἰκίαν (Chio, Ep. 2 εἰς τὴν οἰκίαν ὑποδέχεσθαι αὐτόν) Lk 10: 38; cf. Hs 8, 10, 3; 9, 27, 2 (ὑπ. τινα εἰς as 1 Macc 16: 15). M-M.*

ὑποδέω (Aristot. et al.; 2 Ch 28: 15) predom. mid. in our lit. and elsewh. **ὑποδέομαι** (so Hdt., Aristoph.+) 1 aor. ὑπεδησάμην; pf. ptc. ὑποδεδεμένος; *tie* or *bind beneath, put on* (footwear—so the mid. since Alcaeus 21 Diehl²); w. the acc. either of what is put on the foot (Hdt.+; ὑποδήματα X., Mem. 1, 6, 6; Pla., Gorg. 490E; PGM 4, 934; 2123 σάνδαλα; 7, 729 ὑποδήματα) ὑπόδησαι τὰ σανδάλιά σου Ac 12: 8; cf. Mk 6: 9, or of the foot itself (Thu. 3, 22, 2 τὸν ἀριστερὸν πόδα ὑποδεδεμένος; Lucian, Hist. Conscr. 22; Aelian, V.H. 1, 18) τοὺς πόδας *put shoes on the feet* Eph 6: 15. M-M.*

ὑπόδημα, ατος, τό (Hom.+; inscr., pap., LXX; Jos., Bell. 6, 85; Test. 12 Patr.) *sandal,* a leather sole that is fastened to the foot by means of straps. Pl. (τὰ) ὑποδήματα Mt 3: 11; 10: 10; Mk 1: 7; Lk 3: 16; 10: 4; 15: 22; 22: 35; Hv 4, 2, 1 (on Mt 10: 10; Lk 10: 4 cf. FSpitta, ZWTh 55, '13, 39–45; ibid. 166f; SKrauss, Ἄγγελος I '25, 96–102; JAKleist, The Gospel of St. Mark '36, 257f). The sing. as a collective *footwear* (Test. Zeb. 3: 4f) J 1: 27. W. gen. τῶν ποδῶν (cf. Ps.-Pla., Alc. 1, 128A ποδός) Ac 13: 25. On holy ground τὸ ὑπόδημα τῶν ποδῶν must be taken off 7: 33 (cf. Ex 3: 5; Josh 5: 15.—Dit., Syll.³ 338, 25); cf. JHeckenbach, De Nuditate Sacra '11, 40ff; FPfister, ARW 9, '06, 542; OWeinreich, Hessische Blätter für Volkskunde 10, '11, 212f. M-M. B. 428.*

ὑπόδικος, ον (Aeschyl.+; inscr., pap., Philo; Jos., Vi. 74) *liable to judgment* or *punishment, answerable, accountable* (Pla., Leg. 9 p. 871B et al.; inscr.; PFay. 22, 9 [I BC] τῷ ἀδικουμένῳ) τῷ θεῷ Ro 3: 19. M-M.*

ὑπόδουλος, ον (Physiogn. II 345, 15; Sib. Or. 12, 130) *enslaved, subject as a slave* γίνεσθαί τινι ὑπ. *become enslaved to someone* (Ps.-Clem., Hom. 8, 20) Hm 12, 5, 4.*

ὑποδραμών s. ὑποτρέχω.

ὑποδύομαι pf. ὑποδέδυκα; plpf. ὑποδεδύκειν (Hom.+; Jos., Ant. 15, 282 al.) *get under, take one's place under* ὑπό τι (under) someth. (Hdt. 1, 31) ὑπὸ τὰς γωνίας τοῦ λίθου *under the corners of the stone* Hs 9, 4, 1a. ἐκ τῶν πλευρῶν *along the sides* ibid. b.*

ὑποζύγιον, ου, τό (Theognis, Hdt.+; inscr., pap., LXX, Philo; Jos., Ant. 14, 471 al.) *draught animal, beast of burden* (lit. 'under the yoke'), *pack animal* (acc. to X., Oec. 18, 4 oxen, mules, horses) in our lit. *donkey, ass* (as schol. on Pla. 260c; PHib. 34, 3; 5; 73, 9; s. Mayser II 1, 31; WBauer, JBL 72, '53, 226) Mt 21: 5 (Zech 9: 9); 2 Pt 2: 16. M-M.*

ὑποζώννυμι pres. ptc. ὑποζωννύς (Hdt.+; 2 Macc 3: 19; Jos., Bell. 2, 275, Vi. 293) *undergird, brace,* nautical t.t.: provide a ship w. ὑποζώματα (Pla., Rep. 616c; Athen. 5 p. 204A= funibus Horace, Odes 1, 14, 6), i.e., w. cables that go around the outside of the hull, and in the case of merchantmen, under it (s. Casson below), to give the ship greater firmness in a heavy sea (the verb has this mng. in Polyb. 27, 3, 3; IG I² 73, 9) Ac 27: 17.—ABoeckh, Urkunden über das Seewesen des attischen Staates 1840, 134ff; TDWoolsey, On an Expression in Ac 27: 17, The American Biblical Repository 8, 1842, 405–12; JSmith, The Voyage and Shipwreck of St. Paul⁴ 1880, 107ff; 204ff; Breusing 170–82; HBalmer, Die Romfahrt des Ap. Paulus '05, 160–4; ESchauroth, Harvard Stud. in Class. Philology 22, '11, 173–9; ChVoigt, Die Romfahrt des Ap. Pls.: Hansa 53, '16, 728f; FBrannigan, ThGl 25, '33, 182; HJCadbury, Beginn. I 5, '33, 345–54; LCasson, Ships and Seamanship, etc., '71, 91f, 211; EHaenchen, AG 633, 2. M-M.*

ὑποκάτω adv. *under, below* (Pla.+) in our lit. only as an improper prep. w. gen. (Pla.+; Ocellus Luc. c. 37 ὑ. σελήνης; inscr., pap., LXX, En.; Jos., Bell. 7, 289, Ant. 9, 12; Test. Iss. 1: 5.—Bl-D. §215, 2; 232, 1; Rob. 637) *under, below, down* at Mt 22: 44; Mk 6: 11; 7: 28; 12: 36; Lk 8: 16; J 1: 50 (ὑπὸ τὴν συκῆν 𝔓⁶⁶); Hb 2: 8 (Ps 8: 7); Rv 5: 3, 13; 6: 9; 12: 1. M-M.*

ὑποκάτωθεν adv. *from below* (Pla., Leg. 6 p. 761в; Cyranides p. 61, 9; LXX) as improper prep. w. gen. (*from*) *under* ὑπ. τοῦ οὐρανοῦ 1 Cl 53: 3 (Dt 9: 14).*

ὑπόκειμαι defective dep. (Hom.+; inscr., pap., LXX; Ep. Arist. 105; Philo).
1. lit.—a. *lie* or *be underneath* ὑπέκειτο αὐτοῖς πῦρ AP 7: 22.—b. *lie below, be found* ἐν τῷ ὀφθαλμῷ *in the eye* Lk 6: 42 D.
2. fig. *be subject to, be exposed to* (Philostrat., Vi. Apoll. 6, 41 p. 252, 11 τῷ φόβῳ; Jos., C. Ap. 1, 9) κινδύνῳ 1 Cl 41: 1.*

ὑποκρίνομαι 1 aor. ὑπεκρίθην, Bl-D. §78 (Hom.+ mng. 'answer'=Attic ἀποκρ.; then in Attic 'play a part on the stage'; Ep. Arist. 219; Philo, Conf. Lingu. 48; Joseph.) *pretend, make believe* (since Demosth.; Polyb.; LXX) foll. by the acc. and inf. (w. inf. foll.: Demosth. 31, 8; Polyb. 2, 49, 7; Appian, Hann. 16 §71; 4 Macc 6: 15; Jos., Bell. 1, 520, Ant. 12, 216, Vi. 36) Lk 20: 20 (Bl-D. §157, 2; 397, 2; 406, 1; Rob. 481; 1036; 1038–40). Abs. *play the hypocrite* (Epict. 2, 9, 20; Appian, Bell. Civ. 2, 10, §34; Polyaenus 8, 29; LXX) Hs 9, 19, 3.—UWilckens, TW VIII, 558–71: ὑποκρ. and related words. M-M.*

ὑπόκρισις, εως, ἡ (Hdt.+ = 'answer', then Attic 'playing a part') *hypocrisy, pretense, outward show* (Polyb. 15, 17, 2; 35, 2, 13; Diod. S. 1, 76, 1; Appian, Hann. 19 §83, Syr. 61 §319, Mithrid. 14, 48; Ps.-Lucian, Am. 3; Aesop 284 Halm=166 Hausr.; 2 Macc 6: 25; Philo, Rer. Div. Her. 43, De Jos. 67; Jos., Bell. 1, 628, Ant. 16, 216; Test. Benj. 6: 5) Mt 23: 28; Mk 12: 15; Lk 12: 1; Gal 2: 13; Js 5: 12 t.r.; B 19: 2; 20: 1; 21: 4; D 4: 12; Hm 8: 3. Pl. of the varied forms which hypocrisy assumes 1 Pt 2: 1; D 5: 1.— ἐν ὑποκρίσει ψευδολόγων *by the hypocritical preaching of liars* 1 Ti 4: 2. ἐν ὑποκρίσει *hypocritically* (schol. on Soph., El. 164 p. 111 Papag.) Pol 6: 3; Hv 3, 6, 1; m 2: 5; s 8, 6, 2. Also μεθ᾽ ὑποκρίσεως 1 Cl 15: 1. κατὰ μηδεμίαν ὑπόκρισιν *without any hypocrisy at all* IMg 3: 2 (κατὰ ὑπ. as schol. on Soph., Oed. Col. 1232 p. 451). ἄτερ ὑποκρίσεως *without hypocrisy* Hs 9, 27, 2. M-M.*

ὑποκριτής, οῦ, ὁ (Aristoph., X., Pla.+; inscr.; Zen.-P. 71 [= Sb 6777], 44 mostly in the sense 'play-actor'; so also Ep. Arist. 219) *hypocrite, pretender, dissembler* (Achilles Tat. 8, 8, 14; 8, 17, 3; Artem. 2, 44 p. 148, 3 in the marginal note of a ms.; Jos., Bell. 2, 587 ὑποκριτὴς φιλανθρωπίας.—Job 15: 34 Aquila and Theod. of the godless [= LXX ἀσεβής]; 20: 5 Aquila [=LXX παράνομος]) Mt 6: 2, 5, 16 (in these three passages the mng. 'play-actor' is strongly felt); 7: 5; 15: 7; 16: 3 t.r.; 22: 18; 23: 13–15, 23, 25, 27, 29; 24: 51; Mk 7: 6; Lk 6: 42; 11: 39 v.l.; 12: 56; 13: 15; Hs 8, 6, 5; 9, 18, 3; 9, 19, 2; D 2: 6; 8: 1f.—PJoüon, Ὑποκριτής dans l'Évang.: Rech de Sc rel 20, '30, 312–17; DMatheson, ET 41, '30, 333f; LHMarshall, Challenge of NT Ethics '47, 60f; BZucchelli, ΥΠΟΚΡΙΤΗΣ, Origine e storia del termine '62. M-M.*

ὑπολαμβάνω 2 aor. ὑπέλαβον (Hom.+; inscr., pap., LXX)—1. *take up* τινά *someone* (Jos., Ant. 11, 238) νεφέλη ὑπέλαβεν αὐτὸν ἀπὸ τῶν ὀφθαλμῶν αὐτῶν *a cloud took him up, out of their sight* Ac 1: 9.
2. *receive as a guest, support* (X., An. 1, 1, 7; Diod. S. 19, 67, 1; Jos., C. Ap. 1, 247) 3 J 8.—3. abs. *take up* what is said=*reply* (ὑπολαβὼν ἔφη etc.; Hdt. 7, 101; Thu. 3, 113, 3; Diod. S. 9, 25, 2; 37, 13, 1 al.; 4 Macc 8: 13) ὑπολαβὼν ὁ Ἰησοῦς εἶπεν Lk 10: 30 (ὑπολαβὼν ὁ . . . εἶπεν as Diod. S. 17, 37, 6 ὁ βασιλεὺς ὑπολαβὼν εἶπε

with direct quot.; Prodicus in X., Mem. 2, 1, 29; Job 2: 4; cf. Philostrat., Vi. Apoll. 1, 36 p. 38, 8; Jos., Ant. 7, 184).
4. *assume, think, believe, be of the opinion* (*that*), *suppose* (X., Pla. et al.; inscr., pap., LXX, Philo; Jos., C. Ap. 2, 162; 250) Ac 2: 15. Foll. by ὅτι (Pla., Phaedo 86в; Ps.-Callisth. 1, 46a, 9; En. 106, 6; Ep. Arist. 201; Philo, Rer. Div. Her. 300) Lk 7: 43; 1 Cl 35: 9 (Ps 49: 21); GP 8: 30.—W. inf. and acc. (class.) Papias 2: 4. M-M.*

ὑπολαμπάς, άδος, ἡ occurs as a v.l. at Ac 20: 8 where, instead of ἦσαν λαμπάδες ἱκαναὶ ἐν τῷ ὑπερῴῳ, D reads ἦσαν ὑπολαμπάδες κτλ. In its other occurrences the word seems to mean *window* (or similar opening; s. L-S-J s.v.) and nothing else (Phylarchus [III вc]: 81 fgm. 40 Jac.; inscr. fr. Delos: Dit., Syll.² 588, 219 [II вc].—HSmith, ET 16, '05, 478; Mlt.-H. 328). This may be the mng. in our passage; if so, it would fit in better with a situation in daylight than at night. M-M.*

ὑπόλειμμα (not ὑπόλιμμα, as W-H. spell it; cf. App. 154), ατος, τό (Hippocr., Aristot.+; PSI 860, 8 [III вc]; LXX) *remnant* Ro 9: 27. M-M.*

ὑπολείπω pass.: 1 aor. ὑπελείφθην; 1 fut. ὑπολειφθήσομαι (Hom.+; inscr., pap., LXX, Philo, Joseph.) *leave remaining*; pass. *be left* (*remaining*) (Hom.+; Phlegon: 257 fgm. 36, 1, 4 Jac.; Philo, Aet. M. 99; Jos., Ant. 13, 111, C. Ap. 1, 314) Ro 11: 3 (3 Km 19: 10, 14); 1 Cl 14: 4 (Pr 2: 21). M-M.*

ὑπολήνιον, ου, τό (Demiopr. [cf. on this UKöhler, Her. 23, 1888, 397–401] in Pollux 10, 130; Geopon.; POxy. 1735, 5; LXX.—The adj. Dit., Or. 383, 147) *vat* or *trough* placed beneath the wine-press to hold the wine Mk 12: 1.—AWikenhauser, BZ 8, '10, 273. M-M.*

ὑπόλιμμα s. ὑπόλειμμα.

ὑπολιμπάνω (Dionys. Hal. 1, 23; Themist., Or. 10 p. 139b; inscr.; PHib. 45, 13 [257 вc]; PSI 392, 4), a by-form of ὑπολείπω (on the by-form λιμπάνω cf. Mayser 402) *leave* (*behind*) τινί τι someth. *for someone* 1 Pt 2: 21 (ἀπολιμπάνω 𝔓⁷²). M-M.*

ὑπολύω (Hom.+) lit. *untie*, then *take off one's sandals* or *shoes* (Aeschyl., Aristoph.+; LXX) w. acc. of the pers. whose sandals one takes off τινά (Pla., Symp. 213в; Plut., Pomp. 73, 10; Jos., Ant. 4, 256 ὑπ. αὐτὸν τὰ σάνδαλα; Test. Zeb. 3: 5) ὑπολύειν ἑαυτόν *take off one's own sandals* MPol 13: 2.*

ὑπομειδιάω 1 aor. ὑπεμειδίασα (Anacreontea 45, 14; Polyb. 18, 7, 6; Alciphr. 4, 14, 6 al.; Cat. of the Gk. and Lat. Pap. in the JRyl. Libr. III '38 no. 478, 48; Philo, Abr. 151) *smile quietly* Hv 3, 8, 2.*

ὑπομένω impf. ὑπέμενον; fut. ὑπομενῶ; 1 aor. ὑπέμεινα; pf. ptc. ὑπομεμενηκώς (Hom.+; inscr., pap., LXX; Ep. Arist. 175; Philo, Joseph., Test. 12 Patr.).
1. *remain* or *stay* (*behind*), while others go away ἐν w. dat. of place (Jos., Ant. 18, 328) Lk 2: 43. ἐκεῖ Ac 17: 14.
2. *remain* instead of fleeing (Pla., Theaet. 177в ἀνδρικῶς ὑπομεῖναι—ἀνάνδρως φεύγειν), *stand one's ground, hold out, endure* in trouble, affliction, persecution, abs. Mt 10: 22 (s. PJoüon, Rech de Sc rel 28, '38, 310f); 24: 13; Mk 13: 13 (all three times w. εἰς τέλος); 2 Ti 2: 12; Js 5: 11; 1 Cl 35: 3f; 45: 8 (ἐν πεποιθήσει=full of confidence); 2 Cl 11: 5 (ἐλπίσαντες=in joyful hope); IMg 9: 2 (διὰ τοῦτο, ἵνα); MPol 2: 2 (w. μέχρι and inf.), cf. 3; D 16: 5 (ἐν τῇ πίστει αὐτῶν=in their faith, i.e. endure

the fiery trial). Hence of Christ simply= *submit to, suffer* B 5: 1, 12 (in both cases w. εἰς τοῦτο=for this purpose); cf. 5: 6; 14: 4; IPol 3: 2 (both w. δι' ἡμᾶς); Pol 1: 2 (ὑπὲρ τῶν ἁμαρτιῶν ἡμῶν). κύριος ὑπέμεινεν παθεῖν B 5: 5a; cf. b; 2 Cl 1: 2.—The purpose of the endurance is indicated by εἰς παιδείαν Hb 12: 7 (cf. Nicander in Anton. Lib. 28, 1 εἰς ἀλκήν).—The affliction under which one remains steadfast is expressed in var. ways: τῇ θλίψει *in tribulation* Ro 12: 12; 8: 24 v.l. (here perh. 'put up with', cf. Plut., Mor. 503ʙ). By a ptc. (Jos., Ant. 12, 122) εἰ κολαφιζόμενοι ὑπομενεῖτε 1 Pt 2: 20a; cf. vs. 20b. By the acc. of the thing (Hdt., Thu. et al.; inscr., pap., LXX; Philo, Cher. 2; Jos., Ant. 3, 53; Test. Dan 5: 13) ταῦτα Dg 2: 9. πάντα 1 Cor 13: 7; 2 Ti 2: 10; ISm 4: 2; 9: 2; IPol 3: 1; Dg 5: 5; of Christ πάντα δι' ἡμᾶς Pol 8: 1. σταυρόν Hb 12: 2. τὰς βασάνους 2 Cl 17: 7. δεινὰς κολάσεις MPol 2: 4. τὸ πῦρ 13: 3; cf. Dg 10: 8. τὴν θλῖψιν Hv 2, 2, 7. τὴν ἐπήρειαν IMg 1: 3. ἄθλησιν Hb 10: 32. ἀντιλογίαν 12: 3. παιδείαν vs. 7 t.r. πειρασμόν Js 1: 12. ὑπομονὴν Pol 9: 1 Funk. τὴν ψῆφον τοῦ μαρτυρίου Phlm subscr.

3. *wait for* τινά someone (X., An. 4, 1, 21; Appian, Bell. Civ. 5, 81 §343; Sb 4369 II, 22; Ps 24: 3, 5; 26: 14; Jos., Ant. 5, 121) 1 Cl 34: 8.—PGoicoechea, De conceptu ὑπομονή apud s. Paulum, Diss. Rome '65; FHauck, TW IV 585–93 (ὑ. and ὑπομονή). M-M.*

ὑπομιμνήσκω fut. ὑπομνήσω; 1 aor. ὑπέμνησα, pass. ὑπεμνήσθην (Hom.+; inscr., pap., LXX, Ep. Arist., Philo, Joseph.).

1. act.—a. *remind* τινά someone τὶ *of someth.* (double acc. as Thu. 7, 64, 1; X., Cyr. 3, 3, 37; Pla., Phileb. 67c al.; PFlor. 189, 3 [III ᴀᴅ]; 4 Macc 18: 14; Test. Levi 9: 6) J 14: 26. Also τινα περί τινος (Pla., Phaedr. 275ᴅ; PMich. 100, 2 [III ʙᴄ]; Jos., Ant. 14, 152) 2 Pt 1: 12. W. acc. of the pers. and ὅτι foll. (Jos., Ant. 6, 131) Jd 5; B 12: 2. W. acc. of the pers. and inf. foll. Tit 3: 1. ἑαυτόν *oneself* 1 Cl 7: 1.

b. *call to mind, bring up* τὶ *someth.* (Soph., Philoct. 1170; Hdt. 7, 171; Pla., Phaedr. 241ᴀ al.; Wilcken, Chrest. 238, 1 [II ᴀᴅ] ὑπομιμνήσκω τοῦτο; Wsd 18: 22; Jos., Ant. 14, 384) ταῦτα 2 Ti 2: 14; 1 Cl 62: 3. ὑπομνήσω αὐτοῦ τὰ ἔργα *I will bring up what he is doing* 3 J 10.

c. abs., foll. by acc. and inf. *remind someone that* 1 Cl 62: 2.

2. pass. (Aeschyl.+) *remember, think of* τινός *someth.* (Lucian, Catapl. 4; Philo, Mos. 1, 193) Lk 22: 61. M-M.*

ὑπόμνησις, εως, ἡ (Eur., Thu.+; inscr., pap., LXX)—
1. act., of the (*act of*) *remembering* (Thu., Pla., pap.) Hv 3, 8, 9. ἐν ὑπ. *by a reminder*, i.e. as I remind you 2 Pt 1: 13; 3: 1.

2. pass. (X., Cyr. 3, 3, 38 ὑπόμνησίν τινος ἔχειν; Philo, Poster. Cai. 153; Jos., Ant. 4, 58) ὑπόμνησιν λαμβάνειν τινός *receive a remembrance of*=*remember someth.* 2 Ti 1: 5. M-M.*

ὑπομονή, ῆς, ἡ—1. *patience, endurance, fortitude, steadfastness, perseverance* (Ps.-Pla., Def. 412ᴄ; Aristot., Stoics [Stoic. IV 150 index; Musonius; Epict.—PBarth, D. Stoa⁴ '22, 119ff]; Polyb.; Plut.; LXX; Philo; Jos., Ant. 3, 16 al.; Test. Jos.) esp. as they are shown in the enduring of toil and suffering Lk 21: 19; Rom 5: 3f (on the form of the saying cf. Maximus Tyr. 16, 3b τὴν ἀρετὴν διδόασιν οἱ λόγοι, τοὺς δὲ λόγους ἡ ἄσκησις, τὴν δὲ ἄσκησιν ἡ ἀλήθεια, τὴν δὲ ἀλήθειαν ἡ σχολή); 15: 4f; 2 Cor 6: 4; 1 Th 1: 3; 2 Th 1: 4; 1 Ti 6: 11; 2 Ti 3: 10; Tit 2: 2; Hb 10: 36; Js 1: 3f; 2 Pt 1: 6a, b; Rv 2: 2f, 19; 1 Cl 5: 5, 7; B 2: 2; IEph 3: 1; Hm 8: 9; D 5: 2. πᾶσα ὑπ. *every kind of patience* 2 Cor 12: 12; Col 1: 11. W. the subjective gen. ἡ

ὑπ. Ἰώβ Js 5: 11 (ACarr, The Patience of Job [Js 5: 11]: Exp., 8th Ser. VI '13, 511–17); αὐτοῦ (i.e. Χριστοῦ) *the endurance that Christ showed* Pol 8: 2. Differently ἡ ὑπ. τοῦ Χριστοῦ a *Christ-like fortitude*, i.e. a fortitude that comes fr. communion w. Christ 2 Th 3: 5 (OSchmitz, D. Christusgemeinschaft des Pls im Lichte seines Genetivbrauchs '24, 139f. But s. also 2 below); cf. IRo 10: 3 (s. also 2 below). W. the objective gen. ὑπ. ἔργου ἀγαθοῦ *perseverance in doing what is right* Ro 2: 7 (Polyb. 4, 51, 1 ὑπ. τοῦ πολέμου). ὑπ. τῶν παθημάτων *steadfast endurance of sufferings* 2 Cor 1: 6 (Ps.-Pla., Def. 412ᴄ ὑπ. λύπης; Plut., Pelop. 1, 8 ὑπ. θανάτου; Jos., Ant. 2, 7 πόνων ὑπ.). ὁ λόγος τῆς ὑπομονῆς μου (λόγος 1bβ) Rv 3: 10 (s. also 2 below). δι' ὑπομονῆς *with patience* or *fortitude* Ro 8: 25; Hb 12: 1. διὰ τῆς ὑπομονῆς *through his patient endurance* MPol 19: 2. ἐν ὑπομονῇ (PsSol 2: 36; Test. Jos. 10: 2) Lk 8: 15 (LCerfaux, RB 64, '57, 481–91). ἀσκεῖν πᾶσαν ὑπ. *practice endurance to the limit* Pol 9: 1. ὧδέ ἐστιν ἡ ὑπ. τῶν ἁγίων *here is (an opportunity for) endurance on the part of the saints* (Weymouth) Rv 13: 10 (s. JSchmid, ZNW 43, '50/'51, 112–28); cf. 14: 12.—WMeikle, The Vocabulary of 'Patience' in the OT: Exp. 8th Ser. XIX '20, 219–25, The Voc. etc. in the NT: ibid. 304–13; CSpicq, Patientia: RSphth 19, '30, 95–106; AMFestugière, Rech de Sc rel 21, '31, 477–86; LHMarshall, Challenge of NT Ethics '47, 91f.

2. (*patient*) *expectation* (Ps 9: 19; 61: 6; 2 Esdr [Ezra] 10: 2) Rv 1: 9 (on ὑπ. ἐν Ἰησοῦ cf. IHeikel, StKr 106, '35, 317). Perh. (s. 1 above) 3: 10 and 2 Th 3: 5; IRo 10: 3 might also be classed here.—S. ὑπομένω, end. M-M.**

ὑπομονητικός, ή, όν (Hippocr.+; Philo, Leg. All. 3, 88) *patient, showing endurance* neut. subst. τὸ ὑπομονητικόν *fortitude* MPol 2: 2.*

ὑπονοέω impf. ὑπενόουν; 1 aor. ὑπενόησα (Eur., Hdt. +; pap., LXX, Philo, Joseph.) *suspect, suppose* (Hdt.+; pap.; Sir 23: 21) w. acc. *someth.* (Hdt., Aristoph. et al.) Ac 25: 18 (w. attraction of the rel.; cf. PLond. 1912 [letter of Claudius, 41 ᴀᴅ], 97f ἐξ οὗ μείζονας ὑπονοίας ἀναγκασθήσομαι λαβεῖν). Foll. by acc. and inf. (Bl-D. §397, 2; Rob. 1036.—Hdt. 9, 99 al.; Jos., Ant. 13, 315; PRyl. 139, 14 [34 ᴀᴅ]) 13: 25; 27: 27; cf. Hv 4, 1, 6. M-M.*

ὑπόνοια, ας, ἡ (Thu.+; pap., LXX; Ep. Arist. 316; Philo; Jos., Bell. 1, 227; 631) *suspicion, conjecture* ὑπόνοιαι πονηραί *evil conjectures, false suspicions* 1 Ti 6: 4 (Sir 3: 24 ὑπόνοια πονηρά). M-M. B. 1244.*

ὑποπιάζω s. ὑπωπιάζω.

ὑποπίπτω (Thu., Aristoph. et al.; inscr., pap., LXX; Ep. Arist. 214; Philo; Jos., Bell. 5, 382, Vi. 381; Test. Jos. 7: 8) *fall under* or *within* a classification ὑπό τι (Aristot.; Iambl., Vi. Pythag. 34 §241 ὑπὸ τὴν προειρημένην τάξιν) ὑπὸ τὴν διάνοιάν τινος *fall within someone's comprehension* (διάνοια 1) 1 Cl 35: 2.*

ὑποπλέω 1 aor. ὑπέπλευσα (Dio Chrys., Cass. Dio et al.) *sail under the lee of* an island, i.e. in such a way that the island protects the ship fr. the wind Ac 27: 4, 7. M-M.*

ὑποπνέω 1 aor. ὑπέπνευσα (Aristot., Probl. 8, 6=blow underneath) *blow gently* ὑποπνεύσαντος νότου *when a moderate south(west) wind began to blow* Ac 27: 13.*

ὑποπόδιον, ου, τό (Chares [after 323 ʙᴄ] in Athen. 12 p. 514ꜰ; Lucian, Conscr. H. 27; Athen. 5 p. 192ᴇ; inscr.; PTebt. 45, 38 [113 ʙᴄ]; PRainer 22, 8; 27, 11 [both II ᴀᴅ]; LXX; loanw. in rabb.) *footstool* Js 2: 3. Of the earth as

God's footstool (after Is 66: 1; cf. Philo, Conf. Lingu. 98) Mt 5: 35; Ac 7: 49; B 16: 2. τιθέναι τινὰ ὑποπόδιον τῶν ποδῶν τινος make someone a footstool for someone, i.e. subject him to the other, so that the other can put his foot on the subject's neck (Ps 109: 1) Mt 22: 44 t.r.; Mk 12: 36 v.l.; Lk 20: 43; Ac 2: 35; Hb 1: 13; 10: 13; 1 Cl 36: 5; B 12: 10. M-M.*

ὑποπτεύω 1 aor. ὑπώπτευσα (trag., Thu.+; pap., LXX; Jos., Bell. 2, 617; 3, 367) suspect τινά someone (Soph., Hdt., Thu. et al.) foll. by acc. and inf. IPhld 7: 2.*

ὑπορθόω (Sym.; Dositheus, Ars Gramm. 76, 1 p. 102) support τινά someone GP 10: 39.*

ὑπόστασις, εως, ἡ (Hippocr.+; Polyb. 4, 50, 10; 6, 55, 2; Diod. S. 16, 32, 3; 16, 33, 1; inscr., pap., LXX, in widely different meanings. See Dörrie below)—1. substantial nature, essence, actual being, reality (oft. in contrast to what merely seems to be: Ps.-Aristot., De Mundo 4 p. 395a, 29f; Plut., Mor. 894B; Diog. L., Pyrrh. 9, 91; Artem. 3, 14; Ps 38: 6; Wsd 16: 21; Philo, Aet. M. 88; 92; Jos., C. Ap. 1, 1; Test. Reub. 2: 7) the Son of God is χαρακτὴρ τῆς ὑποστάσεως αὐτοῦ a(n exact) representation of his (= God's) real being Hb 1: 3. Dg 2: 1.
2. situation, condition (Cicero, Ad Attic. 2, 3, 3 ὑπόστασιν nostram= our situation), also specif. frame of mind (Dio Cass. 49, 9; Themist., Or. 13 p. 178B; Jos., Ant. 18, 24) 2 Cor 9: 4; 11: 17; Hb 3: 14 (Dörrie [see below], p. 39: the frame of mind described in Hb 3: 6). The sense 'confidence', 'assurance' must be eliminated, since examples of it cannot be found (acc. to Dörrie and Köster below]). It cannot, therefore, play a role in
3. Hb 11: 1, where it has enjoyed much favor since Luther (also Tyndale, RSV; not KJ). Among the meanings that can be authenticated the one that seems to fit best here is realization (Diod. S. 1, 3, 2 of the realization of a plan; Cornutus 9 p. 9, 3 of the realization of mankind; Jos., C. Ap. 1, 1 that of the Jewish people, both by a divine act): ἔστιν πίστις ἐλπιζομένων ὑπ.= in faith things hoped for become realized, or things hoped for become reality.—ASchlatter, Der Glaube im NT⁴ '27, 614ff; MAMathis, The Pauline πίστις-ὑπόστασις acc. to Hb 11: 1: Washington, Cath. Univ. of Amer. '20; REWitt, Hypostasis: 'Amicitiae Corolla' (RHarris-Festschr.) '33, 319–43; MSchumpp, D. Glaubensbegriff des Hb: Divus Thomas 11, '34, 397–410; FErdin, D. Wort Hypostasis, Diss. Freiburg '39; HDörrie, Ὑπόστασις, Wort- u. Bedeutungsgeschichte: Nachr. der Akad. d. Wissensch. in Göttingen 1955, no. 3, ZNW 46, '55, 196–202; HKöster, TW VIII 571–88 (Köster prefers plan, project [Vorhaben] for the passages in 2 Cor, and reality [Wirklichkeit] for all 3 occurrences in Hb, contrasting the reality of God with the transitory character of the visible world. Cf. also the lit. s.v. πίστις 2a. M-M.*

ὑποστέλλω impf. ὑπέστελλον; 1 aor. mid. ὑπεστειλάμην (Pind.+; inscr., pap., LXX, Philo, Joseph.)—1. act. (Pind.+; Philo, Leg. ad Gai. 71) draw back, withdraw (Polyb. 1, 21, 2 al.; Plut.) ἑαυτόν draw (oneself) back (Polyb. 1, 16, 10; 7, 17, 1 al.) ὑπέστελλεν καὶ ἀφώριζεν ἑαυτόν Gal 2: 12; if ἑαυτόν does not go w. ὑπέστ., ὑποστέλλω is intr. here draw back (Polyb. 6, 40, 14; 10, 32, 3; Plut., Demetr. 47, 6; Philo, Spec. Leg. 1, 5).
2. mid.—a. draw back in fear (Aelian, Nat. An. 7, 19; Philo, Mos. 1, 83; Jos., Vi. 215) Hb 10: 38 (Hab 2: 4).
b. shrink from, avoid because of fear (Demosth. et al.; Jos., Ant. 6, 86 ὑπ. φόβῳ εἰπεῖν) οὐ γὰρ ὑπεστειλάμην

τοῦ μὴ ἀναγγεῖλαι I did not shrink from proclaiming Ac 20: 27.
c. keep silent about τὶ someth. in fear (Demosth. 4, 51; Isocr. 8, 41; Diod. S. 13, 70, 3; Dio Chrys. 10[11], 27 οὐδέν; Lucian, Deor. Conc. 2 οὐδέν; Zen.-P. 59 412, 24 [III BC]; BGU 1303, 10; Philo, Sacr. Abel. 35; Jos., Bell. 1, 387, Vi. 278 οὐδέν al.) οὐδὲν ὑπεστειλάμην τῶν συμφερόντων I have kept silent about nothing that is profitable Ac 20: 20. M-M.*

ὑποστολή, ῆς, ἡ shrinking, timidity (Asclepiodot. Tact. [I BC] 10, 21.—Jos., Bell. 2, 277, Ant. 16, 112 of reserve or timidity in evil-doing) οὐκ ἐσμὲν ὑποστολῆς we do not belong to those who are timid Hb 10: 39. M-M.*

ὑποστρέφω impf. ὑπέστρεφον; fut. ὑποστρέψω; 1 aor. ὑπέστρεψα (Hom.+) in our lit. only intr. (Hom.+; Thu.; pap., LXX, Philo, Joseph.; Test. Gad 1: 5) turn back, return w. εἰς and acc. of place (PGiess. 40 II, 8; Gen 8: 9; Jos., Bell. 1, 229 εἰς Ἱεροσ.) Lk 1: 56; 2: 45; 4: 14 (cf. Jos., Bell. 1, 445); 8: 39 (cf. Jos., Vi. 144 εἰς τὴν οἰκίαν); Ac 8: 25; 13: 13; Gal 1: 17; GP 14: 58. εἰς τὰ ἴδια Ac 21: 6 (ἴδιος 3). εἰς διαφθοράν to corruption, i.e. the grave Ac 13: 34. διά w. gen. of place 20: 3. ἀπό w. gen. of place (Jos., Vi. 139) Lk 4: 1; 24: 9 or a corresp. expr. (Jos., Vi. 329 ἀπὸ τ. πολιορκίας ὑπ.) ἀπὸ τῆς κοπῆς τῶν βασιλέων Hb 7: 1 (Gen 14: 17 Swete). εἰς and ἀπό Ac 1: 12. ἐκ w. gen. of place Ac 12: 25. ἐκ τῆς ἁγίας ἐντολῆς turn away once more (s. ἐντολή 2f) 2 Pt 2: 21. ἐπί τινα to someone Hm 4, 1, 7. Foll. by a final inf. Lk 17: 18. Abs. return (Polyaenus 4, 2, 14; Lucian, Bis Acc. 17; Josh 2: 23; Jos., Ant. 11, 30) Mk 14: 40 v.l.; Lk 2: 20, 43; 8: 37, 40; Ac 8: 28 al. M-M.

ὑποστρωννύω=ὑποστρώννυμι (cf. στρωννύω, beg.— The word occurs Hom.+ [ὑποστορέννυμι, ὑποστόρνυμι]; LXX. In the form ὑποστρωννύω in Athen. 2 p. 48D; in the form ὑποστρώννυμι in Plut., Artax. 22, 10) impf. ὑπεστρώννυον; 1 aor. ὑπέστρωσα; spread τὶ someth. out underneath (PGM 5, 217 σινδόνα; 36, 151) ὑπεστρώννυον τὰ ἱμάτια ἐν τῇ ὁδῷ they were spreading out their cloaks under him in the road Lk 19: 36 (Jos., Ant. 9, 111 ἕκαστος ὑπεστρώννυεν αὐτῷ τὸ ἱμάτιον; 18, 204; Charito 3, 2, 17; Aesop, Fab. 208 P.=378 H. ὑποστρώσας τὸ ἱμάτιον). σποδόν spread out ashes underneath oneself= make one's bed in ashes as a sign of repentance B 3: 2 (Is 58: 5). Pass. κήρυκας ὑποστρωννύμενοι those with trumpet-shells (κῆρυξ 3) under them= those who were laid on trumpet-shells MPol 2: 4. M-M.*

ὑποταγή, ῆς, ἡ (Dionys. Hal. 3, 66, 3 act. 'subjecting') in our lit. only pass. subjection, subordination, obedience (Artem. 1, 73 p. 66, 14; Paradoxogr. p. 218, 7 Westermann ἐν ὑποταγῇ; Vett. Val. 106, 8; 11; 17; 24; 198, 28; BGU 96, 7 [III BC] τὸν ἐν ὑποταγῇ τυγχάνοντα; Wsd 18: 15 A) ἡ ὑποταγὴ τῆς ὁμολογίας ὑμῶν εἰς τὸ εὐαγγέλιον 2 Cor 9: 13 (ὁμολογία 1). ἐν πάσῃ ὑποταγῇ subordinating herself in every respect 1 Ti 2: 11. τέκνα ἔχειν ἐν ὑποταγῇ keep children under control 3: 4. ἐν μιᾷ ὑποταγῇ κατηρτισμένοι made complete in unanimous subjection IEph 2: 2. εἴξαμεν τῇ ὑποταγῇ (dat. of manner) we yielded in submission Gal 2: 5. Of the members of the body ὑποταγῇ μιᾷ χρῆται they experience a mutual subjection 1 Cl 37: 5. ὁ κανὼν τῆς ὑποταγῆς the established norm of obedience (Kleist) 1: 3. M-M.*

ὑποτάσσω 1 aor. ὑπέταξα. Pass.: perf. ὑποτέταγμαι; 2 aor. ὑπετάγην; 2 fut. ὑποταγήσομαι (Aristot., Polyb. et al.; inscr., pap., LXX, Ep. Arist., Philo, Joseph.; Sib. Or. 5, 19).

1. *subject, subordinate*—**a.** act., abs. Ro 8: 20b; 1 Cl 2: 1b. τινά *bring someone to subjection* (Herodian 7, 2, 9) IPol 2: 1. τινί τινα or τι *someone* or *someth.* *to someone* (Epict. 4, 12, 12 of God ὑπ. τί τινι; cf. Da 11: 39 Theod.; Test. Jud. 21: 2; Menander Eph. in Jos., C. Ap. 1, 119; Sib. Or. fgm. 3, 12) 1 Cor 15: 27c, 28c; Phil 3: 21; Hb 2: 5, 8b; Dg 10: 2; Hm 12, 4, 2. In the same sense ὑπ. τι ὑπὸ τοὺς πόδας τινός 1 Cor 15: 27a; Eph 1: 22; also ὑποκάτω τῶν ποδῶν τινος Hb 2: 8a (Ps 8: 7). ὑποτάσσειν ἑαυτόν τινι *subject oneself to someone* (Plut., Mor. 142D to the husband; Simplicius In Epict. p. 33 Düb. to supernatural powers) Hs 9, 22, 3.

b. pass.—**α.** *become subject* τινί to a pers. or a state of being Ro 8: 20a; 1 Cor 15: 28a; Hb 2: 8c; 1 Pt 3: 22; Dg 7: 2; Pol 2: 1; Hm 12, 2, 5. Abs. (Diod. S. 1, 55, 10; Aristobulus in Euseb., Pr. Ev. 8, 10, 10 πάνθ' ὑποτέτακται) 1 Cor 15: 27b.

β. *subject oneself, be subjected* or *subordinated, obey* abs. (Jos., Bell. 4, 175) Ro 13: 5; 1 Cor 14: 34; 1 Cl 2: 1a; 57: 2. W. dat. of actual subordination to persons worthy of respect (Palaeph. 38 p. 56, 15; 57, 2): toward the husband (s. Ps.-Callisth. 1, 22, 4 πρέπον ἐστὶ τὴν γυναῖκα τῷ ἀνδρὶ ὑποτάσσεσθαι, s. 1a above) Eph 5: 22 v.l.; Col 3: 18; Tit 2: 5; 1 Pt 3: 1, 5; parents Lk 2: 51; masters Tit 2: 9; 1 Pt 2: 18; B 19: 7; D 4: 11; secular authorities (1 Ch 29: 24) Ro 13: 1 (CDMorrison, The Powers That Be—Ro 13: 1–13, Diss. Basel '56; EBarnikol, TU 77, '61, 65–133 [non-Pauline]; Tit 3: 1; 1 Pt 2: 13; 1 Cl 61: 1; church officials 1 Cl 1: 3; 57: 1; IEph 2: 2; IMg 2; 13: 2; ITr 2: 1f; 13: 2; IPol 6: 1; Pol 5: 3; νεώτεροι ὑποτάγητε πρεσβυτέροις 1 Pt 5: 5. To God (Epict. 3, 24, 65 τ. θεῷ ὑποτεταγμένος; 4, 12, 11; Ps 61: 2; 2 Macc 9: 12) 1 Cor 15: 28b; Hb 12: 9; Js 4: 7; 1 Cl 20: 1; IEph 5: 3; to Christ Eph 5: 24. To the will of God, the law, etc. Ro 8: 7; 10: 3; 1 Cl 34: 5; Hm 12, 5. 1.—Of submission in the sense of voluntary yielding in love 1 Cor 16: 16; Eph 5: 21; 1 Pt 5: 5b t.r.; 1 Cl 38: 1.—The evil spirits must be subject to the disciples whom Jesus sends out Lk 10: 17, 20. Likew. the prophetic spirits must be subject to the prophets in whom they dwell 1 Cor 14: 32.

2. of literary compositions or documents: *attach* or *append* them to another literary work (oft. inscr., pap.; Jos., Vi. 364, Ant. 16, 161) the letters of Ign. ὑποτεταγμέναι εἰσὶ τῇ ἐπιστολῇ ταύτῃ Pol 13: 2. M-M.*

ὑποτεταγμένως adv. fr. the pf. pass. ptc. of ὑποτάσσω *submissively, obediently* 1 Cl 37: 2.*

ὑποτίθημι 1 aor. ὑπέθηκα; 2 aor. inf. ὑποθεῖναι (Hom. +; inscr., pap., LXX).

1. act. *lay down, risk* τί *someth.* τὸν τράχηλον (Lucian, Enc. Dem. 41 ὑπ. τὴν ψυχὴν ταῖς τῆς πατρίδος τύχαις; cf. Seneca, Ep. 47, 4; POxy. 2722, 35 [commercial]) Ro 16: 4; differently (somewhat as Test. Iss. 5: 3 ὑπ. τὸν νῶτον) *bow in submission* 1 Cl 63: 1 (see s.v. τράχηλος for both passages).

2. mid. (Hom. +) τινί τι *suggest* or *point out someth.* to someone (Hom.; Hdt. 1, 90; Pla., Charm. 155D; pap.) or *enjoin, order someone* (*to do*) *someth.* (Hdt. 4, 134; Philo, Poster. Cai. 12; Jos., Bell. 2, 137, Ant. 1, 76) or *make known, teach someth.* to someone (Pla., Hipp. Maj. 286B) ταῦτα ὑποτιθέμενος τοῖς ἀδελφοῖς 1 Ti 4: 6. M-M.*

ὑποτρέχω 2 aor. ὑπέδραμον (Hom. +; PTebt. 24, 67 [117 BC]; Jos., Ant. 7, 31; 326 al.) *run* or *sail under the lee of* nautical t.t. (Plut., Mor. 243E ὅρμοις 'run in'. Also 'moor under' ἄκραν Heliod. 8, 16; ἄκρα τινί Longus 3, 21) νησίον τι ὑπ. Ac 27: 16. M-M.*

ὑποτύπωσις, εως, ἡ (Diog. L. 9, 78; Sext. Emp., Pyrrh. 2, 79; Pollux 7, 128; Philo, Abr. 71) *model, example,* rather in the sense *prototype* 1 Ti 1: 16. Rather in the sense *standard* 2 Ti 1: 13 (Philod., Mus. p. 77 Kemke [1884] ἀρετῶν; Synes., Dio 1 p. 38 Petav. ὁ λόγος [Δίωνος] ὑποτύπωσίς ἐστιν εὐδαίμονος βίου). EKLee, NTS 8, '61/'62, 171f proposes *outline* for both passages, w. reff. M-M.*

ὑπουργέω *be helpful, assist* (Aeschyl., Hdt. +; pap.; Test. Dan 3, 4; Philo, Vi. Cont. 72; Jos., Ant. 3, 7) εἴς τι *in* or *at someth.* (Eunap., Vi. Soph. p. 108) MPol 13: 1.*

ὑποφέρω (Hom. +; inscr., pap., LXX; Jos., Bell. 6, 197) fut. ὑποίσω; aor. ὑπήνεγκα, inf. ὑπενεγκεῖν (Jos., Ant. 8, 213; for the aor. forms Bl-D. §81, 2 w. app.) *bear* (*up under*), *submit to, endure* τι *someth.* (Hippocr., X., Pla. +; Sb 5238, 22 [12 AD]; LXX) Hv 3, 1, 9a, b; 3, 2, 1. διωγμούς 2 Ti 3: 11. θλίψεις Hs 7: 4–6. λύπας 1 Pt 2: 19; cf. Hm 10, 2, 6. πόνους 1 Cl 5: 4 (cf. X., Hipparch. 1, 3; Pla., Theaet. 173A; Isocr. 4, 64; 2 Macc 7: 36). ὀργήν Hm 12, 4, 1 (cf. Pla., Leg. 9 p. 879c; Mi 7: 9). κίνδυνον *incur danger* (Isocr. 3, 64) 1 Cl 14: 2. ὕβριν *bear up under mistreatment* Hm 8: 10. Abs. 1 Cor 10: 13.—1 Cl 7: 4 Funk for ἐπ. Gebhardt. M-M.*

ὑποχθόνιος, (ία), ιον *under the earth* (Hes. +; Posidon.: 87 fgm. 47 Jac.) οἱ ὑποχθόνιοι *the powers under the earth* w. οἱ ἐπουράνιοι καὶ ἐπίγειοι (ἐπίγειος 2b) ITr 9: 1.*

ὑποχωρέω 1 aor. ὑπεχώρησα (Hom. +; inscr., pap., LXX) *go back, retreat, withdraw,* also in a peaceful sense (as Philo, Abr. 22), *retire.*

1. of persons w. εἰς and acc. (Jos., Vi. 20; 246) εἰς πόλιν Lk 9: 10. Used w. ἐν in the sense 'retire to a place and spend some time there' (cf. Kühner-G. I p. 541) ἦν ὑποχωρῶν ἐν ταῖς ἐρήμοις *he would steal away to* (*the*) *lonely places* 5: 16.—Lk 20: 20 v.l.

2. of things (Jos., Ant. 1, 91; 11, 240) ὁ λίθος ὑπεχώρησεν παρὰ μέρος GP 9: 37 (μέρος 1c, end). M-M.*

ὑπωπιάζω (on the v.l. ὑποπιάζειν cf. W-S. §5, 19 note, end; Mlt.-H. 75) *strike under the eye, give a black eye to* (Aristot., Rhet. 3, 11, 15 p. 1413a, 20; Plut., Mor. 921f; Diog. L. 6, 89).

1. lit. τινά *someone,* of a woman driven to desperation ἵνα μὴ ὑπωπιάζῃ με *in order that she might not fly in my face* Lk 18: 5, unless it is used here in a weakened sense *annoy greatly, wear out* (so L-S-J s.v. II, et al.).—JDM Derrett, NTS 18, '71/'72, 178–91 (esp. 189–91): a symbolic expr. (common throughout Asia), *blacken my face= slander, besmirch* underlies ὑπ. here.

2. symbolically (Aristoph., Fr. 541 πόλεις ὑπωπιασμέναι) *treat roughly, torment, maltreat* 1 Cor 9: 27 (of the apostle's self-imposed discipline. But the expr. is obviously taken fr. the language of prize-fighting vs. 26). M-M.*

ὗς, ὑός, ἡ (Hom. +; inscr., pap., LXX; Jos., Ant. 13, 243 al.) *the female of the swine, sow* (ὁ ὗς is the boar) in a proverb ὗς λουσαμένη εἰς κυλισμὸν βορβόρου *a sow that has bathed herself, only to roll in the mud again* 2 Pt 2: 22 (βόρβορος 2).—On Lk 14: 5 see the editor's introd. to Papyrus Bodmer XIV '61, 18–19; EWiesenberg, HUCA 27, '56, 213–33 (swine). M-M.*

ὑσσός, οῦ, ὁ (Polyb. +; Dionys. Hal. 5, 46, 2 [as long as a spear of moderate length]; Strabo, Plut. et al.) *javelin,* Lat. 'pilum' J 19: 29 v.l. S. ὕσσωπος.*

ὓσσωπος, ου, ἡ and ὁ, also ὓσσωπον, τό (in the secular wr. [Nicander—II bc—, Ther. 872; Alexiph. 603; Chaeremon 44, 6 al.; inscr., pap.] all three genders are quotable; for the LXX the masc. and fem. are certain; Philo, Vi. Cont. 73 excludes the neut. for that author; in Jos., Bell. 6, 201, Ant. 2, 312; 4, 80 the situation is not clear. In our lit. the neut. is certain only in ms. B.— אֵזוֹב) the hyssop, a small bush w. blue flowers and highly aromatic leaves; used in purificatory sacrifices (Ex 12: 22; Lev 14: 4; Num 19: 6, 18.—Dit., Syll.³ 1218, 16 [V bc], where the word is restored [correctly, beyond a doubt], the hyssop serves to purify a house in which a corpse had lain. Chaeremon also mentions its purifying power) Hb 9: 19; 1 Cl 18: 7 (Ps 50: 9); B 8: 1, 6.—In J 19: 29 the hyssop appears as a plant w. a long, firm stem or stalk, which creates a good deal of difficulty. The conjecture by Joachim Camerarius (died 1574), ὑσσῷ (=javelin; ὑσσῷ is actually found in mss. 476 and 1242, both antedating the conjecture) προπεριθέντες, has been accepted by many (e.g. Dalman, Jesus 187; Lagrange, JHBernard; Field, Notes 106–8; M-M.; Gdspd., Probs. 115f; w. reserve, Bultmann). Against the conjecture it has been urged (by WBauer et al.; the cj. is not accepted by Weymouth, CCD, RSV) that the purifying effect of the hyssop (used acc. to Ex 12: 22 specif. at the Passover) is the most important consideration here.—ILöw, Die Flora der Juden II '24, 72f; 84–101, on J 19: 29 esp. 99–101; LFonck, Streifzüge durch die biblische Flora '00, 109; EbNestle, Zum Ysop bei Johannes, Josephus u. Philo: ZNW 14, '13, 263–5; LBaldensperger and GMCrowfoot, Hyssop: PEF 63, '31, 89–98. M-M.*

ὑστερέω 1 aor. ὑστέρησα; pf. ὑστέρηκα; 1 aor. pass. ὑστερήθην (Eur., Hdt.+; inscr., pap., LXX, Joseph.).
1. act.—a. come too late (Phlegon: 257 fgm. 36, 1, 3 Jac.), through one's own fault to miss, fail to reach, be excluded abs. Hb 4: 1. ἀπό τινος be excluded from someth. (Aesop, Fab. 134 H. ἔριφος ὑστερήσας ἀπὸ ποίμνης) 12: 15.
b. be in need of, lack τινός someth. (Demosth. 19, 332 πολλῶν; Phalaris, Ep. 20 H.; Jos., Bell. 2, 617, Ant. 2, 7; Zen.-P. 45 [= Sb 6751], 5 [251/50 bc] ξύλων) Lk 22: 35. Abs. be in need, be poor D 11: 12.
c. be less than, inferior to w. gen. of comparison (Pla., Rep. 7 p. 539E ἐμπειρίᾳ τῶν ἄλλων) τινός be inferior to someone 2 Cor 11: 5; 12: 11.—τί ἔτι ὑστερῶ; in what respect am I still inferior? what do I still lack? Mt 19: 20 (cf. Ps 38: 5). Abs. 1 Cor 12: 24.
d. fail, give out, lack (Socrat., Ep. 14, 9; Diosc. 5, 75, 13 ὑστερούσης πολλάκις σποδοῦ; Is 51: 14 [marginal note in the Cod. Marchal.] καὶ οὐ μὴ ὑστερήσῃ ὁ ἄρτος αὐτοῦ; Zen.-P. 59 311, 5 [250 bc] ἵνα μὴ ὑστερήσῃ τὸ μέλι; BGU 1074, 7 [III ad] μήτε ὑστερεῖν τι ὑμῖν) ὑστερήσαντος οἴνου J 2: 3. ἐν σε ὑστερεῖ you lack one thing Mk 10: 21 (the acc. as Ps 22: 1 οὐδέν με ὑστερήσει).
2. pass. lack, be lacking, go without, come short of w. gen. of the thing (Diod. S. 18, 71, 5; Jos., Ant. 15, 200) Ro 3: 23; Dg 5: 13 (opp. περισσεύειν); IEph 5: 2. Also ἔν τινι 1 Cor 1: 7. Abs. (Sir 11: 11) Lk 15: 14; 1 Cor 8: 8 (opp. περισσεύειν); 2 Cor 11: 9; Phil 4: 12 (opp. περισσ.); B 10: 3. Ptc. 1 Cor 12: 24. ὑστερούμενοι Hb 11: 37. Subst. οἱ ὑστερούμενοι those who are poor or needy Hb 3, 9, 2; 4; 6; m 2: 4. W. χῆραι s 9, 27, 2. W. widow(s) and orphan(s) Hm 8: 10; s 5, 3, 7. M-M.*

ὑστέρημα, ατος, τό (PTebt. 786, 9 [II bc]; LXX; Herm. Wr. 4, 9)—1. need, want, deficiency in contrast to abundance (cf. Judg 18: 10; 19: 19; Ps 33: 10; Achmes 111, 4)

ἐκ τοῦ ὑστερήματος αὐτῆς πάντα τὸν βίον ἔβαλεν Lk 21: 4.—2 Cor 8: 14a, b (opp. περίσσευμα in both instances; Eutecnius 4 p. 37, 17 opp. πλεονέκτημα). Oft. used w. ἀναπληρόω (q.v. 3) or προσαναπληρόω (q.v.) supply the need: ἀναπλ. αὐτοῦ τὸ ὑστ. supply his need 1 Cl 38: 2. τὸ ὑστέρημά μου προσανεπλήρωσαν οἱ ἀδελφοί 2 Cor 11: 9. Also pl. πρ. τὰ ὑστερήματα τῶν ἁγίων 9: 12. Το ἀναπλ. the ὑστέρημα of one person means to make up for his absence, represent him in his absence 1 Cor 16: 17; Phil 2: 30 (λειτουργία 2). Also used w. ἀνταναπληρόω (q.v.) Col 1: 24.
2. lack, shortcoming as a defect which must be removed so that perfection can be attained, in the pl. (Herm. Wr. 13, 1; Test. Benj. 11: 5) τὸ ὑστερήματα τῆς πίστεως ὑμῶν 1 Th 3: 10. Of moral shortcomings 1 Cl 2: 6 (w. παραπτώματα); Hv 3, 2, 2a, b (w. ἁμαρτήματα).*

ὑστέρησις, εως, ἡ (Aq. Job 30: 3; Aesop 105 [ed. GH Schäfer 1810]; Achmes 83, 13f; Cat. Cod. Astr. X 146, 20; 147, 2) need, lack, poverty Mk 12: 44. Pl. deprivations Hs 6, 3, 4.—καθ' ὑστέρησιν because of need or want (κατά II 5aδ) Phil 4: 11.*

ὕστερος, α, ον (Hom.+; inscr., pap., LXX) in our lit. used as comp. and superl. (Bl-D. §62; cf. Rob. 294; 488; 662).
1. as adj.—a. comp. (1 Ch 29: 29) ὁ ὕστερος the second one (of two, as Aristot., Pol. 1312a, 4; Aristopho Com. [IV bc] 5), the latter Mt 21: 31.
b. superl. (ὕστατος is not found in our lit.) ἐν ὑστέροις καιροῖς in the last times 1 Ti 4: 1 (possibly in later, i.e. future times: Pla., Leg. 9 p. 865A ἐν ὑστέροις χρόνοις).
2. neut. ὕστερον as adv. (Hom.+)—a. comp. in the second place, later, then, thereafter (X., Mem. 2, 6, 7; Arrian, An. 7, 14, 10; Dialekt-Inschr. 1222, 4 [Arcadia] ὕστερον δὲ μή=later but no more; Pr 24: 32; Jos., Bell. 7, 285, Ant. 1, 217; Test. Zeb. 10: 7) Mt 4: 2; 21: 30, 32 (μεταμέλ. ὕστερον: Diod. S. 18, 47, 2 ὕστερον μετανοήσαντες ... ἀπέσχοντο=later they changed their minds and refrained; Hierocles, In Carm. Aur. 18 p. 460 Mull.); 25: 11; Mk 16: 14; Lk 4: 2 t.r.; J 13: 36; Hb 12: 11; MPol 18: 1; Papias 2: 15.
b. superl. finally (Theophrast., Char. 5, 10; Aelian, Var. Hist. 9, 33; Jos., Ant. 16, 315; Test. Jos. 3: 8) Mt 21: 37; 26: 60; Lk 20: 32. ὕστερον πάντων last of all Mt 22: 27; Lk 20: 32 t.r. M-M.*

ὑφαίνω (Hom.+; inscr.; POxy. 113, 9 [II ad]; 1414, 11; LXX; Jos., C. Ap. 2, 242 al.) weave Lk 12: 27 (κοπιᾷ 𝔓⁴⁵ 𝔓⁷⁵ et al.). M-M. B. 410.*

ὑφαντός, ή, όν (Hom.+; PAmh. 133, 15 [II ad]; Ex; Jos., Ant. 3, 57) woven J 19: 23. M-M.*

ὑφίστημι fut. mid. ὑποστήσομαι; mid. (Hom.+; inscr., pap., LXX, Philo, Joseph.) resist, face, endure w. acc. (Eur., Cycl. 199; Thu. 1, 144, 5; 7, 66, 2; Diod. S. 16, 51, 1 [τοὺς κινδύνους]; Jdth 6: 3; Pr 13: 8; Jos., Ant. 12, 282) τίς αὐτοῦ τὴν παρουσίαν ὑποστήσεται; Dg 7: 6.*

ὑψηλός, ή, όν (Hom.+; inscr., pap., LXX, Ep. Arist., Philo, Joseph., Test. 12 Patr.) high.
1. lit. ὄρος a high mountain (Epicurus in Diog. L. 10, 103; Ezk 40: 2; Test. Levi 2: 5) Mt 4: 8; 17: 1; Mk 9: 2; Lk 4: 5 t.r.; Rv 21: 10. τεῖχος (cf. Jos., Ant. 20, 191) vs. 12 (in both places w. μέγα). ὑψηλὸν σπήλαιον a lofty cave B 11: 4 (Is 33: 16). Also of human or human-like figures tall (Dio Chrys. 71[21], 1 νεανίσκος; Plut., Aemil. Paul. 18, 3; Jdth 16: 6) Hs 8, 1, 2; 9, 3, 1; ὑψ. τῷ μεγέθει 9, 6, 1.—Comp. ὑψηλότερος w. gen. of comparison (Lucian, Nigr. 25; En.

26, 3) Hs 9, 2, 1. ὑψηλότερος τῶν οὐρανῶν γενόμενος *raised to greater heights than the heavens* Hb 7: 26. Moses stands on two shields ὑψηλότερος πάντων B 12: 2.— μετὰ βραχίονος ὑψηλοῦ Ac 13: 17; cf. 1 Cl 60: 3 (s. βραχίων).—Subst. (Appian, Liby. 130 §620 ἐφ᾿ ὑψηλοῦ = on a high place; Bell. Civ. 3, 28 §110 τὰ ὑψηλά = the high places; likew. Diod. S. 20, 29, 9) τὰ ὑψηλά the *height(s)* (Sb 6797, 33 [255/4 bc]) = heaven ἐν ὑψηλοῖς *on high* (Ps 92: 4; 112: 5, cf. vs. 4) Hb 1: 3.

2. fig. *exalted, proud, haughty,* subst. τὸ ἐν ἀνθρώποις ὑψηλόν *what is considered exalted among men* Lk 16: 15. ὑψηλὰ φρονεῖν *cherish proud thoughts, feel proud* (Quint. Smyrn. [IV ad] 2, 327) Ro 11: 20; 1 Ti 6: 17 v.l. (ὑψ. φρονεῖν = 'think lofty thoughts': Lucian, Hermot. 5; Philo, Ebr. 128). τὰ ὑψηλὰ φρονεῖν *strive after things that are* (too) *high, be too ambitious* Ro 12: 16 (cf. Palaeph., Exc. Vat. p. 94, 6; 1 Km 2: 3, and on the contrast ὑψ.—ταπεινός: Περὶ ὕψους 43, 3). οἱ ὑψηλοί *the proud, the haughty, the high and mighty* (sing.: Philo, Mos. 1, 31) 1 Cl 59: 3; B 19: 6; D 3: 9.—The neut. of the comp. as adv., in a good sense, of richer and higher progress in the fear of God ὀφείλομεν πλουσιώτερον καὶ ὑψηλότερον προσάγειν τῷ φόβῳ αὐτοῦ B 1: 7. M-M. B. 852.*

ὑψηλόφθαλμος, ον (hapax legomenon.—ὑψηλοὶ ὀφθαλμοί in the lit. sense Physiogn. I 327, 2) *lifting up the eyes,* perh. *in pride,* though the context calls rather for *in lust* or *wantonness* D 3: 3 (v.l. in the 7th book of the Apost. Constitutions ῥιψόφθαλμος).*

ὑψηλοφρονέω (Pollux 9, 145; schol. on Pind., Pyth. 2, 91; schol. on Eur., Hippol. 728; Phot. and Suidas s.v. ὑψαυχεῖν; Bl-D. §119, 5 app.; Rob. 163 n.) *be proud, haughty* Ro 11: 20 t.r.; 1 Ti 6: 17.*

ὑψηλοφροσύνη, ης, ἡ (Physiogn. II 225, 6; Hesychius s.v. φυσίωσις; Leontius of Neap. [VII ad] 28 p. 61, 5; 10 HGelzer [1893]) *pride, haughtiness* Hm 8: 3; s 9, 22, 3.*

ὑψηλόφρων, ον, gen. ονος (Eur., Pla., Cass. Dio 72, 8, 3 = 'high-minded, high-spirited') *proud, haughty* (so Pollux 9, 147; Eustath., Opuscula 23, 60 p. 209, 96; the adv. Pel.-Leg. 22, 31) Hs 8, 9, 1.*

ὕψιστος, η, ον (Pind., Aeschyl. +; inscr., pap., LXX, Jewish wr. [s. 2 below]; loanw. in rabb.) superl. of the adv. ὕψι; *highest, most exalted.*

1. in a spatial sense (Diog. L. 8, 31 ὁ ὕψιστος τόπος, acc. to Pythagoras, is the place to which Hermes conducts the pure souls) τὰ ὕψιστα *the highest heights* = heaven (Job 16: 19; Ps 148: 1 = מְרוֹמִים; cf. 1QM 14, 14; 17, 8) ὡσαννὰ ἐν τοῖς ὑψίστοις *grant salvation,* (thou who art) *in the highest heaven* Mt 21: 9; Mk 11: 10 (Gdspd., Probs. 34f). δόξα ἐν ὑψ. Lk 2: 14 (opp. ἐπὶ γῆς); 19: 38 (w. ἐν οὐρανῷ, which means the same). ὁ ὕψιστος ἐν ὑψίστοις *the Most High in the highest* (heaven) 1 Cl 59: 3 (cf. Is 57: 15).

2. ὁ ὕψιστος *the Most High* of God (Ζεὺς ὕψιστος: Pind., Nem. 1, 90; 11, 2; Aeschyl., Eum. 28; CIG 498; 503; 1869 al. [ABCook, Zeus I 2, '25, 876–89; CRoberts, TCSkeat and ADNock, The Guild of Zeus Hypsistos: HTR 29, '36, 39–88]; θεὸς ὕψιστος: inscr. fr. Cyprus in Bull. de corr. hell. 20, 1896 p. 361; Sb 589 [II bc]; 1323, 1 [II ad]; Dit., Or. 378 [I ad] θεῷ ἁγίῳ ὑψίστῳ; 755; 756; PGM 4, 1068 ἱερὸν φῶς τοῦ ὑψίστου θεοῦ; 5, 46; 12, 63; 71. Isis as ὑ. θεός: Isisaretal. v. Kyrene 7 P. Also simply Ὕψιστος CIG 499; 502. On the syncretistic communities of the

σεβόμενοι θεὸν ὕψιστον cf. ESchürer, SAB 1897, 200–25, Gesch. III⁴ '09 p. 174, 70; FCumont, Hypsistos: Suppl. à la Rev. de l'instruction publique en Belgique 1897, Pauly-W. s.v. Hypsistos; APlassart, Mélanges Holleaux '13, 201ff; Clemen² 58–60. Here Jewish influence is unmistakably present, since 'God Most High' belongs above all to the relig. speech of the Jews: LXX; Dit., Or. 96, 5ff [III/II bc]; APF 5, '13, p. 163 [29 bc] θεῷ μεγάλῳ μεγάλῳ ὑψίστῳ; En.; Philo, In Flacc. 46, Ad Gai. 278; 317; Jos., Ant. 16, 163; the Jewish prayers for vengeance fr. Rheneia [Dssm., LO 352ff-LAE 416; Dit., Syll.³ 1181, 1f]; Sib. Or. 3, 519; 719; Ezek. Trag. in Euseb., Pr. Ev. 9, 29, 14, Philo Epicus ibid. 9, 24) ὁ θεὸς ὁ ὑψ. Mk 5: 7; Lk 8: 28; Ac 16: 17; Hb 7: 1 (Gen 14: 18). Also ὁ ὑψ. *the Most High* (oft. Test. 12 Patr.) Ac 7: 48; 1 Cl 29: 2 (Dt 32: 8); 45: 7; 52: 3 (Ps 49: 14). ὁ μόνος ὑψ. 59: 3 (s. 1 above, end). Also without the art. ὕψ. Lk 1: 35, 76. υἱὸς ὑψίστου vs. 32 (of Christ); in the pl. of men (cf. Sir 4: 10) 6: 35. πατὴρ ὕψ. IRo inscr. M-M.*

ὕψος, ους, τό (Aeschyl., Hdt. +; inscr., pap., LXX, En., Ep. Arist., Philo; Jos., C. Ap. 2, 119 ὕ., πλάτος al.; Test. 12 Patr.) *height.*

1. lit.—a. as a dimension 1 Cl 49: 4 (perh. mng. 1b). W. other dimensions (τὸ μῆκος καὶ τὸ πλάτος) Rv 21: 16. (πλάτος καὶ μῆκος καὶ βάθος) Eph 3: 18 (βάθος 1).—Pl. ἀναφέρεσθαι εἰς τὰ ὕψη IEph 9: 1.

b. concrete *height = high place* (Sib. Or. 8, 235), mostly = *heaven* (Ps 17: 17 ἐξ ὕψους; 101: 20; Stephan. Byz. s.v. Λαοδίκεια: ἀφ᾿ ὕψους ὁ θεός) Lk 1: 78 (ἀνατολή 3); 24: 49; Eph 4: 8 (Ps 67: 19). τὰ ὕψη τῶν οὐρανῶν 1 Cl 36: 2 (Diod. S. 4, 7, 4 ὕψος οὐράνιον; Aesop, Fab. 397b τὰ οὐράνια ὕψη).—τὰ ἐν ὕψεσι as someth. different from τὰ ἐν οὐρανοῖς Dg 7: 2 (opp. τὰ ἐν βάθεσι).

2. fig.—a. of rank (Herodian 1, 13, 6; 1 Macc 1: 40; 10: 24.—Of degree: Pla., Ep. 7 p. 351e ὕψος ἀμαθίας the 'height' of ignorance; Ps.-Aristot., De Mundo 6; Plut., Popl. 6, 5; Jos., Ant. 8, 126 ὕψος εὐδαιμονίας) *high position* (opp. ταπεινός and ταπείνωσις) Js 1: 9. τὸν ποιοῦντα ταπεινοὺς εἰς ὕψος *who exalts the humble* (unless εἰς ὑψ. means 'upright', as Apollod. [II bc]: 244 fgm. 107d, e Jac.) 1 Cl 59: 3 (Job 5: 11).

b. of disposition *pride* D 5: 1. ὕψος δυνάμεως *arrogance in one's power* B 20: 1.—JHKühn, Ὕψος '41. GBertram, TW VIII, 600–19: ὕψος and related words. M-M.*

ὑψόω fut. ὑψώσω; 1 aor. ὕψωσα. Pass.: 1 aor. ὑψώθην; 1 fut. ὑψωθήσομαι (Hippocr. +; Dit., Syll.³ 783, 45 [I bc]; LXX; Ep. Arist.; Jos., Bell. 1, 146; 3, 171; Test. 12 Patr.) *lift up, raise high* τινά or τὶ *someone* or *someth.*

1. lit. (Batrach. 81; PGM 4, 2395; 2989f) Μωϋσῆς ὕψωσεν τὸν ὄφιν *Moses lifted up the serpent* by fastening it to a pole in the sight of all J 3: 14a. In the same way Christ is lifted up on the cross vs. 14b (cf. Artem. 4, 49 ὑψηλότατον εἶναι τὸν ἐσταυρωμένον; 1, 76 p. 69, 11; 2, 53; Ps.-Callisth. 2, 21, 26 ἔσεσθε περιφανεῖς κ. διάσημοι πᾶσιν ἀνθρώποις ἐπὶ τὸν σταυρὸν κρεμασθέντες [a play on words w. an ambiguous expr. which, by using the word 'outstanding', can mean social position as well as being lifted up on a cross before the eyes of all]); for J this 'lifting up' is not to be separated fr. the 'exaltation' into heaven, since the heavenly exaltation presupposes the earthly 8: 28; 12: 32 (ἐκ τῆς γῆς; CCTorrey, JBL 51, '32, 320-2)—34 (Hdb. on J 3: 14; CLattey, Le verbe ὑψ. dans St. Jean: Rech de Sc rel 3, '12, 597f; CLindeboom, 'Verhoogd worden'. In Joh. 3: 14: Gereform. Theol. Tijdschrift 15, '15, 491–8; MBlack, Aramaic Approach³

141; OCullmann, ThZ 4, '48, 365f; WThüsing, Die Erhöhung und Verherrlichung Jesu im J, '60). τῇ δεξιᾷ τοῦ θεοῦ ὑψωθείς *exalted* (to heaven) *by the power* (δεξιός 2a, end) *of God* Ac 2: 33. Marking the transition to sense 2 are passages in which ἕως οὐρανοῦ ὑψωθῆναι is a symbol for crowning w. the highest honors (cf. PsSol 1: 5) Mt 11: 23; Lk 10: 15.

2. fig. of enhancement in honor, fame, position, power, fortune, etc. (Polyb. 5, 26, 12 [opp. ταπεινοῦν]; Plut., Mor. 103ε; LXX). God *exalts* τινά *someone* (Test. Jos. 1: 7; 18: 1) ταπεινούς (cf. Ezk 21: 31; Ep. Arist. 263) Lk 1: 52; cf. Js 4: 10; 1 Pt 5: 6. Pass. (Test. Reub. 6: 5; Sib. Or. 3, 582) Mt 23: 12b; Lk 14: 11b; 18: 14b; 2 Cor 11: 7.—τοῦτον (i.e. Christ) ὁ θεὸς ἀρχηγὸν ὕψωσεν *God has exalted him as leader* Ac 5: 31. God τὸν λαὸν ὕψωσεν ἐν γῇ Αἰγύπτου *has made the people great* (in numbers and in power) *in Egypt* 13: 17.—ὑψοῦν ἑαυτόν *exalt oneself, consider oneself better* than others (Test. Jos. 17: 8) Mt 23:

12a; Lk 14: 11a; 18: 14a; B 19: 3; D 3: 9; Hm 11: 12; s 9, 22, 3. M-M.*

ὕψωμα, ατος, τό (Plut., Mor. 782ᴅ; Sext. Emp., Math. 5, 33; 35; LXX; Philo, Praem. 2; Ps.-Phoc. 73; Sib. Or. 8, 234) *height, exaltation.*
1. as an astronomical t.t. (Plut., Mor. 149ᴀ; Ptolem., Apotel. 1, 20, 1ff; oft. Vett. Val.; PLond. 110, 14; Cat. Cod. Astr. XII 102, 25) of the space above the horizon Ro 8: 39 (opp. βάθος, q.v. 1 and cf. Rtzst., Poim. 80; WLKnox, St. Paul and the Church of the Gentiles '39, 106f).—OGerhardt, D. Stern des Messias '22, 15.
2. πᾶν ὕψωμα ἐπαιρόμενον *everything that rises up*, prob. = *all pride* (every proud obstacle, RSV) *that rises up against it* 2 Cor 10: 5 (Euthym.: ὑψηλοφρονία. But Chrysost. X 585ʙ explains it by using πύργωμα, which would mean someth. like 'towering fortress'; cf. PPetr. III 46, 3, 11 τοὺς ἐπαρθέντας τοίχους). M-M.*

Φ

φαγεῖν, φάγομαι s. ἐσθίω.

φάγος (so accented by Hesychius [s.v. τρώκτης] and Eustath., Od. 1630, 15, though Herodian Gr. I 140, 4 prefers φαγός), ου, ὁ (Zenob. Paroem. [II ᴀᴅ] 1, 73) *glutton* w. οἰνοπότης Mt 11: 19; Lk 7: 34.*

φαιλόνης, ου, ὁ is to be spelled so, with t.r. (Bl-D. §25) as against the great uncials and critical editions, which have φελόνης (PFay. 347 [II ᴀᴅ]). This is a Lat. loanw. (paenula. Cf. Hahn p. 10, 8; EFraenkel, Zeitschr. für vergleich. Sprachforschung 42, '09 p. 115, 1; ESchwyzer, Museum Helveticum 3, '46, 50–2; but see B. below), also in rabb. in var. spellings. Its original form was φαινόλας (Rhinthon [III ʙᴄ] in Pollux 7, 61) or φαινόλης (Epict. 4, 8, 34; Artem. 2, 3 p. 88, 10; 5, 29; Athen. 3 p. 97ᴇ; POxy. 736, 4; 1737, 9; 15; PGiess. 10, 21; PHamb. 10, 19 [II ʙᴄ]), also φαινόλιον (POxy. 531, 14 [II ᴀᴅ]; 936, 18; 19). From these by metathesis (cf. CALobeck, Pathologiae Sermonis Graeci Elementa I 1853, 514; Bl-D. §32, 2; Mlt.-H. 81; 106; 155) came φαιλόνης (which is still quotable at least in its dim. form φαιλόνιον [-ώνιον]: POxy. 933, 30; PGiess. 12, 4 [II ᴀᴅ]; BGU 816, 24 [III ᴀᴅ]; cf. Mod. Gk. φελόνι) *cloak* (POxy. 531, 14 τὰ ἱμάτια τὰ λευκὰ τὰ δυνάμενα μετὰ τῶν πορφυρῶν φορεῖσθαι φαινολίων. Likew. Epict.; Athen., loc. cit. Acc. to this the trans. 'valise' is excluded; s. Field, Notes 217f; also excluded is the interpretation in the direction of διφθέρα, the leather cover for papyrus rolls) 2 Ti 4: 13 (cf. on the subject-matter POxy. 1489 [III ᴀᴅ] τὸ κιθώνιν [=χιτώνιον] ἐπιλέλησμαι παρὰ Τεκοῦσαν εἰς τὸν πυλῶνα. πέμψον μοι). M-M. B. 417, where φαινόλα is treated as the original fr. which Lat. paenula is borrowed, and not vice versa; cf. Mlt.-H. 106.*

φαίνω (Hom.+; inscr., pap., LXX, En., Ep. Arist., Philo, Joseph., Test. 12 Patr.) act.: 1 aor. ἔφανα (Bl-D. §72; Mlt.-H. 214f), subj. 3 sing. φάνῃ Rv 8: 12; 18: 23. Pass.: impf. ἐφαινόμην; 2 aor. ἐφάνην; 2 fut. φανήσομαι (cf. Bl-D. §79; Mlt.-H. 262; the older φανοῦμαι only in the LXX-quot. 1 Pt 4: 18).
1. act., in our lit. only intr. *shine, give light, be bright* (Aristoph., Nub. 586 of the sun; Pla., Tim. 39ʙ; Theocr. 2,

11 of the moon; Gen 1: 15, 17; En. 104, 2; Sib. Or. 5, 522; 8, 203) sun Rv 1: 16. Sun and moon 21: 23. Moon PK 2 p. 14, 27; Dg 7: 2. A lamp (1 Macc 4: 50) 2 Pt 1: 19; as a symbol J 5: 35. Light Rv 18: 23; as a symbol J 1: 5; 1 J 2: 8. Day and night *shine*, in so far as the sun, or moon and stars give their light Rv 8: 12 v.l.
2. φαίνομαι—**a.** of light and its sources *shine, flash* (Is 60: 2) of stars, as a symbol Phil 2: 15 (X., Cyr. 1, 6, 1) Mt 24: 27. Of light Rv 18: 23 t.r. Of a star *appear* Mt 2: 7 (FBoll, ZNW 18, '18, 45f). Of the day (Appian, Iber. 35 §143 φαινομένης ἡμέρας) Rv 8: 12 in the text.
b. *appear, be or become visible, be revealed* τότε ἐφάνη καὶ τὰ ζιζάνια Mt 13: 26 (cf. 2 Macc 1: 33 τὸ ὕδωρ ἐφάνη). τὰ ἔργα τῶν ἀνθρώπων 2 Cl 16: 3. τὸ σημεῖον τοῦ υἱοῦ τ. ἀνθρώπου Mt 24: 30. Cf. D 16: 6. ἀτμὶς φαινομένη (opp. ἀφανιζομένη) Js 4: 14. Cf. Hv 3, 2, 6a. ὁ ἀσεβὴς ποῦ φανεῖται; *what will become of the godless man?* 1 Pt 4: 18 (Pr 11: 31). οὐδέποτε ἐφάνη οὕτως *nothing like this was ever seen* (= happened) Mt 9: 33. τὸ φαινόμενον *that which is visible* (Philo, Rer. Div. Her. 270) IRo 3: 3a. τὰ φαινόμενά σου εἰς πρόσωπον *whatever is visible before your face* (opp. τὰ ἀόρατα) IPol 2: 2. φαινόμενα *things which appear* Hb 11: 3 (cf. Sext. Emp., Hypotyp. 1, 138). Ign. explains: I will be a real believer ὅταν κόσμῳ μὴ φαίνωμαι *when I am no longer visibly present in the world* (because I have been devoured by the wild beasts) IRo 3: 2. A play on words is meant to make this clear: Christ also, through the fact that he is ἐν πατρί and hence no longer visibly present in the world, μᾶλλον φαίνεται *is all the more plainly visible* as that which he really is, i.e. ὁ θεὸς ἡμῶν 3: 3b.
c. *appear, make one's appearance, show oneself* (Diod. S. 4, 6, 5 θεὸν φαίνεσθαι παρ' ἀνθρώποις; 5, 2, 4 [divinity]; Charito 5, 7, 10 φάνηθι, δαῖμον ἀγαθέ; Sb 8141, 24 [inscr. I ʙᴄ] δαίμονος τοῦ ἀγαθοῦ υἱός... ἐφάνη; Sib. Or. 5, 152) Hv 1, 4, 3. Elijah (Jos., Ant. 8, 319) ἐφάνη *has made his appearance* (as forerunner of God's kingdom; Mal 3: 22. Some consider that Jesus is Elijah come again) Lk 9: 8. Of the first advent of Jesus Christ, who comes to our world fr. the great Beyond B 14: 5; IMg 6: 1; Dg 11: 2; also w. dat. (X., Cyr. 1, 6, 43; Lucian, Dial. Deor. 20, 5; Ael. Aristid. 51, 25 K. = 27 p.

540 D.: ἡ θεὸς ἐφάνη μοι) κόσμῳ 11: 3. Of the risen Lord, w. dat. Mk 16: 9. Of an angel, w. dat. (2 Macc 3: 33; 10: 29) Mt 1: 20; 2: 13, 19 (cf. Alcaeus [schol. on Nicander, Ther. 613 p. 48 Keil]: φανῆναι τὸν 'Απόλλωνα καθ' ὕπνους; Jos., C. Ap. 1, 289 κατὰ τοὺς ὕπνους ἡ Ἴσις ἐφάνη τῷ 'Α., Ant. 7, 147; 8, 196). ὅπως φανῶσιν τοῖς ἀνθρώποις *in order to be seen by men* Mt 6: 5; w. ptc. to denote the role that one plays before men (Hyperid., fgm. 70, 1; Lucian, Dial. Deor. 4, 1; Ael. Aristid. 47 p. 428 D.) νηστεύοντες *as fasting* vs. 16; cf. 18.—Of the Antichrist φανήσεται ὡς υἱὸς θεοῦ *he will appear* in the same way *as a son of God* D 16: 4.

d. *appear as someth., to be someth.,* made more definite by a predicate nom. (X., Cyr. 1, 4, 19; Cebes 5, 1; Arrian, Anab. 4, 30, 4 πιστὸς ἐφαίνετο= he showed himself to be trustworthy; Test. Reub. 5: 7) φαίνονται ὡραῖοι Mt 23: 27. ἵνα ἡμεῖς δόκιμοι φανῶμεν 2 Cor 13: 7. W. dat. of the pers. *appear to someone as someth.* (Lucian, Dial. Mort. 25, 1) φαίνεσθε τοῖς ἀνθρώποις δίκαιοι Mt 23: 28 (cf. Pr 21: 2). αὕτη ἡ ὁδὸς ἡδυτέρα αὐτοῖς ἐφαίνετο Hs 8, 9, 1. W. ἐνώπιόν τινος instead of the dat.: ἐφάνησαν ἐνώπιον αὐτῶν ὡσεὶ λῆρος τὰ ῥήματα ταῦτα Lk 24: 11.—Foll. by ὡς *look as if* (Test. Jos. 3: 4) Hv 3, 2, 6b; s 9, 9, 7.

e. *to have the outward appearance of being someth. that one actually is* but may not always seem to be, w. predicate nom. εἰ ἦσαν, ἐφαίνοντο ἂν κλάδοι τοῦ σταυροῦ *if they* (the false teachers) *actually were* God's planting, *then they would appear as branches of the cross* ITr 11: 2. οὐ φαίνονται *they are not apparent* Hs 3: 2a, b, 3a, b. ἡ ἁμαρτία ἵνα φανῇ ἁμαρτία *in order that sin might be recognized as sin* Ro 7: 13.

f. *appear to the eyes of the spirit, be revealed* ὅπερ καὶ φανήσεται πρὸ προσώπου ἡμῶν, ἐξ ὧν ἀγαπῶμεν αὐτόν *which also will be revealed before our face by the fact that we love him* IEph 15: 3.

g. *have the appearance, seem* w. dat. and inf. (Hom.+) οἱ τοιοῦτοι οὐκ εὐσυνείδητοί μοι εἶναι φαίνονται IMg 4. W. dat. and ptc. φαίνεσθέ μοι κατὰ ἀνθρώπους ζῶντες ITr 2: 1. τί ὑμῖν φαίνεται; *how does it seem to you? what is your decision?* Mk 14: 64. ἐάν σοι φανῇ *if it seems good to you* Hv 2, 3, 4 (acc. to CHTurner, JTS 21, '20, 198, a Latinism: si tibi videtur. Cf. POxy. 811 [I AD] εἴ σοι φαίνεται). Without a dat. (Jos., C. Ap. 1, 12) οὐδὲν φαίνεται κεκομμένον ἀπ' αὐτοῦ *nothing seems to have been cut from it* (the tree) or *apparently nothing has been cut from it* (cf. Aristoxenus, fgm. 83 φαίνεται "Ολυμπος αὐξήσας μουσικήν=O. has apparently enriched music) Hs 8, 3, 1.—RBultmann/DLührmann, TW IX, 1–11: φαίνω and many related words. M-M. B. 1045f.**

Φάλεκ (also Φαλέκ, Φαλέγ, Φάλεχ 1 Ch 1: 25 B; Hebr. פֶּלֶג, in pause פָּלֶג, Gen 10: 25 al.), ὁ, indecl. (in Joseph. Φάλεγος, ου [Ant. 1, 148]) *Peleg,* son of Eber and father of Reu (Gen 11: 16–19; 1 Ch 1: 25), in the genealogy of Jesus Lk 3: 35.*

φανεροποιέω 1 aor. ἐφανεροποίησα (Hephaestio Astr. [IV AD] 3, 37; schol. on Aristoph., Eq. 1253; Joannes Sardianus, Comm. in Aphthonii Progymn. ed. HRabe '28 p. 161, 23; pap. since VI AD) *reveal, make known* τὶ *someth.* τὴν τοῦ κόσμου σύστασιν 1 Cl 60: 1.*

φανερός, ά, όν (Pind., Hdt.+; inscr., pap., LXX, Ep. Arist., Philo, Joseph.)—**1.** adj. *visible, clear, plainly to be seen, open, plain, evident, known* τὰ φανερὰ ἔργα (opp. κρύφια) 2 Cl 16: 3. Used w. εἶναι (Diod. S. 18, 55, 2 φανεροῦ ὄντος ὅτι=since it was clear that) οἱ καρποὶ

φανεροὶ ἔσονται Hs 4: 3; cf. 4: 4. φανερόν (-ά) ἐστιν Ro 1: 19 (ἐν αὐτοῖς; s. ἐν IV 4a); Gal 5: 19; 1 J 3: 10 (ἐν τούτῳ *by this*); Hm 11: 10; w. the dat. of the pers. in addition 1 Ti 4: 15; B 8: 7 (opp. σκοτεινά). Without the copula, which is to be supplied: w. ὅτι (X., Mem. 3, 9, 2; Teles p. 12, 4; 7) πᾶσιν φανερόν Ac 4: 16 (D has the copula and at the same time the comp.: φανερώτερόν ἐστιν *it is quite well known*). φανερὸν τὸ δένδρον ἀπὸ τοῦ καρποῦ αὐτοῦ *the tree is known by its fruit* (cf. Mt 12: 33) IEph 14: 2 (Vi. Aesopi I c. 3 φανερὸς ἀπὸ τῆς ὄψεως = clearly recognizable by its appearance).—Used w. γίνεσθαι (BGU 1141, 41 [14 BC]; Appian, Bell. Civ. 2, 46 §187 τοῦ κακοῦ φανεροῦ γενομένου; 1 Macc 15: 9; 2 Macc 1: 33; Jos., Ant. 2, 270; 6, 238) φανερὸν ἐγένετο τὸ ὄνομα αὐτοῦ Mk 6: 14. Cf. Lk 8: 17a (opp. κρυπτόν); 1 Cor 3: 13; 11: 19; 14: 25; Hs 9, 12, 3; w. the dat. of the pers. added (Ael. Aristid. 29, 24 K.=40 p. 758 D.: φανεροὶ πᾶσι γίγνεσθαι) Ac 7: 13. ὥστε τοὺς δεσμούς μου φανεροὺς γενέσθαι ἐν ὅλῳ τῷ πραιτωρίῳ καὶ τοῖς λοιποῖς πᾶσιν Phil 1: 13.—Used w. ποιεῖν (Hyperid. 4, 1; Menand., Epitr. 278; POxy. 928, 7; PTebt. 333, 12; 2 Macc 12: 41) *make* (τὶ *someth.*) *known* (Jos., Ant. 12, 189; 204) 1 Cl 21: 7. τινά *make someone known* as what he really is, *reveal the identity of someone* (Jos., Ant. 3, 73) Mt 12: 16; Mk 3: 12.

2. subst. τὸ φανερόν *the open, public notice* (Hyperid. 1, 13, 11 εἰς τὸ φ. φέρειν; Polyb. 2, 46, 1) εἰς φανερὸν ἐλθεῖν *come to light* Mk 4: 22; Lk 8: 17b (a proverb? Constant. Manasse 7, 34f H.: ἐστὶ σκότιον οὐδὲν ὅπερ εἰς φῶς οὐχ ἥκει, οὐκ ἔστι κρύφιον οὐδὲν ὃ μὴ πρὸς γνῶσιν φθάνει). ἐν τῷ φανερῷ (opp. ἐν τῷ κρυπτῷ as Ctesias, Pers. 10) Mt 6: 4 t.r., 6 t.r., 18 t.r. (cf. Aeneas Tact. 426; Jos., Ant. 4, 34); preceded by an art. and used as an adj. ὁ ἐν τῷ φανερῷ 'Ιουδαῖος *the Jew who is one outwardly* by reason of being circumcised Ro 2: 28a; cf. b. M-M. B. 1233.*

φανερόω fut. φανερώσω; 1 aor. ἐφανέρωσα; pf. πεφανέρωκα. Pass.: perf. πεφανέρωμαι; 1 aor. ἐφανερώθην; 1 fut. φανερωθήσομαι (Hdt. 6, 122; Dionys. Hal. 10, 37; Cass. Dio 59, 18; 77, 15; PGdspd. 15, 19 [IV AD]; Jer 40: 6; Philo; Jos., Ant. 20, 76) *reveal, make known, show.*

1. a thing—**a.** act. ἐφανέρωσεν τὴν δόξαν αὐτοῦ J 2: 11 (Jos., Vi. 231 φ. τὴν ὀργήν). ὁ θεὸς αὐτοῖς ἐφανέρωσεν *God has shown them* what can be known about him Ro 1: 19 (cf. AKlöpper, ZWTh 47, '04, 169–80). Cf. 1 Cor 4: 5; Tit 1: 3; 2 Cl 20: 5; Dg 8: 11 (w. ἀποκαλύπτειν); 9: 1, 2b; 11: 5; IRo 8: 2. φανεροῦν τινι ἀποκάλυψιν *disclose a revelation to someone* Hv 3, 1, 2. κατὰ ἀποκάλυψιν φανεροῦν τινι *make known* or *show to someone in a revelation* MPol 22: 3. τῷ θεῷ τὴν ὀσμὴν τῆς γνώσεως αὐτοῦ φανεροῦντι δι' ἡμῶν *to God who makes known through us the fragrance of the knowledge of himself* 2 Cor 2: 14. ὁ πατὴρ πάντα φανεροῖ περὶ τοῦ υἱοῦ 'Ιησοῦ B 12: 8. (ὁ κύριος) πεφανέρωκεν ἡμῖν διὰ τῶν προφητῶν ὅτι κτλ. 2: 4.—*Make known* by word of mouth, *teach* ἐφανέρωσά σου τὸ ὄνομα τοῖς ἀνθρώποις J 17: 6 (though here the teaching is accompanied by a revelation that comes through the deed.—HHHuber, D. Begriff der Offenbarung im Joh. ev. '34). ἐν παντὶ φανερώσαντες ἐν πᾶσιν εἰς ὑμᾶς *in every way we have made this* (i.e. τὴν γνῶσιν) *plain to you, in the sight of all men* 2 Cor 11: 6. Cf. Col 4: 4.

b. pass. *become visible* or *known, be revealed* Mk 4: 22; J 3: 21; 9: 3; Ro 16: 26; 2 Cor 4: 10f; 7: 12; Eph 5: 13f; Col 1: 26; 2 Ti 1: 10; Hb 9: 8; 1 J 4: 9; Rv 3: 18; 15: 4; B 7: 7; IEph 19: 2. Foll. by an indirect quest. 1 J 3: 2a. Foll. by ὅτι

Dg 9: 2a. χωρὶς νόμου δικαιοσύνη θεοῦ πεφανέρωται *apart from the law, the righteousness which is sent from God has been revealed* Ro 3: 21.

2. a person—**a.** act. ἑαυτόν *show* or *reveal oneself*: of God (Philo, Leg. All. 3, 47) διὰ Ἰησοῦ IMg 8: 2.—Of Christ φανέρωσον σεαυτὸν τῷ κόσμῳ J 7: 4. Of the Risen Lord 21: 1a; cf. 1b. Differently ἐφανέρωσεν ἑαυτὸν εἶναι υἱὸν θεοῦ *he revealed that he was the Son of God* B 5: 9.

b. pass.—**α.** *be made known* ἵνα φανερωθῇ τῷ Ἰσραήλ J 1: 31. θεῷ πεφανερώμεθα *we are well known to God* 2 Cor 5: 11a, cf. 11b; 11: 6 t.r. W. ὅτι foll. *become known, be shown (that)* 3: 3; 1 J 2: 19 (logically impersonal, as ἠκούσθη in Mk 2: 1).

β. *show* or *reveal oneself, be revealed, appear* τινί *to someone* Hs 2: 1. ἡμᾶς φανερωθῆναι δεῖ ἔμπροσθεν τοῦ βήματος τοῦ Χριστοῦ 2 Cor 5: 10.—Esp. of Christ; of his appearance in the world ἐφανερώθη ἐν σαρκί 1 Ti 3: 16; cf. B 5: 6; 6: 7, 9, 14; 12: 10. θεοῦ ἀνθρωπίνως φανερουμένου IEph 19: 3.—Hb 9: 26; 1 Pt 1: 20; 1 J 1: 2a, b. The purpose of the appearing is given by a ἵνα clause 1 J 3: 5, 8; B 14: 5; 2 Cl 14: 2.—Of the appearing of the Risen Lord τοῖς μαθηταῖς J 21: 14; cf. Mk 16: 12 (ἐν ἑτέρᾳ μορφῇ), 14. Without a dat. B 15: 9. Of the Second Advent Col 3: 4a; 1 Pt 5: 4; 1 J 2: 28; 3: 2b.—ὑμεῖς σὺν αὐτῷ (i.e. Christ upon his return) φανερωθήσεσθε ἐν δόξῃ Col 3: 4b. Of the church ἡ ἐκκλησία πνευματικὴ οὖσα ἐφανερώθη ἐν τῇ σαρκὶ Χριστοῦ 2 Cl 14: 3. M-M.**

φανερῶς adv. (Aeschyl., Hdt.+; pap.; 2 Macc 3: 28; Philo, Joseph.) *openly, publicly* Mk 1: 45. (Opp. ἐν κρυπτῷ. Cf. Jos., Ant. 5, 213 κρυπτῶς—φ.; Test. Jos. 4: 2) J 7: 10. (Opp. λάθρᾳ, as Pla., Symp. 182D) IPhld 6: 3. *Clearly, distinctly* (Jos., Vi. 277) ἰδεῖν Ac 10: 3. δειχθῆναι Dg 11: 2.—The neut. of the comp. as adv. φανερώτερον *(even) more plainly* λέγειν B 13: 4. M-M.*

φανέρωσις, εως, ἡ (Aristot., De Plant. 2, 1; 9; Herm. Wr. 11, 1; Cat. Cod. Astr. VII 229, 23; 230, 20; VIII 1 p. 165, 6; pap. VIII AD) *disclosure, announcement,* w. objective gen. ἡ φαν. τῆς ἀληθείας *the open proclamation of the truth* 2 Cor 4: 2. The syntax of the gen. in ἡ φανέρωσις τοῦ πνεύματος 1 Cor 12: 7 cannot be determined w. certainty. Whether the gen. is subj. or obj. the expr. means the same thing as χάρισμα. M-M.*

φανός, οῦ, ὁ (Aristoph., X.+; UPZ 5, 18 [163 BC]; 6, 15; loanw. in rabb.) *lamp,* orig.= *torch,* and later, to the great annoyance of the Atticists (Hesychius s.v. Phryn. p. 59 L.; Athen. 15, 58 p. 699Dff; Pollux 6, 103; 10, 116), = *lantern* (λυχνοῦχος); so J 18: 3 beside λαμπάς (q.v. 1). M-M.*

Φανουήλ, ὁ indecl. (פְּנוּאֵל. 1 Ch 4: 4; 8: 25 v.l.; cf. Gen 32: 32, place name; Philo, Conf. Lingu. 129) *Phanuel,* father of Anna the prophetess Lk 2: 36. M-M.*

φαντάζω (Aeschyl., Hdt.+; Sir 34: 5; Wsd 6: 16) *make visible,* usu. in the pass. *become visible, appear* (Philo), esp. of extraordinary phenomena (in nature, etc. Cf. Apollon. Rhod. 4, 1283; Περὶ ὕψους 15, 4; 7; PGM 7, 888) τὸ φανταζόμενον *sight, spectacle,* of a theophany (as Ps.-Aristot., Mirabilia 108 Athena; Herodian 8, 3, 9 of Apollo) Hb 12: 21. M-M.*

φαντασία, ας, ἡ (Aristot., Polyb. et al.; LXX, Philo; Jos., Bell. 6, 69 al.; Test. Reub. 5: 7) *pomp, pageantry* (Polyb. 15, 25, 22; 16, 21, 1 μετὰ φαντασίας; Diod. S. 12, 83, 4; Vett. Val. 38, 26) ἐλθόντος τοῦ Ἀγρίππα μετὰ πολλῆς φαντασίας Ac 25: 23 (πολλὴ φ. as Pel.-Leg. 4, 7f).—Rdm.² 12. M-M.*

φάντασμα, ατος, τό (Aeschyl., Pla.+; LXX; En. 99, 7; Philo; Jos., Bell. 5, 381, Ant. 5, 213) *apparition,* esp. *ghost* (Aeschyl.+; Pla., Phaedo 81D, Tim. 71A; Dionys. Hal. 4, 62; Plut., Dio 2, 4; Lucian, Philops. 29; PGM 4, 2701; 7, 579 φυλακτήριον πρὸς δαίμονας, πρὸς πᾶσαν νόσον καὶ πάθος; Job 20: 8 v.l.; Wsd 17: 14; Jos., Ant. 1, 331; 333) Mt 14: 26; Mk 6: 49; Lk 24: 37 D.—FAltheim, ARW 27, '29, 48. M-M.*

φανῶ s. φαίνω.

φάραγξ, αγγος, ἡ *ravine* (so Alcman [VII BC], Thu.+; LXX [e.g. Is 30: 28; Jer 7: 31]; En.; Ep. Arist. 118; Jos., Bell. 1, 147; 6, 161; Test. Iss. 1: 5; Sib. Or. 3, 682) Lk 3: 5 (Is 40: 4.—Cf. also Diod. S. 20, 36, 2 the laying out of the Appian Way in spite of heights and τόποι φαραγγώδεις), but also *valley* (e.g. Gen 26: 17, 19; Josh 13: 9; Ezk 34: 13; so Vulg. Lk 3: 5). M-M. B. 28.*

Φαραώ, ὁ indecl. (פַּרְעֹה. Gen 12: 15 al.; Ezek. Trag. in Clem. Alex., Strom. 1, 155, 2; Philo; Test. 12 Patr.; Jos., Bell. 5, 379.—As a rule Joseph. has Φαραώθης, ου [Ant. 2, 39]) *Pharaoh,* actually the title of the Egyptian kings (Eg. per-'o= 'great house'), then a proper name; of the *Pharaoh* of the Exodus Ac 7: 10, 13, 21; Ro 9: 17; Hb 11: 24; 1 Cl 4: 10; 51: 5. M-M.*

Φαρές (פֶּרֶץ, in pause פָּרֶץ. Gen 38: 29; 1 Ch 2: 4f; Ruth 4: 18), ὁ indecl. (Jos., Ant. 2, 178 Φάρεσος, ου) *Perez,* son of the patriarch Judah and of Tamar, twin brother of Zerah and father of Hezron; in the genealogy of Jesus Mt 1: 3a, b; Lk 3: 33.*

Φαρισαῖος, ου, ὁ (Hebr. פְּרוּשִׁים = Aram. פְּרִישַׁיָּא, the latter in Gk. transcription Φαρισαῖοι. The Semitic words mean 'the separated ones, separatists'. On the sect of the Pharisees acc. to Josephus and the Mishna s. Schürer II⁴ 449ff, where the pertinent passages are reproduced) *the Pharisee,* though in our lit. it is rarely found in the sing. (Mt 23: 26; Lk 7: 36b, 37, 39; 11: 37f; 18: 10f; Ac 5: 34; 23: 6b; 26: 5; Phil 3: 5); as a rule in the pl. *the Pharisees,* the organized followers of the experts in interpreting the scriptures (scribes). It was the purpose of the Pharisees to take the pattern of the pious Israelite as established by the scribes, and to put it into practice as nearly as possible. They were the most embittered opponents of Jesus and the early Christians. Mentioned w. Sadducees Mt 3: 7; 16: 1, 6, 11f; Ac 23: 6-8. W. Herodians Mk 3: 6; 12: 13; cf. 8: 15; Mk 2: 16 (here οἱ γραμματεῖς τῶν Φ.); 7: 5; Lk 5: 21, 30; 6: 7; 11: 53; 15: 2; J 8: 3; Ac 23: 9 (here γραμματεῖς τοῦ μέρους τῶν Φ.). W. scribes and elders GP 8: 28. As opponents of Jesus Mt 9: 11, 34; 12: 2, 14, 24; 15: 12; 22: 15, 34, 41; Mk 7: 1; 8: 11, 15; 10: 2; 12: 13 al. A Pharisaic high priest GOxy 10. Their fasting Mt 9: 14; Mk 2: 18; (Lk 18: 12). Paul a Ph. Ac 23: 6b; 26: 5 (κατὰ τὴν ἀκριβεστάτην αἵρεσιν τῆς ἡμετέρας θρησκείας ἔζησα Φαρισαῖος); Phil 3: 5.—In addition to the lit. s.v. Σαδδουκαῖος that is pertinent here, cf. also IElbogen, Die Religionsanschauung der Phar. '04; Schürer II⁴ '07, 456ff; IAbrahams, Studies in Pharisaism and the Gospels I '17, II '24; ATRobertson, The Pharisees and Jesus '20; EMeyer II '21, 282ff; RTHerford, The Pharisees '24 (cf. BSEaston, Mr. Herford and the Phar.: ATR 7, '25, 423-37); CGMontefiore, The Synoptic Gospels² '27 II 676a (index s.v. Pharisees); GFMoore, Judaism in the First Centuries of the Christian Era I, II '27; FCBurkitt, Jesus and the 'Pharisees': JTS 28, '27, 392-7; DWRiddle, Jesus and the Ph. '28; JoachJeremias, Jerus. zur Zeit Jesu, ³'62, 279-303; LFinkelstein, The Ph.² '40, The Ph., The Sociol. Background of their Faith, ³'62; IZLauterbach, The Ph. and their Teach.: Hebr. Union Coll. Annual 6, '29, 69-140; OHoltzmann, D. Prophet Mal u. d. Ursprung des Pharisäerbundes: ARW 29, '31, 1-21; LBaeck, Die Pharisäer '34; WFoerster, D. Ursprung des Pharisäismus: ZNW 34, '35, 35-51; SZeitlin, The Pharisees and the Gospels '38; AFinkel, The Pharisees and the Teacher of Nazareth '64.—RMeyer/HFWeiss, TW IX, 11-51.

φαρμακεία, ας, ἡ (X., Pla.+; Vett. Val., pap., LXX; Philo, Spec. Leg. 3, 94; 98) *sorcery, magic* (Polyb. 38, 16, 7; Ex 7: 11, 22; 8: 14; Is 47: 9, 12; Wsd 12: 4; 18: 13; En. 7, 1; Sib. Or. 5, 165) Rv 18: 23. Pl. *magic arts* 9: 21 (v.l. φαρμάκων). In a list of vices Gal 5: 20; B 20: 1; pl. D 5: 1. M-M. B. 1495.*

φαρμακεύς, έως, ὁ (Soph., Trach. 1140; Pla., Symp. 203D γόης καὶ φαρμ.; Philo, Det. Pot. Ins. 38; Jos., Vi. 149f) *mixer of poisons, magician* Rv 21: 8 t.r. (s. φάρμακος).*

φαρμακεύω fut. φαρμακεύσω (Hdt., Pla.+; POxy. 472, 1; 5 [II AD]; LXX; Philo, Det. Pot. Ins. 38) *mix poison, make potions, practice magic* D 2: 2.*

φάρμακον, ου, τό (Hom.+; inscr., pap., LXX, Philo; Jos., Vi. 150)—1. *poison* (Hom.+; Jos., Ant. 16, 253; 17, 62; Test. Jos. 5: 1) Hv 3, 9, 7a (w. φάρμακός); in the symbol of the 'poisoned' heart, ibid. b. θανάσιμον φάρμ. (s. θανάσιμος) ITr 6: 2.

2. *magic potion, charm* (Hom.+; PSI 64, 20 [I BC]; 4 Km 9: 22; Jos., Ant. 15, 93; 19, 193; Test. Reub. 4: 9) Rv 9: 21 v.l. (for φαρμακειῶν).

3. *medicine, remedy, drug* (Hom.+; Dit., Syll.³ 1168, 40; 77; 119; PRyl. 62, 22 [I BC]; PTebt. 117, 22 [I BC]; PGM 5, 247; Philo; Jos., Bell. 4, 573; Test. Jos. 2: 7), also *means of attaining someth.*, w. gen. of the thing desired (Eur., Phoen. 893 φ. σωτηρίας; likew. the teaching of Epicurus: ChJensen, GGAbh. III 5, '33, 81; Kleopatra l. 45; 130 φ. τῆς ζωῆς; Sir 6: 16), the Eucharist as φάρμακον ἀθανασίας *the medicine of* (i.e. *means of attaining*) *immortality* IEph 20: 2 (φ. ἀθαν. Antiphanes Com. 86, 6; Diod. S. 1, 25, 6; Herm. Wr. 460, 13 Sc. The remedy, widely designated by the t.t. φάρμ. ἀθ., whose origin was credited to Isis, was prescribed for the most varied diseases. ThSchermann, ThQ 92, '10, 6ff; Rtzst., Mysterienrel.³ 400). M-M. B. 310f.*

φάρμακος, ου, ὁ (LXX; on the accent and differentiation fr. φαρμακός 'scapegoat' [Hipponax+] see L-S-J under both words, w. ref. to Herodian, Gr. I, 150; s. PKatz, ThLZ 82, '57, 112; Bl-D.-Funk §13; φάρ. is masc. Ex 7: 11; fem. Mal 3: 5) *poisoner* Hv 3, 9, 7a, b; *magician* (Ex 7: 11; 9: 11 al.; Sib. Or. 3, 225) Rv 21: 8 (s. φαρμακεύς); 22: 15. M-M.*

φάσις, εως, ἡ (fr. φημί. Pla.+; inscr., pap., LXX; Philo, Aet. M. 143) *information*, orig. concerning a crime, then gener. *report, announcement, news* (pap.) ἀνέβη φάσις τῷ χιλιάρχῳ ὅτι Ac 21: 31 (ἀνέβη because it went up to the Tower Antonia). M-M.*

φάσκω impf. ἔφασκον (Hom.+; inscr., pap., LXX; Philo; Jos., Ant. 3, 305; 7, 250) *say, assert, claim* foll. by acc. and inf. (PRyl. 117, 19; Philo, Somn. 2, 291; Jos., C. Ap. 2, 145) Ac 24: 9; 25: 19. In an affirmation made concerning the speaker, after the nom. of the ptc. we have the inf. w. predicate nom. φάσκοντες εἶναι σοφοί Ro 1: 22; after the acc. of the ptc., the inf. w. the predicate acc. τοὺς φάσκοντας εἶναι ἀποστόλους Rv 2: 2 t.r. M-M.*

φάτνη, ης, ἡ *manger, stall* (so Hom.+; PLille 17, 15; POxy. 1734; Job 6: 5; 39: 9; Is 1: 3; Hab 3: 17; Philo; Jos., Ant. 8, 41; Sib. Or. 3, 791; loanw. in rabb.) Lk 13: 15. In the Christmas story Lk 2: 7, 12, 16 φ. could perh. be the *stable* (Diod. S. 17, 95, 2 φ. is a place to keep horses, beside κατασκήνωσις, a place for people to stay; Aelian, N.A. 16, 24 p. 402, 10 w. ὁδός) or even a *feeding-place* under the open sky, in contrast to κατάλυμα, the shelter where people stayed (cf. HJCadbury, JBL 45, '26, 317-19; 52, '33, 61f.—Manger: AvanVeldhuizen, NThSt 13, '30, 175-8). Nicol. Dam.: 90 fgm. 3 p. 330, 15 Jac. raises similar doubts.—MDibelius, Jungfrauensohn u. Krippenkind '32, 59ff.—MHengel, TW IX, 51-7. M-M.*

φαῦλος, η, ον (trag., Pre-Socr., Hdt.+; pap., LXX) *worthless, bad, evil, base.*

1. in a moral sense (Soph., X., Pla.+; LXX, Ep. Arist. 142; Philo; Jos., Vi. 41, C. Ap. 1, 53; Sib. Or. 3, 362 [w. ἄδικος]) πρᾶγμα Js 3: 16. ἔργον 1 Cl 28: 1. οἱ φ. *those who are wicked* (Epict. 4, 1, 3; 5; 4, 5, 8; Philo; Jos., Bell. 2, 163 [opp. οἱ ἀγαθοί]) 36: 6. μηδὲν ἔχων λέγειν περὶ ἡμῶν φαῦλον *if he has nothing bad to say about us* Tit 2: 8 (cf. Plut., Mor. 717B φαύλως εἰπεῖν). πράσσειν τι ἀγαθὸν ἢ φαῦλον Ro 9: 11 (the contrast ἀγ. and φαῦλ. as Pla., Protag. 326E τῶν ἀγαθῶν πατέρων πολλοὶ υἱεῖς φαῦλοι γίγνονται); (τὰ) φαῦλα πράσσειν J 3: 20; 5: 29.

2. in a physical sense κομίσασθαι εἴτε ἀγαθὸν εἴτε φαῦλον = receive reward or punishment fr. the judge 2 Cor 5: 10 (cf. X., Symp. 4, 47 τὰ φαῦλα, τὰ ἀγαθά). Yet, in this awkwardly arranged sentence, the idea of the doing of good or evil (mng. 1) also plays a part. M-M.*

φέγγος, ους, τό (Hom. Hymns+; inscr., e.g. Isishymnus v. Andros 39 Peek [I BC]; LXX; Ezek. Trag. in Euseb., Pr. Ev. 9, 29, 14 ἀπ' οὐρανοῦ φ. 16; Philo; Jos., Ant. 2, 308; 11, 285) *light, radiance,* of the moon (Ps.-X., Cyneget. 5, 4; Philo, Somn. 1, 23) Mt 24: 29; Mk 13: 24. Of a λύχνος (Callim. ed vWilam.⁴ '25 no. 55) Lk 11: 33. Of two heavenly beings πολὺ φέγγος ἔχοντες GP 9: 36.*

φείδομαι mid. dep.; fut. φείσομαι; 1 aor. ἐφεισάμην (Hom.+; inscr., pap., LXX, En.; Philo, Leg. All. 1, 66; Jos., Ant. 16, 404, Vi. 328; Test. 12 Patr.).

1. *spare* (Hom.+) τινός *someone* or *someth.* 2 Cor 1: 23. ἐγὼ ὑμῶν φείδομαι *I would like to spare you* a great deal of trouble, by offering good advice 1 Cor 7: 28. φεῖσαί μου τῆς ψυχῆς ἀπὸ ρομφαίας *spare my life* (by protecting me) *from the sword* B 5: 13 (cf. Jer 13: 14 οὐ φείσομαι ἀπὸ διαφθορᾶς αὐτῶν). Mostly w. a neg. *not spare* τινός Ac 20: 29; Ro 8: 32 (Lucian, Syr. Dea 18 οὐδ' . . . γυναικὸς ἐφείσατο, i.e. his own wife); 11: 21a, b; 2 Pt 2: 4f; IRo 1: 2. Abs., but w. οὐδενός understood (Thu. 3, 59, 1; Pr 6: 34; Jos., Ant. 14, 480) 2 Cor 13: 2.

2. *refrain* from doing someth. (X., Cyr. 1, 6, 19; 35; Appian, Basil. 5 §1 πολέμου, Bell. Civ. 5, 120 §498; Dit., Syll.³ 708, 35; Job 16: 5) w. inf. as obj., to be supplied 2 Cor 12: 6 (τοῦ καυχᾶσθαι); ITr 3: 3 (τοῦ γράφειν). M-M.*

φειδομένως (Plut., Alex. 25, 7; Cosmas and Damian 34, 70) adv. of the ptc. φειδόμενος *sparingly* (cf. Theognis, fgm. 1, 931 φείδομαι = be miserly) σπείρειν 2 Cor 9: 6a; θερίζειν b. M-M.*

φελόνης cf. φαιλόνης. M-M.

φέρω (Hom.+; inscr., pap., LXX, En., Ep. Arist., Philo, Joseph., Test. 12 Patr., Sib. Or.) impf. ἔφερον; fut. οἴσω J 21: 18; Rv 21: 26; 1 aor. ἤνεγκα, ptc. ἐνέγκας; 2 aor. inf. ἐνεγκεῖν (Bl-D. §81, 2); 1 aor. pass. ἠνέχθην 2 Pt 1: 17, 21a.

1. *bear, carry*—a. lit. (Aristoph., Frogs 27 τὸ βάρος ὃ φέρεις; X., Mem. 3, 13, 6 φορτίον φέρειν) ἐπέθηκαν αὐτῷ τὸν σταυρὸν φέρειν ὄπισθεν τοῦ Ἰησοῦ Lk 23: 26 (s. σταυρός 1). διὰ τῆς πύλης ἔφερον αὐτούς (=τοὺς λίθους) Hs 9, 4, 1.

b. fig., of the Son of God φέρων τὰ πάντα τῷ ῥήματι τῆς δυνάμεως αὐτοῦ who bears up the universe by his mighty word Hb 1: 3 (cf. Plut., Lucull. 6, 3 φέρειν τὴν πόλιν; Num 11: 14; Dt 1: 9). οὗτος τὰς ἁμαρτίας ἡμῶν φέρει 1 Cl 16: 4 (Is 53: 4).

c. *bear patiently, endure, put up with* (X., An. 3, 1, 23; Appian, Samn. 10 §13 παρρησίαν φ.=put up with candidness, Iber. 78 §337; Jos., Ant. 7, 372; 17, 342) μαλακίαν 1 Cl 16: 3 (Is 53: 3). τὸν ὀνειδισμὸν αὐτοῦ (i.e. Ἰησοῦ) Hb 13: 13 (cf. Ezk 34: 29). τὸ διαστελλόμενον 12: 20. Of God ἤνεγκεν ἐν πολλῇ μακροθυμίᾳ σκεύη ὀργῆς Ro 9: 22.

d. *bring with one, bring along* (Diod. S. 6, 7, 8 γράμματα φέρων; PTebt. 418, 9; 421, 6; 8) φέρουσαι ἃ ἡτοίμασαν ἀρώματα Lk 24: 1. Cf. J 19: 39.—e. τὸ ὄνομα τοῦ κυρίου bear the name of the Lord, i.e. of a Christian Pol 6: 3.

2. *bear, produce* of a plant and its fruits, lit. and symbol. (Hom.+; Diod. S. 9, 11, 1; Aelian, V.H. 3, 18 p. 48, 20; Jo 2: 22; Ezk 17: 8; Jos., Ant. 4, 100) Mt 7: 18a, b; Mk 4: 8; J 12: 24; 15: 2a, b, c, 4f, 8, 16; Hs 2: 3f, 8.

3. *move out of position, drive*; pass. *be moved, be driven, let oneself be driven*—a. lit., by wind and weather (Apollon. Rhod. 4, 1700; Charito 3, 5, 1; Appian, Bell. Civ. 1, 62 §278 in spite of the storm Marius leaped into a boat and ἐπέτρεψε τῇ τύχῃ φέρειν let himself be driven away by fortune; Jer 18: 14; Test. Napht. 6: 5) Ac 27: 15, 17.—*Move, pass* (cf. L-S-J s.v. φέρω B 1) Papias 3.

b. fig., of the Spirit of God, by whom men *are moved* (cf. Job 17: 1 πνεύματι φερόμενος) ὑπὸ πνεύματος ἁγίου φερόμενοι 2 Pt 1: 21b. Cf. Ac 15: 29 D. Of the impulse to do good Hs 6, 5, 7. Of the powers of evil (Ps.-Plut., Hom. 133 ὑπὸ ὀργῆς φερόμενοι; Jos., Bell. 6, 284) PK 2 p. 14, 11; Dg 9: 1.

c. also of the wind itself (Ptolem., Apotel. 1, 11, 3 οἱ φερόμενοι ἄνεμοι; Diog. L. 10, 104 τ. πνεύματος πολλοῦ φερομένου; Quint. Smyrn. 3, 718) φέρεσθαι rush Ac 2: 2. Of fragrance φέρεσθαι ἐπί τινα be borne or wafted to someone (Dio Chrys. 66[16], 6 'rush upon someone') AP 5: 16.—Of writings (Diog. L. 5, 86 φέρεται αὐτοῦ [i.e., Heraclid. Pont.] συγγράμματα κάλλιστα; Marinus, Vi. Procli 38; cf. Arrian, Anab. 7, 12, 6 λόγος ἐφέρετο Ἀλεξάνδρου=a saying of Alexander was circulated) οὗ (=τοῦ Εἰρηναίου) πολλὰ συγγράμματα φέρεται of whom there are many writings in circulation Epil Mosq 1.—Of spiritual development ἐπὶ τὴν τελειότητα φερώμεθα let us move on toward perfection Hb 6: 1.

4. *bring (on), produce*—a. a thing—α. *bring (to), fetch* τὶ someth. Mk 6: 27, 28 (ἐπὶ πίνακι. On the bringing in of a head at a banquet cf. Diog. L. 9, 58.—The presence of a severed head did not necessarily disturb the mood at a meal. Appian, Bell. Civ. 4, 20, §81 relates concerning Antony that he had the head of Cicero placed πρὸ τῆς τραπέζης); Lk 13: 7 D; 15: 22 P75 et al. for ἐξ-; Ac 4: 34, 37; 5: 2; 2 Ti 4: 13; MPol 11: 2; Hs 8, 1, 16 (w. double acc. of the obj. and the pred.); 9, 10, 1. Pass. Mt 14: 11a (ἐπὶ πίνακι; Hv 3, 2, 7; 3, 5, 3; s 8, 2, 1a, b; 9, 4, 7; 9, 6, 5-7; 9, 9, 4f. τινί τι someth. to someone Mt 14: 18 (w. ὧδε); Mk 12: 15. The acc. is supplied fr. the context Mt 14: 11b; J 2: 8a. The dat. and acc. are to be supplied οἱ δὲ ἤνεγκαν Mt 12: 16; J 2: 8b. φέρειν πρός τινα w. acc. of the thing to be supplied (X., Cyr. 8, 3, 47; Ex 32: 2) Hs 8, 4, 3; 9, 10, 2. φ. τι εἰς (1 Km 31: 12) Rv 21: 24, 26. μή τις ἤνεγκεν

αὐτῷ φαγεῖν; *do you suppose that anyone has brought him anything to eat?* J 4: 33.—Fig. *bring (about)* (Hom. +; Mitteis, Chrest. 284, 11 [II BC] αἰσχύνην; PTebt. 104, 30; POxy. 497, 4; 1062, 14; Jos., Vi. 93, C. Ap. 1, 319; Sib. Or. 3, 417) τὸ βάπτισμα τὸ φέρον ἄφεσιν *the baptism which brings (about) forgiveness* B 11: 1.

β. *bring, utter, make* a word, speech, announcement, charge, etc. (Jos., Vi. 359, C. Ap. 1, 251), as a judicial expr. (cf. Demosth. 58, 22; Polyb. 1, 32, 4; PAmh. 68, 62; 69; 72) κατηγορίαν J 18: 29. Cf. Ac 25: 7 t.r., 18 (Field, Notes 140); 2 Pt 2: 11. Perh. this is the place for μᾶλλον ἑαυτῶν καταγνώσιν φερόντων *rather they blame themselves* 1 Cl 51: 2. διδαχήν 2 J 10. ὑποδείγματα *give* or *offer examples* 1 Cl 55: 1 (Polyb. 18, 13, 7 τὰ παραδείγματα). θάνατον ἀνάγκη φέρεσθαι τοῦ διαθεμένου *the death of the one who made the will must be established* Hb 9: 16. τοῦτο φέρεται ἐν *this is brought out*= this is recorded in Epil Mosq 3.—Of a divine proclamation, whether direct or indirect (Diod. S. 13, 97, 7 τ. ἱερῶν φερόντων νίκην) 2 Pt 1: 17, 18, 21a. Perh. also ἐλπίσατε ἐπὶ τὴν φερομένην ὑμῖν χάριν ἐν ἀποκαλύψει Ἰησοῦ Χρ. *hope for the grace that is proclaimed for you at the revelation of Jesus Christ* 1 Pt 1: 13.

γ. φέρειν τὸν δάκτυλον, τὴν χεῖρα *put* or *reach out the finger, the hand* J 20: 27a (ὧδε), vs. 27b.

b. a living being, animal or man—α. *bring* animals Mk 11: 2, 7 (πρός τινα); Lk 15: 23; Ac 14: 13 (ἐπὶ τ. πυλῶνας).

β. *bring* or *lead* people τινά someone ἀσθενεῖς Ac 5: 16. κακούργους GP 4: 10. τινὰ ἐπὶ κλίνης (Jos., Ant. 17, 197) Lk 5: 18. τινὰ τινι *someone to someone* Mt 17: 17 (w. ὧδε); Mk 7: 32; 8: 22. Also τινὰ πρός τινα Mk 1: 32; 2: 3; 9: 17, 19f. φέρουσιν αὐτὸν ἐπὶ τὸν Γολγοθᾶν τόπον 15: 22. ἄλλος οἴσει (σε) ὅπου οὐ θέλεις J 21: 18.

c. of a gate, *lead* somewhere (cf. Hdt. 2, 122; Thu. 3, 24, 1 τὴν ἐς Θήβας φέρουσαν ὁδόν; Ps.-Demosth. 47, 53 θύρα εἰς τὸν κῆπον φέρουσα; Dit., Syll.³ 1118, 5; POxy. 99, 7; 17 [I AD]; 69, 1 [II AD] θύρα φέρουσα εἰς ῥύμην) τὴν πύλην τὴν φέρουσαν εἰς τὴν πόλιν Ac 12: 10 (X., Hell. 7, 2, 7 αἱ εἰς τὴν πόλιν φέρουσαι πύλαι; Diog. L. 6, 78 παρὰ τῇ πύλῃ τῇ φερούσῃ εἰς τὸν Ἰσθμόν; Jos., Ant. 9, 146).—See Fitzmyer s.v. ἄγω.—KWeiss, TW IX, 57–89: φέρω and many related words. M-M. B. 707.**

φεύγω fut. φεύξομαι; 2 aor. ἔφυγον (Hom.+; inscr., pap., LXX, En., Joseph., Test. 12 Patr.).

1. lit. *flee, seek safety in flight* Mt 8: 33; 26: 56; Mk 5: 14; 14: 50, 52 (mng. 2 is also poss.; cf. PTebt. 48, 23f); Lk 8: 34; J 10: 12, 13 t.r.; Ac 7: 29; GP 13: 57. ἀπό (X., Cyr. 7, 2, 4, Mem. 2, 6, 31; Arrian, Ind. 6, 5; Ex 4: 3; 2 Km 19: 10; Jos., Bell. 1, 474; Test. Dan 5: 1) Mk 16: 8; J 10: 5; Js 4: 7= Hm 12, 4, 7; cf. 12, 5, 2; Rv 9: 6; 1 Cl 4: 10; 28: 2; Hm 11: 14; 12, 2, 4 (w. μακράν). ἐκ (Ael. Aristid. 30 p. 583 D.; Jos., Ant. 14, 177) Ac 27: 30. εἰς (X., Mem. 1, 2, 24; Gen 14: 10; Num 24: 11; Jos., Ant. 14, 418 εἰς τὰ ὄρη) Mt 2: 13; 10: 23; 24: 16; Mk 13: 14; Lk 21: 21 (cf. 1 Macc 2: 28); J 6: 15 v.l.; Rv 12: 6. ἐπί w. acc. ἐπὶ τὰ ὄρη Mt 24: 16 v.l. (X., Ages. 2, 11).—RBach, Die Aufforderungen zur Flucht und zum Kampf im alttestamentlichen Prophetenspruch '62.

2. *escape* Mk 14: 52 (mng. 1 is also poss.); Hb 12: 25 t.r. W. the acc. of that which one escapes (Artem. 1, 21; 4, 1 p. 200, 24; Jos., Vi. 94, Ant. 6, 344) ἔφυγον στόματα μαχαίρης 11: 34. πῦρ MPol 2: 3. Cf. 2 Cl 18: 2. ἀπό Mt 3: 7; 23: 33; Lk 3: 7.

3. in a moral sense *flee from, avoid, shun* w. acc. of the thing (Zaleucus in Stob. IV p. 125, 12 H. τ. ἀδικίαν; Cleobulus in Diog. L. 1, 92; Epict. 1, 7, 25; Dit., Syll.³

1268 I, 3 [III BC] ἄδικα φεῦγε; 4 Macc 8: 19) φεύγετε τὴν πορνείαν (Test. Reub. 5: 5) 1 Cor 6: 18; cf. ISm 7: 2. In contrast to διώκειν 1 Ti 6: 11 and 2 Ti 2: 22 (beside διώκειν, φεύγειν τι may have the mng. 'run away from' as schol. on Nicander, Ther. 75).—1 Cl 30: 1; 2 Cl 10: 1; ITr 11: 1; IPhld 2: 1; 6: 2; 7: 2; IPol 5: 1. Also ἀπό τινος (Sir 21: 2 ἀπὸ ἁμαρτίας) 1 Cor 10: 14; B 4: 1, 10; D 3: 1.

4. guard against w. acc. τὰς ἀπειλάς the threats, i.e. the punishments which they hold in prospect 1 Cl 58: 1.—5. vanish, disappear (Ps.-Clem., Hom. 2, 28) πᾶσα νῆσος ἔφυγεν Rv 16: 20. W. ἀπὸ τοῦ προσώπου τινός (as Ps 67: 2; cf. also Dt 28: 7; Josh 8: 5. Yet likew. as early as Ctesias, Pers. 2 φυγεῖν ἀπὸ προσώπου Κύρου and schol. on Nicander, Ther. 377 in a free quot. from Herodas [8, 59] φεύγωμεν ἐκ προσώπου) 20: 11. M-M. B. 698.*

Φῆλιξ, ικος, ὁ (inscr.: Sb 4601, 3 [144 AD]; APF II 442 no. 56, 9 [II AD]; POxford [ed. EPWegener '42] 3, 1 [142 AD]; POxy. 800 [153 AD]; Joseph. index; on the accent Bl-D. §13; Mlt.-H. 57) Antonius Felix, a freedman of the House of the Claudians and brother of Pallas, the favorite of the Emperor Claudius. In 52/53 AD F. became procurator of Palestine. The year of his removal is in dispute (cf. Schürer I, rev. Engl. ed. '73, 465, 42; ESchwartz, NGG '07, 284ff), but was in the neighborhood of 60. The infamous character of his administration helped to lay the ground for the revolt of 66–70 (per omnem saevitiam ac libidinem jus regium servili ingenio exercuit, 'he revelled in cruelty and lust, and wielded the power of a king with the mind of a slave': Tacitus, Hist. 5, 9). Ac 23: 24, 26; 24: 3, 22, 24f, 27; 25: 14.—Zahn, Einl. II³ 647ff; Schürer I, rev. Engl. ed. '73, 460ff; vRohden, Pauly-W. I 261ff; EMeyer III 47ff.—On the question whether Pilate (q.v.), Felix, and Festus were procurators (s. ἐπίτροπος) or prefects (s. ἔπαρχος) see the Lat. inscr. from Caesarea discovered and first publ. by AFrova, Istituto Lombardo Rendiconti 95, '61 (see also Schürer I, rev. Engl. ed. '73, 358 note 22, and 359), which officially refers to Pilate as prefect. The probability is that by the time of Felix and Festus this was officially changed to procurator. The terms were sometimes used interchangeably. M-M.*

φήμη, ης, ἡ (Hom.+; LXX) report, news ἐξῆλθεν ἡ φήμη αὕτη the news of this was spread (Jos., Bell. 2, 416; cf. Philo, Leg. ad Gai. 231) Mt 9: 26. φ. περὶ τινος (Herodian 2, 1, 3; 2, 7, 5) Lk 4: 14. M-M.*

φημί 3 sing. φησίν, 3 pl. φασίν Ro 3: 8; 2 Cor 10: 10 v.l.; 3 sing. of impf. and 2 aor. ἔφη (cf. Kühner-Bl. II 210) (Hom.+; inscr., pap., LXX, Ep. Arist.; Jos., Ant. 20, 8; 10, C. Ap. 1, 12 al.).

1. say, affirm w. direct discourse—a. w. interchange of first and third persons in dialogue Hv 2, 4, 1; 3, 2, 1; 3, 3, 1f and oft.

b. introducing direct discourse—α. preceding it ὁ δέ φησιν· οὔ, μήποτε... Mt 13: 29. Cf. 26: 61; 27: 11, 23; Mk 10: 29; J 9: 38; 18: 29; Ac 7: 2; 8: 36; 10: 30 al. Oft. w. the dat. of the pers. addressed ἔφη αὐτῷ ὁ Ἰησοῦς· πάλιν γέγραπται...Mt 4: 7. Cf. 13: 28; 21: 27; Mk 9: 12; 14: 29; Lk 7: 44; Ac 26: 32. Also πρός τινα Lk 22: 70; Ac 10: 28; 16: 37; 26: 1.—Used w. a ptc., which denotes the nature of the statement ἀποκριθεὶς ὁ ἑκατόνταρχος ἔφη· κύριε...Mt 8: 8. Cf. Lk 23: 3, 40.

β. inserted after the first word or words of the direct discourse (Oenomaus in Euseb., Pr. Ev. 6, 7, 8 ἀγγελῶ, νὴ Δία, φήσει τις, ...17) δός μοι, φησίν, ὧδε...Mt 14: 8. ποίας; φησίν 19: 18 v.l. a. Cf. Lk 7: 40 (here φησίν stands at the close of a direct quot. consisting of only two words); Ac 2: 38 v.l.; 23: 35; 25: 5, 22; 26: 25.

c. without a subj., where it is self-evident ὅρα γάρ φησιν ποιήσεις πάντα (for) see to it, he (i.e. God) says (Ex 25: 40), you must make everything Hb 8: 5. But φησίν is also used impersonally, it is said, so that it can also go w. a plural subject that makes a statement (cf. Demosth. 23, 31; Epict., Enchir. 24, 2; Maximus Tyr. 5, 4a) αἱ ἐπιστολαὶ μέν, φησίν, βαρεῖαι 2 Cor 10: 10 (the subject of this statement is the opposition to Paul in the Corinthian church; hence the v.l. φασίν). W. scripture quotations φησίν it says (φησίν abs. w. a quot. fr. Aratus: Synes., Prov. 2, 5 p. 125A) 1 Cor 6: 16; 1 Cl 30: 2; 2 Cl 7: 6; B 7: 7.

d. φησίν, in introducing scripture quot., can be pred. to a wide variety of subjects (cf. φησὶν ὁ λόγος Pla., Phil. 51c; Maximus Tyr. 22, 5b) φησὶν ὁ ἅγιος λόγος 1 Cl 13: 3. (τὸ πνεῦμα τὸ ἅγιον) 16: 2. αὐτός (=ὁ κύριος) φησιν 16: 15. ὁ θεός 33: 5. ὁ ἐκλεκτὸς Δαυίδ 52: 2.

2. mean by one's statement (Artem. 1, 67 p. 62, 16 φημὶ δὲ ἐγώ=but I mean), w. acc. (Diod. S. 37, 29, 5 Κράσσον φημί; Syntipas p. 10, 12) τοῦτο 1 Cor 7: 29; cf. 10: 15, 19. Foll. by ὅτι 1 Cor 10: 19 (Caecil. Calact., fgm. 103 p. 93, 18 ἀλλὰ τί φημι; ὅτι κτλ.); τοῦτο ὅτι 15: 50. Foll. by acc. and inf. (Synes., Kingship 15 p. 14c) Ro 3: 8.—HFournier, Les verbes 'dire' en Grec ancien '46. M-M. B. 1257.

φημίζω 1 aor. pass. ἐφημίσθην (Hes.+; Sib. Or. 3, 2; 406) spread (a report) by word of mouth or as a rumor (Jos., Bell. 1, 450) pass. (Aeschyl.+; Plut., Mor. 264D oἱ τεθνάναι φημισθέντες='those reported to be dead'; PGiess. 19, 4 [II AD]) Mt 28: 15 v.l.; Ac 13: 43 v.l. M-M.*

Φῆστος, ου, ὁ (PLond. 904, 33 [104 AD]; Josephus index) Porcius Festus, successor to Felix (s. Φῆλιξ) as procurator of Palestine. Neither the beginning nor the end (caused by his death) of his term of office can be determined with full certainty, though it is gener. assumed that he died in the early 60's. During his rule and w. his consent Paul went to the imperial court at Rome. Ac 24: 27; 25: 1, 4, 9, 12–14, 22–4; 26: 24f, 32.—Schürer I, rev. Engl. ed. '73, 467f; Zahn, Einl. II³ 647ff; ESchwartz, NGG '07, 294ff; UHolzmeister, Der hl. Pls vor dem Richterstuhle des Festus: ZkTh 36, '12, 489–511; 742–82; ESpringer, D. Prozess des Ap. Pls: PJ 217, '29, 182–96; RTaubenschlag, Opera Minora II, '59, 721–6 (pap.). M-M.*

φθάνω 1 aor. ἔφθασα (Hom.+; inscr., pap., LXX, Philo, Joseph., Test. 12 Patr.)—1. come before, precede (exx. fr. the later period, incl. inscr. and pap., in Clark [s. below] 375f) w. acc. of the pers. whom one precedes (Diod. S. 15, 61, 4 τοὺς πολεμίους; Appian, Syr. 29 §142, Bell. Civ. 5, 30 §115; Dit., Syll.³ 783, 35 [27 BC] φθάνοντες ἀλλήλους; Wsd 6: 13; Jos., Ant. 7, 247) ἡμεῖς οὐ μὴ φθάσωμεν τοὺς κοιμηθέντας we will by no means precede those who have fallen asleep 1 Th 4: 15.

2. have just arrived, then simply arrive, come (late and Mod. Gk.: Plut., Mor. 210E; 338A; Vett. Val. 137, 35; 174, 12 ἐπὶ ποῖον [ἀστέρα]; Herm. Wr. 9, 10; PPar. 18, 14 [II AD] φθάσομεν εἰς Πελούσιον; PGM 3, 590; LXX [cf. Thackeray p. 288f]; Philo, Op. M. 5, Leg. All. 3, 215 φθάσαι μέχρι θεοῦ, Conf. Lingu. 153, Mos. 1, 2; Test. Reub. 5: 7, Napht. 6: 9 ἐπὶ τ. γῆς [v.l. ἐπὶ τ. γῆν].—JVogeser, Zur Sprache der griech. Heiligenlegenden, Diss. Munich '07, 46; JWittmann, Sprachl. Untersuchungen zu Cosmas Indicopleustes, Diss. Munich '13, 16) ἐπί τινα come upon someone, overtake (in an adverse sense, DDaube, The Sudden in Scripture, '64, 35f). ἄρα ἔφθασεν ἐφ' ὑμᾶς ἡ βασιλεία τοῦ θεοῦ Mt 12: 28; Lk 11: 20 (KWClark, JBL 59, '40, 367–83 ἐγγίζειν and φθ.; HVMartin, ET 52, '40/'41, 270–5). ἔφθασεν ἐπ' αὐτοὺς

ἡ ὀργή 1 Th 2: 16 (cf. Eccl 8: 14; Test. Levi 6: 11). ἄχρι ὑμῶν ἐφθάσαμεν 2 Cor 10: 14. φθ. εἴς τι *come up to, reach, attain someth.* (BGU 522, 6) Ro 9: 31; Phil 3: 16.— GFitzer, TW IX, 90-4. M-M. B. 701f; 703.*

φθαρ- s. φθείρω.

φθαρτός, ή, όν *perishable, subject to decay* or *destruction* (Aristot., Anal. 2, 22; Diod. S. 1, 6, 3 [γεννητὸς καὶ φθαρτός in contrast to ἀγέννητος and ἄφθαρτος]; Plut., Mor. 106D; 717E; Sext. Emp., Math. 9, 141; Philo, Leg. All. 2, 3, Cher. 5; 48 χρυσὸς καὶ ἄργυρος, οὐσίαι φθαρταί; 2 Macc 7: 16) of persons *mortal* ἄνθρωπος (Ps.-Callisth. 2, 22, 12; Philo, Somn. 1, 172) Ro 1: 23; Hs 9, 23, 4. Of things στέφανος 1 Cor 9: 25. σπορά 1 Pt 1: 23. τὰ ἐνθάδε 2 Cl 6: 6. ἀγῶνες *perishable contests*, i.e. *contests for a perishable prize* 7: 1, 4. τὸ κατοικητήριον τῆς καρδίας φθαρτὸν καὶ ἀσθενές B 16: 7. ὕλη (Wsd 9: 15 σῶμα) Dg 2: 3. σάρξ Hs 5, 7, 2 (Philo, Congr. Erud. Grat. 112).—Subst. οἱ φ. *the perishable* of mankind Dg 9: 2. τὸ φ. (Wsd 14: 8; Philo, Op. M. 82) τὸ φθαρτὸν τοῦτο *this perishable* (*nature*) 1 Cor 15: 53f. τὰ φθ. *perishable things* (Test. Benj. 6: 2; Philo, Ebr. 209 [opp. τὰ ἄφθαρτα]) 1 Pt 1: 18; B 19: 8; Dg 6: 8.*

φθέγγομαι mid. dep.; 1 aor. ἐφθεγξάμην (Hom.+; Dit., Syll.³ 1175, 6 ῥῆμα μοχθηρὸν φθ.; 23 [abs.]; PFlor. 309, 10; LXX) lit. 'produce a sound', then *call out loudly*, gener. *speak, utter, proclaim* τὶ someth. (Lucian, Nigr. 3, 11; Iambl. Erot. 21; Sextus 356; Wsd 1: 8 ἄδικα; Test. Dan 5: 2 ἀλήθειαν; Philo; Jos., Bell. 2, 128, C. Ap. 2, 219) ὑπέρογκα *speak bombastically* 2 Pt 2: 18. Of an animal ἐν ἀνθρώπου φωνῇ vs. 16 (Alciphr. 4, 19, 3 εἰ βοῦς μοι τὸ λεγόμενον φθέγξαιτο). Abs., of persons (opp. 'be silent'. —X., An. 6, 6, 28, Cyr. 7, 3, 11; Ael. Aristid. 30, 19 K.= 10 p. 121 D.) Ac 4: 18. M-M.*

φθείρω fut. φθερῶ; 1 aor. ἔφθειρα. Pass.: pf. ἔφθαρμαι, ptc. ἐφθαρμένος; 2 aor. ἐφθάρην; 2 fut. φθαρήσομαι (Hom.+; inscr., pap., LXX, Philo, Test. 12 Patr.) *destroy, ruin, corrupt, spoil.*

1. of outward circumstances—a. *ruin financially* τινά *someone*, so perh. 2 Cor 7: 2 (s. 2a below).—b. The expr. εἴ τις τὸν ναὸν τοῦ θεοῦ φθείρει 1 Cor 3: 17a seems to be derived fr. the idea of the destruction of a house (X., Mem. 1, 5, 3 τὸν οἶκον τὸν ἑαυτοῦ φθείρειν. Oft in marriage contracts: Mitteis, Chrest. 284, 11 [II BC]; PTebt. 104, 29 [92 BC] al.).—ἀγῶνα φθείρειν t.t. for breaking the rules of a contest (Dit., Syll.³ 1076, 3) 2 Cl 7: 4; cf. vs. 5 (here as a symbol).

c. *seduce* a virgin (Eur.+; Diod. S. 1, 23, 4; Jos., Ant. 4, 252) οὐθὲ Εὔα φθείρεται, ἀλλὰ παρθένος πιστεύεται Dg 12: 8 (πιστεύω 1f).—d. pass. *be ruined, be doomed to destruction* by earthly transitoriness or otherw. (Epict. 2, 5, 12 τὸ γενόμενον καὶ φθαρῆναι δεῖ) of idols Dg 2: 4. Of a man bowed bown by old age αὐτοῦ τὸ πνεῦμα τὸ ἤδη ἐφθαρμένον ἀπὸ τῶν προτέρων αὐτοῦ πράξεων *his spirit, which had already degenerated from its former condition* (s. πρᾶξις 6) Hv 3, 12, 2 (cf. Ocellus [II BC] c. 23 Harder ['26] φθείρονται ἐξ ἀλλήλων).

2. in the realm of morals and religion—a. *ruin* or *corrupt* τινά *someone* in his inner life, by erroneous teaching or immorality, so perh. 2 Cor 7: 2 (s. 1a above). ἥτις ἔφθειρεν τὴν γῆν (= τοὺς ἀνθρώπους; cf. γῆ 5b) ἐν τῇ πορνείᾳ αὐτῆς Rv 19: 2. Pass. (UPZ 20, 17 [163 BC]; Test. Jud. 19: 4 ἐν ἁμαρτίαις φθαρείς) τὸν παλαιὸν ἄνθρωπον τὸν φθειρόμενον κατὰ τὰς ἐπιθυμίας Eph 4: 22. Cf. Hs 8, 9, 3 Lake.

b. *ruin* or *corrupt* τὶ someth. by misleading tactics

πίστιν θεοῦ κακῇ διδασκαλίᾳ IEph 16: 2. The church (opp. τηρεῖν) 2 Cl 14: 3a, b. On φθείρουσιν ἤθη χρηστὰ ὁμιλίαι κακαί 1 Cor 15: 33 cf. ἦθος. Pass. *be led astray* (Jos., Bell. 4, 510) μήπως φθαρῇ τὰ νοήματα ὑμῶν ἀπὸ ἀπλότητος (νόημα 1) 2 Cor 11: 3 (φθ. of the seduction of a virgin, s. 1c above).

c. *destroy* in the sense 'punish w. eternal destruction' 1 Cor 3: 17b (= 'punish by destroying' as Jer 13: 9). Pass. 2 Pt 2: 12; Jd 10. ἔφθαρται (w. ἀπώλετο) IPol 5: 2.— GHarder, TW IX, 94-106: φθείρω and many related words. M-M. B. 758.*

φθινοπωρινός, ή, όν *belonging to late autumn* (Aristot., H.A. 5, 11; Polyb. 4, 37, 2; Plut., Mor. 735B ὁ φθινοπωρινὸς ἀήρ, ἐν ᾧ φυλλοχοεῖ τὰ δένδρα; Aelian., N.A. 14, 26 p. 358, 24; PHib. 27, 170 [III BC]). In Jd 12 the false teachers are called δένδρα φθινοπωρινὰ ἄκαρπα *trees in late autumn, without fruit* (w. νεφέλαι ἄνυδροι). The point of the comparison is prob. that trees which have no fruit at the time of harvest (cf. JBMayor, φθινοπωρινός: Exp. 6th Ser. IX '04, 98-104, The Ep. of St. Jude and 2 Pt '07, 55-9) have not fulfilled the purpose for which they exist, any more than waterless clouds. M-M. B. 1015.*

φθόγγος, ου, ὁ (Hom.+; PGM 7, 775; 778; Philo) (clear, distinct) *sound, tone* of musical instruments (Pla., Leg. 812D; Philostrat., Vi. Apoll. 5, 21 p. 181, 19.—Wsd 19: 18) 1 Cor 14: 7. Also of the human *voice* (Hom.+) ἐξῆλθεν ὁ φθόγγος αὐτῶν Ro 10: 18 (cf. Ps 18: 5). M-M.*

φθονέω 1 aor. ἐφθόνησα (Hom.+; inscr.; PFlor. 273, 5; Tob 4: 7; 16; Philo, Test. 12 Patr.) *envy, be jealous* τινί (*of*) *someone* (X., Mem. 3, 5, 16; Chares [IV BC] 1 [Anth. Lyr.² Diehl, suppl. '42]; Herodian 3, 2, 3; Jos., Vi. 230) ἀλλήλοις (Plut., Artax. 24, 7 v.l.) Gal 5: 26 (v.l. ἀλλήλους; the acc. as Aesop 147a, 2 Chambry v.l.); w. inf. (Appian, Bell. Civ. 4, 95 §400 φ. τινι w. inf.=begrudge someone [the chance to]; Jos., C. Ap. 2, 268) μὴ φθονήσωμεν ἑαυτοῖς τυχεῖν τοσούτων ἀγαθῶν *let us not begrudge each other the gaining of such benefits* 2 Cl 15: 5 (Jos., Ant. 4, 235 ἀγαθῶν φθονεῖν τινι).—φ. τινι can also mean *dislike someone, be resentful toward someone* without the connotation of jealousy or a grudge (Appian, Bell. Civ. 1, 79 §360). Absol. Js 4: 2 v.l. M-M.*

φθόνος, ου, ὁ (Pind., Hdt.+; Ael. Aristid. 29, 5 K.=40 p. 752 D.: φθ. as ἔσχατον τῶν ἀνθρωπίνων ἁμαρτημάτων; pap., LXX; Ep. Arist. 224; Philo; Jos., Vi. 80; 122; Test. 12 Patr.) *envy, jealousy,* w. ζῆλος (1 Macc 8: 16; Test. Sim. 4: 5) 1 Cl 3: 2; 4: 7, 13; 5: 2. W. κακία (Test. Benj. 8: 1) Tit 3: 3. In catalogues of vices (in some of which κακία also occurs; cf. also Herm. Wr. 13, 7) Ro 1: 29 (μεστοὺς φθόνου φόνου ἔριδος. The play on words φθόν. φόν. as Eur., Tro. 766ff); 1 Ti 6: 4 (w. ἔρις); φθόνοι Gal 5: 21 (v.l. +φόνοι); 1 Pt 2: 1. διὰ φθόνον *out of envy* (Anaximenes [IV BC]: 72 fgm. 33 Jac.; Philo, Mos. 1, 2; Jos., Vi. 204 ἐπιγνοὺς διὰ φθόνον ἀναιρεθῆναί με προστάξαι, C. Ap. 1, 222) Mt 27: 18; Mk 15: 10; Phil 1: 15 (w. ἔρις). On the difficult and perh. textually damaged pass. πρὸς φθόνον ἐπιποθεῖ τὸ πνεῦμα Js 4: 5 s. ἐπιποθέω; πρός III 6, and cf. FSpitta, Der Brief des Jk [=Zur Gesch. und Lit. des Urchristentums II] 1896, 118ff; PCorssen, GGA 1893, 596f; OKirn, StKr 77, '04, 127ff; 593ff; ChBruston, Rev. de Théol. et des Quest. rel. 11, '07, 368-77; JAFindlay, ET 37, '26, 381f; AMeyer, D. Rätsel des Jk '30, 258f. M-M. B. 1139.*

φθορά, ᾶς, ἡ (Aeschyl., Hdt.+; inscr., pap., LXX, En., Philo; Jos., Ant. 18, 373; Sib. Or. 2, 9) *ruin, destruction, dissolution, deterioration, corruption.*

1. in the world of nature (Galen, In Hippocr. De Natura Hominis Comm. 45 p. 25, 6 Mewaldt γένεσις κ. φθορά= coming into being and passing away; 51 p. 28, 11 γένεσις κ. φθορὰ σώματος.—The reason for the destruction is not found in the word itself, but must be made clear by an addition. Cf. Plut., Artax. 16, 6 Z. concerning Mithridates, who was allowed to decompose while he was still alive: εὐλαὶ κ. σκώληκες ὑπὸ φθορᾶς κ. σηπεδόνος ἀναζέουσιν= maggots and worms swarmed as a result of the destruction and putrefaction [of his body]) τροφὴ φθορᾶς *perishable food* IRo 7: 3. ἅ ἐστιν πάντα εἰς φθορὰν τῇ ἀποχρήσει *all of which are meant for destruction by being consumed* Col 2: 22. Of animals who are destined to be killed 2 Pt 2: 12a (X., Cyr. 7, 5, 64; Artem. 1, 78 p. 74, 27.—Schol. on Nicander, Ther. 795 explains κακόφθορα by saying that it designates animals τὰ ἐπὶ κακῇ φθορᾷ τεχθέντα= born to come to an evil end, i.e., destruction).—Of the *state of being perishable* (opp. ἀφθαρσία as Philo, Mos. 2, 194) 1 Cor 15: 42; also concrete, *that which is perishable* vs. 50. ἡ δουλεία τῆς φθορᾶς *slavery to decay* Ro 8: 21.

2. in specific senses—a. *(destruction by) abortion* (cf. Dit., Syll.³ 1042, 7 [II/III AD] φθορά= miscarriage [which makes the mother unclean for 40 days] and φθόριον= a means of producing abortion) οὐ φονεύσεις ἐν φθορᾷ B 19: 5; D 2: 2.

b. *seduction of a maiden* (Diod. S. 3, 59, 1; 5, 62, 1; Plut., Mor. 712c; Jos., Ant. 17, 309, C. Ap. 2, 202) w. μοιχεία (Philo, Det. Pot. Ins. 102) 2 Cl 6: 4.

3. of religious and moral *depravity* (Ex 18: 18; Mi 2: 10) ἡ ἐν τῷ κόσμῳ ἐν ἐπιθυμίᾳ φθορά *the depravity* that exists *in the world because of passion* (opp. θεία φύσις) 2 Pt 1: 4. δοῦλοι τῆς φθορᾶς 2: 19. Vs. 12b (s. 4 below) scarcely belongs here.

4. of *destruction* in the last days Gal 6: 8 (opp. ζωὴ αἰώνιος). ἐν τῇ φθορᾷ αὐτῶν καὶ φθαρήσονται *when they* (the dumb animals) *are destroyed* in the coming end of the world, *these* (the false teachers), *too, will be destroyed* (so BWeiss, Kühl, JBMayor, Windisch, Knopf, Vrede) 2 Pt 2: 12b. M-M.*

φθορεύς, έως, ὁ *seducer* (Plut., Mor. 18c; Epict. 2, 22, 28 [w. μοιχός]; 4 Macc 18: 8; Philo, Decal. 168 [w. μοιχός]); this mng. is to be preferred for B 10: 7 and prob. also for 20: 2; D 5: 2, where the word is oft. taken to mean *abortionist* (φθορά 2a).—D 16: 3 it is *corrupter* gener.*

φιάλη, ης, ἡ (Hom.+; inscr., pap., LXX, Ep. Arist.; Jos., Ant. 3, 143; 272; loanw. in rabb.) *bowl,* specif. a *bowl used in offerings* (Diod. S. 4, 49, 8) Rv 5: 8 (golden bowl as Ps.-Callisth. 2, 21, 16); 15: 7; 16: 1-4, 8, 10, 12, 17; 17: 1; 21: 9. M-M. B. 346.*

φιλάγαθος, ον (Aristot., Magn. Mor. 2, 14 p. 1212b, 18 φιλάγαθος οὐ φίλαυτος; Polyb. 6, 53, 9; Plut., Mor. 140c, Rom. 30, 7; Vett. Val. 104, 7; inscr.; Wilcken, Chrest. 20 II, 11 [II AD]; POxy. 33 [II AD]; Wsd 7: 22; Ep. Arist.; Philo, Mos. 2, 9) *loving what is good* Tit 1: 8. M-M.*

Φιλαδέλφεια, ας, ἡ (so N.; W-H. Φιλαδέλφια) *Philadelphia,* a city in Lydia (west central Asia Minor; this Philadelphia mentioned in Strabo 12, 8 p. 578; Ptolem. 5, 2, 17; Ael. Aristid. 26, 96 K. al.; inscr.) under Roman rule fr. 133 BC. Significant as a seat of Hellenistic culture. The sixth letter of Rv 1: 11; 3: 7 and one epistle of Ign., IPhld

inscr., are addressed to the Christian church there. MPol 19: 1 mentions eleven martyrs fr. Phil. who were condemned together w. Polycarp in Smyrna.—An inhabitant of the city was called Φιλαδελφεύς title of IPhld (s. Hdb. z. NT on this).—Lghtf., The Apost. Fathers, Part II vol. II² 1889, 237ff; KBuresch, Aus Lydien 1898; Ramsay, Phrygia I 1895, 196ff, Letters ch. 27f; VSchultze, Altchristl. Städte u. Landschaften II 2, '26. M-M.*

φιλαδελφία, ας, ἡ *brotherly love, love of brother* or *sister* (elsewh. in the lit. sense of love for blood brothers or sisters: Alexis Com. [IV BC] 334; Eratosth. [III BC], Cat. p. 12, 18; Plut., περὶ φιλαδελφίας; Lucian, Dial. Deor. 26, 2; Babrius 47, 15; PLond. 1708, 101; 4 Macc 13: 23, 26; 14: 1; Philo, Leg. ad Gai. 87; Jos., Ant. 4, 26) in our literature fig., of love to a brother in the Christian faith (cf. ἀδελφός 2) Ro 12: 10; 1 Th 4: 9; Hb 13: 1; 2 Pt 1: 7a, b; 1 Cl 48: 1. ἀνυπόκριτος 1 Pt 1: 22. περιβόητος 1 Cl 47: 5.—HSedlaczek, φιλαδελφία nach den Schriften des hl. Ap. Pls: ThQ 76, 1894, 272-95. M-M.*

φιλάδελφος, ον *loving one's brother and/or sister* (in the lit. sense [s. φιλαδελφία] Soph., X.+; on gravestones [Sb 6234; 6235; 6653]; 4 Macc 13: 21; 15: 10; Philo, De Jos. 218) in our literature only fig. (cf. Socrat., Ep. 28, 12= sociable; 2 Macc 15: 14= loving one's fellow-countrymen) of love to a brother in the Christian faith 1 Pt 3: 8. M-M.*

φίλανδρος, ον (Aeschyl.+) *loving her husband* (so Phalaris, Ep. 132 φ. καὶ σώφρων; Ep. 58 of Apollonius of Tyana [Philostrat. I 361, 30]; Plut., Mor. 142A φίλανδροι καὶ σώφρονες γυναῖκες; Dit., Syll.³ 783, 39 [I BC]; inscr. fr. Perg. in Dssm., LO 268 [LAE 314]; Maspéro 310, 18; PLond. 1711, 40; Philo, Exs. 139.—Jos., Ant. 18, 159 φιλανδρία.—Dibelius, Hdb. ad loc.) Tit 2: 4. M-M.*

φιλανθρωπία, ας, ἡ (X., Pla.+; inscr., pap., LXX, Ep. Arist., Philo, Joseph.) *love for mankind, (loving) kindness,* of God (Musonius p. 90, 12 H.; Lucian, Bis Accus. 1, end; Philo, Cher. 99; Jos., Ant. 1, 24.—OWeinreich, ARW 18, '15, 25; 50-2.—As a virtue of rulers: Diod. S. 34+35 fgm. 3 [w. χρηστότης]; Dit., Or. 139, 21, Syll.³ 888, 101; Esth 8: 12(l) [w. χρηστότης]; 3 Macc 3: 15, 18; Ep. Arist. 265; 290.—PWendland, ZNW 5, '04 p. 345, 2) and w. χρηστότης (Plut., Aristid. 27, 7 and oft. elsewh.; Philo, Spec. Leg. 2, 141; Jos., Ant. 10, 164) Tit 3: 4; Dg 9: 2. Rather in the sense *hospitality* (cf. ENorden, Die germanische Urgesch. in Tacitus' Germania² '22 p. 137, 2; 138, 1) Ac 28: 2.—Field, Notes 147f; 222f.—On the semantic development: SLorenz, De Progressu Notionis φιλανθρωπίας, Diss. Leipzig '14; STromp de Ruiter, Mnemosyne n. s. 59, '32, 271-306.—CSpicq, La Philanthropie hellénistique (Tit 3: 4), Studia Theologica 12, '58, 169-91. ULuck, TW IX, 107-11. M-M.*

φιλάνθρωπος, ον (Aeschyl., X., Pla.+; inscr., pap., LXX, Ep. Arist., Philo; Jos., Ant. 1, 200) *loving mankind, benevolent* of God (Pla., Symp. 189D, Leg. 4 p. 713D; Plut., Mor. 402A; Lucian, Prom. 6; Xenophon Eph. 5, 4, 10; Aelian, H.A. 9, 33; Philo; Weinreich [s.v. φιλανθρωπία]. Of the Wisdom of God Wsd 1: 6; 7: 23. Also of a ruler [Ep. Arist. 208] 'humane, popular' [Wendland s.v. φιλανθρωπία; Thieme 38]) Dg 8: 7. Of a virtue ἡ φιλόθεος καὶ φιλάνθρωπος ἀγάπη Agr 7 (w. φιλόθεος as Philo, Dec. 110).*

φιλανθρώπως adv. (Isocr., Demosth.+; inscr., LXX, Philo, Joseph.) *benevolently, kindly* φιλανθρώπως χρῆσθαί (τινι) *treat someone in kindly fashion* (Isocr., Ep. 7, 6; Demosth. 19, 225; Aeschin. 3 [C. Ctes.], 57;

Diod. S. 20, 17, 1; Plut., Aemil. 39, 9, Alcib. 4, 6, Mor. 88c; Cass. Dio 71, 14; 27; Jos., C. Ap. 1, 153, Ant. 12, 46; 14, 313 v.l.; Dit., Syll.³ 368, 4f [289/8 BC].—HJCadbury, JBL 45, '26, 202) Ac 27: 3. M-M.*

φιλαργυρέω (Epicurus; Alciphr. 4, 15; Sext. Emp., Math. 11, 122; Dit., Syll.³ 593, 12 [196/4 BC]; 2 Macc 10: 20) *love money, be avaricious* 2 Cl 4: 3.*

φιλαργυρία, ας, ἡ (Isocr.+; Polyb. 9, 25, 4; Diod. S. 7, 14, 5; Cebes 19, 5; Herodian 6, 9, 8; 4 Macc 1: 26; Philo; Test. Judah 18: 2; 19: 1) *love of money, avarice, miserliness* w. other vices 2 Cl 6: 4; Pol 2: 2; 4: 3; 6: 1. As ῥίζα πάντων τῶν κακῶν 1 Ti 6: 10 or ἀρχὴ πάντων χαλεπῶν Pol 4: 1 (cf. Hippocr., Ep. 17, 43 τούτων ἀπάντων αἰτίη ἡ φιλαργυρίη; Democritus in Gnomol. Vatican. 265 Sternbach [Wiener Studien 10, 1888, 231] Δημόκριτος τὴν φιλαργυρίαν ἔλεγε μητρόπολιν πάσης κακίας. Likew. Bion the Sophist in Stob., Eclog. III 417, 5 H.; Diog. L. 6, 50 μητρόπολιν πάντων τῶν κακῶν; Apollod. Com. 4 vol. III p. 280 Kock; also Sib. Or. 2, 111; 8, 17).— JGeffcken, Kynika u. Verwandtes '09, 38ff. M-M.*

φιλάργυρος, ον (Soph., X., Pla.+; Polyb. 9, 22, 8; 9, 25, 1; 9, 26, 11; Diod. S. 5, 27, 4; Epict.; Plut.; Cebes 34, 3; PPetr. III 53j, 14 [III BC]; 4 Macc 2: 8; Philo; Test. Levi 17: 11) *fond of money, avaricious* Lk 16: 14; 2 Ti 3: 2; D 3: 5. M-M.*

φίλαυτος, ον (Aristot. [s. φιλάγαθος and cf. the index of the Berlin ed. IV 818]; Musonius 86, 2 H.; Plut., Epict., Lucian, Sext. Emp.; Philo, Leg. All. 1, 49 φίλαυτος καὶ ἄθεος; Jos., Ant. 3, 190) *loving oneself, selfish* 2 Ti 3: 2. M-M.*

φιλέω impf. ἐφίλουν; 1 aor. ἐφίλησα; pf. πεφίληκα (Hom.+; inscr., pap., LXX, Joseph., Sib. Or.). 1. *love, have affection for, like*—a. w. acc. of the pers.: relatives (X., Mem. 2, 7, 9) Mt 10: 37a, b (on this pass. TArvedson, Svensk Ex. Årsb. 5, '40, 74-82). Good disciples IPol 2: 1. Paul speaks of those who love him in (the) faith Tit 3: 15 (on the greeting here s. UWilcken, APF 6, '20, 379; Sb 7253, 18-20 [296 AD] ἀσπάζομαι τοὺς φιλοῦντας ἡμᾶς κατ᾽ ὄνομα). The world loves those who belong to it J 15: 19. Jesus' disciples love him J 16: 27b; 21: 15-17 (here φ. seems to be=ἀγαπάω, q.v. 1aβ, w. the lit. there, pro and con); so do all true Christians 1 Cor 16: 22 (CSpicq, NovT 1, '56, 200-4). Christ also loves certain persons Rv 3: 19; Lazarus (JLeal, Verb. Dom. 21, '41, 59-64) J 11: 3, 36; the beloved disciple 20: 2. God loves the Son 5: 20 and his disciples 16: 27a (φ. of the love of a deity, Simonides, fgm. 4, 12 οὕς ἂν οἱ θεοὶ φιλέωσιν [i.e. τ. ἀγαθούς]; Dio Chrys. 80[30], 26; Biogr. p. 92; Sib. Or. 3, 711).—SNRoads, A Study of φιλεῖν and ἀγαπᾶν in the NT: Review and Expositor 10, '13, 531-3; CFHogg, Note on ἀγαπ. and φιλέω: ET 38, '27, 379f; BBWarfield, The Terminology of Love in the NT: PTR 16, '18, 1-45; 153-203; FNormann, Diss. Münster, '52; MPaeslack, Theologia Viatorum 5, '53, 51-142; MLattke, Einheit im Wort '75. S. the lit. s.v. ἀγάπη I, end. b. w. acc. of the thing (Hom.+; Wsd 8: 2) τὴν ψυχὴν αὑτοῦ J 12: 25 (Tyrtaeus 7, 18 Diehl² warns about φιλοψυχεῖν). The place of honor Mt 23: 6.—Lk 20: 46; Rv 22: 15 (cf. Pr 29: 3). W. inf. foll. *like* or *love to do someth.*, hence *do someth. often* or *customarily* (Pind., Nem. 1, 15; Aeschyl., Sept. 619, Ag. 763; Soph., Aj. 989; Eur., Iph. T. 1198; Ps.-Eur., Rhes. 394; Hdt. 7, 10, 5; X., Hipparch. 7, 9; Pla., 7th Letter p. 337B; Appian, Liby. 94 §442; Arrian, Anab. 3, 11, 2; Aelian, V.H. 14, 37; PGiess. 84, 13; Is 56:

10; Philo, Op. M. 103; Jos., Ant. 18, 60) φιλοῦσιν προσεύχεσθαι Mt 6: 5. φιλοῦσιν καλεῖσθαι ῥαββὶ they *like to be called 'Rabbi'* 23: 6f. 2. *kiss*, as a special indication of love (Aeschyl., Ag. 1540; Hdt. 1, 134; X., Cyr. 1, 4, 27; Pla., Phaedr. 256A; Aristot., Prob. 30, 1, 8; Plut., Mor. 139D, Alex. 6, 8; Lucian, Ver. Hist. 1, 8; PSI 26, 13; Gen 27: 26f; 29: 11 al.) τινά *someone* Mt 26: 48; Mk 14: 44; Lk 22: 47.—GStählin, TW IX, 112-69: φιλέω and related words. M-M. B. 1110; 1114.*

φίλη, ης, ἡ s. φίλος 2b.

φιλήδονος, ον *loving pleasure, given over to pleasure* (so Polyb. 39, 1, 10; Plut., Mor. 6B; 766B; Epict. in Stob. no. 46 p. 474 Schenkl; Dio Chrys. 4, 115; M. Ant. 6, 51; Maximus Tyr. 24, 4f; Lucian, Herm. 16; Vett. Val. 7, 12; 9, 3; 40, 5; Philo, Agr. 88 al.) 2 Ti 3: 4. M-M.*

φίλημα, ατος, τό (Aeschyl.+; Pr 27: 6; SSol 1: 2; Philo, Rer. Div. Her. 40; Jos., Bell. 7, 391) *a kiss* (φιλέω 2) Lk 22: 48 (JDöller, Der Judaskuss: Korrespondenzblatt f. d. kath. Klerus Österreichs '18; 127-9). φίλημά τινι διδόναι *give someone a kiss* (Nicopho Com. [V/IV BC] 8) Lk 7: 45. The kiss w. which Christian brethren give expression to their intimate fellowship is called φίλημα ἅγιον: ἀσπάσασθε ἀλλήλους ἐν φιλήματι ἁγίῳ Ro 16: 16; 1 Cor 16: 20; 2 Cor 13: 12; cf. 1 Th 5: 26. Also ἀσπάσασθε ἀλλήλους ἐν φιλήματι ἀγάπης 1 Pt 5: 14.—HAchelis, Das Christentum in den ersten drei Jahrhunderten I '12, 292f; Windisch on 2 Cor 13: 12; RSeeberg, Aus Rel. u. Gesch. I '06, 118-22; AWünsche, Der Kuss in Bibel, Talmud u. Midrasch '11; K-MHofmann, Philema Hagion '38; WLowrie, The Kiss of Peace, Theology Today 12, '55, 236-42; KThraede, Jahrb. f. Antike u. Christent. 11f, '68/'69, 124-80. M-M. B. 1114.*

Φιλήμων, ονος, ὁ a name freq. found, *Philemon*, a Christian, prob. at Colossae, a convert of Paul. Philemon's slave, Onesimus, ran away, met Paul, and was also won for Christianity by him. Paul sent him back to his master, and gave him a short letter explaining the circumstances, our Phlm. Phlm 1; subscr.—Zahn, Einl.³ I 312ff; Pölzl (Τιμόθεος, end) 293ff. On the letter s. JKnox, Phlm among the Letters of Paul—a New View of its Place and Importance '35 (²'59), and on this HGreeven, ThLZ 79, '54, 373-8, also WRollins, JBL 78, '59, 277f; WGDoty, Letters in Primitive Christianity '73. M-M.*

Φίλητος (on the accent cf. Kühner-Bl. I 329f; Tdf., Proleg. 103), ου, ὁ (inscr.; POxy. 72, 17 [90 AD]) *Philetus*, an otherw. unknown heretic, mentioned w. Hymenaeus 2 Ti 2: 17. M-M.*

φιλία, ας, ἡ (Theognis, Hdt.+; inscr., pap., LXX, Ep. Arist.; Philo; Jos., Ant. 12, 414, C. Ap. 1, 109; 2, 207 al.) *friendship, love* foll. by the objective gen. (Thu. 1, 91, 1; Sir 27: 18; Philo, Fuga 58 φ. θεοῦ) ἡ φιλία τοῦ κόσμου Js 4: 4 (there is also an αἰσχρὰ φ.: Biogr. p. 112). Pl. φιλίαι ἐθνικαί *friendships with pagans* Hm 10, 1, 4 (φιλία can also= bond of friendship: Diod. S. 10, 4, 6 εἰς τὴν φιλίαν προσλαβέσθαι; 19, 73, 2). M-M.*

Φιλιππήσιος, ου, ὁ *the man from Philippi* (s. Φίλιπποι), *the Philippian*; this form (Stephan. Byz.: ὁ πολίτης Φιλιππεύς [CIG 1578, 13. Cf. Dit., Syll.³ 267A, 3f w. note 4], Φιλιππηνὸς δὲ παρὰ Πολυβίῳ.—WMRamsay, On the Gk. Form of the Name Philippians: JTS 1, '00, 115f) is found Phil 4: 15 and in the titles of Phil and Pol (cf. Irenaeus 3, 3, 4). M-M.*

Φίλιπποι, ων, οἱ (Diod. S. 16, 3, 8; Appian, Bell. Civ. 4, 105 §438; Strabo 7 fgm. 34; 41; 43; Jos., Bell. 1, 242, Ant. 14, 301; 310f; inscr.) *Philippi*, a city in Macedonia, founded on the site of the older Κρηνῖδες by Philip of Macedonia (Diod. S. 16, 8, 6). Under Roman rule fr. about 167 BC. In Ac 16: 12 *Ph*. is called πρώτη τῆς μερίδος Μακεδονίας πόλις, κολωνία (μερίς 1). On the history of Philippi: PCollart, Philippes, ville de Macédoine '37.—Here Paul founded the first church on European soil 16: 12ff; cf. 1 Th 2: 2. Ac also mentions Philippi 20: 6, where Paul touched at the city on his last journey to Jerusalem. ἐγράφη ἀπὸ Φ. [τῆς Μακεδονίας v.l.] 1 and 2 Cor subscr. As a prisoner the apostle sent a letter to the church at Phil.: Phil 1: 1 (among the more recent treatments of the circumstances under which this letter was written, esp. the place of its writing: PFeine, Die Abfassung des Philipper-briefes in Ephesus '16; ADeissmann, Zur ephesin. Gefangenschaft des Ap. Pls: Anatolian Studies for Ramsay '23, 121–7; WMichaelis, D. Datierung des Phil '33; Dibelius, Hdb. exc. on Phil, end; GSDuncan, St. Paul's Ephesian Ministry '30; JSchmid, Zeit u. Ort. d. paulin. Gefangenschaftsbriefe '31; TWManson, Bull. of the JRylands Library 23, '39, 182–200; ELohmeyer, Phil '30, 3; 41, 5; 43, 3; 47].—The name of the city also occurs in the letter of Polycarp to the church at Philippi (on this PNHarrison, Polycarp's Two Epistles to the Philippians '36 [p. 337–51 lit.]), Pol inscr.—Cf. also EdSchweizer, Der 2 Th ein Phil.-brief: ThZ 1, '45, 90–105. M-M. *

Φίλιππος, ου, ὁ (freq. found in lit., inscr., pap.; occurring also in LXX and Joseph.) *Philip*

1. the tetrarch, son of Herod the Great and Cleopatra of Jerusalem (cf. Joseph., index Φίλιππος 6). He was tetrarch of Gaulanitis, Trachonitis, Auranitis, Batanaea and Panias (so Joseph., if the indications he gives in var. passages may thus be brought together), and acc. to Lk 3: 1, also Ituraea (all small districts northeast of Palestine). He rebuilt Panias as Caesarea (Philippi) and Bethsaida as Julias. Joseph. praises his personality and administration (Ant. 18, 106f). He was married to Salome, the daughter of Herodias (cf. Ἡρωδιάς and Σαλώμη, end). He died 33/34 AD, whereupon his territory was joined to the Rom. province of Syria, though only for a short time. Mt 16: 13; Mk 8: 27. Cf. also Mt 14: 3; Mk 6: 17; Lk 3: 19 t.r. and s. Ἡρωδιάς.—Schürer I⁴ 425–31.—2. On the Philip mentioned Mt 14: 3 and Mk 6: 17 s. Ἡρωδιάς.

3. the apostle, one of the Twelve. In the lists of the Twelve (which is the only place where his name is mentioned in the synoptics and Ac), he is found in fifth place, after the two pairs of brothers Peter-Andrew, James-John Mt 10: 3; Mk 3: 18; Lk 6: 14; Ac 1: 13. He is given more prominence in the Fourth Gosp., where he is one of the first to be called, and comes fr. Bethsaida, the city of Simon and Andrew; cf. 1: 43–6, 48; 6: 5, 7; 12: 21f; 14: 8f. Papias 2: 4 he is called one of the πρεσβύτεροι.—On the apostle and the evangelist (s. 4 below), who have oft. been confused, cf. ThZahn, Apostel u. Apostelschüler in der Provinz Asien: Forsch. VI '00 p. 369b (index); EBishop, ATR 28, '46, 154–9 equates 3 and 4.

4. one of the seven 'deacons' at Jerusalem Ac 6: 5; 21: 8; in the latter pass. also called the 'evangelist' (cf. εὐαγγελιστής) to differentiate him fr. the apostle. Ac 8: 5–13 after the death of Stephen he worked in Samaria w. great success; vss. 26–39 he baptized a non-Jew, the chamberlain of the Ethiopian Queen Candace (MvanWanroy, Verb. Dom. '40, 287–93; FBlanke, Kirchenfreund 84, '50, 145–9) and vs. 40 preached the gospel in all the cities fr. Ashdod to Caesarea. Later he lived in Caesarea w. his four

maiden daughters, who possessed the gift of prophecy 21: 8f.—Zahn (3 above); HWaitz, Die Quelle der Philippusgeschichten in der AG 8: 5–40: ZNW 7, '06, 340–55.

5. the Asiarch MPol 12: 2, or high priest MPol 21 Philip, under whom Polycarp suffered martyrdom. M-M. *

φιλοδέσποτος, ον (Theognis, Hdt.+; Diod. S. 17, 66, 5; Lucian; Aelian, N.A. 6, 62; Philo; Jos., Bell. 4, 175) *loving one's master*; the neut. subst. τὸ φιλοδέσποτον *love of their Master* (Lucian, Fug. 16; schol. on Aeschyl., Ag. 3; Philo, Praem. 89) in the Christian sense MPol 2: 2. *

φιλόζωος (w. or without iota subscr.), **ον** (trag.+; Philo) *loving life*, also of plants *tenacious of life* (Theophr., H.Pl. 7, 13, 4; Nicander [II BC], Theriaca 68, Alexipharmaca 274; 591 OSchneider [1856]) Hs 8, 2, 7; 8, 6, 1. *

φιλόθεος, ον (Aristot., Rhet. 2, 17, 6; Diod. S. 1, 95, 4; Lucian, Calumn. 14; Vett. Val. 17, 9; Philo, Agr. 88 al.) *loving God, devout* in a play on words w. φιλήδονος 2 Ti 3: 4 (cf. Porphyr., Ad Marcellam 14 p. 283, 20f N. ἀδύνατον τὸν αὐτὸν φιλόθεόν τε εἶναι καὶ φιλήδονον; Pythagorean saying: Wiener Stud. 8, 1886 p. 279 no. 110). ἀγάπη Agr 7 (w. φιλάνθρωπος, q.v.). M-M. *

Φιλόλογος, ου, ὁ *Philologus*, an otherw. unknown Christian, recipient of a greeting Ro 16: 15. The name is found in Gk. and Lat. inscr. (exx. in Ltzm., Hdb. ad loc.), esp. of slaves and freedmen, and also occurs in the 'familia' of the imperial house (CIL VI 4116 al.). M-M. *

Φιλομήλιον, ου, τό (Strabo 12, 8, 14; Ptolem. 5, 2, 25 al.) *Philomelium*, a city in Phrygia (central Asia Minor), not far fr. Antioch in Pisidia MPol inscr. *

φιλον(ε)ικία, ας, ἡ (Thu.+; inscr., pap., LXX.—On the spelling Bl-D. §23 and L-S-J s.v. φιλόνικος, end; PKatz, ThLZ '36, 282).
1. *contentiousness* (Pla.+; Diod. S. 13, 48, 2; 4 Macc 1: 26; 8: 26; Philo, Leg. ad Gai. 218) MPol 18: 1.—2. *dispute, strife* (Thu. 8, 76, 1; Diod. S. 3, 33, 3; M. Ant. 3, 4; Philo; Jos., Ant. 7, 182, C. Ap. 2, 243; 2 Macc 4: 4) Lk 22: 24 ('emulation': Field, Notes 75f). M-M. B. 1360. *

φιλόν(ε)ικος, ον (on the spelling s.v. φιλον(ε)ικία—1. *quarrelsome, contentious* (Pind., Pla.+; M. Ant. 5, 35; Ezk 3: 7; Philo; Jos., C. Ap. 1, 160, Ant. 15, 166) 1 Cor 11: 16.
2. in a good sense (X., Pla., Plut.; Jos., Ant. 15, 156 al.) *emulous, (in) eager (rivalry)* φιλόν(ε)ικοι ἔστε καὶ ζηλωταὶ περὶ τῶν ἀνηκόντων εἰς σωτηρίαν 1 Cl 45: 1. *

φιλοξενία, ας, ἡ (since Bacchylides 3, 16 Snell; Pla.; Dit., Syll.³ 859A, 4; PLond. 1917, 4) *hospitality* Ro 12: 13; Hm 8: 10. Abraham's *hosp.* 1 Cl 10: 7. Lot's 11: 1. These two men are prob. thought of in Hb 13: 2. Of Rahab 1 Cl 12: 1. Of the Corinthian church 1: 2. DWRiddle, Early Christian Hospitality: JBL 57, '38, 141–54. M-M. *

φιλόξενος, ον (Hom.+; Epict. 1, 28, 23; Philo, Abr. 114; Jos., Vi. 142) *hospitable* 1 Pt 4: 9; 1 Cl 12: 3 (Rahab); Hm 8: 10. The bishop is to be *hosp.* 1 Ti 3: 2 (w. κόσμιος as Epict. 1, 28, 23); Tit 1: 8; cf. ἐπίσκοποι καὶ φιλόξενοι Hs 9, 27, 2. M-M. *

φιλοπονέω (X., Pla.+; pap.; Sir prol. 1. 20) *exert oneself, devote oneself* περί τι *in (to) someth.* (Isocr. 1, 46 τὸ περὶ τὴν ἀρετὴν φιλοπονεῖν; PLond. 130, 5 [I/II AD]) 2 Cl 19: 1. *

φιλοπρωτεύω *wish to be first, like to be leader* (so far only in eccl. usage. But φιλόπρωτος in the same sense in Plut.,

φιλοπρωτεύω – φιμόω

Mor. 471D, Solon 29, 5, Alcib. 2, 1; Artem. 2, 32. Also φιλοπρωτεία in Philod., Herculanensia Volumina coll. 2 vol. I 86, 6; VII 176, 16 [Philod., Rhet. II 159 fgm. 19 Sudh.]; Porphyr., Vi. Plot. 10 [AKirchhoff, Plotini Op. I 1856 p. xxvii]) 3 J 9. M-M.*

φίλος, η, ον (Hom.+; inscr., pap., LXX, Ep. Arist., Philo, Joseph., Test. 12 Patr.)—1. adj., both pass. beloved, dear, and act. loving, kindly disposed, devoted (both Hom.+) in the latter sense w. dat. of the pers. (X., Cyr. 1, 6, 4; Dio Chrys. 52[69], 4 θεοῖς) Ac 19: 31.
   2. subst.—a. ὁ φίλος the friend—a. lit. Lk 7: 6; 11: 5a; 16: 9 (Plut., Mor. 175E ἀφ' ὧν ... φίλον σεαυτῷ πεποίηκας); 23: 12; Ac 16: 39 D; 27: 3; 3 J 15a, b (on φίλοι = Christians cf. J 11: 11; 15: 14f: communication from HJCadbury, '67; Hm 5, 2, 2 (on Ac and 3 J cf. Harnack, Mission⁴ I '23, 435f). φίλοι w. γείτονες Lk 15: 6 (s. γείτων); w. συγγενεῖς 21: 16. Opp. δοῦλοι (unknown comic poet vol. III fgm. 166 Kock; Charito 7, 3, 2 δούλους οὐκ ἂν εἴποιμι τοὺς φίλους) J 15: 15 (ABöhlig, Vom 'Knecht' zum 'Sohn' '68, 63); cf. Hs 5, 2, 6; 11; 5, 4, 1; 5, 5, 3 (in H we have the tetrad δεσπότης, υἱός, δοῦλος, φίλοι). On οἱ ἀναγκαῖοι φίλοι Ac 10: 24 s. ἀναγκαῖος 2 and Jos., Ant. 7, 350. φίλε as familiar address friend Lk 11: 5b; 14: 10. W. subjective gen. (Jos., C. Ap. 1, 109) Lk 11: 6, 8; 12: 4; 14: 12; 15: 29; 3 J 15; 11: 15: 13f cf. EPeterson, Der Gottesfreund: ZKG n.s. 5, '23, 161–202; MDibelius, J 15: 13: Deissmann-Festschr. '27, 168–86; REgenter, Gottesfreundschaft '28; HNeumark, D. Verwendung griech. u. jüd. Motive in den Ged. Philons über d. Stellung Gottes zu s. Freunden, Diss. Würzb. '37; WGrundmann, NovT 3, '59, 62–9. Also AvHarnack, Die Terminologie der Wiedergeburt: TU 42, '18, 97ff. Jesus is τελωνῶν φίλος καὶ ἁμαρτωλῶν Mt 11: 19; Lk 7: 34. Joseph of Arimathaea is ὁ φίλος Πιλάτου καὶ τοῦ κυρίου GP 2: 3. Rarely w. gen. of the thing φίλος τοῦ κόσμου Js 4: 4. Cf. 2 Cl 6: 5.
   β. in a special sense (Hdt. 1, 65=Galen, Protr. 9 p. 28, 26 J.: Lycurgus as φίλος of Zeus; Diod. S. 5, 7, 7 διὰ τὴν ὑπερβολὴν τῆς εὐσεβείας φίλον τῶν θεῶν ὀνομασθῆναι; Ael. Aristid. 27, 36 K.=16 p. 297 D.: θεῶν φίλοι; Sib. Or. 2, 245 Moses as ὁ μέγας φίλος Ὑψίστοιο): on Abraham as φίλος (τοῦ) θεοῦ Js 2: 23; 1 Cl 17: 2; cf. 10: 1 and s. Ἀβραάμ and MDibelius, exc. on Js 2: 23. On ὁ φίλος τοῦ νυμφίου J 3: 29 s. νυμφίος and cf. Sappho, fgm. 124; Paus. Attic. [II AD] ζ, 3 [HErbse '50]. On φίλος τοῦ Καίσαρος J 19: 12 s. Καῖσαρ and EBammel, ThLZ 77, '52, 205–10.
   b. ἡ φίλη the (woman) friend (X., Mem. 2, 1, 23; Jos., Ant. 9, 65 al.) pl. τὰς φίλας her women friends GP 12: 51. W. γείτονες Lk 15: 9 (s. γείτων).—GFuchs, D. Aussagen über d. Freundsch. im NT vergl. m. denen d. Aristot., Diss. Leipzig '14; FHauck, D. Freundschaft b. d. Griechen u. im NT: Festgabe f. ThZahn '28, 211–28. See s.v. ἑταῖρος. M-M.*

φιλοσοφία, ας, ἡ (Pla., Isocr. et al.; 4 Macc; Ep. Arist. 256; Philo; Jos., C. Ap. 1, 54, Ant. 18, 11 al.) philosophy, in our lit. only in one pass. and in an unfavorable sense, w. κενὴ ἀπάτη, of a kind of false teaching Col 2: 8 (perhaps in a bad sense also in the Herm. wr. Κόρη Κόσμου in Stob. I p. 407 W.=494, 7 Sc.=Κόρη Κόσμου 68 (vol. IV p. 22, 9 Nock-Festugière). In 4 Macc 5: 11 the tyrant Antiochus terms the Jewish religion a φλύαρος φιλοσοφία).— GBornkamm, D. Haeresie des Kol: ThLZ 73, '48, 11–20. —OMichel, TW IX, 169–85. M-M.*

φιλόσοφος, ου, ὁ (as subst. X., Pla.+; inscr., pap.; Da 1: 20; Ep. Arist.; Philo; Jos., C. Ap. 1, 176; loanw. in rabb.)

philosopher of Epicureans and Stoics Ac 17: 18 (Jos., C. Ap. 2, 168 ἀπὸ τ. στοᾶς φιλόσοφοι). An ironical judgment on the nature philosophers τοὺς κενοὺς καὶ ληρώδεις λόγους τῶν ἀξιοπίστων φιλοσόφων Dg 8: 2 (on unfavorable judgments concerning philosophers s. Cumont³ '31, 171f; 303, 88). M-M.*

φιλοστοργία, ας, ἡ (X.+; inscr., pap.; 2 Macc 6: 20; 4 Macc 15: 9; Jos., Ant. 8, 193 al.) heartfelt love, strong affection πρός τινα to someone (Polyb. 31, 25, 1 πρὸς ἀλλήλους; Plut., Mor. 962A; Lucian, Tyrann. 1; Philo, Mos. 1, 150) of the love of Christians to each other Dg 1.*

φιλόστοργος, ον (X.+; inscr.; PMich. 148 II, 9 [I AD]; 4 Macc 15: 13; Philo; Jos., Ant. 7, 252 al.) loving dearly τῇ φιλαδελφίᾳ εἰς ἀλλήλους φιλόστοργοι devoted to one another in brotherly love Ro 12: 10.—CSpicq, Φιλόστοργος: RB 62, '55, 497–510. M-M.*

φιλότεκνος, ον (Eur., Hdt.+; PMich. 149, 18, 2 [II AD]; Masp. 20, 10; 4 Macc 15: 4f; Philo, Abr. 179) loving one's children, esp. of women (Aristoph. et al.) w. φίλανδρος (Plut., Mor. 769c; inscr. fr. Perg. [Dssm., LO⁴ 268-LAE 315] γυναικὶ φιλάνδρῳ καὶ φιλοτέκνῳ; Sb 330, 4) Tit 2: 4. Of a father in an unfavorable sense (Synes., Ep. 1 p. 157D φιλότεκνος of an indulgent parent; Lucian, Tyrannic. 4 φ. ἐς ὑπερβολήν) φ. ὢν because you are indulgent Hv 1, 3, 1. M-M.*

φιλοτιμέομαι dep. (Andoc., Pla.+; inscr., pap., 4 Macc 1: 35 v.l.[?]; Philo; Jos., Bell. 1, 206) have an one's ambition, consider it an honor, aspire w. inf. foll. (X., Mem. 2, 9, 3 al.; Ep. Arist. 79; Jos., Ant. 3, 207; 15, 330) Ro 15: 20; 2 Cor 5: 9; 1 Th 4: 11. M-M.*

φιλοτιμία, ας, ἡ (trag., Hdt.+; inscr., pap.; Wsd 14: 18; Ep. Arist. 227; Philo; Jos., Ant. 10, 25 περὶ τὸν θεόν) respect, honor εἰς τὰ κωφὰ τὴν αὐτὴν ἐνδείκνυσθαι φιλοτιμίαν show the same respect to dumb (images) Dg 3: 5.*

φιλόϋλος, ον loving material things (cf. Origen, fgm. in Luc. 71, l. 6 ed. MRauer '30, p. 269 φιλούλων καὶ φιλοσωμάτων λόγοι πιθανοί) symbol. πῦρ φιλόϋλον a fire that longs for material things or that desires to be fed w. material things IRo 7: 2 (ὕλη means 'material things' opposed to God 6: 2, elsewh.='firewood' [ὕλη 1]).*

φιλοφρόνως adv. (Soph., Hdt.+; inscr.; BGU 1009, 3 [II BC]; 2 Macc 3: 9; 4 Macc 8: 5; Ep. Arist. 173; Jos., Ant. 11, 340, C. Ap. 2, 210) in a friendly manner, hospitably Ac 28: 7 (Jos., Bell. 6, 115 φιλοφρόνως ἐδέξατο). M-M.*

φιλόφρων, ον, gen. ονος (Pind., X.+; PGrenf. I 30, 5 [II BC]) well-disposed, friendly, kind 1 Pt 3: 8 t.r.*

Φίλων, ωνος, ὁ (a name freq. found; lit. [e.g., Diod. S. 16, 56, 3; 18, 7, 2], inscr.; PHib. 45, 14 [257 BC]; BGU 1206, 6; 1207, 9 [both 28 BC]) Philo, a deacon fr. Cilicia IPhld 11: 1 who, w. Rheus Agathopus, is following Ign. through Smyrna and Philadelphia, in order to overtake him at Troas (s. Hdb. on IPhld 11: 1). ISm 10: 1; 13: 1.*

φιμόω (Aristoph.+; LXX, Joseph.) inf. φιμοῦν and less well attested φιμοῖν 1 Pt 2:15 ℵ (W-H., App. 166, Introd. §410; Bl-D. §91 app.; W-S. §13, 25); fut. φιμώσω; 1 aor. ἐφίμωσα. Pass.: perf. imperative 2 sing. πεφίμωσο; 1 aor. ἐφιμώθην; tie shut, specif. muzzle.
   1. lit. οὐ φιμώσεις βοῦν ἀλοῶντα (Dt 25: 4=Philo, De Virt. 145) 1 Cor 9: 9 v.l.; 1 Ti 5: 18.—2. fig. (put to) silence (PGM 36, 164; Audollent, Defix. Tab. 15, 24; 22, 42) τινά someone Mt 22: 34; 1 Pt 2: 15. Pass. be silenced

861

or *silent* (Lucian, M. Peregr. 15; Cyranides p. 64, 18; Jos., Bell. 1, 16; 438) ὁ δὲ ἐφιμώθη *but he was silent*=could say nothing Mt 22: 12. In exorcisms (ERohde, Psyche³ II '03, 424) φιμώθητι καὶ ἔξελθε ἐξ (ἀπ᾽) αὐτοῦ Mk 1: 25; Lk 4: 35. Addressed to the raging sea σιώπα, πεφίμωσο Mk 4: 39 (Bl-D. §346 w. app.; Rob. 908). M-M.*

φλαγελλόω (s. φραγέλλιον)=φραγελλόω Mk 15: 15 D.*

φλέγω (Hom.+; inscr.; PSI 28, 12; PGM 4, 1732; LXX, En.; Philo, Op. M. 58; Sib. Or. 3, 761) *burn,* pass. *be burned, burn.*
1. lit. (Alciphr. 1, 2, 1; Jos., Bell. 6, 272) of the mud in hell AP 8: 23.—2. fig. (Charito 8, 8, 7; Dio Chrys. 4, 52 φλεγόμενος ὑπὸ τ. φιλοτιμίας; Achilles Tat. 7, 3, 7; schol. on Nicander, Ther. 151; Anth. Pal. 16, 209 ὅλος φλέγομαι; Philo, Leg. All. 3, 224) ἐφλέγοντο ὑπὸ τῆς ὀργῆς *they were inflamed with anger* GP 12: 50. B. 75.*

Φλέγων, οντος, ὁ (a name freq. found among slaves and freedmen; cf. Ltzm., Hdb. on Ro 16: 14) *Phlegon,* an otherw. unknown Christian, recipient of a greeting Ro 16: 14. M-M.*

φλέψ, φλεβός, ἡ (Hdt., Hippocr.+; PMich. 149, 4, 35 [II AD]; Hos 13: 15; Philo, Jos., Bell. 4, 462) *vein* MPol 2: 2 (on the subj. matter Jos., Bell. 2, 612).*

φλογίζω (Soph.+; LXX) *set on fire* τὶ *someth.* Js 3: 6a. Pass. (Philostrat., Ep. 12 p. 230, 29 by love) ibid. b.—NMacnicol, ET 55, '43/'44, 50-2. M-M.*

φλόξ, φλογός, ἡ (Hom.+; Dit., Syll.³ 1170, 24; PGM 4, 3073; LXX, En.; Philo; Jos., Bell. 6, 272, Ant. 13, 139; Test. Jos. 2: 2) *flame* Lk 16: 24. φ. πυρός (Eur., Bacch. 8 al.; LXX; πῦρ 1a) Ac 7: 30 (Ex 3: 2); Hb 1: 7=1 Cl 36: 3 (cf. LRademacher, Lebende Flamme: Wiener Studien für klass. Philol. 49, '32, 115-18); Rv 1: 14; 2: 18; 19: 12. ἐν πυρὶ φλογός *in flaming fire* (Ex 3: 2 B et al.; Sir 45: 19; PsSol 12: 4; the v.l. ἐν φλογὶ πυρός parallels the text of Is 66: 15; cf. Ex 3: 2 text; PKatz, ἐν πυρὶ φλογός: ZNW 46, '55, 133-8) 2 Th 1: 8. μεγάλη φ. *a high flame* (Lucian, Tim. 6) MPol 15: 1. M-M. B. 72.*

φλυαρέω (Hdt.+; PSI 434, 7; 9 [III BC]; Sb 2266, 12) *talk nonsense (about), bring unjustified charges against* (Isocr. 5, 79 w. βλασφημεῖν; X., Hell. 6, 3, 12; Philo, Somn. 2, 291) w. acc. of the pers. (cf. the pass. Diog. L. 7, 173 τὸν Διόνυσον καὶ Ἡρακλέα φλυαρουμένους ὑπὸ τῶν ποιητῶν) and dat. of the thing λόγοις πονηροῖς φλυαρῶν ἡμᾶς 3 J 10. M-M.*

φλύαρος, ον (Menand., Perinth. 15 J.; Dionys. Hal., Comp. Verbi 26 of pers.; Plut., Mor. 39A; 169E; 701A; Ps.-Pla., Axioch. 365E; 369A; Ps.-Lucian, As. 10; 4 Macc 5: 10; Jos., Vi. 150) *gossipy, foolish* 1 Ti 5: 13.*

φοβερός, ά, όν (Aeschyl.+) in our lit. only in the act. sense *causing fear, fearful, terrible, frightful* (Hdt. et al.; BGU 428, 8 [II AD]; LXX; En. 21, 8f; Ezek. Trag. in Euseb., Pr. Ev. 9, 29, 11; Ep. Arist. 194; Philo; Jos., Bell. 4, 510, Ant. 3, 56; 88; Test. Jos. 6: 2) φοβερὰ ἐκδοχὴ κρίσεως Hb 10: 27 (cf. Sib. Or. 3, 634 φοβ. δίκη). τὸ φανταζόμενον 12: 21. ἄκανθα B 7: 11. ἐπιθυμία Hm 12, 1, 2. φοβερόν (sc. ἐστιν) τὸ ἐμπεσεῖν εἰς χεῖρας θεοῦ Hb 10: 31.*

φοβέω (Hom.+; Wsd 17: 9; Jos., Ant. 14, 456), in out lit. only pass. **φοβέομαι** (Hom.+; Dit., Or. 669, 59, Syll.³ 1268, 17b; pap., LXX, En., Philo, Joseph., Test. 12 Patr.) impf. ἐφοβούμην; 1 aor. ἐφοβήθην; 1 fut. φοβηθήσομαι

(Plut., Brut. 40, 9; M. Ant. 9, 1, 7; Jer 40: 9; Jos., C. Ap. 2. 277; cf. Bl-D. §79).
1. *be afraid,* the aor. oft. in the sense *become frightened*
a. intr., abs. ἐφοβήθησαν σφόδρα *they were terribly frightened* (Ex 14: 10; 1 Macc 12: 52) Mt 17: 6; 27: 54. ἐπεστράφην φοβηθείς *I turned around in terror* Hv 4, 3, 7.—Mt 9: 8; 14: 30; 25: 25; Mk 5: 33; Ac 16: 38. ἐφοβοῦντο γάρ *for they were afraid* Mk 16: 8 (Mk 16: 9-20 is now rarely [e.g. by GHartmann, D. Aufbau des Mk '36, 175-263] considered a part of the original gospel of Mk, though most scholars doubt that the gosp. really ended w. the words ἐφ. γάρ. The original ending may have been lost; among the possible reasons given are the accidental loss of the last page of Mark's own first copy [the same defect, at a very early stage, in the case of the 18th book of the Κεστοί of Jul. Africanus: WBauer, Orthodoxy etc. (Engl. tr. of 2d German ed. '64) '71, 159ff. S. also FGKenyon, Papyrus Rolls and the Ending of St. Mk: JTS 40, '39, 56f; CHRoberts, The Ancient Book and the Ending of St. Mk: ibid. 40, '39, 253-7] or by purposeful suppression, perh. because it may have deviated fr. the other accounts of the resurrection [for the purposeful omission of the end of a document cf. Athen. 4, 61 p. 166D on the 10th book of Theopompus' Philippica, ἀφ᾽ ἧς τινες τὸ τελευταῖον μέρος χωρίσαντες, ἐν ᾧ ἐστιν τὰ περὶ τῶν δημαγωγῶν. S. also Diog. L. 7, 34: a report of Isidorus of Pergamum on the systematic mutilation of books in the library there by Athenodorus the Stoic].—Those who conclude that nothing ever came after ἐφ. γάρ must either assume that the evangelist was prevented fr. finishing his work [Zahn et al.], or that he really intended to close the book w. these words [s. γάρ 1a]. A short sentence, composed of a verb+γάρ also Epict. 3, 9, 19; 4, 8, 4; Artem. 4, 64; 1, 33 p. 35, 6; Oenomaus in Euseb., Pr. Ev. 6, 7, 8; Libanius, Or. 53 p. 65, 20 F.; PMich. 149 VI, 37 [II AD]; Plotinus, Ennead 5, 5, a treatise ending in γάρ; PWvanderHorst, JTS 23, '72, 121-4. So e.g. Wlh., Loisy, Lohmeyer ad loc.; ABauer, Wiener Studien 34, '12, 306ff; Lyder Brun, D. Auferst. Christi '25, 10ff; OLinton, ThBl 8, '29, 229-34; JMCreed, JTS 31, '30, 175-80; MGoguel, La foi à la résurr. de Jésus '33, 176ff; HMosbech, Mkevangeliets Slutning: Sv. Exeg. Årsbok 5, '40, 56-73; WC Allen, JTS 47, '46, 46-9 ['feel reverential awe']; ibid. 48, '47, 201-3. S. also EJGoodspeed, Exp. 8th Ser. XVIII '19, 155-60; reconstruction of the 'lost' ending, in Engl., by Gdspd. in his Introd. to the NT '37, 156; HEProbyn, Exp. 9th Ser. IV '25, 120-5; ROKevin, JBL 45, '26, 81-103; MSEnslin, ibid. 46, '27, 62-8; HJCadbury, ibid. 344f; MRist, ATR 14, '32, 143-51; WLKnox, HTR 35, '42, 13ff; EHelzle, Der Schluss des Mk, '59, Diss. Tübingen; FW Danker, CTM 38, '67, 26f; JLuzarraga, Biblica 50, '69, 497-510; KAland, MBlack-Festschr., '69, 157-80). φοβοῦμαι μᾶλλον *I am all the more fearful* IPhld 5: 1. μὴ φοβηθῆτε *do not be afraid* Mt 10: 31 t.r. (μὴ A III 5a). μὴ φοβοῦ, μὴ φοβεῖσθε *you must no longer be afraid, stop being afraid* (μὴ A III 3b) Mt 10: 31; 14: 27; 17: 7; Mk 5: 36; Lk 1: 13, 30; 2: 10; 5: 10; 8: 50; 12: 7 al. LKöhler, D. Offenbarungsformel 'Fürchte dich nicht!': SchThZ 36, '19, 33ff.—W. acc. of the inner obj. (Bl-D. §153, 1 w. app.; Rob. 468; Pla., Prot. 360B; Ael. Aristid. 30 p. 586 D.: φοβοῦμαι φόβον. On the LXX usage cf. MJohannessohn, Der Gebr. der Kasus in LXX, Diss. Berlin '10, 73) ὁ φόβος ὃν δεῖ σε φοβηθῆναι *the fear which you must have* Hm 7: 1c. ἐφοβήθησαν φόβον μέγαν (Jon 1: 10; 1 Macc 10: 8) *they were very much afraid* Mk 4: 41; Lk 2: 9. In case the nouns are to be taken in the pass. sense, this is also the place for τὸν φόβον αὐτῶν (objective gen.) μὴ

φοβηθῆτε 1 Pt 3: 14 (cf. Is 8: 12) and μὴ φοβούμεναι μηδεμίαν πτόησιν vs. 6 (πτόησις 2); s. 1bγ below.—A class. expr., though favored by the OT (Lev 26: 2; Dt 1: 29; Jer 1: 8, 17; Jdth 5: 23; 1 Macc 2: 62; 8: 12; En. 106, 4; Bl-D. §149; Rob. 577) φοβ. ἀπό τινος be afraid of someone Mt 10: 28a; Lk 12: 4; 1 Cl 56: 11 (Job 5: 22).—Foll. by gen. absol. 56: 10. Foll. by μή and the aor. subj. to denote that which one fears (Thu. 1, 36, 1; Aesop, Fab. 317 H.; Alex. Aphr. 31, II 2 p. 203, 20 τὸν Ἀπόλλω φοβεῖσθαι μή τι παρελθῇ τούτων ἄπρακτον=Apollo is concerned [almost as much as 'sees to it'] that nothing of this remains undone; Jos., Ant. 10, 8, Vi. 252) Ac 23: 10; 27: 17; ITr 5: 1; Hs 9, 20, 2. Foll. by μήποτε (Phlegon: 257 fgm. 36, 2, 4 Jac. φοβοῦμαι περὶ ὑμῶν, μήποτε): Hm 12, 5, 3. φοβηθῶμεν μήποτε δοκῇ τις Hb 4: 1; μήπου Ac 27: 29; μήπως 27: 29 t.r.; 2 Cor 11: 3; 12: 20. A notable feature is the prolepsis of the obj. (cf. Soph., Oed. Rex 767; Thu. 4, 8, 7) φοβοῦμαι ὑμᾶς μήπως εἰκῇ κεκοπίακα εἰς ὑμᾶς I am afraid for you, lest I might have expended my labor on you in vain Gal 4: 11 (Bl-D. §476, 3; Rob. 423).—W. inf. foll. be afraid to do or shrink from doing someth. (Bl-D. §392, 1b.—X., An. 1, 3, 17 al.; Gen 19: 30; 26: 7) Mt 1: 20; 2: 22; Mk 9: 32; Lk 9: 45; 2 Cl 5: 1.—φοβεῖσθαι abs. in the sense take care πλέον φοβεῖσθαι be more careful than usually ITr 4: 1.

b. trans. fear someone or someth.—α. pers. τινά someone (X., An. 3, 2, 19 al.; PGM 4, 2171; Num 21: 34; Dt 3: 2; Jos., Ant. 13, 26) μὴ φοβηθῆτε αὐτούς Mt 10: 26. Ἡρῴδης ἐφοβεῖτο τὸν Ἰωάννην Mt 6: 20. τοὺς Ἰουδαίους J 9: 22.—Gal 2: 12; 2 Cl 5: 4b (saying of Jesus). God Mt 10: 28b; Lk 12: 5a, b, c; 23: 40; 2 Cl 5: 4c (saying of Jesus). The crowd Mt 14: 5; 21: 26, 46; Mk 11: 32; 12: 12; Lk 20: 19; 22: 2; Ac 5: 26 (foll. by μή). τὴν ἐξουσίαν (ἐξουσία 4ca) Ro 13: 3. The angel of repentance Hm 12, 4, 1; s 6, 2, 5. The Christian is to have no fear of the devil Hm 7: 2a; 12, 4, 6f; 12, 5, 2.

β. animals (symbol.) μὴ φοβείσθωσαν τὰ ἀρνία τοὺς λύκους 2 Cl 5: 4a (saying of Jesus, fr. an unknown source).

γ. things τὶ someth. (X., Hell. 4, 4, 8 al.; En. 103, 4; Jos., C. Ap. 1, 90; 2, 232) τὸ διάταγμα τοῦ βασιλέως Hb 11: 23. τὸν θυμὸν τοῦ βασιλέως vs. 27. τὴν κρίσιν 2 Cl 18: 2. τὸν ὄντως θάνατον Dg 10: 7. φοβοῦμαι τὴν ὑμῶν ἀγάπην, μή ... IRo 1: 2. τὰ ὅπλα (symbol.) Hm 12, 2, 4.—1 Pt 3: 14 and 6 belong here in case the nouns in them are to be taken in an act. sense; s. 1a above.—Fear, avoid, shun τὶ someth. (Ps.-Callisth. 1, 41, 9 Δαρεῖος τὸ ἄρμα φοβηθείς) τὴν πλάνην τῶν ἁμαρτωλῶν B 12: 10. τὰ ἔργα τοῦ διαβόλου Hm 7: 3a, c.—AVStröm, Der Hirt des Hermas Allegorie oder Wirklichkeit? Ntl. Sem. Uppsala 3, '36.

2. (have) reverence, respect—a. (for) God, fear (differently 1ba above) him in the sense reverence (Aeschyl., Suppl. 893 δαίμονας; Isocr. 1, 16 τοὺς μὲν θεοὺς φοβοῦ, τοὺς δὲ γονεῖς τίμα; Pla., Leg. 11 p. 927A; Lysias 9, 17; 32, 17; Plut., De Superstit. 2 p. 165B; LXX; Philo, Migr. Abr. 21 [after Gen 42: 18]. Cf. PTebt. 59, 10 [II BC] φοβεῖσθαι καὶ σέβεσθαι τὸ ἱερόν) Lk 1: 50; 18: 2, 4; Ac 10: 35; 1 Pt 2: 17; Rv 14: 7; 19: 5; 1 Cl 21: 7; 23: 1; 28: 1; 45: 6; B 10: 10f (τὸν κύριον); 19: 2, 7; Hm 1: 2; 7: 1, 4f; Hs 5, 1, 5; 8, 11, 2; D 4: 10. Also τὸ ὄνομα τοῦ θεοῦ (2 Esdr 11 [Neh 1]: 11) Rv 11: 18.—φοβούμενοι τὸν θεόν as a t.t.=φοβούμενοι τὸν θεόν (σέβω 2a) Ac 13: 16, 26; sing. 10: 2, 22.—τὸν κύριον (=Christ) Col 3: 22.—WCAllen (s. 1a above) interprets Mk 16: 8 to mean reverence for the divine.

b. for men who command respect (Plut., Galba 3, 4;

Herodian 3, 13, 2; Lev 19: 3 φοβ. πατέρα καὶ μητέρα): of a wife ἵνα φοβῆται τὸν ἄνδρα Eph 5: 33. τὸν ἐπίσκοπον IEph 6: 1.—HBalz, TW IX, 186–216: φοβ. and related words. M-M.

φόβητρον and φόβηθρον (different suffixes; cf. Bl-D. §35, 3; Mlt.-H. 110; Thackeray 104), ου, τό (Hippocr., Morb. Sacr. 1 vol. VI p. 362 L.; Ps.-Pla., Axioch. 367A; Lucian, Alex. 25; Anth. Pal. 11, 189, 3 Düb.; Is 19: 17) terrible sight or event, horror. Pl. φοβητρά τε καὶ σημεῖα ἔσται there will be dreadful portents and signs Lk 21: 11. M-M.*

φόβος, ου, ὁ (Hom. +; inscr., pap., LXX, En., Ep. Arist., Philo, Joseph., Test. 12 Patr., Sib. Or. 3, 679).

1. act. the causing of fear (Appian, Bell. Civ. 3, 27 §104 ἐς φ. τῆς βουλῆς=to intimidate the Senate) so perh. τὸν φόβον αὐτῶν μὴ φοβηθῆτε 1 Pt 3: 14 (Is 8: 12; s. φοβέω 1bγ). Also concrete that which arouses fear, a terror (Soph., Philoct. 1251; Polyb. 11, 30, 2; Appian, Bell. Civ. 2, 135 §565; Dit., Syll.³ 442, 10 [III BC] οὐδένα οὔτε φόβον οὔτε κίνδυνον ὑποστελλόμενοι) οἱ ἄρχοντες οὐκ εἰσὶν φόβος Ro 13: 3. So perh. also εἰδότες οὖν τὸν φόβον τοῦ κυρίου since we know what it is that causes fear of the Lord 2 Cor 5: 11 (i.e. the judgment to come, vs. 10; s. also Field, Notes 183f); s. 2ba below.

2. pass.—a. fear, alarm, fright—a. gener. 2 Cor 7: 11; 1 Pt 1: 17 (mng. fear of the coming judge, unless ἐν φ. here means reverently, as EGSelwyn, 1 Pt '46, 143); Jd 23 (mng. the fear of defiling oneself); Dg 7: 3. W. τρόμος (q.v.) 1 Cor 2: 3; 2 Cor 7: 15; 1 Cl 12: 5. Pl. fears, apprehensions, feelings of anxiety (also class.; Diod. S. 16, 3, 1; 16, 42, 9; Appian, Bell. Civ. 1, 16 §67; 3, 89 §368; Dit., Syll.³ 326, 21 [307/6 BC]; Job 20: 25; Wsd 18: 17; Jos., Ant. 10, 24; 15, 44) ἔξωθεν μάχαι ἔσωθεν φόβοι 2 Cor 7: 5. παράγειν φόβους ἀνθρωπίνους bring in fears of men 2 Cl 10: 3.—W. the obj. gen. of the pers. (Diod. S. 10, 19, 6 ὁ τῶν Περσῶν φόβος), or of the thing (Jos., C. Ap. 1, 259) causing the fear ὁ φόβος τῶν Ἰουδαίων the fear of the Jews J 7: 13; 19: 38; 20: 19. φόβος θανάτου fear of death (Epict. 2, 1, 14; 2, 18, 30 et al.; Philo, Omn. Prob. Lib. 111) Hb 2: 15. τοῦ βασανισμοῦ Rv 18: 10, 15. νόμου Dg 11: 6.—ἀπὸ (τοῦ) φόβου (τινός) because of, out of fear (of someone) Mt 14: 26; 28: 4; Lk 21: 26; Hm 11: 14. Also διὰ τ. φόβον Ac 26: 14 v.l. (Hyperid. 5, 5 διὰ τὸν φ. (Arrian, Anab. 5, 15, 6 διὰ τὸν φ.; Artem. 1, 1 p. 3, 23 διὰ φόβον; Philo, Mos. 1, 164 διὰ φόβον τινός; Jos., Vi. 354 διὰ τὸν φόβον). μετὰ φόβον with or in fear (Aeneas Tact. 1257) of the feeling that accompanies an action Mt 28: 8; Dg 12: 6. —As subject (En. 100, 8): φόβος πίπτει ἐπί τινα fear comes upon someone Ac 19: 17 v.l.; Rv 11: 11 t.r. ἐπιπίπτει ἐπί τινα Lk 1: 12; Ac 19: 17; Rv 11: 11. ἐστὶν ἐπί τινα Ac 2: 43 v.l. γίνεται ἐπί τινα Lk 1: 65; Ac 5: 5, 11 or γίνεταί τινι Ac 2: 43. λαμβάνει τινά (Jos., Vi. 148) Lk 7: 16; Hv 5: 4. πλησθῆναι φόβου Lk 5: 26. φόβῳ συνέχεσθαι 8: 37. φόβον ἔχειν 1 Ti 5: 20; Hm 7: 2c; 12, 4, 7a; s 1: 10. φοβεῖσθαι φόβον (μέγαν) Mk 4: 41; Lk 2: 9; cf. 1 Pt 3: 14 (s. 1 above); Hm 7: 1 (φοβέω 1a).

β. specif. of slavish fear (Diog. Cyn. in Diog. L. 6, 75 δούλου τὸ φοβεῖσθαι), which is not to characterize the Christian's relation to God οὐκ ἐλάβετε πνεῦμα δουλείας εἰς φόβον you have not received a spirit of slavery, to cause you to fear Ro 8: 15. Cf. 1 J 4: 18a, b, c (opp. ἀγάπη. Cf. κόλασις 2, end).

b. reverence, respect—a. toward God (Polyaenus 1, 16, 1; LXX; Ep. Arist. 159 ὁ περὶ θεοῦ φόβος; 189) and Christ, w. τρόμος Phil 2: 12 (s. τρόμος). W. ἀλήθεια 1 Cl

19: 1; Pol 2: 1. W. ἀγάπη 1 Cl 51: 2. W. πίστις, εἰρήνη and other good things and virtues 1 Cl 64. W. ὑπομονή B 2: 2. W. ἐλπὶς εἰς τὸν Ἰησοῦν 11: 11. W. πίστις and ἐγκράτεια Hm 6, 1, 1. W. objective gen. φόβος (τοῦ) θεοῦ (PLond. 1914, 12 φόβον θεοῦ ἔχοντες ἐν τῇ καρδίᾳ; Philo, Spec. Leg. 4, 199; Test. Levi 13: 7, Napht. 2: 9) Ro 3: 18 (Ps 35: 2); 2 Cor 7: 1 (ἀγάπη 𝔓⁴⁶); 1 Cl 3: 4; 21: 6; cf. 8; B 4: 11; 19: 5; 20: 2; Pol 4: 2; Hm 10, 1, 6a; 12, 2, 4b, c; D 4: 9. φόβος (τοῦ) κυρίου (Test. Reub. 4: 1, Sim. 3: 4) Ac 9: 31; 1 Cl 22: 1 (Ps 33: 12); 57: 5 (Pr 1: 29); B 11: 5 (Is 33: 18 v.l.); Hm 7: 4b; 8: 9; 10, 1, 6b; 12, 2, 4a; 12, 3, 1. This may also be the place for 2 Cor 5: 11 (s. 1 above). φόβος Χριστοῦ Eph 5: 21.—For 1 Pt 1: 17 s. 2aα above.

β. toward men, *respect* that is due officials Ro 13: 7a, b (CEBCranfield, NTS 6, '60, 241-9: the ref. may be to God); fr. the slave to his master 1 Pt 2: 18; Eph 6: 5 (w. τρόμος); B 19: 7=D 4: 11 (w. αἰσχύνη); the wife to her husband 1 Pt 3: 2. Gener. 3: 16 (w. πραΰτης).—SFHJ Berkelbach v. der Sprenkel, Vrees en Religie '20; WLütgert, Die Furcht Gottes: MKähler-Festschr. '05, 165ff; RSander, Furcht u. Liebe im palästin. Judentum '35. M-M. B. 1153. **

Φοίβη, ης, ἡ (freq. in mythology, but also e.g. Dit., Syll.³ 805, 10 [c. 54 AD]; PFlor. 50, 61 [III AD]) *Phoebe,* a Christian woman, διάκονος τῆς ἐκκλησίας τῆς ἐν Κεγχρεαῖς (διάκονος 2b), recommended by Paul to the church for which Ro 16: 1 is intended. Cf. Ro subscr.—MDGibson, Phoebe: ET 23, '12, 281; EJGoodspeed, HTR 44, '51, 55-7. M-M. *

Φοινίκη, ης, ἡ (Hom. +; inscr., pap. [e.g. Sb 8008, 34; 51; 56 (261 BC)]; LXX, Ep. Arist., Philo; Joseph., index; Sib. Or.) *Phoenicia,* in NT times the name of the seacoast of central Syria, w. Tyre and Sidon as the most important cities Ac 11: 19; 15: 3; 21: 2. HGuthe, RE XVIII '06, 280-302 (lit.); OEissfeldt, 'Phöniker' and 'Phönikia': Pauly-W. XVII '36. *

Φοινίκισσα s. Συροφοινίκισσα.

φοινικοῦς, ῆ, οῦν *purple-red* (so X. et al.; Dit., Syll.³ 1018, 4; Philo, Leg. All. 3, 57) subst. τὸ φοινικοῦν (w. χρῶμα or ἱμάτιον understood) *purple* (or *red*) *color* or *garment* 1 Cl 8: 4 (Is 1: 18). *

I. φοῖνιξ or **φοίνιξ, ικος, ὁ** *the palm-tree, the date-palm*—**1.** the tree as such (Hom. +; pap., LXX; En. 24, 4; Ep. Arist. 63; Joseph.); at one time evidently a common tree in Palestine, since it is oft. depicted on coins; esp. common in Jericho, the 'city of palms' (Jos., Ant. 14, 54; 15, 96), where there were many more palms at the time of the crusades than at present. τὰ βάϊα τῶν φοινίκων *the branches of palm-trees, the palm-branches* J 12: 13 (s. βάϊον and HBornhäuser, Sukka '35, 106f).—Theobald Fischer, Die Dattelpalme 1881; JTaglicht, Die Dattelpalme in Paläst.: AdSchwarz-Festschr. '17, 403-16; ILöw, Die Flora der Juden II '24, 306-62.

2. *palm-branch, palm-leaf* (Arist., Eth. Magn. 1, 34 p. 1196a, 36 ὁ λαβὼν τὸν φ. ἐν τοῖς ἀγῶσιν; 2 Macc 10: 7; 14: 4; Philo, Agr. 112, Deus Imm. 137 φ. τ. νίκης) φοίνικες ἐν τ. χερσὶν αὐτῶν Rv 7: 9. στέφανοι ἐκ φοινίκων γεγονότες *wreaths made of palm-leaves* Hs 8, 2, 1. M-M. *

II. φοῖνιξ or **φοίνιξ, ικος, ὁ** *the phoenix,* the fabulous bird of Egypt (since Hes., fgm. 171 Rzach³=fgm. 304 Merkelbach-West [Oxford Text]; Hdt. 2, 73; Artem. 4, 47; Achilles Tat. 3, 25; PGM 5, 253; 12, 231; Sib. Or. 8, 139; Celsus 4, 98; cf. RKnopf, Hdb. exc. on 1 Cl 25) 1 Cl 25:

2.—WHRoscher, Lexikon der Mythologie III 2, 3450-72: Phönix; FSchöll, Vom Vogel Phönix 1890; FZimmermann, Die Phönixsage: ThGl 4, '12, 202-23; ThHopfner, D. Tierkult der alten Ägypter: Denkschr. der Wiener Ak. '14; RvdBroek, The Myth of the Phoenix acc. to Class. and Early Christian Trad. '72. *

III. Φοῖνιξ, ικος, ὁ *Phoenix,* a sea-port city on the south coast of Crete, west of Lasaea (Strabo 10, 4, 3; Ptolem. 3, 17, 3; Stadiasmus sive Periplus Maris Magni §328) Ac 27: 12.—HBalmer, D. Romfahrt des Ap. Pls '05, 319ff; Zahn, AG II '21, 825ff; RMOgilvie, JTS 9, '58, 308-14. *

φοιτάω (Hom. +; inscr., pap.; Jos., Ant. 3, 275, C. Ap. 2, 284; Sib. Or. 4, 74) *go back and forth, move about* (*regularly*) of animals upon the earth 1 Cl 33: 3 (Hdt. 1, 78 of horses at pasture). *

φονεύς, έως, ὁ (Hom. +; BGU 1024 VIII, 11; PLeipz. 37, 25; Wsd 12: 5; Joseph.) *murderer* Mt 22: 7 (SvanTilborg, The Jewish Leaders in Mt, '72, 46-72); Ac 7: 52 (w. obj. gen., as Jos., Ant. 1, 57); 28: 4; 1 Pt 4: 15; AP 10: 25. In lists of vices Rv 21: 8; 22: 15; B 20: 2; D 5: 2 (the last two φονεῖς τέκνων). ἀνὴρ φ. Ac 3: 14. M-M. *

φονεύω fut. φονεύσω; 1 aor. ἐφόνευσα; 1 fut. pass. φονευθήσομαι (Pind., Aeschyl., Hdt. +; inscr., pap., LXX; En. 22, 12; Philo, Det. Pot. Ins. 178; Jos., Bell. 2, 654, Ant. 9, 187, C. Ap. 2, 213) *murder, kill,* abs. οὐ φονεύσεις *you shall not commit murder* (Ex 20: 15) Mt 5: 21a (cf. ibid. b); 19: 18; Ro 13: 9; D 2: 2a; also μὴ φονεύσῃς Mk 10: 19; Lk 18: 20; Js 2: 11a. Cf. ibid. b; 4: 2 (where the conjecture φθονεῖτε, originated by Erasmus, has been favored by Calvin, Spitta, JBMayor, Belser, Windisch, Dibelius, Hauck, Moffatt.—De Wette, Beyschlag, Meinertz et al. prefer to take φονεύω in a fig. sense [cf. PLond. 113, 12d, 11 (c. 600 AD) ὁ χρεώστης ἐφόνευσέν με. A similar expr. as early as Herodas 6, 26 αὕτη μ' ἡ γυνή ποτε ἐκτρίψει=this woman will be the death of me yet], of anger; GHRendall, The Ep. of St. James and Judaic Christianity '27, 30f; 113 takes it literally, as do many before him). τινὰ someone Mt 23: 31, 35; Js 5: 6. φ. τέκνον ἐν φθορᾷ B 19: 5; D 2: 2b (cf. φθορά 2a). Pass. *be put to death, die a violent death* 1 Cl 57: 7 (Pr 1: 32); GP 2: 5; 5: 15. M-M. *

φόνος, ου, ὁ (Hom. +; inscr., pap., LXX, Philo; Jos., C. Ap. 2, 205; Sib. Or. 3, 392) *murder, killing* Mk 15: 7; Lk 23: 19, 25; Ac 9: 1. ἐν φόνῳ μαχαίρης (Ex 17: 13; Dt 13: 16; 20: 13) (*by being murdered*) *with the sword* Hb 11: 37. Anger as a cause D 3: 2a. Pl. *bloody deeds* (Diod. S. 13, 48, 2; Ael. Aristid. 35, 7 K.=9 p. 100 D.; Lucian, Catapl. 27 al.; 2 Macc 4: 3; Jos., C. Ap. 2, 269, Vi. 103) 3: 2b. W. other sins Mt 15: 19; Mk 7: 21; Rv 9: 21. In lists of vices (cf. Dio Chrys. 17[34], 19 codd.; Hos 4: 2) Ro 1: 29 (sing. w. φθόνος.—A similar play on words in Appian, Hann. 21 §93 φόνος τε καὶ πόνος); B 20: 1 (sing.); D 5: 1 (pl.). M-M. B. 1455. *

φορά, ᾶς, ἡ (X., Pla.; inscr., pap., Philo) *rapid motion,* fig. *impulse, passion* ἀτάκτοις φοραῖς φέρεσθαι *let oneself be borne along by unbridled passions* Dg 9: 1. *

φορέω fut. φορέσω; 1 aor. ἐφόρεσα; pf. πεφόρηκα (Bl-D. §70, 1; W-S. §13, 3) (Hom. +; inscr., pap., LXX) *bear* (in contrast to φέρω) *for a considerable time* or *regularly,* hence *wear.*

1. lit., clothing (X., An. 7, 4, 4; Herm. Wr. 7, 2b; Jos., Ant. 3, 153 ἔνδυμα; 279; Dit., Syll.³ 736, 177; POxy. 531, 14; 15 [II AD]; 1300, 10; PGiess. 47, 8 [armor]; Sir 11: 5

διάδημα; Ep. Arist.) Mt 11: 8; Js 2: 3. A wreath (Sir 40: 4; Test. Benj. 4: 1) and a purple garment (Jos., Ant. 10, 235) J 19: 5 (Dit., Syll.³ 1018, 1f φορείτω χλαμύδα καὶ στέφανον). Fetters 1 Cl 5: 6. τὴν μάχαιραν Ro 13: 4.

2. fig. ὄνομα φορεῖν *bear a name* (Soph., fgm. 658) Hs 9, 13, 2a, c; 3a, b, c, d; 5; 9, 14, 5f; 9, 15, 2f; 9, 16, 3. δύναμιν 9, 13, 2b. πνεύματα 9, 15, 6; 9, 16, 1; 9, 17, 4. φορ. τὴν εἰκόνα τοῦ χοϊκοῦ *bear the image of the earthly* man, i.e. represent in one's own appearance 1 Cor 15: 49a; cf. b. M-M.*

φόρον, ου, τό cf. Ἀππίου φόρον. M-M.

φόρος, ου, ὁ *tribute, tax* (Hdt., Aristoph.+; inscr., pap., LXX), in our lit. in the expr. *pay taxes* or *tribute* φόρον (φόρους) δοῦναι (1 Macc 8: 4, 7) Lk 20: 22; 23: 2 (cf. Jos., Bell. 2, 403 Καίσαρι δεδώκατε τὸν φόρον); ἀποδοῦναι (Jos., Ant. 14, 203, C. Ap. 1, 119) Ro 13: 7 (φόρ. twice: *pay tribute to the one entitled to receive tribute*); τελεῖν (Jos., Ant. 5, 181; 12, 182) vs. 6 (φόρους). M-M. B. 802.*

φορτίζω (mid. in Hes.; act. and pass. in Lucian, Navig. 45; Babrius 111, 3; Anth. Pal. 10, 5, 5; Ezk 16: 33) pf. pass. ptc. πεφορτισμένος *load, burden* τινά τι *someone with someth.*, more exactly *cause someone to carry someth.* (Bl-D. §155, 7; Rob. 484) symbol., of the burden of keeping the law φορτίζετε τοὺς ἀνθρώπους φορτία δυσβάστακτα Lk 11: 46. Pass. οἱ κοπιῶντες καὶ πεφορτισμένοι (*you who are*) *weary and burdened* Mt 11: 28 (ThHaering, Mt 11: 28–30: ASchlatter-Festschr. '22, 3–15). M-M.*

φορτίον, ου, τό (in form, a dim. of φόρτος.—Hes.+; IG IV² 1, 123, 6 [IV BC], pap., LXX, Joseph.) *burden, load*— **1.** lit. φορτίον βαστάζειν (Teles p. 10 H.; Herm. Wr. 10, 8b) Hs 9, 2, 4. Of the *cargo* of a ship (Hes., X.+; Jos., Ant. 14, 377; POxy. 1153, 9 [I AD]) Ac 27: 10 (t.r. φόρτος). **2.** symbol. (Epict. 2, 9, 22; 4, 13, 16), of the oppressive burden of the law Mt 23: 4; Lk 11: 46a, b. Cf. Mt 11: 30. φορτίον βαστάζειν (Diog. L. 7, 170; Pythagorean in Stob., Flor. 85, 15 V 680 H.) Gal 6: 5 (everyone is to concern himself about his own burden, rather than to compare himself complacently w. others). M-M.*

φόρτος, ου, ὁ (Hom.+; PLond. 307 [II AD]) *burden*, esp. the *cargo* of a ship (Lucian, Nav. 18, V. Hist. 1, 34; Achilles Tat. 3, 2, 9; Jos., C. Ap. 1, 63; Sib. Or. 8, 348) Ac 27: 10 t.r.; s. φορτίον 1.*

Φορτουνᾶτος, ου, ὁ (Lat. name. Dit., Or. 707, 5 Φορτουνᾶτος Σεβαστοῦ ἀπελεύθερος; APF 2, '03, 571 no. 151, 5; Jos., Ant. 18, 247. Cf. Lghtf., The Apost. Fathers, P.I. Vol. I 1890 p. 29, 3; 62, 1, exx. fr. Lat. sources) *Fortunatus.* **1.** an otherw. unknown Christian of Corinth who, w. his Christian fellow-townsmen Stephanas and Achaicus, was w. Paul in Ephesus when 1 Cor was written, 1 Cor 16: 15 v.l., 17; subscr.—**2.** a member of the delegation sent by the Roman church to Corinth 1 Cl 65: 1. M-M.*

φραγ- s. φράσσω.

φραγέλλιον, ου, τό (Lat. loanw.: flagellum [Horace, Sat. 1, 3, 119 horribile flagellum]. In the form φλαγέλλιον PLond. 191, 11 [II AD]; CWessely, Wiener Studien 24, '02 p. 150. Loanw. in rabb. Bl-D. §5, 1b; 41, 2; Mlt.-H. 103; 396; Hahn 261; 265. The spelling φραγέλλιον is found only in very late sources) *whip, lash* J 2: 15. M-M.*

φραγελλόω (in Christian usage [e.g. Πραξεις Παυλου ed. CSchmidt '36, 1, 30]; but cf. Test. Benj. 2, 3 and Aesop fr.

the Cod. Paris. 1277: ChRochefort, Notices et Extraits II 1789 p. 719 no. 19) 1 aor. ἐφραγέλλωσα (Lat. loanw.: flagello; s. φλαγελλόω) *flog, scourge*, a punishment inflicted on slaves and provincials after a sentence of death had been pronounced on them. So in the case of Jesus before the crucifixion (cf. Jos., Bell. 2, 306 οὓς μάστιξιν προαικισάμενος ἀνεσταύρωσεν [sc. Φλῶρος]; 5, 449; Lucian, Pisc. 2) Mt 27: 26; Mk 15: 15 (Mommsen, Röm. Strafrecht 1899, 938f; 983f). M-M.*

φραγμός, οῦ, ὁ (Soph., Hdt.+; BGU 1119, 32 [5 BC]; POxy. 580; LXX, Philo) *fence, wall, hedge*—**1.** lit. (Theocr. 5, 108 the fence around the vineyard) περιέθηκεν φραγμόν (Is 5: 2) Mk 12: 1; w. dat. of the piece of ground enclosed Mt 21: 33. ἄμπελος ἐν φραγμῷ τινι καταλειφθεῖσα *a vine that stands forsaken somewhere along the fence* Hs 9, 26, 4. Vagabonds and beggars frequent the hedges and fences around houses Lk 14: 23. **2.** fig., of the law, that separates Jews and Gentiles, and arouses enmity betw. them τὸ μεσότοιχον τοῦ φραγμοῦ Eph 2: 14 (s. μεσότοιχον and PFeine, Eph 2: 14–16: StKr 72, 1899, 540–74). M-M.*

φράζω 1 aor. ἔφρασα, imper. φράσον (Hom.+; inscr., pap., LXX; Jos., Vi. 331, C. Ap. 2, 211; Sib. Or. 14, 301) in our lit. only in the sense *explain, interpret* someth. mysterious (X., Oec. 16, 8; Cebes 33, 1; Herm. Wr. 380, 2 Sc. θεόν; Job 6: 24 φράσατέ μοι) a parable Mt 13: 36 t.r.; 15: 15. M-M.*

φράσσω 1 aor. ἔφραξα. Pass.: 2 aor. ἐφράγην; 2 fut. φραγήσομαι (Hom.+; inscr., pap., LXX; Jos., Bell. 3, 384). **1.** *shut, close, stop*—**a.** lit. (Herodian 8, 1, 6; Lucian, Nigr. 19 τὰ ὦτα κηρῷ φρ.) στόματα λεόντων *mouths of lions*, so that they can do no harm (cf. Da 6: 17ff; vs. 23 Theod. ἐνέφραξεν τὰ στόματα τῶν λεόντων) Hb 11: 33. **b.** fig., *close* or *stop* the mouth, so that the man must remain silent (Galen, Script. Min. I p. 73, 17 Marquardt; Sib. Or. 8, 420 στόμα ἔφραξαν; 1 Macc 9: 55 ἀπεφράγη τὸ στόμα αὐτοῦ) Ro 3: 19. This mng. may be the correct one for ἡ καύχησις αὕτη οὐ φραγήσεται *this boasting will not be silenced* 2 Cor 11: 10. But φράσσω also means **2.** *stop, block, bar* (Thu. 4, 13, 4 φράξαι τοὺς ἔσπλους; Dio Chrys. 19[36], 2 pass.); in that case 2 Cor 11: 10 means *this boasting will not (let itself) be stopped*. M-M.*

φρέαρ, ατος, τό (Hom. Hymns, Hdt.+; inscr., pap., LXX, Philo) *a well* purposely dug (Appian, Bell. Civ. 4, 107 §448; Arrian, Anab. 6, 18, 1; 6, 20, 4; Jos., Ant. 4, 283 οἱ φρέαρ ὀρύξαντες; Philo, Somn. 1, 8 [after Gen 26: 32]. —Contrast: πηγή—φρέαρ Paus 1, 14; Philo, Poster. Cai. 153) Lk 14: 5; J 4: 11 (Gen 21: 19 φρέαρ ὕδατος ζῶντος; 26: 19), 12 (Hom. Hymns, Demeter 98f the motif of the divine wanderer who sits down near the city φρέατι, ὅθεν ὑδρεύοντο πολῖται).—Also *pit, shaft* (Hero Alex. I p. 32, 12; 15), leading down into the depths of hell (ἄβυσσος 2. —Ps 54: 24 φρέαρ διαφθορᾶς) Rv 9: 1, 2a, b, c. M-M. B. 44.*

φρεναπατάω (in Christian usage; Hesychius; but cf. φρεναπάτης) *deceive* ἑαυτόν *oneself* Gal 6: 3. M-M.*

φρεναπάτης, ου, ὁ (Herodian Gr. II 848, 27; PGrenf. I 1, 10 [II BC]=Coll. p. 178 l. 18; cf. UvWilamowitz, NGG 1896, 209ff; PLond. 1677, 22 [VI AD]) *deceiver, misleader* (w. ματαιολόγος) Tit 1: 10. M-M.*

φρήν, φρενός, ἡ pl. αἱ φρένες (Hom.+; inscr., pap., LXX, Philo) in our lit. only in one place and only in the pl.

as *thinking, understanding* (Hom.+; Plut., Mor. 116в
φρένας ἔχειν; Herm. Wr. 13, 4; 5; Pr 7: 7; 9: 4 al.) 1 Cor
14: 20a, b.—GBertram, TW IX, 216–31: φρήν and
related words. M-M. B. 1198.*

φρίκη, ης, ἡ (Soph., Hdt.+; Dit., Syll.³ 1239, 19; Am 1:
11) *a shudder* caused by fear (Eur. et al.; Plut., Arat. 32,
2; Job 4: 14; Jos., Bell. 5, 565; 6, 123) Hv 3, 1, 5 (w.
τρόμος, as in the Job pass., also Philo, Leg. ad Gai. 267).*

φρίσσω 1 aor. ἔφριξα; pf. ptc. πεφρικώς (Hom.+;
LXX; Sib. Or. 3, 679) *shudder* fr. fear (Hom.+; w. acc. of
the pers. or thing that causes the fear), abs. (Da 7: 15
Theod.; Philo, Det. Pot. Ins. 140) ὅλος ἤμην πεφρικώς
Hv 1, 2, 1. Of demons (who shudder at exorcism: PGM 3,
227; 4, 2541f δαίμονες φρίσσουσί σε; 2829; 12, 118;
Orph. Fgm. in Clem. Alex., Strom. 5, 125, 1; Acta Philippi 132 p. 63 Bonnet; Justin, Dial. 49, 8; Ps.-Clem.,
Hom. 5, 5; Prayer of Manasseh [= Ode 12] 4; Test. Abrah.
[Texts and Studies II 2, 1892] Rec. A 9; 16.—On this subj.
s. the commentaries w. further exx. [without the verb
φρίσσω], esp. Dibelius and JMarty '35, ad loc.; EPeterson, Εἷς Θεός '26, 295–9.—Material and lit. on ὄνομα
φρικτόν in SEitrem, Pap. Osloënses I '25, 98) Js 2: 19.
Symbol. of the earth B 11: 2 (Jer 2: 12). M-M.*

φρονέω impf. ἐφρόνουν; fut. φρονήσω; 1 aor. ἐφρόνησα
(Hom.+; inscr., pap., LXX; Ep. Arist. 236; Philo, Joseph.).
   1. *think, form* or *hold an opinion, judge* ἐφρόνουν ὡς
νήπιος *I thought like a child* 1 Cor 13: 11 (schol. on
Apollon. Rhod. 4, 868a νηπίου ὄντος καὶ νήπια φρο-
νοῦντος). καθὼς φρονοῦσιν *as their opinion is* ISm 2.
καλῶς καὶ ἀληθῶς φρονεῖς *your judgment is right and
true* Hm 3: 4. ταῦτα φρονεῖν 9: 12. ἃ φρονεῖς *the views
that you hold* Ac 28: 22. πολλὰ φρονῶ ἐν θεῷ *many
thoughts are mine when I take God's view of things* (so
Kleist) ITr 4: 1. φρονεῖν τι ὑπέρ τινος *think* or *feel in a
certain way about someone* Phil 1: 7. ὑπέρ τινος φρ. *think
of someone* in the sense *be concerned about him* 4: 10a; cf.
ibid. b. φρ. περί τινος *think of* or *about someone* (Wsd
14: 30) 2 Cl 1: 1a. φρ. τι περί τινος *think someth.
concerning someone* (Isocr. 3, 60; Polyaenus 5, 2, 13;
Lucian, Dial. Mort. 20, 5; Jos., Ant. 12, 125, C. Ap. 2,
168) ISm 5: 2. φρ. μικρὰ περί τινος *think little of
someone* 2 Cl 1: 2 (Philo, Spec. Leg. 2, 256 φρ. περὶ
μοναρχίας τὰ ἄριστα). Cf. 1: 1b. On ἵνα ἀδελφὸς ἰδὼν
ἀδελφὴν οὐδὲν φρονῇ περὶ αὐτῆς θηλυκόν 12: 5a s.
θηλυκός; cf. ibid. b. θεὸν δεσπότην φρ. *think of God as
Master* Dg 3: 2. οὐδὲν ἄλλο φρ. *think nothing different,
not take a different view* Gal 5: 10 (Jos., Bell. 5, 326 φρ.
οὐδὲν ὑγιές). τοῦτο φρ. Phil 3: 15a; τι ἑτέρως φρ. *think
of* or *regard someth. differently* ibid. b; τὸ αὐτὸ φρ. *think
the same thing,* i.e. *be in agreement, live in harmony* (Hdt.
1, 60, 2; Dio Chrys. 17[34], 20; Dit., Or. 669, 36) 2 Cor 13:
11; Phil 2: 2a; 3: 16 t.r.; 4: 2; 2 Cl 17: 3. τὸ αὐτὸ φρονεῖν
ἐν ἀλλήλοις Ro 15: 5; εἰς ἀλλήλους 12: 16a. Also τὰ
αὐτὰ φρ. (Hdt. 5, 72, 2; Appian, Bell. Civ. 1, 65 §295 τὰ
αὐτὰ ἐφρόνουν) Hs 9, 13, 7. τὸ ἓν φρ. Phil 2: 2b.—
Cherish thoughts μὴ ὑπερφρονεῖν παρ᾽ ὃ δεῖ φρονεῖν
not to think more highly than one ought to think Ro 12:
3a. Cf. 1 Cor 4: 6 t.r. (cf. Diod. S. 27, 6, 2 τοὺς ὑπὲρ
ἄνθρωπον φρονοῦντας). ὑψηλὰ φρονεῖν *be proud* Ro 11:
20; 1 Ti 6: 17 v.l.
   2. *set one's mind on, be intent on* foll. by the acc.
(Brutus, Ep. 14 τὰ σὰ φρ.) ἀγαθὰ φρ. Hm 10, 3, 1. τὸ
καλὸν φρ. Hs 5, 2, 7. τέλεια ISm 11: 3. τὰ ὑψηλὰ Ro 12:
16b (cf. 2 Macc 9: 12). τὰ ἐπίγεια Phil 3: 19. τὰ ἐπὶ τῆς

γῆς Col 3: 2 (opp. τὰ ἄνω).—φρ. τά τινος *take someone's
side, espouse someone's cause* (Diod. S. 13, 48, 4 and 7
ἐφρόνουν τὰ Λακεδαιμονίων; 13, 72, 1; 14, 32, 4; 20, 35,
2 and oft.; Appian, Liby. 70 §316, Bell. Civ. 3, 85, §351;
Polyaenus 8, 14, 3 τὰ Ῥωμαίων φρ., cf. HAlmqvist,
Plut. u. das NT '46, 56; Herodian 8, 6, 6; 1 Macc 10: 20;
Jos., Ant. 14, 450 οἱ τὰ Ἡρῴδου φρονοῦντες). τὰ τοῦ
θεοῦ (opp. τὰ τῶν ἀνθρώπων) Mt 16: 23; Mk 8: 33. τὰ
τῆς σαρκός (opp. τὰ τοῦ πνεύματος) Ro 8: 5.—ὁ φρονῶν
τὴν ἡμέραν κυρίῳ φρονεῖ *the one who is intent on the day*
(i.e. a particular day rather than others) Ro 14: 6. φρ. εἰς
τὸ σωφρονεῖν 12: 3b.
   3. *have thoughts* or *(an) attitude(s), be minded* or
disposed τοῦτο φρονεῖτε ἐν ὑμῖν ὃ καὶ ἐν Χριστῷ
Ἰησοῦ *have the same thoughts among yourselves as you
have in your communion with Christ Jesus* (so CHDodd,
The Apost. Preaching '37, 106f) Phil 2: 5 (Christ went so
far as to empty himself of his divine being for the benefit of
mankind). M-M. B. 1198.*

φρόνημα, ατος, τό (Aeschyl., Hdt.+; Vett. Val. 109, 2;
2 Macc 7: 21; 13: 9; Philo, Joseph.) *way of thinking,
mind(-set),* in our lit. (only Ro 8) *aim, aspiration, striving*
(φρονέω 2.—Diod. S. 11, 27, 2 of aspiration for control of
the sea; Jos., Bell. 1, 204; 4, 358 φρόνημα ἐλευθερίου=
striving for freedom, desire for independence) w. subjective gen. (Appian, Ital. 1) τῆς σαρκός Ro 8: 6a, 7. τοῦ
πνεύματος vss. 6b, 27. M-M.*

φρόνησις, εως, ἡ (Soph., Isocr., Pla.+; Dit., Or. 332, 25;
PSI 280; Fluchtaf. 1, 10 p. 6 W.; LXX, Philo, Joseph.)
—1. *way of thinking, (frame of) mind* ἐπιστρέψαι ἀπειθεῖς ἐν φρονήσει (=εἰς φρόνησιν. But with the thought,
so that they have the thought Bl-D. §218) δικαίων Lk 1:
17. W. νοῦς (Dio Chrys. 15[32], 5) Hs 9, 17, 2a, b, 4; 9, 18,
4. διέμειναν ἐν τῇ αὐτῇ φρονήσει 9, 29, 2. συγκεράσαι
ὑμῶν τὴν φρόνησιν ἐπὶ τὸ αὐτό Hv 3, 9, 8 (cf. συγκεράννυμι).
   2. *understanding, insight, intelligence* (Isocr., Pla.,
Aristot.; Dit., l.c.; PGM 5, 313; LXX; Ep. Arist. 124) w.
σοφία (Dio Chrys. 42[59], 1; Synes., Ep. 103 p. 243D; Pr
10: 23; 4 Macc 1: 18; Philo, Praem. 81; Jos., Ant. 2, 87; 8,
171) Eph 1: 8; (opp.: the eyes alone) Dg 2: 1. M-M.*

φρόνιμος, ον (Soph., X., Pla.+; Dit., Or. 383, 106; LXX,
En.; Ep. Arist. 130; Philo; Jos., Ant. 9, 25) *sensible,
thoughtful, prudent, wise* Mt 24: 45; Lk 12: 42 (both w.
πιστός); 1 Cor 10: 15. Opp. μωρός Mt 7: 24; 25: 2, 4, 8f;
1 Cor 4: 10; IEph 17: 2. Opp. ἄφρων (as X., Mem. 2, 3, 1;
Philo, Leg. All. 1, 86) 2 Cor 11: 19; 1 Cl 3: 3. φρόνιμος ὡς
οἱ ὄφεις (cf. Gen 3: 1.—'Shy, timid [scheu]': LKoehler,
Kleine Lichter '45, 76–9) Mt 10: 16=IPol 2: 2. ἐν ἑαυτοῖς
φρόνιμοι *wise in your own estimation=relying on your
own wisdom* Ro 11: 25; also παρ᾽ ἑαυτοῖς (cf. Pr 3: 7) 12:
16 or ἑαυτοῖς 11: 25 p⁴⁶ FG (cf. Ps.-Demetr., El. C. 222
συνετὸς ἑαυτῷ. φρόνιμοι ἐν θεῷ (Test. Napht. 8: 10
σοφοὶ ἐν θεῷ κ. φρόνιμοι) IMg 3: 1; ἐν Χριστῷ 1 Cor 4:
10.—Comp. φρονιμώτερος *shrewder* (Philo; Jos., Bell. 5,
129) Lk 16: 8 (εἰς τὴν γενεὰν τὴν ἑαυτῶν *in relation to
their own generation*).—GDKilpatrick, JTS 48, '47, 63f.
M-M. B. 1213.*

φρονίμως adv. (Aristoph.+; X., Ages. 1, 17; PLond.
1927, 36; Eccl 7: 11 Sym.; Philo; Jos., Ant. 19, 112) *wisely,
shrewdly* Lk 16: 8. M-M.*

φροντίζω (Theognis, Hdt.+; inscr., pap., LXX, Ep.
Arist., Philo, Joseph.) *think of, be intent on, be careful* or
concerned about foll. by gen. (X., Mem. 3, 11, 12; Polyb.

3, 12, 5; BGU 249, 20; 300, 4; Ps 39: 18; 2 Macc 9: 21; 11: 15; Ep. Arist. 121; 245; Jos., Ant. 14, 312, Vi. 94) τῆς ἐνώσεως IPol 1: 2. W. inf. foll. (Achilles Tat. 4, 9, 2; PRyl. 78, 26) ἵνα φροντίζωσιν καλῶν ἔργων προΐστασθαι in order that they might be careful to engage in good works Tit 3: 8. M-M.*

φροντίς, ίδος, ἡ (Pind., Hdt.+; inscr., pap., LXX; Ep. Arist. 8; Philo; Jos., Ant. 5, 236) reflection, thought w. ἐπίνοια Dg 5: 3. In the sense care, concern foll. by εἰς = directed toward 1 Cl 63: 4. Pl. (Dio Chrys. 80[30], 14; Philostrat., Vi. Apoll. 8, 7 p. 304, 25; 316, 15; Jos., Ant. 2, 63) αἱ κεναὶ καὶ μάταιαι φροντίδες empty and idle thoughts or cares 1 Cl 7: 2.*

φροντιστής, οῦ, ὁ (X., Pla. et al.; IG XIV 715; 759; pap. [oft. as a t.t. for 'guardian']; Philo, Somn. 2, 155) protector, guardian w. objective gen. (Jewish inscr. fr. Side in Pamphylia: JHS 28, '08 p. 195f, no. 29 φ. τῆς συναγωγῆς) σὺ αὐτῶν φ. ἔσο IPol 4: 1.*

Φρόντων, ωνος, ὁ (Lat. Fronto. The Gk. form of the name in Jos., Bell. 6, 238; 242; Dit., Or. 533, 34; CIG II add. 2349k; III 5120; IV 9919; Inschr. v. Perg. 511; PGiess. 59 II; POxy. 1188) Fronto IEph 2: 1.*

φρουρά, ᾶς, ἡ (Aeschyl., Hdt.+; inscr., pap., LXX; Philo, Agr. 86 [= bodyguard]; Manetho in Jos., C. Ap. 1, 77; Jos., Ant. 7, 104).
1. guard, sentinel (Lucian, Ver. Hist. 2, 23) φυλάσσειν κατὰ φρουράν stand guard as sentinel GP 9: 35 (κατά II 5bβ).—2. prison (Aeschyl., Prom. 143; BGU 1074, 4 [II AD]) symbol. (Pla., Phaedr. 62B; Aelian, H.A. 4, 41) Χριστιανοὶ κατέχονται ὡς ἐν φρουρᾷ τῷ κόσμῳ Dg 6: 7.*

φρουρέω impf. ἐφρούρουν; fut. φρουρήσω; impf. pass. ἐφρουρούμην (Aeschyl., Hdt.+; inscr., pap., LXX) in our lit. only trans.
1. guard, lit. τὶ someth. (cf. Jdth 3: 6 φ. τ. πόλεις = put garrisons in the cities; Jos., Bell. 3, 12) τὴν πόλιν Δαμασκηνῶν 2 Cor 11: 32. In this case the ref. is surely to the guarding of the city gates fr. within, as a control on all who went out (Jos., Vi. 53 τὰς ἐξόδους δὲ πάσας ἐφρούρει. Cf. Nicol. Dam.: 90 fgm. 130, 51 Jac.) rather than fr. the outside as was sometimes done, e.g. in sieges (Plut., Crassus 9, 2; Jos., Vi. 240); Zahn, NKZ 15, '04, 34ff.
2. hold in custody, confine (Plut., Ant. 84, 4, Mor. 205F; Wsd 17: 15; PGM 4, 2905; 3093) fig., pass.: of mankind before the coming of Jesus ὑπὸ νόμον ἐφρουρούμεθα we were held under custody by the law Gal 3: 23. ἡ ψυχὴ φρουρεῖται τῷ σώματι Dg 6: 4.—3. gener. guard, protect, keep (Soph., Oed. R. 1479 δαίμων σε φρουρήσας τύχοι) the peace of God φρουρήσει τὰς καρδίας ὑμῶν Phil 4: 7. Pass. 1 Pt 1: 5. M-M.*

φρύασσω 1 aor. ἐφρύαξα (the act. only Ps 2: 1 and in the NT use of that pass. Elsewh. always φρυάσσομαι [since Callim., Hymn. 5, 2 Schn.]) snort, fig., of men be arrogant, haughty, insolent (Diod. S. 4, 74, 3; Anth. Pal. 4, 3, 27; 2 Macc 7: 34 v.l.; 3 Macc 2: 2; Philo, Cher. 66) Ac 4: 25 (Ps 2: 1). M-M.*

φρύγανον, ου, τό (Hdt., Aristoph.+; inscr., pap., LXX)
1. bush, shrub (Theophr., H.Pl. 1, 3, 1) B 7: 8.—2. in the pl. thin, dry wood, brushwood, esp. for making fires (X., An. 4, 3, 11 et al. Cf. Is 47: 14; Philo, In Flacc. 68) Ac 28: 3. W. ξύλα (Diod. S. 14, 90, 6; Plut., Mor. 525E) MPol 13: 1. M-M.*

Φρυγία, ας, ἡ Phrygia (Hom.+; inscr., Joseph., Sib. Or.) a large district in Central Asia Minor, whose boundaries varied considerably fr. time to time. Ac 2: 10; 16: 6; 18: 23 (in the last two places w. ἡ Γαλατικὴ χώρα): 1 Ti subscr. (s. Πακατιανός); MPol 4.—Ramsay, Phrygia 1895, 1897 (other publications by Ramsay in Harnack, Mission⁴ II '24 p. 677, 3); JWeiss, RE X 557ff; VSchultze, Altchristl. Städte u. Landschaften II 1, '22; WSchepelern, D. Montanismus u. d. phrygischen Kulte '29. M-M.*

Φρύξ, γός, ὁ (Hom.+; inscr.) a Phrygian (s. Φρυγία) MPol 4.*

φυγαδεύω 1 aor. pass. ἐφυγαδεύθην—1. trans. cause to become a fugitive, banish from the country (X.+; Diod. S. 5, 44, 7; inscr., pap.; Philo, Congr. Erud. Gr. 171) ἐφυγάδευσεν δὲ Μωϋσῆν ἐν τῷ λόγῳ τούτῳ and by this word he drove Moses from the country Ac 7: 29 E. Pass. (Jos., Bell. 1, 661; 4, 504 φυγαδευθείς, Ant. 12, 399) of Paul φυγαδευθείς banished from the country or an exile 1 Cl 5: 6.
2. intr. be a fugitive, live in exile (Polyb. 10, 25, 1; Dit., Syll.³ 175, 20 [IV BC]; 679, 84 [143 BC]; LXX) οὕτως καὶ ἐφυγάδευσεν Μωϋσῆς Ac 7: 29 D.*

Φύγελος (t.r. Φύγελλος), ου, ὁ (on the name and its spelling s. Bl-D. §42, 3 app.; Mlt.-H. 101; OBenndorf, Z. Ortskunde u. Stadtgeschichte v. Ephesus '05, 74) Phygelus, an otherw. unknown Christian in Asia who, acc. to 2 Ti 1: 15, w. Hermogenes turned his back on Paul. M-M.*

φυγή, ῆς, ἡ (Hom.+; inscr., pap., LXX, Philo; Jos., Ant. 18, 324; 20, 4) flight Mt 24: 20; Mk 13: 18 t.r.*

φυλακή, ῆς, ἡ (Hom.+; inscr., pap., LXX, En., Ep. Arist., Philo, Joseph., Test. Jos.; loanw. in rabb.) watch, guard.
1. guarding as an action, in the expr. φυλάσσειν φυλακάς keep watch, do guard duty (X., An. 2, 6, 10; Pla., Leg. 6 p. 758D; Demosth. 7, 14; Plut., Mor. 198A; LXX.—Bl-D. §153, 3) φυλ. φυλακὰς τῆς νυκτὸς ἐπὶ τὴν ποίμνην keep watch over the flock at night (s. φυλ. τῆς νυκτός 4 below) Lk 2: 8.—2. as a pers. guard, sentinel (Hom.+; Dit., Or. 229, 96; 99; PGiess. 19, 16; Jos., Bell. 6, 131) Ac 12: 10 (the πρώτη and δευτέρα φ. as first and second sentinel as Arrian, Anab. 3, 18, 6).
3. the place of guarding, prison (in sing. and pl. Hdt., Thu.+; Dit., Or. 90, 13; 669, 17; pap., LXX; Jos., Vi. 178) οἶκος φυλακῆς Β 14: 7 (Is 42: 7). Also simply φυλακή (Test. Jos. 1: 6) Mt 14: 10; 25: 36, 39, 43f; Mk 6: 27; Lk 22: 33; Ac 5: 19, 21 D, 22; 12: 6, 17; 16: 27, 39 D, 40; Hb 11: 36. The pl. of several prisons (Appian, Bell. Civ. 4, 17 §65) Lk 21: 12; Ac 22: 4; 26: 10; 2 Cor 6: 5; 11: 23; Hv 3, 2, 1. βάλλειν τινὰ εἰς φυλακήν (βάλλω 1b) throw someone into prison Mt 18: 30 (cf. PWSchmidt, Die Gesch. Jesu II '04, 326f); Lk 12: 58; Ac 16: 23f, 37; Rv 2: 10. Pass. Mt 5: 25; Lk 23: 25; J 3: 24, cf. Lk 23: 19. παραδιδόναι εἰς φυλ. (cf. Diod. S. 11, 40, 3 παρέδωκαν εἰς φυλακήν; 12, 31, 2; 17, 32, 2; Dit., Or. 669, 15) Ac 8: 3; cf. Lk 21: 12. τίθεσθαι εἰς φ. (cf. PEleph. 12, 2 [III BC]) Ac 12: 4. ἐν (τῇ) φυλακῇ τίθεσθαι Mt 14: 3 t.r.; Ac 5: 25; ἀποτίθεσθαι Mt 14: 3. δῆσαι Mk 6: 17; κατακλείειν Lk 3: 20; Ac 26: 10. τηρεῖν pass. 5. Of the underworld or the place of punishment in hell (πνεῦμα 2 and 4c) 1 Pt 3: 19 (BReicke, The Disobedient Spirits and Christian Baptism '46, 116f). It is in the φυλ. in the latter sense that Satan will be rendered harmless during the millennium Rv

20: 7. The fallen city of Babylon becomes a φυλακή *haunt* for all kinds of unclean spirits and birds 18: 2a, b.

4. *a watch of the night*, as a division of time (Hdt. 9, 51 al.; Diod. S. 14, 24, 4 δευτέρα φ.; Arrian, Anab. 6, 25, 5 φυλακῇ τῆς νυκτός; PPetr. II 45 II, 18 [246 bc] πρώτης φυλακῆς ἀρχομένης; LXX; Joseph.). Our lit. reflects the Rom. custom of dividing the time betw. 6 p.m. and 6 a.m. into four equal periods or *watches* Mt 14: 25; Mk 6: 48 (Diod. S. 19, 26, 1 περὶ δευτέραν φυλακήν; Jos., Ant. 18, 356 περὶ τετάρτην φυλακήν; for περί cf. also the Freiburg pap. 76, 7 [II bc]: UWilcken, Deissmann-Festschr. '27, 10ff l. 9f περὶ πρώτην φυλακὴν τ. νυκτός). Cf. Mt 24: 43; Lk 12: 38 (here perh. we are to think of only three night-watches, as among the Hebrews and Greeks; cf. Jülicher, Gleichn. 168. So, three night-watches: Diod. S. 19, 38, 3; Polyaenus 4, 8, 4; Jos., Bell. 5, 510). (Mk 13: 35 uses the popular designations ὀψέ, μεσονύκτιον, ἀλεκτοροφωνία, πρωΐ; s. these entries.) M-M. B. 1451.*

φυλακίζω (Wsd 18: 4; Test. Jos. 2: 3; Achmes 84, 3; 87, 12) *imprison* Ac 22: 19; 1 Cl 45: 4.*

φυλακτήριον, ου, τό (Hdt.+; Jos., Ant. 15, 249) *safeguard, means of protection* (Demosth. 6, 24; Philo), esp. *amulet* (Dioscor., Mat. Med. 5, 154; Plut., Mor. 377b al.; Dit., Or. 90, 45; PGM 1, 275; 3, 97; 127; 4, 86; 660; 708; 1071; 2506; 2510; 2694; 2705; 13, 796) as a designation for the *phylacteries* (small boxes containing scripture verses bound on forehead and arm during prayer, in accordance w. Deut 6: 8; s. Webster s.v.) of the Jews, which could be regarded as protections against demonic influences, like amulets: Mt 23: 5.—Schürer II⁴ 567ff [note 81 lit.]; MFriedländer, Der Antichrist '01, 155ff; GKropatscheck, De Amuletorum apud Antiquos Usu, Diss. Greifswald '07; Billerb. IV '28, 250–76; GLanger, Die jüd. Gebetsriemen '31; WLKnox, St. Paul and the Church of the Gentiles '39, 209; GGFox, Journ. of Near Eastern Studies 1, '42, 373–7; Gdspd., Probs. 35f; CBonner, HTR 39, '46, 25–53, esp. 35; JBowman, TU 73, '59, 523–38. M-M.*

φύλαξ, ακος, ὁ (Hom.+; inscr., pap., LXX, Philo; Jos., Ant. 7, 287 al.) *guard, sentinel* Mt 27: 65 D; Ac 5: 23; 12: 6, 19; Dg 2: 7. M-M.*

φύλαρχος, ου, ὁ (X., Pla.+; inscr., pap., LXX) *the ruler of a φυλή, head of a tribe* (X., Cyr. 1, 2, 14; Plut., Crass. 21, 1; Jos., Ant. 17, 56) of the rulers of the 12 Hebrew tribes (Dt 31: 28; 1 Esdr 7: 8; Ep. Arist. 97; Joseph., Ant. 3, 169) 1 Cl 43: 2a, b, 5.*

φυλάσσω fut. φυλάξω; 1 aor. ἐφύλαξα; pf. πεφύλαχα; 1 aor. pass. ἐφυλάχθην (Hom.+; inscr., pap., LXX; En. 100, 7; Ep. Arist., Philo, Test. 12 Patr.; Sib. Or. 3, 33).

1. act. *watch, guard, defend*—**a.** φυλάσσειν φυλακάς Lk 2: 8 (φυλακή 1). φυλάσσειν κατὰ φρουράν GP 9: 35 (φρουρά 1).—**b.** τινά *guard someone* to prevent him fr. escaping (Plut., Mor. 181a) Mk 15: 25 D; Ac 12: 4; 28: 16. Pass. Lk 8: 29; Ac 23: 35.

c. *guard, protect* w. acc. *someone* or *someth.* τινά *someone* (Lind. Tempelchr. D, 47 τοὺς ἀνθρώπους τούτους θεοὶ φυλάσσουσι; Ex 23: 20; Pr 13: 6) J 17: 12 (w. τηρέω as Dio Chrys. 14[31], 150); 2 Pt 2: 5. τινά (Gen 3: 24) αὐλήν Lk 11: 21. τὸν πύργον (Ep. Arist. 102) Hs 9, 5, 1. πάντα τὰ στοιχεῖα Dg 7: 2a. Clothes, to prevent them fr. being stolen Ac 22: 20. τὴν ψυχὴν αὐτοῦ (εἰς ζωὴν αἰώνιον) φυλάσσειν *preserve his life* (for eternal life; cf. Jos., Ant. 3, 199 ἔλαιον φ. εἰς τ. λύχνους) J 12: 25. τὴν παραθήκην *what has been entrusted* so that it is not lost or damaged 1 Ti 6: 20; 2 Ti 1: 14; foll. by an

indication of time (Aelian, V.H. 9, 21 ὦ Ζεῦ, ἐς τίνα με καιρὸν φυλάττεις;) εἰς ἐκείνην τὴν ἡμέραν vs. 12. Cf. B 19: 11; D 4: 13. ἀκακίαν 1 Cl 14: 5 (Ps 36: 37). θνητὴν ἐπίνοιαν Dg 7: 1. τὴν ἀγνείαν Hm 4, 1, 1. τὴν πίστιν κτλ. 6, 1, 1. ὡς ναὸν θεοῦ φυλάσσειν τὴν σάρκα 2 Cl 9: 3. τινά w. a predicate acc. (Wsd 14: 24) φυλάξαι ὑμᾶς ἀπταίστους Jd 24. τινὰ ἀπό τινος (X., Cyr. 1, 4, 7; Menand., Sam. 87f) 2 Th 3: 3 (PGM 4, 2699 φύλαξόν με ἀπὸ παντὸς δαίμονος; 36, 177 ἀπὸ παντὸς πράγματος; Sir 22: 26; Ps 140: 9). ἑαυτὸν ἀπό τινος (Horapollo 2, 94; Herm. Wr. p. 434, 13 Sc.; Test. Reub. 4: 8) 1 J 5: 21. Of an idol χρῄζων ἀνθρώπου τοῦ φυλάξαντος ἵνα μὴ κλαπῇ *needing a man to guard* (it) so that it may not be stolen Dg 2: 2.

d. *stand guard* (Hom.+) GP 8: 33.—**e.** *keep, reserve* pass. (Diod. S. 1, 8, 7) τί τινι *someth. for someone* Dg 10: 7.

f. *keep* a law, etc., fr. being broken, hence *observe, follow* (νόμον Soph., Trach. 616; Dio Chrys. 58[75], 1; νόμους X., Hell. 1, 7, 29; Pla., Rep. 6 p. 484b, Polit. 292a. Cf. Aristoxenus, fgm. 18 p. 13, 31 τὰ ἤθη καὶ τὰ μαθήματα; Dit., Or. 669, 28; PTebt. 407, 9; POxy. 905, 9; PFay. 124, 13; Wsd 6: 4; Sir 21: 11; 4 Macc 5: 29; 15: 10; Jos., C. Ap. 1, 60; Test. Jud. 26: 1, Iss. 5: 1) τί *someth.* Mt 19: 20; Lk 18: 21; 1 Ti 5: 21; Hm 1: 2a; 3: 5a, b; 4, 4, 3; 8: 9; Hs 5, 3, 4. τὸν νόμον (Lucian, Jud. Voc. 5) Ac 7: 53; 21: 24; Gal 6: 13. τὴν ἐντολήν Hm 1: 2b; 8: 12a. τὰς ἐντολάς (Jos., Ant. 6, 336; Test. Zeb. 5: 1, Benj. 10: 3, 5) 2 Cl 8: 4; B 4: 11; Hv 5, 5, 7; m 2: 7; 4, 2, 4a, b; 4, 4, 4a, b; 5, 2, 8; 12, 5, 1; Hs 5, 3, 2f al. Pass. Hm 12, 3, 4f; s 1: 7. τὰ δικαιώματα τοῦ νόμου *the requirements of the law* Ro 2: 26. τὸν λόγον τοῦ θεοῦ Lk 11: 28. τὰ ῥήματα (i.e. of Christ) J 12: 47. τὰ δόγματα Ac 16: 4. φυλ. τὸ σάββατον *keep the Sabbath* B 15: 2 (cf. Ex 31: 16). τὴν Ἰουδαίων δεισιδαιμονίαν φυλ. *practice the superstition of the Jews* Dg 1. τὰ μέτρα τῶν τῆς ἡμέρας δρόμων φυλ. 7: 2b (μέτρον 2a).

2. mid. (Hom.+; LXX)—**a.** (be on one's) *guard against, look out for, avoid* w. acc. of the pers. or thing avoided τινά (Aeschyl., Prom. 717; Appian, Bell. Civ. 2, 25 §96 τὸν Πομπήιον; 5, 8 §32; Ps.-Liban., Charact. Ep. p. 30, 12) 2 Ti 4: 15; IEph 7: 1; ITr 7: 1. τί (Hdt., Aristot. et al.; Jos., Bell. 4, 572) Ac 21: 25; ITr 2: 3. Also ἀπό τινος (PLond. 1349, 35; Dt 23: 10; Test. Sim. 4: 5; 5: 3) Lk 12: 15; Hm 5, 1, 7; s 5, 3, 6. Foll. by ἵνα μή (Bl-D. §392, 1b; cf. Gen 31: 29) 2 Pt 3: 17.

b. OT infl. is prob. felt in the use of the mid. for the act. (cf. Bl-D. §316, 1) in sense 1f above *keep, observe, follow* (Lev 20: 22; 26: 3; Ps 118: 5 al. But as early as Hesiod, Op. 263 ταῦτα φυλασσόμενοι=if you observe this; 765; Ocellus [II bc] c. 56 Harder φυλάττεσθαι τὸ . . . γίνεσθαι) ταῦτα πάντα Mt 19: 20 t.r.; Mk 10: 20; Lk 18: 21 t.r.—**c.** *lay up for oneself* PK 2 p. 15, 2.—GBertram, TW IX, 232–40. M-M. B. 752.**

φυλή, ῆς, ἡ (Pind., Hdt.+; inscr., pap., LXX, Ep. Arist., Philo, Joseph., Test. 12 Patr.; Sib. Or. 3, 288).

1. *tribe*, of the 12 tribes of Israel (Diod. S. 40, 3, 3 δώδεκα φυλαί of the Jews; LXX; Jos., Ant. 11, 133; Test. Benj. 9: 2) Hb 7: 13; Rv 7: 4; 1 Cl 43: 2a, b, 4. Certain tribes are mentioned by name: Ἀσήρ Lk 2: 36. Βενιαμίν Ac 13: 21; Ro 11: 1; Phil 3: 5. Ἰούδα Rv 5: 5; cf. Hb 7: 14; all the tribes Rv 7: 5–8 (except that Manasseh takes the place of Dan, prob. since the latter is the tribe fr. which, because of Gen 49: 17, the Antichrist is to come [WBousset, D. Antichrist 1895, 112ff]). αἱ δώδεκα φυλαὶ τοῦ Ἰσραήλ Mt 19: 28; Lk 22: 30; cf. Rv 21: 12; B 8: 3a, b and the symbolic use Js 1: 1; Hs 9, 17, 1f.

2. *nation, people* (X., Cyr. 1, 2, 5; Dionys. Hal. 2, 7)
πᾶσαι αἱ φυλαὶ τῆς γῆς (Gen 12: 3; 28: 14; Ezk 20: 32)
Mt 24: 30; Rv 1: 7; 1 Cl 10: 3 (Gen 12: 3). W. synonymous
expressions (Test. Ash. 7: 6 χώρα, φυλή, γλῶσσα)
πάντα τὰ ἔθνη, φυλὰς καὶ γλώσσας 2 Cl 17: 4; cf. Rv 5:
9; 7: 9; 11: 9; 13: 7; 14: 6.—CMaurer, TW IX, 240-5.
M-M. B. 1317.*

φύλλον, ου, τό (Hom.+; pap., LXX) *leaf* 1 Cl 23: 4
(scripture quot. of unknown origin). Collectively *foliage* B
11: 6 (Ps 1: 3). Elsewh. in our lit. (as prevailingly in
Lucian) in the pl. (En. 24, 4; Ep. Arist. 70; Jos., Ant. 1,
44; 3, 174; Test. Levi 9: 12) Mt 21: 19; 24: 32; Mk 11: 13a,
b; 13: 28; Rv 22: 2; B 11: 8; Hs 3: 1. ἀποβάλλειν τὰ φ. 3:
3. M-M. B. 525.*

φυλλοροέω (Pherecrates [V BC] in Athen. p. 269D; Plut.,
Mor. 648D; 649C, D; 723E; Epict. 1, 14, 3; 3, 24, 91.
Predom. w. double ρ: φυλλορροέω [X.; Artem. 4, 57;
Aristaen., Ep. 1, 10; Philo, Ebr. 9 al.]) *shed leaves, lose
foliage* 1 Cl 23: 4 = 2 Cl 11: 3 (prophetic saying of unknown
origin).*

φύραμα, ατος, τό *that which is mixed* (fr. φυράω) or
kneaded, (*a lump* or *batch of*) *dough* (Aristot., Probl. 21,
18 p. 929a, 25; Plut., Mor. 693E; PTebt. 401, 27 [I AD];
Num 15: 20f) μικρὰ ζύμη ὅλον τὸ φύραμα ζυμοῖ 1 Cor 5:
6; Gal 5: 9 (ζύμη 1). On Ro 11: 16 cf. Num 15: 20f.
Symbolically (Philo, Sacr. Abel. 108): the Christians are to
be νέον φύραμα *fresh dough,* containing no yeast 1 Cor 5:
7 (cf. Philo, Spec. Leg. 2, 158 φυράματα ἄζυμα).—Of the
dough-like mixture fr. which the potter forms his wares
(Plut., Mor. 811c) *lump* Ro 9: 21. M-M. B. 360.*

φυσικός, ή, όν (X.+; PLeipz. 28, 18; Ep. Arist. 222 al.;
Philo; Jos., Ant. 12, 99; Test. Dan 3: 4) *belonging to
nature.*
1. *natural, in accordance with nature* (Dionys. Hal.,
Plut. et al. φυσικὴ χρῆσις) Ro 1: 26f.—**2.** φυσικὰ creatures *of instinct* γεγεννημένα φυσικὰ εἰς ἅλωσιν καὶ
φθοράν (mere) *creatures of instinct, born to be caught and
killed* 2 Pt 2: 12. M-M.*

φυσικῶς adv. (Aristot., Diod. S., Plut., Philo et al.)
naturally, by instinct Jd 10 (cf. Diog. L. 10, 137 φυσικῶς
καὶ χωρὶς λόγου al.; X., Cyr. 2, 3, 9 μάχην ὁρῶ πάντας
ἀνθρώπους φύσει ἐπισταμένους, ὥσπερ γε καὶ τἆλλα
ζῷα ἐπίσταταί τινα μάχην ἕκαστα οὐδὲ παρ' ἑνὸς
ἄλλου μαθόντα ἢ παρὰ τῆς φύσεως).*

φυσιόω (a later substitute for φυσάω; it is largely limited
to Christian lit. [but also in Philod., Mus. p. 26 JKemke
1884]) pass.: pf. ptc. πεφυσιωμένος; 1 aor. ἐφυσιώθην
blow up, puff up only fig. *puff up, make proud* or *arrogant
τινά someone* ITr 4: 1. τόπος μηδένα φυσιούτω *let no one
be puffed up because of his* (high) *position* ISm 6: 1. Of
knowledge φυσιοῖ *it* (only) *puffs up* 1 Cor 8: 1 = Dg 12: 5.
—Pass. *become puffed up* or *conceited, put on airs* (Test.
Levi 14: 7, 8 v.l.; schol. on Apollon. Rhod. 3, 368b of
anger, that swells the heart; Hesychius; cf. Babrius 114)
1 Cor 4: 18f; 5: 2; 13: 4; IMg 12; ITr 7: 1; IPol 4: 3. εἰκῇ
φυσιούμενος ὑπὸ τοῦ νοὸς τῆς σαρκὸς αὐτοῦ *groundlessly
inflated by his fleshly mind* Col 2: 18. ἵνα μὴ εἷς ὑπὲρ τοῦ
ἑνὸς φυσιοῦσθε (perh. subjunctive; s. ἵνα I 3) κατὰ τοῦ
ἑτέρου *in order that no one of you might be puffed up in
favor of the one* (apostle and thus) *against the other* 1 Cor
4: 6. M-M. B. 684.*

φύσις, εως, ἡ (Hom.+; inscr., pap., LXX, Ep. Arist.,
Philo, Joseph., Test. 12 Patr.; Sib. Or., fgm. 5, 3) *nature.*

1. *natural endowment* or *condition,* inherited fr. one's
ancestors (Isocr. 4, 105 φύσει πολίτης; Isaeus 6, 28 φύσει
υἱός; Pla., Menex. 245D φύσει βάρβαροι, νόμῳ Ἕλληνες; Dit., Syll.³ 720, 3, Or. 472, 4; 558, 6 al.; PFay. 19, 11)
ἡμεῖς φύσει Ἰουδαῖοι Gal 2: 15 (cf. Ptolemaeus, περὶ
Ἡρῴδου τ. βασιλέως: no. 199 Jac. [I AD] Ἰουδαῖοι ...
ἐξ ἀρχῆς φυσικοί; Jos., Ant. 7, 130). ἡ ἐκ φύσεως
ἀκροβυστία the uncircumcision or heathendom that is so
by nature Ro 2: 27 (in contrast to the Jew who becomes a
heathen by violating his law). ἤμεθα τέκνα φύσει ὀργῆς
we were, in our natural condition (as descendants of
Adam), children of wrath Eph 2: 3 (the position of φύσει
betw. the two words as Plut., Mor. 701A). The Christians
of Tralles have a blameless disposition οὐ κατὰ χρῆσιν,
ἀλλὰ κατὰ φύσιν not by usage or habit, but by nature ITr
1: 1. οἱ κατὰ φύσιν κλάδοι the natural branches Ro 11:
21, 24c. ἡ κατὰ φύσιν ἀγριέλαιος a tree which by nature
is a wild olive vs. 24a; opp. παρὰ φύσιν contrary to nature
vs. 24b; s. lit. s.v. ἀγριέλαιος and ἐλαία 2. On κατὰ and
παρὰ φύσιν s. MPohlenz, Die Stoa I '48, 488c.

2. *natural characteristics* or *disposition* ἡ φύσις ἡ
ἀνθρωπίνη (Pla., Theaet. 149B, Tim. 90c; Aristot. p.
1286b, 27; Epict. 2, 20, 18; Philo, Ebr. 166 al.; Aelian,
V.H. 8, 11 τῶν ἀνθρώπων φύσις θνητή) human nature,
unless the sense should be mankind (s. 4 below) Js 3: 7b.
τὸ ἀδύνατον τῆς ἡμετέρας φύσεως the weakness of our
nature Dg 9: 6. θείας κοινωνοὶ φύσεως sharers in the
divine nature 2 Pt 1: 4 (Jos., C. Ap. 1, 232 θείας μετε-
σχηκέναι φύσεως; Himerius, Or. 48 [=Or. 14], 26 of
Dionysus: πρὶν εἰς θεῶν φύσιν ἐλθεῖν=before he attained to the nature of the gods).—Also specif. of sexual
characteristics (Diod. S. 16, 26, 6 originally παρθένοι
prophesied in Delphi διὰ τὸ τῆς φύσεως ἀδιάφθορον=
because their sexuality was uncorrupted. φύσις of sex and
its change Dicaearchus, fgm. 37 W. Obviously φ. also has
the concrete mng. 'sex organ': Nicander, fgm. 107; Diod.
S. 32, 10, 7 φ. ἄρρενος corresponding to φ. θηλείας
following immediately; Anton. Lib. 41, 5; Phlegon: 257
fgm. 36, 2, 1 Jac.). The hyena παρ' ἐνιαυτὸν ἀλλάσσει
τὴν φύσιν changes its nature every year, fr. male to female
and vice versa B 10: 7. The heathen worship τοῖς φύσει μὴ
οὖσιν θεοῖς beings that are by nature no gods at all Gal 4:
8 (cf. CLanger, Euhemeros u. die Theorie der φύσει u.
θέσει θεοί: Ἄγγελος II '26, 53-9; Synes., Prov. 1, 9 p.
97C τοῖς φύσει θεοῖς; Diod. S. 3, 9, 1 differentiates
between two kinds of gods. Some αἰώνιον ἔχειν κ.
ἄφθαρτον τὴν φύσιν. The others θνητῆς φύσεως κεκοι-
νωνηκέναι κ. δι' ἀρετὴν ... τετευχέναι τιμῶν ἀθανάτων).

3. *nature* as the regular natural order μετήλλαξαν τὴν
φυσικὴν χρῆσιν εἰς τὴν παρὰ φύσιν Ro 1: 26 (Diod. S.
32, 11, 1 παρὰ φύσιν ὁμιλία; Appian, Bell. Civ. 1, 109
§511; Athen. 13 p. 605D οἱ παρὰ φύσιν τῇ Ἀφροδίτῃ
χρώμενοι; Philo, Spec. Leg. 3, 39 ὁ παιδεραστὴς τὴν
παρὰ φύσιν ἡδονὴν διώκει; Jos., C. Ap. 2, 273; Test.
Napht. 3: 4). ὅταν ἔθνη φύσει τὰ τοῦ νόμου ποιῶσιν
when Gentiles fulfil the law's demands by following the
natural order (of things) Ro 2: 14 (Ltzm., Hdb., exc. on Ro
2: 14-16); φύσει may mean instinctively, in which case it
belongs under 2 above (cf. WMundle, Theol. Blätter 13,
'34, 249-56 [the Gentile as Christian under direction of the
πνεῦμα]. ἡ φύσις διδάσκει ὑμᾶς 1 Cor 11: 14 (Epict. 1,
16, 9f; Plut., Mor. 478D; Synes., Calv. 14 p. 78C φύσις as
well as νόμος prescribes long hair for women, short hair for
men.—Ltzm., Hdb. ad loc.). τὸ ὄνομα, ὃ κέκτησθε φύσει
δικαίᾳ the name which you bear because of a just natural
order IEph 1: 1 (s. Hdb. ad loc.; for the sense 'natural

disposition' s. JKleist, transl. '46, 119 n. 2).—RMGrant, Miracle and Natural Law '52, 4-18.

4. *natural being, product of nature, creature* (X., Cyr. 6, 2, 29 πᾶσα φύσις=every creature; 3 Macc 3: 29.—Diod. S. 2, 49, 4 plants are called φύσεις καρποφοροῦσαι. It can also mean *species* [X. et al.; 4 Macc 1: 20; Philo] and then at times disappear in translation: Ps.-Pla, Epin. 948D ἡ τῶν ἄστρων φύσις=the stars; X., Lac. 3, 4 ἡ τῶν θηλειῶν φύσις=the women; Aristot., Part. An. 1, 5 περὶ τῆς ζωϊκῆς φυσ.=on animals) πᾶσα φύσις θηρίων κτλ. Js 3: 7a. Also prob. ἡ φ. ἡ ἀνθρωπίνη mankind 3: 7b; s. 2 above.—HKöster, TW IX, 246-71. M-M.*

φυσίωσις, εως, ἡ (in secular wr. as a medical t.t. and in Achmes 153, 6; otherw. a Christian word; Hesychius) *being puffed up, pride, conceit* 2 Cor 12: 20.*

φυτεία, ας, ἡ (X., Theophr.+; pap., LXX and Jos., Ant. 3, 281 in the sense 'planting') *that which is planted, the plant* (Aelian, V.H. 3, 40; Athen. 5 p. 207D; Dit., Or. 606, 7; Philo, Op. M. 41) symbol. (PsSol 14: 4) Mt 15: 13; ITr 11: 1; IPhld 3: 1 (w. Ign. cf. Synes., Prov. 10 p. 100D of the truly good man: ἔστιν ἐπὶ γῆς φυτὸν οὐράνιον after Pla., Tim. 90A). M-M.*

φυτεύω impf. ἐφύτευον; 1 aor. ἐφύτευσα. Pass.: pf. πεφύτευμαι, ptc. πεφυτευμένος; 1 aor. ἐφυτεύθην (Hom.+; inscr., pap., LXX; En. 10, 19 φ. ἀμπέλους; Philo; Jos., Bell. 3, 516, Ant. 11, 50 ἀμπέλους) *plant* τὶ someth. (q.v.; cf. Sib. Or. 3, 397) Mt 15: 13; a tree (since Od. 18, 359) Dg 12: 3; cf. pass. 12: 2, 4; Lk 13: 6 (foll. by ἔν τινι as X., Oec. 20, 3); B 11: 6 (Ps 1: 3. Foll. by παρά τι); sticks Hs 8, 2, 6; 8a, b; pass. 8, 2, 7; 8, 3, 8; 8, 4, 2. φυτεύθητι ἐν τῇ θαλάσσῃ *be planted in the sea* Lk 17: 6. ἀμπελῶνα *a vineyard* (s. ἀμπελών) Mt 21: 33; Mk 12: 1; Lk 20: 9; 1 Cor 9: 7; cf. Hs 5, 5, 2; 5, 6, 2. μέρος τι τοῦ ἀγροῦ ἐφύτευσεν ἀμπελῶνα *he had a part of his field planted as a vineyard* 5, 2, 2. Abs. (X., Mem. 2, 1, 13) Lk 17: 28; as a symbol Dg 12: 6 and of the apostle's work (w. ποτίζειν) 1 Cor 3: 6-8 (Libanius, Or. 13, 52 vol. II p. 82, 2 F.: τὸ καλὸν ἐγὼ μὲν ἐφύτευσα, σὺ δὲ ἔθρεψας, αἱ δὲ πόλεις δρέπονται). M-M.*

φυτόν, οῦ, τό (Hom.+; inscr., pap., LXX; En. 10, 16; Philo; Jos., Ant. 1, 195; Sib. Or. 3, 397) *a plant* AP 5: 15. B. 521.*

φύω (Hom.+; inscr., pap., LXX, Philo, Joseph.) 2 aor. pass. ἐφύην, ptc. φυείς, neut. φυέν (for class. ἔφυν, ptc. φύς, φύν); these forms in Hippocr. and later wr., incl. Joseph. (e.g. Ant. 17, 19; 18, 6.—Beside them φύς Ant. 1, 63; 4, 245; φῦναι 18, 43); CIG 8735.—Bl-D. §76, 2; Mlt.-H. 264; Rob. 350. On the LXX s. Thackeray p. 235, 289f. In our lit. the word has intr. mng., even in the pres. act. (cf. Bl-D. §309, 2; Rob. 800; Sib. Or. 8, 21) *grow* (*up*), *come up* lit. Lk 8: 6, 8. Symbol. ῥίζα πικρίας ἄνω φύουσα Hb 12: 15 (Dt 29: 17). M-M.*

φωλεός, οῦ, ὁ (Aristot.+; Jos., Bell. 4, 507) *den, lair, hole* for animals (Aristot., Plut., Lucian et al.; Herm. Wr. 406, 12 Sc.) of a fox-hole (Neptunianus [II AD] ed. WGemoll, Progr. Striegau 1884, 27) Mt 8: 20; Lk 9: 58 (cf. Plut., Tib. Gr. 9, 5 [828c]: animals have φωλ., but those who are fighting for Italy are without shelter). M-M.*

φωνέω impf. ἐφώνουν; fut. φωνήσω; 1 aor. ἐφώνησα, pass. ἐφωνήθην (Hom.+; inscr., pap. [though not common in either]; LXX; En. 14, 8; Philo, Joseph.).

1. *produce a sound* or *tone*—**a.** of animals (Aristot.; Anton. Lib. 7, 8; Aesop. 225 Halm; Is 38: 14; Jer 17: 11;

Zeph 2: 14) of a cock *crow* (Aesop, Fab. 225; 323b, a cock) Mt 26: 34, 74f; Mk 14: 30, 68 v.l., 72a, b; Lk 22: 34, 60f; J 13: 38; 18: 27.

b. of persons *call* or *cry out, speak loudly, say with emphasis* Lk 8: 8. φ. φωνῇ μεγάλῃ *in a loud voice* Mk 1: 26 (of an evil spirit in a pers.); Lk 23: 46; Ac 16: 28; Rv 14: 18 (w. dat. of the pers. for whom the call is meant). κραυγῇ μεγάλῃ ibid. t.r. ἐφώνησεν λέγων Lk 8: 54; Ac 16: 28; Rv 14: 18 (for a calling angel s. PGM 13, 148). Also φωνήσας εἶπεν Lk 16: 24; 23: 46.

2. *call* someone—**a.** in the sense *address as* ὑμεῖς φωνεῖτέ με· ὁ διδάσκαλος you call me 'Teacher' (nom. w. art. as voc.; cf. Bl-D. §143; 147, 3; Rob. 458; 466) J 13: 13.

b. *call to oneself, summon* (Tob 5: 9) τινά someone (Jos., Vi. 172, Ant. 6, 314) ὁ Ἰησοῦς ἐφώνησεν αὐτούς Mt 20: 32. Cf. 27: 47; Mk 3: 31 t.r.; 9: 35; 10: 49a, b; 15: 35; J 1: 48; 2: 9; 4: 16; 11: 28a; 18: 33; Ac 4: 18 D; 9: 41; 10: 7. τὸν Λάζαρον ἐφώνησεν ἐκ τοῦ μνημείου J 12: 17. —τὰ πρόβατα φωνεῖ κατ' ὄνομα 10: 3. *Have* τινά *someone called* Mk 10: 49c; Lk 16: 2; J 9: 18, 24; 11: 28b. Pass. εἶπεν φωνηθῆναι αὐτῷ τοὺς δούλους *he said the slaves should be called into his presence* Lk 19: 15. W. the obj. omitted φωνήσαντες ἐπυνθάνοντο *they called* (someone) *and inquired* Ac 10: 18.—**c.** in the sense *invite* τινά someone Lk 14: 12. M-M.*

φωνή, ῆς, ἡ (Hom.+; inscr., pap., LXX, En., Ep. Arist., Philo, Joseph., Test. 12 Patr.; Sib. Or. 2, 3).

1. *sound, tone, noise* the source of which is added in the gen.: of musical instruments (Pla., Rep. 3 p. 397A ὀργάνων; Eur., Tro. 127 συρίγγων; Plut., Mor. 713c ψαλτηρίου καὶ αὐλοῦ; Aristoxenus, fgm. 6; Paus. Attic. α, 169; Ex 19: 16, Is 18: 3 and PsSol 8: 1 σάλπιγγος; Is 24: 8 κιθάρας; Aristobul. in Euseb., Pr. Ev. 8, 10, 13) σάλπιγγος Mt 24: 31 v.l.; D 16: 6. φωναὶ τῆς σάλπιγγος *blasts of the trumpet* Rv 8: 13b; or of those who play them κιθαρῳδῶν 14: 2d; 18: 22a; cf. 10: 7. Of the sound of the wind J 3: 8; cf. Ac 2: 6. Of the rolling of thunder (1 Km 7: 10) Rv 6: 1; 14: 2c; 19: 6c. Of the roar of water (Ezk 1: 24b) 1: 15b; 14: 2b; 19: 6b. Of the whirring of wings (Ezk 1: 24a) 9: 9a. Of the clatter of chariots ibid. b (cf. Ezk 3: 13; 26: 10). Of the noise made by a millstone 18: 22b. Of a shout produced by a crowd of people φωνὴ ὄχλου πολλοῦ 19: 1, 6a (Da 10: 6 Theod.). Of the sound caused by spoken words (Da 10: 9) ἡ φωνὴ τοῦ ἀσπασμοῦ σου Lk 1: 44. φωνὴ ῥημάτων *sound of words* Hb 12: 19. Cf. 1 Cl 27: 7 (Ps 18: 4). Abs. of the sound made by a wail of sorrow (cf. Test. Iss. 1: 4) Mt 2: 18 (Jer 38: 15). μεγάλη φωνὴ ἐγένετο ἐν τ. οὐρανῷ GP 9: 35.—Of musical instruments it is said that they φωνὴν διδόναι *produce a sound* 1 Cor 14: 7f.—In Rv we have ἀστραπαὶ καὶ φωναὶ καὶ βρονταί (cf. Ex 19: 16) 4: 5; 8: 5; 11: 19; 16: 18 (are certain other sounds in nature thought of here in addition to thunder, as e.g. the roar of the storm? In Ex 19: 16 φωναὶ κ. ἀστραπαί are surely thunder and lightning. But in Ex 9: 23, 28; 1 Km 12: 18 the mng. of φωναί remains unclear. Cf. also Esth 1: 1d φωναί, βρονταί).

2. *voice*—**a.** gener. Any form of speech or other utterance w. the voice can take place μετὰ φωνῆς μεγάλης Lk 17: 15; ἐν φωνῇ μεγάλῃ Rv 5: 2; 14: 7, 9; mostly φωνῇ μεγάλῃ (Achilles Tat. 8, 1, 1; Sib. Or. 3, 669; 5, 63) Mt 27: 46, 50; Mk 1: 26; 5: 7; 15: 34; Lk 4: 33; 8: 28; 19: 37; J 11: 43; Ac 7: 57, 60; 8: 7; Rv 6: 10; 7: 2, 10 al.; IPhld 7: 1a. μεγάλῃ τῇ φωνῇ (Diod. S. 1, 70, 5; 8, 23, 3; Lucian, Hist. Conscr. 1; Jos., Bell. 6, 188) Ac 14: 10 t.r.; 26: 24; ἐν ἰσχυρᾷ φωνῇ Rv 18: 2. ἐν φωνῇ μιᾷ IEph 4: 2; μιᾷ φ. (Pla., Laws 1 p. 634E; Diod. S. 11, 9, 3; 11, 26, 6;

19, 81, 2; Ael. Aristid. 24, 4 K.=44 p. 825 D.; Lucian, Nigr. 14) AP 5: 19.—αἴρειν φωνήν (αἴρω 1b) Lk 17: 13; πρός τινα Ac 4: 24. ἐπαίρειν φωνήν (ἐπαίρω 1) Lk 11: 27; Ac 2: 14; 14: 11; 22: 22. ἀκούειν τῆς φωνῆς τινος *hear someone speaking* or *calling* (Test. Jos. 9: 4) J 5: 25, 28; 10: 3; Hb 3: 7, 15; 4: 7 (the last three Ps 94: 7); w. a neg. and acc. (φωνήν) Mt 12: 19 (cf. Is 42: 2); J 5: 37. The same expr.=*listen to someone's speech* or *call, follow someone* (Gen 3: 17) 10: 16, 27; 18: 37; Rv 3: 20; B 8: 7; cf. 9: 2 (s. Ex 15: 26).—(ἡ) φωνὴ (τοῦ) νυμφίου (cf. Jer 25: 10) J 3: 29 (cf. Arrian, Cyneg. 17, 1 the dogs χαίρουσιν τὴν φωνὴν τοῦ δεσπότου γνωρίζουσαι); Rv 18: 23.

b. *voice* as it varies from individual to individual or fr. one mood to another (X., An. 2, 6, 9; Gen 27: 22) ἐπιγνοῦσα τὴν φωνὴν τοῦ Πέτρου Ac 12: 14. Cf. J 10: 4f (s. Ael. Aristid. 46 p. 320, horses). ἤθελον ἀλλάξαι τὴν φωνήν μου Gal 4: 20 (ἀλλάσσω 1. φωνή=*tone*: Artem. 4, 56 p. 235, 15).

c. that which the voice gives expression to *call, cry, outcry, loud* or *solemn declaration* (Sb 7251, 21 [III/IV AD] = *order, command*) ὁ Ἰησοῦς ἀφεὶς φωνὴν μεγάλην Mk 15: 37. φωνὴ ἐγένετο μία *a single outcry arose* Ac 19: 34 (cf. Jos., Vi. 133). Cf. 22: 14; 24: 21. Pl. (Ael. Aristid. 52, 3 K.=28 p. 551 D.: ἦσαν φωναί; Jos., Vi. 231, Ant. 15, 52) φωναὶ μεγάλαι *loud cries* Lk 23: 23a; cf. b. ἐλάλησαν αἱ βρονταὶ τὰς ἑαυτῶν φωνάς *the thunders sounded forth their crashing peals* Rv 10: 3b. θεοῦ φωνή (D φωναί) καὶ οὐκ ἀνθρώπου (this is) *the statement of a god and not of a man* Ac 12: 22 (Plut., Mor. 567f: a divine φωνή sounds forth fr. a φῶς μέγα that appears suddenly; Ael. Aristid. 45 p. 11 D.: Πυθίας φωνή; Epict. 3, 23, 20 ἰδοὺ φωναὶ φιλοσόφου; 3, 22, 50; Biogr. p. 454 people received sayings of Hippocr. ὡς θεοῦ φωνὰς κ. οὐκ ἀνθρωπίνου προελθούσας ἐκ στόματος). φωνὴ ἐνεχθεῖσα αὐτῷ *a declaration* (was) *borne to him* 2 Pt 1: 17; cf. 18. Also of sayings in scripture αἱ φωναὶ τῶν προφητῶν Ac 13: 27 (Diod. S. 19, 1, 4 ἡ Σόλωνος φωνή; 20, 30, 2 τῆς τοῦ μάντεως [=τοῦ δαιμονίου] φωνῆς; Diog. L. 8, 14 sayings of Pythagoras).

d. In accordance w. OT and Jewish usage gener. (cf. Bousset, Rel.³ 315. But the Socratic δαιμόνιον=ὁ θεός [Ep. 1, 7] is also called ἡ φωνή: Socrat., Ep. 1, 9 τὸ δαιμόνιόν μοι, ἡ φωνή, γέγονεν, cf. Pla., Apol. 31D) 'the voice' oft. speaks, though the (heavenly) speaker neither appears nor is mentioned (cf. PGM 3, 119 ἐξορκίζω σε κατὰ τῆς ἑβραϊκῆς φωνῆς.—In most cases the divine voice is differentiated fr. the divinity: Theopompus [IV BC] in Diog. L. 1, 115 when Epimenides wishes to build τὸ τῶν Νυμφῶν ἱερόν: ῥαγῆναι φωνὴν ἐξ οὐρανοῦ 'Ἐπιμενίδη, μὴ Νυμφῶν, ἀλλὰ Διός'; Plut., Mor. 355E; 775B; Oenomaus in Euseb., Pr. Ev. 5, 28, 2 Lycurgus receives the laws ὑπὸ τῆς θεοῦ φωνῆς in Delphi; Artapanus in Euseb., Pr. Ev. 9, 27, 21; Jos., Ant. 1, 185 φ. θεία παρῆν; 3, 90 φ. ὑψόθεν . . . 2, 267) ἰδοὺ φωνὴ ἐκ τῶν οὐρανῶν λέγουσα (on the voice fr. heaven s. the lit. s.v. βαπτίζω 2a; also JKosnetter, D. Taufe Jesu '36, esp. 140-90, and FJDölger, Antike u. Christentum V 3, '36, 218-23) Mt 3: 17; cf. 17: 5. ἦλθεν φ. (ἐκ) Mk 9: 7 t.r.; J 12: 28 (Ps.-Callisth. 1, 45, 2f ἦλθεν φωνὴ ἀπὸ τοῦ ἀδύτου· the divine saying follows in direct discourse). ἐξῆλθεν φ. Rv 16: 17 (ἐκ); 19: 5 (ἀπὸ τοῦ θρόνου). γίνεται (ἐγένετο) φ. (ἐκ: Plut., Agis et Cleom. 28, 3 Z.: φωνήν ἐκ τοῦ ἱεροῦ γενέσθαι φράζουσαν; Ael. Aristid. 40, 22 K.=5 p. 62 D.: φωνῆς θείας γενομένης) . . . ἐκ τοῦ μητρῴου [= temple of the Mother of the Gods]) Mk 1: 11; 9: 7; Lk 3: 22; 9: 35f; J 12: 30; Ac 10: 13, 15 (both πρὸς αὐτόν); MPol 9: 1a; GEb 3a (understood), cf. ibid. b; ἐγένετο φ. κυρίου

Ac 7: 31 (cf. Jos., Vi. 259 ἐγένοντο φωναί). ἀπεκρίθη φ. ἐκ τ. οὐρανοῦ 11: 9; ἦχος φωνῆς μοι ἀπεκρίθη Hv 4, 1, 4. ἀκούειν φωνήν *hear a voice* (also w. such additions as λέγουσαν, ἐκ w. gen. of place, μεγάλην, gen. of the speaker) Ac 9: 4; 22: 9; 26: 14; Rv 6: 6f; 9: 13; 10: 4, 8; 12: 10; 14: 2; 18: 4; MPol 9: 1b; Epil Mosq 3; φωνῆς w. the same mng. (w. corresp. additions) Ac 9: 7; 11: 7; 22: 7; Rv 11: 12; 14: 13; 16: 1; 21: 3; GP 10: 41.

e. special cases: ἐπέστρεψα βλέπειν τὴν φωνὴν ἥτις ἐλάλει μετ' ἐμοῦ *I turned around to see* (to whom) *the voice that was speaking to me* (belonged) Rv 1: 12 (cf. X., Hell. 5, 1, 22 σκεψόμενοι τίς ἡ κραυγή; Aesop 248 Halm ἐπεστράφη πρὸς τὴν φωνήν). φωνὴ βοῶντος ἐν τῇ ἐρήμῳ *hark! someone is calling in the desert!* (Is 40: 3; cf. En. 9, 2; Jos., Bell. 6, 301) Mt 3: 3; Mk 1: 3; Lk 3: 4. Referring to the same prophetic pass., John the Baptist applies the same words to himself J 1: 23 *the voice of one calling in the desert* (Ael. Aristid. 49, 5 K.=25 p. 489 D.: φωνὴ λέγοντός του 'τεθεράπευσαι'; Ps.-Pla., Axioch. 1 p. 364A φωνὴ βοῶντός του).—B 9: 3.

3. *language* (Aeschyl., Hdt.+; Cebes 33, 6; Aelian, V.H. 12, 48; Herodian 5, 3, 4; Diog. L. 8, 3; Suppl. Epigr. Gr. VIII 548, 17 [I BC]; PLond. 77, 13; PGM 12, 188 πᾶσα γλῶσσα κ. πᾶσα φωνή; Gen 11: 1; Dt 28: 49; 2 Macc 7: 8, 21, 27; 4 Macc 12: 7; Jos., C. Ap. 1, 1; 50; 73 al.) 1 Cor 14: 10f; 2 Pt 2: 16 (an animal w. ἀνθρώπου φ. as Appian, Bell. Civ. 4, 4 §14 βοῦς φωνὴν ἀφῆκεν ἀνθρώπου; schol. on Apollon. Rhod. 2, 1146 ὁ κριὸς ἀνθρωπίνη χρησάμενος φωνῇ; Philo, Op. M. 156); Dg 5: 1.—OBetz, TW IX, 272-302: φωνή and related words. M-M. B. 1248; 1260.

φῶς, φωτός, τό (trag.+ [in Hom. φάος or φόως]; inscr., pap., LXX, En., Philo, Joseph., Test. 12 Patr., Sib. Or.; loanw. in rabb.) *light*.

1. lit.—a. gener. (opp. σκότος, as Job 18: 18; En. 104, 8; PGM 5, 101; 7, 262; 13, 335) 2 Cor 4: 6 (cf. Gen 1: 3ff); 6: 14; Papias 3. Not present at night J 11: 10. λευκὸς ὡς τὸ φ. Mt 17: 2. νεφέλη φωτός *a bright cloud* vs. 5 v.l. Of the light of the sun (φ. ἡλίου: Dio Chrys. 57[74], 20 fr. Eur., Hippol. 617; Ael. Aristid. 45, 29 K.=8 p. 95 D.) Rv 22: 5b; of a wondrous star IEph 19: 2a, b. Of lamp-light (Jer 25: 10) Lk 8: 16; 11: 33 𝔓⁷⁵ et al.; J 5: 35 (symbol.); Rv 18: 23; 22: 5a. Light fr. a supernatural source (Ael. Aristid. 49, 46 K.= p. 500, 17 D. ἐγένετο φῶς παρὰ τῆς Ἴσιδος; Marinus, Vi. Procli 23: a halo of light around Proclus' head moves the beholder to προσκύνησις): an angel Ac 12: 7; 2 Cor 11: 14 (here ἄγγελος φωτός [cf. IQS 3, 20] is a messenger of the world of light in contrast to Satan); of Paul's conversion experience Ac 9: 3; 22: 6 (both w. ἐκ τοῦ οὐρανοῦ, as X., Cyr. 4, 2, 15; Dio Chrys. 11[12], 29), 9, 11; 26: 13 (οὐρανόθεν); the heavenly city Rv 21: 24. S. 2 below.—Symbolic expressions: ἐν τῷ φωτί *in the open, publicly* (φ. of 'the open' X., Ages. 9, 1.—Opp. ἐν τῇ σκοτίᾳ) Mt 10: 27; Lk 12: 3 (Proverbia Aesopi 104 P.: ἅπερ ἐν νυκτὶ καλύπτεται, ταῦτα εἰς φῶς λαληθέντα . . .). Of an evil-doer it is said that μισεῖ τὸ φῶς καὶ οὐκ ἔρχεται πρὸς τὸ φῶς J 3: 20 (cf. Eur., Iph. T. 1026 κλεπτῶν γὰρ ἡ νύξ, τῆς δ' ἀληθείας τὸ φῶς; Plut., Mor. 82B, Contra Volupt. in Stob., Anthol. 3, 6, 33 vol. III 299 H.; Philo, De Jos. 68, Spec. Leg. 1, 319-23; Test. Napht. 2: 10).

b. by metonymy—a. that which gives light, *light* (*-bearer*): torch, lamp, lantern, etc. (X., Hell. 5, 1, 8 φῶς ἔχειν; Musaeus v. 224 of the λύχνος. Pl., Plut., Ant. 26, 6, Pelop. 12, 3 al.; Lucian, Philops. 31) Ac 16: 29. The *fire*, which furnishes both light and heat (X., Hell. 6, 2, 29,

Cyr. 7, 5, 27; 1 Macc 12: 29) Mk 14: 54 (GWBuchanan, ET 68, '56, 27); Lk 22: 56. Heavenly bodies (Manetho 6, 146 sun and moon δύο φῶτα; likew. Dio Chrys. 23[40], 38; Ptolem., Apotel. 2, 13, 8; 3, 3, 3; 3, 5, 3 al. τὰ φ.=constellations; Vett. Val. index II p. 384; PGM 13, 400; Ps 135: 7; Jer 4: 23): God is the πατὴρ τῶν φώτων Js 1: 17 (cf. Apoc. of Moses 36; 38); the sun as τὸ φῶς τοῦ κόσμου τούτου J 11: 9 (Macrobius, Saturnal. 1, 23, 21 ἥλιε παντοκράτωρ, ... κόσμου φῶς. Cf. Ps.-Demosth. 60, 24). Of the eye as an organ of light (Eur., Cycl. 633 φῶς Κύκλωπος) Mt 6: 23; Lk 11: 35.

β. that which is illuminated by light: πᾶν τὸ φανερούμενον φῶς ἐστιν everything that becomes visible is (=stands in the) light Eph 5: 14.

2. The passages in the central portion of 1a above show that light is the element and sphere of the Divine (Ael. Aristid. 28, 114 K.=49 p. 528 D.: τοῦ θεοῦ φῶς; Sib. Or. 3, 787 ἀθάνατον φ.). God is called φῶς οἰκῶν ἀπρόσιτον 1 Ti 6: 16 (Plut., Pericl. 39, 2 the gods dwell in τὸν τόπον ἀσάλευτον φωτὶ καθαρωτάτῳ περιλαμπόμενον, Mor. 567F: the divine φωνή proceeds fr. a φῶς μέγα that suddenly shines forth), or it is said of him that he is ἐν τῷ φωτί 1 J 1: 7b. In fact, he is described as light pure and simple ὁ θεὸς φῶς ἐστιν vs. 5 (Philo, Somn. 1, 75.— OSchaefer, StKr 105, '33, 467-76). Cf. Dg 9: 6. Likew. the Divine Redeemer in the Fourth Gospel J 1: 7-9, cf. 1 J 2: 8 (FAuer, Wie ist J 1: 9 zu verstehen?: ThGl 28, '36, 397-407); 12: 35a, b, 36a, b (on divinity as light cf. RHCharles, The Book of Enoch '12, 71f; GPWetter, Phos (ΦΩΣ) '15. On this MDibelius, Die Vorstellung v. göttl. Licht: Deutsche Literaturzeitung 36, '15, 1469-83 and MPNilsson, GGA '16, 49ff; FJDölger, Die Sonne der Gerechtigkeit '18, Sol Salutis '20; WBousset, Kyrios Christos² '21, 173; 174, 2 and 3; HJonas, Gnosis u. spätantiker Geist I '34; Dodd 133-6; 183-7 al.; ERGoodenough, By Light, Light: The Mystic Gospel of Hellenistic Judaism '35; RBultmann, Z. Gesch. der Lichtsymbolik im Altertum: Philol. 97, '48, 1-36; IQH 4, 6; 18, 29; BGU 597, 33 [I AD]). He calls himself τὸ φῶς τοῦ κόσμου 8: 12a; 9: 5; 12: 46; cf. 3: 19a (Wetter, 'Ich bin das Licht der Welt': Beiträge zur Religionswissenschaft I 2, '14, 171ff), and is called τὸ φῶς τῶν ἀνθρώπων 1: 4 (Ael. Aristid. 45, 33 K.=8 p. 97 D.: Serapis as κοινὸν ἅπασιν ἀνθρώποις φῶς; hymn to Anubis fr. Kios [WPeek, D. Isishymnus v. Andros '30, p. 139] l. 7: Isis as φῶς πᾶσι βροτοῖσι), and his very being is light and life (ζωή 2aα and β; cf. JPWeisengoff, CBQ 8, '46, 448-51) 1: 4. Cf. also vs. 5; 3: 19b, 21; Lk 2: 32 (Jesus is a φῶς εἰς ἀποκάλυψιν ἐθνῶν). —FJDölger, Lumen Christi: Antike u. Christentum V 1, '35, 1-43. The martyr καθαρὸν φῶς λαμβάνει receives the pure light of heaven IRo 6: 2. This brings us to

3. the fig. mng.—a. light, that illuminates the spirit and soul of man, is gener. the element in which the redeemed person lives, rich in blessings without and within (En. 5, 6 σωτηρία, φῶς ἀγαθόν; 8 φ. καὶ χάρις); of Messianic salvation, the gospel, etc. (opp. σκοτία, σκότος) Mt 4: 16a, b (Is 9: 1a, b; cf. Lucian, Nigr. 4 ἔχαιρον ὥσπερ ἐκ ζοφεροῦ ἀέρος ἐς μέγα φῶς ἀναβλέπων); Ac 26: 18; Eph 5: 13; Col 1: 12; 1 Pt 2: 9; B 3: 4 (Is 58: 8); 1 Cl 16: 12 (Is 53: 11); 36: 2; 59: 2; 2 Cl 1: 4. τὸ φῶς τῆς ζωῆς (cf. IQS 3, 7) J 8: 12b. τὸ φῶς τὸ ἀληθινόν (saying of Pythagoreans: Wiener Stud. 8, 1886 p. 280 no. 118 in contrast to σκότος) 1 J 2: 8, as J 1: 9. φῶς καταγγέλλειν Ac 26: 23. To be filled w. Christian truth means ἐν τῷ φωτὶ περιπατεῖν 1 J 1: 7a, εἶναι 2: 9, μένειν vs. 10. Such persons are called υἱοὶ τοῦ φωτός Lk 16: 8; J 12: 36c (cf. IQS 1, 9 et passim); 1 Th 5: 5; τέκνα φωτός Eph

5: 8b (EGSelwyn, 1 Pt '46, 375-82; KGKuhn, NTS 7, '61, 339: IQS 3, 20; 5, 9; 5, 10); τέκνα φωτὸς ἀληθείας IPhld 2: 1 (Porphyr., Ep. ad Marcellam 20 φῶς τοῦ θεοῦ τῆς ἀληθείας; Simplicius p. 88, 3; 138, 30 Düb. τὸ τῆς ἀληθείας φῶς). They put on τὰ ὅπλα τοῦ φωτός Ro 13: 12, travel the ὁδὸς τοῦ φωτός B 18: 1; 19: 1, 12, and produce the καρπὸς τοῦ φωτός Eph 5: 9.

b. bearers or bringers of this kind of light (φῶς of persons: Od. 16, 23; Anacr. 124 Bergk φάος Ἑλλήνων; Pind., Isthm. 2, 17; trag.; Biogr. p. 453 Hippocr. as ἀστήρ and φῶς of the healing art; Dit., Syll.³ 1238, 2 [c. 160 AD] Φήγιλλα, τὸ φῶς τῆς οἰκίας) Is 49: 6 φῶς ἐθνῶν is referred to Paul and Barnabas Ac 13: 47, and to Christ B 14: 8; cf. 14: 7 (Is 42: 6) and s. 2 above. The Jew considers himself a φῶς τῶν ἐν σκότει Ro 2: 19. Jesus' disciples are τὸ φῶς τοῦ κόσμου Mt 5: 14; cf. vs. 16.—On Is 49: 6 s. HMOrlinsky, The 75th Anniv. Vol. of the Jewish Quarterly Review '67, 409-28.

c. by metonymy, the one who is illuminated or filled w. such light, or who stands in it Eph 5: 8a (s. 1bβ above).— On the dualism of light and darkness, etc., cf. the newly discovered Hebr. texts in the Dead Sea scrolls: KGKuhn, ZThK 47, '50, 192-211; WHBrownlee, Excerpts fr. the Transl. of the Dead Sea Manuals of Discipline: Bull. of the Amer. Schools of Oriental Research no. 121, '51, 8-13; HPreisker, ThLZ 77, '52, 673-8; CGHowie, The Cosmic Struggle: Interpretation 8, '54, 206-17.—ChMugler, Dictionnaire historique de la terminologie optique des Grecs '64; HConzelmann, TW IX, 302-409: φῶς and related words. M.-M. B. 60.*

φωστήρ, ῆρος, ὁ—1. light-giving body, esp. of heavenly bodies, specif. star (Heliod. 2, 24, 6; Vett. Val. 104, 30; 105, 7; Herm. Wr. 496, 2 Sc. [the sun]; Anth. Pal. 15, 17, 3 [Christian]; PGM 13, 298; Fluchtaf. 5, 23; Gen 1: 14, 16; Wsd 13: 2; Sir 43: 7; Sib. Or. 3, 88; Test. Levi 14: 3, Jud. 25: 2) Phil 2: 15 (cf. Da 12: 3; En. 104, 2).—2. splendor, radiance (Anth. Pal. 11, 359, 7; 1 Esdr 8: 76) Rv 21: 11. M.-M.*

φωσφόρος, ον bearing or giving light (Eur.+; pap., Philo); subst. ὁ φ. the morning star, Venus (Eur., Ion 1157; Ps.-Pla., Tim. Locr. 96E; 97A; Plut., Mor. 430A; 601A; 889A al.; Cicero, Nat. Deor. 2, 20; Vett. Val. 236, 6; Sib. Or. 5, 516) fig. 2 Pt 1: 19. JBoehmer, ZNW 22, '23, 228-33; FBoll, Sternglaube u. Sterndeutung⁴ '31, 47f.— FJDölger, Antike u. Christentum V 1, '35, 1ff interprets the 'light-bearer' to mean the sun (this mng. of φ. in Nicetas Eugen. 1, 87; 3, 21; 5, 258 Hercher); cf. HWindisch ad loc. M.-M.*

φωταγωγός, όν (so in Lucian et al.; PGM 5, 190; φωταγωγία in Vett. Val. 301, 22; PGM 4, 955; φωταγωγέω in Celsus 2, 71) light-bringing, light-giving ἄγγελοι φ. light-bringing angels who are set over the way of light B 18: 1.*

φωτεινός, ή, όν (X.+; Sir 17: 31; 23: 19, both comp.) shining, bright, radiant νεφέλη φ. a bright cloud indicating the presence of God Mt 17: 5 (cf. X., Mem. 4, 3, 4 ἥλιος φ.). AP 3: 7 of the radiant garments of the angels. —Opp. σκοτεινός (X., Mem. 3, 10, 1; En. 22, 2) illuminated, full of light (Artem. 1, 64 βαλανεῖα φωτεινά; 2, 36) Mt 6: 22; Lk 11: 34, 36a, b. M.-M.*

φωτίζω (Aristot.+; LXX; En. 5, 8; Philo, Joseph., Test. 12 Patr.) fut. φωτίσω (1 Cor 4: 5; Rv 22: 5) and φωτιῶ (Rv 22: 5 v.l.; Test. Levi 4: 3), cf. Thackeray 228f; 1 aor. ἐφώτισα. Pass.: pf. ptc. πεφωτισμένος; 1 aor. ἐφωτίσθην.

1. intr. (Aristot.; Theophr.; Plut., Num. 4, 9; 8, 2; Sir 42: 16; Philo, Dec. 49) *shine* of God (Ps 75: 5) ἐπί τινα *upon someone* Rv 22: 5.

2. trans.—**a.** lit. *give light to, light (up), illuminate* (Aristarchus of Samos [III BC] p. 358, 20 al. TLHeath ['13]; Diod. S. 3, 48, 4 of the sun ἀκτῖσι τὸν κόσμον; Galen XIX p. 174 K.; PGM 3, 152; 4, 2345; Fluchtaf. 4, 14; 2 Esdr 19 [Neh 9]: 12, 19 τὴν ὁδόν) τινα *someone* Lk 11: 36; Rv 22: 5 t.r.; τὴν πόλιν Rv 21: 23. Pass. (Anaximander in Diog. L. 2, 1 ἀπὸ ἡλίου; Plut., Mor. 1120E; Diog. L. 7, 144 the whole earth ὑπ' αὐτοῦ [the sun] φωτίζεσθαι) 18: 1.

b. fig., of heavenly light (φῶς 2; 3) that is granted the 'enlightened one' (cf. the prayer PGM 4, 990, that calls upon the μέγιστος θεός as τὸν τὰ πάντα φωτίζοντα καὶ διαυγάζοντα τῇ ἰδίᾳ δυνάμει τὸν σύμπαντα κόσμον; Herm. Wr. 1, 32 the inspired one prays to his god for δύναμις and χάρις: ἵνα φωτίσω τοὺς ἐν ἀγνοίᾳ. S. also 13, 18; 19 τὸ πᾶν τὸ ἐν ἡμῖν σῷζε ζωή, φώτιζε φῶς, πνευμάτιζε θεέ; Philo, Fuga and Test. Benj. 6: 4 τ. ψυχήν; Sextus 97.—GAnrich, Das antike Mysterienwesen 1894, 125f; GWobbermin, Religionsgesch. Studien 1896, 155ff; Rtzst., Mysterienrel.³ '27, 44; 264; 292) *enlighten, give light to, shed light upon* τὸ φῶς τὸ ἀληθινὸν (i.e. Christ, the heavenly Redeemer) φωτίζει πάντα ἄνθρωπον J 1: 9 (s. Hdb. ad loc. and s.v. φῶς 2.—For the combination w. φῶς: Cleomedes [II AD] 2, 4 p. 188, 18 HZiegler τὸ φῶς τὸ φωτίζον αὐτόν; Proclus on Pla., Cratyl. p. 103, 28 Pasqu.) φωτίσαι πάντας Eph 3: 9 t.r.

(perh. in the sense 'instruct', cf. 4 Km 17: 27f). God is implored to grant πεφωτισμένους τοὺς ὀφθαλμοὺς τῆς καρδίας 1: 18 (φωτίζειν ὀφθαλμούς: 2 Esdr [Ezra] 9: 8; Ps 18: 9; Bar 1: 12). The Roman church is πεφωτισμένη ἐν θελήματι (i.e. of God) IRo inscr. οἱ ἅπαξ φωτισθέντες Hb 6: 4; cf. 10: 32.

c. *bring to light, reveal* τὶ someth. (Polyb. 22, 5, 10; Epict. 1, 4, 31 τὴν ἀλήθειαν; Plut., Mor. 902c; Jos., Ant. 8, 143 the hidden mng. of the riddle; pass., Lucian, Calum. 32) τὰ κρυπτὰ τοῦ σκότους *that which is hidden in the dark* 1 Cor 4: 5. φ. ζωὴν καὶ ἀφθαρσίαν διὰ τοῦ εὐαγγελίου *bring life and immortality to light through the gospel* 2 Ti 1: 10. Abs., foll. by indir. question φωτίσαι τίς ἡ οἰκονομία τοῦ μυστηρίου *to make clear what the plan of the mystery is* Eph 3: 9. M-M.*

φωτισμός, οῦ, ὁ—1. *illumination, enlightenment, light* (Strato of Lamps. [300 BC] fgm. 76 Wehrli '50; Petosiris, fgm. 12 l. 178 τῆς σελήνης; Sext. Emp., Math. 10, 224 ἐξ ἡλίου; Plut., Mor. 929D; 931A; PMich. 149, 3; 33 [II AD]; Ps 26: 1; 43: 4; Job 3: 9; Philo, Somn. 1, 53) symbol. (Test. Levi 14: 4 τὸ φῶς τοῦ νόμου... εἰς φωτισμὸν παντὸς ἀνθρώπου) εἰς τὸ μὴ αὐγάσαι τὸν φωτισμὸν τοῦ εὐαγγελίου τῆς δόξης τοῦ Χριστοῦ *so that they do not see the light of the gospel of the glory of Christ* 2 Cor 4: 4.

2. *bringing to light, revealing* (φωτίζω 2c) πρὸς φωτισμὸν τῆς γνώσεως vs. 6 (but for other possibilities s. the commentaries. Cf. also Herm. Wr. 10, 21 τὸ τῆς γνώσεως φῶς; 7, 2a). M-M.*

X

χαίρω impf. ἔχαιρον; fut. χαρήσομαι (Bl-D. §77; Mlt.-H. 264); 2 aor. (pass.) ἐχάρην (Hom.+; inscr., pap., LXX, En., Ep. Arist., Philo, Joseph., Test. 12 Patr.).

1. *rejoice, be glad* opp. κλαίειν J 16: 20; Ro 12: 15a, b (Damasc., Vi. Isid. 284 χαίρεις πρὸς τοὺς χαίρεντας) 1 Cor 7: 30a, b. Opp. λύπην ἔχειν J 16: 22. W. ἀγαλλιᾶσθαι (Hab 3: 18) Mt 5: 12; 1 Pt 4: 13b; cf. Rv 19: 7. W. εὐφραίνεσθαι (Jo 2: 23 al. in LXX) Lk 15: 32; Rv 11: 10. W. σκιρτᾶν Lk 6: 23. W. acc. of the inner obj. (Bl-D. §153, 1 w. app.; Rob. 477) χ. χαρὰν μεγάλην *be very glad* (Jon 4: 6) Mt 2: 10. τῇ χαρᾷ ᾗ (by attraction for ἥν) χαίρομεν 1 Th 3: 9. Also χαρᾷ χ., which prob. betrays the infl. of the OT (Is 66: 10), J 3: 29 (Bl-D. §198, 6; Rob. 531; 550). The ptc. is used w. other verbs *with joy, gladly* (Appian, Bell. Civ. 4, 40 §169 ἄπιθι χαίρων; 3 Km 8, 66; Eutecnius 4 p. 43, 7 ἄπεισι χαίρουσα; Laud. Therap. 12 χαίρων ἐστέλλετο) ὑπεδέξατο αὐτὸν χαίρων Lk 19: 6; cf. vs. 37; 15: 5; Ac 5: 41; 8: 39.—The obj. of or reason for the joy is denoted in var. ways: by a prep. χαίρειν ἐπί τινι *rejoice over someone* or *someth.* (Soph.+; X., Cyr. 8, 4, 12, Mem. 2, 6, 35; Pla., Leg. 5 p. 729D; Diod. S. 1, 25, 2; Plut., Mor. 87E; 1088E; BGU 531 I, 4 [I AD]; POxy. 41, 17; Tob 13: 15a, b; Pr 2: 14; 24: 19; Bar 4: 33; Jos., Ant. 1, 294; 3, 32) Mt 18: 13; Lk 1: 14; 13: 17; Ac 15: 31; Ro 16: 19; 1 Cor 13: 6; 16: 17; 2 Cor 7: 13; Rv 11: 10; Hs 5, 2, 5 and 11; 8, 1, 17; 8, 5, 1 and 6; Dg 11: 5. Also διά w. acc. (Appian, Bell. Civ. 4, 102 §428; Ep. Arist. 42) J 3: 29 (11: 15 it is the ὅτι-clause that gives the reason, and δι' ὑμᾶς is *for your sakes = in your interest*); 1 Th 3: 9. ἔν τινι (Soph., Trach. 1118; Pla., Rep. 10 p. 603c; En. 104, 13) ἐν τούτῳ *over that* Phil 1: 18a (for other mngs. of ἐν s. below). περί

τινος *in someth.* (Pla., Ep. 2 p. 310E) 1 Cl 65: 1. ἵνα μὴ λύπην σχῶ ἀφ' ὧν ἔδει με χαίρειν (either ἀπὸ τούτων ἀφ' ὧν or ἀπὸ τούτων οἷς) 2 Cor 2: 3. W. dat. of the pers. Papias 2: 3. The reason or object is given by ὅτι (Lucian, Charon 17; Ex 4: 31) Lk 10: 20b; J 11: 15 (s. above); 14: 28; 2 Cor 7: 9, 16; Phil 4: 10; 2 J 4. χ. ἐν τούτῳ ὅτι Lk 10: 20a. χ. ὅταν 2 Cor 13: 9. χ.... γάρ Phil 1: 18b (19). The reason or obj. is expressed by a ptc. (X., Cyr. 1, 5, 12; Pla., Rep. 5 p. 458A; Dio Chrys. 22[39], 1 al.; PGM 4, 1212 χαίρεις τοὺς σοὺς σῴζων; 1611). ἰδόντες τὸν ἀστέρα ἐχάρησαν Mt 2: 10; cf. Lk 23: 8; J 20: 20; Ac 11: 23; Phil 2: 28; Hv 3, 12, 3; Hs 5, 2, 10; 5, 3, 3; 9, 11, 7. ἀκούσαντες ἐχάρησαν *they were delighted by what they heard* Mk 14: 11; cf. Ac 13: 48.—1 Cl 33: 7; Dg 5: 16. If χαίρειν is also in the ptc., καί comes betw. the two participles: χαίρων καὶ βλέπων (and) *it is with joy that I see* Col 2: 5. ἐχάρην ἐρχομένων ἀδελφῶν καὶ μαρτυρούντων *I was glad when brethren came and testified* 3 J 3.—τῇ ἐλπίδι χαίρ. Ro 12: 12 is not 'rejoice over the hope' (the dat. stands in this mng. X., Mem. 1, 5, 4; Theopompus [IV BC]: 115 fgm. 114 Jac.; Epict., App. D, 3 [p. 479 Sch.] ἀρετῇ χ.; Iambl., Vi. Pyth. 28, 137 οἷς ὁ θεὸς χ.; Pr 17: 19), but rather *rejoice in hope* or *filled with hope* (Bl-D. §196 app.). τὸ ἐφ' ὑμῖν χαίρω *as far as you are concerned, I am glad* Ro 16: 19 t.r. In the majority of cases in our lit. ἐν does not introduce the cause of the joy (s. above): χαίρω ἐν τοῖς παθήμασιν *I rejoice in the midst of* (though *because of* is also poss.) (*the*) *suffering(s)* Col 1: 24 (the Engl. 'in' conveys both ideas). χαίρ. ἐν κυρίῳ Phil 3: 1; 4: 4a, 10 (the imperatives in 3: 1; 4: 4a, b are transl. *good-bye* [so Hom.+] by Gdspd., cf. Probs. 174f; this would class them under 2a below). Abs. Lk 22: 5; J 4: 36; 8: 56 (EbNestle, Abraham Rejoiced: ET 20, '09, 477; JHMoulton, 'Abraham Rejoiced': ibid. 523–8); 2 Cor 6: 10; 7: 7; 13: 11; Phil 2: 17f; 4: 4b (s. Gdspd. above); 1 Th 5: 16; 1 Pt 4: 13a; cf. b; GP 6: 23; Hv 3, 3, 2f; Hs 1: 11; 8, 1, 16.—On the rare mid. χαιρόμενος Ac 3: 8 D cf. Mlt. 161 w. note 1; Bl-D. §307.

2. used as a formula of greeting—**a.** as a form of address, oft. on meeting people (Hom.+; loanw. in rabb.) χαῖρε, χαίρετε *welcome, good day, hail (to you)*, *I am glad to see you*, somet. (e.g. Hermas)= *how do you do?* or even the colloq. *hello*: Mt 26: 49; 27: 29; 28: 9 (here perh. specif. *good morning* [Lucian, Pro Lapsu inter Salutandum 1 τὸ ἑωθινὸν . . . χαίρειν; also scholia p. 234, 13 Rabe; Cass. Dio 69, 18; Nicetas Eugen. 2, 31 H.; so Gdspd., Probs. 45f; he translates Lk 1: 28 and the 2 J and H passages in the same way); Mk 15: 18; Lk 1: 28 (Ps.-Callisth. 1, 4, 2 Nectanebos says to Olympia upon entering her room: χαίροις Μακεδόνων βασίλεια); J 19: 3 (on the sarcastic greeting as king cf. Diod. S. 34+35, fgm. 2, 8f [Eunus]); Hv 1, 1, 4; 1, 2, 2a, b; 4, 2, 2a, b. χαίρειν τινὶ λέγειν *greet someone, bid someone the time of day* (Epict. 3, 22, 64) 2 J 10f.—On the poss. sense *farewell, good-bye* for Phil 3: 1; 4: 4 s. 1 above, end.

b. elliptically at the beginning of a letter (X., Cyr. 4, 5, 27; Theocr. 14, 1; Plut., Ages. 21, 10= Mor. 213A; Aelian, V.H. 1, 25; Jos., Vi. 217; 365; pap. [Wilcken, Chrest. 477–82; HLietzmann, Griech. Pap.: Kl. T. 14², '10; StWitkowski, Epistulae Privatae Graecae² '11; GMilligan, Selections fr. the Gk. Pap.² '11]; LXX.—Bl-D. §389; 480, 5; Rob. 944; 1093. GAGerhard, Untersuchungen zur Gesch. des griech. Briefes, Diss. Heidelb. '03, Philol. 64, '05, 27–65; FZiemann, De Epistularum Graecarum Formulis Sollemnibus: Diss. Philol. Halenses XVIII 4, '11; PWendland, Die urchristl. Literaturformen²،³ '12, 411–17 [suppl. 15: Formalien des Briefes]; WSchubart, Einführung in die Papyruskunde '18; Dssm., LO 116ff=LAE 146ff [lit.]; FXJExler, The Form of the Ancient Gk. Letter '23; ORoller, D. Formular d. paul. Briefe '33; RLArcher, The Ep. Form in the NT: ET 63, '51f, 296–8) τοῖς ἀδελφοῖς . . . χαίρειν *greetings to the brethren* Ac 15: 23; cf. 23: 26; Js 1: 1. Ign. uses the common formula πλεῖστα χαίρειν (πολύς III 2a) IEph inscr.; IMg inscr.; ITr inscr.; IRo inscr.; ISm inscr.; IPol inscr.—The introduction to B is unique: χαίρετε, υἱοὶ καὶ θυγατέρες, ἐν ὀνόματι κυρίου, ἐν εἰρήνῃ 1: 1.—HConzelmann, TW IX 350–404; χαίρω, χάρις, εὐχαριστία et al. M-M.

χάλαζα, ης, ἡ (Hom.+; LXX, En., Philo) *hail* Rv 8: 7 (w. fire as Ex 9: 23–8); 11: 19 (lightning, thunder and hail as a divine manifestation as Jos., Ant. 6, 92; cf. Sib. Or. 3, 691); 16: 21a, b (for the extraordinary size cf. Diod. S. 19, 45, 2 χ. ἄπιστος τὸ μέγεθος, a single hailstone weighed a mina [approx. a pound] or more. The hail caused houses to collapse and killed people: Jos., Ant. 2, 305; deadly hail on the wicked as Ctesias, Pers. 25); *hailstone* Hm 11: 20. M-M.*

χαλάω fut. χαλάσω; 1 aor. ἐχάλασα, pass. ἐχαλάσθην (Pind., Aeschyl.+; PLond. 113*, 12; LXX, Philo) *let down* τὶ *someth.* (Apollon. Rhod. 2, 1267; Jer 45: 6) τὸν κράβαττον *let down the pallet* (through the roof) Mk 2: 4 (see s.v. στέγη). τὰ δίκτυα *let down the nets* into the water (cf. Alciphr. 1, 1, 4) Lk 5: 4f. As a nautical t.t. τὸ σκεῦος (q.v. 1a) Ac 27: 17. τὴν σκάφην εἰς τὴν θάλασσαν vs. 30 (χαλ. εἰς as Jos., Bell. 1, 657; Test. Jos. 1: 4). τινά *someone* (Jer 45: 6) ἐν σπυρίδι *in a hamper* Ac 9: 25; pass. 2 Cor 11: 33 (cf. the escape in Plut., Aemil. Paul. 26, 2). M-M.*

Χαλδαῖος, ου, ὁ (Hdt.+, both as a name for an inhabitant of Χαλδαία and as a designation for astrologers and interpreters of dreams; Philo, Joseph., Test. Napht., Sib. Or.) *Chaldaean*, name of a Semitic nation. γῆ Χαλδαίων (Jer 24: 5) *land of the Chaldaeans*, as the home of Abraham (Gen 11: 28, 31; 15: 7; in these passages: [ἡ] χώρα [τῶν] X.) Ac 7: 4.*

χαλεπός, ή, όν (Hom.+; inscr., pap., LXX, Philo; Jos., Ant. 4, 1 βίος, 13, 422 νόσος) *hard, difficult* καιροὶ χ. *hard times, times of stress* 2 Ti 3: 1. Of words that are hard to bear and penetrate deeply (Hes., Works 332; Dio Chrys. 49[66], 19) Hv 1, 4, 2 (w. σκληρός). Of men (Od. 1, 198; Chio, Ep. 15, 1f; Dit., Syll.³ 780, 31; Ep. Arist. 289; Jos., Ant. 15, 98) *hard to deal with, violent, dangerous* Mt 8: 28. Of animals (Pla., Polit. 274B; Ps.-X., Cyneg. 10, 23; Dio Chrys. 5, 5) B 4: 5 (comp.). In the sense *bad, evil* (Cebes 6, 2 of the πόμα of 'Απάτη) τὰ ἔργα τοῦ ἀγγέλου τῆς πονηρίας χ. ἐστι *the deeds of the angel of wickedness are evil* Hm 6, 2, 10.—Subst. τὰ χ. *(that which is) evil* (X., Mem. 2, 1, 23; POxy. 1242, 36) MPol 11: 1 (opp. τὰ δίκαια). ἀρχὴ πάντων χαλεπῶν φιλαργυρία Pol 4: 1 (cf. 1 Tim 6: 10). M-M. B. 651.*

χαλιναγωγέω fut. χαλιναγωγήσω; 1 aor. ἐχαλιναγώγησα *guide with a bit and bridle, hold in check* (Rhet. Gr. I 425, 19 ἵππον) fig. *bridle, hold in check* (Lucian, Tyrannic. 4 τὰς τῶν ἡδονῶν ὀρέξεις, Salt. 70 πάθη; Poll. 1, 215) τὶ *someth.* γλῶσσαν Js 1: 26 (cf. Philo, Somn. 2, 165). τὸ σῶμα 3: 2 (of the horse also Philo, Op. M. 86). τὴν ἐπιθυμίαν Hm 12, 1, 1. ἑαυτὸν ἀπό τινος *restrain oneself from someth.* Pol 5: 3. M-M.*

χαλινός, οῦ, ὁ (Hom.+; PSI 543, 50 [III BC]; LXX; Jos., Ant. 18, 320; loanw. in rabb.) *bit, bridle* Js 3: 3 (cf. Theognis 551 ἵπποισ' ἔμβαλλε χαλινούς; Soph., Antig. 477; X., Res Equ. 6, 7 ἵνα τὸν χ. ὀρθῶς ἐμβάλῃ; Philo, Agr. 94; cf. the Plut. quot. s.v. πηδάλιον); Rv 14: 20. M-M.*

χαλινόω (X.+) *bridle, hold in check* (Theophr. et al.; Ps.-Phoc. 57 ὀργήν) Js 1: 26 B.*

χάλιξ, ικος, ὁ (Thu., Aristoph.+; pap., LXX) *small, sharp stone, gravel* AP 15: 30.*

χαλκεύς, έως, ὁ (Hom.+; inscr., pap., LXX) *coppersmith*, then gener. *(black)smith, metal-worker* (Aristot., Poet. 25 χαλκέας τοὺς τὸν σίδηρον ἐργαζομένους; Gen 4: 22; 2 Ch 24: 12 χαλκεῖς σιδήρου) 2 Ti 4: 14; Hv 1, 3, 2; making idols Dg 2: 3. M-M. B. 606.*

χαλκεύω pf. pass. ptc. κεχαλκευμένος (Hom.+; 1 Km 13: 20; Jos., Ant. 3, 172, C. Ap. 2, 242) *forge*, first bronze, then metal gener. (Jos., Bell. 7, 429 a golden lamp) Dg 2: 2f.*

χαλκηδών, όνος, ὁ *the chalcedony*, a precious stone (λίθος ὁ χαλκηδόνιος: Les lapidaires Grecs ed. MCh-ERuelle 1898 p. 175; 187; 191) Rv 21: 19. The stones designated by this term in modern times (agate, onyx, carnelian, etc.) are known by other names in ancient writers. On the other hand Pliny (H.N. 37, 7, 92ff) calls a kind of emerald and of jasper Chalcedonian. It is uncertain what is meant by the term in Rv.—S. the lit. s.v. ἀμέθυστος.*

χαλκίον, ου, τό *(copper) vessel, kettle* (Aristoph. in Pollux 10, 109; X., Oec. 8, 19; IG I² 393; UPZ 120, 7 [II BC]; PFay. 95, 11 [II AD]; PTebt. 406, 21; 1 Km 2: 14; 1 Esdr 1: 13) Mk 7: 4. M-M. B. 342.*

χαλκολίβανον, ου, τό (as a neut. in Suidas, Oecumenius) or χαλκολίβανος, ου, ὁ (so the Coptic version and Ausonius [in Salmasius, Exerc. ad Solin. p. 810ᴀ], perh. even fem.: FRehkopf, JoachJeremias-Festschr., '70, 216); someth. like *gold ore*, or *fine brass* or *bronze* (cf. the χαλκός, ὃν τοῦ χρυσοῦ κρεῖττον· ἔλεγον Jos., Ant. 7, 106) Rv 1: 15; 2: 18. Name of a metal or an alloy, the exact nature of which is unknown (since the word is found nowhere independent of Rv). Suidas defines it s.v. χαλκολίβ.: εἶδος ἠλέκτρου τιμιώτερον χρυσοῦ· ἔστι δὲ τὸ ἤλεκτρον ἀλλότυπον χρυσίον μεμιγμένον ὑέλῳ καὶ λιθείᾳ (cf. on ἤλεκτρ. Ezk 1: 27 and Pliny, H.N. 33, 4 where ἤλ. is a natural alloy of gold and silver). The Old Latin versions transl. the word 'aurichalcum' or 'orichalcum' (cf. Vergil, Aen. 12, 87 and Servius' observation on it). The Syrian version and Arethas consider it to be a metal fr. Lebanon (=Libanon in Gk., Lat., et al.)—Cf. the comm. by Bousset, HBSwete ('07), RHCharles, Zahn, ELohmeyer, WHadorn, E-BAllo (³ '33) on Rv 1: 15; also PDiergart, Philol. 64, '05, 150-3.*

χαλκός, οῦ, ὁ (Hom.+; inscr., pap., LXX; Ep. Arist. 119; Philo) *copper, brass, bronze*—1. the metal itself (Jos., Ant. 8, 76 w. gold and silver) Rv 18: 12. As a material (w. others) for making idols PK 2 p. 14, 14; Dg 2: 2.

2. anything that is made of it: (loanw. in rabb. in the sense 'kettle') an idol of brass 2 Cl 1: 6. χαλκὸς ἠχῶν *a noisy* (*brass*) *gong* 1 Cor 13: 1 (cf. ἠχέω; also HRiesenfeld, Coniect. Neot. XII '48, 50-3). *Copper coin, small change* (Lucian, Syr. Dea 29 w. gold and silver money), also simply *money* (Epicharmus in Pollux [who rejects this usage] 9, 90; Artem. 5, 82; PHib. 66, 4 [III ʙᴄ]; PTebt. 79, 8; Sb 4369 II, 26; EpJer 34) Mt 10: 9; Mk 6: 8; 12: 41. M-M. B. 611f.*

χαλκοῦς, ῆ, οῦν (trag., X., Pla.+; inscr., pap., LXX; Test. Levi 6: 1. Contracted fr. χάλκεος, which is found Hom.+; inscr., but rare in pap. and LXX [Thackeray p. 173]; Rv 9: 20 v.l. [Bl-D. §45 app.; Mlt.-H. 121; 347]. Both forms in Joseph. [Schmidt 491f]) *made of copper, brass,* or *bronze* w. χρυσοῦς, ἀργυροῦς Rv 9: 20. Gates πύλη χαλκῆ (Diod. S. 2, 8, 7; 2, 9, 3; 17, 71, 6. Similarly Ps.-Aristot., De Mundo 6, 8 θύραις χαλκαῖς) B 11: 4 (cf. Is 45: 2). Of the bronze serpent of Moses 12: 6 (Num 21: 9; Philo). M-M., -εος.*

χαμαί adv.—1. *on the ground* (Hom.+; pap.; Jdth 12: 15; 14: 18; Jos., Ant. 7, 133) Hv 4, 1, 9; s 2: 3f (ῥίπτω 2); 9, 11, 7; *on the* (level) *ground* (in contrast to 'on the rock and the gate') s 9, 14, 4.

2. *to* (or *on* in the same sense) *the ground* (for χαμᾶζε as early as Hom.; Dionys. Hal. 4, 56, 3; Plut., Marc. 13, 7, Sulla 28, 14; Lucian, Dial. Mort. 20, 2; PLeipz. 40 II, 22; III, 2; Job 1: 20; Jos., Ant. 20, 89; Sib. Or. 3, 685; loanw. in rabb.) J 9: 6; 18: 6; Hm 11: 20. M-M.*

Χανάαν, ἡ indecl. (כְּנַעַן; Gen 11: 31 al.; Philo, Test. 12 Patr.—In Joseph. Χαναναία, ας [Ant. 1, 186]) *Canaan,* in our lit. (i.e. Ac) the land west of the Jordan, where the patriarchs lived Ac 7: 11 (w. Egypt), which God gave to the Hebrews upon their escape fr. Egypt 13: 19 (γῆ X.).—FStähelin, Der Name Kanaan: JWackernagel-Festschr. '23, 150-3.*

Χαναναῖος, α, ον (כְּנַעֲנִי; Gen 12: 6; 13: 7 al. Cf. Philo, Joseph., Test. 12 Patr.; Sib. Or. 13, 56) *belonging to the land and people of Canaan, Canaanite* γυνὴ Χαναναία *a Canaanite woman* fr. the region of Tyre and Sidon Mt 15:

22 (the parall. Mk 7: 26 has Συροφοινίκισσα, q.v.).—KBornhäuser, Pastoralblätter 67, '25, 249-53. M-M.*

χαρά, ᾶς, ἡ (trag., Pla.+; inscr., pap., LXX, En., Ep. Arist., Philo, Joseph., Test. 12 Patr.) *joy.*

1. lit. Gal 5: 22. Opp. λύπη (X., Hell. 7, 1, 32; Philo, Abr. 151; Test. Jud. 25: 4) J 16: 20f; 2 Cor 2: 3; Hb 12: 11. Opp. κατήφεια Js 4: 9. W. ἀγαλλίασις Lk 1: 14; 1 Cl 63: 2; MPol 18: 2. χαρὰ μεγάλη (Jon 4: 6; Jos., Ant. 12, 91) Mt 28: 8; Lk 24: 52; Ac 15: 3. πολλὴ χ. (BGU 1141, 3 [I ʙᴄ] μετὰ πολλῆς χαρᾶς) 8: 8; Phlm 7. πᾶσα χ. (Sb 991, 6 μετὰ πάσης χαρᾶς) Ro 15: 13; Phil 2: 29; Js 1: 2.—W. prep. ἀπὸ τῆς χαρᾶς (Bl-D. §210, 1; Rob. 580) *for joy* Lk 24: 41; Ac 12: 14; ἀπὸ τῆς χαρᾶς αὐτοῦ *in his joy* Mt 13: 44. ἐν χαρᾷ Ro 15: 32; IEph inscr.; MPol 18: 2. μετὰ χαρᾶς (X., Hiero 1, 25; Polyb. 21, 34, 12 v.l.; Diod. S. 16, 79, 4; Plut., Mor. 1095ʙ; Jos., Ant. 8, 124; LXX) *with joy* Mt 13: 20; 28: 8; Mk 4: 16; Lk 8: 13; 10: 17; 24: 52 (Jos., Ant. 11, 67 ὥδευον μετὰ χ. [to Jerus.]); Phil 1: 4; Col 1: 11; Hb 10: 34; 13: 17; 1 Cl 65: 1; Hv 1, 3, 4.—W. subjective gen. J 15: 11b (cf. ibid. a ἡ χ. ἡ ἐμή); 16: 22 (Lycon [III ʙᴄ] fgm. 20 Wehrli '52: τὴν ἀληθινὴν χαρὰν τῆς ψυχῆς τέλος ἔλεγεν εἶναι=he designated the true joy of the soul as the goal); 2 Cor 1: 24; 7: 13; 8: 2. W. gen. to denote the origin of the joy χ. τῆς πίστεως *joy that comes from faith* Phil 1: 25. χ. πνεύματος ἁγίου 1 Th 1: 6; also χ. ἐν πνεύματι ἁγίῳ Ro 14: 17. Used w. verbs: χαρῆναι χαρὰν μεγάλην *be filled with intense joy* Mt 2: 10. Cf. 1 Th 3: 9 (χαίρω 1) χαρᾷ χαίρειν (χαίρω 1) J 3: 29a (foll. by διά τι at someth.). ἀγαλλιᾶσθαι χαρᾷ 1 Pt 1: 8. ἔχειν χαρὰν *have joy, feel pleased* 2 Cor 1: 15 v.l.; Phlm 7; 3 J 4; differently Hs 1: 10 (*have joy* accompanying it). χαρὰν λαμβάνειν *experience joy* Hv 3, 13, 2. χαρὰν ποιεῖν τινι *give someone joy* Ac 15: 3. χαρὰν τινι παρέχειν 1 Cl 63: 2. πληροῦν τινα χαρᾶς *fill someone with joy* (Jos., Bell. 3, 28) Ro 15: 13; pass. πληροῦσθαι χαρᾶς (Diod. S. 3, 17, 3 τέκνα . . . πεπληρωμένα χαρᾶς; Περὶ ὕψους 7, 2 ψυχὴ πληρουμένη χαρᾶς; Ep. Arist. 261; Philo, Mos. 1, 177; Jos., Ant. 15, 421) Ac 13: 52; 2 Ti 1: 4; Dg 10: 3. Also χαρᾶς ἐμπι(μ)πλασθαι (cf. Philo, Det. Pot. Ins. 123; Jos., Ant. 3, 99) MPol 12: 1. χαρᾷ ὑπερπερισσεύεσθαι 2 Cor 7: 4. πᾶσαν χαρὰν ἡγεῖσθαι Js 1: 2 (ἡγέομαι 2). ἔσται χαρά σοι Lk 1: 14; without the dat. *there will be joy* Lk 15: 7 (χ. ἐπί w. dat. as Jos., Ant. 7, 252): also γίνεται χαρά (Tob 11: 18 S) vs. 10, cf. Ac 8: 8. χαρᾶς εἶναι (qualitative gen.) *be pleasant* Hb 12: 11. χαρὰ ὅτι *joy that* J 16: 21.—Ign. provides χαρά w. adjectives to set it off: ἄμωμος IEph inscr.; IMg 7: 1. αἰώνιος κ. παράμονος IPhld inscr.—The Johannine lit. places emphasis on joy as brought to the highest degree (πληρόω 3) ἡ χαρὰ ἡ ἐμὴ πεπλήρωται J 3: 29b; cf. 15: 11b; 16: 24; 17: 13; 1 J 1: 4; 2 J 12. Cf. also the act. πληρώσατέ μου τὴν χαρὰν Phil 2: 2.—As v.l. for χάρις 2 Cor 1: 15.

2. metonymically—a. *the person* or *thing that causes joy,* (*the object of*) *joy* of persons Phil 4: 1 (EPeterson, Nuntius 4, '50, 27f) 1 Th 2: 19f. Of an event that will call forth joy εὐαγγελίζομαι ὑμῖν χαρὰν μεγάλην Lk 2: 10.

b. *a state of joyfulness* (Nicol. Dam.: 90 fgm. 52 p. 354, 3 Jac. οἱ ἀκούοντες ἐν χαρᾷ ἦσαν) εἴσελθε εἰς τὴν χαρὰν τοῦ κυρίου σου Mt 25: 21, 23 (so BWeiss; Jülicher, Gleichn. 475; Zahn, JWeiss, OHoltzmann; but s. c below). Of Christ ὃς ἀντὶ τῆς προκειμένης αὐτῷ χαρᾶς ὑπέμεινεν σταυρόν Hb 12: 2 (πρόκειμαι 2).

c. *festive dinner, banquet* (cf. Dalman, Worte 96; Billerb. I 879; 972) so perh. Mt 25: 21, 23 (but would this have been intelligible to Greeks? S. 2b above).—EGGulin,

Die Freude im NT I (Jesus, early church, Paul) '32; II (John's gosp.) '36; Bultmann on J 17: 13; PJBernadicou, Joy in the Gospel of Lk, Diss. Rome, '70. M-M. B. 1102. **

χάραγμα, ατος, τό (Soph. +)—1. *a mark* or *stamp* engraved, etched, branded, cut, imprinted (Anth. Pal. 6, 63, 6; 7, 220, 2; Anacreontea 27, 2 Preisendanz πυρός brands on horses; BGU 453, 8; PGrenf. II 50a, 3 [both II AD, brands on animals]. For stamps on documents: P Rainer 4, 37; PLond. 277, 20; Sb 5231, 11; 5247, 34; 5275, 11 [all I AD]. The impression on coins: Plut., Ages. 15, 8, Lys. 16, 4, Mor. 211B al.; POxy. 144, 6) in Rv of the mark of the Antichrist, which his adherents bear on hand or forehead (for the subj.-matter cf. 3 Macc 2: 29; UvWilamowitz, Her. 34, 1899, 634f; HLilliebjörn, Über relig. Signierung in d. Antike; mit e. Exkurs über Rv, Diss. Upps. '33): 13: 16; 14: 9; 20: 4. τὸ χάρ. τοῦ θηρίου 15: 2 t.r.; 16: 2; 19: 20. τὸ χάρ. τοῦ ὀνόματος αὐτοῦ 14: 11. τὸ χάρ. τὸ ὄνομα τοῦ θηρίου ἢ τὸν ἀριθμὸν τοῦ ὀνόματος αὐτοῦ 13: 17.—Dssm., NB 68-75 (BS 240-7), LO 289f (LAE 341); JYsebaert, Gk. Baptismal Terminology, '62, esp. 196-204.

2. *thing formed, image* in the representative arts χάρ. τέχνης *an image formed by art* Ac 17: 29 (CIG 6208 Φοῖβον χαράττειν). UWilckens, TW IX, 405-7. M-M. *

χαρακόω 1 aor. ἐχαράκωσα; pf. pass. ptc. κεχαρακωμένος *fence in* (with stakes) (Aeschin. 3, 140; Plut., Cleom. 20, 1; POxy. 729, 23 [II AD]; Jer 39: 2) τὶ someth. a vineyard Hs 5, 2, 2f; 5, 4, 1. Pass. 5, 2, 5 (cf. Is 5: 2, where the verb prob. means 'provide w. stakes [for individual vines]', a sense which is excluded for H by s 5, 5, 3 [cf. συγκρατέω]). *

χαρακτήρ, ῆρος, ὁ (Aeschyl., Hdt. +; inscr., pap., LXX, Ep. Arist., Philo; Jos., Ant. 13, 322; Test. Sim. 5: 4 ['copy' of the Book of Enoch]; loanw. in rabb.).

1. *impress, reproduction, representation*—a. of the impression on coins (Eur., El. 559; Aristot., Pol 1, 6, Oec. 2; Diod. S. 17, 66, 2; Dit., Or. 339, 45; symbol. Polyb. 18, 34, 7; Philo, Plant. 18) symbol. IMg 5: 2a, b.

b. fig., of God ἄνθρωπον ἔπλασεν τῆς ἑαυτοῦ εἰκόνος χαρακτῆρα *he formed man as reproduction of his own form* (s. εἰκών 2) 1 Cl 33: 4 (cf. Dit., Or. 383, 60 of a picture χ. μορφῆς ἐμῆς; 404, 25; Philo, Det. Pot. Ins. 83 calls the soul τύπον τινὰ καὶ χαρακτῆρα θείας δυνάμεως). Christ is χαρ. τῆς ὑποστάσεως αὐτοῦ *an exact representation of his* (=God's) *nature* Hb 1: 3 (ὑπόστασις 1).

2. *characteristic trait* or *manner, distinctive mark* (Hdt. +; Diod. S. 1, 91, 7; Dionys. Hal., Ad Pomp. 3, 16; 2 Macc 4: 10) ἐν ἀποστολικῷ χαρακτῆρι *in apostolic fashion* of an epistolary greeting ITr instr.

3. *outward appearance, form* εὐειδέσταται τῷ χαρακτῆρι *extraordinarily beautiful in appearance* Hs 9, 9, 5.— JGeffcken, Character: ET 21, '10, 426f; AKörte, Her. 64, '29, 69-86 (semantic history).—UWilckens, TW IX, 407-12. M-M. *

χαράκωσις, εως, ἡ (Lycurg. Or. §44 p. 153; Plut., Mar. 7, 4; Dt 20: 20) *fencing in* (s. χαρακόω) a vineyard Hs 5, 2, 3. *

χάραξ, ακος, ὁ (Thu., Aristoph. +; inscr., pap., LXX) *stake*—1. pl. of the stakes used in fencing a vineyard (cf. χαρακόω and s. BGU 830, 5 [I AD]) Hs 5, 4, 1; 5, 5, 3 (the χάρακες are oft. the stakes which support vines and other plants: Thu. 3, 70, 4; Aristoph., Ach. 986, Vesp. 1291;

Theophr., H. Pl. 2, 1, 2; Plut., Mor. 4c; Lucian, Philops. 11; BGU 1122, 17 [I BC]).

2. sing. *palisade* (Philo Mech. 82, 34; Polyb. 1, 80, 11; 3, 45, 5; Plut., Aemil. 17, 5, Marcell. 18, 2, Sulla 17, 5; 28, 3 al.; Arrian, Exp. Alex. 2, 19, 5 Roos; Ep. Arist. 139; Jos., Vi. 214; Dit., Syll.³ 363, 1 [297 BC]; Is 37: 33; Ezk 4: 2; 26: 8) Lk 19: 43 (Theophil. Com. [IV BC], fgm. 9 K. ἐν χάρακι καὶ παρεμβολῇ). M-M. *

χαρήσομαι s. χαίρω.

χαρίζομαι (Hom. +; inscr., pap., LXX, Ep. Arist., Philo, Joseph., Test. 12 Patr.; Sib. Or. 7, 14) mid. dep.: fut. χαρίσομαι Ro 8: 32 (also Lucian, D. Mor. 9, 1; Jos., Ant. 2, 28; for Att. χαριοῦμαι); 1 aor. ἐχαρισάμην; pf. κεχάρισμαι. Pass., w. pass. sense: 1 aor. ἐχαρίσθην Ac 3: 14; 1 Cor 2: 12; Phil 1: 29; 1 fut. χαρισθήσομαι Phlm 22.

1. *give freely* or *graciously as a favor,* of God (so Ael. Aristid. 39, 3 K.=18 p. 409 D.; Herm. Wr. 12, 12; 16, 5 and p. 462, 30; 490, 9; 35; 492, 11 Sc.; 3 Macc 5: 11; Ep. Arist. 196; Test. Sim. 4: 6; Jos., Ant. 3, 87; 4, 317) τινί τι *someth. to someone* (Appian, Bell. Civ. 1, 79 §360 χαρίζεσθαί τινι τὴν σωτηρίαν; Paus. 6, 18, 4 χαρίσασθαί μοι τήνδε ὦ βασιλεῦ τὴν χάριν) Ro 8: 32; Phil 2: 9; 2 Cl 1: 4; Hs 9, 28, 6; D 10: 3. This is also the place for Gal 3: 18 if τὴν κληρονομίαν is to be supplied fr. the context (but s. 3 below). τυφλοῖς ἐχαρίσατο βλέπειν *to the blind he granted the power of sight* Lk 7: 21; t.r. has τὸ βλέπειν (cf. Plut., Mor. 609A; 2 Macc 3: 31, 33). ὁ χαρισάμενος ὑμῖν τοιοῦτον ἐπίσκοπον κεκτῆσθαι *the one who (by his favor) granted you to obtain such a bishop* IEph 1: 3. Pass. 1 Cor 2: 12. ὑμῖν ἐχαρίσθη τὸ ὑπὲρ Χριστοῦ πάσχειν *you have (graciously) been granted the privilege of suffering for Christ* Phil 1: 29.—χ. τινά τινι *give* or *grant someone to someone* (Semonides 7, 93f D.²: Zeus χαρίζεταί τινά τινι=Z. grants one [i.e., a good wife] to someone) κεχάρισταί σοι ὁ θεὸς πάντας τοὺς πλέοντας μετὰ σοῦ *God has given you all those who are sailing with you,* i.e. at your request he has granted them safety fr. deadly danger Ac 27: 24. The one who is 'given' escapes death or further imprisonment by being handed over to those who wish him freed ᾐτήσασθε ἄνδρα φονέα χαρισθῆναι ὑμῖν Ac 3: 14. Cf. Phlm 22 (Diod. S. 13, 59, 3 ἐχαρίσατο αὐτῷ τοὺς συγγενεῖς=he granted him his [captured] relatives [and set them free]; Plut., C. Gracch. 4, 3 χ. τὸν 'Οκτάβιον τῇ μητρί; PFlor. 61, 61 [I AD] cited s.v. ὄχλος 1, end; Jos., Vi. 355.—On the 'giving' of Barabbas s. JMerkel, Die Begnadigung am Passahfeste: ZNW 6, '05, 293-316). On the other hand, the giving of a man to those who wish him ill results in harm to him (cf. Jos., Vi. 53) οὐδείς με δύναται αὐτοῖς χαρίσασθαι Ac 25: 11; cf. vs. 16 (without dat., which is easily supplied; the t.r. adds εἰς ἀπώλειαν to it). Ign. rejects every attempt of others to save his life, because he wishes to leave the world and be with God, and martyrdom opens the way for this: τὸν τοῦ θεοῦ θέλοντα εἶναι κόσμῳ μὴ χαρίσησθε *do not give to the world the one who wishes to belong to God* IRo 6: 2.—The payment of a sum of money which is owed (Ps.-Aeschin., Ep. 12, 14; Philo, Spec. Leg. 2, 39 τὰ δάνεια) Lk 7: 42f is *dispensed with, cancelled*; this forms a transition to sense

2. *give=remit, forgive, pardon* (Dionys. Hal. 5, 4, 3; Jos., Ant. 6, 144 ἁμαρτήματα χαρίζεσθαι) w. dat. of the pers. and acc. of the thing χαρισάμενος ἡμῖν πάντα τὰ παραπτώματα Col 2: 13; cf. 2 Cor 2: 10a; 12: 13. W. dat. of the pers. alone Eph 4: 32a, b; Col 3: 13a, b (Plut., Mor.

488A χαίρειν τῷ χαρίζεσθαι μᾶλλον αὐτοῖς ἢ τῷ νι-κᾶν). W. acc. of the thing alone 2 Cor 2: 10b, c. Abs. (cf. Ep. Arist. 215) 2 Cor 2: 7.

3. χ. τινι show oneself to be gracious to someone (Diod. S. 14, 11, 1; Appian, Bell. Civ. 2, 112 §467; Dit., Syll.³ 354, 4f βουλόμενος χαρίζεσθαι τῷ δήμῳ; Jos., Ant. 17, 222; Eunap. p. 77 Boiss.) Gal 3: 18 (s. 1 above). M-M. B. 1174.*

χάριν acc. of χάρις, used as a prep. (Bl-D. §160; Rob. 488) and (Bl-D. §216, 1 w. app.; Rob. 647) w. the gen. (Hom.+; inscr., pap., LXX); almost always after the word it governs; before it (a tendency in H.Gk.: Dit., Syll.³ index p. 619b; PTebt. 44, 8 [114 BC]; 410, 4 [16 AD]; PGiess. 98, 1 [II AD]. The LXX also has it predom. before: Johannessohn 244, 3) only 1 J 3: 12; for the sake of, on behalf of, on account of.

1. indicating the goal (cf. Hes., Works 709 ψεύδεσθαι γλώσσης χάριν) τῶν παραβάσεων χάριν for the sake of transgressions, i.e. to bring them about Gal 3: 19. αἰσχροῦ κέρδους χ. Tit 1: 11. Cf. 1 Ti 5: 14; Jd 16; 1 Cl 7: 4. τούτου χάριν for this purpose (Appian, Bell. Civ. 4, 89 §375) Tit 1: 5. οὗ χάριν (Appian, Iber. 54 §230; PFlor. 99, 9 [I/II AD]) Dg 11: 3.

2. indicating the reason χάριν τίνος ἔσφαξεν αὐτόν; for what reason (=why) did he kill him? 1 J 3: 12. οὗ χάριν for this reason, therefore (Philo, Op. M. 44) Lk 7: 47 (JCGregg, οὗ χάριν [Lk 7: 47]; ET 37, '26, 525f). τίνος χάριν; for what reason? why? (Polyb. 2, 42, 1; 3, 9, 1; UPZ 5, 42; 6, 29; Ep. Arist. 254; Jos., C. Ap. 2, 263) 1 Cl 31: 2.—The τούτου χάριν (X., Mem. 1, 2, 54; Plut., Mor. 146E; Dit., Syll.³ 888, 70f; BGU 884, 14; 1 Macc 12: 45; Jos., Ant. 4, 197) of Eph 3: 1, 14 may be classed under 1 or 2. M-M.**

χάρις, ιτος, ἡ (Hom.+; inscr., pap., LXX, Ep. Arist., Philo, Joseph., Test. 12 Patr.) acc. quite predom. χάριν, but χάριτα Ac 24: 27; 25: 9 v.l.; Jd 4 and pl. χάριτας Ac 24: 27 t.r.; 1 Cl 23: 1 (Eur., Hel. 1378; Hdt. 6, 41; X., Hell. 3, 5, 16; inscr., pap.; Zech 4: 7; 6: 14; Ep. Arist. 272, pl. 230.—Bl-D. §47, 3 w. app.; W-S. §9, 7; Mayser 271f; Thackeray 150; Helbing 40f; Mlt.-H. 132.—It seems that χάρις is not always clearly differentiated in mng. fr. χαρά; Apollodorus [II BC]: 244 fgm. 90 Jac. says in the second book περὶ θεῶν: κληθῆναι δὲ αὐτὰς ἀπὸ μὲν τ. χαρᾶς Χάριτας· καὶ γὰρ πολλάκις . . . οἱ ποιηταὶ τ. χάριν χαρὰν καλοῦσιν).

1. graciousness, attractiveness (Hom.+; Jos., Ant. 2, 231) of speech (Demosth. 51, 9; Ps.-Demetr. [I AD], Eloc. §127; 133; 135 al.; Eccl 10: 12; Sir 21: 16; Jos., Ant. 18, 208) οἱ λόγοι τῆς χάριτος (gen. of quality) the gracious words Lk 4: 22. ὁ λόγος ὑμῶν πάντοτε ἐν χάριτι Col 4: 6 (cf. Plut., Mor. 514F χάριν τινὰ παρασκευάζοντες ἀλλήλοις, ὥσπερ ἀλσὶ τοῖς λόγοις ἐφηδύνουσι τὴν διατριβήν; cf. further HAlmqvist, Plut. u. das NT '46, 121f; Epict. 3, 22, 90). τὸ πρόσωπον αὐτοῦ χάριτος ἐπληροῦτο MPol 12: 1 can also be placed here in case χάρις means nothing more than graciousness (s. 4 below).

2. favor, grace, gracious care or help, goodwill—a. act., that which one grants to another, the action of one who volunteers to do someth. to which he is not bound χάρις θεοῦ ἦν ἐπ᾽ αὐτό Lk 2: 40. ἡ χάρις τοῦ θεοῦ Ac 11: 2 D; 14: 26. τοῦ κυρίου 15: 40.—Esp. of the gracious intention of God (cf. χ. in relation to God Apollon. Rhod. 3, 1005 σοὶ θεόθεν χάρις ἔσσεται; Dio Chrys. 80[30], 40 χ. τῶν θεῶν; Ael. Aristid. 13 p. 320 D.; 53 p. 620; Sextus 436b; likew. in LXX, Philo, Joseph.; Sib. Or. 4, 46=189; 5, 330;

Ezek. Trag. in Euseb., Pr. Ev. 9, 29, 12.—χ. to denote the gracious dispensations of the emperor: Dit., Or. 669, 44 [I AD]; BGU 19 I, 21 [II AD] χάρ. τοῦ θεοῦ Αὐτοκράτορος; 1085 II, 4) and of Christ, who give (undeserved) gifts to men; God: δικαιούμενοι δωρεὰν τῇ αὐτοῦ χάριτι Ro 3: 24. Cf. 5: 15a, 20f; 6: 1; 11: 5 (ἐκλογή 1), 6a, b, c; Gal 1: 15 (διά III 1e); Eph 1: 6f (KGKuhn, NTS 7, '61, 337 [reff. to Qumran lit.]); 2: 5, 7, 8; cf. Pol 1: 3; 2 Th 1: 12; 2: 16; 2 Ti 1: 9; Tit 2: 11 (ἡ χάρ. τοῦ θεοῦ σωτήριος; cf. Dibelius, Hdb. exc. after Tit 2: 14); 3: 7; Hb 2: 9 (χωρὶς 2aa); 4: 16a; 1 Cl 50: 3; ISm 9: 2; IPol 7: 3. κατὰ χάριν as a favor, out of goodwill (schol. on Soph., Oed. Col. 1751 p. 468 Papag.) Ro 4: 4 (opp. κατὰ ὀφείλημα), 16.—The grace or favor of Christ: διὰ τῆς χάριτος τοῦ κυρίου Ἰησοῦ πιστεύομεν σωθῆναι Ac 15: 11. Cf. Ro 5: 15b; 2 Cor 8: 9; 1 Ti 1: 14; IPhld 8: 1.

b. pass., that which one experiences fr. another (Arrian, Anab. Alex. 3, 26, 4) χάριν ἔχειν have favor 3 J 4 v.l. πρός τινα with someone=win his respect Ac 2: 47; παρά τινι (Appian, Bell. Civ. 2, 89 §376) Hm 10, 3, 1, cf. 5, 1, 5. εὑρεῖν χάριν παρά τινι (Philo, Leg. All. 3, 77, end) Lk 1: 30; Hs 5, 2, 10; ἐνώπιόν τινος Ac 7: 46; ἐν τοῖς μέλλουσι μετανοεῖν among those who are about to repent Hm 12, 3, 3. Ἰησοῦς προέκοπτεν χάριτι παρὰ θεῷ καὶ ἀνθρώποις Lk 2: 52. Cf. Ac 4: 33; 7: 10 (ἐναντίον Φαραώ); Hb 4: 16b.—ποία ὑμῖν χάρις ἐστίν; what credit is that to you? Lk 6: 32-4; s. D 1: 3; 2 Cl 13: 4. Cf. 1 Cor 9: 16 v.l. In these passages the mng. comes close to reward (s. Wetter [below] 209ff w. reff.).—Also by metonymy that which brings someone (God's) favor 1 Pt 2: 19, 20.

c. In Christian epistolary lit. fr. the time of Paul χάρις is found w. the sense (divine) grace or favor in fixed formulas at the beginning and end of letters (Zahn on Gal 1: 3; vDobschütz on 1 Th 1: 1; ELohmeyer, ZNW 26, '27, 158ff; APujol, De Salutat. Apost. 'Gratia vobis et pax': Verb. Dom. 12, '32, 38-40; 76-82; WFoerster, TW II '34, 409ff; Gdspd., Probs. 141f. S. also the lit. s.v. χαίρω 2b). At the beginning of a letter χάρις ὑμῖν καὶ εἰρήνη (w. εἴη to be supplied) Ro 1: 7; 1 Cor 1: 3; 2 Cor 1: 3; Gal 1: 3; Eph 1: 2; Phil 1: 2; Col 1: 2; 1 Th 1: 1; 2 Th 1: 2; Phlm 3; Rv 1: 4; without ὑμῖν Tit 1: 4. χάρις ὑμῖν καὶ εἰρήνη πληθυνθείη 1 Pt 1: 2; 2 Pt 1: 2; 1 Cl inscr. χάρις, ἔλεος, εἰρήνη 1 Ti 1: 2; 2 Ti 1: 2; 2 J 3.—At the end ἡ χάρις (τοῦ κυρίου ἡμῶν Ἰησοῦ Χριστοῦ etc.) μεθ᾽ ὑμῶν (or μετὰ πάντων ὑμῶν etc.) Ro 16: 20, 24 (only in t.r.); 1 Cor 16: 23; 2 Cor 13: 13; Gal 6: 18; Eph 6: 24; Phil 4: 23; Col 4: 18; 1 Th 5: 28; 2 Th 3: 18; 1 Ti 6: 21; 2 Ti 4: 22; Tit 3: 15; Phlm 25; Hb 13: 25; Rv 22: 21; 1 Cl 65: 2. ὁ κύριος τῆς δόξης καὶ πάσης χάριτος μετὰ τοῦ πνεύματος ὑμῶν B 21: 9. χάρις ὑμῖν, ἔλεος, εἰρήνη, ὑπομονὴ διὰ παντός ISm 12: 2. ἔρρωσθε ἐν χάριτι θεοῦ 13: 2.

3. practical application of goodwill, a (sign of) favor, gracious deed or gift, benefaction—a. on the part of men (X., Symp. 8, 36, Ages. 4, 3; Appian, Bell. Civ. 1, 49 §213; Dionys. Hal. 2, 15, 4) χάριν (-ιτα) καταθέσθαι τινι (κατατίθημι 2) Ac 24: 27; 25: 9. αἰτεῖσθαι χάριν 25: 3 (in these passages from Ac χ. approaches the mng. favor, which one does for another. Cf. Appian, Bell. Civ. 1, 108 §506 ἐς χάριν Σύλλα=as a favor to Sulla). ἵνα δευτέραν χάριν σχῆτε that you might have a second proof of my goodwill 2 Cor 1: 15 (unless χάρις here means delight [so in poetry, Pind.+, but also Pla., Isocr.; L-S-J lex. s.v. χάρις IV. Cf. also the quot. fr. Apollodorus at the beg. of the present entry, and the fact that χαρά is v.l. in 2 Cor 1: 15]; in that case δευτέρα means double). Of the collection for Jerusalem (cf. Appian, Bell. Civ. 3, 42 §173 χάριτας

λαμβάνειν=receive gifts) 1 Cor 16: 3; 2 Cor 8: 4, 6f, 19. Cf. B 21: 7.—Eph 4: 29 may suggest a demonstration of human favor (cf. Plut., Mor. 514ε χάριν παρασκευάζοντες ἀλλήλοις), but a ref. to the means by which divine grace is mediated is not to be ruled out (s. b below).

b. on the part of God and Christ; the context will show whether the emphasis is upon the *possession of divine grace* as a source of blessings for the believer, or upon a *store of grace* that is dispensed, or a *state of grace* (i.e. standing in God's favor) that is brought about, or a *deed of grace* wrought by God in Christ, or a *work of grace* that grows fr. more to more. God is called ὁ θεὸς πάσης χάριτος 1 Pt 5: 10; cf. B 21: 9.—χάριν διδόναι τινί (Anacr. 110 Diehl; Appian, Ital. 5 §10): without a dat. Js 4: 6a. ταπεινοῖς δίδωσι χάριν (Pr 3: 34) Js 4: 6b; 1 Pt 5: 5; 1 Cl 30: 2. The Logos is πλήρης χάριτος J 1: 14. Those who belong to him receive of the fulness of his grace, χάριν ἀντὶ χάριτος vs. 16 (ἀντί 2). Cf. vs. 17. τὴν χάριν ταύτην ἐν ᾗ ἑστήκαμεν this state of grace in which we stand Ro 5: 2.—5: 17; 1 Cor 1: 4; 2 Cor 4: 15 (the work of grace in conversion; cf. Ac 11: 23); 6: 1; Gal 1: 6 (*by Christ's deed of grace*); 2: 21; 5: 4; Col 1: 6; 2 Ti 2: 1; Hb 12:15; 13: 9; 1 Pt 1: 10, 13; 3: 7 (συνκληρονόμοι χάριτος ζωῆς *fellow-heirs of the gracious gift that is life*); 5: 12; 2 Pt 3: 18; Jd 4; IPhld 11: 1; ISm 6: 2. The Christians stand ὑπὸ χάριν *under God's gracious will* as expressed in the act of redemption Ro 6: 14f, or they come ὑπὸ τὸν ζυγὸν τῆς χάριτος αὐτοῦ 1 Cl 16: 17 (ζυγός 1). The preaching of salvation is τὸ εὐαγγέλιον τῆς χάριτος τοῦ θεοῦ Ac 20: 24 or ὁ λόγος τῆς χάριτος αὐτοῦ (=τοῦ κυρίου) 14: 3; 20: 32. Even the good news of the gospel can be called ἡ χάρις τοῦ θεοῦ 13: 43; cf. 18: 27; MPol 2: 3. τὸ πνεῦμα τῆς χάριτος *the Spirit from* or *through whom grace is given* Hb 10: 29 (AWArgyle, Grace and the Covenant: ET 60, '48/'49, 26f).—Pl. *favors* (Diod. S. 3, 2, 4; 3, 73, 6; Sb 8139, 4 [inscr. of I BC] of Isis; Jos., C. Ap. 2, 190) 1 Cl 23: 1.—Nelson Glueck, Das Wort chesed im atl. Sprachgebr. als menschl. u. göttl. gemeinschaftsgemässe Verhaltungsweise '27.

4. of exceptional effects produced by divine grace, above and beyond those usu. experienced by Christians (inscr. μεγάλαι χάριτες τοῦ θεοῦ: FCumont, Syria 7, '26, 347ff), in the churches of Macedonia 2 Cor 8: 1 and Corinth 9: 14; cf. vs. 8. The martyr is in full possession of divine grace ISm 11: 1. Paul knows that through the χάρις of God he has been called to be an apostle, and that he has been fitted out w. the powers and capabilities requisite for this office fr. the same source: Ro 1: 5; 12: 3; 15: 15; 1 Cor 3: 10; 15: 10a, b (for the subject matter cf. Polyb. 12, 12b, 3 αὐτὸν [Alex. the Great] ὑπὸ τοῦ δαιμονίου τετευχέναι τούτων ὧν ἔτυχεν=whatever he has received he has received from the god. [For this reason he does not deserve any divine honors.]); 2 Cor 12: 9; Gal 2: 9; Eph 3: 2, 7f; Phil 1: 7.—The χάρις of God manifests itself in various χαρίσματα: Ro 12: 6; Eph 4: 7; 1 Pt 4: 10. This brings us to a number of passages in which χάρις is evidently to be understood in a very concrete sense. It is hardly to be differentiated fr. δύναμις (θεοῦ) or fr. γνῶσις or δόξα (q.v. 1a. On this subj. s. Wetter [below] p. 94ff; esp. 130ff; pap. in the GLumbroso-Festschr. '25, 212ff: χάρις, δύναμις, πνεῦμα w. essentially the same mng.; PGM 4, 2438; 3165; Herm. Wr. 1, 32). οὐκ ἐν σοφίᾳ σαρκικῇ ἀλλ᾽ ἐν χάριτι θεοῦ 2 Cor 1: 12. οὐκ ἐγὼ δὲ ἀλλὰ ἡ χάρις τοῦ θεοῦ σὺν ἐμοί 1 Cor 15: 10c. αὐξάνετε ἐν χάριτι καὶ γνώσει τοῦ κυρίου 2 Pt 3: 18. Cf. 1 Cl 55: 3; B 1: 2 (τῆς δωρεᾶς πνευματικῆς χάρις). Stephen is said to be πλήρης χάριτος καὶ δυνάμεως Ac 6: 8. Divine

power fills the martyr's face w. a radiant glow MPol 12: 1 (but s. 1 above). As the typical quality of the age to come, contrasted w. the κόσμος D 10: 6.

5. *thanks, gratitude* (exx. fr. later times: Diod. S. 11, 71, 4 [χάριτες=proofs of gratitude]; Appian, Syr. 3, 12; 13. Cf. Wetter [below] p. 206f) χάριν ἔχειν τινί *be grateful to someone* (Eur., Hec. 767; X., An. 2, 5, 14; Pla., Phil. 54D; PLeipz. 104, 14 [I BC] χάριν σοι ἔχω) foll. by ὅτι (Epict. 3, 5, 10; Jos., C. Ap. 1, 270; 2, 49) Lk 17: 9 (ERiggenbach, NKZ 34, '23, 439-43); mostly of gratitude to God or Christ; χάρις in our lit. as a whole, in the sense *gratitude*, refers to what we owe the Deity (class.; inscr.; pap., LXX; Jos., Ant. 7, 208) χάριν ἔχω τῷ θεῷ (POxy. 113, 13 [II AD] χάριν ἔχω θεοῖς πᾶσιν.—Epict. 4, 7, 9) 2 Ti 1: 3; foll. by ὅτι *because* 1 Ti 1: 12 (Herm. Wr. 6, 4 κἀγὼ χάριν ἔχω τῷ θεῷ . . ., ὅτι; Jos., Ant. 4, 316); χάριν ἔχειν ἐπί τινι *be grateful for someth.* Phlm 7 t.r. (to men). ἔχωμεν χάριν *let us be thankful* (to God) Hb 12: 28 (the reason for it is given by the preceding ptc. παραλαμβάνοντες. Bl-D. §128, 6 w. app.; cf. Rob. 1201f) χάρις (ἔστω) τῷ θεῷ (X., Oec. 8, 16 πολλὴ χάρις τοῖς θεοῖς; Epict. 4, 4, 7 χάρις τῷ θεῷ; BGU 843, 6 [I/II AD] χάρις τοῖς θεοῖς al. in pap. since III BC.—Philo, Rer. Div. Her. 309) Ro 7: 25; MPol 3: 1. Foll. by ὅτι (X., An. 3, 3, 14 τοῖς θεοῖς χάρις ὅτι; PFay. 124, 16 τοῖς θεοῖς ἐστιν χάρις ὅτι; Epict. 4, 5, 9) Ro 6: 17. Foll. by ἐπί τινι *for someth.* (UPZ 108, 30 [99 BC]) 2 Cor 9: 15. The reason for the thanks is given in the ptc. agreeing w. τῷ θεῷ 2: 14; 8: 16; 1 Cor 15: 57 (cf. Jos., Ant. 6, 145; Philo, Somn. 2, 213). *Thankfulness* (Appian, Bell. Civ. 3, 15 §51 πρός τινα=toward someone) χάριτι *in thankfulness* 10: 30. So prob. also ἐν τῇ χάριτι *in a thankful spirit* Col 3: 16 (Dibelius, Hdb. ad loc.). S. εὐχαριστέω, end. Also PSchubert, Form and Function of the Pauline Thanksgivings '39.—OLoew, Χάρις, Diss., Marburg '08; GPWetter, Charis '13; AvHarnack, Sanftmut, Huld u. Demut in der alten Kirche: JKaftan-Festschr. '20, 113ff; NBonwetsch, Zur Geschichte des Begriffs Gnade in der alten Kirche: Harnack-Festgabe '21, 93-101; EDBurton, Gal ICC '21, 423f; WTWhitley, The Doctrine of Grace '32; JMoffatt, Grace in the NT '31; RWinkler, D. Gnade im NT: Ztschr. f. syst. Theol. 10, '33, 642-80; RHomann, D. Gnade in d. syn. Ev.: ibid. 328-48; J Wobbe, D. Charisgedanke b. Pls '32; RBultmann, Theologie des NT '48, 283-310 (Paul); PRousselot, La Grâce d'après St. Jean et d'après St. Paul: Rech de Sc rel 18, '28, 87-108. Also Christent u. Wissensch. 8, '32, 402-30; JAMontgomery, Hebrew Hesed and Gk. Charis: HTR 32, '39, 97-102; Dodd 61f; TFTorrance, The Doctrine of Grace in the Apost. Fathers, '48; JERenié, Studia Anselmiana 27f, '51, 340-50; CRSmith, The Bible Doctrine of Grace, '56; EEFlack, The Concept of Grace in Bibl. Thought: Bibl. Studies in Memory of HCAlleman, ed. Myers, '60, 137-54; DJDoughty, NTS 19, '73, 163-80. M-M. B. 1166.**

χάρισμα, ατος, τό a gift (*freely and graciously given*), a *favor bestowed* (Sir 7: 33 v.l.; 38: 30 v.l.; Theod. Ps 30: 22; Philo, Leg. All. 3, 78 [twice] δωρεὰ καὶ εὐεργεσία καὶ χάρισμα θεοῦ; Sib. Or. 2, 54 θεοῦ χ.—Alciphr. 3, 17, 4 [it is quite poss. that this comes fr. Attic comedy: Kock III p. 677]; BGU 1044, 4 [IV AD] of benefits bestowed. The other secular exx. of the word come fr. later times: BGU 551, 3; PLond. 77, 24; Sb 4789, 7; Achmes 4, 13; Nicetas Eugen. 6, 537f) in our lit. only of gifts of divine grace.

1. gener., the earthly goods bestowed by God D 1: 5. The privileges granted to the people of Israel Ro 11: 29.

The gracious gift of rescue fr. mortal danger 2 Cor 1: 11. The spiritual possession of the believer Ro 1: 11 (χάρισμα πνευματικόν); 1 Cor 1: 7; ISm inscr.; IPol 2: 2. The gracious gift of redemption Ro 5: 15f; IEph 17: 2. τὸ χάρισμα τοῦ θεοῦ ζωὴ αἰώνιος Ro 6: 23.

2. of special gifts of a non-material sort, bestowed by the grace of God on individual Christians 1 Pt 4: 10; 1 Cl 38: 1. Of the gift of an office, mediated by the laying on of hands 1 Ti 4: 14; 2 Ti 1: 6. Of the power to be continent in matters of sex 1 Cor 7: 7. Of the spiritual gifts in a special sense Ro 12: 6; 1 Cor 12: 4, 9, 28, 30, 31.—S. in addition to the lit. s.v. γλῶσσα 3 also GPWetter, Charis '13, 168–87; EBuonaiuti, I Carismi: Ricerche religiose 4, '28, 259–61; FGrau, Der ntliche Begriff Χάρισμα, Diss. Tübingen '47; HHCharles, The Charismatic Life in the Apost. Church, Diss. Edinburgh, '58; ACPiepkorn, CTM 42, '71, 369–89 (NT and Ap. Fathers). M-M.*

χαριτόω 1 aor. ἐχαρίτωσα; perf. pass. ptc. κεχαριτω-μένος (Sir 18: 17; Sym. Ps 17: 26; Ep. Arist. 225; Test. Jos. 1: 6; BGU 1026 XXIII, 24 [IV AD]; Cat. Cod. Astr. XII 162, 14; Rhet. Gr. I 429, 31; Achmes 2, 18) *bestow favor upon, favor highly, bless,* in our lit. only w. ref. to the divine χάρις: ὁ κύριος ἐχαρίτωσεν αὐτοὺς ἐν πάσῃ πράξει αὐτῶν Hs 9, 24, 3. τῆς χάριτος αὐτοῦ (= τοῦ θεοῦ), ἧς ἐχαρίτωσεν ἡμᾶς ἐν τῷ ἠγαπημένῳ *his great favor, with which he has blessed us through* (or *in*) *his beloved Son* Eph 1: 6. Pass. (Libanius, Progymn. 12, 30, 12 vol. VIII p. 544, 10 F. χαριτούμενος = favored. Cf. Geminus [I BC], Elem. Astronomiae [Manitius 1898] 8, 9 κεχαρισμένον εἶναι τοῖς θεοῖς) in the angel's greeting to Mary κεχαριτωμένη *favored one* (in the sight of God) Lk 1: 28 (SLyonnet, Biblica 20, '39, 131–41; MCambe, RB 70, '63, 193–207). M-M.*

Χαρράν (חָרָן. Gen 11: 31f; 12: 4f; 27: 43; Philo; Test. Levi 2: 1), ἡ indecl. (Jos., Ant. 1, 152; 285 εἰς [τὴν] Χαρράν is surely acc. of Χαρρά) *Haran,* a place in Mesopotamia (= Κάρραι, Carrhae, famous for the defeat of Crassus that took place there in 53 BC), where Abraham lived for a time Ac 7: 2, 4.*

χάρτης, ου, ὁ (since the comic poet Plato [IV BC] in Pollux 7, 210; Theopompus [IV BC] in Περὶ ὕψους 43, 2 χάρται βυβλίων; inscr., pap.; Jer 43: 23; Jos., C. Ap. 1, 307; loanw. in rabb.) mostly taken to mean *a sheet of paper,* i.e. *papyrus* (so Cebes 4, 3; Plut., Mor. 900B; Anth. Pal. 9, 401, 3; 174, 4; 6; Geopon. 13, 5, 4. Oft. pap. Cf. esp. PFlor. 367, 7 χάρτας ἐπιστολικούς letter paper.—On the word s. GGlotz, Bull. soc. arch. Alex. 25, '30, 83–96; Preisigke, Wörterb.). In several pap. (Zen.-P. Cairo 654, 46; 687, 7f; Zen.-P. of Columbia Univ. I no. 4), however, it obviously means a(n unwritten) *papyrus roll* (APF 10, '32, 241; 11, '35, 286f; NLewis, L'industrie du Papyrus '34; Gnomon 12, '36, 48) 2 J 12 (w. μέλαν).—ThBirt, Das antike Buchwesen 1882; KDziatzko, Untersuchungen über ausgewählte Kapitel des antiken Buchwesens '00; VGardt-hausen, Das Buch im Altertum '11; WSchubart, Das Buch bei den Griechen u. Römern² '21, 34; EbNestle, Einfüh-rung in das griechische NT⁴ '23, 32f; 78. M-M. B. 1289.*

χάσμα, ατος, τό (Hes.+; Eur.; Hdt. 4, 85; Philo; Jos., Bell. 5, 566, Ant. 6, 27; 7, 242; 2 Km 18: 17 χ. μέγα; En. 18, 11 χ. μέγα) *chasm* (lit. 'a yawning') of the unbridge-able space betw. Abraham and the place of torture Lk 16: 26 (Diog. L. 8, 31: acc. to Pythagoras the ψυχαὶ ἀκάθαρ-τοι cannot approach the ὕψιστος τόπος to which Hermes has brought the ψυχαὶ καθαραί; cf. 1 Esdr 7: 102–15).*

χεῖλος, ους, τό gen. pl. uncontracted χειλέων (Hb 13: 15 [fr. Hos 14: 3]; Bl-D. §48; Mlt.-H. 139) *lip.*

1. pl. *the lips* (Hom.+; pap., LXX, Philo; Test. Iss. 7: 4) as used in speaking Mt 15: 8; Mk 7: 6; 1 Cl 15: 2; 2 Cl 3: 5; cf. 4 (all Is 29: 13); Ro 3: 13 (Ps 139: 4); Hb 13: 15 (Hos 14: 3); 1 Pt 3: 10 (Ps 33: 14); 1 Cl 15: 5 (Ps 30: 19); 18: 15 (Ps 50: 17); 22: 3 (Ps 33: 14). ἐν χείλεσιν ἑτέρων λαλήσω 1 Cor 14: 21 (Is 28: 11, but significantly differ-ent). In another sense λαλεῖν ἐν χείλεσιν 1 Cl 16: 16 (Ps 21: 8). ἐπὶ τοῖς χείλεσιν ἔχειν τινά *have someone* (i.e. his name) *on the lips* and nothing more (Dio Chrys. 15[32], 50 ἐπὶ τοῖς χείλεσι τὰς ψυχὰς ἔχειν) Hm 12, 4, 4; also ἐπὶ τὰ χείλη Hs 9, 21, 1.

2. sing. *shore, bank* (of a river: Hdt. 2, 94; Polyb. 3, 14, 6 al.; Diod. S. 3, 10, 2; 20, 75, 3; of a lake Aristot., H.A. 6, 16; Jos., Bell. 3, 511) of the sea (Achilles Tat. 2, 18, 2) Hb 11: 12 (Gen 22: 17). τοῦ Ἰορδάνου UGosp 66. M-M.*

χειμάζω (Aeschyl., Thu.+; inscr., pap.; Pr 26: 10) *expose to bad weather, toss in a storm* in our lit. of an actual storm that impedes navigation, and in the pass. (cf. Aeschyl., Prom. 840; Pla., Phil. 29A; Diod. S. 3, 55, 8; 5, 58, 2 κεχειμασμένος ἰσχυρῶς κατὰ τὸν πλοῦν; Ael. Aristid. 44, 13 K.=17 p. 405 D.; χειμαζόμενος; En. 101, 5; Test. Napht. 6: 5; Jos., Ant. 12, 130 al.) σφοδρῶς χειμαζομένων Ac 27: 18. Symbol. (Polystrat. p. 31; Epict., fgm. Stob. 47; Jos., Bell. 3, 195; Test. Jud. 21: 6) IPol 2: 3. M-M.*

χείμαρρος or **χείμαρρους, ου, ὁ** (Hom. [χείμαρροος and χείμαρρος Il. 4, 452; 5, 88]+ predom. in the form χείμαρρους, which also prevails throughout the LXX [χείμαρρος w. certainty only Ps 123: 4, but also Ep. Arist. 117; Sib. Or. 13, 55; cf. Thackeray 144; Helbing 34], as well as in Philo [Rer. Div. Her. 32] and in Joseph. [Ant. 6, 360; w. χείμαρρος 314]) a stream of water that *flows abundantly in the winter* (Suidas defines it: ὁ ἐν τῷ χειμῶνι ῥέων ποταμός; Polyb. 4, 70, 7 and Artem. 2, 27 add ποταμός to χ.), *winter torrent, ravine, wadi* J 18: 1 (cf. Κεδρών and Jos., Ant. 8, 17 τὸν χειμάρρουν Κε-δρῶνα). M-M. B. 42.*

χειμερινός, ή, όν (Hdt.+; inscr., LXX, Philo) *pertaining to winter* καιροὶ χειμερινοί *winter seasons* 1 Cl 20: 9 (Diod. S. 14, 100, 5; 15, 65, 2 χειμερινὴ ὥρα=winter season)*

χειμών, ῶνος, ὁ—**1.** *rainy and stormy weather* (Hom.+; Sb 998 [16/17 AD]; LXX; Jos., Ant. 6, 91) σήμερον χειμών *today it will be stormy* Mt 16: 3. On the sea *storm, bad weather* (Demosth. 18, 194; Diod. S. 11, 13, 1 χ. μέγας=a severe storm; En. 101, 4; Philo, Congr. Erud. Gr. 93 [opp. γαλήνη]; Jos., Ant. 14, 377; Test. Napht. 6: 9) χειμῶνος οὐκ ὀλίγου ἐπικειμένου Ac 27: 20.

2. the season of bad weather, *winter* (Thu., Aristoph.+; inscr., pap.; SSol 2: 11; En. 2, 2; Philo; Jos., Ant. 14, 376; Test. Zeb. 6: 8) J 10: 22 (short clause as Polyaenus 7, 44, 2 πόλεμος ἦν, exc. 36, 8). χειμῶνος *in winter* (Pla., Rep. 3 p. 415E; X., Mem. 3, 8, 9; Appian, Illyr. 24 §70; Dit., Syll.³ 495, 104f) Mt 24: 20; Mk 13: 18. πρὸ χειμῶνος *before winter* (sets in) 2 Ti 4: 21.—Fig. Hs 3: 2f; 4: 2. M-M. B. 1013.*

χείρ, χειρός, ἡ (Hom.+; inscr., pap., LXX, En., Ep. Arist., Philo, Joseph., Test. 12 Patr., Sib. Or.); on the acc. form χεῖραν J 20: 25 v.l.; 1 Pt 5: 6 v.l. cf. JPsichari, Essai sur le Grec de la Septante '08, 164–70. Exx. fr. the pap. in the Hdb. at J 20: 25; *hand.*

1. lit. Mt 12: 10; Mk 3: 1; Lk 6: 6, 8; Ac 12: 7; 20: 34 al. πόδες καὶ χεῖρες Mt 22: 13; cf. Lk 24: 39, 40 𝔓⁷⁵ et al.; Ac 21: 11a. W. other parts of the body in sing. and pl. Mt 5: (29), 30; 18: 8a, b, (9); J 11: 44. In the gen. w. the verbs ἅπτομαι Mt 8: 15; ἐπιλαμβάνομαι (q.v. 1); κρατέω (q.v. 1b). In the acc. w. the verbs αἴρω (q.v. 1a); ἀπονίπτομαι (q.v.); βάλλω J 20: 25b; δέω (q.v. 1b); δίδωμι (q.v. 2); ἐκπετάννυμι (q.v.); ἐκτείνω (q.v. 1); ἐπαίρω (q.v. 1); ἐπιβάλλω (q.v. 1b); ἐπισείω (q.v.); ἐπιτίθημι (q.v. 1aα); cf. ἐπίθεσις (τῶν) χειρῶν (s. ἐπίθεσις); κατασείω (q.v.); νίπτομαι (s. νίπτω 2b and the lit. s.v. βαπτίζω 1; also JDöller, Das rituelle Händewaschen bei den Juden: Theol.-prakt. Quartalschr. 64, '11, 748-58); τίθημι (q.v. I 1aβ); ποιεῖν: ὀπίσω τὰς χεῖρας (ὀπίσω 1b); τὰς χ. ἐναλλάξ (s. ἐναλλάξ).—In the instrumental dat. ἔγραψα τῇ ἐμῇ χειρί (cf. Charito 8, 4, 6; BGU 326 II, 2 al. in pap. —χείρ= handwriting as early as Hyperides in Pollux 2, 152, also Philod., π. ποιημ. 4, 33; 6, 14 Jens.; PMagd. 25, 2 [III вс]; Jos., Ant. 14, 52) Gal 6: 11; Phlm 19. ὁ ἀσπασμὸς τῇ ἐμῇ χειρί (i.e. γέγραπται) 1 Cor 16: 21; Col 4: 18; 2 Th 3: 17 (on the conclusion of a letter written in the sender's own handwriting, which also occurs in pap. letters as well as in the works of the Emperor Julian [Epistulae, Leges etc., ed. Bidez and Cumont '22, nos. 9; 11], cf. CGBruns, Die Unterschriften in den röm. Rechtsurkunden: ABA 1876, 41-138; KDziatzko, art. Brief: Pauly-W. III 1899, 836ff; Dssm., LO 132f; 137f [LAE 166f; 171f]. S. also the lit. s.v. χαίρω 2b). ἐννεύω τῇ χ. (s. ἐννεύω). κατασείω τῇ χ. (s. κατασείω). κρατέω τῇ χ. (κρατέω 1b). Pl. ταῖς χερσίν with the hands (Demetr. Phaler. in Diog. L. 2, 13 ταῖς ἰδίαις χερσίν; Diod. S. 16, 33, 1 τ. ἰδίαις χ. 17, 17, 7 al.; Aesop, Fab. 272 P.=425 H.; Herm. Wr. 5, 2) Lk 6: 1; 1 Cor 4: 12; Eph 4: 28; 1 Th 4: 11 (cf. HPreisker, Das Ethos d. Arbeit im NT '36).— τὸ ἔργον τῶν χειρῶν τινος cf. ἔργον 3 al., also Rv 9: 20.—W. prepositions: the hand on or in which someth. lies or fr. which someth. comes or is taken: ἐν τῇ χειρί Mt 3: 12; Lk 3: 17. (ἔχειν τι εἰς τὰς χεῖρας Hv 1, 2, 2. ἐπὶ τὴν χεῖρα Rv 20: 1. ἐπὶ χειρῶν Mt 4: 6; Lk 4: 11 (both Ps 90: 12). ἐκ (τῆς) χειρός (Diod. S. 2, 8, 6) Rv 8: 4; 10: 10. the hand by which someth. comes about: of pagan gods θεοὶ οἱ διὰ χειρῶν γινόμενοι gods that are made by hand Ac 19: 26. Of an earthly temple οἰκοδομητὸς ναὸς διὰ χειρός B 16: 7. The OT (but cf. Diod. S. 3, 65, 3 ταῖς τῶν γυναικῶν χερσί=by the women; Ael. Aristid. 45 p. 70 D.: μετὰ τῆς χειρὸς τῶν δικαίων; Philostrat., Vi. Apoll. 6, 29; Nicetas Eugen. 7, 165 χειρὶ βαρβάρων) has a tendency to speak of a person's activity as the work of his hand; διὰ χειρός ([τῶν] χειρῶν) τινος ('ם דיַ) through or by someone or someone's activity Mk 6: 2; Ac 2: 23; 5: 12; 7: 25; 11: 30; 14: 3; 15: 23; 19: 11. Also ἐν χειρί Gal 3: 19. Corresp. the hands can represent the pers. who is acting οὐδὲ ὑπὸ χειρῶν ἀνθρωπίνων θεραπεύεται nor does he need to be served by men Ac 17: 25.—The arm may be meant (as Hes., Theog. 150; Hdt. 2, 121, 5 ἐν τῷ ὤμῳ τὴν χεῖρα; Herodas 5, 83 ἐν τῇσι χερσὶ τῇσ'ἐμῇσι =in my arms; Paus. 6, 14, 7; Galen, De Usu Part. 2, 2 vol. I p. 67, 1 Helmreich; Longus 1, 4, 2 χεῖρες εἰς ὤμους γυμναί) in ἐπὶ χειρῶν ἀροῦσίν σε Mt 4: 6; Lk 4: 11 (both Ps 90: 12). Finger Lk 15: 22.

2. fig.—a. The hand of God means his power (Il. 15, 695; Ael. Aristid. 47, 42 K.=23 p. 455 D.: ἐν χερσὶ τοῦ θεοῦ; LXX; Aristobulus in Euseb., Pr. Ev. 8, 10, 1; 7-9; Ezek. Trag. ibid. 9, 29, 14; Sib. Or. 3, 672; 795.—Porphyr. in Euseb., Pr. Ev. 4, 23, 6 ὁ θεὸς ὁ ἔχων ὑπὸ χεῖρα, sc. τ. δαίμονας).

a. as Creator Ac 7: 50 (Is 66: 2). ποίησις χειρῶν αὐτοῦ 1 Cl 27: 7 (Ps 18: 2). τὰ ἔργα τῶν χειρῶν σου Hb 1: 10 (Ps

101: 26); 2: 7 v.l. (Ps 8: 7). Cf. B 5: 10. In connection w. the account of creation the words ἄνθρωπον ταῖς ἱεραῖς χερσὶν ἔπλασεν 1 Cl 33: 4 might almost be taken in the lit. sense.

β. as Ruler, Helper, Worker of Wonders, Regulator of the Universe: χεὶρ κυρίου ἦν μετ' αὐτοῦ Lk 1: 66; Ac 11: 21.—Lk 23: 46 (Ps 30: 6); J 10: 29; Ac 4: 28 (w. βουλή, hence almost='will'; cf. Sir 25: 26), 30; 1 Pt 5: 6 (cf. Gen 16: 9); 1 Cl 60: 3.

γ. as Punisher (schol. on Apollon. Rhod. 4, 1043a ἐν ταῖς χερσὶ τῶν θεῶν νέμεσις) χεὶρ κυρίου ἐπὶ σε (1 Km 12: 15) Ac 13: 11. ἐμπεσεῖν εἰς χεῖρας θεοῦ ζῶντος (s. ἐμπίπτω 2) Hb 10: 31. Cf. 1 Cl 28: 2.

δ. in the same sense also of the hand of Christ or of an angel J 3: 35; 10: 28; 13: 3.—σὺν χειρὶ ἀγγέλου with the help of an angel Ac 7: 35.

b. hostile power (Hom. +; LXX) παραδιδόναι τινὰ εἰς χεῖράς τινος hand over to someone('s power) (s. παραδίδωμι 1b) Ac 21: 11b; pass. Mt 17: 22; 26: 45; Mk 9: 31; Lk 9: 44; 24: 7; Ac 28: 17; D 16: 4. Also παραδίδ. τινὰ ἐν χειρί τινος 1 Cl 55: 5; escape, etc. ἐκ (τῆς) χειρός τινος from someone's power (Gen 32: 12; Ex 18: 10; Jos., Vi. 83) Lk 1: 71, 74; J 10: 39; Ac 12: 11. ἐκ χειρὸς σιδήρου λύσει σε he will free you from the power of the sword 1 Cl 56: 9 (Job 5: 20). ἐκ τῶν χειρῶν ἡμῶν Ac 24: 7 v.l. (cf. X., An. 6, 3, 4; Lucian, Hermot. 9, end). ἐξέφυγον τὰς χεῖρας αὐτοῦ 2 Cor 11: 33. ὑπὸ χειρὸς ἀνθρώπων παθεῖν B 5: 5.

c. distinctive prepositional combinations ἐν χερσίν of someth. that one has in hand, w. which one is concerned at the moment (Hdt. 1, 35 τὸν γάμον ἐν χερσὶν ἔχοντος; Appian, Bell. Civ. 5, 81 §342 τὰ ἐν χερσίν; Ael. Aristid. 45 p. 74 D.; PPetr. II 9[2], 4 [III вс] ἃ εἶχον ἐν ταῖς χερσίν; Jos., Bell. 4, 165) ἐν χερσὶν ὁ ἀγὼν the contest is our concern at present 2 Cl 7: 1. ὑπὸ χεῖρα continually (Ps.-Aristot., Mirabilia c. 52; Jos., Ant. 12, 185) Hv 3, 10, 7; 5: 5; m 4, 3, 6 (Bl-D. §232, 1 app.—In pap. we have the mng. 'privately', 'little by little': PTebt. 71, 15 [II вс]; Gnomon [=BGU V] Prooem. 2f; PAmh. 136, 17).— KGrayston, The Significance of 'Hand' in the NT: B Rigaux-Festschr. '70, 479-87.—ELohse, TW IX, 413-27: χείρ and related words. M-M. B. 237ff.

χειραγωγέω (Diod. S. 13, 20, 4; Plut., Maximus Tyr., Lucian et al.; UPZ 110, 55 [164 вс]; Judg 16: 26 A; Tob 11: 16 S; Jos., Ant. 5, 315) take or lead by the hand (e.g., a man suddenly blinded by an arrow: Appian, Bell. Civ. 2, 60 §248. A blind man in general: Artem. 5, 20) Ac 9: 8. Pass. 22: 11; GP 10: 40. M-M.*

χειραγωγός, οῦ, ὁ one who leads another by the hand, leader (Plut., Mor. 794D; 1063B; Artem. 1, 48; Ael. Aristid. 45 p. 60D; Maximus Tyr. 8, 7h [of God]; Longus 4, 24, 2; Herm. Wr. 7, 2a) Ac 13: 11. M-M.*

χειρόγραφον, ου, τό (since Polyb. 30, 8, 4; Dit., Syll.³ 742, 50f [85 вс]. Oft. in pap. fr. II вс; Tob) a (handwritten) document, specif. a certificate of indebtedness, bond (so plainly Vi. Aesopi I c. 122.—Dssm., LO 281ff [LAE 334ff]) τὸ καθ' ἡμῶν χειρόγραφον the bond that stood against us Col 2: 14 (s. GMegas, ZNW 27, '28, 305-20; OABlanchette, CBQ 23, '61, 306-12: identifies the χ. with Christ). M-M.*

χειροποίητος, ον (Hdt. +; Diod. S. 13, 82, 5; 15, 93, 4; 17, 71, 7; Arrian, Anab. 4, 28, 3; PLond. 854, 4; LXX; Jos., Bell. 1, 419, Ant. 4, 55; Sib. Or. 3, 606; 618, fgm. 3, 29) made by human hands of buildings, specif. temples (Sib. Or. 14, 62 ναῶν χειροποιήτων; Philo, Mos. 2, 88 ἱερόν of the tabernacle) Mk 14: 58; Ac 7: 48 t.r.; 17: 24;

Hb 9: 11, 24. Subst. (Philo, Mos. 2, 168) χειροποίητα *temples built by human hands* Ac 7: 48. Of Jewish circumcision (as opposed to the 'circumcision of the heart') τῆς λεγομένης περιτομῆς ἐν σαρκὶ χειροποιήτου *of the so-called circumcision, brought about in the flesh by human hands* Eph 2: 11. M-M.*

χειροτονέω 1 aor. ἐχειροτόνησα, pass. ἐχειροτονήθην (Aristoph., X., Pla.+; inscr., pap.; Philo, Somn. 2, 243, Spec. Leg. 1, 78; Jos., Vi. 341 al.) *choose, elect by raising hands,* then gener., esp. of election or selection for definite offices or tasks (IG IV² 1, 89, 18 [II/III AD] χ. ἱερέας). The churches *choose* a representative to accompany Paul on his journey to take the collection to Jerusalem 2 Cor 8: 19 (IG II² 1, 1260 χειροτονηθεὶς ὑπὸ τοῦ δήμου στρατηγός.— Cf. Windisch ad loc.). The churches choose envoys to bring congratulations to the church at Antioch IPhld 10: 1; ISm 11: 2; IPol 7: 2. The churches are to elect their own bishops and deacons D 15: 1.—On the other hand the presbyters in Lycaonia and Pisidia were not chosen by the congregations, but it is said of Paul and Barnabas χειροτονήσαντες αὐτοῖς κατ' ἐκκλησίαν πρεσβυτέρους Ac 14: 23. Cf. Tit 1: 9 v.l. and subscr.; 2 Ti subscr. This does not involve a choice by the group; here the word means *appoint, install,* w. the apostles as subj. (Philo, Praem. 54 βασιλεὺς ὑπὸ θεοῦ χειροτονηθείς, De Jos. 248 Joseph βασιλέως ὕπαρχος ἐχειροτονεῖτο, Mos. 1, 198, In Flacc. 109; Jos., Ant. 6, 312 τὸν ὑπὸ τοῦ θεοῦ κεχειροτονημένον βασιλέα; 13, 45). JMRoss, ET 63, '51f, 288f; ELohse, D. Ordination im Spätjudentum u. im NT, '51. M-M.*

χειροτονία, ας, ἡ (Thu.+; inscr., pap., Philo; Jos., Bell. 4, 147, Ant. 3, 192 of choosing and electing; s. χειροτονέω) *the lifting up of the hand* as a hostile or scornful gesture ἐὰν ἀφέλῃς ἀπὸ σοῦ χειροτονίαν *if you stop raising your hand* B 3: 5 (Is 58: 9).*

χείρων, ον, gen. ονος (Hom.+; pap., LXX, Philo, Joseph.) comp. of κακός, *worse, more severe* σχίσμα Mt 9: 16; Mk 2: 21. τιμωρία Hb 10: 29 (Jos., Vi. 172; cf. PGM 2, 54). ἵνα μὴ χεῖρόν σοί τι γένηται *that nothing worse may happen to you* J 5: 14 (cf. Jos., Ant. 4, 142). W. gen. of comparison (1 Km 17: 43; Wsd 15: 18) γίνεται τὰ ἔσχατα χείρονα τῶν πρώτων Mt 12: 45; Lk 11: 26; 2 Pt 2: 20. Cf. Mt 27: 64.—Of a sick woman εἰς τὸ χεῖρον ἐλθεῖν Mk 5: 26.—In the moral realm Hs 9, 17, 5; 9, 18, 1. W. gen. of comparison ἀπίστου χείρων 1 Ti 5: 8. προκόπτειν ἐπὶ τὸ χεῖρον 2 Ti 3: 13 (ἐπὶ τὸ χ. as X., Mem. 3, 5, 13; Pla., Rep. 381B; Diod. S. 15, 88, 4; Strabo 16, 2, 39; Jos., Ant. 16, 207). The Christians know nothing of an ἀπὸ τῶν κρειττόνων ἐπὶ τὰ χείρω μετάνοια MPol 11: 1 (Maximus Tyr. 5, 3a εἰ εἰς τὸ χεῖρον ἐκ τοῦ βελτίστου πονηρῶς (sic) μετέθετο=if [a man turns] to the worse from the best, then the change he makes is an evil one). Of beasts (=soldiers) οἱ χείρους γίνονται who (simply) *become more and more wicked* IRo 5: 1 (cf. Philo, Abr. 129). M-M.*

Χερούβ, τό (Ezk 28: 16) and ὁ (Ex 25: 19; 38: 7: כְּרוּב) indecl. *cherub;* the pl. w. various endings Χερουβείν (PGM 13, 255; 334), -βίν, -βείμ, -βίμ (Sib. Or. 3, 1 τὰ Χερουβίμ; En. 14, 11; 20, 7 [τὰ] Χερουβίν; PGM 4, 634 ἐπὶ τὰ Χερουβίν; Fluchtaf. 3, 24 ἐπὶ τῶν Χερουβί; Ps 79: 2 ἐπὶ τῶν Χερουβίν; En. 20, 7 v.l. Χερουβεί.—As a sing. PGM 4, 3061 τοῦ Χερουβίν; 7, 264 Χερουβίν; predom. neut. τά (Gen 3: 24; Ex 25: 18; 3 Km 6: 27f; 8: 7; 2 Ch 3: 10, 13; Ezk 10: 3, 8, 15; 11: 22; 41: 18, 20; En. 14, 11; Philo, Cher. 1; 25; 28, Fuga 100) more rarely masc. οἱ

(Ex 25: 19; 38: 6f; Jos., Ant. 3, 137.—Elsewh. Joseph. writes Χερουβεῖς; indeed, he used the word as a masc., Ant. 7, 378 and as a fem. 8, 72f), of the two winged figures over the ark of the covenant Χερουβὶν δόξης Hb 9: 5.— AJacoby, ARW 22, '24, 257-65; PDhorme et LHVincent, Les Chérubins: RB 35, '26, 328-58; 481-95; ELohse, TW IX, 427f. M-M.*

χερσόω *make dry and barren* (BGU 195, 21 [II AD]) in our lit. (H) only pass. **χερσόομαι** (Strabo 17, 1, 36; Inscr. Rom. IV 147; PTebt. 5, 94 [118 BC]; 61b, 30; 75, 40; LXX) 1 aor. ἐχερσώθην; pf. ptc. κεχερσωμένος *become barren* or *wild,* lit. of untended vineyards Hm 10, 1, 5. Fig. of Christians who are entangled w. the world 10, 1, 4 or who deny their Lord s 9, 26, 3.*

χέω (Hom.+; inscr., pap., LXX); in its only occurrence in our lit. it stands in the mid. and pass. **χέομαι** *pour out, gush forth* (Philo, Spec. Leg. 4, 26; Jos., Ant. 8, 232; Sib. Or., fgm. 3, 33) ταῦτα τὰ χεόμενα ὕδατα of the waters of the pool of David in contrast to the waters of eternal life GOxy 32. B. 577.*

χήρα, ας, ἡ *the widow* (with and without γυνή Hom.+)— 1. γυνὴ χήρα (Hom.+; BGU 522, 7; POxy. 1120, 12; Jos., Ant. 4, 240; 8, 320; LXX) *a widow* Lk 4: 26 (after 3 Km 17: 9). Elsewh. ἡ χήρα alone, *the widow* (Eur.+; inscr., pap., LXX, Philo; Jos., Ant. 16, 221; Sib. Or. 3, 77); the idea of neediness is oft. prominent in connection w. this word, and it is oft. joined w. orphans (ὀρφανός 1) Mt 23: 14 t.r.; Mk 12: 40, 42f (HHaas, 'Das Scherflein d. Witwe' u. seine Entsprechung im Tripiṭaka '22); Lk 2: 37; 4: 25; 7: 12; 18: 3, 5; 20: 47; 21: 2f; Ac 6: 1; 9: 39, 41; 1 Cor 7: 8; 1 Ti 5: 4, 11, 16a; Js 1: 27; 1 Cl 8: 4 (Is 1: 17); B 20: 2; ISm 6: 2; IPol 4: 1; Pol 6: 1; Hv 2, 4, 3; m 8: 10; s 1: 8; 5, 3, 7; 9, 26, 2; 9, 27, 2. ἡ ὄντως χήρα *the real widow* (ὄντως 2) 1 Ti 5: 3b, 5, 16b.—Symbol. in the proud words of the harlot of Babylon κάθημαι βασίλισσα καὶ χήρα οὐκ εἰμί Rv 18: 7 (cf. La 1: 1).

2. of a special class in the Christian communities, to which not every widow could belong; certain requirements were to be fulfilled. The one who was to belong to it had to be ὄντως χήρα (s. 1 above) 1 Ti 5: 3, 9; ISm 13: 1 (cf. παρθένος); Pol 4: 3.—On the widows in the churches s. LZscharnack, Der Dienst der Frau '02, 100ff; ABludau, D. Versorgung der Witwen (1 Ti 5: 3-16): Der kathol. Seelsorger 19, '07, 165-7; 204-11; 255-60; 305-10; 350-3; ALudwig, Weibl. Kleriker: Theolog.-prakt. Monatsschrift 20, '10, 548-57; 609-17; EvdGoltz, D. Dienst d. Frau in d. christl. Kirche² '14; JViteau, L'institution des Diacres et des Veuves: Revue d'Hist. ecclés. 22, '26, 513-36; AKalsbach, D. Altkirchl. Einrichtung d. Diakonissen '26; JMüller-Bardoff, EFascher-Festschr., '58, 113-33.— GStählin, TW IX, 428-54. S. also s.v. γυνή 1. M-M. B. 131.*

χθές (Hom. Hymns+; the real Attic form; PSI 184, 5 [III AD]; PLond. 983, 2; Jos., Ant. 6, 126, C. Ap. 1, 7; Test. Napht. 1: 4) *yesterday*=ἐχθές (q.v.) J 4: 52 t.r.; Ac 7: 28 t.r. (Ex 2: 14 v.l.); Hb 13: 8 t.r. (of the past [s. ἐχθές] as Diod. S. 2, 5, 5; Jos., Ant. 18, 243; Celsus 6, 10). M-M. B. 1000.*

χιϛʹ s. χξϛʹ.

χιλίαρχος, ου, ὁ (Aeschyl., X.+; inscr., pap., LXX; Jos., Ant. 7, 368; 12, 301; loanw. in rabb.) *the leader of a thousand soldiers,* then also=the Rom. tribunus militum, *military tribune,* the commander of a cohort= about 600 men (so since Polyb. 1, 23, 1; 6, 19, 1; 7ff; also Polyaenus

7, 17; Jos., Ant. 17, 215; inscr., pap.; cf. Hahn 47; 116; 168), in this sense (roughly equivalent to major or colonel) J 18: 12; Ac 21: 31–3, 37; 22: 24, 26–9; 23: 10, 15, 17–19, 22; 24: 7 v.l., 22; 25: 23; 1 Cl 37: 3.—Of high-ranking military officers gener. Mk 6: 21 (but s. EKlostermann, Hdb. ad loc.); Rv 6: 15; 19: 18.—S. the lit. s.v. ἑκατοντάρχης. M-M.*

χιλιάς, άδος, ἡ (Aeschyl., Hdt.+; LXX) (a group of) *a thousand* pl. (En. 10: 17, 19; Jos., Ant. 6, 193) Lk 14: 31a, b; Ac 4: 4; 1 Cor 10: 8; Rv 7: 4–8; 11: 13; 14: 1, 3; 21: 16; 1 Cl 43: 5. χίλιαι χιλιάδες 34: 6 (Da 7: 10). χιλιάδες χιλιάδων *thousands upon thousands* Rv 5: 11 (χιλιάδων also a loanw. in rabb.). In Rv the noun denoting what is counted may stand in the same case as χιλ. (so Theophanes Conf., Chron. 482, 14 de Boor λ´ χιλιάδες νομίσματα; 7, 17 πολλὰς μυριάδας μάρτυρας) instead of the gen. 7: 4, 5a, 8c; 11: 13; 21: 16 v.l.—ELohse, TW IX, 455–60. M-M.*

χίλιοι, αι, α (Hom.+; inscr., pap., LXX, Philo; Jos., Bell. 1, 317, Ant. 11, 15, Vi. 95 al.; Test. Jud. 4: 1; loanw. in rabb.) *a thousand* 2 Pt 3: 8a, b (Ps 89: 4); Rv 11: 3; 12: 6; 14: 20; 1 Cl 34: 6 (Da 7: 10; s. χιλιάς); B 15: 4 (Ps 89: 4). The millennium Rv 20: 2–7 (for the Jewish conceptions JWBailey, JBL 53, ’34, 170–87.—LGry, Le Millénarisme dans ses origines et son développement ’04; JSickenberger, Das Tausendjährige Reich in Apk: SMerkle-Festschr. ’22, 300–16; AWikenhauser, D. Problem d. 1000 jähr. Reiches in Apk: Röm. Quartalschr. 40, ’32, 13–25, D. Herkunft der Idee des 1000j. R. in Apk: ibid. 45, ’38, 1–24, also ThQ 127, ’47, 399–417; HBietenhard, D. 1000j. Reich ’55).*

χιόνινος, η, ον (Ptolem. Euerg. II Histor. no. 234, 10 Jac. =Athen. 9, 17 p. 375D) *snowy, snow-white* ἔρια Hv 1, 2, 2 (s. ἔριον).*

Χίος, ου, ἡ (Hom.+; Jos., Ant. 16, 18; inscr.) *Chios* an island (w. a city by the same name) in the Aegean Sea off the west coast of Asia Minor Ac 20: 15.*

χιτών, ῶνος, ὁ (Hom.+; inscr., pap., LXX, Ep. Arist., Philo; Jos., Ant. 3, 159; 7, 171 [on a woman]; Test. 12 Patr.—On the origin of the word cf. UWilcken, UPZ I p. 390, 1) *tunic, shirt,* a garment worn next to the skin, and by both sexes Mt 10: 10; Mk 6: 9 (on the wearing of two χιτῶνες, one over the other s. Jos., Ant. 17, 136.—The Cynic w. two coats, stick and knapsack: Diog. L. 6, 13.— Polyaenus 4, 14 criticizes τρίβωνα διπλοῦν and βακτηρίαν as signs of effeminacy); Lk 3: 11; 9: 3; Jd 23; Hs 9, 2, 4; 9, 11, 7. W. ἱμάτιον (q.v. 2) Mt 5: 40; Lk 6: 29; D 1: 4 (on these three passages, which belong together, cf. Gerh Kittel, Die Probleme des paläst. Spätjudentums u. d. Urchristentum ’26; J 19: 23a, b (see s.v. ἄραφος); Ac 9: 39.—Mk 14: 63 the pl. prob. does not mean a number of shirts, but *clothes* gener. (the pl. has this mng. Vi. Aesopi W c. 21). M-M. B. 419; 421.*

χιών, όνος, ἡ (Hom.+; PGM 5, 19; 7, 382; LXX; En.; Jos., Ant. 13, 208) *snow* as a symbol of perfect whiteness λευκὸς ὡς χιών Mt 28: 3; Mk 9: 3 t.r.; Rv 1: 14; Hs 8, 2, 3. λευκότερος πάσης χιόνος AP 3: 8 (the same hyperbole as early as Il. 10, 437; Ps.-Demetr., El. C. 124; En. 14, 20; 106, 2).—1 Cl 8: 4 (Is 1: 18); 18: 7 (Ps 50: 9). M-M. B. 69.*

χλαμύς, ύδος, ἡ (acc. to Pollux 10, 164 it occurs in Sappho [56 D.]; elsewh. Aristoph.+; X., An. 7, 4, 4; inscr., pap.; 2 Macc 12: 35; Philo, Leg. ad Gai. 94; Jos., Ant. 5, 33; loanw. in rabb.), a man's outer garment, a *cloak* used by

travelers and soldiers, such as (red in color: χλ. κοκκίνη as PGM 4, 636f) Roman soldiers wore Mt 27: 28, 31 (s. Appian, Bell. Civ. 2, 90 §377 [χ. of the Roman soldier's cloak=2, 150 ἡ πορφύρα]; Philo, In Flacc. 37; Philostrat., Vi. Ap. 5, 38 p. 199, 30). M-M.*

χλευάζω impf. ἐχλεύαζον (Aristoph., Demosth.+; late pap.; Jos., Bell. 6, 365, C. Ap. 2, 137)—1. *mock, sneer, scoff* (Philo, Sacr. Abel. 70; Jos., Ant. 7, 85; Test. Levi 14: 8) Ac 2: 13 t.r.; Ac 17: 32 (cf. Herm. Wr. 1, 29.—Ade Sizoo, Geref. Theol. Tijdschr. 24, ’24, 289–97).

2. trans. *mock, scoff at, sneer at* τινά *someone* (so also Lucian, Prom. in Verb. 33; LXX; Test. Levi 7: 2; Jos., Ant. 12, 170; cf. Philo, Mos. 1, 29) 1 Cl 39: 1. W. ὑβρίζειν (Plut., Artax. 27, 5) Dg 2: 7. M-M.*

χλεύη, ης, ἡ (the pl. as early as Hom. Hymns; the sing. in Dio Chrys. 14[31], 31; Lucian et al.; POxy. 904, 2 [V AD]; Sb 5763, 51; Philo; Jos., Bell. 4, 157, Ant. 7, 61; Sib. Or. 4, 37) *scorn, ridicule* Dg 4: 4.*

χλιαρός, ά, όν (Hdt.+) *lukewarm* (since Hdt. 4, 181; Diod. S. 17, 50, 5; Synes., Ep. 114 p. 254D χ. ὕδωρ.—The unpleasant taste of χ. ὕδ. causes vomiting: Vi. Aesopi I c. 1 p. 230, 7; 18), as a symbol of the church at Laodicea, that is neither hot nor cold and hence is to be spit out Rv 3: 16 (ℵ has the Ionic form χλιερός).—MJSRudwick and EMBGreen, ET 69, ’58, 176–8. M-M.*

Χλόη, ης, ἡ *Chloe* (Semos of Delos [III BC]: no. 396 fgm. 23 Jac. [Χλ. as a surname of Demeter]; Longus 1, 6, 3ff; in Lat.: Horace, Odes 3, 9, 9; Thesaurus Lingu. Lat., Suppl. 1, 401), an otherw. unknown woman who prob. lived in Corinth or Ephesus and may or may not have been a Christian. οἱ Χλόης *Chloe's people* (slaves or freedmen) 1 Cor 1: 11 (FRMHitchcock, JTS 25, ’24, 163–7). M-M.*

χλωρός, ά, όν—1. *yellowish green, (light) green* of plants (Hom.+; inscr., pap., LXX; En. 5, 1; Philo) χλωρὸς χόρτος (PLond. 287, 15 [I AD] al.; Gen 1: 30) Mk 6: 39; Rv 8: 7. Of branches or sticks *green, fresh* Hs 8, 1, 10–18; 8, 2, 2; 4 al. Of vegetation s 9, 1, 6f; 9, 21, 1; 9, 22, 1; 9, 24, 1; cf. 9, 21, 2 w. application to the doubters, who are neither green nor dry.—Subst. τὸ χλωρόν (oft. pap.). πᾶν χλωρόν *everything that is green= every plant* (Gen 2: 5; Dt 29: 22) Rv 9: 4.

2. *pale* as the color of a pers. in sickness as contrasted with his appearance in health (Hippocr., Prognost. 2 p. 79, 18 Kühlew.; Thu. 2, 49, 5; Maximus Tyr. 20, 5b.—Of 'pale' fear Il. 10, 376), so the horse ridden by Death (χλ. of death Sappho, fgm. 2, 14 Diehl²; Artem. 1, 77 p. 71, 27) ἵππος χλωρός Rv 6: 8 (see s.v. πυρρός).—RGradwohl, D. Farben im AT, Beih. ZAW 83, ’63, 27–33. M-M. B. 1058.**

χνοῦς, χνοῦ, ὁ (Hom. [χνόος]+; LXX; Sib. Or. 8, 15 v.l.) *dust, chaff* B 11: 7 (Ps 1: 4).*

χξϛ´ t.r. for ἑξακόσιοι (=χ´) ἑξήκοντα (=ξ´) ἕξ (=ϛ´) *six hundred sixty six* Rv 13: 18. This is the number of the beast, which is the number of a man. On the numerological technique involved here s. ἀριθμός 1 and F Dornseiff, Das Alphabet in Mystik u. Magie² ’26 §7; P Friesenhahn, Hellen. Wortzahlenmystik im NT ’36. The constantly recurring attempts to solve this riddle are based somet. on the Gk., somet. on the Hebr. alphabet; they may yield a name taken fr. mythology (as early as Irenaeus 5, 30, 3 Εὐάνθας, Λατεῖνος, Τειταν, and many others: GHeinrici, Griech.-byz. Gesprächsbücher ’11, p. 60, 3) or fr. history (e.g. Neron Caesar, Ulpius [Trajan] or Domitian [EStauffer, Con. Neot. 11, '47, 237-41], or Jesus in a heretical disguise, CCecchelli: GFunacoli-Festschr., '55, 23-31), the numerical value of whose letters is 666. On the other hand, some prefer to treat the number 666 purely as a number; they suspect a symbolic mng. (GAvan den Bergh van Eysinga, ZNW 13, '12, 293-306, NThT 4, '15, 62-6; ELohmeyer in the Hdb. exc. on Rv 13: 18). Further, cod. C and the Armenian version have the rdg. χιϛ'=616, which is preferred by RSchütz (s. below) and EHirsch, Studien z. 4. Ev. '36, 167; it was known to Irenaeus (5, 30, 1) and rejected by him. The comm. report on the attempts at solution already made; esp. E-BAllo, L'Apocalypse de St. Jean³ '33, exc. 34 p. 232-6; JdeZwaan, De Openbaring van Joh. '25, 46ff; ITBeckwith, Apocalypse '19, 393-411. Cf. also ZNW: PCorssen 3, '02, 238ff; 4, '03, 264ff; 5, '04, 86ff; EVischer 4, '03, 167ff; 5, '04, 84ff; ChBruston 5, '04, 258ff; CClemen 11, '10, 204ff; WHadorn 19, '19/'20, 11-29; SAgrell, Eranos 26, '28, 35-45; GMenken, Geref. Theol. Tijdschr. 36, '36, 136-52; MGoemans, Studia Cath. 13, '37, 28-36; DAvdBosch, 666 het getal eens menschen '40. In general s. LBrun, Die röm. Kaiser in Apk: ZNW 26, '27, 128-51; RSchütz, D. Offb. d. Joh. u. Kaiser Domitian '33; KHolzinger, Ak. d. W. Wien, Phil.-hist. Kl. 216, 3, '36; ABertholet, D. Macht der Schrift im Glauben u. Aberglauben: Abh. der Deutsch. Ak. d. W. zu Berlin '49, esp. p. 30.*

χοϊκός, ή, όν (Rhet. Gr. I 613, 4 γυμνοί τούτους τοῦ χοϊκοῦ βάρους; Hesychius; Suidas) *made of earth* or *dust* (χοῦς), earthy ὁ πρῶτος ἄνθρωπος ἐκ γῆς χοϊκός 1 Cor 15: 47 (cf. Gen 2: 7 ἔπλασεν ὁ θεὸς τὸν ἄνθρωπον χοῦν ἀπὸ τῆς γῆς; Sib. Or. 4, 445 of Adam, the χοϊκῷ πλασθέντι.—Philo, Leg. All. 1, 31 differentiates the οὐράνιος fr. the γήϊνος ἄνθρωπος).—Vss. 48; 49.—ESchweizer, TW IX, 460-8. M-M.*

χοῖνιξ, ικος, ἡ (Hom.+; inscr., pap.; Ezk 45: 10f) *choenix,* a dry measure, oft. used for grain, almost equivalent to a *quart;* a choenix of grain was a daily ration for one man (Hdt. 7, 187; Diog. L. 8, 18 ἡ χοῖνιξ ἡμερήσιος τροφή; Athen. 3, 20 p. 98ε) Rv 6: 6a, b.—FStolle, D. röm. Legionar u. sein Gepäck '14 (the appendix has an explanation of Rv 6: 6). M-M.*

χοιρίον, ου, τό (Aristoph.+; PMagd. 4, 8 [III BC]; Sb 5304, 1) dim. of χοῖρος, lit. *a little swine, piglet,* but also dim. only in form, *swine* and so B 10: 3.*

χοῖρος, ου, ὁ (Hom.+; inscr., pap.; Sym. Is 65: 4; 66: 3) *young pig,* then *swine* gener. (so Epict. 4, 11, 29; Plut., Cicero 7, 6; BGU 92, 7 [II AD]; 649, 7 al. in pap.; Jos., C. Ap. 2, 137; Test. Jud. 2: 5) Mt 8: 30-2; Mk 5: 11-13, 16 (AHarnack, Zu Mk 5: 11-13: ZNW 8, '07, 162; OBauernfeind, Die Worte der Dämonien im Mt '27); Lk 8: 32f; 15: 15f. W. dogs: as unclean animals GOxy 33 (JoachJeremias, Coniect. Neot. 11, '47, 105: fig.); in a proverb Mt 7: 6 (Theophyl. Sim., Ep. 20 τὰ δῶρα τοῖς χοίροις διένειμε; FPerles, ZNW 25, '26, 163f; AMPerry, ET 46, '35, 381). The prohibition against eating pork, and its interpretation B 10: 1, 3a, b, 10.—On swine and the Jews s. Billerb. I 448ff; 492f; KHRengstorf, Rabb. Texte 1. Reihe III '33ff, p. 36f. M-M. B. 161.*

χολάω (Aristoph.+) *be angry* (Artem. 1, 4; Diog. L. 9, 66 al.; inscr. [Ramsay, Phrygia I 2 p. 471 no. 312 of divine wrath]; 3 Macc 3: 1 v.l.) τινί *at someone* J 7: 23 (w. ὅτι foll.). M-M.*

χολή, ῆς, ἡ (Archilochus [VII BC]+; PGM 36, 284; LXX, Philo; Jos., Ant. 17, 173; Test. 12 Patr.; loanw. in rabb.) *gall, bile.*

1. lit., of a substance w. an unpleasant taste (the LXX uses χολή to transl. (a) מְרֵרָה=gall Job 16: 13; (b) מְרֹרָה= poison Job 20: 14; (c) לַעֲנָה=wormwood Pr 5: 4; La 3: 15; (d) רֹאשׁ= poison Dt 29: 17; Ps 68: 22) ἔδωκαν αὐτῷ πιεῖν οἶνον μετὰ χολῆς μεμιγμένον Mt 27: 34 (fr. Ps 68: 22?).—B 7: 3, 5; GP 5: 16 (s. ὄξος).

2. fig., as a designation of Simon Magus (Biogr. p. 153 the tragedian Philocles ἐπεκαλεῖτο Χολὴ διὰ τὸ πικρόν) χολὴ πικρίας *bitter gall* Ac 8: 23 (s. πικρία 1 and cf. Dt 29: 17 ἐν χολῇ καὶ πικρίᾳ; La 3: 15).—ἐν χολῇ has been conjectured by PKatz for ἐνοχλῇ Hb 12: 15 (ZNW 49, '58, 213-23) on the basis of Dt 29: 17 LXX; this is included as a v.l. in N.²⁵. M-M. B. 1134.*

χονδρίζω (hapax legomenon) prob.=χονδρεύω *make groats,* i.e. coarsely crushed grain (Hesychius). εἰς τὸν ἀγρὸν ὅπου χονδρίζεις Hv 3, 1, 2 prob. means a field in which was located an apparatus for preparing groats, where Hermas works.*

χόος s. χοῦς.

Χοραζίν, ἡ indecl. *Chorazin,* a place in Galilee, the location of which may have been the ruins of Kerâzeh, a half hour's walk north-west of Tell Hum. Menachoth 85a mentions a place כרזיים (Billerb. I 605) and Eusebius, Onom. 303, 174 Klosterm. mentions ruins of Chorazin. Mt 11: 21; Lk 10: 13. CKopp, The Holy Places of the Gospels, tr. RWalls '63, 187-9.*

χορδή, ῆς, ἡ (Hom.+; PPetr. III 142, 22 [III BC]; Ps 150: 4; Na 3: 8) *string* (made of gut) pl. w. κιθάρα (Diod. S. 5, 75, 3 τῆς κιθάρας χορδάς; Dio Chrys. 16[33], 57; Ael. Aristid. 28, 121 K.=49 p. 531 D.) IEph 4: 1; IPhld 1: 2.*

χορεύω impf. ἐχόρευον (trag.+; LXX, Philo; Jos., Ant. 17, 235) *dance in chorus* Hs 9, 11, 5. B. 689.*

χορηγέω fut. χορηγήσω; 1 aor. ἐχορήγησα orig. 'lead a chorus' or 'pay the expenses for training a chorus', then gener. *defray the expenses of someth., provide, supply* (in abundance) (Aristoph.+) τὶ *someth.* (Diod. S. 19, 3 ἅπαντα; Jos., Bell. 1, 625) 2 Cor 9: 10 (alternating w. ἐπιχορηγεῖν); 1 Pt 4: 11 (ἧς by attraction for ἥν). τί τινι (Polyb. 22, 26, 2; Dit., Or. 437, 71, Syll.³ 888, 77; PTebt. 51, 9; Sir 1: 10, 26; 1 Macc 14: 10; Ep. Arist. 259; Philo, Mos. 1, 255; Jos., Ant. 7, 279) Dg 1; 3: 4; 10: 6; Hs 2: 5, 8. ἐκ τῶν κόπων αὐτῶν παντὶ ἀνθρώπῳ ἐχορήγησαν they *provided for every man from* (the fruits of) *their labor* Hs 9, 24, 2. M-M.*

χορός, οῦ, ὁ (Hom.+; inscr., pap., LXX, Philo, Joseph.)

1. (*choral*) *dance, dancing* lit. ἤκουσεν συμφωνίας καὶ χορῶν Lk 15: 25.

2. *troop, band, company* (of dancers) of heavenly bodies (Maximus Tyr. 16, 6d; Herm. Wr. 416, 13 Sc. χορὸς ἀστέρων; Himerius, Or. 21, 6 W.; Sib. Or. 8, 450) ἥλιός τε καὶ σελήνη ἀστέρων τε χοροί 1 Cl 20: 3. Cf. IEph 19: 2.

3. *chorus, choir*= group of singers (so prob. Sb 3913, 8 χ. τῶν ἀγγέλων; Jos., Ant. 7, 85. In this sense a χορός of the stars is mentioned: Mesomedes 3, 10; 10, 17; Philo, Mos. 2, 239; ADNock, JTS 31, '30, 310ff) the church is to become a harmonious choir IEph 4: 2. Cf. IRo 2: 2. M-M.*

χορτάζω 1 aor. ἐχόρτασα. Pass.: 1 aor. ἐχορτάσθην; 1 fut. χορτασθήσομαι (Hes.+; pap., LXX) *feed, fill, satisfy;* pass.: *eat one's fill, be satisfied.*

1. of animals πάντα τὰ ὄρνεα ἐχορτάσθησαν ἐκ τῶν σαρκῶν αὐτῶν *all the birds gorged themselves with their flesh* Rv 19: 21 (cf. Test. Jud. 21: 8).

2. of men—**a.** lit. τινά *someone* Mt 15: 33; 1 Cl 59: 4 (τοὺς πεινῶντας). τινά τινος *someone with someth.* Mk 8: 4 (cf. Ps 131: 15). Pass. (Pamphilus [I BC/I AD] in Ael. Dion. χ, 14 ed. HErbse '50; Epict. 1, 9, 19; 3, 22, 66) Mt 14: 20; 15: 37; Mk 6: 42; 7: 27; 8: 8; Lk 6: 21 (οἱ πεινῶντες νῦν); 9: 17; J 6: 26; Phil 4: 12 (opp. πεινᾶν); Js 2: 16. ἀπό τινος (Ps 103: 13) Lk 16: 21. ἔκ τινος 15: 16 v.l.

b. fig.; pass. (Ps.-Callisth. 2, 22, 4 χορτάζεσθαι τῆς λύπης = find satisfaction in grief; Ps 16: 15) *be satisfied* Mt 5: 6 (χ. is also used in connection w. drink and relieves thirst: schol. on Nicander, Alexiph. 225 χόρτασον αὐτὸν οἴνῳ). M-M.*

χόρτασμα, ατος, τό (Polyb.+; pap., LXX, always of fodder for domesticated animals) *food* for men, pl. (Diod. S. 19, 26, 2 χορτάσματα) Ac 7: 11. M-M.*

χόρτος, ου, ὁ (Hom.+) *grass, hay* (Hes.+; pap., LXX, Philo; Jos., Bell. 6, 153, Ant. 20, 85), in our lit. almost always of green grass standing in field or meadow Mt 14: 19 (v.l. has the pl.); J 6: 10. τὸν χόρτον τῆς γῆς Rv 9: 4. ὁ χλωρὸς χόρτος (χλωρός 1) Mk 6: 39; Rv 8: 7. Of wild grass in contrast to cultivated plants ὁ χόρτος τοῦ ἀγροῦ Mt 6: 30; cf. Lk 12: 28; Js 1: 10, 11; 1 Pt 1: 24a, b, c (Is 40: 6, 7.—ἄνθεα ποίης as early as Od. 9, 449). Of stalks of grain in their early, grass-like stages Mt 13: 26; Mk 4: 28. —1 Cor 3: 12 mentions χόρτος *hay* as a building material (of inferior quality, as Diod. S. 20, 65, 1 κάλαμος and χόρτος). M-M. B. 519f.*

Χουζᾶς, ᾶ, ὁ *Chuza* (= אכוזא). The name occurs in a Nabataean [Corpus Inscr. Semiticarum II 1, 227; FC Burkitt, Exp. 5th Ser. IX 1899, 118-22] and in a Syrian [Littmann, Zeitschr. für. Assyriologie 27, '13, 397] inscr.). Borne by an ἐπίτροπος (q.v. 1 and 2) of Herod Antipas; this Chuza was the husband of a follower of Jesus named Joanna Lk 8: 3. M-M.*

χοῦς, χοός, acc. χοῦν, ὁ (Hdt.+; inscr., pap., LXX, Philo; Jos., C. Ap. 1, 192, Ant. 14, 64; Sib. Or. 8, 15; Bl-D. §52; Mlt.-H. 127; 142) *soil, dust,* of the dust of the road (Is 49: 23) ἐκτινάξατε τὸν χοῦν τὸν ὑποκάτω τῶν ποδῶν ὑμῶν Mk 6: 11 (cf. Is 52: 2 and s. ἐκτινάσσω 1). Of the dust that grief-stricken persons scatter upon their heads (Josh 7: 6; La 2: 10) ἔβαλον χοῦν ἐπὶ τὰς κεφαλὰς αὐτῶν Rv 18: 19. M-M.*

χράομαι mid. dep. (Hom.+; inscr., pap., LXX, Philo, Joseph.) 2 sing. χρᾶσαι (Bl-D. §87); 3 sing. pres. indic. and subjunctive χρῆται IRo 9: 1; 1 Ti 1: 8 (cf. Bl-D. §88 w. app.); impf. ἐχρώμην; 1 aor. ἐχρησάμην; pf. κέχρημαι; Mlt.-H. 200; *use.*

1. *make use of, employ*—**a.** w. dat. τινί *someth.* (Appian, Bell. Civ. 4, 102 §427f θαλάσσῃ; Wsd 2: 6; 13: 18; 4 Macc 9: 2; Philo, Aet. M. 70; 71; Jos., Bell. 3, 341; Bl-D. §193, 5; Rob. 532f) βοηθείαις ἐχρῶντο Ac 27: 17 (s. βοήθεια).—1 Cor 7: 31 t.r.; 9: 12, 15; 1 Ti 5: 23 (οἶνος 1); 2 Cl 6: 5; Dg 6: 5; 12: 3 (ᾗ μὴ καθαρῶς χρησάμενοι *not using it in purity*); ITr 6: 1; IPhld 4; Hs 9, 16, 4 (of the use of a seal as PHib. 72, 16 [III BC]). διαλέκτῳ *use a language* Dg 5: 2. Of the law (trag., Hdt.+; Jos., C. Ap. 2, 125) τοῖς νόμοις *live in accordance with the laws* (Jos., Ant. 16, 27) Hs 1: 3f; cf. 6. ἐάν τις αὐτῷ (= τῷ νόμῳ) νομίμως χρῆται 1 Ti 1: 8 (cf. χ. προφήταις Third Corinthians 1: 10). A dat. is to be supplied w. μᾶλλον

χρῆσαι *make the most of, take advantage of* 1 Cor 7: 21, either τῇ δουλείᾳ (so the Peshitta, Chrysostom, Theodoret, Weizsäcker, Heinrici, BWeiss, Schmiedel, Bachmann, Bousset, Lietzmann, JWeiss, Sickenberger, Kiefl, Juncker, H-DWendland, 20th Century, Goodspeed; HBellen, Jahrb. f. Antike u. Christent. 6, '63, 177-80) or τῇ ἐλευθερίᾳ (so Erasmus, Luther, Calvin, FGodet, Lghtf., Zahn, vWalter, Steinmann, Schlatter, Moffatt, RSV); cf. μᾶλλον 2a.—(On this subj.: ThZahn, Sklaverei u. Christentum in d. alten Welt [1879]: Skizzen aus dem Leben d. alten Kirche² 1898, 116-59; ASteinmann, Sklavenlos u. alte Kirche '10¹·⁴ '22, Pls u. d. Sklaven zu Korinth '11; EvDobschütz, Sklaverei u. Christent.: RE³ XVIII 423-33; XXIV 521; JvWalter, Die Sklaverei im NT '14; FXKiefl, Die Theorien des modernen Sozialismus über den Ursprung d. Christentums, Zugleich ein Komm. zu 1 Cor 7: 21, '15, esp. p. 56-109; JWeiss, Das Urchristentum '17, 456-60; ASteinmann, Zur Geschichte der Auslegung v. 1 Cor 7: 21: Théol. Revue 16, '18, 341-8; AJuncker, D. Ethik des Ap. Pls II '19, 175-81; JJKoopmans, De Servitute Antiqua et Rel. Christ., Diss. Amsterdam '20, 119ff; ELohmeyer, Soz. Fragen im Urchrist. '21; FWGrosheide, Exegetica [1 Cor 7: 21]: Geref. Theol. Tijdschr. 24, '24, 298-302; HGreeven [s.v. πλοῦτος 1]; MSEnslin, The Ethics of Paul '30, 205-10; WLWestermann, Enslaved Persons who are Free, AJPh 59, '38, 1-30; HGülzow, Christent. u. Sklaverei [to 300 AD], '69, 177-81. On slavery in antiquity gener.: WLWestermann, Pauly-W. Suppl. VI '35, 894-1068, The Slave Systems of Gk. and Rom. Antiquity, '55; WBKristensen, De antieke opvatting van dienstbaarheid '34; MPohlenz, D. hellen. Mensch '47, 387-96). τινὶ εἴς τι *use someth. for someth.* (Oenomaus in Euseb., Pr. Ev. 5, 33, 14; Simplicius In Epict. p. 27, 52 Düb.) Hv 3, 2, 8. Pass. σὺ αὐτὸς χρᾶσαι ἐκ τῶν αὐτῶν λίθων *you yourself are to be used as one of these stones* 3, 6, 7.—W. a double dat. (trag.+) σχοινίῳ χρώμενοι τῷ πνεύματι *using as a rope the Holy Spirit* IEph 9: 1. W. double dat. of the pers. (Jos., C. Ap. 1, 227) of a church that ποιμένι τῷ θεῷ χρῆται IRo 9: 1.

b. w. acc. (X., Ages. 11, 11; Ps.-Aristot., Oecon. 2, 22 p. 1350a, 7 χρ. τὰ τέλη εἰς διοίκησιν τῆς πόλεως; Ael. Aristid. 13 p. 162D; Dit., Syll.³ 1170, 27 ἄνηθον μετ' ἐλαίου χρ.; PTebt. 273, 28 ὕδωρ χρ.; Wsd 7: 14 v.l.; 2 Macc 4: 19.—Bl-D. §152, 4; Rob. 476) τὸν κόσμον 1 Cor 7: 31 (cf. Simplicius In Epict. p. 29, 30 Düb. τὸ τοῖς μὴ ἐφ' ἡμῖν ὡς ἐφ' ἡμῖν οὖσι κεχρῆσθαι = to use that which is not in our power as if it were in our power. S. also MDibelius, Urchristentum u. Kultur '28).

2. *act, proceed* (Hdt.+; POxy. 474, 38 et al.) w. dat. of the characteristic shown (Aelian, V.H. 2, 15; Jos., Ant. 10, 25) τῇ ἐλαφρίᾳ 2 Cor 1: 17. πολλῇ παρρησίᾳ 3: 12. ὑποταγῇ 1 Cl 37: 5.—W. adv. (PMagd. 6, 12 [III BC] et al.) ἀποτόμως 2 Cor 13: 10.

3. w. dat. of the pers. and an adv. *treat a person in a certain way* (X., Mem. 1, 2, 48 φίλοις καλῶς χρ.; Dit., Or. 51, 8 [III BC] τοῖς τεχνίταις φιλανθρώπως χρῆται; PPetr. III p. 115, 8 [III BC] πικρῶς σοι ἐχρήσατο; POxy. 745, 6; Esth 2: 9; Jos., Ant. 2, 315, C. Ap. 1, 153) φιλανθρώπως ὁ Ἰούλιος τῷ Παύλῳ χρησάμενος Ac 27: 3. Cf. Hs 5, 2, 10. M-M.*

χράω s. κίχρημι.

χρεία, ας, ἡ (Aeschyl.+; inscr., pap., LXX, Ep. Arist., Philo, Joseph.; Test. Zeb. 6: 5) *need, necessity.*

1. χρεία ἐστί τινος *there is need of someth., someth. is needed* (Polyb. 3, 111, 10; 5, 109, 1; Dit., Syll.³ 707, 16f; 736, 63; Sir 3: 22; 11: 9) Lk 10: 42. Without gen. (Diod. S.

1, 19, 5 ὅσον ἂν ᾖ χρεία) ἐὰν ᾖ χρεία *if it is necessary* D 11 : 5. τίς ἔτι χρεία; foll. by acc. w. inf. Hb 7 : 11. χρείαν ἔχειν τινός (*have*) *need* (*of*) *someone or someth.* (class.; inscr., pap.; Is 13 : 17; Wsd 13 : 16; Philo, Plant. 65; Jos., Ant. 8, 228) Mt 6 : 8; 9 : 12; 21 : 3; 26 : 65; Mk 2 : 17; 11 : 3; 14 : 63; Lk 5 : 31; 9 : 11; 15 : 7; 19 : 31, 34; 22 : 71; J 13 : 29; 1 Cor 12 : 21a, b, 24 (w. τιμῆς to be supplied); 1 Th 4 : 12; Hb 5 : 12b; 10 : 36; Rv 21 : 23; 22 : 5. W. gen. of the articular inf. (and acc.) χρείαν ἔχετε τοῦ διδάσκειν ὑμᾶς τινα Hb 5 : 12a (Bl-D. §400, 1; Rob. 1038f; 1061). W. inf. foll. (Da 3 : 16) ἐγὼ χρ. ἔχω ὑπὸ σοῦ βαπτισθῆναι Mt 3 : 14. Cf. 14 : 16; J 13 : 10; 1 Th 1 : 8; 4 : 9 (Bl-D. §393, 5); 5 : 1. W. ἵνα foll. J 2 : 25; 16 : 30; 1 J 2 : 27.

2. *need, lack, want, difficulty* (Diod. S. 3, 16, 2; Appian, Basil. 5 §2 ὑπὸ χρείας = from necessity) χρείαν ἔχειν *be in need, lack someth.* abs. (Diod. S. 17, 77, 2; Dit., Syll.² 857, 12 εἰ χρείαν ἔχοι Διονύσιος) Mk 2 : 25; Ac 2 : 45; 4 : 35; Eph 4 : 28; 1 J 3 : 17; D 1 : 5a, b. οὐδὲν χρείαν ἔχειν *have no lack of anything* (s. οὐδείς 2bγ) Rv 3 : 17 (t.r. οὐδενός). πληροῦν τὴν χρείαν τινός *supply someone's need(s)* (Thu. 1, 70, 7 ἐπλήρωσαν τὴν χρείαν) Phil 4 : 19. εἰς τὴν χρείαν τινὶ πέμψαι *send someth. to someone to supply his need(s)* vs. 16. λειτουργὸς τῆς χρείας μου *the one whose service supplied my need* 2 : 25. Pl. *needs, necessities* (Socrat., Ep. 1, 5 αἱ τῆς πατρίδος χρεῖαι; Geminus [c. 70 BC], Elementa Astronomiae 1, 21 [ed. CManitius 1898] αἱ τοῦ βίου χρεῖαι; Philo, Dec. 99; Jos., Bell. 6, 390, Ant. 13, 225) Ac 20 : 34; 28 : 10 (for πρὸς τὰς χρείας [v.l. τὴν χρείαν] cf. Polyb. 1, 52, 7; Ep. Arist. 11; 258); Ro 12 : 13; Papias 2 : 15. αἱ ἀναγκαῖαι χρεῖαι (ἀναγκαῖος 1) Tit 3 : 14.

3. *the thing that is lacking and* (*therefore*) *necessary* πρὸς οἰκοδομὴν τῆς χρείας (objective gen.) *such as will build up where it is necessary* Eph 4 : 29 (differently JAFindlay, ET 46, '35, 429).

4. *office, duty, service* (Polyb. 4, 87, 9; 10, 21, 1 al. in H.Gk.; inscr., pap.; 2 Macc 8 : 9; Jos., Ant. 13, 65) Ac 6 : 3. M-M. B. 638.*

χρεοφειλέτης and the less well attested form **χρεωφει-λέτης** (due to assimilation, Bl-D. §35, 2 w. app.; 119, 2; Tdf., Prol. 89; W-H., App. 152; Mlt.-H. 73. In the LXX and as v.l. in the NT we have the spelling χρεοφιλέτης), ου, ὁ (Hippocr., Ep. 17, 55; Aeneas Tact. 192; 516; Diod. S. 32, 26, 3; Dionys. Hal.; Plut., Caesar 12, 2, Luc. 20 : 3; Aesop, Fab. 11 H.; Dit., Syll.³ 742, 53; CWessely, Studien z. Paläogr. u. Papyrusk. 20, '21, 129, 4; Job 31 : 37; Pr 29 : 13) *debtor* Lk 7 : 41 (on the parable: PJoüon, Rech de Sc rel 29, '40, 615-19; GMPerrella, Div. Thom. Piac. 42, '40, 553-8); 16 : 5. M-M.*

χρεώστης, ου, ὁ (Plut., Mor. 100c; Dio Chrys. 28[45], 10; Lucian, Abd. 15; Herodian 5, 1, 6; Dit., Syll.³ 833, 9 [120 AD]; BGU 106, 4 [II AD]; 786 II, 6; POxy. 487, 11 al. in pap.; Philo; Jos., Ant. 3, 282) *debtor* χρεώστας θλίβειν *oppress debtors* Hm 8 : 10.*

χρεωφειλέτης s. χρεοφειλέτης.

χρή (Hom.+; inscr., pap.; Pr 25 : 27; 4 Macc 8 : 26A; Ep. Arist. 231; Philo, Joseph.) *it is necessary, it ought* foll. by acc. and inf. Js 3 : 10 (Bl-D. §358, 2; Rob. 319; WSchmid, Attizismus IV 1897, 592). M-M. B. 640.*

χρῄζω (Hom.+; inscr., pap., LXX) (*have*) *need* (*of*) τινός (class.; BGU 37, 7 [50 AD]; PFlor. 138, 6 al.; Jos., Ant. 1, 285; Test. Jud. 14 : 7; Sib. Or. 8, 390) Mt 6 : 32; Lk 11 : 8 (Test. Zeb. 7 : 3); 12 : 30; Ro 16 : 2; 2 Cor 3 : 1; B 2 : 4; Dg 2 : 2; ITr 4 : 2; 12 : 3; Hv 3, 10, 6. οὐδὲν οὐδενὸς χρῄζει

he needs nothing at all 1 Cl 52 : 1. W. inf. foll. (Jos., Ant. 1, 246) Dg 4 : 1. On ὅσον χρῄζει Lk 11 : 8 v.l., s. 1 Km 17 : 18; Dit., Syll.³ 57, 40 [450 BC] and cf. Jülicher, Gleichn. 272. M-M.*

χρῆμα, ατος, τό—1. pl. *property, wealth, means* (Hom. +; inscr., LXX, Philo, Joseph.) οἱ τὰ χρήματα ἔχοντες (X., Mem. 1, 2, 45) Mk 10 : 23; Lk 18 : 24. χρήματα πολλὰ ἔχειν Hs 2 : 5. Cf. Mk 10 : 24 t.r.

2. *money*—a. mostly pl. (Thu., X. et al.; pap.; Job 27 : 17; Ep. Arist. 85; Philo, Poster. Cai. 117; Jos., Bell. 1, 159; Test. Jud. 21 : 7) Ac 8 : 18, 20; 24 : 26 (χρ. διδόναι τινί as Diod. S. 8, 31; Jos., Ant. 7, 393).

b. more rarely sing. (Alcaeus 109+110, 30 D.²; Hdt. 3, 38; Diod. S. 13, 106, 9; 36, fgm. a; POxy. 474, 41; PHermop. 23, 7; Jos., Ant. 11, 56 [property, wealth]) of a definite sum of money Ac 4 : 37.—BReicke, TW IX, 468-71, χρῆμα etc. M-M. B. 634; 769.*

χρηματίζω fut. χρηματίσω; 1 aor. ἐχρημάτισα. Pass.: 1 aor. ἐχρηματίσθην; pf. κεχρημάτισμαι (Hdt.+; inscr., pap., LXX, Ep. Arist., Philo, Joseph.).

1. of God *impart a revelation or injunction or warning* (of oracles, etc., Diod. S. 3, 6, 2; 15, 10, 2; Plut., Mor. 435c; Lucian, Ep. Sat. 2, 25; Ael. Aristid. 50, 5 K. = 26 p. 503 D.; Dit., Syll.³ 663, 13 [200 BC] ὁ θεός μοι ἐχρημά-τισεν κατὰ τὸν ὕπνον; 1110, 8; PFay. 137, 2; 4 [I AD]; PGiess. 20, 18.—Philo, Mos. 2, 238; Jos., Ant. 5, 42; 10, 13; 11, 327 ἐχρημάτισεν αὐτῷ κατὰ τοὺς ὕπνους ὁ θεὸς θαρρεῖν; Jer 32 : 30; 37 : 2).

a. act. Hb 12 : 25.—b. pass.—α. χρηματίζομαι *a revelation or warning is given to me* χρηματισθεὶς κατ' ὄναρ Mt 2 : 22; cf. Hb 8 : 5. περί τινος (Jos., Ant. 3, 212) 11 : 7. Foll. by the inf., which expresses the warning given Mt 2 : 12. ἐχρηματίσθη ὑπὸ ἀγγέλου μεταπέμψασθαί σε *he was directed by an angel to send for you* Ac 10 : 22. Cf. Lk 2 : 26 v.l. (Vett. Val. 67, 5 ὑπὸ δαιμονίων χρηματισθή-σονται).

β. χρηματίζεταί τι *someth. is revealed or prophesied* (UPZ 71, 3 [152 BC] τὰ παρὰ τ. θεῶν σοι χρηματίζεται) ἦν αὐτῷ κεχρηματισμένον ὑπὸ τοῦ πνεύματος Lk 2 : 26.

2. *bear a name, be called or named* (Polyb. 5, 57, 2; Strabo 13, 1, 55; Plut., Ant. 54, 9; Philo, Deus Imm. 121, Leg. ad Gai. 346; Jos., Bell. 2, 488, Ant. 8, 157; 13, 318, C. Ap. 2, 30; Dit., Syll.³ 1150, 4 Καικίλιος ὁ χρηματίζων Βούλων; POxy. 268, 2 [58 AD]; 320; APF 4, '08, 122 V, 15 and oft. in pap.) μοιχαλὶς χρηματίσει Ro 7 : 3. ἐγένετο χρηματίσαι τοὺς μαθητὰς Χριστιανούς Ac 11 : 26.— Mlt.-H. 265 holds that these are two entirely distinct words; that 1 comes fr. an equivalent of χρησμός 'oracle', and 2 fr. χρήματα 'business'. M-M.*

χρηματισμός, οῦ, ὁ (X., Pla.+; inscr., pap., LXX; Philo, Vi. Cont. 17; Jos., Ant. 14, 231) *a divine statement* or *answer* (2 Macc 2 : 4; PGM 4, 2206.—Of a dream, Artem. 1, 2 p. 5, 20) Ro 11 : 4; 1 Cl 17 : 5. M-M.*

χρῆσαι s. χράομαι.

χρήσιμος, η, ον (since Theognis 406; inscr., pap., LXX, Ep. Arist., Philo; Jos., C. Ap. 2, 170; Sib. Or. 3, 230) *useful, beneficial, advantageous* IEph 4 : 2. τινί *for someone* Mt 20 : 28 D=Agr 22. ἐπί τι (Pla., Gorg. 480в, 481в, Leg. 7 p. 796A; Plut., Mar. 10, 10) ἐπ' οὐδέν (Zen.-P. 59 225, 3 [253 BC] ἐπ' οὐθὲν χρήσιμος) 2 Ti 2 : 14. εἴς τι (X., Vect. 4, 42; Pla., Leg. 7 p. 796 D.; Ezk 15 : 4) Hv 4, 3, 4. M-M.*

χρῆσις, εως, ἡ (since Pindar and Democritus 282; inscr., pap., LXX)—1. *use, usage* (Ep. Arist. 143; Philo, Op. M.

42; Jos., Ant. 4, 199, C. Ap. 2, 213; Test. Napht. 2: 4) Dg 2: 2; 4: 2; PK 2 p. 14, 13; 15. οὐ κατὰ χρῆσιν, ἀλλὰ φύσιν *not by usage* or *habit, but by nature* ITr 1: 1.

2. *usefulness* 1 Cl 37: 4. τὴν χρῆσιν ἀπώλεσεν (the honey) *has lost its usefulness* Hm 5, 1, 5.—**3.** *relations, function,* esp. of sexual intercourse (X., Symp. 8, 28; Pla., Leg. 8 p. 841A; Isocr. 19, 11; Ps.-Lucian, Amor. 25 παιδική; Plut., Mor. 905B ὀρέξεις παρὰ τὰς χρήσεις; POxy. 272, 12 al.) ἡ φυσικὴ χρῆσις Ro 1: 26; w. objective gen. τῆς θηλείας vs. 27. M-M.*

χρησμοδοτέω 1 aor. pass. ptc. χρησμοδοτηθείς *give an oracular response* (Ps.-Callisth. p. 3, 13; 52, 9; 81, 14; Lucian, Alex. 43 Jacobitz v.l.; Pollux 1, 17; Etym. Mag. p. 814, 40; inscr. [IV AD]: Ramsay, Phrygia II p. 566), pass. *be given* or *follow an oracular response* 1 Cl 55: 1.*

χρῆσον s. κίχρημι.

χρηστεύομαι mid. dep.; 1 aor. ἐχρηστευσάμην; 1 fut. pass. χρηστευθήσομαι (only in Christian wr.) *be kind, loving, merciful* 1 Cor 13: 4. τινί *to someone* 1 Cl 14: 3. ὡς χρηστεύεσθε, οὕτως χρηστευθήσεται ὑμῖν *as you show kindness, kindness will be shown to you* 13: 2 (saying of Jesus). M-M.*

χρηστολογία, ας, ἡ (Eustath. p. 1437, 53 on Il. 23, 598; eccl. writers) *smooth, plausible speech* (Julius Capitolinus, Pertinax 13 χρηστολόγον eum appellantes qui bene loqueretur et male faceret) Ro 16: 18. M-M.*

χρηστός, ή, όν (trag., Hdt.+; inscr., pap., LXX) *useful, suitable, worthy, good*—**1.** adj.—**a.** of things—**a.** *good, pleasant, kindly, easy* (to wear) (En. 32, 1; Jos., Ant. 3, 98) οἶνος (Plut., Mor. 240D; 1073A; Hippiatr. II 66, 16; Aberciusinschr. 16) Lk 5: 39 (perh. an Aramaism, cf. μέγας 9: 48 and Bl-D. §245; t.r. has the comp. χρηστότερος [Philo, In Flacc. 109; Jos., Ant. 8, 213]). ὁ ζυγός μου Mt 11: 30 (symbolically).

β. (*morally*) *good, reputable* ἤθη χρηστά 1 Cor 15: 33 (cf. ἦθος.—ἦθος χρηστόν also POxy. 642; 1663, 11; Ep. Arist. 290; Philo, Det. Pot. Ins. 38 ἤθη χρηστὰ διαφθείρεται).

b. of persons *kind, loving, benevolent* (Jos., Ant. 6, 92 w. ἐπιεικής; 9, 133 w. δίκαιος; Herodian 4, 3, 3 and Philo, Leg. ad Gai. 67 w. φιλάνθρωπος; Cass. Dio 66, 18; inscr. in FCumont, Études syr. '17 p. 323, 12; POxy. 642).

a. of men (Nicopho Com. [V/IV BC] 16; Ps.-Demosth. 59, 2) 1 Cl 14: 4 (Pr 2: 21) εἴς τινα *to someone* (POxy. 416, 2) Eph 4: 32.—**β.** of God (Hdt. 8, 111; Sb 158, 1; LXX; Philo, Det. Pot. Ins. 46 al.; Sib. Or. 1, 159) 1 Pt 2: 3 (Ps 33: 9), Χριστός 𝔓⁷²; Dg 8: 8. ἐπί τινα *to someone* Lk 6: 35. ἐν τοῖς κτλ. *among those= to those, who* 1 Cl 60: 1.

2. subst. τὸ χρηστόν *kindness* (Philo, Virt. 160; Jos., Ant. 8, 214) τοῦ θεοῦ Ro 2: 4.—JZiegler, Dulcedo Dei '37; CSpicq, RB 54, '47, 321-4.—KWeiss, TW IX, 472-81. M-M.*

χρηστότης, ητος, ἡ (Eur., Isaeus+; inscr., pap., LXX, Philo, Joseph.)—**1.** *goodness, uprightness* (Ps.-Pla., Def. 412E=ἤθους σπουδαιότης) ποιεῖν χρηστότητα *do what is right* (Ps 36: 3) Ro 3: 12 (Ps 13: 3).

2. *goodness, kindness, generosity* (Aristot., De Virt. et Vit. 8 w. ἐπιείκεια [as Philo, Exs. 166] and εὐγνωμοσύνη]; Plut., Demetr. 50, 1 w. φιλανθρωπία [as Philo, Leg. ad Gai. 73]; Dit., Syll.³ 761, 12 w. μεγαλοψυχία; Plut., Galba 22, 7, Mor. 88B; 90E w. μεγαλοφροσύνη.—BGU 372, 18; LXX; opp. πονηρία, Ode of Solomon 11: 20).

a. of men 2 Cor 6: 6; Gal 5: 22 (both w. μακροθυμία; Col 3: 12 (w. σπλάγχνα οἰκτιρμοῦ).—**b.** of God (Ps 30: 20; Philo, Migr. Abr. 122; Jos., Ant. 1, 96; 11, 144) Ro 2: 4 (w. ἀνοχή and μακροθυμία); 9: 23 v.l.; 11: 22c (cf. ἐπιμένω 2); Tit 3: 4 (w. φιλανθρωπία); 1 Cl 9: 1 (w. ἔλεος); 2 Cl 15: 5; 19: 1; Dg 9: 1, 2 (w. φιλανθρωπία and ἀγάπη), 6; 10: 4; IMg 10: 1; ISm 7: 1. (Opp. ἀποτομία) Ro 11: 22a, b. χρηστότης ἐφ' ἡμᾶς (cf. PsSol 5: 18 χ. σου ἐπὶ Ἰσρ.) Eph 2: 7.—LAStachowiak, Chrestotes: Studia Friburgensia, n.s. 17, '57 (Freiburg, Switzerland). M-M.*

χρῖσμα, ατος, τό (X.+; PGM 7, 874; LXX; Philo, Mos. 2, 146; 152; Jos., Ant. 3, 197, mostly=oil for anointing, unguent. For the accent Bl-D. §13; Mlt.-H. 57; Crönert 228, 3) *anointing* (so lit. Ex 29: 7) 1 J 2: 20, 27a, b, usu. taken to mean anointing w. the Holy Spirit (differently Rtzst., Mysterienrel.³ '27, 396f, who thinks of the 'formal equation of the baptismal proclamation w. the χρῖσμα'). M-M.*

χριστέμπορος, ου, ὁ (only in Christian wr.) *a Christ-monger, one who carries on a cheap trade in* (the teachings of) *Christ* D 12: 5.*

Χριστιανισμός, οῦ, ὁ *Christianity* IRo 3: 3; MPol 10: 1. W. Ἰουδαϊσμός IMg 10: 3a, b; IPhld 6: 1. κατὰ Χριστιανισμὸν ζῆν IMg 10: 1.*

Χριστιανός, οῦ, ὁ (formed like Ἡρῳδιανοί [q.v.] or Καισαριανοί Epict. 1, 19, 19; cf. ThMommsen, Her. 34, 1899, 151f; Dssm., LO 323 [LAE 377]; Hahn 263, 9. On the Pompeian inscr. CIL IV 679, the reading of which is quite uncertain, cf. VSchultze, ZKG 5, 1881, 125ff. On the spelling Χρηστιανός אⁱ Ac 11: 26; 26: 28; 1 Pt 4: 16 s. FBlass, Her. 30, 1895, 465ff; Harnack, SAB '15, 762; Bl-D. §24; Mlt.-H. 72) *the Christian* (so also Lucian, Alex. 25; 38, M. Peregr. 11; 12; 13; 16; Tacitus, Ann. 15, 44; Suetonius, Nero 16; Pliny the Younger, Ep. 10, 96, 1; 2; 3 al., also in Trajan's reply) Ac 11: 26; 26: 28; 1 Pt 4: 16 (JKnox, JBL 72, '53, 187–9); IEph 11: 2; IMg 4; IRo 3: 2; IPol 7: 3; MPol 3; 10: 1; 12: 1, 2; D 12: 4; Dg 1: 1; 2: 6, 10; 4: 6; 5: 1; 6: 1-9; PK 2 p. 15, 8.—As an adj. χριστιανός, ή, όν: ἡ χριστιανὴ τροφή ITr 6: 1.—RALipsius, Über den Ursprung u. ältesten Gebr. des Christennamens, Prog. Jena 1873; Zahn, Einl. II³ 41ff; FKattenbusch, Das apostol. Symbol II '00, 557ff; JDaniels, De Naam ΧΡΙ-ΣΤΙΑΝΟΙ: De Studiën 76, '07, 568–80; JLeCoultre, De l'étymologie du mot 'Chrétien': RThPh 40, '07, 188–96; AGercke, Der Christenname ein Scheltname: Festschr. z. Jahrhundertfeier d. Univers. Breslau '11, 360ff; Harnack, Mission I⁴ '23, 424ff; EPeterson, Christianus: Miscellanea Giov. Mercati I '46, 355–72; EJBickerman, HTR 42, '49, 109–24; JMoreau, La Nouvelle Clio 4, '50, 190–2; HBMattingly, JTS 9, '58, 26–37 (cf. Augustiani); CSpicq, Studia Theologica 15, '61, 68–78 (cf. Ciceronianus). M-M.*

χριστομαθία, ας, ἡ (only in Christian wr.) *discipleship with Christ* or *teaching of Christ* κατὰ χριστομαθίαν *in accordance with discipleship to Christ* or *with Christ's teaching* IPhld 8: 2.*

χριστόνομος, ον (only in Ign.) *keeping the law of Christ* IRo inscr.*

Χριστός, οῦ (as an adj. in trag. and LXX; Test. Reub. 6: 8 [the compound νεόχριστος=newly plastered: Diod. S., fgm. one b; 38 and 39, 4; Appian, Bell. Civ. 1, 74 §342]; in our lit. only as a noun.—CCTorrey, Χριστός: Quantulacumque '37, 317-24), ὁ.

1. as an appellative *the Anointed One, the Messiah, the Christ* (cf. Ps 2: 2; PsSol 17: 32; 18: 5, 7.—ESellin, Die israel-jüd. Heilandserwartung '09; EDBurton, ICC Gal '20, 395-9; AvGall, Βασιλεία τ. θεοῦ '26; HGressmann, D. Messias '29; PVolz, D. Eschatol. der jüd. Gemeinde im ntl. Zeitalter '34; Dalman, Worte 237-45; Bousset, Rel.³ 227, Kyrios Christos² '21, 3f; Billerb. I 6-11; MZobel, Gottes Gesalbter: D. Messias u. d. mess. Zeit in Talm. u. Midr. '38; J-JBrierre-Narbonne, Le Messie souffrant dans la littérature rabbinique '40; HRiesenfeld, Jésus Trans-figuré '47, 54-65; 81-96; TNicklin, Gospel Gleanings '50, 265-7; WCvUnnik, NTS 8, '62, 101-16; MdeJonge, The Use of 'Anointed' in the Time of Jesus, NovT 8, '66) ἐπυνθάνετο ποῦ ὁ Χριστὸς γεννᾶται *he inquired where the Messiah was to be born* Mt 2: 4. Cf. 16: 16, 20; 22: 42; 23: 8 t.r., 10; 24: 5, 23; 26: 63; Mk 1: 34 v.l.; 8: 29; 12: 35; 13: 21; 14: 61; Lk 3: 15; 4: 41; 20: 41; 22: 67; 23: 2, 35, 39; 24: 26, 46; J 1: 20, 25; 3: 28; 4: 29, 42 t.r.; 6: 69 t.r.; 7: 26f, 31, 41a, b, 42; 9: 22; 10: 24; 11: 27; 12: 34 (WCvUnnik, NovT 3, '59, 174-9); 20: 31; Ac 2: 30 t.r., 31, 36; 9: 22; 17: 3; 18: 5, 28; 26: 23; 1 J 2: 22; 5: 1 (OAPiper, JBL 66, '47, 445). J translates Μεσσίας as Χριστός 1: 41; 4: 25. ὁ Χριστὸς κυρίου Lk 2: 26; cf. 9: 20; Ac 3: 18; 4: 26 (Ps 2: 2); Rv 11: 15; 12: 10.—Ἰησοῦς ὁ Χριστός *Jesus the Messiah* Ac 5: 42 t.r.; 9: 34 t.r.; 1 Cor 3: 11 t.r.; 1 J 5: 6 t.r.; 1 Cl 42: 1b; IEph 18: 2. ὁ Χριστὸς Ἰησοῦς Ac 5: 42; 19: 4 t.r. Ἰησοῦς ὁ λεγόμενος Χριστός *Jesus, the so-called Messiah* Mt 27: 17, 22.—The transition to sense 2 is marked by certain passages in which Χριστός does not mean the Messiah in general (even when the ref. is to Jesus), but a very definite Messiah, Jesus, who now is called *Christ* not as a title but as a name (cf. Jos., Ant. 20, 200 Ἰησοῦ τοῦ λεγομένου Χριστοῦ. On the art. w. Χρ. cf. Bl-D. §260, 1; Rob. 760f) ἀκούσας τὰ ἔργα τοῦ Χριστοῦ Mt 11: 2; cf. Ac 8: 5; 9: 20 t.r.; Ro 9: 3, 5; 1 Cor 1: 6, 13, 17; 9: 12; 10: 4, 16; 2 Cor 2: 12; 4: 4; Gal 1: 7; 6: 2; Eph 2: 5; 3: 17; 5: 14; Phil 1: 15; Col 1: 7; 2: 17; 2 Th 3: 5; 1 Ti 5: 11; Hb 3: 14; 9: 28; 1 Pt 4: 13; 2 J 9; Rv 20: 4 al.

2. as a personal name; the Gentiles must have understood Χριστός in this way (to them it seemed very much like Χριστός [even in pronunciation—cf. Alex. of Lycopolis, III AD, C. Manich. 24 Brinkmann '05 p. 34, 18ff], a name that is found in lit. [Appian, Mithrid. 10 §32 Σωκράτης . . . , ὅτῳ Χρηστὸς ἐπώνυμον ἦν; 57 §232 Σωκράτη τὸν Χρηστόν; Diod. S. 17, 15, 2 Φωκίων ὁ Χρηστός; Chio, Ep. 4, 3; Philostrat., Vi. Soph. 2, 11, 2: a pupil of Herodes Att. (I BC/I AD): no. 434, fgm. 1, 4, 8; 1, 22, 5 Jac. as surname of a good ruler], in inscr. [e.g. fr. Bithynia ed. FKDörner '41 no. 31 a foundation by Chrestos for the Great Mother; Sb 8819, 5] and pap. [Preisigke, Namenbuch]. Cf. also Suetonius, Claud. 25.—Bl-D. §24 [lit.]; Rob. 192) Ἰησοῦς Χριστός Mt 1: 1, 18; Mk 1: 1; J 1: 17; 17: 3; Ac 2: 38; 3: 6; 4: 10; 8: 12; 9: 34 al. Very oft. in the epistles Ro 1: 4, 6, 8; 3 5: 15 (see s.v. Ἀδάμ); 1 Cor 2: 2 etc.; Hb 10: 10; 13: 8, 21; Js 1: 1; 2: 1; 1 Pt 1: 1-3, 7; 2 Pt 1: 1a, b; 1 J 1: 3; 2: 1; 3: 23; 2 J 7; Jd 1a, b; Rv 1: 1, 2, 5.—Χριστὸς Ἰησοῦς (SV McCasland, JBL 65, '46, 377-83) Ac 24: 24; Ro 3: 24; 6: 3, 11; 8: 1f, 11; 1 Cor 1: 2, 4, 30 etc.; 1 Cl 32: 4; 38: 1; IEph 1: 1; 11: 1; 12: 2; IMg inscr.; ITr 9: 2; IRo 1: 1; IPhld 10: 1; 11: 2; ISm 3: 2; Pol 8: 1 (s. Ltzm., Hdb. exc. on Ro 1: 1).—Χριστός Mk 9: 41; Ro 5: 6, 8; 6: 4, 9; 8: 10 etc.; Hb 3: 6; 9: 11; 1 Pt 2: 21; 3: 18.—On the combination of Χριστός w. κύριος s. κύριος II 2cγ. Cf. on the formulas διὰ Χριστοῦ (Ἰησοῦ): διά A III 2a and b; ἐν Χριστῷ (Ἰησοῦ): ἐν I 5d (also Gdspd., Probs. 146f); σὺν Χριστῷ: σύν 2b. OSchmitz, D. Christusgemeinsch. des Pls

im Lichte s. Genetivgebrauchs '24.—SMowinckel, He that Cometh, tr. GWAnderson '54; HRiesenfeld, The Mytho-logical Background of NT Christology: CHDodd-Festschr. '64, 81-95. θεὸς χριστός Jd 5 𝔓⁷².—On the question of Jesus' Messianic consciousness s. the lit. s.v. Ἰησοῦς 3; υἱός 2, esp. c; also J-BFrey, Le conflit entre le Messia-nisme de Jésus et le Messianisme des Juifs de son temps: Biblica 14, '33, 133-49; 269-93; KGGoetz, Hat sich Jesus selbst für den Messias gehalten u. ausgegeben?: StKr 105, '33, 117-37; GBornkamm, Jesus von Naz. '56, 155-63 (Engl. transl. JMRobinson '60, 169-78).—LCerfaux, Christ in the Theol. of St. Paul, tr. GWebb and AWalker, '59; JMorgenstern, Vetus T 11, '61, 406-31; RHFuller, The Foundations of NT Christology, '65; WThüsing, Per Christum in Deum, '65; HBraun, Qumran u. d. NT II '66, 75-84; DLJones, The Title 'Christos' in Lk-Ac, CBQ 32, '70, 69-76; JDKingsbury, Matthew: Structure, Christol-ogy, Kingdom '75. M-M.

χριστοφόρος, ον *bearing Christ;* subst. ὁ χρ. *the Christ-bearer* IEph 9: 2 (cf. Hdb. ad loc.).*

χρίω 1 aor. ἔχρισα, pass. ἐχρίσθην (Hom.+; inscr., pap., LXX, Philo; Jos., Ant. 2, 221) *anoint* in our lit. only in a fig. sense of an anointing by God (cf. Hom. Hymn to Demeter 237 χρίεσκ' ἀμβροσίῃ: Demeter anoints Demo-phon; Apollon. Rhod. 4, 871). He anoints

1. Jesus, the Christ, for his office Ac 4: 27 (cf. Sib. Or. 5, 68). ἔχρισέν με Lk 4: 18; cf. B 14: 9 (both Is 61: 1). αὐτὸν πνεύματι ἁγίῳ *him with Holy Spirit* Ac 10: 38 (the dat. as Dio Chrys. 66[16], 10; Jos., Ant. 7, 357 ἐλαίῳ χ.). W. double acc. (after LXX) ἔχρισέν σε ἔλαιον ἀγαλ-λιάσεως Hb 1: 9 (Ps 44: 8).

2. David: ἐν ἐλέει αἰωνίῳ ἔχρισα αὐτόν 1 Cl 18: 1 (cf. Ps 88: 21).—3. the prophets: μετὰ τὸ χρισθῆναι αὐτοὺς ἐν πνεύματι ἁγίῳ GH 10b.—4. the apostles, or, more probably, all Christians (at baptism or through the Spirit) 2 Cor 1: 21.—Encycl. of Rel. and Ethics XII 509-16; Reallexikon der Vorgeschichte XI '28, 191ff.—WGrund-mann, TW IX, 482-576: χρίω, χριστός et al. M-M.*

χρόα, ας, ἡ (Aristoph.+) *color* (Pla. et al.; Diod. S. 5, 32, 2; Lucian, LXX, Ep. Arist., Philo; Jos., Ant. 2, 273) Hs 9, 13, 5; 9, 17, 3f. τὰς χρόας ἀλλάσσειν (s. ἀλλάσσω 1 and cf. 2 Macc 3: 16) 9, 4, 5b; 8. χρόαι ποικίλαι 9, 4, 5a.*

χρονίζω fut. χρονίσω and Att. χρονιῶ Hb 10: 37 v.l.; 1 Cl 23: 5; LXX (Aeschyl., Hdt.+; inscr., pap., LXX; Jos., Ant. 16, 403).

1. abs. *take time, linger, fail to come* (or *stay away*) *for a long time* (Thu. 8, 16, 3; Maximus Tyr. 33, 6b; Da 9: 19) χρονίζει μου ὁ κύριος Mt 24: 48. Cf. 25: 5; Hb 10: 37 (Hab 2: 3); 1 Cl 23: 5 (Is 13: 22).

2. w. inf. foll. *delay, take a long time in doing someth.* (Dt 23: 22) Mt 24: 48 t.r.; Lk 12: 45.—3. w. the place indicated by ἐν *stay* (somewhere) *for a long time* (Polyb. 33, 18, 6; Alex. Aphr., Mixt. 9 p. 223, 5 Br.; Pr 9: 18a v.l.) ἐν τῷ ναῷ Lk 1: 21. M-M.*

χρόνος, ου, ὁ (Hom.+; inscr., pap., LXX, En., Ep. Arist., Philo, Joseph., Test. 12 Patr., Sib. Or.) *time,* mostly in the sense *a period of time* πολὺς χρόνος *a long time* (PGiess. 4, 11; PStrassb. 41, 39; Jos., C. Ap. 1, 278) Mt 25: 19; J 5: 6 (πολὺν ἤδη χ. as Jos., Ant. 8, 342; 19, 28). πλείων χρ. *a longer time* (Diod. S. 1, 4, 3; Dio Chrys. 78[29], 15; Dit., Syll.³ 421, 38; 548, 11; PPetr. II 9, 2, 3; Jos., Ant. 9, 228) Ac 18: 20. ἱκανὸς χρόνος *considerable time, a long time* (ἱκανός 1b) Lk 8: 27; Ac 8: 11; 14: 3; 27: 9. μικρὸς χρ. (Is 54: 7) J 7: 33; 12: 35; Rv 6: 11; 20: 3; IEph 5: 1. ὀλίγος χρόνος– χρυσοῦς

(Aristot., Phys. 218b, 15; Dit., Syll.³ 709, 11; PPetr. II 40a, 14) Ac 14: 28; 2 Cl 19: 3; Hs 7: 6. πόσος; Mk 9: 21. τοσοῦτος (Lucian, Dial. Deor. 1, 1; Jos., Bell. 2, 413) J 14: 9 (v.l. has τοσούτῳ χρόνῳ as Epict. 3, 23, 16); Hb 4: 7. ὅσος Mk 2: 19; Ro 7: 1; 1 Cor 7: 39; Gal 4: 1 (ὅσος 1). ὁ πᾶς χρόνος the whole time, all the time (Appian, Bell. Civ. 2, 132 §553; Jos., Ant. 3, 201; Third Corinthians 3: 4) Ac 20: 18; cf. 1: 21. ἐν παντὶ χρόνῳ at every time D 14: 3. χρόνον τινά for a time, for a while (Arrian, Anab. Alex. 6, 6, 5; Synes., Prov. 2, 3 p. 121D) 1 Cor 16: 7; Hs 7: 2. τῷ χρόνῳ in time (Herodas 4, 33 χρόνῳ) 9, 26, 4. στιγμὴ χρόνου (s. στιγμή) Lk 4: 5. τὸ πλήρωμα τοῦ χρόνου (πλήρωμα 5) Gal 4: 4 (cf. Pind., fgm. 147 OSchröder ἐν χρόνῳ δ' ἔγεντ' Ἀπόλλων). Certain special verbs are used w. χρόνος: διαγενέσθαι Ac 27: 9 (s. διαγίνομαι), διατρίβειν (q.v.) Ac 14: 3, 28, πληρωθῆναι 7: 23; 1 Cl 25: 2; Hs 6, 5, 2 (πληρόω 2). χρόνον ἐπέχω (q.v. 2b) Ac 19: 22; ἔχω (q.v. I 2f) J 5: 6; ποιέω (q.v. I 1eδ) Ac 15: 33; 18: 23; βιόω (q.v.) 1 Pt 4: 2.—ὁ χρόνος τῆς ἐπαγγελίας the time for the fulfilment of the promise Ac 7: 17; τῆς παροικίας 1 Pt 1: 17; τῆς πίστεως B 4: 9; D 16: 2; τῆς ἀπάτης καὶ τρυφῆς Hs 6, 5, 1; cf. 6, 4, 4. ὁ χρ. τοῦ φαινομένου ἀστέρος the time when the star appeared Mt 2: 7. ἐπλήσθη ὁ χρ. τοῦ τεκεῖν αὐτήν Lk 1: 57 (πίμπλημι 1bβ.—Ps.-Callisth. 1, 12 τελεσθέντος τοῦ χρόνου τοῦ τεκεῖν). Cf. also Mt 2: 16; Lk 18: 4; Ac 1: 6; 13: 18; Hb 5: 12; 11: 32; 1 Pt 4: 3; Jd 18; Dg 9: 1, 6; Hs 5, 5, 3.— Pl. χρόνοι of a rather long period of time composed of several shorter ones (Diod. S. 1, 5, 1; 5, 9, 4; Ael. Aristid. 46 p. 312 D.; UPZ 42, 45 [162 BC]; Sib. Or. 3, 649; Third Corinthians 3: 10) χρόνοι αἰώνιοι (αἰώνιος 1) Ro 16: 25; 2 Ti 1: 9; Tit 1: 2. ἀρχαῖοι χρ. Pol 1: 2. χρόνοι ἱκανοί (ἱκανός 1b) Lk 8: 27 t.r.; 20: 9; 23: 8. πολλοὶ χρόνοι (πολύς I 1aβ. Yet χρόνοι could somet. =years: Diod. S. 4, 13, 3 ἐκ πολλῶν χρόνων=over a period of many years; 33, 5a μετὰ δέ τινας χρόνους=after a few years; Ps.-Callisth. 2, 33 ed. CMüller of the age of a child ἦν χρόνων ὡσεὶ δώδεκα; Wilcken, Chrest. 129, 14 [346 AD]; Lexicon Vindob. rec. ANauck 1867 p. 19, 104 ἀφήλικες ἄνδρες μέχρι τῶν κε' χρόνων; Philip of Side: Anecdota Gr. Oxon. ed. JACramer IV 1837 p. 246 ἑκατὸν ἔτη ... καὶ μετὰ ἄλλους ἑκατὸν χρόνους; Cyrill. Scyth. 45, 5; 108, 8 and oft. Frequently in later Byzantine writers, e.g., Constantin. Porphyr. ed. GMoravcsik '49 p. 332 [Index]) Lk 8: 29; 1 Cl 42: 5; 44: 3. (οἱ) χρ. τῆς ἀγνοίας Ac 17: 30; ἀποκαταστάσεως πάντων 3: 21. οἱ νῦν χρ. 2 Cl 19: 4. οἱ πρότεροι χρ. Hs 9, 20, 4. οἱ καθ' ἡμᾶς χρ. MPol 16: 2; ἐπ' ἐσχάτου τῶν χρ. 1 Pt 1: 20. χρόνοι w. καιροί (the same juxtaposition: Demosth., Ep. 2, 3; Strato of Lamps. [300 BC], fgm. 10 Wehrli '50; PLond. 42, 23 [168 BC]; Maspéro 159, 36; 167, 45. Cf. Ael. Aristid. 46 p. 291 and 290D. On the difference betw. the two Demosth., Ep. 5, 6) Ac 1: 7; 1 Th 5: 1.—Both sing. and pl. are very oft. governed by prepositions: by ἄχρι (q.v. 1a); διά w. the gen. (διά A II 2), w. the acc. (διά B II 1); ἐκ (q.v. 5a); ἐν (Menand., Per. 296 ἐν τούτῳ τῷ χρόνῳ) PRainer 13, 2; 23, 23; Jer 38: 1) Ac 1: 6; IEph 5: 1; ἐπί w. the dat. (ἐπί II 2) 2 Cl 19: 4, w. the acc. (ἐπί III 2b); κατά w. the acc. (κατά II 5aγ); μετά w. the acc. (μετά B II 1); πρό (πρό 2).—Respite, delay (Aeschyl., Pers. 692; Menand., Dyscolus 186; Diod. S. 10, 4, 3; Lucian, Syr. Dea 20; Vi. Aesopi I c. 21 p. 278, 3 χρόνον ἤτησε; Wsd 12: 20; Jos., Bell. 4, 188 ἂν ἡμεῖς χρόνον δῶμεν, Vi. 370) ἔδωκα αὐτῇ χρόνον ἵνα μετανοήσῃ Rv 2: 21 (Diod. S. 17, 9, 2 διδοὺς μετανοίας χρόνον). χρόνος οὐκέτι ἔσται there should be no more delay 10: 6 (Gdspd., Probs. 200f).—For the history of the word s. KDieterich, RhM n.s. 59, '04,

233ff.—GDelling, D. Zeitverständnis des NTs '40; OCullmann, Christus u. d. Zeit '46, Engl. transl. Christ and Time, FVFilson '50, ³'64, esp. 49f; 51–5; JWilch, Time and Event (OT) '69.—GDelling, TW IX, 576–89. M-M. B. 954.**

χρονοτριβέω (Aristot., Rhet. 3, 3, 3 p. 1406a, 37; Plut., Mor. 225B; D; the mid. UPZ 39, 29; 40 II, 21 [both II BC]. —Cf. Jos., Ant. 12, 368 χρ. ἐτρίβετο) spend time, lose or waste time ἐν τῇ Ἀσίᾳ Ac 20: 16. M-M.*

χρύσεος s. χρυσοῦς. M-M.

χρυσίον, ου, τό (Hdt.+; inscr., pap., LXX, En., Ep. Arist., Philo; Jos., C. Ap. 1, 110 al.; Test. 12 Patr.) gold as a metal of great value 1 Pt 1: 7; MPol 18: 1. Refined in the fire Rv 3: 18; Hv 4, 3, 4a, b. χρ. καθαρόν (Ex 25: 11; 2 Ch 3: 4, 8) pure gold Rv 21: 18, 21. Cf. 1 Cor 3: 12 (Dio Chrys. 30[47], 14 a house of real gold, cf. 62[79], 1); Hb 9: 4.— Gold ornaments, jewelry 1 Ti 2: 9; 1 Pt 3: 3 (pl., as Demosth. 27, 10; 13; Plut., Tim. 15, 10, Artax. 5, 4; Alciphr. 4, 9, 4; Dialekt-Inschr. 4689, 22 [Messenia]; PMich. 214, 32 [296 AD]). κεχρυσωμένη (ἐν) χρυσίῳ adorned with golden jewelry Rv 17: 4; 18: 16.—Coined gold (X., An. 1, 1, 9; Ep. Arist. 319) ἀργύριον καὶ (or ἢ) χρυσίον silver and gold=money (inscr., LXX; Philo, Deus Imm. 169; Jos., Ant. 15, 5) Ac 3: 6; 20: 33; 1 Pt 1: 18. M-M.*

χρυσοδακτύλιος, ον (Hesychius s.v. χρυσοκόλλητος) with a gold ring (or rings) on one's finger(s) Js 2: 2 (cf. Epict. 1, 22, 18). M-M.*

χρυσόλιθος, ου, ὁ chrysolite (Diod. S. 2, 52, 3; PLond. 928, 15 [III AD]; Ex 28: 20; 36: 20; Ezk 28: 13; Jos., Bell. 5, 234, Ant. 3, 168); the ancients (Pliny, N.H. 37, 42) applied the term to the yellow topaz. Rv 21: 20.—Lit. s.v. ἀμέθυστος. M-M.*

χρυσόπρασος, ου, ὁ chrysoprase (Pliny, N.H. 37, 113 chrysoprasus. The Gk. word in Michael Psellus [XI AD] 23: Les lap. Gr. [s. χαλκηδών] p. 204; 208), an apple-green, fine-grained hornstone (variety of quartz), colored by nickel oxide and highly translucent. Rv 21: 20.—Lit. s.v. ἀμέθυστος. M-M.*

χρυσός, οῦ, ὁ (Hom.+; inscr., pap., LXX, Ep. Arist., Philo; Jos., Ant. 3, 135; Test. 12 Patr.) gold, both as a raw material and as a finished product. Rv 9: 7. As an esp. precious material (w. frankincense and myrrh) Mt 2: 11. W. silver PK 2 p. 14, 14 and precious stones 1 Cor 3: 12 t.r.; Rv 18: 12. Refined in the furnace (w. silver) MPol 15: 2. Of coined gold (Demosth. 9, 42), w. ἄργυρος (q.v.) Mt 10: 9. This may also be the mng. in Js 5: 3 and Mt 23: 16f, though vessels of gold may be meant. Gold ornaments 1 Ti 2: 9 v.l.; Rv 17: 4 v.l.; 18: 16 v.l. (s. χρυσίον). Of golden idols Ac 17: 29; 2 Cl 1: 6. M-M. B. 610.*

χρυσοῦς, ῆ, οῦν (trag., Attic wr.; inscr., pap., LXX, Ep. Arist., Philo. Contracted fr. χρύσεος: Hom.+; inscr.; rare in pap. and LXX [Thackeray p. 173]. Both forms in Joseph. [Schmidt 491]. Uncontracted forms are found in our lit. only as v.l. in Rv: χρυσέων 2: 1 AC, χρυσέους 4: 4 ℵ, χρυσέας 5: 8 ℵ); the acc. fem. sing. χρυσᾶν Rv 1: 13 instead of χρυσῆν is formed on the analogy of ἀργυρᾶν (s. PGM 10, 26 χρυσᾶν ἢ ἀργυρᾶν and Bl-D. §45; cf. Mlt.-H. 120f; Psaltes p. 187f) golden= made of or adorned with gold 2 Ti 2: 20; Hb 9: 4a, b; Rv 1: 12f, 20; 2: 1; 4: 4; 5: 8; 8: 3a, b; 9: 13, 20; 14: 14; 15: 6f; 17: 4; 21: 15; Dg 2: 7.—Golden in color or appearance Hv 4, 1, 10; 4, 3, 4. M-M. s.v. -εος.*

χρυσόω (Hdt., Aristoph.+; Dit., Syll.³ 996, 25; POxy. 521, 2; 4; 8; LXX) perf. pass. ptc. κεχρυσωμένος (Jos., Vi. 66) *make golden, gild, adorn with gold,* κεχρυσωμένη, w. (ἐν) χρυσίῳ pleonastically added (cf. Hdt. 2, 132; Ex 26: 32; 2 Ch 3: 8–10), and the further addition of precious stones and pearls, of the harlot Babylon Rv 17: 4; 18: 16. M-M.*

χρῶμα, ατος, τό—1. *color* (Eur., Hdt.+; pap., LXX; En. 18, 7; 98, 2; Ep. Arist. 97; Philo; loanw. in rabb.) Hv 4, 1, 10; 4, 3, 1. τῷ χρώματι *in color* Hs 6, 1, 5. Symbol., of the complete purity of faith among the Roman Christians ἀποδιϋλισμένοι ἀπὸ παντὸς ἀλλοτρίου χρώματος *filtered clear of every alien color* IRo inscr.
    2. *tone-color, melody, key note* in music (Pla., Plut. et al.; Philo, Congr. Erud. Gr. 76) χρῶμα θεοῦ λαβόντες ᾄδετε IEph 4: 2. B. 1050.*

χρώς, χρωτός, ὁ (Hom.+; LXX) *skin, surface of the body* Ac 19: 12; MPol 13: 2. B. 200.*

χωλός, ή, όν (Hom.+; inscr., pap., LXX, Philo; Jos., Bell. 5, 474) *lame, crippled* (also of the hand: Eupolis Com. [V bc] 247; 343; Hippocr., Prorrh. 2, 1) ἀνὴρ χωλὸς ἐκ κοιλίας μητρὸς αὐτοῦ Ac 3: 2; 14: 8. Pl. almost always w. τυφλοί (Antig. Car. 112; Dit., Syll.³ 1168, 36; Job 29: 15; Jos., C. Ap. 2, 23) and in addition oft. w. those subject to other infirmities Mt 11: 5 (also taken symbol., as Pla., Laws 1 p. 634A of ἀνδρεία; Plut., Cim. 16, 10 of Hellas; s. κωφός 2); 15: 30, 31; 21: 14; Lk 7: 22 (also symbol.; s. κωφός 2); 14: 13, 21; J 5: 3.—παραλελυμένοι καὶ χωλοί Ac 8: 7.—*Deprived of one foot* Mt 18: 8; Mk 9: 45.—τὸ χωλόν *what is lame, the lame leg(s)* symbol. Hb 12: 13 (ἐκτρέπω, end). M-M. B. 318.*

χώνευμα, ατος, τό *image made of cast metal, molten image* (Philo of Byzantium, Sept. Orbis Spect. 4, 1 [ed. RHercher 1858 after his Paris ed. of Aelian]; PLeid. X, 21B; LXX) of idols 1 Cl 53: 2; B 14: 3 (both Dt 9: 12).*

χωνευτός, ή, όν (from χωνεύω=melt, pour metal: Polyb. 34, 9, 11; Diod. S. 5, 35, 4; Plut., Lucull. 37, 5; schol. on Nicander, Ther. 257) *cast, poured* (LXX; Eupol. in Euseb., Pr. Ev. 9, 34, 9; Jos., Ant. 8, 77) subst. τὸ χωνευτόν *an image made of cast metal* (Philo, Leg. All. 3, 36) B 12: 6 (Dt 27: 15).*

χώρα, ας, ἡ (Hom.+; inscr., pap., LXX; Ep. Arist., Philo, Joseph., Test. 12 Patr.; Sib. Or.) *country, land.*
    1. *district, region, place*—a. gener. Mk 6: 55; Lk 2: 8; 15: 14f; Ac 13: 49. χώρα μακρά Lk 15: 13; 19: 12. ἡ χώρα ἐγγὺς τῆς ἐρήμου J 11: 54. ἔξω τῆς χώρας *out of that region* Mk 5: 10.
    b. The district is more definitely described ὁ κύριος τῆς χώρας ταύτης *the lord of this country* Hs 1: 4a. The greater definiteness is brought about by a gen. of the ruler 1: 4b; of the inhabitants αὐτῶν (Jos., Ant. 5, 318) Mt 2: 12; Ac 12: 20; 1 Cl 12: 2, mentioned by name (Josh 5: 12; 1 Ch 20: 1; Is 7: 18; Ep. Arist. 107) τῶν Γαδαρηνῶν Mt 8: 28. Cf. Mk 5: 1; Lk 8: 26; Ac 10: 39; of the provincial name (1 Macc 8: 3) ἡ χώρα τῆς Ἰουδαίας Ac 26: 20. Also by a geograph. adj. ἡ Γαλατικὴ χώρα Ac 16: 6; 18: 23; cf. Lk 3: 1; 1 Cl 25: 3 and Mk 1: 5 (here we have ἡ Ἰουδαία χώρα [Jos., Ant. 11, 4] by metonymy for the inhabitants).
    2. *the (open) country* in contrast to the city (Isocr. et al.; Diod. S. 18, 18, 9 πόλιν κ. χώραν; Appian, Iber. 10 §39; PTebt. 416, 11; Ep. Arist. 108f; Sib. Or. 3, 707) εἰς Ἱεροσόλυμα ἐκ τῆς χώρας J 11: 55. κατὰ χώρας καὶ πόλεις κηρύσσοντες 1 Cl 42: 4 (cf. Test. Levi 13: 7). Those who were dispersed by the persecution at Jerusalem διεσπά-

ρησαν κατὰ τὰς χώρας τῆς Ἰουδαίας κ. Σαμαρείας Ac 8: 1. Cf. 11: 2 D.
    3. *(dry) land* in contrast to the sea (Isocr. 7, 1; Diod. S. 3, 40, 2; 20, 61, 4 [opp. θάλασσα]) Ac 27: 27.—4. *field, cultivated land* (X. et al.; Sir 43: 3; Jos., Ant. 7, 191) pl. Lk 21: 21; J 4: 35; Js 5: 4. Sing. *land, farm* (Jos., Ant. 11, 249; 16, 250) Lk 12: 16.—ἐν τῇ χώρᾳ B 7: 8 refers to land which, though uncultivated, grows fruit-bearing bushes.
    5. *place* (Ps.-Tyrtaeus 9, 42 D.² πάντες . . . εἴκουσ᾽ ἐκ χώρης=they all withdraw from the place [which the seasoned soldier claims for himself]) ἐν χώρᾳ καὶ σκιᾷ θανάτου=ἐν χώρᾳ σκιᾶς θανάτου *in the land of the shadow of death* Mt 4: 16 (Is 9: 1).—For the history of the word s. KDieterich, RhM n.s. 59, '04, 226ff. M-M. B. 1302; 1304f.*

Χωραζίν s. Χοραζίν.

χωρέω fut. χωρήσω; 1 aor. ἐχώρησα (Hom.+; inscr., pap., LXX, Ep. Arist., Philo, Joseph., Sib. Or. 3, 18) *make room, give way.*
    1. *go, go out or away, reach* (trag.+; pap.)—a. lit., of food εἰς τὴν κοιλίαν χωρεῖ Mt 15: 17 (=εἰσπορεύεται Mk 7: 19.—Aristot., Probl. 1, 55 the drink εἰς τὰς σάρκας χωρεῖ). ἔκρυσις Papias 3. Of men εἰς τὸν ἴδιον τόπον μέλλει χωρεῖν IMg 5: 1; cf. IEph 16: 2. οὗ μέλλουσι χωρήσειν, τοῦτο that, *to which they are destined to go* Dg 8: 2. εἴς τινα *to someone* (Appian, Bell. Civ. 3, 95 §395 χ. ἐς τὸν ἀδελφόν; 5, 29 §114) of Christ, who has gone to the Father IMg 7: 2. ἔτι κάτω χωρεῖ *go down still farther* Mt 20: 28 D=Agr 22. Of the head of a tall figure χωροῦσα μέχρι τοῦ οὐρανοῦ *it reached up to the sky* GP 10: 40 (like Eris: Il. 4, 443).
    b. fig., of a report (Pla., Ep. 7 p. 333A; 338B λόγος ἐχώρει) εἰς ἡμᾶς ἐχώρησεν *it has reached us* 1 Cl 47: 7. εἰς μετάνοιαν χωρεῖν *come to repentance* 2 Pt 3: 9 (cf. Appian, Bell. Civ. 5, 30 §115 ἐς ἀπόστασιν χ.=turned to revolt). εἴς τι ἀγαθὸν χωρεῖν *lead to some good* B 21: 7 (Soph., El. 615 εἰς ἔργον; Aristoph., Ran. 641 ἐς τὸ δίκαιον).
    2. *be in motion, go forward, make progress* (Pla., Cratyl. 19 p. 402A the saying of Heraclitus πάντα χωρεῖ καὶ οὐδὲν μένει; Hdt. 3, 42; 5, 89; 7, 10; 8, 68; Aristoph., Pax 472; 509, Nub. 907; Polyb. 10, 35, 4; 28, 15, 12; Dionys. Hal. 1, 64, 4; Plut., Galba 10, 1; Jos., Ant. 12, 242; PTebt. 27, 81 ἕκαστα χωρῆσαι κατὰ τὴν ἡμετέραν πρόθεσιν) ὁ λόγος ὁ ἐμὸς οὐ χωρεῖ ἐν ὑμῖν *my word makes no headway among you* J 8: 37 (Moffatt; cf. Weymouth, Eunap., Vi. Soph. p. 103 χωρεῖ λόγος). Or perh. (as in 1b above) *finds no place in you* (RSV; cf. Gdspd. and 20th Cent.; Field, Notes 94f, w. ref. to Alciphr., Ep. 3, 7; Bultmann; DTabachovitz, Till betydelsen av χωρεῖν Joh. 8: 37: Eranos 31, '33, 71f.—Perh. also=χώραν ἔχειν Appian, Bell. Civ. 2, 70 §289 ὀλίγην ἐν αὐτοῖς χώραν ἔχειν; Alex. Aphr., Fat. 6 p. 169, 31 Br. χώραν ἐν αὐτοῖς ἔχει τὸ παρὰ φύσιν *'even that which is contrary to nature has room [to be practiced] among them'*).
    3. *have room for, hold, contain*—a. lit., of vessels that hold a certain quantity (Hdt.+; Diod. S. 13, 83, 3 of stone πίθοι: χ. ἀμφορεῖς χιλίους; 3 Km 7: 24; 2 Ch 4: 5 χ. μετρητάς; Ep. Arist. 76 χωροῦντες ὑπὲρ δύο μετρητάς; Test. Napht. 2: 2) J 2: 6. Cf. Hs 9, 2, 1. In a hyperbolic expr. οὐδ᾽ αὐτὸν τὸν κόσμον χωρήσειν τὰ βιβλία J 21: 25 (Philo, Ebr. 32 οὐδὲ τῶν δωρεῶν ἱκανὸς οὐδεὶς χωρῆσαι τὸ ἄφθονον πλῆθος, ἴσως δὲ οὐδ᾽ ὁ κόσμος. On this subj. cf. ELucius, Die Anfänge des Heiligenkults '04 p. 200, 1; OWeinreich, Antike Heilungswunder '09, 199-

201). Of a space that *holds* people (Thu. 2, 17, 3; Diod. S. 13, 61, ὁ μὴ δυναμένων χωρῆσαι τῶν τριήρων τὸν ὄχλον= be able to hold the crowd; Plut., Mor. 804в; PSI 186, 4 χωρήσει τὸ θέαδρον [sic]; Gen 13: 6; Jos., Bell. 6, 131) without an obj. (cf. οὐ χάρτης χωρεῖ in late pap.= the sheet of paper is not large enough) ὥστε μηκέτι χωρεῖν μηδὲ τὰ πρὸς τὴν θύραν *so that there was no longer any room, even around the door* Mk 2: 2. Cf. Hm 5, 2, 5. Of God πάντα χωρῶν, μόνος δὲ ἀχώρητος ὤν Hm 1: 1; quite sim. PK 2 p. 13, 24.

b. fig.—**α.** of open-heartedness χωρήσατε ἡμᾶς *make room for us* in your hearts 2 Cor 7: 2 (cf. 6: 12; Field, Notes 184).

β. *grasp* in the mental sense, *accept, comprehend, understand* (Περὶ ὕψους 9, 9 τὴν τοῦ θεοῦ δύναμιν; Plut., Cato Min. 64, 5 τὸ Κάτωνος φρόνημα χωρεῖν; Synes., Kingship 29 p. 31ᴅ φιλοσοφία has her abode παρὰ τῷ θεῷ . . . καὶ ὅταν αὐτὴν μὴ χωρῇ κατιοῦσαν ὁ χθόνιος χῶρος, μένει παρὰ τῷ πατρί= and if she comes down and the region of the earth cannot contain her, she remains with the Father; Dit., Syll.³ 814, 11 [67 ᴀᴅ]; Wilcken, Chrest. 238, 8; PGM 4, 729; Jos., C. Ap. 1, 225) τὸν λόγον Mt 19: 11. Pass. Dg 12: 7. W. acc. to be supplied Mt 19: 12a, b=ISm 6: 1. Cf. ITr 5: 1. M-M.*

Χωρήβ (חֹרֵב) indecl. (LXX; but, as it seems, not in Hellenistic Jewish lit.) *Horeb*, the mountain where the law was given ὄρος X. (as Ex 3: 1; 33: 6) PK 2 p. 15, 6.*

χωρίζω fut. χωρίσω; 1 aor. ἐχώρισα. Pass.: pf. ptc. κεχωρισμένος; 1 aor. ἐχωρίσθην (Hdt.+; inscr., pap., LXX, En., Philo, Joseph., Test. 12 Patr.).

1. act. *divide, separate* τὶ someth. (opp. συζεύγνυμι) Mt 19: 6; Mk 10: 9. τινὰ ἀπό τινος (cf. Pla., Phaedo 12 p. 67ᴄ; Diogenes, Ep. 39, 1 χ. τὴν ψυχὴν ἀπὸ τοῦ σώματος; Wsd 1: 3; Philo, Leg. All. 2, 96) Ro 8: 35, 39.

2. pass.—**a.** *separate* (oneself), *be separated* of divorce (Isaeus 8, 36; Polyb. 31, 26 κεχωρίσθαι ἀπὸ τοῦ Λευκίου. Oft. in marriage contracts in the pap. ἀπ᾽ ἀλλήλων χωρισθῆναι: PSI 166, 11 [II вс]; BGU 1101, 5; 1102, 8; 1103, 6 [all I вс] al. Cf. Dssm., NB 67 [BS 247]) ἀπό τινος 1 Cor 7: 10. Abs. vss. 11, 15a, b.

b. *be taken away, take one's departure, go away* of stones that represent people Hs 9, 8, 1. Of people (Jos., Vi. 215), w. ἀπό foll. Ac 1: 4; 18: 2. Foll. by ἐκ (Polyb. 3, 90, 2) 18: 1. Abs. Phlm 15 (Polyb. 3, 94, 9; Dit., Syll.³ 709, 10; 32 [w. εἰς foll.]; PTebt. 50, 9 [II вс]; BGU 1204, 6 al. in pap.; Jos., Bell. 1, 640 al.).

c. In the case of κεχωρισμένος ἀπὸ τῶν ἁμαρτωλῶν Hb 7: 26 the mng. can include not only that Christ has been *separated from sinful men* by being exalted to the heavenly world (s. what follows in the context of Hb 7: 26), but also that because of his attributes (s. what precedes in the context: ὅσιος, ἄκακος, ἀμίαντος) he is *different* from sinful men (for this mng. cf. Hdt. 1, 172; 2, 91; Epict. 2, 9, 2; 2, 10, 2; 4, 11, 1). M-M. B. 845.*

χωρίον, ου, τό (Hdt.+; inscr., pap., LXX, Philo, Joseph.; Test. Jud. 12: 9)—**1.** *place, piece of land, field* (Thu.+; oft. pap.; Jos., Ant. 5, 324; 8, 360) Mt 26: 36; Mk 14: 32; J 4: 5; Ac 1: 18f (Diog. L. 2, 52: Xenophon χωρίον ἐπρίατο); 4: 34, 37 D; 5: 3, 8; 28: 7; MPol 7: 1; Papias 3. Of paradise Dg 12: 2.

2. (a city and its) *environs* (Polyaenus 7, 24), i.e. the region around a city that is closely related to it economically and politically: χωρίον 'Ρωμαίων IRo inscr. (this may correspond to what is called τὰ ὑπὸ 'Ρωμαίοις in Appian, Hann. 29 §123). M-M.*

χωρίς adv. (Hom.+)—**1.** used as an adv. (Hom.+; inscr.; POxy. 1088, 41 [I ᴀᴅ]; Jos., Bell. 1, 586, Ant. 17, 308) *separately, apart, by itself* J 20: 7; ITr 11: 2; Hs 8, 1, 6–17; 8, 4, 4–6.

2. in our lit. quite predom. as an improper prep. w. gen. (coming only after the word it governs οὗ χωρὶς Hb 12: 14; ITr 9: 2; cf. Bl-D. §216, 2; 487; Rob. 425; 647f) *without, apart from* (Pind.+; inscr., pap., LXX; En. 16, 1; Ep. Arist., Philo, Joseph.; the most typical Hellenistic word for 'without', cf. FSolmsen, Beiträge zur griech. Wortforschung '09, 115; Bl-D. §216, 2; Johannessohn 337; 339f; MLMargolis, PHaupt-Festschr. '26, 84ff).

a. w. gen. of the pers.—**α.** *separated from someone, far from someone, without someone* (Vi. Hom. 2 χωρὶς πάντων= apart fr. everyone) ἦτε χωρὶς Χριστοῦ Eph 2: 12; cf. ITr 9: 1f. χωρὶς ἐμοῦ *apart from me* J 15: 5. χ. ἐπισκόπου ITr 7: 2; IPhld 7: 2; ISm 8: 1f; IMg 4: 1. Without Christ 9: 2. οὔτε γυνὴ χωρὶς ἀνδρὸς οὔτε ἀνὴρ χωρὶς γυναικός *neither* (is) *woman* (anything) *apart fr. man, nor man fr. woman* 1 Cor 11: 11. χωρὶς ἡμῶν ἐβασιλεύσατε *without us you have already become kings* 4: 8. Cf. Hb 11: 40.—Hb 2: 9 the v.l. χωρὶς θεοῦ (for χάριτι θεοῦ) *apart fr. God, forsaken by God* (schol. on Apollon. Rhod. 2, 275 χωρὶς τοῦ Διός) is considered the original rdg. by BWeiss (Der Hb in zeitgeschichtl. Beleuchtung: TU 35, 3, '10 p. 12, 1), EKühl (Theol. der Gegenwart 6, '12, 252), AvHarnack (Zwei alte dogm. Korrekturen im Hb: SAB '29, 3ff=Studien I '31, 236–45), and HWMontefiore (The Epistle to the Hebrews '64, 59); this opinion is in contrast to nearly all Gk. mss. beginning w. 𝔓⁴⁶ and to many interpreters, among them Strathmann⁴ '47 and, earlier, JKögel (BFChTh VIII 5/6 '04, 131–41).

β. *without* or *apart from=apart fr. someone's activity* or *assistance* (Appian, Bell. Civ. 1, 65 §298 χωρὶς ὑμῶν; Dionys. Perieg.[?], De Avibus: JACramer, Anecd. Paris. I 1839 p. 33, 13 the phoenix comes into being πατρός τε καὶ μητρὸς χωρίς; Jos., Ant. 15, 226) χωρὶς αὐτοῦ ἐγένετο οὐδὲ ἕν J 1: 3 (cf. IQS 11, 11). πῶς ἀκούσωσιν χωρὶς κηρύσσοντος; *how are they to hear without someone to preach to them?* Ro 10: 14.—Cf. ITr 3: 1.

γ. *besides, in addition to, except* (for) *someone* (Jos., Ant. 7, 352) χωρὶς γυναικῶν καὶ παιδίων *besides women and children* Mt 14: 21; 15: 38. χωρὶς τούτου μηδέν *nothing except him* (i.e. Christ) IEph 11: 2.

b. w. gen. of the thing—**a.** *outside* (of) someth. χ. τοῦ σώματος 2 Cor 12: 3.

β. *without making use of someth., without expressing* or *practicing someth.* (Jos., Ant. 20, 41 χ. τῆς περιτομῆς τὸ θεῖον σέβειν) χωρὶς παραβολῆς οὐδὲν ἐλάλει Mt 13: 34; Mk 4: 34. χωρὶς θεμελίου Lk 6: 49. χωρὶς γογγυσμῶν Phil 2: 14. Cf. 1 Ti 2: 8; 5: 21. χωρὶς τῆς σῆς γνώμης *without having obtained your consent* (Polyb. 3, 21, 1; 2; 7) Phlm 14 (bγ below is also poss.). χωρὶς πάσης ἀντιλογίας Hb 7: 7 (ἀντιλογία 1). χ. οἰκτιρμῶν *without pity* 10: 28 (POxy. 509, 19 χ. ὑπερθέσεως=without delay). Cf. 57: 20a, b; 9: 7, 18, 22. Christ was tempted χ. ἀμαρτίας *without committing any sin* 4: 15. πίστις χ. τῶν ἔργων *faith that does not express itself in deeds* Js 2: 20, 26b, cf. vs. 18. χωρὶς τῆς ἀσφαλείας *without* (making use of) *the security* MPol 13: 3.

γ. *without possessing someth., apart fr. the presence of someth.* χ. νόμου ἁμαρτία νεκρά Ro 7: 8; on ἐγὼ ἔζων χωρὶς νόμου ποτέ vs. 9 cf. [ζάω] 2a. τὸ σῶμα χ. πνεύματος Js 2: 26a. χ. τῆς σῆς γνώμης *without possessing your consent* (cf. POxy. 719, 27) Phlm 14 (though bβ above is also poss.). Cf. Hb 11: 6; 12: 8, 14.

δ. *without relation to* or *connection with someth.*, *independent of someth.* χ. ἁμαρτίας *without any relation to sin*, i.e., not w. the purpose of atoning for it Hb 9: 28. χ. ἔργων νόμου *without regard to the observance of the law* Ro 3: 28; cf. vs. 21; 4: 6.

ε. *besides, in addition to* (Diod. S. 13, 54, 7 χ. τούτων; Appian, Iber. 20 §76 and 64, Illyr. 15 §42; PTebt. 67, 16; POxy. 724, 6; Lev 9: 17; Num 17: 14; Ep. Arist. 165; Jos., Ant. 7, 350) χωρὶς τῶν παρεκτός 2 Cor 11: 28 (s. παρεκτός). M-M.*

χωρισμός, οῦ, ὁ (Aristot.+; Diod. S. 2, 60, 1; LXX) *division* (Hierocles, Carm. Aur. 24 p. 472 Mullach ὁ ἀπὸ θεοῦ χ.) of the situation in the early church οὐκ ἦν χ. αὐτοῖς *there was no division among them* Ac 4: 32 E.*

I. χῶρος, ου, ὁ (Hom.+; inscr., pap.; 4 Macc 18: 23 πατέρων χῶρος v.l.; Philo, Aet. M. 33; Jos., Bell. 5, 402; Sib. Or. 1, 51) *place* μέγιστος *a very large place* AP 5: 15. εὐσεβῶν (Lycurg., Or. §96 p. 160; Socrat., Ep. 27, 1; Ps.-Pla., Ax. 13 p. 371c; Ps.-Plut., Consol. ad Ap. 34 p. 120b; inscr. 9, 8: Eranos 13, '13 p. 87.—Also χ. ἀσεβῶν: Ps.-Pla., Ax. 13 p. 371e; Lucian, Nec. 12, V. Hist. 2, 23; Philo, Cher. 2, Fuga 131) 1 Cl 50: 3.*

II. χῶρος, ου, ὁ (the Lat. corus, caurus=the northwest wind) *the northwest* Ac 27: 12. M-M.*

ψάλλω fut. ψαλῶ (Aeschyl.+; inscr., LXX; Jos., Ant. 11, 67; 12, 349) in our lit., in accordance w. OT usage, *sing, sing praise* w. dat. of the one for whom the praise is intended τῷ ὀνόματί σου ψαλῶ Ro 15: 9 (Ps 17: 50). τῷ κυρίῳ Eph 5: 19; in this pass. a second dat. is added τῇ καρδίᾳ ὑμῶν *in* or *with your heart(s)*; here it is found with ᾄδω (as Ps 26: 6; 32: 3; 56: 8), and the question arises whether a contrast betw. the two words is intended. The original mng. of ψ. was 'pluck', 'play' (a stringed instrument); this persisted at least to the time of Lucian (cf. Parasite 17). In the LXX ψ. freq. means 'sing', whether to the accompaniment of a harp or (as usually) not (Ps 7: 18; 9: 12; 107: 4 al.). This process continued until ψ. in Mod. Gk. means 'sing' exclusively; cf. ψάλτης=singer, chanter, w. no ref. to instrumental accompaniment. Although the NT does not voice opposition to instrumental music, in view of Christian resistance to mystery cults, as well as Pharisaic aversion to musical instruments in worship (s. EWerner, art. 'Music', IDB 3, 466-9), it is likely that some such sense as *make melody* is best here. Those who favor 'play' (e.g. L-S-J; ASouter, Pocket Lexicon, '20; JMoffatt, transl. '13) may be relying too much on the earliest mng. of ψάλλω. B 6: 16 (cf. Ps 107: 4). ψ. τῷ πνεύματι and in contrast to that ψ. τῷ νοΐ *sing praise in spiritual ecstasy* and *in full possession of one's mental faculties* 1 Cor 14: 15. Abs. *sing praise* Js 5: 13. WSSmith, Musical Aspects of the NT, '62. M-M.*

ψαλμός, οῦ, ὁ (Pind., Aeschyl.+; inscr.; PGM 3, 290; LXX; Jos., Ant. 6, 214; 7, 80; 9, 35; loanw. in rabb.) in our lit. only *song of praise, psalm*, in accordance w. OT usage. 1. of the OT Psalms ἐν τῷ νόμῳ Μωϋσέως καὶ τ. προφήταις καὶ ψαλμοῖς Lk 24: 44. ἐν βίβλῳ ψαλμῶν 20: 42; Ac 1: 20. ἐν τῷ ψαλμῷ τῷ δευτέρῳ 13: 33 (D, Or ἐν τῷ πρώτῳ). 2. of Christian songs of praise 1 Cor 14: 26. ψαλμοῖς καὶ ὕμνοις καὶ ᾠδαῖς πνευματικαῖς Eph 5: 19; Col 3: 16.— For lit. see s.v. ὕμνος. M-M.*

ψευδάδελφος, ου, ὁ *false brother*, i.e. one who pretends to be a Christian brother, but whose claim is belied by his unbrotherly conduct. Paul applies the term to his Judaistic opponents 2 Cor 11: 26; Gal 2: 4. Of Christians w. wrong beliefs Pol 6: 3.*

ψευδαπόστολος, ου, ὁ *false apostle*, i.e. one who represents himself to be an apostle without the divine commission necessary for the office (cf. Polyaenus 5, 33, 6 ψευδάγγελοι=false messengers) 2 Cor 11: 13.—Cf. lit. s.v. ψευδόμαρτυς.*

ψευδής, ές (Hom.+; inscr., pap., LXX, En., Philo, Joseph.)—1. of persons (Thu. 4, 27, 4 al.; Jos., Ant. 18, 299) *false, lying* Ac 6: 13 (cf. Pr 19: 5, 9 μάρτυς ψ.); Rv 2: 2. Also of the spirit of man Hm 3: 2. Subst. *the liar* (Pla., Hipp. Min. 365d; 367a; Sir 34: 4) Rv 21: 8.
2. of things *false, lying* λόγος (Phalaris, Ep. 130; Maximus Tyr. 27, 8d; IG I² 700 λόγοι ἄδικοι ψευδεῖς; En. 98, 15; Philo, Mut. Nom. 248; Jos., Ant. 13, 292) D 2: 5. ὅρκος ψευδής *a false oath* B 2: 8 (Zech 8: 17). M-M.*

ψευδοδιδασκαλία, ας, ἡ *false teaching* Pol 7: 2.*

ψευδοδιδάσκαλος, ου, ὁ *false teacher*, prob. *one who teaches falsehoods* (s. the lit. s.v. ψευδόμαρτυς) 2 Pt 2: 1.*

ψευδολόγος, ον (Aristoph.+; Aesop 136 Halm.—Jos., Ant. 8, 410; 17, 105 ψευδολογία) *speaking falsely, lying*; subst. (Polyb. 31, 22, 9; Strabo 2, 1, 9) *liar* 1 Ti 4: 2. M-M.*

ψεύδομαι in our lit. only mid.; fut. ψεύσομαι; 1 aor. ἐψευσάμην (Hom.+; inscr., pap., LXX; En. 104, 9; 10; Ep. Arist., Philo, Joseph.).
1. *lie, tell a falsehood* abs. (X., Mem. 2, 6, 36 al.; Pr 14: 5; Philo, Leg. All. 3, 124; Test. Jos. 13: 9) Mt 5: 11; Hb 6: 18 (θεόν is subj. acc.); 1 J 1: 6; Rv 3: 9; 1 Cl 27: 2a, b, c (Artem. 2, 69 p. 161, 15 ἀλλότριον θεῶν τὸ ψεύδεσθαι); Hm 3: 2. As a formula of affirmation οὐ ψεύδομαι (Jos., Vi. 296; cf. Plut., Mor. 1059a) Ro 9: 1; 2 Cor 11: 31; Gal 1: 20; 1 Ti 2: 7. εἴς τινα *tell lies against someone*, i.e. to his detriment (Sus 55) Col 3: 9. κατά τινος *against someth.* κατὰ τῆς ἀληθείας *against the truth* Js 3: 14 (cf. Bel 11 Theod.). The pers. who is harmed by the lie can be added in the dat. (Ps 17: 45; Josh 24: 27; Jer 5: 12) οὐκ ἀνθρώποις ἀλλὰ τῷ θεῷ Ac 5: 4. πάντα *in every particular* 14: 19 v.l. τί *in any point* Papias 2: 15.
2. *(try to) deceive by lying, tell lies to, impose upon* τινά *someone* (Eur., X.+; Plut., Alcib. 26, 8, Marcell. 27, 7; Jos., Ant. 3, 273; 13, 25; PSI 232, 10) Ac 5: 3 (Appian, Liby. 27 §113 τίς σε δαίμων ἔβλαψε... ψεύσασθαι θεοὺς οὓς ὤμοσας;=what evil spirit beguiled you... to lie to the gods by whom you swore?); 1 Cl 15: 4 (Ps 77: 36, but w. αὐτῷ). M-M.*

ψευδομαρτυρέω impf. ἐψευδομαρτύρουν; fut. ψευδομαρτυρήσω; 1 aor. ἐψευδομαρτύρησα (X., Mem. 4, 4, 11; Pla., Rep. 9 p. 575b, Leg. 11 p. 939c; Aristot., Rhet. 1,

14, 6 p. 1365a, 12, Rhet. ad Alex. 16 p. 1432a, 6; Jos., Ant. 3, 92; 4, 219) *bear false witness, give false testimony* Mt 19: 18; Mk 10: 19; Lk 18: 20; Ro 13: 9 t.r. (all fr. the decalogue Ex 20: 16; Dt 5: 20; cf. Philo, Dec. 138; 172); D 2: 3. κατά τινος *against someone* (so in the two decalogue passages in the OT; also Vi. Aesopi I c. 99; schol. on Soph. Aj. 238 p. 24 Papag. [1888]) Mk 14: 56f. M-M.*

ψευδομαρτυρία, ας, ἡ (Pla.; Attic orators; Plut.; Philo, Rer. Div. Her. 173) *false witness* Mt 15: 19; 26: 59; Pol 2: 2; 4: 3; Hm 8: 5; D 5: 1. M-M. B. 1461.*

ψευδόμαρτυς, υρος, ὁ (ψευδομάρτυς L-S-J, Mod. Gk. et al.) *one who gives false testimony, a false witness* (Pla., Gorg. 472b; Aristot., Rhet. ad Alex. 16 p. 1432a, 6; Heraclides 15; IG V 2, 357, 4; Sus 60f; Philo, Dec. 138) Mt 26: 60; AP 14: 29. ψευδομάρτυρες τοῦ θεοῦ (objective gen.) *men who give false testimony about God* 1 Cor 15: 15.—On ψευδόμαρτυς and the other compounds of ψευδ(ο)- cf. RReitzenstein, NGG '16, 463ff, Her. 52, '17, 446ff; KHoll, ibid. 301ff; ADebrunner, Griech. Wortbildungslehre '17, 37; PCorssen, Sokrates 6, '18, 106–14; Bl-D. §119, 5; Mlt.-H. 280; 285; further lit. in the Indogerm. Jahrb. 5, '18, 123f. CKBarrett in BRigaux-Festschr., '70, 377–96; AATrites, The NT Concept of Witness '77, 75–6.*

ψευδοπροφήτης, ου, ὁ *false prophet,* one who falsely claims to be a prophet of God or who prophesies falsely (Zech 13: 2; Jer 6: 13 al.; Philo, Spec. Leg. 4, 51; Jos., Bell. 6, 285, Ant. 8, 236; 318; 10, 111; Test. Jud. 21: 9; Zosimus: Hermet. IV p. 111, 2) Mt 7: 15; 24: 11, 24; Mk 13: 22; Lk 6: 26; Ac 13: 6; 2 Pt 2: 1; 1 J 4: 1; Rv 16: 13; 19: 20; 20: 10; AP 1: 1; Hm 11: 1f, 4, 7; D 11: 5f, 8–10; 16: 3.—Harnack, Die Lehre der Zwölf Apostel 1884, 119ff, Mission I⁴ '23, 332ff; 362ff; EFascher, Προφήτης '27.*

ψεῦδος, ους, τό (Hom.+; Dit., Syll.³ 1268, 27; Wilcken, Chrest. 110 A, 18 [110 bc]; LXX, En., Ep. Arist., Philo; Jos., Vi. 336; Test. 12 Patr.) *lie, falsehood,* in our lit. predom. w. ref. to relig. matters. Gener. (opp. ἀλήθεια, as Pla., Hippias Minor 370e; Plut., Mor. 16a; Ep. Arist. 206; Philo; Test. Dan 1: 3; 2: 1 al.) ἀποθέμενοι τὸ ψεῦδος λαλεῖτε ἀλήθειαν Eph 4: 25; cf. D 5: 2; B 20: 2 (here the pl. ψεύδη). In a catalogue of vices Hm 8: 5; cf. s 9, 15, 3 (personified). The sing. used collectively τὸ ψεῦδος *lies, lying* (opp. ἀληθές) m 3: 3; but 3: 5 pl. ψεύδη.—Of God (ἀληθινὸς καί) οὐδὲν παρ᾽ αὐτῷ ψεῦδος Hm 3: 1. In contrast, lying is characteristic of the devil J 8: 44 (cf. Porphyr., Abst. 2, 42 of the evil divinities: τὸ ψεῦδος τούτοις οἰκεῖον). For this religiously conceived contrast betw. ψεῦδος and ἀλήθεια cf. 2 Th 2: 11(12); 1 J 2: 21, 27. It is said of the heathen that μετήλλαξαν τὴν ἀλήθειαν τοῦ θεοῦ ἐν τῷ ψεύδει (s. μεταλλάσσω and cf. for the use of ψεῦδος as abstract for concrete Jer 3: 10; 13: 25) Ro 1: 25. On the other hand of the 144,000 sealed ones of Rv ἐν τῷ στόματι αὐτῶν οὐχ εὑρέθη ψεῦδος 14: 5. The Antichrist appears w. τέρατα ψεύδους *deceptive wonders* 2 Th 2: 9. ποιεῖν ψεῦδος *practice (the things that go with) falsehood* (in the relig. sense) Rv 21: 27; 22: 15.—W Luther, 'Wahrheit u. Lüge' im ältesten Griechentum '35. —HConzelmann, TW IX, 590–9, ψεῦδος and cognates. M-M. B. 1170.*

ψευδόχριστος, ου, ὁ *one who, in lying fashion, gives himself out to be the Christ, a false Messiah* (cf. Ψευδοφίλιππος Diod. S. 32, 15, 7; 32, fgm. and in Strabo 13, 4, 2; Ψευδονέρων Lucian, Adv. Indoct. 20; Ψευδομάριος Appian, Bell. Civ. 3, 2 §2) pl. Mt 24: 24; Mk 13: 22 (both w. ψευδοπροφῆται). On the subj. s. Bousset, Rel.³ 223f.*

ψευδώνυμος, ον (Aeschyl.+; Plut., Mor. 479e; Aelian, N.A. 9, 18; Philo, Mos. 2, 171 of pagan gods; Epigr. Gr. 42, 4) *falsely bearing a name, falsely called* of the γνῶσις of heterodox Christians 1 Ti 6: 20. M-M.*

ψεῦσμα, ατος, τό (Pla.+; Plut., Lucian, Aq., Sym., Theod.; Jos., C. Ap. 2, 115 al., Ant. 16, 349) *lie, falsehood,* in our lit. in the sense *lying, untruthfulness, undependability.* (Opp. ἡ ἀλήθεια, q.v. 1; Philo, Aet. M. 56) Ro 3: 7.—Hm 3: 5; 8: 3; D 3: 5.*

ψεύστης, ου, ὁ (Hom.+; LXX) *liar* J 8: 55; Ro 3: 4 (Ps 115: 2); 1 J 2: 4, 22; 4: 20; D 3: 5. W. other sinners (Sib. Or. 2, 257) 1 Ti 1: 10; Tit 1: 9 v.l.; Hs 6, 5, 5. ψεύστην ποιεῖν τινα *make someone a liar* 1 J 1: 10; 5: 10. The devil as a liar J 8: 44 (s. ψεῦδος). The Cretans Tit 1: 12 (s. ἀργός 2 and Κρής). M-M.*

ψηλαφάω 1 aor. ἐψηλάφησα (Hom.+; Polyb. 8, 18, 4; PLond. 1396, 4 [709/14 ad]; LXX; Jos., Ant. 13, 262 v.l.) *feel (about for), touch, handle, grope after* τινά or τί *someone* or *someth.* (Gen 27: 12; Judg 16: 26 al.) ψηλαφήσατέ με Lk 24: 39; ISm 3: 2. Cf. 1 J 1: 1. λίθον Hs 9, 6, 3. In οὐ προσεληλύθατε ψηλαφωμένῳ Hb 12: 18, even if the ὄρει of D t.r. et al. is dropped, the reference is to Mt. Sinai, where God revealed himself in the OT with manifestations that *could be felt* or *touched, were tangible* (ECSelwyn, On ψηλ. in Hb 12: 18: JTS 12, '11, 133f).— Symbol. (Polyb. 8, 18, 4) πάντα τόπον ἐψηλαφήσαμεν *we have touched upon every subject* 1 Cl 62: 2. Of men in their search for God (cf. Philo, Mut. Nom. 126 ψ. τὰ θεῖα) εἰ ἄρα γε ψηλαφήσειαν αὐτὸν καὶ εὕροιεν *if perhaps* (=in the hope that) *they might grope for him and find him* Ac 17: 27 (Norden, Agn. Th. 14–18). M-M. B. 1061.*

ψηφίζω 1 aor. ἐψήφισα (Aeschyl., Hdt.+; inscr.; pap.; 3 Km 3: 8 v.l.; 8: 5 v.l.; Philo; Jos., Ant. 17, 43 al.; Sib. Or. 13, 47) *count (up), calculate, reckon* (lit. 'w. pebbles') (Zen.-P. Cairo III ['28] 59328, 111 [248 bc]; Palaeph. 53 [AWestermann, Mythographi 1843 p. 311, 24] τὰς περιόδους τῶν ἡμερῶν; Plut.) τὴν δαπάνην Lk 14: 28. τὸν ἀριθμὸν τοῦ θηρίου Rv 13: 18. See χξς´ and ἀριθμός 1. M-M.*

ψῆφος, ου, ἡ (Pind., Hdt.+; inscr., pap., LXX. Loanw. in Jewish Aramaic [ZNW 20, '21, 253]) *pebble*—1. used in voting, in juries and elsewh., a black one for conviction, a white one for acquittal (Plut., Mor. 186e, Alcib. 22, 2 al.) καταφέρειν ψῆφον *cast a vote against* Ac 26: 10 (καταφέρω 2.—ψῆφον φέρειν: Philo, Deus Imm. 75; Jos., Ant. 2, 163; 10, 60 [both κατά τινος]). ἡ ψῆφος τ. μαρτυρίου *condemnation to martyrdom* Phlm subscr.

2. as an amulet. This is evidently the sense in which the ψῆφος λευκή (Paroem. Gr.: Diogenianus 6, 9) w. the new name on it (s. Artem. 5, 26 τοῦ Σαράπιδος τὸ ὄνομα ἐγγεγραμμένον λεπίδι χαλκῇ περὶ τὸν τράχηλον δεδέσθαι ὥσπερ σκυτίδα; PGM 5, 449 of a wonder-working stone: ὄπισθε τ. λίθου τὸ ὄνομα) is to be taken Rv 2: 17a, b (WHeitmüller, 'Im Namen Jesu '03, 234; WMRamsay, The White Stone and the 'Gladiatorial' Tessera: ET 16, '05, 558–61).—GBraumann, TW IX, 600–04. M-M.*

ψιθυρισμός, οῦ, ὁ (Plut.; Eccl. 10: 11, but in a neutral sense='hiss, whisper'; likew. Ps.-Lucian, Amor. 15; Philopon., in Aristot., De Anima p. 263, 3; 403, 12 Hayduck 1897; Etym. Mag. p. 818, 55) in our lit. only in a bad sense *whispering, (secret) gossip, tale-bearing* (Philodem., De Ira p. 55 W.; Greek Apocalypse of Baruch [ed. MRJames 1897] 8, 5 [pl.]; 13, 4 [sing.], in the two last passages not far fr. καταλαλιά; Cat. Cod. Astr. VIII 1 p. 170, 8 [pl., near διαβολαί]), always w. καταλαλιά, in the sing. 1 Cl 30: 3, pl. 2 Cor 12: 20; 1 Cl 35: 5.*

ψιθυριστής, οῦ, ὁ (in Athens an epithet of Hermes: [Ps.-] Demosth. 59, 39; Anecd. Gr. p. 317, 11 and Suidas.—Cat. Cod. Astr. X 119, 17; 191, 6; XII 190, 24; Thom. Mag. 403, 7 ψίθυρος οὐ ψιθυριστής) *whisperer, tale-bearer* Ro 1 29. M-M. *

ψιλός, ή, όν (Hom.+; inscr., pap., Philo) *bare,* of land without vegetation (Aesop, Fab. 74 P.=128 H.). A mountain is ψιλόν, βοτάνας μὴ ἔχον Hs 9, 1, 5; cf. 9, 19, 2 (Jos., Bell. 4, 452 ψιλὸν κ. ἄκαρπον ὄρος).*

ψίξ, χός, ἡ (Plut., Aretaeus p. 142, 23; 167, 17; Herodian Gr. I 396, 22 al.; Rhet. Gr. I 646, 16) *bit, crumb,* esp. of bread Mt 15: 27 D; Lk 16: 21 D.*

ψιχίον, ου, τό (dim. of ψίξ [q.v.].—Achmes 46, 22) *a very little bit, crumb* pl. (Soranus: CMG IV p. 86, 10) Mt 15: 27; Mk 7: 28; Lk 16: 21 t.r. M-M.*

ψοφοδεής, ές (Pla.+; Philo, Sacr. Abel. 32 p. 215 l. 15) *easily frightened* (lit. 'by noise'), *timid, anxious* the neut. as subst. τὸ ψοφοδεές *timidity, anxiety* (Plut., Crass. 35, 4) Dg 4: 1.*

ψόφος, ου, ὁ (Eur., Thu.+; inscr. fr. Palestine: JPPeters and HThiersch, Painted Tombs in . . . Marissa '05, 33, 4 [II BC]; PStrassb. 100, 14 [II BC]; Mi 1: 13; Ep. Arist. 91; Philo, Sacr. Abel. 69; Jos., Bell. 4, 108, Ant. 3, 81) *noise, sound* Hv 4, 3, 7.*

ψυγήσομαι s. ψύχω.

ψυχαγωγέω (Pla., X. et al.; PHamb. 91, 22 [167 BC]; PRyl. 128, 12 [c. 30 AD]; Philo) *lead* someone's *soul (astray), attract, beguile* τινά someone (Epict. 3, 21, 23) ὁ πλοῦτος ὁ ψυχαγωγῶν αὐτούς Hv 3, 6, 6.*

ψυχή, ῆς, ἡ (Hom.+; inscr., pap., LXX, En., Ep. Arist., Philo, Joseph., Test. 12 Patr., Sib. Or.) *soul, life;* it is oft. impossible to draw hard and fast lines betw. the meanings of this many-sided word.

1. lit.—a. of life on earth in its external, physical aspects—α. (*breath of) life, life-principle, soul,* of animals (Galen, Protr. 13 p. 42, 27 John; Gen 9: 4) Rv 8: 9. As a rule of human beings (Gen 35: 18; 3 Km 17: 21) Ac 20: 10. When it leaves the body death occurs Lk 12: 20 (cf. Jos., C. Ap. 1, 164). The soul is delivered up to death 1 Cl 16: 13 (Is 53: 12), whereupon it leaves the realm of earth and lives on in Hades (Lucian, Dial. Mort. 17, 2; Jos., Ant. 6, 332) Ac 2: 27 (Ps 15: 10), 31 t.r. or some other place outside the earth Rv 6: 9; 20: 4; AP 10: 25 (Himerius, Or. 8[23]: his consecrated son [παῖς ἱερός 7] Rufinus, when he dies, leaves his σῶμα to the death-demon, while his ψυχή goes into οὐρανός, to live w. the gods 23).—B 5: 13 (s. Ps 21: 21).

β. *earthly life* itself (Diod. S. 1, 25, 6 δοῦναι τὴν ψυχήν =give life back [to the dead Horus]; 3, 26, 2; 14, 65, 2; 16, 78, 5; Jos., Ant. 18, 358 σωτηρία τῆς ψυχῆς; 14, 67) ζητεῖν τὴν ψυχήν τινος Mt 2: 20 (cf. Ex 4: 19); Ro 11: 3 (3 Km 19: 10, 14). δοῦναι τὴν ψυχὴν ἑαυτοῦ (cf. Eur., Phoen. 998) Mt 20: 28; Mk 10: 45; John says for this τιθέναι τὴν ψυχήν J 10: 11, 15, 17, (18); 13: 37f; 15: 13; 1 J 3: 16a, b; παραδιδόναι Ac 15: 26; Hs 9, 28, 2. παραβολεύεσθαι τῇ ψυχῇ Phil 2: 30 (s. παραβολεύομαι). To love one's own life Rv 12: 11; cf. B 1: 4; 4: 6; 19: 5; D 2: 7. Life as prolonged by nourishment Mt 6: 25a, b; Lk 12:

22f. Cf. 14: 26; Ac 20: 24; 27: 10, 22; 28: 19 v.l.; Ro 16: 4. S. also 1d below.

b. *the soul* as seat and center of the inner life of man in its many and varied aspects—α. of the desire for luxurious living (cf. the OT expressions Ps 106: 9; Pr 25: 25; Is 29: 8; 32: 6; Bar 2: 18b. But also X., Cyr. 8, 7, 4; inscr. in Ramsay, Phrygia I 2 p. 477 no. 343, 5 the soul as the seat of enjoyment of the good things in life) of the rich man ἐρῶ τῇ ψυχῇ μου· ψυχή, ἀναπαύου, φάγε, πίε, εὐφραίνου Lk 12: 19 (cf. Aelian, V.H. 1, 32 εὐφραίνειν τὴν ψυχήν; X., Cyr. 6, 2, 28 ἡ ψυχὴ ἀναπαύσεται.—The address to the ψυχή as PsSol 3, 1; Cyranides p. 41, 27). Cf. Rv 18: 14.—β. of evil desires 2 Cl 16: 2; 17: 7.

γ. of feelings and emotions (Anacr., fgm. 4 Diehl²; Diod. S. 8, 32, 3; Sib. Or. 3, 558) περίλυπός ἐστιν ἡ ψυχή μου (cf. Ps 41: 6, 12; 42: 5) Mt 26: 38; Mk 14: 34. ἡ ψυχή μου τετάρακται J 12: 27; cf. Ac 2: 43 (s. 2 below).— Lk 1: 46; 2: 35; J 10: 24; Ac 14: 2, 22; 15: 24; Ro 2: 9; 1 Th 2: 8 (τὰς ἑαυτῶν ψυχάς *our hearts full of love*); Hb 12: 3; 2 Pt 2: 8; 1 Cl 16: 12 (Is 53: 11); 23: 3 (scriptural quot. of unknown origin); B 3: 1, 3, 5b (cf. on these three passages Is 58: 3, 5, 10b); 19: 3; Hm 4, 2, 2; 8: 10; s 1: 8; 7: 4; D 3: 9a, b. It is also said of God in the anthropomorphic manner of expr. used by the OT ὁ ἀγαπητός μου ὃν εὐδόκησεν ἡ ψυχή μου Mt 12: 18 (cf. Is 42: 1); cf. Hb 10: 38 (Hab 2: 4).—One is to love God ἐν ὅλῃ τῇ ψυχῇ Mt 22: 37; Lk 10: 27. Also ἐξ ὅλης τῆς ψυχῆς (Dt 6: 5; 10: 12; 11: 13) Mk 12: 30, 33 t.r.; Lk 10: 27 t.r. (Epict. 2, 23, 42; 3, 22, 18; 4, 1, 131; M. Ant. 12, 29; Sextus 379.—X., Mem. 3, 11, 10 ὅλῃ τῇ ψυχῇ). ἐκ ψυχῆς *from the heart, gladly* (Jos., Ant. 17, 177.—The usual form is ἐκ τῆς ψυχῆς: X., An. 7, 7, 43, Apol. 18 al.; Theocr. 8, 35) Eph 6: 6; Col 3: 23; ἐκ ψυχῆς σου B 3: 5a (Is 58: 10a); 19: 6. μιᾷ ψυχῇ *with one mind* (Dio Chrys. 19[36], 30) Phil 1: 27; cf. Ac 4: 32 (on the combination w. καρδία s. that word 1bη and Ep. Arist. 17); 2 Cl 12: 3 (s. 1 Ch 12: 39b; Diog. L. 5, 20 ἐρωτηθεὶς τί ἐστι φίλος, ἔφη· μία ψυχὴ δύο σώμασιν ἐνοικοῦσα).

c. *the soul* as seat and center of life that transcends the earthly (Pla., Phaedo 28 p. 80A; B; Paus. 4, 32, 4 ἀθάνατός ἐστιν ἀνθρώπου ψ.). As such it can receive divine salvation σῶζου σὺ καὶ ἡ ψυχή σου *be saved, you and your soul* Agr 5 (JoachJeremias, Unknown Sayings of Jesus, tr. Fuller, '57, 61-4). σώζειν τὰς ψυχάς Js 1: 21. ψυχὴν ἐκ θανάτου 5: 20; cf. B 19: 10; Hs 6, 1, 1 (on the death of the soul s. Achilles Tat. 7, 5, 3 τέθνηκας θάνατον διπλοῦν, ψυχῆς κ. σώματος. σωτηρία ψυχῶν 1 Pt 1: 9. περιποίησις ψυχῆς Hb 10: 39. It can also be lost 2 Cl 15: 1; B 20: 1; Hs 9, 26, 3. Men cannot injure it, but God can hand it over to destruction Mt 10: 28a, b. ζημιωθῆναι τὴν ψυχήν (ζημιόω 1) Mt 16: 26a; Mk 8: 36 (FCGrant, Introd. to NT Thought, '50, 162); 2 Cl 6: 2. There is nothing more precious than ψυχή in this sense Mt 16: 26b; Mk 8: 37. It stands in contrast to σῶμα, in so far as it is σάρξ (cf. Dit., Or. 383, 42 [I BC]) Dg 6: 1-9. The believer's soul knows God 2 Cl 17: 1. One Christian expresses the hope that all is well w. another's soul 3 J 2 (s. εὐοδόω). For the soul of the Christian is subject to temptations 1 Pt 2: 11; 2 Pt 2: 14, longs for rest Mt 11: 29, and must be made holy 1 Pt 1: 22 (cf. Jer 6: 16). The soul must be entrusted to God 1 Pt 4: 19; cf. 1 Cl 27: 1. Christ is its ποιμὴν καὶ ἐπίσκοπος (s. ἐπίσκοπος 1) 1 Pt 2: 25; its ἀρχιερεὺς καὶ προστάτης 1 Cl 61: 3; its σωτήρ MPol 19: 2. Apostles and overseers are concerned about the souls of the believers 2 Cor 12: 15; Hb 13: 17. The Christian hope is called the *anchor of the soul* Hb 6: 19. Paul calls God as a witness against his soul; if he is lying, he will forfeit his salvation 2 Cor 1: 23.—Also *life* of this same kind κτήσεσθε τὰς ψυχὰς ὑμῶν *you will gain life for yourselves* Lk 21: 19.

d. Since the soul is the center of both the earthly (1a) and the supernatural (1c) life, a man can find himself facing the question in which character he wishes to preserve it for himself: ὃς ἐὰν θέλῃ τὴν ψυχὴν αὐτοῦ σῶσαι, ἀπολέσει αὐτήν· ὃς δ᾽ ἂν ἀπολέσει τὴν ψυχὴν αὐτοῦ ἕνεκεν ἐμοῦ, σώσει αὐτήν Mk 8: 35. Cf. Mt 10: 39; 16: 25; Lk 9: 24; 17: 33; J 12: 25. The contrast betw. τὴν ψυχὴν εὑρεῖν and ἀπολέσαι is found in Mt 10: 39a, b (cf. HGrimme, BZ 23, '35, 263f); 16: 25b; σῶσαι and ἀπολέσαι vs. 25a; Mk 8: 35a, b; Lk 9: 24a, b; περιποιήσασθαι, ζῳογονῆσαι and ἀπολέσαι 17: 33; φιλεῖν and ἀπολλύναι J 12: 25a; μισεῖν and φυλάσσειν vs. 25b.

e. On the combination of ψυχή and πνεῦμα in 1 Th 5: 23; Hb 4: 12 s. πνεῦμα 3a, end.—A-JFestugière, L'idéal religieux des Grecs et l'Évangile '32, 212-17.—A unique combination is . . . σωμάτων, καὶ ψυχὰς ἀνθρώπων, someth. like *slaves and bondmen* Rv 18: 13 (cf. Ezk 27: 13).

f. In var. Semitic languages the reflexive relationship is paraphrased with נֶפֶשׁ (secular parallels in W-S. §22, 18b note 33); the corresp. use of ψυχή may be detected in certain passages in our lit., esp. in quots. fr. the OT and in places where OT modes of expr. have had considerable influence (Bl-D. §283, 4; W-S. §22, 18b; Mlt. 87; 105 n. 2; Rob. 689; KHuber, Untersuchungen über d. Sprachcharakter des griech. Lev., Zürich Diss., Giessen '16, 67); these may be cited: Mt 11: 29; 26: 38; Mk 10: 45; 14: 34; Lk 12: 19; 14: 26; J 10: 24; 12: 27; 2 Cor 1: 23; 3 J 2; Rv 18: 14; 1 Cl 16: 11 (Is 53: 10); B 3, 1, 3 (Is 58: 3, 5); 4: 2; 17: 1. Cf. also 2 Cor 12: 15; Hb 13: 17.

2. by metonymy *that which possesses life* or a *soul* ψυχὴ ζῶσα (s. Gen 1: 24) a *living creature* Rv 16: 3 t.r. ἐγένετο Ἀδὰμ εἰς ψυχὴν ζῶσαν 1 Cor 15: 45 (Gen 2: 7. S. πνεῦμα 5f). ψυχὴ ζωῆς Rv 16: 3.—πᾶσα ψυχή *everyone* (Lev 7: 27; 23: 29 al.) Ac 2: 43; 3: 23 (Lev 23: 29); Ro 2: 9; 13: 1; 1 Cl 64); Hs 9, 18, 5.—Pl. *persons*, lit. *souls* (class.; PTebt. 56, 11 [II BC] σῶσαι ψυχὰς πολλάς; LXX) ψυχαὶ ὡσεὶ τρισχίλιαι Ac 2: 41; cf. 7: 14 (Ex 1: 5); 27: 37; 1 Pt 3: 20.—This may also be the place for ἔξεστιν ψυχὴν σῶσαι ἢ ἀποκτεῖναι; *is it permissible to save a living person (a human life* is also poss.) *or must we let him die?* Mk 3: 4; Lk 6: 9. t.r. 56 t.r.—EHatch, Essays in Bibl. Gk. 1889, 112-24; ERohde, Psyche⁹⁻¹⁰ '25; JBöhme, D. Seele u. das Ich im homer. Epos '29; EDBurton, Spirit, Soul and Flesh '18; FRüsche, Blut, Leben u. Seele '30; MLichtenstein, D. Wort nefeš in d. Bibel '20; WEStaples, The 'Soul' in the OT: Am. Journ. of Sem. Lang. and Lit. 44, '28, 145-76; FBarth, La notion Paulinienne de ψυχή: RThPh 44, '11, 316-36; ChGuignebert, RHPhr 9, '29, 428-50; NHSnaith, Life After Death: Interpretation 1, '47, 309-25; essays by OCullmann, HAWolfson, WJaeger, HJCadbury in Immortality and Resurrection, ed. KStendahl, '65, 9-53; G Dautzenberg, Sein Leben Bewahren, '66 (gospels); R Jewett, Paul's Anthropological Terms, '71, 334-57.—G Bertram et al., TW IX, 604-67, ψυχή and cognates. M-M. B. 1087. **

ψυχικός, ή, όν (in var. mngs. Diocles, Aristot. +; Ptolem., Apotel. 3, 14, 1 [opp. σωματικός]; Dit., Syll.³ 656, 20 [166 BC]; 4 Macc 1: 32; Philo) *pertaining to the soul* or *life*, in our lit. always denoting the life of the natural world and whatever belongs to it, in contrast to the supernatural world, which is characterized by πνεῦμα (s. PGM 4, 524f and 510= Rtzst., Mysterienrel.³ 175f lines 28 and 20, where the ἀνθρωπίνη ψυχικὴ δύναμις is contrasted w. the ἱερὸν πνεῦμα. On this s. πνευματικός 2aγ; also β and

PGM 4, 725; Herm. Wr. 9, 9; Iambl., Myst. 6, 6 P.: the ἀνθρωπίνη ψυχή in contrast to the gods and to γνῶσις).

1. adj. ψυχικὸς ἄνθρωπος *an unspiritual man*, one who lives on the purely material plane, without being touched by the Spirit of God 1 Cor 2: 14. σῶμα ψυχ. *a physical body* 15: 44a, b. The wisdom that does not come fr. above is called ἐπίγειος, ψυχικός (*unspiritual*), δαιμονιώδης Js 3: 15.

2. subst.—a. τὸ ψυχικόν *the physical* in contrast to τὸ πνευματικόν 1 Cor 15: 46.

b. Jd in vs. 19 calls the teachers of error ψυχικοί, πνεῦμα μὴ ἔχοντες *worldly* (lit. 'psychic') *men, who do not have the Spirit,* thereby taking over the terminology of his Gnostic (on 'psychic' and 'pneumatic' people in the Gnostic view cf. AHilgenfeld, Die Ketzergeschichte des Urchristentums 1884, index) opponents, but applying to the Gnostics the epithets which they used of the orthodox Christians. M-M. *

ψῦχος, ους, τό (Hom. +; Dit., Syll.³ 969, 92; PTebt. 278, 47; LXX; En. 100, 13. On the accent s. Bl-D. §13; Mlt.-H. 57) *cold* J 18: 18; Ac 28: 2; 2 Cor 11: 27 (w. γυμνότης). M-M. *

ψυχρός, ά, όν (Hom. +; inscr., pap., LXX; En. 14, 13; Philo, Joseph.) *cold.*

1. lit.—a. adj. ὕδωρ (Hom. +; Sb 6941, 4; Pr 25: 25; Philo; Jos., Ant. 7, 130) Mt 10: 42 D; D 7: 2. Symbol. of the martyrs τὸ πῦρ ἦν αὐτοῖς ψυχρόν MPol 2: 3 (cf. 4 Macc 11: 26).

b. subst. τὸ ψυχρόν (i.e. ὕδωρ) *cold water* (Hdt. 2, 37 al.; Dit., Syll.³ 1170, 30; ψυχρὸν πίνειν Epict. 3, 12, 17; 3, 15, 3, Ench. 29, 2) Mt 10: 42.

2. fig. (trag., Hdt. +; Jos., Bell. 1, 357; 6, 16, C. Ap. 2, 255) *cool, cold,* i.e. without enthusiasm (Epict. 3, 15, 7; Lucian, Tim. 2 ψ. τὴν ὀργήν) Rv 3: 15a, b, 16 (w. ζεστός and χλιαρός). M-M. B. 1078f. *

ψύχω (Hom. +; inscr., PPetr. II 14(3), 8 [III BC]; LXX) 2 fut. pass. ψυγήσομαι (Galen XI 388 K.—Lob., Phryn. p. 318; Moeris p. 421 P.) *make cool* or *cold* (Philo, Leg. All. 1, 5) pass. *become* or *grow cold* (Hdt. et al.; Philo, Cher. 88; Jos., Ant. 7, 343), *go out, be extinguished* of fire and flame (Pla., Critias 120B) fig. (cf. Jos., Bell. 5, 472 of hope) ψυγήσεται ἡ ἀγάπη Mt 24: 12. M-M. *

ψωμίζω 1 aor. ἐψώμισα (Aristoph., Aristot. +; LXX)—1. w. acc. of the pers. (Antig. Car. 99; Num 11: 4 τίς ἡμᾶς ψωμιεῖ κρέα; Test. Levi 8: 5 ἐψώμισέν με ἄρτον) *feed someone* Ro 12: 20 (Pr 25: 21 v.l.); 1 Cl 55: 2.

2. w. acc. of the thing (s. Num and Test. Levi under 1 above) πάντα τὰ ὑπάρχοντα 1 Cor 13: 3 is either *give away all one's property bit* (cf. ψωμίον) *by bit, dole* it out (so w. double acc. Dt 32: 13; Ps 79: 6), i.e. to feed those who are in need (cf. Gdspd., Probs. 163f), or *divide in small pieces=fritter away.* M-M. *

ψωμίον, ου, τό (since PTebt. 33, 14 [112 BC]; PFay. 119, 34; POxy. 1071, 5 al. pap.; M. Ant. 7, 3, 1; Diog. L. 6, 37) dim. of ψωμός (Hom. +; LXX) (*small*) *piece* or *bit of bread* J 13: 26a, b, 27, 30 (cf. Mod. Gk. ψωμί, 'bread').—PKretschmer, Brot u. Wein im Neugriech.: Glotta 15, '26, 60ff. M-M. B. 357. *

ψωριάω pf. ptc. ἐψωριακώς (Hippocr., Theophr. et al.) *have a rough surface* of stones Hv 3, 2, 8; 3, 6, 2; s 9, 6, 4; 9, 8, 2; 9, 26, 3. *

ψώχω (Hesychius; Etym. Mag. p. 818, 44; as a mid. Nicander, Theriaca 629) *rub so as to thresh,* etc. (Diosc., Mat. Med. 5, 159 pass.) ἤσθιον τοὺς στάχυας ψώχοντες ταῖς χερσίν Lk 6: 1. M-M. *

Ω

Ω omega, last letter of the Gk. alphabet. On ἐγώ (εἰμι) τὸ ἄλφα καὶ τὸ ὦ Rv 1: 8, 11 t.r.; 21: 6; 22: 13 cf. the entry A; also EbNestle, Philol. 70, '11, 155-7.*

ὦ interjection (Hom.+; inscr.; BGU 665 III, 8 [I AD]; LXX; Jos., Ant. 3, 84; 18, 266) O! (oft. before the voc., in accord w. the Koine and w. Semitic usage, but never used when calling upon God. Cf. Bl-D. §146; Rob. 463f; Mlt.-Turner 33).
1. mostly expressing emotion (at the beginning of a clause; Cornutus 14 p. 14, 9 ὦ πονηρέ, κτλ.) ὦ γύναι Mt 15: 28; Hv 1, 1, 7. Cf. Lk 24: 25; Ro 2: 1, 3; 9: 20; Gal 3: 1; 1 Ti 6: 20; Js 2: 20; 1 Cl 23: 4. The nom. takes the place of the voc. (Maximus Tyr. 1, 10g; Philostrat., Ep. 37) Mt 17: 17; Mk 9: 19; Lk 9: 41; Ac 13: 10.
2. without emotion (in accord w. Attic usage, also Ep. Arist. 1; 120) ὦ Θεόφιλε Ac 1: 1. Cf. 18: 14; 27: 21.
3. in exclamations (where it can also be written ὤ)—
a. w. the nom. (Aeschyl.+; Charito 6, 6, 4; Is 6: 5) ὦ βάθος πλούτου Ro 11: 33.
b. w. the gen. (Charito 6, 2, 8; 10; 11; Galen: CMG V 9, 1 p. 387, 2 ὦ τῆς ἀσυνεσίας; Achilles Tat. 5, 11, 2; Philo, Fuga 149 ὦ θαυμαστῆς δοκιμασίας; Jos., Bell. 4, 166, C. Ap. 1, 301 ὦ τῆς εὐχερείας) ὦ τῆς ὑπερβαλλούσης φιλανθρωπίας τοῦ θεοῦ Oh, the surpassing kindness of God to man! Dg 9: 2; cf. 5a, b, c; cf. 1 Cl 53: 5.—MJohannessohn, D. Gebr. der Kasus etc. in LXX, Diss. Berlin '10, 9-13. M-M.*

ὤ s. ὦ 3.

Ὠβήδ t.r. for Ἰωβήδ (q.v.).

ὧδε (Hom.+) adv. of ὅδε, in our lit. adv. of place (Hippocr. [Kühner-G. I p. 444, 3] et al.; Hdt. 1, 49; 5, 48; Pla., Protagoras 328D; Herodas 7, 113; 126; inscr., pap., LXX).
1. here in the sense to this place, hither (as early as Od. 1, 182; PSI 599, 3 [III BC]; POxy. 295, 3; LXX; En. 14, 24 al.) ἦλθες ὧδε Mt 8: 29. Cf. 14: 18; 17: 17; 22: 12; Mk 11: 3; Lk 9: 41; 14: 21; 19: 27; J 6: 25; 20: 27; Ac 9: 21; Rv 4: 1; 11: 12; Hs 5, 1, 1 ab to this place, this far (cf. ἕως II 2b) Lk 23: 5; 1 Cl 20: 7. ὧδε κἀκεῖσε here and there, hither and thither (Aesop 62 Halm) Hm 5, 2, 7; s 6, 1, 6; 6, 2, 7; 9, 3, 1.
2. here in the sense in this place—a. strictly of place (Herodas 2, 98; 3, 96; Dit., Syll.³ 985, 54; PHib. 46, 15 [III BC]; PGrenf. II 36, 17 [95 BC]; BGU 1097, 11; 14; PFay. 123, 10; LXX; Apion in Jos., C. Ap. 2, 10; Bl-D. §103 w. app.; Rob. 299; BKeil, Her. 43, '08 p. 553, 1) Mt 12: 6, 41f; 14: 17; 16: 28; 17: 4a, b; 20: 6; Mk 9: 1, 5; 16: 6; Lk 9: 33; 11: 31f; 15: 17; J 6: 9; Ac 9: 14; Hs 9, 11, 1b. ὧδε= here on earth Hb 13: 14. καθίζειν ὧδε (cf. καθίζω 2a) Mk 14: 32; Hv 3, 1, 8. τὰ ὧδε Col 4: 9. ὧδε—ἐκεῖ here—there (Plut., Mor. 34A; Celsus 2, 43) Mk 13: 21; Lk 17: 21, 23; Js 2: 3. ὧδε—ὧδε Mt 24: 23 (Callim., Epigr. 30 Schn.; Herodas 4, 42 ὧδε καὶ ὧδε). Made more definite by a prepositional phrase ὧδε πρὸς ἡμᾶς Mk 6: 3. Cf. 8: 4; Lk 4: 23.
b. w. the local mng. weakened in this case, at this point, on this occasion, under these circumstances (Herodas 5, 85; Crates, Ep. 6; Quint. Smyrn. 13, 5; PFay. 117, 12 [108 AD]; PMMeyer, Griech. Texte aus Äg. '16, no. 22, 6) ὧδε λοιπόν (cf. Epict. 2, 12, 24) in this case moreover 1 Cor 4: 2. ὧδε ἡ σοφία ἐστίν Rv 13: 18; cf. 17: 9. ὧδέ ἐστιν ἡ

ὑπομονή 13: 10; 14: 12. ὧδε—ἐκεῖ in one case—in the other Hb 7: 8. M-M.

ᾠδή, ῆς, ἡ (Hom. Hymns, Soph., Pla., X.+; inscr., LXX) song, in our lit. only of sacred song, a song of praise to God (εἰς [τὸν] θεόν: Philo, Somn. 2, 34, Virt. 95; Jos., Ant. 7, 305) or to Christ Rv 5: 9; 14: 3a, b (on ᾠ. καινή cf. Ps 143: 9, on worship in heaven gener. EPeterson, Liturgisches Leben '34, 297-306.—Lucian, Zeux. 2 ἡ νέα ᾠ.). ᾄδουσιν τὴν ᾠδὴν Μωϋσέως καὶ τὴν ᾠδὴν τοῦ ἀρνίου 15: 3 (cf. Ex 15: 1 and on Ex 15 as a song in the liturgy of Judaism Elbogen² 23; 86; 113; 117; 136.—ᾄδ. ᾠδήν as Achilles Tat. 3, 15, 3 ὁ ἱερεὺς ᾖδεν ᾠδήν). ψαλμοῖς καὶ ὕμνοις καὶ ᾠδαῖς πνευματικαῖς Eph 5: 19; Col 3: 16 (on the hymn as a means of private edification cf. Hierocles 19 p. 460, where the examination of one's conscience at the close of day [Hierocles 27 p. 484 the golden verses of the Pythagoreans are to be read aloud morning and evening] is designated as ἐπικοίτιον ἆσμα θεῷ= an evening hymn in the presence of God).—Lit. s.v. ὕμνος. M-M.*

ᾠδίν, ῖνος, ἡ (as a nom. in Suidas) 1 Th 5: 3 (Is 37: 3) for the usual form ὠδίς, ῖνος (Hom.+; Suppl. Epigr. Gr. VIII 802; Sb 4312, 4f; LXX, Philo; Jos., Ant. 2, 218.— Bl-D. §46, 4; Mlt.-H. 135) birth-pain(s).
1. lit. 1 Th 5: 3 (sing. as Pind., Ol. 6, 73; Plut., Thes. 20, 5).—2. symbolically (Aeschyl.+; Himerius, Or. 10, 3; 18, 3; Ex 15: 14; Philo)—a. ὠδῖνες τοῦ θανάτου Ac 2: 24 (on the sources of the text s. MWilcox, The Semitisms of Ac, '65, 46-8; s. also s.v. θάνατος 1bβ and λύω 4; RGBratcher, The Bible Translator 10, '59, 18-20: 'cords of death'). ὠδῖνες τοῦ ᾅδου Pol 1: 2 (ᾅδης 1).
b. of the 'Messianic woes', the terrors and torments traditionally viewed as prelude to the coming of the Messianic Age (Billerb. I 950) are associated with the appearance of the Son of Man at the end of history, as the beginning of the (end-time) woes ἀρχὴ ὠδίνων Mt 24: 8; Mk 13: 8; FBusch, Z. Verständnis der syn. Eschatol., Mk 13 neu unters. '38.—GBertram, TW IX, 668-75. M-M.*

ὠδίνω (Hom.+; Epigr. Gr. 321, 12; 1103, 2; UPZ 77 col. 2, 27 [160 BC]; LXX; Philo, Mos. 1, 280 al.; Jos., Bell. 5, 514) suffer birth-pangs, bear amid throes abs. Rv 12: 2 (cf. Is 66: 7; Mi 4: 10). As a voc. ἡ οὐκ ὠδίνουσα you who have no birth-pains Gal 4: 27; 2 Cl 2: 1, 2 (all three Is 54: 1). W. acc. give birth to someone amid throes (trag.; Is 51: 2) symbol. (PGM 2, 92; Philo) τέκνα μου, οὓς πάλιν ὠδίνω Gal 4: 19. M-M.*

ὠθέω impf. ὤθουν (Hom.+; LXX; Philo, Aet. M. 136; Jos., Bell. 1, 250) push, shove τινά someone GP 3: 6. B. 716.*

ὠκεανός, οῦ, ὁ (Hom.+; inscr.; POsl. 3, 14; Philo, Leg. ad Gai. 10; Jos., Bell. 2, 155, Ant. 1, 130; Sib. Or.; loanw. in rabb.) the ocean 1 Cl 20: 8.*

ὠμόλινον, ου, τό (since Cratinus Com. [V BC] 9; Hippocr., Morb. 2, 47 vol. VII p. 70 L.; Sir 40: 4) apron or towel made of coarse linen Hs 8, 4, 1a, b.*

ὦμος, ου, ὁ (Hom.+; inscr., pap., LXX; Ep. Arist. 151; Philo; Jos., Ant. 3, 170; 215; Test. Zeb. 9: 4) shoulder Mt 23: 4 (symbol.); Lk 15: 5; Hv 5: 1; s 6, 2, 5; 9, 2, 4; 9, 9, 5; 9, 13, 8. M-M. B. 235.*

ὠνέομαι mid. dep. (Hes., Hdt.+; inscr., pap., Philo, Test. 12 Patr.) 1 aor. ὠνησάμην (Eupolis [V BC. But cf.

Kühner-Bl. II 577]; Plut., Nic. 10, 2; Paus. 3, 4, 4; Lucian, Herm. 81; inscr. [ESchweizer, Gramm. der perg. Inschr. 1898, 177; Dit., Or. 669, 31]; pap. [UPZ 12, 16, 158 BC; POxy. 1188, 19]; Jos., Ant. 2, 39. Beside it ἐωνησάμην and the class. ἐπριάμην.—Crönert 283) buy τὶ παρά τινος someth. from someone w. gen. of price (Aristoxenus [IV BC], Fgm. 43 Wehrli ἑκατὸν μνῶν; Jos., Ant. 7, 332) Ac 7: 16 (cf. Jos., Ant. 1, 237). M-M. B. 817.*

ᾠόν, οὖ, τό (Hdt.+; inscr., pap., LXX. On the spelling s. Bl-D. §26 app.; Mlt.-H. 84) egg Lk 11: 12. M-M. B. 256.*

ὥρα, ας, ἡ (Hom. [ὥρη]+; inscr., pap., LXX, Ep. Arist., Philo, Joseph., Test. 12 Patr.).

1. time of day ὀψὲ ἤδη οὔσης τῆς ὥρας since it was already late in the day or since the hour was (already) late Mk 11: 11; cf. MPol 7: 1b (s. ὀψέ 1 and 2; Demosth. 21, 84; Polyb. 3, 83, 7 ὀψὲ τῆς ὥρας). ὀψίας οὔσης τῆς ὥρας Mk 11: 11 v.l. (ὄψιος 1). ὥρα πολλή late hour (Polyb. 5, 8, 3; Dionys. Hal. 2, 54; Jos., Ant. 8, 118) 6: 35a, b. ἡ ὥρα ἤδη παρῆλθεν Mt 14: 15 (παρέρχομαι 1aβ).—Mt 24: 42 t.r., 44; Lk 12: 39, 40; Rv 3: 3; D 16: 1. W. ἡμέρα day and time of day, hour Mt 24: 36, 50; 25: 13; Mk 13: 32; Lk 12: 46.

2. hour—a. as a (short) space of time—α. beside year, month, and day Rv 9: 15; the twelfth part of a day (= period of daylight) οὐχὶ δώδεκα ὧραί εἰσιν τῆς ἡμέρας; J 11: 9. μίαν ὥραν ἐποίησαν Mt 20: 12 (s. ποιέω 2c). Cf. Lk 22: 59; Ac 5: 7; 19: 34 (ἐπὶ ὥρας δύο CBurchard, ZNW 61, '70, 167f; Test. Benj. 3, 7, Judah 3, 4); MPol 7: 2b, c; Hv 3, 1, 4. One ὥρα in this world corresponds to a ὥρα thirty days in length in the place of punishment Hs 6, 4, 4. μίαν ὥραν (not even) one hour Mt 26: 40; Mk 14: 37. Such passages help us to understand how ὥρα can acquire the sense

β. a short period of time μιᾷ ὥρᾳ in a single hour= in an unbelievably short time Rv 18: 10, 17, 19. μίαν ὥραν for a very short time 17: 12. Likew. πρὸς ὥραν for a while, for a moment J 5: 35; 2 Cor 7: 8; Gal 2: 5 (cf. on this pass. KLake, Gal 2: 3-5: Exp. 7th Ser. I '06, 236-45; CHWatkins, Der Kampf des Pls um Galatien '13; BWBacon, JBL 42, '23, 69-80); Phlm 15; MPol 11: 2. πρὸς καιρὸν ὥρας 1 Th 2: 17.

b. as a moment of time that takes its name fr. the hour that has just passed (Plut. et al.; Appian, Mithrid. 19 §72 ἑβδόμης ὥρας= at the 7th hour; Dit., Syll.³ 671A, 9 [162/0 BC] ὥρας δευτέρας; 736, 109 [92 BC] ἀπὸ τετάρτας ὥρας ἕως ἑβδόμας; Jos., Vi. 279 ἕκτη ὥ.; Wilcken, Chrest. 1, II, 21 [246 BC] περὶ ὀγδόην ὥραν; PTebt. 15, 2 [II BC]; Sb 5252, 20 [I AD] ἀφ᾽ ὥρας ὀγδόης; Ep. Arist. 303 μέχρι μὲν ὥρας ἐνάτης ἕως ὥρας δευτέρας until eight o'clock in the morning (acc. to our system) Hs 9, 11, 7. ὥρα τρίτη nine o'clock (a.m.) Mk 15: 25 (Gdspd., Probs. 68f); Ac 2: 15 (τῆς ἡμέρας); περὶ τρίτην ὥραν about nine o'clock (Appian, Bell. Civ. 2, 45 §182 περὶ τρίτην ὥραν ἡμέρας) Mt 20: 3; ἀπὸ τρίτης ὥρας τῆς νύκτος by nine o'clock at night (here=tonight) Ac 23: 23 (Jos., Bell. 6, 68; 79 ἀπὸ ἐνάτης ὥ. τῆς νυκτὸς εἰς ἑβδόμην τῆς ἡμέρας). ἀπὸ ὥρας ε᾽ (=πέμπτης) ἕως δεκάτης from eleven o'clock in the morning until four in the afternoon Ac 19: 9 D. περὶ ὥραν πέμπτην (PTebt. 15, 2 [114 BC]; POxy. 1114, 24 περὶ ὥ. τρίτην) at eleven o'clock (a.m.) Hv 3, 1, 2. ὥρα ἕκτη twelve o'clock noon Mt 20: 5; 27: 45a; Mk 15: 33a; Lk 23: 44a; J 4: 6 (ὥρα ὡς ἕκτη about noon; Test. Jos. 8: 1 ὥρα ὡσεὶ ἕκτη); 19: 14 (ὥρα ὡς ἕκτη); Ac 10: 9. ἐχθὲς ὥραν ἑβδόμην yesterday at one o'clock in the afternoon J 4: 52b (on the use of the acc. to express a point of time s. Hdb. ad loc.; Bl-D. §161, 3; Rob. 470). ὥρᾳ

ὀγδόῃ at two o'clock in the afternoon MPol 21. ὥρα ἐνάτη three in the afternoon Mt 20: 5; 27: 45f; Mk 15: 33b, 34; Lk 23: 44b; Ac 3: 1 (ἐπὶ τὴν ὥραν τῆς προσευχῆς τὴν ἐνάτην); 10: 3 (τῆς ἡμέρας); GP 6: 22. ὥρα ὡς δεκάτη about four in the afternoon J 1: 39. ἐνδεκάτῃ ὥρα five o'clock (in the afternoon) Mt 20: (6), 9. ἀπὸ τετάρτης ἡμέρας μέχρι ταύτης τῆς ὥρας ἤμην τὴν ἐνάτην προσευχόμενος four days ago, reckoned from (=at) this very hour, I was praying at three o'clock in the afternoon Ac 10: 30. ἐπύθετο τὴν ὥραν ἐν ᾗ . . . he inquired at what time . . . J 4: 52a; cf. vs. 53 (cf. Ael. Arist. 50, 56 K.=26 p. 519 D.: . . . τὴν ὥραν αἰσθάνομαι . . . ἐκείνην, ἐν ᾗ . . .; 47, 56 K.=23 p. 459 D.: ἀφυπνιζόμην κ. εὗρον ἐκείνην τὴν ὥραν οὖσαν, ᾗπερ . . .).—Less definite are the indications of time in such expressions as ἄχρι τῆς ἄρτι ὥρας up to the present moment 1 Cor 4: 11. πᾶσαν ὥραν hour after hour, every hour, constantly (Ex 18: 22; Lev 16: 2) 15: 30. Also καθ᾽ ὥραν (Strabo 15, 1, 55; Ps.-Clem., Hom. 3, 69) 2 Cl 12: 1. αὐτῇ τῇ ὥρᾳ at that very time, at once, instantly (Pap.; Da 3: 6, 15) Lk 2: 38; 24: 33; Ac 16: 18; 22: 13.

3. the time when someth. took place, is taking place, or will take place (BGU 1816, 12 [I BC] πρὸ ὥρας= before the right time) ἐν ἐκείνῃ τῇ ὥρᾳ Mt 8: 13; 10: 19; 18: 1; 26: 55; Mk 13: 11; Lk 7: 21; Ac 16: 33; Rv 11: 13; MPol 7: 2a. Likew. ἐν αὐτῇ τῇ ὥρᾳ Lk 10: 21; 12: 12; 13: 31; 20: 19 (on both expressions s. JoachJeremias, ZNW 42, '49, 214-17). ἀπὸ τῆς ὥρας ἐκείνης from that time on, at once Mt 9: 22; 15: 28; 17: 18; J 19: 27. ὥρα ἐν ᾗ J 5: 28. ὥρα ὅτε 4: 21, 23; 5: 25; 16: 25. ὥρα ἵνα 16: 2, 32. W. gen. of the thing, the time for which has come (Diod. S. 13, 94, 1; Ael. Aristid. 51, 1 K.=27 p. 534 D.; PGM 1, 221 ἀνάγκης; Jos., Ant. 7, 326 ὥ. ἀρίστου; Sib. Or. 4, 56) ἡ ὥρα τοῦ θυμιάματος Lk 1: 10; τοῦ δείπνου 14: 17; cf. MPol 7: 1a; τοῦ πειρασμοῦ Rv 3: 10; τῆς κρίσεως 14: 7; ἡ ὥρα αὐτῶν the time for them J 16: 4; w. the gen. (of the Passover) to be supplied Lk 22: 14. Also w. the inf. (Hom.+; Lucian, Dial. Deor. 20, 1; Aelian, V.H. 1, 21) ἡ ὥρα θερίσαι the time to reap Rv 14: 15 (cf. Theopomp. [IV BC]: 115 fgm. 31 Jac. θερινὴ ὥ.; Paus. 2, 35, 4 ὥ. θέρους). Also acc. w. inf. (Gen 29: 7) ὥρα (ἐστιν) ὑμᾶς ἐξ ὕπνου ἐγερθῆναι Ro 13: 11.—W. gen. of the pers. the time of or for someone to do or to suffer someth. (cf. Philo, Leg. ad Gai. 168 σὸς νῦν ὁ καιρός ἐστιν, ἐπέγειρε σαυτόν) of a woman who is to give birth ἡ ὥρα αὐτῆς J 16: 21 (ἡμέρα 𝔓⁶⁶ et al.).—Lk 22: 53. Esp. of Jesus, of whose ὥρα J speaks, as the time of his death (Diod. S. 15, 87, 6: the dying Epaminondas says ὥρα ἐστι τελευτᾶν) and of the glorification which is inextricably bound up w. it ἡ ὥρα αὐτοῦ J 7: 30; 8: 20; 13: 1 (foll. by ἵνα); cf. ἡ ὥρα μου 2: 4 (s. Hdb. ad loc.). ἡ ὥρα ἵνα δοξασθῇ 12: 23. ἡ ὥρα αὕτη 12: 27a, b. Also abs. ἐλήλυθεν ἡ ὥρα 17: 1 (AGeorge, 'L'heure' de J 17, RB 61, '54, 392-7); cf. Mt 26: 45; Mk 14: 35, 41.—ἐσχάτη ὥρα the last hour in the present age of the world's existence 1 J 2: 18a, b.—CCCowling, Mark's Use of ὥρα, Australian Biblical Review 5, '56, 153-60.—GDelling, TW IX, 675-81. M-M. B. 954 and esp. 1001.**

ὡραῖος, α, ον (Hes., Hdt.+; inscr., pap., LXX, En., Philo; Jos., Ant. 2, 64; 12, 65 al.; Test. 12 Patr.).—1. happening or coming at the right time ὡς ὡραῖοι οἱ πόδες τῶν εὐαγγελιζομένων how timely is the arrival of those who bring joyful tidings, who proclaim salvation Ro 10: 15 (Is 52: 7 cod. Q a, margin [JZiegler '39 ad loc.]. Cf. KBarth; RBultmann, ThLZ 72, '47, 199). But the πόδες ὡραῖοι Sir 26: 18 are without doubt well-formed feet; see 2 below.

2. beautiful, fair, lovely, pleasant of persons and things, an angel GP 13: 55. Trees (cf. Gen 2: 9; En. 24, 5) B 11: 10

(prophetic saying of uncertain origin). θύρα or πύλη Ac 3: 2, 10 (ESchürer, ZNW 7, '06, 51–68; OHoltzmann, ibid. 9, '08, 71–4; KLake: Beginn. I 5, '33, 479–86.—Of costly and artistic gates of pagan temples Diod. S. 5, 46, 6 θυρώματα τοῦ ναοῦ). Cf. Mt 23: 27. M-M. B. 1191.*

ὥριμος, ον (Aristot.+; Diod. S. et al.; PTebt. 54, 6 [I BC]; LXX) *ripe* σῖτος ὥριμος 1 Cl 56: 15 (Job 5: 26).*

ὠρύομαι mid. dep. (Pind., Hdt.+; LXX) *roar* of lions (Apollon. Rhod. 4, 1339; Dio Chrys., Or. 77+78 §35 Budé; Judg 14: 5; Ps 21: 14; Jer 2: 15; Philo, Somn. 1, 108.—What drives them to it is hunger: Hesychius, ὠρυο-μένων of wolves and lions) 1 Pt 5: 8. M-M.*

ὡς (Hom.+; inscr., pap., LXX, En., Ep. Arist., Philo, Joseph., Test. 12 Patr.; loanw. in rabb.) relative adv. of the relative pron. ὅς. It is used

I. as a comparative particle, indicating the manner in which someth. proceeds *as, like*—1. corresponding to οὕτως='so, in such a way' σωθήσεται, οὕτως ὡς διὰ πυρός *he will be saved,* (but only) *in such a way as* (a man, in an attempt to save himself, must go) *through the fire* (and therefore suffers fr. burns) 1 Cor 3: 15. τὴν ἑαυτοῦ γυναῖκα οὕτως ὡς ἑαυτόν Eph 5: 33; cf. vs. 28. ἡμέρα κυρίου ὡς κλέπτης οὕτως ἔρχεται 1 Th 5: 2. The word οὕτως can also be omitted ἀσφαλίσασθε ὡς οἴδατε *make it as secure as you know how*=*as you can* Mt 27: 65. ὡς οὐκ οἶδεν αὐτός (*in such a way*) *as he himself does not know*= *he himself does not know how, without his know-ing* (*just*) *how* Mk 4: 27. ὡς ἀνῆκεν (*in such a way*) *as is fitting* Col 3: 18. Cf. 4: 4; Eph 6: 20; Tit 1: 5.

2. special uses—a. in ellipses ἐλάλουν ὡς νήπιος *I used to speak as a child* (*is accustomed to speak*) 1 Cor 13: 11a; cf. b, c; Mk 10: 15; Eph 6: 6a; Phil 2: 22; Col 3: 22. ὡς τέκνα φωτὸς περιπατεῖτε *walk as children of the light* (*must walk*) Eph 5: 8; cf. 6: 6b. ὡς ἐν ἡμέρᾳ *as* (*it is one's duty to walk*) *in the daylight* Ro 13: 13. The Israelites went through the Red Sea ὡς διὰ ξηρᾶς γῆς *as* (*one travels*) *over dry land* Hb 11: 29. οὐ λέγει ὡς ἐπὶ πολλῶν ἀλλ' ὡς ἐφ' ἑνός *he speaks not as one would of a plurality* (cf. ἐπί I 1bγ), *but as of a single thing* Gal 3: 16.—Ro 15: 15; 1 Pt 5: 3. Also referring back to οὕτως: οὕτως τρέχω ὡς οὐκ ἀδήλως *I run as* (a man) *with a fixed goal* 1 Cor 9: 26a. Cf. ibid. b; Js 2: 12.

b. ὡς and the words that go w. it can be the subj. or obj. of a clause: γενηθήτω σοι ὡς θέλεις *let it be done* (=*it will be done*) *for you as you wish* Mt 15: 28. Cf. 8: 13; Lk 14: 22 t.r. (cf. ὡς τὸ θέλημά σου, Ode of Solomon 11: 21). The predicate belonging to such a subj. is to be supplied in οὐχ ὡς ἐγὼ θέλω (γενηθήτω) Mt 26: 39a.—ἐποίησεν ὡς προσέταξεν αὐτῷ ὁ ἄγγελος *he did as* (=*that which*) *the angel commanded him* (to do) Mt 1: 24. Cf. 26: 19; 28: 15.—Practically equivalent to ὅ, which is a v.l. for it Mk 14: 72 (JNBirdsall, NovT 2, '58, 272–5).

c. ἕκαστος ὡς *each one as* or *according to what* Ro 12: 3; 1 Cor 3: 5; 7: 17a, b; Rv 22: 12.

d. in indirect questions (X., Cyr. 1, 5, 11 ἀπαίδευτοι ὡς χρὴ συμμάχοις χρῆσθαι) ἐξηγοῦντο ὡς ἐγνώσθη αὐ-τοῖς ἐν τῇ κλάσει τοῦ ἄρτου *they told how he had made himself known to them when they broke bread together* Lk 24: 35. Cf. Mk 12: 26 t.r.; Lk 8: 47; 23: 55; Ac 10: 38; 20: 20; Ro 11: 2; 2 Cor 7: 15.

II. as a conjunction denoting comparison, *as.* This 'as' can have a 'so' expressly corresponding to it or not, as the case may be; further, both sides of the comparison can be expressed in complete clauses, or one or even both may be abbreviated.

1. ὡς is correlative w. οὕτως=*so.* οὕτως . . . ὡς (*so, in such a way*) . . . *as*: οὐδέποτε ἐλάλησεν οὕτως ἄνθρω-πος ὡς οὗτος λαλεῖ ὁ ἄνθρωπος J 7: 46. ὡς . . . οὕτως Ac 8: 32 (Is 53: 7); 23: 11; Ro 5: 15 (ὡς τὸ παράπτωμα, οὕτως καὶ τὸ χάρισμα, both halves to be completed), 18. ὡς κοινωνοί ἐστε τῶν παθημάτων, οὕτως καὶ τῆς παρακλήσεως *as you are comrades in suffering, so* (*shall you be*) *in comfort as well* 2 Cor 1: 7. Cf. 7: 14; 11: 3 t.r.—ὡς . . . καί *as* . . . *so* (Plut., Mor. 39E) Mt 6: 10; Ac 7: 51; 2 Cor 13: 2; Gal 1: 9; Phil 1: 20.

2. The clause beginning w. ὡς can easily be understood and supplied in many cases; when this occurs, the noun upon which the comparison depends can often stand alone, and in these cases ὡς acts as a particle denoting comparison. οἱ δίκαιοι ἐκλάμψουσιν ὡς ὁ ἥλιος *the righteous will shine out as the sun* (*shines*) Mt 13: 43. ὡς ἐπὶ λῃστὴν ἐξήλθατε συλλαβεῖν με *as* (*one goes out*) *against a robber,* (*so*) *you have gone out to arrest me* 26: 55. γίνεσθε φρόνιμοι ὡς οἱ ὄφεις *as serpents* (*are*) 10: 16b. Cf. Lk 12: 27; 21: 35; 22: 31; J 15: 6; 2 Ti 2: 17; 1 Pt 5: 8.

3. Semitic infl. is felt in the manner in which ὡς, combined w. a subst., takes the place of a subst. or an adj.

a. a substantive—α. as subj. (cf. Da 7: 13 ὡς υἱὸς ἀνθρώπου ἤρχετο. Cf. 10: 16, 18) ἐνώπιον τοῦ θρόνου (ἦν) ὡς θάλασσα ὑαλίνη *before the throne there was something like a sea of glass* Rv 4: 6. Cf. 8: 8; 9: 7a. ἀφ' ἑνὸς ἐγενήθησαν ὡς ἡ ἄμμος *from one man they have come into being as the sand,* i.e. countless descendants Hb 11: 12.

β. as obj. ᾄδουσιν ὡς ᾠδὴν καινήν *they were singing, as it were, a new song* Rv 14: 3 t.r. ἤκουσα ὡς φωνήν *I heard what sounded like a shout* 19: 1, 6a, b, c; cf. 6: 1.

b. an adjective, pred. (mostly εἶναι, γίνεσθαι ὡς) ἐὰν μὴ γένησθε ὡς τὰ παιδία *if you do not become child-like* Mt 18: 3. ὡς ἄγγελοί εἰσιν *they are similar to angels* 22: 30. πᾶσα σὰρξ ὡς χόρτος 1 Pt 1: 24. Cf. Mk 6: 34; 12: 25; Lk 22: 26a, b; Ro 9: 27 (Is 10: 22); 29a (Is 1: 9a); 1 Cor 4: 13; 7: 7f, 29–31; 9: 20f; 2 Pt 3: 8a, b (Ps 89: 4); Rv 6: 12a, b al. Sim. also ποίησόν με ὡς ἕνα τῶν μισθίων σου *treat me like one of you day laborers* Lk 15: 19.—The adj. or adjectival expr. for which this form stands may be used as an attribute πίστιν ὡς κόκκον σινάπεως *faith like a mustard seed*=faith no greater than a tiny mustard seed Mt 17: 20; Lk 17: 6. προφήτης ὡς εἷς τῶν προφητῶν Mk 6: 15. Cf. Ac 3: 22; 7: 37 (both Dt 18: 15); 10: 11; 11: 5. ἀρνίον ὡς ἐσφαγμένον *a lamb that appeared to have been slaughtered* Rv 5: 6.—In expressions like τρίχας ὡς τρίχας γυναικῶν 9: 8a the second τρίχας can be omitted as self-evident (Ps 54: 7 v.l.): ἡ φωνὴ ὡς σάλπιγγος 4: 1; cf. 1: 10; 9: 8b; 13: 2a; 14: 2c; 16: 3.

4. Other noteworthy uses—a. ὡς *as* can introduce an example ὡς καὶ Ἠλίας ἐποίησεν Lk 9: 54 t.r. Cf. 1 Pt 3: 6; or, in the combination ὡς γέγραπται, a scripture quotation Mk 1: 2 t.r.; 7: 6; Lk 3: 4; Ac 13: 33. Cf. Ro 9: 25; or even an authoritative human opinion Ac 17: 28; 22: 5; 25: 10; or any other decisive reason Mt 5: 48; 6: 12 (ὡς καί).

b. ὡς introduces short clauses: ὡς εἰώθει *as his custom was* Mk 10: 1. Cf. Hs 5, 1, 2. ὡς λογίζομαι *as I think* 1 Pt 5: 12. ὡς ἐνομίζετο *as was supposed* Lk 3: 23 (Diog. L. 3, 2 ὡς Ἀθήνησιν ἦν λόγος [about Plato's origin]). ὡς ἦν *as he was* Mk 4: 36.

c. The expr. οὕτως ἐστὶν ἡ βασιλεία τοῦ θεοῦ ὡς ἄνθρωπος βάλῃ τὸν σπόρον Mk 4: 26 is gravely irregular fr. a grammatical viewpoint; it is likely that ἄν (=ἐάν, which is read by the t.r.) once stood before ἄνθρωπος and was lost inadvertently. Cf. the comm., e.g. EKlostermann,

Hdb. z. NT⁴ '50 ad loc.; Jülicher, Gleichn. 539; Bl-D. §380, 4; Mlt. 185 w. notes; Rdm.² 154; Rob. 928; 968.

III. ὡς introduces the characteristic quality of a pers., thing, or action, etc., referred to in the context.

1. an actual quality—**a.** *as* τί ἔτι κἀγὼ ὡς ἁμαρτωλὸς κρίνομαι; *why am I still being condemned as a sinner?* Ro 3: 7. ὡς σοφὸς ἀρχιτέκτων 1 Cor 3: 10. ὡς ἀρτιγέννητα βρέφη *as new-born children* (which you really are, if you put away all wickedness) 1 Pt 2: 2. μή τις ὑμῶν πασχέτω ὡς φονεύς 4: 15a; cf. b, 16.—1: 14; 1 Cor 7: 25; 2 Cor 6: 4; Eph 5: 1; Col 3: 12; 1 Th 2: 4, 7a.—In the oblique cases, genitive: τιμίῳ αἵματι ὡς ἀμνοῦ ἀμώμου Χριστοῦ *with the precious blood of Christ, as of a lamb without blemish* 1 Pt 1: 19. δόξαν ὡς μονογενοῦς παρὰ πατρός *glory as of an only-begotten son, coming from the Father* J 1: 14.—Cf. Hb 12: 27. Dative (Stephan. Byz. s.v. Κυνόσαργες: Ἡρακλεῖ ὡς θεῷ θύων): λαλῆσαι ὑμῖν ὡς πνευματικοῖς 1 Cor 3: 1a; cf. b, c; 10: 15; 2 Cor 6: 13; Hb 12: 5; 1 Pt 2: 13f; 3: 7a, b; 2 Pt 1: 19. Accusative: οὐχ ὡς θεὸν ἐδόξασαν Ro 1: 21; 1 Cor 4: 14; 8: 7; Tit 1: 7; Phlm 16; Hb 6: 19; 11: 9; 1 Pt 2: 11.—This is prob. also the place for ὃ ἐὰν ποιῆτε, ἐργάζεσθε ὡς τῷ κυρίῳ *whatever you have to do, do it as work for the Lord* Col 3: 23. Cf. Eph 5: 22. εἴ τις λαλεῖ ὡς λόγια θεοῦ *if anyone preaches,* (let him do so) *as if* (he were proclaiming the) *words of God* 1 Pt 4: 11a; cf. ibid. b; 2 Cor 2: 17b, c; Eph 6: 5, 7.

b. ὡς w. the ptc. gives the reason for an action *as one who, because* (X., Cyr. 7, 5, 13 κατεγέλων τῆς πολιορκίας ὡς ἔχοντες τὰ ἐπιτήδεια; Appian, Liby. 56 §244 μέμφεσθαι τοῖς θεοῖς ὡς ἐπιβουλεύουσι=as being hostile; Polyaenus 2, 1, 1; 3, 10, 3 ὡς ἔχων=just as if he had; Jos., Ant. 1, 251; Dit., Syll.³, 1168, 35); Paul says: I appealed to the Emperor οὐχ ὡς τοῦ ἔθνους μου ἔχων τι κατηγορεῖν *not that I had any charge to bring against my* (own) *people* Ac 28: 19 (Zen.-P. 59 044, 23 [257 BC] οὐχ ὡς μενῶν=not as if it were my purpose to remain there). ὡς foll. by the gen. abs. ὡς τὰ πάντα ἡμῖν τῆς θείας δυνάμεως αὐτοῦ δεδωρημένης *because his divine power has granted us everything* 2 Pt 1: 3.—Only in isolated instances does ὡς show causal force when used w. a finite verb *for* (PLeid. 16, 1, 20; Lucian, Dial. Mort. 17, 2, end, Vit. Auct. 25; Aesop, Fab. 109 P.=148 H.: ὡς εὐθέως ἐξελεύσομαι=because; Tetrast. Iamb. 1, 6, 3; Nicetas Eugen. 6, 131 H. Cf. Herodas 10, 3: ὡς=because [with the copula 'is' to be supplied]) Mt 6: 12 (ὡς καί as Mk 7: 37B; Test. Dan 3: 1; the parallel Lk 11: 4 has γάρ). So, more oft., καθώς (q.v. 3).

c. Almost pleonastic is the use of ὡς before the predicate acc. or nom. w. certain verbs ὡς προφήτην ἔχουσιν τὸν Ἰωάννην Mt 21: 26. Cf. Lk 16: 1. λογίζεσθαί τινα ὡς foll. by acc. *look upon someone as* 1 Cor 4: 1; 2 Cor 10: 2 (for this pass. s. also 3 below). Cf. 2 Th 3: 15a, b; Phil 2: 7; Js 2: 9.

2. a quality that exists only in someone's imagination or is based solely on someone's statement (Jos., Bell. 3, 346) προσηνέγκατέ μοι τὸν ἄνθρωπον τοῦτον ὡς ἀποστρέφοντα τὸν λαόν, καὶ ἰδού . . . *you have brought this man before me as one who* (as you claim) *is misleading the people, and now* . . . Lk 23: 14. τί καυχᾶσαι ὡς μὴ λαβών; *why do you boast, as though you* (as you think) *had not received?* 1 Cor 4: 7. Cf. Ac 3: 12; 23: 15, 20; 27: 30. ὡς μὴ ἐρχομένου μου *as though I were not coming* (acc. to their mistaken idea) 1 Cor 4: 18.

3. a quality wrongly claimed, in any case objectively false ἐπιστολὴ ὡς δι᾽ ἡμῶν *a letter* (falsely) *alleged to be from us* 2 Th 2: 2a (Diod. S. 33, 5, 5 ἔπεμψαν ὡς παρὰ τῶν πρεσβευτῶν ἐπιστολήν they sent a letter which

purported to come from the emissaries; Diog. L. 10: 3 falsified ἐπιστολαὶ ὡς Ἐπικούρου). τοὺς λογιζομένους ἡμᾶς ὡς κατὰ σάρκα περιπατοῦντας 2 Cor 10: 2 (s. also 1c above). Cf. 11: 17; 13: 7. Israel wishes to become righteous οὐκ ἐκ πίστεως ἀλλ᾽ ὡς ἐξ ἔργων *not through faith but through deeds* (the latter way being objectively wrong) Ro 9: 32 (Rdm.² 26f).

IV. Other uses of ὡς—1. as a temporal conjunction (Bl-D. §455, 2; 3 w. app.; Harnack, SAB '08, 392).

a. w. the aor. *when, after* (Hom., Hdt.+; pap. [POxy. 1489, 4 al.]; LXX; Jos., Bell. 1, 445b) ὡς ἐπλήσθησαν αἱ ἡμέραι Lk 1: 23. ὡς ἐγεύσατο ὁ ἀρχιτρίκλινος J 2: 9.—Lk 1: 41, 44; 2: 15, 39; 4: 25; 5: 4; 7: 12; 15: 25; 19: 5; 22: 66; 23: 26; J 4: 1, 40; 6: 12, 16; 7: 10; 11: 6, 20, 29, 32f; 18: 6; 19: 33; 21: 9; Ac 5: 24; 10: 7, 25; 13: 29; 14: 5; 16: 10, 15; 17: 13; 18: 5; 19: 21; 21: 1, 12; 22: 25; 27: 1, 27; 28: 4.

b. w. pres. or impf. *while, when, as long as* (Menand., fgm. 538, 2 K. ὡς ὁδοιπορεῖς; Cyrill. Scyth. [VI AD] ed. ESchwartz '39 p. 143, 1; 207, 22 ὡς ἔτι εἰμί=as long as I live) ὡς ὑπάγεις μετὰ τοῦ ἀντιδίκου σου *while you are going with your opponent* Lk 12: 58. ὡς ἐλάλει ἡμῖν, ὡς διήνοιγεν ἡμῖν τὰς γραφάς *while he was talking, while he was opening the scriptures to us* 24: 32.—J 2: 23; 8: 7; 12: 35f (*as long as*); Ac 1: 10; 7: 23; 9: 23; 10: 17; 13: 25; 19: 9; 21: 27; 25: 14; Gal 6: 10 (*as long as*); 2 Cl 8: 1; 9: 7; IRo 2: 2; ISm 9: 1 (all four *as long as*).—ὡς w. impf., and in the next clause the aor. ind. w. the same subject (Diod. S. 15, 45, 4 ὡς ἐθεώρουν . . . , συνεστήσαντο=when, or as soon as they noticed . . . , they put together [a fleet]; Dit., Syll.³ 1169, 58 ὡς ἐνεκάθευδε, εἶδε='while he was sleeping [in the temple]', or 'when he went to sleep, he saw' [a dream or vision] Mt 28: 9 t.r.; J 20: 11; Ac 8: 36; 16: 4; 22: 11.—*Since* (Soph., Oed. R. 115; Thu. 4, 90, 3) ὡς τοῦτο γέγονεν Mk 9: 21.

c. ὡς ἄν or ὡς ἐάν w. the subjunctive of the time of an event in the future *when, as soon as.*

α. ὡς ἄν (Hyperid. 2, 43, 4; Herodas 5, 50; Lucian, Cronosolon 11; PHib. 59, 1 [c. 245 BC] ὡς ἂν λάβῃς; UPZ 71, 18 [152 BC]; PTebt. 26, 2. Cf. Witkowski² 87; Gen 12: 12; Josh 2: 14; Is 8: 21; Da 3: 15 Theod.) Ro 15: 24; 1 Cor 11: 34; Phil 2: 23.—**β.** ὡς ἐάν (PFay. 111, 16 [95/6 AD] ὡς ἐὰν βλέπῃς) 1 Cl 12: 5f; Hv 3, 8, 9; 3, 13, 2.

2. as a consecutive conj., denoting result=ὥστε *so that* (trag., Hdt.+, though nearly always w. the inf.; so also POxy. 1040, 11; PFlor. 370, 10; Wsd 5: 12; Jos., Ant. 12, 229. W. the indic. X., Cyr. 5, 4, 11 οὕτω μοι ἐβοήθησας ὡς σέσωσμαι; Philostrat., Vi. Apoll. 8, 7 p. 324, 25f; Jos., Bell. 3, 343) Hb 3: 11; 4: 3 (both Ps 94: 11).

3. as a final particle, denoting purpose—**a.** w. subjunctive (Hom.+; Sib. Or. 3, 130; Synes., Hymni 3, 44 [NTerzaghi '39]) ὡς τελειώσω *in order that I might finish* Ac 20: 24 (cf. Mlt. 249).

b. w. inf. (X.; Arrian [very oft.: ABoehner, De Arriani dicendi genere, Diss. Erlangen 1885 p. 56]; PGenève 28, 12 [II AD], ZPE 8, '71, 177: letter of MAurelius 57, cf. 44-6; 3 Macc 1: 2; Joseph.) Lk 9: 52 v.l. ὡς τελειῶσαι Ac 20: 24 v.l. ὡς ἔπος εἰπεῖν Hb 7: 9 (s. ἔπος).

c. used w. prepositions that denote a direction, to indicate the direction intended (class. [Kühner-G. I 472 note 1]; Polyb. 1, 29, 1; LRadermacher, Philol. 60, '01, 495f) πορεύεσθαι ὡς ἐπὶ τὴν θάλασσαν Ac 17: 14 t.r.

4. after verbs of knowing, saying (even introducing direct discourse: Maximus Tyr. 5: 4f), hearing, etc.=ὅτι *that* (X., An. 1, 3, 5; Menand., Per. 137, Sam. 245; Aeneas Tact. 402; 1342; PTebt. 10, 6 [119 BC]; 1 Km 13: 11; Ep. Arist.; Philo, Op. M. 9; Jos., Ant. 7, 39; 9, 162;

15, 249 al.—ORiemann, Revue de Philol. new series 6, 1882, 73-5; HKallenberg, RhM n.s. 68, '13, 465-76; Bl-D. §396 w. app.) ἀναγινώσκειν Mk 12: 26 v.l. (for πῶς); Lk 6: 4 (w. πῶς as v.l.). μνησθῆναι Lk 24: 6 (D ὅσα); cf. 22: 61 (=Lat. quomodo, as in ms. c of the Old Itala; cf. Plautus, Poen. 3, 1, 54-6). ἐπίστασθαι (Jos., Ant. 7, 372) Ac 10: 28; 20: 18b v.l. (for πῶς). εἰδέναι (Mitt. d. dt. arch. Inst. Ath., Abt. 37, '12, 183 [=Kl. T. 110, 81, 10] ἴστε ὡς [131/2 AD]) 1 Th 2: 11a. μάρτυς ὡς Ro 1: 9; Phil 1: 8; 1 Th 2: 10.—ὡς ὅτι s. ὅτι 1dβ.

5. w. numerals *about, approximately, nearly* (Hdt., Thu. et al.; PAmh. 72, 12; PTebt. 381, 4 [VBSchuman, Classical Weekly 28, '34/'35, 95f-pap.]; Jos., Ant. 6, 95; Ruth 1: 4; 1 Km 14: 2) ὡς δισχίλιοι Mk 5: 13. Cf. 8: 9; Lk 1: 56; 8: 42; J 1: 39; 4: 6; 6: 10, 19; 19: 14, 39; 21: 8; Ac 4: 4; 5: 7, 36; 13: 18, 20; Rv 8: 1.

6. in exclamations *how!* (X., Cyr. 1, 3, 2 ὦ μῆτερ, ὡς καλός μοι ὁ πάππος! Himerius, Or. 54 [=Or. 15], 1 ὡς ἡδὺ μοι τὸ θέατρον=how pleasant . . . ! Ps 8: 2; 72: 1) ὡς ὡραῖοι οἱ πόδες τῶν εὐαγγελιζομένων ἀγαθά Ro 10: 15 (cf. Is 52: 7). Cf. 11: 33.

7. w. the superlative ὡς τάχιστα (a literary usage; cf. Bl-D. §244, 1; cf. Rob. 669) *as quickly as possible* Ac 17: 15 (s. ταχέως 3).—WStählin, Symbolon, '58, 99-104. Cf. also ὡσάν, ὡσαύτως, ὡσεί, ὥσπερ, ὡσπερεί, ὥστε. M-M.

ὡσάν or **ὡς, ἄν** *as if, as it were, so to speak* (Bl-D. §453, 3; Rob. 974) Hs 9, 9, 7. W. the inf. ὡσὰν ἐκφοβεῖν 2 Cor 10: 9.—On 1 Cor 12: 2 s. HLietzmann and CKBarrett.*

ὡσαννά=Aram. נָא הוֹשַׁע=Hebr. אָנָּא הוֹשִׁיעָה (Hebr. Ps 118: 25); on the spelling s. W-H., Introd. §408; Tdf., Prol. 107; indecl. *hosanna*='help' or 'save, I pray', an appeal that became a liturgical formula; as a part of the Hallel (Ps 113-18 Hebr.) it was familiar to everyone in Israel. Abs. Mk 11: 9; J 12: 13. W. additions: τῷ υἱῷ Δαυίδ Mt 21: 9a, 15 (FDCoggan, ET 52, '40/'41, 76f; CTWood, ibid. 357). τῷ θεῷ Δ. D 10: 6. ἐν τοῖς ὑψίστοις Mt 21: 9b; Mk 11: 10 (s. ὕψιστος 1).—W-S. p. XV; EKautzsch, Gramm. d. Bibl.-Aram. 1884, 173; Dalman, Gramm.² '05, 249; Billerb. I '22, 845ff; Zahn, Einl. I³ 14; EbNestle, Philol. 68, '09, 462; FSpitta, ZWTh 52, '10, 307-20; FCBurkitt, JTS 17, '16, 139-49; Elbogen² 138f; 219f; HBornhäuser, Sukka '35, 106f; EFFBishop, ET 53, '42, 212-14; Gdspd., Probs. 34f; EWerner, JBL 65, '46, 97-122; JSKennard, Jr., JBL 67, '48, 171-6; ELohse, NovT 6, '63, 183-9, TW IX, 682-4. M-M.*

ὡσαύτως adv. (as one word [cf. MReil, ByzZ 19, '10, 507f] it is post-Homeric; inscr., pap., LXX, Ep. Arist.; Philo, Op. M. 54) (*in*) *the same* (*way*), *similarly, likewise* ἐποίησεν ὡσαύτως Mt 20: 5. Cf. 21: 30, 36; 25: 17; Lk 13: 3 t.r., b; 5: 25; Tit 2: 6; Hs 2: 7; 5, 4, 2; 8, 4, 4; D 11: 11; 13: 2, 6. ὡσαύτως δὲ καί (Strabo 10, 3, 10) Mk 14: 31; Lk 20: 31; Ro 8: 26; 1 Ti 5: 25 v.l. The verb is to be supplied fr. the context (Test. Levi 17: 7) Mk 12: 21; Lk 22: 20; 1 Cor 11: 25; 1 Ti 2: 9 (acc. to vs. 8 βούλομαι is to be supplied); 3: 8 and 11 (sc. δεῖ εἶναι); Tit 2: 3 (λάλει εἶναι); 1 Cl 43: 3.—See ὁμοίως. M-M.*

ὡσεί (Hom. +)—1. particle denoting comparison *as, like,* (*something*) *like,* lit. 'as if' (Hom. +; PSI 343, 10 [256/5 BC]; PTebt. 58, 26; LXX, En., Test. 1 Patr.) in the mss. oft. interchanged w. ὡς (Bl-D. §453, 3; cf. Rob. 968) πνεῦμα καταβαῖνον ὡσεί περιστεράν Mt 3: 16. Cf. 9: 36; Mk 1: 10 t.r.; Ac 2: 3; 6: 15; 9: 18 v.l. (for ὡς); 16: 9 D; Ro 6: 13; Hb 1: 12 (Ps 101: 27); B 6: 6 (Ps 117: 12); Hv 3, 1, 5a, b; 4, 1, 6a, b; s 6, 2, 5. γίνεσθαι ὡσεί Mt 28: 4 t.r.

(for ὡς); Mk 9: 26; Lk 22: 44. εἶναι ὡσεί Mt 28: 3 t.r. (for ὡς); Hs 3: 1f. φαίνεσθαι ὡσεί τι *seem like someth.* Lk 24: 11.

2. w. numbers and measures *about* (X., Hell. 1, 2, 9; 2, 4, 25; PTebt. 15, 2; 25 [114 BC]; Sb 5115, 4 [145 BC]; LXX, Ep. Arist. 13; Jos., Ant. 6, 247; 12, 292) ὡσεὶ πεντακισχίλιοι Mt 14: 21. Cf. Lk 9: 14a, b; J 6: 10 t.r. (for ὡς); Ac 1: 15; 2: 41; 19: 7. ὡσεὶ μῆνας τρεῖς Lk 1: 56 t.r. (for ὡς). Cf. 3, 23; 9: 28; 22: 59. ὡσεὶ ὥρα ἕκτη (Test. Jos. 8: 1) 23: 44; J 4: 6 t.r. (for ὡς); 19: 14 t.r. (for ὡς). Cf. Ac 10: 3. ὡσεὶ στάδια δέκα Hv 4, 1, 2. Cf. 4, 2, 1. ὡσεὶ λίθου βολήν Lk 22: 41. M-M.**

Ὡσηέ or **Ὡσῆε** (הוֹשֵׁעַ; Hos 1: 1f; Philo, Mut. Nominum 121.—In Joseph. the name is written: Ὡσήος, ου, also Ὡσήης [Ant. 9, 277] and Ὡσῆς [278]) ὁ indecl. *Hosea,* one of the 'minor' prophets. Metonymically of his book (Caecilius Calactinus, fgm. 74 p. 56, 20: κεῖσθαι παρὰ τῷ Θουκυδίδῃ, i.e. 3, 13, 3) ἐν τῷ Ὡσηέ Ro 9: 25.*

ὡσί see οὖς.

ὥσπερ (Hom. +; inscr., pap., LXX, Joseph., Test. 12 Patr.) (*just*) *as*—1. in the protasis of a comparison, the apodosis of which begins w. οὕτως (καί) (*just*) *as . . . , so* (X., Mem. 1, 6, 14; Epict., Ench. 27; Dio Chrys. 17[34], 44; 19[36], 20; POxy. 1065, 6) Mt 12: 40; 13: 40; 24: 27, 37; Lk 17: 24; J 5: 21, 26; Ro 5: 19, 21; Js 2: 26; Hv 3, 6, 6; 3, 11, 3; 4, 3, 4a, b; m 10, 3, 3; s 3: 3 al.—ὥσπερ . . . , ἵνα καί w. subjunctive (as a substitute for the imper.) 2 Cor 8: 7. In anacoluthon w. the apodosis to be supplied Ro 5: 12; ὥσπερ γάρ *for it is just like* (Plut., Mor. 7c) Mt 25: 14. Cf. IMg 5: 2.

2. connecting w. what goes before μὴ σαλπίσῃς ὥσπερ οἱ ὑποκριταὶ ποιοῦσιν Mt 6: 2. Cf. 20: 28; 25: 32; Hb 9: 25; Rv 10: 3; IEph 8: 1; 21: 2; IMg 4 (ὥσπερ καί, as PSI 486, 6 [258/7 BC]; PFay. 106, 24). ὥσπερ εἰσὶν θεοὶ πολλοί *just as indeed there are many gods* 1 Cor 8: 5 (s. EvDobschütz, ZNW 24, '25, 50).—The ὥσπερ-clause is somet. shortened and needs to be supplemented: μὴ βατταλογήσητε ὥσπερ οἱ ἐθνικοί (sc. βατταλογοῦσιν) Mt 6: 7. Cf. Ac 3: 17; 11: 15; 1 Th 5: 3; Hb 4: 10; 7: 27; Dg 5: 3; IEph 8: 2. Foll. by gen. abs. ἐγένετο ἦχος ὥσπερ φερομένης πνοῆς βιαίας Ac 2: 2 (Jos., Bell. 2, 556 ὥσπερ βαπτιζομένης νεώς). εἰμὶ ὥσπερ τις *I am like someone* Lk 18: 11. ἔστω σοι ὥσπερ ὁ ἐθνικός *as far as you are concerned, let him be as a Gentile*=treat him like a Gentile Mt 18: 17. γενόμενος ὥσπερ ἐξ ἀρχῆς καινὸς ἄνθρωπος *become, as it were, a new man from the beginning* Dg 2: 1. M-M.

ὡσπερεί (Aeschyl., Pla.+; Diod. S. 5, 31, 4; 10, 3, 2; 17, 112, 5; Ps.-Lucian, Asin. 56; Sym. Ps 57: 9; En. 5, 2) *like, as though, as it were* 1 Cor 4: 13 v.l. (for ὡς); 15: 8. M-M.*

ὥστε (Hom.+; inscr., pap., LXX, En., Ep. Arist., Philo, Joseph., Test. 12 Patr.—Bl-D. §391, 2; 3; Mayser II 1, '26, 297ff).

1. introducing independent clauses *for this reason, therefore, so*—a. foll. by the indic. (X., An. 1, 7, 7; 2, 2, 17 al.) ὥστε ἔξεστιν τοῖς σάββασιν καλῶς ποιεῖν Mt 12: 12. Cf. 19: 6; 23: 31; Mk 2: 28; 10: 8; Ro 7: 4, 12; 13: 2; 1 Cor 3: 7; 7: 38; 11: 27; 14: 22; 2 Cor 4: 12; 5: 16f; Gal 3: 9, 24; 4: 7, 16; Hm 7: 4.

b. foll. by the imperative (X., Cyr. 1, 3, 18; Lucian, Dial. Deor. 6, 1; PLond. 17, 38 [cf. UWilcken, GGA 1894, 721]; Zen.-P. 26 [=Sb 6732], 19 [255 BC] ὥστε φρόντισον; Job 6: 21; Wsd 6: 25; 4 Macc 11: 16) ὥστε ἑδραῖοι γίνεσθε 1 Cor 15: 58. Cf. 10: 12; 11: 33; 14: 39; Phil 2: 12;

4: 1; 1 Th 4: 18; Js 1: 19 t.r.; 1 Pt 4: 19. ὥστε μή w. imper. 1 Cor 3: 21; 4: 5. The hortatory subjunctive can take the place of the imper. ὥστε ἑορτάζωμεν 1 Cor 5: 8. Cf. 2 Cl 4: 3; 7: 1, 3; 10: 1; w. the neg. μή 11: 5.

2. introducing dependent clauses—a. of the actual result *so that*—α. foll. by the indic. (class.; POxy. 471, 89; 1672, 6 [I AD]; Jos., Ant. 12, 124) Gal 2: 13. οὕτως . . . , ὥστε (Epict. 1, 11, 4; 4, 11, 19; Jos., Ant. 8, 206) J 3: 16.

β. foll. by the acc. w. inf. (Ps.-Callisth. 2, 4, 7; BGU 27, 13; POxy. 891, 12; Josh 10: 14; Ep. Arist. 59; 64 al.; Jos., Ant. 12, 124) ὥστε τὸ πλοῖον καλύπτεσθαι Mt 8: 24. Cf. 12: 22; 13: 2, 32, 54; 15: 31; 24: 24 v.l.; 27: 14; Mk 2: 12; 4: 32, 37; 9: 26; 15: 5; Lk 5: 7; Ac 1: 19; 14: 1 (οὕτως ὥστε); 15: 39; Ro 7: 6; 15: 19; 1 Cor 5: 1 (*of such a kind that*, cf. Diod. S. 11, 61, 3 ἄγνοια τοιαύτη ὥστε); 2 Cor 1: 8; 2: 7; 7: 7; Phil 1: 13; 1 Th 1: 7; 2 Th 1: 4; 2: 4; Hb 13: 6; 1 Pt 1: 21; 1 Cl 1: 1; 11: 2; B 4: 2; ITr 1: 1 (οὕτως . . . , ὥστε); MPol 2: 2a; 12: 3; Hv 3, 2, 6 (οὕτως . . . , ὥστε); 4, 1, 8 (οὕτω . . . , ὥστε). ὥστε μή w. acc. and inf. Mt 8: 28; Mk 1: 45; 2: 2; 3: 20; 1 Cor 1: 7; 2 Cor 3: 7; 1 Th 1: 8; MPol 2: 2b.—W. the inf. alone (Aeschyl., Pers. 461; Soph., El. 393; Charito 2, 2, 2; Anth. Pal. 11, 144, 6; POxy. 1279, 14; Gen 1: 17; Ep. Arist. 95; 99; Sib. Or. 5, 413; 475 [οὕτως . . . , ὤ.]) Mt 15: 33; 24: 24; Mk 3: 10; Lk 12: 1; Ac 5: 15; 19: 16; 1 Cor 13: 2; 1 Cl 45: 7.

b. of the intended result, scarcely to be distinguished in mng. fr. ἵνα (Bl-D. §391, 3; Mlt. p. 207; 210; 249; Rdm.² p. 197; Rob. 990) *for the purpose of, with a view to, in order that* w. the inf. foll. (X., Cyr. 3, 2, 16; Ps.-Lucian, Asin. 46; Dit., Syll.³ 736, 114 οἱ κατεσταμένοι ὥστε γράψαι; UPZ 12, 15 [158 BC]; POxy. 501, 14; Gen 9: 15; Job 6: 23; Jos., Ant. 19, 279) Mt 10: 1; 27: 1; Lk 4: 29; 9: 52; 20: 20. M-M.

ὠτάριον, ου, τό dim. of οὖς, but equivalent to it in later Gk. *the* (outer) *ear* (Lucillius [I AD]: Anth. Pal. 11, 75, 2 of the severed ear of a gladiator; Anaxandrides [IV BC] in Athen. 3 p. 95C of an animal's ear.—Elsewh., incl. pap., the word means 'handle') Mk 14: 47 (ὠτίον t.r.); J 18: 10 (ὠτίον 𝔓⁶⁶ et al.). M-M.*

ὠτίον, ου, τό dim. of οὖς (s. PJouon, Rech de Sc rel 24, '34, 473f), but equivalent to it in late Gk.; *the* (outer) *ear* (of man and animal: Eratosth. p. 22, 22; Nicol. Dam.: 90 fgm. 119 Jac. ἀποτέμνει ὠ.; Anth. Pal. 11, 81, 3 [gladiator]; Epict. 1, 18, 18; Athen. 3 p. 95A; 107A; POxy. 108, 17 [II BC]; LXX.—In pap. it means mostly 'handle') Mt 26: 51; Mk 14: 47 t.r.; Lk 22: 51; J 18: 10 𝔓⁶⁶ et al., 26; B 9: 1 (Ps 17: 45). Cf. οὖς 1 and ὠτάριον. M-M. B. 226.*

ὠφέλεια, ας, ἡ (Soph., Hdt.+; inscr., pap., LXX, Ep. Arist., Philo; Jos., Ant. 4, 274; 12, 29 al.—But beside it the spelling ὠφελία is attested as early as Attic Gk.; cf. Bl-D. §23; Mlt.-H. 78) *use, gain, advantage* w. gen. (Ep. Arist. 241) τίς ἡ ὠφέλεια τῆς περιτομῆς; *what is the use of circumcision?* Ro 3: 1 (AFridrichsen, StKr 102, '30, 291–4. Cf. Jos., C. Ap. 2, 143 μηδὲν ὠφεληθεὶς ὑπὸ τῆς περιτομῆς). ὠφελείας χάριν *for the sake of an advantage* (cf. Polyb. 3, 82, 8) Jd 16. M-M.*

ὠφελέω fut. ὠφελήσω; 1 aor. ὠφέλησα. Pass.: 1 aor. ὠφελήθην; 1 fut. ὠφεληθήσομαι *help, aid, benefit, be of use* (*to*).

1. w. personal obj.—a. in the acc. (X., Mem. 1, 2, 61 al.; Herm. Wr. 12, 8; Sb 4305, 10 [III BC]; POxy. 1219, 12; Jos., Ant. 2, 282; Bl-D. §151, 1; Rob. 472) οὐκ ὠφέλησεν ὁ λόγος ἐκείνους Hb 4: 2 (cf. Plut., Mor. 547F). Cf. D 16: 2. Mostly a second acc. is added τινά τι *someone in respect to someth.* (Soph. +; Hdt. 3, 126) τί ὑμᾶς ὠφελήσω; *how will I benefit you?* 1 Cor 14: 6. Cf. Mk 8: 36; ISm 5: 2. Χριστὸς ὑμᾶς οὐδὲν ὠφελήσει Gal 5: 2 (s. PSI 365, 19 [III BC] ὁ σῖτος οὐθὲν ὠφελεῖ ἡμᾶς). Cf. B 4: 9; Papias 2: 4. Pass. *receive help, be benefited* (X., An. 5, 1, 12; Ep. Arist. 294; Philo; Jos., Ant. 2, 81 οὐδὲν ὠφελοῦντο) τί ὠφεληθήσεται ἄνθρωπος; *what good will it do a man?* Mt 16: 26. Cf. Mk 5: 26; Lk 9: 25; 1 Cor 13: 3; Hv 2, 2, 2; s 9, 13, 2. ἔν τινι *by someth.* (cf. Ps 88: 23) Hb 13: 9. τὶ ἔκ τινος ὠφεληθῆναι *be benefited by someone* or *someth. in a certain respect* (Mem. 2, 4, 1 al.; Jer 2: 11) Mt 15: 5; Mk 7: 11 (Gdspd., Probs. 60–2); Pol 13: 2.

b. in the dat. (poets Aeschyl. +; prose wr. since Aristot., Rhetor. 1, 1; inscr.) οὐδέν μοι ὠφελήσει τὰ τερπνὰ τοῦ κόσμου *the joys* (but s. τερπνός) *of the world will not benefit me at all* IRo 6: 1.

2. abs.—a. of a pers. οὐδὲν ὠφελεῖ *he is accomplishing nothing* Mt 27: 24 (s. 2b). Cf. J 12: 19.—b. of a thing ὠφελεῖ *it is of value* Ro 2: 25. W. a neg. J 6: 63 (Jos., Ant. 18, 127.—LTondelli, Biblica 4, '23, 320–7). So perh. οὐδὲν ὠφελεῖ Mt 27: 24 could also mean *nothing does any good, avails* (s. 2a). M-M. B. 1353f.*

ὠφέλιμος, ον (Thu. +; Dit., Syll.³ 1165, 3; PRyl. 153, 11 [II AD]; Philo; Jos., Ant. 16, 25 al.) *useful, beneficial, advantageous* τινί *for someone* or *for someth.* (Polyaenus 8 prooem.) Tit 3: 8; Hv 3, 6, 7. Also πρός τι (Pla., Rep. 10 p. 607D) 1 Ti 4: 8a, b; 2 Tim 3: 16. Heightened ὑπεράγαν ὠφέλιμος 1 Cl 56: 2.—The superl. (Artem. 5 p. 252, 13; Ps.-Lucian, Hipp. 6; Vi. Aesopi II p. 306, 12; Jos., Ant. 19, 206; PMich. 149 XVIII, 20 [II AD]) subst. τὰ ὠφελιμώτατα *what is particularly helpful* 62: 1 (Appian, Bell. Civ. 5, 44 §186 τὰ μάλιστα ὠφελιμώτατα). M-M.*

ὤφθην s. ὁράω.